LIBRARY OF CONGRESS

SUBJECT HEADINGS

Prepared by Subject Cataloging Division
Processing Services

11TH EDITION
VOLUME II
F–O

Cataloging Distribution Service, Library of Congress, Washington, D.C., 1988

Library of Congress Cataloging-in-Publication Data

Library of Congress. Subject Cataloging Division.
  Library of Congress subject headings.

  1. Subject headings, Library of Congress. I. Title.
Z695.L695   1988   025.4′9   87–35390
ISBN 0–8444–0591–4 (v. 1)

**The
National
Bibliographic
Service**

Available from the Cataloging Distribution Service.
Library of Congress, Washington, D.C. 20541

F1 cars
USE Formula One automobiles
F2H (Jet fighter plane)
USE Banshee (Jet fighter plane)
F3D (Jet fighter plane)
USE Skyknight (Jet fighter plane)
F-4 (Fighter planes)
USE Phantom (Fighter planes)
F4D fighter plane
USE Skyray fighter plane
F4F (Fighter plane)
USE Wildcat (Fighter plane)
F4U (Fighter planes)
USE Corsair (Fighter planes)
F-5 (Jet fighter plane)
UF Freedom Fighter (Jet fighter plane)
BT Fighter planes
Jet planes, Military
F7U (Jet fighter plane)
USE Cutlass (Jet fighter plane)
F-8 (Jet fighter plane)
USE Crusader (Jet fighter plane)
F8F (Fighter planes)
USE Bearcat (Fighter planes)
F8U (Jet fighter plane)
USE Crusader (Jet fighter plane)
F9F-2 (Jet fighter plane)
USE Panther (Jet fighter plane)
F9F-3 (Jet fighter plane)
USE Panther (Jet fighter plane)
F9F-4 (Jet fighter plane)
USE Panther (Jet fighter plane)
F9F-5 (Jet fighter plane)
USE Panther (Jet fighter plane)
F9F-6 (Jet fighter plane)
USE Cougar (Jet fighter plane)
F9F-7 (Jet fighter plane)
USE Cougar (Jet fighter plane)
F9F-8 (Jet fighter plane)
USE Cougar (Jet fighter plane)
F9F-9 (Jet fighter plane)
USE Tiger (Jet fighter plane)
F11F (Jet fighter plane)
USE Tiger (Jet fighter plane)
F-15 (Fighter planes)
USE Black widow (Fighter planes)
F-16 (Fighter planes)
BT Fighter planes
Jet planes, Military
F-20 (Chemical)
USE Chloroform
F-23 (Chemical)
USE Fluoroform
F-51 (Fighter planes)
USE Mustang (Fighter planes)
F-86 planes
USE Sabre (Jet fighter planes)
F-94 (Jet fighter plane)
USE Starfire (Jet fighter plane)
F-101 (Jet fighter planes)
USE Voodoo (Jet fighter plane)
F-104 (Fighter plane)
USE Starfighter (Fighter plane)
F-105 fighter plane
USE Thunderchief (Fighter planes)
F-106 (Jet fighter plane)
USE Delta Dart (Jet fighter plane)
F-111 (Fighter planes)
UF TFX (Fighter planes)
BT Fighter planes
F/A-18 (Jet fighter plane)
USE Hornet (Jet fighter plane)
F centers
USE Color centers
F.D. (Jet planes)
USE Fairey Delta (Jet planes)
F-distribution
UF Distribution, F
BT Distribution (Probability theory)
Sampling (Statistics)

F. L. Brinkley Midden (Miss.)
UF Brinkley Midden (Miss.)
F. L. Brinkley Site (Miss.)
BT Kitchen-middens—Mississippi
Mississippi—Antiquities
F. L. Brinkley Site (Miss.)
USE F. L. Brinkley Midden (Miss.)
F layer
USE F region
F.O.B. clause
UF "Free on board"
BT Basing-point system
Commercial law
Contracts, Maritime
Export sales
Maritime law
Risk
Sales
Shipment of goods
F region *(May Subd Geog)*
[QC879]
UF F layer
BT Ionosphere
NT Ionospheric critical frequencies
F stars
BT Cool stars
— Absolute magnitude
USE F stars—Magnitudes
— Magnitudes
UF F stars—Absolute magnitude
— Motion in line of sight
UF F stars—Radial velocity
— Radial velocity
USE F stars—Motion in line of sight
— Spectra
F.T.S.
USE Federal Telecommunications System
Fa-hsiang-tsung
USE Hossō (Sect)
Fa language (Bamileke)
USE Fe'fe' language
FAA (Chemical)
USE Acetylaminofluorene
Faanui (Society Islands)
USE Bora-Bora (Society Islands)
Faba bean *(May Subd Geog)*
[QK495.L52 (Botany)]
[SB205.F3 (Forage plant)]
[SB351.F3 (Food crop)]
UF Broad bean
English bean
European bean
Faba vulgaris
Fava bean
Field bean
Horse bean
Tick bean
Vicia faba
Windsor bean
BT Beans
Forage plants
Vetch
Faba bean as feed *(May Subd Geog)*
[SF99.F3]
BT Feeds
Faba vulgaris
USE Faba bean
Fabbrizi family
USE Fabricius family
Fabelta (Firm) Strike, Zwijnaarde, Belgium, 1983
BT Strikes and lockouts—Textile industry
—Belgium
Faber family
UF Fabre family
Fabian family
UF Fabion family
Fabyan family
RT Faubion family

Fabiano (Fictitious character)
BT Characters and characteristics in literature
RT Ramos, Graciliano, 1892-1953—Characters—Fabiano
Fabii family *(Not Subd Geog)*
UF Gens Fabia
Fabion family
USE Fabian family
Fabius River, Middle (Mo.)
USE Middle Fabius River (Mo.)
Fables
[PN980-PN994]
[PZ8.2]
[PZ14.2]
BT Didactic literature
Exempla
Fiction
Homiletical illustrations
Legends
Literature
Tales
RT Allegories
Parables
NT Bestiaries
Gesta Romanorum
Romances
Fables, African
NT Fables, Zairian
Fables, American *(May Subd Geog)*
UF American fables
Fables, Argentine *(May Subd Geog)*
UF Argentine fables
Fables, Asian
UF Asian fables
Fables, Brazilian *(May Subd Geog)*
UF Brazilian fables
Fables, Byelorussian *(May Subd Geog)*
[PN989.B]
UF Byelorussian fables
Fables, Chinese *(May Subd Geog)*
UF Chinese fables
Fables, Classical
NT Fables, Greek
Fables, Latin
Fables, Congo
USE Fables, Zairian
Fables, Creole *(May Subd Geog)*
UF Creole fables
Fables, Dinka *(May Subd Geog)*
UF Dinka fables
Fables, East Indian
USE Fables, Indic
Fables, English *(May Subd Geog)*
UF English fables
Fables, Estonian *(May Subd Geog)*
UF Estonian fables
Fables, French *(May Subd Geog)*
UF French fables
Fables, French, [German, Italian, etc.]
Fables, German *(May Subd Geog)*
UF German fables
Fables, Greek
BT Fables, Classical
Fables, Greek (Modern) *(May Subd Geog)*
UF Greek fables, Modern
Modern Greek fables
Fables, Hebrew *(May Subd Geog)*
UF Hebrew fables
Fables, Hungarian *(May Subd Geog)*
UF Hungarian fables
Fables, Indic *(May Subd Geog)*
UF East Indian fables
Fables, East Indian
Indic fables
Fables, Italian *(May Subd Geog)*
UF Italian fables
Fables, Korean *(May Subd Geog)*
[PN989.K7]
UF Korean fables

Fables, Latin
  BT Fables, Classical
Fables, Latin (Medieval and modern)
  (May Subd Geog)
  UF Latin fables, Medieval and modern
Fables, Mozambican *(May Subd Geog)*
  UF Mozambican fables
Fables, Oriental
  UF Oriental fables
Fables, Persian *(May Subd Geog)*
  UF Persian fables
Fables, Polish *(May Subd Geog)*
  UF Polish fables
Fables, Romanian *(May Subd Geog)*
  [PN989.R]
  UF Romanian fables
Fables, Scottish *(May Subd Geog)*
  UF Scottish fables
Fables, Spanish *(May Subd Geog)*
  UF Spanish fables
Fables, Spanish American
  UF Spanish American fables
Fables, Thai *(May Subd Geog)*
  UF Thai fables
Fables, Tibetan *(May Subd Geog)*
  [PN989.T]
  UF Tibetan fables
Fables, Ukrainian *(May Subd Geog)*
  UF Ukrainian fables
Fables, Vietnamese *(May Subd Geog)*
  UF Vietnamese fables
Fables, Yiddish *(May Subd Geog)*
  UF Yiddish fables
Fables, Zairian *(May Subd Geog)*
  UF Congo fables
      Fables, Congo
      Zairian fables
  BT Fables, African
Fabliaux
  BT French poetry—To 1500
      Tales—France
Fabre family
  USE Faber family
Fabri family
  USE Fabricius family
Fabric crafts
  USE Textile crafts
Fabric filters *(May Subd Geog)*
  UF Cloth filters
  BT Filters and filtration
Fabric flowers
  [SB449.3.A7 (Flower arrangement)]
  UF Cloth flowers
      Flowers, Fabric
  BT Artificial flowers
  NT Ribbon flowers
      Silk flowers
Fabric pictures *(May Subd Geog)*
  [NK9315]
  BT Collage
      Embroidery
      Needlework
      Tapestry
      Wall hangings
Fabric roofs
  USE Roofs, Fabric
Fabric shops *(May Subd Geog)*
  UF Piece goods shops
      Yard goods shops
  BT Specialty stores
      Textile industry
Fabrica ecclesiae
  USE Church maintenance and repair
Fabrici family
  USE Fabricius family

Fabricius family
  UF Fabbrizi family
      Fabri family
      Fabrici family
      Fabricy family
      Fabriczy family
      Fabrie family
      Fabritius family
Fabrics
  USE Textile fabrics
Fabrics, Bulked woven
  USE Textured woven fabrics
Fabrics, Coated
  USE Coated fabrics
Fabrics, Crease-resistant
  USE Crease-resistant fabrics
Fabrics, Fireproofing of
  USE Fireproofing of fabrics
Fabrics, Industrial
  USE Industrial fabrics
Fabrics, Laminated
  USE Laminated fabrics
Fabrics, Nonwoven
  USE Nonwoven fabrics
Fabrics, Sheer
  USE Sheer fabrics
Fabrics, Stretch woven
  USE Stretch woven fabrics
Fabrics, Synthetic
  USE Synthetic fabrics
Fabrics, Textured woven
  USE Textured woven fabrics
Fabrics, Waterproofing of
  USE Waterproofing of fabrics
Fabrics, Wool
  USE Wool fabrics
Fabricy family
  USE Fabricius family
Fabriczy family
  USE Fabricius family
Fabrie family
  USE Fabricius family
Fabrique nationale automatic rifles
  UF ABL automatic rifles
      FN automatic rifles
  BT Rifles
  NT FAL automatic rifle
Fabritius family
  USE Fabricius family
Fabulous furry Freak brothers (Comic strip)
  UF Freak brothers (Comic strip)
      Shelton, Gilbert. Fabulous furry
        Freak brothers
      Sheridan, Dave. Fabulous furry Freak
        brothers
  BT Comic books, strips, etc.
Fabyan family
  USE Fabian family
Façades *(May Subd Geog)*
  [NA2840-2841]
  UF Architectural fronts
      Fronts (Architecture)
  BT Architecture—Details
      Exterior walls
  NT Cast-iron fronts (Architecture)
      Shop fronts
      Wooden fronts (Architecture)
Facciolella
  [QL638.N46]
  BT Nettastomatidae
Facciolella physonema
  [QL638.N46]
Face
  [NC770 (Drawing)]
  [QL950.5 (Comparative anatomy)]
  [QM535 (Human anatomy)]
  [RL87 (Dermatology)]
  BT Figure drawing
      Head
  RT Pathognomy
      Physiognomy

  NT Beauty, Personal
      Cheek
      Chin
      Eye
      Eyebrows
      Mouth
      Nose
  — **Abnormalities**
      NT Hemifacial microsomia
          Kleeblattschädel syndrome
          Larsen's syndrome
  — **Cancer**
  — **Care and hygiene**
      UF Face care
          Facial care
          Facial treatment
      BT Hygiene
  — **Diseases** *(May Subd Geog)*
      NT Facial pain
          Orofacial pain
          Rosacea
  — — **Diagnosis**
  — **Expression**
      USE Facial expression
  — **Fractures**
      USE Facial bones—Fractures
  — **Innervation**
  — **Muscles**
      USE Facial muscles
  — **Surgery** *(May Subd Geog)*
      [RD523-527]
  — **Wounds and injuries**
      [RD523]
Face (Philosophy)
  [B105.F29]
  BT Philosophy
Face-amount certificate companies
  (May Subd Geog)
  UF Capitalization societies
      Face-amount installment certificate
        companies
      Sociedades de capitalización
      Sociétés de capitalisation
      Sparversicherung
  BT Mutual funds
      Saving and thrift
Face-amount installment certificate companies
  USE Face-amount certificate companies
Face care
  USE Face—Care and hygiene
Face fly
  UF Musca autumnalis
  BT Flies
Face in art
  [N7573.3]
Face of God
  USE God—Face
Face of Jesus Christ
  USE Jesus Christ—Face
Face perception *(May Subd Geog)*
  [BF241]
  UF Face recognition
      Facial perception
      Facial recognition
      Perception, Face
      Recognition, Facial
  BT Visual perception
  RT Facial expression
      Prosopagnosia
Face recognition
  USE Face perception
Face urns
  USE Urns
Facel Vega automobile
  [TL215.F]
  BT Automobiles
Faceted classification
  USE Classification, Faceted

Facetiae
USE American wit and humor, English wit and humor, *and similar headings;* *also subdivision* History, Comic, satirical, etc. *under names of countries, cities, etc.; also subdivisions* Anecdotes *and* Humor *under individual wars and types of animals; and subdivision* Anecdotes, facetiae, satire, etc. *under subjects*
    Anecdotes
    Wit and humor

Facial bones
    BT Skull
    NT Cheek-bone
        Eye-sockets
        Jaws
        Nasal bone
        Turbinate bones
— **Fractures**
    UF Face—Fractures
— **Growth**
Facial care
    USE Face—Care and hygiene
Facial expression
    UF Face—Expression
    BT Emotions
        Expression
        Physiognomy
    RT Face perception
    NT Smile
Facial manifestations of general diseases
    UF Facial symptoms of general diseases
    BT Symptomatology
Facial muscles
    UF Face—Muscles
    BT Muscles
Facial nerve
    BT Nerves, Cranial
— **Diseases** *(May Subd Geog)*
    NT Paralysis, Facial
— **Surgery**
Facial neuralgia
    USE Neuralgia, Facial
Facial pain
    BT Face—Diseases
        Head—Diseases
        Pain
    NT Neuralgia, Facial
Facial paralysis
    USE Paralysis, Facial
Facial perception
    USE Face perception
Facial recognition
    USE Face perception
Facial symptoms of general diseases
    USE Facial manifestations of general diseases
Facial treatment
    USE Face—Care and hygiene
Facies, Stratigraphic
    USE Facies (Geology)
Facies (Geology) *(May Subd Geog)*
    UF Facies, Stratigraphic
        Stratigraphic facies
    BT Geology, Stratigraphic
        Petrology
    NT Lithofacies
Facilitation, Social
    USE Social facilitation
Facilitatory tract
    USE Reticular formation
Facilities, Centralized industrial waste treatment
    USE Centralized industrial waste treatment facilities
Facilities, Meson
    USE Meson factories
Facilities, Nuclear
    USE Nuclear facilities

Facilities, Photon
    USE Photon factories
Facilities, Resource recovery
    USE Resource recovery facilities
Facilities for corn, Postharvest
    USE Corn—Postharvest facilities
Facility layout
    USE Plant layout
Facility management
    Here are entered works on the practice of coordinating the physical workplace with the people and the work of the organization, integrating the principles of business administration, architecture, and behavioral and engineering sciences.
    BT Factory management
        Management
        Work environment
    RT Plant engineering
Facing, Spot
    USE Spot facing
Facing head (in numismatics)
    (May Subd Geog)
    [CJ161.F3]
Facings, Mold (Founding)
    USE Foundry coatings
Facings (Clothing)
    BT Dressmaking
        Sewing
    NT Lapels
Facsimile, Radio
    USE Radio facsimile
Facsimile transmission *(May Subd Geog)*
    [TK6710]
    UF Fax
        Remote facsimile duplicator
        Telefax
    BT Data transmission systems
        Electronics
        Image transmission
        Telecommunication
    NT Electronic mail systems
        Radio facsimile
        Ultrafax
Facsimiles
    SA *subdivision* Facsimiles *under types of printed materials, documents, etc., e.g.* Autographs—Facsimiles; Incunabula—Facsimiles; Newspapers—Facsimiles; *and subdivision* Manuscripts—Facsimiles *under literatures, subjects, and names of individual literary authors and composers*
    NT Radio facsimile
        Reproduction of money, documents, etc.
Fact and law
    USE Law and fact
Factice, Tariff on
    USE Tariff on factice
Factor analysis
    [QA278.5]
    UF Analysis, Factorial
        Factorial analysis
    BT Correlation (Statistics)
        Psychometrics
    RT Path analysis
    NT Factorial experiment designs
        Principal components analysis
        Psychology—Mathematical models
— **Computer programs**
    NT FACTOREP (Computer program)
        SO4B (Computer program)
Factor II
    USE Prothrombin
Factor of safety
    USE Safety factor in engineering
Factor proportions *(May Subd Geog)*
    BT Comparative advantage (Commerce)
        Natural resources

Factor tables
    [QA51]
    UF Prime factors
        Tables, Mathematical
    BT Numbers, Prime
        Numbers, Theory of
        Ready-reckoners
Factor VIII (Blood coagulation)
    USE Blood coagulation factor VIII
Factor VIII antibodies
    USE Blood coagulation factor VIII antibodies
Factor VIII inhibitors
    USE Blood coagulation factor VIII antibodies
Factor XIII (Blood coagulation)
    USE Blood coagulation factor XIII
FACTOREP (Computer program)
    [QA278.5]
    BT Factor analysis—Computer programs
Factorial analysis
    USE Factor analysis
Factorial designs
    USE Factorial experiment designs
Factorial experiment designs
    UF Factorial designs
    BT Experimental design
        Factor analysis
Factorials
    BT Numbers, Theory of
Factories *(May Subd Geog)*
    [HD6068 (Women in)]
    [HD6270 (Junior labor)]
    [HD6974 (Social conditions)]
    [HD7406-HD7510 (Model)]
    [NA6400-NA6510 (Architecture)]
    [TH4511-TH4541 (Building)]
    UF Factory buildings
        Industrial plants
        Mills (Buildings)
        Plants, Industrial
    BT Architecture
        Factory system
        Industrial buildings
        Technology
    RT Mills and mill-work
        Workshops
    SA *headings beginning with the word* Factory
    NT Agricultural processing plants
        Airplane factories
        Asphalt plants
        Canneries
        Chemical plants
        Clothing factories
        Compost plants
        Drug factories
        Employees' buildings and facilities
        Glass factories
        Macaroni factories
        Metallurgical plants
        Pilot plants
        Plant shutdowns
        Printing plants
        Soybean processing plants
        Sugar factories
        Textile factories
— **Accounting**
    [HF5686.M3]
    RT Manufactures—Accounting
— **Air conditioning**
    [TH7684.F2]
    NT Clean rooms
— Automation
    USE Automation
— Clean rooms
    USE Clean rooms
— **Conservation and restoration**
    NT Factories—Remodeling for other use
— **Design and construction**

Factories
— **Design and construction** (Continued)
  [TH4511]
  [TS155]
  UF Factory construction
    Factory design
    Plant design
  NT Floor space, Industrial
    Plant layout
— **Electric equipment**
  NT Industrial electronics
— — **Installation**
    UF Installation of industrial electric
      equipment
— Electronic equipment
  USE Industrial electronics
— **Equipment and supplies**
  [TH4511]
  BT Industrial equipment
— **Fires and fire prevention**
  [TH9445]
— **Heating and ventilation**
  [TH7392.M6]
  [TH7684.F2]
  UF Factories—Ventilation
  BT Factory sanitation
  NT Clean rooms
    Exhaust systems
    Metallurgical plants—Heating and
      ventilation
— Inspection
  USE Factory inspection
— Law and legislation
  USE Factory laws and legislation
— Layout
  USE Plant layout
— **Lighting**
  [TH7975.F2]
  [TK4399.F2 (Electric lighting)]
  UF Factory lighting
    Industrial lighting
— **Location**
  [T56]
  UF Location of factories
  BT Community development
  NT Industrial sites
— Maintenance and repair
  USE Plant maintenance
— Management
  USE Factory management
— Noise
  USE Industrial noise
— **Power supply**
  [TK4035.F3]
  BT Electric power
— **Protection**
  UF Factory protection
    Industrial plant protection
  BT Buildings—Protection
    Police, Private
  RT War damage, Industrial
  NT Food industry and trade—Defense
      measures
    Gas industry—Defense measures
    Industry—Security measures
    Mineral industries—Defense
      measures
    Petroleum industry and trade—
      Defense measures
— **Remodeling for other use**
  UF Factories—Renovation
  BT Factories—Conservation and
      restoration
— Renovation
  USE Factories—Remodeling for other
      use
— **Safety appliances**
  [HD7273]
  RT Employers' liability
— **Safety measures**

BT Factory sanitation
  Industrial hygiene
— Sanitation
  USE Factory sanitation
— **Soundproofing**
  [TH1725]
— **Toilet facilities**
  UF Toilet facilities in factories
  BT Factory sanitation
    Toilets
— Underground
  USE Underground factories
— Ventilation
  USE Factories—Heating and
      ventilation
— Vocational guidance
  USE Industrial arts—Vocational
      guidance
Factories, Meson
  USE Meson factories
Factories, Photon
  USE Photon factories
Factoring (Finance) (May Subd Geog)
  [HG3752.3]
  BT Commercial finance companies
  NT Accounts receivable
— **Law and legislation** (May Subd Geog)
Factorization (Mathematics)
  BT Mathematics
  NT Factorization of operators
    Factors (Algebra)
Factorization of operators
  UF Operators, Factorization of
  BT Factorization (Mathematics)
    Factors (Algebra)
    Operator theory
  RT Wiener-Hopf operators
Factors
  USE Commission merchants
    Manufacturers' agents
Factors (Algebra)
  [QA161 (Algebraic expressions)]
  [QA242 (Numbers)]
  BT Algebra
    Factorization (Mathematics)
    Mathematics
  NT Factorization of operators
    Perfect numbers
Factory and trade waste (May Subd Geog)
  [TD897-9]
  UF Factory waste
    Industrial effluents
    Industrial wastes
    Solid waste management
    Trades-waste
    Waste, Disposal of
    Wastewaters
  BT Plant engineering
  RT Centralized industrial waste treatment
      facilities
    Pollution
    Refuse and refuse disposal
    Waste products
  NT Agricultural wastes
    Animal waste
    Brewery waste
    Canneries—Waste disposal
    Coal mine waste
    Coffee waste
    Coke industry—By-products
    Dairy waste
    Distilling industries—By-products
    Flock
    Flue gases
    Hazardous wastes
    Organic wastes
    Petroleum waste
    Potato waste
    Saline water conversion plants—Waste
      disposal
    Tailings embankments

    Tanning—Waste disposal
    Textile waste
    Waste disposal in the ground
    Waste disposal in the ocean
    Water reuse
    Wood-pulp industry—Waste disposal
— **Environmental aspects**
  (May Subd Geog)
  RT Pollution
— **Law and legislation** (May Subd Geog)
  BT Environmental law
— **Leaching**
  BT Leaching
— **Research** (May Subd Geog)
  BT Research, Industrial
Factory buildings
  USE Factories
Factory canteens
  USE Industrial feeding
Factory construction
  USE Factories—Design and construction
Factory costs
  USE Manufactures—Costs
Factory data acquisition systems, Automatic
  USE Automatic data collection systems
Factory design
  USE Factories—Design and construction
Factory doctors
  USE Occupational physicians
Factory housekeeping
  USE Industrial housekeeping
Factory inspection (May Subd Geog)
  [HD3656-HD3790.9]
  UF Factories—Inspection
    Inspection of factories
  BT Factory laws and legislation
  RT Employers' liability
    Labor inspection
  NT Industrial accidents
Factory laws and legislation
  (May Subd Geog)
  UF Factories—Law and legislation
    Law, Factory
    Law, Industrial
  BT Industrial laws and legislation
  RT Industrial hygiene—Law and
      legislation
    Industrial safety—Law and legislation
  NT Employers' liability
    Factory inspection
    Industrial accidents
    Plant shutdowns—Law and legislation
Factory layout
  USE Plant layout
Factory libraries
  [Z675.F3]
  UF Libraries, Factory
  BT Corporate libraries
Factory lighting
  USE Factories—Lighting
Factory management (May Subd Geog)
  [TS155]
  UF Factories—Management
    Management of factories
    Shop management
  BT Industrial management
  NT Assembly-line methods
    Facility management
    Industrial engineering
    Industrial project management
    Plant engineering
    Production control
    Production engineering
    Quality control
    Stakhanov movement
Factory monitoring systems, Automatic
  USE Automatic data collection systems
Factory noise
  USE Industrial noise
Factory outlets
  USE Outlet stores

Factory physicians
  USE Occupational physicians
Factory press
  USE Employees' magazines, handbooks, etc.
Factory protection
  USE Factories—Protection
Factory sanitation
  [TD895]
  UF Factories—Sanitation
  BT Industrial hygiene
      Plant engineering
      Sanitation
  NT Contamination (Technology)
      Exhaust systems
      Factories—Heating and ventilation
      Factories—Safety measures
      Factories—Toilet facilities
      Food industry and trade—Sanitation
      Industrial housekeeping
  — Law and legislation
        USE Industrial hygiene—Law and
            legislation
Factory schools
  USE Evening and continuation schools
Factory ships in fisheries
  USE Fishery processing ships
Factory sites
  USE Industrial sites
Factory system *(May Subd Geog)*
  [HD2351-6]
  BT Economics
      Industry—History
      Labor and laboring classes
      Machinery in industry
      Manufactures
  NT Factories
Factory tours
  USE Industrial tours
Factory waste
  USE Factory and trade waste
Facts, Miscellaneous
  USE Almanacs
      Curiosities and wonders
      Handbooks, vade-mecums, etc.
      Questions and answers
Facts (Philosophy)
  BT Experience
      Philosophy
Faculties, Canonical
  USE Faculties (Canon law)
Faculties (Canon law)
  [BX1939.F3]
  UF Canonical faculties
      Faculties, Canonical
  NT Absolution (Canon law)
Faculties (Church of England)
Faculty (Education)
  USE *subdivision* Faculty *under names of*
      specific universities, etc., e.g.
        Harvard University—Faculty
      College teachers
      Educators
      Junior colleges—Faculty
      Teachers
      Universities and colleges—Faculty
Faculty advisors *(May Subd Geog)*
  UF Advisors, Faculty
  BT Personnel service in higher education
      Student counselors
Faculty integration *(May Subd Geog)*
  UF Desegregation, Faculty
      Integration, Faculty
      Teachers—Integration
  BT School integration
  — Law and legislation *(May Subd Geog)*
      BT Educational law and legislation
  — United States
      NT Afro-American teachers
Faculty participation in administration
  USE Teacher participation in administration

Faculty-principal relationships
  USE Teacher-principal relationships
Faculty status of college librarians
  USE College librarians—Faculty status
Faculty workload
  USE *subdivision* Faculty—Workload *under*
      types of schools, e.g. Nursing
      schools—Faculty—Workload
      College teachers—Workload
      High school teachers—Workload
      Teachers—Workload
Fading (Radio)
  USE Radio—Transmitters and transmission
      —Fading
Fading channels (Radio)
  USE Radio—Transmitters and transmission
      —Fading
Fading of the color of corn
  USE Corn—Color—Fading
Fading of the color of flowers
  USE Flowers—Color—Fading
Fadner family
Fados
  [M1781-2]
  BT Folk-songs, Portuguese
Fads *(May Subd Geog)*
  UF Crazes
      Fashion (Fad)
  BT Manners and customs
      Popular culture
Faed family
  UF Fead family
      Feader family
Faeroe-Iceland Ridge
  BT Submarine topography—North
      Atlantic Ocean
Faessler family
  USE Fessler family
Fag family
  USE Vagg family
Fagaceae
  [QK495.F14]
  BT Fagales
  NT Beech
      Castanea
      Nothofagus
Fagales
  [QK495.A12 (Botany)]
  BT Dicotyledons
  NT Betulaceae
      Fagaceae
Fagaly family
  UF Fagely family
      Fagley family
      Fagly family
  RT Vogele family
Fagara clava-herculis
  USE Zanthoxylum clava-herculis
Făgăraş Mountains (Romania)
  UF Fogaras Mountains (Romania)
      Munţii Făgăraşului (Romania)
  BT Mountains—Romania
Fagely family
  USE Fagaly family
Fagg family
  USE Vagg family
Fagley family
  USE Fagaly family
Fagly family
  USE Fagaly family
Fagnes (Belgium and Germany)
  USE Hautes Fagnes (Belgium and
      Germany)
Fagopyrum
  [QK495.P78 (Botany)]
  BT Polygonaceae
Fagopyrum emarginatum
  USE Buckwheat
Fagopyrum esculentum
  USE Buckwheat

Fagopyrum sagittatum
  USE Buckwheat
Fagopyrum vulgare
  USE Buckwheat
Fagoters
  USE Fuelwood gatherers
Fagus
  USE Beech
Fagus silvatica
  USE European beech
Fagus sylvatica
  USE European beech
Faher, Tall al- (Syria)
  USE Faher, Tel (Syria)
Faher, Tel (Syria)
  UF Faher, Tall al- (Syria)
      Tall al-Faher (Syria)
      Tel el-Faher (Syria)
      Tel-Faher (Syria)
      Tell el-Faher (Syria)
  BT Syria—Antiquities
Faher, Tel (Syria), Battle of, 1967
  BT Israel-Arab War, 1967—Campaigns—
      Syria
Fahey family
  UF Fahy family
Fahndrich family
  USE Fendrick family
Fahringer family
  USE Farringer family
Fahy family
  USE Fahey family
Faick family
  USE Fike family
Faience *(May Subd Geog)*
  [NK4305-4305.5]
  UF Fayence
  BT Pottery
  NT Delftware
  — Dating
      NT Faience—Marks
  — Marks
      UF Faience—Trade-marks
      BT Faience—Dating
          Pottery—Marks
  — Trade-marks
      USE Faience—Marks
Faience tiles *(May Subd Geog)*
  BT Tiles
Fail family
  USE Fales family
Failaka Island (Kuwait)
  UF Faylakah Island (Kuwait)
      Feilaka Island (Kuwait)
  BT Islands—Kuwait
Faile family
  USE Fales family
Failing family
  USE Fales family
Fails family
  USE Fales family
Failure (Christian theology)
  [BT730.5]
  BT Man (Christian theology)
Failure (Psychology)
  UF Losing (Psychology)
  BT Success
  NT Losers
Failure (Psychology) in literature
Failure Analysis System (Computer system)
  UF FAS (Computer system)
  BT Structural failures—Data processing
Failure in business
  USE Business failures
Failure of banks
  USE Bank failures
Failure of engineering systems
  USE System failures (Engineering)
Failure of metals
  USE Metals—Fracture

Failure of solids
USE Fracture mechanics
Failure of the liver
USE Liver—Failure
Failure time data analysis
UF Data analysis, Failure time
BT Biomathematics
Mathematical statistics
Probabilities
Reliability (Engineering)
System failures (Engineering)
RT Competing risks
Failure to assist in emergencies
USE Assistance in emergencies
Failure to thrive syndrome
(May Subd Geog)
[RJ135]
UF Thrive, Failure to (Syndrome)
BT Child development deviations
Growth disorders
Infants—Diseases
Syndromes in children
Failures, Structural
USE Structural failures
Failures in semiconductors
USE Semiconductors—Failures
Failures in steam-boilers
USE Steam-boilers—Failures
Failures of contraception
USE Contraception—Failures
Fain family
UF Faine family
Fane family
Fawne family
Faine family
USE Fain family
Fainting
USE Syncope (Pathology)
Fair (Painting)
USE Bruegel, Pieter, the Younger, 1564-1637 or 8. Fair
Fair buildings
USE Exhibition buildings
Fair employment practice
USE Discrimination in employment
Fair family
UF Faires family
Fairs family
Fare family
Fayer family
Fair ground art
USE Fairground art
Fair housing
USE Discrimination in housing
Fair Isle (Scotland)
UF Sheep Island (Scotland)
BT Islands—Scotland
Shetland
Fair Oaks, Battle of, 1862
[E473.65]
UF Seven Pines, Battle of, 1862
BT Peninsular Campaign, 1862
United States—History—Civil War, 1861-1865—Campaigns
Fair organ
USE Band organ
Fair trade
USE Competition, Unfair
Price maintenance
Fair trade (Tariff)
USE Free trade and protection
Reciprocity
Fair trial and free press
USE Free press and fair trial
Fair use (Copyright) *(May Subd Geog)*
UF Copyright—Fair use
BT Copyright infringement
NT Copyright and audio-visual education
Copyright and electronic data processing

Magnetic recorders and recording—Fair use (Copyright)
Photocopying processes—Fair use (Copyright)
Video recordings—Fair use (Copyright)
Fair View Park Cemetery (De Kalb, Ill.)
USE Fairview Cemetery (De Kalb, Ill.)
Fairall family
USE Farrell family
Fairchild F-27 (Turboprop transport)
USE Fokker F.27 Friendship (Turboprop transport)
Fairchild family
UF Fairchilds family
Fairchilds family
USE Fairchild family
Faire (The French word)
BT French language—Etymology
Faires family
USE Fair family
Fairey aircraft
[TL686.F]
BT Convertiplanes
Helicopters
Seaplanes
NT Fairey Delta (Jet planes)
Swordfish (Torpedo-bomber)
Fairey Delta (Jet planes)
UF Delta (Jet planes)
F.D. (Jet planes)
BT Fairey aircraft
Jet planes
Supersonic planes
Fairfax City Cemetery (Fairfax, Va.)
UF Cemetery for the Burial of the Confederate Dead (Fairfax, Va.)
BT Cemeteries—Virginia
Fairfield County (Conn.)
— History
— — **Revolution, 1775-1783**
Fairfield family *(Not Subd Geog)*
Fairfield Lake (Tex.)
BT Big Brown Creek (Tex.)
Lakes—Texas
Reservoirs—Texas
Fairground art *(May Subd Geog)*
[NK5030-NK5035]
Here are entered works about amusement rides, showfronts, etc., as art objects.
UF Art, Fairground
Fair ground art
BT Folk art
NT Merry-go-round art
Fairground organ
USE Band organ
Fairies *(May Subd Geog)*
[BF1552 (Occultism)]
[GR549-GR552 (Folklore)]
BT Folklore
NT Elves
Fairy poetry
Gnomes
Goblins
Leprechauns
Melusine (Legendary character)
Morgan le Fay (Legendary character)
Negrinho do pastoreio (Brazilian brownie)
Tengu
Trolls
— Drama
USE Fairy plays
— Poetry
USE Fairy poetry
Fairies in art
Fairings *(May Subd Geog)*
BT Fairs
Souvenirs (Keepsakes)
Fairis family
USE Farris family

Fairiss family
USE Farris family
Fairlane automobile
[TL215.F]
BT Ford automobile
FAIRMODEL (Computer program)
BT Computer programs
Macroeconomics—Computer programs
Fairmont automobile
[TL215.F]
BT Ford automobile
Fairmont Cemetery (Henderson, Ky.)
BT Cemeteries—Kentucky
Fairmount Park (Philadelphia, Pa.)
BT Parks—Pennsylvania
Fairness
[BJ1533.F2]
UF Impartiality
BT Conduct of life
RT Justice
Fairness doctrine (Broadcasting)
(May Subd Geog)
[HE8689.7.F]
Here are entered works dealing with the requirement that broadcasters presenting one side of a controversial issue of public importance must afford reasonable opportunity for the presentation of contrasting views. Works dealing with the requirement that equal opportunities for broadcasting be afforded to all legally qualified candidates for public office if any one such candidate is permitted to broadcast are entered under Equal time rule (Broadcasting).
UF Doctrine of fairness (Broadcasting)
BT Broadcasting—Law and legislation
Broadcasting policy
RT Equal time rule (Broadcasting)
Fairness of God
USE God—Impartiality
Fairntosh Plantation (N.C.)
BT Dwellings—North Carolina
Plantations—North Carolina
Fairs
[GT4580-GT4699 (Manners and customs)]
[HF5470-HF5475 (Markets)]
[HF5481 (Street fairs)]
[HV544 (Charity fairs)]
Here are entered works on public gatherings at a stated time and place at which goods are exhibited and sold. Works on competitive exhibitions of farm products, livestock, baked goods, etc., with prizes for excellence, often combined with carnival-like entertainment, and held annually by states, counties, etc., are entered under Agricultural exhibitions. Works on areas within which or arrangements by which many buyers and sellers are brought into contact with one another in order to exchange goods or services are entered under Markets.
UF Trade fairs
Trade shows
BT Foreign trade promotion
Manners and customs
RT Exhibitions
Markets
SA subdivision Fairs under names of countries, cities, etc.; and names of individual fairs
NT Agricultural exhibitions
Bazaars, Charitable
Bazaars, Oriental
Brome County Fair, Que.
Fairings
— **Law and legislation** *(May Subd Geog)*
Fairs family
USE Fair family
Fairs in art
Fairsted (Brookline, Mass.)
USE Frederick Law Olmsted National Historic Site (Brookline, Mass.)
Fairview Cemetery (De Kalb, Ill.)
UF Fair View Park Cemetery (De Kalb, Ill.)
BT Cemeteries—Illinois

Fairview Cemetery (Gainesville, Tex.)
BT Cemeteries—Texas
Fairview Cemetery (Okla.)
BT Cemeteries—Oklahoma
Fairview Cemetery (Scottsbluff, Neb.)
BT Cemeteries—Nebraska
Fairwell family
USE Farwell family
Fairy chess
[GV1451.2]
BT Chess problems
Fairy lamps
[NK5440.F3]
BT Lamps
Fairy penguin
USE Eudyptula minor
Fairy plays
[PN6120.A4-PN6120.A5 (Juvenile)]
UF Fairies—Drama
Plays, Fairy
BT Drama
Fairy poetry
[PN6110.F3]
UF Fairies—Poetry
BT Fairies
Fairy tales
Poetry
Fairy poetry, American (May Subd Geog)
UF American fairy poetry
BT American poetry
Fairy poetry, English (May Subd Geog)
UF English fairy poetry
BT English poetry
Fairy poetry, English, [etc.]
(May Subd Geog)
Fairy poetry, French (May Subd Geog)
UF French fairy poetry
BT French poetry
Fairy primrose
[QK495.P95 (Botany)]
[SB413.P7 (Ornamental plant)]
UF Primula malacoides
BT Primroses
— Varieties
Fairy shrimps
USE Anostraca
Fairy tales (May Subd Geog)
[GR550-GR552 (Folk-lore)]
[PN3437 (History and criticism)]
BT Children's literature
Children's stories
Fiction
Folk literature
Legends
Literature
RT Tales
NT Fairy poetry
— Classification
[GR550]
[Z5983.F17]
Here are entered lists of fairy tales, or their
types, themes, motifs, variants, etc., compiled
with the aim of arranging them in certain clearly
defined groups, as well as works discussing the
principles upon which systems of classification
may be based.
UF Fairy tales—Themes, motives
Fairy tales—Types
RT Literature, Comparative—Themes,
motives
Plots (Drama, novel, etc.)
— Illustrations
NT Wedgwood fairyland lustre
— Themes, motives
USE Fairy tales—Classification
— Types
USE Fairy tales—Classification
Fairyflies
USE Mymaridae
Faist family
USE Feist family

Faith
[BT770-BT772 (Theology)]
[BV4637 (Moral theology)]
Here are entered works on religious faith and
doubt. Works on belief and doubt from the philosoph-
ical standpoint are entered under the heading Belief
and doubt.
UF Religious belief
Theological belief
BT Belief and doubt
Religion
Salvation
Theological virtues
Trust in God
NT Evidence
Faith, Confessions of
USE Creeds
Faith, Profession of
USE Profession of faith
Faith, Rule of
USE Rule of faith
Faith, Thirteen articles of (Judaism)
USE Thirteen articles of faith (Judaism)
Faith (Buddhism)
BT Buddhism—Doctrines
NT Doubt (Buddhism)
Threefold refuge
Faith (Islam)
[BP166.78]
BT Islam—Doctrines
Salvation (Islam)
NT Kufr (Islam)
— Early works to 1800
— Psychology
BT Islam—Psychology
Faith (Judaism)
[BM729.F3]
BT Judaism—Doctrines
Faith and justification
USE Justification
Faith and reason
[BT50]
Here are entered works on the proper limits, dif-
ferences, similarities, and interaction of the knowl-
edge attained through faith and that attained through
reason. Works more general in scope are entered
under Philosophy and religion, or Religion and
science.
UF Logic and faith
Reason and faith
BT Reason
RT Truth (Christian theology)
NT Double truth theory
Faith and reason (Islam)
BT Islam—Doctrines
Faith and reason (Jewish theology)
Faith-cure
USE Spiritual healing
Faith family
Faith healers
USE Healers
Faith healing
USE Spiritual healing
Faith, hope and charity
USE Theological virtues
Faith in literature
Faithists (May Subd Geog)
[BP605.F34]
BT Cults
Faithless sister (Tale)
USE Prince and the arm bands (Tale)
Faiwol language
UF Faiwolmin language
Fegolmin language
BT Papuan languages
Faiwolmin language
USE Faiwol language
Fajardo family
Fakaofo (Tokelau Islands)
UF Bowditch Island (Tokelau Islands)
Fakaofu (Tokelau Islands)

BT Coral reefs and islands—Tokelau
Islands
Islands—Tokelau Islands
Fakaofu (Tokelau Islands)
USE Fakaofo (Tokelau Islands)
Fake books (Music)
USE Fakebooks (Music)
Fakebooks (Music)
UF Fake books (Music)
BT Jazz music
Popular music
Fakhrabad, Tepe (Iran)
USE Farrokhabad, Tepe (Iran)
Fakirs
[BL2015.F2]
UF Bhikshu
Faqirs
BT Ascetics
FAL automatic rifle
[UD395.F16]
UF Automatic rifle, FAL
BT Fabrique nationale automatic rifles
Rifles
Falaise Gap, Battle of, 1944
BT World War, 1939-1945—Campaigns—
France
Falasha Rescue, 1984-1985
[DT380.4.F3]
UF Airlift of Falashas, 1984-1985
Operation Moses, 1984-1985
BT Search and rescue operations—
Ethiopia
Search and rescue operations—Sudan
Falashas (May Subd Geog)
[DS135.E75]
UF Beta Israel
Ethiopian Jews
Felashas
Fenjas
Foggara
House of Israel
Israel, Beta
Israel, House of
Jews, Ethiopian
Kaila
BT Jews
Falcidian law
USE Legitime
Falcioni family (Not Subd Geog)
Falco
[QL696.F34]
BT Falconidae
Falcons
NT Kestrels
Falco (Fighter plane)
UF Fiat C. R. 42 (Fighter plane)
BT Fighter planes
Falco albicilla
USE White-tailed sea eagle
Falco canorus
[QL696.F34]
Falco cherrug
USE Saker falcon
Falco eleonorae
USE Eleonora's falcon
Falco I (Fighter plane)
USE Reggiane Re 2000 (Fighter plane)
Falco mexicanus
USE Prairie falcon
Falco naumanni
USE Lesser kestrel
Falco pelegrinoides
[QL696.F34]
UF Falco peregrinus pelegrinoides
Falco peregrinus
USE Peregrine falcon
Falco peregrinus pelegrinoides
USE Falco pelegrinoides
Falcò Pio di Savoia family
Falco rufigularis
USE Bat falcon

Falco rusticolus
  USE Gyrfalcon
Falco sacer
  USE Saker falcon
Falco sparverius
  USE American kestrel
Falcon, Peregrine
  USE Peregrine falcon
Falcon (Jet transport)
  USE Dassault Falcon (Jet transport)
Falcon (Missile)
  UF Air-to-air missiles
      Falcon missiles
  BT Antiaircraft missiles
Falcon automobile, Ford
  USE Ford Falcon automobile
Falcon missiles
  USE Falcon (Missile)
Falcon Reservoir (Mexico and Tex.)
  UF Presa Falcón (Mexico and Tex.)
  BT Reservoirs—Mexico
      Reservoirs—Texas
      Rio Grande
Falconberry family
  USE Faulkenberry family
Falconer family
  USE Faulkner family
Falconers *(May Subd Geog)*
  BT Hunters
Falconidae *(May Subd Geog)*
    [QL696.F34]
  BT Falconiformes
  NT Falco
      Falcons
      Kestrels
Falconieri Palace (Rome, Italy)
  USE Palazzo Falconieri (Rome, Italy)
Falconiformes *(May Subd Geog)*
    [QL696.F3]
  UF Accipitres
      Accipitriformes
      Diurnal birds of prey
  BT Birds
      Birds of prey
  NT Accipitridae
      Cathartidae
      Falconidae
      Ospreys
Falconry *(May Subd Geog)*
    [SK321]
  UF Hawking
  BT Game and game-birds
      Hunting
  RT Fowling
Falcons
    [QL696.F34]
  BT Falconidae
  NT American kestrel
      Bat falcon
      Falco
      Gyrfalcon
      Lesser kestrel
      Peregrine falcon
      Prairie falcon
      Saker falcon
Fales family
  UF Fail family
      Faile family
      Failing family
      Fails family
  RT Fehling family
Fali (African people)
  BT Ethnology—East Cameroon
Fali (African people) art
  USE Art, Fali (African people)
Fali language
  UF Falli language
  BT Chadic languages
Falicaine
  BT Anesthetics

Falin family
  USE Fallon family
Faliscan language
    [PA2530]
  BT Italic languages and dialects
Faliscans (Italic people)
  UF Falisci
  BT Ethnology—Italy
      Italic peoples
Falisci
  USE Faliscans (Italic people)
Falkenborough family
  USE Faulkenberry family
Falkener family
  USE Faulkner family
Falkenstein, Counts of
  UF Counts of Falkenstein
  BT Germany—Nobility
Falker family
  USE Felker family
Falkinburgh family
  USE Faulkenberry family
Falkland Islands
    As a geographic subdivision, this heading is used
    directly.
Falkland Islands, Battle of the, 1914
    [D582.F2]
  BT World War, 1914-1918—Naval
      operations
Falkland Islands War, 1982
  UF Anglo-Argentine War, 1982
      Argentine-British War, 1982
      British-Argentine War, 1982
      Falklands War, 1982
      Operation Corporate, 1982
      Operation Rosario, 1982
  BT Argentina—History—1943-
      Great Britain—History—Elizabeth II,
      1952-
Falklands War, 1982
  USE Falkland Islands War, 1982
Falkner family
  USE Faulkner family
Fall
  USE Autumn
Fall army-worms
    [SB945.A8]
  UF Grassworm
  BT Army-worms
Fall color of leaves
  USE Fall foliage
Fall Creek River (Ill.) *(Not Subd Geog)*
  BT Rivers—Illinois
Fall foliage *(May Subd Geog)*
  UF Autumn leaves
      Autumnal coloration of leaves
      Fall color of leaves
      Foliage, Fall
  BT Leaves—Color
  RT Autumn
      Woody plants
Fall of man
    [BT710]
  UF Man, Fall of
  BT Sin
  RT Sin, Original
  NT Forbidden fruit
Fall of man in art
  BT Bible. O.T. Genesis III—Pictorial
      works
Fall of man in literature
Fall River Indians
  USE Pocasset Indians
Fall webworm
  USE Hyphantria cunea
Fallacies (Logic)
    [BC175]
  UF Errors, Logical
      Sophistry (Logic)

  BT Judgment (Logic)
      Logic
      Reasoning
Fallacy, Naturalistic
  USE Naturalistic fallacy
Fallen family
  USE Fallon family
Fallers (Persons)
  USE Loggers
Falli language
  USE Fali language
Fallibility
  BT Philosophical anthropology
  RT Errors
Fallin family
  USE Fallon family
Falling block rifles *(May Subd Geog)*
    [TS536.6.F34]
  UF Rifles, Falling block
  BT Rifles
Falling dominoes
  USE Domino toppling
Falling-stars
  USE Meteors
Falling tower (Sculpture)
  USE Poirier, Anne. Unstable stability
Falling Water (Pa.)
  USE Fallingwater (Pa.)
Fallingwater (Pa.)
  UF Edgar J. Kaufmann House (Pa.)
      Falling Water (Pa.)
      Kaufmann House (Pa.)
  BT Dwellings—Pennsylvania
Fallon family
  UF Falin family
      Fallen family
      Fallin family
      Fallons family
      Falloon family
      Falon family
Fallonia
  USE Anredera
Fallons family
  USE Fallon family
Falloon family
  USE Fallon family
Fallopian tubes
    [QL881 (Comparative anatomy)]
    [QM421 (Human anatomy)]
    [QP265 (Physiology)]
  UF Mammalian oviduct
      Tubes, Fallopian
      Uterine tubes
  BT Adnexa uteri
      Oviduct
  NT Pregnancy, Tubal
— **Innervation**
— Ligature
    USE Tubal sterilization
— **Motility**
    UF Motility of the Fallopian tube
— **Radiography**
    UF Salpingography
    NT Hysterosalpingography
— **Surgery**
    NT Tubal sterilization
Fallot's tetralogy
  USE Tetralogy of Fallot
Fallout, Radioactive
  USE Radioactive fallout
Fallout shelters *(May Subd Geog)*
  UF Shelters, Fallout
  BT Nuclear bomb shelters
  RT Radioactive fallout
Fallow
  USE Fallowing
Fallow deer
  UF Cervus dama
      Dama dama
  BT Deer

Fallowing *(May Subd Geog)*
  UF Fallow
  BT Crop rotation
    Cropping systems
    Tillage
  RT Soil fertility
  NT Shifting cultivation
Falls (Accidents) *(May Subd Geog)*
  BT Accidents
    Impact—Physiological effect
  NT Liability for slip and fall accidents
Falls (Waterfalls)
  USE Waterfalls
Falls Fight, 1676
  [E83.67]
  BT King Philip's War, 1675-1676
Falls of Saint Anthony (Minn.)
  USE Saint Anthony Falls (Minn.)
Falls of St. Anthony (Minn.)
  USE Saint Anthony Falls (Minn.)
Falmouth (Me.). Ledgewood
  USE Ledgewood (Falmouth, Me.)
Falon family
  USE Fallon family
Falsa demonstratio
  USE False demonstration (Law)
False advertising
  USE Advertising, Fraudulent
False alarms *(May Subd Geog)*
  UF Alarms, False
    Alerts, False
    False alerts
  BT Errors
    Warnings
False alerts
  USE False alarms
False asphodel
  USE Tofieldia
False Bay (Cape of Good Hope, South Africa)
  UF Valsbaai (Cape of Good Hope, South
    Africa)
  BT Bays—South Africa
False beech
  USE Nothofagus
False bird-of-paradise plants
  USE Heliconia
False birds of paradise (Plants)
  USE Heliconia
False brinelling
  USE Fretting corrosion
False calamus
  USE Iris pseudacorus
False certification *(May Subd Geog)*
  UF Certification, False
  BT Forgery
    Fraud
    Legal documents
    Misconduct in office
False chinch bug
  UF Nysius ericae
  BT Chinch-bugs
False click beetles
  USE Eucnemidae
False codling moth
  USE Cryptophlebia leucotreta
False Creek (B.C.) *(Not Subd Geog)*
  BT Inlets—British Columbia
False cypress
  USE Chamaecyparis
False demonstration (Law)
  (May Subd Geog)
  UF Demonstration, False (Law)
    Falsa demonstratio
  BT Mistake (Law)
False friends (Lexicology)
  USE Paronyms
False imprisonment *(May Subd Geog)*
  UF Abuse of process
    Imprisonment, False
    Wrongful imprisonment

  BT Imprisonment
    Malicious prosecution
    Offenses against the person
    Torts
  NT Trials (False imprisonment)
False killer whale
  UF Killer whale, False
    Pseudorca
  BT Whales
False Messiahs
  USE Pseudo-Messiahs
False morays
  USE Xenocongridae
False neptis
  USE Archimestra teleboas
False personation *(May Subd Geog)*
  UF Impersonation (Law)
  BT Fraud
    Impersonation
  NT Impersonating an officer
False saffron
  USE Safflower
False spider mites
  [QL458.2.T36]
  UF Phytoptipalpidae
    Pseudoleptidae
    Spider mites, False
    Tenuipalpidae
  BT Mites
  NT Brevipalpus
    Macfarlaniella
False swearing
  USE Perjury
False teeth
  USE Dentures
False testimony *(May Subd Geog)*
  UF False witness
  BT Criminal law
    Witnesses
  RT Perjury
False testimony (Canon law)
False testimony (Greek law)
False white rainbow
  USE Fogbow
False wireworm
  [SB945.F]
False witness
  USE False testimony
Falsecypress
  USE Chamaecyparis
Falsehood
  USE Truthfulness and falsehood
Falsom family
  USE Folsom family
Falster (Denmark)
  BT Islands—Denmark
Falt family
Falven language
  USE Kipchak language
Fama publica
  USE Reputation (Law)
Fame
  UF Celebrity
    Renown
  RT Glory
  — **Religious aspects**
  — — **Buddhism,** [**Christianity, etc.**]
Fame, Halls of
  USE Halls of fame
Familia (Painting)
  USE Velázquez, Diego, 1599-1660. Maids
    of honor
Familia di Dario (Painting)
  USE Veronese, 1528-1588. Family of
    Darius before Alexander
Familial behavior in animals
  [QL761.5]
  UF Kinship behavior in animals
  BT Animal behavior
  NT Animals—Infancy
    Infanticide in animals

    Kin recognition in animals
    Kin selection (Evolution)
    Parental behavior in animals
Familial diseases *(May Subd Geog)*
  UF Diseases in families
  BT Diseases
  NT Adenomatosis, Familial endocrine
    Diseases in twins
    Hypophosphatemia, Familial
Familial dysautonomia
  USE Dysautonomia
Familial endocrine adenomatosis
  USE Adenomatosis, Familial endocrine
Familial hypophosphatemia
  USE Hypophosphatemia, Familial
Familial Mediterranean fever
  USE Periodic peritonitis
Familial splenic anemia
  USE Gaucher's disease
Families
  USE Family
Families, Afro-American
  USE Afro-American families
Families, Asian American
  USE Asian American families
Families, Black
  USE Black families
Families, Cuban American
  USE Cuban American families
Families, Dual-career
  USE Dual-career families
Families, Exponential (Statistics)
  USE Exponential families (Statistics)
Families, Hispanic American
  USE Hispanic American families
Families, Italian American
  USE Italian American families
Families, Japanese American
  USE Japanese American families
Families, Jewish
  USE Jewish families
Families, Mexican American
  USE Mexican American families
Families, Polish American
  USE Polish American families
Families, Puerto Rican
  USE Puerto Rican families
Families, Vietnamese American
  USE Vietnamese American families
Families and libraries
  USE Libraries and families
Families of military personnel
  USE Children of military personnel
    Military dependents
    Missing in action—Family
      relationships
    Prisoners of war—Family relationships
    Soldiers—Family relationships
Families of prisoners of war
  USE Prisoners of war—Family relationships
Families of royal descent
  USE Royal descent, Families of
Families of servicemen missing in action
  USE Missing in action—Family
      relationships
Families of the mentally ill
  USE Mentally ill—Family relationships
Families with problems
  USE Problem families
Familists *(May Subd Geog)*
  [BX7575]
  UF Family of Love (Religious sect)
Famille Bellelli (Portrait)
  USE Degas, Edgar, 1834-1917. Bellelli
    family
Famille rose porcelain *(May Subd Geog)*
  UF Porcelain, Famille rose
  BT China trade porcelain
  — **19th century** *(May Subd Geog)*

Famille Woolsey (Conversation piece)
    USE Berczy, William, 1748-1813.   Woolsey
        family
Family   *(May Subd Geog)*
    ⌐*GN480 (Primitive)*¬
    ⌐*GT2420 (Manners and customs)*¬
    ⌐*HQ (Sociology)*¬
    UF Families
        Family relationships
    BT Sociology
    RT Adult children
        Domestic relations
        Family reunions
        Home
        Households
        Kinship
        Marriage
        Matriarchy
        Patriarchy
    SA *subdivision* Family *under names of*
        individual persons; also subdivision
        Biography—Family *under names of*
        individual literary authors, e.g.
        Shakespeare, William, 1564-1616—
        Biography—Family; *and subdivision*
        Family relationships *under classes*
        of persons
    NT Aunts
        Birth order
        Black families
        Broken homes
        Brothers and sisters
        Children
        Church work with families
        Clans
        Communication in the family
        Computers and family
        Daughters-in-law
        Divorce
        Double bind (Psychology)
        Draw-a-family test
        Dual-career families
        Family life surveys
        Family size
        Fathers
        Fathers-in-law
        Grandparent and child
        Grandparents
        Heads of households
        Heredity, Human
        Host families of foreign students
        Jewish families
        Joint family
        Kinetic family drawing test
        Libraries and families
        Master and servant
        Mentally ill—Family relationships
        Mothers
        Mothers-in-law
        Nieces
        Only child
        Parent and child
        Parenthood
        Parents
        Parents-in-law
        Presidents—Family
        Problem families
        Puerto Rican families
        Rural families
        Single-parent family
        Stepfamilies
        Tribes
        Twins
        Unmarried couples
        Widowers
        Widows
        Work and family
        Youngest child
— **Biblical teaching**
    ⌐*BS680.F3*¬
    NT Fathers in the Bible

— **Effect of strikes and lockouts on**
    (May Subd Geog)
    BT Strikes and lockouts
— **Folklore**
    UF Family customs
        Family lore
    NT Family festivals
— **Health and hygiene**   *(May Subd Geog)*
    ⌐*RA418.5.F3 (Social medicine)*¬
    ⌐*RA777.7 (Personal health)*¬
    UF Family health
    BT Social medicine
    RT Family medicine
    SA *subdivision* Family relationships
        under classes of ill or
        handicapped persons, e.g.
        Critically ill—Family
        relationships
    NT Family psychotherapy
— **Koranic teaching**
    ⌐*BP134.F25*¬
— Law
    USE Domestic relations
— **Longitudinal studies**
— **Mental health**   *(May Subd Geog)*
    ⌐*RC455.4.F3*¬
— Photography
    USE Photography of families
— **Prayer-books and devotions**
    ⌐*BV255-BV259*¬
    ⌐*BX2170.F3 (Catholic)*¬
    Here are entered prayer-books and devotion-
al exercises intended for family worship. For any
denominational aspect duplicate entry is made
under the name of the denomination, with sub-
division Prayer-books and devotions, e.g. Cath-
olic Church—Prayer-books and devotions.
— — **English,** ⌐**French, German, etc.**¬
— Recreation
    USE Family recreation
— **Religious life**
    ⌐*BV4526*¬
    UF Family worship
    NT Family home evenings (Mormon
        Church)
— — **Sermons**
— — **Outlines**
    ⌐*BV4526*¬
— **Religious life (Buddhism)**
— **Religious life (Hinduism)**
    ⌐*BL1228.3.F3*¬
— **Religious life (Islam)**
    ⌐*BP188.3.F3*¬
— **Religious life (Jainism)**
    ⌐*BL1375.F35*¬
— **Religious life (Judaism)**
    BT Jewish way of life
— **Research**   *(May Subd Geog)*
    UF Family research
    NT Family demography
— **Study and teaching**   *(May Subd Geog)*
    NT Family life education
— **Taxation**   *(May Subd Geog)*
    UF Family tax unit
        Family unit, Taxation of
— — **Law and legislation**
    (May Subd Geog)
— Terminology
    USE Kinship—Terminology
— **Testing**
    NT Kvebæk family sculpture technique
— **United States**
    NT Afro-American families
        Asian American families
        Cuban American families
        Hispanic American families
        Italian American families
        Japanese American families
        Mexican American families
        Polish American families
        Vietnamese American families

Family, Holy
    USE Jesus Christ—Family
Family, Patriarchal
    USE Patriarchy
Family allowances   *(May Subd Geog)*
    ⌐*HD4925 (Wages and social insurance)*¬
    ⌐*HV697-HV700.7 (Social welfare)*¬
    UF Allowances, Family
        Child endowment
        Family endowment
        Family wages
    BT Cost and standard of living
        Economic security
        Mothers' pensions
        Wages
    RT Income maintenance programs
    SA *subdivison* Pay, allowances, etc. *under*
        armies, navies, etc., e.g. United
        States.   Army—Pay, allowances,
        etc.; *and subdivison* Officials and
        employees—Salaries, allowances,
        etc. *under countries, cities, etc.*
— **Law and legislation**   *(May Subd Geog)*
Family allowances (Inheritance and succession)
    USE Widow's allowance
Family and communism
    USE Communism and family
Family and computers
    USE Computers and family
Family and state
    USE Family policy
Family and television
    USE Television and family
Family and work
    USE Work and family
Family archives   *(May Subd Geog)*
    ⌐*CD*¬
    Forms and blanks for recording family data are
entered under Family records.
    UF Archives, Family
    BT Family records
    SA *subdivision* Archives *under names of*
        individual families
Family associations
    USE Genealogy—Societies, etc.
Family budgets
    USE Home economics—Accounting
Family case work
    USE Family social work
Family communication
    USE Communication in the family
Family corporations   *(May Subd Geog)*
    UF Family enterprises
    BT Close corporations
        Corporation law
Family counseling
    USE Problem families—Counseling of
Family counselors   *(May Subd Geog)*
    BT Counselors
Family courts
    USE Domestic relations courts
        Juvenile courts
Family customs
    USE Family—Folklore
Family day care   *(May Subd Geog)*
    Here are entered works on the care of children in
private homes by persons other than their parents or
guardians.
    UF Day care, Family
        Home day care
    BT Child care services
— **Law and legislation**   *(May Subd Geog)*
Family demography   *(May Subd Geog)*
    ⌐*HQ759.98*¬
    Here are entered works on the study of the deter-
minants of the number, size, and composition of fami-
lies.
    BT Demography
        Family—Research
Family drawing test
    USE Draw-a-family test
        Kinetic family drawing test

Family endowment
  USE Family allowances
Family enterprises
  USE Family corporations
Family farm operating agreements
  USE Father-son farm operating agreements
Family farms *(May Subd Geog)*
  BT Agriculture
     Farms
  RT Farms, Small
     Private plot agriculture
  — **Finance**
  — — **Law and legislation**
       (May Subd Geog)
  — **Law and legislation** *(May Subd Geog)*
     BT Agricultural laws and legislation
        Farm law
     NT Father-son farm operating
        agreements
  — **Management**
     BT Farm management
  — **Taxation** *(May Subd Geog)*
  — — **Law and legislation**
       (May Subd Geog)
Family festivals *(May Subd Geog)*
  BT Family—Folklore
     Festivals
Family fun
  USE Family recreation
Family group therapy
  USE Family psychotherapy
Family heads
  USE Heads of households
Family health
  USE Family—Health and hygiene
Family Health Maintenance Demonstration
  BT Family medicine—New York (State)
     Health care teams—New York (State)
     Health maintenance organizations—
        New York (State)
Family histories
  USE *subdivision* Genealogy *under countries,
     cities, etc.; and names of individual
     families, e.g.* Lincoln family
Family history
  USE Genealogy
Family home evenings (Mormon Church)
  [BX8643.F3]
  UF Home evenings (Mormon Church)
  BT Family—Religious life
     Family recreation
     Mormon Church
Family in art
  [N8217.F27]
Family in literature
  BT Marriage in literature
Family in mass media *(May Subd Geog)*
  BT Mass media
Family in motion pictures
  BT Moving-pictures
Family in television programs
  USE Television and family
Family in textbooks *(May Subd Geog)*
  BT Text-books
Family in the press
  BT Journalism
     Press
Family law
  USE Domestic relations
Family life education *(May Subd Geog)*
  BT Family—Study and teaching
  NT Home economics
     Parenting—Study and teaching
     Sex instruction

Family life surveys *(May Subd Geog)*
  Here are entered works on the methods and techniques employed, and reports of individual surveys. For the latter the heading may be subdivided by place; in such cases a subject entry is also made under the heading Family—[local subdivision], e.g. 1. Family—United States. 2. Family life surveys—United States. For family life surveys on a special topic the additional subject entry is made under the special topic, e.g. 1. Birth control—United States. 2. Family life surveys—United States.
  BT Family
     Home
     Social surveys
Family lore
  USE Family—Folklore
Family maintenance
  USE Decedents' family maintenance
Family mediation *(May Subd Geog)*
  UF Mediation, Family
  BT Mediation
  NT Divorce mediation
Family medicine *(May Subd Geog)*
  UF Family practice (Medicine)
     General practice (Medicine)
  BT Medicine
  RT Family—Health and hygiene
     Physicians (General practice)
  — **Study and teaching** *(May Subd Geog)*
  — **New York (State)**
     NT Family Health Maintenance
        Demonstration
Family names
  USE Names, Personal
Family of Darius before Alexander (Painting)
  USE Veronese, 1528-1588. Family of
        Darius before Alexander
Family of Love (Religious sect)
  USE Familists
Family of Saltimbanques (Painting)
  USE Picasso, Pablo, 1881-1973. Family of
        Saltimbanques
Family planning
  USE Birth control
Family planning, Natural
  USE Natural family planning
Family planning services
  USE Birth control clinics
Family policy *(May Subd Geog)*
  Here are entered general works on government policies related to the family, e.g. child welfare, family counseling, family planning, income maintenance, tax benefits, housing, etc.
  UF Family and state
     State and family
  BT Public welfare
     Social security
  RT Social policy
  NT Child welfare
     Family social work
     Housing policy
Family practice (Medicine)
  USE Family medicine
Family provision
  USE Legitime
Family psychotherapy *(May Subd Geog)*
  UF Family group therapy
     Family therapy
  BT Family—Health and hygiene
     Group psychotherapy
     Marriage counseling
  RT Mentally ill—Family relationships
     Problem families
  NT Contextual therapy
     Divorce therapy
     Family therapists
     Kvebæk family sculpture technique
     Marital psychotherapy
     Structural-strategic family
        psychotherapy
Family records
  [CS24]

NT Family archives
Family recreation *(May Subd Geog)*
  [GV182.8]
  UF Family—Recreation
     Family fun
  BT Amusements
     Games
     Recreation
  NT Family home evenings (Mormon
     Church)
Family relationships
  USE Family
Family research
  USE Family—Research
Family reunions *(May Subd Geog)*
  UF Reunions, Family
  RT Family
Family rooms
  USE Recreation rooms
Family size *(May Subd Geog)*
  BT Family
  RT Birth control
  NT Birth intervals
     Childlessness
  — **Religious aspects**
  — — **Baptists, [Catholic Church, etc.]**
Family social work *(May Subd Geog)*
  UF Family case work
     Social work with families
  BT Family policy
     Social case work
Family tax unit
  USE Family—Taxation
Family therapists *(May Subd Geog)*
  [RC488.5]
  UF Therapists, Family
  BT Family psychotherapy
     Psychotherapists
  — **Supervision of**
     UF Supervision of family therapists
Family therapy
  USE Family psychotherapy
Family trees
  USE Genealogy
Family unit, Taxation of
  USE Family—Taxation
Family violence *(May Subd Geog)*
  [HQ809-HQ809.3 (Sociology)]
  [RC569.5.F3 (Psychiatry)]
  UF Domestic violence
     Household violence
     Intrafamily violence
  BT Violence
  NT Abused parents
     Child abuse
     Conjugal violence
  — **Cross-cultural studies**
  — **Law and legislation** *(May Subd Geog)*
     BT Domestic relations—Criminal
        provisions
  — **Religious aspects**
  — — **Buddhism, [Christianity, etc.]**
Family wages
  USE Family allowances
Family worship
  USE Family—Religious life
Famine compact, 1765
  [HC275]
Famine victims
  USE Victims of famine
Famines *(May Subd Geog)*
  [HC79.F3 (Economic history)]
  [HV630-HV635 (Famine relief)]
  BT Food supply
     Starvation
Famous Amos Site (Tex.) *(Not Subd Geog)*
  BT Texas—Antiquities
Famous people
  USE Celebrities
Famous people, Halls of
  USE Halls of fame

Famous people, Voices of
  USE Voices of famous people
Famous problems (in geometry)
  USE Geometry—Problems, Famous
FAMULUS (Information retrieval system)
  BT Information storage and retrieval
        systems
Fan (Cameroon people)
  USE Fe'fe' (Cameroon people)
Fan (West African people)
  USE Fang (West African people)
Fan-chiang family
Fan-in-wing aircraft
  BT Airplanes
        Airplanes—Wings
        Lift fans
  NT Short take-off and landing aircraft
        Vertically rising aircraft
Fan language (Bamileke)
  USE Fe'fe' language
Fan language (Bantu)
  USE Fang language
Fan magazines
  USE Moving-pictures—Periodicals
Fan painting (May Subd Geog)
  UF Fan paintings
  BT Fans
        Painting
  — **18th century** (May Subd Geog)
  — **20th century** (May Subd Geog)
Fan painting, Austrian (May Subd Geog)
  UF Austrian fan painting
Fan painting, Chinese
  NT Ch'a hua hu tieh t'u (Fan painting)
        Lin, Ch'un, 12th/13th cent. Bird on
          snowy plum blossoms and bamboo
        Wu, Ping. Bulbul on a bamboo
          branch
  — **Ming-Ch'ing dynasties, 1368-1912**
        ⌈ND1043.5⌉
  — **20th century**
        ⌈ND1045⌉
Fan painting, Italian (May Subd Geog)
  UF Italian fan painting
Fan painting, Japanese
  NT Semmen Hokekyō (Painting)
  — **Edo period, 1600-1868**
Fan painting, Japanese, ⌈etc.⌉
Fan paintings
  USE Fan painting
Fan palm, Miniature
  USE Rhapis excelsa
Fan-shaped Lotus Sūtra
  USE Semmen Hokekyō (Painting)
Fan vaulting (Architecture)
  (May Subd Geog)
  UF Fan vaults (Architecture)
  BT Architecture, Gothic
        Vaults (Architecture), Gothic
Fan vaults (Architecture)
  USE Fan vaulting (Architecture)
Fanagalo
  USE Fanakalo
Fanakalo
        ⌈PM7895.F3⌉
  UF Basic Bantu language
        Fanagalo
        Fanekalo
        Isi-Lololo
        Isi-Piki
        Kitchen Kaffir
        Pidgin Kaffir
  BT Lingua francas
        Xhosa language
Fanariots
  USE Phanariots
Fanaticism
        ⌈BF575.F16 (Psychology)⌉
        ⌈BR114 (Religion)⌉
  UF Intolerance
  BT Enthusiasm

Fancher family
  UF Fansher family
        Fincher family
Fancy dress
  USE Costume
Fancy riding
  USE Trick riding
Fancy work
        ⌈TT740-897⌉
  BT Decoration and ornament
        Sewing
  RT Needlework
        Textile crafts
  NT Appliqué
        Artificial flowers
        Beadwork
        Crocheting
        Drawn-work
        Embroidery
        Hooking
        Knitting
        Lace and lace making
        Netting
        Patchwork
        Pressed flower pictures
        Quilting
        White work embroidery
Fandango Wilderness (Nev.)
  UF Fandango Wilderness Study Area
        (Nev.)
  BT National parks and reserves—Nevada
        Wilderness areas—Nevada
Fandango Wilderness Study Area (Nev.)
  USE Fandango Wilderness (Nev.)
Fandangos
  BT Dance music
Fanders family
  USE Flanders family
Fane family
  USE Fain family
Fanekalo
  USE Fanakalo
Fanfare for Europe Festival
Fanfares
        ⌈M1270⌉
  BT Band music
        Brass band music
        Military music
  RT Military calls
        Trumpet-calls
  NT Bugle-calls
Fang (Cameroon people)
  USE Fe'fe' (Cameroon people)
Fang (West African people)
  UF Fan (West African people)
        Mpangwe (West African people)
        Pahouin (West African people)
        Pahuin (West African people)
        Pamue (West African people)
        Pangwe (West African people)
  BT Ethnology—Africa, West
Fang (West African people) architecture
  USE Architecture, Fang (West African
        people)
Fang (West African people) art
  USE Art, Fang (West African people)
Fang (West African people) arts
  USE Arts, Fang (West African people)
Fang ballads
  USE Ballads, Fang
Fang language
        ⌈PL8167.F3⌉
  UF Fan language (Bantu)
        Fanwe language (Bantu)
        Pahouin language
        Pamue language
        Pangwe language
  BT Cameroon—Languages
        Equatorial Guinea—Languages
        Gabon—Languages
        Yaunde-Fang languages

Fang languages
  USE Yaunde-Fang languages
Fang poetry (May Subd Geog)
Fang songs
  USE Songs, Fang
Faniani family
Fankhauser family
  USE Funkhouser family
Fannia (May Subd Geog)
        ⌈QL537.M8⌉
  BT Muscidae
Fannin family
  USE Fanning family
Fanning family
  UF Fannin family
Fanning-mills
        ⌈S699⌉
  UF Winnowing-machines
  BT Agricultural machinery
        Air classifiers
        Threshing machines
Fanorona
        ⌈GV1469.F34⌉
Fans (May Subd Geog)
        ⌈GT2150 (Manners and customs)⌉
        ⌈NK4870 (Art)⌉
  BT Costume
  NT Fan painting
        Flabella
Fans, Electric
  USE Fans (Machinery)
Fans, Lift
  USE Lift fans
Fans, Mechanical
  USE Fans (Machinery)
Fans, Soccer
  USE Soccer—Fans
Fans, Submarine
  USE Submarine fans
Fans (Machinery)
  UF Blowers
        Blowing-engines
        Exhausters
        Fans, Electric
        Fans, Mechanical
  BT Exhaust systems
        Heating
        Pneumatic-tube transportation
        Ventilation
  NT Ceiling fans
        Ducted fans
        Lift fans
        Punkas
  — Appraisal
        USE Fans (Machinery)—Valuation
  — **Performance**
  — **Valuation**
        UF Fans (Machinery)—Appraisal
Fans (Persons) (May Subd Geog)
  UF Aficionados
        Devotees
        Enthusiasts (Fans)
  BT Persons
  NT Rock music—Fans
        Soccer—Fans
        Sports spectators
Fans in art
Fanshaw family
  USE Fanshawe family
Fanshawe family
  UF Fanshaw family
Fansher family
  USE Fancher family
Fantasia
        ⌈ML448⌉
Fantastic, The (Aesthetics)
        ⌈BH301.F3⌉
  BT Aesthetics
Fantastic drama, English (May Subd Geog)
  UF English fantastic drama
  BT English drama

Fantastic fiction
UF Heroic fantasy
BT Fiction
Literature
RT Supernatural in literature
NT Ghost stories
Magic realism (Literature)
Science fiction
— Collectibles
— Women authors
Fantastic fiction, American
UF American fantastic fiction
BT American fiction
Fantastic fiction, American, ⌈English, etc.⌉
(May Subd Geog)
Fantastic fiction, Argentine
(May Subd Geog)
UF Argentine fantastic fiction
BT Argentine fiction
Fantastic fiction, Bulgarian
(May Subd Geog)
UF Bulgarian fantastic fiction
BT Bulgarian fiction
Fantastic fiction, Canadian
(May Subd Geog)
UF Canadian fantastic fiction
BT Canadian fiction
Fantastic fiction, Chinese (May Subd Geog)
⌈PL2419.F35 (History)⌉
⌈PL2629.F35 (Collections)⌉
UF Chinese fantastic fiction
BT Chinese fiction
Fantastic fiction, Croatian (May Subd Geog)
UF Croatian fantastic fiction
BT Croatian fiction
Fantastic fiction, Dutch (May Subd Geog)
UF Dutch fantastic fiction
BT Dutch fiction
Fantastic fiction, English (May Subd Geog)
UF English fantastic fiction
BT English fiction
— Indic authors
USE Fantastic fiction, Indic (English)
Fantastic fiction, French (May Subd Geog)
UF French fantastic fiction
BT French fiction
Fantastic fiction, French-Canadian
(May Subd Geog)
UF French-Canadian fantastic fiction
BT French-Canadian fiction
Fantastic fiction, German (May Subd Geog)
UF German fantastic fiction
BT German fiction
Fantastic fiction, Indic (English)
(May Subd Geog)
UF Fantastic fiction, English—Indic
authors
Indic fantastic fiction (English)
BT Indic fiction (English)
Fantastic fiction, Italian (May Subd Geog)
⌈PQ4181.F36⌉
UF Italian fantastic fiction
BT Italian fiction
Fantastic fiction, Japanese
(May Subd Geog)
UF Japanese fantastic fiction
BT Japanese fiction
Fantastic fiction, Latin American
(May Subd Geog)
UF Latin American fantastic fiction
BT Latin American fiction
Fantastic fiction, Macedonian
(May Subd Geog)
UF Macedonian fantastic fiction
BT Macedonian fiction
Fantastic fiction, Mexican (May Subd Geog)
UF Mexican fantastic fiction
BT Mexican fiction
Fantastic fiction, Norwegian
(May Subd Geog)
UF Norwegian fantastic fiction

BT Norwegian fiction
Fantastic fiction, Panamanian
(May Subd Geog)
UF Panamanian fantastic fiction
BT Panamanian fiction
Fantastic fiction, Polish (May Subd Geog)
UF Polish fantastic fiction
BT Polish fiction
Fantastic fiction, Romanian
(May Subd Geog)
UF Romanian fantastic fiction
BT Romanian fiction
Fantastic fiction, Russian (May Subd Geog)
UF Russian fantastic fiction
BT Russian fiction
Fantastic fiction, Scottish (May Subd Geog)
UF Scottish fantastic fiction
BT Scottish fiction
Fantastic fiction, Spanish American
(May Subd Geog)
UF Spanish American fantastic fiction
BT Spanish American fiction
Fantastic fiction, Yiddish (May Subd Geog)
UF Yiddish fantastic fiction
BT Yiddish fiction
Fantastic fiction, Yugoslav
(May Subd Geog)
UF Yugoslav fantastic fiction
BT Yugoslav fiction
Fantastic films
UF Moving-pictures—Fantastic films
BT Fantasy in mass media
Feature films
RT Supernatural in moving-pictures
— Religious aspects
Fantastic literature (May Subd Geog)
BT Fantasy in mass media
Literature
RT Supernatural in literature
NT Classification—Books—Fantastic
literature
— Cataloging
USE Cataloging of fantastic literature
— Subject headings
USE Subject headings—Fantastic
literature
Fantastic literature, American
(May Subd Geog)
UF American fantastic literature
BT American literature
Fantastic literature, American, ⌈French, etc.⌉
(May Subd Geog)
Fantastic literature, Bulgarian
(May Subd Geog)
UF Bulgarian fantastic literature
BT Bulgarian literature
Fantastic literature, English
(May Subd Geog)
UF English fantastic literature
BT English literature
Fantastic literature, French
(May Subd Geog)
UF French fantastic literature
BT French literature
Fantastic literature, Spanish
(May Subd Geog)
UF Spanish fantastic literature
BT Spanish literature
Fantastic poetry (May Subd Geog)
BT Poetry
Fantastic poetry, American
(May Subd Geog)
UF American fantastic poetry
BT American poetry
Fantastic poetry, American, ⌈English, etc.⌉
Fantastic poetry, English (May Subd Geog)
UF English fantastic poetry
BT English poetry
Fantastic poetry, Russian (May Subd Geog)
UF Russian fantastic poetry
BT Russian poetry

Fantastic television programs
BT Fantasy in mass media
Television programs
Fantasy
⌈BF408-BF411 (Psychology)⌉
UF Day dreams
Phantasy
BT Defense mechanisms (Psychology)
Dreams
Imagination
Visions
NT Magical thinking
Sexual fantasies
— Religious aspects
— — Buddhism, ⌈Christianity, etc.⌉
— Therapeutic use
BT Psychotherapy
Fantasy football (Game)
⌈GV1202.F⌉
BT Football
Games
Fantasy games (May Subd Geog)
⌈GV1202.F35⌉
UF Fantasy role playing games
BT Games
Role playing
NT Dungeons and dragons (Game)
Heroes Unlimited (Game)
High Fantasy (Game)
Palladium (Game)
RuneQuest (Game)
Sorcery (Game)
Traveller (Game)
— Religious aspects
— — Buddhism, ⌈Christianity, etc.⌉
Fantasy in art
RT Dadaism
Surrealism
Fantasy in children
⌈BF723.F28⌉
BT Child psychology
NT Imaginary conversations in children
Fantasy in literature
Fantasy in mass media (May Subd Geog)
⌈P96.F36⌉
BT Mass media
NT Fantastic films
Fantastic literature
Fantastic television programs
Fantasy role playing games
USE Fantasy games
Fante language
USE Fanti language
Fanti language
⌈PL8167.F4⌉
UF Fante language
Fantsi language
BT Akan language
— Phonetic transcriptions
Fanti poetry (May Subd Geog)
Fantig dialect
USE Lonwolwol dialect
Fantin-Latour family
Fanting dialect
USE Lonwolwol dialect
Fantis
⌈DT511⌉
⌈GN655.F⌉
BT Ethnology—Ghana
RT Akans (African people)
— Medicine
⌈DT510.42⌉
BT Medicine, Primitive
Fantoni family
Fantsi language
USE Fanti language
Fanwe language (Bamileke)
USE Fe'fe' language
Fanwe language (Bantu)
USE Fang language

1311

Fanzines
    BT Little magazines
Faolite
    BT Corrosion and anti-corrosives
FAP (Computer program language)
    UF Fortran assembly program (Computer
            program language)
    BT FORTRAN (Computer program
            language)
Faqirs
    USE Fakirs
Far, Poblado del, Site (Spain)
    USE Turó del Vent Site (Spain)
Far East
    USE East Asia
Far East, Soviet (R.S.F.S.R.)
    USE Soviet Far East (R.S.F.S.R.)
Far Eastern porcelain
    USE Porcelain, East Asian
Far Eastern pottery
    USE Pottery, East Asian
Far Eastern question
    USE Eastern question (Far East)
Far Eastern Textile Group
    USE Yüan tung fang chih Group
Far family
    USE Farr family
Far infrared lasers
    UF Far infrared masers
    BT Infrared sources
            Lasers
Far infrared masers
    USE Far infrared lasers
Far South Egans Wilderness (Nev.)
    UF Far South Egans Wilderness Study
            Area (Nev.)
    BT National parks and reserves—Nevada
            Wilderness areas—Nevada
Far South Egans Wilderness Study Area (Nev.)
    USE Far South Egans Wilderness (Nev.)
Far ultraviolet spectroscopy
    USE Vacuum ultraviolet spectroscopy
Far West (U.S.)
    USE West (U.S.)
Farad
    USE Electric units
Faraday effect
    BT Magneto-optics
            Voigt effect
Faradization
    USE Electrotherapeutics
Fâr‘ah, Tell el-
    USE Fāri‘ah, Tall al-
Farakka Barrage (India)
    USE Farakka Dam (India)
Farakka Dam (India)   *(Not Subd Geog)*
    UF Farakka Barrage (India)
    BT Dams—India
Faral family
    USE Farrell family
Farallon Islands (Calif.)
    BT Islands—California
    RT Point Reyes-Farallon Islands National
            Marine Sanctuary (Calif.)
Farallonophilus
    [QL508.G77]
    BT Gryllacrididae
Farallonophilus cavernicolus
    [QL508.G77]
Faranta's Iron Theatre (New Orleans, La.)
    UF Iron Theatre (New Orleans, La.)
    BT Theaters—Louisiana
Fararanga (Cook Islands)
    USE Penrhyn Atoll (Cook Islands)
Farbentauben
    USE Color pigeons
Farber family
    RT Ferber family
Farbpyramidentest
    USE Color pyramid test

Farce
    [PN1940-PN1949]
        Here are entered works on the farce as a literary
    form. Collections of farces are entered under the
    heading Farces.
    UF Comic literature
            Literature, Comic
    BT Burlesque (Literature)
            Comedy
            Drama
    NT Comedy films
            Commedia dell'arte
            Entremés
            Sainetes
Farces
    [PN6120.F3 (Collections)]
        Here are entered collections of farces. Works on
    the farce as a literary form are entered under Farce.
    BT Drama
    SA French farces; German farces; Spanish
            farces; *and similar headings*
    NT Cuban farces
            Drolls
            French farces
            German farces
            Hindi farces
            Spanish farces
Farcy (Glanders)
    USE Glanders
Farcy (Lymphangitis)
    USE Epizootic lymphangitis
Fare, Bills of
    USE Menus
Fare (The Italian word)
    BT Italian language—Etymology
Fare family
    USE Fair family
Fareinistes
    [BX7577.F3]
    UF Bonjours, Les frères
    BT Catholic Church—France
            Christian sects—France
            Corporal punishment—Religious
                aspects—Catholic Church
            Flagellants and flagellation
            Jansenists
Farel family
    USE Farrell family
Farell family
    USE Farrell family
Farer family
    USE Farrar family
Fares, Bus
    USE Bus lines—Fares
Farewel family
    USE Farwell family
Farewell family
    USE Farwell family
Farewell sermons
    UF Sermons, Farewell
    BT Farewells
            Occasional sermons
Farewells   *(May Subd Geog)*
    UF Adieus
            Good-byes
            Goodbyes
            Leave-takings
            Leavetakings
            Partings (Farewells)
    BT Manners and customs
    RT Separation (Psychology)
    NT Farewell sermons
            Last letters before death
            Last words
Farewells in the Bible
    UF Bible—Farewell addresses
Farey sequences
    USE Series, Farey
Farey series
    USE Series, Farey

Farges Street (Lyon, France)
    USE Rue des Farges (Lyon, France)
Fargurson family
    USE Ferguson family
Fargusen family
    USE Ferguson family
Farguson family
    USE Ferguson family
Farhang (The Persian word)
    BT Persian language—Etymology
Faria family
    UF Farias family
Fāri‘ah, Tall al-
    UF Fâr‘ah, Tell el-
            Khirbat Tall al-Fāri‘ah
            Tall al-Fāri‘ah, Khirbat
            Tell el-Fâr‘ah
    BT West Bank—Antiquities
Farias family
    USE Faria family
Farinaceous products
    USE Starch
Farinati, Paolo, 1524-1606.   Story of Esther
    UF Storia di Ester (Painting)
Faringdon family
    USE Farrington family
Farington family
    USE Farrington family
Farinographs
    BT Mixing machinery
    RT Dough
Farinosae
    USE Commelinales
Faris family
    USE Farris family
Fariss family
    USE Farris family
Farlee family
    USE Farley family
Farley family
    UF Farlee family
            Farly family
Farlin Creek Wilderness (Mont.)
    (Not Subd Geog)
    UF Farlin Creek Wilderness Study Area
            (Mont.)
    BT National parks and reserves—Montana
            Wilderness areas—Montana
Farlin Creek Wilderness Study Area (Mont.)
    USE Farlin Creek Wilderness (Mont.)
Farlow family
Farly family
    USE Farley family
Farm accounting
    USE Agriculture—Accounting
Farm animal babies
    USE Domestic animals—Infancy
Farm animals
    USE Domestic animals
            Livestock
Farm buildings   *(May Subd Geog)*
    [NA8200-NA8260 (Architecture)]
    UF Architecture, Rural
            Buildings, Farm
            Rural architecture
    BT Buildings
    RT Agricultural engineering
            Livestock—Housing
    NT Barns
            Dairy barns
            Farmhouses
            Silos
            Stables
    — Conservation and restoration
        NT Farm buildings—Remodeling for
                other use
    — Contracts and specifications
        (May Subd Geog)
        BT Building—Contracts and
                specifications
    — **Heating and ventilation**

[TH7392.F]
  UF Farm buildings—Ventilation
— **Lighting**
  BT Electricity in agriculture
— **Machinery**
  USE Farm buildings—Mechanical
       equipment
— **Maintenance and repair**
  NT Farm buildings—Remodeling for
      other use
— **Mechanical equipment**
  UF Farm buildings—Machinery
      Mechanical equipment of farm
       buildings
  BT Building fittings
      Machinery
— **Remodeling for other use**
  UF Farm buildings—Renovation
      Remodeling of farm buildings for
       other use
      Renovation of farm buildings for
       other use
  BT Farm buildings—Conservation and
       restoration
      Farm buildings—Maintenance and
       repair
— **Renovation**
  USE Farm buildings—Remodeling for
       other use
— **Thermal properties**
— **Ventilation**
  USE Farm buildings—Heating and
       ventilation
— **Alberta**
  NT Chernochan Machine Shed (Alta.)
Farm corporations *(May Subd Geog)*
  UF Agricultural corporations
      Corporate farms
      Corporation farms
      Farms, Incorporated
      Incorporated farms
  BT Agricultural laws and legislation
      Corporation law
      Corporations
      Farm management
Farm credit
  USE Agricultural credit
Farm crops
  USE Crops
      Field crops
Farm design
  USE Farm layout
Farm engines
[TJ712]
  BT Agricultural machinery
      Engines
      Steam-engines
Farm equipment *(May Subd Geog)*
[S671-S760 *(Agriculture)*]
  UF Agriculture—Equipment and supplies
      Farms—Equipment and supplies
  RT Agricultural engineering
      Agricultural machinery
      Farm supplies
  SA *subdivision* Equipment and supplies
      under individual and groups of
      plants and crops and individual and
      groups of livestock, e.g. Corn—
      Equipment and supplies; Cattle—
      Equipment and supplies
  NT Agricultural implements
      Agricultural instruments
      Farm supply industries
      Gardening—Equipment and supplies
      Haying equipment
      Selling—Farm equipment
      Used farm equipment
Farm equipment operators
  USE Agricultural machinery operators
Farm families
  USE Rural families

Farm forestry
  USE Wood-lots
Farm houses
  USE Farmhouses
Farm implements
  USE Agricultural implements
Farm income *(May Subd Geog)*
  BT Agriculture—Economic aspects
      Income
  RT Agricultural prices
  NT Crop losses
— **Statistical services**
— — **Law and legislation**
     (May Subd Geog)
Farm input industries
  USE Farm supply industries
Farm laborers
  USE Agricultural laborers
Farm law *(May Subd Geog)*
    Here are entered works on farm law for the use of
farmers. General works on agricultural law and legis-
lation are entered under Agricultural laws and legisla-
tion.
  UF Law, Farm
  BT Agricultural laws and legislation
  NT Family farms—Law and legislation
Farm layout *(May Subd Geog)*
[S563]
  UF Farm design
      Farm planning
      Farms—Design
  BT Farm management
Farm life *(May Subd Geog)*
[HT421 *(Sociology)*]
[S521 *(Popular works)*]
    Here are entered popular works on farms and
works on manners and customs on farms. Theoretical
works on the social organization of rural areas are
entered under Sociology, Rural. Works on the social
conditions of rural areas are entered under Rural con-
ditions. Popular works on living in the country and
works on manners and customs in rural areas are
entered under Country life.
  UF Rural life
  BT Country life
  NT Farm life in literature
      Home economics, Rural
— Sounds
    USE Farm sounds
Farm life in art
[N8217.F3]
Farm life in literature
  BT Country life in literature
      Farm life
      Peasants in literature
Farm life in moving-pictures
  BT Moving-pictures
Farm life in the Bible
  UF Bible—Farm life
Farm machinery
  USE Agricultural machinery
Farm management *(May Subd Geog)*
[S560-575]
  UF Farm organization
  BT Agriculture
      Agriculture—Economic aspects
      Farmers
      Farms
      Land tenure
      Management
  RT Agricultural systems
  NT Agricultural productivity
      Agriculture—Accounting
      Agriculture—Custom rates
      Agriculture—Safety measures
      Collective farms—Management
      Family farms—Management
      Farm corporations
      Farm layout
      Farm mechanization
      Farm risks
      Farms, Size of

      State farms—Management
— **Decision making**
[S560-562]
— **Linear programming**
[S566.7]
— **Mathematical models**
  UF Agricultural production functions
      Production functions, Agricultural
— **Records and correspondence**
  UF Farm records
Farm managers *(May Subd Geog)*
  UF Managers, Farm
  BT Agriculturists
Farm manure *(May Subd Geog)*
[S655]
  UF Barnyard manure
      Farm waste
      Farmyard manure
  BT Agricultural wastes
      Animal waste
      Manures
      Organic fertilizers
      Organic wastes as fertilizer
  SA *subdivision* Manure *under names of*
      particular animals, e.g. Cattle—
      Manure; Poultry—Manure
  NT Biogas
      Manure gases
      Manure handling
Farm manure, Liquid *(May Subd Geog)*
  UF Liquid farm manure
  BT Liquid fertilizers
— **Odor control**
  BT Odor control
Farm manure as feed
  BT Animal waste as feed
Farm mechanics
  USE Agricultural mechanics
Farm mechanization *(May Subd Geog)*
  UF Agricultural mechanization
      Mechanization, Agricultural
      Mechanization in agriculture
      Mechanized farming
      Power farming
  BT Agricultural machinery
      Farm management
      Machinery in industry
  NT Electricity in agriculture
Farm mechanization, Cooperative
  (May Subd Geog)
  BT Agriculture, Cooperative
  NT Machine-tractor stations
— **Law and legislation** *(May Subd Geog)*
  BT Agricultural laws and legislation
Farm museums
  USE Agricultural museums
Farm operating agreements, Father and son
  USE Father-son farm operating agreements
Farm organization
  USE Farm management
Farm ownership *(May Subd Geog)*
  BT Farms
      Home ownership
      Land tenure
  NT Farm partnership
Farm partnership *(May Subd Geog)*
  BT Farm ownership
      Partnership
Farm planning
  USE Farm layout
Farm ponds *(May Subd Geog)*
  UF Ponds, Farm
  BT Ponds
Farm population
  USE Rural population
Farm produce *(May Subd Geog)*
[HD9000-HD9019 *(Economics)*]
[S-SB *(Agriculture)*]
  UF Agricultural commodities
      Agricultural products
      Produce

Farm produce *(Continued)*
  BT Agriculture
      Food
      Raw materials
  RT Food industry and trade
      Plant products
      Produce trade
  NT Crops
      Horticultural products
      Surplus agricultural commodities
  — Advertising
      USE Advertising—Farm produce
  — **Grading**
      NT Vegetables—Grading
  — **Handling**
      ⌐S571┐
      BT Materials handling
  — **Marketing**
      ⌐HD9000.6 (Economics)┐
      ⌐HD9006┐
      ⌐S571┐
      UF Agricultural marketing
          Food trade
          Marketing of farm produce
      BT Agricultural prices
          Agriculture—Economic aspects
          Prices
      RT Vegetable trade
      SA *subdivision* Marketing *under*
          specific commodities, e.g. Eggs
           —Marketing; Peach—Marketing
      NT Cooperative marketing of farm
          produce
          Corn—Marketing
          Dairy products—Marketing
          Fiars prices
          Livestock—Marketing
          Pick your own farms
          Roadside marketing
          Vegetables—Marketing
  — — **Law and legislation**
      (May Subd Geog)
  — **Mechanical properties**
      ⌐S589┐
      UF Mechanical properties of farm
          produce
      BT Biomechanics
  — Precooling
      USE Precooling
  — Processing
      USE Agricultural processing
  — **Quality**
      UF Farm produce quality
  — Quality control
      USE Agricultural processing—Quality
          control
          Agriculture—Quality control
  — **Storage**
      ⌐HD9000.9 (Economics)┐
      ⌐SB129┐
      UF Stored products
      RT Cold storage
          Food—Storage
      SA *subdivision* Preservation *under*
          food products, e.g. Butter—
          Preservation; Eggs—
          Preservation; *and subdivision*
          Storage *under specific*
          commodities, e.g. Beans—
          Storage
      NT Grain—Storage
          Vegetables—Storage
  — — **Diseases and injuries**
      (May Subd Geog)
      UF Storage and transportation
          diseases and injuries
      BT Agricultural pests
          Plants—Wounds and injuries
      NT Citrus fruits—Storage—Diseases
          and injuries
          Food storage pests

          Grain—Storage—Diseases and
          injuries
          Vegetables—Storage—Diseases
          and injuries
  — Surpluses
      USE Surplus agricultural commodities
  — Tariff
      USE Tariff on farm produce
  — **Taxation** *(May Subd Geog)*
      ⌐HD9000.8-9019┐
      BT Agriculture—Taxation
  — **Thermal properties**
  — **Transportation**
      ⌐S571┐
      RT Plant quarantine
      NT Fruit—Transportation
          Poultry—Transportation
          Sugar beet—Transportation
          Vegetables—Transportation
  — — **Diseases and injuries**
      UF Storage and transportation
          diseases and injuries
      BT Agricultural pests
          Fungi in agriculture
          Plants—Wounds and injuries
Farm produce quality
  USE Farm produce—Quality
Farm production quotas *(May Subd Geog)*
  UF Agricultural production quotas
      Cropland adjustment program
  BT Agricultural administration
      Agricultural laws and legislation
      Agriculture and state
  RT Acreage allotments
Farm records
  USE Farm management—Records and
      correspondence
Farm rents *(May Subd Geog)*
  UF Rent, Farm
  BT Agriculture—Economic aspects
      Farm tenancy
      Farms
      Rent
Farm risks *(May Subd Geog)*
  UF Risks, Farm
  BT Agriculture
      Farm management
      Insurance, Agricultural
Farm River (Conn.)
  BT Rivers—Connecticut
Farm roads *(May Subd Geog)*
  ⌐TE229.2┐
  UF Roads, Farm
  BT Agricultural engineering
      Private roads
      Rural roads
  — **Law and legislation** *(May Subd Geog)*
Farm shops *(May Subd Geog)*
  ⌐S676┐
  UF Farm workshops
  BT Machine-shops
      Workshops
  NT Agricultural machinery—Maintenance
      and repair
  — **Electric equipment**
      ⌐TK4018┐
      BT Electricity in agriculture
Farm size
  USE Farms, Size of
Farm sounds
  UF Farm life—Sounds
      Farms—Sounds
  BT Country sounds
      Sounds
Farm Strike, United States, 1977-1978
  USE Farmers' Strike, United States, 1977-
      1978
Farm subsidies
  USE Agricultural subsidies

Farm supplies *(May Subd Geog)*
  UF Agricultural supplies
      Agriculture—Equipment and supplies
      Farms—Equipment and supplies
  RT Farm equipment
      Farm supply industries
  SA *subdivision* Equipment and supplies
      under individual and groups of
      plants and crops and individual and
      groups of livestock, e.g. Corn—
      Equipment and supplies; Cattle—
      Equipment and supplies
  NT Agricultural chemicals
      Explosives in agriculture
      Feeds
      Plastics in agriculture
Farm supply industries *(May Subd Geog)*
  ⌐HD9475┐
  UF Farm input industries
  BT Agricultural industries
      Farm equipment
  RT Farm supplies
  SA *specific farm supply industries, e.g.*
      Agricultural machinery industry;
      Fertilizer industry
  NT Agricultural machinery
Farm surpluses
  USE Surplus agricultural commodities
Farm tenancy *(May Subd Geog)*
  UF Leases, Usufructuary
      Tenant farming
      Usufructuary leases
  BT Contracts, Agricultural
      Farms
      Land tenure—Law and legislation
  RT Landlord and tenant
  NT Crofters
      Farm rents
      Métayer system
  — **Economic aspects** *(May Subd Geog)*
      ⌐HD1511┐
      BT Agriculture—Economic aspects
          Land tenure
  — — **United States**
      NT Share-cropping
Farm tenancy (Greek law)
Farm tenancy (Islamic law)
Farm tenancy (Roman law)
  BT Roman law
Farm tools
  USE Agricultural implements
Farm tractors *(May Subd Geog)*
  ⌐S711-S713 (Agriculture)┐
  ⌐TL233-TL233.5 (Manufacture)┐
  UF Agricultural tractors
  BT Agricultural machinery
      Tractors
  NT Used farm tractors
Farm tractors, Used
  USE Used farm tractors
Farm trailers
  BT Agricultural machinery
      Trailers
Farm waste
  USE Animal waste
      Farm manure
Farm wives
  USE Farmers' wives
Farm women
  USE Women in agriculture
Farm wood-lots
  USE Wood-lots
Farm woodlands
  USE Wood-lots
Farm workers
  USE Agricultural laborers
Farm workshops
  USE Farm shops
Farm youth exchange project, International
  USE International farm youth exchange
      project

Farmar family
  USE Farmer family
Farmer family
  UF Farmar family
      Farmor family
Farmers *(May Subd Geog)*
  UF Planters (Persons)
  BT Agriculture
      Agriculturists
      Rural population
  NT Agriculture—Vocational guidance
      Beekeepers
      Cocoa farmers
      Coconut farmers
      Cotton farmers
      Dairy farmers
      Ex-farmers
      Farm management
      Farmers, Part-time
      Goat ranchers
      Minority farmers
      Pesticide applicators (Persons)
      Potato growers
      Ranchers
      Rice farmers
      Sheep ranchers
      Suitcase farming
      Tobacco farmers
      Wheat farmers
      Women farmers
  — Economic conditions
      UF Farmers—Socioeconomic status
  — Education
  — — India
      NT Farmers Training and
          Functional Literacy Project
  — Nutrition
      ₍TX361.F₎
  — Pensions *(May Subd Geog)*
      NT Collective farms—Pensions
  — Political activity
      BT Politics, Practical
  — Prayer-books and devotions
  — — English, ₍French, German, etc.₎
  — Social conditions
      UF Farmers—Socioeconomic status
  — Socioeconomic status
      USE Farmers—Economic conditions
          Farmers—Social conditions
  — Supplementary employment
  — Taxation *(May Subd Geog)*
  — — Law and legislation
      (May Subd Geog)
  — Training of *(May Subd Geog)*
  — — Law and legislation
      (May Subd Geog)
  — India
      NT Farmers Training and Functional
          Literacy Project
  — United States
      NT Chinese American farmers
          Farmers' Strike, United States,
          1977-1978
          Japanese American farmers
Farmers, Afro-American
  USE Afro-American farmers
Farmers, Arab *(May Subd Geog)*
  UF Arab farmers
Farmers, Chinese American
  USE Chinese American farmers
Farmers, Coconut
  USE Coconut farmers
Farmers, Cotton
  USE Cotton farmers
Farmers, Japanese American
  USE Japanese American farmers
Farmers, Jewish *(May Subd Geog)*
  UF Jewish farmers
      Jews as farmers
Farmers, Part-time *(May Subd Geog)*
  UF Part-time farmers

  BT Farmers
      Part-time farming
Farmers, Rice
  USE Rice farmers
Farmers as consumers *(May Subd Geog)*
  BT Consumers
Farmers' cooperatives
  USE Agricultural cooperative credit
      associations
      Agriculture, Cooperative
Farmers Functional Literacy Project
  USE Farmers Training and Functional
      Literacy Project
Farmers' institutes *(May Subd Geog)*
  UF Institutes, Farmers'
  BT Agricultural education
      Agricultural extension work
      Agriculture
Farmer's lung *(May Subd Geog)*
  ₍RC776.F33₎
  UF Harvester's lung
      Thresher's lung
  BT Agricultural laborers—Diseases
      Lungs—Diseases
Farmers' Strike, United States, 1977-1978
  UF Agricultural Strike, United States,
      1977-1978
      Agriculture Strike, United States,
      1977-1978
      Farm Strike, United States, 1977-1978
  BT Demonstrations—United States
      Farmers—United States
      United States—Rural conditions
**Farmers Training and Functional Literacy
Project**
  ₍S544.5.I₎
  UF Farmers Functional Literacy Project
      Farmers Training Programme
  BT Adult education and state—India
      Agricultural extension work—India
      Agriculture and state—India
      Farmers—Education—India
      Farmers—India
      Fundamental education—India
      Radio in agriculture—India
Farmers Training Programme
  USE Farmers Training and Functional
      Literacy Project
Farmers' wives *(May Subd Geog)*
  UF Farm wives
  BT Rural women
      Wives
      Women farmers
      Women in agriculture
  RT Ranchers' wives
Farmers' writings, Austrian, ₍etc.₎
Farmhouses *(May Subd Geog)*
  ₍NA8210 (Architecture)₎
  ₍TH4920 (Building)₎
  UF Farm houses
  BT Dwellings
      Farm buildings
  — Dating
      UF Dating of farmhouses
Farming
  USE Agriculture
Farming, Aquarium fish
  USE Aquarium fish farming
Farming, Butterfly
  USE Butterfly farming
Farming, Crocodile
  USE Crocodile farming
Farming, Dry
  USE Dry farming
Farming, Part-time
  USE Part-time farming
Farming, Snail
  USE Snail farming
Farming of taxes
  USE Taxes, Farming of

Farming on shares
  USE Métayer system
      Share-cropping
Farming systems
  USE Agricultural systems
**Farmington Mine Disaster, Farmington,
W.Va., 1968**
Farmington plan
  BT Acquisitions, Cooperative (Libraries)
      Acquisitions (Libraries)
      Book selection
      Library cooperation
**Farmington River, West Branch (Mass. and
Conn.)**
  UF West Branch Farmington River (Mass.
      and Conn.)
      West Branch of the Farmington River
      (Mass. and Conn.)
  BT Rivers—Connecticut
      Rivers—Massachusetts
Farmlands, Abandoned
  USE Farms, Abandoned
Farmor family
  USE Farmer family
Farms *(May Subd Geog)*
  ₍HD1471 (Large)₎
  ₍HD1476 (Small)₎
  ₍S560-S575₎
  BT Agriculture
      Land use, Rural
      Real property
  NT Dairy farms
      Family farms
      Farm management
      Farm ownership
      Farm rents
      Farm tenancy
      Game farms
      Haciendas
      Historic farms
      Horse farms
      Orchards
      Photography of farms
      Pick your own farms
      Plantations
      Ranches
      School farms
      Sheep ranches
      State farms
      Vineyards
  — Accounting
      USE Agriculture—Accounting
  — Design
      USE Farm layout
  — Equipment and supplies
      USE Farm equipment
          Farm supplies
  — Foreign ownership
      UF Foreign ownership of farms
      BT Alien property
          Investments, Foreign
          Land tenure
  — Location
      UF Farms, Location of
  — Photography
      USE Photography of farms
  — Recreational use *(May Subd Geog)*
      BT Agriculture—Economic aspects
          Outdoor recreation
          Tourist trade
          Vacations
      NT Dude ranches
  — Research
      RT Agriculture—Research—On-farm
  — Sounds
      USE Farm sounds
  — Taxation *(May Subd Geog)*
  — — Law and legislation
      (May Subd Geog)
  — Valuation *(May Subd Geog)*
      ₍HD1393₎

Farms
  — Valuation *(Continued)*
    UF Land valuation
        Valuation of land
  — Alabama
    NT Wadsworth Brothers Farm (Ala.)
  — Andorra
    NT Bernatenea (Andorra)
  — Australia
    NT Melbourne and Metropolitan Board
        of Works Farm (Werribee, Vic.)
  — Connecticut
    NT Caprilands Herb Farm (Coventry,
        Conn.)
  — England
    NT Rushall Farm (England)
        Surrey Docks Farm (Southwark,
        London, England)
  — Finland
    NT Liby (Saltvik, Finland)
  — France
    NT Carrière Farm (France)
  — Iceland
    NT Hlaðir (Iceland)
        Réttarholt (Iceland)
  — Indiana
    NT Merit-Tandy Farm (Switzerland
        County, Ind.)
  — Iowa
    NT Thompson Farm (Boone, Iowa)
  — Italy
    NT Agricola Cornelia (Italy)
  — Kenya
    NT I.C.I.P.E. Farm (Kenya)
        Ithe-wa-Gathoni Farm (Kenya)
        Kelelwa Farm (Kenya)
        Tatton Farm (Kenya)
  — Maryland
    NT Saint Thomas's Manor (Port
        Tobacco, Md.)
        Thornhill Farm (Md.)
  — Massachusetts
    NT Arrowhead Farm (Newburyport,
        Mass.)
  — Michigan
    NT French Farm Lake Site (Mich.)
  — Minnesota
    NT Earle Brown Farm (Brooklyn
        Center, Minn.)
  — New Zealand
    NT Waiora Farm (N.Z.)
        Waipori Farm Settlement (N.Z.)
  — North Carolina
    NT Mason Farm (Chapel Hill, N.C.)
  — Norway
    NT Bruvik gård (Bruvik, Norway)
        Kjeåsen (Norway)
        Tjøtta Gård (Norway)
  — Oregon
    NT Edenbrook Farm (Or.)
        Stauffer-Will Farmstead (Or.)
  — Pennsylvania
    NT Slateford Farm (Pa.)
  — Québec (Province)
    NT Maison Saint-Gabriel (Montréal,
        Québec)
  — Saskatchewan
    NT Early Dawn (Sask.)
        W. R. Motherwell Farmstead
        National Historic Park (Sask.)
  — Sweden
    NT Bälgsjöbodar (Sweden)
  — Vermont
    NT Shelburne Farms (Vt.)
Farms, Abandoned *(May Subd Geog)*
  [S606 (Reclamation)]
  UF Abandoned farms
      Farmlands, Abandoned
Farms, Experimental
  USE Agricultural experiment stations

Farms, Horse
  USE Horse farms
Farms, Incorporated
  USE Farm corporations
Farms, Large *(May Subd Geog)*
  [HD1471]
  UF Large farms
  BT Farms, Size of
Farms, Location of
  USE Farms—Location
Farms, Pick your own
  USE Pick your own farms
Farms, Size of *(May Subd Geog)*
  UF Farm size
      Size of farms
  BT Agriculture—Economic aspects
      Farm management
  NT Economies of scale
      Farms, Large
      Farms, Small
Farms, Small *(May Subd Geog)*
  [HD1476]
  UF Small farms
  BT Farms, Size of
  RT Family farms
  — Government policy *(May Subd Geog)*
    UF Small farm policy
        State and small farms
    BT Agriculture and state
Farms, Stud
  USE Horse farms
Farmsworth family
  USE Farnsworth family
Farmwork rates, Custom
  USE Agriculture—Custom rates
Farmyard manure
  USE Farm manure
Farnam family
  USE Farnham family
Farnborough (Hampshire). Farnborough Hill
  USE Farnborough Hill (Farnborough,
        Hampshire)
Farnborough Hill (Farnborough, Hampshire)
  UF Farnborough (Hampshire).
        Farnborough Hill
  BT Manors—England
Farnese family
Farnese Palace (Rome, Italy)
  USE Palazzo Farnese (Rome, Italy)
Farnese Theater (Parma, Italy)
  USE Teatro Farnese (Parma, Italy)
Farnham family
  UF Farnam family
      Farnum family
Farnswort family
  USE Farnsworth family
Farnsworth family
  UF Farmsworth family
      Farnswort family
      Farnworth family
      Fawnsworth family
Farnum family
  USE Farnham family
Farnworth family
  USE Farnsworth family
Farø (Denmark) *(Not Subd Geog)*
  BT Islands—Denmark
Faro
  BT Gambling
Faroese children's stories
  USE Children's stories, Faroese
Faroese dialect
  [PD2483]
  BT Old Norse language
      Scandinavian languages
  — Texts
    [PD2483]
Faroese fiction *(May Subd Geog)*
  NT Children's stories, Faroese
Faroese folk-songs
  USE Folk-songs, Faroese

Faroese literature
  [PT7581-7599]
  BT Scandinavian literature
Faroese newspapers *(May Subd Geog)*
Faroese philology
Faroese poetry
  [PT7590 (History)]
  [PT7594 (Collections)]
Faroese songs
  USE Songs, Faroese
Farohars
  USE Fravashis
Farr family
  UF Far family
Farrall family
  USE Farrell family
Farran family
  USE Farren family
Farrapos Revolution, Rio Grande do Sul,
    Brazil, 1835-1845
  USE Rio Grande do Sul (Brazil)—History—
        Revolution of the Farrapos, 1835-
        1845
Farrar family
  UF Farer family
      Farrer family
      Farrier family
      Farrior family
      Farror family
Farras family
  USE Farris family
Farrell family
  UF Fairall family
      Faral family
      Farel family
      Farell family
      Farrall family
  RT Farwell family
      Ferrell family
Farren family
  UF Farran family
      Farrin family
      Farron family
      Ferran family
      Ferren family
      Ferrin family
      Ferrins family
      Ferron family
      Pherrin family
Farrer family
  USE Farrar family
Farrier family
  USE Farrar family
Farriery
  USE Horses
      Horseshoeing
      Veterinary medicine
      Veterinary surgery
Farries family
  USE Farris family
Farrin family
  USE Farren family
Farringdon family
  USE Farrington family
Farringer family
  UF Fahringer family
Farrington family
  UF Faringdon family
      Farington family
      Farringdon family
      Ferringdon family
      Ferrington family
      Ffarington family
      Ffaryngton family
Farrior family
  USE Farrar family

Farris family
  UF Fairis family
      Fairiss family
      Faris family
      Fariss family
      Farras family
      Farries family
      Farrise family
      Farriss family
      Farrist family
      Fearis family
      Feris family
      Ferris family
      Ferrise family
      Ferriss family
      Firris family
      Phares family
      Pharis family
Farrise family
  USE Farris family
Farriss family
  USE Farris family
Farrist family
  USE Farris family
Farrokhabad, Tappeh (Iran)
  USE Farrokhabad, Tepe (Iran)
Farrokhabad, Tepe (Iran) *(Not Subd Geog)*
  [DS262.F37]
  UF Fakhrabad, Tepe (Iran)
      Farrokhabad, Tappeh (Iran)
      Farrukhabad, Tepe (Iran)
      Farukhabad, Tepe (Iran)
      Tappeh Farrokhabad (Iran)
      Tepe Fakhrabad (Iran)
      Tepe Farrokhabad (Iran)
      Tepe Farrukhabad (Iran)
      Tepe Farukhabad (Iran)
  BT Cities and towns, Ruined, extinct, etc.
        —Iran
      Iran—Antiquities
Farron family
  USE Farren family
Farror family
  USE Farrar family
Farrukhabad, Tepe (Iran)
  USE Farrokhabad, Tepe (Iran)
Farsi language
  USE Persian language
Farsightedness
  USE Hyperopia
Farster family
  USE Foster family
Farthingales
  USE Crinolines
Farting
  USE Flatulence
Farukhabad, Tepe (Iran)
  USE Farrokhabad, Tepe (Iran)
Farwell family
  UF Fairwell family
      Farewel family
      Farewell family
  RT Farrell family
FAS (Computer system)
  USE Failure Analysis System (Computer
       system)
Fas (The Latin word)
  BT Latin language—Etymology
Fasces
  BT Emblems
      Rome—Antiquities
      Rome—Officials and employees—
        Medals, badges, decorations, etc.
Fascher family
  RT Fosher family
Fascia of Gerota
  USE Gerota's fascia
Fasciae (Anatomy)
  [QM563]
  BT Connective tissues
  NT Gerota's fascia

— Inflammation
    NT Nodular fasciitis
Fasciation *(May Subd Geog)*
  [QK664]
  BT Plants—Abnormalities
Fasciculus atrioventricularis
  USE His bundle
Fasciitis, Nodular
  USE Nodular fasciitis
Fasciitis, Proliferative
  USE Nodular fasciitis
Fasciitis, Pseudosarcomatous
  USE Nodular fasciitis
Fasciola and fascioliasis
  UF Fascioliasis
      Fasciolosis
      Liver-rot
  BT Distomatosis
      Liver flukes
Fascioliasis
  USE Fasciola and fascioliasis
Fasciolosis
  USE Fasciola and fascioliasis
Fascism *(May Subd Geog)*
  [DG571 (Italy)]
  [JC481]
  UF Neo-fascism
  BT Authoritarianism
      Collectivism
  RT Corporate state
      National socialism
      Synarchism
      Totalitarianism
  NT Anti-fascist movements
      Fascist economics
      Fascists
      Propaganda, Fascist
      Trade-unions and fascism
— Biography
    USE Fascists
— Posters
    BT Political posters
— Argentina
    NT Peronism
— Brazil
    UF Integralismo
— Germany
      Here are entered works on post-World War II
      fascist and neo-Nazi movements. Works on fas-
      cism in Germany during the Nazi regime are
      entered under the heading National socialism.
    UF Neo-Nazism
    BT National socialism
— Italy
    NT Partito nazionale fascista
— — 1945-
      UF Neofascism in Italy
      BT Italy—Politics and government
          —1945-
Fascism and architecture *(May Subd Geog)*
  UF Architecture and fascism
  BT Architecture
Fascism and art
  BT Art
  NT Fascism in art
Fascism and culture *(May Subd Geog)*
  BT Culture
      Politics and culture
Fascism and education *(May Subd Geog)*
  BT Education
Fascism and literature *(May Subd Geog)*
  UF Literature and fascism
  BT Literature
Fascism and motion pictures
  (May Subd Geog)
  BT Moving-pictures
Fascism and sex *(May Subd Geog)*
  BT Fascist ethics
      Sex
Fascism and social status *(May Subd Geog)*
  BT Social status

Fascism and the Catholic Church
  (May Subd Geog)
  UF Catholic Church and fascism
  BT Catholic Church
Fascism and women *(May Subd Geog)*
  BT Women
Fascism and youth *(May Subd Geog)*
  BT Youth
Fascism in art
  BT Fascism and art
      National socialism and art
Fascist economics
  BT Economics
      Fascism
Fascist ethics
  UF Ethics, Fascist
  BT Ethics
      Social ethics
      Totalitarian ethics
  NT Fascism and sex
Fascist propaganda
  USE Propaganda, Fascist
Fascists *(May Subd Geog)*
  UF Fascism—Biography
  BT Fascism
— Germany
    NT National socialists
Faselis (Ancient city)
  USE Phaselis (Ancient city)
Fasett family
  USE Fawcett family
Fashion *(May Subd Geog)*
  [GT500-GT2370]
  [TT500-TT645]
  UF Style in dress
  RT Clothing and dress
      Costume
  NT Costume design
      Dressmaking
      Men's clothing
      Tailoring
— Advertising
    USE Advertising—Fashion
— Authorship
    USE Fashion writing
— Forecasting
    BT Forecasting
Fashion (Fad)
  USE Fads
Fashion and art
  [GT529.A7]
  UF Art and fashion
Fashion apparel, Printed
  USE Printed fashion apparel
Fashion artists
  USE Fashion illustrators
Fashion as a topic in art
  USE Fashion in art
Fashion design
  USE Costume design
Fashion design libraries
  USE Costume design libraries
Fashion designers
  USE Costume designers
Fashion dolls *(May Subd Geog)*
  [NK4894.3.F37]
  UF Ladies of fashion dolls
  BT Dolls
Fashion drawing
  [TT509]
  UF Fashion illustration
  BT Drawing
  NT Fashion illustrators
Fashion editors *(May Subd Geog)*
  UF Editors, Fashion
  BT Journalists
Fashion illustration
  USE Fashion drawing

Fashion illustrators *(May Subd Geog)*
  UF Artists, Fashion
    Fashion artists
    Illustrators, Fashion
  BT Fashion drawing
    Illustrators
Fashion in art
  UF Fashion as a topic in art
Fashion marketing
  USE Fashion merchandising
Fashion merchandising *(May Subd Geog)*
  ⌜HD9940⌝
  UF Fashion marketing
  BT Clothing trade
    Merchandising
    Retail trade
Fashion models
  USE Models, Fashion
Fashion photography *(May Subd Geog)*
  ⌜TR679⌝
  UF Photography, Fashion
  BT Photography, Advertising
Fashion shows *(May Subd Geog)*
  ⌜TT502⌝
  UF Style shows
  BT Advertising—Clothing and dress
    Clothing and dress
Fashion writing
  ⌜TT503.5⌝
  UF Fashion—Authorship
  BT Authorship
  NT Newspapers—Sections, columns, etc.—
    Fashion
Fashionable society
  USE Upper classes
Fashoda Crisis, 1898
  ⌜DT156.6⌝
  BT Sudan—History—1862-1899
Fasnacht
  USE Carnival
Fassa Valley (Italy)
  UF Val di Fassa (Italy)
  BT Valleys—Italy
Fassett family
  USE Fawcett family
Fassette family
  USE Fawcett family
Fast and Efficient Evaluation of Derivatives
    (Computer program)
  USE FEED (Computer program)
Fast attack craft
  UF Attack craft, Fast
    Craft, Fast attack
    Ships, Fast attack
  BT Warships
  NT Gunboats
    Torpedo-boats
Fast-day menus
  USE Lenten menus
Fast-day sermons
  ⌜BV4270⌝
  UF Sermons, Fast-day
  BT Fasts and feasts
    Occasional sermons
Fast days
  USE Fasts and feasts
Fast draw pistol shooting *(May Subd Geog)*
  ⌜GV1175.5⌝
  UF Quick draw pistol shooting
    Western pistol shooting
  BT Pistol shooting
Fast Flux Test Facility Program
  BT Materials testing reactors
    Nuclear facilities—Washington (State)
Fast food restaurants *(May Subd Geog)*
  BT Convenience foods
    Restaurants, lunch rooms, etc.
Fast foods
  USE Convenience foods
Fast neutrons
  BT Neutrons

— **Capture**
  ⌜QC721⌝
  BT Neutron capture gamma ray
    spectroscopy
— **Scattering**
  ⌜QC793.5.F328⌝
— **Spectra**
  ⌜QC721⌝
Fast pulsed reactors
  USE Pulsed reactors
Fast reactors
  BT Nuclear reactors
  NT Breeder reactors
    Liquid metal fast breeder reactors
Fast-response data processing
  USE Real-time data processing
Fasteners
  ⌜TJ1320-1340⌝
  UF Fastenings
  BT Joints (Engineering)
    Manufacturing processes
  RT Fasteners industry
  NT Bolts and nuts
    Brackets
    Button loops
    Buttons
    Clasps
    Hooks and eyes
    Keys and keyways (Machinery)
    Locks and keys
    Pins (Engineering)
    Retaining rings
    Rivets and riveting
    Screws
    Sealing (Technology)
    Steel straps
    Zippers
— **Tariff**
  USE Tariff on fastenings
Fasteners industry *(May Subd Geog)*
  ⌜HD9999.F3⌝
  RT Fasteners
— **Collective bargaining**
  USE Collective bargaining—Fasteners
    industry
— **Employees**
  NT Collective bargaining—Fasteners
    industry
Fastenings
  USE Fasteners
Faster reading
  USE Rapid reading
Fasti consulares
  ⌜DG202⌝
  BT Inscriptions, Latin
Fasting
  ⌜BV5055 (Asceticism)⌝
  ⌜RM226-RM228⌝
  Here are entered works on religious fasts and
feasts in general and on Christian fasts and feasts. The
heading may also by divided by religious body or
non-Christian religion, e.g. Fasts and feasts—Cath-
olic Church, ⌜Judaism, etc.⌝. For fasts and feasts of
a religious body occurring in a particular place, add
a second heading Fasts and feasts—⌜local subdivi-
sion⌝ or ⌜city⌝—Festivals, etc.
  UF Abstinence
  BT Asceticism
    Diet
    Penance
  RT Hunger
    Starvation
  NT Fasts and feasts
    Hunger strikes
— **Dispensations**
  ⌜BX2225 (Catholic eucharist)⌝
  BT Catholic Church—Discipline
    Dispensations
Fasting (Buddhism)
  BT Asceticism—Buddhism
    Buddhism
    Spiritual life (Buddhism)

Fasting (Canon law)
  ⌜BX1939.F35⌝
Fasting (Hinduism)
  ⌜BL1215.F3⌝
  BT Asceticism—Hinduism
Fasting (Islam)
  ⌜BP179⌝
  BT Asceticism—Islam
    Pillars of Islam
— **Koranic teaching**
  ⌜BP134.F3⌝
Fasting (Judaism)
  BT Asceticism—Judaism
Fastnacht
  USE Carnival
Fastnachtspiele
  USE Carnival plays
Fastness of color (Textiles)
  USE Colorfastness (Textiles)
Fastnet Yacht Race
  ⌜GV832⌝
  BT Yacht racing
Fasts and feasts *(May Subd Geog)*
  ⌜BL590 (Comparative religion)⌝
  ⌜BV30-BV135 (Christianity)⌝
  ⌜CE81 (Church calendar)⌝
  ⌜GT3930-GT4995 (Manners and
    customs)⌝
  Here are entered works on religious fasts and
feasts in general and on Christian fasts and feasts. The
heading may also be divided by religious body or non-
Christian religion, e.g. Fasts and feasts—Catholic
Church, ⌜Judaism, etc.⌝ For fasts and feasts of a
religious body occurring in a particular place, add a
second heading Fasts and feasts—⌜local subdivi-
sion⌝ or ⌜city⌝—Festivals, etc.
  UF Bible—Festivals
    Church festivals
    Ecclesiastical fasts and feasts
    Fast days
    Feasts
    Heortology
    Holy days
    Religious festivals
  BT Catholic Church
    Christian antiquities
    Days
    Fasting
    Liturgics
    Rites and ceremonies
    Theology, Practical
  RT Church calendar
    Festivals
    Holidays
    Sacred meals
  SA *subdivision* Festivals, etc. *under names
    of cities, towns, etc.; and
    subdivision* Religious life and
    customs *under names of countries,
    states, cities, etc., e.g.* Germany—
    Religious life and customs
  NT Advent
    All Saints' Day
    All Souls' Day
    Ascension Day
    Assumption of the Blessed Virgin
      Mary, Feast of the
    Boy-bishop
    Candlemas
    Christmas
    Church year
    Corpus Christi festival
    Easter
    Elijah the Prophet's Day
    Ember days
    Epiphany
    Fast-day sermons
    Festival-day sermons
    Good Friday
    Holy Innocents, Feast of the
    Holy Saturday
    Immaculate Conception, Feast of the

Jesus Christ the King, Feast of
Lent
Mary, Blessed Virgin, Saint—Feasts
Maundy Thursday
Palm Sunday
Pentecost festival
Presentation of the Blessed Virgin
    Mary, Feast of the
Quinquagesima Sunday
Rogation days
Sacred Heart, Feast of the
Sunday
Thanksgiving Day
Vigils (Liturgy)
Visitation festival
— **Buddhism**
    UF Buddhist fasts and feasts
    NT Uposatha Day
— **Catholic Church**
    NT San Gennaro Festival (New York,
          N.Y.)
— **Catholic Church,** ⌈**Church of England,**
  Presbyterian Church, etc.⌉
— **Egyptian religion**
    UF Egyptian fasts and feasts
— **Greek religion**
    UF Greek fasts and feasts
    NT Religious calendars—Greek
          religion
          Thesmophoria (Festival)
— **Hinduism**
    ⌈*BL1212*⌉
    UF Hindu fasts and feasts
    BT Hinduism
    NT Dasara
          Durgā-pūjā (Hindu festival)
          Holī (Hindu festival)
          Kumbha Melā (Hindu festival)
          Thaipusam
— **Islam**
    ⌈*BP186*⌉
    UF Fasts and feasts, Muslim
          Islamic fasts and feasts
          Muslim fasts and feasts
    BT Islamic religious practice
    SA *names of individual fasts and*
          feasts, e.g. Ramadan
    NT Jum'ah
          Mawlid al-Nabī
— **Jainism**
    ⌈*BL1355.5*⌉
    UF Fasts and feasts, Jaina
          Jaina fasts and feasts
    BT Jainism
— **Jews**
    USE Fasts and feasts—Judaism
— **Judaism**
    UF Fasts and feasts—Jews
          Festivals—Jews
          Holidays—Jews
          Holidays, Jewish
          Jewish holidays
          Jews—Fasts and feasts
          Jews—Festivals
    BT Judaism
    RT Fasts and feasts in the Bible
    SA *names of individual fasts and*
          feasts, e.g. Rosh ha-Shanah;
          Sukkoth
    NT Festival-day sermons, Jewish
          Hanukkah
          High Holidays
          Hol ha-Moed
          Hoshana Rabba
          Purim
          Religious calendars—Judaism
          Sefirah period
          Shavuot
          Tish'ah be-Av
          Tu bi-Shevat
— — **Exercises, recitations, etc.**

⌈*PN4305.J48 (English)*⌉
    BT Recitations
— — **Liturgy**
    NT Mahzorim
— **Samaritan religion**
    ⌈*BM970*⌉
    UF Samaritan fasts and feasts
    BT Samaritans—Religion
    NT Passover (Samaritan)
          Yom Kippur (Samaritan)
— **Shī'ah**
    ⌈*BP194.5*⌉
    UF Shiite fasts and feasts
    NT 'Īd al-Ghadīr
          Tenth of Muḥarram
— **Shinto**
    UF Fasts and feasts, Shinto
    BT Shinto
    NT Gion Festival
Fasts and feasts, Jaina
    USE Fasts and feasts—Jainism
Fasts and feasts, Muslim
    USE Fasts and feasts—Islam
Fasts and feasts, Shinto
    USE Fasts and feasts—Shinto
Fasts and feasts in the Bible
    UF Bible—Fasts and feasts
    RT Fasts and feasts—Judaism
          Rites and ceremonies in the Bible
— **Typology**
    BT Typology (Theology)
Fasu language
    BT Papuan languages
Fat
    ⌈*QP752.F3*⌉
    Here are entered works on fat in its relation to the
    animal organism. Works on the technological aspects
    of oils and fats are entered under Oils and fats. Works
    on the economic aspects of oils and fats are entered
    under Oil industries.
    UF Fats
    BT Lipids
    RT Adipose tissues
    NT Adipocere
          Animal food—Fat content
          Food—Fat content
          Lipemia
          Low-fat diet
          Steapsin
Fat cells
    ⌈*QP88.15 (Physiology)*⌉
    UF Adipocytes
          Adipose cells
    BT Adipose tissues
          Connective tissue cells
Fat dormouse
    USE Edible dormouse
Fat embolism
    UF Embolism, Fat
          Lipid embolism
    BT Embolism
    RT Atheroembolism
Fat emulsions, Intravenous
    (May Subd Geog)
    UF Intravenous fat emulsions
          Intravenous lipid emulsions
          Lipid emulsions, Intravenous
    BT Emulsions (Pharmacy)
          Parenteral feeding
Fat-free diet
    USE Low-fat diet
Făt-Frumos (Legendary character)
    ⌈*GR257-258*⌉
    BT Folklore—Romania
          Romania—Princes and princesses—
          Folklore
Fat globules, Milk
    USE Butterfat—Fat globules
Fat liver of ducks and geese
    USE Foie gras

Fat necrosis
    ⌈*RB149*⌉
    UF Necrosis, Fat
          Steatonecrosis
    BT Necrosis
Fat-rumped sheep
Fat-soluble vitamins
    USE Vitamins, Fat-soluble
Fat suctioning
    USE Suction lipectomy
Fat-tailed sheep
    ⌈*SF373.F3*⌉
Fat tissue
    USE Adipose tissues
Fataia language
    USE Kwaio language
Fataleka (Solomon Islands people)
    ⌈*DU850*⌉
    BT Ethnology—Solomon Islands
          Solomon Islanders
  — **Rites and ceremonies**
    NT Funeral rites and ceremonies,
          Fataleka (Solomon Islands
          people)
Fataleka (Solomon Islands people) funeral rites
  and ceremonies
    USE Funeral rites and ceremonies, Fataleka
          (Solomon Islands people)
Fataleka (Solomon Islands people) philosophy
    USE Philosophy, Fataleka (Solomon Islands
          people)
Fatalism
    USE Fate and fatalism
Fatally ill children
    USE Terminally ill children
Fate and fatalism
    ⌈*BJ1460-BJ1468.5 (Ethics)*⌉
    UF Destiny
          Fatalism
    BT Fortune
          Philosophy
    RT Necessity (Philosophy)
    NT Free will and determinism
          Murphy's law
          Occasionalism
  — **Religious aspects**
    NT Predestination
          Trust in God
  — — **Buddhism,** ⌈**Christianity, etc.**⌉
Fate and fatalism in literature
Fate language
    USE Efate language
Fathead minnow
    ⌈*QL638.C94*⌉
    UF Fatheaded minnow
          Minnow, Fathead
          Pimephales promelas
Fatheaded minnow
    USE Fathead minnow
Father and child   *(May Subd Geog)*
    UF Child and father
          Father-child relationship
    BT Parent and child
    NT Fathers and daughters
          Fathers and sons
          Love, Paternal
          Paternal deprivation
  — **Pictorial works**
Father and son farm operating agreements
    USE Father-son farm operating agreements
Father-child relationship
    USE Father and child
Father Christmas
    USE Santa Claus
Father figures   *(May Subd Geog)*
    UF Figures, Father
    BT Psychology
Father-in-law
    USE Fathers-in-law
Father-search in literature
    ⌈*PN57.F25*⌉

Father-search in literature *(Continued)*
  BT Recognition in literature
Father-separated children
  USE Fatherless family
        Paternal deprivation
Father-son farm operating agreements
  UF Family farm operating agreements
        Farm operating agreements, Father
          and son
        Father and son farm operating
          agreements
  BT Family farms—Law and legislation
Fatherhood (Christian theology)
  BT God—Fatherhood
Fatherland (Theology)
  USE Homeland (Theology)
Fatherland Site (Miss.) *(Not Subd Geog)*
  UF Grand Village of the Natchez Site
        (Miss.)
  BT Mississippi—Antiquities
Fatherless family *(May Subd Geog)*
  UF Father-separated children
  BT Single-parent family
  RT Children of divorced parents
        Paternal deprivation
Fathers *(May Subd Geog)*
  ₍HQ756 (Parenthood)₎
  BT Family
        Parents
  RT Househusbands
  NT Adolescent fathers
        Divorced fathers
        Grandparents
        Love, Paternal
        Patriarchy
        Presidents—United States—Fathers
        Single parents
        Stepfathers
  — Biblical teaching
    USE Fathers in the Bible
  — Biography
  — Mythology
Fathers, Adolescent
  USE Adolescent fathers
Fathers, Apostolic
  USE Apostolic Fathers
Fathers, Cappadocian
  USE Cappadocian Fathers
Fathers, Unmarried
  USE Unmarried fathers
Fathers and daughters *(May Subd Geog)*
  UF Daughters and fathers
  BT Daughters
        Father and child
        Girls
  NT Electra complex
Fathers and sons *(May Subd Geog)*
  UF Sons and fathers
  BT Boys
        Father and child
Fathers and sons in literature
Father's Day
  ₍HQ756₎
  BT Holidays
  — Exercises, recitations, etc.
Fathers-in-law
  UF Father-in-law
  BT Family
        Parents-in-law
Fathers in literature
  NT Fathers in the Bible
Fathers in the Bible
  ₍BS579.F3₎
  UF Bible—Fathers
        Fathers—Biblical teaching
  BT Bible—Biography
        Family—Biblical teaching
        Fathers in literature
Fathers of the church
  ₍BR60-BR67 (Patrology)₎
  ₍BR1705 (Collective biography)₎

Here are entered works on the life and thought of
the leaders of the early church to the time of Gregory
the Great in the West and John of Damascus in the
East. Writings of early Christian authors are entered
under Christian literature, Early.
  UF Church fathers
        Patristics
        Philosophy, Patristic
  BT Christian biography
  NT Apostolic Fathers
        Cappadocian Fathers
        Church history—Primitive and early
          church, ca. 30-600
  — Concordances
    USE Christian literature, Early—
          Concordances
Fathers of the church, Armenian, ₍**Ethiopic,**
Greek, Latin, etc.₎
Fathers of the church, Syriac
  UF Syriac Fathers of the church
Fatigue *(May Subd Geog)*
  ₍BF482 (Psychology)₎
  ₍LB1075 (Educational psychology)₎
  ₍LB3431 (Educational hygiene)₎
  ₍QP321 (Muscle)₎
  ₍T57.72 (Human engineering)₎
  UF Exhaustion
        Tiredness
        Weariness
  BT Physiology
  RT Rest
  NT Rest periods
Fatigue, Intellectual
  USE Fatigue, Mental
Fatigue, Mental
  ₍BF482 (Psychology)₎
  ₍LB1075 (Educational psychology)₎
  ₍QP421 (Physiology)₎
  UF Fatigue, Intellectual
        Mental exhaustion
        Mental fatigue
        Mental overwork
        Overwork, Mental
  BT Attention
        Brain—Diseases
        Mind and body
        Psychology, Pathological
        Psychology, Physiological
        Work—Psychological aspects
  RT Inefficiency, Intellectual
        Neurasthenia
  NT After-images
        Boredom
        Brain—Anemia
        Overpressure (Education)
Fatigue cracking of welded joints in bridges
  USE Bridges—Welded joints—Cracking
Fatigue of airframes
  USE Airframes—Fatigue
Fatigue of bolts and nuts
  USE Bolts and nuts—Fatigue
Fatigue of concrete
  USE Concrete—Fatigue
Fatigue of materials
  USE Materials—Fatigue
Fatigue of metals
  USE *subdivision* Fatigue *under particular*
          metals, e.g. Steel—Fatigue
        Metals—Corrosion fatigue
        Metals—Fatigue
Fatigue of rocks
  USE Rocks—Fatigue
Fatigue of welded joints
  USE Welded joints—Fatigue
Fatigue testing
  USE Fatigue testing machines
        Materials—Fatigue
Fatigue testing machines
  ₍TA413₎
  UF Fatigue testing

  BT Metals—Fatigue
        Testing-machines
Fátima, Nossa Senhora da
  USE Fatima, Our Lady of
Fatima, Our Lady of
  ₍BT660.F3₎
  UF Fátima, Nossa Senhora da
        Nossa Senhora da Fátima
        Our Lady of Fatima
  BT Christian shrines—Portugal
        Mary, Blessed Virgin, Saint—
          Apparitions and miracles
        Mary, Blessed Virgin, Saint—Cult—
          Portugal
Fatimites
  ₍DT173₎
  BT Caliphs
        Egypt—History—640-1250
        Ismailites
Fatness
  USE Obesity
Fats
  USE Fat
        Oils and fats
Fatsizio-jima (Japan)
  USE Hachijō Island (Japan)
Fatty acid synthesis
  USE Acids, Fatty—Synthesis
Fatty acids
  USE Acids, Fatty
Fatty acids, Essential
  USE Vitamin F
Fatty acids, Omega-3
  USE Omega-3 fatty acids
Fatty acids, Unsaturated
  USE Unsaturated fatty acids
Fatty alcohols
  ₍TP248.A5₎
  UF Alcohols, Fatty
  BT Alcohols
  NT Sterols
Fatty degeneration
  USE Degeneration, Fatty
Fatty heart
  USE Heart, Fatty
Fatty liver
  ₍RC848.F3₎
  BT Degeneration, Fatty
        Liver—Diseases
  NT Reye's syndrome
Fatty liver syndrome of chickens
  ₍SF995.6.F3₎
  BT Liver—Diseases
        Poultry—Diseases
Fatty tissue
  USE Adipose tissues
Fatwās
  UF Futwas
  BT Advisory opinions (Islamic law)
        Islamic law—Sources
Fāu Site, Qaryat (Saudi Arabia)
  USE Qaryat al-Fāu Site (Saudi Arabia)
Faubee family
  USE Faubion family
Faubian family
  USE Faubion family
Faubin family
  USE Faubion family
Faubion family
  UF Faubee family
        Faubian family
        Faubin family
        Fawbean family
        Forbee family
        Forbion family
        Forby family
  RT Fabian family
Faubourg Saint-Antoine (Paris, France)
  (Not Subd Geog)
  UF Paris (France). Faubourg Saint-
          Antoine

Faucets *(May Subd Geog)*
  UF Sink faucets
  BT Plumbing fixtures
Faucett family
  USE Fawcett family
Faucette family
  USE Fawcett family
Faucit family
  USE Fawcett family
Faukner family
  USE Faulkner family
Faulconer family
  USE Faulkner family
Fauler family
  USE Fowler family
Faulk family
  UF Faulke family
      Faulks family
      Fawkes family
      Fawks family
      Fawlkes family
      Foalks family
      Folk family
      Folke family
      Folks family
      Foulk family
      Foulke family
      Foulks family
      Fowke family
      Fowkes family
      Fowlkes family
      Fowlks family
Faulke family
  USE Faulk family
Faulkenberry family
  UF Falconberry family
      Falkenborough family
      Falkinburgh family
      Faulkenborough family
      Faulkenburg family
      Faulkenburough family
      Folkenberry family
  RT Fortenberry family
Faulkenborough family
  USE Faulkenberry family
Faulkenburg family
  USE Faulkenberry family
Faulkenburough family
  USE Faulkenberry family
Faulkner, William, 1897-1962
  — Characters
      NT Snopes family (Fictitious
          characters)
  — — Sartoris family
      RT Sartoris family (Fictitious
          characters)
Faulkner Ash Site (Md.)
  USE Faulkner Coal Ash Storage Facility
      (Md.)
Faulkner Coal Ash Storage Facility (Md.)
  UF Faulkner Ash Site (Md.)
  BT Coal ash sites—Maryland
Faulkner family
  UF Falconer family
      Falkener family
      Falkner family
      Faukner family
      Faulconer family
      Forkner family
      Fortner family
Faulks family
  USE Faulk family
Fault gouge
  UF Clay gouge
      Gouge, Fault
      Rock gouge
      Selvage (Geology)
  BT Breccia
      Clay
      Faults (Geology)

Fault location (Electrical engineering)
  USE Electric fault location
Fault location (Engineering)
  [TA169.9]
  UF Location of system faults
      System fault location (Engineering)
  BT Dynamic testing
  NT Electric fault location
Fault-tolerant computing
  UF Computing, Fault-tolerant
  BT Electronic data processing
      Electronic digital computers—
          Reliability
  NT DDLCN (Computer system)
Fault troughs
  USE Grabens (Geology)
Faultfinding
  [BJ1535.F3]
  UF Finding fault
  BT Conduct of life
      Criticism, Personal
Faultrier family
Faults (Geology) *(May Subd Geog)*
  [QE606]
  BT Geology, Structural
  NT Fault gouge
      Nappes (Geology)
      Rifts (Geology)
      Thrust faults (Geology)
  — Scotland
      NT Great Glen (Scotland)
Faulx bourdon
  USE Fauxbourdon
Fauna
  USE Animals
      Zoology
Fauna, Lake
  USE Lake fauna
Fauna, Prehistoric
  USE Paleontology
Faur family
  USE Fore family
Faure family
  USE Fore family
Fauset family
  USE Fawcett family
Fausett family
  USE Fawcett family
Fausset family
  USE Fawcett family
FAUST (Information retrieval system)
  [Z699.4.F23]
  BT Information storage and retrieval
      systems
Faust family
  UF Foost family
      Foust family
Faustar family
  USE Foster family
Fauster family
  USE Foster family
Fautenberry family
  USE Fortenberry family
Fauveliopsis
  [QL391.A6]
  BT Flabelligeridae
Fauves (School of art)
  USE Fauvism
Fauvism *(May Subd Geog)*
  UF Fauves (School of art)
  BT Art, Modern—20th century
      Modernism (Art)
      Painting, French
      Post-impressionism (Art)
Fauxbourdon
  UF Faulx bourdon
  BT Bourdon
Fava bean
  USE Faba bean

Favism
  BT Allergy
      Hemolytic anemia
Favored nation clause *(May Subd Geog)*
  This heading is divided locally by the name of the
  country which grants the favored nation status to
  another country.
  UF Most favored nation clause
  BT Clauses (Law)
      Commercial treaties
  RT Reciprocity
      Tariff
Favorites, Royal *(May Subd Geog)*
  [D107.7]
  UF Court favorites
      Royal favorites
  RT Courts and courtiers
  SA *subdivision* Court and courtiers *under*
      names of countries, e.g. France—
      Court and courtiers
  NT Fools and jesters
      Kings and rulers—Mistresses
Favositacea
  USE Favositidae
Favosites
  BT Favositidae
Favositidae
  [QE778]
  UF Favositacea
  BT Tabulata
  NT Favosites
Favrile glass
  [NK5198.T]
  UF Tiffany Favrile glass
  BT Glass, Colored—United States
Favus
  [RL770]
  UF Tinea favosa
  BT Tinea capitis
Fāw Site, Qaryat (Saudi Arabia)
  USE Qaryat al-Fāu Site (Saudi Arabia)
Fawbean family
  USE Faubion family
Fawcet family
  USE Fawcett family
Fawcett family
  UF Fasett family
      Fassett family
      Fassette family
      Faucett family
      Faucette family
      Faucit family
      Fauset family
      Fausett family
      Fausset family
      Fawcet family
      Fawcette family
      Fawsett family
Fawcette family
  USE Fawcett family
Fawkes family
  USE Faulk family
Fawks family
  USE Faulk family
Fawlkes family
  USE Faulk family
Fawne family
  USE Fain family
Fawning
  USE Toadyism
Fawnsworth family
  USE Farnsworth family
Fawsett family
  USE Fawcett family
Fax
  USE Facsimile transmission
Faxa Bay (Iceland)
  UF Faxa Fjörður (Iceland)
      Faxaflói (Iceland)
      Faxebugt (Iceland)
      Faxi Flói (Iceland)

Faxa Bay (Iceland) *(Continued)*
  BT Bays—Iceland
Faxa Fjörður (Iceland)
  USE Faxa Bay (Iceland)
Faxaflói (Iceland)
  USE Faxa Bay (Iceland)
Faxebugt (Iceland)
  USE Faxa Bay (Iceland)
Faxen family
  USE Faxon family
Faxi Floi (Iceland)
  USE Faxa Bay (Iceland)
Faxin family
  USE Faxon family
Faxon family
  UF Faxen family
     Faxin family
     Faxson family
     Faxton family
Faxson family
  USE Faxon family
Faxton family
  USE Faxon family
Fay family
  UF Faye family
     Fays family
  RT Fayet family
Faye family
  USE Fay family
Fayence
  USE Faience
Fayer family
  USE Fair family
Faye's comet
  [QB723.F2]
Fayet family
  UF de Fayet family
     Fayette family
  RT Fay family
Fayette family
  USE Fayet family
Faylakah Island (Kuwait)
  USE Failaka Island (Kuwait)
Fays family
  USE Fay family
Fayum portraits
  USE Mummy portraits
Fazenda de Santa Cruz (Brazil)
  USE Santa Cruz Fazenda (Brazil)
Fazenda Santo Antonio (Brazil)
  USE Santo Antonio Fazenda (Brazil)
Fazendas
  USE Haciendas
Fazzan (Libya)
  USE Fezzan (Libya)
Fazzini, Pericle, 1913-   Resurrection
  [NB623.F]
  UF Resurrection (Sculpture)
     Resurrezione (Sculpture)
  BT Jesus Christ—Art
FC-groups
  UF Finite conjugate groups
     Groups, FC
     Groups, Finite conjugate
  BT Finite groups
     Infinite groups
Fc receptors
  [QR185.8.F33]
  UF Receptors, Fc
  BT Cell receptors
     Lymphocytes
     Macrophages
Fca language
  USE Balante language
FCHART (Computer program)
  BT Electronic digital computers—
     Programming
Fead family
  USE Faed family
Feader family
  USE Faed family

Feadóg stáin
  USE Penny whistle
Feagan family
  USE Feagans family
Feaganes family
  USE Feagans family
Feagans family
  UF Feagan family
     Feaganes family
     Feagin family
     Feagins family
Feagin family
  USE Feagans family
Feagins family
  USE Feagans family
Fealds family
  USE Field family
Fear, Cape (Smith Island, N.C.)
  UF Cape Fear (Smith Island, N.C.)
  BT Capes (Coasts)—North Carolina
Fear *(May Subd Geog)*
  [BF575.F2 (Psychology)]
  UF Fright
  BT Emotions
  RT Anxiety
     Horror
  NT Bashfulness
     Hysteria (Social psychology)
     Intimidation
     Panic
     Panic attacks
     Phobias
     Stage fright
     Terror
     Timidity
  — Religious aspects
    NT Fear of God
  — — Baptists, [Catholic Church, etc.]
  — — Buddhism, [Christianity, etc.]
Fear (Child psychology)
  USE Fear in children
Fear in children
  [BF723.F4]
  UF Fear (Child psychology)
  BT Child psychology
  NT Fear of the dark
     Phobias in children
Fear in literature
  BT Emotions in literature
  NT Hypochondria in literature
Fear of being alone
  USE Agoraphobia
Fear of crime *(May Subd Geog)*
  BT Crime and criminals
Fear of death
  [RC552.F42]
  UF Death, Fear of
     Thanatophobia
  BT Death—Psychological aspects
     Psychology, Pathological
Fear of diseases
  USE Nosophobia
Fear of enclosed places
  USE Claustrophobia
Fear of flying
  UF Flying, Fear of
  BT Aeronautics—Psychology
Fear of God
  UF Fear of the Lord
     God—Fear
     God, Fear of
  BT Fear—Religious aspects
     God
Fear of God (Judaism)
  BT God (Judaism)
Fear of open space
  USE Agoraphobia
Fear of open spaces
  USE Agoraphobia
Fear of success
  [RC552.F43]

  BT Neuroses
     Success—Psychological aspects
  RT Impostor phenomenon
  NT Impostor phenomenon
Fear of the dark
  [BF723.F4 (Children)]
  UF Dark, Fear of the
  BT Fear in children
Fear of the Lord
  USE Fear of God
Fearal family
  USE Ferrell family
Fearell family
  USE Ferrell family
Fearghaill family
  USE Ferrell family
Fearis family
  USE Farris family
Feasibility appraisals
  USE Feasibility studies
Feasibility studies *(May Subd Geog)*
  UF Feasibility appraisals
     Studies, Feasibility
     Viability studies
  RT Resource allocation
Feast, Parable of
  USE Great supper (Parable)
Feast-day sermons
  USE Festival-day sermons
Feast of Dedication
  USE Hanukkah
Feast of Esther
  USE Purim
Feast of Fools
  USE Fools, Feast of
Feast of Jesus Christ the King
  USE Jesus Christ the King, Feast of
Feast of kingship (Shinto rite)
  USE Ōnie no Matsuri
Feast of Lights
  USE Hanukkah
Feast of Lots
  USE Purim
Feast of Rejoicing over the Law
  USE Simḥat Torah
Feast of Saint Martin
  USE Saint Martin's Day
Feast of Tabernacles
  USE Sukkot
Feast of the Assumption of the Blessed Virgin
  Mary
  USE Assumption of the Blessed Virgin
     Mary, Feast of the
Feast of the Cross
  USE Cross, Feast of the
Feast of the Exaltation of the Cross
  USE Cross, Feast of the
Feast of the Holy Cross
  USE Cross, Feast of the
Feast of the Holy Innocents
  USE Holy Innocents, Feast of the
Feast of the Immaculate Conception
  USE Immaculate Conception, Feast of the
Feast of the Invention of the Holy Cross
  USE Cross, Feast of the
Feast of the Maccabees
  USE Hanukkah
Feast of the Presentation of Jesus Christ
  USE Candlemas
Feast of the Presentation of the Blessed Virgin
  Mary
  USE Presentation of the Blessed Virgin
     Mary, Feast of the
Feast of the Sacred Heart
  USE Sacred Heart, Feast of the
Feast of the Three Hierarchs
  USE Three Hierarchs, Feast of the
Feast of Weeks
  USE Shavuot
Feasts
  USE Fasts and feasts

Feasts at the Valois court (Tapestries)
  [NK3055.V]
  UF Valois tapestries
  BT Tapestry, Flemish
Feather dyeing
  USE Dyes and dyeing—Feathers
Feather family
  UF Featherman family
    Feathers family
    Featherson family
    Vätter family
  RT Featherstone family
    Fetter family
Feather flowers
  [TT891]
  BT Artificial flowers
    Feather-work
Feather grasses
  USE Stipa
Feather industry   (May Subd Geog)
  [HD9999.F4]
  BT Feathers
  NT Wages—Feather industry
Feather River (Calif.)
  BT Rivers—California
Feather tracts
  UF Pterylae
    Pterylography
    Pterylosis
  BT Birds—Anatomy
    Feathers
Feather-wing beetles
  [QL596.P83]
  UF Ptilidae
    Ptiliidae
    Trichopterygidae
  BT Beetles
  NT Porophila
    Xenopteryx
Feather-work   (May Subd Geog)
  [GN434.F3 (Primitive)]
  NT Feather flowers
    Indians of North America—Feather-
      work
Featherbedding (Industrial relations)
  BT Restrictive practices in industrial
    relations
  NT Railroads—Full crew rules
Feathergrasses
  USE Stipa
Featherling, Rush
  USE Tofieldia tenuifolia
Featherman family
  USE Feather family
Feathers
  [QL697]
  UF Down
  BT Birds—Anatomy
    Body covering (Anatomy)
    Poultry industry—By-products
  NT Dyes and dyeing—Feathers
    Feather industry
    Feather tracts
    Hackles (Fly tying)
    Molting
Feathers family
  USE Feather family
Featherson family
  USE Feather family
Featherston family
  USE Featherstone family
Featherstone family   (Not Subd Geog)
  UF Featherston family
  RT Feather family
Feature article writing
  USE Feature writing
Feature films
    Here are entered individual full-length fiction
  films with a running time of 60 minutes or more.
  UF Dramatic films
    Theatrical films

  BT Moving-pictures
  NT Adventure films
    Animal films
    Bible films
    Biographical films
    Comedy films
    Detective and mystery films
    Fantastic films
    Gangster films
    Historical films
    Horror films
    Juvenile delinquency films
    Musical revues, comedies, etc.
    Religious films
    Samurai films
    Short films
    Sports films
    Spy films
    Superman films
    Three Stooges films
    Vampire films
    War films
    Werewolf films
    Western films
Feature story writing
  USE Feature writing
Feature writing
  UF Feature article writing
    Feature story writing
  BT Authorship
    Journalism—Authorship
Feazel family
  USE Feazle family
Feazell family
  USE Feazle family
Feazle family
  UF Feazel family
    Feazell family
Febold Feboldson (Legendary character)
  USE Feboldson, Febold (Legendary
    character)
Feboldson, Febold (Legendary character)
  UF Febold Feboldson (Legendary
    character)
  BT Folklore—United States
Febrerista Revolution, Paraguay, 1936
  USE Paraguay—History—Revolution, 1936
Febrifuge agents
  USE Antipyretics
Febrifuges
  USE Antipyretics
Febrile convulsions
  USE Convulsions, Febrile
Febrile seizures
  USE Convulsions, Febrile
February 11 (Holiday)
  USE Kenkoku Kinen no hi
February Incident, Japan, 1936 (February 26)
  USE Japan—History—February Incident,
    1936 (February 26)
February sixteenth
  USE Sixteenth of February
Fecal impaction
  USE Feces—Impaction
Fecal incontinence
  USE Feces—Incontinence
Fecanes
  USE Fingos
Feces
  [QP159]
  UF Stools (Excrement)
  BT Biological chemistry
    Excretion
  RT Defecation
  NT Meconium
  — **Examination**
    [RB49]
  — **Impaction**   (May Subd Geog)
    UF Fecal impaction
      Impaction of feces
    BT Intestines—Obstructions

  — **Incontinence**
    UF Fecal incontinence
      Incontinence
    BT Defecation disorders
    NT Encopresis
  — **Microbiology**
    [QR171.F4]
  — **Religious aspects**
Feces, Fossil
  USE Coprolites
Fecher family
Fechheim family
  USE Fechheimer family
Fechheimer family   (Not Subd Geog)
  UF Fechheim family
Fechner's law
  USE Weber-Fechner law
Fecht family
Fecundity
  USE Fertility
Fedayeen
  UF Fidā'iyun
  BT Israel-Arab Border Conflicts, 1949-
    Jewish-Arab relations—1949-
    Palestinian Arabs
  NT Entebbe Airport Raid, 1976
    Karāmah (Jordan), Battle of, 1968
Feddersen Wierde Site (Germany)
  (Not Subd Geog)
  BT Germany (West)—Antiquities
Federal aid
  USE Economic assistance, Domestic
Federal aid to adult education
  (May Subd Geog)
  UF Adult education—Federal aid
  BT Adult education—Finance
    Adult education—Law and legislation
    Education and state
Federal aid to alcoholism programs
  (May Subd Geog)
  BT Alcoholism—Prevention—Finance
    Alcoholism—Treatment—Finance
    Grants-in-aid
Federal aid to biology   (May Subd Geog)
  UF Biology—Federal aid
  BT Grants-in-aid
Federal aid to birth control
  (May Subd Geog)
  UF Birth control—Federal aid
  BT Birth control—Finance
    Grants-in-aid
Federal aid to business research
  (May Subd Geog)
  UF Business—Research—Federal aid
  BT Business—Research
    Grants-in-aid
Federal aid to child development
  (May Subd Geog)
  UF Child development—Federal aid
  BT Federal aid to child welfare
    Grants-in-aid
Federal aid to child health services
  (May Subd Geog)
  UF Child health services—Federal aid
  BT Child health services—Finance
    Federal aid to child welfare
    Grants-in-aid
  NT Early and Periodic Screening,
    Diagnosis, and Treatment Program
    Federal aid to infant health services
Federal aid to child welfare
  (May Subd Geog)
  UF Child welfare—Federal aid
  BT Grants-in-aid
  NT Federal aid to child development
    Federal aid to child health services
    Federal aid to day care centers
Federal aid to community development
  (May Subd Geog)
  UF Community development—Federal aid

Federal aid to community development
   (Continued)
   BT Community development
       Grants-in-aid
   NT Community development corporations
Federal aid to community health services
   (May Subd Geog)
   UF Community health services—Federal
       aid
   BT Community health services—Finance
       Federal aid to health facilities
       Grants-in-aid
   NT Federal aid to community mental
       health services
**Federal aid to community mental health
services** *(May Subd Geog)*
   UF Community mental health services—
       Federal aid
   BT Community mental health services—
       Finance
       Federal aid to community health
       services
       Grants-in-aid
Federal aid to dance *(May Subd Geog)*
   UF Dancing—Federal aid
   BT Dancing—Finance
       Federal aid to the arts
       Federal aid to the performing arts
       Grants-in-aid
Federal aid to day care centers
   (May Subd Geog)
   UF Day care centers—Federal aid
   BT Day care centers—Finance
       Federal aid to child welfare
Federal aid to depressed areas
   USE Economic assistance, Domestic
Federal aid to drug abuse treatment programs
   (May Subd Geog)
   UF Drug abuse—Treatment—Federal aid
   BT Drug abuse—Prevention—Finance
       Drug abuse—Treatment—Finance
       Grants-in-aid
Federal aid to education *(May Subd Geog)*
   ₍LB2825₎
   UF Education—Federal aid
       Federal grants for education
   BT Education—Finance
       Education and state
       Educational law and legislation
       Federal aid to youth services
       Grants-in-aid
   NT Educational equalization
       Federal aid to libraries
       Federal aid to private schools
Federal aid to energy development
   (May Subd Geog)
   ₍HD9502₎
   UF Energy development—Federal aid
   BT Energy development—Finance
       Grants-in-aid
Federal aid to fire prevention
   (May Subd Geog)
   UF Fire prevention—Federal aid
   BT Fire prevention—Finance
       Grants-in-aid
Federal aid to fisheries
   USE Fisheries subsidies
Federal aid to handicapped services
   (May Subd Geog)
   UF Handicapped—Services for—Federal
       aid
   BT Grants-in-aid
Federal aid to health facilities
   (May Subd Geog)
   UF Health facilities—Federal aid
   BT Grants-in-aid
       Health facilities—Finance
   NT Federal aid to community health
       services
       Federal aid to health maintenance
       organizations

Federal aid to hospitals
Federal aid to nursing homes
**Federal aid to health maintenance
organizations** *(May Subd Geog)*
   UF Health maintenance organizations—
       Federal aid
   BT Federal aid to health facilities
       Grants-in-aid
       Health maintenance organizations—
       Finance
Federal aid to health planning
   (May Subd Geog)
   UF Health planning—Federal aid
   BT Grants-in-aid
       Health planning—Finance
Federal aid to higher education
   (May Subd Geog)
   BT Education, Higher
       Education and state
       Higher education and state
       Universities and colleges—Finance
   NT Federal aid to medical education
       Federal aid to nursing education
Federal aid to historic sites
   (May Subd Geog)
   BT Grants-in-aid
       Historic sites—Conservation and
       restoration
       Historic sites—Law and legislation
Federal aid to hospitals *(May Subd Geog)*
   UF Hospitals—Federal aid
   BT Federal aid to health facilities
       Grants-in-aid
       Hospitals—Finance
       Hospitals—Law and legislation
Federal aid to infant health services
   (May Subd Geog)
   UF Infant health services—Federal aid
   BT Federal aid to child health services
       Grants-in-aid
       Infant health services—Finance
Federal aid to law enforcement agencies
   (May Subd Geog)
   BT Grants-in-aid
       Law enforcement
Federal aid to libraries *(May Subd Geog)*
   UF Libraries—Federal aid
   BT Federal aid to education
       Grants-in-aid
       Libraries and state
       Library finance
       Library legislation
   NT Federal aid to medical libraries
Federal aid to maternal health services
   (May Subd Geog)
   UF Maternal health services—Federal aid
   BT Grants-in-aid
       Maternal health services—Finance
Federal aid to medical care research
   (May Subd Geog)
   UF Medical care—Research—Federal aid
   BT Federal aid to medical research
       Grants-in-aid
       Medical care—Research—Finance
Federal aid to medical education
   (May Subd Geog)
   UF Medical education—Federal aid
   BT Federal aid to higher education
       Grants-in-aid
       Medical education—Finance
       Medical education policy
   NT Federal aid to paramedical education
       State aid to medical education
Federal aid to medical libraries
   (May Subd Geog)
   UF Medical libraries—Federal aid
   BT Federal aid to libraries
Federal aid to medical research
   (May Subd Geog)
   UF Medicine—Research—Federal aid

   BT Federal aid to research
       Grants-in-aid
       Medicine—Research—Finance
   NT Federal aid to medical care research
Federal aid to minority business enterprises
   (May Subd Geog)
   UF Minority business enterprises—Federal
       aid
   BT Grants-in-aid
       Minority business enterprises—Finance
Federal aid to museums *(May Subd Geog)*
   UF Museums—Federal aid
   BT Grants-in-aid
       Museum finance
       Museums—Law and legislation
Federal aid to nursing education
   (May Subd Geog)
   UF Nursing—Study and teaching—Federal
       aid
   BT Federal aid to higher education
       Grants-in-aid
       Nursing—Study and teaching—
       Finance
Federal aid to nursing homes
   (May Subd Geog)
   UF Nursing homes—Federal aid
   BT Federal aid to health facilities
       Grants-in-aid
       Nursing homes—Finance
Federal aid to outdoor recreation
   (May Subd Geog)
   UF Outdoor recreation—Federal aid
   BT Grants-in-aid
       Outdoor recreation—Finance
       Outdoor recreation—Law and
       legislation
Federal aid to paramedical education
   (May Subd Geog)
   BT Federal aid to medical education
       Paramedical education
   NT State aid to paramedical education
Federal aid to private schools
   (May Subd Geog)
   UF Federal grants for private schools
   BT Educational law and legislation
       Federal aid to education
       Private schools
   RT State aid to private schools
Federal aid to public welfare
   (May Subd Geog)
   UF Public welfare—Federal aid
   BT Grants-in-aid
       Public welfare—Finance
Federal aid to recreation *(May Subd Geog)*
   ₍GV181.6₎
   UF Recreation—Federal aid
   BT Grants-in-aid
       Recreation—Finance
Federal aid to regional planning
   (May Subd Geog)
   UF Regional planning—Federal aid
   BT Grants-in-aid
Federal aid to research *(May Subd Geog)*
   UF Research—Federal aid
   BT Grants-in-aid
       Research, Industrial
   RT Endowment of research
       Research grants
   NT Federal aid to medical research
Federal aid to rural health services
   (May Subd Geog)
   UF Rural health services—Federal aid
   BT Grants-in-aid
       Rural health services—Finance
Federal aid to the arts *(May Subd Geog)*
   UF Art—Federal aid
       Arts—Federal aid
       Federal grants for art
       Federal grants for the arts

BT Art—Finance
Art and state
Arts—Finance
Cultural policy
Grants-in-aid
NT Federal aid to dance
Federal aid to the motion picture
industry
Federal aid to the performing arts
Federal aid to the theater
Federal aid to the motion picture industry
(May Subd Geog)
UF Moving-picture industry—Federal aid
BT Federal aid to the arts
Federal aid to the performing arts
Grants-in-aid
Moving-picture industry—Finance
Federal aid to the performing arts
(May Subd Geog)
UF Performing arts—Federal aid
BT Federal aid to the arts
Grants-in-aid
Performing arts—Finance
NT Federal aid to dance
Federal aid to the motion picture
industry
Federal aid to the theater
Federal aid to the printing industry
(May Subd Geog)
UF Printing industry—Federal aid
BT Grants-in-aid
Printing industry—Finance
Federal aid to the theater *(May Subd Geog)*
UF Theater—Federal aid
BT Federal aid to the arts
Federal aid to the performing arts
Grants-in-aid
Theater—Finance
Federal aid to transportation
(May Subd Geog)
UF Federal grants for transportation
Transportation—Federal aid
BT Grants-in-aid
Transportation—Finance
Transportation and state
Federal aid to vocational education
(May Subd Geog)
UF Federal grants for vocational education
Vocational education—Federal aid
BT Education and state
Vocational education—Finance
Vocational education—Law and
legislation
Federal aid to water quality management
(May Subd Geog)
UF Water quality management—Federal
aid
BT Grants-in-aid
Water quality management—Finance
Federal aid to water resources development
(May Subd Geog)
UF Water resources development—Federal
aid
BT Grants-in-aid
Water resources development—
Finance
**Federal aid to women-owned business
enterprises** *(May Subd Geog)*
UF Women-owned business enterprises—
Federal aid
BT Grants-in-aid
Women-owned business enterprises—
Finance
Federal aid to women's organizations
(May Subd Geog)
BT Grants-in-aid
Women—Societies and clubs—Finance
Federal aid to wood-lots *(May Subd Geog)*
[SD387.W6]
UF Wood-lots—Federal aid

BT Grants-in-aid
Wood-lots—Finance
Federal aid to youth services
(May Subd Geog)
BT Child welfare
Grants-in-aid
NT Federal aid to education
Federal areas within states
(May Subd Geog)
UF Federal enclaves
BT Federal government
Federal-city relations *(May Subd Geog)*
UF City-federal relations
Federal-municipal relations
Urban-federal relations
BT Federal government
Municipal government
Urban policy
NT Urban impact analysis
Federal communications services
USE Federal Telecommunications System
Federal corporation tax
USE Corporations—Taxation
Federal corporations
USE Corporations, Government
Federal defense budget (U.S.)
USE United States. Dept. of Defense—
Appropriations and expenditures
United States—Armed Forces—
Appropriations and expenditures
Federal employees group life insurance
program
USE Insurance, Government employees' life
—United States
Federal enclaves
USE Federal areas within states
Federal funds market (United States)
BT Federal Reserve banks
Federal government *(May Subd Geog)*
[JC355]
[JF751-JF786 (Federal and state
relations)]
Here are entered works on the division of powers
between the central government and state or provin-
cial and local governments in federal systems. Works
on the division of powers between the executive,
legislative, and judicial branches of government are
entered under Separation of powers. Works on the
division of powers between the central government
and state or provincial and local governments in non-
federal systems are entered under Central-local gov-
ernment relations.
UF Division of powers
Federal-state relations
Federalism
BT Constitutional law
Political science
Republics
RT Central-local government relations
Decentralization in government
Democracy
Legislative power
State governments
SA *subdivision* Politics and government
*under names of individual federal
states, e.g.* United States—Politics
and government
NT City-states
Confederation of states
European federation
Exclusive and concurrent legislative
powers
Federal areas within states
Federal-city relations
Federal-state controversies
Imperial federation
Intergovernmental fiscal relations
Intergovernmental tax relations
Interstate controversies
Interstate relations
Intervention (Federal government)
Latin American federation

State rights
— **Information services**
BT Government information
Federal grants
USE Grants-in-aid
Federal grants for art
USE Federal aid to the arts
Federal grants for education
USE Federal aid to education
Federal grants for private schools
USE Federal aid to private schools
Federal grants for the arts
USE Federal aid to the arts
Federal grants for transportation
USE Federal aid to transportation
Federal grants for vocational education
USE Federal aid to vocational education
Federal Hill (Baltimore, Md.)
(Not Subd Geog)
UF Baltimore (Md.). Federal Hill
Federal home loan banks
[HG3729.U4-5]
UF Home loan banks
BT Banks and banking
— **Law and legislation**
BT Banking law
Federal hospitals
USE Hospitals, Public
Federal incorporation
USE Incorporation
Federal intervention
USE Intervention (Federal government)
Federal land banks
[HG2051.U5]
Federal libraries
USE Libraries, Governmental,
administrative, etc.
Federal loyalty-security program, 1947-
USE Loyalty-security program, 1947-
Federal magistrates (U.S.)
USE United States magistrates
Federal-municipal relations
USE Federal-city relations
Federal Palace (Bern, Switzerland)
USE Bundeshaus Bern (Bern, Switzerland)
Federal paperwork
USE Government paperwork
Federal Party
[JK2300-2309]
Subdivided by locality e.g. Federal Party. Mas-
sachusetts.
UF Federalists (U.S.)
Federal preemption
USE Exclusive and concurrent legislative
powers
Federal prose
USE English language—Government jargon
Federal questionnaires
USE Government questionnaires
Federal Reserve banks
[HG2559-2565]
BT Banks of issue—United States
NT Federal funds market (United States)
Federal-state concurrent legislative powers
USE Exclusive and concurrent legislative
powers
Federal-state controversies
(May Subd Geog)
UF Controversies between the United
States and a State
Federal-state disputes
BT Constitutional law
Federal government
Federal-state disputes
USE Federal-state controversies
Federal-state fiscal relations
USE Intergovernmental fiscal relations
Federal-state relations
USE Federal government
Federal-state tax relations
USE Intergovernmental tax relations

1325

Federal style
USE Decoration and ornament—Federal style

Federal Telecommunications System
UF F.T.S.
Federal communications services
United States—Executive departments —Communication systems

Federal theology
USE Covenants (Theology)

Federal Triangle (Washington, D.C.)
(Not Subd Geog)
UF Washington (D.C.). Federal Triangle

Federal War, Colombia, 1860-1862
USE Colombia—History—Civil War, 1860-1862

Federal Wars, Venezuela, 1858-1863
USE Venezuela—History—Federal Wars, 1858-1863

Federalism
USE Federal government

Federalist Revolution, Brazil, 1893-1894
USE Brazil—History—Naval Revolt, 1893-1894

Federalist Revolution, Rio Grande do Sul, Brazil, 1893-1895
USE Rio Grande do Sul (Brazil)—History—Federalist Revolution, 1893-1895

Federalists (U.S.)
USE Federal Party

Federally guaranteed loans
USE Loans—Government guaranty

Federated churches
[BV636]
Here are entered works on local Protestant churches formed by two or more denominations which unite for worship but retain denominational affiliations. Works on independent local Protestant churches with no formal denominational affiliation are entered under Community churches.
UF Churches, Federated
BT Churches
Interdenominational cooperation

Federation, Imperial
USE Imperial federation

Federation, International
USE International organization

Federation of East Africa
USE East Africa Federation

Federation of Europe
USE European federation

Federation of Latin America
USE Latin American federation

Federation of Malaya
USE Malaya

Federations, Financial (Social service)
[HV40-41]
[HV99 (United States: local)]
[national HV97]
UF Community chests
Federations for charity and philanthropy
Financial federations
Welfare federations
BT Charity organization
Community organization
Cooperative societies
Fund raising
Social service

Federations, Local church
USE Local church councils

Federations for charity and philanthropy
USE Federations, Financial (Social service)

Federsee (Germany)
BT Lakes—Germany (West)

Fedotov, Pavel Andreevich, 1815-1852.
Major comes to woo *(Not Subd Geog)*
[ND699.F4]

UF Major comes to woo (Painting)
Request in marriage of the commandant (Painting)
Svatovstvo maı̈ora (Painting)
BT Painting, Russian

Fedritive movement
[HD2961]
BT Cooperation

Fee family

Fe'e Fe'e (Cameroon people)
USE Fe'fe' (Cameroon people)

Fe'e fe'e language
USE Fe'fe' language

Fee system (Taxation)
USE *subdivision* Officials and employees—Salaries, etc. *under names of countries, cities, etc.*
Costs (Law)
Fees, Administrative
Internal revenue
Stamp-duties
Taxation

Feeble-minded
USE Mentally handicapped

Feed
USE Feeds

FEED (Computer program)
UF Fast and Efficient Evaluation of Derivatives (Computer program)
BT Numerical analysis—Computer programs

Feed additive industry *(May Subd Geog)*
BT Feed additives

Feed additive residues *(May Subd Geog)*
[RA1270.F4 (Toxicology)]
UF Residues, Feed additive
BT Food contamination

Feed additives *(May Subd Geog)*
[SF98.A2]
UF Feeds—Additives
NT Feed additive industry
Lysine in animal nutrition
Medicated feeds

Feed conversion efficiency
USE Feed utilization efficiency

Feed grain program *(May Subd Geog)*
UF Feed grain program—United States
BT Agriculture and state—United States
— **Law and legislation** *(May Subd Geog)*
UF Feed grain program—Law and legislation—United States
BT Agricultural laws and legislation—United States
— — United States
USE Feed grain program—Law and legislation
— United States
USE Feed grain program

Feed-grinders
[S709]
BT Agricultural machinery

Feed heads
USE Risers (Founding)

Feed industry and trade
USE Flour and feed trade

Feed mechanisms
BT Machinery
RT Conveying machinery
Orienting mechanisms

Feed mills *(May Subd Geog)*
[TS2158]
BT Feed processing
Flour and feed trade
Milling machinery
— **Equipment and supplies**
— — Appraisal
USE Feed mills—Equipment and supplies—Valuation
— — Valuation
[TS2158]

UF Feed mills—Equipment and supplies—Appraisal
— **Management**
[TS2158]

Feed processing
UF Feeds—Processing
BT Agricultural processing
NT Feed mills

Feed pumps
USE Feed-water pumps

Feed research
USE Feeds—Research

Feed trade
USE Flour and feed trade

Feed utilization efficiency *(May Subd Geog)*
UF Efficiency, Feed utilization
Feed conversion efficiency
Livestock—Feed utilization efficiency
Meat production efficiency
BT Animal nutrition
Feeds
SA *subdivision* Feed utilization efficiency *under names of animals or groups of animals, e.g.* Poultry—Feed utilization efficiency

Feed-water
[TJ375-387]
UF Boiler water
BT Boilers
Steam-boilers
Steam-boilers—Incrustations
Water
NT Steam accumulators

Feed-water heaters
[TJ381-3]

Feed-water pumps
[TJ385]
UF Feed pumps
Pumps, Feed-water
BT Pumping machinery
— **Transmission devices**
BT Gearing

Feed-water purification
[TJ379]
BT Steam-boilers—Incrustations
Water—Purification
NT Deaerators
Water—Softening

Feedback (Electronics)
[TK7835]
BT Amplifiers, Vacuum-tube
Electronics
Feedback control systems
Vacuum-tube circuits
NT Feedback oscillators

Feedback (Psychology)
[BF319.5.F4]
BT Learning, Psychology of
Reinforcement (Psychology)
NT Biofeedback training

Feedback amplifiers
[TK7871.2]

Feedback control systems
[TJ216]
BT Automatic control
Automation
Discrete-time systems
RT Adaptive control systems
Feedforward control systems
NT Biological control systems
Feedback (Electronics)
Man-machine systems—Manual control
Root-locus method
Servomechanisms
Ships—Dynamic positioning systems
— **Dynamics**

Feedback oscillators
[TK7872.O7]
UF Oscillators, Feedback

BT Feedback (Electronics)
    Oscillators, Electric
Feeder air lines
  USE Local service airlines
Feederliners
  USE Commuter aircraft
Feeders
  USE Risers (Founding)
Feeders, Liquid
  USE Liquid feeders
Feedforward control systems
  [TJ216.5]
  BT Automatic control
  RT Feedback control systems
Feedheads
  USE Risers (Founding)
Feeding
  USE Animal nutrition
Feeding, Artificial
  USE Artificial feeding
Feeding, Intravenous
  USE Parenteral feeding
Feeding, Parenteral
  USE Parenteral feeding
Feeding behavior in animals
  USE Animals—Food
Feeding disorders
  USE Ingestion disorders
Feeding of the five thousand (Miracle)
  UF Five thousand, Feeding of the
    (Miracle)
  BT Jesus Christ—Miracles
Feeding of the five thousand (Miracle) in art
Feeding programs (Space flight)
  USE Menus for space flight
Feeding stuffs
  USE Feeds
Feedingstuff
  USE Feeds
Feedlot runoff *(May Subd Geog)*
  [TD811]
  BT Animal waste
    Feedlots
    Runoff
  — Law and legislation *(May Subd Geog)*
Feedlots *(May Subd Geog)*
  BT Animal nutrition
    Livestock factories
  NT Feedlot runoff
Feeds *(May Subd Geog)*
  UF Feed
    Feeding stuffs
    Feedingstuff
    Feedstuff
    Fodder
    Livestock—Feeding and feeds
  BT Farm supplies
  RT Animal nutrition
    Single cell proteins
  SA Grain as feed; Molasses as feed; *and*
    similar headings; and subdivision
    Feeding and feeds *under names of*
    animals and groups of animals, e.g.
    Horses—Feeding and feeds; Poultry
    —Feeding and feeds
  NT Animal waste as feed
    Aquatic plants as feed
    Canola meal as feed
    Corn as feed
    Distillers feeds
    Dried citrus pulp
    Faba bean as feed
    Feed utilization efficiency
    Fish oils as feed
    Forage
    Forage plants
    Grain as feed
    Legumes as feed
    Lupines as feed
    Medicated feeds
    Molasses as feed

    Organic wastes as feed
    Pelleted feed
    Poultry industry—By-products
    Silage
    Sugarcane as feed
    Water hyacinth as feed
  — Additives
    USE Feed additives
  — Amino acid content
    USE Amino acids in animal nutrition
  — Ammonia content
    USE Ammonia in animal nutrition
  — Analysis
    [SF97]
    BT Agricultural chemistry
  — Contamination
    UF Contamination of feeds
    BT Food contamination
      Veterinary toxicology
  — Disinfection
    [RA761]
  — Flavor and odor
    [SF97.7]
    UF Feeds—Odor
    BT Flavor
      Odors
  — Grading
    UF Feeds—Standards
  — Law and legislation *(May Subd Geog)*
  — Marketing
    BT Flour and feed trade
  — Microbiology
  — Mineral content
    USE Minerals in animal nutrition
  — Odor
    USE Feeds—Flavor and odor
  — Processing
    USE Feed processing
  — Protein content
    USE Proteins in animal nutrition
  — Research *(May Subd Geog)*
    UF Feed research
  — Standards
    USE Feeds—Grading
  — Transportation
  — Weight and measurement
Feeds, Antenna
  USE Antenna feeds
Feedstock
  BT Raw materials
Feedstuff
  USE Feeds
Feeling
  USE Perception
    Touch
Feelings
  USE Emotions
Feemster family
  UF Feimster family
Feep, Lefty (Fictitious character)
  UF Lefty Feep (Fictitious character)
  BT Characters and characteristics in
    literature
  RT Bloch, Robert, 1917- —Characters—
    Lefty Feep
Feero family
  USE Ferro family
Fees, Administrative *(May Subd Geog)*
  UF Administrative fees
    Fee system (Taxation)
  BT Administrative law
  RT Costs (Law)
    Stamp-duties
  NT Fees, Consular
    Impact fees
    Passports—Fees
    Tonnage fees
    User charges
Fees, Adult education
  USE Adult education fees

Fees, Bank
  USE Banks and banking—Service charges
Fees, Consular
  UF Consular fees
    Diplomatic and consular service—Fees
  BT Diplomatic and consular service
    Fees, Administrative
  SA *subdivision* Diplomatic and consular
    service—Fees *under names of*
    countries, e.g. Cuba—Diplomatic
    and consular service—Fees
Fees, Development
  USE Impact fees
Fees, Ecclesiastical
  [BX1939.F (Canon law)]
  UF Ecclesiastical fees
  BT Church finance
  NT Annates
    Mass stipends
    Tithes
Fees, Impact
  USE Impact fees
Fees, Import
  USE Tariff
Fees, Legal
  USE Costs (Law)
    Lawyers—Fees
Fees, Medical
  USE Medical fees
Fees, Passport
  USE Passports—Fees
Fees, Professional *(May Subd Geog)*
  UF Professional fees
  SA *subdivision* Fees *under names of*
    professional groups, e.g. Architects
    —Fees; Lawyers—Fees
  NT Costs (Law)
    Dental fees
    Medical fees
Fees, User
  USE User charges
Fees (Law)
  USE Costs (Law)
    Lawyers—Fees
Feet
  USE Foot
Feet, Washing of
  USE Foot washing (Rite)
Feet in the Bible
  [BS680.F43]
  UF Bible—Feet
  BT Foot
    Foot—Religious aspects
    Foot washing (Rite)
Feet Kune Do
  USE Karate
Feet of fines
  USE Fines and recoveries
Feet washing
  USE Foot washing (Rite)
Fe'fe' (Cameroon people)
  [DT570]
  UF Bafang (Cameroon people)
    Fan (Cameroon people)
    Fang (Cameroon people)
    Fe'e Fe'e (Cameroon people)
  BT Bamileke (African people)
    Ethnology—Cameroon
Fe'fe' language
  UF Bafang language
    Bakou language
    Bana language
    Fa language (Bamileke)
    Fan language (Bamileke)
    Fanwe language (Bamileke)
    Fe'e fe'e language
    Kuu language
    Nufi language
  BT Bamileke languages
    Cameroon—Languages

Fegley family
  UF Voegeli family
Fegolmin language
  USE Faiwol language
Fehan (Indonesian people)
  USE Tetum (Indonesian people)
Fehling family
  UF Feling family
  RT Fales family
Fehling's solution
  ₎QD321₎
  ₎TP382₎
  BT Chemical tests and reagents
Fehmarn (Germany)
  UF Insel Fehmarn (Germany)
  BT Islands—Germany (West)
Fehmarn, Battle of, 1644
  ₎DL190₎
  BT Dano-Swedish War, 1643-1645
Fehmic courts
  ₎JN3269₎
  UF Vehmgerichte
  BT Courts
     Criminal courts
Fehndrich family
  USE Fendrick family
Fehnel family
  USE Fennell family
Fehrbellin, Battle of, 1675
  ₎DD394.3₎
  BT Prussia (Germany)—History—
     Frederick William, the Great
     Elector, 1640-1688
Fei-ts'ui Dam (Taiwan)
  BT Dams—Taiwan
Feia
  ₎QL638.G7₎
  BT Gobiidae
Feick family
  USE Fike family
Feicke family
  USE Fike family
Feigned diseases
  USE Blindness, Feigned
     Malingering
Feik family
  USE Fike family
Feike family
  USE Fike family
Feil family
  USE Feiler family
Feilaka Island (Kuwait)
  USE Failaka Island (Kuwait)
Feild family
  USE Field family
Feilds family
  USE Field family
Feiler family
  UF Feil family
     Filer family
  RT Fieler family
Feimster family
  USE Feemster family
Feisst family
  USE Feist family
Feist family
  UF Faist family
     Feisst family
Félalime family
Feland family
Felashas
  USE Falashas
Felata
  USE Fulahs
Felbertauernstrasse (Austria)
  BT Roads—Austria
Felchli family
  UF Felchlia family
Felchlia family
  USE Felchli family

Feldshers
  USE Physicians' assistants
Feldspar *(May Subd Geog)*
  ₎QE391.F3₎
  BT Rock-forming minerals
  NT Adularia
     Anorthosite
     Plagioclase
Feldspar industry *(May Subd Geog)*
Feldspathide
  USE Feldspathoid
Feldspathoid *(May Subd Geog)*
  UF Feldspathide
     Felspathoid
  BT Silicate minerals
  NT Cancrinite
     Leucite
     Melilite
     Nephelite
Feldt family
  USE Felts family
Felidae
  ₎QL737.C23₎
     Here are entered works on the family of cats.
  Works on domestic breeds of cats are entered under
  Cats.
  UF Cat family
     Wildcats
  BT Carnivora
     Cats
  NT Felis
     Mayailurus
Felidae, Fossil
  NT Ischyrosmilus
     Smilodon
Feline dirofilariasis
  USE Feline heartworm disease
Feline heartworm
  USE Dirofilaria immitis
Feline heartworm disease *(May Subd Geog)*
  ₎SF986.H₎
  UF Cat heartworm disease
     Dirofilariasis, Feline
     Feline dirofilariasis
     Heartworm disease in cats
  BT Cats—Diseases
  RT Dirofilaria immitis
Feline leukemia *(May Subd Geog)*
  ₎SF986.L48₎
  UF Cat leukemia
     Feline leukosis
     Leukemia, Feline
  BT Cats—Diseases
     Leukemia in animals
Feline leukemia virus
  UF Feline lymphoma virus
     Leukemia virus, Feline
  BT Retroviruses
Feline leukosis
  USE Feline leukemia
Feline lymphoma virus
  USE Feline leukemia virus
Feline sarcoma virus
  UF Sarcoma virus, Feline
  BT Retroviruses
     Sarcoma
Feling family
  USE Fehling family
Felis
  ₎QL737.C23₎
  BT Felidae
  NT Panthera
Felis capensis
  USE Serval
Felis catus
  USE Cats
Felis catus silvestris
  USE European wildcat
Felis domestica
  USE Cats

Felis libyca
  USE Felis lybica
Felis lybica
  ₎QL737.C23₎
  UF African wild cat
     Felis libyca
Felis marmorata
  USE Marbled cat
Felis nebulosa
  USE Clouded leopard
Felis pardalis
  USE Ocelots
Felis serval
  USE Serval
Felis uncia
  USE Snow leopard
Felix (Comic strip)
  UF Lööf, Jan, 1940-   Felix (Comic
        strip)
     Wejp-Olsen, Werner.   Felix (Comic
        strip)
  BT Comic books, strips, etc.
FELIX C-256 (Computer)
  ₎QA76.8.F₎
  BT Electronic digital computers
  — Programming
     ₎QA76.8.F₎
     NT SIRIS (Computer system)
Felix the Cat (Fictitious character)
  BT Comic books, strips, etc.
Felker family
  UF Falker family
     Folker family
     Folkers family
     Fulcher family
     Voelckel family
     Voelkel family
     Volckel family
  RT Fulkerson family
Felkner family
  USE Feltner family
Fell family
  UF Fells family
     Fels family
Fellans
  USE Fulahs
Fellatio
  USE Oral intercourse
Feller family
  UF Fellerman family
     Felman family
Fellerman family
  USE Feller family
Felling cull trees
  USE Cull tree felling
Fellodistomidae
  ₎QL391.P7₎
  UF Monascidae
     Steringophoridae
     Xenoperidae
  BT Digenea
Fellow family
  USE Fellows family
Fellowes family
  USE Fellows family
Fellows family
  UF Fellow family
     Fellowes family
Fellowship
  UF Companionship
     Comradeship
  BT Friendship
  — Religious aspects
  — — Baptists, ₎Catholic Church, etc.₎
  — — Buddhism, ₎Christianity, etc.₎
Fellowship Movement
  USE Gemeinschaftsbewegung
Fellowships
  USE *subdivision* Scholarships, fellowships,
     etc. *under subjects, e.g.* Medicine—
     Scholarships, fellowships, etc.

Scholarships
Fells family
USE Fell family
Felman family
USE Feller family
Felon (Disease)
UF Whitlow
Felony
USE Criminal law
Felpel family
RT Voelpel family
Felps family
USE Phelps family
Fels family
USE Fell family
Felsenmeer *(May Subd Geog)*
UF Block field
Stone field
BT Patterned ground
Felsenthal National Wildlife Refuge (Ark.)
BT National parks and reserves—Arkansas
Wildlife refuges—Arkansas
Felspathoid
USE Feldspathoid
Felt
[TS1825]
NT Felting machines
Hatter's fur
Papermaking machinery felts
Felt boots *(May Subd Geog)*
UF Boots, Felt
Boots and shoes, Felt
BT Boots
Felt family
USE Felts family
Felt making
USE Felting
Felt marker decoration
[TT386]
UF Felt tip marker decoration
Felt tip pen decoration
Marker decoration, Felt
BT Decoration and ornament
Handicraft
Felt marker drawing *(May Subd Geog)*
UF Marker drawing, Felt
BT Drawing
Felt tip marker decoration
USE Felt marker decoration
Felt tip pen decoration
USE Felt marker decoration
Felt work
Here are entered works on the use of felt in handi-
craft. Works on the process of felt making are entered
under Felting.
UF Feltwork
BT Textile crafts
Feltch family
USE Felts family
Felte family
USE Felts family
Felteh family
USE Felts family
Felten family
USE Felton family
Feltin family
USE Felton family
Felting
[TT849.5]
Here are entered works on the process of felt mak-
ing. Works on the use of felt in handicraft are entered
under Felt work.
UF Felt making
BT Textile industry
Felting machines
[TS1825]
BT Felt
Textile machinery
Feltinore family
USE Feltner family

Feltner family
UF Felkner family
Feltinore family
Voelckner family
Voelkner family
Völckner family
Völkner family
Felton family
UF Felten family
Feltin family
Feltrinelli prize
Felts (Papermaking)
USE Papermaking machinery felts
Felts family
UF Feldt family
Felt family
Feltch family
Felte family
Felteh family
Feltz family
Felz family
Feltwork
USE Felt work
Feltz family
USE Felts family
Felz family
USE Felts family
Female apprentices
USE Women apprentices
Female bodybuilders
USE Women bodybuilders
Female change of life
USE Menopause
Female climacteric
USE Menopause
Female detectives
USE Women detectives
Female generative organs
USE Generative organs, Female
Female gods
USE Goddesses
Female homosexuals
USE Lesbians
Female impersonators
USE Impersonators, Female
Female infertility
USE Infertility, Female
Female offenders *(May Subd Geog)*
UF Delinquent women
Offenders, Female
Women—Crime
Women criminals
Women offenders
BT Crime and criminals
Women
NT Delinquent girls
Reformatories for women
Women outlaws
Women prisoners
— **Rehabilitation** *(May Subd Geog)*
— — **Minnesota**
NT Genesis II Program
Female orgasm
USE Orgasm, Female
Female prostitution
USE Prostitution
Female sex hormone
USE Hormones, Sex
Female sterility
USE Infertility, Female
Female sterilization
USE Sterilization of women
Female studies
USE Women's studies
Female Union Band Society Burying Ground
(Washington, D.C.)
USE Mount Zion Cemetery (Washington,
D.C.)

Females *(May Subd Geog)*
Here are entered works on female organisms in
general. Works on the human female are entered
under Women.
BT Sex
NT Cows
Ewes
Mares
Sows
Women
— **Evolution**
BT Evolution
— **Physiology**
BT Physiology
Females, Human
USE Women
Feminine beauty (Aesthetics)
(May Subd Geog)
Here are entered works on the attractiveness of
women as a philosophic or artistic concept. Practical
works on personal grooming and appearance are en-
tered under Beauty, Personal.
UF Ideal beautiful women
BT Aesthetics
Women in art
NT Beauty, Personal
Femininity (Philosophy)
[BD450]
BT Philosophical anthropology
Philosophy
Femininity (Psychology)
BT Sex (Psychology)
Women—Psychology
Femininity of God
UF God—Femininity
BT God
RT God—Motherhood
Feminism *(May Subd Geog)*
[HQ1101-2030.7]
UF Women's lib
Women's liberation movement
BT Women
NT Feminist motion pictures
Feminist therapy
Feminists
International Women's Decade, 1976-
1985
International Women's Year, 1975
Radical therapy
Sex discrimination against women
Women—History
Women—Legal status, laws, etc.
Women—Social conditions
Women's rights
— **Bibliography**
RT Feminist literature
— **Religious aspects**
NT Bible and feminism
— — **Baptists, [Catholic Church, etc.]**
— — **Buddhism, [Christianity, etc.]**
Feminism and art *(May Subd Geog)*
BT Art
Feminism and the arts
Feminism and literature *(May Subd Geog)*
BT Literature
RT Literature—Women authors
NT Feminist literary criticism
Feminist poetry
Feminism and motion pictures
(May Subd Geog)
[PN1995.9.W6]
BT Moving-pictures
NT Feminist motion pictures
Feminism and music *(May Subd Geog)*
[ML82]
BT Feminism and the arts
Music
Feminism and the arts *(May Subd Geog)*
[NX180.F4]
UF Arts and feminism
NT Feminism and art
Feminism and music

Feminism and theater (May Subd Geog)
  ⌜PN1590.W64⌝
  UF Theater and feminism
  BT Theater
Feminist cinema
  USE Feminist motion pictures
Feminist consultants (May Subd Geog)
  BT Consultants
Feminist criticism (May Subd Geog)
  UF Criticism, Feminist
  BT Criticism
  NT Feminist literary criticism
Feminist literary criticism (May Subd Geog)
  UF Literary criticism, Feminist
  BT Feminism and literature
      Feminist criticism
Feminist literature (May Subd Geog)
  UF Literature, Feminist
  RT Feminism—Bibliography
Feminist motion pictures (May Subd Geog)
  ⌜PN1995.9.W6⌝
  UF Feminist cinema
  BT Feminism
      Feminism and motion pictures
      Moving-pictures
      Women in the motion picture industry
Feminist poetry (May Subd Geog)
  BT Feminism and literature
      Poetry
Feminist poetry, Italian (May Subd Geog)
  UF Italian feminist poetry
  BT Italian poetry
Feminist poetry, Spanish (May Subd Geog)
  UF Spanish feminist poetry
  BT Spanish poetry
Feminist poetry, Spanish American
  (May Subd Geog)
  UF Spanish American feminist poetry
  BT Spanish American poetry
Feminist studies
  USE Women's studies
Feminist theater (May Subd Geog)
  ⌜PN2270.F45 (United States)⌝
  UF Women's theater
  BT Theater
Feminist therapy
  ⌜RC489.F45⌝
  Here are entered works on psychotherapy for
  women which focuses on the effects of sexism on
  their mental health.
  UF Therapy, Feminist
  BT Feminism
      Psychotherapy
      Women—Mental health
Feminists (May Subd Geog)
  BT Feminism
      Social reformers
  NT Suffragettes
      Women social reformers
Femme (Tapestry)
  USE Miró, Joan, 1893-   Woman
Femmes fatales (May Subd Geog)
  UF Adventuresses
      Seductresses
      Vamps
  BT Women
Femmes fatales in art
  ⌜NX650.F46⌝
Femoral artery
  UF Femur—Artery
  BT Arteries
Femoral epiphysis
  USE Femur—Epiphysis
Femoral hernia
  BT Hernia
Femoral nerve
  — Surgery
Femoral triangle
  USE Scarpa's triangle
Femoral trigone
  USE Scarpa's triangle

Femoral vein
  ⌜QL835 (Anatomy, Comparative)⌝
  ⌜QM191 (Anatomy, Human)⌝
Femur
  ⌜QL821 (Anatomy, Comparative)⌝
  ⌜QM117 (Anatomy, Human)⌝
  UF Thighbone
  BT Leg
  NT Iliofemoral joint
  — Artery
      USE Femoral artery
  — **Diseases** (May Subd Geog)
      NT Femur—Radiography
          Idiopathic femoral necrosis
  — **Epiphysis**
      UF Femoral epiphysis
  — **Radiography**
      BT Femur—Diseases
  — **Surgery**
  — **Wounds and injuries**
Femur neck
Fen Country (England)
  USE Fens, The (England)
Fen family
  USE Fenn family
Fen Ho (China)
  USE Fen River (China)
Fen River (China)
  UF Fen Ho (China)
      Fen Shui (China)
  BT Rivers—China
Fen Shui (China)
  USE Fen River (China)
Fence lizard
  USE Sceloporus undulatus
Fence lizard, European
  USE Lacerta agilis
Fencers (May Subd Geog)
  ⌜GV1144⌝
Fences (May Subd Geog)
  ⌜NA8390-NA8392 (Gates and fences)⌝
  ⌜S723-S725 (Agriculture)⌝
  BT Garden structures
  RT Hedges
  NT Cattle guards
      Electric fences
      Gates
      Roads—Guard fences
      Snow fences
      Stone walls
      Wire fencing
  — **Law and legislation** (May Subd Geog)
      RT Boundaries (Estates)
Fences, Anti-dazzle
  USE Roads—Glare screens
Fences (Receivers of stolen goods)
  USE Receiving stolen goods
Fenchel-Orlicz spaces
  BT Function spaces
      Orlicz spaces
Fencing (May Subd Geog)
  ⌜GV1143-GV1150.6 (Sports)⌝
  ⌜U860-U863 (Military science)⌝
  UF Fighting
  BT Athletics
      Dueling
      Hand-to-hand fighting
      Swords
  RT Swordplay
  NT Kendo
      Sabers
      Single-stick
      Stage fencing
      Swordsmen
  — **Rules**
      ⌜GV1149⌝
Fencing, Oriental
  UF Oriental fencing
Fencing in art
  ⌜N8217.F4⌝

Fenclofenac
  UF Dichlorophenoxyphenylacetic acid
  BT Anti-inflammatory agents
      Antirheumatic agents
      Phenylacetic acid
Fenclonine
  USE Chlorophenylalanine
Fender-Rhodes (Musical instrument)
  USE Electronic piano
Fenders, Automobile
  USE Automobiles—Fenders
Fenders for automobiles
  USE Automobiles—Fenders
Fenders for docks, piers, etc.
  UF Docks—Fenders
      Piers—Fenders
  BT Harbors
  NT Ships—Fenders
Fenders for street-cars
  USE Car fenders
Fendiline
  ⌜RC684.F44⌝
  BT Calcium—Antagonists
      Myocardial depressants
      Phenethylamines
      Vasodilators
Fendrich family
  USE Fendrick family
Fendrick family
  UF Fahndrich family
      Fehndrich family
      Fendrich family
Fenecchio River (Italy) (Not Subd Geog)
  UF Rio Fenecchio (Italy)
  BT Rivers—Italy
Fenel family
  USE Fennell family
Fenell family
  USE Fennell family
Fenemore family
  USE Fenimore family
Fener family
  USE Fenner family
Fenestra rotunda
  ⌜QL948⌝
  ⌜QM507⌝
  ⌜QP461⌝
  BT Ear
Feng-huang Hill Site (Chiang-ling hsien, China)
  ⌜DS793.F⌝
  UF Feng-huang Shan Site (Chiang-ling
          hsien, China)
      Feng-hwang Hill Site (Chiang-ling
          hsien, China)
  BT China—Antiquities
Feng-huang Shan Site (Chiang-ling hsien, China)
  USE Feng-huang Hill Site (Chiang-ling
          hsien, China)
Feng-hwang Hill Site (Chiang-ling hsien, China)
  USE Feng-huang Hill Site (Chiang-ling
          hsien, China)
Feng River (China)
  UF Feng shui (China)
  BT Rivers—China
Feng shui (China)
  USE Feng River (China)
Feng-shui (May Subd Geog)
  ⌜BF1779.F4⌝
  BT Divination
      Geomancy
Fengate Site (England) (Not Subd Geog)
  BT England—Antiquities
      Peterborough (Cambridgeshire)—
          Antiquities
Fenger family
Fenians
  ⌜DA954⌝

BT Canada—History—Fenian invasions,
　　1866-1870
　　Home rule (Ireland)
　　Ireland—History—1837-1901
　　Irish question
Fenil family
　USE Fennell family
Fenimore family
　UF Fenemore family
　　Fennimore family
　　Finamore family
　　Finemore family
　　Finnemore family
Fenis Castle (Comune di Fenis, Italy)
　USE Castello di Fenis (Comune di Fenis,
　　Italy)
Fenite *(May Subd Geog)*
　[QE475]
　BT Rocks, Igneous
Fenitoin
　USE Phenytoin
Fenitrothion
　[SB952.F]
　UF Dimethylmethylnitrop
　　henylphosphorothioate
　　Dimethylnitrotolyl phosphorothioate
　BT Organophosphorus compounds
　　Thiophosphates
Fenjas
　USE Falashas
Fenland (England)
　USE Fens, The (England)
Fenn family
　UF De Fenne family
　　DeFenne family
　　Fen family
　　Fenne family
　　Venn family
Fenne family
　USE Fenn family
Fennecs
　[QL737.C22]
　UF Fennecus zerda
　BT Foxes
Fennecus zerda
　USE Fennecs
Fennel
　[QK495.U48]
　UF Foeniculum
　BT Umbelliferae
Fennel family
　USE Fennell family
Fennell family
　UF Fehnel family
　　Fenel family
　　Fenell family
　　Fenil family
　　Fennel family
　　Fennil family
Fenner family
　UF Fener family
　　Fennir family
　　Venner family
Fennil family
　USE Fennell family
Fennimore family
　USE Fenimore family
Fennir family
　USE Fenner family
Fenno-Ugric languages
　USE Finno-Ugric languages
Fennoscandia
　USE Scandinavia
Fennoscandian shield
　USE Baltic Shield
Fenoterol
　UF Dihydroxyhydroxymeth
　　ylphenethylaminometh
　　ylbenzylalcohol

BT Bronchodilator agents
　　Ethanolamines
　　Sympathomimetic agents
Fens, The (England) *(Not Subd Geog)*
　UF Fen Country (England)
　　Fenland (England)
　　The Fens (England)
Fens *(May Subd Geog)*
　[DA670.F33 (England)]
　BT Drainage
　　Wetlands
　RT Bogs
　　Marshes
　　Moors and heaths
　　Waste lands
Fensch family
　USE Fenske family
Fenske family
　UF Fensch family
Fenster family
　UF Fensterer family
　　Fenstermacher family
　　Fenstermaker family
　　Finster family
Fensterer family
　USE Fenster family
Fenstermacher family
　USE Fenster family
Fenstermaker family
　USE Fenster family
Fentanyl
　[RD86.F45]
　UF Phenethylpiperidylpropionanilide
　　citrate
　　Phentanyl
　BT Analgesics
　　Anesthetics
　　Citrates
　　Narcotics
　　Piperidine
　　Tranquilizing drugs
Fentem family
Fenton family
　UF Fentons family
　　Phenton family
Fentons family
　USE Fenton family
Fentress family
　UF Fentriss family
Fentriss family
　USE Fentress family
Fenua Iti (Cook Islands)
　USE Takutea (Cook Islands)
Feragen family
Feral animals *(May Subd Geog)*
　[SF140.F47]
　UF Animals, Feral
　BT Animals
　RT Domestic animals
　NT Feral livestock
　　Feral mammals
Feral cats *(May Subd Geog)*
　[SF450]
　BT Cats
　　Feral mammals
Feral children *(May Subd Geog)*
　[GN372 (Anthropology)]
　[RJ507.F47 (Child psychiatry)]
　UF Wild children
　　Wolf children
　BT Exceptional children
　　Wild men
Feral dogs *(May Subd Geog)*
　[SF810.7.D65]
　　Here are entered works on domesticated dogs that
　have returned to the wild. Works on undomesticated
　mammals of the family Canidae that resemble domes-
　tic dogs are entered under Wild dogs.
　UF Stray dogs
　BT Dogs
　　Feral mammals

　RT Wild dogs
Feral horses
　USE Wild horses
Feral livestock *(May Subd Geog)*
　UF Livestock, Feral
　　Wild livestock
　BT Feral animals
　　Livestock
　NT Feral swine
　　Wild horses
Feral mammals *(May Subd Geog)*
　[SF140.F47]
　BT Feral animals
　　Mammals
　NT Feral cats
　　Feral dogs
　　Feral swine
　　Wild horses
Feral swine *(May Subd Geog)*
　[SF397.8-SF397.83]
　UF Hogs, Wild
　　Pigs, Wild
　　Swine, Feral
　　Swine, Wild
　　Wild hogs
　　Wild pigs
　　Wild swine
　BT Feral livestock
　　Feral mammals
　　Swine
　RT Wild boar
Ferber family
　RT Farber family
Ferberite
　[QE391.F4]
　RT Tungsten
**Ferdinand the faithful and Ferdinand the
　unfaithful (Tale)**
　[BR75.F4]
　UF Clever horse (Tale)
　　Ferdinand true and Ferdinand untrue
　　(Tale)
　BT Tales
Ferdinand true and Ferdinand untrue (Tale)
　USE Ferdinand the faithful and Ferdinand
　　the unfaithful (Tale)
Ferdinandina Site (Okla.) *(Not Subd Geog)*
　UF Deer Creek Site (Okla.)
　　Fernandina Site (Okla.)
　BT Oklahoma—Antiquities
Ferdinandy family
Fere family
　USE Ferry family
Feree family
　USE Ferry family
Ferel family
　USE Ferrell family
Ferenc family
　USE Ferenczy family
Ference family
　USE Ferenczy family
Ferenci family
　USE Ferenczy family
Ferencz family
　USE Ferenczy family
Ferenczy family
　UF Ferenc family
　　Ference family
　　Ferenci family
　　Ferencz family
　　Ferenz family
　　Ferenzi family
Ferenz family
　USE Ferenczy family
Ferenzi family
　USE Ferenczy family
Feresa attenuata
　USE Pygmy killer whale
Feresa occulta
　USE Pygmy killer whale

Feret family
  USE Ferry family
Fergana Range (Kirghiz S.S.R.)
  UF Ferganskiĭ khrebet (Kirghiz S.S.R.)
  BT Mountains—Kirghiz S.S.R.
Fergana Valley
  UF Ferganskaĭa dolina
  BT Valleys—Kirghiz S.S.R.
      Valleys—Tajik S.S.R.
      Valleys—Uzbek S.S.R.
Ferganskaĭa dolina
  USE Fergana Valley
Ferganskiĭ khrebet (Kirghiz S.S.R.)
  USE Fergana Range (Kirghiz S.S.R.)
Fergason family
  USE Ferguson family
Fergerson family
  USE Ferguson family
Fergison family
  USE Ferguson family
Fergus family
  USE Ferguson family
Ferguson family
  UF Fargurson family
      Fargusen family
      Farguson family
      Fergason family
      Fergerson family
      Fergison family
      Fergus family
      Fergusson family
      Forgason family
      Forgerson family
      Forgeson family
      Forgison family
      Forguson family
      Furgason family
      Furgerson family
      Furgeson family
      Furgison family
      Furguson family
Fergusson family
  USE Ferguson family
Ferir (The French word)
  [PC2886.9.F]
  BT French language—Etymology
Feris family
  USE Farris family
Ferlo (Senegal)
Fermat's last theorem
  UF Last theorem, Fermat's
  BT Diophantine analysis
      Numbers, Theory of
  RT Fermat's theorem
Fermat's theorem
  [QA244]
  BT Variational principles
  RT Congruences and residues
      Fermat's last theorem
Ferme de la Carrière (France)
  USE Carrière Farm (France)
Fermentation
  [QK896 (Plant physiology)]
  [QP601 (Physiological chemistry)]
  [QR151 (Micro-organisms)]
  [TP500-TP618 (Fermentation
      industries)]
  UF Ferments
  BT Biochemical engineering
      Chemistry
      Industrial microbiology
      Microbiological synthesis
  NT Brewing
      Fermentation products industry
      Fish, Fermented
      Food, Fermented
      Molds (Botany)
      Nattō
      Penicillium
      Rumen fermentation
      Silage—Fermentation

      Sugars
Fermentation gum
  USE Dextran
Fermentation products industry
  (May Subd Geog)
  [HD9660.F48]
  BT Fermentation
Fermentation tube
  [QR66]
  BT Bacteriology—Technique
Fermented cream
  USE Sour cream
Fermented fish
  USE Fish, Fermented
Fermented food
  USE Food, Fermented
Ferments
  USE Enzymes
      Fermentation
Fermi-Dirac particles
  USE Fermions
Fermi gas
  USE Electron gas
Fermi surfaces
  [QC176]
  UF Surfaces, Fermi
  BT Electrons
      Energy-band theory of solids
      Free electron theory of metals
      Quantum statistics
Fermi-Thomas theory
  USE Thomas-Fermi theory
Fermions
  UF Fermi-Dirac particles
  BT Quantum statistics
  RT Leptons (Nuclear physics)
Fern, Adder's
  USE Polypodium vulgare
Fern, Wall
  USE Polypodium vulgare
Fern allies
  USE Pteridophyta
Fern rhapis
  USE Rhapis excelsa
Fernandes family
  USE Fernandez family
Fernández de Córdoba family
Fernandez family
  UF Fernandes family
      Fernando family
Fernandian language
  USE Bube language
Fernandina Site (Okla.)
  USE Ferdinandina Site (Okla.)
Fernando family
  USE Fernandez family
Fernando Po (Equatorial Guinea)
  UF Bioco (Equatorial Guinea)
      Bioko (Equatorial Guinea)
      Fernando Póo (Equatorial Guinea)
      Isla de Bioco (Equatorial Guinea)
      Isla de Bioko (Equatorial Guinea)
      Macias Nguema (Equatorial Guinea)
  BT Islands—Equatorial Guinea
Fernando Póo (Equatorial Guinea)
  USE Fernando Po (Equatorial Guinea)
Fernico
  USE Iron-nickel-cobalt alloys
Ferns (May Subd Geog)
  [QK520-QK532]
  [SB429 (Culture)]
  UF Acrogens
      Filicineae
  BT Botany
      Cryptogams
      Foliage plants
      Pteridophyta
  NT Cut ferns
      Dennstaedtiaceae
      Ferns, Ornamental
      Filicales

      Marsileales
      Salviniales
      Thelypteridaceae
      Water ferns
  — **Anatomy**
      [QK521]
  — **Spores**
  — **Type specimens**
      [QK523]
      BT Type specimens (Natural history)
Ferns, Cut
  USE Cut ferns
Ferns, Fossil
  [QE961]
  BT Paleobotany
  NT Archaeopteris
      Coenopteridales
      Glossopteris
Ferns, Garden
  USE Ferns, Ornamental
Ferns, Maidenhair
  USE Maidenhair ferns
Ferns, Mosquito
  USE Azolla
Ferns, Ornamental (May Subd Geog)
  [SB429 (Culture)]
  UF Ferns, Garden
      Garden ferns
      Ornamental ferns
  BT Ferns
      Foliage plants
  NT Platycerium
Fero family
  USE Ferro family
Fero language
  USE Pero language
Feroe family
  USE Ferro family
Feroge languages
  BT Niger-Congo languages
Feroll family
  USE Ferrell family
Feronidae
  USE Carabidae
Ferradura Site (Spain)
  UF La Ferradura Site (Spain)
  BT Spain—Antiquities
Ferral family
  USE Ferrell family
Ferrall family
  USE Ferrell family
Ferralsols (May Subd Geog)
  [S592.17.F45]
  UF Krasnozems
      Latosols
      Oxisols
      Sols ferrallitiques
  BT Soils
Ferran family
  USE Farren family
Ferrant Pegasus computer
  USE Pegasus computer
Ferrari automobile
Ferrassie Rock-shelter (France)
  (Not Subd Geog)
  UF La Ferrassie Rock-shelter (France)
  BT Caves—France
      France—Antiquities
Ferrates
  USE Ferrites (Magnetic materials)
Ferre family
  USE Ferry family
Ferree family
  USE Ferry family
Ferrel family
  USE Ferrell family

Ferrell family
  UF Fearal family
      Fearell family
      Fearghaill family
      Ferel family
      Feroll family
      Ferral family
      Ferrall family
      Ferrel family
      Ferril family
      Ferrile family
      Ferrill family
      Ferrol family
  RT Farrell family
Ferren family
  USE Farren family
Ferrer family
Ferret, Black-footed
  USE Black-footed ferret
Ferreting *(May Subd Geog)*
  ⌐SK293¬
  UF Hunting with ferrets
  BT Hunting
  RT Ferrets
Ferrets
  ⌐QL737.C2 (Zoology)¬
  ⌐SB994.R2 (Rat-catching)¬
  RT European polecat
      Ferreting
      Weasels
  — Physiology
Ferrets as laboratory animals
Ferrets as pets
  ⌐SF459.F47¬
Ferrey family
  USE Ferry family
Ferric chloride
  ⌐QD181.F4¬
  UF Ferric trichloride
      Flores martis
      Iron 3-chloride
      Iron chloride
      Iron perchloride
      Iron trichloride
      Ironic chloride
  BT Chlorides
Ferric hydrates
  USE Ferric hydroxides
Ferric hydroxides
  ⌐QD181.F4¬
  UF Ferric hydrates
  BT Hydroxides
Ferric ions
  USE Iron ions
Ferric nitrate
  ⌐QD181.F4¬
  UF Nitrate of iron
Ferric salts
  ⌐QD181.F4¬
  BT Salts
Ferric trichloride
  USE Ferric chloride
Ferrie family
  USE Ferry family
Ferrierite *(May Subd Geog)*
  ⌐QE391.F45¬
Ferries *(May Subd Geog)*
  ⌐HE5751-5870¬
  BT Passenger ships
      River boats
      Roll-on/roll-off ships
      Transportation
      Work boats
  NT Train ferries
  — Access roads *(May Subd Geog)*
      UF Access roads to ferries
      BT Roads
  — Law and legislation *(May Subd Geog)*
      BT Highway law

Ferries in art
  NT Fox, Emanuel Phillips, 1865-1915.
      Ferry
Ferril family
  USE Ferrell family
Ferrile family
  USE Ferrell family
Ferrill family
  USE Ferrell family
Ferrimagnetism
  BT Magnetism
Ferrin family
  USE Farren family
Ferrinatrite
  BT Iron salts
Ferringdon family
  USE Farrington family
Ferrington family
  USE Farrington family
Ferrins family
  USE Farren family
Ferris family
  USE Farris family
Ferris wheels *(May Subd Geog)*
  ⌐GV1860.F45¬
  BT Amusement rides
      Wheels
Ferrise family
  USE Farris family
Ferriss family
  USE Farris family
Ferrite
  ⌐TN693.I7 (Metallography)¬
  RT Ferrites (Magnetic materials)
  NT Copper ferrite
Ferrite cores
  UF Cores, Ferrite
  BT Ferrite devices
      Magnetic cores
Ferrite devices
  ⌐TK7872.F4¬
  BT Electronic apparatus and appliances
      Magnetic devices
  NT Ferrite cores
Ferrite isolators
  ⌐TK7872.F4¬
  UF Isolators, Ferrite
  BT Wave guides
Ferrites (Magnetic materials)
  UF Ferrates
  BT Gyrators
      Magnetic materials
  RT Ferrite
  NT Orthoferrites
      Yttrium iron garnet
  — Heat treatment
  — Thermal properties
Ferritic stainless steel
  USE Ferritic steel
Ferritic steel
  UF Ferritic stainless steel
      Stainless steel, Ferritic
      Steel, Ferritic
  BT Steel, Stainless
Ferritin
  BT Carrier proteins
      Iron in the body
      Iron proteins
  RT Hemosiderin
      Isoferritin
Ferro (Canary Islands)
  USE Hierro (Canary Islands)
Ferro family
  UF Feero family
      Fero family
      Feroe family
      Ferrone family
      Ferroni family
Ferro-vanadium
  USE Ferrovanadium

Ferroboron
  BT Boron
Ferrocarril de Antioquia
  ⌐HE2950 (Economics)¬
  BT Railroads—Colombia
Ferrocarriles Catalanes
  BT Railroads—Spain
Ferrocement
  USE Reinforced concrete
Ferrocement boats
  USE Concrete boats
Ferrocement tanks
  USE Concrete tanks
Ferrocene
  UF Dicyclopentadienyl iron
  BT Metallocenes
      Organoiron compounds
Ferrocyanides
  NT Sodium nitroferricyanide
Ferroelectric crystals
  UF Ferroelectrics
  NT Ferroelectric storage cells
Ferroelectric devices
  BT Dielectric devices
      Electronic apparatus and appliances
      Ferroelectricity
      Solid state electronics
  RT Piezoelectric devices
  NT Ferroelectric storage cells
Ferroelectric effect
  USE Ferroelectricity
Ferroelectric storage cells
  UF Memory devices
  BT Ferroelectric crystals
      Ferroelectric devices
Ferroelectricity
  ⌐QC595¬
  UF Ferroelectric effect
      Seignette-electricity
  BT Crystals—Electric properties
      Dielectrics
      Polarization (Electricity)
  NT Domain structure
      Ferroelectric devices
      Photoferroelectric effect
Ferroelectrics
  USE Ferroelectric crystals
Ferrofluids
  USE Magnetic fluids
Ferrography (Photomechanical process)
  USE Ferromagnetography
Ferrol family
  USE Ferrell family
Ferromagnetic domain
  USE Domain structure
Ferromagnetic materials
  ⌐TK454.4.M3 (Electric engineering)¬
  ⌐TK7871.15.M3 (Electronics)¬
  BT Ferromagnetism
      Magnetic materials
  — Fluctuations
      UF Fluctuations in ferromagnetic
          materials
Ferromagnetic resonance
  UF Resonance, Ferromagnetic
  BT Ferromagnetism
      Magnetic resonance
Ferromagnetism
  BT Magnetism
  NT Antiferromagnetism
      Barkhausen effect
      Domain structure
      Ferromagnetic materials
      Ferromagnetic resonance
      Ising model
      Magnetization
      Spin waves

Ferromagnetography
    UF Ferrography (Photomechanical
            process)
        Magnetography (Photomechanical
            process)
    BT Electrophotography
        Photomechanical processes
Ferromanganese
    [TN757.F3]
    BT Iron-manganese alloys
Ferron family
    USE Farren family
Ferrone family
    USE Ferro family
Ferroni family
    USE Ferro family
Ferroproteins
    USE Iron proteins
Ferrosilicon
    [TN757.F4]
    UF Silicon-iron
    BT Iron-silicon alloys
        Silicon steel
Ferrotitanium alloys
    USE Titanium-iron alloys
Ferrotungsten
    BT Iron-tungsten alloys
Ferrotype
    USE Tintype
Ferrous ions
    USE Iron ions
Ferrous metal industries
    USE Iron industry and trade
        Steel industry and trade
Ferrous oxide
    NT Limonite
Ferrous salts
    [QD181.F4]
    BT Salts
Ferrous sulphate
    [QD181.F4]
    UF Iron sulphate
Ferrovanadium
    UF Ferro-vanadium
    BT Vanadium alloys
Ferrovia del San Gottardo
    USE Gotthardbahn
Ferrovie Federali Svizzere
    USE Schweizerische Bundesbahnen
Ferry (Painting)
    USE Fox, Emanuel Phillips, 1865-1915.
        Ferry
Ferry Boat du Nuit (Express train)
    USE Night Ferry (Express train)
Ferry-bridges
    [TG435]
    UF Bridges, Ferry
Ferry family
    UF Fere family
        Feree family
        Feret family
        Ferre family
        Ferree family
        Ferrey family
        Ferrie family
        Ferrys family
Ferry flying
    USE Airplanes—Ferrying
Ferrying of airplanes
    USE Airplanes—Ferrying
Ferryor family
    RT Verry family
Ferrys family
    USE Ferry family
Fertile crescent
    USE Middle East
Fertility
    [QP273 (Physiology)]
    UF Fecundity
    BT Reproduction
    RT Infertility in animals

    NT Cattle—Fertility
        Fishes—Fertility
        Heterosis
        Sterilization reversal
    — **Effect of drugs on**
        UF Fertility, Effect of drugs on
        BT Drugs—Physiological effect
    — **Endocrine aspects**
        UF Endocrine aspects of fertility
            Fertility—Hormonal aspects
            Hormonal aspects of fertility
    — **Hormonal aspects**
        USE Fertility—Endocrine aspects
Fertility, Effect of drugs on
    USE Fertility—Effect of drugs on
Fertility, Human (May Subd Geog)
    [GN241 (Physiological anthropology)]
    [HB903.F4 (Statistics)]
    [QP273 (Physiology)]
    UF Human fertility
        Natality
    BT Demography
        Human reproduction
    RT Infertility
    SA subdivision Population under names of
            countries, e.g. United States—
            Population
    NT Birth intervals
        Conception
        PROJTARG (Computer program)
    — **Immunological aspects**
    — **Nutritional aspects**
    — **Statistics**
        UF Birth-rate
Fertility cults (May Subd Geog)
    UF Cults, Fertility
    BT Cults
    NT Rice planting rites
    — **Japan**
        NT Taasobi
Fertility of eggs
    USE Eggs—Hatchability
Fertilization, Human
    USE Conception
Fertilization, In vitro
    USE Fertilization in vitro
Fertilization, Laboratory
    USE Fertilization in vitro
Fertilization, Test tube
    USE Fertilization in vitro
Fertilization (Biology)
    [QH485]
    UF Amphimixis
    BT Biology
        Cells
        Embryology
        Physiology
        Reproduction
    NT Conception
Fertilization in vitro (May Subd Geog)
    UF Ectogenesis, Preimplantational
        Fertilization, In vitro
        Fertilization, Laboratory
        Fertilization, Test tube
        In vitro fertilization
        IVF
        Laboratory fertilization
        Preimplantational ectogenesis
        Test tube fertilization
    BT Genetic engineering
Fertilization in vitro, Human
    (May Subd Geog)
    [RG135]
    UF Babies, Test tube
        Human fertilization in vitro
        Human in vitro fertilization
        Test tube babies
    BT Conception
        Embryology, Human
        Human reproduction
    — **Law and legislation** (May Subd Geog)

        BT Medical laws and legislation
            Parent and child (Law)
    — **Religious aspects**
    — — **Baptists,** [Catholic Church, etc.]
    — — **Buddhism,** [Christianity, etc.]
Fertilization in vitro, Human (Islamic law)
    (May Subd Geog)
    BT Islamic law
Fertilization of lakes
    USE Lakes—Fertilization
Fertilization of plants
    [QK828]
    BT Botany
        Plant physiology
        Plants
        Plants—Reproduction
    NT Cleistogamy
        Pollination
Fertilization of plants by insects
    [QK926]
    BT Insect-plant relationships
        Insects
    NT Pollination by insects
Fertilization of sea-water
    USE Sea-water—Fertilization
Fertilization of soils
    USE Fertilizers
Fertilizer equipment (May Subd Geog)
    [S693.5]
    UF Fertilizers—Equipment and supplies
    BT Agricultural machinery
        Fertilizers
    NT Fertilizer spreaders
Fertilizer industry (May Subd Geog)
    [HD9483-9484]
    BT Fertilizers
        Nitrogen industries
    NT Compost plants
        Wages—Fertilizer industry
    — **Equipment and supplies**
Fertilizer-pesticide mixtures
    (May Subd Geog)
    UF Pesticide-fertilizer mixtures
    BT Fertilizers
        Mixtures
        Pesticides
    — **Application**
        UF Application of fertilizer-pesticide
            mixtures
Fertilizer spreaders
    UF Spreaders of fertilizers
    BT Fertilizer equipment
Fertilizers (May Subd Geog)
    [S631-S667 (Agriculture)]
    UF Artificial fertilizers
        Chemical fertilizers
        Fertilization of soils
        Soils—Fertilization
    BT Agricultural chemicals
        Plants—Nutrition
        Soil amendments
    RT Soil fertility
    SA subdivision Fertilizers under individual
            crops, e.g. Corn—Fertilizers
    NT Ammonia as fertilizer
        Aquatic plants as fertilizer
        Ashes as fertilizer
        Calcium fertilizers
        Corn—Fertilizers
        Cyanamid
        Fertilizer equipment
        Fertilizer industry
        Fertilizer-pesticide mixtures
        Fish-scrap fertilizer
        Forest soils—Fertilization
        Garden fertilizers
        Lakes—Fertilization
        Liming of soils
        Liquid fertilizers
        Magnesium fertilizers
        Manures

1334

Marl
Meadows—Fertilizers
Micronutrient fertilizers
Molasses as fertilizer
Nitrogen fertilizers
Nitrogen-fixing algae as fertilizer
Organic fertilizers
Organic wastes as fertilizer
Phosphatic fertilizers
Potassium fertilizers
Salt as fertilizer
Sea-water—Fertilization
Sewage as fertilizer
Sewage irrigation
Sewage sludge as fertilizer
Slag as fertilizer
Soils—Fertilizer movement
Straw as fertilizer
Sulphur fertilizers
Urea as fertilizer
Waste products as fertilizer
Wood waste as mulch, soil conditioner,
etc.
Zinc fertilizers
— Application
UF Application of fertilizers
RT Spraying and dusting in agriculture
NT Aerial fertilizing
— Equipment and supplies
USE Fertilizer equipment
— Tariff
USE Tariff on fertilizers
Fertő tó (Austria and Hungary)
USE Neusiedler Lake (Austria and
Hungary)
Ferula
⌈QK495.U48⌉
UF Silphium
BT Umbelliferae
Ferverda family
UF Ferwerda family
Ferwerda family
USE Ferverda family
Fescue *(May Subd Geog)*
⌈QK495.G74 (Botany)⌉
UF Festuca
BT Grasses
NT Arizona fescue
Meadow fescue
Red fescue
Tall fescue
Fescue foot
BT Cattle—Diseases
Fesher family
USE Fisher family
Fesler family
USE Fessler family
Fesmire family
Fessler family
UF Faessler family
Fesler family
Festa de Bon Jesus de Pirapora
BT Blacks—Brazil
Fester family
Festival-day sermons
⌈BV4254.3⌉
UF Feast-day sermons
Sermons, Festival-day
BT Church year sermons
Fasts and feasts
NT All Saints' Day sermons
All Souls' Day sermons
Christmas sermons
— Jewish authors
USE Festival-day sermons, Jewish
Festival-day sermons, Jewish
UF Festival-day sermons—Jewish authors
Jewish festival-day sermons
BT Fasts and feasts—Judaism
Jewish sermons
NT Rosh ha-Shanah sermons

Sukkot sermons
Festival of American Music, Rochester, N.Y.
USE Eastman School Festival of American
Music
Festivals *(May Subd Geog)*
⌈GT3930-GT4995 (Manners and
customs)⌉
⌈LB3560-LB3575 (Educational)⌉
BT Days
Manners and customs
RT Anniversaries
Fasts and feasts
Pageants
Processions
SA *names of individual festivals, e.g.*
Fools, Feast of
NT Art festivals
Boy-bishop
Craft festivals
Dance festivals
Drama festivals
Family festivals
Folk festivals
Harvest festivals
Holidays
Moving-picture festivals
Music festivals
Parades
Rice planting rites
Tournaments
— Jews
USE Fasts and feasts—Judaism
— India
NT Gambhira Festival
Mopin
— Japan
NT Gion Festival
Mikoshi
Taasobi
— Spain
NT Fiesta de San Fermín, Pamplona,
Spain
— United States
NT Fourth of July celebrations
Festivals, Craft
USE Craft festivals
Festivals in art
Festivals in literature
Festivals of Male Voice Praise
BT Music festivals
Festschriften *(May Subd Geog)*
UF Anniversary volumes
Commemorative volumes
Homage volumes
Jubilee volumes
Wedding publications
RT Essays
NT Speeches, addresses, etc.
Festuca
USE Fescue
Festuca arizonica
USE Arizona fescue
Festuca arundinacea
USE Tall fescue
Festuca elatior
USE Meadow fescue
Tall fescue
Festuca pratensis
USE Meadow fescue
Festuca rubra
USE Red fescue
Festuca viridis
USE Red fescue
FESWMS-TX (Computer program)
UF Finite-Element Surface-Water
Modeling System-Texas (Computer
program)
BT Hydrodynamics—Computer programs

Fetal alcohol syndrome *(May Subd Geog)*
BT Abnormalities, Human
Alcoholism in pregnancy
Fetus—Diseases
Syndromes
Fetal anoxia *(May Subd Geog)*
UF Fetal hypoxia
BT Anoxemia
Fetus—Diseases
NT Asphyxia neonatorum
Fetal behavior
USE Behavioral embryology
Fetal blood
UF Cord blood
Umbilical cord blood
BT Blood
Fetal brain *(May Subd Geog)*
BT Brain
Fetal cardiography
USE Fetal heart rate monitoring
Fetal death *(May Subd Geog)*
⌈RG631-633⌉
UF Fetus, Death of the
BT Death
Mortality
Pregnancy, Complications of
NT Abortion
Lithopedion
Still-birth
Fetal distress *(May Subd Geog)*
UF Distress, Fetal
BT Fetus—Diseases
Stress (Physiology)
Fetal erythroblastosis
USE Erythroblastosis fetalis
Fetal globulins
USE Alpha fetoproteins
Fetal growth
USE Fetus—Growth
Fetal growth retardation
USE Fetus—Growth retardation
Fetal heart
BT Heart
NT Fetal heart rate monitoring
— Blood-vessels
NT Truncus arteriosus
— — Abnormalities
NT Truncus arteriosus, Persistent
Fetal heart rate monitoring
(May Subd Geog)
⌈RG628.3.H42⌉
UF Cardiotocography
Fetal cardiography
Heart rate monitoring, Fetal
BT Cardiography
Fetal heart
Fetus—Diseases—Diagnosis
Heart beat
Patient monitoring
— Equipment and supplies
NT Fetal heart rate monitoring
equipment industry
**Fetal heart rate monitoring equipment
industry** *(May Subd Geog)*
⌈HD9995.F48⌉
BT Fetal heart rate monitoring—
Equipment and supplies
Fetal hypoxia
USE Fetal anoxia
Fetal immunity, Maternally acquired
USE Maternally acquired immunity
Fetal liver cells *(May Subd Geog)*
BT Liver cells
Fetal malnutrition *(May Subd Geog)*
⌈RG627.6.M34⌉
UF Prenatal malnutrition
BT Fetus—Diseases
Fetus—Nutrition
Malnutrition in children
Malnutrition in pregnancy

Fetal membranes
  UF Membranes, Fetal
  BT Membranes (Biology)
  NT Amnion
      Chorioallantois
      Chorion
Fetal nerve tissue *(May Subd Geog)*
  BT Nerve tissue
Fetal offering rites
  USE Fetal propitiatory rites
Fetal passive immunity
  USE Maternally acquired immunity
Fetal pharmacology
  USE Fetus—Effect of drugs on
Fetal pig
  USE Pig embryo
Fetal presentation
  ₍RG671-693₎
  UF Labor presentation (Obstetrics)
      Lie (Obstetrics)
      Presentation, Fetal
      Presentation (Obstetrics)
  BT Delivery (Obstetrics)
  NT Breech delivery
Fetal propitiatory rites *(May Subd Geog)*
  UF Fetal offering rites
      Propitiatory rites, Fetal
  BT Abortion—Religious aspects
      Fetus—Religious aspects
      Liturgies
      Rites and ceremonies
  — Baptists, ₍Catholic Church, etc.₎
  — Buddhism
      UF Mizugo kuyō
          Mizuko kuyō
  — Buddhism, ₍Christianity, etc.₎
Fetal rickets
  USE Achondroplasia
Fetal transfusion
  USE Blood—Transfusion, Intrauterine
Fetal visualization, Direct
  USE Fetoscopy
Feterita
  USE Durra
Fetiales
  ₍JX2025₎
  BT Ambassadors
Fetichism
  USE Fetishism
Feticide
  USE Abortion
Fetishism *(May Subd Geog)*
  ₍GN472 (Ethnology)₎
  ₍HQ79 (Sex)₎
  UF Fetichism
  BT Psychosexual disorders
      Worship
  NT Animism
      Idols and images
      Voodooism
Fetoplacental function tests
  USE Placental function tests
Fetoproteins, Alpha
  USE Alpha fetoproteins
Fetoscopy *(May Subd Geog)*
  ₍RG628.3.F47₎
  UF Direct fetal visualization
      Direct intrauterine visualization
      Fetal visualization, Direct
      Intrauterine visualization, Direct
      Visualization, Direct fetal
  BT Endoscopy
      Prenatal diagnosis
Fetter family
  UF Fetterman family
      Fetters family
      Vetter family
      Vetterman family
  RT Feather family
Fetterman family
  USE Fetter family

Fetterman Fight, 1866
  UF Hundred in the Hands, Battle of the,
      1866
      Philip Kearny, Fort—Massacre, 1866
  BT Cheyenne Indians—Wars
      Dakota Indians—Wars
      Indians of North America—Wars—
      1866-1895
Fetters family
  USE Fetter family
Fettes family
Fetuins
  USE Alpha fetoproteins
Fetus
  ₍RG600 (Physiology)₎
  UF Foetus
      Unborn child
  BT Embryology
      Reproduction
  SA *headings beginning with the word*
      Fetal
  NT Carcinoembryonic antigens
      Docimasia pulmonum
      Ductus arteriosus
      Gestational age
      Maternal-fetal exchange
      Obstetrics
      Prenatal influences
      Urachus
      Wolffian body
  — Abnormalities *(May Subd Geog)*
      ₍QM691-QM695 (Teratology)₎
      ₍RG626-RG629 (Obstetrics)₎
      BT Abnormalities, Human
  — Anatomy
      BT Anatomy, Human
  — Behavior
      USE Behavioral embryology
  — Diseases *(May Subd Geog)*
      ₍RG626-629₎
      UF Embryopathies
      BT Pregnancy, Complications of
      NT Achondroplasia
          Blood—Transfusion, Intrauterine
          Cytomegalic inclusion disease
          Dysostosis
          Erythroblastosis fetalis
          Fetal alcohol syndrome
          Fetal anoxia
          Fetal distress
          Fetal malnutrition
          Fetus—Effect of radiation on
          Fetus—Growth retardation
  — — Diagnosis
      BT Prenatal diagnosis
      NT Amniocentesis
          Fetal heart rate monitoring
  — Effect of drugs on
      ₍RG627.6.D79₎
      UF Fetal pharmacology
      BT Drugs—Physiological effect
          Obstetrical pharmacology
          Pharmacology
  — Effect of radiation on
      ₍RG627.6.R33₎
      UF Fetus—Radiation effects
          Fetus, Effect of radiation on the
      BT Fetus—Diseases
          Radiation—Physiological effect
  — Growth
      ₍RG613₎
      UF Fetal growth
          Intrauterine growth
      NT Birth size
  — Growth retardation *(May Subd Geog)*
      UF Fetal growth retardation
          Growth retardation, Fetal
          Growth retardation, Intrauterine
          Intrauterine growth retardation

      BT Birth size
          Fetus—Diseases
          Growth disorders
      NT Birth weight, Low
  — Metabolism
      ₍RG615₎
      BT Fetus—Physiology
          Metabolism
  — Nutrition
      ₍RG615₎
      BT Pregnancy—Nutritional aspects
      NT Fetal malnutrition
  — Physiology
      ₍RG610-620₎
      NT Fetus—Metabolism
  — Radiation effects
      USE Fetus—Effect of radiation on
  — Religious aspects
      UF Fetus (Theology)
      BT Man (Theology)
      NT Fetal propitiatory rites
  — — Buddhism, ₍Christianity, etc.₎
  — Research
  — — Law and legislation
      (May Subd Geog)
      BT Medical laws and legislation
          Unborn children (Law)
  — Respiration and cry
      ₍RG620₎
      BT Adaptation (Physiology)
      NT Apnea neonatorum
Fetus, Death of the
  USE Fetal death
Fetus, Effect of radiation on the
  USE Fetus—Effect of radiation on
Fetus (Theology)
  USE Fetus—Religious aspects
Fetzpattreck family
  USE Fitzpatrick family
Feu family
  USE Few family
Feudal castles
  USE Castles
Feudal courts *(May Subd Geog)*
  BT Courts
      Feudal law
  RT Manorial courts
Feudal domains
  USE Fiefs
Feudal estates
  USE Fiefs
Feudal law *(May Subd Geog)*
  UF Droit féodal
      Feudalism—Law
      Law, Feudal
  BT Land tenure—Law and legislation
  NT Allodium
      Banality (Law)
      Feudal courts
      Homage (Feudal law)
      Incorporation (Feudal law)
      Landfriede
Feudal tenure
  USE Feudalism
      Land tenure
Feudalism *(May Subd Geog)*
  ₍D131₎
  ₍JC109-JC116 (Feudal state)₎
  UF Feudal tenure
  BT Civilization, Medieval
      Land tenure
      Land use
      Land use, Rural
      Middle Ages—History
  RT Chivalry
      Estates (Social orders)
  NT Duchies
      Fiefs
      Homage (Feudal law)
      Immunity (Feudalism)
      Jus primae noctis

Ministerials
Scutage
— **Historiography**
  BT Middle Ages—Historiography
— **Law**
  USE Feudal law
— **Japan**
  UF Shogunate
  NT Daimyo
— **Turkey**
  NT Timar
Feuds
  USE Vendetta
Feuds, Literary
  USE Literary quarrels
Feuerbach family
  UF Feuerbacher family
    Firebacher family
Feuerbacher family
  USE Feuerbach family
Feuilletons
  BT Fiction
    Journalism
    Newspapers
    Serialized fiction
  NT Newspapers—Sections, columns, etc.—
    Fiction
Feuilletons, Bulgarian *(May Subd Geog)*
  UF Bulgarian feuilletons
Feuilletons, French *(May Subd Geog)*
  UF French feuilletons
Feuilletons, German, ₍Russian, etc.₎
Feuilletons, Polish *(May Subd Geog)*
  UF Polish feuilletons
Feuilletons, Swedish
  UF Swedish feuilletons
Feuilletons, Uzbek *(May Subd Geog)*
  UF Uzbek feuilletons
  BT Uzbek fiction
Feurstein family
Fever *(May Subd Geog)*
  ₍RC106₎
  UF Hyperthermia
    Pyrexia
  RT Body temperature
    Exanthemata
  SA *names of fevers, e.g.* Scarlatina;
    Typhoid fever; Typhus fever;
    Yellow fever
  NT Antipyretics
    Lassa fever
    Malaria
    Malignant hyperthermia
    Pyrogens
    Relapsing fever
— **Eclectic treatment**
  ₍RV211₎
— **Homeopathic treatment**
  ₍RX211₎
Fever, Artificial
  USE Fever therapy
Fever, Enteric
  USE Typhoid fever
Fever, Eruptive
  USE Exanthemata
Fever, Hemoglobinuric
  USE Blackwater fever
Fever, Puerperal
  USE Puerperal septicemia
Fever, Therapeutic
  USE Fever therapy
Fever, Traumatic
  USE Traumatic fever
Fever in children *(May Subd Geog)*
  BT Children—Diseases
  NT Convulsions, Febrile
Fever reducing drugs
  USE Antipyretics
Fever therapy
  ₍RM868₎

UF Artificial fever
  Fever, Artificial
  Fever, Therapeutic
BT Therapeutics, Physiological
  Thermotherapy
NT Malariotherapy
Feverfew *(May Subd Geog)*
  ₍QK495.C74 (Botany)₎
  ₍RM666.F44 (Therapeutics)₎
  UF Chrysanthemum parthenium
    Feverfew chrysanthemum
    Matricaria capensis
    Matricaria parthenium
    Pyrethrum parthenium
    Tanacetum parthenium
  BT Tanacetum
Feverfew, Bastard
  USE Parthenium hysterophorus
Feverfew chrysanthemum
  USE Feverfew
Fevrier family
Few-body problem
  UF Problem of few bodies
  BT Nuclear physics
    Quantum theory
  RT Many-body problem
  NT Three-body problem
    Two-body problem
Few family
  UF Feu family
Fewtrell family
  USE Futrell family
Feynman diagrams
  BT Many-body problem
    Matrices
    Quantum theory
  NT Feynman integrals
Feynman integrals
  UF Integrals, Feynman
  BT Feynman diagrams
    Integrals, Multiple
Fezzan (Libya)
  UF Fazzan (Libya)
    Phazania (Libya)
  BT Deserts—Libya
Ffarington family
  USE Farrington family
Ffaryngton family
  USE Farrington family
FFF (Chromatographic analysis)
  USE Field-flow fractionation
FGGE
  USE First GARP Global Experiment
Fia (African people)
  USE Bafia (African people)
Fialds family
  USE Field family
Fiars prices
  ₍HB233.A3 (Agricultural prices)₎
  BT Farm produce—Marketing
    Grain trade
    Prices
Fiat 124 automobile
  ₍TL215.F₎
  UF 124 automobile
  BT Fiat automobile
Fiat 850 automobile
  ₍TL215.F₎
  UF 850 automobile
  BT Fiat automobile
Fiat automobile
  ₍TL215.F₎
  NT Fiat 124 automobile
    Fiat 850 automobile
    Fiat X1/9 automobile
Fiat C. R. 42 (Fighter plane)
  USE Falco (Fighter plane)
Fiat CR-32 (Fighter plane)
  ₍UG1242.F5₎
  BT Fighter planes

Fiat machine-gun
  ₍UF620.F₎
  BT Machine-guns
Fiat money
  USE Currency question
    Legal tender
    Paper money
Fiat trucks
  ₍TL230.5.F₎
  BT Trucks
Fiat X1/9 automobile
  BT Fiat automobile
Fiber bundles (Mathematics)
  UF Bundles, Fiber (Mathematics)
  BT Fiber spaces (Mathematics)
    Groups, Continuous
  NT Classifying spaces
    Fiberings (Mathematics)
    Vanishing theorems
Fiber content of food
  USE Food—Fiber content
Fiber deficiency diseases *(May Subd Geog)*
  ₍RC627.F5₎
  UF Dietary fiber deficiency
  BT Deficiency diseases
  RT High-fiber diet
  NT Diverticulosis
— Diet therapy
  USE High-fiber diet
Fiber glass
  USE Glass fibers
Fiber glass craft
  USE Fiberglass craft
Fiber glass reinforced plastics
  USE Glass reinforced plastics
Fiber in human nutrition
  ₍TX553.F53₎
  UF Dietary fiber
    Fiber in the diet
    Roughage in the diet
  BT Nutrition
  NT Food—Fiber content
    High-fiber diet
Fiber in the diet
  USE Fiber in human nutrition
Fiber industry, Plant
  USE Plant fiber industry
Fiber optics
  UF Optics, Fiber
  BT Integrated optics
    Optical communications
    Optoelectronic devices
    Photonics
  NT Light pens
    Optical fibers
Fiber optics industry *(May Subd Geog)*
Fiber plants *(May Subd Geog)*
  ₍SB241-261₎
  BT Botany, Economic
  RT Plant fiber industry
    Plant fibers
  SA *specific fiber plants, e.g.* Cotton, Flax,
    Hemp
  NT Chamaerops humilis
    Date palm
    Fique
    Furcraea
    Matwork plants
    Rattan palms
    Sunn hemp
Fiber-reactive dyes
  USE Reactive dyes
Fiber reclamation
  UF Fibers—Reclamation
    Reclamation of fibers
Fiber-reinforced ceramic matrix composites
  USE Fiber-reinforced ceramics
Fiber-reinforced ceramics
  ₍TA455.C43₎

Fiber-reinforced ceramics *(Continued)*
- UF Ceramic-fiber composites
-     Ceramic matrix composites, Fiber-reinforced
-     Composites, Ceramic-fiber
-     Composites, Fiber-reinforced ceramic matrix
-     Fiber-reinforced ceramic matrix composites
-     Reinforced ceramics, Fiber
- BT Ceramics
-     Fibrous composites

Fiber reinforced composites
- USE Fibrous composites

Fiber reinforced concrete
- USE Reinforced concrete, Fiber

Fiber reinforced plastics
- BT Fibrous composites
-     Plastics
-     Reinforced plastics
- NT Glass reinforced plastics
- **— Joints**
-     BT Joints (Engineering)

Fiber sculpture
- USE Soft sculpture
-     Tapestry
-     Wall hangings

Fiber spaces (Mathematics)
- UF Fibre spaces (Mathematics)
- BT Algebraic topology
- NT Classifying spaces
-     Fiber bundles (Mathematics)
-     Fiberings (Mathematics)
-     Vector bundles

Fiber work
- USE Fiberwork

Fiberboard
- UF Building board
-     Insulating board
- BT Paperboard
-     Wall board
-     Wood waste
- NT Glass fiberboard
-     Hardboard
-     Particle board
- **— Permeability**

Fiberboard, Glass
- USE Glass fiberboard

Fiberboard industry *(May Subd Geog)*
- [TS875]

Fiberglass
- USE Glass fibers

Fiberglass boats
- BT Boats and boating
-     Glass reinforced plastics

Fiberglass craft *(May Subd Geog)*
- [NB1270.G5 (Sculpture)]
- [TT297.8 (Handicraft)]
- UF Fiber glass craft
-     Glass fiber craft
- BT Plastics craft

Fiberings (Mathematics)
- [QA612.6]
- BT Fiber bundles (Mathematics)
-     Fiber spaces (Mathematics)
-     Mathematics

Fiberlily, New Zealand
- USE Phormium tenax

Fibers *(May Subd Geog)*
- [HD9155-HD9156 (Industry)]
- BT Cordage
- SA *headings beginning with the word Fiber*
- NT Cellulose fibers
-     Crystal whiskers
-     Fibrous composites
-     Kenaf
-     Man-made fibers industry
-     Metal fibers
-     Optical fibers
-     Paper

    Phormium tenax
    Plant fibers
    Sanseviera
    Textile fibers
    Thread
    Vulcanized fiber
- **— Reclamation**
-     USE Fiber reclamation

Fibers, Carbon
- USE Carbon fibers

Fibers, Ceramic
- USE Ceramic fibers

Fibers, Glass
- USE Glass fibers

Fibers, Graphite
- USE Graphite fibers

Fibers, Inorganic
- USE Inorganic fibers

Fibers, Polyester
- USE Polyester fibers

Fibers, Quartz
- USE Quartz fibers

Fibers, Silicate
- USE Silicate fibers

Fibers in art
- USE Fiberwork

Fiberwork *(May Subd Geog)*
- [N7433.9 (Fine arts)]
- UF Fiber work
-     Fibers in art
- RT Textile crafts
- NT Grasswork
-     Lauhala weaving
-     Rattan work

Fibonacci numbers
- UF Fibonacci sequence
-     Sequence, Fibonacci
- BT Numbers, Theory of

Fibonacci sequence
- USE Fibonacci numbers

Fibre spaces (Mathematics)
- USE Fiber spaces (Mathematics)

Fibrin
- [QP91]
- NT Blood coagulation factor XIII
-     Fibrinolysis

Fibrin stabilizing factor
- USE Blood coagulation factor XIII

Fibrinogen
- [QP93.5]
- BT Blood
-     Hemostatics

Fibrinogenase
- USE Thrombin

Fibrinokinase
- USE Plasminokinase

Fibrinolysin
- BT Fibrinolytic agents
- USE Plasmin
- NT Antifibrinolytic agents

Fibrinolysis
- BT Blood—Coagulation
-     Enzymes
-     Fibrin
- NT Fibrinolytic agents

Fibrinolysis inhibitors
- USE Antifibrinolytic agents

Fibrinolytic agents
- UF Antithrombotic agents
-     Fibrinolytic enzymes
-     Thrombolytic agents
- BT Enzymes
-     Fibrinolysis
- NT Ceruloplasmin
-     Fibrinolysin
-     Plasmin
-     Plasminogen
-     Plasminogen activators

Fibrinolytic enzymes
- USE Fibrinolytic agents

Fibroblast intermediate filament proteins
- USE Intermediate filament proteins

Fibroblasts
- UF Desmocytes
-     Fibrocytes
- BT Cells
-     Connective tissue cells

Fibrocystic disease of breast
- USE Breast—Fibrocystic disease

Fibrocystic disease of pancreas
- USE Cystic fibrosis

Fibrocytes
- USE Fibroblasts

Fibroid tumor
- USE Leiomyoma uteri

Fibroids
- USE Leiomyoma uteri

Fibrolite
- USE Sillimanite

Fibromas
- BT Tumors
- NT Neurofibroma

Fibromyoma uteri
- USE Leiomyoma uteri

Fibronectins
- [QP552.F53]
- UF Cold-insoluble globulins
- BT Blood proteins
-     Globulin
-     Glycoproteins

Fibroplasia, Retrolental
- USE Retrolental fibroplasia

Fibrosis, Cystic
- USE Cystic fibrosis

Fibrosis, Pulmonary
- USE Pulmonary fibrosis

Fibrosis, Retroperitoneal
- USE Retroperitoneal fibrosis

Fibrosis of the heart
- USE Heart—Fibrosis

Fibrous cavernitis
- USE Penile induration

Fibrous ceramics
- USE Ceramic fibers

Fibrous composites
- UF Composites, Fibrous
-     Fiber reinforced composites
-     Filament reinforced composites
-     Reinforced fibrous composites
- BT Composite materials
-     Fibers
- NT Fiber-reinforced ceramics
-     Fiber reinforced plastics
- **— Fatigue**
-     [TA418.9.C6]
- **— Fracture**
-     BT Fracture mechanics

Fibrous composites industry
(May Subd Geog)

Fibrous concrete
- USE Reinforced concrete, Fiber

Fibrous crystals
- USE Crystal whiskers

Fibrous dysplasia of bone
- [RC931.F5]
- BT Bones—Diseases
-     Phakomatoses

Fibrous glass board
- USE Glass fiberboard

Fibrous glass industry
- USE Glass fiber industry

Fibrous graphite
- USE Graphite fibers

Fibula
- BT Leg

Fibula (Archaeology) *(May Subd Geog)*
- [CC400 (Archaeology)]
- [NK7306-NK7308 (Art)]
- BT Archaeology
-     Jewelry

RT Brooches
    Clasps
— **Italy**
    NT Fibula Praenestina
Fibula Praenestina
    UF Fibula Prenestina
        Praenestina, Fibula
        Praenestine Fibula
    BT Fibula (Archaeology)—Italy
Fibula Prenestina
    USE Fibula Praenestina
Ficana (Ancient city) *(Not Subd Geog)*
    [DG70.F53]
    BT Cities and towns, Ruined, extinct, etc.
        —Italy
        Italy—Antiquities
Fichardt family *(Not Subd Geog)*
Fichgerrel family
    USE Fitzgerald family
Fichpatrick family
    USE Fitzpatrick family
Fichtel-Berg (Karl-Marx-Stadt, Germany :
    Bezirk)
    USE Fichtelberg (Karl-Marx-Stadt,
        Germany : Bezirk)
Fichtelberg (Karl-Marx-Stadt, Germany :
    Bezirk)
    UF Fichtel-Berg (Karl-Marx-Stadt,
        Germany : Bezirk)
    BT Erzgebirge (Czechoslovakia and
        Germany)
        Mountains—Germany (East)
Fichtelgebirge (Germany and Czechoslovakia)
    UF Smrčiny (Germany and
        Czechoslovakia)
        Smrky (Germany and Czechoslovakia)
    BT Mountains—Czechoslovakia
        Mountains—Germany (West)
Fichtelite
Fick (Name)
    BT Names, Personal
Fick family *(Not Subd Geog)*
    UF Fickas family
        Ficke family
        Fickes family
    RT Fickle family
Fickas family
    USE Fick family
Ficke family
    USE Fick family
Fickes family
    USE Fick family
Fickle family *(Not Subd Geog)*
    RT Fick family
Ficoidaceae
    USE Aizoaceae
Ficoll
    BT Centrifugation, Density gradient
        Epichlorohydrin
        Glucose
        Polymers and polymerization
Fiction
    [PN3311-3503]
    UF Metafiction
        Novellas (Short novels)
        Novels
        Stories
    BT Literature
        Prose literature
    SA *subdivision* Fiction *under particular*
        topics for collections of stories or
        novels on those topics, and under
        historical subjects or characters for
        individual works of historical or
        biographical fiction, e.g. Children—
        Fiction; Stalingrad, Battle of, 1942-
        1943—Fiction
    NT Adventure stories
        Allegories
        Baseball stories
        Bildungsroman

        Biographical fiction
        Children's stories
        Christian fiction
        Christmas stories
        Code and cipher stories
        College stories
        Confession stories
        Detective and mystery stories
        Didactic fiction
        Dime novels
        Domestic fiction
        Easter stories
        Epistolary fiction
        Erotic stories
        Experimental fiction
        Fables
        Fairy tales
        Fantastic fiction
        Feuilletons
        Fishing stories
        Ghost stories
        Historical fiction
        Horror tales
        Humorous stories
        Hunting stories
        Islamic stories
        Legal novels
        Legends
        Love stories
        Martial arts fiction
        Musical fiction
        Nature stories
        Nonfiction novel
        Novelists
        Novelle
        Oral interpretation of fiction
        Pastoral fiction
        Picaresque literature
        Plot-your-own stories
        Radio stories
        Railroad stories
        Religious fiction
        Romances
        Romanticism
        Science fiction
        Sea stories
        Serialized fiction
        Short stories
        Sports stories
        Spy stories
        Tales
        Three-decker novels
        War stories
        Western stories
        Young adult fiction
— **15th and 16th centuries**
— **18th century**
— **19th century**
— **20th century**
— — **History and criticism**
    NT Black humor (Literature)
— — **Stories, plots, etc.**
— **Authorship**
    UF Fiction writing
        Writing, Fiction
    BT Authorship
— **Black authors**
    UF Black fiction
— **Collections**
    [PZ1 (Fiction in English)]
— **Computer programs**
    NT ROALD (Computer program)
— Dramatic production
    USE Chamber theater
— **History and criticism**
    [PN3329-3503]
    NT Psychological fiction
— Male authors
    USE Fiction—Men authors
— **Men authors**
    UF Fiction—Male authors

— Oral interpretation
    USE Oral interpretation of fiction
— Plots
    USE Plots (Drama, novel, etc.)
— **Religious aspects**
— — **Buddhism, [Christianity, etc.]**
— **Stories, plots, etc.**
— **Technique**
    [PN3355-3383]
    UF Fiction writing
        Metafiction
        Writing, Fiction
    BT Authorship
    NT Children's stories—Technique
        Detective and mystery stories—
            Technique
        First person narrative
        Free indirect speech
        Plots (Drama, novel, etc.)
        Point of view (Literature)
        Psychological fiction
        Setting (Literature)
        Western stories—Technique
Fiction, Autobiographic
    USE Autobiographical fiction
Fiction, Autobiographical
    USE Autobiographical fiction
Fiction, Biographical
    USE Biographical fiction
Fiction, Epistolary
    USE Epistolary fiction
Fiction, Gothic
    USE Gothic revival (Literature)
Fiction, Historical
    USE Historical fiction
Fiction, Juvenile
    USE *subdivision* Juvenile fiction *under*
        historical events and characters, etc.
Fiction, Medieval
    [PN692 (History)]
    UF European fiction—Medieval, 500-1500
        Medieval fiction
Fiction, Political
    USE Political fiction
Fiction, Psychological
    USE Psychological fiction
Fiction, Renaissance
    USE European fiction—Renaissance, 1450-
        1600
Fiction, Serialized
    USE Serialized fiction
Fiction, Western
    USE Western stories
Fiction in libraries
    [Z711.5]
    UF Libraries, Fiction in
    BT Libraries
Fiction reading
    USE Oral interpretation of fiction
Fiction writing
    USE Fiction—Authorship
        Fiction—Technique
Fictions, Theory of
    [B1574.B (Bentham)]
    [B3354.V (Vaihinger)]
    [BC199.F5 (Logic)]
    [BL51 (Philosophy and religion)]
    BT Knowledge, Theory of
        Reality
        Truth
    NT Illusion in literature
Fictions (Law)
    UF Legal fictions
    RT Presumptions (Law)
Fictions (Roman law)
    BT Roman law
Fictitious animals
    USE Animals, Mythical
Fictitious names
    USE Anonyms and pseudonyms

Fictitious places
  USE Geographical myths
Fictitious societies
  USE Imaginary societies
Ficus (Plants) *(May Subd Geog)*
    ⌜*QK495.M73 (Botany)*⌝
    ⌜*SB317.F52 (Economic botany)*⌝
  UF Fig (Genus)
  BT Moraceae
  NT Banyan tree
      Ficus religiosa
      Fig
Ficus benghalensis
  USE Banyan tree
Ficus carica
  USE Fig
Ficus religiosa
    ⌜*QK495.M73 (Botany)*⌝
    ⌜*RM666.F47 (Therapeutics)*⌝
  UF Bo tree (Species)
      Botree
      Peepal tree
      Peepul tree
      Pipal tree
      Pipul tree
      Sacred fig
  BT Ficus (Plants)
  NT Bodhi Tree
Fidā'iyun
  USE Fedayeen
Fidden family
  USE Finden family
Fiddle
  USE Violin
Fiddle playing
  USE Fiddling
Fiddle tunes *(May Subd Geog)*
  BT Country music
      Violin music
  NT Fiddling
Fiddleheads *(May Subd Geog)*
    ⌜*QK524.P7 (Botany)*⌝
    ⌜*SB351.F (Culture)*⌝
  UF Ostrich fern
Fiddler-crabs
    ⌜*QL444.D3*⌝
  UF Uca
  BT Crabs
Fiddlers *(May Subd Geog)*
  BT Violinists
Fiddling
    ⌜*MT279 (Instruction and study)*⌝
  UF Fiddle playing
  BT Fiddle tunes
      Folk music
      Violin
Fideicommissum *(May Subd Geog)*
    ⌜*HD1236-9*⌝
  BT Inheritance and succession
      Trusts and trustees
  RT Entail
Fideicommissum (Roman-Dutch law)
Fideicommissum (Roman law)
Fidejussio
  USE Suretyship and guaranty (Roman law)
Fidelia
    ⌜*QL568.F47*⌝
  BT Fideliidae
Fidelia villosa
    ⌜*QL568.F47*⌝
Fideliidae
    ⌜*QL568.F47*⌝
  BT Hymenoptera
  NT Fidelia
      Neofidelia
Fidelity bonds
  USE Insurance, Surety and fidelity
Fidelity insurance
  USE Insurance, Surety and fidelity
Fidonidae
  USE Geometridae

Fiducia
  BT Mortgages (Roman law)
      Pledges (Roman law)
      Roman law
      Sales (Roman law)
  RT Trusts and trustees
  NT Constitutum possessorium
Fiefdoms
  USE Fiefs
Fiefs *(May Subd Geog)*
  UF Feudal domains
      Feudal estates
      Fiefdoms
  BT Feudalism
Field, Crystalline electric
  USE Crystalline electric field
Field, Depth of (Photography)
  USE Depth of field (Photography)
Field artillery
  USE Artillery, Field and mountain
Field astronomy
  USE Geodetic astronomy
Field athletes
  USE Track and field athletes
Field athletics
  USE Track-athletics
Field bean
  USE Faba bean
Field biology
  USE Biology—Field work
Field borders
  USE Windbreaks, shelterbelts, etc.
Field cameras
  USE View cameras
Field coils (Electric generators)
  USE Electric generators—Field coils
Field-coupled surface waves
  UF Surface-coupled electrohydrodynamic
        systems
      Surface-coupled magnetohydrodynamic
        systems
  BT Electrodynamics
      Magnetohydrodynamics
      Surface waves
Field crops *(May Subd Geog)*
    ⌜*SB183-SB317*⌝
  UF Farm crops
  BT Crops
  RT Food crops
      Tree crops
  SA *specific crops, e.g.* Cotton; Hay; Wheat
  NT Companion crops
      Cover crops
      Double cropping
      Energy crops
      Field experiments
      Forage plants
      Grain
      Irrigation farming
      Oilseed plants
      Planting time
  — Breeding
      ⌜*SB185.7*⌝
  — Disease and pest resistance
      (May Subd Geog)
  — Diseases and pests *(May Subd Geog)*
      SA *names of diseases and pests, e.g.*
            European chafer
  — Ecology
      BT Agricultural ecology
  — Field experiments
      USE Field experiments
  — Genetics
  — Harvesting time
      USE Harvesting time
  — Physiology
      ⌜*SB185.5*⌝
  — Planting time
      USE Planting time
  — Seeds
      ⌜*SB113.2-SB118.45*⌝

      BT Seeds
  — Soils
      USE Crops and soils
            Soil science
            Soils
  — Spacing
      USE Plant spacing
  — Varieties
  — Water requirements
  — Tropics
      NT Tropical crops
Field dependence (Psychology)
  UF Field independence (Psychology)
  BT Cognition
      Perception
Field desorption mass spectrometry
  BT Mass spectrometry
Field-effect transistors
  UF Unipolar transistors
  BT Transistors
  NT Metal oxide semiconductor field-effect
        transistors
      Metal semiconductor field-effect
        transistors
Field emission
  UF Emission, Field
  BT Electron work function
      Electrons—Emission
  NT Field emission cathodes
      Field ion microscope
Field emission cathodes
  BT Cathodes
      Field emission
  NT Photocathodes
Field equations, Einstein
  USE Einstein field equations
Field experiments *(May Subd Geog)*
  UF Agriculture—Field experiments
      Crops—Field experiments
      Field crops—Field experiments
      Field plot technique
      Field tests
      Field trials in agriculture
  BT Agriculture—Experimentation
      Field crops
  RT Agriculture—Research—On-farm
  SA *subdivision* Field experiments *under
        names of crops, e.g.* Fruit—Field
        experiments
Field extensions (Mathematics)
  UF Extension fields (Mathematics)
  BT Fields, Algebraic
  NT Theory of descent (Mathematics)
Field family
  UF Fealds family
      Feild family
      Feilds family
      Fialds family
      Fieldes family
      Fields family
  RT Fielding family
Field fauna
  USE Meadow fauna
Field-flow fractionation
  UF FFF (Chromatographic analysis)
      Fractionation, Field-flow
  BT Liquid chromatography
Field fortification
  USE Fortification, Field
Field garlic
  USE Allium vineale
Field glasses
  USE Binoculars
Field handball
  USE Fieldball
Field hockey *(May Subd Geog)*
    ⌜*GV1017.H7*⌝
  BT Hockey
  NT Field hockey players
  — Coaching
      UF Field hockey coaching

Field hockey coaching
  USE Field hockey—Coaching
Field hockey players *(May Subd Geog)*
  BT Field hockey
        Hockey players
Field hospitals
  USE Hospitals, Military
        Medicine, Military
        Red Cross
        War—Relief of sick and wounded
Field houses
  ₍GV405₎
  BT Sports facilities
  RT Gymnasiums
Field independence (Psychology)
  USE Field dependence (Psychology)
Field ion emission microscope
  USE Field ion microscope
Field ion microscope
  UF Field ion emission microscope
        Ion microscope
  BT Field emission
        Microscope and microscopy
Field ionization mass spectrometry
  BT Mass spectrometry
Field marshals
  USE Marshals
Field mice
  USE Microtus
Field names *(May Subd Geog)*
  BT Names, Geographical
Field of Cloth of Gold, France, 1520
  UF Cloth of Gold, Field of, France, 1520
        Field of Cloth of Gold, 1520
  BT France—History—Francis I, 1515-
        1547
        Great Britain—History—Henry VIII,
        1509-1547
Field of Cloth of Gold, 1520
  USE Field of Cloth of Gold, France, 1520
Field of view from airplanes
  USE Airplanes—Field of view
Field of view from helicopters
  USE Helicopters—Field of view
Field of vision
  USE Visual fields
Field of vision, Measurement of
  USE Perimetry
Field orders
  USE Orders, Preparation of (Military
        science)
Field photography
  USE Outdoor photography
Field plot technique
  USE Field experiments
Field plotters
  ₍GA150.5₎
  BT Electronic analog computers
        Geography—Methodology
Field rations
  USE Operational rations (Military supplies)
        Survival and emergency rations
Field reeves *(May Subd Geog)*
  BT Police, Rural
Field service (Military science)
  ₍U170-175₎
  BT Military art and science
        Tactics
  SA *subdivsion* Field service *under armies,*
        e.g. United States. Army—Field
        service
Field sports
  USE Hunting
        Sports
Field telegraph
  USE Military telegraph
Field tests
  USE Field experiments
Field theories, Unified
  USE Unified field theories

Field theory, Quantized
  USE Quantum field theory
Field theory (Linguistics)
  BT Linguistics
        Semantics
Field theory (Physics)
  UF Classical field theory
        Continuum physics
  BT Physics
  RT Continuum mechanics
        Electromagnetic theory
  NT Einstein field equations
        Electric fields
        Electromagnetic fields
        Gauge fields (Physics)
        Gauge invariance
        Gravitation
        Gravitational fields
        Instantons
        Magnetic fields
        Quantum field theory
        Self-consistent field theory
        Twistor theory
        Unified field theories
Field theory (Social psychology)
  BT Social psychology
Field trial dogs *(May Subd Geog)*
  BT Dogs
Field trials
  ₍SF425₎
  BT Dog shows
Field trials in agriculture
  USE Field experiments
Field trips by air
  USE Aeronautics in education
Field vole, European
  USE Microtus agrestis
Field work
  USE *subdivision* Field work *under*
        disciplines for discussions of the
        techniques of carrying out work in
        the field to gain practical experience
        through firsthand observation, e.g.
        Biology—Field work
Field work (Educational method)
  ₍LB2394₎
  RT Education, Cooperative
        Project method in teaching
        School excursions
  NT Aeronautics in education
        Industrial tours
Fieldball
  UF Field handball
        Handball, Field
  NT Team handball
  — Refereeing
        USE Fieldball officiating
  — Rules
Fieldball officiating
  ₍GV1017.F5₎
  UF Fieldball—Refereeing
  BT Sports officiating
Fieldes family
  USE Field family
Fielding (Baseball)
  ₍GV870₎
  UF Infield (Baseball)
        Outfield (Baseball)
  BT Baseball
Fielding family
  RT Field family
Fields, Algebraic
  ₍QA247₎
  UF Algebraic fields
        Algebraic numbers
  BT Algebra, Abstract
  RT Numbers, Theory of
        Rings (Algebra)
  NT Adeles
        Algebra, Differential
        Algebraic number theory

        Division algebras
        Field extensions (Mathematics)
        Finite fields (Algebra)
        Formally real fields
        Ideals (Algebra)
        Jacobi sums
        Local fields (Algebra)
        Near-fields
        p-adic fields
        Quadratic fields
        Quaternions
        Skew fields
        Topological fields
        Witt group
  — Units
        UF Units of algebraic fields
Fields, Baseball
  USE Baseball fields
Fields, Electromagnetic
  USE Electromagnetic fields
Fields, Formally real
  USE Formally real fields
Fields, Gas
  USE Gas fields
Fields, Gauge (Physics)
  USE Gauge fields (Physics)
Fields, Gravitational
  USE Gravitational fields
Fields, Local (Algebra)
  USE Local fields (Algebra)
Fields, Magnetic
  USE Magnetic fields
Fields, Quadratic
  USE Quadratic fields
Fields, Random
  USE Random fields
Fields, Valued
  USE Valued fields
Fields, Vector
  USE Vector fields
Fields family
  USE Field family
Fields prizes
  BT Mathematics—Awards
Fieler family
  RT Feiler family
Fiero automobile
  ₍TL215.F₎
  BT Pontiac automobile
Fiero family
Fieseler Fi-156 Storch (Military airplane)
  BT Aeronautics, Military—Germany
        Airplanes, Military
Fiesta automobile
  ₍TL215.F₎
  BT Ford automobile
Fiesta de San Fermín, Pamplona, Spain
  UF Fiesta de San Fermín (Spain)
        San Fermin Festival, Pamplona, Spain
  BT Festivals—Spain
Fiesta de San Fermín (Spain)
  USE Fiesta de San Fermín, Pamplona,
        Spain
Fife
  ₍ML935 (History)₎
  BT Flute
        Woodwind instruments
Fife and drum bands
  USE Fife and drum corps
Fife and drum corps *(May Subd Geog)*
  UF Drum and fife corps
        Fife and drum bands
  BT Bands (Music)
Fife and drum music
  ₍M1270₎
  UF Drum and fife music
  BT Fife music
        Percussion music
Fife family
  USE Fyffe family

Fife music
  ⌐M60-62┐
  NT Fife and drum music
Fife music (Fifes (2))
  ⌐M288-9┐
Fifer family
  USE Fyffe family
FIFOTRAN-G1 (Computer program)
Fifteen puzzle
  ⌐GV1511.F4┐
Fifteenth century
  BT Middle Ages—History
     Renaissance
  — Biography
     USE Biography—15th century
  — **Forecasts**
Fifteenth of Shevat
  USE Tu bi-Shevat
Fifth column
  USE Subversive activities
     World War, 1939-1945—
       Collaborationists
Fifth generation computers
  (May Subd Geog)
  ⌐QA76.85┐
    Here are entered works on a family of computers
  developed especially for artificial intelligence ap-
  plications.
  BT Computers
  RT Artificial intelligence
Fifth grade (Education)
  BT Education, Elementary
Fifth Monarchy Men
  ⌐DA420-429┐
  BT Christian sects—England
     Great Britain—Politics and
       government—1649-1660
Fifth of May (Mexican holiday)
  USE Cinco de Mayo (Mexican holiday)
Fifth Republic, French
  USE France—History—1958-
     France—Politics and government—
       1958-
Fifth wheels (Couplings)
  USE Truck tractors—Fifth wheels
Fifty-two stages (Mahayana Buddhism)
  USE Bodhisattva stages (Mahayana
     Buddhism)
Fig *(May Subd Geog)*
  ⌐QK495.M73 (Botany)┐
  ⌐SB365 (Culture)┐
  UF Caprifig
     Common fig
     Ficus carica
     Fig tree
  BT Ficus (Plants)
  NT Cookery (Figs)
  — **Religious aspects**
  — — Buddhism, ⌐Christianity, etc.┐
  — — **Christianity**
     NT Barren fig tree (Parable)
  — Tariff
     USE Tariff on figs
  — **Varieties**
Fig, Banyan
  USE Banyan tree
Fig (Genus)
  USE Ficus (Plants)
Fig caprifier
  USE Fig wasp
Fig chalcid
  USE Fig wasp
Fig-eater
  USE Green June beetle
Fig insect
  USE Fig wasp
Fig-moth
  ⌐SB608.F35┐
  UF Almond moth
Fig tree
  USE Fig

Fig tree, Barren
  USE Barren fig tree (Parable)
Fig tree in art
Fig tree in literature
  BT Trees in literature
Fig wasp
  ⌐QL568.A23┐
  UF Blastophagus grossorum
     Blastophagus psenes
     Fig caprifier
     Fig chalcid
     Fig insect
Fig wasp family
  USE Agaonidae
Figeater
  USE Green June beetle
Figg family
  UF Figge family
     Figgers family
     Figgs family
Figge family
  USE Figg family
Figgers family
  USE Figg family
Figgs family
  USE Figg family
Fighter-bomber sabres
  USE Sabre (Jet fighter planes)
Fighter-bombers
  USE Attack planes
Fighter pilots *(May Subd Geog)*
  ⌐UG626-UG626.2 (Biography)┐
  UF Aces (Fighter pilots)
     Air aces
     Pilots, Fighter
  BT Air pilots, Military
Fighter plane combat *(May Subd Geog)*
  ⌐UG700-705┐
  UF Combat, Fighter plane
     Dogfighting (Military aeronautics)
     Fighter-to-fighter plane combat
  BT Air warfare
Fighter plane sounds
  BT Airplane sounds
     Fighter planes
     Sounds
Fighter planes *(May Subd Geog)*
  ⌐TL685.3 (Manufacture)┐
  ⌐UG1242.F5 (Military science)┐
  UF Pursuit planes
  BT Airplanes
     Airplanes, Military
  RT Attack planes
  NT 97 Sen (Fighter planes)
     Aermacchi MB326 (Jet fighter plane)
     Airacobra (Fighter plane)
     Albatros D. (Fighter plane)
     Avro Arrow (Turbojet fighter plane)
     BAC Lightning (Fighter plane)
     BAC TSR 2 (Turbojet fighter planes)
     Banshee (Jet fighter plane)
     Bearcat (Fighter planes)
     Black widow (Fighter planes)
     Boeing P-26 (Fighter plane)
     Bristol Beaufighter (Fighter plane)
     Camel (Fighter planes)
     Canuck (Jet fighter plane)
     Corsair (Fighter planes)
     Cougar (Jet fighter plane)
     Crusader (Jet fighter plane)
     Curtiss Hawk (Fighter planes)
     Cutlass (Jet fighter plane)
     Delta Dart (Jet fighter plane)
     Eagle (Jet fighter plane)
     F-5 (Jet fighter plane)
     F-16 (Fighter planes)
     F-111 (Fighter planes)
     Falco (Fighter plane)
     Fiat CR-32 (Fighter plane)
     Fighter plane sounds
     Focke-Wulf 190 (Fighter planes)

     Folgore (Fighter plane)
     Gladiator (Fighter planes)
     Harrier (Jet fighter plane)
     Hayabusa (Fighter planes)
     Hayate (Fighter planes)
     Heinkel 100 (Fighter planes)
     Heinkel 112 (Fighter planes)
     Heinkel 162 (Jet fighter planes)
     Hellcat (Fighter planes)
     Hien (Fighter planes)
     Hornet (Jet fighter plane)
     Hunter (Turbojet fighter planes)
     Hurricane (Fighter planes)
     Javelin (Jet fighter plane)
     Kikka (Jet fighter plane)
     Kingcobra (Fighter plane)
     Lightning (Fighter planes)
     Messerschmitt 109 (Fighter planes)
     Messerschmitt 110 (Fighter planes)
     Messerschmitt 163 (Fighter planes)
     Messerschmitt 262 (Fighter planes)
     Meteor (Fighter planes)
     MIG (Fighter planes)
     MIG-25 (Jet fighter plane)
     Mirage (Fighter planes)
     Moskito (Fighter plane)
     Mustang (Fighter planes)
     Nieuport-Macchi 11 (Fighter plane)
     Nieuport-Macchi 17 (Fighter plane)
     Night fighter planes
     Orione (Fighter plane)
     P-40 (Fighter planes)
     Panther (Jet fighter plane)
     Pfeil (Fighter planes)
     Phantom (Fighter planes)
     Raiden (Fighter plane)
     Reggiane Re 2000 (Fighter plane)
     Sabre (Jet fighter planes)
     Scimitar (Fighter planes)
     Shiden (Fighter plane)
     Shooting Star (Jet fighter plane)
     Skyknight (Jet fighter plane)
     Skyray fighter plane
     Spad (Fighter planes)
     Spitfire (Fighter planes)
     Starfighter (Fighter plane)
     Starfire (Jet fighter plane)
     Super Etendard (Jet fighter plane)
     Tempest (Fighter plane)
     Thunderbolt (Fighter planes)
     Thunderchief (Fighter planes)
     Thunderstreak (Fighter planes)
     Tiger (Jet fighter plane)
     Tomcat (Jet fighter plane)
     Tornado (Jet fighter plane)
     Toryu (Fighter plane)
     Typhoon (Fighter plane)
     Vampire (Turbojet fighter planes)
     Veltro (Fighter plane)
     Viggen (Jet fighter plane)
     Voodoo (Jet fighter plane)
     Wildcat (Fighter planes)
     Zero (Fighter planes)
  — **Flight testing**
  — **Piloting**
  — **Tail surfaces**
  — **Turbojet engines**
  — **Wings**
Fighter-to-fighter plane combat
  USE Fighter plane combat
Fighting
  USE Animal fighting
     Battles
     Boxing
     Bullfights
     Combat
     Dogfighting
     Dueling
     Fencing
     Gladiators
     Military art and science

Naval art and science
Night fighting (Military science)
Street fighting (Military science)
Swordplay
Tournaments
War
Fighting, Cock
USE Cockfighting
Fighting, Hand-to-hand
USE Hand-to-hand fighting
Fighting, Knife
USE Knife fighting
Fighting (Psychology)
[BF723.F5 (Child study)]
UF Combativeness
Pugnacity
BT Hostility (Psychology)
Psychology
Violence
RT Aggressiveness (Psychology)
Fighting bull
[SF199.F5]
BT Bulls
RT Bullfights
Fighting chickens
USE Game fowl
Fighting cocks
USE Game fowl
Fighting dog, Chinese
USE Chinese Shar-Pei
Fighting dogs *(May Subd Geog)*
[SF428.85]
UF Pit dogs
BT Dogfighting
Dogs
Fighting fishes
USE Betta
Fighting of fires
USE Fire extinction
Fighting on stage
USE Stage fighting
Fights, Church
USE Church controversies
Figural aftereffects
[BF241]
UF Aftereffects, Figural
BT Imagery (Psychology)
Perception
Psychology, Physiological
Vision
Figurate numbers
USE Numbers, Polygonal
Figuration
USE Figurative art
Figurative art *(May Subd Geog)*
UF Art, Figurative
Figuration
BT Realism in art
NT Human figure in art
Tableaux (Art)
Figure (Horse)
USE Justin Morgan (Horse)
Figure and background perception
USE Figure-ground perception
Figure and ground perception
USE Figure-ground perception
Figure-background perception
USE Figure-ground perception
Figure drawing
BT Drawing
Nude in art
RT Human figure in art
NT Face
Head
Figure-ground perception *(May Subd Geog)*
UF Figure and background perception
Figure and ground perception
Figure-background perception
BT Gestalt psychology
Visual discrimination

RT Form perception
Pattern perception
Space perception
Figure in wood
USE Wood—Figure
Figure of the earth
USE Earth—Figure
Figure painting
[ND1290]
BT Nude in art
Painting
RT Human figure in art
Portrait painting
NT Genre painting
Figure sculpture *(May Subd Geog)*
[NB1930-NB1936]
BT Human figure in art
Sculpture
Figure skaters
USE Skaters
Figure skating
USE Skating
Figured bass
USE Continuo *used as part of the specification of medium in headings, e.g.,* Trio-sonatas (Violins (2), continuo)
Thorough bass
Figureheads of ships
[VM308]
UF Ships—Figureheads
BT Decoration and ornament
Ship decoration
Ships
Figurengruppe (Sculpture)
USE Steiner, Rudolf, 1861-1925. Group of Three Figures
Figures, Father
USE Father figures
FIGURES II (Computer program)
UF Finite Element Interactive Graphics Users Routines (Computer program)
BT Finite element method—Computer programs
Figures of speech
[PN227-PN228]
Here are entered general works and works on figures of speech in the English language. Works treating of figures of speech in other languages are entered under the name of the language, with subdivision Figures of speech.
UF English language—Figures of speech
Imagery
Speech, Figures of
Tropes
BT Rhetoric
Symbolism
SA *particular figures of speech, e.g.* Metaphor; Simile
NT Antonomasia
Aposiopesis (Rhetoric)
Apostrophe (Rhetoric)
Chiasmus
Enallage
English language—Metonyms
English language—Parallelism
Metonyms
Oxymoron
Personification in literature
Understatement
Figurines *(May Subd Geog)*
UF Statuettes
BT Decorative arts
Small sculpture
NT Bronze figurines
Chalkware
Clay figurines
Dolls
Glass figurines
Gold figurines
Lead figurines

Ming ch'i
Netsukes
Pincushion dolls
Porcelain figures
Pottery figures
Silver figurines
Terra-cotta figurines
Ushabti
Wood-carved figurines
— **England**
NT Royal Doulton figurines
— **Germany (West)**
NT Hummel figurines
— **Greece**
NT Tanagra figurines
Figurines, Bronze
USE Bronze figurines
Figurines, Clay
USE Clay figurines
Figurines, Glass
USE Glass figurines
Figurines, Tanagra
USE Tanagra figurines
Figworts
USE Scrophulariaceae
Fiil family
Fiji
As a geographic subdivision, this heading is used directly.
— **Antiquities**
NT Sigatoka Dune Site (Viti Levu, Fiji)
— **Languages**
NT Bislama language
Fijian language
[PL6235]
UF Viti language
BT Melanesian languages
Fijian periodicals *(May Subd Geog)*
Fijian poetry
Fijian poetry (English)
UF English poetry—Fijian authors
Fijian proverbs
USE Proverbs, Fijian
Fijians
[DU600]
BT Ethnology—Fiji
Fike family
UF Faick family
Feick family
Feicke family
Feik family
Feike family
Fikes family
Fyke family
Fikes family
USE Fike family
Fila Brasileiro
[SF429.F38]
UF Brazilian mastiff
BT Dog breeds
Mastiff
Fila language
USE Mele-Fila language
Filament reinforced composites
USE Fibrous composites
Filamentary crystals
USE Crystal whiskers
Filaments, Cytoplasmic
USE Cytoplasmic filaments
Filaments, Metal
USE Metal fibers
Filaments, Solar
USE Sun—Filaments
Filaments for electric lamps
USE Electric lamps, Incandescent—Filaments
Filaria denticulata
USE Haemonchus contortus
Filarial worms
USE Filarioida

Filariasis *(May Subd Geog)*
  [*RA644.F5 (Public health)*]
  [*RC142.5 (Internal medicine)*]
  UF Filarioida diseases
  BT Helminthiasis
  NT Elephantiasis
      Loaiasis
      Onchocerciasis
Filarioida
  [*QL391.N4*]
  UF Filarial worms
      Filarioidea
  BT Nematoda
  NT Dipetalonematidae
Filarioida diseases
  USE Filariasis
Filarioidea
  USE Filarioida
Filbert *(May Subd Geog)*
  [*QK495.B56 (Botany)*]
  [*SB401.F5 (Culture)*]
  UF Corylus
      Filbert tree
      Hazel
      Hazelnut
  BT Betulaceae
  — Tariff
      USE Tariff on filberts
Filbert industry *(May Subd Geog)*
  [*HD9259.F5-53*]
Filbert tree
  USE Filbert
Filbrick family
  USE Philbrick family
File compression (Computer science)
  USE Data compression (Computer science)
File family
  UF Files family
      Fyle family
      Fyles family
      Phyle family
File organization (Computer science)
  [*QA76.9.F5*]
  UF Organization, File (Computer science)
  BT Data base management
      Electronic data processing
      Electronic digital computers—
        Programming
      Information storage and retrieval
        systems
  NT Data compression (Computer science)
      Data structures (Computer science)
      Hashing (Computer science)
      List processing (Electronic computers)
      LITMAS (Computer program)
  — Computer programs
      NT VU-FILE (Computer program)
Filefishes
  USE Balistidae
Filer family
  USE Feiler family
Files, Computer program
  USE Computer programs
Files, Data
  USE Data bases
Files (Records)
  BT Records—Management
  NT Authority files (Cataloging)
      Collectanea files
      Computer files
      Library records
      Vertical files (Libraries)
Files and filing (Documents)
  USE Filing systems
Files and rasps
  [*TJ1285-7*]
  UF Rasps
  BT Hardware
Files family
  USE File family

FILESTAT (Computer programs)
  BT Statistics—Computer programs
Fili (Irish poets)
  [*PB1321*]
  BT Irish poetry
      Poets, Irish
Filial love
  USE Filial piety
Filial piety *(May Subd Geog)*
  [*BJ1639*]
  UF Filial love
      Piety, Filial
  BT Conduct of life
      Parent and child
      Piety
  — Biblical teaching
      NT Ten commandments—Parents
Filiation (Law)
  USE Paternity
Filibuster War, Nicaraguan
  USE Nicaragua—History—Filibuster War,
        1855-1860
Filibusters *(May Subd Geog)*
  [*G539*]
  UF Freebooters
  BT Buccaneers
      Pirates
      War, Maritime (International law)
  RT Soldiers of fortune
  NT Cuba—History—Insurrection, 1849-
        1851
      Nicaragua—History—Filibuster War,
        1855-1860
Filibusters (Political science)
  (May Subd Geog)
  [*JF519*]
  BT Parliamentary practice
      Political science
Filibusters (West Indian buccaneers)
  USE Buccaneers
Filicales
  BT Ferns
  NT Adiantaceae
      Aspidiaceae
      Aspleniaceae
      Athyriaceae
      Cyatheaceae
      Gleicheniaceae
      Hymenophyllaceae
      Lomariopsidaceae
      Parkeriaceae
      Polypodiaceae
      Schizaeaceae
Filicide *(May Subd Geog)*
  [*HV6542 (Crimes and offenses)*]
  [*KF9305 (Criminal law)*]
  BT Homicide
      Infanticide
      Murder
      Parricide
Filicide in literature
Filicineae
  USE Ferns
Filicollidae
  USE Polymorphidae
Filigrains
  USE Water-marks
Filigree *(May Subd Geog)*
  BT Art metal-work
Filigree, Paper
  USE Paper quillwork
Filigree lettering
  [*NK3625.F*]
  BT Lettering
Filing, Saw
  USE Saw filing
Filing rules, Library
  USE Library filing rules
Filing systems
  [*HF5735-5746*]
  UF Files and filing (Documents)

  BT Information retrieval
      Office practice
  RT Alphabetizing
      Indexing
  NT Electronic filing systems
      Library filing rules
  — Computer programs
Filioque
  USE Holy Spirit—Procession
Filipino American business people
  USE Filipino Americans in business
Filipino Americans *(May Subd Geog)*
  BT Ethnology—United States
  NT Missions to Filipino Americans
  — Economic conditions
      NT Filipino Americans—Employment
  — Employment *(May Subd Geog)*
      BT Filipino Americans—Economic
          conditions
Filipino Americans in business
  (May Subd Geog)
  UF Businessmen, Filipino American
      Filipino American business people
  BT Minority business enterprises—United
      States
Filipinos *(May Subd Geog)*
  UF Philippinos
      Pilipinos
  BT Ethnology—Philippines
Filippi family
  USE De Filippo family
Filippis family
  USE De Filippo family
Filippo family
  USE De Filippo family
Ffilippoi (City)
  USE Philippi (City)
Filiya language
  USE Pero language
Fill (Earthwork)
  USE Fills (Earthwork)
Fill and scour (Geomorphology)
  USE Scour and fill (Geomorphology)
Filled foods (Cookery)
  USE Stuffed foods (Cookery)
Filler metal
  BT Metals
  NT Brazing alloys
      Solder and soldering
      Welding rods
Fillers (in paper, paint, etc.)
  [*TN948.F45*]
  BT Paint
      Paper
      Textile chemicals
  NT Elastomers—Reinforcement
      Rubber—Reinforcement
Fillet lines (Bookbinding)
  USE Fillets (Bookbinding)
Fillets, Fish
  USE Fish fillets
Fillets (Bookbinding)
  UF Fillet lines (Bookbinding)
      Roulettes (Bookbinding)
  BT Bookbinding
Fillets (Engineering)
  BT Engineering
Filling stations
  USE Automobiles—Service stations
Fillings (Dentistry) *(May Subd Geog)*
  [*RK517-519*]
  UF Dental fillings
  BT Dentistry, Operative
  NT Dental amalgams
      Inlays (Dentistry)
Fillips family
  USE Phillips family
Fillmore family
  UF Filmore family
      Phillimore family
      Philmore family

Fillo dough cookery
  USE Cookery (Filo dough)
Fillpot family
  USE Philpott family
Fillpott family
  USE Philpott family
Fills, Rock
  USE Rockfills
Fills, Sanitary
  USE Sanitary landfills
Fills (Earthwork) *(May Subd Geog)*
  UF Earth fills
      Fill (Earthwork)
      Land fills
      Landfills
  BT Earthwork
      Soil mechanics
  NT Embankments
      Hydraulic filling
      Sanitary landfills
  — Law and legislation *(May Subd Geog)*
    BT Engineering law
Film, Television
  USE Television film
Film acting
  USE Moving-picture acting
Film actors
  USE Moving-picture actors and actresses
Film adaptations
  [PN1997.85]
  UF Adaptations, Film
      Books, Filmed
      Filmed books
      Films from books
      Literature—Film and video adaptations
      Moving-picture adaptations
  BT Literature—Adaptations
      Moving-picture plays
  SA *subdivision* Film and video adaptations
      *under individual literatures and
      under names of individual literary
      authors, e.g.* English literature—
      Film and video adaptations;
      Shakespeare, William, 1564-1616—
      Film and video adaptations
  NT Operas—Film and video adaptations
Film audiences
  USE Moving-picture audiences
Film authorship
  USE Moving-picture authorship
Film badge dosimetry
  USE Photographic dosimetry
Film boiling
  [QC320.22.F5]
  UF Boiling, Film
      Leidenfrost effect
  BT Ebullition
      Evaporation
      Heat—Transmission
Film catalogs
  USE Moving-pictures—Catalogs; *and
      subdivision* Film catalogs *under
      specific subjects, e.g.* Geology—
      Film catalogs
      Moving-pictures—Catalogs
Film coefficients (Physics)
  BT Boundary layer
      Diffusion
      Heat—Transmission
      Surface energy
      Surface tension
Film collections
  USE Moving-picture film collections
Film coupons, UNESCO
  USE UNESCO film coupons
Film credits of motion picture actors and
    actresses
  USE Moving-picture actors and actresses—
      Credits

Film credits of motion picture producers and
    directors
  USE Moving-picture producers and
      directors—Credits
Film critics
  USE Moving-picture critics
Film directors
  USE Moving-picture producers and
      directors
Film dosimetry
  USE Photographic dosimetry
Film editing (Cinematography)
  USE Moving-pictures—Editing
Film festivals
  USE Moving-picture festivals
Film genres *(May Subd Geog)*
      Here are entered works on the theory of film
  genres and works discussing film genres collectively.
  Works on a specific film genre are entered under the
  heading for the genre, e.g. Western films.
  UF Genre films
      Moving-picture genres
  BT Moving-pictures
  RT Moving-pictures—Plots, themes, etc.
Film industry (Motion pictures)
  USE Moving-picture industry
Film kinesics
  USE Nonverbal communication in motion
      pictures
Film libraries
  USE Moving-picture film collections
Film literature
  USE Moving-picture literature
Film loops
  USE Moving-pictures, Loop
Film make-up
  UF Moving-picture make-up
  BT Make-up, Theatrical
Film music
  USE Moving-picture music
Film posters
  UF Moving-picture posters
      Moving-pictures—Posters
  BT Playbills
      Posters
Film posters, American *(May Subd Geog)*
  UF American film posters
Film posters, Czech, [etc.]
  (May Subd Geog)
Film posters, French *(May Subd Geog)*
  UF French film posters
Film posters, German *(May Subd Geog)*
  UF German film posters
Film posters, Italian *(May Subd Geog)*
  UF Italian film posters
Film posters, Japanese *(May Subd Geog)*
  UF Japanese film posters
Film posters, Russian *(May Subd Geog)*
  UF Russian film posters
Film posters, Ukrainian *(May Subd Geog)*
  UF Ukrainian film posters
Film producers and directors
  USE Moving-picture producers and
      directors
Film programs
  USE Moving-picture programs
Film resistors
  USE Electric resistors, Film
Film slides
  USE Filmstrips
Film stars
  USE Moving-picture actors and actresses
Film strip projectors
  USE Projectors
Film strips
  USE Filmstrips
Filmed books
  USE Film adaptations

Filmer family
  UF Filmere family
      Fylmer family
      Fylmere family
Filmere family
  USE Filmer family
Filmgoers
  USE Moving-picture audiences
Filming on location
  USE Moving-picture locations
Filmography
  USE *subdivision* Film catalogs *under
      subjects*
      Moving-pictures—Catalogs
Filmore family
  USE Fillmore family
Films
  USE Filmstrips
      Microfilms
      Moving-pictures
      Photography—Films
Films, Cinematographic
  USE Moving-picture film
Films, Color
  USE Color photography—Films
Films, Dielectric
  USE Dielectric films
Films, Instant photography
  USE Instant photography—Films
Films, Liquid
  USE Liquid films
Films, Magnetic
  USE Magnetic films
Films, Metallic
  USE Metallic films
Films, Monomolecular
  USE Monomolecular films
Films, Optical
  USE Optical films
Films, Polyester
  USE Polyester films
Films, Powdered
  USE Powder film
Films, Radiographic
  USE Radiography—Films
Films, Semiconductor
  USE Semiconductor films
Films, Thick
  USE Thick films
Films, Thin
  USE Thin films
Films, Western
  USE Western films
Films by children
  BT Children
      Moving-pictures
      Moving-pictures and children
Films for foreign speakers
  USE *subdivisions* Films for foreign speakers;
      and Films for French, [Spanish,
      etc.] speakers *under individual and
      groups of languages for instructional
      films about a language or languages
      designed for speakers of other
      languages, e.g.* English language—
      Films for French, [Spanish, etc.]
      speakers
Films for the deaf
  USE Films for the hearing impaired
Films for the hearing impaired
  (May Subd Geog)
  UF Deaf, Films for the
      Films for the deaf
      Moving-pictures for the deaf
      Moving-pictures for the hearing
      impaired
  BT Hearing impaired
Films for TV commercials
  USE Television commercial films
Films for young adults
  USE Young adult films

Films from books
USE Film adaptations
Films noirs *(May Subd Geog)*
[PN1995.9.F54]
UF Crime films
BT Moving-pictures
Films on art
USE Art in moving-pictures
Filmscripts
USE Moving-picture plays
Filmstrip collections
[Z692.F5]
UF Collections, Filmstrip
Filmstrip libraries
Libraries, Filmstrip
BT Libraries, Special
Filmstrip libraries
USE Filmstrip collections
Filmstrips
UF Film slides
Film strips
Films
Slidefilms
BT Audio-visual materials
Microphotography
RT Slides (Photography)
NT English language—Study and teaching
—Audio-visual aids
Newspapers on filmstrips
— Cataloging
USE Cataloging of filmstrips
Filmstrips, Newsreel
USE Newsreels
Filmstrips in education *(May Subd Geog)*
BT Education—Audio-visual aids
Filmstrips in religious education
[BV1535.3]
BT Religious education—Audio-visual aids
NT Christian education—Filmstrips
Filo dough cookery
USE Cookery (Filo dough)
Filps family
USE Phelps family
Filter cloth
[TS1781]
BT Filters and filtration
Textile fabrics
— **Acoustic properties**
Filter family
Filter industry *(May Subd Geog)*
[HD9999.F46-HD9999.F464]
Filter-presses
[TJ1470-1475]
BT Filters and filtration
Filter tips
USE Cigarette filters
Filtered laminar airflow systems
USE Laminar flow clean rooms
Filtered modules
BT Modules (Algebra)
Filtered rings
BT Rings (Algebra)
Filtering, Kalman
USE Kalman filtering
Filters, Acoustic
USE Acoustic filters
Filters, Acoustic surface wave
USE Acoustic surface wave filters
Filters, Adaptive
USE Adaptive filters
Filters, Crystal
USE Electric filters, Crystal
Filters, Digital electric
USE Electric filters, Digital
Filters, Digital (Mathematics)
USE Digital filters (Mathematics)
Filters, Light
USE Light filters
Filters, Photographic
USE Photography—Light filters

Filters, Radio
USE Radio filters
Filters, Wave-guide
USE Electric filters, Wave-guide
Filters (Mathematics)
BT Mathematics
NT Digital filters (Mathematics)
Ultrafilters (Mathematics)
Filters and filtration
[QD63.F5 (Chemistry)]
[TD441-TD449 (Water-supply)]
[TP156.F5 (Chemical technology)]
BT Porous materials
Sanitary engineering
Separation (Technology)
RT Separators (Machines)
NT Acoustic filters
Air filters
Automobiles—Motors—Oil filters
Blood—Filtration
Chemistry—Manipulation
Cigarette filters
Coal preparation—Filtration
Dialysis
Diatomaceous earth
Diesel motor—Oil filters
Fabric filters
Filter cloth
Filter-presses
Fuel filters
Hydraulic fluid filters
Membrane filters
Oil filters
Sewage—Purification—Filtration
Tractors—Motors—Oil filters
Trickling filters
Ultrafiltration
Vacuum filters
Water—Purification—Direct filtration
Water—Purification—Filtration
Wine and wine making—Filtration
Filtration, Membrane
USE Membrane separation
Filtration of blood
USE Blood—Filtration
Filtration plants
USE Water—Purification—Filtration
FIM-929 (Missile)
USE Stinger (Missile)
Fimbriae (Microbiology)
USE Pili (Microbiology)
Fimbristylis
[QK495.C997]
BT Cyperaceae
Fimetaria
USE Sordaria
Fimetariaceae
USE Sordariaceae
Fin family
USE Finn family
Fin rays
USE Fins
Fin whale
USE Finback whale
Finafrock family
USE Finfrock family
Final cause
USE Causation
Teleology
Final offer arbitration *(May Subd Geog)*
Here are entered works on a type of interest arbitration in which the arbitrator selects either the union's or the employer's final proposal.
UF Arbitration, Final offer
Last best offer arbitration
BT Interest arbitration
Final utility
USE Marginal utility
Finalism (Philosophy)
[B1018.F54]

BT Philosophy
Teleology
Finamore family
USE Fenimore family
Finance *(May Subd Geog)*
UF Funds
BT Economics
RT Currency question
Money
SA *subdivision* Finance *under subjects and under names of individual nongovernmental corporate bodies*
NT Amortization
Banks and banking
Bonds
Budget in business
Business losses
Capital
Capital market
Capitalists and financiers
Church finance
Commerce
Contingencies in finance
Controllership
Credit
Debt
Default (Finance)
Deflation (Finance)
Disinvestment
Finance, Personal
Flow of funds
Income
Inflation (Finance)
Insurance
Intermediation (Finance)
International finance
Investments
Lease or buy decisions
Liquidity (Economics)
Loans
Money market
Museum finance
Open market operations
Prices
Profit
Securities
Self-financing
Sinking-funds
Speculation
Stock-exchange
Syndicates (Finance)
War finance
Wealth
Women in finance
— **Bibliography**
RT Finance literature
— **Computer programs**
NT PIRAL (Computer program)
— **Law and legislation** *(May Subd Geog)*
NT Financial planners—Malpractice
— **Mathematical models**
NT Capital assets pricing model
— **Mathematics**
USE Business mathematics
— **Statistics**
UF Financial statistics
— **Vocational guidance**
UF Finance as a profession
Finance, Buddhist temple
USE Buddhist temple finance
Finance, Church
USE Church finance
Finance, International
USE International finance
Finance, Local
USE Local finance
Finance, Military
USE War, Cost of
Finance, Municipal
USE Municipal finance

Finance, Personal (May Subd Geog)
⌐HG179¬
  UF Personal finance
  BT Finance
  SA *subdivision* Finance, Personal *under*
       classes of persons and under names
       of individual persons
  NT Astrology and personal finance
       Budgets, Personal
       Children's allowances
       Estate planning
       Financial disclosure
       Financial security
       Home economics—Accounting
       Insurance
       Saving and thrift
  — **Calendars**
  — **Computer programs**
      NT Dollars and Sense (Computer
          program)
         Home Accountant (Computer
          program)
         Home Accountant Plus (Computer
          program)
         Home Money Manager (Computer
          program)
         Managing Your Money (Computer
          program)
         Payroll (Computer program)
         PFP (Computer program)
  — **Marketing**
      UF Marketing of personal financial
          planning services
  — **Religious aspects**
      NT Tithes
  — — **Buddhism,** ⌐**Christianity, etc.**¬
  — — **Christianity**
      BT Stewardship, Christian
      NT Christian giving
Finance, Public (May Subd Geog)
  UF Cameralistics
      Public finance
  RT Currency question
      Money
  SA *subdivision* Appropriations and
       expenditures *under names of*
       countries, cities, government
       agencies, institutions, etc.
  NT Bonds
       Budget
       Claims
       Customs administration
       Debts, Public
       Default (Finance)
       Deficit financing
       Expenditures, Public
       Fiscal policy
       Government lending
       Government monopolies
       Government spending policy
       Intergovernmental fiscal relations
       Internal revenue
       Investment of public funds
       Local finance
       Metropolitan finance
       Public depositaries
       Public goods
       Revenue
       Sinking-funds
       Special funds
       State bankruptcy
       Sunset reviews of government
         programs
       Tariff
       Taxation
       User charges
       War, Cost of
       War finance
  — **Accounting**
      ⌐HJ9701-9995¬

      UF Government accounting
         Public accounting
      NT Debts, Public—Accounting
         Government business enterprises—
          Accounting
         Legislative auditing
         Tax accounting
  — — **Law and legislation**
      (May Subd Geog)
  — **Auditing**
  — — **Law and legislation**
      (May Subd Geog)
  — **Law and legislation** (May Subd Geog)
  — — **Criminal provisions**
  — **France**
  — — **To 1789**
  — — **1789-1871**
  — — **1871-1918**
  — — **1918-**
  — **Great Britain**
  — — **To 1688**
  — — **1688-1815**
  — — **1815-1918**
  — — **1918-1945**
  — — **1945-**
  — — **Accounting**
  — **Islamic countries**
      ⌐HJ233¬
      UF Islamic public finance
         Muslim public finance
  — **United States**
      UF Specie payments
  — — **To 1789**
  — — **1789-1800**
  — — **1801-1861**
  — — **1861-1875**
  — — **1875-1900**
  — — **1901-1933**
  — — **1933-**
  — — **States**
      NT Budget—United States—States
         Taxation, State
  — **Washington Metropolitan Area**
Finance, Public (Islamic law)
  (May Subd Geog)
  BT Islamic law
Finance, War
  USE War finance
Finance as a profession
  USE Finance—Vocational guidance
Finance charges (May Subd Geog)
  BT Consumer credit
      Credit
      Loans, Personal
  NT Interest
  — **Law and legislation** (May Subd Geog)
      BT Usury laws
Finance companies, Commercial
  USE Commercial finance companies
      Instalment plan
Finance departments (May Subd Geog)
  BT Management
Finance houses
  USE Commercial finance companies
Finance literature
  UF Literature, Finance
  RT Finance—Bibliography
Financial accounting
  USE Accounting
Financial aid, Student
  USE Student aid
Financial aid administration, Student
  USE Student financial aid administration
Financial aid contracts (May Subd Geog)
    Here are entered works on a type of contract such
  as "contrats d'aide financière" in France, whereby a
  business enterprise receives governmental financial
  aid in exchange for its following the government's
  directives within the area of national economic plan-
  ning.

      BT Economic policy
         Public contracts
Financial aid to students
  USE Student aid
Financial disclosure (May Subd Geog)
    Here are entered works on the disclosure of per-
  sonal finances of public officials and of candidates
  and appointees for public office.
      UF Disclosure of personal finances
         Government in the sunshine
         Sunshine, Government in the
      BT Finance, Personal
         Political ethics
  — **Law and legislation** (May Subd Geog)
Financial District (New York, N.Y.)
  USE Wall Street (New York, N.Y.)
Financial federations
  USE Federations, Financial (Social service)
Financial futures (May Subd Geog)
  ⌐HG6024.3¬
  UF Futures, Financial
  RT Forward exchange
      Hedging (Finance)
  NT Interest rate futures
      Stock index futures
Financial institutions (May Subd Geog)
  UF Financial intermediaries
      Financial services
  NT Agricultural credit corporations
      Banks and banking
      Building and loan associations
      Capital market
      Commercial finance companies
      Communication in financial
        institutions
      Discount houses (Finance)
      Government financial institutions
      Insurance companies
      Lenders of last resort
      Money market
      Pension trusts
      Trading rooms (Finance)
  — **Investments**
      BT Investments
  — **Law and legislation** (May Subd Geog)
      BT Banking law
  — **Real estate investments**
      BT Real estate investment
Financial institutions, International
  UF International financial institutions
  BT International finance
  NT Banks and banking, International
Financial intermediaries
  USE Financial institutions
Financial intermediation
  USE Intermediation (Finance)
Financial journalism
  USE Journalism, Commercial
Financial libraries (May Subd Geog)
  ⌐Z675.F5¬
  UF Libraries, Financial
  BT Business libraries
Financial Management System (Information
  retrieval system)
  USE FMS (Information retrieval system)
Financial news
  USE Journalism, Commercial
      Newspapers—Sections, columns, etc.—
        Finance
Financial planners (May Subd Geog)
  ⌐HG179.5¬
  UF Planners, Financial
  BT Planners
  RT Investment advisers
  — **Malpractice** (May Subd Geog)
      UF Malpractice by financial planners
         Tort liability of financial planners
      BT Finance—Law and legislation
         Malpractice
  — **Marketing**

Financial planners
— **Marketing** *(Continued)*
    UF Marketing of financial planning
          services
Financial security
    UF Security, Financial
    BT Finance, Personal
Financial services
    USE Financial institutions
Financial statements *(May Subd Geog)*
    [HF5681.B2 (Balance sheet)]
    UF Balance sheets
        Income statements
        Operating statements
        Profit and loss statements
    BT Accounting
        Auditing
        Bookkeeping
        Business
        Business records
        Corporation reports
    SA *subdivision* Accounting *under special*
        subjects, e.g. Insurance, Life—
        Accounting; Universities and
        colleges—Accounting
    NT Accounts receivable
        Auditors' reports
        Disclosure in accounting
        Financial statements, Consolidated
        Funds-flow statements
        Line of business reporting
        Pro forma statements (Accounting)
        Ratio analysis
— **Law and legislation** *(May Subd Geog)*
Financial statements, Compilation and review
of
    USE Financial statements, Unaudited
Financial statements, Consolidated
  (May Subd Geog)
  [HF5681.B2]
    UF Combined financial statement
        Consolidated balance sheet
        Consolidated financial statements
    BT Financial statements
        Holding companies—Accounting
— **Law and legislation** *(May Subd Geog)*
Financial statements, Interim
  (May Subd Geog)
  [HF5681.B2]
    UF Interim financial statements
        Interim statements, Financial
Financial statements, Misleading
  (May Subd Geog)
    UF Misleading financial statements
        Misrepresentations in financial
        statements
        Negligence in financial statements
Financial statements, Unaudited
  (May Subd Geog)
  [HF5681.B2]
    UF Compilation and review of financial
        statements
        Financial statements, Compilation and
        review of
        Unaudited financial statements
Financial statistics
    USE Finance—Statistics
Financial Times Clipper Race
  [GV832]
    BT Yacht racing
Financiers
    USE Capitalists and financiers
Financing, Compensatory
    USE Compensatory financing
Financing, Deficit
    USE Deficit financing
Finback whale
    UF Balaenoptera physalis
        Fin whale
        Finner
        Razorback

    BT Whales
Finch, Gouldian
    USE Gouldian finch
Finch, Zebra
    USE Zebra finch
Finch family
Fincher family
    USE Fancher family
Finches
  [QL696.P2]
    BT Passeriformes
    NT Drepanididae
        Emberizidae
        Fringillidae
        Grosbeaks
Finches, Grass
    USE Grass finches
Finck family
    USE Fink family
Fincke family
    USE Fink family
Finckley family
    USE Finklea family
Finden family
    UF Fidden family
        Finnen family
Finding fault
    USE Faultfinding
Finding lists
    USE Library catalogs
Finding lost property
    USE Lost articles (Law)
Finding of Christ in the Temple (Painting)
    USE Hunt, William Holman, 1827-1910.
        Finding of the Saviour in the
        Temple
Finding of the Saviour in the Temple
  (Painting)
    USE Hunt, William Holman, 1827-1910.
        Finding of the Saviour in the
        Temple
Findlay family
    USE Finley family
Findley family
    USE Finley family
Findly family
    USE Finley family
Fine arts
    USE Art
        Arts
Fine editions
    USE Bibliography—Fine editions
Fine family
    USE Finn family
Fine-rolls
  [DA25]
Fine-structure constant
    UF Constant, Fine-structure
        Constant, Sommerfeld fine-structure
        Sommerfeld fine-structure constant
    BT Constants, Physical
Finefrock family
    USE Finfrock family
Finemore family
    USE Fenimore family
Fines (Land titles)
    USE Fines and recoveries
Fines (Penalties) *(May Subd Geog)*
    UF Penalties (Criminal law)
    BT Costs (Law)
        Criminal law
        Punishment
    NT Penalties, Contractual
        Tax penalties
Fines and recoveries *(May Subd Geog)*
    UF Feet of fines
        Fines (Land titles)
        Pedes finium
        Recoveries (Law)
    BT Real property
    NT Repossession

Finey family
    USE Finney family
Finfrock family *(Not Subd Geog)*
    UF Finafrock family
        Finefrock family
        Finifrock family
        Finnefrock family
        Finneyfrock family
        Fivecoat family
        Fivecoate family
        Fivecoats family
        Fünffrock family
        Fünfrock family
Fingar family
    USE Finger family
Finger alphabet
    USE Deaf—Means of communication
Finger calculation
    UF Calculation, Finger
        Finger mathematics
        Mathematics, Finger
    BT Arithmetic
        Fingers
Finger family
    UF Fingar family
Finger games
    USE Finger play
Finger joint
— **Surgery**
Finger Lakes (N.Y.)
    BT Lakes—New York (State)
    NT Cayuga Lake (N.Y.)
        Keuka Lake (N.Y.)
        Skaneateles Lake (N.Y.)
Finger marks
    USE Fingerprints
Finger mathematics
    USE Finger calculation
Finger millet
    USE Ragi
Finger painting
    UF Painting, Finger
        Painting without a brush
    BT Children as artists
        Painting
Finger play
  [GV1218.F5]
    UF Finger games
    BT Play
Finger pressure therapy
    USE Acupressure
Finger prints
    USE Fingerprints
Finger rings
    USE Rings
Finger-sucking
    UF Sucking of fingers
    BT Oral habits
    NT Thumb sucking
Fingering (Piano playing)
    USE Piano—Instruction and study—
        Fingering
        Piano—Studies and exercises—
        Fingering
Fingernail biting
    USE Nail-biting
Fingernails
    BT Fingers
        Nails (Anatomy)
Fingernails in rabbinical literature
    BT Rabbinical literature
Fingerprints
  [GN192 (Anthropology)]
  [HV6074 (Criminology)]
    UF Dactylography
        Dactyloscopy
        Finger marks
        Finger prints

BT Anthropometry
    Crime and criminals—Identification
    Dermatoglyphics
    Identification
NT Artificial satellites in fingerprint
     transmission
    Bertillon system
    Fortune-telling by fingerprints
    Thumbprints
— **Laser use in**
    [HV6074]
    BT Lasers

Fingers
    [QM548]
    BT Hand
    NT Finger calculation
      Fingernails
      Thumb
— **Abnormalities** *(May Subd Geog)*
    NT Camptodactyly
      Dupuytren's contracture
— **Diseases** *(May Subd Geog)*
    NT Vibration syndrome
— **Wounds and injuries**

Fingos
    UF Aba-Mbos
      Abambos
      Amafengos
      Amafingos
      Fecanes
      Fingus
      Mfengos
    BT Bantus
      Ethnology—South Africa
    NT Missions to Fingos

Fingus
    USE Fingos

Finials
    [TH2495]
    BT Architectural metal-work
      Building
    NT Roof crestings

Finifrock family
    USE Finfrock family

Finishes and finishing
    [TP934-TP944 (Finishes)]
    [TT300-TT345 (Finishing)]
    UF Finishing
      Finishing materials
    BT Coating processes
      Coatings
      Manufacturing processes
      Materials
    NT Concrete—Finishing
      Cotton finishing
      Jewelry—Finishing
      Lacquer and lacquering
      Metals—Finishing
      Paint
      Painting, Industrial
      Paper finishing
      Soil repellents
      Stains and staining
      Surface preparation
      Textile finishing
      Textile finishing agents
      Varnish and varnishing
      Wood finishing

Finishing
    USE Finishes and finishing

Finishing, Furniture
    USE Furniture finishing

Finishing materials
    USE Finishes and finishing

Finishing processes, Print
    USE Print finishing processes

Finisterre-Huon languages
    UF Huon-Finisterre languages
    BT Papuan languages
    NT Kate language
      Komba language

    Nabak language
    Selepet language
    Wantoat language

Finite, The
    UF Finiteness
      Finitude
      Finity
    BT Ontology
      Philosophy
    RT Infinite

Finite arithmetic
    USE Modular arithmetic

Finite automata
    USE Sequential machine theory

Finite conjugate groups
    USE FC-groups

Finite difference method
    USE Finite differences

Finite differences
    UF Differences, Finite
      Finite difference method
    BT Numerical analysis

Finite Element Interactive Graphics Users
   Routines (Computer program)
    USE FIGURES II (Computer program)

Finite element method
    BT Numerical analysis
    RT Galerkin methods
    NT Finite strip method
— **Computer programs**
    NT ADINA (Computer program)
      FIGURES II (Computer program)
      SKYSOL (Computer program)
      STARS (Computer program)
      WAPPP (Computer program)
      WECAN (Computer program)

Finite Element Program for Automatic
   Dynamic Incremental Nonlinear Analysis
   (Computer program)
    USE ADINA (Computer program)

Finite-Element Surface-Water Modeling
   System-Texas (Computer program)
    USE FESWMS-TX (Computer program)

Finite fields (Algebra)
    [QA247.3]
    UF Modular fields (Algebra)
    BT Algebra, Abstract
      Fields, Algebraic
      Galois theory
      Modules (Algebra)

Finite generalized quadrangles
    UF Generalized quadrangles, Finite
      Quadrangles, Generalized finite
    BT Finite geometries

Finite geometries
    [QA167.2]
    UF Geometries, Finite
    BT Combinatorial geometry
    NT Finite generalized quadrangles

Finite groups
    UF Groups, Finite
    BT Groups, Theory of
    RT Modules (Algebra)
    NT Burnside problem
      Characters of groups
      FC-groups
      Finite simple groups
      Groups, Multiply transitive
      Groups, Nilpotent
      Mathieu groups
      Q-groups
      Sporadic groups (Mathematics)
      Sylow subgroups

Finite nuclei
    UF Nuclei, Finite
    BT Nuclear physics

Finite number systems
    USE Modules (Algebra)

Finite simple groups
    UF Simple groups, Finite

    BT Finite groups
      Linear algebraic groups

Finite strip method
    BT Finite element method
      Numerical analysis
      Structures, Theory of
    NT Plates (Engineering)
      Slabs

Finitely pseudo-Frobenius rings
    USE FPF rings

Finiteness
    USE Finite, The

Finitude
    USE Finite, The

Finity
    USE Finite, The

Fink family
    UF Finck family
      Fincke family
      Finke family

Finke family
    USE Fink family

Finklea family
    UF Finckley family

Finland
    NT Finns
— **Church history**
— — **20th century**
— **Civilization**
— **Description and travel**
— — **1945-1980**
— — **1981-**
— **Economic conditions**
— — **1918-**
— — **1945-**
— **Foreign relations**
— — **1917-1945**
— — **1945-**
— **History**
    [DK445-465]
— — **To 1523**
— — **1523-1611**
— — **Gustavus II Adolphus, 1611-1632**
— — **Charles X Gustavus, 1654-1660**
— — **18th century**
— — **19th century**
    USE Finland—History—1809-1917
— — **Russian Conquest, 1808-1809**
    BT Russo-Swedish War, 1808-1809
— — **1809-1917**
    [DL1065-1065.8]
    UF Finland—History—19th century
— — **20th century**
— — **Revolution, 1917-1918**
— — — **Casualties (Statistics, etc.)**
— — — **Literature and the Revolution**
— — — **Personal narratives**
— — — **Pictorial works**
— — — **Prisoners and prisons**
— — **1918-1939**
    [DL1084]
— — **1939-**
    [DK459.45]
— **Politics and government**
— — **1809-1917**
— — **20th century**
— — **1917-1945**
— — **1945-**
— **Public buildings**
    USE Public buildings—Finland
— **Social conditions**
— — **1945-**

Finland, Gulf of
    UF Finskiĭ zaliv
      Finskiy zaliv
      Gulf of Finland
      Soomelaht
      Suomenlahti

Finland, Gulf of *(Continued)*
　BT　Baltic Sea
　　　Bays—Estonia
　　　Bays—Finland
　　　Bays—Russian S.F.S.R.
Finland Proper (Finland)
　USE　Varsinais-Suomi (Finland)
Finlason family
　USE　Finlayson family
Finlay family
　USE　Finley family
Finlay Mountains (Tex.)
　BT　Mountains—Texas
Finlayson family
　UF　Finlason family
Finless porpoise
　　[QL737.C434]
　UF　Neomeris phocaenoides
　　　Neophocaena phocaenoides
　BT　Porpoises
Finley family
　UF　Findlay family
　　　Findley family
　　　Findly family
　　　Finlay family
　　　Finly family
Finly family
　USE　Finley family
FINMARC
　USE　MARC System—Finland
Finn family
　UF　Fin family
　　　Fine family
　　　Finne family
　RT　Finney family
Finne family
　USE　Finn family
Finnefrock family
　USE　Finfrock family
Finnemore family
　USE　Fenimore family
Finnen family
　USE　Finden family
Finner
　USE　Finback whale
Finnerud family
Finney family
　UF　Finey family
　　　Finny family
　　　Phiney family
　　　Phinney family
　　　Phinny family
　RT　Finn family
Finneyfrock family
　USE　Finfrock family
Finng language
　USE　Bobo Fing language
Finnish abbreviations
　USE　Abbreviations, Finnish
Finnish agricultural assistance
　USE　Agricultural assistance, Finnish
Finnish-American newspapers
　BT　American newspapers
　　　Finnish newspapers
Finnish Americans *(May Subd Geog)*
　BT　Ethnology—United States
　　　Finns—United States
Finnish art
　USE　Art, Finnish
Finnish arts
　USE　Arts, Finnish
Finnish authors
　USE　Authors, Finnish
Finnish baths
　USE　Sauna
Finnish book-plates
　USE　Book-plates, Finnish
Finnish children's literature
　USE　Children's literature, Finnish
Finnish children's periodicals
　USE　Children's periodicals, Finnish

Finnish children's plays
　USE　Children's plays, Finnish
Finnish children's stories
　USE　Children's stories, Finnish
Finnish Christian literature
　USE　Christian literature, Finnish
Finnish Christian poetry
　USE　Christian poetry, Finnish
Finnish coins
　USE　Coins, Finnish
Finnish corporations
　USE　Corporations, Finnish
Finnish detective and mystery stories
　USE　Detective and mystery stories, Finnish
Finnish document writing
　USE　Document writing, Finnish
Finnish drama *(May Subd Geog)*
　　[PH311 (History)]
　　[PH347 (Collections)]
　NT　Children's plays, Finnish
　　　Radio plays, Finnish
Finnish drawing
　USE　Drawing, Finnish
Finnish economic assistance
　USE　Economic assistance, Finnish
Finnish educational assistance
　USE　Educational assistance, Finnish
Finnish encyclopedias and dictionaries
　USE　Encyclopedias and dictionaries,
　　　Finnish
Finnish epic poetry
　USE　Epic poetry, Finnish
Finnish fiction *(May Subd Geog)*
　NT　Children's stories, Finnish
　　　Detective and mystery stories, Finnish
　　　Historical fiction, Finnish
　　　Horror tales, Finnish
　　　Sea stories, Finnish
　　　Short stories, Finnish
Finnish folk literature
　USE　Folk literature, Finnish
Finnish folk poetry
　USE　Folk poetry, Finnish
Finnish folk-songs
　USE　Folk-songs, Finnish
Finnish historical fiction
　USE　Historical fiction, Finnish
Finnish horror tales
　USE　Horror tales, Finnish
Finnish hymns
　USE　Hymns, Finnish
Finnish imprints *(May Subd Geog)*
Finnish laboring class writings
　USE　Laboring class writings, Finnish
Finnish language *(May Subd Geog)*
　　[PH101-293]
　BT　Baltic-Finnic languages
　— Abbreviations
　　　USE　Abbreviations, Finnish
　— **Etymology**
　　　NT　Pärnä (The Finnish word)
　— **Style**
　　　NT　Document writing, Finnish
　— **Writing**
　　　NT　Document writing, Finnish
Finnish literature *(May Subd Geog)*
　　[PH300-405]
　NT　Children's literature, Finnish
　　　Christian literature, Finnish
　　　Folk literature, Finnish
　　　Laboring class writings, Finnish
　　　Young adult literature, Finnish
Finnish literature (American)
　USE　American literature—Finnish authors
Finnish literature (Swedish)
　　Duplicate entry is made under Swedish literature
　—Finnish authors.
　— **20th century**
Finnish lithography
　USE　Lithography, Finnish

Finnish love poetry
　USE　Love poetry, Finnish
Finnish manuscripts
　USE　Manuscripts, Finnish
Finnish missions
　USE　Missions, Finnish
Finnish mural painting and decoration
　USE　Mural painting and decoration, Finnish
Finnish mythology
　USE　Mythology, Finno-Ugrian
Finnish national characteristics
　USE　National characteristics, Finnish
Finnish newspapers *(May Subd Geog)*
　NT　Finnish-American newspapers
Finnish orations
　USE　Speeches, addresses, etc., Finnish
Finnish painting
　USE　Painting, Finnish
Finnish periodicals
　　[PN5355.F5 (History)]
　NT　Children's periodicals, Finnish
Finnish philology
Finnish poetry *(May Subd Geog)*
　　[PH310 (History)]
　　[PH345-PH346 (Collections)]
　NT　Christian poetry, Finnish
　　　Epic poetry, Finnish
　　　Folk poetry, Finnish
　　　Love poetry, Finnish
Finnish poetry (Swedish)
　　Duplicate entry is made under Swedish poetry—
　Finnish authors.
Finnish poets
　USE　Poets, Finnish
Finnish posters
　USE　Posters, Finnish
Finnish pottery
　USE　Pottery, Finnish
Finnish prints
　USE　Prints, Finnish
Finnish prose literature *(May Subd Geog)*
Finnish proverbs
　USE　Proverbs, Finnish
Finnish quotations
　USE　Quotations, Finnish
Finnish radio plays
　USE　Radio plays, Finnish
Finnish reference books
　USE　Reference books, Finnish
Finnish riddles
　USE　Riddles, Finnish
Finnish sculpture
　USE　Sculpture, Finnish
Finnish sea stories
　USE　Sea stories, Finnish
Finnish short stories
　USE　Short stories, Finnish
Finnish shorthand
　USE　Shorthand, Finnish
Finnish songs
　USE　Songs, Finnish
Finnish speeches
　USE　Speeches, addresses, etc., Finnish
Finnish spitz
　　[SF429.F4]
　UF　Spitz, Finnish
　BT　Spitz dogs
Finnish students *(May Subd Geog)*
　BT　Students
Finnish technical assistance
　USE　Technical assistance, Finnish
Finnish wit and humor *(May Subd Geog)*
　　Here are entered collections from several authors
　and individual authors who have not written in other
　literary forms.
Finnish wit and humor, Pictorial
　(May Subd Geog)
Finnish women authors
　USE　Women authors, Finnish
Finnish young adult literature
　USE　Young adult literature, Finnish

Finno-Russian War, 1939-1940
  USE Russo-Finnish War, 1939-1940
Finno-Ugrian folk art
  USE Folk art, Finno-Ugrian
Finno-Ugrian jewelry
  USE Jewelry, Finno-Ugrian
Finno-Ugrian languages
  USE Finno-Ugric languages
Finno-Ugrians *(May Subd Geog)*
  UF Ugro-Finns
  BT Uralic peoples
  NT Bulgars (Turkic people)
      Estonians
      Finns
      Hungarians
      Karelians
      Khanty
      Komi
      Lapps
      Livonians
      Mansi
      Mari
      Mordvins
      Permians
      Udmurts
      Veps
      Votes (People)
  — **Anthropometry**
Finno-Ugric folk poetry
  USE Folk poetry, Finno-Ugric
Finno-Ugric folk-songs
  USE Folk-songs, Finno-Ugric
Finno-Ugric languages
  [PH]
  UF Fenno-Ugric languages
      Finno-Ugrian languages
      Ugro-Finnic languages
  BT Uralic languages
  NT Baltic-Finnic languages
      Hungarian language
      Lapp language
      Mari language
      Mordvin language
      Ob-Ugric languages
      Permic languages
  — **Study and teaching** *(May Subd Geog)*
      NT Finno-Ugrists
Finno-Ugric philology
Finno-Ugric poetry *(May Subd Geog)*
  NT Folk poetry, Finno-Ugric
Finno-Ugricists
  USE Finno-Ugrists
Finno-Ugrists *(May Subd Geog)*
  UF Finno-Ugricists
  BT Finno-Ugric languages—Study and
      teaching
Finns *(May Subd Geog)*
  BT Ethnology—Finland
      Finland
      Finno-Ugrians
  — **United States**
      NT Finnish Americans
Finny family
  USE Finney family
Finontok language
  USE Bontoc language
Fins
  [QL639]
  UF Fin rays
      Rays on fish
  BT Fishes—Anatomy
Finsen rays
  USE Phototherapy
Finsen therapy
  USE Phototherapy
Finskiĭ zaliv
  USE Finland, Gulf of
Finskiy zaliv
  USE Finland, Gulf of
Finsler spaces
  [QA689]

UF Spaces, Finsler
BT Geometry, Differential
Finstad family *(Not Subd Geog)*
Finster family
  USE Fenster family
Finvold family *(Not Subd Geog)*
Fionia (Denmark)
  USE Fyn (Denmark)
Fionie (Denmark)
  USE Fyn (Denmark)
Fiordland National Park (N.Z.)
  BT National parks and reserves—New
      Zealand
      Parks—New Zealand
Fiords
  USE Fjords
Fiorentino (City)
  UF Torre Fiorentina (City)
  BT Cities and towns, Ruined, extinct, etc.
      —Italy
      Italy—Antiquities
Fiorinia
  [QL527.D5]
  BT Diaspididae
  NT Fiorinia externa
Fiorinia externa
  [QL527.D5]
  UF Hemlock scale
  BT Fiorinia
Fioriture
  USE Embellishment (Vocal music)
Fiote language
  USE Kituba language
      Kongo language
      Koongo dialect (Western Kongo)
Fipa (African people)
  BT Ethnology—Tanzania
      Ethnology—Zambia
Fipa folk literature
  USE Folk literature, Fipa
Fique *(May Subd Geog)*
  [QK495.A26 (Botany)]
  [SB261.F56 (Fiber plant)]
  UF Furcraea macrophylla
      Sisal, Wild
      Wild sisal
  BT Fiber plants
Fir *(May Subd Geog)*
  [QK494.5.P66 (Botany)]
  [SD397.F5 (Culture)]
  UF Abies
      Firs
  BT Pinaceae
  NT Abies alba
      Abies concolor
      Abies grandis
      Abies lasiocarpa
      Abies magnifica
      Balsam fir
      Bornmueller fir
      Cilician fir
      Noble fir
      Siberian fir
      Spanish fir
  — **Diseases and pests** *(May Subd Geog)*
      NT Douglas-fir tussock moth
          Scolytus ventralis
          Semanotus litigiosus
Fir, China
  USE China fir
Fir, Douglas
  USE Douglas fir
Fir, Silver
  USE Cathaya argyrophylla
Fir engraver beetle
  USE Scolytus ventralis
Fir tree borer
  USE Semanotus litigiosus
Firat River
  USE Euphrates River

Firdaws, Khirbat
  USE Herodium
Fire, Valley of (Nev.)
  UF Valley of Fire (Nev.)
  BT Valleys—Nevada
  RT Valley of Fire State Park (Nev.)
Fire
  [GN416-GN417 (Ethnology)]
  [GR495 (Folk-lore)]
  [TP265 (Chemistry)]
  BT Chemistry
  RT Combustion
      Heat
  NT Fires
      Flame
      Fuel
      Heating
      Indians of North America—Fire use
      Pyromania
      Smoke
      Will-o'-the-wisp
  — Environmental aspects
      USE Fire ecology
  — **Mythology**
  — **Psychological aspects**
      NT Fire behavior in children
  — **Religious aspects**
      NT Candles and lights
          Fire walking
          Fire-worshipers
  — — **Buddhism**
      NT Homa (Rite)
  — — **Buddhism, [Christianity, etc.]**
  — — **Hinduism**
      NT Agnihotra (Hindu rite)
          Homa (Rite)
          Timiti (Hindu rite)
Fire, Greek
  USE Greek fire
Fire-alarms *(May Subd Geog)*
  [TK7271]
  UF Fire warning systems
      Warning systems, Fire
  BT Electric apparatus and appliances
  RT Electric alarms
  NT Stench fire-warning system in mines
Fire ant venom
  USE Fire ants—Venom
Fire ants *(May Subd Geog)*
  [QL568.F7]
  UF Solenopsis
  BT Ants
  NT Solenopsis invicta
      Solenopsis richteri
  — **Venom**
      UF Fire ant venom
          Solamine
          Solenopsin
      BT Alkaloids
Fire assay
  USE Assaying
Fire balls
  USE Meteors
Fire bean
  USE Scarlet runner bean
Fire behavior in children *(May Subd Geog)*
  UF Child firesetting
      Fire curiosity in children
      Firesetting by children
  BT Child psychology
      Fire—Psychological aspects
  NT Pyromania in children
Fire-blight *(May Subd Geog)*
  [SB741.F6 (Plant disease)]
  UF Fireblight
      Pear-blight
  BT Bacterial diseases of plants
Fire-boats
  USE Fireboats
Fire bombs
  USE Incendiary bombs

Fire-boxes
  USE Locomotives—Fire-boxes
Fire-brick
  [TP832.F5]
  BT Bricks
      Refractory materials
  NT Alumina brick
      Magnesia brick
Fire casualties
  USE Fires—Casualties
Fire-clay (May Subd Geog)
  [TA455.F5 (Testing)]
  [TN941-TN943 (Mineral resources)]
  [TP838 (Technology)]
  BT Clay
Fire companies
  USE Fire-departments
Fire control (Aerial gunnery)
  BT Aerial gunnery
  NT United States. Navy—Aviation fire
      control technicians
  — **Equipment**
      UF Airborne fire control systems
      BT Airplanes, Military—Armament
Fire control (Gunnery)
  [UF848]
  UF Gun fire control
  BT Gunnery
      Tracking radar
  NT Position-finders
      Range-finding
      Target acquisition
  — **Equipment**
  — **Optical equipment**
      [UF849]
      UF Fire control optics
      BT Artillery
          Optical instruments
          Ordnance
      NT Range-finding
          Telescopic sights
Fire control (Naval gunnery)
  [VF520]
  BT Naval gunnery
      Ordnance, Naval
      Remote control
  NT Range-finding
      United States. Navy—Fire control
          technicians (Missile)
  — **Equipment**
  — **Radar equipment**
      [VF530]
      UF Fire control radar
          Radar, Fire control
      BT Range-finding
          Tracking radar
Fire control optics
  USE Fire control (Gunnery)—Optical
      equipment
Fire control radar
  USE Fire control (Naval gunnery)—Radar
      equipment
Fire control technicians (Ballistic missile fire
  control) (United States Navy)
  USE United States. Navy—Fire control
      technicians (Ballistic missile fire
      control)
Fire control technicians (Missile) (United
  States Navy)
  USE United States. Navy—Fire control
      technicians (Missile)
Fire controlmen (United States Navy)
  USE United States. Navy—Fire
      controlmen
Fire-crested wren
  USE Regulus ignicapillus
Fire curiosity in children
  USE Fire behavior in children
Fire damages, Liability for
  USE Liability for fire damages

Fire-damp
  [TN305]
      Here are entered works on methane as a combus-
  tible gas formed in coal mines. Works on methane
  present in a stratum of coal are entered under
  Coalbed methane.
  UF Marsh-gas
  BT Gases, Asphyxiating and poisonous
      Mine gases
  RT Coalbed methane
Fire deaths
  USE Fires—Casualties
Fire department chemical engines
  USE Chemical fire engines
Fire-department paraphernalia
  USE Fire-departments—Collectibles
Fire-departments (May Subd Geog)
  [TH9500-9599]
  UF Fire companies
  SA official reports of fire-departments
      under names of cities and towns
  NT Fire fighters—Residence requirements
      Fire stations
      Police-fire integration
  — **Collectibles** (May Subd Geog)
      UF Fire-department paraphernalia
      BT Fire-departments—Equipment and
          supplies
  — **Communication systems**
      BT Public safety radio service
      NT Radio in fire prevention
  — **Equipment and supplies**
      [TH9361-9383]
      NT Fire-departments—Collectibles
          Ladders, Aerial
  — — **Appraisal**
      USE Fire-departments—Equipment
          and supplies—Valuation
  — — **Valuation**
      UF Fire-departments—Equipment
          and supplies—Appraisal
  — **Law and legislation** (May Subd Geog)
  — **Uniforms**
      BT Uniforms, Civil
Fire detectors (May Subd Geog)
  [TH9271]
  UF Smoke detectors
  BT Detectors
      Fires
      Remote sensing—Equipment and
          supplies
Fire districts
  USE Fire protection districts
Fire dogs
  USE Dalmatian dogs
Fire-eating
  [GV1559]
  BT Conjuring
Fire ecology (May Subd Geog)
  UF Ecology, Fire
      Ecopyrology
      Fire—Environmental aspects
  BT Ecology
      Forest fires
      Forest management
      Grassland fires
  RT Prescribed burning
Fire engine driving
  BT Motor vehicle driving
Fire engines (May Subd Geog)
  [TH9371-TH9377]
  UF Fire-fighting vehicles
      Fire trucks
  BT Emergency vehicles
      Fire extinction—Equipment and
          supplies
  NT Chemical fire engines
  — **Appraisal**
      USE Fire engines—Valuation
  — **Dispatching**
      UF Dispatching of fire engines

  — — **Data processing**
      NT CADS (Computer system)
  — **Valuation**
      UF Fire engines—Appraisal
Fire-escapes (May Subd Geog)
  [TH2274]
  BT Building laws
  NT Life-saving at fires
      Life-saving nets
Fire etching
  USE Pyrography
Fire extinction (May Subd Geog)
  [TH9111-TH9599]
  UF Buildings—Fires and fire prevention
      Extinction of fires
      Fighting of fires
      Fire fighting
      Firefighting
  BT Fire prevention
  RT Insurance engineering
  NT Fire extinguishers
      Fire fighters
      Fire protection districts
      Fire sprinklers
      Fire streams
      Fireboats
      Forest fires—Prevention and control
      Grassland fires—Prevention and
          control
      Ground cover fires—Prevention and
          control
      Hose-couplings
      Mine fires—Prevention and control
      Wildfires—Prevention and control
  — **Chemical systems**
      [TH9338]
      RT Fire extinguishing agents
  — **Equipment and supplies**
      NT Fire engines
  — **Explosion systems**
      [TH9339]
  — **Vocational guidance** (May Subd Geog)
      BT Fire fighters
  — **Water-supply**
      [TH9311-9334]
      NT Fire hose
Fire extinguishers
  [TH9362]
  UF Extinguishers, Fire
  BT Fire extinction
  NT Fire extinguishing agents
Fire extinguishing agents
  [TP266]
  BT Chemicals
      Fire extinguishers
  RT Fire extinction—Chemical systems
  NT Bromotrifluoromethane
Fire fighters (May Subd Geog)
  UF Firefighters
      Firemen
  BT Fire extinction
      Fire prevention
  NT Afro-American fire fighters
      Collective labor agreements—Fire
          fighters
      Fire extinction—Vocational guidance
      Fire prevention—Vocational guidance
      Forest fire fighters
      Smokejumpers
      Trade-unions—Fire fighters
      Wildfire fighters
  — Collective bargaining
      USE Collective bargaining—Fire
          fighters
  — **Pensions** (May Subd Geog)
      UF Fire fighters—Salaries, pensions,
          etc.
  — — **Law and legislation**
      (May Subd Geog)
  — **Physical training**
      [TH9128]

— **Residence requirements**
  UF Residence requirements for fire
       fighters
  BT Fire-departments
— **Salaries, etc.** *(May Subd Geog)*
  UF Fire fighters—Salaries, pensions,
       etc.
— — **Law and legislation**
     (May Subd Geog)
— Salaries, pensions, etc.
  USE Fire fighters—Pensions
        Fire fighters—Salaries, etc.
Fire fighters, Afro-American
  USE Afro-American fire fighters
Fire fighting
  USE Fire extinction
Fire fighting equipment industry
  (May Subd Geog)
  ⌐HD9999.F5⌐
Fire-fighting vehicles
  USE Fire engines
Fire hose
  ⌐TH9380⌐
  BT Fire extinction—Water-supply
       Hose
       Hydrants
Fire in art
  ⌐N8217.F5⌐
Fire in literature
Fire inspection
  USE Fire prevention—Inspection
**Fire Inspection Reporting System (Computer
system)**
  USE FIRS (Computer system)
Fire insurance
  USE Insurance, Fire
Fire investigation *(May Subd Geog)*
  ⌐TH9180⌐
  BT Fires
       Investigations
  NT Arson investigation
Fire Island (N.Y.)
  BT Islands—New York (State)
Fire Island National Seashore (N.Y.)
  BT National parks and reserves—New
       York (State)
       Recreation areas—New York (State)
Fire liability law
  USE Liability for fire damages
Fire lilies
  USE Cyrtanthus
Fire lookout stations *(May Subd Geog)*
  ⌐SD421.375⌐
  UF Firewatch towers
       Forest fire lookout stations
       Lookout stations, Fire
       Lookout towers, Fire
       Stations, Fire lookout
  BT Forest fire detection
Fire lookouts *(May Subd Geog)*
  ⌐SD421.375⌐
  UF Fire spotters
       Fire watchers, Forest
       Firewatchers, Forest
       Forest fire lookouts
       Forest fire watchers
       Lookouts, Fire
       Spotters, Fire
  BT Forest fire detection
Fire losses
  USE Fires
       Insurance, Fire
Fire-making
  ⌐GN416-GN417 (Ethnology)⌐
Fire-marks
  ⌐HG9799 (British insurance)⌐
  UF Fire-plates
       Insurance, Fire—Office marks
  BT Insurance, Fire
Fire-plates
  USE Fire-marks

Fire pot cookery
  UF Cookery, Fire pot
  BT Cookery, Oriental
Fire prevention *(May Subd Geog)*
  ⌐TH9111-9599⌐
  UF Buildings—Fires and fire prevention
       Fire safety
       Prevention of fires
  BT Fires
  RT Insurance engineering
  SA *subdivision* Fires and fire prevention
      under individual types of
      institutions, buildings, industries,
      and vehicles, e.g. Psychiatric
      hospitals—Fires and fire prevention;
      Warehouses—Fires and fire
      prevention; Construction industry—
      Fires and fire prevention;
      Automobiles—Fires and fire
      prevention
  NT Building, Fireproof
       Electric apparatus and appliances—
         Fires and fire prevention
       Fire extinction
       Fire fighters
       Fireproofing
       Fireproofing agents
       Forest fires—Prevention and control
       Grassland fires—Prevention and
         control
       Ground cover fires—Prevention and
         control
       Lightning-arresters
       Lightning-conductors
       Lightning protection
       Mine fires—Prevention and control
       Radio in fire prevention
       Wildfires—Prevention and control
— **Data processing**
  NT FIRS (Computer system)
— **Equipment and supplies**
  NT Fire prevention equipment industry
— **Federal aid**
  USE Federal aid to fire prevention
— **Finance**
  NT Federal aid to fire prevention
— **Inspection**
  UF Fire inspection
— **Law and legislation** *(May Subd Geog)*
  BT Safety regulations
— **Research** *(May Subd Geog)*
  ⌐TH9120⌐
  UF Fire research
  BT Research, Industrial
  NT Fire-testing
— **Study and teaching** *(May Subd Geog)*
  UF Fire prevention education
— **Vocational guidance**
  BT Fire fighters
Fire prevention education
  USE Fire prevention—Study and teaching
Fire prevention equipment industry
  (May Subd Geog)
  ⌐HD9999.F5-54⌐
  BT Fire prevention—Equipment and
       supplies
Fire proofing
  USE Fireproofing
Fire protection districts *(May Subd Geog)*
  UF Fire districts
  BT Fire extinction
       Special districts
— **Finance**
— — **Law and legislation**
     (May Subd Geog)
— **Law and legislation** *(May Subd Geog)*
— **Maine**
  NT Maine Forestry District
Fire research
  USE Fire prevention—Research

Fire resistant materials *(May Subd Geog)*
  ⌐TH1065⌐
  UF Flame resistant materials
  BT Fireproofing
  NT Fire resistant plastics
       Fire resistant polymers
Fire resistant materials industry
  (May Subd Geog)
  ⌐HD9999.F55-554⌐
Fire resistant plastics
  ⌐TH1074⌐
  UF Flame retardant plastics
  BT Fire resistant materials
       Fireproofing
       Plastics
Fire resistant polymers
  ⌐TH1074.5⌐
  UF Fire retardant polymers
       Flame retardant polymers
  BT Fire resistant materials
       Fireproofing
       Polymers and polymerization
Fire resisting agents
  USE Fireproofing agents
Fire retardant polymers
  USE Fire resistant polymers
Fire retardants
  USE Fireproofing agents
Fire safety
  USE Fire prevention
Fire ships
  USE Fireships
Fire spotters
  USE Fire lookouts
Fire sprinklers
  ⌐TH9336⌐
  UF Automatic sprinklers
       Sprinkling systems
  BT Fire extinction
       Sprinklers
— **Law and legislation** *(May Subd Geog)*
  BT Building laws
Fire stations *(May Subd Geog)*
  UF Firehouses
       Houses, Fire
       Stations, Fire
  BT Fire-departments
Fire streams
  ⌐TH9323⌐
  BT Fire extinction
       Nozzles
Fire-testing
  ⌐TH1091-1098⌐
  UF Flammability testing
  BT Building, Fireproof
       Building materials—Testing
       Fire prevention—Research
       Fireproofing
       Testing
  NT Concrete—Fire-testing
       Conveyor belts—Fire-testing
       Flame spread
       House furnishings—Fire-testing
       Oxygen index of materials
       Textile fabrics—Fire-testing
       Upholstery—Fire-testing
— **Computer programs**
  NT RAPID (Computer program)
Fire trucks
  USE Fire engines
Fire use by Indians of North America
  USE Indians of North America—Fire use
Fire victims
  USE Fires—Casualties
Fire walking *(May Subd Geog)*
  UF Firewalking
       Walking on fire
  BT Fire—Religious aspects
  NT Timiti (Hindu rite)
Fire warning systems
  USE Fire-alarms

Fire watchers, Forest
  USE Fire lookouts
Fire weather *(May Subd Geog)*
  BT Forest meteorology
      Weather
  RT Forest fires
Fire-worshipers *(May Subd Geog)*
  ₍BL453₎
  BT Fire—Religious aspects
      Religion, Primitive
      Religions
      Worship
  RT Parsees
  NT Zoroastrianism
Firearms *(May Subd Geog)*
  ₍TS532-TS537.5 (Manufacture)₎
  ₍U (Military science)₎
  ₍V (Naval science)₎
      Covers works on weapons from which a missile, as
  a bullet, ball, or shell, is hurled by the action of explo-
  sives.
  UF Gun
      Guns
      Small arms
      Weapons
  BT Arms and armor
  RT Gunnery
      Shooting
      Shooting, Military
  SA *subdivision* Firearms *under armies,*
      navies, etc., e.g. United States.
      Army—Firearms; United States.
      Navy—Firearms
  NT Air guns
      Allen and Wheelock firearms
      AR-7 carbine
      Browning firearms
      Colt firearms
      Commemorative firearms
      Espingoles
      Firearms theft
      Flame throwers
      Gun control
      Gunpowder
      Gunstocks
      Holsters
      Hunting guns
      Husqvarna firearms
      Machine-guns
      Mountain guns
      Muzzle-loading firearms
      Muzzles (Firearms)
      Ordnance
      Paraffin test
      Pinfire firearms
      Pistols
      Presentation firearms
      Revolvers
      Rifles
      Sharps firearms
      Shotguns
      Silencers (Firearms)
      Smith and Wesson firearms
      Sporting guns
      Winchester firearms
  — Accidents
      NT Hunting—Accidents and injuries
  — Design and construction
      NT Firearms designers
  — Identification
      ₍HV8077₎
      UF Identification of firearms
      NT Forensic ballistics
  — Law and legislation *(May Subd Geog)*
          Here are entered works on the legal aspects of
      gun control. General and non-legal works on the
      control of guns are entered under Gun control.
      UF Firearms control
          Gun control—Law and legislation
      BT Safety regulations
      NT Products liability—Firearms

  — Locks
      ₍TS535₎
      UF Percussion-lock
  — Maintenance and repair
      ₍TS535₎
      BT Gunsmithing
  — Markings
      UF Markings on firearms
  — Modification
      UF Modification of firearms
  — Private collections *(May Subd Geog)*
  — Products liability
      USE Products liability—Firearms
  — Sights
      ₍TS535₎
      ₍UD390 (Military rifles)₎
      ₍UF854 (Artillery)₎
      UF Sights for firearms
      BT Ordnance
      RT Telescopic sights
  — Taxation *(May Subd Geog)*
      UF Pistols—Taxation
          Revolvers—Taxation
  — — Law and legislation
      (May Subd Geog)
  — Testing
      NT Proofmarks
  — Use in crime prevention
      UF Use of firearms in crime prevention
      BT Crime prevention
Firearms, Presentation
  USE Presentation firearms
Firearms control
  USE Firearms—Law and legislation
      Gun control
Firearms designers *(May Subd Geog)*
  BT Designers
      Firearms—Design and construction
  RT Gunsmiths
Firearms industry and trade
  (May Subd Geog)
  ₍HD9743₎
      Here are entered works on the small-arms indus-
  try. Works on heavy firearms are entered under the
  heading Ordnance.
  BT Armaments
      Munitions
  NT Gunsmithing
Firearms owners *(May Subd Geog)*
  UF Gun owners
      Owners, Firearms
Firearms ownership *(May Subd Geog)*
  ₍HV8059₎
  UF Gun ownership
      Ownership of firearms
Firearms theft *(May Subd Geog)*
  UF Theft, Firearms
  BT Crime and criminals
      Firearms
      Larceny
Firebacher family
  USE Feuerbach family
Firebacks *(May Subd Geog)*
  BT Ironwork
      Plaques, plaquettes
Firebird (Ballet)
  ₍GV1790.F₎
  BT Ballets
Firebird automobile
  ₍TL215.F₎
  BT Pontiac automobile
Fireblight
  USE Fire-blight
Fireboards
  USE Dummy board figures
Fireboats
  ₍TH9391₎
      Here are entered works on boats equipped with
  pumps and other equipment for fighting fires. Works
  on ships carrying combustibles or explosives sent
  among enemy ships to set them on fire are entered
  under Fireships.

  UF Fire-boats
  BT Fire extinction
      Ships
      Work boats
Firebrat
  ₍QL503.8.L4₎
  UF Thermobia domestica
  BT Thermobia
Firebreaks (Fuelbreaks)
  USE Fuelbreaks
Firecrackers *(May Subd Geog)*
  ₍TP300₎
  BT Fireworks
Firecrest
  USE Regulus ignicapillus
Firefighters
  USE Fire fighters
Firefighting
  USE Fire extinction
Fireflies
  ₍QL596.L28₎
  UF Glow-worms
      Lampyridae
      Lightning bugs
      Lightningbugs
      Malacodermidae
      Telephoridae
  BT Beetles
      Bioluminescence
  NT Photinus
      Photuris
      Pyractonema
Firehole River (Wyo.)
  BT Rivers—Wyoming
Firehouses
  USE Fire stations
Firelands (Ohio)
Fireless cookers
  ₍TX831₎
  UF Cookers, Fireless
      Cookery, Fireless
      Hay-boxes
  BT Cookery
      Stoves
Firemen
  USE Fire fighters
Firemen, Locomotive
  USE Locomotive firemen
Firemen (United States Navy)
  USE United States. Navy—Firemen
Fireplace cookery
  ₍TX840.F5₎
  BT Cookery
      Fireplaces
  RT Barbecue cookery
Fireplace industry *(May Subd Geog)*
  ₍HD9715.9.F57-HD9715.9.F574₎
Fireplaces *(May Subd Geog)*
  ₍NA3050-NA3055 (Architecture)₎
  ₍TH7421-TH7434 (Heating)₎
  UF Chimneypieces
      Grates
  BT Architecture—Details
      Heating
      Space heaters
  RT Chimneys
  NT Andirons
      Barbecues (Fireplaces)
      Fireplace cookery
      Mantels
  — Aerodynamics
Fireproof building
  USE Building, Fireproof
Fireproof paint
  USE Paint, Fireproof
Fireproofing
  ₍TH1061-TH1093 (Building)₎
  ₍TP267 (Fabrics)₎
  UF Fire proofing
      Flameproofing

BT Building, Fireproof
   Fire prevention
   Insurance, Fire
NT Fire resistant materials
   Fire resistant plastics
   Fire resistant polymers
   Fire-testing
   Fireproofing of wood
   Paint, Fireproof
Fireproofing agent industry
   (May Subd Geog)
   [HD9999.F55-554]
BT Fireproofing agents
Fireproofing agents   (May Subd Geog)
   [TP266.5]
UF Chemical fire retardants
   Fire resisting agents
   Fire retardants
   Flame retardants
   Flameproofing agents
BT Fire prevention
NT Dibromopropanol phosphate
   Fireproofing agent industry
   Polybrominated biphenyls
— **Mixing**
   BT Mixing
Fireproofing of fabrics
UF Fabrics, Fireproofing of
NT Children's clothing—Fires and fire
      prevention
   Clothing and dress—Fires and fire
      prevention
   Infants—Clothing—Fires and fire
      prevention
Fireproofing of wood
UF Wood—Fireproofing
BT Fireproofing
   Wood—Preservation
Fires   (May Subd Geog)
   [TH9448-9]
UF Buildings—Fires and fire prevention
   Conflagrations
   Fire losses
BT Accidents
   Disasters
   Fire
SA subdivision Fire, [date] under names
      of individual institutions, structures,
      etc.; and subdivision Fires and fire
      prevention under individual types of
      institutions, buildings, industries,
      and vehicles, e.g. Psychiatric
      hospitals—Fires and fire prevention;
      Warehouses—Fires and fire
      prevention; Construction industry—
      Fires and fire prevention;
      Automobiles—Fires and fire
      prevention
NT Arson
   Campfires
   Fire detectors
   Fire investigation
   Fire prevention
   Forest fires
   Ground cover fires
   Insurance, Fire—Statistics
   Liability for fire damages
   Life-saving at fires
   Mine fires
   Wildfires
— **Casualties**
   UF Casualties in fires
      Fire casualties
      Fire deaths
      Fire victims
   BT Mass casualties
— **Photography**
   USE Photography of fires
Fires in literature
Fires in ships
   USE Ships—Fires and fire prevention

Fire's on, Lapstone Tunnel (Painting)
   USE Streeton, Arthur, Sir, 1867-1943.
      Fire's on, Lapstone Tunnel
Firesetting, Pathological
   USE Pyromania
Firesetting by children
   USE Fire behavior in children
Fireships   (May Subd Geog)
   [V827-V827.5]
   Here are entered works on ships carrying combustibles or explosives sent among enemy ships to set them on fire. Works on boats equipped with pumps and other equipment for fighting fires are entered under Fireboats.
   UF Fire ships
   BT Warships
Firetree
   USE Chamaecyparis obtusa
      Myrica faya
Firewalking
   USE Fire walking
Firewalking (Hindu rite)
   USE Timiti (Hindu rite)
Firewatch towers
   USE Fire lookout stations
Firewatchers, Forest
   USE Fire lookouts
Firewood
   USE Fuelwood
Firewood crops
   USE Fuelwood crops
Fireworks   (May Subd Geog)
   [TP300-301]
UF Pyrotechnics
NT Firecrackers
   Flares
   Military fireworks
— **Accidents and injuries**
   UF Fireworks—Injuries
— **Injuries**
   USE Fireworks—Accidents and
      injuries
— **Law and legislation**   (May Subd Geog)
Firing of employees
   USE Employees, Dismissal of
Firing ranges
   USE Bombing and gunnery ranges
      Rifle-ranges
Firm names
   USE Business names
Firmeza (Dance)
Firmin family
   USE Furman family
Firmont family
   USE Virmond family
Firms
   USE Business enterprises
Firms, Accounting
   USE Accounting firms
Firms, Architectural
   USE Architectural firms
Firms, Law
   USE Law firms
Firmund family
   USE Virmond family
Firris family
   USE Farris family
Firs
   USE Fir
FIRS (Computer system)
UF Fire Inspection Reporting System
      (Computer system)
BT Electronic digital computers—
      Programming
   Fire prevention—Data processing
First aid for animals
   [SF911]
UF Animal first aid
   Emergency treatment for animals
   Veterinary first aid

BT Veterinary emergencies
   Veterinary medicine
   Veterinary surgery
   Wildlife rescue
RT Veterinary traumatology
First aid in illness and injury
   [RC86-88]
UF Ambulance drill
   Emergencies
   Emergencies, Medical
   Injuries
   Wounded, First aid to
BT Assistance in emergencies
   Rescue work
   Wounds and injuries—Treatment
RT Medical emergencies
NT Accidents
   Artificial respiration
   Asphyxia
   Bandages and bandaging
   Burns and scalds
   Drowning, Restoration from
   Emergency medical services
   Heimlich maneuver
   Resuscitation
   Transport of sick and wounded
First and second branchial arch syndrome
   USE Hemifacial microsomia
First arch syndrome
   USE Hemifacial microsomia
First-born children
   USE Children, First-born
First century, A.D.
BT History, Ancient
First Century Christian Fellowship
   USE Oxford Group
First Choice (Computer program)
   [HF5548.4.F57]
BT Computer programs
First Coalition, War of the, 1792-1797
UF War of the First Coalition, 1792-1797
BT Europe—History—1789-1815
   Napoleonic Wars, 1800-1814
— **Campaigns**
— — **France**
      NT Hondschoote, Battle of, 1793
— — **Netherlands**
      NT Camperdown, Battle of, 1797
— — **Portugal**
      NT Saint Vincent, Cape (Portugal),
         Battle of, 1797
First communion
   [BX2237]
UF Communion, First
   Lord's Supper—First communion
BT Initiation rites—Religious aspects—
      Christianity
   Lord's Supper
   Lord's Supper—Admission age
NT First communion sermons
First communion sermons
UF Sermons, First communion
BT First communion
   Occasional sermons
First contact of aboriginal peoples with
Occidental civilization
   USE Man, Primitive—First contact with
      Occidental civilization
First day covers (Philately)
   (May Subd Geog)
   [HE6184.F57]
BT Covers (Philately)
   Postage-stamps
   Postmarks
First editions
   USE subdivision Bibliography—First
      editions under Literature and under
      names of literatures, e.g. English
      literature—Bibliography—First
      editions
      Bibliography—First editions

First fruits
  USE Annates
      Seven species (Jewish law)
      Tithes
First GARP Global Experiment
  UF FGGE
      GARP Global Experiment, First
      Global Atmospheric Research
        Programme Global Experiment,
        First
  BT Meteorology—Research
First generation children
  USE Children of immigrants
First German Lutheran Cemetery (Chicago,
  Ill.)
  USE Wunders Cemetery (Chicago, Ill.)
First grade (Education)
  BT Education, Primary
First impression (Psychology)
  ₍BF323.F5₎
First issues
  USE *subdivision* Bibliography—First issues
      under types of periodicals, e.g.
      English periodicals—Bibliography—
      First issues
First ladies (United States)
  USE Presidents—United States—Wives
First lines (Rhetoric)
  USE Openings (Rhetoric)
First loves *(May Subd Geog)*
  UF Loves, First
  BT Persons
  RT Love
First-mortgage bonds
  USE Mortgage bonds
First of June, 1794, Battle of
  ₍DA87.5 1794₎
  UF Prairial, Battle of, 1794
First of May
  USE May Day (Labor holiday)
First-order logic
  ₍BC128₎
  BT Logic, Modern
      Logic, Symbolic and mathematical
First performances of musical works
  USE Music—First performances
First person narrative
  UF Narrative, First person
  BT Fiction—Technique
      Literature
      Narration (Rhetoric)
      Point of view (Literature)
  RT Persona (Literature)
First philosophy
  ₍BD331₎
  BT Metaphysics
First strike (Nuclear strategy)
      Here are entered works on preemptive strategic
  nuclear attacks designed to destroy an enemy's
  strategic forces before they can be used against one's
  own strategic forces. Works on the principle that a
  military power, in the event of war, would not be the
  first to resort to the tactical or strategic use of nuclear
  weapons are entered under No first use (Nuclear
  strategy).
  BT Preemptive attack (Military science)
      Targeting (Nuclear strategy)
  RT Deterrence (Strategy)
      No first use (Nuclear strategy)
First Texas Revolution, Tex., 1813
  USE Medina River (Tex.), Battle of, 1813
First trimester of pregnancy
  USE Pregnancy—Trimester, First
First Triumvirate, 60-53 B.C.
  USE Rome—History—First Triumvirate,
      60-53 B.C.
First World War
  USE World War, 1914-1918
First year teachers *(May Subd Geog)*
  UF Beginning teachers
      Teachers, First year
  BT Teachers

— **Attitudes**
    BT Attitude (Psychology)
Firth of Clyde (Scotland)
  USE Clyde, Firth of (Scotland)
Firth of Forth (Scotland)
  USE Forth, Firth of (Scotland)
Firth of Tay (Scotland)
  USE Tay, Firth of (Scotland)
Fiscal evasion
  USE Tax evasion
Fiscal limitations
  USE Tax and expenditure limitations
Fiscal policy *(May Subd Geog)*
  BT Economic policy
      Finance, Public
  RT Monetary policy
  NT Inflation (Finance)—Effect of taxation
      on
Fiscal relations, Intergovernmental
  USE Intergovernmental fiscal relations
Fiscal relations, International
  USE Intergovernmental fiscal relations
Fiscal restraints
  USE Tax and expenditure limitations
Fiscal year *(May Subd Geog)*
  UF Year, Fiscal
  BT Accounting
      Bookkeeping
— **Law and legislation** *(May Subd Geog)*
Fisch family
  USE Fish family
Fischborn family
  USE Fishburne family
Fischer family
  USE Fisher family
Fischer-Tropsch process
  BT Carbon monoxide
      Coal liquefaction
      Hydrogenation
      Petroleum, Synthetic
  NT Gasoline, Synthetic
      Methanation
Fischl, Eric, 1948-   Floating islands
  (Not Subd Geog)
  UF Floating islands (Etchings)
  BT Etching, American
**Fischl, Eric, 1948-   Year of the drowned
dog**
  UF Year of the drowned dog (Etchings)
  BT Etching, American
Fiscus (Roman law)
Fiset family
Fish
  USE Fishes
Fish, Canned
  UF Canned fish
  BT Fishery products, Canned
      Food, Canned
  NT Salmon, Canned
      Sardines, Canned
      Tuna, Canned
Fish, Dried
  UF Dried fish
  BT Fishery products, Dried
Fish, Fermented *(May Subd Geog)*
  ₍SH336.F45₎
  UF Fermented fish
      Fish silage
  BT Fermentation
      Fish as feed
      Fishery products—Preservation
Fish, Frozen
  UF Frozen fish
  BT Fishery products, Frozen
      Food, Frozen
Fish, Irradiated
  UF Irradiated fish
  BT Fishery products—Preservation
      Food, Irradiated
      Seafood, Irradiated

Fish, Preserved
  USE Fishery products—Preservation
Fish, Salted *(May Subd Geog)*
  ₍SH336.S3₎
  UF Salt fish
      Salt preservation of fish
  BT Fishery products—Preservation
      Salting of food
Fish, Smoked
  UF Food, Smoked
      Smoked fish
  BT Fishery products—Preservation
  NT Eels, Smoked
Fish and game, Dressing of
  USE Fishes, Dressing of
      Game and game-birds, Dressing of
Fish and game licenses *(May Subd Geog)*
  UF Fishing—Licenses
      Fishing licenses
      Hunting—Licenses
      Hunting licenses
  BT Fishery law and legislation
      Licenses
Fish as carriers of disease
  BT Animals as carriers of disease
Fish as feed
  NT Fish, Fermented
Fish as food
  ₍TX385 (Food sources)₎
  ₍TX556.5 (Food values)₎
  BT Fishery technology
      Fishes
      Food
      Seafood
  NT Cookery (Fish)
      Fish protein concentrate
— **Analysis**
  ₍TX556.5₎
  BT Fishes—Composition
— **Contamination**
  UF Contamination of fish
  BT Food contamination
— Spoilage
  USE Fishery products—Spoilage
Fish as laboratory animals
Fish attracting by light
  USE Light fishing
Fish breeding *(May Subd Geog)*
  ₍SH155.5₎
  BT Fish-culture
  NT Fishes—Sexing
      Fishes—Spawning, Artificial
      Fishes—Spawning, Induced
Fish conservation
  USE Fishery conservation
Fish control
  USE Fishes—Control
Fish counters
  USE Fishes—Counting
Fish Creek Mountains Wilderness (Calif.)
  (Not Subd Geog)
  UF Fish Creek Mountains Wilderness
      Study Area (Calif.)
  BT National parks and reserves—
      California
      Wilderness areas—California
Fish Creek Mountains Wilderness Study Area
  (Calif.)
  USE Fish Creek Mountains Wilderness
      (Calif.)
Fish-culture *(May Subd Geog)*
  ₍SH₎
  UF Artificial propagation of fishes
      Fish farming
      Pisciculture
  BT Animal culture
      Aquaculture
      Fishes
      Mariculture
  RT Aquariums
  NT Animal introduction

Aquarium fish farming
Fish breeding
Fish culturists
Fish hatcheries
Fish ponds
Fish stocking
Fishery resources—Hatchery vs. wild
    stocks
Fishes—Control
Fishes—Feeding and feeds
Fishes—Spawning, Artificial
Fishes—Spawning, Induced
— **Equipment and supplies**
    NT Fishes—Eggs—Incubation
— **Water-supply**
    [SH154]
    UF Fish hatcheries—Water-supply
— — **Recycling**
      [SH154]
      UF Closed system fish culture
      BT Recycling (Waste, etc.)
         Water reuse
Fish culturists *(May Subd Geog)*
    [SH20]
    UF Pisciculturists
    BT Fish-culture
Fish detection
    [SH344.2]
    UF Detection of fish
    BT Fisheries
        Fisheries—Equipment and supplies
    NT Echo sounding in fishing
        Sonar in fishing
Fish distribution
    USE Fishes—Geographical distribution
        Fishes—Seasonal distribution
        Fishes—Vertical distribution
Fish eagle, African
    USE African fish eagle
Fish-eating bat
    USE Myotis vivesi
Fish eggs
    USE Fishes—Eggs
Fish family *(Not Subd Geog)*
    UF Fisch family
    RT Fisher family
Fish farming
    USE Fish-culture
Fish fillets
    UF Fillets, Fish
    BT Fish trade
        Fishery products
Fish flour
    USE Fish protein concentrate
Fish genetics
    USE Fishes—Genetics
Fish habitat
    USE Fishes—Habitat
Fish habitat improvement *(May Subd Geog)*
    [SH157.8]
    BT Fishery management
        Wildlife habitat improvement
    RT Stream conservation
    NT Artificial reefs
        Fish screens
        Fishways
Fish handling *(May Subd Geog)*
    BT Fishery products
        Fishery technology
    NT Fishes, Dressing of
— **Loading and unloading**
    [SH337]
    UF Fish loading
        Fish unloading
        Fishes—Loading and unloading
    BT Loading and unloading
— **Odor control**
    BT Odor control
Fish hatcheries *(May Subd Geog)*
    UF Hatcheries, Fish
    BT Fish-culture

RT Aquaculture stations
— Incubators
    USE Fishes—Eggs—Incubation
— **Law and legislation** *(May Subd Geog)*
    BT Fishery law and legislation
— Water-supply
    USE Fish-culture—Water-supply
Fish hatchery stock vs. wild stock
    USE Fishery resources—Hatchery vs. wild
        stocks
Fish-hawks
    USE Ospreys
Fish hooks
    USE Fishhooks
Fish House (Tucson, Ariz.)
    USE Edward Nye Fish House (Tucson,
        Ariz.)
Fish impressions
    USE Fish prints
Fish inspection *(May Subd Geog)*
    [SH335 (Practice)]
    UF Fisheries—Inspection
        Fishes—Inspection
        Inspection of fish
    BT Fishery law and legislation
        Food adulteration and inspection
Fish kills *(May Subd Geog)*
    [SH171-179]
    UF Mass mortality of fishes
    BT Die-off (Zoology)
        Fishes—Mortality
        Wildlife conservation
    RT Fishes—Diseases
        Fishes—Effect of water pollution on
Fish ladders
    USE Fishways
Fish Lake Site (Ill.) *(Not Subd Geog)*
    BT Illinois—Antiquities
Fish law
    USE Fishery law and legislation
Fish leeches
    USE Piscicolidae
Fish liver oils
    USE Fish oils
Fish loading
    USE Fish handling—Loading and unloading
Fish management
    USE Fishery management
Fish marking
    USE Fish tagging
Fish-meal *(May Subd Geog)*
    [HD9469.F5-HD9469.F512
      (Economics)]
    [SF99.F5 (Feed)]
    [SH336.F55 (Processing)]
    BT Fishery products
        Meal
Fish-meal as feed
Fish-meal as food
    BT Food
Fish milt
    USE Fishes—Spermatozoa
Fish mosaic (Palestrina)
    [NA3770]
    UF Fish mosaic of Palestrina
    BT Fishes in art
        Mosaics—Italy
        Mosaics, Roman—Italy
        Pavements, Mosaic—Italy
Fish mosaic of Palestrina
    USE Fish mosaic (Palestrina)
Fish mounting
    USE Fishes—Collection and preservation
Fish movement (Christianity)
    BT Church work
        Laity
Fish names
    USE Fishes—Nomenclature (Popular)
Fish nets
    USE Fishing nets

Fish-oil
    USE Fish oils
Fish-oil as feed
    USE Fish oils as feed
Fish oils *(May Subd Geog)*
    [TP676 (Chemical technology)]
    UF Fish liver oils
        Fish-oil
    BT Fishery products
        Marine animal oils
    NT Cod-liver oil
Fish oils as feed *(May Subd Geog)*
    UF Fish-oil as feed
    BT Feeds
Fish oils in human nutrition
    (May Subd Geog)
    BT Nutrition
Fish passages
    USE Fishways
Fish planting
    USE Fish stocking
Fish poisons (Piscicides)
    USE Piscicides
Fish ponds *(May Subd Geog)*
    [SH159]
    UF Fishponds
        Ponds, Fish
    BT Fish-culture
Fish populations *(May Subd Geog)*
    UF Fish stocks
        Fishes—Population
        Fishes—Population dynamics
        Population dynamics in fisheries
        Populations, Fish
    BT Animal populations
        Fisheries
        Fishes—Geographical distribution
    NT Fishery resources—Hatchery vs. wild
        stocks
        Fishes—Counting
        Fishes—Racial analysis
— **Computer programs**
— **Thinning**
      UF Thinning of fish populations
      BT Fishery management
         Fishes—Control
Fish prints
    [NE1340]
    UF Fish impressions
        Fish rubbings
        Gyotaku
    BT Fishes in art
        Prints
Fish processing
    USE Fishery processing
Fish processing ships
    USE Fishery processing ships
Fish protein concentrate
    UF Fish flour
        FPC
    BT Fish as food
        Fishery products
Fish remains (Archaeology)
    (May Subd Geog)
    [CC79.5.A5]
    UF Fishes in archaeology
    BT Animal remains (Archaeology)
        Archaeology—Methodology
Fish roe
    USE Fishes—Eggs
Fish rubbings
    USE Fish prints
Fish sanitation
    USE Fishery products—Sanitation
Fish-scrap fertilizer
    [S659]
    BT Fertilizers
        Fishery products
        Organic wastes as fertilizer
Fish screens *(May Subd Geog)*
    [SH157.85.F54]

Fish screens *(Continued)*
  UF Screens, Fish
  BT Fish habitat improvement
Fish sexing
  USE Fishes—Sexing
Fish silage
  USE Fish, Fermented
Fish sounds
  BT Animal sounds
      Sounds
Fish spoilage
  USE Fishery products—Spoilage
Fish Springs National Wildlife Refuge (Utah)
(Not Subd Geog)
  BT National parks and reserves—Utah
      Wildlife refuges—Utah
Fish stocking *(May Subd Geog)*
  UF Fish planting
      Stocking of fish
      Stocking of streams, etc.
  BT Fish-culture
      Fishery management
Fish stocks
  USE Fish populations
Fish tagging *(May Subd Geog)*
  [SH156.8]
  UF Fish marking
      Fishes—Marking
      Fishes—Tagging
      Tagging of fish
  BT Animal marking
      Fisheries—Research
  NT Shellfish tagging
Fish tapeworm
  USE Diphyllobothrium latum
Fish trade *(May Subd Geog)*
  [HD9450-HD9469]
  [HF2651.F5 (Tariff)]
  [SH]
  BT Fisheries
      Fisheries—Economic aspects
  NT Fish fillets
      Fishery products
      Fishery products—Cooperative
        marketing
      Ornamental fish trade
      Shellfish trade
      Strikes and lockouts—Fish trade
      Wages—Fish trade
  — Law and legislation *(May Subd Geog)*
      BT Fishery law and legislation
Fish traps *(May Subd Geog)*
  [GN423 (Primitive)]
  [SH344.6.T (Fisheries)]
  UF Trap fishing
  BT Fisheries
      Fishing nets
Fish unloading
  USE Fish handling—Loading and unloading
Fish waste
  USE Fisheries—By-products
Fish wheels
  USE Fishwheels
Fishack family
  UF Fishok family
Fishback family
Fishbed (Jet fighter planes)
  UF MIG-21 (Jet fighter planes)
  BT MIG (Fighter planes)
Fishburn family
  USE Fishburne family
Fishburne family
  UF Fischborn family
      Fishburn family
Fisher (Animal)
  [QL737.C25]
  UF Fishers (Animal)
      Martes pennanti
  BT Martens

Fisher exact test
  UF Exact test, Fisher
      Test, Fisher exact
  BT Statistical hypothesis testing
Fisher family
  UF Fesher family
      Fischer family
      Fysher family
  RT Fish family
Fisher Valley (Utah)
  BT Valleys—Utah
Fisheries *(May Subd Geog)*
  [SH]
  UF Commercial fishing
      Fishery industry
      Fishery methods
      Fishing industry
      Sea-fisheries
  BT Aquatic resources
      Natural resources
  RT Fishes
  NT Anchovy fisheries
      Artificial reefs
      Atlantic croaker fisheries
      Baitfish fisheries
      Billfish fisheries
      Bonito fisheries
      Capelin fisheries
      Carp fisheries
      Channel bass fisheries
      Cod-fisheries
      Coral fisheries
      Crab fisheries
      Eel fisheries
      Electric fishing
      Estuarine fisheries
      Fish detection
      Fish populations
      Fish trade
      Fish traps
      Fishery innovations
      Fishery management
      Fishery processing industries
      Fishery scientists
      Fishery technology
      Fishways
      Flatfish fisheries
      Galaxias fisheries
      Gillnetting
      Grouper fisheries
      Grunt fisheries
      Haddock fisheries
      Hake fisheries
      Halibut fisheries
      Herring fisheries
      Krill fisheries
      Lift net fishing
      Light fishing
      Lingcod fisheries
      Lobster fisheries
      Longlining (Fisheries)
      Lumpfish fisheries
      Lutjanidae fisheries
      Mackerel fisheries
      Marlin fisheries
      Menhaden fisheries
      Mullet fisheries
      Octopus fisheries
      Pacific ocean perch fisheries
      Pacific saury fisheries
      Plastics in fisheries
      Pump fishing
      Salmon-fisheries
      Sardine fisheries
      Seining
      Shad fisheries
      Shellfish fisheries
      Smelt fisheries
      Sponge fisheries
      Squid fisheries
      Strikes and lockouts—Fisheries

      Striped bass fisheries
      Sturgeon fisheries
      Trammel netting
      Trawls and trawling
      Trepang fisheries
      Trout fisheries
      Tuna fisheries
      Turtle fisheries
      White seabass fisheries
      Yellowtail fisheries
  — By-products
      [TP996.F5]
      UF Fish waste
  — Catch effort
      UF Catch per unit of effort in fisheries
          CPUE in fisheries
          Fishery catch effort
          Fishing catch effort
      BT Fisheries—Statistics
          Fishery management
      SA *subdivision* Catch effort *under
          types of fisheries and methods
          of fishing, e.g.* Halibut fisheries
          —Catch effort; Trawls and
          trawling—Catch effort
  — Climatic factors
      UF Climatic factors on fisheries
          Fisheries—Meteorological factors
      BT Bioclimatology
          Climatology
          Hydrometeorology
  — Collective bargaining
      USE Collective bargaining—Fisheries
  — Collective labor agreements
      USE Collective labor agreements—
          Fisheries
  — Computer programs
  — Economic aspects *(May Subd Geog)*
      NT Fish trade
          Fishery policy
  — Equipment and supplies
      UF Fishery gear
          Fishing gear, Commercial
      BT Fishery technology
      NT Electric fishing
          Fish detection
          Fisheries—Gear selectivity
          Fishery equipment industry
          Fishhooks
          Fishing boats
          Fishing nets
          Fishwheels
          Longlining (Fisheries)
          Trawls and trawling
  — Fishing effort
      UF Effort in fisheries
          Fishery effort
          Fishing effort
      BT Fisheries—Statistics
          Fishery management
      SA *subdivision* Fishing effort *under
          types of fisheries and methods
          of fishing, e.g.* Halibut fisheries
          —Fishing effort; Purse seining—
          Fishing effort
  — Gear selectivity
      [SB344.15]
      UF Fishing gear selectivity,
          Commercial
          Gear selectivity in fisheries
          Selectivity of fishery gear
      BT Fisheries—Equipment and supplies
          Fishery management
  — Hydrologic factors
      UF Fisheries—Limnological factors
          Fisheries—Oceanographic factors
          Fisheries limnology
          Hydrologic factors on fisheries

BT Fishery oceanography
    Hydrology
    Limnology
    Oceanography
— Inspection
    USE Fish inspection
— Law
    USE Fishery law and legislation
— **Licenses** *(May Subd Geog)*
    BT Fishery law and legislation
    NT Foreign fishing
— — **Limited entry**
      UF Limited entry in fisheries
      BT Fishery management
— Limnological factors
    USE Fisheries—Hydrologic factors
— Meteorological factors
    USE Fisheries—Climatic factors
— Navigation
    USE Fisheries navigation
— Oceanographic factors
    USE Fisheries—Hydrologic factors
— **Research** *(May Subd Geog)*
    UF Sport fishery research
    NT Exploratory fishing
      Fish tagging
      Fishery research stations
      Fishery research vessels
— **Statistics**
    NT Fisheries—Catch effort
      Fisheries—Fishing effort
— **Terminology**
    NT English language—Conversation
      and phrase books (for fishers)
— **Vocational guidance**
Fisheries, Cooperative *(May Subd Geog)*
  UF Cooperative fisheries
    Fishery cooperatives
  BT Cooperation
  NT Fishery products—Cooperative
    marketing
— **Law and legislation** *(May Subd Geog)*
    BT Fishery law and legislation
Fisheries conservation
  USE Fishery conservation
Fisheries for baitfish
  USE Baitfish fisheries
Fisheries limnology
  USE Fisheries—Hydrologic factors
Fisheries management
  USE Fishery management
Fisheries navigation *(May Subd Geog)*
  [SH343.8]
  UF Fisheries—Navigation
  BT Fishery technology
    Fishing boats
    Navigation
Fisheries oceanography
  USE Fishery oceanography
Fisheries resources
  USE Fishery resources
Fisheries subsidies *(May Subd Geog)*
  [SH334]
  UF Federal aid to fisheries
    Fishery subsidies
  BT Fishery policy
    Subsidies
— **Law and legislation** *(May Subd Geog)*
    BT Fishery law and legislation
Fisheries technology
  USE Fishery technology
Fisherman's knots
  USE Fishing knots
Fishermen
  USE Fishers
Fishermen's wives
  USE Fishers' wives
Fishers *(May Subd Geog)*
  [HD8039.F65 (Labor)]
  UF Fishermen
  RT Fishing

NT English language—Conversation and
    phrase books (for fishers)
    Sealers (Persons)
    Whalers (Persons)
    Women fishers
— Records
    USE Fishing—Records
— **Supplementary employment**
— Trade-unions
    USE Trade-unions—Fishers
— Wages
    USE Wages—Fishers
Fishers (Animal)
  USE Fisher (Animal)
Fishers Island (N.Y. : Island)
  BT Islands—New York (State)
Fishers' wives *(May Subd Geog)*
  UF Fishermen's wives
  BT Wives
Fisherwomen
  USE Women fishers
Fishery catch effort
  USE Fisheries—Catch effort
Fishery colleges
  USE Fishery schools
Fishery conservation *(May Subd Geog)*
  [SH327.7]
  UF Fish conservation
    Fisheries conservation
    Fishery resources conservation
  BT Conservation of natural resources
    Fishery resources
    Marine resources conservation
    Wildlife conservation
Fishery cooperatives
  USE Fisheries, Cooperative
Fishery effort
  USE Fisheries—Fishing effort
Fishery equipment industry
(May Subd Geog)
  [HD9488-9489]
  BT Fisheries—Equipment and supplies
  NT Strikes and lockouts—Fishery
    equipment industry
Fishery experts
  USE Fishery scientists
Fishery extension work *(May Subd Geog)*
  BT Agricultural extension work
Fishery gear
  USE Fisheries—Equipment and supplies
Fishery harbors
  USE Fishing ports
Fishery industry
  USE Fisheries
Fishery innovations *(May Subd Geog)*
  UF Innovations, Fishery
    Technological change in fisheries
  BT Fisheries
    Fishery technology
Fishery laboratories
  USE Fishery research stations
Fishery law and legislation
(May Subd Geog)
  [SH323-SH327]
  [SK355-SK579 (Fish and game laws)]
  UF Fish law
    Fisheries—Law
    Fishery regulations
    Fishing—Law
    Fishing regulations
    Law, Fishery
  BT Fishery policy
    Fishing
    International law
    Territorial waters
    Water—Law and legislation
    Wildlife conservation—Law and
      legislation
  NT Aquaculture—Law and legislation
    Artificial reefs—Law and legislation

    Channel bass fisheries—Law and
      legislation
    Diving, Submarine—Law and
      legislation
    Endangered species—Law and
      legislation
    Fish and game licenses
    Fish hatcheries—Law and legislation
    Fish inspection
    Fish trade—Law and legislation
    Fisheries—Licenses
    Fisheries, Cooperative—Law and
      legislation
    Fisheries subsidies—Law and
      legislation
    Fishery products—Law and legislation
    Fishery products—Marketing—Law
      and legislation
    Fishes—Control—Law and legislation
    Halibut fisheries—Law and legislation
    Indians of North America—Fishing—
      Law and legislation
    Lobster fisheries—Law and legislation
    Marine mammals—Law and legislation
    Oyster-culture—Law and legislation
    Pacific halibut fishing—Law and
      legislation
    Piscicides—Law and legislation
    Salmon-fisheries—Law and legislation
    Sealing—Law and legislation
    Shellfish fisheries—Law and legislation
    Shrimp fisheries—Law and legislation
    Steelhead fishing—Law and legislation
    Trawls and trawling—Law and
      legislation
    Tuna fisheries—Law and legislation
    Whaling—Law and legislation
Fishery libraries *(May Subd Geog)*
  UF Libraries, Fishery
  BT Technical libraries
Fishery management *(May Subd Geog)*
  [SH328-329]
  UF Fish management
    Fisheries management
  BT Fisheries
    Wildlife management
  NT Exploratory fishing
    Fish habitat improvement
    Fish populations—Thinning
    Fish stocking
    Fisheries—Catch effort
    Fisheries—Fishing effort
    Fisheries—Gear selectivity
    Fisheries—Licenses—Limited entry
    Fishery resources—Commercial vs.
      recreational use
    Fishery resources—Hatchery vs. wild
      stocks
    Fishes—Control
    Fishes—Counting
    Fishes—Racial analysis
    Fishing—Catch effort
    Foreign fishing
— International cooperation
    USE Fishery management,
      International
Fishery management, International
(May Subd Geog)
  [SH328]
  UF Fishery management—International
    cooperation
    High seas fishery management
    International fishery management
    World fishery management
Fishery methods
  USE Fisheries
Fishery oceanography *(May Subd Geog)*
  [SH343.2]
  UF Fisheries oceanography
  BT Marine biology
    Oceanography

Fishery oceanography *(Continued)*
 NT Fisheries—Hydrologic factors
Fishery policy *(May Subd Geog)*
 [SH328-329]
 BT Economic policy
  Fisheries—Economic aspects
  Industry and state
  Marine resources and state
 NT Fisheries subsidies
  Fishery law and legislation
  Fishery resources—Commercial vs.
   recreational use
Fishery processing *(May Subd Geog)*
 [SH335-336.5]
 UF Fish processing
  Seafood processing
 BT Fishery products
  Fishery technology
 NT Fishery products—Preservation
Fishery processing industries
 (May Subd Geog)
 BT Fisheries
  Fishery products
— **Odor control**
  BT Odor control
Fishery processing ships *(May Subd Geog)*
 [SH335.6]
 UF Factory ships in fisheries
  Fish processing ships
 BT Fishery products
  Fishing boats
Fishery products *(May Subd Geog)*
 [HD9450-HD9469 (Fishery products)]
 [SH335-SH337 (Fisheries)]
 UF Seafood products
 BT Aquatic resources
  Fish trade
 NT Fish fillets
  Fish handling
  Fish-meal
  Fish oils
  Fish protein concentrate
  Fish-scrap fertilizer
  Fishery processing
  Fishery processing industries
  Fishery processing ships
  Klipfish
  Seafood
— **Cooperative marketing**
  UF Cooperative marketing of fishery
   products
   Fishes—Cooperative marketing
  BT Fish trade
   Fisheries, Cooperative
— **Freshness**
  USE Fishery products—Spoilage
— **Law and legislation** *(May Subd Geog)*
  BT Fishery law and legislation
— **Marketing**
— — **Law and legislation**
   (May Subd Geog)
  BT Fishery law and legislation
— **Microbiology**
— **Preservation**
  [SH335-SH337 (Fisheries)]
  [TX612.F5]
  UF Fish, Preserved
  BT Cold storage
   Fishery processing
  NT Fish, Fermented
   Fish, Irradiated
   Fish, Salted
   Fish, Smoked
   Fishery products, Canned
   Fishery products, Dried
   Fishery products, Frozen
   Shrimps, Irradiated
— **Research** *(May Subd Geog)*
  UF Fishery products research
— **Sanitation**
  [QR118]

 UF Fish sanitation
— **Spoilage**
  UF Fish as food—Spoilage
   Fish spoilage
   Fishery products—Freshness
   Freshness of fish
   Spoilage of fish
  BT Food spoilage
— **Storage**
Fishery products, Canned
 UF Canned fishery products
 BT Fishery products—Preservation
  Food, Canned
 NT Crabs, Canned
  Fish, Canned
  Lobsters, Canned
  Oysters, Canned
  Shrimps, Canned
Fishery products, Dried *(May Subd Geog)*
 UF Dried fishery products
  Seafood, Dried
 BT Fishery products—Preservation
 NT Fish, Dried
Fishery products, Frozen *(May Subd Geog)*
 UF Frozen fishery products
 BT Fishery products—Preservation
  Food, Frozen
 NT Crabs, Frozen
  Fish, Frozen
  Seafood, Frozen
  Shrimps, Frozen
Fishery products research
 USE Fishery products—Research
Fishery regulations
 USE Fishery law and legislation
Fishery research stations *(May Subd Geog)*
 [SH332-332.2]
 UF Fishery laboratories
  Stations, Fishery research
 BT Fisheries—Research
  Laboratories
Fishery research vessels *(May Subd Geog)*
 [SH343.4 (General)]
 BT Fisheries—Research
  Fishing boats
  Marine biology research vessels
  Research vessels
  Ships
 RT Exploratory fishing
 SA *names of individual fishery research
  vessels*
Fishery resources *(May Subd Geog)*
 [SH327.5]
 UF Fisheries resources
 BT Aquatic resources
  Marine resources
 NT Exploratory fishing
  Fishery conservation
— **Commercial vs. recreational use**
  UF Commercial vs. recreational use of
   fishery resources
   Fishery resources—Recreational vs.
   commercial use
   Recreational vs. commercial use of
   fishery resources
   Resource allocation for commercial
   and recreational fishing
  BT Fishery management
   Fishery policy
   Recreation and state
— **Hatchery vs. wild stocks**
  UF Fish hatchery stock vs. wild stock
   Fishery resources—Wild vs.
   hatchery stocks
   Hatchery vs. wild stocks of fish
  BT Fish-culture
   Fish populations
   Fishery management
   Fishes—Genetics
— **Recreational vs. commercial use**

  USE Fishery resources—Commercial
   vs. recreational use
— **Wild vs. hatchery stocks**
  USE Fishery resources—Hatchery vs.
   wild stocks
Fishery resources conservation
 USE Fishery conservation
Fishery schools *(May Subd Geog)*
 [SH332]
 UF Fishery colleges
 BT Schools
  Universities and colleges
Fishery scientists *(May Subd Geog)*
 [SH20]
 UF Fishery experts
 BT Fisheries
  Scientists
 RT Ichthyologists
Fishery subsidies
 USE Fisheries subsidies
Fishery technology *(May Subd Geog)*
 [SH334.5-344.8]
 UF Fisheries technology
 BT Fisheries
  Technology
 NT Fish as food
  Fish handling
  Fisheries—Equipment and supplies
  Fisheries navigation
  Fishery innovations
  Fishery processing
  Fishing ports
Fishes *(May Subd Geog)*
 [GR745 (Folk-lore)]
 [QL614-QL639]
 UF Fish
  Pisces
 BT Aquatic animals
  Vertebrates
 RT Fisheries
  Fishing
  Ichthyology
 SA *names of orders, families, etc. of
  fishes, e.g.* Perciformes, Salmonidae,
  Tarpon
 NT Aquarium fishes
  Aquariums
  Baitfish
  Chondrichthyes
  Dangerous fishes
  Exploratory fishing
  Fish as food
  Fish-culture
  Forage fish
  Marine fishes
  Ornamental fishes
  Osteichthyes
  Poisonous fishes
  Tropical fish
— **Abnormalities** *(May Subd Geog)*
— **Age**
  UF Fishes—Age and growth studies
   Fishes, Age of
— **Age and growth studies**
  USE Fishes—Age
   Fishes—Growth
— **Age determination**
  [QL639.15]
— **Anatomy**
  [QL639]
  SA *subdivision* Fishes *under* Digestive
   organs, Nervous system, Sense-
   organs
  NT Air-bladder (in fishes)
   Barbel (Anatomy)
   Branchial arch
   Branchiostegals
   Chloride cells
   Electric organs in fishes
   Fins
   Gills

Interrenal gland
Saccus vasculosus
Scales (Fishes)
Weberian apparatus
— — Atlases
— Anecdotes
    UF Fishes—Anecdotes, facetiae, satire,
        etc.
    BT Anecdotes
— Anecdotes, facetiae, satire, etc.
    USE Fishes—Anecdotes
          Fishes—Humor
— Autopsy
— Bacteriology
    USE Fishes—Microbiology
— Behavior
    SA *subdivision* Behavior *under names*
        of particular fishes, e.g.
        Sticklebacks—Behavior
— — Climatic factors
— Biography
— Biological control *(May Subd Geog)*
    BT Fishes—Control
          Pests—Biological control
— Body form
    USE Fishes—Morphology
— Catalogs and collections
    (May Subd Geog)
— Classification
    ₜQL618ₗ
    NT Fishes—Identification
— Cleaning
    USE Fishes, Dressing of
— Collection and preservation
    ₜQL618.6ₗ
    UF Fish mounting
    NT Aquarium fish collecting
— Color
    UF Color of fishes
— Composition
    BT Fishes—Physiology
    NT Fish as food—Analysis
— Control *(May Subd Geog)*
    UF Coarse fish control
          Fish control
          Rough fish control
    BT Fish-culture
          Fishery management
          Pests—Control
    NT Fish populations—Thinning
          Fishes—Biological control
          Fishes—Integrated control
          Piscicides
— — Law and legislation
    (May Subd Geog)
    BT Fishery law and legislation
— Cooperative marketing
    USE Fishery products—Cooperative
          marketing
— Counting
    UF Counting of fish
          Fish counters
    BT Fish populations
          Fishery management
          Fishes—Migration
— Cytology
— Development
    ₜQL639.25ₗ
    NT Embryology—Fishes
          Fishes—Larvae
— Diseases *(May Subd Geog)*
    ₜSH171-179ₗ
    RT Fish kills
    NT Bacterial gill disease
          Channel catfish virus disease
          Columnaris disease
          Fishes—Parasites
          Furunculosis
          Gas bubble disease in fish
— — Chemotherapy
    BT Chemotherapy

— — Epidemiology
— Distribution, Geographical
    USE Fishes—Geographical distribution
— Distribution, Seasonal
    USE Fishes—Seasonal distribution
— Distribution, Vertical
    USE Fishes—Vertical distribution
— Ecology
    NT Fishes—Effect of habitat
          modification on
          Fishes—Effect of water levels on
— Effect of dams on
    ₜSH173ₗ
    BT Dams
— Effect of habitat modification on
    ₜSH171ₗ
    BT Fishes—Ecology
— Effect of light on
— Effect of logging on
    ₜSH177.L63ₗ
    BT Logging
— Effect of radiation on
    BT Radiation—Physiological effect
— Effect of sediments on
    UF Sediment effect on fish
    BT Sediment, Suspended
          Silt
— Effect of water levels on
    ₜSH177.W38ₗ
    UF Streamflow alteration effect on fish
          Water level effect on fish
    BT Fishes—Ecology
    NT Fishes—Stranding
— Effect of water pollution on
    ₜSH174ₗ
    BT Water—Pollution
    RT Fish kills
— Effect of water quality on
    ₜSH154 (Culture)ₗ
    ₜSH173 (Diseases)ₗ
    BT Water quality
— Effect of water temperature on
    ₜSH177.T45ₗ
    UF Temperature tolerance in fishes
          Thermal stress in fishes
          Water temperature effect on fishes
    BT Fishes—Physiology
          Temperature—Physiological effect
— Eggs
    UF Fish eggs
          Fish roe
          Fishes—Roe
          Ichthyoplankton
          Roe of fishes
    NT Caviar
          Fishes—Fertility
— — Counting
    UF Counting of fish eggs
          Fishes—Fecundity measurement
    BT Counting
          Fishes—Fertility
— — Incubation
    ₜSH155.8ₗ
    UF Fish hatcheries—Incubators
          Incubation of fish eggs
    BT Fish-culture—Equipment and
          supplies
          Incubators
— Evolution
    ₜQL618.2ₗ
    BT Vertebrates—Evolution
— Fecundity
    USE Fishes—Fertility
— Fecundity measurement
    USE Fishes—Eggs—Counting
— Feeding and feeds
    ₜSH156ₗ
    BT Fish-culture
    RT Fishes—Food
— Fertility
    ₜQL639.2ₗ

    UF Fishes—Fecundity
    BT Fertility
          Fishes—Eggs
          Fishes—Reproduction
    NT Fishes—Eggs—Counting
— Fiction
— Field guides
    USE Fishes—Identification
— Folklore
— Food
    ₜQL639ₗ
    RT Fishes—Feeding and feeds
    NT Forage fish
— Genetics
    ₜQL638.99ₗ
    UF Fish genetics
    NT Fishery resources—Hatchery vs.
          wild stocks
          Fishes—Germplasm resources
— Geographical distribution
    ₜQL619-637ₗ
    UF Fish distribution
          Fishes—Distribution, Geographical
          Fishes—Zoogeography
    NT Fish populations
          Fishes—Racial analysis
— Germplasm resources
    BT Fishes—Genetics
— Growth
    UF Fishes—Age and growth studies
          Fishes—Length-weight
          relationships
    NT Fishes—Size
— Habitat
    UF Fish habitat
— Hibernation
    ₜQL639.1ₗ
— Histology
— Homing
    BT Fishes—Migration
— Host plants
    BT Host plants
— Humor
    UF Fishes—Anecdotes, facetiae, satire,
          etc.
    BT Wit and humor
— Identification
    UF Fishes—Field guides
          Fishes—Keys
    BT Fishes—Classification
    NT Fishes—Nomenclature (Popular)
          Fishes—Racial analysis
— Immunology
    ₜQL638.97ₗ
— Infancy
    UF Infancy of fishes
    NT Fishes—Larvae
— Inspection
    USE Fish inspection
— Integrated control *(May Subd Geog)*
    BT Fishes—Control
— Keys
    USE Fishes—Identification
— Larvae
    ₜQL639.25ₗ
    UF Ichthyoplankton
          Larvae—Fishes
    BT Fishes—Development
          Fishes—Infancy
    NT Leptocephalous larvae
— Length-weight relationships
    USE Fishes—Growth
— Loading and unloading
    USE Fish handling—Loading and
          unloading
— Locomotion
    ₜQL639.4ₗ
    UF Fishes—Swimming
    BT Animal swimming
— Marking
    USE Fish tagging

Fishes (Continued)
— **Microbiology**
    UF Fishes—Bacteriology
— **Migration**
    [QL639]
    UF Migration of fishes
    NT Fishes—Counting
          Fishes—Homing
          Fishes—Seasonal distribution
          Smolting
—— **Climatic factors**
— Milt
    USE Fishes—Spermatozoa
— **Morphology**
    [QL639]
    UF Fishes—Body form
— **Mortality**
    NT Fish kills
          Fishes—Stranding
— **Mythology**
— Nests
    UF Fishes—Redds
          Nests of fishes
          Redds of fishes
    BT Nest building
— **Nomenclature**
    [QL618]
— **Nomenclature (Popular)**
    [QL618]
    For common names of fish of a particular lo-
    cality, two headings are used: 1. Fishes—
    [place]. 2. Fishes—Nomenclature (Popular)
    UF Fish names
    BT Fishes—Identification
— **Odor**
    UF Odor of fishes
    BT Odors
— **Parasites** (May Subd Geog)
    [SH175]
    UF Parasites—Fishes
    BT Fishes—Diseases
          Parasites
—— **Biological control** (May Subd Geog)
—— **Control** (May Subd Geog)
— Photography
    USE Photography of fishes
— **Physiology**
    NT Electric organs in fishes
          Fishes—Composition
          Fishes—Effect of water
             temperature on
          Fishes—Reproduction
          Smolting
— **Pictorial works**
— Population
    USE Fish populations
— Population dynamics
    USE Fish populations
— **Prices** (May Subd Geog)
— **Psychology**
— **Racial analysis**
    UF Racial analysis of fish
    BT Fish populations
          Fishery management
          Fishes—Geographical distribution
          Fishes—Identification
          Fishes, Anadromous
— Redds
    USE Fishes—Nests
— **Religious aspects**
—— **Buddhism,** [**Christianity, etc.**]
— **Reproduction**
    BT Fishes—Physiology
    NT Fishes—Fertility
          Fishes—Spawning
—— **Climatic factors**
—— **Endocrine aspects**
— **Research** (May Subd Geog)
    [QL618.5]
    UF Ichthyological research
          Ichthyology—Research

— Roe
    USE Fishes—Eggs
— Scales
    USE Scales (Fishes)
— **Seasonal distribution**
    UF Fish distribution
          Fishes—Distribution, Seasonal
          Seasonal distribution of fishes
    BT Fishes—Migration
— **Sexing**
    UF Fish sexing
          Sex determination of fishes
          Sexing of fish
    BT Fish breeding
— **Size**
    UF Size of fishes
    BT Fishes—Growth
— **Spawning**
    [QL639.2]
    UF Natural spawning of fishes
    BT Fishes—Reproduction
          Spawning
— **Spawning, Artificial**
    [SH155.6]
    UF Artificial spawning of fishes
          Fishes—Stripping
          Spawn collection from fish
          Stripping of fish spawn
    BT Fish breeding
          Fish-culture
— **Spawning, Induced**
    [SH155.7]
    UF Induced spawning of fishes
    BT Fish breeding
          Fish-culture
— **Speciation**
    UF Speciation of fishes
    BT Species
— **Spermatozoa**
    UF Fish milt
          Fishes—Milt
          Milt of fishes
    BT Spermatozoa
— **Stranding**
    UF Stranding of fish
    BT Fishes—Effect of water levels on
          Fishes—Mortality
— Stripping
    USE Fishes—Spawning, Artificial
— **Surgery** (May Subd Geog)
— Swimming
    USE Fishes—Locomotion
— Tagging
    USE Fish tagging
— Tariff
    USE Tariff on fishes
— **Therapeutic use**
    BT Materia medica, Animal
— **Training**
    BT Animals, Training of
— **Transportation**
— **Variation**
    UF Variation in fishes
    BT Variation (Biology)
— Venom
    USE Poisonous fishes—Venom
— **Vertical distribution**
    UF Fish distribution
          Fishes—Distribution, Vertical
          Vertical distribution of fishes
    BT Vertical distribution (Aquatic
          biology)
— **Weight**
    BT Body weight
— **Wintering**
    UF Wintering-over in fishes
— **Wounds and injuries** (May Subd Geog)
— Zoogeography
    USE Fishes—Geographical distribution
— **Tropics**

Here are entered works on fishes of tropical
regions. Works on exotic aquarium fish are en-
tered under Tropical fish.
    NT Tropical fish
Fishes, Age of
    USE Fishes—Age
Fishes, Anadromous
    UF Anadromous fishes
    NT Atlantic salmon
          Cutthroat trout, Sea-run
          Fishes—Racial analysis
          Pacific salmon
          Shad
          Smolting
          Steelhead (Fish)
Fishes, Apodal, Fossil
    USE Eels, Fossil
Fishes, Cleaning of
    USE Fishes, Dressing of
Fishes, Deep-sea (May Subd Geog)
    UF Deep-sea fishes
    BT Marine fishes
Fishes, Draught of (Miracle)
    USE Miraculous draught of fishes (Miracle)
Fishes, Dressing of
    [SH446.D]
    UF Cleaning of fish
          Dressing of fish
          Fish and game, Dressing of
          Fishes—Cleaning
          Fishes, Cleaning of
    BT Fish handling
          Fishing
          Game and game-birds, Dressing of
Fishes, Electric
    USE Electric organs in fishes
Fishes, Fossil
    [QE851-2]
    NT Acanthodii
          Chondrichthyes, Fossil
          Cosmine
Fishes, Fresh-water (May Subd Geog)
    UF Freshwater fishes
    BT Freshwater fauna
    SA names of classes, orders, etc. of fresh-
          water fishes
Fishes, Poisonous
    USE Poisonous fishes
Fishes and civilization
    UF Civilization and fishes
    BT Civilization
Fishes as pets
    USE Ornamental fishes
Fishes in archaeology
    USE Fish remains (Archaeology)
Fishes in art
    [7668.F57]
    NT Fish mosaic (Palestrina)
          Fish prints
Fishhooks (May Subd Geog)
    [SH344.8.H6 (Commercial fishing)]
    [SH452.9.H (Sportfishing)]
    UF Fish hooks
          Fishing hooks
    BT Fisheries—Equipment and supplies
          Fishing rigs
          Fishing tackle
Fishhooks Wilderness (Ariz.)
    UF Fishhooks Wilderness Study Area
          (Ariz.)
    BT National parks and reserves—Arizona
          Wilderness areas—Arizona
Fishhooks Wilderness Study Area (Ariz.)
    USE Fishhooks Wilderness (Ariz.)
Fishing (May Subd Geog)
    [SH401-691]
    UF Angling
          Recreational fishing
          Sport fishing
    BT Aquatic sports

RT Fishers
    Fishes
NT Aeronautics in fishing
    Arctic char fishing
    Artificial reefs
    Atlantic cod fishing
    Ayu fishing
    Backpack fishing
    Bait
    Bait fishing
    Barbel fishing
    Bass fishing
    Big game fishing
    Billfish fishing
    Black bass fishing
    Bluefishing
    Bluegill fishing
    Bonefishing
    Bottom fishing
    Bream fishing
    Brook trout fishing
    Brown trout fishing
    Burbot fishing
    Carp fishing
    Casting (Fishing)
    Channel bass fishing
    Charter boat fishing
    Chinook salmon fishing
    Chub fishing
    Coho salmon fishing
    Crabbing
    Crappie fishing
    Eel fishing
    Electric fishing
    Fishery law and legislation
    Fishes, Dressing of
    Flatfish fishing
    Fly fishing
    Fugu fishing
    Golden trout fishing
    Grayling fishing
    Halibut fishing
    Hunting and fishing clubs
    Ice fishing
    Largemouth bass fishing
    Mackerel fishing
    Mahseer fishing
    Marlin fishing
    Mullet fishing
    Muskellunge fishing
    Needlefish fishing
    Pacific halibut fishing
    Panfish fishing
    Perch fishing
    Pickerel fishing
    Pike fishing
    Plug fishing
    Rainbow trout fishing
    Ray fishing
    Roach fishing
    Sailfish fishing
    Salmon-fishing
    Saltwater fishing
    Sea bass fishing
    Sea trout fishing
    Shad fishing
    Shark fishing
    Sheatfish fishing
    Shellfish gathering
    Skate fishing
    Smallmouth bass fishing
    Spear fishing
    Spin-fishing
    Steelhead fishing
    Striped bass fishing
    Sturgeon fishing
    Sunfish fishing
    Swordfish fishing
    Tarpon fishing
    Tench fishing
    Tope fishing

Tournament fishing
Trolling (Fishing)
Trout fishing
Tuna fishing
Walleye fishing
Weakfish fishing
Zander fishing
— Access roads
    UF Access roads to fishing
        Public access roads to fishing
    BT Roads
— Anecdotes, facetiae, satire, etc.
    RT Fishing stories
— Catch effort
    BT Fishery management
        Fishing—Statistics
        Fishing surveys
— Equipment and supplies
    [SH447-453]
    NT Fishing tackle
— — Taxation   (May Subd Geog)
— — Law and legislation
    (May Subd Geog)
— Law
    USE Fishery law and legislation
— Licenses
    USE Fish and game licenses
— Literary collections
— Pictorial works
    NT Fishing in art
— Records
    [SH455]
    UF Fishers—Records
        Fishing records
        Fishing trophies
— Religious aspects
    NT Fishing in the Bible
— Statistics
    NT Fishing—Catch effort
— Terminology
    NT English language—Conversation
        and phrase books (for fishers)
Fishing, Electric
    USE Electric fishing
Fishing, Prehistoric   (May Subd Geog)
    UF Prehistoric fishing
    BT Archaeology
Fishing, Primitive   (May Subd Geog)
    [GN423]
    UF Primitive fishing
    BT Industries, Primitive
    NT Harpoons
        Indians of North America—Fishing
— New Zealand
    NT Maoris—Fishing
Fishing bat
    USE Myotis vivesi
Fishing boat industry   (May Subd Geog)
    [HD9489.B63-634]
    BT Fishing boats
Fishing boats   (May Subd Geog)
    BT Boats and boating
        Fisheries—Equipment and supplies
        Ships
        Work boats
    NT Bisquines
        Bragozzos
        Bugeyes (Boats)
        Coracles
        Dories (Boats)
        Fisheries navigation
        Fishery processing ships
        Fishery research vessels
        Fishing boat industry
        Friendship sloops
        Hookers (Fishing boats)
        Schuyts
        Sharpies (Sailboats)
        Skipjacks
        Trabacolos
— Crew accommodations

    UF Crew accommodations on fishing
        boats
        Crew's accommodations on fishing
        boats
— Electric equipment
    BT Electricity on ships
— Electronic equipment
    UF Electronics in fisheries
— Finance
— — Law and legislation
    (May Subd Geog)
— Flags, insignia, etc.
    BT Flags
        Insignia
— Fuel consumption
— Hydraulic equipment
— Refrigeration
    [SH344.8.R4]
    UF Chilling fish at sea
        Freezing fish at sea
    BT Cold storage on shipboard
        Marine refrigeration
        Refrigerator ships
— Safety measures
    BT Merchant marine—Safety measures
Fishing bobbers
    [SH452.9.B6]
    UF Bobbers, Fishing
        Fishing floats
        Floats, Fishing
    BT Bait fishing
        Fishing rigs
        Fishing tackle
Fishing camps
    USE Fishing lodges
Fishing catch effort
    USE Fisheries—Catch effort
Fishing clubs
    USE Hunting and fishing clubs
Fishing contests
    USE Tournament fishing
Fishing Creek, Battle of, 1862
    USE Mill Springs, Battle of, 1862
Fishing Creek Lake (S.C.)
    USE Fishing Creek Reservoir (S.C.)
Fishing Creek Reservoir (S.C.)
    UF Fishing Creek Lake (S.C.)
    BT Catawba River (N.C. and S.C.)
        Lakes—South Carolina
        Reservoirs—South Carolina
Fishing effort
    USE Fisheries—Fishing effort
Fishing-flies
    USE Flies, Artificial
Fishing floats
    USE Fishing bobbers
Fishing gear, Commercial
    USE Fisheries—Equipment and supplies
Fishing gear selectivity, Commercial
    USE Fisheries—Gear selectivity
Fishing hackles
    USE Hackles (Fly tying)
Fishing hooks
    USE Fishhooks
Fishing in art
    BT Fishing—Pictorial works
        Sports in art
Fishing in book-plates
    [Z994.5.F57]
    BT Book-plates
Fishing in literature
    NT Fishing in the Bible
Fishing in the Bible
    BT Fishing—Religious aspects
        Fishing in literature
        Sea in the Bible
Fishing industry
    USE Fisheries
Fishing knots   (May Subd Geog)
    [SH452.9.K6]
    UF Fisherman's knots

Fishing knots *(Continued)*
  BT Fishing rigs
      Fishing tackle
      Knots and splices
Fishing licenses
  USE Fish and game licenses
Fishing lodges *(May Subd Geog)*
  UF Fishing camps
      Fishing resorts
      Hunting and fishing camps
  BT Architecture, Domestic
      Camps
      Club-houses
      Dwellings
      Resorts
— **Catch effort**
Fishing lures
  UF Lures, Fishing
  BT Bait
      Fishing rigs
      Fishing tackle
  NT Flies, Artificial
      Jigs (Fishing lures)
Fishing nets *(May Subd Geog)*
  [SH344.8.N4]
  UF Fish nets
      Fishnets
  BT Fisheries—Equipment and supplies
      Nets
  NT Fish traps
      Gillnetting
      Glass fishing floats
      Lift net fishing
      Purse seining
      Seining
      Trammel netting
      Trawls and trawling
Fishing nets industry *(May Subd Geog)*
  [HD9489.N48]
Fishing ports *(May Subd Geog)*
  [SH337.5]
  UF Fishery harbors
  BT Fishery technology
      Harbors
Fishing records
  USE Fishing—Records
Fishing reels *(May Subd Geog)*
  [SH452.5]
  UF Reels (Fishing)
  BT Fishing tackle
Fishing regulations
  USE Fishery law and legislation
Fishing resorts
  USE Fishing lodges
Fishing rigs
  [SH452.9.R5]
  UF Rigs, Fishing
      Terminal tackle for fishing
  BT Fishing tackle
  NT Fishhooks
      Fishing bobbers
      Fishing knots
      Fishing lures
Fishing rods *(May Subd Geog)*
  [SH452]
  UF Fly rods
      Rods, Fishing
  BT Fishing tackle
— **Tariff**
      USE Tariff on fishing rods
— **Wrapping**
      [SH452.2]
      UF Interlacing fishing rods
          Rod wrapping (Fishing)
          Wrapping of fishing rods
      BT Thread
Fishing spiders, Giant
  USE Dolomedes
Fishing stories
  BT Fiction
      Sports stories

  RT Fishing—Anecdotes, facetiae, satire,
      etc.
Fishing stories, American *(May Subd Geog)*
  UF American fishing stories
  BT American fiction
Fishing surveys *(May Subd Geog)*
  Here are entered works on the methods and tech-
niques employed, and reports of individual surveys.
For the latter the heading may be subdivided by
place; in such cases a subject entry is also made under
the heading Fishing—[local subdivision], e.g. 1.
Fishing—United States. 2. Fishing surveys—United
States. For fishing surveys on a special topic the addi-
tional subject entry is made under the special topic,
e.g. 1. Salmon-fishing—United States. 2. Fishing sur-
veys—United States.
  UF Angling surveys
      Creel censusing (Fishing)
  BT Surveys
  NT Fishing—Catch effort
Fishing tackle
  [SH447-453]
  BT Fishing—Equipment and supplies
  NT Fishhooks
      Fishing bobbers
      Fishing knots
      Fishing lures
      Fishing reels
      Fishing rigs
      Fishing rods
Fishing tackle industry *(May Subd Geog)*
  [HD9489.T33]
Fishing trophies
  USE Fishing—Records
Fishing villages *(May Subd Geog)*
  BT Maritime anthropology
      Villages
Fishing with natural bait
  USE Bait fishing
Fishnets
  USE Fishing nets
Fishok family
  USE Fishack family
Fishplates
  USE Railroads—Rails—Fastenings
Fishponds
  USE Fish ponds
Fishways *(May Subd Geog)*
  [SH153]
  UF Fish ladders
      Fish passages
  BT Dams
      Fish habitat improvement
      Fisheries
      Flood dams and reservoirs
Fishwheels *(May Subd Geog)*
  UF Fish wheels
      Salmon wheels
  BT Fisheries—Equipment and supplies
Fisk family
  UF Fiske family
Fisk Site (Ont.) *(Not Subd Geog)*
  BT Ontario—Antiquities
Fiske family
  USE Fisk family
Fisker family
Fissiculata
  [QE783.B6]
  BT Blastoidea
Fission, Nuclear
  USE Nuclear fission
Fission, Spontaneous
  USE Spontaneous fission
Fission (Biology)
  BT Reproduction, Asexual
Fission cross sections
  BT Cross sections (Nuclear physics)
      Nuclear fission
  NT Elastic cross sections
      Inelastic cross sections
      Neutron cross sections

Fission dating method
  USE Radioactive dating
Fission gases
  BT Fission products
      Gases
  NT Krypton—Isotopes
      Xenon—Isotopes
Fission products
  BT Nuclear fission
      Radioactive substances
  NT Fission gases
      Radioactive fallout
      Reactor fuel reprocessing
— **Computer programs**
— **Decay**
— **Spectra**
Fission track dating
  [QE508]
  BT Radioactive dating
Fissionable materials
  USE Radioactive substances
Fissure sealants (Dentistry)
  USE Pit and fissure sealants (Dentistry)
Fistula
  [RD643]
  BT Abnormalities, Human
Fistula, Anal
  [RD643]
Fistula, Antral-oral
  USE Fistula, Oroantral
Fistula, Antro-oral
  USE Fistula, Oroantral
Fistula, Arteriovenous
  UF Aneurysms, Arteriovenous
      Arteriovenous aneurysms
      Arteriovenous fistula
      Arteriovenous shunts, Abnormal
  BT Blood-vessels—Abnormalities
  NT Arteriovenous anastomosis
Fistula, Biliary
  UF Biliary fistula
  BT Biliary tract—Diseases
Fistula, Branchial cleft
  UF Branchial cleft fistula
  BT Aorta—Diseases
Fistula, Gastric
  UF Gastric fistula
Fistula, Intestinal
  UF Intestinal fistula
Fistula, Labyrinthine
  UF Labyrinthine fistula
  BT Labyrinth (Ear)
Fistula, Lacrimal
  [RD643]
  UF Lacrimal fistula
  BT Lacrimal organs—Diseases
Fistula, Oroantral
  UF Antral-oral fistula
      Antro-oral fistula
      Fistula, Antral-oral
      Fistula, Antro-oral
      Oroantral fistula
  BT Maxillary sinus—Diseases
      Mouth—Diseases
Fistula, Recto-urethral
  UF Recto-urethral fistula
  BT Rectum—Diseases
      Urethra—Diseases
Fistula, Tracheal
  USE Fistula, Tracheoesophageal
Fistula, Tracheoesophageal
  UF Fistula, Tracheal
  BT Trachea—Diseases
Fistula, Urinary
  UF Urinary fistula
Fistula, Uterine
  BT Uterus—Diseases
Fistula, Vesico-vaginal
  UF Vesicovaginal fistula
  BT Bladder—Diseases

Fitch family

Fitchia
  ⌜QK495.C74⌝
  BT Compositae

Fitchpattareck family
  USE Fitzpatrick family

Fitkin family

Fitness, Physical
  USE Physical fitness

Fitness to stand trial
  USE Competency to stand trial

Fitness training, Nautilus
  USE Nautilus training

Fits, Press
  USE Press fits

Fits (Engineering)
  USE Tolerance (Engineering)

Fitsgerald family
  USE Fitzgerald family

Fitshaw family
  USE Titshaw family

Fitspatrick family
  USE Fitzpatrick family

Fitting, Curve
  USE Curve fitting

Fitting, Shrink
  USE Shrink fitting

Fitting (Engineering)
  USE Machine-shop practice

Fitting family

Fitting of hearing aids
  USE Hearing aids—Fitting

Fitting of shoes
  USE Shoes—Fitting

Fitting out of boats
  USE Boats and boating—Equipment and
       supplies

Fitting subgroup
  USE Maximal subgroups

Fittings, Building
  USE Building fittings

Fitz Randolph family
  USE Randolph family

Fitz Warin family
  UF Fitzwarine family

Fitzgarald family
  USE Fitzgerald family

Fitzgeoffrey, Cormac (Fictitious character)
  UF Cormac Fitzgeoffrey (Fictitious
      character)
  BT Characters and characteristics in
      literature
  RT Howard, Robert Ervin, 1906-1936—
      Characters—Cormac Fitzgeoffrey

Fitzgerald family
  UF Fichgerrel family
      Fitsgerald family
      Fitzgarald family
      Fitzgerrald family
      Fitzgerrel family
      Fitzjerald family

Fitzgerrald family
  USE Fitzgerald family

Fitzgerrel family
  USE Fitzgerald family

Fitzhugh's Woods, Battle of, 1864
  ⌜E476.35⌝
  BT Arkansas—History—Civil War, 1861-
      1865
      United States—History—Civil War,
      1861-1865—Campaigns

Fitzjerald family
  USE Fitzgerald family

Fitzner family
  USE Pfitzner family

Fitzpaterick family
  USE Fitzpatrick family

Fitzpatrick family
  UF Fetzpattreck family
      Fichpatrick family
      Fitchpattareck family
      Fitspatrick family
      Fitzpaterick family

Fitzroy River (Qld.)
  BT Rivers—Australia

Fitzroya
  ⌜QK494.5.C975⌝
  BT Cupressaceae

Fitzsimmonds family
  USE Fitzsimmons family

Fitzsimmons family
  UF Fitzsimmonds family
      Fitzsimons family

Fitzsimons family
  USE Fitzsimmons family

Fitzwarine family
  USE Fitz Warin family

Fiu language
  BT Melanesian languages

Fiumara Buonamico (Italy)
  USE Buonamico River (Italy)

Fiumara di Amendolea (Italy)
  USE Amendolea River (Italy)

Fiume Agri (Italy)
  USE Agri River (Italy)

Fiume Arno (Italy)
  USE Arno River (Italy)

Fiume Belice (Sicily)
  USE Belice River (Sicily)

Fiume Brenta (Italy)
  USE Brenta River (Italy)

Fiume Conca (Italy)
  USE Conca River (Italy)

Fiume Elsa (Italy)
  USE Elsa River (Italy)

Fiume Flumendosa (Sardinia)
  USE Flumendosa River (Sardinia)

Fiume Isarco (Italy)
  USE Isarco River (Italy)

Fiume Isonzo (Slovenia and Italy)
  USE Isonzo River (Slovenia and Italy)

Fiume Mavone (Italy)
  USE Mavone River (Italy)

Fiume Nievole (Italy)
  USE Nievole River (Italy)

Fiume Orcia (Italy)
  USE Orcia River (Italy)

Fiume Panaro (Italy)
  USE Panaro River (Italy)

Fiume Reno (Italy)
  USE Reno River (Italy)

Fiume Sacco (Italy)
  USE Sacco River (Italy)

Fiume Secchia (Italy)
  USE Secchia River (Italy)

Fiume Sele (Italy)
  USE Sele River (Italy)

Fiume Sieve (Italy)
  USE Sieve River (Italy)

Fiume Tammaro (Italy)
  USE Tammaro River (Italy)

Fiume Tevere (Italy)
  USE Tiber River (Italy)

Fiume Ticino (Switzerland and Italy)
  USE Ticino River (Switzerland and Italy)

Fiume Verzasca (Switzerland)
  USE Verzasca River (Switzerland)

Five (The number)
  BT Symbolism of numbers

Five (The number) in art

Five agents (Chinese philosophy)
  ⌜B127.F58⌝
  UF Agents, Five (Chinese philosophy)
      Elements, Five (Chinese philosophy)
      Five elements (Chinese philosophy)
      Wu-hsing (Chinese philosophy)
  BT Agent (Philosophy)
      Philosophy, Chinese

Five-and-ten-cent stores
  USE Variety stores

Five Civilized Tribes
  ⌜E78.I5⌝
  ⌜E78.O45⌝
  UF Indians of North America—Five
      Civilized Tribes
  BT Indians of North America—Indian
      Territory
      Indians of North America—Oklahoma
  RT Cherokee Indians
      Chickasaw Indians
      Choctaw Indians
      Creek Indians
  NT Seminole Indians
  — Government relations
  — Land tenure
  — Land transfers
  — Tribal citizenship

Five Commandments (Buddhism)
  USE Five Precepts (Buddhism)

Five dynasties and the Ten kingdoms, China,
  907-979
  USE China—History—Five dynasties and
       the Ten kingdoms, 907-979

Five elements (Chinese philosophy)
  USE Five agents (Chinese philosophy)

Five-gaited horse
  USE American saddlebred horse

Five Hu and the Sixteen kingdoms, China,
  304-439
  USE China—History—Five Hu and the
       Sixteen kingdoms, 304-439

Five hundred (Game)
  ⌜GV1295.F5⌝

Five Islands (La.)
  BT Islands—Louisiana
  NT Avery Island (La.)

Five Nations
  USE Iroquois Indians

Five-needle pine, Japanese
  USE Japanese five-needle pine

Five pillars of Islam
  USE Pillars of Islam

Five Precepts (Buddhism)
  ⌜BQ5485-5525⌝
  UF Five Commandments (Buddhism)
      Precepts, Five (Buddhism)
  BT Buddhism—Discipline
      Buddhist laymen—Discipline
      Buddhist precepts

Five Sacred Wounds
  UF Five Wounds
      Wounds, Five Sacred
  BT Jesus Christ—Crucifixion
  NT Sacred Heart, Devotion to
      Wound in the Side

Five-spined engraver
  USE Ips confusus

Five-suit bridge
  ⌜GV1282.9.F5⌝
  BT Bridge whist
      Contract bridge

Five thousand, Feeding of the (Miracle)
  USE Feeding of the five thousand (Miracle)

Five Towns Region (England)
  USE Potteries (England)

Five Wounds
  USE Five Sacred Wounds

Fivecoat family
  USE Finfrock family

Fivecoate family
  USE Finfrock family

Fivecoats family
  USE Finfrock family

Fives (Game)
  ⌜GV1003⌝

Fix-point estimation
  UF Point estimation
  BT Estimation theory

1365

Fixation (Histology)
  UF Tissue fixation
      Tissues—Fixation
  BT Cytology—Technique
      Histology—Technique
      Tissues—Preservation
Fixation of nitrogen
  USE Nitrogen—Fixation
Fixed base operators industry
  (May Subd Geog)
  [HD9711]
  BT Aircraft industry
      Airports
      Private flying
Fixed costs
  USE Overhead costs
Fixed exchange rates
  USE Foreign exchange
Fixed-film biological process (Sewage
    purification)
  USE Sewage—Purification—Fixed-film
          biological process
Fixed ideas
  USE Eccentrics and eccentricities
       Monomania
       Obsessive-compulsive neurosis
Fixed partial dentures
  USE Bridges (Dentistry)
Fixed point theory
  [QA329.9]
  BT Nonlinear operators
  RT Coincidence theory (Mathematics)
  NT Degree, Topological
Fixed storage
  USE Read-only storage
Fixed wing aircraft
  USE Airplanes
Fixing, Price
  USE Price fixing
Fixtures (Law) *(May Subd Geog)*
  BT Landlord and tenant
      Things (Law)
  RT Appurtenances
      Real property
  NT Personal property
Fixtures (Mechanical devices)
  USE Jigs and fixtures
Fjöllum (Iceland)
  USE Jökulsá á Fjöllum (Iceland)
Fjord horse
Fjords *(May Subd Geog)*
  [GB454.F5]
  UF Fiords
  BT Coasts
  — Alaska
      NT Kenai Fjords (Alaska)
  — Germany (West)
      NT Kiel Fjord (Germany)
  — Iceland
      NT Eyjafjörður (Iceland)
          Ísafjörður (Iceland)
  — Norway
      NT Oslofjorden (Norway)
Fjort (African people)
  USE Bakongo (African people)
Flabella
  [NK4870]
  BT Christian art and symbolism
      Fans
Flabellidae
  [QL377.C5]
  BT Scleractinia
Flabelligerida *(May Subd Geog)*
  [QL391.A6]
  BT Polychaeta
  NT Acrocirridae
      Flabelligeridae
Flabelligeridae
  [QL391.A6]
  BT Flabelligerida
  NT Fauveliopsis

Flabellorhagidia
  [QL458.2.R45]
  BT Rhagidiidae
Flabellula
FLAC computer
  USE Seac computer
Flaccidity, Muscle
  USE Muscle hypotonia
Flach family
  USE Flack family
Flack family
  UF Flach family
      Flacke family
Flacke family
  USE Flack family
Flacourtiaceae
  NT Casearia
Flag Day
  [JK1761]
  [LB3531]
  BT Holidays
Flag family
  USE Flagg family
Flag football *(May Subd Geog)*
  UF Tail football
  BT Football
Flag football for women *(May Subd Geog)*
  BT Sports for women
Flag of convenience
  USE Flags of convenience
Flag-waving (Exercise)
  [GV488]
  BT Drill (not military)
Flagella (Microbiology)
  BT Cilia and ciliary motion
      Micro-organisms—Motility
Flagellants and flagellation
  [HV8613-8621]
  UF Flagellation
      Flogging
      Whipping
  BT Asceticism
      Corporal punishment
  NT Disciplinati
      Fareinistes
      Scourging of Christ, Devotion to
Flagellariaceae
  [QK495.F58]
  BT Commelinales
Flagellata
  [QL368.F5]
  UF Mastigophora
  BT Infusoria
      Protozoa
  NT Dinoflagellata
      Diplomonadida
      Ebriida
      Kinetoplastida
      Protomonadida
      Silicoflagellata
Flagellation
  USE Corporal punishment
       Flagellants and flagellation
Flagellation of Christ, Devotion to
  USE Scourging of Christ, Devotion to
Flagelloserranus
  [QL638.S48]
  BT Serranidae
Flageolet
  [ML935-6]
  BT Flute
      Woodwind instruments
  RT Recorder (Musical instrument)
  NT Galoubet
      Melody flute
      Penny whistle
Flageolet and continuo music
  UF Continuo and flageolet music
  NT Sonatas (Flageolet and continuo)
Flageolet and piano music
  [M240-242]

  UF Piano and flageolet music
Flageolet and violin music
  [M290]
  UF Violin and flageolet music
Flageolet and violin music, Arranged
  [M290]
Flageolet music
  [M60-62]
  BT Flute music
      Recorder music
Flageolet music, Arranged
  [M63-64]
Flageolet music (Flageolets (2))
  [M288-9]
Flageolet music (Flageolets (2)), Arranged
  [M288-9]
Flageolet Rockshelter (France)
  UF Le Flageolet Rockshelter (France)
  BT Caves—France
      France—Antiquities
Flageolet tones
  USE Harmonics (Music)
Flagg family
  UF Flag family
      Flagge family
      Flogg family
Flagge family
  USE Flagg family
Flagrans crimen *(May Subd Geog)*
  UF Flagrant délit
  BT Criminal law
      Criminal procedure
      Evidence, Criminal
Flagrant délit
  USE Flagrans crimen
Flags *(May Subd Geog)*
  [CR101-115 (Heraldry)]
  [JC345-347 (Emblems of state)]
  [TT850.2 (Handicraft)]
  [UC590-595 (Military science, U360-
      365)]
  [V300-305 (Naval science)]
  [VK385 (Merchant marine signalling)]
  UF Banners
      Colors (Flags)
      Ensigns
  BT Heraldry
  RT Emblems, National
      Signals and signaling
      Standards, Military
  SA *subdivision* Flags *under names of
      individual military services and
      under individual wars, e.g.* United
      States. Army—Flags; United
      States—History—Civil War, 1861-
      1865—Flags
  NT Church pennants
      Fishing boats—Flags, insignia, etc.
      Guidons
      Postage-stamps—Topics—Flags
      Steamboat lines—Flags, insignia, etc.
      Tankas (Tibetan scrolls)
      United Nations—Emblem and flag
      Yacht flags
  — Law and legislation *(May Subd Geog)*
  — Germany
  — Great Britain
      UF Union Jack
  — United States
      UF United States—Flags
      NT United States. Army—Flags
          United States. Navy—Flags
          United States—History—Civil War,
          1861-1865—Flags
  —— States
      [CR113.1 (Heraldry)]
      [JC346.A3 (Political science)]
      UF State flags (United States)
Flags, Corn
  USE Gladiolus

Flags in art
Flags of convenience *(May Subd Geog)*
Here are entered works on the practice of register-
ing a merchant vessel with a country that has less
restrictive safety requirements, registration fees, etc.
UF Flag of convenience
BT Ships—Registration and transfer
RT Ship transfers to foreign registry
Flags of truce
UF Bearers of a flag of truce
Truce, Flags of
BT Armistices
Protective signs (International law)
War (International law)
Flake board
USE Particle board
Flake family
UF Flakes family
Flake-glass laminates
UF Glass-flake laminates
BT Glass reinforced plastics
Laminated plastics
Flakes family
USE Flake family
Flambouron Mountains (Greece)
USE Pieria Mountains (Greece)
Flame
[QC241 (Sound)]
[QD516 (Chemistry)]
BT Combustion
Fire
Flame deposition
USE Flame spraying
Flame hardening
[TN752.F]
BT Metals—Heat treatment
Surface hardening
Flame monitoring systems
[TH6882]
BT Gas-burners
Flame photometry
BT Photometry
Spectrum analysis
Flame resistant materials
USE Fire resistant materials
Flame retardant plastics
USE Fire resistant plastics
Flame retardant polymers
USE Fire resistant polymers
Flame retardants
USE Fireproofing agents
Flame scarfing
USE Scarfing (Metals)
Flame spectroscopy
BT Spectrum analysis
NT Arc spectra
Flame spraying
UF Flame deposition
Spraying, Flame
BT Protective coatings
Flame spread
[TH1091-1093]
UF Spread of flames
Surface flame spread
BT Fire-testing
Flame throwers
[UG447]
BT Firearms
Incendiary weapons
Flamenco
[GV1796.F55 (Dancing)]
[ML3712 (Music literature)]
UF Cante hondo
Flamenco music
UF Cante flamenco
Cante hondo
BT Dance music—Spain
Folk dance music—Spain
Folk music—Spain
Folk-songs, Spanish
Gypsies—Music

Flamens
USE Priests, Roman
Flameproofing
USE Fireproofing
Flameproofing agents
USE Fireproofing agents
Flamicell River (Spain)
USE Flamisell River (Spain)
Flamines
USE Priests, Roman
Fläming, Hoher (Germany)
USE Hoher Fläming (Germany)
Flaming Gorge Reservoir (Wyo. and Utah)
BT Green River (Wyo.-Utah)
Reservoirs—Utah
Reservoirs—Wyoming
Flamingo flower
USE Anthuriums
Flamingo lilies
USE Anthuriums
Flamingos
[QL696.C56]
UF Odontoglossae
Flaminia, Via (Italy)
USE Via Flaminia (Italy)
Flamisell River (Spain)
UF Flamicell River (Spain)
Rio Flamisell (Spain)
BT Rivers—Spain
Flammability
USE *subdivision* Flammability *under*
individual materials and types of
materials, e.g. Metals—Flammability
Flammability testing
USE Fire-testing
Oxygen index of materials
Flammable materials
USE Inflammable materials
Flammable textiles
USE Inflammable textiles
Flancs-de-Chien Indians
USE Thlingchadinne Indians
Flander family
USE Flanders family
Flanders
Here are entered works on the Flemish region in
its greatest geographical extension, from the French
departement of Nord north of Dunkirk, through the
Dutch-speaking area of Belgium, including all the
former lands of the County of Flanders, to the Dutch
province of Zeeland south of the West Scheldt.
As a geographic subdivision, this heading is used
directly.
— Civilization
NT Drawing, Spanish—Flemish
influences
Painting, French—Flemish
influences
Painting, Italian—Flemish
influences
Painting, Modern—17th-18th
centuries—Flemish influences
— History *(Not Subd Geog)*
NT Cassel (France), Battle of, 1328
Flanders family
UF Fanders family
Flander family
Flandreau Indians
USE Santee Indians
Flandrin family
Flaneurs *(May Subd Geog)*
UF Idlers
Loungers
Saunterers
BT Characters and characteristics
Flanges
[TA492.F5]
NT Pipe flanges
Flannel
BT Textile fabrics
Flannel boards
USE Flannelgraphs

Flannelgraphs
UF Flannel boards
BT Teaching—Aids and devices
Flannellet
[TH9446.F6 (Fire protection)]
[TS1580]
BT Cotton fabrics
Flap-footed lizards
USE Pygopodidae
Flapjacks
USE Pancakes, waffles, etc.
Flaps (Airplanes)
[TL673.F6]
UF Airplanes—Flaps
BT Aerofoils
Ailerons
Airplanes—Control surfaces
Lift (Aerodynamics)
RT Spoilers (Airplanes)
NT Jet flaps (Airplanes)
Flaps (Surgery)
UF Surgical flaps
BT Autografts
Surgery, Plastic
RT Skin-grafting
Flare gas systems (Chemical engineering)
(May Subd Geog)
[TP159.F52]
UF Flare stacks (Chemical engineering)
Flares (Chemical engineering)
Systems, Flare gas (Chemical
engineering)
BT Chemical plants—Safety appliances
Petroleum refineries—Safety
appliances
RT Waste gases—Combustion
Flare projector pistol
USE Liberator pistol
Flare stacks (Chemical engineering)
USE Flare gas systems (Chemical
engineering)
Flare stars
[QB843.F55]
UF UV Ceti stars
BT Cataclysmic variable stars
Cool stars
RT Red dwarfs
Flares
BT Fireworks
Lighting
Signals and signaling
Flares, Proton
USE Proton flares
Flares, Solar
USE Solar flares
Flares (Chemical engineering)
USE Flare gas systems (Chemical
engineering)
Flash cards
USE Word recognition
Flash distillation process (Saline water
conversion)
USE Saline water conversion—Flash
distillation process
Flash-light photography
USE Photography, Flash-light
Flash photolysis
[QP519.9.F52 (Biochemistry)]
UF Photolysis, Flash
BT Biological chemistry—Technique
Photochemistry—Technique
Flash radiography
UF Instantaneous radiography
Radiography, Flash
BT Radiography
Flashlights
UF Electric flashlights
Torches (Flashlights)
BT Electric lamps, Portable
Lamps

Flasks
  USE Bottles
Flat bark beetles
  USE Cucujidae
Flat Bayou (Ark.)
  BT Bayous—Arkansas
Flat bugs
  USE Aradidae
Flat-coated retriever
  [SF429.F]
  BT Retrievers
Flat-footed flies
  [QL537.P63]
  UF Clythiidae
      Platypezidae
  BT Diptera
  NT Callomyia
      Calotarsa
      Platypeza
      Protoclythia
Flat-headed snake
  UF Tantilla gracilis
Flat income tax
  USE Flat-rate income tax
Flat pea
  [SB205.F]
  BT Forage plants
      Peas
Flat racing
  USE Horse-racing
Flat-rate income tax   *(May Subd Geog)*
  UF Flat income tax
      Flat-rate tax
      Flat tax
      Income tax, Flat-rate
      Tax, Flat
  BT Income tax
Flat-rate tax
  USE Flat-rate income tax
Flat Rock Creek (Va.)
  BT Rivers—Virginia
Flat roofs
  [TH2409]
  UF Roofs, Flat
  — Thermal properties
Flat silver
  USE Silver flatware
      Silver-plated flatware
Flat springs
  USE Leaf springs
Flat tax
  USE Flat-rate income tax
Flatboats   *(May Subd Geog)*
  BT Boats and boating
      River life
Flatfish fisheries   *(May Subd Geog)*
  [SH351.F5]
  UF Flounder fisheries
      Sole fisheries
  BT Fisheries
  NT Halibut fisheries
Flatfish fishing
  [SH691.F5]
  BT Fishing
Flatfishes
  [QL637.9.P5]
  UF Flounders
      Heterosomata
      Pleuronectiformes
      Soles
      Turbots
  BT Osteichthyes
  NT Bothidae
      Citharidae
      Cynoglossidae
      Gymnachirus
      Halibut
      Pleuronectidae
      Soleidae
Flatfoot
  [RD785]

  UF Pes planus
  BT Foot—Abnormalities
Flathead fishes
  USE Platycephalidae
Flathead Indian Reservation (Mont.)
  BT Indians of North America—Montana
      —Reservations
      Kutenai Indians—Reservations
      Salish Indians—Reservations
Flathead Indians
  USE Salish Indians
Flathead National Forest (Mont.)
  (Not Subd Geog)
  BT Forest reserves—Montana
      National parks and reserves—Montana
Flathead River (B.C. and Mont.)
  BT Rivers—British Columbia
      Rivers—Montana
Flathead sole
  [QL638.P7]
  UF Hippoglossoides elassodon
      Sole, Flathead
Flatheaded adders
  USE Hognose snakes
Flatheads
  USE Platycephalidae
Flatirons
  USE Irons (Pressing)
Flatness measurement
  BT Mensuration
      Surfaces (Technology)
Flats
  USE Apartments
Flats, Tidal
  USE Tidal flats
Flattery, Servile
  USE Toadyism
Flatulence
  UF Farting
  BT Gastrointestinal gas
      Stomach—Diseases
Flatvaer Islands (Antarctic regions)
  (Not Subd Geog)
  BT Islands—Antarctic regions
Flatware   *(May Subd Geog)*
  BT Tableware
  NT Forks
      Knives
      Silver flatware
      Silver-plated flatware
      Spoons
Flatware, Stainless steel
  USE Tableware, Stainless steel
Flatworms
  USE Platyhelminthes
Flavel family
  UF Flavell family
      Flavelle family
      Flaville family
      Flayville family
Flavell family
  USE Flavel family
Flavelle family
  USE Flavel family
Flavian Amphitheater (Rome, Italy)
  USE Colosseum (Rome, Italy)
Flavian family
  UF Flavius family
Flaville family
  USE Flavel family
Flavins
  BT Coenzymes
      Pigments
  NT Flavoproteins
      Quercetin
Flavius family
  USE Flavian family
Flaviviridae
  USE Flaviviruses

Flaviviruses
  UF Flaviviridae
      Group B arboviruses
  BT Arthropod-borne viruses
      Togaviruses
  NT Dengue viruses
      Tick-borne encephalitis viruses
Flavonoids
  NT Bioflavonoids
  — Spectra
Flavoproteins
  BT Dehydrogenases
      Flavins
Flavor
  UF Tastes
  BT Food—Analysis
      Taste
  NT Alcoholic beverages—Flavor and odor
      Beer—Flavor and odor
      Butter—Flavor and odor
      Dairy products—Flavor and odor
      Feeds—Flavor and odor
      Food—Sensory evaluation
      Fruit—Flavor and odor
      Fruit juices—Flavor and odor
      Liquors—Flavor and odor
      Meat, Precooked—Flavor and odor
      Milk—Flavor and odor
      Milk, Remade—Flavor and odor
      Oils and fats—Flavor and odor
      Orange juice—Flavor and odor
Flavor dynamics, Quantum
  USE Quantum flavor dynamics
Flavoring essences
  [TP450-453]
  BT Cookery
      Food
  RT Essences and essential oils
  NT Cookery (Vanilla)
      Sweeteners
      Vanilla
Flavoring essences industry
  (May Subd Geog)
  [HD9212-9212.5]
Flawlessness
  USE Perfection
Flax   *(May Subd Geog)*
  [HF5716.F4 (Trade, HD9155,
      HE7677.F55)]
  [QK495.L74 (Botany)]
  [SB253 (Culture)]
  [TS1700-1731 (Technology)]
  UF Baltic hemp
      Linum usitatissimum
  BT Oilseed plants
      Yarn
  RT Linen
  NT Flax straw
      Flaxseed
  — Disease and pest resistance
      (May Subd Geog)
  — Diseases and pests   *(May Subd Geog)*
      SA *specific diseases and pests, e.g.*
          Flax rust; Flaxwilt
  — Harvesting
  — Microbiology
  — Seed
      USE Flaxseed
  — Varieties
      UF Flaxseed—Varieties
Flax, New Zealand
  USE Phormium tenax
Flax as feed
  BT Flax straw
Flax industry   *(May Subd Geog)*
  BT Textile industry
  NT Wages—Flax and hemp trade
Flax rust
  UF Melampsora lini
Flax spinning
  [TS1727]

BT Spinning
Flax straw
  BT Flax
     Straw
  NT Flax as feed
Flaxseed *(May Subd Geog)*
  ⌈SB299.F6 (Culture)⌉
  UF Flax—Seed
     Linseed
  BT Flax
     Oilseeds
  NT Linseed-oil
  — Varieties
     USE Flax—Varieties
Flaxseed oil
  USE Linseed-oil
Flaxwilt
Flay family
  USE Fleay family
Flaye family
  USE Fleay family
Flayville family
  USE Flavel family
Flea-beetles
  ⌈QL596.C5⌉
  ⌈SB608⌉
  ⌈SB945 (Pests)⌉
  BT Beetles
     Chrysomelidae
  NT Alder flea-beetle
     Purslane flea-beetle
     Tobacco flea-beetle
Flea-borne typhus
  USE Typhus, Endemic flea-borne
Flea family
  USE Fleay family
Flea markets *(May Subd Geog)*
  BT Junk trade
     Markets
     Secondhand trade
  RT Rummage sales
Fleas *(May Subd Geog)*
  ⌈QL599.5-599.82⌉
  UF Aphaniptera
     Rophoteira
     Siphonaptera
     Suctoria (Insects)
  BT Insects
  NT Beach-flea
     Ceratophyllidae
     Hystrichopsyllidae
     Ischnopsyllidae
     Monopsyllus
     Pulicidae
     Stephanocircidae
  — Control *(May Subd Geog)*
     ⌈RA641.F5⌉
     UF Fleas—Extermination
  — Extermination
     USE Fleas—Control
Fleas as carriers of disease
  ⌈RA641.F5⌉
  BT Insects as carriers of disease
  NT Typhus, Endemic flea-borne
Fleas in literature
Fleay family
  UF Flay family
     Flaye family
     Flea family
     Flee family
Flecher family
  USE Fletcher family
Fleck family *(Not Subd Geog)*
  UF Flecke family
     Flecken family
Flecke family
  USE Fleck family
Flecken family
  USE Fleck family
Fledglings (Birds)
  USE Birds—Nestlings

Flee family
  USE Fleay family
Fleece
  USE Wool
Fleeing from scene of accident
  USE Hit-and-run drivers
Fleeing in the Bible
  UF Bible—Fleeing
Fleer family
  UF Fleher family
Fleet, American Bicentennial
  USE American Bicentennial Fleet
Fleet ballistic missile weapons systems
  ⌈V990-995⌉
  BT Ballistic missiles
     Strategic forces
     United States. Navy—Weapons
      systems
     Weapons systems
  RT Nuclear submarines
  NT Polaris (Missile)
     Poseidon (Weapons system)
     Trident (Weapons systems)
Fleet family
  RT Fleetwood family
Fleet train
  USE Naval auxiliary vessels
Fleets, Motor vehicle
  USE Motor vehicle fleets
Fleetwood, Battle of, 1863
  USE Brandy Station, Battle of, 1863
Fleetwood family
  RT Fleet family
Flegel family *(Not Subd Geog)*
  UF Flegle family
Flegle family
  USE Flegel family
Fleher family
  USE Fleer family
Fleischer family
  UF Fleisher family
     Flesch family
     Flescher family
     Flesher family
Fleischman family
  USE Fleshman family
Fleischmann family
  USE Fleshman family
Fleisher family
  USE Fleischer family
Fleishman family
  USE Fleshman family
Fleming, Ian, 1908-1964
  — Characters
    — — **James Bond**
       RT Bond, James (Fictitious
          character)
Fleming family
  UF Flemming family
     Flemyng family
Flemings *(May Subd Geog)*
  BT Ethnology—Belgium
Flemish alabaster sculpture
  USE Alabaster sculpture, Flemish
Flemish architecture
  USE Architecture, Flemish
Flemish art
  USE Art, Flemish
Flemish arts
  USE Arts, Flemish
Flemish authors
  USE Authors, Flemish
Flemish bronze fonts
  USE Bronze fonts, Flemish
Flemish children's literature
  USE Children's literature, Flemish
Flemish children's stories
  USE Children's stories, Flemish
Flemish Christian poetry
  USE Christian poetry, Flemish

Flemish drama *(May Subd Geog)*
  — 19th century
  — 20th century
Flemish dramatists
  USE Dramatists, Flemish
Flemish drawing
  USE Drawing, Flemish
Flemish engraving
  USE Engraving, Flemish
Flemish fiction *(May Subd Geog)*
  NT Children's stories, Flemish
     Science fiction, Flemish
     Short stories, Flemish
Flemish folk literature
  USE Folk literature, Flemish
Flemish genre painting
  USE Genre painting, Flemish
Flemish illumination of books and manuscripts
  USE Illumination of books and manuscripts,
     Flemish
Flemish landscape drawing
  USE Landscape drawing, Flemish
Flemish language
  USE Dutch language
Flemish letters
Flemish literature *(May Subd Geog)*
  ⌈PT6000-PT6199 (History)⌉
  ⌈PT6215-PT6397 (Collections)⌉
  For literature in the Flemish language from 1830
  on. The older literature is entered under the heading
  Dutch literature.
  UF Belgian literature (Flemish)
  BT Dutch literature
  NT Belgian literature
     Children's literature, Flemish
Flemish marine painting
  USE Marine painting, Flemish
Flemish movement
  ⌈DH491⌉
  NT Aldietsche Beweging
Flemish narrative painting
  USE Narrative painting, Flemish
Flemish newspapers
  ⌈PN5261-PN5269 (History)⌉
  BT Belgian newspapers
Flemish painting
  USE Painting, Flemish
Flemish panel painting
  USE Panel painting, Flemish
Flemish periodicals
  ⌈PN5261-PN5270 (History)⌉
  BT Belgian periodicals
Flemish philology
Flemish poetry
  ⌈PT6140 (History)⌉
  ⌈PT6330-PT6340 (Collections)⌉
  Cf. note under Flemish literature.
  NT Christian poetry, Flemish
  — 20th century
Flemish prints
  USE Prints, Flemish
Flemish prose literature
  — 19th century
  — 20th century
Flemish relief (Sculpture)
  USE Relief (Sculpture), Flemish
Flemish science fiction
  USE Science fiction, Flemish
Flemish sculpture
  USE Sculpture, Flemish
Flemish short stories
  USE Short stories, Flemish
Flemish still-life painting
  USE Still-life painting, Flemish
Flemish wit and humor
  ⌈PN6222.B4⌉
  BT Belgian wit and humor
Flemish wit and humor, Pictorial
Flemish wood-engraving
  USE Wood-engraving, Flemish

Flemming family
USE Fleming family
Flemyng family
USE Fleming family
Flesch family
USE Fleischer family
Flescher family
USE Fleischer family
Flesh (Theology)
BT Man (Christian theology)
Flesh flies
USE Sarcophagidae
Flesh foods
USE Animal food
Flesher family
USE Fleischer family
Fleshman family *(Not Subd Geog)*
UF Fleischman family
Fleischmann family
Fleishman family
Fletch (Fictitious character)
UF Fletcher, Irwin Maurice (Fictitious character)
Irwin Maurice Fletcher (Fictitious character)
RT Mcdonald, Gregory, 1937- — Characters—Fletch
Fletchall family
Fletcher, Irwin Maurice (Fictitious character)
USE Fletch (Fictitious character)
Fletcher Cemetery (Brown, Miami County, Ohio)
BT Cemeteries—Ohio
Fletcher family
UF Flecher family
Flitcher family
RT Flowers family
Fletcher Site (Mich.)
BT Michigan—Antiquities
Fleur-de-lis
[CR41.F6]
Fleurance family
USE Florence family
Fleurieu Peninsula (S. Aust.)
(Not Subd Geog)
BT Peninsulas—Australia
Fleurons
USE Type ornaments
Fleurus, Battle of, 1690
[D280.F6]
BT Grand Alliance, War of the, 1689-1697—Campaigns—Belgium
Fleurus, Battle of, 1794
[DC222.F6]
BT France—History—Revolution, 1794—Campaigns
Fleury family
UF De Fleur family
De Fleury family
DeFleur family
DeFleury family
Flory family
Fleuve Senegal
USE Senegal River
Flexamia
[QL527.C49]
BT Leafhoppers
FLEXCURVE (Computer program)
[QA297.6]
BT Curve fitting—Computer programs
Flexibacter columnaris
USE Chondrococcus columnaris
Flexibility (Psychology)
USE Adaptability (Psychology)
Flexibility of joints
USE Joints—Range of motion
Flexible benefit plans
USE Cafeteria benefit plans
Flexible circuits
USE Flexible printed circuits

Flexible contact lenses
USE Contact lenses, Hydrophilic
Flexible couplings
USE Couplings, Flexible
Flexible exchange rates
USE Foreign exchange
Flexible fringe benefits
USE Cafeteria benefit plans
Flexible gunnery
USE Aerial gunnery
Flexible hours of labor
USE Hours of labor, Flexible
Flexible manufacturing systems
(May Subd Geog)
UF FMS
Manufacturing systems, Flexible
BT Automation
Production engineering
RT Computer integrated manufacturing systems
Flexible pavements
USE Pavements, Flexible
Flexible printed circuits
UF Flexible circuits
BT Printed circuits
Flexible shafting
[TJ1057]
BT Shafting
Flexible surfaces, Equilibrium of
USE Equilibrium of flexible surfaces
Flexible weapons (Hand-to-hand fighting)
(May Subd Geog)
[U167.5.H3]
UF Weapons, Flexible (Hand-to-hand fighting)
BT Hand-to-hand fighting
Flexible work hours
USE Hours of labor, Flexible
Flexitime
USE Hours of labor, Flexible
Flexography
[Z252.5.F6]
UF Aniline printing
BT Printing, Practical
Flexometer
[TS1449 (Textile testing)]
Flextime
USE Hours of labor, Flexible
Flexure
[QB154 (Astronomical adjustments)]
[TG265 (Beams)]
Here are entered works on the bending behavior of materials. Works dealing with bending as a forming process are entered under Bending.
NT Elasticity
Girders
Strains and stresses
Strength of materials
Flick Trial, Nuremberg, Germany, 1947-1949
UF Subsequent proceedings, Nuremberg War Crime Trials, case no. 5
BT Nuremberg War Crime Trials, 1946-1949
Flicker, Common
USE Colaptes auratus
Flicker fusion
UF Critical flicker frequency
Fusion (Vision)
BT Vision
Flickers
USE Colaptes
Flicorno
USE Fluegelhorn
Fliers, Advertising
USE Advertising fliers
Flies
[QL531-8]
UF Fly
RT Diptera
NT Blowflies
Bombyliidae

Botflies
Cuterebridae
Drosophilidae
Face fly
Fruit-flies
Hessian flies
Horn fly
Horseflies
Housefly
Maggots
Mayflies
Robber flies
Sawflies
Stoneflies
Tsetse-flies
Warble-flies
— **Control** *(May Subd Geog)*
[RA641.F6 (Public health)]
UF Fly control
Flies, Artificial *(May Subd Geog)*
[SH451]
UF Artificial flies
Fishing-flies
BT Fishing lures
Fly fishing
RT Fly tying
NT Hackles (Fly tying)
Flies, True
USE Diptera
Flies as carriers of disease
(May Subd Geog)
[RA641.F6]
BT Insects as carriers of disease
Flight
[QL698 (Bird flight)]
[TL570-TL578 (Mechanics of flight)]
UF Flying
BT Locomotion
RT Aeronautics
Wings
NT Animal flight
Flying-machines
Stability of airplanes
— Medical aspects
USE Aviation medicine
— **Physiological aspects**
[RC1075]
UF Aviation physiology
Physiological aspects of flight
BT Aviation medicine
Aviation toxicology
NT Jet lag
— — **Age factors**
— Psychological aspects
USE Aeronautics—Psychology
Flight, Unpowered
USE Gliding and soaring
Flight 007 Incident, 1983
USE Korean Air Lines Incident, 1983
Flight attendants *(May Subd Geog)*
UF Air hostesses
Air stewardesses
Air stewards
Airline hostesses
Airline stewardesses
Airline stewards
Airlines—Flight attendants
Airlines—Hostesses
Airlines—Stewardesses
Airlines—Stewards
Hostesses, Airline
Stewardesses, Airline
Stewards, Airline
BT Flight crews
Flight control
[TL589.4]

Here are entered works on systems that govern aircraft and space vehicle attitude, stability, and direction of motion. Works on systems for supervising the navigation of aircraft and space vehicles from one location to another are entered under Guidance systems (Flight)
- UF Control systems (Flight)
- BT Automatic control
  Guidance systems (Flight)
- NT Airplanes—Control systems
  Artificial satellites—Control systems
  Automatic pilot (Airplanes)
  Automatic pilot (Helicopters)
  Balloons—Control systems
  Guided missiles—Control systems
  Helicopters—Control systems
  Rockets (Aeronautics)—Control systems
  Space vehicles—Control systems

Flight crews (May Subd Geog)
- UF Air crews
  Aircraft crews
  Aircrews
  Airplanes—Crews
  Flying personnel
- BT Airlines—Employees
- NT Air pilots
  Bombardiers
  Flight attendants
  Flight engineers
  Flight navigators
  Flight radio operators
- — Anthropometry
Flight data recorders
- USE Flight recorders
Flight decks, Aircraft carrier
- USE Aircraft carriers—Flight decks
Flight easements
- USE Avigation easements
Flight engineering
- BT Aeronautical instruments
  Airplanes—Motors
Flight engineers (May Subd Geog)
- BT Flight crews
- — Strikes and lockouts
  - USE Strikes and lockouts—Flight engineers
Flight in art
  ⌈N8217.F6⌉
Flight in motion pictures
  ⌈PN1995.9.F58⌉
- UF Aeronautics in motion pictures
- BT Moving-pictures
Flight instruction
- USE Flight training
Flight into Egypt
- USE Jesus Christ—Flight into Egypt
Flight navigators (May Subd Geog)
- UF Air navigators
- BT Flight crews
Flight navigators, Military
  (May Subd Geog)
- UF Military flight navigators
- BT Aeronautics, Military
Flight of ideas
  ⌈RC553.F55⌉
- UF Ideas, Flight of
- BT Mentally ill—Language
  Psychology, Pathological
  Thought and thinking
Flight of Louis XVI to Varennes, 1791
- USE Louis XVI, King of France, 1754-1793 —Flight to Varennes, 1791
Flight officers
- USE subdivision Flight officers under armies, navies, etc., e.g. United States. Navy—Flight officers
Flight radio operators (May Subd Geog)
- UF Airplanes—Radio operators

- BT Flight crews
  Radio in aeronautics
  Radio operators
Flight recorders
  ⌈TL589.2.F5⌉
- UF Airplanes—Flight recorders
  Black boxes (Flight recorders)
  Data recorders, Flight
  Flight data recorders
  Recorders, Flight
- BT Aeronautical instruments
Flight simulator industry (May Subd Geog)
- BT Flight simulators
Flight simulators
- UF OFT (Flight simulator)
- BT Aeronautics, Military—Study and teaching
  Airplanes—Piloting
  Flight training
  Synthetic training devices
  Training planes
- NT Flight simulator industry
  Helicopter flight trainer
  Link trainers
Flight testing of airplanes
- USE Airplanes—Flight testing
  Airplanes, Military—Flight testing
Flight testing of helicopters
- USE Helicopters—Flight testing
Flight to Jupiter
- USE Space flight to Jupiter
Flight to Mars
- USE Space flight to Mars
Flight to Mercury
- USE Space flight to Mercury
Flight to the moon
- USE Space flight to the moon
Flight tracking
- USE Artificial satellites—Tracking
  Balloons—Tracking
  Guided missiles—Tracking
  Space vehicles—Tracking
Flight training (May Subd Geog)
  ⌈TL710-713⌉
- UF Flight instruction
  Flying classes
- BT Aeronautics—Study and teaching
- RT Airplanes—Piloting
- NT Flight simulators
  Link trainers
  Space flight training
  Training planes
Flightless cormorant
  ⌈QL696.P4745⌉
- UF Nannopterum harrisi
Flights, Endurance
- USE Endurance flights
Flights, Transatlantic
- USE Transatlantic flights
Flights, Transpacific
- USE Transpacific flights
Flights around the world
  ⌈G445⌉
- UF World flights
- BT Aeronautics—Flights
  Geography, Aerial
  Voyages around the world
Flinders Island (Tas.)
- BT Furneaux Islands (Tas.)
  Islands—Australia
Flinders Range (S. Aust.)
- BT Flinders Ranges (S. Aust.)
  Mountains—Australia
Flinders Ranges (S. Aust.)
- BT Mountains—Australia
- NT Flinders Range (S. Aust.)
Flindt family
- USE Flint family
Flinn family
- USE Flynn family

Flint (May Subd Geog)
  ⌈QE391.Q2 (Mineralogy)⌉
  ⌈TN948.F5 (Mining)⌉
- BT Quartz
- RT Chert
Flint china
- USE Ironstone china
Flint family
- UF Flindt family
  Flynt family
Flint implements
- USE Stone implements
Flint industry (May Subd Geog)
  ⌈HD9585.F5-54⌉
Flint knapping
- USE Flintknapping
Flint Ridge Cave System (Ky.)
- BT Caves—Kentucky
Flint Schools' Experimental Program for the Emotionally Handicapped
- BT Mentally ill children—Education
Flintholm (Denmark)
- BT Manors—Denmark
Flintknapping
  ⌈GN799.T6 (Prehistoric tools)⌉
  ⌈TT293 (Rock craft)⌉
- UF Flint knapping
  Knapping of flint
- BT Rock craft
Flitch beams
  ⌈TA660.F57⌉
- UF Beams, Flitch
  Flitch plate beams
- BT Girders
Flitch of Dunmow
- USE Dunmow flitch
Flitch plate beams
- USE Flitch beams
Flitcher family
- USE Fletcher family
Float, Check
- USE Check float
Float (Banking)
- USE Bank float
Float (Swimming)
- USE Swimming—Float
Float fishing, British
- USE Bait fishing
Floaters (Bottles)
- USE Drift bottles
Floaters (Securities)
- USE Floating rate notes
Floating (Swimming)
- USE Swimming—Float
Floating batteries
  ⌈V890⌉
- BT Artillery
  Batteries
  Coast defenses
  Fortification
  Naval art and science
- RT Gunboats
Floating bodies
  ⌈QA907⌉
  ⌈QC147⌉
- BT Hydrostatics
- NT Archimedes' principle
Floating breakwaters
- USE Breakwaters, Mobile
Floating charges
Floating cranes
  ⌈TJ1363⌉
- BT Cranes, derricks, etc.
  Work boats
- — Tariff
  - USE Tariff on floating cranes
Floating exchange rates
- USE Foreign exchange
Floating ferns
- USE Water ferns

Floating harbors *(May Subd Geog)*
  [TC363]
  UF Floating marine terminals
      Floating ports
      Harbors, Floating
      Marine terminals, Floating
      Ports, Floating
  BT Harbors
Floating hospitals
  USE Hospital ships
Floating ice stations
  USE Drifting ice stations
Floating instrument platforms
  USE Oceanographic buoys
Floating islands (Etchings)
  USE Fischl, Eric, 1948-   Floating
        islands
Floating marine terminals
  USE Floating harbors
Floating-point arithmetic
  [QA76.6]
  UF Arithmetic, Floating-point
  BT Computer arithmetic
      Electronic digital computers—
        Programming
Floating ports
  USE Floating harbors
Floating prisons
  USE Prison hulks
Floating rate instruments
  USE Floating rate notes
Floating rate notes *(May Subd Geog)*
  [HG4755]
      Here are entered works on securities, such as vari-
    able rate mortgage loans, with variable interest rates
    which are indexed to some pre-established money
    market rate.
  UF Floaters (Securities)
      Floating rate instruments
      Floating rate securities
      Instruments, Floating rate
      Notes, Floating rate
      Securities, Floating rate
  BT Securities
  RT Variable rate loans
  NT Mortgage loans, Variable rate
Floating rate securities
  USE Floating rate notes
Floating theaters
  USE Showboats
Floats, Fishing
  USE Fishing bobbers
Floats (Hydraulic engineering)
  USE Pontoons
Floats (Parades) *(May Subd Geog)*
  BT Parades
      Vehicles
Flocculants
  [TP159.F54]
  BT Flocculation
  NT Polyethylene oxide
Flocculation
  [QC183 (Physics)]
  [QD547 (Theory of solution)]
  [TP156.F55 (Chemical engineering)]
  BT Chemistry, Physical and theoretical
      Matter—Properties
      Sedimentation and deposition
  NT Coagulation
      Flocculants
      Sewage—Purification—Flocculation
      Sonic coagulation
Flocculi
  USE Sun—Flocculi
Flocculi, Bright
  USE Solar plages
Flocculi, Calcium
  USE Solar plages

Flock
  BT Factory and trade waste
      Rags
      Upholstery
  NT Flocking, Electrostatic
Flocking, Electrostatic
  [TS1512.5]
  UF Electrostatic flocking
  BT Flock
      Nonwoven fabrics
Flod family
  USE Flood family
Flodden, Battle of, 1513
  [DA784.6]
  BT Scotland—History—James IV, 1488-
        1513
Flodeen family
  USE Floden family
Floden family
  UF Flodeen family
      Flodin family
      Floen family
Flodh family
  USE Flood family
Flodin family
  USE Floden family
Floen family
  USE Floden family
Flogg family
  USE Flagg family
Flogging
  USE Corporal punishment
      Flagellants and flagellation
Flona de São Francisco de Paula (Brazil)
  USE Floresta Nacional de São Francisco de
        Paula (Brazil)
Flood, Biblical
  USE Deluge
Flood (Hinduism)
  USE Deluge (Hinduism)
Flood (Painting)
  USE Uccello, Paolo di Dono, known as,
        1396 or 7-1475.   Flood
Flood control *(May Subd Geog)*
  UF Flood prevention
      Flood protection
      Prevention of floods
  BT Floods
      Hurricane protection
      Rivers—Regulation
  RT Forest influences
  NT Flood damage prevention
      Flood dams and reservoirs
      Flood forecasting
      Lakes—Regulation
      Levee districts
      Reservoirs—Regulation
      Stream channelization
      Water diversion
  — Law and legislation *(May Subd Geog)*
      UF Flood dams and reservoirs—Law
            and legislation
  — Social aspects *(May Subd Geog)*
      UF Society and flood control
Flood control dams
  USE Flood dams and reservoirs
Flood damage *(May Subd Geog)*
  BT Floods
  SA subdivision Flood damage *under*
        subjects, e.g. Bridges—Flood
        damage; Roads—Flood damage
Flood damage prevention *(May Subd Geog)*
  UF Flood proofing
      Flood protection
  BT City planning
      Flood control
      Floods
Flood damages, Liability for
  USE Liability for flood damages
Flood dams and reservoirs *(May Subd Geog)*
  [TC167 (Hydraulics)]

  [TC540-TC555 (Dams)]
  UF Flood control dams
  BT Dams
      Diversion structures (Hydraulic
        engineering)
      Flood control
      Reservoirs
  NT Dikes (Engineering)
      Fishways
      Levee districts
      Sluice gates
  — Law and legislation
      USE Flood control—Law and
            legislation
Flood family
  UF Flod family
      Flodh family
      Floud family
      Fludd family
Flood forecasting *(May Subd Geog)*
  UF Floods—Forecasting
  BT Flood control
      Flood routing
      Floods
      Geophysical prediction
      Hydrological forecasting
      Stream measurements
Flood icings
  USE Aufeis
Flood insurance
  USE Insurance, Flood
Flood-plain icings
  USE Aufeis
Flood plain management
  USE Floodplain management
Flood plains
  USE Floodplains
Flood prevention
  USE Flood control
Flood proofing
  USE Flood damage prevention
Flood protection
  USE Flood control
      Flood damage prevention
Flood routing
  [GB1203]
  UF Routing, Flood
  BT Floods
      Stream measurements
  NT Flood forecasting
Flood Site (B.C.) *(Not Subd Geog)*
  BT British Columbia—Antiquities
Floodgates
  USE Sluice gates
Flooding ice
  USE Aufeis
Floodlighting
  [TK4399.F55]
  BT Electric lighting
      Lighting
Floodplain ecology *(May Subd Geog)*
  UF Floodplain pool ecology
      Floodwater ecology
  BT Freshwater ecology
      Valley ecology
  NT Floodplain flora
Floodplain flora *(May Subd Geog)*
  [QK108-QK474.5 (Local)]
  BT Botany
      Botany—Ecology
      Floodplain ecology
      Valley flora
  RT Plants, Effect of floods on
Floodplain management *(May Subd Geog)*
  UF Flood plain management
      Management of flood plains
      Management of floodplains
  BT Floodplains
      Watershed management
Floodplain pool ecology
  USE Floodplain ecology

Floodplains *(May Subd Geog)*
  ₍GB562₎
    Works on floodplains of individual rivers are entered under the name of the river valley, e.g. Rhine River Valley.
  UF Flood plains
      River flood plains
  BT Plains
      Valleys
  NT Floodplain management
— **Law and legislation** *(May Subd Geog)*
— **California**
    NT Barton Flats (Calif.)
— **Illinois**
    NT American Bottom (Ill.)
— **Zambia**
    NT Kafue Flats (Zambia)
Floods *(May Subd Geog)*
  ₍GB1201-GB1397 (Physical geography)₎
  ₍HV610 (Relief work)₎
  ₍SD425 (Floods and forests)₎
  ₍TC404-TC535 (Engineering)₎
  UF Inundations
  BT Meteorology
      Natural disasters
      Rain and rainfall
      Water
  RT Rivers
  NT Flood control
      Flood damage
      Flood damage prevention
      Flood forecasting
      Flood routing
      Forest influences
      Plants, Effect of floods on
      Storm surges
— Forecasting
    USE Flood forecasting
— **Religious aspects**
    NT Deluge
Floodwater ecology
  USE Floodplain ecology
Floor area, Industrial
  USE Floor space, Industrial
Floor cleaning machines
  UF Floor machines
  BT Floors—Maintenance and repair
Floor coverings *(May Subd Geog)*
  ₍HD9937₎
  BT Flooring
      Interior decoration
  NT Carpets
      Linoleum
      Rugs
Floor coverings industry *(May Subd Geog)*
  ₍HD9937₎
Floor hockey
  USE Indoor hockey
Floor machines
  USE Floor cleaning machines
Floor materials
  USE Flooring
Floor of mouth
  USE Mouth floor
Floor plans
  USE Architecture, Domestic—Designs and plans
Floor polishers
  USE Floor polishing machines
Floor polishing machines
  UF Floor polishers
  BT Floors—Maintenance and repair
      Household appliances, Electric
— Tariff
    USE Tariff on floor polishing machines
Floor rock (Dance)
  USE Break dancing
Floor space, Industrial *(May Subd Geog)*
  UF Floor area, Industrial

BT Business
    Factories—Design and construction
    Industry
    Interior architecture
Floor traders (Finance) *(May Subd Geog)*
  ₍HG4621₎
  UF Traders, Floor (Finance)
  BT Brokers
      Commodity exchanges
      Stock-exchange
Flooring
  ₍TH2521₎
  UF Floor materials
  BT Building materials
      Floors
  NT Floor coverings
— Costs
    USE Flooring—Estimates and costs
— **Estimates and costs**
    UF Flooring—Costs
— **Skid resistance**
Flooring, Asphalt
  UF Asphalt flooring
Flooring, Concrete
  UF Concrete flooring
  BT Concrete construction
Flooring, Plastic
  UF Plastic flooring
  BT Plastics
Flooring, Tile
  UF Tile flooring
  BT Tiles
Flooring, Wooden
  UF Wood flooring
  NT Parquet floors
Floors *(May Subd Geog)*
  ₍NA2970 (Architecture)₎
  ₍TH2521 (Building)₎
  BT Architecture—Details
      Building
      Carpentry
  NT Bridges—Floors
      Cold-storage lockers—Floors
      Flooring
      Industrial buildings—Floors
      Packing-houses—Floors
      Pavements, Mosaic
      Slaughtering and slaughter-houses—Floors
— **Maintenance and repair**
    NT Floor cleaning machines
        Floor polishing machines
— **Thermal properties**
Floors, Concrete
  ₍TH2521₎
  BT Concrete construction
Floors, Mosaic
  UF Mosaic floors
  BT Mosaics
Floors, Terrazzo
  USE Terrazzo
Floors, Wooden
  UF Wood floors
  BT Building, Wooden
Floors (Bridges)
  USE Bridges—Floors
Flophouses
  USE Lodging-houses
Floppy mitral valve syndrome
  USE Mitral valve—Displacement
Flora
  USE Botany
       Plants
Flora, Antarctic
  USE Botany—Antarctic regions
Flora, Arctic
  USE Botany—Arctic regions
Flora, Estuarine
  USE Estuarine flora
Flora, Hot spring
  USE Hot spring flora

Flora, Hurricane, 1963
  USE Hurricane Flora, 1963
Floral arrangers
  USE Flower arrangers
Floral decoration
  USE Flower arrangement
Floral decoration and ornament
  USE Decoration and ornament—Plant forms
Floral designers
  USE Flower arrangers
Floral games *(May Subd Geog)*
  UF Games, Floral
      Jeux floraux
  BT Literature—Competitions
      Poetry—Competitions
Floral potpourris
  USE Potpourris (Scented floral mixtures)
Florances family
  USE Florence family
Floreana (Galapagos Islands)
  USE Santa María Island (Galapagos Islands)
Florence (Italy)
— **Description**
— — **1981-**
— **History**
— — **To 1421**
      NT Ciompi, Revolt of the, 1378
— — **1421-1737**
      NT Orti Oricellari Conspiracy, 1522
          Orti Oricellari Group
          Pazzi Conspiracy, 1478
— — **1737-1860**
        ₍DG738.3-738.6₎
— — **1860-1945**
        ₍DG738.5-738.79₎
— — **1945-**
        ₍DG738.7-738.79₎
— **Intellectual life**
    NT Orti Oricellari Group
— **Politics and government**
— — **To 1421**
— — **1421-1737**
— — **1737-1860**
— — **1860-1945**
— — **1945-**
Florence (Italy). Lion Rosso
  USE Lion Rosso (Florence, Italy)
Florence (Italy). Rifredi
  USE Rifredi (Florence, Italy)
Florence (Italy). Riofredi
  USE Rifredi (Florence, Italy)
Florence (Italy). Riofredo
  USE Rifredi (Florence, Italy)
Florence family
  UF Fleurance family
      Florances family
      Florences family
      Florrence family
      Flourance family
      Flowrance family
Florence Street Site (Cahokia, Ill.)
  (Not Subd Geog)
  BT Illinois—Antiquities
Florences family
  USE Florence family
Florentine football
  UF Calcio fiorentino, Gioco del
      Gioco del calcio fiorentino
  BT Football
      Rugby football
Flores, Battle of, 1591
  ₍DA87.5 1591₎
  BT Azores—History
      Great Britain—History, Naval—Tudors, 1485-1603
Flores complex-toothed rat
  USE Papagomys armandvillei
Flores family
  USE Flórez family

Flores giant rat
USE Papagomys armandvillei
Flores Island (Indonesia)
UF Floris Island (Indonesia)
Mangarai Island (Indonesia)
Pulau Flores (Indonesia)
Pulau Floris (Indonesia)
Pulau Mangarai (Indonesia)
BT Islands—Indonesia
Sunda Islands, Lesser (Indonesia)
Flores Island giant tree rat
USE Papagomys armandvillei
Flores martis
USE Ferric chloride
Floresta Nacional de São Francisco de Paula (Brazil)
UF Flona de São Francisco de Paula (Brazil)
Joaquim Francisco de Assis Brasil, Parque Florestal (Brazil)
Parque Florestal Joaquim Francisco de Assis Brasil (Brazil)
São Francisco de Paula, Floresta Nacional de (Brazil)
BT Forest reserves—Brazil
National parks and reserves—Brazil
Flórez family
UF Flores family
Floriculture *(May Subd Geog)*
[SB403-SB450]
Here are entered works on the commercial growing of flowers and ornamental plants. Works on home flower growing are entered under Flower gardening.
BT Botany
Horticulture
Ornamental horticulture
Plants
RT Flowers
Ornamental plant industry
SA *particular types of plants and flowers, e.g. Aquatic plants; Chrysanthemums; Climbing plants; Dahlias; Peonies*
NT Annuals (Plants)
Biennials (Plants)
Bulbs
Cold-frames
Corms
Cut flowers
Floriculturists
Florists
Flowers—Marketing
Greenhouses
House plant industry
Orchid culture
Perennials
Plant-breeding
Plants, Ornamental
Rose culture
Window-gardening
— Exhibitions
USE Flower shows
Floriculturists *(May Subd Geog)*
BT Floriculture
Florida
— Antiquities
NT Cypress Creek Site (Fla.)
Deerstand Site (Fla.)
Fort Center Site (Fla.)
Granada Site (Miami, Fla.)
Harney Flats Site (Fla.)
Josslyn Island Mound (Fla.)
McKeithen Site (Fla.)
— Capital and capitol
NT Florida State Capitol (Tallahassee, Fla.)
— Description and travel
— — To 1865
— — 1865-1950
— — 1951-1980
— — 1981-

— History
[F306-320]
— — To 1565
— — Cession to the United States, 1819
— — To 1821
— — Huguenot colony, 1562-1565
BT Huguenots—Florida
— — Spanish colony, 1565-1763
NT St. Augustine Expedition, 1743
— — English colony, 1763-1784
— — Revolution, 1775-1783
— — Spanish colony, 1784-1821
— — War of 1812
— — Seminole Wars, 1817-1858
USE Seminole War, 1st, 1817-1818
Seminole War, 2d, 1835-1842
Seminole War, 3d, 1855-1858
— — 1821-1865
— — Civil War, 1861-1865
[E558]
— — — Centennial celebrations, etc.
— — 1865-
— — War of 1898
— Languages
NT Mikasuki language
— Politics and government
— — 1565-1763
— — 1821-1865
— — Civil War, 1861-1865
— — 1865-1950
— — 1951-
— Public buildings
USE Public buildings—Florida
Florida automatic computer
USE Seac computer
Florida beggarweed
USE Beggar-weed
Florida crocodile
USE American crocodile
Florida Everglades (Fla.)
USE Everglades (Fla.)
Florida fern caterpillar
[SB945.F6]
Florida gallinule
USE Gallinula chloropus
Florida Interlibrary Loan Improvement Project
BT Inter-library loans—Florida
Florida Islands (Solomon Islands)
BT Islands—Solomon Islands
Florida Keys (Fla.)
UF Keys, Florida (Fla.)
BT Islands—Florida
Florida language
[PL6240]
UF Anudha language
Gela language
Nggela language
BT Melanesian languages
Florida Library Information Network
BT Library information networks—Florida
Florida manatee
USE Trichechus manatus
Florida moss
USE Spanish moss
Florida Panther National Wildlife Refuge (Fla.)
BT National parks and reserves—Florida
Wildlife refuges—Florida
Florida poisontree
USE Metopium toxifera
Florida pompano
[QL638.C25 (Zoology)]
[SH167.P7 (Culture)]
UF Pompano, Florida
Trachinotus carolinus
Florida State Capitol (Tallahassee, Fla.)
UF State Capitol (Tallahassee, Fla.)
BT Florida—Capital and capitol

Florida Street (Buenos Aires, Argentina)
USE Calle Florida (Buenos Aires, Argentina)
Florida velvet bean
[SB205.B3]
BT Beans
Florida War, 1835-1842
USE Seminole War, 2d, 1835-1842
Florida water rat
USE Neofiber alleni
Florida wax scale
[QL527.C6 (Entomology)]
[SB945.F64 (Pest)]
UF Ceroplastes floridensis
Wax scale, Florida
BT Citrus fruits—Diseases and pests
Florida worm lizard
USE Rhineura floridana
Floridan Aquifer
BT Aquifers—Southern States
Florideae
USE Red algae
Florideophyceae
USE Red algae
Florideophycidae
USE Red algae
Florin
Florio family *(Not Subd Geog)*
Floris Island (Indonesia)
USE Flores Island (Indonesia)
Florissant Valley (Mo.)
BT Valleys—Missouri
Florist suppliers *(May Subd Geog)*
UF Suppliers, Florist
RT Florists
Florists *(May Subd Geog)*
[SB443]
BT Floriculture
Flowers—Marketing
Ornamental horticulture
Ornamental plant industry
RT Florist suppliers
Garden centers (Retail trade)
Nursery dealers
— Credit guides
[HF5585.F6]
Florist's cyclamen *(May Subd Geog)*
[QK495.P95 (Botany)]
[SB413.C9 (Ornamental plant)]
UF Cyclamen indicum
Cyclamen persicum
Cyclamen vernale
Shooting star flower
BT Cyclamen
Flornoy family
USE Flournoy family
Florrence family
USE Florence family
Flory family
USE Fleury family
Floss, Dental
USE Dental floss
Flotation
[TN523]
BT Ore-dressing
Separation (Technology)
NT Sewage—Purification—Flotation
— Equipment and supplies
NT Flotation reagents
Flotation reagents
[TN523]
BT Chemical tests and reagents
Flotation—Equipment and supplies
Flötenuhr
USE Musical clock
Flötenwerk
USE Musical clock
Flotilla, Freedom, 1980
USE Mariel Boatlift, 1980
Floud family
USE Flood family

Flounder, Gulf
USE Gulf flounder
Flounder, Southern
USE Southern flounder
Flounder, Starry
USE Starry flounder
Flounder, Winter
USE Winter flounder
Flounder fisheries
USE Flatfish fisheries
Flounders
USE Flatfishes
Flounders, Left-eyed
USE Bothidae
Flounders, Right-eyed
USE Pleuronectidae
Flour
[TS2120-TS2159 (Manufacture)]
[TX393 (Food supply)]
[TX558.W5 (Food values)]
[TX595.F6 (Adulteration)]
UF Breadstuffs
BT Cereal products
Wheat products
RT Grain—Milling
Wheat
NT Banana flour
Barley
Batters (Food)
Bread
Dough
Graham flour
Grain
Oats
Soybean flour
— **Effect of radiation on**
UF Flour, Effect of radiation on
BT Radiation
— **Microbiology**
Flour, Effect of radiation on
USE Flour—Effect of radiation on
Flour and feed trade (May Subd Geog)
[HD2769.M58 (Trusts)]
[HD9056]
[HF2651.F6 (Tariff)]
UF Feed industry and trade
Feed trade
Milling trade
NT Feed mills
Feeds—Marketing
Pet food industry
— **Seasonal variations**
Flour as feed
Flour as food (May Subd Geog)
[TX558.W5]
BT Food
Flour beetles
USE Tribolium
Flour-mills (May Subd Geog)
[TS2120-2159]
UF Grist-mills
BT Food processing plants
Grain—Milling
Milling machinery
— **Electric equipment**
— **Employees** (May Subd Geog)
NT Trade-unions—Flour-mill
employees
Wages—Flour-mill employees
— — Collective labor agreements
USE Collective labor agreements—
Flour-mill employees
— **Equipment and supplies**
— — Appraisal
USE Flour-mills—Equipment and
supplies—Valuation
— — — **Valuation**
[TS2149]
UF Flour-mills—Equipment and
supplies—Appraisal
— **Fumigation**

BT Fumigation
— **Industrial capacity**
— **Law and legislation** (May Subd Geog)
— **Management**
[TS2149]
Flourance family
USE Florence family
Flourensia
[QK495.C74]
BT Compositae
Flournois family
USE Flournoy family
Flournoy family
UF Flornoy family
Flournois family
Flournoys family
Flournoys family
USE Flournoy family
Flours family
USE Flowers family
Flow, Axoplasmic
USE Axonal transport
Flow, Base (Aerodynamics)
USE Base flow (Aerodynamics)
Flow, Groundwater
USE Groundwater flow
Flow, Irrigation return
USE Irrigation—Tailwater recovery systems
Flow, Multiphase
USE Multiphase flow
Flow, One-dimensional
USE One-dimensional flow
Flow, Polyphase
USE Multiphase flow
Flow, Shear
USE Shear flow
Flow, Stratified
USE Stratified flow
Flow, Stream
USE Streamflow
Flow, Transient (Aerodynamics)
USE Unsteady flow (Aerodynamics)
Flow, Transition
USE Transition flow
Flow, Two-phase
USE Two-phase flow
Flow, Unsteady (Aerodynamics)
USE Unsteady flow (Aerodynamics)
Flow blue china
USE Blue and white transfer ware
Flow chart generators
UF Automatic flowcharting
Flowcharting, Automatic
Generators, Flow chart
BT Electronic data processing
documentation
Electronic digital computers—
Programming
Flow charts
Generators (Computer programs)
Flow charts
UF Flow diagrams
Flow process charts
Flowcharts
BT Graphic methods
System analysis
NT Flow chart generators
Flow cytofluorometry
USE Flow cytometry
Flow cytometry
UF Cell counting, Laser
Cell separation, Laser
Cell sorting, Laser
Flow cytofluorometry
Flow cytophotometry
Laser cell counting
Laser cell separation
Laser cell sorting

BT Cancer—Diagnosis
Cytology—Technique
Hematology—Technique
Immunology—Technique
— **Diagnostic use**
[RC270.3.F56 (Cancer diagnosis)]
BT Diagnosis, Cytologic
Flow cytophotometry
USE Flow cytometry
Flow diagrams
USE Flow charts
Flow graphs
USE Flowgraphs
Flow measurement
USE Flow meters
Flow meter industry (May Subd Geog)
BT Flow meters
Flow meters
[TC177]
UF Current meters (Fluid dynamics)
Flow measurement
Flowmeters
Fluid meters
Meters, Flow
BT Hydraulic engineering—Instruments
Hydraulic measurements
Stream-gaging stations
Stream measurements
Water-meters
NT Acoustic velocity meters
Blood flow—Measurement
Flow meter industry
Gas-meters
Metering pumps
Parshall flumes
Pitot tubes
Rheometers
Rotameters
Steam-meters
Water current meters
— **Calibration**
Flow of bulk solids
USE Bulk solids flow
Flow of funds (May Subd Geog)
BT Finance
NT National income
— **Accounting**
Flow of gas
USE Gas flow
Flow of news, International
USE Communication—International
cooperation
Foreign news
Flow of water
USE Hydraulics
Flow process charts
USE Flow charts
Flow turning (Metalwork)
USE Metal-spinning
Flow visualization
UF Visualization of flow
BT Fluid dynamics
SA subdivision Flow visualization under
subjects, e.g. Wind tunnels—Flow
visualization
Flow visualization in wind tunnels
USE Wind tunnels—Flow visualization
Flowcharting, Automatic
USE Flow chart generators
Flowcharts
USE Flow charts
Flower arrangement (May Subd Geog)
[SB445-449]
UF Floral decoration
Flowers—Arrangement
BT Cut flowers
Decoration and ornament
Flowers
Table setting and decoration
NT Bridal bouquets
Corsages

Flower arrangement (Continued)
    Dried flower arrangement
    Driftwood arrangement
    Flower leis
    Miniature flower arrangement
— Exhibitions
    USE Flower arrangement shows
Flower arrangement, Chinese
  (May Subd Geog)
  [SB450.7]
  UF Chinese flower arrangement
Flower arrangement, Chinese, [Japanese, etc.]
— History
Flower arrangement, Japanese
  (May Subd Geog)
  [SB450-450.65]
  UF Ikebana
    Japanese flower arrangement
— Ichiyo school
  UF Ichioyo ikebana
— Ikenobō school
  [SB450.5.I4]
  UF Ikenobō ikebana
— Koryū school
  UF Koryū ikebana
— Koryū Sōkenryū school
  [SB450.5.K]
  UF Koryū Sōkenryū ikebana
— Mishōryū school
  [SB450.5.M]
  UF Kyōto Mishōryū ikebana
    Mishōryū ikebana
— Ohara school
  [SB450.5.O]
  UF Ohara ikebana
— Omuro school
  UF Omuro ikebana
    Omuroryū ikebana
— Rikyū Koryū school
  UF Rikyū Koryū ikebana
— Ryūsei school
  [SB450.5.R]
  UF Ryūseiha ikebana
— Senkei school
  UF Senkei ikebana
    Senkeiryū ikebana
— Shōgetsudō Koryū school
  UF Shōgetsudō Koryū ikebana
— Shōka style
  UF Shōka ikebana
— Sōbi school
  [SB450.5.S]
  UF Sōbi ikebana
    Sōbiryū ikebana
— Sōgetsu school
  [SB450.5.S6]
  UF Sōgetsu ikebana
Flower arrangement, Korean
  (May Subd Geog)
  [SB450.8]
  UF Korean flower arrangement
Flower arrangement, Thai (May Subd Geog)
  [SB450.87]
  UF Thai flower arrangement
Flower arrangement in art
Flower arrangement in churches
  (May Subd Geog)
  [SB449.5.C4]
  UF Church flower arrangement
  BT Church decoration and ornament
Flower arrangement shows
  (May Subd Geog)
  [SB449.15]
  UF Flower arrangement—Exhibitions
  BT Flower shows

Flower arrangers (May Subd Geog)
  UF Arrangers, Flower
    Designers, Floral
    Floral arrangers
    Floral designers
    Flower masters
    Masters, Flower
Flower bugs
  USE Anthocoridae
Flower cookery
  USE Cookery (Flowers)
Flower drawing
  USE Flower painting and illustration
Flower family
  USE Flowers family
Flower Festival in Genzano (Ballet)
  UF Blomsterfesten i Genzano (Ballet)
    Blumenfest von Genzano (Ballet)
  BT Ballets
Flower flies
  USE Syrphidae
Flower-Garden Peninsula (Spitsbergen Island, Norway)
  USE Blomesletta Peninsula (Spitsbergen Island, Norway)
Flower gardening (May Subd Geog)
  [SB403-SB413]
    Here are entered works on home flower growing. Works on the commercial growing of flowers and ornamental plants are entered under Floriculture.
  BT Flowers
    Gardening
  NT Bedding plants
    Wild flower gardening
Flower judging
  USE Flower shows—Judging
Flower language
  [GR780-790]
  UF Flowers, Language of
    Language of flowers
  BT Plants—Folklore
  RT Flowers in literature
    Symbolism of flowers
Flower leis (May Subd Geog)
  [SB449.5.L4]
  BT Flower arrangement
    Leis
Flower masters
  USE Flower arrangers
Flower painting and illustration
  (May Subd Geog)
  UF Flower drawing
    Flowers, Painting of
  BT Botanical illustration
    Drawing
    Painting
  RT Flowers in art
  NT Rosemaling
Flower prints
  USE Flowers in art
Flower shows (May Subd Geog)
  [SB441]
  UF Floriculture—Exhibitions
  BT Exhibitions
    Horticultural exhibitions
  NT Flower arrangement shows
— Judging
  UF Flower judging
    Flowers—Judging
Flowering bean
  USE Scarlet runner bean
Flowering bulbs
  USE Bulbs
Flowering cherries (May Subd Geog)
  [QK495.R78 (Botany)]
  [SB413.C5 (Ornamental plants)]
  UF Cherries, Flowering
  BT Flowering trees
  NT Japanese flowering cherry
Flowering cornel
  USE Flowering dogwood

Flowering dogwood
  UF American dogwood
    Cornus florida
    Flowering cornel
  BT Dogwood
    Flowering trees
Flowering of plants
  USE Plants, Flowering of
Flowering plants
  USE Angiosperms
    Flowers
Flowering plums (May Subd Geog)
  [QK495.R78 (Botany)]
  BT Flowering trees
    Plum
    Prunus
  NT Prunus triloba
Flowering plums in art
  UF Plum blossoms in art
Flowering shrubs (May Subd Geog)
  BT Flowering woody plants
    Ornamental shrubs
  NT Bougainvillea
    Crape myrtle, Common
    Hibiscus syriacus
Flowering time
  USE Plants, Flowering of—Flowering time
Flowering trees (May Subd Geog)
  UF Trees, Flowering
  BT Flowering woody plants
    Ornamental trees
  NT Crape myrtle, Common
    Flowering cherries
    Flowering dogwood
    Flowering plums
    Plumeria
Flowering woody plants (May Subd Geog)
  [SB435]
  BT Ornamental woody plants
  NT Flowering shrubs
    Flowering trees
Flowerpeckers
  [QL696.P242]
  UF Dicaeidae
  BT Passeriformes
Flowerpots
  BT Plant containers
    Plants, Potted
    Pottery
Flowers (May Subd Geog)
  [GT5160 (Manners and customs)]
  [QK (Botany)]
  [SB403-SB450 (Culture)]
  UF Flowering plants
  BT Botany
    Horticultural crops
    Inflorescence
    Plants
    Plants, Cultivated
  RT Floriculture
  SA names of flowers, e.g. Carnations, Roses, Violets
  NT Annuals (Plants)
    Anthuriums
    Bedding plants
    Biennials (Plants)
    Cleistogamy
    Cookery (Flowers)
    Cut flowers
    Double flowers
    Everlasting flowers
    Flower arrangement
    Flower gardening
    National flowers
    Nectaries
    Oil flower plants
    Plants, Flowering of
    Plants, Flowering of—Flowering time
    Pollinaria
    Pollination
    Prefectural flowers

Provincial flowers
State flowers
Wild flowers
— **Anatomy**
[QK653-QK659]
[QK692-QK698]
BT Botany—Anatomy
RT Flowers—Morphology
— Arrangement
USE Flower arrangement
— **Collection and preservation**
BT Plants—Collection and
preservation
NT Flowers—Drying
Preserved flower pictures
— **Color**
[QK669 (Nomenclature)]
UF Color of flowers
RT Color in gardening
— — **Fading**
UF Color fading of flowers
Fading of the color of flowers
— — — **Control**
[SB442.5]
UF Control of the color fading of
flowers
— **Drying**
BT Flowers—Collection and
preservation
NT Dried flower arrangement
— **Gift-books**
— Judging
USE Flower shows—Judging
— **Marketing**
BT Floriculture
NT Florists
— — **Periodicals**
— **Morphology**
[QK653-9]
BT Botany—Morphology
RT Flowers—Anatomy
NT Calyx (Botany)
— **Odor**
UF Fragrance of flowers
BT Odors
RT Aromatic plants
NT Gardens, Fragrant
— **Religious aspects**
NT Flowers in the Bible
— — **Buddhism,** [**Christianity, etc.**]
— Tariff
USE Tariff on cut flowers
Flowers, Artificial
USE Artificial flowers
Flowers, Bead
USE Bead flowers
Flowers, Bread
USE Bread flowers
Flowers, Ceramic
USE Ceramic flowers
Flowers, Clay
USE Ceramic flowers
Flowers, Fabric
USE Fabric flowers
Flowers, Forcing of
USE Forcing (Plants)
Flowers, Language of
USE Flower language
Flowers, Painting of
USE Flower painting and illustration
Flowers, Papier-mâché
USE Papier-mâché flowers
Flowers, Ribbon
USE Ribbon flowers
Flowers, Silk
USE Silk flowers
Flowers, Symbolism of
USE Symbolism of flowers
Flowers, Wax
USE Wax flowers

Flowers, Wild
USE Wild flowers
Flowers (in heraldry)
Flowers family *(Not Subd Geog)*
UF Flours family
Flower family
RT Fletcher family
Flowers in art
UF Flower prints
BT Plants in art
RT Flower painting and illustration
SA *names of specific flowers in art, e.g.*
Carnations in art
NT Decoration and ornament—Plant
forms
Flowers in literature
UF Flowers in poetry
BT Plants in literature
RT Flower language
NT Roses in literature
Flowers in poetry
USE Flowers in literature
Flowers in the Bible
UF Bible—Flowers
BT Flowers—Religious aspects
Plants in the Bible
Flowers of tin
USE Stannic oxide
Flowgraphs
UF Flow graphs
Signal flowgraphs
BT Graphic methods
System analysis
Flowmeter, Laser
USE Laser Doppler velocimeter
Flowmeters
USE Flow meters
Flowoff
USE Runoff
Flowrance family
USE Florence family
Flows, Anosov
USE Anosov flows
Floyd family
Flu
USE Influenza
Fluck family
UF Flucke family
Flucker family
Flucke family
USE Fluck family
Flucker family
USE Fluck family
Fluctuating exchange rates
USE Foreign exchange
Fluctuations, Cross section (Nuclear physics)
USE Cross section fluctuations (Nuclear
physics)
Fluctuations, Rainfall
USE Rainfall anomalies
Fluctuations, Valence
USE Valence fluctuations
Fluctuations (Physics)
[QC6.4.F58]
UF Variations (Physics)
BT Stochastic processes
SA *subdivision* Fluctuations *under*
subjects, e.g. Semiconductors—
Fluctuations; Solids—Fluctuations
NT Brownian motion processes
Cross section fluctuations (Nuclear
physics)
Oscillations
Fluctuations in ferromagnetic materials
USE Ferromagnetic materials—Fluctuations
Fluctuations in semiconductors
USE Semiconductors—Fluctuations
Fluctuations in solids
USE Solids—Fluctuations
Fludd family
USE Flood family

Flue dust
USE Fly ash
Flue gases *(May Subd Geog)*
[TD885]
UF Stack gases
BT Combustion gases
Factory and trade waste
NT Ships—Inert gas systems
— **Desulphurization**
BT Desulphuration
— **Measurement**
— **Physiological effect**
NT Plants, Effect of flue gases on
— **Purification**
— — **Equipment and supplies**
BT Pollution control equipment
Flue pipes (Organ pipes)
UF Flues (Organ pipes)
BT Organ-pipes
Fluegelhorn
[ML975-7]
UF Flicorno
Flugelhorn
BT Brass instruments
NT Alto horn
— **Studies and exercises (Jazz)**
[MT493.3]
Fluegelhorn and organ music
UF Organ and fluegelhorn music
NT Chorale preludes (Fluegelhorn and
organ)
Fluegelhorn and piano music
[M270.F]
[M271.F]
UF Piano and fluegelhorn music
Fluegelhorn and piano music, Arranged
[M270.F]
[M271.F]
NT Fluegelhorn with string orchestra—
Solo with piano
Fluegelhorn music
[M110.F53]
NT Brass quartets (Baritone, fluegelhorn,
horn, trumpet)
Fluegelhorn with band *(May Subd Geog)*
[M1205-M1206]
Fluegelhorn with string orchestra
[M1134.F7]
[M1135.F7]
RT Concertos (Fluegelhorn with string
orchestra)
— **Solo with piano**
[M1135.F7]
BT Fluegelhorn and piano music,
Arranged
Flueggea
[QK495.E9 (Botany)]
UF Flueggia
Fluggea
BT Euphorbiaceae
Flueggia
USE Flueggea
Flues
[TH2281]
UF Smoke-pipes
BT Ventilation
RT Chimneys
NT Gas appliances—Vents
Flues (Organ pipes)
USE Flue pipes (Organ pipes)
Fluetsch family
UF Flutsch family
Flugelhorn
USE Fluegelhorn
Fluggea
USE Flueggea
Fluhart family
UF Fluharty family
Fluharty family
USE Fluhart family

Fluid amplifiers
  UF Amplifiers, Fluid
  BT Fluid dynamics
      Fluidic devices
Fluid balance disorders
  USE Body fluid disorders
Fluid bed processes
  USE Fluidization
Fluid copying processes
  [Z48]
  UF Liquid copying processes
      Spirit duplicating
  BT Copying processes
Fluid couplings
  USE Hydraulic couplings
Fluid dynamic measurements
  UF Fluid dynamics—Measurement
      Measurements, Fluid dynamic
  BT Physical measurements
  NT Laser Doppler velocimeter
      Radioactive tracers in fluid dynamic
        measurements
Fluid dynamics
  BT Fluid mechanics
      Fluids
  SA *subdivisions* Fluid dynamics *and* Fluid
        models *under subjects, e.g.*
        Turbomachines—Fluid dynamics;
        Geophysics—Fluid models
  NT Acceleration potential
      Acoustic streaming
      Aerodynamics
      Blades
      Body fluid flow
      Boundary layer
      Boundary layer control
      Bulk solids flow
      Cascades (Fluid dynamics)
      Darcy's law
      Diffusers
      Eddies
      Electrohydrodynamics
      Flow visualization
      Fluid amplifiers
      Fluid-film bearings
      Fluidization
      Gas dynamics
      Heat—Convection, Natural
      Hydrodynamics
      Ion flow dynamics
      Laminar flow
      Magnetohydrodynamics
      Mass transfer
      Mixing
      Molecular acoustics
      Multiphase flow
      Navier-Stokes equations
      Newtonian fluids
      One-dimensional flow
      Plumes (Fluid dynamics)
      Rayleigh waves
      Relativistic fluid dynamics
      Rossby number
      Shear flow
      Shock waves
      Smoke plumes
      Stratified flow
      Surface waves
      Transition flow
      Two-phase flow
      Viscous flow
      Vortex-motion
      Wakes (Fluid dynamics)
  — **Approximation methods**
  — **Computer programs**
      NT PHOENICS (Computer program)
  — **Measurement**
      USE Fluid dynamic measurements

Fluid dynamics (Space environment)
  UF Space flight—Fluid dynamics
      Space fluid dynamics
      Space vehicles—Fluid dynamics
  BT Space environment
  NT Rarefied gas dynamics
Fluid energy mills
  USE Jet mills
Fluid fertilizers
  USE Liquid fertilizers
Fluid-film bearings
  UF Bearings, Fluid-film
      Hydrostatic bearings
  BT Bearings (Machinery)
      Fluid dynamics
      Lubrication and lubricants
  NT Gas-lubricated bearings
Fluid fuel reactors
  [TK9203.F5]
  BT Nuclear reactors
Fluid inclusions *(May Subd Geog)*
  [QE364.2.F47]
  UF Inclusions, Fluid
      Liquid inclusions
  BT Mineralogy
Fluid ingestion
  USE Drinking (Physiology)
Fluid jet cutting
  USE Jet cutting
Fluid logic
  UF Fluidic logic
  BT Automatic control
      Fluidic devices
      Logic design
      Switching theory
Fluid mechanics
  UF Hydromechanics
  BT Continuum mechanics
  RT Fluids
  NT Contact angle
      Diaphragms (Mechanical devices)
      Fluid dynamics
      Fluid power technology
      Hodograph equations
      Hydraulic engineering
      Hydraulics
      Hydrometer
      Hydrostatics
      Pascal's law
      Splashes
Fluid meters
  USE Flow meters
Fluid power technology
  BT Fluid mechanics
  SA *subdivision* Hydraulic drive *under
        subjects, e.g.* Diesel locomotives—
        Hydraulic drive
  NT Fluidic devices
      Hydraulic control
      Hydraulic machinery
      Jet cutting
      Pneumatic control
      Pneumatic machinery
Fluid rotor gyroscopes
  [TJ209]
  UF Hydrodynamic gyroscopes
  BT Gyroscopes
Fluid therapy
  [RM170]
  UF Fluids—Therapeutic use
  BT Body fluids
      Water-electrolyte balance (Physiology)
  NT Hypertonic solutions—Therapeutic use
  — **Computer programs**
      NT Fluidmod (Computer program)
Fluid therapy for children *(May Subd Geog)*
  [RJ53.F5]
  BT Children—Diseases—Treatment
Fluid trench construction
  USE Slurry trench construction

Fluidic computers
  [TJ853]
  UF Hydraulic computers
      Pneumatic computers
  BT Computers
      Fluidic devices
Fluidic devices
  BT Fluid power technology
  NT Fluid amplifiers
      Fluid logic
      Fluidic computers
      Pneumatic control valves
Fluidic logic
  USE Fluid logic
Fluidization
  [TP156.F65]
  UF Fluid bed processes
      Fluidized systems
  BT Bulk solids flow
      Catalysis
      Chemical engineering
      Cracking process
      Fluid dynamics
      Particles
      Separation (Technology)
  NT Fluidized-bed furnaces
      Fluidized reactors
      Spouted bed processes
Fluidized-bed combustion
  BT Combustion
  RT Fluidized-bed furnaces
Fluidized-bed furnaces
  [TH7140]
  UF Furnaces, Fluidized-bed
  BT Fluidization
      Furnaces
  RT Fluidized-bed combustion
Fluidized reactors
  UF Reactors, Fluidized
  BT Fluidization
      Nuclear reactors
Fluidized systems
  USE Fluidization
Fluidmod (Computer program)
  BT Computer programs
      Fluid therapy—Computer programs
Fluids
  [QA901-QA930 (Analytical
      mechanics)]
  [QC141-QC168 (Physics)]
  BT Hydraulics
      Mechanics
      Physics
  RT Fluid mechanics
      Hydrostatics
      Permeability
  NT Drops
      Fluid dynamics
      Gases
      Hydraulic fluids
      Jets
      Liquids
      Magnetic fluids
      Newtonian fluids
      Osmosis
      Rotating masses of fluid
      Solvents
  — **Acoustic properties**
      NT Underwater acoustics
  — **Migration**
      UF Migration of fluids
      BT Petroleum—Geology
      RT Groundwater flow
  — Therapeutic use
      USE Fluid therapy
  — **Thermal properties**
Fluids, Body
  USE Body fluids
Fluids, Drilling
  USE Drilling muds

1378

Fluids and humors, Animal
  USE Body fluids
Flukes, Liver
  USE Liver flukes
Flumendosa River (Sardinia)
  UF Fiume Flumendosa (Sardinia)
  BT Rivers—Italy
Flumes
    [TC175 (Hydraulics)]
    [TC933 (Irrigation)]
    [TJ847 (Water-power)]
  BT Channels (Hydraulic engineering)
     Diversion structures (Hydraulic
       engineering)
     Water-power
  NT Irrigation canals and flumes
     Parshall flumes
  — **Models**
  — — **Calibration**
Flunitrazepam *(May Subd Geog)*
    [RM666.F52]
  UF Fluorophenyldihydrom
       ethylnitrobenzodiazepine
     Fluridrazepam
  BT Benzodiazepines
     Hypnotics
     Tranquilizing drugs
Fluoborates
Fluorene
  UF Benzindene
     Diphenylenemethane
  BT Methane
  NT Cycloheptafluorene
Fluorenylacetamide
  USE Acetylaminofluorene
Fluorescein
    [QD441 (Chemistry)]
  UF Resorcinolphthalein
  BT Dyes and dyeing
     Phthaleins
  NT Fluorescence angiography
     Sulphonfluorescein
Fluorescein angiography
  USE Fluorescence angiography
Fluorescence
    [QC477]
  BT Luminescence
     Radioactivity
  NT Fluorescent lighting
     Fluorescent screens
     Fluorimeter
     Fluorimetry
     Immunofluorescence
     Mössbauer effect
     Optical brighteners
     Superfluorescence
Fluorescence, Sensitized
    [QC477.4]
  UF Sensitized fluorescence
Fluorescence analysis
  USE Fluorimetry
Fluorescence angiography
    [RE79.A5]
  UF Fluorescein angiography
     Fundus fluorescence photography
  BT Angiography
     Eye—Blood-vessels—Radiography
     Fluorescein
     Fundus oculi
     Photography, Ophthalmic
Fluorescence cytophotometry
  USE Cytofluorometry
Fluorescence microscopy
  BT Immunofluorescence
     Microscope and microscopy
  NT Direct epifluorescent filter technique
     Fluorescent antibody technique
Fluorescence spectrometry
  USE Fluorescence spectroscopy
Fluorescence spectroscopy
    [QD96.F56 (Chemistry)]

    [QH324.9.F4 (Biochemistry)]
  UF Fluorescence spectrometry
     Spectrometry, Fluorescence
     Spectroscopy, Fluorescence
  BT Luminescence spectroscopy
     Spectrum analysis
Fluorescent antibody technique
  BT Fluorescence microscopy
     Immunofluorescence
     Immunoglobulins
Fluorescent antigen technique
  BT Immunofluorescence
Fluorescent bleaches
  USE Optical brighteners
Fluorescent brighteners
  USE Optical brighteners
Fluorescent excitation analysis
  USE X-ray spectroscopy
Fluorescent lamp industry *(May Subd Geog)*
Fluorescent lamps
    [TK4386]
  UF Electric lamps, Fluorescent
  BT Fluorescent lighting
Fluorescent lighting
    [TK4386]
  UF Electric lighting, Fluorescent
  BT Electric discharge lighting
     Fluorescence
  NT Fluorescent lamps
  — **Health aspects** *(May Subd Geog)*
      UF Fluorescent lighting—Hygienic
           aspects
  — Hygienic aspects
      USE Fluorescent lighting—Health
           aspects
Fluorescent screens
  UF Cathode ray tube screens
     Screens, Cathode ray tube
     Screens, Fluorescent
     Screens, Phosphorescent
  BT Fluorescence
     Phosphorescence
     Phosphors
  RT Fluoroscopy
Fluorescent whitening agents
  USE Optical brighteners
Fluorescent x-ray spectroscopy
  USE X-ray spectroscopy
Fluoridation of milk
  USE Milk—Fluoridation
Fluoridation of water
  USE Water—Fluoridation
Fluoride poisoning, Chronic
  USE Fluorosis
Fluorides
    [QD181.F1]
  BT Fluorine compounds
  NT Cobaltous fluoride
     Cryolite
     Hydrogen fluoride
     Manganous fluoride
     Milk—Fluoridation
     Platinum hexafluoride
     Rare earth fluorides
     Sodium fluoride
     Uranium fluorides
     Water—Fluoridation
  — **Physiological effect**
      NT Plants, Effect of fluorides on
Fluorimeter
  UF Fluorometer
  BT Fluorescence
Fluorimetric analysis
  USE Fluorimetry
Fluorimetric cell analysis
  USE Cytofluorometry

Fluorimetry
  UF Fluorescence analysis
     Fluorimetric analysis
     Fluorometric analysis
     Fluorometry
     Luminescence analysis
  BT Chemistry, Analytic
     Fluorescence
  NT Cytofluorometry
     Fluoroscopy
Fluorination
    [QD281.F55]
  BT Chemical reactions
     Halogenation
Fluorine
    [QD181.F1]
  BT Halogens
  NT Liquid fluorine
  — **Isotopes**
  — — **Decay**
  — — **Spectra**
  — **Physiological effect**
      NT Milk—Fluoridation
         Mottled enamel
         Plants, Effect of fluorine on
         Water—Fluoridation
  — **Spectra**
  — **Toxicology**
      UF Fluorine compounds—Toxicology
      RT Fluorosis
Fluorine compounds
  NT Fluorides
     Organofluorine compounds
  — **Spectra**
  — Toxicology
      USE Fluorine—Toxicology
Fluorine industry *(May Subd Geog)*
    [HD9660.F54-544]
Fluorine mica
  UF Fluormica
     Fluoromica
  BT Mica
Fluorine organic compounds
  USE Organofluorine compounds
Fluorite
  USE Fluorspar
Fluormica
  USE Fluorine mica
Fluorocarbons
  BT Organofluorine compounds
     Polycyclic aromatic hydrocarbons
  NT Chlorofluorocarbons
     Isoflurane
     Polytef
  — **Law and legislation** *(May Subd Geog)*
Fluorocarbons industry *(May Subd Geog)*
    [HD9660.F56-58]
Fluorodihydroxymethylethylidenebisoxypre
  gnadienedione
  USE Triamcinolone acetonide
Fluoroethylene
  UF Vinyl fluoride
  BT Fluorohydrocarbons
     Vinyl halides
Fluoroform
    [QD305.H6]
  UF F-23 (Chemical)
     Freon-23
     R-23 (Chemical)
     Trifluoromethane
  BT Fluorohydrocarbons
     Methane
Fluorohydrocarbons
  NT Fluoroethylene
     Fluoroform
Fluorometer
  USE Fluorimeter
Fluoromethylmethylsulfinylbenzylideneindene
  acetic acid
  USE Sulindac

Fluoromethylmethylsulfinylphenylmethylen
  eindene acetic acid
  USE Sulindac
Fluorometric analysis
  USE Fluorimetry
Fluorometry
  USE Fluorimetry
Fluoromica
  USE Fluorine mica
Fluorophenyldihydromethylnitrobenzodiazepine
  USE Flunitrazepam
Fluoropyrimidinedione
  USE Fluorouracil
Fluoropyrimidines
  ₍RC271.F55 (Cancer chemotherapy)₎
  BT Organofluorine compounds
     Pyrimidines
  NT Fluorouracil
Fluoroscopic diagnosis
  USE Diagnosis, Fluoroscopic
Fluoroscopy
  BT Fluorimetry
     X-rays
  RT Fluorescent screens
  NT Diagnosis, Fluoroscopic
Fluorosis (May Subd Geog)
  ₍RC627.F57₎
  UF Chronic endemic fluorosis
     Chronic fluoride poisoning
     Chronic fluorine poisoning
     Fluoride poisoning, Chronic
  BT Chronic diseases
  RT Fluorine—Toxicology
  NT Mottled enamel
Fluorotetrahydroxypregnadienedione
  cyclicacetal with acetone
  USE Triamcinolone acetonide
Fluorouracil
  UF Dioxofluoropyrimidine
     Fluoropyrimidinedione
  BT Antineoplastic agents
     Fluoropyrimidines
     Uracil—Antagonists
  — Analogs
     UF Analogs of fluorouracil
        Fluorouracil—Congeners
        Fluorouracil—Derivatives
  — Congeners
     USE Fluorouracil—Analogs
  — Derivatives
     USE Fluorouracil—Analogs
Fluorspar (May Subd Geog)
  ₍QE391.F6 (Mineralogy)₎
  ₍TN948.F6 (Mineral resources)₎
  UF Fluorite
  NT Blue john
  — Inclusions
     ₍QE391.F6₎
     UF Enclaves in fluorspar
        Inclusions in fluorspar
Fluosilicates
  ₍SB951 (Insecticides)₎
Fluothane
  USE Halothane
Flurazepam (May Subd Geog)
  UF Chlorodiethylaminoet
     hylfluorophenyldihyd
     robenzodiazepinone
  BT Benzodiazepines
     Hypnotics
     Tranquilizing drugs
Fluridrazepam
  USE Flunitrazepam
Flurothyl (May Subd Geog)
  ₍RC483.5.F58₎
  UF Bistrifluoroethyl ether
     Hexafluorodiethyl ether
  BT Ethers
     Shock therapy
     Stimulants

Flush (Dog)
  BT Cocker spaniels
     Dogs
Flushing (New York, N.Y.)
  (Not Subd Geog)
  UF New York (N.Y.). Flushing
Flute
  ₍ML935-ML937 (History)₎
  UF Alto flute
     Boehm flute
  BT Woodwind instruments
  NT Bānsurī
     Czakan
     Fife
     Flageolet
     Galoubet
     Hsiao
     Hsüan (Musical instrument)
     Huang chung (Musical instrument)
     Nāy
     Piccolo
     Recorder (Musical instrument)
     Ryūteki
     Shakuhachi
     Shinobue
     Taegŭm
     Tanso
     Ti tzu
     Tibia (Musical instrument)
  — Construction
     ₍ML936₎
  — Fingering charts
     ₍MT348₎
  — Orchestra studies
     ₍MT346₎
     BT Flute—Studies and exercises
  — Studies and exercises
     ₍MT345₎
     NT Flute—Orchestra studies
Flute and accordion music
  ₍M298₎
  UF Accordion and flute music
Flute and banjo music
  ₍M296-297₎
  UF Banjo and flute music
Flute and bassoon music
  USE Bassoon and flute music
Flute and celesta music
  ₍M298₎
  UF Celesta and flute music
Flute and chime music
  ₍M298₎
  UF Chime and flute music
Flute and cimbalom music
  ₍M298₎
  UF Cimbalom and flute music
Flute and clarinet music
  USE Clarinet and flute music
Flute and continuo music
  UF Continuo and flute music
  NT Marches (Flute and continuo)
     Minuets (Flute and continuo)
     Rondos (Flute and continuo)
     Sonatas (Flute and continuo)
     Suites (Flute and continuo)
     Variations (Flute and continuo)
Flute and double-bass music
  ₍M290-291₎
  UF Double-bass and flute music
Flute and electronic organ music
  ₍M182-186₎
  UF Electronic organ and flute music
  BT Flute and organ music
Flute and English-horn music
  USE English horn and flute music
Flute and guitar music
  ₍M296-7₎
  UF Guitar and flute music
  NT Potpourris (Flute and guitar)
     Sonatas (Flute and guitar)
     Suites (Flute and guitar)

     Variations (Flute and guitar)
Flute and guitar music, Arranged
  ₍M296-7₎
Flute and guitar with orchestra
  ₍M1040-1041₎
  RT Concertos (Flute and guitar)
Flute and guitar with string orchestra
  ₍M1140-1141₎
  RT Concertos (Flute and guitar with string
     orchestra)
Flute and harp music
  ₍M296-7₎
  UF Harp and flute music
  NT Concertos (Flute and harp)
     Concertos (Flute and harp with string
        orchestra)
     Flute and harp with orchestra
     Flute and harp with string orchestra
     Rondos (Flute and harp)
     Sonatas (Flute and harp)
     Suites (Flute and harp)
     Variations (Flute and harp)
Flute and harp music, Arranged
  ₍M296-7₎
Flute and harp with orchestra
  ₍M1040-1041₎
  BT Flute and harp music
  RT Concertos (Flute and harp)
Flute and harp with string ensemble
  RT Concertos (Flute and harp with string
     ensemble)
Flute and harp with string orchestra
  ₍M1105-6₎
  UF Harp and flute with string orchestra
  BT Flute and harp music
  RT Concertos (Flute and harp with string
     orchestra)
Flute and harpsichord music
  ₍M240-242₎
  UF Harpsichord and flute music
  NT Concertos (Flute and harpsichord with
     string orchestra)
     Flute and harpsichord with string
        orchestra
     Minuets (Flute and harpsichord)
     Sonatas (Flute and harpsichord)
     Suites (Flute and harpsichord)
     Variations (Flute and harpsichord)
Flute and harpsichord with string ensemble
  NT Concertos (Flute and harpsichord with
     string ensemble)
Flute and harpsichord with string orchestra
  ₍M1105-6₎
  BT Flute and harpsichord music
  RT Concertos (Flute and harpsichord with
     string orchestra)
  NT Suites (Flute and harpsichord with
     string orchestra)
  — Scores
     ₍M1105₎
Flute and horn music
  ₍M288-9₎
  UF Horn and flute music
  NT Concertos (Flute and horn with string
     orchestra)
     Flute and horn with string orchestra
Flute and horn with string orchestra
  ₍M1105-6₎
  BT Flute and horn music
     String-orchestra music
  RT Concertos (Flute and horn with string
     orchestra)
  NT Variations (Flute and horn with string
     orchestra)
Flute and hurdy-gurdy music
  ₍M298₎
  UF Hurdy-gurdy and flute music
Flute and keyboard instrument music
  ₍M240-M242₎
  UF Keyboard instrument and flute music

Flute and koto music
[M296-7]
UF Koto and flute music
Flute and lute music
[M296-297]
UF Lute and flute music
NT Sonatas (Flute and lute)
Flute and marimba music
[M298]
UF Marimba and flute music
NT Suites (Flute and marimba)
Flute and oboe d'amore with string orchestra
[M1140-1141]
RT Concertos (Flute and oboe d'amore
with string orchestra)
Flute and oboe music
[M288-9]
UF Oboe and flute music
NT Concertos (Flute and oboe)
Concertos (Flute and oboe with
chamber orchestra)
Concertos (Flute and oboe with string
orchestra)
Flute and oboe with chamber orchestra
Flute and oboe with orchestra
Flute and oboe with string orchestra
Suites (Flute and oboe)
Flute and oboe with chamber orchestra
[M1040-1041]
BT Flute and oboe music
RT Concertos (Flute and oboe with
chamber orchestra)
Flute and oboe with orchestra
[M1040-1041]
BT Flute and oboe music
RT Concertos (Flute and oboe)
— Solos with piano
[M1041]
BT Trios (Piano, flute, oboe), Arranged
Flute and oboe with string orchestra
[M1105-6]
BT Flute and oboe music
RT Concertos (Flute and oboe with string
orchestra)
NT Variations (Flute and oboe with string
orchestra)
— Scores
[M1105]
— Solos with piano
[M1141]
BT Trios (Piano, flute, oboe), Arranged
**Flute and oboe with string orchestra,
Arranged**
[M1105-6]
Flute and organ music
[M182-186]
UF Organ and flute music
NT Chorale preludes (Flute and organ)
Flute and electronic organ music
Sonatas (Flute and organ)
Suites (Flute and organ)
Variations (Flute and organ)
Flute and percussion music
[M298]
UF Percussion and flute music
NT Concertos (Flute and percussion with
string orchestra)
Flute and percussion with string
orchestra
Sonatas (Flute and percussion)
Suites (Flute and percussion)
Flute and percussion with string orchestra
[M1105-6]
BT Flute and percussion music
RT Concertos (Flute and percussion with
string orchestra)
Flute and piano music
[M240-242]
UF Piano and flute music
NT Canons, fugues, etc. (Flute and piano)

Concertos (Flute and piano with string
orchestra)
Flute and piano with string orchestra
Marches (Flute and piano)
Passacaglias (Flute and piano)
Polkas (Flute and piano)
Recorder and harpsichord music
Rondos (Flute and piano)
Sonatas (Flute and piano)
Suites (Flute and piano)
Variations (Flute and piano)
Waltzes (Flute and piano)
Flute and piano music, Arranged
[M243-4]
NT Ballets arranged for flute and piano
Concertos (Flute)—Solo with piano
Concertos (Flute with chamber
orchestra)—Solo with piano
Concertos (Flute with string orchestra)
—Solo with piano
Concertos (Flute with string
orchestra), Arranged—Solo with
piano
Flute with chamber orchestra—Solo
with piano
Flute with orchestra—Solo with piano
Flute with string ensemble—Solo with
piano
Flute with string orchestra—Solo with
piano
Rondos (Flute with orchestra)—Solo
with piano
Suites (Flute with orchestra)—Solo
with piano
Suites (Flute with string orchestra)—
Solo with piano
Suites (Flute with string orchestra),
Arranged—Solo with piano
Variations (Flute with orchestra)—Solo
with piano
Flute and piano with orchestra
[M1040-1041]
RT Concertos (Flute and piano)
Flute and piano with string ensemble
NT Concertos (Flute and piano with string
ensemble)
Flute and piano with string orchestra
[M1105-6]
BT Flute and piano music
RT Concertos (Flute and piano with string
orchestra)
— Scores
[M1105]
Flute and piccolo music
[M288-289]
UF Piccolo and flute music
Flute and piccolo with flute ensemble
Flute and recorder music
[M288-9]
UF Recorder and flute music
NT Concertos (Flute and recorder with
string orchestra)
Flute and recorder with string
orchestra
Sonatas (Flute and recorder)
Flute and recorder with string orchestra
[M1105-6]
BT Flute and recorder music
RT Concertos (Flute and recorder with
string orchestra)
Flute and saxophone music
[M288-289]
UF Saxophone and flute music
Flute and tabla music
[M298]
UF Tabla and flute music
Flute and trombone music
[M288-9]
UF Trombone and flute music
NT Concertos (Flute and trombone with
chamber orchestra)

Flute and trombone with chamber
orchestra
Flute and trombone with chamber orchestra
[M1040-1041]
BT Flute and trombone music
RT Concertos (Flute and trombone with
chamber orchestra)
NT Suites (Flute and trombone with
chamber orchestra)
Flute and trumpet music
[M288-9]
UF Trumpet and flute music
NT Concertos (Flute and trumpet with
string orchestra)
Flute and trumpet with string
orchestra
Flute and trumpet with string orchestra
[M1105-6]
BT Flute and trumpet music
RT Concertos (Flute and trumpet with
string orchestra)
NT Canons, fugues, etc. (Flute and
trumpet with string orchestra)
Flute and unspecified instrument music
USE Duets (Unspecified instrument and
flute)
Flute and vibraphone music
[M298]
UF Vibraphone and flute music
Flute and viola d'amore music
[M290-291]
UF Viola d'amore and flute music
NT Concertos (Flute and viola d'amore
with string orchestra)
Flute and viola d'amore with string
orchestra
Flute and viola d'amore with string orchestra
[M1105-6]
BT Flute and viola d'amore music
String-orchestra music
RT Concertos (Flute and viola d'amore
with string orchestra)
Flute and viola music
[M290-291]
UF Viola and flute music
NT Sonatas (Flute and viola)
Flute and viola with instrumental ensemble
RT Concertos (Flute and viola with
instrumental ensemble)
Flute and viola with string ensemble
RT Concertos (Flute and viola with string
ensemble)
Flute and violin music
[M290-291]
UF Violin and flute music
NT Canons, fugues, etc. (Flute and violin)
Concertos (Flute and violin)
Concertos (Flute and violin with string
orchestra)
Flute and violin with orchestra
Flute and violin with string orchestra
Sonatas (Flute and violin)
Suites (Flute and violin)
Variations (Flute and violin)
Flute and violin with orchestra
[M1040-1041]
BT Flute and violin music
RT Concertos (Flute and violin)
— Solos with piano
[M1041]
BT Trios (Piano, flute, violin),
Arranged
Flute and violin with string orchestra
[M1105-6]
BT Flute and violin music
String-orchestra music
RT Concertos (Flute and violin with string
orchestra)
NT Suites (Flute and violin with string
orchestra)

Flute and violoncello music
[M290-291]
  UF Violoncello and flute music
  NT Canons, fugues, etc. (Flute and
      violoncello)
    Concertos (Flute and violoncello with
      string orchestra)
    Flute and violoncello with string
      orchestra
    Minuets (Flute and violoncello)
    Sonatas (Flute and violoncello)
    Suites (Flute and violoncello)
Flute and violoncello with string orchestra
[M1105-6]
  BT Flute and violoncello music
  RT Concertos (Flute and violoncello with
      string orchestra)
  — Scores
      [M1105]
Flute clock
  USE Musical clock
Flûte enchantée (Ballet)
  USE Magic flute (Ballet)
Flute ensembles
[M955-956]
[M957.2]
[M958-959]
    Here are entered compositions for ten or more
    flutes and collections of compositions for a varying
    number of flutes.
    When used in conjunction with specific solo in-
    strument(s), the designation flute ensemble may
    stand for any number of flutes.
  SA Concertos ([Solo instrument(s)] with
      flute ensemble); [Solo
      instrument(s)] with flute ensemble;
      Suites, Variations, Waltzes, and
      similar headings with specifications
      of instruments which include the
      specification Flute ensemble
Flute, horn, harp with string orchestra
[M1105-6]
  BT String-orchestra music
    Trios (Flute, horn, harp)
  RT Concertos (Flute, horn, harp with
      string orchestra)
Flute makers
  BT Woodwind instrument makers
Flute music
[M60-64]
  SA Concertos, Minuets, Sonatas, Suites,
      and similar headings with
      specification of instruments; Trios
      [Quartets, etc.], Wind trios
      [quartets, etc.], and Woodwind
      trios [quartets, etc.] followed by
      specifications which include the
      flute; also Wind ensembles,
      Woodwind ensembles, and headings
      that begin with the words flute or
      flutes
  NT English horn and flute music
    Flageolet music
    Marches (Flute)
    Passacaglias (Flute)
    Potpourris (Flute)
    Recorded accompaniments (Flute)
    Rondos (Flute)
    Sonatas (Flute)
    Suites (Flute)
    Variations (Flute)
  — Interpretation (Phrasing, dynamics, etc.)
      [MT140]
      [MT145]
Flute music, Arranged
[M63-64]
  NT Operas arranged for flute
Flute music (Flutes (2))
[M288-9]
  NT Canons, fugues, etc. (Flutes (2))
    Concertos (Flutes (2))

Concertos (Flutes (2) with chamber
  orchestra)
Concertos (Flutes (2) with string
  orchestra)
Flutes (2) with chamber orchestra
Flutes (2) with orchestra
Flutes (2) with string orchestra
Marches (Flutes (2))
Minuets (Flutes (2))
Sonatas (Flutes (2))
Suites (Flutes (2))
Variations (Flutes (2))
Flute music (Flutes (2)), Arranged
[M288-9]
  NT Overtures arranged for flutes (2)
Flute music (Flutes (3))
  USE Woodwind trios (Flutes (3))
Flute music (Flutes (4))
  USE Woodwind quartets (Flutes (4))
Flute music (Flutes (5))
  USE Woodwind quintets (Flutes (5))
Flute music (Flutes (6))
  USE Woodwind sextets (Flutes (6))
Flute music (Flutes (7))
  USE Woodwind septets (Flutes (7))
Flute music (Flutes (8))
  USE Woodwind octets (Flutes (8))
Flute music (Flutes (9))
  USE Woodwind nonets (Flutes (9))
Flute music (Jazz)
[M60-64]
**Flute, oboe d'amore, viola d'amore with string
  orchestra**
[M1105-6]
  BT Trios (Flute, oboe d'amore, viola
      d'amore)
  RT Concertos (Flute, oboe d'amore, viola
      d'amore with string orchestra)
**Flute, oboe d'amore, violin with string
  orchestra**
[M1140-1141]
  BT Trios (Flute, oboe d'amore, violin)
  RT Concertos (Flute, oboe d'amore, violin
      with string orchestra)
Flute, oboe, trumpet with string orchestra
[M1105-6]
  BT String-orchestra music
    Wind trios (Flute, oboe, trumpet)
  RT Concertos (Flute, oboe, trumpet with
      string orchestra)
Flute, oboe, violin, violoncello with orchestra
[M1040-1041]
  BT Quartets (Flute, oboe, violin,
      violoncello)
  RT Concertos (Flute, oboe, violin,
      violoncello)
Flute, oboe, violin with string orchestra
[M1140-1141]
  BT Trios (Flute, oboe, violin)
  RT Concertos (Flute, oboe, violin with
      string orchestra)
Flute-players (May Subd Geog)
[ML937]
  UF Flutists
    Music—Biography
  BT Musicians
Flute-playing clock
  USE Musical clock
Flute, saxophone, harp with string orchestra
[M1105-6]
  BT Trios (Flute, saxophone, harp)
  RT Concertos (Flute, saxophone, harp
      with string orchestra)
Flute, timpani, violin with string orchestra
[M1140-1141]
  BT Trios (Flute, timpani, violin)
  RT Concertos (Flute, timpani, violin with
      string orchestra)
Flute, viola, violoncello with string orchestra
[M1105-6]
  BT Trios (Flute, viola, violoncello)

  RT Concertos (Flute, viola, violoncello
      with string orchestra)
Flute with accordion ensemble
  BT Accordion ensembles
  RT Concertos (Flute with accordion
      ensemble)
Flute with band
[M1205-6]
  RT Concertos (Flute with band)
  NT Suites (Flute with band)
Flute with band, Arranged
[M1257]
  — Scores and parts
      [M1257]
Flute with brass ensemble
  RT Concertos (Flute with brass ensemble)
Flute with chamber orchestra
[M1020-1021]
  RT Concertos (Flute with chamber
      orchestra)
  NT Rondos (Flute with chamber orchestra)
    Suites (Flute with chamber orchestra)
    Variations (Flute with chamber
      orchestra)
  — Solo with piano
      [M1021]
      BT Flute and piano music, Arranged
Flute with chamber orchestra, Arranged
[M1020-1021]
Flute with flute ensemble
  RT Concertos (Flute with flute ensemble)
Flute with instrumental ensemble
  RT Concertos (Flute with instrumental
      ensemble)
  NT Rondos (Flute with instrumental
      ensemble)
    Variations (Flute with instrumental
      ensemble)
Flute with jazz ensemble
[M1366]
  RT Concertos (Flute with jazz ensemble)
Flute with orchestra
[M1020-1021]
  BT Orchestral music
  RT Concertos (Flute)
  NT Polonaises (Flute with orchestra)
    Recorder with orchestra
    Rondos (Flute with orchestra)
    Suites (Flute with orchestra)
    Symphonies (Flute with orchestra)
    Variations (Flute with orchestra)
  — Solo with piano
      [M1021]
      BT Flute and piano music, Arranged
Flute with orchestra, Arranged
[M1020-1021]
  — Scores
      [M1020]
Flute with percussion ensemble
  RT Concertos (Flute with percussion
      ensemble)
  NT Suites (Flute with percussion
      ensemble)
Flute with string ensemble
  RT Concertos (Flute with string ensemble)
  — Solo with piano
      BT Flute and piano music, Arranged
Flute with string orchestra
[M1105-6]
  RT Concertos (Flute with string orchestra)
  NT Canons, fugues, etc. (Flute with string
      orchestra)
    Rondos (Flute with string orchestra)
    Suites (Flute with string orchestra)
    Variations (Flute with string orchestra)
  — Solo with piano
      [M1106]
      BT Flute and piano music, Arranged
Flute with string orchestra, Arranged
[M1105-6]

Flute with wind ensemble
  RT Concertos (Flute with wind ensemble)
Flute with woodwind ensemble
  RT Concertos (Flute with woodwind
    ensemble)
Flutes (2), glockenspiel with string orchestra
  [M1105-6]
  UF Two flutes and glockenspiel with string
    orchestra
  BT String-orchestra music
    Trios (Flutes (2), glockenspiel)
  RT Concertos (Flutes (2), glockenspiel
    with string orchestra)
Flutes (2), marimba with string orchestra
  [M1105-6]
  UF Two flutes, marimba with string
    orchestra
  BT String-orchestra music
    Trios (Flutes (2), marimba)
  RT Concertos (Flutes (2), marimba with
    string orchestra)
  — Scores
    [M1105]
**Flutes (2), viola, violoncello with string
  orchestra**
  [M1140-1141]
  BT Quartets (Flutes (2), viola, violoncello)
  RT Concertos (Flutes (2), viola,
    violoncello with string orchestra)
**Flutes (2), violin, violoncello with string
  orchestra**
  [M1140-1141]
  BT Quartets (Flutes (2), violin,
    violoncello)
  RT Concertos (Flutes (2), violin,
    violoncello with string orchestra)
Flutes (2), violin with string orchestra
  [M1140-1141]
  BT Trios (Flutes (2), violin)
  RT Concertos (Flutes (2), violin with
    string orchestra)
Flutes (2), violoncello with string orchestra
  [M1140-1141]
  BT Trios (Flutes (2), violoncello)
  RT Concertos (Flutes (2), violoncello with
    string orchestra)
Flutes (2) with chamber orchestra
  [M1020-1021]
  UF Two flutes with chamber orchestra
  BT Chamber-orchestra music
    Flute music (Flutes (2))
  RT Concertos (Flutes (2) with chamber
    orchestra)
Flutes (2) with flute ensemble
  RT Concertos (Flutes (2) with flute
    ensemble)
Flutes (2) with orchestra
  [M1020-1021]
  UF Two flutes with orchestra
  BT Flute music (Flutes (2))
  RT Concertos (Flutes (2))
  — Solos with piano
    [M1021]
    BT Trios (Piano, flutes (2)), Arranged
Flutes (2) with string ensemble
Flutes (2) with string orchestra
  [M1105-6]
  UF Two flutes with string orchestra
  BT Flute music (Flutes (2))
  RT Concertos (Flutes (2) with string
    orchestra)
  NT Canons, fugues, etc. (Flutes (2) with
    string orchestra)
    Suites (Flutes (2) with string orchestra)
Flutes (3) and harp with orchestra
  [M1040-1041]
  BT Quartets (Flutes (3), harp)
  RT Concertos (Flutes (3) and harp)
Flutes (3) with band
  [M1205-1206]
  BT Woodwind trios (Flutes (3))

  RT Concertos (Flutes (3) with band)
  — Scores and parts
    [M1205]
Flutes (3) with string orchestra
  [M1120-1121]
  BT Woodwind trios (Flutes (3))
  RT Concertos (Flutes (3) with string
    orchestra)
  NT Suites (Flutes (3) with string orchestra)
Flutes (4) with band
  [M1205-6]
  BT Woodwind quartets (Flutes (4))
  RT Concertos (Flutes (4) with band)
Flutes (4) with band, Arranged
  [M1257]
  — Scores and parts
    [M1257]
Flutes (4) with chamber orchestra
  [M1020-1021]
  BT Woodwind quartets (Flutes (4))
  RT Concertos (Flutes (4) with chamber
    orchestra)
Flutes (4) with orchestra
  [M1020-1021]
Flutists
  USE Flute-players
Flutsch family
  USE Fluetsch family
Flutter (Aerodynamics)
  [TL574.F6]
  BT Aerodynamics
    Oscillations
    Vibration (Aeronautics)
  NT Oscillating wings (Aerodynamics)
Fluvents
  USE Fluvisols
Fluvial deposits
  USE Alluvium
Fluvial sediment transport
  USE Sediment transport
Fluvisols (May Subd Geog)
  [S592.17.F55]
  UF Alluvial soils
    Auenböden
    Fluvents
    Om soils
    Warp soils
  BT Soils
  RT Alluvium
Flux, Magnetic
  USE Magnetic flux
Flux, Neutron
  USE Neutron flux
Flux (Metallurgy)
  RT Slag
Flux compression, Magnetic
  USE Magnetic flux compression
Flux of water vapor
  USE Water vapor transport
Flux pinning
  UF Pinning, Flux
  BT Dislocations in crystals
    Point defects
    Superconductors—Magnetic properties
Fluxgate magnetometer
  [QC819]
  UF Saturable core magnetometer
  BT Magnetometer
Fluxions
  USE Calculus
Fluxmeter
  BT Electric apparatus and appliances
    Electric measurements
    Galvanometer
Fly
  USE Flies
Fly ash
  UF Ash, Pulverized fuel
    Flue dust
    Fuel ash, Pulverized
    Pulverized fuel ash

  BT Coal, Pulverized
    Coal ash
    Dust
    Furnaces
    Waste products
Fly casting
  [SH454.2]
  BT Casting (Fishing)
    Fly fishing
Fly control
  USE Flies—Control
Fly disease
  USE Trypanosomiasis
Fly dressing
  USE Fly tying
Fly fishing (May Subd Geog)
  [SH456]
  BT Fishing
  NT Flies, Artificial
    Fly casting
    Saltwater fly fishing
Fly rods
  USE Fishing rods
Fly tying
  [SH451]
  UF Fly dressing
  RT Flies, Artificial
  — Equipment and supplies
    NT Hackles (Fly tying)
Fly tying hackles
  USE Hackles (Fly tying)
Fly-wheels
  USE Flywheels
Flycatcher, Acadian
  USE Acadian flycatcher
Flycatcher, Pied
  USE Pied flycatcher
Flycatchers
  [QL696.P2 (Birds)]
  BT Passeriformes
  NT Tyrannidae
Flyers, Advertising
  USE Advertising fliers
Flying
  USE Flight
Flying, Cross-country
  USE Cross-country flying
Flying, Fear of
  USE Fear of flying
Flying, Mountain
  USE Mountain flying
Flying, Night
  USE Night flying
Flying, Overwater
  USE Overwater flying
Flying, Private
  USE Private flying
Flying boats
  USE Seaplanes
Flying bombs
  USE Guided missiles
Flying classes
  USE Aeronautics in education
    Flight training
Flying clubs
  USE Private flying—Societies, etc.
Flying discs (Game) (May Subd Geog)
  [GV1097.F7]
  UF Flying saucers (Game)
    Frisbee (Registered trademark)
    Plastic disc throwing
    Plastic saucers (Game)
  NT Ultimate (Game)
Flying doctor services
  USE Aeronautics in medicine
Flying Dutchman
  BT Ocean—Folklore
Flying Fortress (Bombers)
  USE B-17 bomber
Flying foxes
  [QL737.C575]

Flying foxes *(Continued)*
  UF Fox bats
  BT Frugivores
       Pteropodidae
Flying lemurs
  [QL737.D35]
  UF Colugos
       Cynocephalidae
       Dermoptera
       Gliding lemurs
  BT Mammals
  NT Cynocephalus
Flying lemurs, Fossil
  [QE882.F]
  BT Mammals, Fossil
Flying-machines
  [TL670-724]
  BT Flight
  RT Aeronautics
       Airplanes
  NT Autogiros
       Gliders (Aeronautics)
       Helicopters
       Human powered aircraft
       Ornithopters
       Propellers, Aerial
       Rockets (Aeronautics)
       Strongmobile (Flying automobile)
Flying over water
  USE Overwater flying
Flying personnel
  USE Flight crews
Flying phalangers
  [QL737.M3]
  UF Phalangers, Flying
  BT Marsupialia
Flying qualities of airplanes
  USE Airplanes—Handling characteristics
Flying qualities of helicopters
  USE Helicopters—Handling characteristics
Flying saucers
  USE Unidentified flying objects
Flying saucers (Game)
  USE Flying discs (Game)
Flying spot scanners
  UF Scanners, Flying spot
  BT Cathode ray tubes
       Optical data processing
       Scanning systems
Flying squirrel, Southern
  USE Glaucomys volans
Flying squirrels
  [QL737.R68]
  UF Petauristinae
  BT Sciuridae
  NT Glaucomys
Flying wing airplanes
  USE Airplanes, Tailless
Flyingfish, Fourwing
  USE Hirundichthys affinis
Flyingfishes
  [QL638.E9]
  BT Atheriniformes
       Exocoetidae
  NT Exocoetus
Flyleaf
  USE Endpapers
Flyn family
  USE Flynn family
Flynn family
  UF Flinn family
       Flyn family
Flynt family
  USE Flint family
Flysch *(May Subd Geog)*
  BT Geology, Stratigraphic—Cretaceous
       Geology, Stratigraphic—Tertiary
       Sandstone
Flywheels *(May Subd Geog)*
  [TJ541]

  UF Balance wheels
       Fly-wheels
  BT Rotors
       Wheels
  RT Energy storage
FM (Fighter plane)
  USE Wildcat (Fighter plane)
FM broadcasting
  UF FM radio broadcasting
       Frequency modulation broadcasting
       Frequency modulation radio
         broadcasting
  BT Radio broadcasting
       Radio frequency modulation
FM detectors
  USE Frequency modulation detectors
FM radio
  USE Radio frequency modulation
FM radio broadcasting
  USE FM broadcasting
FM stereophonic receivers
  USE Stereophonic receivers
FMS
  USE Flexible manufacturing systems
FMS (Information retrieval system)
  UF Financial Management System
         (Information retrieval system)
  BT Information storage and retrieval
         systems—Accounting
       Information storage and retrieval
         systems—Finance
FN automatic rifles
  USE Fabrique nationale automatic rifles
Fō dialect
  USE Fon dialect
Foà-Kurlov cells
  BT Lymphocytes
Foalks family
  USE Faulk family
Foals *(May Subd Geog)*
  [SF277-303]
  UF Baby horses
       Horses—Infancy
  BT Animals—Infancy
       Horses
Foam
  BT Colloids
  NT Antifoaming agents
       Foamed materials
       Plastic foams
Foam fractionation (Sewage purification)
  USE Sewage—Purification—Foam
         fractionation
Foam fractionation (Water purification)
  USE Water—Purification—Foam
         fractionation
Foam glass
  USE Cellular glass
Foam inhibitors
  USE Antifoaming agents
Foam regulators
  USE Antifoaming agents
Foam rubber
  UF Rubber, Foamed
       Rubber foam
  BT Foamed materials
       Rubber
Foamed materials
  BT Foam
       Materials
       Porous materials
  NT Cellular glass
       Foam rubber
       Plastic foams
       Urethane foam
Foard family
  USE Ford family
Fobb family
  USE Fobes family
Fobbs family
  USE Fobes family

Fobes family
  UF Fobb family
       Fobbs family
       Fobs family
  RT Forbes family
Fobs
  USE Watch fobs
Fobs family
  USE Fobes family
Foca camera
  [TR263.F]
Focal infection
  UF Infection, Focal
  BT Communicable diseases
       Infection
Focal infection, Dental
  [RK305]
  [RK351]
  UF Dental focal infection
  BT Teeth—Diseases
Focal planes
  UF Planes, Focal
  BT Optics
Foch Avenue (Paris, France)
  USE Avenue Foch (Paris, France)
Focillidae
  USE Noctuidae
Focke-Wulf 190 (Fighter planes)
  UF FW-190 (Fighter planes)
  BT Fighter planes
       Focke-Wulf airplanes
Focke-Wulf airplanes
  [TL686.F62]
  NT Focke-Wulf 190 (Fighter planes)
       Moskito (Fighter plane)
Focke-Wulf Moskito (Fighter plane)
  USE Moskito (Fighter plane)
Focke-Wulf Ta 154 (Fighter plane)
  USE Moskito (Fighter plane)
FOCUS (Computer program language)
  [QA76.73.F]
  BT Programming languages (Electronic
         computers)
Focusing, Isoelectric
  USE Isoelectric focusing
Fodder
  USE Feeds
Fodder beet
  USE Mangel-wurzel
Foden trucks
  [TL230.5.F]
  BT Trucks
Foelsch family
  UF Foelsche family
       Folsch family
       Voelsch family
       Volsch family
Foelsche family
  USE Foelsch family
Foeniculum
  USE Fennel
Foetus
  USE Fetus
Fog *(May Subd Geog)*
  [QC929.F7 (Meteorology)]
  [RA575 (Hygiene of atmosphere)]
  BT Meteorology
       Water
  NT Automobile driving in bad weather
       Ice fog
       Smog
  — Control
     [QC929.F7 (Meteorology)]
     [TL557.F6 (Airports)]
     UF Fog control
          Fog dispersal
          Fog modification
          Fog seeding
     BT Weather control
Fog, Mountain *(May Subd Geog)*
  UF Mountain fog

BT Clouds
    Mountains
    Weather, Influence of mountains on
Fog-bells
    [VK383]
    BT Aids to navigation
        Navigation
Fog control
    USE Fog—Control
Fog dispersal
    USE Fog—Control
Fog modification
    USE Fog—Control
Fog seeding
    USE Fog—Control
Fog-signals *(May Subd Geog)*
    [VK383]
    BT Aids to navigation
        Navigation
        Signals and signaling
Fogaras Mountains (Romania)
    USE Făgăraş Mountains (Romania)
Fogbe dialect
    USE Fon dialect
Fogbow
    [QC976.R2]
    UF False white rainbow
        Mistbow
        White rainbow
    BT Meteorological optics
        Rainbow
Fogel family
    USE Vogel family
Fogelar family
    USE Voegler family
Foggara
    USE Falashas
        Qanat
Foggia, Madonna Incoronata di
    USE Foggia, Vergine Incoronata di
Foggia, Vergine Incoronata di
    [BT660.F585]
    UF Foggia, Madonna Incoronata di
        Madonna Incoronata di Foggia
        Vergine Incoronata di Foggia
    BT Mary, Blessed Virgin, Saint—Cult—
        Italy
Fogle family
    USE Vogel family
Fogler family
    USE Voegler family
Fogous
    USE Cave-dwellings
Fogwell family
    UF Fogwill family
Fogwill family
    USE Fogwell family
Fohanagh (Ireland)
    USE Fohenagh (Ireland)
Fohenagh (Ireland)
    UF Fohanagh (Ireland)
Föhn *(May Subd Geog)*
    [QC939.F6]
    BT Winds
    RT Santa Ana winds
Fohn family
Föhr (Germany)
    UF Insel Föhr (Germany)
    BT Islands—Germany (West)
        North Frisian Islands (Denmark and
        Germany)
Foie gras
    UF Fat liver of ducks and geese
        Liver, Fat, of ducks and geese
    BT Ducks—Anatomy
        Geese—Anatomy
        Liver
Foie gras industry *(May Subd Geog)*
    [HD9330.F63-HD9330.F634]
Foil, Gold
    USE Gold foil

Foil craft, Aluminum
    USE Aluminum foil craft
Foilage plant industry *(May Subd Geog)*
Foils, Metal
    USE Metal foils
Fokker airplanes
    NT Fokker F.27 Friendship (Turboprop
        transport)
Fokker F.27 Friendship (Turboprop transport)
    [TL686.F]
    UF Fairchild F-27 (Turboprop transport)
    BT Fokker airplanes
        Turboprop transports
Fokker-Planck equation
    UF Equation, Fokker-Planck
        Planck-Fokker equation
    BT Differential equations, Partial
    RT Stochastic differential equations
Folate antagonists
    USE Folic acid—Antagonists
Folded plate structures
    [TA660.P63]
    UF Hipped plate structures
        Plate structures, Folded
        Structures, Folded plate
    BT Building
        Plates (Engineering)
        Structural engineering
    — Vibration
Foldi family
Folding chairs *(May Subd Geog)*
    BT Chairs
Folding knives
    USE Pocketknives
Folding-machines
    [Z261]
    BT Printing machinery and supplies
    NT Baumfolder (Folding machine)
Folding of napkins
    USE Napkin folding
Folds (Geology) *(May Subd Geog)*
    [QE606-606.5]
    BT Geology, Structural
    NT Diapirs
        Geosynclines
        Nappes (Geology)
Folex
    USE Tributylphosphorotrithioite
Foley family
Folgore (Fighter plane)
    UF C.202 (Fighter plane)
        Macchi C.202 (Fighter plane)
    BT Fighter planes
Foliage
    USE Leaves
Foliage, Artificial
    USE Artificial leaves
Foliage, Cut
    USE Cut foliage
Foliage, Fall
    USE Fall foliage
Foliage-eating animals
    USE Folivores
Foliage plants *(May Subd Geog)*
    [SB431]
    UF Leaf plants
        Plants, Foliage
    BT Plants, Ornamental
    SA *names of individual plants, e.g.*
        Begonias
    NT Ferns
        Ferns, Ornamental
Foliar application of agricultural chemicals
    USE Agricultural chemicals—Foliar
        application
Foliar application of plant regulators
    USE Plant regulators—Foliar application
Foliar diagnosis
    UF Leaf analysis
        Leaves—Analysis

    BT Plants—Analysis
        Plants—Nutrition
Foliar feeding
    [S662.5]
    UF Foliar fertilization
        Leaf feeding
        Leaves—Fertilization
        Leaves, Feeding of
        Spray application of liquid fertilizers
    BT Liquid fertilizers—Application
Foliar fertilization
    USE Foliar feeding
Folias (Music)
    This heading is used without specification of
    medium. For works for a specific medium, a second
    heading is assigned, e.g. 1. Folias (Music) 2. Guitar
    music.
    UF Follias (Music)
    BT Dance music
        Songs
        Variations
Foliate head (Sculpture) *(May Subd Geog)*
    UF Head, Foliate (Sculpture)
    BT Christian art and symbolism—
        Medieval, 500-1500
        Head in art
        Sculpture, Medieval—Themes, motives
Foliated structures
    USE Foliations (Mathematics)
Foliations (Mathematics)
    [QA613.62]
    UF Foliated structures
    BT Differential topology
Folic acid
    [QP772.F6 (Physiology)]
    [RM666.F57 (Therapeutics)]
    UF Pteroylglutamic acid
        Vitamin B10
        Vitamin Bc
        Vitamin M
    BT Pteridines
        Vitamin B complex
    NT Folinic acid
    — Antagonists
        [RM666.F58 (Therapeutics)]
        UF Folate antagonists
            Folic acid antagonists
            Vitamin M antagonists
        BT Antimetabolites
        NT Methotrexate
Folic acid antagonists
    USE Folic acid—Antagonists
Folic acid deficiency *(May Subd Geog)*
    [RC627.F6]
    UF Vitamin M deficiency
    BT Avitaminosis
Folic acid in animal nutrition
    (May Subd Geog)
    [SF98.V5]
    UF Vitamin M in animal nutrition
    BT Animal nutrition
Folic acid in human nutrition
    (May Subd Geog)
    [QP772.F6]
    UF Vitamin M in human nutrition
    BT Nutrition
Folie à deux
    [RC528.F6]
    BT Psychoses
Folinic acid
    UF Citrovorum factor
        Leucovorin
    BT Antineoplastic agents
        Folic acid
Folisols
    USE Histosols
Folivores *(May Subd Geog)*
    UF Foliage-eating animals
        Leaf-eating animals
    BT Herbivores

Folk architecture
  USE Vernacular architecture
Folk art *(May Subd Geog)*
    [N5311-N5313 (General works)]
    [NK801-NK1094 (by country, A-Z)]
  UF Art, Folk
      Art, Popular
      Peasant art
  BT Art
      Art and society
  RT Art, Primitive
      Arts and crafts movement
      Children as artists
      Decorative arts
  NT Bodhidharma dolls
      Fairground art
      Glass underpainting
      Jewelry, Rustic
      Santos (Art)
      Tole painting
  — **India**
      NT Alpana (Art)
          Mandana (Art)
  — **Pennsylvania**
      NT Art, Pennsylvania Dutch
  — **Russian S.F.S.R.**
      NT Folk art, Veps
  — **Taiwan**
  — — **Awards**
          NT Min tsu i shu hsin ch'uan chiang
  — **United States**
      NT Mexican American folk art
Folk art, Afro-American
  USE Afro-American folk art
Folk art, Aromanian *(May Subd Geog)*
    [NK608.A78]
  UF Aromanian folk art
Folk art, Cape Verdean American
  USE Cape Verdean American folk art
Folk art, Dogra *(May Subd Geog)*
  UF Dogra folk art
  BT Dogras (Indic people)
Folk art, Finno-Ugrian *(May Subd Geog)*
  UF Finno-Ugrian folk art
Folk art, Jewish
  UF Jewish folk art
      Jews—Folk art
  BT Art, Jewish
      Jewish art and symbolism
Folk art, Lapp *(May Subd Geog)*
  UF Lapp folk art
Folk art, Mexican American
  USE Mexican American folk art
Folk art, Mongolian *(May Subd Geog)*
    [NK608.M65]
  UF Mongolian folk art
Folk art, Veps *(May Subd Geog)*
  UF Veps folk art
  BT Folk art—Russian S.F.S.R.
Folk artists *(May Subd Geog)*
  BT Artists
Folk beliefs
  USE Folklore
      Superstition
Folk classification *(May Subd Geog)*
    [GN468.4]
    Here are entered works on the systematic division
  of the universe into groups, classes, or families by
  preliterate or folk societies.
  UF Classification, Primitive
      Primitive classification
  BT Classification
      Ethnophilosophy
Folk costume
  USE Costume
Folk dance music *(May Subd Geog)*
    [M1627]
    Here are entered collections of miscellaneous folk
  dance music. Music for individual dances is entered
  under dance form, e.g. Square dance music.

    If the collection also contains dance instruction,
  two headings are used, e.g. 1. Folk dancing. 2. Folk
  dance music.
    If the collection is for a medium other than piano,
  an additional heading is used for the medium, e.g. 1.
  Folk dance music. 2. Orchestral music, Arranged.
    For works consisting of Folk dance music of an
  individual ethnic group, an additional subject entry is
  made under the heading [ethnic group]—[place]
  —Music.
  UF National dances
  BT Dance music
      Folk music
      Music
  — **Poland**
      NT Krakowiaks
  — **Spain**
      NT Flamenco music
Folk dancing *(May Subd Geog)*
    [GV1580-GV1799]
    Here are entered collections of miscellaneous folk
  dances which include instructions for the dances.
    If the collection also contains the dance music,
  two headings are used, e.g. 1. Folk dancing. 2. Folk
  dance music.
  UF National dances
  BT Dancing
      National music
  RT Folk music
  NT Play-party
      Square dancing
  — **Brazil**
      NT Bumba-Meu-Boi
          Capoeira (Dance)
          Caroço (Dance)
          Lelê (Dance)
          Lundu (Dance)
          Moçambique (Dance)
          Quilombo (Dance)
  — **India**
      NT Chhau (Dance)
  — **Thailand**
      NT Nōrā (Dance)
Folk dancing, Adyghe *(May Subd Geog)*
  UF Adyghe folk dancing
Folk dancing, Argentine, [**French, German,
  etc.**]
    Subdivided by locality.
  SA *names of individual folk dances*
Folk dancing, Austrian
  NT Schuhplattler
Folk dancing, Bashkir *(May Subd Geog)*
  UF Bashkir folk dancing
Folk dancing, Brazilian *(May Subd Geog)*
  UF Brazilian folk dancing
Folk dancing, Buriat *(May Subd Geog)*
  UF Buriat folk dancing
Folk dancing, Byelorussian
  (May Subd Geog)
  UF Byelorussian folk dancing
Folk dancing, Chinese *(May Subd Geog)*
  UF Chinese folk dancing
Folk dancing, Embu *(May Subd Geog)*
  UF Embu folk dancing
Folk dancing, German
  NT Schuhplattler
Folk dancing, Japanese *(May Subd Geog)*
  UF Japanese folk dancing
Folk dancing, Kalmyk *(May Subd Geog)*
  UF Kalmyk folk dancing
Folk dancing, Karelian *(May Subd Geog)*
  UF Karelian folk dancing
Folk dancing, Korean *(May Subd Geog)*
  UF Korean folk dancing
Folk dancing, Latvian *(May Subd Geog)*
  UF Latvian folk dancing
Folk dancing, Lithuanian *(May Subd Geog)*
  UF Lithuanian folk dancing
Folk dancing, Moldavian *(May Subd Geog)*
  UF Moldavian folk dancing
Folk dancing, Nepali *(May Subd Geog)*
  UF Nepali folk dancing

Folk dancing, Polish *(May Subd Geog)*
  UF Polish folk dancing
Folk dancing, Russian *(May Subd Geog)*
  UF Russian folk dancing
Folk dancing, Serbian *(May Subd Geog)*
  UF Serbian folk dancing
Folk dancing, Slovak *(May Subd Geog)*
  UF Slovak folk dancing
Folk dancing, Ukrainian *(May Subd Geog)*
  UF Ukrainian folk dancing
Folk dancing, Uzbek *(May Subd Geog)*
  UF Uzbek folk dancing
Folk dancing, Yakut *(May Subd Geog)*
  UF Yakut folk dancing
Folk dentistry *(May Subd Geog)*
    [GR880]
  UF Dentistry folklore
      Folklore, Dental
  BT Dentistry
      Folk medicine
      Medicine, Magic, mystic, and spagiric
      Medicine, Primitive
Folk-drama
    [PN1008.D7 (History)]
  UF Folk-plays
  BT Drama
      Folk literature
  RT Pastoral drama
  NT Carnival plays
      Drama—Origin
      Puppets and puppet-plays
Folk-drama, American *(May Subd Geog)*
  UF American folk-drama
  BT American drama
Folk-drama, Azerbaijani *(May Subd Geog)*
  UF Azerbaijani folk-drama
  BT Azerbaijani drama
Folk-drama, Bengali *(May Subd Geog)*
  UF Bengali folk-drama
  BT Bengali drama
Folk-drama, Braj *(May Subd Geog)*
  UF Braj folk-drama
  BT Braj drama
Folk-drama, Byelorussian *(May Subd Geog)*
  UF Byelorussian folk-drama
  BT Byelorussian drama
Folk-drama, Chinese *(May Subd Geog)*
    [PL2357 (History)]
    [PL2567 (Collections)]
  UF Chinese folk-drama
  BT Chinese drama
Folk-drama, English
  UF English folk-drama
  NT Mumming plays
Folk-drama, German *(May Subd Geog)*
  UF German folk-drama
  BT German drama
Folk-drama, German, [**Italian, etc.**]
  (May Subd Geog)
Folk-drama, Greek (Modern)
  (May Subd Geog)
  UF Greek folk-drama, Modern
      Modern Greek folk-drama
  BT Greek drama, Modern
Folk-drama, Gujarati *(May Subd Geog)*
  UF Gujarati folk-drama
  BT Gujarati drama
Folk-drama, Hausa *(May Subd Geog)*
  UF Hausa folk-drama
  BT Hausa drama
Folk-drama, Hindi *(May Subd Geog)*
  UF Hindi folk-drama
  BT Hindi drama
Folk-drama, Hungarian *(May Subd Geog)*
  UF Hungarian folk-drama
  BT Hungarian drama
Folk-drama, Igbo *(May Subd Geog)*
  UF Igbo folk-drama
  BT Igbo drama
Folk-drama, Indic *(May Subd Geog)*
  UF Indic folk-drama

BT Indic drama
Folk-drama, Indonesian *(May Subd Geog)*
  UF Indonesian folk-drama
  BT Indonesian drama
Folk-drama, Kannada *(May Subd Geog)*
  UF Kannada folk-drama
  BT Kannada drama
Folk-drama, Korean *(May Subd Geog)*
  UF Korean folk-drama
  BT Korean drama
  NT Sandae plays
Folk-drama, Malayalam *(May Subd Geog)*
  UF Malayalam folk-drama
  BT Malayalam drama
Folk-drama, Manipuri *(May Subd Geog)*
  UF Manipuri folk-drama
  BT Manipuri drama
Folk-drama, Marathi *(May Subd Geog)*
  UF Marathi folk-drama
  BT Marathi drama
Folk-drama, Oriya *(May Subd Geog)*
  UF Oriya folk-drama
  BT Oriya drama
Folk-drama, Panjabi *(May Subd Geog)*
  UF Panjabi folk-drama
  BT Panjabi drama
Folk-drama, Rajasthani *(May Subd Geog)*
  UF Rajasthani folk-drama
  BT Rajasthani drama
Folk-drama, Romanian *(May Subd Geog)*
  UF Romanian folk-drama
  BT Romanian drama
Folk-drama, Spanish *(May Subd Geog)*
  UF Spanish folk-drama
  BT Spanish drama
Folk-drama, Spanish American
  (May Subd Geog)
  UF Spanish American folk-drama
  BT Spanish American drama
Folk-drama, Tamil *(May Subd Geog)*
  UF Tamil folk-drama
  BT Tamil drama
Folk-drama, Telugu *(May Subd Geog)*
  UF Telugu folk-drama
  BT Telugu drama
Folk family
  USE Faulk family
Folk festivals *(May Subd Geog)*
  BT Festivals
     Folklore
  — Austria
    NT Salzburger Adventsingen, Salzburg,
      Austria
  — Botswana
    NT Laedza Batanani, Botswana
Folk high schools *(May Subd Geog)*
  UF People's high schools
  BT Adult education
     Education, Secondary
Folk literature *(May Subd Geog)*
  [PN905-1008]
  UF Folk-tales
     Literature, Primitive
     Oral literature
     Primitive literature
  BT Folklore
     Literature
  NT Chap-books
     Dialect literature
     Fairy tales
     Folk-drama
     Folk poetry
     Folk-songs
     Legends
     Nursery rhymes
     Proverbs
     Riddles
     Semiotics and folk literature
     Symbolism in folk literature
     Tales
     Tongue twisters

— History and criticism
  UF Folklore—History and criticism
  NT Oral-formulaic analysis
— Themes, motives
  [PN57.A1]
    Here are entered works on typical plots, mo-
    tives, etc. found in folk literature.
  BT Folklore—Classification
  NT Pharaoh's army (in religion, folk-
     lore, etc.)
Folk literature, African *(May Subd Geog)*
  UF African folk literature
  BT African literature
Folk literature, Albanian *(May Subd Geog)*
  UF Albanian folk literature
  BT Albanian literature
Folk literature, American, [etc.]
  (May Subd Geog)
Folk literature, Arabic *(May Subd Geog)*
  UF Arabic folk literature
  BT Arabic literature
  — Libya
    UF Libyan literature
Folk literature, Aramaic *(May Subd Geog)*
  UF Aramaic folk literature
  BT Aramaic literature
Folk literature, Argentine *(May Subd Geog)*
  UF Argentine folk literature
Folk literature, Aromanian
  (May Subd Geog)
  UF Aromanian folk literature
  BT Aromanian literature
Folk literature, Assamese *(May Subd Geog)*
  UF Assamese folk literature
  BT Assamese literature
Folk literature, Azerbaijani
  (May Subd Geog)
  UF Azerbaijani folk literature
  BT Azerbaijani literature
Folk literature, Bajjika *(May Subd Geog)*
  UF Bajjika folk literature
  BT Bajjika literature
Folk literature, Bamileke *(May Subd Geog)*
  [GR351.2.B35]
  UF Bamileke folk literature
Folk literature, Bantu *(May Subd Geog)*
  [GR350.2]
  UF Bantu folk literature
Folk literature, Bashkir *(May Subd Geog)*
  UF Bashkir folk literature
  BT Bashkir literature
Folk literature, Basque *(May Subd Geog)*
  [GR137.7]
  UF Basque folk literature
  BT Basque literature
Folk literature, Bengali *(May Subd Geog)*
  UF Bengali folk literature
  BT Bengali literature
Folk literature, Bhojpuri *(May Subd Geog)*
  [GR302.2.B]
  UF Bhojpuri folk literature
Folk literature, Braj *(May Subd Geog)*
  UF Braj folk literature
Folk literature, Brazilian *(May Subd Geog)*
  UF Brazilian folk literature
  BT Brazilian literature
Folk literature, Bulgarian *(May Subd Geog)*
  UF Bulgarian folk literature
  BT Bulgarian literature
Folk literature, Bunak *(May Subd Geog)*
  UF Bunak folk literature
Folk literature, Bundeli *(May Subd Geog)*
  UF Bundeli folk literature
  BT Bundeli literature
Folk literature, Buriat *(May Subd Geog)*
  UF Buriat folk literature
  BT Buriat literature
Folk literature, Byelorussian
  (May Subd Geog)
  UF Byelorussian folk literature
     White Russian folk literature

  BT Byelorussian literature
Folk literature, Byzantine
  UF Byzantine folk literature
  BT Byzantine literature
Folk literature, Celtic *(May Subd Geog)*
  UF Celtic folk literature
  BT Celtic literature
Folk literature, Chhattisgarhi
  (May Subd Geog)
  UF Chhattisgarhi folk literature
  BT Chhattisgarhi literature
Folk literature, Chinese *(May Subd Geog)*
  [PL2445 (History)]
  [PL2446 (Collections)]
  UF Chinese folk literature
  BT Chinese literature
  NT Pien wen (Buddhist song-tales)
Folk literature, Chuvash *(May Subd Geog)*
  UF Chuvash folk literature
  BT Chuvash literature
Folk literature, Circassian *(May Subd Geog)*
  UF Circassian folk literature
Folk literature, Colombian
  (May Subd Geog)
  UF Colombian folk literature
  BT Colombian literature
Folk literature, Croatian *(May Subd Geog)*
  UF Croatian folk literature
  BT Croatian literature
Folk literature, Dogri *(May Subd Geog)*
  UF Dogri folk literature
  BT Dogri literature
Folk literature, Dyak *(May Subd Geog)*
  UF Dyak folk literature
  BT Dyak literature
Folk literature, Efik *(May Subd Geog)*
  UF Efik folk literature
Folk literature, English *(May Subd Geog)*
  UF English folk literature
  BT English literature
  NT Folk poetry, English
Folk literature, Finnish *(May Subd Geog)*
  UF Finnish folk literature
  BT Finnish literature
Folk literature, Fipa *(May Subd Geog)*
  [GR356.72.F58]
  UF Fipa folk literature
Folk literature, Flemish *(May Subd Geog)*
  UF Flemish folk literature
Folk literature, French *(May Subd Geog)*
  UF French folk literature
  BT French literature
Folk literature, German *(May Subd Geog)*
  UF German folk literature
Folk literature, Greek *(May Subd Geog)*
  UF Greek folk literature
  BT Greek literature
Folk literature, Gujarati *(May Subd Geog)*
  UF Gujarati folk literature
  BT Gujarati literature
Folk literature, Hebrew *(May Subd Geog)*
  UF Hebrew folk literature
  BT Hebrew literature
     Jewish literature
Folk literature, Himachali
  (May Subd Geog)
  UF Himachali folk literature
  BT Himachali literature
Folk literature, Hindi *(May Subd Geog)*
  UF Hindi folk literature
  BT Hindi literature
Folk literature, Hungarian
  (May Subd Geog)
  UF Hungarian folk literature
  BT Hungarian literature
Folk literature, Iban *(May Subd Geog)*
  UF Iban folk literature
  BT Iban literature
Folk literature, Igbo (African people)
  (May Subd Geog)
  UF Igbo (African people) folk literature

Folk literature, Indic *(May Subd Geog)*
  UF Indic folk literature
  BT Indic literature
Folk literature, Irish *(May Subd Geog)*
  UF Irish folk literature
Folk literature, Israeli *(May Subd Geog)*
  UF Israeli folk literature
  BT Israeli literature
Folk literature, Italian *(May Subd Geog)*
  UF Italian folk literature
  BT Italian literature
Folk literature, Jamaican *(May Subd Geog)*
  UF Jamaican folk literature
  BT Jamaican literature
Folk literature, Japanese *(May Subd Geog)*
  UF Japanese folk literature
  BT Japanese literature
Folk literature, Jewish
  USE Jewish folk literature
Folk literature, Judeo-Arabic
  (May Subd Geog)
  UF Judeo-Arabic folk literature
  BT Judeo-Arabic literature
Folk literature, Kannada *(May Subd Geog)*
  UF Kannada folk literature
  BT Kannada literature
Folk literature, Karelian *(May Subd Geog)*
  UF Karelian folk literature
  BT Karelian literature
Folk literature, Kazakh *(May Subd Geog)*
  UF Kazakh folk literature
  BT Kazakh literature
Folk literature, Khanty *(May Subd Geog)*
  UF Khanty folk literature
  BT Khanty literature
Folk literature, Korean *(May Subd Geog)*
  UF Korean folk literature
  BT Korean literature
Folk literature, Krio *(May Subd Geog)*
  UF Krio folk literature
  BT Krio literature
Folk literature, Kumauni *(May Subd Geog)*
  UF Kumauni folk literature
  BT Kumauni literature
Folk literature, Kurukh *(May Subd Geog)*
  UF Kurukh folk literature
  BT Kurukh literature
Folk literature, Laadi *(May Subd Geog)*
  ⌐GR357.52.L33¬
  UF Laadi folk literature
Folk literature, Ladino *(May Subd Geog)*
  UF Ladino folk literature
  BT Ladino literature
Folk literature, Lithuanian
  (May Subd Geog)
  UF Lithuanian folk literature
  BT Lithuanian literature
Folk literature, Low German
  (May Subd Geog)
  UF Low German folk literature
  BT Low German literature
Folk literature, Luba *(May Subd Geog)*
  UF Luba folk literature
Folk literature, Luyana *(May Subd Geog)*
  UF Luyana folk literature
Folk literature, Macedonian
  (May Subd Geog)
  UF Macedonian folk literature
  BT Macedonian literature
Folk literature, Malay *(May Subd Geog)*
  UF Malay folk literature
  BT Malay literature
Folk literature, Malvi *(May Subd Geog)*
  UF Malvi folk literature
  BT Malvi literature
Folk literature, Mandeali *(May Subd Geog)*
  UF Mandeali folk literature
Folk literature, Mandingo *(May Subd Geog)*
  ⌐GR350.32.M33¬
  UF Mandingo folk literature

Folk literature, Mansi *(May Subd Geog)*
  UF Mansi folk literature
  BT Mansi literature
Folk literature, Marathi *(May Subd Geog)*
  UF Marathi folk literature
  BT Marathi literature
Folk literature, Mari *(May Subd Geog)*
  UF Mari folk literature
  BT Mari literature
Folk literature, Masai *(May Subd Geog)*
  UF Masai folk literature
  BT Masai literature
Folk literature, Mbosi *(May Subd Geog)*
  UF Mbosi folk literature
  BT Mbosi literature
Folk literature, Meru *(May Subd Geog)*
  UF Meru folk literature
  BT Meru literature
Folk literature, Minangkabau
  (May Subd Geog)
  UF Minangkabau folk literature
Folk literature, Moldavian
  NT Folk poetry, Moldavian
Folk literature, Mongolian
  (May Subd Geog)
  UF Mongolian folk literature
  BT Mongolian literature
Folk literature, Ndebele (Zimbabwe)
  (May Subd Geog)
  UF Ndebele folk literature (Zimbabwe)
  BT Ndebele literature (Zimbabwe)
Folk literature, Nemi *(May Subd Geog)*
  UF Nemi folk literature
  BT Nemi literature
Folk literature, Nengone *(May Subd Geog)*
  UF Nengone folk literature
Folk literature, Nepali *(May Subd Geog)*
  UF Nepali folk literature
  BT Nepali literature
Folk literature, Ngonde *(May Subd Geog)*
  ⌐GR356.72.N47¬
  UF Ngonde folk literature
Folk literature, Norwegian
  (May Subd Geog)
  UF Norwegian folk literature
  BT Norwegian literature
Folk literature, Ogan *(May Subd Geog)*
  UF Ogan folk literature
  BT Ogan literature
Folk literature, Oriya *(May Subd Geog)*
  UF Oriya folk literature
  BT Oriya literature
Folk literature, Ossetic *(May Subd Geog)*
  UF Ossetic folk literature
  BT Ossetic literature
Folk literature, Paite *(May Subd Geog)*
  UF Paite folk literature
  BT Paite literature
Folk literature, Pamir *(May Subd Geog)*
  UF Pamir folk literature
  BT Pamir literature
Folk literature, Panjabi *(May Subd Geog)*
  UF Panjabi folk literature
  BT Panjabi literature
Folk literature, Pawari *(May Subd Geog)*
  UF Pawari folk literature
Folk literature, Persian *(May Subd Geog)*
  UF Persian folk literature
  BT Persian literature
Folk literature, Philippine *(May Subd Geog)*
  UF Philippine folk literature
  BT Philippine literature
Folk literature, Polish *(May Subd Geog)*
  UF Polish folk literature
  BT Polish literature
Folk literature, Portuguese
  (May Subd Geog)
  UF Portuguese folk literature
  BT Portuguese literature

Folk literature, Raeto-Romance
  (May Subd Geog)
  UF Raeto-Romance folk literature
  BT Raeto-Romance literature
Folk literature, Rajasthani
  (May Subd Geog)
  UF Rajasthani folk literature
  BT Rajasthani literature
Folk literature, Rapanui *(May Subd Geog)*
  ⌐GR385.E2¬
  UF Rapanui folk literature
Folk literature, Romanian *(May Subd Geog)*
  UF Romanian folk literature
  BT Romanian literature
Folk literature, Romany *(May Subd Geog)*
  UF Romany folk literature
  BT Romany literature
Folk literature, Russian *(May Subd Geog)*
  UF Russian folk literature
  BT Russian literature
Folk literature, Ryukyu *(May Subd Geog)*
  UF Ryukyu folk literature
Folk literature, Sakata *(May Subd Geog)*
  ⌐GR357.82.S24¬
  UF Sakata folk literature
Folk literature, Sambalpuri
  (May Subd Geog)
  UF Sambalpuri folk literature
  BT Sambalpuri literature
Folk literature, Scottish *(May Subd Geog)*
  UF Scottish folk literature
  BT Scottish literature
Folk literature, Serbian *(May Subd Geog)*
  UF Serbian folk literature
  BT Serbian literature
Folk literature, Simelungun
  (May Subd Geog)
  UF Simelungun folk literature
  BT Simelungun literature
Folk literature, Sindhi *(May Subd Geog)*
  UF Sindhi folk literature
  BT Sindhi literature
Folk literature, Sinhalese *(May Subd Geog)*
  UF Sinhalese folk literature
  BT Sinhalese literature
Folk literature, Slavic *(May Subd Geog)*
  UF Slavic folk literature
  BT Slavic literature
Folk literature, Somali *(May Subd Geog)*
  UF Somali folk literature
  BT Somali literature
Folk literature, Sotho *(May Subd Geog)*
  ⌐GR359.52.S68¬
  UF Sotho folk literature
Folk literature, Spanish *(May Subd Geog)*
  UF Spanish folk literature
  BT Spanish literature
Folk literature, Subiya *(May Subd Geog)*
  UF Subiya folk literature
Folk literature, Sundanese
  (May Subd Geog)
  UF Sundanese folk literature
  BT Sundanese literature
Folk literature, Swahili *(May Subd Geog)*
  UF Swahili folk literature
  BT Swahili literature
Folk literature, Tajik *(May Subd Geog)*
  UF Tajik folk literature
  BT Tajik literature
Folk literature, Tamashek *(May Subd Geog)*
  UF Tamashek folk literature
Folk literature, Tamil *(May Subd Geog)*
  UF Tamil folk literature
  BT Tamil literature
Folk literature, Tangkhul *(May Subd Geog)*
  UF Tangkhul folk literature
  BT Tangkhul literature
Folk literature, Tatar *(May Subd Geog)*
  UF Tatar folk literature
  BT Tatar literature

Folk literature, Telugu *(May Subd Geog)*
  UF Telugu folk literature
  BT Telugu literature
Folk literature, Thai *(May Subd Geog)*
  UF Thai folk literature
  BT Thai literature
Folk literature, Tonga (Zambesi)
  (May Subd Geog)
  UF Tonga folk literature (Zambesi)
  BT Tonga literature (Zambesi)
Folk literature, Turkish *(May Subd Geog)*
  UF Turkish folk literature
  BT Turkish literature
Folk literature, Turkmen *(May Subd Geog)*
  UF Turkmen folk literature
  BT Turkmen literature
Folk literature, Tuvinian *(May Subd Geog)*
  UF Tuvinian folk literature
  BT Tuvinian literature
Folk literature, Udmurt *(May Subd Geog)*
  UF Udmurt folk literature
  BT Udmurt literature
Folk literature, Uea *(May Subd Geog)*
  UF Uea folk literature
Folk literature, Ukrainian *(May Subd Geog)*
  UF Ukrainian folk literature
  BT Ukrainian literature
Folk literature, Uzbek *(May Subd Geog)*
  UF Uzbek folk literature
  BT Uzbek literature
Folk literature, Vietnamese
  (May Subd Geog)
  UF Vietnamese folk literature
  BT Vietnamese literature
Folk literature, Wolio *(May Subd Geog)*
  UF Wolio folk literature
  BT Wolio literature
Folk literature, Yakut *(May Subd Geog)*
  UF Yakut folk literature
  BT Yakut literature
Folk literature, Yiddish *(May Subd Geog)*
  UF Yiddish folk literature
  BT Yiddish literature
Folk literature, Yugoslav *(May Subd Geog)*
  UF Yugoslav folk literature
  BT Yugoslav literature
Folk literature, Yui *(May Subd Geog)*
  UF Yui folk literature
Folk-lore
  USE Folklore
Folk-lore, Applied
  USE Applied folklore
Folk-lore and education
  USE Folklore and education
Folk medicine *(May Subd Geog)*
  UF Ethnic medicine
      Ethnomedicine
      Folklore, Medical
      Medical folk-lore
  BT Folklore
      Medical anthropology
      Medicine, Magic, mystic, and spagiric
      Medicine, Primitive
      Therapeutic systems
  NT Folk dentistry
      Healers
      Healing
  — **Cross-cultural studies**
  — **Formulae, receipts, prescriptions**
Folk models *(May Subd Geog)*
  ⌈GN468.5⌉
    Here are entered works on ethnological investiga-
  tions into a people's own concepts of their actions,
  their reasons and explanations for them, and more
  generally the whole range of their own notions about
  the social and natural world.
    BT Ethnology—Methodology
Folk music *(May Subd Geog)*
    For works consisting of folk music of an individual
  ethnic group, an additional subject entry is made
  under the heading ⌈ethnic group⌉—⌈place⌉—Music.

  BT Folklore
      Music
      National music
  RT Folk dancing
  NT Fiddling
      Folk dance music
      Folk-songs
  — **Mexico**
      NT Mariachi
  — **Spain**
      NT Flamenco music
  — **Thailand**
      NT Pīphāt music
  — **United States**
      NT Blues (Music)
          Country music
          Folk-rock music
Folk music groups *(May Subd Geog)*
  BT Musical groups
Folk philosophy
  USE Ethnophilosophy
Folk-plays
  USE Folk-drama
Folk poetry *(May Subd Geog)*
  ⌈PN1347 (Collections, PN1345)⌉
  ⌈PN1347 (History, PN1341)⌉
  UF Oral poetry
  BT Folk literature
      Folk-songs
  NT Indian poetry
      Nursery rhymes
Folk poetry, African
  UF African folk poetry
  BT African poetry
Folk poetry, Ainu *(May Subd Geog)*
  UF Ainu folk poetry
  BT Ainu poetry
Folk poetry, Albanian *(May Subd Geog)*
  UF Albanian folk poetry
  BT Albanian poetry
Folk poetry, American *(May Subd Geog)*
  UF American folk poetry
  BT American poetry
  NT Toasts (Afro-American folk poetry)
Folk poetry, American, ⌈etc.⌉
  (May Subd Geog)
  ⌈PS476 (History)⌉
  ⌈PS477-PS478 (Collections)⌉
Folk poetry, Amharic *(May Subd Geog)*
  UF Amharic folk poetry
  BT Amharic poetry
Folk poetry, Anglo-Saxon
  USE Folk poetry, English (Old)
Folk poetry, Arabic *(May Subd Geog)*
  UF Arabic folk poetry
  BT Arabic poetry
Folk poetry, Argentine *(May Subd Geog)*
  UF Argentine folk poetry
  BT Agentine poetry
Folk poetry, Australian *(May Subd Geog)*
  UF Australian folk poetry
  BT Australian poetry
Folk poetry, Azerbaijani *(May Subd Geog)*
  UF Azerbaijani folk poetry
  BT Azerbaijani poetry
Folk poetry, Balinese *(May Subd Geog)*
  UF Balinese folk poetry
  BT Balinese poetry
Folk poetry, Bengali *(May Subd Geog)*
  UF Bengali folk poetry
  BT Bengali poetry
Folk poetry, Bhili *(May Subd Geog)*
  UF Bhili folk poetry
  BT Bhili poetry
Folk poetry, Bhojpuri *(May Subd Geog)*
  UF Bhojpuri folk poetry
  BT Bhojpuri poetry
Folk poetry, Brazilian *(May Subd Geog)*
  UF Brazilian folk poetry
  BT Brazilian poetry

Folk poetry, Bulgarian *(May Subd Geog)*
  UF Bulgarian folk poetry
  BT Bulgarian poetry
Folk poetry, Byelorussian *(May Subd Geog)*
  UF Byelorussian folk poetry
  BT Byelorussian poetry
Folk poetry, Chinese *(May Subd Geog)*
  ⌈PL2309.F65 (History)⌉
  ⌈PL2519.F6 (Collections)⌉
  UF Chinese folk poetry
  BT Chinese poetry
Folk poetry, Chuang *(May Subd Geog)*
  UF Chuang folk poetry
  BT Chuang poetry
Folk poetry, Croatian *(May Subd Geog)*
  UF Croatian folk poetry
  BT Croatian poetry
Folk poetry, Dogri *(May Subd Geog)*
  UF Dogri folk poetry
  BT Dogri poetry
Folk poetry, Dravidian *(May Subd Geog)*
  UF Dravidian folk poetry
  BT Dravidian poetry
Folk poetry, English *(May Subd Geog)*
  UF English folk poetry
  BT English poetry
      Folk literature, English
  — Subjects
      USE Folk poetry, English—Themes,
           motives
  — **Themes, motives**
      UF Folk poetry, English—Subjects
Folk poetry, English (Old)
  (May Subd Geog)
  UF Anglo-Saxon folk poetry
      English folk poetry, Old
      Folk poetry, Anglo-Saxon
      Old English folk poetry
  BT English poetry—Old English, ca. 450-
      1100
Folk poetry, Finnish *(May Subd Geog)*
  UF Finnish folk poetry
  BT Finnish poetry
Folk poetry, Finno-Ugric *(May Subd Geog)*
  UF Finno-Ugric folk poetry
  BT Finno-Ugric poetry
Folk poetry, Gayo *(May Subd Geog)*
  UF Gayo folk poetry
  BT Gayo poetry
Folk poetry, Georgian *(May Subd Geog)*
  UF Georgian folk poetry
  BT Georgian poetry
Folk poetry, German *(May Subd Geog)*
  UF German folk poetry
  BT German poetry
Folk poetry, Greek *(May Subd Geog)*
  UF Greek folk poetry
  BT Greek poetry
Folk poetry, Greek (Modern)
  (May Subd Geog)
  UF Greek folk poetry, Modern
      Modern Greek folk poetry
  BT Greek poetry, Modern
Folk poetry, Gujarati *(May Subd Geog)*
  UF Gujarati folk poetry
  BT Gujarati poetry
Folk poetry, Hindi *(May Subd Geog)*
  UF Hindi folk poetry
  BT Hindi poetry
Folk poetry, Iban *(May Subd Geog)*
  UF Iban folk poetry
  BT Iban poetry
Folk poetry, Igbo *(May Subd Geog)*
  UF Igbo folk poetry
  BT Igbo poetry
Folk poetry, Irish *(May Subd Geog)*
  UF Irish folk poetry
  BT Irish poetry
Folk poetry, Italian *(May Subd Geog)*
  UF Italian folk poetry
  BT Italian poetry

Folk poetry, Japanese *(May Subd Geog)*
  UF Japanese folk poetry
  BT Japanese poetry
Folk poetry, Kannada *(May Subd Geog)*
  UF Kannada folk poetry
  BT Kannada poetry
Folk poetry, Karelian *(May Subd Geog)*
  UF Karelian folk poetry
  BT Karelian poetry
Folk poetry, Kazakh *(May Subd Geog)*
  UF Kazakh folk poetry
  BT Kazakh poetry
Folk poetry, Komi *(May Subd Geog)*
  UF Komi folk poetry
  BT Komi poetry
Folk poetry, Korean *(May Subd Geog)*
  UF Korean folk poetry
  BT Korean poetry
Folk poetry, Kurdish *(May Subd Geog)*
  UF Kurdish folk poetry
  BT Kurdish poetry
Folk poetry, Latvian *(May Subd Geog)*
  UF Latvian folk poetry
  BT Latvian poetry
Folk poetry, Macedonian *(May Subd Geog)*
  UF Macedonian folk poetry
  BT Macedonian poetry
Folk poetry, Malagasy *(May Subd Geog)*
  UF Malagasy folk poetry
  BT Malagasy poetry
Folk poetry, Mandailing *(May Subd Geog)*
  UF Mandailing folk poetry
  BT Mandailing poetry
Folk poetry, Mangyan *(May Subd Geog)*
  UF Mangyan folk poetry
Folk poetry, Minangkabau
  (May Subd Geog)
  UF Minangkabau folk poetry
  BT Minangkabau poetry
Folk poetry, Moldavian *(May Subd Geog)*
  UF Moldavian folk poetry
  BT Folk literature, Moldavian
Folk poetry, Mongolian *(May Subd Geog)*
  UF Mongolian folk poetry
  BT Mongolian poetry
Folk poetry, Munda *(May Subd Geog)*
  UF Munda folk poetry
  BT Munda poetry
Folk poetry, Mundari *(May Subd Geog)*
  UF Mundari folk poetry
  BT Mundari poetry
Folk poetry, Muong *(May Subd Geog)*
  UF Muong folk poetry
  BT Muong poetry
Folk poetry, Nigerian *(May Subd Geog)*
  UF Nigerian folk poetry
  BT Nigerian poetry
Folk poetry, Pai *(May Subd Geog)*
  UF Pai folk poetry
  BT Pai poetry
Folk poetry, Panjabi *(May Subd Geog)*
  UF Panjabi folk poetry
  BT Panjabi poetry
Folk poetry, Persian *(May Subd Geog)*
  UF Persian folk poetry
  BT Persian poetry
Folk poetry, Peruvian *(May Subd Geog)*
  UF Peruvian folk poetry
  BT Peruvian poetry
Folk poetry, Polynesian
  UF Polynesian folk poetry
  BT Polynesian poetry
Folk poetry, Portuguese *(May Subd Geog)*
  UF Portuguese folk poetry
  BT Portuguese poetry
Folk poetry, Puerto Rican
  (May Subd Geog)
  UF Puerto Rican folk poetry
  BT Puerto Rican poetry

Folk poetry, Raeto-Romance
  (May Subd Geog)
  [PC947.8]
  UF Raeto-Romance folk poetry
  BT Raeto-Romance poetry
Folk poetry, Romanian *(May Subd Geog)*
  UF Romanian folk poetry
  BT Romanian poetry
Folk poetry, Russian *(May Subd Geog)*
  UF Russian folk poetry
  BT Russian poetry
  NT Skaz
Folk poetry, Serbian *(May Subd Geog)*
  UF Serbian folk poetry
  BT Serbian poetry
Folk poetry, Shona *(May Subd Geog)*
  UF Shona folk poetry
  BT Shona poetry
Folk poetry, Simelungun *(May Subd Geog)*
  UF Simelungun folk poetry
  BT Simelungun poetry
Folk poetry, Sinhalese *(May Subd Geog)*
  UF Sinhalese folk poetry
  BT Sinhalese poetry
Folk poetry, Slavic
  UF Slavic folk poetry
  BT Slavic poetry
Folk poetry, Slovak *(May Subd Geog)*
  UF Slovak folk poetry
  BT Slovak poetry
Folk poetry, Slovenian *(May Subd Geog)*
  UF Slovenian folk poetry
  BT Slovenian poetry
Folk poetry, Spanish *(May Subd Geog)*
  UF Spanish folk poetry
  BT Spanish poetry
Folk poetry, Swedish *(May Subd Geog)*
  UF Swedish folk poetry
  BT Swedish poetry
Folk poetry, Tamil *(May Subd Geog)*
  UF Tamil folk poetry
  BT Tamil poetry
Folk poetry, Tatar *(May Subd Geog)*
  UF Tatar folk poetry
  BT Tatar poetry
Folk poetry, Telugu *(May Subd Geog)*
  UF Telugu folk poetry
  BT Telugu poetry
Folk poetry, Thai *(May Subd Geog)*
  UF Thai folk poetry
  BT Thai poetry
Folk poetry, Tibetan *(May Subd Geog)*
  UF Tibetan folk poetry
  BT Tibetan poetry
Folk poetry, Turkish *(May Subd Geog)*
  UF Turkish folk poetry
  BT Turkish poetry
Folk poetry, Turkmen *(May Subd Geog)*
  UF Turkmen folk poetry
  BT Turkmen poetry
Folk poetry, Udmurt *(May Subd Geog)*
  UF Udmurt folk poetry
  BT Udmurt poetry
Folk poetry, Ukrainian *(May Subd Geog)*
  UF Ukrainian folk poetry
  BT Ukrainian poetry
Folk poetry, Uzbek *(May Subd Geog)*
  UF Uzbek folk poetry
  BT Uzbek poetry
Folk poetry, Vietnamese *(May Subd Geog)*
  UF Vietnamese folk poetry
  BT Vietnamese poetry
Folk poetry, Welsh *(May Subd Geog)*
  UF Welsh folk poetry
  BT Welsh poetry
Folk poetry, Xhosa *(May Subd Geog)*
  UF Xhosa folk poetry
  BT Xhosa poetry
Folk poetry, Yao (Southeastern Asia)
  (May Subd Geog)
  UF Yao folk poetry (Southeastern Asia)

  BT Yao poetry (Southeastern Asia)
Folk poetry, Yoruba *(May Subd Geog)*
  UF Yoruba folk poetry
  BT Yoruba poetry
Folk-psychology
  USE Ethnopsychology
Folk-rock music *(May Subd Geog)*
  UF Ecology rock music
      Folkrock music
      Soft rock music
  BT Folk music—United States
      Rock music—United States
Folk singers *(May Subd Geog)*
  UF Folksingers
  BT Singers
  — Japan
    NT Goze
Folk-songs *(May Subd Geog)*
  [M1627 (Music)]
  [ML3545 (Music literature)]
  [PN1341-PN1345 (Folk poetry)]
    Here are entered collections of folk-songs in vari-
  ous unrelated languages. Works in a single language
  or group of languages are entered under this heading
  with language qualifier, e.g. Folk-songs, English;
  Folk-songs, Slavic. For works consisting of folk-songs
  of an individual ethnic group, additional subject en-
  tries are made under the heading [ethnic group]—
  Music and under the heading Folk music—[place]
  or Music—[place].
  BT Folk literature
      Folk music
      Music
      National music
      Songs
      Vocal music
  RT Ballads
      National songs
  NT Carols
      Dumy
      Folk poetry
      Lays
      Play-party
      Rice—Planting—Songs and music
      Work-songs
  — Accompaniment
    [MT68]
    BT Musical accompaniment
  — Criticism, Textual
  — Instrumental settings
Folk-songs, Abkhaz *(May Subd Geog)*
  [M1766-1767]
  UF Abkhaz folk-songs
Folk-songs, Acoli *(May Subd Geog)*
  UF Acoli folk-songs
Folk-songs, Adyghe *(May Subd Geog)*
  [M1766-1767]
  UF Adyghe folk-songs
Folk-songs, Adzhar *(May Subd Geog)*
  [M1766.A3]
  [M1767.A3]
  UF Adzhar folk-songs
Folk-songs, Agri *(May Subd Geog)*
  UF Agri folk-songs
Folk-songs, Ainu *(May Subd Geog)*
  UF Ainu folk-songs
Folk-songs, Aka (Central African Republic)
  (May Subd Geog)
  UF Aka folk-songs (Central African
      Republic)
Folk-songs, Akan *(May Subd Geog)*
  UF Akan folk-songs
Folk-songs, Albanian *(May Subd Geog)*
  UF Albanian folk-songs
Folk-songs, Ambo (Zambia)
  (May Subd Geog)
  UF Ambo (Zambia) folk-songs
Folk-songs, Antandroy *(May Subd Geog)*
  UF Antandroy folk-songs
Folk-songs, Arabic *(May Subd Geog)*
  UF Arabic folk-songs

Folk-songs, Armenian *(May Subd Geog)*
    UF Armenian folk-songs
Folk-songs, Aromanian *(May Subd Geog)*
    UF Aromanian folk-songs
Folk-songs, Australian (Aboriginal)
    (May Subd Geog)
    UF Australian (Aboriginal) folk-songs
Folk-songs, Awadhi *(May Subd Geog)*
    UF Awadhi folk-songs
Folk-songs, Bamileke *(May Subd Geog)*
    UF Bamileke folk-songs
Folk-songs, Banjarese *(May Subd Geog)*
    UF Banjarese folk-songs
Folk-songs, Bantu *(May Subd Geog)*
    UF Bantu folk-songs
Folk-songs, Basque *(May Subd Geog)*
    UF Basque folk-songs
Folk-songs, Bassari *(May Subd Geog)*
    UF Bassari folk-songs
Folk-songs, Béarnais *(May Subd Geog)*
    UF Béarnais folk-songs
Folk-songs, Bella Coola *(May Subd Geog)*
    UF Bella Coola folk-songs
Folk-songs, Bengali *(May Subd Geog)*
    UF Bengali folk-songs
Folk-songs, Bhili *(May Subd Geog)*
    UF Bhili folk-songs
Folk-songs, Bhojpuri *(May Subd Geog)*
    UF Bhojpuri folk-songs
Folk-songs, Bohemian
    USE Folk-songs, Czech
Folk-songs, Bosavi *(May Subd Geog)*
    UF Bosavi folk-songs
Folk-songs, Breton *(May Subd Geog)*
    UF Breton folk-songs
Folk-songs, Buin *(May Subd Geog)*
    UF Buin folk-songs
Folk-songs, Bulgarian *(May Subd Geog)*
    UF Bulgarian folk-songs
    BT Folk-songs, Slavic
Folk-songs, Bundeli *(May Subd Geog)*
    UF Bundeli folk-songs
Folk-songs, Burgundian *(May Subd Geog)*
    UF Burgundian folk-songs
Folk-songs, Burmese *(May Subd Geog)*
    UF Burmese folk-songs
Folk-songs, Byelorussian *(May Subd Geog)*
    UF Byelorussian folk-songs
Folk-songs, Cajun French *(May Subd Geog)*
    UF Cajun French folk-songs
Folk-songs, Catalan *(May Subd Geog)*
    UF Catalan folk-songs
    NT Goigs
Folk-songs, Chakma *(May Subd Geog)*
    UF Chakma folk-songs
Folk-songs, Chechen *(May Subd Geog)*
    ₍M1766-1767₎
    UF Chechen folk-songs
Folk-songs, Chhattisgarhi *(May Subd Geog)*
    UF Chhattisgarhi folk-songs
Folk-songs, Chinese *(May Subd Geog)*
    UF Chinese folk-songs
Folk-songs, Chuvash *(May Subd Geog)*
    ₍M1766-1767₎
    UF Chuvash folk-songs
Folk-songs, Cornish *(May Subd Geog)*
    UF Cornish folk-songs
Folk-songs, Creole *(May Subd Geog)*
    UF Creole folk-songs
Folk-songs, Croatian *(May Subd Geog)*
    UF Croatian folk-songs
    BT Folk-songs, Slavic
Folk-songs, Czech *(May Subd Geog)*
    UF Czech folk-songs
        Folk-songs, Bohemian
    BT Folk-songs, Slavic
Folk-songs, Dakota *(May Subd Geog)*
    UF Dakota folk-songs
Folk-songs, Danish *(May Subd Geog)*
    UF Danish folk-songs
    BT Folk-songs, Scandinavian

Folk-songs, Dargwa *(May Subd Geog)*
    UF Dargwa folk-songs
Folk-songs, Dimasa *(May Subd Geog)*
    UF Dimasa folk-songs
Folk-songs, Dinka *(May Subd Geog)*
    UF Dinka folk-songs
Folk-songs, Dogri *(May Subd Geog)*
    UF Dogri folk-songs
Folk-songs, Dutch *(May Subd Geog)*
    UF Dutch folk-songs
Folk-songs, Embu *(May Subd Geog)*
    UF Embu folk-songs
Folk-songs, English *(May Subd Geog)*
    UF English folk-songs
    — United States
        NT Spirituals (Songs)
Folk-songs, Eskimo *(May Subd Geog)*
    UF Eskimo folk-songs
    BT Eskimos—Music
Folk-songs, Estonian *(May Subd Geog)*
    UF Estonian folk-songs
Folk-songs, Ethiopian *(May Subd Geog)*
    UF Ethiopian folk-songs
Folk-songs, Faroese *(May Subd Geog)*
    UF Faroese folk-songs
    BT Folk-songs, Scandinavian
Folk-songs, Finnish *(May Subd Geog)*
    UF Finnish folk-songs
Folk-songs, Finno-Ugric *(May Subd Geog)*
    UF Finno-Ugric folk-songs
Folk-songs, French *(May Subd Geog)*
    UF French folk-songs
Folk-songs, Friesian *(May Subd Geog)*
    UF Friesian folk-songs
Folk-songs, Friulian *(May Subd Geog)*
    UF Friulian folk-songs
Folk-songs, Fulah *(May Subd Geog)*
    UF Fulah folk-songs
Folk-songs, Gã *(May Subd Geog)*
    UF Gã folk-songs
Folk-songs, Gaelic *(May Subd Geog)*
    UF Gaelic folk-songs
Folk-songs, Ganda *(May Subd Geog)*
    UF Ganda folk-songs
Folk-songs, Garhwali *(May Subd Geog)*
    UF Garhwali folk-songs
Folk-songs, Garo *(May Subd Geog)*
    UF Garo folk-songs
Folk-songs, Gascon *(May Subd Geog)*
    UF Gascon folk-songs
Folk-songs, Gayo *(May Subd Geog)*
    UF Gayo folk-songs
Folk-songs, Gbaya *(May Subd Geog)*
    UF Gbaya folk-songs
Folk-songs, German *(May Subd Geog)*
    UF German folk-songs
    NT Folk-songs, Low German
    — Switzerland
        NT Yodels
Folk-songs, Gondi *(May Subd Geog)*
    UF Gondi folk-songs
Folk-songs, Greek *(May Subd Geog)*
    UF Greek folk-songs
Folk-songs, Greek (Modern)
    (May Subd Geog)
    UF Greek folk-songs, Modern
        Modern Greek folk-songs
Folk-songs, Guarani *(May Subd Geog)*
    UF Guarani folk-songs
Folk-songs, Gujarati *(May Subd Geog)*
    UF Gujarati folk-songs
Folk-songs, Gujuri *(May Subd Geog)*
    UF Gujuri folk-songs
Folk-songs, Hebrew *(May Subd Geog)*
    UF Hebrew folk-songs
Folk-songs, Himachali *(May Subd Geog)*
    UF Himachali folk-songs
Folk-songs, Hindi *(May Subd Geog)*
    UF Hindi folk-songs
Folk-songs, Hungarian *(May Subd Geog)*
    UF Hungarian folk-songs

Folk-songs, Iatmul *(May Subd Geog)*
    UF Iatmul folk-songs
Folk-songs, Icelandic *(May Subd Geog)*
    UF Icelandic folk-songs
    BT Folk-songs, Scandinavian
Folk-songs, Indic *(May Subd Geog)*
    UF Indic folk-songs
Folk-songs, Ingush *(May Subd Geog)*
    ₍M1766-1767₎
    UF Ingush folk-songs
Folk-songs, Irish *(May Subd Geog)*
    UF Irish folk-songs
Folk-songs, Italian *(May Subd Geog)*
    UF Italian folk-songs
Folk-songs, Japanese *(May Subd Geog)*
    UF Japanese folk-songs
        Saibara
Folk-songs, Javanese *(May Subd Geog)*
    UF Javanese folk-songs
Folk-songs, Kalmyk *(May Subd Geog)*
    UF Kalmyk folk-songs
Folk-songs, Kamba *(May Subd Geog)*
    UF Kamba folk-songs
Folk-songs, Kangri *(May Subd Geog)*
    UF Kangri folk-songs
Folk-songs, Kannada *(May Subd Geog)*
    UF Kannada folk-songs
Folk-songs, Karamojong *(May Subd Geog)*
    UF Karamojong folk-songs
Folk-songs, Karelian *(May Subd Geog)*
    UF Karelian folk-songs
Folk-songs, Karo-Batak *(May Subd Geog)*
    UF Karo-Batak folk-songs
Folk-songs, Kashubian *(May Subd Geog)*
    UF Kashubian folk-songs
Folk-songs, Kazakh *(May Subd Geog)*
    UF Kazakh folk-songs
Folk-songs, Kemak *(May Subd Geog)*
    UF Kemak folk-songs
Folk-songs, Khakass *(May Subd Geog)*
    UF Khakass folk-songs
Folk-songs, Khanty *(May Subd Geog)*
    UF Khanty folk-songs
Folk-songs, Kikuyu *(May Subd Geog)*
    UF Kikuyu folk-songs
Folk-songs, Kimbundu *(May Subd Geog)*
    UF Kimbundu folk-songs
Folk-songs, Kodagu *(May Subd Geog)*
    UF Kodagu folk-songs
Folk-songs, Konkani *(May Subd Geog)*
    UF Konkani folk-songs
Folk-songs, Korean *(May Subd Geog)*
    UF Korean folk-songs
Folk-songs, Kpelle *(May Subd Geog)*
    UF Kpelle folk-songs
Folk-songs, Kuanua *(May Subd Geog)*
    UF Kuanua folk-songs
Folk-songs, Kului *(May Subd Geog)*
    UF Kului folk-songs
Folk-songs, Kurdish *(May Subd Geog)*
    UF Kurdish folk-songs
Folk-songs, Kurukh *(May Subd Geog)*
    UF Kurukh folk-songs
Folk-songs, Ladakhi *(May Subd Geog)*
    UF Ladakhi folk-songs
Folk-songs, Ladino *(May Subd Geog)*
    UF Ladino folk-songs
Folk-songs, Langue d'oc *(May Subd Geog)*
    UF Langue d'oc folk-songs
Folk-songs, Lao *(May Subd Geog)*
    UF Lao folk-songs
Folk-songs, Latvian *(May Subd Geog)*
    UF Latvian folk-songs
Folk-songs, Lepcha *(May Subd Geog)*
    UF Lepcha folk-songs
Folk-songs, Lithuanian *(May Subd Geog)*
    UF Lithuanian folk-songs
Folk-songs, Livonian *(May Subd Geog)*
    UF Livonian folk-songs
Folk-songs, Lobi *(May Subd Geog)*
    UF Lobi folk-songs

Folk-songs, Low German (May Subd Geog)
  UF Low German folk-songs
  BT Folk-songs, German
Folk-songs, Lunda (May Subd Geog)
  UF Lunda folk-songs
Folk-songs, Lushai (May Subd Geog)
  UF Lushai folk-songs
Folk-songs, Macedonian (May Subd Geog)
  [M1724-1725]
  UF Macedonian folk-songs
Folk-songs, Maithili (May Subd Geog)
  UF Maithili folk-songs
Folk-songs, Malagasy (May Subd Geog)
  UF Malagasy folk-songs
Folk-songs, Malay (May Subd Geog)
  UF Malay folk-songs
Folk-songs, Malayalam (May Subd Geog)
  UF Malayalam folk-songs
Folk-songs, Mandailing (May Subd Geog)
  UF Mandailing folk-songs
Folk-songs, Mandingo (May Subd Geog)
  UF Mandingo folk-songs
Folk-songs, Mansi (May Subd Geog)
  UF Mansi folk-songs
Folk-songs, Manx (May Subd Geog)
  UF Manx folk-songs
Folk-songs, Maori (May Subd Geog)
  UF Maori folk-songs
Folk-songs, Marathi (May Subd Geog)
  UF Marathi folk-songs
Folk-songs, Mari (May Subd Geog)
  UF Mari folk-songs
Folk-songs, Marwari (May Subd Geog)
  UF Marwari folk-songs
Folk-songs, Moldavian (May Subd Geog)
  UF Moldavian folk-songs
Folk-songs, Mongolian (May Subd Geog)
  UF Mongolian folk-songs
Folk-songs, Mundari (May Subd Geog)
  UF Mundari folk-songs
Folk-songs, Ngbaka ma'bo (May Subd Geog)
  UF Ngbaka ma'bo folk-songs
Folk-songs, Nimadi (May Subd Geog)
  UF Nimadi folk-songs
Folk-songs, Norwegian (May Subd Geog)
  UF Norwegian folk-songs
  BT Folk-songs, Scandinavian
Folk-songs, Nuer (May Subd Geog)
  UF Nuer folk-songs
Folk-songs, Old French (May Subd Geog)
  UF Old French folk-songs
Folk-songs, Oriya (May Subd Geog)
  UF Oriya folk-songs
Folk-songs, Paite (May Subd Geog)
  UF Paite folk-songs
Folk-songs, Panjabi (May Subd Geog)
  UF Panjabi folk-songs
Folk-songs, Papuan (May Subd Geog)
  UF Papuan folk-songs
Folk-songs, Pennsylvania German
  (May Subd Geog)
  UF Pennsylvania German folk-songs
Folk-songs, Polish (May Subd Geog)
  UF Polish folk-songs
  BT Folk-songs, Slavic
Folk-songs, Portuguese (May Subd Geog)
  UF Portuguese folk-songs
  NT Fados
  — Brazil
    NT Congadas
Folk-songs, Provençal (May Subd Geog)
  UF Provençal folk-songs
Folk-songs, Punu (May Subd Geog)
  UF Punu folk-songs
Folk-songs, Quechua (May Subd Geog)
  UF Quechua folk-songs
Folk-songs, Raeto-Romance
  (May Subd Geog)
  UF Raeto-Romance folk-songs
Folk-songs, Rajasthani (May Subd Geog)
  UF Rajasthani folk-songs

Folk-songs, Romanian (May Subd Geog)
  UF Romanian folk-songs
Folk-songs, Romany (May Subd Geog)
  UF Romany folk-songs
Folk-songs, Ruanda (May Subd Geog)
  UF Ruanda folk-songs
Folk-songs, Rundi (May Subd Geog)
  UF Rundi folk-songs
Folk-songs, Russian (May Subd Geog)
  UF Russian folk-songs
  BT Folk-songs, Slavic
  NT Byliny
      Chastushki
Folk-songs, Salampasu (May Subd Geog)
  UF Salampasu folk-songs
Folk-songs, Sambalpuri (May Subd Geog)
  UF Sambalpuri folk-songs
Folk-songs, Samoan (May Subd Geog)
  UF Samoan folk-songs
Folk-songs, Santali (May Subd Geog)
  UF Santali folk-songs
Folk-songs, Sardinian (May Subd Geog)
  UF Sardinian folk-songs
Folk-songs, Scandinavian (May Subd Geog)
  UF Scandinavian folk-songs
  NT Folk-songs, Danish
      Folk-songs, Faroese
      Folk-songs, Icelandic
      Folk-songs, Norwegian
      Folk-songs, Swedish
Folk-songs, Serbo-Croatian
  (May Subd Geog)
  UF Serbo-Croatian folk-songs
Folk-songs, Simelungun (May Subd Geog)
  UF Simelungun folk-songs
Folk-songs, Sinhalese (May Subd Geog)
  UF Sinhalese folk-songs
Folk-songs, Slavic (May Subd Geog)
  UF Slavic folk-songs
  NT Folk-songs, Bulgarian
      Folk-songs, Croatian
      Folk-songs, Czech
      Folk-songs, Polish
      Folk-songs, Russian
      Folk-songs, Slovak
      Folk-songs, Slovenian
      Folk-songs, Sorbian
      Folk-songs, Ukrainian
Folk-songs, Slovak (May Subd Geog)
  UF Slovak folk-songs
  BT Folk-songs, Slavic
Folk-songs, Slovenian (May Subd Geog)
  UF Slovenian folk-songs
  BT Folk-songs, Slavic
Folk-songs, Somali (May Subd Geog)
  UF Somali folk-songs
Folk-songs, Sorbian (May Subd Geog)
  UF Sorbian folk-songs
  BT Folk-songs, Slavic
Folk-songs, Southern Slavic
  (May Subd Geog)
  UF Southern Slavic folk-songs
Folk-songs, Spanish (May Subd Geog)
  UF Spanish folk-songs
  NT Coplas
      Flamenco music
  — Mexico
    NT Corridos
  — Peru
    NT Mulizas
Folk-songs, Sranan (May Subd Geog)
  UF Sranan folk-songs
Folk-songs, Sundanese (May Subd Geog)
  UF Sundanese folk-songs
Folk-songs, Swedish (May Subd Geog)
  UF Swedish folk-songs
  BT Folk-songs, Scandinavian
Folk-songs, Tahitian (May Subd Geog)
  UF Tahitian folk-songs
Folk-songs, Tamazight (May Subd Geog)
  UF Tamazight folk-songs

Folk-songs, Tamil (May Subd Geog)
  UF Tamil folk-songs
Folk-songs, Tatar (May Subd Geog)
  UF Tatar folk-songs
Folk-songs, Teda (May Subd Geog)
  UF Teda folk-songs
Folk-songs, Teke (May Subd Geog)
  UF Teke folk-songs
Folk-songs, Telugu (May Subd Geog)
  UF Telugu folk-songs
Folk-songs, Tewa (May Subd Geog)
  UF Tewa folk-songs
Folk-songs, Thai (May Subd Geog)
  UF Thai folk-songs
Folk-songs, Tibetan (May Subd Geog)
  UF Tibetan folk-songs
Folk-songs, Tlingit (May Subd Geog)
  UF Tlingit folk-songs
Folk-songs, Tsogo (May Subd Geog)
  UF Tsogo folk-songs
Folk-songs, Tsonga (May Subd Geog)
  UF Tsonga folk-songs
Folk-songs, Tswana (May Subd Geog)
  UF Tswana folk-songs
Folk-songs, Tuvinian (May Subd Geog)
  UF Tuvinian folk-songs
Folk-songs, Ukrainian (May Subd Geog)
  UF Ukrainian folk-songs
  BT Folk-songs, Slavic
  NT Kolomyĭky
Folk-songs, Urdu (May Subd Geog)
  UF Urdu folk-songs
Folk-songs, Uzbek (May Subd Geog)
  UF Uzbek folk-songs
Folk-songs, Vietnamese (May Subd Geog)
  UF Vietnamese folk-songs
Folk-songs, Walloon (May Subd Geog)
  UF Walloon folk-songs
Folk-songs, Welsh (May Subd Geog)
  UF Welsh folk-songs
Folk-songs, Yiddish (May Subd Geog)
  UF Yiddish folk-songs
Folk-songs, Yoruba (May Subd Geog)
  UF Yoruba folk-songs
Folk-songs, Zande (May Subd Geog)
  UF Zande folk-songs
Folk-songs, Zarma (May Subd Geog)
  UF Zarma folk-songs
Folk-tales
  USE Folk literature
       Legends
       Tales
Folke family
  USE Faulk family
Folkenberry family
  USE Faulkenberry family
Folker family
  USE Felker family
Folkers family
  USE Felker family
Folklore (May Subd Geog)
  [GR]
  UF Folk beliefs
      Folk-lore
      Traditions
  BT Ethnology
      Manners and customs
      Religion, Primitive
  RT Material culture
      Mythology
      Oral tradition
      Storytelling
  SA subdivision Folklore under ethnic,
      national or occupational groups; and
      under topics for discussions of those
      topics as themes in folklore
  NT Applied folklore
      Cinderella (Legendary character)
      Communication in folklore
      Ethnic folklore
      Fairies

Folk festivals
Folk literature
Folk medicine
Folk music
Folklorists
Graffiti
Grail
Literature and folklore
Monsters
Pregnant Man (Legendary character)
Psychoanalysis and folklore
Public folklore
Trickster
Urban folklore
— **Classification**
    Here are entered lists of types, themes, motifs, variants, etc. of folklore material compiled with the aim of arranging them in certain clearly defined groups, as well as works discussing the principles upon which systems of classification may be based.
  UF Folklore—History and criticism
       Folklore—Themes, motives
  RT Folklore archives
  NT Folk literature—Themes, motives
— **Government policy** *(May Subd Geog)*
  RT Public folklore
— History and criticism
  USE Folk literature—History and criticism
       Folklore—Classification
       Folklore—Structural analysis
— **Methodology**
  NT Folklore—Structural analysis
       Oral-formulaic analysis
— **Performance**
  UF Performance of folklore
  BT Oral communication
— **Structural analysis**
  UF Folklore—History and criticism
       Structural analysis (Folklore)
       Structuralism (Folklore analysis)
  BT Folklore—Methodology
       Structural anthropology
— Themes, motives
  USE Folklore—Classification
— **Africa, East**
  NT Liyongo (Legendary character)
— **Africa, West**
  NT Anansi (Legendary character)
— **Argentina**
  NT Difunta Correa (Legendary character)
— **Australia**
  NT Bunyips
— **Azerbaijan S.S.R.**
— — **Uzbek influences**
    BT Uzbek S.S.R.—Civilization
— **Belgium**
— **Brazil**
— **Byzantine Empire**
  NT Digenis Akritas (Legendary character)
— **Caribbean Area**
  NT Anansi (Legendary character)
— **China**
  NT Chung, Tzu-ch'i (Legendary character)
       Meng-chiang-nü (Legendary character)
       Po, Ya (Legendary character)
       Ts'ang, Chieh (Legendary character)
       Uncle Tompa (Legendary character)
— **Europe**
  NT Astyanax (Legendary character)
       Gregorius (Legendary character)
       Iseult (Legendary character)
       Joan (Legendary Pope)

       Reynard the Fox (Legendary character)
       Sibille, Queen (Legendary character)
       Swan-knight
       Tristan (Legendary character)
— **France**
  NT Hervis de Metz (Legendary character)
       Melusine (Legendary character)
       Renaud de Montauban (Legendary character)
       Roland (Legendary character)
— **Germany**
  NT Pied Piper of Hamelin (Legendary character)
— **Germany (West)**
  NT Pua Moders (Legendary character)
— **Great Britain**
  NT Brutus the Trojan (Legendary character)
       Lear, King (Legendary character)
       Robin Hood (Legendary character)
— **Greece**
  NT Aeneas (Legendary character)
       Andromache (Legendary character)
       Antenor (Legendary character)
       Antigone (Legendary character)
       Astyanax (Legendary character)
       Caeneus (Legendary character)
       Danaus (Legendary character)
       Hector (Legendary character)
       Hecuba (Legendary character)
       Laocoön (Legendary character)
       Philoctetes (Legendary character)
       Theano (Legendary character)
       Thyestes (Legendary character)
— **Hawaii**
  NT Hale-mano (Legendary character)
— **India**
  NT Āmrapālī (Legendary character)
       Candrabhāna (Legendary character)
       Cucīlavaḷḷal (Legendary character)
       Cūdāla (Legendary character)
       Maitonphi (Legendary character)
       Mantharā (Legendary character)
       Mohanārāṇī (Legendary character)
       Pannā (Legendary character)
       Rāja Bībī (Legendary character)
       Salesa (Legendary character)
       Ṭimikkindyen (Legendary character)
       Vijayamala (Legendary character)
— **Indonesia**
  NT Ratu Adil (Legendary character)
— **Ireland**
  NT Amergin (Legendary character)
       Cuchulain (Legendary character)
— **Italy**
  NT Giufà (Legendary character)
       Griselda (Legendary character)
— **Japan**
  NT Kappa (Japanese water goblin)
       Oshira-sama
       Seven gods of fortune
       Tekona (Legendary character)
       Urashima Tarō (Legendary character)
— **Latin America**
  NT Llorona (Legendary character)
— **Middle East**
  UF Folklore—Near East
  NT Nasreddin Hoca (Legendary character)
       Scheherazade (Legendary character)
— Near East
  USE Folklore—Middle East
— **North America**
  NT Coyote (Legendary character)

— **Poland**
  NT Lech (Legendary character)
— **Puerto Rico**
  NT Juan Bobo (Legendary character)
— **Romania**
  NT Făt-Frumos (Legendary character)
       Harap Alb (Legendary character)
       Păcală (Legendary character)
— **Rome**
  NT Aeneas (Legendary character)
       Roman she-wolf (Legendary character)
       Turnus (Legendary character)
— **Soviet Union**
  NT Baba Yaga (Legendary character)
— **Spain**
  NT Cucafera
       Don Juan (Legendary character)
— **Turkey**
  NT Nasreddin Hoca (Legendary character)
— **United States**
  NT Bunyan, Paul (Legendary character)
       Feboldson, Febold (Legendary character)
       John Henry (Legendary character)
       Magarac, Joe (Legendary character)
       Pecos Bill (Legendary character)
       Smith, Windwagon
— **Uzbek S.S.R.**
— — **Azerbaijani influences**
    BT Azerbaijan S.S.R.—Civilization
— **Venezuela**
  NT Lionza, María (Legendary character)
— **West Indies**
  NT Anansi (Legendary character)
— **Zaire**
  NT Kabundji (Legendary character)
Folklore, Applied
USE Applied folklore
Folklore, Biblical
USE Folklore in the Bible
Folklore, Dental
USE Folk dentistry
Folklore, Medical
USE Folk medicine
Folklore, Public
USE Public folklore
Folklore and children *(May Subd Geog)*
  [GR43.C4]
    Here are entered works which discuss the relationship between children and folklore. Works on folklore produced by or for children and works on children as a theme in folklore are entered under Children—Folklore.
  UF Folklore and youth
  BT Children
       Youth
Folklore and education *(May Subd Geog)*
  [LB1583.8]
  UF Education and folklore
       Folk-lore and education
  BT Education
Folklore and history *(May Subd Geog)*
  BT History
Folklore and nationalism *(May Subd Geog)*
  BT Nationalism
Folklore and youth
USE Folklore and children
Folklore archives *(May Subd Geog)*
  BT Archives
  RT Folklore—Classification
       Folklore libraries

Folklore in rabbinical literature
    BT Folklore in the Bible
         Jews in literature
         Midrash—Folklore
         Rabbinical literature
         Talmud—Folklore
Folklore in the Bible
      Here are entered works on folklore as a theme in
    the Bible. Works on the Bible as a theme in folklore
    are entered under Bible—Folklore.
    UF Folklore, Biblical
    NT Folklore in rabbinical literature
Folklore libraries *(May Subd Geog)*
    UF Libraries, Folklore
    BT Humanities libraries
    RT Folklore archives
Folkloric communication
    USE Communication in folklore
Folklorists *(May Subd Geog)*
    [GR50]
    BT Folklore
    NT Ethnomusicologists
Folklorists, Women
Folkrock music
    USE Folk-rock music
Folks family
    USE Faulk family
Folksingers
    USE Folk singers
Folkways
    USE Manners and customs
         Social norms
Follet family
    USE Follett family
Follett family *(Not Subd Geog)*
    UF Follet family
         Follette family
    RT La Follette family
Follette family
    USE Follett family
Follias (Music)
    USE Folias (Music)
Follicle-stimulating hormone
    BT Gonadotropin
Follicle stimulating hormone release inhibiting
  factor
    USE Somatostatin
Follicles, Hair
    USE Hair follicles
Follicular hormone
    USE Estrone
Folliculin
    USE Estrone
Folliculina
    BT Folliculinidae
Folliculinidae
    [QL368.A22]
    BT Spirotricha
    NT Folliculina
Follies (Architecture) *(May Subd Geog)*
    UF Folly (Architecture)
    BT Architecture
         Pavilions
Follies (Etchings)
    USE Goya, Francisco, 1746-1828.
         Proverbs
Follis (Coin) *(May Subd Geog)*
    BT Coins, Roman
Follmar family
    USE Follmer family
Follmer family
    UF Follmar family
         Folmar family
         Folmer family
         Fullmer family
         Fulmer family
         Volkmar family
         Vollmar family
         Vollmer family
         Volmar family
         Volmer family

Follow-up in teacher training
    (May Subd Geog)
    UF Teachers colleges—Follow-up service
    BT Teachers—Training of
Folly
    BT Conduct of life
    RT Pride and vanity
    — **Religious aspects**
    — — **Baptists,** [Catholic Church, etc.]
    — — **Buddhism,** [Christianity, etc.]
Folly (Architecture)
    USE Follies (Architecture)
Folly in art
Folmar family
    USE Follmer family
Folmer family
    USE Follmer family
Folsch family
    USE Foelsch family
Folsom culture
Folsom family
    UF Falsom family
         Folsome family
         Folsum family
Folsom points
    [E98.I4]
    BT Indians of North America—
             Implements
         Paleo-Indians
         Projectile points
         Stone implements
Folsome family
    USE Folsom family
Folsum family
    USE Folsom family
Foma (Bantu people)
    BT Ethnology—Zaire
Fomes lignosus
Fomes pini
    BT Conifers—Diseases and pests
Fon (African people)
    [DT541.42]
    UF Dahomans
         Dahomeans
         Dahomey (African people)
         Dahomeyans
    BT Ethnology—Benin
         Ethnology—Nigeria
         Ewe (African people)
    NT Aja (African people)
Fon (African people) art
    USE Art, Fon (African people)
Fon dialect
    [PL8164.Z9]
    UF Dahoman language
         Djedji dialect
         Fō dialect
         Fogbe dialect
         Fongbe dialect
         Jeji dialect
    BT Ewe language
    — **Etymology**
        NT Gbè (The Fon word)
            Xó (The Fon word)
Fon poetry *(May Subd Geog)*
Fon proverbs
    USE Proverbs, Fon
Fondi-Grabmal Fresko (Mural painting and
  decoration)
    USE Neroni, Bartolomeo, ca. 1505-1571.
         Fondi Monument fresco
Fondi Monument fresco (Mural painting and
  decoration)
    USE Neroni, Bartolomeo, ca. 1505-1571.
         Fondi Monument fresco
Fondue
    BT Chafing dish cookery
         Cookery (Cheese)
Fongbe dialect
    USE Fon dialect

Fonseca, Gulf of
    UF Fonseca Bay
         Golfo de Fonseca
         Gulf of Fonseca
    BT Bays—El Salvador
         Bays—Honduras
         Bays—Nicaragua
Fonseca Bay
    USE Fonseca, Gulf of
Fonseca family
Fonstad family
Fontaine family
    UF Delafontaine family
         La Fontaine family
         Lafond family
         Lafont family
         Lafontant family
Fontainebleau, Forest of (France)
    UF Bière Forest (France)
         Bierre Forest (France)
         Forest of Fontainebleau (France)
         Forêt de Bière (France)
         Forêt de Bierre (France)
         Forêt de Fontainebleau (France)
    BT Forest reserves—France
Fontainebleau Palace (Fontainebleau, France)
    USE Château de Fontainebleau
         (Fontainebleau, France)
Fontainebleau school of art
    [N6845.5.M3]
    UF Ecole de Fontainebleau
         School of Fontainebleau
    BT Art, French
Fontana di Trevi (Rome, Italy)
    [DG815.4.F]
    UF Trevi Fountain (Rome, Italy)
    BT Fountains—Italy
Fontanel
    USE Skull
Fontanelle
    USE Skull
FONTASY (Computer program)
    BT Computer graphics—Computer
            programs
Fontenay family
    USE Fontenot family
Fonteneau family
    USE Fontenot family
Fontenot family *(Not Subd Geog)*
    UF Fontenay family
         Fonteneau family
Fontenoy, Battle of, 1745
    [D293.7.F6]
    BT Austrian Succession, War of, 1740-
         1748
Fontibón (Bogotá, Colombia)
    (Not Subd Geog)
    UF Bogotá (Colombia). Fontibón
Fonticola
    USE Phagocata
Fonts *(May Subd Geog)*
    [NA5070]
    UF Baptismal fonts
    BT Baptism
         Baptisteries
         Christian antiquities
         Christian art and symbolism
         Church decoration and ornament
         Church furniture
    NT Bronze fonts
Fonts, Romanesque *(May Subd Geog)*
    UF Romanesque fonts
Fonts baptismaux de Liège
    USE Renier, de Huy, d. 1150. Liège font
Food
    [GT2860 (Manners and customs)]
    [HD9000-HD9490 (Trade)]
    [QH521 (Biology)]
    [RA601-RA602 (Public health)]
    [RM214-RM261 (Diet)]
    [TP370-TP465 (Chemical technology)]

[TX341-TX641 (Home economics)]
UF Foods
BT Digestion
    Dinners and dining
    Home economics
    Table
RT Cookery
    Diet
    Dietaries
    Gastronomy
    Nutrition
SA *subdivision* Food *under subjects, e.g.*
    Birds—Food; Indians—Food; also
    headings beginning with the word
    Food; and particular foods and
    beverages, e.g. Bread, Milk
NT Acorns as food
    Agar as food
    Animal food
    Animals—Food
    Aquatic plants as food
    Baby foods
    Bantus—Food
    Beverages
    Cassava as food
    Cereals as food
    Coloring matter in food
    Condiments
    Convenience foods
    Corn as food
    Courts and courtiers—Food
    Eggs as food
    Farm produce
    Fish as food
    Fish-meal as food
    Flavoring essences
    Flour as food
    Food, Junk
    Food, Natural
    Food, Pickled
    Food crops
    Food mixes
    Food presentation
    Fruit
    Grain
    Hay as food
    Hispanic Americans—Food
    Honey as food
    Igbo (African people)—Food
    Insects as food
    Kikuyu (African people)—Food
    Kosher food
    Legumes as food
    Lupines as food
    Macaroni products
    Meat
    Milk as food
    Nguni (African people)—Food
    Nuts
    Oats as food
    Operational rations (Military supplies)
    Plant proteins as food
    Plants, Edible
    Pollen as food
    Poultry as food
    Seafood
    Seeds as food
    Sorghum as food
    Soybean as food
    Straw as food
    Stuffed foods (Cookery)
    Survival and emergency rations
    Vegetarianism
    Wildlife as food
    Wola (Papua New Guinea people)—
      Food
    Zande (African people)—Food
— Adulteration
    USE Food adulteration and inspection
— **Analysis**
    [TX541-5]

UF Analysis of food
    Chemistry of food
    Food—Chemistry
    Food, Chemistry of
    Food chemistry
BT Chemistry, Technical
    Sanitary chemistry
RT Food—Composition
NT Flavor
    Food—Sensory evaluation
    Food—Water activity
    Food additives
— **Bacteriology**
    [QR115-129]
BT Food—Microbiology
— — **Laboratory manuals**
    BT Bacteriology—Laboratory
        manuals
— **Caloric content**
    [TX551]
UF Caloric content of foods
    Calories (Food)
    Food calories
BT Food—Composition
— **Carbohydrate content**
    [TX553.C28]
BT Carbohydrates
    Food—Composition
NT Complex carbohydrate diet
    High-carbohydrate diet
— Chemistry
    USE Food—Analysis
        Food—Composition
— **Cholesterol content**
    [TX553.C43]
UF Cholesterol content of food
BT Cholesterol
    Food—Composition
— Color
    USE Color of food
— **Composition**
UF Chemistry of food
    Food—Chemistry
    Food, Chemistry of
    Food chemistry
RT Food—Analysis
NT Food—Caloric content
    Food—Carbohydrate content
    Food—Cholesterol content
    Food—Fat content
    Food—Fiber content
    Food—Mineral content
    Food—Polysaccharide content
    Food—Potassium content
    Food—Protein content
    Food—Sodium content
    Food—Sugar content
    Food—Vitamin content
    Food—Water activity
— Conservation
    USE Food conservation
— Containers
    USE Food containers
— Contamination
    USE Food contamination
— **Cooling**
UF Cooling of food
BT Food—Preservation
— Dehydration
    USE Food—Drying
— Desiccation
    USE Food—Drying
— **Drying**
UF Dehydration of food
    Desiccation of food
    Evaporation of food
    Food—Dehydration
    Food—Desiccation
    Food—Evaporation
BT Food—Preservation
RT Food, Dried

— — Patents
    USE Food, Dried—Patents
— **Effect of heat on**
    UF Food—Heat effects
    BT Cookery
        Heat
— Evaporation
    USE Food—Drying
— **Fat content**
    BT Fat
        Food—Composition
        Oils and fats, Edible
— **Fiber content**
    UF Fiber content of food
        Roughage
    BT Fiber in human nutrition
        Food—Composition
        High-fiber diet
— **Folklore**
    NT Food habits
— Freezing
    USE Food, Frozen
— **Fumigation**
    BT Fumigation
— Heat effects
    USE Food—Effect of heat on
— Inspection
    USE Food adulteration and inspection
— **International cooperation**
    NT Food and Agriculture Organization
        of the United Nations
— **Iron content**
— Irradiation
    USE Radiation preservation of food
— **Labeling**
    NT Food—Shelf-life dating
— — **Law and legislation**
    (May Subd Geog)
    BT Food law and legislation
— Law and legislation
    USE Food law and legislation
— **Microbiology**
    UF Micro-organisms in food
    BT Sanitary microbiology
    SA *subdivision* Microbiology *under*
        types of food, e.g. Fishery
        products—Microbiology; Meat—
        Microbiology
    NT Food—Bacteriology
        Food poisoning
        Food spoilage
— **Mineral content**
    UF Mineral content of food
    BT Food—Composition
        Minerals in nutrition
— **Moisture**
    NT Food—Water activity
— **Odor**
    UF Aroma of food
    BT Odors
    NT Food—Sensory evaluation
— **Optical properties**
— **Packaging**
    UF Groceries—Packaging
    NT Edible coatings
        Food containers
— — **Law and legislation**
    (May Subd Geog)
    BT Food law and legislation
— Photography
    USE Photography of food
— **Pictorial works**
— **Polysaccharide content**
    [TX553.P65]
    BT Food—Composition
        Polysaccharides
— **Potassium content**
    BT Food—Composition
        Potassium
— **Preservation**
    [TX599-613]

1395

Food

— **Preservation** *(Continued)*
    UF Food preservation
          Preservation of food
    BT Food supply
    RT Food, Dried
          Food preservatives
    SA *subdivision* Preservation *under*
          various food products, e.g.
          Butter—Preservation; Fishery
          products—Preservation
    NT Antibiotics in food preservation
          Canning and preserving
          Chemical preservatives
          Cold storage
          Drying apparatus—Food
          Food—Cooling
          Food—Drying
          Food, Canned
          Food, Frozen
          Food additives
          Food spoilage
          Meat—Preservation
          Precooling
          Radiation preservation of food
          Salting of food
          Vegetables—Preservation

— **Prices**
    USE Food prices
— **Products liability**
    USE Products liability—Food
— **Protein content**
    BT Food—Composition
          Proteins
— **Purchasing**
    USE Marketing (Home economics)
— **Radiation preservation**
    USE Radiation preservation of food
— **Radioactive contamination**
    USE Radioactive contamination of
          food
— **Religious aspects**
    NT Food in the Bible
          Monasticism and religious orders—
          Dietary rules
— — **Black Muslims**
    NT Black Muslims—Dietary laws
— — **Buddhism**
    NT Monasticism and religious
          orders, Buddhist—Dietary
          rules
— — **Buddhism, [Christianity, etc.]**
— — **Islam**
    NT Food in the Koran
          Muslims—Dietary laws
— — **Jainism**
    NT Jains—Dietary laws
— — **Judaism**
    NT Jews—Dietary laws
— — **Sikhism**
    NT Sikhs—Dietary laws
— **Sensory evaluation**
    [TX546]
    UF Food—Taste testing
          Food tasting
          Organoleptic analysis of food
          Taste testing of food
    BT Flavor
          Food—Analysis
          Food—Odor
          Food—Testing
          Sensory evaluation
          Taste
    NT Tea tasting
          Wine tasting
— **Shelf-life dating**

    UF Date marking of food
          Food dating
          Freshness dating of food
          Open code dating of food
          Open dating of food
          Open shelf-life dating of food
          Pull dates of food
          Shelf-life dating of food
    BT Food—Labeling
          Food spoilage
— **Sodium content**
    [TX553.S65]
    BT Food—Composition
          Sodium
— **Spectra**
— **Storage**
    UF Stored products
    RT Farm produce—Storage
    NT Food storage pests
— **Sugar content**
    BT Food—Composition
          Sugar
— **Taste testing**
    USE Food—Sensory evaluation
— **Testing**
    NT Food—Sensory evaluation
— **Texture**
    USE Food texture
— **Therapeutic use**
    USE Diet therapy
— **Thermal properties**
— **Toxicology**
    USE Food poisoning
— **Tunguses**
    USE Tunguses—Food
— **Vitamin content**
    UF Vitamin content of food
    BT Food—Composition
          Vitamins in human nutrition
— **Water activity**
    [TX553.W3]
    UF Water activity of food
    BT Food—Analysis
          Food—Composition
          Food—Moisture
          Vapor pressure

Food, Artificial
    [RM258-RM261 (Diet)]
    [TX357]
    UF Artificial food
          Substitutes for food
          Synthetic food
    BT Diet in disease
    NT Food substitutes
Food, Baby
    USE Baby foods
Food, Canned
    [TX552]
    UF Canned foods
    BT Canning and preserving
          Food—Preservation
          Packing-house products
    RT Canned foods industry
    NT Cookery (Canned foods)
          Fish, Canned
          Fishery products, Canned
          Fruit, Canned
          Meat, Canned
          Poultry, Canned
          Vegetables, Canned
— **Labeling**
— **Sterilization**
Food, Chemistry of
    USE Food—Analysis
          Food—Composition
Food, Convenience
    USE Convenience foods
Food, Cost of
    USE Cost and standard of living
Food, Dehydrated
    USE Food, Dried

Food, Dehydrofrozen
    USE Food, Frozen
Food, Dietetic
    UF Dietetic food
    BT Diet
          Diet in disease
    NT Confectionery, Sugar-free
Food, Dried
    [TX609]
    UF Dehydrated foods
          Desiccated foods
          Dried foods
          Food, Dehydrated
    BT Drying apparatus—Food
    RT Food—Drying
          Food—Preservation
    NT Cookery (Dried foods)
          Dried food industry
          Eggs, Dried
          Food, Freeze-dried
          Fruit, Dried
          Meat, Dried
          Vegetables, Dried
— **Microbiology**
— **Patents**
    UF Food—Drying—Patents
Food, Enriched
    UF Enriched food
          Fortified food
    RT Food additives
    NT Cereal products, Enriched
          Salt, Iodized
          Sugar, Enriched
Food, Fermented
    [TP371.44]
    UF Fermented food
    BT Fermentation
Food, Freeze-dried
    UF Freeze-dried food
    BT Food, Dried
          Freeze-drying
Food, Fried
    UF Fried food
    BT Frying
    NT Skillet cookery
Food, Frozen
    [TP493.5]
    UF Dehydrofrozen food
          Food—Freezing
          Food, Dehydrofrozen
          Freezing of food
          Frozen food
    BT Food—Preservation
    NT Apple, Frozen
          Baked products, Frozen
          Chickens, Frozen
          Cookery (Frozen foods)
          Desserts, Frozen
          Eggs, Frozen
          Fish, Frozen
          Fishery products, Frozen
          Frozen foods industry
          Fruit, Frozen
          Meat, Frozen
          Milk, Frozen
          Poultry, Frozen
          Shrimps, Frozen
          Vegetables, Frozen
          Yogurt, Frozen
Food, Health
    USE Food, Natural
Food, Irradiated
    UF Irradiated foods
    BT Radiation preservation of food
    NT Fish, Irradiated
          Seafood, Irradiated
          Shrimps, Irradiated
Food, Junk
    [TX370]
    UF Junk food
    BT Food

RT Snack foods
Food, Kasher
  USE Kosher food
Food, Kosher
  USE Kosher food
Food, Natural
  ₍TX369₎
  UF Food, Health
      Food, Organically grown
      Health food
      Natural food
      Organically grown food
  BT Food
      Health products
  RT Natural food restaurants
  NT Cookery (Natural foods)
      Natural foods industry
      Wild plants, Edible
Food, Organically grown
  USE Food, Natural
Food, Pickled *(May Subd Geog)*
  UF Pickled food
  BT Food
  NT Kimch'i
      Pickles
Food, Precooked
  UF Precooked food
  NT Meat, Precooked
Food, Pure
  USE Food adulteration and inspection
      Food law and legislation
Food, Raw
  ₍TX392₎
  UF Raw food
      Uncooked food
      Unfired food
  BT Diet
      Vegetables
  RT Vegetarianism
  NT Raw food diet
  — **Therapeutic use**
      BT Raw food diet
Food, Smoked
  USE Cookery (Smoked foods)
      Fish, Smoked
      Meat, Smoked
Food, Wild *(May Subd Geog)*
  UF Foraging for wild food
      Gathering wild food
      Wild edibles
      Wild food gathering
      Wild foods
  BT Outdoor life
      Wilderness survival
  NT Cookery (Wild foods)
      Game and game-birds
      Seafood gathering
      Wild plants, Edible
      Wildlife as food
Food additives
  ₍TX553.A3₎
  UF Additive compounds
      Additives, Food
      Chemical additives in food
  BT Food—Analysis
      Food—Preservation
      Food industry and trade
  RT Food, Enriched
  NT Dietary supplements
      Edible coatings
      Food preservatives
      Monosodium glutamate
      Sweeteners
  — **Law and legislation** *(May Subd Geog)*
      BT Food law and legislation
Food additives industry *(May Subd Geog)*
  ₍HD9205₎
Food adulteration and inspection
  (May Subd Geog)
  ₍HD9000.9 (Economics)₎
  ₍TX501-TX595 (Technical works)₎

UF Analysis of food
    Food—Adulteration
    Food—Inspection
    Food, Pure
    Food inspection
    Inspection of food
    Pure food
BT Adulterations
    Consumer protection
    Public health
    Sanitary chemistry
NT Fish inspection
    Food contamination
    Food spoilage
    Meat inspection
    Milk commissions, Medical
    Milk hygiene
— **Law and legislation** *(May Subd Geog)*
    BT Food law and legislation
Food aid programs
  USE Food relief
Food allergy
  ₍RC596₎
  BT Allergy
— **Diet therapy**
  ₍RC588.D53₎
  UF Allergy—Diet therapy
  NT Egg-free diet
— — **Recipes**
  ₍RC588.D53₎
  UF Cookery for allergics
  BT Cookery for the sick
Food allergy in children *(May Subd Geog)*
  ₍RJ386.5₎
  BT Pediatric allergy
**Food and Agriculture Organization of the
  United Nations** *(May Subd Geog)*
  ₍HD9000.1 (Food supply)₎
  ₍S401 (Agriculture)₎
  ₍TX341 (Food and nutrition)₎
  Here are entered works on the Food and Agricul-
  ture Organization of the United Nations as an inter-
  national body. This heading may be subdivided geo-
  graphically to indicate relationships with specific re-
  gions or countries, e.g. Food and Agriculture Organi-
  zation of the United Nations—United States.
  BT Agriculture—International cooperation
      —Societies, etc.
      Food—International cooperation
      Rural development—International
      cooperation
— **United States**
Food animals
  USE Animal food
Food assistance programs
  USE Food relief
Food binge-purge behavior
  USE Bulimia
Food brokers
  BT Grocery trade
      Produce trade
Food buying
  USE Marketing (Home economics)
Food calories
  USE Food—Caloric content
Food chains (Ecology) *(May Subd Geog)*
  UF Food webs (Ecology)
  BT Animals—Food
      Biological productivity
      Ecology
      Niche (Ecology)
  NT Detritus
Food chemistry
  USE Food—Analysis
      Food—Composition
Food color
  USE Color of food
Food colorings
  USE Coloring matter in food
Food colors
  USE Coloring matter in food

Food conservation
  ₍TX357₎
  Here are entered works on the preservation and
  careful use of food, especially in war time. Economic
  works on the availability of food are entered under
  Food supply.
  UF Conservation of food
      Food—Conservation
  BT Food supply
  NT Canning and preserving
      Food contamination
Food consultants *(May Subd Geog)*
  BT Consultants
Food consumption *(May Subd Geog)*
  UF Consumption of food
  BT Cost and standard of living
      Food supply
  NT Engel's law
Food consumption forecasting
  (May Subd Geog)
  UF Forecasting, Food consumption
  BT Economic forecasting
Food consumption surveys
  USE Nutrition surveys
Food container industry *(May Subd Geog)*
  BT Food containers
Food containers
  UF Food—Containers
  BT Containers
      Food—Packaging
  SA *subdivisions* Containers *and* Packaging
      under specific foods, e.g. Milk—
      Containers; Apple—Packaging
  NT Aluminum cans
      Food container industry
      Glass candy containers
      Retort pouches
      Tin cans
Food contamination *(May Subd Geog)*
  UF Contaminated food
      Food—Contamination
      Foods, Contaminated
  BT Contamination (Technology)
      Decontamination (from gases,
      chemicals, etc.)
      Food adulteration and inspection
      Food conservation
      Public health
  NT Animal food—Contamination
      Antibiotic residues
      Baby foods—Contamination
      Dairy products—Contamination
      Feed additive residues
      Feeds—Contamination
      Fish as food—Contamination
      Infant formulas—Contamination
      Meat—Contamination
      Milk contamination
      Pesticide residues in food
      Radioactive contamination of food
      Rice oil—Contamination
      Seafood—Contamination
      Veterinary drug residues
Food control
  USE Food supply
Food crops *(May Subd Geog)*
  ₍SB175-SB177₎
  BT Food
      Plants, Edible
  RT Agroforestry
      Field crops
      Horticultural crops
  NT Fruit
      Grain
      Legumes
      Nuts
      Oilseed plants
      Quinoa
      Root-crops
      Vegetables

Food customs
    USE Food habits
Food dating
    USE Food—Shelf-life dating
Food decoration
    USE Cookery (Garnishes)
Food-drug interactions
    USE Drug-nutrient interactions
Food dyes
    USE Coloring matter in food
Food engineers (May Subd Geog)
    [TP369.5-369.6]
    BT Engineers
Food exchange lists (May Subd Geog)
        Here are entered works dealing with lists of foods
    grouped according to similarities in composition so
    that foods within a group may be used interchangea-
    bly in diet planning.
    UF Dietary exchange lists
        Exchange lists, Food
        Lists, Food exchange
        Nutritional exchange lists
    BT Diet therapy
Food for invalids
    USE Cookery for the sick
Food for school children
    USE School children—Food
Food gathering societies
    USE Hunting and gathering societies
Food habits (May Subd Geog)
    [GT2850-GT2955]
    [TX357]
    UF Eating
        Food customs
        Foodways
        Man—Food habits
    BT Food—Folklore
        Habit
    RT Diet
        Nutrition
        Nutrition—Psychological aspects
        Oral habits
    NT Animals—Food
        Children—Nutrition—Psychological
            aspects
        Food preferences
Food handling
    [TX537]
    UF Food sanitation
        Handling of food
    BT Sanitation, Household
    SA subdivision Sanitation under subjects,
        e.g. Food service—Sanitation;
        Restaurants, lunch rooms, etc.—
        Sanitation
    — Research grants (May Subd Geog)
Food in art
Food in literature
Food in the Bible
    UF Bible—Food
    BT Food—Religious aspects
Food in the Koran
    [BP134.F58]
    UF Koran—Food
    BT Food—Religious aspects—Islam
Food industry and trade (May Subd Geog)
        Here are entered works on the processing of food
    in general and on the marketing of processed food
    products. Works on the processing of specific kinds
    of food products are entered under the heading for
    the specific product with the subdivision Processing
    or under the heading for the industry. General works
    on the processing of agricultural products are entered
    under Agricultural processing. Works on a specific
    aspect or method of processing are entered under the
    heading for the specific process.
    UF Food preparation
        Food processing
        Food trade
    BT Agricultural processing
    RT Farm produce

    SA individual processed foods and
        industries, e.g. Butter; Flour and
        feed trade; also subdivision
        Postharvest technology under
        individual food crops, e.g. Corn—
        Postharvest technology; and
        subdivision Processing under
        individual food animals and crops,
        e.g. Cattle—Processing; Corn—
        Processing
    NT Carbohydrates, Refined
        Dairy processing
        Ethnic food industry
        Food additives
        Food prices
        Kosher food industry
        Produce trade
        Snack foods
        Strikes and lockouts—Food industry
            and trade
        Wages—Food industry and trade
    — Advertising
        USE Advertising—Food
    — By-products
        NT Food processing by-products
            industry
    — Collective labor agreements
        USE Collective labor agreements—
            Food industry
    — Credit guides
    — Defense measures
        BT Factories—Protection
            War damage, Industrial
    — Dust control
    — Electric equipment
    — Employees
        UF Food processing workers
        NT Collective labor agreements—Food
            industry
    — Energy consumption
    — Equipment and supplies
        NT Amylograph
            Food processing machinery
    — — Appraisal
        USE Food industry and trade—
            Equipment and supplies—
            Valuation
    — — Maintenance and repair
    — — Valuation
        UF Food industry and trade—
            Equipment and supplies—
            Appraisal
    — Law and legislation
        USE Food law and legislation
    — Management
    — Production control
    — Quality control
    — Sanitation
        [TP370]
        UF Food-plant sanitation
        BT Factory sanitation
    — Seasonal variations
    — Technology transfer
        BT Technology transfer
    — Netherlands
    — — Employees
        NT Calvé (Firm) Strike, 1977
Food inspection
    USE Food adulteration and inspection
Food insurance
    USE Insurance, Food supply
Food intake
    USE Ingestion
Food irradiation
    USE Radiation preservation of food

Food law and legislation (May Subd Geog)
    UF Food—Law and legislation
        Food, Pure
        Food industry and trade—Law and
            legislation
        Law, Food
        Pure food
    BT Commercial law
        Consumer protection—Law and
            legislation
    RT Produce trade—Law and legislation
    SA subdivision Law and legislation under
        individual foods, e.g. Potatoes—Law
        and legislation
    NT Advertising—Food—Law and
            legislation
        Canning and preserving—Law and
            legislation
        Coloring matter in food—Law and
            legislation
        Desserts, Frozen—Law and legislation
        Dietary supplements—Law and
            legislation
        Eggs—Inspection—Law and legislation
        Food—Labeling—Law and legislation
        Food—Packaging—Law and legislation
        Food additives—Law and legislation
        Food adulteration and inspection—
            Law and legislation
        Food service—Sanitation—Law and
            legislation
        Food supply—Law and legislation
        Fruit juices—Law and legislation
        Grocery trade—Law and legislation
        Infant formulas—Law and legislation
        Margarine—Law and legislation
        Meat industry and trade—Law and
            legislation
        Pesticide residues in food—Law and
            legislation
        Poultry—Inspection—Law and
            legislation
        Products liability—Food
        Restaurants, lunch rooms, etc.—Law
            and legislation
        Supermarkets—Sanitation—Law and
            legislation
    — Criminal provisions
Food mixes
    UF Mixes (Cookery)
        Prepared food
    BT Food
        Mixers (Cookery)
Food of wild animals
    USE Animals—Food
Food packets, Survival
    USE Survival and emergency rations
Food pages of newspapers
    USE Newspapers—Sections, columns, etc.—
        Food
Food-plant sanitation
    USE Food industry and trade—Sanitation
Food plants
    USE Plants, Edible
Food poisoning (May Subd Geog)
    [RA1258-RA1260 (General)]
    [RC143 (Bacterial)]
    UF Food—Toxicology
    BT Food—Microbiology
        Poisoning
        Putrefaction
    RT Ptomaine poisoning
    NT Animal food—Toxicology
        Botulism
        Salmonellosis
Food policy
    USE Nutrition policy
Food preferences (May Subd Geog)
    UF Food selection
    BT Food habits
        Nutrition

RT Nutrition—Psychological aspects
    Taste
NT Pica (Pathology)
Food preparation
  USE Cookery
    Food industry and trade
Food presentation
  UF Presentation of food
  BT Cookery
    Food
    Gastronomy
    Table
  NT Cookery (Garnishes)
Food preservation
  USE Food—Preservation
Food preservatives
  [TX607-8]
  UF Preservatives, Food
  BT Food additives
  RT Food—Preservation
  NT Subtilin
Food prices *(May Subd Geog)*
  UF Food—Prices
  BT Agricultural prices
    Cost and standard of living
    Food industry and trade
    Produce trade
Food processing
  USE Food industry and trade
Food processing by-products industry
(May Subd Geog)
  [HD9495]
  BT Food industry and trade—By-products
Food processing machinery
  BT Food industry and trade—Equipment
    and supplies
    Food processing plants—Equipment
    and supplies
    Machinery
Food processing machinery industry
(May Subd Geog)
  [HD9025]
Food processing plants *(May Subd Geog)*
  [TP373]
  BT Agricultural processing plants
  NT Bakers and bakeries
    Beverage processing plants
    Canneries
    Cheese factories
    Creameries
    Dairy plants
    Flour-mills
    Fruit processing plants
    Gluten plants
    Macaroni factories
    Packing-houses
    Poultry plants
    Soybean processing plants
    Sugar factories
    Vegetable processing plants
  — Equipment and supplies
    NT Food processing machinery
Food processing workers
  USE Food industry and trade—Employees
Food processor cookery
  [TX840.F6]
  BT Cookery
    Kitchen utensils
Food relief *(May Subd Geog)*
  [HV696.F6]
  UF Food aid programs
    Food assistance programs
  BT Charities
    Disaster relief
    Public welfare
    Surplus agricultural commodities
    Unemployed
  RT Emergency food supply

SA *subdivisions* Civilian relief *and* Food
    supply *under individual wars, e.g.*
    World War, 1939-1945—Civilian
    relief; World War, 1939-1945—
    Food supply
NT Diet-kitchens
    Emergency mass feeding
    Meals on wheels programs
— Law and legislation *(May Subd Geog)*
— United States
    NT Food stamp program
Food relief, American *(May Subd Geog)*
Food relief, Canadian *(May Subd Geog)*
  UF Canadian food relief
Food relief, Italian *(May Subd Geog)*
  UF Italian food relief
Food requirements, Dietary
  USE Nutrition—Requirements
Food sanitation
  USE *subdivision* Sanitation *under subjects,*
    e.g. Food service—Sanitation;
    Restaurants, lunch rooms, etc.—
    Sanitation
    Food handling
Food sections of newspapers
  USE Newspapers—Sections, columns, etc.—
    Food
Food selection
  USE Food preferences
Food service *(May Subd Geog)*
  [TX901-TX946.5]
    Here are entered works on quantity preparation
and service of food for outside the home. Works deal-
ing solely with quantity food preparation are entered
under Quantity cookery.
  UF Mass feeding
    Volume feeding
  RT Quantity cookery
  SA *subdivision* Food service *under types*
    of institutions, organized activities,
    etc., for provisions for meals and
    food in those enterprises, e.g.
    Airlines—Food service; Hospitals—
    Food service
  NT Caterers and catering
    Emergency mass feeding
    Industrial feeding
    Restaurants, lunch rooms, etc.
    School lunchrooms, cafeterias, etc.
    Table service
    United States. Congress—Food
    service
    Wine service
— Advertising
  USE Advertising—Food service
— Collective labor agreements
  USE Collective labor agreements—
    Food service
— Contracting out
  BT Contracting out
— Employees
  USE Food service employees
— Equipment and supplies
  NT Food service equipment industry
— Management
  USE Food service management
— Personnel management
  [TX911.3.P4]
  RT Food service employees
— Research *(May Subd Geog)*
  UF Food service research
— Sanitation
— — Law and legislation
    (May Subd Geog)
    BT Food law and legislation
    Public health laws
— Study and teaching *(May Subd Geog)*
Food service employees
  UF Food service—Employees
    Food service workers
  RT Food service—Personnel management

NT Collective labor agreements—Food
    service
    Food service hostesses
    Food service hosts
    School food service directors
    Waitresses
Food service equipment industry
(May Subd Geog)
  [HD9999.R54]
  BT Food service—Equipment and supplies
Food service hostesses
  [TX930]
  UF Hostesses, Food service
  BT Food service employees
Food service hosts
  [TX930]
  UF Hosts, Food service
  BT Food service employees
Food service management *(May Subd Geog)*
  [TX911.3.M27]
  UF Food service—Management
Food service research
  USE Food service—Research
Food service specialists (United States Armed
Forces)
  USE United States—Armed Forces—Food
    service specialists
Food service workers
  USE Food service employees
Food spoilage
  UF Spoilage of food
  BT Food—Microbiology
    Food—Preservation
    Food adulteration and inspection
  NT Fishery products—Spoilage
    Food—Shelf-life dating
Food stamp fraud *(May Subd Geog)*
  UF Food stamp program—Law and
    legislation—Criminal provisions
  BT Food stamp program
    Welfare fraud
Food stamp plan
  USE Food stamp program
Food stamp program *(May Subd Geog)*
  [HV696.F6]
  UF Food stamp plan
  BT Food relief—United States
  NT Food stamp fraud
— Law and legislation *(May Subd Geog)*
— — Criminal provisions
    USE Food stamp fraud
Food storage pests *(May Subd Geog)*
  [SB937]
  UF Storage pests of food
    Stored food pests
  BT Farm produce—Storage—Diseases and
    injuries
    Food—Storage
    Pests
— Control *(May Subd Geog)*
Food substitutes
  [HC286.2 (European War, 1914-1918:
    Germany)]
  [TX357]
  UF Milk substitutes
    Substitutes for food
  BT Food, Artificial
    Substitute products
  NT Coffee substitutes
    Meat substitutes
Food supplements
  USE Dietary supplements
Food supply *(May Subd Geog)*
  [HD9000-HD9019 (Economics)]
    Here are entered economic works on the availabil-
ity of food. Works on the preservation and careful use
of food, especially in war time are entered under
Food conservation.
  UF Food control
  BT Produce trade

Food supply (Continued)
RT Agriculture
Single cell proteins
SA subdivision Food supply under
individual wars, e.g. World War,
1939-1945—Food supply
NT Emergency food supply
Famines
Food—Preservation
Food conservation
Food consumption
Green Revolution
Meat industry and trade
— **International cooperation**
NT Insurance, Food supply
— **Law and legislation** (May Subd Geog)
BT Food law and legislation
— **Religious aspects**
— — **Baptists,** ⌈**Catholic Church, etc.**⌉
— — **Buddhism,** ⌈**Christianity, etc.**⌉
Food supply insurance
USE Insurance, Food supply
Food tasting
USE Food—Sensory evaluation
Food texture
UF Food—Texture
Texture of food
Food trade
USE Farm produce—Marketing
Food industry and trade
Produce trade
Food warmers
⌈NK4695.F6⌉
UF Veilleuses (Pottery)
Warmers, Food
BT Cookware
Porcelain
Pottery
Food webs (Ecology)
USE Food chains (Ecology)
Food writers (May Subd Geog)
UF Cookery writers
Writers, Cookery
Writers, Food
BT Authors
Foods
USE Food
Foods, Baby
USE Baby foods
Foods, Contaminated
USE Food contamination
Foods, Infant
USE Baby foods
Foodways
USE Food habits
Fool hen
USE Spruce grouse
Fools, Feast of (May Subd Geog)
⌈GT4995.F6⌉
UF Feast of Fools
Fools and jesters (May Subd Geog)
⌈GT3670⌉
UF Court fools
Jesters
BT Courts and courtiers
Favorites, Royal
Joking
NT Badḥanim
Clowns
Hanswurst
Motley
Pierrot (Fictitious character)
Punchinello (Fictitious character)
Fools and jesters in art
Fools and jesters in literature
Fools for Christ
USE Holy fools
Foord family
USE Ford family
Foords family
USE Ford family

Foore family
USE Fore family
Foosball (Game) (May Subd Geog)
⌈GV1469.4⌉
UF Soccer, Table
Table soccer
Foost family
USE Faust family
Foot
⌈QL950.7⌉
⌈QM549⌉
UF Feet
Paw
BT Extremities, Lower
NT Chopart's joint
Feet in the Bible
Foot—Acupuncture
Heel bone
Podiatry
Tendon of Achilles
Toes
— **Abnormalities** (May Subd Geog)
RT Orthopedic shoes
NT Clubfoot
Flatfoot
Foot—Dislocation
Footbinding
Larsen's syndrome
— **Abscess** (May Subd Geog)
BT Foot—Diseases
— **Acupuncture**
BT Foot
— **Adaptation**
BT Adaptation (Biology)
Adaptation (Physiology)
— **Aging**
— Amputation
USE Amputations of foot
— **Anatomy**
⌈QL950.7 (Comparative anatomy)⌉
⌈QM549 (Human anatomy)⌉
— **Ankylosis**
— Artificial deformities
USE Footbinding
— **Biopsy**
⌈RD563⌉
BT Foot—Examination
Foot—Surgery
— **Blood-vessels**
— **Calcification** (May Subd Geog)
BT Foot—Diseases
— **Cancer** (May Subd Geog)
⌈RC280.F⌉
BT Foot—Tumors
— — **Etiology**
— **Care and hygiene** (May Subd Geog)
BT Podiatry
NT Foot—Protection
— **Cysts** (May Subd Geog)
BT Foot—Tumors
— **Cytology**
— **Diseases** (May Subd Geog)
⌈RC951⌉
BT Podiatry
NT Drop foot
Foot—Abscess
Foot—Calcification
Foot—Infections
Foot—Necrosis
Foot—Radiography
Foot—Tumors
Foot—Ulcers
Foot manifestations of general
diseases
Nails, Ingrowing
— — **Diagnosis**
NT Foot—Examination
— **Dislocation** (May Subd Geog)
⌈RD781⌉
BT Foot—Abnormalities
Foot—Wounds and injuries

— **Dissection**
— **Effect of drugs on**
— **Effect of radiation on**
UF Foot—Radiation effects
BT Radiation—Physiological effect
— **Evolution**
— **Examination**
⌈RD563⌉
BT Foot—Diseases—Diagnosis
NT Foot—Biopsy
— **Fractures** (May Subd Geog)
⌈RD563⌉
BT Foot—Wounds and injuries
— **Growth**
— **Hemorrhage**
— **Infections** (May Subd Geog)
BT Communicable diseases
Foot—Diseases
NT Athlete's foot
Foot—Tuberculosis
Mycetoma
— **Innervation**
— **Measurement**
— **Microbiology**
⌈QR171.F⌉
— **Movements**
UF Foot motility
Foot movements
Motility, Foot
Movements, Foot
— **Muscles**
— **Necrosis**
BT Foot—Diseases
— **Paralysis**
BT Paralysis
— **Protection** (May Subd Geog)
BT Accidents—Prevention
Foot—Care and hygiene
— Radiation effects
USE Foot—Effect of radiation on
— **Radiography** (May Subd Geog)
BT Foot—Diseases
— — **Positioning**
BT Radiography, Medical—
Positioning
— **Reimplantation**
⌈RD563⌉
UF Foot—Replantation
BT Foot—Surgery
Reimplantation (Surgery)
— **Religious aspects**
NT Feet in the Bible
Foot washing (Rite)
— — **Buddhism,** ⌈**Christianity, etc.**⌉
— Replantation
USE Foot—Reimplantation
— **Surgery** (May Subd Geog)
⌈RD563⌉
BT Podiatry
NT Amputations of foot
Excision of ankle
Foot—Biopsy
Foot—Reimplantation
— — **Patients** (May Subd Geog)
— **Tuberculosis** (May Subd Geog)
⌈RC312.5.F⌉
BT Foot—Infections
— **Tumors** (May Subd Geog)
⌈RC280.F⌉
BT Foot—Diseases
NT Foot—Cancer
Foot—Cysts
— **Ulcers** (May Subd Geog)
BT Foot—Diseases
— **Weight**
— **Wounds and injuries** (May Subd Geog)
⌈RD563⌉
NT Foot—Dislocation
Foot—Fractures
— — **Chemotherapy**
— — **Chiropractic treatment**

— — **Complications and sequelae**
(*May Subd Geog*)
Foot, Washing of
USE Foot washing (Rite)
Foot-and-mouth disease (*May Subd Geog*)
[SF793]
UF Aftosa fever
Aphthous fever
Hoof-and-mouth disease
BT Cattle—Diseases
Veterinary virology
— **Epidemiology**
Foot-and-mouth disease virus
BT Rhinoviruses
Foot-ball
USE Football
Foot-binding
USE Footbinding
Foot bridges
USE Footbridges
Foot family
USE Foote family
Foot manifestations of general diseases
BT Foot—Diseases
Symptomatology
Foot motility
USE Foot—Movements
Foot movements
USE Foot—Movements
Foot-powered mechanisms
USE Pedal-powered mechanisms
Foot prints
USE Footprints
Foot races
USE Running races
Foot rot in sheep
[SF968]
Foot soldiers
USE Infantry
Foot trails
USE Trails
Foot washing (Rite)
[BV873.F7]
UF Feet, Washing of
Feet washing
Foot, Washing of
Washing of feet
BT Cults
Foot—Religious aspects
Lustrations
Rites and ceremonies
Sacraments
Water—Religious aspects—Christianity
NT Feet in the Bible
Foot wear
USE Footwear
Footbag (*May Subd Geog*)
[GV960.F66]
BT Football
Football (*May Subd Geog*)
[GV937-GV960]
Here are entered general works and works on
American football.
UF American football
Foot-ball
BT College sports
SA *subdivision* Football *under names of
schools, colleges, etc.*
NT All-Star Football Game
Australian football
Backfield play (Football)
Blocking (Football)
Canadian football
Eight-man football
End play (Football)
Fantasy football (Game)
Flag football
Florentine football
Footbag
Football scouting
Footballs

Kemari
Kicking (Football)
Line play (Football)
Passing (Football)
Quarterback (Football)
Rugby football
Six-man football
Soccer
Sugar Bowl Game, New Orleans, La.
Super Bowl Game (Football)
Tackling (Football)
Touch football
— **Accidents and injuries**
UF Football—Injuries
Football accidents
— **Attendance**
USE Football attendance
— **Defense**
[GV951.18]
UF Defensive football
— **History**
— **Injuries**
USE Football—Accidents and injuries
— **Offense**
[GV951.8]
UF Offensive football
— **Records**
UF Football players—Records
— **Rules**
[GV955]
— **Songs and music**
[M1977.S718]
[M1978.S718]
BT Sports—Songs and music
— **Training**
[GV951.85]
UF Football training
Training, Football
— **California**
NT Rose Bowl Game, Pasadena, Calif.
— **Florida**
NT Orange Bowl Game, Miami, Fla.
— **United States**
— — **Awards**
NT Heisman Trophy
Football accidents
USE Football—Accidents and injuries
Football attendance
UF Attendance, Football
Football—Attendance
Football cards (*May Subd Geog*)
BT Sports cards
Football kickers
USE Placekickers (Football)
Football players (*May Subd Geog*)
[GV939]
NT Placekickers (Football)
Running backs (Football)
Tight ends (Football)
Wide receivers (Football)
— **Collective labor agreements**
USE Collective labor agreements—
Football players
— **Records**
USE Football—Records
— **United States**
NT Afro-American football players
Football players, Afro-American
USE Afro-American football players
Football scouting
[GV959]
UF Scouting, Football
BT Football
Football stories
BT Sports stories
Football training
USE Football—Training
Footballs
BT Balls (Sporting goods)
Football

Footbinding (*May Subd Geog*)
UF Foot—Artificial deformities
Foot-binding
BT Deformities, Artificial
Foot—Abnormalities
Footbridges (*May Subd Geog*)
[TG428]
UF Foot bridges
BT Bridges
Foote family
UF Foot family
Fout family
Fouts family
Foutz family
Pfautz family
Footings, Concrete
USE Concrete footings
Footnotes, Bibliographical
USE Bibliographical citations
Footpaths
USE Trails
Footprints (*May Subd Geog*)
[HV8077.5.F6 (Criminology)]
UF Foot prints
Footwear impressions
BT Anthropometry
Crime and criminals—Identification
Dermatoglyphics
Identification
Footprints, Fossil (*May Subd Geog*)
[QE845]
UF Fossil footprints
Fossil tracks
Ichnology
Tracks, Fossil
Trackways, Fossil
BT Paleontology
Sedimentary structures
Footprints of Gautama Buddha
USE Gautama Buddha—Footprints
Footraces
USE Running races
Foot's resolution, 1829
[E381]
BT United States—Politics and
government—1829-1837
United States—Public lands
Footwear (*May Subd Geog*)
[TS989-1025]
UF Boots and shoes
Foot wear
BT Clothing and dress
NT Ballet slippers
Boots
Plastic footwear
Rubber footwear
Shoes
— **Tariff**
USE Tariff on footwear
Footwear, Plastic
USE Plastic footwear
Footwear, Protective
USE Safety shoes
Footwear, Rubber
USE Rubber footwear
Footwear impressions
USE Footprints
Footwear industry (*May Subd Geog*)
[HD9787]
NT Strikes and lockouts—Footwear
industry
Wages—Footwear industry
For profit health facilities
USE Health facilities, Proprietary
For profit hospitals
USE Hospitals, Proprietary
For profit nursing homes
USE Nursing homes, Proprietary
Fora, Italian
USE Forums, Roman

Fora, Roman
  USE Forums, Roman
Forage
    [SF95-SF99 (Animal culture)]
    [UC660-UC665 (Military science)]
    BT Armies—Commissariat
        Feeds
    SA *subdivision* Forage *under armies, e.g.*
        France. Armée—Forage
Forage fish *(May Subd Geog)*
    BT Fishes
        Fishes—Food
        Predation (Biology)
    NT Baitfish
Forage harvesting machinery
    (May Subd Geog)
    [S695]
    UF Choppers
        Forage plant harvesters
    BT Forage plants—Harvesting
        Harvesting machinery
Forage plant harvesters
  USE Forage harvesting machinery
Forage plants *(May Subd Geog)*
    [SB193-207]
    BT Feeds
        Field crops
        Grazing
        Plants
    RT Grasses
        Pastures
    NT Alfalfa
        Atriplex repanda
        Beans
        Big trefoil
        Bromegrasses
        Browse
        Bur clover
        Cactus
        Clover
        Corn
        Cowpea
        Faba bean
        Flat pea
        Hardinggrass
        Hay
        Heather
        Kafir corn
        Kikuyu grass
        Kudzu
        Legumes
        Lespedeza
        Lotus
        Mangel-wurzel
        Millet
        Narrowleaf trefoil
        Pangolagrass
        Peas
        Prickly-pear
        Range plants
        Rape (Plant)
        Rhodes grass
        Sainfoin
        Serradella
        Silage
        Sorghum
        Soybean
        Sudan grass
        Sweet clover
        Symphoricarpos rotundifolius
        Tall fescue
        Tamarugo
        Timothy-grass
        Velvet-bean
        Vetch
    — Drying
        [SB198]
        UF Green crop drying
    — Harvesting
        NT Forage harvesting machinery
    — Seed

— Soils
    [S597.F]
    BT Crops and soils
        Soils
        Soils and animal nutrition
— Varieties
— Water requirements
Foraging for seafood
  USE Seafood gathering
Foraging for wild food
  USE Food, Wild
Foraker act, 1900 (Puerto Rico)
Foraminifera *(May Subd Geog)*
    [QL368.F6]
    UF Thalamophora
    BT Protozoa
    NT Microspheres
— Geographical distribution
Foraminifera, Fossil *(May Subd Geog)*
    [QE772]
    BT Protozoa, Fossil
    NT Discocyclinidae
        Fusulinidae
        Globorotaliidae, Fossil
        Hyperammina
        Miliolidae, Fossil
        Nummulitidae, Fossil
        Orbitoididae, Fossil
        Uvigerinidae
Forbee family
  USE Faubion family
Forbes Expedition against Fort Duquesne,
1758
    [E199]
    BT United States—History—French and
        Indian War, 1755-1763—Campaigns
Forbes family
    UF Forbis family
        Forbs family
    RT Fobes family
Forbidden City (Peking, China)
    UF Imperial Palace (Peking, China)
        Ku-kung (Peking, China)
        Tzu-chin-ch'eng (Peking, China)
    BT Palaces—China
Forbidden-combination check
  USE Error-correcting codes (Information
        theory)
Forbidden fruit
    [BS1237]
    UF Fruit, Forbidden
    BT Eden
        Fall of man
        Fruit in the Bible
        Tree of life
Forbin family
Forbion family
  USE Faubion family
Forbis family
  USE Forbes family
Forbs, Range
  USE Range plants
Forbs family
  USE Forbes family
Forbush decreases
    [QC485]
    UF Forbush effect
    BT Cosmic rays
        Solar flares
Forbush effect
  USE Forbush decreases
Forby family
  USE Faubion family
Force, Centrifugal
  USE Centrifugal force
Force, Centripetal
  USE Centripetal force
Force, Electromotive
  USE Electromotive force
Force, Vital
  USE Vital force

Force (Law)
  USE Violence (Law)
Force and energy
    [QC73]
    UF Conservation of energy
        Correlation of forces
        Energy
    BT Physics
        Power (Mechanics)
        Variational principles
    RT Dynamics
        Mechanics
        Motion
        Quantum theory
    NT Energy budget (Geophysics)
        Energy storage
        Energy transfer
        Heat, Mechanical equivalent of
        Mass (Physics)
        Mechanical efficiency
        Nuclear energy
        Pressure
        Virial theorem
        Virtual work
        Vital force
        Work (Mechanics)
Force fits
  USE Press fits
Force majeure
  USE Vis major (Civil law)
Force pumps
  USE Pumping machinery
Forced heirs
  USE Legitime
        Widow's share
Forced indoctrination
  USE Brainwashing
Forced labor *(May Subd Geog)*
    UF Compulsory labor
        Conscript labor
        Labor, Compulsory
        Labor, Forced
    BT Crimes against humanity
        Labor and laboring classes
        Native labor
    SA *subdivision* Conscript labor *under*
        individual wars, e.g. World War,
        1939-1945—Conscript labor
    NT Contract labor
        Convict labor
        Peonage
        Serfdom
        Service, Compulsory non-military
        Slave labor
Forced labor (International law)
    BT International law
Forced landings (over water)
  USE Airplanes—Ditching
Forced loans *(May Subd Geog)*
    [HJ8047]
    UF Compulsory loans
        Loans, Compulsory
        Loans, Forced
    BT Debts, Public
        Loans
— **Law and legislation** *(May Subd Geog)*
Forced removal of Indians
  USE Indians of North America—Removal
Forceps
    [RD73.F7]
Forceps, Obstetric
    [RG739]
    BT Obstetrics—Apparatus and instruments
Forces, Intermolecular
  USE Intermolecular forces
Forces, Paramilitary
  USE Paramilitary forces
Forces and couples
    [QA823]
    [QA831]
    UF Couples (Mechanics)

BT Mechanics
Statics
Forces nouvelles (Group of artists)
⌜N6848.5.F67⌟
BT Art, Modern—20th century—France
Forcible entry and detainer
(May Subd Geog)
UF Usurpation (Law)
BT Actions and defenses
Eviction
Landlord and tenant
Offenses against property
Possession (Law)
Possessory actions
Real property
Remedies (Law)
Trespass
Forcible entry and detainer (Islamic law)
(May Subd Geog)
Forcing (Model theory)
⌜QA9.7⌟
BT Model theory
Forcing (Plants)
⌜SB127⌟
UF Flowers, Forcing of
Fruit, Forcing of
Vegetables, Forcing of
BT Gardening
Greenhouses
Horticulture
Plants
RT Greenhouse gardening
Greenhouse management
NT Cloche gardening
Hotbeds
Seeds—Stratification
Vernalization
Forcum family
Ford automobile
⌜TL215.F7⌟
UF Ford automobiles
BT Automobiles
NT Anglia automobile
Capri automobile
Cobra automobile
Consul automobile
Cortina automobile
Edsel automobile
Escort automobile
Fairlane automobile
Fairmont automobile
Fiesta automobile
Ford Falcon automobile
Ford Model A automobile
Ford Model T automobile
Ford Tempo automobile
Ford trucks
Granada automobile
Maverick automobile
Mercury automobile
Mustang automobile
Pinto automobile
Popular automobile
Prefect automobile
Ranchero automobile
Taunus automobile
Thunderbird automobile
Torino automobile
Zephyr automobile
Zodiac automobile
Ford automobiles
USE Ford automobile
Ford Courier truck
⌜TL230.5.F⌟
UF Courier truck
BT Ford trucks
Trucks
Ford do Brasil Strike, 1981
⌜HD5354.A82 1981⌟

BT Automobile industry workers—Brazil
Strikes and lockouts—Automobile
industry—Brazil
Strikes and lockouts—Brazil
Ford Falcon automobile
⌜TL215.F⌟
UF Falcon automobile, Ford
BT Ford automobile
Ford family
UF Foard family
Foord family
Foords family
Forde family
Fordes family
Fords family
Fouarde family
RT Fore family
Ford Model A automobile
⌜TL215.F7⌟
UF Model A Ford automobile
BT Ford automobile
Ford Model T automobile
⌜TL215.F⌟
UF Model T automobile
BT Ford automobile
**Ford Motor Company Strike, Windsor, Ont.,
1943**
Ford mural (Painting)
USE Collins, Paul. Gerald R. Ford mural
Ford Powder Mill Site (Morristown, N.J.)
(Not Subd Geog)
UF Powder Mill Site (Morristown, N.J.)
BT Morristown National Historical Park
(N.J.)
New Jersey—Antiquities
Ford Ranchero automobile
USE Ranchero automobile
Ford Ranger truck
⌜TL230.5.F⌟
UF Ranger truck
BT Ford trucks
Ford Tempo automobile
⌜TL215.F⌟
UF Tempo automobile, Ford
BT Ford automobile
**Ford Three-engined Monoplane (Transport
plane)**
⌜TL686.F⌟
UF Ford Tri-motor (Transport plane)
Three-engined Monoplane, Ford
(Transport plane)
Tin Goose (Transport plane)
Tri-motor, Ford (Transport plane)
Trimotor, Ford (Transport plane)
BT Transport planes
Ford Tri-motor (Transport plane)
USE Ford Three-engined Monoplane
(Transport plane)
Ford trucks
⌜TL230.5.F⌟
BT Ford automobile
Trucks
NT Bronco truck
Ford Courier truck
Ford Ranger truck
Ford vans
⌜TL230.5.F⌟
BT Vans
NT Aerostar van
Forde family
USE Ford family
Fordes family
USE Ford family
Fords (Stream crossings) *(May Subd Geog)*
UF Crossings, Low water
Low water crossings
Rivers—Fords
Stream fords
— **Virginia**
NT Kelly's Ford (Va.)

Fords family
USE Ford family
Ford's Theatre (Washington, D.C.)
BT Theaters—Washington (D.C.)
Fore (New Guinea people)
BT Ethnology—New Guinea
— **Medicine**
⌜DU740.42⌟
BT Medicine, Primitive—Papua New
Guinea
Fore-edge painting
⌜ND2370⌟
UF Decoration, Fore-edge
Painting, Fore-edge
BT Book ornamentation
Decoration and ornament
Watercolor painting
Fore family
UF Faur family
Faure family
Foore family
Foree family
RT Ford family
Fore language
BT Papuan languages
Forearm
⌜QL950.7 (Comparative anatomy)⌟
⌜QM548 (Human anatomy)⌟
BT Arm
Forebrain
USE Prosencephalon
Forecasting
⌜CB158⌟
UF Futurology
Prediction
SA *subdivision* Forecasting *under names
of countries, cities, etc., and under
subjects; and subdivision* Forecasts
under individual centuries, e.g.
Twentieth century—Forecasts
NT Agricultural prices—Forecasting
Agriculture—Forecasting
Air—Pollution—Forecasting
Automobile ownership—Forecasting
Cattle—Forecasting
Corn—Forecasting
Education—Forecasting
Electric power consumption—
Forecasting
Energy consumption—Forecasting
Fashion—Forecasting
Forests and forestry—Forecasting
Future in popular culture
Geophysical prediction
Hospital utilization—Forecasting
Housing forecasting
International relations—Forecasting
Prognosis
Prophecy
Social prediction
Solar activity—Forecasting
Warnings
— **Study and teaching** *(May Subd Geog)*
⌜CB158⌟
UF Future research
Future studies
Futures research
Futures studies
Forecasting, Business
USE Business forecasting
Forecasting, Cloud
USE Cloud forecasting
Forecasting, Crime
USE Crime forecasting
Forecasting, Cyclone
USE Cyclone forecasting
Forecasting, Drought
USE Drought forecasting
Forecasting, Economic
USE Economic forecasting

Forecasting, Election
  USE Election forecasting
Forecasting, Employment
  USE Employment forecasting
Forecasting, Food consumption
  USE Food consumption forecasting
Forecasting, Forest fire
  USE Forest fire forecasting
Forecasting, Housing
  USE Housing forecasting
Forecasting, Hydrological
  USE Hydrological forecasting
Forecasting, Income
  USE Income forecasting
Forecasting, Ionospheric
  USE Ionospheric forecasting
Forecasting, Minimum temperature
  USE Temperature forecasting, Minimum
Forecasting, Population
  USE Population forecasting
Forecasting, Precipitation
  USE Precipitation forecasting
Forecasting, Public expenditures
  USE Expenditures, Public—Forecasting
Forecasting, Sales
  USE Sales forecasting
Forecasting, Stock price
  USE Stock price forecasting
Forecasting, Technological
  USE Technological forecasting
Forecasting, Thunderstorm
  USE Thunderstorm forecasting
Forecasting, Traffic
  USE Traffic estimation
Forecasting, Weather
  USE Weather forecasting
Forecasting, Wind
  USE Wind forecasting
Forecasting theory
  USE Prediction theory
Forecasts, Long-range weather
  USE Long-range weather forecasts
Forecasts (Meteorology), Probability
  USE Probability forecasts (Meteorology)
Foreclosure *(May Subd Geog)*
  UF Foreclosure sales
      Mechanics' lien foreclosure
      Mortgage foreclosure
      Statutory foreclosure
      Strict foreclosure
  BT Executions (Law)
      Judicial sales
      Mechanics' liens
      Mortgages
  NT Tax-sales
Foreclosure sales
  USE Foreclosure
Foree family
  USE Fore family
Foregrounding
      ₍PN226 (Literary style)₎
  BT Language and languages—Style
      Style, Literary
Foregut
      ₍QL861 (Comparative anatomy)₎
      ₍QM331 (Human anatomy)₎
      ₍QP146 (Physiology)₎
  UF Stomodeum
  BT Alimentary canal
Foreign accent
  USE *subdivision* Pronunciation by foreign
        speakers *under individual languages
        and groups of languages, e.g.*
        English language—Pronunciation by
        foreign speakers
Foreign affairs
  USE *subdivisions* Foreign relations *and*
        Foreign relations administration
        under names of countries
        International relations

Foreign agents *(May Subd Geog)*
      ₍JX1896 (International law)₎
  UF Agents, Foreign
      Foreign propagandists
      Propagandists, Foreign
  BT Diplomatic and consular service
      Lobbyists
      Propaganda
  NT Commercial agents
Foreign agricultural laborers
  USE Agricultural laborers, Foreign
Foreign aid program
  USE Economic assistance
      Military assistance
      Technical assistance
Foreign aid to agriculture
  USE Agricultural assistance
Foreign aid to education
  USE Educational assistance
Foreign aid to population programs
  USE Population assistance
Foreign area studies
  USE Area studies
Foreign assistance
  USE Economic assistance
      Military assistance
      Technical assistance
Foreign associations, institutions, etc.
  USE Associations, institutions, etc., Foreign
Foreign automobiles
  USE Automobiles, Foreign
Foreign banks and banking
  USE Banks and banking, Foreign
Foreign bodies (Surgery)
  BT Accidents
      Surgery
      Surgery, Operative
  SA *subdivision* Foreign bodies *under
        names of organs, e.g.* Eye—Foreign
        bodies
  NT Bezoar
Foreign business enterprises
  USE Business enterprises, Foreign
Foreign cars
  USE Automobiles, Foreign
Foreign chemical compounds
  USE Xenobiotics
Foreign coins
  USE Coins, Foreign
Foreign college graduates
  USE College graduates, Foreign
Foreign commerce
  USE Commerce
Foreign compounds
  USE Xenobiotics
Foreign corporations
  USE Corporations, Foreign
Foreign correspondents *(May Subd Geog)*
  UF Correspondents, Foreign
  BT Reporters and reporting
  — **Legal status, laws, etc.**
      (May Subd Geog)
      BT Press law
Foreign debts
  USE Debts, External
Foreign economic policy
  USE International economic relations
Foreign economic relations
  USE International economic relations
Foreign educational aid
  USE Educational assistance
Foreign engineering students
  USE Engineering students, Foreign
Foreign enlistment *(May Subd Geog)*
  UF Enlistment
  BT Military offenses
  RT Mercenary troops
Foreign exchange
      ₍HG3810-HG4000₎

      Here are entered works on foreign currencies and
  on the mechanisms or instruments for settling financial transactions between nations. Works on the economic theory of the acceptance of one thing for
  another are entered under Exchange.
  UF Cambistry
      Capital exports
      Capital imports
      Exchange, Foreign
      Exchange rates
      Fixed exchange rates
      Flexible exchange rates
      Floating exchange rates
      Fluctuating exchange rates
      International exchange
  BT Commerce
      International finance
      Money
  NT Asian dollar market
      Balance of payments
      Black market—Foreign exchange
      Capital flight tax
      Capital movements
      Currency convertibility
      Emigrant remittances
      Euro-bond market
      Euro-dollar market
      Foreign exchange administration
      Foreign exchange problem
      Forward exchange
      International clearing
      Purchasing power parity
      Sterling area
      Valuta clause
  — **Accounting**
      UF Foreign exchange accounting
      BT Accounting
  — Conflict of laws
      USE Conflict of laws—Foreign
            exchange
  — **Law and legislation** *(May Subd Geog)*
      UF Exchange control
      BT Commercial law
          Foreign trade regulation
          International travel regulations
  — — **Criminal provisions**
  — Tables
      USE Money—Tables
Foreign exchange accounting
  USE Foreign exchange—Accounting
Foreign exchange administration
  (May Subd Geog)
  BT Foreign exchange
Foreign-exchange brokers *(May Subd Geog)*
  BT Brokers
Foreign exchange futures
  USE Forward exchange
Foreign exchange problem *(May Subd Geog)*
  BT Currency question
      Foreign exchange
      International liquidity
  NT Devaluation of currency
      French franc area
      Sterling area
Foreign fishing *(May Subd Geog)*
      Here are entered works on fishing within a na-
  tion's territorial waters by vessels of foreign national-
  ity.
  BT Economic zones (Maritime law)
      Fisheries—Licenses
      Fishery management
      Foreign licensing agreements
  — **Surveillance of**
      UF Surveillance of foreign fishing
Foreign freight forwarders
  USE Ocean freight forwarders
Foreign heads of state, Crimes against
  USE Offenses against foreign heads of state
Foreign heads of state, Offenses against
  USE Offenses against foreign heads of state
Foreign income, Taxation of
  USE Income tax—Foreign income

Foreign institutions, associations, etc.
  USE Associations, institutions, etc., Foreign
Foreign insurance companies
  USE Insurance companies, Foreign
Foreign investments
  USE Investments, Foreign
Foreign judgments
  USE Judgments, Foreign
Foreign labor
  USE Alien labor
Foreign language camps
  USE Language camps
Foreign language competency of businessmen
  USE Businessmen—Foreign language
        competency
Foreign language competency of officials and
    employees in foreign countries
  USE *subdivision* Officials and employees—
        Foreign countries—Foreign
        language competency *under*
        countries, etc.
Foreign language laboratories
  USE Language laboratories
Foreign language newspapers, American
  USE American newspapers—Foreign
        language press
Foreign language newspapers, Canadian
  USE Canadian newspapers—Foreign
        language press
Foreign language newspapers, Chinese
  USE Chinese newspapers—Foreign language
        press
Foreign language periodicals, American
  USE American periodicals—Foreign
        language press
Foreign language periodicals, Canadian
  USE Canadian periodicals—Foreign
        language press
Foreign language periodicals, Swedish
  USE Swedish periodicals—Foreign language
        press
Foreign language press
  USE *subdivision* Foreign language press
        under types of newspapers and
        periodicals, e.g. American
        newspapers—Foreign language press
Foreign language press, French
  USE French newspapers—Foreign language
        press
Foreign language publications
  — Cataloging
        USE Cataloging of foreign language
              publications
Foreign language study
  USE Language and languages—Study and
        teaching
Foreign language testing
  USE *subdivision* Examinations *under names*
        of languages or groups of languages,
        e.g. English language—
        Examinations; Languages, Modern
        —Examinations
Foreign languages
  USE Language and languages
        Languages, Modern
Foreign law, Pleading and proof of
  (May Subd Geog)
      BT Conflict of laws
          Evidence (Law)
          Judicial notice
          Pleading
Foreign lawyers
  USE Lawyers, Foreign
Foreign licensing agreements
      UF Joint-venture agreements
          Know-how assistance agreements
          Technical assistance agreements

      BT Commerce
          International business enterprises
          International economic relations
          Investments, Foreign
          License agreements
      RT Exclusive licenses
          Patent licenses
          Technology transfer
      NT Foreign fishing
Foreign loan insurance
  USE Insurance, Foreign loan
Foreign loans
  USE Loans, Foreign
Foreign mail
  USE Postal service—Foreign mail
Foreign medical graduates
  USE Physicians, Foreign
Foreign medical personnel
  USE Medical personnel, Foreign
Foreign medical students
  USE Medical students, Foreign
Foreign merchants
  USE Merchants, Foreign
Foreign military sales
  USE Military assistance
        Munitions
Foreign news *(May Subd Geog)*
      Here are entered works on journalistic practices in
    reporting news about foreign events. When the head-
    ing is subdivided by place, the subdivision refers to
    the locality where the news is released.
      UF Flow of news, International
          International flow of news
          International news
          News, Foreign
          News flow, International
          World news
      BT Journalism
          News agencies
          Press
  — **Censorship**
        BT Freedom of information
Foreign nurses
  USE Nurses, Foreign
Foreign nursing students
  USE Nursing students, Foreign
Foreign Office (London, England : Building)
      BT Great Britain—Diplomatic and
          consular service—Buildings
Foreign offices
      BT Diplomatic and consular service
          International law
          International relations
      SA *names of individual foreign offices, e.g.*
          United States. Dept. of State
Foreign opinion
  USE *subdivision* Foreign public opinion
        under names of countries, etc.; and
        under individual wars, e.g. United
        States—History—Civil War, 1861-
        1865—Foreign public opinion
Foreign ownership of farms
  USE Farms—Foreign ownership
Foreign ownership of real property
  USE Real property—Foreign ownership
Foreign ownership of the construction industry
  USE Construction industry—Foreign
        ownership
Foreign pest introduction
  USE Pest introduction
Foreign physicians
  USE Physicians, Foreign
Foreign policy
  USE *subdivision* Foreign relations *under*
        names of countries
        International relations
Foreign policy and trade-unions
  USE Trade-unions and foreign policy
Foreign population
  USE Aliens
        Immigrants

          Minorities
Foreign prisoners
  USE Prisoners, Foreign
Foreign propagandists
  USE Foreign agents
Foreign property
  USE Alien property
Foreign public opinion
  USE *subdivision* Foreign public opinion
        under names of countries, etc.; and
        under individual wars, e.g. United
        States—History—Civil War, 1861-
        1865—Foreign public opinion
Foreign publications, Acquisition of
  USE Acquisition of foreign publications
Foreign radio stations *(May Subd Geog)*
      UF Alien radio stations
          Radio stations, Foreign
Foreign relations
  USE *subdivision* Foreign relations *under*
        names of countries, e.g. France—
        Foreign relations
        International relations
Foreign relations administration
  USE *subdivision* Foreign relations
        administration *under names of*
        countries, e.g. United States—
        Foreign relations administration
Foreign relations law (United States)
  USE United States—Foreign relations—Law
        and legislation
Foreign relations specialists
  USE International relations specialists
Foreign sales corporations *(May Subd Geog)*
      UF Corporations, Foreign sales
      BT Corporations, Foreign
          Subsidiary corporations
      RT Domestic international sales
          corporations
          Export sales
Foreign service
  USE Diplomatic and consular service
Foreign students
  USE Students, Foreign
Foreign study *(May Subd Geog)*
      BT Education
      RT Students, Foreign
Foreign tax credit *(May Subd Geog)*
      BT Corporations—Taxation
          Income tax—Foreign income
          Tax credits
          Taxation, Double
Foreign tax havens
  USE Tax havens
Foreign teachers
  USE Teachers, Foreign
Foreign teaching positions
  USE Teachers, Foreign—Employment
Foreign television programs
  USE Television programs, Foreign
Foreign trade
  USE Commerce, *and pertinent subjects*
          referred to under that heading
        Commerce
Foreign trade and employment
  (May Subd Geog)
      UF Employment and foreign trade
      BT Commerce
          Labor supply
      RT Investments, Foreign, and employment
          Trade adjustment assistance
          Unemployed
Foreign trade control
  USE Foreign trade regulation
Foreign trade enterprises
  USE Trading companies
Foreign trade policy
  USE Commercial policy
Foreign trade promotion *(May Subd Geog)*
      UF Export promotion
          Export trade promotion

Foreign trade promotion *(Continued)*
  BT Commercial policy
      Export sales
      Industry and state
  RT Foreign trade regulation
      Subsidies
  NT Export credit
      Export premiums
      Export processing zones
      Fairs
      Import substitution
      Insurance, Export credit
      Trade missions
      Trading companies
  — **Evaluation**
  — **Law and legislation** *(May Subd Geog)*
  — **United States**
      NT Domestic international sales
          corporations
Foreign trade regulation *(May Subd Geog)*
  UF Export and import controls
      Foreign trade control
      Import and export controls
      Import restrictions
      International trade control
      International trade regulation
      Prohibited exports and imports
  BT Commercial law
      Commercial policy
      Trade adjustment assistance
  RT Foreign trade promotion
  NT Antidumping duties—Law and
          legislation
      Commercial treaties
      Customs administration—Law and
          legislation
      Export controls
      Foreign exchange—Law and legislation
      Free ports and zones—Law and
          legislation
      Import quotas
      International clearing
      Producers' associations—Law and
          legislation
      Trading companies—Law and
          legislation
  — Conflict of laws
      USE Conflict of laws—Foreign trade
          regulation
  — **Criminal provisions**
  — **United States**
      NT Export associations—Law and
          legislation
Foreign trade routes
  USE Trade routes
Foreign trade zones
  USE Free ports and zones
Foreign-trained lawyers
  USE Lawyers, Foreign
Foreign-trained medical personnel
  USE Medical personnel, Foreign
Foreign-trained physicians
  USE Physicians, Foreign
Foreign visitors
  USE Visitors, Foreign
Foreign workers
  USE Alien labor
Foreigners
  USE *subdivision* Foreign population *under*
      names of countries, cities, etc.
      Aliens
      Immigrants
      Naturalization
      Visitors, Foreign
Foreigners, Visiting
  USE Visitors, Foreign
Forelimbs
  USE Extremities, Upper

Foreman family
  UF Foremon family
      Forman family
      Formon family
      Fourman family
Foremen
  USE Supervisors, Industrial
Foremen's unions
  USE Trade-unions—Industrial supervisors
Foremon family
  USE Foreman family
Forenames
  USE Names, Personal
Forensic accounting *(May Subd Geog)*
  BT Accounting
      Accounting—Law and legislation
Forensic anthropology
  [GN69.8]
  UF Anthropology, Forensic
      Medicolegal anthropology
  BT Human skeleton
      Identification
      Law and anthropology
      Medical jurisprudence
      Physical anthropology
  NT Forensic osteology
Forensic applications of mass spectrometry
  USE Mass spectrometry—Forensic
      applications
Forensic audiology
  [RA1062.8]
  UF Audiology, Forensic
      Medicolegal audiology
  BT Medical jurisprudence
Forensic ballistics
  [HV8077]
  UF Ballistics, Forensic
  BT Criminal investigation
      Evidence, Criminal
      Evidence, Expert
      Evidence (Law)
      Firearms—Identification
Forensic cardiology *(May Subd Geog)*
  [RA1170.H4]
  UF Cardiology, Forensic
      Medicolegal cardiology
  BT Cardiology
      Medical jurisprudence
  NT Heart—Diseases—Law and legislation
Forensic chemistry
  USE Chemistry, Forensic
Forensic dentistry
  USE Dental jurisprudence
Forensic dermatology
  UF Dermatology—Jurisprudence
      Dermatology, Forensic
      Medicolegal dermatology
  BT Medical jurisprudence
Forensic economics *(May Subd Geog)*
  BT Economics
Forensic engineering *(May Subd Geog)*
  BT Engineering law
Forensic entomology *(May Subd Geog)*
  [RA1063.45]
  BT Entomology
      Medical jurisprudence
Forensic genetics *(May Subd Geog)*
  UF Genetics, Forensic
  BT Genetics
      Medical jurisprudence
Forensic gynecology
  UF Gynecology—Jurisprudence
      Gynecology, Forensic
      Medicolegal gynecology
  BT Medical jurisprudence
  NT Forensic obstetrics
Forensic hematology
  UF Medicolegal hematology
  BT Hematology
      Medical jurisprudence
  NT Forensic serology

Forensic hypnotism
  BT Hypnotism
  RT Hypnotism—Law and legislation
Forensic mass spectrometry
  USE Mass spectrometry—Forensic
      applications
Forensic medicine
  USE Medical jurisprudence
Forensic neurology
  [RA1147]
  UF Forensic neuropathology
      Medicolegal neurology
      Neurology—Jurisprudence
      Neurology, Forensic
  BT Medical jurisprudence
  NT Forensic neuropsychology
      Forensic psychiatry
Forensic neuropathology
  USE Forensic neurology
Forensic neuropsychology *(May Subd Geog)*
  [RA1147.5]
  UF Medicolegal neuropsychology
  BT Forensic neurology
      Neuropsychology
      Psychology, Forensic
Forensic obstetrics
  UF Medicolegal obstetrics
      Obstetrics—Jurisprudence
      Obstetrics, Forensic
  BT Forensic gynecology
      Medical jurisprudence
  NT Docimasia pulmonum
Forensic odontology
  USE Dental jurisprudence
Forensic oncology *(May Subd Geog)*
  [RA1170.C35]
  UF Medicolegal oncology
      Oncology, Forensic
  BT Medical jurisprudence
      Oncology
Forensic ophthalmology *(May Subd Geog)*
  [RA1062.5]
  UF Medicolegal ophthalmology
      Ophthalmology—Jurisprudence
      Ophthalmology, Forensic
  BT Medical jurisprudence
Forensic orations
  UF Arguments, Legal
      Legal arguments
  BT Oral pleading
      Speeches, addresses, etc.
      Trial practice
  RT Forensic oratory
Forensic orations, Imaginary
  UF Imaginary forensic orations
Forensic orations in the Bible
  UF Bible—Forensic orations
Forensic oratory
  BT Forensics (Public speaking)
      Oral pleading
      Oratory
  RT Forensic orations
  NT Summation (Law)
Forensic osteology
  UF Medicolegal osteology
      Osteology, Forensic
  BT Bones
      Forensic anthropology
      Medical jurisprudence
Forensic pathologists *(May Subd Geog)*
  BT Forensic pathology
      Forensic scientists
      Medical examiners (Law)
      Pathologists
Forensic pathology *(May Subd Geog)*
  [RA1063.4]
  UF Pathology, Forensic
  BT Medical jurisprudence
  RT Coroners
      Medical examiners (Law)
  NT Forensic pathologists

Forensic photography
  USE Photography, Legal
Forensic psychiatrists *(May Subd Geog)*
  ₍RA1151₎
    BT Psychiatrists
Forensic psychiatry *(May Subd Geog)*
  ₍RA1151₎
    Here are entered works on psychiatry as applied
  in courts of law. Works on the legal status of persons
  of unsound mind are entered under the heading In-
  sanity—Jurisprudence.
    UF Psychiatry, Forensic
    BT Criminal psychology
        Forensic neurology
        Insanity—Jurisprudence
        Medical jurisprudence
        Psychology, Forensic
    RT Insane, Criminal and dangerous
    NT Litigious paranoia
        Traumatic neuroses
Forensic psychology
  USE Psychology, Forensic
Forensic radiography
  ₍RA1058.5₎
    UF Medicolegal radiography
        Radiography—Jurisprudence
        Radiography, Forensic
    BT Medical jurisprudence
Forensic scientists *(May Subd Geog)*
    BT Criminal investigation
        Scientists
    NT Forensic pathologists
        Medical examiners (Law)
Forensic serology *(May Subd Geog)*
    UF Medicolegal serology
    BT Forensic hematology
        Serology
Forensic statistics *(May Subd Geog)*
    BT Statistics
Forensic thermography *(May Subd Geog)*
  ₍RA1058.7₎
    UF Medicolegal thermography
        Thermography, Forensic
    BT Medical jurisprudence
        Medical thermography
Forensic toxicology *(May Subd Geog)*
  ₍RA1228₎
    UF Medicolegal toxicology
        Toxicology—Jurisprudence
    BT Chemistry, Forensic
        Medical jurisprudence
        Toxicology
    NT Poisoning
        Self-poisoning
Forensics (Public speaking)
    UF Argumentation
    BT Oratory
        Public speaking
    RT Persuasion (Rhetoric)
    NT Debates and debating
        Forensic oratory
Foreordination
  USE Predestination
Forest administrative districts
  USE Forest districts
Forest animals
  USE Forest fauna
Forest Avenue Historical District (Vermillion, S.D.)
    BT Historic districts—South Dakota
Forest birds *(May Subd Geog)*
    UF Woodland birds
    BT Birds
        Forest fauna
Forest Cemetery (Coeur d'Alene, Idaho)
    BT Cemeteries—Idaho
Forest clearcutting
  USE Clear-cutting
Forest conservation *(May Subd Geog)*
  ₍SD411-428₎

    UF Conservation of forests
        Forest preservation
        Preservation of forests
    BT Conservation of natural resources
        Forest management
        Plant conservation
    NT Forest genetic resources conservation
        Forest influences
        Forest protection
        Forest reserves
        Reforestation
  — **Citizen participation**
  — **Himalaya Mountains**
      NT Chipko movement
Forest consultants
  USE Forestry consultants
Forest cooperatives
  USE Forests and forestry, Cooperative
Forest credit *(May Subd Geog)*
    UF Credit, Forest
    BT Agricultural credit
        Credit
  — **Law and legislation** *(May Subd Geog)*
      BT Banking law
          Forestry law and legislation
Forest depletion
  USE Deforestation
Forest districts *(May Subd Geog)*
    UF Districts, Forest
        Divisions, Forest
        Forest administrative districts
        Forest divisions
    BT Forests and forestry
  — **British Columbia**
      NT Kamloops Forest Region (B.C.)
          Prince Rupert Forest Region (B.C.)
Forest divisions
  USE Forest districts
Forest drainage *(May Subd Geog)*
  ₍SD408.2₎
    BT Drainage
        Forestry engineering
Forest ecology *(May Subd Geog)*
    UF Forests and forestry—Ecology
    BT Botany—Ecology
        Ecology
    NT Forest flora
        Forest meteorology
        Forest microclimatology
        Forest site quality
        Jungle ecology
        Old growth forests
        Rain forests
        Taiga ecology
        Timberline
        Trees—Growth
Forest economics
  USE Forests and forestry—Economic
      aspects
Forest engineering
  USE Forestry engineering
Forest entomology
  USE Forest insects
Forest extension work
  USE Forestry extension work
Forest fallow cultivation
  USE Shifting cultivation
Forest family
  USE Forrest family
Forest farming
  USE Tree crops
Forest fauna *(May Subd Geog)*
  ₍QL112₎
    UF Forest animals
    BT Zoology
    NT Forest birds
        Forest insects
        Jungle fauna
Forest fertilization
  USE Forest soils—Fertilization

Forest fire control
  USE Forest fires—Prevention and control
Forest fire detection *(May Subd Geog)*
  ₍SD421₎
    UF Forest fires—Detection
    BT Forest fires—Prevention and control
    NT Fire lookout stations
        Fire lookouts
Forest fire fighters *(May Subd Geog)*
    BT Fire fighters
        Forest fires—Prevention and control
        Wildfire fighters
    NT Smokejumpers
  — **Training of** *(May Subd Geog)*
Forest fire fighting
  USE Forest fires—Prevention and control
Forest fire forecasting *(May Subd Geog)*
    UF Forecasting, Forest fire
    BT Forest fires—Prevention and control
  — **Computer programs**
Forest fire insurance
  USE Insurance, Forest
Forest fire lookout stations
  USE Fire lookout stations
Forest fire lookouts
  USE Fire lookouts
Forest fire research
  USE Forest fires—Research
Forest fire watchers
  USE Fire lookouts
Forest fires *(May Subd Geog)*
  ₍SD421₎
    BT Fires
        Natural disasters
        Wildfires
    RT Deforestation
        Fire weather
    NT Fire ecology
        Insurance, Forest
        Prescribed burning
  — Control
      USE Forest fires—Prevention and
           control
  — Detection
      USE Forest fire detection
  — Extinction
      USE Forest fires—Prevention and
           control
  — **Law and legislation** *(May Subd Geog)*
      UF Forest fires—Prevention and
          control—Law and legislation
      BT Forestry law and legislation
  — **Prevention and control**
      ₍SD421₎
      UF Forest fire control
          Forest fire fighting
          Forest fires—Control
          Forest fires—Extinction
          Lumbering—Fires and fire
            prevention
      BT Fire extinction
          Fire prevention
          Forest protection
      RT Smokey Bear
      NT Aeronautics in forest fire control
          Forest fire detection
          Forest fire fighters
          Forest fire forecasting
          Fuelbreaks
  — — Advertising
        USE Advertising—Forest fire
             prevention
  — — **Citizen participation**
        NT Volunteer workers in forest fire
            prevention
  — — **Data processing**
        NT INFORMAP (Information
            retrieval system)
  — — Law and legislation
        USE Forest fires—Law and
             legislation

1407

Forest fires *(Continued)*
— **Research** *(May Subd Geog)*
  UF Forest fire research
— **Oregon**
  NT Tillamook Burn, Or., 1933
Forest flora *(May Subd Geog)*
  [QK108-475.5 (General, QK938.F6)]
  [QK475-493.5 (Woody plants)]
  UF Forest plants
    Woodland plants
  BT Botany
    Forest ecology
    Forests and forestry
    Plants
  RT Woody plants
  NT Mangrove plants
    Rain forest plants
Forest genetic resources conservation
  (May Subd Geog)
  [SD399.7]
  UF Conservation of forest genetic
    resources
    Genetic resources conservation, Forest
  BT Forest conservation
    Forest genetics
    Germplasm resources, Plant
Forest genetics
  UF Forests and forestry—Genetic research
    Trees—Genetics
  BT Plant genetics
  NT Forest genetic resources conservation
    Poplar—Genetics
    Seed orchards
Forest Hills (New York, N.Y.)
  (Not Subd Geog)
  UF New York (N.Y.). Forest Hills
Forest hydrology
  USE Hydrology, Forest
Forest industries
  USE Forest products industry
Forest influences *(May Subd Geog)*
  [SD416-SD416.3 (General)]
  UF Forests and floods
    Forests and rainfall
    Forests and water-supply
  BT Floods
    Forest conservation
    Rain and rainfall
    Water-supply
  RT Botany—Ecology
    Flood control
  NT Forest meteorology
    Forest microclimatology
    Forests and forestry
    Hydrology, Forest
Forest insects *(May Subd Geog)*
  [SB761]
  UF Forest entomology
  BT Forest fauna
    Forest protection
    Insects
    Trees—Diseases and pests
  SA *names of insects, e.g.* Pine-moth
  NT Bark beetles
    Wood borers
— **Biological control** *(May Subd Geog)*
  BT Forest insects—Control
— **Control** *(May Subd Geog)*
  NT Forest insects—Biological control
— **Host plants**
Forest insurance
  USE Insurance, Forest
Forest inventories
  USE Forest surveys
Forest irrigation
  USE Forests and forestry—Irrigation
Forest land owners
  USE Forest landowners
Forest landowners *(May Subd Geog)*
  [SD387.L33]

  UF Forest land owners
    Forest owners
    Landowners, Forest
    Owners, Forest
    Timber landowners
    Woodland owners
  BT Forests and forestry
    Landowners
    Wood-lots
Forest law
  USE Forestry law and legislation
Forest litter *(May Subd Geog)*
  BT Forest soils
    Humus
    Leaf-mold
— **Biodegradation**
  UF Decay of forest litter
    Decomposition of forest litter
Forest machinery *(May Subd Geog)*
  BT Forestry engineering
  NT Logging—Machinery
— **Hydraulic equipment**
— Safety measures
  USE Forests and forestry—Safety
    measures
— **Traction**
Forest management *(May Subd Geog)*
  BT Forest policy
    Management
  RT Watershed management
  NT Clear-cutting
    Fire ecology
    Forest conservation
    Forest protection
    Forest rangers
    Forest thinning
    Tree farms
— **Citizen participation**
— **Computer programs**
  NT MANAGD (Computer program)
    TEVAP (Computer program)
Forest mapping *(May Subd Geog)*
  [SD387.M3]
  UF Forests and forestry—Mapping
  BT Cartography
    Forest surveys
    Forests and forestry—Maps
    Vegetation mapping
Forest mensuration
  USE Forests and forestry—Mensuration
Forest meteorology *(May Subd Geog)*
  [SD390.5-390.6]
  UF Meteorology, Forest
  BT Forest ecology
    Forest influences
    Meteorology
  RT Forest microclimatology
  NT Fire weather
Forest microclimatology *(May Subd Geog)*
  [SD390.5-390.6]
  UF Climate and forests
    Forests and climate
  BT Forest ecology
    Forest influences
    Microclimatology
    Vegetation and climate
  RT Forest meteorology
Forest nurseries *(May Subd Geog)*
  [SD398-398.43]
  UF Nurseries, Forest
    Nurseries (Forestry)
  RT Trees—Seedlings
Forest of Ardennes
  USE Ardennes
Forest of Dean (England)
  USE Dean, Forest of (England)
Forest of Fontainebleau (France)
  USE Fontainebleau, Forest of (France)
Forest of Orléans (France)
  USE Orléans, Forest of (France)

Forest of Rambouillet (France)
  USE Rambouillet Forest (France)
Forest owners
  USE Forest landowners
Forest Park (New York, N.Y. : Park)
  BT Parks—New York (State)
Forest Park (Portland, Or.)
  (Not Subd Geog)
  BT Parks—Oregon
Forest Park (Saint Louis, Mo.)
  BT Parks—Missouri
Forest plantations
  USE Tree farms
Forest planting
  USE Afforestation
    Forests and forestry
Forest plants
  USE Forest flora
Forest plants, Rain
  USE Rain forest plants
Forest policy *(May Subd Geog)*
  [SD561-668]
  UF Forestry and state
    Government and forestry
    State and forestry
  BT Forests and forestry—Economic
    aspects
    Industry and state
  RT Forest reserves
    Forestry projects
  NT Forest management
    Forestry law and legislation
    Forests and forestry—Government
    ownership
Forest preservation
  USE Forest conservation
Forest Preserve of New York State (N.Y.)
  USE New York State Forest Preserve
    (N.Y.)
Forest production
  USE Forest productivity
    Forest products
    Forests and forestry
    Forests and forestry—Economic
    aspects
    Timber
Forest productivity *(May Subd Geog)*
  UF Forest production
    Productivity, Forest
  BT Agricultural productivity
    Forests and forestry
    Primary productivity (Biology)
  RT Forest site quality
Forest products *(May Subd Geog)*
  [HD9750-HD9769 (Economics)]
  [SD (Forestry)]
  [TS (Technology)]
  UF Forest production
  BT Botany, Economic
    Commercial products
    Raw materials
  NT Pine wool
    Rubber
    Timber
    Wood
    Wood products
— Information storage and retrieval systems
  USE Information storage and retrieval
    systems—Forest products
— **Quarantine** *(May Subd Geog)*
  BT Plant quarantine
— **Taxation** *(May Subd Geog)*
  RT Forests and forestry—Taxation
Forest products industry *(May Subd Geog)*
  [HD9750-9769]
  UF Forest industries
    Forestry industry
    Wood products industry
    Wood-using industries
  NT Strikes and lockouts—Forest products
    industry

Wages—Forest products industry
— Public relations
    USE Public relations—Forest products
        industry
Forest protection *(May Subd Geog)*
    UF Protection of forests
    BT Forest conservation
        Forest management
    RT Plants, Protection of
    NT Forest fires—Prevention and control
        Forest insects
        Trees—Diseases and pests
        Trees—Wounds and injuries
— Law and legislation
    USE Forestry law and legislation
— **Maine**
    NT Maine Forestry District
Forest radiography
    USE Radiography in forestry
Forest rangers *(May Subd Geog)*
    UF Rangers, Forest
    BT Forest management
        Forest reserves
    RT Park rangers
Forest recreation
    USE Forest reserves—Recreational use
Forest red gum tree
    USE Eucalyptus tereticornis
Forest regeneration
    USE Forest reproduction
Forest reproduction *(May Subd Geog)*
    Here are entered works on the reproduction of
forests by natural processes. Works on artificial re-
production of forests are entered under Reforesta-
tion.
    UF Forest regeneration
        Regeneration (Forestry)
    BT Reforestation
Forest research laboratories
    USE Forestry laboratories
Forest reserves *(May Subd Geog)*
    ⌜SD426-8⌟
    UF Forests, National
        Forests, State
        National forests
        State forests
    BT Forest conservation
        Natural monuments
        Public lands
        Wildlife conservation
    RT Forest policy
        Forests and forestry—Government
            ownership
        National parks and reserves
    NT Forest rangers
        Forests, County
        Forests and forestry
        Royal forests
        Wilderness areas
— **Accounting**
— — **Law and legislation**
        (May Subd Geog)
— **Finance**
— — **Law and legislation**
        (May Subd Geog)
— **Law and legislation** *(May Subd Geog)*
    BT Forestry law and legislation
— **Multiple use**
    ⌜SD427.M8 (United States)⌟
    ⌜SD428 (States)⌟
    ⌜SD567-SD662 (Other countries)⌟
    UF Multiple use of forest reserves
— **Recreational use**
    ⌜GV191.67.F6⌟
    UF Forest recreation
    BT Outdoor recreation
— **Alabama**
    NT Talladega National Forest (Ala.)
        Tuskegee National Forest (Ala.)
        William B. Bankhead National
            Forest (Ala.)

— **Alaska**
    NT Chugach National Forest (Alaska)
        Tongass National Forest (Alaska)
— **Arizona**
    NT Apache National Forest (Ariz.)
        Coconino National Forest (Ariz.)
        Coronado National Forest (Ariz.
            and N.M.)
        Sitgreaves National Forest (Ariz.)
— **Arkansas**
    NT Ouachita National Forest (Ark.
            and Okla.)
        Ozark National Forest (Ark.)
        Saint Francis National Forest
            (Ark.)
— **Australia**
    NT Barmah State Forest (Vic.)
        Brisbane Forest Park (Qld.)
        Kulkyne State Forest (Vic.)
        Lorne Forest Park (Vic.)
        Macedon Forest Park (Vic.)
        Shannon Forest and
            D'Entrecasteaux National Park
            (W.A.)
        Sherbrooke Forest Park (Vic.)
        Wombat State Forest (Vic.)
— **Brazil**
    NT Floresta Nacional de São Francisco
            de Paula (Brazil)
— **California**
    NT Cleveland National Forest (Calif.)
        Los Padres National Forest (Calif.)
        Modoc National Forest (Calif.)
        Rogue River National Forest (Or.
            and Calif.)
        Siskiyou National Forest (Or. and
            Calif.)
        Stanislaus National Forest (Calif.)
        Toiyabe National Forest (Nev. and
            Calif.)
— **Colorado**
    NT Arapaho National Forest (Colo.)
        Colorado State Forest (Colo.)
        Grand Mesa National Forest
            (Colo.)
        Manitou Experimental Forest
            (Colo.)
        Manti La Sal National Forest
            (Utah and Colo.)
        Pike National Forest (Colo.)
        Roosevelt National Forest (Colo.)
        Routt National Forest (Colo.)
        San Isabel National Forest (Colo.)
        San Juan National Forest (Colo.)
— **England**
    NT Charnwood Forest (England)
— **Florida**
    NT Apalachicola National Forest (Fla.)
        Ocala National Forest (Fla.)
        Osceola National Forest (Fla.)
— **France**
    NT Fontainebleau, Forest of (France)
        Rambouillet Forest (France)
— **Georgia**
    NT Chattahoochee National Forest
            (Ga.)
        Oconee National Forest (Ga.)
— **Germany (East)**
    NT Dübener Heide (Germany)
        Tharandter Wald (Germany)
— **Germany (West)**
    NT Bannwald "Steinhäusle"
            (Germany)
        Naturpark Arnsberger Wald
            (Germany)
        Naturpark Eggegebirge-Südlicher
            Teutoburger Wald (Germany)
        Naturpark Kottenforst-Ville
            (Germany)
        Naturpark Pfälzerwald (Germany)

        Naturpark Rothaargebirge
            (Germany)
— **Idaho**
    NT Boise National Forest (Idaho)
        Cache National Forest (Utah and
            Idaho)
        Caribou National Forest
        Clearwater National Forest (Idaho)
        Coeur d'Alene National Forest
            (Idaho)
        Kaniksu National Forest
        Nezperce National Forest (Idaho)
        Payette National Forest (Idaho)
        Saint Joe National Forest (Idaho)
        Salmon National Forest (Idaho)
        Targhee National Forest (Idaho
            and Wyo.)
— **Illinois**
    NT Palos Forest Preserve (Ill.)
        Shawnee National Forest (Ill.)
— **India**
    NT Bori Forest Range (India)
        Pachmarhi Forest Range (India)
— **Indiana**
    NT Hoosier National Forest (Ind.)
— **Ivory Coast**
    NT Parc National du Banco (Ivory
            Coast)
— **Japan**
    NT Asakawa Forest (Japan)
        Kenminno Forest (Japan)
— **Kentucky**
    NT Daniel Boone National Forest
            (Ky.)
— **Kenya**
    NT Kakamega Forest Reserve (Kenya)
— **Maine**
    NT White Mountain National Forest
            (N.H. and Me.)
— **Massachusetts**
    NT Harvard Forest (Mass. : Forest)
        Leominster State Forest (Mass.)
— **Michigan**
    NT Hiawatha National Forest (Mich.)
        Huron National Forest (Mich.)
        Ottawa National Forest (Mich.)
        Pigeon River Country State Forest
            (Mich.)
— **Minnesota**
    NT Chippewa National Forest (Minn.)
        Superior National Forest (Minn.)
— **Mississippi**
    NT Bienville National Forest (Miss.)
        De Soto National Forest (Miss.)
        Delta National Forest (Miss.)
        Homochitto National Forest
            (Miss.)
        Tombigbee National Forest (Miss.)
— **Missouri**
    NT Mark Twain National Forest (Mo.)
— **Montana**
    NT Deerlodge National Forest (Mont.)
        Flathead National Forest (Mont.)
        Helena National Forest (Mont.)
        Kaniksu National Forest
— **Netherlands**
    NT Boswachterij Dorst (Netherlands)
— **Nevada**
    NT Toiyabe National Forest (Nev. and
            Calif.)
— **New Hampshire**
    NT White Mountain National Forest
            (N.H. and Me.)
— **New Jersey**
    NT Watchung Reservation (N.J.)
— **New Mexico**
    NT Cibola National Forest (N.M.)
        Coronado National Forest (Ariz.
            and N.M.)
        Santa Fe National Forest (N.M.)
— **New York (State)**

Forestry innovations *(May Subd Geog)*
 UF Forests and forestry—Innovations
  Forests and forestry—Technological
   innovations
  Innovations, Forestry
  Technical change in forests and
   forestry
 BT Forests and forestry
  Technological innovations
 NT Logging—Technological innovations
Forestry journalism
 USE Journalism, Forestry
Forestry laboratories *(May Subd Geog)*
 ₍SD356.7-356.72₎
 UF Forest research laboratories
  Forestry sciences laboratories
  Forests and forestry—Laboratories
  Laboratories, Forestry
 BT Laboratories
Forestry law and legislation
 (May Subd Geog)
 ₍SD561-668₎
 UF Forest law
  Forest protection—Law and legislation
  Forests and forestry—Law
  Government and forestry
  Law, Forestry
  Timber laws and legislation
 BT Forest policy
  Natural resources—Law and legislation
  Wildlife conservation—Law and
   legislation
 RT Plants, Protection of—Law and
   legislation
 NT Endangered species—Law and
   legislation
  Forest credit—Law and legislation
  Forest fires—Law and legislation
  Forest reserves—Law and legislation
  Logging—Law and legislation
  Reforestation—Law and legislation
  Trees—Diseases and pests—Law and
   legislation
  Trees in cities—Law and legislation
  Wood waste—Law and legislation
 — Colonies
  USE Forestry law and legislation,
   Colonial
 — **Criminal provisions**
 — ₍country₎
 — — **Colonies**
Forestry law and legislation, Colonial
  Here are entered general and comparative works
 only. Works on forestry law and legislation of the
 colonies of an individual country are entered under
 the heading Forestry law and legislation with subdivi-
 sion ₍country₎—Colonies. Works dealing with a
 specific colony are entered under the same heading,
 subdivided by the name of the colony.
 UF Colonial forestry law
  Colonies—Forestry law and legislation
  Forestry law and legislation—Colonies
Forestry law and legislation (Roman law)
Forestry libraries *(May Subd Geog)*
 ₍Z675.F₎
 UF Libraries, Forestry
 BT Technical libraries
Forestry literature
 ₍SD387.D6₎
 UF Forests and forestry—Literature
 RT Forests and forestry—Bibliography
Forestry projects *(May Subd Geog)*
 ₍SD387.P74 (General)₎
 UF Development projects, Forestry
  Forestry development projects
  Projects, Forestry
 BT Agricultural development projects
  Forests and forestry
 RT Forest policy
 NT Social forestry programs
 — **Rwanda**
  NT Projet pilote forestier

Forestry schools and education
 (May Subd Geog)
 ₍SD251-356₎
 UF Forestry education
  Forests and forestry—Study and
   teaching
 BT Agricultural education
  Agriculture—Study and teaching
  Schools
  Technical education
  Vocational education
 NT Forestry teachers
Forestry sciences laboratories
 USE Forestry laboratories
Forestry teachers *(May Subd Geog)*
 BT Forestry schools and education
  Teachers
Forestry wives
 USE Foresters' wives
Forests, County *(May Subd Geog)*
 ₍SD426-428₎
 UF County forests
 BT Community forests
  Forest reserves
Forests, Exotic
 USE Exotic forests
Forests, National
 USE Forest reserves
Forests, Old growth
 USE Old growth forests
Forests, Petrified
 USE Petrified forests
Forests, State
 USE Forest reserves
Forests, Submerged
 UF Submerged forests
 BT Forests and forestry
Forests, Virgin
 USE Old growth forests
Forests and climate
 USE Forest microclimatology
Forests and floods
 USE Forest influences
Forests and forestry *(May Subd Geog)*
 ₍HJ3805 (Income from state forests)₎
 ₍HJ4167 (Taxation)₎
 ₍SD₎
 UF Forest planting
  Forest production
  Forestation
  Forestry industry
  Silviculture
  Sylviculture
 BT Agriculture
  Forest influences
  Forest reserves
  Natural resources
  Water-supply
 RT Afforestation
  Arboriculture
  Logging
  Timber
  Tree crops
  Trees
  Wood
 SA *headings beginning with the words*
  Forest *and* Forestry
 NT Aeronautics in forestry
  Agroforestry
  Brush
  Chaparral
  Community forests
  Cut-over lands
  Energy crops
  Exotic forestry
  Exotic forests
  Explosives in forestry
  Forest districts
  Forest flora
  Forest landowners
  Forest productivity

  Forest site quality
  Forestry innovations
  Forestry projects
  Forests, Submerged
  Hardwoods
  Hydrology, Forest
  Insurance, Forest
  Landscape gardening
  Lumber
  Lumber trade
  Lumbering
  Moving-pictures in forestry
  Natural history—Outdoor books
  Old growth forests
  Planting (Plant culture)
  Plastics in forestry
  Pruning
  Radioactive tracers in forestry
  Rain forests
  Reforestation
  Slash (Logging)
  Taigas
  Tree farms
  Tree felling
  Tree planting
  Trees—Growth
  Urban forestry
  Wood-lots
 — **Accidents** *(May Subd Geog)*
  NT Forests and forestry—Safety
   measures
 — **Appropriate technology**
  ₍SD387.A66₎
  BT Appropriate technology
 — **Bibliography**
  RT Forestry literature
 — **Computer programs**
 — Ecology
  USE Forest ecology
 — **Economic aspects** *(May Subd Geog)*
  ₍SD₎
  UF Forest economics
   Forest production
  BT Agriculture—Economic aspects
  NT Forest policy
 — Engineering
  USE Forestry engineering
 — **Experimental areas**
  ₍SD359₎
 — **Forecasting**
  ₍SD387.F58₎
  BT Forecasting
 — Genetic research
  USE Forest genetics
 — **Government ownership**
  (May Subd Geog)
  UF Government ownership of forests
  BT Forest policy
  RT Forest reserves
 — Information storage and retrieval systems
  USE Information storage and retrieval
   systems—Forestry
 — Innovations
  USE Forestry innovations
 — **Irrigation**
  ₍SD408.15-SD408.154₎
  UF Forest irrigation
   Irrigated forestry
   Irrigation, Forest
  BT Irrigation
 — Laboratories
  USE Forestry laboratories
 — Law
  USE Forestry law and legislation
 — Literature
  USE Forestry literature
 — Mapping
  USE Forest mapping
 — **Maps**
  NT Forest mapping
 — **Mensuration**

Forests and forestry
  — Mensuration *(Continued)*
    ₍SD551-7₎
    UF Forest mensuration
        Log scaling
        Timber—Mensuration
        Timber cruising
    NT Dendrometer
  — — Computer programs
  — Multiple use
    UF Multiple use of forest lands
  — — Law and legislation
      (May Subd Geog)
  — Safety measures
    ₍SD411₎
    UF Forest machinery—Safety measures
    BT Forests and forestry—Accidents
  — Social aspects *(May Subd Geog)*
    ₍SD387.S55₎
    UF Social forest management
        Society and forests and forestry
    RT Social forestry programs
  — Study and teaching
    USE Forestry schools and education
  — Subject headings
    USE Subject headings—Forestry
  — Surveying
    USE Forest surveys
  — Taxation *(May Subd Geog)*
    ₍HJ4167₎
    UF Timber—Taxation
    BT Real property tax
        Severance tax
    RT Forest products—Taxation
  — — Law and legislation
      (May Subd Geog)
  — Technological innovations
    USE Forestry innovations
  — Thermographic methods
  — Thinning
    USE Forest thinning
  — Tools and implements
    BT Tools
  — Valuation
    ₍SD551-7₎
    UF Forest valuation
        Timber cruising
  — Vocational guidance *(May Subd Geog)*
    ₍SD387.F6₎
    BT Foresters
  — Weed control *(May Subd Geog)*
  — Austria
    NT Bohemian Forest
        Wienerwald (Austria)
  — Belgium
    NT Soignes Forest (Belgium)
  — Byelorussian S.S.R.
    NT Bialowieza Forest (Poland and
        Byelorussian S.S.R.)
  — Colorado
    NT Manitou Experimental Forest
        (Colo.)
  — Czechoslovakia
    NT Bohemian Forest
  — Denmark
    NT Svinkløv Plantation (Denmark)
  — England
    NT Ashdown Forest (England)
        Dean, Forest of (England)
        Epping Forest (England)
        New Forest (England)
  — France
    NT Chantilly Forest (France)
        Compiègne Forest (France)
        Ermenonville Forest (France)
        Halatte Forest (France)
        Laigue Forest (France)
        Marly Forest (France)
        Orléans, Forest of (France)
        Paimpont, Forest of (France)
        Trois Pignons Forest (France)

  — Germany (East)
    NT Spree Forest (Germany)
        Thuringian Forest (Germany)
  — Germany (West)
    NT Bavarian Forest (Germany)
        Black Forest (Germany)
        Bohemian Forest
        Frankenwald (Germany)
        Nationalpark Bayerischer Wald
        (Germany)
        Reinhardswald (Germany)
        Spessart (Germany)
        Steigerwald (Germany)
        Teutoburg Forest (Germany)
  — Indonesia
    NT Maria Forest (Sumbawa, Indonesia)
        Tololai Forest (Sumbawa,
        Indonesia)
  — Italy
    NT Val di Canneto Forest (Italy)
  — Kenya
    NT Nguruman Forest (Kenya)
  — Manitoba
    NT Sandilands Provincial Forest
        (Man.)
  — Massachusetts
  — — Experimental areas
    NT Harvard Forest (Mass. : Forest)
  — New Jersey
    NT Wharton State Forest (N.J.)
  — New York (State)
    NT Hector Land Use Area (N.Y.)
  — Poland
    NT Bialowieza Forest (Poland and
        Byelorussian S.S.R.)
        Kampinoska Forest (Poland)
        Kurpiowska Forest (Poland)
        Niepolomice Forest (Poland)
        Zielonka Forest (Poland)
  — Scotland
    NT Achray Forest (Scotland)
Forests and forestry, Cooperative
  (May Subd Geog)
    UF Cooperative forestry
        Cooperative forests
        Forest cooperatives
        Forestry cooperatives
    BT Agriculture, Cooperative
        Cooperation
    NT Community forests
Forests and rainfall
    USE Forest influences
Forests and water-supply
    USE Forest influences
Forests in art
Forests in literature
    BT Nature in literature
    RT Trees in literature
Foresyth family
    USE Forsyth family
Forêt de Bière (France)
    USE Fontainebleau, Forest of (France)
Forêt de Bierre (France)
    USE Fontainebleau, Forest of (France)
Forêt de Chantilly (France)
    USE Chantilly Forest (France)
Forêt de Compiègne (France)
    USE Compiègne Forest (France)
Forêt de Fontainebleau (France)
    USE Fontainebleau, Forest of (France)
Forêt de Laigle (France)
    USE Laigue Forest (France)
Forêt de Laigue (France)
    USE Laigue Forest (France)
Forêt de Marly (France)
    USE Marly Forest (France)
Forêt de Paimpont (France)
    USE Paimpont, Forest of (France)
Forêt de Rambouillet (France)
    USE Rambouillet Forest (France)

Forêt de Soignes (Belgium)
    USE Soignes Forest (Belgium)
Forêt d'Ermenonville (France)
    USE Ermenonville Forest (France)
Forêt des Trois Pignons (France)
    USE Trois Pignons Forest (France)
Forêt d'Halatte (France)
    USE Halatte Forest (France)
Forêt domaniale de Soignes (Belgium)
    USE Soignes Forest (Belgium)
Forêt domaniale des Trois Pignons (France)
    USE Trois Pignons Forest (France)
Forêt d'Orléans (France)
    USE Orléans, Forest of (France)
Forêt Noire (Germany)
    USE Black Forest (Germany)
Forey family
    UF Fury family
Forez (France)
Forez, Parc naturel régional Livradois (France)
    USE Parc naturel régional Livradois-Forez
    (France)
Forfang family *(Not Subd Geog)*
Forfeiture *(May Subd Geog)*
    RT Attainder
    NT Escheat
        Lapse (Law)
Forficula
    ₍QL510.3.F6₎
    BT Forficulidae
Forficulidae
    ₍QL510.3.F6₎
    BT Dermaptera
    NT Forficula
Forgason family
    USE Ferguson family
Forge shops *(May Subd Geog)*
    ₍TS225₎
    UF Forges
    BT Forging
  — Equipment and supplies
    NT Forging machinery
  — Health aspects
    USE Forging—Health aspects
  — Safety measures
    USE Forging—Safety measures
Forge shops in art
Forge welding *(May Subd Geog)*
    UF Welding, Forge
    BT Pressure welding
Forged aluminum
    USE Aluminum forgings
Forged steel flanges, Tariff on
    USE Tariff on forged steel flanges
Forged titanium
    USE Titanium forgings
Forgers *(May Subd Geog)*
    BT Forgery
    NT Art forgers
Forgerson family
    USE Ferguson family
Forgery *(May Subd Geog)*
    ₍HG1696-HG1698 (Checks)₎
    ₍HV6675-HV6685₎
    ₍Z41 (Autographs)₎
    BT Criminal law
        Fraud
        Offenses against property
        Swindlers and swindling
    SA *subdivision* Forgeries *under names of*
        individual persons and under types
        of art, objects, documents, etc., e.g.
        Postage-stamps—Forgeries
    NT Arts—Forgeries
        Blanks in legal documents
        Cancellations (Philately)—Forgeries
        Checks—Criminal provisions
        Counterfeits and counterfeiting
        Drawing—Forgeries
        False certification
        Forgers

Glassware—Forgeries
Hallmarks—Forgeries
Literary forgeries and mystifications
Painting—Forgeries
Pewter—Forgeries
Postmarks—Forgeries
Reproduction of money, documents,
etc.—Law and legislation
Signatures (Writing)
Trials (Forgery)
Vienna porcelain—Forgeries
Forgery (Canon law)
Forgery (Roman law)
Forgery of antiquities *(May Subd Geog)*
ㄷCC140ㄱ
UF Antiquities, Forgery of
Archaeological forgeries
BT Antiquities
RT Art—Forgeries
NT Kensington Rune Stone
Pottery—Forgeries
Swords—Forgeries
— England
NT Piltdown forgery
— New York (State)
NT Cardiff giant
Forgery of hall-marks
USE Hallmarks—Forgeries
Forgery of hallmarks
USE Hallmarks—Forgeries
Forgery of inscriptions
ㄷCN99ㄱ
UF Inscriptions—Forgeries
Forgery of manuscripts *(May Subd Geog)*
ㄷBX875 (Catholic Church documents)ㄱ
ㄷPN171.F6-PN171.F7 (Literature)ㄱ
ㄷZ41 (Autographs)ㄱ
UF Manuscripts—Forgeries
Manuscripts, Forgery of
NT Manuscripts—Certification
Forgery of paintings
USE Painting—Forgeries
Forgery of pottery
USE Pottery—Forgeries
Forgery of works of art
USE Art—Forgeries
Forges
USE Forge shops
Forgeson family
USE Ferguson family
Forget-me-nots
ㄷSB413 (Culture)ㄱ
Forgetfulness
USE Memory
Forging
ㄷTS225 (Manufacture)ㄱ
ㄷTT215-TT240 (Shop work)ㄱ
UF Drop-forging
BT Metal-work
RT Blacksmithing
Ironwork
Metal stamping
NT Aluminum forgings
Brass forgings
Dies (Metal-working)
Drawing (Metal-work)
Explosive forming
Eye-bars
Forge shops
Forging machinery
High energy forming
Punching machinery
Rolling (Metal-work)
Steel forgings
Titanium forgings
Upset forging
Welding
— Health aspects *(May Subd Geog)*
UF Forge shops—Health aspects
Forging—Hygienic aspects
— Hygienic aspects

USE Forging—Health aspects
— Safety measures
UF Forge shops—Safety measures
Forging, Upset
USE Upset forging
Forging industry *(May Subd Geog)*
ㄷHD9510-9529ㄱ
BT Iron industry and trade
Metal trade
Steel industry and trade
— Netherlands
— — Employees
NT Nederlandsche Grofsmederij
Strike, 1978
Forging machinery
BT Forge shops—Equipment and supplies
Forging
Metal-working machinery
— Appraisal
USE Forging machinery—Valuation
— Construction
USE Forging machinery—Design and
construction
— Design and construction
UF Forging machinery—Construction
— Drawing
USE Forging machinery—Drawings
— Drawings
UF Forging machinery—Drawing
BT Mechanical drawing
— Electric driving
— Electric equipment
— Foundations
— — Vibration
— Hydraulic drive
— Valuation
ㄷTS225ㄱ
UF Forging machinery—Appraisal
Forgings, Titanium
USE Titanium forgings
Forgison family
USE Ferguson family
Forgiveness
ㄷBJ1476ㄱ
BT Conduct of life
RT Pardon
— Religious aspects
NT Forgiveness of sin
— — Baptists, ㄷCatholic Church, etc.ㄱ
— — Buddhism, ㄷChristianity, etc.ㄱ
Forgiveness of sin
ㄷBT795ㄱ
UF Sin, Forgiveness of
BT Forgiveness—Religious aspects
Sin
RT Absolution
NT Confession
Penance
Forgiveness of sin (Islam)
ㄷBP134.F6 (Koran)ㄱ
BT Islam—Doctrines
Sin (Islam)
Forgiveness of sin in art
Forgue family
USE Forgues family
Forgues family
UF Forgue family
Forguson family
USE Ferguson family
Fori Imperiali Road (Rome, Italy)
USE Via dei Fori Imperiali (Rome, Italy)
Forissier family
Forist family
USE Forrest family
Forister family
USE Foster family

Fork lift trucks
BT Conveying machinery
Hoisting machinery
Industrial electric trucks
Industrial power trucks
Lifting-jacks
Trucks
Forked Deer River (Tenn.)
BT Rivers—Tennessee
Forkner family
USE Faulkner family
Forkner shorthand
USE Shorthand—Forkner
Forks *(May Subd Geog)*
ㄷNK7230-NK7240 (Silver)ㄱ
ㄷTX298-TX299 (Household utensils)ㄱ
BT Flatware
Forligelse (The Danish word)
BT Danish language—Etymology
Form, Jordan
USE Jordan matrix
Form, Jordan normal
USE Jordan matrix
Form, Literary
USE Literary form
Form, Musical
USE Musical form
Form (Aesthetics)
ㄷBH301.F6ㄱ
UF Aesthetic form
BT Aesthetics
NT Symmetry (Art)
Form (Logic)
ㄷBC199.F6ㄱ
UF Logical form
BT Logic
Form (Philosophy)
BT Idealism
Matter
Metaphysics
RT Structuralism
NT Formalization (Philosophy)
Form and matter
USE Hylomorphism
Form criticism (Bible)
USE Bible—Criticism, Form
Form discrimination
USE Form perception
Form factor (Nuclear physics)
ㄷQC794ㄱ
BT Approximation theory
Scattering (Physics)
RT Bootstrap theory (Nuclear physics)
Form in biology
USE Morphology
Form letters
BT Commercial correspondence
Letter-writing
Form of contract *(May Subd Geog)*
UF Contract, Form of
BT Contracts
Formalities (Law)
RT Statute of frauds
Form of juristic acts
USE Formalities (Law)
Locus regit actum
Form perception
UF Form discrimination
Shape discrimination
BT Perception
Visual discrimination
Visual perception
RT Figure-ground perception
NT Color and form recognition test
Pattern perception
Picture perception
— Cross-cultural studies
Form perception in children
ㄷBF723.P36ㄱ
BT Perception in children

Form psychology
  USE Gestalt psychology
Form requirements (Law)
  USE Formalities (Law)
Forma pauperis
  USE In forma pauperis
Formability of metals
  USE Metals—Formability
Formal culture
  USE Formal discipline
Formal discipline
  UF Culture, Formal
      Discipline, Formal
      Formal culture
  BT Discipline
      Education
      Educational psychology
      Habit
      Teaching
  RT Transfer of training
  NT Memory
Formal gardens
  USE Gardens
Formal groups
  USE Groups, Formal
Formal language semantics
  USE Formal languages—Semantics
Formal languages
    ₍QA267.3₎
  BT Formalization (Linguistics)
      Language and languages
      Machine theory
  NT AUTOMATH (Formal language)
      Graph grammars
      L systems
      PARIS (Formal language)
      Parsing (Computer grammar)
      SYNTOL (Formal language)
  — Semantics
      UF Formal language semantics
          Logical semantics
          Semantics (Logic)
      BT Semantics
  — Syntax
Formal semantics
  USE Semantics
Formaldehyde
    ₍QD305.A6 (Chemistry)₎
    ₍RA766.F6 (Disinfectants)₎
    ₍TP248.F6 (Chemical technology)₎
  UF Formalin
  BT Disinfection and disinfectants
  NT Wood products—Formaldehyde release
  — **Dipole moments**
  — **Spectra**
Formalin
  USE Formaldehyde
Formalism (Art) *(May Subd Geog)*
      Here are entered works discussing art emphasiz-
    ing its structure, style or artistic means rather than its
    contents.
  BT Art
  RT Art for art's sake (Movement)
Formalism (Literary analysis)
    (May Subd Geog)
    ₍PN98.F6₎
  UF Russian formalism (Literary analysis)
  BT Criticism
Formalities (Jewish law)
Formalities (Law) *(May Subd Geog)*
      Here are entered works on general legal form re-
    quirements, including writing, notarization and per-
    formance before witnesses. Works containing general
    collections of legal forms are entered under Forms
    (Law).
  UF Form of juristic acts
      Form requirements (Law)
  NT Form of contract
      Insinuation (Civil law)
  — Conflict of laws
      USE Conflict of laws—Formalities

Formalities (Roman law)
  UF Subtilitas legum
Formalization (Linguistics)
    ₍P128.F67₎
  BT Linguistic analysis (Linguistics)
      Linguistics
  NT Formal languages
Formalization (Philosophy)
    ₍BD258₎
  BT Form (Philosophy)
      Knowledge, Theory of
      Logic
      Methodology
      Philosophy
Formally real fields
  UF Fields, Formally real
      Real fields, Ordering of
  BT Fields, Algebraic
Forman family
  USE Foreman family
Formants (Speech)
  UF Speech formants
  BT Sound
      Speech
      Voice
      Vowels
Format of books
  USE Books—Format
Format of microfiches
  USE Microfiches—Format
Format of periodicals
  USE Periodicals—Format
Formation, Character
  USE Personality development
Formation, Heat of
  USE Heat of formation
Formation, Star
  USE Stars—Formation
Formation, Stellar
  USE Stars—Formation
Formation damage (Petroleum engineering)
  BT Drilling muds
      Oil sands—Permeability
      Oil well drilling
      Petroleum—Geology
Formation of corporations
  USE Incorporation
Formation of spectral lines
  USE Spectral line formation
Formation waters (Oil fields)
  USE Oil field brines
Formations (Geology) *(May Subd Geog)*
  UF Geologic formations
      Geological formations
      Stratigraphic formations
  BT Geology, Stratigraphic
  NT Aquifers
  — Arizona
      NT Toreva Formation (Ariz.)
          Winterhaven Formation (Calif. and
              Ariz.)
  — **British Colombia**
  — **British Columbia**
      NT Queen Charlotte Group (B.C.)
  — California
      NT Sespe Formation (Calif.)
          Winterhaven Formation (Calif. and
              Ariz.)
  — Colorado
      NT Creede Formation (Colo.)
          Green River Formation
  — Florida
      NT Hawthorn Formation
          Sunniland Formation (Fla.)
  — Georgia
      NT Hawthorn Formation
          Pumpkinvine Creek Formation
              (Ga.)
  — Idaho
      NT Hoodoo Quartzite (Idaho)
          Yellowjacket Formation (Idaho)

  — **Kentucky**
      NT Breathitt Formation (Ky. and
              Tenn.)
  — **Louisiana**
      NT Frio Clay (Tex. and La.)
  — **Middle West**
      NT Sioux Quartzite
          Wedron Formation
  — **Montana**
      NT Blackleaf Formation (Mont.)
          Heath Formation (Mont.)
          Livingston Formation (Mont.)
          Spokane Formation (Mont.)
  — **Nevada**
      NT Popovich Formation (Nev.)
          Roberts Mountains Formation
              (Nev. and Utah)
  — **New Jersey**
      NT Kirkwood Formation (N.J. and
              Pa.)
  — **New Mexico**
      NT Popotosa Formation (N.M.)
          Santa Rosa Formation (N.M. and
              Tex.)
  — **Pennsylvania**
      NT Kirkwood Formation (N.J. and
              Pa.)
  — **South Carolina**
      NT Hawthorn Formation
  — **Tennessee**
      NT Breathitt Formation (Ky. and
              Tenn.)
  — **Texas**
      NT Frio Clay (Tex. and La.)
          Santa Rosa Formation (N.M. and
              Tex.)
  — **Utah**
      NT Green River Formation
          Roberts Mountains Formation
              (Nev. and Utah)
  — **West (U.S.)**
      NT Fort Union Formation
          Frontier Formation
          Morrison Formation
          Navajo Sandstone
          Niobrara Formation
          Phosphoria Formation
          Wasatch Formation
  — **Wyoming**
      NT Blair Formation (Wyo.)
          Colter Formation (Wyo.)
          Green River Formation
Formatting of information display systems
  USE Information display systems—
      Formatting
Formazza Valley (Italy)
  BT Valleys—Italy
FormDesigner (Computer program)
    ₍HF5371₎
  BT Business—Forms—Computer programs
Forme uniche della continuita nello spazio
    (Sculpture)
  USE Boccioni, Umberto, 1882-1916.
      Unique forms of continuity in space
Formentera (Spain)
  UF Isla de Formentera (Spain)
      Ophiusa (Spain)
  BT Islands—Spain
      Pityusic Islands (Spain)
Former clergy
  USE Ex-clergy
Former farmers
  USE Ex-farmers
Former jeopardy
  USE Double jeopardy
Former mental patients
  USE Ex-mental patients
Former mentally ill
  USE Ex-mental patients
Former monks
  USE Ex-monks

1414

Former nuns
  USE Ex-nuns
Former presidents
  USE Ex-presidents
Former prisoners of war
  USE Ex-prisoners of war
Former Sung dynasty, China, 420-479
  USE China—History—Liu Sung dynasty,
       420-479
Formic acid
  [QD305.A2 (Chemistry)]
  [RM666.F6 (Therapeutics)]
Formica (Insect) *(May Subd Geog)*
  [QL568.F7]
  BT Ants
  NT Formica exsectoides
Formica exsectoides *(May Subd Geog)*
  [QL568.F7]
  BT Formica (Insect)
Formicariidae
  [QL696.P2455]
  UF Ant thrushes
     Antbirds
  BT Passeriformes
  NT Formicarius
     Gymnopithys
     Hylophylax
     Phaenostictus
     Terenura
Formicarius
  [QL696.P2455]
  BT Formicariidae
  NT Formicarius rufifrons
Formicarius rufifrons
  [QL696.P2455]
  UF Rufous-fronted ant thrush
  BT Formicarius
Formicidae
  USE Ants
Forming of aluminum
  USE Aluminum forming
Formon family
  USE Foreman family
Formosa (Government general of Taiwan,
    1895-1945)
  USE Taiwan
Formosa pine
  USE Pinus taiwanensis
Formosa serow
  USE Japanese serow
Formosan . . .
  USE *subject headings beginning with the
       word* Taiwan
Formosan cypress
  USE Chamaecyparis formosensis
Formosans
  USE Taiwanese
Forms, Automorphic
  USE Automorphic forms
Forms, Bilinear
  UF Bilinear forms
  NT Inner product spaces
Forms, Binary
  UF Binary forms
  NT Forms, Quadratic
Forms, Cusp (Mathematics)
  USE Cusp forms (Mathematics)
Forms, Differential
  USE Differential forms
Forms, Dirichlet
  UF Dirichlet forms
  BT Forms (Mathematics)
     Potential, Theory of
Forms, Dress
  USE Dress forms
Forms, Exterior
  USE Exterior forms
Forms, Hermitian
  USE Hermitian forms
Forms, Jacobi
  USE Jacobi forms

Forms, Modular
  UF Modular forms
  BT Forms (Mathematics)
  NT Curves, Modular
     Cusp forms (Mathematics)
     Hecke operators
     Hilbert modular surfaces
     Jacobi forms
Forms, Normal (Mathematics)
  USE Normal forms (Mathematics)
Forms, Pfister
  UF Pfister forms
  BT Forms, Quadratic
Forms, Quadratic
  UF Quadratic forms
  BT Forms, Binary
     Numbers, Theory of
  RT Diophantine analysis
  NT Forms, Pfister
     Maslov index
     Witt group
Forms, Quadrilinear
  [QA201]
  UF Quadrilinear forms
Forms, Quaternary
  UF Quaternary forms
Forms, Ternary
  UF Ternary forms
Forms, Trilinear
  UF Trilinear forms
Forms (Canon law)
  [BX1939.F6]
Forms (Concrete construction)
  USE Concrete construction—Formwork
Forms (Frankish law)
Forms (Germanic law)
Forms (Hindu law)
Forms (Jewish law)
Forms (Law) *(May Subd Geog)*
  [HF1243 (Commercial law: United
   States)]
    Here are entered works containing general collec-
  tions of legal forms. Works on general legal form
  requirements, including writing, notarization and
  performance before witnesses, are entered under For-
  malities (Law).
  UF Legal forms
     Precedents (Law)
  BT Acknowledgments
     Actions and defenses
     Business law
     Commercial law
     Pleading
  RT Conveyancing
     Legal composition
  SA *subdivision* Forms *under legal subjects*
  NT Contracts—Forms
     Formularies (Diplomatics)
     Interrogatories
     Legal correspondence
     Letters patent
Forms (Mathematics)
  [QA201]
  [QA243-QA244]
  UF Quantics
  BT Algebra
     Mathematics
  NT Automorphic forms
     Forms, Dirichlet
     Forms, Modular
     Hermitian forms
     Partitions (Mathematics)
Forms (Precast concrete)
  USE Precast concrete—Formwork

Forms (Roman law)
Forms, blanks, etc.
  USE *subdivision* Forms *under names of
       individual corporate bodies, and
       under topical headings for works
       consisting of, or containing,
       substantial numbers of blank forms,
       e.g.* Business—Forms
Forms of address *(May Subd Geog)*
  [CR3499-4420]
  UF Address, Forms of
     Address, Titles of
     Titles of address
  BT Etiquette
     Letter-writing
     Salutations
     Titles of honor and nobility
  SA *subdivision* Address, Forms of *under
       names of languages, e.g.* English
       language—Address, Forms of
Formula Atlantic automobiles
  BT Automobiles, Racing
Formula diet
  USE Elemental diet
Formula One automobiles
  UF F1 cars
  BT Automobiles, Racing
Formula Super Vee automobiles
  BT Automobiles, Racing
     Volkswagen automobile
Formula translation (Computer program
  language)
  USE FORTRAN (Computer program
       language)
Formulaic analysis, Oral
  USE Oral-formulaic analysis
Formularies, Medical
  USE Medicine—Formulae, receipts,
       prescriptions
Formularies (Diplomatics)
  [CD80]
  BT Diplomatics
     Forms (Law)
  NT Letters patent
Formulas, Biotechnological
  USE Biotechnology—Formulae
Formulas, Cubature
  USE Cubature formulas
Formulas, Infant
  USE Infant formulas
Formulas, Product
  USE Product formulas (Operator theory)
Formulas, Trace
  USE Trace formulas
Formulas (Mathematics)
  USE Mathematics—Formulae
Formulas for artists' materials
  USE Artists' materials—Formulae
Formulas for ceramics
  USE Ceramics—Formulae
Formulas for glazes
  USE Glazes—Formulae
Formulas for photography
  USE Photography—Formulae
Formulas for pottery
  USE Pottery—Formulae
Formulated food
  USE Elemental diet
Formulation of cases in psychiatry
  USE Psychiatry—Case formulation
Fornall family
  USE Fornell family
Fornarina (Portrait painting)
  USE Raphael, 1483-1520. Portrait of la
       Fornarina
Fornel House (Québec, Québec)
  USE Maison Fornel (Québec, Québec)
Fornell family
  UF Fornall family
Fornio Indians
  USE Fulnio Indians

Fornovo, Battle of, 1495
  [DG541]
  BT Italy—History—Expedition of Charles
        VIII, 1494-1496
Foro Romano (Rome, Italy)
  USE Roman Forum (Rome, Italy)
Forress family
  USE Forrest family
Forrest family
  UF Forest family
        Forist family
        Forress family
        Forriss family
        Forust family
Forrester family
  USE Foster family
Forriss family
  USE Forrest family
Forrister family
  USE Foster family
Forristor family
  USE Foster family
Forsaith family
  USE Forsyth family
Forseth family
Forseyth family
  USE Forsyth family
Forsight family
  USE Forsyth family
Forsith family
  USE Forsyth family
Forsithe family
  USE Forsyth family
Forsoning (The Danish word)
  BT Danish language—Etymology
Forster family
  USE Foster family
Forsterite (May Subd Geog)
  UF Boltonite
        White olivine
  BT Olivine
Forsyth family
  UF Foresyth family
        Forsaith family
        Forseyth family
        Forsight family
        Forsith family
        Forsithe family
        Forsythe family
        Forsythes family
Forsythe family
  USE Forsyth family
Forsythes family
  USE Forsyth family
Forsythia (May Subd Geog)
  [QK495.O44 (Botany)]
  [SB413.F6 (Culture)]
  BT Oleaceae
Fort Alexander Indian Reserve (Man.)
  UF Maple River Indian Reserve (Man.)
  BT Chippewa Indians—Reservations
Fort Ancient culture (May Subd Geog)
  [E99.F]
  BT Ohio River Valley—Antiquities
Fort Apache Indian Reservation (Ariz.)
  BT Apache Indians—Reservations
        Indians of North America—Arizona—
          Reservations
Fort Belknap (Tex.)
  UF Belknap, Fort (Tex.)
  BT Fortification—Texas
Fort Belknap Indian Reservation (Mont.)
  BT Assiniboin Indians—Reservations
        Indians of North America—Montana
          —Reservations
Fort Berthold Indian Reservation (N.D.)
  BT Arikara Indians—Reservations
        Hidatsa Indians—Reservations
        Indians of North America—North
          Dakota—Reservations
        Mandan Indians—Reservations

Fort Branch (N.C.)
  UF Branch Fort (N.C.)
  BT Fortification—North Carolina
Fort Bridger (Wyo.)
  UF Bridger, Fort (Wyo.)
  BT Fortification—Wyoming
Fort Carillon (N.Y.)
  USE Fort Ticonderoga (N.Y.)
Fort Center Site (Fla.) (Not Subd Geog)
  UF Fort Centre Site (Fla.)
  BT Florida—Antiquities
Fort Centre Site (Fla.)
  USE Fort Center Site (Fla.)
Fort Chambly (Chambly, Québec)
  BT Fortification—Québec (Province)
Fort Chiswell Mansion (Max Meadows, Va.)
  BT Dwellings—Virginia
Fort Dallas (Miami, Fla.)
  UF Dallas, Fort (Miami, Fla.)
  BT Fortification—Florida
  RT Granada Site (Miami, Fla.)
Fort Dallas Park (Miami, Fla.)
  (Not Subd Geog)
  UF Miami (Fla.). Fort Dallas Park
Fort Dalles (Dalles, Or.) (Not Subd Geog)
  UF Dalles, Fort (Dalles, Or.)
  BT Fortification—Oregon
Fort Davis National Historic Site (Tex.)
  BT Historic sites—Texas
        National parks and reserves—Texas
Fort Dearborn Massacre, 1812
  USE Chicago (Ill.)—Massacre, 1812
Fort Dodge-Fort Griffin Trail
  USE Texas Cattle Trail
Fort family
  UF Forte family
        Fourt family
Fort George (New York, N.Y.)
  UF George, Fort (New York, N.Y.)
  BT Fortification—New York (State)
Fort Gibson Lake (Okla.)
  UF Fort Gibson Reservoir (Okla.)
  BT Lakes—Oklahoma
        Reservoirs—Oklahoma
Fort Gibson Reservoir (Okla.)
  USE Fort Gibson Lake (Okla.)
Fort Griffin (Tex.)
  UF Griffin, Fort (Tex.)
  BT Fortification—Texas
Fort Griffin-Fort Dodge Trail
  USE Texas Cattle Trail
Fort Griswold, Massacre of, 1781
  USE Groton Heights, Battle of, 1781
Fort Guijarros (San Diego, Calif.)
  UF Guijarros, Fort (San Diego, Calif.)
  BT Fortification—California
Fort, Gwalior (Gwalior, India)
  USE Gwalior Fort (Gwalior, India)
Fort Hale (New Haven, Conn.)
  USE Fort Nathan Hale (New Haven,
          Conn.)
Fort Hope Indian Reserve (Ont.)
  BT Chippewa Indians—Reservations
        Indians of North America—Ontario—
          Reservations
Fort Huachuca (Ariz.)
  UF Huachuca Fort (Ariz.)
  BT Fortification—Arizona
Fort Jefferson (Dry Tortugas, Fla.)
  UF Jefferson, Fort (Dry Tortugas, Fla.)
  BT Fortification—Florida
Fort Krzesławicki (Kraków, Poland)
  UF Krzesławice Fort (Kraków, Poland)
  BT Fortification—Poland
Fort Laramie (Wyo. : Fort)
  UF Laramie, Fort (Wyo. : Fort)
  BT Fort Laramie National Historic Site
        (Wyo.)
        Fortification—Wyoming

Fort Laramie National Historic Site (Wyo.)
  BT Fortification—Wyoming
        Historic sites—Wyoming
        National parks and reserves—United
          States
        Parks—Wyoming
  NT Fort Laramie (Wyo. : Fort)
Fort Laramie, Treaty of, 1851
  UF Treaty of Fort Laramie, 1851
Fort Larned (Larned, Kan.)
  UF Larned, Fort (Larned, Kan.)
  BT Fort Larned National Historic Site
        (Larned, Kan.)
        Fortification—Kansas
**Fort Larned National Historic Site (Larned,
Kan.)**
  BT Fortification—Kansas
        Historic sites—Kansas
        National parks and reserves—United
          States
        Parks—Kansas
  NT Fort Larned (Larned, Kan.)
Fort Leaton (Tex.)
  UF Leaton, Fort (Tex.)
  BT Fortification—Texas
Fort Lee (N.J.)
  — History
  — — Revolution, 1775-1783
        [F144.F]
Fort Louisbourg National Historic Park (Cape
  Breton Island, N.S.)
  USE Fortress of Louisbourg National
          Historic Park (Cape Breton Island,
          N.S.)
Fort Louisburg National Historic Park (Cape
  Breton Island, N.S.)
  USE Fortress of Louisbourg National
          Historic Park (Cape Breton Island,
          N.S.)
Fort Mackinac (Mackinac Island, Mich.)
  UF Mackinac, Fort (Mackinac Island,
          Mich.)
  BT Fortification—Michigan
Fort Macon (N.C.)
  UF Macon, Fort (N.C.)
  BT Fortification—North Carolina
Fort Manuel (S.D.)
  UF Manuel Fort (S.D.)
  BT Fortification—South Dakota
        Indians of North America—South
          Dakota—Trading posts
Fort Marion (Saint Augustine, Fla.)
  USE Castillo de San Marcos (Saint
          Augustine, Fla.)
Fort Marion National Monument (Saint
  Augustine, Fla.)
  USE Castillo de San Marcos National
          Monument (Saint Augustine, Fla.)
Fort Massachusetts (Ship Island, Miss.)
  UF Massachusetts, Fort (Ship Island,
          Miss.)
  BT Fortification—Mississippi
Fort Maurepas (Ocean Springs, Miss.)
  UF Maurepas Fort (Ocean Springs, Miss.)
  BT Fortification—Mississippi
Fort McHenry (Baltimore, Md.)
  UF McHenry, Fort (Baltimore, Md.)
  BT Fortification—Maryland
  RT Fort McHenry National Monument
        and Historic Shrine (Baltimore,
        Md.)
Fort McHenry, Md., Bombardment of
  USE Baltimore, Battle of, 1814
**Fort McHenry National Monument and
Historic Shrine (Baltimore, Md.)**
  BT Historic sites—Maryland
        National monuments—Maryland
  RT Fort McHenry (Baltimore, Md.)
Fort Michilimackinac (Mich.)
  UF Michilimackinac, Fort (Mich.)
  BT Fortification—Michigan

Fort Mifflin (Philadelphia, Pa.)
  (Not Subd Geog)
  UF Mifflin, Fort (Philadelphia, Pa.)
      Old Fort Mifflin (Philadelphia, Pa.)
  BT Fortification—Pennsylvania
Fort Mississauga (Niagara-on-the-Lake, Ont.)
  UF Mississauga Fort (Niagara-on-the-
      Lake, Ont.)
  BT Fortification—Ontario
Fort Myers (Fla.). Landings at Fort Myers
  USE Landings at Fort Myers (Fort Myers,
      Fla.)
Fort Nathan Hale (New Haven, Conn.)
  UF Fort Hale (New Haven, Conn.)
      Hale, Fort (New Haven, Conn.)
      Nathan Hale, Fort (New Haven,
      Conn.)
  BT Fortification—Connecticut
Fort Niagara (N.Y.)
  USE Old Fort Niagara (N.Y.)
Fort Osage (Mo.)
  UF Osage, Fort (Mo.)
  BT Fortification—Missouri
Fort Oswego (Oswego, N.Y.)
  (Not Subd Geog)
  UF Oswego, Fort (Oswego, N.Y.)
  BT Fortification—New York (State)
  — Capture, 1756 *(Not Subd Geog)*
      [E199]
      UF Oswego, Fort, Capture of, 1756
      BT United States—History—French
          and Indian War, 1755-1763—
          Campaigns
Fort Pillow, Battle of, 1864
  [E476.17]
  BT United States—History—Civil War,
      1861-1865—Campaigns
Fort Piute Wilderness (Calif.)
  (Not Subd Geog)
  UF Fort Piute Wilderness Study Area
      (Calif.)
  BT National parks and reserves—
      California
      Wilderness areas—California
Fort Piute Wilderness Study Area (Calif.)
  USE Fort Piute Wilderness (Calif.)
Fort Point Channel Area (Boston, Mass.)
  (Not Subd Geog)
  UF Boston (Mass.). Fort Point Channel
      Area
Fort Príncipe da Beira (Brazil)
  USE Forte Príncipe da Beira (Brazil)
Fort Pulaski National Monument (Ga.)
  BT National monuments—Georgia
Fort Raleigh (Roanoke Island, N.C.)
  UF Raleigh, Fort (Roanoke Island, N.C.)
  BT Fortification—North Carolina
  RT Fort Raleigh National Historic Site
      (Roanoke Island, N.C.)
Fort Raleigh National Historic Site (Roanoke Island, N.C.)
  BT Historic sites—North Carolina
      National parks and reserves—North
      Carolina
  RT Fort Raleigh (Roanoke Island, N.C.)
Fort Richardson (Tex.) *(Not Subd Geog)*
  UF Richardson, Fort (Tex.)
  BT Fortification—Texas
Fort Rock Valley (Or.)
  BT Valleys—Oregon
Fort Sage Drift Fence Site (Nev.)
  (Not Subd Geog)
  BT Nevada—Antiquities
Fort Saint Anthony (Minn.)
  USE Fort Snelling (Minn.)
Fort Saint Charles Archaeological Site (Magnusons Island, Minn.)
  (Not Subd Geog)
  UF Fort St. Charles Archaeological Site
      (Magnusons Island, Minn.)
  BT Minnesota—Antiquities

Fort Saint George (Madras, India)
  UF Saint George, Fort (Madras, India)
      St. George, Fort (Madras, India)
  BT Fortification—India
Fort Saint Mary (La.)
  UF Batterie de la Pointe (La.)
      Fort Sainte Mary (La.)
      Fort St. Mary (La.)
      Fort Ste. Mary (La.)
  BT Fortification—Louisiana
Fort Sainte-Marie among the Hurons (Ont.)
  UF Sainte-Marie among the Hurons, Fort
      (Ont.)
  BT Fortification—Ontario
Fort Sainte Mary (La.)
  USE Fort Saint Mary (La.)
Fort San Lorenza (Panama), Battle of, 1740
  BT Panama—History—To 1903
Fort San Lorenzo (Panama)
  UF Castillo de San Lorenzo (Panama)
      Fuerte San Lorenzo (Panama)
      San Lorenzo, Fort (Panama)
  BT Fortification—Panama
Fort Sanders, Battle of, 1863
  BT United States—History—Civil War,
      1861-1865—Campaigns
Fort Saybrook (Old Saybrook, Conn.)
  UF Saybrook, Fort (Old Saybrook, Conn.)
  BT Fortification—Connecticut
Fort Schuyler (Rome, N.Y.)
  USE Fort Stanwix (Rome, N.Y.)
Fort Sherman (Panama)
  UF Ft. Sherman (Panama)
      Sherman, Fort (Panama)
  BT Fortification—Panama
Fort Snelling (Minn.)
  UF Fort Saint Anthony (Minn.)
      Fort St. Anthony (Minn.)
      Saint Anthony, Fort (Minn.)
      Snelling, Fort (Minn.)
      St. Anthony, Fort (Minn.)
  BT Fortification—Minnesota
Fort St. Anthony (Minn.)
  USE Fort Snelling (Minn.)
Fort St. Charles Archaeological Site
  (Magnusons Island, Minn.)
  USE Fort Saint Charles Archaeological Site
      (Magnusons Island, Minn.)
Fort St. Mary (La.)
  USE Fort Saint Mary (La.)
Fort Stanwix (Rome, N.Y.)
  UF Fort Schuyler (Rome, N.Y.)
      Schuyler, Fort (Rome, N.Y.)
      Stanwix, Fort (Rome, N.Y.)
  BT Fortification—New York (State)
Fort Ste. Mary (La.)
  USE Fort Saint Mary (La.)
Fort Sturgeon (Sask.)
  USE Sturgeon Fort (Sask.)
Fort Sumter (Charleston, S.C.)
  UF Sumter, Fort (Charleston, S.C.)
  BT Fortification—South Carolina
  RT Fort Sumter National Monument
      (Charleston, S.C.)
Fort Sumter National Monument (Charleston, S.C.)
  BT National monuments—South Carolina
  RT Fort Sumter (Charleston, S.C.)
Fort Ticonderoga (N.Y.)
  UF Carillon, Fort (N.Y.)
      Fort Carillon (N.Y.)
      Ticonderoga, Fort (N.Y.)
  BT Fortification—New York (State)
Fort Tilden (New York, N.Y.)
  UF Tilden, Fort (New York, N.Y.)
  BT Fortification—New York (State)
      Gateway National Recreation Area
      (N.J. and N.Y.)
Fort Union Coal Region (Mont.)
  BT Coal—Montana

Fort Union Formation *(Not Subd Geog)*
  BT Formations (Geology)—West (U.S.)
      Geology, Stratigraphic—Tertiary
Fort Vancouver National Historic Site (Wash.)
  BT Historic sites—Washington (State)
      National parks and reserves—United
      States
      Parks—Washington (State)
Fort Victoria (Alta.)
  UF Pakan (Alta.)
      Victoria Post (Alta.)
  BT Fortification—Alberta
Fort Washington (Md.)
  UF Washington Fort (Md.)
  BT Fortification—Maryland
Fort Washington State Park (Pa.)
  BT Parks—Pennsylvania
Fort Wayne and Southern Railroad
  BT Railroads—United States
Fort Wellington (Prescott, Ont.)
  UF Wellington Fort (Prescott, Ont.)
  BT Fortification—Ontario
Fort William Henry (N.Y.)
  (Not Subd Geog)
  UF William Henry, Fort (N.Y.)
  BT Fortification—New York (State)
  — Capture, 1757 *(Not Subd Geog)*
      [E199]
      UF Fort William Henry, N.Y., Capture
          of, 1757
      BT United States—History—French
          and Indian War, 1755-1763—
          Campaigns
Fort William Henry, N.Y., Capture of, 1757
  USE Fort William Henry (N.Y.)—Capture,
      1757
Fort Worth Basin (Tex.)
  BT Geology—Texas
Fort Worth Water Garden (Fort Worth, Tex.)
  UF Water Garden of Fort Worth (Fort
      Worth, Tex.)
  BT Water gardens—Texas
Fortaleza River (Peru)
  UF Río Fortaleza (Peru)
  BT Rivers—Peru
Forte das Cinco Pontas (Recife, Brazil)
  UF Castrum Frederici Henrici (Recife,
      Brazil)
      Cinco Pontas Fort (Recife, Brazil)
      Forte de São Tiago das Cinco Pontas
      (Recife, Brazil)
      Vesting Frederik Hendrik (Recife,
      Brazil)
      Vijfhoek Vesting (Recife, Brazil)
  BT Fortification—Brazil
Forte de São Tiago das Cinco Pontas (Recife, Brazil)
  USE Forte das Cinco Pontas (Recife, Brazil)
Forte di Longone (Porto Azzurro, Italy)
  USE Piazza di Longone (Porto Azzurro,
      Italy)
Forte di San Giacomo (Porto Azzurro, Italy)
  USE Piazza di Longone (Porto Azzurro,
      Italy)
Forte family
  USE Fort family
Forte Príncipe da Beira (Brazil)
  UF Fort Príncipe da Beira (Brazil)
      Príncipe da Beira Fort (Brazil)
      Real Forte Príncipe da Beira (Brazil)
  BT Fortification—Brazil
Fortenberry family
  UF Fautenberry family
      Fortenbury family
      Fortinberry family
      Fortinbury family
  RT Faulkenberry family
Fortenbury family
  USE Fortenberry family

Fortepiano
  USE Piano
Fortezza della Brunella (Aulla, Italy)
  UF Brunella Fortress (Aulla, Italy)
  BT Castles—Italy
Fortezza di San Giovanni Battista (Florence, Italy)
  UF San Giovanni Battista Fort (Florence, Italy)
  BT Fortification—Italy
Forth, Firth of (Scotland)   *(Not Subd Geog)*
  UF Bodotria (Scotland)
      Firth of Forth (Scotland)
      Forth Estuary (Scotland)
      Forth River Estuary (Scotland)
  BT Estuaries—Scotland
FORTH (Computer program language)
  ⌐QA76.73.F⌐
  BT Programming languages (Electronic computers)
Forth Estuary (Scotland)
  USE Forth, Firth of (Scotland)
Forth River Estuary (Scotland)
  USE Forth, Firth of (Scotland)
Fortification   *(May Subd Geog)*
  ⌐UG400-409⌐
  UF Forts
  BT Military art and science
  RT Earthwork
      Military architecture
      Military engineering
  SA *subdivision* Defenses *under names of countries and names of individual forts*
  NT Attack and defense (Military science)
      Castles
      City walls
      Coast defenses
      Floating batteries
      Intrenchments
      Limes (Roman boundary)
      Martello towers
      Mines, Military
      Sapping
  — Models
      BT Military miniatures
  — Alaska
      NT Kolmakovskiy Redoubt (Alaska)
  — Alberta
      NT Fort Victoria (Alta.)
  — Antigua
      NT Shirley Heights (Antigua)
  — Argentina
      NT Fuerte Sancti Spiritus (Argentina)
  — Arizona
      NT Fort Huachuca (Ariz.)
  — Arkansas
      NT Arkansas Post National Memorial (Ark.)
  — Australia
      NT Eureka Stockade (Ballarat, Vic.)
  — Belgium
      NT Atlantic Wall (France and Belgium)
  — Brazil
      NT Forte das Cinco Pontas (Recife, Brazil)
          Forte Príncipe da Beira (Brazil)
  — Bulgaria
      NT Aulŭt na Khan Omurtag (Bulgaria)
          Shumenskata krepost (Bulgaria)
  — Byelorussian S.S.R.
      NT Brestskaiā krepost'-geroĭ memorialnyĭ kompleks (Brest, Byelorussian S.S.R.)
  — California
      NT Fort Guijarros (San Diego, Calif.)
          Sutter's Fort (Sacramento, Calif.)
  — China
      NT Great Wall of China (China)
  — Connecticut

  NT Fort Nathan Hale (New Haven, Conn.)
      Fort Saybrook (Old Saybrook, Conn.)
  — England
      NT Hadrian's Wall (England)
          Offa's Dyke (Wales and England)
          Tower of London (London, England)
  — Florida
      NT Castillo de San Marcos (Saint Augustine, Fla.)
          Fort Dallas (Miami, Fla.)
          Fort Jefferson (Dry Tortugas, Fla.)
  — France
      NT Atlantic Wall (France and Belgium)
          Maginot Line (France)
  — Georgia
  — Germany (West)
      NT Siegfried Line (Germany)
          Veste Coburg (Coburg, Germany)
  — Greece
      NT Acropolis (Athens, Greece)
  — Guatemala
      NT Castillo de Matamoros (Guatemala, Guatemala)
  — Hungary
      NT Egri vár (Eger, Hungary)
  — India
      NT Chitor Fort (India)
          Fort Saint George (Madras, India)
          Gwalior Fort (Gwalior, India)
  — Israel
      NT Crusaders' Castle (Tsefat, Israel)
  — Italy
      NT Acropolis of Lipari (Lipari, Lipari Islands, Italy)
          Fortezza di San Giovanni Battista (Florence, Italy)
          Nuraghi
          Piazza di Longone (Porto Azzurro, Italy)
  — Japan
      NT Asada Jin'ya (Toyonaka-shi, Japan)
          Ishinomakijō (Ishinomaki-shi, Japan)
          Kaneta no ki (Mitsushima-chō, Japan)
          Kukuchijō (Kikuka-machi, Japan)
          Takayasujō (Yao-shi, Japan)
          Tatsuokajō (Usuda-machi, Japan)
          Tottorijō (Tottori-shi, Japan)
          Tsukiorijō (Daigo-machi, Japan)
  — Jordan
      NT Qaṣr Kharāna (Jordan)
  — Kansas
      NT Fort Larned (Larned, Kan.)
          Fort Larned National Historic Site (Larned, Kan.)
  — Korea
      NT Samnyŏn Sansŏng (Poŭn-gun, Korea)
  — Korea (South)
      NT Kongsansŏng (Kongju-up, Korea)
  — Libya
      NT Qaṣr aṣ-Ṣaḥābī (Libya)
  — Louisiana
      NT Camp Moore (La.)
          Fort Saint Mary (La.)
  — Manitoba
      NT Pine Fort (Man.)
  — Maryland
      NT Fort McHenry (Baltimore, Md.)
          Fort Washington (Md.)
  — Mexico
      NT Castillo de San Juan de Ulúa (San Juan de Ulúa Island, Mexico)
  — Michigan
      NT Fort Mackinac (Mackinac Island, Mich.)

      Fort Michilimackinac (Mich.)
  — Minnesota
      NT Fort Snelling (Minn.)
  — Mississippi
      NT Fort Massachusetts (Ship Island, Miss.)
          Fort Maurepas (Ocean Springs, Miss.)
  — Missouri
      NT Fort Osage (Mo.)
  — New York (State)
      NT Fort George (New York, N.Y.)
          Fort Oswego (Oswego, N.Y.)
          Fort Stanwix (Rome, N.Y.)
          Fort Ticonderoga (N.Y.)
          Fort Tilden (New York, N.Y.)
          Fort William Henry (N.Y.)
          Old Fort Niagara (N.Y.)
  — North Carolina
      NT Fort Branch (N.C.)
          Fort Macon (N.C.)
          Fort Raleigh (Roanoke Island, N.C.)
  — Norway
      NT Fredriksten Fortress (Halden, Norway)
          Stavern Fort (Stavern, Norway)
  — Nova Scotia
      NT Fortress of Louisbourg National Historic Park (Cape Breton Island, N.S.)
  — Ontario
      NT Fort Mississauga (Niagara-on-the-Lake, Ont.)
          Fort Sainte-Marie among the Hurons (Ont.)
          Fort Wellington (Prescott, Ont.)
  — Oregon
      NT Fort Dalles (Dalles, Or.)
  — Panama
      NT Fort San Lorenzo (Panama)
          Fort Sherman (Panama)
  — Pennsylvania
      NT Fort Mifflin (Philadelphia, Pa.)
  — Poland
      NT Fort Krzesławicki (Kraków, Poland)
  — Québec (Province)
      NT Fort Chambly (Chambly, Québec)
  — Rome
      NT Rome—Military antiquities
  — Russian S.F.S.R.
      NT Kremlin (Moscow, R.S.F.S.R.)
          Kremlin (Novgorod, R.S.F.S.R.)
  — Saskatchewan
      NT Sturgeon Fort (Sask.)
  — South Carolina
      NT Fort Sumter (Charleston, S.C.)
  — South Dakota
      NT Fort Manuel (S.D.)
  — Spain
      NT Talayots
  — Sri Lanka
      NT Sigiriya (Sri Lanka)
  — Texas
      NT Alamo (San Antonio, Tex.)
          Fort Belknap (Tex.)
          Fort Griffin (Tex.)
          Fort Leaton (Tex.)
          Fort Richardson (Tex.)
  — Tunisia
      NT Byrsa (Carthage)
  — Ukraine
  — United States
      UF United States—Fortifications
  — Wales
      NT Offa's Dyke (Wales and England)
  — West Bank
      NT Herodium
  — Wyoming
      NT Fort Bridger (Wyo.)

Fort Laramie (Wyo. : Fort)
Fort Laramie National Historic
   Site (Wyo.)
— Yugoslavia
  NT Belgrade Fortress (Belgrade,
       Serbia)
Fortification, Field
  [UG403]
  UF Field fortification
  BT Intrenchments
      Military engineering
  NT Tanks (Military science)
Fortification, Greek *(May Subd Geog)*
  UF Greek fortification
  BT Architecture, Greek
      Classical antiquities
Fortification, Prehistoric *(May Subd Geog)*
  UF Hill-forts
      Prehistoric fortification
  BT Archaeology
  NT Earthworks (Archaeology)
— England
Fortification, Primitive *(May Subd Geog)*
  [GN789]
  BT Industries, Primitive
      Warfare, Primitive
  NT Mounds
— Yugoslavia
Fortification, Roman *(May Subd Geog)*
  UF Roman fortification
  BT Architecture, Roman
      Classical antiquities
Fortifications, Attack and defense of
  USE Attack and defense (Military science)
Fortified cereal products
  USE Cereal products, Enriched
Fortified food
  USE Food, Enriched
Fortified sugar
  USE Sugar, Enriched
Fortified wine industry *(May Subd Geog)*
  BT Fortified wines
Fortified wines *(May Subd Geog)*
  UF Dessert wines
      Wines, Fortified
  BT Wine and wine making
  NT Fortified wine industry
      Madeira wine
      Marsala wine
      Port wine
      Sherry
Fortín Boquerón, Battle of, 1932
  USE Boquerón, Battle of, 1932
Fortin family
  UF Forton family
Fortín Toledo, Battle of, 1933
  USE Toledo, Battle of, 1933
Fortinberry family
  USE Fortenberry family
Fortinbury family
  USE Fortenberry family
Fortitude
  [BV4647.F6]
  BT Courage
      Morale
Fortna family
Fortner family
  USE Faulkner family
Forton family
  USE Fortin family
FORTRAN (Computer program language)
  UF Formula translation (Computer
        program language)
  NT AUTOSATE
      DIVERSE (Computer program)
      FAP (Computer program language)
      GASP (Computer program language)
      ROCKET (Computer program)
      SIMSCRIPT (Computer program
        language)
      SLAM (Computer program language)

Fortran assembly program (Computer program
  language)
  USE FAP (Computer program language)
FORTRAN Simulated BASIC Interpretive
  Compiler (Computer program)
  USE FOSBIC (Computer program)
Fortress, Crusaders' (Tsefat, Israel)
  USE Crusaders' Castle (Tsefat, Israel)
Fortress of Belgrade (Belgrade, Serbia)
  USE Belgrade Fortress (Belgrade, Serbia)
Fortress of Louisbourg National Historic Park
(Cape Breton Island, N.S.)
  UF Fort Louisbourg National Historic
       Park (Cape Breton Island, N.S.)
      Fort Louisburg National Historic Park
       (Cape Breton Island, N.S.)
      Louisbourg National Historic Park
       (Cape Breton Island, N.S.)
      Louisburg National Historic Park
       (Cape Breton Island, N.S.)
      Parc Historique National Forteresse de
       Louisbourg (Cape Breton Island,
       N.S.)
  BT Fortification—Nova Scotia
      National parks and reserves—Canada
      Parks—Nova Scotia
Fortress warfare
  USE Attack and defense (Military science)
Fortresses (Bombers)
  USE Boeing bombers
Forts
  USE Fortification
Fortuna (Roman deity)
  [BL820.F7]
  BT Gods, Roman
      Mythology, Roman
Fortune
  NT Chance
      Fate and fatalism
      Success
Fortune, Seven gods of
  USE Seven gods of fortune
Fortune, Soldiers of
  USE Soldiers of fortune
Fortune hunters *(May Subd Geog)*
  [HQ756]
  UF Gigolos
  BT Marriage
Fortune teller (Painting)
  USE Caravaggio, Michelangelo Merisi da,
       1573-1610. Fortune teller
      La Tour, Georges du Mesnil de, 1593-
       1652. Fortune teller
Fortune-tellers *(May Subd Geog)*
  BT Fortune-telling
Fortune-telling
  [BF1850-BF1891]
  UF Fortunetelling
  BT Amusements
      Occultism
  NT Choice by lot
      Crystal gazing
      Fortune-tellers
      Magic mirrors
      Palmistry
Fortune telling by birds
  [BF1891.B5]
  BT Divination
Fortune-telling by birthdays
  BT Birthdays
      Divination
Fortune-telling by cards
  UF Cartomancy
  BT Card tricks
      Cards
      Divination
  NT Tarot
Fortune-telling by Chinese characters
  [BF1891.C48]
  BT Chinese characters
      Divination

Fortune-telling by dice
  [BF1891.D5]
  BT Dice
      Divination
Fortune-telling by fingerprints
  [BF1891.F5]
  BT Divination
      Fingerprints
Fortune-telling by moles
  [BF1891.M65]
  BT Birthmarks
      Divination
      Mole (Dermatology)
Fortune-telling by names
  BT Divination
      Names, Personal
Fortune-telling by numbers
  UF Arithmomancy
      Numbers, Fortune-telling by
  BT Symbolism of numbers
Fortune-telling by pendulum
  [BF1779.P45]
  BT Divination
      Pendulum
Fortune-telling by precious stones
  [BF1891.P74]
  BT Precious stones
Fortune-telling by runes
  [BF1891.R85]
  BT Divination
      Runes
Fortune-telling by seals
  UF Fortune-telling by signets
  BT Seals (Numismatics)
Fortune-telling by signets
  USE Fortune-telling by seals
Fortune-telling by tea leaves
  [BF1881]
  BT Divination
Fortune telling in art
Fortunes
  USE Income
      Wealth
Fortunetelling
  USE Fortune-telling
Forty (The number)
  BT Symbolism of numbers
Forty-five (Game)
  [GV1295.F7]
Forty hours' adoration
  USE Forty hours' devotion
Forty hours' devotion
  [BX2169]
  UF Forty hours' adoration
      Forty hours' prayer
  BT Lord's Supper—Catholic Church—
        Prayer-books and devotions
Forty hours' prayer
  USE Forty hours' devotion
Forty-seven Rōnin
  UF Akō gishi
      Chūshingura Incident, 1703
  BT Japan—History—Tokugawa period,
       1600-1868
      Rōnin
  NT Japan—History—Akō Vendetta, 1703
Forum, Open
  USE Forums (Discussion and debate)
Forum non conveniens *(May Subd Geog)*
  UF Inconvenient forum
  BT Conflict of laws—Jurisdiction
      Jurisdiction
Forum prorogatum
  USE Prorogated jurisdiction
Forum Romanum (Rome, Italy)
  USE Roman Forum (Rome, Italy)
Forums, Roman *(May Subd Geog)*
  UF Fora, Italian
      Fora, Roman
      Roman forums

Forums, Roman *(Continued)*
    BT Courts—Rome
        Local government—Rome
        Markets—Rome
        Plazas—Rome
    — Italy
      NT Roman Forum (Rome, Italy)
Forums (Discussion and debate)
    [LC6501-LC6560]
    [PN4177-PN4191 (Debating)]
    UF Conferences
        Forum, Open
        Group discussion
        Open forum
        Public forums
        Workshops (Group discussion)
    BT Debates and debating
        Discussion
        Meetings
    RT Radio addresses, debates, etc.
    NT Catholic academies
        Evangelical academies
        Group reading
        Seminars
        Workshops (Adult education)
Forust family
    USE Forrest family
Forward exchange *(May Subd Geog)*
    [HG3853]
    UF Foreign exchange futures
        Futures exchange
    BT Foreign exchange
    RT Financial futures
    — Law and legislation *(May Subd Geog)*
Forward Swept Wing Demonstrator, Grumman
    Model 712 (Jet plane)
    USE Grumman X-29A (Jet plane)
Forwarders, Freight
    USE Freight forwarders
Forwarding agents
    USE Freight forwarders
Forwarding merchants
    USE Freight forwarders
Forwarding services, Mail
    USE Mail receiving and forwarding services
Forwards (Basketball) *(May Subd Geog)*
    BT Basketball players
FOSBIC (Computer program)
    UF FORTRAN Simulated BASIC
        Interpretive Compiler (Computer
        program)
    BT Compilers (Computer programs)
Foscari Villa (Mira, Italy)
    USE Villa Foscari (Mira, Italy)
Fosfomycin *(May Subd Geog)*
    [RM666.F64]
    UF Fosfonomycin
        Phosphonomycin
    BT Antibacterial agents
        Antibiotics
        Epoxy compounds
        Phosphonic acids
Fosfonomycin
    USE Fosfomycin
Fosher family
    UF Foshiers family
    RT Fascher family
Foshiers family
    USE Fosher family
Fosie family
Fossa, Popliteal
    USE Popliteal fossa
Fossa (Mammals)
    [QL737.C28]
    UF Cryptoprocta ferox
    BT Cryptoprocta
Fossa axillaris
    USE Axilla
Fossa cranii posterior
    USE Cranial fossa, Posterior

Fosselman family
    USE Fosselmann family
Fosselmann family
    UF Fosselman family
        Fusselman family
        Vosselmann family
Fossil apes
    USE Apes, Fossil
Fossil botany
    USE Paleobotany
Fossil coelacanthiformes
    USE Coelacanthiformes, Fossil
Fossil dust
    USE Diatomaceous earth
Fossil eggs
    USE Eggs, Fossil
Fossil energy
    USE Fossil fuels
Fossil excrement
    USE Coprolites
Fossil feces
    USE Coprolites
Fossil footprints
    USE Footprints, Fossil
Fossil fuel power plants *(May Subd Geog)*
    BT Power-plants
    NT Coal-fired power plants
        Gas power plants
Fossil fuels *(May Subd Geog)*
    UF Fossil energy
    BT Fuel
        Power resources
    RT Energy minerals
    NT Coal
        Gas, Natural
        Oil-shales
        Peat
        Petroleum
Fossil man *(May Subd Geog)*
    UF Early man
        Hominidae, Fossil
        Hominids, Fossil
        Human paleontology
        Man, Fossil
    BT Human evolution
        Man, Prehistoric
        Physical anthropology
    SA *names of fossil hominids by genera*
        and species, e.g. Zinjanthropus,
        Pithecanthropus erectus
    NT Australopithecines
        Cro-Magnon man
        Neanderthal race
        Paranthropus
        Piltdown forgery
        Solo man
    — Craniology
    — Alberta
    — China
      NT Peking man
    — Ethiopia
      NT Australopithecus afarensis
    — Greece
      NT Petralona man
    — Zambia
      NT Rhodesian man
Fossil plants
    USE Paleobotany
Fossil pollen
    USE Pollen, Fossil
Fossil Priapulida
    USE Priapulida, Fossil
Fossil resins
    USE Resins, Fossil
Fossil soils
    USE Paleopedology
Fossil spores (Botany)
    USE Spores (Botany), Fossil
Fossil teeth
    USE Teeth, Fossil

Fossil tracks
    USE Footprints, Fossil
Fossil voles
    USE Voles, Fossil
Fossil wood
    USE Trees, Fossil
Fossils
    USE Paleontology
Fossils, Living
    USE Living fossils
Fossils, Trace
    USE Trace fossils
Fosso Arno (Italy)
    USE Arno River (Italy)
Fosso Lanzo (Italy)
    USE Lanzo River (Italy)
Fosster family
    USE Foster family
Foster care, Home
    USE Foster home care
Foster care, Institutional
    USE Children—Institutional care
Foster children *(May Subd Geog)*
    BT Children
Foster day care
    USE Day care centers
Foster families
    USE Foster parents
Foster family
    UF Farster family
        Faustar family
        Fauster family
        Forester family
        Forister family
        Forrester family
        Forrister family
        Forristor family
        Forster family
        Fosster family
        Fosters family
        Fostor family
Foster family care
    USE Foster home care
Foster grandparents *(May Subd Geog)*
    UF Grandparents, Foster
    BT Aged volunteers in social service
        Grandparent and child
Foster home care *(May Subd Geog)*
    UF Child placing
        Foster care, Home
        Foster family care
    BT Child care services
        Child welfare
        Children—Institutional care
        Group homes
    NT Adoption
        Children, Adopted
        Group homes for children
        Group homes for the developmentally
          disabled
        Group homes for the handicapped
        Group homes for youth
    — Law and legislation *(May Subd Geog)*
      BT Guardian and ward
        Parent and child (Law)
Foster parents *(May Subd Geog)*
    UF Foster families
    BT Parents
Fosters family
    USE Foster family
Fostor family
    USE Foster family
Fotonovela *(May Subd Geog)*
    UF Fotoromanzo
        Photo novels
        Photoroman
    BT Comic books, strips, etc.
        Popular literature
        Stories without words

Fotonovela industry (May Subd Geog)
  BT Book industries and trade
      Publishers and publishing
Fotoromanzo
  USE Fotonovela
Fouarde family
  USE Ford family
Foucault's pendulum
  [QB633]
  BT Pendulum
  RT Earth—Rotation
Foul brood, American
  UF American foul brood
  BT Bees—Diseases
Foul brood, European
  UF European foul brood
  BT Bees—Diseases
Foula Island (Scotland)
  [DA880.F]
  BT Islands—Scotland
      Shetland
Foulahs
  USE Fulahs
Foulbé
  USE Fulahs
Fouler family
  USE Fowler family
Fouling
  UF Biofouling
      Microbial fouling
      Particulate fouling
      Precipitation fouling
  BT Surfaces (Technology)
  RT Fouling organisms
  SA *subdivision* Fouling *under subjects, e.g.*
      Heat exchangers—Fouling
  NT Corrosion and anti-corrosives
      Incrustations
      Marine fouling organisms
      Paint, Antifouling
Fouling of ship bottoms
  USE Ships—Fouling
Fouling organisms
  BT Aquatic animals
      Aquatic plants
      Hydraulic structures
  RT Fouling
  NT Marine fouling organisms
Foulk family
  USE Faulk family
Foulke family
  USE Faulk family
Foulks family
  USE Faulk family
Foulse language
  USE Kurumba language
Found art
  USE Found objects (Art)
Found objects (Art)
  UF Found art
      Objects, Found (Art)
  BT Art, Modern—20th century
  NT Assemblage (Art)
      Collage
Found objects (Art) in interior decoration
  [NK2115.5.F68]
  BT Interior decoration
Foundation garment industry
  (May Subd Geog)
  [HD9969.F65-653]
  BT Underwear industry
  NT Corset industry
Foundation garments
  [TT677]
  UF Corsetry
      Foundations (Clothing)
      Garments, Foundation
  BT Underwear
  NT Brassieres
      Bustles
      Corsets

Foundation sacrifices (May Subd Geog)
  UF Building foundation sacrifices
  BT Manners and customs
      Rites and ceremonies
      Sacrifice
  NT Corner stones, Laying of
Foundation stones, Laying of
  USE Corner stones, Laying of
Foundations (May Subd Geog)
  [TA775-TA787 (Engineering)]
  [TC197 (Hydraulic engineering)]
  [TH2101 (Building design)]
  [TH5201 (Building construction)]
  BT Architecture—Details
      Building
      Civil engineering
      Structural engineering
      Underground construction
  RT Caissons
      Earthwork
      Masonry
      Soil consolidation
      Soil mechanics
      Walls
  NT Anchorage (Structural engineering)
      Basements
      Bridges—Foundations and piers
      Bridges, Concrete—Foundations and
        piers
      Columns—Foundations
      Compressed air
      Concrete
      Concrete dams—Foundations
      Concrete footings
      Cribwork
      Dams—Foundations
      Electric lines—Poles and towers—
        Foundations
      Electric substations—Foundations
      Hydraulic structures—Foundations
      Industrial buildings—Foundations
      Kilns, Rotary—Foundations
      Machine-tools—Foundations
      Machinery—Foundations
      Marine engines—Foundations
      Mobile homes—Foundations
      Open caissons
      Pagodas—Foundations
      Piling (Civil engineering)
      Railroad bridges—Foundations and
        piers
      Railroads—Buildings and structures—
        Foundations
      Railroads—Track—Foundations
      Roads—Foundations
      Rock bolts
      Rolling-mill machinery—Foundations
      Settlement of structures
      Slurry trench construction
      Steam-boilers, Marine—Foundations
      Steam-turbines—Foundations
      Towers—Foundations
      Turbogenerators—Foundations
      Vibrators—Foundations
      Wooden pagodas—Foundations
Foundations (Clothing)
  USE Foundation garments
Foundations (Endowments)
  USE Charitable uses, trusts, and foundations
      Endowments
Foundations of arithmetic
  USE Arithmetic—Foundations
Foundations of geometry
  USE Geometry—Foundations
Foundations of mathematical analysis
  USE Mathematical analysis—Foundations
Foundations of projective geometry
  USE Geometry, Projective—Foundations
Founding
  [TS228.99-TS240]

Here are entered general works on melting and
casting metals.
  UF Casting
      Foundry practice
  BT Metal-work
  RT Pattern-making
  SA *subdivision* Founding *under groups of*
      metals, e.g. Nonferrous metals—
      Founding
  NT Aluminum founding
      Bell founding
      Brass founding
      Bronze founding
      Centrifugal casting
      Continuous casting
      Copper founding
      Cupola-furnaces
      Die-casting
      Foundry chemistry
      Foundry research
      Gating system (Founding)
      Inoculation (Founding)
      Iron-founding
      Magnesium founding
      Metal castings
      Metals—Rapid solidification processing
      Molding (Founding)
      Pattern-making machinery
      Precision casting
      Risers (Founding)
      Slip casting
      Steel founding
      Titanium founding
      Type and type-founding
— **Health aspects** (May Subd Geog)
  [RC965.F6]
  UF Founding—Hygienic aspects
— Hygienic aspects
  USE Founding—Health aspects
— Subject headings
  USE Subject headings—Founding
— **Vocational guidance**
  UF Founding as a profession
Founding as a profession
  USE Founding—Vocational guidance
Foundlings (May Subd Geog)
  [HV835-847]
  BT Abandoned children
      Child welfare
  RT Orphans
  NT Adoption
Foundries (May Subd Geog)
  [TS229-238]
  NT Coremakers
      Die-casting industry
      Iron foundries
      Iron molders
      Steel foundries
— **Dust control**
— **Equipment and supplies**
  UF Foundry supplies
— — Appraisal
  USE Foundries—Equipment and
      supplies—Valuation
— — Drawing
  USE Foundries—Equipment and
      supplies—Drawings
— — **Drawings**
  UF Foundries—Equipment and
      supplies—Drawing
  BT Mechanical drawing
— — **Valuation**
  [TS237]
  UF Foundries—Equipment and
      supplies—Appraisal
— **Quality control**
Foundry chemistry
  [QD133]
  UF Chemistry, Foundry
  BT Chemistry
      Founding

Foundry coatings *(May Subd Geog)*
  UF Core coatings (Founding)
      Core washes (Founding)
      Dressings, Mold (Founding)
      Facings, Mold (Founding)
      Mold coatings (Founding)
      Mold dressings (Founding)
      Mold facings (Founding)
      Mold washes (Founding)
      Washes, Core (Founding)
      Washes, Mold (Founding)
  BT Coatings
      Molding (Founding)
      Refractory coating
Foundry ladles
  UF Ladles, Foundry
  BT Metallurgical plants—Equipment and
      supplies
  — Linings
      UF Linings of foundry ladles
      BT Refractory materials
Foundry practice
  USE Founding
Foundry research
  BT Founding
      Research, Industrial
Foundry sand
  USE Sand, Foundry
Foundry supplies
  USE Foundries—Equipment and supplies
Foundry workers
  USE Foundrymen
Foundrymen *(May Subd Geog)*
  [HD8039.F75]
  UF Foundry workers
  BT Metal-workers
  NT Trade-unions—Foundrymen
      Wages—Foundrymen
  — Collective bargaining
      USE Collective bargaining—
          Foundrymen
Fountain pens
  [TS1266 (Manufacture)]
  BT Pens
Fountains *(May Subd Geog)*
  [NA9400-NA9425]
  UF Garden fountains
  BT Hydraulic structures
      Water in landscape architecture
  NT Drinking fountains
  — Germany (West)
      NT Elwedritsche-Brunnen (Neustadt
          an der Weinstrasse, Germany)
  — Italy
      NT Fontana di Trevi (Rome, Italy)
Fountains, Renaissance *(May Subd Geog)*
  UF Renaissance fountains
Fountains in art
Fouquet family
Fouquieriaceae
  [QK495.F6 (Botany)]
  BT Tubiflorae
Four (The number)
  BT Symbolism of numbers
Four-channel sound systems
  USE Quadraphonic sound systems
Four-color problem
  BT Color in cartography
      Graph theory
      Map-coloring problem
Four Corners-Ambrosia-Pajarito 500 kV
  Transmission Project
  BT Electric power transmission—New
      Mexico
Four Corners Region
  BT Southwest, New
Four cornets with band
  USE Cornets (4) with band
Four-day week *(May Subd Geog)*
  UF Alternative work schedules
  BT Hours of labor

  RT Hours of labor, Flexible
  — Law and legislation *(May Subd Geog)*
      BT Labor laws and legislation
Four dimensional manifolds (Topology)
  USE Four-manifolds (Topology)
Four elements (Philosophy)
  UF Elements, Four (Philosophy)
  BT Cosmology
      Matter
      Ontology
      Philosophy
      Substance (Philosophy)
Four Forest Cantons, Lake of (Switzerland)
  USE Lucerne Lake (Switzerland)
Four golden horses in the sun (Venice, Italy)
  USE Cavalli di San Marco (Venice, Italy)
Four harpsichords with orchestra
  USE Harpsichords (4) with orchestra
Four harpsichords with string orchestra
  USE Harpsichords (4) with string orchestra
Four horns with band
  USE Horns (4) with band
Four horns with orchestra
  USE Horns (4) with orchestra
Four Horsemen of the Apocalypse
  UF Apocalypse, Four Horsemen of the
  BT Horses—Religious aspects—
      Christianity
      Symbolism in the Bible
Four Hundred, Revolution of the, Athens,
  Greece, 411 B.C.
  USE Athens (Greece)—History—Revolution
      of the Four Hundred, 411 B.C.
Four-manifolds (Topology)
  UF 4-dimensional manifolds (Topology)
      4-manifolds (Topology)
      Four dimensional manifolds
        (Topology)
      Manifolds, Four dimensional
  BT Low-dimensional topology
      Topological manifolds
Four Noble Truths
  UF Noble Truths, Four
      Truths, Four Noble
  BT Buddhism—Doctrines
  NT Eightfold Path
Four picture test
  BT Picture interpretation tests
      Projective techniques
      Thematic apperception test
Four Satipaṭṭhānāni (Buddhism)
  USE Satipaṭṭhāna (Buddhism)
Four-sided jellyfish
  USE Cubomedusae
Four Smṛty-upasthānāni (Buddhism)
  USE Satipaṭṭhāna (Buddhism)
Four times daily (Sculpture)
  USE Ellison, Robert. Four times daily
Four toed elephant shrew
  USE Petrodromus tetradactylus
Four violins with string orchestra
  USE Violins (4) with string orchestra
Four-wheel drive automobiles
  USE Automobiles—Four-wheel drive
Fourcade family
Fourche La Fave River (Ark.)
  UF Fourche Lafave River (Ark.)
      Fourche River (Ark.)
  BT Rivers—Arkansas
  NT Nimrod Lake (Ark.)
Fourche Lafave River (Ark.)
  USE Fourche La Fave River (Ark.)
Fourche River (Ark.)
  USE Fourche La Fave River (Ark.)
Fourcroea
  USE Furcraea
Fourcroya
  USE Furcraea
Fourie family
Fourier analysis
  [QA403.5]

  UF Analysis, Fourier
  BT Mathematical analysis
  NT Fourier integral operators
      Fourier series
      Fourier transformations
      Functions, Orthogonal
      Maximal functions
      Orthogonal polynomials
      Series, Orthogonal
Fourier integral operators
  BT Fourier analysis
      Integral operators
Fourier integrals
  USE Fourier series
Fourier optics
  USE Fourier transform optics
Fourier series
  [QA404]
  UF Fourier integrals
      Series, Fourier
      Series, Trigonometric
      Trigonometric series
  BT Calculus
      Fourier analysis
  RT Harmonic analysis
      Harmonic functions
  NT Almost periodic functions
      Helson sets
      Integrals, Dirichlet
      Pseudofunctions
  — Computer programs
Fourier transform interferometry
  USE Fourier transform spectroscopy
Fourier transform optics
  UF Fourier optics
  BT Fourier transformations
      Optics
  NT Fourier transform spectroscopy
Fourier transform spectroscopy
  [QC451]
  UF Fourier transform interferometry
      Interference spectrometry
      Multiplex spectrometry
      Spectroscopy, Fourier transform
  BT Fourier transform optics
      Fourier transformations
      Hadamard transform spectroscopy
      Interferometer
      Spectrum analysis
Fourier transformations
  UF Transformations, Fourier
      Transforms, Fourier
  BT Fourier analysis
      Groups, Theory of
      Harmonic analysis
      Transformations (Mathematics)
  NT Digital filters (Mathematics)
      Fourier transform optics
      Fourier transform spectroscopy
      Optical transfer function
  — Computer programs
Fourman family
  USE Foreman family
Fournier family
  UF Fournière family
Fournière family
  USE Fournier family
Fourt family
  USE Fort family
Fourteen holy helpers
  UF Auxiliary saints, Christian
      Christian auxiliary saints
      Helpers, Fourteen holy
      Holy helpers, Fourteen
  BT Christian saints
Fourteenth century
  BT Middle Ages—History
  NT Civilization, Medieval—14th century
Fourteenth of July
  USE Bastille Day

Fourth dimension
  [QA699]
  Here are entered philosophical and imaginative works. Mathematical works are entered under Hyperspace.
  UF Space of more than three dimensions
  BT Mathematics
  NT Space and time
Fourth disease
  USE Rubella
Fourth Estate (Painting)
  USE Pellizza da Volpedo, 1868-1907.
      Fourth estate
Fourth grade (Education)
  BT Education, Primary
Fourth Lake (Wis.)
  USE Mendota, Lake (Wis.)
Fourth of July
  UF Independence Day (United States)
      July Fourth
  BT Holidays—United States
      United States—Anniversaries, etc.
  — Songs and music
      [M1629.3.F6]
Fourth of July celebrations
  (May Subd Geog)
    [E286 (United States history)]
    [PN4305.H7 (Recitations)]
  UF Celebrations, Fourth of July
  BT Festivals—United States
Fourth of July orations
  [E286]
  BT Speeches, addresses, etc.
      Speeches, addresses, etc., American
Fourth of July Valley Site (Colo.)
  (Not Subd Geog)
  BT Colorado—Antiquities
Fourth World
  USE Developing countries
Fourwing flyingfish
  USE Hirundichthys affinis
Foust family
  USE Faust family
Fout family
  USE Foote family
Fouta cattle
  USE N'Dama cattle
Fouts family
  USE Foote family
Foutz family
  USE Foote family
Foval
  USE Pearl art glass
Fowble family
Fowke family
  USE Faulk family
Fowkes family
  USE Faulk family
Fowl, Game
  USE Game fowl
Fowl cholera
  USE Chicken cholera
Fowl paralysis
  USE Marek's disease
Fowl pest
  USE Fowl plague
      Newcastle disease
Fowl plague *(May Subd Geog)*
  [SF995.6.F59]
  UF Fowl pest
  BT Virus diseases in poultry
  NT Duck plague
Fowl plague virus
  BT Myxoviruses
Fowl pox *(May Subd Geog)*
  [SF995.6.F]

  UF Avian contagious epithelioma
      Avian diphtheria
      Avian pox
      Bird pox
      Chicken pox in poultry
      Epithelioma contagiosum
      Fowlpox
  BT Poultry—Diseases
      Poxvirus diseases
Fowl tick
  USE Argas persicus
Fowl typhoid
  [SF995]
  BT Poultry—Diseases
      Salmonellosis in poultry
Fowlar family
  USE Fowler family
Fowler family
  UF Fauler family
      Fouler family
      Fowlar family
      Fowlers family
Fowlerite *(May Subd Geog)*
  BT Rhodonite
Fowlers family
  USE Fowler family
Fowling *(May Subd Geog)*
  [SK311-333]
  UF Bird hunting
      Game bird hunting
      Wildfowling
  BT Game and game-birds
      Hunting
      Shooting
  RT Falconry
  NT Bird trapping
      Decoys (Hunting)
      Pigeon shooting
      Sandhill crane shooting
      Shooting preserves
      Upland game bird shooting
      Waterfowl shooting
  — **Law and legislation** *(May Subd Geog)*
Fowlkes family
  USE Faulk family
Fowlks family
  USE Faulk family
Fowlpox
  USE Fowl pox
Fowls
  USE Poultry
Fox, Emanuel Phillips, 1865-1915. Ferry
  [ND1105.F6]
  UF Ferry (Painting)
  BT Ferries in art
Fox
  USE Foxes
Fox automobile
  USE Audi Fox automobile
Fox Basin (N.W.T.)
  USE Foxe Basin (N.W.T.)
Fox bats
  USE Flying foxes
Fox family
  UF Foxe family
      Foxx family
Fox-hunting *(May Subd Geog)*
  [SK284-7]
  BT Horse sports
  RT Hunt riding
  NT Hunters (Horses)
      Melbourne Hunt
      Quorn Hunt
  — **England**
      NT Puckeridge and Thurlow Hunt
  — **Gibraltar**
      NT Royal Calpe Hunt
Fox-hunting in literature
Fox Indians
  [E99.F7]

  UF Meskwaki Indians
      Mesquakie Indians
      Muskwaki Indians
      Musquakie Indians
      Outagami Indians
  BT Algonquian Indians
      Indians of North America
  RT Sauk Indians
Fox Island (Alaska)
  USE Renard Island (Alaska)
Fox Islands (Alaska)
  BT Islands—Alaska
Fox language
  [PM1195]
  BT Algonquian languages
Fox River (Wis.)
  BT Rivers—Wisconsin
Fox River (Wis. and Ill.)
  BT Rivers—Illinois
      Rivers—Wisconsin
Fox squirrel
  [QL737.R68]
  UF Eastern fox squirrel
      Sciurus niger
  BT Squirrels
  — **Food**
Fox terrier, Wirehaired
  [SF429.F52]
  UF Wire fox terrier
      Wire-haired fox terrier
      Wirehaired fox terrier
  BT Fox terriers
Fox terriers
  [SF429.F5]
  UF Foxterriers
  BT Terriers
  NT Fox terrier, Wirehaired
Fox Theatre (Saint Louis, Mo.)
  [PN2277.S]
  BT Theaters—Missouri
Fox trot
  [GV1796.F6]
Fox trots
  BT Dance music
Foxberry
  USE Vaccinium vitis-idaea
Foxe Basin (N.W.T.)
  UF Fox Basin (N.W.T.)
  BT Atlantic Ocean
Foxe family
  USE Fox family
Foxes
  [QL737.C2 (Zoology)]
  [QL795.F8 (Stories and anecdotes)]
  UF Fox
  NT Arctic fox
      Fennecs
      Gray fox
      Kit fox
      Red fox
      Silver fox
      Vulpes
  — **Behavior**
  — **Feeding and feeds**
  — **Folklore**
      NT Reynard the Fox (Legendary
          character)
  — **Religious aspects**
      NT Inari
Foxes as pets
  [SF459.F68]
Foxes in art
Foxglove, Common
  USE Digitalis purpurea
Foxglove, Rusty
  USE Digitalis ferruginea
Foxglove, Straw
  USE Digitalis lutea

Foxglove aphid
  UF Acyrthosiphon solani
      Aphis solani
      Myzus pseudosolani
      Myzus solani
Foxgloves
  [QK495.S43]
  UF Digitalis (Genus)
  BT Scrophulariaceae
Foxhall Crescents (Washington, D.C.)
  (Not Subd Geog)
  UF Washington (D.C.). Foxhall
        Crescents
Foxholes
  USE Intrenchments
Foxhounds
  [SF429.F6]
  NT American foxhounds
Foxiphalus
  [QL444.M315]
  BT Phoxocephalidae
Fox's H-function
  UF G-functions, Generalized
      Generalized G-functions
      Generalized Mellin-Barnes functions
      H-functions, Fox's
      Mellin-Barnes functions, Generalized
  BT Functions, Hypergeometric
Foxtail
  [QK495.G74 (Botany)]
  [SB201.F (Agriculture)]
  [SB608.F7 (Diseases and pests)]
Foxterriers
  USE Fox terriers
Foxwell family
Foxworth family (Not Subd Geog)
  UF Foxworthy family
Foxworthy family
  USE Foxworth family
Foxx family
  USE Fox family
Foyers
  USE Entrance halls
FP-45 pistol
  USE Liberator pistol
FPC
  USE Fish protein concentrate
FPF rings
  UF Finitely pseudo-Frobenius rings
      Rings, Finitely pseudo-Frobenius
      Rings, FPF
  BT Associative rings
fra(X) syndrome
  USE Fragile X syndrome
Fra Mauro Crater (Moon)
  BT Lunar craters
      Moon
Frable family
  USE Fravel family
Frache family
  UF Frash family
Frack family
  USE Frock family
Fractal sets
  USE Fractals
Fractals
  UF Fractal sets
      Sets, Fractal
      Sets of fractional dimension
  BT Dimension theory (Topology)
      Geometry
      Mathematical models
      Set theory
Fractional distillation
  USE Distillation, Fractional
Fractional horsepower electric motors
  USE Electric motors, Fractional horsepower
Fractional integrals
  USE Integrals, Fractional
Fractionation, Field-flow
  USE Field-flow fractionation

Fractionation of amino acids
  USE Amino acids—Separation
Fractionation of blood proteins
  USE Blood proteins—Separation
Fractionation of cells
  USE Cell fractionation
Fractionation of nucleic acids
  USE Nucleic acids—Separation
Fractionation of nucleotides
  USE Nucleotides—Separation
Fractionation of peptides
  USE Peptides—Separation
Fractionation of proteins
  USE Proteins—Separation
Fractions
  [QA117]
  [QA137 (Methods of teaching)]
  BT Arithmetic
      Mathematics
      Numbers, Rational
  NT Series, Farey
Fractions, Continued
  [QA295]
  UF Continued fractions
  RT Processes, Infinite
  NT Padé approximant
Fractions, Decimal
  [QA242 (Theory of numbers)]
  UF Decimal fractions
Fractography
  UF Microfractography
  BT Electron microscopy
      Fracture mechanics
      Metallography
      Metals—Fracture
Fracture compression plates
  USE Bone plates (Orthopedics)
Fracture fixation
  UF Skeletal fixation (Surgery)
  BT Fractures—Treatment
  NT Bonesetters
      External skeletal fixation (Surgery)
      Internal fixation in fractures
  — **Complications and sequelae**
Fracture fixation, External
  USE External skeletal fixation (Surgery)
Fracture fixation, Internal
  USE Internal fixation in fractures
Fracture fixation, Intramedullary
  USE Intramedullary fracture fixation
Fracture mechanics
  [TA409]
  UF Failure of solids
      Fracture of materials
      Fracture of solids
      Materials—Fracture
      Mechanics, Fracture
      Solids—Fracture
  BT Deformations (Mechanics)
      Strength of materials
  RT Brittleness
      Materials—Fatigue
      Penetration mechanics
      Structural failures
  NT Ceramics—Fracture
      Continuum damage mechanics
      Fibrous composites—Fracture
      Fractography
      Glass—Fracture
      Metals—Fracture
      Pavements—Cracking
      Pipe lines—Cracking
      Polymers and polymerization—
        Fracture
      Pressure vessels—Cracking
      R-curves
      Yield-line analysis
Fracture of materials
  USE Fracture mechanics
Fracture of metals
  USE Metals—Fracture

Fracture of polymeric materials
  USE Polymers and polymerization—
        Fracture
Fracture of solids
  USE Fracture mechanics
Fractures (May Subd Geog)
  [RD101-103]
  UF Bones—Fractures
  BT Bones—Wounds and injuries
  RT Callus
  SA subdivision Fractures under names of
        bones and regions of the body, e.g.
        Maxilla—Fractures; Foot—Fractures
  NT Osteoclasis
  — **Treatment**
      NT Fracture fixation
Fractures, Compound
  USE Fractures, Open
Fractures, Open (May Subd Geog)
  UF Compound fractures
      Fractures, Compound
      Open fractures
Fractures, Pathologic
  USE Fractures, Spontaneous
Fractures, Spontaneous
  [RD101]
  UF Fractures, Pathologic
      Pathologic fractures
      Spontaneous fractures
  BT Bones—Diseases
      Osteopsathyrosis
Fractures, Ununited (May Subd Geog)
  UF Ununited fractures
  BT Wound healing
  NT Pseudarthrosis
Fractures in animals
  [SF914.4]
  BT Veterinary surgery
      Veterinary traumatology
Fractures in children (May Subd Geog)
  BT Children—Wounds and injuries
Fracturing, Hydraulic
  USE Hydraulic fracturing
Frafra language
  USE Nankanse language
Fragaria
  USE Strawberries
Fragile X syndrome (May Subd Geog)
  [RJ506.F73 (Pediatrics)]
  UF fra(X) syndrome
  BT Human chromosome abnormalities
      Mental retardation
      Syndromes
      X chromosome—Abnormalities
Fragmentary books
  USE Unfinished books
Fragmentation, Storage (Computer science)
  USE Storage fragmentation (Computer
        science)
Fragmentation bombs
  [UG1282.F7]
  BT Bombs
Fragrance of flowers
  USE Flowers—Odor
Fragrances
  USE Odors
Fragrances in the Bible
  USE Odors in the Bible
Fragrant gardens
  USE Gardens, Fragrant
Frahm family (Not Subd Geog)
  UF Frahmke family
Frahmke family
  USE Frahm family
Fraim family
  USE Frame family
Fraiser family
  USE Fraser family
Fraisier family
  USE Fraser family

Fraisor family
USE Fraser family
Fraizer family
USE Fraser family
Fraktur art
USE Illumination of books and manuscripts,
Mennonite
"Fram" Expedition, 1st, 1893-1896
⌐G700 1893⌐
"Fram" Expedition, 2d, 1898-1902
⌐G670 1898⌐
Framboesia
USE Yaws
Frame drums
BT Drum
NT Ḍaph
Frame family
UF Fraim family
Frames family
Frame houses, Wooden
USE Wooden-frame houses
Frame-stories
⌐PN3383.F7⌐
BT Prologues and epilogues
Short story
Tales
Frame Work (Computer program)
USE Framework (Computer program)
Framed structures
USE Structural frames
Frames, Eyeglass
USE Eyeglass frames
Frames (Information theory)
BT Data structures (Computer science)
Information theory
Frames (Structures)
USE Structural frames
Frames family
USE Frame family
Framework (Computer program)
UF Frame Work (Computer program)
BT Computer programs
Framework II (Computer program)
⌐HF5548.4.F72⌐
BT Business—Computer programs
Frameworks (Structures)
USE Structural frames
Framing (Building) *(May Subd Geog)*
⌐TH2301⌐
BT Building
Structural frames
NT Half-timbered buildings
House framing
Roofs
Wooden-frame buildings
Framing of pictures
USE Picture frames and framing
Framiré
USE Terminalia ivorensis
Franc area, French
USE French franc area
France
NT French
— **Antiquities**
NT Bastion de Solidor Site (Saint-
Malo, France)
Bois l'Abbé Site (France)
Cassons Site (France)
Château de Schoeneck Site
(France)
Combe Grenal Cave (France)
Crêt-Châtelard Site (France)
Ferrassie Rock-shelter (France)
Flageolet Rockshelter (France)
Fritsch Rockshelter (France)
Graufesenque Site (Millau, France)
Laouza Rock Shelter (France)
Lascaux Cave (France)
Liquière Site (France)
Pincevent Site (France)
Rouffignac Cave (France)

Sources de la Seine Site (France)
Terra Amata Site (France)
Vénat Site (France)
— **Armed Forces**
— — **Medals, badges, decorations, etc.**
NT Medaille de Sainte-Hélène
— **Bio-bibliography**
— **Capital and capitol**
— **Church history**
— — **To 987**
— — **Middle Ages, 987-1515**
— — **16th century**
— — **17th century**
— — **18th century**
— — **19th century**
— — **20th century**
— — **1945-**
— **Civilization**
NT Africa—Civilization—French
influences
Africa, West—Civilization—French
influences
America—Civilization—French
influences
Art, American—French influences
Art, German—French influences
Art, Italian—French influences
Art, Scottish—French influences
Art, Ukrainian—French influences
Arts, American—French influences
Arts, Norwegian—French
influences
Arts, Portuguese—French
influences
Arts, Russian—French influences
Brazil—Civilization—French
influences
Bulgaria—Civilization—French
influences
Civilization, Modern—French
influences
Civilization, Slavic—French
influences
English literature—French
influences
Europe—Civilization—French
influences
Germany—Civilization—French
influences
Impressionism (Art)—Japan—
French influences
Indian Ocean Region—Civilization
—French influences
Italy—Civilization—French
influences
Painting, Japanese—French
influences
Romania—Civilization—French
influences
Sculpture, Belgian—French
influences
Turkey—Civilization—French
influences
United States—Civilization—
French influences
— — **To 700**
— — **700-1000**
— — **1000-1328**
— — **1328-1600**
— — **17th-18th centuries**
— — **1789-1830**
— — **1830-1900**
— — **1901-**
— — **1901-1945**
— — **1945-**
— — **American influences**
BT United States—Civilization
— — **Arab influences**
— — **German influences**
BT Germany—Civilization
— — **Italian influences**

BT Italy—Civilization
— — **Turkish influences**
BT Turkey—Civilization
— — **West African influences**
BT Africa, West—Civilization
— **Colonies**
— — **Administration**
— **Commerce**
— **Commercial policy**
— **Constitutional law**
NT Lit de justice
— **Court and courtiers**
— **Description and travel**
— — **To 1600**
— — **1600-1799**
⌐DC24-25⌐
— — **1800-1918**
— — **1919-1944**
⌐DC28⌐
— — **1945-1974**
⌐DC29⌐
— — **1975-**
⌐DC29.3⌐
— — **Guide-books**
— — **Maps**
USE France—Maps
— **Dictionaries and encyclopedias**
— **Economic conditions**
— — **17th century**
— — **19th century**
— — **20th century**
⌐HC276⌐
— — **1918-**
— — **1918-1945**
— — **1945-**
— — **1981-** *(Not Subd Geog)*
⌐HC276.3⌐
— **Economic policy**
— — **20th century**
⌐HC276⌐
— — **1918-1945**
— — **1945-**
— — **1981-** *(Not Subd Geog)*
⌐HC276.3⌐
— **Empresses**
UF Empresses, French
French empresses
BT France—Kings and rulers
— **Encyclopedias and dictionaries**
— **Foreign relations** *(May Subd Geog)*
— — **To 987**
— — **16th century**
— — **1589-1610**
— — **1589-1789**
— — **1610-1643**
— — **1643-1715**
— — **1715-1774**
— — **1715-1793**
— — **1774-1793**
— — **1789-1815**
— — **1792-1815**
— — **19th century**
— — **1814-1830**
— — **1815-1848**
— — **1815-1870**
— — **1830-1848**
— — **1848-1870**
— — **1852-1870**
— — **1870-1940**
— — **1914-1940**
— — **1940-1945**
— — **1945-1958**
— — **1958-1969**
— — **1969-1981**
— — **1981-**
— — **Germany**
NT Agadir Incident, 1911
— **Gazetteers**
— **Historical geography**
— **History**
⌐DC⌐

Franceschi family (Not Subd Geog)
  UF De Franceschi family
    Franceski family
    Francesoni family
Franceski family
  USE Franceschi family
Francesoni family
  USE Franceschi family
Franch family
  USE Frank family
Franchise
  USE Elections
    Suffrage
Franchises, Municipal
  USE Municipal franchises
Franchises, Retail
  USE Franchises (Retail trade)
Franchises, Sports
  USE Sports franchises
Franchises, Taxation of
  USE Corporations—Taxation
Franchises (Retail trade) (May Subd Geog)
  [HF5429.23-HF5429.235]
  UF Franchises, Retail
    Retail franchises
  BT Retail trade
    Small business
  — **Law and legislation** (May Subd Geog)
    BT Agency (Law)
      Trade regulation
Franchthi Cave (Greece)
  USE Franchthi Cave Site (Greece)
Franchthi Cave Site (Greece)
  UF Franchthi Cave (Greece)
    Franchthi Site (Greece)
  BT Caves—Greece
    Greece—Antiquities
Franchthi Site (Greece)
  USE Franchthi Cave Site (Greece)
Francies family
  USE Francis family
Francigena Road (Italy and France)
  USE Strada di Francia (Italy and France)
Francis, of Assisi, Saint, 1182-1226
  — **Art**
    NT Bellini, Giovanni, d. 1516. Saint
      Francis in ecstasy
  — **Friends and associates**
FRANCIS (Information retrieval system)
  UF French Retrieval Automated Network
    for Current Information in Social
    and Human Sciences (Information
    retrieval system)
  BT Information storage and retrieval
    systems—Humanities
    Information storage and retrieval
    systems—Social sciences
Francis Case, Lake (S.D.)
  UF Lake Francis Case (S.D.)
  BT Lakes—South Dakota
Francis family (Not Subd Geog)
  UF Frances family
    Francies family
    Franciss family
    Franses family
Francis Marion National Forest (S.C.)
  BT Forest reserves—South Carolina
    National parks and reserves—United
    States
Francisca Road (Italy and France)
  USE Strada di Francia (Italy and France)
Franciscan architecture
  USE Architecture, Franciscan
Franciscan art
  USE Art, Franciscan
Franciscan convents and nunneries
  USE Convents and nunneries, Franciscan
Franciscan crown
  [BX2163]

  UF Crown, Franciscan
    Rosary, Seraphic
    Seraphic rosary
  BT Franciscans
    Rosary
Franciscan monasteries
  USE Monasteries, Franciscan
Franciscan movement (Anglican Communion)
  (May Subd Geog)
  UF Anglican Franciscan movement
    Anglican Franciscans
    Franciscans, Anglican
  BT Monasticism and religious orders,
    Anglican
Franciscan Recollects (May Subd Geog)
  [BX3980]
  UF Franciscan Recollets
    Recollects (Franciscan)
    Recollets (Franciscan)
  BT Franciscans
  — **Missions**
Franciscan Recollets
  USE Franciscan Recollects
Franciscan tertiaries
  USE Secular Franciscans
Franciscan ware
  [NK4340.F68]
  BT Ceramic tableware—California
    Pottery—20th century—California
    Pottery, American
Franciscana dolphin
  USE La Plata dolphin
Franciscans
  NT Secular Franciscans
  [BX3601-BX3605 (Men)]
  [BX4361-BX4364 (Women)]
  UF Friars, Gray
    Friars Minor
    Gray Friars
    Grey Friars
    Minorites
    St. Francis, Order of
  BT Friars
    Monasticism and religious orders
  NT Franciscan crown
    Franciscan Recollects
    Fraticelli
  — **Bio-bibliography**
    [Z7840.F8]
  — **Manuscripts**
  — **Missions**
    [BV2280]
    NT Missions of Piritu
Franciscans, Anglican
  USE Franciscan movement (Anglican
    Communion)
Franciscans in literature
Francisco Gómez House (Montevideo,
  Uruguay)
  USE Casa de Francisco Gómez
    (Montevideo, Uruguay)
Francisco I. Madero Avenue (Mexico City,
  Mexico)
  USE Avenida Francisco I. Madero (Mexico
    City, Mexico)
Franciss family
  USE Francis family
Francium
  BT Alkali metals
    Radioactive substances
Franck family
  USE Frank family
Francke family
  USE Frank family
Franco-Chinese War, 1884-1885
  USE Chinese-French War, 1884-1885
Franco family (Not Subd Geog)
  RT Frank family
Franco-German War, 1870-1871
  [DC281-326]

  UF France—History—Franco-German
    War, 1870-1871
    Franco-Prussian War, 1870-1871
    Germany—History—Franco-German
    War, 1870-1871
  NT Alsace-Lorraine question
    Amiens, Battle of, 1870
    Beaune-la-Rolande, Battle of, 1870
    Belfort, Battle of, 1871
    Champigny-sur-Marne, France, Battle
    of, 1870
    Coulmiers, Battle of, 1870
    Épinal, Battle of, 1870
    France—History—Occupation and
    evacuation, 1871-1873
    Gravelotte, Battle of, 1870
    Le Mans, Battle of, 1871
    Loigny-Poupry, Battle of, 1870
    Noisseville, Battle of, 1870
    Orléans, Battle of, 1870
    Rambervillers, Battle of, 1870
    Sedan Campaign, 1870
    Spicheren, Battle of, 1870
    Thiais, France, Battle of, 1870
    Vionville, Battle of, 1870
    Weissenburg, Battle of, 1870
    Wörth, Battle of, 1870
  — **Aerial operations**
  — **Campaigns** (May Subd Geog)
  — — **France**
    NT Cussey, Battle of, 1870
  — **Causes**
  — **Fiction**
    NT Franco-German War, 1870-1871—
      Juvenile fiction
  — **Juvenile fiction**
    BT Franco-German War, 1870-1871—
      Fiction
  — **Literature and the war**
  — **Postal service**
  — **Prisoners and prisons**
  — **Regimental histories**
  — **Reparations**
Franco-Provençal dialects (May Subd Geog)
  [PC3081-3148]
  UF Dialects
  BT Provençal language—Dialects
  NT Provençal language
Franco-Prussian War, 1870-1871
  USE Franco-German War, 1870-1871
Franco-Russian Alliance
  [D397]
  UF Russo-French Alliance
  BT Europe—Politics and government—
    1871-1918
Franco-Soviet pact, 1935
  UF Pacte franco-soviétique, 1935
Franco-Spanish War, 1635-1659
  [DC124.45]
  UF French-Spanish War, 1635-1659
    Spanish-French War, 1635-1659
  BT France—History—17th century
    Thirty Years' War, 1618-1648
  NT Pyrenees, Peace of the, 1659
  — **Campaigns** (May Subd Geog)
  — — **France**
    NT Dunes, Battle of the, 1658
Franco-Spanish War, 1667-1668
  USE Devolution, War of, 1667-1668
Franco-Syrian treaty, 1936
  UF Damascus, Treaty of, 1936
Francoism
  BT Spain—Politics and government—
    1939-1975
    Spain—Politics and government—
    1975-
Francolins
  UF Francolinus
  BT Partridges
  NT Erckel francolin

Francolinus
  USE Francolins
Francolinus erckelii
  USE Erckel francolin
Franconia, House of
  USE Franconian House
Franconia (Duchy)
  USE Franconia (Germany)
Franconia (Germany)
  UF Franconia (Duchy)
    Franken (Germany)
Franconian emperors
  USE Germany—History—Franconian
    House, 1024-1125
    Holy Roman Empire—History—
    Franconian House, 1024-1125
Franconian Forest (Germany)
  USE Frankenwald (Germany)
Franconian House *(Not Subd Geog)*
  UF Franconia, House of
    Salian House
  RT Germany—History—Franconian
    House, 1024-1125
    Holy Roman Empire—History—
    Franconian House, 1024-1125
Franconian Jura (Germany)
  USE Fränkische Alb (Germany)
Franconian law
  USE Law, Frankish
Franconian Switzerland (Germany)
  USE Fränkische Schweiz (Germany)
Francs-tireurs
  USE Guerrillas
Frangipane family *(Not Subd Geog)*
  NT Palazzo Frangipane (Licata, Sicily)
Frangipane Palace (Licata, Sicily)
  USE Palazzo Frangipane (Licata, Sicily)
Frangipani
  USE Plumeria
Frangula
  *[QP981.F (Experimental
    pharmacology)]*
  [RM666.F (Therapeutics)]
  RT Buckthorn
Frank (Fighter planes)
  USE Hayate (Fighter planes)
Frank family *(Not Subd Geog)*
  UF Franch family
    Franck family
    Francke family
    Franke family
    Franken family
    Franks family
  RT Franco family
Frank Lloyd Wright House (Oak Park, Ill.)
  BT Dwellings—Illinois
    Wright, Frank Lloyd, 1867-1959—
    Homes and haunts—Illinois
Frank Lloyd Wright Studio (Oak Park, Ill.)
  BT Office buildings—Illinois
    Wright, Frank Lloyd, 1867-1959—
    Homes and haunts—Illinois
Franke family
  USE Frank family
Franken (Germany)
  USE Franconia (Germany)
Franken family
  USE Frank family
Frankenhöhe (Germany)
Frankenstein (Fictitious character)
  UF Doctor Frankenstein (Fictitious
    character)
    Dr. Frankenstein (Fictitious character)
  BT Characters and characteristics in
    literature
  RT Shelley, Mary Wollstonecraft, 1797-
    1851—Characters—Frankenstein
Frankenstein family *(Not Subd Geog)*
Frankenstein films
  [PN1995.9.F8]

  BT Characters and characteristics in
    moving-pictures
    Horror films
    Moving-pictures
Frankenthal porcelain
  [NK4399.F8]
  UF Porcelain, Frankenthal
  BT Porcelain, German
  RT Strasbourg porcelain
Frankenwald (Germany)
  UF Franconian Forest (Germany)
  BT Forests and forestry—Germany (West)
    Mountains—Germany (West)
Frankfurt rite of Judaism
  USE Judaism—Frankfurt rite
Frankfurt school
  USE Frankfurt school of sociology
Frankfurt school of sociology
  (May Subd Geog)
  UF Critical theory (Sociology)
    Frankfurt school
    Frankfurt sociologists
  BT Schools of sociology
  RT Marxian school of sociology
Frankfurt sociologists
  USE Frankfurt school of sociology
Frankfurt vocabulary tests
  BT Vocabulary tests
Frankfurter Gruppe
  USE Quadriga (Group of artists)
Frankfurter Hauptbahnhof (Frankfurt am Main,
    Germany)
  USE Hauptbahnhof (Frankfurt am Main,
    Germany)
Frankfurter Kopf (Statue)
  USE Liebieghaus kouros head (Statue)
Frankfurter Kuroskopf (Statue)
  USE Liebieghaus kouros head (Statue)
Frankfurter Rathaus (Frankfurt am Main,
    Germany)
  USE Frankfurter Römer (Frankfurt am
    Main, Germany)
**Frankfurter Römer (Frankfurt am Main,
    Germany)**
  UF Frankfurter Rathaus (Frankfurt am
    Main, Germany)
    Römer (Frankfurt am Main, Germany)
  BT City halls—Germany (West)
  — Kaisersaal
    UF Kaisersaal, Frankfurter Römer
      (Frankfurt am Main, Germany)
    BT Coronations—Germany (West)
      Halls—Germany (West)
Frankfurters *(May Subd Geog)*
  [TS1974.S3 (Manufacture)]
  [TX749 (Cookery)]
  UF Hot dogs
    Weenies
    Wieners
  BT Sausages
  NT Cookery (Frankfurters)
Frankia
  [QR82.F7]
  BT Frankiaceae
Frankiaceae
  [QR82.F7]
  BT Actinomycetales
  NT Frankia
Franking privilege *(May Subd Geog)*
  [HE6148]
  [HE6448 (United States)]
  UF Penalty mail
    Postal service—Franking privilege
    Postal service—Penalty mail
  BT Postal service
    Postal service—Rates
  — United States
    UF Penalty mail
Fränkische Alb (Germany)
  UF Franconian Jura (Germany)
    Fränkischer Jura (Germany)

  BT Alps
    Mountains—Germany (West)
Fränkische Schweiz (Germany)
  UF Franconian Switzerland (Germany)
Fränkischer Jura (Germany)
  USE Fränkische Alb (Germany)
Frankish decorative arts
  USE Decorative arts, Frankish
Frankish law
  USE Law, Frankish
Franklin (Tenn.), Battle of, 1864
  [E477.52]
  BT Tennessee—History—Civil War, 1861-
    1865
    United States—History—Civil War,
    1861-1865—Campaigns
Franklin Ace 1000 (Computer)
  [QA76.8.F]
  BT Franklin computer
    Microcomputers
  — Programming
Franklin automobile
  [TL215.F]
Franklin computer
  [QA76.8.F]
  BT Electronic digital computers
  NT Franklin Ace 1000 (Computer)
  — Programming
Franklin Court (Philadelphia, Pa.)
  BT Streets—Pennsylvania
Franklin family *(Not Subd Geog)*
  UF Frankling family
Franklin River (Tas.)
  BT Rivers—Australia
Frankling family
  USE Franklin family
Frankliniella
  [QL598.3.T4]
  BT Thripidae
  NT Frankliniella occidentalis
Frankliniella occidentalis
  [QL598.3.T4]
  BT Frankliniella
Franklin's grouse
  USE Spruce grouse
Franklin's gull
  [QL696.C46]
  UF Larus pipixan
Frankopan family *(Not Subd Geog)*
Franks *(May Subd Geog)*
  [DC64-DC81 (France)]
  [DD127-DD134 (Germany)]
  [DG515 (Italy)]
  [DH151 (Netherlands)]
  [DH576 (Belgium)]
  BT Germanic tribes
    Germany—History—To 843
  — History
  — — To 768
  — — 768-814
  — — 814-843
  — — 843-987
  — Nobility
    UF Nobility, Frankish
Franks family
  USE Frank family
Frans family
  USE Frantz family
Fransen family
  USE Franson family
Franses family
  USE Francis family
Franson family *(Not Subd Geog)*
  UF Fransen family
    Franzen family
Frantz family *(Not Subd Geog)*
  UF Frans family
    Franz family
    Franze family
    Frens family

Franz family
USE Frantz family
Franz Josef Land (R.S.F.S.R.)
UF Fridtjof Nansen Land (R.S.F.S.R.)
Zemlîâ Frantsa-Iosifa (R.S.F.S.R.)
Zemlya Frantsa-Iosifa (R.S.F.S.R.)
BT Islands—Russian S.F.S.R.
Islands of the Arctic
Franze family
USE Frantz family
Franzen family
USE Franson family
Frapper (The French word)
[PC2886.9.F]
BT French language—Etymology
Frarey family
USE Frary family
Frary family *(Not Subd Geog)*
UF Frarey family
Frasch process
[TN890]
BT Sulphur mines and mining
Fraser, Antonia, 1932- *(Not Subd Geog)*
1932-
— **Characters**
— — **Jemima Shore**
RT Shore, Jemima (Fictitious
character)
Fraser Canyon (B.C.)
UF Canyon of the Fraser River (B.C.)
Fraser River Canyon (B.C.)
BT Canyons—British Columbia
Fraser family *(Not Subd Geog)*
UF Fraiser family
Fraisier family
Fraisor family
Fraizer family
Frasher family
Frashier family
Frasier family
Frasior family
Frasure family
Frasyier family
Frayser family
Frayzier family
Frazair family
Frazer family
Frazier family
Frazir family
Frazire family
Frazor family
RT Frizzell family
Fraser Island (Qld.)
UF Great Sandy Island (Qld.)
BT Islands—Australia
Fraser River (B.C.)
BT Rivers—British Columbia
Fraser River Canyon (B.C.)
USE Fraser Canyon (B.C.)
Fraser's dolphin
USE Lagenodelphis hosei
Frash family
USE Frache family
Frasher family
USE Fraser family
Frashier family
USE Fraser family
Frasier family
USE Fraser family
Frasior family
USE Fraser family
Frasure family
USE Fraser family
Frasyier family
USE Fraser family
Fratercula
[QL696.C42]
BT Alcidae
Puffins
Fratercula arctica
USE Atlantic puffin

Fraternal benefit societies
USE Friendly societies
Fraternal insurance
USE Insurance, Fraternal
Fraternal organizations
USE Friendly societies; Greek letter
societies; *and similar headings*
Friendly societies
Greek letter societies
Fraternities
USE Greek letter societies
Initiations (into trades, societies, etc.)
Secret societies
Fraternity libraries *(May Subd Geog)*
[Z675.F7]
UF Chapter-house libraries
Club-house libraries
Greek letter society libraries
Libraries, Chapter-house
Libraries, Club-house
Libraries, Fraternity
Libraries, Greek letter society
Libraries, Sorority
Sorority libraries
BT Libraries, University and college
Fraternity songs
[M1960]
UF Sorority songs
BT Greek letter societies
Students' songs—United States
SA *subdivision* Songs and music *under
names of fraternities, e.g.* Phi Kappa
Psi—Songs and music
Fraticelli
[BX3602]
BT Franciscans
Fratres arvales
BT Cults—Rome
Fratricide *(May Subd Geog)*
BT Homicide
Murder
Fraud *(May Subd Geog)*
[HV6691-6699]
UF Deceit
Misrepresentation (Law)
BT Commercial crimes
Criminal law
Deception
Offenses against property
Simulation (Civil law)
Torts
Undue influence
White collar crimes
RT Dolus (Civil law)
Impostors and imposture
Mistake (Law)
Swindlers and swindling
NT Automobile repair fraud
Bad faith (Law)
Blanks in legal documents
Cardsharping
Checks—Criminal provisions
Commercial credit fraud
Credit card fraud
Diploma mills
False certification
False personation
Forgery
Fraud investigation
Fraudulent conveyances
Insurance crimes
Medicaid fraud
Medicare fraud
Reformation of instruments
Restitutio in integrum
Securities fraud
Statute of frauds
Trials (Fraud)
Welfare fraud
Whiskey frauds

Fraud (Germanic law)
Fraud (Islamic law) *(May Subd Geog)*
Fraud (Jewish law)
Fraud (Roman-Dutch law)
Fraud (Roman law)
Fraud in science *(May Subd Geog)*
[Q172.5.F7]
UF Scientific fraud
Fraud investigation
BT Criminal investigation
Fraud
NT Welfare fraud investigation
Frauds, Literary
USE Literary forgeries and mystifications
Frauds, Statute of
USE Statute of frauds
Fraudulent advertising
USE Advertising, Fraudulent
Fraudulent conveyances *(May Subd Geog)*
UF Actio pauliana
Bankruptcy, Fraudulent
BT Bankruptcy
Contracts, Gratuitous
Fraud
Torts
RT Assignments for benefit of creditors
Creditors' bills
Debtor and creditor
Simulation (Civil law)
NT Bulk sales
Fraudulent conveyances (Hindu law)
RT Benami transactions
Fraudulent conveyances (Roman-Dutch law)
Fraudulent conveyances (Roman law)
NT Exceptio doli (Roman law)
Frauenberg (Germany)
BT Mountains—Germany (West)
Fraunhofer lines
BT Absorption spectra
Spectrum, Solar
Fraust family
USE Frost family
Fravashis
[BL1590.F73]
UF Farohars
BT Angels
Spirits
Zoroastrianism
Fravel family *(Not Subd Geog)*
UF Frable family
Frevel family
Fraxinus
USE Ash (Tree)
Fraxinus americana
USE White ash
Fray
USE Affray
Frayser family
USE Fraser family
Frayzier family
USE Fraser family
Frazair family
USE Fraser family
Frazer family
USE Fraser family
Frazer Nash automobile
UF Frazernash automobile
Frazernash automobile
USE Frazer Nash automobile
Frazier family
USE Fraser family
Frazil ice *(May Subd Geog)*
UF Crystals, Frazil
Ice, Frazil
Ice, Lolly
Ice, Needle
Lolly ice
Needle ice
BT Ice crystals
Ice on rivers, lakes, etc.

Frazir family
USE Fraser family
Frazire family
USE Fraser family
Frazor family
USE Fraser family
Freak brothers (Comic strip)
USE Fabulous furry Freak brothers (Comic strip)
Freaks
USE Monsters
Frease family
USE Freese family
Fréchet spaces
UF Spaces, Fréchet
BT Linear topological spaces
Fred (Computer program)
[QA76.76.T49]
UF Fred text editor (Computer program)
BT Text editors (Computer programs)
FRED (Computer program language)
[QA76.73.F]
BT Programming languages (Electronic computers)
Fred text editor (Computer program)
USE Fred (Computer program)
Frederic family
USE Frederick family
Frederick II, Holy Roman Emperor, 1194-1250
— **Homes and haunts** *(May Subd Geog)*
UF Frederick II, Holy Roman Emperor, 1194-1250—Homes
— — **Italy**
— **Homes**
USE Frederick II, Holy Roman Emperor, 1194-1250—Homes and haunts
Frederick family *(Not Subd Geog)*
UF Frederic family
Fredericks family
Fredrich family
Fredrick family
Frederick Law Olmsted National Historic Site (Brookline, Mass.)
UF Fairsted (Brookline, Mass.)
Olmsted National Historic Site (Brookline, Mass.)
BT Dwellings—Massachusetts
Historic sites—Massachusetts
National parks and reserves—Massachusetts
Frederick Ringer House (Nagasaki-shi, Japan)
USE Kyū Ringā (Otōto) Jūtaku (Nagasaki-shi, Japan)
Fredericks family
USE Frederick family
Fredericksburg, Battle of, 1862
[E474.85]
BT United States—History—Civil War, 1861-1865—Campaigns
Frederikssundsbanen
BT Railroads—Denmark
Fredholm equations
UF Equations, Fredholm
BT Integral equations
— **Numerical solutions**
BT Numerical analysis
Fredholm operators
UF Operators, Fredholm
BT Linear operators
Fredonian Insurrection, 1826-1827
[F389 (Texas)]
BT Texas—History—To 1846
Fredrich family
USE Frederick family
Fredrick family
USE Frederick family
Fredrikssten Fortress (Halden, Norway)
USE Fredriksten Fortress (Halden, Norway)

Fredriksten Fortress (Halden, Norway)
UF Fredrikssten Fortress (Halden, Norway)
Friederich Stein Fortress (Halden, Norway)
BT Fortification—Norway
Fredriksvern (Stavern, Norway)
USE Stavern Fort (Stavern, Norway)
Free agency
USE Free will and determinism
Free association (Psychology)
UF Association, Free (Psychology)
BT Association of ideas
Psychoanalysis
Psychotherapy
Free banking *(May Subd Geog)*
BT Banks and banking
Free choice of employment
(May Subd Geog)
[HD4903]
UF Employment, Free choice of
Freedom of employment
Freedom of occupation
Liberty of employment
Liberty of occupation
Occupation, Free choice of
BT Civil rights
Labor supply
Personality (Law)
Free Church of Scotland
[BX9084]
Free churches *(May Subd Geog)*
Here are entered works on churches free from state relationship or control, as distinguished from established churches.
UF Believers' church
Churches, Free
Nonconformity (Religion)
BT Christian sects
Church and state
Protestant churches
RT Dissenters, Religious
Established churches
— **Clergy**
BT Clergy
— **Hymns**
Free circulation newspapers and periodicals
(May Subd Geog)
[PN4784.F74 (General)]
UF Free newspapers
Free periodicals
Shoppers (Publications)
BT Newspapers
Periodicals
Free cities
USE Internationalized territories
Free coinage
USE Currency question
Silver question
Free computer software *(May Subd Geog)*
UF Free software
Public domain software
Software, Free computer
BT Computer software
Free material
Free convection
USE Heat—Convection, Natural
Free diving
USE Skin diving
Free earth oscillations
[QE539]
UF Earth oscillations
Free oscillations of the earth
BT Oscillations
Seismology
Free electron lasers
BT Electrons
Lasers
Free electron theory of metals
UF Metals, Free electron theory of

BT Electron gas
Electrons
Energy-band theory of solids
Metals
RT Conduction band
NT Anderson model
Charge density waves
Effective mass (Physics)
Electric conductivity
Electron mobility
Electron transport
Electrons—Emission
Fermi surfaces
Magnetism, Band theory of
Metal-insulator transitions
One-dimensional conductors
Pseudopotential method
Free energy, Gibbs'
USE Gibbs' free energy
Free energy relationship, Linear
USE Linear free energy relationship
Free enterprise
USE Laissez-faire
Free enthalpy
USE Gibbs' free energy
Free fall, Physiological effect of
USE Weightlessness
Free-floating ferns
USE Water ferns
Free groups
BT Groups, Theory of
NT Free metabelian groups
Free harbors
USE Free ports and zones
Free indirect speech
[PN3383.F74]
UF Free indirect style
Indirect speech, Free
Speech, Free indirect
BT Fiction—Technique
Narration (Rhetoric)
RT Indirect discourse in literature
Free indirect style
USE Free indirect speech
Free lance photography
USE Photography, Freelance
Free-lancers
USE Self-employed
Free-law movement
BT Law—Interpretation and construction
Law—Philosophy
Natural law
Free love *(May Subd Geog)*
[HQ961-HQ967 (Sociology)]
[HX546 (Socialism and free love)]
BT Marriage
Sexual ethics
RT Concubinage
Unmarried couples
NT Cuckolds
Free material
UF Freebies
Give-aways
Giveaways
RT Gifts
Samples (Commerce)
NT Free computer software
Free metabelian groups
UF Groups, Free metabelian
Meta-abelian groups, Free
Metabelian groups, Free
BT Abelian groups
Free groups
Free newspapers
USE Free circulation newspapers and periodicals
"Free on board"
USE F.O.B. clause
Free oscillations of the earth
USE Free earth oscillations

Free periodicals
  USE Free circulation newspapers and
        periodicals
Free piston engines
  [TJ779]
  BT Engines
      Gas-turbines
      Internal combustion engines
Free ports and zones *(May Subd Geog)*
  [HF1418]
  UF Foreign trade zones
      Free harbors
      Free trade zones
      Free zones
      Zones, Free trade
  BT Free trade and protection
      Harbors
      Tariff
  NT Harbors—Port charges
  — **Law and legislation** *(May Subd Geog)*
      BT Customs administration
          Foreign trade regulation
      RT Bonded warehouses and goods
      NT Duty-free transit
  — **China**
      NT Chu-hai Special Economic Zone
          (Chu-hai shih, China)
          Shen-chen Special Economic Zone
          (Shen-chen shih, China)
  — **Greece**
      NT Free Zone of Thessalonikē
          (Thessalonikē, Greece)
  — **Venezuela**
      NT Paraguaná Industrial Free Zone
          (Venezuela)
Free press and fair trial *(May Subd Geog)*
  UF Fair trial and free press
      Prejudicial publicity and free press
      Pretrial publicity
      Publicity, Pretrial
      Trial by newspaper
  BT Conduct of court proceedings
      Freedom of information
      Freedom of the press
      Journalistic ethics
  NT Newspaper court reporting
Free products (Group theory)
  UF Products, Free (Group theory)
  BT Groups, Theory of
Free-radical polymerization
  USE Addition polymerization
Free radical reactions
  UF Radical reactions, Free
      Reactions, Free radical
  BT Chemical reactions
  RT Free radicals (Chemistry)
  NT Membrane lipids—Peroxidation
Free radicals (Chemistry)
  [QD471 (Chemistry)]
  [QP527 (Biochemistry)]
  BT Radicals (Chemistry)
  RT Free radical reactions
  NT Active oxygen
Free schools *(May Subd Geog)*
  UF Alternative schools
  BT Education—Experimental methods
  RT Open plan schools
Free seed distribution
  USE Seed distribution
Free software
  USE Free computer software
Free-Soil Party
  [JK2336]
      Subdivided by locality, e.g. Free-Soil Party. Mas-
      sachusetts.
Free-Soil Party. Massachusetts
Free speech
  USE Freedom of speech
Free Spirit, Brethren of the
  USE Brethren of the Free Spirit

Free State-Sotho War, 1865-1866
  USE Sotho-Free State War, 1865-1866
Free style stroke (Swimming)
  USE Swimming—Crawl stroke
Free surfaces (Crystallography)
  UF Crystal surfaces, Free
      Crystals—Free surfaces
  BT Crystallography
      Surfaces
Free-tailed bat, Giant African
  USE Tadarida africana
Free-tailed bats
  USE Molossidae
Free thought *(May Subd Geog)*
  [BL2700-BL2790]
  UF Freethought
      Thought, Free
  RT Rationalism
  NT Bible—Evidences, authority, etc.
  — **Hymns**
Free time (Leisure)
  USE Leisure
Free-to-choose movement
  USE Pro-choice movement
Free trade and protection
  [HF1701-2701]
  UF Fair trade (Tariff)
      Protection
  BT Commercial policy
      Economic policy
      Economics
  RT Mercantile system
      Tariff
  SA *subdivisions* Commercial policy *and*
      Economic policy *under names of*
      countries
  NT Balance of trade
      Free ports and zones
      Import quotas
      Laissez-faire
      Reciprocity
      Second best, Theory of
      Shipping bounties and subsidies
      Supply and demand
      Tolls
  — **Free trade**
      [HF1701-2580]
      For free trade arguments. Works on the tariff
      question in a particular country may take this or
      the succeeding heading in addition to the head-
      ing Tariff, e.g. 1. Tariff—United States. 2. Free
      trade and protection—Free trade.
  — **Protection**
      [HF1701-2580]
      For arguments in favor of protection.
Free trade areas
  USE Customs unions
Free trade zones
  USE Free ports and zones
Free verse
  [PN1059.F]
  UF Vers libre
  BT English language—Versification
      Poetry
  RT Imagist poetry
  NT Enjambement
Free verse, Urdu *(May Subd Geog)*
  UF Urdu free verse
  BT Urdu poetry
Free will and determinism
  [BF620-BF628 (Psychology)]
  [BJ1460-BJ1468 (Ethics)]
  UF Determinism and indeterminism
      Free agency
      Freedom of the will
      Indeterminism
      Liberty of the will

      BT Autonomy (Psychology)
          Conscience
          Ethics
          Fate and fatalism
          Law—Philosophy
          Philosophy
          Predestination
          Sin
          Theology, Doctrinal
          Will
      RT Human acts
          Necessity (Philosophy)
          Responsibility
      NT Ajivikas
          Decision-making (Ethics)
          Freedom (Theology)
          God—Omniscience
          God—Will
          Inhibition
          Libertines (French philosophers)
          Life and death, Power over
          Molinism
  — **Biblical teaching**
      BT Bible—Theology
Free will and determinism (Islam)
  [BP166.3]
  BT Islam—Doctrines
      Islamic ethics
  NT God (Islam)—Will
      Predestination (Islam)
Free will and determinism in literature
Free Zone of Thessalonikē (Thessalonikē,
  Greece) *(Not Subd Geog)*
  UF Eleuthera Zōnē Thessalonikēs
      (Thessalonikē, Greece)
      Thessalonikē (Greece). Eleuthera
        Zōnē Thessalonikēs
      Thessalonikē (Greece). Free Zone of
        Thessalonikē
  BT Free ports and zones—Greece
Free zones
  USE Free ports and zones
Freebies
  USE Free material
Freeboard, Tables of
  USE Load-line
      Ships—Measurement
Freebooters
  USE Buccaneers
      Filibusters
      Pirates
Freeborn family
  USE Freeburn family
Freeborne family
  USE Freeburn family
Freeburn family *(Not Subd Geog)*
  UF Freeborn family
      Freeborne family
Freed family *(Not Subd Geog)*
  UF Frid family
      Fried family
Freed slaves
  USE Freedmen
Freedman's Savings Bank Building
  (Washington, D.C.)
  BT Bank buildings—Washington (D.C.)
Freedmen *(May Subd Geog)*
  [E185.2 (United States)]
  [HT731 (General)]
  UF Freed slaves
      Refugees, Afro-American
  BT Afro-Americans
      Reconstruction
      Slavery—United States
      Slavery—United States—Emancipation
  RT Slavery
  — **France**
      NT Colliberts
Freedmen (Roman law)
Freedom
  USE Freedom (Jewish theology)

Liberty
Slavery
Freedom, Academic
USE Academic freedom
Freedom, Degree of
USE Degree of freedom
Freedom (Islam)
⌜BP190.5.F7⌝
UF Liberty (Islam)
Freedom (Jewish theology)
UF Freedom
Freedom (Psychology)
USE Autonomy (Psychology)
Freedom (Theology)
UF Liberty (Theology)
BT Free will and determinism
Law and gospel
Theology, Doctrinal
NT Liberation theology
— **History of doctrines**
Freedom and art *(May Subd Geog)*
UF Artistic freedom
BT Art
Communication in art
Creation (Literary, artistic, etc.)
RT Art—Censorship
NT Dissenters, Artistic
Dissident art
Freedom Fighter (Jet fighter plane)
USE F-5 (Jet fighter plane)
Freedom Flotilla, 1980
USE Mariel Boatlift, 1980
Freedom marches (Civil rights)
USE Civil rights demonstrations
Freedom of assembly
USE Assembly, Right of
Freedom of association *(May Subd Geog)*
⌜JK-JQ (JC607)⌝
UF Association, Freedom of
Association, Right of
Freedom of coalition
Liberty of association
Right of association
BT Associations, institutions, etc.
Civil rights
Liberty
Personality (Law)
RT Assembly, Right of
NT Trade-unions—Law and legislation
Freedom of association (Canon law)
Freedom-of-choice movement
USE Pro-choice movement
Freedom of coalition
USE Freedom of association
Freedom of contract
USE Liberty of contract
Freedom of debate (Legislative bodies)
USE Legislative bodies—Freedom of debate
Freedom of decision (Ethics)
USE Decision-making (Ethics)
Freedom of employment
USE Free choice of employment
Freedom of information *(May Subd Geog)*
UF Information, Freedom of
Intellectual freedom
Liberty of information
Right to know
BT Civil rights
RT Freedom of speech
Telecommunication—Law and legislation
NT Academic freedom
Executive privilege (Government information)
Foreign news—Censorship
Free press and fair trial
Government and the press
Government information
Moving-pictures—Censorship
Radio—Censorship
Radio broadcasting

Freedom of information (International law)
BT International law
Freedom of information in the church
(May Subd Geog)
⌜BV740⌝
UF Secrecy in the church
BT Church
Freedom of movement *(May Subd Geog)*
UF Movement, Freedom of
BT Civil rights
Domicile
Emigration and immigration law
Industrial laws and legislation
Labor laws and legislation
Liberty
Personality (Law)
Freedom of movement (International law)
BT International law
Freedom of occupation
USE Free choice of employment
Freedom of religion *(May Subd Geog)*
⌜BV741⌝
UF Freedom of worship
Intolerance
Liberty of religion
Religious freedom
Religious liberty
BT Civil rights
Liberty
NT Indians of North America—Freedom of religion
— **History**
UF Freedom of religion—History of doctrines
— — **16th century**
— History of doctrines
USE Freedom of religion—History
Freedom of religion (Canon law)
UF Religious liberty (Canon law)
Freedom of religion (International law)
UF Religious liberty (International law)
BT International law
Freedom of speech *(May Subd Geog)*
UF Free speech
Intellectual freedom
Liberty of speech
Speech, Freedom of
BT Civil rights
RT Assembly, Right of
Freedom of information
NT Blasphemy
Legislative bodies—Freedom of debate
Libel and slander
Sedition
Freedom of speech in Judaism
⌜BM645.F73⌝
UF Liberty of speech in Judaism
BT Judaism—Discipline
Religious tolerance
Freedom of speech in the church
UF Liberty of speech in the church
BT Church—Authority
Religious tolerance
Freedom of teaching
USE Teaching, Freedom of
Freedom of testation *(May Subd Geog)*
UF Liberty of testation
Testation, Freedom of
BT Inheritance and succession
Right of property
Wills
NT Dower
Legitime
Freedom of the air
USE Airspace (International law)
Freedom of the press *(May Subd Geog)*
UF Censorship of the press
Liberty of the press
Press—Censorship
Press censorship

BT Censorship
Civil rights
Journalism
Press
Press law
NT Free press and fair trial
Libel and slander
Freedom of the seas
⌜D580 (European War)⌝
⌜JX4423-JX4425 (International law)⌝
⌜JX5203-JX5268 (Maritime war: International law)⌝
Here are entered works dealing with political aspects and theories, also popular controversial literature. Works of technical or predominantly legal character are entered under Maritime law. Historical works and discussions of both political and legal aspects are entered under both headings.
UF Closed sea (Mare clausum)
Open sea (Mare liberum)
Sea, Freedom of the
Seas, Freedom of the
BT International law
Maritime law
Sea-power
War, Maritime (International law)
NT Jurisdiction over ships at sea
Freedom of the will
USE Free will and determinism
Freedom of worship
USE Freedom of religion
Freedom Railway
USE Tan-Zam Railway
Freedom Trail (Boston, Mass.)
BT Trails—Massachusetts
Freedom Train
⌜JK4⌝
Freehand technical sketching
⌜T359⌝
UF Sketching, Technical
Technical freehand sketching
Technical sketching, Freehand
BT Engineering graphics
Mechanical drawing
Technical illustration
Freehold
USE Land tenure
Real property
Freelan family
USE Freeland family
Freelance photography
USE Photography, Freelance
Freelancers
USE Self-employed
Freeland family *(Not Subd Geog)*
UF Freelan family
Freland family
Freeman family *(Not Subd Geog)*
UF Freemon family
Freman family
Freeman's Farm, Battle of, 1777
USE Saratoga Campaign, 1777
Freemasonry *(May Subd Geog)*
⌜HS351-929⌝
UF Masonic orders
Masonry (Secret order)
RT Freemasons
SA *subdivision* Freemasonry *under names of individuals, e.g.* Washington, George, 1732-1799—Freemasonry
NT Women and freemasonry
— **Law and legislation** *(May Subd Geog)*
— **Lodges**
— **Religious aspects**
— — **Baptists, ⌜Catholic Church, etc.⌝**
— — **Buddhism, ⌜Christianity, etc.⌝**
— — **Catholic Church**
— **Rituals**
— **Symbolism**
BT Symbolism

1433

Freemasonry, Afro-American
  USE Afro-American freemasonry
Freemasons *(May Subd Geog)*
    ₍HS351-929₎
  UF Masons (Secret order)
  RT Freemasonry
  SA *subdivision* Freemasonry *under names*
      of persons
  — Charities
      ₍HS471₎
Freemasons, Afro-American
  USE Afro-American freemasons
Freemen *(May Subd Geog)*
  BT Citizenship
      Municipal government
Freemen (American colonies)
  BT New England—Politics and
      government—Colonial period, ca.
      1600-1775
Freemen (Greek law)
Freemen (Roman law)
Freemon family
  USE Freeman family
Freer Medal
  USE Charles Lang Freer Medal
Freerks family *(Not Subd Geog)*
Frees family
  USE Freese family
Freese family *(Not Subd Geog)*
  UF Frease family
      Frees family
      Freesen family
      Freeze family
      Freezy family
  RT Fries family
Freesen family
  USE Freese family
Freesia
    ₍QK495.I75₎
  BT Iridaceae
Freestyle stroke (Swimming)
  USE Swimming—Crawl stroke
Freethought
  USE Free thought
Freeway airspace utilization
  USE Express highways—Airspace utilization
Freeway driving
  USE Automobile driving on highways
Freeways
  USE Express highways
Freeze-dried food
  USE Food, Freeze-dried
Freeze-drying
  UF Lyophilization
  BT Cryobiology
      Drying apparatus
      Refrigeration and refrigerating
          machinery
      Sublimation (Chemistry)
  NT Food, Freeze-dried
Freeze-etching
    ₍QH231₎
  BT Microscope and microscopy—
      Technique
Freeze family
  USE Freese family
Freeze fracture replication
  USE Freeze fracturing
Freeze fracturing
    ₍QH236.2₎
  UF Freeze fracture replication
  BT Electron microscopy—Technique
      Histology—Technique
Freezers, Home
  USE Home freezers
Freezing
  USE Cryobiology
      Frost
      Ice
      Plants, Effect of cold on

Refrigeration and refrigerating
    machinery
  Soil freezing
  Temperature—Physiological effect
  Water-pipes—Freezing
Freezing and opening of rivers, lakes, etc.
  USE Ice on rivers, lakes, etc.
Freezing fish at sea
  USE Fishing boats—Refrigeration
Freezing of corn
  USE Corn, Frozen
Freezing of drugs
  USE Drugs, Frozen
Freezing of food
  USE Food, Frozen
Freezing of human bodies
  USE Cryonics
Freezing of semen
  USE Semen, Frozen
Freezing points
    ₍QD545₎
  NT Anti-freeze solutions
Freezing points of solutions
  USE Cryoscopy
      Molecular weights
Freezing precipitation *(May Subd Geog)*
  BT Precipitation (Meteorology)
  RT Icing (Meteorology)
  NT Glaze (Meteorology)
      Ice fog
Freezing process (Civil engineering)
  USE Soil freezing
Freezing process (Saline water conversion)
  USE Saline water conversion—Freezing
      process
Freezing process (Water purification)
  USE Water—Purification—Freezing process
Freezy family
  USE Freese family
Fregatidae
  USE Frigate-birds
Fregellae (Ancient city) *(Not Subd Geog)*
    ₍DG70.F73₎
  BT Cities and towns, Ruined, extinct, etc.
      —Italy
      Italy—Antiquities
Fregilupus *(May Subd Geog)*
    ₍QL676.8₎
  BT Birds, Extinct
Frei family
  USE Frye family
Freiberg am Kärpf (Switzerland)
  UF Freiberg Kärpf (Switzerland)
  BT Natural areas—Switzerland
Freiberg family
  USE Friberg family
Freiberg Kärpf (Switzerland)
  USE Freiberg am Kärpf (Switzerland)
Freiberger family
  USE Friberg family
Freibig family
  USE Treybig family
Freiburg i. B., Battle of, 1644
    ₍D267.F85₎
  BT Thirty Years' War, 1618-1648
Freie family
  USE Frye family
Freight-absorption system
  USE Delivered pricing
Freight and freightage *(May Subd Geog)*
    ₍HE593-HE597 (Shipping)₎
    ₍HE2301-HE2500 (Railroads)₎
  UF Affreightment
      Cargo
      Freight handling
      Transportation—Freight

  BT Carriers
      Commerce
      Contracts, Maritime
      Maritime law
      Materials handling
      Railroads
      Transportation
  RT Railroads—Freight
      Tonnage
  NT Aeronautics, Commercial—Freight
      Bills of lading
      Cargo theft
      Charter-parties
      Containerization
      Demurrage
      Electric railroads—Freight
      Freight forwarders
      Inland water transportation—Freight
          traffic
      Insurance, Freight
      Lighterage
      Refrigerated transport
      Seatrains
      Stowage
      Tare
      Truck terminals
      Trucking
  — Claims
      ₍HE1795₎
    UF Claims, Freight
  — Classification
    UF Freight classification
    BT Commercial products—
        Classification
    SA *subdivision* Freight classification
        under means of transportation,
        e.g. Railroads—Freight
        classification
  — Rates
    UF Freight rates
  — Tables
      ₍TF664₎
    UF Freight and freightage—Tables and
        ready-reckoners
  — Tables and ready-reckoners
    USE Freight and freightage—Tables
  — Taxation *(May Subd Geog)*
    BT Transportation—Taxation
Freight-car service
  USE Demurrage (Car service)
      Railroads—Freight
      Railroads—Freight-cars
Freight-cars
  USE Railroads—Freight-cars
Freight-cars on truck trailers
  UF Truck trailers, Freight cars on
  BT Piggyback transportation
      Railroads—Freight
      Transportation, Automotive
Freight classification
  USE *subdivision* Freight classification *under*
      means of transportation, e.g.
      Railroads—Freight classification
      Freight and freightage—Classification
Freight forwarders *(May Subd Geog)*
  UF Forwarders, Freight
      Forwarding agents
      Forwarding merchants
  BT Bailments
      Commercial law
      Freight and freightage
      Hire
      Shipping
  RT Carriers
  NT Ocean freight forwarders
Freight handling
  USE Freight and freightage
      Railroads—Freight
Freight insurance
  USE Insurance, Freight

Freight planes
  USE Transport planes
Freight rates
  USE *subdivision* Rates *under means of*
      transportation, e.g. Railroads—Rates
      Freight and freightage—Rates
Freight ships
  USE Cargo ships
Freight vessels
  USE Cargo ships
Freighters
  USE Cargo ships
Freiligrath family *(Not Subd Geog)*
Freiling family *(Not Subd Geog)*
  UF Freyling family
      Friling family
      Frilingk family
Freland family
  USE Freeland family
Freman family
  USE Freeman family
Fremont culture
Frémont House (Tucson, Ariz.)
  UF Casa del Gobernador (Tucson, Ariz.)
      John Charles Frémont House (Tucson,
      Ariz.)
  BT Dwellings—Arizona
French *(May Subd Geog)*
  BT Ethnology—France
      France
— **Algeria**
  RT Pieds-Noirs
— **Foreign countries**
  ₍DC33.9₎
  UF French in foreign countries
— **Italy**
  NT Rome (Italy)—History—Revolution
      of 1848-1849—Participation,
      French
— **Soviet Union**
  BT Émigrés
— **United States**
  BT Émigrés
  NT French Americans
French abbreviations
  USE Abbreviations, French
French adventure stories
  USE Adventure stories, French
French aesthetics
  USE Aesthetics, French
French agricultural assistance
  USE Agricultural assistance, French
French-Algerian War, 1954-1962
  USE Algeria—History—Revolution, 1954-
      1962
French alien labor
  USE Alien labor, French
French almanacs
  USE Almanacs, French
French Alps (France)
  USE Alps, French (France)
French-American literature
  (May Subd Geog)
  UF American literature (French)
      French literature—American authors
  BT French literature
French-American newspapers
  ₍PN4885.F72₎
  BT American newspapers
      French newspapers
French-American periodicals
  ₍PN4885.F72₎
  BT American periodicals
      French periodicals
French-American poetry *(May Subd Geog)*
  UF American poetry (French)
      French poetry—American authors
  BT French poetry
— **Creole authors**
  UF Creole poetry (French-American)

French Americans *(May Subd Geog)*
  UF French Americans—United States
  BT Ethnology—United States
      French—United States
— United States
  USE French Americans
French and Indian War
  USE United States—History—French and
      Indian War, 1755-1763
French anonymous writings
  USE Anonymous writings, French
French anonyms and pseudonyms
  USE Anonyms and pseudonyms, French
French architecture
  USE Architecture, French
French art
  USE Art, French
French arts
  USE Arts, French
French atlases
  USE Atlases, French
French authors
  USE Authors, French
French autobiographical fiction
  USE Autobiographical fiction, French
French ballads
  USE Ballads, French
French banks and banking
  USE Banks and banking, French
French Bible stories
  USE Bible stories, French
French book-plates
  USE Book-plates, French
French bronze sculpture
  USE Bronze sculpture, French
French bulldogs
  ₍S429.F8₎
  BT Bulldogs
French-Canadian aged, Writings of the
  USE Aged, Writings of the, French-
      Canadian
French-Canadian alien labor
  USE Alien labor, French-Canadian
French-Canadian art
  USE Art, French-Canadian
French-Canadian arts
  USE Arts, French-Canadian
French-Canadian authors
  USE Authors, French-Canadian
French-Canadian children's literature
  USE Children's literature, French-Canadian
French-Canadian college verse
  USE College verse, French-Canadian
French-Canadian detective stories
  USE Detective and mystery stories, French-
      Canadian
French-Canadian dialect
  USE French language—Canada
French-Canadian drama *(May Subd Geog)*
  ₍PQ3911 (History)₎
  ₍PQ3916 (Collections)₎
  NT One-act plays, French-Canadian
French-Canadian espionage stories
  USE Spy stories, French-Canadian
French-Canadian essays *(May Subd Geog)*
  ₍PR3912 (History)₎
  ₍PR3916.D8 (Collections)₎
French-Canadian fantastic fiction
  USE Fantastic fiction, French-Canadian
French-Canadian fiction
  ₍PQ3912 (History)₎
  ₍PQ3916.F (Collections)₎
  NT Detective and mystery stories, French-
      Canadian
      Fantastic fiction, French-Canadian
      Historical fiction, French-Canadian
      Humorous stories, French-Canadian
      Political fiction, French-Canadian
      Science fiction, French-Canadian
      Short stories, French-Canadian
      Spy stories, French-Canadian

French-Canadian haiku
  USE Haiku, French-Canadian
French-Canadian historical fiction
  USE Historical fiction, French-Canadian
French-Canadian humorous stories
  USE Humorous stories, French-Canadian
French-Canadian letters *(May Subd Geog)*
  ₍PQ3912 (History)₎
  ₍PQ3916 (Collections)₎
  BT Letters
French-Canadian literature
  (May Subd Geog)
  ₍PQ3900-PQ3912 (History)₎
  ₍PQ3913-PQ3916 (Collections)₎
  UF French literature—Canada
  BT Canadian literature
      French literature
  NT Children's literature, French-Canadian
      Mentally ill, Writings of the, French-
      Canadian
— **20th century**
French-Canadian love poetry
  USE Love poetry, French-Canadian
French-Canadian manuscripts
  USE Manuscripts, French-Canadian
French-Canadian mystery stories
  USE Detective and mystery stories, French-
      Canadian
French-Canadian newspapers
  (May Subd Geog)
  BT Canadian newspapers
French-Canadian novelists
  USE Novelists, French-Canadian
French-Canadian one-act plays
  USE One-act plays, French-Canadian
French-Canadian paleography
  USE Paleography, French-Canadian
French-Canadian periodicals
  (May Subd Geog)
  BT French periodicals
  NT Women's periodicals, French-Canadian
French-Canadian poetry *(May Subd Geog)*
  ₍PQ3912 (History)₎
  ₍PQ3916 (Collections)₎
  BT Canadian poetry
      French poetry
  NT College verse, French-Canadian
      Haiku, French-Canadian
      Sonnets, French-Canadian
      War poetry, French-Canadian
French-Canadian poets
  USE Poets, French-Canadian
French-Canadian political fiction
  USE Political fiction, French-Canadian
French-Canadian prisoners' writings
  USE Prisoners's writings, French-Canadian
French-Canadian prose literature
  (May Subd Geog)
  ₍PQ3912 (History)₎
  ₍PQ3916 (Collections)₎
  BT Canadian prose literature
French-Canadian proverbs
  USE Proverbs, French-Canadian
French-Canadian science fiction
  USE Science fiction, French-Canadian
French-Canadian short stories
  USE Short stories, French-Canadian
French-Canadian sonnets
  USE Sonnets, French-Canadian
French-Canadian spy stories
  USE Spy stories, French-Canadian
French-Canadian students *(May Subd Geog)*
  BT Students
French-Canadian war poetry
  USE War poetry, French-Canadian
French-Canadian wit and humor
  (May Subd Geog)
  ₍PN6178.C3 (Collections)₎
  ₍PQ3912 (History)₎
  NT Humorous stories, French-Canadian

French-Canadian wit and humor, Pictorial
  (May Subd Geog)
French-Canadian women novelists
  USE Women novelists, French-Canadian
French-Canadian women's periodicals
  USE Women's periodicals, French-Canadian
French-Canadian writings of the mentally ill
  USE Mentally ill, Writings of the, French-
       Canadian
French-Canadians *(May Subd Geog)*
  ⌈F1027⌉
  BT Canadians
  NT Acadians
      Canada—English-French relations
      Canada—History—Rebellion, 1837-
        1838
      Missions to French-Canadians
  — **Intellectual life**
French Canal (Panama)
  UF Canal Francés (Panama)
      Canal French (Panama)
  BT Canals—Panama
French-Candian youth
  USE Youth, French-Canadian
French Catholic nonjurors
  USE Nonjurors, French Catholic
French chap-books
  USE Chap-books, French
French children's encyclopedias and
    dictionaries
  USE Children's encyclopedias and
       dictionaries, French
French children's literature
  USE Children's literature, French
French children's plays
  USE Children's plays, French
French children's stories
  USE Children's stories, French
French children's writings
  USE Children's writings, French
French Christian literature
  USE Christian literature, French
French Christian poetry
  USE Christian poetry, French
French civics
  USE Civics, French
French clover
  USE Alfalfa
French coins
  USE Coins, French
French college and school drama
  USE College and school drama, French
French college prose
  USE College prose, French
French college verse
  USE College verse, French
French color prints
  USE Color prints, French
French commercial correspondence
  USE Commercial correspondence, French
French complaint poetry
  USE Complaint poetry, French
French cookery
  USE Cookery, French
French corporations
  USE Corporations, French
French Cree language
  USE Michif language
French Creek State Park (Pa.)
  BT Parks—Pennsylvania
French Creole children's stories, Mauritian
  USE Children's stories, Mauritian (French
       Creole)
French Creole fiction, Mauritian
  USE Mauritian fiction (French Creole)
French Creole fiction, Réunion
  USE Réunion fiction (French Creole)
French Creole languages
  USE Creole dialects, French
French Creole literature, Haitian
  USE Haitian literature (French Creole)

French Creole literature, Martinique
  USE Martinique literature (French Creole)
French Creole literature, Réunion
  USE Réunion literature (French Creole)
French Creole poetry
  USE Creole poetry, French
French Creole poetry, Guadeloupe
  USE Guadeloupe poetry (French Creole)
French Creole poetry, Haitian
  USE Haitian poetry (French Creole)
French Creole poetry, Réunion
  USE Réunion poetry (French Creole)
French Creole short stories, Réunion
  USE Short stories, Réunion (French Creole)
French crescent rolls
  USE Croissants
French criminals' writings
  USE Criminals' writings, French
French detective stories
  USE Detective and mystery stories, French
French dialect, Louisiana
  USE Cajun French dialect
French dialect literature
  USE Dialect literature, French
French dialogues
  USE Dialogues, French
French diaries
  ⌈PQ1284 (Collections)⌉
  BT Diaries
French didactic drama
  USE Didactic drama, French
French didactic fiction
  USE Didactic fiction, French
French didactic literature
  USE Didactic literature, French
French Directory, 1795-1799
  USE France—History—Revolution, 1795-
       1799
French document writing
  USE Document writing, French
French domestic fiction
  USE Domestic fiction, French
French drama *(May Subd Geog)*
  ⌈PQ500-PQ591 (History)⌉
  ⌈PQ1211-PQ1241 (Collections)⌉
  BT Drama
  NT Children's plays, French
      College and school drama, French
      Didactic drama, French
      Historical drama, French
      Moralities, French
      Mysteries and miracle-plays, French
      Pastoral drama, French
      Radio plays, French
      Religious drama, French
  — **To 1500**
      ⌈PQ511-PQ515 (History)⌉
      ⌈PQ1341-PQ1385 (Collections)⌉
  — **16th century**
      ⌈PQ521-PQ523 (History)⌉
      ⌈PQ1219 (Collections)⌉
  — **17th century**
      ⌈PQ526-PQ528 (History)⌉
      ⌈PQ1220 (Collections)⌉
  — **18th century**
      ⌈PQ536-PQ538 (History)⌉
      ⌈PQ1221 (Collections)⌉
  — **19th century**
      ⌈PQ541-PQ553 (History)⌉
      ⌈PQ1222 (Collections)⌉
  — **20th century**
      ⌈PQ556-PQ558 (History)⌉
      ⌈PQ1223 (Collections)⌉
  — African authors
      USE African drama (French)
  — Algerian authors
      USE Algerian drama (French)
  — **Belgian authors**
      ⌈PQ3830 (History)⌉
      ⌈PQ3846 (Collections)⌉
  — Caribbean authors

      USE Caribbean drama (French)
  — Haitian authors
      USE Haitian drama
French drama (Comedy)
  ⌈PQ566-PQ568 (History)⌉
  ⌈PQ1229-PQ1231 (Collections)⌉
  BT Comedy
French drama (Tragedy)
  ⌈PQ561-PQ563 (History)⌉
  ⌈PQ1227 (Collections)⌉
  BT Tragedy
French dramatists
  USE Dramatists, French
French economic assistance
  USE Economic assistance, French
French economic sanctions
  USE Economic sanctions, French
French emblem books
  USE Emblem books, French
French empresses
  USE France—Empresses
French encyclopedias and dictionaries
  USE Encyclopedias and dictionaries, French
French endive
  USE Belgian endive
French-English War . . .
  USE *subject headings beginning with the*
       words Anglo-French War
French engraving
  USE Engraving, French
French epic literature
  USE Epic literature, French
French epic poetry
  USE Epic poetry, French
French epigrams
  USE Epigrams, French
French Equatorial Africa
  USE Africa, French-speaking Equatorial
French erotic literature
  USE Erotic literature, French
French erotic painting
  USE Erotic painting, French
French erotic poetry
  USE Erotic poetry, French
French erotic stories
  USE Erotic stories, French
French essays
  ⌈PQ731 (History)⌉
  ⌈PQ1290-PQ1291 (Collections)⌉
  Here are entered collections of essays by several
  authors.
  BT Essays
French etching
  USE Etching, French
French Expedition to Ireland, 1796-1797
  UF Bantry Bay Expedition, 1796-1797
      Brest Expedition, 1796-1797
  BT France—History—1789-1815
      Great Britain—History—Invasions
      Ireland—History—1760-1820
French Expedition to Jersey, 1781
  USE Jersey, Battle of, 1781
French Expedition to Wales, 1797
  BT France—History—1789-1815
      Great Britain—History—Invasions
      Wales—History
French fables
  USE Fables, French
French fairy poetry
  USE Fairy poetry, French
French family *(Not Subd Geog)*
French fantastic fiction
  USE Fantastic fiction, French
French fantastic literature
  USE Fantastic literature, French
French farces
  ⌈PQ584 (History)⌉
  ⌈PQ1237.F2 (Collections)⌉
  BT Farces

French Farm Lake Site (Mich.)
  (Not Subd Geog)
  BT Farms—Michigan
      Michigan—Antiquities
French feuilletons
  USE Feuilletons, French
French fiction *(May Subd Geog)*
  [PQ631-PQ671 (History)]
  [PQ1261-PQ1279 (Collections)]
  NT Adventure stories, French
      Autobiographical fiction, French
      Children's stories, French
      Detective and mystery stories, French
      Didactic fiction, French
      Domestic fiction, French
      Erotic stories, French
      Fantastic fiction, French
      Historical fiction, French
      Horror tales, French
      Humorous stories, French
      Love stories, French
      Pastoral fiction, French
      Picaresque literature, French
      Sea stories, French
      Short stories, French
      Spy stories, French
      Young adult fiction, French
  — **To 1500**
    [PQ221 (History)]
    [PQ1391 (Collections)]
  — **16th century**
    [PQ643 (History)]
    [PQ1266 (Collections)]
  — **17th century**
    [PQ645 (History)]
    [PQ1267 (Collections)]
  — **18th century**
    [PQ648 (History)]
    [PQ1268 (Collections)]
  — **19th century**
    [PQ651-PQ661 (History)]
    [PQ1269 (Collections)]
  — **20th century**
    [PQ671 (History)]
    [PQ1271 (Collections)]
  — African authors
    USE African fiction (French)
  — Algerian authors
    USE Algerian fiction (French)
  — **Belgian authors**
    [PQ3842 (History)]
    [PQ3848 (Collections)]
    Duplicate entry is made under Belgian fiction
    (French).
  — **British influences**
    BT Great Britain—Civilization
  — Cameroon authors
    USE Cameroon fiction (French)
  — Caribbean authors
    USE Caribbean fiction (French)
  — French Guiana authors
    USE French Guiana fiction (French)
  — Guadeloupe authors
    USE Guadeloupe fiction (French)
  — Haitian authors
    USE Haitian fiction
  — Ivory Coast authors
    USE Ivory Coast fiction (French)
  — Martinique authors
    USE Martinique fiction (French)
  — Mauritian authors
    USE Mauritian fiction (French)
  — Niger authors
    USE Niger fiction (French)
  — Nigerien authors
    USE Niger fiction (French)
  — North African authors
    USE North African fiction (French)
  — Réunion authors
    USE Réunion fiction (French)
  — Senegalese authors

    USE Senegalese fiction (French)
  — Vietnamese authors
    USE Vietnamese fiction (French)
  — West African authors
    USE West African fiction (French)
  — West Indian authors
    USE West Indian fiction (French)
French Fifth Republic
  USE France—History—1958-
      France—Politics and government—
      1958-
French film posters
  USE Film posters, French
French folk literature
  USE Folk literature, French
French folk-songs
  USE Folk-songs, French
French franc area
  UF Franc area, French
      Zone franc
  BT Currency question
      Foreign exchange problem
      Monetary unions
French gardens
  USE Gardens, French
French genre painting
  USE Genre painting, French
French Guiana
  BT Guiana
  — **Description and travel**
  — — **1951-1980** *(Not Subd Geog)*
  — — **1981-** *(Not Subd Geog)*
  — **History**
  — — **To 1814**
  — — **1814-1947**
  — — **1947-**
  — **Languages**
    NT Oyampi language
      Palicur language
  — **Politics and government**
  — — **To 1814**
  — — **1814-1947**
  — — **1947-**
French Guiana fiction (French)
  UF French fiction—French Guiana
      authors
French Guiana literature (French)
  (May Subd Geog)
  UF French literature—French Guiana
      authors
French Guiana poets
  USE Poets, French Guiana
French Guinea
  USE Guinea
French haiku
  USE Haiku, French
French Hindu hymns
  USE Hindu hymns, French
French historical drama
  USE Historical drama, French
French historical fiction
  USE Historical fiction, French
French horn
  USE Horn (Musical instrument)
French horror tales
  USE Horror tales, French
French humorous poetry
  USE Humorous poetry, French
French humorous stories
  USE Humorous stories, French
French hymns
  USE Hymns, French
French illumination of books and manuscripts
  USE Illumination of books and manuscripts,
      French
French imprints *(May Subd Geog)*
  UF Imprints (Publications)
  — **Translations from Spanish**
French in foreign countries
  USE French—Foreign countries

French Indochina
  USE Indochina
French Invasion of Ireland, 1798
  USE Ireland—History—Rebellion of 1798
French invasion of Madagascar, 1895
  USE Madagascar—History—French
      invasion, 1895
French investments
  USE Investments, French
French laboring class writings
  USE Laboring class writings, French
French landscape prints
  USE Landscape prints, French
French language *(May Subd Geog)*
  [PC2001-3761]
  UF Langue d'oïl
  NT Cajun French dialect
  — **To 1500**
    [PC2801-2896]
    UF French language—Old French
      language
      Old French language
  — **Early modern, 1500-1700**
    [PC2201-PC2693]
    [PC2901-PC2908]
  — — **Vocabulary**
  — Abbreviations
    USE Abbreviations, French
  — **Acronyms**
  — **Business French**
    [HF5728.F8 (Correspondence)]
    [PC2120.C6]
  — Canadianisms, French
    USE Canadianisms, French
  — **Conversation and phrase books**
  — — **English**
  — **Dialects**
    NT Dialect literature, French
  — — **Canada**
    NT Canadianisms, French
  — **Dictionaries**
    NT Picture dictionaries, French
  — **Epithets**
  — **Etymology**
    NT Coeur (The French word)
      Comme (The French word)
      Comment (The French word)
      Et (The French word)
      Faire (The French word)
      Ferir (The French word)
      Frapper (The French word)
      Galant (The French word)
      Homme (The French word)
      Ire (The French word)
      Mettre (The French word)
      Sang (The French word)
      Si (The French word)
  — — **Names**
  — **Figures of speech**
  — **Films for English speakers**
  — **Gerundive**
    [PC2312]
  — **Grammar**
  — **Lexicology**
  — **Medical French**
    UF Medical French
    BT Medicine—Language
      Medicine—Terminology
  — Old French language
    USE French language—To 1500
  — **Orthography and spelling**
  — **Phonetics**
  — **Readers**
  — — **Civilization, Geography, [etc.]**
  — — **Science**
  — — **Science fiction**
  — **Readers for new literates**
  — **Rhetoric**
  — Scientific French
    USE French language—Technical
      French

French language (Continued)
— **Semantics**
— **Slang**
— **Technical French**
    UF French language—Scientific French
        Scientific French
        Technical French
    BT Technical writing
        Technology—Language
— **Terms and phrases**
    NT Gallicisms
— **Text-books for foreign speakers**
— — **English**
— **Vocabulary**
    NT Gallicisms
— **Writing**
    NT Document writing, French
— **Canada**
        Here are entered works on the French language in Canada as a whole. Its history, structure, orthography, pronunciation, etc. are indicated by addition of a second subject heading under French language with appropriate subdivision. Works dealing with the usage of words and idiomatic expressions peculiar to Canada are entered under Canadianisms, French.
    UF French-Canadian dialect
French letter-writing
  USE Letter-writing, French
French letters
    ₍PQ711 (History)₎
    ₍PQ1285-PQ1288 (Collections)₎
    BT Letters
    NT Anglo-Norman letters
French literature *(May Subd Geog)*
    ₍PQ1-PQ841 (History)₎
    ₍PQ1101-PQ1297 (Collections)₎
    NT Anonymous writings, French
        Belgian literature
        Children's literature, French
        Children's writings, French
        Christian literature, French
        Corsican literature
        Criminals' writings, French
        Dialect literature, French
        Didactic literature, French
        Encyclopedists
        Epic literature, French
        Erotic literature, French
        Fantastic literature, French
        Folk literature, French
        French-American literature
        French-Canadian literature
        Laboring class writings, French
        Pastoral literature, French
        Provençal literature
        Revolutionary literature, French
        Swiss literature
        Young adult literature, French
— **To 1500**
    ₍PQ151-PQ221 (History)₎
    ₍PQ1300-PQ1391 (Collections)₎
    UF Old French literature
    NT Anglo-Norman literature
— **16th century**
    ₍PQ230-PQ239 (History)₎
    ₍PQ1121-PQ1125 (Collections)₎
    NT Pléiade
— **17th century**
    ₍PQ241-PQ251 (History)₎
    ₍PQ1126-PQ1130 (Collections)₎
    NT Ancients and moderns, Quarrel of
        Précieuses
— **18th century**
    ₍PQ261-PQ276 (History)₎
    ₍PQ1131-PQ1135 (Collections)₎
    NT Ancients and moderns, Quarrel of
— **19th century**
    ₍PQ281-PQ299 (History)₎
    ₍PQ1136-PQ1139 (Collections)₎
— **20th century**
    ₍PQ301-PQ307 (History)₎

    ₍PQ1141 (Collections)₎
— African authors
  USE African literature (French)
— Algerian authors
  USE Algerian literature (French)
— American authors
  USE French-American literature
— **Belgian authors**
    ₍PQ3810-PQ3838 (History)₎
    ₍PQ3840-PQ3853 (Collections)₎
    UF Belgian literature (French)
— Benin authors
  USE Benin literature (French)
— **Bibliography**
    ₍Z2161-2189₎
— — **Early**
    ₍Z2162₎
    ₍Z2172₎
— **Black authors**
    UF Black literature (French)
— Cameroon authors
  USE Cameroon literature (French)
— Caribbean authors
  USE Caribbean literature (French)
— **Competitions**
    NT Prix Goncourt
— Congo (Brazzaville) authors
  USE Congo (Brazzaville) literature
      (French)
— Egyptian authors
  USE Egyptian literature, Modern
      (French)
— **English influences**
    BT England—Civilization
— **Foreign authors**
— French Guiana authors
  USE French Guiana literature
      (French)
— Gabon authors
  USE Gabon literature (French)
— Haitian authors
  USE Haitian literature
— Ivory Coast authors
  USE Ivory Coast literature (French)
— **Jewish authors**
    UF Jewish literature (French)
— Lebanese authors
  USE Lebanese literature (French)
— **Libyan authors**
    UF Libyan literature
— Malagasy authors
  USE Malagasy literature (French)
— Martinique authors
  USE Martinique literature (French)
— Mauritian authors
  USE Mauritian literature (French)
— Moroccan authors
  USE Moroccan literature (French)
— North African authors
  USE North African literature (French)
— **North Vietnamese authors**
    UF North Vietnamese literature
      (French)
— **Protestant authors**
— Réunion authors
  USE Réunion literature (French)
— Senegalese authors
  USE Senegalese literature (French)
— **Swiss authors** *(May Subd Geog)*
    UF Swiss literature (French)
— **Translations into English**
— Tunisian authors
  USE Tunisian literature (French)
— West Indian authors
  USE West Indian literature (French)
— Zairian authors
  USE Zairian literature (French)
— Canada
  USE French-Canadian literature
— **Foreign countries**
    ₍PQ3809₎

    UF French literature in foreign
        countries
French literature in foreign countries
  USE French literature—Foreign countries
French lithography
  USE Lithography, French
French loans
  USE Loans, French
French love poetry
  USE Love poetry, French
French love stories
  USE Love stories, French
French lullabies
  USE Lullabies, French
French manuscripts
  USE Manuscripts, French
French maxims
  USE Maxims, French
French medals
  USE Medals, French
French medical assistance
  USE Medical assistance, French
French metal sculpture
  USE Metal sculpture, French
French military assistance
  USE Military assistance, French
French miniature painting
  USE Miniature painting, French
French miracle-plays
  USE Mysteries and miracle-plays, French
French missions
  USE Missions, French
French monarchy
  USE Monarchy—France
French monologues
  USE Monologues, French
French moving-picture cartoons
  USE Moving-picture cartoons, French
French mysteries and miracle-plays
  USE Mysteries and miracle-plays, French
French mystery stories
  USE Detective and mystery stories, French
French narrative art
  USE Narrative art, French
French narrative painting
  USE Narrative painting, French
French narrative poetry
  USE Narrative poetry, French
French national characteristics
  USE National characteristics, French
French newspapers *(May Subd Geog)*
    ₍PN5171-PN5189 (History)₎
    BT Newspapers
    NT French-American newspapers
— **Circulation**
— **Foreign language press**
    UF Foreign language press, French
    BT Ethnic press—France
— **Sections, columns, etc.**
    BT Newspapers—Sections, columns,
        etc.
French newspapers (Belgian)
  USE Belgian newspapers
French newspapers (Swiss)
  USE Swiss newspapers
French novelists
  USE Novelists, French
French nuclear weapons information
  USE Nuclear weapons information, French
French orations
  USE Speeches, addresses, etc., French
French painting
  USE Painting, French
French paleography
  USE Paleography, French
French parodies
  USE Parodies, French
French part-songs
  USE Part-songs, French
French pastel drawing
  USE Pastel drawing, French

French pastoral drama
  USE Pastoral drama, French
French pastoral fiction
  USE Pastoral fiction, French
French pastoral literature
  USE Pastoral literature, French
French pastoral poetry
  USE Pastoral poetry, French
French patriotic poetry
  USE Patriotic poetry, French
French periodicals *(May Subd Geog)*
  [PN5171-PN5190 (History)]
  BT Periodicals
  NT French-American periodicals
    French-Canadian periodicals
    Women's periodicals, French
  — Foreign language press
    BT Ethnic press—France
    RT Foreign language periodicals,
      French
  — Foreign countries
    UF French periodicals in foreign
      countries
French periodicals (Belgian)
  USE Belgian periodicals
French periodicals (Swiss)
  USE Swiss periodicals
French periodicals in foreign countries
  USE French periodicals—Foreign countries
French philology *(May Subd Geog)*
  [PC2001-2071]
French picaresque literature
  USE Picaresque literature, French
French picture dictionaries
  USE Picture dictionaries, French
French poetry *(May Subd Geog)*
  [PQ400-PQ491 (History)]
  [PQ1161-PQ1201 (Collections)]
  BT Poetry
  NT Chansons de geste
    Christian poetry, French
    College verse, French
    Complaint poetry, French
    Epic poetry, French
    Erotic poetry, French
    Fairy poetry, French
    French-American poetry
    French-Canadian poetry
    Haiku, French
    Humorous poetry, French
    Lays
    Love poetry, French
    Narrative poetry, French
    Pastoral poetry, French
    Patriotic poetry, French
    Political poetry, French
    Religious poetry, French
    Renga, French
    Revolutionary poetry, French
    Romances
    School verse, French
    Sea poetry, French
    Sonnets, French
    Troubadours
    Trouvères
    Visual poetry, French
    War poetry, French
  — To 1500
    [PQ151-PQ216 (History)]
    [PQ1300-PQ1391 (Collections)]
    UF Old French poetry
    BT Trouvères
    NT Anglo-Norman poetry
      Fabliaux
      Rhétoriqueurs (Group of poets)
      Rondeaus
  — 16th century
    [PQ416-PQ418 (History)]
    [PQ1173 (Collections)]
    NT Pléiade
      Rhétoriqueurs (Group of poets)

  — 17th century
    [PQ421-PQ423 (History)]
    [PQ1175 (Collections)]
  — 18th century
    [PQ426-PQ428 (History)]
    [PQ1177 (Collections)]
  — 19th century
    [PQ431-PQ439 (History)]
    [PQ1181-PQ1183 (Collections)]
    NT Parnassianism
  — 20th century
    [PQ441-PQ443 (History)]
    [PQ1184 (Collections)]
  — African authors
    USE African poetry (French)
  — Algerian authors
    USE Algerian poetry (French)
  — Alsatian authors
    UF Alsatian poetry (French)
  — American authors
    USE French-American poetry
  — Belgian authors *(May Subd Geog)*
    [PQ3826-PQ3829 (History)]
    [PQ3843 (Collections)]
    UF Belgian poetry (French)
    NT Prix Max Rose de poésie
  — Benin authors
    USE Benin poetry (French)
  — Black authors
    UF Black poetry (French)
  — Burkinabe authors
    USE Burkinabe poetry (French)
  — Cameroon authors
    USE Cameroon poetry (French)
  — Congo (Brazzaville) authors
    USE Congo (Brazzaville) poetry
      (French)
  — East Cameroon authors
    UF East Cameroon poetry (French)
  — Egyptian authors
    USE Egyptian poetry, Modern
      (French)
  — Guadeloupe authors
    USE Guadeloupe poetry (French)
  — Guinean authors
    USE Guinean poetry (French)
  — Haitian authors
    USE Haitian poetry
  — Malagasy authors
    USE Malagasy poetry (French)
  — Martinique authors
    USE Martinique poetry (French)
  — Mauritian authors
    USE Mauritian poetry (French)
  — Moroccan authors
    USE Moroccan poetry (French)
  — Niger authors
    USE Niger poetry (French)
  — Nigerien authors
    USE Niger poetry (French)
  — North African authors
    USE North African poetry (French)
  — Réunion authors
    USE Réunion poetry (French)
  — Swiss authors *(May Subd Geog)*
    UF Swiss poetry (French)
  — Togolese authors
    USE Togolese poetry (French)
  — Tunisian authors
    USE Tunisian poetry (French)
  — West Indian authors
    USE West Indian poetry (French)
  — Women authors
  — Zairian authors
    USE Zairian poetry (French)
French political poetry
  USE Political poetry, French
French political posters
  USE Political posters, French
French political satire
  USE Political satire, French

French portrait drawing
  USE Portrait drawing, French
French portrait painting
  USE Portrait painting, French
French portrait sculpture
  USE Portrait sculpture, French
French portraits
  USE Portraits, French
French posters
  USE Posters, French
French prints
  USE Prints, French
French prisoners' writings
  USE Prisoners' writings, French
French propaganda
  USE Propaganda, French
French property *(May Subd Geog)*
  UF Property, French
  BT Alien property
  — Foreign countries
French prose literature
  [PQ601-PQ771 (History)]
  [PQ1243-PQ1297 (Collections)]
  NT College prose, French
  — To 1500
    [PQ607 (History, PQ221)]
    [PQ1391 (Collections)]
  — West Indian authors
    USE West Indian prose literature
      (French)
French Protestants
  USE Huguenots
French proverbs
  USE Proverbs, French
French radio plays
  USE Radio plays, French
French relief (Sculpture)
  USE Relief (Sculpture), French
French religious drama
  USE Religious drama, French
French religious poetry
  USE Religious poetry, French
French religious satire
  USE Religious satire, French
French renga
  USE Renga, French
French Retrieval Automated Network for
  Current Information in Social and Human
  Sciences (Information retrieval system)
  USE FRANCIS (Information retrieval
    system)
French Revolution
  USE France—History—Revolution, 1789-
    1799
French revolutionary literature
  USE Revolutionary literature, French
French revolutionary poetry
  USE Revolutionary poetry, French
French reweaving
  USE Reweaving
French River (Mass. and Conn.)
  BT Rivers—Connecticut
    Rivers—Massachusetts
French Riviera (France)
  USE Riviera (France)
French salons
  USE Salons
French satire
  USE Satire, French
French school verse
  USE School verse, French
French sculpture
  USE Sculpture, French
French sea poetry
  USE Sea poetry, French
French sea stories
  USE Sea stories, French
French sermons
  USE Sermons, French
French short stories
  USE Short stories, French

French small art works
    USE Small art works, French
French small painting
    USE Small painting, French
French sociologists (Durkheimian school)
    USE Durkheimian school of sociology
French Somaliland
    USE Djibouti
French songs
    USE Songs, French
French sonnets
    USE Sonnets, French
French-Spanish War, 1635-1659
    USE Franco-Spanish War, 1635-1659
French-Spanish War, 1667-1668
    USE Devolution, War of, 1667-1668
French-speaking Equatorial Africa
    USE Africa, French-speaking Equatorial
French-speaking Switzerland
    USE Switzerland, French-speaking
French-speaking West Africa
    USE Africa, French-speaking West
French speeches
    USE Speeches, addresses, etc., French
French spinach
    USE Orach
French spoliation claims
    [E336]
    [JX238.F72-JX238.F75]
    BT Claims
French spy stories
    USE Spy stories, French
French still-life painting
    USE Still-life painting, French
French students *(May Subd Geog)*
    BT Students
French studies
    USE France—Study and teaching
French subject headings
    USE Subject headings, French
French Sudan
    USE Mali
French surplus agricultural commodities
    USE Surplus agricultural commodities,
        French
French technical assistance
    USE Technical assistance, French
French terra-cotta sculpture
    USE Terra-cotta sculpture, French
French Territory of the Afars and Issas
    USE Djibouti
French visual poetry
    USE Visual poetry, French
French walnut
    USE Walnut, English
French war poetry
    USE War poetry, French
French watercolor painting
    USE Watercolor painting, French
French West Africa
    USE Africa, French-speaking West
French West Indian Expedition, 1790
    BT West Indies, French—History
French West Indies
    USE West Indies, French
French wit and humor *(May Subd Geog)*
    [PN6183-PN6185]
    [PQ751 (History)]
    [PQ1295 (Collections)]
    Here are entered collections from several authors
    and individual authors who have not written in other
    literary forms.
    NT Humorous stories, French
        Political satire, French
French wit and humor, Pictorial
    [NC1490-1499]
French women authors
    USE Women authors, French
French women's periodicals
    USE Women's periodicals, French

French wood-engraving
    USE Wood-engraving, French
French young adult fiction
    USE Young adult fiction, French
French young adult literature
    USE Young adult literature, French
French youths' writings
    USE Youths' writings, French
Frenchman Cap (Tas.)
    USE Frenchmans Cap (Tas.)
Frenchman River (Sask. and Mont.)
    BT Rivers—Montana
        Rivers—Saskatchewan
Frenchmans Cap (Tas.) *(Not Subd Geog)*
    UF Frenchman Cap (Tas.)
    BT Mountains—Australia
Frenchtown, Battle of, 1813
    USE Raisin River, Battle of, 1813
Frennesson family
    USE Frennsson family
Frennson family
    USE Frennsson family
Frennsson family *(Not Subd Geog)*
    UF Frennesson family
        Frennson family
Frens family
    USE Frantz family
Frentani (Italic people) *(May Subd Geog)*
    [DG225.F73]
    BT Ethnology—Italy
        Italic peoples
    RT Oscans
Frenulum labii
    USE Labial frenulum
Frenulum linguae
    USE Lingual frenum
Frenum linguae
    USE Lingual frenum
Frenum of tongue
    USE Lingual frenum
Freon-20
    USE Chloroform
Freon-23
    USE Fluoroform
Frequencies, Langmuir
    USE Plasma frequencies
Frequencies, Plasma
    USE Plasma frequencies
Frequencies, Rainfall
    USE Rainfall frequencies
Frequencies of oscillating systems
    UF Frequencies of vibrating systems
        Frequency analysis (Dynamics)
        Frequency of oscillation
        Frequency of vibration
        Vibration frequencies
    BT Oscillations
        Vibration
    NT Audio frequency
        Doppler effect
        Frequency response (Dynamics)
        Frequency response (Electrical
            engineering)
        Frequency stability
        Plasma frequencies
        Radio frequency
    — Measurement
        [QC661]
        BT Frequency standards
        NT Electric measurements
            Electromagnetic measurements
            Frequency meters
Frequencies of vibrating systems
    USE Frequencies of oscillating systems
Frequency, Maximum usable (Radio)
    USE Maximum usable frequency (Radio)
Frequency, Speech
    USE Voice frequency
Frequency, Voice
    USE Voice frequency

Frequency analysis (Dynamics)
    USE Frequencies of oscillating systems
Frequency changers
    [TK2799]
    UF Frequency converters
    BT Electric current converters
        Electric motors
    NT Frequency dividers
        Frequency multipliers
        Frequency synthesizers
Frequency converters
    USE Frequency changers
Frequency counts of words
    USE *subdivision* Word frequency *under
        individual languages, e.g.* English
        language—Word frequency
        Language and languages—Word
        frequency
Frequency curves
    [HA31]
    BT Correlation (Statistics)
        Curves
        Distribution (Probability theory)
        Probabilities
        Statistics
Frequency detectors
    USE Frequency discriminators
Frequency deviation (Radio frequency
    modulation)
    USE Radio frequency modulation—
        Transmitters and transmission—
        Frequency deviation
Frequency-deviation meters
    UF Meters, Frequency-deviation
    BT Frequency meters
        Radio frequency
        Radio measurements
Frequency discriminators
    [TK6565.D4]
    UF Discriminators, Frequency
        Frequency detectors
    BT Frequency modulation detectors
        Radio detectors
        Radio frequency modulation
Frequency distribution
    USE Distribution (Probability theory)
Frequency dividers
    BT Frequency changers
Frequency effectiveness of advertising
    USE Advertising—Effective frequency
Frequency meters
    UF Meters, Frequency
    BT Electric meters
        Frequencies of oscillating systems—
            Measurement
    NT Frequency-deviation meters
        Harmonic analyzers
Frequency modulation, Pulse
    USE Pulse frequency modulation
Frequency modulation, Radio
    USE Radio frequency modulation
Frequency modulation broadcasting
    USE FM broadcasting
Frequency modulation detectors
    UF Demodulators, Frequency modulation
        Detectors, Frequency modulation
        FM detectors
    BT Demodulation (Electronics)
        Radio detectors
        Radio frequency modulation
    NT Frequency discriminators
Frequency modulation radio broadcasting
    USE FM broadcasting
Frequency modulation radios
    USE Radio frequency modulation—
        Receivers and reception
Frequency modulation receivers
    USE Radio frequency modulation—
        Receivers and reception
Frequency multipliers
    [TK2799]

UF Static frequency changers
BT Frequency changers
Frequency of oscillation
USE Frequencies of oscillating systems
Frequency of vibration
USE Frequencies of oscillating systems
Frequency relays
[TK872.R38]
BT Electric relays
Frequency response (Dynamics)
BT Frequencies of oscillating systems
Oscillations
Vibration
Frequency response (Electrical engineering)
UF Amplitude-frequency response
Response, Frequency (Electrical
engineering)
BT Electric engineering
Frequencies of oscillating systems
Frequency spectra
[QC454.F85]
UF Spectra, Frequency
Spectrum, Frequency
BT Spectrum analysis
Frequency stability
BT Frequencies of oscillating systems
Radio frequency
Stability
NT Radio frequency modulation—
Transmitters and transmission—
Frequency deviation
Frequency standards
UF Standard frequencies
BT Standards, Engineering
RT Time—Systems and standards
NT Atomic clocks
Atomic frequency standards
Frequencies of oscillating systems—
Measurement
National Measurement System for
Time and Frequency
Oscillators, Crystal
Frequency synthesizers
UF Synthesizers, Frequency
BT Frequency changers
Oscillators, Crystal
Signal generators
Frequency word lists
USE *subdivision* Word frequency *under*
individual languages, e.g. English
language—Word frequency
Language and languages—Word
frequency
Frequent flier programs
USE Frequent flyer programs
Frequent flyer bonus programs
USE Frequent flyer programs
Frequent flyer programs *(May Subd Geog)*
UF Airlines—Frequent flyer programs
Bonus programs, Frequent flyer
Frequent flier programs
Frequent flyer bonus programs
BT Advertising—Airlines
Freschwiller, Battle of, 1870
USE Wörth, Battle of, 1870
Fresco painting
USE Mural painting and decoration
Fresel family
USE Frizzell family
Fresh-air charity *(May Subd Geog)*
[HV931-941]
BT Charities
Child welfare
Children—Institutional care
Public welfare
Social settlements
NT Camping
Fresh water
BT Water
NT Drinking water
Saline water conversion

— **Law and legislation** *(May Subd Geog)*
Fresh-water biology
USE Freshwater biology
Fresh-water drum
[QL638.S34]
UF Aplodinotus grunniens
Bubbler (Fish)
Drum, Fresh-water
Gaspergou
Perch, White
Sheepshead (Fish)
White perch, Freshwater
Fresh-water ecology
USE Freshwater ecology
Fresh-water fauna
USE Freshwater fauna
Fresh-water flora
USE Freshwater flora
Fresh-water mussels
USE Mussels, Fresh-water
Unionidae
Fresh-water turtles
USE Turtles
Freshman class (High school)
USE Ninth grade (Education)
Freshmen, College
USE College freshmen
Freshness dating of food
USE Food—Shelf-life dating
Freshness of fish
USE Fishery products—Spoilage
Freshwater algae *(May Subd Geog)*
BT Algae
Freshwater flora
Freshwater phytoplankton
Freshwater barriers
USE Saline water barriers
Freshwater biology *(May Subd Geog)*
[QH96-100]
UF Fresh-water biology
Hydrobiology
BT Aquatic biology
Biology
RT Freshwater ecology
Limnology
NT Freshwater fauna
Freshwater flora
Freshwater microbiology
Mineral water biology
Radioactive tracers in freshwater
biology
Freshwater ecology *(May Subd Geog)*
[QH541.5.F7]
UF Fresh-water ecology
BT Aquatic ecology
Ecology
RT Freshwater biology
NT Floodplain ecology
Freshwater productivity
Lake ecology
Marsh ecology
Pond ecology
Reservoir ecology
Spring ecology
Stream ecology
Freshwater fauna *(May Subd Geog)*
[QL141-149]
UF Fresh-water fauna
BT Aquatic animals
Freshwater biology
NT Fishes, Fresh-water
Freshwater invertebrates
Freshwater zooplankton
Lake fauna
Marsh fauna
Freshwater fishes
USE Fishes, Fresh-water
Freshwater flora *(May Subd Geog)*
[QK105 (Botany)]
[QK108-QK474.5 (Local)]
[QK932 (Ecology)]

UF Fresh-water flora
BT Aquatic plants
Freshwater biology
RT Wetland flora
NT Aquarium plants
Bog flora
Freshwater algae
Freshwater fungi
Freshwater phytoplankton
Lake flora
Marsh flora
Pond flora
Reservoir flora
Stream flora
Freshwater fungi *(May Subd Geog)*
[QK618.2]
BT Freshwater flora
Fungi
Freshwater invertebrates *(May Subd Geog)*
BT Aquatic invertebrates
Freshwater fauna
Invertebrates
Freshwater microbiology *(May Subd Geog)*
[QR105.5]
BT Aquatic microbiology
Freshwater biology
Microbiology
Water—Microbiology
NT Water—Bacteriology
Freshwater phytoplankton
(May Subd Geog)
[QK935]
BT Freshwater flora
Freshwater plankton
Phytoplankton
NT Freshwater algae
Freshwater plankton *(May Subd Geog)*
[QH96.8.P5]
BT Plankton
NT Freshwater phytoplankton
Freshwater zooplankton
Freshwater production rate
USE Freshwater productivity
Freshwater productivity *(May Subd Geog)*
UF Freshwater production rate
BT Biological productivity
Freshwater ecology
Freshwater tanker ballasting
USE Tankers—Freshwater ballasting
Freshwater turtles
USE Turtles
Freshwater zooplankton *(May Subd Geog)*
[QL143]
BT Freshwater fauna
Freshwater plankton
Zooplankton
Freskenzyklus von Urschalling (Mural)
UF Urschalling Church frescoes (Mural
painting and decoration)
BT Christian art and symbolism—
Medieval, 500-1500
Fresnel integrals
USE Integrals, Fresnel
Fresnel lenses
BT Lenses
Frette family *(Not Subd Geog)*
UF Fretty family
Fretting (Geomorphology)
USE Honeycomb weathering
Fretting corrosion
[TA407]
UF False brinelling
Friction oxidation
Rubbing corrosion
Wear oxidation
BT Corrosion and anti-corrosives
Friction
Mechanical wear
Oxidation
Fretts family
USE Fretz family

Fretty family
  USE Frette family
Fretum Gallicum
  USE Dover, Strait of
Fretum Siculum (Italy)
  USE Messina, Strait of (Italy)
Fretwork
  ⌈*NK9930*⌉
  UF Scrollwork
     Sorrento work
  BT Decoration and ornament
     Wood-carving
     Woodwork
Fretwork weathering
  USE Honeycomb weathering
Fretz family *(Not Subd Geog)*
  UF Fretts family
  RT Fritz family
Freud, Sigmund, 1856-1939
  — Humor, satire, etc.
  — Political and social views
  — Relations with women
Frevel family
  USE Fravel family
Frevo (Dance)
  ⌈*GV1796.F7*⌉
Frevos
  BT Dance music
Frey family
  USE Frye family
Freycinet National Park (Tas.)
  BT National parks and reserves—Australia
Freye family
  USE Frye family
Freyer's purple emperor butterfly
  ⌈*QL561.N9*⌉
  UF Apatura metis
     Purple emperor butterfly, Freyer's
Freyfogle family *(Not Subd Geog)*
Freyling family
  USE Freiling family
Frezel family
  USE Frizzell family
Friars, Black
  USE Dominicans
Friars, Gray
  USE Franciscans
Friars *(May Subd Geog)*
  ⌈*BX2820*⌉
  UF Mendicant orders
  BT Christian biography
  RT Monasticism and religious orders
  NT Augustinians
     Carmelites
     Dominicans
     Franciscans
Friars Minor
  USE Franciscans
Friars preachers
  USE Dominicans
Friaul (Italy)
  USE Friuli (Italy)
Friberg family *(Not Subd Geog)*
  UF Freiberg family
     Freiberger family
     Fribourgh family
Fribourgh family
  USE Friberg family
Frick family *(Not Subd Geog)*
  UF Fricke family
     Fricks family
     Frix family
Fricke family
  USE Frick family
Fricks family
  USE Frick family
Friction
  ⌈*QC197*⌉
  BT Machinery
     Mechanics
     Physics

  RT Bearings (Machinery)
     Tribology
  NT Aerodynamic heating
     Fretting corrosion
     Friction materials
     Frictional resistance (Hydrodynamics)
     Internal friction
     Lubrication and lubricants
     Mechanical wear
     Rolling contact
     Seizing (Metals)
     Skin friction (Aerodynamics)
     Surface roughness
     Surfaces (Technology)
     Tires, Rubber—Traction
Friction clutches
  USE Clutches (Machinery)
Friction gearing
  ⌈*TJ202*⌉
  BT Gearing
Friction layer (Meteorology)
  USE Planetary boundary layer
Friction materials
  ⌈*TN693.F7 (Metallography)*⌉
  BT Friction
     Materials
  RT Brakes
Friction oxidation
  USE Fretting corrosion
Friction welding
  BT Pressure welding
Frictional resistance (Hydrodynamics)
  UF Skin friction (Hydrodynamics)
  BT Friction
     Hydrodynamics
     Ship resistance
     Ships—Hydrodynamics
     Surfaces (Technology)
Frictional unemployment
  USE Unemployment, Frictional
Frid family
  USE Freed family
Friday menus
  USE Lenten menus
Friday prayer (Islam)
  USE Jum'ah
Fridtjof Nansen Land (R.S.F.S.R.)
  USE Franz Josef Land (R.S.F.S.R.)
Fridtorp Site (Sweden) *(Not Subd Geog)*
  BT Sweden—Antiquities
Fried family
  USE Freed family
Fried food
  USE Food, Fried
Friedel-Crafts reaction
  ⌈*QD341.A2 (Aromatic anhydrides)*⌉
  ⌈*QD501*⌉
  BT Chemical reactions
Friedensfahrt (Bicycle race)
  ⌈*GV1049*⌉
  BT Bicycle racing—Germany (East)
Friederich Stein Fortress (Halden, Norway)
  USE Fredriksten Fortress (Halden, Norway)
Friedhof am Hörnli (Basel, Switzerland)
  USE Basel-Städtischer Friedhof am Hörnli
     (Basel, Switzerland)
Friedland, Battle of, 1807
  ⌈*DC230.F7*⌉
Friedreich's ataxia *(May Subd Geog)*
  ⌈*RC406.F7*⌉
  UF Degeneration, Spinocerebellar
     Friedreich's disease
     Hereditary ataxia
     Hereditary spinal sclerosis
     Sclerosis, Hereditary spinal
     Spinal sclerosis, Hereditary
     Spinocerebellar degeneration
  BT Ataxia
     Cerebellum—Diseases
     Genetic disorders
     Spinal cord—Diseases

Friedreich's disease
  USE Friedreich's ataxia
Friel family *(Not Subd Geog)*
  UF Friele family
     O'Friel family
Friele family
  USE Friel family
Frieling test
  ⌈*BF698.8.F7*⌉
  BT Color—Psychological aspects
     Personality tests
Friemoth family *(Not Subd Geog)*
Friend (Quaker) poetry (American)
  USE American poetry—Quaker authors
Friend (Quaker) poetry (English)
  USE English poetry—Quaker authors
Friend at midnight (Parable)
  ⌈*BT378.F*⌉
Friend cookery
  USE Cookery, Quaker
Friend leukemia virus
  USE Friend virus
Friend virus
  UF Friend leukemia virus
     Rowson-Parr virus
     Swiss mouse leukemia virus
     Virus, Friend
  BT Mouse leukemia viruses
Friendliness
  USE Friendship
Friendly casualties due to friendly fire
  (Military science)
  USE Amicicide (Military science)
Friendly fire, Friendly casualties due to
  (Military science)
  USE Amicicide (Military science)
Friendly societies *(May Subd Geog)*
  ⌈*HG9201-HG9245 (Fraternal
     insurance)*⌉
  ⌈*HS1501-HS1510*⌉
  UF Benefit societies
     Fraternal benefit societies
     Fraternal organizations
     Mutual aid societies
     Mutual benefit associations
     Societies, Benefit
  BT Charities
     Labor and laboring classes
     Social security
     Societies
     Trade-unions
     Welfare work in industry
  RT Insurance, Assessment
  NT Insurance, Fraternal
  — Law and legislation *(May Subd Geog)*
Friendly visiting
  ⌈*HV43*⌉
  BT Social service
     Social settlements
  RT Social case work
  NT Elberfeld system
Friends (Quakers)
  USE Quakers
**Friends' Burial Ground Site (Staines,
  Middlesex)**
  BT England—Antiquities
Friends of God ("Gottesfreunde")
  ⌈*BV5070.F73*⌉
  NT Brothers of the Common Life
Friends of the library *(May Subd Geog)*
  ⌈*Z681.5*⌉
  BT Libraries—Societies, etc.
     Public relations—Libraries
Friendship *(May Subd Geog)*
  ⌈*BF575.F66 (Psychology)*⌉
  ⌈*BJ1533.F8 (Ethics)*⌉
  ⌈*GN486.3 (Ethnology)*⌉
  UF Affection
     Friendliness
  BT Conduct of life
     Interpersonal relations

RT Love
SA *subdivision* Friends and associates
under names of individual persons
NT Childhood friendship
Fellowship
Neighborliness
Pen pals
— **Religious aspects**
— — **Buddhism,** ⌐**Christianity, etc.**⌐
Friendship Hill National Historic Site (Pa.)
BT Dwellings—Pennsylvania
Historic sites—Pennsylvania
National parks and reserves—United
States
Friendship in art
BT Art
Friendship in literature
Friendship letters
USE International correspondence
Pen pals
**Friendship Pentecostal Holiness Church
Cemetery (Greenwood County, S.C.)**
BT Cemeteries—South Carolina
Friendship quilts *(May Subd Geog)*
BT Quilts
Friendship sloops
BT Fishing boats
Sloops
Frierson family *(Not Subd Geog)*
Fries family *(Not Subd Geog)*
UF Friese family
Friesen family
Friess family
Friesz family
Riesen family
Von Riesen family
RT Freese family
Friis family
Fries Rebellion, 1798-1799
⌐*E326*⌐
BT Pennsylvania Dutch—History—18th
century
United States—History—1783-1815
Frieschi family *(Not Subd Geog)*
Friese Eilanden
USE Frisian Islands
Friese family
USE Fries family
Friesen family
USE Fries family
Friesian Americans *(May Subd Geog)*
UF Friesian Americans—United States
BT Ethnology—United States
Friesians—United States
— **United States**
USE Friesian Americans
Friesian ballads
USE Ballads, Friesian
Friesian cattle
USE Holstein-Friesian cattle
Friesian cattle, Portuguese
USE Turino cattle
Friesian drama
Friesian essays
Friesian fiction *(May Subd Geog)*
Friesian folk-songs
USE Folk-songs, Friesian
Friesian horse
⌐*SF293.F9*⌐
Friesian Islands
USE Frisian Islands
Friesian language
⌐*PF1401-1497*⌐
UF Frisian language
BT Germanic languages
Low German language
— **To 1500**
Friesian law
USE Law, Friesian

Friesian letters *(May Subd Geog)*
Friesian literature
⌐*PF1501-1558*⌐
UF Frisian literature
— **20th century**
Friesian movement
Here are entered works on a movement, which
originated in the nineteenth century among the Frie-
sians, to preserve and strengthen Friesian culture,
language and literature.
BT Friesians
Friesian newspapers *(May Subd Geog)*
Friesian philology
⌐*PF1401-1414*⌐
BT Germanic philology
Friesian poetry *(May Subd Geog)*
⌐*PF1513 (Collections)*⌐
— **To 1500**
Friesian proverbs
USE Proverbs, Friesian
Friesians *(May Subd Geog)*
⌐*DJ401.F5-DJ401.F59*⌐
BT Ethnology—Netherlands
NT Friesian movement
— **United States**
NT Friesian Americans
Friesische Inseln
USE Frisian Islands
Friesland
— **History**
NT Staveren, Netherlands, Battle of,
1345
Friesland, East (Germany)
USE East Friesland (Germany)
Friesland, North (Germany)
USE North Friesland (Germany)
Friess family
USE Fries family
Friesz family
USE Fries family
Friezes *(May Subd Geog)*
⌐*NA2965 (Architecture)*⌐
⌐*NK2120 (Decoration)*⌐
BT Architecture—Details
Decoration and ornament
NT Metopes
Friezes, Doric
⌐*NA2965*⌐
UF Doric friezes
BT Architecture—Greece
Frigano Jate language
USE Yagaria language
Frigate-birds
⌐*QL696.S6*⌐
UF Fregatidae
Frigatebirds
Man-of-war birds
BT Pelecaniformes
Frigate-birds, Fossil
⌐*QE872.P4*⌐
BT Pelecaniformes, Fossil
NT Limnofregata
Frigatebirds
USE Frigate-birds
Frigates *(May Subd Geog)*
BT Anti-submarine warfare
— **Models**
BT Ship models
Fright
USE Fear
Frigidity (Psychology)
BT Psychosexual disorders
Sexual disorders
RT Orgasm, Female
Frigorimeter
BT Bioclimatology
Meteorological instruments
Temperature—Physiological effect
Friis family *(Not Subd Geog)*
RT Fries family

Friling family
USE Freiling family
Frilingk family
USE Freiling family
Frillfin goby
USE Bathygobius soporator
Fringe benefits
USE Employee fringe benefits
Fringe method, Moiré
USE Moiré method
Fringe parking *(May Subd Geog)*
UF Park and ride systems
BT Automobile parking
Commuting
Fringe patterns
USE Diffraction patterns
Fringe theater
USE Experimental theater—Great Britain
Fringes (Jewish cultus)
USE Zizith
Fringillidae
⌐*QL696.P246*⌐
UF Geospizidae
BT Finches
Passeriformes
NT Carduelis
Chaffinches
Coccothraustes
Goldfinches
Serinus
Frink family *(Not Subd Geog)*
UF Frinkle family
Frinkle family
USE Frink family
Frio Clay (Tex. and La.)
UF Frio Formation (Tex. and La.)
BT Formations (Geology)—Louisiana
Formations (Geology)—Texas
Geology, Stratigraphic—Oligocene
Frio Formation (Tex. and La.)
USE Frio Clay (Tex. and La.)
Frío River (Costa Rica)
UF Río Frío (Costa Rica)
BT Rivers—Costa Rica
Frio River (Tex.)
BT Rivers—Texas
NT Choke Canyon Reservoir (Tex.)
Frioulian dialect
USE Friulian dialect
Frisbe family
USE Frisby family
Frisbee (Registered trademark)
USE Flying discs (Game)
Frisbee family
USE Frisby family
Frisbey family
USE Frisby family
Frisbie family
USE Frisby family
Frisby family *(Not Subd Geog)*
UF Frisbe family
Frisbee family
Frisbey family
Frisbie family
Frisell family
USE Frizzell family
Frisia cattle
USE Turino cattle
Frisian Islands
UF Friese Eilanden
Friesian Islands
Friesische Inseln
Frisiske Øer
Waddeneilanden
BT Islands—Denmark
Islands—Germany (West)
Islands—Netherlands
NT North Frisian Islands (Denmark and
Germany)
West Frisian Islands (Netherlands)

Frisian Islands, North (Denmark and
    Germany)
    USE North Frisian Islands (Denmark and
        Germany)
Frisian language
    USE Friesian language
Frisian literature
    USE Friesian literature
Frisiske Øer
    USE Frisian Islands
Frissel family
    USE Frizzell family
Frissell family
    USE Frizzell family
Frit-flies
    [SB608.G6]
    UF Oscinella frit
Fritch family
    USE Fritz family
Fritchey family
    USE Fritz family
Fritchie family
    USE Fritz family
Frits family
    USE Fritz family
Fritsch family
    USE Fritz family
Fritsch Rockshelter (France)
    UF Abri Fritsch (France)
    BT Caves—France
        France—Antiquities
Fritschen family
    USE Fritz family
Fritscher family
    USE Fritz family
Fritschi family
    USE Fritz family
Fritts family
    USE Fritz family
Fritz family *(Not Subd Geog)*
    UF Fritch family
        Fritchey family
        Fritchie family
        Frits family
        Fritsch family
        Fritschen family
        Fritscher family
        Fritschi family
        Fritts family
        Fritzsch family
    RT Fretz family
Fritzinger family *(Not Subd Geog)*
Fritzsch family
    USE Fritz family
Friuli (Italy)
    UF Friaul (Italy)
Friulian dialect *(May Subd Geog)*
    [PC947]
    UF Frioulian dialect
        Rhaetian dialects
    BT Italy—Languages
        Raeto-Romance language
Friulian drama *(May Subd Geog)*
    [PC947.74 (Collections)]
    BT Friulian literature
    NT Radio plays, Friulian
Friulian folk-songs
    USE Folk-songs, Friulian
Friulian literature *(May Subd Geog)*
    [PC947.5 (History)]
    [PC947.6-PC947.9 (Collections)]
    BT Italy—Literatures
    NT Friulian drama
        Friulian poetry
Friulian philology
    [PC947]
Friulian poetry *(May Subd Geog)*
    [PC947.7 (Collections)]
    BT Friulian literature
Friulian radio plays
    USE Radio plays, Friulian

Friulians
    [DG457.F7]
    UF Furlans
    BT Ethnology—Italy
Frivolity
    [BV4627.F7]
Frivolous suits (Civil procedure)
    (May Subd Geog)
    UF Vexatious suits (Civil procedure)
    BT Actions and defenses
Frix family
    USE Frick family
Frizel family
    USE Frizzell family
Frizell family
    USE Frizzell family
Frizle family
    USE Frizzell family
Frizzel family
    USE Frizzell family
Frizzell family *(Not Subd Geog)*
    UF Fresel family
        Frezel family
        Frisell family
        Frissel family
        Frissell family
        Frizel family
        Frizell family
        Frizle family
        Frizzel family
        Frizzelle family
    RT Fraser family
Frizzelle family
    USE Frizzell family
Frô (The word)
    BT German language—Old High German,
        750-1050—Etymology
Frobenius algebras
    [QA251.5]
    UF Algebras, Frobenius
    BT Associative algebras
Frobenius groups
    BT Groups, Theory of
Frobisher Bay (N.W.T.)
    BT Bays—Northwest Territories
Frock family *(Not Subd Geog)*
    UF Frack family
Frodesham family
    USE Frodsham family
Frodsham family *(Not Subd Geog)*
    UF De Frodesham family
        Frodesham family
Froebel system of education
    USE Kindergarten
Froehner family *(Not Subd Geog)*
    UF Frohner family
Froeschwiller, Battle of, 1870
    USE Wörth, Battle of, 1870
FROG (Computer program language)
    [QH541.15.E45]
Frog culture *(May Subd Geog)*
    [SH185]
    UF Frog raising
    BT Small animal culture
    NT Frog legs trade
Frog kick (Swimming)
    USE Swimming—Kick
Frog Lake Massacre, 1885
    [F1060.9]
    BT Riel Rebellion, 1885
Frog legs trade *(May Subd Geog)*
    [HD9469.F7-712]
    BT Frog culture
Frog Level Road (Ala.)
    USE Huntsville Road (Ala.)
Frog raising
    USE Frog culture
Frogfishes
    USE Antennariidae
Froghoppers
    USE Cercopidae

Frogmen
    USE Underwater demolition teams
Frogs *(May Subd Geog)*
    [QL668.E2 (Zoology)]
    BT Anura
    NT Brevicipitidae
        Cookery (Frogs)
        Dendrobatidae
        Hylidae
        Hyperoliidae
        Leiopelmatidae
        Leptodactylidae
        Microhylidae
        Myobatrachidae
        Pseudidae
        Ranidae
        Rhacophoridae
        Tadpoles
    — Anatomy
    — Food
    — Physiology
Frogs as laboratory animals
Frogs as pets
    BT Amphibians as pets
Frohner family
    USE Froehner family
Froides, Iles
    USE Prince Edward Islands
Frolovia
    USE Saussurea
From family
    USE Froom family
Frome (Somerset). Trinity
    USE Trinity (Frome, Somerset)
Frome family
    USE Froom family
Fromm family
    USE Froom family
Fronde
    [DC124.4]
    NT Bordeaux (France)—History—
        Uprising, 1652-1653
        Mazarinades
Froneman family *(Not Subd Geog)*
    UF Fronemann family
Fronemann family
    USE Froneman family
Front-end alignment (Automobile wheels)
    USE Automobiles—Wheels—Alignment
Front jack-knife dive
    USE Diving—Jackknife dive
Front Morges
    UF Morges, Front
Front pages of newspapers
    USE Newspapers—Sections, columns, etc.—
        Front pages
Front Range (Colo. and Wyo.)
    BT Mountains—Colorado
        Mountains—Wyoming
        Rocky Mountains
    NT Laramie Mountains (Wyo. and Colo.)
        Longs Peak (Colo.)
        Medicine Bow Mountains (Colo. and
            Wyo.)
        Pikes Peak (Colo.)
        Tarryall Mountains (Colo.)
Front-screen projection
    [TR859]
    UF Alekon-Gerard process
        Jenkins process
        Scotchlite process
    BT Cinematography
        Lantern projection
Front Street (Appleton, Wis.)
    BT Streets—Wisconsin
Front-wheel drive (Automobiles)
    USE Automobiles—Front-wheel drive
Frontage roads *(May Subd Geog)*
    [TE228.7]
    UF Service roads
    BT Roads

Frontal leukotomy
   USE Frontal lobotomy
Frontal lobes
   BT Cerebral cortex
   NT Motor cortex
Frontal lobotomy   *(May Subd Geog)*
   ⌈*RD594*⌉
   UF Frontal leukotomy
      Leucotomy
      Leukotomy
      Lobotomy, Frontal
      Lobotomy, Prefrontal
      Prefrontal lobotomy
   BT Brain—Surgery
      Psychosurgery
Frontal occlusion (Meteorology)
   USE Occluded fronts (Meteorology)
Frontal sinus
   ⌈*QL947 (Comparative anatomy)*⌉
   ⌈*QM505 (Human anatomy)*⌉
   UF Sinus, Frontal
   BT Nose
      Paranasal sinuses
   — Surgery
      ⌈*RF421*⌉
Frontenac family   *(Not Subd Geog)*
Frontier and pioneer life   *(May Subd Geog)*
   ⌈*F596 (United States)*⌉
   UF Border life
      Frontier and pioneer life—History
      Homesteading
      Pioneer life
   BT Adventure and adventurers
      Manners and customs
   RT Pioneers
   NT Cowboys
      Cowgirls
      Frontier thesis
      Indians of North America—Captivities
      Land claim associations
      Overland journeys to the Pacific
      Ranch life
      Wild men
   — History
      USE Frontier and pioneer life
   — Pennsylvania
      NT Susquehanna claim
Frontier and pioneer life in art
Frontier children
   USE Pioneer children
Frontier formalities
   USE International travel regulations
Frontier Formation   *(Not Subd Geog)*
   BT Formations (Geology)—West (U.S.)
      Geology, Stratigraphic—Cretaceous
Frontier hypothesis
   USE Frontier thesis
Frontier patrols
   USE Border patrols
Frontier thesis
   ⌈*E179.5*⌉
   UF Frontier hypothesis
      Turner hypothesis
      Turner thesis
      Turner's frontier hypothesis
   BT Frontier and pioneer life
      History—Philosophy
Frontier Wars, South Africa, 1811-1878
   USE South Africa—History—Frontier Wars,
      1811-1878
Frontier women
   USE Women pioneers
Frontier workers   *(May Subd Geog)*
   UF Border traffic
      Border workers
      Boundary traffic
   BT Alien labor
      Aliens
      Emigration and immigration

Frontiers
   USE *subdivisions* Boundaries *and* Frontier
      troubles *under names of countries,*
      states, etc.
      Boundaries
Frontispiece
   ⌈*Z242*⌉
Frontons
   USE Pediments
Fronts, Cast-iron (Architecture)
   USE Cast-iron fronts (Architecture)
Fronts, Shop
   USE Shop fronts
Fronts, Wooden (Architecture)
   USE Wooden fronts (Architecture)
Fronts (Architecture)
   USE Façades
Fronts (Meteorology)   *(May Subd Geog)*
   BT Meteorology
      Weather
   RT Air masses
   NT Intertropical convergence zone
      Occluded fronts (Meteorology)
      Squall lines
Froom family   *(Not Subd Geog)*
   UF From family
      Frome family
      Fromm family
      Froome family
Froome family
   USE Froom family
Frøslevlejren (Frøslev, Sønderjyllands amt,
   Denmark : Concentration camp)
   (Not Subd Geog)
   ⌈*D805.D3*⌉
   BT Concentration camps—Denmark
      World War, 1939-1945—
         Concentration camps—Denmark
Frost   *(May Subd Geog)*
   ⌈*QC929.H6*⌉
   UF Freezing
   BT Meteorology
      Temperature—Physiological effect
      Water
   RT Glaze (Meteorology)
   SA *subdivision* Frost damage *under*
      subjects, e.g. Pavements—Frost
      damage; Roads—Frost damage
   NT Cryopedology
      Depth hoar
      Frost hazard
      Frost protection
      Frozen ground
      Ice
      Ice crystals
      Irrigation canals and flumes—Linings
         —Frost damage
      Plants, Effect of cold on
      Refrigeration and refrigerating
         machinery
      Thawing
Frost damage
   USE *subdivision* Frost damage *under*
      subjects, e.g. Pavements—Frost
      damage
Frost family   *(Not Subd Geog)*
   UF Fraust family
      Frostt family
Frost flakes
   USE Ice fog
Frost fog
   USE Ice fog
Frost hazard   *(May Subd Geog)*
   ⌈*QC929.H6*⌉
   UF Hazard, Frost
   BT Frost
Frost heaving
   BT Frozen ground
Frost mist
   USE Ice crystals

Frost protection   *(May Subd Geog)*
   BT Frost
      Horticulture
      Plants—Winter protection
      Plants, Effect of cold on
      Plants, Effect of temperature on
      Plants, Protection of
   SA *subdivision* Frost protection *under*
      particular crops, e.g. Corn—Frost
      protection; Fruit—Frost protection
Frost resistance of plants
   USE Plants—Frost resistance
Frost resistant concrete
   UF Concrete—Freezing and thawing
      Concrete, Frost resistant
   BT Concrete
   RT Concrete, Effect of temperature on
Frost snow
   USE Ice crystals
Frostbite
   BT Cold—Physiological effect
   NT Chilblains
Frostings, Cake
   USE Icings, Cake
Frøstrup family
Frostt family
   USE Frost family
Frottage
   USE Rubbing
Frottola
   Here are entered works on the frottola as a musi-
   cal form. Musical works composed in the form of the
   frottola are entered under the heading Frottole.
   UF Strambotto (Music)
Frottole
   Here are entered musical works composed in the
   form of the frottola. Works on the frottola as a musi-
   cal form are entered under the heading Frottola. A
   second heading for medium is assigned if a specific
   medium of performance is given in the work.
   UF Strambotto (Music)
Frozen apple
   USE Apple, Frozen
Frozen assets
   USE Liquidity (Economics)
Frozen baked products
   USE Baked products, Frozen
Frozen berries
   USE Berries, Frozen
Frozen blood
   UF Blood—Freezing
      Blood, Frozen
   BT Blood—Collection and preservation
      Cryopreservation of organs, tissues,
         etc.
   NT Erythrocytes, Frozen
Frozen concentrated apple juice
   USE Apple juice, Frozen concentrated
Frozen concentrated orange juice
   USE Orange juice, Frozen concentrated
Frozen crabs
   USE Crabs, Frozen
Frozen desserts
   USE Desserts, Frozen
Frozen desserts, Non-dairy
   USE Non-dairy frozen desserts
Frozen drugs
   USE Drugs, Frozen
Frozen erythrocytes
   USE Erythrocytes, Frozen
Frozen fish
   USE Fish, Frozen
Frozen fishery products
   USE Fishery products, Frozen
Frozen fog
   USE Ice fog
Frozen food
   USE Food, Frozen
Frozen food cookery
   USE Cookery (Frozen foods)
Frozen-food lockers
   USE Cold-storage lockers

Frozen foods industry *(May Subd Geog)*
  BT Food, Frozen
Frozen fruit
  USE Fruit, Frozen
Frozen fruit juices
  USE Fruit juices, Frozen
Frozen ground *(May Subd Geog)*
  UF Frozen soil
      Permafrost
      Soils, Frozen
  BT Cold regions
      Cryopedology
      Frost
      Soils
      Soils, Effect of temperature on
  NT Aufeis
      Frost heaving
      Ice mechanics
      Ice-wedge polygons
      Patterned ground
      Rock glaciers
      Sanitary engineering, Low temperature
      Soil freezing
      Thermokarst
  — Research *(May Subd Geog)*
      UF Frozen ground research
  — Thermal properties
Frozen ground research
  USE Frozen ground—Research
Frozen histological sections
  USE Frozen tissue sections
Frozen human embryos *(May Subd Geog)*
  UF Human embryo, Frozen
  BT Cryobiology
      Human embryo—Preservation
Frozen milk
  USE Milk, Frozen
Frozen peas
  USE Peas, Frozen
Frozen potatoes
  USE Potatoes, Frozen
Frozen seafood
  USE Seafood, Frozen
Frozen sections (Histology)
  USE Frozen tissue sections
Frozen semen
  USE Semen, Frozen
Frozen shrimps
  USE Shrimps, Frozen
Frozen soil
  USE Frozen ground
Frozen sperm
  USE Semen, Frozen
Frozen stars
  USE Black holes (Astronomy)
Frozen tissue sections
  UF Frozen histological sections
      Frozen sections (Histology)
      Histological sections, Frozen
      Tissue sections, Frozen
  BT Cryopreservation of organs, tissues,
        etc.
      Microtomy
Frozen vegetables
  USE Vegetables, Frozen
Frozen yogurt
  USE Yogurt, Frozen
Fructivorous animals
  USE Frugivores
Fructofuranosidase
  USE Invertase
Fructofuranosylglucopyranoside
  USE Sucrose
Fructosans
  [QD321]
  BT Fructose
Fructose
  [QD321]
  BT Glycosides
      Monosaccharides
      Sucrose

  NT Cookery (Fructose)
      Fructosans
      Sugar—Inversion
Fructose in human nutrition
  (May Subd Geog)
  BT Nutrition
Fructus
  USE Fruits (Civil law)
Fructus cynosbati
  USE Rose hips
Frugé family *(Not Subd Geog)*
Frugivores *(May Subd Geog)*
  UF Fructivorous animals
      Frugivorous fauna
      Fruit-eating animals
  BT Herbivores
  NT Flying foxes
Frugivorous fauna
  USE Frugivores
Fruit *(May Subd Geog)*
  [HD9240-HD9259 (Trade)]
  [SB354-SB399 (Culture)]
  UF Fruits
      Pomology
  BT Botany
      Food
      Food crops
      Horticultural crops
      Horticultural products
  SA *particular fruits, e.g.* Apple, Orange
  NT Berries
      Citrus fruits
      Cones (Botany)
      Cookery (Fruit)
      Date
      Fruit, Dried
      Fruit-culture
      Fruit juices
      Fruit wines
      Parthenocarpy
      Passion fruit
      Pods (Botany)
      Stone fruit
      Tropical fruit
  — Anatomy
      [QK660]
      [QK699]
      BT Botany—Anatomy
      RT Fruit—Morphology
          Seeds—Anatomy
  — Breeding
      [SB357.3]
      UF Fruit breeding
      BT Plant-breeding
      RT Fruit breeders
  — Canning
      USE Fruit—Preservation
  — Chemical composition
      USE Fruit—Composition
  — Color
      UF Color of fruit
      BT Color of food
  — Composition
      UF Fruit—Chemical composition
  — Cooperative marketing
      BT Fruit—Marketing
  — Disease and pest resistance
      (May Subd Geog)
      [SB608.F8]
  — Disease-free stock
      UF Disease-free fruit stock
          Fruit trees—Disease-free stock
      BT Fruit—Diseases and pests
          Stocks (Horticulture)
  — Diseases and pests *(May Subd Geog)*
      [SB608.F8]
      UF Fruit—Pests
          Fruit pests
          Fruit trees—Diseases and pests
      BT Trees—Diseases and pests

      SA *subdivision* Diseases and pests
            under particular fruits, e.g.
            Grapes—Diseases and pests; *and*
            names of diseases and pests, e.g.
            Pear thrips, Codling-moth
      NT Brown rot of fruit
          Fruit—Disease-free stock
          Fruit—Storage—Diseases and
            injuries
          Fruit-flies
          Grapolitha woeberiana
          Plant diseases
          Scale-insects
  — Dispersal
      UF Dispersal of fruit
  — Drying
      UF Drying of fruit
          Evaporation of fruit
          Fruit—Evaporation
      BT Fruit—Preservation
  — — Patents
      USE Fruit, Dried—Patents
  — Evaporation
      USE Fruit—Drying
  — Field experiments
  — Flavor and odor
      UF Fruit—Odor
      BT Flavor
          Odors
  — Frost protection
  — Genetics
  — Grading
  — Handling
      [SB360]
      UF Fruit handling
          Handling of fruit
  — Harvesting
  — — Machinery
      [S715.F]
      BT Fruit—Machinery
          Harvesting machinery
  — Irrigation
  — Law and legislation *(May Subd Geog)*
      UF Fruit—Marketing—Law and
            legislation
          Fruit trade—Law and legislation
  — Machinery
      NT Fruit—Harvesting—Machinery
  — Marketing
      [SB360]
      UF Marketing of fruit
      RT Fruit trade
      SA *subdivision* Marketing *under names*
            of fruits, e.g. Apple—Marketing;
            Citrus fruits—Marketing
      NT Fruit—Cooperative marketing
  — — Law and legislation
      USE Fruit—Law and legislation
  — Microbiology
  — Morphology
      [QK660]
      BT Botany—Morphology
      RT Fruit—Anatomy
  — Odor
      USE Fruit—Flavor and odor
  — Packaging
  — — Law and legislation
      (May Subd Geog)
  — Pests
      USE Fruit—Diseases and pests
  — Physiology
  — Planting time
  — Precooling
      BT Fruit—Preservation
  — Preservation
      UF Fruit—Canning
          Preservation of fruit
      NT Fruit—Drying
          Fruit—Precooling
          Fruit—Waxing
  — Prices *(May Subd Geog)*

UF Fruit trade—Prices
— **Pruning**
    UF Fruit trees—Pruning
— **Quality**
    UF Fruit quality
— **Research**
—— **Law and legislation**
    (May Subd Geog)
— **Ripening**
    [SB354-399]
    UF Ripening of fruit
— **Sampling**
— **Seed**
— **Soils**
    [S597.F]
— **Spacing**
— **Storage**
    [SB360]
    SA *subdivision* Storage *under names of*
      fruits, e.g. Apple—Storage;
      Citrus fruits—Storage
    NT Root cellars
—— **Diseases and injuries**
    (May Subd Geog)
    [SB608.F8]
    BT Fruit—Diseases and pests
— **Tariff**
    USE Tariff on fruit
— **Thinning**
    USE Fruit thinning
— **Transplanting**
    UF Transplanting of fruit
    BT Fruit-culture
— **Transportation**
    BT Farm produce—Transportation
    SA *subdivision* Transportation *under*
      names of fruits, e.g. Apple—
      Transportation; Citrus fruits—
      Transportation
—— **Diseases and injuries**
    (May Subd Geog)
— **Varieties**
    BT Botany—Variation
    SA *subdivision* Varieties *under names*
      of fruits, e.g. Peach—Varieties
— **Water requirements**
— **Waxing**
    BT Fruit—Preservation
    Waxes
— **Weed control** *(May Subd Geog)*
Fruit, Artificial
    USE Artificial fruit
Fruit, Canned
    UF Canned fruit
    BT Food, Canned
    NT Grapefruit juice, Canned
      Orange juice, Canned
Fruit, Dehydrated
    USE Fruit, Dried
Fruit, Dried *(May Subd Geog)*
    UF Dehydrated fruit
      Dried fruit
      Fruit, Dehydrated
    BT Food, Dried
      Fruit
    RT Dried fruit industry
    NT Cookery (Dried fruit)
      Grapefruit juice, Dried
— **Patents**
    UF Fruit—Drying—Patents
Fruit, Effect of ozone on
    USE Plants, Effect of ozone on
Fruit, Forbidden
    USE Forbidden fruit
Fruit, Forcing of
    USE Forcing (Plants)
Fruit, Fossil
    [QE995]
    BT Paleobotany
Fruit, Frozen
    [TP493.5]

UF Frozen fruit
BT Food, Frozen
SA *specific frozen fruits, e.g.* Cranberries,
    Frozen
NT Fruit juices, Frozen
Fruit, Tropical
    USE Tropical fruit
Fruit bat, Relict collared
    USE Myonycteris relicta
Fruit bat, Straw-colored
    USE Straw-colored fruit bat
Fruit bats, Little collared
    USE Myonycteris
Fruit bats, Old World
    USE Pteropodidae
Fruit breeders *(May Subd Geog)*
    UF Breeders, Fruit
    BT Plant breeders
    RT Fruit—Breeding
Fruit breeding
    USE Fruit—Breeding
Fruit carving
    UF Carving, Fruit
    BT Carving (Decorative arts)
      Cookery (Garnishes)
      Table setting and decoration
Fruit-culture *(May Subd Geog)*
    [SB354-399]
    UF Pomology
    BT Fruit
      Gardening
      Horticulture
    RT Arboriculture
    SA *names of fruits*
    NT Apple growers
      Berries
      Dwarf fruit trees
      Fruit—Transplanting
      Fruit thinning
      Fruit trees
      Fungi in agriculture
      Grafting
      Horticulturists
      Nurseries (Horticulture)
      Olive industry and trade
      Pruning
      Stocks (Horticulture)
      Stone fruit
      Viticulture
— **Research** *(May Subd Geog)*
— **British Columbia**
    NT Certified Budwood Program
Fruit-eating animals
    USE Frugivores
Fruit family
    USE Fruits family
Fruit-flies
    [QL537.M6 (Zoology)]
    [SB945.F8 (Fruit pests)]
    BT Flies
      Fruit—Diseases and pests
    NT Drosophila
      Mediterranean fruit-fly
      Mexican fruit-fly
      Tephritidae
— **Biological control** *(May Subd Geog)*
    [SB945.F8]
    BT Fruit-flies—Control
— **Control** *(May Subd Geog)*
    [SB945.F8]
    NT Fruit-flies—Biological control
Fruit grading machinery
    BT Agricultural machinery
Fruit handling
    USE Fruit—Handling
Fruit in art
    UF Fruit prints
Fruit in literature
Fruit in the Bible
    UF Bible—Fruit
    BT Plants in the Bible

NT Forbidden fruit
Fruit jars, Glass
    USE Glass fruit jars
Fruit juice industry *(May Subd Geog)*
    [HD9348.5]
    BT Fruit juices
Fruit juices
    [TP562]
    UF Juices, Fruit
    BT Fruit
      Fruit wines
    NT Apple juice
      Citrus juices
      Fruit juice industry
      Grape juice
      Grapefruit juice, Canned
      Grapefruit juice, Dried
      Lemon juice
      Must
      Orange juice
      Orange juice, Canned
      Passion fruit juice
— **Flavor and odor**
    UF Fruit juices—Odor
    BT Flavor
      Odors
— **Law and legislation** *(May Subd Geog)*
    BT Food law and legislation
— **Odor**
    USE Fruit juices—Flavor and odor
— **Pasteurization**
    UF Pasteurization of fruit juices
Fruit juices, Canned
Fruit juices, Concentrated
    NT Apple juice, Frozen concentrated
      Orange juice, Frozen concentrated
Fruit juices, Frozen
    UF Frozen fruit juices
    BT Fruit, Frozen
    NT Apple juice, Frozen concentrated
      Orange juice, Frozen concentrated
Fruit lecanium
    [SB945.F]
Fruit of the Spirit
    Here are entered works dealing collectively with
these qualities induced by the Holy Spirit such as
love, joy, peace, faith, meekness, and temperance.
Works on extraordinary phenomena such as glosso-
lalia, visions, prophecies and interpretations, heal-
ings, discernment of spirits, etc. are entered under
Gifts, Spiritual.
    UF Fruits of the Spirit
      Spirit, Fruit of the
    BT Spiritual life
Fruit painting and illustration
    (May Subd Geog)
    BT Botanical illustration
      Painting
Fruit pests
    USE Fruit—Diseases and pests
Fruit prints
    USE Fruit in art
Fruit processing plants *(May Subd Geog)*
    [TP440]
    BT Food processing plants
Fruit quality
    USE Fruit—Quality
Fruit thinning
    UF Fruit—Thinning
    BT Fruit-culture
Fruit trade *(May Subd Geog)*
    [HD9240-HD9259]
    BT Produce trade
    RT Fruit—Marketing
    NT Apple industry
      Citrus fruit industry
      Coconut industry
      Olive industry and trade
— **Law and legislation**
    USE Fruit—Law and legislation
— **Prices**
    USE Fruit—Prices

Fruit-tree leaf roller
Fruit tree red spider
  USE European red mite
Fruit trees *(May Subd Geog)*
  BT Fruit-culture
    Trees
  SA *particular fruit trees, e.g.* Apple,
    Cherry
  NT Dwarf fruit trees
    Lime tree
    Tree crops
  — Disease-free stock
    USE Fruit—Disease-free stock
  — Diseases and pests
    USE Fruit—Diseases and pests
  — Pruning
    USE Fruit—Pruning
Fruit trees, Training of
  USE Espaliers
Fruit wines
  [*TP561*]
  BT Fruit
  RT Wine and wine making
  NT Cider
    Fruit juices
    Perry
Fruits
  USE Fruit
Fruits (Civil law) *(May Subd Geog)*
  UF Fructus
  BT Possession (Law)
    Real property
    Usufruct
Fruits family *(Not Subd Geog)*
  UF Fruit family
    Frute family
Fruits of the Spirit
  USE Fruit of the Spirit
Fruitworm, Tomato
  USE Heliothis zea
Frullaniaceae
  [*QK555.F9*]
  BT Jungermanniales
Frushka Gora (Serbia)
  USE Fruška Mountains (Serbia)
Fruška Gora (Serbia)
  USE Fruška Mountains (Serbia)
Fruška Mountains (Serbia)
  UF Frushka Gora (Serbia)
    Fruška Gora (Serbia)
  BT Mountains—Yugoslavia
Frustration
  [*BF575.F7*]
  UF Futility
  BT Attitude (Psychology)
    Emotions
  NT Control (Psychology)
    Rosenzweig picture-frustration test
  — Testing
    BT Psychological tests
Frustration in children
  [*BF723.F7*]
  BT Child psychology
Frustration in literature
  BT Emotions in literature
Frustration of contracts
  USE Impossibility of performance
Frustules, Diatom
  USE Diatoms—Frustules
Frute family
  USE Fruits family
Fry family
  USE Frye family
Fry symbolic profile
  USE Symbolic profile (Personality test)
Frye family *(Not Subd Geog)*
  UF Frei family
    Freie family
    Frey family
    Freye family
    Fry family

  RT Fryman family
Fryers, Deep fat
  [*TX657.F7*]
  UF Deep fat fryers
  BT Kitchen utensils
Frying
  BT Cookery
  NT Food, Fried
    Skillet cookery
    Stir frying
    Wok cookery
Frying, Stir
  USE Stir frying
Frying pan cookery
  USE Skillet cookery
Frying Pan Lake (N.Z.)
  BT Lakes—New Zealand
Frykensjöarna (Sweden)
  UF Mellan Fryken Lake (Sweden)
    Nedre Fryken Lake (Sweden)
    Övre Fryken Lake (Sweden)
  BT Lakes—Sweden
Fryman family *(Not Subd Geog)*
  RT Frye family
Frypan cookery
  USE Skillet cookery
Fry's art glass
  USE Pearl art glass
Fryxell family *(Not Subd Geog)*
FSW Demonstrator, Grumman Model 712 (Jet
  plane)
  USE Grumman X-29A (Jet plane)
FT-1 (Fighter planes)
  USE Black widow (Fighter planes)
Ft. Sherman (Panama)
  USE Fort Sherman (Panama)
Fu
  [*PL2519.F8*]
  BT Chinese poetry
    Chinese prose literature
Fu-ch'un Mountains (China)
  (Not Subd Geog)
  UF Fu-ch'un shan (China)
  BT Mountains—China
Fu-ch'un shan (China)
  USE Fu-ch'un Mountains (China)
Fu-ch'un shan chü hsin t'u (Watercolor
  painting)
  USE Yeh, Ch'ien-yü, 1907-   New
    painting of the mountains around
    Fu-ch'un
Fu-ch'un shan chü t'u (Scroll)
  USE Huang, Kung-wang, 1269-1358.
    Dwelling in the Fu-ch'un Mountains
Fu ling Site (Shen-yang shih, China)
  BT Sepulchral monuments—China
Fuca, Strait of (B.C. and Wash.)
  USE Juan de Fuca Strait (B.C. and Wash.)
Fucales *(May Subd Geog)*
  [*QK569.F*]
  BT Brown algae
    Kelps
Fuchs family *(Not Subd Geog)*
Fuchsia *(May Subd Geog)*
  [*QK495.O46 (Botany)*]
  [*SB413.F8 (Ornamental plants)*]
  BT Onagraceae
  — Varieties
Fuchsian functions
  USE Functions, Automorphic
Fuchsite
  [*QE391.F*]
Fucus digitatus
  USE Laminaria digitata
Fucus pyriferus
  USE Giant kelp
Fucus virsoides
  [*QK569.F95 (Botany)*]
Fudge family *(Not Subd Geog)*
Fudō myōō (Buddhist deity)
  USE Acala (Buddhist deity)

Fueger family
  USE Fugger family
Fuegians
  [*F2986*]
  UF Indians of South America—Tierra del
    Fuego
  BT Indians of South America
  NT Alacaluf Indians
    Ona Indians
    Yahgan Indians
  — Antiquities
Fuel *(May Subd Geog)*
  [*TP315-TP360 (Technology)*]
  BT Boilers
    Combustion
    Engines
    Fire
    Home economics
    Power resources
    Smoke prevention
  RT Briquets (Fuel)
    Heating
  SA *subdivision* Fuel *under armies, navies,*
    etc., e.g. United States. Navy—
    Fuel; *subdivision* Fuel supplies
    under wars, e.g. World War, 1939-
    1945—Fuel supplies; *and*
    subdivisions Fuel, Fuel consumption
    and Fuel systems *under subjects,*
    e.g. Jet planes—Fuel; Steam-boilers
    —Fuel consumption; Automobiles—
    Fuel systems
  NT Agricultural wastes as fuel
    Anthracite coal
    Asphalt as fuel
    Bark as fuel
    Benzene as fuel
    Biomass energy
    Charcoal
    Coal
    Coal-fired power plants—Fuel
    Coal-water fuel
    Coke
    Combustion deposits in engines
    Corn stover as fuel
    Diesel motor—Alternate fuels
    Electric power-plants—Conversion to
      coal
    Energy crops
    Fossil fuels
    Fuelwood
    Furnaces—Conversion to coal
    Gas as fuel
    Hecter fuel
    Hydrogen as fuel
    Internal combustion engines, Spark
      ignition—Alternate fuels
    Lignite
    Liquid fuels
    Mennonite grass-burner
    Metal-base fuel
    Methanol as fuel
    Motor fuels
    Mud fuel
    Peat
    Petroleum as fuel
    Refuse as fuel
    Rice hulls as fuel
    Sewage-sludge fuel
    Smoke
    Straw as fuel
    Synthetic fuels
    Vegetable oils as fuel
    Waste products as fuel
  — Testing
    [*TP321-2*]
    NT Heat of combustion
Fuel, Colloidal
  [*TP360*]
  UF Colloidal fuel

BT Coal, Pulverized
   Liquid fuels
   Petroleum
   Petroleum as fuel
Fuel, Liquid
   USE Liquid fuels
Fuel ash, Pulverized
   USE Fly ash
Fuel assistance for the aged
   USE Aged—Energy assistance
Fuel assistance for the handicapped
   USE Handicapped—Energy assistance
Fuel assistance for the poor
   USE Poor—Energy assistance
Fuel breaks
   USE Fuelbreaks
Fuel-briquet plants
   UF Briquet plants
   BT Coal preparation plants
   — Electric equipment
Fuel burnup (Nuclear engineering)
   [TK9360]
   UF Burnup, Fuel (Nuclear engineering)
   BT Nuclear fuels
Fuel cell industry (May Subd Geog)
   BT Fuel cells
Fuel cells
   [TK2920]
   BT Direct energy conversion
      Electric batteries
      Electric power production from
         chemical action
      Electrochemistry
   NT Fuel cell industry
   — Electrodes
      BT Electrodes
   — Law and legislation (May Subd Geog)
Fuel claddings, Nuclear
   USE Nuclear fuel claddings
Fuel consumption
   USE subdivision Fuel consumption under
      subjects, e.g. Steam-boilers—Fuel
      consumption
Fuel crops
   USE Energy crops
Fuel elements
   USE Nuclear fuel elements
Fuel filters
   BT Filters and filtration
Fuel injection pumps
   USE Fuel pumps
Fuel oil
   USE Petroleum as fuel
Fuel oil burners
   USE Oil burners
Fuel pumps
   UF Fuel injection pumps
   BT Automobiles—Motors
      Internal combustion engines
      Pumping machinery
   RT Internal combustion engines—Fuel
      systems
   NT Arc-jet rocket engines—Fuel systems
      Automobiles—Fuel systems
      Diesel motor—Fuel systems
      Motor vehicles—Fuel systems
      Rocket engines—Fuel systems
Fuel rods, Nuclear
   USE Nuclear fuel rods
Fuel systems
   USE subdivision Fuel systems under
      subjects, e.g. Automobiles—Fuel
      systems
Fuel tanks of airplanes
   USE Airplanes—Fuel tanks
Fuel tanks of rockets
   USE Rockets (Aeronautics)—Fuel tanks
Fuel trade (May Subd Geog)
   [HD9540-HD9559]
   [TP315]
   NT Coal trade

Coke
Degree days
Wood
Fuel wood
   USE Fuelwood
Fuelbreaks (May Subd Geog)
   Here are entered works on strategically located
   wide strips, on which a cover of dense vegetation has
   been changed to that of lower flammability as an aid
   to fire control.
   UF Firebreaks (Fuelbreaks)
      Fuel breaks
   BT Forest fires—Prevention and control
      Wildfires—Prevention and control
Fuels, Thermonuclear
   USE Thermonuclear fuels
Fuelwood (May Subd Geog)
   [TP324]
   UF Firewood
      Fuel wood
      Wood as fuel
      Wood fuel
   BT Fuel
      Wood products
   NT Fuelwood crops
      Wood—Combustion
   — Burning
      UF Burning of fuelwood
Fuelwood consumption (May Subd Geog)
   UF Consumption of fuelwood
Fuelwood crops (May Subd Geog)
   [SD536.5-536.6]
   UF Firewood crops
   BT Energy crops
      Fuelwood
      Tree crops
      Woody plants
   NT Fuelwood cutting
Fuelwood cutting (May Subd Geog)
   [SD536.5-536.6]
   UF Chopping of fuelwood
      Splitting fuelwood
      Woodcutting (Fuelwood)
   BT Cutting
      Fuelwood crops
Fuelwood gatherers (May Subd Geog)
   UF Fagoters
      Gatherers, Fuelwood
      Wood gatherers
Fuelwood industry (May Subd Geog)
   [HD9769.F84]
Fuerstenberg family
   USE Fürstenberg family
Fuerte de San Rafael de Matamoros
   (Guatemala, Guatemala)
   USE Castillo de Matamoros (Guatemala,
      Guatemala)
Fuerte River (Mexico) (Not Subd Geog)
   UF Río del Fuerte (Mexico)
      Río Fuerte (Mexico)
   BT Rivers—Mexico
Fuerte San Lorenzo (Panama)
   USE Fort San Lorenzo (Panama)
Fuerte Sancti Spiritus (Argentina)
   [F2841]
   UF Sancti Spiritus Fort (Argentina)
   BT Argentina—History—1515-1535
      Fortification—Argentina
Fuga toxin
   USE Tetrodotoxin
Fugalia
   USE Regifugium
Fugat family
   USE Fugatt family
Fugate family
   USE Fugatt family

Fugatt family (Not Subd Geog)
   UF Fugat family
      Fugate family
      Fuget family
      Fugit family
      Fugitt family
Füger family
   USE Fugger family
Fuget family
   USE Fugatt family
Fugger family (Not Subd Geog)
   UF Fueger family
      Füger family
Fugi cherry
   USE Prunus incisa
Fuging tunes
   USE Hymns, English
Fugio cent
   USE Cent
Fugit family
   USE Fugatt family
Fugitive serfs
   USE Runaway serfs
Fugitive slave law of 1793
   BT Fugitive slaves—United States
Fugitive slave law of 1850
   BT Compromise of 1850
      Fugitive slaves—United States
   NT Christiana (Pa.)—Riot, 1851
Fugitive slaves (May Subd Geog)
   UF Runaway slaves
      Slavery—Fugitive slaves
   BT Slaves
   — Ohio
   — — History
      NT Oberlin-Wellington Rescue,
         1858
   — Pennsylvania
      NT Christiana (Pa.)—Riot, 1851
   — United States
      UF Refugees, Afro-American
      RT Underground railroad
      NT Fugitive slave law of 1793
         Fugitive slave law of 1850
   — West Indies
      NT Maroons
Fugitives from justice (May Subd Geog)
   BT Arrest
      Contumacy
      Crime and criminals
      Criminal procedure
   NT Escape (Law)
      Escapes
      Executions in effigy
Fugitt family
   USE Fugatt family
Fuglei family
   USE Fuglie family
Fuglestad family (Not Subd Geog)
Fuglie family (Not Subd Geog)
   UF Fuglei family
Fuglsang family (Not Subd Geog)
Fugu
   [QL638.T32]
   BT Poisonous fishes
      Tetraodontidae
   NT Cookery (Fugu)
      Fugu rubripes
Fugu fishing (May Subd Geog)
   [SH691.F83]
   BT Fishing
Fugu rubripes
   [QL638.T32]
   BT Fugu
Fugue
   [ML448]
   [MT59]
   Here are entered works on the fugue as a musical
   form. Scores are entered under the heading Canons,
   fugues, etc.
   UF Ricercare

Fugue (Continued)
  BT Counterpoint
  RT Canon (Music)
Fugue (Psychology)
    ₍RJ506.F85 (Child psychiatry)₎
  BT Memory, Disorders of
      Psychology, Pathological
Fugues
  USE Canons, fugues, etc.
Fuguing tunes
  USE Hymns, English
Fuhrman family
  USE Furman family
Fuhrmann family
  USE Furman family
Fuji, Mount (Japan)
  UF Fuji-san (Japan)
      Fuji-yama (Japan)
      Fujiyama (Japan)
      Mount Fuji (Japan)
      Suji Mountain (Japan)
  BT Mountains—Japan
      Volcanoes—Japan
  — Eruptions
      ₍QE523.F₎
Fuji (Sect)
  USE Nichiren Shōshū
Fuji cherry
  USE Prunus incisa
Fuji-Hakone-Izu-Kokuritsu Kōen (Japan)
  UF Fuji-Hakone National Park (Japan)
      Hakone National Park (Japan)
  BT National parks and reserves—Japan
Fuji-Hakone National Park (Japan)
  USE Fuji-Hakone-Izu-Kokuritsu Kōen
      (Japan)
Fuji River (Japan)
  UF Fujigawa (Japan)
      Fujikawa (Japan)
  BT Rivers—Japan
Fuji-san (Japan)
  USE Fuji, Mount (Japan)
Fuji-yama (Japan)
  USE Fuji, Mount (Japan)
Fujica camera
Fujigawa (Japan)
  USE Fuji River (Japan)
Fujikawa (Japan)
  USE Fuji River (Japan)
Fujimarujō (Yumesaki-chō, Japan)
  USE Okishiojō (Yumesaki-chō, Japan)
Fujiwara Capital (City)
  USE Fujiwara-kyō (City)
Fujiwara family (Not Subd Geog)
Fujiwara-kyō (City) (Not Subd Geog)
  UF Fujiwara Capital (City)
      Fujiwarakyō (City)
      Shin'yakuno no Miyako (City)
  BT Cities and towns, Ruined, extinct, etc.
      —Japan
      Japan—Antiquities
Fujiwara Sumitomo Revolt, Japan, 936-941
  USE Japan—History—Shōhei Revolt, 936-
      941
Fujiwarakyō (City)
  USE Fujiwara-kyō (City)
Fujiyama (Japan)
  USE Fuji, Mount (Japan)
Fuju-fuse (Sect)
  UF Fujufuse (Sect)
  BT Buddhist sects
      Nichiren (Sect)
Fujufuse (Sect)
  USE Fuju-fuse (Sect)
Fukagawa Shimbokuen (Tokyo, Japan)
  USE Kiyosumi Teien (Tokyo, Japan)
Fuke (Sect)
  UF Fukeshū
      Komushū
      P'u hua tsung

  BT Buddhist sects
      Zen Buddhism
Fukeshū
  USE Fuke (Sect)
Fukiage Gyoen (Tokyo, Japan)
  UF Fukiage Imperial Garden (Tokyo,
      Japan)
  BT Gardens—Japan
      Kōkyo (Tokyo, Japan)
Fukiage Imperial Garden (Tokyo, Japan)
  USE Fukiage Gyoen (Tokyo, Japan)
Fuksa family (Not Subd Geog)
  UF Fuxa family
Fukuchiin family (Not Subd Geog)
Fukuhara family (Not Subd Geog)
Fukuizumi family (Not Subd Geog)
Fukumoto family (Not Subd Geog)
Fukuoka 14 (Nagasaki-shi, Japan :
  Concentration camp) (Not Subd Geog)
    ₍D805.J3₎
  BT Concentration camps—Japan
      World War, 1939-1945—
      Concentration camps—Japan
Fukuoka-ken (Japan)
  — History
  —— Peasant Uprising, 1873
        USE Chikuzen Peasant Uprising,
        1873
Fukuoka-shi (Japan). Shikanoshima
  USE Shikanoshima (Fukuoka-shi, Japan)
Fukurodajō (Daigo-machi, Japan)
  USE Tsukiorijō (Daigo-machi, Japan)
Fukusa (May Subd Geog)
  BT Embroidery—Japan
      Gift wrapping
Fukushima Castle (Jōetsu-shi, Japan)
  USE Fukushimajō (Jōetsu-shi, Japan)
Fukushima Incident, Japan, 1882
  UF Fukushima jiken, Japan, 1882
  BT Japan—History—Meiji period, 1868-
      1912
      Peasant uprisings—Japan
Fukushima jiken, Japan, 1882
  USE Fukushima Incident, Japan, 1882
Fukushimajō (Jōetsu-shi, Japan)
  UF Echigo Fukushimajō (Jōetsu-shi,
      Japan)
      Fukushima Castle (Jōetsu-shi, Japan)
  BT Castles—Japan
Fūl, Tall (Not Subd Geog)
    ₍DS110.F8₎
  UF Tall al Fūl
  BT Cities and towns, Ruined, extinct, etc.
      —Jordan
      Jordan—Antiquities
Ful language
  USE Fulah language
Fulah Empire
    ₍DT515.9.F8₎
  UF Sokoto Empire
  BT Fulahs
Fulah folk-songs
  USE Folk-songs, Fulah
Fulah language
    ₍PL8181-4₎
  UF Adamawa dialect
      Ful language
      Fulani language
      Fulbe language
      Fulde language
      Fulfulde language
      Peul language
      Poul language
  BT Africa, West—Languages
      Niger-Congo languages
  NT Pular dialect
Fulah law
  USE Law, Fulah

Fulah literature (May Subd Geog)
Fulah poetry
Fulah proverbs
  USE Proverbs, Fulah
Fulahs
    ₍GN652.F9₎
  UF Felata
      Fellans
      Foulahs
      Foulbé
      Fulani
      Fulbe
      Fulfulde
      Peulhs
  BT Ethnology—Africa, West
      Ethnology—Sudan (Region)
  RT Toucouleurs
  NT Bororo (African people)
      Fulah Empire
      Jaawambe (African people)
Fulani
  USE Fulahs
Fulani cattle, Senegal
  USE Gobra zebu
Fulani cattle, White
  USE Gobra zebu
Fulani language
  USE Fulah language
Fulbe
  USE Fulahs
Fulbe language
  USE Fulah language
Fulbright family (Not Subd Geog)
Fulcher family
  USE Felker family
Fulcidacidae
  USE Chrysomelidae
Fulcomer family (Not Subd Geog)
Fulda River (Germany)
  BT Rivers—Germany (West)
Fulde language
  USE Fulah language
Fulenwider family (Not Subd Geog)
  UF Fullenwider family
      Fullewider family
      Fullinwider family
  RT Vollenweider family
Fulfillment (Ethics)
  USE Self-realization
Fulford family (Not Subd Geog)
Fulfulde
  USE Fulahs
Fulfulde language
  USE Fulah language
Fulgoridae
    ₍QL527.F9₎
  BT Homoptera
      Planthoppers
  NT Phrictus
      Sogata
Fulgoroidea
  USE Planthoppers
Fulica
  USE Coots
Fulica americana
  USE American coot
Fulkerson family (Not Subd Geog)
  RT Felker family
Full crew rules
  USE Railroads—Full crew rules
Full-day kindergarten (May Subd Geog)
  UF All-day kindergarten
  BT Kindergarten
Full dentures
  USE Complete dentures
Full employment policies
  BT Economic policy
      Economic security
      Industry and state
      Manpower policy

RT Employment stabilization
      Unemployment
SA *subdivision* Full employment policies
      under names of countries, etc.
NT Deficit financing
      Employment subsidies
      Government spending policy
      Labor supply
      Public service employment
Full family *(Not Subd Geog)*
RT Fuller family
Full-moon maple
USE Fullmoon maple
Full-pressure suits (Space environment)
USE Extravehicular space suits
Full-wave rectifiers
      ⌈TK7872.R35⌉
UF Rectifiers, Full-wave
BT Electric current rectifiers
Fullar family
USE Fuller family
Fullarton family
USE Fullerton family
Fullear family
USE Fuller family
Fulleborn's black boubou
USE Laniarius fulleborni
Fullenwider family
USE Fulenwider family
Fuller family *(Not Subd Geog)*
UF Fullar family
      Fullear family
      Fullier family
RT Full family
      Fullerton family
Fuller projection (Cartography)
BT Map-projection
Fuller's earth *(May Subd Geog)*
      ⌈TN948.F9⌉
UF Attapulgite
      Attapulgus clay
BT Silicates
Fullerton family *(Not Subd Geog)*
UF Fullarton family
      Fulleton family
      Fullington family
      Fullonton family
RT Fuller family
Fulleton family
USE Fullerton family
Fullewider family
USE Fulenwider family
Fullier family
USE Fuller family
Fulling (Textiles)
USE Textile finishing
Fullington family
USE Fullerton family
Fullinwider family
USE Fulenwider family
Fullmer family
USE Follmer family
Fullmoon maple
      ⌈QK495.A17 (Botany)⌉
      ⌈SB413.F (Ornamental plant)⌉
UF Acer japonicum
      Full-moon maple
BT Japanese maple
      Maple
      Ornamental shrubs
      Ornamental trees
Fullonton family
USE Fullerton family
Fulls (Beaches)
USE Beach ridges
Fullton family
USE Fulton family
Fulmar, Northern
USE Fulmarus glacialis
Fulmars
      ⌈QL696.P665⌉

BT Procellariidae
NT Fulmarus
Fulmarus
BT Fulmars
      Procellariidae
Fulmarus glacialis
      ⌈QL696.P665⌉
UF Atlantic fulmar
      Fulmar, Northern
      Fulmarus minor
      Fulmarus rodgersii
      Northern fulmar
      Procellaria glacialis
Fulmarus minor
USE Fulmarus glacialis
Fulmarus rodgersii
USE Fulmarus glacialis
Fulmer family
USE Follmer family
Fulminant hyperthermia
USE Malignant hyperthermia
Fulmodeston Site (England)
BT England—Antiquities
Fulnio Indians
UF Carijó Indians
      Carnijó Indians
      Fornio Indians
      Iate Indians
BT Indians of South America
      Tapuya Indians
Fulnio language
UF Carnijo language
      Iate language
      Yahthe language
BT Indians of South America—Languages
Fulse language
USE Kurumba language
Fulten family
USE Fulton family
Fultin family
USE Fulton family
Fulton County (Pa.)
— History
— — Civil War, 1861-1865
      ⌈F157.F9⌉
Fulton County Narrow Gauge Railway
UF Peavine Railway
BT Railroads—United States
Fulton family *(Not Subd Geog)*
UF Fullton family
      Fulten family
      Fultin family
Fulvic acids
BT Acids, Organic
Fulvous tree duck
UF Dendrocygna bicolor
      Tree duck, Fulvous
BT Ducks
Fumarate reductase
USE Succinate dehydrogenase
Fumarhydrogenase
USE Succinate dehydrogenase
Fumariaceae
USE Papaveraceae
Fumaric acid
      ⌈QD305.A2⌉
Fumaric hydrogenase
USE Succinate dehydrogenase
Fumarolic gases
USE Volcanic gases
Fume, Silica
USE Silica fume
Fume control
UF Control of fumes
BT Aerosols
      Air—Pollution
      Contamination (Technology)
      Gases, Asphyxiating and poisonous
      Smoke

SA *subdivision* Fume control *under types
      of industries, plants, and processes,
      e.g.* Construction industry—Fume
      control
NT Smoke prevention
Fumée Mountain (French Guiana)
      (Not Subd Geog)
UF La Fumée Mountain (French Guiana)
BT Mountains—French Guiana
Fumes, Welding
USE Welding fumes
Fumigants
BT Disinfection and disinfectants
      Fumigation
      Gases, Asphyxiating and poisonous
      Pesticides
SA *specific fumigants, e.g.* Hydrocyanic
      acid
NT Ethylene dibromide
Fumigation
      ⌈RA761-RA766 (Public health)⌉
      ⌈SB955 (Plant culture)⌉
RT Disinfection and disinfectants
SA *subdivision* Fumigation *under
      individual and types of plants and
      crops, e.g.* Corn—Fumigation
NT Buildings—Fumigation
      Flour-mills—Fumigation
      Food—Fumigation
      Fumigants
      Greenhouses—Fumigation
      Refrigerator cars—Fumigation
      Ships—Fumigation
      Soil fumigation
Funado family
USE Funato family
Funafuti Atoll (Tuvalu)
BT Coral reefs and islands—Tuvalu
Funambulation
USE Tightrope walking
Funato family *(Not Subd Geog)*
UF Funado family
Funck family
USE Funk family
Function, Greatest integer
USE Greatest integer function
Function, Möbius
USE Möbius function
Function, Optical transfer
USE Optical transfer function
Function, Patterson
USE Patterson function
Function, Secondary
USE Secondary function (Psychology)
Function algebras
UF Algebras, Function
BT Analytic functions
      Banach algebras
NT Hardy classes
      Uniform algebras
**Function generators (Electronic analog
computers)**
      ⌈TK7895.F8⌉
BT Electronic analog computers
      Potentiometer
NT Space card (Analog computers)
Function generators (Electronic instruments)
UF Generators, Function
BT Signal generators
Function spaces
UF Spaces, Function
BT Functional analysis
NT Besov spaces
      Fenchel-Orlicz spaces
      Functionals
      Interpolation spaces
      Lorentz spaces
      Lp spaces
      Orlicz spaces
      Sobolev spaces
      Spaces of measures

Function tests, Endocrine
  USE Endocrine function tests
Function tests, Pulmonary
  USE Pulmonary function tests
Function tests (Medicine)
  [RC71.8]
  BT Diagnosis
    Physiology, Pathological
  RT Diagnosis, Noninvasive
  NT Endocrine function tests
    Exercise tests
    Gastrointestinal function tests
    Handicapped—Functional assessment
    Heart function tests
    Kidney function tests
    Liver function tests
    Pituitary-adrenal function tests
    Placental function tests
    Provocation tests (Medicine)
    Pulmonary function tests
    Reflexes—Testing
    Thyroid gland function tests
    Vestibular function tests
Function theory, Geometric
  USE Geometric function theory
Functional analysis
  [QA320]
  UF Functional calculus
  BT Calculus of variations
  RT Functional equations
    Integral equations
  NT Approximation theory
    Density functionals
    Digital filters (Mathematics)
    Distributions, Theory of (Functional
      analysis)
    Function spaces
    Functionals
    Functor theory
    Hardy spaces
    Hilbert algebras
    Integration, Functional
    Invariant subspaces
    Linear topological spaces, Ordered
    Lp spaces
    Multipliers (Mathematical analysis)
    Nonlinear functional analysis
    Normed linear spaces
    Operator theory
    Perturbation (Mathematics)
    Rings with involution
    Schauder bases
    Spectral theory (Mathematics)
    Topological algebras
    Vector spaces
    Vector valued functions
Functional analysis, Nonlinear
  USE Nonlinear functional analysis
Functional analysis (Linguistics)
  USE Functionalism (Linguistics)
Functional analysis (Social sciences)
  USE Functionalism (Social sciences)
Functional assessment of the handicapped
  USE Handicapped—Functional assessment
Functional asymmetry (Brain)
  USE Cerebral dominance
Functional bowel disease
  USE Irritable colon
Functional burden (Linguistics)
  USE Functional load (Linguistics)
Functional calculus
  USE Functional analysis
Functional change (Linguistics)
  USE Transmutation (Linguistics)
Functional competencies
  USE Life skills
Functional determinants
  USE Jacobians
Functional differential equations
  UF Differential equations, Functional

  BT Differential equations
    Functional equations
  NT Point mappings (Mathematics)
  — Asymptotic theory
    UF Asymptotic theory in functional
      differential equations
    BT Asymptotic expansions
  — Delay equations
    UF Delay equations (Functional
      differential equations)
      Delay functional differential
      equations
      Retarded argument (Functional
      differential equations)
      Time-lag systems (Functional
      differential equations)
  — Numerical solutions
    BT Numerical analysis
Functional equations
  [QA431]
  UF Equations, Functional
  RT Functional analysis
  NT Differential-difference equations
    Functional differential equations
    Integral equations
    Invariant imbedding
    Programming (Mathematics)
  — Numerical solutions
    [QA431]
    BT Numerical analysis
    NT Degree, Topological
Functional integration
  USE Integration, Functional
Functional linguistics
  USE Functionalism (Linguistics)
Functional literacy *(May Subd Geog)*
  [LC149.7]
  UF Literacy, Functional
    Occupational literacy
  BT Literacy
Functional load (Linguistics)
  UF Functional burden (Linguistics)
  BT Phonemics
Functional methods, Density
  USE Density functionals
Functional programming languages
  BT Programming languages (Electronic
    computers)
Functional representation
  [JF1057-9]
  UF Occupational representation
    Representation, Functional
    Vocational representation
  BT Representative government and
    representation
  RT Corporate state
  NT Guild socialism
    Pressure groups
Functional sentence perspective (Grammar)
  USE Grammar, Comparative and general—
    Topic and comment
Functional somatic symptoms
  USE Somatoform disorders
Functional-structural analysis (Linguistics)
  USE Functionalism (Linguistics)
Functionalism (Architecture)
  (May Subd Geog)
  UF Functionalism in architecture
  BT Architecture, Modern—20th century
    International style (Architecture)
Functionalism (Linguistics)
  [P147]
  UF Functional analysis (Linguistics)
    Functional linguistics
    Functional-structural analysis
    (Linguistics)
  BT Linguistics
    Structural linguistics
Functionalism (Psychology)
  BT Psychology

Functionalism (Social sciences)
  [GN363 (Ethnology)]
  UF Functional analysis (Social sciences)
    Structural-functional analysis (Social
    sciences)
  BT Ethnology—Philosophy
    Social sciences
    Social systems
Functionalism in architecture
  USE Functionalism (Architecture)
Functionalism in art
Functionals
  BT Function spaces
    Functional analysis
    Functions
  NT Statistical functionals
Functionals, Density
  USE Density functionals
Functions
  [QA331-351]
  UF Analysis (Mathematics)
  BT Differential equations
    Mathematical analysis
    Mathematics
    Numbers, Complex
    Set theory
  RT Calculus
  NT Additive functions
    Approximation theory
    Asymptotic expansions
    Cluster set theory
    Convergence
    Convolutions (Mathematics)
    Distributions, Theory of (Functional
      analysis)
    Functionals
    Germs (Mathematics)
    Homomorphisms (Mathematics)
    Mappings (Mathematics)
    Mathematical constants
    Matrix derivatives
    Numerical differentiation
    Pseudofunctions
    Riemann surfaces
    Smoothness of functions
    Wave function
  — Computer programs
Functions, Abelian
  [QA345]
  UF Abelian functions
    Integrals, Abelian
  RT Geometry, Algebraic
Functions, Airy
  USE Airy functions
Functions, Algebraic
  [QA341]
  UF Algebraic functions
  NT Riemann-Roch theorems
Functions, Almost periodic
  USE Almost periodic functions
Functions, Analytic
  USE Analytic functions
Functions, Arithmetic
  USE Arithmetic functions
Functions, Automorphic
  [QA353.A9]
  UF Automorphic functions
    Fuchsian functions
    Functions, Fuchsian
  NT Eisenstein series
Functions, Bernoulli's
  USE Bernoullian numbers
Functions, Besselian
  USE Bessel functions
Functions, Beta
  UF Beta functions
Functions, Characteristic
  UF Characteristic functions
  BT Probabilities
  NT Distribution (Probability theory)

Functions, Chebyshev's
  USE Chebyshev polynomials
Functions, Circular
  USE Trigonometrical functions
Functions, Closure of
  USE Closure of functions
Functions, Computable
  USE Computable functions
Functions, Concave
  USE Concave functions
Functions, Concentration
  USE Concentration functions
Functions, Continuous
  UF Continuous functions
  NT Banach-Stone theorem
      Chebyshev systems
      Closure of functions
      Helson sets
      Lattices, Continuous
      Mappings (Mathematics)
Functions, Convex
  USE Convex functions
Functions, Coulomb
  USE Coulomb functions
Functions, Demand (Economic theory)
  USE Demand functions (Economic theory)
Functions, Differentiable
  USE Differentiable functions
Functions, Discontinuous
  [QA351]
  UF Discontinuous functions
Functions, Elliptic
  [QA343]
  UF Elliptic functions
      Integrals, Elliptic
  RT Functions of complex variables
      Integrals, Hyperelliptic
  NT Functions, Modular
      Jacobi forms
Functions, Entire
  [QA353.E5]
  UF Entire functions
      Functions, Integral
      Integral functions
  BT Functions of complex variables
  NT Value distribution theory
Functions, Error
  USE Error functions
Functions, Exponential
  [QA342]
  UF Exponential functions
      Functions, Hyperbolic
      Hyperbolic functions
  BT Exponents (Algebra)
      Logarithms
  RT Logarithmic functions
Functions, Fuchsian
  USE Functions, Automorphic
Functions, Gamma
  [QA351]
  UF Gamma functions
Functions, Generalized
  USE Distributions, Theory of (Functional
      analysis)
Functions, Generating
  USE Generating functions
Functions, Green's
  USE Green's functions
Functions, Harmonic
  USE Harmonic functions
Functions, Holomorphic
  USE Holomorphic functions
Functions, Hough
  USE Hough functions
Functions, Hyperbolic
  USE Functions, Exponential
Functions, Hyperelliptic
  USE Integrals, Hyperelliptic
Functions, Hypergeometric
  [QA351]
  UF Hypergeometric functions

  RT Hypergeometric series
  NT Fox's H-function
      Hypergeometric distribution
      Weber functions
Functions, Implicit
  UF Implicit functions
Functions, Incidence
  USE Incidence functions
Functions, Integral
  USE Functions, Entire
Functions, Inverse
  UF Inverse functions
Functions, Kernel
  USE Kernel functions
Functions, L-
  USE L-functions
Functions, Lagrangian
  USE Lagrangian functions
Functions, Lamé's
  USE Lamé's functions
Functions, Legendre's
  USE Legendre's functions
Functions, Liapunov
  USE Liapunov functions
Functions, Logarithmic
  USE Logarithmic functions
Functions, Lommel
  USE Lommel functions
Functions, Mathieu
  USE Mathieu functions
Functions, Meromorphic
  [QA331]
  UF Meromorphic functions
  NT Nevanlinna theory
      Value distribution theory
Functions, Modular
  [QA343]
  UF Modular functions
  BT Functions, Elliptic
      Groups, Theory of
      Numbers, Theory of
  NT Functions, Polyhedral
Functions, Monogenic
  USE Analytic functions
      Monogenic functions
Functions, Monotonic
  USE Monotonic functions
Functions, Nondifferentiable
  USE Nondifferentiable functions
Functions, Numerical
  USE Numerical functions
Functions, Orthogonal
  [QA404.5]
  UF Orthogonal functions
  BT Fourier analysis
  RT Series, Orthogonal
  NT Orthogonal polynomials
      Walsh functions
Functions, Painlevé
  USE Painlevé equations
Functions, Parabolic cylinder
  USE Weber functions
Functions, Patterson
  USE Patterson functions
Functions, Periodic
  USE Periodic functions
Functions, Polyharmonic
  USE Polyharmonic functions
Functions, Polyhedral
  UF Polyhedral functions
  BT Functions, Modular
  NT Groups, Theory of
Functions, Potential
  USE Differential equations, Partial
      Harmonic analysis
      Potential, Theory of
      Spherical harmonics
Functions, Production (Economic theory)
  USE Production functions (Economic
      theory)

Functions, Proper
  USE Eigenfunctions
Functions, Quasianalytic
  USE Quasianalytic functions
Functions, Quaternion
  UF Quaternion functions
  BT Functions of complex variables
      Quaternions
Functions, Recursive
  USE Recursive functions
Functions, Regular
  USE Analytic functions
Functions, Schlicht
  USE Univalent functions
Functions, Set
  USE Set functions
Functions, Simple
  USE Univalent functions
Functions, Special
  [QA351]
  UF Special functions
  BT Mathematical analysis
  SA *names of special functions, e.g.*
      Functions, Orthogonal;
      Trigonometrical functions
  NT C-functions
Functions, Spherical
  [QA406]
  UF Spherical functions
  BT Spherical harmonics
  RT Functions, Spheroidal
Functions, Spheroidal
  UF Spheroidal functions
  BT Ellipsoid
      Harmonic functions
  RT Functions, Spherical
  NT Mathieu functions
Functions, Star-like
  USE Star-like functions
Functions, Subharmonic
  [QA405]
  UF Subharmonic functions
  BT Functions of real variables
      Potential, Theory of
  RT Harmonic functions
Functions, Symmetric
  USE Symmetric functions
Functions, Theta
  [QA345]
  UF Theta functions
  NT Series, Theta
Functions, Toroidal
  USE Toroidal harmonics
Functions, Transcendental
  [QA351]
  UF Transcendental functions
  SA *names of specific transcendental*
      functions, e.g. Bessel functions;
      Functions, Gamma; Functions,
      Hypergeometric
  NT Dilogarithms
Functions, Transfer
  USE Transfer functions
Functions, Trigonometrical
  USE Trigonometrical functions
Functions, Univalent
  USE Univalent functions
Functions, Vector
  USE Vector valued functions
Functions, Vector valued
  USE Vector valued functions
Functions, Walsh
  USE Walsh functions
Functions, Weber
  USE Weber functions
Functions, Zeta
  [QA351]
  UF Zeta functions
  NT Euler products
      Gaussian sums
      Selberg trace formula

Functions of bounded variation
    UF Bounded variation, Functions of
    BT Functions of real variables
Functions of complex variables
    [QA331]
    UF Complex variables
    RT Functions, Elliptic
        Functions of real variables
    NT Analytic functions
        Arithmetic functions
        Banach spaces
        Blaschke products
        Bloch constant
        Boundary value problems
        Calculus of residues
        Closure of functions
        Conformal invariants
        Discontinuous groups
        Functions, Entire
        Functions, Quaternion
        Functions of several complex variables
        Geometric function theory
        Global analysis (Mathematics)
        Hardy classes
        Hardy spaces
        Kernel functions
        Laurent series
        Monogenic functions
        Quasiconformal mappings
        Series, Lie
        Star-like functions
        Univalent functions
Functions of real variables
    [QA331.5]
    UF Real variables
    RT Functions of complex variables
    NT Concave functions
        Concentration functions
        Convex functions
        Differentiable functions
        Functions, Subharmonic
        Functions of bounded variation
        Functions of several real variables
        Henstock integrals
        Integrals, Denjoy
        Jacobians
        Monotonic functions
        Nondifferentiable functions
        Set functions
        Vector valued functions
Functions of several complex variables
    UF Complex variables
        Several complex variables, Functions of
    BT Functions of complex variables
    NT Analytic continuation
        Analytic mappings
        Analytic spaces
        Automorphic forms
        Domains of holomorphy
        Eisenstein series
        Holomorphic functions
        Holomorphic mappings
        Jacobians
        Moduli theory
        Pseudoconvex domains
        Stein spaces
        Symmetric domains
        Teichmüller spaces
Functions of several real variables
    UF Real variables
        Several real variables, Functions of
    BT Functions of real variables
    NT Maximal functions
Functor theory
    UF Functorial representation
    BT Algebra, Homological
        Functional analysis
        Transformations (Mathematics)
    RT Categories (Mathematics)

Functorial representation
    USE Functor theory
Fund accounting *(May Subd Geog)*
    [HF5681.F84]
    BT Accounting
        Special funds
Fund-flow statements
    USE Funds-flow statements
Fund raisers (Persons) *(May Subd Geog)*
    BT Capitalists and financiers
    RT Fund raising
Fund raising *(May Subd Geog)*
    [HG177-HG177.5 (General fund raising)]
    [HV41.2-HV41.9 (Charitable and philanthropic fund raising)]
    UF Fundraising
        Money raising
    RT Fund raisers (Persons)
        Social service—Finance
    NT Arts fund raising
        Benefit performances
        Church fund raising
        Educational fund raising
        Federations, Financial (Social service)
        Library fund raising
        Raffles
        Telephone fund raising
  — **Law and legislation** *(May Subd Geog)*
Fund raising consultants *(May Subd Geog)*
    [HG177 (General)]
    [HV41.5 (Charities)]
    UF Consultants, Fund raising
    BT Consultants
Fundamental constants, Physical
    USE Constants, Physical
Fundamental education *(May Subd Geog)*
    Here are entered works on training to develop minimum performance ability in practical skills essential to community development in socio-economically deprived areas and developing countries. Works on training to develop mastery of the basic subject areas in school programs are entered under Basic education.
    BT Community development
        Education
    NT Competency based education
        Wardha scheme of education
  — **India**
        NT Farmers Training and Functional Literacy Project
Fundamental groups (Mathematics)
    BT Groups, Theory of
Fundamental life skills
    USE Life skills
Fundamental option (Ethics)
    [BJ1278.F]
    UF Option, Fundamental (Ethics)
    BT Christian ethics
        Ethics
Fundamental physical constants
    USE Constants, Physical
Fundamental rights
    USE Civil rights
Fundamental theology
    USE Apologetics
        Theology, Doctrinal
Fundamentalism
    [BT82.2]
    Here are entered works on a movement in American Protestantism that arose early in the 20th century in reaction to modernism stressing the inerrancy of the Bible in matters of faith and morals and as a literal historical record and holding as essential to Christian faith belief in the virgin birth, physical resurrection, Second Coming, etc. Works on Protestant denominations of the fundamentalist type and on fundamentalist congregations for which a particular denomination cannot be identified are entered under Fundamentalist churches.
    BT Theology, Doctrinal—History—20th century

    RT Evangelicalism
        Modernist-fundamentalist controversy
    NT Mormon Fundamentalism
Fundamentalist churches *(May Subd Geog)*
    Here are entered works on Protestant denominations of the fundamentalist type and on fundamentalist congregations for which a particular denomination cannot be identified. Works on a movement in American Protestantism that arose early in the 20th century in reaction to modernism stressing the inerrancy of the Bible in matters of faith and morals as a literal historical record and holding as essential to Christian faith belief in the virgin birth, physical resurrection, Second Coming, etc. are entered under Fundamentalism.
    BT Christian sects
Funday, Bay of
    USE Fundy, Bay of
Fundella *(May Subd Geog)*
    [QL561.P9]
    BT Pyralidae
Fundos
    USE Haciendas
Fundraising
    USE Fund raising
Funds
    USE Finance
Funds, Electronic transfers of
    USE Electronic funds transfers
Funds, Money market
    USE Money market funds
Funds, Revolving
    USE Revolving funds
Funds, Scholarship
    USE Scholarships
Funds, Special
    USE Special funds
Funds-flow statements *(May Subd Geog)*
    [HF5681.B2]
    UF Fund-flow statements
        Funds statements
    BT Financial statements
Funds management, Bank
    USE Asset-liability management (Banking)
Funds statements
    USE Funds-flow statements
Fundulus
    [QL638.C96]
    BT Cyprinodontidae
    NT Barrens topminnow
        Fundulus albolineatus
Fundulus albolineatus
    [QL638.C96]
    UF Topminnow, White line
        Topminnow, Whiteline
        White line topminnow
        Whiteline topminnow
    BT Fundulus
Fundulus blairae
    [QL638.C96]
Fundulus heteroclitus
    [QL638.C96]
Fundulus julisia
    USE Barrens topminnow
Fundulus nottii
    [QL638.C96]
    UF Starhead topminnow
        Topminnow, Starhead
        Western starhead topminnow
Fundus fluorescence photography
    USE Fluorescence angiography
Fundus oculi
    UF Eyegrounds
        Ocular fundus
    BT Eye
        Ophthalmoscope and ophthalmoscopy
    NT Fluorescence angiography
Fundy, Bay of
    UF Bay of Funday
        Bay of Fundy
        Funday, Bay of

BT Bays—Maine
   Bays—New Brunswick
   Bays—Nova Scotia
NT Minas Basin (N.S.)
Fundy National Park (N.B.)
   BT National parks and reserves—New
       Brunswick
Fünen (Denmark)
   USE Fyn (Denmark)
Funérailles de Patrocle (Drawing)
   USE David, Jacques Louis, 1748-1825.
       Burial of Patroclus
Funeral at Ornans (Painting)
   USE Courbet, Gustave, 1819-1877.
       Funeral at Ornans
Funeral cars
   USE Hearses (Vehicles)
Funeral coaches
   USE Hearses (Vehicles)
Funeral directors
   USE Undertakers and undertaking
Funeral etiquette
   USE Mourning etiquette
Funeral hymns
   BT Funeral music
       Hymns
   NT Dirges
Funeral industry
   USE Undertakers and undertaking
Funeral Mountains Wilderness (Calif.)
   UF Funeral Mountains Wilderness Study
       Area (Calif.)
   BT National parks and reserves—
       California
       Wilderness areas—California
Funeral Mountains Wilderness Study Area
   (Calif.)
   USE Funeral Mountains Wilderness (Calif.)
Funeral music
   BT Church music
       Music
       Sacred vocal music
   RT Memorial music
   NT Death in music
       Funeral hymns
       Requiems
Funeral of a warrior (Drawing)
   USE David, Jacques Louis, 1748-1825.
       Burial of Patroclus
Funeral orations
   ₍PA3482 (Greek, PA3264)₎
   BT Speeches, addresses, etc.
   NT Funeral sermons
Funeral rites and ceremonies
   (May Subd Geog)
   ₍GN486 (Ethnology)₎
   ₍GT3150-GT3390 (Manners and
       customs)₎
   UF Burial customs
       Graves
       Mortuary customs
       Obsequies
   BT Archaeology
       Burial
       Manners and customs
       Rites and ceremonies
   RT Cremation
       Dead
       Mourning customs
   NT Color in funerals
       Dokhmas
       Funeral service
       Indians of North America—Mortuary
           customs
       Indians of South America—Mortuary
           customs
       Lanterns of the dead
       Military funerals
       Orientation (Religion)
       Scaffold burial
       Stone pillows

       Urns
   — Early church, ca. 30-600
       USE Funeral rites and ceremonies,
           Early Christian
   — Hittites
       USE Funeral rites and ceremonies,
           Hittite
   — Jews
       USE Funeral rites and ceremonies,
           Jewish
   — Egypt
       NT Canopic jars
Funeral rites and ceremonies, Acoli
   ₍DT433.242₎
   UF Acoli funeral rites and ceremonies
   BT Acoli (African people)—Rites and
       ceremonies
Funeral rites and ceremonies, Akan
   (May Subd Geog)
   UF Akan funeral rites and ceremonies
   BT Akans (African people)—Rites and
       ceremonies
Funeral rites and ceremonies, Ancient
   (May Subd Geog)
   ₍GT3170₎
   UF Ancient funeral rites and ceremonies
**Funeral rites and ceremonies, Australian
   aboriginal** *(May Subd Geog)*
   UF Australian aboriginal funeral rites and
       ceremonies
   BT Australian aborigines—Rites and
       ceremonies
**Funeral rites and ceremonies, Bakongo
   (African people)**
   ₍DT650.B33₎
   UF Bakongo funeral rites and ceremonies
   BT Bakongo (African people)—Rites and
       ceremonies
**Funeral rites and ceremonies, Balinese
   (Indonesian people)** *(May Subd Geog)*
   UF Balinese (Indonesian people) funeral
       rites and ceremonies
   BT Balinese (Indonesian people)—Rites
       and ceremonies
**Funeral rites and ceremonies, Bamileke
   (African people)** *(May Subd Geog)*
   UF Bamileke (African people) funeral rites
       and ceremonies
   BT Bamileke (African people)—Rites and
       ceremonies
Funeral rites and ceremonies, Basque
   UF Basque funeral rites and ceremonies
**Funeral rites and ceremonies, Bayaka (African
   people)**
   UF Bayaka (African people) funeral rites
       and ceremonies
   BT Bayaka (African people)—Rites and
       ceremonies
**Funeral rites and ceremonies, Berawan
   (Malaysian people)**
   ₍DS597.367.B47₎
   UF Berawan (Malaysian people) funeral
       rites and ceremonies
   BT Berawan (Malaysian people)—Rites
       and ceremonies
Funeral rites and ceremonies, Black
   (May Subd Geog)
   UF Black funeral rites and ceremonies
**Funeral rites and ceremonies, Bobo (African
   people)** *(May Subd Geog)*
   ₍DT555.45.B63₎
   UF Bobo (African people) funeral rites and
       ceremonies
   BT Bobo (African people)—Rites and
       ceremonies
Funeral rites and ceremonies, Bonpo
   (May Subd Geog)
   ₍BQ7982.3₎
   UF Bonpo (Sect)—Funeral rites and
       ceremonies
       Bonpo funeral rites and ceremonies

   BT Bonpo (Sect)—Rituals
       Funeral rites and ceremonies, Buddhist
Funeral rites and ceremonies, Buddhist
   (May Subd Geog)
   ₍BL1477.8.F8₎
   UF Buddhist funeral rites and ceremonies
   BT Buddhism—Rituals
   NT Buddhist posthumous names
       Funeral rites and ceremonies, Bonpo
       Funeral rites and ceremonies, Zen
Funeral rites and ceremonies, Confucian
   (May Subd Geog)
   UF Confucian funeral rites and ceremonies
   BT Confucianism—Rituals
**Funeral rites and ceremonies, Dan (African
   people)**
   ₍DT630.5.G (Liberia)₎
   UF Dan (African people) funeral rites and
       ceremonies
       Funeral rites and ceremonies, Gere
Funeral rites and ceremonies, Early Christian
   (May Subd Geog)
   UF Early Christian funeral rites and
       ceremonies
       Funeral rites and ceremonies—Early
       church, ca. 30-600
   BT Church history—Primitive and early
       church, ca. 30-600
Funeral rites and ceremonies, Etruscan
   (May Subd Geog)
   UF Etruscan funeral rites and ceremonies
**Funeral rites and ceremonies, Fataleka
   (Solomon Islands people)**
   ₍DU850₎
   UF Fataleka (Solomon Islands people)
       funeral rites and ceremonies
   BT Fataleka (Solomon Islands people)—
       Rites and ceremonies
Funeral rites and ceremonies, Gere
   USE Funeral rites and ceremonies, Dan
       (African people)
**Funeral rites and ceremonies, Giryama
   (African people)** *(May Subd Geog)*
   UF Giryama (African people) funeral rites
       and ceremonies
   BT Giryama (African people)—Rites and
       ceremonies
Funeral rites and ceremonies, Hawaiian
   (May Subd Geog)
   ₍DU624.65₎
   UF Hawaiian funeral rites and ceremonies
   BT Hawaiians—Rites and ceremonies
Funeral rites and ceremonies, Hindu
   (May Subd Geog)
   UF Hindu funeral rites and ceremonies
   BT Hinduism—Rituals
Funeral rites and ceremonies, Hittite
   (May Subd Geog)
   UF Funeral rites and ceremonies—Hittites
       Hittite funeral rites and ceremonies
   BT Hittites—Rites and ceremonies
**Funeral rites and ceremonies, Idoma (African
   people)**
   UF Idoma (African people) funeral rites
       and ceremonies
   BT Idoma (African people)—Rites and
       ceremonies
Funeral rites and ceremonies, Illyrian
   UF Illyrian funeral rites and ceremonies
Funeral rites and ceremonies, Indo-European
   UF Indo-European funeral rites and
       ceremonies
Funeral rites and ceremonies, Islamic
   (May Subd Geog)
   ₍BP184.9.F8₎
   UF Funeral rites and ceremonies, Muslim
       Islamic funeral rites and ceremonies
       Muslim funeral rites and ceremonies
   BT Islamic religious practice

Funeral rites and ceremonies, Jewish
(*May Subd Geog*)
[BM712]
　UF　Funeral rites and ceremonies—Jews
　　　Jewish funeral rites and ceremonies
　　　Jews—Funeral rites and ceremonies
　BT　Judaism—Customs and practices
　NT　Mourning customs, Jewish
Funeral rites and ceremonies, Kumu (Zairian people)
　UF　Kumu (Zairian people) funeral rites and ceremonies
　BT　Kumu (Zairian people)—Rites and ceremonies
Funeral rites and ceremonies, Lappish
　UF　Lappish funeral rites and ceremonies
Funeral rites and ceremonies, Luyia (African people)
　UF　Luyia (African people) funeral rites and ceremonies
　BT　Luyia (African people)—Rites and ceremonies
Funeral rites and ceremonies, Mahafaly (Malagasy people) (*May Subd Geog*)
　UF　Mahafaly (Malagasy people) funeral rites and ceremonies
　BT　Mahafaly (Malagasy people)—Rites and ceremonies
Funeral rites and ceremonies, Maori
(*May Subd Geog*)
　UF　Maori funeral rites and ceremonies
　BT　Maoris—Rites and ceremonies
Funeral rites and ceremonies, Minoan
(*May Subd Geog*)
　UF　Minoan funeral rites and ceremonies
　BT　Minoans—Rites and ceremonies
Funeral rites and ceremonies, Murngin (Australian people) (*May Subd Geog*)
[DU125.M8 (Australian aborigines)]
　UF　Murngin (Australian people) funeral rites and ceremonies
　BT　Murngin (Australian people)—Rites and ceremonies
Funeral rites and ceremonies, Muslim
　USE　Funeral rites and ceremonies, Islamic
Funeral rites and ceremonies, Ngadju (Indonesian people)
　USE　Funeral rites and ceremonies, Ngaju (Indonesian people)
Funeral rites and ceremonies, Ngaju (Indonesian people) (*May Subd Geog*)
[DS646.32.N45]
　UF　Funeral rites and ceremonies, Ngadju (Indonesian people)
　　　Ngaju (Indonesian people) funeral rites and ceremonies
　BT　Ngaju (Indonesian people)—Rites and ceremonies
Funeral rites and ceremonies, Roman
(*May Subd Geog*)
　UF　Roman funeral rites and ceremonies
Funeral rites and ceremonies, Senufo (African people) (*May Subd Geog*)
　UF　Senufo (African people) funeral rites and ceremonies
　BT　Senufo (African people)—Rites and ceremonies
Funeral rites and ceremonies, Shinto
(*May Subd Geog*)
[BL2224.25.F8]
　UF　Shinto funeral rites and ceremonies
　BT　Shinto—Rituals
Funeral rites and ceremonies, Slavic
(*May Subd Geog*)
　UF　Slavic funeral rites and ceremonies
Funeral rites and ceremonies, Yakut
(*May Subd Geog*)
　UF　Yakut funeral rites and ceremonies
　BT　Yakuts—Rites and ceremonies

Funeral rites and ceremonies, Yoruba
(*May Subd Geog*)
　UF　Yoruba funeral rites and ceremonies
　BT　Yorubas—Rites and ceremonies
Funeral rites and ceremonies, Zen
(*May Subd Geog*)
[BQ9271.F8]
　UF　Zen Buddhism—Funeral rites and ceremonies
　　　Zen funeral rites and ceremonies
　BT　Funeral rites and ceremonies, Buddhist
Funeral rites and ceremonies in art
Funeral rites and ceremonies in literature
Funeral sermons
[BV4275 (Collections)]
　UF　Sermons, Funeral
　BT　Funeral orations
　　　Funeral service
　　　Occasional sermons
— History and criticism
— Outlines
Funeral sermons, Jewish
　BT　Jewish sermons
Funeral service (*May Subd Geog*)
[BV199.F8]
　UF　Burial service
　　　Service, Funeral
　BT　Funeral rites and ceremonies
　　　Liturgies
　　　Worship programs
　NT　Funeral sermons
— Baptists, [Catholic Church, etc.]
Funeral vehicles
　USE　Hearses (Vehicles)
Funerary cones (*May Subd Geog*)
　UF　Cones, Funerary
　BT　Pottery, Egyptian
　　　Seals (Numismatics)—Egypt
　　　Tombs—Egypt
Fünffrock family
　USE　Finfrock family
Fünfrock family
　USE　Finfrock family
Fungal antigens
[QR186.5.F]
　BT　Antigens
　　　Fungi
Fungal biotechnology
　USE　Fungi—Biotechnology
Fungal cell walls
[QK601]
　UF　Cell walls, Fungal
　BT　Cell membranes
　　　Fungi
Fungal cultures
　USE　Fungi—Cultures and culture media
Fungal differentiation
　USE　Fungi—Differentiation
Fungal diseases
　USE　Mycoses
Fungal diseases of plants (*May Subd Geog*)
[SB733]
　UF　Fungous diseases of plants
　BT　Plant diseases
　RT　Fungi, Phytopathogenic
　　　Plants, Effect of mycotoxins on
　NT　Barley leaf stripe disease
　　　Barley net-spot blotch disease
　　　Brown rot of fruit
　　　Charcoal rot
　　　Downy mildew diseases
　　　Eutypella canker
　　　Powdery mildew diseases
　　　Scleroderris canker
　　　Silver leaf disease
　　　Smut diseases
　　　Soybean rust disease
　　　Take-all disease
Fungal enzymes
　BT　Enzymes

Fungal genetics
　USE　Fungi—Genetics
Fungal lung diseases
　USE　Lungs—Diseases, Fungal
Fungal metabolites (*May Subd Geog*)
　BT　Fungi—Physiology
　　　Plant metabolites
　RT　Microbial metabolites
　NT　Mycotoxins
Fungal molecular biology (*May Subd Geog*)
　UF　Molecular biology, Fungal
　BT　Molecular biology
Fungal protoplasts
[QK601]
　UF　Protoplasts, Fungal
　BT　Fungi—Cytology
　　　Protoplasts
Fungal skin diseases
　USE　Dermatomycoses
Fungal toxins
　USE　Mycotoxins
Fungal viruses
[QR343]
　UF　Mycoviruses
　　　Viruses, Fungal
　BT　Plant viruses
Fungal zoospores
　USE　Fungi—Zoospores
Fungi (*May Subd Geog*)
[QK600-635]
　BT　Cryptogams
　　　Micro-organisms
　　　Parasitic plants
　　　Unicellular organisms
　RT　Molds (Botany)
　　　Mushrooms
　　　Mycology
　NT　Acrasiomycetes
　　　Aquatic fungi
　　　Ascomycetes
　　　Basidiomycetes
　　　Coenobic plants
　　　Dermatophytes
　　　Discomycetes
　　　Freshwater fungi
　　　Fungal antigens
　　　Fungal cell walls
　　　Gasteromycetes
　　　Hydromyxomycetes
　　　Hypocreales
　　　Mildew
　　　Mycotrophy
　　　Myxomycetes
　　　Peronosporales
　　　Pleomorphic fungi
　　　Pyrenomycetes
　　　Soil fungi
　　　Trichomycetes
　　　Wood-decaying fungi
　　　Wood-staining fungi
　　　Yeast fungi
　　　Zygomycetes
— Anatomy
[QK601]
　NT　Plasmodium (Myxomycetes)
— Biotechnology
[TP248.27.F86]
　UF　Fungal biotechnology
　BT　Biotechnology
— Catalogs and collections
　USE　Mycology—Catalogs and collections
— Collection and preservation
　BT　Plants—Collection and preservation
— Color
[QK601 (Botanical chemistry)]
— Cultures and culture media
　UF　Fungal cultures
　　　Mycology—Cultures and culture media

BT Cultures (Biology)
RT Plant growing media
NT Mushrooms—Soils
— Cytology
 [QK601]
 NT Fungal protoplasts
— Development
— Differentiation
 UF Differentiation, Fungal
  Fungal differentiation
 BT Microbial differentiation
  Plant cell differentiation
— Dispersal
 UF Dispersal of fungi
— Dormancy
— Ecology
— Economic aspects
 BT Botany, Economic
 NT Fungi—Industrial applications
  Fungi—Therapeutic use
  Fungi, Edible
  Fungi, Pathogenic
  Fungi, Phytopathogenic
  Fungi in agriculture
  Medical mycology
  Mushrooms, Edible
— Genetics
 [QK602]
 UF Fungal genetics
  Mycogenetics
— Geographical distribution
 BT Phytogeography
— Host plants
 USE Fungi, Phytopathogenic—Host
  plants
— Hyphae
 [QK601]
 UF Hyphae of fungi
 BT Mycelium
— Identification
— Industrial applications
 UF Industrial mycology
 BT Biochemical engineering
  Fungi—Economic aspects
  Fungi—Physiology
— Morphogenesis
 [QK601]
 BT Plant morphogenesis
— Morphology
 BT Botany—Morphology
— Parasites
 UF Parasites—Fungi
— Photography
 USE Photography of fungi
— Physiology
 [QK601]
 NT Fungal metabolites
  Fungi—Industrial applications
— Pictorial works
 NT Mushrooms—Pictorial works
— Reproduction
 [QK601]
 BT Plants—Reproduction
— Spores
 NT Fungi—Zoospores
— — Morphology
— Therapeutic use
 BT Fungi—Economic aspects
— Toxicology
 USE Mycotoxicoses
— Type specimens
 BT Type specimens (Natural history)
— Zoospores
 UF Fungal zoospores
 BT Fungi—Spores
Fungi, Aquatic
 USE Aquatic fungi
Fungi, Edible (May Subd Geog)
 [SB353-SB353.5 (Culture)]
 UF Edible fungi

BT Fungi—Economic aspects
 Plants, Edible
NT Auricularia auricula-judae
 Mushrooms, Edible
 Poria cocos
 Tremella fuciformis
 Truffles
 Yeast
Fungi, Fossil
 [QE958]
 BT Paleobotany
Fungi, Marine
 USE Marine fungi
Fungi, Nematode-destroying
 (May Subd Geog)
 [QK604 (Botany)]
 UF Nematode-destroying fungi
  Nematode-trapping fungi
  Nematophagous fungi
 BT Fungi, Predatory
Fungi, Pathogenic (May Subd Geog)
 [QR245]
 UF Fungi, Poisonous
  Pathogenic fungi
 BT Fungi—Economic aspects
  Micro-organisms, Pathogenic
  Parasites
 RT Medical mycology
  Mycoses
  Veterinary mycology
 NT Fungi, Phytopathogenic
  Pithomyces chartarum
  Toxigenic fungi
Fungi, Phytopathogenic (May Subd Geog)
 UF Phytopathogenic fungi
  Plant fungi
 BT Fungi—Economic aspects
  Fungi, Pathogenic
  Fungi in agriculture
  Micro-organisms, Phytopathogenic
 RT Fungal diseases of plants
 NT Alternaria
  Botryodiplodia theobromae
  Botryotinia
  Brown rot fungi of fruit
  Ceratocystis ulmi
  Damping-off diseases
  Eutypella parasitica
  Gaeumannomyces graminis
  Gremmeniella abietina
  Macrophomina phaseolina
  Peronosporaceae
  Phytophthora
  Phytophthora palmivora
  Pyrenophora graminea
  Rusts (Fungi)
  Sclerospora
  Sclerotium cepivorum
  Smut fungi
— Host plants
 UF Fungi—Host plants
Fungi, Pleomorphic
 USE Pleomorphic fungi
Fungi, Poisonous
 USE Fungi, Pathogenic
Fungi, Predatory
 UF Predacious fungi
  Predatory fungi
 BT Fungi in agriculture
 NT Fungi, Nematode-destroying
Fungi, Thermophilic
 UF Thermophilic fungi
 BT Micro-organisms, Thermophilic
 NT Bacteria, Thermophilic
Fungi, Toxigenic
 USE Toxigenic fungi
Fungi, Wood-decaying
 USE Wood-decaying fungi
Fungi, Wood-staining
 USE Wood-staining fungi

Fungi as feed
Fungi imperfecti
 [QK625]
 UF Deuteromycetes
  Imperfect fungi
 NT Alternaria
  Blastomycetes
  Coelomycetes
  Hyphomycetes
Fungi in agriculture
 [SB733 (Fungus diseases)]
 BT Agricultural microbiology
  Agricultural pests
  Fruit-culture
  Fungi—Economic aspects
 NT Anthracnose
  Farm produce—Transportation—
   Diseases and injuries
  Fungi, Phytopathogenic
  Fungi, Predatory
  Fungicides
  Plant diseases
  Wood-staining fungi
Fungibles (May Subd Geog)
 UF Res fungibiles
 BT Civil law
Fungicides
 [SB951]
 UF Germicides
 BT Agricultural chemicals
  Fungi in agriculture
  Pesticides
  Trees—Diseases and pests
  Wood preservatives
 RT Seeds—Disinfection
 NT Antifungal agents
  Benomyl
  Bordeaux mixture
  Soil fungicides
  Systemic fungicides
— Law and legislation
 USE Pesticides—Law and legislation
— Physiological effect
 NT Plants, Effect of fungicides on
Fungiform papilla
 [QL945 (Comparative anatomy)]
 [QM503 (Human anatomy)]
 UF Papilla fungiformis
 BT Tongue
Fungiidae
 [QL377.C7]
 UF Mushroom corals
 BT Scleractinia
Fungivoridae
 USE Mycetophilidae
Fungoid mycosis
 USE Mycosis fungoides
Fungous diseases
 USE Mycoses
Fungous diseases in animals
 USE Veterinary mycology
Fungous diseases of plants
 USE Fungal diseases of plants
Fungous ear diseases
 USE Ear—Fungi
Fungous eye diseases
 USE Eye—Fungi
Fungous lung diseases
 USE Lungs—Diseases, Fungal
Fungs
 [DT132]
 BT Ethnology—Sudan
Fungus ants
 UF Fungus-growing ants
  Gardening ants
  Trachymyrmex
 BT Ants
 NT Acromyrmex
Fungus gnats
 USE Mycetophilidae

Fungus gnats, Dark-winged
  USE Sciaridae
Fungus-growing ants
  USE Fungus ants
Funicular railroads
  USE Railroads, Cable
Funk family (Not Subd Geog)
  UF Funck family
     Funke family
Funke family
  USE Funk family
Funkhouser family (Not Subd Geog)
  UF Fankhauser family
Funkia
  USE Hosta
Funnel-beaker culture (May Subd Geog)
  [GN776.2-5.F8]
  UF TRB culture
  BT Neolithic period
Funnel weavers
  USE Agelenidae
Funnel-web spiders
  USE Agelenidae
Funnels (Naval architecture)
  USE Stacks (Naval architecture)
Funnies
  USE Comic books, strips, etc.
Funryū (Missile)
  BT Surface-to-air missiles
Fuodno (Lapp deity)
  USE Ruto (Lapp deity)
Fur
  [QL942 (Anatomy)]
  [QP88.3 (Physiology)]
  [TS1060-TS1067 (Technology)]
  BT Body covering (Anatomy)
  RT Hides and skins
  NT Artificial fur
     Hatter's fur
     Molting
     Rabbit fur
  — **Dressing and dyeing**
     [TS1061]
     UF Dyes and dyeing—Fur
        Fur dressing
        Fur dyeing
  — **Storage**
     UF Fur storage
     BT Fur trade
  — **Taxation** (May Subd Geog)
     BT Luxuries—Taxation
  — **Thermal properties**
Fur, Artificial
  USE Artificial fur
Fur-bearing animals (May Subd Geog)
  [SF403-SF405 (Animal culture)]
  [SK283 (Trapping)]
  BT Mammals
     Trapping
     Zoology
     Zoology, Economic
  SA names of fur-bearing animals, e.g.
     Arctic fox, Beavers, Seals (Animals)
  NT Coypu
     Fur trade
  — **Feeding and feeds**
     [SF403]
Fur coats
  USE Fur garments
Fur dressing
  USE Fur—Dressing and dyeing
Fur dyeing
  USE Fur—Dressing and dyeing
Fur farming (May Subd Geog)
  [SF402-SF405]
  BT Animal culture
  NT Mink farming
Fur garments (May Subd Geog)
  [GT2070 (Manners and customs)]
  [TT525 (Manufacture)]

  UF Clothing, Fur
     Fur coats
     Furriery
     Furs (Clothing)
  BT Clothing and dress
Fur garments in art
  [N8217.F8]
Fur language
  BT Chad—Languages
     Nilo-Saharan languages
     Sudan—Languages
Fur money (May Subd Geog)
  BT Money, Primitive
Fur seal, Northern
  USE Northern fur seal
Fur-seal arbitration
  USE Bering Sea controversy
Fur Seal Islands (Alaska)
  USE Pribilof Islands (Alaska)
Fur seals, Southern
  USE Southern fur seals
Fur storage
  USE Fur—Storage
Fur trade (May Subd Geog)
  [HD9944]
  UF Furriers
  BT Fur-bearing animals
     Trapping
  SA names of fur-bearing animals
  NT Bering Sea controversy
     Fur—Storage
     Fur traders
     Fur workers
     Mink fur industry
  — **Law and legislation** (May Subd Geog)
Fur traders (May Subd Geog)
  UF Traders, Fur
     Voyageurs
  BT Fur trade
Fur traders' wives (May Subd Geog)
  BT Wives
Fur workers (May Subd Geog)
  UF Furriers
  BT Fur trade
  NT Trade-unions—Fur workers
     Wages—Fur workers
Furaldelhyde industry (May Subd Geog)
  [HD9660.F85]
Furan resins
  [TP1180.F8]
  BT Furans
     Gums and resins, Synthetic
Furanes
  USE Furans
Furans
  UF Furanes
     Furfuranes
     Tetroles
  BT Heterocyclic compounds
  NT Dibenzofurans
     Furan resins
     Nitrofurans
     Ranitidine
     Tetrahydrofuran
Furāt River
  USE Euphrates River
Furazans
  UF Furoxanes
     Furoxans
  BT Heterocyclic compounds
Furca
  [QL445 (Crustacea)]
  [QL494 (Insects)]
  BT Crustacea—Anatomy
     Insects—Anatomy
Furcation of teeth roots
  USE Teeth—Roots—Furcation
Furcraea
  [QK495.A26 (Botany)]
  [SB261.F98 (Fiber plants)]

  UF Fourcroea
     Fourcroya
     Furcroea
     Furcroya
  BT Agavaceae
     Fiber plants
Furcraea macrophylla
  USE Fique
Furcroea
  USE Furcraea
Furcroya
  USE Furcraea
Fureman family
  USE Furman family
Furfuranes
  USE Furans
Furgason family
  USE Ferguson family
Furgerson family
  USE Ferguson family
Furgeson family
  USE Ferguson family
Furgison family
  USE Ferguson family
Furguson family
  USE Ferguson family
Furiants
  BT Dance music
Furies
  [BL820.F8]
  BT Mythology
     Mythology, Classical
Furies (Greek mythology)
  USE Erinyes (Greek mythology)
Furka-Oberalp-Bahn
  BT Electric railroads—Switzerland
     Railroads—Switzerland
     Railroads, Narrow-gage—Switzerland
Furlans
  USE Friulians
Furlough from prison
  USE Prison furloughs
Furloughs
  USE subdivision Armed Forces—Leaves
     and furloughs under names of
     countries, etc.; and subdivision
     Leaves and furloughs under names
     of individual military services
     Civil service—Furloughs
     Missionaries—Leaves and furloughs
     Prison furloughs
Furman family (Not Subd Geog)
  UF Firmin family
     Fuhrman family
     Fuhrmann family
     Fureman family
     Fyrmyn family
Furnace atmospheres
  USE Metallurgical furnaces—Protective
     atmospheres
Furnaces
  UF Grates
     Steam-boilers—Furnaces
  BT Heating
     Smoke prevention
     Steam-boilers
  RT Kilns
  NT Coal-fired furnaces
     Electric furnaces
     Fluidized-bed furnaces
     Fly ash
     Glass furnaces
     Image furnaces
     Metallurgical furnaces
     Roller hearth furnaces
     Solar furnaces
     Tube-still heaters
  — **Combustion**
     UF Steam-boilers—Combustion
  — **Conversion to coal**
     UF Conversion of furnaces to coal

BT Coal
   Fuel
— **Conversion to natural gas**
   UF Conversion of furnaces to natural
      gas
   BT Gas, Natural
— **Efficiency**
— **Fuel consumption**
— **Fuel systems**
   [TJ324.5]
— **Grates**
   [TJ322-TJ324 (Steam-boilers)]
Furnaces, Continuous
   USE Continuous furnaces
Furnaces, Cyclone
   USE Cyclone furnaces
Furnaces, Fluidized-bed
   USE Fluidized-bed furnaces
Furnaces, Salt bath
   USE Salt bath furnaces
Furnariidae
   [QL696.P2464]
   UF Ovenbirds, Neotropical
   BT Passeriformes
   NT Furnarius
Furnarius
   [QL696.P2464]
   BT Furnariidae
Furnarius leucopus
   USE Pale-legged hornero
Furnarius rufus
   [QL696.P2464]
   UF Baker bird
      Hornero, Rufous
      Rufous hornero
Furneaux Islands (Tas.)
   BT Islands—Australia
   NT Flinders Island (Tas.)
Furniture *(May Subd Geog)*
   [GT450 (Manners and customs)]
   [NK2200-NK2750 (Art)]
   [TS880-TS889 (Technology)]
   [TT194-TT199.4 (Handicraft)]
   UF Wood furniture
      Wooden furniture
   BT Arts and crafts movement
      Decoration and ornament
      Decorative arts
      House furnishings
   RT Interior decoration
      Upholstery
   NT Architect-designed furniture
      Bamboo furniture
      Bars (Furniture)
      Bedroom furniture
      Benches
      Bentwood furniture
      Built-in furniture
      Chairs
      Chests
      Children's furniture
      Church furniture
      Computer furniture
      Country furniture
      Cupboards
      Desks
      Dining room furniture
      Dormitories—Furniture, equipment,
         etc.
      Garden ornaments and furniture
      Gilt furniture
      High schools—Furniture, equipment,
         etc.
      Hospitals—Furniture, equipment, etc.
      Implements, utensils, etc.
      Junior high schools—Furniture,
         equipment, etc.
      Library fittings and supplies
      Living room furniture
      Metal furniture
      Miniature furniture

      Mirrors
      Office furniture
      Outdoor furniture
      Painted furniture
      Plastic furniture
      Printers' furniture
      Public buildings—Furniture,
         equipment, etc.
      Rattan furniture
      Rosewood furniture
      Schools—Furniture, equipment, etc.
      Seating (Furniture)
      Shelving (Furniture)
      Stands (Furniture)
      Stools
      Tables
      Unit furniture
      United States. Army—Barracks and
         quarters—Furniture
      Upholstered furniture
      Used furniture
      Veneers and veneering
      Wicker furniture
      Workbenches
— **Attribution**
   UF Attribution of furniture
      Furniture—Reattribution
   BT Furniture—Expertising
— Building
   USE Furniture making
— Conservation and restoration
   USE Furniture—Repairing
— Design
   USE Furniture design
— Drawing
   USE Furniture—Drawings
— **Drawings**
   UF Furniture—Drawing
   BT Furniture design
      Mechanical drawing
— **Exhibitions**
— **Expertising**
   NT Furniture—Attribution
— Finishing
   USE Furniture finishing
— **Marks**
   UF Cabinet-workers' marks
      Marks, Cabinet-workers'
      Marks, Furniture
   BT Marks of origin
— Models
   USE Doll furniture
      Miniature furniture
— **Private collections**
   [NK2220]
— Reattribution
   USE Furniture—Attribution
— Refinishing
   USE Furniture finishing
— **Repairing**
   [TT199]
   UF Furniture—Conservation and
        restoration
      Restoration of furniture
   BT Furniture making
   RT Furniture finishing
— **Reproduction**
   UF Reproduction of furniture
   BT Antiques—Reproduction
      Art—Reproduction
— Restoration
   USE Furniture finishing
— **Styles** *(Not Subd Geog)*
   [NK2235]
   UF Furniture styles
      Styles of furniture
   NT Furniture, Amana
      Furniture, Baroque
      Furniture, Colonial
      Furniture, Edwardian
      Furniture, Etruscan

      Furniture, Georgian
      Furniture, Gothic
      Furniture, Medieval
      Furniture, Mennonite
      Furniture, Mission
      Furniture, Mormon
      Furniture, Pennsylvania Dutch
      Furniture, Regency
      Furniture, Renaissance
      Furniture, Rococo
      Furniture, Shaker
      Furniture, Victorian
— **China**
   UF Furniture, Chinese
— — **History**
— — — **Ming-Ch'ing dynasties, 1368-1912**
— **Japan**
— — **History**
— — — **Edo period, 1600-1868**
— **Korea**
— — **History**
— — — **Yi dynasty, 1392-1910**
— **United States**
— — **English influences**
   BT England—Civilization
— — **History**
— — — **19th century**
— — — **20th century**
Furniture, Amana *(May Subd Geog)*
   UF Amana furniture
   BT Furniture—Styles
Furniture, Ancient *(May Subd Geog)*
   UF Ancient furniture
Furniture, Baroque *(May Subd Geog)*
   [NK2365]
   UF Baroque furniture
   BT Furniture—Styles
Furniture, Bentwood
   USE Bentwood furniture
Furniture, Built-in
   USE Built-in furniture
Furniture, Children's
   USE Children's furniture
Furniture, Chinese
   USE Furniture—China
Furniture, Church
   USE Church furniture
Furniture, Colonial *(May Subd Geog)*
   UF Colonial furniture
   BT Furniture—Styles
   NT Furniture, Dutch colonial
      Furniture, Spanish colonial
— **United States**
   NT Furniture, Early American
Furniture, Computer
   USE Computer furniture
Furniture, Country
   USE Country furniture
Furniture, Dutch colonial *(May Subd Geog)*
   UF Company furniture
      Dutch colonial furniture
      Dutch East India Company furniture
   BT Furniture, Colonial
Furniture, Early American
   (May Subd Geog)
   UF Early American furniture
   BT Furniture, Colonial—United States
Furniture, Edwardian *(May Subd Geog)*
   UF Edwardian furniture
   BT Furniture—Styles
Furniture, Etruscan *(May Subd Geog)*
   [NK2310]
   UF Etruscan furniture
   BT Furniture—Styles
Furniture, Georgian *(May Subd Geog)*
   UF Georgian furniture
   BT Furniture—Styles
Furniture, Gothic *(May Subd Geog)*
   [NK2345]
   UF Gothic furniture
   BT Furniture—Styles

Furniture, Koa *(May Subd Geog)*
  BT Koa
Furniture, Medieval *(May Subd Geog)*
  [NK2335-NK2345]
  UF Medieval furniture
  BT Furniture—Styles
Furniture, Mennonite *(May Subd Geog)*
  UF Mennonite furniture
  BT Furniture—Styles
Furniture, Mission *(May Subd Geog)*
  UF Mission furniture
     Mission oak furniture
  BT Arts and crafts movement
     Furniture—Styles
     Furniture, Oak—United States
Furniture, Mormon *(May Subd Geog)*
  UF Mormon furniture
  BT Furniture—Styles
Furniture, Oak *(May Subd Geog)*
  BT Oak
  — **United States**
     NT Furniture, Mission
Furniture, Painted
  USE Painted furniture
Furniture, Painted country
  USE Painted country furniture
Furniture, Pennsylvania Dutch
  UF Pennsylvania Dutch furniture
  BT Furniture—Styles
Furniture, Pine *(May Subd Geog)*
  BT Pine
Furniture, Regency *(May Subd Geog)*
  [NK2375]
  UF Regency furniture
  BT Furniture—Styles
Furniture, Renaissance *(May Subd Geog)*
  [NK2355]
  UF Renaissance furniture
  BT Furniture—Styles
Furniture, Rococo *(May Subd Geog)*
  [NK2375]
  UF Rococo furniture
  BT Furniture—Styles
Furniture, Rosewood
  USE Rosewood furniture
Furniture, Shaker *(May Subd Geog)*
  UF Shaker furniture
  BT Furniture—Styles
  NT Chairs, Shaker
Furniture, Spanish colonial
  (May Subd Geog)
  UF Spanish colonial furniture
  BT Furniture, Colonial
Furniture, Used
  USE Used furniture
Furniture, Victorian *(May Subd Geog)*
  [NK2390]
  UF Victorian furniture
  BT Furniture—Styles
Furniture beetle
  USE Anobium punctatum
Furniture building
  USE Furniture making
Furniture carpet beetle
  USE Anthrenus vorax
Furniture design *(May Subd Geog)*
  [TT196]
  UF Furniture—Design
  BT Design
  RT Furniture designers
  NT Chair design
     Color in furniture design
     Furniture—Drawings
Furniture designers *(May Subd Geog)*
  UF Designers, Furniture
  BT Designers
  RT Furniture design
Furniture finishing
  [TS885 (Wood industries)]
  [TT199.4 (Woodworking crafts)]

  UF Finishing, Furniture
     Furniture—Finishing
     Furniture—Refinishing
     Furniture—Restoration
     Furniture refinishing
     Refinishing, Furniture
     Restoration of furniture
  BT Furniture making
     Wood finishing
  RT Furniture—Repairing
  NT Furniture painting
Furniture fittings
  USE Cabinet hardware
Furniture hardware
  USE Cabinet hardware
Furniture in art
Furniture industry and trade
  (May Subd Geog)
  [HD9773]
  [TS840-TS887]
  NT Furniture workers
     Kitchen cabinet industry
  — **Capital productivity**
     BT Capital productivity
  — Collective labor agreements
     USE Collective labor agreements—
        Furniture industry
Furniture making
  [TS880-TS887 (Wood industries)]
  [TT194-TT199 (Woodworking crafts)]
  UF Furniture—Building
     Furniture building
  BT Joinery
     Woodwork
  RT Cabinet-work
  NT Furniture—Repairing
     Furniture finishing
     Upholstery
Furniture painting
  BT Furniture finishing
     Painting, Industrial
Furniture refinishing
  USE Furniture finishing
Furniture styles
  USE Furniture—Styles
Furniture workers *(May Subd Geog)*
  BT Furniture industry and trade
     Woodworkers
  RT Cabinet-workers
  NT Chair-makers
     Trade-unions—Furniture workers
     Wages—Furniture workers
Furomonazoles
  USE Oxazoles
Furosemide
  BT Diuretics
Furoxanes
  USE Furazans
Furoxans
  USE Furazans
Furriers
  USE Fur trade
     Fur workers
Furriery
  USE Fur garments
Furrow family *(Not Subd Geog)*
Furrow irrigation
  USE Irrigation, Furrow
Furs (Clothing)
  USE Fur garments
Fürstenberg family *(Not Subd Geog)*
  UF Fuerstenberg family
     Von Fürstenberg family
Fürstenberg porcelain
  [NK4399.F87]
  UF Porcelain, Fürstenberg
  BT Porcelain, German
Furtum usus
  USE Unauthorized use
Furu Iseki (Tenri-shi, Japan)
  USE Furu Site (Tenri-shi, Japan)

Furu Site (Tenri-shi, Japan)
  (Not Subd Geog)
  UF Furu Iseki (Tenri-shi, Japan)
  BT Japan—Antiquities
Furuhashi family *(Not Subd Geog)*
Furuike Iseki (Izumiōtsu-shi, Japan)
  USE Furuike Site (Izumiōtsu-shi, Japan)
Furuike Site (Izumiōtsu-shi, Japan)
  (Not Subd Geog)
  UF Furuike Iseki (Izumiōtsu-shi, Japan)
  BT Japan—Antiquities
Furuncle
  UF Boil
Furunculosis
  BT Fishes—Diseases
Furuseto pottery
  USE Seto pottery
Furusund (Sweden)
  BT Islands—Sweden
Fury (Jet fighter planes)
  USE Sabre (Jet fighter planes)
Fury family
  USE Forey family
Furylbenzimidazole
  [QP801.F87 (Biochemistry)]
  BT Benzimidazoles
Furze
  USE Gorse
Fusa Yomado Iseki (Abiko-shi, Japan)
  USE Fusa Yomado Site (Abiko-shi, Japan)
Fusa Yomado Site (Abiko-shi, Japan)
  (Not Subd Geog)
  UF Fusa Yomado Iseki (Abiko-shi, Japan)
  BT Japan—Antiquities
Fusain
Fusain (Art)
  USE Charcoal drawing
Fusarium
  [QK625.T8 (Botany)]
  [SB741.F9 (Phytopathogens)]
  BT Tuberculariaceae
Fusarium cubense
  USE Banana wilt
Fusarium nivale
  USE Snow mold
Fusarium oxysporum
  RT Oil palm wilt
Fusarium wilt of cotton
  USE Cotton fusarium wilt
Fusarium wilt of oil palm
  USE Oil palm wilt
Fusarium wilt of tomatoes
  USE Tomato wilt
Fuse wire arc tester
  UF Arc tester, Fuse wire
     Tester, Fuse wire arc
     Wire arc tester, Fuse
  BT Electric apparatus and appliances
     Surface discharges (Electricity)—
        Instruments
Fused bath electrolysis
  USE Fused salt electrolysis
Fused quartz
  USE Silica, Vitreous
Fused quartz fibers
  USE Quartz fibers
Fused salt electrolysis
  UF Fused bath electrolysis
     Molten salt electrolysis
  BT Electrolysis
     Electrometallurgy
Fused salts
  UF Molten salts
     Salts, Fused
  BT Salts
Fused silica
  USE Silica, Vitreous
Fused silica fibers
  USE Quartz fibers
Fusel-oil
  [TP593 (Alcohol)]

Fuselage (Airplanes)
  USE Airplanes—Fuselage
Fuselier family
  USE Fusilier family
Fuses, Electric
  USE Electric fuses
Fuses (Ordnance)
  UF Fuzes (Ordnance)
  BT Electric fuses
    Projectiles
  NT Proximity fuzes
Fusible interfacings
  USE Fusible materials in sewing
Fusible materials in sewing
  ₁TT557₁
  UF Bonding materials, Iron-on
    Fusible interfacings
    Interfacings, Fusible
    Iron-on bonding materials
    Materials, Fusible, in sewing
    Webbing, Fusible, in sewing
  BT Hems
    Interfacings (Clothing)
    Sewing
Fusible plugs
  BT Steam-boilers
Fusiform rust of pines
  USE Pine fusiform rust
Fusilier de la Claire family
  USE Fusilier family
Fusilier family *(Not Subd Geog)*
  UF Fuselier family
    Fusilier de la Claire family
    Fusilier la Claire family
    Fuzelier family
    Fuzelle family
    Fuzilier family
    Fuzlle family
Fusilier la Claire family
  USE Fusilier family
Fusion
  ₁QC303₁
    Here are entered works on the change of the state
  of a substance from the solid phase to the liquid
  phase. Works on the nuclear reaction between two
  light nuclei to form a heavier nucleus with release of
  binding energy are entered under Nuclear fusion.
  Works on the transition from a frozen to an unfrozen
  state by warming are entered under Thawing.
  UF Melting
  BT Chemistry, Physical and theoretical
  NT Liquation
    Nuclear fusion
    Thawing
Fusion, Gene
  USE Gene fusion
Fusion, Inertial confinement
  USE Pellet fusion
Fusion, Laser
  USE Laser fusion
Fusion, Latent heat of
  ₁QC303₁
  UF Latent heat of fusion
  BT Heat
Fusion, Membrane
  USE Membrane fusion
Fusion, Nuclear
  USE Nuclear fusion
Fusion, Pellet
  USE Pellet fusion
Fusion (Vision)
  USE Flicker fusion
Fusion of corporations
  USE Consolidation and merger of
    corporations
Fusion piercing drilling
  ₁TN279₁
  BT Boring
    Jet cutting
    Rock-drills
Fusion reactions
  USE Controlled fusion

Nuclear fusion
Fusion reactions, Controlled
  USE Controlled fusion
Fusion reactions, Heavy ion
  USE Heavy ion fusion reactions
Fusion reactors
  ₁TK9204₁
  UF Controlled fusion reactors
    Controlled thermonuclear reactors
    Thermonuclear reactors, Controlled
  BT Controlled fusion
    Nuclear reactors
  NT Thermonuclear fuels
    Tokamaks
  — Fuels
    USE Thermonuclear fuels
  — **Refueling**
    UF Refueling of fusion reactors
  — **Walls**
    UF Thermonuclear reactor walls
      Walls, Fusion reactor
      Walls, Thermonuclear reactor
Fuson family *(Not Subd Geog)*
Fusselman family
  USE Fosselmann family
Füssen, Treaty of, 1745
  ₁DD407.F8₁
  BT Austrian Succession, War of, 1740-
    1748
Fusulinidae
  ₁QE772₁
  BT Foraminifera, Fossil
Futa cattle
  USE N'Dama cattle
Futa Toro
  USE Toucouleurs
Futako Kaidō (Japan)
  USE Ōyama Kaidō (Japan)
Futakuchi Rokuchō Iseki (Kanazawa-shi,
  Japan)
  USE Futakuchi Rokuchō Site (Kanazawa-
    shi, Japan)
**Futakuchi Rokuchō Site (Kanazawa-shi,
  Japan)** *(Not Subd Geog)*
  UF Futakuchi Rokuchō Iseki (Kanazawa-
    shi, Japan)
  BT Japan—Antiquities
Futankobe
  USE Toucouleurs
Futatsu-iwa Iseki (Abashiri-shi, Japan)
  USE Futatsuiwa Site (Abashiri-shi, Japan)
Futatsu-iwa Site (Abashiri-shi, Japan)
  USE Futatsuiwa Site (Abashiri-shi, Japan)
Futatsuiwa Iseki (Abashiri-shi, Japan)
  USE Futatsuiwa Site (Abashiri-shi, Japan)
Futatsuiwa Site (Abashiri-shi, Japan)
  (Not Subd Geog)
  UF Futatsu-iwa Iseki (Abashiri-shi, Japan)
    Futatsu-iwa Site (Abashiri-shi, Japan)
    Futatsuiwa Iseki (Abashiri-shi, Japan)
  BT Japan—Antiquities
Futility
  USE Frustration
Futral family
  USE Futrell family
Futrall family
  USE Futrell family
Futrell family *(Not Subd Geog)*
  UF Fewtrell family
    Futral family
    Futrall family
    Futrelle family
    Futrill family
Futrelle family
  USE Futrell family
Futrill family
  USE Futrell family
Futuḥ
  USE Islamic Empire
Futuna-Aniwa language *(May Subd Geog)*
  ₁PL6436₁

  UF Erronan language
    West Futuna language
    Western Futuna language
  BT Polynesian languages
    Vanuatu—Languages
Futuna language
  ₁PL6435₁
  UF East Futuna language
    Eastern Futuna language
  RT Polynesian languages
Future as a theme in literature
  USE Future in literature
Future contingents (Logic)
  UF Contingentia futura (Logic)
    Contingents, Future (Logic)
  BT Logic
    Many-valued logic
Future estates
  USE Future interests
Future in literature
  ₁PN56.F₁
  UF Future as a theme in literature
  BT Future in popular culture
  RT Science fiction
    Time in literature
  NT Eschatology in literature
Future in popular culture *(May Subd Geog)*
    Here are entered works that discuss the represen-
  tation of the future in popular culture.
  BT Forecasting
    Popular culture
  NT Future in literature
Future interests *(May Subd Geog)*
  UF Future estates
  BT Estates (Law)
    Property
  RT Expectancies (Law)
  NT Executory interests
    Perpetuities
    Remainders (Estates)
    Reversion
Future life
  ₁BL535-BL547 (Comparative religion)₁
  ₁BT899-BT904 (Theology)₁
  UF Afterlife
    Eternal life
    Hades
    Life, Future
    Life after death
    Retribution
  BT Eschatology
  RT Eternity
    Immortality
    Near-death experiences—Religious
      aspects
  NT Children—Death—Religious aspects
    Elysium
    Future punishment
    Heaven
    Hell
    Intermediate state
    Paradise
    Rebirth in Western Paradise
      (Buddhism)
    Resurrection
    Soul
  — **Baptists, ₁Catholic Church, etc.₁**
  — **Buddhism, ₁Christianity, etc.₁**
  — **History of doctrines**
  — **Islam**
    NT Paradise (Islam)
  — **Koranic teaching**
Future punishment
  ₁BT834-8₁
  UF Endless punishment
    Eternal punishment
    Everlasting punishment
    Retribution
  BT Future life
    Punishment
  NT Annihilationism

Future punishment *(Continued)*
    Hell
    Purgatory
    Reprobation
  — **Buddhism,** [**Christianity, etc.**]
Future research
  USE Forecasting—Study and teaching
Future studies
  USE Forecasting—Study and teaching
Future time perspective
  USE Time perspective
Futures
  USE Commodity exchanges
    Hedging (Finance)
    Put and call transactions
    Short selling
    Speculation
Futures, Financial
  USE Financial futures
Futures, Interest rate
  USE Interest rate futures
Futures exchange
  USE Forward exchange
Futures research
  USE Forecasting—Study and teaching
Futures studies
  USE Forecasting—Study and teaching
Futurism (Art) *(May Subd Geog)*
  [ND1265]
  BT Aesthetics
    Art
    Art, Modern—20th century
    Modernism (Art)
    Painting
  RT Action in art
    Post-impressionism (Art)
  NT Kinetic sculpture
    Letter-pictures
Futurism (Literary movement)
  (May Subd Geog)
  UF Cubo-futurism
  BT Literature, Modern
  NT Constructivism (Russian literature)
Futurology
  USE Forecasting
Futūwah (Islamic order)
  USE Futuwwa (Islamic order)
Futuwwa (Islamic order) *(May Subd Geog)*
  UF Futūwah (Islamic order)
  BT Civilization, Islamic
    Orders of knighthood and chivalry,
      Islamic
    Sufism
Futwas
  USE Fatwās
Fuxa family
  USE Fuksa family
Fuyuge
  USE Mafulus
Fuyuge language
  [PL6621.F8]
  UF Mafulu language
  BT Papuan languages
Fuzelier family
  USE Fusilier family
Fuzelle family
  USE Fusilier family
Füzéri vár (Füzér, Hungary)
  BT Castles—Hungary
Fuzes, Proximity
  USE Proximity fuzes
Fuzes (Ordnance)
  USE Fuses (Ordnance)
Fuzilier family
  USE Fusilier family
Fuzlle family
  USE Fusilier family
Fuzzy algorithms
  BT Algorithms
    Cluster set theory
  RT Fuzzy sets

Fuzzy arithmetic
  BT Arithmetic
    Fuzzy sets
Fuzzy numbers
  UF Numbers, Fuzzy
  BT Fuzzy sets
Fuzzy sets
  UF Sets, Fuzzy
  BT Set theory
  RT Fuzzy algorithms
  NT Fuzzy arithmetic
    Fuzzy numbers
Fuzzy systems
  UF Systems, Fuzzy
  BT System analysis
FW-190 (Fighter planes)
  USE Focke-Wulf 190 (Fighter planes)
Fyen (Denmark)
  USE Fyn (Denmark)
Fyfe family
  USE Fyffe family
Fyffe family *(Not Subd Geog)*
  UF Fife family
    Fifer family
    Fyfe family
    Phyfe family
    Phyffe family
  RT Pfeiffer family
Fyke family
  USE Fike family
Fylde (England)
  [DA670.F99]
Fyle family
  USE File family
Fyles family
  USE File family
Fylfot
  USE Swastika
Fylmer family
  USE Filmer family
Fylmere family
  USE Filmer family
Fyn (Denmark)
  UF Fionia (Denmark)
    Fionie (Denmark)
    Fünen (Denmark)
    Fyen (Denmark)
  BT Islands—Denmark
Fyrmyn family
  USE Furman family
Fysher family
  USE Fisher family
G6PD (Enzyme)
  USE Glucosephosphate dehydrogenase
G6PD deficiency
  USE Glucosephosphate dehydrogenase
    deficiency
G-8 (Fictitious character)
  BT Characters and characteristics in
    literature
  RT Hogan, Robert J.—Characters—G-8
G.A.R. Cemetery (Homer, Ill.)
  UF GAR Cemetery (Homer, Ill.)
    Grand Army of the Republic
      Cemetery (Homer, Ill.)
  BT Cemeteries—Illinois
G.A.R. Cemetery (Miami, Okla.)
  USE GAR Cemetery (Miami, Okla.)
G//ana-khwe language
  USE G//ana language
G//ana language
  UF G//ana-khwe language
    Gana language
    //Ganakhoe language
    Kanakhoe language
  BT Botswana—Languages
    Khoisan languages
G-functions, Generalized
  USE Fox's H-function
G.I. loans
  USE Veterans—Loans

G-machine (Computer)
  [QA76.8.G]
  BT Electronic digital computers
G/PL/I (Computer program language)
  BT Graph theory—Data processing
    PL/I (Computer program language)
    Programming languages (Electronic
      computers)
G-spaces
  [QA689]
  UF Geodesic spaces
    Spaces, G
    Spaces, Geodesic
  BT G-structures
    Metric spaces
G stars
  BT Cool stars
  — Absolute magnitude
    USE G stars—Magnitudes
  — **Distribution**
  — **Magnitudes**
    UF G stars—Absolute magnitude
G-structures
  [QA649]
  UF Structures, G
  BT Geometry, Differential
  NT G-spaces
G.W. Parkway
  USE George Washington Memorial
    Parkway
G/wi (African people)
  [DT797]
  UF Gewi (African people)
  BT Ethnology—Botswana
    San (African people)
G/wi-khwe language
  USE G/wi language
G/wi language
  UF G/wi-khwe language
    /Guikhoe language
    Gwi language
  BT Botswana—Languages
    Khoisan languages
Gã (African people)
  [DT511]
  BT Ethnology—Ghana
Gã folk-songs
  USE Folk-songs, Gã
Gã language
  [PL8191]
  UF Accra language
    Acra language
    Akra language
    Incran language
  BT Kwa languages
Gaabell family
  USE Göbel family
Gaanda (African people)
  [DT515.45.G32]
  UF Gabin (African people)
    Ganda (Nigerian people)
    Kabin (African people)
    Kanda (African people)
    Mokar (African people)
  BT Ethnology—Nigeria
GAAP
  USE Accounting—Standards
Gaardhøje family *(Not Subd Geog)*
Gaasti family
  USE Gosti family
Gab (Artificial language)
  [PM8360.G2]
  BT Languages, Artificial
GABA
  [QP563.G32]
  UF Gamma-aminobutyric acid
  BT Aminobutyric acid
    Neurotransmitters
  — **Agonists**

UF Agonists, GABA
GABA agonists
GABA mimetics
Mimetics, GABA
BT GABA—Receptors
RT Progabide
— **Antagonists**
UF Antagonists, GABA
GABA antagonists
BT GABA—Receptors
— **Receptors**
UF GABA receptors
Receptors, GABA
BT Cell receptors
Neurotransmitter receptors
NT GABA—Agonists
GABA—Antagonists
GABA agonists
USE GABA—Agonists
GABA antagonists
USE GABA—Antagonists
GABA mimetics
USE GABA—Agonists
GABA receptors
USE GABA—Receptors
Gabbel family
USE Gable family
Gabble family
USE Gable family
Gabbra (African people)
[DT433.545.G32]
UF Gabra (African people)
BT Ethnology—Kenya
Oromo (African people)
Gabbro (May Subd Geog)
[QE461]
Gabel
USE Salt—Taxation
Salt—Taxation—France
Gabel family
USE Gable family
Göbel family
Gabele family
USE Göbel family
Gabelsberger-Noĕ shorthand
USE Shorthand, Italian—Gabelsberger-Noĕ
Gabelsberger-Poliński shorthand
USE Shorthand, Polish—Gabelsberger-Poliński
Gabelsberger shorthand
USE Shorthand—Gabelsberger
Gabelsberger shorthand, Armenian
USE Shorthand, Armenian—Gabelsberger
Gabelsberger shorthand, German
USE Shorthand, German—Gabelsberger
Gabelsberger shorthand, Serbo-Croatian
USE Shorthand, Serbo-Croatian—Gabelsberger
Gabelsberger shorthand, Spanish
USE Shorthand, Spanish—Gabelsberger
Gabii (Ancient city)
[DG70.G3]
BT Cities and towns, Ruined, extinct, etc.
—Italy
Italy—Antiquities
Gabii, Arch of the (Verona, Italy)
USE Arch of the Gabii (Verona, Italy)
Gabin (African people)
USE Gaanda (African people)
Gabl family
USE Gable family
Gable family (Not Subd Geog)
UF Gabbel family
Gabble family
Gabel family
Gabl family
Gaebel family
RT Gabler family
Gabler family (Not Subd Geog)
RT Gable family

Gables (May Subd Geog)
[NA2920]
BT Architecture—Details
Gabo Island (Vic.)
BT Islands—Australia
Gabon
— **Description and travel**
— — 1981-
[DT546.128]
— **Economic conditions**
— — 1960-
— **History**
— — To 1839
[DT546.165]
— — 1839-1960
[DT546.165-546.175]
— — 1960-
[DT546.18-546.183]
— **Languages**
NT Fang language
Tsogo language
Yaunde-Fang languages
Gabon literature (French) (May Subd Geog)
UF French literature—Gabon authors
Gabon painting
USE Painting, Gabon
Gabon sculpture
USE Sculpture, Gabon
Gaboon mahogany
USE Aucoumea klaineana
Gaboon viper
[QL666.O69]
UF Bitis gabonica
Gabra (African people)
USE Gabbra (African people)
Gabriel (Archangel)
[BT968.G2]
BT Angels
Gabriel family (Not Subd Geog)
Gabrieleño Indians
[E99.G15]
UF Kizh Indians
Tobikhar Indians
BT Indians of North America
Shoshonean Indians
— **Antiquities**
Gabrieleño language
[PM1201]
UF Tobikhar language
RT Shoshonean languages
Gabrielsonite (May Subd Geog)
Gabriola Island (B.C.)
BT Islands—British Columbia
Gach family
USE Gachet family
Gache family
USE Gachet family
Gachet family (Not Subd Geog)
UF Gach family
Gache family
Gada River (Nigeria and Niger)
USE Maradi River (Nigeria and Niger)
Gadaba (Indic people)
[DS432.G27]
UF Gadba (Indic people)
Hallar (Indic people)
Ollar (Indic people)
BT Ethnology—India
Gadaba language (Dravidian)
UF Gadba language (Dravidian)
Gudwa language (Dravidian)
Gutob language (Dravidian)
Koṇekor Gadaba language
Ollari language
Salur language
BT Dravidian languages
India—Languages
Gadah ha-ma'aravit
USE West Bank
Ga'dang language
USE Gaddang language

Gadarene demoniac (Miracle)
USE Healing of the Gerasene demoniac (Miracle)
Gadba (Indic people)
USE Gadaba (Indic people)
Gadba language (Dravidian)
USE Gadaba language (Dravidian)
Gaddang (Philippine people)
BT Ethnology—Philippines
Gaddang language
[PL5671]
UF Ga'dang language
BT Philippine languages
Gaddang literature (May Subd Geog)
BT Philippines—Literatures
Gaddis (Indic people)
[DS432.G]
BT Ethnology—India
Gade (African people)
UF Gade (African tribe)
BT Ethnology—Nigeria
Gade (African tribe)
USE Gade (African people)
Gade family
USE Gadson family
Gader River (Czechoslovakia)
UF Gaderský potok (Czechoslovakia)
BT Rivers—Czechoslovakia
Gaderský potok (Czechoslovakia)
USE Gader River (Czechoslovakia)
Gadflies
USE Horseflies
Gadgets
USE Implements, utensils, etc.
Gadi Lohars
USE Lohars
Gadiculus
[QL638.G2]
BT Codfish
Gadiculus argenteus
[QL638.G2]
Gadiculus thori
[QL638.G2]
Gadidae
USE Codfish
Gadidae, Fossil
USE Codfish, Fossil
Gadie family
USE Gowdy family
Gadiformes
[QL637.9.G3]
UF Anacanthini
Macruriformes
BT Osteichthyes
NT Carapidae
Codfish
Macrouridae
Moridae
Ophidiidae
Zoarcidae
Gadiformes, Fossil
[QE852.G26]
BT Osteichthyes, Fossil
NT Codfish, Fossil
Gadjerong (Australian people)
[DU125.G33]
UF Kadjeroen (Australian people)
Kadjerong (Australian people)
BT Australian aborigines
Ethnology—Australia
Gadner family
USE Gardner family
Gadolinite
[QE391.G]
Gadolinium
— **Isotopes**
— — **Spectra**
Gadolinium earths
[QD181.G4]
Gadow family (Not Subd Geog)
UF Gardow family

Gadsden family
USE Gadson family
Gadsden Purchase
[F786]
BT Southwest, New—History—1848-
Gadsden treaty, 1853
[F786]
Gadsen family
USE Gadson family
Gadson family (Not Subd Geog)
UF Gade family
Gadsden family
Gadsen family
Gadsup (Papuan people)
[DU740.42]
BT Ethnology—Papua New Guinea
Papuans
Gadsup language
BT Papuan languages
NT Agarabe language
Gaduliya Lohars
USE Lohars
Gadus
[QL638.G2]
BT Codfish
NT Gadus merlangus
Gadus aeglefinus
USE Haddock
Gadus callarias
USE Atlantic cod
Gadus esmarkii
USE Norway pout
Gadus macrocephalus
USE Pacific cod
Gadus merlangus
[QL638.G2]
UF Merlangius merlangus
Merlangus merlangus
Whiting (Fish)
BT Gadus
Gadus morhua macrocephalus
USE Pacific cod
Gadus morrhua
USE Atlantic cod
Gadus poutassou
[QL638.G2]
UF Blue whiting
Micromesistius poutassou
Whiting, Blue (Fish)
Gadus virens
USE Pollachius virens
Gaebel family
USE Gable family
Gaebu Timikkindyen (Legendary character)
USE Ṭimikkindyen (Legendary character)
Gaedschalk family
USE Gottschalk family
Gaekwad dynasty (Not Subd Geog)
Gaelic fiction (May Subd Geog)
NT Short stories, Gaelic
Gaelic folk-songs
USE Folk-songs, Gaelic
Gaelic imprints (May Subd Geog)
Gaelic language
[PB1501-1599]
UF Erse
Scottish language
BT Celtic languages
Goidelic languages
RT Irish language
NT Manx language
Gaelic language (Irish)
USE Irish language
Gaelic literature
[PB1605-1709]
BT British literature
Celtic literature
Gaelic philology
Gaelic poetry
[PB1605-PB1607]
[PB1631-PB1634]

[PB1648]
NT Political poetry, Gaelic
— 20th century
[PB1605 (History)]
[PB1631 (Collections)]
Gaelic political poetry
USE Political poetry, Gaelic
Gaelic short stories
USE Short stories, Gaelic
Gaelic songs
USE Songs, Gaelic
Gaels
USE Celts
Gaembs family
USE Gambs family
Gaerber family
USE Garber family
Gaertner family
USE Gardner family
Gaeta (Italy), Battle of, 1806
BT Napoleonic Wars, 1800-1814—
Campaigns—Italy
Gaetz family
USE Getz family
Gaeumannomyces
[QK623.D]
BT Diaporthaceae
Gaeumannomyces graminis
[QK623.D (Mycology)]
[SB608.G6 (Pathogen)]
UF Cereal take-all
Ophiobolus graminis
Ophiochaeta graminis
Rhaphidophora graminis
Take-all fungus
BT Fungi, Phytopathogenic
Grain—Diseases and pests
Grasses—Diseases and pests
NT Take-all disease
Gafat language
[PJ9285]
BT Ethiopian languages
Extinct languages
Gafeney family
USE Gaffney family
Gaff family
USE Goff family
Gaff-topsails (Fishes)
[QL638.A75]
BT Catfishes
Gaffney family (Not Subd Geog)
UF Gafeney family
Gaffs, Penny
USE Penny theaters
Gafuku (Papua New Guinea people)
USE Gahuku (Papua New Guinea people)
Gafuku language
USE Gahuku language
Gag (Fish)
UF Mycteroperca microlepis
BT Sea bass
Gag (Surgical instrument)
UF Mouth gag
BT Mouth—Surgery
Gag rule
USE subdivision Freedom of debate under
names of specific legislative bodies,
e.g. United States. Congress—
Freedom of debate
Legislative bodies—Freedom of debate
Newspaper court reporting
Gagá (Cult)
[BL2532.G33]
BT Cults—Dominican Republic
RT Voodooism
Gagaku
BT Music—Japan
NT Bugaku
Tōgaku
Gagauz
USE Gagauzi

Gagauz language
UF Gagauzi language
BT Bulgaria—Languages
Romania—Languages
Soviet Union—Languages
Turkic languages
Turkic languages, Southwest
Gagauzi
UF Gagauz
BT Ethnology—Balkan Peninsula
Oghuz
Turks
Gagauzi language
USE Gagauz language
Gage blocks
[TJ1166]
BT Gages
Measuring instruments
— Calibration
Gage family (Not Subd Geog)
UF Gaige family
Gaugi family
Gaugy family
Gawge family
Gage fields (Physics)
USE Gauge fields (Physics)
Gage invariance
USE Gauge invariance
Gager family (Not Subd Geog)
RT Jager family
Gages
[TJ1166]
UF Gauges
BT Measuring instruments
Weights and measures
RT Thickness measurement
NT Beta gages
Depth gage
Dial indicator
Drain-gages
Electric gages
Gage blocks
Indexing (Machine-shop practice)
Level indicators
Miter-gages
Pneumatic gages
Pressure gages
Radioactive gages
Rain gauges
Screw-thread gages
Strain gages
Surface gages
Vacuum-gages
— Calibration
Gages, Bourdon
USE Bourdon gages
Gages (Railroads)
USE Railroads—Gages
Gaging
[TP609]
UF Gauging
BT Mensuration
RT Liquors—Gaging and testing
NT Wine and wine making—Gaging and
testing
Gagliarde
USE Galliards
Gagou (African people)
[DT545.42]
UF Gban (African people)
Kagou (African people)
BT Ethnology—Ivory Coast
Gagou language
USE Gagu language
Gagu language
[PL8193]
UF Gagou language
Gban language
BT Ivory Coast—Languages
Kweni language
Southern Mande languages

Gaguedi
  USE Protea
Gagyū Hill (Japan)
  UF Gagyū-san (Japan)
     Gagyū-zan (Japan)
     Hakodate-yama (Japan)
  BT Mountains—Japan
  NT Hakodateyama Kōen (Hakodate-shi, Japan)
Gagyū-san (Japan)
  USE Gagyū Hill (Japan)
Gagyū-zan (Japan)
  USE Gagyū Hill (Japan)
Gagyūjō (Watari-chō, Japan)
  USE Watarijō (Watari-chō, Japan)
Gahan family *(Not Subd Geog)*
  UF Gahen family
Gahen family
  USE Gahan family
Gahom language
  USE Bahinemo language
Gahu
  BT Dance music—Africa, West
     Percussion ensembles
Gahuku (Papua New Guinea people)
  UF Gafuku (Papua New Guinea people)
  BT Ethnology—Papua New Guinea
     Papuans
Gahuku language
  UF Gafuku language
  BT Papuan languages
  RT Asaro language
Gaiac, Essence de bois
  USE Guaiac wood oil
Gaidamaks
  USE Haidamaks
Gaidropsarus
  [QL638.G2]
  BT Codfish
Gaige family
  USE Gage family
Gaigle (Game)
  [GV1299.G2]
Gailiunaite family
  USE Gailiunas family
Gailiunas family *(Not Subd Geog)*
  UF Gailiunaite family
Gaillard family
  USE Gillard family
Gaillarde family
  USE Gillard family
Gaillardes
  USE Galliards
Gain family
  USE Gaines family
Gain of weight in pregnancy
  USE Pregnant women—Weight gain
Gain sharing *(May Subd Geog)*
  [HD4928.G34]
     Here are entered works on any of a variety of wage payment methods in which workers receive additional earnings solely due to increases in productivity. Works on the distribution of money in the form of a bonus to employees as an outright gift or as a reward for outstanding achievement are entered under Bonus system. Works on the sharing of all profits or a predetermined percentage of them among all employees are entered under Profit-sharing.
  UF Gainsharing
     Productivity gain sharing
  BT Incentives in industry
     Wages
     Wages and labor productivity
Gaine family
  USE Gaines family
Gaines family *(Not Subd Geog)*
  UF Gain family
     Gaine family
     Gains family
     Ganes family
     Gaynes family
     Geans family

Gainesville Lake (Ala.)
  BT Lakes—Alabama
Gaingbe (African people)
  USE Mina (African people)
Gains family
  USE Gaines family
Gainsborough, Thomas, 1727-1788. Giovanna Baccelli
  [ND1329.G]
  UF Giovanna Baccelli (Portrait painting)
Gainsborough, Thomas, 1727-1788. Painter's daughters chasing a butterfly
  [ND1329.G]
  UF Painter's daughters chasing a butterfly (Portrait painting)
  BT Children—Portraits
     Children in art
Gainsharing
  USE Gain sharing
Gairdner, Lake (S. Aust.) *(Not Subd Geog)*
  UF Lake Gairdner (S. Aust.)
  BT Lakes—Australia
Gairfowl
  USE Great auk
Gaiser family *(Not Subd Geog)*
  UF Guiser family
Gait disorders
  USE Locomotion, Disordered
Gait in animals *(May Subd Geog)*
  UF Animal gaits
  BT Animal locomotion
  NT Horses—Paces, gaits, etc.
Gait in horses
  USE Horses—Paces, gaits, etc.
Gait in humans *(May Subd Geog)*
  UF Human gaits
  BT Human locomotion
     Running
     Walking
Gaita
  [ML980]
  UF Spanish bagpipe
  BT Bagpipe
Gaites family
  USE Gates family
Gajapati dynasty, 1435-1550
  USE Sūryavaṁśi Gajapati dynasty, 1435-1550
Gajili dialect
  USE Hazili dialect
Gajo language
  USE Gayo language
Gala (African people)
  USE Oromo (African people)
Galaaen family *(Not Subd Geog)*
Galactic center
  BT Galaxies
     Milky Way
  RT Galactic nuclei
Galactic clusters
  USE Stars—Open clusters
Galactic cosmic rays
  [QC485.9.G34]
  BT Cosmic rays
     Galaxies
  NT Solar cosmic rays
Galactic evolution
  USE Galaxies—Evolution
Galactic magnetic fields
  USE Interstellar magnetic fields
Galactic nebulae
  USE Nebulae
Galactic nuclei
  UF Nuclei, Galactic
  BT Galaxies
  RT Galactic center
Galactic orbits of K stars
  USE K stars—Orbits
Galactic orbits of stars
  USE Stars—Orbits

Galactic windows
  UF Windows, Galactic
  BT Milky Way
Galactic X-ray sources
  USE X-ray sources, Galactic
Galactin
  USE Prolactin
Galactopoietic hormone
  USE Prolactin
Galactorrhea
  USE Lactation disorders
Galactose
  [QD321]
  BT Glycosides
     Monosaccharides
  NT Plants, Effect of galactose on
Galactosemia
  BT Mental retardation
Galago
  [QL737.P955]
  BT Lorisidae
Galago demidovii
  USE Demidoff's bushbaby
Galago senegalensis
  USE Lesser bushbaby
Galagoides demidovii
  USE Demidoff's bushbaby
Galagos
  USE Lorisidae
Galahad
  UF Sir Galahad
  BT Arthurian romances
Galaher family
  USE Gallagher family
Galali dialect (Wilson River)
  USE Wangkumara (Galali) dialect
Galan family
  USE Galen family
Galant (The French word)
  BT French language—Etymology
Galant automobile
  USE Colt Galant automobile
Galante family
  USE Gallant family
Galantines
  BT Cookery (Meat)
     Cookery (Molded dishes)
     Cookery (Poultry)
Galapagos albatross
  [QL696.P63]
  UF Diomedea irrorata
Galapagos Islands
  NT Santa María Island (Galapagos Islands)
Galapagos Rift
  BT Rifts (Geology)—Pacific Ocean
Galapagos storm-petrel
  USE Oceanodroma tethys
Galapagos tortoise
  [QL666.C584]
  UF Testudo porteri
Galard family *(Not Subd Geog)*
  UF Gallard family
     Goalard family
     Golard family
Galatea (Greek deity)
  BT Goddesses, Greek
Galatians
  RT Celts
     Gauls
  NT Greece—History—Galatian Invasion, 279-278 B.C.
Galatians in art
Galawa language
  USE Alawa language
Galaway family
  USE Galloway family
Galaxias
  [QL638.G25]
  BT Galaxiidae
Galaxias fisheries *(May Subd Geog)*
  [SH351.G35]

Galaxias fisheries *(Continued)*
  UF New Zealand whitebait fisheries
      Whitebait fisheries, New Zealand
  BT Fisheries
Galaxies
  [QB856-QB858.8]
  UF Extragalactic nebulae
      Nebulae, Extragalactic
  BT Astronomy
  NT Active galaxies
      Density wave theory
      Dwarf galaxies
      Elliptical galaxies
      Emission-line galaxies
      Galactic center
      Galactic cosmic rays
      Galactic nuclei
      Magellanic Clouds
      Milky Way
      Nebulae
      Radio sources (Astronomy)
      Seyfert galaxies
      Stars
      X-ray sources, Galactic
  — Clusters
    [QB858.7]
    UF Clusters of galaxies
        Galaxies—Groups
        Galaxy clusters
        Groups of galaxies
    NT Virgo Cluster
  — Evolution
    UF Evolution, Galactic
        Galactic evolution
    BT Astronomy
  — Groups
    USE Galaxies—Clusters
  — Motion in the line of sight
    [QB857]
    UF Galaxies—Radial velocity
  — Problems exercises, etc.
  — Radial velocity
    USE Galaxies—Motion in the line of
         sight
  — Spectra
Galaxies, Active
  USE Active galaxies
Galaxiidae
  NT Galaxias
Galaxiiformes
  USE Salmoniformes
Galaxy (Milky Way)
  USE Milky Way
Galaxy clusters
  USE Galaxies—Clusters
Galaz Ruin (N.M.)
  USE Galaz Site (N.M.)
Galaz Site (N.M.) *(Not Subd Geog)*
  UF Galaz Ruin (N.M.)
  BT New Mexico—Antiquities
Galbraith family *(Not Subd Geog)*
  UF Galbreath family
      Galbreth family
      Gelbrith family
      Gilberth family
      Gilbraith family
      Gilbreath family
      Gilbreth family
      Gillbreath family
      Kilbraith family
      Kilbreath family
  RT Culbreth family
Galbreath family
  USE Galbraith family
Galbreth family
  USE Galbraith family
Galbulidae
  USE Jacamars
Gald family
  USE Gault family

Galeazzi family *(Not Subd Geog)*
Galeener family *(Not Subd Geog)*
  UF Galener family
      Galenor family
      Goleanor family
      Golenor family
Galeher family
  USE Gallagher family
Galela (Indonesian people)
  [DS632.G25]
  UF Galelarese (Indonesian people)
  BT Ethnology—Indonesia
Galela language
  USE Galelarese language
Galelarese (Indonesian people)
  USE Galela (Indonesian people)
Galelarese language
  [PL5323]
  UF Galela language
  BT Malayan languages
Galemys
  [QL737.I57]
  BT Moles (Animals)
Galemys pyrenaicus
  USE Pyrenean desman
Galen family *(Not Subd Geog)*
  UF Galan family
Galena *(May Subd Geog)*
  [QE391.G3]
  [TN452.G3]
  UF Blue lead
      Galenite
      Lead glance
  BT Lead ores
      Sulphide minerals
Galener family
  USE Galeener family
Galenite
  USE Galena
Galenor family
  USE Galeener family
Galeocerdo
  [QL638.95.C3]
  BT Carcharhinidae
Galeocerdo arcticus
  USE Tiger shark
Galeocerdo cuvieri
  USE Tiger shark
Galeodidae
  [QL458.82.G3]
  BT Solpugida
  NT Othoes
Galeopithecus
  USE Cynocephalus
Galeopterus
  USE Cynocephalus
Galeorhinus
  [QL638.95.C3]
  BT Carcharhinidae
Galeorhinus australis
  USE Galeorhinus galeus
Galeorhinus galeus
  [QL638.95.C3]
  UF Galeorhinus australis
      Liver-oil shark
      School shark
      Tope
  RT Tope fishing
Galeorhinus zyopterus
  USE Soupfin shark
Galerida cristata
  USE Crested lark
Galerkin methods
  BT Numerical analysis
  RT Finite element method
Galeruca
  [QL596.C5]
  UF Adimonia
  BT Chrysomelidae
Galerucella
  [QL596.C5]

  BT Chrysomelidae
  NT Galerucella nymphaeae
Galerucella nymphaeae
  [QL596.C5]
  BT Galerucella
Galerucidae
  USE Chrysomelidae
Galerum
  USE Galerus
Galerus
  UF Galerum
  BT Head-gear
Gales
  USE Windstorms
Gales family *(Not Subd Geog)*
  UF Gayles family
Galeta Point (Panama) *(Not Subd Geog)*
  UF Punta Galeta (Panama)
  BT Capes (Coasts)—Panama
Galford family *(Not Subd Geog)*
Galga
  USE Ingush
Galga River (Hungary) *(Not Subd Geog)*
  BT Rivers—Hungary
Galgadung language
  USE Kalkatungu language
Galgulidae
  USE Gelastocoridae
Galgulus
  USE Gelastocoris
Galiano Island (B.C.)
  BT Islands—British Columbia
Galibi Indians
  [F2460]
  BT Carib Indians
      Indians of South America
Galibi language
  [PM5976]
  BT Cariban languages
      Indians of South America—Languages
Galicia (Poland and Ukraine)
  UF Galicja (Poland and Ukraine)
      Galizien (Poland and Ukraine)
      Halichina (Poland and Ukraine)
  — History
  — — Peasant Uprising, 1846
    (Not Subd Geog)
    BT Peasant uprisings—Galicia
        (Poland and Ukraine)
  — — Uprising, 1848
  — — Revolution, 1863-1864
    (Not Subd Geog)
  — — Revolution, 1917-1921
    (Not Subd Geog)
Galicia (Spain : Region) *(Not Subd Geog)*
  — Politics and government
    (Not Subd Geog)
  — — 20th century *(Not Subd Geog)*
Galicia, Eastern (Ukraine)
  UF Eastern Galicia (Ukraine)
      Galicja Wschodnia (Ukraine)
      Skhidna Halychyna (Ukraine)
  BT Ukraine, Western
Galician dialect
  USE Gallegan dialect
Galicians (Spanish)
  USE Gallegans
Galicja (Poland and Ukraine)
  USE Galicia (Poland and Ukraine)
Galicja Wschodnia (Ukraine)
  USE Galicia, Eastern (Ukraine)
Galil (Israel)
  USE Galilee (Israel)
Galilean group
  UF Group, Galilean
  BT Groups, Continuous
      Transformation groups
Galilee (Israel)
  [DS110.G2]
  UF Galil (Israel)

Galilee, Sea of (Israel)
  USE Tiberias Lake (Israel)
Galileo Galilei Prize
  USE Premio internazionale Galileo Galilei
Galileo Project
  BT Jupiter probes
Galin-Paris-Chevé method (Music)
  [MT20]
  BT Music—Instruction and study
      Musical notation
      Sight-reading (Music)
      Sight-singing
      Singing—Methods
Galiteuthis
  [QL430.3.C72]
  BT Cranchiidae
Galiteuthis galacialis
  [QL430.3.C72]
Galium
  [QK495.R85]
  UF Bedstraw (Plant)
      Catchweed
      Cleavers (Plant)
      Cleaverwort
      Clivers (Plant)
      Goose grass
  BT Rubiaceae
Galium odorata
  USE Sweet woodruff
Galiway family
  USE Galloway family
Galizien (Poland and Ukraine)
  USE Galicia (Poland and Ukraine)
Gall
  USE Bile
Gall-bladder
  USE Gallbladder
Gall crabs
  USE Cryptochiridae
Gall-ducts
  USE Bile-ducts
Gall-flies
  USE Gallflies
Gall-gnats
  USE Gall midges
  NT Cecidomyia
      Contarinia
      Dasyneura
      Haplodiplosis
      Janetiella
      Miastor
      Retinodiplosis
      Rye gall-gnat
      Saddle gall midge
      Sitodiplosis
Gall midges *(May Subd Geog)*
  [QL537.C33 (Entomology)]
  UF Cecidomyiidae
      Gall-gnats
      Gnats, Gall
      Itonididae
      Midges, Gall
  BT Diptera
  NT Asphondylia
      Asteromyia
      Heteropeza
      Mayetiola
      Thecodiplosis
Gall mites
  USE Eriophyidae
Gall sickness
  USE Anaplasmosis
Gall wasps
  USE Gallflies
Galla (African people)
  USE Oromo (African people)
Galla language
  USE Oromo language
Gallady family
  USE Galloway family

Gallagher family *(Not Subd Geog)*
  UF Galaher family
      Galeher family
      Gallaher family
      Gallegher family
      Galleher family
      Gallehew family
      Galliger family
      Galligher family
      Galliher family
      Galloher family
      Gelaher family
      O'Gallagher family
Gallaher family
  USE Gallagher family
Galland family
  USE Gallant family
Gallant family *(Not Subd Geog)*
  UF Galante family
      Galland family
Gallanty-shows
  USE Shadow pantomimes and plays
Gallaratese (Milan, Italy)
  USE Quartiere Gallaratese (Milan, Italy)
Gallard family
  USE Galard family
Gallas
  USE Oromo (African people)
Gallaway family
  USE Galloway family
Gallbladder
  [QL867 (Comparative anatomy)]
  [QM351 (Human anatomy)]
  [QP185 (Physiology)]
  UF Gall-bladder
  BT Biliary tract
  — **Blood-vessels**
  — Calculi
      USE Gallstones
  — **Diseases** *(May Subd Geog)*
      [RC849-RC853]
      NT Cholecystitis
         Cholecystoses
         Gallstones
  — Inflammation
      USE Cholecystitis
  — **Radiography** *(May Subd Geog)*
      UF Cholecystography
  — **Surgery** *(May Subd Geog)*
      [RD546-RD547]
      NT Cholecystectomy
  — — **Complications and sequelae**
      (May Subd Geog)
Gallega Island (Mexico)
  USE San Juan de Ulúa Island (Mexico)
Gallegan authors
  USE Authors, Gallegan
Gallegan ballads
  USE Ballads, Gallegan
Gallegan dialect *(May Subd Geog)*
  [PC5411-5414]
  UF Galician dialect
  BT Portuguese language
Gallegan drama *(May Subd Geog)*
Gallegan fiction *(May Subd Geog)*
  NT Short stories, Gallegan
Gallegan imprints *(May Subd Geog)*
Gallegan literature
  [PQ9450-PQ9462 (History)]
  [PQ9463-PQ9468 (Collections)]
  BT Spanish literature
Gallegan national characteristics
  USE National characteristics, Gallegan
Gallegan newspapers *(May Subd Geog)*
Gallegan periodicals *(May Subd Geog)*
Gallegan philology
Gallegan poetry
  [PQ9460]
  [PQ9464]
  NT Quatrains, Gallegan
  — To 1500

  USE Portuguese poetry—To 1500
Gallegan prose literature *(May Subd Geog)*
Gallegan quatrains
  USE Quatrains, Gallegan
Gallegan riddles
  USE Riddles, Gallegan
Gallegan short stories
  USE Short stories, Gallegan
Gallegan songs
  USE Songs, Gallegan
Gallegan wit and humor *(May Subd Geog)*
Gallegan wit and humor, Pictorial
  (May Subd Geog)
  [NC1630-1639]
Gallegans *(May Subd Geog)*
  [DP302.G11-DP302.G12 (Spain)]
  [F1789.G3 (Cuba)]
  UF Galicians (Spanish)
      Gallegos
Gallegez family
  USE Gallegos family
Gallegher family
  USE Gallagher family
Gallego family
  USE Gallegos family
Gállego River (Spain)
  UF Río Gállego (Spain)
  BT Rivers—Spain
Gallegos
  USE Gallegans
Gallegos family *(Not Subd Geog)*
  UF Gallegez family
      Gallego family
Gallegos Mesa (N.M.)
  BT Mesas—New Mexico
Galleher family
  USE Gallagher family
Gallehew family
  USE Gallagher family
Gallein
  [QD441]
  BT Coal-tar colors
Galleons *(May Subd Geog)*
  BT Sailing ships
  RT Galleys
Gallep family
  USE Gallup family
Galleria
  [QL561.P9]
  BT Pyralidae
  NT Galleria mellonella
Galleria mellonella *(May Subd Geog)*
  [QL561.P9]
  UF Bee moth
      Larger wax moth
      Wax moth, Larger
  BT Galleria
Galleridae
  USE Pyralidae
Galleries, Art
  USE Art museums
Galleries (Architecture) *(May Subd Geog)*
Galleriidae
  USE Pyralidae
Galleway family
  USE Galloway family
Galleys
  [VM15-17]
  BT Prisons
      Ships
  RT Galleons
Galleys (Ship kitchens)
  UF Ship kitchens
      Ships' kitchens
  BT Kitchens
Gallflies
  [QL568.C9]
  UF Cynipidae
      Gall-flies
      Gall wasps

Gallflies (Continued)
  BT Hymenoptera
      Wasps
  RT Galls (Botany)
  NT Violet gallfly
Galliambic
  [PA188.G]
  [PA416.G]
  [PA2337.G]
Galliards
  UF Gagliarde
      Gaillardes
  BT Dance music
Galliari family *(Not Subd Geog)*
Gallic acid
  [QD341.A2 (Chemistry)]
  [RM666.G (Therapeutics)]
Gallic coins
  USE Coins, Gallic
Gallic language
  USE Gaulish language
Gallic Wars, 58-51 B.C.
  USE Gaul—History—Gallic Wars, 58-51
      B.C.
Gallican rite (Catholic Church)
  USE Catholic Church—Gallican rite
Gallicanism
  BT Catholic Church—France—
      Government
      Church and state—France—History
  RT Pragmatic sanction of Charles VII,
      1438
Gallicisms
  [PB307]
  BT French language—Terms and phrases
      French language—Vocabulary
  SA *subdivision* Gallicisms *under names of*
      languages, e.g. English language—
      Gallicisms
Galliformes *(May Subd Geog)*
  [QL696.G2]
  UF Gallinae
  BT Birds
  NT Cracidae
      Hoactzin
      Megapodiidae
      Phasianidae
      Pheasants
      Tetraonidae
      Turkeys
  — **Anatomy**
Galliger family
  USE Gallagher family
Galligher family
  USE Gallagher family
Galliher family
  USE Gallagher family
Gallinae
  USE Galliformes
Gallinago gallinago
  USE Wilson's snipe
Gallinula
  [QL696.G876]
  BT Rallidae
Gallinula chloropus
  [QL696.G876]
  UF Common gallinule
      Florida gallinule
      Gallinule, Common
      Gray moorhen
      Moorhen, Gray
Gallinule, Common
  USE Gallinula chloropus
Gallinya language
  USE Oromo language
Gallipoli Campaign, 1915
  USE World War, 1914-1918—Campaigns—
      Turkey—Gallipoli Peninsula
Gallipoli Peninsula (Turkey)
  UF Gelibolu Peninsula (Turkey)
  BT Peninsulas—Turkey

Gallison family *(Not Subd Geog)*
Gallium
  [QD181.G2]
  — **Electrometallurgy**
    [TN799.G3]
  — **Isotopes**
    UF Gallium isotopes
  — — **Spectra**
  — **Metallurgy**
    [TN799.G3]
  — **Spectra**
Gallium alloys
  NT Gallium-tin alloys
Gallium arsenide semiconductors
  BT Semiconductors
Gallium compounds
Gallium isotopes
  USE Gallium—Isotopes
Gallium organic compounds
  USE Organogallium compounds
Gallium-tin alloys
  UF Tin-gallium alloys
  BT Gallium alloys
      Tin alloys
Galliway family
  USE Galloway family
Gallo-Italian dialects
  [PC1851-1874]
  UF Dialects
Gallo language
  USE Gallong language
Gallo-Roman architecture
  USE Architecture, Gallo-Roman
Gallo-Roman art
  USE Art, Gallo-Roman
Gallo-Roman bronzes
  USE Bronzes, Gallo-Roman
Gallo-Roman gods
  USE Gods, Gallo-Roman
Gallo-Roman mural painting and decoration
  USE Mural painting and decoration, Gallo-
      Roman
Gallo-Roman pottery
  USE Pottery, Gallo-Roman
Gallo-Roman relief (Sculpture)
  USE Relief (Sculpture), Gallo-Roman
Gallo-Roman sculpture
  USE Sculpture, Gallo-Roman
Gallo-Roman terra-cotta sculpture
  USE Terra-cotta sculpture, Gallo-Roman
Galloa (African people)
  USE Galwa (African people)
Gallodeoxycholic acid
  USE Chenodeoxycholic acid
Gallóglaigh
  USE Galloglasses
Galloglasses
  [DA933-DA937 (Ireland)]
  UF Gallóglaigh
      Gallowglasses
  BT Mercenary troops
Galloher family
  USE Gallagher family
Gallolestes
  [QE882.T49]
  BT Mammals, Fossil
Gallolestes pachymandibularis
  [QE882.T49]
Gallong language
  [PL4001.G16]
  UF Gallo language
      Galo language
  BT Tibeto-Burman languages
Gallongs
  UF Galongs
  BT Abors
      Ethnology—India
Gallop family
  USE Gallup family
Gallopamil
  [RC684.G34]

  UF Dimethoxyphenethylme
      thylaminoisopropyltr
      imethoxyphenylvaleronitrile
  BT Calcium—Antagonists
      Hypotensive agents
      Myocardial depressants
      Nitriles
      Phenethylamines
      Vasodilators
Galloperdix
  USE Spur fowl
Galloup family
  USE Gallup family
Galloupe family
  USE Gallup family
Gallowary family
  USE Galloway family
Galloway (Scotland)
Galloway cattle
  [SF199.G (SF193.G2)]
  NT Belted Galloway
Galloway family *(Not Subd Geog)*
  UF Galaway family
      Galiway family
      Gallady family
      Gallaway family
      Galleway family
      Galliway family
      Gallowary family
      Galode family
      Galoway family
      Galway family
      Golaway family
      Golladay family
      Golliday family
Gallowglasses
  USE Galloglasses
Gallows *(May Subd Geog)*
  BT Hanging
      Law—Antiquities
Galls (Botany) *(May Subd Geog)*
  [SB767]
  UF Cecidology
      Insect galls
      Plant galls
  BT Tumors, Plant
  RT Gallflies
      Insect pests
  — **Anatomy**
Gallstones *(May Subd Geog)*
  [RC850 (Medicine)]
  [RD547 (Surgery)]
  UF Bile-ducts—Calculi
      Biliary calculi
      Calculi, Biliary
      Cholelith
      Cholelithiasis
      Gallbladder—Calculi
  BT Bile-ducts—Diseases
      Calculi
      Gallbladder—Diseases
  NT Chenodeoxycholic acid
Gallup family *(Not Subd Geog)*
  UF Gallep family
      Gallop family
      Galloup family
      Galloupe family
      Gallupe family
      Galop family
      Galup family
      Galut family
Gallupe family
  USE Gallup family
Gallus
  USE Jungle fowl
Gallus domesticus
  USE Chickens
Gallus gallus
  USE Chickens
      Red junglefowl

Galo language
USE Gallong language
Galoa (African people)
USE Galwa (African people)
Galode family
USE Galloway family
Galois correspondences
UF Correspondences, Galois
BT Set theory
RT Closure operators
Galois theory
⌈QA171 (Groups)⌉
⌈QA214 (Equations, QA211)⌉
BT Equations, Theory of
Groups, Theory of
Numbers, Theory of
NT Finite fields (Algebra)
Galongs
USE Gallongs
Galop family
USE Gallup family
Galops
BT Dance music
Galoubet
⌈ML935-7⌉
UF Txistu
BT Flageolet
Flute
Recorder (Musical instrument)
Woodwind instruments
Galoubet and tambourin music
⌈M298⌉
UF Tambourin and galoubet music
Galoubet music
⌈M110.G⌉
Galoubet music (Galoubets (2))
⌈M288-9⌉
Galoway family
USE Galloway family
Galphin, George, d. 1780
— **Homes and haunts**
— — **South Carolina**
NT Silver Bluff (S.C.)
Galt family
USE Gault family
Galtung family (Not Subd Geog)
Galum Creek (Ill.) (Not Subd Geog)
BT Rivers—Illinois
Galumnidae
⌈QL458.2.G34⌉
BT Mites
Galup family
USE Gallup family
Galut family
USE Gallup family
Galuth
USE Jews—Diaspora
Galvaginus (Legendary character)
USE Gawain (Legendary character)
Galvanic batteries
USE Electric batteries
Galvanic corrosion
USE Electrolytic corrosion
Galvanic skin response
UF Electrodermal response
Psychogalvanic reflex
Skin conductance response
Skin potential response
Skin response, Galvanic
BT Electrophysiology
Reflexes
Skin
Galvanism
USE Electricity
Galvanized iron
USE Iron, Galvanized
Galvanized steel
USE Steel, Galvanized
Galvanizing
⌈TS660⌉
BT Plating

RT Zinc coating
NT Iron, Galvanized
Metals—Pickling
Steel, Galvanized
Zinc plating
Galvanoionization
USE Iontophoresis
Galvanomagnetic effects
BT Electric currents
Magnetic fields
Thermomagnetism
Transport theory
NT Hall effect
Magnetoresistance
Galvanometer
⌈QC544.G2⌉
BT Electric apparatus and appliances
RT Electric measurements
NT Fluxmeter
Galvanoplastic process
USE Electrotyping
Galvanoplasty
USE Electrometallurgy
Electroplating
Electrotyping
Galvanosurgery
USE Electrosurgery
Galvanotropism
UF Electropism
BT Plants, Effect of electricity on
Galveston Bay (Tex.)
BT Bays—Texas
Galveston-Houston Electric Railway
BT Railroads—United States
Galveston Island (Tex.)
UF Island of Galveston (Tex.)
BT Islands—Texas
Galvezia
⌈QK495.S43⌉
BT Scrophulariaceae
Galvezia leucantha
⌈QK495.S43⌉
Galwa (African people)
UF Galloa (African people)
Galoa (African people)
Igulua (African people)
Ngaloi (African people)
BT Ethnology—Gabon
Myene (African people)
Galway Bay (Ireland)
BT Bays—Ireland
Galway family
USE Galloway family
Gamala (Ancient city)
USE Gamla (Ancient city)
Gamant language
USE Kemant language
Gamasidae
NT Parasitus
Gamba players
USE Viol players
Gambai dialect
⌈PL8197⌉
UF Kabba Laka dialect
Ngambai dialect
Sara Gambai dialect
Sara Ngambay dialect
BT Chad—Languages
Sara languages
Gamball family
USE Gamble family
Gambaye (African people)
UF Ngambaye (African people)
BT Ethnology—Chad
Gambel family
USE Gamble family
Gambel quail
USE Gambel's quail
Gambell family
USE Gamble family

Gambel's quail
UF Gambel quail
Lophortyx gambelii
BT Quails
Gambesian sleeping sickness
USE African trypanosomiasis
Gambhira Festival
BT Festivals—India
Gambia
— **Economic conditions**
— — **1965-**
— **History**
NT Niumi (Kingdom)
— — **Coup d'état, 1981** (Not Subd Geog)
BT Coups d'état—Gambia
— **Languages**
NT Diola language
Serer language
Wolof language
— **Politics and government**
— — **1965-**
Gambía Indians
USE Moguex Indians
Gambian black-headed weaver
USE Ploceus melanocephalus
Gambiano Indians
USE Moguex Indians
Gambill family
USE Gamble family
Gambists
USE Viol players
Gamble family (Not Subd Geog)
UF Gamball family
Gambel family
Gambell family
Gambill family
Gambol family
Gimbold family
Gimpel family
Gamble House (Pasadena, Calif.)
USE David B. Gamble House (Pasadena, Calif.)
Gamblers (May Subd Geog)
BT Gambling
NT Lottery winners
Gambling (May Subd Geog)
⌈GV1245 (Card-playing, Ethics of)⌉
⌈HV6708-HV6722 (Crimes and offenses)⌉
UF Betting
Games of chance
Gaming
BT Contracts, Aleatory
Crimes without victims
Criminal law
Ethics
Organized crime
RT Wagers
NT Bingo—Law and legislation
Blackjack (Game)
Book-making (Betting)
Boule (Game)
Cards
Cardsharping
Casinos
Compulsive gambling
Dice
Faro
Gamblers
Horse race betting
Indians of North America—Gambling
Lotteries
Pari-mutuel betting
Raffles
Roulette
Slot machines
Soccer—Betting
Speculation
Sports betting
Trente-et-quarante
— **Religious aspects**

Gambling
— **Religious aspects** *(Continued)*
— — **Buddhism, [Christianity, etc.]**
— **Taxation** *(May Subd Geog)*
    NT Horse-racing—Taxation
Gambling, Compulsive
    USE Compulsive gambling
Gambling (Canon law)
Gambling chips *(May Subd Geog)*
    [NK4696.35 (Decorative arts)]
    UF Chips, Gambling
    BT Tokens
Gambling literature
    UF Literature, Gambling
Gambling problem (Mathematics)
    USE Games of chance (Mathematics)
Gambling systems
    [GV1302]
    UF Betting systems
        Systems,, Gambling
    BT Chance
        Probabilities
        Statistics
Gambo hemp
    USE Kenaf
Gambol family
    USE Gamble family
Gambs family *(Not Subd Geog)*
    UF Gaembs family
        Gams family
        Gems family
        Gemse family
Gambusia
    [QL638.P73]
    BT Poeciliidae
Gambusia affinis
    [QL638.P73]
    UF Mosquitofish
Gambusiformes
    USE Atheriniformes
Game and game-bird stocking
    (May Subd Geog)
    UF Restocking of game and game-birds
        Stocking of game and game-birds
    BT Animal culture
        Game bird culture
        Wildlife management
Game and game-birds *(May Subd Geog)*
    [QL696.G2 (Ornithology)]
    [SK (Hunting)]
    UF Wild-fowl
    BT Birds
        Food, Wild
        Zoology
    RT Hunting
        Trapping
    SA *particular animals and birds, e.g.* Deer,
        Grouse, Rabbits
    NT Animal introduction
        Band-tailed pigeon
        Big game animals
        Cookery (Game)
        Decoys (Hunting)
        Falconry
        Fowling
        Game bird culture
        Game fowl
        Game-laws
        Game protection
        Shore birds
        Tinamiformes
        Upland game birds
        Waterfowl
        Wildlife as food
    — **Age determination**
    — **Control**
        USE Wildlife pests—Control
    — **Diseases** *(May Subd Geog)*
        BT Birds—Diseases
    — **Feeding and feeds**
        BT Game protection

Game and game-birds, Dressing of
    UF Dressing of game
        Fish and game, Dressing of
    BT Hunting
        Slaughtering and slaughter-houses
    NT Fishes, Dressing of
Game bird culture *(May Subd Geog)*
    [SF508]
    BT Animal culture
        Aviculture
        Game and game-birds
    NT Game and game-bird stocking
        Upland game bird culture
        Waterfowl culture
    — **United States**
        NT National poultry improvement plan
Game bird hunting
    USE Fowling
Game bird management *(May Subd Geog)*
    BT Wildlife management
    NT Upland game bird management
Game birds, Upland
    USE Upland game birds
Game boards
    USE Gameboards
Game breeders *(May Subd Geog)*
    UF Breeders, Game
    BT Animal breeders
Game calling (Hunting)
    BT Animal sounds
        Calls (for animals)
        Hunting
Game chickens
    USE Game fowl
Game cocks
    USE Game fowl
        Old English Game (Chickens)
Game control
    USE Wildlife pests—Control
Game depredation
    USE Wildlife depredation
Game farms *(May Subd Geog)*
    BT Farms
Game fowl *(May Subd Geog)*
    [SF502.8-503.52]
    UF Fighting chickens
        Fighting cocks
        Fowl, Game
        Game chickens
        Game cocks
    BT Chicken breeds
        Chickens
        Game and game-birds
    RT Cockfighting
        Roosters
    NT Old English Game (Chickens)
        Old English Game bantams
Game keepers
    USE Gamekeepers
Game-laws *(May Subd Geog)*
    [SK355-579]
    UF Game protection—Law and legislation
        Hunting—Law and legislation
        Hunting law
    BT Game and game-birds
        Game protection
        Wildlife conservation—Law and
            legislation
    RT Game wardens
    NT Birds, Protection of—Law and
            legislation
        Endangered species—Law and
            legislation
        Hunting with bow and arrow—Law
            and legislation
        Indians of North America—Hunting—
            Law and legislation
        Marine mammals—Law and legislation
        Trapping—Law and legislation
Game management
    USE Wildlife management

Game meat
    USE Wildlife as food
Game pests
    USE Wildlife pests
Game-preserves *(May Subd Geog)*
    [SK357]
    UF Game reserves
    BT Hunting
        Wildlife management areas
    NT Royal forests
        Shooting preserves
    — **Bhutan**
        NT Manas Game Sanctuary (Bhutan)
    — **Kenya**
        NT Masai Mara Game Reserve
            (Kenya)
            Tsavo National Park (Kenya)
    — **Michigan**
        NT Isle Royale National Park (Mich.)
    — **South Africa**
        NT Timbavati Game Reserve (South
            Africa)
    — **Tanzania**
        NT Ngorongoro Game Control Area
            Reserve (Tanzania)
            Selous Game Reserve (Tanzania)
Game protection *(May Subd Geog)*
    [SK351-579]
    UF Protection of game
    BT Game and game-birds
        Wildlife conservation
    NT Birds, Protection of
        Game and game-birds—Feeding and
            feeds
        Game-laws
        Gamekeepers
    — **Law and legislation**
        USE Game-laws
Game reeves
    USE Game wardens
Game reserves
    USE Game-preserves
Game rooms
    USE Recreation rooms
Game shows
    UF Television game shows
    BT Contests
        Radio programs
        Rewards (Prizes, etc.)
        Television programs
    RT Quiz shows
Game theory
    [QA269]
    UF Games, Theory of
        Theory of games
    BT Mathematical models
        Mathematics
    NT Decision-making
        Differential games
        Games of chance (Mathematics)
        Games of strategy (Mathematics)
        Simulation games in education
        Statistical decision
    — **Computer programs**
        NT SMS (Computer program)
Game wardens *(May Subd Geog)*
    UF Game reeves
    BT Police, Rural
    RT Game-laws
Gameboards *(May Subd Geog)*
    UF Boards, Game
        Game boards
    RT Board games
Gamekeepers *(May Subd Geog)*
    UF Game keepers
    BT Game protection
    NT Riverkeepers
Gamel family
    USE Gemmell family
Gamelan
    [ML1251]

UF Gamelang
BT Orchestra
    Percussion instruments
NT Khjai Mendung (Gamelan)
Gamelan music
Gamelang
  USE Gamelan
Gamell family
  USE Gemmell family
Games *(May Subd Geog)*
    [*BF717 (Psychology of play)*]
    [*GN454-GN456 (Ethnology)*]
    [*GR480-GR485 (Folk-lore)*]
    [*GV1200-GV1511*]
    [*LB1137 (Psychology, Educational)*]
    [*LB1177 (Kindergarten)*]
    [*LB3031 (School management)*]
  UF Children—Recreation
    Children's games
    Games for children
    Pastimes
    Recreations
  BT Children's paraphernalia
    Entertaining
    Physical education and training
  RT Amusements
    Play
    Sports
  SA *specific games, e.g.* Backgammon,
    Baseball, Billiards, Chess,
    Dominoes, Tennis, Whist
  NT Adventure games
    Ball games
    Bible games and puzzles
    Board games
    Booster (Game)
    Cards
    Dancing—Children's dances
    Drinking games
    Educational games
    Electronic games
    Family recreation
    Fantasy football (Game)
    Fantasy games
    Games for travelers
    Games for two
    Geographical recreations
    Group games
    Hand games
    Highland games
    Indoor games
    Letter writing recreations
    Matchstick games
    Ouija board
    Pencil games
    Philosophical recreations
    Pinball machines
    Play-party
    Psychological games
    Puzzles
    Quoits
    Reading games
    Rotisserie League Baseball (Game)
    Schools—Exercises and recreations
    Secular games
    Senior Olympics
    Singing games
    Targets (Sports)
    Traveller (Game)
    Turkmen—Games
    Video games
    Word games
    World Cup (Track-athletics)
  — Data processing
    Here are entered works on the application of
  computers and data processing techniques to
  games in general, including recording statistics,
  setting up tournaments, etc. Works on games
  played on a computer are entered under Computer games.
    NT Computer games

— **Symbolic aspects**
    [*GV1201.35*]
  UF Games, Symbolism of
    Symbolism of games
  BT Symbolism
— **Afghanistan**
  NT Buzkashi
— **United States**
  NT Afro-American children's games
    Mexican American children's
    games
Games, Adventure
  USE Adventure games
Games, Bible
  USE Bible games and puzzles
Games, Chinese, [Mexican, Oriental, etc.]
Games, Computer adventure
  USE Computer adventure games
Games, Differential
  USE Differential games
Games, Floral
  USE Floral games
Games, Greek and Roman
  UF Games, Roman
    Roman games
  NT Secular games
Games, Japanese
  NT Sugoroku (Game)
Games, Olympic
  USE Olympics
Games, Political
  USE Political games
Games, Primitive *(May Subd Geog)*
    [*GN454-457*]
  NT Dan (African people)—Games
    Indians of Central America—Games
    Indians of Mexico—Games
    Indians of North America—Games
    Indians of South America—Games
— **Australia**
  NT Australian aborigines—Games
— **New Zealand**
  NT Maoris—Games
Games, Psychic
  USE Psychic games
Games, Rhythmic
  USE Games with music
Games, Roman
  USE Games, Greek and Roman
Games, Russian
  UF Russian games
Games, Secular
  USE Secular games
Games, Symbolism of
  USE Games—Symbolic aspects
Games, Theory of
  USE Game theory
Games, Tibetan
  NT Rebirth (Game)
Games for backpackers
  USE Games for campers
Games for campers *(May Subd Geog)*
    [*GV1202.C36*]
  UF Backpackers' games
    Campers' games
    Games for backpackers
  BT Amusements
    Backpacking
    Camping
Games for children
  USE Games
Games for travelers *(May Subd Geog)*
    [*GV1206*]
  UF Travelers, Games for
  BT Automobiles—Touring
    Games
    Travel
Games for two *(May Subd Geog)*
    [*GV1201.4*]
  UF Two, Games for
  BT Games

Games in art
Games in art education *(May Subd Geog)*
  BT Art—Study and teaching
    Educational games
Games in Buddhist education
    [*BQ190*]
  BT Buddhist education
  NT Rebirth (Game)
Games in Christian education
    [*BV1536.3*]
  BT Christian education
Games in gerontology
  USE Gerontology—Simulation games
Games in Jewish religious education
  BT Jewish religious education
Games in literature
Games in mathematics education
    [*QA20.G35*]
  BT Educational games
    Mathematics—Study and teaching
  RT Mathematical recreations
Games in religious education
  BT Religious education
Games of chance
  USE Gambling
Games of chance (Mathematics)
    [*QA273*]
  UF Gambling problem (Mathematics)
  BT Chance
    Game theory
    Probabilities
  NT Monte Carlo method
Games of strategy (Mathematics)
    [*QA270*]
  UF Games with rational pay-off
    (Mathematics)
    Rational games (Mathematics)
    Strategy, Games of (Mathematics)
  BT Game theory
    Groups, Theory of
    Mathematical optimization
    Matrices
    Topology
  NT Management games
Games with music
    [*M1993*]
  UF Action songs
    Games, Rhythmic
    Rhythmic games
  BT Children's songs
    Play-party
  RT Singing games
  NT Musical card games
Games with rational pay-off (Mathematics)
  USE Games of strategy (Mathematics)
Gametes
  BT Embryology
    Reproduction
  NT Ovum
    Spermatozoa
Gametogenesis
  BT Embryology
  NT Oogenesis
    Spermatogenesis
Gameway Ajilee (Navajo rite)
  USE Ajilee (Navajo rite)
Gamgee family *(Not Subd Geog)*
Gaming
  USE Gambling
Gaming, Educational
  USE Simulation games in education
Gamla (Ancient city) *(Not Subd Geog)*
    [*DS99.G35*]
  UF Gamala (Ancient city)
  BT Cities and towns, Ruined, extinct, etc.
    —Syria
    Syria—Antiquities

Gamla Stan (Stockholm, Sweden)
  (Not Subd Geog)
  UF Old Town (Stockholm, Sweden)
      Staden (Stockholm, Sweden)
      Staden Mellan Broarna (Stockholm,
        Sweden)
      Stockholm (Sweden).   Gamla Stan
      Stockholm (Sweden).   Old Town
GAMMA (Electronic computer system)
  UF Graphically Aided Mathematical
      Machine
  BT On-line data processing
Gamma-aminobutyric acid
  USE GABA
Gamma-cystathionase
  USE Cystathionine gamma-lyase
Gamma decay
  UF Decay, Gamma
  BT Gamma rays
      Radioisotopes—Decay
Gamma fission reaction
  USE Photofission
Gamma functions
  USE Functions, Gamma
Gamma-gamma interactions
  USE Photon-photon interactions
Gamma globulin
  [QP552.G3]
  BT Blood proteins
      Globulin
  NT Hypergammaglobulinemia
Gamma globulin deficiency
  USE Agammaglobulinemia
Gamma particle (Cytology)
  UF Particle, Gamma (Cytology)
  BT Cell organelles
      Cytoplasm
      Plant cells and tissues
Gamma ray angular correlations
  [QC793.5.G327]
  BT Angular correlations (Nuclear physics)
      Gamma rays
Gamma ray astronomy
  [QB471]
  BT Astronomy
      Gamma rays
      Space astronomy
  NT Gamma ray bursts
Gamma ray bursts
  [QB471.7.B85]
  UF Bursts, Cosmic gamma ray
      Bursts, Gamma ray
      Cosmic gamma ray bursts
      Transients, Gamma ray
  BT Gamma ray astronomy
      X-ray bursts
Gamma ray lasers
  BT Gamma rays
      Lasers
Gamma ray production
  USE Gamma ray sources
Gamma ray sources
  [QC793.5.G322]
  UF Gamma ray production
      Gamma sources
      Sources, Gamma ray
  BT Gamma rays
      Radiation sources
Gamma ray spectrometer
  [QC787.S6]
  BT Spectrometer
  — **Calibration**
Gamma ray spectrometry
  UF Spectrometry, Gamma ray
  BT Angular correlations (Nuclear physics)
      Gamma rays
      Nuclear spectroscopy
      Radiochemistry
      Spectrometer
      Spectrum analysis
  NT In-beam gamma ray spectroscopy

Neutron capture gamma ray
    spectroscopy
— **Computer programs**
Gamma rays
  [QC490]
  BT Electromagnetic waves
      Ionizing radiation
      Radiation
      X-rays
  NT Gamma decay
      Gamma ray angular correlations
      Gamma ray astronomy
      Gamma ray lasers
      Gamma ray sources
      Gamma ray spectrometry
— **Industrial applications**
  NT Radiography, Industrial
— **Measurement**
  BT Electromagnetic measurements
— **Physiological effect**
  NT Plants, Effect of gamma rays on
— **Polarization**
— **Scattering**
— **Therapeutic use**
  BT Radiotherapy
Gamma sources
  USE Gamma ray sources
Gammaglobulinopathies, Monoclonal
  USE Gammopathies, Monoclonal
Gammarus pseudolimnaeus
  [QL444.M315]
Gammelgaard family (Not Subd Geog)
  UF Gammelgard family
Gammelgard family
  USE Gammelgaard family
Gammill family
  USE Gemmell family
Gammopathies, Monoclonal
  (May Subd Geog)
  [RC647.H9]
  UF Gammaglobulinopathies, Monoclonal
      Immunoglobulinopathies, Monoclonal
      M-component
        hypergammaglobulinemia
      Monoclonal gammopathies
      Monoclonal immunoglobulinopathies
  BT Hypergammaglobulinemia
      Immunoglobulins
      Plasma cell diseases
  RT Antibodies, Monoclonal
  NT Multiple myeloma
Gamō (Sendai-shi, Miyagi-ken, Japan)
  (Not Subd Geog)
  UF Sendai-shi (Miyagi-ken, Japan).
      Gamō
Gamopetalae
  [QK495.G]
Gamow barrier
  USE Potential barrier
Gamper family (Not Subd Geog)
Gams family
  USE Gambs family
Gamzigrad (City) (Not Subd Geog)
  BT Cities and towns, Ruined, extinct, etc.
      —Yugoslavia
      Yugoslavia—Antiquities
Gan ha-omanut ʻa. sh. Bili Roz (Jerusalem)
  UF Billy Rose Art Garden (Jerusalem)
      Billy Rose Sculpture Garden
        (Jerusalem)
      Gan ha-omanut ʻal shem Bili Roz
        (Jerusalem)
  BT Sculpture gardens—Israel
Gan ha-omanut ʻal shem Bili Roz (Jerusalem)
  USE Gan ha-omanut ʻa. sh. Bili Roz
      (Jerusalem)
Gana language
  USE G//ana language
Gaṇagaura
  USE Gangaur

//Ganakhoe language
  USE G//ana language
Ganana River (Ehtiopia and Somalia)
  USE Juba River (Ethiopia and Somalia)
Ganaphosidae
  NT Neozimiris
Gaṇapule family (Not Subd Geog)
Ganda (African people)
  UF Baganda (African people)
      Waganda (African people)
  BT Bantus
      Ethnology—Uganda
Ganda (Nigerian people)
  USE Gaanda (African people)
Ganda fiction (May Subd Geog)
Ganda folk-songs
  USE Folk-songs, Ganda
Ganda language
  [PL8201]
  UF Lu-ganda
      Luganda language
  BT Bantu languages
— **Etymology**
  NT Obugezi (The Ganda word)
Ganda proverbs
  USE Proverbs, Ganda
Gander River (Nfld.) (Not Subd Geog)
  BT Rivers—Newfoundland
Gandey family
  USE Gandy family
Gandhara (Pakistan) (Not Subd Geog)
Gandhara art
  USE Art, Gandhara
Gandhara sculpture
  USE Sculpture, Gandhara
Gandharvas (Buddhist deities)
  (May Subd Geog)
  [BQ4780-4785]
  BT Angels (Buddhism)
      Gods, Buddhist
Gandja language
  USE Narak language
Gandrup family (Not Subd Geog)
Gandy family (Not Subd Geog)
  UF Gandey family
Ganelon (Legendary character)
  UF Gano (Legendary character)
  BT Characters and characteristics in
      literature
Ganes family
  USE Gaines family
Gaṇeśa (Hindu deity) (May Subd Geog)
  [BL1225.G34]
  UF Ganesha (Hindu deity)
  BT Gods, Hindu
Ganesha (Hindu deity)
  USE Gaṇeśa (Hindu deity)
Ganet family
  USE Gannett family
Gang language
  USE Acoli language
Gang of Four Trial, Peking, China, 1980-1981
  BT China—Politics and government—
      1976-
      Chung-kuo kung chʻan tang—Purges
      Trials (Political crimes and offenses)—
      China
Ganga dynasty
  USE Gangas
Gangā River (India and Bangladesh)
  USE Ganges River (India and Bangladesh)
Ganga-Yamuna Doab (India)
  USE Ganges-Yamuna Doab (India)
Gangas (Not Subd Geog)
  UF Ganga dynasty
  BT India—History—324 B.C.-1000 A.D.
      India—History—1000-1526
Gangaur
  [BL1213.G3]
  UF Gaṇagaura
  BT Moon—Religious aspects—Hinduism

Gangdisê Shan (China)
  USE Kailas Mountain (China)
Ganges-Jumna Doab (India)
  USE Ganges-Yamuna Doab (India)
Ganges Plain (India and Bangladesh)
  USE Gangetic Plain (India and Bangladesh)
Ganges River (India and Bangladesh)
  UF Gangā River (India and Bangladesh)
    Padma River (Bangladesh)
  BT Rivers—Bangladesh
    Rivers—India
Ganges-Yamuna Doab (India)
  UF Doab (India)
    Ganga-Yamuna Doab (India)
    Ganges-Jumna Doab (India)
  BT Alluvial plains—India
Gangetic Plain (India and Bangladesh)
  UF Ganges Plain (India and Bangladesh)
  BT Plains—Bangladesh
    Plains—India
Gangleron
  UF Ganglerone
  BT Ganglionic blocking agents
Ganglerone
  USE Gangleron
Ganglia, Autonomic
  UF Autonomic ganglia
  BT Nervous system, Parasympathetic
    Nervous system, Sympathetic
  NT Ciliary ganglion
    Myenteric plexus
    Pterygopalatine ganglion
    Solar plexus
Ganglia, Basal
  USE Basal ganglia
Ganglia, Sensory
  UF Sensory ganglia
  BT Neurons
    Sense-organs
  NT Retinal ganglion cells
Ganglia, Spinal
  USE Spinal ganglia
Ganglion, Gasserian
  USE Gasserian ganglion
Ganglion cells of retina
  USE Retinal ganglion cells
Ganglion pterygopalatinum
  USE Pterygopalatine ganglion
Ganglion semilunare
  USE Gasserian ganglion
Ganglionic blocking agents
  BT Autonomic drugs
  NT Gangleron
    Parasympatholytic agents
    Sympatholytic agents
Ganglionic crest
  USE Neural crest
Ganglionic ridge
  USE Neural crest
Ganglionic stimulating agents
  BT Autonomic drugs
  NT Parasympathomimetic agents
    Sympathomimetic agents
Ganglioside lipidosis
  USE Gangliosidoses
Ganglioside storage diseases
  USE Gangliosidoses
Gangliosides
  ⌜QP752.G3 (Biochemistry)⌝
  BT Glycosphingolipids
Gangliosidoses
  UF Ganglioside lipidosis
    Ganglioside storage diseases
  BT Mental retardation
    Metabolism, Inborn errors of
    Nervous system—Diseases
    Sphingolipidoses
  NT Tay-Sachs disease
Gangliosidosis GM2 type 1
  USE Tay-Sachs disease

Gangrene
  ⌜RD153 (Military surgery)⌝
  ⌜RD628 (Pathology)⌝
  UF Mortification (Pathology)
  RT Necrosis
Gangrene, Presenile
  USE Thromboangiitis obliterans
Gangs (May Subd Geog)
  ⌜HV6437-HV6439 (Crime and
    criminals)⌝
  UF Crime syndicates
    Gangsters
    Street gangs
    Youth gangs
  BT Boys—Societies and clubs
    Crime and criminals
    Girls—Societies and clubs
    Juvenile delinquency
    Social psychology
  RT Hoodlums
  NT Prison gangs
    Yakuza
Gangs, Motorcycle
  USE Motorcycle gangs
Gangster films
  UF Crime films
  BT Feature films
    Moving-pictures
Gangsters
  USE Gangs
    Hoodlums
Gangte language
  ⌜PL4001.G17⌝
  UF Gante language
  BT Tibeto-Burman languages
Ganguela language
  ⌜PL8202⌝
  UF Ngangela language
  BT Bantu languages
Ganguella (Bantu people)
  USE Ngangela (Bantu people)
Ganier family (Not Subd Geog)
Ganière River (France)
  UF Rivière Ganière (France)
  BT Rivers—France
Ganja
  USE Bhang (Drug)
    Marihuana
Ganja language (Papua New Guinea)
  USE Narak language
Gannagaro Historic Site (N.Y.)
  USE Ganondagan State Historic Site (N.Y.)
Ganne family (Not Subd Geog)
Gannemer family
  USE Kennamer family
Gannet family
  USE Gannett family
Gannets
  ⌜QL696.P48⌝
  BT Sulidae
  NT Northern gannet
Gannets, Fossil
Gannett family (Not Subd Geog)
  UF Ganet family
    Gannet family
Gano (Legendary character)
  USE Ganelon (Legendary character)
Ganoderma
  ⌜QK629.G (Botany)⌝
  ⌜SB295.G35 (Medicinal plant)⌝
  BT Botany, Medical
    Ganodermataceae
Ganoderma lucidum
Ganodermataceae
  ⌜QK629.G (Botany)⌝
  BT Aphyllophorales
  NT Ganoderma
Ganondagan State Historic Site (N.Y.)
  (Not Subd Geog)
  ⌜E99.S3⌝

  UF Boughton Hill Historic Site (N.Y.)
    Gannagaro Historic Site (N.Y.)
  BT Historic sites—New York (State)
    New York (State)—Antiquities
Ganser family
  USE Gonser family
Gansert family
  USE Gonser family
Ganshorn family
  USE Goshorn family
Gansshorn family
  USE Goshorn family
Gant family
  USE Gantt family
Gantai-to Island (Korea)
  USE Amt'ae Island (Korea)
Gante language
  USE Gangte language
Gantley family (Not Subd Geog)
Gantrees
  USE Gantries
Gantries
  ⌜TA660.F7⌝
  UF Gantrees
  BT Structural frames
Gantrisch (Switzerland)
  BT Mountains—Switzerland
Gantry cranes
  ⌜TJ1365⌝
  BT Bridge cranes
    Cranes, derricks, etc.
    Traveling cranes
Gants family
  USE Gantt family
Gantt charts
  BT Graphic methods
    Scheduling (Management)
Gantt family (Not Subd Geog)
  UF Gant family
    Gants family
    Gantz family
    Gaunt family
    Gaunts family
    Gauntt family
    Gent family
    Gontz family
Gantvoort family (Not Subd Geog)
Gantz family
  USE Gantt family
Gantzer family
  USE Gonser family
Gantzhorn family
  USE Goshorn family
Ganymede (Greek mythology)
  UF Ganymedes (Greek mythology)
  BT Mythology, Greek
Ganymedes (Greek mythology)
  USE Ganymede (Greek mythology)
Ganzheit (Philosophy)
  USE Whole and parts (Philosophy)
Ganzheit (Psychology)
  USE Whole and parts (Psychology)
Gaô Empire
  USE Songhai Empire
Gaols
  USE Jails
    Prisons
Gaonic literature
  USE Geonic literature
Gap, Energy
  USE Energy gap (Physics)
Gap, Generation
  USE Conflict of generations
Gape worm
  USE Gapeworm
Gapeworm (May Subd Geog)
  ⌜QL391.N4 (Zoology)⌝
  UF Gape worm
    Syngamus trachea
    Syngamus trachealis

Gapeworm *(Continued)*
  BT Birds—Parasites
    Syngamus
Gapfill family
  USE Gibble family
Gapper red-backed mouse
  USE Clethrionomys gapperi
Gaps, Electric spark
  USE Electric spark gaps
GAR Cemetery (Homer, Ill.)
  USE G.A.R. Cemetery (Homer, Ill.)
GAR Cemetery (Miami, Okla.)
  UF G.A.R. Cemetery (Miami, Okla.)
    Grand Army of the Republic
      Cemetery (Miami, Okla.)
    Grand Old Army of the Republic
      Cemetery (Miami, Okla.)
  BT Cemeteries—Oklahoma
Garage doors
  BT Doors
  — Radio control
    UF Radio-controlled garage-door
      operators
    BT Mechanically-operated doors
Garage sales *(May Subd Geog)*
  [HF5482.3]
  UF Yard sales
  BT Sales
    Secondhand trade
  RT Rummage sales
Garages *(May Subd Geog)*
  [NA8348]
  NT Automobile parking
    Automobiles—Service stations
    Carports
    Parking garages
  — Equipment and supplies
    — — Appraisal
      USE Garages—Equipment and
        supplies—Valuation
    — — Valuation
      UF Garages—Equipment and
        supplies—Appraisal
  — Law and legislation *(May Subd Geog)*
Garages, Cooperative *(May Subd Geog)*
  UF Cooperative garages
Garam River (Czechoslovakia)
  USE Hron River (Czechoslovakia)
Garamszentbenedek altarpiece (Panel painting)
  USE Kolozsvári, Tamás, fl. 1427. Calvary
    altarpiece
Garand rifle
  BT Rifles
Garard family
  USE Gerard family
Garasia (Indic people)
  USE Grasia (Indic people)
Garatt family
  USE Garrett family
Garavance
  USE Chickpea
Garawa language
  [PL7101.G37]
  UF Karawa language (Australia)
    Karrawar language
    Karwa language
    Korrawa language
    Kurrawar language
    Leearrawa language
  BT Australia—Languages
    Australian languages
Garawi
  USE Sudan grass
Garbage
  USE Organic wastes
    Refuse and refuse disposal
Garbage Analysis Programme
  BT Refuse and refuse disposal—Australia
Garbage as feed
  UF Refuse as feed

  BT Organic wastes as feed
    Refuse and refuse disposal
Garbage as fuel
  USE Refuse as fuel
Garbage can models of decision making
  Here are entered works on models of organiza-
  tional decision making that are based on the analogy
  of the various factors affecting the mix of garbage that
  occurs in a single can.
  BT Decision-making—Mathematical
    models
Garbage collection
  USE Refuse collection
Garbage trucks
  USE Refuse collection vehicles
Garbagemen
  USE Refuse collectors
Garbanzo
  USE Chickpea
Garber family *(Not Subd Geog)*
  UF Gaerber family
    Garbers family
    Garbrecht family
    Garver family
  RT Gerber family
Garber shorthand
  USE Shorthand—International
Garberg family *(Not Subd Geog)*
Garbers family
  USE Garber family
Garbillon family *(Not Subd Geog)*
Garbrecht family
  USE Garber family
Garcinia
  [QK495.G87]
  BT Guttiferae
Garcinia mangostana
  USE Mangosteen
Garda, Lake (Italy)
  UF Benaco, Lake (Italy)
    Gardasee (Italy)
    Lago Benaco (Italy)
    Lago di Garda (Italy)
    Lake Garda (Italy)
  BT Lakes—Italy
Gardasee (Italy)
  USE Garda, Lake (Italy)
Garden animals
  USE Garden fauna
Garden apartments *(May Subd Geog)*
  BT Apartment houses
Garden archaeology *(May Subd Geog)*
  [SB466.7-466.75]
  UF Archaeology of gardens
  BT Archaeology
    Gardens
Garden architecture
  USE Garden structures
    Gardens—Design
Garden beet
  USE Beets
Garden borders
  UF Borders (Gardening)
    Ornamental borders (Gardening)
  BT Landscape architecture
    Plants, Ornamental
Garden centers (Retail trade)
  (May Subd Geog)
  [SB454.6]
  BT House plant industry
    Ornamental horticulture
    Ornamental plant industry
  RT Florists
    Gardening
    Nurseries (Horticulture)
    Nursery dealers
  NT Gardening—Equipment and supplies—
    Marketing
    Nursery stock—Marketing
Garden cities *(May Subd Geog)*
  [HT161-HT165]

  BT Cities and towns
    Greenbelts
Garden clubs
  USE Gardening—Societies, etc.
Garden contracting
  USE Landscape gardening—Contracts and
    specifications
Garden design
  USE Gardens—Design
Garden dormouse
  [QL737.R656]
  UF Dormouse, Garden
    Eliomys
    Eliomys melanurus
    Eliomys quercinus
  BT Dormice
Garden ecology *(May Subd Geog)*
  [QH541.5.G37]
  BT Agricultural ecology
    Ecology
    Gardens
Garden egg
  USE Eggplant
Garden farming
  USE Truck farming
Garden fauna *(May Subd Geog)*
  UF Garden animals
  BT Gardens
    Zoology
Garden ferns
  USE Ferns, Ornamental
Garden fertilizers
  [S633]
  UF Gardening—Fertilizers and manures
  BT Fertilizers
Garden fixtures
  USE Garden ornaments and furniture
Garden fountains
  USE Fountains
Garden geraniums
  USE Geraniums
    Pelargoniums
Garden historians *(May Subd Geog)*
  [SB470]
  BT Gardening—History
    Gardens—History
    Historians
    Landscape gardening—History
Garden Island (W.A.)
  BT Islands—Australia
Garden lighting
  [SB476]
  UF Lighting, Garden
  BT Electric lighting
    Exterior lighting
    Garden ornaments and furniture
    Landscape architecture
    Lighting, Architectural and decorative
Garden literature
  USE Horticultural literature
Garden lizard, Indian
  USE Calotes versicolor
Garden nasturtiums
  USE Nasturtiums
Garden of delights (Painting)
  USE Bosch, Hieronymus, d. 1516. Garden
    of delights
Garden of earthly delights (Painting)
  USE Bosch, Hieronymus, d. 1516. Garden
    of delights
Garden of Eden
  USE Eden
Garden of love (Painting)
  USE Rubens, Peter Paul, Sir, 1577-1640.
    Garden of love
Garden of love in art
  BT Allegories
    Gardens in art
    Love in art
    Symbolism in art

Garden orach
USE Orach
Garden ornaments and furniture
(*May Subd Geog*)
⌈SB473.5⌉
UF Garden fixtures
BT Decoration and ornament
Furniture
Garden structures
Gardens
Landscape architecture
Outdoor furniture
NT Benches
Garden lighting
Stone lanterns
Trellises
Garden paths
USE Garden walks
Garden pests (*May Subd Geog*)
⌈SB603.5⌉
BT Agricultural pests
Gardening
RT Plant diseases
NT Helix aspersa
Garden photography
USE Photography of gardens
Garden plants
USE Plants, Ornamental
Garden plants, Alpine
USE Alpine garden plants
Garden ponds
USE Water gardens
Garden pools
USE Water gardens
Garden Range 1 Site (Vic.)
UF Garden Range No. 1 Site (Vic.)
BT Australia—Antiquities
Garden Range No. 1 Site (Vic.)
USE Garden Range 1 Site (Vic.)
Garden rhubarb
USE Rhubarb
Garden rooms (*May Subd Geog*)
UF Conservatories, Home
Home conservatories
Rooms, Garden
BT Conservatories
RT Greenhouses
House plants
Garden shows
USE Horticultural exhibitions
Garden shrubs
USE Ornamental shrubs
Garden Site (Man.)
UF Beauchamp Farm Site (Man.)
BT Manitoba—Antiquities
Garden snail
USE Helix aspersa
Garden spider
USE Aranea diadematus
Garden State Parkway (N.J.)
BT Parkways—New Jersey
Garden structures (*May Subd Geog*)
⌈TH4961-4962⌉
UF Garden architecture
Structures, Garden
BT Building
Gardens
Landscape architecture
NT Fences
Garden ornaments and furniture
Garden walks
Patios
Toolshed
Garden supplies
USE Gardening—Equipment and supplies
Garden therapy
USE Gardening—Therapeutic use
Garden tools (*May Subd Geog*)
⌈SB454.8⌉
BT Agricultural implements
Gardening—Equipment and supplies

NT Hoes
Toolshed
Garden tractors, Used
USE Used lawn tractors
Garden trees
USE Ornamental trees
Garden vines
USE Ornamental climbing plants
Garden walks
UF Garden paths
Paths, Garden
Walks, Garden
BT Garden structures
Gardens
Landscape architecture
Trails
Garden warbler
⌈QL696.P279⌉
UF Sylvia borin
BT Sylvia (Bird)
Garden webworm
Gardena River (Italy)
UF Grödner Bach (Italy)
Rio di Gardena (Italy)
Rio Gardena (Italy)
BT Rivers—Italy
Gardener family
USE Gardner family
Gardeners (*May Subd Geog*)
BT Gardening
NT English language—Conversation and
phrase books (for gardeners)
Wages—Gardeners
Women gardeners
Gardenia (*May Subd Geog*)
UF Cape jasmine
Gardenia virginica
USE Triadenum virginicum
Gardening (*May Subd Geog*)
⌈SB451-SB466⌉
Here are entered works on the practical opera-
tions in the cultivation of fruits, vegetables, flowers
and ornamental plants.
UF Bedding (Horticulture)
BT Agriculture
Plants
Plants, Cultivated
RT Garden centers (Retail trade)
Horticulture
NT Acclimatization (Plants)
Aquatic plants
Artificial light gardening
Autumn gardening
Balcony gardening
Bulbs
Circle gardening
Climbing plants
Cloche gardening
Cold-frames
Color in gardening
Community gardens
Container gardening
Corms
Cottage gardens, English
Desert gardening
Flower gardening
Forcing (Plants)
Fruit-culture
Garden pests
Gardeners
Gardens
Gardens, Chalk
Gardens, Limestone
Grafting
Greenhouse gardening
Greenhouses
Grounds maintenance
Herb gardening
Hillside gardening
Indoor gardening
Landscape gardening

Mulching
Native plant gardening
Organic gardening
Patio gardening
Pit gardening
Plant growing media
Plant propagation
Planting (Plant culture)
Plants—Training
Plants, Ornamental
Plants, Potted
Prairie gardening
Pruning
Raised bed gardening
Roof gardening
Seaside gardening
Square foot gardening
Topiary work
Truck farming
Vegetable gardening
Weeds
Window-gardening
Winter gardening
— **Competitions** (*May Subd Geog*)
NT Victory Garden Contest
— **Equipment and supplies**
⌈SB133⌉
UF Garden supplies
BT Agricultural implements
Agricultural machinery
Farm equipment
Horticultural machinery
Tools
NT Garden tools
Gardening equipment industry
Spraying equipment
— — **Marketing**
BT Garden centers (Retail trade)
— Exhibitions
USE Horticultural exhibitions
— Fertilizers and manures
USE Garden fertilizers
— **History**
NT Garden historians
— **Juvenile literature**
⌈SB55⌉
⌈SB455-SB457⌉
Here are entered general works on gardening
written for children. Works on gardens planted
and cultivated with the participation of children
are entered under Children's gardens.
— **Societies, etc.**
UF Garden clubs
— **Terminology**
NT English language—Conversation
and phrase books (for gardeners)
— **Therapeutic use**
UF Garden therapy
Horticultural therapy
BT Occupational therapy
Gardening, Meadow
USE Meadow gardening
Gardening ants
USE Fungus ants
Gardening equipment industry
(*May Subd Geog*)
⌈HD9486.5⌉
BT Gardening—Equipment and supplies
Gardening for color
USE Color in gardening
Gardening for fragrance
USE Gardens, Fragrant
Gardening for the aged
⌈SB455.A⌉
BT Aged
Gardening for the physically handicapped
⌈SB455.P58⌉
BT Physically handicapped
Gardening in the shade (*May Subd Geog*)
⌈SB434.7⌉

Gardening in the shade *(Continued)*
  UF Gardens, Shade
      Shade gardens
      Shady gardens
  RT Shade-tolerant plants
Gardening literature
  USE Horticultural literature
Gardening on chalk
  USE Gardens, Chalk
Gardening on limestone
  USE Gardens, Limestone
Gardening to attract wildlife
  (May Subd Geog)
  UF Gardening with wildlife
  BT Wildlife attracting
Gardening under glass
  USE Greenhouse gardening
Gardening with wildlife
  USE Gardening to attract wildlife
Gardening without soil
  USE Hydroponics
Gardenor family
  USE Gardner family
Gardens *(May Subd Geog)*
  ⌈SB451-466⌉
  UF Formal gardens
  BT Gardening
  NT Backyard gardens
      Botanical gardens
      Children's gardens
      Church gardens
      Community gardens
      Cottage gardens, English
      Courtyard gardens
      Garden archaeology
      Garden ecology
      Garden fauna
      Garden ornaments and furniture
      Garden structures
      Garden walks
      Herb gardens
      Historic gardens
      Indoor gardens
      Knot gardens
      Maze gardens
      Peat gardens
      Photography of gardens
      Rock gardens
      Rose gardens
      School gardens
      Sculpture gardens
      Wall gardens
      Water gardens
      Working-men's gardens
  — Design
      ⌈SB471-SB472 (General)⌉
      ⌈SB473 (Home grounds)⌉
      UF Garden architecture
          Garden design
      BT Landscape architecture
      RT Landscape gardening
      SA *special styles of gardens, e.g.*
          Gardens, Japanese; Gardens,
          Mogul
  — History
      NT Garden historians
  — **Law and legislation** *(May Subd Geog)*
  — **Mythology**
  — **Symbolic aspects**
      ⌈SB470.7⌉
      BT Symbolism
      NT Gardens in literature
  — **Arkansas**
      NT Arkansas Territorial Restoration
          Gardens (Little Rock, Ark.)
  — **British Columbia**
      NT Butchart Gardens (Victoria, B.C.)
  — **China**
      NT Yüan Ming Yüan (Peking, China)
  — **Delaware**

        NT Henry Francis du Pont Winterthur
            Museum Gardens (Del.)
  — **England**
      NT Attingham Park (England)
          Cottesbrooke Kitchen Garden
          (England)
          East Lambrook Garden (Somerset)
          Gravetye Manor Gardens (West
          Sussex)
          Great Comp Garden (Kent)
          Leasowes Garden (Halesowen,
          Worcestershire)
          Renishaw Gardens (South
          Yorkshire)
          Sherringham Gardens (England)
          Stowe Gardens (Buckinghamshire)
          University of Oxford Gardens
          (Oxford, Oxfordshire)
          Wakehurst Place (Ardingly, West
          Sussex)
          Wilton House Garden (Wiltshire)
  — **France**
      NT Parc de Versailles (Versailles,
          France)
          Parc Monceau (Paris, France)
  — **Germany (West)**
      NT Steinhorst Garten (Germany)
  — **Hawaii**
      NT Walker Gardens (Honolulu,
          Hawaii)
  — **India**
      NT Gardens, Mogul
  — **Italy**
      NT Hadrian's Villa (Tivoli, Italy)—
          Stadium
  — **Japan**
      NT Adachi Bijutsukan Teien (Yasugi-
          shi, Japan)
          Eiheiji Teien (Eiheiji-chō, Japan)
          Fukiage Gyoen (Tokyo, Japan)
          Hama Rikyū Teien (Tokyo, Japan)
          Heian no Sono (Kyoto, Japan)
          Horikiri Shōbuen (Tokyo, Japan)
          Kairakuen (Mito-shi, Japan)
          Kiyosumi Teien (Tokyo, Japan)
          Koishikawa Kōrakuen (Tokyo,
          Japan)
          Kōkyo gaien (Tokyo, Japan)
          Shinjuku Gyoen (Tokyo, Japan)
  — **Maine**
      NT Celia Thaxter's Garden (Appledore
          Island, Me.)
  — **Massachusetts**
      NT Public Garden (Boston, Mass.)
  — **New York (State)**
      NT Cloisters Gardens (New York,
          N.Y.)
          Hoyt Street Garden (New York,
          N.Y.)
          Kijkuit Gardens (N.Y.)
  — **North Carolina**
      NT Elizabethan Gardens (Roanoke
          Island, N.C.)
  — **Pennsylvania**
      NT Deerfield Garden (Pa.)
          Longwood Gardens (Pa.)
  — **Scotland**
      NT Belgrave Crescent Gardens
          (Edinburgh, Lothian)
          Inverewe Garden (Scotland)
  — **South Carolina**
      NT Magnolia Gardens (Charleston,
          S.C.)
  — **Taiwan**
      NT Chih Shan Yüan (Taipei, Taiwan)
  — **Virginia**
      NT Italian Garden (Richmond, Va.)
  — **Wales**
      NT Bodnant Garden (Gwynedd)
  — **Washington (D.C.)**

        NT Enid A. Haupt Garden
            (Washington, D.C.)
            Watergate Gardens (Washington,
            D.C.)
            White House Gardens
            (Washington, D.C.)
Gardens, American *(May Subd Geog)*
  UF American gardens
Gardens, Australian *(May Subd Geog)*
  ⌈SB457.534⌉
  UF Australian gardens
Gardens, Backyard
  USE Backyard gardens
Gardens, Baroque *(May Subd Geog)*
  UF Baroque gardens
Gardens, British *(May Subd Geog)*
  ⌈SB457.54⌉
  UF British gardens
Gardens, Chalk *(May Subd Geog)*
  ⌈SB456.8⌉
  UF Alkaline gardens
      Chalk gardens
      Chalky gardens
      Gardening on chalk
  BT Alkali lands
      Chalk
      Gardening
Gardens, Chinese *(May Subd Geog)*
  ⌈SB457.55⌉
  UF Chinese gardens
Gardens, Color
  USE Color in gardening
Gardens, English *(May Subd Geog)*
  ⌈SB457.6⌉
  UF Bric-a-brac gardens, English poetic
      English gardens
      English landscape gardens
      English natural gardens
      English picturesque gardens
      English poetic bric-a-brac gardens
      Landscape gardens, English
      Natural gardens, English
      Picturesque gardens, English
      Poetic bric-a-brac gardens, English
  BT Landscape architecture
      Landscape gardening
  — **Italian influences**
      BT Italy—Civilization
Gardens, European *(May Subd Geog)*
  UF European gardens
  — **Chinese influences**
      BT China—Civilization
Gardens, Fragrant *(May Subd Geog)*
  ⌈SB454.3.F7⌉
  UF Fragrant gardens
      Gardening for fragrance
      Scented gardens
  BT Aromatic plants
      Flowers—Odor
Gardens, French *(May Subd Geog)*
  ⌈SB457.65⌉
  UF French gardens
Gardens, Georgian *(May Subd Geog)*
  ⌈SB457.68⌉
  UF Georgian gardens
Gardens, Glass
  USE Glass gardens
Gardens, Indoor
  USE Indoor gardens
Gardens, Islamic *(May Subd Geog)*
  ⌈SB457.8⌉
  UF Islamic gardens
  BT Gardens, Persian
Gardens, Italian *(May Subd Geog)*
  ⌈SB457.85⌉
  UF Italian gardens
Gardens, Japanese *(May Subd Geog)*
  — **Buddhist influences**
      ⌈SB458⌉
      BT Civilization, Buddhist
  — **Chinese influences**

BT China—Civilization
— **Zen influences**
[*SB458*]
BT Zen Buddhism
Gardens, Latin *(May Subd Geog)*
[*SB458.3*]
UF Latin gardens
Gardens, Limestone *(May Subd Geog)*
[*SB456.8*]
UF Alkaline gardens
Gardening on limestone
Limestone gardens
BT Alkali lands
Gardening
Limestone
Gardens, Medieval *(May Subd Geog)*
[*SB458.35*]
UF Medieval gardens
Gardens, Miniature
[*SB419 (Indoor)*]
[*SB433.5 (General)*]
UF Dish gardening
Miniature gardens
Tray gardens
BT Container gardening
House plants
Indoor gardening
Miniature objects
RT Miniature plants
NT Bonkei
Glass gardens
Gardens, Mogul *(May Subd Geog)*
UF Mogul gardens
BT Gardens—India
Gardens, Persian
Gardens, Oriental *(May Subd Geog)*
[*SB466 (Local)*]
UF Oriental gardens
Gardens, Persian *(May Subd Geog)*
[*SB458.5*]
UF Persian gardens
NT Gardens, Islamic
Gardens, Mogul
Gardens, Regency *(May Subd Geog)*
UF Regency gardens
Gardens, Renaissance *(May Subd Geog)*
UF Renaissance gardens
Gardens, Rococo *(May Subd Geog)*
UF Rococo gardens
Gardens, Roman *(May Subd Geog)*
[*SB458.55*]
UF Roman gardens
Gardens, Rose
USE Rose gardens
Gardens, Sculpture
USE Sculpture gardens
Gardens, Shade
USE Gardening in the shade
Gardens, Theater
USE Roof garden theaters
Gardens, Victorian *(May Subd Geog)*
[*SB458.7*]
UF Victorian gardens
Gardens, Zoological
USE Zoos
Gardens in art
[*N8217.G36*]
NT Garden of love in art
Mi, Wan-chung, chin shih 1595.
Shao yüan hsiu hsi t'u
Gardens in literature
BT Gardens—Symbolic aspects
Gardens of the Cloisters (New York, N.Y.)
USE Cloisters Gardens (New York, N.Y.)
Gardiken Reservoir (Sweden)
BT Lakes—Sweden
Reservoirs—Sweden
Umeälven (Sweden)
Gardiner family
USE Gardner family

Gardiners family
USE Gardner family
Gardner family *(Not Subd Geog)*
UF Gadner family
Gaertner family
Gardener family
Gardenor family
Gardiner family
Gardiners family
Gardnier family
Gardnir family
Gardnor family
Gartiner family
Gartner family
Guardner family
RT Garner family
Gardner machine-gun
[*VF410.G2-VF410.G24 (Naval)*]
BT Machine-guns
Gardnier family
USE Gardner family
Gardnir family
USE Gardner family
Gardnor family
USE Gardner family
Gardow family
USE Gadow family
Garduno family *(Not Subd Geog)*
Gare Saint-Lazare (Painting)
USE Manet, Edouard, 1832-1883. Gare
Saint-Lazare
Garefowl
USE Great auk
Garehart family
USE Gearhart family
Garell family
USE Jarrell family
Garelli moped
[*TL443*]
BT Mopeds
Garen family *(Not Subd Geog)*
Garet family
USE Garrett family
Gareth family
USE Garrett family
Garett family
USE Garrett family
Garey family
USE Gary family
Garfagnana (Italy)
UF Carfagnana (Italy)
Garfield Home (Mentor, Ohio)
USE James A. Garfield Home (Mentor,
Ohio)
Garfishes
USE Garpikes
Garforth family
USE Goforth family
Garfowl
USE Great auk
Gargano Peninsula (Italy)
USE Gargano Promontory (Italy)
Gargano Promontory (Italy)
UF Gargano Peninsula (Italy)
Monte Gargano (Italy)
Promontorio del Gargano (Italy)
BT Mountains—Italy
Peninsulas—Italy
Garganus family
USE Gruganus family
Gargaphia
[*QL523.T5*]
Gargaphia solani
USE Eggplant lace bug
Gargar (Papua New Guinea people)
BT Ethnology—Papua New Guinea
Gargoyles *(May Subd Geog)*
[*NA3683.G37*]

BT Architecture—Details
Decoration and ornament,
Architectural
Grotesque in art
Garhwal (India : Region)
Garhwali dialect
BT Pahari languages
Garhwali folk-songs
USE Folk-songs, Garhwali
Garhwali literature *(May Subd Geog)*
Garhwali philology
Garhwali poetry *(May Subd Geog)*
Garhwali proverbs
USE Proverbs, Garhwali
Garia (Papua New Guinea people)
[*DU740.42*]
BT Ethnology—Papua New Guinea
Garibaldi, Giuseppe, 1807-1882
— **Retreat from Rome, 1849**
BT Rome (Italy)—History—Revolution
of 1848-1849
Garibaldi Park (B.C.)
USE Garibaldi Provincial Park (B.C.)
Garibaldi Provincial Park (B.C.)
UF Garibaldi Park (B.C.)
BT Parks—British Columbia
Garibaldi Square (Sassuolo, Italy)
USE Piazza Garibaldi (Sassuolo, Italy)
Garibaldi Street (Genoa, Italy)
USE Via Garibaldi (Genoa, Italy)
Garif Indians
USE Black Carib Indians
Garffuna language
USE Black Carib language
Garigliano Valley, Battle of, 1944
BT World War, 1939-1945—Campaigns—
Italy
Garison family
USE Garrison family
Garisson family
USE Garrison family
Garitson family
USE Garrison family
Garlach family
USE Gerlach family
Garland family *(Not Subd Geog)*
UF Garlind family
Gartland family
MacGartlan family
MacGartland family
McGartlan family
McGartland family
Garlands
USE Wreaths
Garlands of Rāgas (Paintings)
USE Rāgamālā painting
Garlech family
USE Gerlach family
Garlic *(May Subd Geog)*
[*QK495.L72 (Botany)*]
[*SB351.G3 (Vegetables)*]
[*TX407.G (Food)*]
UF Allium sativum
BT Allium
RT Cookery (Garlic)
Garlic, Crow
USE Allium vineale
Garlic, Field
USE Allium vineale
Garlic family
USE Gerlach family
Garlic industry *(May Subd Geog)*
[*HD9235.G36-362*]
Garlick family
USE Gerlach family
Garlind family
USE Garland family
Garlington family *(Not Subd Geog)*
UF Girlington family
Gyrlyngton family

Garlock family
USE Gerlach family
Garmager family *(Not Subd Geog)*
Garman family *(Not Subd Geog)*
UF Garmon family
RT Garmann family
German family
Garmann family *(Not Subd Geog)*
RT Garman family
German family
Garmannia
[QL638.G7]
BT Gobiidae
Garment cutting
[TT520 (Women's clothing)]
[TT590 (Men's clothing)]
BT Cutting
Tailoring
RT Dressmaking—Pattern design
NT Children's clothing—Pattern design
Shirts, Men's—Pattern design
Garment factories
USE Clothing factories
Garment workers
USE Clothing workers
**Garment Workers' Strike, New York, N.Y.,
1912-1913**
BT Strikes and lockouts—Clothing trade—
New York (State)
Garments
USE Clothing and dress
Garments, Foundation
USE Foundation garments
Garments, Leather
USE Leather garments
Garmire family *(Not Subd Geog)*
Garmon family
USE Garman family
Garnar family
USE Garner family
Garner family *(Not Subd Geog)*
UF Garnar family
Garnier family
Garnur family
RT Gardner family
Grenier family
Garness family *(Not Subd Geog)*
Garnet *(May Subd Geog)*
[TN997.G3]
NT Yttrium iron garnet
Garnet family
USE Garnett family
Garnet jewelry *(May Subd Geog)*
UF Jewelry, Garnet
BT Jewelry
Garnett family *(Not Subd Geog)*
UF Garnet family
Garni computer
BT Electronic digital computers
Machine translating
Translating machines
Garnier family
USE Garner family
Garnishes in cookery
USE Cookery (Garnishes)
Garnishment
USE Attachment and garnishment
Garnsey Bison Kill Site (N.M.)
USE Garnsey Site (N.M.)
Garnsey Site (N.M.) *(Not Subd Geog)*
UF Garnsey Bison Kill Site (N.M.)
BT New Mexico—Antiquities
RT Garnsey Spring Site (N.M.)
Garnsey Spring Site (N.M.)
BT New Mexico—Antiquities
RT Garnsey Site (N.M.)
Garnur family
USE Garner family
Garo (Indic people)
[DS432.G34]

UF Alchik (Indic people)
Garos
Garrow (Indic people)
BT Ethnology—India
NT Missions to Garo (Indic people)
Garo folk-songs
USE Folk-songs, Garo
Garo language
[PL4001.G2]
UF Garrow language
BT Bodo languages
Tibeto-Burman languages
Garo law
USE Law, Garo
Garo literature *(May Subd Geog)*
Garo philology
Garona River (Spain and France)
USE Garonne River (Spain and France)
Garonne River (Spain and France)
(Not Subd Geog)
UF Garona River (Spain and France)
Garumna River (Spain and France)
La Garonne Fleuve (Spain and France)
Río Garona (Spain and France)
BT Rivers—France
Rivers—Spain
Garos
USE Garo (Indic people)
Garoute family
USE Garoutte family
Garoutte family *(Not Subd Geog)*
UF Garoute family
GARP Global Experiment, First
USE First GARP Global Experiment
Garpikes
[QL638.5]
UF Garfishes
Garpipes
Gars
Lepisosteus
Garpipes
USE Garpikes
Garrald family
USE Jarrell family
Garrard family
USE Gerard family
Garrat family
USE Garrett family
Garred family
USE Jarrett family
Garreld family
USE Jarrell family
Garret family
USE Garrett family
Garrets
USE Attics
Garretson family
USE Garrison family
Garrett family *(Not Subd Geog)*
UF Garatt family
Garet family
Gareth family
Garett family
Garrat family
Garret family
Garrot family
Garrott family
RT Garrison family
Gerard family
Jarrett family
Garrettson family
USE Garrison family
Garrey family
USE Gary family
Garrigan family *(Not Subd Geog)*
Garrigers family
USE Garrigues family
Garrigue family
USE Garrigues family

Garrigues family *(Not Subd Geog)*
UF Garrigers family
Garrigue family
Garrigus family
Garriques family
Garrigues Region (Spain) *(Not Subd Geog)*
UF Comarca de Les Garrigues (Spain)
Les Garrigues Region (Spain)
Garrigus family
USE Garrigues family
Garriques family
USE Garrigues family
Garrison Dam (N.D.)
BT Dams—North Dakota
Garrison Diversion Unit (Missouri River
Watershed)
USE Missouri River Basin project.
Garrison Diversion Unit
Garrison family *(Not Subd Geog)*
UF Garison family
Garisson family
Garitson family
Garretson family
Garrettson family
Garrisson family
Garritson family
Gerison family
Gerrison family
Gerritson family
RT Garrett family
Garrison Gilman House (Exeter, N.H.)
USE Gilman Garrison House (Exeter, N.H.)
Garrison House (Exeter, N.H.)
USE Gilman Garrison House (Exeter, N.H.)
Garrison towns
USE Military towns
Garrisons *(May Subd Geog)*
[U370-375]
Garrisons, British *(May Subd Geog)*
UF British garrisons
Garrisson family
USE Garrison family
Garritson family
USE Garrison family
Garrod family
USE Gerard family
Garrone family *(Not Subd Geog)*
Garrot family
USE Garrett family
Garrote
[HV8696]
BT Capital punishment
Garrott family
USE Garrett family
Garrotxa (Spain)
Garrow (Indic people)
USE Garo (Indic people)
Garrow language
USE Garo language
Garrulax
[QL696.P285]
UF Laughingthrushes
BT Timaliidae
NT Garrulax affinis
Garrulax affinis
[QL696.P285]
UF Black-faced laughingthrush
BT Garrulax
Garrulus
[QL696.P2367]
BT Corvidae
Jays
NT Garrulus gladarius
Garrulus gladarius
[QL696.P2367]
UF Common jay
Eurasian jay
BT Garrulus
Garry family
USE Gary family

Gars
USE Garpikes
Garten family (*Not Subd Geog*)
UF Garton family
Gartenstadion, Hadrian's Villa (Tivoli, Italy)
USE Hadrian's Villa (Tivoli, Italy)—
Stadium
Garter snakes
[QL666.O636]
UF Thamnophis
BT Colubridae
NT Eastern ribbonsnake
Thamnophis couchii
Thamnophis cyrtopsis
Thamnophis elegans
Thamnophis exsul
Thamnophis marcianus
Thamnophis ordinoides
Thamnophis radix
Thamnophis sirtalis
Western ribbonsnake
Garth family (*Not Subd Geog*)
UF Garthe family
Garthe family
USE Garth family
Garthia
[QL666.L245]
BT Geckos
Gartiner family
USE Gardner family
Gartland family
USE Garland family
Gartner family
USE Gardner family
Gartok Expedition, 1904-1905
[DS785]
Garton family
USE Garten family
Garumna River (Spain and France)
USE Garonne River (Spain and France)
Garusi Site (Tanzania)
USE Laetoli Site (Tanzania)
Garvan family
USE Garvin family
Garven family
USE Garvin family
Garver family
USE Garber family
Garvey family (*Not Subd Geog*)
UF Garvie family
Garvie family
USE Garvey family
Garvin family (*Not Subd Geog*)
UF Garvan family
Garven family
Garvis family
USE Jarvis family
Garwood family (*Not Subd Geog*)
Gary family (*Not Subd Geog*)
UF Garey family
Garrey family
Garry family
RT Gery family
Garza family (*Not Subd Geog*)
UF De la Garza family
Garza-Little Elm Reservoir (Tex.)
UF Lake Lewisville (Tex.)
Lewisville, Lake (Tex.)
BT Lakes—Texas
Reservoirs—Texas
Garza-Sada family (*Not Subd Geog*)
Gas
[TP700]
[TP751-TP764]
UF Coal-gas
Illuminating gas
Producer gas
BT Gases, Asphyxiating and poisonous
RT Coal-tar products
Distillation, Destructive
NT Acetylene

Gas manufacture and works
Gases
Mineral oils
Petroleum
Scrubber (Chemical technology)
Synthesis gas
Water-gas
— Analysis
USE Gases—Analysis
— **Electric ignition**
[TK7291]
UF Electric ignition of gas
BT Electric apparatus and appliances
— **Heating and cooking** (*May Subd Geog*)
[TH7453-TH7457 (Gas-stoves)]
BT Gas appliances
Gas as fuel
— **Law and legislation** (*May Subd Geog*)
UF Gas industry—Law and legislation
— **Odorizing**
[TP754]
UF Odorizing of gas
BT Gas industry—Safety measures
Odors
— **Pipe lines**
UF Gas pipe lines
— Research
USE Gas research
— **Toxicology**
[RA1247.G2]
NT Plants, Effect of gases on
— War use
USE Gases, Asphyxiating and
poisonous—War use
Gas, Blast furnace
USE Blast furnace gas
Gas, Bose-Einstein
USE Bose-Einstein gas
Gas, Bottled
USE Liquefied petroleum gas
Gas, Casinghead
USE Casinghead gas
Gas, Gastrointestinal
USE Gastrointestinal gas
Gas, Lattice
USE Lattice gas
Gas, Natural (*May Subd Geog*)
[HD242.5 (Gas lands)]
[TN880 (Mineral industries)]
[TP350 (Fuel)]
UF Natural gas
Sour gas
BT Energy minerals
Fossil fuels
Geology, Economic
Wells
RT Gas fields
Gas industry
NT Casinghead gas
Compressed natural gas
Condensate oil wells
Furnaces—Conversion to natural gas
Gas, Natural, in submerged lands
Gas condensate reservoirs
Gas reservoirs
Gas seepage
Liquefied natural gas
Liquefied petroleum gas
— **Cleaning**
[TN880.5]
— Companies
USE Gas companies
— **Conservation**
UF Conservation of natural gas
Natural gas conservation
BT Energy conservation
Mineral resources conservation
— Dehydration
USE Gas, Natural—Drying
— **Drying**
UF Gas, Natural—Dehydration

BT Gases—Drying
— **Geology** (*May Subd Geog*)
BT Geology
NT Carbonate reservoirs
Gas, Natural—Migration
— **Hydrates**
BT Hydrates
— **Law and legislation** (*May Subd Geog*)
UF Oil and gas law
NT Oil and gas leases
— **Migration**
UF Gas migration
Migration of natural gas
BT Gas, Natural—Geology
— **Pipe line failures**
UF Gas, Natural—Pipe lines—Failures
Pipe line failures (Natural gas)
BT Disasters
— **Pipe lines**
BT Gas, Natural—Transportation
— — **Cathodic protection**
— — **Communication systems**
— — — **Power supply**
BT Electric power
— — **Compressor stations**
BT Compressors
Pumping stations
— — — Appraisal
USE Gas, Natural—Pipe lines—
Compressor stations—
Valuation
— — — **Valuation**
[TN880.5]
UF Gas, Natural—Pipe lines—
Compressor stations—
Appraisal
— — — **Vibration**
[TN880.5]
— — **Design and construction**
[TN880.5]
— — **Electric equipment**
[TK4035.P55]
— — Failures
USE Gas, Natural—Pipe line
failures
— — **Joints**
BT Joints (Engineering)
Pipe joints
— — **Law and legislation**
(*May Subd Geog*)
— — **Power supply**
— — **Taxation** (*May Subd Geog*)
BT Gas, Natural—Taxation
— — — **Law and legislation**
(*May Subd Geog*)
— — **Valves**
BT Valves
— — **Welding**
— **Reserves**
UF Gas reserves
Natural gas reserves
Reserves of natural gas
— **Storage**
NT Gas, Natural—Underground
storage
— **Sweetening**
[TP754]
UF Sweetening of natural gas
RT Deodorization
Desulphuration
Hydrogen sulphide
— **Taxation** (*May Subd Geog*)
NT Gas, Natural—Pipe lines—Taxation
— — **Law and legislation**
(*May Subd Geog*)
— **Thermal properties**
— **Transportation**
[HD9580]
[TN880]
NT Gas, Natural—Pipe lines
— **Underground storage** (*May Subd Geog*)

1479

Gas, Natural
— Underground storage *(Continued)*
    BT Gas, Natural—Storage
        Underground storage
— — Models
— Viscosity
— Well drilling
    USE Gas well drilling
— Alaska
— — Pipe lines
    NT Alaska Highway Gas Pipeline
— Algeria
— — Pipe lines
    NT Algeria-Italy Natural Gas
            Pipeline
— Canada
— — Pipe lines
    NT Alaska Highway Gas Pipeline
— Italy
— — Pipe lines
    NT Algeria-Italy Natural Gas
            Pipeline
— Northwest Territories
— — Pipe lines
    NT Mackenzie Valley Pipeline
            (N.W.T.)
— Soviet Union
— — Pipe lines
    NT Urengoï Pipeline
— United States
— — Pipe lines
    NT Northern Border Pipeline
— Wyoming
    NT Project Wagon Wheel
Gas, Natural, in submerged lands
(May Subd Geog)
    UF Gas in submerged lands
        Offshore gas fields
    BT Gas, Natural
        Mineral resources in submerged lands
        Ocean energy resources
        Submerged lands
    RT Offshore gas industry
— Law and legislation *(May Subd Geog)*
Gas, Poisonous
    USE Gases, Asphyxiating and poisonous
Gas and oil engines
    USE Internal combustion engines
Gas and oil leases
    USE Oil and gas leases
Gas apparatus and appliances
    USE Gas appliances
        Gas manufacture and works—
            Equipment and supplies
Gas appliance vent systems
    USE Gas appliances—Vents
Gas appliances
    [TP758]
    UF Gas apparatus and appliances
        Gas equipment and appliances
    BT Gas industry
    NT Gas—Heating and cooking
        Gas-burners
        Gas-fixtures
        Gas flow
        Gas-meters
        Gas ovens
        Gas toasters
        Stoves, Gas
        Water heaters, Gas
— Flues
    USE Gas appliances—Vents
— Vents
    [TH6835]
    UF Gas appliance vent systems
        Gas appliances—Flues
        Gas vents
        Vents (Gas appliances)
    BT Flues
Gas as fuel
    [TP345-350]

    BT Fuel
    NT Acetylene as fuel
        Automobiles—Gas-producers
        Automobiles—Motors (Compressed-
            gas)
        Combined combustion of coal and gas
        Gas—Heating and cooking
        Liquefied petroleum gas
        Oil gas
        Tractors—Gas-producers
— Rates
    USE Gas companies—Rates
Gas bearings
    USE Gas-lubricated bearings
Gas bladder
    USE Air-bladder (in fishes)
Gas bubble disease in fish *(May Subd Geog)*
    [SH177.G3]
    BT Decompression sickness
        Fishes—Diseases
        Nitrogen supersaturation
Gas-burners
    [TH6880]
    BT Gas appliances
    NT Argand burner
        Bunsen burner
        Flame monitoring systems
Gas bursts
    UF Bursts, Gas
        Outbursts, Gas
    BT Mine accidents
        Mine gases
    RT Rock bursts
Gas calorimeters
    [QC293.G3 (General)]
    [QC787.G34 (Nuclear physics)]
    UF Calorimeters, Gas
        Calorimeters, Gas-sampling
        Gas-sampling calorimeters
    BT Calorimeters and calorimetry
Gas chromatography
    [QD79.C45 (Analytical chemistry)]
    [QD117.C515 (Quantitative inorganic
        chemistry)]
    [QD272.C44 (Organic chemistry)]
    UF Gas-liquid chromatography
        Vapor-phase chromatography
    BT Chromatographic analysis
— Industrial applications
    BT Chemistry, Technical
Gas cleaning
    USE Gases—Cleaning
Gas companies *(May Subd Geog)*
    [HF6161.G2 (Advertising)]
    [HG4029.G2 (Finance)]
    [HG4841.G2 (Securities)]
    UF Gas, Natural—Companies
    BT Public utilities
    RT Gas manufacture and works
— Law and legislation *(May Subd Geog)*
— Rates
    UF Gas as fuel—Rates
        Gas rates
Gas condensate reservoirs *(May Subd Geog)*
    UF Condensate reservoirs, Gas
        Reservoirs, Gas condensate
    BT Gas, Natural
        Oil fields
    NT Condensate oil wells
Gas-condensate wells
    USE Condensate oil wells
Gas condensers
    [TP764]
Gas cooled reactors
    UF Reactors, Gas cooled
    BT Nuclear reactors
Gas cyaniding
    USE Carbonitriding
Gas cylinders
    UF Compressed gas containers

    BT Containers
        Cylinders
        Pressure vessels
Gas-detectors
    [HD7264]
    BT Chemical detectors
        Gas leakage
        Leak detectors
— Calibration
Gas discharges
    USE Glow discharges
Gas distribution *(May Subd Geog)*
    [TP757]
    RT Gas-governors
        Gas-pipes
    NT Gas leakage
        Gases, Compressed
Gas drilling (Petroleum engineering)
(May Subd Geog)
    BT Boring
        Gas well drilling
        Oil well drilling
Gas dynamic lasers
    USE Gasdynamic lasers
Gas dynamics
    UF Gasdynamics
    BT Fluid dynamics
        Thermodynamics
    NT Aerodynamics
        Density wave theory
        Gas flow
        Gasdynamic lasers
        Jets—Fluid dynamics
        Rarefied gas dynamics
        Relaxation (Gas dynamics)
        Thermomolecular pressure
Gas engineering
    BT Engineering
Gas engines
    USE Internal combustion engines
Gas engines, Automotive
    USE Automobiles—Motors (Compressed-
        gas)
Gas equipment and appliances
    USE Gas appliances
        Gas manufacture and works—
            Equipment and supplies
Gas exchange, Pulmonary
    USE Pulmonary gas exchange
Gas expanders
    USE Expanders, Gas
Gas extraction *(May Subd Geog)*
    BT Extraction (Chemistry)
Gas field chemicals
    UF Chemicals, Gas field
    BT Chemicals
Gas field chemicals industry
(May Subd Geog)
Gas field equipment industry
(May Subd Geog)
    [HD9581]
Gas fields *(May Subd Geog)*
    UF Fields, Gas
        Natural gas fields
    BT Mines and mineral resources
    RT Gas, Natural
— Alberta
    NT Elmworth Gas Field (Alta.)
Gas-filled cables
    USE Electric cables—Gas insulation
Gas-fitting
    [TH7920-7930]
    RT Pipe-fitting
        Plumbing
    NT Gas-fixtures
— Law and legislation *(May Subd Geog)*
Gas-fixtures
    [TH7960-7967]
    BT Gas appliances
        Gas-fitting
    NT Gas light fixtures

Gas flow
  UF Flow of gas
       Gases, Flow of
  BT Aerodynamics
       Gas appliances
       Gas dynamics
  RT Air flow
  NT Gas-lubricated bearings
       Gas-meters
       Schlieren photography
Gas gangrene
  [RC144.G3]
  BT Clostridium diseases
Gas gangrene antitoxin
  BT Bacterial antitoxins
Gas-governors
  [TH7945]
  UF Gas-regulators
  BT Gas-meters
       Governors (Machinery)
  RT Gas distribution
Gas holders
  USE Gasholders
Gas in submerged lands
  USE Gas, Natural, in submerged lands
Gas in war
  USE Gases, Asphyxiating and poisonous—
         War use
Gas industry *(May Subd Geog)*
  [TP751-764]
    Here are entered general works on industries based on natural or manufactured gas. Works on municipal or other agencies which distribute to consumers are entered under the heading Gas companies. Technical treatises on the manufacture of gas are entered under the heading Gas manufacture and works.
  BT Energy industries
       Gas manufacture and works
  RT Coke industry
       Gas, Natural
  SA *other headings beginning with the word* Gas
  NT Gas appliances
       Offshore gas industry
  — **Defense measures**
      BT Factories—Protection
         War damage, Industrial
  — **Equipment and supplies**
  — — Appraisal
      USE Gas industry—Equipment and
         supplies—Valuation
  — — **Valuation**
      UF Gas industry—Equipment and
         supplies—Appraisal
  — Law and legislation
      USE Gas—Law and legislation
  — **Safety measures**
      [TP751.1]
      NT Gas—Odorizing
Gas-insulated cables
  USE Electric cables—Gas insulation
Gas lasers
  [TA1695]
  BT Lasers
  RT Plasma lasers
  NT Argon lasers
       Carbon dioxide lasers
       Carbon monoxide lasers
       Excimer lasers
       Gasdynamic lasers
       Helium-mercury lasers
       Helium-neon lasers
       Molecular gas lasers
Gas law
  USE Ideal gas law
Gas law, Ideal
  USE Ideal gas law
Gas leakage
  UF Leakage, Gas
  BT Gas distribution
  NT Gas-detectors

Gas leases
  USE Oil and gas leases
Gas lenses
  [QC165.3]
  BT Gases
       Lenses
Gas-lift (Petroleum)
  USE Oil wells—Gas lift
Gas lift pumps
  UF Pumps, Gas lift
  BT Pumping machinery
  RT Air lift pumps
       Oil wells—Gas lift
Gas light fixtures *(May Subd Geog)*
  UF Gaslight fixtures
  BT Gas-fixtures
       Gas-lighting
  NT Gas street lamps
       Incandescent gas-lighting—Fixtures
Gas light fixtures, Victorian
  (May Subd Geog)
  UF Victorian gas light fixtures
Gas light fixtures industry *(May Subd Geog)*
Gas-lighting *(May Subd Geog)*
  [TH7910-7970]
  RT Lighting
  NT Acetylene
       Gas light fixtures
       Incandescent gas-lighting
Gas-liquid chromatography
  USE Gas chromatography
Gas-lubricated bearings
  [TJ1073.5]
  UF Bearings, Gas-lubricated
       Gas bearings
  BT Fluid-film bearings
       Gas flow
Gas-machines
  [TP764]
  BT Gas manufacture and works
  NT Gas-producers
Gas manufacture and works
  (May Subd Geog)
  [HD4486-HD4495 (Public ownership)]
  [TP700-TP764]
  UF Producer gas
  BT Gas
  RT Gas companies
       Gas-producers
  NT Coal gasification
       Coal gasification, Underground
       Gas industry
       Gas-machines
       Oil gasification
       Synthesis gas
       Water-gas
  — Apparatus
      USE Gas manufacture and works—
         Equipment and supplies
  — **By-products**
      [TP755]
  — **Equipment and supplies**
      UF Gas apparatus and appliances
        Gas equipment and appliances
        Gas manufacture and works—
          Apparatus
      NT Gas-retorts
        Scrubber (Chemical technology)
  — **Pilot plants**
Gas masks
  [HD7275 (Labor hygiene)]
  [TN297 (Mining)]
  [UG447 (Military science)]
  BT Respirators
Gas metal arc welding
  [TK4660]
  UF Carbon dioxide arc welding
       Electrogas welding
       Magnetic flux welding
       Metal inert gas welding
       MIG welding

  BT Electric welding
  — **Electrodes**
      BT Electrodes
Gas-meters
  [TH7940]
  UF Meters, Gas
  BT Flow meters
       Gas appliances
       Gas flow
  NT Gas-governors
Gas migration
  USE Gas, Natural—Migration
Gas myelography
  USE Pneumomyelography
Gas ovens
  UF Ovens, Gas
  BT Gas appliances
       Stoves, Gas
Gas pipe lines
  USE Gas—Pipe lines
Gas-pipes
  [TP757]
  BT Pipe
  RT Gas distribution
  NT Electrolytic corrosion
       Pipe flanges
  — **Cathodic protection**
  — **Cleaning**
      [TP751.1]
      UF Gas-pipes—Purging
        Purging of gas-pipes
  — **Corrosion**
      BT Electrolytic corrosion
  — Purging
      USE Gas-pipes—Cleaning
  — **Welding**
Gas pools
  USE Gas reservoirs
Gas power plants *(May Subd Geog)*
  [TJ768]
  UF Power plants, Gas
  BT Fossil fuel power plants
Gas-producers
  [TP762]
  UF Producer gas
  BT Gas-machines
  RT Gas manufacture and works
  NT Acetylene generators
       Automobiles—Gas-producers
       Biogas
       Coal gasification
Gas producers
  NT Internal combustion engines
Gas-producers
  NT Tractors—Gas-producers
Gas purification
  USE Gases—Purification
Gas purifier
  USE Scrubber (Chemical technology)
Gas ranges
  USE Stoves, Gas
Gas rates
  USE Gas companies—Rates
Gas-regulators
  USE Gas-governors
Gas research *(May Subd Geog)*
  UF Gas—Research
  BT Chemistry, Technical—Research
       Research, Industrial
Gas reserves
  USE Gas, Natural—Reserves
Gas reservoirs *(May Subd Geog)*
  UF Gas pools
       Pools, Gas
  BT Gas, Natural
       Reservoirs
  — **Permeability**
Gas-retorts
  [TP764]
  BT Gas manufacture and works—
       Equipment and supplies

Gas-sampling calorimeters
  USE Gas calorimeters
Gas seep
  USE Gas seepage
Gas seepage *(May Subd Geog)*
  UF Gas seep
  BT Gas, Natural
     Seepage
Gas stations
  USE Automobiles—Service stations
Gas stoves
  USE Stoves, Gas
Gas street lamps *(May Subd Geog)*
  BT Gas light fixtures
     Lamps
     Street-lighting
Gas toasters
  UF Toasters, Gas
  BT Gas appliances
     Kitchen utensils
Gas tubes
  BT Electron tubes
  NT Diodes
     Ignitrons
     Thyratrons
     Transmit-receive tubes
Gas tubing
  ⌈TP757⌉
Gas tungsten arc welding
  ⌈TK4660⌉
  UF TIG-welding
     Tungsten arc welding
     Tungsten inert gas welding
  BT Electric welding
Gas-turbine automobiles
  USE Automobiles, Gas-turbine
Gas-turbine cars
  USE Automobiles, Gas-turbine
Gas-turbine disks
  ⌈TJ778⌉
  UF Gas-turbine wheels
     Gas-turbines—Disks
  BT Disks, Rotating
     Gas-turbines
Gas-turbine industry *(May Subd Geog)*
  ⌈HD9705.5.T87-874⌉
  BT Gas-turbines
Gas-turbine locomotives
  UF Locomotives, Gas-turbine
  BT Gas-turbines
     Locomotives
  — Electric driving
Gas-turbine materials
  USE Gas-turbines—Materials
Gas-turbine motor-cars
  BT Railroad motor-cars
Gas-turbine power-plants *(May Subd Geog)*
  ⌈TK1076⌉
  UF Air storage power-plants
     Power-plants, Gas-turbine
  BT Electric power-plants
  — Ericsson cycle
    UF Ericsson cycle gas-turbine power-
      plants
    BT Thermodynamics
Gas turbine system technicians (Mechanical)
  (United States Navy)
  USE United States. Navy—Gas turbine
     system technicians (Mechanical)
Gas-turbine wheels
  USE Gas-turbine disks
Gas-turbines
  ⌈TJ778⌉
  BT Ducted fans
     Turbines
  NT Aircraft gas-turbines
     Automotive gas turbines
     Free piston engines
     Gas-turbine disks
     Gas-turbine industry
     Gas-turbine locomotives

    Marine gas-turbines
— Aerodynamics
  BT Aerodynamics
— Blades
— Ceramic materials
  BT Ceramic materials
— Combustion
— Combustion chambers
  UF Combustion chambers, Gas-turbine
     Combustors, Gas-turbine
  BT Combustion chambers
     Combustion engineering
— Disks
  USE Gas-turbine disks
— Drawing
  USE Gas-turbines—Drawings
— Drawings
  UF Gas-turbines—Drawing
  BT Mechanical drawing
— Dynamics
  ⌈TJ778⌉
— Erecting work
  ⌈TJ778⌉
  BT Installation of industrial equipment
— Fuel
— Incrustations
— Lubrication
— Materials
  ⌈TJ778⌉
  UF Gas-turbine materials
  RT Metals at high temperatures
— Vibration
  ⌈TJ778⌉
— Welding
Gas-turbines, Aircraft
  USE Aircraft gas-turbines
Gas vents
  USE Gas appliances—Vents
Gas warfare
  USE Gases, Asphyxiating and poisonous—
     War use
Gas water heaters
  USE Water heaters, Gas
Gas welding
  USE Oxyacetylene welding and cutting
Gas well blowouts
  USE Gas wells—Blowouts
Gas well drilling *(May Subd Geog)*
  UF Drilling, Gas well
     Gas, Natural—Well drilling
     Well drilling, Gas
  BT Boring
     Gas wells
  NT Air drilling (Petroleum engineering)
     Gas drilling (Petroleum engineering)
     Gas wells—Blowouts
— Finance
— — Law and legislation
    (May Subd Geog)
— Law and legislation *(May Subd Geog)*
Gas wells *(May Subd Geog)*
  ⌈TN880-883⌉
  UF Natural gas wells
     Wells, Gas
  RT Oil wells
  NT Gas well drilling
— Acidization
  UF Acidization of gas wells
— Blowouts
  UF Blow outs, Gas well
     Blowouts, Gas well
     Gas well blowouts
  BT Gas well drilling
— Equipment and supplies
  NT Well packers
— Testing
  NT Drill stem testing
Gascogne, Golfe de (France and Spain)
  USE Biscay, Bay of (France and Spain)
Gascon Christian poetry
  USE Christian poetry, Gascon

Gascon dialect *(May Subd Geog)*
  ⌈PC3421-3428⌉
  BT Langue d'oc
     Provençal language
  NT Béarnais dialect
Gascon folk-songs
  USE Folk-songs, Gascon
Gascon literature *(May Subd Geog)*
  ⌈PC3347 (To 1500)⌉
  ⌈PC3411.G4⌉
Gascon philology *(May Subd Geog)*
  ⌈PC3421-3428⌉
Gascon poetry *(May Subd Geog)*
  ⌈PC3347 (To 1500)⌉
  ⌈PC3411.G4⌉
  NT Christian poetry, Gascon
Gasconade River (Mo.)
  BT Rivers—Missouri
Gascony, Gulf of (France and Spain)
  USE Biscay, Bay of (France and Spain)
Gascoyne River (W.A.) *(Not Subd Geog)*
  BT Rivers—Australia
Gasdynamic lasers
  ⌈TA1695⌉
  UF Gas dynamic lasers
     Lasers, Gasdynamic
  BT Gas dynamics
     Gas lasers
Gasdynamics
  USE Gas dynamics
Gasel
  USE Ghazals
Gaseous dielectrics
  USE Dielectrics, Gaseous
Gaseous diffusion plants *(May Subd Geog)*
  BT Isotope separation
     Nuclear facilities
Gaseous discharge
  USE Plasma (Ionized gases)
Gaseous environment (Space environment)
  USE Artificial atmospheres (Space
     environment)
Gaseous nebulae
  USE Nebulae
Gaseous plasma
  USE Plasma (Ionized gases)
Gases
  ⌈QC161-QC168 (Mechanics)⌉
  ⌈QC241 (Vibrations in tubes)⌉
  ⌈QC286 (Expansion)⌉
  ⌈QC297 (Specific heats)⌉
  ⌈QD531 (Manipulation)⌉
  ⌈TP242-TP244 (Chemical technology)⌉
  BT Diffusion
     Fluids
     Gas
     Hydrostatics
     Matter—Properties
     Mechanics
     Physics
     Vapors
  RT Pneumatics
  SA *specific gases, e.g.* Acetylene, Argon,
     Helium, Hydrogen, Nitrogen,
     Oxygen
  NT Artificial atmospheres (Space
     environment)
     Avogadro's hypothesis
     Balloon gases
     Bubbles
     Combustion gases
     Dalton's law
     Diesel motor exhaust gas
     Electric insulators and insulation—
      Gases
     Fission gases
     Gas lenses
     Gases, Real
     Gibbs' paradox
     Ideal gas law
     Manostat

Osmosis
Plants, Gases in
Protective atmospheres
Virial coefficients
— **Absorption and adsorption**
[QC182]
UF Absorption of gases
Adsorption of gases
Sorption of gases
BT Absorption
Plate towers
NT Accommodation coefficient
Getters
— **Acoustic properties**
— **Analysis**
[QD121]
[TP754 (Illuminating gas)]
UF Gas—Analysis
NT Eudiometer
— **Cleaning**
UF Gas cleaning
BT Dust—Removal
NT Scrubber (Chemical technology)
— Dehydration
USE Gases—Drying
— Diffusion
USE Diffusion
— **Drying**
UF Gases—Dehydration
NT Gas, Natural—Drying
— Expansion
USE Expansion of gases
— Ionization
USE Ionization of gases
— **Liquefaction**
[QD535]
UF Liquefaction of gases
BT Chemistry
Chemistry, Physical and theoretical
Heat
Low temperature engineering
Thermochemistry
RT Low temperature research
NT Expanders, Gas
Hydrogen
Liquefied gases
Liquefied natural gas
Liquefied petroleum gas
Liquid air
Liquid argon
Liquid fluorine
Liquid helium
Liquid hydrogen
Liquid nitrogen
Liquid oxygen
— **Occlusion**
[QC182]
UF Occlusion of gases
— **Physiological effect**
[RA576 (Air pollution)]
[RA1245-RA1247 (Toxicology)]
NT Asphyxia
Gases, Asphyxiating and poisonous
Plants, Effect of gases on
— **Purification**
UF Gas purification
NT Air—Purification
— — **Adsorption**
— **Separation**
UF Air—Separation
BT Separation (Technology)
— **Spectra**
[QC454]
— **Therapeutic use**
[RM666.G2]
UF Pneumatology (Medicine)
NT Pneumoperitoneum, Artificial
— **Thermal properties**
NT Charles' law
— Viscosity
USE Viscosity

Gases, Asphyxiating and poisonous
(May Subd Geog)
[RA577 (Public health)]
[RA1245-RA1247 (Toxicology)]
UF Asphyxiating gases
Gas, Poisonous
Gases, Irrespirable, offensive, and
poisonous
Gases, Poisonous
Poison gas
Poisonous gases
BT Gases—Physiological effect
Hazardous substances
Poisons
RT Asphyxia
NT Aerosol sniffing
Carbon dioxide
Carbon monoxide
Fire-damp
Fume control
Fumigants
Gas
Glue-sniffing
Hydrogen sulphide
Lewisite (Poison gas)
Mine gases
Mustard gas
Tear gas
Volcanic gases
Waste gases
Welding fumes
— **Law and legislation** (May Subd Geog)
BT Nuisances
— **Toxicology**
[RA1245]
UF Inhalation toxicology
— **War use**
[UG447]
UF Gas—War use
Gas in war
Gas warfare
BT Air defenses
Military art and science
War (International law)
RT Chemical warfare
NT Decontamination (from gases,
chemicals, etc.)
Tear gas munitions
Gases, Combustion
USE Combustion gases
Gases, Compressed
[TP761.C65]
UF Compressed gas
BT Gas distribution
NT Automobiles—Motors (Compressed-
gas)
Compressed natural gas
Liquefied petroleum gas
— **Law and legislation** (May Subd Geog)
Gases, Electric discharges through
USE Electric discharges through gases
Gases, Expansion of
USE Expansion of gases
Gases, Flow of
USE Gas flow
Gases, Ionization of
USE Ionization of gases
Gases, Ionized
UF Ionized gases
BT Electromagnetism
Gases, Kinetic theory of
Ionization of gases
Particles
NT Air, Ionized
H II regions (Astrophysics)
Ion flow dynamics
Magneto-ionic theory
Plasma (Ionized gases)
Rockets (Aeronautics)—Ionization
phenomena

Gases, Irrespirable, offensive, and poisonous
USE Gases, Asphyxiating and poisonous
Gases, Kinetic theory of
[QC175]
UF Kinetic theory of gases
BT Mathematical physics
Matter, Kinetic theory of
Molecular dynamics
Molecular theory
Statistical physics
NT Gases, Ionized
Joule-Thomson effect
Krook equation
Maxwell-Boltzmann distribution law
Virial theorem
Gases, Liquefied
USE Liquefied gases
Gases, Noble
USE Gases, Rare
Gases, Photoionization of
USE Photoionization of gases
Gases, Poisonous
USE Gases, Asphyxiating and poisonous
Gases, Rare
UF Elements, Inert
Gases, Noble
Inert elements
Noble gases
Rare gases
BT Nonmetals
NT Argon
Helium
Krypton
Neon
Radon
Rare gas compounds
Solid rare gases
Xenon
— **Optical properties**
— **Thermal properties**
Gases, Real
UF Imperfect gases
Real gases
BT Gases
Gases, Volcanic
USE Volcanic gases
Gases, Waste
USE Waste gases
Gases at high temperatures
BT High temperatures
NT High temperature plasmas
Gases in manure
USE Manure gases
Gases in marine sediments
USE Marine sediments—Gas content
Gases in metals
UF Metals, Gases in
BT Metals—Analysis
NT Aluminum alloys—Hydrogen content
Degassing of metals
Iron—Hydrogen content
Metals—Hydrogen content
Metals—Nitrogen content
Metals—Oxygen content
Nonferrous metals—Hydrogen content
Steel—Hydrogen content
Steel—Nitrogen content
Steel—Oxygen content
Titanium—Hydrogen content
Gases in mines
USE Mine gases
Gases in plants
USE Plants, Gases in
Gases in rocks
[QE511]
UF Rocks, Gases in
BT Geophysics
Petrology
Gases in the blood
USE Blood gases

Gases industry *(May Subd Geog)*
  ⌐HD9660.G37¬
Gasherbrum I (Pakistan)
  UF Gasherbrum Mountain (Pakistan)
      Gusharbrum (Pakistan)
      Hidden Peak (Pakistan)
  BT Karakoram Range
      Mountains—Pakistan
Gasherbrum Mountain (Pakistan)
  USE Gasherbrum I (Pakistan)
Gasholders
  UF Gas holders
  BT Tanks
  — **Welding**
Gasification of coal
  USE Coal gasification
Gasification of coal, Underground
  USE Coal gasification, Underground
Gasification of oil
  USE Oil gasification
Gaskets
  BT Machinery
      Packing (Mechanical engineering)
      Sealing (Technology)
      Washers (for bolts and screws)
Gaslight fixtures
  USE Gas light fixtures
Gasner family
  USE Gessner family
GASNTI classification
  USE Classification, GASNTI
Gasohol
  ⌐TP358¬
  BT Alcohol as fuel
      Gasoline
  — **Law and legislation** *(May Subd Geog)*
Gasohol industry *(May Subd Geog)*
  ⌐HD9502.5.A43¬
Gasoline *(May Subd Geog)*
  ⌐TP692.2¬
  BT Catalytic reforming
      Cracking process
      Liquid fuels
  NT Airplanes—Fuel
      Automobiles—Fuel consumption
      Automobiles—Fuel systems—Vapor
        lock
      Gasohol
      Inflammable liquids
  — **Anti-knock and anti-knock mixtures**
      ⌐TP692.2¬
    UF Anti-knock compounds
        High-octane gasoline
        Octane number
    BT Motor fuels—Anti-knock and anti-
          knock mixtures
    NT Ethylene dibromide
  — — **Law and legislation**
        (May Subd Geog)
  — **Law and legislation** *(May Subd Geog)*
  — **Pipe lines**
    UF Gasoline pipe lines
    BT Gasoline—Transportation
  — **Prices** *(May Subd Geog)*
  — **Research** *(May Subd Geog)*
    UF Gasoline research
  — **Storage**
    UF Gasoline storage
  — **Supply**
    USE Gasoline supply
  — **Taxation** *(May Subd Geog)*
      ⌐HD9579.G3-HD9579.G5¬
      Here are entered general works on the taxa-
      tion of gasoline. Works on the taxation of gaso-
      line as a motor fuel are entered under Motor fuels
      —Taxation.
    UF Gasoline tax
  — **Transportation**
      ⌐TP692.2¬
    NT Gasoline—Pipe lines

Gasoline, Synthetic
  ⌐TP692.2¬
  UF Synthetic gasoline
  BT Fischer-Tropsch process
      Petroleum, Synthetic
      Synthetic fuels
Gasoline automobiles
  USE Automobiles
Gasoline consumption of automobiles
  USE Automobiles—Fuel consumption
Gasoline engines
  USE Internal combustion engines, Spark
        ignition
Gasoline industry *(May Subd Geog)*
  ⌐HD9579.G3-5¬
Gasoline inspection
  USE Oil inspection
Gasoline locomotives
  ⌐TN338 (Mining)¬
  BT Locomotives
      Mine haulage
Gasoline motors
  USE Internal combustion engines, Spark
        ignition
Gasoline pipe lines
  USE Gasoline—Pipe lines
Gasoline pump industry *(May Subd Geog)*
  BT Automobile industry and trade
      Petroleum industry and trade
Gasoline pumps
  UF Pumps, Gasoline
  BT Automobiles—Service stations—
        Equipment and supplies
      Pumping machinery
Gasoline research
  USE Gasoline—Research
Gasoline stations
  USE Automobiles—Service stations
Gasoline storage
  USE Gasoline—Storage
Gasoline stoves
  USE Stoves, Gasoline
Gasoline supply *(May Subd Geog)*
  UF Gasoline—Supply
  BT Petroleum industry and trade
Gasoline tax
  USE Gasoline—Taxation
GASP (Computer program language)
  UF General activity simulation program
  BT Digital computer simulation
      FORTRAN (Computer program
        language)
Gaspar Strait (Indonesia)
  USE Gelasa Strait (Indonesia)
Gaspar Straten (Indonesia)
  USE Gelasa Strait (Indonesia)
Gaspé Peninsula (Québec)
  UF Gaspésie (Québec)
      Peninsula of Gaspé (Québec)
      Péninsule de la Gaspésie (Québec)
      Péninsule Gaspésienne (Québec)
  BT Peninsulas—Québec (Province)
Gaspé shrew
  ⌐QL737.I56¬
  UF Sorex gaspensis
Gaspergou
  USE Fresh-water drum
Gaspésie (Québec)
  USE Gaspé Peninsula (Québec)
Gasquière family
  USE Ghesquières family
Gass family *(Not Subd Geog)*
  UF Gasse family
      Gasser family
      Gassert family
      Gassie family
  RT Gassman family
Gassandō Iseki (Kahoku-machi, Japan)
  USE Gassandō Site (Kahoku-machi, Japan)

Gassandō Site (Kahoku-machi, Japan)
  (Not Subd Geog)
  UF Gassandō Iseki (Kahoku-machi, Japan)
  BT Japan—Antiquities
Gassaway family *(Not Subd Geog)*
Gasse family
  USE Gass family
Gasser family
  USE Gass family
Gasserian ganglion
  UF Ganglion, Gasserian
      Ganglion semilunare
  BT Trigeminal nerve
Gassert family
  USE Gass family
Gasset family
  USE Gossett family
Gassett family
  USE Gossett family
Gassie family
  USE Gass family
Gassman family *(Not Subd Geog)*
  UF Gassmann family
  RT Gass family
Gassmann family
  USE Gassman family
Gassner family
  USE Gessner family
Gasteier family *(Not Subd Geog)*
Gasten family
  USE Gaston family
Gaster (Switzerland)
Gasteracantha
  ⌐QL458.42.A7¬
  BT Araneidae
Gasteracantha versicolor
  ⌐QL458.42.A7¬
Gasterochismidae
  USE Scombridae
Gasteromycetes *(May Subd Geog)*
  ⌐QK626-QK629¬
  BT Basidiomycetes
      Fungi
  NT Lycoperdales
      Nidulariales
      Phallales
Gasteropoda *(May Subd Geog)*
  ⌐QL430.4-QL430.5¬
  Here are entered systematic studies. Popular
  works on the shelled species of gasteropods are en-
  tered under Snails.
  UF Gastropoda
  BT Mollusks
  NT Abalones
      Amphineura
      Archaeogastropoda
      Endodontidae
      Heteropoda
      Olividae
      Opisthobranchia
      Pectinibranchiata
      Prosobranchiata
      Pulmonata
      Snails
      Tentaculitida
      Thecosomata
  — **Anatomy**
    UF Snails—Anatomy
  — **Food**
    UF Snails—Food
  — **Physiology**
Gasteropoda, Fossil
  ⌐QE808-9¬
  UF Snails, Fossil
  BT Mollusks, Fossil
  NT Murchisoniata
      Neritidae, Fossil
      Opisthobranchia, Fossil
      Pectinibranchiata, Fossil
      Prosobranchiata, Fossil
      Turritellidae, Fossil

Gasteropoda as carriers of disease
(May Subd Geog)
  UF Snails as carriers of disease
  BT Mollusks as carriers of disease
Gasterosteidae
  USE Sticklebacks
Gasterosteidae, Fossil
  BT Gasterosteiformes, Fossil
  NT Gasterosteus, Fossil
Gasterosteiformes
  ₍QL637.9.G37₎
  UF Hemibranchii
      Lophobranchii
      Solenichthyes
      Thoracostei
  BT Osteichthyes
  NT Indostomidae
      Sticklebacks
      Syngnathidae
Gasterosteiformes, Fossil
  BT Teleostei, Fossil
  NT Gasterosteidae, Fossil
Gasterosteus
  ₍QL638.G27₎
  BT Sticklebacks
Gasterosteus, Fossil
  BT Gasterosteidae, Fossil
Gasterosteus aculeatus
  USE Three-spined stickleback
Gasteruptiidae (May Subd Geog)
  ₍QL568.G3₎
  BT Hymenoptera
  NT Gasteruption
Gasteruption (May Subd Geog)
  ₍QL568.G3₎
  BT Gasteruptiidae
Gasti family
  USE Gosti family
Gastin family
  USE Gaston family
Gaston, Lake (N.C. and Va.)
  UF Lake Gaston (N.C. and Va.)
  BT Lakes—North Carolina
      Lakes—Virginia
      Reservoirs—North Carolina
      Reservoirs—Virginia
      Roanoke River (Va. and N.C.)
Gaston family (Not Subd Geog)
  UF Gasten family
      Gastin family
      Gesting family
      Gostin family
      Gusten family
      Gustin family
      Gustion family
      Guston family
Gastrectomy (May Subd Geog)
  ₍RD540.5₎
  UF Gastric resection
  BT Stomach—Surgery
  — Complications and sequelae
      NT Postgastrectomy syndromes
Gastric anacidity
  USE Achlorhydria
Gastric antacids
  USE Antacids
Gastric biopsy
  USE Stomach—Biopsy
Gastric diseases
  USE Stomach—Diseases
Gastric fistula
  USE Fistula, Gastric
Gastric hypoacidity
  USE Achlorhydria
Gastric intubation
  USE Stomach—Intubation
Gastric juice
  ₍QP193₎

  BT Body fluids
      Digestion
      Exocrine glands—Secretions
      Stomach—Secretions
  NT Pepsin
      Pepsinogen
      Rennet
Gastric lavage
  UF Stomach—Irrigation
  BT Irrigation (Medicine)
      Stomach—Intubation
      Stomach-pump
Gastric motility
  USE Stomach—Motility
Gastric mucosa
  UF Mucosa, Gastric
  BT Mucous membrane
      Stomach
Gastric resection
  USE Gastrectomy
Gästrikland (Sweden)
Gastrimargus
  ₍QL508.A2₎
  BT Acrididae
Gastrimargus africanus
  ₍QL508.A2₎
Gastrin
  ₍QP801.H7₎
  BT Gastrointestinal hormones
      Stomach—Secretions
  — Receptors
Gastritis
  USE Stomach—Inflammation
Gastro-esophageal reflux
  USE Gastroesophageal reflux
Gastrochaenidae
  ₍QL430.7.G23₎
  BT Teleodesmacea
Gastrodes (Ctenophora) (May Subd Geog)
  ₍QL380.5.T47₎
  BT Gastrodidae
  NT Gastrodes parasiticum
Gastrodes (Insect)
  ₍QL523.L9₎
  BT Lygaeidae
Gastrodes parasiticum (May Subd Geog)
  ₍QL380.5.T47₎
  BT Gastrodes (Ctenophora)
Gastrodia
  ₍QK495.O64₎
  BT Orchids
  NT Gastrodia elata
Gastrodia elata
  ₍QK495.O64 (Botany)₎
  ₍SB295.G37 (Culture)₎
  UF T'ien ma
  BT Gastrodia
Gastrodidae (May Subd Geog)
  ₍QL380.5.T47₎
  BT Platyctenida
  NT Gastrodes (Ctenophora)
Gastroduodenostomy
  BT Duodenum—Surgery
      Stomach—Surgery
  — Complications and sequelae
Gastroenteritis
  ₍RC840.G3₎
  BT Gastrointestinal system—Diseases
  NT Enteritis
      Stomach—Inflammation
Gastroenteritis in cattle (May Subd Geog)
  BT Cattle—Diseases
      Veterinary gastroenterology
Gastroenteritis in children
  (May Subd Geog)
  ₍RJ456.G₎
  BT Pediatric gastroenterology
Gastroenteritis of swine, Transmissible
  USE Transmissible gastroenteritis of swine
Gastroenterologic emergencies
  USE Gastrointestinal emergencies

Gastroenterological endocrinology
  USE Gastrointestinal hormones
Gastroenterologists (May Subd Geog)
  BT Internists
Gastroenterology
  ₍RC799-RC869₎
  BT Internal medicine
  SA headings beginning with the word
      Gastrointestinal
  NT Gastrointestinal system
      Geriatric gastroenterology
      Hospitals—Gastroenterology services
      Pediatric gastroenterology
      Proctology
      Radioisotopes in gastroenterology
      Veterinary gastroenterology
Gastroenteropathies, Protein-losing
  USE Protein-losing enteropathies
Gastroesophageal junction
  USE Esophagogastric junction
Gastroesophageal reflux (May Subd Geog)
  UF Esophageal reflux
      Esophagitis, Reflux
      Gastro-esophageal reflux
      Reflux esophagitis
  BT Esophagus—Diseases
  RT Heartburn
  NT Gastroesophageal reflux in children
Gastroesophageal reflux, Pediatric
  USE Gastroesophageal reflux in children
Gastroesophageal reflux in children
  (May Subd Geog)
  ₍RJ456.G33₎
  UF Gastroesophageal reflux, Pediatric
      Pediatric gastroesophageal reflux
  BT Gastroesophageal reflux
      Pediatric gastroenterology
Gastroesophageal sphincter
  USE Cardioesophageal sphincter
Gastrointestinal agents
  ₍RM355₎
  UF Drugs, Gastrointestinal
  BT Gastrointestinal system—Diseases
      Pharmacology
  NT Antacids
      Anthelmintics
      Antidiarrheals
      Antiemetics
      Antiperistaltics
      Bile acids
      Cholagogues
      Emetics
      Pancreopepsine
      Proglumide
      Purgatives
      Ranitidine
Gastrointestinal angiography
  USE Digestive organs—Blood-vessels—
      Radiography
Gastrointestinal emergencies
  (May Subd Geog)
  UF Emergencies, Gastroenterologic
      Emergencies, Gastrointestinal
      Gastroenterologic emergencies
  BT Gastrointestinal system—Diseases
      Medical emergencies
Gastrointestinal enzymes
  USE Digestive enzymes
Gastrointestinal function tests
  BT Function tests (Medicine)
Gastrointestinal gas
  UF Gas, Gastrointestinal
      Intestinal gas
      Intestines, Gases in
  BT Gastrointestinal system—Diseases
  NT Flatulence
Gastrointestinal hemorrhage
  UF Alimentary canal—Hemorrhage
  BT Hemorrhage

Gastrointestinal hormones
  UF Endocrinological gastroenterology
       Gastroenterological endocrinology
       Gut hormones
  BT Hormones
  NT Cholecystokinin
       Gastrin
       Neurotensin
       Secretin
       Somatostatin
       Vasoactive intestinal peptides
Gastrointestinal motility
  USE Gastrointestinal system—Motility
Gastrointestinal motility disorders
  USE Gastrointestinal system—Motility—
        Disorders
Gastrointestinal services in hospitals
  USE Hospitals—Gastroenterology services
Gastrointestinal system
  [QM341-QM345 (Anatomy)]
  [QP151-QP156 (Physiology)]
  [RC799-RC869 (Disease)]
  UF Gastrointestinal tract
  BT Alimentary canal
       Digestive organs
       Gastroenterology
  NT Intestines
       Stomach
  — **Diseases** *(May Subd Geog)*
    NT Gastroenteritis
       Gastrointestinal agents
       Gastrointestinal emergencies
       Gastrointestinal gas
       Indigestion
       Nausea
       Protein-losing enteropathies
  — **Motility**
    [QP180]
    UF Gastrointestinal motility
       Motility, Gastrointestinal
    BT Biomechanics
       Digestion
    RT Peristalsis
  — — **Disorders** *(May Subd Geog)*
      [RC811]
      UF Gastrointestinal motility
         disorders
         Motility disorders,
          Gastrointestinal
Gastrointestinal tract
  USE Gastrointestinal system
Gastroliths
  UF Gizzard stones
       Stomach stones
  BT Vertebrates
Gastronema
  USE Cyrtanthus
Gastronomy
  [TX631-641]
  UF Eating
  BT Diet
  RT Cookery
       Dinners and dining
       Food
  NT Drinking behavior
       Food presentation
       Gluttony
       Menus
       Picnicking
Gastrophotography
  BT Gastroscope and gastroscopy
       Photography, Medical
Gastropoda
  USE Gasteropoda
Gastroscope and gastroscopy
  USE Gastroscopes
       Gastroscopy
  NT Gastrophotography
Gastroscopes *(May Subd Geog)*
  UF Gastroscope and gastroscopy
  BT Endoscopes

Gastroscopy *(May Subd Geog)*
  [RC804.G3]
  UF Gastroscope and gastroscopy
  BT Endoscopy
       Stomach—Examination
Gastrosericus
  [QL568.S7]
  BT Sphecidae
Gastrostomy *(May Subd Geog)*
  [RD540.5]
  BT Stomach—Surgery
Gastrotaenia
  BT Aporidea
Gastrotheca
  [QL668.E24]
  BT Hylidae
Gastrotheca orophylax
  [QL668.E24]
Gastrotheca walkeri
  [QL668.E24]
Gastrotomy
  USE Stomach—Surgery
Gastrotricha
  [QL391.G2]
  BT Aschelminthes
  NT Chaetonotoidea
       Macrodasyoidea
Gastrulation
  BT Embryology
Gasur (Ancient city)
  USE Nuzi (Ancient city)
GAT (Computer program)
  UF General analysis technique (Computer
        program)
       Georgetown automatic translation
  BT Electronic digital computers—
        Programming
       Russian language—Machine translating
Gatche family
  USE Geitgey family
Gate array circuits
  [TK7895.G36]
  UF Gate arrays
  BT Integrated circuits
Gate arrays
  USE Gate array circuits
Gate family
  USE Gates family
Gate money (Prisons)
  USE Prison release gratuities
Gate receipts, Taxation of
  USE Amusements—Taxation
Gaterinidae
  USE Grunts (Fishes)
Gates *(May Subd Geog)*
  [NA493-NA495 (Military
    architecture)]
  [NA8385-NA8392 (Architecture)]
  [S723 (Agriculture)]
  BT Fences
       Walls
  SA *names of individual gates*
  NT Lich-gates
       Torii
  — **Iraq**
    NT Ishtar Gate (Babylon)
  — **Netherlands**
    NT Sabelspoort (Arnhem, Netherlands)
  — **Sweden**
    NT Norre Port (Halmstad, Sweden)
  — **Ukraine**
    NT Zoloti vorota (Kiev, Ukraine)
Gates, Coincidence
  USE Coincidence circuits
Gates, Hydraulic
  USE Hydraulic gates
Gates (Work of art)
  USE Christo, 1935-   Gates
Gates family *(Not Subd Geog)*
  UF Gaites family
       Gate family

  RT Getz family
       Goetz family
Gates Learjet aircraft
  USE Lear jet aircraft
Gates of hell (Sculpture)
  USE Rodin, Auguste, 1840-1917.   Gates of
        hell
**Gates of the Arctic National Park and
  Preserve (Alaska)**
  BT National parks and reserves—United
        States
       Parks—Alaska
Gateway Arch (Saint Louis, Mo.)
  BT Arches—Missouri
       Saint Louis (Mo.)—Monuments
Gateway Center (Pittsburgh, Pa.)
  (Not Subd Geog)
  UF Pittsburgh (Pa.).   Gateway Center
**Gateway National Recreation Area (N.J. and
  N.Y.)**
  BT National parks and reserves—United
        States
       Recreation areas—New Jersey
       Recreation areas—New York (State)
  NT Fort Tilden (New York, N.Y.)
       Sandy Hook Proving Ground (N.J.)
Gatewood family *(Not Subd Geog)*
  UF Gatwood family
Gatherers, Fuelwood
  USE Fuelwood gatherers
Gathering and hunting societies
  USE Hunting and gathering societies
Gathering of Traditional Indiana Fiddlers and
  Other Folks
  USE Battle Ground Fiddlers' Gathering,
        Battle Ground, Ind.
Gathering seafood
  USE Seafood gathering
Gathering wild food
  USE Food, Wild
Gatherings, Religious
  USE Religious gatherings
Gathers (Sewing)
  BT Clothing and dress
       Sewing
Gathmann torpedo gun
  [UF630]
Gathright Lake (Va.)
  USE Moomaw Lake (Va.)
Gâtinais (France)
Gatineau Park (Québec)
  UF Parc de Gatineau (Québec)
  BT National parks and reserves—Canada
       Parks—Québec (Province)
Gating system (Founding)
  BT Founding
  RT Risers (Founding)
Gatliff family *(Not Subd Geog)*
Gatling guns
  [UF620.G3]
  [VF410.G3-VF410.G34 (Naval)]
  BT Machine-guns
       Mitrailleuses
Gato (Dance)
  [GV1796.G]
Gattermann reaction
  BT Chemical reactions
Gattes family
  USE Getty family
Gatti family *(Not Subd Geog)*
Gattis family
  USE Getty family
Gatun Dam (Panama) *(Not Subd Geog)*
  BT Dams—Panama
Gatun Lake (Panama)
  UF Lago Gatún (Panama)
  BT Chagres River (Panama)
       Lakes—Panama
       Reservoirs—Panama
  RT Gatun Dam (Panama)

Gatun River (Panama)
  UF Río Gatún (Panama)
  BT Rivers—Panama
Gatwood family
  USE Gatewood family
Gaucher-Schlagenhaufer syndrome
  USE Gaucher's disease
Gaucher's disease (May Subd Geog)
  ⌐RC632.G36⌐
  UF Cerebroside lipidosis
      Familial splenic anemia
      Gaucher-Schlagenhaufer syndrome
      Splenic anemia, Familial
  BT Anemia
      Cerebrosides—Metabolism—Disorders
      Mental retardation
      Reticuloendotheliosis
      Sphingolipidoses
Gaucho (The word)
Gaucho poetry (Argentine)
  USE Argentine poetry—Gaucho authors
Gauchos (May Subd Geog)
  ⌐F2217 (General)⌐
  ⌐F2621 (Brazil)⌐
  ⌐F2682.9 (Paraguay)⌐
  ⌐F2722.9 (Uruguay)⌐
  ⌐F2926 (Argentina)⌐
  BT Herders
      Horsemen and horsewomen
  RT Cowboys
  NT Cowgirls
Gauchos in art
Gauchos in literature
Gaudian languages
  USE Indo-Aryan languages, Modern
Gaudie family
  USE Gowdy family
Gaudier, Henri. Hieratic head of Ezra Pound
  UF Hieratic head of Ezra Pound (Portrait
      sculpture)
  BT Pound, Ezra, 1885-1972—Portraits
      Sculpture, French
      Sculpture, Modern—20th century—
      France
Gaudiès Castle (Gaudiès, France)
  USE Château de Gaudiès (Gaudiès, France)
Gaudreau family
  USE Godreau family
Gaudy family
  USE Gowdy family
Gaudy ware (May Subd Geog)
  ⌐NK4340.G38⌐
  UF Gaudy Welsh china
      Gawdy ware
  BT Pottery, English
      Pottery, Welsh
Gaudy Welsh china
  USE Gaudy ware
Gauff family
  USE Goff family
Gaugamela, Battle of, 331 B.C.
  ⌐DF234.5⌐
  UF Arbela, Battle of, 331 B.C.
  BT Iran—History—Macedonian Conquest,
      334-325 B.C.
      Macedonia—History—To 168 B.C.
Gauge fields (Physics)
  ⌐QC793.3.F5⌐
  UF Fields, Gauge (Physics)
      Gage fields (Physics)
      Gauge theories (Physics)
  BT Field theory (Physics)
      Groups, Theory of
      Physics
      Symmetry (Physics)
  RT Gauge invariance
  NT Grand unified theories (Nuclear
      physics)
      Instantons

Gauge invariance
  UF Gage invariance
      Invariance, Gauge
  BT Conservation laws (Physics)
      Electric charge and distribution
      Field theory (Physics)
      Potential, Theory of
      Quantum electrodynamics
      Symmetry (Physics)
      Transformations (Mathematics)
  RT Gauge fields (Physics)
Gauge theories (Physics)
  USE Gauge fields (Physics)
Gauges
  USE Gages
Gauges, Precipitation
  USE Precipitation gauges
Gauges, Pressure
  USE Pressure gages
Gaugh family
  USE Goff family
Gaughenor family
  USE Coughenour family
Gaugi family
  USE Gage family
Gauging
  USE Gaging
Gaugy family
  USE Gage family
Gauīā River (Latvia and Estonia)
  USE Gauja River (Latvia and Estonia)
Gauja National Park (Latvia)
  USE Gaujas nacionālais parks (Latvia)
Gauja River (Latvia and Estonia)
  UF Aa River (Latvia and Estonia)
      Aha River (Latvia and Estonia)
      Gauīā River (Latvia and Estonia)
      Gaujas upe (Latvia and Estonia)
      Gauya River (Latvia and Estonia)
      Giuja River (Latvia and Estonia)
      Koiva River (Latvia and Estonia)
      Livländische Aa River (Latvia and
      Estonia)
      Livonian Aa River (Latvia and
      Estonia)
      Treider Aa (Latvia and Estonia)
  BT Rivers—Estonia
      Rivers—Latvia
Gaujas nacionālais parks (Latvia)
  UF Gauja National Park (Latvia)
      Natsional'nyĭ park Gauīā (Latvia)
  BT National parks and reserves—Soviet
      Union
      Parks—Latvia
Gaujas upe (Latvia and Estonia)
  USE Gauja River (Latvia and Estonia)
Gauker family (Not Subd Geog)
Gaul
  — History
      ⌐DC21⌐
      ⌐DC62⌐
  — — To 58 B.C.
  — — Gallic Wars, 58-51 B.C.
        ⌐DC62 (France)⌐
        ⌐DG264 (Rome)⌐
      UF Gallic Wars, 58-51 B.C.
      BT Rome—History—Republic, 265-
          30 B.C.
      NT Alesia, Battle of, 52 B.C.
          Gergovie, Battle of, 52 B.C.
          Haute Alsace, Battle of, 58 B.C.
  — — 58 B.C.-511 A.D.
Gaul family
  USE Gault family
Gauler family
  USE Gault family
Gauley River (W. Va.)
  BT Rivers—West Virginia
  NT Summersville Lake (W. Va.)

Gaulin family (Not Subd Geog)
Gaulish calendar
  USE Calendar, Celtic
Gaulish inscriptions
  USE Inscriptions, Gaulish
Gaulish language
  ⌐PB3001-3029⌐
  UF Gallic language
  BT Celtic languages
      Celtic languages, Continental
Gaulos Island (Malta)
  USE Gozo Island (Malta)
Gauls (May Subd Geog)
  ⌐DC62-63⌐
  RT Celts
      Galatians
  NT Arverni
      Salassi (Gallic people)
Gauls in literature
Gault family (Not Subd Geog)
  UF Gald family
      Galt family
      Gaul family
      Gauler family
      Golt family
Gaulus Island (Malta)
  USE Gozo Island (Malta)
Gaumer family (Not Subd Geog)
Gauna language
  USE Kaurna language
Gaunt family
  USE Gantt family
Gaunts family
  USE Gantt family
Gauntt family
  USE Gantt family
Gauntzer family
  USE Gonser family
Gaura
  ⌐QK495.O46⌐
  UF Gauridium
      Schizocarya
  BT Onagraceae
Gaurī (Hindu deity)
  BT Gods, Hindu
  NT Annapūrṇā (Hindu deity)
Gauridium
  USE Gaura
Gaurna language
  USE Kaurna language
Gaurthny family
  USE Gwartney family
Gaus family
  USE Goss family
Gause family
  USE Goss family
Gauss-Bonnet theorem
  BT Algebraic topology
      Geometry, Differential
      Polygons
Gauss conformal projection (Cartography)
  USE Transverse Mercator projection
      (Cartography)
Gauss error function
  USE Error functions
Gauss-Krüger projection (Cartography)
  USE Transverse Mercator projection
      (Cartography)
Gauss maps
  UF Maps, Gauss
  BT Mappings (Mathematics)
      Surfaces, Minimal
Gauss' quadrature formulas
  USE Gaussian quadrature formulas
Gauss sums
  USE Gaussian sums
Gaussian basis sets (Quantum mechanics)
  BT Basis sets (Quantum mechanics)

Gaussian beams
  UF Beams, Gaussian
      Gaussian light
      Light, Gaussian
  BT Beam optics
      Gaussian processes
Gaussian distribution
  UF Distribution, Gaussian
      Distribution, Normal
      Normal distribution
  BT Distribution (Probability theory)
Gaussian hypergeometric series
  USE Hypergeometric series
Gaussian light
  USE Gaussian beams
Gaussian measures
  UF Measures, Gaussian
  BT Gaussian processes
      Measure theory
Gaussian mechanical quadrature formulas
  USE Gaussian quadrature formulas
Gaussian noise
  USE Random noise theory
Gaussian processes
  BT Distribution (Probability theory)
      Stochastic processes
  NT Gaussian beams
      Gaussian measures
      Ornstein-Uhlenbeck process
Gaussian quadrature formulas
  ₁QA299.4.G3₁
  UF Gauss' quadrature formulas
      Gaussian mechanical quadrature
        formulas
  BT Numerical integration
Gaussian series
  USE Hypergeometric series
Gaussian sums
  UF Gauss sums
      Sums, Gaussian
  BT Functions, Zeta
      Numerical functions
      Sequences (Mathematics)
Gauss's series
  USE Hypergeometric series
Gautama Buddha
  — Bodhi
      USE Gautama Buddha—
        Enlightenment
  — **Cult**
      NT Gautama Buddha—Footprints
  — **Enlightenment**
      ₁BQ935₁
      UF Gautama Buddha—Bodhi
      BT Enlightenment (Buddhism)
  — **Footprints** (May Subd Geog)
      ₁BQ922₁
      UF Footprints of Gautama Buddha
      BT Buddhist cults
          Gautama Buddha—Cult
  — **Hindu interpretations**
      UF Gautama Buddha—Interpretations,
            Hindu
          Gautama Buddha in Hinduism
      BT Buddhism—Relations—Hinduism
          Hinduism—Relations—Buddhism
  — **History of doctrines**
      BT Buddhism—Doctrines
  — Interpretations, Hindu
      USE Gautama Buddha—Hindu
        interpretations
  — **Pre-existence**
      BT Buddhism—Doctrines
  — **Shrines** (May Subd Geog)
      ₁BQ6460₁
      BT Buddhist shrines
          Stūpas
  — **Teachings**
      BT Buddhism—Doctrines
          Buddhism—Doctrines—History—
            Early period, to ca. 250 B.C.

Gautama Buddha in Hinduism
  USE Gautama Buddha—Hindu
    interpretations
Gautherot family
  USE Godreau family
Gauthier family (Not Subd Geog)
  UF Gautier family
Gautier family
  USE Gauthier family
Gauvain (Legendary character)
  USE Gawain (Legendary character)
Gauya River (Latvia and Estonia)
  USE Gauja River (Latvia and Estonia)
Gavage
  USE Tube feeding
Gavan family
  USE Givens family
Gavdo (Island), Battle of, 1941
  USE Matapan, Battle of, 1941
Gavelkind
Gaven family
  USE Givens family
Gavet family
  USE Gavitt family
Gavett family
  USE Gavitt family
Gavey family
  USE Gavitt family
Gavi, Arco dei (Verona, Italy)
  USE Arch of the Gabii (Verona, Italy)
Gavia immer
  USE Common loon
Gaviae
  USE Laridae
Gaviiformes
  USE Loons
Gavilanes Site (Peru) (Not Subd Geog)
  UF Huarmey Norte 1 Site (Peru)
      Los Gavilanes Site (Peru)
  BT Peru—Antiquities
Gavin family
  USE Givens family
Gaving family
  USE Givens family
Gaviões Indians
  ₁F2520.1.G37₁
  UF Augutge Indians
      Parkateyê Indians
      Piocobgês Indians
      Pukóbye Indians
      Western Gaviões Indians
  BT Indians of South America
      Timbira Indians
Gavit family
  USE Gavitt family
Gavitt family (Not Subd Geog)
  UF Gavet family
      Gavett family
      Gavey family
      Gavit family
      Govett family
      Govit family
Gavon family
  USE Givens family
Gavottes
  BT Dance music
Gawain
  USE Gawain (Legendary character)
Gawain (Legendary character)
  UF Galvaginus (Legendary character)
      Gauvain (Legendary character)
      Gawain
      Gawayne (Legendary character)
      Gwalchmei (Legendary character)
      Walgainus (Legendary character)
      Walwain (Legendary character)
      Walwen (Legendary character)
  BT Arthurian romances
Gawayne (Legendary character)
  USE Gawain (Legendary character)

Gawdie family
  USE Gowdy family
Gawdy family
  USE Gowdy family
Gawdy ware
  USE Gaudy ware
Gawędy
  BT Polish literature
      Polish wit and humor
      Tales—Poland
Gawge family
  USE Gage family
Gawigl language
  UF Gawil language
      Kaugel language
      Kauil language
  BT Papuan languages
Gawil language
  USE Gawigl language
Gaws family
  USE Goss family
Gawurna language
  USE Kaurna language
Gay bars (May Subd Geog)
  BT Homosexuality
      Hotels, taverns, etc.
Gay couples
  USE Homosexual couples
Gay family (Not Subd Geog)
  UF Gaye family
Gay Head Indians
  ₁F74.G25₁
  BT Algonquian Indians
      Indians of North America
      Wampanoag Indians
Gay lib
  USE Gay liberation movement
Gay liberation movement (May Subd Geog)
  ₁HQ76.5-8₁
  UF Gay lib
      Homophile movement
      Homosexual liberation movement
  BT Homosexuality
Gay-Lussac's law
  USE Charles' law
Gay parents
  USE Homosexual parents
Gay people
  USE Homosexuals
Gay persons
  USE Homosexuals
Gaya language
  USE Luo language (Kenya and Tanzania)
Gayal
  UF Mithan
  BT Cattle
Gayana
  USE Guiana
Gāyatrī (Hindu deity)
  BT Gods, Hindu
Gāyatrī Parivāra
  ₁BL1253₁
  BT Arya-Samaj
      Hindu sects
Gaye family
  USE Gay family
Gayles family
  USE Gales family
Gaynes family
  USE Gaines family
Gayo (Indonesian people) marriage customs
    and rites
  USE Marriage customs and rites, Gayo
    (Indonesian people)
Gayo folk poetry
  USE Folk poetry, Gayo
Gayo folk-songs
  USE Folk-songs, Gayo
Gayo Islamic poetry
  USE Islamic poetry, Gayo

Gayo language
　UF　Gajo language
　BT　Malayan languages
Gayo poetry *(May Subd Geog)*
　NT　Folk poetry, Gayo
　　　Islamic poetry, Gayo
Gayo proverbs
　USE　Proverbs, Gayo
Gayos (Indonesian people)
　BT　Ethnology—Indonesia
　— Rites and ceremonies
　　　NT　Marriage customs and rites, Gayo
　　　　　(Indonesian people)
Gays
　USE　Homosexuals
Gays, Female
　USE　Lesbians
Gays, Male
　USE　Homosexuals, Male
Gays' writings
　USE　Homosexuals' writings
Gaza, Battles of, 1917
　[D568.7]
　BT　World War, 1914-1918—Campaigns—
　　　Palestine
Gaza Strip *(Not Subd Geog)*
　　As a geographic subdivision, this heading is used
　directly. Headings for entities located within the
　Gaza Strip are used indirectly through Gaza Strip as
　geographic subdivisions.
　BT　Palestine
Gaze
　[QP491]
　BT　Visual perception
　— Psychological aspects
　　　[BF637.C45]
　　　BT　Nonverbal communication
　　　　　(Psychology)
　　　　　Social perception
　— Regulation
　　　UF　Regulation of gaze
　　　BT　Biological control systems
Gaze hounds
　USE　Gazehounds
Gazehounds
　[SF429.G3]
　UF　Coursers (Dogs)
　　　Gaze hounds
　　　Sight hounds
　　　Sighthounds
　NT　Afghan hounds
　　　Borzoi
　　　Deer-hounds
　　　Greyhounds
　　　Irish wolfhound
　　　Lurcher
　　　Saluki
　　　Whippets
Gazelle Peninsula (New Britain Island, Papua New Guinea
　BT　Peninsulas—Papua New Guinea
Gazelle River (Sudan)
　USE　Bahr al-Ghazāl (Sudan : River)
Gazelles
　[QL737.U5]
Gazels
　USE　Ghazals
Gazetteers
　UF　Names, Geographical—Dictionaries
　BT　Geography—Dictionaries
　　　Toponymy
　SA　subdivision Gazetteers *under names of*
　　　countries, states, etc. for
　　　dictionaries of geographic names of
　　　those places with descriptions
Gazettes *(May Subd Geog)*
　UF　Government gazettes
　　　Official gazettes
　BT　Government publications
　　　Periodicals

Gazettes in microform
　BT　Microforms
　NT　Gazettes on microfilm
Gazettes on microfilm
　BT　Gazettes in microform
　　　Microfilms
Gazili dialect
　USE　Hazili dialect
Gazing into a crystal ball
　USE　Crystal gazing
Gazoo
　USE　Kazoo
Gbagyi language
　[PL8203.G35]
　BT　Kwa languages
　　　Nigeria—Languages
Gbaka (African people)
　USE　Ngbaka (African people)
Gban (African people)
　USE　Gagou (African people)
Gban language
　USE　Gagu language
Gbande (Liberian people)
　USE　Gbandi (Liberian people)
Gbandi (Liberian people)
　UF　Bandi (Liberian people)
　　　Gbande (Liberian people)
　　　Gbassi (Liberian people)
　BT　Ethnology—Liberia
Gbandi language
　[PL8204]
　UF　Bandi language
　BT　Liberia—Languages
　　　Mande languages
Gbandi language (Zaire)
　USE　Ngbandi language
Gbanja kola tree
　USE　Kola tree
Gbanya (African people)
　USE　Gonja (African people)
Gbanzili (African people)
　USE　Banziri (African people)
Gbanziri (African people)
　USE　Banziri (African people)
Gbari (African people)
　USE　Gwari (African people)
Gbari language
　USE　Gwari language
Gbasa (Liberian people)
　USE　Bassa (Liberian people)
Gbasa language
　USE　Bassa language (Liberia)
Gbassi (Liberian people)
　USE　Gbandi (Liberian people)
Gbaya (African people)
　UF　Baya (African people)
　　　Bwaka (African people)
　　　Gbeya (African people)
　BT　Ethnology—Africa, West
　NT　Kara (Gbayan people)
Gbaya folk-songs
　USE　Folk-songs, Gbaya
Gbaya language
　[PL8205]
　UF　Baya language
　　　Gbea language
　　　Gbeya language
　　　Ngbaka Gbaya language
　BT　Cameroon—Languages
　　　Central African Republic—Languages
　　　Congo (Brazzaville)—Languages
　　　Niger-Congo languages
　NT　Yaayuwee dialect
Gbè (The Fon word)
　BT　Fon dialect—Etymology
Gbe language
　USE　Ewe language
Gbea language
　USE　Gbaya language
Gbeya (African people)
　USE　Gbaya (African people)

Gbeya language
　USE　Gbaya language
Gboare (African people)
　USE　Bachama (African people)
GCA
　USE　Ground controlled approach
GCARS II (Information retrieval system)
　[TE206]
　UF　Generalized Computer-Aided Route
　　　Selection System
　BT　Information storage and retrieval
　　　systems—Roads—Location
Gciriku language
　USE　Diriku language
Gcod (Bonpo rite)
　[BQ7982.3]
　BT　Bonpo (Sect)—Rituals
　　　Gcod (Buddhist rite)
Gcod (Buddhist rite)
　[BQ7699.G36]
　BT　Buddhism—Rituals
　NT　Gcod (Bonpo rite)
Gdańsk, Gulf of (Poland and R.S.F.S.R.)
　(Not Subd Geog)
　UF　Danzig, Bay of (Poland and
　　　R.S.F.S.R.)
　　　Danzig, Gulf of (Poland and
　　　R.S.F.S.R.)
　　　Danziger Bucht (Poland and
　　　R.S.F.S.R.)
　　　Gdanskaiā bukhta (Poland and
　　　R.S.F.S.R.)
　　　Gulf of Gdańsk (Poland and
　　　R.S.F.S.R.)
　　　Zatoka Gdańska (Poland and
　　　R.S.F.S.R.)
　BT　Bays—Poland
　　　Bays—Russian S.F.S.R.
Gdańsk Pomerania (Poland)
　USE　Pomerelia (Poland)
Gdanskaiā bukhta (Poland and R.S.F.S.R.)
　USE　Gdańsk, Gulf of (Poland and
　　　R.S.F.S.R.)
Gdebo language
　USE　Grebo language
GDPS (Computer system)
　UF　Global Data-processing System
　　　(Computer system)
Ge (African people)
　USE　Mina (African people)
GE 600 series (Computers)
　BT　Electronic digital computers
　— Programming
Gẽ dialect
　USE　Mina dialect
Gê Indians
　[F2520.1.G4]
　BT　Indians of South America
　　　Indians of South America—Brazil
GE Mark III (Electronic computer system)
　BT　Computer networks
　　　Time-sharing computer systems
GE Plot (Schenectady, N.Y.)
　USE　General Electric Realty Plot Historic
　　　District (Schenectady, N.Y.)
GE Realty Plot (Schenectady, N.Y.)
　USE　General Electric Realty Plot Historic
　　　District (Schenectady, N.Y.)
Gea
　[QL458.42.A7]
　BT　Araneidae
Gea family
　USE　Gee family
Geac (Computer system)
　[Z678.93.G43]
　UF　Geac Library Information System
　BT　Libraries—Automation
Geac Library Information System
　USE　Geac (Computer system)
Gean
　USE　Sweet cherry

Geans family
  USE Gaines family
Gear-cutting machines
  [TJ187]
  BT Gearing
  NT Gear-shaping machines
     Gear-shaving machines
     Gearing—Manufacture
— **Maintenance and repair**
     UF Gear-cutting machines—Repairing
— Repairing
     USE Gear-cutting machines—
          Maintenance and repair
Gear family
  USE Geer family
Gear industry *(May Subd Geog)*
  [HD9705.5.G42-424]
  RT Gearing
— Collective bargaining
     USE Collective bargaining—Gear
          industry
— **Employees**
     NT Collective bargaining—Gear
          industry
Gear pumps
  [TJ917]
  UF Pumps, Gear
  BT Rotary pumps
Gear rolling
  [TJ184]
  UF Roll forming of gears
  BT Gearing—Manufacture
     Rolling (Metal-work)
Gear selectivity in fisheries
  USE Fisheries—Gear selectivity
Gear-shaping machines
  [TJ187]
  BT Gear-cutting machines
     Shapers
Gear-shaving machines
  BT Gear-cutting machines
     Gearing—Manufacture
Gearhart family *(Not Subd Geog)*
  UF Garehart family
     Gearheart family
     Gearhert family
     Geerhart family
     Gehrhart family
     Gerhard family
     Gerhardt family
     Gerhart family
     Gerhartt family
  RT Gebhardt family
Gearheart family
  USE Gearhart family
Gearhert family
  USE Gearhart family
Gearing
  [TJ184-204]
  UF Cog-wheels
     Gears
  BT Machinery
     Power transmission
     Rolling contact
     Wheels
  RT Gear industry
     Mechanical movements
  NT Automobiles—Steering-gear
     Automobiles—Transmission devices
     Automobiles, Military—Transmission
        devices
     Boring machinery—Transmission
        devices
     Clutches (Machinery)
     Coal-mining machinery—Transmission
        devices
     Construction equipment—Transmission
        devices
     Conveying machinery—Transmission
        devices
     Couplings

     Diesel locomotives—Transmission
        devices
     Electric locomotives—Transmission
        devices
     Feed-water pumps—Transmission
        devices
     Friction gearing
     Gear-cutting machines
     Gearing, Reduction
     Hoisting machinery—Transmission
        devices
     Indexing (Machine-shop practice)
     Locomotives—Transmission devices
     Machine-tools—Transmission devices
     Marine turbines—Transmission devices
     Mining machinery—Transmission
        devices
     Motor vehicles—Transmission devices
     Odontograph
     Oil well pumps—Transmission devices
     Road machinery—Transmission
        devices
     Rolling-mill machinery—Transmission
        devices
     Ships—Transmission devices
     Sprockets
     Tracklaying vehicles—Transmission
        devices
     Tractors—Transmission devices
— Drawing
     USE Gearing—Drawings
— **Drawings**
     UF Gearing—Drawing
     BT Mechanical drawing
— **Dynamics**
     [TJ184]
— **Interference**
     UF Interference, Gearing
     BT Rolling contact
— **Lubrication**
— **Manufacture**
     BT Gear-cutting machines
     NT Gear rolling
        Gear-shaving machines
— **Vibration**
Gearing, Bevel
  [TJ193-6]
  UF Bevel-gearing
Gearing, Helical
  USE Gearing, Spiral
Gearing, Hypoid
  UF Hypoid gearing
Gearing, Involute
  USE Gearing, Spur
Gearing, Novikov
  UF Novikov gearing
Gearing, Planetary
  UF Epicyclic gearing
     Planetary gearing
  NT Harmonic drives
Gearing, Plastic
  [TP1185.M3]
  UF Plastic gearing
  BT Plastics
Gearing, Reduction
  UF Reduction gearing
  BT Gearing
  NT Speed reducers
— **Vibration**
Gearing, Spiral
  [TJ192]
  UF Gearing, Helical
     Spiral gearing
  NT Spiral milling
Gearing, Spur
  [TJ189]
  UF Gearing, Involute
     Spur gearing
Gearing, Worm
  [TJ200]
  UF Worm-gear

Gears
  USE Gearing
Gears family
  USE Geer family
Geary family
  USE Gery family
Geastraceae
  [QK629.G4]
  BT Lycoperdales
Geats
  BT Ethnology—Scandinavia
Gebel 'Atāqa (Egypt)
  USE Ataqa Mountains (Egypt)
Gebel el Achdar (Libya)
  USE Akhdar Mountains (Libya)
Gebel el Akhdar (Libya)
  USE Akhdar Mountains (Libya)
Gebert family
  USE Gebhardt family
Gebfall family
  USE Gibble family
Gebhard family
  USE Gebhardt family
Gebhardt family *(Not Subd Geog)*
  UF Capehart family
     Gebert family
     Gebhard family
     Gebhart family
     Kephart family
  RT Gearhart family
Gebhart family
  USE Gebhardt family
**Gebrüder Hofmann Strike, Eibelstadt,
Germany, 1983-1984**
  BT Strikes and lockouts—Agricultural
     machinery industry—Germany
     (West)
Gebusi (Papua New Guinea people)
  [DU740.42]
  BT Ethnology—Papua New Guinea
Gecarcinidae
  [QL444.M33]
  UF Burrowing land crabs
     Land crabs, Burrowing
  BT Crabs
     Decapoda (Crustacea)
  NT Cardisoma
     Gecarcinus
Gecarcinus
  [QL444.M33]
  BT Gecarcinidae
Gecarcinus lateralis
  [QL444.M33]
Geck family *(Not Subd Geog)*
Geckner family
  USE Goeckner family
Geckobia
  [QL458.2.P87]
  BT Pterygosomatidae
Geckos
  [QL666.L245]
  UF Gekkonidae
  BT Lizards
  NT Anarbylus
     Cyrtodactylus
     Eublepharis
     Garthia
     Gekko
     Gonatodes
     Hemidactylus
     Kaokogecko
     Lepidodactylus
     Lygodactylus
     Pachydactylus
     Perochirus
     Pseudothecadactylus
     Sphaerodactylus
     Tarentola
Geckos as pets
  [SF459.G35]

GED tests
  USE General educational development tests
Gedaged language
  UF Graged language
  BT Melanesian languages
GEDANKEN (Computer program language)
Geddes' comet
  ₍QB723.G₎
Geddes family *(Not Subd Geog)*
  UF Geddis family
Gedding family
  USE Giddings family
Geddings family
  USE Giddings family
Geddis family
  USE Geddes family
Gedebo language
  USE Grebo language
Gederaas family
  USE Gederos family
Gederos family *(Not Subd Geog)*
  UF Gederaas family
Gediminas aikštė (Vilnius, Lithuania)
  UF Gediminas Square (Vilnius, Lithuania)
  BT Plazas—Lithuania
Gediminas Square (Vilnius, Lithuania)
  USE Gediminas aikštė (Vilnius, Lithuania)
Gee-Bee (Racing plane)
  BT Airplanes, Racing
Gee family *(Not Subd Geog)*
  UF Gea family
     Gehe family
Geekie family *(Not Subd Geog)*
Geelvinkia
  ₍QL444.M33₎
  BT Sundathelphusidae
Geer family *(Not Subd Geog)*
  UF Gear family
     Gears family
     Geers family
Geerhart family
  USE Gearhart family
Geers family
  USE Geer family
Geese *(May Subd Geog)*
  ₍QL696.A52 (Zoology)₎
  ₍SF505 (Culture)₎
  ₍SK333.G6 (Hunting)₎
  UF Goose
  BT Poultry
     Waterfowl
  NT Bar-headed goose
     Barnacle goose
     Bean goose
     Blue goose
     Branta
     Brent-goose
     Canada goose
     Greylag goose
     Ross's goose
     Snow goose
     Swan goose
     White-fronted goose
  — Anatomy
     NT Foie gras
Geese, Fossil
Geese in art
Geez language
  USE Ethiopic language
Geffereys family
  USE Jeffries family
Gefries family
  USE Jeffries family

Gegam Range (Armenian S.S.R.)
  UF Agmaganskiĭ khrebet (Armenian S.S.R.)
     Agmaganskiy khrebet (Armenian S.S.R.)
     Gegamskiĭ khrebet (Armenian S.S.R.)
     Gegamskiy khrebet (Armenian S.S.R.)
     Ghegham Range (Armenian S.S.R.)
     Gueghamian Range (Armenian S.S.R.)
  BT Mountains—Armenian S.S.R.
Gegamskiĭ khrebet (Armenian S.S.R.)
  USE Gegam Range (Armenian S.S.R.)
Gegamskiy khrebet (Armenian S.S.R.)
  USE Gegam Range (Armenian S.S.R.)
Gegenschein
  USE Counterglow
Gegs
  USE Ghegs
Gehe family
  USE Gee family
Gehlert family *(Not Subd Geog)*
Gehrhart family
  USE Gearhart family
Gehrig's disease
  USE Amyotrophic lateral sclerosis
Gehringiidae
  USE Carabidae
Geidel family *(Not Subd Geog)*
Geier family
  USE Geyer family
Geigar family
  USE Geiger family
Geiger counters
  USE Geiger-Müller counters
Geiger family *(Not Subd Geog)*
  UF Geigar family
     Gieger family
     Gigar family
     Giger family
     Gigher family
     Guiger family
     Gyger family
     Gygir family
     Gygor family
Geiger-Müller counters
  ₍QC476₎
  UF Counting tubes
     Geiger counters
  BT Ionization chambers
     Nuclear counters
     Radiation
     Radioactivity
     Radioactivity—Instruments
     Radioactivity—Measurement
     Transducers
     Vacuum-tubes
Geigle family
  USE Geitgey family
Geijer family *(Not Subd Geog)*
  UF Geijerstam family
Geijerstam family
  USE Geijer family
Geikie Gorge National Park (W.A.)
  BT National parks and reserves—Australia
Geikie River (Sask.)
  BT Rivers—Saskatchewan
Geikielite
  USE Ilmenite
Geisel River (Germany)
  BT Rivers—Germany (East)
Geisendörfer family
  USE Geissendörfer family
Geisha girl porcelain
  ₍NK4399.G45₎
  UF Porcelain, Geisha girl
  BT Porcelain, Japanese
Geishas *(May Subd Geog)*
  ₍GT3412₎
  BT Entertainers

Geisinger family *(Not Subd Geog)*
Geissdörfer family
  USE Geissendörfer family
Geissendörfer family *(Not Subd Geog)*
  UF Geisendörfer family
     Geissdörfer family
Geissolomaceae
  USE Geissolomataceae
Geissolomataceae
  ₍QK495.G27₎
  UF Geissolomaceae
  BT Thymelaeales
Geist family
  USE Gist family
Geistfeld family *(Not Subd Geog)*
Geitchey family
  USE Geitgey family
Geitgey family *(Not Subd Geog)*
  UF Catchey family
     Gatche family
     Geigle family
     Geitchey family
     Geitty family
     Getchey family
     Getge family
     Getgen family
     Getgey family
     Gethey family
     Gethge family
     Gitgen family
     Goettge family
     Göttge family
     Gottgen family
Geitty family
  USE Geitgey family
Geiyo Islands (Japan)
  UF Geiyo shotō (Japan)
  BT Islands—Japan
Geiyo shotō (Japan)
  USE Geiyo Islands (Japan)
Gekeler family *(Not Subd Geog)*
Gékkerre family
  USE Ghesquières family
Gekko
  ₍QL666.L245₎
  BT Geckos
  NT Phyllodactylus
Gekkō (Night fighter plane)
  USE Irving (Night fighter plane)
Gekkonidae
  USE Geckos
Gekū Shintō
  USE Ise Shintō
Gel diffusion tests
  USE Immunodiffusion
Gel electrophoresis
  ₍QP519.9.G42 (Biochemistry)₎
  UF Electrophoresis, Gel
  BT Electrophoresis
  NT Electrophoresis, Polyacrylamide gel
Gel filtration chromatography
  USE Gel permeation chromatography
Gel permeation chromatography
  UF Chromatography, Gel permeation
     Chromatography, Size exclusion
     Gel filtration chromatography
     SEC (Chromatographic analysis)
     Size exclusion chromatography
     Steric exclusion liquid chromatography
  BT Chromatographic analysis
  NT Sepharose
Gela, Battle of, 1943
  ₍D763.S5₎
  BT World War, 1939-1945—Campaigns—Italy
Gela language
  USE Florida language
Gelada baboon
  ₍QL737.P93₎
  UF Theropithecus gelada

Gelada baboon *(Continued)*
  BT Baboons
      Theropithecus
Gelaher family
  USE Gallagher family
Gelaki language
  USE Gilaki language
Gelasa Strait (Indonesia)
  UF Gaspar Strait (Indonesia)
      Gaspar Straten (Indonesia)
      Kelasa Strait (Indonesia)
      Selat Gaspar (Indonesia)
      Selat Gelasa (Indonesia)
      Straits of Gaspar (Indonesia)
  BT Straits—Indonesia
Gelasinospora
  [QK623.S6]
  BT Sordariaceae
Gelastocoridae
  [QL523.G36]
  UF Galgulidae
      Mononychidae
      Nerthridae
  BT Hemiptera
  NT Gelastocoris
Gelastocoris *(May Subd Geog)*
  [QL523.G36]
  UF Galgulus
  BT Gelastocoridae
  NT Gelastocoris oculatus
Gelastocoris oculatus *(May Subd Geog)*
  [QL523.G36]
  BT Gelastocoris
Gelatin
  NT Cookery (Gelatin)
      Photographic gelatin
Gelatin (Jewish law)
  [BM710]
  BT Jewish law
      Jews—Dietary laws
Gelatin industry *(May Subd Geog)*
  [HD9429.G4-43]
Gelatinization
  USE Gelation
Gelation
  UF Gelatinization
      Gelling
  BT Coagulation
      Colloids
Gelbrith family
  USE Galbraith family
Gelder family *(Not Subd Geog)*
Gelderland (Netherlands)
  — Capital and capitol
        NT Huis der Provincie (Arnhem,
            Netherlands)
Gelderse Achterhoek (Netherlands)
  USE Graafschap (Netherlands)
Geleba (African people)
  USE Dasanetch (African people)
Gelechia
  [QL561.G4]
  BT Gelechiidae
Gelechia dodecella
  USE Pine bud moth
Gelechia gossypiella
  USE Pink bollworm
Gelechidae
  USE Gelechiidae
Gelechiidae
  [QL561.G4]
  UF Anacampsidae
      Chrysoesthiidae
      Dichomeridae
      Gelechidae
      Physoptilidae
      Timyridae
  BT Lepidoptera
      Moths
  NT Exoteleia
      Gelechia

Gnorimoschema
Keiferia
Pectinophora
Phthorimaea
Recurvaria
Sitotroga
Gelibolu Peninsula (Turkey)
  USE Gallipoli Peninsula (Turkey)
Gelidiaceae
  NT Gelidium
      Pterocaldia
Gelididae
  USE Nototheniidae
Gelidium
  [QK569.G4 (Botany)]
  BT Gelidiaceae
Gelidium robustum
  [QK569.G5 (Botany)]
  [SH391.G (Fisheries)]
Gelidium sesquipedale
  [QK569.G4 (Botany)]
  [SH391.G44 (Fisheries)]
Gelling
  USE Gelation
Gelochelidon
  [QL696.C46]
  BT Gulls
Gelochelidon nilotica
  USE Gull-billed tern
Gelre's Hof (Arnhem, Netherlands)
  USE Huis der Provincie (Arnhem,
      Netherlands)
Gels
  USE Colloids
Gels (Pharmacy)
  [RS201.G]
  BT Colloids in medicine
      Drugs—Dosage forms
      Pharmacy
Gelsemium
  [RM666.G3 (Therapeutics)]
Gelukpa (Sect)
  USE Dge-lugs-pa (Sect)
GEM (Computer operating system)
  BT Operating systems (Computers)
GEM (Computer program)
  [HB139]
  UF General Econometric Matrix
      (Computer program)
  BT Econometrics—Computer programs
Gem carving *(May Subd Geog)*
  BT Carving (Decorative arts)
      Gems
      Glyptics
      Sculpture
Gem cutting
  [TS752.5]
  UF Cutting of gems
      Lapidary art
  BT Cutting
      Gems
      Precious stones
  NT Diamond cutting
Gematria
  [BM525 (Judaism)]
  [BS1187 (Old Testament)]
  [BS2390 (New Testament)]
  Here are entered works on the substitution of
  numbers for letters of the Hebrew alphabet as a meth-
  od of exegesis employed to derive mystical insights
  into sacred writings or to obtain new interpretations
  of the texts.
  BT Hermeneutics
      Symbolism of numbers
Gembloux, Battle of, 1940
  [D756.5.G]
  BT World War, 1939-1945—Campaigns—
      Belgium
Gembrook State Forest (N.Z.)
  (Not Subd Geog)
  BT Forest reserves—New Zealand

Gemeinschaftsbewegung
  [BR856]
  UF Fellowship Movement
  BT Evangelicalism
      Germany—Church history—19th
        century
      Germany—Church history—20th
        century
      Pietism
Gemell family
  USE Gemmell family
Gemeprost
  [RG734.5.G45 (Abortifacients)]
  UF Methylhydroxyhydroxy
      dimethyloctenyloxocy
      clopentylheptenoate
  BT Synthetic prostaglandins E
Gemil family
  USE Gemmell family
Gemination
  BT Consonants
      Grammar, Comparative and general—
        Phonology
  SA *subdivision* Gemination *under names*
      of languages and groups of
      languages, e.g. English language—
      Gemination
Gemini project
  USE Project Gemini
Gemmation (Botany)
  USE Plants—Reproduction
Gemmation (Zoology)
  USE Reproduction, Asexual
Gemmel family
  USE Gemmell family
Gemmell family *(Not Subd Geog)*
  UF Gamel family
      Gamell family
      Gammill family
      Gemell family
      Gemil family
      Gemmel family
      Gemmil family
      Gemmill family
Gemmil family
  USE Gemmell family
Gemmill family
  USE Gemmell family
Gempei Wars, 1180-1185
  USE Japan—History—Gempei Wars, 1180-
      1185
Gempei Wars in literature
  USE Japan—History—Gempei Wars, 1180-
      1185—Literature and the war
Gempylidae
  [QL638.G4]
  UF Mackerels, Snake
      Snake mackerels
  BT Perciformes
  NT Lepidocybium
      Lepidocybium flavobrunneum
Gems *(May Subd Geog)*
  [GT2250-GT2280 (Manners and
      customs)]
  [NK5505-NK5735 (Glyptics)]
  [NK7650-NK7690 (Art industries)]
  [TS750-TS757 (Manufacture)]
  Here are entered books on engraved stones and
  jewels, interesting from the point of view of antiqui-
  ties or art. Works of mineralogical interest are en-
  tered under Precious stones.
  UF Jewels
  BT Archaeology
      Art
      Classical antiquities
      Decoration and ornament
      Engraving
      Mineralogy

RT Cameos
      Glyptics
      Intaglios
      Jewelry
      Precious stones
NT Astrology and gems
      Birthstones
      Chalchihuitl
      Crown jewels
      Gem carving
      Gem cutting
      Ilmenite
      Jet (Precious stone)
      Lapidaries (Medieval literature)
      Portraits on gems
      Scarabs
— **Collectors and collecting**
    [NK5530]
    NT Gems as an investment
— **Prices**
    NT Gems as an investment
— **Private collections**
    [NK5515]
— **Religious aspects**
    NT Minerals in the Bible
— **Reproductions, facsimiles, etc.**
Gems, Ancient
— **Reproduction**
    [NK5735]
    UF Reproduction of ancient gems
Gems, Artificial
  USE Precious stones, Artificial
Gems, Classical *(May Subd Geog)*
  [NK5565]
  UF Classical gems
  BT Classical antiquities
Gems, Etruscan *(May Subd Geog)*
  UF Etruscan gems
GEMS (Computer program language)
  USE SIMSCRIPT (Computer program
        language)
Gems as an investment
  [NK5530]
  BT Gems—Collectors and collecting
      Gems—Prices
      Investments
Gems family
  USE Gambs family
Gems in literature
Gems in the Bible
  USE Minerals in the Bible
GEMS Landfill (N.J.) *(Not Subd Geog)*
  BT Hazardous waste sites—New Jersey
      Sanitary landfills—New Jersey
Gems of art (Game)
  [GV1299.G3]
Gemsbok
  UF Cape oryx
      Gemsbuck
      Oryx gazella
  BT Oryx
Gemsbuck
  USE Gemsbok
Gemse family
  USE Gambs family
Gemstone collecting
  USE Mineralogy—Collectors and collecting
      Precious stones—Collectors and
        collecting
Gemstones
  USE Precious stones
Gemüt (The German word)
  BT German language—Etymology
Gen dialect
  USE Mina dialect
Gen Movement *(May Subd Geog)*
  BT Youth—Religious life
Genatropin
  USE Atropine
Gendarmes
  USE Police

      Police, Rural
Gende (Papuan people)
  UF Yonu (Papuan people)
  BT Ethnology—New Guinea
      Papuans
Gender
  USE *subdivision* Gender *under names of*
      languages and groups of languages
      Grammar, Comparative and general—
        Gender
Gender (Musical instrument)
  UF Demung gantung
      Kliningan
      Slentem gantung
  BT Musical instruments—Indonesia
      Percussion instruments
Gender differences
  USE Sex differences
Gender discrimination
  USE Sex discrimination
Gender dysphoria
  USE Gender identity disorders
Gender identity disorders *(May Subd Geog)*
  [RC560.G45 (Psychiatry)]
  UF Dysphoria, Gender
      Gender dysphoria
  BT Identity (Psychology)
      Psychosexual disorders
  NT Sex change
Gene, Lethal
  USE Lethal mutation
Gene amplification
  UF Amplification, Gene
  BT Gene expression
Gene banks, Plant *(May Subd Geog)*
  [QK981 (Plant genetics)]
  [SB123.3 (Plant-breeding)]
  UF Plant gene banks
  BT Germplasm resources, Plant
      Seeds
Gene cloning
  USE Molecular cloning
Gene expression
  [QH450]
  RT Genetic regulation
  NT Gene amplification
      Genetic code
      Genetic vectors
      Sex determination, Genetic
— **Regulation**
    USE Genetic regulation
Gene expression regulation
  USE Genetic regulation
Gene frequency
  BT Population genetics
Gene fusion
  [QH462.G46]
  UF Fusion, Gene
  BT Microbial mutation
      Transduction
      Translocation (Genetics)
Gene mapping
  USE Chromosome mapping
Gene rearrangement theory
  USE Antibody diversity
Gene resources
  USE Germplasm resources
Gene Site (Sweden)
  UF Genesmon Site (Sweden)
  BT Sweden—Antiquities
Gene splicing
  USE Genetic engineering
Gene therapy *(May Subd Geog)*
  [RB155]
  UF Therapy, Gene
  BT Genetic engineering
      Therapeutics
Genealogical correspondence
  [CS15]
  UF Correspondence

  BT Genealogy
      Letter-writing
Genealogical instructors
  USE Genealogy teachers
Genealogical literature *(May Subd Geog)*
  UF Literature, Genealogical
  RT Genealogy—Bibliography
Genealogical research
  USE Genealogy
Genealogists *(May Subd Geog)*
  [CS8]
  BT Genealogy
Genealogy
  [CS]
  UF Ancestry
      Descent
      Family history
      Family trees
      Genealogical research
      Genealogy—Handbooks, manuals, etc.
      Genealogy—Research
      Pedigrees
  BT Auxiliary sciences of history
      History
  RT Biography
      Heraldry
      Precedence
  SA *subdivision* Family *under names of*
      individual persons; also subdivision
      Genealogy *under names of*
      countries, cities, etc., and under
      classes of persons and ethnic
      groups; and names of individual
      families, e.g. Lincoln family
  NT Aerial photography in genealogy
      Cemeteries—Recording
      Daimyo—Genealogy
      Genealogical correspondence
      Genealogists
      Indians of North America—Genealogy
      Interviewing in genealogy
      Jesus Christ—Genealogy
      Jews—Genealogy
      Kings and rulers—Genealogy
      Newspapers—Sections, columns, etc.—
        Genealogy
      Newspapers in genealogy
      Nobility—Genealogy
      Peerage
      Photographs in genealogy
      Probate records
      Registers of births, etc.
      Royal descent, Families of
— **Bibliography**
    RT Genealogical literature
— Handbooks, manuals, etc.
    USE *subdivision* Genealogy—
        Handbooks, manuals, etc.
        under names of countries,
        cities, etc. and classes of
        persons
        Genealogy
— **Law and legislation** *(May Subd Geog)*
    NT Copyright
      Recording and registration
— **Religious aspects** *(Not Subd Geog)*
    SA *subdivision* Genealogy—Religious
      aspects *under names of*
      countries, cities, etc.
— — **Baptists,** [**Catholic Church, etc.**]
      (May Subd Geog)
— **Research**
    USE Genealogy
— **Societies, etc.**
    UF Family associations
Genealogy in literature
Genealogy in the Bible
  [BS569]
  UF Bible—Genealogy
  NT Jesus Christ—Genealogy

Genealogy teachers *(May Subd Geog)*
  UF Genealogical instructors
      Instructors, Genealogical
      Teachers, Genealogy
  BT Teachers
General activity simulation program
  USE GASP (Computer program language)
General analysis technique (Computer
  program)
  USE GAT (Computer program)
General aptitude test battery
  BT Ability—Testing
General average
  USE Average (Maritime law)
General aviation
  USE Private flying
**General certificate of education examination
  (Great Britain)**
General Certificate of Secondary Education
      Here are entered works on an examination for
    children over 16 years old in England and Wales that
    combines aspects of the General Certificate of Edu-
    cation with those of the Certificate of Secondary
    Education.
  BT High schools—Great Britain—
      Examinations
General chapters *(May Subd Geog)*
  UF Chapters, General
  BT Monasticism and religious orders—
      Government
General confession (Prayer)
  BT Confession (Prayer)
      Prayers
General Convention of the Christian Church
  (May Subd Geog)
      [BX6751-6793]
  BT Christian sects
  — United States
      NT Afro-American Christians (General
          Convention of the Christian
          Church)
General Dynamics B-58
  USE B-58 bomber
General Econometric Matrix (Computer
  program)
  USE GEM (Computer program)
General educational development tests
  UF GED tests
  BT Achievement tests
      United States. Army—Examinations
  NT High school equivalency examinations
**General Electric Realty Plot Historic District
  (Schenectady, N.Y.)** *(Not Subd Geog)*
  UF GE Plot (Schenectady, N.Y.)
      GE Realty Plot (Schenectady, N.Y.)
      Schenectady (N.Y.). General Electric
        Realty Plot Historic District
  BT Historic districts—New York (State)
General equilibrium (Economics)
  USE Equilibrium (Economics)
General Game Playing Program
  USE GGPP (Computer program)
General Information Processing System
  USE GIPSY (Information retrieval system)
General Integrated Programming System
  USE GIPS (Electronic computer system)
General intercessions
  UF Prayer of the faithful
      Prayers of the people
  BT Liturgies
  — Baptists, [Catholic Church, etc.]
General judgment
  USE Judgment Day
General Ledger (Computer program)
  BT Accounting—Computer programs
General Ledger Accounting System (Computer
  system)
  USE GLAS (Computer system)
General Ledger Accounting System for
  Osborne Computers (Computer system)
  USE OSGLAS (Computer system)

General Motors automobiles
      [TL215.G]
  UF GM automobiles
  BT Automobiles
  NT Buick automobile
      Cadillac automobile
      Chevrolet automobile
      General Motors C-cars
      General Motors J-cars
      General Motors X-cars
      La Salle automobile
      Oldsmobile automobile
      Pontiac automobile
General Motors C-cars
      [TL215.G]
  UF C-cars
  BT General Motors automobiles
**General Motors Corporation Sit-Down Strike,
  1936-1937**
General Motors J-cars
      [TL215.G]
  UF J-cars
  BT Automobiles
      General Motors automobiles
  NT Chevrolet Cavalier automobile
General Motors X-cars
      [TL215.G]
  UF X-cars
  BT Automobiles
      General Motors automobiles
  NT Citation automobile
      Omega automobile
      Phoenix automobile
      Skylark automobile
General Patton (Tank)
  USE M48 (Tank)
      M60 (Tank)
General practice (Medicine)
  USE Family medicine
      Physicians (General practice)
General practitioners
  USE Physicians (General practice)
General problem solver (Computer program)
  USE GPS (Computer program)
General property tax
  USE Property tax
General Purpose Simulation System
  USE GPSS (Computer program language)
General relativity (Physics)
      [QC173.6]
  UF Relativistic theory of gravitation
      Relativity theory, General
  BT Gravitation
      Physics
      Relativity (Physics)
  NT Einstein field equations
      Equivalence principle (Physics)
      Gravitational radiation
      Quantum gravity
      Supergravity
General Robert E. Lee Mansion (Va.)
  USE Arlington House, the Robert E. Lee
      Memorial (Va.)
General semantics
      [B820]
  UF Non-Aristotelian philosophy
      Semantics, General
  BT Education
      Semantics (Philosophy)
  NT Epistemics
      Pragmatics
General staffs
  USE *names of individual general staffs*
      Armies—Staffs
General stores *(May Subd Geog)*
  UF Country stores
  BT Stores, Retail
General strike
      [HD5307]
      [HD6477 (Direct action)]

      Here are entered works dealing with the concept
    of the general strike. For works dealing with an in-
    dividual general strike in a particular place the name
    of the place and the date of the strike are included in
    the heading, e.g. General Strike, Great Britain, 1926;
    General Strike, Seattle, Wash., 1919.
  BT Strikes and lockouts
General Strike, Arequipa, Peru, 1919
  BT Strikes and lockouts—Peru
General Strike, Austria, 1950
      [HD5370]
  UF Austria—General Strike, 1950
  BT Strikes and lockouts—Austria
General Strike, Basel, Switzerland, 1919
  BT Strikes and lockouts—Switzerland
General Strike, Belgium, 1960-1961
General Strike, Buenos Aires, Argentina, 1919
  BT Strikes and lockouts—Argentina
General Strike, Castilblanco, Spain, 1931
  BT Strikes and lockouts—Spain
General Strike, Colombia, 1977
  (May Subd Geog)
      [HD5357]
  BT Strikes and lockouts—Colombia
General Strike, Costa Rica, 1947
  BT Strikes and lockouts—Costa Rica
General Strike, Denmark, 1920
  (May Subd Geog)
  BT Strikes and lockouts—Denmark
General Strike, Denmark, 1925
  BT Strikes and lockouts—Denmark
General Strike, Ecuador, 1922
  BT Strikes and lockouts—Ecuador
General Strike, El Salvador, 1967
  BT Strikes and lockouts—El Salvador
General Strike, Elche, Spain, 1903
  BT Strikes and lockouts—Spain
General Strike, France, 1968
General Strike, Galaţi, Romania, 1916
  BT Strikes and lockouts—Romania
General Strike, Genoa, Italy, 1900
  BT Strikes and lockouts—Italy
General Strike, Germany, 1920
  (May Subd Geog)
  UF Germany—General Strike, 1920
  RT Germany—History—Kapp Putsch,
      1920
General Strike, Great Britain, 1926
  (May Subd Geog)
      [HD5366]
General Strike, Honduras, 1954
      [HD5336]
  UF Honduras—General Strike, 1954
  BT Strikes and lockouts—Honduras
General Strike, Hong Kong, 1925
  BT Canton (China)—General Strike, 1925
      Strikes and lockouts—Hong Kong
General Strike, Kraków, Poland, 1936
  BT Strikes and lockouts—Poland
General Strike, Lisbon, Portugal, 1944
  BT Strikes and lockouts—Portugal
General Strike, Madrid, Spain, 1976
  BT Strikes and lockouts—Spain
General Strike, Medellín, Colombia, 1934
  BT Strikes and lockouts—Colombia
General Strike, Northern Ireland, 1974
      [HD5368]
General Strike, Pamplona, Spain, 1973
  BT Strikes and lockouts—Spain
General Strike, Peru, 1919
  BT Strikes and lockouts—Peru
General Strike, Rosario, Argentina, 1969
  BT Strikes and lockouts—Argentina
General Strike, Russia, 1903
General Strike, Sabadell, Spain, 1976
  BT Strikes and lockouts—Spain
General Strike, Saint Louis, Mo., 1877
  BT Strikes and lockouts—Missouri
General Strike, São Paulo, Brazil, 1953
  BT Strikes and lockouts—Brazil

General Strike, Seattle, Wash., 1919
  BT Strikes and lockouts—Washington
      (State)
General Strike, Spain, 1917
General Strike, Spain, 1976
  UF Spain—General Strike, 1976
  BT Strikes and lockouts—Spain
General Strike, Sri Lanka, 1953
  BT Strikes and lockouts—Sri Lanka
General Strike, Sweden, 1909
General Strike, Sweden, 1971
General Strike, Transvaal, 1913
  UF Transvaal (South Africa)—General
      Strike, 1913
  BT Strikes and lockouts—South Africa
General Strike, Uruguay, 1973
  UF Uruguay—General Strike, 1973
General Strike, Varnsdorf, Czechoslovakia,
1947
  BT Strikes and lockouts—Czechoslovakia
General Strike, Vitoria, Spain, 1976
  BT Strikes and lockouts—Spain
General Strike, Winnipeg, Man., 1919
  BT Strikes and lockouts—Manitoba
General Strike, York, England, 1926
  BT Strikes and lockouts—England
General Strike, Zanzibar, Zanzibar, 1948
  BT Strikes and lockouts—Tanzania
General vicars
  USE Vicars-general
General warrants
  USE Warrants (Law)
General well-being schedule
  UF NCHS' general well-being schedule
  BT Psychological tests
General will
  ⌈JC328.2⌉
  UF Will, General
  BT Authority
  RT Consensus (Social sciences)
      Legitimacy of governments
General Zionism
  ⌈DS150.G4-6⌉
  UF Zionism, General
  BT Zionism
Generalized coherent states
  USE Coherent states
Generalized Computer-Aided Route Selection
  System
  USE GCARS II (Information retrieval
      system)
Generalized Data Base Planning System
  USE GPLAN (Electronic computer system)
Generalized data management systems
  USE Data base management
Generalized functions
  USE Distributions, Theory of (Functional
      analysis)
Generalized G-functions
  USE Fox's H-function
Generalized inverses of linear operators
  USE Linear operators—Generalized inverses
Generalized Mellin-Barnes functions
  USE Fox's H-function
Generalized phrase structure grammar
  UF GPSG (Linguistics)
  BT Generative grammar
      Phrase structure grammar
Generalized quadrangles, Finite
  USE Finite generalized quadrangles
Generalized spaces
  USE Spaces, Generalized
Generalized system of preferences (Tariff)
  USE Tariff preferences
Generally accepted accounting principles
  USE Accounting—Standards
Generals (May Subd Geog)
  ⌈D507 (European War)⌉
  ⌈U51-U54 (Military biography)⌉

Works dealing with the lives, etc. of generals of a
particular nationality are entered here and also under
the name of the country in question with subheading
Army—Biography, e.g. United States.   Army—Bi-
ography.
  BT Soldiers
  RT Military biography
  NT Marshals
      Military inspectors general
      Strategi, Greek
Generals' wives (May Subd Geog)
  BT Officers' wives
      Wives
Generating functions
  ⌈QA164.8 (Combinatorial analysis)⌉
  ⌈QA353.G44 (Special functions)⌉
  UF Functions, Generating
  BT Combinatorial analysis
Generating functions, Exponential
  ⌈QA164.8⌉
  UF Exponential generating functions
Generation
  USE Reproduction
Generation, Baby boom
  USE Baby boom generation
Generation, Spontaneous
  USE Spontaneous generation
Generation gap
  USE Conflict of generations
Generation of geometric forms
  UF Geometric forms, Generation of
  BT Geometrical drawing
      Geometry, Descriptive
  NT Body of revolution
      Revolutions (Descriptive geometry)
Generation of numerical grids (Numerical
analysis)
  USE Numerical grid generation (Numerical
      analysis)
Generations (May Subd Geog)
  BT Age groups
  NT Conflict of generations
Generations, Alternating
  ⌈QH489⌉
  UF Alternating generations
      Heterogenesis
Generative Exam System (Computer system)
  BT Electronic data processing—Computer-
      assisted instruction
      PLATO (Electronic computer system)
Generative grammar
  UF Grammar, Comparative and general—
      Derivation
      Grammar, Generative
      Grammar, Transformational
      Transformational grammar
  BT Grammar, Comparative and general
      Psycholinguistics
  SA subdivision Grammar, Generative
      under names of languages, e.g.
      English language—Grammar,
      Generative
  NT Competence and performance
      (Linguistics)
      Deep structure (Linguistics)
      Generalized phrase structure grammar
      Government-binding theory
      (Linguistics)
      Lexical-functional grammar
      Lexical grammar
      Markedness (Linguistics)
      Montague grammar
      Parsing (Computer grammar)
      Phrase structure grammar
      Relational grammar
      Surface structure (Linguistics)
Generative organs
  ⌈QL876-QL881 (Comparative
      anatomy)⌉
  ⌈QM416-QM421 (Human anatomy)⌉
  ⌈QP251-QP285 (Physiology)⌉

  UF Genital organs
      Genitalia
      Reproductive organs
      Sex organs
      Sexual organs
  BT Genitourinary organs
  RT Reproduction
  NT Gonads
      Orgasm
      Sex change
— Abnormalities (May Subd Geog)
      NT Laurence-Moon-Biedl syndrome
— Amphibians, ⌈Birds, Insects, etc.⌉
      Works on the generative organs of a particu-
      lar class, order, family, genus, or species are en-
      tered under Generative organs, subdivided by
      the larger zoological groups only. When the
      monograph treats of one of the smaller divisions,
      additional entry is made under the specific
      group, e.g. 1. Generative organs—Amphibians.
      2. Frogs.
— Bacteriology
      ⌈QR171⌉
— Cancer
      NT Disgerminoma
— Diseases (May Subd Geog)
      RT Theriogenology
      NT Infertility
— — Diagnosis
— Surgery
      NT Sterilization (Birth control)
— Transplantation
      ⌈QP90⌉
      ⌈QP251⌉
Generative organs, Female
  ⌈QL881 (Comparative anatomy)⌉
  ⌈QM421 (Human anatomy)⌉
  ⌈QP261-QP281 (Physiology)⌉
  UF Female generative organs
  SA names of individual organs
  NT Obstetrics
      Oviduct
      Spermatheca
— Blood-vessels
— Cancer
— — Diagnosis
— Diseases (May Subd Geog)
      RT Gynecology
      NT Endometriosis
          Generative organs, Female—
          Radiography
          Gynecologic emergencies
          Infertility, Female
          Menstruation disorders
— — Diagnosis
      NT Vaginal smears
— Examination
      NT Vaginal smears
— Innervation
— Radiography
      UF Generative organs, Female—X-ray
          examination
      BT Generative organs, Female—
          Diseases
— Secretions
— Surgery
      USE Gynecology, Operative
— Tumors
— X-ray examination
      USE Generative organs, Female—
          Radiography
Generative organs, Male
  ⌈QL878 (Comparative anatomy)⌉
  ⌈QM416 (Human anatomy)⌉
  ⌈QP255-QP257 (Physiology)⌉
  UF Male generative organs
  RT Andrology
  SA names of individual organs
  NT Aedeagus
      Prostate gland
      Seminal vesicles
      Testis

Generative organs, Male *(Continued)*
  Vas deferens
  — **Diseases** *(May Subd Geog)*
    NT Infertility, Male
      Spermatorrhea
  — **Surgery**
  — **Tuberculosis**
Generator, Van de Graaff
  USE Van de Graaff generator
Generators, Electric
  USE Electric generators
Generators, Electrostatic
  USE Electrostatic accelerators
Generators, Flow chart
  USE Flow chart generators
Generators, Function
  USE Function generators (Electronic
    instruments)
Generators, Hall
  USE Hall generators
Generators, Hydroelectric
  USE Hydroelectric generators
Generators, Magnetohydrodynamic
  USE Magnetohydrodynamic generators
Generators, Pulse
  USE Pulse generators
Generators, Radionuclide
  USE Radionuclide generators
Generators, Random number
  USE Random number generators
Generators, Sawtooth
  USE Sawtooth generators
Generators, Superconducting
  USE Superconducting generators
Generators, Vortex
  USE Vortex generators
Generators (Computer programs)
  UF Program generators (Computer
    programs)
  BT Automatic programming (Computer
    science)
    Computer programs
  NT ATLAS (Computer program)
    Code generators
    Flow chart generators
    PAC (Computer program)
    RPG (Computer program language)
Generators of groups
  USE Groups, Theory of—Generators
Generators of ideals (Algebra)
  USE Ideals (Algebra)—Generators
Generic drug substitution
  USE Drugs—Generic substitution
Generic drugs
  USE Drugs—Generic substitution
Generic products *(May Subd Geog)*
  UF Products, Generic
  BT Business names
    Commercial products
    Manufactures
  NT Drugs—Generic substitution
Generosity
  [BJ1533.G4]
  UF Giving
  RT Magnanimity
  NT Gifts
Genes
  USE Heredity
Genes, Cancer
  USE Oncogenes
Genes, Complementary
  USE Complementation (Genetics)
Genesee River (Pa. and N.Y.)
  BT Rivers—New York (State)
    Rivers—Pennsylvania
Genesis II Program
  BT Community-based corrections—
    Minnesota
    Female offenders—Rehabilitation—
    Minnesota

Genesmon Site (Sweden)
  USE Gene Site (Sweden)
Genetic algebras
  UF Algebras, Genetic
  BT Algebra, Abstract
    Biomathematics
Genetic code
  BT Gene expression
    Molecular biology
    Molecular genetics
  NT Genetic transcription
    Genetic translation
Genetic counseling *(May Subd Geog)*
  BT Health counseling
    Human genetics
    Medical genetics
    Prenatal diagnosis
  NT Genetic counselors
Genetic counselors *(May Subd Geog)*
  UF Counselors, Genetic
  BT Counselors
    Genetic counseling
    Geneticists
Genetic determination of sex
  USE Sex determination, Genetic
Genetic diagnosis
  USE Human chromosome abnormalities—
    Diagnosis
Genetic diseases
  USE Genetic disorders
Genetic disorders *(May Subd Geog)*
  [RB155]
  UF Congenital diseases
    Disorders, Genetic
    Disorders, Inherited
    Genetic diseases
    Hereditary diseases
    Inherited diseases
  BT Diseases
  RT Medical genetics
  SA subdivision Genetic aspects *under*
    individual diseases, e.g. Cancer—
    Genetic aspects; and subdivision
    Diseases—Genetic aspects under
    organs and regions of the body, e.g.
    Heart—Diseases—Genetic aspects
  NT Adenomatosis, Familial endocrine
    Ataxia telangiectasia
    Basal cell nevus syndrome
    Charcot-Marie-Tooth disease
    Cystic fibrosis
    Dysraphia
    Ehlers-Danlos syndrome
    Friedreich's ataxia
    Human chromosome abnormalities
    Huntington's chorea
    Klein-Waardenburg syndrome
    Laurence-Moon-Biedl syndrome
    Lipomembranous polycystic
      osteodysplasia
    Marfan syndrome
    Metabolism, Inborn errors of
    Norrie's disease
    Phakomatoses
    Usher's syndrome
    Von Willebrand's disease
Genetic engineering *(May Subd Geog)*
  [QH442-QH442.2 (Genetics)]
  [TP248.6 (Chemical technology)]
  UF Designed genetic change
    Engineering, Genetic
    Gene splicing
    Genetic intervention
    Genetic surgery
  BT Genetic recombination
  RT Biotechnology
  NT Animal genetic engineering
    Cell nuclei—Transplantation
    Cloning
    Fertilization in vitro
    Gene therapy

    Microbial genetic engineering
    Molecular cloning
    Plant genetic engineering
    Protein engineering
    Recombinant DNA
  — **Government policy** *(May Subd Geog)*
    UF Genetic engineering and state
      Genetic engineering policy
      State and genetic engineering
    BT Science and state
  — **Law and legislation** *(May Subd Geog)*
    BT Medical laws and legislation
  — **Religious aspects**
  — — **Baptists, [Catholic Church, etc.]**
  — — **Buddhism, [Christianity, etc.]**
Genetic engineering, Animal
  USE Animal genetic engineering
Genetic engineering, Microbial
  USE Microbial genetic engineering
Genetic engineering and state
  USE Genetic engineering—Government
    policy
Genetic engineering industry
  (May Subd Geog)
  [HD9995.G]
Genetic engineering policy
  USE Genetic engineering—Government
    policy
Genetic epidemiology *(May Subd Geog)*
  UF Epidemiology, Genetic
  BT Epidemiology
Genetic intervention
  USE Genetic engineering
Genetic literature *(May Subd Geog)*
  UF Genetics literature
    Literature, Genetic
Genetic load
  BT Mutation (Biology)
    Population genetics
Genetic polymorphisms
  UF Polymorphism, Genetic
  NT Chromosome polymorphism
    Hemoglobin polymorphisms
    Immunoglobulin allotypes
    Immunoglobulin idiotypes
Genetic psychology *(May Subd Geog)*
  [BF699-BF711]
  Here are entered works on the evolutionary psy-
  chology of man in terms of origin and development,
  whether in the individual or in the species. Works on
  the psychological development of the individual from
  infancy to old age are entered under Developmental
  psychology.
  UF Evolutionary psychology
    Psychology, Genetic
  BT Evolution
    Human evolution
    Human genetics
    Psychology
  NT Adulthood
    Age (Psychology)
    Critical periods (Biology)
    Culture conflict
    Emotional maturity
    Intelligence levels
    Maturation (Psychology)
    Sociobiology
Genetic recombination
  UF Recombination, Genetic
  BT Chromosomes
  NT Bacterial transformation
    Crossing over (Genetics)
    Genetic engineering
    Genetic transformation
    Recombinant DNA
  — **Research**
  — — **Law and legislation**
    (May Subd Geog)
    BT Medical laws and legislation
Genetic regulation
  [QH450]

Here are entered works on the control of the type and rate of cellular processes by regulation of the activity of specific genes controlling individual biochemical reactions. Works on the various mechanisms of cellular control such as structural control, biochemical control, cell differentiation, etc., are entered under Cellular control mechanisms.
- UF Gene expression—Regulation
  Gene expression regulation
- BT Biosynthesis
  Cellular control mechanisms
  Molecular genetics
- RT Gene expression
- NT Enzyme induction
  Genetic transcription—Regulation
  Genetic translation
  Operons
  Repressors, Genetic

Genetic repressors
- USE Repressors, Genetic

Genetic research
- USE Genetics—Research

Genetic resources
- USE Germplasm resources

Genetic resources conservation, Forest
- USE Forest genetic resources conservation

Genetic screening
- USE Human chromosome abnormalities—Diagnosis

Genetic sex determination
- USE Sex determination, Genetic

Genetic surgery
- USE Genetic engineering

Genetic toxicology *(May Subd Geog)*
  [RA1224.3 (Toxicology)]
- UF Genotoxicology
  Toxicology—Genetic aspects
- BT Biochemical genetics
  Medical genetics
  Toxicology
- RT Carcinogenesis
  Chemical mutagenesis

Genetic transcription
  [QH450.2]
- UF Transcription (Genetics)
- BT Genetic code
- NT Messenger ribonucleic acid
  Operons
  Promoters (Genetics)
— **Regulation**
  BT Genetic regulation

Genetic transduction
- USE Transduction

Genetic transformation
- UF Transformation (Genetics)
- BT Genetic recombination
  Microbial genetics
  Nucleic acids
- RT Transfection
- NT Bacterial transformation

Genetic translation
  [QH450.5]
- UF Translation (Genetics)
- BT Genetic code
  Genetic regulation
  Messenger ribonucleic acid
- NT Nonsense suppression (Genetics)
  Ribonucleic acid, Transfer

Genetic variation in humans
- USE Human genetics—Variation

Genetic vectors
- UF Vectors, Genetic
- BT Gene expression
  Molecular cloning
- RT Recombinant DNA
- NT Plasmids
  Viruses

Genetical imaging systems
- USE Imaging systems in genetics

Geneticists *(May Subd Geog)*
- BT Biologists
  Microbiologists

- NT Genetic counselors
  Plant geneticists
  Women geneticists

Genetics
- BT Biology
  Embryology
  Eugenics
  Hybridization
  Life (Biology)
  Mendel's law
  Reproduction
- RT Adaptation (Biology)
  Breeding
  Chromosomes
  Evolution
  Heredity
  Mutation (Biology)
  Variation (Biology)
- SA *subdivision* Genetic aspects *under subjects, e.g.* Color vision—Genetic aspects; *and headings beginning with the word* Genetic
- NT Allelomorphism
  Animal genetics
  Behavior genetics
  Cell populations
  Complementation (Genetics)
  Crossing over (Genetics)
  Cytogenetics
  Cytoplasmic inheritance
  Developmental genetics
  Ecological genetics
  Endocrine genetics
  Epigenesis
  Forensic genetics
  Genomes
  Germplasm resources
  Gynecology—Genetic aspects
  Human genetics
  Immunogenetics
  Karyotypes
  Linkage (Genetics)
  Microbial genetics
  Molecular genetics
  Mosaicism
  Natural selection
  Nature and nurture
  Neurogenetics
  Pharmacogenetics
  Plant genetics
  Population genetics
  Quantitative genetics
  Radiogenetics
  Somatic hybrids
  Species
  Translocation (Genetics)
— Drug effects
  USE Pharmacogenetics
— Immunological aspects
  USE Immunogenetics
— **Instruments**
  NT Imaging systems in genetics
— **Mathematical models**
  BT Biomathematics
— **Research** *(May Subd Geog)*
  UF Genetic research
— Subject headings
  USE Subject headings—Genetics
— **Technique**
  NT Imaging systems in genetics

Genetics, Experimental
- UF Experimental genetics
- BT Biology, Experimental

Genetics, Forensic
- USE Forensic genetics

Genetics, Medical
- USE Medical genetics

Genetics and environment
- USE Nature and nurture

Genetics literature
- USE Genetic literature

Genetta
  [QL737.C28]
- BT Viverridae

Genetta genetta
  [QL737.C28]
- UF Small-spotted genet

Genetta tigrina
  [QL737.C28]
- UF Blotched genet
  Large-spotted genet

Geneva (Switzerland)
— **History**
—— **1536-1603**
    [DQ458]

Geneva (Switzerland). Rues basses
- USE Rues basses (Geneva, Switzerland)

Geneva, Lake (Switzerland and France)
- UF Genève Lake (Switzerland and France)
  Genfersee (Switzerland and France)
  Lac de Genève (Switzerland and France)
  Lac Léman (Switzerland and France)
  Lake Geneva (Switzerland and France)
  Léman Lake (Switzerland and France)
  Lemannus (Switzerland and France)
  Lemanus (Switzerland and France)
- BT Lakes—France
  Lakes—Switzerland

Geneva award
- USE Alabama claims

Geneva mechanisms
  [TJ181.7]
- BT Mechanical movements

Geneva protocol, 1922
- BT Arbitration, International

Geneva protocol, 1924
- BT Arbitration, International

Geneva PX-8 (Computer)
- USE Epson Geneva PX-8 (Computer)

Genève Lake (Switzerland and France)
- USE Geneva, Lake (Switzerland and France)

Genfersee (Switzerland and France)
- USE Geneva, Lake (Switzerland and France)

Gengbe dialect
- USE Mina dialect

Geniculate bodies
- UF Bodies, Geniculate
  Corpus geniculatum
- BT Hearing
  Thalamus

Genii
- USE Jinn

Genil River (Spain)
- UF Río Genil (Spain)
- BT Rivers—Spain

Genital herpes
- USE Herpes genitalis

Genital organs
- USE Generative organs

Genitalia
- USE Generative organs

Genito-urinary organs
- USE Genitourinary organs

Genitourinary diseases in animals
- USE Veterinary urology

Genitourinary organs
  [QL871-QL881 (Comparative anatomy)]
  [QM401-QM421 (Human anatomy)]
  [QP247-QP285 (Physiology)]
- UF Genito-urinary organs
  Urogenital organs
- BT Anatomy
- NT Cloaca (Zoology)
  Generative organs
  Urinary organs
— **Abnormalities** *(May Subd Geog)*
— Bacteriology

Genitourinary organs
— Bacteriology *(Continued)*
  USE Genitourinary organs—
    Microbiology
— **Blood-vessels**
— **Diseases** *(May Subd Geog)*
  [RC870-RC923 *(General and male)*]
  [RG *(Gynecology)*]
  RT Urology
  NT Veterinary urology
— — **Diagnosis**
  [RC874]
  NT Genitourinary organs—
    Radiography
— — **Eclectic treatment**
  [RV281-RV286]
— — **Homeopathic treatment**
  [RX351-RX356]
— **Foreign bodies**
— **Infections** *(May Subd Geog)*
  NT Gonorrhea
— **Microbiology**
  UF Genitourinary organs—
    Bacteriology
— **Radiography** *(May Subd Geog)*
  UF Urography
  BT Genitourinary organs—Diseases—
    Diagnosis
— **Surgery** *(May Subd Geog)*
  [RD571-RD592]
  UF Operative urology
    Urological surgery
    Urology, Operative
  NT Gynecology, Operative
— **Tuberculosis** *(May Subd Geog)*
  [RC312.5.G4-RC312.5.G5]
— **Tumors** *(May Subd Geog)*
  [RC280.G4-RC280.G52]
— **Wounds and injuries** *(May Subd Geog)*
Genius *(May Subd Geog)*
  [BF412-BF426 *(Psychology)*]
  UF Gifted adults
    Greatness
  BT Psychology
  NT Creation (Literary, artistic, etc.)
    Gifted children
    Gifted women
    Mental calculators
    Originality
Genius (Companion spirit)
  UF Companion spirits
  BT Mythology, Roman
    Spirits
  RT Jinn
  NT Guardian angels
Genius and insanity
  USE Genius and mental illness
Genius and mental illness *(May Subd Geog)*
  [BF423]
  UF Genius and insanity
    Insanity and genius
  BT Mental illness
Genizah
  BT Manuscripts
    Synagogues
  NT Cairo Genizah
Genji monogatari emaki (Scrolls)
  [ND1059.6]
  BT Murasaki Shikibu, b. 978? Genji
    monogatari—Illustrations
    Painting, Japanese—Kamakura-
      Momoyama periods, 1185-1600
    Painting, Japanese—Heian period, 794-
      1185
    Scrolls, Japanese
GENMIX (Computer program)
Genn family
  USE Ginn family
Gennaken language
  USE Pampa language

Gennaro Festival (New York, N.Y.)
  USE San Gennaro Festival (New York,
    N.Y.)
Gennesaret, Lake of (Israel)
  USE Tiberias Lake (Israel)
Gennings family
  USE Jennings family
Genoa (Italy)
— **History**
— — **To 1339**
— — **1339-1528**
— — **1528-1789**
— — **Uprising, 1746**
      BT Austrian Succession, War of,
        1740-1748
— — **1789-1815**
— — **1815-**
Genocide *(May Subd Geog)*
  BT Crimes against humanity
    International offenses
    Race relations
    Racism
    Terrorism
  NT Holocaust, Jewish (1939-1945)
    Trials (Genocide)
Genodermatology
  USE Skin—Diseases—Genetic aspects
Genodermatoses
  USE Skin—Diseases—Genetic aspects
Genomes
  [QH447]
  BT Genetics
  RT Haploidy
Genotoxicology
  USE Genetic toxicology
Genre (Art)
  BT Art
  NT Narrative art
Genre (Literature)
  USE Literary form
Genre films
  USE Film genres
Genre painting *(May Subd Geog)*
  [ND1450-ND1452 *(Genre painting)*]
  [ND2350-ND2352 *(Water-color)*]
  UF Genre paintings
  BT Figure painting
    Painting
  NT Conversation piece (Portrait painting)
    Narrative painting
    Ukiyoe
— **17th century** *(May Subd Geog)*
— **18th century** *(May Subd Geog)*
— **19th century** *(May Subd Geog)*
  NT Genre painting, Victorian
— **20th century** *(May Subd Geog)*
Genre painting, Austrian *(May Subd Geog)*
  UF Austrian genre painting
Genre painting, Chinese *(May Subd Geog)*
  UF Chinese genre painting
— **20th century**
Genre painting, Danish *(May Subd Geog)*
  UF Danish genre painting
Genre painting, Dutch *(May Subd Geog)*
  UF Dutch genre painting
Genre painting, Dutch, [German, etc.]
Genre painting, European *(May Subd Geog)*
  UF European genre painting
Genre painting, Flemish *(May Subd Geog)*
  UF Flemish genre painting
Genre painting, French *(May Subd Geog)*
  UF French genre painting
Genre painting, German *(May Subd Geog)*
  UF German genre painting
Genre painting, Hungarian
  (May Subd Geog)
  UF Hungarian genre painting
Genre painting, Japanese
  NT Hōkoku sairei zu (Screen painting)
    Semmen Hokekyō (Painting)
— **Edo period, 1600-1868**

— **1868-**
Genre painting, Korean *(May Subd Geog)*
  [ND1452]
  UF Korean genre painting
Genre painting, Russian *(May Subd Geog)*
  UF Russian genre painting
  NT Plastov, Arkadiĭ Aleksandrovich, 1893-
    1972. Summer
Genre painting, Spanish *(May Subd Geog)*
  UF Spanish genre painting
Genre painting, Victorian *(May Subd Geog)*
  UF Victorian genre painting
  BT Genre painting—19th century
Genre paintings
  USE Genre painting
Genrich family
  USE Gingrich family
Genroku Period, Japan, 1688-1704
  USE Japan—History—Genroku period,
    1688-1704
Gens Claudia
  USE Claudii family
Gens Fabia
  USE Fabii family
Gens Julia
  USE Julii family
Gens Volusia
  USE Volusii Saturnini family
Genseng
  USE Ginseng
Genson family *(Not Subd Geog)*
  RT Jensen family
Genstat (Computer system)
  BT Electronic digital computers—
    Programming
    Mathematical statistics—Data
      processing
    Statistics—Data processing
Gent family
  USE Gantt family
Gentamicin
  BT Aminoglycosides
    Antibacterial agents
Gentianaceae
  BT Gentianales
Gentianales
  [QK495.A12 *(Botany)*]
  UF Apocynales
    Contortae
    Loganiales
  BT Dicotyledons
  NT Apocynaceae
    Asclepiadaceae
    Gentianaceae
    Loganiaceae
    Rubiaceae
Gentians
  [QK495.G35 *(Botany)*]
  [SB413.G3 *(Culture)*]
Gentiles, Righteous
  USE Righteous Gentiles
Gentiles in rabbinical literature
  BT Rabbinical literature
Gentiles in the New Testament
  UF Bible. N.T.—Gentiles
  NT Strangers in the Bible
Gentiles in the Old Testament
  [BS1199.N6]
  UF Bible. O.T.—Gentiles
  BT Aliens (Jewish law)
  NT Strangers in the Bible
Gentle Jungle (Colton, Calif.)
  BT Animals, Training of—California
    Ranches—California
Gentleman Usher of the Black Rod
  USE Black Rod
Gentlemen's agreements
  USE Consensual contracts
Gentoo language
  USE Telugu language

Gentoo penguin
[Ql696.S473]
UF Penguin, Gentoo
Pygoscelis papua
BT Penguins
Gentrification (May Subd Geog)
BT Urban renewal
Gentry
UF Gentry, Landed
Landed gentry
BT Upper classes
SA subdivision Gentry under names of
countries, regions, etc., e.g. Great
Britain—Gentry
Gentry, Landed
USE Gentry
Gentry family (Not Subd Geog)
Genya (African people)
[DT650.G46]
UF Baenya (African people)
Bagenya (African people)
Eenya (African people)
Enya (African people)
Ouénya (African people)
Vouaghénia (African people)
Wagenia (African people)
Waggenia (African people)
Wainya (African people)
Wenya (African people)
BT Ethnology—Zaire
Genya language
USE Enya language
Geo-codes
USE Geographical location codes
Geo-electric prospecting
USE Electric prospecting
Geoarchaeology
USE Archaeological geology
Geobotanical prospecting
UF Biological prospecting
Botanical prospecting
BT Plant indicators
Prospecting
RT Biogeochemical prospecting
Geobotany
USE Phytogeography
Geocalycaceae
[QK555.G44]
BT Jungermanniales
NT Stolonophora
Geocapromys
USE Capromys
Geocaryum
[QK495.U48 (Botany)]
BT Umbelliferae
Geocells
USE Geogrids
Geochemical analysis
USE Geochemistry, Analytic
Geochemical prospecting (May Subd Geog)
BT Prospecting
NT Biogeochemical prospecting
Geochemistry (May Subd Geog)
[QE514-QE516.5]
UF Chemical composition of the earth
Chemical geology
Earth—Chemical composition
Geological chemistry
Geology, Chemical
BT Chemistry
Earth sciences
NT Biogeochemical cycles
Biogeochemistry
Cementation (Petrology)
Chemical denudation
Chemical oceanography
Chemical weathering
Geochemists
Mineralogical chemistry
Mineralogy, Determinative
Organic geochemistry

Rocks—Analysis
Sediments (Geology)—Analysis
— **Computer programs**
— Information storage and retrieval systems
USE Information storage and retrieval
systems—Geochemistry
Geochemistry, Analytic
[QE516.3]
UF Analytical geochemistry
Geochemical analysis
BT Chemistry, Analytic
Geochemists (May Subd Geog)
BT Chemists
Geochemistry
Geologists
Scientists
Geochronology
USE Geological time
Geochrony
USE Geological time
Geocoridae
USE Lygaeidae
Geocoris
[QL523.L9]
BT Lygaeidae
Geodecists
USE Geodesists
Geodes
[QE495]
BT Concretions
Paleontology
Rocks
Rocks, Sedimentary
Sedimentary structures
Geodesic domes
BT Domes
Geodesic spaces
USE G-spaces
Geodesics (Mathematics)
BT Geometry, Differential
Global analysis (Mathematics)
Mathematics
Geodesists (May Subd Geog)
[QB35-36]
UF Geodecists
BT Astronomers
Earth scientists
Geophysicists
Geodesy (May Subd Geog)
[QB281-341]
UF Degrees of latitude and longitude
Geodetics
BT Astronomy
Earth
Mensuration
RT Arc measures
Earth—Figure
Geography, Mathematical
Surveying
SA subdivision Surveys under names of
countries, cities, etc., e.g. France—
Surveys; Massachusetts—Surveys
NT Aeronautics in geodesy
Area measurement
Astronautics in geodesy
Azimuth
Base measuring
Electronics in surveying
Geodetic astronomy
Geodetic satellites
Geographical positions
Gravimeter (Geophysical instrument)
Gravity
Isostasy
Latitude
Least squares
Longitude
Marine geodesy
Moon—Figure
Prismatic astrolabe
Radar in geodesy

Sea level
Triangulation
— **Computer programs**
[QB297]
— **Observations**
UF Geodetic observations
Observations, Geodetic
Geodesy, Lunar
USE Selenodesy
Geodetic astronomy (May Subd Geog)
[QB201-237]
UF Celestial geodesy
Field astronomy
BT Astronomy, Spherical and practical
Geodesy
NT Azimuth
Geographical positions
Latitude
Longitude
Time
Geodetic observations
USE Geodesy—Observations
Geodetic satellites
[TL798.G4]
UF Satellites, Geodetic
BT Artificial satellites
Astronautics in geodesy
Geodesy
Geodetics
USE Geodesy
Geodimeter
BT Distances—Measurement
Kerr cell shutters
Geoduck
UF Goeduck
Gooeyduck
BT Clams
Geodynamics
[QE500-505]
UF Geology, Dynamic
Tectonophysics
BT Geophysics
NT Cryopedology
Expanding earth
Metamorphism (Geology)
Polar wandering
Rayleigh waves
Sea-floor spreading
Geofabrics
USE Geosynthetics
Geoffroy tamarin
USE Saguinus oedipus
Geoffroy's dolphin
USE Inia geoffrensis
Geoffroy's long-nosed bats
USE Anoura (Mammals)
Geognosy
USE Geology
Geographers (May Subd Geog)
[G67-69]
BT Earth scientists
Geography
NT Geography—Vocational guidance
Government geographers
Women geographers
Geographic Incremental Plotting System
USE GIPSY (Computer program)
Geographic models
USE Geography, Economic—Mathematical
models
Geographical area codes
USE Geographical location codes
Geographical atlases
USE Atlases
Geographical boundaries
USE Boundaries
Geographical dictionaries
USE Geography—Dictionaries
Geographical distribution of animals
USE Zoogeography

Geographical distribution of animals and plants
  USE Biogeography
Geographical distribution of diseases
  USE Medical geography
Geographical distribution of fossil animals and
    plants
  USE Paleobiogeography
Geographical distribution of man
  USE Anthropo-geography
      Ethnology
      Man—Migrations
Geographical distribution of plants
  USE Phytogeography
Geographical location codes
  UF Geo-codes
      Geographical area codes
  NT Grids (Cartography)
Geographical models
  USE Geography—Mathematical models
Geographical museums
  BT Museums
Geographical myths
  ⌐G100⌐
  ⌐GR650-GR690 (Folk-lore)⌐
  UF Cities, Imaginary
      Fictitious places
      Imaginary cities
      Imaginary islands
      Imaginary places
      Islands, Imaginary
      Mythical places
      Places, Imaginary
  BT Geography—History
      Mythology
      Voyages, Imaginary
  NT Atlantis
      Beklan Empire
      Bellville (Imaginary place)
      Central City (Imaginary place)
      Cibola, Seven Cities of
      Civilization, Subterranean
      Cockaigne
      Dorsai (Imaginary place)
      Dragon Pass
      El Dorado
      Harrisonville, N.J. (Imaginary place)
      Kenoska (Imaginary place)
      Lemuria
      Lost continents
      Middle Earth (Imaginary place)
      San Borondon (Imaginary place)
      Shambhala
      Yoknapatawpha County (Imaginary
        place)
Geographical myths in mass media
  ⌐P96.G46⌐
  BT Mass media
Geographical names
  USE Names, Geographical
Geographical pathology
  USE Medical geography
Geographical perception
    Here are entered general works on people's men-
  tal images of the physical environment around them
  or in distant lands.
  UF Cognitive maps
      Environmental perception
      Maps, Mental
      Mental maps
      Perceptual cartography
      Perceptual maps
  BT Geography
      Perception
      Spatial behavior
  RT Orientation (Psychology)
      Space perception
  SA subdivision Maps, Mental under the
        names of cities, countries, etc.
Geographical perception in children
  ⌐HQ784.G45⌐

  BT Children
      Perception in children
Geographical photography
  USE Photography in geography
Geographical positions (May Subd Geog)
  ⌐G109-G110⌐
  ⌐QB201-QB237 (Determination of)⌐
  BT Geodesy
      Geodetic astronomy
  RT Geography, Mathematical
      Grids (Cartography)
      Latitude
      Longitude
  NT Astronautics in navigation
      Horizons, Artificial
      Raydist
Geographical recreations (May Subd Geog)
  ⌐GV1485⌐
  UF Geography—Games
      Recreations, Geographical
  BT Games
      Geography—Study and teaching
Geographical research
  USE Geography—Research
Geography (May Subd Geog)
  ⌐G-GF (Geography)⌐
  ⌐GN476.4 (Ethnology)⌐
    Here and with local subdivision are entered works
  on the discipline of geography. Works on the geogra-
  phy of particular places are entered under the name
  of the place with the subdivision Description and
  travel under names of regions, countries, etc.; and
  Description under names of cities.
  BT Cosmography
      Earth sciences
      World history
  SA subdivision Description and travel
        under names of countries; and
        subdivision Maps under names of
        places
  NT Anthropo-geography
      Astronomical geography
      Biogeography
      Boundaries
      Classification—Books—Geography
      Communism and geography
      Ethnology
      Geographers
      Geographical perception
      Local geography
      Man—Influence of environment
      Maps
      Medical geography
      Military geography
      Physical geography
      Quotations about places
      Religion and geography
      Rural geography
      Surveying
      Voyages and travels
  — To 400 A.D.
      USE Geography, Ancient
  — 400-1400
      USE Geography, Medieval
  — **15th-16th centuries**
      ⌐G113⌐
      UF Geography—Early works
  — **17th-18th centuries**
      ⌐G114⌐
      ⌐G120-G121⌐
      UF Geography—Early works
  — Atlases
      USE Atlases
  — **Computer programs**
  — **Dictionaries**
      ⌐G101-8⌐
      UF Geographical dictionaries
          Geography—Gazetteers
      SA subdivision Gazetteers under
            names of countries, etc., e.g.
            France—Gazetteers

      NT Gazetteers
  — — History
        USE Toponymy
  — Early works
        USE Classical geography
            Geography—15th-16th centuries
            Geography—17th-18th centuries
            Geography, Ancient
            Geography, Medieval
  — Games
        USE Geographical recreations
  — Gazetteers
        USE Geography—Dictionaries
  — **History**
      ⌐G80-G99⌐
        Here are entered works on the history of
      geography as a discipline.
      NT Buddhist geography
          Geographical myths
          Geography, Medieval
          Maps, Early
  — **Mathematical models**
      UF Geographical models
      BT Geography—Mathematics
  — **Mathematics**
        Here are entered works on the use of math-
      ematics in geography. Works on the branch of
      physical geography dealing with the attributes of
      the Earth, such as size, slope, and movements,
      and with those relations to heavenly bodies
      which affect the Earth's features, are entered
      under Geography, Mathematical.
      BT Geography—Methodology
      NT Geography—Mathematical models
          Geography—Statistical methods
  — **Methodology**
      NT Field plotters
          Geography—Mathematics
          Geography—Network analysis
          Photography in geography
  — Models
        USE Relief models
  — **Network analysis**
      ⌐G70.25⌐
      UF Network analysis (Geography)
      BT Geography—Methodology
  — Nomenclature
        USE Geography—Terminology
  — **Pictorial works**
      ⌐G136-9⌐
      UF Geography—Views
          Voyages and travels—Views
      RT Views
  — Punched card systems
        USE Punched card systems—Names,
          Geographical
  — **Radio scripts**
  — **Research** (May Subd Geog)
      UF Geographical research
      NT Astronautics in geographical
            research
  — **Societies, etc.**
  — **Statistical methods**
      BT Geography—Mathematics
  — **Study and teaching** (May Subd Geog)
      ⌐G72-76⌐
      RT Area studies
      NT Geographical recreations
          Geography rooms and equipment
  — — **Audio-visual aids**
  — **Tables**
      ⌐G109-G110⌐
      UF Geography—Tables, etc.
  — Tables, etc.
        USE Geography—Tables
  — **Terminology**
      ⌐G104-8⌐
      UF Geography—Nomenclature
          Topographical terms
      RT Names, Geographical
  — Text-books
        USE Geography—Textbooks

1500

— **Textbooks**
  Here are entered works discussing geography textbooks. Individual geography textbooks are entered under specific headings according to time of authorship, e.g. Geography (for 19th and 20th century works); Geography—17th-18th centuries; Geography, Medieval.
  UF Geography—Text-books
— **Views**
  USE Geography—Pictorial works
        Views
— **Vocational guidance** *(May Subd Geog)*
  ⌞G65⌟
  BT Geographers
  NT Interns (Geography)
Geography, Aerial
  ⌞G142⌟
  Here are entered works on the effect of aviation on geography, as well as works on geographical factors in aeronautics.
  UF Aerial geography
        Air-age geography
        Aviation and geography
        Geography and aviation
  SA *subdivisions* Description and travel—
        Aerial *under countries, regions, etc.,*
        or Description—Aerial *under cities*
  NT Aeronautics, Commercial
        Flights around the world
Geography, Agricultural
  USE Agricultural geography
Geography, Ancient
  ⌞G82-G88⌟
  Here are entered works on the geography of the ancient world. Works on the geography of Greece and Rome treated together are entered under Classical geography.
  UF Ancient geography
        Geography—To 400 A.D.
        Geography—Early works
  SA *subdivision* Description and travel
        under names of countries
  NT Cities and towns, Ancient
        Classical geography
        Vedas—Geography
— **Maps**
  ⌞G1033⌟
  ⌞GA205-GA213⌟
  UF Atlases, Historical
        Historical atlases
        History—Atlases
        Maps, Historical
        War maps
  BT Maps, Early
  NT Peutinger table
Geography, Arabic
  ⌞G93⌟
  UF Arabic geography
  BT Geography, Medieval
Geography, Astronomical
  USE Astronomical geography
Geography, Biblical
  USE Bible—Geography
Geography, Buddhist
  USE Buddhist geography
Geography, Classical
  USE Classical geography
Geography, Commercial
  ⌞HF1021-HF1029⌟
  Here are entered text-books of commercial geography and treatises on the natural resources, commerce, and industries of several countries or of the world, from the standpoint of commerce.
  UF Commercial geography
        World economics
  BT Commerce
        Commercial products
  RT Geography, Economic
  NT Trade routes
Geography, Cultural
  USE Anthropo-geography
Geography, Ecclesiastical
  USE Ecclesiastical geography

Geography, Economic
  ⌞HC⌟
  ⌞HD⌟
  Here are entered works which discuss in a general way the natural resources, commerce, and industries of several countries or of the world. Similar works concerning one country are entered under name of country with subdivision Economic conditions. Cf. note under Geography, Commercial.
  UF Economic geography
        World economics
  BT Agriculture—Economic aspects
        Commerce
        Commercial products
        Space in economics
  RT Agricultural geography
        Geography, Commercial
— **Maps**
  SA *subdivision* Economic conditions—
        Maps *under names of countries,*
        etc.
— **Mathematical models**
  UF Geographic models
Geography, Historical
  ⌞D-F⌟
  ⌞G141⌟
  Here are entered works which take a historical approach to the geography of countries, regions, etc. at a particular period in the past.
  Works limited to an individual country, region, etc. are entered under the name of that country or region with the subdivision Historical geography.
  Works on the branch of geography that deals with human governments, the boundaries and subdivisions of political units and the situations of cities are entered under Geography, Political.
  UF Historical geography
  BT Ecclesiastical geography
        History
  NT Buddhist geography
        Geography, Medieval
— **Maps**
  UF Atlases, Historical
        Historical atlases
        History—Atlases
        Maps, Historical
        War maps
Geography, Human
  USE Anthropo-geography
Geography, Islamic
  USE Koran—Geography
Geography, Linguistic
  USE Linguistic geography
Geography, Local
  USE Local geography
Geography, Mathematical
  ⌞GA⌟
  Here are entered works on the branch of physical geography that deals with attributes of the Earth, such as its size, shape, and movements, and with those relations to heavenly bodies which affect the features of the Earth. Works on the use of mathematics in geography are entered under Geography—Mathematics.
  UF Mathematical geography
  BT Mathematics
  RT Astronomical geography
        Geodesy
        Geographical positions
  NT Area measurement
        Cartography
        Cartometry
        Cosmography
        Latitude
        Longitude
        Map-projection
        Nautical astronomy
        Surveying
        Surveys
— **Tables**
  ⌞GA4⌟
  UF Geography, Mathematical—Tables,
        etc.

— **Tables, etc.**
  USE Geography, Mathematical—
        Tables
Geography, Medical
  USE Medical geography
Geography, Medieval
  ⌞G89-G95⌟
  Here are entered geographical works written during the Middle Ages, as well as works dealing with the geography of that period.
  UF Geography—400-1400
        Geography—Early works
  BT Geography—History
        Geography, Historical
        Middle Ages
  NT Geography, Arabic
— **Maps**
  UF Atlases, Historical
        Historical atlases
        History—Atlases
        Maps, Historical
        Middle Ages—History—Maps
        War maps
Geography, Military
  USE Military geography
Geography, Physical
  USE Physical geography
Geography, Political
  Here are entered works on the branch of geography that deals with human governments, the boundaries and subdivisions of political units and the situations of cities.
  Works which take a historical approach to the geography of countries, regions, etc. at a particular period in the past are entered under Geography, Historical.
  UF Political geography
  BT Anthropo-geography
        International relations
        World politics
  NT Boundaries
        Cities and towns
        Geopolitics
        Territory, National
Geography, Rural
  USE Rural geography
Geography, Social
  USE Anthropo-geography
Geography, Soil
  USE Soil geography
Geography, Talmudic
  USE Talmud—Geography
Geography, Urban
  USE Cities and towns
Geography, Vedic
  USE Vedas—Geography
Geography and aviation
  USE Geography, Aerial
Geography and religion
  USE Religion and geography
Geography of population
  USE Population geography
Geography rooms and equipment
  ⌞LB3325.G4⌟
  UF Rooms, Geography
  BT Geography—Study and teaching
        Schools—Furniture, equipment, etc.
Geogrids
  ⌞TA455.G44⌟
  UF Geocells
        Geowebs
        Polymer grids
  BT Geosynthetics
Geohydrology
  USE Hydrogeology
Geoid
  USE Earth—Figure
Geolabididae
  ⌞QE882.I5⌟
  BT Insectivora, Fossil
  NT Centetodon

Geologic erosion
  USE Erosion
Geologic formations
  USE Formations (Geology)
Geologic mapping
  USE Geological mapping
Geologic shells
  USE Shields (Geology)
Geological archaeology
  USE Archaeological geology
Geological chemistry
  USE Geochemistry
Geological cycles
  USE Geology—Periodicity
Geological exhibitions
  USE Geology—Exhibitions
Geological formations
  USE Formations (Geology)
Geological literature searching
  USE Information storage and retrieval
      systems—Geology
Geological mapping *(May Subd Geog)*
  [QE36]
  UF Geologic mapping
  BT Cartography
  RT Geology—Maps
Geological maps
  USE Geology—Maps
Geological microbiology
  USE Geomicrobiology
Geological modeling
  [QE43]
  UF Modeling, Geological
  BT Models and modelmaking
Geological museums *(May Subd Geog)*
  [QE51]
  BT Museums
Geological oceanography
  USE Submarine geology
Geological periodicity
  USE Geology—Periodicity
Geological physics
  USE Geophysics
Geological research
  USE Geology—Research
Geological specimens
  — Collection and preservation
      [QE50]
Geological statistics
  USE Geology—Statistical methods
Geological surveys
  [QE61-350]
  BT Surveys
  SA Geology—[local subdivision]—
      Surveys, *e.g.* Geology—United
      States—Surveys
  — Employees
      NT Wages—Geological survey
          employees
Geological time
  [QE508]
  UF Age of rocks
      Dating of rocks
      Geochronology
      Geochrony
      Rocks—Age
      Time, Geological
  BT Chronology
      Historical geology
  RT Earth—Age
  NT Hydration rind dating
      Paleoclimatology
      Radioactive dating
      Thermoluminescence dating
Geological unconformities
  USE Unconformities (Geology)
Geologists *(May Subd Geog)*
  [QE21-22]

  BT Earth scientists
      Geophysicists
      Naturalists
      Scientists
  NT Engineering geologists
      Geochemists
      Geology—Vocational guidance
      Paleontologists
      Petroleum geologists
      Women geologists
Geologists, Engineering
  USE Engineering geologists
Geology *(May Subd Geog)*
  [QE]
  UF Geognosy
      Geoscience
  BT Earth sciences
      Natural history
  NT Aerial photography in geology
      Aeronautics in geology
      Archaeological geology
      Astronautics in geology
      Bitumen—Geology
      Classification—Books—Geology
      Coal—Geology
      Deluge
      Gas, Natural—Geology
      Geysers
      Gondwana (Geology)
      Historical geology
      Hydrogeology
      Iron ores—Geology
      Manganese ores—Geology
      Mars (Planet)—Geology
      Military geology
      Mountains
      Oceanography
      Ore-deposits
      Outcrops (Geology)
      Paleoclimatology
      Paleogeography
      Paleohydrology
      Paleolimnology
      Paleontology
      Pediments (Geology)
      Petroleum—Geology
      Physical geology
      Planets—Geology
      Sedimentology
      Sediments (Geology)
      Slopes (Physical geography)
      Speleology
      Submarine geology
      Submarine topography
      Troilite ores—Geology
      Tungsten ores—Geology
      Uranium ores—Geology
      Urban geology
      Volcanism
      Volcanoes
  — Bibliography
      NT Information storage and retrieval
          systems—Geology
  — Computer programs
      NT JKDIGIT (Computer program)
          NCHARAN (Computer program)
  — Exhibitions
      UF Geological exhibitions
  — Film catalogs
      [QE40]
      BT Visual education
  — Guide-books
  — History
      [QE11-13]
      BT Catastrophes (Geology)
  — Maps
      [QE33]
      UF Geological maps
          Maps, Geological
      RT Geological mapping
          Magnetism, Terrestrial—Maps

  — Mathematics
      [QE33]
      UF Mathematical geology
      NT Perspective correlation in geology
  — Nomenclature
      [QE7]
      RT Geology—Terminology
  — Periodicity
      UF Geological cycles
          Geological periodicity
      BT Cycles
      NT Varves
  — Research *(May Subd Geog)*
      UF Geological research
  — Societies, etc.
  — Statistical methods
      UF Geological statistics
  — Study and teaching (Higher)
      (May Subd Geog)
  — Terminology
      RT Geology—Nomenclature
  — Vocational guidance *(May Subd Geog)*
      [QE34]
      BT Geologists
  — Alabama
      NT Black Warrior Basin (Ala. and
          Miss.)
  — Alaska
      NT Orca Group (Alaska)
          Sitka Graywacke (Alaska)
          Valdez Group (Alaska)
  — Alberta
      NT Athabasca Basin (Sask. and Alta.)
  — Arctic Ocean
      NT Greenland Basin
          Norwegian Basin
  — Arizona
      NT Gila Conglomerate (Ariz. and
          N.M.)
          Pedregosa Basin
  — Arkansas
      NT Arkoma Basin (Ark. and Okla.)
  — Australia
      NT Bangemall Basin (W.A.)
          Canning Basin (W.A.)
          Carnarvon Basin (W.A.)
          Eucla Basin (W.A. and S. Aust.)
          Longford Basin (Tas.)
          Ngalia Basin (N.T.)
          Pedirka Basin (S. Aust. and N.T.)
  — Brazil
      NT Recôncavo Basin (Brazil)
  — British Columbia
      NT Princeton Basin (B.C.)
  — California
      NT Owens Valley Group (Calif.)
          Raymond Basin (Calif.)
  — China
      NT Chiu-ch'üan Basin (China)
          Ku-yang Basin (China)
          Tsaidam Basin (China)
  — Colorado
      NT Cheyenne Basin (Colo. and Wyo.)
          Raton Basin (Colo. and N.M.)
          Ridges Basin (Colo.)
          San Juan Basin (N.M. and Colo.)
          Uinta Basin (Utah and Colo.)
  — Czechoslovakia
      NT Dąbrowa Basin (Poland and
          Czechoslovakia)
          Liptov Basin (Czechoslovakia)
  — Egypt
      NT Dakhla Basin (Egypt)
  — Germany (West)
      NT Mainz Basin (Germany)
  — Kansas
      NT Anadarko Basin
  — Mali
      NT Taoudenni Basin (Mali)
  — Maryland
      NT Culpeper Basin (Va. and Md.)

— Mexico
  NT Maverick Basin (Tex. and Mexico)
      Pedregosa Basin
— Michigan
  NT Michigan Basin (Mich. and Ont.)
— Mississippi
  NT Black Warrior Basin (Ala. and
      Miss.)
— Montana
  NT Bighorn Basin (Mont. and Wyo.)
— Moon
  USE Lunar geology
— Nevada
  NT Needles Range Group (Utah and
      Nev.)
— New Brunswick
  NT Windsor Group (N.B. and N.S.)
— New Mexico
  NT Delaware Basin (Tex. and N.M.)
      Gila Conglomerate (Ariz. and
        N.M.)
      Midland Basin (Tex. and N.M.)
      Pedregosa Basin
      Raton Basin (Colo. and N.M.)
      San Juan Basin (N.M. and Colo.)
— Nova Scotia
  NT Windsor Group (N.B. and N.S.)
— Oklahoma
  NT Anadarko Basin
      Arkoma Basin (Ark. and Okla.)
— Ontario
  NT Medina Group
      Michigan Basin (Mich. and Ont.)
— Poland
  NT Dąbrowa Basin (Poland and
      Czechoslovakia)
— Russian S.F.S.R.
  NT Bureya Basin (R.S.F.S.R.)
      Kansk-Achinsk Basin (R.S.F.S.R.)
      Kuznetsk Basin (R.S.F.S.R.)
— Saskatchewan
  NT Athabasca Basin (Sask. and Alta.)
— Southwest, New
  NT Paradox Basin
— Texas
  NT Anadarko Basin
      Delaware Basin (Tex. and N.M.)
      East Texas Basin (Tex.)
      Fort Worth Basin (Tex.)
      Maverick Basin (Tex. and Mexico)
      Midland Basin (Tex. and N.M.)
      Palo Duro Basin (Tex.)
— Ukraine
  NT Krivoĭ Rog Basin (Ukraine)
      Lvov-Volyn Basin (Ukraine)
— United States
  NT Denver Basin
      Medina Group
— — Surveys
— Utah
  NT Needles Range Group (Utah and
      Nev.)
      Uinta Basin (Utah and Colo.)
— Venezuela
  NT Maracaibo Basin (Venezuela)
— Virginia
  NT Barboursville Basin (Va.)
      Culpeper Basin (Va. and Md.)
— Wyoming
  NT Bighorn Basin (Mont. and Wyo.)
      Cheyenne Basin (Colo. and Wyo.)
      Hanna Basin (Wyo.)
      Laramie Basin (Wyo.)
      Shirley Basin (Wyo.)
Geology, Biblical
  USE Bible and geology
Geology, Chemical
  USE Geochemistry
      Mineralogical chemistry
      Mineralogy, Determinative
      Rocks—Analysis

Geology, Dynamic
  USE Geodynamics
Geology, Economic *(May Subd Geog)*
  [TN260]
  UF Economic geology
  BT Physical geology
  SA *other geological products, e.g.*
      Asbestos, Graphite, Gypsum,
      Limestone, Peat
  NT Building stones
      Coal
      Engineering geology
      Gas, Natural
      Mineral oils
      Mines and mineral resources
      Mining geology
      Ores
      Petroleum
      Quarries and quarrying
      Soils
Geology, Historical
  USE Historical geology
Geology, Lunar
  USE Lunar geology
Geology, Martian
  USE Mars (Planet)—Geology
Geology, Military
  USE Military geology
Geology, Mining
  USE Mining geology
Geology, Photography in
  USE Photography in geology
Geology, Stratigraphic
  [QE651-699]
  UF Age of rocks
      Rocks—Age
      Stratigraphic geology
  RT Historical geology
  NT Borings
      Cratons
      Facies (Geology)
      Formations (Geology)
      Lithofacies
      Lunar stratigraphy
      Oil well logging
      Paleontology, Stratigraphic
      Pluvial periods
      Stratigraphic correlation
      Unconformities (Geology)
— Algonkian
  [QE655]
  UF Algonkian period
  NT Geology, Stratigraphic—Huronian
— Archaean
  [QE653]
  UF Archaean period
      Archaeozoic period
      Archean period
      Archeozoic period
      Geology, Stratigraphic—
        Archaeozoic
  BT Geology, Stratigraphic—Pre-
      Cambrian
  NT Geology, Stratigraphic—Laurentian
      Schists
— Archaeozoic
  USE Geology, Stratigraphic—
      Archaean
— Caenozoic
  USE Geology, Stratigraphic—Cenozoic
— Caledonian
  USE Geology, Stratigraphic—Paleozoic
— Cambrian
  [QE656]
  UF Cambrian period
      Geology, Stratigraphic—Primordial
  BT Geology, Stratigraphic—Paleozoic
  NT Pumpkinvine Creek Formation
      (Ga.)
— Carboniferous
  [QE671-3]

  UF Carboniferous period
  BT Geology, Stratigraphic—Paleozoic
  NT Geology, Stratigraphic—
      Mississippian
      Geology, Stratigraphic—
      Pennsylvanian
— Cenozoic
  [QE690-699]
  UF Caenozoic period
      Cenozoic period
      Geology, Stratigraphic—Caenozoic
  NT Columbia Aquifer
      Geology, Stratigraphic—
      Quaternary
      Geology, Stratigraphic—Tertiary
      Molasse
— Cretaceous
  [QE685-8]
  UF Cretaceous period
      Laramie formation
      Montana formation
  BT Geology, Stratigraphic—Mesozoic
  NT Blackleaf Formation (Mont.)
      Blair Formation (Wyo.)
      Flysch
      Frontier Formation
      Niobrara Formation
      Queen Charlotte Group (B.C.)
      Sitka Graywacke (Alaska)
      Sunniland Formation (Fla.)
      Valdez Group (Alaska)
— Devonian
  [QE665]
  UF Devonian period
      Old red sandstone (Geology)
      Oriskany formation
  BT Geology, Stratigraphic—Paleozoic
— Diluvial
  USE Geology, Stratigraphic—Recent
— Eocene
  [QE692]
  UF Eocene period
  BT Geology, Stratigraphic—Tertiary
  NT Green River Formation
      Orca Group (Alaska)
      Sespe Formation (Calif.)
      Wasatch Formation
— Gothlandian
  USE Geology, Stratigraphic—Silurian
— Holocene
  USE Geology, Stratigraphic—Recent
— Huronian
  UF Huronian epoch
  BT Geology, Stratigraphic—Algonkian
      Geology, Stratigraphic—Pre-
      Cambrian
— Jurassic
  [QE681-3]
  UF Geology, Stratigraphic—Liassic
      Jurassic period
      Lias
  BT Geology, Stratigraphic—Mesozoic
      Oolite
  NT Morrison Formation
      Navajo Sandstone
      Sitka Graywacke (Alaska)
      Winterhaven Formation (Calif. and
      Ariz.)
— Laurentian
  [QE653]
  BT Geology, Stratigraphic—Archaean
— Liassic
  USE Geology, Stratigraphic—Jurassic
— Lower Carboniferous
  USE Geology, Stratigraphic—
      Mississippian
— Lower Silurian
  USE Geology, Stratigraphic—
      Ordovician
— Mesozoic
  [QE675-688]

Geology, Stratigraphic
— **Mesozoic** *(Continued)*
  UF Mesozoic period
  NT Geology, Stratigraphic—Cretaceous
      Geology, Stratigraphic—Jurassic
      Geology, Stratigraphic—Triassic
— **Miocene**
  [QE694]
  UF Miocene period
  BT Geology, Stratigraphic—Neocene
      Geology, Stratigraphic—Tertiary
  NT Colter Formation (Wyo.)
      Creede Formation (Colo.)
      Kirkwood Formation (N.J. and
        Pa.)
      Sespe Formation (Calif.)
— **Mississippian**
  [QE672]
  UF Geology, Stratigraphic—Lower
      Carboniferous
      Geology, Stratigraphic—
        Subcarboniferous
      Mississippian epoch
  BT Geology, Stratigraphic—
      Carboniferous
  NT Heath Formation (Mont.)
      Windsor Group (N.B. and N.S.)
— **Neocene**
  [QE694-5]
  UF Neocene epoch
  BT Geology, Stratigraphic—Tertiary
  NT Geology, Stratigraphic—Miocene
      Geology, Stratigraphic—Pliocene
— **Oligocene**
  [QE693]
  UF Oligocene period
  BT Geology, Stratigraphic—Tertiary
  NT Creede Formation (Colo.)
      Frio Clay (Tex. and La.)
      Needles Range Group (Utah and
        Nev.)
      Sespe Formation (Calif.)
— **Ordovician**
  [QE662]
  UF Geology, Stratigraphic—Lower
      Silurian
      Geology, Stratigraphic—Silurian,
      Lower
      Lower Silurian period
      Ordovician formation
      Silurian period, Lower
  BT Geology, Stratigraphic—Paleozoic
  NT Medina Group
— **Paleocene**
  UF Paleocene period
  BT Geology, Stratigraphic—Tertiary
  NT Orca Group (Alaska)
      Wasatch Formation
— Paleogene
  USE Geology, Stratigraphic—Tertiary
— **Paleozoic**
  [QE654-674]
  UF Geology, Stratigraphic—
      Caledonian
      Paleozoic period
  NT Geology, Stratigraphic—Cambrian
      Geology, Stratigraphic—
      Carboniferous
      Geology, Stratigraphic—Devonian
      Geology, Stratigraphic—Ordovician
      Geology, Stratigraphic—Permian
      Geology, Stratigraphic—Silurian
— **Pennsylvanian**
  [QE673]
  UF Pennsylvanian epoch
  BT Geology, Stratigraphic—
      Carboniferous
  NT Ada Aquifer (Okla.)
      Breathitt Formation (Ky. and
        Tenn.)
      Vamoosa Aquifer (Okla.)

— **Permian**
  [QE674]
  UF Permian formation
  BT Geology, Stratigraphic—Paleozoic
  NT Deep-Basin Brine Aquifer (Tex.)
      Owens Valley Group (Calif.)
      Phosphoria Formation
— **Pleistocene**
  [QE696-8]
  UF Pleistocene period
  BT Geology, Stratigraphic—
      Quaternary
      Glacial climates
  RT Glacial epoch
  NT Drift
      Gila Conglomerate (Ariz. and
        N.M.)
      Wedron Formation
— **Pliocene**
  [QE695]
  UF Pleiocene period
      Pliocene period
  BT Geology, Stratigraphic—Neocene
      Geology, Stratigraphic—Tertiary
  NT Gila Conglomerate (Ariz. and
        N.M.)
— Postglacial
  USE Geology, Stratigraphic—Recent
— **Pre-Cambrian**
  [QE655]
  UF Geology, Stratigraphic—
      Proterozoic
      Pre-Cambrian period
      Proterozoic period
  NT Geology, Stratigraphic—Archaean
      Geology, Stratigraphic—Huronian
      Hoodoo Quartzite (Idaho)
      Pumpkinvine Creek Formation
        (Ga.)
      Shields (Geology)
      Sioux Quartzite
      Spokane Formation (Mont.)
      Yellowjacket Formation (Idaho)
— Primordial
  USE Geology, Stratigraphic—
      Cambrian
— Proterozoic
  USE Geology, Stratigraphic—Pre-
      Cambrian
— **Quaternary**
  [QE696-9]
  UF Quaternary period
  BT Geology, Stratigraphic—Cenozoic
  NT Geology, Stratigraphic—
      Pleistocene
      Geology, Stratigraphic—Recent
      Glacial epoch
— **Recent**
  UF Geology, Stratigraphic—Diluvial
      Geology, Stratigraphic—Holocene
      Geology, Stratigraphic—Postglacial
      Recent epoch (Stratigraphic
        geology)
  BT Geology, Stratigraphic—
      Quaternary
  NT Hydration rind dating
— **Silurian**
  [QE661-3]
  UF Geology, Stratigraphic—
      Gothlandian
      Silurian period
  BT Geology, Stratigraphic—Paleozoic
  NT Medina Group
— Silurian, Lower
  USE Geology, Stratigraphic—
      Ordovician
— Subcarboniferous
  USE Geology, Stratigraphic—
      Mississippian
— **Tertiary**
  [QE691-5]

  UF Geology, Stratigraphic—Paleogene
      Tertiary period
  BT Geology, Stratigraphic—Cenozoic
  NT Flysch
      Fort Union Formation
      Geology, Stratigraphic—Eocene
      Geology, Stratigraphic—Miocene
      Geology, Stratigraphic—Neocene
      Geology, Stratigraphic—Oligocene
      Geology, Stratigraphic—Paleocene
      Geology, Stratigraphic—Pliocene
      Popotosa Formation (N.M.)
— **Triassic**
  [QE676-9]
  UF Triassic period
  BT Geology, Stratigraphic—Mesozoic
  NT Navajo Sandstone
      Santa Rosa Formation (N.M. and
        Tex.)
— **Cretaceous**
  NT Livingston Formation (Mont.)
      Toreva Formation (Ariz.)
— **Devonian**
  NT Popovich Formation (Nev.)
— **Nomenclature** *(May Subd Geog)*
  [QE645]
— **Silurian**
  NT Roberts Mountains Formation
      (Nev. and Utah)
Geology, Structural
  [QE601-611]
  UF Geotectonics
      Structural geology
      Tectonics (Geology)
  BT Physical geology
  RT Mountains
      Rocks—Cleavage
  NT Cap rock
      Cryptoexplosion structures
      Diagenesis
      Domes (Geology)
      Eskar
      Faults (Geology)
      Folds (Geology)
      Grabens (Geology)
      Intrusions (Geology)
      Island arcs
      Joints (Geology)
      Orogeny
      Placer deposits
      Plate tectonics
      Rifts (Geology)
      Rock deformation
      Roof pendants (Geology)
      Schistosity
      Stylolites
Geology, Submarine
  USE Submarine geology
Geology, Urban
  USE Urban geology
Geology and Bible
  USE Bible and geology
Geology and religion
  USE Bible and geology
      Religion and science
Geomagnetic fields
  USE Magnetism, Terrestrial
Geomagnetic indexes
  UF Geomagnetic indices
      Indexes, Geomagnetic
  BT Geophysics
      Magnetism, Terrestrial
Geomagnetic indices
  USE Geomagnetic indexes
Geomagnetic maps
  USE Magnetism, Terrestrial—Maps
Geomagnetic micropulsations
  (May Subd Geog)
  [QC809.M25]
  UF Micropulsations, Geomagnetic
      Telluric current micropulsations

BT Earth currents
    Ionospheric drift
    Magnetism, Terrestrial
    Oscillations
NT Microwaves
Geomagnetic polarity reversals
  USE Geomagnetic reversals
Geomagnetic reversals
  UF Earth's polarity reversals
    Geomagnetic polarity reversals
    Polarity reversals, Geomagnetic
    Reversals, Geomagnetic
  BT Magnetism, Terrestrial
Geomagnetism
  USE Magnetism, Terrestrial
Geomancy *(May Subd Geog)*
  [BF1745-BF1773]
    Here are entered works on divination by means of
figures or lines, such as natural or artificial configura-
tions of earth or connecting dots jotted at random on
paper.
  UF Geomanty
  BT Divination
  NT Feng-shui
    Ifa
Geomanty
  USE Geomancy
Geomedicine
  USE Medical geography
Geomembranes
  [TA455.G44]
  BT Geosynthetics
Geometra
  [QL561.G6]
  BT Geometridae
Geometra boreata
  USE Operophthera fagata
Geometra brumata
  USE Winter moth
Geometric constructions
  USE Geometrical constructions
Geometric forms, Generation of
  USE Generation of geometric forms
Geometric function theory
  UF Function theory, Geometric
  BT Functions of complex variables
  NT Conformal mapping
    Extremal problems (Mathematics)
    Kernel functions
    Quasiconformal mappings
    Univalent functions
Geometric measure theory
  [QA312]
  UF Measure theory, Geometric
  BT Measure theory
Geometric period, Greece, ca. 900-700 B.C.
  USE Greece—History—Geometric period,
    ca. 900-700 B.C.
Geometric probabilities
  BT Probabilities
Geometric programming
  BT Programming (Mathematics)
Geometric quantization
  [QC174.17.G46]
  UF Quantization, Geometric
  BT Geometry, Differential
    Quantum theory
Geometric series
  USE Series, Geometric
Geometric vases
  USE Vases, Geometric
Geometrical constructions
  UF Constructions, Geometric
    Constructions, Geometrical
    Geometric constructions
  BT Geometry
Geometrical drawing
  [QA464]
  [QA497]
  UF Mathematical drawing
    Plans

BT Drawing
    Geometry
RT Mechanical drawing
    Projection
NT Design
    Generation of geometric forms
    Geometry, Descriptive
    Graphic methods
    Perspective
Geometrical models
  UF Geometry—Models
  BT Geometry
    Models and modelmaking
  NT Polyhedra—Models
Geometrical optics
  USE Optics, Geometrical
Geometrical theory of diffraction
  USE Diffraction, Geometrical
Geometridae
  [QL561.G6]
  UF Acidalidae
    Acidaliidae
    Boarmiidae
    Brephidae
    Chlorochromatidae
    Chlorochromidae
    Chlorometridae
    Cimeliidae
    Cyclophoridae
    Cyllopodidae
    Dendrometridae
    Desmobathridae
    Ectropidae
    Ephyridae
    Erosiidae
    Fidonidae
    Geometroidae
    Hazidae
    Hedylidae
    Hemitheidae
    Hydriomenidae
    Idaeidae
    Idoeidae
    Larentidae
    Larentiidae
    Lyrceidae
    Mecoceridae
    Melanalophidae
    Micronidae
    Monoctenidae
    Monocteniidae
    Oenochromidae
    Oenochromiidae
    Orthostixidae
    Palyadae
    Selidosematidae
    Selidosemidae
    Sterrhidae
    Terpnidae
    Zonosomatidae
    Zonosomidae
  BT Lepidoptera
    Moths
  NT Abraxas
    Anacamptodes
    Annaphila
    Ascotis
    Biston
    Bupalus
    Ceratonyx
    Chesiadodes
    Cleora
    Ennomos
    Geometra
    Hesperumia
    Hulstina
    Hydriomena
    Lambdina
    Mericisca
    Meris (Moth)
    Nemeris

    Nepterotaea
    Operophthera
    Oporinia
    Pero
    Plataea
    Pseudoboarmia
    Pterotaea
    Sabulodes
    Somatolophia
    Stenoporpia
    Xanthotype
    Zamarada
Geometries, Continuous
  USE Continuous geometries
Geometries, Finite
  USE Finite geometries
Geometrodynamics
  [QC173.59.G44]
  BT Geometry
    Relativity (Physics)
Geometroidae
  USE Geometridae
Geometry *(May Subd Geog)*
  [QA440-699]
  BT Mathematics
  RT Euclid's Elements
  NT Angle
    Complexes
    Congruences (Geometry)
    Curves
    Envelopes (Geometry)
    Fractals
    Geometrical constructions
    Geometrical drawing
    Geometrical models
    Geometrodynamics
    Hyperspace
    Locus (Mathematics)
    Porisms
    Pyramid (Geometry)
    Ratio and proportion
    Similarity (Geometry)
    Sphere
    Stochastic geometry
    Surfaces
    Topology
    Transformations (Mathematics)
    Trigonometry
  — **Early works to 1800**
    [QA31-35]
    RT Mathematics, Greek
  — Famous problems
    USE Geometry—Problems, Famous
  — **Foundations**
    [QA681]
    UF Foundations of geometry
    BT Mathematics—Philosophy
    RT Geometry, Non-Euclidean
      Parallels (Geometry)
    NT Axioms
      Hyperspace
  — Models
    USE Geometrical models
  — **Problems, exercises, etc.**
    [QA459 (Elementary)]
    [QA555 (Analytical)]
    NT Pythagorean proposition
  — **Problems, Famous**
    [QA466-9]
    UF Famous problems (in geometry)
      Geometry—Famous problems
      Problems, Famous (in geometry)
    NT Circle-squaring
      Cube, Duplication of
      Trisection of angle
  — **Study and teaching** *(May Subd Geog)*
Geometry, Affine
  UF Affine geometry
  BT Geometry, Modern
  NT Affine differential geometry
    Desarguesian planes

Geomorphic geology
  USE Geomorphology
Geomorphological mapping
  (May Subd Geog)
  ⌐GB400.42.M3⌐
  BT Cartography
      Geomorphology—Maps
Geomorphological research
  USE Geomorphology—Research
Geomorphology *(May Subd Geog)*
  ⌐GB400-GB649⌐
  UF Geomorphic geology
      Physiography
  BT Physical geography
  NT Aerial photography in geomorphology
      Astronautics in geomorphology
      Climatic geomorphology
      Cratering
      Earth pyramids
      Eolian processes
      Inlets
      Landforms
      Volcanism
  — Instruments
      UF Instruments, Geomorphological
  — Maps
      NT Geomorphological mapping
  — Research *(May Subd Geog)*
      UF Geomorphological research
Geomyidae
  USE Pocket gophers
Geomys
  ⌐QL737.R654⌐
  BT Pocket gophers
  NT Geomys bursarius
Geomys bursarius
  ⌐QL737.R654⌐
  UF Plains pocket gopher
  BT Geomys
Geomyzidae
  USE Opomyzidae
Geonic literature
  UF Gaonic literature
  BT Hebrew literature
      Jewish literature
      Talmud
  RT Geonim
  NT Rabbinical literature
      Responsa—To 1040
Geonic responsa
  USE Responsa—To 1040
Geonim
  BT Rabbis
      Talmud
  RT Geonic literature
Geonoma
  ⌐QK495.P17⌐
  BT Palms
Geonoma molinae
  ⌐QK495.P17⌐
Geopelia
  ⌐QL696.C63⌐
  BT Columbidae
  NT Barred dove
Geopelia striata
  USE Barred dove
Geophagus
  ⌐QL638.C55⌐
  BT Cichlidae
Geophagy
  USE Pica (Pathology)
Geophis
  ⌐QL666.O636⌐
  BT Colubridae
Geophone
  ⌐TN297 (Mine-rescue work)⌐
  BT Mine safety—Equipment and supplies
      Seismometers
  NT Hydrophone
Geophysical instruments
  UF Instruments, Geophysical

  BT Physical instruments
      Scientific apparatus and instruments
  RT Meteorological instruments
  NT Magnetic instruments
      Riometer
      Tiltmeter
Geophysical methods in soil surveys
  USE Soil surveys—Geophysical methods
Geophysical Monitoring for Climatic Change
  BT Atmosphere
      Climatic changes
      Meteorology—Research
Geophysical observatories *(May Subd Geog)*
  ⌐QC808⌐
  UF Geophysics—Observatories
      Observatories, Geophysical
      Stations, Geophysical
  BT Geophysics—Observations
      Observatories
  SA *individual observatories*
  NT Gravity stations
      Hydrometeorological stations
      Magnetism, Terrestrial—Observatories
      Meteorological stations
      Orbiting geophysical observatories
      Seismological stations
      Seismology—Observatories
Geophysical prediction
  UF Geophysics—Forecasts
      Prediction, Geophysical
  BT Forecasting
      Natural disasters
  NT Earthquake prediction
      Flood forecasting
      Hydrological forecasting
      Weather forecasting
Geophysical prospecting
  USE Prospecting—Geophysical methods
Geophysical radiography
  USE Radiography in geophysics
Geophysical well logging *(May Subd Geog)*
  UF Logging, Geophysical well
      Well logging, Geophysical
  BT Prospecting—Geophysical methods
  NT Radiation well logging
Geophysicists *(May Subd Geog)*
  BT Earth scientists
      Geophysics
  NT Geodesists
      Geologists
      Meteorologists
      Oceanographers
      Seismologists
      Volcanologists
Geophysics *(May Subd Geog)*
  ⌐QC801-QC809 (Physics)⌐
  ⌐QE500-QE511.7 (Geology)⌐
  UF Geological physics
      Physics, Terrestrial
      Terrestrial physics
  BT Earth sciences
      Physics
  NT Astronautics in geophysics
      Atmospheric physics
      Auroras
      Counterglow
      Dynamo theory (Cosmic physics)
      Earth currents
      Earth resistance
      Earth tides
      Electronics in geophysics
      Energy budget (Geophysics)
      Gases in rocks
      Geodynamics
      Geomagnetic indexes
      Geophysicists
      Gravimeter (Geophysical instrument)
      Information theory in geophysics
      Magnetism, Terrestrial
      Magnetohydrodynamics
      Marine geophysics

      Mass budget (Geophysics)
      Meteorology
      Oceanography
      Paleogeophysics
      Plate tectonics
      Prospecting—Geophysical methods
      Radiative transfer
      Rock pressure
      Seismology
      Soil surveys—Geophysical methods
      Solifluction
      Terrestrial heat flow
      Thermoremanent magnetization
      Van Allen radiation belts
  — Computer programs
  — Fluid models
      ⌐QC809.F5⌐
      UF Rotating dishpan
  — Forecasts
      USE Geophysical prediction
  — International cooperation
      NT International Geophysical Year,
          1957-1958
          International Years of the Quiet
          Sun, 1964-1965
          Solar Maximum Year, 1979-1981
  — Methodology
      NT Radiography in geophysics
  — Observations
      UF Observations, Geophysical
      NT Geophysical observatories
  — Observatories
      USE Geophysical observatories
Geophysics, Electronics in
  USE Electronics in geophysics
Geophysics in archaeology
  (May Subd Geog)
  ⌐CC79.G46⌐
  BT Archaeology—Methodology
Geopolitics *(May Subd Geog)*
  ⌐JC319-323⌐
  BT Geography, Political
      International relations
      Political science
  RT Anthropo-geography
      Boundaries
      Demography
      Territory, National
      World politics
  NT Buffer states
Geoprumnon
  USE Astragalus (Plants)
Georg-Büchner-Preis
  UF Büchner-Preis
Georg family
  USE George family
George (Lusaka, Zambia) *(Not Subd Geog)*
  UF Lusaka (Zambia). George
George, Cape (N.S.)
  UF Cape George (N.S.)
  BT Capes (Coasts)—Nova Scotia
George, Fort (New York, N.Y.)
  USE Fort George (New York, N.Y.)
George, Lake (N.Y.)
  UF Lake George (N.Y.)
  BT Lakes—New York (State)
      Reservoirs—New York (State)
George, Lake, Battle of, 1755
  ⌐E199⌐
  BT Crown Point Expedition, 1755
GEORGE 3 (Computer system)
George Cross
  ⌐CR4880⌐
George family *(Not Subd Geog)*
  UF Georg family
      Georges family
      Jorge family
George Fourth Sea (Antarctic regions)
  USE Weddell Sea (Antarctic regions)
George IV Sea (Antarctic regions)
  USE Weddell Sea (Antarctic regions)

George junior republics
  USE Junior republics
George Kleine Film Collection
  UF Kleine, George—Film collections
    Library of Congress George Kleine
      Film Collection
  BT Moving-picture film collections
George Medal
  ₍CR4887₎
  BT Decorations of honor—Great Britain
George Reeves Site (Ill.)
  BT Illinois—Antiquities
George Reservoir (Ala. and GA.)
  USE Walter F. George Reservoir (Ala. and
    Ga.)
George Smiley (Fictitious character)
  USE Smiley, George (Fictitious character)
George Sound (N.Z.)
  BT Sounds (Geomorphology)—New
    Zealand
George Street (Sydney, N.S.W.)
  (Not Subd Geog)
  BT Streets—Australia
George Street (Toronto, Ont.)
  BT Streets—Ontario
George Washington Bridge (New York, N.Y.)
  BT Bridges—New Jersey
    Bridges—New York (State)
    Hudson River (N.Y. and N.J.)—
      Bridges
George Washington Memorial Parkway
  UF G.W. Parkway
    George Washington Parkway
    Washington Memorial Parkway
  BT National parks and reserves—
      Maryland
    National parks and reserves—Virginia
    National parks and reserves—
      Washington (D.C.)
    Parkways—Maryland
    Parkways—Virginia
    Parkways—Washington (D.C.)
  NT Mount Vernon Memorial Highway
      (Va.)
    Mount Vernon Trail (Va.)
**George Washington National Forest (Va. and
  W. Va.)**
  BT Forest reserves—Virginia
    Forest reserves—West Virginia
    National parks and reserves—United
      States
George Washington Parkway
  USE George Washington Memorial
    Parkway
Georges Bank
  BT Banks (Oceanography)—North
    Atlantic Ocean
Georges family
  USE George family
Georgetown automatic translation
  USE GAT (Computer program)
**Georgetown Loop Historic Mining and
  Railroad Park (Colo.)**
  BT Parks—Colorado
    Railroad museums—Colorado
    Silver mines and mining—Museums
Georgetown Square (Washington, D.C.)
  (Not Subd Geog)
  UF Washington (D.C.). Georgetown
    Square
Georgia
  — Antiquities
    NT Cannon's Point Plantation Site
        (Ga.)
      Cemochechobee Archaeological
        District (Ga.)
      Little Egypt Site (Ga.)
      Potts' Tract Site (Ga.)
      Tunacunnhee Site (Ga.)
      Walter F. George Dam Mound
        Site (Ga.)

— **Description and travel**
— — **Colonial period, ca. 1600-1775**
— — **1775-1950**
— — **1951-1980**
— — **1981-**
— **History**
    ₍F281-295₎
— — **Colonial period, ca. 1600-1775**
    NT St. Augustine Expedition, 1740
      St. Augustine Expedition, 1743
— — — **Juvenile literature**
— — **Revolution, 1775-1783**
    ₍E263.G3₎
— — **1775-1865**
— — **War of 1812**
    ₍E359.5.G4₎
— — Creek War, 1836
    USE Creek War, 1836
— — **Civil War, 1861-1865**
    ₍E503₎
    ₍E559₎
    NT Sherman's March to the Sea
      Wilson's Cavalry Raid, 1865
— — — **Campaigns** (Not Subd Geog)
— — — **Centennial celebrations, etc.**
— — **1865-**
— **Politics and government**
— — **Colonial period, ca. 1600-1775**
— — **1775-1865**
    NT Yazoo Fraud
— — **Civil War, 1861-1865**
— — **1865-1950**
— — **1951-**
— **Public lands**
    NT Yazoo Fraud
— **Social life and customs**
— — **Colonial period, ca. 1600-1775**
    ₍F289₎
Georgia (Republic)
  USE Georgian S.S.R.
Georgia (Transcaucasia)
  USE Georgian S.S.R.
Georgia, Gulf of (B.C.)
  USE Georgia, Strait of (B.C.)
Georgia, Strait of (B.C.)
  UF Georgia, Gulf of (B.C.)
    Gulf of Georgia (B.C.)
    Strait of Georgia (B.C.)
  BT Straits—British Columbia
Georgia Embayment
  BT Bays—Florida
    Bays—Georgia
    Bays—South Carolina
Georgia pine
  USE Longleaf pine
Georgiadi, Dimitŭr
— **Homes and haunts**
— — **Bulgaria**
    NT Kŭshta na Dimitŭr Georgiadi
      (Plovdiv, Bulgaria)
Georgian (Georgian S.S.R.) art
  USE Art, Georgian (Georgian S.S.R.)
Georgian (Georgian S.S.R.) coins
  USE Coins, Georgian (Georgian S.S.R.)
Georgian (Georgian S.S.R.) illumination of
  books and manuscripts
  USE Illumination of books and manuscripts,
    Georgian (Georgian S.S.R.)
Georgian (Georgian S.S.R.) mural painting and
  decoration
  USE Mural painting and decoration,
    Georgian (Georgian S.S.R.)
Georgian (Georgian S.S.R.) pottery
  USE Pottery, Georgian (Georgian S.S.R.)
Georgian architecture
  USE Architecture, Georgian
Georgian art
  USE Art, Georgian
Georgian Bay (Ont.)
  BT Bays—Ontario
    Huron, Lake (Mich. and Ont.)

Georgian children's literature
  USE Children's literature, Georgian
Georgian decoration and ornament
  (Transcaucasia)
  USE Decoration and ornament, Georgian
    (Transcaucasia)
Georgian embroidery
  USE Embroidery, Georgian
Georgian epic literature
  USE Epic literature, Georgian
Georgian epic poetry
  USE Epic poetry, Georgian
Georgian fiction (May Subd Geog)
  NT Short stories, Georgian
Georgian folk poetry
  USE Folk poetry, Georgian
Georgian furniture
  USE Furniture, Georgian
Georgian gardens
  USE Gardens, Georgian
Georgian glassware
  USE Glassware, Georgian
Georgian hymns
  USE Hymns, Georgian
Georgian incantations
  USE Incantations, Georgian
Georgian language
  ₍PK9101-9151₎
  BT Caucasian languages
    Kartvelian languages
  NT Adzhar dialect
    Imeretian dialect
— **Dialects**
    NT Gurian dialect
Georgian literature
  ₍PK9160-9178₎
  UF Grusian literature
  NT Children's literature, Georgian
    Epic literature, Georgian
Georgian Military Road (Georgian S.S.R. and
  R.S.F.S.R.)
  USE Voenno-Gruzinskaia doroga (Georgian
    S.S.R. and R.S.F.S.R.)
Georgian mural painting and decoration
  USE Mural painting and decoration,
    Georgian
Georgian philology
  BT Caucasian philology
Georgian philosophy
  USE Philosophy, Georgian
Georgian poetry
  ₍PK9162₎
  ₍PK9166₎
  NT Epic poetry, Georgian
    Folk poetry, Georgian
Georgian prose literature (May Subd Geog)
— **To 1500**
Georgian riddles
  USE Riddles, Georgian
Georgian S.S.R.
  UF Georgia (Republic)
    Georgia (Transcaucasia)
— **History**
— — **To 1801**
    NT Didgora Mountain (Georgian
      S.S.R.), Battle of, 1121
— — **1801-1917**
— — **1917-**
— — **Revolution, 1917-1921**
    ₍DK265.8.G4₎
— **Languages**
    NT Imeretian dialect
    Svan language
Georgian short stories
  USE Short stories, Georgian
Georgian silverwork
  USE Silverwork, Georgian
Georgian style (Decoration and ornament)
  USE Decoration and ornament—Georgian
    style

Georgian type
  USE Type and type-founding—Georgian
       type
Georgian wood-carving
  USE Wood-carving, Georgian
Georgians (Transcaucasians)
  (May Subd Geog)
  UF Grusinians
      Ibernians
      Karthveli
  BT Ethnology—Georgian S.S.R.
Georychus
  ₍QL737.R628₎
  BT Bathyergidae
GEOS (Computer operating system)
  BT Operating systems (Computers)
Geoscience
  USE Geology
Geoscience electronics
  USE Electronics in earth sciences
Geoscopaeus
  ₍QL596.S75₎
  BT Staphylinidae
Geospizidae
  USE Fringillidae
Geostationary satellites
  UF Geosynchronous satellites
      Satellites, Geostationary
      Satellites, Geosynchronous
      Satellites, Synchronous
      Synchronous satellites
  BT Artificial satellites in
       telecommunication
  RT Earth—Rotation
  NT Syncom (Communications satellite)
  — **Attitude control systems**
      UF Attitude control systems
          (Astronautics)
  — **Orbital spacing**
      USE Geostationary satellites—Spacing
  — **Spacing**
      UF Geostationary satellites—Orbital
          spacing
          Orbital spacing of geostationary
          satellites
          Spacing of geostationary satellites
Geostrophic wind
  BT Winds
      Winds aloft
Geosynchronous satellites
  USE Geostationary satellites
Geosynclines *(May Subd Geog)*
  ₍QE607₎
  BT Folds (Geology)
      Subsidences (Earth movements)
  — **United States**
      NT Mississippi Embayment
Geosynthetics *(May Subd Geog)*
  ₍TA455.G44₎
  UF Geofabrics
  BT Materials
      Synthetic fabrics
  NT Geogrids
      Geomembranes
      Geotextiles
Geotechnique
  USE Rock mechanics
       Soil mechanics
Geotechnique, Marine
  USE Marine geotechnique
Geotectonics
  USE Geology, Structural
Geotextiles
  ₍TA455.G44₎
  BT Geosynthetics
Geothermal brines *(May Subd Geog)*
  UF Brines, Geothermal
  BT Geothermal resources
      Saline waters

Geothermal-coal hybrid power plants
  (May Subd Geog)
  UF Coal-geothermal hybrid power plants
      Hybrid power plants, Geothermal-coal
      Power plants, Geothermal-coal hybrid
  BT Coal-fired power plants
      Electric power-plants
      Geothermal power plants
Geothermal engineering *(May Subd Geog)*
  BT Chemical engineering
      Electric engineering
      Heat engineering
  NT Geothermal power plants
      Hawaii Geothermal Project
Geothermal leases *(May Subd Geog)*
  UF Geothermal steam leases
  BT Leases
Geothermal power plants *(May Subd Geog)*
  UF Power plants, Geothermal
  BT Electric power-plants
      Geothermal engineering
  NT Geothermal-coal hybrid power plants
Geothermal Project, Hawaii
  USE Hawaii Geothermal Project
Geothermal resources *(May Subd Geog)*
  ₍GB1199.5-GB1199.8₎
  UF Thermal waters
  BT Natural resources
  NT Geothermal brines
      Geysers
      Hot springs
      Springs
  — **Law and legislation** *(May Subd Geog)*
  — **Multiple use**
      UF Multiple use of geothermal
          resources
  — **Hawaii**
      NT Hawaii Geothermal Project
Geothermal steam leases
  USE Geothermal leases
Geothlypis trichas
  USE Maryland yellowthroat
Geotropism
  ₍QH511 (Biology)₎
  ₍QK776 (Botany)₎
  Here are entered works on geotropic movements
in both animals and plants.
  UF Plants, Effect of gravity on
  BT Growth (Plants)
      Irritability
      Plants—Irritability and movements
      Tropisms
  RT Plants, Effect of weightlessness on
Geotrupidae
  USE Scarabaeidae
Geotrygon
  ₍QL696.C63₎
  UF Quail-doves
  BT Columbidae
  NT Geotrygon frenata
Geotrygon frenata
  ₍QL696.C63₎
  UF White-throated quail-dove
  BT Geotrygon
Geotrypidae
  USE Scarabaeidae
Geowebs
  USE Geogrids
Gephyrea
  USE Echiura
       Sipuncula
Gepidae
  ₍DD78.G5₎
  BT Germanic tribes
      Goths
Geradon family *(Not Subd Geog)*
Gerakan Tigapuluh September
  USE Indonesia—History—Coup d'etat, 1965
Gerald family
  USE Jarrell family

Gerald R. Ford mural (Painting)
  USE Collins, Paul. Gerald R. Ford mural
Geraniaceae *(May Subd Geog)*
  ₍QK495.G38₎
  BT Geraniales
  NT Pelargoniums
Geraniales
  ₍QK495.A12₎
  BT Dicotyledons
  NT Erythroxylaceae
      Euphorbiaceae
      Geraniaceae
      Linaceae
      Tropaeolaceae
Geranium collinum
  USE Upland geranium
Geraniums *(May Subd Geog)*
  ₍SB413.G35₎
  UF Garden geraniums
  NT Upland geranium
  — **Varieties**
Geraniums, Garden
  USE Pelargoniums
Gerard family *(Not Subd Geog)*
  UF Garard family
      Garrard family
      Garrod family
      Gerrard family
  RT Garrett family
      Gerardi family
      Girard family
Gerardi family *(Not Subd Geog)*
  UF Gerardy family
  RT Gerard family
Gerardy family
  USE Gerardi family
Gerasa (Ancient city) *(Not Subd Geog)*
  UF Jerash (Ancient city)
  BT Cities and towns, Ruined, extinct, etc.
      —Jordan
      Jordan—Antiquities
Gerasene demoniac (Miracle)
  USE Healing of the Gerasene demoniac
       (Miracle)
Gerbah Island (Tunisia)
  USE Jarbah Island (Tunisia)
Gerber family *(Not Subd Geog)*
  UF Gerberich family
      Gerver family
      Gervers family
  RT Garber family
Gerbera
  ₍QK495.C74 (Botany)₎
  ₍SB413.G36 (Floriculture)₎
  UF African daisy
      Barberton daisy
      Transvaal daisy
  BT Compositae
      Daisies
  — **Diseases and pests** *(May Subd Geog)*
      NT Cyclamen mite
Gerberich family
  USE Gerber family
Gerbils
  ₍QL737.R638₎
  BT Cricetidae
Gerbils as laboratory animals
Gerbils as pets
  ₍SF459.G4₎
Gerde family
  USE Gjerde family
Gere (African people)
  UF Dan (African people)
      Guere (African people)
      Ngere (African people)
      We (Ivory Coast people)
  BT Ethnology—Ivory Coast
      Ethnology—Liberia
Gere (Kru-speaking African people)
  USE Wobe (African people)

Gere language (Kru)
  USE Wobe language
Gere language (Mande)
  USE Dan language
Gerecse Mountains (Hungary)
  (Not Subd Geog)
  BT Mountains—Hungary
Gereme (Ancient city)
  USE Keramos (Ancient city)
Gergovie, Battle of, 52 B.C.
  ₊DC62₊
  BT Gaul—History—Gallic Wars, 58-51
    B.C.
Gerhard family
  USE Gearhart family
Gerhardt family
  USE Gearhart family
Gerhart family
  USE Gearhart family
Gerhartt family
  USE Gearhart family
Geriatric anesthesia
  ₊RD145₊
  BT Anesthesia
    Geriatrics
  — **Complications and sequelae**
Geriatric cardiology *(May Subd Geog)*
  BT Cardiology
Geriatric dentistry
  USE Aged—Dental care
Geriatric dermatology *(May Subd Geog)*
  ₊RL73.A35₊
  BT Dermatology
Geriatric gastroenterology *(May Subd Geog)*
  ₊RC802.4.A34₊
  BT Gastroenterology
Geriatric gynecology *(May Subd Geog)*
  BT Aged women—Diseases
    Gynecology
Geriatric nephrology *(May Subd Geog)*
  BT Nephrology
Geriatric neurology *(May Subd Geog)*
  ₊RC346₊
  BT Geriatrics
    Neurology
  NT Communicative disorders in the aged
Geriatric nursing *(May Subd Geog)*
  ₊RC954₊
  BT Nursing
Geriatric occupational therapy
  USE Occupational therapy for the aged
Geriatric oncology *(May Subd Geog)*
  ₊RC281.A34₊
  UF Aged—Tumors
    Tumors in the aged
  BT Oncology
Geriatric ophthalmology
  ₊RE48.2.A5₊
  BT Ophthalmology
  NT Aged, Blind
    Aged, Visually handicapped
Geriatric orthopedics *(May Subd Geog)*
  ₊RD732.3.A44₊
  BT Aged—Surgery
    Orthopedia
  RT Aged, Physically handicapped
Geriatric otolaryngology *(May Subd Geog)*
  ₊RF47.A35₊
  BT Otolaryngology
  NT Aged, Deaf
Geriatric pathology
  ₊RC953₊
  BT Pathology
Geriatric pharmacology *(May Subd Geog)*
  ₊RC953.7₊
  BT Pharmacology
  NT Geriatric psychopharmacology
    Geriatrics—Formulae, receipts,
      prescriptions
Geriatric physical therapy
  USE Physical therapy for the aged

Geriatric psychiatry *(May Subd Geog)*
  ₊RC451.4.A5₊
  UF Aged—Psychiatric care
    Gerontopsychiatry
    Psychiatry, Geriatric
    Psychogeriatrics
  BT Psychiatry
  RT Aged—Mental health
  NT Cognition disorders in the aged
    Depression in the aged
    Schizophrenia in the aged
  — **Documentation**
    NT AGP System
Geriatric psychopharmacology
  ₊RC451.4.A5₊
  BT Geriatric pharmacology
    Psychopharmacology
Geriatric recreational therapy
  USE Recreational therapy for the aged
Geriatric surgery
  USE Aged—Surgery
Geriatric urology *(May Subd Geog)*
  BT Urology
Geriatrics *(May Subd Geog)*
  ₊RC952-RC954.6₊
  BT Medicine
  RT Gerontology
  SA *headings beginning with the word*
    Geriatric
  NT Aged—Diseases
    Aged—Health and hygiene
    Aged—Medical care
    Aged—Wounds and injuries
    Aged women—Surgery
    Geriatric anesthesia
    Geriatric neurology
    Veterinary geriatrics
  — **Diagnosis**
    ₊RC953₊
  — **Formulae, receipts, prescriptions**
    ₊RC953.7₊
    BT Geriatric pharmacology
  — **Law and legislation** *(May Subd Geog)*
    BT Medical laws and legislation
  — **Psychological aspects**
    BT Medicine and psychology
Gering language
  USE Anem language
Gerisa, Tel (Israel)
  USE Gerisah Site (Israel)
Gerisah, Tel- (Israel)
  USE Gerisah Site (Israel)
Gerisah Site (Israel) *(Not Subd Geog)*
  UF Gerisa, Tel (Israel)
    Gerisah, Tel- (Israel)
    Jarishe, Tell (Israel)
    Jerishe, Tell (Israel)
    Tel Gerisa (Israel)
    Tel-Gerisah (Israel)
    Tell Jarishe (Israel)
    Tell Jerishe (Israel)
  BT Israel—Antiquities
Gerison family
  USE Garrison family
Gerlach family *(Not Subd Geog)*
  UF Carlock family
    Garlach family
    Garlech family
    Garlic family
    Garlick family
    Garlock family
    Gerlich family
Gerlich family
  USE Gerlach family
Germ, Wheat
  USE Wheat germ
Germ cells
  ₊QL964₊
  UF Reproductive cells
    Sex cells

  BT Cells
    Embryology
    Germplasm resources
    Heredity
  RT Oogenesis
    Spermatogenesis
  NT Ovum
    Spermatozoa
Germ-free life
  USE Germfree life
Germ letters
  USE Bijas
Germ line theory
  USE Antibody diversity
Germ plasm resources
  USE Germplasm resources
Germ theory
  USE Life—Origin
    Spontaneous generation
Germ theory of disease
  ₊RB214₊
  UF Disease germs
    Germs
    Microbes
  BT Communicable diseases
    Diseases—Causes and theories of
      causation
  RT Bacteriology
  NT Air—Microbiology
    Bacteria, Pathogenic
Germ warfare
  USE Biological warfare
Germain family
  USE German family
Germaine family
  USE German family
German (Dance)
  ₊GV1757₊
  UF Cotillion
German abbreviations
  USE Abbreviations, German
German adventure stories
  USE Adventure stories, German
German aesthetics
  USE Aesthetics, German
German agricultural assistance
  USE Agricultural assistance, German
German almanacs
  USE Almanacs, German
German altarpieces
  USE Altarpieces, German
German-American literature
  (May Subd Geog)
  ₊PT3900-PT3912 (History)₊
  ₊PT3913-PT3916 (Collections)₊
  BT American literature
    German literature
    United States—Literatures
  NT Literature, Comparative—German and
    American
  — **Catholic authors**
German-American newspapers
  (May Subd Geog)
  ₊PN4885.G3₊
  BT American newspapers
    German newspapers
  NT Austrian-American newspapers
German-American periodicals
  BT American periodicals
    German periodicals
German-American poetry
  ₊PT3910 (History)₊
  ₊PT3914 (Collections)₊
  BT American poetry
    German poetry
German-American wit and humor
  BT American wit and humor
    German wit and humor
German Americans *(May Subd Geog)*
  UF German Americans—United States

BT Ethnology—United States
    Germans—United States
SA *subdivision* German Americans *under*
    individual wars, e.g. World War,
    1939-1945—German Americans
  — Missouri
    NT Saxon emigration, 1838-1839
  — Pennsylvania
    NT Pennsylvania Dutch
  — United States
    USE German Americans
German architecture
  USE Architecture, German
German art
  USE Art, German
German art objects
  USE Art objects, German
German arts
  USE Arts, German
German atlases
  USE Atlases, German
German-Austrian Monetary Union of 1857
  USE Austrian-German Monetary Union of
    1857
German-Austrian Pact, July 1936
  [DB97]
  UF Austrian-German Pact, July 1936
  BT Austria—Foreign relations—Germany
    Austria—History—1918-1938
    Germany—Foreign relations—Austria
    Germany—History—1933-1945
German authors
  USE Authors, German
German autobiographical fiction
  USE Autobiographical fiction, German
German ballads
  USE Ballads, German
German banks and banking
  USE Banks and banking, German
German Baptist Brethren
  USE Church of the Brethren
German Baptist Meeting House Cemetery
  (Washington, York County, Pa.)
  USE Bermudian Church of the Brethren
    Cemetery (Washington, York
    County, Pa.)
German Bible stories
  USE Bible stories, German
German Bight (Germany)
  USE Helgoland Bight (Germany)
German block-books
  USE Block-books, German
German-Bohemian literature
  USE German literature—Czechoslovakia—
    Bohemia
German book-plates
  USE Book-plates, German
German-British naval agreement, 1935
  USE Anglo-German naval agreement, 1935
German bronze sculpture
  USE Bronze sculpture, German
German bronzes
  USE Bronzes, German
German calligraphy
  USE Calligraphy, German
German camomile
  USE Matricaria chamomilla
German Catholicism
  [BX4740]
  Here are entered works on an antipapal, national-
  istic movement among Catholics in Germany started
  by J. Ronge and J. Czerski in 1844.
  UF Deutschkatholizismus
    German Catholics (Sect)
  BT Catholic Church—Germany—History
    —19th century
German Catholics (Sect)
  USE German Catholicism
German chamaedrys
  USE Wall germander

German chamomile
  USE Matricaria chamomilla
German children's literature
  USE Children's literature, German
German children's periodicals
  USE Children's periodicals, German
German children's plays
  USE Children's plays, German
German children's poetry
  USE Children's poetry, German
German children's stories
  USE Children's stories, German
German Christian drama
  USE Christian drama, German
German Christian literature
  USE Christian literature, German
German-Christian movement
  [BR856]
  UF German-Christians (Movement)
  BT Church and state—Germany—History
    —1933-1945
    Germany—Church history—1933-1945
    National socialism
German Christian poetry
  USE Christian poetry, German
German-Christians (Movement)
  USE German-Christian movement
German clergymen's writings
  USE Clergymen's writings, German
German cockroach
  USE Blattella germanica
German collage
  USE Collage, German
German college and school drama
  USE College and school drama, German
German concrete poetry
  USE Concrete poetry, German
German cookery
  USE Cookery, German
German corporations
  USE Corporations, German
German court epic
  USE Court epic, German
German Day celebrations
  BT Germans—Foreign countries
German Democratic Republic
  USE Germany (East)
German detective stories
  USE Detective and mystery stories, German
German dialect literature
  USE Dialect literature, German
German diaries *(May Subd Geog)*
  BT Diaries
German didactic literature
  USE Didactic literature, German
German drama *(May Subd Geog)*
  [PT605-PT709 (History)]
  [PT1251-PT1299 (Collections)]
  BT Drama
  NT Carnival plays
    Children's plays, German
    Christian drama, German
    College and school drama, German
    Folk-drama, German
    Historical drama, German
    Jesuit drama, German
    Political plays, German
    Radio plays, German
    Singspiel
  — To 1500
    [PT621 (History)]
    [PT1435-PT1477 (Collections)]
  — Early modern, 1500-1700
    [PT636-8 (History, PT631-3)]
    [PT1263-4 (Collections)]
  — 18th century
    [PT636-PT643 (History)]
    [PT1265 (Collections)]
  — 19th century
    [PT651-PT663 (History)]
    [PT1266 (Collections)]

  — 20th century
    [PT666-PT668 (History)]
    [PT1268 (Collections)]
  — Austrian authors
    [PT3821 (History)]
    [PT3826.D8 (Collections)]
    UF Austrian drama (German)
  — Microcard catalogs
  — Stories, plots, etc.
    [PT626]
  — Swiss authors
    USE Swiss drama (German)
German drama (Comedy)
  [PT676 (History)]
  [PT1275-PT1277 (Collections)]
  NT Carnival plays
German drama (Tragedy)
  [PT671 (History)]
  [PT1271-PT1273 (Collections)]
German drawing
  USE Drawing, German
German East Africa
  Here are entered works on the former German
  colony whose territory corresponds to present-day
  Rwanda, Burundi, the continental portion of Tan-
  zania, and a small section of Mozambique. Works on
  this territory for the period after 1919 when the colo-
  ny ceased to exist are entered under one or more of
  the names, as appropriate, of the countries now occu-
  pying the territory.
  UF Africa, German East
German elegiac poetry
  USE Elegiac poetry, German
German encyclopedias and dictionaries
  USE Encyclopedias and dictionaries,
    German
German engraving
  USE Engraving, German
German epic literature
  USE Epic literature, German
German epigrams
  USE Epigrams, German
German epistolary poetry
  USE Epistolary poetry, German
German erotic literature
  USE Erotic literature, German
German erotic poetry
  USE Erotic poetry, German
German espionage
  USE Espionage, German
German essays *(May Subd Geog)*
  [PT831 (History)]
  [PT1354 (Collections)]
  Here are entered collections of essays by several
  authors.
German etching
  USE Etching, German
German exchange of persons programs
  USE Exchange of persons programs,
    German
German Expedition to China, 1900-1901
  [DS771.5]
German fables
  USE Fables, German
German family *(Not Subd Geog)*
  UF Germain family
    Germaine family
    Germann family
    Germen family
  RT Garman family
    Garmann family
German fantastic fiction
  USE Fantastic fiction, German
German farces
  [PT696 (History)]
  [PT1283.F2 (Collections)]
  BT Farces
German Federal Republic
  USE Germany (West)
German fiction *(May Subd Geog)*
  [PT741-PT772 (History)]
  [PT1321-PT1340 (Collections)]

German fiction *(Continued)*
　NT　Adventure stories, German
　　　Autobiographical fiction, German
　　　Bildungsroman
　　　Children's stories, German
　　　Detective and mystery stories, German
　　　Dime novels, German
　　　Fantastic fiction, German
　　　Historical fiction, German
　　　Love stories, German
　　　Pastoral fiction, German
　　　Picaresque literature, German
　　　Psychological fiction, German
　　　Science fiction, German
　— Middle High German, 1050-1500
　　　［PT230］
　— Early modern, 1500-1700
　　　［PT753-PT756 (History)］
　　　［PT1313-PT1314 (Collections)］
　— 18th century
　　　［PT759 (History)］
　　　［PT1315 (Collections)］
　— 19th century
　　　［PT763-PT771 (History)］
　　　［PT1332 (Collections)］
　— 20th century
　　　［PT772 (History)］
　　　［PT1334 (Collections)］
　— Austrian authors
　　　［PT3822 (History)］
　　　［PT3826 (Collections)］
　　　UF　Austrian fiction (German)
　　　NT　Children's stories, German—
　　　　　Austrian authors
　— Swiss authors
　　　USE　Swiss fiction (German)
German film posters
　USE　Film posters, German
German folk-drama
　USE　Folk-drama, German
German folk literature
　USE　Folk literature, German
German folk poetry
　USE　Folk poetry, German
German folk-songs
　USE　Folk-songs, German
German genre painting
　USE　Genre painting, German
German Grand Prix Race
　UF　Grand Prix, German
　BT　Automobile racing
　　　Grand Prix racing
German guided missile bases
　USE　Guided missile bases, German
German haiku
　USE　Haiku, German
German Hebrew
　USE　Yiddish language
German historical drama
　USE　Historical drama, German
German historical fiction
　USE　Historical fiction, German
German hunt terrier
　　［SF429.G36］
　UF　Hunt terrier, German
　BT　Dog breeds
　　　Terriers
German hymns
　USE　Hymns, German
German idealism
　USE　Idealism, German
German illumination of books and manuscripts
　USE　Illumination of books and manuscripts,
　　　German
German imprints *(May Subd Geog)*
German investments
　USE　Investments, German
German Jesuit drama
　USE　Jesuit drama, German
German Jewish religious poetry
　USE　Jewish religious poetry, German

German Jews
　USE　Jews, German
German laboring class writings
　USE　Laboring class writings, German
German landscape painting
　USE　Landscape painting, German
German landscape prints
　USE　Landscape prints, German
German language *(May Subd Geog)*
　　［PF3001-5999］
　BT　Germanic languages
　NT　Low German language
　— Old High German, 750-1050
　　　［PF3801-3991］
　　　UF　Old High German language
　— — Etymology
　　　　NT　Balder (The word)
　　　　　　Frô (The word)
　　　　　　Hêrro (The word)
　　　　　　Milti (The word)
　　　　　　Truhtin (The word)
　— Middle High German, 1050-1500
　　　［PF4043-4350］
　　　UF　Middle High German language
　— — Etymology
　　　　NT　Êre (The word)
　　　　　　Scande (The word)
　　　　　　Tumpheit (The word)
　　　　　　Wellen (The Middle High
　　　　　　　German word)
　— Early modern, 1500-1700
　　　［PF4501-4596］
　— — Foreign words and phrases
　— — — French
　　　　　USE　German language—Early
　　　　　　modern, 1500-1700—
　　　　　　Gallicisms
　— — Gallicisms
　　　　UF　German language—Early
　　　　　modern, 1500-1700—Foreign
　　　　　words and phrases—French
　— Abbreviations
　　　USE　Abbreviations, German
　— Business German
　　　［HF5728.G3 (Correspondence)］
　　　［PF3120.C7］
　— Dialects
　　　NT　Pidgin German
　— Dictionaries
　　　NT　Picture dictionaries, German
　— Etymology
　　　NT　Auf (The German word)
　　　　　Bauer (The German word)
　　　　　Bleiben (The German word)
　　　　　Bocksbeutel (The German word)
　　　　　Deutsch (The German word)
　　　　　Doch (The German word)
　　　　　Eigentlich (The German word)
　　　　　Erlösen (The German word)
　　　　　Gemüt (The German word)
　　　　　Geschehen (The German word)
　　　　　Grab (The German word)
　　　　　Grabhügel (The German word)
　　　　　Hügel (The German word)
　　　　　Intellektueller (The German word)
　　　　　Ja (The German word)
　　　　　Klassiker (The German word)
　　　　　Laune (The German word)
　　　　　Lernen (The German word)
　　　　　Liberal (The German word)
　　　　　Machen (The German word)
　　　　　Marotte (The German word)
　　　　　Mâze (The German word)
　　　　　Pumpernickel (The German word)
　　　　　Schon (The German word)
　　　　　Sehen (The German word)
　　　　　Sein (The German word)
　　　　　Sollen (The German word)
　　　　　Stube (The German word)
　　　　　Tick (The German word)
　　　　　Tun (The German word)

　　　　　Überhaupt (The German word)
　　　　　Wandel (The German word)
　— Names
　　　USE　Names, German
　— Orthography and spelling
　— Slang
　　　NT　Pidgin German
German letter-writing
　USE　Letter-writing, German
German letters
　　［PT811 (History)］
　　［PT1348-PT1352 (Collections)］
German literature *(May Subd Geog)*
　　［PT1-PT951 (History)］
　　［PT1100-PT1485 (Collections)］
　RT　Authors, German
　NT　Austrian literature
　　　Children's literature, German
　　　Christian literature, German
　　　Dialect literature, German
　　　Didactic literature, German
　　　Epic literature, German
　　　Erotic literature, German
　　　German-American literature
　　　Laboring class writings, German
　　　Low German literature
　　　Pastoral literature, German
　　　Prisoners' writings, German
　　　Revolutionary literature, German
　　　Swiss literature
　　　Young adult literature, German
　　　Youths' writings, German
　— Old High German, 750-1050
　　　［PF3985-PF3991 (Collections)］
　　　［PT183 (History)］
　　　UF　German poetry—Old High
　　　　　German, 750-1050
　　　　　Old High German literature
　— Middle High German, 1050-1500
　　　［PT175-PT230 (History)］
　　　［PT1375-PT1479 (Collections)］
　　　UF　Middle High German literature
　— Early modern, 1500-1700
　　　［PT238-PT281 (History)］
　　　［PT1121-PT1126 (Collections)］
　— 18th century
　　　［PT1131 (Collections)］
　— — History and criticism
　　　　［PT285-321］
　　　　NT　Sturm und Drang movement
　— 19th century
　　　［PT1136 (Collections)］
　— — History and criticism
　　　　［PT341-395］
　　　　RT　Young Germany
　　　　NT　Biedermeier
　— 20th century
　　　［PT401-PT403 (History)］
　　　［PT1141 (Collections)］
　— Austrian authors
　　　［PT3810-PT3822 (History)］
　　　［PT3823-PT3829 (Collections)］
　　　UF　Austrian literature (German)
　— Bibliography
　　　［Z2221-2249］
　— — Early
　　　　［Z2222］
　　　　［Z2232］
　— Catholic authors
　　　［PT89］
　　　［PT1109.C3］
　— Film adaptations
　　　USE　German literature—Film and
　　　　　video adaptations
　— Film and video adaptations
　　　UF　German literature—Film
　　　　　adaptations
　— Jewish authors
　　　UF　Jewish literature (German)
　— Swiss authors
　　　USE　Swiss literature (German)

— Czechoslovakia
— — Bohemia
　UF　German-Bohemian literature
— Foreign countries
　[PT3808-3809]
　UF　German literature in foreign
　　　countries
— Germany
— — Bavaria
　UF　Bavarian literature
— — Swabia
　UF　Swabian literature
— Germany (East)
　UF　East German literature
— Germany, Northern
　BT　Low German literature
— Switzerland
　BT　Swiss literature
German literature (English)
　USE　English literature—German authors
German literature in foreign countries
　USE　German literature—Foreign countries
German lithography
　USE　Lithography, German
German loans
　USE　Loans, German
German love poetry
　USE　Love poetry, German
German love stories
　USE　Love stories, German
German lullabies
　USE　Lullabies, German
German Lutherans
　USE　Lutherans, German
German manuscripts
　USE　Manuscripts, German
German marble sculpture
　USE　Marble sculpture, German
German marine art
　USE　Marine art, German
German marine painting
　USE　Marine painting, German
German mathematics
　USE　Mathematics, German
German maxims
　USE　Maxims, German
German measles
　USE　Rubella
German mercenaries
　[DD102.7]
　UF　Landsknechte
　BT　Mercenary troops
　NT　Hanoverian mercenaries
　　　Hessian mercenaries
　　　United States—History—Revolution,
　　　　1775-1783—German mercenaries
German metal sculpture
　USE　Metal sculpture, German
German Methodists
　USE　Methodists, German
German missions
　USE　Missions, German
German mural painting and decoration
　USE　Mural painting and decoration,
　　　German
German mystery stories
　USE　Detective and mystery stories, German
German names
　USE　Names, German
German narrative poetry
　USE　Narrative poetry, German
German national characteristics
　USE　National characteristics, German
German newspapers　(May Subd Geog)
　[PN5201-PN5219 (History)]
　NT　Austrian newspapers
　　　German-American newspapers
　　　Swiss newspapers
— Taxation
　BT　Newspapers—Taxation
— Foreign countries

— Poland
　Duplicate entry is made under Polish newspa-
　pers (German)
German novelists
　USE　Novelists, German
German nursery rhymes
　USE　Nursery rhymes, German
German occupation, Albania, 1943-1944
　USE　Albania—History—Axis occupation,
　　　1939-1944
German occupation of Denmark, 1940-1945
　USE　Denmark—History—German
　　　occupation, 1940-1945
German occupation of Netherlands, 1940-1945
　USE　Netherlands—History—German
　　　occupation, 1940-1945
German occupation of Norway, 1940-1945
　USE　Norway—History—German
　　　occupation, 1940-1945
German orations
　USE　Speeches, addresses, etc., German
German paleography
　USE　Paleography, German
German panel painting
　USE　Panel painting, German
German parodies
　USE　Parodies, German
German part-songs
　USE　Part-songs, German
German pastel drawing
　USE　Pastel drawing, German
German pastoral fiction
　USE　Pastoral fiction, German
German pastoral literature
　USE　Pastoral literature, German
German penmanship
　USE　Penmanship, German
German periodicals　(May Subd Geog)
　[PN5201-PN5220 (History)]
　NT　Austrian periodicals
　　　Children's periodicals, German
　　　German-American periodicals
　　　Silesian periodicals
　　　Swiss periodicals
　　　Women's periodicals, German
— Foreign countries
German philology
　[PF3001-3095]
　BT　Germanic philology
— Middle High German, 1050-1500
German picaresque literature
　USE　Picaresque literature, German
German picture dictionaries
　USE　Picture dictionaries, German
German poetry　(May Subd Geog)
　[PT500-PT597 (History)]
　[PT1151-PT1241 (Collections)]
　NT　Children's poetry, German
　　　Christian poetry, German
　　　Concrete poetry, German
　　　Elegiac poetry, German
　　　Epistolary poetry, German
　　　Erotic poetry, German
　　　Folk poetry, German
　　　German-American poetry
　　　Haiku, German
　　　Jewish religious poetry, German
　　　Love poetry, German
　　　Narrative poetry, German
　　　Political poetry, German
　　　Prose poems, German
　　　Protest poetry, German
　　　Renga, German
　　　Sonnets, German
　　　Verse satire, German
　　　Waka, German
　　　War poetry, German
— Old High German, 750-1050
　USE　German literature—Old High
　　　German, 750-1050
— Middle High German, 1050-1500

　[PT175-PT227 (History)]
　[PT1391-PT1429 (Collections)]
　NT　Court epic, German
— Early modern, 1500-1700
　[PT525-PT531 (History)]
　[PT1163-PT1165 (Collections)]
— 18th century
　[PT533-PT535 (History)]
　[PT1167-PT1169 (Collections)]
— 19th century
　[PT541-PT547 (History)]
　[PT1171-PT1173 (Collections)]
— 20th century
　[PT551-PT553 (History)]
　[PT1174-PT1175 (Collections)]
— Austrian authors
　[PT3820 (History)]
　[PT3824 (Collections)]
　Duplicate entry is made under Austrian poe-
　try (German)
— Czech authors
　[PT3836]
　UF　Czech poetry (German)
— Polish authors
　UF　Polish poetry (German)
— Swiss authors
　USE　Swiss poetry (German)
German pointer, Shorthaired
　USE　German shorthaired pointer
German pointer, Wirehaired
　USE　German wirehaired pointers
German police dogs
　USE　German shepherd dogs
German-Polish pact, 1934
　USE　Polish-German pact, 1934
German political plays
　USE　Political plays, German
German political poetry
　USE　Political poetry, German
German political posters
　USE　Political posters, German
German political satire
　USE　Political satire, German
German portrait painting
　USE　Portrait painting, German
German portraits
　USE　Portraits, German
German posters
　USE　Posters, German
German prints
　USE　Prints, German
German prisoners' writings
　USE　Prisoners' writings, German
German propaganda
　USE　Propaganda, German
German property　(May Subd Geog)
German prose literature　(May Subd Geog)
　[PT711-PT871 (History)]
　[PT1301-PT1360 (Collections)]
　NT　Prose poems, German
— Swiss authors
　USE　Swiss prose literature (German)
German prose poems
　USE　Prose poems, German
German protest poetry
　USE　Protest poetry, German
German proverbs
　USE　Proverbs, German
German psychological fiction
　USE　Psychological fiction, German
German question (1949-　　)
　USE　German reunification question (1949-
　　　)
German quotations
　USE　Quotations, German
German radio plays
　USE　Radio plays, German
German rampion
　USE　Evening primrose
German rearmament
　USE　Germany—Defenses

German reference books
  USE Reference books, German
German Reformed Church (U.S.)
  USE Reformed Church in the United States
German renga
  USE Renga, German
German resistance movement
  USE Anti-Nazi movement
German reunification question (1949-   )
  [DD257.25]
  UF German question (1949-   )
     German unification question (1949-
)
     Reunification of Germany, Proposed
        (1949-   )
     Unification of Germany, Proposed
        (1949-   )
  BT Germany—History—Allied
        occupation, 1945-
     World War, 1939-1945—Peace
  NT Berlin question (1945-   )
     Rapacki plan
**German reunification question (1949-   ) in
motion pictures**
  BT Moving-pictures
German revolutionary literature
  USE Revolutionary literature, German
German riddles
  USE Riddles, German
German Russians
  USE Russian Germans
German saltpeter
  USE Ammonium nitrate
German satire
  USE Satire, German
German schools
  USE Schools—Germany
     Schools, German
German science fiction
  USE Science fiction, German
German sculpture
  USE Sculpture, German
German self-portraits
  USE Self-portraits, German
German shepherd dogs
  [SF429.G37]
  UF Alsatian wolf dogs
     German police dogs
     Police dogs (Breed)
  RT White German shepherd dog
German short-haired pointer
  USE German shorthaired pointer
German shorthaired pointer
  [SF429.G4]
  UF German pointer, Shorthaired
     German short-haired pointer
     Short-haired pointer, German
     Shorthaired pointer, German
  BT Dog breeds
     Pointers (Dogs)
German silver
  USE Nickel silver
German songs
  USE Songs, German
German sonnets
  USE Sonnets, German
German Southwest Africa
  USE Namibia
German-speaking Europe
  USE Europe, German-speaking
German-speaking Switzerland
  USE Switzerland, German-speaking
German speeches
  USE Speeches, addresses, etc., German
German students *(May Subd Geog)*
  BT Students
  NT Prussian students
German subject headings
  USE Subject headings, German
German technical assistance
  USE Technical assistance, German

German theatrical posters
  USE Theatrical posters, German
German unification question (1949-   )
  USE German reunification question (1949-
)
German verse satire
  USE Verse satire, German
German waka
  USE Waka, German
German war poetry
  USE War poetry, German
German Warehouse (Richland Center, Wis.)
  USE A.D. German Warehouse (Richland
        Center, Wis.)
German watercolor painting
  USE Watercolor painting, German
German West Africa
  USE Cameroon
German wirehaired pointers
  [SF429.G43]
  UF German pointer, Wirehaired
     Wire-haired pointer, German
     Wirehaired pointer, German
  BT Pointers (Dogs)
German wit and humor *(May Subd Geog)*
  [PN6193-PN6195 (Collections)]
  [PT851 (History)]
  Here are entered collections from several authors
  and individual authors who have not written in other
  literary forms.
  NT Bavarian wit and humor
     German-American wit and humor
     Low German wit and humor
     Political satire, German
     Schnaderhüpfel
     Silesian wit and humor
     Swabian wit and humor
German wit and humor, Pictorial
  [NC1500-1509]
German women's periodicals
  USE Women's periodicals, German
German young adult literature
  USE Young adult literature, German
German youths' writings
  USE Youths' writings, German
Germanasca River (Italy)
  UF Torrente Germanasca (Italy)
  BT Rivers—Italy
Germander *(May Subd Geog)*
  [QK495.L25 (Botany)]
  UF Teucrium
  BT Lamiaceae
  NT Cat thyme
     Teucrium oxylepis
     Wall germander
Germander, Chamaedrys
  USE Wall germander
Germander, Common
  USE Wall germander
Germander, Wall
  USE Wall germander
Germania Building (Milwaukee, Wis.)
  BT Office buildings—Wisconsin
Germanic antiquities
  [DD51-55]
  UF Antiquities, Germanic
     Germanic tribes—Antiquities
  BT Antiquities
  SA *subdivision* Antiquities, Germanic
        *under names of countries, cities,
        etc.*
Germanic architecture
  USE Architecture, Germanic
Germanic art
  USE Art, Germanic
Germanic art metal-work
  USE Art metal-work, Germanic
Germanic art objects
  USE Art objects, Germanic
Germanic arts
  USE Arts, Germanic

Germanic ballads
  USE Ballads, Germanic
Germanic calendar
  USE Calendar, Germanic
Germanic civilization
  USE Civilization, Germanic
Germanic cults *(May Subd Geog)*
  BT Cults
Germanic decoration and ornament
  USE Decoration and ornament, Germanic
Germanic decorative arts
  USE Decorative arts, Germanic
Germanic fiction
  [PN836 (History and criticism)]
Germanic gods
  USE Gods, Germanic
Germanic invasions of Rome
  USE Rome—History—Germanic Invasions,
        3d-6th centuries
Germanic jewelry
  USE Jewelry, Germanic
Germanic languages
  [PD-PF]
  UF Teutonic languages
  BT Indo-European languages
  NT Danish language
     Dutch language
     English language
     English language—Old English, ca.
        450-1100
     Friesian language
     German language
     Germanic philology
     Gothic language
     Low German language
     Norwegian language
     Scandinavian languages
     Scots language
     Swedish language
  — History
     NT Proto-Germanic language
  — Names
     USE Names, Germanic
  — Phonology
     UF Verner's law
Germanic law
  USE Law, Germanic
Germanic literature
  [PN821-840]
  Here are entered chiefly treatises on the early
  literature of the Germanic tribes, Goths, Anglo-Sax-
  ons, Scandinavians, etc.
  SA *names of the various literatures which
        form the Germanic group, e.g.*
        Dutch literature, English literature,
        Swedish literature
Germanic mythology
  USE Mythology, Germanic
Germanic names
  USE Names, Germanic
Germanic philology
  [PD1-71]
  BT Germanic languages
  SA *names of various languages and
        literatures which form the Germanic
        group, i.e.* Danish, Dutch, English,
        Friesian, Gothic, Icelandic and Old
        Norse, Low German, Norwegian,
        Swedish
  NT Dutch philology
     English philology
     Friesian philology
     German philology
     Scandinavian philology
Germanic poetry
  [PN834]
Germanic tribes *(May Subd Geog)*
  [GN585.G4 (Ethnography)]
  [JC41 (Political institutions, JC29)]

1514

BT Germany—History—To 843
    Indo-Europeans
    Migrations of nations
    Teutonic race
RT Goths
NT Alemanni
    Bajuwarii
    Bastarnae
    Batavians
    Bavarians
    Caninefates
    Chauci (Germanic people)
    Cimbri
    Franks
    Gepidae
    Jutes
    Lygii
    Marcomanni
    Missions—Germanic tribes
    Quadi
    Rome—History—Germanic Invasions,
      3d-6th centuries
    Saxons
    Sithones
    Suevi
    Swabians
    Tervingi
    Ubii
    Vandals
    Visi
— Agriculture
    USE Agriculture—Germanic tribes
— Antiquities
    USE Germanic antiquities
— Civilization
    USE Civilization, Germanic
— **History, Military**
— **Religion**
    [BL830-875]
    NT Irminsul
      Mythology, Germanic
      Mythology, Norse
      Salvation (Germanic religion)
— Weaving
    USE Weaving—Germanic tribes
Germanic women
    USE Women, Germanic
Germanides
    BT Germanium compounds
Germanists *(May Subd Geog)*
    BT Philologists
Germanium
    [QD181.G5]
    NT Germanium compounds
— **Electric properties**
— **Isotopes**
    UF Germanium isotopes
      Isotopic germanium
— **Quenching**
    UF Quenching of germanium
    BT Cooling
      Metals—Heat treatment
— **Spectra**
Germanium alloys
    BT Germanium compounds
    NT Silver-germanium alloys
Germanium compounds
    BT Germanium
    NT Germanides
      Germanium alloys
Germanium crystals
— **Electric properties**
— **Magnetic properties**
Germanium detectors
    USE Germanium diodes
Germanium diodes
    [TK6565.V3 (Radio)]
    [TK7872.V3]
    UF Germanium detectors

BT Crystals
    Diodes
    Electron tubes
    Tunnel diodes
Germanium isotopes
    USE Germanium—Isotopes
Germanium organic compounds
    USE Organogermanium compounds
Germanium-silver alloys
    USE Silver-germanium alloys
Germanization
    BT Assimilation (Sociology)
      Civics
Germann family
    USE German family
Germanophone Europe
    USE Europe, German-speaking
Germanophone Switzerland
    USE Switzerland, German-speaking
Germans *(May Subd Geog)*
    BT Ethnology—Germany
    NT Hessians
      Missions to Germans
      Russian Germans
— **Brazil**
— **Foreign countries**
    NT German Day celebrations
— **Soviet Union**
    Here are entered works on Germans in the
    Soviet Union. Works on emigrants from the Ger-
    man-speaking colonies in the Soviet Union estab-
    lished in the 18th and early 19th centuries along
    the Volga River and the Black Sea are entered
    under Russian Germans.
    BT Ethnology—Soviet Union
— **United States**
    NT German Americans
Germans in literature
Germantown, Battle of, 1777
    [E241.G3]
    BT Pennsylvania—History—Revolution,
      1775-1783
      United States—History—Revolution,
      1775-1783—Campaigns
Germany
    Here are entered works on Germany for the pre-
    1949 period, the Territories under Allied Occupa-
    tion, and East Germany and West Germany, collec-
    tively, for the post-1949 period.
    NT Germany (East)
      Germany (West)
— **Antiquities, Roman**
— **Armed Forces**
— — **Medals, badges, decorations, etc.**
    NT Orden Pour le Mérite
— **Capital and capitol**
    NT Reichstagsgebäude (Berlin,
      Germany)
— **Church history**
— — **To 843**
— — **Middle Ages, 843-1517**
    NT Stedingers
— — **16th century**
— — **17th century**
— — **18th century**
— — **19th century**
    NT Gemeinschaftsbewegung
— — **20th century**
    NT Gemeinschaftsbewegung
— — **1933-1945**
    NT German-Christian movement
— — **1945-**
    NT Church and state—Germany—
      History—1945-
— **Civilization**
    NT Art, British—German influences
      Art, Danish—German influences
      Art, English—German influences
      Art, French—German influences
      Art, Italian—German influences
      Art, Russian—German influences
      Art, Ukrainian—German influences

      Arts, Dutch—German influences
      Brazil—Civilization—German
        influences
      English fiction—German influences
      English literature—German
        influences
      France—Civilization—German
        influences
      Italy—Civilization—German
        influences
      Medicine—Netherlands—German
        influences
      Medicine—United States—German
        influences
      Painting, American—German
        influences
      United States—Civilization—
        German influences
— — **French influences**
    BT France—Civilization
— — **Indic influences**
    BT India—Civilization
— — **Italian influences**
    BT Italy—Civilization
— — **Jewish influences**
    BT Jews—Civilization
— **Constitutional history**
    NT Mediatized states
— **Defenses**
    UF German rearmament
      Germany—Rearmament
— **Denazification**
    USE Denazification
— **Description and travel**
— — **1919-1944**
— — **1945-**
— **Economic conditions**
— — **19th century**
— — **1888-1918**
    [HC285]
— — **20th century**
— — **1918-1945**
— — **1945-**
— **Economic policy**
— — **1888-1918**
    [HC285]
— — **1918-1933**
    [HC286.3]
— — **1933-1945**
— — **1945-**
— **Emigration and immigration**
— — **History**
— — — **1933-1945**
— **Foreign relations** *(May Subd Geog)*
— — **To 1517**
— — **1517-1648**
— — **1648-1740**
— — **1789-1900**
— — **1848-1870**
— — **1871-**
— — **1871-1888**
— — **1871-1918**
— — **1888-1918**
— — **20th century**
— — **1918-**
— — **1918-1933**
— — **1933-1945**
— — **1945-**
— — **Austria**
    NT German-Austrian Pact, July
      1936
— — **France**
    NT Agadir Incident, 1911
— **General Strike, 1920**
    USE General Strike, Germany, 1920
— **History**
    [DD]
— — **To 843**
    NT Franks
      Germanic tribes
      Marcomannic War, 167-180

— — Modern period, 1517-
— Social conditions
— — 18th century
— — 1871-1918
— — 1918-1933
— — 1933-1945
— Social life and customs
— — 20th century
Germany. Reichstag
— **Dissolution**
Germany (Democratic Republic, 1949-)
USE Germany (East)
Germany (East)
Here are entered works on the Democratic Republic established in 1949, and works on the eastern part of the former jurisdiction, Germany.
UF East Germany
Eastern Germany
German Democratic Republic
Germany (Democratic Republic, 1949-)
Germany (Territory under Allied occupation, 1945-1955)
Germany, Democratic Republic of
Germany, East
Germany, Eastern
BT Germany
— **Antiquities** *(Not Subd Geog)*
NT Gommerstedt Site (Germany)
Oelknitz Site (Germany)
— **Boundaries**
— — **Poland**
NT Oder-Neisse Line (Germany and Poland)
— **History**
— — **Uprising, 1953 (June)**
BT Germany—History—Allied occupation, 1945-
Germany—Politics and government—1945-
Germany (Federal Republic, 1949-)
USE Germany (West)
Germany (Territory under Allied occupation, 1945-1955)
USE Germany (East)
Germany (West)
Germany (West)
Here are entered works on the Federal Republic established in 1949, and works on the western part of the former jurisdiction, Germany.
UF German Federal Republic
Germany (Federal Republic, 1949-)
Germany (Territory under Allied occupation, 1945-1955)
Germany, Federal Republic of
Germany, West
Germany, Western
West Germany
Western Germany
BT Germany
NT Ruhr (Germany : Region)
— **Antiquities**
NT Bilzingsleben Site (Germany)
Burgerroth Site (Germany)
Feddersen Wierde Site (Germany)
Grosse Grotte (Germany)
Hascherkeller Site (Germany)
Heuneburg Site (Germany)
Liebenau Site (Germany)
Schernau Site (Germany)
Speckberg bei Meilenhofen Site (Germany)
— **Economic conditions**
— — **1974-**
[HC286.7]
— **Economic policy**
— — **1974-**
[HC286.7]
— **Politics and government**
— — **1982-**

Germany, Democratic Republic of
USE Germany (East)
Germany, East
USE Germany (East)
Germany, Eastern
USE Germany (East)
Germany, Federal Republic of
USE Germany (West)
Germany, Northern
As a geographic subdivision, this heading is used directly.
UF Northern Germany
Germany, Southern
As a geographic subdivision, this heading is used directly.
UF South Germany
Southern Germany
Germany, West
USE Germany (West)
Germany, Western
USE Germany (West)
Germany (East) in mass media
(May Subd Geog)
[P96.G]
BT Mass media
Germar family
USE Gumaer family
Germe X
USE Yersinia enterocolitica
Germen family
USE German family
Germfree life
UF Disease-free life
Germ-free life
Gnotobiology
Gnotobiotics
Life, Germfree
Specific pathogen free life
BT Microbiology
Germicidal lamps
BT Air—Purification
Electric lamps
Germicides
USE Bactericides
Disinfection and disinfectants
Fungicides
Germinal layers
[QL971]
BT Embryology
NT Parablast
Germinal membrane
USE Blastoderm
Germination
[QK740]
UF Seeds—Germination
BT Botany—Embryology
Plant physiology
RT Seeds—Viability
SA *subdivision* Preharvest sprouting *under individual crops and groups of crops, e.g.* Corn—Preharvest sprouting
NT Corn—Preharvest sprouting
Potatoes—Sprouting
Seeds—Stratification
Vernalization
Germinoblastomas
USE Lymphomas
Germo alalunga
USE Albacore
Germplasm resources *(May Subd Geog)*
[QH75-QH77 (General)]
[S494.3 (Breeding)]
UF Conservation of germplasm
Gene resources
Genetic resources
Germ plasm resources

BT Breeding
Conservation of natural resources
Genetics
Natural resources
Nature conservation
NT Germ cells
Germplasm resources, Animal
(May Subd Geog)
[QH432 (Animal genetics)]
[SF105.3 (Breeding)]
UF Animal germplasm resources
BT Animal genetics
SA *subdivision* Germplasm resources *under particular animals, e.g.* Cattle—Germplasm resources; Fishes—Germplasm resources
NT Sperm banks
Germplasm resources, Plant
(May Subd Geog)
[QK981 (Plant genetics)]
[SB123.3 (Plant-breeding)]
UF Conservation of plant genetic resources
Conservation of plant germplasm resources
Plant genetic resources
Plant germplasm resources
BT Plant-breeding
Plant genetics
SA *subdivision* Germplasm resources *under particular plants, e.g.* Corn—Germplasm resources
NT Crops—Germplasm resources
Forest genetic resources conservation
Gene banks, Plant
— **Storage**
— — **In vitro**
UF In vitro storage of plant germplasm resources
BT Plant cell culture
Plant tissue culture
Germs
USE Bacteria
Bacteriology
Germ theory of disease
Micro-organisms
Germs (Mathematics)
BT Equivalence classes (Set theory)
Functions
Gernsbacher Altes Rathaus (Gernsbach, Germany)
BT City halls—Germany (West)
Geroĭ Sovetskogo Soĭuza
UF Hero of the Soviet Union
BT Decorations of honor—Soviet Union
Heroes—Soviet Union
Medals—Soviet Union
Geroldseck family *(Not Subd Geog)*
Gerontocracy
[GN492.1]
BT Aged
Gerontologists *(May Subd Geog)*
BT Social scientists
— **Supply and demand**
Gerontology *(May Subd Geog)*
[HQ1060-HQ1064]
Here and with local subdivision are entered works on the discipline of gerontology. Works on the conditions of the aged in general and in particular places are entered under Aged.
BT Social sciences
RT Geriatrics
NT Aged
Aging
Old age
— **Bibliography**
RT Gerontology literature
— **Biographical methods**
Here are entered works on the analysis of biographical materials such as life histories, diaries, oral histories, films, correspondence, or other personal documents in gerontology.

Gerontology
— **Biographical methods** *(Continued)*
    UF Biographical methods in
            gerontology
        Biography in gerontology
        Personal documents in gerontology
    BT Biography
— **Collected works**
— **Congresses**
— **Periodicals**
        Here are entered periodicals on the subject of
    the aged and their problems. Periodicals issued
    for the aged on the problems of the aged are
    entered under Aged—Periodicals.
    UF Gerontology—Yearbooks
— **Simulation games**
    UF Games in gerontology
    BT Simulation methods
— **Yearbooks**
    USE Gerontology—Periodicals
Gerontology literature
  UF Literature, Gerontology
  RT Gerontology—Bibliography
Gerontopsychiatry
  USE Geriatric psychiatry
Gerota's capsule
  USE Gerota's fascia
Gerota's fascia
  UF Fascia of Gerota
      Gerota's capsule
      Perirenal fascia
      Renal fascia
  BT Fasciae (Anatomy)
      Kidneys
Gerow family *(Not Subd Geog)*
  UF Giraud family
Gerrand family *(Not Subd Geog)*
Gerrard family
  USE Gerard family
Gerrauld family
  USE Jarrell family
Gerretsen family *(Not Subd Geog)*
  UF Gerretson family
Gerretson family
  USE Gerretsen family
Gerrhonotus
  [QL666.L2254]
  UF Alligator lizards
  BT Anguidae
  NT Gerrhonotus panamintinus
Gerrhonotus panamintinus
  [QL666.L2254]
  UF Alligator lizard, Panamint
      Panamint alligator lizard
  BT Gerrhonotus
Gerridae
  [QL523.G4]
  UF Water striders, Long-legged
  BT Hemiptera
  NT Halobates
Gerrie family
  USE Gery family
Gerris odontogaster
  [QL523.G4]
Gerrison family
  USE Garrison family
Gerritson family
  USE Garrison family
Gerry family
  USE Gery family
Gerrymander
  [JK1347-8]
  BT Administrative and political divisions
      Election districts
      Legislative bodies
      Representative government and
        representation
Gersch family
  USE Gersh family
Gersh family *(Not Subd Geog)*
  UF Gersch family

Gerstenberg family
  USE Gerstenberger family
Gerstenberger family *(Not Subd Geog)*
  UF Gerstenberg family
Gerstl family
  USE Gerstle family
Gerstle family *(Not Subd Geog)*
  UF Gerstl family
      Gerstley family
Gerstley family
  USE Gerstle family
GERT (Network analysis)
  UF Graphical evaluation and review
        technique
  BT Network analysis (Planning)
Gerulata (Bratislava, Czechoslovakia)
  USE Rusovce (Bratislava, Czechoslovakia)
Gerundive (Grammar)
  USE Grammar, Comparative and general—
       Gerundive
Gervais' beaked whale
  USE Mesoplodon europaeus
Gervais family
  USE Jarvis family
Gervase family
  USE Jarvis family
Gerver family
  USE Gerber family
Gervers family
  USE Gerber family
Gervis family
  USE Jarvis family
Gery family *(Not Subd Geog)*
  UF Geary family
      Gerrie family
      Gerry family
      Guerry family
  RT Gary family
Geryon (Classical mythology)
  [BL820.G47]
  BT Monsters
      Mythology, Classical
Geryoniidae *(May Subd Geog)*
  [QL377.H9]
  BT Trachylina
  NT Liriope (Coelenterata)
Ges languages
  USE Tapuyan languages
Gesandten (Painting)
  USE Holbein, Hans, 1497-1543.
      Ambassadors
Geschehen (The German word)
  BT German language—Etymology
Gesell family *(Not Subd Geog)*
  UF Gessel family
      Gessell family
  RT Sell family
Gesell incomplete man test
  UF Incomplete man test
  BT Psychological tests
Gesenke Mountains (Czechoslovakia)
  USE Jeseníky Mountains (Czechoslovakia)
Geshur Mountain (Israel)
  USE Karkom Mountain (Israel)
Gesler family
  USE Gessner family
Gesme family *(Not Subd Geog)*
  UF Gjesme family
Gesneriaceae
  [QK495.G4 (Botany)]
  [SB413.G37 (Ornamental plants)]
  UF Gesneriads
  NT Saintpaulia
Gesneriads
  USE Gesneriaceae
Gesquière family
  USE Ghesquières family
Gess family
  USE Guest family
Gessel family
  USE Gesell family

Gessell family
  USE Gesell family
Gessenay (Switzerland)
  USE Saanenland (Switzerland)
Gessler family
  USE Gessner family
Gessner family *(Not Subd Geog)*
  UF Gasner family
      Gassner family
      Gesler family
      Gessler family
Gesso
  [NK5080]
  BT Decoration and ornament
      Plaster of Paris
Gesst family
  USE Gist family
Gest family
  USE Gist family
Gesta Romanorum
  [PA8320-8325]
  BT Fables
Gestagens
  USE Progestational hormones
Gestalt completion test
  USE Street gestalt completion test
Gestalt psychology
  [BF203]
  UF Configuration (Psychology)
      Form psychology
      Psychology, Structural
      Structural psychology
  BT Consciousness
      Ejection (Psychology)
      Knowledge, Theory of
      Perception
      Psychology
      Senses and sensation
  NT Attribution (Social psychology)
      Bender gestalt test
      Figure-ground perception
      Street gestalt completion test
      Whole and parts (Psychology)
Gestalt test
  USE Bender gestalt test
Gestalt therapy
  [RC489.G4]
  BT Psychotherapy
Gestation
  USE Pregnancy
Gestation age
  USE Gestational age
Gestational age *(May Subd Geog)*
  UF Gestation age
  BT Age
      Embryology
      Fetus
      Infants (Premature)
  RT Pregnancy—Duration
— **Testing**
    BT Age determination (Zoology)
      Man—Age determination
Gestational mothers
  USE Surrogate mothers
Gesting family
  USE Gaston family
Gestogens
  USE Progestational hormones
Gestosis
  USE Toxemia of pregnancy
Gests family
  USE Gist family
Gesture *(May Subd Geog)*
  [PN4165 (Public speaking)]
  UF Mudra
  BT Acting
      Elocution
      Movement (Acting)
      Nonverbal communication
      Oratory
  RT Sign language

NT Shanghai gesture
Gesture, Shanghai
 USE Shanghai gesture
Gesture in art
Gesture in dance *(May Subd Geog)*
 UF Dance gesture
 BT Dancing
Gesture in literature
Gesture in worship
 BT Worship
 NT Cross, Sign of the
Gesture language
 USE Deaf—Means of communication
  Indians of North America—Sign
   language
  Sign language
Gestures (Buddhism)
 USE Mudrās (Buddhism)
Gesu (African people)
 USE Gisu (African people)
Getae
 — Religion
  NT Zalmoxis
Getas
 USE Sabots
Getchey family
 USE Geitgey family
Getge family
 USE Geitgey family
Getgen family
 USE Geitgey family
Getgey family
 USE Geitgey family
Gethey family
 USE Geitgey family
Gethge family
 USE Geitgey family
Gethsemane, Prayer of
 USE Jesus Christ—Prayer in Gethsemane
Getman family *(Not Subd Geog)*
 UF Gettman family
Getter-ion pumps
 USE Ion pumps
Getters
 BT Gases—Absorption and adsorption
  Metals
  Vacuum-tubes
 NT Ion pumps
Gettes family
 USE Getty family
Gettess family
 USE Getty family
Getteys family
 USE Getty family
Getting up early
 USE Early rising
Gettis family
 USE Getty family
Gettman family
 USE Getman family
Getty bronze (Statue)
 BT Bronzes—Greece
  Bronzes, Greek
Getty family *(Not Subd Geog)*
 UF Gattes family
  Gattis family
  Gettes family
  Gettess family
  Getteys family
  Gettis family
  Gettys family
Getty Museum Herb Garden (Malibu, Calif.)
 USE J. Paul Getty Museum Herb Garden
  (Malibu, Calif.)
Gettys family
 USE Getty family
Gettysburg, Battle of, 1863
 ₍E475.53₎
 BT Gettysburg Campaign, 1863
  United States—History—Civil War,
   1861-1865—Campaigns

NT Gettysburg National Military Park
 (Pa.)
Gettysburg Campaign, 1863
 ₍E475.51-53₎
 UF Lee's 2d Northern Invasion
  Maryland Campaign, 1863
  Pennsylvania Invasion, 1863
 BT United States—History—Civil War,
   1861-1865—Campaigns
  Virginia—History—Civil War, 1861-
   1865
 NT Gettysburg, Battle of, 1863
Gettysburg National Military Park (Pa.)
 BT Gettysburg, Battle of, 1863
  Military parks—Pennsylvania
  National parks and reserves—United
   States
  Parks—Pennsylvania
Gettysburg Reunion, 1913
 ₍E475.57₎
Gettysburg Reunion, 1938
 ₍E475.58₎
 UF Blue and Gray Reunion, 1938
Getwezi
 USE Jaćwież
Getz family *(Not Subd Geog)*
 UF Gaetz family
 RT Gates family
  Goetz family
Getzandanner family
 USE Getzendanner family
Getzendaner family
 USE Getzendanner family
Getzendanner family *(Not Subd Geog)*
 UF Getzandanner family
  Getzendaner family
  Giessendanner family
  Giezendanner family
  Giezentanner family
 RT Danner family
Geul River (Belgium and Netherlands)
 (Not Subd Geog)
 UF Göhl River (Belgium and Netherlands)
  Guele River (Belgium and
   Netherlands)
 BT Rivers—Belgium
  Rivers—Netherlands
Geurin family *(Not Subd Geog)*
 UF Geurins family
  Guarin family
  Guerant family
  Guerin family
  Guering family
  Guerrin family
  Guran family
  Gurin family
  Gurrin family
 RT Guérin d'Agon family
Geurins family
 USE Geurin family
Geven family
 USE Givens family
Gevin family
 USE Givens family
Gewi (African people)
 USE G/wi (African people)
Geyer family
 UF Geier family
  Gier family
  Guyer family
  Gyer family
Geyser Basin, Lower (Wyo.)
 USE Lower Geyser Basin (Wyo.)
Geysers, The (Calif.)
 UF Big Geysers (Calif.)
  The Geysers (Calif.)
 BT Geysers—California
Geysers *(May Subd Geog)*
 ₍QE528₎
 UF Thermal waters

BT Geology
 Geothermal resources
 Physical geography
 Water
 Water, Underground
RT Springs
— California
 NT Geysers, The (Calif.)
— Wyoming
 NT Lower Geyser Basin (Wyo.)
  Norris Geyser Basin (Wyo.)
Geyst family
 USE Gist family
Gezerot taḥ ve-tat, 1648-1649
 BT Ukraine—History—1648-1654
Gezira (Sudan)
GG 1 (Electric locomotive)
 BT Electric locomotives—United States
GGPP (Computer program)
 UF General Game Playing Program
Ghadīr
 BT 'Alī ibn Abī Ṭālib, Caliph, 600 (ca.)-
   661—Imamate
  Shī'ah—Doctrines
 NT 'Īd al-Ghadīr
Ghadīr al-Khumm
 USE 'Īd al-Ghadīr
Ghadr movement
 BT East Indians—North America—
   Politics and government
  India—Politics and government—
   1857-1919
Ghalchah languages
 USE Pamir languages
Ghana
 — Economic conditions
 — — To 1957
 — — 1957-1979
 — — 1979-
 — History
  NT Denkyira (Kingdom)
 — — To 1957
  ₍DT511-511.3₎
  NT Ashanti War, 1822-1831
   Ashanti War, 1873-1874
   Ashanti War, 1900
 — — Portuguese rule, 1469-1637
  ₍DT511₎
  UF Mina, Portuguese
   Portuguese Mina
 — — Danish Settlements, 1659-1850
  UF Danish Settlements, Ghana,
    1659-1850
  BT Denmark—Colonies—Africa
 — — 1957-
  ₍DT512₎
 — — Coup d'état, 1966
 — — Coup d'état, 1972
 — — Coup d'état, 1979
  ₍DT512.32₎
 — — Coup d'état, 1981
  BT Coups d'état—Ghana
 — Languages
  NT Akan language
   Hanga language (Ghana)
   Mo language (Ghana and Ivory
    Coast)
 — Politics and government
 — — To 1957
 — — 1957-1979
 — — 1979-
 — Social conditions
 — — 17th century
Ghana Empire
 ₍DT532.15₎
Ghanaian art
 USE Art, Ghanaian
Ghanaian arts
 USE Arts, Ghanaian
Ghanaian children's stories (English)
 USE Children's stories, Ghanaian (English)

Ghanaian children's writings (English)
  USE Children's writings, Ghanaian
        (English)
Ghanaian college prose (English)
  USE College prose, Ghanaian (English)
Ghanaian college verse (English)
  USE College verse, Ghanaian (English)
Ghanaian literature
Ghanaian literature (English)
    (May Subd Geog)
      ⌐9379.85 (History, PR9379-9379.4)¬
      ⌐PR9379.45-9379.85 (Collections)¬
  UF English literature—Ghanaian authors
Ghanaian newspapers *(May Subd Geog)*
Ghanaian periodicals *(May Subd Geog)*
Ghanaian poetry (English)
    (May Subd Geog)
      ⌐PR9379.2 (History)¬
      ⌐PR9379.6-PR9379.65 (Collections)¬
  UF English poetry—Ghanaian authors
  NT Revolutionary poetry, Ghanaian
        (English)
Ghanaian prose literature (English)
    (May Subd Geog)
  UF English prose literature—Ghanaian
        authors
  NT College prose, Ghanaian (English)
Ghanaian revolutionary poetry (English)
  USE Revolutionary poetry, Ghanaian
        (English)
Ghanaian short stories (English)
  USE Short stories, Ghanaian (English)
Ghanaian students *(May Subd Geog)*
  BT Students
Ghanaian wit and humor, Pictorial
    (May Subd Geog)
Ghanaians *(May Subd Geog)*
  BT Ethnology—Ghana
Ghanchīs
      ⌐DS432.G43¬
  UF Ghãñcīs
  BT Caste—India
        Ethnology—India
Ghãñcīs
  USE Ghanchīs
Gharapuri Island (India)
  USE Elephanta Island (India)
Ghasel
  USE Ghazals
Ghasquière family
  USE Ghesquières family
Ghassul culture
      ⌐GN775.5.G5¬
  BT Man, Prehistoric
        Neolithic period
Ghassul Site (Jordan) *(Not Subd Geog)*
      ⌐GN778.3.G48¬
  UF Teleilāt Ghassūl (Jordan)
        Tell Ghassul (Jordan)
        Tulaylāt al Ghassūl (Jordan)
  BT Jordan—Antiquities
Ghats, Western (India)
  USE Western Ghats (India)
Ghaudesh Island (Malta)
  USE Gozo Island (Malta)
Ghaudex Island (Malta)
  USE Gozo Island (Malta)
Ghawex Island (Malta)
  USE Gozo Island (Malta)
Ghawr (Jordan)
  UF Ghor (Jordan)
        Ghur (Jordan)
        Kikar ha-Yarden (Jordan)
        Kikkar ha-Yarden (Jordan)
Ghazāl, Baḥr al- (Sudan : River)
  USE Baḥr al-Ghazāl (Sudan : River)
Ghazal River (Sudan)
  USE Baḥr al-Ghazāl (Sudan : River)

Ghazals *(May Subd Geog)*
  UF Gasel
        Gazels
        Ghasel
        Ghazels
  BT Poetry
Ghazals, Arabic *(May Subd Geog)*
      ⌐PJ7542.G4¬
  UF Arabic ghazals
  BT Arabic poetry
Ghazals, Bhojpuri *(May Subd Geog)*
  UF Bhojpuri ghazals
  BT Bhojpuri poetry
Ghazals, Chagatai *(May Subd Geog)*
  UF Chagatai ghazals
  BT Chagatai poetry
Ghazals, Dakhini Hindustani
    (May Subd Geog)
  UF Dakhini Hindustani ghazals
  BT Dakhini Hindustani poetry
Ghazals, Gujarati *(May Subd Geog)*
  UF Gujarati ghazals
  BT Gujarati poetry
Ghazals, Nepali *(May Subd Geog)*
  UF Nepali ghazals
  BT Nepali poetry
Ghazals, Panjabi *(May Subd Geog)*
  UF Panjabi ghazals
  BT Panjabi poetry
Ghazals, Persian *(May Subd Geog)*
  UF Persian ghazals
  BT Persian poetry
Ghazals, Sindhi *(May Subd Geog)*
  UF Sindhi ghazals
  BT Sindhi poetry
Ghazals, Turkish *(May Subd Geog)*
  UF Turkish ghazals
  BT Turkish poetry
Ghazals, Urdu *(May Subd Geog)*
  UF Urdu ghazals
  BT Urdu poetry
Ghazels
  USE Ghazals
Ghaznawids
  USE Ghaznevids
Ghaznevids
      ⌐DS288.7¬
  UF Ghaznawids
GHC (Computer program language)
      ⌐QA76.73.G¬
  UF Guarded Horn Clauses (Computer
        program language)
  BT Programming languages (Electronic
        computers)
Ghec-chi language
  USE Kekchi language
Ghee
  BT Butter
        Butterfat
  — Grading and standardization
Ghegham Range (Armenian S.S.R.)
  USE Gegam Range (Armenian S.S.R.)
Gheghids
  USE Ghegs
Ghegs
  UF Gegs
        Gheghids
  BT Albanians
Ghent altarpiece (Panel painting)
  USE Eyck, Jan van, 1390-1440. Ghent
        altarpiece
Ghent family *(Not Subd Geog)*
Ghent, Treaty of, 1814
      ⌐E358¬

Ghesquières family *(Not Subd Geog)*
  UF Gasquière family
        Gékkerre family
        Gesquière family
        Ghasquière family
        Ghieskières family
        Ghiesquire family
        Gieskière family
        Guesquières family
        Quéquière family
Ghettos
  USE *names of minority groups in individual
        places*
        Afro-Americans—Housing
        Afro-Americans—Segregation
        Blacks—Segregation
        Jews—Segregation
Gheyn family *(Not Subd Geog)*
Ghibellines
  USE Guelfs and Ghibellines
Ghieskières family
  USE Ghesquières family
Ghiesquire family
  USE Ghesquières family
Ghiliaks
  USE Gilyaks
Ghillies
  USE Hunting guides
        Riverkeepers
GHO, Conn.
  USE Greater Hartford Open, Conn.
Ghomala language
  USE Bandjoun language
Ghoorkas
  USE Gurkhas
Ghor (Jordan)
  USE Ghawr (Jordan)
Ghorapaḍe, House of *(Not Subd Geog)*
Ghorids
  USE Ghurids
Ghoss family
  USE Goss family
Ghost crabs
  UF Ocypode
  BT Crabs
Ghost dance
      ⌐E98.D2¬
  BT Indians of North America—Dances
        Nativistic movements
Ghost-faced bats
  USE Mormoops
Ghost plays
  BT Drama
Ghost plays, English *(May Subd Geog)*
  UF English ghost plays
  BT English drama
Ghost plays, Japanese *(May Subd Geog)*
  UF Japanese ghost plays
  BT Japanese drama
Ghost River Wilderness (Alta.)
    (Not Subd Geog)
  UF Ghost River Wilderness Area (Alta.)
  BT Wilderness areas—Alberta
Ghost River Wilderness Area (Alta.)
  USE Ghost River Wilderness (Alta.)
Ghost sharks
  USE Chimaeridae
Ghost stories
      ⌐BF1445-BF1486 (Occult sciences)¬
      ⌐PN3435 (History and criticism)¬
      ⌐PZ1-PZ3 (Fiction in English)¬
  UF Ghosts—Fiction
  BT Detective and mystery stories
        Fantastic fiction
        Fiction
  RT Horror tales
Ghost stories, American *(May Subd Geog)*
  UF American ghost stories
  BT American fiction
Ghost stories, Canadian *(May Subd Geog)*
  UF Canadian ghost stories

BT Canadian fiction
Ghost stories, Chinese   *(May Subd Geog)*
[*PL2419.G5 (History)*]
[*PL2629.G5 (Collections)*]
UF Chinese ghost stories
BT Chinese fiction
Ghost stories, Dutch   *(May Subd Geog)*
UF Dutch ghost stories
BT Dutch fiction
Ghost stories, English   *(May Subd Geog)*
UF English ghost stories
BT English fiction
Ghost stories, German, [etc.]
(May Subd Geog)
Ghost stories, Japanese   *(May Subd Geog)*
UF Japanese ghost stories
BT Japanese fiction
Ghost stories, Marathi   *(May Subd Geog)*
UF Marathi ghost stories
BT Marathi fiction
Ghost stories, Norwegian   *(May Subd Geog)*
UF Norwegian ghost stories
BT Norwegian fiction
Ghost towns
USE Cities and towns, Ruined, extinct, etc.
Ghost writing
USE Ghostwriting
Ghosts, Cave of (Vic.)   *(Not Subd Geog)*
UF Cave of Ghosts (Vic.)
BT Australia—Antiquities
Caves—Australia
Ghosts   *(May Subd Geog)*
[*BF1445-BF1486 (Occult sciences)*]
[*GR580 (Folk-lore)*]
UF Haunted houses
Phantoms
Specters
RT Apparitions
NT Hiding-places (Secret chambers, etc.)
Materialization
Poltergeists
— Fiction
USE Ghost stories
Ghosts in art
Ghosts in literature
[*PN56.S8*]
NT Shakespeare, William, 1564-1616—
Characters—Ghosts
Ghostwriting
UF Ghost writing
BT Authorship—Collaboration
NT Speechwriting
Ghoulie
[*GV1282.9.G5*]
UF Train-bridge
BT Contract bridge
Ghouls and ogres
[*GR525*]
[*GR560*]
UF Ogres
BT Monsters
Vampires
NT Tengu
Ghoya (African people)
UF Ghoya (Bantu tribe)
Kubung (African people)
Leghoya (African people)
BT Bantus
Ethnology—South Africa
Ghoya (Bantu tribe)
USE Ghoya (African people)
Ghur (Jordan)
USE Ghawr (Jordan)
Ghurids
[*DS358*]
UF Ghorids
Ghurkas
USE Gurkhas
Ghuzz
USE Oghuz

Gi-Tonga language
USE Tonga language (Inhambane)
Giacometti, Alberto, 1901-1966.   Portrait of James Lord
[*ND553.G56*]
Giali Island (Greece)
BT Dodecanese
Islands—Greece
Giannuzzi's semilunar bodies
USE Salivary glands
Giant African free-tailed bat
USE Tadarida africana
Giant anteater
USE Myrmecophaga
Giant arborvitae
USE Thuja plicata
Giant arum
USE Amorphophallus
Giant bird's nest
USE Pterospora andromedea
Giant cabbage
[*QK495.C9*]
Giant cactus
USE Saguaro
Giant cell arteritis   *(May Subd Geog)*
[*RC694.5.G5*]
UF Arteritis, Cranial
Arteritis, Giant cell
Arteritis, Temporal
Cranial arteritis
Horton's arteritis
Temporal arteritis
BT Arteritis
RT Polymyalgia rheumatica
Giant cell tumors
BT Tumors
Giant chromosomes
[*QH605*]
UF Polytene chromosomes
BT Chromosomes
NT Chromosome underreplication
Lambrush chromosomes
Giant cockroaches
USE Blaberus
Giant eagle owl
USE Bubo lacteus
Giant fir
USE Abies grandis
Giant fishing spiders
USE Dolomedes
Giant garter snake
USE Thamnophis couchii
Giant gourami
USE Gourami
Giant hairy scorpions
USE Hadrurus
Giant kangaroo
USE Grey kangaroo
Giant kelp   *(May Subd Geog)*
[*QK569.L53 (Algology)*]
[*SH391.G5 (Fisheries)*]
UF Fucus pyriferus
Kelp, Giant
Macrocystis pyrifera
BT Macrocystis
Giant multipole resonance
UF Multipole resonance, Giant
Resonance, Giant multipole
BT Nuclear magnetic resonance
Giant nuclear magnetic resonance
USE Nuclear magnetic resonance, Giant
Giant nuthatch
UF Sitta magna
BT Nuthatches
Giant oyster
USE Crassostrea gigas
Giant Pacific oyster
USE Crassostrea gigas
Giant panda
[*QL737.C214*]
UF Ailuropoda melanoleuca

BT Pandas
Giant perch
USE Barramundi
Giant pied-billed grebe
BT Grebes
Giant reed
UF Arundo donax
Giant resonance (Nuclear physics)
USE Nuclear magnetic resonance, Giant
Giant saguaro
USE Saguaro
Giant salamander
USE Megalobatrachus japonicus
Giant scallop
[*QL430.7.P3 (Zoology)*]
[*SH372 (Fisheries)*]
UF Atlantic sea scallop
Pecten magellanicus
Placopecten magellanicus
Sea scallop, Atlantic
BT Scallops
Giant sensitive plant
USE Mimosa pigra
Giant sequoia
[*QK494.5.T3 (Botany)*]
[*SD397.G (Forestry)*]
UF Big tree
Bigtree
Mammoth tree
Redwood, Sierra
Sequoia
Sequoia, Giant
Sequoia gigantea
Sequoia washingtoniana
Sequoia wellingtonia
Sequoiadendron
Sequoiadendron giganteum
Sierra redwood
Wellingtonia gigantea
BT Taxodiaceae
NT Sequoia National Park (Calif.)
Giant squids
[*QL430.3.O*]
UF Architeuthis
BT Squids
Giant sugarcane borer
USE Castnia licus
Giant toad
USE Bufo marinus
Giant water bugs
USE Belostomatidae
Giant water lily
USE Victoria (Plants)
Giants   *(May Subd Geog)*
[*GN69 (Somatology)*]
BT Abnormalities, Human
Monsters
Stature, Tall
NT Cyclopes (Greek mythology)
— **Mythology**
— **Religious aspects**
NT Giants in the Bible
Giant's cauldrons
USE Potholes
Giants in the Bible
[*BS1199.G5*]
BT Giants—Religious aspects
Giardia
[*QL368.D65 (Zoology)*]
[*QR201.G45 (Pathogenic protozoa)*]
BT Hexamitidae
NT Giardia lamblia
Giardia enterica
USE Giardia lamblia
Giardia intestinalis
USE Giardia lamblia
Giardia lamblia
[*QL368.D65 (Zoology)*]
[*QR201.G45 (Pathogenic protozoa)*]

Giardia lamblia *(Continued)*
  UF Giardia enterica
      Giardia intestinalis
      Giardia mesnili
      Lamblia intestinalis
  BT Giardia
Giardia mesnili
  USE Giardia lamblia
Giardiasis *(May Subd Geog)*
  UF Lambliasis
      Liambliasis
  BT Medical protozoology
Giardino Puccini (Pistoia, Italy)
  UF Puccini Garden (Pistoia, Italy)
  BT Parks—Italy
Giarung language
  USE Gyarung language
Gib family
  USE Gibbs family
Gibans family
  USE Gibbons family
Gibb family
  USE Gibbs family
Gibbel family
  USE Gibble family
Gibbels family
  USE Gibble family
Gibberellins
  [QK898.G45 (Botanical chemistry)]
  BT Plant hormones
      Plant regulators
  — Physiological effect
    NT Plants, Effect of gibberellins on
Gibberichthyidae
  [QL638.G45]
  UF Kasidoridae
      Kasidoroidae
  BT Beryciformes
Gibbes family
  USE Gibbs family
Gibbins family
  USE Gibbons family
Gibble family *(Not Subd Geog)*
  UF Gapfill family
      Gebfall family
      Gibbel family
      Gibbels family
      Gibfel family
      Gipel family
      Gipfel family
      Gipple family
      Kipple family
Gibbon family
  USE Gibbons family
Gibbons
  [QL737.P9]
  UF Hylobates
  BT Apes
  NT Whitehanded gibbon
Gibbons as pets
  [SF459.G53]
Gibbons Burying Ground (S.C.)
  USE Gibbons Family Cemetery (S.C.)
Gibbons Cemetery (S.C.)
  USE Gibbons Family Cemetery (S.C.)
Gibbons Creek Reservoir (Tex.)
  BT Reservoirs—Texas
Gibbons family *(Not Subd Geog)*
  UF Gibans family
      Gibbins family
      Gibbon family
      Gibeons family
      Gibins family
      Gibons family
  RT Gibbs family
Gibbons Family Cemetery (S.C.)
  UF Gibbons Burying Ground (S.C.)
      Gibbons Cemetery (S.C.)
  BT Cemeteries—South Carolina
Gibbs' equation
  UF Equation, Gibbs'

  BT Differential equations
      Phase rule and equilibrium
      Thermodynamics
Gibbs family *(Not Subd Geog)*
  UF Gib family
      Gibb family
      Gibbes family
      Gibes family
      Gibs family
  RT Gibbons family
Gibbs' free energy
  UF Free energy, Gibbs'
      Free enthalpy
      Gibbs' function
  BT Enthalpy
      Entropy
  RT Surface energy
      Thermodynamic potentials
  NT Linear free energy relationship
Gibbs' function
  USE Gibbs' free energy
Gibbs' Hill Lighthouse and Park (Bermuda Island, Bermuda Islands)
  (Not Subd Geog)
  UF Gibbs' Hill Park (Bermuda Island, Bermuda Islands)
  BT Parks—Bermuda Islands
Gibbs' Hill Park (Bermuda Island, Bermuda Islands)
  USE Gibbs' Hill Lighthouse and Park (Bermuda Island, Bermuda Islands)
Gibbs' paradox
  [QC174.17.G5]
  UF Paradox, Gibbs'
  BT Entropy
      Gases
Gibeonites
  BT Ethnology—Palestine
Gibeons family
  USE Gibbons family
Gibert's disease
  USE Pityriasis rosea
Gibes family
  USE Gibbs family
Gibfel family
  USE Gibble family
Gibins family
  USE Gibbons family
Giblin family *(Not Subd Geog)*
Gibons family
  USE Gibbons family
Gibraltar
  As a geographic subdivision, this heading is used directly.
  — Siege, 1779-1783
    [DA87.5 1779]
Gibraltar, Strait of
  UF Détroit de Gibraltar
      Estrecho de Gibraltar
      Strait of Gibraltar
      Strait of Hercules
  BT Straits
Gibs family
  USE Gibbs family
Gibson, Walter Brown, 1897-
  — Characters
  — — Shadow
      RT Shadow (Fictitious character)
Gibson Desert (W.A.)
  BT Deserts—Australia
Gibson family *(Not Subd Geog)*
  UF Gibsone family
      Gip family
      Gipp family
      Gips family
      Gipson family
Gibson paradox
  BT Interest rates
      Paradox
      Prices

Gibsone family
  USE Gibson family
Gibsoniothamnus
  [QK495.S43]
  BT Scrophulariaceae
Gidabal dialect
  UF Gidjabal dialect
      Kitabul dialect
  BT Australia—Languages
      Bandjalang language
Gidayū
  USE Jōruri
Giddens family *(Not Subd Geog)*
Giddig family
  USE Giddings family
Gidding family
  USE Giddings family
Giddings family *(Not Subd Geog)*
  UF Gedding family
      Geddings family
      Giddig family
      Gidding family
      Gidings family
      Gittings family
      Gittins family
Gidings family
  USE Giddings family
Gidjabal dialect
  USE Gidabal dialect
Gidjingali (Australian people)
  USE Burera (Australian people)
Gidlow family
  USE Goodloe family
Gidra (Papua New Guinea people)
  UF Oriomo (Papua New Guinea people)
      Wipitungam (Papua New Guinea people)
  BT Ethnology—Papua New Guinea
      Papuans
Gieger family
  USE Geiger family
Giegerich family *(Not Subd Geog)*
Gieltz family
  USE Kilts family
Gien language
  USE Tchien language
GIER (Computer)
  BT Electronic digital computers
  — Programming
Gier family
  USE Geyer family
Gier River (France)
  BT Rivers—France
Gieseler family
  USE Giesler family
Gieskière family
  USE Ghesquières family
Giesler family *(Not Subd Geog)*
  UF Gieseler family
Giessen test
  [BF698.8.G5]
  BT Personality tests
Giessendanner family
  USE Getzendanner family
Giest family
  USE Gist family
Giezendanner family
  USE Getzendanner family
Giezentanner family
  USE Getzendanner family
Giffard family
  USE Gifford family
Giffen family *(Not Subd Geog)*
  UF Giffens family
  RT Giffin family
      Griffin family
      Griffith family
Giffens family
  USE Giffen family
Giffin family *(Not Subd Geog)*
  UF Giffins family

RT Giffen family
    Griffin family
    Griffith family
Giffins family
  USE Giffin family
Gifford family *(Not Subd Geog)*
  UF Giffard family
    Giffords family
Giffords family
  USE Gifford family
Gift-books (Annuals, etc.)
  ⌜AY10-19⌝
  UF Annuals
    Christmas books
    Keepsakes (Books)
  BT Anthologies
    Souvenirs (Keepsakes)
  SA *subdivision* Gift-books *under subjects,*
    e.g. Marriage—Gift-books
Gift exchange
  USE Ceremonial exchange
Gift Lake (Alta.)
  BT Lakes—Alberta
Gift of the USSR to UNESCO (Mural
  painting)
  USE Glazunov, Il'ĩa Sergeevich. Gift of
    the USSR to UNESCO
Gift of tongues
  USE Glossolalia
Gift shops *(May Subd Geog)*
  BT Specialty stores
  NT Hospital gift shops
Gift tax
  USE Gifts—Taxation
Gift wrapping
  ⌜TT870⌝
  UF Wrapping of gifts
  BT Packaging
  NT Fukusa
Gift wrapping materials
  USE Gift wraps
Gift wraps *(May Subd Geog)*
  UF Gift wrapping materials
    Giftwraps
    Wraps, Gift
  BT Wrapping materials
Gifted adults
  USE Genius
Gifted children *(May Subd Geog)*
  ⌜LC3991-LC4000⌝
  UF Bright children
    Child prodigies
    Precocity
    Prodigies, Child
    Superior children
    Talented children
  BT Exceptional children
    Genius
  RT Talented students
  NT Children as actors
    Children as artists
    Children as musicians
    Educational acceleration
    Gifted girls
  — **Education** *(May Subd Geog)*
    NT High schools—Honors courses
      Teachers of gifted children
  — — **Law and legislation**
    (May Subd Geog)
    BT Educational law and legislation
  — — **Reading,** ⌜etc.⌝
  — — **Research** *(May Subd Geog)*
  — — **Science**
  — **Education (Preschool)**
    (May Subd Geog)
    ⌜LC3993.218⌝
  — **Identification**
    BT Ability—Testing
  — **Mental health** *(May Subd Geog)*
    ⌜RJ507.G55⌝

Gifted children, Teachers of
  USE Teachers of gifted children
Gifted girls *(May Subd Geog)*
  ⌜BF723.G52 (Psychology)⌝
  UF Girls, Gifted
  BT Gifted children
    Girls
Gifted women *(May Subd Geog)*
  UF Women, Gifted
  BT Genius
    Women
Gifts *(May Subd Geog)*
  ⌜GT3050 (Manners and customs)⌝
  UF Donations
    Presents
  BT Contracts, Gratuitous
    Generosity
    Manners and customs
  RT Collation (Law)
    Free material
  NT Benefactors
    Deferred giving
    Diplomatic gifts
    Donation of organs, tissues, etc.
    Gifts to minors
    Indians of North America—Gifts
    Insinuation (Civil law)
    Modus (Civil law)
  — **Taxation** *(May Subd Geog)*
    UF Gift tax
    BT Inheritance and transfer tax
      Wealth tax
    NT Real property and taxation
  — — **Deductions**
    NT Marital deduction
  — — — **Law and legislation**
    (May Subd Geog)
  — — **Law and legislation**
    (May Subd Geog)
  — — **Rates and tables**
  — — **Treaties**
    USE Taxation, Double—Treaties
Gifts, Spiritual
  ⌜BT767.3⌝
  Here are entered works on extraordinary
  phenomena such as glossolalia, visions, prophecies
  and interpretations, healings, discernment of spirits,
  etc. Works dealing collectively with those qualities
  induced by the Holy Spirit such as love, joy, peace,
  faith, meekness, and temperance are entered under
  Fruit of the Spirit.
  UF Charismata
    Gifts of grace
    Gifts of the Holy Spirit
    Grace, Gifts of
    Spiritual gifts
  BT Grace (Theology)
  NT Baptism in the Holy Spirit
    Glossolalia
    Prophecy (Christianity)
  — **Baptists,** ⌜**Catholic Church, etc.**⌝
Gifts (Canon law)
Gifts (Greek law)
Gifts (Hittite law)
Gifts (Islamic law)
  BT Islamic law
Gifts (Kindergarten)
  USE Kindergarten—Methods and manuals
Gifts (Roman-Dutch law)
Gifts (Roman law)
Gifts causa mortis *(May Subd Geog)*
  UF Donatio mortis causa
    Gifts mortis causa
Gifts causa mortis (Greek law)
Gifts causa mortis (Jewish law)
Gifts causa mortis (Roman law)
Gifts mortis causa
  USE Gifts causa mortis
Gifts of grace
  USE Gifts, Spiritual
Gifts of money to minors
  USE Gifts to minors

Gifts of securities to minors
  USE Gifts to minors
Gifts of the Holy Spirit
  USE Gifts, Spiritual
Gifts to minors *(May Subd Geog)*
  UF Gifts of money to minors
    Gifts of securities to minors
  BT Gifts
    Securities
Giftware industry *(May Subd Geog)*
  ⌜HD9999.G49-494⌝
  RT Giftwares
Giftwares *(May Subd Geog)*
  RT Giftware industry
Giftwraps
  USE Gift wraps
Gigant (Transport planes)
  USE Messerschmitt 323 (Transport planes)
Gigantobilharzia
  ⌜QL391.P7⌝
  BT Schistosomatidae
Gigantobilharzia huronensis
  ⌜QL391.P7⌝
Giganturidae
  ⌜QL638.G5⌝
  BT Salmoniformes
Gigar family
  USE Geiger family
Gigartina
  ⌜QK569.G5 (Botany)⌝
  BT Gigartinaceae
Gigartina canaliculata
  ⌜QK569.G5 (Botany)⌝
  ⌜SH391.G (Fisheries)⌝
Gigartinaceae
  NT Gigartina
Gigartinales *(May Subd Geog)*
  ⌜QK569.G⌝
  BT Red algae
  NT Rhodophyllidaceae
Giger family
  USE Geiger family
Giggard family *(Not Subd Geog)*
Gigging (Textiles)
  USE Napping (Textiles)
Gigher family
  USE Geiger family
Giglio Island (Italy)
  UF Igilium Island (Italy)
    Isola del Giglio (Italy)
  BT Islands—Italy
Gigolos
  USE Fortune hunters
Giguère family *(Not Subd Geog)*
Gigues
  USE Jigs
Gihi language
  USE Kissi language
Gii language
  USE Kissi language
Gijidō, Kokkai (Tokyo, Japan)
  USE Kokkai Gijidō (Tokyo, Japan)
Gikuyu (African people)
  USE Kikuyu (African people)
Gikuyu language
  USE Kikuyu language
Gikwezo language
  USE Kwese language
Gila (Fish)
  ⌜QL638.C94⌝
  BT Cyprinidae
Gila bicolor
  USE Tui chub
Gila Conglomerate (Ariz. and N.M.)
  UF Gila Formation (Ariz. and N.M.)
  BT Geology—Arizona
    Geology—New Mexico
    Geology, Stratigraphic—Pleistocene
    Geology, Stratigraphic—Pliocene
Gila Formation (Ariz. and N.M.)
  USE Gila Conglomerate (Ariz. and N.M.)

Gila monster
  UF Heloderma suspectum
Gila River (N.M. and Ariz.)
  BT Rivers—Arizona
      Rivers—New Mexico
  NT Buttes Reservoir (Ariz.)
Gila trout
  [QL638.S2]
  UF Salmo gilae
  BT Salmo
      Trout
Gilaki language
  [PK6996.G54]
  UF Gelaki language
      Gilan language
  BT Iran—Languages
      Iranian languages
Gilan language
  USE Gilaki language
Gilardi family (Not Subd Geog)
Gilasby family
  USE Gillespie family
Gilaspy family
  USE Gillespie family
Gilbart family
  USE Gilbert family
Gilbert family (Not Subd Geog)
  UF Gilbart family
      Gilberts family
      Gilbertson family
Gilbert Islands
  USE Kiribati
Gilbertese language
  [PL6245]
  UF Arorai language
      I-Kiribati language
      Kiribatese language
      Kiribati language
  BT Micronesian languages
Gilberth family
  USE Galbraith family
Gilbertines
  [BX3670]
  BT Monasticism and religious orders
Gilberts family
  USE Gilbert family
Gilbertson family
  USE Gilbert family
Gilbraith family
  USE Galbraith family
Gilbreath family
  USE Galbraith family
Gilbreth family
  USE Galbraith family
Gilchrest family
  USE Gilchrist family
Gilchriest family
  USE Gilchrist family
Gilchrist family (Not Subd Geog)
  UF Gilchrest family
      Gilchriest family
      Gilcrest family
Gilcrest family
  USE Gilchrist family
Gild socialism
  USE Guild socialism
Gilden family
  USE Golden family
Gildersleave family
  USE Gildersleeve family
Gildersleeve family (Not Subd Geog)
  UF Gildersleave family
Gilding
  [TS715 (Metal manufactures)]
  [TT380 (Mechanical trades)]
  BT Goldwork
      Painting, Industrial
      Plating
      Stains and staining
  RT Metals—Coloring
  NT Bookbinding—Gilding

Electroplating
      Gilt bronzes
      Gold-plating
Gilds
  USE Guilds
Gile family
  USE Giles family
Giles family (Not Subd Geog)
  UF Gile family
      Guile family
      Jiles family
Gilfillan family
  USE Gillfillan family
Gilford family
  USE Guilford family
Gilgo family (Not Subd Geog)
  UF Gilgoe family
      Gilgow family
Gilgoe family
  USE Gilgo family
Gilgow family
  USE Gilgo family
Gilham family
  USE Gilliam family
Giliak
  USE Gilyaks
Giliak language
  USE Gilyak language
Giliaks
  USE Gilyaks
Gilis family
  USE Gilley family
Gill arch
  USE Branchial arch
Gill disease, Bacterial
  USE Bacterial gill disease
Gill family (Not Subd Geog)
  UF Gille family
      Gills family
      Guil family
      Guill family
  RT Giller family
Gill nets
  USE Gillnetting
Gill netting
  USE Gillnetting
Gill-over-the-ground
  USE Ground ivy
Gillam family
  USE Gilliam family
Gillard family (Not Subd Geog)
  UF Gaillard family
      Gaillarde family
      Gillarde family
      Gilliard family
Gillarde family
  USE Gillard family
Gillasby family
  USE Gillespie family
Gillaspey family
  USE Gillespie family
Gillaspie family
  USE Gillespie family
Gillaspy family
  USE Gillespie family
Gillat family
  USE Gillette family
Gillbreath family
  USE Galbraith family
Gille family
  USE Gill family
Gillelan family
  USE Gilliland family
Gilleland family
  USE Gilliland family
Gillelen family
  USE Gilliland family
Giller family (Not Subd Geog)
  UF Gillers family
  RT Gill family

Gillers family
  USE Giller family
Gilles de la Tourette's syndrome
  (May Subd Geog)
  [RC375]
  UF Guinon's disease
      Tic syndrome
      Tourette syndrome
  BT Central nervous system—Diseases
      Syndromes
      Tic
Gillesby family
  USE Gillespie family
Gillespie family (Not Subd Geog)
  UF Gilasby family
      Gilaspy family
      Gillasby family
      Gillaspey family
      Gillaspie family
      Gillaspy family
      Gillesby family
      Gillespy family
Gillespy family
  USE Gillespie family
Gillet family
  USE Gillette family
Gillett family
  USE Gillette family
Gillette family (Not Subd Geog)
  UF Gillat family
      Gillet family
      Gillett family
      Gillit family
      Gillitt family
      Jellet family
      Jillet family
      Jillitt family
Gilley family
  UF Gilis family
      Gillie family
      Gillies family
      Gillis family
      Guillis family
Gillfillan family (Not Subd Geog)
  UF Gilfillan family
Gillford family
  USE Guilford family
Gillham family
  USE Gilliam family
Gilliam family (Not Subd Geog)
  UF Gilham family
      Gillam family
      Gillham family
      Gilliams family
      Guillam family
      Guilliams family
  RT Gullett family
Gilliams family
  USE Gilliam family
Gilliard family
  USE Gillard family
Gillichthys
  [QL638.G7]
  BT Gobiidae
  NT Gillichthys mirabilis
Gillichthys mirabilis
  [QL638.G7]
  UF Long-jawed goby
      Longjaw mudsucker
  BT Gillichthys
Gillie family
  USE Gilley family
Gillies
  USE Hunting guides
      Riverkeepers
Gillies family
  USE Gilley family
Gillilan family
  USE Gilliland family

Gilliland family (Not Subd Geog)
   UF Gillelan family
       Gilleland family
       Gillelen family
       Gillilan family
Gillis family
   USE Gilley family
Gillit family
   USE Gillette family
Gillitt family
   USE Gillette family
Gillman family
   USE Gilman family
Gillmor family
   USE Gilmore family
Gillmore family
   USE Gilmore family
Gillnets
   USE Gillnetting
Gillnetting
   ⌈SH344.6.G5⌉
   UF Gill nets
       Gill netting
       Gillnets
   BT Fisheries
       Fishing nets
Gilloch family
   USE Gillock family
Gillock family (Not Subd Geog)
   UF Gilloch family
Gillott family
   USE Gullett family
Gills
   ⌈QL846 (Anatomy)⌉
   BT Fishes—Anatomy
       Respiratory organs
   RT Branchial arch
   NT Branchiostegals
       Chloride cells
Gills family
   USE Gill family
Gillson family
   USE Gilson family
Gilman family (Not Subd Geog)
   UF Gillman family
       Gilmon family
Gilman Garrison House (Exeter, N.H.)
   UF Garrison Gilman House (Exeter, N.H.)
       Garrison House (Exeter, N.H.)
   BT Dwellings—New Hampshire
Gilmer family
   USE Gilmore family
Gilmon family
   USE Gilman family
Gilmor family
   USE Gilmore family
Gilmore family (Not Subd Geog)
   UF Gillmor family
       Gillmore family
       Gilmer family
       Gilmor family
       Gilmour family
Gilmour family
   USE Gilmore family
Giloca River (Spain)
   USE Jiloca River (Spain)
Gilolo (Indonesia)
   USE Halmahera (Indonesia)
Gilot family
   USE Gullett family
Gilpichthys
   ⌈QE852.A33⌉
   BT Agnatha, Fossil
Gilpichthys greenei
   ⌈QE852.A33⌉
Gilpinia
   ⌈QL568.D5⌉
   BT Diprionidae
Gilson family (Not Subd Geog)
   UF Gillson family

Gilsonite
   ⌈QE391.G⌉
   UF Uintaite
   BT Hydrocarbons
Gilt bronzes (May Subd Geog)
   BT Bronzes
       Gilding
Gilt bronzes, Buddhist (May Subd Geog)
   UF Buddhist gilt bronzes
Gilt bronzes, Chinese (May Subd Geog)
   UF Chinese gilt bronzes
Gilt bronzes, Japanese (May Subd Geog)
   UF Japanese gilt bronzes
   BT Bronzes, Japanese
   — To 794
   — To 1600
Gilt furniture (May Subd Geog)
   BT Furniture
Gilts
   USE Sows
Giltz family
   USE Kilts family
Gilyak
   USE Gilyaks
Gilyak language
   ⌈PM67⌉
   UF Giliak language
       Guiliak language
       Nivkh language
   BT Hyperborean languages
Gilyaks
   ⌈DK759.G5⌉
   UF Ghiliaks
       Giliak
       Giliaks
       Gilyak
       Nivkh
       Nivkhi
   BT Ethnology—Russian S.F.S.R.
   — Implements
Gimarra (African people)
   USE Gimira (African people)
Gimbala (Bantu people)
   USE Mbala (Bantu people)
Gimbala language
   USE Mbala language (Bandundu region, Zaire)
Gimbold family
   USE Gamble family
Gimbunda language
   USE Mbunda language (Zambia)
Gimi language (May Subd Geog)
   BT Papua New Guinea—Languages
       Papuan languages
Gimini (African people)
   USE Djimini (African people)
Gimira (African people)
   ⌈DT380.4.G35⌉
   UF Chimira (African people)
       Gimarra (African people)
   BT Cushites
       Ethnology—Ethiopia
GIML (Computer program language)
   ⌈QA76.73.G⌉
   UF Graphical interactive machine
       language (Computer program
       language)
   BT Computer graphics
       Interactive computer systems
Gimpel family
   USE Gamble family
Gin
   ⌈TP607.G4⌉
Gin (Cotton machinery)
   USE Cotton gins and ginning
Gin family
   USE Ginn family
Gin rummy
   USE Rummy (Game)
Gines family
   USE Joines family

Ginetta automobile
   ⌈TL215.G⌉
   BT Sports cars
Ginger (May Subd Geog)
   UF Amomum zingiber
       Canton ginger
       Common ginger
       True ginger
       Zingiber officinale
       Zingiber officinalis
       Zingiber zingeber
       Zingiber zingiber
   NT Cookery (Ginger)
Ginger beer bottles (May Subd Geog)
   BT Beverage containers
       Bottles
Ginger industry (May Subd Geog)
   ⌈HD9211.G55-554⌉
Gingerbread
   BT Cake
   NT Gingerbread houses
Gingerbread houses
   UF Houses, Gingerbread
   BT Christmas cookery
       Christmas decorations
       Cookery (Ginger)
       Cookies
       Gingerbread
Gingerich family
   USE Gingrich family
Gingin Brook (W.A.)
   BT Rivers—Australia
Gingiva
   USE Gums
Gingival curettage
   USE Subgingival curettage
Gingival fluid
   UF Crevicular fluid
   BT Body fluids
       Gums
Gingival hyperplasia (May Subd Geog)
   UF Gingival overgrowth
   BT Gums—Diseases
       Hyperplasia
Gingival overgrowth
   USE Gingival hyperplasia
Gingivectomy (May Subd Geog)
   BT Gums—Surgery
Gingivitis (May Subd Geog)
   ⌈RK410⌉
   UF Gums—Inflammation
   BT Gums—Diseases
Gingivitis, Necrotizing ulcerative
   (May Subd Geog)
   ⌈RK410⌉
   UF Necrotizing ulcerative gingivitis
       Trench mouth
       Ulcerative gingivitis
       Ulceromembranous gingivitis
       Vincent's gingivitis
       Vincent's infection
Gingko
   USE Ginkgo
Gingras family (Not Subd Geog)
Gingrich family
   UF Genrich family
       Gingerich family
       Guengerich family
       Güngerich family
   RT Kingery family
Gini coefficient
   UF Coefficient, Gini
   BT Income distribution—Mathematical
       models
Ginkgo
   ⌈QK495.G48⌉

Ginkgo (Continued)
  UF Gingko
      Ginkgo biloba
      Ginkgoaceae
      Ginkgoales
      Ginkyo
      Maidenhair tree
      Salisburia
  BT Gymnosperms
Ginkgo, Fossil
  UF Ginkgoaceae, Fossil
Ginkgo biloba
  USE Ginkgo
Ginkgoaceae
  USE Ginkgo
Ginkgoaceae, Fossil
  USE Ginkgo, Fossil
Ginkgoales
  USE Ginkgo
Ginks family
  USE Jenkins family
Ginkyo
  USE Ginkgo
Ginn family (Not Subd Geog)
  UF Genn family
      Gin family
      Gyn family
      Gynn family
Ginnings family
  USE Jennings family
Ginny dolls (May Subd Geog)
  [NK4894.3.G55]
  BT Dolls—United States
Ginori family (Not Subd Geog)
Ginseng (May Subd Geog)
  [QK495.A6853 (Botany)]
  [SB295.G5 (Medicinal plants)]
  UF Aralia ginseng
      Chinese ginseng
      Genseng
      Panax ginseng
      Panax pseudoginseng
      Panax schinseng
  NT American ginseng
Ginseng industry (May Subd Geog)
  [HD9019.G55-HD9019.G552
    (Agricultural industry)]
  [HD9675.G5-HD9675.G7 (Drug
    trade)]
Ginukh dialect
  [PK9201.G5]
  BT Daghestan languages
Ginza (Tokyo, Japan) (Not Subd Geog)
  UF Tokyo (Japan). Ginza
Ginzan-ko (Japan)
  USE Okutadami Lake (Japan)
Ginzan Lake (Japan)
  USE Okutadami Lake (Japan)
Gio language
  USE Dan language
Gioco del calcio fiorentino
  USE Florentine football
Gion family
  USE Guion family
Gion Festival
  UF Gion Matsuri
      Gionmatsuri
  BT Fasts and feasts—Shinto
      Festivals—Japan
Gion Matsuri
  USE Gion Festival
Giong
  USE Moso (Tribe)
Gionmatsuri
  USE Gion Festival
Giorgi family (Not Subd Geog)
Giorgio, Monte San (Switzerland)
  USE San Giorgio Mountain (Switzerland)
Giorgione, 1477-1511. Nativity
  [ND623.G]

UF Natività (Painting)
    Nativity (Painting)
  BT Jesus Christ—Art
Giovanna (Legendary Pope)
  USE Joan (Legendary Pope)
Giovanna Baccelli (Portrait painting)
  USE Gainsborough, Thomas, 1727-1788.
      Giovanna Baccelli
Giovanni (Name)
  USE John (Name)
Gip family
  USE Gibson family
Gipel family
  USE Gibble family
Gipende language
  USE Pende language
Gipfel family
  USE Gibble family
Gipp family
  USE Gibson family
Gipple family
  USE Gibble family
Gippsland (Vic.)
Gippsland Lakes (Vic.)
  BT Lakes—Australia
Giprus
  [QL527.C49]
GIPS (Electronic computer system)
  UF General Integrated Programming
      System
Gips family
  USE Gibson family
Gipsies
  USE Gypsies
Gipson family
  USE Gibson family
GIPSY (Computer program)
  UF Geographic Incremental Plotting
      System
GIPSY (Information retrieval system)
  UF General Information Processing
      System
  BT Information storage and retrieval
      systems
Gipsy moth
  USE Gypsy moth
Gipsy musicians
  USE Musicians, Gypsy
Giraffes
  [QL737.U5]
  BT Ruminants
  NT Daisy Rothschild (Giraffe)
      Okapi
Giraffes, Fossil
  [QE882.U3]
Girard family (Not Subd Geog)
  RT Gerard family
Girasia (Indic people)
  USE Grasia (Indic people)
Giraud family
  USE Gerow family
Gîrbova Mountains (Romania)
  USE Baiului Mountains (Romania)
Girders
  [TA891 (Riveting)]
  [TG350-TG360]
  UF Beams
  BT Bars (Engineering)
      Building
      Engineering
      Flexure
      Structural frames
  RT Bridges
      Graphic statics
  NT Box beams
      Building, Iron and steel
      Castellated beams
      Concrete beams
      Diaphragms (Structural engineering)
      Flitch beams
      Grillages (Structural engineering)

      Influence lines
      Plate girders
      Roofs
      Spandrel beams
      Steel, Structural
      Steel I-beams
      Steel joists
      Steel-wood I-beams
      Thin-walled structures
      Wooden beams
  — Testing
  — Vibration
  — Welding
Girders, Composite
  USE Composite construction
Girders, Continuous
  [TG355]
  UF Continuous girders
  BT Graphic statics
      Strains and stresses
  NT Bridges, Continuous
      Influence lines
  — Vibration
Girders, Plate
  USE Plate girders
Girdle, Shoulder
  USE Shoulder girdle
Girdle-tailed lizards
  USE Cordylidae
Girdles of chastity
  USE Chastity belts
Giriama (African people)
  USE Giryama (African people)
Giriama language
  USE Giryama language
Girl apprentices
  USE Women apprentices
Girl preferences of parents
  USE Sex of children, Parental preferences
      for
Girl Scouts (May Subd Geog)
  [HS3353.G5]
  BT Girls—Societies and clubs
  SA subdivision War work—Girl Scouts
      under individual wars, e.g. World
      War, 1939-1945—War work—Girl
      Scouts
  — Public relations
      UF Public relations—Girl Scouts
Girl victims of crimes
  USE Girls—Crimes against
Girlie magazines (May Subd Geog)
  UF Girly magazines
  BT Erotica
      Sex oriented periodicals
Girlington family
  USE Garlington family
Girls (May Subd Geog)
  [BJ1651-BJ1658 (Ethics)]
  [GT2540 (Manners and customs)]
  [HQ777 (Care of)]
  [HV879-HV887 (Aids and homes for)]
  BT Parent and child
      Women
  RT Children
      Young women
      Youth
  SA subdivision Participation, Juvenile
      under individual wars, e.g. World
      War, 1939-1945—Participation,
      Juvenile
  NT Adolescent girls
      Christian education of girls
      Daughters
      Delinquent girls
      Etiquette for girls
      Fathers and daughters
      Gifted girls
      Mothers and daughters
      Religious education of girls
      Sex instruction for girls

Sisters
— **Anthropometry**
— **Biography**
  [CT3205]
    RT Children—Biography
    NT Children in the Bible
— **Crimes against**
  [HV6250.4.G57]
    UF Crimes against girls
        Girl victims of crimes
        Girls, Crimes against
    BT Child abuse
        Child molesting
— **Diseases** *(May Subd Geog)*
— **Education**
    USE Coeducation
         Women—Education
— Education, Medieval
    USE Women—Education, Medieval
— Employment
    USE Children—Employment
         Youth—Employment
— Etiquette
    USE Etiquette for girls
— **Health and hygiene**
    BT Hygiene
— **Nutrition**
— **Portraits**
    BT Children—Portraits
        Children in art
— **Prayer-books and devotions**
— — **English,** [**French, German,** etc.]
— **Sexual behavior**
    BT Children—Sexual behavior
— **Societies and clubs** *(May Subd Geog)*
  [HS3341-3365]
    UF Girls' clubs
    BT Clubs
        Social settlements
        Societies
    NT 4-H clubs
        Gangs
        Girl Scouts
        Science clubs
        Working-women's clubs
        Young farmers' clubs
— **Diseases**
    NT Rett syndrome
Girls, Crimes against
    USE Girls—Crimes against
Girls, Delinquent
    USE Delinquent girls
Girls, Gifted
    USE Gifted girls
Girls as criminals
    USE Delinquent girls
Girls' basketball
    USE Basketball for women
Girls' clubs
    USE Girls—Societies and clubs
Girls in art
Girls in literature
    BT Children in literature
Girls in the Bible
    USE Children in the Bible
Girls' softball
    USE Softball for women
Girls' volleyball
    USE Volleyball for women
Girly magazines
    USE Girlie magazines
Girney family
    USE Gurney family
Giro d'Italia (Bicycle race)
Girón, Playa Invasion, 1961
    USE Cuba—History—Invasion, 1961
Girondists
  [DC179]
  [JN2474.G5 (Constitutional history)]

    BT France—History—Revolution, 1789-
        1799
        France—History—Revolution, 1789-
        1799—Clubs
Girsu (Ancient city) *(Not Subd Geog)*
    UF Tello (Iraq)
        Telloh (Iraq)
    BT Cities and towns, Ruined, extinct, etc.
        —Iraq
        Iraq—Antiquities
Giryama (African people)
  [DT433.545.G55]
    UF Agiryama (African people)
        Giriama (African people)
        Kigiriama (African people)
        Wagiliama (African people)
    BT Ethnology—Kenya
        Nika (African people)
— **Rites and ceremonies**
    NT Funeral rites and ceremonies,
        Giryama (African people)
Giryama (African people) funeral rites and
ceremonies
    USE Funeral rites and ceremonies, Giryama
         (African people)
Giryama (African people) sculpture
    USE Sculpture, Giryama (African people)
Giryama language
    UF Giriama language
        Kigiryama language
    BT Bantu languages
        Nika language
Giselle (Ballet)
  [GV1790.G5]
    BT Ballets
Gisert family
    USE Gossett family
Gishō Gengyō e (Scrolls)
    USE Kegon engi (Scrolls)
Gisi language
    USE Kissi language
Gisiga language
    UF Guissiga language
    BT Chadic languages
Gisira language
    USE Shira language
Gissar Mountains (Tajik S.S.R. and Uzbek
S.S.R.)
    USE Gissar Range (Tajik S.S.R. and Uzbek
         S.S.R.)
Gissar Range (Tajik S.S.R. and Uzbek S.S.R.)
    UF Gissar Mountains (Tajik S.S.R. and
        Uzbek S.S.R.)
        Gissarskiĭ khrebet (Tajik S.S.R. and
        Uzbek S.S.R.)
        Gissarskiy khrebet (Tajik S.S.R. and
        Uzbek S.S.R.)
        Khrebet Gissarskiy (Tajik S.S.R. and
        Uzbek S.S.R.)
    BT Mountains—Tajik S.S.R.
        Mountains—Uzbek S.S.R.
Gissar Valley (Tajik S.S.R.)
    UF Gissarskaĭa dolina (Tajik S.S.R.)
        Gissarskaya dolina (Tajik S.S.R.)
    BT Valleys—Tajik S.S.R.
Gissarskaĭa dolina (Tajik S.S.R.)
    USE Gissar Valley (Tajik S.S.R.)
Gissarskaya dolina (Tajik S.S.R.)
    USE Gissar Valley (Tajik S.S.R.)
Gissarskiĭ khrebet (Tajik S.S.R. and Uzbek
S.S.R.)
    USE Gissar Range (Tajik S.S.R. and Uzbek
         S.S.R.)
Gissarskiy khrebet (Tajik S.S.R. and Uzbek
S.S.R.)
    USE Gissar Range (Tajik S.S.R. and Uzbek
         S.S.R.)

Gist family *(Not Subd Geog)*
    UF Geist family
        Gesst family
        Gest family
        Gests family
        Geyst family
        Giest family
        Guist family

    RT Guest family

Gisu (African people)
    UF Bagesu (African people)
        Bagishu (African people)
        Gesu (African people)
        Gisu (Bantu tribe)

    BT Bantus
        Ethnology—Uganda
        Kavirondo (African people)

Gisu (Bantu tribe)
    USE Gisu (African people)
Gisu language
  [PL8207.G55]

    UF Lugisu language
        Lumasaaba language
        Masaba language

    BT Bantu languages

    NT Bukusu language

Gitgen family
    USE Geitgey family

Gitksan Indians
    USE Kitksan Indians

Gitonga (African people)
    USE Chopi (African people)

Gitonga language
    USE Tonga language (Inhambane)

Gittings family
    USE Giddings family

Gittins family
    USE Giddings family

Giuba River (Ethiopia and Somalia)
    USE Juba River (Ethiopia and Somalia)

Giudizio universale (Painting)
    USE Michelangelo Buonarroti, 1475-1564.
         Last judgment

         Miroglio, Valerio.   Last judgment

Giufà (Legendary character)
  [GR175-177]

    BT Folklore—Italy

Giuja River (Latvia and Estonia)
    USE Gauja River (Latvia and Estonia)

Giur language
    USE Lwo language (Sudan)

Givan family
    USE Givens family

Givans family
    USE Givens family

Givaro Indians
    USE Jivaro Indians

Give-aways
    USE Free material

Giveaways
    USE Free material

Given family
    USE Givens family

Givenn family
    USE Givens family

Givens family (Not Subd Geog)
  UF Gavan family
     Gaven family
     Gavin family
     Gaving family
     Gavon family
     Geven family
     Gevin family
     Givan family
     Givans family
     Given family
     Givenn family
     Givin family
     Givins family
     Givon family
     Givons family
     Givvins family
     Govan family
     Guivens family
Givin family
  USE Givens family
Giving
  USE Generosity
Giving, Buddhist
  USE Buddhist giving
Giving, Charitable
  USE subdivision Charitable contributions
       under classes of persons, ethnic
       groups, and types of organizations
Giving, Christian
  USE Christian giving
Giving, Deferred
  USE Deferred giving
Giving, Hindu
  USE Hindu giving
Giving, Jaina
  USE Jaina giving
Giving, Planned
  USE Deferred giving
Givins family
  USE Givens family
Givon family
  USE Givens family
Givons family
  USE Givens family
Givvins family
  USE Givens family
Giza Pyramids (Egypt)
  USE Pyramids of Giza (Egypt)
Gizi language
  USE Kissi language
Gizii (African people)
  USE Gusii (African people)
Gizima language
  USE Kissi language
Gizo (Legendary character)
  USE Anansi (Legendary character)
Gizzard
     ⌜QL862⌝
  BT Birds—Anatomy
     Stomach
Gizzard shad
  UF Dorosoma cepedianum
  BT Shad
Gizzard stones
  USE Gastroliths
Gjæslingan
Gjende (Norway)
  BT Lakes—Norway
Gjerde family (Not Subd Geog)
  UF Gerde family
     Jerdee family
Gjesme family
  USE Gesme family
Gjønnes family (Not Subd Geog)
Glaama River (Norway)
  USE Glomma River (Norway)
Glacial climates (May Subd Geog)
  UF Climates, Glacial
     Glacials
  BT Paleoclimatology

NT Geology, Stratigraphic—Pleistocene
Glacial cosmogony
  USE Cosmogony, Glacial
Glacial drift
  USE Drift
Glacial epoch (May Subd Geog)
     ⌜QE697-QE698⌝
  UF Ice age
  BT Geology, Stratigraphic—Quaternary
  RT Geology, Stratigraphic—Pleistocene
  NT Drumlins
     Loess
     Varves
— Arctic regions
     NT Bering Land Bridge
— California
— Canada
— Idaho
— Nevada
— United States
— Utah
— Wisconsin
     NT Ice Age National Scientific
        Reserve (Wis.)
Glacial erosion (May Subd Geog)
     ⌜QE575-6⌝
  UF Ice erosion
  BT Erosion
Glacial ice covers
  USE Ice sheets
Glacial Lake Agassiz
  USE Agassiz, Lake
Glacial Lake Algonquin
  USE Algonquin, Lake
Glacial Lake Missoula
  USE Missoula, Lake
Glacial lakes (May Subd Geog)
  BT Glacial landforms
     Lakes
— Canada
     NT Agassiz, Lake
— Idaho
     NT Missoula, Lake
— Montana
     NT Missoula, Lake
— Ontario
     NT Algonquin, Lake
— United States
     NT Agassiz, Lake
        Algonquin, Lake
— Washington (State)
     NT Missoula, Lake
Glacial landforms (May Subd Geog)
     ⌜GB581-588⌝
  UF Glaciated terrain
  BT Landforms
  NT Glacial lakes
     Moraines
     Rock glaciers
— California
— Canada
— United States
Glacials
  USE Glacial climates
Glaciares National Park (Argentina)
  USE Parque Nacional Los Glaciares
       (Argentina)
Glaciated terrain
  USE Glacial landforms
Glacicavicola
     ⌜QL596.L43⌝
  BT Leptodiridae
Glacicavicola bathyscioides
     ⌜QL596.L43⌝
Glacier Bay (Alaska)
  BT Bays—Alaska
  NT Glacier Bay National Park and
     Preserve (Alaska)
Glacier Bay National Monument (Alaska)
  USE Glacier Bay National Park and
       Preserve (Alaska)

Glacier Bay National Park and Preserve
(Alaska)
  UF Glacier Bay National Monument
     (Alaska)
  BT Glacier Bay (Alaska)
     Glaciers—Alaska
     National parks and reserves—United
       States
     Natural monuments—Alaska
     Parks—Alaska
Glacier bear
  UF Blue bear
     Euarctos emmonsi
     Ursus emmonsi
  BT Bears
     Black bear
Glacier caves (May Subd Geog)
  BT Caves
Glacier du Rhône (Switzerland)
  USE Rhone Glacier (Switzerland)
Glacier Express (Express train)
  BT Railroads—Switzerland—Express-trains
Glacier National Park (B.C.)
  UF Parc national de Glacier (B.C.)
     Parc national Glacier (B.C.)
  BT National parks and reserves—British
     Columbia
Glacier National Park (Mont.)
  BT Glaciers—Montana
     National parks and reserves—United
       States
     Parks—Montana
  NT Going-to-the-Sun Road (Mont.)
Glaciers, The (Argentina)
  USE Parque Nacional Los Glaciares
       (Argentina)
Glaciers (May Subd Geog)
     ⌜GB2401-GB2598⌝
  BT Ice
  RT Glaciology
  NT Ice mechanics
     Ice sheets
     Surging glaciers
— Alaska
     NT Columbia Glacier (Alaska)
        Glacier Bay National Park and
          Preserve (Alaska)
        Matanuska Glacier (Alaska)
— Alberta
     NT Athabasca Glacier (Alta.)
        Columbia Icefield (B.C. and Alta.)
        Peyto Glacier (Alta.)
        Saskatchewan Glacier (Alta.)
— Antarctic regions
     NT Beardmore Glacier (Antarctic
          regions)
        Hays Glacier (Antarctic regions)
        Shackleton Glacier (Antarctic
          regions)
        Taylor Glacier (Antarctic regions)
— Argentina
     NT Parque Nacional Los Glaciares
          (Argentina)
— Austria
     NT Hochkönig Glacier (Austria)
— British Columbia
     NT Columbia Icefield (B.C. and Alta.)
— Iceland
     NT Langjökull Glacier (Iceland)
        Mýrdalsjökull (Iceland)
— Montana
     NT Glacier National Park (Mont.)
— Peru
     NT Broggi Glacier (Peru)
— Russian S.F.S.R.
     NT Kolka Glacier (R.S.F.S.R.)
— Switzerland
     NT Grindelwald Glacier (Switzerland)
        Rhone Glacier (Switzerland)
Glaciers, Rock
  USE Rock glaciers

Glaciology
  [GB2401-GB2598]
  BT Hydrology
  RT Glaciers
  NT Aerial photography in glaciology
      Astronautics in glaciology
      Ice caps
      Ice mechanics
      Radar in glaciology
      Radioisotopes in glaciology
Gladden family (Not Subd Geog)
  UF Gladdin family
      Gladding family
      Gladdon family
      Glade family
      Gladen family
      Glading family
      Gladney family
Gladdin family
  USE Gladden family
Gladding family
  USE Gladden family
Gladdishe family
  USE Gladwish family
Gladdon family
  USE Gladden family
Glade family
  USE Gladden family
Gladen family
  USE Gladden family
Gladiator (Fighter planes)
  UF Gloster Gladiator
  BT Fighter planes
      Gloster aircraft
Gladiatorial War, 73-71 B.C.
  USE Rome—History—Servile Wars, 135-71
      B.C.
Gladiators
  [DG95]
  [GV35]
  UF Fighting
  NT Auctorati
Gladiators, War of the, 73-71 B.C.
  USE Rome—History—Servile Wars, 135-71
      B.C.
Gladiators in art
Gladieux family (Not Subd Geog)
Gladigau family (Not Subd Geog)
  UF Gladigow family
Gladigow family
  USE Gladigau family
Glading family
  USE Gladden family
Gladiolus (May Subd Geog)
  [QK495.I75 (Botany)]
  [SB413.G5 (Ornamental plants)]
  UF Corn flags
      Flags, Corn
      Lilies, Sword
      Sword lilies
  BT Iridaceae
Gladish family
  USE Gladwish family
Gladishe family
  USE Gladwish family
Gladness
  USE Cheerfulness
      Contentment
      Happiness
Gladney family
  USE Gladden family
Gladstone, Port of (Qld.) (Not Subd Geog)
  UF Curtis, Port (Qld.)
      Gladstone Harbour (Qld.)
      Port Curtis (Qld.)
      Port of Gladstone (Qld.)
  BT Harbors—Australia
Gladstone Harbour (Qld.)
  USE Gladstone, Port of (Qld.)

Gladwish family (Not Subd Geog)
  UF De Gladwyshe family
      Gladdishe family
      Gladish family
      Gladishe family
      Gladwishe family
      Gladwyshe family
      Gladyshe family
      Gleddish family
      Gledwishe family
Gladwishe family
  USE Gladwish family
Gladwyshe family
  USE Gladwish family
Gladyshe family
  USE Gladwish family
Glagolitic alphabet
  [PG91]
  BT Alphabet
      Slavic languages—Alphabet
Glagolitic diplomatics
  USE Diplomatics, Glagolitic
Glagolitic imprints (May Subd Geog)
Glagolitic inscriptions
  USE Inscriptions, Glagolitic
Glagolitic literature
  USE Church Slavic literature
Glagolitic manuscripts
  USE Manuscripts, Glagolitic
Glagolitic paleography
  USE Paleography, Glagolitic
Glåma River (Norway)
  USE Glomma River (Norway)
Glamor photography
  USE Glamour photography
Glamour photography
  [TR678]
  UF Cheesecake photography
      Glamor photography
      Photography, Glamour
      Pin-up photography
      Pinup photography
  BT Photography—Portraits
      Photography, Artistic
      Photography, Erotic
  NT Pinup art
Glance
  USE Chalcocite
Glancey family
  USE Clancy family
Glancy family
  USE Clancy family
Gland of Bartholin
  USE Bartholin's gland
Gland of internal secretion
  USE Endocrine glands
Gland of Luschka
  USE Coccygeal gland
Glanders
  [RC146 (Human)]
  [SF796]
  UF Farcy (Glanders)
  BT Horses—Diseases
  RT Epizootic lymphangitis
  NT Melioidosis
Glands
  [QL865-QL868 (Comparative
      anatomy)]
  [QM325-QM371 (Human anatomy)]
  [QP190-QP246 (Physiology)]
  RT Secretion
  SA particular glands, e.g. Cowper's glands;
      Hemolymph glands; Kidneys; Liver
  NT Endocrine glands
      Exocrine glands
      Salt gland
  — Diseases (May Subd Geog)
      [RC633]
      [RC648-RC659]
      NT Cystic fibrosis
  — Transplantation

Glands, Cutaneous
  USE Cutaneous glands
Glands, Ductless
  USE Endocrine glands
Glands, Lacrimal
  USE Lacrimal organs
Glands, Mammary
  USE Mammary glands
Glands, Odoriferous
  [QL494-QL496 (Insects)]
  [QL943]
  BT Animal defenses
      Odors
Glands, Salivary
  USE Salivary glands
Glands, Sebaceous
  USE Sebaceous glands
Glands (Botany)
  [QK650]
  [QK703]
Glands of Brunner
  USE Brunner's glands
Glandula uropygalis
  USE Uropygial gland
Glandular fever
  USE Mononucleosis
Glanencheli
  USE Cypriniformes
Glaphyridae
  USE Scarabaeidae
Glaphyriidae
  USE Pyralidae
Glare, Headlight
  USE Headlight glare
Glare screens
  USE Roads—Glare screens
Glareolidae
  [QL696.C448]
  BT Charadriiformes
  NT Pluvianus
Glarner Alpen (Switzerland)
  USE Glarner Alps (Switzerland)
Glarner Alps (Switzerland)
  UF Glarner Alpen (Switzerland)
      Glärnisch (Switzerland)
      Glaurus Alps (Switzerland)
  BT Alps
      Mountains—Switzerland
Glärnisch (Switzerland)
  USE Glarner Alps (Switzerland)
GLAS (Computer system)
  UF General Ledger Accounting System
      (Computer system)
  BT Accounting—Data processing
      Electronic digital computers—
      Programming
      SuperCalc (Computer program)
Glas automobile
  [TL215.G5]
  UF Goggomobil automobile
      Isar automobile
Glascock family (Not Subd Geog)
  UF Glascocke family
      Glasscock family
Glascocke family
  USE Glascock family
Glaser family
  USE Glass family
Glasgow (Strathclyde). Gorbals
  USE Gorbals (Glasgow, Strathclyde)
Glasgow school of painters
  USE Glasgow school of painting
Glasgow school of painting
  [ND481.G5]
  UF Glasgow school of painters
  BT Painting, Modern—19th century—
      Scotland
      Painting, Scottish
Glaskasten Marl (Marl, Germany)
  USE Skulpturenmuseum Glaskasten (Marl,
      Germany)

Glaspalast (Munich, Germany)
  UF Crystal Palace (Munich, Germany)
  BT Exhibition buildings—Germany (West)
Glass
    [NK5100-NK5430 (Decorative art)]
    [QC375 (Optical instruments)]
    [TA450 (Materials of engineering and
      construction)]
  BT Amorphous substances
      Ceramics
      Optical instruments
  NT Crystal glass
      Electric insulators and insulation—
        Glass
      Glass-ceramics
      Glass coatings
      Glass-metal sealing
      Glassware
      Jena glass
      Silica, Vitreous
  — **Bonding**
     [TP858]
    NT Glass-metal sealing
  — **Defects**
  — **Electric properties**
  — **Fracture**
    BT Fracture mechanics
  — Grinding
    USE Glass grinding and polishing
  — Melting
    USE Glass melting
  — Polishing
    USE Glass grinding and polishing
  — Recycling
    USE Glass waste—Recycling
  — **Research** (May Subd Geog)
    UF Glass research
  — **Standards**
Glass, Cameo
  USE Cameo glass
Glass, Carnival
  USE Carnival glass
Glass, Cellular
  USE Cellular glass
Glass, Colored (May Subd Geog)
  UF Colored glass
  BT Glass, Ornamental
  RT Glass painting and staining
  NT Pâte de verre
  — **United States**
    NT Favrile glass
Glass, Custard
  USE Custard glass
Glass, Cut
  USE Cut glass
Glass, Depression
  USE Depression glass
Glass, Enameled
  USE Enameled glass
Glass, Engraved
  USE Engraved glass
Glass, Foam
  USE Cellular glass
Glass, Milk
  USE Milk glass
Glass, Millefiori
    [NK5430]
  UF Millefiori glass
Glass, Opal
  USE Opal glass
Glass, Opaque
  USE Milk glass
Glass, Optical
    [QC375]
  UF Optical glass
  BT Lenses
      Optical instruments
  NT Glass grinding and polishing
Glass, Ornamental
    [TP863-TP864]

    Here are entered works on cut, embossed, sand-
blast, and other ornamental glass used in building.
  BT Cut glass
      Decoration and ornament
  NT Engraved glass
      Glass, Colored
      Glass construction
      Glass embossing
      Glass engraving
      Glass etching
      Glass painting and staining
      Sand-blast
Glass, Pearl art
  USE Pearl art glass
Glass, Photosensitive
  UF Photosensitive glass
Glass, Plate
  USE Plate-glass
Glass, Pressed
  USE Pressed glass
Glass, Safety
    [TP862]
  UF Laminated glass
      Non-shatterable glass
      Safety glass
      Shatter-proof glass
  BT Laminated materials
  — Tariff
    USE Tariff on safety glass
Glass, Soluble
  USE Soluble glass
Glass, Spun
  USE Glass fibers
Glass, Stained
  USE Glass painting and staining
Glass architecture
  USE Glass construction
Glass art (May Subd Geog)
    [NK5100-5440]
  BT Art
      Decorative arts
  NT Engraved glass
      Glass chandeliers
      Glass craft
      Glass figurines
      Glass painting and staining
      Glass sculpture
      Glass underpainting
Glass as structural material
  USE Glass construction
Glass baskets
  USE Baskets, Glass
Glass beads (May Subd Geog)
  BT Beads
      Granular materials
  — **Italy**
  —— **Murano**
      UF Venetian beads
Glass bells (May Subd Geog)
    [NK5440.B37]
  BT Bells
      Glassware
Glass blocks (May Subd Geog)
    [TH1560 (Glass construction)]
  BT Blocks (Building materials)
Glass blowing and working
  (May Subd Geog)
    [TP859]
  BT Chemical apparatus
      Chemistry—Laboratory manuals
      Chemistry—Manipulation
      Glass craft
      Glass manufacture
Glass bottom boats
  BT Boats and boating
Glass candlesticks (May Subd Geog)
    [NK5440.C26]
  UF Candlesticks, Glass
  BT Candlesticks
      Glassware

Glass candy containers (May Subd Geog)
    [NK5440.C3]
  UF Candy containers, Glass
  BT Food containers
      Glass containers
Glass canopies, Architectural
  (May Subd Geog)
  UF Architectural glass canopies
  BT Canopies, Architectural
      Glass construction
Glass-ceramic pipe
  USE Pipe, Glass-ceramic
Glass-ceramics
  UF Devitrified glass
      Pyroceram
      Pyroceramics
  BT Ceramics
      Glass
  NT Pipe, Glass-ceramic
Glass chandeliers (May Subd Geog)
    [NK5440.C48]
  BT Chandeliers
      Glass art
Glass Christmas decorations
  (May Subd Geog)
    [NK5440.C4]
  BT Christmas decorations
      Glassware
Glass cloth
  UF Cloth, Glass
  BT Glass fibers
Glass coatings
    Here are entered works on coatings applied to the
surfaces of glass objects.
  UF Coatings, Glass
  BT Coatings
      Glass
      Thin films
Glass construction (May Subd Geog)
    [NA4140 (Architecture)]
    [TH1560 (Building)]
  UF Glass architecture
      Glass as structural material
      Glass in architecture
  BT Architecture
      Building
      Glass, Ornamental
  RT Conservatories
  NT Glass canopies, Architectural
      Glass doors
Glass container industry (May Subd Geog)
    [HD9624.C66-664]
  BT Glass containers
Glass containers
  BT Containers
      Glassware
  NT Bottles
      Glass candy containers
      Glass container industry
      Glass fruit jars
Glass craft (May Subd Geog)
    [TT298]
  BT Glass art
      Handicraft
  NT Glass blowing and working
      Glass embossing
      Glass engraving
      Glass etching
      Glass figurines
      Glass grinding and polishing
      Glass painting and staining
  — **Patterns**
Glass doors (May Subd Geog)
  BT Doors
      Glass construction
  NT Revolving doors
Glass doors, Sliding
  UF Sliding-glass doors
  BT Doors
Glass electrodes
  USE Electrodes, Glass

Glass embossing
[TP863]
UF Embossing of glass
BT Glass, Ornamental
Glass craft
Glass engraving
BT Engraving
Glass, Ornamental
Glass craft
NT Engraved glass
Glass etching *(May Subd Geog)*
BT Etching
Glass, Ornamental
Glass craft
NT Heisey Rose (Glass etching)
Heisey's Orchid (Glass etching)
— Patterns
Glass factories *(May Subd Geog)*
BT Factories
Glass family *(Not Subd Geog)*
UF Glaser family
Glasser family
Glass fiber board
USE Glass fiberboard
Glass fiber craft
USE Fiberglass craft
Glass fiber industry *(May Subd Geog)*
UF Fibrous glass industry
BT Glass manufacture
Glass trade
Man-made fibers industry
NT Glass reinforced plastics
Glass fiber sculpture *(May Subd Geog)*
[NB1270.G5]
BT Glass reinforced plastics
Plastic sculpture
Sculpture
Glass fiberboard
[TA450]
UF Fiberboard, Glass
Fibrous glass board
Glass fiber board
BT Fiberboard
Glass fibers
UF Fiber glass
Fiberglass
Fibers, Glass
Glass, Spun
Spun glass
RT Silicate fibers
NT Electric insulators and insulation—
Glass fibers
Glass cloth
Glass reinforced plastics
Quartz fibers
— Dyeing
USE Dyes and dyeing—Glass fibers
— Tariff
USE Tariff on glass fibers
Glass figurines *(May Subd Geog)*
UF Figurines, Glass
BT Figurines
Glass art
Glass craft
Glassware
Glass fishing floats *(May Subd Geog)*
UF Glass floats
BT Fishing nets
Glassware
Glass-flake laminates
USE Flake-glass laminates
Glass floats
USE Glass fishing floats
Glass fruit jars *(May Subd Geog)*
[NK5440.F7]
UF Fruit jars, Glass
BT Canning and preserving—Equipment
and supplies
Glass containers

Glass furnaces
UF Glass melting furnaces
Glass tank furnaces
BT Furnaces
Glass manufacture
Glass melting
Glass gardens
[SB417]
UF Bottle gardens
Gardens, Glass
Plant terrariums
BT Container gardening
Gardens, Miniature
Indoor gardening
Indoor gardens
Terrariums
RT Wardian cases
NT Miniature plants
Glass grinding and polishing
UF Glass—Grinding
Glass—Polishing
Glass polishing
BT Glass, Optical
Glass craft
Glass manufacture
Grinding and polishing
NT Turning, Diamond
Glass harmonica
[ML1055]
UF Glasses, Musical
Harmonica, Glass
Musical glasses
Glass-harmonica and lute music
[M298]
UF Lute and glass-harmonica music
Glass-harmonica and piano music
[M284.G6]
[M285.G6]
UF Piano and glass-harmonica music
Glass-harmonica music
[M165]
SA Concertos, Minuets, Sonatas, Suites,
*and similar headings with
specification of instruments; Trios
[Quartets, etc.] followed by
specifications which include the
glass harmonica; also headings that
begin with the words glass
harmonica or glass harmonicas*
Glass in architecture
USE Glass construction
Glass in literature
Glass in medicine *(May Subd Geog)*
[R857.G55]
BT Biomedical materials
Glass industry
USE Glass manufacture
Glass trade
Glass-joining to metals
USE Glass-metal sealing
Glass kerosene lamps *(May Subd Geog)*
[NK5440.K44]
UF Kerosene lamps, Glass
BT Glassware
Kerosene lamps
Glass knives *(May Subd Geog)*
[NK5440.K54 (Art industries)]
BT Glassware
Knives
Glass lampshades
USE Lampshades, Glass
Glass lizards
USE Ophisaurus
Glass manufacture *(May Subd Geog)*
[TP845-869]
UF Glass industry
BT Ceramic industries
NT Annealing of glass
Bottle industry
Glass blowing and working
Glass fiber industry

Glass furnaces
Glass grinding and polishing
Glass melting
Glass-workers
Optical instruments
Precious stones, Artificial
Pressed glass
Sand, Glass
— Chemistry
— Collective labor agreements
USE Collective labor agreements—
Glass manufacture
— **Equipment and supplies**
— — Appraisal
USE Glass manufacture—
Equipment and supplies—
Valuation
— — **Valuation**
UF Glass manufacture—Equipment
and supplies—Appraisal
— **Molds**
[TP859.5]
UF Glassmaking molds
Molds, Glassmaking
BT Molding materials
Glass melting
UF Glass—Melting
BT Glass manufacture
NT Glass furnaces
Glass melting furnaces
USE Glass furnaces
Glass-metal sealing
[TS718]
UF Glass-joining to metals
Glass-to-metal sealing
Metal-bonding to glass
Metal-glass sealing
Metal-to-glass sealing
BT Glass
Glass—Bonding
Metal bonding
Metals
Sealing (Technology)
Welding
Glass Mountain (Mono County, Calif.)
(Not Subd Geog)
BT Mountains—California
Glass painters *(May Subd Geog)*
UF Glasspainters
BT Glass painting and staining
Painters
Glass painting and staining
(May Subd Geog)
[NK5300-5410]
UF Glass, Stained
Painted glass
Stained glass
Windows, Stained glass
BT Art
Arts and crafts movement
Church decoration and ornament
Color in the ceramic industries
Decoration and ornament
Glass, Ornamental
Glass art
Glass craft
Painting
RT Glass, Colored
NT Glass painters
Lumiprints
— **Patterns**
[TT298]
Glass painting and staining, Baroque
(May Subd Geog)
UF Baroque glass painting and staining
Glass painting and staining, Cistercian
(May Subd Geog)
UF Cistercian glass painting and staining
Glass painting and staining, Gothic
(May Subd Geog)
UF Gothic glass painting and staining

Glass painting and staining, Gothic
  (Continued)
  NT Rose windows
Glass painting and staining, Islamic
  (May Subd Geog)
  UF Islamic glass painting and staining
Glass painting and staining, Medieval
  (May Subd Geog)
  NT Rose windows
Glass painting and staining, Renaissance
  (May Subd Geog)
  UF Renaissance glass painting and staining
Glass painting and staining, Romanesque
  (May Subd Geog)
  UF Romanesque glass painting and
      staining
Glass painting and staining, Victorian
  (May Subd Geog)
  UF Victorian glass painting and staining
Glass painting and staining industry
  (May Subd Geog)
  [HD9624.S72-724]
Glass pipe
  USE Pipe, Glass
Glass plastics
  USE Glass reinforced plastics
Glass polishing
  USE Glass grinding and polishing
Glass print
  USE Cliché-verre
Glass recycling
  USE Glass waste—Recycling
Glass reinforced plastics
  UF Fiber glass reinforced plastics
      Glass plastics
  BT Fiber reinforced plastics
      Glass fiber industry
      Glass fibers
      Plastics
      Reinforced plastics
  RT Pultrusion
  NT Fiberglass boats
      Flake-glass laminates
      Glass fiber sculpture
  — Thermal properties
    [TA455.P55]
Glass reinforced plastics industry
  (May Subd Geog)
  [HD9662.G5-53]
Glass research
  USE Glass—Research
Glass sand
  USE Sand, Glass
Glass sculpture *(May Subd Geog)*
  [NB1270.G4]
  UF Sculpture, Glass
  BT Glass art
      Sculpture
  NT Neon sculpture
Glass tank furnaces
  USE Glass furnaces
Glass-to-metal sealing
  USE Glass-metal sealing
Glass trade *(May Subd Geog)*
  [HD9623]
  [HF2651.G5 (Tariff)]
  UF Glass industry
  NT Bottle industry
      Glass fiber industry
      Strikes and lockouts—Glass trade
Glass underpainting *(May Subd Geog)*
  [NK5431-5436]
  UF Hinterglasmalerei
      Painting, Underglass
      Peinture sous verre
      Pictures on glass
      Reverse-painted glass
  BT Folk art
      Glass art
      Painting

Glass underpainting, Medieval
  (May Subd Geog)
  UF Medieval glass underpainting
Glass underpainting, Renaissance
  (May Subd Geog)
  UF Renaissance glass underpainting
Glass waste
  UF Waste glass
  BT Waste products
  — Recycling *(May Subd Geog)*
    [TP859.7]
    UF Glass—Recycling
        Glass recycling
Glass weights
  [CJ3413]
  BT Weights and measures, Arabic
Glass-workers *(May Subd Geog)*
  [HD8039.G5]
  BT Glass manufacture
  NT Collective labor agreements—Glass
      manufacture
      Trade-unions—Glass-workers
      Wages—Glass-workers
  — Belgium
    NT Glaverbel-Gilly (Firm) Strike,
        1974-1975
Glassboro Conference, 1967
Glasscock family
  USE Glascock family
Glasser family
  USE Glass family
Glasses, Eye
  USE Eyeglasses
Glasses, Magnetic
  USE Spin glasses
Glasses, Metallic
  USE Metallic glasses
Glasses, Musical
  USE Glass harmonica
Glasses, Spin
  USE Spin glasses
Glasseyed pike
  USE Walleye (Fish)
Glasshouse crops
  USE Greenhouse plants
Glasshouse plants
  USE Greenhouse plants
Glassites
  USE Sandemanianism
Glassmaking molds
  USE Glass manufacture—Molds
Glasspainters
  USE Glass painters
Glassware *(May Subd Geog)*
  [NK5101-NK5430 (Art)]
  [TP865-TP868 (Technology)]
  BT Glass
      House furnishings
      Table setting and decoration
      Vases
  NT Baskets, Glass
      Cameo glass
      Crackle
      Crystal glass
      Cup plates
      Custard glass
      Cut glass
      Depression glass
      Enameled glass
      Engraved glass
      Glass bells
      Glass candlesticks
      Glass Christmas decorations
      Glass containers
      Glass figurines
      Glass fishing floats
      Glass kerosene lamps
      Glass knives
      Lamp-chimneys, globes, etc.
      Lampshades, Glass
      Milk glass

      Miniature glassware
      Opal glass
      Paperweights
      Pattern glass
      Portraits on glassware
      Pressed glass
      Salt shakers
      Saltcellars
      Stemware
      Sulphides (Art)
  — Catalogs
  — Collectors and collecting
    [NK5101-5199]
    NT Glassware as an investment
  — Forgeries *(May Subd Geog)*
    BT Forgery
  — History
  — — 16th century
    NT Glassware, Renaissance
  — — 18th century
    NT Glassware, Rococo
  — — 19th century
  — — 20th century
  — Oriental influences
    BT Civilization, Oriental
  — Prices
    NT Glassware as an investment
  — Private collections
    [NK5101-5196]
  — Trade-marks
  — — Forgeries
  — Venetian influences
    BT Venice (Italy)—Civilization
  — Japan
  — — History
  — — — Edo period, 1600-1868
  — — — 1868-
  — United States
  — — History
  — — — 20th century
    NT Depression glass
      Swankyswig tumblers
Glassware, Ancient *(May Subd Geog)*
  [NK5107]
  UF Ancient glassware
Glassware, Baroque *(May Subd Geog)*
  UF Baroque glassware
Glassware, Byzantine *(May Subd Geog)*
  UF Byzantine glassware
Glassware, Classical *(May Subd Geog)*
  UF Classical glassware
Glassware, Colonial *(May Subd Geog)*
  UF Colonial glassware
Glassware, Early Christian
  (May Subd Geog)
  UF Early Christian glassware
Glassware, Georgian
  UF Georgian glassware
Glassware, Greco-Roman *(May Subd Geog)*
  UF Greco-Roman glassware
Glassware, Islamic *(May Subd Geog)*
  [NK5108.9]
  UF Glassware, Muslim
      Islamic glassware
      Muslim glassware
Glassware, Medieval *(May Subd Geog)*
Glassware, Muslim
  USE Glassware, Islamic
Glassware, Renaissance *(May Subd Geog)*
  UF Renaissance glassware
  BT Glassware—History—16th century
Glassware, Rococo *(May Subd Geog)*
  UF Rococo glassware
  BT Glassware—History—18th century
Glassware, Sassanid *(May Subd Geog)*
  UF Sassanid glassware
Glassware, Victorian *(May Subd Geog)*
  UF Victorian glassware
  — Venetian influences
    BT Venice (Italy)—Civilization

Glassware as an investment
    BT Glassware—Collectors and collecting
        Glassware—Prices
        Investments
Glassware in literature
Glassy alloys
    USE Metallic glasses
Glassy metals
    USE Metallic glasses
Glaucidium
    ⌐QL696.S83¬
    BT Strigidae
Glaucidium passerinum
    ⌐QL696.S83¬
Glaucionetta clangula
    USE Goldeneye
Glaucoma *(May Subd Geog)*
    ⌐RE871¬
    UF High intraocular pressure
        Intraocular pressure, High
    BT Eye—Diseases and defects
    NT Cyclodialysis
    — Diagnosis
        NT Tonometry
    — Surgery
Glaucoma, Chronic simple
    USE Glaucoma, Open angle
Glaucoma, Open angle *(May Subd Geog)*
    UF Chronic simple glaucoma
        Glaucoma, Chronic simple
        Glaucoma, Simple
        Glaucoma, Wide-angle
        Glaucoma simplex
        Open angle glaucoma
        Simple glaucoma
        Wide-angle glaucoma
Glaucoma, Simple
    USE Glaucoma, Open angle
Glaucoma, Wide-angle
    USE Glaucoma, Open angle
Glaucoma in children
    UF Congenital glaucoma
        Pediatric glaucoma
    BT Pediatric ophthalmology
Glaucoma simplex
    USE Glaucoma, Open angle
Glaucomys
    ⌐QL737.R68¬
    BT Flying squirrels
        Sciuridae
    NT Glaucomys volans
Glaucomys volans
    ⌐QL737.R68¬
    UF Flying squirrel, Southern
        Southern flying squirrel
    BT Glaucomys
Glauconiidae
    USE Leptotyphlopidae
Glauconite
    ⌐QE391.G5¬
Glaucopsyche
    ⌐QL561.L8¬
    BT Lycaenidae
Glaucous-winged gull
    UF Larus glaucescens
    BT Gulls
Glaukos (The Greek word)
    BT Greek language—Etymology
Glaurus Alps (Switzerland)
    USE Glarner Alps (Switzerland)
Glavda language
    ⌐PL8207.G6¬
    BT Chadic languages
        Mandara language
Glaverbel-Gilly (Firm) Strike, 1974-1975
    BT Glass-workers—Belgium
        Strikes and lockouts—Glass trade—
            Belgium
        Strikes and lockouts—Belgium
Glaze (Meteorology) *(May Subd Geog)*
    ⌐QC929.G4¬

    UF Glaze ice
        Glazed frost
    BT Freezing precipitation
        Ice
        Icing (Meteorology)
    RT Frost
Glaze ice
    USE Glaze (Meteorology)
Glazed brick
    ⌐TP832.G6¬
    BT Bricks
Glazed frost
    USE Glaze (Meteorology)
Glazes
    ⌐TP812¬
    ⌐TP823¬
    BT Ceramics
        Color in the ceramic industries
        Glazing (Ceramics)
        Pottery
    NT Crystalline glazes
        Engobes
        Luster-ware
    — Formulae
        UF Formulas for glazes
            Glazes—Formulae, tables, etc.
    — Formulae, tables, etc.
        USE Glazes—Formulae
            Glazes—Tables
    — Tables
        UF Glazes—Formulae, tables, etc.
Glazes, Crystalline
    USE Crystalline glazes
Glazing
    ⌐TH8251-8275¬
    NT Sealed double glazing
Glazing (Ceramics)
    BT Ceramics
        Pottery
    NT Glazes
Glazunov, Il'ia Sergeevich. Gift of the USSR to UNESCO
    UF Contribution of the peoples of the
        USSR to culture and world
        civilization (Mural painting)
        Dar SSSR IUNESKO (Mural painting)
        Gift of the USSR to UNESCO (Mural
        painting)
    BT Mural painting and decoration,
        Russian
GLC automobile
    USE Mazda GLC automobile
Gleaning *(May Subd Geog)*
    ⌐HD1549¬
    BT Agriculture
        Charity laws and legislation
        Harvesting
Gleasonia
    ⌐QK495.R85¬
    BT Rubiaceae
Glebes
    USE Church lands
Glebo (African people)
    USE Grebo (African people)
Glebo language
    USE Grebo language
Glecoma hederacea
    USE Ground ivy
Gleddish family
    USE Gladwish family
Gleditsia
    USE Honey locust
Gledwishe family
    USE Gladwish family
Glees, catches, rounds, etc.
    UF Catches
        Rounds
    BT Song-books
        Vocal music
    RT Canons, fugues, etc. (Vocal)

Gleichenia
    BT Gleicheniaceae
Gleicheniaceae
    ⌐QK524.G¬
    BT Filicales
    NT Gleichenia
Gleichoma hederacea
    USE Ground ivy
Glen Albin (Scotland)
    USE Great Glen (Scotland)
Glen Albyn (Scotland)
    USE Great Glen (Scotland)
Glen Canyon (Utah and Ariz.)
    BT Canyons—Arizona
        Canyons—Utah
    RT Glen Canyon National Recreation
        Area (Utah and Ariz.)
Glen Canyon National Recreation Area (Utah and Ariz.)
    BT National parks and reserves—United
        States
        Recreation areas—Arizona
        Recreation areas—Utah
    RT Glen Canyon (Utah and Ariz.)
Glen family *(Not Subd Geog)*
    UF Glenn family
    RT Glynn family
Glen More Albin (Scotland)
    USE Great Glen (Scotland)
Glénan Islands (France)
    UF Glénans Islands (France)
        Iles de Glénan (France)
        Iles de Glénans (France)
        Iles-Glénans (France)
        Les Glénans (France)
    BT Islands—France
Glénans Islands (France)
    USE Glénan Islands (France)
Glenbrook Site (Ont.) *(Not Subd Geog)*
    BT Ontario—Antiquities
Glencoe (Va.)
    BT Plantations—Virginia
Glencoe Massacre, 1692
    ⌐DA804.7¬
    BT Scotland—History—1689-1745
Glendale Lake (Pa.)
    BT Lakes—Pennsylvania
        Reservoirs—Pennsylvania
Glendale Memorial Park Cemetery (Glendale, Ariz.)
    BT Cemeteries—Arizona
Glendening family *(Not Subd Geog)*
    UF Glendenning family
        Glendinning family
Glendenning family
    USE Glendening family
Glendinning family
    USE Glendening family
Glendower's Way (Wales)
    USE Owain Glyndŵr's Way (Wales)
Glenfinnan Estate (Highland Region, Scotland) *(Not Subd Geog)*
    BT Manors—Scotland
Glenn family
    USE Glen family
Glenn Highway (Alaska)
    BT Roads—Alaska
Glensax Burn (Scotland)
    BT Rivers—Scotland
Glerup family *(Not Subd Geog)*
Gleysteen family *(Not Subd Geog)*
Glial cells
    USE Neuroglia
Glibenclamide
    BT Hypoglycemic agents
        Hypoglycemic sulphonylureas

Glick family (Not Subd Geog)
  UF Click family
      Glicker family
      Glickerman family
      Glickman family
      Gliukmann family
      Gluck family
      Gluckman family
      Glueck family
      Glueckman family
Glicker family
  USE Glick family
Glickerman family
  USE Glick family
Glickman family
  USE Glick family
Gliclazide
  [RC661.G56 (Diabetes therapy)]
  UF Hexahydrocyclopentap
      yrroltolylsulphonylurea
  BT Hypoglycemic sulphonylureas
Glide (Crystallography)
  [QD921]
  UF Translation glide (Crystallography)
  BT Crystals—Defects
Glide path systems
  [TL696.L33]
  UF Glide slope
      Landing path
  BT Airplanes—Landing
      Instrument landing systems
      Radio in aeronautics
Glide slope
  USE Glide path systems
Glider mail
  USE Glider post
Glider post (May Subd Geog)
  [HE6239.G54]
  UF Glider mail
      Post, Glider
  BT Air mail service
Glider recognition
  USE Gliders (Aeronautics)—Recognition
Glider troops
  USE Airborne troops
Gliders (Aeronautics)
  [TL760-769]
  UF Sailplanes (Aeronautics)
  BT Airplanes
      Flying-machines
      Sailing
  RT Gliding and soaring
  NT Gotha gliders
      Hang gliders
      Messerschmitt 321 (Glider)
  — Law and legislation (May Subd Geog)
  — Models
      NT Paper airplanes
  — — Radio control
  — Piloting
      [TL765]
  — Recognition
      UF Aircraft identification
          Aircraft recognition
          Glider recognition
          Recognition of gliders
Gliders (Mammals) (May Subd Geog)
  [QL737.M3]
  BT Marsupialia
  NT Petauridae
Gliding and soaring (May Subd Geog)
  [GV764-GV766 (Sport)]
  [TL760]
  UF Flight, Unpowered
      Motorless flight
      Soaring (Aeronautics)
      Soaring flight
  BT Aeronautical sports
      Aeronautics
  RT Gliders (Aeronautics)
  NT Hang gliding

  — Facilities
Gliding bacteria
  USE Cytophagales
       Myxobacterales
Gliding lemurs
  USE Flying lemurs
Glinn family
  USE Glynn family
Glins family
  USE Glynn family
Glinus
  [QK495.M6]
  BT Molluginaceae
Glinus lotoides
  [QK495.M6]
  UF Mollugo hirta
      Pharnaceum pentagynum
Glinus oppositifolius
  [QK495.M6]
  UF Mollugo oppositifolia
      Mollugo spergula
Glioblastoma, Retinal
  USE Retinoblastoma
Glioma, Retinal
  USE Retinoblastoma
Gliomas
  BT Nervous system—Tumors
  NT Medulloblastoma
      Pseudoglioma
Gliomastix
  [QK625.D4]
  BT Dematiaceae
Gliridae
  USE Dormice
Glis
  USE Edible dormouse
Glis glis
  USE Edible dormouse
Gliukmann family
  USE Glick family
Global analysis (Mathematics)
  [QA614]
  UF Analysis, Global (Mathematics)
  BT Differential topology
      Functions of complex variables
      Geometry, Algebraic
  NT Anosov flows
      Critical point theory (Mathematical
          analysis)
      Differentiable dynamical systems
      Geodesics (Mathematics)
      Index theorems
      Infinite-dimensional manifolds
      Jet bundles (Mathematics)
      Pseudogroups
Global Atmospheric Research Programme
  Global Experiment, First
  USE First GARP Global Experiment
Global Data-processing System (Computer
  system)
  USE GDPS (Computer system)
Global differential geometry
  UF Differential geometry, Global
  BT Geometry, Differential
Global learning
  USE Global method of teaching
Global method of teaching
  [LB1029.G55]
  UF Global learning
      Globalism (Education)
  BT Education, Elementary
      Teaching
  NT Reading (Elementary)—Whole-word
      method
Global Observing System (Meteorology)
  UF GOS (Meteorology)
  BT Meteorology—International
      cooperation
      Meteorology—Observations
      Meteorology—Research

Global Positioning System
  UF GPS (Navigational system)
      Navigation Satellite Timing and
          Ranging Global Positioning System
      NAVSTAR GPS
  BT Artificial satellites in navigation
Global radiation (May Subd Geog)
  [QC912.55]
  UF Radiation, Global
  BT Atmospheric radiation
      Solar radiation
Global satellite communications systems
  USE Artificial satellites in
       telecommunication
Global temperature changes
  [QC903]
  UF Temperature changes, Global
      World temperature changes
  BT Atmospheric temperature
Global Weather Experiment Project
  BT Meteorology—Research
      Weather
Globalism (Education)
  USE Global method of teaching
Globe artichoke
  USE Artichokes
Globe Derby (Race horse)
Globe Mutiny, 1824
  [DU710]
Globe tulip
  USE Calochortus
Globes (May Subd Geog)
  [G3170]
  UF Globes, Terrestrial
      Terrestrial globes
  RT Orbs
      World maps
  SA subdivision Globes under names of
      moons and planets (other than
      Earth) and under certain subjects,
      e.g. Mars (Planet)—Globes;
      Submarine topography—Globes
  NT Blind, Globes for the
      Rubik's World
  — Trade and manufacture
Globes, Celestial
  UF Celestial globes
  BT Astronomical models
  RT Astronomy—Charts, diagrams, etc.
Globes, Lunar
  USE Moon—Globes
Globes, Terrestrial
  USE Globes
Globicephala
  [QL737.C432]
  UF Blackfish whales
  BT Delphinidae
Globicephala brachyptera
  USE Globicephala macrorhynchus
Globicephala edwardii
  USE Globicephala melaena
Globicephala leucosagmaphora
  USE Globicephala melaena
Globicephala macrorhyncha
  USE Globicephala macrorhynchus
Globicephala macrorhynchus
  [QL737.C432]
  UF Globicephala brachyptera
      Globicephala macrorhyncha
      Globicephala scammonii
      Globicephala sieboldii
      Indian pilot whale
      Pacific pilot whale
      Pilot whale, Shortfin
      Short-finned pilot whale
      Shortfin pilot whale
Globicephala melaena
  [QL737.C432]

UF Caaing whale
 Globicephala edwardii
 Globicephala leucosagmaphora
 Long-finned pilot whale
 Longfin pilot whale
 Pilot whale, Longfin
 Pothead whale
 Southern pilot whale
Globicephala scammonii
 USE Globicephala macrorhynchus
Globicephala sieboldii
 USE Globicephala macrorhynchus
Globiceps
 [QL523.M5]
 BT Miridae
Globidens
 [QE862.L2]
 BT Mosasauridae
Globidens dakotensis
 [QE862.L2]
Globidiosis
 USE Besnoitiosis
Globin
 [QP552.G5]
 BT Hemoglobin
 Histones
 Proteins
 NT Haptoglobin
Globoid cell leukodystrophy
 USE Leukodystrophy, Globoid cell
Globoid leukodystrophy
 USE Leukodystrophy, Globoid cell
Globorotalia, Fossil
 [QE772]
 UF Astrorotalia, Fossil
 Planorotalia, Fossil
 Planorotalites, Fossil
 Planulina, Fossil
 Pulvinulina, Fossil
 Rotalina, Fossil
 Truncorotalia, Fossil
 BT Globorotaliidae, Fossil
Globorotaliidae, Fossil
 [QE772]
 UF Marginolamellidae, Fossil
 BT Foraminifera, Fossil
 NT Globorotalia, Fossil
Globular clusters of stars
 USE Stars—Globular clusters
Globular proteins
Globules, Milk fat
 USE Butterfat—Fat globules
Globulin
 NT Alpha fetoproteins
 Alpha globulin
 C-reactive protein
 Fibronectins
 Gamma globulin
 Haptoglobin
 Immunoglobulins
 Macroglobulins
 Myosin
 Thyroglobulin
 Transferrin
Globus pallidus
 UF Pallidum
 BT Basal ganglia
 Brain
Glockenspiel
 [ML1040 (History)]
 UF Bell-lyra
 Orchestral bells
 BT Percussion instruments
Glockenspiel and celesta music
 [M284.G65]
 [M285.G65]
 UF Celesta and glockenspiel music
Glockenspiel and harpsichord music
 [M284.G65]
 [M285.G65]
 UF Harpsichord and glockenspiel music

Glockenspiel music
 [M147]
 SA Concertos, Minuets, Sonatas, Suites,
 *and similar headings with
 specification of instruments;* Trios
 [Quartets, etc.] *followed by
 specifications which include the
 glockenspiel; also* Percussion
 ensembles, Percussion music, *and
 headings that begin with the words
 glockenspiel or glockenspiels*
 NT Glockenspiel with string orchestra
 Quartets (Piano, flute, harp,
 glockenspiel)
 Quintets (Pianos (4), glockenspiel)
 Quintets (Trombone, glockenspiel,
 percussion)
 Trios (Piano, clarinet, glockenspiel)
Glockenspiel with string orchestra
 [M1105-6]
 BT Glockenspiel music
 RT Concertos (Glockenspiel with string
 orchestra)
Gloeocantharellus
 [QK629.G6]
 BT Gomphaceae
Gloeosporium
 BT Melanconiaceae
Glomerular filtration rate
 BT Kidney function tests
 Kidney glomerulus
Glomeruli renis
 USE Kidney glomerulus
Glomerulonephritis
 BT Immune complex diseases
 Kidney glomerulus—Diseases
 NT IgA glomerulonephritis
 — Immunological aspects
Glomerulus, Kidney
 USE Kidney glomerulus
Glomfjord Raid, 1942
 BT World War, 1939-1945—Campaigns—
 Norway
Glomma River (Norway) *(Not Subd Geog)*
 UF Glaama River (Norway)
 Glåma River (Norway)
 BT Rivers—Norway
Glomus caroticum
 USE Carotid body
Glomus jugulare
 [QL939 (Comparative anatomy)]
 [QM471 (Human anatomy)]
 [QP368.8 (Physiology)]
 UF Jugular body
 Jugular paraganglia
 Paraganglia, Jugular
 BT Chemoreceptors
 Nonchromaffin paraganglia
 — Tumors
 BT Nonchromaffin paraganglioma
Glonoin
 USE Nitroglycerin
Gloominess
 USE Pessimism
 Sadness
Gloria in excelsis Deo (Music)
 BT Masses
Gloria in excelsis Deo
Glorification (Theology)
 USE Glory of God
Glory
 RT Fame
Glory, Divine
 USE Glory of God
Glory-bush
 USE Tibouchina
Glory in literature
Glory of God
 [BT180.G6]

UF Divine glory
 Glorification (Theology)
 Glory, Divine
 God—Glory
 God, Glory of
 BT God
Glory of God (Judaism)
Glorybush
 USE Tibouchina
Glosa (Artificial language)
 (May Subd Geog)
 [PM8365]
 BT Languages, Artificial
Glossaries
 USE *subdivision* Glossaries, vocabularies,
 etc. *under individual languages for
 incomplete lists of the words of a
 language which may or may not be
 alphabetically arranged, with or
 without definitions*
Glossators
 BT Canon law—History
 Roman law—History
Glossematics
 UF Glossemes
 BT Linguistic analysis (Linguistics)
 Mathematical linguistics
 SA *subdivision* Glossematics *under names
 of languages and groups of
 languages*
Glossemes
 USE Glossematics
Glossidae
 [QL430.7.G55]
 BT Veneroida
 NT Glossus
Glossina
 USE Tsetse-flies
Glossina palpalis
 [QL537.G4]
 BT Tsetse-flies
Glossiphoniidae
 [QL391.A6]
 BT Leeches
Glossocoma
 USE Votomita
Glossocrinus
 [QE782]
 BT Poteriocrinitidae
Glossocrinus bellitubatus
 [QE782]
Glossoderma
 USE Glossus
Glossolalia
 [BL54]
 UF Gift of tongues
 Speaking with tongues
 Tongues, Gift of
 BT Gifts, Spiritual
 RT Baptism in the Holy Spirit
 Pentecostalism
 Xenoglossy
Glossoma
 USE Votomita
Glossopharyngeal nerve
 [QL939]
 [QM471]
 [QP366]
 BT Nerves, Cranial
 Pharynx
 Tongue
Glossopharyngeal respiration
 BT Respiration
Glossopteris
 [QE961]
 BT Ferns, Fossil
 NT Vertebraria
Glossus
 [QL430.7.G55]

Glossus (Continued)
  UF Bucardia
      Buccardium
      Glossoderma
      Isocardia
      Tychocardia
  BT Glossidae
Glossus humanus
  [QL430.7.G55]
Gloster aircraft
  [TL686.G]
  NT Gladiator (Fighter planes)
      Javelin (Jet fighter plane)
      Meteor (Fighter planes)
Gloster Gladiator
  USE Gladiator (Fighter planes)
Gloster Meteor
  USE Meteor (Fighter planes)
Glottis
  [QL853 (Comparative anatomy)]
  [QM255 (Human anatomy)]
  BT Larynx
  NT Vocal cords
  — Spasm
      USE Laryngismus stridulus
Glottochronology
  [P143.3]
  BT Comparative linguistics
      Lexicology
      Linguistic change
      Mathematical linguistics
  NT Lexicostatistics
Glottopolitics
  USE Language policy
Glove boxes (Safety devices)
  BT Manipulators (Radioactive substances)
      Radioisotopes—Safety measures
Glove industry (May Subd Geog)
  NT Trade-unions—Glove industry
      Wages—Glove industry
Glover family
Gloves (May Subd Geog)
  [GT2170 (Costume)]
  [HD9947 (Trade)]
  [TS2160 (Manufacture)]
  NT Mittens
Gloves, Baseball
  USE Baseball gloves
Gloves (Surgery)
  [RD73.G5]
  BT Surgical instruments and apparatus
Glow discharges
  [QC711.8.G5]
  UF Cold cathode discharges
      Discharges, Cold cathode
      Discharges, Gas
      Discharges, Glow
      Gas discharges
      Joshi effect
  BT Electric discharges
      Electric discharges through gases
Glow-lamps
  USE Electric lamps
Glow-worms
  USE Fireflies
Gloxinias
Głubczyce Plateau (Poland and Czechoslovakia)
  UF Płaskowyż Głubczycki (Poland and
        Czechoslovakia)
  BT Plateaus—Czechoslovakia
      Plateaus—Poland
Glubokoe Lake (R.S.F.S.R.)
  UF Glubokoye Lake (R.S.F.S.R.)
      Lake Glubokoe (R.S.F.S.R.)
      Ozero Glubokoe (R.S.F.S.R.)
  BT Lakes—Russian S.F.S.R.
Glubokoye Lake (R.S.F.S.R.)
  USE Glubokoe Lake (R.S.F.S.R.)
Glucagon
  BT Pancreas—Secretions

Glucagonoma (May Subd Geog)
  [RC280.P25]
  UF Alpha cell tumor
  BT Islands of Langerhans—Tumors
Glucan glucanohydrolase
  USE Dextranase
Glucans
  UF Polyglucoses
  BT Polysaccharides
  NT Cellulose
      Dextran
      Dextrine
      Glycogen
Glucic acid
  USE Reductones
Glucides
  RT Glucosides
Glucinium
  USE Beryllium
Glucinum
  USE Beryllium
Glucitol
  USE Sorbitol
Gluck family
  USE Glick family
Gluck-Piccinni controversy
  [ML1727.35]
  BT Opera
  RT Guerre des Bouffons
Gluckman family
  USE Glick family
Glucocorticoid receptors
  USE Glucocorticoids—Receptors
Glucocorticoids
  [QP572.G54]
  BT Adrenocortical hormones
      Anti-inflammatory agents
  NT Corticosterone
      Hydrocortisone
      Triamcinolone
  — Receptors
      UF Glucocorticoid receptors
          Receptors, Glucocorticoid
Glucolysis
  USE Glycolysis
Gluconeogenesis
  [QP702.G56]
  UF Glyconeogenesis
  BT Glucose—Synthesis
      Metabolism
  — Regulation
      UF Regulation of gluconeogenesis
      BT Cellular control mechanisms
Glucose
  [QD321 (Chemistry)]
  [TP414 (Chemical technology)]
  BT Monosaccharides
      Sucrose
      Sugar
  NT Blood sugar
      Dextran
      Ficoll
      Glucuronic acid
      Metrizamide
      Streptozotocin
      Sugar—Inversion
  — Synthesis
      UF Glucose synthesis
      NT Gluconeogenesis
Glucose in blood
  USE Blood sugar
Glucose industry (May Subd Geog)
  [TP414]
  NT Corn-starch
Glucose synthesis
  USE Glucose—Synthesis
Glucose tolerance tests
  BT Blood—Analysis
      Blood sugar
      Diabetes—Diagnosis

Glucosephosphate dehydrogenase
  [QP603.G57]
  UF G6PD (Enzyme)
  BT Dehydrogenases
Glucosephosphate dehydrogenase deficiency
  (May Subd Geog)
  [RC632.G55]
  UF G6PD deficiency
  BT Hemolytic anemia
      Metabolism, Inborn errors of
Glucosidase antagonists
  USE Glucosidase inhibitors
Glucosidase inhibitors
  UF Antagonists, Glucosidase
      Glucosidase antagonists
      Inhibitors, Glucosidase
  BT Enzyme inhibitors
  NT Acarbose
Glucosidase synthesis
  USE Glucosidases—Synthesis
Glucosidases
  [QP609.G4]
  BT Glycosidases
  — Synthesis
      UF Glucosidase synthesis
Glucosides
  [QD325 (Chemistry)]
  [QP925 (Pharmacology)]
  RT Glucides
      Glycosides
  NT Anthocyanin
      Betuloside
      Etoposide
      Glucosinolates
      Oligosaccharides
      Saponins
Glucosinolates
  BT Glucosides
Glucosuria
  USE Glycosuria
Glucosyltransferases
  USE Glycosyltransferases
Glucuronates
  USE Glucuronides
Glucuronic acid
  [QP702.G57]
  BT Glucose
      Uronic acids
  NT Glucuronides
      Laetrile
  — Synthesis
      UF Glucuronic acid synthesis
Glucuronic acid synthesis
  USE Glucuronic acid—Synthesis
Glucuronidase
Glucuronide synthesis
  USE Glucuronides—Synthesis
Glucuronides
  [QP702.G572]
  UF Conjugated glucuronates
      Glucuronates
      Glycuronides
  BT Glucuronic acid
      Glycosides
  — Synthesis
      UF Glucuronide synthesis
Glue
  [TP967-8]
  BT Binders (Materials)
  RT Adhesives
      Bone products
  NT Gluing
      Soybean glue
Glue ear
  USE Otitis media with effusion
Glue-sniffing (May Subd Geog)
  [HV5822.G5]
  BT Gases, Asphyxiating and poisonous
      Solvent abuse
Glueck family
  USE Glick family

Glueckman family
  USE Glick family
Glued joints
  USE Adhesive joints
Gluing
  BT Cabinet-work
      Glue
      Joinery
      Woodwork
Glumac family (Not Subd Geog)
Gluons
  ⌐QC793.5.G552-5529⌐
  BT Particles (Nuclear physics)
      Quarks
  RT Quark-gluon interactions
Glutaconaldehyde
  ⌐QD305.A6⌐
  UF Pentenedial
  BT Aldehydes
      Glutaconic acid
Glutaconic acid
  BT Carboxylic acids
  NT Glutaconaldehyde
Glutamate decarboxylase
  UF Glutamic acid decarboxylase
      Glutamic decarboxylase
  BT Decarboxylases
Glutamic acid
  BT Neurotransmitters
  NT Monosodium glutamate
Glutamic acid decarboxylase
  USE Glutamate decarboxylase
Glutamic acid esters
  BT Esters
Glutamic acid polymers
  ⌐QD383.G57⌐
  BT Polymers and polymerization
Glutamic decarboxylase
  USE Glutamate decarboxylase
Glutamine
  BT Amino acids
  NT Proglumide
Glutamine synthetase
  BT Ligases
Glutaminyl-peptide glutamyltransferase
  USE Transglutaminases
Glutamyl T RNA synthetase
  USE Glutamyl-tRNA synthetase
Glutamyl-transfer ribonucleate synthetase
  USE Glutamyl-tRNA synthetase
Glutamyl-tRNA synthetase
  UF Glutamyl T RNA synthetase
      Glutamyl-transfer ribonucleate
        synthetase
  BT Ligases
Glutaredoxin
  BT Proteins
      Thiols
Glutathione
  BT Oligopeptides
Glutathione transferase
  BT Transferases
Gluteal region
  USE Buttocks
Gluten
  ⌐QD431 (Chemistry)⌐
  ⌐TS2149 (Milling)⌐
  NT Cookery (Gluten)
Gluten-free diet
  BT Celiac disease
      Diet in disease
  — Recipes
      BT Cookery
Gluten plants (May Subd Geog)
  UF Plants, Gluten
  BT Food processing plants
Gluttons (Animals)
  USE Wolverines
Gluttony
  BT Deadly sins
      Gastronomy

  NT Obesity—Psychological aspects
Glyceridae
  ⌐QL391.A6⌐
  BT Phyllodocida
Glycerides
  ⌐QD305.A4⌐
  NT Monoglycerides
      Triglycerides
Glycerin
  ⌐HD9660.G57-HD9660.G6 (Trade)⌐
  ⌐RA766.G6 (Disinfectants)⌐
  ⌐RM666.G (Therapeutics)⌐
  ⌐TP973 (Chemical technology)⌐
  BT Alcohols
  NT Nitroglycerin
Glyceryl trinitrate
  USE Nitroglycerin
Glycin
  USE Glycine
Glycine
  UF Aminoacetic acid
      Glycin
      Glycocoll
  BT Acetic acid
      Amino acids
      Neurotransmitters
  NT Diethylenetriaminepentaacetic acid
      Glyphosate
  — Metabolism
      UF Glycine metabolism
Glycine (Plant)
  UF Ground-nuts
Glycine max
  USE Soybean
Glycine metabolism
  USE Glycine—Metabolism
Glycine subterra
  USE Bambarra groundnut
Glyciphagus
  USE Glycyphagus
Glycocoll
  USE Glycine
Glycogen
  ⌐QP701⌐
  BT Glucans
  RT Polysaccharides
  NT Glycogenosis
      Liver—Glycogenic function
  — Synthesis
      UF Glycogen synthesis
Glycogen disease
  USE Glycogenosis
Glycogen synthesis
  USE Glycogen—Synthesis
Glycogen synthetase a kinase
  USE Protein kinase
Glycogenosis
  ⌐RJ456.G⌐
  UF Glycogen disease
      Hepatonephromegalia glycogenica
      Thesaurimosis glycogenica
      Von Gierche's disease
  BT Children—Diseases
      Glycogen
      Liver—Diseases
      Liver—Glycogenic function
Glycol dibromide
  USE Ethylene dibromide
Glycol dichloride
  USE Ethylene dichloride
Glycol dicyanide
  USE Succinonitrile
Glycol ethylene ether
  USE Dioxane
Glycolipids
  ⌐QD301 (Organic chemistry)⌐
  ⌐QP752.G56 (Biochemistry)⌐
  NT Glycosphingolipids
Glycols
  ⌐QD305.A4⌐

  UF Ethylene alcohol
      Ethylene glycol
  NT Methoxyhydroxyphenylglycol
Glycolysis
  ⌐QP701⌐
  UF Glucolysis
  BT Blood—Examination
      Pathology
      Sugar in the body
Glyconeogenesis
  USE Gluconeogenesis
Glycoprotein synthesis
  USE Glycoproteins—Synthesis
Glycoproteins
  NT Colony-stimulating factors
        (Physiology)
      Elastin
      Fibronectins
      Glycosylated hemoglobin
      Ia antigens
      Interferon
      Interphotoreceptor retinoid-binding
        protein
      Proteoglycans
      Prothrombin
      Thyroglobulin
      Tumor necrosis factor
  — Synthesis
      UF Glycoprotein synthesis
Glycosaminoglycans
  BT Mucopolysaccharides
Glycosaminopeptides
  USE Peptidoglycans
Glycosidases
  UF Glycoside hydrolases
  BT Hydrolases
  NT Amylases
      Dextranase
      Glucosidases
Glycoside hydrolases
  USE Glycosidases
Glycosides
  RT Glucosides
  NT Aminoglycosides
      Cardiac glycosides
      Fructose
      Galactose
      Glucuronides
      Xyloside
Glycosphingolipids
  UF Asialogangliosides
      Sphingoglycolipids
  BT Glycolipids
      Sphingolipids
  NT Cerebrosides
      Gangliosides
Glycosuria
  ⌐RC909⌐
  UF Glucosuria
  BT Diabetes
      Sugar in the body
      Urine—Analysis
Glycosyl hemoglobin
  USE Glycosylated hemoglobin
Glycosylated hemoglobin
  ⌐QP99.3.G55⌐
  UF Glycosyl hemoglobin
      Hemoglobin, Glycosyl
      Hemoglobin, Glycosylated
  BT Glycoproteins
      Hemoglobin polymorphisms
  RT Diabetes
Glycosyltransferases
  UF Glucosyltransferases
      Transglucosylases
      Transglycosylases
  BT Enzymes
  NT Phosphorylase
Glycozone
  ⌐RM671.G⌐
  BT Antiseptics

Glycuronides
  USE Glucuronides
Glycyphagidae
  [QL458.2.G4]
  BT Mites
Glycyphagus
  [QL458.2.G4]
  UF Glyciphagus
  NT Glycyphagus spinipes
Glycyphagus spinipes
  [QL458.2.G4]
  BT Glycyphagus
Glyndŵr's Way (Wales)
  USE Owain Glyndŵr's Way (Wales)
Glynn family (Not Subd Geog)
  UF Glinn family
    Glins family
  RT Glen family
Glyoxalase
Glyoxyldiureide
  USE Allantoin
Glyoxysomes
  BT Cell organelles
Glyphipterigidae
  USE Glyphipterygidae
Glyphipterygidae
  [QL561.G65]
  UF Glyphipterigidae
    Hemerophilidae
    Simaethidae
  BT Lepidoptera
  NT Homadaula
Glyphography
  [NE2570]
  BT Pictures—Printing
    Plate-printing
  RT Electrotyping
Glyphosate
  [SB952.G58]
  UF Phosphonomethylglycine
  BT Glycine
    Herbicides
    Isopropylamine
    Organophosphorus compounds
    Plant regulators
  NT Plants, Effect of glyphosate on
Glyphs (Graphic methods)
  BT Graphic methods
GLYPLIT (Computer program)
  BT Computer programs
    Translators (Computer programs)
GLYPNIR (Computer program language)
  BT Illiac computer—Programming
    Programming languages (Electronic
      computers)
Glyptemoda
  [QL430.5.H45]
  BT Helicinidae
Glyptics
  [NK5500-6050]
  UF Glyptography
  BT Art
    Carving (Decorative arts)
    Engraving
    Sculpture
  RT Gems
  NT Cameos
    Gem carving
    Intaglios
    Medals
    Netsukes
    Plaques, plaquettes
    Seal makers
    Seals (Numismatics)
Glyptidae
  USE Carabidae
Glyptocephalus
  [QL638.P7]
  BT Pleuronectidae
Glyptocoileus
  USE Glyptodon

Glyptodon
  [QE882.E2]
  UF Glyptocoileus
    Glyptopedius
    Glyptostracon
    Stromatherium
    Xenoglyptodon
  BT Glyptodontidae
Glyptodontidae
  [QE882.E2]
  UF Hoplophoridae
  BT Edentata, Fossil
  NT Glyptodon
Glyptogluteus
  [QL458.87.T4]
  BT Thelyphonidae
Glyptography
  USE Glyptics
Glyptolith
  USE Ventifact
Glyptonotus
  [QL444.M34]
  BT Idoteidae
Glyptopedius
  USE Glyptodon
Glyptosaurus
  [QE862.L2]
  BT Anguidae, Fossil
Glyptoscellis
  [QL596.C5]
  BT Chrysomelidae
Glyptostracon
  USE Glyptodon
Glyptotendipes
  [QL537.C456]
  BT Chironomidae
GM2 gangliosidosis, Type 1
  USE Tay-Sachs disease
GM automobiles
  USE General Motors automobiles
GMAT
  USE Graduate Management Admission Test
Gmbwaga (African people)
  USE Ngbaka (African people)
GMC Jimmy truck
  UF Jimmy truck
  BT GMC trucks
    Trucks
GMC trucks
  [TL230.5.G]
  BT Trucks
  NT GMC Jimmy truck
    GMC vans
GMC vans
  [TL230.5.G]
  BT GMC trucks
    Vans
  NT Safari van
GMDH algorithms
  UF Group method of data handling
    algorithms
  BT Nonparametric statistics—Data
    processing
    Regression analysis—Data processing
    Self-organizing systems—Data
    processing
    System analysis—Data processing
Gmelina
  [QK495.V48]
  BT Verbenaceae
  NT Gmelina arborea
Gmelina arborea (May Subd Geog)
  [QK495.V48 (Botany)]
  [SD397.G56 (Forestry)]
  BT Gmelina
Gñāni yoga
  USE Yoga, Jñāna
Gnaphosa
  [QL458.42.G5]
  BT Gnaphosidae

Gnaphosidae
  [QL458.42.G5]
  BT Spiders
  NT Apodrassodes
    Callilepis
    Camillina
    Cesonia
    Drassyllus
    Echemus
    Eilica
    Gnaphosa
    Haplodrassus
    Herpyllus
    Litopyllus
    Lygromma
    Nodocion
    Orodrassus
    Rachodrassus
    Scopodes
    Scotophaeus
    Sergiolus
    Sosticus
    Synaphosus
    Zelotes
    Zimiromus
Gnatcatchers
  [QL696.P2]
  SA names of specific gnatcatchers, e.g.
    Blue-gray gnatcatcher
Gnathonemus
  [QL638.M676]
  BT Mormyridae
Gnathophis
  [QL638.C66]
  BT Congridae
Gnathophis capensis
  [QL638.C66]
Gnathophis mystax
  [QL638.C66]
Gnathostoma (May Subd Geog)
  [QL391.N4]
  UF Chiranthus
    Gnathostomum
  BT Gnathostomatidae
Gnathostomatidae (May Subd Geog)
  [QL391.N4]
  BT Spirurida
  NT Gnathostoma
Gnathostomiasis (May Subd Geog)
  UF Gnathostomosis
  BT Helminthiasis
Gnathostomosis
  USE Gnathostomiasis
Gnathostomulida
Gnathostomum
  USE Gnathostoma
Gnathotrichus
  [QL596.S35]
  BT Scolytidae
Gnathypops
  [QL638.O65]
  BT Opisthognathidae
Gnats, Gall
  USE Gall midges
Gnau (Papua New Guinea people)
  [DU740.42]
  BT Ethnology—Papua New Guinea
— **Medicine**
    BT Medicine, Primitive
Gneisenau Mine (Germany)
  (Not Subd Geog)
  UF Bergwerk Gneisenau (Germany)
  BT Coal mines and mining—Germany
    (West)
Gneiss (May Subd Geog)
  [QE461]
  [QE475]
Gnetaceae
  [QK494.5.G565]
  BT Gnetales
  NT Gnetum

Gnetales
[QK494]
BT Gymnosperms
NT Ephedraceae
Gnetaceae
Gnetum
[QK494.5.G565 (Botany)]
BT Gnetaceae
Gnetum gnemon
[QK494.5.G565 (Botany)]
Gnidus (Ancient city)
USE Cnidus (Ancient city)
Gnome project
USE Project Gnome
Gnomes (May Subd Geog)
BT Fairies
Gnomes (Maxims)
USE Aphorisms and apothegms
Maxims
Proverbs
Gnomic poetry
BT Poetry
RT Priamel
Gnomic poetry, Anglo-Saxon
USE Gnomic poetry, English (Old)
Gnomic poetry, Balinese (May Subd Geog)
UF Balinese gnomic poetry
BT Balinese poetry
Gnomic poetry, English (Old)
(May Subd Geog)
UF Anglo-Saxon gnomic poetry
English gnomic poetry, Old
Gnomic poetry, Anglo-Saxon
Old English gnomic poetry
BT English poetry—Old English, ca. 450-
1100
Gnomic poetry, Greek
[PA3125]
[PA3453]
[PA3623]
Gnomic poetry, Hebrew
[BS1455]
Gnomic poetry, Hindi (May Subd Geog)
UF Hindi gnomic poetry
BT Hindi poetry
Gnomic poetry, Kawi (May Subd Geog)
UF Kawi gnomic poetry
BT Kawi poetry
Gnomic poetry, Latin
[PA6059.G6]
[PA6135.G6]
[PA6164]
Gnomic poetry, Sanskrit (May Subd Geog)
UF Sanskrit gnomic poetry
BT Sanskrit poetry
Gnomic poetry, Welsh
[PB2281]
Gnomonia
[QK623.G55 (Botany)]
BT Gnomoniaceae
Gnomoniaceae
[QK623.G55 (Botany)]
BT Diaporthales
NT Endothia
Gnomonia
Gnomonics
USE Sundials
Gnorimoschema
[QL561.G4]
BT Gelechiidae
Gnorimoschema lycopersicella
USE Tomato pinworm
Gnossus (Ancient city)
USE Knossos (Ancient city)
Gnostic ethics
UF Ethics, Gnostic
Gnostic literature
BT Gnosticism
Gnosticism
[B638]
[BT1390 (Theology)]

BT Heresies, Christian—History—Early
church, ca. 30-600
Philosophy, Ancient
Religions
NT Gnostic literature
Naassenes
Ophites
Valentinians
Wisdom (Gnosticism)
Gnostidae
USE Ptinidae
Gnotobiology
USE Germfree life
Gnotobiotics
USE Germfree life
GNP
USE Gross national product
Gntare (Indic people)
USE Didayi (Indic people)
Gnu, Brindled
USE Brindled gnu
Gnu, White-tailed
USE White-tailed gnu
GNU Emacs (Computer program)
BT Text editors (Computer programs)
Gnus
UF Connochaetes
Gorgon (Genus)
Wildebeests
BT Antelopes
Bovidae
NT Brindled gnu
White-tailed gnu
Go (Game) (May Subd Geog)
[GV1459-1460.8]
UF Gobang (Game)
Igo (Game)
Patuk
Wei chi (Game)
Wei-ki (Game)
— Collections of games
— End games
[GV1460.4]
UF End games
Endgames
— Handicap games
[GV1460.5]
— Jōseki
[GV1460]
— Middle games
[GV1460.3]
— Openings
[GV1460.2]
UF Openings (Games)
— Rules
— Tesuji
[GV1460.43]
UF Tesuji
— Tournaments
Go (Game) players (May Subd Geog)
[GV1459.4-.42]
Go (Game) problems
[GV1460.6]
Go-cart racing
USE Karting
Go dialect (Ivory Coast)
USE Godye dialect
Go-ichigo jiken, 1932
USE Japan—History—May Incident, 1932
(May 15)
Go-Kart North Site (Ill.) (Not Subd Geog)
BT Illinois—Antiquities
Go-Kart racing
USE Karting
Go-Karts (Midget cars)
USE Karts (Midget cars)
Go Kinai (Japan)
USE Kinai Region (Japan)
Go-moku
USE Gomoku

Go-moku narabe
USE Gomoku
Gò Mun Site (Vietnam) (Not Subd Geog)
[DS559.93]
BT Vietnam—Antiquities
Go-Preachers (Christian sect)
USE Two-by-Two's (Christian sect)
Goad family
USE Good family
Goafing (Mining)
USE Mine filling
Goagiro language
USE Goajiro language
Goajiro Indians
[F2270.2.G6]
UF Guajiro Indians
BT Indians of South America
Goajiro language
[PM5981]
UF Goagiro language
Guajira language
BT Arawakan languages
Indians of South America—Languages
Goal (Philosophy)
[B105.G63]
BT Philosophy
Goal (Psychology)
BT Motivation (Psychology)
Goal-directed action
USE Action theory
Goal-directed behavior
USE Action theory
Goal setting in personnel management
(May Subd Geog)
[HF5549.5.G6]
UF Setting of goals in personnel
management
BT Management by objectives
Personnel management
Supervision of employees
RT Employee motivation
Incentives in industry
Performance standards
Goalard family
USE Galard family
Goalies (Soccer)
USE Soccer—Goalkeepers
Goalkeepers (Soccer)
USE Soccer—Goalkeepers
Goalkeeping (Soccer)
USE Soccer—Goalkeeping
Goals (Sports)
USE Targets (Sports)
Goaltenders (Soccer)
USE Soccer—Goalkeepers
Goan family
USE Gohn family
Goanese (May Subd Geog)
UF Goans
BT Ethnology—India
Goannas
USE Monitor lizards
Goans
USE Goanese
Goar family
USE Gore family
Goat breeding
UF Goats—Breeding
Goat breeds (May Subd Geog)
[SF383.4-SF383.5 (Local)]
[SF383 (General)]
[SF385-SF386 (Individual)]
UF Breeds of goats
BT Goats
NT Adal goat
Angora goat
Granada goat
Nubian goats
Pygmy goat
Goat cheese (May Subd Geog)
[SF271.87-272]

Goat cheese *(Continued)*
  UF Goat's milk cheese
  BT Cheese
  NT Cookery (Goat cheese)
Goat industry *(May Subd Geog)*
  BT Goats
Goat Island (N.S.W.) *(Not Subd Geog)*
  UF Memel Island (N.S.W.)
  BT Islands—Australia
Goat lice
  BT Lice
Goat lymph
  ₍RM800.L9₎
Goat milk
  USE Goat's milk
Goat moth, American
  USE Prionoxystus robiniae
Goat nut
  USE Jojoba
Goat ranchers *(May Subd Geog)*
  BT Farmers
      Goats
      Ranchers
Goatfishes
  USE Mullidae
Goats *(May Subd Geog)*
  ₍SF380-SF388₎
  UF Dairy goats
      Goats, Domestic
      Milk goats
  BT Livestock
  NT Goat breeds
      Goat industry
      Goat ranchers
      Kids (Goats)
  — Breeding
      USE Goat breeding
  — **Diseases** *(May Subd Geog)*
      ₍SF968-970₎
      SA *names of specific diseases, e.g.*
          Scrapie
      NT Brucellosis in goats
          Udder—Bacteriology
          Udder—Diseases
  — **Feeding and feeds**
  — **Herd-books**
      UF Herd-books
Goats, Domestic
  USE Goats
Goats, Fossil
Goats, Wild
  USE Capra
Goats as laboratory animals
Goats in art
Goat's milk
  UF Goat milk
  BT Milk
Goat's milk cheese
  USE Goat cheese
Gob piles
  USE Coal mine waste
      Spoil banks
Goba (Shona-speaking people)
  USE Gova (Shona-speaking people)
Goba language
  USE Mbukushu language
Gobang (Game)
  USE Go (Game)
Gobar gas
  USE Biogas
Gobbel family
  USE Göbel family
Gobbing (Mining)
  USE Mine filling
Gobble family
  USE Göbel family
Gobbledygook
  USE English language—Government jargon
      Jargon (Terminology)
      Languages, Mixed

Göbel family *(Not Subd Geog)*
  UF Gaabell family
      Gabel family
      Gabele family
      Gobbel family
      Gobble family
      Goble family
Gobelin tapestry
  ₍NK3049.G7₎
  BT Tapestry—France
Gober
  USE Gobir
Gobi Desert (Mongolia and China)
  UF Ku-pi Sha-mo (Mongolia and China)
  BT Deserts—China
      Deserts—Mongolia
Gobies
  USE Gobiidae
Gobiesocidae
  USE Clingfishes
Gobiesociformes
  ₍QL638.G6₎
  UF Xenopterygii
  BT Osteichthyes
  NT Clingfishes
Gobiidae
  ₍QL638.G7₎
  UF Apocrypteidae
      Benthophilidae
      Doliichthyidae
      Dollichthyidae
      Eleotridae
      Gobies
      Gobiomoridae
      Goby
      Milyeringidae
      Oxudercidae
      Periophthalmidae
      Sicydiaphiidae
  BT Perciformes
  NT Bathygobius
      Boleophthalmus
      Bollmannia
      Brachygobius
      Coryphopterus
      Eviota
      Feia
      Garmannia
      Gillichthys
      Gobiomorphus
      Gobiopsis
      Gobius
      Kelloggella
      Microgobius
      Mistichthys
      Monishia
      Pycnomma
      Tyson
Gobiomoridae
  USE Gobiidae
Gobiomorphus
  ₍QL638.G7₎
  BT Gobiidae
Gobiopsis
  ₍QL638.G7₎
  BT Gobiidae
Gobir
  UF Gober
      Gobirawa
  BT Ethnology—Nigeria
      Hausa (African people)
Gobirawa
  USE Gobir
Gobius
  ₍QL638.G7₎
  BT Gobiidae
  NT Gobius fluviatilis
Gobius fluviatilis
  ₍QL638.G7₎
  BT Gobius

Gobius saldanha
  ₍QL638.G7₎
  UF Bathygobius saldanha
Goble family
  USE Göbel family
Goblet cells
  USE Exfoliative cytology
Goblets *(May Subd Geog)*
  BT Drinking vessels
      Stemware
Goblin shark
  ₍QL638.95.M58₎
  UF Mitsukurina
      Scapanorhynchus
  BT Mitsukurinidae
Goblins *(May Subd Geog)*
  UF Hobgoblins
  BT Fairies
Gobra zebu
  ₍SF199.G62₎
  UF Fulani cattle, Senegal
      Fulani cattle, White
      Senegal Fulani cattle
      Senegal zebu
      White Fulani cattle
  BT Cattle breeds
      Zebus
Goby
  USE Gobiidae
Gocart racing
  USE Karting
Gochenour family
  USE Coughenour family
Gochinor family
  USE Coughenour family
Gochnatia
  ₍QK495.C74₎
  BT Compositae
Gochnatia hatschbachii
  ₍QK495.C74 (Botany)₎
Göcsej Hills (Hungary) *(Not Subd Geog)*
  BT Mountains—Hungary
God
  ₍BM610 (Judaism)₎
  ₍BT98-BT180₎
  BT Agnosticism
      Atheism
      Theology, Doctrinal
  RT Metaphysics
      Monotheism
      Religion
      Theism
      Trinity
  NT Anthropomorphism
      Appropriation (Christian theology)
      Beatific vision
      Causation
      Creation
      Desire for God
      Dispensationalism
      Fear of God
      Femininity of God
      Glory of God
      Hidden God
      Holy, The
      Holy Spirit
      Image of God
      Immanence of God
      Jesus Christ
      Judgment of God
      Kingdom of God
      Miracles
      Myth
      Mythology
      Natural theology
      Occasionalism
      Pantheism
      Polytheism
      Praise of God
      Presence of God
      Providence and government of God

Revelation
Teleology
Theocracy
Theodicy
Theology
Transcendence of God
Trinities
Tritheism
Trust in God
— Absence
　USE Hidden God
— Anger
　USE God—Wrath
— **Art**
　[N8040]
　NT Gods in art
　　　Holy Spirit—Art
　　　Jesus Christ—Art
　　　Trinity—Art
— **Attributes**
　[BL205 (Comparative religion)]
　[BT130-BT153 (Doctrinal
　　theology)]
　UF Attributes of God
　NT God—Incomparability
　　　God—Simplicity
　　　Suffering of God
— **Beauty**
　[BT153.B4]
— **Biblical teaching**
　[BT99]
　NT God—Worship and love—Biblical
　　　teaching
　　　Ten commandments—God
— Dispensations
　USE Dispensationalism
— **Face**
　UF Face of God
— Fairness
　USE God—Impartiality
— **Fatherhood**
　[BT153.F3]
　BT Kingdom of God
　RT Children of God
　NT Adoption (Theology)
　　　Fatherhood (Christian theology)
— Fear
　USE Fear of God
— Femininity
　USE Femininity of God
— Glory
　USE Glory of God
— **Goodness**
　[BT137]
— **History of doctrines**
　[BT98]
— — **Early church, ca. 30-600**
　　[BT98]
— — **Middle Ages, 600-1500**
— — **16th century**
— — **17th century**
— — **19th century**
　　[BT98]
— — **20th century**
— **Holiness**
　[BT147]
　UF Holiness of God
— Image
　USE Image of God
— Immanence
　USE Immanence of God
— **Immutability**
　[BT153.I47]
— — **History of doctrines**
　　[BT153.I47]
— **Impartiality**
　[BT153.I49]
　UF Fairness of God
　　　God—Fairness
　　　Impartiality of God
— Impassibility

　USE Suffering of God
— **Incomparability**
　[BT153.I6]
　UF Incomparability of God
　BT God—Attributes
　　　Monotheism
— **Jealousy**
　[BT153.J4]
　UF God, Jealousy of
　　　Jealousy of God
　BT Jealousy—Religious aspects
— Judgment
　USE Judgment of God
— Justice
　USE God—Righteousness
— **Knowableness**
　[BT98-108]
　UF God—Knowledge
　　　God, Knowledge of
　　　God (Theory of knowledge)
　　　Knowableness of God
　　　Knowledge of God
　BT Knowledge, Theory of (Religion)
— — **History of doctrines**
— Knowledge
　USE God—Knowableness
　　　God—Omniscience
— **Love**
　[BT140]
　Here are entered works on God's love toward
　man. Works on the love and worship which man
　accords to God are entered under the heading
　God—Worship and love.
　BT Love—Religious aspects
— **Mercy**
　[BT153.M4]
　BT Mercy
— **Motherhood**
　[BT153.M6]
　UF Motherhood of God
　RT Femininity of God
— **Name**
　[BT180.N2]
　BT Names in the Bible
　NT Basmalah
　　　God (Judaism)—Name
　　　Holy Name, Devotion to
　　　Memra (The word)
— — **Biblical teaching**
　　UF Jehovah
　　　　Yahveh
　　　　Yahweh
　　　　Yehovah
　　　　Yhwh
　　NT Ten commandments—Name of
　　　　God
— **Omnipotence**
　[BT133]
— **Omnipresence**
　[BT132]
　Here are entered works on the general pres-
　ence of God in all creation. Works on the special
　presence of God in a particular place, or with a
　particular object or group of people are entered
　under Presence of God.
　UF Shekinah
　RT Jesus Christ—Presence
　　　Presence of God
— **Omniscience**
　[BT131]
　UF God—Knowledge
　　　God, Knowledge of
　　　Knowledge of God
　　　Omniscience of God
　BT Free will and determinism
　　　Predestination
— Oneness
　USE God—Simplicity
— Pain
　USE Suffering of God
— Passibility
　USE Suffering of God

— **Patience**
　[BT153.P36]
　UF Patience of God
　BT Patience—Religious aspects
— Permissive will
　USE Theodicy
— Praise
　USE Praise of God
— Presence
　USE Presence of God
— **Promises**
　[BT180.P7]
　BT Promises—Religious aspects
— **Proof**
— — **History of doctrines**
— Proof, Axiological
　USE God—Proof, Moral
— **Proof, Cosmological**
　[BT98-102]
　UF Cosmological argument
　BT Cosmology
— Proof, Deontological
　USE God—Proof, Moral
— **Proof, Empirical**
　[BT98-101]
　UF Empirical argument
　BT Experience
　　　Experience (Religion)
— **Proof, Moral**
　UF Axiological proof of God
　　　Deontological proof of God
　　　God—Proof, Axiological
　　　God—Proof, Deontological
　　　Moral proof of God
　BT Ethics
— — **History of doctrines**
　　[BT98]
— **Proof, Ontological**
　[BT98-101]
　UF Ontological argument
　BT Ontology
— **Proof, Teleological**
　[BT98-101]
　UF Teleological argument
　BT Teleology
— Providence and government
　USE Providence and government of
　　　God
— Revelation
　USE Revelation
— **Righteousness**
　[BT145]
　UF God—Justice
　　　Righteousness of God
— — **History of doctrines**
— **Simplicity**
　[BT148]
　UF Actus purus
　　　God—Oneness
　　　God—Unicity
　　　God—Unity
　　　Oneness of God
　　　Simplicity of God
　　　Unicity of God
　　　Unity of God
　BT God—Attributes
— Sovereignty
　USE Providence and government of
　　　God
— Suffering
　USE Suffering of God
— Throne
　USE Throne of God
— Transcendence
　USE Transcendence of God
— Unicity
　USE God—Simplicity
— Unity
　USE God—Simplicity
— **Will**
　UF Will of God

God
— **Will** *(Continued)*
BT Free will and determinism
— — **History of doctrines**
— Will, Permissive
USE Theodicy
— **Wisdom**
[BT150]
BT Wisdom—Religious aspects
— **Worship and love**
[BV4817]
Here are entered works on the worship and love which man accords to God. Works on the love which God has toward man are entered under the heading God—Love.
BT Love—Religious aspects
Worship
NT Bhakti
— — **Biblical teaching**
[BS1199.W73]
BT God—Biblical teaching
— **Wrath**
UF Anger of God
God—Anger
Wrath of God
God, Children of
USE Children of God
God, Desire for
USE Desire for God
God, Fear of
USE Fear of God
God, Glory of
USE Glory of God
God, Hidden
USE Hidden God
God, Image of
USE Image of God
God, Immanence of
USE Immanence of God
God, Jealousy of
USE God—Jealousy
God, Kingdom of
USE Kingdom of God
God, Knowledge of
USE God—Knowableness
God—Omniscience
God, Pain of
USE Suffering of God
God, People of
USE People of God
God, Providence and government of
USE Providence and government of God
God, Suffering of
USE Suffering of God
God (African religion)
God (Brahmanism)
USE God (Hinduism)
God (Chinese religion)
[BL1800-1810]
God (Egyptian religion)
NT Gods, Egyptian
God (Greek religion)
[B398.G6]
[BL795.G6]
God (Hinduism)
[BL1200-1225]
UF God (Brahmanism)
BT Hinduism
NT Brahman
Trimūrti
God (Islam)
[BP166.2]
UF Allah
Monotheism (Islam)
BT Islam—Doctrines
NT Word of God (Islam)
— **Attributes**
— **Knowableness**
— **Koranic teaching**
— **Mercy**
BT Mercy

— Most beautiful names
USE God (Islam)—Name
— **Name**
Here are entered works on the various terms for God, including the 99 Most Beautiful Names of God. Prayer-books and devotional literature using the names of God mainly as an inspirational device or focal point for worship are entered under Sufism—Prayer-books and devotions, etc. Works on the theological meaning of the names as characteristics of God are entered under God (Islam)—Attributes.
UF God (Islam)—Most beautiful names
God (Islam)—Ninety-nine names
— Ninety-nine names
USE God (Islam)—Name
— **Proof**
— Throne
USE Throne of God (Islam)
— **Will**
BT Free will and determinism (Islam)
— **Worship and love**
BT Worship (Islam)
God (Jainism)
[BL1356]
UF Paramadevatā
BT Jainism
— **Omniscience**
God (Judaism)
[BM610]
BT Judaism—Doctrines
NT Fear of God (Judaism)
Holy Spirit (Judaism)
Providence and government of God (Judaism)
— **Attributes**
— **Knowableness**
— **Name**
UF Jehovah
Yahveh
Yahweh
Yehovah
Yhwh
BT God—Name
— **Omniscience**
— **Worship and love**
God (Sikhism)
[BL2018.22]
BT Sikhism
God (Theory of knowledge)
USE God—Knowableness
God (Theosophy)
[BP573.G6]
BT Theosophy
God and man, Mystical union of
USE Mystical union
God in literature
BT Religion in literature
RT Gods in literature
God is dead theology
USE Death of God theology
Godaizan (Korea)
USE Odae Mountain (Korea)
Godall family
USE Goodall family
Godard family
USE Goddard family
Godars family
USE Goddard family
Godart family
USE Goddard family
Godāvari River (India)
BT Rivers—India
Godbey family *(Not Subd Geog)*
UF Godby family
Godby family
USE Godbey family

Goddard family *(Not Subd Geog)*
UF Godard family
Godars family
Godart family
Goddart family
Goddeard family
Godderd family
Goddhart family
Godeard family
Godhard family
Godward family
Goodard family
Goodhard family
Goodhart family
Goodheart family
Goddart family
USE Goddard family
Goddeard family
USE Goddard family
Godderd family
USE Goddard family
Goddes de Varennes family
USE Goddes family
Goddes family *(Not Subd Geog)*
UF De Goddes de Varennes family
De Goddes family
Goddes de Varennes family
Godes family
Goddesses *(May Subd Geog)*
UF Female gods
BT Gods
NT Cybele (Goddess)
Grain goddesses
Mother-goddesses
Goddesses, Greek
UF Greek goddesses
NT Artemis (Greek deity)
Astraea (Greek deity)
Atropos (Greek deity)
Daphne (Greek deity)
Diktynna (Greek deity)
Galatea (Greek deity)
Hecate (Greek deity)
Hestia (Greek deity)
Lachesis (Greek deity)
Muses (Greek deities)
Goddesses, Hindu
[BL1216]
UF Hindu goddesses
Goddesses, Mother
USE Mother-goddesses
Goddesses, Roman
[BL805]
UF Roman goddesses
BT Gods, Roman
NT Diana (Roman deity)
Goddesses, Yoruba
UF Yoruba goddesses
NT Oya (Yoruba deity)
Goddesses in art
USE Gods in art
Goddesses in literature
USE Gods in literature
Goddhart family
USE Goddard family
Godeanu Mountains (Romania)
UF Munții Godeanu (Romania)
BT Mountains—Romania
Godeard family
USE Goddard family
Godefroid family *(Not Subd Geog)*
Godel family
USE Goodall family
Gödel numbers
UF Numbers, Gödel
BT Logic, Symbolic and mathematical
Numbers, Theory of
Gödel's theorem
UF Undecidable theories

BT Arithmetic—Foundations
   Completeness theorem
   Incompleteness theorems
   Logic, Symbolic and mathematical
   Numbers, Theory of
RT Decidability (Mathematical logic)
Godes family
USE Goddes family
Godesburg (Bonn, Germany)
UF Godesburg Castle (Bonn, Germany)
BT Castles—Germany (West)
Godesburg Castle (Bonn, Germany)
USE Godesburg (Bonn, Germany)
Godetia
USE Clarkia
Godetia amoena
USE Clarkia amoenia
Godetia grandiflora
USE Clarkia amoenia
Godetia lindleyana
USE Clarkia amoenia
Godetia whitneyi
USE Clarkia amoenia
Godfathers
USE Sponsors
Godferey family
USE Godfrey family
Godfray family
USE Godfrey family
Godfree family
USE Godfrey family
Godfrey family *(Not Subd Geog)*
UF Godferey family
   Godfray family
   Godfree family
   Godfry family
Godfry family
USE Godfrey family
Godhard family
USE Goddard family
Godi family
USE Godoi family
Godia dialect
USE Godye dialect
Godianism (Cult) *(May Subd Geog)*
BT Cults—Nigeria
   Nigeria—Religion
Godié dialect
USE Godye dialect
Godmothers
USE Sponsors
Godoberi language
   ₍PK9201.G63₎
BT Daghestan languages
Godoi family *(Not Subd Geog)*
UF De Godoi family
   Godi family
   Godoy family
Godoy family
USE Godoi family
Godreau family *(Not Subd Geog)*
UF Gaudreau family
   Gautherot family
   Gottreau family
   Goudreau family
Godridge family
USE Goodrich family
Gods
   ₍BL473₎
UF Deities
BT Mythology, Classical
RT Mythology
   Religions
SA *names of deities, e.g.* Athena (Greek
   deity), Baal (Deity)
NT Attis (God)
   Dente (African deity)
   Goddesses
   Healing gods
   Kings and rulers—Religious aspects
   Mountain-gods

Myth
Rain gods
Rice-gods
Sacred marriage (Mythology)
Sea gods
Sky-gods
Titans (Mythology)
Venus deities
Water-gods
Wind gods
— **Biblical teaching**
   ₍BS1199.G63₎
BT Idolatry
   Idols and images—Worship
NT Ten commandments—Other gods
— Costume
   USE Idols and images—Costume and
      adornment
— Dictionaries
   USE Mythology—Dictionaries
Gods, African
UF African gods
NT Nyabingi (African deity)
Gods, Anatolian *(May Subd Geog)*
UF Anatolian gods
Gods, Assyro-Babylonian
UF Assyro-Babylonian gods
BT Assyro-Babylonian religion
NT Anu (Assyro-Babylonian deity)
   Marduk (Babylonian deity)
Gods, Bonpo *(May Subd Geog)*
   ₍BQ7981.2-7981.4₎
UF Bonpo gods
BT Bonpo (Sect)
   Gods, Buddhist
NT Dbal-gsas (Bonpo deity)
   Ma-tri (Bonpo deity)
   Me-ri (Bonpo deity)
   Sitātapatrā (Bonpo deity)
   Stag-lha-me-'bar (Bonpo deity)
Gods, Buddhist *(May Subd Geog)*
UF Buddhist gods
BT Buddhism
NT Acala (Buddhist deity)
   Akṣobhya (Buddhist deity)
   Amitābha (Buddhist deity)
   Angels (Buddhism)
   Avalokiteśvara (Buddhist deity)
   Bhaiṣajyaguru (Buddhist deity)
   Bodhisattvas
   Buddhas
   Cakrasamvara (Buddhist deity)
   Ḍākinī (Buddhist deity)
   Dam-tshig-rdo-rje (Buddhist deity)
   Gandharvas (Buddhist deities)
   Gods, Bonpo
   Gods, Japanese
   Hachiman (Shinto deity)
   Hayagrīva (Buddhist deity)
   Kṣitigarbha (Buddhist deity)
   Kun-dga'-gźon-nu (Buddhist deity)
   Kurukullā (Buddhist deity)
   Mahākāla (Buddhist deity)
   Mahāyakṣa (Buddhist deity)
   Maitreya (Buddhist deity)
   Mañjuśrī (Buddhist deity)
   Mgon-po Bse-khrab-can (Buddhist
      deity)
   Pañjara (Buddhist deity)
   Pattini (Buddhist deity)
   Rdo-rje-śugs-ldan-rtsal (Buddhist deity)
   Uṣṇīṣavijayā (Buddhist deity)
   Vajradhara (Buddhist deity)
   Vajrakīla (Buddhist deity)
   Vajrapāṇi (Buddhist deity)
   Vajrasattva (Buddhist deity)
   Vajravārāhi (Buddhist deity)
   Vajrayoginī (Buddhist deity)
   Viśrāvaṇa (Buddhist deity)
   Yakṣas (Buddhist deities)
   Yama (Buddhist deity)

   Yamāntaka (Buddhist deity)
Gods, Buddhist, in art
NT Jūnitenzō (Painting)
Gods, Canaanite
UF Canaanite gods
NT Rešep (Canaanite deity)
Gods, Carthaginian
USE Gods, Punic
Gods, Celtic
UF Celtic gods
NT Borvo (Celtic deity)
   Damona (Celtic deity)
Gods, Chinese *(May Subd Geog)*
UF Chinese gods
NT Gods, Taoist
   Ma-tsu (Chinese goddess)
Gods, Dacian
UF Dacian gods
Gods, Egyptian
   ₍BL2450.G6₎
UF Egyptian gods
BT God (Egyptian religion)
NT Amon (Egyptian deity)
   Anubis (Egyptian deity)
   Apedemak (Egyptian deity)
   Aten (Egyptian deity)
   Atum (Egyptian deity)
   Horus (Egyptian deity)
   Isis (Egyptian deity)
   Min (Egyptian deity)
   Neith (Egyptian deity)
   Osiris (Egyptian deity)
   Serapis (Egyptian deity)
   Shai (Egyptian deity)
   Tatenen (Egyptian deity)
   Teneniyt (Egyptian deity)
Gods, Gallo-Roman
UF Gallo-Roman gods
Gods, Germanic
UF Germanic gods
NT Mannus (Germanic deity)
Gods, Greek
UF Greek gods
NT Achelous (Greek deity)
   Adonis (Greek deity)
   Aesculapius (Greek deity)
   Aphrodite (Greek deity)
   Apollo (Greek deity)
   Ares (Greek deity)
   Aristaeus (Greek deity)
   Athena (Greek deity)
   Cronus (Greek deity)
   Demeter (Greek deity)
   Dionysus (Greek deity)
   Eileithyia (Greek deity)
   Eris (Greek deity)
   Eros (Greek deity)
   Gods, Minoan
   Gods, Mycenaean
   Gods, Samothracian
   Hephaestus (Greek deity)
   Hera (Greek deity)
   Hermes (Greek deity)
   Inachus (Greek deity)
   Marsyas (Greek deity)
   Mother goddesses, Greek
   Nike (Greek deity)
   Pan (Greek deity)
   Persephone (Greek deity)
   Pluto (Greek deity)
   Poseidon (Greek deity)
   Psyche (Greek deity)
   Themis (Greek deity)
   Zephyrus (Greek deity)
   Zeus (Greek deity)
Gods, Greek, in art
Gods, Hawaiian *(May Subd Geog)*
UF Hawaiian gods
NT Kamapua'a (Hawaiian deity)
Gods, Healing
USE Healing gods

Gods, Hindu *(May Subd Geog)*
  UF Hindu gods
  BT Hinduism
  NT Aatimna (Hindu deity)
        Aditi (Hindu deity)
        Ādityas (Hindu deities)
        Agni (Hindu deity)
        Aiyanār (Hindu deity)
        Annapūrṇā (Hindu deity)
        Bagalāmukhī (Hindu deity)
        Balarāma (Hindu deity)
        Bāṭa Ṭhākurāṇī (Hindu deity)
        Bhādū (Hindu deity)
        Bhagavati (Hindu deity)
        Bhairava (Hindu deity)
        Bōre Dēvaru (Hindu deity)
        Brahmā (Hindu deity)
        Cāmuṇḍā (Hindu deity)
        Caṇḍi (Hindu deity)
        Candra (Hindu deity)
        Dattāreya (Hindu deity)
        Devanārāyana (Hindu deity)
        Durgā (Hindu deity)
        Gaṇeśa (Hindu deity)
        Gaurī (Hindu deity)
        Gāyatrī (Hindu deity)
        Gods, Vedic
        Gosānī (Hindu deity)
        Hanumān (Hindu deity)
        Hayagrīva (Hindu deity)
        Indra (Hindu deity)
        Jagannātha (Hindu deity)
        Jyotibā (Hindu deity)
        Kāma (Hindu deity)
        Kaṇṇaki (Hindu deity)
        Kanyakāparameśvari (Hindu deity)
        Kārttikeya (Hindu deity)
        Karumāri (Hindu deity)
        Karumari Amman (Hindu deity)
        Khamlāmba (Hindu deity)
        Khōḍiyāra Mātā (Hindu deity)
        Krishna (Hindu deity)
        Lakshmi (Hindu deity)
        Lakṣmaṇa (Hindu deity)
        Manasā (Hindu deity)
        Mārtaṇḍa (Hindu deity)
        Matsya (Hindu deity)
        Mīnākṣī (Hindu deity)
        Mitra (Hindu deity)
        Murugan (Hindu deity)
        Nabagraha (Hindu deity)
        Narasiṃha (Hindu deity)
        Nārāyaṇa (Hindu deity)
        Paccaināyaki (Hindu deity)
        Paraśurāma (Hindu deity)
        Parvati (Hindu deity)
        Pattini (Hindu deity)
        Pattisvarar (Hindu deity)
        Pradyumna (Hindu deity)
        Pūlaṅkoṇṭāḷamman (Hindu deity)
        Puvaṇēsvari (Hindu deity)
        Rādhā (Hindu deity)
        Rāma (Hindu deity)
        Raṇachoḍarāya (Hindu deity)
        Śakti (Hindu deity)
        Sampatkumāra (Hindu deity)
        Śani (Hindu deity)
        Santoshī Mātā (Hindu deity)
        Sarasvatī (Hindu deity)
        Sāvitrī (Hindu deity)
        Shambulinga (Hindu deity)
        Sītā (Hindu deity)
        Śītalā (Hindu deity)
        Siva (Hindu deity)
        Soma (Hindu deity)
        Sonārāya (Hindu deity)
        Sri Venkatesvara (Hindu deity)
        Śrīvidyā (Hindu deity)
        Tejājī (Hindu deity)
        Tripurasundarī (Hindu deity)
        Tulasī (Hindu deity)

        Tushu (Hindu deity)
        Tusu (Hindu deity)
        Uṣas (Hindu deity)
        Vāmana (Hindu deity)
        Varāha (Hindu deity)
        Varuṇa (Hindu deity)
        Vāyu (Hindu deity)
        Vēlāpuri Kaṟuppaṇṇacāmi (Hindu
          deity)
        Vishnu (Hindu deity)
        Viśvakarman (Hindu deity)
        Viṭhobā (Hindu deity)
        Yakṣas (Hindu deities)

Gods, Hittite
  UF Hittite gods
  BT Hittites—Religion

Gods, Indic
    [BL2015.G63]
  UF Indic gods
  BT India—Religion

Gods, Jaina *(May Subd Geog)*
  UF Jaina gods
  BT Jainism
  NT Nāgakumāra (Jaina deity)
        Padmāvatī (Jaina deity)

Gods, Japanese
    [BL2211.G6]
  UF Japanese gods
  BT Gods, Buddhist
        Gods, Shinto
  NT Dōsojin
        Kamagami
        Kōshin

Gods, Lapp
  UF Lapp gods
  NT Ruto (Lapp deity)

Gods, Latvian
  NT Jumis (Latvian deity)

Gods, Lusitanian
  USE Gods, Portuguese

Gods, Minoan
    [BL793.C7]
  UF Minoan gods
  BT Gods, Greek

Gods, Mycenaean
    [BL793.M8]
  UF Mycenaean gods
  BT Gods, Greek

Gods, Norse
  UF Norse gods
  NT Loki (Norse deity)

Gods, Phoenician
  UF Phoenician gods
  BT Phoenicians—Religion

Gods, Phrygian
  UF Phrygian gods
  NT Sabazius (Thraco-Phrygian deity)

Gods, Portuguese
  UF Gods, Lusitanian
        Lusitanian gods
        Portuguese gods

Gods, Punic
  UF Carthaginian gods
        Gods, Carthaginian
        Punic gods
  NT Caelestis (Punic deity)

Gods, Roman
  UF Roman gods
  NT Cacus (Roman deity)
        Ceres (Roman deity)
        Cupid (Roman deity)
        Fortuna (Roman deity)
        Goddesses, Roman
        Juno (Roman deity)
        Jupiter (Roman deity)
        Liber Pater (Roman deity)
        Mars (Roman deity)
        Mater Matuta (Roman deity)
        Mefitis (Roman deity)
        Mercury (Roman deity)
        Minerva (Roman deity)

        Neptune (Roman deity)
        Ops (Roman deity)
        Proserpina (Roman deity)
        Saturn (Roman deity)
        Venus (Roman deity)
        Victoria (Roman deity)
        Vulcan (Roman deity)

Gods, Rundi
  UF Rundi gods
  NT Imana (Rundi deity)

Gods, Samothracian
    [BL793.S3]
  UF Samothracian gods
  BT Gods, Greek

Gods, Semitic
  UF Semitic gods
  BT Semites—Religion
  NT Asherah (Semitic deity)
        Mot (Semitic god)

Gods, Seven lucky
  USE Seven gods of fortune

Gods, Shinto
    [BL2226]
  BT Shinto
  NT Amaterasu Ōmikami (Shinto deity)
        Gods, Japanese
        Hachiman (Shinto deity)
        Ōkuninushi no kami
        Susanoo no Mikoto (Shinto deity)

Gods, Slavic
  UF Slavic gods
  BT Slavs—Religion
  NT Svantovit (Slavic deity)

Gods, Sumerian
    [BL1615]
  NT Inanna (Sumerian deity)

Gods, Syrian
  UF Syrian gods

Gods, Taoist *(May Subd Geog)*
  UF Taoist gods
  BT Gods, Chinese

Gods, Thracian
  UF Thracian gods
  NT Bendida (Thracian deity)
        Sabazius (Thraco-Phrygian deity)

Gods, Ugaritic
  UF Ugaritic gods

Gods, Umbanda
    [BL2592.U514G6]
  UF Umbanda gods
  BT Umbanda (Cultus)
  RT Gods, Yoruba

Gods, Vedic
    [BL1216-1225]
  UF Vedic gods
  BT Gods, Hindu
        Vedas—Criticism, interpretation, etc.
  NT Ādityas (Hindu deities)

Gods, Yoruba *(May Subd Geog)*
  UF Yoruba gods
  BT Yorubas—Religion
  RT Gods, Umbanda

Gods, Zoroastrian
  UF Zoroastrian gods
  BT Zoroastrianism
  NT Sraosha (Zoroastrian deity)

Gods (in numismatics)
  BT Art and mythology
        Gods in art
        Numismatics

God's eye (Talisman)
  USE Ojo de Dios (Talisman)

Gods in art
  UF Goddesses in art
  BT Art and religion
        God—Art
  RT Idols and images
  NT Gods (in numismatics)

Gods in literature
  UF Goddesses in literature
  BT Religion in literature

RT God in literature
Gods in rabbinical literature
  [BM509.G63]
  BT Idols and images—Worship
      Rabbinical literature
Gods of fortune, Seven
  USE Seven gods of fortune
God's truce
  USE Truce of God
God's Word (Theology)
  USE Word of God (Theology)
Godshal family
  USE Goodsell family
Godshalk family
  USE Gottschalk family
Godshall family
  USE Goodsell family
Godshalt family
  USE Gottschalk family
Godshell family
  USE Gottschalk family
Godshul family
  USE Gottschalk family
Godward family
  USE Goddard family
Godwin, William, 1756-1836
  — Characters
  — — Caleb Williams
          RT Williams, Caleb (Fictitious
              character)
Godwin Austen, Mount (Pakistan)
  USE K2 (Pakistan : Mountain)
Godwin family
  USE Goodwin family
Godwine family
  USE Goodwin family
Godwit, Black-tailed
  USE Black-tailed godwit
Godwits
  UF Limosa
  BT Scolopacidae
  NT Black-tailed godwit
Godwyn family
  USE Goodwin family
Godye dialect
  UF Go dialect (Ivory Coast)
      Godia dialect
      Godié dialect
  BT Bete language
      Ivory Coast—Languages
Godzilla films
  [PN1995.9.G63 (History and
   criticism)]
  BT Characters and characteristics in
      moving-pictures
      Horror films
Goe family (Not Subd Geog)
  RT Goes family
Goeckner family (Not Subd Geog)
  UF Geckner family
Goeduck
  USE Geoduck
Goeldi's marmoset
  USE Callimico goeldii
Goeldi's monkey
  USE Callimico goeldii
Goeler family
  USE Göler family
Goeler von Ravensburg family
  USE Göler family
Goeller family
  USE Göler family
Goering family (Not Subd Geog)
  UF Goring family
Goertner family
  USE Curtner family
Goertzen family (Not Subd Geog)
**Goes, Hugo van der, 1435?-1482. Adoration
  of the shepherds**
    [ND673.G6]

UF Aanbidding van de herders (Painting)
    Adoration of the shepherds (Painting)
BT Altarpieces, Flemish
    Altarpieces, Gothic—Belgium
    Christmas in art
    Jesus Christ—Art
    Shepherds in art
Goes family (Not Subd Geog)
  RT Goe family
Goethe family (Not Subd Geog)
Goethe prize
  UF Goethepreis
Goethepreis
  USE Goethe prize
Goethite (May Subd Geog)
  [QE391.G]
  UF Xanthosiderite
  BT Iron oxides
Goetsch family
  USE Goetz family
Goetschi family
  USE Goetschius family
Goetschius family (Not Subd Geog)
  UF Goetschi family
      Goetschy family
  RT Goetz family
Goetschy family
  USE Goetschius family
Goettge family
  USE Geitgey family
Goettsche family
  USE Goetz family
Goetz family (Not Subd Geog)
  UF Goetsch family
      Goettsche family
      Goetze family
  RT Gates family
      Getz family
      Goetschius family
Goetze family
  USE Goetz family
Goff family (Not Subd Geog)
  UF Gaff family
      Gauff family
      Gaugh family
      Goffe family
      Goph family
      Gough family
      McGoff family
Goffe family
  USE Goff family
Goffering-machines
  [TJ1530]
  BT Textile machinery
Goforth family (Not Subd Geog)
  UF Garforth family
      Gofourth family
Gofourth family
  USE Goforth family
Goggles, Safety
  USE Safety goggles
Goggomobil automobile
  USE Glas automobile
**Gogh, Vincent van, 1853-1890.
  Hogeschoolrijdster**
    [ND653.G7]
  UF Hogeschoolrijdster (Painting)
Gogir Feng (Pakistan)
  USE K2 (Pakistan : Mountain)
Gogo language
  [PL8208]
  UF Chigogo language
  BT Bantu languages
Gogodala (Papua New Guinea people)
  UF Gogodara (Papua New Guinea people)
  BT Ethnology—Papua New Guinea
Gogodala language
  UF Gogodara language
  BT Papuan languages
Gogodara (Papua New Guinea people)
  USE Gogodala (Papua New Guinea people)

Gogodara language
  USE Gogodala language
Gogstad ship
  USE Viking ships
Goguel family (Not Subd Geog)
Gogynfeirdd (Welsh poets)
  BT Poets, Welsh
      Welsh poetry—To 1550
Göhl River (Belgium and Netherlands)
  USE Geul River (Belgium and Netherlands)
Gohn family (Not Subd Geog)
  UF Goan family
  RT Kuhn family
Goho family (Not Subd Geog)
Goidelic languages
  BT Celtic languages
  NT Gaelic language
      Irish language
      Manx language
Goigs
  [ML3086]
  BT Christian poetry, Catalan
      Folk-songs, Catalan
      Hymns, Spanish
Going away to school
  USE Residence and education
Going concern (Accounting)
  [HF5681.G55]
  BT Accounting
      Business enterprises—Valuation
Going public (Securities) (May Subd Geog)
  [HG4028.S7]
  UF Public ownership of close corporations
  RT Close corporations—Finance
      Corporations—Finance
      Stocks
  — Law and legislation (May Subd Geog)
Going-to-the-Sun Highway (Mont.)
  USE Going-to-the-Sun Road (Mont.)
Going-to-the-Sun Road (Mont.)
  UF Going-to-the-Sun Highway (Mont.)
      Transmountain Highway (Mont.)
      Transmountain Road (Mont.)
  BT Glacier National Park (Mont.)
      Roads—Montana
Gois Causeway (France)
  UF Le Gois (France)
      Passage du Gois (France)
  BT Causeways—France
Goiter (May Subd Geog)
  [RC656-RC656.3]
  UF Bronchocele
      Goitre
  BT Iodine deficiency diseases
      Thyroid gland—Diseases
  NT Endemic goiter
      Graves' disease
      Substernal goiter
  — Nutritional aspects
Goiter, Exophthalmic
  USE Graves' disease
Goiter, Substernal
  USE Substernal goiter
Goitre
  USE Goiter
Gojari language
  USE Gujuri language
Gojō family (Not Subd Geog)
Gojōnome Kaidō (Japan)
  BT Roads—Japan
Gojri language
  USE Gujuri language
Goken Yashiki Iseki (Nankoku-shi, Japan)
  USE Goken Yashiki Site (Nankoku-shi,
       Japan)
Goken Yashiki Site (Nankoku-shi, Japan)
  (Not Subd Geog)
  UF Goken Yashiki Iseki (Nankoku-shi,
      Japan)
  BT Japan—Antiquities

Gokenin
  BT Samurai
Gokhale family
Gokin family
  USE Gookin family
Gokō family *(Not Subd Geog)*
Gokstad ship
  USE Viking ships
Gola language
  [PL8211]
  UF Gora language
      Gura language
  BT Liberia—Languages
      Niger-Congo languages
      Sierra Leone—Languages
Golan Heights *(Not Subd Geog)*
    As a geographic subdivision, this heading is used
  directly.
  UF Djaulân region
      Djolan region
      Golan Plateau
      Jaulân Region
      Jawlān Region
      Julan Region
      Murtafa‘āt al Jawlān
      Syria (Territory under Israeli
          occupation, 1967-   )
  BT Palestine
Golan Plateau
  USE Golan Heights
Golard family
  USE Galard family
Golaway family
  USE Galloway family
Gold *(May Subd Geog)*
  [HG289-HG297 (Finance)]
  [HG551 (Coinage)]
  [QD181.A9 (Chemistry)]
  [TN410-TN429 (Mineral resources)]
  UF Specie
  BT Currency question
      Precious metals
  RT Coinage
      Money
      Silver question
  NT Gold clause
      Gold foil
      Gold mines and mining
      Gold standard
      Goldwork
      Monetary gold confiscations
      Quantity theory of money
      Spun gold
  — Assaying
    [TN580.G6]
  — Electrometallurgy
    [TN768]
  — Isotopes
    UF Gold isotopes
  —— Decay
  —— Spectra
  — Law and legislation *(May Subd Geog)*
  — Metallurgy
    [TN760-769]
    UF Gold metallurgy
    NT Chlorination
        Cyanide process
        Gold—Milling
  — Milling
    [TN762]
    BT Gold—Metallurgy
  — Minting
    [HG321]
  — Protective coatings
    USE Gold coatings
  — Spectra
  — Standards of fineness
    [HD9747]
    BT Coinage
    RT Hallmarks

Gold, Cloth of
  USE Cloth of gold
Gold alloys
  [RK653 (Dentistry)]
  [TS729]
  NT Gold-cadmium alloys
      Gold-chromium alloys
      Gold-cobalt alloys
      Gold-copper alloys
      Gold-platinum alloys
      Silver-gold alloys
Gold and ivory sculpture
  USE Sculpture, Chryselephantine
Gold articles
  USE Goldwork
Gold beryl
  USE Chrysoberyl
Gold boxes *(May Subd Geog)*
  BT Boxes
      Boxes, Ornamental
      Goldwork
Gold boxes, Rococo *(May Subd Geog)*
  UF Rococo gold boxes
Gold-cadmium alloys
  UF Cadmium-gold alloys
  BT Cadmium alloys
      Gold alloys
Gold-chromium alloys
  UF Chromium-gold alloys
  BT Chromium alloys
      Gold alloys
Gold clause *(May Subd Geog)*
  BT Bonds
      Contracts
      Currency question
      Debtor and creditor
      Escalator clause
      Gold
      Payment
  NT Valuta clause
Gold coatings
  UF Gold—Protective coatings
  BT Protective coatings
  — Optical properties
Gold-cobalt alloys
  UF Cobalt-gold alloys
  BT Cobalt alloys
      Gold alloys
Gold coins *(May Subd Geog)*
  BT Coins
  NT Beaver (Coin)
      Burgerspond (Coin)
      Gulden (Coin)
  — Law and legislation *(May Subd Geog)*
  — South Africa
    NT Krugerrand (Coin)
Gold compounds
  [QD412.A9]
Gold-copper alloys
  UF Copper-gold alloys
  BT Copper alloys
      Gold alloys
Gold discoveries
  USE Gold mines and mining
Gold dredging *(May Subd Geog)*
  [TN422]
  UF Dredging (Gold mining)
  BT Gold mines and mining
Gold embroidery *(May Subd Geog)*
  BT Embroidery
Gold exchange standard
  USE Gold standard
Gold-eye
  [QL638.H5]
  UF Goldeye (Fish)
Gold family
  USE Gould family
Gold figurines *(May Subd Geog)*
  BT Figurines
      Goldwork

Gold figurines, Classical
  UF Classical gold figurines
  BT Classical antiquities
Gold figurines, Gothic *(May Subd Geog)*
  UF Gothic gold figurines
Gold films
  [TN693.G6]
  BT Metallic films
Gold foil
  UF Foil, Gold
  BT Gold
      Metal foils
  NT Gold-leaf
Gold in art
  [N8217.G6]
Gold industry *(May Subd Geog)*
  [HD9536]
Gold isotopes
  USE Gold—Isotopes
Gold jewelry *(May Subd Geog)*
  BT Goldwork
      Jewelry
Gold jewelry, Ancient *(May Subd Geog)*
  UF Ancient gold jewelry
Gold-leaf
  [TS260]
  BT Gold foil
Gold Medal (American Institute of Architects)
  USE AIA Gold Medal
Gold metallurgy
  USE Gold—Metallurgy
Gold miners *(May Subd Geog)*
  BT Miners
  — Biography
    UF Gold mines and mining—Personal
        narratives
  — Ontario
**Gold Miners' Strike, Kirkland Lake, Ont.,
1941-1942**
  BT Strikes and lockouts—Gold mining—
      Ontario
Gold mines and mining *(May Subd Geog)*
  [HD9536 (Economics)]
  [TN410-TN429 (Mineral industries)]
  UF Gold discoveries
      Gold rush
      Gold rushes
  BT Gold
  RT Hydraulic mining
  SA *subdivision* Gold discoveries *under
      names of countries, etc.*
  NT Gold dredging
      Prospecting
      Strikes and lockouts—Gold mining
  — Personal narratives
    USE Gold miners—Biography
  — California
    NT Los Burros Mining District (Calif.)
  — Nevada
    NT Carlin Mine (Nev.)
        Comstock Lode (Nev.)
  — South Africa
    NT Malmani gold fields
Gold ores *(May Subd Geog)*
Gold organic compounds
  USE Organogold compounds
Gold plate
  USE Plate
Gold-plating
  [TS692.G64]
  BT Gilding
      Plating
Gold-platinum alloys
  UF Platinum-gold alloys
  BT Gold alloys
      Platinum alloys
**Gold Restoration of the Rose Building (Little
Rock, Ark.)**
  UF Rose Building (Little Rock, Ark.)
  BT Commercial buildings—Arkansas

Gold rush
  USE Gold mines and mining
Gold rushes
  USE Gold mines and mining
Gold-silver alloys
  USE Silver-gold alloys
Gold standard
  ₍HG297₎
  UF Gold exchange standard
  BT Currency question
       Gold
       International liquidity
       Money
  RT Bimetallism
  NT Currency convertibility
Gold thread
  BT Thread
  RT Spun gold
Gold-weights
  USE Goldweights
Gold work
  USE Goldwork
Goldblatt hypertension
  USE Renovascular hypertension
Goldcrest
  USE Regulus regulus
Goldegg Castle (Goldegg im Pongau, Austria)
  USE Schloss Goldegg (Goldegg im Pongau,
       Austria)
Golden age (Mythology)
  BT Mythology, Classical
Golden age (Mythology) in literature
  BT Utopias in literature
Golden apple
  USE Bael (Tree)
Golden aspen
  USE Populus tremuloides
Golden bull, 1356
  ₍JN3270.G8₎
  UF Bull, Golden
  BT Electors (Kurfürsten)
Golden calf (Bible)
  UF Calf, Golden (Bible)
  BT Idols and images
Golden-cheeked warbler
  ₍QL696.P2618₎
  UF Dendroica chrysoparia
       Warbler, Golden-cheeked
Golden-crested kinglet
  USE Regulus regulus
Golden eagle
  ₍QL696.F32₎
  UF Aquila chrysaetos
  BT Eagles
  NT Himalayan golden eagle
Golden family *(Not Subd Geog)*
  UF Gilden family
       Goldin family
       Golding family
       Goldon family
       Goldwin family
       Goldwyn family
       Goldyn family
       Goulding family
Golden Fleece (Greek mythology)
  USE Argonauts (Greek mythology)
Golden-fronted woodpecker
  UF Centurus aurifrons
  BT Woodpeckers
Golden Gate (Kiev, Ukraine)
  USE Zoloti vorota (Kiev, Ukraine)
Golden Gate Bridge (San Francisco, Calif.)
  BT Bridges—California
Golden Gate National Recreation Area (Calif.)
  BT National parks and reserves—United
       States
       Recreation areas—California
Golden Gate Park (San Francisco, Calif.)
  BT Parks—California

Golden Globe Race, 1968-1969
  USE Sunday Times Golden Globe Race,
       1968-1969
Golden hamster *(May Subd Geog)*
  ₍QL737.R638₎
  UF Hamster, Golden
       Hamster, Syrian
       Mesocricetus auratus
       Syrian hamster
  BT Mesocricetus
Golden-headed manakin
  ₍QL696.P263₎
  UF Pipra erythrocephala
Golden Hill Reservation (Conn.)
  BT Indians of North America—
       Connecticut—Reservations
       Paugusset Indians—Reservations
Golden Horde
  ₍DS22.7₎
  UF Kipchak (Khanate)
       Kiptchak (Khanate)
  BT Mongols—History
Golden Horseshoe (Ont.)
  BT Ontario, Lake, Region (N.Y. and Ont.)
Golden Isles (Ga.)
  ₍F292.G58₎
  BT Islands—Georgia
       Sea Islands
  NT Saint Catherine Island (Ga.)
       Saint Simon's Island (Ga.)
       Sapelo Island (Ga.)
       Sea Island (Ga.)
Golden jackal
  USE Canis aureus
Golden lion tamarin
  USE Leontopithecus rosalia
Golden-mantled ground squirrel
  ₍QL737.R68₎
  UF Callospermophilus lateralis
       Spermophilus lateralis
  BT Ground squirrels
Golden mean
  USE Moderation
Golden monkey
  USE Rhinopithecus roxellanae
Golden Mound Site (Afghanistan)
  USE Tillya-tepe Site (Afghanistan)
Golden orb-weaving spider
  USE Nephila maculata
Golden oriole *(May Subd Geog)*
  ₍QL696.P2585₎
  UF Oriolus oriolus
  BT Oriolus
Golden plovers
  ₍QL696.C43₎
  UF Plovers, Golden
       Pluvialis
  BT Charadriidae
       Plovers
Golden poppy
  USE California poppy
Golden retrievers
  ₍SF429.G63₎
  BT Retrievers
Golden robin
  USE Northern oriole
Golden rose (Papal award)
  BT Decorations of honor, Papal
Golden Rose of Montreux
  UF Goldene Rose von Montreux
       Rose d'Or de Montreux
  BT Television broadcasting—Awards
Golden rule
  ₍BL85 (Comparative religion)₎
  ₍BV4715 (Moral theology)₎
  UF Rule, Golden
  BT Christian ethics
Golden section
  ₍QA466₎
  UF Extreme and mean ratio

  BT Geometry, Plane
       Ratio and proportion
Golden Temple Assault, Amritsar, India, 1984
  USE India—History—Golden Temple
       (Amritsar) Assault, 1984
Golden Triangle (Pittsburgh, Pa.)
  (Not Subd Geog)
  UF Pittsburgh (Pa.). Golden Triangle
Golden Triangle (Southeastern Asia)
  Here are entered works on the region consisting
  of northeastern Burma, northern Thailand, northern
  Laos, and southern Yunnan Province in China.
  UF Chin-san-chiao (Southeastern Asia)
Golden trout
  ₍QL638.S2₎
  UF Salmo aquabonita
  BT Trout
Golden trout fishing
  BT Fishing
       Trout fishing
Golden Trout Wilderness (Calif.)
  (Not Subd Geog)
  BT National parks and reserves—
       California
       Wilderness areas—California
Golden Valley Wilderness (Calif.)
  BT Wilderness areas—California
Goldene Rose von Montreux
  USE Golden Rose of Montreux
Goldeneye
  ₍QL696.A5₎
  UF Bucephala clangula
       Glaucionetta clangula
Goldenlined blenny
  USE Malacoctenus aurolineatus
Goldenrod
  ₍QK495.S (Solidago)₎
  BT Rubber plants
  NT Sweet goldenrod
Goldeye (Fish)
  USE Gold-eye
Goldfield Strike, 1907
  ₍HD5325.M8 1907.G₎
Goldfinches
  ₍QL696.P246₎
  BT Fringillidae
Goldfinches in art
  BT Birds in art
Goldfish *(May Subd Geog)*
  ₍QL638.C94 (Zoology)₎
  ₍SF458.G6 (Aquarium fish)₎
  BT Aquarium fishes
       Ornamental carp
       Ornamental fishes
Goldi
  USE Golds
Goldi language
  USE Nanai language
Goldian language
  USE Nanai language
Goldilocks and the three bears (Tale)
  USE Three bears (Tale)
Goldin family
  USE Golden family
Golding family
  USE Golden family
Goldklang family *(Not Subd Geog)*
Goldline blenny
  USE Malacoctenus aurolineatus
Goldman family *(Not Subd Geog)*
  UF Goldmann family
Goldmann family
  USE Goldman family
Goldman's wood rat
  UF Neotoma goldmani
  BT Wood rats
Goldner family *(Not Subd Geog)*
  UF Guldner family
Goldon family
  USE Golden family

Golds
  [DK759.G6]
  UF Goldi
  BT Ethnology—China
     Ethnology—Russian S.F.S.R.
     Tunguses
Goldsberry family
  USE Goldsborough family
Goldsborough family *(Not Subd Geog)*
  UF Goldsberry family
     Goldsbury family
Goldsbury family
  USE Goldsborough family
Goldscheider's disease
  USE Epidermolysis bullosa
Goldschmidt family
  USE Goldsmith family
Goldschmidtine
  USE Stephanite
Goldschmitt family
  USE Goldsmith family
Goldsmith family *(Not Subd Geog)*
  UF Goldschmidt family
     Goldschmitt family
     Gouldsmith family
Goldsmithing
  USE Goldwork
Goldsmiths *(May Subd Geog)*
  BT Art metal-workers
Goldstein rays
  USE Canal rays
Goldwasser family
  USE Goldwater family
Goldwater family *(Not Subd Geog)*
  UF Goldwasser family
Goldweights *(May Subd Geog)*
  UF Gold-weights
  BT Art metal-work
     Brasswork
     Weights and measures
Goldweights, Akan (African people)
  UF Akan (African people) goldweights
  NT Goldweights, Ashanti
Goldweights, Ashanti
  BT Goldweights, Akan (African people)
Goldweights, Ashanti, [etc.]
Goldwin family
  USE Golden family
Goldwork *(May Subd Geog)*
  [NK7100-NK7695 (Art industries)]
  [TS720-TS761 (Manufactures)]
  UF Gold articles
     Gold work
     Goldsmithing
  BT Art metal-work
     Arts and crafts movement
     Gold
     Metal-work
  RT Jewelry making
  SA Indians of North America—Goldwork;
     and similar headings
  NT Engraving (Metal-work)
     Gilding
     Gold boxes
     Gold figurines
     Gold jewelry
     Indians of North America—Goldwork
     Plate
     Vinaigrettes
  — China
  — — History
  — — — T'ang-Five dynasties, 618-960
Goldwork, Ancient *(May Subd Geog)*
  UF Ancient goldwork
Goldwork, Baroque *(May Subd Geog)*
  UF Baroque goldwork
Goldwork, Colonial *(May Subd Geog)*
  UF Colonial goldwork
Goldwork, Gothic *(May Subd Geog)*
  UF Gothic goldwork

Goldwork, Hellenistic *(May Subd Geog)*
  UF Hellenistic goldwork
Goldwork, Medieval *(May Subd Geog)*
  UF Medieval goldwork
Goldwork, Merovingian *(May Subd Geog)*
  UF Merovingian goldwork
Goldwork, Minoan *(May Subd Geog)*
  UF Minoan goldwork
Goldwork, Mycenaean *(May Subd Geog)*
  UF Mycenaean goldwork
Goldwork, Ottonian *(May Subd Geog)*
  UF Ottonian goldwork
Goldwork, Prehistoric *(May Subd Geog)*
  [GN799.G6]
  UF Prehistoric goldwork
  BT Antiquities
Goldwork, Renaissance *(May Subd Geog)*
  UF Renaissance goldwork
Goldwork, Rococo *(May Subd Geog)*
  UF Rococo goldwork
Goldwork, Romanesque *(May Subd Geog)*
  UF Romanesque goldwork
Goldwork, Sassanid *(May Subd Geog)*
  UF Sassanid goldwork
Goldwork, Thracian *(May Subd Geog)*
  UF Thracian goldwork
Goldwyn family
  USE Golden family
Goldyn family
  USE Golden family
Gole (African people)
  USE Zarma (African people)
Goleanor family
  USE Galeener family
Golem
  BT Legends, Jewish
     Mysticism—Judaism
GOLEM (Information retrieval system)
  UF Grossspeicherorientierte,
     listenorientierte Ermittlungsmethode
     (Information retrieval system)
  BT Information storage and retrieval
     systems
     Interactive computer systems
Golem Iskar River (Bulgaria)
  USE Iskŭr River (Bulgaria)
Golema Mountains (Bulgaria)
  UF Golyama planina (Bulgaria)
     Golyema planina (Bulgaria)
  BT Mountains—Bulgaria
Golenor family
  USE Galeener family
Göler family *(Not Subd Geog)*
  UF Goeler family
     Goeler von Ravensburg family
     Goeller family
     Göler von Ravensburg family
Göler von Ravensburg family
  USE Göler family
Golf *(May Subd Geog)*
  [GV961-987]
  NT Caddies
     Caddying
     Golf for women
     Golfers
     Grip (Golf)
     Putting (Golf)
     Swing (Golf)
  — Drive
     [GV979.D74]
     UF Drive (Golf)
        Driving (Golf)
  — Equipment and supplies
     NT Golf clubs (Sporting goods)
        Golf equipment industry
  — Rules
     [GV971]
  — Tournaments *(May Subd Geog)*
     [GV970]

  Individual tournaments by name, or place,
  and date, e.g. Canadian Open Golf Champion-
  ship Tournament, Winnipeg, 1952.
  — — **Arizona**
     NT Phoenix Open, Phoenix, Ariz.
  — — **Connecticut**
     NT Greater Hartford Open, Conn.
  — — **Great Britain**
     NT British Open Golf
        Championship
Golf, Miniature
  [GV987]
  UF Miniature golf
  NT Bilgo (Game)
Golf automobile
  [TL215.G]
  BT Volkswagen automobile
Golf balls
  BT Balls (Sporting goods)
Golf clubs (Sporting goods)
  (May Subd Geog)
  [GV976]
  UF Clubs, Golf (Sporting goods)
  BT Golf—Equipment and supplies
     Sporting goods
Golf courses *(May Subd Geog)*
  UF Golf-links
     Links, Golf
  BT Sports facilities
Golf-croquet
  [GV1017.G]
Golf equipment industry *(May Subd Geog)*
  [HD9993.G65]
  BT Golf—Equipment and supplies
Golf for women
  [GV966]
  BT Golf
     Sports for women
Golf-links
  USE Golf courses
Golfe de Gascogne (France and Spain)
  USE Biscay, Bay of (France and Spain)
Golfe du Morbihan (France)
  USE Morbihan Gulf (France)
Golfe du Saint-Laurent
  USE Saint Lawrence, Gulf of
Golfers *(May Subd Geog)*
  BT Golf
  NT Women golfers
Golfo de California (Mexico)
  USE California, Gulf of (Mexico)
Golfo de Fonseca
  USE Fonseca, Gulf of
Golfo de Guayaquil
  USE Guayaquil, Gulf of
Golfo de Honduras
  USE Honduras, Gulf of
Golfo de Maracaibo (Venezuela)
  USE Maracaibo Lake (Venezuela)
Golfo de San Blas (Panama)
  USE San Blas Gulf (Panama)
Golfo de Urabá (Colombia)
  USE Urabá, Gulf of (Colombia)
Golfo de Vizcaya (France and Spain)
  USE Biscay, Bay of (France and Spain)
Golfo di Napoli (Italy)
  USE Naples, Bay of (Italy)
Golfo di Policastro (Italy)
  USE Policastro Gulf (Italy)
Golfo di Pozzuoli (Italy)
  USE Pozzuoli Gulf (Italy)
Golgi apparatus
  UF Golgi bodies
     Golgi elements
     Golgi material
  BT Cell organelles
     Protoplasm
Golgi bodies
  USE Golgi apparatus
Golgi elements
  USE Golgi apparatus

Golgi material
    USE Golgi apparatus
Goliards
    ﹝PA8065.S8 (Latin verse)﹞
    UF Vagantes
        Vagi scholares
Goliath (Airplane)
Golin dialect
    BT Dom dialects
        Marigl dialect
Göll, Hoher (Austria and Germany)
    USE Hoher Göll (Austria and Germany)
Golladay family
    USE Galloway family
Gollahon family (Not Subd Geog)
    UF Gollehon family
Gollehon family
    USE Gollahon family
Gollety family (Not Subd Geog)
Golliday family
    USE Galloway family
Gollum
    ﹝QL638.95.C3﹞
    BT Carcharhinidae
Gólo language
    BT Banda languages
Golodnaĭa step' (Kazakh S.S.R.)
    USE Betpak-Dala (Kazakh S.S.R.)
Golodnaya step' (Kazakh S.S.R.)
    USE Betpak-Dala (Kazakh S.S.R.)
Golt family
    USE Gault family
Golyama planina (Bulgaria)
    USE Golema Mountains (Bulgaria)
Golyem Iskŭr River (Bulgaria)
    USE Iskŭr River (Bulgaria)
Golyema planina (Bulgaria)
    USE Golema Mountains (Bulgaria)
Goma (Rite)
    USE Homa (Rite)
Gomadj language
    USE Gumatj language
Gomaidj language
    USE Gumatj language
Gombē pottery
    USE Rakuzan pottery
Gombe Rama
    USE Killekyatha
Gombe Stream National Park (Tanzania)
    UF Gombe Stream Reserve (Tanzania)
    BT National parks and reserves—Tanzania
Gombe Stream Reserve (Tanzania)
    USE Gombe Stream National Park
        (Tanzania)
Gomberg-Bachmann reaction
    BT Chemical reactions
Gombert family
    USE Gompert family
Gomera (Canary Islands)
    UF Isla de la Gomera (Canary Islands)
        La Gomera (Canary Islands)
    BT Islands—Canary Islands
Gómez House (Montevideo, Uruguay)
    USE Casa de Francisco Gómez
        (Montevideo, Uruguay)
Gommerstedt Site (Germany)
    BT Germany (East)—Antiquities
Gomoku
    ﹝GV1469.G7﹞
    UF Go-moku
        Go-moku narabe
        Gomoku narabe
        Renju
    BT Board games
Gomoku narabe
    USE Gomoku
Gömör-Szepesi Érchegység (Czechoslovakia)
    USE Slovak Ore Mountains
        (Czechoslovakia)

Gompert family (Not Subd Geog)
    UF Gombert family
        Gumbert family
        Gumpert family
        Gumprecht family
        Gumprect family
Gomphaceae
    ﹝QK629.G6﹞
    BT Aphyllophorales
    NT Gloeocantharellus
        Gomphus
        Ramaria
Gomphidae
    ﹝QL520.3.G6﹞
    UF Clubtails
    BT Dragonflies
        Odonata
Gomphocarpus
    ﹝QK495.A815﹞
    BT Asclepiadaceae
Gomphocarpus fruticosus
    ﹝QK495.A815﹞
    UF Asclepias fruticosa
Gomphonema
    BT Naviculaceae
Gomphotherium angustidens
    ﹝QE882.P8﹞
    UF Hemimastodon annectens
        Mastodon angustidens
        Serridentinus mongoliensis
        Trilophodon angustidens
        Trilophodon cooperi
        Trilophodon inopinatus
Gomphus
    ﹝QK629.G6﹞
    BT Gomphaceae
Gonadal dysgenesis
    USE Turner's syndrome
Gonadectomy
    USE Castration
Gonadotrophin
    USE Gonadotropin
Gonadotropin
    UF Gonadotrophin
    BT Pituitary hormones
    NT Chorionic gonadotropins
        Follicle-stimulating hormone
        Hebin
        Luteinizing hormone
        Prolactin
Gonads
    UF Sex glands
    BT Endocrine glands
        Generative organs
    NT Ovaries
        Testis
Gonapodyaceae
    ﹝QK621﹞
    UF Gonopodyaceae
    BT Monoblepharidales
    NT Monoblepharella
Gonatodes
    ﹝QL666.L245﹞
    BT Geckos
Gonatopus bifarius
    USE Haplogonatopus bifarius
Gonatopus oratorius
    USE Donisthorpina formicicola
Gonatozygaceae
    USE Mesotaeniaceae
Gonce family (Not Subd Geog)
Goncourt Prize
    USE Prix Goncourt
Gond language
    USE Gondi language
Gondi folk-songs
    USE Folk-songs, Gondi
Gondi language
    ﹝PL4631-4﹞
    UF Gond language
    BT Dravidian languages

    NT Abujhmaria dialect
Gondi Palace (Florence, Italy)
    USE Palazzo Gondi (Florence, Italy)
Gondi poetry
    ﹝PL4634 (Texts)﹞
Gondolas
    BT Canal-boats
    RT Gundalows
Gondolella
    BT Conodonts
Gondra, Battle of, 1933
    UF Batalla de Gondra, 1933
    BT Chaco War, 1932-1935
Gonds
    ﹝DS432.G6﹞
    NT Dorla (Indic people)
        Kolams
        Maria (Indic people)
        Muria
Gondwana (Geology)
    ﹝QE511.5﹞
    UF Gondwanaland
    BT Geology
        Physical geography
    RT Continental drift
Gondwanaland
    USE Gondwana (Geology)
Gonepteryx
    ﹝QL561.P5﹞
    BT Pieridae
Gong
    USE Tamtam
Gonga (African people)
    ﹝DT380.4.G66﹞
    BT Ethnology—Ethiopia
Gongabula language
    USE Gungabula language
Gongga Mountains (China)
    USE Minya Konka (China)
Gongorism
    ﹝PQ6066﹞
    UF Culteranismo
        Cultism
    BT Baroque literature
        Spanish literature—History and
            criticism
Goniadidae
    ﹝QL391.A6﹞
    BT Phyllodocida
Gonin-gumi
    USE Goningumi
Goningumi
    UF Gonin-gumi
    RT Tonarigumi
Goniometry
    ﹝QC103﹞
    BT Angle
Gonionema
    USE Gonionemus
Gonionemus (May Subd Geog)
    ﹝QL377.H9﹞
    UF Gonionema
    BT Petasidae
    NT Gonionemus murbachii
        Gonionemus vertens
Gonionemus murbachii (May Subd Geog)
    ﹝QL377.H9﹞
    BT Gonionemus
Gonionemus vertens (May Subd Geog)
    ﹝QL377.H9﹞
    BT Gonionemus
Gonioscopy
    ﹝RE79.G﹞
    BT Eye—Examination
Gonja (African people)
    UF Gbanya (African people)
        Gonya (African people)
        Ngbanya (African people)
        Ngbanyito (African people)
    BT Ethnology—Ghana

Gonja language
  ₍PL8215₎
  UF Guang language
  BT Kwa languages
  NT Nchumburu language
      Nkunya language
Gonja Region (Ghana)
Gonococcus
  USE Neisseria gonorrhoeae
Gonodactylidae
  ₍QL444.M375₎
  BT Stomatopoda
  NT Gonodactylus
Gonodactylus
  ₍QL444.M375₎
  BT Gonodactylidae
Gonodonta
  ₍QL561.N7₎
  BT Noctuidae
Gonopodyaceae
  USE Gonapodyaceae
Gonopteridae
  USE Noctuidae
Gonorrhea *(May Subd Geog)*
  ₍RC202₎
  BT Bacterial diseases
      Genitourinary organs—Infections
      Sexually transmitted diseases
      Urethritis
  RT Neisseria gonorrhoeae
  NT Conjunctivitis, Infantile
Gonorynchiformes
  ₍QL637.9.G6₎
  UF Chanoiformes
  BT Osteichthyes
  NT Chanidae
      Kneriidae
Gonosomes
  USE Sex chromosomes
Gonostomatidae
  ₍QL638.G8₎
  UF Bristlemouth fishes
      Gonostomidae
      Lightfishes
      Maurolicidae
  BT Salmoniformes
  NT Sonoda
      Vinciguerria
Gonostomidae
  USE Gonostomatidae
Gonser family *(Not Subd Geog)*
  UF Ganser family
      Gansert family
      Gantzer family
      Gauntzer family
  RT Conser family
Gonter family
  USE Gunther family
Gontz family
  USE Gantt family
Gonya (African people)
  USE Gonja (African people)
Gonyaulax tamarensis
  ₍QL368.D6₎
Gonyaulax toxin
  USE Saxitoxin
Gonzaga cameo
  ₍NK5722₎
  UF Ptolemy II and Arsinoë (Cameo)
  BT Cameos—Egypt
      Egypt—Antiquities
Gonzaga family *(Not Subd Geog)*
  UF Gonzague family
Gonzague family
  USE Gonzaga family
Gonzales (Tex.), Battle of, 1835
  BT Texas—History—Revolution, 1835-
      1836—Campaigns
  NT Come and Take It Cannon
Goober, Congo
  USE Bambarra groundnut

Gooch family *(Not Subd Geog)*
  UF Gouch family
Good, Common
  USE Common good
Good and evil
  ₍BJ1400-1408₎
  UF Evil
      Wickedness
  BT Ethics
      Philosophy
      Polarity
      Religious thought
  NT Evil in literature
      Good in literature
      Guilt
      Theodicy
      Three monkeys (Motif)
Good and evil (Hinduism)
  ₍BJ1400-1408₎
  BT Hinduism
      Polarity—Religious aspects—Hinduism
Good and evil (Islam)
  ₍BJ1400-1405₎
  BT Islam—Doctrines
      Islamic ethics
      Polarity—Religious aspects—Islam
  — Koranic teaching
    ₍BP134.G65₎
Good and evil (Judaism)
  BT Ethics, Jewish
      Judaism—Doctrines
      Polarity—Religious aspects—Judaism
  NT Holocaust (Jewish theology)
      Yetzer hara (Judaism)
Good and evil in art
  NT Good in literature
Good as a theme in literature
  USE Good in literature
Good behavior, Security for
  USE Surety of the peace
Good behavior (Law) *(May Subd Geog)*
  UF Behavior, Good (Law)
  BT Certificates of good conduct
      Surety of the peace
Good-byes
  USE Farewells
Good faith (Canon law)
Good faith (International law)
  BT International law
Good faith (Jewish law)
Good faith (Law) *(May Subd Geog)*
  UF Bona fides (Law)
  RT Bad faith (Law)
      Ignorance (Law)
      Mistake (Law)
  NT Strict law
Good faith (Roman law)
Good family *(Not Subd Geog)*
  UF Goad family
      Goode family
      Goods family
      Guth family
Good Friday
  ₍BV95₎
  BT Fasts and feasts
      Holy Week
  RT Jesus Christ—Crucifixion
  NT Good Friday sermons
Good Friday music
  ₍M2098.G5 (Part-songs, M2078.G5,
    M2088.G5)₎
  ₍M2149.4.G7 (Catholic liturgical
    music)₎
  BT Holy-Week music
      Lenten music
  RT Passion-music
Good Friday sermons
  ₍BV95₎
  UF Sermons, Good Friday

  BT Good Friday
      Holy-Week sermons
      Jesus Christ—Passion—Sermons
  NT Jesus Christ—Seven last words—
      Sermons
Good Hope, Cape of (South Africa : Cape)
  USE Cape of Good Hope (South Africa :
      Cape)
Good in literature
  UF Good as a theme in literature
  BT Good and evil
      Good and evil in art
Good neighbor policy
  USE Latin America—Foreign relations—
      United States
      United States—Foreign relations—
      Latin America
Good offices
  USE Mediation, International
Good Samaritan (Parable)
  ₍BT378.G6₎
Good Samaritan (Parable) in art
Good Samaritan laws
  USE Assistance in emergencies
Good Samaritan shilling
  UF Samaritan shilling
  BT Shilling
Good-will (in business, etc.)
  (May Subd Geog)
  ₍HF5353₎
  BT Business
      Industrial property
      Intangible property
Good works (Judaism)
  USE Commandments (Judaism)
Good works (Theology)
  BT Salvation
  RT Merit (Christianity)
      Reward (Theology)
  NT Corporal works of mercy
Goodal family
  USE Goodall family
Goodale family
  USE Goodall family
Goodall family *(Not Subd Geog)*
  UF Godall family
      Godel family
      Goodal family
      Goodale family
      Goodals family
      Goodell family
  RT Goodwill family
Goodals family
  USE Goodall family
Goodard family
  USE Goddard family
Goodbar family *(Not Subd Geog)*
Goodbary family *(Not Subd Geog)*
  UF Goodberry family
Goodberry family
  USE Goodbary family
Goodbyes
  USE Farewells
Goode family
  USE Good family
Goodeidae
  ₍QL638.G82₎
  UF Characodontidae
  BT Atheriniformes
      Killifishes
  NT Allodontichthys
      Xenoophorus
Goodell family
  USE Goodall family
Goodeniaceae
  ₍QK495.G655 (Botany)₎
  BT Campanulales
  NT Scaevola
Goodenough draw-a-man test
  (May Subd Geog)
  ₍BF432.5.G64₎

UF Draw-a-man test
BT Draw-a-person test
Drawing, Psychology of
Intelligence tests
RT Goodenough-Harris drawing test
Goodenough family *(Not Subd Geog)*
UF Goodenow family
Goodnough family
Goodenough-Harris drawing test
(May Subd Geog)
⌜BF432.5.G64⌝
BT Draw-a-person test
Drawing, Psychology of
Intelligence tests
RT Goodenough draw-a-man test
Goodenough Island (Papua New Guinea)
UF Morata (Papua New Guinea)
Nidula Island (Papua New Guinea)
BT D'Entrecasteaux Islands (Papua New
Guinea)
Islands—Papua New Guinea
Goodenow family
USE Goodenough family
Gooderham family *(Not Subd Geog)*
Goodhard family
USE Goddard family
Goodhart family
USE Goddard family
Goodheart family
USE Goddard family
Goodier family *(Not Subd Geog)*
Goodill family
USE Goodwill family
**Gooding City of Rocks East Wilderness
(Idaho)**
UF Gooding City of Rocks East
Wilderness Study Area (Idaho)
BT National parks and reserves—Idaho
Wilderness areas—Idaho
Gooding City of Rocks East Wilderness Study
Area (Idaho)
USE Gooding City of Rocks East
Wilderness (Idaho)
**Gooding City of Rocks West Wilderness
(Idaho)**
UF Gooding City of Rocks West
Wilderness Study Area (Idaho)
BT National parks and reserves—Idaho
Wilderness areas—Idaho
Gooding City of Rocks West Wilderness Study
Area (Idaho)
USE Gooding City of Rocks West
Wilderness (Idaho)
Goodlet family *(Not Subd Geog)*
UF Goodlett family
Goodlett family
USE Goodlet family
Goodloe family *(Not Subd Geog)*
UF Gidlow family
Goodlow family
Goodlowe family
Guddelowe family
Gudlawe family
Gudloe family
Goodlow family
USE Goodloe family
Goodlowe family
USE Goodloe family
Goodness-of-fit tests
UF Tests, Goodness-of-fit
BT Statistical hypothesis testing
Goodnews Bay (Alaska : Bay)
BT Bays—Alaska
Goodnight family *(Not Subd Geog)*
RT Gutknecht family
Goodnough family
USE Goodenough family
Goodredge family
USE Goodrich family

Goodrich family *(Not Subd Geog)*
UF Godridge family
Goodredge family
Goodrick family
Goodridg family
Goodridge family
Goodrigde family
Goodrige family
Goodruch family
Goodwich family
Goodrick family
USE Goodrich family
Goodridg family
USE Goodrich family
Goodridge family
USE Goodrich family
Goodrigde family
USE Goodrich family
Goodrige family
USE Goodrich family
Goodruch family
USE Goodrich family
Goods, Confusion of
USE Confusion of goods
Goods, Ecclesiastical
USE Church supplies
Goods, Intermediate
USE Intermediate goods
Goods, Public
USE Public goods
Goods, Woolen
USE Woolen goods
Goods family
USE Good family
Goods in transit, Tariff on
USE Duty-free transit
Goodsell family *(Not Subd Geog)*
UF Godshal family
Godshall family
Goodwell family
USE Goodwill family
Goodwhill family
USE Goodwill family
Goodwich family
USE Goodrich family
Goodwill family *(Not Subd Geog)*
UF Goodill family
Goodwell family
Goodwhill family
Goodwille family
Goodwilley family
Goodwillie family
RT Goodall family
Goodwille family
USE Goodwill family
Goodwilley family
USE Goodwill family
Goodwillie family
USE Goodwill family
Goodwin family *(Not Subd Geog)*
UF Godwin family
Godwine family
Godwyn family
Goodwine family
Goodwyn family
Goodwine family
USE Goodwin family
Goodwood (West Sussex) International
Dressage Championship
USE International Dressage Championship,
Goodwood, West Sussex
Goodwood Operation
USE Operation Goodwood
Goodwyn family
USE Goodwin family
Goodyear family *(Not Subd Geog)*
UF Gudger family
RT Gutjahr family
Goodyera
⌜QK495.O64⌝
BT Orchids

Gooeyduck
USE Geoduck
Goofus glass
⌜NK5439.G64⌝
BT Pressed glass—United States
Goofy (Comic strip)
⌜PN6728.G⌝
BT Comic books, strips, etc.
Gooi (Netherlands : Region)
UF Gooiland (Netherlands)
Het Gooi (Netherlands)
't Gooi (Netherlands)
Gooiland (Netherlands)
USE Gooi (Netherlands : Region)
Gookens family
USE Gookin family
Gookin family *(Not Subd Geog)*
UF Coogkins family
Gokin family
Gookens family
Gooking family
Gookins family
Gooking family
USE Gookin family
Gookins family
USE Gookin family
Gool family
USE Gould family
Goold family
USE Gould family
Goolsby family *(Not Subd Geog)*
Gooney bird (Transport plane)
USE Douglas DC-3 (Transport plane)
Goor languages
USE Gur languages
Goorals
USE Gorals
Goorkhas
USE Gurkhas
Goose
USE Geese
Goose (Game)
⌜GV1469.G⌝
Goose Creek (Clay County, Ky.)
BT Rivers—Kentucky
Goose grass
USE Galium
Goose hunting
USE Goose shooting
Goose Lake (Calif. and Or.)
BT Lakes—California
Lakes—Oregon
Goose shooting
UF Goose hunting
BT Waterfowl shooting
Gooseberries
⌜SB386.G6⌝
BT Ribes
Gooseberry, Chinese
USE Kiwi fruit
Gooseberry, Ichang
USE Kiwi fruit
Goosefishes
USE Lophiidae
Goosefoots
USE Chenopodium
Goosehorn family
USE Goshorn family
Gooshorn family
USE Goshorn family
Goower family
USE Gower family
Goowers family
USE Gower family
Gopal (Hindu deity)
USE Krishna (Hindu deity)
Goph family
USE Goff family
Gopher snake
USE Pituophis melanoleucus

Gopher tortoise
  [QL666.C584]
  UF Gopher turtle
      Gopherus polyphemus
Gopher turtle
  USE Gopher tortoise
Gophers
  USE Pocket gophers
Gopherus
  [QL666.C584]
  BT Testudinidae
  NT Gopherus berlandieri
Gopherus agassizi
  USE Desert tortoise
Gopherus berlandieri
  [QL666.C584]
  UF Texas tortoise
  BT Gopherus
Gopherus polyphemus
  USE Gopher tortoise
Gora Alkhanai (R.S.F.S.R.)
  USE Alkhanai Mountain (R.S.F.S.R.)
Gora Alkhanay (R.S.F.S.R.)
  USE Alkhanai Mountain (R.S.F.S.R.)
Gora Goverla (Ukraine)
  USE Goverla, Mount (Ukraine)
Gora Goverlya (Ukraine)
  USE Goverla, Mount (Ukraine)
Góra Howerla (Ukraine)
  USE Goverla, Mount (Ukraine)
Gora language
  USE Gola language
Gorals
  [QL737.U53]
  UF Goorals
      Naemorhedus
      Nemorhaedus
  BT Bovidae
Goramy
  USE Gourami
Goran family
  USE Goranson family
Gorandji (Australian people)
  USE Gurindji (Australian people)
Goranson family (Not Subd Geog)
  UF Goran family
      Göransson family
Göransson family
  USE Goranson family
Gorbals (Glasgow, Strathclyde)
  (Not Subd Geog)
  UF Glasgow (Strathclyde).   Gorbals
Gorbet family
  USE Gorbett family
Gorbett family (Not Subd Geog)
  UF Gorbet family
Gorby family (Not Subd Geog)
Gordale Scar (Painting)
  USE Ward, James, 1769-1859.   Gordale
      Scar
Gordan family
  USE Gordon family
Gorden family
  USE Gordon family
Gordiacea
  [QL391.N5]
  UF Horse-hair worms
      Horsehair worms
  BT Nemathelminthes
      Worms
  NT Nematomorpha
Gordididea
  USE Gordioida
Gordiidae
  [QL391.N5]
  BT Gordioida
Gordin family
  USE Gordon family
Gording family
  USE Gordon family

Gordioida
  [QL391.N5]
  UF Gordididea
  BT Nematomorpha
  NT Gordiidae
Gordioidea
  USE Nematomorpha
Gordion (Turkey) (Not Subd Geog)
  [DS156.G6]
  UF Gordium (Turkey)
  BT Cities and towns, Ruined, extinct, etc.
      —Turkey
      Turkey—Antiquities
Gordium (Turkey)
  USE Gordion (Turkey)
Gordius robustus
  [QL391.N5]
Gordon, Lake (Tas.)
  UF Lake Gordon (Tas.)
  BT Lakes—Australia
Gordon Bennett Cup Race
  [GV759.2.G67]
  UF Gordon Bennett Race
  BT Airplane racing
Gordon Bennett Race
  USE Gordon Bennett Cup Race
Gordon family (Not Subd Geog)
  UF Gordan family
      Gorden family
      Gordin family
      Gording family
      Gorton family
      Gourdin family
      Gourdon family
Gordon Relief Expedition, 1884-1885
  BT Egypt—History—British occupation,
      1882-1936
Gordon Riots, 1780
  [DA510]
  UF No-Popery Riots, 1780
  BT Catholic emancipation
      Riots—England
Gordon setters
  [SF429.G67]
  BT Setters (Dogs)
Gore family (Not Subd Geog)
  UF Goar family
Gorenjsko (Slovenia)
  UF Carniola, Upper (Slovenia)
      Oberkrain (Slovenia)
      Upper Carniola (Slovenia)
Gorge-purge syndrome
  USE Bulimia
Gorges (May Subd Geog)
  UF Ravines
  BT Canyons
  NT Coulees
— **China**
  NT Yangtze River Gorges (China)
— **England**
  NT Creswell Crags (England)
— **Germany (East)**
  NT Rabenauer Grund (Germany)
— **Japan**
  NT Kurobe River Gorge (Japan)
— **Kentucky**
  NT Red River Gorge (Ky.)
— **Ohio**
  NT Raven Rocks (Ohio)
— **Ontario**
  NT Brookbanks Ravine (Ont.)
— **Oregon**
  NT Columbia River Gorge (Or. and
      Wash.)
— **Romania**
  NT Iron Gates (Romania and Serbia)
— **Washington (State)**
  NT Columbia River Gorge (Or. and
      Wash.)
— **Yugoslavia**
  NT Iron Gates (Romania and Serbia)

Gorges family (Not Subd Geog)
Gorgets
  UF Hausse-col
  BT Armies—Insignia
      Arms and armor
      Uniforms, Military
Gorgon (Genus)
  USE Gnus
Gorgonacea (May Subd Geog)
  [QL377.C6]
  UF Gorgonaria
      Gorgoniaceae
  BT Alcyonaria
  NT Chrysogorgiidae
      Isididae
      Paramuriceidae
Gorgonaria
  USE Gorgonacea
Gorgoniaceae
  USE Gorgonacea
Gorgons
  [BL820.G7]
  BT Monsters
      Mythology
      Mythology, Classical
Gorgons in art
Gorhambury House (Hertfordshire)
  BT Dwellings—England
Gori language
  USE Laal language
Gorillas
  [QL737.P9]
  BT Apes
  NT Koko (Gorilla)
— **Behavior**
Gorillas as pets
Gorin C Iseki (Japan)
  USE Gorin C Site (Japan)
Gorin C Site (Japan) (Not Subd Geog)
  UF Gorin C Iseki (Japan)
  BT Japan—Antiquities
Gorindji (Australian people)
  USE Gurindji (Australian people)
Goring family
  USE Goering family
Goriška (Slovenia and Italy)
  UF Goriško in Gradiščansko (Slovenia and
      Italy)
      Gorizia e Gradisca (Slovenia and
      Italy)
      Görz and Gradiska (Slovenia and
      Italy)
Goriško in Gradiščansko (Slovenia and Italy)
  USE Goriška (Slovenia and Italy)
Goriūnov machine-gun
  UF Goryunov machine-gun
  BT Machine-guns
Gorizia, Battle of, 1916
  [D569.G7]
  BT Isonzo, Battles of the, 1915-1917
      World War, 1914-1918—Campaigns—
      Italy
Gorizia e Gradisca (Slovenia and Italy)
  USE Goriška (Slovenia and Italy)
Gorkhali language
  USE Nepali language
Gorkhas
  USE Gurkhas
Gorkio Gatvė (Vilnius, Lithuania)
  (Not Subd Geog)
  UF Aušros Vartų Gatvė (Vilnius,
      Lithuania)
      Didžioji Gatvė (Vilnius, Lithuania)
      M. Gorkio Gatvė (Vilnius, Lithuania)
      Pilies Gatvė (Vilnius, Lithuania)
  BT Streets—Lithuania
Gorky Street (Leningrad, R.S.F.S.R.)
  USE Prospekt Gor'kogo (Leningrad,
      R.S.F.S.R.)
Gorlice-Tarnow, Battle of, 1915
  [D557.G6]

BT World War, 1914-1918—Campaigns—
Poland
Gorlin-Goltz syndrome
USE Basal cell nevus syndrome
Gorlin syndrome
USE Basal cell nevus syndrome
Gorlin's syndrome
USE Basal cell nevus syndrome
Gormally family
USE Gormley family
Gorman family (Not Subd Geog)
UF O'Gorman family
Gormelly family
USE Gormley family
Gormely family
USE Gormley family
Gormley family (Not Subd Geog)
UF Gormally family
Gormelly family
Gormely family
Gormly family
Gormolly family
Gormly family
USE Gormley family
Gormogons
[HS247.G6]
Gormolly family
USE Gormley family
Gormont family
USE Gourmont family
Gornaia Shoriia (R.S.F.S.R.)
UF Gornaya Shoria (R.S.F.S.R.)
Gornaya Shoriya (R.S.F.S.R.)
BT Mountains—Russian S.F.S.R.
Gornaya Shoria (R.S.F.S.R.)
USE Gornaia Shoriia (R.S.F.S.R.)
Gornaya Shoriya (R.S.F.S.R.)
USE Gornaia Shoriia (R.S.F.S.R.)
Gornje Primorje (Slovenia)
USE Slovensko Primorje (Slovenia)
Gornji Birač (Bosnia and Hercegovina)
USE Birač (Bosnia and Hercegovina)
Górnośląskie Zagłębie Węglowe (Poland and
Czechoslovakia)
USE Dąbrowa Basin (Poland and
Czechoslovakia)
Górny Śląsk (Poland and Czechoslovakia)
USE Silesia, Upper (Poland and
Czechoslovakia)
Gorod nauki (Novosibirsk, R.S.F.S.R.)
USE Akademgorodok (Novosibirsk,
R.S.F.S.R.)
Gorodki (Game)
[GV903]
Gorona
USE Korana (African people)
Gorontalo language
[PL5327]
UF Gunongtello language
Gurantala language
Holontalo language
BT Malayan languages
Gorostiaga family (Not Subd Geog)
Gorre and Daphetid Railroad (Model railroad)
BT Railroads—Models
Gorsage family
USE Gorsuch family
Gorse (May Subd Geog)
[QK495.L52 (Botany)]
[SB615.G67 (Weed)]
UF Furze
Ulex europaeus
Whin
BT Weeds
Gorski kotar (Croatia)
Gorsuch family (Not Subd Geog)
UF Gorsage family
Gossadge family
Gossage family
Gortner family
USE Curtner family

Gorton family
USE Gordon family
Gortroe Massacre, Ireland, 1834
UF Rathcormac Massacre, Ireland, 1834
BT Massacres—Ireland
Tithe War, 1829-1838
Gortynia (Greece)
[DF901.G6]
Gortynidae
USE Noctuidae
Gorum language
USE Parengi language
Gofy Bardzkie (Poland)
USE Bardo Mountains (Poland)
Góry Bialskie (Poland and Czechoslovakia)
USE Bialskie Mountains (Poland and
Czechoslovakia)
Góry Bystrzyckie (Poland)
USE Bystrzyca Mountains (Poland)
Góry Izerskie (Poland and Czechoslovakia)
USE Izerskie Mountains (Poland and
Czechoslovakia)
Góry Kaczawskie (Poland)
USE Kaczawa Mountains (Poland)
Góry Kamienne (Poland)
USE Kamienne Mountains (Poland)
Gory Orlické (Czechoslovakia)
USE Orlické Mountains (Czechoslovakia)
Gory Pamir
USE Pamir
Gory Putorana (R.S.F.S.R.)
USE Putorana Plateau (R.S.F.S.R.)
Góry Sowie (Poland)
USE Sowie Mountains (Poland)
Góry Stołowe (Poland)
USE Stołowe Mountains (Poland)
Góry Świętokrzyskie (Poland)
USE Świętokrzyskie Mountains (Poland)
Gory Talysh (Azerbaijan S.S.R. and Iran)
USE Talish Mountains (Azerbaijan S.S.R.
and Iran)
Góry Wałbrzyskie (Poland)
USE Wałbrzych Mountains (Poland)
Gory Zemplen (Czechoslovakia and Hungary)
USE Tokaj-Eperjes Mountains
(Czechoslovakia and Hungary)
Góry Złote (Poland and Czechoslovakia)
USE Złote Mountains (Poland and
Czechoslovakia)
Góry Złotostockie (Poland and
Czechoslovakia)
USE Złote Mountains (Poland and
Czechoslovakia)
Goryōkaku (Usuda-machi, Japan)
USE Tatsuokajō (Usuda-machi, Japan)
Goryōkaku, Battle of, 1868-1869
USE Hakodate, Battle of, 1868-1869
Gorytidae
USE Sphecidae
Gorytodes
USE Plataea
Goryunov machine-gun
USE Goriŭnov machine-gun
Görz and Gradiska (Slovenia and Italy)
USE Goriška (Slovenia and Italy)
GOS (Meteorology)
USE Global Observing System
(Meteorology)
Gosainthan (China)
USE Hsi-hsia-pang-ma Peak (China)
Gosānī (Hindu deity)
BT Gods, Hindu
Gosannen gunki (Scrolls)
USE Gosannen kassen ekotoba (Scrolls)
Gosannen kassen ekotoba (Scrolls)
[ND1053.4]
UF Gosannen gunki (Scrolls)
Hachiman Tarō ekotoba (Scrolls)

BT Japan—History—Later Three Years
War, 1083-1087—Pictorial works
Painting, Japanese—Kamakura-
Momoyama periods, 1185-1600
Scrolls, Japanese
Goshawk
UF Accipiter gentilis
BT Hawks
Goshorn family (Not Subd Geog)
UF Ganshorn family
Gansshorn family
Gantzhorn family
Goosehorn family
Gooshorn family
Gosorn family
Gosshorn family
Goshute Indians
USE Gosiute Indians
Goshute Peak Wilderness (Nev.)
(Not Subd Geog)
UF Goshute Peak Wilderness Study Area
(Nev.)
BT National parks and reserves—Nevada
Wilderness areas—Nevada
Goshute Peak Wilderness Study Area (Nev.)
USE Goshute Peak Wilderness (Nev.)
Gosiute Indians
[E99.G67]
UF Goshute Indians
BT Indians of North America
Numic Indians
Shoshonean Indians
Goslin family
USE Gosselin family
Gosorn family
USE Goshorn family
Gospel, Social
USE Social gospel
Gospel and law
USE Law and gospel
Gospel music (May Subd Geog)
[M2198-M2199 (Music)]
[ML3186.8-ML3187 (History and
criticism)]
UF Music, Gospel
BT Afro-Americans—Music
Popular music
Sacred songs
NT Contemporary Christian music
Revivals—Hymns
Gospel musicians (May Subd Geog)
[ML385-403]
BT Country musicians
Musicians
Gospel passion narratives
USE Passion narratives (Gospels)
Gospels enthroned
USE Enthronement of the Gospels
Goss family (Not Subd Geog)
UF Gaus family
Gause family
Gaws family
Ghoss family
Gosse family
Gossadge family
USE Gorsuch family
Gossage family
USE Gorsuch family
Gossan family (Not Subd Geog)
Gosse family
USE Goss family
Gosselin family (Not Subd Geog)
UF Goslin family
Gosset family
USE Gossett family

Gossett family *(Not Subd Geog)*
  UF Gasset family
      Gassett family
      Gisert family
      Gosset family
      Gossit family
      Gossitt family
      Guset family
  RT Goswick family
Gosshorn family
  USE Goshorn family
Gossip
  [BJ1535.G6]
  RT Slander
  NT Talebearing
Gossip in mass media *(May Subd Geog)*
  [P96.G65]
  UF Gossip industry
  BT Mass media
Gossip industry
  USE Gossip in mass media
Gossit family
  USE Gossett family
Gossitt family
  USE Gossett family
Gossypein
  USE Gossypol
Gossypium hirsutum
  USE Cotton
Gossypium raimondii
  [QK495.M27 (Botany)]
  BT Cotton
Gossypol
  [QD441 (Pigment)]
  [RG137.6.G68 (Medicine)]
  [SF99 (Cottonseed feeds)]
  [TP681 (Cottonseed oil)]
  UF Gossypein
Gosti family *(Not Subd Geog)*
  UF Gaasti family
      Gasti family
Gostin family
  USE Gaston family
Gosudarstvennaia avtomatizirovannaia sistema nauchno-technicheskoĭ informatsii classification
  USE Classification, GASNTI
Got family
  USE Gott family
Göta Canal (Sweden)
  BT Canals—Sweden
Gotaizan (Korea)
  USE Odae Mountain (Korea)
Götaland (Sweden)
  UF Götarike (Sweden)
Götarike (Sweden)
  USE Götaland (Sweden)
Gotelli Dwarf Conifer Collection (Washington, D.C.)
  BT Dwarf conifers—Catalogs and collections—Washington (D.C.)
Gotha gliders
  BT Gliders (Aeronautics)
Gothenburg system
  [HV5092-5]
  BT Liquor laws
      Temperance
Gothic altarpieces
  USE Altarpieces, Gothic
Gothic altars
  USE Altars, Gothic
Gothic architecture
  USE Architecture, Gothic
Gothic art
  USE Art, Gothic
Gothic art metal-work
  USE Art metal-work, Gothic
Gothic arts
  USE Arts, Gothic
Gothic capitals (Architecture)
  USE Capitals (Architecture), Gothic

Gothic choir-stalls
  USE Choir-stalls, Gothic
Gothic decoration and ornament
  USE Decoration and ornament, Gothic
Gothic decorative arts
  USE Decorative arts, Gothic
Gothic doorways
  USE Doorways, Gothic
Gothic drawing
  USE Drawing, Gothic
Gothic engraving
  USE Engraving, Gothic
Gothic furniture
  USE Furniture, Gothic
Gothic glass painting and staining
  USE Glass painting and staining, Gothic
Gothic gold figurines
  USE Gold figurines, Gothic
Gothic goldwork
  USE Goldwork, Gothic
Gothic illumination of books and manuscripts
  USE Illumination of books and manuscripts, Gothic
Gothic ivories
  USE Ivories, Gothic
Gothic language
  [PD1101-1211]
  BT Germanic languages
Gothic law
  USE Law, Gothic
Gothic literature *(May Subd Geog)*
  UF Literature, Gothic
  BT Literature
Gothic majolica
  USE Majolica, Gothic
Gothic mural painting and decoration
  USE Mural painting and decoration, Gothic
Gothic narrative painting
  USE Narrative painting, Gothic
Gothic novel
  USE Gothic revival (Literature)
Gothic painting
  USE Painting, Gothic
Gothic panel painting
  USE Panel painting, Gothic
Gothic philology
Gothic relics and reliquaries
  USE Relics and reliquaries, Gothic
Gothic revival (Architecture)
  (May Subd Geog)
  BT Architecture, Gothic
      Gothic revival (Art)
      Revival movements (Art)
  RT Architecture, Victorian
Gothic revival (Art) *(May Subd Geog)*
  Here are entered works on the revival of Gothic principles in art during the late 18th and early 19th centuries.
  BT Art, Modern
      Arts, Modern
      Revival movements (Art)
      Romanticism in art
  NT Gothic revival (Architecture)
Gothic revival (Literature)
  (May Subd Geog)
  UF Fiction, Gothic
      Gothic novel
      Literature, Gothic
  BT Literature, Modern
      Revival movements (Art)
      Romanticism
  NT Penny dreadfuls
Gothic-roman type controversy
  [Z250.5.G6]
  UF Roman-gothic type controversy
  BT Type and type-founding
      Type and type-founding—Gothic type
      Type and type-founding—Roman type
Gothic sculpture
  USE Sculpture, Gothic

Gothic sepulchral monuments
  USE Sepulchral monuments, Gothic
Gothic tapestry
  USE Tapestry, Gothic
Gothic type
  USE Type and type-founding—Gothic type
Gothic vaults (Architecture)
  USE Vaults (Architecture), Gothic
Gothic War, Italy, 535-555
  USE Italy—History—Gothic War, 535-555
Gothic wood-carving
  USE Wood-carving, Gothic
Gothic writing
  USE Writing, Gothic
Gothland (Sweden)
  USE Gotland (Sweden)
Goths *(May Subd Geog)*
  [D137-D138 (Migrations)]
  UF East Goths
      Ostgoths
      Ostrogoths
  RT Germanic tribes
  NT Gepidae
      Italy—Civilization—Germanic influences
      Visigoths
  — **Italy**
      BT Italy—History—To 476
      NT Italy—History—476-774
          Italy—History—Gothic War, 535-555
Goths in literature
Gótico, Barrio (Barcelona, Spain)
  USE Barrio Gótico (Barcelona, Spain)
Gotland (Sweden)
  UF Gothland (Sweden)
      Gottland (Sweden)
  BT Islands—Sweden
Gotō family *(Not Subd Geog)*
Gotō Islands (Japan)
  UF Gotō-rettō (Japan)
  BT Islands—Japan
Gotō-rettō (Japan)
  USE Gotō Islands (Japan)
Gotō Shishaku Kinen Shiminshō
  BT Rewards (Prizes, etc.)—Japan
Gotra (Buddhism)
  [BQ4285]
  BT Buddhism—Doctrines
Gotschalk family
  USE Gottschalk family
Gott family *(Not Subd Geog)*
  UF Got family
Göttge family
  USE Geitgey family
Gottgen family
  USE Geitgey family
Gotthard Pass (Switzerland)
  USE Saint Gotthard Pass (Switzerland)
Gotthard Railway
  USE Gotthardbahn
Gotthardbahn
  UF Chemin de fer du Saint-Gothard
      Ferrovia del San Gottardo
      Gotthard Railway
  BT Railroads—Switzerland
Gotthelft family *(Not Subd Geog)*
Göttingen Altes Rathaus (Göttingen, Germany)
  USE Altes Rathaus (Göttingen, Germany)
Gottland (Sweden)
  USE Gotland (Sweden)
Gottorf, Treaty of, May 27, 1768
  [DD901.H27 (Hamburg)]
  UF Treaty of Gottorf, May 27, 1768
Gottreau family
  USE Godreau family

Gottschalk family *(Not Subd Geog)*
  UF Gaedschalk family
      Godshalk family
      Godshalt family
      Godshell family
      Godshul family
      Gotschalk family
      Gottschall family
      Gottshalk family
      Gottshall family
Gottschall family
  USE Gottschalk family
Gottshalk family
  USE Gottschalk family
Gottshall family
  USE Gottschalk family
Gottwald family *(Not Subd Geog)*
Gotwezi
  USE Jaćwież
Gouache painting
  BT Painting
      Watercolor painting
Gouache painting, Chinese
  (May Subd Geog)
  UF Chinese gouache painting
  — 20th century
Gouberville family *(Not Subd Geog)*
Gouch family
  USE Gooch family
Goudey family
  USE Gowdy family
Goudie family
  USE Gowdy family
Goudreau family
  USE Godreau family
Goudy bas-relief
  USE Emmons, Earl H., 1888-   Goudy
      bas-relief
Goudy family
  USE Gowdy family
Gouen family
  USE Gowen family
Gouge, Fault
  USE Fault gouge
Gougerot-Sjogren's syndrome
  USE Sjogren's syndrome
Gouges (Woodworking)
  USE Chisels
Gough family
  USE Goff family
Gouhard family
Gouin (African people)
  UF Guen (African people)
      Guin (African people)
      Gwin (African people)
      Mbouin (African people)
  BT Ethnology—Burkina Faso
      Senufo (African people)
Gouin family *(Not Subd Geog)*
Goul family
  USE Gould family
Goulasch (Contract bridge)
  [GV1282.8.G68]
  UF Hollandaise (Contract bridge)
      Mayonnaise (Contract bridge)
  BT Contract bridge
Goulbin Maradi (Nigeria and Niger)
  USE Maradi River (Nigeria and Niger)
Goulburn River (Vic.)
  BT Rivers—Australia
Gould family *(Not Subd Geog)*
  UF Gold family
      Gool family
      Goold family
      Goul family .
  RT Guild family
Gouldian finch
  [QL696.P244 (Zoology)]
  [SF473.G68 (Culture)]

  UF Chloebia gouldiae
      Finch, Gouldian
      Poephila gouldiae
  BT Chloebia
Goulding family
  USE Golden family
Gouldsboro Bay (Me.)
  BT Bays—Maine
Gouldsmith family
  USE Goldsmith family
Goum (African people)
  USE Gun (African people)
Goun family
  USE Gowen family
Goura (Musical instrument)
  BT Musical instruments—Africa
Gourague language
  USE Gurage language
Gourami
  [QL638.A5 (General)]
  [SH167.G64 (Culture)]
  UF Giant gourami
      Goramy
      Osphronemus goramy
  BT Anabantidae
Gourd, Bottle
  USE Lagenaria siceraria
Gourd, Calabash
  USE Lagenaria siceraria
Gourd, Club
  USE Trichosanthes anguina
Gourd, Snake
  USE Trichosanthes anguina
Gourd, White-flowered
  USE Lagenaria siceraria
Gourd craft *(May Subd Geog)*
  [TT873.5]
  BT Handicraft
Gourdin family
  USE Gordon family
Gourdon family
  USE Gordon family
Gourds *(May Subd Geog)*
  [QK495.C96 (Botany)]
  [SB413.G6 (Culture)]
  NT Lagenaria
      Trichosanthes
Gourmantché (African people)
  USE Gurma (African people)
Gourmantché language
  USE Gurma language
Gourmont family *(Not Subd Geog)*
  UF Gormont family
Gournay family
  USE Gurney family
Gouro (African people)
  USE Guro (African people)
Gouro language
  USE Kweni language
Gourounsi (African people)
  USE Gurunsi (African people)
Gourounsi dialects
  USE Gurunsi dialects
Gout
  [RC629-629.5]
  UF Podagra
  BT Arthritis
      Metabolism, Inborn errors of
      Rheumatism
  — Nutritional aspects
Gova (Shona-speaking people)
  UF Cova (Shona-speaking people)
      Goba (Shona-speaking people)
  BT Ethnology—Zambia
      Ethnology—Zimbabwe
      Mashona
Gova language
  USE Mbukushu language
Govan family
  USE Givens family

Gove family
  USE Gowen family
Gover family *(Not Subd Geog)*
Goverla, Mount (Ukraine)
  UF Gora Goverla (Ukraine)
      Gora Goverlya (Ukraine)
      Góra Howerla (Ukraine)
      Hora Hoverla (Ukraine)
      Mount Goverla (Ukraine)
  BT Carpathian Mountains
      Mountains—Ukraine
Governesses *(May Subd Geog)*
  [LC41]
  BT Child care workers
      Domestic education
Governesses in literature
Government
  USE Political science
Government, Comparative
  USE Comparative government
Government, Neighborhood
  USE Neighborhood government
Government, Primitive
  USE Political anthropology
Government, Resistance to
  (May Subd Geog)
  [JC328.3]
  UF Civil disobedience
      Civil obedience
      Higher law
      Non-resistance to government
      Political violence
      Resistance to government
  BT Direct action
      Evil, Non-resistance to
      Political crimes and offenses
      Political ethics
      Political science
  RT Insurgency
      Revolutions
  SA *subdivision* Protest movements *under
      individual wars, e.g.* World War,
      1939-1945—Protest movements
  NT Anarchism
      Anomy
      Civil war
      Coups d'état
      Hunger strikes
  — Religious aspects
      BT Religion and state
  — — Buddhism, [Christianity, etc.]
  — — Christianity
Government, Resistance to, in literature
Government (Grammar)
  UF Grammar, Comparative and general—
          Government
      Grammar, Comparative and general—
          Prepositions—Government
      Grammar, Comparative and general—
          Verb—Government
      Regimen (Grammar)
  SA *subdivision* Government *under names
      of individual languages and groups
      of languages, e.g.* English language
      —Government
Government accounting
  USE Finance, Public—Accounting
Government advertising *(May Subd Geog)*
  UF Advertising—Government
      Advertising, Government
  BT Government publicity
  NT Minorities in government advertising
Government advisory boards
  USE Executive advisory bodies
Government agencies
  USE Administrative agencies
Government aircraft *(May Subd Geog)*
  [TL723]

Government aircraft *(Continued)*
- UF Aircraft, Government
  - Airplanes, Government
  - Government airplanes
  - Government-owned aircraft
- BT Airplanes
- NT Airplanes, Military

Government airplanes
- USE Government aircraft

Government and binding (Linguistics)
- USE Government-binding theory
  - (Linguistics)

Government and business
- USE Industry and state

Government and forestry
- USE Forest policy
  - Forestry law and legislation

Government and the press *(May Subd Geog)*
- UF Press and government
  - Press policy
  - State and the press
- BT Executive privilege (Government
  - information)
  - Freedom of information
  - Government information
  - Government publicity
  - Journalism
  - Press
  - Press law
  - Press releases
  - Reporters and reporting
- RT Press and politics
- NT Local government and the press
  - Official secrets

Government architects
- USE Architects in government

Government assistance
- USE Economic assistance, Domestic

Government attorneys *(May Subd Geog)*
- UF Attorneys, Government
  - Government lawyers
  - Lawyers, Government
- BT Lawyers
- SA *subdivision* Lawyers *under particular*
  - *branches of the armed forces, e.g.*
  - United States. Army—Lawyers
- NT Attorneys-general
  - City attorneys
  - County attorneys
  - Government litigation
  - Judge advocates
  - Police legal advisors
  - Public prosecutors

Government banking
- USE Postal savings-banks

Government-binding theory (Linguistics)
- UF Binding theory (Linguistics)
  - Government and binding (Linguistics)
- BT Generative grammar
  - Linguistics

Government body headings
- USE Government headings (Cataloging)

Government bonds
- USE Government securities

Government buildings
- USE Public buildings

Government business enterprises
(May Subd Geog)
- UF Business enterprises, Government
  - Parastatals
  - Public enterprises
- BT Government competition
  - Industry and state
  - Public utilities
  - Public works
- RT Corporations, Government
- NT Government holding companies
  - Government monopolies
  - Government ownership
  - Government trading
  - Municipal ownership

Off-budget government entities
- **— Accounting**
  - BT Finance, Public—Accounting
- **— Auditing**
  - BT Auditing
- — Collective bargaining
  - USE Collective bargaining—
    - Government business
    - enterprises
- — Collective labor agreements
  - USE Collective labor agreements—
    - Government business
    - enterprises
- — Conflict of laws
  - USE Conflict of laws—Government
    - business enterprises
- **— Costs**
- — — **Law and legislation**
  - *(May Subd Geog)*
- **— Employees**
  - BT Civil service
  - NT Trade-unions—Government
    - business enterprise employees
- **— Finance**
  - NT Revolving funds
- **— Law and legislation** *(May Subd Geog)*

Government by commission
- USE Municipal government by commission

Government cars
- USE Automobiles, Government

Government centralization
- USE Decentralization in government

Government communication systems
(May Subd Geog)
- UF Communication systems, Government
  - Public administration—Communication
    - systems
  - State communication systems
- BT Telecommunication systems
- **— Law and legislation** *(May Subd Geog)*

Government competition *(May Subd Geog)*
- UF Competition, Government
- BT Competition
  - Corporations, Government
  - Government ownership
  - Industry and state
- NT Government business enterprises

Government consultants *(May Subd Geog)*
- BT Consultants
- RT Policy scientists
- NT Architects in government
  - Engineers in government
  - Political scientists in government
  - Scientists in government
  - Social scientists in government
  - Without-compensation personnel

Government contracts
- USE Public contracts

Government corporations
- USE Corporations, Government

Government correspondence
(May Subd Geog)
- UF Correspondence
- BT Letter-writing
  - Public records
- SA *subdivision* Records and
  - correspondence *under subjects or*
  - *names of government agencies*
- NT Memorandums

Government crisis management
- USE Crisis management in government

Government debts
- USE Debts, Public

Government decentralization
- USE Decentralization in government

Government departments
- USE *subdivision* Executive departments
  - *under names of countries, cities,*
  - *etc.*
  - Administrative agencies

Government depositories
- USE Public depositaries

Government-developed inventions and patents
- USE Patents and government-developed
  - inventions

Government dissolution (Parliamentary
practice)
- USE No confidence motions

Government documents
- USE Government publications

Government documents, Local
- USE Local government documents

Government economists *(May Subd Geog)*
- BT Economists

Government employee strikes
- USE Strikes and lockouts—Civil service

Government employees
- USE *subdivision* Officials and employees
  - *under names of countries, cities,*
  - *etc., e.g.* United States—Officials
  - and employees; *and subdivision*
  - Government employees *under*
  - *specific subjects, e.g.* Collective
  - bargaining—Government
  - employees; Collective labor
  - agreements—Government
  - employees
  - Civil service

Government employees, Volunteer
- USE Volunteer workers in government

Government employees' dental insurance
- USE Insurance, Government employees'
  - dental

Government employees' health insurance
- USE Insurance, Government employees'
  - health

Government employees' life insurance
- USE Insurance, Government employees' life

Government employees' literary writings
- BT Literature

Government employees' literary writings,
Brazilian *(May Subd Geog)*
- UF Brazilian government employees'
  - literary writings
- BT Brazilian literature

Government employees' political activities
- USE Civil service—Political activity
  - United States—Officials and
  - employees—Political activity

Government engineers
- USE Engineers in government

Government etiquette *(May Subd Geog)*
- UF Government protocol
  - Protocol, Government
- BT Etiquette
- NT Diplomatic etiquette

Government executives *(May Subd Geog)*
- BT Executives
  - Public officers
- NT Colonial administrators
  - Women government executives

Government executives, Afro-American
- USE Afro-American government executives

Government executives, Women
- USE Women government executives

Government expenditures
- USE Expenditures, Public

Government financial institutions
(May Subd Geog)
- UF Public financial institutions
- BT Financial institutions

Government formation process (Parliamentary
practice)
- USE Confidence voting

Government gazettes
- USE Gazettes

Government geographers *(May Subd Geog)*
- BT Geographers

Government guaranty of deposits in banks
- USE Banks and banking—Government
  - guaranty of deposits

Government guaranty of loans
  USE Loans—Government guaranty
Government headings (Cataloging)
  (May Subd Geog)
    [Z695.8]
    Works on headings designating government bo-
    dies of particular jurisdictions are entered here subdi-
    vided by the name of the jurisdiction.
  UF Government body headings
  BT Cataloging of government publications
      Corporate headings (Cataloging)
Government Hill (Anchorage, Alaska)
  (Not Subd Geog)
  UF Anchorage (Alaska). Government
      Hill
Government holding companies
  (May Subd Geog)
  BT Corporations, Government
      Government business enterprises
      Government ownership
      Holding companies
Government hospitals
  USE Hospitals, Public
Government House (Calcutta, India)
  USE Raj Bhavan (Calcutta, India)
Government House (Ottawa, Ont.)
  USE Rideau Hall (Ottawa, Ont.)
Government housing
  USE Public housing
Government immunity
  USE Government liability
Government in the sunshine
  USE subdivision Executive departments—
      Public meetings under names of
      countries, cities, etc., e.g. United
      States—Executive departments—
      Public meetings
    Financial disclosure
    Legislative bodies—Public meetings
Government information (May Subd Geog)
  UF Government secrecy
      Information, Government
  BT Freedom of information
  RT Public records
  NT Executive privilege (Government
      information)
      Federal government—Information
      services
      Government and the press
      Official secrets
      Security classification (Government
      documents)
  — Copyright
      USE Copyright—Official information
Government information services
  USE Government publicity
Government institutions
  USE Public institutions
Government insurance
  USE Insurance, Government
Government interns (Legislation)
  USE Interns (Legislation)
Government investigations
  USE Governmental investigations
Government investments
  USE Public investments
Government jargon
  USE subdivision Government jargon under
      names of languages, e.g. English
      language—Government jargon
Government jobs
  USE Civil service positions
Government lawyers
  USE Government attorneys
Government lending (May Subd Geog)
  UF Government loans
      Loans, Government

  BT Credit
      Economic assistance, Domestic
      Economic policy
      Finance, Public
      Industry and state
      Loans
  NT Insurance, Government
      Veterans—Loans
— **Law and legislation** (May Subd Geog)
Government liability (May Subd Geog)
    [JF1621]
    [JK-JQ]
    Here are entered works on the liability of the state
    for wrongful acts of officials. Works on criminal of-
    fenses committed by government officials in the per-
    formance of their duties are entered under Miscon-
    duct in office. Works on offenses against professional
    ethics or against discipline are entered under names
    of countries, cities, government departments, etc.
    with subdivision Officials and employees—Disci-
    pline. Works on specific offenses are entered under
    the name of the offense, e.g. Bribery. Works on the
    personal liability of government officials to the state
    or to individuals for wrongful acts committed in of-
    fice are entered under Administrative responsibility.
  UF Government immunity
      Government responsibility
      Liability, Government
      Liability, Public
      Liability of the state
      Public liability
      Sovereign immunity
      State liability
      State responsibility
      Tort liability of the government
      Tort liability of the state
  BT Administrative law
      Administrative responsibility
      Constitutional law
      Liability (Law)
      Misconduct in office
      Public law
      Torts
  RT Act of state
      Constitutional torts
  NT Compensation for judicial error
      De facto doctrine
      Denial of justice
      Insurance, Government risks
      Liability for school accidents
      Tort liability of highway departments
      Tort liability of municipal corporations
      Tort liability of school districts
  — Conflict of laws
      USE Conflict of laws—Government
          liability
  — **Great Britain**
      UF Crown proceedings
  — **United States**
      RT State action (Civil rights)
Government liability (International law)
  UF International claims
  BT International law
      Sovereignty
  RT Claims
      State succession
  NT Exhaustion of local remedies
      (International law)
      Immunities of foreign states
      Tort liability of international agencies
  — **Cases**
      NT Corfu Channel case
Government liability insurance
  USE Insurance, Government risks
Government librarians (May Subd Geog)
  UF Librarians, Government
  BT Special librarians
Government libraries
  USE Libraries, Governmental,
      administrative, etc.
Government life insurance
  USE Insurance, Government life

Government litigation (May Subd Geog)
  UF Litigation, Government
  BT Attorneys-general
      Government attorneys
      Procedure (Law)
Government loans
  USE Government lending
Government marketing (May Subd Geog)
    [JF1525.M37]
  UF Marketing, Government
      Marketing, Public sector
      Public sector marketing
  BT Marketing
Government missions (May Subd Geog)
  UF Missions, Government
  BT International relations
      Public administration
  NT Diplomatic and consular service
      Economic assistance
      Military missions
      Technical assistance
      Trade missions
Government missions, American, [etc.]
  (May Subd Geog)
Government missions, Taiwan
  (May Subd Geog)
  UF Taiwan government missions
Government monopolies (May Subd Geog)
    [HD3853-6]
  UF Monopolies, Government
      State monopolies
  BT Finance, Public
      Government business enterprises
      Government ownership
      Monopolies
      Revenue
      Taxation
  SA names of products, e.g. Salt, Tobacco
  — **Law and legislation** (May Subd Geog)
      BT Internal revenue law
Government office practice
  USE Office practice in government
Government officials
  USE Public officers
Government-owned aircraft
  USE Government aircraft
Government-owned automobiles
  USE Automobiles, Government
Government-owned corporations
  USE Corporations, Government
Government-owned patents
  USE Patents, Government-owned
Government ownership (May Subd Geog)
    [HD3840-4420]
  UF Nationalization
      Public ownership
      Socialization of industry
      State ownership
  BT Collectivism
      Economic policy
      Government business enterprises
      Industry and state
      Socialism
  RT Privatization
  SA subdivision Government ownership
      under types of industries, e.g.
      Construction industry—Government
      ownership
  NT Corporations, Government
      Government competition
      Government holding companies
      Government monopolies
      Government trading
      Land, Nationalization of
      Municipal ownership
      Railroads and state
      Socialist property
  — **Law and legislation** (May Subd Geog)
      RT Eminent domain

1557

Government ownership of coal mines
USE Coal mines and mining—Government
ownership
Government ownership of electric utilities
USE Electric utilities—Government
ownership
Government ownership of forests
USE Forests and forestry—Government
ownership
Government ownership of insurance companies
USE Insurance—Government ownership
Government ownership of mines
USE Mines and mineral resources—
Government ownership
Government ownership of railroads
USE Railroads and state
Government ownership of retail trade
USE Retail trade—Government ownership
Government ownership of the meat industry
USE Meat industry and trade—Government
ownership
Government ownership of the petroleum
industry
USE Petroleum industry and trade—
Government ownership
Government ownership of the potash industry
USE Potash industry and trade—
Government ownership
Government ownership of the printing industry
USE Printing industry—Government
ownership
Government ownership of wireless telegraph
USE Telegraph, Wireless—Government
ownership
Government Palace (La Paz, Bolivia)
USE Palacio Quemado (La Paz, Bolivia)
Government Palace (Salvador, Brazil)
USE Palácio Rio Branco (Salvador, Brazil)
Government paperwork *(May Subd Geog)*
UF Federal paperwork
Paper work, Government
Paperwork, Government
Records management, Government
BT Office practice in government
Paperwork (Office practice)
Public records
NT Government questionnaires
Government report writing
Inflation (Finance)—Effect of
government paperwork on
— **Law and legislation** *(May Subd Geog)*
BT Administrative law
Government patents
USE Patents, Government-owned
Government policy
USE *subdivision* Government policy *under
subjects; and headings of the type
[Topic] and state and [Topic]
policy, e.g.* Science and state;
Economic policy
Government political scientists
USE Political scientists in government
Government positions
USE Civil service positions
Government price control
USE Price regulation
Government price policy
USE Prices—Government policy
Government price regulation
USE Price regulation
Government procurement
USE Government purchasing
Government productivity *(May Subd Geog)*
UF Productivity, Government
BT Production (Economic theory)
Public administration
RT Capital productivity
NT Civil service—Labor productivity
Local government—Labor productivity
Government professional employees
USE Professional employees in government

Government programs, Sunset reviews of
USE Sunset reviews of government
programs
Government property
UF Public property
BT Property
Public administration
RT Socialist property
SA *subdivision* Government property
*under names of countries, cities,
etc.*
NT Surplus government property
— **Vandalism**
BT Vandalism
Government property, Surplus
USE Surplus government property
Government property and taxation
USE Taxation and government property
Government protocol
USE Government etiquette
Government publications
UF Documents
Government documents
Official publications
Public documents
BT Communication in politics
Library materials
RT Government publicity
Printing, Public
SA *subdivision* Government publications
*under names of countries, states,
counties, cities, etc., e.g.* United
States—Government publications
NT Acquisition of government publications
Exchanges, Literary and scientific
Gazettes
Local government documents
Maps
Municipal documents
Security classification (Government
documents)
— Cataloging
USE Cataloging of government
publications
— Classification
USE Classification—Government
publications
— **Use studies**
BT Library use studies
Government publicity *(May Subd Geog)*
Here are entered works on the dissemination of
information by government agencies on their activi-
ties.
UF Government information services
Information services, Government
Public relations—Public administration
Publicity, Government
BT Communication in politics
Propaganda
Public administration
RT Government publications
NT Government advertising
Government and the press
Public relations—Courts
Public relations—Municipal
government
Radio broadcasting
— **Law and legislation** *(May Subd Geog)*
Government purchasing *(May Subd Geog)*
UF Government procurement
Procurement, Government
Public procurement
Public purchasing
Purchasing, Government
BT Nontariff trade barriers
Purchasing
SA *subdivision* Procurement *under names
of individual government agencies*
NT Buy national policy
Purchasing agents
— **Law and legislation** *(May Subd Geog)*

BT Public contracts
Sales
Government purchasing of real property
(May Subd Geog)
UF Real property, Government purchasing
of
BT Public contracts
Vendors and purchasers
NT Eminent domain
Government questionnaires
(May Subd Geog)
UF Federal questionnaires
Questionnaires, Government
BT Government paperwork
Industry and state
Public administration
Public records
Questionnaires
RT Census
Government R and D contracts
USE Research and development contracts,
Government
Government records
USE Public records
Government regulation of commerce
USE *methods of regulation, e.g.* Bounties,
Tariff
Commercial policy
Industrial laws and legislation
Industry and state
Interstate commerce
Trade regulation
Government regulation of railroads
USE Interstate commerce
Railroad law
Railroads and state
Government reorganization
USE Administrative agencies—
Reorganization
Government report writing
[JF1525.R]
BT Government paperwork
Report writing
Government research and development
contracts
USE Research and development contracts,
Government
Government responsibility
USE Government liability
Government risks insurance
USE Insurance, Government risks
Government salaries
USE Civil service—Salaries, etc.
Government sale of real property
(May Subd Geog)
UF Real property, Government sale of
BT Vendors and purchasers
NT Public land sales
Government scientific agencies
USE Scientific bureaus
Government scientists
USE Scientists in government
Government secrecy
USE Executive privilege (Government
information)
Government information
Official secrets
Security classification (Government
documents)
Government securities *(May Subd Geog)*
[HG4701-4726]
UF Government bonds
Public securities
Securities, Government
BT Bonds
Debts, Public
Securities
NT Municipal bonds
State bonds
Treasury bills
— **Effect of inflation on**

BT Inflation (Finance)
— **Law and legislation** *(May Subd Geog)*
Government service
　USE Civil service
Government social scientists
　USE Social scientists in government
Government spending, Waste in
　USE Waste in government spending
Government spending policy
(May Subd Geog)
　UF Public spending policy
　BT Economic policy
　　Finance, Public
　　Full employment policies
　RT Expenditures, Public
　SA *subdivision* Appropriations and
　　expenditures *under names of*
　　countries ₍for descriptive and
　　statistical works on government
　　spending₎
　NT Employment subsidies
　　Tax and expenditure limitations
　— United States
　　NT Entitlement spending
Government subsidies
　USE Subsidies
Government surveys
　USE Surveys
Government trading *(May Subd Geog)*
　UF State trading
　BT Commerce
　　Commercial policy
　　Government business enterprises
　　Government ownership
Government transfer payments
　USE Transfer payments
Government vessels
　UF State ships
　　State vessels
　BT Exterritoriality
　　Immunities of foreign states
　　Maritime law
　　Ships
　SA *subdivision* Government vessels *under*
　　names of countries, e.g. United
　　States—Government vessels
　NT Lighthouse tenders
　　Warships
Governmental investigations
(May Subd Geog)
　Here are entered works on investigations initiated
by the ᴧᴘgislative, executive, or judicial branches of
the government and usually conducted by ad hoc or
permanent bodies for the purpose of investigating
some particular problem of public interest.
　UF Commissions of inquiry
　　Executive investigations
　　Government investigations
　　Investigations, Governmental
　　Judicial investigations
　　Legislative investigations
　BT Investigations
　　Justice, Administration of
　　Legislation
　　Legislative bodies—Committees
　　Legislative oversight
　　Public administration
　SA *names of specific investigative bodies*
　NT Criminal investigation
　　Executive privilege (Government
　　information)
　　Legislative hearings
　— United States
　　UF Congressional investigations
Governments, Legitimacy of
　USE Legitimacy of governments
Governments in exile
　UF Refugee governments

BT Exiles
　International law
　International relations
　Refugees, Political
　Sovereignty
　State, The
SA *subdivision* Governments in exile
　under names of wars, e.g. World
　War, 1939-1945—Governments in
　exile
Governor-General's Residence (Ottawa, Ont.)
　USE Rideau Hall (Ottawa, Ont.)
Governor John Wentworth Historic Site
(Wolfeboro, N.H.) *(Not Subd Geog)*
　UF Governor's Farm (Wolfeboro, N.H.)
　　Wentworth Estate (Wolfeboro, N.H.)
　　Wentworth Plantation (Wolfeboro,
　　N.H.)
　BT Historic sites—New Hampshire
Governor Nelson A. Rockefeller Empire State
　Plaza (Albany, N.Y.)
　USE Empire State Plaza (Albany, N.Y.)
Governor Shirley's War
　USE United States—History—King
　　George's War, 1744-1748
Governor Thomas E. Dewey Thruway (N.Y.)
　USE New York State Thruway (N.Y.)
Governors
　Works on governors of the United States are en-
tered under the heading Governors—United States.
Works on governors in other countries are entered
under the name of the country with subdivision Gov-
ernors.
　Works on governors of a state or province are
entered under the name of the state or province with
subdivision Governors, e.g. Louisiana—Governors.
　BT Kings and rulers
　— Children
　　Works on the children of governors of all ju-
　risdictions except the United States are entered
　under the name of the jurisdiction with subdivi-
　sion Governors—Children, e.g. New York
　(State)—Governors—Children. Works discuss-
　ing collectively the children of the governors of
　the United States are entered under Governors—
　United States—Children.
　　BT Children
　— Election
　　Works on the election of governors of all ju-
　risdictions except the United States are entered
　under the name of the jurisdiction with the sub-
　division Governors—Election, e.g. New York
　(State)—Governors—Election. Works discuss-
　ing collectively the election of the governors of
　the United States are entered under Governors—
　United States—Election.
　　BT Elections
　　SA *subdivision* Governors—Election
　　　under names of jurisdictions
　　　other than the United States
　　NT Governors—United States—
　　　Election
　— Wives
　　Works on the wives of governors of all juris-
　dictions except the United States are entered
　under the name of the jurisdiction with subdivi-
　sion Governors—Wives, e.g. New York (State)
　—Governors—Wives. Works discussing collec-
　tively the wives of the governors of the United
　States are entered under Governors—United
　States—Wives.
　　UF Governors' wives
　　　Wives of governors
　　BT Statesmen's wives
　　　Wives
　　　Women in politics
　　NT Governors—United States—Wives
　— United States
　　BT State governments
　— — **Children**
　— — **Election**
　　　BT Governors—Election
　— — Inability

　USE Governors—United States—
　　Succession
— — **Nomination**
　　UF Nomination of governors
　　BT Nominations for office
— — **Powers and duties**
　　₍JK2447-2458₎
　　SA *subdivision* Governors—Powers
　　　and duties *under names of*
　　　individual states, e.g.
　　　Louisiana—Governors—
　　　Powers and duties
— — **Staff**
— — **Succession**
　　UF Governors—United States—
　　　Inability
　　SA *subdivision* Governors—
　　　Succession *under names of*
　　　individual states, e.g.
　　　Massachusetts—Governors—
　　　Succession
— — **Transition periods**
　　₍JK2447₎
　　UF Gubernatorial transitions
　　　Transitions, Gubernatorial
— — **Wives**
　　BT Governors—Wives
Governors (Machinery)
　₍TJ1055₎
　Here are entered works on governing mechanisms
used in general machinery.
　UF Centrifugal regulators
　　Regulators
　BT Automatic control
　NT Electronic control
　　Gas-governors
　　Governors (Steam-engine)
Governors (Steam-engine)
　₍TJ550-TJ551₎
　Here are entered works on governing mechanisms
applied particularly to steam-engines.
　BT Governors (Machinery)
　　Steam-engines
Governor's Farm (Wolfeboro, N.H.)
　USE Governor John Wentworth Historic
　　Site (Wolfeboro, N.H.)
Governor's House (Uxmal Site, Mexico)
　USE Governor's Palace (Uxmal Site,
　　Mexico)
Governor's Mansion (Austin, Tex.)
　USE Texas Governor's Mansion (Austin,
　　Tex.)
Governor's Mansion (Carson City, Nev.)
　USE Nevada Governor's Mansion (Carson
　　City, Nev.)
Governor's Mansion (Frankfort, Ky.)
　USE Kentucky Governor's Mansion
　　(Frankfort, Ky.)
Governor's Palace (Uxmal Site, Mexico)
　₍F1435.1.U7₎
　UF Governor's House (Uxmal Site,
　　Mexico)
　　House of the Governor (Uxmal Site,
　　Mexico)
　BT Dwellings—Mexico
Governor's Palace (Williamsburg, Va.)
　BT Dwellings—Virginia
Governors' wives
　USE Governors—Wives
Govett family
　USE Gavitt family
Govit family
　USE Gavitt family
Gow family
　USE Gowen family
Gowan family
　USE Gowen family
Gowans family
　USE Gowen family
Gowar family
　USE Gower family

Gowars family
USE Gower family
Gowda dialect
USE Kannada language—Dialects—Gowda
Gowday family
USE Gowdy family
Gowdey family
USE Gowdy family
Gowdy family *(Not Subd Geog)*
UF Gadie family
Gaudie family
Gaudy family
Gawdie family
Gawdy family
Goudey family
Goudie family
Goudy family
Gowday family
Gowdey family
Gowen family *(Not Subd Geog)*
UF Gouen family
Goun family
Gove family
Gow family
Gowan family
Gowans family
Gowens family
Gowin family
Gowing family
Gowns family
Gowens family
USE Gowen family
Gower (Wales)
UF Gwyr (Wales)
BT Peninsulas—Wales
Gower family *(Not Subd Geog)*
UF Goower family
Goowers family
Gowar family
Gowars family
Gowers family
Leveson-Gower family
Gowers family
USE Gower family
Gowin family
USE Gowen family
Gowing family
USE Gowen family
Gowns, College
USE Academic costume
Gowns, Wedding
USE Wedding costume
Gowns family
USE Gowen family
Gowrie Conspiracy, 1600
[DA789]
Goya, Francisco, 1746-1828
Goya, Francisco, 1746-1828. Caprichos
UF Caprichos (Etching)
BT Etching—18th century—Spain
Etching, Spanish
Goya, Francisco, 1746-1828. Disasters of war
[NE2062.5.G6]
UF Desastres de la guerra (Etchings)
Disasters of war (Etchings)
BT Etching—19th century—Spain
Etching, Spanish
Goya, Francisco, 1746-1828. Proverbs
UF Disparates (Etchings)
Follies (Etchings)
Proverbios (Etchings)
Proverbs (Etchings)
BT Etching—19th century—Spain
Etching, Spanish
Goya, Francisco, 1746-1828. Regina Martirum
UF Regina Martirum (Mural)
Reina de los mártires (Mural)
Virgen Reina de los mártires (Mural)
BT Mary, Blessed Virgin, Saint—Art

Goya, Francisco, 1746-1828
— Adaptations
Goyana
USE Guiana
Goyen family
USE Guynes family
Goyne family
USE Guynes family
Goynes family
USE Guynes family
Gozaisho Kaidō (Japan) *(Not Subd Geog)*
BT Roads—Japan
Gozan literature
USE Japanese literature—Zen authors
Goze *(May Subd Geog)*
BT Blind musicians—Japan
Folk singers—Japan
Minstrels—Japan
Women musicians—Japan
Gozo Island (Malta)
UF Calypso's Island (Malta)
Gaulos Island (Malta)
Gaulus Island (Malta)
Ghaudesh Island (Malta)
Ghaudex Island (Malta)
Ghawex Island (Malta)
Gozzo Island (Malta)
BT Islands—Malta
Gozzo Island (Malta)
USE Gozo Island (Malta)
GPLAN (Electronic computer system)
UF Generalized Data Base Planning
System
GPS (Computer program)
UF General problem solver (Computer
program)
BT Artificial intelligence
Problem solving
GPS (Navigational system)
USE Global Positioning System
GPSG (Linguistics)
USE Generalized phrase structure grammar
GPSS (Computer program language)
UF General Purpose Simulation System
BT Digital computer simulation
GR-5 (Trail)
USE Grande Randonée Cinq (Trail)
Graabaek family
USE Grobeck family
Graafian follicle
[QL965]
[QM611]
BT Embryology
Ovaries
NT Corpus luteum
Graafschap (Netherlands)
UF Achterhoek (Netherlands)
De Graafschap (Netherlands)
Gelderse Achterhoek (Netherlands)
Graal
USE Grail
Graap family *(Not Subd Geog)*
Grab (The German word)
BT German language—Etymology
Grabel family
USE Graybill family
Grabell family
USE Graybill family
Grabens (Geology) *(May Subd Geog)*
UF Fault troughs
BT Geology, Structural
Rifts (Geology)
Graber family *(Not Subd Geog)*
UF Greber family
RT Gruber family
Grabhügel (The German word)
BT German language—Etymology
Grabil family
USE Graybill family
Grabill family
USE Graybill family

Grabl family
USE Graybill family
Grable family
USE Graybill family
Grabow altarpiece
USE Bertram, of Minden, ca. 1340-ca.
1415. Grabow altarpiece
Grabower Altar
USE Bertram, of Minden, ca. 1340-ca.
1415. Grabow altarpiece
Grace, Gifts of
USE Gifts, Spiritual
Grace (Aesthetics)
Grace (Theology)
[BT760-761]
BT Salvation
RT Law and gospel
NT Gifts, Spiritual
Molinism
Regeneration (Theology)
Sacraments
Supernatural (Theology)
Virtue, Infused
Grace at meals
[BV283.G7]
UF Blessings, Table
Prayers, Table
Table blessings
Table prayers
BT Prayers
— Buddhism, [Christianity, etc.]
Grace-Reynolds Application and Study of
PETO
USE GRASP System
Graceland Mansion (Memphis, Tenn.)
BT Dwellings—Tennessee
Graces, Expectative
USE Benefices, Ecclesiastical
Graces, The
[BL820.G8 (Mythology)]
[PN57.G6 (Literature)]
Gracey family *(Not Subd Geog)*
UF Gracie family
Gracy family
Gracia Street (Barcelona, Spain)
USE Paseo de Gracia (Barcelona, Spain)
Gracie family
USE Gracey family
Gracie Mansion (New York, N.Y.)
UF Archibald Gracie Mansion (New York,
N.Y.)
BT Dwellings—New York (State)
New York (N.Y.)—Mayors—
Dwellings
Gracilariidae
USE Gracillariidae
Gracillariidae
[QL561.G7]
UF Eucestidae
Gracilariidae
Leaf blotch miners
Leafblotch miners
Leafmining moths
Lithocolletidae
Phyllocnistidae
Phyllonorycteridae
Phyllorycteridae
Phylloryctidae
BT Lepidoptera
Moths
NT Cameraria
Graciosa Island (Azores)
UF Ilha Graciosa (Azores)
BT Azores
Grackles
Gracy family
USE Gracey family
Grad Rihemberk (Branik, Slovenia)
UF Rihemberk Castle (Branik, Slovenia)
BT Castles—Yugoslavia

Gradation (Linguistics)
  USE Grammar, Comparative and general—
       Gradation
Gradchany (Prague, Czechoslovakia)
  USE Hradčany (Prague, Czechoslovakia)
Grade crossings
  USE Railroads—Crossings
Grade family (Not Subd Geog)
  RT Winogradsky family
Grade labeling
  USE Labels
Grade placement, School
  USE School grade placement
Grade repetition (May Subd Geog)
  UF Non-promotion (School)
       Repetition, Grade
  BT Promotion (School)
       Slow learning children
       Underachievers
Grade schools
  USE Elementary schools
Grade separation (Highway engineering)
  USE Roads—Interchanges and intersections
Graded modules
  BT Modules (Algebra)
Graded rings
  BT Rings (Algebra)
Graded schools
  USE Ability grouping in education
       Grading and marking (Students)
Gradehede, Battle of, 1157
  [DL170.8]
  BT Denmark—History—To 1241
Graders (Earthmoving machinery)
  UF Grading machinery
       Motor graders
       Road graders
  BT Earthmoving machinery
       Motor vehicles
       Road machinery
       Scrapers (Earthmoving machinery)
  — Lubrication
Gradey family
  USE Grady family
Gradie family
  USE Grady family
Gradient methods, Conjugate
  USE Conjugate gradient methods
Grading
    Here are entered works on the division of com-
  mercial products into categories of uniform quality to
  facilitate marketing.
  UF Commercial products—Grading
  RT Specifications
       Standardization
       Testing
  SA subdivisions Grading and Grading and
       standardization under specific
       commodities, e.g. Cotton—Grading;
       Farm produce—Grading; Milk—
       Grading and standardization
  NT Labels
Grading and marking (Students)
  (May Subd Geog)
  [LB3051-LB3063]
    Here are entered works concerned solely with
  evaluation of academic achievement. Works concerned with testing student academic achievement
  and aptitudes are entered under Educational tests
  and measurements. Works on evaluating students on
  their total performance, including academic achievement, behavior, attitudes, interest, motivation, participation, etc., are entered under Students—Rating
  of.
  UF Graded schools
       Marking (Students)
       Students—Grading and marking
  BT Educational tests and measurements
       Examinations—Interpretation
       Personnel records in education
       Students—Rating of
  RT School reports

  NT Ability grouping in education
       College credits—Outside work
       Pass-fail grading system
       Promotion (School)
       School credits
       School credits—Outside work
       School grade placement
Grading machinery
  USE Graders (Earthmoving machinery)
Grading of coins
  USE Coins—Grading
Grado Lagoon (Italy)
  UF Laguna di Grado (Italy)
  BT Lagoons—Italy
Graduals (Liturgical books)
  [BX2043 (Roman Catholic, primarily
       non-musical)]
  [M2148-M2148.5 (Roman Catholic,
       primarily musical)]
  BT Liturgies
Graduals (Music)
  [M2079.L416]
  BT Propers (Music)
Graduate education
  USE Universities and colleges—Graduate
       work
Graduate education of women
  USE Universities and colleges—Graduate
       work of women
Graduate examinations
  USE Universities and colleges—Graduate
       work—Examinations
Graduate Management Admission Test
  [HF1118]
  UF GMAT
  BT Business—Examinations
       Management—Examinations
       Universities and colleges—Graduate
       work—Examinations
Graduate programs
  USE Universities and colleges—Graduate
       work
Graduate record examination
  BT Scholastic aptitude test
       Universities and colleges—
       Examinations
       Universities and colleges—Graduate
       work
       Universities and colleges—Graduate
       work—Examinations
Graduate schools
  USE Universities and colleges—Graduate
       work
Graduate student mobility
  UF Migration of graduate students
       Mobility
  BT Student mobility
Graduate students (May Subd Geog)
  UF Students, Graduate
  BT College students
       Universities and colleges—Graduate
       work
  SA subdivision Graduate students under
       names of universities, e.g. Columbia
       University—Graduate students
  NT Graduate teaching assistants
       Women graduate students
  — Political activity
       BT College students—Political activity
       Politics, Practical
  — Science (May Subd Geog)
Graduate study in education
  USE Education—Graduate work
Graduate study in special education
  USE Special education teachers—Training
       of—Graduate work
Graduate teaching assistants
  (May Subd Geog)
  UF College teacher aides
       College teacher assistants

  BT College teachers
       Graduate students
Graduate work
  USE subdivision Study and teaching
       (Graduate) under topical headings
       Universities and colleges—Graduate
       work
Graduate work in biology
  USE Biology—Study and teaching
       (Graduate)
Graduate work in education
  USE Education—Graduate work
Graduate work in psychology
  USE Psychology—Study and teaching
       (Graduate)
Graduate work in special education
  USE Special education teachers—Training
       of—Graduate work
Graduate work of women
  USE Universities and colleges—Graduate
       work of women
Graduated payment mortgage loans
  USE Mortgage loans, Variable rate
Graduated taxation
  USE Taxation, Progressive
Graduates, College
  USE College graduates
Graduates, Elementary school
  USE Elementary school graduates
Graduates, High school
  USE High school graduates
Graduates, Junior high school
  USE Junior high school graduates
Graduation (Statistics)
  BT Statistics
  RT Smoothing (Statistics)
Graduation sermons
  USE Baccalaureate addresses
Grady family (Not Subd Geog)
  UF Gradey family
       Gradie family
       O'Grady family
  RT McGrady family
Graeco-Roman law
  USE Law, Byzantine
Graeter family
  USE Crider family
Graetz family
  USE Gratz family
Graf family
  USE Graff family
Graf-Wellhausen hypothesis (Pentateuchal
  criticism)
  USE Documentary hypothesis (Pentateuchal
       criticism)
Graff family (Not Subd Geog)
  UF Graf family
  RT Groff familu
       Grove family
Graffiti (May Subd Geog)
  [GT3912]
  BT Folklore
       Inscriptions
  RT Street art
  SA subdivision Graffiti under individual
       wars, e.g. World War, 1939-1945—
       Graffiti
Graffito decoration (May Subd Geog)
  UF Decoration, Graffito
       Sgraffito decoration
  BT Arts and crafts movement
       Decoration and ornament
       Mural painting and decoration
       Plastering
GRAFIK (Computer program language)
  [QA76.73.G]
Grafil languages
  USE Bamileke languages
Graflex camera
  NT Graphic camera

Graft (Game)
  [GV1299.G7]
Graft (in politics)
  USE Corruption (in politics)
Graft copolymers
  UF Graft polymers
  BT Polymers and polymerization
Graft polymers
  USE Graft copolymers
Graft rejection *(May Subd Geog)*
    Here are entered works on the immunological response of a host against grafted tissue leading to destruction of the graft. Works on the reaction of an immunocompetent graft against the tissues of an immunologically immature or deficient recipient are entered under Graft versus host reaction.
  UF Rejection of grafts
    Rejection of transplants
    Transplant rejection
  BT Transplantation immunology
Graft versus host reaction *(May Subd Geog)*
    Here are entered works on the reaction of an immunocompetent graft against the tissues of an immunologically immature or deficient recipient. Works on the immunological response of a host against grafted tissue leading to destruction of the graft are entered under Graft rejection.
  UF Runt disease
  BT Immunologic diseases
    Transplantation immunology
Grafting
    [S691-S693 (Implements)]
    [SB123.5 (General)]
  BT Fruit-culture
    Gardening
    Horticulture
    Plant-breeding
    Plant propagation
    Trees
  NT Budding
    Stocks (Horticulture)
Grafting of bone
  USE Bone-grafting
Grafting of nerves
  USE Nerve grafting
Grafting of skin
  USE Skin-grafting
Grafton family *(Not Subd Geog)*
Grafton House (Grafton Regis, Northamptonshire)
  UF Grafton Regis Manor House (Grafton Regis, Northamptonshire)
  BT Dwellings—England
    Manors—England
Grafton portrait of Shakespeare (Painting)
  BT Portrait painting—16th century—England
    Portrait painting, English
Grafton Regis Manor House (Grafton Regis, Northamptonshire)
  USE Grafton House (Grafton Regis, Northamptonshire)
Gragary family
  USE Gregory family
Graged language
  USE Gedaged language
Graham family *(Not Subd Geog)*
  UF Grahame family
    Grahams family
    Grame family
    Grames family
  RT Grimes family
Graham flour
    [TS2149 (Milling)]
    [TX558.W5 (Food values)]
  BT Flour
Graham shorthand
  USE Shorthand—Graham
Graham shorthand, Spanish
  USE Shorthand, Spanish—Graham

Graham-Tewksbury Feud
  UF Pleasant Valley Vendetta
    Tewksbury-Graham Feud
  BT Vendetta—Arizona
Grahame family
  USE Graham family
Grahamite
    [TN885]
Grahamites
    [TX392]
  BT Vegetarianism
Grahams family
  USE Graham family
Graham's law
    [QC163.5]
  UF Law of diffusion, Graham's
  BT Chemistry, Physical and theoretical
    Diffusion
Grahovac, Battle of, 1858
  BT Turco-Montenegrin War, 1858
Graian Alps (France and Italy)
  UF Alpes Grées (France and Italy)
    Alpi Graie (France and Italy)
    Graies Alpes (France and Italy)
  BT Alps, Western
    Mountains—France
    Mountains—Italy
Graies Alpes (France and Italy)
  USE Graian Alps (France and Italy)
Grail
  UF Graal
    Gral
    Gréal
    Holy Grail
  BT Chalices
    Folklore
GRAIL (Electronic computer system)
  UF Graphical Input Language
  BT Computer graphics
    Electronic digital computers—Programming
    On-line data processing
Grail movement (Bernhardt)
    [BP605.B4]
Grail movement (Catholic)
  BT Catholic Church—Societies, etc.
Grain *(May Subd Geog)*
    [SB189-SB191 (Culture)]
  UF Breadstuffs
    Cereals
  BT Botany, Economic
    Field crops
    Flour
    Food
    Food crops
    Seed crops
  SA *names of the various cereal plants, e.g.* Corn; Rye; Wheat
  NT Green Revolution
    Lodging of grain
    Oats
    Sorghum
    Winter grain
— **Cooperative marketing**
  BT Grain trade
— **Diseases and pests** *(May Subd Geog)*
    [SB608.G6]
  UF Grain pests
  SA *subdivision* Diseases and pests *under names of cereal plants, e.g.* Millet—Diseases and pests; Wheat—Diseases and pests; *also names of pests, e.g.* Chinchbugs, Mediterranean flour-moth, Rye gall-gnat
  NT Cereal rusts
    Cereal smut diseases
    Cereal smut fungi
    Dinoderus truncatus
    Draeculacephala mollipes
    Gaeumannomyces graminis

    Grain—Storage—Diseases and injuries
    Oulema melanopa
    Puccinia graminis
    Puccinia recondita
    Take-all disease
— **Drying**
  UF Drying apparatus—Grain
    Grain drying
  SA *subdivision* Drying *under names of grains, e.g.* Corn—Drying
— **Field experiments**
— **Grading**
  SA *subdivision* Grading *under names of cereal plants*
— **Harvesting**
— **History**
— **Irrigation**
— **Losses** *(May Subd Geog)*
— **Microbiology**
— **Milling**
  UF Grain milling
    Milling of grain
  RT Flour
    Meal
  SA *subdivision* Milling *under names of grains, e.g.* Corn—Milling
  NT Flour-mills
    Milling machinery
— **Ripening**
  UF Ripening of grain
  BT Plant physiology
— **Storage**
  BT Farm produce—Storage
  SA *subdivision* Storage *under names of grains, e.g.* Wheat—Storage
  NT Grain aeration
— — **Diseases and injuries**
    (May Subd Geog)
  BT Farm produce—Storage—Diseases and injuries
    Grain—Diseases and pests
  NT Granary weevil
    Khapra beetle
    Oryzaephilus mercator
    Sawtoothed grain beetle
    Sitophilus
— **Threshing**
  USE Threshing
— **Varieties**
— **Weight and measurement**
— **Weights and measures**
    [HF5716.G7]
    [QC89]
  BT Weights and measures
Grain aeration *(May Subd Geog)*
    [SB190]
  UF Aeration of grain
    Granaries—Aeration
  BT Grain—Storage
Grain-aphis
  USE Grain-louse
Grain as feed
  BT Feeds
Grain beetle, Sawtoothed
  USE Sawtoothed grain beetle
Grain beetles
  USE Sitophilus
Grain bins
  USE Granaries
Grain borer, Larger
  USE Dinoderus truncatus
Grain boundaries
    [QD921 (Crystallography)]
    [TN690 (Metallography)]
  UF Crystal grain boundaries
  BT Crystallography
  RT Crystals—Growth
    Dislocations in crystals
    Twinning (Crystallography)

Grain boundary diffusion
  USE Kirkendall effect
Grain drying
  USE Grain—Drying
Grain dust
  BT Dust
  NT Dust explosion
Grain elevator managers *(May Subd Geog)*
  UF Elevator managers, Grain
       Managers, Grain elevator
  BT Grain elevators—Employees
       Grain elevators—Management
Grain elevators *(May Subd Geog)*
  [TH4461]
  UF Country elevators
       Elevators, Grain
  NT Granaries
  — **Electric equipment**
  — **Employees**
     NT Grain elevator managers
  — **Equipment and supplies**
  — — Appraisal
       USE Grain elevators—Equipment
            and supplies—Valuation
  — — **Valuation**
       UF Grain elevators—Equipment and
            supplies—Appraisal
  — **Law and legislation** *(May Subd Geog)*
  — **Management**
     [SB190]
     NT Grain elevator managers
  — **Ventilation**
Grain elevators, Cooperative
  BT Agriculture, Cooperative
Grain goddesses *(May Subd Geog)*
  BT Goddesses
Grain growth in metals
  USE Metal crystals—Growth
Grain-handling machinery
Grain in art
Grain itch
  USE Straw itch
Grain-louse
  [QL523.A6 (Zoology)]
  [SB945.G7]
  UF Grain-aphis
       Green bug
       Schizaphis graminum
       Spring grain-aphis
       Wheat aphid
  — **Biological control** *(May Subd Geog)*
     BT Grain-louse—Control
  — **Control** *(May Subd Geog)*
     NT Grain-louse—Biological control
Grain milling
  USE Grain—Milling
Grain pests
  USE Grain—Diseases and pests
Grain products
  USE Cereal products
Grain rusts
  USE Cereal rusts
Grain sorghum
  USE Sorghum
Grain trade *(May Subd Geog)*
  [HD9030-HD9049]
  [HF2651.G8 (Tariff)]
  BT Produce trade
  NT Corn industry
       Fiars prices
       Grain—Cooperative marketing
       Wheat trade
  — **Law and legislation** *(May Subd Geog)*
  — **Tables**
     [HF5716.G7 (General)]
     [HG3875.G7 (Foreign exchange)]
     UF Grain trade—Tables and ready-
          reckoners
  — Tables and ready-reckoners
     USE Grain trade—Tables

Grain tribute (China)
Grain weevils
  USE Granary weevil
       Sitophilus
Graineries
  USE Granaries
Grainger family
  USE Granger family
Graining
  [TT330]
  BT Stains and staining
       Wood finishing
  RT Painting, Industrial
       Simulated wood
Grains of paradise
  [QK495.Z65 (Botany)]
  UF Aframomum grana-paradisi
       Aframomum melegueta
       Amomum melegueta
       Guinea grains
       Guinea pepper
       Malagueta pepper
       Melegueta pepper
       Paradise, Grains of
       Paradise meleguetapepper
       Pepper, Guinea
       Pepper, Malagueta
       Pepper, Melegueta
  BT Plants, Edible
Graisivaudan Valley (France)
  UF Grésivaudan Valley (France)
  BT Valleys—France
Graiste family
  USE Grasty family
Graisty family
  USE Grasty family
Grajos Cave (Spain) *(Not Subd Geog)*
  UF Cueva de los Grajos (Spain)
  BT Caves—Spain
       Spain—Antiquities
Gral
  USE Grail
Gram (Legume)
  USE Chickpea
Gram (Unit)
  [QC106]
  UF Gramme (Unit)
  BT Mass (Physics)
       Metric system
       Units
Gram-atom
  USE Mole (Chemistry)
Gram-atomic weight
  USE Mole (Chemistry)
Gram family *(Not Subd Geog)*
  UF Gramm family
       Grams family
Gram-formula weight
  USE Mole (Chemistry)
Gram-molecular weight
  USE Mole (Chemistry)
Gram-molecule
  USE Mole (Chemistry)
Gram negative bacteria
  UF Bacteria, Gram negative
       Bacteria gram negative
  BT Bacteria
       Gram's stain
  NT Azotobacteraceae
       Bdellovibrio
       Chlamydiales
       Endotoxins
       Halobacterium
       Legionella pneumophila
       Methylomonadaceae
       Rhizobiaceae
       Rhodospirillaceae
Gram pea
  USE Chickpea
Gram stain
  USE Gram's stain

Grama grass, Blue
  USE Blue grama grass
Grame family
  USE Graham family
Grames family
  USE Graham family
Gramicidins
  BT Antibiotics
       Ionophores
       Peptides
Graminaceae
  USE Grasses
Gramineae
  USE Grasses
Gramling family *(Not Subd Geog)*
Gramm family
  USE Gram family
Grammar
  USE *subdivision* Grammar *under names of*
       languages, e.g. English language—
       Grammar
       Grammar, Comparative and general
       Language and languages—Grammars
Grammar, Applicative
  USE Applicative grammar
Grammar, Arc pair
  USE Arc pair grammar
Grammar, Case
  USE Case grammar
Grammar, Categorial
  USE Categorial grammar
Grammar, Comparative and general
  [P151-295]
     Here are entered: 1. Works comparing and classi-
  fying the grammatical structure of genetically un-
  related languages or groups of languages; 2. Works in
  which the principles of grammar in general are dis-
  cussed, i.e. general, philosophical or universal gram-
  mar. Works which present a specific comparison of
  the grammars of two or more languages or groups of
  languages are entered under the name of the language, with the subdivision Grammar, Comparative,
  e.g. 1. Slavic languages—Grammar, Comparative; or,
  1. Russian language—Grammar, Comparative—
  English. 2. English language—Grammar,
  Comparative—Russian; or, 1. Slavic languages—
  Grammar, Comparative—Germanic. 2 Germanic
  languages—Grammar, Comparative—Slavic.
  UF Comparative grammar
       Dialects
       Grammar
       Grammar, Philosophical
       Grammar, Universal
       Language and languages—Grammar,
          Comparative
       Philosophical grammar
  BT Linguistics
       Philology
  SA *subdivision* Grammar, Comparative
       under names of languages
  NT Ambiguity
       Anaphora (Linguistics)
       Applicative grammar
       Cartesian linguistics
       Categorial grammar
       Cognitive grammar
       Conditionals (Logic)
       Emphasis (Linguistics)
       Generative grammar
       Grammaticality (Linguistics)
       Language and languages
       Lexical grammar
       Linguistic analysis (Linguistics)
       Linguistic String Parser (Computer
          grammar)
       Markedness (Linguistics)
       Network grammar
       Order (Grammar)
       Parenthesis (Rhetoric)
       Parsing (Computer grammar)
       Relational grammar
       Speculative grammar

Grammar, Comparative and general
  (Continued)
    Stratificational grammar
    Systemic grammar
    Tagmemics
    Transmutation (Linguistics)
  — Accents and accentuation
    USE Accents and accentuation
  — Adjectival constructions
    USE Grammar, Comparative and
       general—Adjectivals
  — **Adjectivals**
    UF Adjectivals
      Grammar, Comparative and
        general—Adjectival
        constructions
      Grammar, Comparative and
        general—Adjective groups
    SA *subdivision* Adjectivals *under*
      individual languages and groups
      of languages, e.g. English
      language—Adjectivals
  — **Adjective**
    [P273]
    UF Adjective
    BT Grammar, Comparative and
       general—Nominals
    NT Grammar, Comparative and
       general—Possessives
  — Adjective groups
    USE Grammar, Comparative and
       general—Adjectivals
  — **Adverb**
    [P284]
    UF Adverb
    BT Grammar, Comparative and
       general—Connectives
  — **Adverbials**
    UF Adverbials
    SA *subdivision* Adverbials *under*
      names of languages or groups of
      languages, e.g. English language
      —Adverbials
  — **Affixes**
    UF Affixes
    SA *subdivision* Affixes *under names of*
      languages, e.g. English language
      —Affixes
    NT Grammar, Comparative and
       general—Infixes
      Grammar, Comparative and
       general—Suffixes and prefixes
  — **Agreement**
    UF Agreement (Grammar)
      Concord (Grammar)
      Grammar, Comparative and
       general—Concord
    BT Grammar, Comparative and
       general—Case
      Grammar, Comparative and
       general—Gender
      Grammar, Comparative and
       general—Number
      Grammar, Comparative and
       general—Person
      Grammar, Comparative and
       general—Syntax
    SA *subdivision* Agreement *under*
      names of languages, e.g. English
      language—Agreement
  — Analogy
    USE Analogy (Linguistics)
  — **Animacy**
    UF Animacy (Grammar)
      Grammar, Comparative and
       general—Animateness
    BT Grammar, Comparative and
       general—Grammatical categories

    SA *subdivision* Animacy *under*
      individual languages and groups
      of languages, e.g. English
      language—Animacy
  — Animateness
    USE Grammar, Comparative and
       general—Animacy
  — **Apposition**
    UF Apposition (Grammar)
  — **Article**
    [P277]
    UF Article
  — **Aspect**
    UF Aspect (Linguistics)
      Grammar, Comparative and
       general—Verbal aspect
    BT Grammar, Comparative and
       general—Temporal constructions
      Grammar, Comparative and
       general—Verb
    SA *subdivision* Aspect *under particular*
      languages, e.g. English language
      —Aspect
  — Asymmetry
    USE Asymmetry (Linguistics)
  — **Attribute**
    UF Attribute (Grammar)
  — **Auxiliaries**
    UF Auxiliaries (Grammar)
    BT Grammar, Comparative and
       general—Grammatical categories
    SA *subdivisions* Auxiliary verbs,
      Conjunctions, *and* Prepositions
      under individual languages and
      groups of languages, e.g. English
      language—Auxiliary verbs;
      English language—Conjunctions;
      English language—Prepositions
    NT Grammar, Comparative and
       general—Prepositions
  — **Case**
    [P253]
    UF Case
    NT Case grammar
      Grammar, Comparative and
       general—Agreement
      Grammar, Comparative and
       general—Ergative constructions
      Grammar, Comparative and
       general—Possessives
  — Causative constructions
    USE Causative (Linguistics)
  — Classifiers
    USE Classifiers (Linguistics)
  — **Clauses**
    UF Clauses
    BT Grammar, Comparative and
       general—Sentences
      Grammar, Comparative and
       general—Syntax
    NT Grammar, Comparative and
       general—Comparative clauses
      Grammar, Comparative and
       general—Concessive clauses
      Grammar, Comparative and
       general—Relative clauses
      Grammar, Comparative and
       general—Temporal clauses
  — Clicks
    USE Clicks (Phonetics)
  — **Clitics**
    UF Clitics (Grammar)
    BT Accents and accentuation
      Tagmemics
    SA *subdivision* Clitics *under names of*
      languages and groups of
      languages, e.g. English language
      —Clitics
    NT Grammar, Comparative and
       general—Enclitics
  — **Collective nouns**

    [P271]
    BT Grammar, Comparative and
       general—Noun
    SA *subdivision* Collective nouns *under*
      names of languages and groups
      of languages, e.g. English
      language—Collective nouns
  — **Comparative clauses**
    UF Comparative clauses (Grammar)
    BT Comparison (Grammar)
      Grammar, Comparative and
       general—Clauses
    SA *subdivision* Comparative clauses
      under individual languages and
      groups of languages, e.g. English
      language—Comparative clauses
  — Comparison
    USE Comparison (Grammar)
  — **Compensatory lengthening**
    [P217.8]
    UF Compensatory lengthening
       (Phonetics)
    BT Duration (Phonetics)
      Grammar, Comparative and
       general—Phonology
  — **Complement**
    [P299.C59]
    UF Complement (Grammar)
    BT Grammar, Comparative and
       general—Verb phrase
    SA *subdivision* Complement *under*
      individual languages and groups
      of languages, e.g. English
      language—Complement
  — Complex nominals
    USE Grammar, Comparative and
       general—Noun phrase
  — Composition
    USE Grammar, Comparative and
       general—Compound words
  — **Compound words**
    UF Composition (Grammar)
      Compound words
      Grammar, Comparative and
       general—Composition
      Words, Compound
    BT Grammar, Comparative and
       general—Word formation
    SA *subdivision* Compound words
      under individual languages and
      groups of languages, e.g. English
      language—Compound words
  — **Concessive clauses**
    [P292.3]
    UF Clauses, Concessive
      Concessive clauses
    BT Grammar, Comparative and
       general—Clauses
    SA *subdivision* Concessive clauses
      under individual languages and
      groups of languages, e.g. English
      language—Concessive clauses
  — Concord
    USE Grammar, Comparative and
       general—Agreement
  — Conditional clauses
    USE Grammar, Comparative and
       general—Conditionals
  — Conditional constructions
    USE Grammar, Comparative and
       general—Conditionals
  — Conditional sentences
    USE Grammar, Comparative and
       general—Conditionals
  — **Conditionals**
    [P292.5]

UF Conditionals (Grammar)
　　Grammar, Comparative and
　　　general—Conditional clauses
　　Grammar, Comparative and
　　　general—Conditional
　　　constructions
　　Grammar, Comparative and
　　　general—Conditional sentences
　　Grammar, Comparative and
　　　general—Hypothetical clauses
　　Grammar, Comparative and
　　　general—Protasis
　　Hypothetical clauses (Grammar)
　　Protasis (Grammar)
BT Grammar, Comparative and
　　　general—Mood
　　Grammar, Comparative and
　　　general—Sentences
SA *subdivision* Conditionals *under*
　　individual languages and groups
　　of languages, e.g. English
　　language—Conditionals

— **Conjunctions**
　　[P286]
UF Conjunctions (Linguistics)
BT Grammar, Comparative and
　　　general—Connectives
SA *subdivision* Conjunctions *under*
　　individual languages and groups
　　of languages, e.g. English
　　language—Conjunctions
— Conjunctive mood
USE Grammar, Comparative and
　　　general—Subjunctive
— **Connectives**
　　[P286]
UF Connectives (Linguistics)
　　Grammar, Comparative and
　　　general—Sentence connectors
　　Sentence connectors
BT Grammar, Comparative and
　　　general—Syntax
SA *subdivision* Connectives *under*
　　individual languages and groups
　　of languages, e.g. English
　　language—Connectives
NT Grammar, Comparative and
　　　general—Adverb
　　Grammar, Comparative and
　　　general—Conjunctions
— Consonants
USE Consonants
— Context
USE Context (Linguistics)
— **Coordinate constructions**
　　[P299.C6]
UF Coordination (Linguistics)
BT Grammar, Comparative and
　　　general—Syntax
　　Parallelism (Linguistics)
SA *subdivision* Coordinate
　　constructions *under names of*
　　languages and groups of
　　languages, e.g. English language
　　—Coordinate constructions
— Deictic function
USE Grammar, Comparative and
　　　general—Deixis
— **Deixis**
　　[P299.D44]
UF Deixis (Linguistics)
　　Grammar, Comparative and
　　　general—Deictic function
SA *subdivision* Deixis *under names of*
　　languages and groups of
　　languages, e.g. English language
　　—Deixis
— **Deletion**
UF Deletion (Linguistics)
　　Deletion transformation
　　　(Linguistics)

BT Grammar, Comparative and
　　　general—Syntax
SA *subdivision* Deletion *under names*
　　of languages and groups of
　　languages, e.g. English language
　　—Deletion
— **Denominative**
UF Denominative
— Derivation
USE Generative grammar
　　Grammar, Comparative and
　　　general—Word formation
　　Language and languages—
　　　Etymology
— **Determiners**
　　[P299.D]
UF Determinatives (Linguistics)
　　Determiners (Linguistics)
BT Classifiers (Linguistics)
RT Definiteness (Linguistics)
SA *subdivision* Determiners *under*
　　names of languages and groups
　　of languages, e.g. English
　　language—Determiners
— Duration
USE Duration (Phonetics)
— **Ellipsis**
　　[P291.3]
UF Ellipsis (Grammar)
　　Grammar, Comparative and
　　　general—Elliptical constructions
BT Grammar, Comparative and
　　　general—Syntax
— Elliptical constructions
USE Grammar, Comparative and
　　　general—Ellipsis
— **Enclitics**
UF Enclitics (Grammar)
BT Accents and accentuation
　　Grammar, Comparative and
　　　general—Clitics
SA *subdivision* Enclitics *under names*
　　of languages and groups of
　　languages, e.g. English language
　　—Enclitics
— Ergative case
USE Grammar, Comparative and
　　　general—Ergative
　　　constructions
— **Ergative constructions**
　　[P291.5]
UF Ergative (Linguistics)
　　Grammar, Comparative and
　　　general—Ergative case
BT Grammar, Comparative and
　　　general—Case
　　Grammar, Comparative and
　　　general—Syntax
SA *subdivision* Ergative constructions
　　under names of languages and
　　groups of languages, e.g. English
　　language—Ergative
　　constructions
— **Exclamations**
UF Exclamations (Linguistics)
　　Exclamatory (Linguistics)
BT Grammar, Comparative and
　　　general—Syntax
SA *subdivision* Exclamations *under*
　　individual languages and groups
　　of languages, e.g. English
　　language—Exclamations
— **Exercises**
— **Existential constructions**
UF Existential constructions
　　　(Grammar)
BT Grammar, Comparative and
　　　general—Sentences
　　Grammar, Comparative and
　　　general—Verb phrase

SA *subdivision* Existential
　　constructions *under names of*
　　languages and groups of
　　languages, e.g. English language
　　—Existential constructions
— **Gender**
　　[P271]
UF Gender
BT Language and languages—Sex
　　　differences
NT Grammar, Comparative and
　　　general—Agreement
— **Gerundive**
UF Gerundive (Grammar)
SA *subdivision* Gerundive *under*
　　names of languages and groups
　　of languages, e.g. French
　　language—Gerundive
— Government
USE Government (Grammar)
— **Gradation**
　　Here are entered works on expressions which
　　describe the relative amount of a quality in two
　　or more objects, as in comparison, diminution,
　　etc. Works on the change of one vowel to another
　　accompanying a change in the degree of stress
　　are entered under the heading Grammar, Com-
　　parative and general—Vowel gradation.
UF Gradation (Linguistics)
RT Grammar, Comparative and
　　　general—Vowel gradation
SA *subdivision* Gradation *under names*
　　of languages and groups of
　　languages, e.g. English language
　　—Gradation
— **Grammatical categories**
　　[P204.5]
UF Categories, Grammatical
　　Grammar, Comparative and
　　　general—Major form classes
　　Grammatical categories
BT Componential analysis (Linguistics)
SA *subdivision* Grammatical categories
　　under names of languages and
　　groups of languages, e.g. English
　　language—Grammatical
　　categories
NT Grammar, Comparative and
　　　general—Animacy
　　Grammar, Comparative and
　　　general—Auxiliaries
　　Parts of speech
— **Grammaticalization**
UF Grammaticalization
BT Grammar, Comparative and
　　　general—Syntax
　　Semantics
SA *subdivision* Grammaticalization
　　under individual languages and
　　groups of languages, e.g. English
　　language—Grammaticalization
— **Honorific**
UF Grammar, Comparative and
　　　general—Polite form
　　Honorific
　　Polite form (Grammar)
— Hypothetical clauses
USE Grammar, Comparative and
　　　general—Conditionals
— **Ideophone**
UF Ideophone
SA *subdivision* Ideophone *under*
　　names of languages and groups
　　of languages, e.g. English
　　language—Ideophone
— **Imperative**
UF Imperative (Grammar)
　　Jussive (Grammar)
BT Grammar, Comparative and
　　　general—Mood
　　Grammar, Comparative and
　　　general—Verb

Grammar, Comparative and general
  — **Imperative** *(Continued)*
    SA *subdivision* Imperative *under*
      names of languages and groups
      of languages, e.g. English
      language—Imperative
  — Impersonal constructions
    USE Grammar, Comparative and
      general—Subjectless
      constructions
  — **Indicative**
    UF Indicative mood
    BT Grammar, Comparative and
      general—Mood
    SA *subdivision* Indicative *under names*
      of languages and groups of
      languages, e.g. English language
      —Indicative
  — **Indirect discourse**
    UF Grammar, Comparative and
      general—Indirect quotation
      Grammar, Comparative and
      general—Reported speech
      Indirect discourse (Grammar)
      Indirect quotation (Grammar)
      Indirect speech (Grammar)
      Reported speech (Grammar)
    BT Discourse analysis
      Narration (Rhetoric)
    SA *subdivision* Indirect discourse
      under names of languages and
      groups of languages, e.g. English
      language—Indirect discourse
  — Indirect quotation
    USE Grammar, Comparative and
      general—Indirect discourse
  — **Infinitive**
    UF Infinitive
    BT Grammar, Comparative and
      general—Verbals
  — **Infixes**
    [P245]
    UF Infixes
    BT Grammar, Comparative and
      general—Affixes
    SA *subdivision* Infixes *under individual*
      languages and groups of
      languages, e.g. English language
      —Infixes
  — **Inflection**
    [P251-9]
    UF Inflection
      Inflectional morphology
      Language and languages—
      Inflection
    BT Grammar, Comparative and
      general—Morphology
    NT Grammar, Comparative and
      general—Reduplication
  — **Interjections**
    [P287]
    BT Grammar, Comparative and
      general—Particles
    SA *subdivision* Interjections *under*
      individual languages and groups
      of languages, e.g. English
      language—Interjections
  — **Interrogative**
    UF Interrogative (Grammar)
      Questions and answers
      (Linguistics)
    SA *subdivision* Interrogative *under*
      names of languages, e.g.
      Romance languages—
      Interrogative
  — Intonation
    USE Intonation (Phonetics)
  — Major form classes
    USE Grammar, Comparative and
      general—Grammatical
      categories

  — **Mass nouns**
    [P271]
    UF Grammar, Comparative and
      general—Mass terms
      Grammar, Comparative and
      general—Non-count nouns
      Grammar, Comparative and
      general—Quantifiable nouns
      Grammar, Comparative and
      general—Unbounded nouns
      Grammar, Comparative and
      general—Uncountable nouns
      Mass nouns
      Nouns, Mass
    BT Grammar, Comparative and
      general—Noun
      Grammar, Comparative and
      general—Number
  — Mass terms
    USE Grammar, Comparative and
      general—Mass nouns
  — **Mathematical models**
    [P151]
    BT Mathematical linguistics
  — **Mood**
    UF Mode (Grammar)
      Mood (Grammar)
    BT Grammar, Comparative and
      general—Verb
    NT Grammar, Comparative and
      general—Conditionals
      Grammar, Comparative and
      general—Imperative
      Grammar, Comparative and
      general—Indicative
      Grammar, Comparative and
      general—Subjunctive
  — **Morphology**
    [P241]
    Here are entered works on the study and
  analysis of the structure, forms and classes of
  words in languages, including inflection, derivation and compounding. Works on the formation
  of words in languages by the processes of derivation and compounding only are entered under
  the heading Grammar, Comparative and general
  —Word formation.
    UF Morphology (Linguistics)
    SA *subdivision* Morphology *under*
      names of languages and groups
      of languages, e.g. English
      language—Morphology
    NT Autosegmental theory (Linguistics)
      Grammar, Comparative and
      general—Inflection
      Grammar, Comparative and
      general—Word formation
      Morphemics
  — Mutation
    USE Mutation (Phonetics)
  — **Negatives**
    UF Negatives (Grammar)
  — **Nominals**
    [P271]
    UF Nominals (Grammar)
      Noun-equivalents (Grammar)
      Substantives (Grammar)
    RT Grammar, Comparative and
      general—Noun phrase
    SA *subdivision* Nominals *under names*
      of languages and groups of
      languages, e.g. English language
      —Nominals
    NT Grammar, Comparative and
      general—Adjective
      Grammar, Comparative and
      general—Noun
      Grammar, Comparative and
      general—Numerals
      Grammar, Comparative and
      general—Pronoun
  — Non-count nouns

    USE Grammar, Comparative and
      general—Mass nouns
  — **Noun**
    UF Noun
    BT Grammar, Comparative and
      general—Nominals
    NT Grammar, Comparative and
      general—Collective nouns
      Grammar, Comparative and
      general—Mass nouns
  — **Noun phrase**
    UF Grammar, Comparative and
      general—Complex nominals
      Grammar, Comparative and
      general—Subject
      Noun phrase
      Subject (Grammar)
    RT Grammar, Comparative and
      general—Nominals
    SA *subdivision* Noun phrase *under*
      names of languages and groups
      of languages, e.g. English
      language—Noun phrase
  — **Number**
    UF Dual (Grammar)
      Number (Grammar)
      Plural (Grammar)
    NT Grammar, Comparative and
      general—Agreement
      Grammar, Comparative and
      general—Mass nouns
  — **Numerals**
    [P275]
    BT Grammar, Comparative and
      general—Nominals
  — **Particles**
    UF Particles (Grammar)
    NT Grammar, Comparative and
      general—Interjections
      Grammar, Comparative and
      general—Sentence particles
  — **Passive voice**
    UF Passive voice
      Voice, Passive
    BT Grammar, Comparative and
      general—Voice
    SA *subdivision* Passive voice *under*
      names of languages and groups
      of languages, e.g. English
      language—Passive voice
  — **Person**
    UF Grammar, Comparative and
      general—Pronoun—Person
      Grammar, Comparative and
      general—Verb—Person
      Person (Grammar)
    BT Grammar, Comparative and
      general—Pronoun
      Grammar, Comparative and
      general—Verb
    SA *subdivision* Person *under names of*
      languages and groups of
      languages, e.g. English language
      —Person
    NT Grammar, Comparative and
      general—Agreement
  — **Phonology**
    [P215-240]
    UF Phonology
    NT Autosegmental theory (Linguistics)
      Consonants
      Distinctive features (Linguistics)
      Gemination
      Grammar, Comparative and
      general—Compensatory
      lengthening
      H (The sound)
      Juncture (Linguistics)
      Labiality (Phonetics)
      Mutation (Phonetics)
      Nasality (Phonetics)

Neutralization (Linguistics)
Phonemics
Prosodic analysis (Linguistics)
Tone (Phonetics)
Vowels
— **Phonology, Comparative**
UF Comparative phonology
Contrastive phonetics
Contrastive phonology
Grammar, Comparative and
general—Phonology, Contrastive
Phonetics, Contrastive
Phonology, Comparative
Phonology, Contrastive
BT Contrastive linguistics
SA *subdivision* Phonology,
Comparative *under individual
languages and groups of
languages, e.g.* English language
—Phonology, Comparative
— Phonology, Contrastive
USE Grammar, Comparative and
general—Phonology,
Comparative
— Phrasal verb
USE Grammar, Comparative and
general—Verb phrase
— Phrases
USE Phraseology
— Polite form
USE Grammar, Comparative and
general—Honorific
— Possessive adjective
USE Grammar, Comparative and
general—Possessives
— Possessive case
USE Grammar, Comparative and
general—Possessives
— Possessive pronoun
USE Grammar, Comparative and
general—Possessives
— **Possessives**
[P273 (Adjectives)]
[P279 (Pronouns)]
UF Grammar, Comparative and
general—Possessive adjective
Grammar, Comparative and
general—Possessive case
Grammar, Comparative and
general—Possessive pronoun
Possessives (Grammar)
BT Grammar, Comparative and
general—Adjective
Grammar, Comparative and
general—Case
Grammar, Comparative and
general—Pronoun
SA *subdivision* Possessives *under
names of languages and groups
of languages, e.g.* English
language—Possessives
— **Postpositions**
UF Postpositions
SA *subdivision* Postpositions *under
languages and groups of
languages, e.g.* English language
—Postpositions
— Predicate
USE Grammar, Comparative and
general—Verb phrase
— Prefixes
USE Grammar, Comparative and
general—Suffixes and prefixes
— **Prepositional phrases**
[P285]
UF Prepositional phrases
SA *subdivision* Prepositional phrases
*under names of languages and
groups of languages, e.g.* English
language—Prepositional phrases

NT Grammar, Comparative and
general—Prepositions
— **Prepositions**
[P285]
UF Prepositions
BT Grammar, Comparative and
general—Auxiliaries
Grammar, Comparative and
general—Prepositional phrases
— — Government
USE Government (Grammar)
— **Pronoun**
[P279]
BT Grammar, Comparative and
general—Nominals
RT Grammar, Comparative and
general—Reflexives
NT Grammar, Comparative and
general—Person
Grammar, Comparative and
general—Possessives
— — Person
USE Grammar, Comparative and
general—Person
— Protasis
USE Grammar, Comparative and
general—Conditionals
— Quantifiable nouns
USE Grammar, Comparative and
general—Mass nouns
— **Quantifiers**
UF Language and languages—
Quantifiers
Quantifiers (Linguistics)
SA *subdivision* Quantifiers *under
names of languages, e.g.* English
language—Quantifiers
— **Reduction**
[P299.R4]
UF Reduction (Linguistics)
— **Reduplication**
[P245]
UF Reduplication (in language)
BT Grammar, Comparative and
general—Inflection
— **Reflexives**
UF Reflexivity (Grammar)
Reflexivization (Grammar)
RT Grammar, Comparative and
general—Pronoun
Grammar, Comparative and
general—Verb
SA *subdivision* Reflexives *under
individual languages and groups
of languages, e.g.* English
language—Reflexives
— **Relative clauses**
UF Clauses, Relative
Relative clauses
BT Grammar, Comparative and
general—Clauses
SA *subdivision* Relative clauses *under
individual languages and groups
of languages, e.g.* English
language—Relative clauses
— Reported speech
USE Grammar, Comparative and
general—Indirect discourse
— Semantics
USE Semantics, Comparative
— Sentence connectors
USE Grammar, Comparative and
general—Connectives
— **Sentence particles**
BT Grammar, Comparative and
general—Particles
SA *subdivision* Sentence particles
*under names of languages and
groups of languages, e.g.*
Japanese language—Sentence
particles

— **Sentences**
UF Language and languages—
Sentences
Sentences (Grammar)
NT Grammar, Comparative and
general—Clauses
Grammar, Comparative and
general—Conditionals
Grammar, Comparative and
general—Existential
constructions
— Subject
USE Grammar, Comparative and
general—Noun phrase
— Subject and predicate
USE Grammar, Comparative and
general—Topic and comment
— **Subjectless constructions**
UF Grammar, Comparative and
general—Impersonal
constructions
Impersonal constructions
(Grammar)
Subjectless constructions
(Grammar)
BT Grammar, Comparative and
general—Syntax
SA *subdivision* Subjectless
constructions *under individual
languages and groups of
languages, e.g.* English language
—Subjectless constructions
— **Subjunctive**
UF Conjunctive mood
Grammar, Comparative and
general—Conjunctive mood
Subjunctive mood
BT Grammar, Comparative and
general—Mood
SA *subdivision* Subjunctive *under
languages and groups of
languages, e.g.* English language
—Subjunctive
— **Subordinate constructions**
[P294]
UF Subordination (Linguistics)
BT Grammar, Comparative and
general—Syntax
SA *subdivision* Subordinate
constructions *under names of
languages and groups of
languages, e.g.* English language
—Subordinate constructions
— **Substitution**
UF Substitution (Linguistics)
— **Suffixes and prefixes**
[P245]
UF Grammar, Comparative and
general—Prefixes
Prefixes
Suffixes and prefixes
BT Grammar, Comparative and
general—Affixes
SA *subdivision* Suffixes and prefixes
*under names of languages and
groups of languages, e.g.* English
language—Suffixes and prefixes
— **Suppletion**
[P241]
NT English language—Suppletion
— **Switch-reference**
UF Switch-reference (Grammar)
BT Reference (Linguistics)
SA *subdivision* Switch-reference *under
individual languages and groups
of languages, e.g.* English
language—Switch-reference
— **Syllable**
[P236]
UF Language and languages—Syllable
Syllable

Grammar, Comparative and general
(Continued)
— **Syntax**
  ₍P291-5₎
  UF Language and languages—Syntax
      Syntax
  NT Case grammar
      Causative (Linguistics)
      Dependency grammar
      Grammar, Comparative and
        general—Agreement
      Grammar, Comparative and
        general—Clauses
      Grammar, Comparative and
        general—Connectives
      Grammar, Comparative and
        general—Coordinate
        constructions
      Grammar, Comparative and
        general—Deletion
      Grammar, Comparative and
        general—Ellipsis
      Grammar, Comparative and
        general—Ergative constructions
      Grammar, Comparative and
        general—Exclamations
      Grammar, Comparative and
        general—Grammaticalization
      Grammar, Comparative and
        general—Subjectless
        constructions
      Grammar, Comparative and
        general—Subordinate
        constructions
      Grammar, Comparative and
        general—Temporal constructions
      Grammar, Comparative and
        general—Topic and comment
      Phraseology
— **Temporal clauses**
  UF Temporal clauses
  BT Grammar, Comparative and
        general—Clauses
      Grammar, Comparative and
        general—Temporal constructions
  SA *subdivision* Temporal clauses *under*
        names of languages, e.g. English
        language—Temporal clauses
— **Temporal constructions**
  ₍P294.5₎
  UF Temporal constructions (Grammar)
  BT Grammar, Comparative and
        general—Syntax
  SA *subdivision* Temporal constructions
        under names of languages and
        groups of languages, e.g. English
        language—Temporal
        constructions
  NT Grammar, Comparative and
        general—Aspect
      Grammar, Comparative and
        general—Temporal clauses
      Grammar, Comparative and
        general—Tense
— **Tense**
  UF Tense (Grammar)
  BT Grammar, Comparative and
        general—Temporal constructions
  NT Tense (Logic)
— **Theme and rheme**
  USE Grammar, Comparative and
        general—Topic and comment
— **Tone**
  USE Tone (Phonetics)
— **Topic and comment**
  ₍P291₎
      Here are entered works on the concept, close-
  ly related to that of the traditional notion of sub-
  ject and predicate, that most sentences consist of
  two basic elements, the subject that is announced
  and the statement that is made about it.

  UF Functional sentence perspective
        (Grammar)
      Grammar, Comparative and
        general—Subject and predicate
      Grammar, Comparative and
        general—Theme and rheme
      Predicate and subject (Grammar)
      Subject and predicate (Grammar)
      Theme and rheme
      Topic and comment (Grammar)
  BT Grammar, Comparative and
        general—Syntax
  SA *subdivision* Topic and comment
        under individual languages and
        groups of languages, e.g. English
        language—Topic and comment
— **Transitivity**
  UF Grammar, Comparative and
        general—Verb—Transitivity
      Transitivity (Grammar)
  BT Grammar, Comparative and
        general—Verb phrase
  SA *subdivision* Transitivity *under*
        names of languages and groups
        of languages, e.g. English
        language—Transitivity
— **Typology**
  USE Typology (Linguistics)
— **Unbounded nouns**
  USE Grammar, Comparative and
        general—Mass nouns
— **Uncountable nouns**
  USE Grammar, Comparative and
        general—Mass nouns
— **Verb**
  ₍P259₎
  ₍P281₎
  UF Verb
  BT Grammar, Comparative and
        general—Verb phrase
      Grammar, Comparative and
        general—Verbals
  RT Grammar, Comparative and
        general—Reflexives
  NT Grammar, Comparative and
        general—Aspect
      Grammar, Comparative and
        general—Imperative
      Grammar, Comparative and
        general—Mood
      Grammar, Comparative and
        general—Person
— — **Government**
  USE Government (Grammar)
— — **Person**
  USE Grammar, Comparative and
        general—Person
— — **Transitivity**
  USE Grammar, Comparative and
        general—Transitivity
— **Verb phrase**
  UF Grammar, Comparative and
        general—Phrasal verb
      Grammar, Comparative and
        general—Predicate
      Predicate (Grammar)
  RT Grammar, Comparative and
        general—Verbals
  SA *subdivision* Verb phrase *under*
        names of languages and groups
        of languages, e.g. English
        language—Verb phrase
  NT Grammar, Comparative and
        general—Complement
      Grammar, Comparative and
        general—Existential
        constructions
      Grammar, Comparative and
        general—Transitivity
      Grammar, Comparative and
        general—Verb

— **Verbal aspect**
  USE Grammar, Comparative and
        general—Aspect
— **Verbals**
  ₍P281₎
  UF Verbals (Grammar)
      Verbids (Grammar)
  RT Grammar, Comparative and
        general—Verb phrase
  NT Grammar, Comparative and
        general—Infinitive
      Grammar, Comparative and
        general—Verb
— **Voice**
  ₍P281₎
  UF Voice (Grammar)
  NT Grammar, Comparative and
        general—Passive voice
— **Vowel gradation**
      Here are entered works on the change of one
  vowel to another accompanying a change in the
  degree of stress. Works on expressions which de-
  scribe the relative amount of a quality in two or
  more objects, as in comparison, diminution, etc.
  are entered under the heading Grammar, Com-
  parative and general—Gradation.
  UF Ablaut
      Apophony
      Vowel gradation
  BT Vowels
  RT Grammar, Comparative and
        general—Gradation
  SA *subdivision* Vowel gradation *under*
        languages and groups of
        languages, e.g. English language
        —Vowel gradation
— **Vowel harmony**
  UF Vowel harmony
  BT Vowels
  NT Okpe language—Vowel harmony
— **Vowels**
  USE Vowels
— **Word formation**
  ₍P245₎
      Here are entered works on the formation of
  words in languages by the processes of derivation
  and compounding. Works on the study and anal-
  ysis of the structure, forms, and classes of words
  in languages, including inflection, derivation and
  compounding are entered under the heading
  Grammar, Comparative and general—Mor-
  phology.
  UF Derivational morphology
      Grammar, Comparative and
        general—Derivation
      Word formation
  BT Grammar, Comparative and
        general—Morphology
  NT Amalgams (Linguistics)
      Calques
      Grammar, Comparative and
        general—Compound words
      Portmanteau words
— **Word order**
  UF Language and languages—Word
        order
      Word order
  BT Order (Grammar)
  NT Languages, Modern—Word order
Grammar, Generative
  USE Generative grammar
Grammar, Philosophical
  USE Grammar, Comparative and general
Grammar, Phrase structure
  USE Phrase structure grammar
Grammar, Polyglot
  USE Language and languages—Grammars
Grammar, Relational
  USE Relational grammar
Grammar, Transformational
  USE Generative grammar

Grammar, Universal
 USE Grammar, Comparative and general
Grammar schools
 USE Public schools
Grammars, Graph
 USE Graph grammars
Grammatical categories
 USE Grammar, Comparative and general—
  Grammatical categories
Grammatical speech disorders
 USE Agrammatism
Grammaticality (Linguistics)
 ₁P299.G7₁
 UF Grammaticalness (Linguistics)
 BT Grammar, Comparative and general
  Linguistics
 RT Acceptability (Linguistics)
 NT Agrammatism
Grammaticalization
 USE Grammar, Comparative and general—
  Grammaticalization
Grammaticalness (Linguistics)
 USE Grammaticality (Linguistics)
Gramme (Unit)
 USE Gram (Unit)
Gramme dynamos
 ₁TK2441₁
 BT Electric generators
Grammemes
 USE Tagmemics
Grammicolepidae
 ₁QL638.G843₁
 UF Diamond dories
  Dories, Diamond
  Grammicolepididae
 BT Zeiformes
 NT Grammicolepis
Grammicolepididae
 USE Grammicolepidae
Grammicolepis
 ₁QL638.G843₁
 BT Grammicolepidae
Grammistidae
 ₁QL638.G848₁
 UF Rypticidae
  Soapfishes
 BT Perciformes
 NT Rypticus
Grammogale
 USE Mustela
Grammos-Vitsi, Battle of, 1949
 UF Vitsi-Grammos, Battle of, 1949
 BT Greece—History—Civil War, 1944-
  1949
Grammostola
 ₁QL458.42.T5₁
 BT Tarantulas
Grammy Awards
 BT Rewards (Prizes, etc.)—United States
  Sound recordings—Awards
Grammysiidae
 ₁QE812.G43₁
 BT Pholadomyoida, Fossil
 NT Ennirostra
Gramophone
 USE Phonograph
Grampian Hills (Scotland)
 USE Grampians (Scotland)
Grampian Mountains (Scotland)
 USE Grampians (Scotland)
Grampians (Scotland)
 UF Grampian Hills (Scotland)
  Grampian Mountains (Scotland)
 BT Mountains—Scotland
 NT Cairngorms (Scotland)
Grampus orca
 USE Killer whale
Grams family
 USE Gram family
Gram's stain
 UF Gram stain

 BT Stains and staining (Microscopy)
 NT Gram negative bacteria
Gran Lago de Maracaibo (Venezuela)
 USE Maracaibo Lake (Venezuela)
Gran Monticulo de la Culebra (Guatemala,
  Guatemala)
 USE Culebra, Gran Monticulo de la
  (Guatemala, Guatemala)
Gran Paradiso National Park (Italy)
 USE Parco nazionale del Gran Paradiso
  (Italy)
Gran River (Czechoslovakia)
 USE Hron River (Czechoslovakia)
Granada (Kingdom)
 — History
  ₁DP115-118₁
 — — Spanish Conquest, 1476-1492
   ₁DP121-123₁
 — Kings and rulers
  NT Zīrid dynasty
Granada automobile
 ₁TL215.G₁
 BT Ford automobile
Granada goat
 BT Goat breeds
Granada Site (Miami, Fla.)
 BT Florida—Antiquities
 RT Fort Dallas (Miami, Fla.)
Granaries *(May Subd Geog)*
 ₁NA8240₁
 ₁TH4461 (Construction)₁
 UF Grain bins
  Graineries
 BT Grain elevators
 — Aeration
  USE Grain aeration
 — Law and legislation *(May Subd Geog)*
 — China
  NT Han-chia Granary (Lo-yang shih,
   China)
Granary weevil *(May Subd Geog)*
 ₁QL596.C9 (Zoology)₁
 ₁SB945.G53 (Pest)₁
 UF Calandra granaria
  Grain weevils
  Sitophilus granarius
  Weevil, Granary
  Weevils, Grain
 BT Beetles
  Grain—Storage—Diseases and injuries
Grand Alliance, War of the, 1689-1697
 ₁D279-D280₁
 UF League of Augsburg, War of the, 1689-
  1697
  Nine Years' War, 1689-1697
  War of the Grand Alliance, 1689-1697
  War of the League of Augsburg, 1689-
  1697
 BT Europe—History—1648-1715
  France—History—Louis XIV, 1643-
  1715
 NT United States—History—King
  William's War, 1689-1697
 — Campaigns
 — — Belgium
  NT Fleurus, Battle of, 1690
 — — France
  NT Hogue, La, Battle of, 1692
Grand Am automobile
 ₁TL215.G₁
 BT Pontiac automobile
Grand Army of the Republic Cemetery
  (Homer, Ill.)
 USE G.A.R. Cemetery (Homer, Ill.)
Grand Army of the Republic Cemetery
  (Miami, Okla.)
 USE GAR Cemetery (Miami, Okla.)
Grand Bahama (Bahamas)
 UF Bahama Ile (Bahamas)
  Great Bahama Island (Bahamas)
 BT Islands—Bahamas

Grand Banks of Newfoundland
 BT Banks (Oceanography)—North
  Atlantic Ocean
Grand Beach Provincial Park (Man.)
 BT Parks—Manitoba
Grand Camée de France
 BT Cameos
Grand Canal (China)
 UF Yün Ho (China)
 BT Canals—China
Grand Canyon (Ariz.)
 BT Canyons—Arizona
 RT Grand Canyon National Park (Ariz.)
 NT Powell Plateau (Ariz.)
  Walhalla Plateau (Ariz.)
Grand Canyon National Park (Ariz.)
 BT National parks and reserves—United
  States
  Parks—Arizona
 RT Grand Canyon (Ariz.)
Grand Central Terminal (New York, N.Y.)
 BT Railroad terminals—New York (State)
Grand Coulee Dam (Wash.)
 (Not Subd Geog)
 BT Dams—Washington (State)
Grand Council, Italy, 1943
 USE Italy—History—Grand Council, 1943
Grand Detour Cemetery (Grand Detour, Ill.)
 BT Cemeteries—Illinois
Grand du Bonnet Falls Site (Man.)
 USE Sinnock Site (Man.)
Grand fir
 USE Abies grandis
Grand Gulf Nuclear Powerplant (Miss.)
 BT Nuclear power plants—Mississippi
Grand Island (N.Y. : Island)
 BT Islands—New York (State)
Grand Island (Ont.)
 USE Wolfe Island (Ont.)
Grand jury *(May Subd Geog)*
 BT Criminal procedure
  Jury
 RT Indictments
  Informations
Grand Liverpool Steeplechase
 USE Grand National Handicap Steeplechase
Grand Manitou Island (Ont.)
 USE Manitoulin Island (Ont.)
Grand Manitoulin Island (Ont.)
 USE Manitoulin Island (Ont.)
Grand Mesa National Forest (Colo.)
 BT Forest reserves—Colorado
  National parks and reserves—Colorado
Grand-Morin River (France)
 (Not Subd Geog)
 BT Rivers—France
Grand National Handicap Steeplechase
 ₁SF359.7.G7₁
 UF Grand Liverpool Steeplechase
  Grand National Steeplechase
  Liverpool and National Steeplechase
  National Steeplechase, Grand
 BT Steeplechasing—England
Grand National Steeplechase
 USE Grand National Handicap Steeplechase
Grand Old Army of the Republic Cemetery
  (Miami, Okla.)
 USE GAR Cemetery (Miami, Okla.)
Grand Prix, German
 USE German Grand Prix Race
Grand Prix automobile
 USE Pontiac Grand Prix automobile
Grand Prix Brno
 ₁GV1029₁
 BT Automobile racing
  Grand Prix racing
Grand Prix de Dressage
 BT Dressage tests
  Olympics
Grand Prix de Rome
 USE Prix de Rome

Grand Prix d'endurance, France
　USE　Le Mans Endurance Race, France
Grand Prix of Canada
　USE　Canadian Grand Prix Race
Grand Prix racing
　　[GV1029]
　　BT　Automobile racing
　　　　British Grand Prix Race
　　NT　Canadian Grand Prix Race
　　　　German Grand Prix Race
　　　　Grand Prix Brno
　　　　Italian Grand Prix Race
　　　　Monaco Grand Prix Race
　　　　Sebring Grand Prix Race
　　　　United States Grand Prix Race
　　　　Watkins Glen Grand Prix Race
Grand Prix racing in motion pictures
　　BT　Moving-pictures
Grand Rapids Project (Environment (Art))
　USE　Morris, Robert, 1931-　Grand
　　　　Rapids Project
Grand Remonstrance, 1641
　　[DA397]
　　BT　Great Britain—Politics and
　　　　government—1625-1649
Grand River (Kan. and Okla.)
　USE　Neosho River (Kan. and Okla.)
Grand River (Mich.)
　　BT　Rivers—Michigan
Grand River (Ont.)
　　BT　Rivers—Ontario
Grand River Canal (Ont.)
　　BT　Canals—Ontario
Grand River Ute Indians
　USE　Yampa Indians
Grand Temple (Abū Sunbul, Egypt)
　USE　Great Temple (Abū Sunbul, Egypt)
Grand Terre Island (La.)　(Not Subd Geog)
　　BT　Islands—Lousiana
Grand Teton Mountains (Wyo. and Idaho)
　USE　Teton Range (Wyo. and Idaho)
Grand Teton National Park (Wyo.)
　　BT　Mountains—Wyoming
　　　　National parks and reserves—United
　　　　　States
　　　　Parks—Wyoming
　　　　Teton Range (Wyo. and Idaho)
　　NT　Jackson Hole (Wyo.)
Grand Tetons (Wyo. and Idaho)
　USE　Teton Range (Wyo. and Idaho)
Grand Theatre (Swansea, West Glamorgan)
　　BT　Theaters—Wales
Grand Trianon (Versailles, France)
　　[DC801.V55-57]
　　UF　Trianon, Grand (Versailles, France)
　　BT　Palaces—France
Grand Trunk Canal (England)
　USE　Trent and Mersey Canal (England)
Grand unification theories (Nuclear physics)
　USE　Grand unified theories (Nuclear
　　　　physics)
Grand unified theories (Nuclear physics)
　　[QC794.6.G7]
　　UF　Grand unification theories (Nuclear
　　　　physics)
　　　　Unification of fundamental particle
　　　　　interactions (Nuclear physics)
　　　　Unified theories
　　BT　Gauge fields (Physics)
　　　　Nuclear reactions
　　　　Supergravity
　　　　Supersymmetry
　　　　Unified field theories
　　NT　Electroweak interactions
　　　　Protons—Decay
Grand Union Canal (England)
　　UF　Regents Canal (England)
　　BT　Canals—England
Grand Village of the Natchez Site (Miss.)
　USE　Fatherland Site (Miss.)

Grandadilla, Purple
　USE　Passion fruit
Grandchild and grandparent
　USE　Grandparent and child
Grandchildren of alcoholics
　　(May Subd Geog)
　　UF　Alcoholics' grandchildren
　　BT　Alcoholics
Granddaddy longlegs
　USE　Opiliones
Grande Chartreuse Mountains (France)
　USE　Chartreuse Mountains (France)
Grande Randonée Cinq (Trail)
　　UF　Europe-2 (Trail)
　　　　GR-5 (Trail)
　　　　Great Ramble-5 (Trail)
　　BT　Trails—Europe
Grande River (Alajuela, Costa Rica)
　　(Not Subd Geog)
　　UF　Río Grande (Alajuela, Costa Rica)
　　BT　Rivers—Costa Rica
Grande River (Guatemala)
　USE　Motagua River (Guatemala)
Grande River (Peru)
　　UF　Río Grande (Peru)
　　BT　Rivers—Peru
Grandee family
　USE　Grandy family
Grandeur, Delusions of
　USE　Megalomania
Grandfather clocks
　USE　Longcase clocks
Grandfathers
　　BT　Grandparents
Grandfather's clock
　USE　Longcase clocks
Grandglaize Creek (Mo.)
　　BT　Rivers—Missouri
Grandjeanicidae
　　[QL458.2.G]
Grandlienard family　(Not Subd Geog)
　　UF　Grandlinard family
Grandlinard family
　USE　Grandlienard family
Grandmothers　(May Subd Geog)
　　BT　Grandparents
Grandparent and child　(May Subd Geog)
　　[BF723.G68 (Psychology)]
　　UF　Child and grandparent
　　　　Children and grandparents
　　　　Grandchild and grandparent
　　　　Grandparent and grandchild
　　BT　Child psychology
　　　　Children and the aged
　　　　Family
　　　　Grandparents
　　　　Interpersonal relations
　　NT　Foster grandparents
Grandparent and grandchild
　USE　Grandparent and child
Grandparents　(May Subd Geog)
　　BT　Family
　　　　Fathers
　　　　Mothers
　　　　Parents
　　NT　Grandfathers
　　　　Grandmothers
　　　　Grandparent and child
Grandparents, Foster
　USE　Foster grandparents
Grands Causses (France)
　USE　Causses (France)
Grandsaigne, family of printers
　　(Not Subd Geog)
Grandstands　(May Subd Geog)
　　[TH4711]
　　BT　Stadia
Grandy family　(Not Subd Geog)
　　UF　Grandee family
　　　　Grandys family

Grandys family
　USE　Grandy family
Graneger family
　USE　Granger family
Grange (Wimbledon, Surrey)
　　UF　Grange Road (Wimbledon, Surrey)
　　BT　Streets—England
Grange
　USE　Patrons of Husbandry
Grange family
　USE　Granger family
Grange Road (Wimbledon, Surrey)
　USE　Grange (Wimbledon, Surrey)
Granger family　(Not Subd Geog)
　　UF　Grainger family
　　　　Graneger family
　　　　Grange family
　　　　Grenger family
Grangerism
　USE　Illustrated books—Extra-illustrated
Granicus, Battle of the, 334 B.C.
　　[DF234.35]
　　BT　Greece—History—Macedonian
　　　　　Expansion, 359-323 B.C.
　　　　Iran—History—Macedonian Conquest,
　　　　　334-325 B.C.
Granier family
　USE　Grenier family
Granite　(May Subd Geog)
　　[QE462.G7 (Petrology)]
　　[TN970 (Building stones)]
　　NT　Granite outcrops
　　　　Rapakivi
　—　Inclusions
　　　　[QE462.G7]
　　　　UF　Enclaves in granite
　　　　　　Inclusions in granite
Granite Building (Rochester, N.Y.)
　　BT　Office buildings—New York (State)
Granite cutters
　USE　Stone-cutters
Granite industry and trade
　　(May Subd Geog)
　　UF　Granite quarrying
　　BT　Stone industry and trade
Granite outcrops　(May Subd Geog)
　　BT　Granite
　　　　Outcrops (Geology)
Granite quarrying
　USE　Granite industry and trade
Granite Reef Aqueduct (Ariz.)
　　BT　Aqueducts—Arizona
Granite sculpture　(May Subd Geog)
　　BT　Sculpture
Granite sculpture, Romanesque
　　(May Subd Geog)
　　UF　Romanesque granite sculpture
Graniteware
　USE　Enameled ware
Granivores　(May Subd Geog)
　　UF　Granivorous animals
　　　　Seed-eating animals
　　　　Seedeaters
　　BT　Herbivores
Granivorous animals
　USE　Granivores
Granodiorite　(May Subd Geog)
　　[QE461]
　　BT　Rocks, Igneous
Granola cookery
　USE　Cookery (Granola)
Grant Center Cemetery (Iowa)
　　BT　Cemeteries—Iowa
Grant family　(Not Subd Geog)
　　UF　Grante family
　　　　Grants family
Grant-Kohrs Ranch National Historic Site
　　(Mont.)
　　BT　Historic sites—Montana
　　　　Ranches—Montana

Grant proposals, Peer review of
USE Peer review of research grant proposals
Grante family
USE Grant family
Grants
USE Grants-in-aid
Research grants
Subsidies
Grants, Block
USE Block grants
Grants, Land
USE Land grants
Grants, Research
USE Research grants
Grants family
USE Grant family
Grants-in-aid *(May Subd Geog)*
Here are entered works on grants of money made by a central to a local government.
UF Federal grants
Grants
BT Intergovernmental fiscal relations
RT Economic assistance, Domestic
Local finance
SA subdivision Finance *under particular subjects, e.g.* Roads—Finance
NT Block grants
Federal aid to alcoholism programs
Federal aid to biology
Federal aid to birth control
Federal aid to business research
Federal aid to child development
Federal aid to child health services
Federal aid to child welfare
Federal aid to community development
Federal aid to community health services
Federal aid to community mental health services
Federal aid to dance
Federal aid to drug abuse treatment programs
Federal aid to education
Federal aid to energy development
Federal aid to fire prevention
Federal aid to handicapped services
Federal aid to health facilities
Federal aid to health maintenance organizations
Federal aid to health planning
Federal aid to historic sites
Federal aid to hospitals
Federal aid to infant health services
Federal aid to law enforcement agencies
Federal aid to libraries
Federal aid to maternal health services
Federal aid to medical care research
Federal aid to medical education
Federal aid to medical research
Federal aid to minority business enterprises
Federal aid to museums
Federal aid to nursing education
Federal aid to nursing homes
Federal aid to outdoor recreation
Federal aid to public welfare
Federal aid to recreation
Federal aid to regional planning
Federal aid to research
Federal aid to rural health services
Federal aid to the arts
Federal aid to the motion picture industry
Federal aid to the performing arts
Federal aid to the printing industry
Federal aid to the theater
Federal aid to transportation

Federal aid to water quality management
Federal aid to water resources development
Federal aid to women-owned business enterprises
Federal aid to women's organizations
Federal aid to wood-lots
Federal aid to youth services
Research grants
State aid to education
State aid to hospitals
— **Accounting**
— — **Law and legislation**
(May Subd Geog)
— **Auditing**
— — **Law and legislation**
(May Subd Geog)
— **Law and legislation** *(May Subd Geog)*
Grants-in-aid, Colonial
UF Colonies—Grants-in-aid
BT Colonies—Finance
Grants-in-aid, International
USE Economic assistance
International relief
Grant's line (Game)
[GV1469.G3]
Granturco (The Italian word)
BT Italian language—Etymology
Gräntzdörffer family
USE Grenzdörfer family
Granular conjunctivitis
USE Trachoma
Granular leucocytes
USE Granulocytes
Granular lids
USE Trachoma
Granular materials
BT Bulk solids
Materials
NT Compacting
Glass beads
— **Permeability**
— **Plastic properties**
[TA418.78]
— **Sampling**
Granulation, Photospheric
USE Solar granulation
Granulation, Solar
USE Solar granulation
Granulation tissue
BT Wound healing
NT Cicatrices
Granulite *(May Subd Geog)*
UF Leptite
BT Rocks, Metamorphic
Granulocyte antigens
[QR186.6.G73]
BT Granulocytes
Tissue specific antigens
Granulocytes
UF Granular leucocytes
Leucocytes, Granular
BT Leucocytes
NT Basophil leucocytes
Eosinophiles
Granulocyte antigens
Neutrophils
Granulocytopenia
UF Granulopenia
NT Agranulocytosis
Granuloma
BT Inflammation
NT Chronic granulomatous disease
Eosinophilic granuloma
Granuloma, Dental
USE Granuloma, Periapical
Granuloma, Periapical
UF Dental granuloma
Granuloma, Dental
Periapical granuloma

BT Dental pulp—Diseases
Periapical diseases
Granuloma benignum
USE Sarcoidosis
Granuloma fungoides
USE Mycosis fungoides
Granuloma inguinale
USE Granuloma venereum
Granuloma venereum *(May Subd Geog)*
[RC203.G]
UF Donovanosis
Granuloma inguinale
Venereal granuloma
BT Bacterial diseases
Sexually transmitted diseases
Skin—Infections
Granulomatosis, Lipophagic intestinal
USE Whipple's disease
Granulomatous disease, Chronic
USE Chronic granulomatous disease
Granulopenia
USE Granulocytopenia
Gränzdörfer family
USE Grenzdörfer family
Gränzdörffer family
USE Grenzdörfer family
Graomys pearsoni
USE Andalgalomys pearsoni
Grape
USE Grapes
Grape berry moth
Grape culture
USE Viticulture
Grape cure
USE Grapes—Therapeutic use
Grape industry *(May Subd Geog)*
[HD9259.G68-7]
BT Grapes
Grape juice *(May Subd Geog)*
BT Fruit juices
Grape juice industry *(May Subd Geog)*
[HD9348.5.G]
Grape leaf-folder
[SB945.G58]
Grape leaf-hopper
[SB945.G6]
Grape-leaf skeletonizer
[SB945.G]
Grape pests
USE Grapes—Diseases and pests
Grape products *(May Subd Geog)*
NT Raisins
Wine and wine making
Grape-scale
[SB945.G]
Grape-vine aphis
[SB945.G]
Grape-vine root-worm
[SB608.G7]
Grapefruit *(May Subd Geog)*
[SB370.G7]
UF Grapefruit tree
Pomelo
BT Citrus fruits
NT Cookery (Grapefruit)
Grapefruit juice, Canned
BT Citrus juices
Fruit, Canned
Fruit juices
Grapefruit juice, Dried
BT Citrus juices
Fruit, Dried
Fruit juices
Grapefruit tree
USE Grapefruit
Grapes *(May Subd Geog)*
[HD9259.G68-HD9259.G7 (Trade)]
[QK495.V84 (Botany)]
[SB387-SB399 (Culture)]
UF Grape
Vitis

1571

Grapes *(Continued)*
　BT　Wine and wine making
　RT　Viticulture
　SA　*headings beginning with the word*
　　　Grape
　NT　Currant grapes
　　　Grape industry
　　　Muscadine grape
　— **Disease and pest resistance**
　　　(May Subd Geog)
　— **Diseases and pests**　*(May Subd Geog)*
　　　[SB608.G7]
　　UF　Grape pests
　　　　Raisins—Diseases and pests
　　BT　Black rot
　　SA　*names of diseases and pests, e.g.*
　　　　　Black rot, Grape leaf-hopper,
　　　　　Grape-scale, Phylloxera
　　NT　Janetiella oenophila
　　　　Sparganothis pilleriana
　— **Harvesting**
　— **Irrigation**
　— **Pruning**
　　UF　Grapes—Training
　　　　Grapevine pruning and training
　— **Therapeutic use**
　　UF　Grape cure
　— **Training**
　　　USE　Grapes—Pruning
　— **Varieties**
　— **Water requirements**
Grapes in art
Grapevine pruning and training
　USE　Grapes—Pruning
Graph grammars
　UF　Grammars, Graph
　BT　Formal languages
　　　Graph theory
Graph-PAD (Computer program)
　BT　Computer graphics—Computer
　　　　programs
Graph rewriting systems (Computer science)
　USE　Rewriting systems (Computer science)
Graph theorems, Closed
　USE　Closed graph theorems
Graph theory
　　　[QA166]
　UF　Graphs, Theory of
　　　Theory of graphs
　BT　Combinatorial analysis
　　　Topology
　NT　Bond graphs
　　　Closed graph theorems
　　　Complete graphs
　　　Directed graphs
　　　Four-color problem
　　　Graph grammars
　　　Hypergraphs
　　　Lattice paths
　　　Map-coloring problem
　　　Matroids
　　　Network analysis (Planning)
　　　Paths and cycles (Graph theory)
　　　Perfect graphs
　　　Petri nets
　　　Ramsey theory
　　　Random graphs
　　　Representations of graphs
　　　Trees (Graph theory)
　— **Data processing**
　　NT　G/PL/I (Computer program
　　　　　language)
Graphemic analysis
　USE　Graphemics
Graphemics
　　　[P211.5]
　UF　Graphemic analysis
　BT　Graphology
　　　Linguistics
　　　Writing
　NT　English language—Graphemics

Graphic algebra
　USE　Algebra—Graphic methods
Graphic arts　*(May Subd Geog)*
　UF　Art, Graphic
　　　Arts, Graphic
　　　Graphics
　BT　Art
　　　Visual communication
　NT　Calendar art
　　　Commercial art
　　　Drawing
　　　Engraving
　　　Lasers in the graphic arts
　　　Micrographics
　　　Nameplates of publications
　　　Painting
　　　Picture-books
　　　Printing
　　　Prints
　　　Scribing (Cartography)
　　　Television graphics
　— **Awards**
　　BT　Rewards (Prizes, etc.)
　— **Cataloging**
　　　USE　Cataloging of graphic materials
　— **Equipment and supplies**
　　NT　Graphic arts equipment industry
Graphic arts, English, [French, Lithuanian,
　etc.]　*(May Subd Geog)*
Graphic arts, Italian　*(May Subd Geog)*
　UF　Italian graphic arts
Graphic arts equipment industry
　(May Subd Geog)
　　　[HD9790]
　BT　Graphic arts—Equipment and supplies
Graphic camera
　BT　Graflex camera
Graphic communication
　USE　Visual communication
Graphic data processing
　USE　Computer graphics
Graphic differentiation
　USE　Numerical differentiation
Graphic materials, Cataloging of
　USE　Cataloging of graphic materials
Graphic methods
　　　[QA90]
　　　[QA277 (Discussion of observations)]
　UF　Graphics
　　　Graphs
　BT　Geometrical drawing
　　　Least squares
　　　Mathematics
　　　Mechanical drawing
　SA　*subdivision* Graphic methods *under*
　　　names of disciplines, types of
　　　technical processes, scientific
　　　phenomena, etc., for the technique
　　　of solving problems by means of
　　　graphs, e.g. Physics—Graphic
　　　methods
　NT　Decision logic tables
　　　Flow charts
　　　Flowgraphs
　　　Gantt charts
　　　Glyphs (Graphic methods)
　　　Graphic statics
　　　Line of balance (Management)
　　　Mathematics—Charts, diagrams, etc.
　　　Nomography (Mathematics)
　　　Organization charts
　　　Regge trajectories
　— **Computer programs**
　　NT　Plot Pak (Computer program)
Graphic Programming System
　USE　PAGE-1 (Electronic computer system)
Graphic statics
　　　[TG270]
　　　[TJ235 (Machinery)]

　BT　Bridge construction
　　　Graphic methods
　　　Statics
　　　Structures, Theory of
　RT　Girders
　　　Mechanical drawing
　　　Strains and stresses
　　　Strength of materials
　NT　Bridges
　　　Building, Iron and steel
　　　Girders, Continuous
　　　Influence lines
　　　Nomography (Mathematics)
　　　Roofs
Graphical evaluation and review technique
　USE　GERT (Network analysis)
Graphical Input Language
　USE　GRAIL (Electronic computer system)
Graphical interactive machine language
　(Computer program language)
　USE　GIML (Computer program language)
Graphical Remote Access Support System
　USE　GRASS (Electronic computer system)
Graphically Aided Mathematical Machine
　USE　GAMMA (Electronic computer
　　　　　system)
Graphics
　USE　Graphic arts
　　　Graphic methods
Graphics, Cataloging of
　USE　Cataloging of graphic materials
Graphics, Computer
　USE　Computer graphics
Graphics, Engineering
　USE　Engineering graphics
Graphics, Television
　USE　Television graphics
Graphidaceae
　BT　Graphidales
Graphidales
　　　[QK585.G (Botany)]
　BT　Ascolichens
　NT　Graphidaceae
Graphipterus
　　　[QL596.C2]
　BT　Carabidae
Graphite　*(May Subd Geog)*
　　　[TN845]
　　　[TP261.G7 (Artificial)]
　UF　Black-lead
　　　Plumbago
　BT　Carbon
　NT　Graphitization
Graphite fibers
　UF　Fibers, Graphite
　　　Fibrous graphite
　BT　Carbon fibers
　　　Inorganic fibers
　　　Refractory materials
Graphite fibers industry　*(May Subd Geog)*
Graphite industry　*(May Subd Geog)*
　　　[HD9559.G73]
Graphite miners　*(May Subd Geog)*
　BT　Miners
Graphitization
　　　[TN710 (Cast-iron)]
　　　[TN845 (Naturally occurring carbon)]
　　　[TP261.G7 (Chemical engineering)]
　BT　Graphite
Graphium ulmi
　USE　Ceratocystis ulmi
Graphognathus
　USE　White-fringed beetles
Grapholitha
　　　[QL561.T8]
　BT　Tortricidae
　NT　Cherry fruit worm
　　　Oriental fruit moth
Grapholitha molesta
　USE　Oriental fruit moth

Grapholitha packardi
  USE Cherry fruit worm
Grapholitha woeberiana
  ₍QL561.T8₎
  UF Cherry tree stem-borer
    Laspeyresia woeberiana
    Plum tree stem-borer
  BT Fruit—Diseases and pests
Grapholithidae
  USE Tortricidae
Graphologists *(May Subd Geog)*
  UF Handwriting analysts
  BT Graphology
Graphology
  ₍BF889-905₎
  UF Handwriting analysis
  BT Penmanship
    Writing
  RT Drawing, Psychology of
  SA *subdivision* Autographs *under names*
    of persons and groups of
    individuals, e.g. Composers—
    Autographs
  NT Astrology and graphology
    Graphemics
    Graphologists
Graphology and astrology
  USE Astrology and graphology
Graphophone
  USE Phonograph
Graphops
  ₍QL596.C5₎
  BT Chrysomelidae
Graphoscopic Scale, Pikunas
  USE Pikunas Graphoscopic Scale
Graphosomatidae
  USE Pentatomidae
Graphotyping
  ₍NE2280₎
  UF Chalk engraving
  BT Engraving
    Printing, Practical
Graphs
  USE Graphic methods
Graphs, Complete
  USE Complete graphs
Graphs, Directed
  USE Directed graphs
Graphs, Perfect
  USE Perfect graphs
Graphs, Random
  USE Random graphs
Graphs, Representations of
  USE Representations of graphs
Graphs, Theory of
  USE Graph theory
Grappa
  ₍TP599₎
  BT Brandy
Grapsidae
  ₍QL444.M33₎
  UF Burrowing land crabs
    Land crabs, Burrowing
  BT Decapoda (Crustacea)
Graptemys
  ₍QL666.C547₎
  BT Emydidae
Graptemys pulchra
  USE Alabama map turtle
Graptolites
  ₍QE840.5₎
  NT Dendroidea
    Graptoloidea
    Mastigograptus
Graptolithidae
  USE Noctuidae
Graptoloidea
  ₍QE840.5₎
  BT Graptolites
Grasia (Indic people)
  ₍DS432.G7₎

  UF Garasia (Indic people)
    Girasia (Indic people)
    Grassia (Indic people)
  BT Ethnology—India
    India—Scheduled tribes
  NT Bhils
GRASP System
  ₍RT89₎
  UF Grace-Reynolds Application and Study
    of PETO
  BT Hospitals—Administration
    Nursing services—Administration
Grass, Cotton
  USE Eriophorum
Grass, Reed
  USE Phragmites australis
GRASS (Electronic computer system)
  UF Graphical Remote Access Support
    System
  BT Computer graphics
    On-line data processing
Grass-burner
  USE Mennonite grass-burner
Grass carp
  USE Ctenopharyngodon idella
Grass finches
  UF Finches, Grass
    Poephilinae
    Spermestidae
  BT Waxbills
Grass fires
  USE Grassland fires
Grass huts *(May Subd Geog)*
  UF Straw huts
  BT Huts
Grass parakeet
  USE Budgerigars
Grass pickerel
  ₍QL638.E7₎
  UF Esox americanus vermiculatus
    Esox vermiculatus
  BT Pickerel
Grass research
  USE Grasses—Research
Grass River (Man. : River)
  BT Rivers—Manitoba
Grass seed
  USE Grasses—Seed
Grass seed industry *(May Subd Geog)*
  ₍HD9019.S43-432₎
  BT Grasses—Seed
Grass skiing
  USE Skiing, Grass
Grass snake, European
  USE Natrix natrix
Grass spiders
  USE Agelenidae
Grass staggers
  USE Grass tetany
Grass tetany
  ₍SF967.G7₎
  UF Grass staggers
    Hypomagnesemia
    Staggers, Grass
    Tetany, Grass
  BT Deficiency diseases in domestic
    animals
    Magnesium—Metabolism
    Ruminants—Diseases
**Grass Valley (Lander County and Eureka
County, Nev.)**
  BT Valleys—Nevada
Grass voles
  USE Microtus
Grass waterways
  USE Grassed waterways
Grass weaving
  BT Grasswork
    Hand weaving
Grass work
  USE Grasswork

Grass writing
  USE Chinese language—Writing, Cursive
Grassed channels
  USE Grassed waterways
Grassed waterways
  UF Grass waterways
    Grassed channels
    Vegetated channels
    Vegetated waterways
    Waterways, Grassed
    Waterways, Vegetated
  BT Ditches
    Drainage
    Grasses
    Soil-binding
    Soil conservation
Grasseichthyidae
  USE Kneriidae
Grasses *(May Subd Geog)*
  ₍QK495.G74 (Botany)₎
  ₍SB197-SB201 (Culture)₎
  UF Agrostology
    Graminaceae
    Gramineae
    Herbage
    Poaceae
  BT Botany, Economic
    Lawns
    Range plants
  RT Forage plants
    Hay
    Meadows
    Pastures
    Prairie flora
  SA *particular grasses, e.g.* Esparto, Quitch-
    grass; *and headings beginning with*
    the word Grass
  NT Apera
    Bamboo
    Bambusa
    Bromegrasses
    Ehrharta
    Fescue
    Grassed waterways
    Grasslands
    Grazing
    Hordeum
    Oats
    Ornamental grasses
    Oryza
    Otachyrium
    Panicum
    Paspalum
    Pennisetum
    Phragmites
    Saccharum
    Soil-binding
    Stipa
    Taeniatherum
    Turfgrasses
    Wheat
    Zizania
  — Diseases and pests *(May Subd Geog)*
    ₍SB608.G8₎
    NT Asiatic beetle
      Claviceps
      Gaeumannomyces graminis
      Maize rough dwarf virus disease
      Puccinia graminis
      Puccinia rubigo-vera
      Puccinia tomipara
      Rhodes grass scale
      Sclerospora
      Snow mold
      Stripe rust
      Take-all disease
      Wheat streak mosaic disease
  — Drying
    USE Hay—Drying
  — **Harvesting**
  — **Research** *(May Subd Geog)*

1573

Grasses
  — **Research** *(Continued)*
    UF Grass research
  — **Seed**
    UF Grass seed
    NT Grass seed industry
  — Tariff
    USE Tariff on grass seed
  — **Varieties**
Grasses, Fossil
  BT Paleobotany
Grasses, Sea
  USE Seagrasses
Grassfield languages
  USE Bamileke languages
Grasshopper mice
  USE Onychomys
Grasshopper mouse
  [QL737.R638]
  UF Onychomys leucogaster
Grasshopper Pueblo (Ariz.)
  (Not Subd Geog)
  UF Grasshopper Ruin (Ariz.)
  BT Arizona—Antiquities
    Pueblos—Arizona
Grasshopper Ruin (Ariz.)
  USE Grasshopper Pueblo (Ariz.)
Grasshoppers
  USE Locusts
Grasshoppers, Shorthorned
  USE Acrididae
Grassia (Indic people)
  USE Grasia (Indic people)
Grassland ecology *(May Subd Geog)*
  [QH541.5.P7]
  BT Ecology
  NT Veld flora
Grassland farming
  USE Meadows
    Pastures
Grassland fauna *(May Subd Geog)*
  [QL115]
  BT Zoology
Grassland fires *(May Subd Geog)*
  UF Grass fires
  BT Ground cover fires
  NT Fire ecology
    Prescribed burning
  — **Prevention and control**
    BT Fire extinction
    Fire prevention
Grasslands *(May Subd Geog)*
  [QH541.5.P7]
  [QK938.P7]
  Here are entered works on the natural regions of
  the world in which the characteristic plants are
  grasses and forbs. Works on the management and
  farming of natural or cultivated grassland areas are
  entered under Meadows, Pastures, Rangelands, and
  Range management.
  BT Grasses
  NT Llanos
    Prairies
    Rangelands
    Savannas
    Steppes
  — **Africa, Southern**
    NT Veld
  — **Argentina**
    NT Pampas (Argentina)
  — **Colorado**
    NT Comanche National Grassland
      (Colo.)
      Pawnee National Grassland (Colo.)
  — **Idaho**
    NT Curlew National Grassland (Idaho)
  — **New Mexico**
    NT Kiowa National Grassland (N.M.)
  — **Oklahoma**
    NT Black Kettle National Grassland
      (Okla. and Tex.)

Rita Blanca National Grassland
  (Okla. and Tex.)
  — **Saskatchewan**
    NT Grasslands National Park (Sask.)
  — **Texas**
    NT Black Kettle National Grassland
      (Okla. and Tex.)
      McClellan Creek National
      Grassland (Tex.)
      Rita Blanca National Grassland
      (Okla. and Tex.)
  — Tropics
    USE Savannas
Grasslands Bantu languages
  [PL8219]
  UF Bantu languages, Grasslands
    Grasslands languages
    Plateau Bantoid languages
  BT Benue-Congo languages
    Cameroon—Languages
  NT Limbum language
    Yamba language (Cameroon and
    Nigeria)
Grasslands languages
  USE Grasslands Bantu languages
Grasslands National Park (Sask.)
  BT Grasslands—Saskatchewan
    National parks and reserves—Canada
    Parks—Saskatchewan
Grassmann manifolds
  UF Grassmannians
    Manifolds, Grassmann
  BT Differential topology
    Manifolds (Mathematics)
Grassmannians
  USE Grassmann manifolds
Grassmann's theory of extension
  USE Ausdehnungslehre
Grassnut
  USE Triteleia laxa
Grasswork
  [TT876.3]
  UF Grass work
  BT Fiberwork
    Nature craft
  NT Bamboo work
    Grass weaving
Grassworm
  USE Fall army-worms
Grassy bog
  USE Muskeg
Grassy Narrows Indian Reservation (Ont.)
  BT Chippewa Indians—Reservations
    Indians of North America—Ontario—
    Reservations
Grastie family
  USE Grasty family
Grasty family *(Not Subd Geog)*
  UF Graiste family
    Graisty family
    Grastie family
    Greesty family
    Greste family
    Grestie family
    Gresty family
    Greysty family
    Griesty family
Gratefulness
  USE Gratitude
Gräter family
  USE Crider family
Graters, Nutmeg
  USE Nutmeg graters
Grates
  USE Fireplaces
    Furnaces
Grates, Culvert
  USE Culverts—Grates
Gratings
  USE Grilles

Gratings, Diffraction
  USE Diffraction gratings
Gratitude
  [BJ1533.G8 (Ethics)]
  [BV4647.G8 (Theology)]
  UF Gratefulness
    Thankfulness
  BT Conduct of life
  — **Religious aspects**
  — — **Buddhism,** [**Christianity, etc.**]
Gratuitous contracts
  USE Contracts, Gratuitous
Gratz family *(Not Subd Geog)*
  UF Graetz family
    Gratzer family
    Gretz family
    Gretzer family
Gratzer family
  USE Gratz family
Grauch family *(Not Subd Geog)*
Graucob family *(Not Subd Geog)*
Graufesenque Site (Millau, France)
  (Not Subd Geog)
  UF La Graufesenque Site (Millau, France)
  BT France—Antiquities
Grauvieh
  USE Grey Tirolean cattle
Grauwacke
  USE Graywacke
Grave family
  USE Graves family
Grave-posts
  USE Graveposts
Gravel *(May Subd Geog)*
  [TN939]
  BT Aggregates (Building materials)
Gravel (Pathology)
  USE Calculi, Urinary
Gravel family *(Not Subd Geog)*
  UF Gravell family
    Gravelle family
Gravel industry
  USE Sand and gravel industry
Gravel plants
  USE Sand and gravel plants
Gravel roads
  USE Roads, Gravel
Gravelin family
  USE Graveline family
Graveline family *(Not Subd Geog)*
  UF Gravelin family
Gravelines, Battle of, 1558
  BT France—History—Henry II, 1547-
    1559
    Spain—History—Philip II, 1556-1598
Gravell family
  USE Gravel family
Gravelle family
  USE Gravel family
Gravelotte, Battle of, 1870
  [DC303.4]
  UF Rezonville, Battle of, Aug. 18, 1870
    St. Privat, Battle of, 1870
  BT Franco-German War, 1870-1871
Graveposts *(May Subd Geog)*
  UF Grave-posts
  BT Sepulchral monuments
Graves (France : Region)
Graves
  USE Burial
    Cemeteries
    Epitaphs
    Funeral rites and ceremonies
    Mounds
    Sepulchral monuments
    Tombs
Graves, Military
  USE Soldiers' bodies, Disposition of
Graves' disease *(May Subd Geog)*
  [RC657.5.G7]

UF Basedow's disease
        Exophthalmic goiter
        Goiter, Exophthalmic
    BT Autoimmune diseases
        Goiter
        Hyperthyroidism
    RT Thyroid eye disease
Graves family *(Not Subd Geog)*
    UF Grave family
        Greaves family
    RT Grayson family
        Grieve family
Gravestones
    USE Sepulchral monuments
Gravette points
    BT Gravettian culture
        Man, Prehistoric
Gravettian culture *(May Subd Geog)*
    BT Europe—Antiquities
        Paleolithic period—Europe
        Perigordian culture
    NT Gravette points
Gravetye Gardens (West Sussex)
    USE Gravetye Manor Gardens (West
        Sussex)
Gravetye Manor (West Sussex)
    BT Manors—England
Gravetye Manor Gardens (West Sussex)
    UF Gravetye Gardens (West Sussex)
    BT Gardens—England
Graveyards
    USE Cemeteries
Gravid uterus
    USE Uterus, Pregnant
Gravida
    USE Pregnant women
GRAVIK (Computer program)
    BT Gravity—Measurement—Computer
        programs
Gravimeter (Geophysical instrument)
    ₍QB331₎
    UF Gravity balance
        Gravity meter
    BT Geodesy
        Geophysics
        Gravity
        Gravity—Measurement
    — Calibration
Gravimetric analysis
    USE Chemistry, Analytic—Quantitative
Graving-docks
    USE Dry-docks
Graviscae (Ancient city)
    ₍DG70.G73₎
    BT Cities and towns, Ruined, extinct, etc.
        —Italy
        Italy—Antiquities
Gravitation
    ₍QB341 (Constant of)₎
    ₍QC178 (Theories of)₎
    Here are entered theoretical works on the phe-
nomenon of gravitation, i.e. the attraction between
masses anywhere in the universe, and on determinations of the constant of gravitation. Works relating to
measurement of the resultant effect of the gravitational attraction and centrifugal repulsion between
any body and a planet or other celestial body, including works on earth's gravity are entered under the
heading Gravity.
    BT Field theory (Physics)
        Matter—Properties
        Physics
    RT Antigravity
        Centrifugal force
        Relativity (Physics)
    SA *subdivision Gravity under names of
        bodies, e.g.* Moon—Gravity
    NT Earth—Density
        Ether (of space)
        General relativity (Physics)
        Gravitational fields
        Gravitational potential

        Gravitational radiation
        Lagrangian points
        Mass (Physics)
        Matter
        Potential, Theory of
        Quantum gravity
        Reduced gravity environments
        Virial theorem
        Weightlessness
Gravitational collapse
    UF Collapse, Gravitational
    BT Stars
    NT Black holes (Astronomy)
        White holes (Astronomy)
Gravitational convection
    USE Density currents
Gravitational field of the moon
    USE Moon—Gravity
Gravitational fields
    ₍QC178₎
    UF Fields, Gravitational
    BT Field theory (Physics)
        Gravitation
        Gravity
    NT Einstein field equations
Gravitational lenses
    BT Lenses
Gravitational mass
    USE Mass (Physics)
Gravitational potential
    BT Gravitation
        Potential, Theory of
Gravitational radiation
    BT General relativity (Physics)
        Gravitation
        Radiation
Gravity *(May Subd Geog)*
    ₍QB331-9₎
    Here are entered works relating to measurement
of the resultant effect of the gravitational attraction
and centrifugal repulsion between any body and a
planet or other celestial body, including works on
earth's gravity. Theoretical works on the phenomenon of gravitation, i.e. the attraction between masses
anywhere in the universe, and on determinations of
the constant of gravitation are entered under the
heading Gravitation.
    UF Earth—Gravity
    BT Geodesy
        Specific gravity
        Weights and measures
    RT Pendulum
    SA *subdivision Gravity under names of
        bodies, e.g.* Moon—Gravity
    NT Earth—Figure
        Gravimeter (Geophysical instrument)
        Gravitational fields
        Gravity anomalies
        Gravity stations
        Gravity waves
        Weight (Physics)
    — Measurement
        NT Gravimeter (Geophysical
            instrument)
    — — Computer programs
            NT ARKhIV (Computer program)
                GRAVIK (Computer program)
                MAGELLAN (Computer
                programs)
    — Physiological effect
        ₍QH657₎
        ₍QP82₎
        NT Weightlessness
Gravity, Center of
    USE Center of mass
Gravity, Local disturbance of
    USE Gravity anomalies
Gravity, Quantum
    USE Quantum gravity
Gravity, Specific
    USE Specific gravity

Gravity anomalies *(May Subd Geog)*
    ₍QB331₎
    UF Anomalies, Gravity
        Bouguer anomalies
        Gravity, Local disturbance of
        Isostatic anomalies
    BT Gravity
        Plumb-line deflections
        Prospecting—Geophysical methods
Gravity balance
    USE Gravimeter (Geophysical instrument)
Gravity concentrators
    ₍TN520₎
    UF Concentrators, Gravity
    BT Coal preparation plants
        Ore-dressing
        Separators (Machines)
Gravity dams *(May Subd Geog)*
    ₍TC547₎
    UF Dams, Gravity
    BT Concrete dams
Gravity-free state, Physiological effect of
    USE Weightlessness
Gravity gradient booms
    UF Booms, Gravity gradient
    BT Artificial satellites—Attitude control
        systems
        Space vehicles—Attitude control
        systems
Gravity meter
    USE Gravimeter (Geophysical instrument)
Gravity prospecting *(May Subd Geog)*
    ₍TN269₎
    BT Prospecting—Geophysical methods
Gravity railroads
    USE Railroads, Gravity
Gravity stations *(May Subd Geog)*
    UF Stations, Gravity
    BT Geophysical observatories
        Gravity
Gravity switching yards
    USE Railroads—Hump yards
Gravity waves
    ₍QA927 (Mathematics)₎
    UF Waves, Gravity
    BT Gravity
        Hydrodynamics
        Waves
Gravure printing
    USE Intaglio printing
Grawi language
    USE Shauri language
Gray
    UF Grey
Gray bat
    USE Myotis grisescens
Gray birch
    USE Yellow birch
Gray-cheeked parakeet
    ₍QL696.P7 (Ornithology)₎
    ₍SF473.G74 (Cage-bird)₎
    UF Brotogeris pyrrhopteris
        Grey-cheeked parakeet
        Orange-flanked parakeet
        Orange-winged parakeet
        Parakeet, Gray-cheeked
        Parakeet, Orange-flanked
        Parakeet, Orange-winged
    BT Brotogeris
Gray-cheeked thrush, Bicknell's
    USE Bicknell's thrush
Gray duiker
    USE Sylvicapra grimmia
Gray family *(Not Subd Geog)*
    UF Graye family
        Grey family
        Greye family
    RT Grayson family
Gray fox
    BT Foxes

Gray Friars
  USE Franciscans
Gray gull
  rQL696.C46ı
  UF Larus modestus
Gray hair _(May Subd Geog)_
  UF Silver hair
    White hair
  BT Hair
Gray-headed dove
  rQL696.C63ı
  UF Leptotila plumbeiceps
  BT Leptotila
Gray heron
  rQL696.C52ı
  UF Ardea cinerea
    Grey heron
  BT Herons
Gray in art
  NT Grisaille painting
Gray market
  USE Black market
Gray mold of strawberries
  USE Strawberry gray mold
Gray moorhen
  USE Gallinula chloropus
Gray mullets
  rQL638.M8ı
  UF Grey mullets
    Mugilidae
    Mullets, Gray
  NT Agonostomus
    Mugil
    Mullet fisheries
Gray parrot, African
  USE African gray parrot
Gray partridge
  USE Perdix perdix
Gray peppermint eucalyptus
  USE Eucalyptus radiata
Gray pike
  USE Walleye (Fish)
Gray pine
  USE Jack-pine
    Pinus sabiniana
Gray power
  USE Senior power
Gray reef shark
  USE Carcharhinus menisorrah
Gray sea eagle
  USE White-tailed sea eagle
Gray snapper
  rQL638.L9ı
  UF Lutjanus griseus
    Snapper, Gray
Gray squeteague
  USE Cynoscion regalis
Gray squirrel
  UF Eastern grey squirrel
    Sciurus carolinensis
  BT Squirrels
  — Control _(May Subd Geog)_
    rSB994.Sı
Gray whale
  USE Pacific gray whale
Gray white eye
  USE Zosterops borbonica
Gray widow spider
  USE Latrodectus geometricus
Graybil family
  USE Graybill family

Graybill family _(Not Subd Geog)_
  UF Grabel family
    Grabell family
    Grabil family
    Grabill family
    Grabl family
    Grable family
    Graybil family
    Grebiel family
    Greybill family
    Kraybill family
  RT Crabill family
    Krehbiel family
Graydon family _(Not Subd Geog)_
Graye family
  USE Gray family
Grayfish
  NT Cookery (Grayfish)
Graygreen blenny
  USE Malacoctenus erdmani
Grayling
  rQL638.S2ı
  rSH167.G8 (Culture)ı
  UF Grayling, European
Grayling, Arctic
  USE Arctic grayling
Grayling, European
  USE Grayling
Grayling, Michigan
  USE Arctic grayling
Grayling, Montana
  USE Arctic grayling
Grayling fishing
  rSH691.Gı
  BT Fishing
Grays Harbor (Wash.)
  BT Harbors—Washington (State)
    Inlets—Washington (State)
Gray's monitor lizard
  rQL666.L29ı
  UF Butaan
    Varanus grayi
    Varanus olivaceous
  BT Varanus
Graysby
  rQL638.S48ı
  UF Cephalopholis cruentatus
    Epinephelus cruentatus
    Petrometopon cruentatus
Grayson family _(Not Subd Geog)_
  RT Graves family
    Gray family
Graystoke Plateau (B.C.)
  BT Plateaus—British Columbia
Graywacke _(May Subd Geog)_
  UF Grauwacke
    Greywacke
  BT Sandstone
Graz-Köflacher Bahn
  BT Railroads—Austria
Graz Künstlerhaus (Graz, Austria)
  USE Künstlerhaus (Graz, Austria)
Grazier family _(Not Subd Geog)_
Grazing _(May Subd Geog)_
  rHD241 (Public lands)ı
  rSD427.G8 (Forests)ı
  BT Agricultural systems
    Cattle
    Grasses
    Range management
  RT Pastures
    Rangelands
  NT Forage plants
    Grazing districts
Grazing districts _(May Subd Geog)_
  BT Grazing
    Pastures
    Public lands
    Rangelands
    Special districts

Grazing incidence
  rQC437ı
  UF Incidence, Grazing
  BT Optics
Grazing rights
  USE Pasture, Right of
Gréal
  USE Grail
Grear family
  USE Greer family
Grease
  USE Lubrication and lubricants
    Oils and fats
Greason family
  USE Creason family
Greasy cutworm
  USE Black cutworm
Great, The (Epithet)
  BT Epithets
Great Alföld
  UF Alföld, Great
    Great Hungarian Plain
    Hungarian Plain
    Nagy Alföld
    Nagy Magyar Alföld
  BT Plains—Hungary
    Plains—Romania
    Plains—Yugoslavia
Great anteater
  USE Myrmecophaga
Great apes
  USE Apes
Great arteries, Transposition of
  USE Transposition of great vessels
Great auk
  rQL696.A3ı
  UF Gairfowl
    Garefowl
    Garfowl
Great Awakening
  rBR520ı
  Here are entered works dealing with the revival of
religion that occurred in the American colonies in the
18th century.
  UF Awakening, Great
  BT Religious awakening—Christianity
    United States—Church history—
      Colonial period, ca. 1600-1775
  RT Evangelical Revival
Great Bahama Island (Bahamas)
  USE Grand Bahama (Bahamas)
Great barbet
  USE Megalaima virens
Great barracuda
  rQL638.S77ı
  UF Sphyraena barracuda
  BT Barracudas
Great Barrier Reef (Qld.)
  BT Coral reefs and islands—Australia
  NT Dunk Island (Qld.)
    One Tree Island (Qld.)
Great Basin
  UF Basin and Range Province
    Intermontane region
  BT United States
Great Basin kangaroo rat
  USE Dipodomys microps
Great Basin tent caterpillar
  UF Malacosoma fragile
Great Bath (Corinth, Greece)
  USE Roman Bath (Corinth, Greece)
Great Bear
  USE Ursa Major
Great Bear Lake (N.W.T.)
  BT Lakes—Northwest Territories
Great Belt (Denmark)
  USE Store Bælt (Denmark)
Great Bermuda (Bermuda Islands)
  USE Bermuda Island (Bermuda Islands)
Great bittern
  USE European bittern

Great Blood Purge, 1934
  USE Germany—History—Great Blood
      Purge, 1934
Great blue heron
  UF Ardea herodias
  BT Herons
Great blue shark
  USE Blue shark
Great books program
  USE Group reading
Great Brak River (South Africa)
  (Not Subd Geog)
  UF Groot-Brakrivier (South Africa)
      Grootbrakrivier (South Africa)
  BT Rivers—South Africa
Great Britain
      Here are entered works on the United Kingdom of
  Great Britain and Northern Ireland, which comprises
  England, Northern Ireland, Scotland, and Wales, as
  well as works on the island of Great Britain. Works
  on the Republic of Ireland and on the island of the
  British Isles called Ireland are entered under Ireland.
  Works on the non-jurisdictional island group com-
  prising the islands of Great Britain, Ireland, and
  smaller adjacent islands are entered under British
  Isles.
  NT Commonwealth of Nations
  — **Antiquities**
      NT Sutton Hoo Ship Burial (England)
  — **Antiquities, Roman**
  — **Biography**
  — **Church history**
  — — **To 449**
  — — **Anglo Saxon period, 449-1066**
      (Not Subd Geog)
  — — **Medieval period, 1066-1485**
  — — **Modern period, 1485-**
  — — **16th century**
  — — **17th century**
  — — **18th century**
  — — **19th century**
  — — **20th century**
  — **Civilization**
      NT Architecture—India—New Delhi—
          British influences
      Armenian literature—British
          influences
      Art, German—British influences
      French fiction—British influences
      Indic fiction (English)—British
          influences
      Landscape painting, American—
          British influences
      Painting, Indic—British influences
      South Africa—Civilization—British
          influences
  — — **To 1066**
      NT Civilization, Anglo-Saxon
  — — **Medieval period, 1066-1485**
  — — **16th century**
  — — **17th century**
  — — **18th century**
  — — **19th century**
  — — **20th century**
  — — **1945-**
  — — **American influences**
      BT United States—Civilization
  — — **Greek influences**
      BT Greece—Civilization
  — — **Hindu influences**
      [DA115]
      BT Civilization, Hindu
  — — **Mediterranean influences**
      (Not Subd Geog)
      BT Mediterranean Region—
          Civilization
  — — **Roman influences**
      BT Rome—Civilization
  — **Coast defenses**
  — **Colonies**
      NT Imperial federation
  — — **Administration**

  UF Great Britain—Colonies—
      Politics and government
  — — **Boundaries** *(May Subd Geog)*
  — — **Commerce** *(May Subd Geog)*
  — — **Constitutional history**
  — — **Constitutional law**
  — — **Defenses**
  — — **Description and travel**
  — — **Discovery and exploration**
  — — **Economic conditions**
  — — **Economic policy**
  — — **Emigration and immigration**
  — — **Government publications**
  — — **History**
  — — **Industries**
  — — **Manufactures**
  — — **Native races**
  — — **Officials and employees**
  — — Politics and government
      USE Great Britain—Colonies—
          Administration
  — — **Population**
  — — **Public lands**
  — — **Public works**
  — — **Race relations**
  — — **Religion**
  — — **Religious life and customs**
  — — **Rural conditions**
  — — **Social conditions**
  — — **Social life and customs**
  — — **Social policy**
  — — **Africa**
  — — **America**
      UF Great Britain—Colonies—North
          America
      RT United States—History—
          Colonial period, ca. 1600-
          1775
  — — **Asia**
  — — North America
      USE Great Britain—Colonies—
          America
  — — **Oceania**
  — **Commercial treaties**
  — **Constitutional history**
  — **Description and travel**
  — — **To 1600**
  — — **1601-1700**
  — — **1701-1800**
  — — **1801-1900**
  — — **1901-1945**
  — — **1946-1970**
  — — **1971-**
  — **Diplomatic and consular service**
      (May Subd Geog)
  — — **Buildings** *(Not Subd Geog)*
      NT Foreign Office (London,
          England : Building)
  — **Economic conditions**
  — — **17th century**
  — — **18th century**
      [HC254.5]
  — — **1760-1860**
  — — **19th century**
  — — **20th century**
  — — **1918-1945**
  — — **1945-**
  — **Economic policy**
  — — **1918-1945**
  — — **1945-**
  — Foreign population
      USE Aliens—Great Britain
          Immigrants—Great Britain
  — — Housing
      USE Aliens—Great Britain—
          Housing
          Immigrants—Great Britain—
          Housing
  — **Foreign relations**
  — — **1066-1485**
  — — **1154-1399**

  — — **1422-1461**
  — — **1485-1603**
  — — **16th century**
  — — **1509-1547**
  — — **1558-1603**
  — — **1603-1625**
  — — **1603-1688**
  — — **1625-1649**
  — — **1649-1660**
  — — **1660-1688**
  — — **1660-1714**
  — — **1689-1702**
  — — **1689-1714**
  — — **18th century**
  — — **1702-1714**
  — — **1714-1727**
  — — **1714-1837**
  — — **1727-1760**
  — — **1760-1789**
  — — **1760-1820**
  — — **1789-1820**
  — — **1800-1837**
  — — **19th century**
  — — **1820-1830**
  — — **1837-1901**
  — — **20th century**
  — — **1901-1910**
  — — **1901-1936**
  — — **1910-1936**
  — — **1936-1945**
  — — **1945-**
  — **Gentry**
      UF Squires
  — **History**
      [DA]
      UF England—History
  — — **To 55 B.C.**
  — — **To 449**
  — — **To 1066**
  — — — **Historiography**
  — — — **Juvenile literature**
  — — **To 1485**
  — — — **Historiography**
      [DA129.5]
  — — — **Juvenile literature**
  — — **Roman period, 55 B.C.-449 A.D.**
  — — — **Juvenile literature**
  — — **Anglo Saxon period, 449-1066**
      (Not Subd Geog)
      NT England—Church history—
          Anglo Saxon period, 449-
          1066
  — — — **Juvenile literature**
      (Not Subd Geog)
  — — **Edmund, 855-870**
  — — **Alfred, 871-899**
  — — **Ethelred II, 979-1016**
      NT Meldon, Eng., Battle of, 991
  — — **Canute, 1017-1035**
  — — **Edward, the Confessor, 1042-1066**
  — — **William I, 1066-1087**
      NT Hastings, Battle of, 1066
  — — **Norman period, 1066-1154**
  — — — **Juvenile literature**
  — — **Medieval period, 1066-1485**
  — — — **Juvenile literature**
  — — **1066-1687**
  — — **William II, Rufus, 1087-1100**
  — — **Henry I, 1100-1135**
  — — **Stephen, 1135-1154**
  — — **Henry II, 1154-1189**
  — — **Angevin period, 1154-1216**
  — — — **Juvenile literature**
  — — **Plantagenets, 1154-1399**
  — — **Richard I, 1189-1199**
  — — **John, 1199-1216**
  — — **13th century**
  — — **Henry III, 1216-1272**
      NT Lincoln, Battle of, 1217
  — — **Barons' War, 1263-1267**
      (Not Subd Geog)

Great Britain
— History
— — **Barons' War, 1263-1267**
(Continued)
[DA227.5]
UF Barons' War, 1263-1267
— — — **Campaigns**
NT Lewes (East Sussex), Battle
of, 1264
— — **Edward I, 1272-1307**
— — **Edward I, II, 1272-1327**
(Not Subd Geog)
— — **14th century**
— — — **Juvenile literature**
— — **Edward II, 1307-1327**
— — **Edward II, III, 1307-1377**
(Not Subd Geog)
— — **Edward III, 1327-1377**
— — **Richard II, 1377-1399**
— — **Peasants' Revolt, 1381**
USE Tyler's Insurrection, 1381
— — **Henry IV, 1399-1413**
— — **House of Lancaster, 1399-1461**
— — **Lancaster and York, 1399-1485**
UF Great Britain—History—15th
century
— — — **Juvenile literature**
— — **15th century**
USE Great Britain—History—
Lancaster and York, 1399-
1485
— — **Henry V, 1413-1422**
— — **Henry VI, 1422-1461**
NT Cade's Rebellion, 1450
— — **Wars of the Roses, 1455-1485**
UF Roses, Wars of the, 1455-1485
Wars of the Roses, 1455-1485
— — — **Campaigns** (Not Subd Geog)
NT Bosworth Field, Battle of,
1485
— — — **Juvenile literature**
— — **Edward IV, 1461-1483**
— — **House of York, 1461-1485**
— — **Richard III, 1483-1485**
— — **Modern period, 1485-**
— — **Henry VII, 1485-1509**
NT Stoke, Battle of, England, 1487
— — **Tudors, 1485-1603**
UF Great Britain—History—16th
century
NT Babington Plot, 1586
— — — **Juvenile literature**
— — **16th century**
USE Great Britain—History—
Tudors, 1485-1603
— — **Henry VIII, 1509-1547**
NT Field of Cloth of Gold, France,
1520
Pilgrimage of Grace, 1536-1537
— — **Edward VI, 1547-1553**
NT Kett's Rebellion, 1549
— — **Edward VI and Mary, 1547-1558**
— — **Mary I, 1553-1558**
— — **Elizabeth, 1558-1603**
NT Armada, 1588
— — — **Pamphlets**
— — **Rebellion of 1569**
— — **17th century**
USE Great Britain—History—
Stuarts, 1603-1714
— — **James I, 1603-1625**
NT Gunpowder Plot, 1605
— — **Early Stuarts, 1603-1649**
— — — **Juvenile literature**
— — **Stuarts, 1603-1714**
UF Great Britain—History—17th
century
— — — **Juvenile literature**
— — **Charles I, 1625-1649**
— — **Civil War, 1642-1649**
UF Civil war—Great Britain

NT Roundway Down, Battle of,
1643
— — — **Campaigns** (Not Subd Geog)
NT Marston Moor, Battle of,
1644
Preston, Battle of, 1648
— — — **Causes**
— — — **Juvenile literature**
— — **Puritan Revolution, 1642-1660**
BT Puritans
— — — **Juvenile literature**
— — **Commonwealth and Protectorate,
1649-1660**
UF Commonwealth of England
NT Worcester, Battle of, 1651
— — — **Juvenile literature**
— — **Charles II, 1660-1685**
NT Monmouth's Rebellion, 1685
Popish Plot, 1678
Rye House Plot, 1683
— — **Restoration, 1660-1688**
UF Restoration, 1660-1688
BT Restorations, Political
NT Dutch War, 1672-1678
— — **1660-1714**
— — — **Pamphlets**
— — **James II, 1685-1688**
— — **Revolution of 1688**
— — **William and Mary, 1689-1702**
NT Aughrim, Battle of, 1691
Lancashire Plot, 1689-1694
— — **1689-1714**
— — **18th century**
— — — **Juvenile literature**
— — **Anne, 1702-1714**
— — **George I, 1714-1727**
— — **George I, II, 1714-1760**
(Not Subd Geog)
— — **1714-1837**
— — **George II, 1727-1760**
— — **1760-1789**
— — **George III, 1760-1820**
— — **1789-1820**
NT Napoleonic Wars, 1800-1814—
Proposed invasion of
England, 1793-1805
— — **1800-1837**
NT Chesapeake-Leopard Affair,
1807
Copenhagen, Battle of, 1801
Luddites
— — **19th century**
— — — **Juvenile literature**
— — **George IV, 1820-1830**
NT Cato Street Conspiracy, 1820
— — **William IV, 1830-1837**
— — **Victoria, 1837-1901**
NT Abyssinian Expedition, 1867-
1868
— — **Crimean War, 1853-1856**
USE Crimean War, 1853-1856
— — **20th century**
— — — **Juvenile literature**
— — **Edward VII, 1901-1910**
— — **George V, 1910-1936**
— — **Edward VIII, 1936**
— — **George VI, 1936-1952**
— — **Elizabeth II, 1952-**
NT Falkland Islands War, 1982
— — **Invasions**
UF Invasions of Great Britain
NT French Expedition to Ireland,
1796-1797
French Expedition to Wales,
1797
Jersey, Battle of, 1781
— — — **Juvenile literature**
— — **Philosophy**
— **History, Military**
— — **Roman period, 55 B.C.-449 A.D.**

— — **Anglo-Saxon period, 449-1066**
(Not Subd Geog)
— — **Medieval period, 1066-1485**
— — **Tudors, 1485-1603**
[DA66]
— — **Stuarts, 1603-1714**
— — **18th century**
NT Jersey, Battle of, 1781
— — **1789-1820**
NT Rosetta, Battle of, 1807
Walcheren Expedition, 1809
— — **19th century**
— — **20th century**
— **History, Naval**
— — **Tudors, 1485-1603**
NT Flores, Battle of, 1591
Lisbon Expedition, 1589
— — **Stuarts, 1603-1714**
NT Cadiz, Battle of, 1656
Santa Cruz de Tenerife, Battle
of, 1657
— — **18th century**
NT Camperdown, Battle of, 1797
Saint Vincent, Cape (Portugal),
Battle of, 1797
Santa Cruz de Tenerife, Battle
of, 1797
Sicilian Expedition, 1718-1720
— — **19th century**
— — **20th century**
— — **Juvenile literature**
— — **Intellectual life**
— — **To 1066**
— — **Medieval period, 1066-1485**
— — **16th century**
— — **17th century**
— — **18th century**
— — **19th century**
— — **20th century**
— — **1945-**
— **Kings and rulers**
NT Anglo-Saxons—Kings and rulers
Hanover, House of
Lancaster, House of
Monarchy—Great Britain
Plantagenet, House of
Royal Ascot
Tudor, House of
Windsor, House of
— — **Art collections**
BT Art—Private collections
— — **Art patronage**
— — **Autographs**
— — **Biography**
— — **Collectibles**
— — **Juvenile literature**
— — **Succession**
— **Literatures**
USE British literature
— **National Health Service**
USE National Health Service (Great
Britain)
— **Nobility**
NT Normandy, Dukes of
— **Peerage**
— **Politics and government**
UF England—Politics and government
— — **To 1485**
— — **449-1066**
— — **1066-1154**
— — **1066-1485**
— — **1154-1189**
— — **1154-1399**
— — **1216-1272**
— — **1272-1307**
— — **1307-1327**
— — **1327-1377**
[DA233]
— — **1377-1399**
— — **1399-1485**
— — **1461-1483**

— — 1485-
— — 1485-1509
— — 1485-1603
— — 1509-1547
— — 1547-1553
— — 1553-1558
— — 1558-1603
— — 1603-1625
— — 1603-1649
— — 1603-1714
— — 1625-1649
    NT Grand Remonstrance, 1641
— — 1642-1649
— — 1642-1660
— — 1649-1660
    NT Fifth Monarchy Men
— — 1660-1688
— — 1660-1714
— — Revolution of 1688
— — 1689-1702
— — 18th century
— — 1702-1714
— — 1714-1727
— — 1714-1760
— — 1714-1820
— — 1714-1837
— — 1727-1760
— — 1760-1789
— — 1760-1820
— — 1789-1820
— — 1800-1837
— — 19th century
— — 1820-1830
— — 1830-1837
— — 1837-1901
    NT Chartism
— — 20th century
— — 1901-1910
— — 1901-1936
— — 1910-1936
— — 1936-
— — 1936-1945
— — 1945-
— — 1945-1964
— — 1964-1979
— — 1979-
— Popular culture
    NT Punk culture
— Princes and princesses
— — Juvenile literature
— Proclamations
— Queens
— — Autographs
— — Juvenile literature
— Religion
— — To 449
— — 17th century
— — 19th century
— — 20th century
— Royal household
— Rural conditions
— — 19th century
— Social conditions
— — 17th century
— — 18th century
— — 19th century
— — 20th century
— — 1945-
— Social life and customs
— — To 1066
— — Medieval period, 1066-1485
— — 16th century
— — 17th century
— — 18th century
— — 19th century
    [DA533]
— — 20th century
    [DA566.4]
— — 1945-
    [DA588]
— Surveys (Not Subd Geog)

Great Britain. Army
— Boys
    USE Great Britain. Army—Boys'
        units
— Boys' units
    [U549.2]
    UF Great Britain. Army—Boys
— Camel troops
— Cavalry
    BT Cavalry—Great Britain
— — Drill and tactics
— Colonial forces (May Subd Geog)
— Drill and tactics
— Mascots
    NT Rats (Dog)
— Medals, badges, decorations, etc.
    NT Distinguished conduct medal
        (Great Britain)
        South Africa Medal (1834-1853)
— Scottish regiments
— Swiss regiments
    UF Swiss regiments of the British
        Army
— Welsh regiments
    [UA663]
Great Britain. Parliament
— Rules and practice
— University representation
    UF Great Britain. Parliament.
        House of Commons—University
        representation
        University representation (British
        parliament)
    BT Great Britain. Parliament.
        House of Commons—Election
        districts
        Voting, Plural
Great Britain. Parliament. House of
Commons
— Election districts
    UF Boroughs, Parliamentary
    NT Great Britain. Parliament—
        University representation
— University representation
    USE Great Britain. Parliament—
        University representation
Great chain of being (Philosophy)
    USE Chain of being (Philosophy)
Great Church at Haarlem (1648) (Painting)
    USE Saenredam, Pieter Jansz, 1597-1665.
        Sint Bavo-kerk te Haarlem (1648)
Great circle (Geometry)
    BT Circle
        Sphere
Great-circle sailing
    [VK571]
    BT Navigation
        Sailing
Great Comanche Raid, 1840
    USE Comanche Indians—Wars, 1840
Great Commission (Bible)
    [BV2074]
    UF Commission, Great (Bible)
    BT Evangelistic work
        Missions—Biblical teaching
Great Comp Garden (Kent)
    (Not Subd Geog)
    UF Comp Garden, Great (Kent)
    BT Gardens—England
Great cormorant
    [QL696.P4]
    UF Common cormorant
        European cormorant
        Phalacrocorax carbo
Great crested grebe
    UF Columbus cristatus
        Podiceps cristatus
    BT Grebes
Great Danes
    [SF429.G7]

Great Dipper
    USE Ursa Major
Great Dismal Swamp Canal (N.C. and Va.)
    USE Dismal Swamp Canal (N.C. and Va.)
Great Divide (Australia)
    USE Great Dividing Range
Great Dividing Range
    UF Eastern Highlands (Australia)
        Great Divide (Australia)
    BT Mountains—Australia
    NT Australian Alps (N.S.W. and Vic.)
        Blue Mountains (N.S.W.)
Great eagle owl
    USE Bubo bubo
Great Emigration, Serbia, 1690
    USE Serbia—History—Great Emigration,
        1690
Great Falls of the Potomac (Md. and Va.)
    (Not Subd Geog)
    BT Potomac River
        Waterfalls—Maryland
        Waterfalls—Virginia
Great Falls Park (Va.)
    BT National parks and reserves—United
        States
        Parks—Virginia
Great feast (Parable)
    USE Great supper (Parable)
Great Fish River (N.W.T.)
    USE Back River (N.W.T.)
Great Glen (Scotland)
    UF Glen Albin (Scotland)
        Glen Albyn (Scotland)
        Glen More Albin (Scotland)
        Great Glen of Albin (Scotland)
    BT Faults (Geology)—Scotland
Great Glen of Albin (Scotland)
    USE Great Glen (Scotland)
Great gray owl
    [QL696.S83]
    UF Strix nebulosa
Great grey kangaroo
    USE Grey kangaroo
Great Hogoheeche River (Ga.)
    USE Ogeechee River (Ga.)
Great horned owl
    USE Horned owl
Great Hungarian Plain
    USE Great Alföld
Great Indian Desert (India and Pakistan)
    USE Thar Desert (India and Pakistan)
Great International Paper Airplane Contest
    BT Paper airplanes—Competitions
Great Karoo (South Africa)
    USE Great Karroo (South Africa)
Great Karroo (South Africa)
    UF Central Karroo (South Africa)
        Great Karoo (South Africa)
        Groot Karroo (South Africa)
        Karoo, Great (South Africa)
        Karroo, Great (South Africa)
    BT Plateaus—South Africa
Great Lake (China)
    USE T'ai Lake (China)
Great Lake (Tas.)
    BT Lakes—Australia
Great Lakes
    RT Lake States
    NT Erie, Lake
        Huron, Lake (Mich. and Ont.)
        Michigan, Lake
        Ontario, Lake (N.Y. and Ont.)
        Superior, Lake
— Level
    USE Great Lakes—Water level
— Neutrality
— Storm, 1913
— Temperature
— Water level
    UF Great Lakes—Level
        Water level of the Great Lakes

Great Lakes cisco
USE Lake herring
Great Lakes States
USE Lake States
Great Meadows, Battle of, 1754
USE Necessity, Fort, Battle of, 1754
Great Miami River (Ohio)
USE Miami River (Ohio)
Great monad (Symbol)
USE Yin Yang symbol
Great Moravia (Czechoslovakia)
USE Moravia (Czechoslovakia)
Great Mother of the Gods
USE Cybele (Goddess)
Great National Pike
USE Cumberland Road
Great nebula of Orion
USE Orion Nebula
Great Northern Railway (Ireland)
BT Railroads—Northern Ireland
Great Northern Railway (U.S.)
BT Railroads—United States
Great Northern War, 1700-1721
USE Northern War, 1700-1721
Great Ocean Road (Vic.)
BT Roads—Australia
Great Ogeechee River (Ga.)
USE Ogeechee River (Ga.)
Great Ouse River (England)
UF Ouse, Great, River (England)
Ouse, River (Northamptonshire-
Norfolk, England)
River Ouse (Northamptonshire-
Norfolk, England)
BT Rivers—England
Great Plains
UF Plains, The Great
BT Northwest, Canadian
West (U.S.)
NT High Plains (U.S.)
— Antiquities
NT Mill Creek culture
Great Plains Conservation Program
Great Plains toad
USE Bufo cognatus
Great Poland (Poland)
USE Wielkopolska (Poland)
Great powers
UF Powers, Great
BT Balance of power
International law
International relations
States, Size of
World politics
RT Equality of states
Middle powers
States, Small
NT Concert of Europe
Great Proletarian Cultural Revolution, China,
1966-1969
USE China—History—Cultural Revolution,
1966-1969
Great Pyramid (Egypt)
UF Cheops, Pyramid of (Egypt)
Khufu, Pyramid of (Egypt)
Pyramid of Cheops (Egypt)
Pyramid of Khufu (Egypt)
BT Egypt—Antiquities
Pyramids—Egypt
Pyramids of Giza (Egypt)
Great Pyrenees (Dogs)
[SF429.G75]
UF Pyrenean Mountain dogs
Great Ramble-5 (Trail)
USE Grande Randonée Cinq (Trail)
Great Rift Valley
UF Rift Valley
BT Rifts (Geology)—Africa
Rifts (Geology)—Middle East
Valleys—Africa
Valleys—Middle East

Great River Road
UF Mississippi River Parkway
BT Roads—Manitoba
Roads—Ontario
Roads—United States
Great Sacandaga Lake (N.Y.)
UF Great Sacandaga Reservoir (N.Y.)
BT Lakes—New York (State)
Reservoirs—New York (State)
Great Sacandaga Reservoir (N.Y.)
USE Great Sacandaga Lake (N.Y.)
Great Salt Lake (Utah)
BT Lakes—Utah
Saline waters—Utah
Great Salt Lake Desert (Utah)
BT Deserts—Utah
**Great Sand Dunes National Monument
(Colo.)** (Not Subd Geog)
BT National monuments—Colorado
Great Sandy Desert (W.A.)
(Not Subd Geog)
BT Deserts—Australia
Great Sandy Island (Qld.)
USE Fraser Island (Qld.)
Great Sanhedrin
USE Sanhedrin
Great Saturday
USE Holy Saturday
Great Schism
USE Schism—Eastern and Western Church
Schism, The Great Western, 1378-
1417
Great Slave River (Alta. and N.W.T.)
USE Slave River (Alta. and N.W.T.)
Great Smokies (N.C. and Tenn.)
USE Great Smoky Mountains (N.C. and
Tenn.)
Great Smoky Mountains (N.C. and Tenn.)
UF Great Smokies (N.C. and Tenn.)
Smokies (N.C. and Tenn.)
Smoky Mountains (N.C. and Tenn.)
BT Mountains—North Carolina
Mountains—Tennessee
**Great Smoky Mountains National Park (N.C.
and Tenn.)**
UF Smoky Mountains National Park (N.C.
and Tenn.)
BT National parks and reserves—United
States
Parks—North Carolina
Parks—Tennessee
Great South Bay (N.Y.)
BT Bays—New York (State)
Great Southern & Western Railway
BT Railroads—Ireland
Great spotted woodpecker
[QL696.P56]
UF Dendrocopos major
Picoides major
Picus major
BT Picoides
Great Stone Face (N.H.)
USE Old Man of the Mountain (N.H.)
Great supper (Parable)
[BT378.G7]
UF Feast, Parable of
Great feast (Parable)
Guests who made excuses (Parable)
King's son, Marriage of (Parable)
Marriage of the king's son (Parable)
Supper, Parable of
Unwilling guests (Parable)
Wedding feast (Parable)
Wedding garment (Parable)

Great Temple (Abū Sunbul, Egypt)
UF Abu Simbel, Great Temple of (Abū
Sunbul, Egypt)
Grand Temple (Abū Sunbul, Egypt)
Great Temple of Ramses II (Abū
Sunbul, Egypt)
Rameses II, Great Temple of (Abū
Sunbul, Egypt)
Ramses II, Great Temple of (Abū
Sunbul, Egypt)
BT Temples—Egypt
Great Temple of Amun (Karnak, Egypt)
USE Temple of Amon (Karnak, Egypt)
Great Temple of Ramses II (Abū Sunbul,
Egypt)
USE Great Temple (Abū Sunbul, Egypt)
Great Thanksgiving (Liturgy)
USE Eucharistic prayers
Great tit
[QL696.P2615]
UF Parus major
Great Trek
USE South Africa—History—Great Trek,
1836-1840
Great Tribulation (Christian eschatology)
USE Tribulation (Christian eschatology)
Great Uhuru Railway
USE Tan-Zam Railway
Great Valley (Calif.)
USE Central Valley (Calif. : Valley)
Great vessels, Transposition of
USE Transposition of great vessels
Great Wall of China (China)
[DS793.G67]
UF China—Great Wall
China—Wall
China, Great Wall of (China)
Chinese Wall (China)
Wall of China (China)
BT Fortification—China
Walls—China
Great War, Uruguay, 1843-1852
USE Uruguay—History—Great War, 1843-
1852
Great Western Railway (Colorado)
BT Railroads—United States
Great Western Schism
USE Schism, The Great Western, 1378-
1417
Great White Brotherhood
[BP605.G68]
BT Cults—United States
Great white shark
USE White shark
Great Zimbabwe (City) (Not Subd Geog)
UF Zimbabwe, Great (City)
BT Cities and towns, Ruined, extinct, etc.
—Zimbabwe
Zimbabwe—Antiquities
Greater Antilles
USE West Indies
Greater crested tern
[QL696.C46]
UF Sterna bergii
Thalasseus bergii
BT Sterna
Greater East Asia co-prosperity sphere
UF Asia co-prosperity sphere
East Asia co-prosperity sphere
BT East Asia—Economic conditions
Greater Hartford Open
USE Greater Hartford Open, Conn.
Greater Hartford Open, Conn.
UF GHO, Conn.
Greater Hartford Open
Greater Hartford Open Golf
Tournament, Conn.
Greater Hartford Tournament, Conn.
BT Golf—Tournaments—Connecticut

Greater Hartford Open Golf Tournament,
  Conn.
  USE Greater Hartford Open, Conn.
Greater Hartford Tournament, Conn.
  USE Greater Hartford Open, Conn.
Greater Khingan Range (China)
  UF Ta-hsing-an-ling (China)
  BT Mountains—China
Greater kudu
  [QL737.U53]
  UF Koodoo
        Koudou
        Kudu, Greater
        Strepsiceros strepsiceros
        Tragelaphus strepsiceros
Greater prairie chicken
  UF Tympanuchus cupido
  BT Prairie-hens
Greater vehicle
  USE Mahayana Buddhism
Greater weever
  USE Trachinus draco
Greater whitethroat
  [QL696.P279]
  UF Sylvia communis
        Whitethroat, Greater
  BT Sylvia (Bird)
Greatest integer function
  UF Function, Greatest integer
  BT Diophantine analysis
        Numbers, Natural
        Numbers, Theory of
Greatness
  USE Genius
Greaver family
  USE Greever family
Greaves family
  USE Graves family
Greber family
  USE Graber family
Grebes (May Subd Geog)
  [QL696.P9]
  UF Podicipedidae
        Podicipediformes
  BT Birds
        Divers (Birds)
  NT Giant pied-billed grebe
        Great crested grebe
        Little grebe
        Pied-billed grebe
Grebiel family
  USE Graybill family
Grebo (African people)
  [DT630.5.G6]
  UF Glebo (African people)
        Grebo (African tribe)
        Gweabo (African people)
        Krebo (African people)
  BT Ethnology—Ivory Coast
        Ethnology—Liberia
        Kru (African people)
Grebo (African tribe)
  USE Grebo (African people)
Grebo language
  [PL8221]
  UF Gdebo language
        Gedebo language
        Glebo language
        Krebo language
  BT Kru languages
        Liberia—Languages
Grecale
  USE Gregale
Grecian . . .
  USE headings beginning with the word
        Greek
Grecian fire
  USE Greek fire
Greco-Bactrian art
  USE Art, Greco-Bactrian

Greco-Italian War, 1940-1941
  USE World War, 1939-1945—Campaigns—
        Greece
Greco-Roman art
  USE Art, Greco-Roman
Greco-Roman civilization
  USE Civilization, Greco-Roman
Greco-Roman eschatology
  USE Eschatology, Greco-Roman
Greco-Roman glassware
  USE Glassware, Greco-Roman
Greco-Roman law
  USE Law, Byzantine
Greco-Roman painting
  USE Painting, Greco-Roman
Greco-Roman Schism
  USE Schism—Eastern and Western Church
        Schism, Acacian, 484-519
Greco-Roman sculpture
  USE Sculpture, Greco-Roman
Greco-Roman terra-cotta sculpture
  USE Terra-cotta sculpture, Greco-Roman
Greco-Roman vases
  USE Vases, Greco-Roman
Greco-Turkish War, 1897
  [DF827]
  [DR575 (Period in Turkey)]
  UF Greece—History—War with Turkey,
        1897
        Turco-Greek War, 1897
  BT Turkey—History—1878-1909
Greco-Turkish War, 1921-1922
  UF Turco-Greek War, 1921-1922
  BT Greece—History—1917-1944
        Turkey—History—Revolution, 1918-
        1923
  NT Dumlupınar, Battle of, 1922
        İnönü, Battle of, 1921
— **Peace**
— **Treaties**
Greder family
  USE Crider family
Gredos (Spain)
  USE Gredos Mountains (Spain)
Gredos Mountains (Spain)
  UF Gredos (Spain)
        Sierra de Gredos (Spain)
  BT Mountains—Spain
Greece
— **Antiquities**
      UF Antiquities, Grecian
      NT Agios Petros Site (Greece)
            Agora (Athens, Greece)
            Aliki Site (Thasos Island, Greece)
            Aplomata Site (Naxos Island,
              Greece)
            Asine (Argolis, Greece : Ancient
              city)
            Ayia Irini Site (Kea Island,
              Greece)
            Chorsiai (Ancient city)
            Delphi (Ancient city)
            Demetrias (City)
            Dimini Site (Greece)
            Elis (Ancient city)
            Emporio (Ancient city)
            Epidaurus (Ancient city)
            Eretria (Ancient city)
            Franchthi Cave Site (Greece)
            Hagia Triada (Ancient city)
            Halieis (Ancient city)
            Ialysos (Ancient city)
            Kameiros (Ancient city)
            Kastanas Site (Greece)
            Kitsos Cave (Greece)
            Knossos (Ancient city)
            Kommos Site (Crete)
            Kore statues
            Lathouresa Site (Greece)
            Lithares Site (Greece)
            Mália Site (Crete)

            Manika (Ancient city)
            Megalopolis (Ancient city)
            Mycenae (Ancient city)
            Olympia (Greece : Ancient
              sanctuary)
            Paradimi Site (Greece)
            Phialae
            Philippi (City)
            Pydna (Greece)
            Pylos Site (Ēleia, Greece)
            Sanctuary of Artemis (Thasos
              Island, Greece)
            Sanctuary of Poseidon and
              Amphitrite (Greece)
            Sanctuary of the Kabeiroi (Voiõtia,
              Greece)
            Sicyon (Ancient city)
            Sitagroi Site (Greece)
            Sparta (Ancient city)
            Stoas
            Tanagra (Ancient city)
            Thesmophorion (Eretria)
            Tower of the Winds (Athens,
              Greece)
            Vases, Greek
— —**Juvenile literature**
— **Biography**
      BT Classical biography
— **Civilization**
      UF Civilization, Greek
      NT Art, Byzantine—Greek influences
            Art, Etruscan—Greek influences
            Art, German—Greek influences
            Art, Medieval—Greek influences
            Bronzes, Etruscan—Greek
              influences
            Civilization, Islamic—Greek
              influences
            Civilization, Medieval—Greek
              influences
            Civilization, Occidental—Greek
              influences
            Civilization, Oriental—Greek
              influences
            Egypt—Civilization—Greek
              influences
            English literature—Greek
              influences
            Europe—Civilization—Greek
              influences
            Great Britain—Civilization—Greek
              influences
            India—Civilization—Greek
              influences
            Iran—Civilization—Greek
              influences
            Ireland—Civilization—Greek
              influences
            Italy, Southern—Civilization—
              Greek influences
            Jewelry—India—Greek influences
            Norway—Civilization—Greek
              influences
            Philosophy, German—Greek
              influences
            Pottery, Iberian—Greek influences
            Psychoanalysis—Greek influences
            Romania—Civilization—Greek
              influences
            Rome—Civilization—Greek
              influences
            Salentina Peninsula (Italy)—
              Civilization—Greek influences
            Sculpture, Etruscan—Greek
              influences
            Sicily—Civilization—Greek
              influences
            Spain—Civilization—Greek
              influences
            Thrace—Civilization—Greek
              influences

— — Occupation, 1941-1944
    BT World War, 1939-1945—Greece
— — Civil War, 1944-1949
    [DF849.5]
    UF Civil War, Greece, 1944-1949
    NT Grammos-Vitsi, Battle of, 1949
— — 1950-1967
    [DF850]
— — Coup d'état, 1967 (April 21)
    [DF853]
    BT Coups d'état—Greece
— — Coup d'état, 1967 (December 13)
    [DF853]
    BT Coups d'état—Greece
— — 1967-1974
    [DF853]
— — 1974-
    [DF854]
    NT Cyprus—History—Cyprus Crisis, 1974-
— — Coup d'état, 1973 (May 22-23)
    (Not Subd Geog)
    [DF853]
    BT Coups d'état—Greece
— Intellectual life
— — To 146 B.C. (Not Subd Geog)
— — 1453-1821
— — 19th century
— — 20th century
— Languages (Not Subd Geog)
    NT Aeolic Greek dialect
    Attic Greek dialect
    Doric Greek dialect
    Ionic Greek dialect
— Officials and employees
    NT Proxenies (Greek officials)
— Politics and government
— — To 146 B.C.
    NT Synoecism
— — 146 B.C.-323 A.D.
— — 1453-1821
— — 19th century
— — 1821-
— — 1821-1832
— — 1832-1862
    [DF823-823.7]
— — 1863-1913
— — 20th century
— — 1913-1917
— — 1917-1935
— — 1935-1967
— — 1967-1974
— — 1974-
— Public buildings
    USE Public buildings—Greece
— Religion
    NT Anastenaria
— Social conditions
— — To 146 B.C.
— — 19th century
— — 1974-
— Social life and customs
— — 20th century
Greece, Medieval
  USE Greece—History—323-1453
Greece, Seven sages of
  USE Seven wise men of Greece
Greed
  USE Avarice
Greegory family
  USE Gregory family
Greek abbreviations
  USE Abbreviations, Greek
Greek alien labor
  USE Alien labor, Greek
Greek American artists (May Subd Geog)
  UF Artists, Greek American
  BT Artists—United States

Greek American drama (May Subd Geog)
  UF American drama (Modern Greek)
  Greek drama, Modern—American authors
  BT American drama
  Greek drama, Modern
Greek-American wit and humor
  BT Greek wit and humor, Modern
Greek American women (May Subd Geog)
  UF Women, Greek American
Greek American youth (May Subd Geog)
  [E184.G7]
  UF Youth, Greek American
  BT Youth—United States
Greek Americans (May Subd Geog)
  BT Ethnology—United States
  Greeks—United States
Greek architecture
  USE Architecture, Greek
Greek art
  USE Art, Greek
Greek arts
  USE Arts, Greek
Greek astrology
  USE Astrology, Greek
Greek astronomy
  USE Astronomy, Greek
Greek atlases
  USE Atlases, Greek
Greek authors
  USE Authors, Greek
Greek authors, Modern
  USE Authors, Greek (Modern)
Greek bronze sculpture
  USE Bronze sculpture, Greek
Greek bronzes
  USE Bronzes, Greek
Greek Byzantine rite (Catholic Church)
  USE Catholic Church—Byzantine rite, Greek
Greek chap-books, Modern
  USE Chap-books, Greek (Modern)
Greek children's literature, Modern
  USE Children's literature, Greek (Modern)
Greek children's plays, Modern
  USE Children's plays, Greek (Modern)
Greek children's poetry, Modern
  USE Children's poetry, Greek (Modern)
Greek children's stories, Modern
  USE Children's stories, Greek (Modern)
Greek children's writings, Modern
  USE Children's writings, Greek (Modern)
Greek Christian poetry
  USE Christian poetry, Greek
Greek Christian poetry, Modern
  USE Christian poetry, Greek (Modern)
Greek chronology
  USE Chronology, Greek
Greek Church
  USE Orthodox Eastern Church
Greek civics
  USE Civics, Greek
Greek corporations
  USE Corporations, Greek
Greek costume
  USE Costume—Greece
Greek dialect, Aeolic
  USE Aeolic Greek dialect
Greek dialect, Doric
  USE Doric Greek dialect
Greek dialect, Ionic
  USE Ionic Greek dialect
Greek dialogues
  USE Dialogues, Greek
Greek didactic drama
  USE Didactic drama, Greek
Greek drama
  [PA3131-PA3239 (History)]
  [PA3461-PA3468 (Collections)]
  BT Classical drama
  NT Didactic drama, Greek

  Historical drama, Greek
— Chorus
  USE Drama—Chorus (Greek drama)
— Incidental music
  BT Music, Greek and Roman
  Music, Incidental
  Opera
— Presentation, Ancient
  USE Theater—Greece
— Presentation, Modern
  [PA3238]
Greek drama, Modern (May Subd Geog)
  NT Children's plays, Greek (Modern)
  Folk-drama, Greek (Modern)
  Greek American drama
  One-act plays, Greek (Modern)
— 1453-1800
— American authors
  USE Greek American drama
Greek drama (Comedy)
  [PA3161-PA3199 (History)]
  [PA3465-PA3466 (Collections)]
  BT Comedy
Greek drama (Satyr play)
  [PA3160]
  [PA3464]
  UF Satyric drama, Greek
  BT Dionysia
Greek drama (Tragedy)
  [PA3131-PA3159 (History)]
  [PA3461-PA3463 (Collections)]
  BT Tragedy
— Themes, motives
  NT Cassiope (Mythical queen)
Greek dramatists, Modern
  USE Dramatists, Greek (Modern)
Greek education
  USE Education, Greek
Greek elegiac poetry
  USE Elegiac poetry, Greek
Greek elegiac poetry, Modern
  USE Elegiac poetry, Greek (Modern)
Greek encyclopedias and dictionaries
  USE Encyclopedias and dictionaries, Greek
Greek epic poetry
  USE Epic poetry, Greek
Greek epigrams
  USE Epigrams, Greek
Greek erotic poetry
  USE Erotic poetry, Greek
Greek erotic poetry, Modern
  USE Erotic poetry, Greek (Modern)
Greek erotic stories, Modern
  USE Erotic stories, Greek (Modern)
Greek essays, Modern (May Subd Geog)
Greek ethics
  USE Ethics, Greek
Greek fables, Modern
  USE Fables, Greek (Modern)
Greek fasts and feasts
  USE Fasts and feasts—Greek religion
Greek fiction
  [PA3267 (History)]
  [PA3487.E7 (Collections)]
  BT Classical fiction
  NT Love stories, Greek
Greek fiction, Modern (May Subd Geog)
  NT Children's stories, Greek (Modern)
  Detective and mystery stories, Greek (Modern)
  Erotic stories, Greek (Modern)
  Sea stories, Greek (Modern)
  Short stories, Greek (Modern)
  War stories, Greek (Modern)
Greek fire
  [TP268-TP269 (Ancient)]
  [TP300 (Modern)]
  UF Fire, Greek
  Grecian fire
  BT Combustion
  Explosives, Military

Greek folk-drama, Modern
  USE Folk-drama, Greek (Modern)
Greek folk literature
  USE Folk literature, Greek
Greek folk poetry
  USE Folk poetry, Greek
Greek folk poetry, Modern
  USE Folk poetry, Greek (Modern)
Greek folk-songs
  USE Folk-songs, Greek
Greek folk-songs, Modern
  USE Folk-songs, Greek (Modern)
Greek fortification
  USE Fortification, Greek
Greek goddesses
  USE Goddesses, Greek
Greek gods
  USE Gods, Greek
Greek historical drama
  USE Historical drama, Greek
Greek historical poetry
  USE Historical poetry, Greek
Greek hymns
  USE Hymns, Greek
     Hymns, Greek (Classical)
Greek iambic poetry
  USE Iambic poetry, Greek
Greek icons
  USE Icons, Greek
Greek imprints *(May Subd Geog)*
 — Cataloging
    USE Cataloging of Greek imprints
Greek inscriptions
  USE Inscriptions, Greek
Greek landscape painting (Modern)
  USE Landscape painting, Greek (Modern)
Greek language
  ⌈PA201-1179⌉
  BT Classical languages
    Indo-European languages
  RT Classical philology
    Greek philology
  NT Aeolic Greek dialect
    Attic Greek dialect
    Doric Greek dialect
    Inscriptions, Greek
    Ionic Greek dialect
    Manuscripts, Greek
 — **Alphabet**
  NT Inscriptions, Linear B
    Tau (The Greek letter)
 — **Dialects**
 — **Etymology**
  NT Aisa (The Greek word)
    Amechania (The Greek word)
    Anachoresis (The Greek word)
    Anamnēsis (The Greek word)
    Anapausis (The Greek word)
    Aryballos (The Greek word)
    Astheneia (The Greek word)
    Atē (The Greek word)
    Baptizein (The Greek word)
    Charopos (The Greek word)
    Daimonie (The Greek word)
    Dikē (The Greek word)
    Doulos (The Greek word)
    Drakōn (The Greek word)
    Drósos (The Greek word)
    Dynamis (The Greek word)
    Eérsē (The Greek word)
    Ekbasis (The Greek word)
    Élthon (The Greek word)
    Encheiridion (The Greek word)
    Euchesthai (The Greek word)
    Euchomai (The Greek word)
    Eulogein (The Greek word)
    Eusebēs (The Greek word)
    Glaukos (The Greek word)
    Hieros (The Greek word)
    Hosios (The Greek word)
    Isopoliteia (The Greek word)

Kai (The Greek word)
Kairós (The Greek word)
Mellein (The Greek word)
Moira (The Greek word)
Mysterion (The Greek word)
Noos (The Greek word)
Nosēma (The Greek word)
Nousos (The Greek word)
Parrhēsia (The Greek word)
Penia (The Greek word)
Pistis (The Greek word)
Pistos (The Greek word)
Ploutos (The Greek word)
Pneuma (The Greek word)
Psychē (The Greek word)
Skopos (The Greek word)
Teleō (The Greek word)
Telos (The Greek word)
Words, New—Greek
 — **Medical Greek**
  UF Medical Greek
  BT Medicine—Language
    Medicine—Terminology
 — **Metrics and rhythmics**
 — **Reduplication**
 — **Study and teaching** *(May Subd Geog)*
 — **Terms and phrases**
  NT Allote allos (The Greek phrase)
    Kalos kagathos (The Greek phrase)
Greek language, Biblical
  ⌈PA695-PA895⌉
  Here are entered works on the language of the
Septuagint and the New Testament. Works on Helle-
nistic Greek are entered under Greek language,
Hellenistic (300 B.C.-600 A.D.).
  UF Bible—Philology
    Biblical Greek
    New Testament Greek
  BT Bible—Language, style
    Languages—Religious aspects
  NT Greek language, Hellenistic (300 B.C.-
    600 A.D.)
 — **Dictionaries**
  UF Bible. Greek—Dictionaries
 — **Etymology**
  NT Apokatastasis (The Greek word)
    Diathēkē (The Greek word)
    Eirēnē (The Greek word)
    Oikos (The Greek word)
 — **Terms and phrases**
  NT Einai en (The Greek phrase)
    Menein en (The Greek phrase)
Greek language, Byzantine
  USE Greek language, Medieval and late
**Greek language, Hellenistic (300 B.C.-600
A.D.)**
  ⌈PA600-PA691⌉
  Here are entered works on Hellenistic Greek.
Works on the language of the Septuagint and the
New Testament are entered under Greek language,
Biblical.
  UF Greek language (Koinē)
    Hellenistic Greek
    Koinē (Greek language)
  BT Greek language, Biblical
Greek language, Medieval and late
  ⌈PA1001-1179⌉
  Covers the period, ca. 600-1821.
  UF Greek language, Byzantine
Greek language, Modern *(May Subd Geog)*
  ⌈PA1001-1179⌉
  UF Romaic language
Greek language (Koinē)
  USE Greek language, Hellenistic (300 B.C.-
    600 A.D.)
Greek language in Rome
Greek laudatory poetry
  USE Laudatory poetry, Greek
Greek law
  USE Law, Greek
Greek letter societies
  ⌈LJ⌉

  UF College fraternities
    Fraternal organizations
    Fraternities
    Sororities, Greek letter
  BT Secret societies
    Societies
    Universities and colleges
  RT Hazing
    Initiations (into trades, societies, etc.)
  SA *names of individual societies, e.g.*
    Delta Kappa Epsilon
  NT Fraternity songs
Greek letter society libraries
  USE Fraternity libraries
Greek letter-writing
  USE Letter-writing, Greek
Greek letters
  ⌈PA3042 (History)⌉
  ⌈PA3403.E6 (Teubner collections)⌉
  ⌈PA3487.E4 (Collections)⌉
  ⌈PA3601-PA3671 (Translations)⌉
  BT Classical letters
  RT Byzantine letters
Greek letters, Modern
Greek literature *(May Subd Geog)*
  ⌈PA3051-4505⌉
  BT Balkan Peninsula—Literatures
  RT Byzantine literature
    Classical literature
    Classical philology
    Greek philology
  NT Folk literature, Greek
    Romances, Greek
 — **Criticism, Textual**
 — **Jewish authors**
    ⌈PA3421.G8⌉
  UF Jewish literature (Hellenistic)
 — **Relation to the New Testament**
  UF Bible. N.T.—Relation to Greek
    literature
  BT Bible and literature
 — **Study and teaching** *(May Subd Geog)*
 — **Themes, motives**
Greek literature, Byzantine
  USE Byzantine literature
Greek literature, Hellenistic
  UF Hellenistic Greek literature
  NT Greek poetry, Hellenistic
Greek literature, Medieval and late
  USE Byzantine literature
    Greek literature, Modern—1453-1800
Greek literature, Modern *(May Subd Geog)*
  ⌈PA5201-5660⌉
  UF Neo-Greek literature
    Romaic literature
  NT Athenian school (Literary movement)
    Children's literature, Greek (Modern)
    Revolutionary literature, Greek
    (Modern)
 — **1453-1800**
  UF Greek literature, Medieval and late
 — **20th century**
Greek love poetry
  USE Love poetry, Greek
Greek love poetry, Modern
  USE Love poetry, Greek (Modern)
Greek love stories
  USE Love stories, Greek
Greek Macedonia
  USE Macedonia (Greece)
Greek manuscripts
  USE Manuscripts, Greek
Greek mathematics
  USE Mathematics, Greek
Greek maxims
  USE Maxims, Greek
Greek medals
  USE Medals, Greek
Greek medicine
  USE Medicine, Greek and Roman

Greek mercenaries
  ₍DF89₎
  BT Mercenary troops
Greek mosaics
  USE Mosaics, Greek
Greek mother goddesses
  USE Mother goddesses, Greek
Greek mural painting and decoration
  USE Mural painting and decoration, Greek
Greek music
  USE Music, Greek and Roman
Greek narrative poetry (Modern)
  USE Narrative poetry, Greek (Modern)
Greek national characteristics
  USE National characteristics, Greek
Greek newspapers *(May Subd Geog)*
  ₍PN5231-PN5239 (History)₎
Greek one-act plays, Modern
  USE One-act plays, Greek (Modern)
Greek oracles
  USE Oracles, Greek
Greek orations
  USE Speeches, addresses, etc., Greek
Greek painting
  USE Painting, Greek
Greek papyri
  USE Manuscripts, Greek (Papyri)
Greek pastoral poetry
  USE Pastoral poetry, Greek
Greek pastoral poetry (Modern)
  USE Pastoral poetry, Greek (Modern)
Greek periodicals *(May Subd Geog)*
  ₍PN5231-PN5240 (History)₎
  — Special numbers
Greek philology
  ₍PA1-99₎
  RT Classical philology
     Greek language
     Greek literature
  NT Inscriptions, Greek
     Manuscripts, Greek
Greek philology, Medieval and late
  (May Subd Geog)
Greek philology, Modern
Greek philosophy
  USE Philosophy, Ancient
Greek philosophy (Modern)
  USE Philosophy, Greek (Modern)
Greek poetry *(May Subd Geog)*
  ₍PA3092-PA3129 (History)₎
  ₍PA3431-PA3459 (Collections)₎
  NT Byzantine poetry
     Christian poetry, Greek
     Dithyramb
     Elegiac poetry, Greek
     Epic poetry, Greek
     Erotic poetry, Greek
     Folk poetry, Greek
     Historical poetry, Greek
     Iambic poetry, Greek
     Laudatory poetry, Greek
     Love poetry, Greek
     Pastoral poetry, Greek
Greek poetry, Hellenistic *(May Subd Geog)*
  UF Hellenistic Greek poetry
  BT Greek literature, Hellenistic
Greek poetry, Modern *(May Subd Geog)*
  ₍PA5250-PA5255 (History)₎
  ₍PA5280-PA5289 (Collections)₎
  NT Children's poetry, Greek (Modern)
     Christian poetry, Greek (Modern)
     Elegiac poetry, Greek (Modern)
     Erotic poetry, Greek (Modern)
     Folk poetry, Greek (Modern)
     Love poetry, Greek (Modern)
     Narrative poetry, Greek (Modern)
     Pastoral poetry, Greek (Modern)
     Sonnets, Greek (Modern)
     Verse satire, Greek (Modern)
  — 1453-1800

Greek poets
  USE Poets, Greek
Greek poets, Modern
  USE Poets, Greek (Modern)
Greek portrait sculpture
  USE Portrait sculpture, Greek
Greek pottery
  USE Pottery, Greek
Greek printing
  USE Printing, Greek
Greek prints
  USE Prints, Greek
Greek prose literature *(May Subd Geog)*
  ₍PA3255-PA3281 (History)₎
  ₍PA3473-PA3515 (Collections)₎
Greek prose literature, Modern
  (May Subd Geog)
  ₍PA5265 (History)₎
  ₍PA5295 (Collections)₎
Greek proverbs
  USE Proverbs, Greek
Greek proverbs, Modern
  USE Proverbs, Greek (Modern)
Greek quotations
  USE Quotations, Greek
Greek quotations, Modern
  USE Quotations, Greek (Modern)
Greek relief (Sculpture)
  USE Relief (Sculpture), Greek
Greek revival (Architecture)
  (May Subd Geog)
  BT Architecture, Greek
     Neoclassicism (Architecture)
Greek rhetoric
  USE Rhetoric, Ancient
Greek romances
  USE Romances, Greek
Greek sarcophagi
  USE Sarcophagi, Greek
Greek satire
  USE Satire, Greek
Greek scene painting
  USE Scene painting, Greek
Greek sea stories, Modern
  USE Sea stories, Greek (Modern)
Greek sermons
  USE Sermons, Greek
Greek short stories, Modern
  USE Short stories, Greek (Modern)
Greek songs, Modern
  USE Songs, Greek (Modern)
Greek speeches
  USE Speeches, addresses, etc., Greek
Greek strategi
  USE Strategi, Greek
Greek students *(May Subd Geog)*
  BT Students
Greek Tatar language *(May Subd Geog)*
  UF Urum language
  BT Soviet Union—Languages
     Turkic languages, Northwest
Greek temples
  USE Temples, Greek
Greek terra-cotta figurines
  USE Terra-cotta figurines, Greek
Greek terra-cotta sculpture
  USE Terra-cotta sculpture, Greek
Greek Theater (Syracuse, Sicily)
  UF Teatro antico (Syracuse, Sicily)
     Teatro greco di Siracusa (Syracuse,
        Sicily)
  BT Theaters—Italy
Greek tribes
  ₍DF251₎
Greek type
  USE Type and type-founding—Greek type
Greek urns
  USE Urns, Greek
Greek vase-painting
  USE Vase-painting, Greek

Greek vases
  USE Vases, Greek
Greek verse satire, Modern
  USE Verse satire, Greek (Modern)
Greek war stories, Modern
  USE War stories, Greek (Modern)
Greek wit and humor
  ₍PA3249 (History)₎
  ₍PA3469.W5 (Collections)₎
  BT Classical wit and humor
Greek wit and humor, Modern
  NT Greek-American wit and humor
Greek wit and humor, Modern, Pictorial
Greeks *(May Subd Geog)*
  BT Ethnology—Greece
     Indo-Europeans
     Mediterranean race
  — Egypt
  — Italy
  — Libya
  — Turkey
  — United States
     NT Greek Americans
Greele family
  USE Greeley family
Greeley family *(Not Subd Geog)*
  UF Creeley family
     Creely family
     Creilly family
     Greele family
     Greely family
Greely family
  USE Greeley family
Green
Green alder
  USE European green alder
Green algae *(May Subd Geog)*
  ₍QK569.C6₎
  UF Algae, Green
     Chlorophyceae
     Chlorophyta
     Isokontae
  BT Algae
  NT Caulerpales
     Chaetophorales
     Chlorococcales
     Cladophorales
     Oedogoniales
     Ulotrichales
     Ulvales
     Volvocales
     Zygnematales
Green algae, Fossil *(May Subd Geog)*
  ₍QE955₎
  BT Algae, Fossil
Green almond
  USE Pistachio
Green anole
  USE Anolis carolinensis
Green barley essence
  USE Dried green barley juice
Green barley juice *(May Subd Geog)*
  UF Barley juice, Green
  BT Barley
     Vegetable juices
  NT Dried green barley juice
Green barley juice, Dried
  USE Dried green barley juice
Green barley powder
  USE Dried green barley juice
Green bell pepper
  USE Bell pepper
Green belts
  USE Greenbelts
Green-bottle flies
  ₍QL537.C24₎
  UF Greenbottle flies
     Greenbottles (Insects)
  BT Blowflies
  NT Lucilia

Green bug
  USE Grain-louse
Green cancer
  USE Chloroma
Green-cap eremomela
  USE Eremomela scotops
Green citrus aphid
  USE Aphis spiraecola
Green cod
  USE Lingcod
        Pollachius virens
Green cormorant
  USE Shag
Green crab
  USE Carcinus maenas
Green Creek (Tex.)
  BT Rivers—Texas
Green crop drying
  USE Forage plants—Drying
Green darner
  ₍QL520.3.A4₎
  UF Anax junius
        Anax spiniferus
Green-eyed skimmers
  USE Corduliidae
Green family *(Not Subd Geog)*
  UF Greene family
        Greens family
  RT Gruenhagen family
Green flash
  UF Blue flash
        Blue-green flame
        Green ray
        Green segment
  BT Meteorological optics
        Sunset phenomena
Green frog
  UF Rana clamitans
        Spring frog
Green gram
  USE Mung bean
Green heron
  ₍QL696.C52₎
  UF Butorides
        Butorides striatus
        Butorides virescens
        Striated heron
  BT Ardeidae
        Herons
Green iguana
  USE Iguana iguana
Green June beetle
  ₍QL596.S3₎
  UF Allorhina nitida
        Cotinis flagranticeps
        Cotinis nitida
        Fig-eater
        Figeater
        June beetle, Green
        Scarabaeus nitidus
  BT Beetles
        Cotinus
Green lacewing flies
  USE Chrysopidae
Green linnet
  USE Greenfinch
Green mallee
  ₍QK495.E86 (Botany)₎
  ₍SD397.G (Culture)₎
  UF Eucalyptus viridis
        Mallee, Green
  BT Eucalyptus
Green manure crops *(May Subd Geog)*
  ₍S661 (Manures)₎
  ₍SB284-SB284.4 (Culture)₎
  UF Crops, Green manure
        Green manures
        Manure crops, Green
  BT Green manuring
  NT Serradella
        Sunn hemp

Green manures
  USE Green manure crops
Green manuring *(May Subd Geog)*
  ₍S661₎
  BT Cover crops
        Manures
        Nitrogen—Fixation
        Organic fertilizers
        Soil inoculation
  NT Green manure crops
Green monkey
  USE Cercopithecus aethiops
Green Mountain Reservoir (Colo.)
  (Not Subd Geog)
  BT Reservoirs—Colorado
Green peach aphid
  ₍SB945₎
  UF Myzus persicae
  — **Insecticide resistance**
Green pigeons
  USE Treron
Green plovers
  USE Lapwings
Green Point Site (Mich.)
  USE Schultz Site (Mich.)
Green ray
  USE Green flash
Green Revolution *(May Subd Geog)*
  ₍HD1415-HD2210 (Economics)₎
  ₍S439-S481 (Local)₎
  ₍S494.5.I5 (General)₎
  UF Revolution, Green
  BT Agricultural innovations
        Agriculture
        Agriculture and state
        Food supply
        Grain
Green River (Ky. : River)
  BT Rivers—Kentucky
Green River (Wyo.-Utah)
  BT Rivers—Colorado
        Rivers—Utah
        Rivers—Wyoming
  NT Flaming Gorge Reservoir (Wyo. and
        Utah)
Green River Cemetery (Green River, Wyo.)
  USE Greenriver Cemetery (Green River,
        Wyo.)
Green River Formation *(Not Subd Geog)*
  BT Formations (Geology)—Colorado
        Formations (Geology)—Utah
        Formations (Geology)—Wyoming
        Geology, Stratigraphic—Eocene
Green River Lake (Ky.)
  UF Green River Reservoir (Ky.)
  BT Lakes—Kentucky
        Reservoirs—Kentucky
Green River language
  USE Abau language
Green River Reservoir (Ky.)
  USE Green River Lake (Ky.)
Green River Valley (Wyo.-Utah)
  BT Valleys—Colorado
        Valleys—Utah
        Valleys—Wyoming
Green sandpiper
  ₍QL696.C48₎
  UF Tringa ochropus
Green sea turtle
  USE Green turtle
Green segment
  USE Green flash
Green soldier-bug
  ₍SB945.G₎
Green Spring Plantation, Va., Battle of, 1781
Green-striped maple worm
  USE Maple worm
Green sucker
  USE Catostomus discobolus
Green sunfish
  ₍QL638.C3₎

  UF Lepomis cyanellus
Green swordtail
  USE Xiphophorus helleri
Green-throated mountain gem
  USE Lamporis viridipallens
Green turtle
  ₍QL666.C536₎
  UF Chelonia japonica
        Chelonia mydas
        Green sea turtle
  BT Chelonia
Green Turtle Cay (Bahamas : Island)
  BT Islands—Bahamas
Greenager family
  USE Grinager family
Greenback Party
  USE National Greenback Party
"Greenbackers"
  USE National Greenback Party
Greenbacks
  ₍HG604-5₎
  BT Inflation (Finance)—United States
        Legal tender
        Paper money—United States
  RT National Greenback Party
Greenbelt Park (Md.)
  BT Parks—Maryland
Greenbelts *(May Subd Geog)*
  UF Green belts
  BT Open spaces
  NT Garden cities
Greenbottle flies
  USE Green-bottle flies
Greenbottles (Insects)
  USE Green-bottle flies
Greenbrier River (W. Va.)
  BT Rivers—West Virginia
Greene family
  USE Green family
Greenell family
  USE Grinnell family
Greenewall family
  USE Greenwell family
Greenewalt family
  USE Greenwell family
Greenex (Firm) Strike, 1977
  BT Miners—Greenland
        Strikes and lockouts—Miners—
          Greenland
        Strikes and lockouts—Greenland
Greenfeild family
  USE Greenfield family
Greenfeld family
  USE Greenfield family
Greenfield family *(Not Subd Geog)*
  UF Greenfeild family
        Greenfeld family
Greenfinch
  ₍QL696.P246₎
  UF Carduelis chloris
        Green linnet
  BT Carduelis
Greenhagen family
  USE Gruenhagen family
Greenhead
  USE Striped bass
Greenhouse climate
  USE Greenhouses—Climate
Greenhouse crops
  USE Greenhouse plants
Greenhouse culture
  USE Greenhouse gardening
        Greenhouse management
Greenhouse effect, Atmospheric
  (May Subd Geog)
  UF Atmospheric greenhouse effect
  BT Atmospheric temperature
        Carbon dioxide
        Heat budget (Geophysics)
        Infrared albedo
        Solar radiation

Greenhouse gardening *(May Subd Geog)*
 [SB415 (General)]
   Here are entered works on home greenhouse plant
 culture. Works on the commercial growing of plants
 in greenhouses and on the management of the green-
 houses themselves are entered under Greenhouse
 management.
   UF Gardening under glass
      Greenhouse culture
   BT Gardening
      Greenhouses
      Indoor gardening
   RT Artificial light gardening
      Forcing (Plants)
      Greenhouse plants
      Greenhouses, Window
 — **Equipment and supplies**
   NT Potting soils
Greenhouse management *(May Subd Geog)*
 [SB415]
   Here are entered works on the commercial grow-
 ing of plants in greenhouses and on the management
 of the greenhouses themselves. Works on home
 greenhouse plant culture are entered under Green-
 house gardening.
   UF Greenhouse culture
      Greenhouses—Management
   BT Greenhouses
      Horticulture
      Ornamental horticulture
   RT Forcing (Plants)
      Greenhouse plants
   NT Artificial light gardening
      Greenhouses—Climate
      Pit gardening
Greenhouse plants *(May Subd Geog)*
 [SB415]
   UF Glasshouse crops
      Glasshouse plants
      Greenhouse crops
   BT Horticultural crops
      Horticulture
      Plants, Ornamental
   RT Greenhouse gardening
      Greenhouse management
Greenhouse thrips
 [SB945.T]
Greenhouse white fly
   UF Whitefly, Greenhouse
Greenhouses *(May Subd Geog)*
 [SB415-416]
   UF Hothouses
   BT Floriculture
      Gardening
      Horticulture
   RT Conservatories
      Garden rooms
      Phytotron
   NT Cold-frames
      Forcing (Plants)
      Greenhouse gardening
      Greenhouse management
      Growth cabinets and rooms
      Solar greenhouses
      Wardian cases
 — **Climate**
   [SB415]
   UF Climate, Greenhouse
      Greenhouse climate
   BT Greenhouse management
      Microclimatology
 — **Environmental engineering**
   [SB415-416]
 — **Fumigation**
   BT Fumigation
 — **Heating and ventilation**
   [SB416]
 — Management
   USE Greenhouse management
 — **Roofs**
   [SB416]
   BT Roofs

 — **Shading**
   UF Shading of greenhouses
Greenhouses, Solar
 USE Solar greenhouses
Greenhouses, Window
 [SB416.3]
   UF Window greenhouses
      Windowsill greenhouses
   BT Windows
   RT Greenhouse gardening
      Window-gardening
Greenland
   As a geographic subdivision, this heading is used
 directly.
 — **Strategic aspects**
   BT Military geography
      Strategy
Greenland Basin
   UF Arctic Basin
   BT Geology—Arctic Ocean
      Submarine topography—Arctic Ocean
Greenland collared lemming
 USE Collared lemming
Greenland halibut
 [QL638.P7]
   UF Halibut, Greenland
      Reinhardtius hippoglossoides
Greenland-Iceland Rise
   BT Submarine topography—North
      Atlantic Ocean
Greenland right whale
 USE Bowhead whale
Greenland Sea
   BT Arctic Ocean
Greenland whale
 USE Bowhead whale
Greenlanders *(May Subd Geog)*
   BT Ethnology—Greenland
Greenlandic language
 USE Eskimo language
Greenler family *(Not Subd Geog)*
Greenling fishes
 USE Hexagrammidae
Greenlings
 USE Hexagrammidae
Greenman family *(Not Subd Geog)*
Greenock and Port Glasgow Tramways
   BT Railroads—Great Britain
Greenriver Cemetery (Green River, Wyo.)
   UF Green River Cemetery (Green River,
      Wyo.)
   BT Cemeteries—Wyoming
Greens, Edible *(May Subd Geog)*
   UF Leafy vegetables
      Pot-herbs
      Potherbs
      Vegetables, Leafy
   BT Plants, Edible
      Vegetable gardening
      Vegetables
   RT Cookery (Greens)
   NT Dandelions
      Salad greens
      Spinach
      Watercress
Greens, Salad
 USE Salad greens
Greens family
 USE Green family
Green's functions
   UF Functions, Green's
   BT Differential equations
      Potential, Theory of
Green's operators
 USE Potential, Theory of
Green's theorem
 USE Potential, Theory of
Greensand
 [QE685 (Geology, QE471)]
 [S643 (Fertilizers)]
   BT Sandstone

Greenshank
 [QL696.C48]
   UF Common greenshank
      Tringa nebularia
Greensickness
 USE Chlorosis
Greenslad family
 USE Greenslit family
Greenslate family
 USE Greenslit family
Greensledge family
 USE Greenslit family
Greenslet family
 USE Greenslit family
Greenslett family
 USE Greenslit family
Greenslid family
 USE Greenslit family
Greenslit family *(Not Subd Geog)*
   UF Greenslad family
      Greenslate family
      Greensledge family
      Greenslet family
      Greenslett family
      Greenslid family
      Greenslitt family
      Grinslet family
Greenslitt family
 USE Greenslit family
Greenstone belts *(May Subd Geog)*
   UF Belts, Greenstone
   BT Rocks, Metamorphic
Greenstreet family *(Not Subd Geog)*
Greentail prawn
 USE Metapenaeus bennettae
Greenville and French Broad Railroad
   BT Railroads—United States
Greenville, Treaty of, 1795
 [E83.794]
Greenwall family
 USE Greenwell family
Greenwalt family
 USE Greenwell family
Greenwater Lake Provincial Park (Sask.)
   BT Parks—Saskatchewan
Greenwater Valley Wilderness (Calif.)
   UF Greenwater Valley Wilderness Study
      Area (Calif.)
   BT National parks and reserves—
      California
      Wilderness areas—California
Greenwater Valley Wilderness Study Area
 (Calif.)
 USE Greenwater Valley Wilderness (Calif.)
Greenway Plaza (Houston, Tex.)
   BT Plazas—Texas
Greenwell family *(Not Subd Geog)*
   UF Greenewall family
      Greenewalt family
      Greenwall family
      Greenwalt family
      Greenwill family
      Grenewell family
      Grenwall family
      Grenwell family
      Grenwill family
Greenwich (New York, N.Y.)
 USE Greenwich Village (New York, N.Y.)
Greenwich Island (Caroline Islands)
 USE Kapingamarangi Atoll (Caroline
      Islands)
Greenwich Village (New York, N.Y.)
 (Not Subd Geog)
   UF Greenwich (New York, N.Y.)
      New York (N.Y.). Greenwich Village
Greenwill family
 USE Greenwell family
Greenwood Cemetery (Fowlerville, Mich.)
   BT Cemeteries—Michigan

Greenwood Cemetery (Greenwood, S.C.)
    UF Methodist Cemetery (Greenwood, S.C.)
          Old Methodist Cemetery (Greenwood, S.C.)
    BT Cemeteries—South Carolina
Greenwood Cemetery (Pittsburgh, Pa.)
    BT Cemeteries—Pennsylvania
Greenwood family *(Not Subd Geog)*
Greenwood Lake (N.J. and N.Y.)
    UF Long Pond (N.J. and N.Y.)
    BT Lakes—New Jersey
          Lakes—New York (State)
Greer family *(Not Subd Geog)*
    UF Grear family
          Greir family
          Greyer family
          Grier family
Greers Ferry Lake (Ark.)
    UF Greers Ferry Reservoir (Ark.)
    BT Lakes—Arkansas
          Little Red River (Ark.)
          Reservoirs—Arkansas
Greers Ferry Reservoir (Ark.)
  USE Greers Ferry Lake (Ark.)
Greesty family
  USE Grasty family
Greeting cards *(May Subd Geog)*
    ⌐BJ2095.G7 (Etiquette)¬
    ⌐NC1860 (Art)¬
    ⌐TX872 (Handicraft)¬
    UF Cards, Greeting
    NT Christmas cards
          New Year cards
          Valentines
Greeting cards industry *(May Subd Geog)*
    ⌐HD9839.G7-.G74¬
Greetings
  USE Salutations
Greever family *(Not Subd Geog)*
    UF Greaver family
          Griever family
Greeves, R. V. (Richard V.) **Unknown**
    UF Unknown (Sculpture)
    BT Bronze sculpture, American
Greff (Dog)
    BT Dogs
          Guide dogs
          Labrador retriever
Greffeth family
  USE Griffith family
Grefsenmarka (Oslo, Norway)
  USE Lillomarka (Oslo, Norway)
Greg family
  USE Gregg family
Gregal
  USE Gregale
Gregale
    ⌐QC939.G73¬
    UF Euroaquilo
          Euroclydon
          Grecale
          Gregal
          Gregau
          Guergal
    BT Winds—Mediterranean Region
Gregarines
    UF Gregarinida
    BT Sporozoa
Gregarinida
  USE Gregarines
Gregary family
  USE Gregory family
Gregau
  USE Gregale
Gregersen family *(Not Subd Geog)*
    UF Gregerson family
          Gregorson family
Gregerson family
  USE Gregersen family

Gregg family *(Not Subd Geog)*
    UF Greg family
          Greggs family
          Grigg family
          Griggs family
          Grigs family
    RT Grigsby family
Gregg shorthand
  USE Shorthand—Gregg
Gregg shorthand, French
  USE Shorthand, French—Gregg
Gregg shorthand, Italian
  USE Shorthand, Italian—Gregg
Gregg shorthand, Portuguese
  USE Shorthand, Portuguese—Gregg
Gregg shorthand, Russian
  USE Shorthand, Russian—Gregg
Gregg shorthand, Spanish
  USE Shorthand, Spanish—Gregg
Greggery family
  USE Gregory family
Greggory family
  USE Gregory family
Greggs family
  USE Gregg family
Grégoire (Legendary character)
  USE Gregorius (Legendary character)
Gregor family
  USE Gregory family
Gregorey family
  USE Gregory family
Gregorian calendar
  USE Calendar, Gregorian
Gregorian chant
  USE Chants (Plain, Gregorian, etc.)
Gregorius (Legendary character)
    UF Grégoire (Legendary character)
          Gregory (Legendary character)
    BT Folklore—Europe
Gregorson family
  USE Gregersen family
Gregory (Legendary character)
  USE Gregorius (Legendary character)
Gregory family *(Not Subd Geog)*
    UF Gragary family
          Greegory family
          Gregary family
          Greggery family
          Greggory family
          Gregor family
          Gregorey family
          Gregrey family
          Griggery family
          Griggory family
          Grigory family
          Grigrey family
    RT McGregor family
Gregrey family
  USE Gregory family
Greib family *(Not Subd Geog)*
Grein family
  USE Greiner family
Greindl family *(Not Subd Geog)*
Greiner family *(Not Subd Geog)*
    UF Grein family
          Greinke family
          Griner family
          Gruener family
          Gruner family
Greinke family
  USE Greiner family
Greir family
  USE Greer family
Grekul family *(Not Subd Geog)*
Grekul House (Smoky Lake, Alta.)
    BT Dwellings—Alberta
Gremaux family
  USE Grimard family
Gremillion family *(Not Subd Geog)*
    UF Gremillon family

Gremillon family
  USE Gremillion family
Gremlin automobile
    BT American Motors automobiles
Gremmeniella
Gremmeniella abietina
    ⌐SB741.S38 (Control)¬
    BT Fungi, Phytopathogenic
    NT Scleroderris canker
Gremmeniella canker
  USE Scleroderris canker
Gremore family
  USE Grimard family
Gremour family
  USE Grimard family
Grenada
  — History
  — — Coup d'état, 1979
        BT Coups d'état—Grenada
  — — **American invasion, 1983**
        UF American invasion of Grenada, 1983
           Operation Urgent Fury, 1983
        BT United States—History, Military—20th century
  — **Politics and government**
  — — **To 1974**
  — — **1974-**
Grenada, Battle of, 1779
    ⌐E271¬
    BT United States—History—Revolution, 1775-1783—Naval operations
          West Indies—History—1775-1783
Grenades *(May Subd Geog)*
    ⌐UF765¬
    UF Hand-grenades
          Rampart-grenades
          Rifle grenades
    BT Bombs
          Projectiles
Grenadian Americans *(May Subd Geog)*
    ⌐E184.G75¬
    UF Grenadian Americans—United States
    BT Ethnology—United States
          Grenadians—United States
  — United States
      USE Grenadian Americans
Grenadian poetry (English)
  (May Subd Geog)
    UF English poetry—Grenadian authors
    NT Revolutionary poetry, Grenadian (English)
Grenadian revolutionary poetry (English)
  USE Revolutionary poetry, Grenadian (English)
Grenadians *(May Subd Geog)*
    BT Ethnology—Grenada
  — **United States**
      NT Grenadian Americans
Grenadiers (Fishes)
  USE Macrouridae
Grenager family
  USE Grinager family
Grenell family
  USE Grinnell family
Grenelle family
  USE Grinnell family
Grenewell family
  USE Greenwell family
Grenfell family *(Not Subd Geog)*
Grenger family
  USE Granger family
Grenier family
    UF Granier family
    RT Garner family
Grennell family
  USE Grinnell family
Grenville family *(Not Subd Geog)*
Grenville Island (Fiji)
  USE Rotuma Island (Fiji)

Grenwall family
  USE Greenwell family
Grenwell family
  USE Greenwell family
Grenwill family
  USE Greenwell family
Grenz rays
  UF Infraroentgen rays
      Rays, Grenz
      Soft radiation
      Soft x radiation
      Soft x-rays
  BT X-rays
Grenzdörfer family *(Not Subd Geog)*
  UF Gräntzdörffer family
      Gränzdörfer family
      Gränzdörffer family
      Grenzdörffer family
      Grenzendörfer family
      Kreinsdorff family
      Krenzdörffer family
Grenzdörffer family
  USE Grenzdörfer family
Grenzendörfer family
  USE Grenzdörfer family
Gresham family *(Not Subd Geog)*
  UF Grisham family
      Grissam family
      Grissham family
Gresham's law
  ₍HG225₎
  BT Money
Grésivaudan Valley (France)
  USE Graisivaudan Valley (France)
Gresson family
  USE Creason family
Gressoney Valley (Italy)
  UF Cressoney Valley (Italy)
      Val di Gressoney (Italy)
  BT Valleys—Italy
Greste family
  USE Grasty family
Grestie family
  USE Grasty family
Gresty family
  USE Grasty family
Greswold family
  USE Griswold family
Gretz family
  USE Gratz family
Gretzer family
  USE Gratz family
Greup family *(Not Subd Geog)*
Greuter family
  USE Crider family
Greve family
  USE Grieve family
Greves family
  USE Grieve family
Greville family *(Not Subd Geog)*
Grex (The Latin word)
  BT Latin language—Etymology
Grey
  USE Gray
Grey-cheeked parakeet
  USE Gray-cheeked parakeet
Grey duiker
  USE Sylvicapra grimmia
Grey family
  USE Gray family
Grey Friars
  USE Franciscans
Grey heron
  USE Gray heron
Grey kangaroo
  ₍QL737.M35₎

  UF Eastern grey kangaroo
      Forester (Kangaroo)
      Giant kangaroo
      Great grey kangaroo
      Macropus canguru
      Macropus giganteus
      Macropus major
  BT Kangaroos
Grey-lag goose
  USE Greylag goose
Grey larch bud moth
  USE Zeiraphera diniana
Grey larch tortrix
  USE Zeiraphera diniana
Grey long-eared bat
  USE Plecotus austriacus
Grey mullets
  USE Gray mullets
Grey River (N.Z.)
  BT Rivers—New Zealand
Grey seal
  UF Halichoerus grypus
  BT Seals (Animals)
Grey shrew, Pale
  USE Pale grey shrew
Grey Sindhi cattle
  USE Tharparkar cattle
Grey Tirolean cattle
  ₍SF199.G74₎
  UF Grauvieh
      Oberinntal cattle
Greybill family
  USE Graybill family
Greye family
  USE Gray family
Greyer family
  USE Greer family
Greyhound racing *(May Subd Geog)*
  ₍SF440₎
  BT Dog racing
      Greyhounds
  — **Law and legislation** *(May Subd Geog)*
Greyhounds
  ₍SF429.G8₎
  UF Long dogs
      Longdogs
  BT Gazehounds
  NT Greyhound racing
      Italian greyhound
      Pharaoh hound
      Whippets
Greylag goose
  ₍QL696.A5₎
  UF Anser anser
      Grey-lag goose
  BT Geese
Greylock Reservation (Mass.)
  USE Mount Greylock State Reservation
      (Mass.)
Greysty family
  USE Grasty family
Greywacke
  USE Graywacke
Grid generation, Numerical (Numerical
    analysis)
  USE Numerical grid generation (Numerical
      analysis)
Grid lines
  USE Grids (Cartography)
GRID-P (Computer program)
  ₍T385₎
  BT Computer graphics
      Computer programs
Grid reference systems
  USE Grids (Cartography)
Grid systems
  USE Grids (Cartography)
Griddle cakes
  USE Pancakes, waffles, etc.
Grider family *(Not Subd Geog)*
  UF Kreiter family

  RT Crider family
Grids, Cattle
  USE Cattle guards
Grids (Cartography) *(May Subd Geog)*
  UF Grid lines
      Grid reference systems
      Grid systems
      Map grids
      Military grid system
  BT Cartography
      Coordinates
      Geographical location codes
      Maps
  RT Geographical positions
Grids (Cartography) in art
Grids (Electronics)
  USE Electron tubes—Grids
      Vacuum-tubes—Grids
Gridwork (Structural engineering)
  USE Grillages (Structural engineering)
Grieder family
  USE Crider family
Grief
  UF Mourning
      Sorrow
  BT Bereavement
      Emotions
      Loss (Psychology)
  NT Church work with the bereaved
      Consolation
      Crying
Grief in art
Grief in children
  ₍BF723.G75₎
  BT Bereavement in children
      Child psychology
Grief in literature
Griego family *(Not Subd Geog)*
Griep family
  USE Griepp family
Griepe family
  USE Griepp family
Griepentrog family *(Not Subd Geog)*
Griepp family *(Not Subd Geog)*
  UF Griep family
      Griepe family
      Grip family
      Gripp family
Grier family
  USE Greer family
Grierson's Cavalry Raid, 1863
  ₍E475.23₎
  BT Mississippi—History—Civil War,
      1861-1865
Griesemer family *(Not Subd Geog)*
  UF Griesheimer family
      Griesmer family
      Grisamore family
      Grismer family
      Grismore family
Grieser Altar
  USE Pacher, Michael, 15th cent. Gries
      Altar
Griesheimer family
  USE Griesemer family
Griesmer family
  USE Griesemer family
Griesty family
  USE Grasty family
Grievance arbitration *(May Subd Geog)*
  UF Arbitration, Grievance
      Arbitration, Judicable
      Judicable arbitration
  BT Arbitration, Industrial
Grievance procedures *(May Subd Geog)*
  ₍HD6972.5 (Industrial relations)₎
  ₍HF5549.5.G7 (Personnel
      management)₎
  UF Labor grievances
  BT Collective labor agreements
      Personnel management

Grievance procedures (Military law)
    USE Complaints (Military law)
Grieve family *(Not Subd Geog)*
    UF Greve family
        Greves family
        Grieves family
    RT Graves family
Griever family
    USE Greever family
Grieves family
    USE Grieve family
Grifeth family
    USE Griffith family
Griffan family
    USE Griffin family
Griffen family
    USE Griffin family
Griffes family
    USE Griffis family
Griffeth family
    USE Griffith family
Griffeths family
    USE Griffith family
Griffin, Fort (Tex.)
    USE Fort Griffin (Tex.)
Griffin family *(Not Subd Geog)*
    UF Griffan family
        Griffen family
        Griffine family
        Griffing family
        Griffinn family
        Griffins family
        Griffn family
        Grifin family
        Grifing family
        Griphin family
        Gryffin family
        Gryffyn family
        Gryfyn family
    RT Giffen family
        Giffin family
        Griffith family
Griffine family
    USE Griffin family
Griffing family
    USE Griffin family
Griffinn family
    USE Griffin family
Griffins
    UF Gryphons
    BT Animals, Mythical
Griffins family
    USE Griffin family
Griffins in art
Griffis family *(Not Subd Geog)*
    UF Griffes family
        Griffiss family
    RT Griffith family
Griffiss family
    USE Griffis family
Griffith family *(Not Subd Geog)*
    UF Greffeth family
        Grifeth family
        Griffeth family
        Griffeths family
        Griffiths family
        Griffits family
        Griffitts family
        Grifith family
        Grifiths family
    RT Giffen family
        Giffin family
        Griffin family
        Griffis family
Griffiths family
    USE Griffith family
Griffits family
    USE Griffith family
Griffitts family
    USE Griffith family

Griffn family
    USE Griffin family
Griffon, Brussels
    USE Brussels griffon
Grifin family
    USE Griffin family
Grifing family
    USE Griffin family
Grifith family
    USE Griffith family
Grifiths family
    USE Griffith family
Grigg family
    USE Gregg family
Griggery family
    USE Gregory family
Griggory family
    USE Gregory family
Griggs family
    USE Gregg family
Grignard reaction
    USE Grignard reagents
Grignard reagents
    ₍QD77₎
    UF Grignard reaction
    BT Chemical tests and reagents
    RT Organomagnesium compounds
Grigory family
    USE Gregory family
Grigrey family
    USE Gregory family
Grigs family
    USE Gregg family
Grigsby family *(Not Subd Geog)*
    RT Gregg family
Gṛihyasūtras
    ₍PK3057₎
    ₍PK3157₎
    ₍PK3257₎
    ₍PK3357₎
    ₍PK3457₎
    BT Vedas
Grijalva River (Mexico)
    UF Chaipa River (Mexico)
        Mezcalapa River (Mexico)
        Rio Grande de Chiapa (Mexico)
        Tabasco River (Mexico)
    BT Rivers—Mexico
Grill family *(Not Subd Geog)*
    UF Grille family
        Grills family
        Grylls family
Grillages (Structural engineering)
    ₍TA660.G7₎
    UF Gridwork (Structural engineering)
    BT Girders
        Structural frames
Grille family
    USE Grill family
Grilles *(May Subd Geog)*
    ₍NA3030₎
    UF Gratings
    BT Architecture—Details
        Doors
        Ironwork
        Windows
    NT Automobiles—Grilles
        Culverts—Grates
    — Patterns
Grilling (Cookery)
    USE Barbecue cookery
        Broiling
Grills family
    USE Grill family
Grim family
    USE Grimm family
Grima-Hermann House (New Orleans, La.)
    USE Hermann-Grima House (New Orleans,
        La.)
Grimaldi family *(Not Subd Geog)*
    UF Grimaldo family

Grimaldo family
    USE Grimaldi family
Grimani family *(Not Subd Geog)*
Grimard family *(Not Subd Geog)*
    UF Gremaux family
        Gremore family
        Gremour family
Grimes family *(Not Subd Geog)*
    RT Graham family
Grimilds hævn (Ballad)
    ₍PT8050.G₎
    BT Ballads, Danish
Grimm family *(Not Subd Geog)*
    UF Grim family
        Grimme family
Grimme family
    USE Grimm family
Grimmett family *(Not Subd Geog)*
    UF Grimmitt family
        Grimmitte family
Grimmiaceae
    ₍QK539.G7₎
    BT Grimmiales
    NT Racomitrium
Grimmiales
    ₍QK539.G₎
    BT Mosses
    NT Grimmiaceae
Grimmitt family
    USE Grimmett family
Grimmitte family
    USE Grimmett family
Grimsby Park (Grimsby, Ont.)
    BT Parks—Ontario
Grimsehl family *(Not Subd Geog)*
    UF Grimsel family
        Grimsell family
Grimsel family
    USE Grimsehl family
Grimsell family
    USE Grimsehl family
Grimsley family *(Not Subd Geog)*
Grimston family *(Not Subd Geog)*
Grimwood family *(Not Subd Geog)*
Grinager family *(Not Subd Geog)*
    UF Greenager family
        Grenager family
Grindall family
    USE Grinnell family
Grindel family
    USE Grinnell family
Grindeland family *(Not Subd Geog)*
Grindelia
    ₍QK495.C74₎
    BT Compositae
Grindelia squarrosa
    ₍QK495.C74₎
Grindell family
    USE Grinnell family
Grindelwald Glacier (Switzerland)
    UF Grindelwald Gletscher (Switzerland)
    BT Glaciers—Switzerland
Grindelwald Gletscher (Switzerland)
    USE Grindelwald Glacier (Switzerland)
Grinders, Centerless
    USE Centerless grinders
Grinders, Meat
    USE Meat grinders
Grinding, Autogenous
    USE Autogenous grinding
Grinding, Internal
    USE Internal grinding
Grinding (Size reduction)
    USE Size reduction of materials
Grinding and polishing
    ₍TJ1280-1298₎
    UF Buffing
        Lapping
        Polishing
    BT Machining
        Surface preparation

1590

NT Burnishing
    Centerless grinding
    Concrete—Finishing
    Deburring
    Electrolytic grinding
    Electrolytic polishing
    Emery-wheels
    Glass grinding and polishing
    Grinding machines
    Grinding wheels
    Honing
    Internal grinding
    Liquid honing
    Metallographic specimens
    Metals—Finishing
    Polishing wheels
    Sand-blast
    Sharpening of tools
    Stone polishing machinery
    Teeth—Polishing
    Tumbling (Metal finishing)
    Vibratory finishing (Metal work)
— Computer programs
   [TJ1280]

Grinding machinery industry
(May Subd Geog)
  BT Grinding machines

Grinding machines
  BT Grinding and polishing
  NT Centerless grinders
    Grinding machinery industry
    Grinding wheels
    Meat grinders
— Drawing
  USE Grinding machines—Drawings
— Drawings
  UF Grinding machines—Drawing
  BT Mechanical drawing
— Electric equipment
— Vibration

Grinding media in ball mills
  USE Ball mills—Grinding media
Grinding of occlusal tooth surfaces, Selective
  USE Occlusal adjustment
Grinding of teeth (Habit)
  USE Bruxism

Grinding wheels
  UF Abrasive wheels
    Grindstones
  BT Abrasives
    Grinding and polishing
    Grinding machines
  NT Diamond wheels
Grindle family
  USE Grinnell family
Grindol family
  USE Grinnell family
Grindoll family
  USE Grinnell family
Grindstone Creek (Mo.)
  BT Rivers—Missouri
Grindstones
  USE Grinding wheels
Griner family
  USE Greiner family
Grini (Norway : Concentration camp)
(Not Subd Geog)
  [D805.N8]
  BT Concentration camps—Norway
    World War, 1939-1945—
      Concentration camps—Norway
Grinley family (Not Subd Geog)
Grinnal family
  USE Grinnell family

Grinnell family (Not Subd Geog)
  UF Greenell family
    Grenell family
    Grenelle family
    Grennell family
    Grindall family
    Grindel family
    Grindell family
    Grindle family
    Grindol family
    Grindoll family
    Grinnal family
    Grinols family
Grinols family
  USE Grinnell family
Grinslet family
  USE Greenslit family
Grip (Golf)
  [GV979.G7]
  BT Golf
Grip family
  USE Griepp family
Gripe family
  USE Cripe family
Griphin family
  USE Griffin family
Griphosaurus
  USE Archaeopteryx
Gripman family (Not Subd Geog)
Gripon family (Not Subd Geog)
Gripp family
  USE Griepp family
Grippe
  USE Influenza
Grips (Machines, tools, etc.)
  USE Handles
Griquas
  [DT764.G]
  UF Bastaards
  BT Colored people (South Africa)
    Ethnology—South Africa
    Khoikhoi (African people)
    Miscegenation
Grisaille painting (May Subd Geog)
  BT Gray in art
    Painting—Technique
Grisak family (Not Subd Geog)
Grisamore family
  USE Griesemer family
Grisbåda question
  [DL658.8]
  UF Grisebaa question
Griscom family (Not Subd Geog)
Grisdale (Wash.)
  USE Camp Grisdale (Wash.)
Grisebaa question
  USE Grisbåda question
Griselda (Legendary character)
  UF Patient Griselda (Legendary character)
  BT Folklore—Italy
Grisham family
  USE Gresham family
Grismer family
  USE Griesemer family
Grismore family
  USE Griesemer family
Grisons in literature
Grissam family
  USE Gresham family
Grissham family
  USE Gresham family
Grist-mills
  USE Flour-mills
Gristle
  USE Cartilage
Griswald family
  USE Griswold family
Griswall family
  USE Griswold family
Griswell family
  USE Griswold family

Griswold Cemetery (Little Rock, Ill.)
  BT Cemeteries—Illinois
Griswold family (Not Subd Geog)
  UF Greswold family
    Griswald family
    Griswall family
    Griswell family
    Griswould family
Griswould family
  USE Griswold family
Grit
  USE Shot (Pellets)
Gritberry
  USE Arctostaphylos
Gritman family (Not Subd Geog)
  UF Gritmon family
    Grittman family
Gritmon family
  USE Gritman family
Grito de Ipiranga, Brazil, 1822
  USE Brazil—History—Revolution, 1822
Grito de Lares, Puerto Rico, 1868
  USE Puerto Rico—History—Insurrection,
    1868
Grito de Yara, Cuba, 1868
  USE Cuba—History—Insurrection, 1868-
    1878
Grits
  UF Hominy grits
  BT Cereals as food
    Corn as food
Gritti's amputation
  USE Amputations of leg
Grittman family
  USE Gritman family
Grivet monkey
  USE Cercopithecus aethiops
Grizzly bear
  [QL737.C27]
  UF Ursus arctos horribilis
    Ursus horribilis
  BT Bears
    Brown bear
Groase family
  USE Gross family
Groats
  [TX558.G67]
  BT Cereal products
Grobeck family (Not Subd Geog)
  UF Graabaek family
Grobin Davis Site (Okla.)
  UF Applegate Mounds (Okla.)
    White Oak Creek Site (Okla.)
  BT Oklahoma—Antiquities
Grobler family (Not Subd Geog)
Groce family
  USE Gross family
Groceries
  [HD9320-HD9330 (Economics)]
  [TX341-TX357 (Home economics)]
— Packaging
  USE Food—Packaging
— Purchasing
  USE Marketing (Home economics)
Grocers
  [HD9320-HD9330 (Economics)]
  [TX341-TX357 (Home economics)]
Grocery shopping
  USE Marketing (Home economics)
Grocery trade (May Subd Geog)
  [HD9320-HD9330 (Economics)]
  [HF5716.G8 (Cost tables)]
  [HF5849.G8 (Window displays)]
  [HF6161.G8 (Advertising)]
  [HF6201.G73 (Business)]
  NT Convenience stores
    Delicatessens
    Food brokers
    Product coding
    Self-service stores
    Supermarkets

Grocery trade (Continued)
  Wages—Grocery trade
  — Law and legislation (May Subd Geog)
    BT Food law and legislation
        Trade regulation
Grochów (Warsaw, Poland)
    (Not Subd Geog)
  UF Warsaw (Poland). Grochów
Grochów, Poland (Warsaw), Battle of, 1831
  USE Grochów (Warsaw, Poland), Battle of,
        1831
Grochów (Warsaw, Poland), Battle of, 1831
    [DK4362.5.G75]
  UF Grochów, Poland (Warsaw), Battle of,
        1831
  BT Poland—History—Revolution, 1830-
        1832—Campaigns
Grödner Bach (Italy)
  USE Gardena River (Italy)
Groenendael sheepdog
  USE Belgian sheepdog
Groeneveld family
  USE Gruenwald family
Groenewald family
  USE Gruenwald family
Groenewold family
  USE Gruenwald family
Groenincks family
  USE Groeninx family
Groeninx family (Not Subd Geog)
  UF Groenincks family
Groenveld family
  USE Gruenwald family
Groenvold family
  USE Gruenwald family
Groesbeck family (Not Subd Geog)
  UF Grossbeck family
        Grusbeck family
Grofe family
  USE Groff family
Groff family (Not Subd Geog)
  UF Grofe family
        Groffe family
        Groffman family
        Grofman family
        Groof family
  RT Graff family
        Grove family
Groffe family
  USE Groff family
Groffman family
  USE Groff family
Grofman family
  USE Groff family
Grog ration (United States Navy)
  USE United States. Navy—Rum ration
Groin
    [QM161 (Muscles)]
    [QM543]
  UF Inguen
        Inguinal region
        Regio inguinales
  BT Abdomen
        Thigh
  — Surgery
  — Tumors
Groins (Shore protection)
  UF Groynes (Shore protection)
  BT Hydraulic structures
        Shore protection
Groix Island (France)
  UF Croix Island (France)
        Ile de Croix (France)
        Ile de Groix (France)
  BT Islands—France
Groll family (Not Subd Geog)
Grølsted family (Not Subd Geog)
Gromada family (Not Subd Geog)
Grommets (Metal-work)
  USE Eyelets (Metal-work)

Grönland-wal (Airplane)
Grønningsæter family (Not Subd Geog)
Grøntved family (Not Subd Geog)
  UF Grøntvedt family
Grøntvedt family
  USE Grøntved family
Gronwall inequalities
  UF Inequalities, Gronwall
  BT Integral inequalities
Groof family
  USE Groff family
Groom family
  USE Grooms family
Groome family
  USE Grooms family
Groomes family
  USE Grooms family
Grooming, Personal
  USE Beauty, Personal
        Grooming for men
Grooming for men
    [RA777.8]
  UF Grooming, Personal
        Male grooming
        Toilet (Grooming)
  BT Men—Health and hygiene
  NT Men's clothing
Grooming for women
  USE Beauty, Personal
Grooming of cattle
  USE Cattle—Grooming
Grooming of horses
  USE Horses—Grooming
Grooming of sheep
  USE Sheep—Grooming
Grooms family (Not Subd Geog)
  UF Groom family
        Groome family
        Groomes family
Groot-Brakrivier (South Africa)
  USE Great Brak River (South Africa)
Groot family
  USE De Groot family
Groot Fortuin (Indonesia)
  USE Siberut (Indonesia)
Groot Karroo (South Africa)
  USE Great Karroo (South Africa)
Grootbrakrivier (South Africa)
  USE Great Brak River (South Africa)
Grootdraai Dam (South Africa)
  UF Grootdraaidam (South Africa)
  BT Dams—South Africa
Grootdraaidam (South Africa)
  USE Grootdraai Dam (South Africa)
Groote Eylandt (N.T.)
  BT Islands—Australia
Groote family
  USE De Groot family
Groote Schuur (Cape Town, South Africa)
  BT Dwellings—South Africa
        Prime ministers—South Africa—
        Dwellings
Grootfaam family (Not Subd Geog)
Groover family
  USE Grover family
Gröpelingen family (Not Subd Geog)
Gros family
  USE Gross family
Gros Ventre Wilderness (Wyo.)
  BT Wilderness areas—Wyoming
Gros Ventres of Montana
  USE Atsina Indians
Gros Ventres of the Missouri
  USE Hidatsa Indians
Gros Ventres of the Prairie
  USE Atsina Indians
Grosbeaks
    [QL696.P2]
  BT Finches
        Passeriformes
  SA names of grosbeaks, e.g. Cardinal-birds

Groschen (Coin) (May Subd Geog)
    [CJ2721]
  BT Coins, German
Groschenromane
  USE Dime novels, German
Grose family
  USE Gross family
Groseclose family (Not Subd Geog)
  UF Grosklaus family
  RT Gross family
Grosklaus family
  USE Groseclose family
Gross Clinic (Painting)
  USE Eakins, Thomas, 1844-1916. Gross
        Clinic
Gross family (Not Subd Geog)
  UF Groase family
        Groce family
        Gros family
        Grose family
        Grosse family
  RT Groseclose family
Gross national product (May Subd Geog)
  UF GNP
        National product, Gross
  BT Economics
        Statistics
        Wealth
  RT Income
        National income
Grossbeck family
  USE Groesbeck family
Grossbeeren, Battle of, 1813
  BT Napoleonic Wars, 1800-1814—
        Campaigns—Germany (East)
Grosse family
  USE Gross family
Grosse Grotte (Germany) (Not Subd Geog)
  BT Caves—Germany (West)
        Germany (West)—Antiquities
Grosse Ile (Québec)
  BT Islands—Québec (Province)
Grosser Feldberg (Germany)
  BT Mountains—Germany (West)
        Taunus (Germany)
Grossherzoglich Oldenburgische Eisenbahn
  BT Railroads—Germany (West)
Grossman family (Not Subd Geog)
  UF Grossmann family
Grossmann family
  USE Grossman family
Grossouvrinae
  USE Pseudoperisphinctinae
Grossspeicherorientierte, listenorientierte
    Ermittlungsmethode (Information retrieval
    system)
  USE GOLEM (Information retrieval
        system)
Grossvenor family
  USE Grosvenor family
Grosswetterlagen (May Subd Geog)
    [QC880.4.A8]
  BT Synoptic climatology
        Synoptic meteorology
  RT Atmospheric circulation
Grosvener family
  USE Grosvenor family
Grosvenor family (Not Subd Geog)
  UF Grossvenor family
        Grosvener family
        Grovener family
        Grovenor family
        Grovner family
Grosventre language
  USE Atsina language
        Hidatsa language
Grosventres of the Missouri
  USE Hidatsa Indians
Grosventres of the Prairie
  USE Atsina Indians

Grotelueschen family (Not Subd Geog)
Grotepass family (Not Subd Geog)
Grotesque (May Subd Geog)
 [BH301.G74 (Aesthetics)]
  BT Aesthetics
     Arabesques
     Burlesque (Literature)
     Caricature
     Comedy
     Satire
  NT Photography of the grotesque
Grotesque in architecture (May Subd Geog)
 [NA208.5]
  BT Architecture
Grotesque in art
 [N8217.G8]
  NT Gargoyles
Grotesque in literature
  NT Ugliness in literature
Groth family (Not Subd Geog)
  UF Grothe family
Grothe family
  USE Groth family
Grothendieck categories
  UF Categories, Grothendieck
  BT Abelian categories
Grothendieck groups
  BT Groups, Theory of
     Rings (Algebra)
Grothite
  USE Sphene
Groton Heights, Battle of, 1781
 [E241.G8]
  UF Fort Griswold, Massacre of, 1781
  BT Connecticut—History—Revolution,
     1775-1783
     United States—History—Revolution,
     1775-1783—Campaigns
Grotrian diagrams
  UF Diagrams, Grotrian
  BT Spectrum analysis
Grotta di Porto Badisco (Italy)
  USE Porto Badisco Cave (Italy)
Grotte de Lascaux (France)
  USE Lascaux Cave (France)
Grotto architecture
  USE Cave architecture
Grotto dei Cervi (Italy)
  USE Porto Badisco Cave (Italy)
Grottoes
  USE Caves
Grötzinger Malerkolonie
 [N6867.5.G7]
  BT Artist colonies—Germany (West)
Ground, Patterned
  USE Patterned ground
Ground anchors
  USE Guy anchors
Ground attack planes
  USE Attack planes
Ground bass
 [ML448]
  UF Basso ostinato
     Ostinato
  BT Composition (Music)
     Variation (Music)
Ground bean
  USE Bambarra groundnut
Ground beetles
  USE Carabidae
Ground cedar
  USE Juniperus communis
Ground control (Mining) (May Subd Geog)
 [TN288]
  UF Control of ground in mining
     Ground support (Mining)
  BT Mine subsidences
     Mining engineering
     Rock mechanics
  NT Concrete mine supports
     Gypsum-bonded mine roof bolts

     Kettlebottoms (Mining)
     Mine roof bolting
     Mine roof control
     Mine timbering
     Pillaring (Mining)
     Stoping (Mining)
Ground controlled approach
 [TL696.L33]
  UF Blind landing
     GCA
     Talk-down system
  BT Airplanes—Landing
     Instrument landing systems
     Landing aids (Aeronautics)
     Radar in aeronautics
Ground cover fires (May Subd Geog)
 [SD421.47]
  Here are entered works on fires involving any natural vegetation, particularly near or on the ground.
  BT Fires
     Wildfires
  NT Grassland fires
     Moors and heaths—Fires and fire
     prevention
  — **Prevention and control**
     [SD421.47]
     BT Fire extinction
       Fire prevention
Ground cover plants (May Subd Geog)
 [SB432]
  UF Cover plants
  BT Lawns
     Plants, Ornamental
  NT Paspalum hieronymii
Ground-cushion phenomenon
 [TA352]
 [TL574.G7 (Aeronautics)]
  UF Air-bearing lift
     Ground effect (Aerodynamics)
     Ground pressure (Aerodynamics)
  BT Aerodynamics
     Air jets
     Compressibility
     Lift (Aerodynamics)
     Pneumatics
  NT Ground-effect machines
Ground effect (Aerodynamics)
  USE Ground-cushion phenomenon
Ground-effect machine mail
  USE Hovermail
Ground-effect machines
  UF Air-bearing vehicles
     Air-cushion vehicles
     Ground pressure vehicles, Minimum
     Ground proximity machines
     Hovercraft
  BT Ground-cushion phenomenon
     Motor vehicles
  RT Lift fans
  NT Helicopters
     Vertically rising aircraft
  — **Dynamics**
     [TL574.G7]
  — **Vibration**
Ground handling of aircraft
  USE Airplanes—Ground handling
Ground-hogs
  USE Marmots
Ground ivy
  UF Gill-over-the-ground
     Glecoma hederacea
     Gleichoma hederacea
     Nepeta hederacea
Ground leases
  USE Building leases
Ground-nut oil
  USE Peanut oil
Ground-nuts
  USE Glycine (Plant)
     Peanuts

Ground penetrating radar
  UF Ground probing radar
     Subsurface radar
  BT Radar
Ground pressure (Aerodynamics)
  USE Ground-cushion phenomenon
Ground pressure vehicles, Minimum
  USE Ground-effect machines
Ground probing radar
  USE Ground penetrating radar
Ground proximity machines
  USE Ground-effect machines
Ground radioactive waste disposal
  USE Radioactive waste disposal in the
     ground
Ground-rent
  USE Rent
     Rent (Economic theory)
Ground simulators (Wind tunnels)
  USE Wind tunnels—Ground simulators
Ground skink
  USE Lygosoma laterale
Ground-speed indicator
 [TL696.G7]
  BT Aeronautical instruments
Ground squirrels
 [QL737.R68]
  UF Citellus
  BT Sciuridae
  NT California ground squirrel
     European souslik
     Golden-mantled ground squirrel
     Richardson ground squirrel
     Thirteen-lined ground squirrel
Ground squirrels as carriers of disease
 (May Subd Geog)
 [RA641.G7]
Ground stations (Satellite telecommunication)
  USE Earth stations (Satellite
     telecommunication)
Ground substance (Anatomy)
  USE Extracellular matrix
Ground support (Aeronautics, Military)
  USE United States. Navy—Aviation—
     Ground support
Ground support (Mining)
  USE Ground control (Mining)
Ground support equipment (Ordnance
  rocketry)
  USE Ground support systems (Ordnance
     rocketry)
Ground support operations (Ordnance
  rocketry)
  USE Ground support systems (Ordnance
     rocketry)
Ground support systems (Astronautics)
  BT Astrionics
     Astronautics
     Electricity in astronautics
  NT Earth stations (Satellite
     telecommunication)
     Launch complexes (Astronautics)
     Space vehicles—Tracking
     Space vehicles—Transportation
Ground support systems (Ordnance rocketry)
  UF Ground support equipment (Ordnance
     rocketry)
     Ground support operations (Ordnance
     rocketry)
  BT Rockets (Ordnance)
Ground temperature
  USE Earth temperature
Ground tits
  USE Wren tits
Ground-to-air missiles
  USE Surface-to-air missiles
Ground vibration
  USE Soils—Vibration
Ground water
  USE Water, Underground

Ground water level
  USE Water table
Ground-water recharge
  USE Water, Underground—Artificial
      recharge
Ground water surface
  USE Water table
Ground water table
  USE Water table
Ground-water tracers
  USE Groundwater tracers
Ground wood pulping process
  USE Mechanical pulping process
Grounded-anode amplifiers
  USE Cathode followers
Groundhog Day
  [GT4995.G]
  BT Holidays
Grounding (Electricity)
  USE Electric currents—Grounding
Grounding of ships
  USE Stranding of ships
Groundnut, Bambara
  USE Bambarra groundnut
Groundnut, Bambarra
  USE Bambarra groundnut
Groundnut, Madagascar
  USE Bambarra groundnut
Groundnut, Stone
  USE Bambarra groundnut
Groundnuts
  USE Peanuts
Grounds maintenance *(May Subd Geog)*
  Here are entered works on the maintenance of
  public, industrial, and institutional grounds and large
  estates.
  BT Gardening
     Horticultural service industry
     Landscape gardening
     Landscaping industry
     Maintenance
     Ornamental horticulture
  RT Landscape nurseries
  SA *subdivision* Maintenance *under special*
     subjects, e.g. Parks—Maintenance;
     Recreation areas—Maintenance
  NT Roadside improvement
     Turf management
Groundwater
  USE Water, Underground
Groundwater barriers
  USE Saline water barriers
Groundwater flow *(May Subd Geog)*
  [TC176]
  UF Base flow
     Flow, Groundwater
  BT Water, Underground
  RT Fluids—Migration
     Subsurface drainage
  NT Darcy's law
     Seepage
Groundwater quality
  USE Water, Underground—Quality
Groundwater tracers *(May Subd Geog)*
  UF Ground-water tracers
     Tracers, Groundwater
     Tracers (Hydrogeology)
  BT Hydrogeology—Methodology
  NT Radioactive tracers in hydrogeology
Groundwood pulping process
  USE Mechanical pulping process
Group, Brauer
  USE Brauer group
Group, Galilean
  USE Galilean group
Group, Renormalization
  USE Renormalization group
Group, Weil
  USE Weil group
Group, Witt
  USE Witt group

Group actions (Mathematics)
  UF Actions, Group (Mathematics)
  BT Algebraic varieties
     Topological transformation groups
Group algebras
  UF Algebras, Group
  BT Abelian groups
     Algebra
     Locally compact groups
Group B arboviruses
  USE Flaviviruses
Group characters
  USE Characters of groups
Group communication, Small
  USE Communication in small groups
Group counseling
  [BF637.C6]
  BT Counseling
  RT Group psychotherapy
  NT Group guidance in education
     Group intelligence tests
     Self-help groups
Group creditors insurance
  USE Insurance, Group creditors
Group decision-making
  USE Decision-making, Group
Group dental practice *(May Subd Geog)*
  UF Dental group practice
     Group practice in dentistry
  BT Dental clinics
     Dental economics
     Dentistry—Practice
Group discussion
  USE Discussion
     Forums (Discussion and debate)
Group divisibility
  USE Groups of divisibility
Group dynamics
  USE Social groups
Group extensions (Mathematics)
  [QA171]
  UF Extensions, Group (Mathematics)
  BT Groups, Theory of
  NT Weil group
Group games
  UF Group sports
     Sports for groups
     Team games
  BT Games
Group guidance in education
  BT Group counseling
     Personnel service in education
  NT Group intelligence tests
Group homes *(May Subd Geog)*
  Here are entered works on planned, single
  housekeeping units in residential dwellings that pro-
  vide care for small groups of unrelated residents liv-
  ing together as families, but requiring supervision.
  UF Community-based residences
  BT Institutional care
     Rehabilitation centers
     Social service
  NT Foster home care
     Halfway houses
  — Law and legislation *(May Subd Geog)*
  — Location
  — — Law and legislation
     (May Subd Geog)
Group homes for children *(May Subd Geog)*
  BT Children—Institutional care
     Foster home care
     Halfway houses
  NT Orphanages
  — Law and legislation *(May Subd Geog)*
     BT Children—Legal status, laws, etc.
Group homes for the developmentally disabled
  (May Subd Geog)
  BT Developmentally disabled—Housing
     Foster home care
     Halfway houses

Group homes for the handicapped
  (May Subd Geog)
  BT Foster home care
     Halfway houses
     Handicapped—Housing
Group homes for youth *(May Subd Geog)*
  BT Foster home care
     Halfway houses
     Youth—Housing
Group hospitalization
  USE Insurance, Hospitalization
Group identity *(May Subd Geog)*
  UF Collective identity
     Community identity
     Identity, Collective
     Identity, Community
     Identity, Group
     Identity, Social
     Social identity
  BT Identity (Psychology)
  NT Ethnicity
Group identity, Ethnic
  USE Ethnicity
Group insurance
  USE Insurance, Group
Group intelligence tests *(May Subd Geog)*
  [LB1130.G76]
  BT Group counseling
     Group guidance in education
     Intelligence tests
Group legal services
  USE Prepaid legal services
Group medical practice *(May Subd Geog)*
  [R729.5.G6]
  UF Group practice in medicine
     Medical group practice
  BT Medical cooperation
     Medical economics
     Medicine—Practice
  RT Clinics
  NT Clinic managers
     Health maintenance organizations
     Medical corporations
  — Law and legislation *(May Subd Geog)*
     BT Medical laws and legislation
  — Sociological aspects
     BT Sociology
Group medical practice, Prepaid
  USE Health maintenance organizations
Group method in teaching
  USE Group work in education
Group method of data handling algorithms
  USE GMDH algorithms
Group ministry
  [BV675]
  UF Co-ministry
     Ministry, Group
     Multiple staff ministry
     Team ministry
  BT Cooperative ministry
Group of three Figures (Sculpture)
  USE Steiner, Rudolf, 1861-1925. Group of
     Three Figures
Group parents
  USE Child care workers
Group portraits
  USE Portraits, Group
Group practice in dentistry
  USE Group dental practice
Group practice in medicine
  USE Group medical practice
Group prayer
  USE Prayer groups
Group presentations (Mathematics)
  USE Presentations of groups (Mathematics)
Group problem solving
  USE Problem solving, Group
Group psychoanalysis
  [RC510]
  BT Group psychotherapy
     Psychoanalysis

Group psychotherapists
[RC488]
BT Psychotherapists
Group psychotherapy
[RC488]
UF Collective psychotherapy
BT Psychotherapy
RT Group counseling
NT Family psychotherapy
Group psychoanalysis
Moving-pictures in psychotherapy
Psychodrama
Group reading *(May Subd Geog)*
[LC6601-6660]
UF Book-study groups
Great books program
Reading circles
Reading groups
BT Forums (Discussion and debate)
RT Book clubs
Books and reading
Group relations training
UF Consciousness-raising groups
Encounter groups
Sensitivity training
T-groups
BT Interpersonal relations
Small groups
Social interaction
Social perception
Group representation (Mathematics)
USE Representations of groups
Group rings
BT Groups, Theory of
Rings (Algebra)
Group schemes (Mathematics)
UF Schemes, Group (Mathematics)
BT Geometry, Algebraic
Groups, Theory of
Schemes (Algebraic geometry)
NT Groups, Formal
p-divisible groups
Group selection (Evolution)
[QH376]
BT Evolution
Population biology
Group sex *(May Subd Geog)*
UF Orgies
Swinging (Sexual behavior)
BT Sex
Sex customs
Group sports
USE Group games
Group suicide
USE Mass suicide
Group teaching
USE Group work in education
Group technology
[TS155]
BT Production management
Group theory, Combinatorial
USE Combinatorial group theory
Group work, Church
USE Church group work
Group work, Social
USE Social group work
Group work in architecture
(May Subd Geog)
UF Team work in architecture
BT Architectural practice
Architecture
Group work in art *(May Subd Geog)*
UF Teamwork in art
Group work in education
UF Group method in teaching
Group teaching
BT Education
Teaching
NT Team learning approach in education
Workshops (Adult education)

Groupe Finistère (Group of artists)
[ND548.5.F56]
BT Painting, French
Groupe Témoignage
USE Témoignage (Group of artists)
Groupement d'interêt economique
BT Corporations, Nonprofit—France
Juristic persons—France
Partnership—France
Grouper fisheries *(May Subd Geog)*
BT Fisheries
Groupers
[QL638.S48]
BT Serranidae
NT Cookery (Groupers)
Epinephelus
Groupies *(May Subd Geog)*
BT Rock music—Fans
Youth
Grouping, Homogeneous
USE Ability grouping in education
Grouping by ability
USE Ability grouping in education
Groupoids
BT Groups, Theory of
NT Lie groupoids
Groups, Age
USE Age groups
Groups, Bieberbach
USE Bieberbach groups
Groups, Chamber music
USE Chamber music groups
Groups, Characters of
USE Characters of groups
Groups, Chevalley
USE Chevalley groups
Groups, Class (Mathematics)
USE Class groups (Mathematics)
Groups, Combinatorial
USE Combinatorial group theory
Groups, Compact
USE Compact groups
Groups, Compact Abelian
USE Compact Abelian groups
Groups, Continuous
[QA385]
UF Continuous groups
BT Differential equations
Lie algebras
NT Differential forms
Differential invariants
Ergodic theory
Fiber bundles (Mathematics)
Galilean group
Lorentz groups
Topological groups
Transformations, Infinitesimal
Groups, Diagnosis related
USE Diagnosis related groups
Groups, Dimensionless
USE Dimensionless numbers
Groups, Discrete
USE Discrete groups
Groups, Ethnic
USE Ethnic groups
Groups, Existentially closed
USE Existentially closed groups
Groups, FC
USE FC-groups
Groups, Finite
USE Finite groups
Groups, Finite conjugate
USE FC-groups
Groups, Formal
UF Formal groups
BT Group schemes (Mathematics)
Groups, Theory of
Groups, Free metabelian
USE Free metabelian groups
Groups, Holonomy
USE Holonomy groups

Groups, Hopfian
USE Hopfian groups
Groups, Infinite
USE Infinite groups
Groups, Janko
USE Janko groups
Groups, Kleinian
USE Kleinian groups
Groups, Lie
USE Lie groups
Groups, Lorentz
USE Lorentz groups
Groups, Mathieu
USE Mathieu groups
Groups, Multiply transitive
[QA171]
UF Multiply transitive groups
Transitive groups, Multiply
BT Finite groups
Permutation groups
Groups, Musical
USE Musical groups
Groups, Nilpotent
UF Nilpotent groups
BT Finite groups
NT Lie groups, Nilpotent
Localization theory
Polycyclic groups
Groups, Non-Abelian
USE Non-Abelian groups
Groups, Non-Hopfian
USE Non-Hopfian groups
Groups, Nonabelian
USE Non-Abelian groups
Groups, Orderable
USE Orderable groups
Groups, Picard
USE Picard groups
Groups, Prayer
USE Prayer groups
Groups, Q
USE Q-groups
Groups, Rational
USE Q-groups
Groups, Representation theory of
USE Representations of groups
Groups, Rock
USE Rock groups
Groups, Self-help
USE Self-help groups
Groups, Small
USE Small groups
Groups, Social
USE Social groups
Groups, Sporadic (Mathematics)
USE Sporadic groups (Mathematics)
Groups, Symmetry
USE Symmetry groups
Groups, Symplectic
USE Symplectic groups
Groups, Theory of
[QA171]
UF Substitutions
BT Algebra
Algebra, Abstract
Equations, Theory of
Functions, Polyhedral
Mathematics
Numbers, Theory of
NT Abelian groups
Algebra, Boolean
Arithmetic groups
Automorphisms
Bieberbach groups
Categories (Mathematics)
Combinatorial group theory
Crystallography, Mathematical
Differential algebraic groups
Discontinuous groups
Eightfold way (Nuclear physics)
Finite groups

Groups, Theory of *(Continued)*
    Fourier transformations
    Free groups
    Free products (Group theory)
    Frobenius groups
    Functions, Modular
    Fundamental groups (Mathematics)
    Galois theory
    Games of strategy (Mathematics)
    Gauge fields (Physics)
    Grothendieck groups
    Group extensions (Mathematics)
    Group rings
    Group schemes (Mathematics)
    Groupoids
    Groups, Formal
    Heaps (Mathematics)
    Homotopy groups
    Hopfian groups
    Hypergroups
    Infinite groups
    Isomorphisms (Mathematics)
    Lattice ordered groups
    Lattice theory
    Linear algebraic groups
    Loops (Group theory)
    Lorentz groups
    Lorentz transformations
    Matrix groups
    Maximal subgroups
    Modular groups
    Non-Abelian groups
    Non-Hopfian groups
    Ordered groups
    p-adic groups
    Permutation groups
    Pregroups
    Presentations of groups (Mathematics)
    Profinite groups
    Quasigroups
    Representations of groups
    Rotation groups
    Rubik's Cube
    Rubik's Revenge
    Semigroups
    Solvable groups
    Space groups
    Spectral synthesis (Mathematics)
    Transformation groups
    Transformations (Mathematics)
    Unitary groups
    Weil group
    Witt group
    Word problems (Mathematics)
  — **Generators**
    UF Generators of groups
    NT Burnside problem
  — **Reflections**
    UF Reflections of groups
  — **Relations**
    UF Relations in group theory
    NT Burnside problem
Groups, Topological
  USE Topological groups
Groups, Torsion free Abelian
  USE Torsion free Abelian groups
Groups, Whitehead
  USE Whitehead groups
Groups, Work
  USE Work groups
Groups of divisibility
  UF Divisibility groups
     Divisible groups
     Group divisibility
  BT Algebra
     Ordered groups
Groups of galaxies
  USE Galaxies—Clusters
Groups of points
    [QA603]
  BT Set theory

    NT Convex domains
Groups of rotations
  USE Rotation groups
Groups of stars
  USE Stars—Clusters
Groups of transformations
  USE Transformation groups
Groups, p-adic
  USE p-adic groups
Groups, p-divisible
  USE p-divisible groups
Grouse
    [QL696.G2 (Zoology)]
    [SK325.G (Hunting)]
  BT Upland game birds
  NT Black grouse
     Bonasa
     Capercaillie
     Dusky grouse
     Ptarmigans
     Rock ptarmigan
     Ruffed grouse
     Sage grouse
     Sharp-tailed grouse
     Spruce grouse
     Willow ptarmigan
Grouse, Ruffed
  USE Ruffed grouse
Grouse hunting
  USE Grouse shooting
Grouse shooting *(May Subd Geog)*
  UF Grouse hunting
  BT Upland game bird shooting
  NT Ruffed grouse shooting
Grout (Mortar)
    [TA434]
  UF Cement grout
  BT Grouting
     Mortar
Grouting
  UF Pressure grouting
  BT Concrete construction
     Masonry
     Mortar
  NT Grout (Mortar)
Grov family
  USE Grove family
Grove, Battle of the, Va., 1864
  USE Wilson-Kautz Raid, Va., 1864
Grove family *(Not Subd Geog)*
  UF Grov family
     Groves family
     Grovs family
  RT Graff family
     Groff family
     Grover family
Grovener family
  USE Grosvenor family
Grovenor family
  USE Grosvenor family
Grover family *(Not Subd Geog)*
  UF Groover family
     Grovier family
  RT Grove family
Groves, Sacred
  USE Sacred groves
Groves family
  USE Grove family
Groveton, Battle of, 1862
  USE Bull Run, 2d Battle, 1862
Grovier family
  USE Grover family
Grovner family
  USE Grosvenor family
Grovs family
  USE Grove family
Grow frames, Solar
  USE Solar growing frames
Growers, Apple
  USE Apple growers

Growers, Coconut
  USE Coconut farmers
Growers, Cotton
  USE Cotton farmers
Growers, Potato
  USE Potato growers
Growing frames, Solar
  USE Solar growing frames
Growing media, Plant
  USE Plant growing media
Growing of Christmas trees
  USE Christmas tree growing
Growlers (Electrical engineering)
    [TK2799]
  BT Electric apparatus and appliances
     Electric testing
     Electric transformers
Grown-up abused children
  USE Adult child abuse victims
Grown-up children
  USE Adult children
     Young adults
Growth
    [QH511 (Biology)]
    [QP84 (Physiology)]
  BT Morphology (Animals)
     Physiology
  RT Developmental biology
  SA *subdivision* Growth *under subjects, e.g.*
     Cities and towns—Growth; Crystals
     —Growth; Fishes—Growth; Foot—
     Growth
  NT Allometry
     Bacterial growth
     Chemotaxis
     Developmental genetics
     Growth (Plants)
     Heterosis
     Human growth
     Microbial growth
     Ossification
     Regeneration (Biology)
  — **Research** *(May Subd Geog)*
    [QP84]
Growth, Personal
  USE Self-actualization (Psychology)
Growth (Bacteria)
  USE Bacterial growth
Growth (Plants)
    [QK731-769]
  UF Plant growth
     Plants—Growth
  BT Botany
     Growth
     Plant physiology
     Plants
  RT Diosmosis
     Meristem
     Plants—Development
     Rejuvenescence (Botany)
  SA *subdivision* Growth *under particular*
    plants, e.g. Algae—Growth; Corn—
    Growth; *etc.*
  NT Algae—Growth
     Bacterial growth
     Crops—Growth
     Geotropism
     Growth cabinets and rooms
     Heterosis
     Hydrotropism
     Microbial growth
     Plant growing media
     Plant hormones
     Plant regulators
     Plants—Photomorphogenesis
     Regeneration (Botany)
     Tree-rings
     Trees—Growth
     Vernalization
Growth (Psychology)
  USE Maturation (Psychology)

Success

Growth cabinets and rooms
  [QK715.5 (General)]
  UF Growth chambers
      Rooms, Growth
  BT Greenhouses
      Growth (Plants)
  RT Phytotron
— **Environmental engineering**
Growth chambers
  USE Growth cabinets and rooms
Growth disorders
  BT Metabolism—Disorders
  NT Dwarfism
      Failure to thrive syndrome
      Fetus—Growth retardation
Growth factors
  USE Growth promoting substances
Growth hormone
  USE Somatotropin
Growth hormone deficiency
  USE Dwarfism, Pituitary
Growth hormone inhibitory hormone
  USE Somatostatin
Growth hormone release inhibiting factor
  USE Somatostatin
Growth inhibiting substances
  BT Agricultural chemicals
      Plant regulators
  NT Plant hormones
Growth promoting substances
  [QK731 (Botany)]
  UF Growth factors
      Growth substances
  BT Agricultural chemicals
      Plant regulators
  NT Colony-stimulating factors
        (Physiology)
      Indoleacetic acid
      Nerve growth factor
      Plant hormones
      Somatomedin
— **Implantation**
  UF Implantation of growth promoting
      substances
Growth regulating substances
  USE Growth regulators
Growth regulators
  UF Growth regulating substances
  NT Plant regulators
Growth retardation
  USE Dwarfism
Growth retardation, Fetal
  USE Fetus—Growth retardation
Growth retardation, Intrauterine
  USE Fetus—Growth retardation
Growth substances
  USE Growth promoting substances
Groynes (Shore protection)
  USE Groins (Shore protection)
Grub family
  USE Grubb family
Grubb family *(Not Subd Geog)*
  UF Grub family
      Grubbs family
      Grubs family
Grubbiaceae
  [QK495.G76 (Botany)]
  BT Santalales
Grubbs family
  USE Grubb family
Grube family
  USE Gruber family
Gruben family *(Not Subd Geog)*
Grubenmann family *(Not Subd Geog)*
Gruber family *(Not Subd Geog)*
  UF Grube family
      Grubman family
      Grubner family
  RT Graber family

Gruber-Widal reaction
  USE Typhoid fever—Diagnosis—
      Agglutination reaction
Grubman family
  USE Gruber family
Grubner family
  USE Gruber family
Grubs family
  USE Grubb family
Gruel
  USE Porridge
Gruel, Rice
  USE Congee
Gruener family
  USE Greiner family
Gruenhagen family *(Not Subd Geog)*
  UF Greenhagen family
      Grunhagen family
  RT Green family
Gruenigen family
  USE Von Grunigen family
Gruenwald family *(Not Subd Geog)*
  UF Groeneveld family
      Groenewald family
      Groenewold family
      Groenveld family
      Groenvold family
      Grunewald family
      Grunwald family
Gruganus family *(Not Subd Geog)*
  UF Garganus family
      Gurganey family
      Gurgany family
      Gurgeyney family
Gruidae
  USE Cranes (Birds)
Gruiformes *(May Subd Geog)*
  [QL696.G8]
  BT Birds
  NT Aramidae
      Bustards
      Cranes (Birds)
      Psophiidae
      Rallidae
Gruinse
  USE Gurunsi (African people)
Grumman airplanes
  [TL686.G]
  NT Albatross (Amphibian planes)
      Cougar (Jet fighter plane)
      EA-6 (Electronic warfare aircraft)
      Grumman Avenger (Bombers)
      Grumman X-29A (Jet plane)
      Hellcat (Fighter planes)
      Panther (Jet fighter plane)
      Tiger (Jet fighter plane)
      Wildcat (Fighter plane)
Grumman Albatross
  USE Albatross (Amphibian planes)
Grumman Avenger (Bombers)
  BT Bombers
      Grumman airplanes
Grumman F6F Hellcat
  USE Hellcat (Fighter planes)
Grumman Model 712 Forward Swept Wing
  Demonstrator (Jet plane)
  USE Grumman X-29A (Jet plane)
Grumman Tomcat (Fighter plane)
  USE Tomcat (Jet fighter plane)
Grumman X-29A (Jet plane)
  UF Forward Swept Wing Demonstrator,
      Grumman Model 712 (Jet plane)
      FSW Demonstrator, Grumman Model
      712 (Jet plane)
      Grumman Model 712 Forward Swept
      Wing Demonstrator (Jet plane)
  BT Grumman airplanes
      Jet planes
Grundlast
  USE Reallast

Grundtvigianism
  [BR986]
  UF Grundtvigians
  BT Lutheran Church—Denmark
      Theology, Doctrinal—Denmark—
      History
Grundtvigians
  USE Grundtvigianism
Grundy (Race horse)
  [SF355.G]
Gruner family
  USE Greiner family
**Grünewald, Matthias, 16th cent.   Mocking of
Christ**
  [ND588.G7]
  UF Mocking of Christ (Painting)
      Verspottung Christi (Painting)
  BT Jesus Christ—Art
Grunewald family
  USE Gruenwald family
Grunhagen family
  USE Gruenhagen family
Grunigen family
  USE Von Grunigen family
Grunion
  [QL638.A8]
  UF Leuresthes tenuis
  BT Silversides
Grunshi
  USE Gurunsi (African people)
Grunt fisheries *(May Subd Geog)*
  [SH351.G78]
  BT Fisheries
  RT Grunts (Fishes)
— **Catch effort**
Grunts (Fishes)
  [QL638.P772]
  UF Gaterinidae
      Haemulidae
      Haemulonidae
      Plectorhynchidae
      Pomadasidae
      Pomadasyidae
      Pristipomatidae
      Pristipomidae
      Xenichthyidae
  BT Perciformes
  RT Grunt fisheries
  NT Pomadasys
Grunwald, Battle of, 1410
  USE Tannenberg, Battle of, 1410
Grunwald family
  USE Gruenwald family
Grunwick (Firm) Strike, 1976-1977
  [HD5366.P43]
  BT Photographic industry—Employees
      Strikes and lockouts—Photographic
      industry—Great Britain
      Strikes and lockouts—Great Britain
Grupa Śnieżnika (Poland and Czechoslovakia)
  USE Śnieżnik Mountains (Poland and
      Czechoslovakia)
Grupa Toruńska (Group of artists)
  UF Toruńska, Grupa (Group of artists)
  BT Art, Polish
Grupa Zacheta (Group of artists)
  UF Zacheta, Grupa (Group of artists)
  BT Art, Polish
Grupe family *(Not Subd Geog)*
Grupo Grimm (Group of artists)
  BT Landscape painting, Brazilian
Gruppo della Marmolada (Italy)
  USE Marmolada Mountains (Italy)
Gruppo dell'Adamello (Italy)
  USE Adamello Mountains (Italy)
Grus
  [QL696.G84]
  BT Cranes (Birds)
  NT Japanese crane
Grus americana
  USE Whooping cranes

Grus canadensis
USE Sandhill crane
Grus grus
USE Common crane
Grus japonensis
USE Japanese crane
Grus nigricolis
USE Black-necked crane
Grusbeck family
USE Groesbeck family
Grusi
USE Gurunsi (African people)
Grusi dialects
USE Gurunsi dialects
Grusian literature
USE Georgian literature
Grusinians
USE Georgians (Transcaucasians)
Grussi
USE Gurunsi (African people)
Grussi dialects
USE Gurunsi dialects
Grüter family
USE Crider family
Grütter family
USE Crider family
Gryffin family
USE Griffin family
Gryffyn family
USE Griffin family
Gryfyn family
USE Griffin family
Gryllacrididae
[QL508.G77]
BT Orthoptera
NT Farallonophilus
Stenopelmatus
Gryllidae
USE Crickets
Gryllotalpa
[QL508.G87]
BT Mole-crickets
Gryllotalpa gryllotalpa
[QL508.G87]
Gryllotalpidae
USE Mole-crickets
Gryllotalpinae
USE Mole-crickets
Grylls family
USE Grill family
Grynderup family (Not Subd Geog)
UF Grynnerup family
Grynnerup family
USE Grynderup family
Grynszpan family (Not Subd Geog)
Gryphaea angulata
USE American oyster
Gryphons
USE Griffins
Gryphornis
USE Archaeopteryx
Gryposis penis
USE Chordee
Grystidae
USE Centrarchidae
Grzbiet Tomaszowski-Lwowski (Poland and
Ukraine)
USE Roztocze Range (Poland and Ukraine)
Gsell family
USE Sell family
Gśin-rje (Buddhist deity)
USE Yama (Buddhist deity)
GSP (Tariff)
USE Tariff preferences
GTI automobile
[TL215.G]
BT Volkswagen automobile
GTO automobile
[TL215.G]
BT Pontiac automobile

Gtor-ma (Buddhist liturgical object)
BT Buddhist liturgical objects—Lamaism
Gu Achi Site (Ariz.) (Not Subd Geog)
BT Arizona—Antiquities
Gu Mountain (China)
USE Ku Mountain (China)
Gu-shan (China)
USE Ku Mountain (China)
Guacanahua Indians
USE Ese Ejje Indians
Guacanahua language
USE Ese Ejja language
Guachichile Indians
[F1219]
BT Indians of Mexico
Guadalajara, Battle of, 1937
[DP269.2.G]
BT Spain—History—Civil War, 1936-1939
—Campaigns
Guadalaviar River (Spain)
USE Turia River (Spain)
Guadalcanal Island (Solomon Islands)
BT Islands of the Pacific
Solomon Islands
**Guadalcanal Island (Solomon Islands), Battle
of, 1942-1943**
[D767.98]
BT World War, 1939-1945—Campaigns—
Pacific Ocean
Guadalquivir River (Spain)
UF Baetis River (Spain)
Betis River (Spain)
Kebir Wadi (Spain)
Río Guadalquivir (Spain)
Wadi el Kebir (Spain)
BT Rivers—Spain
Wadis—Spain
Guadalupe, Nuestra Señora de
USE Guadalupe, Our Lady of
Guadalupe, Our Lady of
[BT660.G8-82]
UF Guadalupe, Nuestra Señora de
Nuestra Señora de Guadalupe
Our Lady of Guadalupe
BT Christian shrines—Mexico
Mary, Blessed Virgin, Saint—
Apparitions and miracles—Mexico
Mary, Blessed Virgin, Saint—Cult—
Mexico
Guadalupe fur seal
[QL737.P63]
UF Arctocephalus philippii
Arctocephalus townsendi
Juan Fernandez fur seal
Philippi fur seal
BT Eared seals
Guadalupe Island (Mexico)
UF Isla de Guadalupe (Mexico)
Isla Guadalupe (Mexico)
BT Islands—Mexico
Guadalupe Mountains National Park (Tex.)
BT National parks and reserves—United
States
Parks—Texas
Guadalupe River (Tex.)
BT Rivers—Texas
NT Canyon Lake (Tex.)
Guadalupe Ruin (N.M.)
UF Guadalupe Site (N.M.)
BT New Mexico—Antiquities
Pueblos—Mexico
Guadalupe Site (N.M.)
USE Guadalupe Ruin (N.M.)
Guadarrama Mountains (Spain)
UF Sierra de Guadarrama (Spain)
BT Mountains—Spain
Guadeloupe children's poetry (French)
USE Children's poetry, Guadeloupe
(French)

Guadeloupe children's writings (French)
USE Children's writings, Guadeloupe
(French)
Guadeloupe fiction (French)
[PQ3948.5.G8 (History)]
[PQ3948.5.G82 (Collections)]
UF French fiction—Guadeloupe authors
Guadeloupe poetry (French)
(May Subd Geog)
[PQ3948.5.G]
UF French poetry—Guadeloupe authors
NT Children's poetry, Guadeloupe
(French)
Guadeloupe poetry (French Creole)
(May Subd Geog)
UF Creole poetry, Guadeloupe French
French Creole poetry, Guadeloupe
Guadelupe woodpecker
[QL696.P56]
UF Melanerpes herminieri
Guadiamar River (Spain)
UF Río Guadiamar (Spain)
BT Rivers—Spain
Guadiana River (Spain and Portugal)
UF Rio Guadiana (Spain and Portugal)
BT Rivers—Portugal
Rivers—Spain
Guaharibo Indians
UF Aharaibu Indians
Vajaribo Indians
BT Indians of South America
Yanoama Indians
Guahibo Indians
[F2319.2.G8]
UF Guaibo Indians
BT Indians of South America
NT Cuiva Indians
Guahibo language
[PM6013]
UF Guaigua language
Wa-jibi language
BT Arawakan languages
Indians of South America—Languages
NT Cuiva language
Sicuane dialect
Guahibo law
USE Law, Guahibo
Guaiac
USE Guaiacum
Guaiac wood oil (May Subd Geog)
UF Bois gaiac essence
Champaca wood oil
Esencia de guayacán
Esencia de palo santo
Essence de bois gaiac
Gaiac, Essence de bois
Guaiacum wood oil
Guayacán, Esencia de
Ligni guaiaci, Oleum
Oil of guaiac wood
Oleum ligni guaiaci
Palo santo, Esencia de
BT Bulnesia sarmienti
Essences and essential oils
Guaiac wood oil industry (May Subd Geog)
[HD9999.E78]
Guaiacum
UF Guaiac
Guaiacum wood oil
USE Guaiac wood oil
Guaiaqui language
USE Guayaki language
Guaibo Indians
USE Guahibo Indians
Guaica Indians
USE Waica Indians
Guaicuruan languages
USE Guaycuruan languages
Guaigua language
USE Guahibo language

1598

Guaiño
USE Huayno
Guajajara Indians
USE Tenetehara Indians
Guajajara language
USE Tenetehara language
Guajira language
USE Goajiro language
Guajiro Indians
USE Goajiro Indians
Gualán (Guatemala), Battle of, 1954
[F1466.5]
BT Guatemala—History—Revolution,
1954—Campaigns
Gualtney family
USE Gwartney family
Guamanian cookery
USE Cookery, Guamanian
Guambia Indians
USE Moguex Indians
Guambia language
USE Moguex language
Guambiano Indians
USE Moguex Indians
Guambiano language
USE Moguex language
Guana Indians
[F2230.2.G]
BT Indians of South America
NT Tereno Indians
Guana language
[PM6051]
BT Indians of South America—Languages
Guanabara Bay (Brazil)
UF Baia de Guanabara (Brazil)
Rio de Janeiro Bay (Brazil)
BT Bays—Brazil
Guanaco
[QL737.U54]
UF Huanaco
Lama guanicoe
BT Lama (Genus)
Guanajuatite
Guanano language
[PM6058]
UF Anano language
Kotiria language
Uanana language
Wanana language
Guanare River (Venezuela)
UF R'io Guanare (Venezuela)
BT Rivers—Venezuela
Guanche language
[PJ2371]
UF Canarian language (Canary Islands)
Teneriffan language
BT Berber languages
Extinct languages
Guanches
[DP302.C36-DP302.C51 (Canary
Islands)]
[GN661.C2 (Ethnology)]
BT Berbers
Guang language
USE Gonja language
Guanidine
[QP801.G8 (Biochemistry)]
UF Aminoformamidine
Aminomethanamidine
Carbamamidine
Carbamidine
Carbondiamide imide
Iminourea
Uramine
BT Amidines
RT Guanidino compounds
Guanidine compounds
USE Guanidino compounds
Guanidines
USE Guanidino compounds

Guanidino compounds
[QP801.G83]
UF Guanidine compounds
Guanidines
Guanido compounds
RT Guanidine
NT Cimetidine
Mercaptoethylguanidine
Guanido compounds
USE Guanidino compounds
Guano
[HD9484.G9 (Trade)]
[S649]
BT Manures
Organic fertilizers
Organic wastes as fertilizer
Guano industry *(May Subd Geog)*
[HD9484.G8-9]
Guanosine cyclic monophosphate
USE Cyclic guanylic acid
Guanylic acid, Cyclic
USE Cyclic guanylic acid
Guar
UF Camposia teragonolobus
Cyamopsis psoralioides
Cyamopsis tetragonoloba
Cyanopsis psoralioides
Cyanopsis tetragonoloba
BT Legumes
Guar gum industry *(May Subd Geog)*
[HD9235.G8-82]
Guarana *(May Subd Geog)*
[QK495.S19 (Botany)]
[SB295.G8 (Medicinal plant)]
UF Paullinia cupana
BT Psychotropic plants
Guarani drama *(May Subd Geog)*
Guarani folk-songs
USE Folk-songs, Guarani
Guarani imprints *(May Subd Geog)*
[Z7122.G9]
Guarani Indians
[F2230.2.G72]
BT Indians of Central America
Indians of South America
NT Apapocuva Indians
Asurini Indians
Caingua Indians
Guayaqui Indians
Héta Indians
Pauserna Indians
Seven Reductions, War of the, 1754-
1756
— Antiquities
— Missions
Guarani language
[PM7171-9]
BT Indians of South America—Languages
Tupi languages
RT Guarayo language
NT Guayaki language
Guarani literature *(May Subd Geog)*
Guarani proverbs
USE Proverbs, Guarani
Guarani songs
USE Songs, Guarani
Guaranine
USE Caffeine
Guaranteed annual income
(May Subd Geog)
UF Annual income guarantee
Guaranteed income
BT Economic security
Income
Income maintenance programs
NT Negative income tax
Wages—Annual wage
Guaranteed annual wage
USE Wages—Annual wage
Guaranteed income
USE Guaranteed annual income

Guaranteed loans, Federally
USE Loans—Government guaranty
Guaranteed wages
USE Wages—Annual wage
Guaranty
USE Suretyship and guaranty
Warranty
Guaranty, Treaties of
[JX4171.G8]
UF Treaties of guaranty
BT International relations
Neutrality
Sovereignty
Treaties
Guaranty insurance
USE Insurance, Surety and fidelity
Guaranty of bank deposits
USE Banks and banking—Government
guaranty of deposits
Guarao
USE Warrau Indians
Guarapo
BT Sugarcane products
Guararapes, Battle of, 1648
BT Brazil—History—Dutch Conquest,
1624-1654
Guararapes, Battle of, 1649
BT Brazil—History—Dutch Conquest,
1624-1654
Guaraŝu Indians
USE Pauserna Indians
Guaratinguetá family *(Not Subd Geog)*
Guaraúna language
[PM6091]
BT Indians of South America—Languages
RT Cariban languages
Guarauno Indians
USE Warrau Indians
Guarauno language
USE Warrau language
Guarayo Indians
BT Indians of South America
Guarayo Indians (Tacanan)
USE Ese Ejje Indians
Guarayo language
[PM6096]
BT Indians of South America—Languages
Tupi languages
RT Guarani language
Guarayo language (Tacanan)
USE Ese Ejja language
Guarayú-tá Indians
USE Pauserna Indians
Guard, Advanced (Military science)
USE Advanced guard (Military science)
Guard dogs
USE Watchdogs
Guard duty
[U190-195]
UF Advance guards
Outposts
Patrols
Picket duty
Sentinels
BT Military art and science
SA *subdivision* Guard duty *under armies,*
e.g. United States. Army—Guard
duty
Guard family *(Not Subd Geog)*
Guard fences (Roads)
USE Roads—Guard fences
Guard hair
[QL942]
BT Hair
Guarded Horn Clauses (Computer program
language)
USE GHC (Computer program language)
Guardian and ward *(May Subd Geog)*
UF Tutelage
Wards

Guardian and ward *(Continued)*
    BT Domestic relations
          Trusts and trustees
    RT Capacity and disability
          Conservatorships
          Interdiction (Civil law)
    NT Adoption—Law and legislation
          Custody of children
          Foster home care—Law and legislation
          Ordinaries
          Parent and child (Law)
          Prodigals (Law)
— Conflict of laws
    USE Conflict of laws—Guardian and
             ward
— Domicile
    USE Domicile in domestic relations
Guardian and ward (Byzantine law)
Guardian and ward (Canon law)
Guardian and ward (Islamic law)
    RT Interdiction (Islamic law)
Guardian and ward (Jewish law)
Guardian and ward (Roman law)
Guardian angels
    BT Angels
          Genius (Companion spirit)
Guardner family
  USE Gardner family
Guardrails (Roads)
  USE Roads—Guard fences
Guards, Body
  USE Bodyguards
Guards, Cattle
  USE Cattle guards
Guards, Inmate
  USE Inmate guards
Guards, Papal
  USE Papal guards
Guards, Royal
  USE Guards troops
Guards (Basketball) *(May Subd Geog)*
    BT Basketball players
Guards troops *(May Subd Geog)*
    [UA12.8]
    UF Guards, Royal
          Royal guards
          Troops, Guards
    BT Soldiers
    SA *names of military or para-military*
          units bearing the title Guards or its
          equivalents
    NT Papal guards
Guarequena Indians
  USE Arekena Indians
Guarequena language
  USE Arekena language
Guarin family
  USE Geurin family
Guarinite
    UF Hiordahlite
    BT Silicates
Guarino Indians
    [F2270.2.G83]
    BT Indians of South America
          Indians of South America—Colombia
          —Mixed bloods
Guarpe Indians
    [F2823.G]
    UF Huarpe Indians
    BT Indians of South America
Guarpe language
  USE Allentiac language
Guartney family
  USE Gwartney family
Guasco River (Chile)
  USE Huasco River (Chile)
Guastec Indians
  USE Huastec Indians
Guastec language
  USE Huastec language

Guatemala
— **Antiquities**
    NT Chaculá Site (Guatemala)
          Culebra, Gran Montículo de la
             (Guatemala, Guatemala)
          Kaminaljuyu Site (Guatemala)
          Macanché Island Site (Guatemala)
          Naranjo Site (Guatemala)
          Quiriguá Site (Guatemala)
          Seibal Site (Guatemala)
          Tikal Site (Guatemala)
          Uaxactún Site (Guatemala)
— **Boundaries**
— — **Belize**
    NT Belize question
— **Description and travel**
— — **1951-1980**
— — **1981-**
— **Economic conditions**
— — **1918-1945**
— — **1945-**
— — **1945-1985** *(Not Subd Geog)*
— — **1985-** *(Not Subd Geog)*
— **Foreign relations**
— — **1945-**
— **History**
    [F1461-1477]
— — **To 1821**
— — **1821-1945**
— — **Revolution, 1871**
    [F1466.45]
— — **October Revolution, 1944**
    [F1466.45]
    UF October Revolution, Guatemala,
          1944
— — **1945-**
— — **Revolution, 1954**
    [F1466.5]
— — — **Campaigns** *(Not Subd Geog)*
    NT Gualán (Guatemala), Battle
          of, 1954
— **Languages**
    NT Aguacatec language
          Chuj language
          Cubulco Achi language
          Kanjobal language
          Rabinal Achi language
— **Politics and government**
— — **To 1821**
— — **1821-**
— — **1821-1945**
— — **1945-1985**
— — **1985-**
Guatemala-British Honduras dispute
  USE Belize question
Guatemala prize
  USE Premio Guatemala
Guatemalan art
  USE Art, Guatemalan
Guatemalan authors
  USE Authors, Guatemalan
Guatemalan cookery
  USE Cookery, Guatemalan
Guatemalan cotton boll weevil ant
  USE Kelep
Guatemalan drama *(May Subd Geog)*
    [PQ7493 (History)]
    [PQ7497 (Collections)]
    NT One-act plays, Guatemalan
Guatemalan fiction
    NT Short stories, Guatemalan
Guatemalan grey squirrel
  USE Sciurus aureogaster
Guatemalan howler monkey
  USE Mantled howler monkey
Guatemalan landscape painting
  USE Landscape painting, Guatemalan
Guatemalan literature
    [PQ7490-7499]
    BT Spanish American literature

Guatemalan one-act plays
  USE One-act plays, Guatemalan
Guatemalan periodicals
    [PN4989.G]
Guatemalan poetry
    [PQ7492 (History)]
    [PQ7496 (Collections)]
Guatemalan poets
  USE Poets, Guatemalan
Guatemalan prints
  USE Prints, Guatemalan
Guatemalan sculpture
  USE Sculpture, Guatemalan
Guatemalan short stories
  USE Short stories, Guatemalan
Guatemalan wit and humor, Pictorial
Guato Indians
    [F2520.1.G]
    UF Vuato Indians
    BT Indians of South America
Guatuso Indians
    [F1545.2.G77]
    UF Corobici Indians
          Huatuso Indians
    BT Indians of Central America—Costa
          Rica
Guava *(May Subd Geog)*
    [QK495.M9 (Botany)]
    [SB379.G8 (Culture)]
    UF Apple guava
          Common guava
          Psidium guajava
          Yellow guava
Guava industry *(May Subd Geog)*
    [HD9259.G8-83]
Guayabera shirts *(May Subd Geog)*
    UF Guayaberas
          Shirts, Guayabera
    BT Shirts, Men's
Guayaberas
  USE Guayabera shirts
Guayabero language
    UF Jiw language
    BT Colombia—Languages
          Indians of South America—Colombia
          —Languages
Guayacán, Esencia de
  USE Guaiac wood oil
Guayaki-Ache language
  USE Guayaki language
Guayaki Indians
  USE Guayaqui Indians
Guayaki language
    UF Guaiaqui language
          Guayaki-Ache language
          Guayaqui language
          Guoyagui language
    BT Guarani language
          Paraguay—Languages
Guayana
  USE Guiana
Guayana Highlands
  USE Guiana Highlands
Guayana Indians
    [F2230.2.G75]
    BT Indians of South America
Guayana Region (Venezuela)
    UF Región de Guayana (Venezuela)
Guayanés River (Humacao, P.R.)
    BT Rivers—Puerto Rico
Guayaqui Indians
    [F2679]
    UF Aché Indians
          Guayaki Indians
    BT Guarani Indians
          Indians of South America
Guayaqui language
  USE Guayaki language
Guayaquil, Gulf of
    UF Golfo de Guayaquil
          Gulf of Guayaquil

BT Bays—Ecuador
    Bays—Peru

Guayaquil Interview, Guayaquil, Ecuador, 1822
    [F2235.36]
    UF Conferencia de Guayaquil, Guayaquil, Ecuador, 1822
        Entrevista de Guayaquil, Guayaquil, Ecuador, 1822
        Guayaquil Meeting, Guayaquil, Ecuador, 1822
    BT South America—History—Wars of Independence, 1806-1830
Guayaquil Meeting, Guayaquil, Ecuador, 1822
    USE Guayaquil Interview, Guayaquil, Ecuador, 1822

Guayas River (Ecuador)
    UF Río de Zapotal (Ecuador)
        Río Guayas (Ecuador)
        Río Zapotal (Ecuador)
        Zapotal River (Ecuador)
    BT Rivers—Ecuador

Guaycuru Indians
    [F2230.2.G78]
    BT Indians of South America
    NT Abipone Indians
        Cadioéo Indians
        Mbaya Indians
        Mocobi Indians
        Pilaga Indians
        Tereno Indians
        Toba Indians
   — Religion and mythology
Guaycuruan languages
    [PM6116]
    UF Guaicuruan languages
    BT Indians of South America—Languages
    RT Abipone language
        Mbaya language
        Toba language (Indian)
    NT Pilaga language
Guaycururú language
    USE Mbaya language
Guaymi hymns
    USE Hymns, Guaymi
Guaymi Indians
    [F1434]
    BT Chibcha Indians
        Indians of Central America
Guaymi language
    [PM3806]
    BT Indians of Central America—Languages
Guayule (May Subd Geog)
    [QK495.C74 (Botany)]
    [SB291.G8 (Culture)]
    UF Parthenium argentatum
    BT Rubber plants
    RT Guayule rubber
   — Harvesting
Guayule rubber (May Subd Geog)
    BT Rubber
    RT Guayule
        Guayule rubber industry
Guayule rubber industry (May Subd Geog)
    [HD9161.5.G82-824]
    RT Guayule rubber
Gubala family
    USE Gublo family
Gubernatorial transitions
    USE Governors—United States—Transition periods
Gublo family (Not Subd Geog)
    UF Gubala family
Gudbrandsdal (Norway)
    USE Gudbrandsdalen (Norway)
Gudbrandsdalen (Norway)
    UF Gudbrandsdal (Norway)
    BT Valleys—Norway
Guddelowe family
    USE Goodloe family

Gude language
    UF Cheke language
        Mapodi language
        Mapuda language
        Shede language
    BT Chadic languages
Gudela (African people)
    USE Hadiya (African people)
Gudgen family
    USE Gudgeon family
Gudgeon family (Not Subd Geog)
    UF Gudgen family
        Gudgin family
Gudger family
    USE Goodyear family
Gudgin family
    USE Gudgeon family
Gudknecht family
    USE Gutknecht family
Gudlawe family
    USE Goodloe family
Gudloe family
    USE Goodloe family
Gudovius family
    USE Gusovius family
Gŭdulka
    [ML927.G]
Gudwa language (Dravidian)
    USE Gadaba language (Dravidian)
Gueghamian Range (Armenian S.S.R.)
    USE Gegam Range (Armenian S.S.R.)
Guelaia (Berber people)
    USE Iqar'iyen (Berber people)
Guele River (Belgium and Netherlands)
    USE Geul River (Belgium and Netherlands)
Guelf, House of (Not Subd Geog)
    UF Guelph, House of
        House of Guelf
        House of Guelph
        House of Welf
        Welf, House of
    BT Germany—Kings and rulers
    RT Guelfs and Ghibellines
Guelfs and Ghibellines
    [DD147 (Germany)]
    [DG522-DG523]
    UF Ghibellines
        Guelphs
    RT Guelf, House of
    NT Colle di Val d'Elsa, Italy, Battle of, 1269
Guelph, House of
    USE Guelf, House of
Guelphs
    USE Guelfs and Ghibellines
Guen (African people)
    USE Gouin (African people)
Guen dialect
    USE Mina dialect
Guenevere, Queen (Legendary character)
    UF Guinevere, Queen (Legendary character)
        Queen Guenevere (Legendary character)
    BT Arthurian romances
Guengerich family
    USE Gingrich family
Güenoa language
    [PM6126]
    BT Chana language
        Charrua language
        Indians of South America—Languages
Guenons
    USE Cercopithecus
Guérande Peninsula (France)
    UF Presqu'île de Guérande (France)
    BT Peninsulas—France
Guerant family
    USE Geurin family

Guerard family (Not Subd Geog)
Guere (African people)
    USE Gere (African people)
Guere (Kru-speaking African people)
    USE Wobe (African people)
Guere language (Kru)
    USE Wobe language
Guere language (Mande)
    USE Dan language
Gueren Indians
    USE Tapuya Indians
Guergal
    USE Gregale
Guerillas
    USE Guerrillas
Guérin d'Agon family (Not Subd Geog)
    RT Geurin family
Guerin family
    USE Geurin family
Guérin-Stern syndrome
    USE Arthrogryposis
Guering family
    USE Geurin family
Guerney family
    USE Gurney family
Guernica (Painting)
    USE Picasso, Pablo, 1881-1973. Guernica
Guernsey cattle
    [SF193.G9 (Herd-books)]
    [SF199.G8]
    BT Dairy cattle
Guéroult family (Not Subd Geog)
Guerra Chiquita, Cuba, 1879-1880
    USE Cuba—History—Revolution, 1879-1880
Guerra de Castas, Yucatán, Mexico, 1847-1855
    USE Yucatán (Mexico : State)—History—Caste War, 1847-1855
Guerra de los Mil Días, Colombia, 1899-1903
    USE Colombia—History—Revolution, 1899-1903
Guerra de Paquisha, 1981
    USE Ecuador-Peru Conflict, 1981
Guerra del Pacífico, 1879-1884
    USE War of the Pacific, 1879-1884
Guerra dos Cabanos, Alagoas (Brazil), 1832-1835
    USE Alagoas (Brazil)—History—Revolution, 1832-1835
Guerra Grande, Uruguay, 1843-1852
    USE Uruguay—History—Great War, 1843-1852
Guerrand family
    USE Guerrant family
Guerrant family (Not Subd Geog)
    UF Guerrand family
Guerre des Bouffons
    [ML1727.33]
    UF Bouffons, Guerre des
    BT Opera
    RT Gluck-Piccinni controversy
Guerrilla warfare
    [U240]
    UF Unconventional warfare
    BT Insurgency
        Military art and science
        Strategy
        Tactics
        War
    NT Commando troops
        Counterinsurgency
        Special forces (Military science)
Guerrillas (May Subd Geog)
    [D25.5]
    Here are entered general and historical works. Works on the military aspects of guerrilla warfare are entered under the heading Guerrilla warfare. International legal aspects of guerrilla warfare are entered under the heading Guerrillas (International law) Municipal criminal law is entered under the heading Guerrillas—Law and legislation.

Guerrillas *(Continued)*
  UF Bushwhackers
       Francs-tireurs
       Guerillas
       Maquis
       Partisans
  BT National liberation movements
  SA *subdivision* Underground movements
       under individual wars, e.g. World
       War, 1939-1945—Underground
       movements
  NT Haiduks
       Women guerrillas
  — Law and legislation *(May Subd Geog)*
     BT Military offenses
Guerrillas, Women
  USE Women guerrillas
Guerrillas (International law)
  [*JX5123*]
  BT Combatants and noncombatants
       (International law)
       War (International law)
       War crimes
Guerrillas as artists *(May Subd Geog)*
  BT Artists
Guerrin family
  USE Geurin family
Guerry family
  USE Gery family
Guerze (African people)
  USE Kpelle (African people)
Guerzé language
  USE Kpelle language
Guesquières family
  USE Ghesquières family
Guess family
  USE Guest family
Guesst family
  USE Guest family
Guest (Game)
  [*GV1295.G9*]
Guest family *(Not Subd Geog)*
  UF Gess family
       Guess family
       Guesst family
       Gueste family
       Guests family
  RT Gist family
Guest ranches
  USE Dude ranches
Guest workers
  USE Alien labor
Gueste family
  USE Guest family
Guests
  USE Entertaining
       Hospitality
Guests family
  USE Guest family
Guests who made excuses (Parable)
  USE Great supper (Parable)
Guestworkers
  USE Alien labor
Guetar Indians
  UF Huetar Indians
  BT Indians of Central America
Gueux
  [*DH187-193*]
  UF Beggars, The
  — Songs and music
     [*PT5484*]
     BT Dutch poetry—1500-1800
        Netherlands—History—Wars of
        Independence, 1556-1648—
        Poetry
        Patriotic poetry, Dutch
        Songs, Dutch
Gueyraud family *(Not Subd Geog)*
Gugada dialect
  [*PL7101.G76*]
  UF Kukota dialect

  BT Australia—Languages
       Australian languages
Gugenheim family
  USE Guggenheim family
Guggenheim family *(Not Subd Geog)*
  UF Gugenheim family
Guglielmo (Name)
  USE William (Name)
Gugu Yalanji language
  [*PL7101.G77*]
  UF Guguyalanji language
       Jalandji language
       Koko Jelandji language
       Koko Yalanji language
       Kuku Yalanji language
  BT Australia—Languages
       Australian languages
Guguyalanji language
  USE Gugu Yalanji language
Guha (Mythological character)
  BT Mythology, Indic
Guhu-Samane language
  UF Mid-Waria language
  BT Papuan languages
Guiana
  UF Gayana
       Goyana
       Guayana
  NT Brazil, North
       French Guiana
       Guyana
       Surinam
       Venezuela
Guiana Highlands
  UF Guayana Highlands
  BT Plateaus—South America
Guianan cock of the rock
  USE Rupicola rupicola
Guichola language
  USE Huichol language
Guidance, Student
  USE Personnel service in education
       Vocational guidance
Guidance, Vocational
  USE Vocational guidance
Guidance counselors
  USE Student counselors
Guidance in education
  USE Personnel service in education
Guidance systems (Flight)
  [*TL589.4*]
    Here are entered works on systems for supervising
the navigation of aircraft and space vehicles from one
location to another. Works on systems which govern
aircraft and space vehicle attitude, stability, and di-
rection of motion are entered under Flight control.
  BT Aeronautical instruments
       Automatic control
       Navigation (Aeronautics)
       Remote control
  SA *subdivision* Guidance systems *under*
       types of aircraft, e.g. Guided
       missiles—Guidance systems
  NT Flight control
       Proportional navigation
Guide (Electronic computer system)
Guide-boats, Adirondack
  USE Adirondack guide-boats
Guide-books
  USE *subdivision* Guide-books *under*
       subjects, e.g. Geology—Guide-
       books; *and subdivisions* Description
       and travel—Guide-books *under*
       names of regions, countries, etc., or
       Description—Guide-books *under*
       names of cities
Guide dog schools *(May Subd Geog)*
  [*HV1780-HV1780.6*]
  UF Schools for guide dogs
       Schools for seeing eye dogs
       Seeing eye dog schools

  BT Schools
Guide dogs
  UF Dog guides
       Seeing Eye dogs
  BT Blind—Travel
       Working dogs
  NT Greff (Dog)
GUIDE-O (Information retrieval system)
  BT Information storage and retrieval
       systems
Guide-posts
  USE Signs and signboards
Guidebooks
  USE *subdivision* Guide-books *under*
       subjects, e.g. Geology—Guide-
       books; *and subdivisions* Description
       and travel—Guide-books *under*
       names of regions, countries, etc., or
       Description—Guide-books *under*
       names of cities
Guided bombs
  [*UG1282.G8*]
  UF Bombs, Guided
  BT Precision guided munitions
  NT Azon bombs
Guided missile bases
  UF Missile bases
  BT Guided missiles
       Military bases
  NT Guided missile silos
Guided missile bases, German
  (May Subd Geog)
  UF German guided missile bases
Guided missile frigates
  USE Guided missile ships
Guided missile industries *(May Subd Geog)*
  UF Guided missile production
       Guided missiles industry
       Missile industry
  BT Aerospace industries
  NT Strikes and lockouts—Guided missile
       industries
Guided missile production
  USE Guided missile industries
Guided missile ranges *(May Subd Geog)*
  UF Missile ranges
       Ranges, Guided missile
  BT Guided missiles—Testing
       Proving grounds
Guided missile ships
  UF Guided missile frigates
  BT Guided missiles
       Warships
  NT AEGIS (Weapons system)
       United States. Navy—Gunner's
       mates (Missiles)
Guided missile silos
  UF Missile silos
       Silos, Guided missile
  BT Guided missile bases
Guided missile sounds
  UF Guided missiles—Sounds
  BT Sounds
       Space flight sounds
Guided missiles
  UF Bombs, Flying
       Flying bombs
       Missiles, Guided
       Pilotless aircraft
  BT Airplanes
       Bombs
       Precision guided munitions
       Projectiles, Aerial
       Rocketry
       Rockets (Aeronautics)
       Rockets (Ordnance)
       United States. Air Force—Weapons
       systems
       United States. Navy—Weapons
       systems
       Vehicles, Remotely piloted

RT Surface-to-surface missiles
SA *names of specific missiles, e.g.* Bomarc
(Missile); Nike rocket; V-1 bomb;
V-2 rocket
NT Air-to-surface missiles
Antiaircraft missiles
Antimissile missiles
Antitank missiles
Ballistic missiles
Cruise missiles
Exocet (Guided missile)
Guided missile bases
Guided missile ships
MX (Weapons system)
Roland (Missile)
Surface-to-air missiles
Trident (Weapons systems)
United States. Army—Guided missile
personnel
United States. Navy—Fire control
technicians (Missile)
United States. Navy—Gunner's
mates (Missiles)
— **Aerodynamics**
— **Control systems**
UF Missile control systems
BT Flight control
NT Guided missiles—Radio control
— **Electric equipment**
— **Electronic equipment**
BT Electronic control
— **Guidance systems**
UF Missile guidance systems
— **Optical equipment**
— **Pneumatic equipment**
— **Radar equipment**
— **Radio control**
BT Guided missiles—Control systems
— Sounds
USE Guided missile sounds
— **Testing**
NT Guided missile ranges
— **Tracking**
UF Flight tracking
Missile tracking
Tracking
BT Tracking radar
NT Range instrumentation ships
— **Wings**
BT Wings
Guided missiles industry
USE Guided missile industries
Guided munitions, Precision
USE Precision guided munitions
Guided vehicle systems, Automated
USE Automated guided vehicle systems
Guideposts
USE Signs and signboards
Guides, Hunting
USE Hunting guides
Guides, Tour (Persons)
USE Tour guides (Persons)
Guides for hunters, fishermen, etc.
USE Hunting guides
Guides for mountaineering (Persons)
USE Mountaineering guides (Persons)
Guido, Don (Fictitious character)
USE Don Guido (Fictitious character)
GUIDON (Computer program)
BT Computer-assisted instruction—
Computer programs
Guidons
₍UC590-595₎
BT Flags
Standards, Military
Guiger family
USE Geiger family
Guijarros, Fort (San Diego, Calif.)
USE Fort Guijarros (San Diego, Calif.)
/Guikhoe language
USE G/wi language

Guil family
USE Gill family
Guilá Naquitz Cave (Mexico)
BT Caves—Mexico
Mexico—Antiquities
Guild family *(Not Subd Geog)*
RT Gould family
Guild socialism
₍HD6479₎
UF Gild socialism
BT Corporate state
Functional representation
Socialism
Syndicalism
NT Management—Employee participation
Guildhall (Swansea, West Glamorgan)
BT Municipal buildings—Wales
Guilds *(May Subd Geog)*
₍HD6456-6473₎
UF Craft guilds
Gilds
Labor organizations
Merchant companies
Workers' associations
BT Brotherhoods
Confraternities
Labor and laboring classes
Societies
RT Employers' associations
Trade and professional associations
Trade-unions
SA *names of individual guilds*
NT Building guilds
Compagnonnages
Jewish guilds
Journey workers—Societies, etc.
Women in guilds
— **Italy**
NT Comacine Masters (Builders)
— **Spain**
Guilds, Altar
USE Altar guilds
Guilds, Building
USE Building guilds
Guilds, Jewish
USE Jewish guilds
Guile family
USE Giles family
Guile in literature
USE Deception in literature
Guilford Court House, Battle of, 1781
₍E241.G9₎
BT North Carolina—History—Revolution,
1775-1783
United States—History—Revolution,
1775-1783—Campaigns
Guilford family *(Not Subd Geog)*
UF Gilford family
Gillford family
Gulliford family
Guilford-Zimmerman temperament survey
₍BF698.8.G8₎
BT Psychological tests
Temperament
Guilherme de Melo family *(Not Subd Geog)*
UF Melo family, Guilherme de
Guilhermo (Name)
USE William (Name)
Guiliak language
USE Gilyak language
Guilielma
₍QK495.P17₎
BT Palms
Guilielma gasipaes
USE Peach palm
Guilielma speciosa
USE Peach palm
Guilielma utilis
USE Peach palm
Guill family
USE Gill family

Guillain-Barré syndrome
USE Polyradiculoneuritis
Guillam family
USE Gilliam family
Guillaume (Name)
USE William (Name)
Guilleminia
USE Votomita
Guillen family
USE Gullett family
Guillet family
USE Gullett family
Guilliams family
USE Gilliam family
Guillier family
USE Gullett family
Guillios family
USE Gullett family
Guilliot family
USE Gullett family
Guilliott family
USE Gullett family
Guillis family
USE Gilley family
Guillot family
USE Gullett family
Guillotin family
USE Gullett family
Guillotine
₍HV8555₎
BT Capital punishment
Executions and executioners
Guillott family
USE Gullett family
Guillotte family
USE Gullett family
Guilloz family *(Not Subd Geog)*
Guilotte family
USE Gullett family
Guilt
₍BF575.G8 (Psychology)₎
₍BJ1471.5 (Ethics)₎
BT Christian ethics
Conscience
Emotions
Ethics
Good and evil
Sin
Super-ego
RT Shame
— **Religious aspects**
— — **Buddhism,** ₍**Christianity, etc.**₎
Guilt (Adat law)
Guilt (Canon law)
Guilt (Jewish law)
Guilt (Law) *(May Subd Geog)*
BT Criminal law
Criminal liability
NT Criminal intent
Dolus (Civil law)
Ignorance (Law)
Negligence
Pleas (Criminal procedure)
Guilt (Roman law)
Guilt and culture *(May Subd Geog)*
BT Culture
Ethnopsychology
Guilty, Pleas of
USE Pleas of guilty
Guilty pleas
USE Pleas of guilty
Guimar family
USE Gumaer family
Guin (African people)
USE Gouin (African people)
Guin family
USE Gum family
Guinea
UF French Guinea
Guinea, French
— **Antiquities**

Guinea
— Antiquities (Continued)
  NT Niani (Guinea)
— Economic conditions
— — 1958-1984
— — 1984-
— Foreign relations
— — 1958-
— History
— — Portuguese Invasion, 1970
    ⌈DT543.8⌉
    UF Portuguese Invasion of Guinea,
        1970
    BT Guinea-Bissau—History,
        Military
        Portugal—History, Military
— — Coup d'état, 1984
    BT Coups d'état—Guinea
— Languages
  NT Badyaranke language
      Balante language
      Diola language
      Kissi language
      Kono language
      Kpelle language
      Limba language
      Loma language
      Mandjak language
      Mankanya language
      Mano language
      Susu language
— Politics and government
— — To 1958
— — 1958-1984
— — 1984-
Guinea, French
  USE Guinea
Guinea, Gulf of
  UF Gulf of Guinea
  BT Atlantic Ocean
Guinea, Portuguese
  USE Guinea-Bissau
Guinea, Spanish
  USE Equatorial Guinea
Guinea (Coin)
    ⌈CJ2484 (Numismatics)⌉
    ⌈HG935 (Finance)⌉
  BT Sovereign (Coin)
Guinea-Bissau
  UF Guinea, Portuguese
      Portuguese Guinea
— Economic conditions
— — To 1974
— — 1974-
— History
— — Revolution, 1963-1974
    ⌈DT613.78⌉
— — Coup d'état, 1980
    BT Coups d'état—Guinea-Bissau
— History, Military
  NT Guinea—History—Portuguese
      Invasion, 1970
— Politics and government
— — To 1974
— — 1974-
Guinea Current
    ⌈GC296.G8⌉
  BT Ocean currents
Guinea-fowl
    ⌈SF506⌉
  BT Birds, Ornamental
      Poultry
Guinea grains
  USE Grains of paradise
Guinea grass (May Subd Geog)
    ⌈QK495.G74 (Botany)⌉
    ⌈SB201.G8 (Forage plant)⌉
  UF Panicum maximum
  BT Panicum
Guinea pepper
  USE Grains of paradise

Guinea pig breeds (May Subd Geog)
  UF Guinea pigs—Breeds
  BT Animal breeds
Guinea pigs (May Subd Geog)
    ⌈SF459.G9⌉
  BT Caviidae
— Breeds
  USE Guinea pig breeds
Guinea pigs as laboratory animals
  BT Laboratory animals
Guinea pigs as pets
    ⌈SF459.G9⌉
  BT Pets
Guinea yam
  USE Dioscorea rotundata
Guinea yam, Yellow
  USE Dioscorea cayenensis
Guinean poetry (French) (May Subd Geog)
  UF French poetry—Guinean authors
  NT Revolutionary poetry, Guinean
      (French)
Guinean revolutionary poetry (French)
  USE Revolutionary poetry, Guinean
      (French)
Guinebauld family (Not Subd Geog)
  UF Guinebault family
Guinebault family
  USE Guinebauld family
Guines family
  USE Guinness family
Guiness family
  USE Guinness family
Guinevere, Queen (Legendary character)
  USE Guenevere, Queen (Legendary
      character)
Guing family
  USE Guion family
Guingbe (African people)
  USE Mina (African people)
Guinigi family (Not Subd Geog)
Guinness family (Not Subd Geog)
  UF Guines family
      Guiness family
      MacGinnis family
      MacGuinness family
      McGinnis family
      McGuinness family
Guinon's disease
  USE Gilles de la Tourette's syndrome
Guio family (Not Subd Geog)
Guion family (Not Subd Geog)
  UF Gion family
      Guing family
      Guyon family
      Gyon family
Guiraud family (Not Subd Geog)
Guise, House of (Not Subd Geog)
  BT France—Nobility
Guiser family
  USE Gaiser family
Guissiga language
  USE Gisiga language
Guist family
  USE Gist family
Guitar
    ⌈ML1015-ML1018⌉
  UF Spanish guitar
  RT Vihuela
  NT Balalaika
      Bandurria
      Charango
      Cithern
      Dobro
      Electric guitar
      English guitar
      Harp-lute guitar
      Hawaiian guitar
      Lyre-guitar
      Ukulele
      Yüeh ch'in
— Construction

  NT Guitar—Customizing
— Customizing
  UF Customizing of guitars
  BT Guitar—Construction
— Electronic equipment
  UF Electronic equipment for guitars
  BT Electronic apparatus and
      appliances
— Group instruction
  USE Guitar—Methods—Group
      instruction
— Instruction and study
    ⌈MT580⌉
  NT Guitar music—Teaching pieces
— Methods
    ⌈MT582⌉
— — Group instruction
    ⌈MT582⌉
  UF Guitar—Group instruction
— — Self-instruction
    ⌈MT588⌉
  UF Guitar—Self-instruction
— Methods (Bluegrass)
    ⌈MT582 (General)⌉
    ⌈MT588 (Self-instructors)⌉
— Methods (Blues)
    ⌈MT582⌉
  BT Blues (Music)
— Methods (Country)
    ⌈MT582 (General)⌉
    ⌈MT588 (Self-instructors)⌉
  BT Country music
— Methods (Ragtime)
    ⌈MT582⌉
  BT Ragtime music
— Self-instruction
  USE Guitar—Methods—Self-
      instruction
— Tuning
    ⌈ML3809 (History)⌉
    ⌈MT165 (Instruction)⌉
Guitar, Electric
  USE Electric guitar
Guitar, Harp-lute
  USE Harp-lute guitar
Guitar, Hawaiian
  USE Hawaiian guitar
Guitar, Steel
  USE Hawaiian guitar
Guitar and accordion music
  USE Accordion and guitar music
Guitar and Appalachian dulcimer music
  USE Appalachian dulcimer and guitar music
Guitar and banjo music
  USE Banjo and guitar music
Guitar and bassoon music
  USE Bassoon and guitar music
Guitar and clarinet music
  USE Clarinet and guitar music
Guitar and concertina music
  USE Concertina and guitar music
Guitar and continuo music
  UF Continuo and guitar music
  NT Sonatas (Guitar and continuo)
Guitar and double-bass music
  USE Double-bass and guitar music
Guitar and drum music
    ⌈M298⌉
  UF Drum and guitar music
Guitar and dulcimer music
  USE Dulcimer and guitar music
Guitar and English horn music
  USE English horn and guitar music
Guitar and flute music
  USE Flute and guitar music
Guitar and harp music
    ⌈M292-293⌉
  UF Harp and guitar music
Guitar and harp with chamber orchestra
    ⌈M1040-1041⌉

RT Concertos (Guitar and harp with
   chamber orchestra)
Guitar and harpsichord music
   [M276-7]
   UF Harpsichord and guitar music
   NT Concertos (Guitar and harpsichord
      with string orchestra)
      Guitar and harpsichord with string
         orchestra
      Sonatas (Guitar and harpsichord)
      Suites (Guitar and harpsichord)
Guitar and harpsichord music, Arranged
   [M276-7]
Guitar and harpsichord with string orchestra
   [M1140-1141]
   BT Guitar and harpsichord music
   RT Concertos (Guitar and harpsichord
      with string orchestra)
Guitar and horn music
   USE Horn and guitar music
Guitar and mandolin music
   UF Mandolin and guitar music
Guitar and oboe d'amore music
   USE Oboe d'amore and guitar music
Guitar and oboe music
   USE Oboe and guitar music
Guitar and organ music
   [M182-186]
   UF Organ and guitar music
Guitar and penny whistle music
   USE Penny whistle and guitar music
Guitar and percussion music
   USE Percussion and guitar music
Guitar and percussion music, Arranged
   [M298]
Guitar and piano music
   [M276-7]
   UF Piano and guitar music
   NT Concertos (Guitar and piano with
      string orchestra)
      Guitar and piano with string orchestra
      Marches (Guitar and piano)
      Polonaises (Guitar and piano)
      Potpourris (Guitar and piano)
      Rondos (Guitar and piano)
      Sonatas (Guitar and piano)
      Suites (Guitar and piano)
      Variations (Guitar and piano)
      Waltzes (Guitar and piano)
Guitar and piano music, Arranged
   [M276-7]
   NT Concertos (Guitar)—Solo with piano
      Concertos (Guitar), Arranged—Solo
         with piano
      Concertos (Guitar with chamber
         orchestra)—Solo with piano
      Concertos (Guitar with string
         orchestra)—Solo with piano
      Guitar with orchestra—Solo with
         piano
      Overtures arranged for guitar and
         piano
      Suites (Guitar with chamber orchestra)
         —Solo with piano
      Suites (Guitar with orchestra)—Solo
         with piano
Guitar and piano with jazz ensemble
   RT Concertos (Guitar and piano with jazz
      ensemble)
Guitar and piano with string orchestra
   [M1140-1141]
   BT Guitar and piano music
   RT Concertos (Guitar and piano with
      string orchestra)
Guitar and piccolo music
   USE Piccolo and guitar music
Guitar and recorder music
   USE Recorder and guitar music
Guitar and saxophone music
   USE Saxophone and guitar music

Guitar and trumpet music
   USE Trumpet and guitar music
Guitar and unspecified instrument music
   USE Duets (Unspecified instrument and
      guitar)
Guitar and viola d'amore music
   USE Viola d'amore and guitar music
Guitar and viola music
   USE Viola and guitar music
Guitar and violin music
   USE Violin and guitar music
Guitar and violoncello music
   USE Violoncello and guitar music
Guitar band
   USE Plectral ensembles
Guitar music
   [M125-129]
   SA Concertos, Minuets, Sonatas, Suites,
      *and similar headings with
      specification of instruments;* Trios
      [Quartets, etc.] *followed by
      specifications which include the
      guitar; also* Plectral ensembles *and
      headings that begin with the words
      guitar or guitars*
   NT Canons, fugues, etc. (Guitar)
      Dobro music
      Hawaiian-guitar music
      Minuets (Guitar)
      Overtures (Guitar)
      Passacaglias (Guitar)
      Potpourris (Guitar)
      Recorded accompaniments (Guitar)
      Rondos (Guitar)
      Sonatas (Guitar)
      Suites (Guitar)
      Tablature (Musical notation)
      Variations (Guitar)
      Waltzes (Guitar)
   — Teaching pieces
      [MT585]
      BT Guitar—Instruction and study
Guitar music (Guitars (2))
   [M292-3]
   NT Concertos (Guitars (2))
      Concertos (Guitars (2) with chamber
         orchestra)
      Guitars (2) with chamber orchestra
      Guitars (2) with orchestra
      Passacaglias (Guitars (2))
      Rondos (Guitars (2))
      Sonatas (Guitars (2))
      Suites (Guitars (2))
      Variations (Guitars (2))
      Waltzes (Guitars (2))
Guitar music (Guitars (2)), Arranged
   [M292-3]
   NT Overtures arranged for guitars (2)
Guitar music (Guitars (3))
   USE Trios (Guitars (3))
Guitar music (Guitars (4))
   USE Quartets (Guitars (4))
Guitar music (Guitars (5))
   USE Quintets (Guitars (5))
Guitar music (Jazz)
   [M125-129]
   NT Guitar with jazz ensemble
Guitar music (Ragtime)
   [M125-129]
   BT Ragtime music
Guitar violoncello
   USE Arpeggione
Guitar with chamber orchestra
   [M1037.4.G8]
   BT Chamber-orchestra music
   RT Concertos (Guitar with chamber
      orchestra)
   NT Suites (Guitar with chamber orchestra)
Guitar with instrumental ensemble
   RT Concertos (Guitar with instrumental
      ensemble)

Guitar with jazz ensemble
   [M1366]
   BT Guitar music (Jazz)
Guitar with orchestra
   [M1037.4.G8]
   BT Orchestral music
   RT Concertos (Guitar)
   NT Suites (Guitar with orchestra)
      Variations (Guitar with orchestra)
   — Solo with piano
      [M1037.4.G8]
      BT Guitar and piano music, Arranged
Guitar with orchestra, Arranged
   [M1037.4.G8]
Guitar with plectral ensemble
   NT Concertos (Guitar with plectral
      ensemble)
Guitar with string ensemble
   RT Concertos (Guitar with string
      ensemble)
Guitar with string orchestra
   [M1105-6]
   RT Concertos (Guitar with string
      orchestra)
   NT Variations (Guitar with string
      orchestra)
Guitar with string orchestra, Arranged
   [M1105-6]
Guitare d'amour
   USE Arpeggione
Guitarfishes
   [QL638.85.R4]
   UF Rhinobatidae
   BT Rajiformes
Guitarists *(May Subd Geog)*
   [ML399 (Biography: collective)]
   [ML419 (individual)]
Guitars (2) with chamber orchestra
   [M1037.4.G8]
   UF Two guitars with chamber orchestra
   BT Guitar music (Guitars (2))
   RT Concertos (Guitars (2) with chamber
      orchestra)
Guitars (2) with jazz ensemble
   [M1366]
   RT Concertos (Guitars (2) with jazz
      ensemble)
Guitars (2) with orchestra
   [M1037.4.G8]
   BT Guitar music (Guitars (2))
   RT Concertos (Guitars (2))
Guitars (3) with chamber orchestra
   [M1037.4.G8]
   BT Trios (Guitars (3))
   RT Concertos (Guitars (3) with chamber
      orchestra)
Guitars (4) with orchestra
   [M1037.4.G8]
   BT Orchestral music
      Quartets (Guitars (4))
   RT Concertos (Guitars (4))
Guiting Power Site (England)
   (Not Subd Geog)
   BT England—Antiquities
Guivens family
   USE Givens family
Guiziga (African people)
   BT Ethnology—Cameroon
Gujar language
   USE Gujuri language
Gujaratees (Indic people)
   USE Gujaratis (Indic people)
Gujarati authors
   USE Authors, Gujarati
Gujarati children's literature
   USE Children's literature, Gujarati
Gujarati drama *(May Subd Geog)*
   NT Folk-drama, Gujarati
      One-act plays, Gujarati
      Radio plays, Gujarati

1605

Gujarati essays *(May Subd Geog)*
Gujarati fiction *(May Subd Geog)*
    NT Historical fiction, Gujarati
        Short stories, Gujarati
Gujarati folk-drama
    USE Folk-drama, Gujarati
Gujarati folk literature
    USE Folk literature, Gujarati
Gujarati folk poetry
    USE Folk poetry, Gujarati
Gujarati folk-songs
    USE Folk-songs, Gujarati
Gujarati ghazals
    USE Ghazals, Gujarati
Gujarati historical fiction
    USE Historical fiction, Gujarati
Gujarati imprints *(May Subd Geog)*
Gujarati Jaina hymns
    USE Jaina hymns, Gujarati
Gujarati Jaina poetry
    USE Jaina poetry, Gujarati
Gujarati language
    [PK1841-7]
    BT Indo-Aryan languages, Modern
    NT Halari dialect
        Parsi-Gujarati dialect
Gujarati literature
    [PK1850-1888]
    NT Children's literature, Gujarati
        Folk literature, Gujarati
  — 20th century
  — Arab influences
    BT Civilization, Arab
  — Iranian influences
    BT Iran—Civilization
Gujarati love poetry
    USE Love poetry, Gujarati
Gujarati manuscripts
    USE Manuscripts, Gujarati
Gujarati marriage customs and rites
    USE Marriage customs and rites, Gujarati
Gujarati narrative poetry
    USE Narrative poetry, Gujarati
Gujarati newspapers
Gujarati one-act plays
    USE One-act plays, Gujarati
Gujarati periodicals
Gujarati philology
Gujarati poetry
    [PK1856 (Collections)]
    NT Folk poetry, Gujarati
        Ghazals, Gujarati
        Jaina poetry, Gujarati
        Love poetry, Gujarati
        Narrative poetry, Gujarati
        Prose poems, Gujarati
        Religious poetry, Gujarati
        Sonnets, Gujarati
  — To 1500
  — 1500-1800
  — 20th century
Gujarati poets
    USE Poets, Gujarati
Gujarati political satire
    USE Political satire, Gujarati
Gujarati prose literature *(May Subd Geog)*
    NT Prose poems, Gujarati
  — To 1500
Gujarati prose poems
    USE Prose poems, Gujarati
Gujarati proverbs
    USE Proverbs, Gujarati
Gujarati radio plays
    USE Radio plays, Gujarati
Gujarati religious poetry
    USE Religious poetry, Gujarati
Gujarati sheep
    [SF373.G84]
    UF Patanwadi sheep
        Pattanwadi sheep
    BT Sheep breeds

Gujarati short stories
    USE Short stories, Gujarati
Gujarati shorthand
    USE Shorthand, Gujarati
Gujarati songs
    USE Songs, Gujarati
Gujarati sonnets
    USE Sonnets, Gujarati
Gujarati wit and humor
    BT Indic wit and humor
    NT Political satire, Gujarati
Gujaratis
  — Rites and ceremonies
Gujaratis (Indic people)
    [DS432.G85]
    UF Gujaratees (Indic people)
        Gujratis (Indic people)
    BT Ethnology—India
  — Rites and ceremonies
      NT Marriage customs and rites, Gujarati
Gujari language
    USE Gujuri language
Gujars
    BT Caste—India
        Ethnology—India
Gujer language
    USE Gujuri language
Gujingalia (Australian people)
    USE Burera (Australian people)
Gujjari language
    USE Gujuri language
Gujowski family
    USE Gusovius family
Gujratis (Indic people)
    USE Gujaratis (Indic people)
Gujri language
    USE Gujuri language
        Urdu language
Gujuri folk-songs
    USE Folk-songs, Gujuri
Gujuri language
    [PK1911]
    UF Gojari language
        Gojri language
        Gujar language
        Gujari language
        Gujer language
        Gujjari language
        Gujri language
    BT India—Languages
        Rajasthani language
Gujuri literature *(May Subd Geog)*
Gujuri songs
    USE Songs, Gujuri
Gula language (Lake Iro, Chad)
    USE Kùláál language
Gulaker family *(Not Subd Geog)*
Gulbin Maradi (Nigeria and Niger)
    USE Maradi River (Nigeria and Niger)
Guldager family *(Not Subd Geog)*
Gulden (Coin) *(May Subd Geog)*
    BT Coins, Austrian
        Coins, Dutch
        Coins, German
        Gold coins
        Silver coins
Guldhammer family *(Not Subd Geog)*
Guldner family
    USE Goldner family
Guleo (African people)
    USE Kulebele (African people)
Guler painting *(May Subd Geog)*
    BT Miniature painting, Indic
        Pahari painting
Gulf brook lamprey
    [QL638.25.P48]
    UF Brook lamprey, Gulf
        Lamprey, Gulf brook
        Lethenteron meridionale

Gulf Coast (Mexico) *(Not Subd Geog)*
    BT Coasts—Mexico
Gulf Coast (U.S.)
    BT Coasts—United States
        Gulf States
Gulf flounder
    [QL638.B65]
    UF Flounder, Gulf
        Gulf fluke
        Paralichthys albigutta
Gulf fluke
    USE Gulf flounder
Gulf Intracoastal Waterway
    (Not Subd Geog)
    UF Intracoastal Waterway, Gulf Section
    BT Intracoastal waterways—Gulf States
Gulf Islands National Seashore (Fla. and Miss.)
    BT Islands—Florida
        Islands—Mississippi
        National parks and reserves—United States
        Parks—Florida
        Parks—Mississippi
Gulf of Aden
    USE Aden, Gulf of
Gulf of Aegina (Greece)
    USE Saronic Gulf (Greece)
Gulf of Alaska (Alaska)
    USE Alaska, Gulf of (Alaska)
Gulf of Amatique
    USE Honduras, Gulf of
Gulf of Aqaba
    USE Aqaba, Gulf of
Gulf of Arta (Greece)
    USE Arta, Gulf of (Greece)
Gulf of Bothnia
    USE Bothnia, Gulf of
Gulf of California (Mexico)
    USE California, Gulf of (Mexico)
Gulf of Campeche (Mexico)
    USE Campeche, Bay of (Mexico)
Gulf of Chihli (China)
    USE Po Hai (China)
Gulf of Darien (Colombia)
    USE Urabá, Gulf of (Colombia)
Gulf of Finland
    USE Finland, Gulf of
Gulf of Fonseca
    USE Fonseca, Gulf of
Gulf of Gascony (France and Spain)
    USE Biscay, Bay of (France and Spain)
Gulf of Gdańsk (Poland and R.S.F.S.R.)
    USE Gdańsk, Gulf of (Poland and R.S.F.S.R.)
Gulf of Georgia (B.C.)
    USE Georgia, Strait of (B.C.)
Gulf of Guayaquil
    USE Guayaquil, Gulf of
Gulf of Guinea
    USE Guinea, Gulf of
Gulf of Honduras
    USE Honduras, Gulf of
Gulf of Kotor (Montenegro)
    USE Kotor, Gulf of (Montenegro)
Gulf of Mexico
    USE Mexico, Gulf of
Gulf of Morbihan (France)
    USE Morbihan Gulf (France)
Gulf of Oman
    USE Oman, Gulf of
Gulf of Pagasai (Greece)
    USE Volos, Gulf of (Greece)
Gulf of Saint Lawrence
    USE Saint Lawrence, Gulf of
Gulf of Saint Vincent (S.A.)
    USE Saint Vincent, Gulf (S.A.)
Gulf of Siam
    USE Thailand, Gulf of
Gulf of Sidra, Battle of, 1942
    USE Sidra, Gulf of, Battle of, 1942

Gulf of Sirte, Battle of, 1942
  USE Sidra, Gulf of, Battle of, 1942
Gulf of Suez
  USE Suez, Gulf of
Gulf of Tatary (R.S.F.S.R.)
  USE Tatar Strait (R.S.F.S.R.)
Gulf of Thailand
  USE Thailand, Gulf of
Gulf of Urabá (Colombia)
  USE Urabá, Gulf of (Colombia)
Gulf of Volos (Greece)
  USE Volos, Gulf of (Greece)
Gulf pipefish
  ₍QL638.S9₎
  UF Syngnathus scovelli
Gulf Region (La.)
Gulf Region (Miss.)
  BT Gulf States
Gulf Region (Tex.)
  BT Gulf States
Gulf Saint Vincent (S.A.)
  USE Saint Vincent, Gulf (S.A.)
Gulf States
  NT Gulf Coast (U.S.)
       Gulf Region (Miss.)
       Gulf Region (Tex.)
  — **History**
       ₍F296₎
  — — **To 1803**
  — — **Revolution, 1775-1783**
Gulf Stream
  ₍GC296.G9₎
  BT Ocean currents
Gulf Stream (Painting)
  USE Homer, Winslow, 1836-1910. Gulf
       Stream
Gulf Stream beaked whale
  USE Mesoplodon europaeus
Gulf Stream in art
  NT Homer, Winslow, 1836-1910. Gulf
       Stream
Gulf Stream of Japan
  USE Kuroshio
Gulf-weed crab, Portunid
  USE Portunus sayi
Gulfs
  USE Bays
Gull-billed tern
  ₍QL696.C46₎
  UF Gelochelidon nilotica
       Sterna nilotica
Gullah dialect
  ₍PM7875.G8₎
  BT Black English
       Creole dialects, English—South
       Carolina
Gullett family *(Not Subd Geog)*
  UF Gillott family
       Gilot family
       Guillen family
       Guillet family
       Guillier family
       Guillios family
       Guilliot family
       Guilliott family
       Guillot family
       Guillotin family
       Guillott family
       Guillotte family
       Guilotte family
       Gullette family
  RT Gilliam family
Gullette family
  USE Gullett family
Gullies (Arroyas)
  USE Arroyos
Gulliford family
  USE Guilford family
Gulls
  ₍QL696.C46₎

  BT Charadriiformes
       Sea birds
  NT Black-headed gull
       Black-tailed gull
       California gull
       Chlidonias
       Gelochelidon
       Glaucous-winged gull
       Herring-gull
       Larus
       Laughing gull
       Lesser black-backed gull
       Ring-billed gull
Gullwing automobile
  USE Mercedes 300SL automobile
Gulma (African people)
  USE Gurma (African people)
Gulmance language
  USE Gurma language
Gulmanceba (African people)
  USE Gurma (African people)
Gulo
  ₍QL737.C25₎
  BT Mustelidae
  NT Wolverines
Gulo gulo
  USE Wolverines
Gum (City) *(Not Subd Geog)*
  UF Gumi (City)
  BT Cities and towns, Ruined, extinct, etc.
       —Sweden
       Sweden—Antiquities
Gum, Chewing
  USE Chewing gum
Gum, Poplar
  USE Eucalyptus alba
Gum, Timor white
  USE Eucalyptus alba
Gum arabic *(May Subd Geog)*
  ₍TP978₎
  UF Acacia (Gum)
       Senegal gum
  BT Adhesives
  RT Acacia senegal
Gum arabic acacia
  USE Acacia senegal
Gum arabic tree
  USE Acacia senegal
Gum bands
  USE Rubber bands
Gum-bichromate process
  USE Photography—Printing processes—
       Gum-bichromate
Gum-copal
  USE Copal
Gum disease, Java
  USE Sugarcane leaf scald
Gum elastic
  USE Rubber
Gum family *(Not Subd Geog)*
  UF Guin family
       Gumm family
Gum plastics
  UF Rubber-modified plastics
  BT Plastics
Gum trees, Australian
  USE Eucalyptus
Gum-wood
  ₍QK495.N98₎
Gumadji language
  USE Gumatj language
Gumaer family *(Not Subd Geog)*
  UF Germar family
       Guimar family
Gumaidji language
  USE Gumatj language
Gumait language
  USE Gumatj language
Gumatj language
  ₍PL7101.G79₎

  UF Gomadj language
       Gomaidj language
       Gumadji language
       Gumaidji language
       Gumait language
       Kainyao language
       Komaits language
       Kumait language
       Kumatj language
  BT Australia—Languages
       Australian languages
Gumbáingar language
  ₍PL7101.G8₎
  UF Kumbainggeri language
  BT Australia—Languages
       Australian languages
Gumbert family
  USE Gompert family
Gumbo
  USE Okra
Gumbrin
  USE Bentonite
Gumby (Fictitious character)
Gumi (City)
  USE Gum (City)
Gumla
  ₍MT725.G8 (Instruction)₎
  BT Musical instruments—Nepal
       Percussion instruments
Gumm family
  USE Gum family
Gummosis
  ₍SB741.G8₎
Gump family *(Not Subd Geog)*
  UF Gumpp family
       Gumps family
Gumpert family
  USE Gompert family
Gumpp family
  USE Gump family
Gumprecht family
  USE Gompert family
Gumprect family
  USE Gompert family
Gumps family
  USE Gump family
Gums
  ₍QM306₎
  UF Gingiva
  BT Periodontium
  NT Gingival fluid
  — **Care and hygiene**
       ₍RK61₎
       BT Hygiene
       RT Teeth—Care and hygiene
  — **Diseases** *(May Subd Geog)*
       ₍RK401-410₎
       BT Mouth—Diseases
            Periodontal disease
       NT Gingival hyperplasia
            Gingivitis
            Oral manifestations of general
            diseases
  — **Inflammation**
       USE Gingivitis
  — **Surgery**
       NT Gingivectomy
            Subgingival curettage
Gums and resins *(May Subd Geog)*
  ₍QD419-QD419.7 (Chemistry)₎
  ₍SB289-SB291 (Culture)₎
  ₍TP977-TP979.5 (Chemical
       technology)₎
  UF Resins
       Rosin
  BT Plant exudates
       Protective coatings
  SA *specific gums and resins, e.g.* Copal;
       Kauri gum; Kino
  NT Ion exchange resins
       Naval stores

1607

Gums and resins *(Continued)*
    Oleoresins
    Resinography
    Resins, Fossil
    Rosin-oil
    Turpentining
 — Microscopic structure
    USE Resinography
— Permeability
— Spectra
Gums and resins, Artificial
  USE Gums and resins, Synthetic
Gums and resins, Synthetic
  (May Subd Geog)
  ⌐*TP977-TP978 (General)*¬
  ⌐*TP1180 (Plastics)*¬
  UF Artificial resins
    Gums and resins, Artificial
    Resins, Synthetic
    Synthetic resins
  BT Chemistry, Technical
    Plastics
    Protective coatings
    Synthetic products
  NT Acetal resins
    Acrylic resins
    Alkyd resins
    Dental resins
    Epoxy resins
    Furan resins
    Indene resins
    Lucite
    Phenolic resins
    Polyesters
    Resin concrete
    Synthetic gums and resins industry
    Thermoplastics
    Thermosetting plastics
    Urea-formaldehyde resins
Gums and resins industry *(May Subd Geog)*
  ⌐*HD9769.R4-HD9769.R44*¬
Gun
  USE Firearms
    Ordnance
    Rifles
    Shotguns
Gun, Mountain
  USE Mountain guns
Gun (African people)
  ⌐*DT541.42*¬
  UF Goum (African people)
  BT Ethnology—Benin
Gun-carriages
  ⌐*UF640-642*¬
  BT Ordnance
Gun-carriages, Disappearing
  ⌐*UF650*¬
Gun control *(May Subd Geog)*
  ⌐*HV7435-HV7439*¬
  Here are entered general and non-legal works on
the control of guns. Works on the legal aspects of gun
control are entered under Firearms—Law and legis-
lation.
  UF Control of guns
    Firearms control
    Handgun control
  BT Firearms
 — Law and legislation
    USE Firearms—Law and legislation
Gun dogs
  USE Hunting dogs
Gun family
  USE Gunn family
Gun fire control
  USE Fire control (Gunnery)
Gun-flints
  ⌐*U888*¬
Gun holsters
  USE Holsters
Gun motor carriages
  USE Tank destroyers

Gun owners
  USE Firearms owners
Gun ownership
  USE Firearms ownership
Gun stocks
  USE Gunstocks
Gun turrets
  USE Airplanes, Military—Turrets
    Warships—Turrets
Gunantuna (Melanesian people)
  ⌐*DU550 (Bismarck Archipelago)*¬
  ⌐*GN671.B5 (Anthropology)*¬
  BT Melanesians
Gunantuna language
  USE Kuanua language
Gunawitji (Australian people)
  USE Gunwinggu (Australian people)
Gunboats
  BT Fast attack craft
    Warships
  RT Floating batteries
Gunce family
  USE Gunn family
Guncotton
  ⌐*TP276*¬
  BT Explosives
  RT Gunpowder
    Nitrocellulose
  NT Pyroxylin
Guncrete
  USE Gunite
Gundalows *(May Subd Geog)*
  UF Gundelows
  RT Barges
    Gondolas
    Scows
Gundelows
  USE Gundalows
Gunder family
  USE Gunderman family
Gunderman family *(Not Subd Geog)*
  UF Gunder family
    Gundermann family
Gundermann family
  USE Gunderman family
Gundestrup caldron (Silverwork)
  ⌐*NK7233.G77*¬
  UF Caldron of Gundestrup (Silverwork)
    Cauldron of Gundestrup (Silverwork)
    Gundestrup cauldron (Silverwork)
    Gundestrup silver caldron (Silverwork)
    Gundestrup silver cauldron
      (Silverwork)
  BT Silverwork—Denmark
Gundestrup cauldron (Silverwork)
  USE Gundestrup caldron (Silverwork)
Gundestrup silver caldron (Silverwork)
  USE Gundestrup caldron (Silverwork)
Gundestrup silver cauldron (Silverwork)
  USE Gundestrup caldron (Silverwork)
Gundjun dialects
  ⌐*PL7101.G82*¬
  UF Koonjan dialects
    Kunjen dialects
    Ngundjan dialects
  BT Australia—Languages
    Australian languages
Gundo (African people)
  USE Nkundu (African people)
Güneş theory (Turkish language)
  USE Turkish language—History—Güneş
    theory
Gung fu
  USE Kung fu
Gungabula language
  UF Gongabula language
    Kongabula language
  BT Australia—Languages
    Australian languages
Güngerich family
  USE Gingrich family

Guniam Indians
  USE Itenez Indians
Gunite
  ⌐*TA446*¬
  UF Guncrete
    Shotcreting
    Sprayed concrete
  BT Concrete
    Mortar
  RT Cement gun
Gunja
  USE Bhang (Drug)
Gunkel family
  USE Kunkel family
Gunkle family
  USE Kunkel family
Gunks (N.Y.)
  USE Shawangunk Mountains (N.Y.)
Gunn diodes
  USE Diodes, Gunn
Gunn effect
  BT Oscillators, Microwave
    Semiconductors
  NT Diodes, Gunn
Gunn family *(Not Subd Geog)*
  UF Gun family
    Gunce family
    Guns family
Gunn oscillators
  USE Oscillators, Microwave
Gunnell family *(Not Subd Geog)*
  UF Gunnells family
    Gunnels family
Gunnells family
  USE Gunnell family
Gunnels
  ⌐*QL638.P56*¬
  UF Opisthocentridae
    Pholidae
    Pholididae
  BT Perciformes
  NT Pholis
Gunnels family
  USE Gunnell family
Gunners
  USE *subdivision* Gunners *under individual
    armed forces, armies, navies, etc.,
    e.g.* United States—Armed Forces—
    Gunners; United States. Navy—
    Gunners
Gunners, Aerial
  USE *subdivision* Aerial gunners *under
    individual armed forces, armies,
    navies, etc., e.g.* United States—
    Armed Forces—Aerial gunners
Gunners, Naval
  USE *subdivision* Gunners *under names of
    individual navies, e.g.* United States.
    Navy—Gunners
Gunner's mate technicians (United States
  Navy)
  USE United States. Navy—Gunner's mate
    technicians
Gunner's mates (Missiles)
  USE United States. Navy—Gunner's
    mates (Missiles)
Gunner's mates (United States Navy)
  USE United States. Navy—Gunner's
    mates
Gunnery
  ⌐*UF150-302 (Manuals, drill books)*¬
  ⌐*UF800*¬
  ⌐*VF150-302 (Naval, VF144-7)*¬
  Here are entered general works, and also hand-
books, manuals, and regulations of a general charac-
ter.
  BT Artillery drill and tactics
    Military art and science
    Shooting

RT Ballistics
    Firearms
    Ordnance
    Projectiles
    Shooting, Military
NT Aerial gunnery
    Ammunition
    Artillery
    Artillerymen
    Bombing and gunnery ranges
    Explosives
    Fire control (Gunnery)
    Gunpowder
    Naval gunnery
    Position-finders
    Range-finding
    Rifle practice
    Tank gunnery
    Target acquisition
    Target practice
    Telescopic sights

Gunnery ranges
USE Bombing and gunnery ranges

Gunning
USE Hunting
    Shooting

Gunnison River (Colo.)
BT Rivers—Colorado

Gunnysack industry
USE Burlap bag industry

Gunongtello language
USE Gorontalo language

Gunpowder
    ₍HD9663 (Industry)₎
    ₍TP272 (Chemical technology)₎
BT Explosives
    Firearms
    Gunnery
    Powders
    Propellants
    Shooting, Military
RT Ammunition
    Guncotton
NT Compensating-powder
    Saltpeter
— History
— Safety measures

Gunpowder, Smokeless
    ₍TP273₎
UF Powder, Smokeless
    Smokeless powder

Gunpowder Plot, 1605
    ₍DA392₎
BT Great Britain—History—James I,
      1603-1625

Guns
USE Firearms
    Ordnance
    Rifles
    Shotguns

Guns, Hunting
USE Hunting guns

Guns, Line-throwing
USE Line-throwing guns

Guns, Mountain
USE Mountain guns

Guns, Sporting
USE Sporting guns

Guns, Submachine
USE Submachine guns

Guns family
USE Gunn family

Gunships (Military aircraft)
  (May Subd Geog)
BT Airplanes, Military

Gunshot wounds
    ₍RD156₎

Here are entered works on gunshot wounds in general and of particular organs or regions of the body. For the latter, a first subject heading is made for the wounds of the part of the body, e.g. 1. Heart—Wounds and injuries. 2. Gunshot wounds.

UF Bullet wounds
BT Surgery, Military
    Wounds and injuries

Gunsmithing
    ₍TS535₎
BT Firearms industry and trade
NT Firearms—Maintenance and repair
    Pistols—Customizing
— Tools and implements
    BT Tools

Gunsmiths *(May Subd Geog)*
RT Firearms designers
NT Trade-unions—Gunsmiths

Gunstocks
UF Gun stocks
    Stocks, Gun
BT Firearms

Gunter family
USE Gunther family

Gunter's line
USE Slide-rule

Guntersville Lake (Ala. and Tenn.)
BT Lakes—Alabama
    Lakes—Tennessee
    Reservoirs—Alabama
    Reservoirs—Tennessee

Gunther family *(Not Subd Geog)*
UF Gonter family
    Gunter family

Gunther's tree-shrew
USE Tupaia minor

Gunther's vole
USE Microtus guentheri

Guntzelman family
USE Gunzelman family

Gunu language *(May Subd Geog)*
UF Nugunu language
BT African languages
    Cameroon—Languages

Gunua-Kena language
USE Pampa language

Güntüna küne language
USE Pampa language

Gunung Mulu National Park (Sarawak)
UF Mulu National Park, Gunung
      (Sarawak)
BT National parks and reserves—Malaysia
    Parks—Malaysia
    Rain forests—Malaysia

Gunung Tambora (Sumbawa, Indonesia)
USE Tambora, Mount (Sumbawa,
      Indonesia)

Gunwiggu (Australian people)
USE Gunwinggu (Australian people)

Gunwinggu (Australian people)
UF Gunawitji (Australian people)
    Gunwiggu (Australian people)
    Koorungo (Australian people)
    Kulunglutji (Australian people)
    Mayali (Australian people)
    Winggu (Australian people)
BT Australian aborigines
    Ethnology—Australia

Gunwinggu (Australian people) bark painting
USE Bark painting, Gunwinggu (Australian
      people)

Gunwinggu language
    ₍PL7101.G83₎
BT Australia—Languages
    Australian languages

Gunzelman family *(Not Subd Geog)*
UF Guntzelman family
    Kuntzelmann family

Gunzenhauser family *(Not Subd Geog)*

Guoyagui language
USE Guayaki language

Gupapuyngu language
BT Australia—Languages
    Australian languages

Guppies
    ₍QL638.P73 (Zoology)₎
    ₍SF458.G8 (Culture)₎
UF Guppy
    Lebistes reticulatus
    Poecilia reticulata
BT Aquarium fishes

Guppy
USE Guppies

Guppy family *(Not Subd Geog)*

Gupta architecture
USE Architecture, Gupta

Gupta dynasty *(Not Subd Geog)*
BT India—History—324 B.C.-1000 A.D.

Gupta sculpture
USE Sculpture, Gupta

Guptill family *(Not Subd Geog)*
Gupton family *(Not Subd Geog)*

Gur languages *(May Subd Geog)*
    ₍PL8222₎
UF Goor languages
    Voltaic languages
BT Niger-Congo languages
NT Bobo dialects
    Dogon language
    Dompago dialect
    Gurma language
    Gurunsi dialects
    Hanga language (Ghana)
    Konkomba language
    Kulango language
    Kurumba language
    Lele dialect
    Lobi dialects
    Mampruli language
    Moba language
    Mossi languages
    Nankanse language
    Senufo language
    Somba language
    Tagbana language
    Tobote language
    Tusia language
    Vige language

Gura language
USE Gola language

Gurage language
    ₍PJ9288₎
UF Gourague language
BT Ethiopian languages

Gurages
    ₍DT380₎
BT Ethnology—Ethiopia

Guran family
USE Geurin family

Gurantala language
USE Gorontalo language

Gurenne language
USE Nankanse language

Gurganey family
USE Gruganus family

Gurgany family
USE Gruganus family

Gurgeyney family
USE Gruganus family

Gurian dialect
    ₍PK9132₎
UF Guric dialect
    Gurish dialect
BT Georgian language—Dialects

Guric dialect
USE Gurian dialect

Gurin family
USE Geurin family

Gurindji (Australian people)
  UF Gorandji (Australian people)
      Gorindji (Australian people)
      Kurintji (Australian people)
      Kutandji (Australian people)
  BT Australian aborigines
  — Government relations
Gurish dialect
  USE Gurian dialect
Gurjara-Pratihara dynasty *(Not Subd Geog)*
  [DS451.8]
  UF Prathiharas
      Pratiharas
  BT India—History—324 B.C.-1000 A.D.
Gurjari language
  USE Urdu language
Gurkha dynasty, 1768-
  USE Shah dynasty, 1768-
Gurkha soldiers *(May Subd Geog)*
  BT Gurkhas
      Mercenary troops
Gurkhali language
  USE Nepali language
Gurkhas
  [DS485.N4]
  UF Ghoorkas
      Ghurkas
      Goorkhas
      Gorkhas
  BT Ethnology—Nepal
  NT Gurkha soldiers
Gurma (African people)
  [DT555.45.G85]
  UF Gourmantché (African people)
      Gulma (African people)
      Gulmanceba (African people)
  BT Ethnology—Burkina Faso
Gurma (African people) philosophy
  USE Philosophy, Gurma (African people)
Gurma language
  UF Gourmantché language
      Gulmance language
  BT Gur languages
  NT Moba language
Gurmukhi alphabet
  [PK2632]
  BT Alphabet
      Panjabi language—Alphabet
Gurnea family
  USE Gurney family
Gurnee family
  USE Gurney family
Gurney family *(Not Subd Geog)*
  UF Girney family
      Gournay family
      Guerney family
      Gurnea family
      Gurnee family
      Gurnie family
Gurnie family
  USE Gurney family
Guro (African people)
  UF Gouro (African people)
      Kweni (African people)
      Lo (African people)
  BT Ethnology—Ivory Coast
Guro language
  USE Kweni language
Gurob (Ancient city) *(Not Subd Geog)*
  BT Cities and towns, Ruined, extinct, etc.
      —Egypt
      Egypt—Antiquities
Gurrin family
  USE Geurin family
Gurtner family
  USE Curtner family
Guru (Computer program)
  [HF5548.4.G87]
  BT Computer programs
Guru-pūja
  USE Guru worship (Rite)

Guru-sādhana
  USE Guru worship (Rite)
Guru worship (Rite) *(May Subd Geog)*
  UF Guru-pūja
      Guru-sādhana
      Guru-yoga
  BT Cults
      Gurus
      Worship
  — **Buddhism** *(May Subd Geog)*
      [BQ5030.G87 (General)]
      [BQ7699.G87 (Tibetan Buddhism)]
      BT Buddhism—Rituals
Guru-yoga
  USE Guru worship (Rite)
Gurumbu (New Guinea tribe)
  USE Gururumba (New Guinea tribe)
Gurumsi
  USE Gurunsi (African people)
Gurumsi dialects
  USE Gurunsi dialects
Gurune language
  USE Nankanse language
Gurung language
  [PL3801.G8]
  BT Tibeto-Burman languages
Gurunga
  USE Gurunsi (African people)
Gurungs
  BT Bhotias (Tibetan people)
      Ethnology—Nepal
Gurunsi (African people)
  UF Gourounsi (African people)
      Gruinse
      Grunshi
      Grusi
      Grussi
      Gurumsi
      Gurunga
  BT Ethnology—Burkina Faso
  NT Builsa (African people)
Gurunsi dialects
  UF Gourounsi dialects
      Grusi dialects
      Grussi dialects
      Gurumsi dialects
  BT Gur languages
  NT Kasena dialect
      Mo language (Ghana and Ivory Coast)
      Nunuma dialect
      Sisala language
      Tamprusi dialect
      Vagala language
Gurupi River (Brazil)
  UF Gurupy River (Brazil)
      Rio Gurupi (Brazil)
      Rio Gurupy (Brazil)
  BT Rivers—Brazil
Gurupy River (Brazil)
  USE Gurupi River (Brazil)
Gururumba (New Guinea tribe)
  UF Gurumbu (New Guinea tribe)
  BT Ethnology—New Guinea
Gurus *(May Subd Geog)*
  BT Hinduism
  NT Guru worship (Rite)
      Sikh gurus
Gurus, Nirankari
  USE Nirankari gurus
Gurus, Sikh
  USE Sikh gurus
Gusains
  [BL1245.G8]
  BT Hindu sects
Gusen (Austria : Concentration camp)
  BT World War, 1939-1945—
      Concentration camps—Austria
Guset family
  USE Gossett family
Gusewski family
  USE Gusovius family

Gusharbrum (Pakistan)
  USE Gasherbrum I (Pakistan)
Gushers
  [TN871]
  UF Oil gushers
  BT Oil wells
Gusii (African people)
  [DT433.545.G86]
  UF Gizii (African people)
      Kisii (African people)
      Kosova (African people)
  BT Bantus
      Ethnology—Kenya
Gusii language
  UF Ekegusii language
      Guzii language
      Kisii language
  BT Bantu languages
Gusli
  [ML1015.G8 (Russian)]
  BT Dulcimer
  NT Kanklès
      Kantele (Musical instrument)
Gusli music (Guslis (2))
  [M292-293]
Guslis (2) with chamber orchestra
  [M1037.4.G85]
  RT Concertos (Guslis (2) with chamber
      orchestra)
Gusovius family *(Not Subd Geog)*
  UF Gudovius family
      Gujowski family
      Gusewski family
      Gusovski family
      Guzewski family
Gusovski family
  USE Gusovius family
Gust loads
  BT Aerodynamic load
      Atmospheric turbulence
      Wind-pressure
  — **Measurement**
      BT Aerodynamic measurements
Gustafson family *(Not Subd Geog)*
  UF Gustavson family
Gustation
  USE Taste
Gustation disorders
  USE Taste disorders
Gustavson family
  USE Gustafson family
Gusten family
  USE Gaston family
Gustin family
  USE Gaston family
Gustion family
  USE Gaston family
Guston family
  USE Gaston family
Gustorfer Chorschranken (Sculpture)
  [NB586.C]
  UF Chorschranken in Gustorf (Sculpture)
  BT Sculpture—Germany (West)
Gut hormones
  USE Gastrointestinal hormones
Gut industries
  USE Animal gut industries
Gut of Canso (N.S.)
  USE Canso, Strait of (N.S.)
Gutenberg-Preis der Stadt Leipzig
  BT Book design
Guth family
  USE Good family
Guthrie family *(Not Subd Geog)*
  UF Guttery family
Gutierrez-Magee Expedition, 1812-1813
  UF Magee-Gutierrez Expedition, 1812-
      1813
  BT Texas—History—1810-1821
  NT Medina River (Tex.), Battle of, 1813

Gutîi Mountains (Romania)
  UF Munţii Gutâiului (Romania)
      Munţii Gutîi (Romania)
      Munţii Gutîiului (Romania)
      Munţii Gutinului (Romania)
  BT Mountains—Romania
Gutjahr family *(Not Subd Geog)*
  RT Goodyear family
Gutknecht family *(Not Subd Geog)*
  UF Gudknecht family
  RT Goodnight family
Gutob language (Dravidian)
  USE Gadaba language (Dravidian)
Gutsch family
  USE Kutsch family
Gutsul Alps (Ukraine)
  USE Hutsul Alps (Ukraine)
Gutsul'skie Al'py (Ukraine)
  USE Hutsul Alps (Ukraine)
Gutsul'skiye Al'py (Ukraine)
  USE Hutsul Alps (Ukraine)
Gutta-percha
  ₁HD9161 (Trade)₁
  ₁SB291.I5 (Culture)₁
  ₁TS1930 (Manufacture)₁
  BT Rubber, Cyclized
  RT Rubber
Gutters
  ₁TH2493₁
  BT Building
      Roof drainage
      Roofs
Guttery family
  USE Guthrie family
Guttiferae
  ₁QK495.G87₁
  UF Clusiaceae
  BT Guttiferales
  NT Garcinia
      Hypericum
      Triadenum
Guttiferales
  ₁QK495.A12₁
  UF Parietales
  BT Dicotyledons
  NT Actinidiaceae
      Caryocaraceae
      Dipterocarpaceae
      Guttiferae
      Quiinaceae
Guttis
  USE Guttus
Gutto Riot, Reykjavík, Iceland, 1932
  USE Reykjavík (Iceland)—Gúttó Riot, 1932
Guttus *(May Subd Geog)*
  UF Guttis
  BT Vases, Etruscan
      Vases, Greek
Guttuso, Renato, 1912-   Bosco d'amore
  (Not Subd Geog)
  ₁ND623.G86₁
  UF Bosco d'amore (Painting)
  BT Erotic painting, Italian
Guy anchors
  ₁TA777₁
  UF Anchors, Deadman
      Anchors, Ground
      Anchors, Guy
      Deadman anchors
      Ground anchors
      Tiebacks (Anchors)
  BT Anchorage (Structural engineering)
Guyan River (W. Va.)
  USE Guyandotte River (W. Va.)
Guyana
  BT Guiana
  — Description and travel
  — — 1951-1980
  — — 1981-
  — Economic conditions
  — — 1918-1966

— — 1966-
— History
    ₁F2361-2391₁
— — To 1803
        NT English West Indian Expedition, 1795-1796
— — 1803-1966
— — 1966-
— Languages
    NT Surinam Hindustani language
— Politics and government
— — To 1803
— — 1803-1966
— — 1966-
— Social conditions
— — 1966-
Guyandot River (W. Va.)
  USE Guyandotte River (W. Va.)
Guyandotte River (W. Va.)
  UF Guyan River (W. Va.)
      Guyandot River (W. Va.)
  BT Rivers—West Virginia
Guyanese *(May Subd Geog)*
  BT Ethnology—Guyana
  — United States
      NT Guyanese Americans
Guyanese Americans *(May Subd Geog)*
  ₁E184.G86₁
  UF Guyanese Americans—United States
  BT Ethnology—United States
      Guyanese—United States
  — United States
      USE Guyanese Americans
Guyanese children's poetry
  USE Children's poetry, Guyanese
Guyanese cookery
  USE Cookery, Guyanese
Guyanese drama *(May Subd Geog)*
  ₁PR9320.3 (History)₁
  ₁PR9320.7 (Collections)₁
  UF English drama—Guyanese authors
Guyanese fiction *(May Subd Geog)*
  UF English fiction—Guyanese authors
  NT Short stories, Guyanese
Guyanese literature *(May Subd Geog)*
  ₁PR9320.45-PR9320.8 (Collections)₁
  ₁PR9320-PR9320.4 (History)₁
  UF English literature—Guyanese authors
Guyanese poetry *(May Subd Geog)*
  ₁PR9320.2 (History)₁
  ₁PR9320.6 (Collections)₁
  UF English poetry—Guyanese authors
  NT Children's poetry, Guyanese
      Revolutionary poetry, Guyanese
Guyanese poets
  USE Poets, Guyanese
Guyanese revolutionary poetry
  USE Revolutionary poetry, Guyanese
Guyanese short stories
  USE Short stories, Guyanese
Guyer family
  USE Geyer family
Guynes family *(Not Subd Geog)*
  UF Goyen family
      Goyne family
      Goynes family
Guyon family
  USE Guion family
Guyton family *(Not Subd Geog)*
Guyuk dialect
  BT Longuda language
      Nigeria—Languages
Guzewski family
  USE Gusovius family
Guzii language
  USE Gusii language
Guzy
  USE Oghuz
Guzzi motorcycle
  USE Moto Guzzi motorcycle

Gvozdena vrata (Romania and Serbia)
  USE Iron Gates (Romania and Serbia)
GVS 100 (Computer)
  ₁QA76.8.G₁
  BT Hybrid computers
— Programming
    ₁QA76.6₁
Gwa dialect (Ghana)
  ₁PL8215.95.G₁
  UF Anum dialect
  BT Kwa languages
Gwaka (African people)
  USE Ngbaka (African people)
Gwalchmei (Legendary character)
  USE Gawain (Legendary character)
Gwali language
  USE Gwari language
Gwalior Fort (Gwalior, India)
  UF Fort, Gwalior (Gwalior, India)
  BT Fortification—India
Gwalthney family
  USE Gwartney family
Gwaltney family
  USE Gwartney family
Gwamba language
  USE Tsonga language
Gwandara language
  UF Kwandara language
  BT Chadic languages
Gwari (African people)
  UF Gbari (African people)
      Gwari (African tribe)
  BT Ethnology—Nigeria
Gwari (African tribe)
  USE Gwari (African people)
Gwari language
  UF Gbari language
      Gwali language
  BT Kwa languages
Gwartney family *(Not Subd Geog)*
  UF Gaurthny family
      Gualtney family
      Guartney family
      Gwalthney family
      Gwaltney family
      Gwatney family
Gwatkin family *(Not Subd Geog)*
  UF Gwatkins family
  RT Watkins family
Gwatkins family
  USE Gwatkin family
Gwatney family
  USE Gwartney family
Gwazum language
  USE Ngizim language
Gwe language
  USE Sukuma language
Gweabo (African people)
  USE Grebo (African people)
Gweabo language
  USE Jabo language
Gwembe (African people)
  USE Tonga (Zambian people)
GWF airplanes
  ₁TL686.G₁
Gwi language
  USE G/wi language
Gwich'in language
  USE Kutchakutchin language
Gwin (African people)
  USE Gouin (African people)
Gwynn Island (Va.) *(Not Subd Geog)*
  UF Gwynn's Island (Va.)
  BT Islands—Virginia
Gwynns Falls (Md.)
  BT Rivers—Maryland
      Waterfalls—Maryland
Gwynn's Island (Va.)
  USE Gwynn Island (Va.)
Gwyr (Wales)
  USE Gower (Wales)

Gxon language
USE !Xõ language
Gyalopion
[QL666.O636]
BT Colubridae
Gyan chaupar (Game)
USE Leela (Game)
Gyaros Island (Greece) (Not Subd Geog)
UF Nísos Yíaros (Greece)
Nísos Yioúra (Greece)
Yiaros Island (Greece)
Yioura Island (Greece)
BT Cyclades (Greece)
Islands—Greece
Gyarung language
[PL3651.G9]
UF Giarung language
BT Tibetan language—Dialects
Gyebu Timikkindyen (Legendary character)
USE Ṭimikkindyen (Legendary character)
Gyer family
USE Geyer family
Gyge
[QL444.M34]
BT Bopyridae
Gyge branchialis
[QL444.M34]
Gyger family
USE Geiger family
Gygir family
USE Geiger family
Gygor family
USE Geiger family
Gyitkshan Indians
USE Kitksan Indians
Gyldendahl family
USE Gyldendal family
Gyldendal family (Not Subd Geog)
UF Gyldendahl family
Gyldensteen (Denmark)
UF Enggård (Denmark)
BT Manors—Denmark
Gylling family (Not Subd Geog)
Gymkhanas, Mounted
USE Gymkhanas (Horsemanship)
Gymkhanas (Horsemanship)
(May Subd Geog)
[SF296.G9]
UF Gymkhanas, Mounted
Horse-shows—Gymkhana division
BT Horse-shows
Horse sports
Horsemanship
Gymnachirus
[QL638.S7]
BT Flatfishes
Soleidae
Gymnarchidae
[QL638.G87]
BT Mormyriformes
NT Gymnarchus
Gymnarchus
[QL638.G87]
BT Gymnarchidae
NT Gymnarchus niloticus
Gymnarchus niloticus
[QL638.G87]
BT Gymnarchus
Gymnarthridae
BT Microsauria
NT Euryodus
Gymnasion (Samos Island, Greece)
UF Gymnasium (Samos Island, Greece)
BT Gymnasiums—Greece
Gymnasium (Samos Island, Greece)
USE Gymnasion (Samos Island, Greece)
Gymnasium-Bath Complex (Sardis)
USE Bath-Gymnasium Complex (Sardis)
Gymnasiums (May Subd Geog)
[GV403-405]

BT Physical education facilities
Sports facilities
RT Field houses
— Apparatus and equipment
USE Gymnasiums—Equipment and
supplies
— **Equipment and supplies**
[GV407-410]
UF Gymnasiums—Apparatus and
equipment
NT Pangymnastikon
— **Greece**
NT Gymnasion (Samos Island, Greece)
— **Turkey**
NT Bath-Gymnasium Complex (Sardis)
Gymnastics (May Subd Geog)
[GV461-475]
BT Athletics
Exercise
Sports
RT Callisthenics
Physical education and training
NT Acrobatics
Balance beam
Chest weights
Gymnastics for men
Gymnastics for women
Horizontal bar
Indian clubs
Parallel bars
Pyramids (Gymnastics)
Rings (Gymnastics)
Schools—Exercises and recreations
Swedish gymnastics
Vaulting-horse
— **Judging**
BT Sports officiating
— **Rules**
Gymnastics, Medical
USE Exercise therapy
Gymnastics for children
[GV464.5]
BT Physical education for children
NT Exercise therapy for children
Gymnastics for men (May Subd Geog)
[GV463.5]
UF Men's gymnastics
BT Gymnastics
Gymnastics for women (May Subd Geog)
[GV464]
BT Gymnastics
Physical education for women
— **Rules**
[GV464]
Gymnastics in literature
Gymnasts (May Subd Geog)
BT Athletes
Gymnidae
USE Lymantriidae
Gymnoascaceae
BT Eurotiales
Gymnobranchiata
USE Nudibranchiata
Gymnocladus canadensis
USE Kentucky coffeetree
Gymnocladus dioicus
USE Kentucky coffeetree
Gymnocypris
[QL638.C94]
BT Cyprinidae
Gymnocypris przewalskii
[QL638.C94]
Gymnodontidae
USE Tetraodontidae
Gymnodraco acuticeps
[QL638.B2]
Gymnodraco victori
[QL638.B2]
Gymnogyps californianus
USE California condor

Gymnolaemata (May Subd Geog)
[QL396-397.96]
BT Bryozoa
NT Cheilostomata
Ctenostomata
Cyclostomata (Bryozoa)
Gymnolaemata, Fossil
BT Bryozoa, Fossil
NT Cheilostomata, Fossil
Cryptostomata
Ctenostomata, Fossil
Cyclostomata, Fossil (Bryozoa)
Cystoporata
Gymnonoti
USE Cypriniformes
Gymnophiona
USE Caecilians
Gymnopithys
[QL696.P2455]
BT Formicariidae
Gymnopleurus
[QL596.S3]
BT Scarabaeidae
Gymnosomata
[QL430.4]
Gymnosomatidae
USE Tachinidae
Gymnosperms
[QK494]
BT Phanerogams
NT Conifers
Cycadales
Ginkgo
Gnetales
Taxopsida
Gymnosperms, Fossil
BT Paleobotany
NT Conifers, Fossil
Cordaitales
Resins, Fossil
Gymnothorax
[QL638.M875]
UF Rabula
BT Morays
Gymnothorax bathyphilus
[QL638.M875]
Gymnotidae
[QL638.G9]
BT Cypriniformes
NT Eigenmannia
Gymnurus
USE Echinosorex
Gyn family
USE Ginn family
Gynandromorphism
BT Hermaphroditism
Sex (Biology)
Sex differentiation disorders
NT Virilism
Gynecocracy
USE Matriarchy
Gynecologic diagnosis
USE Gynecology—Diagnosis
Gynecologic drugs (May Subd Geog)
[RG131]
BT Drugs
Gynecology—Formulae, receipts,
prescriptions
NT Emmenagogues
Oral contraceptives
Gynecologic emergencies (May Subd Geog)
[RG158]
UF Emergencies, Gynecologic
BT Generative organs, Female—Diseases
Gynecology
Medical emergencies
Gynecologic endocrinology
USE Endocrine gynecology
Gynecologic examination
[RG107-RG107.5]

BT Gynecology—Diagnosis
    Physical diagnosis
    Women—Medical examinations
Gynecologic nursing
  [RG105]
BT Gynecology
    Nursing
NT Hysterectomy—Nursing
Gynecologic practice
USE Gynecology—Practice
Gynecological pathology
USE Pathology, Gynecological
Gynecologist and patient *(May Subd Geog)*
UF Gynecologist-patient relationship
    Patient and gynecologist
BT Physician and patient
Gynecologist-patient relationship
USE Gynecologist and patient
Gynecologists *(May Subd Geog)*
— **Attitudes**
    BT Attitude (Psychology)
— **Legal status, laws, etc.**
    NT Gynecologists—Malpractice
— **Malpractice** *(May Subd Geog)*
    UF Tort liability of gynecologists
    BT Gynecologists—Legal status, laws,
        etc.
        Gynecology—Law and legislation
        Malpractice
Gynecology *(May Subd Geog)*
  [RG]
BT Medicine
RT Generative organs, Female—Diseases
    Women—Diseases
NT Endocrine gynecology
    Geriatric gynecology
    Gynecologic emergencies
    Gynecologic nursing
    Pathology, Gynecological
    Pediatric gynecology
    Veterinary gynecology
    Women's health services
— **Diagnosis**
    [RG107-RG107.5]
    UF Diagnosis, Gynecologic
        Gynecologic diagnosis
    BT Diagnosis
    NT Gynecologic examination
— **Formulae, receipts, prescriptions**
    [RG131]
    NT Gynecologic drugs
— **Genetic aspects**
    BT Genetics
        Medical genetics
— Hospitals
    USE Hospitals, Gynecologic and
        obstetric
— **Immunological aspects**
— Jurisprudence
    USE Forensic gynecology
— **Law and legislation** *(May Subd Geog)*
    BT Medical laws and legislation
    NT Gynecologists—Malpractice
— **Practice**
    UF Gynecologic practice
— **Psychological aspects**
    [RG103.5]
    BT Medicine and psychology
— **Psychosomatic aspects**
    BT Medicine, Psychosomatic
— **Social aspects** *(May Subd Geog)*
    UF Society and gynecology
Gynecology, Forensic
USE Forensic gynecology
Gynecology, Operative *(May Subd Geog)*
  [RG104]
UF Generative organs, Female—Surgery
    Operative gynecology
BT Genitourinary organs—Surgery
NT Clitoridectomy
    Curettage, Vacuum

    Gynoplasty
    Obstetrics—Surgery
— **Complications and sequelae**
Gynecology, Osteopathic
  [RZ386]
BT Osteopathy
Gynecology, Pediatric
USE Pediatric gynecology
Gynn family
USE Ginn family
Gynogenesis
BT Parthenogenesis
    Reproduction
Gynoplasty
  [RG104.5]
BT Gynecology, Operative
    Surgery, Plastic
Gynt, Peer (Fictitious character)
UF Peer Gynt (Fictitious character)
BT Characters and characteristics in
    literature
RT Ibsen, Henrik, 1828-1906—Characters
    —Peer Gynt
Gyon family
USE Guion family
Győr-Sopron-Ebenfurti Vasút
BT Railroads—Austria
    Railroads—Hungary
Gyotaku
USE Fish prints
Gyp Hill (Tex.)
BT Mountains—Texas
Gypaetus barbatus
USE Lammergeier
Gypona
  [QL527.C49]
BT Leafhoppers
Gyponidae
USE Leafhoppers
Gypsic soils
USE Soils—Gypsum content
Gypsies *(May Subd Geog)*
  [DX]
UF Gipsies
    Romanies
BT Nomads
SA *subdivision* Gypsies *under individual*
    wars, e.g. World War, 1939-1945—
    Gypsies
NT Missions to Gypsies
    Nawar
    Tinkers
— **Language**
    NT Romany language
— **Music**
    NT Flamenco music
— **India**
    NT Sikligars
Gypsiferous soils
USE Soils—Gypsum content
Gypsum *(May Subd Geog)*
  [TN946]
BT Evaporites
RT Plaster of Paris
NT Gypsum-bonded mine roof bolts
    Phosphogypsum
    Soils—Gypsum content
— **Inclusions**
    [QE391.G93]
    UF Enclaves in gypsum
        Inclusions in gypsum
Gypsum Cliffs (Alta.) *(Not Subd Geog)*
BT Cliffs—Alberta
Gypsum industry *(May Subd Geog)*
  [HD9585.G9-93]

Gypsum mines and mining
  (May Subd Geog)
BT Mines and mineral resources
Gypsy and soldier (Painting)
USE Caravaggio, Michelangelo Merisi da,
    1573-1610. Fortune teller
Gypsy caravans
USE Wagons, Gypsy
Gypsy language
USE Romany language
Gypsy magic
USE Magic, Gypsy
Gypsy medicine
USE Medicine, Gypsy
Gypsy moth *(May Subd Geog)*
  [QL561.L9 (Entomology)]
  [SB945.G9 (Pest)]
UF Gipsy moth
    Lymantria dispar
    Porthetria dispar
Gypsy musicians
USE Musicians, Gypsy
Gypsy poetry
Gypsy wagons
USE Wagons, Gypsy
Gyr falcon
USE Gyrfalcon
Gyrators
BT Electric networks
    Microwave circuits
NT Ferrites (Magnetic materials)
    Hall effect
    Wave guides
Gyrfalcon
UF Falco rusticolus
    Gyr falcon
BT Falcons
Gyrinidae
  [QL596.G8]
UF Whirligig beetles
Gyrinophilus
  [QL668.C274]
BT Plethodontidae
Gyrlyngton family
USE Garlington family
Gyro compass
  [QA862.G9]
  [TL589.C6]
  [VK577]
UF Compass, Gyroscopic
    Gyrocompass
    Gyrostatic compass
BT Aeronautical instruments
    Automatic pilot (Ships)
    Gyroscopes
NT Automatic pilot (Airplanes)
Gyro horizon
USE Artificial horizons (Aeronautical
    instruments)
Gyro pilot
USE Automatic pilot (Airplanes)
    Automatic pilot (Ships)
Gyro stabilizers
USE Gyrostabilizers
Gyro vertical (Instruments)
USE Artificial horizons (Aeronautical
    instruments)
Gyrocompass
USE Gyro compass
Gyrocotylidea
  [QL391.P7]
BT Cestoda
Gyrodynamics
USE Rotational motion
    Rotational motion (Rigid dynamics)
Gyropilot
USE Automatic pilot (Airplanes)
    Automatic pilot (Ships)
Gyroplanes
USE Autogiros

Gyros (Gyroscopes)
  USE Gyroscopes
Gyroscopes *(May Subd Geog)*
  ⌐QA862.G9 (Dynamics)¬
  UF Gyros (Gyroscopes)
  BT Rotational motion (Rigid dynamics)
    Tops
  NT Artificial horizons (Aeronautical
      instruments)
    Cryogenic gyroscopes
    Fluid rotor gyroscopes
    Gyro compass
    Gyroscopic instruments
    Gyrostabilizers
    Optical gyroscopes
    Rate gyroscopes
Gyroscopic instruments
  BT Aeronautical instruments
    Gyroscopes
    Nautical instruments
    Physical instruments
  SA *names of specific instruments and uses,*
      e.g. Automatic pilot (Airplanes);
      Gyro compass; Horizons, Artificial;
      Inertial navigation
  NT Astronautical instruments
Gyrostabilizers
  UF Gyro stabilizers
  BT Gyroscopes
    Stability
Gyrostachys cernua
  USE Spiranthes cernua
Gyrostatic compass
  USE Gyro compass
Gyrostemonaceae
  ⌐QK495.G877 (Botany)¬
  BT Centrospermae
Gyrothrix
  ⌐QK625.D4¬
  UF Campsotrichum
  BT Dematiaceae
Gyrotrons
  ⌐TK7871.79.G95¬
  UF Cyclotron resonance masers
  BT Microwave tubes
Gyrus suprasylvius
  USE Suprasylvian gyrus
H (The sound)
  ⌐P235.5¬
  BT Grammar, Comparative and general—
      Phonology
    Phonetics
H-2 locus
  UF H-2 system
  BT Immunogenetics
H 2 regions (Astrophysics)
  USE H II regions (Astrophysics)
H-2 system
  USE H-2 locus
H-8 (Computer)
  USE Heathkit H-8 (Computer)
H-bomb
  USE Hydrogen bomb
H-functions, Fox's
  USE Fox's H-function
H-guide
  USE Dielectric wave guides
H II regions (Astrophysics)
  UF H 2 regions (Astrophysics)
    H regions (Astrophysics)
  BT Astrophysics
    Gases, Ionized
    Interstellar hydrogen
    Nebulae
    Stars—Formation
H.P. 80 (Jet planes)
  USE Victor (Jet planes)
H.P. 115 (Jet planes)
  USE Handley Page 115 (Jet planes)
H.R. 10 plans
  USE Keogh plans

H.R.D. motorcycle
  USE Vincent H.R.D. motorcycle
H-R diagrams
  USE HR diagrams
H regions (Astrophysics)
  USE H II regions (Astrophysics)
H-spaces
  UF Hopf spaces
    Spaces, Hopf
  BT Topological groups
H-T-P Technique
  USE House-Tree-Person Technique
H-Y antigen
  ⌐QR184.35¬
  UF HY antigen
    Sex determinant antigen
  BT Histocompatibility antigens
    Immunogenetics
    Immunology, Developmental
H/Z-100 (Computer)
  USE Zenith Z-100 (Computer)
Ha 'Ivri (The Hebrew word)
  USE 'Ivri (The Hebrew word)
Ha-le-ma-no (Legendary character)
  USE Hale-mano (Legendary character)
ha-Yarden
  USE Jordan River
Haabai (Tonga)
  USE Ha'apai Group (Tonga)
Haafuluhoa (Tonga)
  USE Vava'u Island (Tonga)
Haag family *(Not Subd Geog)*
Haag Site (Ind.)
  USE Leonard Haag Site (Ind.)
Haagenstad family *(Not Subd Geog)*
Haagsche Tramweg
  BT Railroads—Netherlands
    Street-railroads—Netherlands
Haagse school of painting
  ⌐N6947.5.H3 (Art)¬
  ⌐ND647.5.H3 (Painting)¬
  UF Hague school of painting
  BT Painting, Dutch
    Painting, Modern—19th century—
      Netherlands
Haahr family
  USE Haar family
Ha'apai Group (Tonga)
  UF Haabai (Tonga)
    Hapai (Tonga)
  BT Islands—Tonga
Haapasaari (Finland : Island)
  BT Islands—Finland
Haar family *(Not Subd Geog)*
  UF Haahr family
    Haarman family
    Haarmann family
Haar integral
  USE Integrals, Haar
Haar measure
  USE Integrals, Haar
Haarlem Stadhuis (Haarlem, Netherlands)
  BT City halls—Netherlands
Haarman family
  USE Haar family
Haarmann family
  USE Haar family
Haar's measure
  USE Integrals, Haar
Haas family *(Not Subd Geog)*
  UF Haase family
    Hase family
Haase family
  USE Haas family
Haatvedt family *(Not Subd Geog)*
Haavara
  UF Ha'avarah
  BT Investments, German—Palestine
    Jewish property—Germany
    Palestine—Emigration and immigration

Ha'avarah
  USE Haavara
Habad *(May Subd Geog)*
  UF Chabad
    Lubavitch-Chabad
  BT Hasidism
Habaner ware
  ⌐NK4340.H3¬
Habans
  USE Anabaptists
Habe (African people)
  USE Dogons (African people)
Habe language
  USE Dogon language
Habeas corpus *(May Subd Geog)*
  BT Civil rights
    Constitutional law
    Criminal procedure
    Detention of persons
    Extraordinary remedies
    Martial law
    Post-conviction remedies
    Writs
  NT Amparo (Writ)
Habeas corpus (International law)
  BT International law
Habel family *(Not Subd Geog)*
  UF Habell family
Habell family
  USE Habel family
Habelschwerdt Mountains (Poland)
  USE Bystrzyca Mountains (Poland)
Habelschwerdter Gebirge (Poland)
  USE Bystrzyca Mountains (Poland)
Habenaria
  ⌐QK495.O64 (Botany)¬
  BT Orchids
Habenaria andrewsii
  ⌐QK495.O64¬
Habenaria multicaudata
  ⌐QK495.O64¬
Haberdashery
  USE Men's furnishing goods
Habermehl family
  USE Hovermale family
Haberu (The Japanese word)
  BT Japanese language—Etymology
Habiri
  USE Habiru
Habiru
  UF Chabiroe
    Habiri
    Khabiri
  BT Ethnology—Iraq
    Jews—Origin
Habit
  ⌐BF335-7¬
  BT Conduct of life
    Psychology
  NT Food habits
    Formal discipline
    Health behavior
    Inhibition
    Instinct
    Narcotic habit
    Oral habits
    Tobacco habit
Habit, Clerical
  USE Clergy—Costume
Habit, Ecclesiastical
  USE Clergy—Costume
Habit, Monastic
  USE Monasticism and religious orders—
      Habit
    Monasticism and religious orders,
      Buddhist—Habit
Habit, Riding
  USE Riding habit
Habit (Philosophy)
  ⌐B105.H32¬
  BT Philosophy

Habit breaking (May Subd Geog)
 ⌐BF337.B74┐
  Here are entered works on reduction or elimination of unwanted habits in general. Works on reduction or elimination of specific habits are entered under specific headings with appropriate subdivision, e.g. Tobacco habit—Treatment.
 UF Breaking, Habit
   Breaking habits
 BT Behavior modification
   Self-control
Habitable atmospheres (Space environment)
 USE Artificial atmospheres (Space environment)
Habitant farm (Painting)
 USE Krieghoff, Cornelius, 1815-1872.
   Habitant farm
Habitat, Human
 USE Human settlements
Habitat (Ecology)
 UF Wildlife habitat
 BT Ecology
 SA subdivision Habitat under names of organisms, e.g. Corn—Habitat; Fishes—Habitat
 NT Habitat partitioning (Biology)
   Habitat selection
   Niche (Ecology)
   Wildlife habitat improvement
 — Modification
  UF Habitat modification (Ecology)
    Modification of habitat (Ecology)
  BT Man—Influence on nature
  SA subdivision Effect of habitat modification on under individual animals and groups of animals, e.g. Fishes—Effect of habitat modification on
  NT Wildlife habitat improvement
Habitat improvement, Wildlife
 USE Wildlife habitat improvement
Habitat modification (Ecology)
 USE Habitat (Ecology)—Modification
Habitat partitioning (Biology)
 BT Competition (Biology)
   Ecology
   Habitat (Ecology)
   Habitat selection
   Resource partitioning (Ecology)
Habitat selection
 UF Selection of habitat
 BT Animal ecology
   Habitat (Ecology)
   Resource partitioning (Ecology)
 NT Habitat partitioning (Biology)
Habitations of domestic animals
 USE Animal housing
Habitations of wild animals
 USE Animals—Habitations
Habitats, Space
 USE Space colonies
Habitual criminals
 USE Recidivists
Habituation (Neuropsychology)
 ⌐QP374┐
 RT Conditioned response
   Extinction (Psychology)
Habrocytus (May Subd Geog)
 ⌐QL568.P94┐
 BT Pteromalidae
 NT Habrocytus cerealellae
Habrocytus cerealellae (May Subd Geog)
 ⌐QL568.P94┐
 BT Habrocytus
Habronattus (May Subd Geog)
 ⌐QL458.42.S24┐
 BT Jumping spiders
Habsburg, House of (Not Subd Geog)
 UF Austria, House of
   Hapsburg, House of
 BT Austria—Kings and rulers

Ḥabshush family (Not Subd Geog)
 UF Hibshoosh family
   Ḥibshush family
Habu
 USE Trimeresurus flavoviridis
Ḥabūba Kabira Site (Syria)
 (Not Subd Geog)
 ⌐DS99.H25┐
 BT Cities and towns, Ruined, extinct, etc.—Syria
   Syria—Antiquities
Habutsu family (Not Subd Geog)
Hachi-hachi
 USE Hachi-ju-hachi (Game)
Hachi-ju-hachi (Game)
 ⌐GV1299.H3┐
 UF Eighty-eight (Game)
   Hachi-hachi
   Hana
   Hana-karuta
Hachidaishū
 BT Waka
 NT Sandaishū
Hachigaminejō (Jōetsu-shi, Japan)
 USE Kasugayamajō (Jōetsu-shi, Japan)
Hachijō Island (Japan)
 UF Fatsizio-jima (Japan)
   Hachijō-jima (Japan)
 BT Islands—Japan
   Izu Islands (Japan)
Hachijō-jima (Japan)
 USE Hachijō Island (Japan)
Hachiman (Shinto deity) (May Subd Geog)
 ⌐BL2226.2.H3┐
 UF Hachiman Daibosatsu (Buddhist deity)
   Hachiman Daibosatsu (Shinto deity)
 BT Gods, Buddhist
   Gods, Shinto
Hachiman Daibosatsu (Buddhist deity)
 USE Hachiman (Shinto deity)
Hachiman Daibosatsu (Shinto deity)
 USE Hachiman (Shinto deity)
Hachiman Tarō ekotoba (Scrolls)
 USE Gosannen kassen ekotoba (Scrolls)
Hachimantai Kokuritsu Kōen (Japan)
 USE Towada-Hachimantai National Park (Japan)
Hachimantai Plateau (Japan)
 BT Plateaus—Japan
 NT Towada-Hachimantai National Park (Japan)
Hachisuka family (Not Subd Geog)
Hacienda de Jalpa (Mexico)
 USE Jalpa Hacienda (Mexico)
Hacienda de La Concha (Mexico)
 USE Concha Hacienda (Mexico)
Hacienda de Ojocaliente (Mexico)
 USE Ojocaliente Hacienda (Mexico)
Hacienda de San Antonio Tochatlaco (Mexico)
 USE San Antonio Tochatlaco Hacienda (Mexico)
Hacienda de San Carlos Borromeo (Mexico)
 USE San Carlos Borromeo Hacienda (Mexico)
Hacienda de San Juan de los Otates (Mexico)
 USE San Juan de los Otates Hacienda (Mexico)
Hacienda Serrana (Ecuador)
 USE Serrana Hacienda (Ecuador)
Hacienda Yerbabuena (Colombia)
 USE Yerbabuena Hacienda (Colombia)
Haciendas (May Subd Geog)
 ⌐HD1471 (Land tenure)┐
 UF Estancias
   Fazendas
   Fundos
 BT Farms
   Land tenure
   Land tenure—Latin America
   Plantations
   Ranches

 RT Latifundio
 — Bolivia
  NT Siporo Hacienda (Bolivia)
 — Brazil
  NT Santa Cruz Fazenda (Brazil)
    Santo Antonio Fazenda (Brazil)
 — Colombia
  NT Yerbabuena Hacienda (Colombia)
 — Ecuador
  NT Serrana Hacienda (Ecuador)
 — Mexico
  NT Concha Hacienda (Mexico)
    Jalpa Hacienda (Mexico)
    Ojocaliente Hacienda (Mexico)
    San Antonio Tochatlaco Hacienda (Mexico)
    San Carlos Borromeo Hacienda (Mexico)
    San Juan de los Otates Hacienda (Mexico)
Hack Lake (Colo.)
 BT Lakes—Colorado
Hack saws
 USE Hacksaws
Hack writers
 BT Authors
Hackamore
 BT Harness
Hackathorn family
 USE Heckathorn family
Hackberry
 ⌐QK495.C (Celtis)┐
Hackbrett
 USE Dulcimer
Hackedorn family
 USE Heckathorn family
Hackemoeller family
 USE Hakemoller family
Hackendorn family
 USE Heckathorn family
Hackensack Indians
 ⌐E99.H15┐
 BT Delaware Indians
   Indians of North America
Hackensack Meadowlands (N.J.)
 USE Meadowlands (N.J.)
Hackensack Meadows (N.J.)
 USE Meadowlands (N.J.)
Hacker family (Not Subd Geog)
Hacker's Creek (W. Va.) (Not Subd Geog) .
 BT Rivers—West Virginia
Hackle (Fly tying)
 USE Hackles (Fly tying)
Hackleback sturgeon
 USE Shovelnose sturgeon
Hackles (Fly tying) (May Subd Geog)
 ⌐SH451┐
 UF Artificial fly hackles
   Fishing hackles
   Fly tying hackles
   Hackle (Fly tying)
 BT Feathers
   Flies, Artificial
   Fly tying—Equipment and supplies
Hackley family (Not Subd Geog)
Hackmatack
 USE Juniperus communis
Hackney family (Not Subd Geog)
Hackney horse
 ⌐SF293.H2┐
 BT Coach horses
   Horse breeds
Hacks, Tie
 USE Tie hacks
Hacks (Carriages)
 USE Cab and omnibus service
   Carriages and carts
Hacksaws
 ⌐TJ1233┐
 UF Hack saws

Hacksaws *(Continued)*
  BT Metal-cutting
      Saws
Hackthorn family
  USE Heckathorn family
Hadamard matrices
  ₜQA166.4ₗ
  BT Combinatorial analysis
      Combinatorial designs and
        configurations
      Matrices
Hadamard transform optics
  USE Hadamard transform spectroscopy
Hadamard transform spectroscopy
  ₜQC454.H33ₗ
  UF Hadamard transform optics
      Multiplex spectrometry
      Optics, Hadamard transform
      Spectroscopy, Hadamard transform
  BT Imaging systems
      Matrices
      Spectrum analysis
  NT Fourier transform spectroscopy
Hadas
  UF Hārās
  BT Chauhan dynasties
      Rajputs
Haḍbat Mustaghānim (Algeria)
  USE Mostaganem Plateau (Algeria)
Haddan family
  USE Hadden family
Hadden family *(Not Subd Geog)*
  UF Haddan family
      Haddin family
      Haddon family
      Hedden family
      Heddin family
      Heddon family
      Heden family
Haddin family
  USE Hadden family
Haddock
  ₜQL638.G2ₗ
  ₜSH351.H18 (Fisheries)ₗ
  UF Gadus aeglefinus
      Melanogrammus aeglefinus
  NT Cookery (Haddock)
Haddock family *(Not Subd Geog)*
  UF Haddox family
Haddock fisheries *(May Subd Geog)*
  ₜSH351.H18ₗ
  BT Fisheries
Haddon family
  USE Hadden family
Haddox family
  USE Haddock family
Hadeley family
  USE Hadley family
Haden family
  USE Hayden family
Hadenidae
  USE Noctuidae
Hadensee (Germany)
  USE Hiddensee (Germany)
Haderiis family
  USE Haderis family
Haderis family *(Not Subd Geog)*
  UF Haderiis family
Hades
  USE Future life
      Hell
Hades (Greek deity)
  USE Pluto (Greek deity)
Hadges family
  USE Hodges family

Hadhramaut (Yemen : People's Democratic Republic)
  UF Hadhramawt (Yemen : People's
        Democratic Republic)
      Hadramaut (Yemen : People's
        Democratic Republic)
      Hadramawt (Yemen : People's
        Democratic Republic)
Hadhramawt (Yemen : People's Democratic
  Republic)
  USE Hadhramaut (Yemen : People's
        Democratic Republic)
Hadhrami inscriptions
  USE Inscriptions, Hadrami
Hadia (African people)
  USE Hadiya (African people)
Hadiah Adinegoro
  UF Adinegoro prize
  BT Journalism—Awards
      Rewards (Prizes, etc.)
Hadidi, Tall (Syria)
  UF Hadidi Site (Syria)
      Tall Hadidi (Syria)
      Tell Hadidi (Syria)
  BT Syria—Antiquities
Hadidi Site (Syria)
  USE Hadidi, Tall (Syria)
Hadin family
  USE Hayden family
Hading family
  USE Hayden family
Hadith
  ₜBP135ₗ
    Here are entered works on the oral traditions concerning the deeds and sayings of Muḥammad, the prophet, solely. Works on the oral traditions concerning the deeds and sayings of Imams and Muḥammad, the prophet, are entered under Hadith (Shiites). Works on the traditions of individual Imams are entered under the name of the Imam with subdivision Hadith.
  UF Tradition (Islam)
  BT Islamic law—Sources
      Islamic literature
  RT Sunna
  NT Iran in the Hadith
      Jews in the Hadith
      Women in the Hadith
      Yemen in the Hadith
  — Abrogator and abrogated Hadith
    ₜBP136.78ₗ
  — Authorities
    ₜBP136.4-BP136.6ₗ
    UF Authorities of the Hadith
        Hadith—Transmitters
        Transmitters of Hadith
    NT Muḥammad, Prophet, d. 632—
        Companions
  — Commentaries
    USE Hadith—Criticism, interpretation,
        etc.
  — Criticism, interpretation, etc.
    ₜBP135ₗ
    UF Hadith—Commentaries
  — — History
    NT Hadith scholars
  — Criticism, Textual
  — Early works to 1800
  — Evidences, authority, etc.
    ₜBP136.4-BP136.6ₗ
    UF Evidences of the Hadith
  — Forgeries
    ₜBP136.74ₗ
  — Language, style
  — Transmitters
    USE Hadith—Authorities
Hadith (Shiites)
  ₜBP193.25-BP193.28ₗ

    Here are entered works on the oral traditions concerning the deeds and sayings of Imams and Muḥammad, the prophet. Works on the oral traditions concerning the deeds and sayings of Muḥammad, the prophet, solely, are entered under Hadith. Works on the traditions of individual Imams are entered under the name of the Imam with subdivision Hadith.
  UF Imams—Hadith
      Imams—Traditions
      Tradition (Shiites)
  BT Imams
  — Authorities
    ₜBP193.28ₗ
    UF Hadith (Shiites)—Transmitters
  — Transmitters
    USE Hadith (Shiites)—Authorities
Hadith scholars *(May Subd Geog)*
  UF Scholars, Hadith
  BT Hadith—Criticism, interpretation, etc.
      —History
      Scholars, Muslim
Hadith stories
Hadiya (African people)
  ₜDT380.4.H33ₗ
  UF Gudela (African people)
      Hadia (African people)
  BT Ethnology—Ethiopia
Hadjerai (African people)
  UF Hadjerai (African tribe)
  BT Ethnology—Chad
Hadjerai (African tribe)
  USE Hadjerai (African people)
Hadley family *(Not Subd Geog)*
  UF Hadeley family
      Hadly family
      Headlee family
      Headley family
      Headly family
      Hedley family
      Hedly family
Hadlock family *(Not Subd Geog)*
Hadly family
  USE Hadley family
Hadon family
  USE Hayden family
Hadramaut (Yemen : People's Democratic
  Republic)
  USE Hadhramaut (Yemen : People's
        Democratic Republic)
Hadramawt (Yemen : People's Democratic
  Republic)
  USE Hadhramaut (Yemen : People's
        Democratic Republic)
Hadrami inscriptions
  USE Inscriptions, Hadrami
Hadran
  BT Jewish sermons
      Talmud
Hadrian's Villa (Tivoli, Italy)
  UF Adriana Villa (Tivoli, Italy)
      Villa Adriana (Tivoli, Italy)
  BT Italy—Antiquities, Roman
      Palaces—Italy
  — Stadium
    UF Gartenstadion, Hadrian's Villa
        (Tivoli, Italy)
    BT Gardens—Italy
        Stadia—Italy
Hadrian's Wall (England)
  BT Fortification—England
      Walls—England
Hadron collisions
  USE Hadron interactions
Hadron interactions
  UF Collisions, Hadron
      Hadron collisions
      Interactions, Hadron
  BT Hadrons
      Nuclear reactions
Hadron production, Multiple
  USE Hadrons—Multiplicity

Hadron spectroscopy
  [QC793.5.H327]
  UF Spectroscopy, Hadron
  BT Nuclear spectroscopy
      Spectrum analysis
Hadrons
      [QC793.5.H32-QC793.5.H329]
  UF Strongly interacting particles
  BT Particles (Nuclear physics)
  RT Partons
  NT Baryons
      Exotic atoms
      Hadron interactions
      Mesons
  — **Decay**
  — **Multiplicity**
      UF Hadron production, Multiple
          Multihadron production
          Multiparticle hadrodynamics
          Multiple generation of hadrons
          Multiple production of hadrons
          Multiplicity of hadrons
      BT Collisions (Nuclear physics)
          Nuclear reactions
  — **Scattering**
      [QC721]
  — **Spectra**
Hadrurus
  [QL458.72.I95]
  UF Giant hairy scorpions
  BT Iuridae
Hadzapi (African people)
  USE Tindiga (African people)
Haedong (Sect)
  USE Wŏnhyo (Sect)
Haefer family
  USE Hafer family
Haegele family
  USE Hagler family
Haegelin family
  USE Hagler family
Haeger family
  USE Hagler family
Haegler family
  USE Hagler family
Haegŭm
  [ML927.H]
  BT Musical instruments—Korea
      Stringed instruments, Bowed
Haegŭm music
  [M59.H3]
Hael family
  USE Hale family
Haeltzuk language
  USE Heiltsuk language
Haemaphysalis
  [QL458.2.I9]
  BT Ixodidae
Haemaphysalis longicornis
  [QL458.2.I9]
Haematobia
  [QL537.M8]
  BT Muscidae
Haematobia irritans
  USE Horn fly
Haematobia serrata
  USE Horn fly
Haematomyzidae
  [QL540.3.H33]
  UF Rhynchophthirina
  BT Mallophaga
  NT Haematomyzus
Haematomyzus
  [QL540.3.H33]
  UF Idolocoris
      Phantasmocoris
  BT Haematomyzidae
  NT Haematomyzus elefantis
Haematomyzus elefantis
  [QL540.3.H33]
  UF Elephant louse

  BT Haematomyzus
Haematopinidae
  [QL570.3.H37]
  BT Anoplura
  NT Haematopinus
Haematopinus
  [QL570.3.H37]
  UF Hematopinus
  BT Haematopinidae
Haematopinus suis
  USE Hog lice
Haematopodidae
  [QL696.C452]
  BT Charadriiformes
  NT Haematopus
Haematopus
  [QL696.C452]
  BT Haematopodidae
Haematopus chathamensis
  USE Chatham Islands oystercatcher
Haematopus ostralegus
  USE Oystercatcher
Haematopus unicolor
  USE Variable oystercatcher
Haemerosidae
  USE Noctuidae
Haemmel family
  USE Hamel family
Haemocytes
  USE Blood cells
Haemolaelaps
  [QL458.2.L33]
  BT Laelapidae
  NT Haemolaelaps travisi
Haemolaelaps travisi
  [QL458.2.L33]
  BT Haemolaelaps
Haemolytic plaque technique
  USE Hemolytic plaque technique
Haemonchus (May Subd Geog)
  [QL391.N4]
  BT Trichostrongylidae
  NT Haemonchus contortus
Haemonchus contortus (May Subd Geog)
  [QL391.N4]
  UF Abomesi ovis
      Filaria denticulata
      Strongylus contortus
      Strongylus filicollis
      Strongylus placei
  BT Haemonchus
Haemophilus
  USE Hemophilus
Haemophilus diseases
  USE Hemophilus diseases
Haemosporidia
  BT Sporozoa
Haemostasis
  USE Hemostasis
Haemulidae
  USE Grunts (Fishes)
Haemulonidae
  USE Grunts (Fishes)
Haera-kino Harbour (N.Z.)
  USE Herekino Harbour (N.Z.)
Haesbreucq family
  USE Hasbrouck family
Haese family (Not Subd Geog)
Haesleakaer (Denmark)
  USE Hesselagergård (Denmark)
Haet'ae
  USE Nori
Hafer family (Not Subd Geog)
  UF Haefer family
      Haffer family
Haffer family
  USE Hafer family
Hafirs (May Subd Geog)
  BT Ponds
      Reservoirs
      Water-storage

Hafiz (May Subd Geog)
  BT Islam—Functionaries
      Koran—Memorizing
      Koran—Recitation
Hafling horse
  UF Hafling mountain pony
Hafling mountain pony
  USE Hafling horse
Hafman family
  USE Hoffman family
Hafnia
  USE Hafnium oxide
Hafnium
  [QD181.H5]
  BT Titanium group
  — **Isotopes**
  — — **Decay**
  — **Metallography**
Hafnium chloride
  USE Hafnium tetrachloride
Hafnium compounds
Hafnium dioxide
  USE Hafnium oxide
Hafnium ores (May Subd Geog)
Hafnium organic compounds
  USE Organohafnium compounds
Hafnium oxide
  UF Hafnia
      Hafnium dioxide
  BT Oxides
Hafnium tetrachloride
  UF Hafnium chloride
  BT Tetrachlorides
Hafoulou-Hou (Tonga)
  USE Vava'u Island (Tonga)
Hafsides (Not Subd Geog)
  [DT199]
  UF Hafsite dynasty
  BT Africa, North—History—1517-1882
Hafsite dynasty
  USE Hafsides
Haga family (Not Subd Geog)
Hagadot
  USE Haggadot
Hagaers family
  USE Hagaerts family
Hagaerts family (Not Subd Geog)
  UF Hagaers family
      Hagarts family
      Hagers family
      Hagerts family
      Haghaerts family
      Hagharts family
Hagan family (Not Subd Geog)
  UF Hagans family
      Hagen family
      Hagens family
      Hagon family
      Heagen family
      Heagon family
      Heagons family
Hagano (Medieval literary character)
  USE Hagen (Medieval literary character)
Hagans family
  USE Hagan family
Hagar family
  USE Hager family
Hagarts family
  USE Hagaerts family
Hagarty family
  USE Haggerty family
Hagavatn (Iceland)
  BT Lakes—Iceland
Hagel family
  USE Hagler family
Hagele family
  USE Hagler family
Hagelin family
  USE Hagler family

Hageman family *(Not Subd Geog)*
  UF Hagemann family
      Hagerman family
Hagemann family
  USE Hageman family
Hagen (Medieval literary character)
  UF Hagano (Medieval literary character)
      Hogni (Medieval literary character)
Hagen (Papua New Guinea people)
  USE Medlpa (Papua New Guinea people)
Hagen family
  USE Hagan family
Hagen Gebirge (Austria)
  USE Hagengebirge (Austria)
Hagen language
  USE Medlpa language
Hagengebirge (Austria)
  UF Hagen Gebirge (Austria)
  BT Mountains—Austria
Hagens family
  USE Hagan family
Hager family *(Not Subd Geog)*
  UF Hagar family
      Heaga family
      Heager family
Hagerman family
  USE Hageman family
Hagers family
  USE Hagaerts family
Hager's Grove Sites (Salem, Or.)
  BT Oregon—Antiquities
Hagerstown Valley (Md.)
  USE Cumberland Valley (Md. and Pa.)
Hagert family
  USE Haggart family
Hagerts family
  USE Hagaerts family
Hagerty family
  USE Haggerty family
Hagfishes
  [QL638.14]
  UF Hyperotreta
      Myxiniformes
      Myxinoidei
  BT Agnatha
  NT Myxinidae
      Paramyxinidae
Haggadot
  [BM675.P4]
  UF Hagadot
      Haggadoth
  BT Seder—Liturgy
Haggadot, Kibbutz
  [BM675.P45]
  UF Kibbutz Haggadot
  BT Haggadot, Secular
      Passover
Haggadot, Secular
  [BM675.P45]
  UF Secular Haggadot
  BT Passover
  NT Haggadot, Kibbutz
Haggadoth
  USE Haggadot
Haggag Wadi (Egypt)
  USE Ḥajjāj Wadi (Egypt)
Haggard family
  USE Haggart family
Haggart family *(Not Subd Geog)*
  UF Hagert family
      Haggard family
Haggarty family
  USE Haggerty family
Haggerty family *(Not Subd Geog)*
  UF Hagarty family
      Hagerty family
      Haggarty family
Haghaerts family
  USE Hagaerts family
Hagharts family
  USE Hagaerts family

Haghia Irini Site (Kea Island, Greece)
  USE Ayia Irini Site (Kea Island, Greece)
Haghia Triada (Ancient city)
  USE Hagia Triada (Ancient city)
Hagi pottery *(May Subd Geog)*
  [NK4168.H]
  UF Pottery, Hagi
  BT Pottery, Japanese
Hagi Rebellion, 1876
  BT Japan—History—Meiji period, 1868-
      1912
Hagia Eikōn tēs Megalochares Tēnou (Icon)
  BT Icons
Hagia Triada (Ancient city)
  (Not Subd Geog)
  UF Ayía Triádha (Ancient city)
      Haghia Triada (Ancient city)
  BT Cities and towns, Ruined, extinct, etc.
      —Greece
      Greece—Antiquities
Hagihara Site (Aira-chō, Japan)
  UF Hagihawa Iseki (Aira-cho, Japan)
  BT Japan—Antiquities
Hagihawa Iseki (Aira-cho, Japan)
  USE Hagihara Site (Aira-chō, Japan)
Hagiography
  [BX4662]
  Here are entered works on the writing and critical
  study of the lives of the saints.
  UF Hagiology
  BT Saints
  NT Buddhist hagiography
      Christian hagiography
      Synaxarion
Hagiography, Buddhist
  USE Buddhist hagiography
Hagiography, Christian
  USE Christian hagiography
Hagiology
  USE Hagiography
Hagler family *(Not Subd Geog)*
  UF Haegele family
      Haegelin family
      Haeger family
      Haegler family
      Hagel family
      Hagele family
      Hagelin family
      Haigler family
Hagon family
  USE Hagan family
Hagood family *(Not Subd Geog)*
  UF Haguewood family
      Haigwood family
      Haygood family
  RT Hayward family
      Haywood family
      Hogwood family
Hagoromo-chō (Tachikawa-shi, Japan)
  (Not Subd Geog)
  UF Tachikawa-shi (Japan). Hagoromo-
      chō
Hague (Netherlands). Houtwijk
  USE Houtwijk (Hague, Netherlands)
Hague (Netherlands). Nieuw-Waldeck
  USE Nieuw-Waldeck (Hague, Netherlands)
Hague in art
Hague porcelain
  [NK4399.H3]
  UF Porcelain, Hague
Hague school of painting
  USE Haagse school of painting
Hague, Treaty of, 1717
  [D283.5]
  UF Treaty of the Hague, 1717
Haguewood family
  USE Hagood family
Haguro Mountain (Japan)
  UF Hagurosan (Japan)
  BT Mountains—Japan

Hagurosan (Japan)
  USE Haguro Mountain (Japan)
Hahl family *(Not Subd Geog)*
Hahn family *(Not Subd Geog)*
  UF Hahne family
Hahne family
  USE Hahn family
Hahniidae
  [QL458.42.H33]
  BT Spiders
Hai He (China)
  USE Hai River (China)
Hai Ho (China)
  USE Hai River (China)
Hai-Nan (China)
  USE Hainan Island (China)
Hai prose
  USE Haibun
Hai River (China)
  UF Hai He (China)
      Hai Ho (China)
  BT Rivers—China
Haibun *(May Subd Geog)*
  UF Hai prose
      Haibun, Japanese
Haibun, Canadian *(May Subd Geog)*
  UF Canadian haibun
  BT Canadian poetry
Haibun, Japanese
  USE Haibun
Haida artists
  USE Artists, Haida
Haida Indians
  [E99.H2]
  UF Skittagetan Indians
  BT Indians of North America
  — Antiquities
Haida language
  [PM1271-4]
  UF Skittagetan languages
  BT Na-Dene languages
Haidamaks
  [DK508.7]
  UF Gaidamaks
      Haydamaks
  BT Brigands and robbers
      Peasant uprisings
Haiden family
  USE Hayden family
Haiduks *(May Subd Geog)*
  UF Haiduti
      Hajduks
      Heyducks
      Khaiduti
  BT Bulgaria—History—1393-1878
      Guerrillas
      Macedonia—History—1389-1912
      Serbia—History—1456-1804
Haiduti
  USE Haiduks
Haifa (Israel). Kiryat Haim
  USE Ḳiryat Ḥayim (Haifa, Israel)
Haifa (Israel). Kiryat Haiyim
  USE Ḳiryat Ḥayim (Haifa, Israel)
Haifa (Israel). Ḳiryat Ḥayim
  USE Ḳiryat Ḥayim (Haifa, Israel)
Haifa (Israel). Kiryat Ḥayyim
  USE Ḳiryat Ḥayim (Haifa, Israel)
Haifa (Israel). Qiryat Haim
  USE Ḳiryat Ḥayim (Haifa, Israel)
Haifa (Israel). Qiryat Haiyim
  USE Ḳiryat Ḥayim (Haifa, Israel)
Haifa (Israel). Qiryat Hayim
  USE Ḳiryat Ḥayim (Haifa, Israel)
Haifa (Israel). Qiryat Ḥayyim
  USE Ḳiryat Ḥayim (Haifa, Israel)
Haig family
  USE Haight family
Haig-Thomas Island (N.W.T.)
  BT Islands—Northwest Territories
      Queen Elizabeth Islands (N.W.T.)

Haiga

⌐ND2462⌐

UF Haikai painting

Haiku painting

BT Painting, Japanese

Haigh family

USE Haight family

Haighs family

USE Hayes family

Haight-Ashbury (San Francisco, Calif.)

(Not Subd Geog)

UF San Francisco (Calif.). Haight-Ashbury

Haight family (Not Subd Geog)

UF Haig family

Haigh family

Hait family

Haite family

Haitt family

Hayt family

Hayte family

RT Hight family

NT Hoyt family

Haigler family

USE Hagler family

Haigwood family

USE Hagood family

Haihin Plain (Laos)

USE Jars, Plain of (Laos)

Haikai

BT Japanese literature

Japanese poetry

Renga

RT Haiku

NT Bashō school

Danrin School

Renku

Haikai painting

USE Haiga

Haiku

UF Haiku, Japanese

Hokku

BT Japanese poetry

Poetry

RT Haikai

NT Renga

Senryu

— Explication

— Women authors

Haiku, American (May Subd Geog)

UF American haiku

BT American poetry

Haiku, American, ⌐English, etc.⌐

Haiku, Canadian (May Subd Geog)

UF Canadian haiku

BT Canadian poetry

Haiku, English (May Subd Geog)

UF English haiku

BT English poetry

Haiku, French (May Subd Geog)

UF French haiku

BT French poetry

Haiku, French-Canadian (May Subd Geog)

UF French-Canadian haiku

BT French-Canadian poetry

Haiku, German (May Subd Geog)

UF German haiku

BT German poetry

Haiku, Japanese

USE Haiku

Haiku, Urdu (May Subd Geog)

UF Urdu haiku

BT Urdu poetry

Haiku in photography

BT Photography

Haiku painting

USE Haiga

Hail (May Subd Geog)

⌐QC929.H1⌐

UF Hailstones

BT Meteorology

Precipitation (Meteorology)

Storms

Water

NT Ice crystals

Plants, Effect of hail on

Hail control (May Subd Geog)

BT Weather control

NT Technology Assessment of the Suppression of Hail Study

Hail family

USE Hale family

Hail insurance

USE Insurance, Hail

Hailam dialect

USE Chinese language—Dialects—Hainan

Haile family

USE Hale family

Hailes family

USE Hale family

Hailey family

USE Haley family

Hailey National Park (India)

USE Corbett National Park (India)

Hailman family

USE Heilman family

Hails family

USE Hale family

Hailstone National Wildlife Refuge (Mont.)

(Not Subd Geog)

BT National parks and reserves—Montana

Wildlife refuges—Montana

Hailstones

USE Hail

Hailtsa language

USE Heiltsuk language

Hailtsuk language

USE Heiltsuk language

Hailuoto Island (Finland)

UF Karlö (Finland)

BT Islands—Finland

Haimes family

USE Hames family

Haimtsu

USE Pinus pumila

Hain family

USE Haynes family

Hainan Dao (China)

USE Hainan Island (China)

Hainan Island (China)

UF Hai-Nan (China)

Hainan Dao (China)

Hainan Tao (China)

BT Islands—China

Hainan Tao (China)

USE Hainan Island (China)

Hainds family

USE Haynes family

Haine family

USE Haynes family

Hainer family

USE Hayner family

Haines family

USE Haynes family

Hainhofer, Philipp, 1578-1647. Uppsala Kunstschrank (Not Subd Geog)

UF Uppsala Cabinet (Furniture)

Uppsala Kunstschrank (Furniture)

Upsala Kunstschrank (Furniture)

BT Chests—Germany

Wood-carving—Germany

Hainline family (Not Subd Geog)

RT Henlein family

Hains family

USE Haynes family

Hainsworth family (Not Subd Geog)

Hair

⌐GN193 (Anthropology)⌐

⌐QL942 (Anatomy, Comparative)⌐

⌐QM488 (Anatomy, Human)⌐

BT Beauty, Personal

Body covering (Anatomy)

Color of man

Head

RT Scalp

NT Beard

Bristles

Eyebrows

Eyelashes

Gray hair

Guard hair

Molting

Mustache

Redheads

Wigs

— Bleaching

USE Hair—Dyeing and bleaching

— **Care and hygiene**

⌐RL91⌐

NT Combs

Hair dryers

— Coloring

USE Hair—Dyeing and bleaching

— **Conditioning**

UF Conditioning of hair

Hair conditioning

BT Hairdressing

— **Diseases** (May Subd Geog)

⌐RL91 (Popular works)⌐

⌐RL151-RL159 (General)⌐

NT Baldness

Hair manifestations of general diseases

Hypertrichosis

Plica polonica

— **Dyeing and bleaching**

⌐TT973⌐

UF Coloring of hair

Hair—Bleaching

Hair—Coloring

Hair—Tinting

Tinting of hair

BT Bleaching

Hairdressing

— **Erotic aspects**

BT Erotica

— Permanent waving

USE Permanent waving

— **Relaxing**

UF Hair relaxing

Relaxing of hair

BT Hairdressing

— **Removal**

⌐RL92 (Popular works)⌐

⌐RL115.5 (By electrolysis)⌐

UF Depilation

Hair, Removal of

Hair removal

Removal of hair

NT Electrolysis in surgery

Shaving

— **Shampooing**

UF Hair—Washing

Hair shampooing

Hair washing

Shampooing of hair

Washing of hair

BT Hairdressing

RT Shampoos

— Tinting

USE Hair—Dyeing and bleaching

— **Transplantation**

— Washing

USE Hair—Shampooing

Hair, Removal of

USE Hair—Removal

Hair (Botany)

USE Trichomes

Hair-balls

⌐SF851 (Veterinary medicine)⌐

Hair blowers
USE Hair dryers
Hair conditioners *(May Subd Geog)*
⌐TP984 (Chemical technology)⌐
UF Conditioners, Hair
Conditioning rinses, Hair
Hair conditioning rinses
Rinses, Hair conditioning
BT Hair preparations
Hair conditioning
USE Hair—Conditioning
Hair conditioning rinses
USE Hair conditioners
Hair-dos
USE Hairstyles
Hair-dressing
USE Hairdressing
Hair dryers
UF Blowers, Hair
Dryers, Hair
Hair blowers
Hairblowers
Hairdryers
BT Drying apparatus
Electric apparatus and appliances
Hair—Care and hygiene
Hair dyes *(May Subd Geog)*
⌐TP984 (Chemical technology)⌐
⌐TT969 (Hairdressing)⌐
UF Dyes and dyeing—Hair
Hair tints
Tints, Hair
BT Hair preparations
— **Law and legislation** *(May Subd Geog)*
Hair family *(Not Subd Geog)*
UF Haire family
Hairs family
Hare family
Hares family
Hear family
Heare family
Heere family
Heir family
Heire family
Hair follicles
UF Follicles, Hair
BT Epithelium
Hair in art
Hair in literature
Hair manifestations of general diseases
UF Hair symptoms of general diseases
BT Hair—Diseases
Symptomatology
Hair preparations *(May Subd Geog)*
⌐TP984 (Chemical technology)⌐
⌐TT969 (Hairdressing)⌐
BT Toilet preparations
NT Hair conditioners
Hair dyes
Shampoos
Hair relaxing
USE Hair—Relaxing
Hair removal
USE Hair—Removal
Hair shampooing
USE Hair—Shampooing
Hair sheep *(May Subd Geog)*
⌐SF373.H17⌐
UF Hairsheep
Hairy sheep
BT Sheep
Sheep breeds
Hair styles
USE Hairstyles
Hair symptoms of general diseases
USE Hair manifestations of general diseases
Hair tints
USE Hair dyes
Hair washing
USE Hair—Shampooing

Hair-work
⌐TT975-6⌐
UF Hairwork
NT Hair-work, Ornamental
Hair-work, Ornamental *(May Subd Geog)*
⌐NK6076⌐
UF Ornamental hair-work
BT Hair-work
Hairblowers
USE Hair dryers
Haircutting
BT Barbering
Hairdressing
Hairdos
USE Hairstyles
Hairdressers
USE Beauty operators
Hairdressing *(May Subd Geog)*
UF Hair-dressing
Hairstyling
Headdress
BT Beauty, Personal
Beauty culture
RT Barbering
NT Braids (Hairdressing)
Hair—Conditioning
Hair—Dyeing and bleaching
Hair—Relaxing
Hair—Shampooing
Haircutting
Hairstyles
Permanent waving
— Collective labor agreements
USE Collective labor agreements—
Hairdressing
— **Equipment and supplies**
NT Combs
— **Health aspects** *(May Subd Geog)*
UF Hairdressing—Hygienic aspects
— Hygienic aspects
USE Hairdressing—Health aspects
— **United States**
NT Hairdressing of Afro-Americans
Hairdressing of Afro-Americans
UF Afro (Hair style)
Afro-American hairdressing
Afro-Americans—Hairdressing
BT Hairdressing—United States
Hairdressing of Blacks
UF Afro (Hair style)
Black hairdressing
Blacks—Hairdressing
Hairdryers
USE Hair dryers
Haire family
USE Hair family
Hairless dogs *(May Subd Geog)*
⌐SF429.H27⌐
BT Dogs
NT Xoloitzcuintli
Hairpalm
USE Chamaerops humilis
Hairpin lace
⌐TT805⌐
BT Crocheting
Lace and lace making
Hairs family
USE Hair family
Hairsheep
USE Hair sheep
Hairsprings
USE Balance springs
Hairstyles *(May Subd Geog)*
UF Coiffures
Hair-dos
Hair styles
Hairdos
BT Hairdressing
Hairstyling
USE Hairdressing

Hairwork
USE Hair-work
Hairy cell leukemia
USE Leukemia, Hairy cell
Hairy chestnut
USE Chinese chestnut
Hairy-legged vampire bat
USE Diphylla ecaudata
Hairy moued collie
USE Bearded collie
Hairy-root disease
⌐SB741.H3⌐
Hairy sheep
USE Hair sheep
Hairy woodpecker
⌐QL696.P56⌐
UF Picoides villosus
BT Picoides
Haiselwood family
USE Hazelwood family
Haisla Indians
⌐E99.H23⌐
UF Kitamat Indians
Kitimat Indians
Kitlope Indians
BT Indians of North America
Kwakiutl Indians
Wakashan Indians
Haisla language
⌐PM1282⌐
UF Kitamat language
Kitimaat language
Kitimat language
BT British Columbia—Languages
Wakashan languages
Haislewood family
USE Hazelwood family
Haislip family *(Not Subd Geog)*
UF Haslip family
Haslop family
Haslope family
Haslup family
Hazelip family
Hazeloop family
Heaslip family
Heslep family
Heslop family
Hislop family
Hyslop family
Hyslup family
Haisten family
USE Hastings family
Haiston family
USE Hastings family
Hait family
USE Haight family
Haite family
USE Haight family
Haithcock family
USE Hathcock family
Haiti
— **Civilization**
— — **African influences**
BT Africa—Civilization
— — **American influences**
BT United States—Civilization
— **Description and travel**
— — **1951-1980**
— — **1981-**
— **Economic conditions**
— — **1971-**
— **Foreign relations**
— — **1804-1844**
— **History**
⌐F1901-1939⌐
— — **To 1791**
— — **Revolution, 1791-1804**
NT Vertières, Battle of, 1803
— — — **Juvenile literature**
— — **1804-**
— — **1804-1844**

—— **Revolution, 1843**
  [F1938.3]
    UF Haitian Revolution, 1843
—— **1844-1915**
  [F1926]
    NT Las Carreras, Battle of, 1849
       Santomé, Battle of, 1855
—— **American occupation, 1915-1934**
  [F1927]
—— **1934-1986** *(Not Subd Geog)*
  [F1928]
—— **1986-** *(Not Subd Geog)*
— **Politics and government**
—— **To 1791**
—— **1791-1804**
—— **1804-**
—— **1804-1844**
—— **1844-1934**
—— **1934-1971**
—— **1971-1986**
—— **1986-**
— **Social conditions**
—— **1971-**
Haiti (Island)
  USE Hispaniola
Haitian alien labor
  USE Alien labor, Haitian
Haitian Americans *(May Subd Geog)*
  [E184.H27]
    UF Haitian Americans—United States
    BT Ethnology—United States
       Haitians—United States
  — United States
       USE Haitian Americans
Haitian art
  USE Art, Haitian
Haitian arts
  USE Arts, Haitian
Haitian authors
  USE Authors, Haitian
Haitian children's writings
  USE Children's writings, Haitian
Haitian cookery
  USE Cookery, Haitian
Haitian drama *(May Subd Geog)*
  [PQ3943 (History and criticism)]
  [PQ3947 (Collections)]
    UF French drama—Haitian authors
Haitian fiction *(May Subd Geog)*
  [PQ3944 (History and criticism)]
  [PQ3947.5 (Collections)]
    UF French fiction—Haitian authors
       Haitian fiction (French)
Haitian fiction (French)
  USE Haitian fiction
Haitian literature *(May Subd Geog)*
  [PQ3940-3949.2]
    UF French literature—Haitian authors
    NT Haitian literature (French Creole)
Haitian literature (French Creole)
  (May Subd Geog)
  [PM7854.H3]
    UF Creole literature, Haitian French
       French Creole literature, Haitian
    BT Haitian literature
Haitian orations
  USE Speeches, addresses, etc., Haitian
Haitian painting
  USE Painting, Haitian
Haitian poetry *(May Subd Geog)*
  [PQ3942 (History and criticism)]
  [PQ3946 (Collections)]
    UF French poetry—Haitian authors
    NT Haitian poetry (French Creole)
       School verse, Haitian
Haitian poetry (French Creole)
  (May Subd Geog)
  [PM7854.H3]
    UF Creole poetry, Haitian French
       French Creole poetry, Haitian

    BT Creole poetry, French
       Haitian poetry
Haitian proverbs
  USE Proverbs, Haitian
Haitian publications, Acquisition of
  USE Acquisition of Haitian publications
Haitian Revolution, 1843
  USE Haiti—History—Revolution, 1843
Haitian school verse
  USE School verse, Haitian
Haitian speeches
  USE Speeches, addresses, etc., Haitian
Haitians *(May Subd Geog)*
    BT Ethnology—Haiti
  — United States
       NT Haitian Americans
Haitt family
  USE Haight family
Hajduks
  USE Haiduks
Haji no Sato Iseki (Fujiidera-shi, Japan)
  USE Haji no Sato Site (Fujiidera-shi, Japan)
Haji no Sato Site (Fujiidera-shi, Japan)
  (Not Subd Geog)
    UF Haji no Sato Iseki (Fujiidera-shi,
       Japan)
    BT Japan—Antiquities
Hajj
  USE Muslim pilgrims and pilgrimages—
       Saudi Arabia—Mecca
Ḥajjāj Wadi (Egypt)
    UF Haggag Wadi (Egypt)
       Wadi Haggag (Egypt)
       Wadi Ḥajjāj (Egypt)
    BT Wadis—Egypt
Ḥajjat al-wadāʿ
  [BP77.68]
    UF Ḥijjat al-wadāʿ
Hajji Firuz Site (Iran)
  USE Hajji Firuz Tepe (Iran)
Hajji Firuz Tepe (Iran) *(Not Subd Geog)*
    UF Hajji Firuz Site (Iran)
    BT Iran—Antiquities
Haka dialect
  USE Lai language
Hakafot
  USE Hakafoth
Hakafoth
    UF Hakafot
       Hakkafot
       Hakkafoth
    BT Judaism—Customs and practices
       Processions, Religious—Judaism
Hakanochō Iseki (Kusatsu-shi, Japan)
  USE Hakanochō Site (Kusatsu-shi, Japan)
Hakanochō Site (Kusatsu-shi, Japan)
  (Not Subd Geog)
    UF Hakanochō Iseki (Kusatsu-shi, Japan)
    BT Japan—Antiquities
Hakas (Tribe)
  [DS432.H]
    BT Chin tribes
Hake
  [QL638.M (Zoology)]
    UF Merlucciidae
    BT Codfish
    NT Merluccius
       Pacific hake
Hake fisheries *(May Subd Geog)*
  [SH351.H185]
    BT Fisheries
Hakemoller family *(Not Subd Geog)*
    UF Hackemoeller family
Hakestad family *(Not Subd Geog)*
Ḥakétia language *(May Subd Geog)*
  [PC4813]
    UF Ḥakétie language
       Ḥakitía language

    BT Arabic language
       Hebrew language
       Jews—Morocco—Languages
       Ladino language—Dialects—Morocco
       Morocco—Languages
       Spanish language
Ḥakétie language
  USE Ḥakétia language
Hakhamanishiya
  USE Achaemenid dynasty, 559-330 B.C.
Ḥakili language
  USE Sḫauri language
Ḥakitía language
  USE Ḥakétia language
Hakka dialects *(May Subd Geog)*
  [PL1851-1860]
    BT Chinese language—Dialects
Hakkafot
  USE Hakafoth
Hakkafoth
  USE Hakafoth
Hakkas
    NT Missions to Hakkas
Hakke Shintō
  USE Shirakawa Shintō
Hakkōda Mountain (Japan)
    UF Hakkōda-san (Japan)
       Hakkōda-yama (Japan)
    BT Mountains—Japan
Hakkōda-san (Japan)
  USE Hakkōda Mountain (Japan)
Hakkōda-yama (Japan)
  USE Hakkōda Mountain (Japan)
Hakodate, Battle of, 1868-1869
    UF Goryōkaku, Battle of, 1868-1869
    BT Japan—History—Civil War, 1868
Hakodate Strait (Japan)
  USE Tsugaru Strait (Japan)
Hakodate-yama (Japan)
  USE Gagyū Hill (Japan)
Hakodateyama Kōen (Hakodate-shi, Japan)
    UF Hakodateyama Park (Hakodate-shi,
       Japan)
    BT Gagyū Hill (Japan)
       Parks—Japan
Hakodateyama Park (Hakodate-shi, Japan)
  USE Hakodateyama Kōen (Hakodate-shi,
       Japan)
Hakone, Mount (Japan)
    UF Hakone-yama (Japan)
       Mount Hakone (Japan)
    BT Mountains—Japan
       Volcanoes—Japan
Hakone Ekiden
  [GV1065.23]
    BT Marathon running—Japan
Hakone National Park (Japan)
  USE Fuji-Hakone-Izu-Kokuritsu Kōen
       (Japan)
Hakone-yama (Japan)
  USE Hakone, Mount (Japan)
Hakra Valley (Pakistan) *(Not Subd Geog)*
    BT Valleys—Pakistan
Haku Mountain (Japan)
    UF Haku-san (Japan)
       Hakusan (Japan)
    BT Mountains—Japan
Haku-san (Japan)
  USE Haku Mountain (Japan)
Hakusai
  USE Chinese cabbage
Hakusan (Japan)
  USE Haku Mountain (Japan)
Hakutōsan (Korea)
  USE Paektu Mountain (Korea)
Hala leaf weaving
  USE Lauhala weaving
Hala Sultan Tekke Site (Cyprus)
  (Not Subd Geog)
    BT Cyprus—Antiquities

Hala tree *(May Subd Geog)*
   [QK495.P18]
   UF Pandanus odoratissimus
         Pandanus odoriferous
         Pandanus tectorius
         Textile screw pine
         Thatch screw pine
   NT Lauhala weaving
Ḥalabīyah Site (Syria)
   USE Zenobia (City)
Ḥalabiyya Site (Syria)
   USE Zenobia (City)
Halacaridae
   [QL458.2.H3]
   BT Mites
Halacha
   USE Jewish law
         Talmud
         Tradition (Judaism)
Halachic Midrashim
   USE Halakhic Midrashim
Halaelurus
   [QL638.95.S38]
   BT Scyliorhinidae
Halakha
   USE Jewish law
         Talmud
         Tradition (Judaism)
Halakhic Midrashim
   UF Halachic Midrashim
         Midrash Halakah
         Midrashim, Halakhic
         Midrashim, Tannaitic
         Tannaitic Midrashim
Halam family
   USE Hallam family
Halams (Indic people)
   [DS432.H33]
   UF Hallams (Indic people)
         Kaipengs (Indic people)
         Khephongs (Indic people)
   BT Ethnology—India
         India—Scheduled tribes
         Tipura (Indic people)
Halari dialect *(May Subd Geog)*
   BT Gujarati language
         India—Languages
Halates
   BT Halogens
   NT Alkaline earth halates
Halatte Forest (France)
   UF Forêt d'Halatte (France)
   BT Forests and forestry—France
Halavah
   USE Halvah
Halberstadt family *(Not Subd Geog)*
Halbert family
   USE Holbert family
Halbi language
   [PK1914]
   UF Bastari language
   BT Indo-Aryan languages, Modern
   RT Marathi language
         Oriya language
Halbrook family
   USE Holbrook family
Halbturn Castle (Halbturn, Austria)
   USE Schloss Halbturn (Halbturn, Austria)
Halbud family
   USE Holbert family
Halburton family
   USE Halliburton family
Halcom family
   USE Holcomb family
Halcomb family
   USE Holcomb family
Hald family *(Not Subd Geog)*
Haldane family *(Not Subd Geog)*
   UF Haldean family
Halde family
   USE Haldeman family

Haldean family
   USE Haldane family
Haldebrand family
   USE Hildebrand family
Haldeman family *(Not Subd Geog)*
   UF Halde family
         Haldemann family
Haldemann family
   USE Haldeman family
Haldner family *(Not Subd Geog)*
Hale, Fort (New Haven, Conn.)
   USE Fort Nathan Hale (New Haven, Conn.)
Hale family *(Not Subd Geog)*
   UF Hael family
         Hail family
         Haile family
         Hailes family
         Hails family
         Hales family
         Hayle family
         Hayles family
         Hayls family
         Heyl family
Hale-mano (Legendary character)
   UF Ha-le-ma-no (Legendary character)
         Halemano (Legendary character)
   BT Folklore—Hawaii
Haleakala National Park (Hawaii)
   BT National parks and reserves—Hawaii
Halechinischidae
   [QL447.5]
   BT Tardigrada
   NT Styraconyx
Haleciidae
   [QL377.H9]
   BT Hydroida
Halecostomi
   USE Pholidophoriformes
Halemano (Legendary character)
   USE Hale-mano (Legendary character)
Haler
   USE Heller (Coin)
Hales family
   USE Hale family
Halesus
   [QL518.L5]
   BT Limnephilidae
Haley family *(Not Subd Geog)*
   UF Hailey family
         Hayley family
         Hayli family
   RT Halley family
Half-breed Indians
   USE Indians—Mixed bloods
Half-cent
   [CJ1836]
   BT Cent
Half-columns *(May Subd Geog)*
   BT Architecture
         Columns
Half court basketball
   USE Halfcourt basketball
Half-dime
   [CJ1835]
Half-dollar
   [CJ1835 (United States)]
Half-dolls
   USE Pincushion dolls
Half-hose
   USE Socks
Half-life (Nuclear physics)
   [QC795]
   UF Radioactive half-life
         Radioisotopes—Half-life
   BT Radioactivity
         Radioisotopes
   RT Radioactive decay

   SA *subdivision* Half-life *under names of*
         radioactive substance, e.g. Lutetium
         —Isotopes—Half-life; *and*
         subdivision Decay *under names of*
         radioactive substances, e.g. Fission
         products—Decay; Radium—Decay
Half-open door in art *(May Subd Geog)*
   BT Doors in art
         Symbolism in art
Half-parent
   USE Stepparents
Half-timber work
   USE Half-timbered buildings
Half-timbered buildings *(May Subd Geog)*
   UF Buildings, Half-timbered
         Half-timber work
   BT Building, Wooden
         Buildings
         Framing (Building)
   NT Half-timbered churches
         Half-timbered houses
Half-timbered churches *(May Subd Geog)*
   BT Church architecture
         Churches
         Half-timbered buildings
Half-timbered houses *(May Subd Geog)*
   [NA7175]
   UF Houses, Half-timbered
   BT Architecture, Domestic
         Half-timbered buildings
         House framing
Half-tone process
   USE Photoengraving—Halftone process
Half-track vehicles
   USE Tracklaying vehicles
Half-track vehicles, Military
   [UG446.5]
   UF Half-tracks (Military science)
         Military half-tracks
   BT Armored vehicles, Military
         Automobiles, Military
         Tracklaying vehicles
   NT SdKfz 251 (Half-track)
Half-tracks (Military science)
   USE Half-track vehicles, Military
Half-wave rectifiers
   [TK7872.R35]
   UF Rectifiers, Half-wave
   BT Electric current rectifiers
Half-way covenant
   USE Covenants (Church polity)
Halfbeaks
   [QL638.H5]
   UF Hemiramphidae
         Hemirhamphidae
   BT Exocoetidae
   NT Hemiramphus
Halfbreed Lake National Wildlife Refuge (Mont.) *(Not Subd Geog)*
   BT National parks and reserves—Montana
         Wildlife refuges—Montana
Halfcourt basketball *(May Subd Geog)*
   [GV887]
   UF Half court basketball
         One-basket basketball
   BT Basketball
  — Rules
Halfrubber (Game) *(May Subd Geog)*
   [GV881.6]
Halftone process
   USE Photoengraving—Halftone process
Halfway houses *(May Subd Geog)*
   BT Community-based corrections
         Correctional institutions
         Group homes
         Health facilities
         Mental health services
         Mentally ill—Rehabilitation
         Rehabilitation centers
   NT Group homes for children

Group homes for the developmentally
disabled
Group homes for the handicapped
Group homes for youth
Halhaiin Gol, Battle of, 1939
UF Nomonhan Incident, 1939
BT Russo-Japanese Border Conflicts,
1932-1941
Halia language
BT Melanesian languages
Haliaeetus
BT Accipitridae
Sea eagles
Haliaeetus albicilla
USE White-tailed sea eagle
Haliaeetus leucocephalus
USE Bald eagle
Haliaeetus vocifer
USE African fish eagle
Halias (Ancient city)
USE Halieis (Ancient city)
Haliburntoun family
USE Halliburton family
Haliburton family
USE Halliburton family
Haliburtoun family
USE Halliburton family
Haliburtun family
USE Halliburton family
Halibut
BT Flatfishes
NT Atlantic halibut
California halibut
Pacific halibut
Halibut, Greenland
USE Greenland halibut
Halibut fisheries *(May Subd Geog)*
⌐SH351.H2¬
BT Atlantic halibut
California halibut
Fisheries
Flatfish fisheries
Pacific halibut
— **Catch effort**
— **Fishing effort**
— **Law and legislation** *(May Subd Geog)*
BT Fishery law and legislation
Halibut fishing *(May Subd Geog)*
⌐SH691.H3¬
BT Fishing
Halibut fishing, Pacific
USE Pacific halibut fishing
Halicarnassus (Ancient city)
(Not Subd Geog)
⌐DS156.H3¬
UF Halikarnassos (Ancient city)
BT Cities and towns, Ruined, extinct, etc.
—Turkey
Turkey—Antiquities
Halichina (Poland and Ukraine)
USE Galicia (Poland and Ukraine)
Halichoerus grypus
USE Grey seal
Haliclystidae
USE Eleutherocarpidae
Haliclystus *(May Subd Geog)*
⌐QL377.S4¬
BT Eleutherocarpidae
NT Haliclystus stejnegeri
Haliclystus stejnegeri *(May Subd Geog)*
⌐QL377.S4¬
BT Haliclystus
Halictidae
⌐QL568.H3¬
UF Sweat bees
BT Bees
Hymenoptera
NT Conanthalictus
Dufourea
Halictus
Homalictus

Lasioglossum
Urohalictus
Halictus
⌐QL568.H3¬
BT Halictidae
Halictus ligatus
⌐QL568.H3¬
Haliday family
USE Holliday family
Halides
⌐QD165¬
NT Alkali metal halides
Allyl halides
Aluminum halides
Hydrogen fluoride
Iodides
Metal halides
Molybdenum halides
Silver halides
Transition metal halides
Zinc halides
Halidragon
USE Plesiosaurus
Halieis (Ancient city) *(Not Subd Geog)*
UF Halias (Ancient city)
BT Cities and towns, Ruined, extinct, etc.
—Greece
Greece—Antiquities
Halifax (Bomber)
BT Bombers
Handley Page airplanes
Halikarnassos (Ancient city)
USE Halicarnassus (Ancient city)
Haliotidae
USE Abalones
Haliotis
USE Abalones
Haliotis diversicolor
⌐QL430.5.H34¬
UF Sulculus diversicolor
Haliplidae
⌐QL596.H2¬
BT Beetles
Halisidota
⌐QL561.A8¬
UF Halysidota
BT Arctiidae
Halite
USE Salt
Ḥalitsah
⌐BM720.H3¬
UF Chaliza
BT Levirate
Marriage (Jewish law)
Hāliya Kaibarttas
USE Mahisyas
Halkomelem Indians
USE Stalo Indians
Halkomelem language
USE Stalo language
Halkow family *(Not Subd Geog)*
Halkyard family *(Not Subd Geog)*
Hall, Satan (Fictitious character)
UF Satan Hall (Fictitious character)
RT Daly, Carroll John, 1889-1958—
Characters—Satan Hall
Hall effect
⌐QC611¬
BT Electric currents
Electricity
Galvanomagnetic effects
Gyrators
NT Hall generators
Hall family *(Not Subd Geog)*
UF Halle family
Halls family
Hawl family
RT Haller family
Hallman family
Hall generators
UF Generators, Hall

BT Hall effect
Hall Héroult process
UF Hall process
Heroult process
BT Aluminum—Electrometallurgy
Electrolysis
Hall Land (Greenland)
Hall-marks
USE Hallmarks
Hall polynomials
BT Abelian groups
Partitions (Mathematics)
Polynomials
Hall process
USE Hall Héroult process
Hall scale
USE Nilotaspis halli
Halla Mountain (Korea)
UF Auckland, Mount (Korea)
Halla-san(Korea)
Hallasan (Korea)
Halna-san (Korea)
Hanna San (Korea)
Kanra-san (Korea)
Mount Auckland (Korea)
Mount Halla (Korea)
Mountain Hanra (Korea)
BT Mountains—Korea
Volcanoes—Korea
Halla-san(Korea)
USE Halla Mountain (Korea)
Hallabrin family *(Not Subd Geog)*
UF Hallabrinyi family
Hallabrinyi family
USE Hallabrin family
Halladay family
USE Holliday family
Hallade family
USE Holliday family
Hallah
BT Priests, Jewish
Tithes—Jews
Tithes (Jewish law)
Hallam family *(Not Subd Geog)*
UF Halam family
Hallem family
Hallim family
Hallom family
Hallum family
Hallums family
Halm family
Halum family
Helam family
Hellum family
Hollam family
Hollim family
Hollum family
Van Hallum family
Hallams (Indic people)
USE Halams (Indic people)
Hallar (Indic people)
USE Gadaba (Indic people)
Hallasan (Korea)
USE Halla Mountain (Korea)
Hallaway family
USE Holloway family
Hallawell family
USE Hallowell family
Hallberg family *(Not Subd Geog)*
Hallbert family
USE Holbert family
Hallbrook family
USE Holbrook family
Halle family
USE Hall family
Hallem family
USE Hallam family
Hallenbeck family *(Not Subd Geog)*
RT Hollenbeck family
Hallensworth family
USE Hollingsworth family

Haller
USE Heller (Coin)
Haller family (Not Subd Geog)
    RT Hall family
        Hollar family
Hallerud family (Not Subd Geog)
Halles, Quartier des (Paris, France)
    USE Quartier des Halles (Paris, France)
Halley family (Not Subd Geog)
    UF Hally family
    RT Haley family
        Hawley family
Halley's comet (Not Subd Geog)
    [QB723.H2]
    BT Comets
Halliburton family (Not Subd Geog)
    UF Halburton family
        Haliburntoun family
        Haliburton family
        Haliburtoun family
        Haliburtun family
        Hallyburton family
        Hallyburtoun family
        Halyborton family
        Halybourton family
        Halyburton family
        Halyburtoun family
        Halyburtoune family
        Healyburton family
        Heleburtone family
        Helibourtone family
        Hollyburton family
Halliday family
    USE Holliday family
Hallim family
    USE Hallam family
Halling (Dance)
    [GV1796.H2]
Halliwell family
    USE Hallowell family
Halliwill family
    USE Hallowell family
Hallman family (Not Subd Geog)
    UF Hallmann family
    RT Hall family
Hallmann family
    USE Hallman family
Hallmark Cards, Inc.
    — **Collectibles** (May Subd Geog)
Hallmarks (May Subd Geog)
    [NK7210]
    UF Hall-marks
        Marks on plate
    BT Plate
    RT Gold—Standards of fineness
        Silver—Standards of fineness
    NT Pewter—Marks
        Silver ingots—Marks
    — **Forgeries** (May Subd Geog)
        UF Forgery of hall-marks
            Forgery of hallmarks
        BT Forgery
    — **Law and legislation** (May Subd Geog)
Hallo family (Not Subd Geog)
    UF Hallow family
        Holla family
        Hollo family
        Hollow family
Hallom family
    USE Hallam family
Hallow-Eve
    USE Halloween
Hallow family
    USE Hallo family
Hallowall family
    USE Hallowell family
Halloway family
    USE Holloway family
Halloween (May Subd Geog)
    [GT4965]

UF All Hallows' Eve
    Hallow-Eve
BT Manners and customs
NT Halloween decorations
    Jack-o-lanterns
Halloween decorations
    [TT900.H32]
    BT Halloween
        Holiday decorations
Hallowel family
    USE Hallowell family
Hallowell family (Not Subd Geog)
    UF Hallawell family
        Halliwell family
        Halliwill family
        Hallowall family
        Hallowel family
        Hollawel family
        Hollawell family
        Hollowell family
        Hollwell family
        Hollywell family
Hallowing Point Site (Md.)
    BT Kitchen-middens—Maryland
        Maryland—Antiquities
Halloysite (May Subd Geog)
Halls (May Subd Geog)
    NT Auditoriums
        City halls
        Entrance halls
        Music-halls
    — **Egypt**
        NT Temple of Amon (Karnak, Egypt)
            —Hypostyle Hall
    — **England**
        NT Royal Albert Hall (London,
            England)
    — **Germany (West)**
        NT Frankfurter Römer (Frankfurt am
            Main, Germany)—Kaisersaal
            Rathaus zu Münster (Münster in
            Westfalen, Germany)—
            Friedenssaal
    — **Washington (D.C.)**
        NT Constitution Hall (Washington,
            D.C.)
            Memorial Continental Hall
            (Washington, D.C.)
Halls family
    USE Hall family
Halls of fame (May Subd Geog)
    UF Celebrity, Halls of
        Fame, Halls of
        Famous people, Halls of
    BT Biography
        Heroes
        Museums
Halls of residence
    USE Dormitories
Halls of the Ancients (Washington, D.C.)
    BT Museum buildings—Washington (D.C.)
Hall's rifle
    BT Rifles
Hallstatt period (May Subd Geog)
    [GN779-780]
    BT Iron age
        Man, Prehistoric
    NT Mounds—Rhine River Valley
    — **Germany (West)**
Hallstatt Site (Austria) (Not Subd Geog)
    BT Austria—Antiquities
Hallucinations and illusions
    [BF491-BF493 (Psychology)]
    [RC553.H3 (Psychiatry and
    psychopathology)]
    UF Delusions
        Illusions
    BT Psychology, Pathological
        Subconsciousness
    NT Deathbed hallucinations
        Hallucinations and illusions in children

Illusion (Philosophy)
        Insanity
        Lysergic acid diethylamide—
            Physiological effect
        Maggid (Cabala)
        Megalomania
        Mirages
        Optical illusions
Hallucinations and illusions in children
    (May Subd Geog)
    [RJ506.H34]
    BT Hallucinations and illusions
        Psychoses in children
Hallucinogenic drugs
    UF Consciousness-expanding drugs
        Hallucinogens
        Mind-distorting drugs
        Psychedelic drugs
        Psychotomimetic drugs
    BT Drug abuse
        Psychotropic drugs
    RT Hallucinogenic plants
        Mushrooms, Hallucinogenic
    NT Cannabinoids
        Lysergic acid diethylamide
        Mescaline
        Phencyclidine
Hallucinogenic drugs and religious experience
    [BL65.D7]
    UF Experience (Religion) and
        hallucinogenic drugs
    NT Mushroom ceremony
    — **Cross-cultural studies**
Hallucinogenic mushrooms
    USE Mushrooms, Hallucinogenic
Hallucinogenic plants (May Subd Geog)
    [QK99 (General)]
    [SB293-SB295 (Culture)]
    UF Hallucinogens
        Plants, Hallucinogenic
        Plants, Psychedelic
        Psychedelic plants
    BT Psychotropic plants
    RT Hallucinogenic drugs
    SA names of hallucinogenic plants, e.g.
        Cannabis; Datura; Peyote
    NT Ayahuasca
        Belladonna
        Mandrake
        Mushrooms, Hallucinogenic
    — **Cross-cultural studies**
Hallucinogens
    USE Hallucinogenic drugs
        Hallucinogenic plants
Hallum family
    USE Hallam family
        Helms family
Hallums family
    USE Hallam family
Hallunda Site (Sweden) (Not Subd Geog)
    BT Sweden—Antiquities
Hallux valgus
    BT Toes—Abnormalities
Hallways
    USE Corridors
Hallwil, Lake (Switzerland)
    UF Hallwiler See (Switzerland)
        Hallwilersee (Switzerland)
        Lac d'Hallwil (Switzerland)
        Lake Hallwil (Switzerland)
    BT Lakes—Switzerland
Hallwiler See (Switzerland)
    USE Hallwil, Lake (Switzerland)
Hallwilersee (Switzerland)
    USE Hallwil, Lake (Switzerland)
Hally family
    USE Halley family
Hallyburton family
    USE Halliburton family
Hallyburtoun family
    USE Halliburton family

Halm family
  USE Hallam family
Halmahera (Indonesia)
  UF Djailolo (Indonesia)
      Gilolo (Indonesia)
      Pulau Halmahera (Indonesia)
  BT Islands—Indonesia
Halmaheran languages
  UF North Halmaheran languages
  BT Papuan languages
  NT Ternate language
      Tobelo language
      West Makian language
Halna-san (Korea)
  USE Halla Mountain (Korea)
Halo (Art)
  USE Nimbus (Art)
Halo-blight
    [SB608.O2]
Halobacterium
    [QR82.P78]
  UF Salt bacteria
  BT Archaebacteria
      Bacteria, Aerobic
      Gram negative bacteria
      Micro-organisms, Halophilic
  RT Salt—Bacteriology
  NT Bacteriorhodopsin
Halobates
    [QL523.G4]
  BT Gerridae
Halobates sewelli
    [QL523.G4]
Halocarbons
    [QD305.H15 (Chemistry)]
    [TD887.H3 (Air pollution)]
    [TP248.H3 (Chemical technology)]
  UF Halogenated hydrocarbons
  BT Carbon
      Halogens
      Organohalogen compounds
  NT Chlorofluorocarbons
      Dibromodifluoromethane
Halochromism
    [QD441]
Halocypridae
  USE Halocyprididae
Halocyprididae
    [QL444.O85]
  UF Halocypridae
  BT Myodocopida
  NT Archiconchoecia
Halodactylus
  USE Alcyonidium
Halodactylus diaphanus
  USE Alcyonidium diaphanus
Halogen organic compounds
  USE Organohalogen compounds
Halogenated hydrocarbons
  USE Halocarbons
Halogenation
    [QD281.H3]
  NT Blood proteins—Radioiodination
      Fluorination
Halogens
    [QD165]
  BT Nonmetals
  NT Astatine
      Bromine
      Carnallite
      Chlorine
      Fluorine
      Halates
      Halocarbons
      Iodine
      Organohalogen compounds
  — Spectra
Halogeton glomeratus
  BT Livestock poisoning plants
Halon 1301
  USE Bromotrifluoromethane

Halonnesos Island (Greece)
  USE Alónnisos Island (Greece)
Halophilic micro-organisms
  USE Micro-organisms, Halophilic
Halophils
  USE Micro-organisms, Halophilic
Halophytes *(May Subd Geog)*
  BT Botany—Ecology
      Coastal flora
      Plant communities
  RT Tidemarsh flora
  NT Mangrove plants
      Salt-tolerant crops
Halophytic crops
  USE Salt-tolerant crops
Haloporphyrus
  USE Lepidion
Halos (Meteorology)
    [QC976.H1]
  BT Meteorological optics
Halosauriformes
  USE Notacanthiformes
Halothane
    [RD86.H3]
  UF Fluothane
  BT Anesthetics
      Ethanes
Halotydeus
    [QL458.2.P35]
  UF Sand mites
  BT Penthaleidae
Haloveliidae
  USE Veliidae
Halperin family
  USE Halpern family
Halpern family *(Not Subd Geog)*
  UF Halperin family
      Halprin family
      Heilbron family
      Heilbronn family
      Heilbronner family
      Heilbrunn family
Halprin family
  USE Halpern family
Hälsingland (Sweden)
  UF Helsingland (Sweden)
Halstead Battery (Neuropsychology)
  USE Halstead-Reitan Neuropsychological
      Test Battery
Halstead family *(Not Subd Geog)*
  UF Halsted family
Halstead Neuropsychological Test Battery
  USE Halstead-Reitan Neuropsychological
      Test Battery
Halstead-Reitan Battery (Neuropsychology)
  USE Halstead-Reitan Neuropsychological
      Test Battery
**Halstead-Reitan Neuropsychological Test
Battery**
    [RC386.6.H34]
  UF Halstead Battery (Neuropsychology)
      Halstead Neuropsychological Test
      Battery
      Halstead-Reitan Battery
      (Neuropsychology)
      Halstead-Reitan Test Battery
      (Neuropsychology)
  BT Neuropsychological tests
Halstead-Reitan Test Battery
(Neuropsychology)
  USE Halstead-Reitan Neuropsychological
      Test Battery
Halsted family
  USE Halstead family
Halter horse classes
  USE Horse-shows—Halter classes
Haltica
  USE Altica
Halticidae
  USE Chrysomelidae

Halton House (Halton, Buckinghamshire)
  UF Halton Mansion (Halton,
      Buckinghamshire)
  BT Manors—England
Halton Mansion (Halton, Buckinghamshire)
  USE Halton House (Halton,
      Buckinghamshire)
Halukkah
  BT Jews—Palestine—Charities
Halum family
  USE Hallam family
Halun family *(Not Subd Geog)*
Halur
  USE Bānsurī
Ḥalutsim
  USE Halutzim
Halutzim
  UF Chalutzim
      Ḥalutsim
  BT Pioneers—Israel
Halvah
  UF Halavah
  BT Candy
Halvorsen family *(Not Subd Geog)*
  RT Alverson family
Halyborton family
  USE Halliburton family
Halybourton family
  USE Halliburton family
Halyburton family
  USE Halliburton family
Halyburtoun family
  USE Halliburton family
Halyburtoune family
  USE Halliburton family
Halys River (Turkey)
  USE Kizil River (Turkey)
Halysidota
  USE Halisidota
Ham
    [TS1962 (Meat industry)]
    [TX373 (Food supply)]
    [TX556.H (Food values)]
  BT Pork
  NT Cookery (Ham)
  — Microbiology
Ham family
  USE Hamm family
Ham House (Surrey)
  BT Manors—England
Ham industry *(May Subd Geog)*
Ham of the knee
  USE Popliteal fossa
Ham radio
  USE Amateur radio stations
      Radio—Amateurs' manuals
Ham television
  USE Amateur television stations
Hama Detached Palace Garden (Tokyo, Japan)
  USE Hama Rikyū Teien (Tokyo, Japan)
Hama-dōri (Japan)
  USE Hama Kaidō (Japan)
Hama family
  USE Hammer family
Hama Kaidō (Japan) *(Not Subd Geog)*
  UF Hama-dōri (Japan)
      Higashi Kaidō (Japan)
  BT Roads—Japan
Hama Rikyū Teien (Tokyo, Japan)
  (Not Subd Geog)
  UF Hama Detached Palace Garden
      (Tokyo, Japan)
  BT Gardens—Japan
      Parks—Japan
Hamadōri Iseki (Higashidōri-mura, Japan)
  USE Hamadōri Site (Higashidōri-mura,
      Japan)
Hamadōri Site (Higashidōri-mura, Japan)
  UF Hamadōri Iseki (Higashidōri-mura,
      Japan)
  BT Japan—Antiquities

Hamadryad
  USE King cobra
Hamadryas baboon
  UF Comopithecus hamadryas
     Papio hamadryas
  BT Baboons
Hamaguchi family *(Not Subd Geog)*
Hamamelidaceae
  [QK495.H3 (Botany)]
  UF Altingiaceae
  BT Rosales
  NT Altingia
     Hamamelis
Hamamelis
  [QK495.H3 (Botany)]
  BT Hamamelidaceae
Haman family
  USE Hammond family
Hamana Lake (Japan)
  UF Hamanako (Japan)
  BT Lakes—Japan
Hamanako (Japan)
  USE Hamana Lake (Japan)
Hamar (African people)
  [DT380.4.H36]
  BT Baggara (African tribe)
     Ethnology—Sudan
Hamar family
  USE Hammer family
Hamar language
  USE Hmar language
Hamarr family
  USE Hammer family
Hamartite
  USE Bastnaesite
Ḥamat (Ancient city) *(Not Subd Geog)*
  UF Ḥamat Ṭeveryah (Ancient city)
     Ḥame Ṭeveryah (Ancient city)
     Ḥammat (Ancient city)
     Ḥammat Ṭveria (Ancient city)
     Ḥammata (Ancient city)
     Ḥammath Tiberias (Ancient city)
     Ḥammei Ṭveria (Ancient city)
     Ḥummām Ṭubariya (Ancient city)
     Tiberias Hotspring (Ancient city)
  BT Cities and towns, Ruined, extinct, etc.
     —Israel
     Israel—Antiquities
Ḥamat Ṭeveryah (Ancient city)
  USE Ḥamat (Ancient city)
Hamataliva
  [QL458.42.O9]
  UF Hamataliwa
  BT Oxyopidae
Hamataliwa
  USE Hamataliva
Hambelton family
  USE Hamilton family
Hambey family
  USE Hamby family
Hamble family
  USE Hamel family
Hamble River (England)
  BT Rivers—England
Hambledon Hill Site (England)
  BT England—Antiquities
Hamblen familu
  USE Hamlin family
Hamblet family
  USE Hamlett family
     Hamlin family
Hambleton family
  USE Hamilton family
Hambletonian, Du Quoin, Ill.
  [SF345.H35]
  BT Harness racing—Illinois
Hambletonian 10 (Horse)
  UF Rysdyk's Hambletonian
  RT Standardbred horse
Hambletoniola
  [QL523.M5]

  BT Miridae
Hamblett family
  USE Hamlett family
Hambley family
  USE Hamley family
Hamblie family
  USE Hamley family
Hamblin family
  USE Hamlin family
Hambly family
  USE Hamley family
Hamblyn family
  USE Hamley family
Hambro family *(Not Subd Geog)*
Hambukuhu (African people)
  USE Hambukushu (African people)
Hambukushu (African people)
  [DT797]
  UF Hambukuhu (African people)
  BT Bantus
     Ethnology—Botswana
Hamburg (Germany)
  — History
  — — **Revolution, 1848-1849**
  — — **Revolution, 1918-1919**
Hamburg (Germany). Vierlande
  USE Vierlande (Hamburg, Germany)
Hamburger
  USE Cookery (Beef)
Hamburgisches Planungsinformation- und
  Analysesystem (Computer system)
  USE HAMPAS (Computer system)
Hamburgs (Poultry)
  [SF489.H2]
Hamby family *(Not Subd Geog)*
  UF Hambey family
     Hanby family
     Hemby family
Hamdanids
  [DS76]
  BT Iraq—History—634-1534
     Muslims
     Syria—History—750-1260
Hame family
  USE Hames family
Ḥame Ṭeveryah (Ancient city)
  USE Ḥamat (Ancient city)
Hämeen Linna (Hämeenlinna, Finland)
  BT Castles—Finland
Hameister family *(Not Subd Geog)*
Hamel family *(Not Subd Geog)*
  UF Haemmel family
     Hamble family
     Hamil family
     Hammel family
     Hammell family
     Hammill family
     Hampel family
     Hembell family
     Hempble family
     Hempel family
     Hemphill family
     Hempl family
     Hemple family
Hamelin, Pied Piper of (Legendary character)
  USE Pied Piper of Hamelin (Legendary
     character)
Hameln, Pied Piper of (Legendary character)
  USE Pied Piper of Hamelin (Legendary
     character)
Hamelton family
  USE Hamilton family
Hamelyn family
  USE Hamley family
Hamer family
  USE Hammer family
Hamersley family
  USE Hammerly family
Hamersly family
  USE Hammerly family

Hames family *(Not Subd Geog)*
  UF Haimes family
     Hame family
     Hammes family
     Haymes family
Hamesucken
  USE Hamsocn
Hamfare
  USE Hamsocn
Hamil family
  USE Hamel family
Hamileton family
  USE Hamilton family
Hamilton, N.Z., in art
Hamilton-Burr Duel
  USE Burr-Hamilton Duel
Hamilton-Cayley theorem
  USE Cayley-Hamilton theorem
Hamilton family *(Not Subd Geog)*
  UF Hambelton family
     Hambleton family
     Hamelton family
     Hamileton family
     Hammelton family
     Hammilton family
Hamilton-Jacobi equations
  UF Equations, Hamilton-Jacobi
     Equations, Jacobi-Hamilton
     Jacobi-Hamilton equations
  BT Calculus of variations
     Differential equations, Partial
     Hamiltonian systems
     Mechanics
  — Numerical solutions
     BT Numerical analysis
Hamilton Range, Mount (Calif.)
  UF Mount Hamilton Range (Calif.)
  BT Coast Ranges
     Mountains—California
Hamilton Site (Ont.) *(Not Subd Geog)*
  BT Ontario—Antiquities
Hamiltonian dynamical systems
  USE Hamiltonian systems
Hamiltonian operator
  UF Operator, Hamiltonian
  BT Differential operators
     Quantum theory
Hamiltonian systems
  [QA614.83]
  UF Hamiltonian dynamical systems
     Systems, Hamiltonian
  BT Differentiable dynamical systems
  NT Hamilton-Jacobi equations
Ḥamishah 'Asar bi-Shevat
  USE Tu bi-Shevat
Hamites
  [GN545 (Anthropology)]
  [HT1581-HT1589 (Races)]
  BT Mediterranean race
     Nilo-Hamitic tribes
  RT Berbers
  NT Boran (African people)
     Cushites
     Masai
     Somalis
Hamitic languages
  [PJ2301-2651]
  BT Afroasiatic languages
  NT Berber languages
     Cushitic languages
     Egyptian language
     Nilo-Hamitic languages
Hamito-Semitic languages
  USE Afroasiatic languages
Hamlet
  RT Shakespeare, William, 1564-1616—
     Characters—Hamlet
Hamlet family
  USE Hamlett family

Hamlett family (Not Subd Geog)
　UF　Hamblet family
　　　Hamblett family
　　　Hamlet family
　　　Hamlette family
　RT　Hamlin family
Hamlette family
　USE　Hamlett family
Hamley family (Not Subd Geog)
　UF　Hambley family
　　　Hamblie family
　　　Hambly family
　　　Hamblyn family
　　　Hamelyn family
　　　Hamli family
　　　Hamlyn family
　RT　Hamlin family
Hamli family
　USE　Hamley family
Hamlin family (Not Subd Geog)
　UF　Hamblen familu
　　　Hamblet family
　　　Hamblin family
　RT　Hamlett family
　　　Hamley family
Hamlyn family
　USE　Hamley family
Hamm family (Not Subd Geog)
　UF　Ham family
　　　Hamn family
　RT　Hamming family
Hammack family (Not Subd Geog)
Hammadidas
　USE　Hammudid dynasty
Hamman family
　USE　Hammond family
Hammand family
　USE　Hammond family
Hammar family
　USE　Hammer family
Ḥammat (Ancient city)
　USE　Ḥamat (Ancient city)
Hammat family
　USE　Hammett family
Ḥammat Ṭveria (Ancient city)
　USE　Ḥamat (Ancient city)
Ḥammata (Ancient city)
　USE　Ḥamat (Ancient city)
Ḥammath Tiberias (Ancient city)
　USE　Ḥamat (Ancient city)
Hammatt family
　USE　Hammett family
Ḥammei Ṭveria (Ancient city)
　USE　Ḥamat (Ancient city)
Hammel family
　USE　Hamel family
Hammell family
　USE　Hamel family
Hammelton family
　USE　Hamilton family
Hammen family
　USE　Hammond family
Hammer, Mike (Fictitious character)
　UF　Mike Hammer (Fictitious character)
　RT　Spillane, Mickey, 1918-　—
　　　　Characters—Mike Hammer
Hammer family (Not Subd Geog)
　UF　Hama family
　　　Hamar family
　　　Hamarr family
　　　Hamer family
　　　Hammar family
　　　Hammers family
　　　Hamor family
　RT　Hemmer family
Hammer throwing
　BT　Weight throwing
Hammer toe
　USE　Hammertoe
Hammered dulcimer
　USE　Dulcimer

Hammered metalwork
　USE　Chasing (Metalwork)
Hammered stringed instruments
　USE　Stringed instruments
Hammerhead sharks
　_[QL638.95.S7]_
　UF　Sphyrnidae
　BT　Carcharhiniformes
　NT　Smooth hammerhead
Hammerli family
　USE　Hammerly family
Hammerly family (Not Subd Geog)
　UF　Hamersley family
　　　Hamersly family
　　　Hammerli family
　　　Hammersley family
Hammers
　_[TJ1201.H3]_
　[TJ1305 (Power tool)]
　BT　Carpentry—Tools
　　　Metal-work
Hammers family
　USE　Hammer family
Hammersley family
　USE　Hammerly family
Hammersmith Teenage Project
　BT　Community-based corrections—
　　　　England
　　　Juvenile corrections—England
　　　Rehabilitation of juvenile delinquents
　　　　—England
　　　Social work with delinquents and
　　　　criminals—England
Hammertoe
　UF　Hammer toe
　BT　Toes—Abnormalities
Hammes family
　USE　Hames family
Hammet family
　USE　Hammett family
Hammett equation
　UF　Hammett rule
　BT　Linear free energy relationship
Hammett family (Not Subd Geog)
　UF　Hammat family
　　　Hammatt family
　　　Hammet family
　　　Hammit family
　　　Hammitt family
　　　Hammot family
　　　Hemmit family
Hammett rule
　USE　Hammett equation
Hammill family
　USE　Hamel family
Hammilton family
　USE　Hamilton family
Hamminck family
　USE　Hamming family
Hamming family (Not Subd Geog)
　UF　Hamminck family
　　　Hamminga family
　　　Hamminge family
　　　Hammingh family
　　　Hammings family
　　　Hammink family
　RT　Hamm family
Hamminga family
　USE　Hamming family
Hamminge family
　USE　Hamming family
Hammingh family
　USE　Hamming family
Hammings family
　USE　Hamming family
Hammink family
　USE　Hamming family
Hammit family
　USE　Hammett family
Hammitt family
　USE　Hammett family

Hammock industry (May Subd Geog)
　BT　Hammocks
Hammocks
　[GN415.H (Ethnology)]
　[TS1781 (Manufacture)]
　NT　Hammock industry
Hammon family
　USE　Hammond family
Hammond electric organ
　USE　Hammond organ
Hammond family (Not Subd Geog)
　UF　Haman family
　　　Hamman family
　　　Hammand family
　　　Hammen family
　　　Hammon family
　　　Hammonds family
　　　Hammons family
　　　Hamon family
　　　Hamond family
　　　Hamons family
Hammond organ
　_[ML597]_
　UF　Hammond electric organ
　BT　Electronic organ
　　　Organ
　— Registration
　　_[MT192]_
Hammond organ music
　USE　Electronic organ music (Hammond
　　　　registration)
Hammonds family
　USE　Hammond family
Hammons family
　USE　Hammond family
Hammory family
　USE　Hemry family
Hammot family
　USE　Hammett family
Hammudid dynasty (Not Subd Geog)
　UF　Hammadidas
　　　Hammudids
　　　Hammudies
　　　Hammudites
　BT　Berbers—Spain
　　　Spain—History—711-1516
Hammudids
　USE　Hammudid dynasty
Hammudies
　USE　Hammudid dynasty
Hammudites
　USE　Hammudid dynasty
Hamn family
　USE　Hamm family
Hamon family
　USE　Hammond family
Hamond family
　USE　Hammond family
Hamons family
　USE　Hammond family
Hamor family
　USE　Hammer family
Hamosa
　USE　Astragalus (Plants)
HAMPAS (Computer system)
　_[JS78]_
　UF　Hamburgisches Planungsinformation-
　　　　und Analysesystem (Computer
　　　　system)
　BT　Electronic digital computers—
　　　　Programming
　　　Local government—Data processing
Hampden family
　USE　Hampton family
Hampel family
　USE　Hamel family
Hampshire sheep
Hampshire swine
　_[SF393.H3]_
Hampson liquefier
　_[QD535]_

Hampton, James, 1909-1964. Throne of the
Third Heaven of the Nations Millenium
General Assembly
  ₍NB237.H₎
  UF Throne of the Third Heaven of the
      Nations Millenium General
      Assembly (Sculpture)
  BT Sculpture, American
Hampton Court (Hampton, Middlesex)
  UF Hampton Court Palace (Hampton,
      Middlesex)
  BT Palaces—England
Hampton Court Palace (Hampton, Middlesex)
  USE Hampton Court (Hampton, Middlesex)
Hampton family (Not Subd Geog)
  UF Hampden family
      Hamton family
      Hempton family
Hampton Plantation (S.C.)
  (Not Subd Geog)
  BT Plantations—South Carolina
  RT Hampton Plantation State Park (S.C.)
Hampton Plantation State Park (S.C.)
  BT Parks—South Carolina
  RT Hampton Plantation (S.C.)
Hampton Roads (Va.)
  BT Roadsteads—Virginia
Hampton Roads, Battle of, 1862
  ₍E473.2₎
  BT United States—History—Civil War,
      1861-1865—Campaigns
      United States—History—Civil War,
      1861-1865—Naval operations
Hamptons (Long Island, N.Y.)
Hamrick family (Not Subd Geog)
  UF Hemrick family
Hamsocn
  "The right of security and privacy in a man's
  home."—Black, Law dictionary, 4th ed., 1951.
  UF Hamesucken
      Hamfare
      Hausfrieden
  BT Criminal law
      Privacy, Right of
  RT Unlawful entry
Hamster, Dwarf
  USE Phodopus sungorus
Hamster, Golden
  USE Golden hamster
Hamster, Striped hairy-footed
  USE Phodopus sungorus
Hamster, Syrian
  USE Golden hamster
Hamsters (May Subd Geog)
  ₍QL737.R638₎
  UF Cricetini
  BT Cricetidae
  NT Mesocricetus
      Phodopus
Hamsters as laboratory animals
  BT Laboratory animals
Hamsters as pets
  ₍SF459.H3₎
Hamtiknon language
  USE Kinaray-a language
Hamton family
  USE Hampton family
Hamung (Indonesian people)
  USE Uhunduni (Indonesian people)
Hamyaritic inscriptions
  USE Inscriptions, Sabaean
Han-chia Granary (Lo-yang shih, China)
  UF Han-chia ts'ang (Lo-yang shih, China)
  BT Granaries—China
Han-chia ts'ang (Lo-yang shih, China)
  USE Han-chia Granary (Lo-yang shih,
      China)
Han dynasty
  USE China—History—Han dynasty, 202
      B.C.-220 A.D.

Han-gang (Korea)
  USE Han River (Korea)
Han kung ch'un hsiao (Scroll)
  USE Ch'iu, Ying, ca. 1494-ca. 1552.
      Spring morning in the Han Palace
Han River (Korea) (Not Subd Geog)
  UF Han-gang (Korea)
      Han'gang (Korea)
  BT Rivers—Korea (South)
Han River (Shensi Province and Hupeh
Province, China)
  UF Han Shui (Shensi Province and Hupeh
      Province, China)
  BT Rivers—China
Han Shui (Shensi Province and Hupeh
Province, China)
  USE Han River (Shensi Province and
      Hupeh Province, China)
Hana
  USE Hachi-ju-hachi (Game)
Hana family
  USE Hanna family
Hana-karuta
  USE Hachi-ju-hachi (Game)
Hanafis
  BT Islamic law
      Islamic sects
      Sunnites
Hanami Iseki (Koga-machi, Japan)
  USE Hanami Site (Koga-machi, Japan)
Hanami Site (Koga-machi, Japan)
  UF Hanami Iseki (Koga-machi, Japan)
  BT Japan—Antiquities
Hanamure Ōtohara Iseki (Japan)
  USE Ōtohara Site (Japan)
Hanan family
  USE Hannon family
Hanaoka Iseki (Kudamatsu-shi, Japan)
  USE Hanaoka Site (Kudamatsu-shi, Japan)
Hanaoka Site (Kudamatsu-shi, Japan)
  (Not Subd Geog)
  UF Hanaoka Iseki (Kudamatsu-shi, Japan)
  BT Japan—Antiquities
Hanau (Germany)
  — History
  — — Revolution, 1848-1849
      ₍DD209.H₎
      BT Germany—History—Revolution,
          1848-1849
Hanbalites
  BT Islamic law
      Islamic sects
      Sunnites
Hanbury family
  USE Hansborough family
Hanby family
  USE Hamby family
Hanchen family
  USE Hanchett family
Hanchet family
  USE Hanchett family
Hanchett family (Not Subd Geog)
  UF Hanchen family
      Hanchet family
      Hansett family
      Hantchet family
      Hantichet family
Hancock family (Not Subd Geog)
  UF Hancok family
      Hancox family
      Handcock family
      Handcox family
      Hankok family
      Hencock family
      Hendcock family
Hancok family
  USE Hancock family
Hancox family
  USE Hancock family
Hand
  ₍BF908-BF940 (Psychology)₎

  ₍MT221 (Piano)₎
  ₍NC774 (Art)₎
  ₍QM548 (Anatomy)₎
  UF Paw
  BT Extremities, Upper
  RT Left- and right-handedness
  NT Fingers
      Thumb
— Abnormalities (May Subd Geog)
  NT Syndaktylia
— Anatomy
— Care and hygiene
  NT Hand washing
— Diseases (May Subd Geog)
  ₍RC951₎
  NT Hand—Radiography
— Mythology
— Photography
  USE Photography of hands
— Pictorial works
— Radiography
  BT Hand—Diseases
— Religious aspects
— — Buddhism, ₍Christianity, etc.₎
— — Judaism
  NT Hand washing (Jewish rite)
— Surgery
— Words for
  UF Words for hand
  BT Language and languages—
      Etymology
— Wounds and injuries
Hand (The English word)
  BT English language—Etymology
Hand-bags
  USE Handbags
Hand bell ringing
  USE Handbell ringing
Hand cars
  USE Handcars
Hand family (Not Subd Geog)
  UF Hander family
      Handerer family
      Hands family
      Hanner family
      Hanners family
Hand games
  BT Games
Hand-grenades
  USE Grenades
Hand in art
  ₍N8217.H3₎
Hand irons
  USE Irons (Pressing)
Hand lenses
  UF Lenses, Hand
      Lenses, Pocket
      Loupes
      Magnifying glasses
      Pocket lenses
  BT Lenses
Hand looms
  USE Handlooms
Hand-operated pumps
  USE Hand pumps
Hand-organ
  USE Barrel organ
Hand planes
  USE Planes (Hand tools)
Hand press
  USE Handpress
Hand-printed Book Project
  (May Subd Geog)
  UF HPB Project
      Project HPB
  BT Bibliography—Early printed books
      Bibliography, Universal
Hand-printed books (May Subd Geog)
  UF Bibliography—Hand-printed books
      Books, Hand-printed
      Handprinted books

BT Books
Hand pumps *(May Subd Geog)*
[TJ903]
UF Hand-operated pumps
Handpumps
Pumps, Hand
BT Pumping machinery
Hand-railing
[TH5675-7]
UF Railing
BT Carpentry
Stair building
Hand-Schueller-Christian syndrome
UF Schueller-Christian disease
BT Reticuloendotheliosis
Hand shadows
USE Shadow-pictures
Hand spinning *(May Subd Geog)*
[TT847]
BT Arts and crafts movement
Spinning
Textile crafts
Hand stamps
UF Stamps, Hand
RT Rubber stamps
Hand stamps (Philately) *(May Subd Geog)*
BT Postage-stamps—Collectors and
collecting
NT Maritime postal hand stamps
Hand test
[BF205.H3]
BT Projective techniques
Hand-to-hand fighting
[GV1111-1141]
UF Fighting, Hand-to-hand
Man-to-man combat
Personal combat
BT Combat
Martial arts
RT Self-defense
NT Boxing
Commando troops
Fencing
Flexible weapons (Hand-to-hand
fighting)
Stick fighting
Wrestling
Hand-to-hand fighting, Oriental
UF Hap Ki-do
Oriental hand-to-hand fighting
Shaolin martial arts
NT Aikido
Hwarangdo
Jiu-jitsu
Judo
Karate
Kendo
Kung fu
Martial artists
San-jitsu
Hand-to-hand fighting, Oriental, in motion pictures
BT Moving-pictures
Hand tools
USE Tools
Hand washing
UF Handwashing
Washing of hands
BT Hand—Care and hygiene
Hygiene
NT Surgical scrub
Hand washing (Jewish rite)
[BM720.H34]
BT Hand—Religious aspects—Judaism
Judaism—Customs and practices
Water—Religious aspects—Judaism
Hand weaving *(May Subd Geog)*
UF Weaving, Hand
BT Arts and crafts movement
Textile crafts
Weaving

NT Card weaving
Grass weaving
Inkle weaving
Lauhala weaving
Palm frond weaving
Reweaving
— **Patterns**
Handayama Iseki (Hamamatsu-shi, Japan)
USE Handayama Site (Hamamatsu-shi,
Japan)
Handayama Site (Hamamatsu-shi, Japan)
(Not Subd Geog)
UF Handayama Iseki (Hamamatsu-shi,
Japan)
BT Japan—Antiquities
Handbag industry *(May Subd Geog)*
[HD9947.5]
BT Handbags
Handbags *(May Subd Geog)*
UF Hand-bags
Pocket books (Handbags)
Pocketbooks (Handbags)
Purses
BT Dress accessories
NT Handbag industry
Tote bags
Handball *(May Subd Geog)*
[GV1017.H2]
NT Paddleball
Racquetball
Handball, Field
USE Fieldball
Handball, Team
USE Team handball
Handbell and organ music
[M183-4]
UF Organ and handbell music
Handbell and organ music, Arranged
[M185-6]
Handbell music
[M147]
BT Handbell ringing
Handbell ringing
[MT710]
UF Bell ringing
Hand bell ringing
BT Bells
Carillons
NT Handbell music
Handbells *(May Subd Geog)*
BT Bells
Handbills, Advertising
USE Advertising fliers
Handbooks, vade-mecums, etc.
[AG103-AG190]
Here are entered works of general miscellaneous
information arranged for ready reference and consul-
tation.
UF Facts, Miscellaneous
Miscellaneous facts
Pocket companions
Vade-mecums, etc.
BT Commonplace-books
Encyclopedias and dictionaries
SA *subdivision* Handbooks, manuals, etc.
under topical headings and under
names of individual corporate
bodies, and names of countries,
cities, etc.
NT Recipes
Technical manuals
Textbooks
Handcars
UF Hand cars
Railroads—Handcars
BT Railroads—Cars
Handcarts *(May Subd Geog)*
UF Pushcarts
BT Carriages and carts
Handcock family
USE Hancock family

Handcox family
USE Hancock family
Handcuffs
[HV7936.E7]
BT Police—Equipment and supplies
Handedness
USE Left- and right-handedness
Hander family
USE Hand family
Handerer family
USE Hand family
Handerson family
USE Henderson family
Handey family
USE Handy family
Handford family
USE Hanford family
Handforde family
USE Hanford family
Handgun control
USE Gun control
Handgun shooting
USE Pistol shooting
Handgunning
USE Pistol shooting
Handguns
USE Pistols
Handicapped *(May Subd Geog)*
UF Disabled
RT Invalids
NT Camps for the handicapped
Children of handicapped parents
Christian education of the handicapped
Church work with the handicapped
Computers and the handicapped
Dancing for handicapped persons
Day care centers for the handicapped
Developmentally disabled
Disability evaluation
Handicapped and the arts
Handicapped parents
International Year of Disabled
Persons, 1981
Libraries and the handicapped
Meetings and the handicapped
Mentally handicapped
Monkeys as aids for the handicapped
Museums and the handicapped
Musical instruments for the
handicapped
Parks and the handicapped
Pastoral care of the handicapped
Physically handicapped
Recreation areas and the handicapped
Sex instruction for the handicapped
Sick
Social work with the handicapped
Socially handicapped
Veterans, Disabled
Wages—Handicapped
— Assessment of function
USE Handicapped—Functional
assessment
— **Care** *(May Subd Geog)*
UF Handicapped—Care and treatment
— Care and treatment
USE Handicapped—Care
— **Clothing**
[TT648]
UF Clothing for the handicapped
BT Clothing and dress
— **Employment** *(May Subd Geog)*
RT Vocational rehabilitation
NT Handicapped in the civil service
Sheltered workshops
Vocational guidance for the
handicapped
— — **Law and legislation**
(May Subd Geog)
BT Labor laws and legislation
— **Energy assistance**

Handicapped
— **Energy assistance** *(Continued)*
    UF Energy assistance for the
           handicapped
        Energy cost assistance for the
           handicapped
        Fuel assistance for the handicapped
    BT Economic assistance, Domestic
        Energy policy
— — **Law and legislation**
    (May Subd Geog)
— **Functional assessment**
    [*RM930.8 (Rehabilitation therapy)*]
    UF Assessment of function of the
           handicapped
        Functional assessment of the
           handicapped
        Handicapped—Assessment of
           function
    BT Function tests (Medicine)
        Psychological tests
        Rehabilitation
— **Home care** *(May Subd Geog)*
— — **Law and legislation**
    (May Subd Geog)
— **Housing** *(May Subd Geog)*
    BT Housing
    NT Group homes for the handicapped
— **Institutional care** *(May Subd Geog)*
— **Legal status, laws, etc.**
    (May Subd Geog)
    NT Legal assistance to the
           handicapped
— **Life skills guides**
— **Long term care** *(May Subd Geog)*
    UF Long term care of the handicapped
    BT Long-term care of the sick
— **Marriage**
    [*HQ1036-1043*]
    BT Marriage
— **Means of communication**
    NT Communication devices for the
           disabled
— **Nutrition**
    [*TX361.H35*]
— **Printing and writing systems**
— **Psychology**
    UF Psychological aspects of disability
— **Recreation**
    UF Invalids—Recreation
    NT Horsemanship for the handicapped
        Sports for the handicapped
— **Rehabilitation**
    USE Rehabilitation
        Vocational rehabilitation
— **Research** *(May Subd Geog)*
— **Services for** *(May Subd Geog)*
    NT Communication in handicapped
        services
— — Federal aid
        USE Federal aid to handicapped
           services
— **Sexual behavior**
    [*HQ30.5*]
— **Taxation** *(May Subd Geog)*
— — **Law and legislation**
    (May Subd Geog)
— **Travel** *(May Subd Geog)*
    [*HV1568.6*]
— **United States**
    NT Hispanic American handicapped
Handicapped, School library services to
  USE School libraries—Services to the
        handicapped
Handicapped and architecture
  USE Architecture and the handicapped
Handicapped and art museums
  USE Art museums and the handicapped
Handicapped and computers
  USE Computers and the handicapped

Handicapped and libraries
  USE Libraries and the handicapped
Handicapped and the arts *(May Subd Geog)*
  [*NX180.H34*]
  BT Arts
      Handicapped
Handicapped and the performing arts
(May Subd Geog)
  BT Performing arts
Handicapped as consumers
(May Subd Geog)
  BT Consumers
Handicapped automobile drivers
  USE Automobile drivers, Physically
        handicapped
Handicapped bus drivers
  USE Bus drivers, Physically handicapped
Handicapped children *(May Subd Geog)*
  UF Abnormal children
      Children, Abnormal and backward
  BT Children
      Exceptional children
  NT Aphasic children
      Architecture and handicapped children
      Brain-damaged children
      Christian education of handicapped
        children
      Church work with handicapped
        children
      Dancing for handicapped children
      Developmentally disabled children
      Handicapped youth
      Hyperactive children
      Indians of North America—
        Handicapped children
      Learning disabled children
      Libraries and handicapped children
      Mentally handicapped children
      Parents of handicapped children
      Perceptually handicapped children
      Physical education for handicapped
        children
      Physically handicapped children
      Social work with handicapped children
      Socially handicapped children
— **Care** *(May Subd Geog)*
    UF Handicapped children—Care and
        treatment
— — **Moral and ethical aspects**
— Care and treatment
    USE Handicapped children—Care
— **Development**
    [*RJ137*]
    Here are entered works on how mental and
    physical handicaps affect the physical, psycho-
    logical, and social growth of children.
    UF Development and handicaps
        (Pediatrics)
        Handicaps and child development
    BT Child development
— **Education** *(May Subd Geog)*
    [*LC4001-LC4100*]
    NT Portage for handicapped children
        Teachers of handicapped children
— — **Art,** [etc.]
— — **Law and legislation**
    (May Subd Geog)
    BT Educational law and legislation
— — **Music**
    BT Music—Instruction and study—
        Juvenile
— — **Research** *(May Subd Geog)*
— — **Social sciences**
— **Education (Elementary)**
    (May Subd Geog)
— **Education (Preschool)**
    (May Subd Geog)
    [*LC4019.2*]
— **Home care** *(May Subd Geog)*
— **Hospital care** *(May Subd Geog)*
    [*RJ138*]

    BT Hospital care
— **Identification**
    BT Children—Medical examinations
— **Institutional care** *(May Subd Geog)*
— **Psychological testing**
    UF Handicapped children—Testing
    BT Psychological tests for children
— **Services for** *(May Subd Geog)*
    [*HV888*]
    UF Services for handicapped children
— Testing
    USE Handicapped children—
        Psychological testing
    NT Bankson language screening test
        Illinois test of psycholinguistic
        abilities
— **Vocational education**
    BT Vocational education
Handicapped children, Parents of
  USE Parents of handicapped children
Handicapped children, Teachers of
  USE Teachers of handicapped children
Handicapped children and libraries
  USE Libraries and handicapped children
Handicapped Hispanic Americans
  USE Hispanic American handicapped
Handicapped in mass media
  (May Subd Geog)
  Here are entered works discussing the portrayal of
  handicapped in mass media.
Handicapped in the civil service
  (May Subd Geog)
  BT Civil service
      Handicapped—Employment
Handicapped librarians
  USE Librarians, Physically handicapped
Handicapped-owned business enterprises
  (May Subd Geog)
  BT Business enterprises
Handicapped parents *(May Subd Geog)*
  [*HQ759.912*]
  UF Disabled parents
      Exceptional parents
      Parents, Handicapped
  BT Handicapped
      Parents
Handicapped scientists
  USE Scientists, Physically handicapped
Handicapped teachers *(May Subd Geog)*
  UF Disabled teachers
      Teachers, Disabled
      Teachers, Handicapped
  BT Teachers
Handicapped truck drivers
  USE Truck drivers, Physically handicapped
Handicapped women *(May Subd Geog)*
  BT Women
  NT Physically handicapped women
      Socially handicapped women
Handicapped youth *(May Subd Geog)*
  BT Handicapped children
      Youth
  NT Learning disabled youth
      Mentally handicapped youth
      Physically handicapped youth
      Socially handicapped youth
— **Education** *(May Subd Geog)*
— — **Science** *(May Subd Geog)*
— **Life skills guides**
— **Vocational education** *(May Subd Geog)*
    [*LC4019.7*]
    BT Vocational education
Handicapping
  USE Horse race betting
      Sports betting
Handicaps and child development
  USE Handicapped children—Development
Handicraft *(May Subd Geog)*
  [*NK (Artistic crafts)*]
  [*TT*]
  UF Crafts (Handicrafts)

BT Occupational therapy
RT Arts and crafts movement
   Manual training
   Occupations
   Sloyd
NT Aluminum foil craft
   Artisans
   Artists' studios
   Balloon sculpture
   Balsa wood craft
   Bast work
   Bible crafts
   Bread dough craft
   Burlap craft
   Button craft
   Camps—Decoration
   Candlemaking
   Collage
   Cork craft
   Cornhusk craft
   Craft festivals
   Creative activities and seat work
   Cut-out craft
   Decorative balls
   Earth casting
   Egg carton craft
   Egg decoration
   Eggshell craft
   Eskimo craft
   Felt marker decoration
   Glass craft
   Gourd craft
   Hobbies
   Indian craft
   Indians of North America—Industries
   Industrial arts
   Jackets for bottles, vases, etc.
   Jewelry making
   Jewish crafts
   Lace craft
   Leather work
   Macaroni craft
   Miniature craft
   Models and modelmaking
   Nail craft
   Nature craft
   Panty hose craft
   Paper, Handmade
   Peanut craft
   Photography of handicraft
   Pincushions
   Pine cone craft
   Pine needle crafts
   Pipe cleaner craft
   Plaster craft
   Plastics craft
   Plywood craft
   Pottery craft
   Puppet making
   Quillwork
   Raffia work
   Ribbon work
   Rock craft
   Rubber stamp printing
   Rush-work
   Sand casting
   Sand craft
   Selling—Handicraft
   Shellcraft
   Sprang
   Straw work
   String craft
   Textile crafts
   Tile craft
   Toy making
   Wire craft
   Women artisans
   Wreaths
— Cooperative marketing
   UF Cooperative marketing of
      handicrafts

BT Handicraft—Marketing
— Equipment and supplies
— Law and legislation (May Subd Geog)
— Marketing
   NT Handicraft—Cooperative marketing
— Therapeutic use
   [RM735.7.H]
   BT Occupational therapy
      Therapeutics
— Vocational guidance (May Subd Geog)
   BT Artisans
— New Mexico
— — Marketing
   NT Native Market, Santa Fe, N.M.
Handicraft for the mentally handicapped
   BT Mentally handicapped
Handicraft for the physically handicapped
   BT Physically handicapped
Handicraft in the Bible
   [BS680.H35]
   UF Bible—Handicraft
Handicraft industries (May Subd Geog)
   [HD2340.8-HD2346.5]
Handicraft photography
   USE Photography of handicraft
Handicraft surveys (May Subd Geog)
      Here are entered works on the methods and tech-
   niques employed, and reports of individual surveys.
   For the latter the heading may be subdivided by
   place; in such cases a subject entry is also made under
   the heading Handicraft—[local subdivision], e.g. 1.
   Handicraft—United States.   2. Handicraft surveys—
   United States.
      For handicraft surveys on a special topic the addi-
   tional subject entry is made under the special topic,
   e.g. 1. Hand weaving—United States.   2. Handicraft
   surveys—United States.
   BT Surveys
Handkerchiefs
   [HD9930 (Trade)]
   [TS1725 (Manufacture)]
   BT Clothing and dress
      Costume
   NT Bandannas
Handle bodies
   USE Handlebodies
Handle body
   USE Handlebodies
Handle of a surface
   USE Handlebodies
Handlebodies
   [QA613.658]
   UF Handle bodies
      Handle body
      Handle of a surface
      Handlebody
      Handles (Topology)
   BT Differential topology
Handlebody
   USE Handlebodies
Handles
   UF Grips (Machines, tools, etc.)
   BT Implements, utensils, etc.
      Machinery
      Tools
Handles (Topology)
   USE Handlebodies
Handley Page 80 (Jet planes)
   USE Victor (Jet planes)
Handley Page 115 (Jet planes)
   UF H.P. 115 (Jet planes)
   BT Handley Page airplanes
      Jet planes
      Supersonic planes
Handley Page airplanes
   NT Halifax (Bomber)
      Handley Page 115 (Jet planes)
      Victor (Jet planes)
Handling, Remote (Radioactive substances)
   USE Remote handling (Radioactive
      substances)

Handling characteristics of airplanes
   USE Airplanes—Handling characteristics
Handling of art
   USE Art—Handling
Handling of bulk solids
   USE Bulk solids handling
Handling of cotton
   USE Cotton handling
Handling of food
   USE Food handling
Handling of fruit
   USE Fruit—Handling
Handling of materials
   USE Materials handling
Handling of snakes (Holiness churches)
   USE Snake cults (Holiness churches)
Handloading of ammunition
   [TS538.3]
   UF Reloading of ammunition
   BT Ammunition
      Cartridges
Handloom industry (May Subd Geog)
   BT Textile industry
Handlooms (May Subd Geog)
   [TT848.5]
   UF Hand looms
   BT Looms
Handmade paper
   USE Paper, Handmade
Handorf family
   USE Von Handorf family
Handorff family
   USE Von Handorf family
Handpress (May Subd Geog)
   UF Hand press
   BT Printing, Practical
      Printing-press
Handprinted books
   USE Hand-printed books
Handpumps
   USE Hand pumps
Hands, Imposition of
   USE Imposition of hands
Hands, Laying on of
   USE Imposition of hands
Hands family
   USE Hand family
Handson family
   USE Hansen family
Handwashing
   USE Hand washing
Handworked photography
   USE Photography, Handworked
Handwriting
   USE Autographs
      Paleography
      Penmanship
      Writing
Handwriting analysis
   USE Graphology
Handwriting analysts
   USE Graphologists
Handy family (Not Subd Geog)
   UF Handey family
      Hendee family
      Hendy family
      Hendyman family
Handyman's manuals
   USE Repairing—Amateurs' manuals
Hane family
   USE Haynes family
Hanen family
   USE Hannon family
Haner family
   USE Hayner family
Hanes family
   USE Haynes family
Hanford family (Not Subd Geog)
   UF Handford family
      Handforde family
      Hansford family

1631

Hang glider pilots
  USE Air pilots
Hang gliders
  BT Gliders (Aeronautics)
Hang gliding
  UF Sky sailing
    Skysurfing
  BT Gliding and soaring
Hanga dialect (Kenya)
  UF Kawanga dialect
    Luhanga dialect
    Oluhanga dialect
    Oluwanga dialect
    Wanga dialect
  BT Kenya—Languages
    Luyia language
Hanga language (Ghana)
  UF Anga language (Ghana)
  BT Ghana—Languages
    Gur languages
Han'gang (Korea)
  USE Han River (Korea)
Hangars
  [TL730]
  BT Airports—Buildings
Hangay Mountains (Mongolia)
  USE Khangai Mountains (Mongolia)
Hangayn Nuruu (Mongolia)
  USE Khangai Mountains (Mongolia)
Hangers, Plant
  USE Plant hangers
Hanging
  [HV8579-8581]
  BT Capital punishment
    Executions and executioners
  NT Gallows
Hanging baskets
  [SB418]
    Here are entered works on hanging baskets in-
  cluding the planting and the care of plants used in
  them.
  BT Baskets
    Container gardening
  RT Hanging plants
  NT Plant hangers
Hanging flies
  USE Bittacidae
Hanging gardens in spring (Painting)
  USE Li, Ssu-hsün, 651-716. Hanging
    gardens in spring
Hanging in effigy
  USE Executions in effigy
Hanging plants
  [SB432.5]
  UF Plants, Hanging
    Trailing plants
  BT Container gardening
    House plants
    Plants, Ornamental
  RT Hanging baskets
    Ornamental climbing plants
    Plant hangers
Hanging Rock (Ohio)
  USE Hanging Rock Iron Region (Ohio)
Hanging Rock Iron Region (Ohio)
  UF Hanging Rock (Ohio)
Hanging roofs
  USE Roofs, Suspension
Hangingflies
  USE Bittacidae
Hangnest
  USE Northern oriole
Hangö, Battle of, 1714
  [DL743.H]
  BT Northern War, 1700-1721
Hangö, Battle of, 1941
  USE Hanko (Finland), Battle of, 1941
Hangover cures
  UF Cures, Hangover
  BT Alcohol—Physiological effect
    Drugs—Physiological effect

Hanha (African people)
  USE Hanya (African people)
Hani family
  USE Hannie family
Hanin family
  USE Hannon family
Haniwa *(May Subd Geog)*
  [NB159.J]
  BT Terra-cotta sculpture, Japanese
Hanka, Battle of, 1936
  USE Khanka, Battle of, 1936
Hankel functions
  [QA408]
  UF Bessel functions (Third kind)
  BT Bessel functions
Hankel operators
  UF Operators, Hankel
  BT Integral operators
Hankin family
  USE Hankins family
Hankins family *(Not Subd Geog)*
  UF Hankin family
    Hankinson family
Hankinson family
  USE Hankins family
Hanko (Finland), Battle of, 1941
  UF Hangö, Battle of, 1941
  BT World War, 1939-1945—Campaigns—
    Finland
Hankok family
  USE Hancock family
Hankyū Dentetsu
  BT Railroads—Japan
    Street-railroads—Japan
Hanlon family *(Not Subd Geog)*
Hanna Basin (Wyo.)
  BT Geology—Wyoming
Hanna family *(Not Subd Geog)*
  UF Hana family
    Hannah family
    Hannay family
Hanna-Honeycomb House (Stanford, Calif.)
  USE Paul R. Hanna House (Stanford, Calif.)
Hanna House (Stanford, Calif.)
  USE Paul R. Hanna House (Stanford, Calif.)
Hanna San (Korea)
  USE Halla Mountain (Korea)
Hannaford family *(Not Subd Geog)*
Hannah family
  USE Hanna family
Hannam family
  USE Hannum family
Hannan family
  USE Hannon family
Hannay, Richard (Fictitious character)
  UF Richard Hannay (Fictitious character)
  BT Characters and characteristics in
    literature
  RT Buchan, John, 1875-1940—Characters
    —Richard Hannay
Hannay family
  USE Hanna family
Hanneman family *(Not Subd Geog)*
  UF Hannemann family
Hannemann family
  USE Hanneman family
Hannen family
  USE Hannon family
Hanner family
  USE Hand family
Hanners family
  USE Hand family
Hannie family *(Not Subd Geog)*
  UF Hani family
Hännig family
  USE Hennig family
Hanning family
  USE Henning family
Hannings family
  USE Henning family

Hannokihara Iseki (Ōtsu-shi, Japan)
  USE Hannokihara Site (Ōtsu-shi, Japan)
Hannokihara Site (Ōtsu-shi, Japan)
  (Not Subd Geog)
  UF Hannokihara Iseki (Ōtsu-shi, Japan)
  BT Japan—Antiquities
Hannon family *(Not Subd Geog)*
  UF Hanan family
    Hanen family
    Hanin family
    Hannan family
    Hannen family
    Hanon family
    Hanoun family
    Hanoune family
Hannover (Name)
  USE Hanover (Name)
Hannover Kubus (Hannover, Germany)
  USE Kubus Hannover (Hannover,
    Germany)
Hannum family *(Not Subd Geog)*
  UF Hannam family
Hanon family
  USE Hannon family
Hanor family
  USE Hayner family
Hanoun family
  USE Hannon family
Hanoune family
  USE Hannon family
Hanover, House of *(Not Subd Geog)*
  UF House of Hanover
  BT Great Britain—Kings and rulers
Hanover (Name)
  UF Hannover (Name)
  BT Names, Geographical
Hanover horse
  USE Hanoverian horse
Hanover Junction (Va.), Battle of, 1864
  USE North Anna River (Va.), Battle of,
    1864
Hanover, Treaty of, 1725
  [D287.7]
  UF Treaty of Hanover, 1725
Hanoverian horse
  [SF293.H35]
  UF Hanover horse
Hanoverian mercenaries
  [DA500]
  [DA503]
  BT German mercenaries
    Mercenary troops
Hanrahan family *(Not Subd Geog)*
  UF O'Hanrahan family
Hans (Horse)
  USE Clever Hans (Horse)
Hans Christian Andersen Medal
Hansa towns
    Here are entered works that discuss collectively
  the medieval cities belonging to the Hanseatic
  League.
    As a geographic subdivision, this heading is used
  directly.
  UF Hanse towns
  BT Cities and towns
Hansard family *(Not Subd Geog)*
  UF Hanserd family
    Hansird family
Hansberry family
  USE Hansborough family
Hansborough family *(Not Subd Geog)*
  UF Hanbury family
    Hansberry family
    Hansbro family
    Hansbrough family
    Hansbury family
Hansbro family
  USE Hansborough family
Hansbrough family
  USE Hansborough family

Hansbury family
USE Hansborough family
Hanscom family (Not Subd Geog)
UF Anscombe family
Hanscomb family
Hanscombe family
Hanscum family
Hanscomb family
USE Hanscom family
Hanscombe family
USE Hanscom family
Hanscum family
USE Hanscom family
Hanse towns
USE Hansa towns
Hansen family (Not Subd Geog)
UF Handson family
Hanson family
Hanssen family
Hansson family
RT Laurentze-Hansen family
Hansen's disease
USE Leprosy
Hanserd family
USE Hansard family
Hansett family
USE Hanchett family
Hansford family
USE Hanford family
Hanshin Denki Tetsudō
BT Railroads—Japan
Street-railroads—Japan
Hansird family
USE Hansard family
Hanslow family (Not Subd Geog)
Hansmeier family (Not Subd Geog)
UF Hansmeyer family
Hansmeyer family
USE Hansmeier family
Hanson family
USE Hansen family
Hanssen family
USE Hansen family
Hansson family
USE Hansen family
Hanswurst
BT Fools and jesters
Hantchet family
USE Hanchett family
Hantichet family
USE Hanchett family
Hanukah
USE Hanukkah
Ḥanukka
USE Hanukkah
Hanukkah
[BM695.H3]
UF Chanukah
Chanukkah
Dedication, Feast of
Feast of Dedication
Feast of Lights
Feast of the Maccabees
Hanukah
Ḥanukka
Lights, Feast of
Maccabees, Feast of the
BT Fasts and feasts—Judaism
Light—Religious aspects—Judaism
Maccabees
NT Hanukkah decorations
Hanukkah lamp
Hanukkah cookery
[TX724]
UF Cookery, Hanukkah
BT Cookery, Jewish
Holiday cookery
Hanukkah decorations
[TT900.H34]

BT Hanukkah
Holiday decorations
Jewish crafts
Hanukkah in rabbinical literature
BT Rabbinical literature
Hanukkah lamp
[BM657.H3]
BT Art, Jewish
Candles and lights
Hanukkah
Jews—Antiquities
Judaism—Liturgical objects
Menorah
Symbolism
Hanumān (Hindu deity)
BT Gods, Hindu
Hanuman langur
USE Presbytis entellus
Hanunóo
BT Ethnology—Philippines
Hanunóo language
BT Mangyan language
Philippine languages
Hanwa Denki Tetsudō
UF Hanwasen
BT Railroads—Japan
Street-railroads—Japan
Hanwasen
USE Hanwa Denki Tetsudō
Hanya (African people)
UF Hanha (African people)
Hanya (Bantu tribe)
Muhanha (African people)
BT Bantus
Ethnology—Angola
Hanya (Bantu tribe)
USE Hanya (African people)
Hanyū no Sato Iseki (Tomika-chō, Japan)
USE Hanyū no Sato Site (Tomika-chō, Japan)
Hanyū no Sato Site (Tomika-chō, Japan)
(Not Subd Geog)
UF Hanyū no Sato Iseki (Tomika-chō, Japan)
BT Japan—Antiquities
Haole koa
USE Lead tree
Haoma
[BL1590.H36]
BT Indo-Iranians—Religion
Zoroastrianism
RT Soma
Hap Ki-do
USE Hand-to-hand fighting, Oriental
Hapai (Tonga)
USE Ha'apai Group (Tonga)
Hapax legomenon
BT Lexicology
Haplochilus latipes
USE Oryzias latipes
Haplochromis
[QL638.C55]
BT Cichlidae
Haplochromis buysi
[QL638.C55]
Haplodiplosis
[QL537.C33]
BT Gall-gnats
Haplodiplosis equestris
USE Saddle gall midge
Haplodoci
USE Toadfishes
Haplodrassus
[QL458.42.G5]
BT Gnaphosidae
Haplogonatopus
[QL568.D7]
BT Dryinidae
Haplogonatopus bifarius
[QL568.D7]

UF Gonatopus bifarius
Platygonatopus bifarius
Trigonatopus bifarius
Haplographium
[QK625.D4]
BT Dematiaceae
Haplographium calophylli
[QK625.D4]
Haploids
USE Haploidy
Haploidy
UF Haploids
BT Chromosome numbers
RT Genomes
Haplology
BT Phonetics
SA subdivision Haplology under names of languages and groups of languages, e.g. English language—Haplology
Haplomi
USE Salmoniformes
Haplomycosis
USE Adiaspiromycosis
Haplopappus
[QK495.C74]
BT Compositae
Haplopappus gracilis
[QK495.C74]
Haplopharyngidae
[QL391.P7]
BT Rhabdocoelida
NT Haplopharynx
Haplopharynx
[QL391.P7]
BT Haplopharyngidae
Haplopharynx quadristimulus
[QL391.P7]
Haploptilia
USE Coleophora
Haploptiliidae
USE Coleophoridae
Haplopus
[QL508.P5]
BT Phasmidae
Haplorhini
USE Monkeys
Haplosclerida
[QL373.D4]
BT Demospongiae
Haplothrips
[QL598.3.P45]
BT Phlaeothripidae
Haplothrips verbasci
USE Mullein thrips
Hapner family (Not Subd Geog)
Håpnes family (Not Subd Geog)
Happening (Art) (May Subd Geog)
BT Art, Modern—20th century
Pantomime
NT Performance art
Street theater
Happes family
USE Hoppes family
Happiness
[B491.H36 (Philosophy, B187.H3)]
[BF575.H27 (Psychology)]
[BJ1480-1486 (Ethics)]
UF Gladness
BT Emotions
RT Cheerfulness
Contentment
Joy
Pleasure
NT Mental health
— **Religious aspects**
— — Buddhism, [Christianity, etc.]
— **Testing**
[BF575.H27]
BT Psychological tests

Happiness in literature
Happy Colony
  BT Utopias
Happy Land (Buddhism)
  USE Western Paradise (Buddhism)
Haprolepis
  [QL568.E6]
  BT Encyrtidae
Haprolepis dalmanni
  [QL568.E6]
Haps family
  USE Hoppes family
Hapsburg, House of
  USE Habsburg, House of
Haptal
  USE Ephthalites
Haptens
  BT Antigens
Haptic sense
  USE Touch
Haptics
  USE Touch
Haptoglobin
  [QP552.H3]
  BT Alpha globulin
    Blood proteins
    Carrier proteins
    Globin
    Globulin
Har Geshur (Israel)
  USE Karkom Mountain (Israel)
Har ha-bayit (Jerusalem)
  USE Temple Mount (Jerusalem)
Har ha-Zetim (Jerusalem)
  USE Mount of Olives (Jerusalem)
Har Ḥorev (Egypt)
  USE Sinai, Mount (Egypt)
Har Karkom (Israel)
  USE Karkom Mountain (Israel)
Har Sinai (Egypt)
  USE Sinai, Mount (Egypt)
Hara Iseki (Tosayamada-chō, Japan)
  USE Hara Site (Tosayamada-chō, Japan)
Hara-kiri
  USE Seppuku
Hara Site (Tosayamada-chō, Japan)
  (Not Subd Geog)
  UF Hara Iseki (Tosayamada-chō, Japan)
  BT Japan—Antiquities
Harada family *(Not Subd Geog)*
Harada House (Riverside, Calif.)
  BT Dwellings—California
Harae (Shinto)
  USE Harai (Shinto)
Haragure language
  USE Aragure language
Harai (Shinto)
  UF Harae (Shinto)
  BT Shinto—Rituals
Harakiri
  USE Seppuku
Harakmbet Indians
  USE Mashco Indians
Harakmbet language
  USE Mashco language
Haral family
  USE Harrell family
Harald family
  USE Harrell family
Haraldson family
  USE Harrell family
Ḥaram al-Sharīf (Jerusalem)
  USE Temple Mount (Jerusalem)
Ḥaram esh-Sherīf (Jerusalem)
  USE Temple Mount (Jerusalem)
Haramosh (Pakistan)
  BT Karakoram Range
    Mountains—Pakistan
Harap Alb (Legendary character)
  [GR257]

  UF White Arab (Legendary character)
    White Moor (Legendary character)
  BT Folklore—Romania
Harappa culture
  USE Indus civilization
Harappa Site (Pakistan) *(Not Subd Geog)*
  [DS392.2.H3]
  BT Pakistan—Antiquities
Harari language
  [PJ9293]
  UF Adari language
    Ararge language
    Harrarjie language
  BT Ethiopian languages
Hararis
  [DT443 (Tanganyika)]
Hārās
  USE Hadas
Harassment, Sexual
  USE Sexual harassment
Harassment of women, Sexual
  USE Sexual harassment of women
Haratajino Iseki (Tomioka-shi, Japan)
  USE Haratajino Site (Tomioka-shi, Japan)
Haratajino Site (Tomioka-shi, Japan)
  UF Haratajino Iseki (Tomioka-shi, Japan)
  BT Japan—Antiquities
Harauti language
  [PK1921-4]
  BT Rajasthani language
Harauti literature *(May Subd Geog)*
Harauti philology
  [PK1921]
Harauti poetry *(May Subd Geog)*
  [PK1923.5 (History)]
  [PK1924.A2 (Collections)]
Harayama 1-gōfun Site (Izumizaki-mura, Japan) *(Not Subd Geog)*
  BT Japan—Antiquities
Harbansus
  [QL444.085]
  BT Philomedidae
Harber family
  USE Harbor family
Harbert family *(Not Subd Geog)*
  UF Harberts family
Harberts family
  USE Harbert family
Harbeson family
  USE Harbin family
Harbigny family
  USE Herbigny family
Harbin family *(Not Subd Geog)*
  UF Harbeson family
    Harbinson family
    Harbison family
Harbinson family
  USE Harbin family
Harbison family
  USE Harbin family
Harbor access
  USE Harbors—Access
Harbor defenses
  USE Coast defenses
Harbor family *(Not Subd Geog)*
  UF Harber family
    Harbour family
Harbor Islands (Mass.)
  USE Boston Harbor Islands (Mass.)
Harbor masters *(May Subd Geog)*
  BT Harbors
Harbor of Refuge Lighthouse (Del.)
  [VK1025.H]
  BT Lighthouses—Delaware
Harbor police *(May Subd Geog)*
  BT Police
  NT Police divers
Harbor porpoise
  [QL737.C434]
  UF Phocoena phocoena
  BT Porpoises

Harbor seal
  [QL737.P64]
  UF Phoca richardii
    Phoca vitulina
  BT Seals (Animals)
Harbor sounds
  USE Waterfront sounds
Harbors *(May Subd Geog)*
  [HE550-HE560 (Transportation)]
  [JX4138 (International law)]
  [TC203-TC326 (General)]
  [TC353-TC365 (Engineering)]
  [VK321-VK369.8 (Navigation)]
  UF Ports
    Seaports
  BT Channels (Hydraulic engineering)
    Hydraulic structures
    Terminals (Transportation)
    Transportation
  NT Breakwaters
    Docks
    Dredging
    Fenders for docks, piers, etc.
    Fishing ports
    Floating harbors
    Free ports and zones
    Harbor masters
    Harbors of refuge
    Jetties
    Marinas
    Marine terminals
    Mooring of ships
    Petroleum shipping terminals
    Piers
    Pilots and pilotage
    Port districts
    Roadsteads
    Wharves
  — **Access**
    UF Access to harbors
      Harbor access
      Transportation to harbors
  — **Access roads**
    UF Access roads to harbors
    BT Roads
  — **Anchorage**
    BT Anchorage
  — **Communication systems**
  — **Computer programs**
  — **Design and construction**
  — — **Finance**
  — — — **Law and legislation**
      (May Subd Geog)
  — — **Law and legislation**
      (May Subd Geog)
  — **Earthquake effects**
    UF Earthquakes and harbors
    BT Earthquakes and hydraulic
      structures
  — **Electric equipment**
    [TK4035.H3]
  — **Finance**
  — **Hydrodynamics**
    BT Hydrodynamics
  — **Law and legislation** *(May Subd Geog)*
    BT Maritime law
  — **Maintenance and repair**
    [TC205]
  — **Port charges**
    [HE951-3]
    UF Port charges
    BT Free ports and zones
      Maritime law
      Shipping
      Tariff
      Tolls
      User charges
  — **Traffic control**
    UF Ship traffic control
      Traffic control in harbors
      Vessel traffic control

BT Electronics in navigation
— Views
— **Australia**
   NT Gladstone, Port of (Qld.)
      Port Dalrymple (Tas.)
— **Hawaii**
   NT Pearl Harbor (Hawaii)
— **Hong Kong**
   NT Victoria Harbor (Hong Kong)
— **Massachusetts**
   NT Salem Maritime National Historic
      Site (Mass.)
— **New Jersey**
   NT Little Egg Harbor (N.J.)
— **New York (State)**
   NT Henderson Harbor (N.Y. : Harbor)
— **New Zealand**
   NT Hokianga Harbor (N.Z.)
      Manukau Harbor (N.Z.)
      Otago Harbor (N.Z.)
      Porirua Harbour (N.Z.)
      Waitemata Harbor (N.Z.)
— **Panama**
   NT Darien Harbor (Panama)
— **Russian S.F.S.R.**
   NT Korsakov Harbor (R.S.F.S.R.)
— **United States**
   UF United States—Harbors
— **Washington (State)**
   NT Grays Harbor (Wash.)
Harbors, Floating
   USE Floating harbors
Harbors in art
Harbors of refuge *(May Subd Geog)*
   [VK369-VK369.8]
     Here are entered works on harbors provided on
stormy coasts for the shelter of vessels or small craft
in distress or seeking safety from storms.
   UF Ports of refuge
      Refuge harbors
   BT Harbors
Harbour Bridge (Sydney, N.S.W.)
   USE Sydney Harbour Bridge (Sydney,
      N.S.W.)
Harbour family
   USE Harbor family
Harbour of Otago (N.Z.)
   USE Otago Harbor (N.Z.)
Harburger Berge, Naturpark (Germany)
   USE Naturpark Harburger Berge (Germany)
Harcourt's storm-petrel
   USE Oceanodroma castro
Hard-core unemployed *(May Subd Geog)*
   [HD5708.8-HD5708.85 (Labor
     market)]
   [HF5549.5.H3 (Personnel
     management)]
   UF Socially handicapped—Employment
   BT Labor supply
      Unemployed
Hard-facing
   [TS227.3]
   UF Hard-surfacing
      Metals—Hard-facing
   BT Metals—Finishing
      Surface hardening
      Welding
   NT Hard-facing alloys
      Pressure vessels—Linings
Hard-facing alloys
   UF Hard-surfacing alloys
   BT Alloys
      Hard-facing
Hard family *(Not Subd Geog)*
   UF Hardt family
   RT Hart family
Hard materials
   [TA418.45]
   BT Hardness
      Materials
   RT Mechanical wear

— **Machining**
   BT Machining
Hard-of-hearing
   USE Hearing impaired
Hard palate
   USE Palate
Hard plastic dolls *(May Subd Geog)*
   [NK4894.4.H37]
   UF Dolls, Hard plastic
   BT Dolls
Hard superconductors
   USE Superconductors, Type II
Hard-surfacing
   USE Hard-facing
Hard-surfacing alloys
   USE Hard-facing alloys
Hard ticks
   USE Ixodidae
Hard water
   USE Water—Hardness
Hard woods
   USE Hardwoods
Hardanger (Norway)
   USE Hardangervidda (Norway)
Hardanger fiddle
   [ML760]
   UF Hardangerfele
      Hardingfele
   BT Violin
Hardanger-fiddle music
   [M59]
Hardanger fiddle with string orchestra
   [M1119.H37]
   RT Concertos (Hardanger fiddle with
      string orchestra)
Hardanger needlework
   [TT787]
   UF Norwegian drawn work
   BT Drawn-work
      Embroidery
      Needlework
Hardanger Plateau (Norway)
   USE Hardangervidda (Norway)
Hardanger Vidda (Norway)
   USE Hardangervidda (Norway)
Hardangerfele
   USE Hardanger fiddle
Hardangervidda (Norway) *(Not Subd Geog)*
   UF Hardanger (Norway)
      Hardanger Plateau (Norway)
      Hardanger Vidda (Norway)
      Vidda (Norway)
   BT Plateaus—Norway
Hardboard
   BT Fiberboard
   NT Particle board
Hardboard industry *(May Subd Geog)*
   [HD9769.H37-373]
Harde family
   USE Hardy family
Hardee family
   USE Hardy family
Hardeman family *(Not Subd Geog)*
   UF Hardemon family
      Hardiman family
   RT Hardman family
Hardemon family
   USE Hardeman family
Harden family
   USE Harding family
Hardenability of metals
   USE Metals—Hardenability
Hardenberg family
   USE Hardenbergh family
Hardenbergh family *(Not Subd Geog)*
   UF Hardenberg family
      Hardenberghe family
      Hardenburg family
      Hardenburghe family
Hardenberghe family
   USE Hardenbergh family

Hardenbrook family *(Not Subd Geog)*
Hardenburg family
   USE Hardenbergh family
Hardenburghe family
   USE Hardenbergh family
Hardening, Explosive
   USE Explosive hardening
Hardening, Strain
   USE Strain hardening
Hardening, Surface
   USE Surface hardening
Hardening of the arteries
   USE Arteriosclerosis
Harder family
   USE Herder family
Hardesty family *(Not Subd Geog)*
   UF Hardister family
      Hardisty family
      Hardofsty family
Hardey family
   USE Hardy family
Hardgrave family
   USE Hargrave family
Hardgrove family
   USE Hargrave family
Hardi family
   USE Hardy family
Hardie family
   USE Hardy family
Hardig Brook (R.I.)
   BT Rivers—Rhode Island
Hardiman family
   USE Hardeman family
Hardin family
   USE Harding family
Hardiness of plants
   USE Plants—Hardiness
Harding family *(Not Subd Geog)*
   UF Harden family
      Hardin family
      Hardinge family
      Harting family
      Hartting family
      Harttung family
      Hartung family
   RT Hardinger family
Harding grass
   USE Hardinggrass
Harding River (W.A.)
   BT Rivers—Australia
Hardinge family
   USE Harding family
Hardinger family *(Not Subd Geog)*
   UF Hartinger family
      Hedinger family
      Hepinger family
      Hettinger family
   RT Harding family
Hardingfele
   USE Hardanger fiddle
Hardinggrass
   [QK495.G74 (Botany)]
   [SB201.H (Culture)]
   UF Harding grass
   BT Forage plants
Hardison family *(Not Subd Geog)*
   UF Hardiston family
      Hardyson family
Hardister family
   USE Hardesty family
Hardiston family
   USE Hardison family
Hardisty family
   USE Hardesty family
Hardman family *(Not Subd Geog)*
   UF Herdman family
   RT Hardeman family
Hardness
   [TA407 (Engineering tests)]
   NT Brinell test
      Concrete—Penetration resistance

Hardness *(Continued)*
    Hard materials
    Metals—Hardenability
    Microhardness
    Precipitation hardening
  — **Testing**
    NT Rockwell hardness
Hardness of heart
  UF Obduracy
  BT Obstinacy
Hardness of water
  USE Water—Hardness
Hardofsty family
  USE Hardesty family
Hardreshulle family *(Not Subd Geog)*
Hardt family
  USE Hard family
Hardtack, Operation, 1958
  USE Operation Hardtack, 1958
Hardware *(May Subd Geog)*
  [HD9745 (Trade)]
  [TS400-TS455 (Manufacture)]
  BT Iron industry and trade
    Metal trade
  NT Bolts and nuts
    Building fittings
    Cabinet hardware
    Clamps (Engineering)
    Crowbars
    Cutlery
    Door fittings
    Files and rasps
    Knives
    Locks and keys
    Nails and spikes
    Saws
    Screws
    Strikes and lockouts—Hardware
      industry
    Tools
    Washers (for bolts and screws)
  — **Credit guides**
    [HF5585.H3]
Hardware, Cabinet
  USE Cabinet hardware
Hardware, Computer
  USE Computer input-output equipment
    Computers
Hardware industry *(May Subd Geog)*
  [HD9745]
Hardware industry workers
  (May Subd Geog)
Hardware stores *(May Subd Geog)*
  BT Specialty stores
  — **Credit guides**
Hardwood industry *(May Subd Geog)*
  [HD9769.H39-HD9769.H394]
Hardwoods *(May Subd Geog)*
  UF Hard woods
  BT Forests and forestry
    Lumber
    Wood
  SA *names of hardwoods, e.g.* Walnut
  — **Diseases and pests** *(May Subd Geog)*
    BT Trees—Diseases and pests
  — **Labeling**
    NT Mahogany—Labeling
Hardy Boys (Fictitious characters)
  BT Characters and characteristics in
      literature
  RT Stratemeyer, Edward, 1862-1930—
      Characters—Hardy Boys
Hardy classes
  UF Classes, Hardy
    Hp classes
  BT Function algebras
    Functions of complex variables

Hardy family *(Not Subd Geog)*
  UF Harde family
    Hardee family
    Hardey family
    Hardi family
    Hardie family
    Hardyes family
Hardy herbaceous perennials
  USE Perennials
Hardy-Littlewood method
  BT Diophantine analysis
    Equations—Numerical solutions
    Numbers, Theory of
Hardy spaces
  UF Spaces, Hardy
  BT Functional analysis
    Functions of complex variables
Hardy-Weinberg equilibrium principle
  USE Hardy-Weinberg formula
Hardy-Weinberg formula
  UF Hardy-Weinberg equilibrium principle
    Hardy-Weinberg law
  BT Biomathematics
    Population genetics—Mathematical
      models
    Stochastic processes
Hardy-Weinberg law
  USE Hardy-Weinberg formula
Hardyes family
  USE Hardy family
Hardyson family
  USE Hardison family
Hare (Helicopters)
  USE Mi-1 (Helicopters)
Hare and hounds
  [GV1063 (Games)]
  UF Paper-chasing
Hare breeding
  [SF454.2]
  UF Hares—Breeding
Hare family
  USE Hair family
Hare hunting *(May Subd Geog)*
  [SK341.H3]
  BT Hunting
Hare Indians
  USE Kawchottine Indians
Hare Krishnas *(May Subd Geog)*
  BT Hindus
  — **Biography**
    UF International Society for Krishna
      Consciousness—Biography
Hare language
  USE Kawchottine language
Harebell
  USE Campanula rotundifolia
Haregrave family
  USE Hargrave family
Harel family
  USE Harrell family
Harelip
  [RD524]
  UF Cleft lip
  BT Lips—Abnormalities
    Surgery, Plastic
Harelson family
  USE Harrell family
Harem
  [DT70 (Egypt)]
  [DT192 (Barbary States)]
  [HQ1170 (Women in the Orient)]
  [HQ1707 (Turkey, DR432)]
  BT Polygamy
Harengula
  [QL638.C64]
  BT Clupeidae
    Sardines
Harengula humeralis
  USE Redear sardine
Hares *(May Subd Geog)*
  [QL737.L32 (Zoology)]

  [SF451-SF455 (Breeding)]
  [SK341.H3 (Hunting)]
  BT Leporidae
  NT Belgian hare
    Coursing
    European hare
  — **Breeding**
    USE Hare breeding
Hares, Fossil
  [QE882.R6]
Hares family
  USE Hair family
Hare's Hill, Va., Battle of, 1865
  USE Stedman, Fort, Battle of, 1865
Hare's syndrome
  USE Pancoast's syndrome
Hareson family
  USE Harrison family
Harewell family
  USE Harwell family
Harewelle family
  USE Harwell family
Harewood family
  USE Harwood family
Harewood House (Harewood, West Yorkshire)
  BT Dwellings—England
Harget family
  USE Hargett family
Hargett family *(Not Subd Geog)*
  UF Harget family
    Hargitt family
    Hargrett family
    Hergert family
    Herget family
    Hergett family
    Hergott family
    Herigodt family
Hargis family *(Not Subd Geog)*
Hargitt family
  USE Hargett family
Hargrave family *(Not Subd Geog)*
  UF Hardgrave family
    Hardgrove family
    Haregrave family
    Hargraves family
    Hargreaves family
    Hargrove family
Hargraves family
  USE Hargrave family
Hargreaves family
  USE Hargrave family
Hargrett family
  USE Hargett family
Hargrove family
  USE Hargrave family
Hari Kebangsaan Malaysia
  USE Independence Day (Malaysia)
Hariana cattle
  [SF199.H37]
Hariani dialect
  USE Bangaru dialect
Haridasas
  [BL1285.7-1285.792]
  BT Vaishnavism
    Vedanta
Hariegawa Kita Iseki (Shin'asahi-chō, Japan)
  USE Hariegawa Kita Site (Shin'asahi-chō,
    Japan)
Hariegawa Kita Site (Shin'asahi-chō, Japan)
  (Not Subd Geog)
  UF Hariegawa Kita Iseki (Shin'asahi-chō,
    Japan)
  BT Japan—Antiquities
Harijans
  USE Untouchables
Harilson family
  USE Harrell family
Haring family
  USE Herring family
Harington family
  USE Harrington family

Haringvliet (Netherlands)
    BT Inlets—Netherlands
Hariri, Tall (Syria)
    USE Mari (Ancient city)
Haris family
    USE Harris family
Hariścandra (Hindu mythology)
    UF Harischandra (Hindu mythology)
        Harishchandra (Hindu mythology)
    BT Mythology, Hindu
Harischandra (Hindu mythology)
    USE Hariścandra (Hindu mythology)
Harishchandra (Hindu mythology)
    USE Hariścandra (Hindu mythology)
Harison family
    USE Harrison family
Hariss family
    USE Harris family
Harisson family
    USE Harrison family
Härjedalen (Sweden)
Harjehausen family (Not Subd Geog)
    UF Harjehusen family
        Harriehausen family
        Harringehusen family
Harjehusen family
    USE Harjehausen family
Harju Uprising, 1343
    UF Estonia—History—Harju Uprising,
        1343
    BT Peasant uprisings—Estonia
        Peasantry—Estonia
Harker family (Not Subd Geog)
Harkness family (Not Subd Geog)
Harknessia
    ₍QK625.Z9₎
    BT Zythiaceae
Harlem, East (New York, N.Y.)
    USE East Harlem (New York, N.Y.)
Harlem Heights, Battle of, 1776
    ₍E241.H2₎
    BT New York (N.Y.)—History—
        Revolution, 1775-1783
        New York (State)—History—
        Revolution, 1775-1783
        United States—History—Revolution,
        1775-1783—Campaigns
Harlem Renaissance
    UF New Negro Movement
        Renaissance, Harlem
    BT Afro-American arts
        American literature—Afro-American
        authors
Harlequin
    ₍PN1988.H3₎
    BT Pantomime
        Puppets and puppet-plays
Harley-Davidson motorcycle
Harley family (Not Subd Geog)
    UF Harllee family
        Harly family
    RT Hartley family
Harllee family
    USE Harley family
Harloe family
    USE Harlow family
Harlow family (Not Subd Geog)
    UF Harloe family
        Harlowe family
    RT Penhallow family
Harlowe family
    USE Harlow family
Harly family
    USE Harley family
Harmal
    USE Peganum harmala
Harmaloga fumiferana
    USE Spruce budworm
Harman family
    USE Harmon family

Harmann family
    USE Harmon family
Harmar's Expedition, 1790
    ₍E83.79₎
    BT Indians of North America—Wars—
        1790-1794
Hármashatár, Mount (Budapest, Hungary)
    UF Hármashatár-hegy (Budapest,
        Hungary)
        Hármashatárhegy (Budapest, Hungary)
        Mount Hármashatár (Budapest,
        Hungary)
    BT Mountains—Hungary
Hármashatár-hegy (Budapest, Hungary)
    USE Hármashatár, Mount (Budapest,
        Hungary)
Hármashatárhegy (Budapest, Hungary)
    USE Hármashatár, Mount (Budapest,
        Hungary)
Harmel
    USE Peganum harmala
Harmen family
    USE Harmon family
Harmer family (Not Subd Geog)
    RT Harmon family
Harmin family
    USE Harmon family
Harmolita
    ₍QL568.E85₎
    UF Isosoma
        Joint-worms
    BT Eurytomidae
Harmon family (Not Subd Geog)
    UF Harman family
        Harmann family
        Harmen family
        Harmin family
        Harmond family
    RT Harmer family
Harmond family
    USE Harmon family
Harmonic analysis
    ₍QA403₎
    UF Analysis (Mathematics)
        Functions, Potential
        Potential functions
    BT Banach algebras
        Calculus
        Mathematical analysis
        Mathematics
    RT Bessel functions
        Fourier series
        Harmonic functions
        Time-series analysis
    NT Fourier transformations
        Jacobi series
        L1 algebras
        Lamé's functions
        Measure algebras
        Multipliers (Mathematical analysis)
        Sidon sets
        Spectral synthesis (Mathematics)
        Spherical harmonics
        Toroidal harmonics
Harmonic analysis (Music)
    ₍MT50₎
    UF Music—Harmonic analysis
    BT Harmony
        Music—Theory
        Musical analysis
    NT Schenkerian analysis
Harmonic analyzers
    UF Analyzers, Harmonic
    BT Electric meters
        Electronic instruments
        Frequency meters
        Harmonics (Electric waves)
Harmonic dictation
    USE Musical dictation
Harmonic drives
    ₍TJ202₎

    UF Harmonic speed changers
    BT Gearing, Planetary
        Power transmission
    RT Splines
Harmonic functions
    ₍QA405₎
    UF Functions, Harmonic
        Laplace's equations
    BT Differential equations, Partial
    RT Bessel functions
        Fourier series
        Functions, Subharmonic
        Harmonic analysis
        Lamé's functions
        Spherical harmonics
        Toroidal harmonics
    NT Functions, Spheroidal
        Maximum principles (Mathematics)
        Polyharmonic functions
Harmonic maps
    ₍QA614.73₎
    UF Maps, Harmonic
    BT Mappings (Mathematics)
Harmonic motion
    BT Motion
    NT Harmonic oscillators
Harmonic oscillators
    UF Linear oscillators
        Oscillators, Harmonic
        Oscillators, Linear
        Oscillators, Simple
        Simple oscillators
    BT Harmonic motion
Harmonic spaces
    UF Spaces, Harmonic
    BT Locally compact spaces
        Sheaves, Theory of
Harmonic speed changers
    USE Harmonic drives
Harmonica
    ₍ML1088₎
    UF Mouth harmonica
        Mouth organ
    BT Mouth organs
Harmonica, Glass
    USE Glass harmonica
Harmonica and harp music
    ₍M296-M297₎
    UF Harp and harmonica music
Harmonica and harpsichord music
    ₍M284.M6₎
    ₍M285.M6₎
    UF Harpsichord and harmonica music
    NT Sonatas (Harmonica and harpsichord)
Harmonica and piano music
    ₍M284.M6₎
    ₍M285.M6₎
    UF Piano and harmonica music
    NT Sonatas (Harmonica and piano)
        Suites (Harmonica and piano)
Harmonica and piano music, Arranged
    ₍M284.M6₎
    ₍M285.M6₎
    NT Concertos (Harmonica)—Solo with
        piano
Harmonica band
    USE Harmonica ensembles
Harmonica ensembles
    Here are entered works for three or more har-
    monicas and collections of compositions for a varying
    number of harmonicas.
    UF Harmonica band
    NT Waltzes (Harmonica ensemble)
Harmonica music
    ₍M175.M8₎

Harmonica music *(Continued)*
  SA Concertos, Sonatas, Suites, Waltzes,
      and similar headings with
      specification of instruments; Trios
      ₍Quintets, etc.₎ *followed by*
      specifications which include the
      harmonica; also headings that begin
      with the words Harmonica or
      Harmonicas
Harmonica players *(May Subd Geog)*
  BT Musicians
Harmonica with chamber orchestra
    ₍M1039.4.M6₎
  RT Concertos (Harmonica with chamber
      orchestra)
Harmonica with orchestra
    ₍M1039.4.M6₎
  RT Concertos (Harmonica)
  NT Suites (Harmonica with orchestra)
Harmonica with string orchestra
    ₍M1139.4.M6₎
  RT Concertos (Harmonica with string
      orchestra)
  NT Suites (Harmonica with string
      orchestra)
Harmonicon, Chemical
  USE Pyrophone
Harmonics (Electric waves)
  BT Electric waves
  NT Harmonic analyzers
Harmonics (Music)
  UF Flageolet tones
      Overtones (Music)
      Partials (Music)
  BT Music—Acoustics and physics
  NT Bass guitar—Instruction and study—
      Harmonics
Harmonie (Information retrieval system)
    ₍Z699.4.H36₎
  BT Information storage and retrieval
      systems
Harmonie State Park (Ind.)
  UF Harmonie State Recreation Area (Ind.)
  BT Parks—Indiana
      Recreation areas—Indiana
Harmonie State Recreation Area (Ind.)
  USE Harmonie State Park (Ind.)
Harmonists
  UF Rappists
  BT Christian sects
      Collective settlements
      Communism
Harmonium
  USE Reed-organ
Harmonium, Bichromatic
  USE Bichromatic harmonium
Harmonization of law
  USE Law—International unification
Harmonized chant
  USE Chants (Anglican)
Harmonometer (Mechanical musical
  instrument)
Harmony
    ₍ML444 (History)₎
    ₍ML3815 (Acoustics)₎
    ₍ML3836 (Psychology)₎
    ₍ML3852 (Aesthetics)₎
    ₍MT50 (Instruction)₎
  BT Composition (Music)
      Music
      Music—Instruction and study
      Music—Theory
  RT Thorough bass
      Tonality
  SA *subdivision* Harmony *under names of*
      composers, e.g. Wagner, Richard,
      1813-1883—Harmony
  NT Bourdon
      Cadence (Music)
      Chromatic alteration (Music)
      Harmonic analysis (Music)

      Melody
      Modulation (Music)
      Musical intervals and scales
      Organ-point
      Solmization
      Suspension (Music)
      Symmetrical inversion (Music)
      Twelve-tone system
  — **Mechanical aids**
      ₍MT50₎
    UF Chromophone
Harmony, Keyboard
    ₍MT224₎
  UF Keyboard harmony
  BT Improvisation (Music)
      Piano—Instruction and study
Harmony (Aesthetics)
    ₍BH301.H3₎
  BT Aesthetics
      Music
      Music—Philosophy and aesthetics
Harmony (Aesthetics) as a theme in literature
  USE Harmony (Aesthetics) in literature
Harmony (Aesthetics) in literature
  UF Harmony (Aesthetics) as a theme in
      literature
Harmony (Cosmology)
  USE Harmony of the spheres
Harmony (Philosophy)
    ₍B105.H37₎
  BT Philosophy
Harmony in Blue and Gold Room
  USE Peacock Room
Harmony of the spheres
    ₍BD645₎
  UF Cosmic harmony
      Harmony (Cosmology)
      Music of the spheres
  BT Cosmology
Harmsen family *(Not Subd Geog)*
  UF Harmssen family
      Harmston family
Harmssen family
  USE Harmsen family
Harmston family
  USE Harmsen family
Harnden family
  USE Herndon family
Harndon family
  USE Herndon family
Harned family *(Not Subd Geog)*
Harnes family
  USE Harness family
Harness
    ₍GT5888 (Manners and customs)₎
    ₍S720-S721 (Farm implements)₎
  BT Horses
      Saddlery
  NT Bridle
      Check-rein
      Curb-bit
      Hackamore
      Horse brasses
      Yokes
Harness drivers *(May Subd Geog)*
  UF Drivers, Harness
  BT Horsemen and horsewomen
Harness family *(Not Subd Geog)*
  UF Harnes family
      Harnish family
      Harniss family
Harness horses
  USE Driving horses
      Harness racehorses
Harness making and trade
  (May Subd Geog)
    ₍HD9780 (Trade)₎
    ₍TS1030-TS1035 (Manufacture)₎
  BT Leather industry and trade
      Saddlery

  NT Trade-unions—Harness making and
      trade
Harness racehorses *(May Subd Geog)*
    ₍SF343₎
  UF Harness horses
      Pacers and trotters
      Trotters and pacers
  BT Harness racing
      Race horses
  SA *names of individual racehorses*
  NT Rambling Willie (Race horse)
  — **Training**
      ₍SF341₎
Harness racing *(May Subd Geog)*
    ₍SF338.7-345₎
  UF Sulky racing
      Trotting-races
  BT Horse-racing
  NT Harness racehorses
  — **Law and legislation** *(May Subd Geog)*
  — **Vocational guidance**
  — **Illinois**
      NT Hambletonian, Du Quoin, Ill.
  — **Kentucky**
      NT Red Mile (Lexington, Ky.)
  — **New Zealand**
      NT Interdominion Championship
          New Zealand Trotting Cup
Harney family *(Not Subd Geog)*
  UF Hartney family
Harney Flats Site (Fla.) *(Not Subd Geog)*
  BT Florida—Antiquities
Harnish family
  USE Harness family
Harniss family
  USE Harness family
Haroi language
    ₍PL4498.H37₎
  UF Bahnar Cham language
      Hrway language
  BT Austroasiatic languages
      Chamic languages
Harold family
  USE Harrell family
Haroldson family
  USE Harrell family
Haroué Castle (Haroué, France)
  USE Château d'Haroué (Haroué, France)
Harp
    ₍ML1005-ML1006 (History and
    construction)₎
  UF Celtic harp
      Irish harp
  NT Aeolian harp
      Clavi-harp
      Harp-lute guitar
      Harp zither
      Kantele (Musical instrument)
      Kokle
  — **Construction**
      ₍ML1006₎
  — **Instruction and study**
      ₍MT540-548₎
      NT Harp music—Teaching pieces
  — **Orchestra studies**
      ₍MT546₎
      BT Harp—Studies and exercises
  — **Studies and exercises**
      NT Harp—Orchestra studies
Harp and alpenhorn music
  USE Alpenhorn and harp music
Harp and clarinet music
  USE Clarinet and harp music
Harp and clarinet with string orchestra
  USE Clarinet and harp with string orchestra
Harp and dulcimer music
  USE Dulcimer and harp music
Harp and English horn music
  USE English horn and harp music
Harp and flute music
  USE Flute and harp music

Harp and flute with string orchestra
USE Flute and harp with string orchestra
Harp and guitar music
USE Guitar and harp music
Harp and harmonica music
USE Harmonica and harp music
Harp and harpsichord music
[M272-273]
UF Harpsichord and harp music
NT Sonatas (Harp and harpsichord)
Harp and horn music
USE Horn and harp music
Harp and lute music
[M292-3]
UF Lute and harp music
NT Concertos (Harp and lute)
Harp and lute with orchestra
Harp and lute with orchestra
[M1040-1041]
BT Harp and lute music
RT Concertos (Harp and lute)
Harp and oboe music
USE Oboe and harp music
Harp and organ music
[M182-4]
UF Organ and harp music
NT Harp and organ with string orchestra
Harp and organ with string orchestra
[M1105-6]
BT Harp and organ music
RT Concertos (Harp and organ with string orchestra)
Harp and percussion music
USE Percussion and harp music
Harp and piano music
[M272-3]
UF Piano and harp music
NT Concertos (Harp and piano)
Harp and piano with orchestra
Sonatas (Harp and piano)
Variations (Harp and piano)
Harp and piano music, Arranged
[M272-3]
NT Chaconnes (Harp with string orchestra)—Solo with piano
Concertos (Harp)—Solo with piano
Concertos (Harp with string orchestra)—Solo with piano
Concertos (Harp with string orchestra), Arranged—Solo with piano
Harp with band—Solo with piano
Harp with orchestra—Solo with piano
Harp with string orchestra—Solo with piano
Harp and piano with orchestra
[M1040-1041]
BT Harp and piano music
RT Concertos (Harp and piano)
Harp and recorder music
USE Recorder and harp music
Harp and saxophone music
USE Saxophone and harp music
Harp and trumpet music
USE Trumpet and harp music
Harp and vibraphone music
[M298]
UF Vibraphone and harp music
Harp and viola music
USE Viola and harp music
Harp and violin music
USE Violin and harp music
Harp and violoncello music
USE Violoncello and harp music
Harp ensembles
[M965-M969]
Here are entered compositions for ten or more harps and collections of compositions for a varying number of harps.
BT Plectral ensembles

Harp family *(Not Subd Geog)*
RT La Harpe family
Harp-lute
USE Kora (Musical instrument)
Harp-lute guitar
[ML1015-1018]
UF Guitar, Harp-lute
BT Guitar
Harp
Lute
Harp-lute guitar and piano music
[M282-3]
UF Piano and harp-lute guitar music
Harp-lute guitar music
[M142.H2]
NT Suites (Harp-lute guitar)
Harp music
[M115-119]
SA Concertos, Minuets, Sonatas, Suites, *and similar headings with specification of instruments;* Trios [Quartets, etc.] *followed by specifications which include the harp; also* Plectral ensembles *and headings that begin with the words* harp *or* harps
NT Chaconnes (Harp)
Marches (Harp)
Potpourris (Harp)
Sonatas (Harp)
Suites (Harp)
Variations (Harp)
Waltzes (Harp)
— **Bibliography**
[ML128.H3]
— — **Graded lists**
[ML132.H3]
UF Harp music—Graded lists
— Graded lists
USE Harp music—Bibliography—Graded lists
— **Teaching pieces**
[MT545]
BT Harp—Instruction and study
Harp music (Harps (2))
[M292-3]
NT Concertos (Harps (2))
Concertos (Harps (2) with string orchestra)
Harps (2) with orchestra
Harps (2) with string orchestra
Sonatas (Harps (2))
Suites (Harps (2))
Harp music (Harps (2)), Arranged
[M292-3]
Harp music (Harps (3))
USE Trios (Harps (3))
Harp music (Harps (4))
USE Quartets (Harps (4))
Harp music (Harps (5))
USE Quintets (Harps (5))
Harp music (Jazz)
[M115-M119]
Harp seal
UF Phoca groenlandica
BT Seals (Animals)
Harp, violin, violoncello with orchestra
[M1040-1041]
BT Trios (Harp, violin, violoncello)
RT Concertos (Harp, violin, violoncello)
— Scores
[M1040]
Harp with band
[M1205-1206]
RT Concertos (Harp with band)
— Solo with piano
[M1206]
BT Harp and piano music, Arranged
Harp with brass ensemble
RT Concertos (Harp with brass ensemble)
NT Variations (Harp with brass ensemble)

Harp with chamber orchestra
[M1036-7]
RT Concertos (Harp with chamber orchestra)
NT Suites (Harp with chamber orchestra)
Variations (Harp with chamber orchestra)
Harp with chamber orchestra, Arranged
[M1036-7]
— Scores
[M1036]
Harp with instrumental ensemble
RT Concertos (Harp with instrumental ensemble)
Harp with orchestra
[M1036-7]
RT Concertos (Harp)
NT Suites (Harp with orchestra)
Symphonies (Harp with orchestra)
Variations (Harp with orchestra)
— Solo with piano
[M1037]
BT Harp and piano music, Arranged
Harp with string orchestra
[M1105-6]
RT Concertos (Harp with string orchestra)
NT Chaconnes (Harp with string orchestra)
— Solo with piano
[M1106]
BT Harp and piano music, Arranged
Harp with string orchestra, Arranged
[M1105-6]
— Scores
Harp zither
[ML1015.H (History)]
[MT634.H37 (Instruction)]
UF MacArthur harp
BT Harp
Zither
Harpacticoida
[QL444.C74]
BT Crustacea
NT Tisbidae
Harpadon
[QL638.H3]
UF Harpodon
BT Harpadontidae
Harpadon nehereus
USE Bombay duck (Fish)
Harpadontidae
[QL638.H3]
UF Harpodontidae
BT Myctophiformes
NT Harpadon
Harpagiferidae
[QL638.H28]
BT Perciformes
NT Pogonophryne
Harpalidae
USE Carabidae
Harpalus
[QL596.C2]
BT Carabidae
Harpar family
USE Harper family
Harper family *(Not Subd Geog)*
UF Harpar family
Harpir family
Harpur family
Harpers Ferry (W. Va.)
— **History**
— — **John Brown's Raid, 1859**
[E451]
UF Harpers Ferry Raid, Harpers Ferry, W. Va., 1859
John Brown's Raid, Harpers Ferry, W. Va., 1859

Harpers Ferry National Historical Park
    BT Historic sites—Maryland
        Historic sites—Virginia
        Historic sites—West Virginia
        National parks and reserves—United
          States
        Parks—Maryland
        Parks—Virginia
        Parks—West Virginia
Harpers Ferry Raid, Harpers Ferry, W. Va.,
    1859
    USE Harpers Ferry (W. Va.)—History—
          John Brown's Raid, 1859
Harpham family *(Not Subd Geog)*
Harpir family
    USE Harper family
Harpists *(May Subd Geog)*
    ⌐*ML399 (Biography: collective)*⌐
    ⌐*ML419 (individual)*⌐
Harpodon
    USE Harpadon
Harpodon nehereus
    USE Bombay duck (Fish)
Harpodontidae
    USE Harpadontidae
Harpoons
    ⌐*GN447.H29 (Primitive)*⌐
    ⌐*SH387*⌐
    BT Fishing, Primitive
        Indians of North America—
          Implements
    NT Harpoons, Prehistoric
Harpoons, Prehistoric *(May Subd Geog)*
    UF Prehistoric harpoons
    BT Harpoons
        Man, Prehistoric—Tools
Harps (2), percussion with string orchestra
    ⌐*M1140-1141*⌐
    BT Sextets (Harps (2), percussion)
    RT Concertos (Harps (2), percussion with
          string orchestra)
Harps (2) with chamber orchestra
    ⌐*M1036-1037*⌐
    RT Concertos (Harps (2) with chamber
          orchestra)
Harps (2) with orchestra
    ⌐*M1036-7*⌐
    BT Harp music (Harps (2))
    RT Concertos (Harps (2))
Harps (2) with string ensemble
    RT Concertos (Harps (2) with string
          ensemble)
Harps (2) with string orchestra
    ⌐*M1105-6*⌐
    BT Harp music (Harps (2))
    RT Concertos (Harps (2) with string
          orchestra)
    NT Suites (Harps (2) with string orchestra)
Harps (4) with string orchestra
    ⌐*M1136-1137*⌐
    BT Quartets (Harps (4))
    RT Concertos (Harps (4) with string
          orchestra)
    NT Suites (Harps (4) with string orchestra)
Harpsichord
    ⌐*ML650-ML697 (History and*
      construction)⌐
    UF Cembalo
        Clavecin
        Clavicembalo
        Spinet
        Virginal
    RT Piano
    NT Claviorganum
        Keyboards
Harpsichord, Electronic
    USE Electronic harpsichord
Harpsichord and bassoon music
    USE Bassoon and harpsichord music
Harpsichord and celesta music
    USE Celesta and harpsichord music

Harpsichord and clarinet music
    USE Clarinet and harpsichord music
Harpsichord and double-bass music
    USE Double-bass and harpsichord music
Harpsichord and English horn music
    USE English horn and harpsichord music
Harpsichord and flute music
    USE Flute and harpsichord music
Harpsichord and glockenspiel music
    USE Glockenspiel and harpsichord music
Harpsichord and guitar music
    USE Guitar and harpsichord music
Harpsichord and harmonica music
    USE Harmonica and harpsichord music
Harpsichord and harp music
    USE Harp and harpsichord music
Harpsichord and lute music
    USE Lute and harpsichord music
Harpsichord and mandolin music
    USE Mandolin and harpsichord music
Harpsichord and oboe d'amore music
    USE Oboe d'amore and harpsichord music
Harpsichord and oboe music
    USE Oboe and harpsichord music
Harpsichord and organ music
    ⌐*M182-4*⌐
    UF Organ and harpsichord music
    NT Passacaglias (Harpsichord and organ)
        Sonatas (Harpsichord and organ)
Harpsichord and organ music, Arranged
    ⌐*M185-6*⌐
Harpsichord and organ with chamber
** orchestra**
    ⌐*M1040-1041*⌐
    RT Concertos (Harpsichord and organ
          with chamber orchestra)
Harpsichord and percussion music
    USE Percussion and harpsichord music
Harpsichord and piano music
    ⌐*M214*⌐
    UF Piano and harpsichord music
    NT Concertos (Harpsichord and piano)
        Concertos (Harpsichord and piano
          with dance orchestra)
        Harpsichord and piano with dance
          orchestra
        Harpsichord and piano with orchestra
        Harpsichord and piano with wind
          ensemble
Harpsichord and piano music, Arranged
    ⌐*M215*⌐
    NT Concertos (Harpsichord)—Solo with
          piano
        Concertos (Harpsichord with chamber
          orchestra)—Solo with piano
        Concertos (Harpsichord with
          instrumental ensemble)—Solo with
          piano
        Concertos (Harpsichord with string
          orchestra)—Solo with piano
        Variations (Harpsichord with string
          orchestra)—2-piano scores
Harpsichord and piano with dance orchestra
    ⌐*M1353*⌐
    BT Harpsichord and piano music
    RT Concertos (Harpsichord and piano
          with dance orchestra)
Harpsichord and piano with orchestra
    ⌐*M1010-1011*⌐
    BT Harpsichord and piano music
    RT Concertos (Harpsichord and piano)
Harpsichord and piano with wind ensemble
    ⌐*M915-917*⌐
    BT Harpsichord and piano music
    RT Concertos (Harpsichord and piano
          with wind ensemble)
    NT Wind ensembles
Harpsichord and piccolo music
    USE Piccolo and harpsichord music
Harpsichord and recorder music
    USE Recorder and harpsichord music

Harpsichord and trumpet music
    USE Trumpet and harpsichord music
Harpsichord and viola da gamba music
    USE Viola da gamba and harpsichord music
Harpsichord and viola d'amore music
    USE Viola d'amore and harpsichord music
Harpsichord and viola music
    USE Viola and harpsichord music
Harpsichord and viola pomposa music
    USE Viola pomposa and harpsichord music
Harpsichord and violin music
    USE Violin and harpsichord music
Harpsichord and violoncello music
    USE Violoncello and harpsichord music
Harpsichord and violone music
    USE Violone and harpsichord music
Harpsichord duets
    USE Harpsichord music (4 hands)
        Harpsichord music (Harpsichords (2))
Harpsichord, flute, harp with string orchestra
    ⌐*M1105-6*⌐
    BT Trios (Harpsichord, flute, harp)
    RT Concertos (Harpsichord, flute, harp
          with string orchestra)
    NT Suites (Harpsichord, flute, harp with
          string orchestra)
Harpsichord, flute, oboe with string orchestra
    ⌐*M1105-6*⌐
    BT Trios (Harpsichord, flute, oboe)
    RT Concertos (Harpsichord, flute, oboe
          with string orchestra)
    NT Suites (Harpsichord, flute, oboe with
          string orchestra)
  — Scores
    ⌐*M1105-6*⌐
Harpsichord, flute, violin with string orchestra
    ⌐*M1105-6*⌐
    BT String-orchestra music
        Trios (Harpsichord, flute, violin)
    RT Concertos (Harpsichord, flute, violin
          with string orchestra)
Harpsichord, flutes (2) with string orchestra
    ⌐*M1105-6*⌐
    UF Two flutes, harpsichord with string
          orchestra
    BT String-orchestra music
        Trios (Harpsichord, flutes (2))
    RT Concertos (Harpsichord, flutes (2) with
          string orchestra)
Harpsichord, guitars (2), harp, double bass
** with orchestra**
    ⌐*M1040-1041*⌐
    BT Quintets (Harpsichord, guitars (2),
          harp, double bass)
    RT Concertos (Harpsichord, guitars (2),
          harp, double bass)
Harpsichord makers *(May Subd Geog)*
    BT Musical instrument makers
Harpsichord music
    ⌐*M20-39*⌐
    UF Virginal music
    BT Keyboard instrument music
        Piano music
    SA Concertos, Minuets, Sonatas, Suites,
        and similar headings with
        specification of instruments; Trios
        ⌐Quartets, etc.⌐ *followed by*
        specifications which include the
        harpsichord; also headings that
        begin with the words harpsichord or
        harpsichords
    NT Canons, fugues, etc. (Harpsichord)
        Chaconnes (Harpsichord)
        Chorale preludes (Harpsichord)
        Claviorganum music
        Minuets (Harpsichord)
        Polonaises (Harpsichord)
        Rondos (Harpsichord)
        Sonatas (Harpsichord)
        Suites (Harpsichord)
        Thorough bass—Realizations

Variations (Harpsichord)
— **Instructive editions**
   [MT245-7]
   BT Piano music—Instructive editions
Harpsichord music, Arranged
   NT Chaconnes (Harpsichord), Arranged
      Overtures arranged for harpsichord
Harpsichord music, Arranged (Jazz)
   USE Harpsichord music (Jazz)
Harpsichord music (4 hands)
   [M200-M204]
   [M207-M212]
   UF Harpsichord duets
Harpsichord music (Harpsichords (2))
   [M214-215]
   UF Harpsichord duets
   NT Canons, fugues, etc. (Harpsichords (2))
      Concertos (Harpsichords (2))
      Concertos (Harpsichords (2) with
         string orchestra)
      Harpsichords (2) with orchestra
      Harpsichords (2) with string orchestra
      Sonatas (Harpsichords (2))
      Suites (Harpsichords (2))
Harpsichord music (Harpsichords (2)),
   Arranged
   [M215]
   NT Concertos (Harpsichord)—2-
      harpsichord scores
Harpsichord music (Harpsichords (3))
   [M216]
   UF Harpsichord trios (Harpsichords (3))
   NT Concertos (Harpsichords (3) with
         string orchestra)
      Harpsichords (3) with string orchestra
Harpsichord music (Harpsichords (4))
   [M216]
   UF Harpsichord quartets (Harpsichords
         (4))
   NT Concertos (Harpsichords (4))
      Concertos (Harpsichords (4) with
         string orchestra)
      Harpsichords (4) with orchestra
      Harpsichords (4) with string orchestra
      Variations (Harpsichords (4))
Harpsichord music (Jazz)
   [M20-32]
   UF Harpsichord music, Arranged (Jazz)
Harpsichord, piano, harp with string orchestra
   [M1140-1141]
   BT Trios (Harpsichord, piano, harp)
   RT Concertos (Harpsichord, piano, harp
         with string orchestra)
Harpsichord, piano, violin with orchestra
   [M1040-1041]
   BT Trios (Harpsichord, piano, violin)
   RT Concertos (Harpsichord, piano, violin)
Harpsichord players
   USE Harpsichordists
Harpsichord quartets (Harpsichords (4))
   USE Harpsichord music (Harpsichords (4))
Harpsichord realizations of thorough bass
   USE Thorough bass—Realizations
Harpsichord trios (Harpsichords (3))
   USE Harpsichord music (Harpsichords (3))
Harpsichord, violin, violoncello with string
   orchestra
   [M1140-1141]
   BT Trios (Harpsichord, violin, violoncello)
   RT Concertos (Harpsichord, violin,
         violoncello with string orchestra)
Harpsichord, violins (2), violoncello with
   orchestra
   [M1040-M1041]
   BT Quartets (Harpsichord, violins (2),
         violoncello)
   NT Concertos (Harpsichord, violins (2),
         violoncello)
Harpsichord with chamber orchestra
   [M1010-1011]

   RT Concertos (Harpsichord with chamber
         orchestra)
Harpsichord with instrumental ensemble
   BT Concertos (Harpsichord with chamber
         orhcestra)
   NT Concertos (Harpsichord with chamber
         orchestra)
Harpsichord with orchestra
   [M1010-1011]
   BT Orchestral music
   RT Concertos (Harpsichord)
Harpsichord with percussion ensemble
Harpsichord with string ensemble
   [M910-912]
   BT String ensembles
   RT Concertos (Harpsichord with string
         ensemble)
Harpsichord with string orchestra
   [M1105-6]
   RT Concertos (Harpsichord with string
         orchestra)
   NT Variations (Harpsichord with string
         orchestra)
   — **Scores**
      [M1105]
Harpsichordists *(May Subd Geog)*
   UF Harpsichord players
   BT Musicians
Harpsichords (2) with orchestra
   [M1010-1011]
   UF Two harpsichords with orchestra
   BT Harpsichord music (Harpsichords (2))
   RT Concertos (Harpsichords (2))
Harpsichords (2) with string orchestra
   [M1105-6]
   UF Two harpsichords with string orchestra
   BT Harpsichord music (Harpsichords (2))
   RT Concertos (Harpsichords (2) with
         string orchestra)
Harpsichords (3) with string orchestra
   [M1105-6]
   UF Three harpsichords with string
         orchestra
   BT Harpsichord music (Harpsichords (3))
   RT Concertos (Harpsichords (3) with
         string orchestra)
Harpsichords (4) with orchestra
   [M1010-1011]
   UF Four harpsichords with orchestra
   BT Harpsichord music (Harpsichords (4))
   RT Concertos (Harpsichords (4))
Harpsichords (4) with string orchestra
   [M1105-6]
   UF Four harpsichords with string
         orchestra
   BT Harpsichord music (Harpsichords (4))
   RT Concertos (Harpsichords (4) with
         string orchestra)
Harpur family
   USE Harper family
Harpuridae
   USE Surgeonfishes
Harpyionycteris
   [QL737.C575]
   BT Pteropodidae
Harrad family
   USE Harrell family
Harrah family
   USE O'Hara family
Harral family
   USE Harrell family
Harrall family
   USE Harrell family
Harrallson family
   USE Harrell family
Harralson family
   USE Harrell family
Harranians
   [BL1635]
   UF Sabians

Harrarjie language
   USE Harari language
Harras family
   USE Harris family
Harrel family
   USE Harrell family
Harrell family *(Not Subd Geog)*
   UF Haral family
      Harald family
      Haraldson family
      Harel family
      Harelson family
      Harilson family
      Harold family
      Haroldson family
      Harrad family
      Harral family
      Harrall family
      Harrallson family
      Harralson family
      Harrel family
      Harrelson family
      Harrillson family
      Harrod family
      Harrol family
      Harry family
   RT Henry family
Harrelson family
   USE Harrell family
Harreson family
   USE Harrison family
Harriehausen family
   USE Harjehausen family
Harrier (Jet fighter plane)
   BT Fighter planes
      Jet planes
      Short take-off and landing aircraft
      Vertically rising aircraft
Harriers
   [QL696.F32]
   UF Circinae
      Circus (Birds)
   BT Accipitridae
   NT Circus cyaneas
Harries family
   USE Harris family
Harrillson family
   USE Harrell family
Harriman, Edward Henry, 1848-1909
   — **Homes and haunts**
   — — **New York (State)**
         NT Arden House (Harriman, N.Y.)
Harriman family *(Not Subd Geog)*
Harriman State Park (N.Y.)
   BT Parks—New York (State)
Harrin family
   USE Herring family
Harring family
   USE Herring family
Harringehusen family
   USE Harjehausen family
Harrington family *(Not Subd Geog)*
   UF Harington family
      Haryngton family
      Hearington family
      Herington family
      Herrington family
   RT Herring family
Harrington Sound (Bermuda Islands)
   BT Lagoons—Bermuda Islands
      Sounds (Geomorphology)—Bermuda
         Islands
Harris, Joel Chandler, 1848-1908
   (Not Subd Geog)
   — **Characters**
   — — **Uncle Remus**
         RT Remus, Uncle (Fictitious
               character)

Harris family *(Not Subd Geog)*
  UF Haris family
      Hariss family
      Harras family
      Harries family
      Harriss family
      Harrisse family
Harris Island (Scotland)
  USE Lewis with Harris Island (Scotland)
Harrisburg Insurrection, 1838
  USE Buckshot War, 1838
Harrisburg Seven (Trial)
  [KF224.H27]
Harrisen family
  USE Harrison family
Harrisina
  [QL561.Z9]
  BT Zygaenidae
Harrisina brillians
  USE Western grape-leaf skeletonizer
Harrison, Fort, Battle of, 1812
  [E356.H3]
  BT Indians of North America—Wars—
      1812-1815
      United States—History—War of 1812
      —Campaigns
Harrison, Fort, Capture of, 1864
  [E477.21]
  BT United States—History—Civil War,
      1861-1865—Campaigns
Harrison family *(Not Subd Geog)*
  UF Hareson family
      Harison family
      Harisson family
      Harreson family
      Harrisen family
      Harrisson family
      Herison family
      Herrison family
Harrisonville, N.J. (Imaginary place)
  BT Geographical myths
Harriss family
  USE Harris family
Harrisse family
  USE Harris family
Harrisson family
  USE Harrison family
Harrod family
  USE Harrell family
Harrol family
  USE Harrell family
Harrower psychodiagnostic inkblot test
  [BF698.8.H35]
  UF Inkblot test, Harrower
      psychodiagnostic
  BT Personality tests
      Projective techniques
      Rorschach test
Harrows
  [TJ1482 (Mechanical engineering and
  machinery)]
  BT Agricultural machinery
Harry family
  USE Harrell family
Harry S. Truman Dam (Mo.)
  (Not Subd Geog)
  BT Dams—Missouri
Harry S. Truman Reservoir (Mo.)
  (Not Subd Geog)
  UF Truman Lake (Mo.)
  BT Lakes—Missouri
      Reservoirs—Missouri
Harsey family
  USE Hersey family
Harshbarger family *(Not Subd Geog)*
  UF Harshberger family
      Hirschberg family
      Hirschberger family
Harshberger family
  USE Harshbarger family

Harshey family
  USE Hershey family
Harshy family
  USE Hershey family
Harsit River (Turkey) *(Not Subd Geog)*
  BT Rivers—Turkey
Harstad family *(Not Subd Geog)*
Ḥarsūsī language
  [PJ7141-7144]
  BT Mahri language
      South Arabic language
Hart family *(Not Subd Geog)*
  UF Harte family
      Harts family
      Hartt family
      Heart family
  RT Dehart family
      Hard family
      Herzog family
Harte family
  USE Hart family
Hartebeest, Lichtenstein's
  USE Lichtenstein's hartebeest
Hartebeest, Red
  USE Red hartebeest
Hartebeests
  [QL737.U53]
  BT Bovidae
  NT Alcelaphus
      Lichtenstein's hartebeest
      Red hartebeest
Hartford & Springfield Street Railway
  BT Street-railroads—United States
Hartford Cemetery (Kan.)
  BT Cemeteries—Kansas
Hartge family *(Not Subd Geog)*
  UF Hartje family
Harthope Burn (England)
  BT Rivers—England
Harthorn family
  USE Hawthorne family
Harting family
  USE Harding family
Hartinger family
  USE Hardinger family
Hartje family
  USE Hartge family
Hartley family *(Not Subd Geog)*
  UF Hartly family
      Heartley family
      Heartly family
  RT Harley family
Hartley transforms
  UF Transforms, Hartley
  BT Transformations (Mathematics)
Hartly family
  USE Hartley family
Hartman family *(Not Subd Geog)*
  UF Hartmann family
      Heartman family
Hartmann family
  USE Hartman family
Hartmannellidae
  [QL368.A5]
  BT Amoebida
  NT Saccamoeba
Hartney family
  USE Harney family
Hartree approximation
  USE Hartree-Fock approximation
Hartree-Fock approximation
  [QC176.8.E4]
  UF Hartree approximation
      Hartree-Fock-Slater approximation
  BT Approximation theory
      Atoms
      Energy-band theory of solids
      Many-body problem
      Self-consistent field theory
  NT Pairing correlations (Nuclear physics)

Hartree-Fock-Slater approximation
  USE Hartree-Fock approximation
Hartree units
  USE Atomic units
Harts family
  USE Hart family
Hartsdale Canine Cemetery (Hartsdale, N.Y.)
  BT Pet cemeteries—New York (State)
Hartsel family
  USE Hartzell family
Hartsell family
  USE Hartzell family
Härtsfeldbahn
  BT Railroads—Germany (West)
Hartsoe family
  USE Herzog family
Hartt family
  USE Hart family
Hartting family
  USE Harding family
Harttung family
  USE Harding family
Hartung family
  USE Harding family
Hartwell Lake (S.C. and Ga.)
  BT Lakes—Georgia
      Lakes—South Carolina
      Reservoirs—Georgia
      Reservoirs—South Carolina
      Savannah River (Ga. and S.C.)
Hartz Mountains (Germany)
  USE Harz Mountains (Germany)
Hartzel family
  USE Hartzell family
Hartzell family *(Not Subd Geog)*
  UF Hartsel family
      Hartsell family
      Hartzel family
      Hartzil family
      Hertsel family
      Hertzel family
      Herzel family
      Hirtzel family
      Hirzel family
Hartziella
  [QE983]
  BT Onagraceae, Fossil
  NT Hartziella rosenkjaeri
Hartziella rosenkjaeri
  UF Carpolithes rosenkjaeri
  BT Hartziella
Hartzil family
  USE Hartzell family
Haru Island (Micronesia)
  USE Moen Island (Micronesia)
Haru Kofun (Yoshii-machi, Fukuoka-ken,
  Japan)
  USE Haru Site (Yoshii-machi, Fukuoka-ken,
      Japan)
Haru Site (Yoshii-machi, Fukuoka-ken, Japan)
  UF Haru Kofun (Yoshii-machi, Fukuoka-
      ken, Japan)
  BT Japan—Antiquities
Harvard (Training planes)
  USE T-6 (Training planes)
Harvard Chiapas Project
  UF Chiapas Project
      Harvard University Chiapas Project
  BT Indians of Mexico—Chiapas
      Tzeltal Indians
      Tzotzil Indians
Harvard Forest (Mass. : Forest)
  BT Forest reserves—Massachusetts
      Forests and forestry—Massachusetts—
      Experimental areas
Harvard Mark I (Calculator)
  USE Mark I (Calculator)
Harvard University
  — Accounting
  — Administration
  — Admission

Hasamiyama Site (Fujiidera-shi, Japan)
(Not Subd Geog)
   UF Hasamiyama Iseki (Fujiidera-shi,
         Japan)
   BT Japan—Antiquities
Hasang Incident, 1938
   USE Changkufeng Incident, 1938
Hasashima Iseki (Sakaide-shi, Japan)
   USE Hasashima Site (Sakaide-shi, Japan)
Hasashima Site (Sakaide-shi, Japan)
   UF Hasashima Iseki (Sakaide-shi, Japan)
   BT Japan—Antiquities
Hasbrauck family
   USE Hasbrouck family
Hasbrook family
   USE Hasbrouck family
Hasbrouck family (Not Subd Geog)
   UF D'Hazebrouck family
         Haesbreucq family
         Hasbrauck family
         Hasbrook family
         Hasebrock family
         Hassebrouk family
         Hazebreucq family
         Hazebrouck family
         Van Hazebrouck family
         Von Asbroeck family
Hascherkeller Site (Germany)
(Not Subd Geog)
   BT Germany (West)—Antiquities
Hase family
   USE Haas family
Hasebrock family
   USE Hasbrouck family
Hasegawa family (Not Subd Geog)
Hasel family
   USE Hasell family
Hasell family (Not Subd Geog)
   UF Hasel family
         Hassel family
         Hassell family
         Hazel family
         Hazell family
         Hazle family
Haselwood family
   USE Hazelwood family
Haselwoode family
   USE Hazelwood family
Hash coding (Computer science)
   USE Hashing (Computer science)
Hash family (Not Subd Geog)
   RT Ash family
Hashab tree
   USE Acacia senegal
Hasheesh
   USE Hashish
Hashemite Kingdom, 1921-1958
   USE Iraq—History—Hashemite Kingdom,
         1921-1958
Hashemites
   USE Hashimites
Hashim family (Not Subd Geog)
   UF Hasim family
Hashimites
   UF Banū Hāshim
         Hashemites
   BT Arabs
Hashing (Computer science)
   [QA76.9.H36]
   UF Hash coding (Computer science)
   BT File organization (Computer science)
Hashirae
   USE Ukiyoe
Hashish
   [RC568.C2 (Intoxications)]
   [RS165.H3 (Materia medica)]
   UF Dagga
         Hasheesh
         Hemp, Indian
   BT Cannabis
         Narcotics

— **Psychological aspects**
   [BF209.H3]
   BT Psychopharmacology
Hashizu family (Not Subd Geog)
Hashknife Ranch (Ariz.)
   BT Ranches—Arizona
Ḥashwīya
   BT Islamic sects
Ḥaside umot ha-'olam
   USE Righteous Gentiles
Ḥasidei ummot ha-olam
   USE Righteous Gentiles
Hasidic legends
   USE Hasidim—Legends
Hasidic parables
   USE Parables, Hasidic
Hasidic rite
   USE Judaism—Hasidic rite
Hasidim (May Subd Geog)
   UF Chasidim
         Hassidim
   BT Hasidism
         Jews
— **Biography**
   UF Hasidism—Biography
— **Legends**
   UF Hasidic legends
         Legends, Hasidic
         Tales, Hasidic
   BT Legends, Jewish
Hasidism (May Subd Geog)
   [BM198]
   UF Chasidism
         Hassidism
   BT Jewish sects
         Mysticism—Judaism
   NT Belz Hasidim
         Bratslav Hasidim
         Habad
         Hasidim
         Judaism—Hasidic rite
         Parables, Hasidic
         Satmar Hasidim
         Zaddikim
— **Apologetic works**
— **Biography**
   USE Hasidim—Biography
— **Philosophy**
   BT Philosophy, Jewish
Hasidism, Medieval
   BT Judaism—Germany
Hasim family
   USE Hashim family
Hasinai Indians
   BT Caddo Indians
         Indians of North America
— **Antiquities**
Haskal family
   USE Haskell family
Haskalah (May Subd Geog)
   BT Enlightenment
         Judaism
         Liberalism (Religion)
         Reform Judaism
Haskall family
   USE Haskell family
Haskamah
   USE Approbations (Hebrew literature)
Haskel family
   USE Haskell family
Haskell family (Not Subd Geog)
   UF Haskal family
         Haskall family
         Haskel family
         Haskill family
         Haskill family
Haskil family
   USE Haskell family
Haskill family
   USE Haskell family

Haskin family
   USE Haskins family
Haskings family
   USE Haskins family
Haskins family (Not Subd Geog)
   UF Haskin family
         Haskings family
         Hasskins family
   RT Hoskins family
Hasle family (Not Subd Geog)
Hasle Valley (Switzerland)
   USE Haslital (Switzerland)
Haslegrave family
   USE Hesselgrave family
Hasler family
   USE Hassler family
Hasletal (Switzerland)
   USE Haslital (Switzerland)
Haslewood family
   USE Hazelwood family
Hasli Valley (Switzerland)
   USE Haslital (Switzerland)
Hasliberg (Switzerland)
   BT Plateaus—Switzerland
Haslip family
   USE Haislip family
Haslital (Switzerland)
   UF Hasle Valley (Switzerland)
         Hasletal (Switzerland)
         Hasli Valley (Switzerland)
   BT Valleys—Switzerland
Haslop family
   USE Haislip family
Haslope family
   USE Haislip family
Haslup family
   USE Haislip family
Hasmonaeans
   USE Maccabees
Hassebrouk family
   USE Hasbrouck family
Hassel family
   USE Hasell family
Hasselbalch family (Not Subd Geog)
Hasselblad camera
Hassell family
   USE Hasell family
Hasseltse Virga Jesse (Sculpture)
   USE Virga Jesse (Sculpture)
Hassidim
   USE Hasidim
Hassidism
   USE Hasidism
Hasskama
   USE Approbations (Hebrew literature)
Hasskins family
   USE Haskins family
Hassler family (Not Subd Geog)
   UF Hasler family
   RT Hosler family
         Hostler family
Hasta (Unit of measure)
   USE Cubit
Hastain family
   USE Hastings family
Hasteens family
   USE Hastings family
Hasten family
   USE Hastings family
Hastey family
   USE Hasty family
Hasti family (Not Subd Geog)
   RT Hasty family
Hastie family
   USE Hasty family
Hastin family
   USE Hastings family
Hasting family
   USE Hastings family
Hastings, Battle of, 1066
   [DA196]

BT Great Britain—History—William I,
1066-1087
Hastings embroidery
Hastings family *(Not Subd Geog)*
UF Haisten family
Haiston family
Hastain family
Hasteens family
Hasten family
Hastin family
Hasting family
Hastins family
Haston family
Hastons family
Hystings family
Hastins family
USE Hastings family
Haston family
USE Hastings family
Hastons family
USE Hastings family
Hasty family *(Not Subd Geog)*
UF Hastey family
Hastie family
RT Hasti family
Hasumi family *(Not Subd Geog)*
Hat trade *(May Subd Geog)*
[HD9948]
NT Trade-unions—Hat trade
Wages—Hat trade
Hatamoto *(May Subd Geog)*
[DS827.H37]
BT Daimyo
Samurai
Hatboxes *(May Subd Geog)*
BT Boxes
Hats
RT Bandboxes
Hatch covers
BT Ships—Equipment and supplies
Hatch davits
USE Davits
Hatch family *(Not Subd Geog)*
Hatchability of eggs
USE Eggs—Hatchability
Hatchazawa Iseki (Rokkasho-mura, Japan)
USE Hatchazawa Site (Rokkasho-mura,
Japan)
Hatchazawa Site (Rokkasho-mura, Japan)
(Not Subd Geog)
UF Hatchazawa Iseki (Rokkasho-mura,
Japan)
BT Japan—Antiquities
Hatchee River (Miss. and Tenn.)
USE Hatchie River (Miss. and Tenn.)
Hatcher family *(Not Subd Geog)*
UF Hetcher family
Hatcheries, Chicken
USE Chickens—Hatcheries
Hatcheries, Fish
USE Fish hatcheries
Hatcheries, Poultry
USE Poultry—Hatcheries
Hatcheries, Turkey
USE Turkeys—Hatcheries
Hatchery vs. wild stocks of fish
USE Fishery resources—Hatchery vs. wild
stocks
Hatchetfishes, Marine
USE Sternoptychidae
Hatchettin
[QE391.H]
Hatchie River (Miss. and Tenn.)
UF Big Hatchie River (Miss. and Tenn.)
Hatchee River (Miss. and Tenn.)
BT Rivers—Mississippi
Rivers—Tennessee
Hatching of eggs
USE Eggs—Incubation
Hatchments
BT Heraldry

RT Achievements (Heraldry)
Hatcliff family *(Not Subd Geog)*
UF Hatcliffe family
Hatclyffe family
Hateclyf family
Hatteclyf family
Hatcliffe family
USE Hatcliff family
Hatclyffe family
USE Hatcliff family
Hate
[BF575.H]
UF Hatred
BT Emotions
NT Misanthropy
Self-hate (Psychology)
Hate letters
USE Hate mail
Hate mail
[PN6140.H38]
UF Hate letters
Mail, Hate
BT Invective
Letters
RT Anonymous letters
Hateclyf family
USE Hatcliff family
Hatfeild Chase (England)
USE Hatfield Chase (England)
Hatfield Chase (England)
UF Hatfeild Chase (England)
BT Polders—England
Hatfield family *(Not Subd Geog)*
UF Hotfield family
NT Hatfield-McCoy Feud
Hatfield House (Hertfordshire)
BT Manors—England
Hatfield, Luton and Dunstable Railway
BT Railroads—Great Britain
Hatfield-McCoy Feud
UF McCoy-Hatfield Feud
BT Hatfield family
McCoy family
Vendetta—Kentucky
Vendetta—West Virginia
Hath (Unit of measure)
USE Cubit
Haṭha yoga
USE Yoga, Haṭha
Hathaway family *(Not Subd Geog)*
UF Hatheway family
Hathway family
Hathwey family
Hathcock family *(Not Subd Geog)*
UF Haithcock family
Heathcock family
Hatheway family
USE Hathaway family
Hathorn family
USE Hawthorne family
Hathorne family
USE Hawthorne family
Hathway family
USE Hathaway family
Hathwey family
USE Hathaway family
Hatigoria (Indic people)
USE Ao (Indic people)
Hatigorria language
USE Ao language
Hatikva Neighbourhood (Tel Aviv, Israel)
USE Shekhunat-ha-Tiḳyah (Tel Aviv, Israel)
Hatikva Quarter (Tel Aviv, Israel)
USE Shekhunat-ha-Tiḳyah (Tel Aviv, Israel)
Hatmacher family
USE Hatmaker family
Hatmacker family
USE Hatmaker family

Hatmaker family *(Not Subd Geog)*
UF Hatmacher family
Hatmacker family
Heutmacher family
Huthmacher family
Hutmacher family
Hatnen-nesut (Ancient city)
USE Heracleopolis Magna (Ancient city)
Haton family
USE Hatton family
Hatpin holders *(May Subd Geog)*
BT Hatpins
Hatpins *(May Subd Geog)*
[NK7695]
BT Jewelry
Pins and needles
NT Hatpin holders
Hatred
USE Hate
Hats *(May Subd Geog)*
[GT2110 (Manners and customs)]
[TS2180-TS2193 (Manufacture)]
BT Clothing and dress
Head-gear
RT Millinery
NT Hatboxes
Hatter's fur
Safety hats
Straw industries
Hatsang Incident, 1938
USE Changkufeng Incident, 1938
Hatsukarijō (Kawagoe-shi, Japan)
USE Kawagoejō (Kawagoe-shi, Japan)
Hatt family *(Not Subd Geog)*
UF Hott family
RT Hutt family
Hatta family *(Not Subd Geog)*
Hattah Lakes National Park (Vic.)
BT National parks and reserves—Australia
Hattan family
USE Hatton family
Hattanda kofun (Sera-chō, Japan)
USE Hattanda Site (Sera-chō, Japan)
Hattanda Site (Sera-chō, Japan)
(Not Subd Geog)
UF Hattanda kofun (Sera-chō, Japan)
BT Japan—Antiquities
Hatteclyf family
USE Hatcliff family
Hatten family
USE Hatton family
Hatteras, Cape (N.C.)
UF Cape Hatteras (N.C.)
BT Capes (Coasts)—North Carolina
Hatteras Indians
USE Lumbee Indians
Hatters *(May Subd Geog)*
NT Trade-unions—Hat trade
Hatter's fur
UF Hatter's plush
BT Felt
Fur
Hats
Hatter's plush
USE Hatter's fur
Hattic language
UF Khattili language
Khattish language
BT Anatolian languages
Hattin family
USE Hatton family
Hatton family *(Not Subd Geog)*
UF Haton family
Hattan family
Hatten family
Hattin family
RT Hutton family
Hatton Garden (London, England)
BT Streets—England

Hattori family (Not Subd Geog)
Hattstein family (Not Subd Geog)
Hatzfeldt family (Not Subd Geog)
Haubargs family
  USE Hauberg family
Hauberg family (Not Subd Geog)
  UF Haubargs family
Hauer family
  USE Hower family
Hauert family
  USE Hower family
Haug family (Not Subd Geog)
  UF Hauge family
      Haugen family
Haugaard family (Not Subd Geog)
Haugdahl family
  USE Hodal family
Haugdal family
  USE Hodal family
Hauge family
  USE Haug family
Haugen family
  USE Haug family
Hauger family (Not Subd Geog)
  RT Hower family
Haught family (Not Subd Geog)
  UF Haut family
      Haute family
      Hawt family
  RT Hoyt family
Haugseggen family (Not Subd Geog)
Hauhungaroa Range (N.Z.)
  BT Mountains—New Zealand
Haukes family
  USE Hawk family
Hauling, Log
  USE Log transportation
Hauling tests
  [TE450]
Haultefeuille family
  USE D'Hautefeuille family
Haunted houses
  USE Ghosts
Haunts
  USE subdivision Homes and haunts under
        classes of persons and under names
        of individual persons
Haupt Garden (Washington, D.C.)
  USE Enid A. Haupt Garden (Washington,
        D.C.)
Hauptbahnhof (Frankfurt am Main, Germany)
  UF Frankfurter Hauptbahnhof (Frankfurt
        am Main, Germany)
  BT Railroads—Germany (West)—Stations
Hauptbahnhof (Hamburg, Germany)
  BT Railroads—Germany (West)—Stations
Hauraki Gulf Maritime Park (N.Z.)
  BT Marine parks and reserves—New
        Zealand
      National parks and reserves—New
        Zealand
      Parks—New Zealand
Hauran (Syria)
  UF Hawrān (Syria)
Haurangi State Forest Park (N.Z.)
  BT Forest reserves—New Zealand
      Parks—New Zealand
Hauritz family (Not Subd Geog)
Haus am Checkpoint Charlie (Berlin,
    Germany)
  UF Checkpoint Charlie House (Berlin,
        Germany)
  BT Municipal buildings—Germany (West)
Haus Bitz (Frechen, Germany)
  UF Bitz House (Frechen, Germany)
  BT Municipal buildings—Germany (West)
Haus Dr. Nolden (Mayen, Germany)
  UF Doktor Nolden House (Mayen,
        Germany)
      Dr. Nolden House (Mayen, Germany)
      Nolden House (Mayen, Germany)

  BT Dwellings—Germany (West)
Haus family (Not Subd Geog)
  RT House family
Haus Rüschhaus (Münster in Westfalen,
    Germany)
  UF Rüsch Haus (Münster in Westfalen,
        Germany)
      Rüsch House (Münster in Westfalen,
        Germany)
      Rüschhaus (Münster in Westfalen,
        Germany)
  BT Dwellings—Germany (West)
Haus zum Kiel (Zurich, Switzerland)
  [NA7393.Z]
  UF Kiel House (Zurich, Switzerland)
  BT Dwellings—Switzerland
Haus zum Rechberg (Zurich, Switzerland)
  UF Rechberg Haus (Zurich, Switzerland)
      Zürich Rechberg Haus (Zurich,
        Switzerland)
  BT Municipal buildings—Switzerland
Hausa (African people) (May Subd Geog)
  [DT515.45.H38]
  UF Hausas
      Haussa (African people)
  BT Ethnology—Nigeria
  NT Gobir
      Mawri (African people)
— Religion
      [BL2480.H3]
  NT Bori (Cult)
Hausa (African people) pottery
  USE Pottery, Hausa (African people)
Hausa architecture
  USE Architecture, Hausa
Hausa art
  USE Art, Hausa
Hausa decoration and ornament
  USE Decoration and ornament, Hausa
Hausa drama (May Subd Geog)
  BT Hausa literature
  NT Folk-drama, Hausa
Hausa folk-drama
  USE Folk-drama, Hausa
Hausa imprints (May Subd Geog)
  [Z7108.H38]
Hausa language
  [PL8231-4]
  UF Hawsa language
  BT Chadic languages
  RT Angas language
  NT Uwana language
Hausa literature (May Subd Geog)
  [PL8233.5-8234]
  NT Hausa drama
Hausa love poetry
  USE Love poetry, Hausa
Hausa poetry (May Subd Geog)
  NT Love poetry, Hausa
Hausa women
  USE Women, Hausa
Hausas
  USE Hausa (African people)
Hausbuch (Sketch-book)
  USE Master of the Housebook, 15th cent.
      Housebook
Hausdorff compactifications
  [QA611.23]
  UF Compactifications, Hausdorff
  BT Topology
Hausdorff measures
  BT Measure theory
Hauser family (Not Subd Geog)
  UF Heuser family
  RT Houser family
Hausfrieden
  USE Hamsocn
Hausfriedensbruch
  USE Unlawful entry

Hausman family (Not Subd Geog)
  UF Haussman family
      Haussmann family
      Houseman family
      Housemon family
      Housman family
      Housmon family
Haussa (African people)
  USE Hausa (African people)
Hausse-col
  USE Gorgets
Haussman family
  USE Hausman family
Haussmann family
  USE Hausman family
Haustorium
  BT Parasitic plants
Hauswirth family (Not Subd Geog)
Haut family
  USE Haught family
Haut-Saintois (France)
Haute Alsace, Battle of, 58 B.C.
  BT Gaul—History—Gallic Wars, 58-51
        B.C.
Haute école (Horsemanship)
  (May Subd Geog)
  [SF309.57]
  UF High school (Horsemanship)
  BT Horsemanship
      Horses—Training
  RT Dressage
      Riding schools
Haute family
  USE Haught family
Haute-Sûre Nature Park (Luxembourg)
  USE Parc naturel de la Haute-Sûre
        (Luxembourg)
Hautefeuille family
  USE D'Hautefeuille family
Hautes Fagnes (Belgium and Germany)
  (Not Subd Geog)
  UF Fagnes (Belgium and Germany)
      Hoge Venen (Belgium and Germany)
      Hohe Venn (Belgium and Germany)
      Hohes Venn (Belgium and Germany)
  BT Moors and heaths—Belgium
      Moors and heaths—Germany (West)
      Mountains—Belgium
      Mountains—Germany (West)
Hauthorn family
  USE Hawthorne family
Havasu Canyon (Ariz.)
  UF Cactus Canyon (Ariz.)
  BT Canyons—Arizona
Havasupai Indians
  [E99.H3]
  UF Supai Indians
  BT Indians of North America
— Religion and mythology
Havasupai language
  [PM1311]
  BT Yuman languages
Havbo family (Not Subd Geog)
Havel Lake (Germany)
  UF Havel See (Germany)
      Havelsee (Germany)
  BT Lakes—Germany (East)
Havel See (Germany)
  USE Havel Lake (Germany)
Havelsee (Germany)
  USE Havel Lake (Germany)
Haven family (Not Subd Geog)
  UF Havens family
      Havins family
Havener family
  USE Heavener family
Havens family
  USE Haven family
Haver (The Portuguese word)
  BT Portuguese language—Etymology

Haverland family
USE Haviland family
Haverty family *(Not Subd Geog)*
Haviland china
BT Porcelain
Haviland family *(Not Subd Geog)*
UF Haverland family
Havins family
USE Haven family
Havner family
USE Heavener family
HAVOC (Information retrieval system)
[Z699.5.A9]
UF Humberside Audio Visual Catalogue
BT Audio-visual materials
Cataloging of non-book materials—
Data processing
Information storage and retrieval
systems—Audio-visual materials
Havoc bomber
USE A-20 bomber
Havsfjord, Battle of, 872
[DL464]
BT Norway—History—To 1030
Havu (African people)
[DT650.H38]
UF Bahavu (African people)
BT Ethnology—Zaire
Havunese language
USE Sawu language
Havyaka dialect *(May Subd Geog)*
UF Kannada language—Dialects—
Havyaka
BT India—Languages
Kannada language
Hawaii
NT Hawaii Island (Hawaii)
Kauai (Hawaii)
Lanai (Hawaii)
Maui (Hawaii)
Molokai (Hawaii)
Niihau (Hawaii)
Oahu (Hawaii)
— **Antiquities** *(Not Subd Geog)*
NT Keopu Burial Site (Hawaii)
— **Description and travel**
— — **To 1950**
— — **1951-1980**
— — **1981-**
— **Economic conditions**
— — **1918-1959**
— — **1959-**
— **History**
[DU620-629]
— — **To 1893**
[DU627]
— — **Revolution of 1893**
— — **1893-1900**
— — **1900-1959**
— — **1959-**
— **Juvenile literature**
— **Kings and rulers**
NT Kalakaua, House of
Kamehameha, House of
Kawananakoa, House of
— **Politics and government**
— — **To 1893**
— — **1893-1898**
— — **1900-1959**
— — **1959-**
Hawaii County (Hawaii)
USE Hawaii Island (Hawaii)
Hawaii Geothermal Project
UF Geothermal Project, Hawaii
BT Geothermal engineering
Geothermal resources—Hawaii
Renewable energy sources
Hawaii in art
Hawaii Island (Hawaii)
UF Big Island (Hawaii)
Hawaii County (Hawaii)

BT Hawaii
Islands—Hawaii
Hawaiian beet web-worm
[SB608.B4]
Hawaiian cookery
USE Cookery, Hawaiian
Hawaiian cosmogony
USE Cosmogony, Hawaiian
Hawaiian duck
[QL696.A52]
UF Anas platyrhynchos wyvilliana
Anas wyvilliana
Koloa-maoli
BT Anas
Mallard
Hawaiian funeral rites and ceremonies
USE Funeral rites and ceremonies,
Hawaiian
Hawaiian gods
USE Gods, Hawaiian
Hawaiian goose
USE Nene
Hawaiian guitar
[ML1015]
UF Guitar, Hawaiian
Guitar, Steel
Steel guitar
BT Guitar
— **Instruction and study**
[MT590]
NT Hawaiian-guitar music—Teaching
pieces
Hawaiian-guitar band
USE Plectral ensembles
Hawaiian-guitar music
[M142.H3]
BT Guitar music
NT Plectral ensembles
— **Teaching pieces**
[MT590.5]
BT Hawaiian guitar—Instruction and
study
Hawaiian honeycreepers
USE Drepanididae
Hawaiian hymns
USE Hymns, Hawaiian
Hawaiian imprints *(May Subd Geog)*
Hawaiian language
[PL6441-9]
BT Polynesian languages
— **Dictionaries**
NT Picture dictionaries, Hawaiian
Hawaiian literature *(May Subd Geog)*
BT United States—Literatures
Hawaiian monk seal
[QL737.P64]
UF Monachus schauinslandi
BT Monk seals
Hawaiian newspapers
[PN5621-PN5629]
Here are entered works on newspapers in the Ha-
waiian language. General works about newspapers
issued in the state of Hawaii are entered under
American newspapers—Hawaii.
Hawaiian picture dictionaries
USE Picture dictionaries, Hawaiian
Hawaiian poetry
Hawaiian proverbs
USE Proverbs, Hawaiian
Hawaiian rat
UF Rattus hawaiiensis
BT Rats
Rattus
Hawaiian shirts
USE Aloha shirts
Hawaiian songs
USE Songs, Hawaiian
Hawaiian wood-carving
USE Wood-carving, Hawaiian
Hawaiians *(May Subd Geog)*
UF Owyhees

BT Ethnology—Hawaii
Polynesians
— **Anthropometry**
— **Food**
— **Medicine**
BT Medicine, Primitive
— **Rites and ceremonies**
NT Funeral rites and ceremonies,
Hawaiian
Ḥawār (Bahrain)
UF Djezira Hawar (Bahrain)
Howar (Bahrain)
BT Islands—Bahrain
Haward family
USE Hayward family
Hawarde family
USE Hayward family
Hawarth family
USE Haworth family
Hawash River (Ethiopia)
USE Awash River (Ethiopia)
Hawawish Site (Egypt)
[DT73.H34]
BT Egypt—Antiquities
Hawea, Lake (N.Z.) *(Not Subd Geog)*
UF Lake Hawea (N.Z.)
BT Lakes—New Zealand
Hawel family
USE Howell family
Hawell family
USE Howell family
Hawes family
USE Hayes family
Hawfinch
[QL696.P246]
UF Coccothraustes coccothraustes
Hawk (Missile)
BT Surface-to-air missiles
Hawk automobile
USE Studebaker Hawk automobile
Hawk family *(Not Subd Geog)*
UF Haukes family
Hawke family
Hawkes family
Hawks family
Hoakes family
Hawk moths
USE Sphingidae
Hawke family
USE Hawk family
Hawken family
USE Hawkins family
Hawken rifle
BT Rifles
Hawkens family
USE Hawkins family
Hawker airplanes
[TL686.H32]
NT Buccaneer (Bomber)
Tempest (Fighter plane)
Typhoon (Fighter plane)
Hawker Hunter (Turbojet fighter planes)
USE Hunter (Turbojet fighter planes)
Hawkers and hawking
USE Peddlers and peddling
Hawkes family
USE Hawk family
Hawkes House (Salem, Mass.)
USE Benjamin Hawkes House (Salem,
Mass.)
Hawkesbury River (N.S.W.)
UF Hawksbury River (N.S.W.)
BT Rivers—Australia
Hawkesworth family *(Not Subd Geog)*
UF Hawksworth family
Hawkfishes
USE Cirrhitidae
Hawkin family
USE Hawkins family
Hawking
USE Falconry

Hawking family
  USE Hawkins family
Hawkings family
  USE Hawkins family
Hawkins family *(Not Subd Geog)*
  UF Hawken family
     Hawkens family
     Hawkin family
     Hawking family
     Hawkings family
     Hawkinson family
Hawkinson family
  USE Hawkins family
Hawkmoths
  USE Sphingidae
Hawks
  ₍QL696.A2₎
  UF Sparrow-hawks
  NT Goshawk
     Red-tailed hawk
Hawks family
  USE Hawk family
Hawks Nest Tunnel (W. Va.)
  BT Tunnels—West Virginia
Hawksbury River (N.S.W.)
  USE Hawkesbury River (N.S.W.)
Hawksworth family
  USE Hawkesworth family
Hawkwood Site (Alta.) *(Not Subd Geog)*
  BT Alberta—Antiquities
Hawl family
  USE Hall family
Hawley family *(Not Subd Geog)*
  UF Hawly family
  RT Halley family
     Holley family
Hawly family
  USE Hawley family
Hawood family
  USE Haywood family
Haworth family *(Not Subd Geog)*
  UF Hawarth family
     Hayworth family
Haworthia
  ₍QK495.L72 (Botany)₎
  ₍SB413.H38 (Ornamental plants)₎
  UF Aloe, Cushion
     Cactus, Star
     Cushion aloe
     Star cactus
     Wart plants
  BT Liliaceae
     Plants, Ornamental
Hawrān (Syria)
  USE Hauran (Syria)
Hawsa language
  USE Hausa language
Hawser family
  USE Houser family
Hawt family
  USE Haught family
Hawthorn, Chinese
  USE Chinese hawthorn
Hawthorn family
  USE Hawthorne family
Hawthorn Formation
  UF Hawthorne Formation
  BT Formations (Geology)—Florida
     Formations (Geology)—Georgia
     Formations (Geology)—South Carolina
Hawthorne, Nathaniel, 1804-1864
  — Homes and haunts
  — — Massachusetts
        NT Old Manse (Concord, Mass.)

Hawthorne family *(Not Subd Geog)*
  UF Harthorn family
     Hathorn family
     Hathorne family
     Hauthorn family
     Hawthorn family
     Haythorn family
     Haythorne family
     Heythorn family
     Heythorne family
Hawthorne Formation
  USE Hawthorn Formation
Hawthorns
  ₍QK495.R78 (Botany)₎
  UF Crataegus
  BT Rosaceae
  NT Chinese hawthorn
Hawu language
  USE Sawu language
Haxton family *(Not Subd Geog)*
  UF Haxtun family
Haxtun family
  USE Haxton family
Hay *(May Subd Geog)*
  ₍SB198₎
  BT Forage plants
  RT Grasses
  SA *names of hay crops, e.g.* Alfalfa,
     Clover
  NT Haying equipment
     Pelleted hay
     Stacks (Hay, grain, etc.)
  — Drying
     UF Grasses—Drying
  — — Equipment and supplies
        USE Haying equipment
  — Equipment and supplies
        USE Haying equipment
  — Handling
  — Harvesting
  — — Equipment and supplies
        USE Haying equipment
Hay as feed
Hay as food
  BT Food
Hay-boxes
  USE Fireless cookers
Hay family
  USE Hayes family
Hay-fever *(May Subd Geog)*
  ₍RC590₎
  UF Allergic rhinitis
     Autumnal catarrh
     Catarrh, Autumnal
     Rhinitis, Allergic
     Rhinitis, Vasomotor
     Rose-cold
     Vasomotor rhinitis
  BT Nose—Diseases
     Respiratory allergy
  NT Hay-fever plants
  — Homeopathic treatment
     ₍RX326.H3₎
Hay-fever in children *(May Subd Geog)*
  BT Pediatric allergy
Hay-fever plants *(May Subd Geog)*
  ₍QK100₎
  BT Allergens
     Hay-fever
     Medicinal plants
     Poisonous plants
Hay making equipment
  USE Haying equipment
Hay-Pauncefote treaty, 1901
  ₍JX1398.7₎
Hay-scented fern
  ₍QK524.D5₎
  UF Dennstaedtia punctilobula
Hay trade *(May Subd Geog)*
  ₍HD9030-9049₎

Haya (African people)
  ₍DT443₎
  UF Basiba (African people)
     Baziba (African people)
     Ekihaya (African people)
     Heia (African people)
     Kiziba (African people)
     Wahaya (African people)
     Wassiba (African people)
     Ziba (African people)
  BT Ethnology—Tanzania
     Ethnology—Uganda
Haya language
  USE Ziba language
Haya law
  USE Law, Haya
Hayabusa (Fighter planes)
  UF Nakajima Ki 43 (Fighter planes)
  BT Fighter planes
Hayachine Mountain (Japan)
  UF Hayachine-san (Japan)
     Hayatsune-san (Japan)
  BT Mountains—Japan
Hayachine-san (Japan)
  USE Hayachine Mountain (Japan)
Hayagrīva
  BT Horses—Mythology
     Horses—Religious aspects
     Mythology, Chinese
Hayagrīva (Buddhist deity)
  ₍BQ4860.H37₎
  BT Gods, Buddhist
  RT Hayagrīva (Hindu deity)
Hayagrīva (Hindu deity)
  ₍BL1225.H34₎
  BT Gods, Hindu
  RT Hayagrīva (Buddhist deity)
Hayakawa Tenjinmori Iseki (Ayase-shi, Japan)
  USE Hayakawa Tenjinmori Site (Ayase-shi,
     Japan)
Hayakawa Tenjinmori Site (Ayase-shi, Japan)
  (Not Subd Geog)
  UF Hayakawa Tenjinmori Iseki (Ayase-shi,
     Japan)
  BT Japan—Antiquities
Hayasa language
  USE Khayasa language
Hayashi Iseki (Fujiidera-shi, Japan)
  USE Hayashi Site (Fujiidera-shi, Japan)
Hayashi Site (Fujiidera-shi, Japan)
  (Not Subd Geog)
  UF Hayashi Iseki (Fujiidera-shi, Japan)
  BT Japan—Antiquities
Hayate (Fighter planes)
  ₍TL685.3₎
  UF Frank (Fighter planes)
     Ki 84 (Fighter planes)
     Nakajima Hayate (Fighter planes)
     Nakajima Ki 84 (Fighter planes)
  BT Fighter planes
Hayato (Japanese people)
  ₍DS831.H₎
  BT Ethnology—Japan
Hayatsune-san (Japan)
  USE Hayachine Mountain (Japan)
Haybarger family
  USE Hybarger family
Haycraft family *(Not Subd Geog)*
Haydamaks
  USE Haidamaks

Hayden family (*Not Subd Geog*)
  UF Haden family
      Hadin family
      Hading family
      Hadon family
      Haiden family
      Haydin family
      Haydon family
      Headen family
      Headin family
      Headon family
      Heyden family
      Heydon family
      Hiden family
      Hyden family
Haydin family
  USE Hayden family

Haydon family
  USE Hayden family

Haye family
  USE Hayes family

Hayers family
  USE Ayers family

Hayes family (*Not Subd Geog*)
  UF Haighs family
      Hawes family
      Hay family
      Haye family
      Hays family
      Hey family
      Heyes family

Hayes River (Man.)
  BT Rivers—Manitoba

Haygood family
  USE Hagood family

Haying equipment (*May Subd Geog*)
  UF Hay—Drying—Equipment and
        supplies
      Hay—Equipment and supplies
      Hay—Harvesting—Equipment and
        supplies
      Hay making equipment

  BT Farm equipment
      Harvesting machinery
      Hay

Hayle family
  USE Hale family

Hayles family
  USE Hale family

Hayley family
  USE Haley family

Hayli family
  USE Haley family

Hayls family
  USE Hale family

Haymarket Square Riot, Chicago, Ill., 1886
  ₁HX846.C4₁

  UF Chicago (Ill.)—Haymarket Square
        Riot, 1886

  BT Riots—Illinois

Haymes family
  USE Hames family

Hayn family
  USE Haynes family

Hayner family (*Not Subd Geog*)
  UF Hainer family
      Haner family
      Hanor family
      Heiner family
      Hiner family
      Hyner family

Haynes automobile
Haynes family (*Not Subd Geog*)
  UF Hain family
      Hainds family
      Haine family
      Haines family
      Hains family
      Hane family
      Hanes family
      Hayn family
      Hayns family
      Hean family
      Heans family
      Hehn family
      Hehns family
      Heyn family
      Heyns family
Hayns family
  USE Haynes family
Hays family
  USE Hayes family
Hays Glacier (Antarctic regions)
  BT Glaciers—Antarctic regions
Hayson family
  USE Hazen family
Hayt family
  USE Haight family
Hayte family
  USE Haight family
Haythorn family
  USE Hawthorne family
Haythorne family
  USE Hawthorne family
Hayu dialect
  ₁PL3801.V2₁
  NT Tibeto-Burman languages
      Vayu dialect
Hayward family (*Not Subd Geog*)
  UF Haward family
      Hawarde family
      Hegward family
      Hegwood family
      Heyward family
  RT Hagood family
      Haywood family
      Hogwood family
      Howard family
Haywood family (*Not Subd Geog*)
  UF Hawood family
      Heywood family
  RT Hagood family
      Hayward family
      Hogwood family
Hayworth family
  USE Haworth family
Ḥazaḳah
  BT Jewish law
      Possession (Jewish law)
      Presumptions (Jewish law)
Hazalwood family
  USE Hazelwood family
Hazan family
  USE Hazen family
Hazan Incident, 1938
  USE Changkufeng Incident, 1938
Ḥazanim
  USE Cantors, Jewish
Hazara language
  ₁PK6996.H3₁
  UF Khazara language
      Khezare language
  BT Iranian languages
      Persian language
Hazāras
  BT Ethnology—Afghanistan
      Mongols
Hazard, Frost
  USE Frost hazard
Hazard (Law)
  USE Danger (Law)

Hazardous geographic environments
  (*May Subd Geog*)
  ₁GF85₁
  UF Environments, Hazardous geographic
  BT Human ecology
  RT Disasters
Hazardous goods
  USE Hazardous substances
Hazardous materials
  USE Hazardous substances
Hazardous substances (*May Subd Geog*)
  ₁T55.3.H3₁
  UF Dangerous goods
      Dangerous materials
      Hazardous goods
      Hazardous materials
      Toxic and inflammable goods
  BT Industrial safety
      Materials
  NT Carcinogens
      Chemicals—Safety measures
      Explosives—Safety measures
      Gases, Asphyxiating and poisonous
      Hazardous wastes
      Inflammable materials
      Poisons
      Radioactivity—Safety measures
  —Labeling (*May Subd Geog*)
  ——Law and legislation
        (*May Subd Geog*)
  —Law and legislation (*May Subd Geog*)
      RT Toxic torts
      NT Hazardous substances—
            Transportation—Law and
            legislation
          Liability for hazardous substances
            pollution damages
  —Packaging
  ——Law and legislation
        (*May Subd Geog*)
  —Transportation
  ——Law and legislation
        (*May Subd Geog*)
        BT Hazardous substances—Law and
              legislation
Hazardous substances damages, Liability for
  USE Toxic torts
Hazardous substances pollution damages,
  Liability for
  USE Liability for hazardous substances
        pollution damages
Hazardous waste disposal
  USE Hazardous wastes
Hazardous waste disposal sites
  USE Hazardous waste sites
Hazardous waste management industry
  (*May Subd Geog*)
  BT Hazardous wastes
Hazardous waste sites (*May Subd Geog*)
  UF Chemical landfills
      Dumps, Toxic
      Hazardous waste disposal sites
      Toxic dumps
  BT Hazardous waste treatment facilities
      Sanitary landfills
      Waste disposal sites
  NT Radioactive waste disposal in the
        ground
      Radioactive waste sites
  —Law and legislation (*May Subd Geog*)
  —Leaching
      BT Leachate
          Leaching
  —Location
  ——Law and legislation
        (*May Subd Geog*)
        BT Environmental law
  —Zone of aeration
      BT Zone of aeration
  ——Monitoring
        BT Environmental monitoring

Hazardous waste sites *(Continued)*
  — **New Jersey**
    NT GEMS Landfill (N.J.)
  — **New York (State)**
    NT Love Canal Chemical Waste
        Landfill (Niagara Falls, N.Y.)
Hazardous waste treatment facilities
  (May Subd Geog)
  UF Toxic waste treatment facilities
  BT Hazardous wastes
  NT Hazardous waste sites
    Hazardous wastes—Incineration
  — **Law and legislation** *(May Subd Geog)*
  — **Location**
  — — **Law and legislation**
    (May Subd Geog)
    BT Environmental law
  — **Taxation** *(May Subd Geog)*
  — — **Law and legislation**
    (May Subd Geog)
Hazardous wastes *(May Subd Geog)*
  UF Hazardous waste disposal
    Poisonous wastes
    Toxic wastes
    Waste, Disposal of
    Wastes, Hazardous
  BT Factory and trade waste
    Hazardous substances
    Refuse and refuse disposal
  RT Pollution
  NT Hazardous waste management industry
    Hazardous waste treatment facilities
  — **Incineration**
    BT Hazardous waste treatment
      facilities
      Incineration
  — — **Law and legislation**
    (May Subd Geog)
  — **Law and legislation** *(May Subd Geog)*
  — **Transportation**
  — — **Law and legislation**
    (May Subd Geog)
Haze, Smoke
  USE Smaze
Hazebreucq family
  USE Hasbrouck family
Hazebrouck family
  USE Hasbrouck family
Hazel
  USE Filbert
Hazel dormouse
  USE Hazel mouse
Hazel family
  USE Hasell family
Hazel grouse
  USE Hazel hen
Hazel hen
  [QL696.G285]
  UF Bonasa bonasia
    Hazel grouse
    Tetrastes bonasia
Hazel mouse
  [QL737.R656]
  UF Hazel dormouse
    Mouse, Hazel
    Muscardinus
    Muscardinus avellanarius
    Red dormouse
  BT Dormice
Hazelgrave family
  USE Hesselgrave family
Hazelgrove family
  USE Hesselgrave family
Hazelia (Frogs)
  USE Edwardtayloria
Hazelip family
  USE Haislip family
Hazell family
  USE Hasell family
Hazelnut
  USE Filbert

Hazeloop family
  USE Haislip family
Hazelwood family *(Not Subd Geog)*
  UF Haiselwood family
    Haislewood family
    Haselwood family
    Haselwoode family
    Haslewood family
    Hazalwood family
    Hazlewood family
    Hazzlewood family
    Hesilwoode family
    Hezlwood family
Hazen, Lake (Ellesmere Island, N.W.T.)
  UF Lake Hazen (Ellesmere Island,
    N.W.T.)
  BT Lakes—Northwest Territories
Hazen family *(Not Subd Geog)*
  UF Hayson family
    Hazan family
    Hazens family
    Hazon family
    Hazzen family
Hazens family
  USE Hazen family
Hazidae
  USE Geometridae
Hazili dialect
  UF Gajili dialect
    Gazili dialect
  BT Kunimaipa language
Hazing *(May Subd Geog)*
  [LB3604-LB3615 (Student life)]
  [U410.E9 (West Point)]
  [V415.E9 (Annapolis)]
  UF Ragging
  BT Students—Conduct of life
  RT Greek letter societies
    Initiations (into trades, societies, etc.)
  NT Secret societies
Hazle family
  USE Hasell family
Hazlewood family
  USE Hazelwood family
Hazon family
  USE Hazen family
Hazuki no monogatari emaki (Scrolls)
  [ND1059.6]
  BT Painting, Japanese—Kamakura-
    Momoyama periods, 1185-1600
    Scrolls, Japanese
Ḥazzanim
  USE Cantors, Jewish
Hazzen family
  USE Hazen family
Hazzlewood family
  USE Hazelwood family
HCMM Program
  USE Heat Capacity Mapping Mission
    Program
HDL
  USE High density lipoproteins
Hē Athenaikē Scholē (Literary movement)
  USE Athenian school (Literary movement)
He-Hg lasers
  USE Helium-mercury lasers
He-Ne lasers
  USE Helium-neon lasers
Heabler family
  USE Hepler family
Head
  [NC770-NC773 (Anatomy, Artistic)]
  [QM535 (Anatomy, Human)]
  BT Figure drawing
  RT Skull
  NT Brain
    Ear
    Eye
    Face
    Hair
    Jaws

    Mouth
    Nose
    Phrenology
    Retromaxillary space
    Scalp
  — **Abnormalities** *(May Subd Geog)*
    NT Dicephalism
      Microcephaly
  — Artificial deformities
    USE Skull—Artificial deformities
  — **Cancer**
  — **Diseases** *(May Subd Geog)*
    [RC936]
    NT Facial pain
      Head—Radiography
      Headache
  — — **Homeopathic treatment**
    [RX637]
  — Measurement
    USE Cephalometry
  — **Mythology**
  — **Radiography**
    BT Head—Diseases
  — **Religious aspects**
  — **Surgery**
    [RD521-RD529]
    [RD763 (Orthopedic)]
    NT Brain—Surgery
      Skull—Surgery
      Trephining
  — **Tumors**
    [RC280.H]
    [RD661-RD663]
    NT Cephalaematoma
  — **Wounds and injuries**
    [RD521]
  — — **Complications and sequelae**
Head, Foliate (Sculpture)
  USE Foliate head (Sculpture)
Head banging
  BT Child psychology
    Child psychopathology
Head-binding
  USE Skull—Artificial deformities
Head capsule
  [QL494]
  BT Insects—Anatomy
Head family *(Not Subd Geog)*
  UF Heade family
    Heads family
Head-gear *(May Subd Geog)*
  [GN419.1 (Anthropology)]
  [GT2110 (Manners and customs)]
  UF Headdress
  RT Costume
    Millinery
  NT Berets
    Galerus
    Hats
    Headbands
    Kerchiefs
    Miters
    Turbans
  — **Religious aspects**
    NT Kamelaukions
Head-hunters *(May Subd Geog)*
  BT Ethnology
Head in art
  [N8217.H5]
  NT Foliate head (Sculpture)
Head masters
  USE School principals
Head mistresses
  USE School principals
Head nurses
  USE Nurse administrators
Head offices (Corporations)
  USE Corporations—Headquarters
Head process
  USE Notochord

Head-Smashed-In Bison Jump Site (Alta.)
USE Head-Smashed-In Buffalo Jump Site (Alta.)
Head-Smashed-In Buffalo Jump Site (Alta.)
UF Head-Smashed-In Bison Jump Site (Alta.)
BT Alberta—Antiquities
Buffalo jump—Alberta
Head-spar trees
USE Spartrees
Head Start programs *(May Subd Geog)*
BT Socially handicapped children—Education (Preschool)—United States
Head tax
USE Poll-tax
Head teachers
USE School principals
Head trees (Logging)
USE Spartrees
Head waves
UF Conical waves
Lateral waves
Refracted waves
Refraction arrivals
BT Elastic waves
Seismic waves
Headache
[RB128]
[RC392 (Migraine)]
BT Head—Diseases
Pain
NT Cluster headache
Migraine
— **Homeopathic treatment**
[RX301.H5]
— **Psychosomatic aspects**
Headbands *(May Subd Geog)*
[GT2111]
BT Head-gear
Headbands (Bookbinding)
[Z271.3.H43]
BT Bookbinding
Headboat fishing
USE Charter boat fishing
Headdress
USE Hairdressing
Head-gear
Heade family
USE Head family
Headen family
USE Hayden family
Headin family
USE Hayden family
Headings, Subject
USE Subject headings
Headington family *(Not Subd Geog)*
Headlee family
USE Hadley family
Headley family
USE Hadley family
Headlight glare
UF Automobile headlight glare
Glare, Headlight
BT Automobile driving at night
Automobiles—Lighting
Reflection (Optics)
NT Roads—Glare screens
Headlights
USE Automobiles—Lighting
Locomotives—Headlights
Headline writing
USE Newspapers—Headlines
Headly family
USE Hadley family
Headmasters
USE School principals
Headmistresses
USE School principals
Headon family
USE Hayden family

Headquarters, Corporate
USE Corporations—Headquarters
Headquarters, Military
USE *subdivision* Headquarters *under armies, navies, etc., e.g.* United States—Armed Forces—Headquarters
Heads family
USE Head family
Heads of departments (High schools)
USE Departmental chairmen (High schools)
Heads of households *(May Subd Geog)*
UF Family heads
Households, Heads of
BT Family
NT Women heads of households
Heads of state *(May Subd Geog)*
[JF251 (Political science)]
UF Rulers
State, Heads of
BT Executive power
Statesmen
NT Caliphs
Dictators
Emperors
Kings and rulers
Offenses against foreign heads of state
Offenses against heads of state
Presidents
Prime ministers
Prytanes
Women heads of state
— **Mothers**
— **Succession**
[JF285]
UF Political succession
Succession, Political
— **Term of office**
[JF286]
UF Term of office of heads of state
— **Wives**
BT Wives
— **Canada**
— — **Dwellings**
NT Rideau Hall (Ottawa, Ont.)
— **China**
— — **Dwellings**
NT Chung-nan-hai (Peking, China)
Headstamps (Cartridges)
USE Cartridges—Headstamps
Headstander (Fish)
USE Chilodus punctatis
Headteachers
USE School principals
Headwaiters
USE Maître d's
Heaga family
USE Hager family
Heagen family
USE Hagan family
Heager family
USE Hager family
Heagon family
USE Hagan family
Heagons family
USE Hagan family
Heald family *(Not Subd Geog)*
Healers *(May Subd Geog)*
[RZ407-RZ408 (Mental healing)]
UF Faith healers
Mental healers
Psychic healers
Spiritual healers
Traditional healers
BT Folk medicine
Healing
Medicine, Primitive
Mental healing
Spiritual healing
NT Bonesetters
Herbalists
Naturopaths

Shamans
Women healers
Healers in mass media *(May Subd Geog)*
[P96.H42]
BT Mass media
Healey automobile
USE Austin-Healey automobile
Healey family
USE Healy family
Healing *(May Subd Geog)*
UF Curing (Medicine)
BT Folk medicine
Medicine
Therapeutics
NT Healers
Mental healing
Nature, Healing power of
Wound healing
— **Religious aspects**
NT Healing gods
Healing in the Bible
Spiritual healing
Healing, Spiritual
USE Spiritual healing
Healing arts licensing boards
USE Health occupations licensing boards
Healing Buddha (Buddhist deity)
USE Bhaiṣajyaguru (Buddhist deity)
Healing gods
[BL325.H4]
UF Gods, Healing
BT Gods
Healing—Religious aspects
Medicine, Magic, mystic, and spagiric
Mental healing
Mythology
Spiritual healing
Healing in the Bible
[BS680.H4]
BT Healing—Religious aspects
Medicine in the Bible
Spiritual healing
Healing of Peter's mother-in-law (Miracle)
UF Peter's mother-in-law, Healing of (Miracle)
BT Jesus Christ—Miracles
Healing of the epileptic boy (Miracle)
[BT367.H]
UF Epileptic boy, Healing of (Miracle)
BT Jesus Christ—Miracles
Healing of the Gerasene demoniac (Miracle)
UF Gadarene demoniac (Miracle)
Gerasene demoniac (Miracle)
BT Jesus Christ—Miracles
Healing of the lame man (Miracle)
UF Lame man (Miracle)
BT Jesus Christ—Miracles
Healing of the man born blind (Miracle)
UF Man blind from his birth (Miracle)
Man born blind (Miracle)
BT Jesus Christ—Miracles
Healing of the man sick of the palsy (Miracle)
[BT367.H]
UF Healing of the paralytic (Miracle)
Man sick of the palsy (Miracle)
Palsy, Healing of the man sick of the (Miracle)
Paralytic, Healing of the (Miracle)
BT Jesus Christ—Miracles
Healing of the nobleman's son (Miracle)
UF Nobleman's son (Miracle)
BT Jesus Christ—Miracles
Healing of the paralytic (Miracle)
USE Healing of the man sick of the palsy (Miracle)
Healing of the ten lepers (Miracle)
UF Cleansing of the ten lepers (Miracle)
Ten lepers, Cleansing of (Miracle)
Ten lepers, Healing of (Miracle)
BT Leprosy in the Bible

Healing of wounds
  USE Wound healing
Healing systems
  USE Therapeutic systems
Health
      [RA773-RA790]
      Here are entered works on optimal physical, mental, and social well-being, as well as how to achieve and preserve it. Works on personal body care and cleanliness are entered under Hygiene. Works on muscular efficiency and physical endurance are entered under Physical fitness.
  UF Personal health
      Wellness
  BT Medicine
      Physiology
  RT Diseases
      Holistic medicine
      Hygiene
  SA subdivision Biography—Health under names of individual literary authors, e.g. Shakespeare, William, 1564-1616—Biography—Health; also subdivision Health under names of other individual persons; also subdivision Care and hygiene under parts of the body, e.g. Foot—Care and hygiene; also subdivision Health and hygiene under classes of persons and ethnic groups; and subdivision Health aspects under subjects
  NT Alexander technique
      Astrology and health
      Climatology, Medical
      Diet
      Environmental health
      Executives—Health programs
      Exercise
      Health attitudes
      Health products
      Health status indicators
      Longevity
      Mental health
      Nutrition
      Periodic health examinations
      Physical fitness
      Presidents—United States—Health
      Public health
      Relaxation
      Rest
      Rural health
      Self-care, Health
      Shakespeare, William, 1564-1616—Biography—Health
      Sleep
      Statesmen—Health
      Vitality
  — Economic aspects
      USE Medical economics
  — Environmental aspects
      USE Environmental health
  — Public opinion
      USE Health attitudes
  — **Religious aspects**
  — — **Baptists, [Catholic Church, etc.]**
  — — **Buddhism, [Christianity, etc.]**
  — — **Hinduism**
          NT Hygiene, Hindu
  — — **Islam**
          NT Hygiene, Islamic
  — — **Judaism**
          NT Hygiene, Jewish
  — — **Mormon Church**
          NT Hygiene, Mormon
  — — **Taoism**
          NT Hygiene, Taoist
  — Study and teaching
      USE Health education
Health, Bills of
  USE Bills of health

Health, Community
  USE Public health
Health, International
  USE World health
Health, Military
  USE Military hygiene
Health, Public
  USE Public health
Health, World
  USE World health
Health administration
  USE Health services administration
      Public health administration
Health agencies, Voluntary
  USE Voluntary health agencies
Health and housing
  USE Housing and health
Health and Nutrition Examination Survey
  BT Health surveys—United States
      Nutrition surveys—United States
Health and race (May Subd Geog)
  BT Medical anthropology
      Race
Health and welfare federations
  USE Community welfare councils
Health attitudes (May Subd Geog)
  UF Health—Public opinion
      Hygiene—Public opinion
  BT Attitude (Psychology)
      Health
  RT Health behavior
  NT Patient satisfaction
Health auxiliaries
  USE Allied health personnel
Health behavior (May Subd Geog)
      [RA776.9]
  UF Behavior, Health
      Health habits
  BT Diseases—Causes and theories of causation
      Habit
      Human behavior
      Medicine and psychology
  RT Health attitudes
  NT Patient compliance
      Self-care, Health
Health boards (May Subd Geog)
      [RA5]
      [RA11-RA388 (Reports)]
  UF Boards of health
      Public health boards
  BT Public health
      Public health administration
      Public health laws
  NT Health occupations licensing boards
      Mental health boards
  — **Appropriations and expenditures**
Health care
  USE Medical care
Health care, Self
  USE Self-care, Health
Health care administration
  USE Health services administration
      Public health administration
Health care administrators
  USE Health services administrators
Health care auxiliaries
  USE Allied health personnel
Health care costs
  USE Medical care, Cost of
Health care delivery
  USE Medical care
Health care delivery organizations, Comprehensive
  USE Health maintenance organizations
Health care institutions
  USE Health facilities
Health care personnel
  USE Medical personnel
Health care planning
  USE Health planning

Health care surveys
  USE Medical care surveys
Health care teams (May Subd Geog)
      [R729.5.H4]
  UF Health teams
      Medical care teams
      Patient care teams
      Team work in medicine
  BT Medical cooperation
      Medical personnel
  NT Burn care teams
      Dental teams
      Mental health care teams
      Nurse-physician joint practice
      Team nursing
  — **Training of** (May Subd Geog)
      UF Training of health care teams
      BT Medical education
          Paramedical education
  — **New York (State)**
      NT Family Health Maintenance Demonstration
Health care technology
  USE Medical technology
Health catchment areas
  USE Health service areas
Health clubs
  USE Physical fitness centers
Health communication
  USE Communication in medicine
Health counseling (May Subd Geog)
      [R727.4]
  BT Counseling
      Health education
      Medical personnel and patient
      Patient education
  NT Abortion counseling
      Alcoholism counseling
      Drug abuse counseling
      Genetic counseling
      Mental health counseling
      Sex counseling
Health ecology
  USE Environmental health
Health economics
  USE Medical economics
Health education (May Subd Geog)
  UF Health—Study and teaching
      Hygiene—Study and teaching
  BT Communication in medicine
      Education
      Preventive health services
  RT Health promotion
  NT Childbirth—Study and teaching
      Dental health education
      Drama in health education
      Health counseling
      Mass media in health education
      Mental health education
      Patient education
      Radio in health education
      Sexually transmitted diseases—Study and teaching
  — **Law and legislation** (May Subd Geog)
      BT Educational law and legislation
Health education (Elementary)
      (May Subd Geog)
Health education (Preschool)
      (May Subd Geog)
      [LB1140.5.H4]
Health education (Secondary)
      (May Subd Geog)
Health education of women
      (May Subd Geog)
  BT Women—Education
  RT Women—Health and hygiene
Health examinations
  USE Periodic health examinations
Health facilities (May Subd Geog)
  UF Health care institutions
      Medical facilities

BT Medical care
   Public health
NT Ambulances
   Clinics
   Dispensaries
   Halfway houses
   Health resorts, watering-places, etc.
   Hospitals
   Long-term care facilities
   Medical centers
   Medical laboratories
   Medical offices
   Mental health facilities
   Mental retardation facilities
   Poison control centers
   Rehabilitation centers
   Religious health facilities
   Tissue banks
   Vaccination centers
— **Administration**
   BT Health services administration
   NT Health facilities—Affiliations
      Health facilities—Business
         management
      Health facilities—Materials
         management
— **Affiliations**
   UF Affiliations between health
         facilities
      Cooperation between health
         facilities
      Health facilities—Relationships
      Relationships between health
         facilities
   BT Health facilities—Administration
      Medical cooperation
   NT Hospitals—Regional alliances
      Multihospital systems
— **Business management**
   ₁RA971.3₁
   UF Business management of health
         facilities
      Health facility business
         management
   BT Health facilities—Administration
— **Certificate of need**
   UF Certificate of need for health
         facilities
      Certification of need for health
         facilities
      Health facilities—Need
         certification
      Need certification for health
         facilities
   BT Health facilities—Planning
— — **Law and legislation**
      (May Subd Geog)
      BT Health facilities—Law and
            legislation
         Medical laws and legislation
— Collective bargaining
   USE Collective bargaining—Health
         facilities
— Collective labor agreements
   USE Collective labor agreements—
         Health facilities
— **Complaints against**
   UF Complaints against health facilities
— **Cost of construction**
— **Disinfection**
   BT Disinfection and disinfectants
— **Employees**
   NT Collective bargaining—Health
         facilities
      Trade-unions—Health facilities
— **Endowments**
   BT Charities, Medical
— **Energy consumption**
   BT Energy consumption
— Federal aid
   USE Federal aid to health facilities

— **Finance**
   NT Federal aid to health facilities
— — **Law and legislation**
      (May Subd Geog)
— — **Reporting** (May Subd Geog)
— **Fires and fire prevention**
— — **Law and legislation**
      (May Subd Geog)
— **Law and legislation** (May Subd Geog)
   NT Health facilities—Certificate of
         need—Law and legislation
— **Licenses** (May Subd Geog)
   BT Medical laws and legislation
— **Location**
   BT Medically underserved areas
— **Materials management**
   ₁RA971.33₁
   BT Health facilities—Administration
      Materials management
— Need certification
   USE Health facilities—Certificate of
         need
— **Planning**
   NT Health facilities—Certificate of
         need
— **Power supply**
   ₁RA969.48₁
   BT Electric power
— Relationships
   USE Health facilities—Affiliations
— **Soundproofing**
— **Taxation** (May Subd Geog)
— — **Law and legislation**
      (May Subd Geog)
— **Utilization**
   UF Utilization of health facilities
   NT Hospital utilization
— **Waste disposal**
   RT Medical supplies, Disposable
Health facilities, Investor-owned
   USE Health facilities, Proprietary
Health facilities, Private for profit
   USE Health facilities, Proprietary
Health facilities, Proprietary
   (May Subd Geog)
   UF For profit health facilities
      Health facilities, Investor-owned
      Health facilities, Private for profit
      Investor-owned health facilities
      Private for profit health facilities
      Proprietary health facilities
   BT Medical corporations
   NT Hospitals, Proprietary
      Nursing homes, Proprietary
Health facilities, Religious
   USE Religious health facilities
Health facility business management
   USE Health facilities—Business
         management
Health food
   USE Food, Natural
Health foods industry
   USE Natural foods industry
Health habits
   USE Health behavior
Health hazard appraisal
   USE Health risk assessment
Health in mass media (May Subd Geog)
   ₁P96.H43₁
   BT Mass media
Health indicators
   USE Health status indicators
Health insurance
   USE Insurance, Health
Health maintenance organization patients
   (May Subd Geog)
   UF Patients, Health maintenance
         organization
   BT Health maintenance organizations
      Sick

Health maintenance organizations
   (May Subd Geog)
   ₁RA413-RA413.7₁
   UF Comprehensive health care delivery
         organizations
      Group medical practice, Prepaid
      Health care delivery organizations,
         Comprehensive
      Health plans, Prepaid
      HMOs
      Prepaid group medical practice
      Prepaid health plans
   BT Group medical practice
      Insurance, Health
      Managed care plans (Medical care)
   NT Health maintenance organization
         patients
      Social health maintenance
         organizations
— **Citizen participation**
— Federal aid
   USE Federal aid to health
            maintenance organizations
— **Finance**
   NT Federal aid to health maintenance
         organizations
— **Law and legislation** (May Subd Geog)
— **New York (State)**
   NT Family Health Maintenance
         Demonstration
Health manpower
   USE Medical personnel
      Public health personnel
Health Manpower Pilot Projects Program
   ₁RA396.A4.C2₁
   UF California Health Manpower Pilot
         Projects Program
      Experimental Health Manpower Pilot
         Projects Program
   BT Allied health personnel—Licenses—
         California
      Medical personnel—Licenses—
         California
      Paramedical education—California
Health misconceptions
   USE Medical misconceptions
Health occupations examining boards
   USE Health occupations licensing boards
Health occupations licensing boards
   (May Subd Geog)
   ₁RA396₁
   UF Boards of examiners for health
         occupations
      Examining boards for health
         occupations
      Healing arts licensing boards
      Health occupations examining boards
      Health professions licensing boards
      Licensing boards for health
         occupations
   BT Health boards
   RT Medical personnel—Licenses
      Public health personnel—Licenses
Health occupations schools
   (May Subd Geog)
   ₁R735-R832 (General)₁
   ₁R847-R847.7 (Paramedical)₁
   UF Health professions schools
      Medical occupations schools
      Medical professions schools
   BT Medical education
      Paramedical education
      Schools
      Universities and colleges
   NT Chiropractic schools
      Dental schools
      Health occupations students
      Hospitals, Teaching
      Medical colleges
      Naturopathic schools
      Nursing schools

1653

Health occupations schools
  (Continued)
      Osteopathic schools
      Pharmacy colleges
      Physical therapy schools
      Schools of public health
      Teaching nursing homes
      Veterinary colleges
  — **United States**
    NT Area Health Education Centers
        Program
Health occupations students
  (May Subd Geog)
    BT Health occupations schools
      Medical personnel
      Students
    NT Dental students
      Medical students
      Nursing students
      Osteopathic students
      Women veterinary students
Health of children
  USE Children—Health and hygiene
Health of women
  USE Women—Health and hygiene
Health of workers
  USE Industrial hygiene
Health-officers *(May Subd Geog)*
  [RA5]
  [RA440.8]
    UF Public health officers
    BT Health services administrators
      Medicine—Biography
      Public health
      Public health administration
      Public health laws
      Public health personnel
  — **Training of** *(May Subd Geog)*
    [RA440.8]
Health officers, Environmental
  USE Sanitarians
Health personnel
  USE Medical personnel
    Public health personnel
Health planning *(May Subd Geog)*
  [RA393-395]
    UF Comprehensive health planning
      Health care planning
      Health services planning
      Medical care—Planning
      Medical care planning
      Public health—Planning
    BT Medical policy
      Planning
      Public health
    RT Health services administration
    NT Environmental health—Planning
      Health service areas
      Medical care—Needs assessment
      Mental health planning
  — **Citizen participation**
  — **Federal aid**
    USE Federal aid to health planning
  — **Finance**
    NT Federal aid to health planning
  — **Law and legislation** *(May Subd Geog)*
  — **Public relations**
    USE Public relations—Health planning
Health planning areas
  USE Health service areas
Health plans, Prepaid
  USE Health maintenance organizations
    Insurance, Health
Health policy
  USE Medical policy
Health products *(May Subd Geog)*
    UF Health supplies
    BT Commercial products
      Health
    RT Medical supplies
    NT Allergy products

      Drugs, Nonprescription
      Food, Natural
      Oral hygiene products
      Toilet preparations
Health professions
  USE Medical personnel
Health Professions Career Opportunity
Program
    BT Medicine—Vocational guidance—
      California
      Minorities—Education (Graduate)—
      California
      Minorities in medicine—California
Health professions licensing boards
  USE Health occupations licensing boards
Health professions schools
  USE Health occupations schools
Health program evaluation
  USE Public health—Evaluation
Health programs
  USE *subdivision* Health programs *under*
    subjects, e.g. Executives—Health
    programs
Health promotion *(May Subd Geog)*
  [RA427.8]
    UF Promotion of health
      Wellness programs
    BT Preventive health services
    RT Health education
    NT Executives—Health programs
      Hospitals—Health promotion services
Health promotion services in hospitals
  USE Hospitals—Health promotion services
Health psychology, Clinical
  USE Clinical health psychology
Health records
  USE Medical records
    Public health records
Health reformers *(May Subd Geog)*
    BT Medical innovations
      Public health personnel
      Reformers
      Therapeutic systems
Health resorts, watering-places, etc.
(May Subd Geog)
  [RA791-954]
    UF Health spas
      Spas
      Watering-places
    BT Climatotherapy
      Health facilities
      Hydrotherapy
      Resorts
    NT Labor rest homes
      Mineral waters
      Sanatoriums
      Seaside resorts
      Summer resorts
      Visitors' taxes
      Winter resorts
  — **Law and legislation** *(May Subd Geog)*
  — **Utilization**
    UF Utilization of health resorts,
      watering-places, etc.
  — **China**
    NT Chung-shan wen ch'üan pin kuan
      (China)
  — **Romania**
    NT Băile Bálványos (Romania)
Health resorts, watering-places, etc., Ancient
(May Subd Geog)
  — **Israel**
Health risk appraisal
  USE Health risk assessment
Health risk assessment *(May Subd Geog)*
  [RA427.3]
    Here are entered works on the process of deter-
  mining the health effects of exposure of individuals or
  of a population to hazardous materials and/or situa-
  tions, or on the adverse consequences that may result
  from the use of a technology or some other action.

    UF Assessment, Health risk
      Health hazard appraisal
      Health risk appraisal
      HRA (Public health)
      Human risk assessment
    BT Medicine, Preventive
      Public health
      Risk assessment
    RT Environmental health
    NT Medical screening
Health sciences administration
  USE Health services administration
    Public health administration
Health sciences libraries
  USE Medical libraries
Health sciences personnel
  USE Medical personnel
    Public health personnel
Health scientists
  USE Medical scientists
Health self-care
  USE Self-care, Health
Health service areas *(May Subd Geog)*
    UF Areas, Health service
      Catchment areas, Health
      Health catchment areas
      Health planning areas
    BT Health planning
      Medical care
      Medical geography
      Regional medical programs
      Special districts
    NT Medically underserved areas
Health service shortage areas
  USE Medically underserved areas
Health services
  USE Medical care
    Public health
Health services administration
(May Subd Geog)
    UF Health administration
      Health care administration
      Health sciences administration
      Medical care—Administration
      Medical care—Management
    RT Health planning
      Public health administration
    NT Community mental health services—
      Administration
      Environmental health—Administration
      Health facilities—Administration
      Health services administrators
      Hospitals—Administration
      Medical centers—Administration
      Nursing homes—Administration
      Nursing services—Administration
      Pharmacy management
Health services administrators
(May Subd Geog)
  [RA424.4-RA424.5 (Biography)]
    UF Administrators, Health services
      Health care administrators
      Medical care administrators
    BT Executives
      Health services administration
      Medical personnel
      Public health personnel
    NT Clinic managers
      Health-officers
      Hospital administrators
      Nurse administrators
      Nursing home administrators
  — **Job stress**
  — **Time management**
Health services for women
  USE Women's health services
Health services personnel
  USE Medical personnel
    Public health personnel
Health services planning
  USE Health planning

Health spas
USE Health resorts, watering-places, etc.
Physical fitness centers
Health status indexes
USE Health status indicators
Health status indicators *(May Subd Geog)*
[RA407-409.5]
UF Health indicators
Health status indexes
Indexes, Health status
Indicators, Health status
BT Health
Health surveys
Medical statistics
Public health—Methodology
Quality of life
Social indicators
NT APACHE (Disease classification
system)
Nottingham Health Profile
Sickness Impact Profile
Health supplies
USE Health products
Health surveys *(May Subd Geog)*
Here are entered works on the methods and tech-
niques employed in conducting health surveys, and
reports of individual surveys. For the latter the head-
ing may be subdivided by place; in such cases an
additional subject entry is made under the heading
Public health—[local subdivision], e.g. 1. Public
health—United States. 2. Health surveys—United
States. For health surveys on a special topic, the addi-
tional subject entry is made under the special topic,
e.g. 1. Youth—Health and hygiene—United States.
2. Health surveys—United States.
UF Public health—Surveys
Public health surveys
BT Public health
Surveys
NT Dental surveys
Health status indicators
Medical care surveys
Mental health surveys
— **Data tape catalogs**
— **Statistical methods**
BT Medical statistics
— **United States**
NT Health and Nutrition Examination
Survey
Health systems agencies *(May Subd Geog)*
UF Agencies, Health systems
HSAs (Health planning)
BT Public health advisory groups
Health teams
USE Health care teams
Health technicians
USE Biomedical technicians
Health technologists, Animal
USE Animal health technicians
Health technology
USE Medical technology
Health technology, Animal
USE Animal health technology
Health testing, Multiphasic
USE Multiphasic health screening
Health thoughts
USE Mental healing
Health visitors
USE Visiting nurses
Health workers, Primary
USE Community health aides
Health workers, Village
USE Community health aides
Health/Zenith Z-100 (Computer)
USE Zenith Z-100 (Computer)
Healths, Drinking of
USE Drinking customs
Toasts
Healthshire Hills (Jamaica)
USE Hellshire Hills (Jamaica)
Healthshire Hummock (Jamaica)
USE Hellshire Hills (Jamaica)

Healy family *(Not Subd Geog)*
UF Healey family
Hely family
Healyburton family
USE Halliburton family
Hean family
USE Haynes family
Heans family
USE Haynes family
HEAO (Artificial satellite)
UF High energy astronomy observatory
(Artificial satellite)
BT Astronomical observatories
Orbiting astronomical observatories
Scientific satellites
X-ray astronomy
Heaphy Track (N.Z.)
UF Heaphy Trail (N.Z.)
BT Trails—New Zealand
Heaphy Trail (N.Z.)
USE Heaphy Track (N.Z.)
Heaps (Mathematics)
BT Groups, Theory of
Hear family
USE Hair family
Hear no evil (Motif)
USE Three monkeys (Motif)
Heard family
USE Hurd family
Heare family
USE Hair family
Hearing
[BF251 (Psychology)]
[GN275 (Anthropology)]
[QP461-QP469 (Physiology)]
UF Acoustics
Audition (Physiology)
Ear—Physiology
Physiological acoustics
BT Bioacoustics
Music—Physiological aspects
Senses and sensation
Sound
RT Audiology
Auditory pathways
Deafness
Ear
Listening
NT Audiometry
Auditory adaptation
Auditory perception
Bone conduction
Directional hearing
Echolocation (Physiology)
Geniculate bodies
Hearing levels
Labyrinth (Ear)
Psychoacoustics
Tympanal organ
— **Religious aspects**
— — **Buddhism, [Christianity, etc.]**
— Testing
USE Audiometry
Hearing aid industry *(May Subd Geog)*
BT Medical instruments and apparatus
industry
Hearing aids *(May Subd Geog)*
[RF300-RF310]
Here are entered works on devices to improve
hearing ability. Works on synthetic replicas of the ear
used to restore cosmetic harmony to the face are
entered under Ear prostheses.
BT Deafness
Prosthesis
NT Cochlear implants
Earmolds (Hearing aids)
— **Fitting**
UF Fitting of hearing aids
Hearing aids—Selection
Selection of hearing aids
— **Purchasing**

— Selection
USE Hearing aids—Fitting
Hearing aids, Binaural *(May Subd Geog)*
UF Binaural hearing aids
Hearing clinics *(May Subd Geog)*
[RF5-6]
UF Audiology clinics
BT Clinics
Hearing disorders
Hearing defects
USE Hearing disorders
Hearing disorders *(May Subd Geog)*
[RF290]
UF Auditory disorders
Defective hearing
Disorders of hearing
Hearing defects
Hearing impairments
BT Communicative disorders
Ear—Diseases
Perception, Disorders of
Sense-organs—Diseases
NT Deafness
Hearing clinics
Ototoxic agents
Tinnitus
Word deafness
— **Diagnosis**
NT Electrocochleography
— Prevention
USE Deafness—Prevention
Hearing disorders in children
(May Subd Geog)
[RF291.5.C45]
BT Communicative disorders in children
Pediatric otolaryngology
NT Children, Deaf
Hearing impaired children
Word deafness in children
— **Diagnosis**
NT Discrimination by Identification of
Pictures Test
Threshold by Identification of
Pictures Test
Hearing ear dogs *(May Subd Geog)*
[HV2509]
UF Dogs for the deaf
BT Deaf
Working dogs
— **Law and legislation** *(May Subd Geog)*
Hearing examiners
USE Examiners (Administrative procedure)
Hearing family
USE Herring family
Hearing impaired *(May Subd Geog)*
[HV2350-HV2990.5]
UF Hard-of-hearing
Partial hearing
Partially hearing
BT Physically handicapped
NT Deaf
Films for the hearing impaired
Libraries and the hearing impaired
Video recordings for the hearing
impaired
Hearing impaired, Libraries for the
USE Libraries and the hearing impaired
Hearing-impaired aged
USE Aged, Deaf
Hearing impaired and libraries
USE Libraries and the hearing impaired
Hearing impaired children
(May Subd Geog)
[HV2391-2392.2]
UF Children, Hearing impaired
BT Hearing disorders in children
Perceptually handicapped children
RT Children, Deaf
Hearing impairments
USE Hearing disorders

Hearing levels *(May Subd Geog)*
  UF Hearing threshold levels
  BT Audiometry
      Hearing
Hearing loss
  USE Deafness
Hearing loss, Central
  USE Word deafness
Hearing threshold levels
  USE Hearing levels
Hearings, Legislative
  USE Legislative hearings
Hearington family
  USE Harrington family
Hearn family *(Not Subd Geog)*
  UF Hearne family
      Heerin family
      Hern family
      Herne family
      Heron family
      Hurn family
  RT Herndon family
Hearndon family
  USE Herndon family
Hearne family
  USE Hearn family
Hearon family
  USE Herring family
Hearring family
  USE Herring family
Hearsay evidence
  USE Evidence, Hearsay
Hearsay family
  USE Hersey family
Hearses (Vehicles)
  [TL235.8]
  UF Funeral cars
      Funeral coaches
      Funeral vehicles
  BT Carriages and carts
      Motor vehicles
      Undertakers and undertaking
Hearsey family
  USE Hersey family
Hearst Castle (Calif.)
  USE Hearst-San Simeon State Historical
       Monument (Calif.)
Hearst family *(Not Subd Geog)*
  UF Herst family
      Hirst family
      Hurst family
**Hearst-San Simeon State Historical
  Monument (Calif.)**
  UF Cuesta Encantada (Calif.)
      Enchanted Hill (Calif.)
      Hearst Castle (Calif.)
      San Simeon Estate (Calif.)
  BT Dwellings—California
      Historic sites—California
Hearsy family
  USE Hersey family
Heart
  [QP111-QP114 (Physiology)]
  BT Cardiovascular system
      Chest
  SA *headings beginning with the words*
      Cardiac *or* Cardiogenic
  NT Cardiac receptors
      Cardiography
      Fetal heart
      Heart atrium
      Heart conduction system
      Pericardium
      Pulse
  — Abnormalities *(May Subd Geog)*
      [RC687]
      UF Congenital heart disease
          Heart—Diseases, Congenital
          Heart defects
          Heart diseases, Congenital
      NT Atrial septal defects

Ebstein's anomaly
      Tetralogy of Fallot
      Total anomalous pulmonary venous
        connection
      Transposition of great vessels
      Truncus arteriosus, Persistent
      Ventricular septal defects
  — — Complications and sequelae
      (May Subd Geog)
  — — Psychological aspects
      BT Sick—Psychology
  — — Radiography
      BT Heart—Radiography
  — — Surgery *(May Subd Geog)*
  — Aging
  — Anatomy
      [QL838 (Comparative anatomy)]
      [QM181 (Human anatomy)]
      NT Heart septum
  — Atlases
  — Biopsy
      [RC683.5.B5]
      BT Heart—Examination
  — Biopsy, Needle
      UF Heart—Needle biopsy
      BT Heart—Diseases—Diagnosis
  — Blood-vessels
      UF Cardiac blood-vessels
      NT Coronary arteries
  — — Abnormalities
      NT Patent ductus arteriosus
  — — Transposition
      USE Transposition of great vessels
  — Calcification
      UF Cardiac calcification
  — Conduction system
      USE Heart conduction system
  — Contraction
      [QP113]
      UF Contraction of the heart
          Heart—Muscle—Contraction
          Heart contraction
          Myocardial contraction
          Systole (Cardiology)
          Systolic time interval
      BT Muscle contraction
      RT Heart beat
  — Cryopreservation
      BT Heart—Preservation
  — Cultures and culture media
  — Cytology
      NT Heart cells
  — Diastolic relaxation
      USE Diastole (Cardiac cycle)
  — Differentiation
  — Dilatation
      [RC685.D55]
      UF Cardiomegaly
          Dilatation of the heart
          Enlargement of the heart
          Heart—Enlargement
          Heart enlargement
      BT Heart—Diseases
          Heart—Size
      NT Heart—Measurement
          Orthodiagraphy
  — Diseases *(May Subd Geog)*
      [RC681-688]
      UF Cardiac diseases
          Heart attack
          Heart diseases
      RT Cardiology
      NT Arrhythmia
          Blood—Circulation, Disorders of
          Carcinoid heart disease
          Cardiac arrest
          Cardiac tamponade
          Congestive heart failure
          Cor pulmonale
          Coronary heart disease
          Endocarditis

Heart—Dilatation
      Heart—Fibrosis
      Heart—Hypertrophy
      Heart—Infections
      Heart—Muscle—Diseases
      Heart—Parasites
      Heart, Fatty
      Heart block
      Heart failure
      Postpericardiotomy syndrome
  — — Case studies
  — — Chemotherapy
      [RC684.C48]
      RT Cardiovascular agents
  — — Diagnosis
      [RC683]
      NT Angiocardiography
          Ballistocardiography
          Cardiac catheterization
          Cardiography
          Electrocardiography
          Electrokymography
          Heart—Biopsy, Needle
          Heart murmurs
          Percussion
          Pulse
          Sphygmograph
  — — — Equipment and supplies
      NT Heart disease diagnostic
          equipment industry
  — — Diet therapy
      [RC684.D5]
      BT Heart—Diseases—Nutritional
          aspects
      NT Low-cholesterol diet
          Salt-free diet
  — — — Recipes
      [RC684.D5]
      UF Cardiacs, Cookery for
          Cookery for cardiacs
      BT Cookery for the sick
  — — Environmental aspects
      (May Subd Geog)
      UF Environmentally induced heart
          diseases
  — — Epidemiology
  — — Etiology
  — — Genetic aspects
      UF Congenital heart disease
  — — Homeopathic treatment
      [RX311-316]
  — — Immunotherapy
      BT Heart—Diseases—Treatment
  — — Law and legislation
      (May Subd Geog)
      BT Forensic cardiology
          Medical jurisprudence
          Medical laws and legislation
  — — Mortality
  — — Nutritional aspects
      NT Heart—Diseases—Diet therapy
  — — Patients *(May Subd Geog)*
      UF Cardiac patients
          Cardiacs
          Heart patients
      BT Sick
  — — — Employment *(May Subd Geog)*
  — — — Rehabilitation *(May Subd Geog)*
      UF Cardiac rehabilitation
  — — Pictorial works
      USE Heart—Pictorial works
  — — Popular works
  — — Prevention
  — — Psychosomatic aspects
  — — Public opinion
  — — Relapse *(May Subd Geog)*
      UF Recrudescence of heart disease
          Recurrence of heart disease
          Relapse of heart disease
  — — Research *(May Subd Geog)*
      UF Heart research

— — Social aspects *(May Subd Geog)*
    UF Society and heart diseases
— — Treatment *(May Subd Geog)*
    NT Heart—Diseases—
        Immunotherapy
— Diseases, Congenital
    USE Heart—Abnormalities
— Displacement
    UF Cardioptosis
— Dissection
— Drug effects
    USE Heart—Effect of drugs on
— Effect of drugs on
    ⌜RM345-RM349⌝
    UF Heart—Drug effects
    RT Cardiovascular agents
— Effect of radiation on
    UF Heart—Radiation effects
    BT Radiation—Physiological effect
— Enlargement
    USE Heart—Dilatation
        Heart—Hypertrophy
— Evolution
— Examination
    NT Heart—Biopsy
— Fibrosis *(May Subd Geog)*
    UF Cardiac fibrosis
        Fibrosis of the heart
    BT Collagen diseases
        Heart—Diseases
— Foreign bodies
— Growth
— Hemorrhage
— Histology
— Histopathology
— Hydatids
    SA *Example under* Echinococcosis
— Hypertrophy
    ⌜RC685.H9⌝
    UF Cardiomegaly
        Enlargement of the heart
        Heart—Enlargement
        Heart enlargement
        Hypertrophic cardiomyopathy
    BT Heart—Diseases
        Heart—Size
    NT Heart—Measurement
        Orthodiagraphy
— Imaging
    ⌜RC683.5.I42⌝
    UF Cardiac diagnostic imaging
        Cardiac imaging
        Diagnostic cardiac imaging
        Imaging of the heart
    NT Ultrasonic cardiography
— Infarction *(May Subd Geog)*
    ⌜RC685.I6⌝
    UF Heart attack
        Myocardial infarction
    BT Coronary heart disease
    NT Cardiogenic shock
— — Complications and sequelae
    (May Subd Geog)
— — Diagnosis
— — Mortality
— — Psychosomatic aspects
— Infections *(May Subd Geog)*
    UF Cardiac infections
        Heart—Infectious diseases
        Heart infections
    BT Communicable diseases
        Heart—Diseases
    NT Endocarditis, Bacterial
        Rheumatic heart disease
— Infectious diseases
    USE Heart—Infections
— Innervation
    UF Cardiac nerves
— Magnetic fields
— Massage
    USE Cardiac massage

— Mathematical models
— Measurement
    ⌜QM181 (Human anatomy)⌝
    BT Heart—Dilatation
        Heart—Hypertrophy
    NT Orthodiagraphy
— Metabolism
    UF Cardiac metabolism
        Heart—Muscle—Metabolism
        Heart metabolism
        Myocardial metabolism
— — Regulation
    UF Regulation of heart metabolism
    BT Biological control systems
— Microbiology
— Models
— Muscle
    UF Cardiac muscle
        Heart muscle
        Myocardium
    BT Muscles
— — Contraction
    USE Heart—Contraction
— — Diseases *(May Subd Geog)*
    UF Cardiomyopathy
        Myocardial diseases
    BT Heart—Diseases
    NT Myocarditis
— — Inflammation
    USE Myocarditis
— — Metabolism
    USE Heart—Metabolism
— — Regeneration
    UF Regeneration, Heart muscle
        Regeneration, Myocardium
    BT Regeneration (Biology)
— Mythology
— Necrosis
    UF Cardiac necrosis
— Needle biopsy
    USE Heart—Biopsy, Needle
— Palpitation
    ⌜RC685.A65⌝
    UF Palpitation of the heart
    RT Arrhythmia
— Paralysis, Induced
    USE Cardiac arrest, Induced
— Parasites *(May Subd Geog)*
    UF Parasites—Heart
    BT Heart—Diseases
— Pictorial works
    UF Heart—Diseases—Pictorial works
— Preservation
    UF Preservation of heart
    NT Heart—Cryopreservation
— Psychophysiology
— Radiation effects
    USE Heart—Effect of radiation on
— Radiography *(May Subd Geog)*
    ⌜RC683.5.R3⌝
    UF Heart—X-ray examination
    NT Heart—Abnormalities—
        Radiography
        Orthodiagraphy
— — Positioning
    BT Radiography, Medical—
        Positioning
— Relaxation, Diastolic
    USE Diastole (Cardiac cycle)
— Research
    USE Cardiology—Research
— Rupture
    ⌜RC685.R9⌝
— Secretions
— Sex differences
— Size
    UF Size of heart
    NT Heart—Dilatation
        Heart—Hypertrophy
— Sounds
    ⌜QP111⌝

    UF Auscultation of the heart
        Heart sounds
        Heart tones
    BT Sounds
    NT Heart murmurs
        Phonocardiography
— Sounds, Abnormal
    USE Heart murmurs
— Surgery *(May Subd Geog)*
    UF Cardiac surgery
        Open-heart surgery
    NT Anesthesia in cardiology
        Cardiac arrest, Induced
        Cardiac catheterization
        Cardiomyoplasty
        Cardiopulmonary bypass
        Coronary heart disease—Surgery
        Myocardial revascularization
— — Case studies
— — Complications and sequelae
    (May Subd Geog)
— — Instruments
    BT Surgical instruments and
        apparatus
    NT Heart, Mechanical
— — — Sterilization
— — Nursing *(May Subd Geog)*
    ⌜RD598⌝
    UF Cardiosurgical nursing
    BT Cardiovascular disease nursing
— — Nutritional aspects
    BT Nutrition
— — Patients *(May Subd Geog)*
— — Psychological aspects
    BT Medicine and psychology
— Syphilis *(May Subd Geog)*
— Terminology
    USE Cardiology—Terminology
— Transplantation *(May Subd Geog)*
    ⌜RD598⌝
    UF Heart transplantation
— — Immunological aspects
— — Patients *(May Subd Geog)*
    BT Sick
— — Psychological aspects
— — Social aspects *(May Subd Geog)*
    UF Society and heart
        transplantation
— Tumors *(May Subd Geog)*
— Ultrastructure
— Valves
    UF Cardiac valves
        Heart valves
        Valves, Heart
    NT Aortic valve
        Heart valve prosthesis
        Mitral valve
        Tricuspid valve
— — Diseases *(May Subd Geog)*
    ⌜RC685.V2⌝
    UF Aortic regurgitation
        Cardiac valve diseases
        Heart valve diseases
        Valvular diseases
        Valvular heart diseases
    NT Heart valve diseases in children
        Pulmonary stenosis
— — Transplantation *(May Subd Geog)*
— — — Patients *(May Subd Geog)*
— Ventricles
    UF Cardiac ventricles
        Ventricles, Heart
— — Diseases *(May Subd Geog)*
— Wounds and injuries *(May Subd Geog)*
    ⌜RD598⌝
— — Chemotherapy
— — Complications and sequelae
    (May Subd Geog)
— X-ray examination
    USE Heart—Radiography

Heart, Artificial (May Subd Geog)
 ₍RD598.35.A78₎
   Here are entered works on intracorporeal pump-
 ing mechanisms that duplicate the function of the
 natural heart. Works on extracorporeal pumping
 mechanisms that duplicate the function of the
 natural heart are entered under Heart, Mechanical.
   UF Artificial heart
       Intracorporeal artificial heart
   BT Artificial organs
       Blood—Circulation, Artificial
       Cardiovascular instruments, Implanted
   NT Pacemaker, Artificial (Heart)
 — **Complications and sequelae**
   (May Subd Geog)
 — **Power supply**
     BT Electric power
         Medical electronics
Heart, Fatty
 ₍RC685.F₎
 ₍SF811₎
   UF Fatty heart
   BT Heart—Diseases
   RT Degeneration, Fatty
Heart, Mechanical (May Subd Geog)
 ₍RD598.35.M42₎
   Here are entered works on extracorporeal pump-
 ing mechanisms that duplicate the function of the
 natural heart. Works on intracorporeal pumping
 mechanisms that duplicate the function of the natural
 heart are entered under Heart, Artificial.
   UF Extracorporeal artificial heart
       Heart-lung machine
       Mechanical heart
       Perfusion pump (Heart)
   BT Blood—Circulation, Artificial
       Heart—Surgery—Instruments
   NT Cardiopulmonary bypass
       Intra-aortic balloon counterpulsation
       Oxygenators
Heart arrest
   USE Cardiac arrest
Heart atrium
   UF Atrium cordis
       Cardiac atrium
   BT Heart
   NT Atrial natriuretic peptides
Heart attack
   USE Coronary heart disease
       Heart—Diseases
       Heart—Infarction
Heart beat
   UF Cardiac cycle
       Cycle, Cardiac
       Heart cycle
       Heart rate
   BT Heart conduction system
       Hemodynamics
   RT Heart—Contraction
       Pulse
   NT Arrhythmia
       Diastole (Cardiac cycle)
       Fetal heart rate monitoring
Heart block
   UF Cardiac block
   BT Arrhythmia
       Heart—Diseases
   NT Adams-Stokes syndrome
       Bundle-branch block
Heart catheterization
   USE Cardiac catheterization
Heart cells
 ₍QP114.C44₎
   UF Cardiac cells
       Cardiocytes
       Cardiomyocytes
   BT Cells
       Heart—Cytology
Heart cherry
   USE Sweet cherry
Heart circulation
   USE Coronary circulation

Heart conduction system
   UF Cardiac conduction system
       Conducting system of the heart
       Conduction system of the heart
       Conductive system of the heart
       Connecting system of the heart
       Heart—Conduction system
   BT Heart
   NT Heart beat
       His bundle
       Sinoatrial node
Heart contraction
   USE Heart—Contraction
Heart cycle
   USE Heart beat
Heart defects
   USE Heart—Abnormalities
Heart disease diagnostic equipment industry
   (May Subd Geog)
 ₍HD9995.C36-364₎
   BT Heart—Diseases—Diagnosis—
             Equipment and supplies
Heart diseases
   USE Heart—Diseases
Heart diseases, Congenital
   USE Heart—Abnormalities
Heart enlargement
   USE Heart—Dilatation
       Heart—Hypertrophy
Heart failure
 ₍RC682₎
   UF Cardiac insufficiency
   BT Heart—Diseases
       Surgery, Operative
   RT Cardiac arrest
   NT Congestive heart failure
Heart family
   USE Hart family
Heart function tests (May Subd Geog)
 ₍RC683.5.H4₎
   UF Cardiac function tests
   BT Function tests (Medicine)
   NT Indicator dilution
       Pulse—Measurement
       Treadmill exercise tests
Heart in art
Heart infections
   USE Heart—Infections
Heart-lung bypass
   USE Cardiopulmonary bypass
Heart-lung machine
   USE Heart, Mechanical
Heart massage
   USE Cardiac massage
Heart metabolism
   USE Heart—Metabolism
Heart murmurs
   UF Cardiac murmurs
       Heart—Sounds, Abnormal
       Murmurs, Heart
   BT Heart—Diseases—Diagnosis
       Heart—Sounds
Heart murmurs in children
   (May Subd Geog)
   BT Pediatric cardiology
Heart muscle
   USE Heart—Muscle
Heart of Jesus, Devotion to
   USE Sacred Heart, Devotion to
Heart of Mary, Devotion to
   USE Sacred Heart of Mary, Devotion to
Heart pacing
   USE Cardiac pacing
Heart patients
   USE Heart—Diseases—Patients
Heart rate
   USE Heart beat
Heart rate monitoring, Fetal
   USE Fetal heart rate monitoring
Heart receptors
   USE Cardiac receptors

Heart research
   USE Cardiology—Research
       Heart—Diseases—Research
Heart resuscitation
   USE Cardiac resuscitation
Heart septum
   UF Septum cordis
   BT Heart—Anatomy
 — **Abnormalities**
     NT Endocardial cushion defects
Heart sounds
   USE Heart—Sounds
Heart surgery instruments industry
   (May Subd Geog)
 ₍HD9995.C36-364₎
Heart tones
   USE Heart—Sounds
Heart transplantation
   USE Heart—Transplantation
Heart valve diseases
   USE Heart—Valves—Diseases
Heart valve diseases in children
   (May Subd Geog)
 ₍RJ426.V3₎
   BT Heart—Valves—Diseases
       Pediatric cardiology
Heart valve prosthesis
 ₍RD598₎
   UF Prosthetic heart valves
   BT Heart—Valves
       Prosthesis
Heart valve prosthesis industry
   (May Subd Geog)
 ₍HD9995.C36-HD9995.C364₎
Heart valves
   USE Heart—Valves
Heart worm, Canine
   USE Dirofilaria immitis
Heart worm, Feline
   USE Dirofilaria immitis
Heartburn
   UF Cardialgia
       Pyrosis
   BT Indigestion
       Symptomatology
   RT Gastroesophageal reflux
Hearth Cat (Legendary character)
   USE Cinderella (Legendary character)
Hearth-money (May Subd Geog)
 ₍HJ2612 (English tax)₎
   UF Chimney-money
       Hearth tax
       Taxation of hearths
   BT Taxation
Hearth tax
   USE Hearth-money
Heartley family
   USE Hartley family
Heartly family
   USE Hartley family
Heartman family
   USE Hartman family
Hearts (Game)
 ₍GV1295.H4₎
Heartwater
 ₍SF809.H4₎
   BT Cattle—Diseases
       Rickettsial diseases
Heartwood (May Subd Geog)
 ₍QK647 (Botany)₎
   UF Duramen
   BT Wood
Heartworm, Canine
   USE Dirofilaria immitis
Heartworm, Feline
   USE Dirofilaria immitis
Heartworm disease in cats
   USE Feline heartworm disease
Heartworm disease in dogs
   USE Canine heartworm disease

Heaslip family
  USE Haislip family
Heat
    [QC251-338]
  BT Electromagnetic waves
     Physics
  RT Cold
     Combustion
     Fire
     Temperature
     Thermochemistry
     Thermodynamics
  NT Aerodynamic heating
     Animal heat
     Atmospheric temperature
     Calorimeters and calorimetry
     Cogeneration of electric power and
      heat
     Entropy
     Expansion (Heat)
     Expansion of gases
     Expansion of liquids
     Expansion of solids
     Food—Effect of heat on
     Fusion, Latent heat of
     Gases—Liquefaction
     Heat engineering
     High temperatures
     Liquid air
     Metals at high temperatures
     Pyrometers and pyrometry
     Solidification
     Steam
     Surfaces, Isothermic
     Temperature control
     Thawing
     Thermoelectricity
     Thermography
     Thermography (Copying process)
     Thermomagnetism
     Thermometers and thermometry
     Waste heat
  — Absorption
    USE Heat—Radiation and absorption
  — Conduction
     [QC321-3]
    UF Conduction of heat
    NT Thermal diffusivity
  — — Computer programs
  — Convection
     [QC327]
    UF Convection of heat
    NT Convection (Astrophysics)
      Convection (Meteorology)
  — Convection, Natural
     [QC330]
    UF Convection, Free
      Convection, Natural
      Free convection
      Natural convection
    BT Fluid dynamics
  — Experiments
  — Laboratory manuals
     [QC263]
    BT Calorimeters and calorimetry
  — Physiological effect
     [QH653 (Cells)]
     [QP82 (Physiology)]
    UF Heat stress (Biology)
      High temperatures—Physiological
       effect
      Hyperthermia
    BT Temperature—Physiological effect
    NT Heat shock proteins
      Heatstroke
      Plants, Effect of heat on
  — Radiation and absorption
     [QC331-8]

    UF Absorption (Heat)
      Heat—Absorption
      Heat absorption
      Radiative heat transfer
    BT Absorption spectra
      Radiation
    RT Radiative transfer
    NT Cooling
  — Religious aspects
  — — Buddhism, [Christianity, etc.]
  — Storage devices
    USE Heat storage devices
  — Therapeutic use
    USE Thermotherapy
  — Transmission
     [QC320-338]
    UF Heat transfer
      Thermal transfer
      Transmission of heat
    BT Energy transfer
    NT Ablation (Aerothermodynamics)
      Ceilings—Thermal properties
      Doors—Thermal properties
      Exterior walls—Thermal properties
      Film boiling
      Film coefficients (Physics)
      Heat exchangers
      Heat pipes
      Heat pulses
      Heat sinks (Electronics)
      Heat-transfer media
      Rayleigh number
      Terrestrial heat flow
      Windows—Thermal properties
  — — Computer programs
  — — Instruments
     [QC323]
    UF Instruments, Heat transfer
    NT Heat flux transducers
Heat, Mechanical equivalent of
    [QC312]
  UF Mechanical equivalent of heat
  BT Force and energy
     Thermodynamics
Heat, Specific
  USE Specific heat
Heat absorption
  USE Heat—Radiation and absorption
Heat accumulators
  USE Heat regenerators
Heat and electric power cogeneration
  USE Cogeneration of electric power and
    heat
Heat as a disinfectant
    [RA766.H4]
  BT Disinfection and disinfectants
Heat balance (Engineering)
  UF Balance, Heat (Engineering)
  BT Heating
     Thermodynamics
Heat barrier
  USE Aerodynamic heating
    High temperatures
Heat budget (Geophysics) *(May Subd Geog)*
    [QC809.E6]
  UF Budget, Heat (Geophysics)
     Thermal budget (Geophysics)
  BT Energy budget (Geophysics)
  RT Atmospheric temperature
     Ocean temperature
  NT Atmospheric thermodynamics
     Greenhouse effect, Atmospheric
     Soil temperature
     Terrestrial heat flow
Heat Capacity Mapping Mission Program
  UF HCMM Program
  BT Astronautics in earth sciences
     Earth sciences—Remote sensing
     Earth temperature—Remote sensing
     Infrared albedo—Measurement

Heat content
  USE Enthalpy
Heat developable paper
  USE Thermographic paper
Heat engineering *(May Subd Geog)*
  BT Heat
     Mechanical engineering
     Thermodynamics
  NT Combustion engineering
     Geothermal engineering
     Heat-engines
     Heat recovery
     Heat storage
     Heating
  — Instruments
    UF Instruments, Heat engineering
  — — Appraisal
     USE Heat engineering—Instruments
        —Valuation
  — — Valuation
     [TJ260]
    UF Heat engineering—Instruments
      —Appraisal
  — Safety regulations *(May Subd Geog)*
    BT Engineering law
  — Standards
    BT Standards, Engineering
Heat engineering laboratories
  USE Thermodynamics laboratories
Heat-engines
    [TJ255-TJ265 (Mechanical
     engineering)]
  BT Engines
     Heat engineering
  RT Thermodynamics
  NT Heat pumps
     Internal combustion engines
     Satz engine
     Steam-engines
     Stirling engines
  — Thermodynamics
     [TJ265]
Heat equation
    [QA377]
  UF Diffusion equation
     Heat flow equation
  BT Differential equations, Parabolic
  NT Burgers equation
     Terrestrial heat flow
  — Numerical solutions
    BT Numerical analysis
Heat exchanger industry *(May Subd Geog)*
  BT Heat exchangers
Heat exchangers
    [TP363]
  BT Chemical engineering—Apparatus and
     supplies
     Heat—Transmission
     Refrigeration and refrigerating
      machinery
  NT Air heaters
     Heat exchanger industry
  — Fluid dynamics
  — Fouling
  — Vibration
  — Welding
Heat flow, Terrestrial
  USE Terrestrial heat flow
Heat flow equation
  USE Heat equation
Heat flow equation, Nonlinear
  USE Burgers equation
Heat flux transducers
  UF Transducers, Heat flux
  BT Heat—Transmission—Instruments
     Transducers
Heat function
  USE Enthalpy
Heat in animals
  USE Estrus

Heat insulating materials
USE Insulation (Heat)
Heat island, Urban
USE Urban heat island
Heat of adsorption
BT Adsorption
Heat of combustion
UF Combustion, Heat of
BT Fuel—Testing
Thermochemistry
Heat of dilution
USE Heat of solution
Heat of formation
UF Enthalpy of formation
Formation, Heat of
BT Thermochemistry
Thermodynamics
Heat of hydration
BT Hydration
Thermochemistry
Heat of immersion
USE Heat of wetting
Heat of mixing
BT Mixing
Heat of solution
_[QC310]_
UF Heat of dilution
Solution, Heat of
BT Calorimeters and calorimetry
Solubility
Solution (Chemistry)
Thermochemistry
Heat of wetting
_[QC310]_
UF Energy of immersion
Heat of immersion
Immersion, Heat of
BT Wetting
Heat pipes
Here are entered works on heat transfer cylinders
that absorb heat at one end by vaporization of a liquid
and release heat by condensation of the liquid at the
other end. Works on pipes which are components of
heating installations in structures are entered under
Heating-pipes.
BT Heat—Transmission
Heat-transfer media
Pipe
Heat pollution of rivers, lakes, etc.
USE Thermal pollution of rivers, lakes, etc.
Heat production in plants
USE Plants, Heat production in
Heat pulses
UF Pulses, Heat
BT Heat—Transmission
Heat pump industry _(May Subd Geog)_
_[HD9683]_
BT Heat pumps
Heat pumps _(May Subd Geog)_
[TH7638 (Heating)]
[TJ262 (Mechanical engineering)]
BT Heat-engines
Pumping machinery
Thermodynamics
NT Heat pump industry
— Thermodynamics
Heat recovery
UF Recovery of waste heat
Waste heat recovery
BT Cogeneration of electric power and
heat
Heat engineering
Waste heat
RT Heat regenerators
NT Total energy systems (On-site electric
power production)
— Equipment and supplies
NT Heat recovery equipment industry
Heat recovery equipment industry
(May Subd Geog)
_[HD9683.5.H46-464]_

BT Heat recovery—Equipment and
supplies
Heat regenerators
UF Heat accumulators
BT Heat storage devices
Stoves
Waste heat
RT Heat recovery
Heat release in the atmosphere, Latent
USE Atmosphere—Latent heat release
Heat resistant alloys
_[TN700]_
UF Alloys, Heat resistant
High temperature metals
Metals, Heat resistant
Refractory metals
Superalloys
BT Alloys
Heat resistant materials
Metals at high temperatures
Powder metallurgy
NT Chromium-cobalt-nickel-molybdenum
alloys
Nimonic alloys
Nitrides
Steel, Heat resistant
Tantalum alloys
— Welding
Heat resistant concrete
UF Concrete, Heat resistant
BT Concrete
Heat resistant materials
RT Concrete, Effect of temperature on
Heat resistant materials
_[TA418.26]_
UF High temperature materials
BT Materials
Materials at high temperatures
NT Ceramic metals
Heat resistant alloys
Heat resistant concrete
Heat resistant plastics
Refractory materials
Heat resistant plastics
BT Heat resistant materials
Plastics
NT Polyimidazopyrrolone
Heat resistant steel
USE Steel, Heat resistant
Heat sensitive copying processes
USE Thermography (Copying process)
Heat shielding
USE Shielding (Heat)
Heat shock proteins
_[QP552.H43]_
BT Heat—Physiological effect
Proteins
Heat sinks (Electronics)
_[TK7872.H4]_
UF Dissipators (Electronics)
BT Heat—Transmission
RT Electronic apparatus and appliances—
Cooling
Semiconductors—Cooling
Heat storage
UF Storage, Heat
Thermal energy storage
BT Energy storage
Heat engineering
Thermodynamics
Heat storage devices
UF Heat—Storage devices
Storage devices, Heat
Thermal storage devices
BT Heating
NT Heat regenerators
Heat stress (Biology)
USE Heat—Physiological effect
Heat stroke
USE Heatstroke

Heat transfer
USE Heat—Transmission
Heat transfer, Terrestrial
USE Terrestrial heat flow
Heat transfer coefficient
USE Nusselt number
Heat transfer images
USE Thermography (Copying process)
Heat-transfer media
UF Heat-transmission media
Thermal-transfer media
BT Heat—Transmission
NT Heat pipes
Refrigerants
Heat-transmission media
USE Heat-transfer media
Heat treatment of aluminum alloys
USE Aluminum alloys—Heat treatment
Heat treatment of metals
USE Metals—Heat treatment
Heat treatment of steel
USE Steel—Heat treatment
Heated water discharges into rivers, lakes, etc.
USE Thermal pollution of rivers, lakes, etc.
Heaten family
USE Heaton family
Heater family _(Not Subd Geog)_
UF Heatter family
Heeter family
Heaters, Air
USE Air heaters
Heaters, Kerosene
USE Kerosene heaters
Heaters, Space
USE Space heaters
Heaters, Tube-still
USE Tube-still heaters
Heath (Botany)
USE Erica
Heather
Heath berry, Baby
USE Empetrum nigrum
Heath ecology
USE Moor ecology
Heath family _(Not Subd Geog)_
UF Heathe family
Heth family
Heath fauna
USE Moor fauna
Heath flora
USE Moor flora
Heath Formation (Mont.) _(Not Subd Geog)_
BT Formations (Geology)—Montana
Geology, Stratigraphic—Mississippian
Heath H-8 (Computer)
USE Heathkit H-8 (Computer)
Heathcock
USE Black grouse
Heathcock family
USE Hathcock family
Heathcote National Park (N.S.W.)
BT National parks and reserves—Australia
Heathe family
USE Heath family
Heathenism
USE Paganism
Heather
_[QK495.E68]_
UF Calluna
Heath (Botany)
BT Ericaceae
Forage plants
Heathkit H-8 (Computer)
UF H-8 (Computer)
Heath H-8 (Computer)
BT Microcomputers
— Programming
Heaths
USE Moors and heaths

Heating
⌐GT420-GT425 *(Manners and customs)*⌐
⌐TH7010-TH7641 *(Building construction)*⌐
BT Buildings—Environmental engineering
Fire
Heat engineering
Home economics
Sanitation, Household
RT Boilers
Fuel
Stoves
Ventilation
SA *subdivision* Heating and ventilation *under types of buildings, factories, vehicles, or other constructions, e.g.* Factories—Heating and ventilation; Railroads—Cars—Heating and ventilation
NT Air curtains
Braziers
Buildings—Airtightness
Chimneys
Cogeneration of electric power and heat
Degree days
Electric heating
Fans (Machinery)
Fireplaces
Furnaces
Heat balance (Engineering)
Heat storage devices
Heating load
Hot-air heating
Hot-water heating
Insulation (Heat)
Oil burners
Radiant heating
Radiators
Soil heating
Solar heating
Space heaters
Steam-heating
Waste heat
— Climatic factors
⌐TH7015⌐
BT Engineering meteorology
— Control
⌐TH7466.5⌐
UF Heating—Regulators
BT Heating—Equipment and supplies
Temperature control
Thermostat
SA *subdivision* Heating and ventilation—Control *under subjects, e.g.* Dwellings—Heating and ventilation—Control
NT Hot-water heating—Regulators
Induction heating—Regulators
Steam-heating—Regulators
— Equipment and supplies
NT Heating—Control
— Law and legislation *(May Subd Geog)*
UF Dwellings—Heating and ventilation—Law and legislation
BT Building laws
NT Heating and ventilation industry—Law and legislation
— Panel system
USE Radiant heating
— Regulators
USE Heating—Control
Heating, Aerodynamic
USE Aerodynamic heating
Heating, Dielectric
USE Dielectric heating
Heating, Infrared
USE Infrared heating
Heating, Microwave
USE Microwave heating

Heating, Plasma
USE Plasma heating
Heating and ventilation control in dwellings
USE Dwellings—Heating and ventilation—Control
Heating and ventilation industry
(May Subd Geog)
BT Ventilation
NT Air conditioning industry
Heating equipment industry
— **Law and legislation** *(May Subd Geog)*
BT Building laws
Heating—Law and legislation
NT Air conditioning industry—Law and legislation
— Strikes and lockouts
USE Strikes and lockouts—Plumbing and heating industry
Heating equipment industry
(May Subd Geog)
BT Heating and ventilation industry
Heating from central stations
(May Subd Geog)
⌐TH7641⌐
UF Central heating plants
Central station heating
District heating
BT Heating plants
NT Cogeneration of electric power and heat
Heating load
BT Heating
Thermodynamics
Heating of petroleum products
USE Petroleum products—Heating
Heating-pipes
⌐TH7478⌐
Here are entered works on pipes which are components of heating installations in structures. Works on heat transfer cylinders that absorb heat at one end by vaporization of a liquid and release heat by condensation of the liquid at the other end are entered under Heat pipes.
BT Pipe
Plumbing
Heating plants
⌐TH7461⌐
⌐TJ395⌐
NT Heating from central stations
— Collective labor agreements
USE Collective labor agreements—Heating plants
— **Equipment and supplies**
Heating research
BT Building research
Heaton family *(Not Subd Geog)*
UF Heaten family
Heats of vaporization
USE Vaporization, Heats of
Heatstroke
UF Heat stroke
BT Heat—Physiological effect
Heatter family
USE Heater family
Heatwole family *(Not Subd Geog)*
Heaven
⌐BT844-BT849⌐
⌐N8150 *(Art)*⌐
BT Future life
NT Beatific vision
Empyrean
Heavenly recognition
Intermediate state
Takamagahara
Translation to heaven
— **Buddhism,** ⌐**Christianity, etc.**⌐
— Islam
USE Paradise (Islam)

Heaven in art
Heavener family *(Not Subd Geog)*
UF Havener family
Havner family
Heavner family
Heevner family
Hevener family
Hevner family
Hivner family
RT Huebner family
Heavenly recognition
⌐BT847⌐
Here are entered works on the Christian belief that in heaven the redeemed will recognize those whom they knew on earth.
UF Recognition, Heavenly
BT Heaven
Heavenly sanctuary doctrine (Seventh-Day Adventists)
USE Sanctuary doctrine (Seventh-Day Adventists)
Heaviside layer
USE Ionosphere
Heavner family
USE Heavener family
Heavy electrons
USE Mesons
Heavy elements
UF Elements, Heavy
BT Chemical elements
Radioactive substances
NT Actinide elements
Superheavy elements
Transuranium elements
Heavy elements, Super
USE Superheavy elements
Heavy harness horses
USE Coach horses
Heavy horses
USE Draft horses
Heavy hydrogen
USE Hydrogen—Isotopes
Heavy ion accelerators
⌐QC787.L5⌐
UF Accelerators, Heavy ion
Heavy ion linac
Heavy ion linear accelerators
Hilac
Linac, Heavy ion
BT Heavy ions
Ion accelerators
Linear accelerators
Heavy ion collisions
⌐QC794.8.H4⌐
BT Collisions (Nuclear physics)
Deep inelastic collisions
Heavy ions
RT Ion bombardment
— **Spectra**
Heavy ion fusion reactions
⌐QC794.8.H4⌐
UF Fusion reactions, Heavy ion
BT Nuclear fusion
Heavy ion linac
USE Heavy ion accelerators
Heavy ion linear accelerators
USE Heavy ion accelerators
Heavy ions
⌐QC702.7.H42⌐
BT Ions
NT Heavy ion accelerators
Heavy ion collisions
Heavy metal (Music) *(May Subd Geog)*
BT Rock music
Heavy metals
BT Metals
NT Plants, Effect of heavy metals on
Soils—Heavy metal content
Heavy metals removal (Sewage purification)
USE Sewage—Purification—Heavy metals removal

Heavy minerals *(May Subd Geog)*
　UF　Minerals, Heavy
　BT　Mineralogy
　　　Rocks, Sedimentary
Heavy particles (Nuclear physics)
　BT　Particles (Nuclear physics)
　NT　Baryons
　　　Hyperons
　　　Kaons
Heavy water
　USE　Deuterium oxide
Heavy water piles
　USE　Heavy water reactors
Heavy water reactors
　　[TK9203.H4]
　UF　Heavy water piles
　BT　Deuterium oxide
　　　Nuclear reactors
　　　Solid fuel reactors
　NT　Steam generating heavy water reactors
　— **Exponential measurements**
　　　UF　Reactor lattices
　　　BT　Neutrons
　　　　　Nuclear engineering
　　　　　Nuclear fuels
Heb family
　USE　Hebb family
Hebard family
　USE　Hibbert family
Hebb family *(Not Subd Geog)*
　UF　Heb family
Hebbard family
　USE　Hibbert family
Hebeloma
　　[QK629.C787]
　UF　Hebelomatis
　BT　Cortinariaceae
Hebelomatis
　USE　Hebeloma
Heber-Reno Stock Trail (Ariz.)
　UF　Heber-Reno Trail (Ariz.)
　　　Reno-Heber Stock Trail (Ariz.)
　BT　Trails—Arizona
Heber-Reno Trail (Ariz.)
　USE　Heber-Reno Stock Trail (Ariz.)
Heberlein family *(Not Subd Geog)*
Hebert family
　USE　Hibbert family
Hebertella
　BT　Plectorthidae
Hebin
　　[QP187]
　BT　Gonadotropin
　　　Pituitary hormones
Hebler family
　USE　Hepler family
Hebot family
　USE　Hibbert family
Hebraists *(May Subd Geog)*
　BT　Hebrew philology
　　　Philologists
　　　Scholars
Hebraists, Christian *(May Subd Geog)*
　UF　Christian Hebraists
Hebrew art
　USE　Art, Jewish
Hebrew artists
　USE　Artists, Jewish
Hebrew astrology
　USE　Astrology, Hebrew
Hebrew astronomy
　USE　Astronomy, Jewish
Hebrew authors
　USE　Authors, Hebrew
Hebrew ballads
　USE　Ballads, Hebrew
Hebrew calendar
　USE　Calendar, Jewish
Hebrew calligraphy
　USE　Calligraphy, Hebrew

Hebrew children's encyclopedias and
　dictionaries
　USE　Children's encyclopedias and
　　　　dictionaries, Hebrew
Hebrew children's literature
　USE　Children's literature, Hebrew
Hebrew children's plays
　USE　Children's plays, Hebrew
Hebrew children's poetry
　USE　Children's poetry, Hebrew
Hebrew children's prose poems
　USE　Children's prose poems, Hebrew
Hebrew Christians
　USE　Jewish Christians
Hebrew chronology
　USE　Chronology, Jewish
Hebrew commercial correspondence
　USE　Commercial correspondence, Hebrew
Hebrew day schools
　USE　Jewish day schools
Hebrew detective stories
　USE　Detective and mystery stories, Hebrew
Hebrew drama *(May Subd Geog)*
　BT　Bible plays
　　　Jewish drama
　RT　Israeli drama
　NT　Children's plays, Hebrew
　　　Moralities, Hebrew
　— Israel
　　　USE　Israeli drama
Hebrew elegiac poetry
　USE　Elegiac poetry, Hebrew
Hebrew encyclopedias and dictionaries
　USE　Encyclopedias and dictionaries,
　　　　Hebrew
Hebrew essays
　　Here are entered collections of essays by several
　authors.
Hebrew fables
　USE　Fables, Hebrew
Hebrew fiction *(May Subd Geog)*
　NT　Detective and mystery stories, Hebrew
　　　Love stories, Hebrew
　　　Sea stories, Hebrew
　　　Short stories, Hebrew
　— Israel
　　　USE　Israeli fiction
Hebrew folk literature
　USE　Folk literature, Hebrew
Hebrew folk-songs
　USE　Folk-songs, Hebrew
Hebrew hymns
　USE　Hymns, Hebrew
Hebrew illumination of books and manuscripts
　USE　Illumination of books and manuscripts,
　　　　Jewish
Hebrew imprints *(May Subd Geog)*
　— Cataloging
　　　USE　Cataloging of Hebrew imprints
Hebrew incantations
　USE　Incantations, Hebrew
Hebrew inscriptions
　USE　Inscriptions, Hebrew
Hebrew language *(May Subd Geog)*
　　[PJ4501-PJ4937]
　UF　Bible—Philology
　　　Jewish language
　BT　Bible—Language, style
　　　Jews—Languages
　　　Languages—Religious aspects
　　　Semitic languages, Northwest
　NT　Hakétia language
　　　Italian language—Dialects—Judeo-
　　　　Italian
　　　Ladino language
　　　Yiddish language
　— **Accents and accentuation**
　　　NT　Bible. O.T.—Accents and
　　　　　accentuation
　— **Etymology**
　　　NT　'Am (The Hebrew word)

　　　　Arakh (The Hebrew word)
　　　　'Avad (The Hebrew word)
　　　　Dam (The Hebrew word)
　　　　Drakon (The Hebrew word)
　　　　Emet (The Hebrew word)
　　　　Hesed (The Hebrew word)
　　　　'Ir (The Hebrew word)
　　　　'Ivri (The Hebrew word)
　　　　Kodesh (The Hebrew word)
　　　　Lev (The Hebrew word)
　　　　Mal'akh (The Hebrew word)
　　　　Na'ar (The Hebrew word)
　　　　Nefesh (The Hebrew word)
　　　　Ruah (The Hebrew word)
　　　　Shem (The Hebrew word)
　　　　Shema' (The Hebrew word)
　　　　Shim'u (The Hebrew word)
　　　　Torah (The Hebrew word)
　　　　Tsedek (The Hebrew word)
　— **Metrics and rhythmics**
　　　Here are entered works on the meter and
　　rhythm of the Hebrew Bible and other ancient
　　Hebrew literature. Works on the versification of
　　medieval and modern Hebrew poetry are entered
　　under Hebrew language—Versification.
　— **Particles**
　　　NT　Ki (The Hebrew particle)
　— **Punctuation**
　　　NT　Bible. O.T.—Accents and
　　　　　accentuation
　— **Roots**
　　　NT　Brk (The Hebrew root)
　　　　　Hyh (The Hebrew root)
　　　　　Hzh (The Hebrew root)
　　　　　Kpr (The Hebrew root)
　　　　　Myt (The Hebrew root)
　　　　　Ntn (The Hebrew root)
　　　　　Pkd (The Hebrew root)
　　　　　'Rk (The Hebrew root)
　　　　　Shb' (The Hebrew root)
　　　　　Tsdk (The Hebrew root)
　　　　　'Vd (The Hebrew root)
　— **Versification**
　　　Here are entered works on the versification of
　　medieval and modern Hebrew poetry. Works on
　　the meter and rhythm of the Hebrew Bible and
　　other ancient Hebrew literature are entered
　　under Hebrew language—Metrics and rhyth-
　　mics.
　— **Vocalization**
　— **Writing**
　　　NT　Scribes, Jewish—Handbooks,
　　　　　manuals, etc.
Hebrew language, Mishnaic
　USE　Hebrew language, Talmudic
Hebrew language, Post-Biblical
　　[PJ4901-4950]
　UF　Hebrew language, Rabbinic
　— **Particles**
　　　NT　Ela (The Hebrew particle)
Hebrew language, Rabbinic
　USE　Hebrew language, Post-Biblical
Hebrew language, Talmudic
　　[PJ4901-4950]
　UF　Hebrew language, Mishnaic
Hebrew law
　USE　Jewish law
Hebrew letters
Hebrew libraries
　USE　Jewish libraries
Hebrew literature
　　[PJ5001-PJ5060]
　UF　Jews—Literature
　RT　Jewish literature
　NT　Approbations (Hebrew literature)
　　　Bible
　　　Children's literature, Hebrew
　　　Children's stories, Hebrew
　　　Folk literature, Hebrew
　　　Geonic literature
　　　Hebrew prose literature
　　　Rabbinical literature

Talmud
— Cataloging
USE Cataloging of Jewish literature
Hebrew literature, Medieval
⌐PJ5016 (History)⌐
⌐PJ5037 (Collections)⌐
Hebrew literature, Modern
(May Subd Geog)
⌐PJ5017-PJ5021 (History)⌐
⌐PJ5038 (Collections)⌐
— Israel
USE Israeli literature
Hebrew love poetry
USE Love poetry, Hebrew
Hebrew love stories
USE Love stories, Hebrew
Hebrew manuscripts
USE Manuscripts, Hebrew
Hebrew maqamah
USE Maqamah, Hebrew
Hebrew medicine
USE Medicine, Jewish
Hebrew moralities
USE Moralities, Hebrew
Hebrew music
USE Jews—Music
Hebrew mystery stories
USE Detective and mystery stories, Hebrew
Hebrew newspapers
⌐PN5650⌐
BT Jewish newspapers
Hebrew paleography
USE Paleography, Hebrew
Hebrew periodicals
⌐PN5650⌐
Hebrew philology
⌐PJ4501-4541⌐
NT Hebraists
Hebrew poetry *(May Subd Geog)*
⌐PJ5022-PJ5025 (History)⌐
⌐PJ5039-PJ5042 (Collections)⌐
UF Bible—Poetry
BT Jewish poetry
NT Azharot
Children's poetry, Hebrew
Elegiac poetry, Hebrew
Jewish religious poetry, Hebrew
Love poetry, Hebrew
Maqamah, Hebrew
Prose poems, Hebrew
Samaritan religious poetry, Hebrew
Hebrew poetry, Biblical
⌐BS1401-BS1405.5⌐
UF Bible—Poetry
NT Psalmody
Hebrew poetry, Medieval
NT Piyutim
Hebrew poetry, Modern *(May Subd Geog)*
— Israel
USE Israeli poetry
Hebrew poets
USE Poets, Hebrew
Hebrew prose literature *(May Subd Geog)*
BT Hebrew literature
NT Prose poems, Hebrew
Hebrew prose poems
USE Prose poems, Hebrew
Hebrew quotations
USE Quotations, Hebrew
Hebrew satire
USE Satire, Hebrew
Hebrew sea stories
USE Sea stories, Hebrew
Hebrew short stories
USE Short stories, Hebrew
Hebrew songs
USE Songs, Hebrew
Hebrew wit and humor
RT Jewish wit and humor
NT Israeli wit and humor

Hebrews
USE Jews
Hebridae
⌐QL523.H4⌐
UF Naeogaeidae
Velvet water bugs
Water bugs, Velvet
BT Hemiptera
Hebrides (Scotland)
UF Ebudae (Scotland)
Hebudae (Scotland)
Western Islands (Scotland)
BT Islands—Scotland
NT Inner Hebrides (Scotland)
Western Isles (Scotland)
Hebrides, Outer (Scotland)
USE Western Isles (Scotland)
Hebudae (Scotland)
USE Hebrides (Scotland)
Hecalidae
USE Leafhoppers
Hecate (Greek deity)
⌐BL820.H43⌐
BT Goddesses, Greek
Hecate Strait (B.C.)
BT Straits—British Columbia
Hecathorn family
USE Heckathorn family
Heck family *(Not Subd Geog)*
RT Hicks family
Heckathorn family *(Not Subd Geog)*
UF Hackathorn family
Hackedorn family
Hackendorn family
Hackthorn family
Hecathorn family
Heckendorn family
Hecke operators
UF Operators, Hecke
BT Forms, Modular
Operator theory
Heckelphone
⌐ML990.H4⌐
BT Oboe
Heckelphone music
⌐M110.H4⌐
NT Quintets (Harpsichord, English horn, heckelphone, oboe, oboe d'amore)
Quintets (Piano, English horn, heckelphone, oboe, oboe d'amore)
Woodwind quartets (English horn, heckelphone, oboe, oboe d'amore)
Woodwind trios (English horn, heckelphone, oboe)
Heckendorn family
USE Heckathorn family
Heckman family
USE Hickman family
Heckmann family
USE Hickman family
Hecla (Iceland)
USE Hekla (Iceland)
Hecla Provincial Park (Man.)
BT Parks—Manitoba
Hecter fuel
⌐TL704.7⌐
BT Fuel
Liquid fuels
Hectograph
⌐Z48⌐
BT Copying processes
Hector (Legendary character)
BT Folklore—Greece
Hector Land Use Area (N.Y.)
BT Forests and forestry—New York (State)
Parks—New York (State)
Hector Mountains (New Zealand)
(Not Subd Geog)
BT Mountains—New Zealand

Hecuba (Legendary character)
BT Folklore—Greece
Hedden family
USE Hadden family
Heddin family
USE Hadden family
Heddon family
USE Hadden family
Hedelund family *(Not Subd Geog)*
Heden family
USE Hadden family
Hedenbergite
⌐QE391.H34⌐
BT Pyroxene
Heder
UF Cheder
BT Jewish day schools
Jews—Education
Hedera senticosa
USE Acanthopanax senticosus
Hederelloidea
USE Cyclostomata, Fossil (Bryozoa)
Hedge clippers
⌐SB454.8⌐
UF Clippers, Hedge
Hedge shears
Hedge trimmers
Shears, Hedge
Trimmers, Hedge
BT Pruning shears
Hedge family
USE Hedges family
Hedge nettles
USE Stachys
Hedge shears
USE Hedge clippers
Hedge-sparrow
USE Dunnock
Hedge trimmers
USE Hedge clippers
Hedgehogs
⌐QL737.I53⌐
BT Erinaceidae
Hedgehogs, Fossil
⌐QE882.I5⌐
UF Erinaceidae, Fossil
BT Insectivora, Fossil
NT Brachyericinae
Erinaceinae
Hedgepath family
USE Hedgpeth family
Hedgepeth family
USE Hedgpeth family
Hedger family
USE Hedges family
Hedgerow ecology *(May Subd Geog)*
BT Ecology
Windbreaks, shelterbelts, etc.
Hedgerows
USE Windbreaks, shelterbelts, etc.
Hedges *(May Subd Geog)*
⌐SB437⌐
BT Landscape architecture
Trees
RT Fences
Screens (Plants)
Shrubs
NT Evergreens
Landscape gardening
Maze gardens
Hedges family *(Not Subd Geog)*
UF Hedge family
Hedger family
Hedging (Finance)
UF Futures
BT Commodity exchanges
Put and call transactions
Speculation
Stock-exchange
RT Financial futures
— **Law and legislation** *(May Subd Geog)*

Hedgpeth family *(Not Subd Geog)*
　UF　Hedgepath family
　　　Hedgepeth family
　　　Hedgspeth family
　　　Hudspeth family
Hedgspeth family
　USE　Hedgpeth family
Hedinger family
　USE　Hardinger family
Hedley family
　USE　Hadley family
Hedly family
　USE　Hadley family
Hedonal
　[QP981.H5 (Physiology)]
　[RM666.H (Therapeutics)]
Hedonism
　[B279 (Greek philosophy)]
　[BJ1491 (Ethics)]
　UF　Eudemonism
　BT　Asceticism
　　　Ethics
　　　Philosophy
　RT　Pleasure
　　　Utilitarianism
　NT　Lokāyata
Hedreadge family
　USE　Hildreth family
Hedstrom family *(Not Subd Geog)*
Hedylepta
　[QL561.P9]
　BT　Pyralidae
Hedylepta accepta
　USE　Sugarcane leafroller
Hedylidae
　USE　Geometridae
Heekeren family *(Not Subd Geog)*
　UF　Van Heekeren family
Heel bone
　UF　Calcaneal bone
　　　Calcaneum
　　　Calcaneus
　　　Os calcis
　　　Os tarsi fibulare
　BT　Foot
　— Fracture
Heel flies
　USE　Warble-flies
Heeler, Australian
　USE　Australian cattle dog
Heeler, Blue
　USE　Australian cattle dog
Heeler, Queensland
　USE　Australian cattle dog
Heemskerk, Martin van, 1498-1574.　Saint
　Luke painting the portrait of the Virgin
　[ND653.H]
　UF　Saint Luke painting the portrait of the
　　　　Virgin (Painting)
　　　Sant Lucas-altaar (Painting)
Heere family
　USE　Hair family
Heerin family
　USE　Hearn family
Heerman family
　USE　Herman family
Heesbeen family *(Not Subd Geog)*
Heeter family
　USE　Heater family
Heevner family
　USE　Heavener family
Hegau (Germany)
Hegele family *(Not Subd Geog)*
Hegeman family *(Not Subd Geog)*
Hegeter
　[QL596.T2]
　BT　Tenebrionidae
Hegetotheriidae
　[QE882.N6]
　BT　Notoungulata
　NT　Raulringueletia

Heggins family
　USE　Higgins family
Hegins family
　USE　Higgins family
Hegirah
　USE　Muḥammad, Prophet, d. 632—Hijrah
Hegue language
　USE　Eudeve language
Hegward family
　USE　Hayward family
Hegwood family
　USE　Hayward family
Hegyköz (Hungary)
Hehe law
　USE　Law, Wahehe
Hehn family
　USE　Haynes family
Hehns family
　USE　Haynes family
Hei Ho (China and R.S.F.S.R.)
　USE　Amur River (China and R.S.F.S.R.)
Hei-kom (African people)
　USE　Heikum (African people)
Hei-lung Chiang (China and R.S.F.S.R.)
　USE　Amur River (China and R.S.F.S.R.)
Hei-lung Kiang (China and R.S.F.S.R.)
　USE　Amur River (China and R.S.F.S.R.)
Hei Miao dialect
　USE　Black Hmong dialect
Heia (African people)
　USE　Haya (African people)
Heian Jingū (Kyoto, Japan)
　NT　Heian no Sono (Kyoto, Japan)
Heian no Sono (Kyoto, Japan)
　(Not Subd Geog)
　BT　Botanical gardens—Japan
　　　Gardens—Japan
　　　Heian Jingū (Kyoto, Japan)
Heibel family *(Not Subd Geog)*
Heiberg family
　USE　Heiberger family
Heiberger family *(Not Subd Geog)*
　UF　Heiberg family
Heidel family *(Not Subd Geog)*
Heidelberg family *(Not Subd Geog)*
　UF　Heidelberger family
Heidelberg school
　[ND1100.17.I45]
　BT　Impressionism (Art)—Australia
　　　Painting, Australian
　　　Painting, Modern—19th century—
　　　　Australia
Heidelberger family
　USE　Heidelberg family
Heiden family
　USE　Heider family
Heidenhain pouch
　UF　Heidenhain's pouch
　BT　Physiology, Experimental
　　　Stomach
Heidenhain syndrome
　USE　Jakob-Creutzfeldt disease
Heidenhain's pouch
　USE　Heidenhain pouch
Heidenreich family *(Not Subd Geog)*
　UF　Heidenrich family
　　　Heidenrick family
　　　Heidenriech family
　　　Heidenright family
　　　Heitenrick family
Heidenrich family
　USE　Heidenreich family
Heidenrick family
　USE　Heidenreich family
Heidenriech family
　USE　Heidenreich family
Heidenright family
　USE　Heidenreich family

Heider family *(Not Subd Geog)*
　UF　Heiden family
　　　Heidinger family
　　　Van Heiden family
　　　Von Heiden family
Heidinger family
　USE　Heider family
Heifer Project
　BT　Agricultural assistance, American
　　　Church charities—United States
Heifers
　BT　Cows
　— Feeding and feeds
Height, Body
　USE　Stature
Height family
　USE　Hight family
　　　Hite family
Height requirements for police
　USE　Police—Height requirements
Height requirements for soldiers
　USE　Soldiers—Height requirements
Height restrictions for buildings
　USE　Buildings—Height restrictions
Heights
　USE　Altitudes
Heights, The (New York, N.Y.)
　UF　The Heights (New York, N.Y.)
　BT　Single-room occupancy hotels—New
　　　　York (State)
Heiji Civil War, 1159
　USE　Japan—History—Hōgen and Heiji
　　　　Insurrections, 1156-1159
Heiji monogatari emaki (Paintings)
　[ND1059.6.H]
　BT　Scrolls, Japanese
Heiji Uprising, 1159
　USE　Japan—History—Hōgen and Heiji
　　　　Insurrections, 1156-1159
Heijō Palace (Nara-shi, Japan)
　USE　Heijōkyū (Nara-shi, Japan)
Heijōkyū (Nara-shi, Japan)
　UF　Heijō Palace (Nara-shi, Japan)
　　　Heijōkyūseki (Nara-shi, Japan)
　　　Nara Imperial Palace (Nara-shi, Japan)
　　　Nara no Miya (Nara-shi, Japan)
　BT　Japan—Antiquities
　　　Palaces—Japan
Heijōkyūseki (Nara-shi, Japan)
　USE　Heijōkyū (Nara-shi, Japan)
Heikal family
　USE　Heikel family
Heike family
　USE　Taira family
Heikel family *(Not Subd Geog)*
　UF　Heikal family
Heiken family
　USE　Heikens family
Heikens family *(Not Subd Geog)*
　UF　Heiken family
Heikum (African people)
　UF　Hei-kom (African people)
　BT　Ethnology—Namibia
　　　Khoikhoi (African people)
Heilbron family
　USE　Halpern family
Heilbronn, Union of, 1633
　[D267.H3]
　BT　Thirty Years' War, 1618-1648
Heilbronn family
　USE　Halpern family
Heilbronner family
　USE　Halpern family
Heilbrunn family
　USE　Halpern family
Heiligenbergerbeek (Netherlands)
　BT　Rivers—Netherlands
Heiligerlee, Battle of, 1568
　BT　Netherlands—History—Wars of
　　　　Independence, 1556-1648—
　　　　Campaigns

Heilman family (Not Subd Geog)
  UF Hailman family
      Heilmann family
      Heylman family
      Hileman family
      Hyleman family
Heilmann family
  USE Heilman family
Heilsberg Castle (Lidzbark Warmiński, Poland)
  USE Zamek biskupów warmińskich
          (Lidzbark Warmiński, Poland)
Heiltsuk language
  [PM1321]
  UF Haeltzuk language
      Hailtsa language
      Hailtsuk language
  NT Wakashan languages
Heilung Jiang (China and R.S.F.S.R.)
  USE Amur River (China and R.S.F.S.R.)
Heim family (Not Subd Geog)
Heimleck family
  USE Heimlich family
Heimlich family (Not Subd Geog)
  UF Heimleck family
      Hemlic family
      Himbeck family
      Himelick family
      Himelock family
      Himley family
      Hymlich family
      Hymlick family
Heimlich maneuver
  UF Abdominal thrust maneuver
  BT First aid in illness and injury
      Respiratory organs—Foreign bodies—
        Treatment
      Respiratory organs—Obstructions—
        Treatment
Hein family (Not Subd Geog)
  UF Heine family
      Heinen family
      Heins family
  RT Hines family
Heinary family
  USE Henry family
Heine family
  USE Hein family
Heineman family
  USE Heinemann family
Heinemann family (Not Subd Geog)
  UF Heineman family
      Heinzelman family
      Heinzelmann family
      Heinzleman family
      Heinzlemann family
      Hentzelman family
      Hentzelmann family
Heinen family
  USE Hein family
Heiner family
  USE Hayner family
Heinger family
  USE Henninger family
Heinkel 100 (Fighter planes)
  [TL686.H35]
  UF Heinkel 113 (Fighter planes)
  BT Fighter planes
Heinkel 111 (Bomber)
  [TL685.3]
  BT Bombers
Heinkel 112 (Fighter planes)
  [TL686.H35]
  BT Fighter planes
Heinkel 113 (Fighter planes)
  USE Heinkel 100 (Fighter planes)
Heinkel 162 (Jet fighter planes)
  BT Fighter planes
      Jet planes
Heinkel 177 (Bombers)
  BT Bombers

Heinkel airplanes
  [TL686.H]
Heinlein family
  USE Henlein family
Heinlen family
  USE Henlein family
Heinrich family (Not Subd Geog)
  UF Heinrichs family
  RT Hendricks family
      Henriques family
Heinrichs family
  USE Heinrich family
Heins family
  USE Hein family
Heinz bodies
  BT Erythrocytes
Heinzelman family
  USE Heinemann family
Heinzelmann family
  USE Heinemann family
Heinzleman family
  USE Heinemann family
Heinzlemann family
  USE Heinemann family
Heir apparent (May Subd Geog)
  BT Inheritance and succession
Heir family
  USE Hair family
Heire family
  USE Hair family
Heirlooms (May Subd Geog)
  BT Entail
      Inheritance and succession
      Property
      Restraints on alienation
Heironimus family
  USE Hieronymus family
Heironymus family
  USE Hieronymus family
Heirs
  USE Inheritance and succession
Heirs, Unworthiness of
  USE Unworthiness of heirs
Heirs family
  USE Ayers family
Heis family
  USE Heiss family
Heiselberg family (Not Subd Geog)
  RT Heissel family
Heisenberg uncertainty principle
  [QC174.17.H4]
  UF Indeterminancy principle
      Uncertainty principle
  BT Quantum theory
  NT Causality (Physics)
Heiser family (Not Subd Geog)
  UF Heizer family
Heisey pressed glass (May Subd Geog)
  BT Pressed glass—United States
Heisey Rose (Glass etching)
  BT Glass etching
Heisey's Orchid (Glass etching)
  BT Glass etching
Heisman Memorial Trophy
  USE Heisman Trophy
Heisman Trophy
  UF Heisman Memorial Trophy
  BT College sports—United States—
        Awards
      Football—United States—Awards
Heisner family (Not Subd Geog)
Heiss family (Not Subd Geog)
  UF Heis family
      Heisse family
      Heist family
      Hise family
      Hist family
      Hyst family
  RT Heuss family
Heisse family
  USE Heiss family

Heissel family (Not Subd Geog)
  RT Heiselberg family
Heist family
  USE Heiss family
Heisteriaceae
  USE Olacaceae
Heitenrick family
  USE Heidenreich family
Heiwa Kaidō (Japan) (Not Subd Geog)
  UF Hirawa Kaidō (Japan)
      Komatsukawa Kaidō (Japan)
      Nanbumichi (Japan)
  BT Roads—Japan
Heizer family
  USE Heiser family
Hejira
  USE Muḥammad, Prophet, d. 632—Hijrah
Hekaib, Temple of (Elephantine, Egypt)
  USE Sanctuary of Heqaib (Elephantine,
          Egypt)
Hekayeb, Temple of (Elephantine, Egypt)
  USE Sanctuary of Heqaib (Elephantine,
          Egypt)
Heke's Rebellion, 1844-1846
  USE Hone Heke's Rebellion, 1844-1846
Hekla (Iceland)
  UF Hecla (Iceland)
  BT Mountains—Iceland
      Volcanoes—Iceland
Hektorović family (Not Subd Geog)
HeLa cells
  BT Cancer cells
      Clone cells
      Uterus—Cancer
Helam family
  USE Hallam family
Helarctos malayanus
  USE Sun bear
Helbert family
  USE Holbert family
Heldebrand family
  USE Hildebrand family
Heldensage
  [PN684]
  [PT204-PT212]
  UF Heroic saga
  BT Epic literature
      Heroes
      Legends
  RT Chansons de geste
  NT Byliny
Heldreth family
  USE Hildreth family
Heldridge family
  USE Hildreth family
Hele Kaivartas
  USE Mahisyas
Heleburtone family
  USE Halliburton family
Heleidae
  USE Ceratopogonidae
Helems family
  USE Helms family
Helen (Greek mythology)
  USE Helen of Troy (Greek mythology)
Helen of Troy (Greek mythology)
  [BL820.H45]
  UF Helen (Greek mythology)
  BT Mythology, Greek
Helena (Ark.), Battle of, 1863
  [E474.9]
  BT Arkansas—History—Civil War, 1861-
        1865
      United States—History—Civil War,
        1861-1865—Campaigns
Helena National Forest (Mont.)
  (Not Subd Geog)
  BT Forest reserves—Montana
      National parks and reserves—Montana
Helenium
  USE Sneezeweed

Helenium hoopesii
  ⌐QK495.C74¬
  UF Orange sneezeweed
      Western sneezeweed
  BT Livestock poisoning plants
      Sneezeweed
Helenium mexicanum
  ⌐QK495.C74 (Botany)¬
  BT Medicinal plants
      Sneezeweed
Heleodytes
  USE Cactus wrens
Heleomyzidae
  ⌐QL537.H44¬
  UF Helomyzidae
  BT Diptera
  NT Cairnsimyia
Helfer family (Not Subd Geog)
  UF Helfre family
  RT Elfert family
Helferich family
  USE Helfrich family
Helfferich family
  USE Helfrich family
Helfferig family
  USE Helfrich family
Helffrich family
  USE Helfrich family
Helfre family
  USE Helfer family
Helfrich family (Not Subd Geog)
  UF Helferich family
      Helfferich family
      Helfferig family
      Helffrich family
      Helfrick family
      Helfrig family
      Hellferich family
Helfrick family
  USE Helfrich family
Helfrig family
  USE Helfrich family
Helgason family
  USE Helgeson family
Helgeandsholmen (Stockholm, Sweden)
  (Not Subd Geog)
  UF Stockholm (Sweden).
        Helgeandsholmen
  BT Islands—Sweden
Helgesen family
  USE Helgeson family
Helgeson family (Not Subd Geog)
  UF Helgason family
      Helgesen family
Helgö (Sweden)
  USE Lillön (Sweden)
Helgoland, Battle of, 1914
  ⌐D582.H¬
  BT World War, 1914-1918—Naval
      operations
Helgoland Bight (Germany)
  UF Deutsche Bucht (Germany)
      German Bight (Germany)
      Helgoländer Bight (Germany)
      Heligoland Bight (Germany)
  BT Inlets—Germany (West)
Helgoländer Bight (Germany)
  USE Helgoland Bight (Germany)
Helianthus
  ⌐QK495.C74¬
  BT Compositae
Helianthus annuus
  USE Sunflowers
Helianthus tuberosus
  USE Jerusalem artichoke
Helibourtone family
  USE Halliburton family
Helical springs
  ⌐TJ210¬
  BT Springs (Mechanism)

Helicidae (May Subd Geog)
  ⌐QL430.5.H4¬
  BT Stylommatophora
  NT Helix (Mollusks)
Helicinidae
  ⌐QL430.5.H45¬
  BT Archaeogastropoda
  NT Emoda
      Glyptemoda
      Stoastoma
Heliconis
  ⌐QL513.C65¬
  BT Coniopterygidae
Helicolenus
  ⌐QL638.S42¬
  UF Blackbelly rosefish
      Rosefish, Blackbelly
  BT Scorpaenidae
  NT Helicolenus avius
Helicolenus avius
  ⌐QL638.S42¬
  BT Helicolenus
Helicoliths
  ⌐QE955¬
  UF Ahmuellerellaceae
      Helicosphaeraceae
      Pontosphaeraceae
  BT Coccoliths, Fossil
Helicon bass
  USE Tuba
Heliconia
  ⌐QK495.M78 (Botany)¬
  UF Bihai
      Bird-of-paradise plants, False
      Birds of paradise, False (Plants)
      False bird-of-paradise plants
      False birds of paradise (Plants)
      Lobster-claw plants
  BT Musaceae
Heliconia caribaea
  USE Balisier
Heliconia sampaiona
  ⌐QK495.M78 (Botany)¬
Helicops
  ⌐QL666.O636¬
  BT Colubridae
Helicops pastazae
  ⌐QL666.O636¬
Helicops petersi
  ⌐QL666.O636¬
Helicopter ambulances (May Subd Geog)
  ⌐RA996.5¬
  BT Aeronautics—Relief service
      Aeronautics in medicine
      Ambulances
Helicopter amphibious assault ships
  USE Amphibious assault ships
Helicopter auto-pilot
  USE Automatic pilot (Helicopters)
Helicopter flight simulator
  USE Helicopter flight trainer
Helicopter flight trainer
  UF Helicopter flight simulator
      Helicopter simulator
  BT Flight simulators
      Helicopters—Piloting
Helicopter industry (May Subd Geog)
  BT Helicopters
Helicopter pilots (May Subd Geog)
  UF Helicopters—Pilots
  BT Air pilots
  — Training of (May Subd Geog)
      UF Training of helicopter pilots
Helicopter recognition
  USE Helicopters—Recognition
Helicopter rotors
  USE Rotors (Helicopters)
Helicopter simulator
  USE Helicopter flight trainer
Helicopter transportation (May Subd Geog)
  BT Aeronautics, Commercial

Helicopters
  ⌐TL716¬
  BT Aeronautics
      Airplanes
      Flying-machines
      Ground-effect machines
  NT Automatic pilot (Helicopters)
      Convertiplanes
      Fairey aircraft
      Helicopter industry
      Heliports
      HueyCobra (Helicopter)
      Jet helicopters
      Ka-26 (Helicopter)
      Metropolitan helicopter services
      Mi-1 (Helicopters)
      Mi-6A (Helicopter)
      Mi-8 (Helicopters)
      Military helicopters
      Rotors (Helicopters)
      Sea King (Helicopter)
      Sikorsky helicopter
  — Aerodynamics
  — Airworthiness
      UF Airworthiness requirements
      NT Airworthiness certificates
  — Cargo
      BT Cargo handling
  — Cold weather operation
  — Control systems
      BT Flight control
  — Electric equipment
  — Field of view
      UF Field of view from helicopters
          Helicopters—Range of vision
          Range of vision from helicopters
          Visual span (Helicopters)
  — Flight testing
      UF Flight testing of helicopters
      BT Helicopters—Testing
  — Flying qualities
      USE Helicopters—Handling
          characteristics
  — Handling characteristics
      ⌐TL716¬
      UF Flying qualities of helicopters
          Helicopters—Flying qualities
      BT Stability of helicopters
  — Landing
  — Law and legislation (May Subd Geog)
  — Models
  — Motors
  — Piloting
      ⌐TL716.5¬
      NT Helicopter flight trainer
      — — Human factors
          UF Human factors in helicopter
              piloting
          BT Human engineering
  — Pilots
      USE Helicopter pilots
  — Radio equipment
  — Range of vision
      USE Helicopters—Field of view
  — Recognition
      UF Aircraft identification
          Aircraft recognition
          Helicopter recognition
          Recognition of helicopters
  — Rotors
      USE Rotors (Helicopters)
  — Stability
      USE Stability of helicopters
  — Testing
      NT Helicopters—Flight testing
  — Turbojet engines
      ⌐TL709.3.T83¬
      UF Turbojet helicopter engines
      BT Aircraft gas-turbines
          Jet helicopters

Helicopters, Home-built
  UF Home-built helicopters
Helicopters, Used
  USE Used aircraft
Helicosphaeraceae
  USE Helicoliths
Helicoverpa zea
  USE Heliothis zea
Heligmosomidae
    [QL391.N4]
  BT Rhabditoidea
Heligoland Bight (Germany)
  USE Helgoland Bight (Germany)
Heliochromy
  USE Color photography
Heliodon
    [QC912]
  BT Architecture and climate
      Astronomical instruments
Heliofugus
    [QL596.T2]
  BT Tenebrionidae
Heliograph
    [UG582.H4]
  UF Heliotrope (Engineering instrument)
  NT Photoheliograph
      Spectroheliograph
Heliogravure
  USE Photogravure
Heliometer
    [QB97]
  BT Astronomical instruments
  NT Parallax
      Planets—Diameters
      Sun—Diameters
Heliomicrometer
    [QB97]
  BT Astronomical instruments
Heliophobus plants
  USE Shade-tolerant plants
Heliopolis (Ancient city)
    [DT73.H42]
  UF Iunu (Ancient city)
      On (Ancient city)
      Onu (Ancient city)
      Ounû (Ancient city)
      Tall Hisn (Egypt)
      Tell Hisn (Egypt)
  BT Cities and towns, Ruined, extinct, etc.
        —Egypt
      Egypt—Antiquities
Heliosphere
    [QC881.2.H43]
  BT Helium ions
      Ionosphere
Heliostat
    [QB97 (Sun observations)]
    [QC373.H5 (Optical)]
  BT Astronomical instruments
Heliotherapy
  USE Sun-baths
Heliothidae
  USE Noctuidae
Heliothis
    [QL561.N7]
  BT Noctuidae
Heliothis armigera
    [QL561.N7 (General)]
    [SB945.H28 (Pest)]
  UF Bollworm, Old World
      Corn earworm
      Earworm, Corn
Heliothis umbrosus
  USE Heliothis zea
Heliothis zea
    [QL561.N7 (General)]
    [SB945.H28 (Pest)]

  UF Bollworm, New World
      Bombyx obsoleta
      Budworm, Tobacco
      Chloridea obsoleta
      Corn earworm
      Cotton bollworm
      Earworm, Corn
      Fruitworm, Tomato
      Helicoverpa zea
      Heliothis umbrosus
      Tobacco budworm
      Tomato fruitworm
Heliothripidae
  USE Thripidae
Heliotrope (Engineering instrument)
  USE Heliograph
Heliotropism
  USE Phototropism
Heliotype
    [TR937]
  BT Collotype
      Photography
      Photomechanical processes
Heliozoa
    [QL368.H5]
  BT Protozoa
Heliports (May Subd Geog)
    [TL725.5]
  BT Aeronautics, Commercial
      Airports
      Helicopters
Heliscomys
    [QE882.R6]
  BT Heteromyidae
      Heteromyidae, Fossil
Helium (May Subd Geog)
    [QD181.H4 (Chemistry)]
    [TL666 (Aeronautics)]
    [TP245.H4 (Chemical technology)]
  BT Gases, Rare
      Radioactivity
  NT Liquid helium
      Solid helium
  — **Electric properties**
  — **Isotopes**
    UF Helium isotopes
      Isotopic helium
  — — **Decay**
  — **Spectra**
  — **Thermal properties**
Helium, Solid
  USE Solid helium
Helium at low temperatures
  BT Low temperatures
  NT Liquid helium
      Solid helium
Helium ions
  BT Ions
  NT Heliosphere
  — **Scattering**
  — **Spectra**
Helium isotopes
  USE Helium—Isotopes
Helium-mercury lasers
  UF He-Hg lasers
      Lasers, Helium-mercury
      Mercury-helium lasers
  BT Gas lasers
Helium-neon lasers
    [TA1695]
  UF He-Ne lasers
      Lasers, Helium-neon
      Neon-helium lasers
  BT Gas lasers
Helium stars
  USE B stars
Helix, Spherical
  USE Loxodrome
Helix (Mollusks)
    [QL430.5.H4]
  BT Helicidae

  NT Helix aspersa
      Helix pomatia
Helix aspersa
    [QL430.5.H4 (Zoology)]
    [SF597.S6 (Culture)]
  UF Brown snail
      Garden snail
  BT Garden pests
      Helix (Mollusks)
      Snails, Edible
Helix pomatia
    [QL430.5.H4 (Zoology)]
    [SF597.S6 (Snail farming)]
  UF Roman snail
      Snail, Roman
      Snail, Vineyard
      Vineyard snail
  BT Helix (Mollusks)
      Snails, Edible
Helix thyroidus
  USE Mesodon thyroidus
Hell
    [BL545 (Comparative religion)]
    [BL735 (Classical mythology)]
    [BT834-BT838 (Theology)]
  UF Endless punishment
      Eternal punishment
      Everlasting punishment
      Hades
      Retribution
      Sheol
  BT Future life
      Future punishment
  NT Intermediate state
      Reprobation
  — **Buddhism, [Christianity, etc.]**
Hellams family
  USE Helms family
Hellcat (Fighter planes)
  UF Grumman F6F Hellcat
  BT Fighter planes
      Grumman airplanes
Helle family
  USE Heller family
Hellebrant family
  USE Hildebrand family
Hellem family
  USE Helms family
Hellems family
  USE Helms family
Hellenic Trough
  BT Submarine trenches—Mediterranean
      Sea
Hellenism
    [DF77 (History)]
    [PN56.H4 (Literature)]
    Here are entered works on the spread of Greek civilization and influence throughout the ancient world following the conquests of Alexander the Great. Works on the combined civilizations of Greece and Rome following the conquest of Greece in 146 B.C. are entered under Civilization, Greco-Roman. Works on both ancient Greek and Roman civilization are entered under Civilization, Classical.
  BT Greece—Civilization—To 146 B.C.
  SA *headings beginning with the word*
      Hellenistic
  NT Neoplatonism
Hellenistic architecture
  USE Architecture, Hellenistic
Hellenistic art
  USE Art, Hellenistic
Hellenistic bronzes
  USE Bronzes, Hellenistic
Hellenistic goldwork
  USE Goldwork, Hellenistic
Hellenistic Greek
  USE Greek language, Hellenistic (300 B.C.-
      600 A.D.)
Hellenistic Greek literature
  USE Greek literature, Hellenistic

Hellenistic Greek poetry
USE Greek poetry, Hellenistic
Hellenistic Judaism
USE Jews—Civilization—Greek influences
Judaism—History—Post-exilic period,
586 B.C.-210 A.D.
Hellenistic lamps
USE Lamps, Hellenistic
Hellenistic mosaics
USE Mosaics, Hellenistic
Hellenistic mural painting and decoration
USE Mural painting and decoration,
Hellenistic
Hellenistic portrait sculpture
USE Portrait sculpture, Hellenistic
Hellenistic portraits
USE Portraits, Hellenistic
Hellenistic pottery
USE Pottery, Hellenistic
Hellenistic sculpture
USE Sculpture, Hellenistic
Hellenistic terra-cotta sculpture
USE Terra-cotta sculpture, Hellenistic
Hellenists
USE Classicists
Heller (Coin) *(May Subd Geog)*
UF Haler
Haller
BT Coins, German
Heller family *(Not Subd Geog)*
UF Helle family
Hellerman family
Hellermann family
Hellerman family
USE Heller family
Hellermann family
USE Heller family
Hellesøe family *(Not Subd Geog)*
Helleson family *(Not Subd Geog)*
Hellespont (Turkey)
USE Dardanelles Strait (Turkey)
Hellferich family
USE Helfrich family
Hellims family
USE Helms family
Hellmack family
USE Helmick family
Hellmer family
USE Helmers family
Hellmers family
USE Helmers family
Hellms family
USE Helms family
Helloms family
USE Helms family
**Hells Canyon National Recreation Area (Or.
and Idaho)** *(Not Subd Geog)*
BT National parks and reserves—Idaho
National parks and reserves—Oregon
Recreation areas—Idaho
Recreation areas—Oregon
Hell's Half Acre (Valley View, Cuyahoga
County, Ohio)
USE Locktender's House (Valley View,
Cuyahoga County, Ohio)
Hell's Half Acre Wilderness (Idaho)
(Not Subd Geog)
UF Hell's Half Acre Wilderness Study
Area (Idaho)
BT National parks and reserves—Idaho
Wilderness areas—Idaho
Hell's Half Acre Wilderness Study Area
(Idaho)
USE Hell's Half Acre Wilderness (Idaho)
Hellshire Hills (Jamaica)
UF Healthshire Hills (Jamaica)
Healthshire Hummock (Jamaica)
Helshire (Jamaica)
BT Mountains—Jamaica
Hellum family
USE Hallam family

Hellums family
USE Helms family
Hellweg family
USE Helwig family
Hellwig family
USE Helwig family
Helm family
USE Helms family
Helmack family
USE Helmick family
Helmand River (Afghanistan)
(Not Subd Geog)
UF Helmund River (Afghanistan)
Hilmand River (Afghanistan)
BT Rivers—Afghanistan
Helme family
USE Helms family
Helmeck family
USE Helmick family
Helmer family
USE Helmers family
Helmers family *(Not Subd Geog)*
UF Hellmer family
Hellmers family
Helmer family
Helmes family
USE Helms family
Helmeted hornbill
[QL696.C729]
UF Rhinoplax vigil
BT Hornbills
Helmets *(May Subd Geog)*
[N6600-N6699 (Art)]
[U825 (Military science)]
NT Riot helmets
Safety hats
— **Japan**
— — **History**
— — — **Kamakura-Momoyama periods,
1185-1600**
— — — **Edo period, 1600-1868**
Helmholtz double layer
USE Electric double layer
Helmholtz equation
UF Reduced wave equation
Wave equation, Reduced
BT Differential equations, Elliptic
Wave equation
— **Numerical solutions**
BT Numerical analysis
Helmich family
USE Helmick family
Helmick family *(Not Subd Geog)*
UF Hellmack family
Helmack family
Helmeck family
Helmich family
Helmidae
USE Elmidae
Helminthiasis *(May Subd Geog)*
BT Medical helminthology
Parasitic diseases
NT Angiostrongylosis
Ascariasis
Cestode diseases
Filariasis
Gnathostomiasis
Hookworm disease
Opisthorchiasis
Oxyuriasis
Paragonimiasis
Schistosomiasis
Trichinosis
Trichuriasis
Helminthiasis in children *(May Subd Geog)*
[RJ406.H]
BT Communicable diseases in children
NT Ascariasis in children
Helminthidae
USE Elmidae

Helminthology *(May Subd Geog)*
[QL386-394]
BT Worms
Worms, Intestinal and parasitic
Zoology
NT Helminths
Medical helminthology
Veterinary helminthology
Helminthomorpha
USE Enteropneusta
Helminthosporium gramineum
USE Pyrenophora graminea
Helminthosporium stripe disease of barley
USE Barley leaf stripe disease
Helminths *(May Subd Geog)*
[QL392]
BT Helminthology
Intestines—Parasites
Worms, Intestinal and parasitic
NT Annelida
Nemathelminthes
Platyhelminthes
— **Hosts**
UF Host animals to helminths
BT Parasitism
Helmka family
USE Helmke family
Helmkay family
USE Helmke family
Helmke family *(Not Subd Geog)*
UF Helmka family
Helmkay family
Helmkey family
Helmkey family
USE Helmke family
Helmn family
USE Helms family
Helms family *(Not Subd Geog)*
UF Hallum family
Helems family
Hellams family
Hellem family
Hellems family
Hellims family
Hellms family
Helloms family
Hellums family
Helm family
Helme family
Helmes family
Helmn family
Hiloms family
RT Elmes family
Helmund River (Afghanistan)
USE Helmand River (Afghanistan)
Helobiae
[QK495.A14 (Botany)]
UF Alismales
Alismatales
Hydrocharitales
Naiadales
Potamogetonales
BT Aquatic plants
Monocotyledons
NT Aponogetonaceae
Hydrocharitaceae
Ruppiaceae
Heloderma
[QL666.L247]
BT Helodermatidae
Lizards
Heloderma, Fossil
[QE862.L2]
BT Helodermatidae, Fossil
Heloderma matthewi
[QE862.L2]
Heloderma suspectum
USE Gila monster
Helodermatidae
[QL666.L247]
BT Lizards

NT Heloderma
Helodermatidae, Fossil
[QE862.L2]
BT Lizards, Fossil
NT Heloderma, Fossil
Helogale
[QL737.C28]
UF Dwarf mongooses
Mongooses, Dwarf
Mongooses, Pigmy
Pigmy mongooses
Pygmy mongooses
BT Viverridae
NT Helogale undulata
Helogale undulata
[QL737.C28]
BT Helogale
Helogeneidae
[QL638.H444]
UF Helogenidae
Hologenidae
BT Catfishes
NT Helogenes
Helogenes
[QL638.H444]
BT Helogeneidae
Helogenes unidorsalis
[QL638.H444]
Helogenidae
USE Helogeneidae
Helomyzidae
USE Heleomyzidae
Helonias
[QK495.L72]
BT Liliaceae
Helonias bullata
[QK495.L72]
UF Pink, Swamp
Swamp pink
Heloniopsis
[QK495.L72]
BT Liliaceae
Heloniopsis breviscapa
USE Heloniopsis orientalis
Heloniopsis japonica
USE Heloniopsis orientalis
Heloniopsis orientalis
[QK495.L72]
UF Heloniopsis breviscapa
Heloniopsis japonica
Helopeltis (May Subd Geog)
[QL523.M5]
BT Miridae
Helopheridae
USE Hydrophilidae
Helophoridae
USE Hydrophilidae
Helophorus
[QL596.H8]
BT Hydrophilidae
Helopidae
USE Tenebrionidae
Heloridae
[QL568.H4]
BT Hymenoptera
HELOS (Artificial satellite)
USE EXOSAT (Artificial satellite)
Helos Plain (Greece)
UF Elos Plain (Greece)
BT Plains—Greece
Helotiaceae
BT Helotiales
NT Cenangium
Helotiales
[QK623.H (Botany)]
BT Discomycetes
NT Dermateaceae
Helotiaceae
Hyaloscyphaceae
Leotiaceae
Sclerotiniaceae

Helots (May Subd Geog)
BT Serfdom—Greece
Slavery—Greece
Social classes—Greece
NT Perioeci
HELP (Computer program)
UF Hybrid Executive Linkage Program
BT Hybrid computers—Programming
Help-seeking behavior (May Subd Geog)
UF Assistance seeking behavior
Behavior, Help seeking
Seeking help
BT Interpersonal relations
Help-wanted advertising (May Subd Geog)
[HF6125.5]
BT Advertising
Advertising, Classified
Job hunting
Helpers, Fourteen holy
USE Fourteen holy helpers
Helpers of Muḥammad, Prophet, d. 632
USE Ansar
Helping behavior
UF Behavior, Helping
BT Human behavior
Interpersonal relations
RT Altruism
Caring
NT Counseling
Encouragement
Psychotherapy
— **Religious aspects**
— — **Buddhism,** [Christianity, etc.]
Helping behavior in animals
USE Altruistic behavior in animals
Helping behavior in children
(May Subd Geog)
[BF723.H45 (Psychology)]
BT Child psychology
Helplessness (Psychology)
[BF575.H4]
BT Emotions
— **Religious aspects**
— — **Buddhism,** [Christianity, etc.]
Helshire (Jamaica)
USE Hellshire Hills (Jamaica)
Helsingborg, Battle of, 1710
[DL743.H3]
BT Northern War, 1700-1721—Campaigns
—Sweden
Helsingland (Sweden)
USE Hälsingland (Sweden)
Helson sets
UF Sets, Helson
BT Fourier series
Functions, Continuous
Set theory
Helstrup family (Not Subd Geog)
Heltebran family
USE Hildebrand family
Heltebrand family
USE Hildebrand family
Helton family
USE Hilton family
Heltzel family
USE Hutzel family
Helvetii (Celtic people)
[DQ34]
BT Celts
Ethnology—Switzerland
Helvey family
USE Hulvey family
Helwich family
USE Helwig family
Helwig family (Not Subd Geog)
UF Hellweg family
Hellwig family
Helwich family
Hely family
USE Healy family

Helzel family
USE Hutzel family
Hemacytometer
USE Hemocytometer
Hemagglutinating virus of Japan
USE Sendai virus
Hemagglutination
USE Blood—Agglutination
Hemagglutination tests
[QR187.H38]
BT Agglutination tests
Antigen-antibody reactions
Blood—Agglutination
Hemagglutinin
Immunoassay
NT Coomb's test
Hemagglutinin
[QP91 (Blood)]
[QR185 (Immunity)]
BT Agglutination
Agglutinins
Blood—Agglutination
Immunity
NT Hemagglutination tests
Lectins
Phytohemagglutinins
Heman family
USE Hemann family
Hemangioendothelioma, Malignant
USE Angiosarcoma
Hemangioma
BT Angioma
Blood-vessels—Tumors
Hemangiosarcoma
USE Angiosarcoma
Hemann family (Not Subd Geog)
UF Heman family
Hemapheresis (May Subd Geog)
[RM173]
UF Blood—Apheresis
Blood—Pheresis
Blood component separation
BT Blood—Collection and preservation
Blood—Transfusion
NT Leukapheresis
Plasmapheresis
Hemarthrosis
BT Hemorrhage
Joints—Diseases
Hematemesis
BT Stomach—Diseases
Stomach—Ulcers
Hematin
USE Heme
Hematite (May Subd Geog)
UF Raddle
BT Iron ores
Hematite crystals
Hematocele
Hematochyluria
[RC918.H4]
Hematocrit
BT Blood—Examination
Erythrocytes
Hematoencephalic barrier
USE Blood-brain barrier
Hematogenic shock
USE Hemorrhagic shock
Hematologic diseases
USE Blood—Diseases
Hematologic equipment industry
(May Subd Geog)
[HD9995.H42-424]
BT Hematology—Equipment and supplies
Hematological manifestations of general diseases
[RB145]
UF Hematological symptoms of general
diseases
BT Blood—Diseases
Symptomatology

Hematological symptoms of general diseases
  USE Hematological manifestations of
       general diseases
Hematologists (May Subd Geog)
  BT Medical scientists
      Physicians
  RT Hematology
Hematology
  BT Internal medicine
  RT Hematologists
  NT Blood
      Forensic hematology
      Immunohematology
      Pediatric hematology
      Radioisotopes in hematology
      Serology
  — **Equipment and supplies**
      NT Hematologic equipment industry
  — **Technique**
      NT Flow cytometry
Hematology, Comparative
  ₍QP91₎
  UF Comparative hematology
Hematology, Experimental
  (May Subd Geog)
  ₍QP91 (Physiology)₎
  ₍RB145 (Pathology)₎
  ₍RC636 (Medicine)₎
  UF Experimental hematology
  BT Medicine, Experimental
      Physiology, Experimental
Hematology, Veterinary
  USE Veterinary hematology
Hematoma
  UF Blood tumor
  BT Hemorrhage
      Tumors
  NT Subdural hematoma
Hematophilia
  USE Hemophilia
Hematopinus
  USE Haematopinus
Hematopoiesis
  UF Blood formation
      Hemopoiesis
  BT Blood
  NT Blood cells
      Erythropoiesis
      Hematopoietic agents
      Hematopoietic system
      Monocytopoiesis
Hematopoietic agents
  ₍RM335₎
  BT Hematopoiesis
      Pharmacology
Hematopoietic stem cells
  BT Blood cells
      Bone marrow cells
      Hematopoietic system
      Stem cells
  — **Growth**
Hematopoietic system
  UF Hemopoietic system
  BT Hematopoiesis
  NT Bone marrow
      Hematopoietic stem cells
      Reticulo-endothelial system
      Spleen
  — **Cancer**
Hematoporphyrin
  ₍QP671₎
  UF Photodyn
  BT Blood—Pigments
      Porphyrin and porphyrin compounds
Hematuria
  ₍RC918.H4₎
  ₍SF961₎
  BT Hemorrhage
      Urinary organs—Diseases
      Urine—Analysis
  NT Hematuria in children

Hematuria in children (May Subd Geog)
  ₍RJ476.H44₎
  BT Hematuria
      Pediatric nephrology
Hemba (African people)
  UF Babuye (African people)
      Bahemba (African people)
      Buye (African people)
      Luba-Hemba (African people)
      Wabuyu (African people)
      Waruwa (African people)
  BT Bantus
      Ethnology—Zaire
      Luba (African people)
Hemba (African people) art
  USE Art, Hemba (African people)
Hemba (African people) sculpture
  USE Sculpture, Hemba (African people)
Hemba (African people) wood-carving
  USE Wood-carving, Hemba (African
       people)
Hembell family
  USE Hamel family
Hembre family
  USE Hembree family
Hembree family (Not Subd Geog)
  UF Hembre family
      Hembrees family
      Hembres family
      Hembry family
  RT Emery family
Hembrees family
  USE Hembree family
Hembres family
  USE Hembree family
Hembry family
  USE Hembree family
Hemby family
  USE Hamby family
Heme
  UF Hematin
  BT Hemoglobin
      Porphyrin and porphyrin compounds
      Tetrapyrroles
  NT Hemoproteins
Heme proteins
  USE Hemoproteins
Hemel Hempstead and Harpenden Railway
  BT Railroads—Great Britain
Hemenway family
  USE Hemingway family
**Hemenway Southwestern Archaeological
  Expedition, 1886-1894**
Hemer family
  USE Hemmer family
Hēmera tou Ochi (Greek holiday)
  UF Ochi Day (Greek holiday)
      October twenty-eighth (Greek holiday)
      Twenty-eighth of October (Greek
       holiday)
  BT Holidays—Greece
Hemerobiidae
  ₍QL513.H5₎
  UF Brown lacewing flies
      Sympherobiidae
  BT Lacewing flies
      Neuroptera
  NT Boriomyia
      Micromus
Hemerocalis
  USE Daylilies
Hemerocallis
  USE Daylilies
Hemerocampa
  ₍QL561.L9₎
  BT Lymantriidae
Hemerophilidae
  USE Glyphipterygidae
Hemeroplanes (May Subd Geog)
  ₍QL561.S7₎
  BT Sphingidae

  NT Hemeroplanes elainae
Hemeroplanes elainae (May Subd Geog)
  ₍QL561.S7₎
  BT Hemeroplanes
Hemerosidae
  USE Noctuidae
Hemery family
  USE Hemry family
Hemianopsia
  ₍RE94₎
  BT Blindness
Hemibelideus
  USE Ring-tailed phalangers
Hemibranchii
  USE Gasterosteiformes
Hemic cells
  USE Blood cells
Hemicellulose
  ₍QK865₎
  BT Cellulose
Hemiceridae
  USE Notodontidae
Hemichaena
  ₍QK495.S43₎
  BT Scrophulariaceae
Hemichordata
  ₍QL612₎
  BT Animal colonies
  NT Enteropneusta
      Pterobranchia
Hemichromis
  ₍QL638.C55₎
  BT Cichlidae
Hemicoccidae
  USE Kermesidae
Hemicolectomy (May Subd Geog)
  ₍RD543.C57₎
  BT Colectomy
  NT Left hemicolectomy
      Right hemicolectomy
Hemicolectomy, Left
  USE Left hemicolectomy
Hemicolectomy, Right
  USE Right hemicolectomy
Hemicycliophora
  BT Hemicycliophoridae
Hemicycliophoridae
  ₍QL391.N4₎
  BT Nematoda
  NT Hemicycliophora
Hemicyclostoma
  USE Stoastoma
Hemidactylium
  ₍QL668.C274₎
  BT Plethodontidae
Hemidactylus
  ₍QL666.L245₎
  BT Geckos
Hemidiscaceae
  ₍QK569.H44 (Botany)₎
  BT Centrales
  NT Azpeitia
Hemifacial microsomia (May Subd Geog)
  UF Branchial arch syndrome
      First and second branchial arch
       syndrome
      First arch syndrome
      Microsomia, Hemifacial
  BT Face—Abnormalities
      Jaws—Abnormalities
Hemigrammus
  ₍QL638.C5₎
  BT Characidae
  NT Hemigrammus caudovittatus
Hemigrammus caudovittatus
  ₍QL638.C5₎
  BT Hemigrammus
Hemileia
  ₍QK627.P97₎
  UF Hemileiopsis
  BT Pucciniaceae

NT Hemileia vastatrix
Hemileia coffeicola
  [QK627.P97 (Botany)]
  [SB608.C6 (Agricultural pest)]
  UF Uredo coffeicola
  BT Coffee—Diseases and pests
Hemileia vastatrix
  [QK627.P97 (Mycology)]
  [SB608.C6 (Control)]
  UF Coffee leaf rust fungus
    Coffee rust fungus
  BT Hemileia
    Rusts (Fungi)
  RT Coffee leaf rust
Hemileiopsis
  USE Hemileia
Hemileucidae
  USE Saturniidae
Hemimastodon annectens
  USE Gomphotherium angustidens
Hemingsway family
  USE Hemingway family
Hemingway, Ernest, 1899-1961
  (Not Subd Geog)
  — **Characters**
  — — **Nick Adams**
      RT Adams, Nick (Fictitious
        character)
Hemingway family *(Not Subd Geog)*
  UF Hemenway family
    Hemingsway family
    Hemmenway family
    Hemmingway family
    Hemminway family
Hemiodontidae
  [QL638.H45]
  BT Cypriniformes
Hemionus
  USE Equus
Hemipelvectomy *(May Subd Geog)*
  BT Amputation
    Pelvis—Surgery
  — **Nursing** *(May Subd Geog)*
Hemipeplidae
  USE Cucujidae
Hemiphractus
  [QL668.E24]
  BT Hylidae
Hemiplegia
  BT Paralysis
Hemiplegics
  BT Paralytics
Hemiptera *(May Subd Geog)*
  [QL521-524.2]
  UF Heteroptera
    Rhynchota
    Siphonata
  BT Insects
  NT Anthocoridae
    Aradidae
    Belostomatidae
    Berytidae
    Cimicidae
    Coreidae
    Corixidae
    Cydnidae
    Dipsocoridae
    Drepanosiphidae
    Enicocephalidae
    Gelastocoridae
    Gerridae
    Hebridae
    Homoptera
    Lace bugs
    Leptopodidae
    Lygaeidae
    Mesoveliidae
    Microphysidae
    Miridae
    Naucoridae
    Ochteridae

Pentatomidae
Phymatidae
Planthoppers
Plataspidae
Polyctenidae
Pyrrhocoridae
Reduviidae
Rhopalidae
Scale-insects
Scutelleridae
Veliidae
Water-scorpions
Hemiramphidae
  USE Halfbeaks
Hemiramphus
  [QL638.E9 (Zoology)]
  [SH351.H195 (Fish culture)]
  BT Exocoetidae
    Halfbeaks
Hemiramphus balao
  [QL638.E9 (Zoology)]
  [SH351.H195 (Fish culture)]
Hemiramphus brasiliensis
  [QL638.E9 (Zoology)]
  [SH351.H195 (Fish culture)]
Hemirhamphidae
  USE Halfbeaks
Hemisia *(May Subd Geog)*
  [QL568.A53]
  UF Centris
  BT Anthophoridae
Hemisphaeriales
  [QK623.H (Botany)]
  UF Microthyriales
  BT Loculoascomycetes
  NT Microthyriaceae
Hemisphere, Eastern
  USE Eastern Hemisphere
Hemisphere, Northern
  USE Northern Hemisphere
Hemisphere, Southern
  USE Southern Hemisphere
Hemisphere, Western
  USE Western Hemisphere
Hemispheric dominance (Brain)
  USE Cerebral dominance
Hemisus
  [QL668.E225]
  BT Brevicipitidae
Hemitheidae
  USE Geometridae
Hemitragus
  USE Tahrs
Hemitragus jemlahicus
  USE Himalayan tahr
Hemleben family *(Not Subd Geog)*
Hemlic family
  USE Heimlich family
Hemlock, Black
  USE Mountain hemlock
Hemlock, Canada
  USE Eastern hemlock
Hemlock, Canadian
  USE Eastern hemlock
Hemlock, Eastern
  USE Eastern hemlock
Hemlock, Mountain
  USE Mountain hemlock
Hemlock, Pacific
  USE Western hemlock
Hemlock, Sargent's weeping
  USE Sargent's weeping hemlock
Hemlock, West coast
  USE Western hemlock
Hemlock, Western
  USE Western hemlock
Hemlock (Materia medica)
  USE Conium
Hemlock borer
  USE Melanophila fulvoguttata

Hemlock looper
  [QL561.G6]
  [SB945.H]
  UF Hemlock spanworm
    Lambdina fiscellaria
Hemlock sawfly
Hemlock scale
  USE Fiorinia externa
Hemlock spanworm
  USE Hemlock looper
Hemlock spruce
  USE Eastern hemlock
Hemlocks (Trees)
  USE Tsuga
Hemlocks (Trees), Fossil
  USE Tsuga, Fossil
Hemm family
  USE Hemmer family
Hemme family
  USE Hemmer family
Hemmenway family
  USE Hemingway family
Hemmer family *(Not Subd Geog)*
  UF Hemer family
    Hemm family
    Hemme family
  RT Hammer family
Hemmery family
  USE Hemry family
Hemmingstedt, Battle of, 1500
  BT Denmark—History—1448-1660
Hemmingway family
  USE Hemingway family
Hemminway family
  USE Hemingway family
Hemmit family
  USE Hammett family
Hemochromatosis *(May Subd Geog)*
  [RC632.H4]
  UF Bronze diabetes
    Diabetes, Bronze
    Iron storage disease
  BT Hemosiderosis
    Metabolism, Inborn errors of
    Pigmentation disorders
Hemocuprein
  USE Superoxide dismutase
Hemocyanin
  BT Blood—Pigments
    Copper proteins
Hemocytes
  USE Blood cells
Hemocytometer
  UF Hemacytometer
  BT Blood cell count
Hemodialysis *(May Subd Geog)*
  UF Blood—Dialysis
    Blood dialysis
    Extracorporeal dialysis
    Kidney dialysis
    Renal dialysis
  BT Dialysis
    Therapeutics
  RT Blood—Filtration
  NT Artificial kidney
    Peritoneal dialysis
  — **Equipment and supplies**
      NT Hemodialysis equipment industry
  — **Home therapy**
      UF Home dialysis
        Home hemodialysis
      BT Home care services
  — **Patients** *(May Subd Geog)*
      UF Dialysis patients
        Hemodialysis patients
  — **Psychological aspects**
      BT Sick—Psychology
  — **Social aspects** *(May Subd Geog)*
      UF Society and hemodialysis

Hemodialysis, Continuous arteriovenous
  USE Continuous arteriovenous
     hemofiltration
Hemodialysis equipment industry
  (May Subd Geog)
  [HD9995.H42-424]
  BT Hemodialysis—Equipment and
     supplies
Hemodialysis patients
  USE Hemodialysis—Patients
Hemodialyzer reprocessing
  USE Hemodialyzers—Reuse
Hemodialyzer reuse
  USE Hemodialyzers—Reuse
Hemodialyzer reutilization
  USE Hemodialyzers—Reuse
Hemodialyzers *(May Subd Geog)*
  [RC901.7.H45]
  UF Dialyzers (Artificial kidney)
  BT Artificial kidney
  — Reuse
    UF Hemodialyzer reprocessing
      Hemodialyzer reuse
      Hemodialyzer reutilization
      Reuse of hemodialyzers
Hemodynamics
  BT Blood—Circulation
    Hydrodynamics
  RT Cardiac output
  NT Blood—Filtration
    Blood—Viscosity
    Blood flow
    Blood pressure
    Blood volume
    Heart beat
    Regional blood flow
Hemoerythrin
  BT Blood—Pigments
Hemofiltration
  USE Blood—Filtration
Hemofiltration, Continuous arteriovenous
  USE Continuous arteriovenous
     hemofiltration
Hemoglobin
  [QP96.5]
  UF Hemoglobulin
  BT Blood—Pigments
    Blood proteins
    Erythrocytes
    Hemoproteins
  RT Hemoglobin polymorphisms
  NT Anoxemia
    Bile pigments
    Globin
    Heme
    Oxyhemoglobin
  — Synthesis
  — — Regulation
    UF Regulation of hemoglobin
      synthesis
    BT Biological control systems
Hemoglobin, Abnormal
  USE Hemoglobin polymorphisms
    Hemoglobinopathy
Hemoglobin, Glycosyl
  USE Glycosylated hemoglobin
Hemoglobin, Glycosylated
  USE Glycosylated hemoglobin
Hemoglobin abnormalities
  USE Hemoglobin polymorphisms
Hemoglobin polymorphisms
  [GN264 (Anthropology)]
  [QP96.5 (Physiology)]
  [RC641.7.H35 (Disease)]
  UF Abnormal hemoglobin
    Hemoglobin, Abnormal
    Hemoglobin abnormalities
    Hemoglobin variants
    Polymorphisms, Hemoglobin
    Variants, Hemoglobin
  BT Genetic polymorphisms

  RT Hemoglobin
    Hemoglobinopathy
  NT Glycosylated hemoglobin
Hemoglobin variants
  USE Hemoglobin polymorphisms
Hemoglobinometry
  BT Blood—Analysis
Hemoglobinopathy
  [RC641.7.H35]
  UF Abnormal hemoglobin
    Hemoglobin, Abnormal
  BT Anemia
  RT Hemoglobin polymorphisms
  NT Sickle cell anemia
    Thalassemia
  — Diagnosis
  — Genetic aspects
Hemoglobinopathy in children
  (May Subd Geog)
  [RJ416.H43]
  BT Pediatric hematology
Hemoglobinuric fever
  USE Blackwater fever
Hemoglobulin
  USE Hemoglobin
Hemogram
  USE Blood cell count
Hemolymph
  BT Blood
    Lymphatics
Hemolymph glands
  [QL841]
Hemolysis and hemolysins
  [QR185]
  BT Antigen-antibody reactions
    Blood
    Immunity
    Serum
  NT Hemolytic anemia
    Hemolytic plaque technique
    Lysolecithin
Hemolytic anemia *(May Subd Geog)*
  [RC641.7.H4]
  UF Anemia, Hemolytic
  BT Anemia
    Hemolysis and hemolysins
  NT Erythroblastosis fetalis
    Favism
    Glucosephosphate dehydrogenase
     deficiency
    Hemolytic anemia, Autoimmune
    Hemolytic-uremic syndrome
    Sickle cell anemia
    Thalassemia
Hemolytic anemia, Autoimmune
  (May Subd Geog)
  [RC641.7.H4]
  UF Autoimmune hemolytic anemia
    Autoimmune hemolytic disorder
    Hemolytic disorder, Autoimmune
  BT Autoimmune diseases
    Hemolytic anemia
Hemolytic disease of newborn
  USE Erythroblastosis fetalis
Hemolytic disorder, Autoimmune
  USE Hemolytic anemia, Autoimmune
Hemolytic plaque technique
  [QR187.H45]
  UF Haemolytic plaque technique
    Jerne's plaque technique
  BT Complement fixation
    Hemolysis and hemolysins
    Plaque assay technique
Hemolytic-uremic syndrome
  BT Hemolytic anemia
    Uremia
Hemopericardium
  USE Cardiac tamponade
Hemophilia *(May Subd Geog)*
  [RC642]

  UF Hematophilia
    Hemorrhagic diathesis
  BT Blood—Coagulation, Disorders of
  NT Blood coagulation factor VIII
    Hemophiliacs
  — Complications and sequelae
Hemophilia in children *(May Subd Geog)*
  [RJ416.H45]
  BT Pediatric hematology
Hemophiliacs *(May Subd Geog)*
  UF Hemophilics
  BT Chronically ill
    Hemophilia
Hemophilics
  USE Hemophiliacs
Hemophilus
  [QR82.B95]
  UF Haemophilus
  BT Brucellaceae
Hemophilus diseases
  UF Haemophilus diseases
  BT Bacterial diseases
  NT Chancroid
    Hemophilus meningitis
Hemophilus influenzae
  [QR82.B95]
  UF Bacillus influenzae
    Bacterium influenzae
    Pfeiffer bacillus
Hemophilus meningitis
  BT Hemophilus diseases
    Meningitis
Hemophilus pertussis
  USE Bordetella pertussis
Hemopneumothorax
  BT Hemorrhage
    Pleural effusions
Hemopoiesis
  USE Hematopoiesis
Hemopoietic system
  USE Hematopoietic system
Hemoproteins
  [QP552.H46]
  UF Heme proteins
  BT Heme
    Metalloproteins
  NT Catalase
    Cytochrome c
    Cytochrome oxidase
    Cytochrome P-450
    Hemoglobin
    Myoglobin
    Oxygenases
    Peroxidase
Hemoptysis
  USE Hemorrhage
Hemorrhage
  [RB144]
  [RD33.3]
  UF Bleeding
    Hemoptysis
  BT Anemia
    Blood
    Surgery, Operative
  RT Arteries—Wounds and injuries
  SA *subdivision* Hemorrhage *under names*
    of organs and regions of the body,
    e.g. Heart—Hemorrhage; Foot—
    Hemorrhage; etc.
  NT Bloodletting
    Gastrointestinal hemorrhage
    Hemarthrosis
    Hematoma
    Hematuria
    Hemopneumothorax
    Hemorrhagic diseases
    Hemostasis
    Hemostatics
    Infarction
    Nosebleed
    Oral hemorrhage

— **Complications and sequelae**
  NT Anemia, Hypovolemic
Hemorrhage, Uterine
  ⌈RG573 (Pregnancy)⌉
  ⌈RG711 (Labor)⌉
  ⌈RG821 (Puerperal state)⌉
  UF Uterus—Hemorrhage
  BT Labor, Complicated
      Uterus—Diseases
  NT Menorrhagia
Hemorrhagic bronchitis
  USE Bronchopulmonary spirochaetosis
Hemorrhagic diathesis
  USE Hemophilia
Hemorrhagic disease of newborn
  ⌈RJ271⌉
  UF Morbus haemolyticus neonatorum
  BT Hemorrhagic diseases in children
Hemorrhagic diseases
  ⌈RC633⌉
  UF Hemorrhagic disorders
  BT Diseases
      Hemorrhage
  NT Blood—Coagulation, Disorders of
      Von Willebrand's disease
Hemorrhagic diseases in children
  (May Subd Geog)
  ⌈RJ416.H46⌉
  BT Pediatric hematology
  NT Hemorrhagic disease of newborn
Hemorrhagic disorders
  USE Hemorrhagic diseases
Hemorrhagic encephalitis
  UF Encephalitis, Hemorrhagic
      Strümpell-Leichtenstern encephalitis
Hemorrhagic fever (May Subd Geog)
  BT Arenavirus diseases
  NT Dengue
      Ebola virus disease
      Hemorrhagic fever, Omsk
Hemorrhagic fever, Omsk (May Subd Geog)
  ⌈RC147.H44⌉
  UF Omsk hemorrhagic fever
  BT Arbovirus diseases
      Hemorrhagic fever
Hemorrhagic septicemia of cattle
  ⌈SF967.H⌉
  UF Corn-stalk disease
      Shipping fever of cattle
      Stockyards fever
      Stockyards pneumonia
  BT Buffaloes—Diseases
      Cattle—Diseases
      Septicemia
Hemorrhagic septicemia of swine
  USE Swine plague
Hemorrhagic shock
  UF Hematogenic shock
  BT Shock
Hemorrhoids
  ⌈RC865⌉
  UF Piles (Disease)
  BT Rectum—Diseases
      Varicose veins
— **Homeopathic treatment**
  ⌈RX343⌉
Hemory family
  USE Hemry family
Hemosiderin
  ⌈QP551⌉
  BT Blood—Pigments
      Iron proteins
  RT Ferritin
Hemosiderosis (May Subd Geog)
  ⌈RC632.H45⌉
  BT Iron—Metabolism—Disorders
  NT Hemochromatosis
Hemospasia
  ⌈RZ999⌉
  UF Hemospasis
  BT Therapeutics, Cutaneous and external

  RT Cupping
  NT Hyperemia, Artificial
Hemospasis
  USE Hemospasia
Hemostasis
  UF Haemostasis
  BT Hemorrhage
  NT Blood—Coagulation
      Hemostatics
Hemostasis, Surgical (May Subd Geog)
  ⌈RD33.3⌉
  UF Surgical hemostasis
  BT Surgery, Operative
Hemostatics
  ⌈RD33.3⌉
  UF Styptics
  BT Hemorrhage
      Hemostasis
  NT Fibrinogen
      Kino
Hemotherapy
  USE Blood—Transfusion
Hemp (May Subd Geog)
  ⌈HD9155 (Trade)⌉
  ⌈SB255 (Culture)⌉
  ⌈TS1733 (Technology)⌉
    Here are entered general works on hemp plants
  and on Cannabis sativa as a fiber plant. Works on
  Cannabis sativa as a drug plant are entered under
  Cannabis.
  UF Cannabis sativa
  BT Plant fibers
  RT Ramie
      Rope
  NT Cordage
      Jute
      Kenaf
      Roselle
      Sisal hemp
      Sunn hemp
      Twine
— **Control** (May Subd Geog)
  ⌈SB615.H⌉
Hemp, Indian
  USE Hashish
Hemp, Manila
  USE Manila hemp
Hemp industry (May Subd Geog)
  NT Wages—Flax and hemp trade
Hemp industry workers (May Subd Geog)
Hempble family
  USE Hamel family
Hempel family
  USE Hamel family
Hempfield Railroad
  BT Railroads—United States
Hemphill family
  USE Hamel family
Hempl family
  USE Hamel family
Hemple family
  USE Hamel family
Hemprich's coral snake
  USE Micrurus hemprichi
Hempton family
  USE Hampton family
Hempweed, Climbing
  USE Climbing hempweed
Hemrey family
  USE Hemry family
Hemrick family
  USE Hamrick family
Hemry family (Not Subd Geog)
  UF Hammory family
      Hemery family
      Hemmery family
      Hemory family
      Hemrey family
  RT Emery family
      Henry family

Hems
  BT Dressmaking
      Sewing
  NT Fusible materials in sewing
Hen harrier
  USE Circus cyaneas
Henager family
  USE Henninger family
Henary family
  USE Henry family
Henbane, Black
  USE Hyoscyamus niger
Hench family (Not Subd Geog)
  UF Henche family
Henche family
  USE Hench family
Hencke family
  USE Henkel family
Henckel family
  USE Henkel family
Hencock family
  USE Hancock family
Hendcock family
  USE Hancock family
Hendecasyllable
  UF Endecasyllable
Hendee family
  USE Handy family
Hender family
  USE Henders family
Hendereck family
  USE Hendricks family
Henders family (Not Subd Geog)
  UF Hender family
Henderson family (Not Subd Geog)
  UF Handerson family
      Hendorson family
      Hendreson family
Henderson Harbor (N.Y. : Harbor)
  BT Harbors—New York (State)
Henderson Site (N.M.) (Not Subd Geog)
  BT New Mexico—Antiquities
Hendleman family (Not Subd Geog)
Hendorson family
  USE Henderson family
Hendreck family
  USE Hendricks family
Hendreson family
  USE Henderson family
Hendrexson family
  USE Hendricks family
Hendric family
  USE Hendricks family
Hendrich family
  USE Hendricks family
Hendrick family
  USE Hendricks family
Hendricks family (Not Subd Geog)
  UF Hendereck family
      Hendreck family
      Hendrexson family
      Hendric family
      Hendrich family
      Hendrick family
      Hendricksen family
      Hendrickson family
      Hendrik family
      Hendriks family
      Hendrix family
      Hendrixson family
      Hendryx family
      Henrick family
      Henricks family
      Henrickson family
      Henriksen family
      Henrikson family
      Henrixon family
      Hindricks family
  RT Heinrich family
      Henriques family

Hendricksen family
  USE Hendricks family
Hendrickson family
  USE Hendricks family
Hendrie family
  USE Hendry family
Hendries family
  USE Hendry family
Hendrik family
  USE Hendricks family
Hendriks family
  USE Hendricks family
Hendrix family
  USE Hendricks family
Hendrixson family
  USE Hendricks family
Hendry family *(Not Subd Geog)*
  UF Hendrie family
    Hendries family
Hendryx family
  USE Hendricks family
Hendy family
  USE Handy family
Hendyman family
  USE Handy family
Heneary family
  USE Henry family
Henegar family
  USE Henninger family
Heneger family
  USE Henninger family
Henegor family
  USE Henninger family
Henen family
  USE Henning family
Henenger family
  USE Henninger family
Henequen *(May Subd Geog)*
  ⌐QK495.A484 (Botany)⌐
  ⌐SB261.H4 (Culture)⌐
  UF Mexican sisal
  NT Twine
Henequen industry *(May Subd Geog)*
  ⌐HD9156.H46-463⌐
Henery family
  USE Henry family
Heng Mountains (China)
  UF Heng Shan (China)
    Hengshan (China)
  BT Mountains—China
Heng Shan (China)
  USE Heng Mountains (China)
Hengshan (China)
  USE Heng Mountains (China)
Hengst family *(Not Subd Geog)*
  UF Hengster family
Hengster family
  USE Hengst family
Henicocephalidae
  USE Enicocephalidae
Henig family
  USE Henning family
Henigar family
  USE Henninger family
Heniger family
  USE Henninger family
Henin family
  USE Henning family
Hening family
  USE Henning family
Heningar family
  USE Henninger family
Heninger family
  USE Henninger family
Henins family
  USE Henning family
Henk family
  USE Henkel family
Henke family
  USE Henkel family

Henkel family *(Not Subd Geog)*
  UF Hencke family
    Henckel family
    Henk family
    Henke family
    Henkes family
    Henkle family
  RT Hinkle family
Henkersmahl
  USE Last meal before execution
Henkes family
  USE Henkel family
Henkle family
  USE Henkel family
Henkley family
  USE Hinkley family
Henlein family *(Not Subd Geog)*
  UF Heinlein family
    Heinlen family
  RT Hainline family
Henley Royal Regatta (England)
  ⌐GV798⌐
  BT Regattas—England
    Rowing—England
Henna
  UF Alhenna
    Egyptian henna
  BT Dyes and dyeing
Hennager family
  USE Henninger family
Hennary family
  USE Henry family
Henneberg, Counts of *(Not Subd Geog)*
  UF Counts of Henneberg
  BT Germany—Nobility
Hennecke family *(Not Subd Geog)*
Hennefeld family *(Not Subd Geog)*
Hennegar family
  USE Henninger family
Henneger family
  USE Henninger family
Hennepin Avenue (Minneapolis, Minn.)
  BT Streets—Minnesota
Hennery family
  USE Henry family
Hennig family *(Not Subd Geog)*
  UF Hännig family
  RT Henning family
    Henninger family
Hennigar family
  USE Henninger family
Henniger family
  USE Henninger family
Henning family *(Not Subd Geog)*
  UF Hanning family
    Hannings family
    Henen family
    Henig family
    Henin family
    Hening family
    Henins family
    Hennings family
    Henon family
    Hining family
    Hinings family
    Hinnings family
  RT Hennig family
    Henningsen family

Henninger family *(Not Subd Geog)*
  UF Heinger family
    Henager family
    Henegar family
    Heneger family
    Henegor family
    Henenger family
    Henigar family
    Heniger family
    Heningar family
    Heninger family
    Hennager family
    Hennegar family
    Henneger family
    Hennigar family
    Henniger family
  RT Hennig family
Hennings family
  USE Henning family
Henningsen family *(Not Subd Geog)*
  UF Henningson family
    Henningsson family
  RT Henning family
Henningson family
  USE Henningsen family
Henningsson family
  USE Henningsen family
Hennry family
  USE Henry family
Henon family
  USE Henning family
Henopidae
  USE Acroceridae
Henrey family
  USE Henry family
Henri family
  USE Henry family
Henrick family
  USE Hendricks family
Henricks family
  USE Hendricks family
Henrickson family
  USE Hendricks family
Henriksen family
  USE Hendricks family
Henrikson family
  USE Hendricks family
Henriques family *(Not Subd Geog)*
  RT Heinrich family
    Hendricks family
    Henry family
Henriquezia
  ⌐QK495.R85⌐
  BT Rubiaceae
Henriqueziaceae
  USE Rubiaceae
Henrixon family
  USE Hendricks family
Henry, Fort, Battle of, 1862
  ⌐E472.96⌐
  BT United States—History—Civil War,
    1861-1865—Campaigns
Henry (Horse)
  BT Horses
    Horses in moving-pictures
Henry family *(Not Subd Geog)*
  UF Heinary family
    Henary family
    Heneary family
    Henery family
    Hennary family
    Hennery family
    Hennry family
    Henrey family
    Henri family
  RT Emery family
    Harrell family
    Hemry family
    Henriques family

Henry Francis du Pont Winterthur Museum
   Gardens (Del.)   (Not Subd Geog)
      UF Du Pont Winterthur Museum Gardens
            (Del.)
         Winterthur Museum Gardens (Del.)
      BT Gardens—Delaware
Henry II style (Decoration and ornament)
   USE Decoration and ornament—Henry II
            style
Henry IV style (Decoration and ornament)
   USE Decoration and ornament—Henry IV
            style
Henry Lloyd Manor House (Huntington,
   N.Y.)
      UF Lloyd Manor House (Huntington,
            N.Y.)
      BT Caumsett State Park (N.Y.)
         Dwellings—New York (State)
Henry Moore Grand Prize
      BT Rewards (Prizes, etc.)—Japan
         Sculpture—Awards
Henry Turnbuckle (Fictitious character)
   USE Turnbuckle, Henry (Fictitious
            character)
Henrys Fork (Idaho)
      BT Rivers—Idaho
Hens
   USE Chickens
         Poultry
Henselian rings
      UF Rings, Henselian
      BT Commutative rings
Hensely family
   USE Hensley family
Hensen family
   USE Henson family
Henshaw family   (Not Subd Geog)
      UF Hindshaw family
         Hinshaw family
Henslee family
   USE Hensley family
Hensley family   (Not Subd Geog)
      UF Hensely family
         Henslee family
         Hensly family
         Hinseley family
         Hinsely family
         Hinsley family
         Hinsly family
         Hynsley family
Henslow's sparrow
   ⌜QL696.P2438⌝
      UF Ammodramus henslowii
      BT Ammodramus
Hensly family
   USE Hensley family
Henson family   (Not Subd Geog)
      UF Hensen family
Henstock integrals
      UF Integrals, Henstock
      BT Functions of real variables
Henton family
   USE Hinton family
Henty family   (Not Subd Geog)
Hentzelman family
   USE Heinemann family
Hentzelmann family
   USE Heinemann family
Heortology
   USE Church calendar
         Church year
         Fasts and feasts
         Saints—Calendar
HEP (Computer)
   USE Denelcor HEP (Computer)
Hepar calcis
   USE Calcium sulphide
Heparin
   ⌜QP702.H4⌝
      BT Anticoagulants (Medicine)
         Polysaccharides

Hepatectomy
      BT Liver—Surgery
Hepatic artery
   — Surgery
Hepatic cells
   USE Liver cells
Hepatic cirrhosis
   USE Liver—Cirrhosis
Hepatic coma
   ⌜RC848⌝
      UF Porto-hepatic encephalopathy
      BT Coma
         Liver—Diseases
      RT Liver—Failure
Hepatic encephalopathy
   USE Reye's syndrome
Hepatic failure
   USE Liver—Failure
Hepatic function tests
   USE Liver function tests
Hepatic insufficiency
   USE Liver—Failure
Hepatic puncture
   USE Liver—Puncture
Hepatic regeneration
   USE Liver—Regeneration
Hepatic transplantation
   USE Liver—Transplantation
Hepaticae
   USE Liverworts
Hepaticorenal syndrome
   USE Hepatorenal syndrome
Hepatidae
   USE Surgeonfishes
Hepatitis   (May Subd Geog)
   ⌜RC848.H42⌝
      UF Liver—Inflammation
      BT Liver—Diseases
      NT Toxic hepatitis
Hepatitis, Delta
   USE Delta infection
Hepatitis, Homologous serum
   USE Hepatitis B
Hepatitis, Infectious
   USE Hepatitis A
Hepatitis, Neonatal   (May Subd Geog)
   ⌜RJ272⌝
      UF Neonatal hepatitis
      BT Hepatitis in children
         Infants (Newborn)—Diseases
Hepatitis, Non-A, non-B   (May Subd Geog)
   ⌜RC848.H425⌝
      UF Hepatitis C
         Non-A, non-B hepatitis
      BT Hepatitis, Viral
Hepatitis, Serum
   USE Hepatitis B
Hepatitis, Toxic
   USE Toxic hepatitis
Hepatitis, Viral   (May Subd Geog)
   ⌜RC848.H43⌝
      UF Viral hepatitis
         Virus hepatitis
      BT Liver—Diseases
         Virus diseases
      NT Delta infection
         Hepatitis, Non-A, non-B
         Hepatitis A
         Hepatitis B
         Rift Valley fever
Hepatitis, Viral, in children
   (May Subd Geog)
   ⌜RJ456.H46⌝
      BT Hepatitis in children
         Virus diseases in children
Hepatitis A   (May Subd Geog)
   ⌜RC848.I6⌝

      UF Acute catarrhal jaundice
         Epidemic hepatitis
         Hepatitis, Infectious
         Infectious hepatitis
         Infectious jaundice
      BT Hepatitis, Viral
Hepatitis associated antigen
      UF Australia antigen
         Hepatitis B antigen
         Serum hepatitis antigen
      BT Antigens
         Hepatitis B virus
Hepatitis B   (May Subd Geog)
   ⌜RC848.H44⌝
      UF Hepatitis, Homologous serum
         Hepatitis, Serum
         Homologous serum hepatitis
         Serum hepatitis
      BT Hepatitis, Viral
         Liver—Diseases
   — Preventive innoculation
      NT Hepatitis B vaccine
Hepatitis B antigen
   USE Hepatitis associated antigen
Hepatitis B vaccine
   ⌜QR189.5.H46 (Immunology)⌝
   ⌜RA644.H4 (Public health)⌝
      BT Hepatitis B—Preventive innoculation
         Viral vaccines
Hepatitis B virus   (May Subd Geog)
   ⌜QR201.H46⌝
      UF Dane particle
         Homologous serum hepatitis virus
         Serum hepatitis virus
      BT Hepatitis viruses
      NT Hepatitis associated antigen
Hepatitis C
   USE Hepatitis, Non-A, non-B
Hepatitis D
   USE Delta infection
Hepatitis D virus
   USE Delta-associated agent
Hepatitis delta virus
   USE Delta-associated agent
Hepatitis in children   (May Subd Geog)
   ⌜RJ456.H⌝
      BT Pediatric gastroenterology
      NT Hepatitis, Neonatal
         Hepatitis, Viral, in children
Hepatitis viruses
      UF Viruses, Hepatitis
      BT Viruses
      NT Delta-associated agent
         Hepatitis B virus
Hepatocellular carcinoma
   USE Liver—Cancer
Hepatocytes
   USE Liver cells
Hepatolenticular degeneration
   ⌜RC394.H4⌝
      UF Degeneration, Hepatolenticular
         Lenticular degeneration
         Progressive lenticular degeneration
         Wilson's disease
      BT Brain—Diseases
         Copper—Metabolism—Disorders
         Liver—Diseases
Hepatoma
      BT Liver—Tumors
Hepatonephritis serosa acuta
   USE Hepatorenal syndrome
Hepatonephromegalia glycogenica
   USE Glycogenosis
Hepatoptosis
   USE Liver—Displacement
Hepatorenal syndrome   (May Subd Geog)
   ⌜RC848.H46⌝

Hepatorenal syndrome *(Continued)*
  UF Bile nephrosis
      Cholemic nephrosis
      Hepaticorenal syndrome
      Hepatonephritis serosa acuta
      Hepatourologic syndrome
      Heyd's syndrome
      Urohepatic syndrome
  BT Biliary tract—Diseases
      Liver—Diseases
      Renal insufficiency, Acute
      Syndromes
Hepatourologic syndrome
  USE Hepatorenal syndrome
Hephaesteum (Athens, Greece)
  USE Hephaisteion (Athens, Greece)
Hephaestus (Fish)
  [QL638.T27]
  BT Teraponidae
Hephaestus (Greek deity)
  BT Gods, Greek
      Mythology, Greek
  RT Vulcan (Roman deity)
Hephaestus epirrhinos
  [QL638.T27]
Hephaestus, Temple of (Athens, Greece)
  USE Hephaisteion (Athens, Greece)
Hephaisteion (Athens, Greece)
  [DF287.H4]
  UF Hephaesteum (Athens, Greece)
      Hephaestus, Temple of (Athens, Greece)
      Hephaistos, Temple of (Athens, Greece)
      Temple of Hephaestus (Athens, Greece)
      Temple of Hephaistos (Athens, Greece)
      Theseion (Athens, Greece)
      Theseum (Athens, Greece)
  BT Temples—Greece
Hephaistos, Temple of (Athens, Greece)
  USE Hephaisteion (Athens, Greece)
Hephthalite language
  USE Ephthalite language
Hephthalites
  USE Ephthalites
Hepialidae
  [QL561.H47]
  BT Lepidoptera
  NT Callipielus
Hepinger family
  USE Hardinger family
Hepler family *(Not Subd Geog)*
  UF Heabler family
      Hebler family
      Heppeler family
      Heppler family
      Hoeppler family
Hepner family *(Not Subd Geog)*
  UF Hoepfner family
      Hoepner family
      Hoeppener family
      Hoeppner family
Heppeler family
  USE Hepler family
Heppler family
  USE Hepler family
Heptachlor
  UF Heptachlorodicyclopentadiene
      Heptachlorotetrahydromethanoindene
  BT Cyclic compounds
      Insecticides
      Organochlorine compounds
Heptachlorodicyclopentadiene
  USE Heptachlor
Heptachlorotetrahydromethanoindene
  USE Heptachlor
Heptageniidae
  [QL505.3.H4]
  UF Stream mayflies

  BT Mayflies
  NT Afronurus
      Stenonema
Heptagon
  UF Seven-sided polygon
  BT Polygons
Heptamycin
  BT Antibiotics
Heptane
  NT Amoxicillin
Heqaib, Sanctuary of (Elephantine, Egypt)
  USE Sanctuary of Heqaib (Elephantine, Egypt)
Heqaib, Shrine of (Elephantine, Egypt)
  USE Sanctuary of Heqaib (Elephantine, Egypt)
Hequembourg family *(Not Subd Geog)*
Hera (African people)
  UF Hera (African tribe)
  BT Ethnology—Zimbabwe
Hera (African tribe)
  USE Hera (African people)
Hera (Greek deity)
  BT Gods, Greek
      Mythology, Greek
  RT Juno (Roman deity)
Heraclean tablets
  [CN397.H4]
  UF Tablets, Heraclean
  BT Inscriptions, Greek
Heracleopolis (Ancient city)
  USE Heracleopolis Magna (Ancient city)
Heracleopolis Magna (Ancient city)
  (Not Subd Geog)
  [DT73.H44]
  UF Hatnen-nesut (Ancient city)
      Heracleopolis (Ancient city)
      Herakleopolis Magna (Ancient city)
      Neni-nesu (Ancient city)
  BT Cities and towns, Ruined, extinct, etc.—Egypt
      Egypt—Antiquities
Heracles (Greek mythology)
  [BL820.H5]
  BT Mythology, Greek
  RT Hercules (Roman mythology)
  — Art
      NT Herkules-Bauwerk (Kassel, Germany)
Heracleum *(May Subd Geog)*
  [QK495.U48]
  BT Umbelliferae
Heraclidae, Return of the
  USE Greece—History—Dorian invasions, ca. 1125-1025 B.C.
Herakleia (Ancient city)
  USE Carteia (Ancient city)
Herakleopolis Magna (Ancient city)
  USE Heracleopolis Magna (Ancient city)
Heraldia
  [QL638.S9]
  BT Pipefishes
      Syngnathidae
Heraldia nocturna
  [QL638.S9]
Heraldic book-plates
  USE Book-plates, Heraldic
Heraldic models
  USE Miniature heraldic porcelain
Heraldic porcelain, Miniature
  USE Miniature heraldic porcelain
Heraldic visitations
  USE Visitations, Heraldic
Heraldists *(May Subd Geog)*
Heraldry *(May Subd Geog)*
  [CR (National)]
  [JC345 (National: theory)]
  UF Arms, Coats of
      Blazonry
      Coats of arms
      Pedigrees

  BT Auxiliary sciences of history
      Signs and symbols
  RT Chivalry
      Crests
      Decorations of honor
      Devices
      Emblems, National
      Genealogy
      Knights and knighthood
      Precedence
      Titles of honor and nobility
  SA *subdivision* Heraldry *under topical headings, types of industries, and names of individual corporate bodies for the devising, granting, or use of armorial insignia, e.g.* Book industries and trade—Heraldry; Popes—Heraldry; *also particular heraldic devices, e.g.* Collar (in heraldry); Coq gaulois (Heraldic device); Eagle (in heraldry); Elephant (in heraldry); Fleur-de-lis
  NT Achievements (Heraldry)
      Badges
      Battle-cries
      Bear (in heraldry)
      Canting arms (Heraldry)
      Color in heraldry
      Crosses (in heraldry)
      Emblems
      Escutcheons
      Flags
      Hatchments
      Insignia
      Kings and rulers—Heraldry
      Livery buttons
      Mottoes
      Nobility—Heraldry
      Orders of knighthood and chivalry
      Seals (Numismatics)
      Visitations, Heraldic
  — Law and legislation *(May Subd Geog)*
  — United States
      UF United States—Heraldry
Heraldry, Ecclesiastical
  USE Heraldry, Sacred
Heraldry, Ornamental
  [CR29-69]
  UF Ornamental heraldry
  BT Decoration and ornament
Heraldry, Sacred *(May Subd Geog)*
  [CR1101-1131]
  UF Ecclesiastical heraldry
      Heraldry, Ecclesiastical
      Sacred heraldry
  BT Christian antiquities
      Christian art and symbolism
  NT Popes—Heraldry
      Shinto shrines—Heraldry
Heraldry, School
  USE School heraldry
Heraldry in literature
Heralds *(May Subd Geog)*
  [CR183-CR185 (General)]
  [GT5020 (Manners and customs)]
  BT Courts and courtiers
Heran family
  USE Herring family
Herb doctors
  USE Herbalists
Herb farming *(May Subd Geog)*
  [SB351.H5]
  BT Agriculture
Herb gardening *(May Subd Geog)*
  [SB351.H5]
  BT Gardening
      Herbs
  RT Herb gardens
Herb gardens *(May Subd Geog)*
  [SB351.H5]
  BT Gardens

RT Herb gardening
— California
NT Huntington Herb Garden (San
Marino, Calif.)
J. Paul Getty Museum Herb
Garden (Malibu, Calif.)
— New York (State)
NT Robison York State Herb Garden
(Ithaca, N.Y.)
Herb pastes
USE Pestos
Herb remedies
USE Herbs—Therapeutic use
Herb teas
USE Herbal teas
Herbage
USE Grasses
Herbal cosmetics   (May Subd Geog)
BT Cosmetics
Herbs
Herbal medicine
USE Herbs—Therapeutic use
Herbal potpourris
USE Potpourris (Scented floral mixtures)
Herbal teas
UF Herb teas
Teas, Herb
Teas, Herbal
BT Herbs
Tea substitutes
NT Black drink
Herbalists   (May Subd Geog)
UF Herb doctors
BT Healers
Materia medica, Vegetable
Herbals   (May Subd Geog)
Here are entered manuals describing useful plants,
primarily those used for medicinal purposes.
BT Botanical literature
Botany—Pre-Linnean works
Herbs
Medicinal plants
Plants, Useful
Herbaria   (May Subd Geog)
[QK75-QK77]
Here are entered works on collections of dried
plant specimens, usually mounted and arranged for
botanical reference. Works on individual herbaria are
entered under the name of the herbarium.
UF Herbariums
BT Botany
RT Botanical museums
Plants—Collection and preservation
SA subdivision Herbarium under names of
individual persons, families, and
corporate bodies
NT Botany—Type specimens
Herbaria on microfiche   (May Subd Geog)
BT Microfiches
Herbariums
USE Herbaria
Herbert family   (Not Subd Geog)
UF Herberts family
Herberts family
USE Herbert family
Herbicide
USE Herbicides
Herbicide antagonists
USE Herbicide antidotes (Plant protection)
Herbicide antidotes (Plant protection)
(May Subd Geog)
[SB951.45]
UF Antagonists, Herbicide
Antidotes, Herbicide (Plant protection)
Herbicide antagonists
Herbicide safeners
Safeners, Herbicide
BT Agricultural chemicals
Plants, Protection of
RT Herbicides

Herbicide injuries to crops
USE Crops—Herbicide injuries
Herbicide Orange
USE Agent Orange
Herbicide resistance   (May Subd Geog)
[SB951.4]
UF Resistance to herbicides
Weeds—Herbicide resistance
BT Herbicides
Pesticide resistance
Herbicide safeners
USE Herbicide antidotes (Plant protection)
Herbicides   (May Subd Geog)
[SB951.4 (Agriculture)]
Here are entered descriptive works on herbicides
and their use in weed control. Works on the physio-
logical effect of herbicides on plants are entered
under Plants, Effect of herbicides on.
UF Herbicide
Weed killers
Weedicides
BT Agricultural chemicals
Pesticides
Weeds—Control
RT Herbicide antidotes (Plant protection)
NT Agent Orange
Aquatic herbicides
Dichlorophenoxyacetic acid
Diuron
Glyphosate
Herbicide resistance
MCPA (Herbicide)
Metribuzin
Paraquat
Pendimethalin
Pentachlorophenol
Picloram
Sodium pentachlorophenate
Soils—Herbicide content
Soils—Herbicide movement
Trichlorophenoxyacetic acid
— Application
UF Application of herbicides
—— Climatic factors
— Biodegradation
— Law and legislation
USE Pesticides—Law and legislation
— Toxicology
BT Spraying and dusting residues in
agriculture
NT Plants, Effect of herbicides on
— War use
UF War use of herbicides
BT Biological warfare
Chemical warfare
NT Agent Orange
Operation Ranch Hand
Herbicides, Aquatic
USE Aquatic herbicides
Herbicides industry   (May Subd Geog)
Herbigny family   (Not Subd Geog)
UF De Harbigny family
De Herbigny family
D'Herbigny family
Harbigny family
Herbivora
USE Herbivores
Herbivora, Fossil
USE Herbivores, Fossil
Herbivores   (May Subd Geog)
UF Herbivora
Herbivorous animals
Plant-eating animals
BT Animals
SA individual herbivorous animals
NT Folivores
Frugivores
Granivores
Herbivores, Fossil   (May Subd Geog)
UF Herbivora, Fossil
BT Paleontology

Herbivorous animals
USE Herbivores
Herbs   (May Subd Geog)
[SB351.H5 (Culture)]
[TX406 (Food)]
[TX819.H4 (Cookery)]
BT Plants
Plants, Useful
NT Anise
Botany—Pre-Linnean works
Cookery (Herbs)
Dill
Herb gardening
Herbal cosmetics
Herbal teas
Herbals
Lavender (Plant)
Rosemary
Selling—Herbs
— Catalogs and collections
— Religious aspects
— Therapeutic use
UF Herb remedies
Herbal medicine
Medicinal herbs
BT Botany, Medical
Materia medica, Vegetable
RT Medicine, Botanic
Hercamp family
USE Huerkamp family
Hercegovina (Bosnia and Hercegovina)
UF Herzegovina (Bosnia and Hercegovina)
Hum (Bosnia and Hercegovina)
Zahumlje (Bosnia and Hercegovina)
— History
—— Insurrection, 1882
Herculaneum (Ancient city)
(Not Subd Geog)
[DG70.H5]
UF Ercolano (Ancient city)
Scavi di Ercolano (Ancient city)
BT Cities and towns, Ruined, extinct, etc.
—Italy
Italy—Antiquities
Hercules (Roman mythology)
[BL820.H5]
BT Mythology, Roman
RT Heracles (Greek mythology)
Hercules (Turboprop transports)
UF C-130 (Transport plane)
Lockheed Hercules
BT Airplanes, Military
Jet transports
Turboprop transports
Hercules'-club
USE Zanthoxylum clava-herculis
Hercules, Temple of (Sabratha)
USE Temple of Hercules (Sabratha)
Herculesclub ash
USE Zanthoxylum clava-herculis
Herculesclub pricklyash
USE Zanthoxylum clava-herculis
Herd-books
USE Cattle—Herd-books
Goats—Herd-books
Swine—Herd-books
Herd family
USE Hurd family
Herder family   (Not Subd Geog)
UF Harder family
Herders   (May Subd Geog)
UF Herdsmen
RT Livestock
Nomads
Pastures
Rangelands
Transhumance
NT Cowboys
Cowgirls
Gauchos
Shepherds

Herders *(Continued)*
— **Training of** *(May Subd Geog)*
   ⌈SF81-83⌉
— **Australia**
   NT Jackeroos
Herding, Reindeer
   USE Reindeer herding
Herding behavior in animals
   UF Congregation in animals
      Herding instinct
   BT Animal behavior
      Instinct
Herding instinct
   USE Herding behavior in animals
Herdman family
   USE Hardman family
Herdsmen
   USE Herders
Heredia family *(Not Subd Geog)*
Hereditary ataxia
   USE Friedreich's ataxia
Hereditary chorea
   USE Huntington's chorea
Hereditary cutaneomandibular polyoncosis
   USE Basal cell nevus syndrome
Hereditary diseases
   USE Genetic disorders
Hereditary dyskeratosis follicularis
   USE Keratosis follicularis
Hereditary ectodermal dysplasia
   USE Ectodermal dysplasia
Hereditary metabolic disorders
   USE Metabolism, Inborn errors of
Hereditary opalescent dentin
   USE Dentinogenesis imperfecta
Hereditary pseudohemophilia
   USE Von Willebrand's disease
Hereditary spinal sclerosis
   USE Friedreich's ataxia
Hereditary succession
   USE Inheritance and succession
Heredity
   ⌈BF341-BF346 (Psychology)⌉
   ⌈BF418 (Heredity and genius)⌉
   ⌈HM121 (Sociology)⌉
   ⌈HQ753 (Eugenics)⌉
   ⌈HV5133 (Heredity and alcoholism)⌉
   ⌈HV6121-HV6125 (Heredity and crime)⌉
   ⌈QH431 (Biology)⌉
   ⌈RJ91 (Heredity and child culture)⌉
   UF Ancestry
      Descent
      Genes
      Inheritance (Biology)
      Pangenesis
   BT Biology
      Breeding
      Children
      Diseases—Causes and theories of causation
      Man
      Sociology
   RT Atavism
      Eugenics
      Genetics
      Mendel's law
      Natural selection
   NT Biometry
      Blood groups
      Chromosomes
      Consanguinity
      Crossing over (Genetics)
      Cytoplasmic inheritance
      Evolution
      Germ cells
      Hybridization
      Inheritance of acquired characters
      Linkage (Genetics)
      Man—Constitution
      Nature and nurture

Population genetics
Variation (Biology)
Heredity, Human
   ⌈HQ753⌉
   ⌈QH431⌉
   UF Heredity in man
   BT Eugenics
      Family
      Man—Constitution
      Prenatal influences
   NT Deaf—Marriage
      Degeneration
      Education and heredity
      Human genetics
      Mentally handicapped—Marriage
Heredity and environment
   USE Nature and nurture
Heredity in man
   USE Heredity, Human
Heredity of acquired characters
   USE Inheritance of acquired characters
Heredity of disease
   USE Medical genetics
Heredo-retinopathia congenitalis
   USE Norrie's disease
Hereford cattle
   ⌈SF193.H5 (Herd-books)⌉
   ⌈SF199.H4⌉
   BT Beef cattle
   NT Polled Hereford cattle
Herekamp family
   USE Huerkamp family
Herekino Harbour (N.Z.)
   UF Haera-kino Harbour (N.Z.)
      Herikina Harbour (N.Z.)
   BT Bays—New Zealand
Herem
   USE Excommunication (Jewish law)
Heren Canal (Amsterdam, Netherlands)
   USE Herengracht (Amsterdam, Netherlands)
Herengracht (Amsterdam, Netherlands)
   UF Heren Canal (Amsterdam, Netherlands)
      Lords' Canal (Amsterdam, Netherlands)
   BT Canals—Netherlands
Herero language
   ⌈PL8241⌉
   UF Otjiherero language
   BT Bantu languages
Herero Revolt, Namibia, 1904-1907
   USE Namibia—History—Herero Revolt, 1904-1907
Hereros
   ⌈DT709⌉
   ⌈GN657.H⌉
   UF Damaras
      Herreros
      Ovaherero
   NT Himba (Bantu people)
— **History**
   NT Namibia—History—Herero Revolt, 1904-1907
Heresies
   USE Heresy
Heresies, Buddhist *(May Subd Geog)*
   UF Buddhist heresies
   BT Buddhism—Doctrines
      Buddhist sects
      Heresy
   NT Kakushi Nembutsu
Heresies, Christian *(May Subd Geog)*
   ⌈BT1313-1480⌉
   UF Christian heresies
   BT Heresy
      Theology, Doctrinal
   RT Christian sects
   NT Antinomianism
      In Coena Domini bulls
— **History**

— — **Early church, ca. 30-600**
   ⌈BT1319-1475⌉
   NT Adamites
      Adoptionism
      Alogi
      Amalricians
      Arianism
      Circumcellions
      Donatists
      Ebionism
      Elkesaites
      Encratites
      Eunomianism
      Eutychians
      Gnosticism
      Mandaeans
      Manichaeism
      Messalians
      Monarchianism
      Monophysites
      Monothelitism
      Montanism
      Nestorians
      Pelagianism
      Pneumatomachi
      Priscillianism
      Quartodecimans
      Sabellianism
      Subordinationism
      Tritheism
      Valentinians
— — **Middle Ages, 600-1500**
   ⌈BT1319-1475⌉
   NT Bogomiles
      Brethren of the Free Spirit
      Nihilianism
      Paulicians
— — **Modern period, 1500-**
   ⌈BT1476-1480⌉
Heresies, Islamic *(May Subd Geog)*
   ⌈BP167.5⌉
   UF Heresies, Muslim
      Islamic heresies
      Muslim heresies
   BT Heresy
      Islam—Doctrines
      Islamic sects
      Kufr (Islam)
Heresies, Jewish *(May Subd Geog)*
   UF Jewish heresies
   BT Heresy
      Jewish sects
      Judaism—Doctrines
Heresies, Muslim
   USE Heresies, Islamic
Heresy
   ⌈BT1313-1490⌉
   UF Heresies
   BT Offenses against religion
   RT Apostasy
   NT Heresies, Buddhist
      Heresies, Christian
      Heresies, Islamic
      Heresies, Jewish
      Schism
      Trials (Heresy)
Heresy (Canon law)
   ⌈BX1939.H4⌉
Heretics, Buddhist *(May Subd Geog)*
   UF Buddhist heretics
Heretics, Christian *(May Subd Geog)*
   UF Christian heretics
Heretics, Islamic
   USE Heretics, Muslim
Heretics, Jewish *(May Subd Geog)*
   UF Jewish heretics
Heretics, Muslim *(May Subd Geog)*
   UF Heretics, Islamic
      Islamic heretics
      Muslim heretics

Hergert family
USE Hargett family
Herget family
USE Hargett family
Hergett family
USE Hargett family
Hergott family
USE Hargett family
Herick family
USE Herrick family
Herigodt family
USE Hargett family
Herikina Harbour (N.Z.)
USE Herekino Harbour (N.Z.)
Herin family
USE Herring family
Hering family
USE Herring family
Heringa family (Not Subd Geog)
Heringia dodecella
USE Pine bud moth
Heringiola dodecella
USE Pine bud moth
Herington family
USE Harrington family
Herison family
USE Harrison family
Heritiera
 [QK495.S8]
 UF Argyrodendron
 Tarrietia
 BT Sterculiaceae
Herkules (Kassel, Germany)
USE Herkules-Bauwerk (Kassel, Germany)
Herkules-Bauwerk (Kassel, Germany)
 UF Herkules (Kassel, Germany)
 Herkules Denkmal (Kassel, Germany)
 Herkules Oktogon (Kassel, Germany)
 Oktogon (Kassel, Germany)
 BT Heracles (Greek mythology)—Art
 Monuments—Germany (West)
Herkules Denkmal (Kassel, Germany)
USE Herkules-Bauwerk (Kassel, Germany)
Herkules Oktogon (Kassel, Germany)
USE Herkules-Bauwerk (Kassel, Germany)
Herlin family
USE Herlinger family
Herling family
USE Herlinger family
Herlinger family (Not Subd Geog)
 UF Herlin family
 Herling family
 Herrlinger family
Herly family
USE Hurley family
Hermae
 BT Cults—Greece
Herman family (Not Subd Geog)
 UF Heerman family
 Hermann family
 Herrman family
 Herrmann family
Hermandades (May Subd Geog)
 [JS6306.Z7H]
Hermann family
USE Herman family
Hermann-Grima House (New Orleans, La.)
 UF Grima-Hermann House (New Orleans, La.)
 BT Dwellings—Louisiana
 — Stables
 BT Stables—Louisiana
Hermannia (Animal)
 [QL458.2.H47]
 BT Hermanniidae
 NT Hermannia convexa
Hermannia (Plant)
 [QK495.S8]
 BT Sterculiaceae
Hermannia convexa
 [QL458.2.H47]

BT Hermannia (Animal)
Hermanniidae
 [QL458.2.H47]
 BT Mites
 NT Hermannia (Animal)
Hermannite
USE Rhodonite
Hermaphroditism
 [RC883]
 UF Intersexuality
 BT Sex (Biology)
 Sex differentiation disorders
 Sexual disorders
 NT Bisexuality
 Gynandromorphism
Hermeneutics
 [BD240-BD241 (Methodology)]
 [PA49 (Classics)]
 UF Interpretation
 BT Criticism
 SA subdivision Hermeneutics under
 individual sacred books, e.g. Bible—
 Hermeneutics; and subdivision
 Sacred books—Hermeneutics under
 individual religions, e.g. Buddhism
 —Sacred books—Hermeneutics
 NT Gematria
 — Religious aspects
 — — Buddhism, [Christianity, etc.]
 — — Christianity
 NT Preunderstanding (Theology)
Hermeneutics, Biblical
USE Bible—Hermeneutics
Hermeneutics, Talmudic
USE Talmud—Hermeneutics
Hermes (Communications satellite)
 [TK5104.2.H46]
 BT Artificial satellites in
 telecommunication
 Astronautics—Canada
 Telecommunication—Canada
Hermes (Greek deity)
 BT Gods, Greek
 Mythology, Greek
 RT Mercury (Roman deity)
Hermetic philosophers (May Subd Geog)
 BT Philosophers
Hermetically sealed double glazing
USE Sealed double glazing
Hermeticism
USE Hermetism
Hermetism (May Subd Geog)
 UF Hermeticism
 BT Occultism
Herminidae
USE Noctuidae
Hermione Mutiny, 1797
 [DA87.7]
Hermit-crabs
 [QL444.D3]
 UF Anomura
 Paguridea
 BT Crabs
 NT Aeglidae
 Coenobitidae
Hermit-crabs as pets
 [SF459.H47]
Hermit spadefoot
USE Scaphiopus holbrookii
Hermit-thrush
USE Thrushes
Hermitages (May Subd Geog)
 UF Cells of hermits
 Hermits' cells
 BT Monasteries
 RT Hermits
Hermite polynomials
 UF Polynomials, Hermite
 BT Differential equations—Numerical
 solutions
 Orthogonal polynomials

Hermitian forms
 UF Forms, Hermitian
 BT Forms (Mathematics)
Hermitian inner product spaces
USE Inner product spaces
Hermitian structures
 UF Structures, Hermitian
 BT Complex manifolds
 Geometry, Differential
 RT Kählerian structures
Hermitian symmetric spaces
USE Symmetric spaces, Hermitian
Hermits (May Subd Geog)
 [BX2845-BX2847 (Monasticism)]
 [CT9990-CT9991 (Biography)]
 UF Anchorites
 Eremites
 BT Christian biography
 Eccentrics and eccentricities
 Monastic and religious life
 Saints
 RT Hermitages
 Recluses
 NT Augustinians
 Buddhist hermits
 Camaldolites
 Pillar saints
Hermits' cells
USE Hermitages
Hermits in art
Hermits in literature
Hermodactyl
 [RS165.H5 (Drugs)]
Hermopolis Magna (City) (Not Subd Geog)
 [DT73.A85]
 UF al-Ashmunayn Site (Egypt)
 el-Ashmunein Site (Egypt)
 Eshmunein Site (Egypt)
 Hermoupolis (City)
 Khmun (City)
 Khmunu (City)
 Shmun (City)
 Wenu (City)
 BT Cities and towns, Ruined, extinct, etc.
 —Egypt
 Egypt—Antiquities
Hermoupolis (City)
USE Hermopolis Magna (City)
Hermundson family (Not Subd Geog)
Hern family
USE Hearn family
Hernád River (Czechoslovakia and Hungary)
 UF Hornád River (Czechoslovakia and
 Hungary)
 BT Rivers—Czechoslovakia
 Rivers—Hungary
Hernandiaceae
 [QK495.H42]
 BT Magnoliales
Hernani (Fictitious character)
 BT Characters and characteristics in
 literature
 RT Hugo, Victor, 1802-1885—Characters
 —Hernani
Herndon family (Not Subd Geog)
 UF Harnden family
 Harndon family
 Hearndon family
 RT Hearn family
Herne family
USE Hearn family
Hernhutters
USE Moravians
Hernia
 [RD621-6]
 UF Abdomen—Hernia
 Abdominal hernia
 Bubonocele
 Rupture
 BT Intestines—Surgery
 RT Trusses (Surgery)

Hernia *(Continued)*
  SA *subdivision* Hernia *under names of*
      organs, e.g. Lungs—Hernia
  NT Femoral hernia
      Hiatal hernia
      Inguinal hernia
      Ventral hernia
  — **Surgery**
      UF Herniotomy
Herningsholm (Denmark)
  BT Manors—Denmark
Herniotomy
  USE Hernia—Surgery
Hero
  BT Mythology, Greek
  RT Leander
  — **Art**
      NT Hero and Leander (Tapestries)
Hero and Leander (Tapestries)
  UF Bratislava Hero and Leander tapestries
  BT Hero—Art
      Leander—Art
      Tapestry—Czechoslovakia
      Tapestry, Baroque—Czechoslovakia
Hero of the Soviet Union
  USE Geroĭ Sovetskogo Soĭuza
Hero-worship
  USE Heroes
Herodion
  USE Herodium
Herodiones
  USE Herons
      Storks
Herodium *(Not Subd Geog)*
  UF Firdaws, Khirbat
      Herodion
      Herodyon
      Khirbat Firdaws
  BT Castles—West Bank
      Fortification—West Bank
      West Bank—Antiquities
Herodyon
  USE Herodium
Heroes *(May Subd Geog)*
  UF Hero-worship
      Heroism
      Superheroes
  BT Adventure and adventurers
      History
      Mythology, Classical
  RT Antiheroes
      Apotheosis
      Courage
      Heroines
      Mythology
  SA *particular civilian and military awards,*
      e.g. George Cross; Medal of Honor
  NT Bogatyrs
      Boys as soldiers
      Explorers
      Halls of fame
      Heldensage
      Martyrs
  — **Mythology**
  — **Religious aspects**
      ₍BL815.H47₎
  — **Soviet Union**
      NT Geroĭ Sovetskogo Soĭuza
Heroes (in numismatics)
  BT Heroes in art
      Numismatics
Heroes in art
  NT Heroes (in numismatics)
Heroes in literature
  NT Shakespeare, William, 1564-1616—
      Characters—Heroes
Heroes in mass media *(May Subd Geog)*
  ₍P96.H46₎
  BT Mass media
Heroes in motion pictures
  BT Moving-pictures

Heroes Unlimited (Game)
  ₍GV1469.62.H45₎
  BT Fantasy games
Heroi-comical literature
  USE Mock-heroic literature
Heroic couplet
  USE Heroic verse, English
Heroic fantasy
  USE Fantastic fiction
Heroic poetry
  USE Epic poetry
Heroic saga
  USE Heldensage
Heroic verse, English
  ₍PE1515₎
  UF Heroic couplet
  BT Couplets
      English language—Versification
Heroic virtue
  Here are entered works dealing with the exercise
  of virtue in a pre-eminent degree, a prerequisite for
  beatification and canonization.
  UF Virtue, Heroic
  BT Virtue
  RT Beatification
Heroid
  ₍PN1415₎
  ₍PT581.H5 (German)₎
  BT Imaginary letters
Heroids
  BT Poetry
Heroin
  ₍HV5822.H4₎
  BT Morphine
      Narcotics
Heroin dependency
  USE Heroin habit
Heroin habit *(May Subd Geog)*
  ₍HV5822.H4 (Social pathology)₎
  ₍RC568.H4 (Psychopathology)₎
  UF Heroin dependency
  BT Narcotic habit
  — **Treatment** *(May Subd Geog)*
      ₍RC568.H4₎
Heroines *(May Subd Geog)*
  UF Heroism
  BT Women
      Women in the Bible
  RT Heroes
Heroines in literature
  NT Shakespeare, William, 1564-1616—
      Characters—Heroines
Heroines of Jericho, Afro-American
  UF Afro-American Heroines of Jericho
Heroism
  USE Courage
      Heroes
      Heroines
Heron (Transport plane)
  BT Transport planes
Heron family
  USE Hearn family
Herons
  ₍QL696.C52₎
  UF Egrets
      Herodiones
  BT Ardeidae
  NT Ardea
      Black-crowned night heron
      Cattle egret
      European bittern
      Gray heron
      Great blue heron
      Green heron
      Nycticorax
      Rufous night heron
Heroult process
  USE Hall Héroult process
Héroux family *(Not Subd Geog)*
Herpes
  USE Herpesvirus diseases

Herpes genitalis *(May Subd Geog)*
  ₍RA644.H45 (Public health)₎
  ₍RC203.H45 (Internal medicine)₎
  UF Genital herpes
      Herpes progenitalis
      Herpes simplex, Genital
  BT Herpes simplex
      Sexually transmitted diseases
Herpes progenitalis
  USE Herpes genitalis
Herpes simplex
  ₍RC147.H6₎
  BT Herpesvirus diseases
      Skin—Infections
  NT Herpes genitalis
Herpes simplex, Genital
  USE Herpes genitalis
Herpes simplex virus
  UF Herpes virus hominis
  BT Herpesviruses
Herpes tonsurans maculosus
  USE Pityriasis rosea
Herpes virus hominis
  USE Herpes simplex virus
Herpes zoster
  ₍RC147.H6₎
  UF Shingles (Disease)
  BT Herpesvirus diseases
Herpes zoster virus
  USE Varicella-zoster virus
Herpestes
  ₍QL737.C28₎
  BT Viverridae
Herpestes ichneumon
  ₍QL737.C28₎
  UF African mongoose
      Egyptian mongoose
Herpestinae
  USE Mongooses
Herpesviridae
  USE Herpesviruses
Herpesvirus diseases
  UF Herpes
  BT Virus diseases
  NT Chickenpox
      Cytomegalic inclusion disease
      Epstein-Barr virus diseases
      Herpes simplex
      Herpes zoster
      Pseudorabies
Herpesvirus diseases in animals
  (May Subd Geog)
  ₍SF809.H47₎
  BT Veterinary virology
  NT Channel catfish virus disease
      Equine herpesvirus diseases
      Infectious bovine rhinotracheitis
      Marek's disease
Herpesvirus diseases in horses
  USE Equine herpesvirus diseases
Herpesvirus vaccines
  ₍QR189.5.H48₎
  BT Viral vaccines
Herpesviruses
  UF Herpesviridae
  BT Viruses
      Viruses, DNA
  NT Cytomegaloviruses
      Duck plague virus
      Epstein-Barr virus
      Herpes simplex virus
      Pseudorabies virus
      Varicella-zoster virus
Herpetodryas serra
  USE Tropidodryas serra
Herpetologists *(May Subd Geog)*
  ₍QL26-35₎
  BT Herpetology
      Zoologists
Herpetology *(May Subd Geog)*
  BT Zoology

NT Amphibians
    Herpetologists
    Reptiles
Herpothamnus
  USE Vaccinium
Herpyllus
    ⌐QL458.42.G5⌐
  BT Gnaphosidae
Herran family
  USE Herring family
Herreen family *(Not Subd Geog)*
Herren family
  USE Herring family
Herren Street (Vienna, Austria)
  USE Herrengasse (Vienna, Austria)
Herrengasse (Vienna, Austria)
  UF Herren Street (Vienna, Austria)
  BT Streets—Austria
Herrenhaus Steinhorst (Germany)
  UF Steinhorst Manor (Germany)
  BT Manors—Germany (West)
Herrenhausen (Hannover, Germany)
  BT Castles—Germany (West)
Herreroland (Namibia)
  USE Damaraland (Namibia : Region)
Herreros
  USE Hereros
Herreros Street (Villafranca del Panadés,
  Spain)
  USE Calle de los Herreros (Villafranca del
      Panadés, Spain)
Herrick family *(Not Subd Geog)*
  UF Herick family
    Heyrick family
Herrin family
  USE Herring family
Herring
    ⌐QL638.C64⌐
    ⌐SH167.H5 (Fish-culture)⌐
  UF Atlantic herring
    Clupea harengus pallasii
    Clupea pallasii
    Pacific herring
  NT Cookery (Herring)
Herring, Blueback
  USE Blueback herring
Herring, Lake
  USE Lake herring
Herring family *(Not Subd Geog)*
  UF Haring family
    Harrin family
    Harring family
    Hearing family
    Hearon family
    Hearring family
    Heran family
    Herin family
    Hering family
    Herran family
    Herren family
    Herrin family
    Herrown family
  RT Harrington family
Herring fisheries *(May Subd Geog)*
    ⌐SH351.H5⌐
  BT Fisheries
Herring-gull
    ⌐QL696.L3⌐
  BT Gulls
Herring industry *(May Subd Geog)*
    ⌐HD9469.H4-43⌐
Herrington family
  USE Harrington family
Herrington Lake (Ky.)
  BT Dix River (Ky.)
    Lakes—Kentucky
    Reservoirs—Kentucky
Herrington Manor State Park (Md.)
  BT Parks—Maryland
Herrison family
  USE Harrison family

Herrlinger family
  USE Herlinger family
Herrman family
  USE Herman family
Herrmann family
  USE Herman family
Herrnhuter
  USE Bohemian Brethren
    Moravians
Hêrro (The word)
  BT German language—Old High German,
     750-1050—Etymology
Herrown family
  USE Herring family
Herrscher family
  USE Hershey family
Hersch family
  USE Hershey family
Herschy family
  USE Hershey family
Herset family *(Not Subd Geog)*
Hersey family *(Not Subd Geog)*
  UF Harsey family
    Hearsay family
    Hearsey family
    Hearsy family
  RT Hershey family
Hersfelder Kreisbahn
  BT Railroads—Germany (West)
Hersh family
  USE Hershey family
Hershey family *(Not Subd Geog)*
  UF Harshey family
    Harshy family
    Herrscher family
    Hersch family
    Herschy family
    Hersh family
    Hershy family
  RT Hersey family
    Hirsch family
Hershy family
  USE Hershey family
Herst family
  USE Hearst family
Hertel family *(Not Subd Geog)*
  UF Hertle family
  RT Hertler family
Herter family *(Not Subd Geog)*
Hertle family
  USE Hertel family
Hertler family *(Not Subd Geog)*
  RT Hertel family
Hertsel family
  USE Hartzell family
Hertsgaard family *(Not Subd Geog)*
Hertzel family
  USE Hartzell family
Hertzian waves
  USE Electric waves
    Microwaves
    Radio waves
Hertzog family
  USE Herzog family
Hertzogprys
  BT Afrikaans literature—Competitions—
     South Africa
    Literary prizes—South Africa
Hertzsprung-Russell diagrams
  USE HR diagrams
Heruis de Mes (Legendary character)
  USE Hervis de Metz (Legendary character)
Hervey Bay (Qld.)
  BT Bays—Australia
Hervey family
  USE Harvey family
Hervey Island (Cook Islands)
  USE Manuae (Cook Islands)
Hervis de Metz (Legendary character)
  UF Heruis de Mes (Legendary character)
  BT Folklore—France

Hervy family
  USE Harvey family
Herzegovina (Bosnia and Hercegovina)
  USE Hercegovina (Bosnia and Hercegovina)
Herzel family
  USE Hartzell family
Herzog family *(Not Subd Geog)*
  UF Hartsoe family
    Hertzog family
  RT Hart family
Hese family
  USE Hess family
Ḥesed (The Hebrew word)
  UF Ḥäsäd (The Hebrew word)
  BT Hebrew language—Etymology
Hesilwoode family
  USE Hazelwood family
Hesionidae
    ⌐QL391.A6⌐
  BT Phyllodocida
  NT Microphthalmus
Hesitation form (Linguistics)
  BT Linguistics
Heslep family
  USE Haislip family
Hesler family *(Not Subd Geog)*
Heslop family
  USE Haislip family
Hesperia *(May Subd Geog)*
    ⌐QL561.H5⌐
  BT Hesperiidae
Hesperidae
  USE Hesperiidae
Hesperidin
  BT Bioflavonoids
Hesperiidae
    ⌐QL561.H5⌐
  UF Achylodidae
    Cyclopididae
    Erynnidae
    Eudamidae
    Hesperidae
    Hesperioidea
    Skippers (Butterflies)
    Telegonidae
    Thamyrididae
    Thymelidae
  BT Butterflies
    Lepidoptera
  NT Autochton
    Erynnis
    Hesperia
    Onespa
    Pyrgus
    Wallengrenia
Hesperinidae
  USE Bibionidae
Hesperioidea
  USE Hesperiidae
Hesperoctenes
    ⌐QL523.P64⌐
  BT Polyctenidae
Hesperomys
  USE Calomys
Hesperonesian languages
  USE Malayan languages
Hesperoptenus
    ⌐QL737.C595⌐
  BT Vespertilionidae
Hesperumia
    ⌐QL561.G6⌐
  BT Geometridae
Hess family *(Not Subd Geog)*
  UF Hese family
    Hesse family
    Hesser family
    Hest family
  RT Hiss family
Hess Site (Mo.) *(Not Subd Geog)*
  BT Missouri—Antiquities

Hesse (Germany)
— History
— — To 1247
— — 1247-1567
— — Landgraviate, 1567-1806
— — Grand duchy, 1806-1918
— — Revolution, 1848-1849
      BT Germany—History—Revolution,
          1848-1849
— — 1918-
— Politics and government
— — 1945-
Hesse family
  USE Hess family
Hesse in art
Hesselagergård (Denmark)
  UF Haesleakaer (Denmark)
  BT Manors—Denmark
Hesselgrave family *(Not Subd Geog)*
  UF Haslegrave family
     Hazelgrave family
     Hazelgrove family
     Hesselgreaves family
     Hezelgrave family
Hesselgreaves family
  USE Hesselgrave family
Hesser family
  USE Hess family
Hessian flies
  [SB945.H3]
  BT Flies
Hessian mercenaries
  BT German mercenaries
     Mercenary troops
  NT United States—History—Revolution,
     1775-1783—German mercenaries
Hessians *(May Subd Geog)*
  BT Germans
Hessians in the American Revolution
  USE United States—History—Revolution,
     1775-1783—German mercenaries
Hessle Road (Hull, Humberside)
  BT Streets—England
Hest family
  USE Hess family
Hester family *(Not Subd Geog)*
  UF Hesters family
     Hesther family
Hesters family
  USE Hester family
Hesther family
  USE Hester family
Hestia (Greek deity)
  BT Goddesses, Greek
Hesychasm
  [BX384.5]
  BT Mysticism—Orthodox Eastern Church
Het Gooi (Netherlands)
  USE Gooi (Netherlands : Region)
Het Loo (Apeldoorn, Netherlands)
  UF Loo Palace (Apeldoorn, Netherlands)
  BT Palaces—Netherlands
Héta Indians
  [F2520.1.H48]
  UF Aré Indians
     Ivaparé Indians
     Setá Indians
     Sheta Indians
     Xetá Indians
     Yvaparé Indians
  BT Botocudo Indians
     Guarani Indians
     Indians of South America
     Indians of South America—Brazil
Hetch Hetchey Valley (Calif.)
  USE Hetch Hetchy Valley (Calif.)
Hetch Hetchy Valley (Calif.)
  UF Hetch Hetchey Valley (Calif.)
  BT Valleys—California
Hetcher family
  USE Hatcher family

Hetep Senwosret (Ancient city)
  USE Kahun (Ancient city)
Heteralocha
  [QL696.P224]
  BT Callaeidae
Heteralocha acutirostris
  USE Huia
Heterandria
  [QL638.P73]
  UF Pseudoxiphophorus
  BT Poeciliidae
Heteroauxin
  USE Indoleacetic acid
Heterocampa
  [QL561.N8]
  BT Notodontidae
Heterocera
  USE Moths
Heteroceridae
  [QL596.H45]
  BT Beetles
Heterocheylidae
  [QL458.2.H4]
  BT Mites
Heterochromatin
  [QH599]
  BT Chromatin
Heterochromic uveitis
  USE Iridocyclitis
Heterocycles
  USE Heterocyclic compounds
Heterocyclic chemistry
  [QD399-QD406]
  UF Chemistry, Heterocyclic
  BT Chemistry, Organic
Heterocyclic compounds
  [QD399-QD406]
  UF Cycloids, Mixed (Chemistry)
     Heterocycles
     Mixed cycloids (Chemistry)
  BT Cyclic compounds
  NT Auranofin
     Azepines
     Bromocriptine
     Carbolines
     Cytochalasins
     Dithiolylium
     Doxepin
     Etomidate
     Furans
     Furazans
     Indocyanine green
     Ivermectin
     Lactams
     Lisuride
     Methotrexate
     Naphthacridinone
     Nomifensine
     Oxazoles
     Piperidine
     Polymethines
     Prazosin
     Pteridines
     Pyran
     Pyridine
     Pyrimidines
     Pyrrole
     Pyrylium compounds
     Tetrachlorodibenzodioxin
     Tetrahydroisoquinolines
     Timolol maleate
     Tioconazole
     Trimipramine
     Uracil
     Xanthene
— Spectra
Heterodera glycines
  UF Soybean cyst nematode
  BT Soybean—Diseases and pests
Heterodon nasicus
  USE Western hognose snake

Heterodon platyrhinos
  USE Eastern hognose snake
Heterodontidae
  [QL638.95.H4]
  BT Heterodontiformes
  NT Heterodontus
Heterodontiformes
  [QL638.95.H4]
  UF Bullhead sharks
  BT Chondrichthyes
     Sharks
  NT Heterodontidae
Heterodontus
  [QL638.95.H4]
  BT Heterodontidae
  NT Horn shark
Heterodontus bonae-spei
  USE Port Jackson shark
Heterodontus francisci
  USE Horn shark
Heterodontus japonicus
  USE Port Jackson shark
Heterodontus phillipi
  USE Port Jackson shark
Heterodontus portusjacksoni
  USE Port Jackson shark
Heterodyne reception (Radio)
  USE Radio—Receivers and reception—
     Heterodyne reception
Heterodyning (Electronics)
  BT Electronics
  NT Superheterodyne receivers
Heterogeneous catalysis
  [QD505]
  BT Catalysis
Heterogeneous Element Processor (Computer)
  USE Denelcor HEP (Computer)
Heterogenesis
  USE Generations, Alternating
     Life—Origin
     Spontaneous generation
Heterogeomys
  USE Orthogeomys
Heterognathi
  USE Cypriniformes
Heterografts
  USE Xenografts
Heterologous transplants
  USE Xenografts
Heterometry
  BT Chemistry, Analytic—Quantitative
Heteromi
  USE Notacanthiformes
Heteromodal effects
  USE Intersensory effects
Heteromyidae
  NT Heliscomys
     Heteromys
     Kangaroo rats
     Liomys
     Perognathus
     Pocket mice
Heteromyidae, Fossil
  [QE882.R6]
  BT Rodents, Fossil
  NT Heliscomys
Heteromys
  [QL737.R66]
  UF Spiny pocket mice
  BT Heteromyidae
     Pocket mice
Heteromys anomalus
  [QL737.R66]
  UF Forest spiny pocket mouse
Heteroneura
  USE Clusiodes
Heteroneuridae
  USE Clusiidae
Heteronyms
  BT Lexicology
     Semantics

SA *subdivision* Heteronyms *under names*
of languages or groups of languages,
e.g. English language—Heteronyms
Heteropelma
⌐QL568.I2⌐
BT Ichneumonidae
Heteropeza *(May Subd Geog)*
⌐QL537.C33⌐
BT Gall midges
Heterophoria *(May Subd Geog)*
⌐RE776⌐
UF Phoria
BT Eye—Movement disorders
Heteroplastic grafts
USE Xenografts
Heteropoda
⌐QL430.4 *(Mollusks)*⌐
BT Gasteropoda
NT Atlantidae
Heteropodidae
⌐QL458.42.H48⌐
UF Eusparassidae
Sparassidae
BT Crab spiders
Spiders
NT Polybetes
Heteropsammia *(May Subd Geog)*
⌐QL377.C7⌐
BT Dendrophylliidae
Heteroptera
USE Hemiptera
Heteroptera, Fossil
BT Insects, Fossil
Heterorthina
BT Dalmanellidae
Heterosarus *(May Subd Geog)*
⌐QL568.A4⌐
BT Andrenidae
Heteroscedasticity
BT Analysis of variance
Econometrics
Least squares
RT Homoscedasticity
Heterosis
⌐QH421 *(Biology)*⌐
⌐S494 *(Breeding)*⌐
⌐SB123 *(Plant breeding)*⌐
⌐SF105 *(Animal breeding)*⌐
UF Hybrid vigor
BT Breeding
Fertility
Growth
Growth (Plants)
Hybridization
Heterosomata
USE Flatfishes
Heterosporium
⌐QK625.D4⌐
BT Dematiaceae
Heterostraci
⌐QE852.A33⌐
BT Agnatha, Fossil
Heterostylism
⌐QK926⌐
BT Plants—Reproduction
Plants, Sex in
Pollination
Heterotherms
USE Poikilotherms
Heterotricha
USE Spirotricha
Heterotrichum
USE Saussurea
Heterotrophic bacteria
USE Bacteria, Heterotrophic
Heterotropia
USE Strabismus
Heterozygosis
⌐QH21-QH25 *(Biology)*⌐
⌐SB123 *(Plant breeding)*⌐

Heth family
USE Heath family
Hetizel family
USE Hutzel family
Hetmans *(May Subd Geog)*
BT Cossacks
Hetol
⌐RM666.H⌐
Hettinger family
USE Hardinger family
Heuchera
⌐QK495.S3⌐
UF Alumroot
BT Saxifragaceae
Heudebourg family
USE Hudiburgh family
Heugh family
USE Hughes family
Heulandite
⌐QE391.H55⌐
Heuneburg Site (Germany)
(Not Subd Geog)
BT Germany (West)—Antiquities
Heuristic
⌐BD260⌐
BT Methodology
Philosophy
Heuristic programming
⌐T57.84⌐
BT Artificial intelligence
Programming (Mathematics)
Heuscheuer Mountains (Poland)
USE Stołowe Mountains (Poland)
Heuser family
USE Hauser family
Heuss family *(Not Subd Geog)*
RT Heiss family
Heutmacher family
USE Hatmaker family
Hève, Cap de la (France)
UF Cap de la Hève (France)
BT Capes (Coasts)—France
Heve language
USE Eudeve language
Hevea *(May Subd Geog)*
⌐QK495.E9 *(Botany)*⌐
⌐SB291.H4 *(Culture)*⌐
UF Hevea brasiliensis
Para rubber tree
Siphonia ridleyana
BT Euphorbiaceae
Rubber plants
— **Diseases and pests** *(May Subd Geog)*
NT Ceratostomella fimbriata
— **Weed control** *(May Subd Geog)*
⌐SB608.H5⌐
Hevea brasiliensis
USE Hevea
Hevea seed oil
⌐TP684.R83⌐
UF Pará rubber seed oil
Rubber-seed oil
Hevener family
USE Heavener family
Hevner family
USE Heavener family
Hewen family
USE Hewins family
Hewes family
USE Hughes family
Hewgley family
USE Huguley family
Hewings family
USE Hewins family
Hewins family *(Not Subd Geog)*
UF Hewen family
Hewings family
Huen family
Hughins family

**Hewitt Lake National Wildlife Refuge
(Mont.)** *(Not Subd Geog)*
BT National parks and reserves—Montana
Wildlife refuges—Montana
Hewitt-Nachbin spaces
⌐QA611.234⌐
UF Hewitt Q-spaces
Nachbin-Hewitt spaces
Q-spaces, Hewitt spaces
Spaces, Hewitt-Nachbin
Spaces, Nachbin-Hewitt
BT Realcompact spaces
Hewitt Q-spaces
USE Hewitt-Nachbin spaces
Hewlett family
USE Hulett family
Hewlett-Packard 33E (Calculator)
USE HP33E (Calculator)
Hewlett-Packard 41 (Calculator)
USE HP-41 (Calculator)
Hewlett-Packard 41C (Calculator)
USE HP41C (Calculator)
Hewlett-Packard 41C/CV (Calculator)
USE HP-41C/CV (Calculator)
Hewlett-Packard 41CV (Calculator)
USE HP-41CV (Calculator)
Hewlett-Packard 41CX (Calculator)
USE HP-41CX (Calculator)
Hewlett-Packard 67 (Calculator)
USE HP-67/97 (Calculator)
Hewlett-Packard 67/97 (Calculator)
USE HP-67/97 (Calculator)
Hewlett-Packard 71 (Calculator)
USE HP-71 (Calculator)
Hewlett-Packard 110 Portable Computer
USE HP 110 Portable Computer
Hewlett-Packard 150 (Computer)
USE HP 150 (Computer)
Hewlett-Packard computers
⌐QA76.8.H⌐
UF HP computers
BT Electronic digital computers
NT HP 110 Portable Computer
HP 150 (Computer)
HP/1000 (Computer)
HP 2000 (Computer)
HP 3000 (Computer)
HP Touchscreen computers
— **Programming**
Hewlett-Packard HP-12C (Calculator)
USE HP-12C (Calculator)
Hewlett-Packard HP-18C (Calculator)
USE HP-18C (Calculator)
Hewlett-Packard programmable calculators
⌐QA75⌐
BT Programmable calculators
NT HP-18C (Calculator)
HP25 (Calculator)
HP33E (Calculator)
HP-41 (Calculator)
HP41C (Calculator)
HP-41C/CV (Calculator)
HP-41CV (Calculator)
HP-41CX (Calculator)
Hewlett Packard programmable calculators
NT HP-67/97 (Calculator)
Hewlett-Packard programmable calculators
NT HP-71 (Calculator)
Hewlett-Packard Touchscreen computers
USE HP Touchscreen computers
Hewlin family
USE Hulen family
Hewlings family
USE Hulen family
Hews family
USE Hughes family

Hewson family (Not Subd Geog)
- UF Hooson family
- Hoosun family
- Howson family
- Hughson family
- Huson family
- RT Hughes family

Hex signs (May Subd Geog)
- BT Decoration and ornament
- Signs and symbols
- Talismans
- Witchcraft in art
- NT Barn symbols

Hexachlorocyclopentadiene
- BT Cyclopentadiene
- Organochlorine compounds

Hexachlorocyclopentadiene dimer
- USE Mirex

Hexachlorohexahydrom
ethanobenzodioxathiepin oxide
- USE Endosulfan

Hexachlorotrinorbornenylenedimethyl sulphite
- USE Endosulfan

Hexacreusia
- [QL444.C58]
- BT Balanidae

Hexacreusia durhami
- [QL444.C58]

Hexactinellida
- [QL373.H6]

Hexactinellida, Fossil
- [QE775]
- UF Hyalospongea, Fossil
- BT Sponges, Fossil
- NT Lychniskida, Fossil

Hexadecimal system
- USE Sexadecimal system

Hexafluorodiethyl ether
- USE Flurothyl

Hexagenia
- [QL505.3.E65]
- BT Ephemeridae
- NT Hexagenia limbata
- Hexagenia recurvata

Hexagenia limbata
- [QL505.3.E65]
- BT Hexagenia

Hexagenia recurvata
- [QL505.3.E65]
- BT Hexagenia

Hexagons
- BT Polygons
- NT Pascal's theorem

Hexagram (Coin)
- [CJ1249]
- BT Coins, Byzantine

Hexagrammidae
- [QL638.H49]
- UF Chiridae
- Greenling fishes
- Greenlings
- Ophiodontidae
- Oxylebiidae
- BT Perciformes
- Scorpaeniformes
- NT Lingcod

Hexahydrobenzene
- USE Cyclohexane

Hexahydrocyclopentapyrroltolylsulphonylurea
- USE Gliclazide

Hexahydrodimethylmethylbutenylmethanoben
zazocinol
- USE Pentazocine

Hexameter
- [P311]
- [PA416.H6 (Greek)]
- [PA2337.H6 (Latin)]
- [PE1531.H6 (English)]

Hexamethylene
- USE Cyclohexane

Hexamethylenebischlorophenylbiguanide
- USE Chlorhexidine

Hexamethyleneimines
- USE Azepines

Hexamitidae
- [QL368.D65]
- BT Diplomonadida
- NT Giardia

Hexanaphthene
- USE Cyclohexane

Hexanchidae
- [QL638.95.H48]
- UF Cow sharks
- BT Hexanchiformes
- NT Hexanchus

Hexanchiformes
- [QL638.95.H48]
- BT Chondrichthyes
- Sharks
- NT Hexanchidae

Hexanchus
- [QL638.95.H48]
- BT Hexanchidae

Hexane
- NT Cyclacillin

Hexapoda
- USE Insects

Hexosaminidase A deficiency (Tay-Sachs)
- USE Tay-Sachs disease

Hexose monophosphate pathway
- USE Pentose phosphate pathway

Hexose monophosphate shunt
- USE Pentose phosphate pathway

Hexose phosphates
- [QP702.H (Animal biochemistry)]
- BT Sugar phosphates
- — Metabolism
- NT Pentose phosphate pathway

Hexosemonophosphate shunt
- USE Pentose phosphate pathway

Hexyloxyphenyl decyloxybenzoate
- [QD923]
- UF HOPDOB (Chemical)
- BT Benzoates
- Liquid crystals

Hey family
- USE Hayes family

Heyd family
- USE Hite family

Heyden family
- USE Hayden family

Heydon family
- USE Hayden family

Heydrich family
- USE Hydrick family

Heydrick family
- USE Hydrick family

Heyd's syndrome
- USE Hepatorenal syndrome

Heydt family
- USE Hite family

Heyducks
- USE Haiduks

Heyer family
- USE Ayers family

Heyerdahl family (Not Subd Geog)

Heyes family
- USE Hayes family

Heyl family
- USE Hale family

Heylman family
- USE Heilman family

Heyn family
- USE Haynes family

Heyns family
- USE Haynes family

Heyrick family
- USE Herrick family

Heysen Trail (S. Aust.)
- BT Trails—Australia

Heythorn family
- USE Hawthorne family

Heythorne family
- USE Hawthorne family

Heyward family
- USE Hayward family

Heywood family
- USE Haywood family

Hezelgrave family
- USE Hesselgrave family

Hezlewood family
- USE Hazelwood family

HFB airplanes
- [TL686.H]

HHC (Computer)
- UF Olympia HHC (Computer)
- Panasonic HHC (Computer)
- Quasar HHC (Computer)
- BT Microcomputers
- Portable computers
- — Programming

Hi-fi systems
- USE High-fidelity sound systems

Hiang te
- USE So na

Hiantoporidae
- [QL398.C5]
- BT Cheilostomata
- NT Tremogasterina

Hiaqui Indians
- USE Yaqui Indians

Hiatal hernia
- UF Esophageal hernia
- BT Diaphragm—Hernia
- Hernia

Hiawatha (Express train)
- BT Railroads—United States—Express-
trains

Hiawatha National Forest (Mich.)
- BT Forest reserves—Michigan
- National parks and reserves—United
States
- NT Rock River Canyon Wilderness
(Mich.)

Hiba, Tall (Iraq)
- USE Lagash (Ancient city)

Hiba arborvitae
- [QK494.5.C975 (Botany)]
- [SD397.H57 (Forestry)]
- UF Hiba falsearborvitae

Hiba falsearborvitae
- USE Hiba arborvitae

Hibakusha
- USE Atomic bomb victims

Hibard family
- USE Hibbert family

Ḥibat Tsiyon
- USE Ḥibbat Zion

Hibbard family
- USE Hibbert family

Hibbards family
- USE Hibbert family

Hibbart family
- USE Hibbert family

Ḥibbat Zion
- UF Ḥibat Tsiyon
- BT Zionism

Hibberd family
- USE Hibbert family

Hibbert family (Not Subd Geog)
　UF　Hebard family
　　　Hebbard family
　　　Hebert family
　　　Hebot family
　　　Hibard family
　　　Hibbard family
　　　Hibbards family
　　　Hibbart family
　　　Hibberd family
　　　Hibbird family
　　　Hibbord family
　　　Hibert family
Hibbird family
　USE　Hibbert family
Hibbord family
　USE　Hibbert family
Hibernation
　[QL755]
　BT　Animal behavior
　　　Dormancy (Biology)
　　　Sleep
　　　Zoology
　RT　Winter
　SA　*subdivision* Hibernation *under*
　　　individual animals, e.g. Fishes—
　　　Hibernation
　NT　Artificial hibernation
Hibert family
　USE　Hibbert family
Hibiscus
　[QK495.M27 (Botany)]
　[SB413.H6 (Ornamental plant)]
　BT　Malvaceae
Hibiscus cannabinus
　USE　Kenaf
Hibiscus mealy bug
　USE　Phenacoccus hirsutus
Hibiscus syriacus
　[QK495.M27 (Botany)]
　[SB413.H6 (Flowering shrub)]
　UF　Althea, Shrub
　　　Rose of Sharon
　　　Shrub althea
　BT　Flowering shrubs
Hibiya (Tokyo, Japan) (Not Subd Geog)
　UF　Tokyo (Japan).　Hibiya
Hibiya Kōen (Tokyo, Japan)
　UF　Hibiya Park (Tokyo, Japan)
　BT　Parks—Japan
Hibiya Kōtō Gakkō
Hibiya Park (Tokyo, Japan)
　USE　Hibiya Kōen (Tokyo, Japan)
Hibon de Frohen family
　USE　Hibon family
Hibon family (Not Subd Geog)
　UF　Hibon de Frohen family
Hibshoosh family
　USE　Ḥabshush family
Ḥibshush family
　USE　Ḥabshush family
Hican trees
　USE　Hicans
Hicans (May Subd Geog)
　[QK495.J85 (Botany)]
　UF　Hican trees
　BT　Hickories
　RT　Pecan
Hiccough
　USE　Hiccups
Hiccups
　UF　Hiccough
　　　Singultus
　BT　Diaphragm
　　　Spasms
　　　Symptomatology
Hichcock family
　USE　Hitchcock family
Hichcox family
　USE　Hitchcock family

Hichiriki
　[ML990.H5]
　BT　Musical instruments—Japan
　　　Oboe
Hichiriki music
　[M110.H]
　NT　Quintets (Piano, hichiriki, harp, violin,
　　　violoncello)
Hichishūjō (Toyota-shi, Japan)
　USE　Koromojō (Toyota-shi, Japan)
Hick family
　USE　Hicks family
Hickcox family (Not Subd Geog)
　UF　Hickock family
　　　Hickok family
　　　Hickox family
　　　Hicock family
　　　Hicox family
Hickel family
　USE　Hickle family
Hickes family
　USE　Hicks family
Hickey family (Not Subd Geog)
　UF　Hickland family
　　　Hicklin family
　　　Hickling family
Hickey Plot, 1776
　[E277]
　BT　American loyalists
　　　New York (N.Y.)—History—
　　　　Revolution, 1775-1783
　　　United States—History—Revolution,
　　　　1775-1783
Hickinbotham family
　USE　Higginbotham family
Hickinbottom family
　USE　Higginbotham family
Hickland family
　USE　Hickey family
Hickle family (Not Subd Geog)
　UF　Hickel family
Hicklin family
　USE　Hickey family
Hickling family
　USE　Hickey family
Hickman family (Not Subd Geog)
　UF　Heckman family
　　　Heckmann family
　　　Hickmann family
　　　Hickmon family
Hickmann family
　USE　Hickman family
Hickmon family
　USE　Hickman family
Hickock family
　USE　Hickcox family
Hickok family
　USE　Hickcox family
Hickon Creek (Pa.)
　USE　Tohickon Creek (Pa.)
Hickories (May Subd Geog)
　[QK495.J85 (Botany)]
　[SD397.H6 (Forestry)]
　UF　Carya
　　　Hickory
　　　Hickory trees
　　　Hicoria
　BT　Juglandaceae
　NT　Hicans
　　　Pecan
Hickory
　USE　Hickories
Hickory shad
　[QL638.C64]
　UF　Alosa mediocris
　BT　Shad
Hickory trees
　USE　Hickories
Hickory wattle
　USE　Mangium

Hickox family
　USE　Hickcox family
**Hicks, Edward, 1780-1849.　Peaceable
Kingdom**
　[ND237.H58]
　UF　Peaceable Kingdom (Painting)
　BT　Animals in art
　　　Bible.　O.T.　Isaiah—Illustrations
　　　Penn's treaty with the Indians, 1682,
　　　　in art
Hicks family (Not Subd Geog)
　UF　Hick family
　　　Hickes family
　　　Hix family
　　　Hixs family
　　　Hyx family
　RT　Heck family
　　　Hixson family
Hicksford Raid, 1864
　[E477.21]
　BT　Emporia (Va.)—History—Civil War,
　　　　1861-1865
　　　United States—History—Civil War,
　　　　1861-1865—Campaigns
Hicksites (May Subd Geog)
　[BX7751-BX7752]
　BT　Society of Friends
Hickson family
　USE　Hixson family
Hicock family
　USE　Hickcox family
Hicoria
　USE　Hickories
Hicoria pecan
　USE　Pecan
Hicox family
　USE　Hickcox family
Hid treasure (Parable)
　USE　Hidden treasure (Parable)
Hida-Kaidō (Japan)
　USE　Nakasendō (Japan)
Hida Region (Japan)
Hidage
　[HJ4337 (Taxation: Great Britain)]
　BT　Land value taxation—Great Britain
Hidaka family (Not Subd Geog)
Hidaka Iseki (Takasaki-shi, Japan)
　USE　Hidaka Site (Takasaki-shi, Japan)
Hidaka Mountain Range (Japan)
　UF　Hidaka Mountains (Japan)
　　　Hidaka-sammyaku (Japan)
　　　Hitaka Mountain Range (Japan)
　BT　Mountains—Japan
Hidaka Mountains (Japan)
　USE　Hidaka Mountain Range (Japan)
Hidaka-sammyaku (Japan)
　USE　Hidaka Mountain Range (Japan)
Hidaka Site (Takasaki-shi, Japan)
　(Not Subd Geog)
　UF　Hidaka Iseki (Takasaki-shi, Japan)
　BT　Japan—Antiquities
Hidalgoa
　[QK495.C74]
　BT　Compositae
Hidatsa Indians
　[E99.H6]
　UF　Gros Ventres of the Missouri
　　　Grosventres of the Missouri
　　　Minitaree Indians
　　　Minnetaree Indians
　BT　Indians of North America
　　　Siouan Indians
　NT　Crow Indians
　— Reservations
　　　NT　Fort Berthold Indian Reservation
　　　　(N.D.)
Hidatsa language
　[PM1331]
　UF　Grosventre language
　BT　Siouan languages

Hidden economy
  USE Informal sector (Economics)
Hidden God
  UF Deus Absconditus
      God—Absence
      God, Hidden
  BT God
Hidden Peak (Pakistan)
  USE Gasherbrum I (Pakistan)
Hidden reserves (Accounting)
  USE Reserves, Secret (Accounting)
Hidden treasure (Parable)
  [BT378.H54]
  UF Hid treasure (Parable)
      Treasure (Parable)
      Treasure in the field (Parable)
Hidden unemployment
  USE Disguised unemployment
Hiddensee (Germany)
  UF Hadensee (Germany)
      Hiddensö (Germany)
  BT Islands—Germany (East)
Hiddensö (Germany)
  USE Hiddensee (Germany)
Hiddeser Bent-Donoper Teich,
    Naturschutzgebiet (Germany)
  USE Naturschutzgebiet Hiddeser Bent-
      Donoper Teich (Germany)
Hide family
  USE Hyde family
Hide powder
  [TS985]
  BT Collagen
      Hides and skins
      Tanning
  RT Tannins
Ḥideḳel River
  USE Tigris River
Hiden family
  USE Hayden family
Hides and skins (May Subd Geog)
  [HD9778 (Trade)]
  [TS967 (Manufactures)]
  UF Pelts
      Skins
  RT Fur
      Leather
      Tanning
  NT Buckskin
      Hide powder
  — **Defects**
      RT Leather—Defects
  — **Disinfection**
      [RA761]
  — **Dressing and dyeing**
      UF Dyes and dyeing—Hides and skins
  — **Effect of radiation on**
      UF Hides and skins, Effect of radiation
          on
      BT Radiation
  — **Religious aspects**
      NT Hides and skins in the Bible
  — **Tariff**
      USE Tariff on hides
Hides and skins, Effect of radiation on
  USE Hides and skins—Effect of radiation
      on
Hides and skins in the Bible
  UF Bible—Hides and skins
  BT Hides and skins—Religious aspects
Hides and skins in the Talmud
  [BM509.H54]
  UF Talmud—Hides and skins
Hides and skins industry (May Subd Geog)
  [HD9778]
  — **Collective labor agreements**
      USE Collective labor agreements—
          Hides and skins industry
Hides family
  USE Hyde family

Hiding-places (Secret chambers, etc.)
  (May Subd Geog)
  [DA380 (17th century, England)]
  UF Priest's holes
      Secret chambers
      Subterranean passages
  BT Caves
      Ghosts
      Historic buildings
      Labyrinths
      Persecution
      Secrecy
Hidinger family (Not Subd Geog)
Hie Daichi Site (Fukuoka-shi, Japan)
  USE Mizuho Site (Fukuoka-shi, Japan)
Hiebert family (Not Subd Geog)
  RT Hubbard family
Hiedaichi Site (Fukuoka-shi, Japan)
  USE Mizuho Site (Fukuoka-shi, Japan)
Hien (Fighter planes)
  UF Kawasaki Ki 61 (Fighter planes)
      Kawasaki Ki 100 (Fighter planes)
      Ki 61 (Fighter plane)
      Swallow (Japanese fighter plane)
      Tony (Japanese fighter plane)
  BT Fighter planes
      Kawasaki airplanes
Hiep Duc Valley (Vietnam)
  BT Valleys—Vietnam
Hieraaetus
  [QL696.F32]
  BT Accipitridae
Hieraaetus fasciatus
  USE Bonelli's eagle
Hierarchies (May Subd Geog)
  BT Order
  NT Hierarchy (Linguistics)
Hierarchy (Linguistics)
  UF Stratification (Linguistics)
  BT Hierarchies
      Linguistic analysis (Linguistics)
      Linguistics
  NT Stratificational grammar
Hierarchy, plus Input, Process, Output
    technique
  USE HIPO technique
Hieratic head of Ezra Pound (Portrait
    sculpture)
  USE Gaudier, Henri. Hieratic head of
      Ezra Pound
Hieratic inscriptions
  USE Egyptian language—Inscriptions
Hieratic writing
  USE Egyptian language—Papyri, Hieratic
      Egyptian language—Writing, Hieratic
Hieroglyphic Bibles
  [BS560]
  UF Bible—Hieroglyphic Bibles
  BT Bible—Picture Bibles
      Children's literature
      Picture-books for children
Hieroglyphic inscriptions
  USE Inscriptions, Hieroglyphic
Hieroglyphic type
  USE Type and type-founding—Hieroglyphic
      type
Hieroglyphics
  [PJ1091-PJ1097 (Egyptian)]
  UF Ideography
  BT Inscriptions
      Paleography
      Writing
  RT Picture-writing
  NT Alphabet
      Writing—History
Hieroglyphics, Aztec
  USE Aztecs—Writing
Hieroglyphics, Egyptian
  USE Egyptian language—Writing,
      Hieroglyphic

Hieroglyphics, Maya
  USE Mayas—Writing
Hieroglyphics, Mexican
  USE Indians of Mexico—Writing
Hieroglyphodes
  [QL508.A2]
  BT Acrididae
Hieroglyphus
  [QL508.A2]
  BT Acrididae
Hieronimus family
  USE Hieronymus family
Hieronymi family
  USE Hieronymus family
Hieronymites
  [BX3680.H5]
Hieronymites in Spain
  [BX3680.H5]
Hieronymus family (Not Subd Geog)
  UF Heironimus family
      Heironymus family
      Hieronimus family
      Hieronymi family
      Rhonemus family
      Ronemous family
      Ronemus family
      Ronimous family
Hieros (The Greek word)
  BT Greek language—Etymology
Hieroxestidae
  USE Lyonetiidae
Hierro (Canary Islands)
  UF Estaca, Puerto de la (Canary Islands)
      Ferro (Canary Islands)
      Puerto de la Estaca (Canary Islands)
      Puerto del Hierro (Canary Islands)
  BT Islands—Canary Islands
Higan family
  USE Higgins family
Higaonan (Philippine people)
  USE Bukidnon (Philippine people)
Higashi Kaidō (Japan)
  USE Hama Kaidō (Japan)
Higashi Kōya Kaidō (Japan)
  (Not Subd Geog)
  BT Roads—Japan
Higashi Nikkō Kaidō (Japan)
  USE Nikkō Kaidō (Japan)
Higashi Ōta Iseki (Maebaru-shi, Japan)
  USE Ōta Site (Maebaru-machi, Japan)
Higashiarai Iseki (Ichinomiya-ch-o, Yamanashi-
    ken, Japan)
  USE Higashiarai Site (Ichinomiya-ch-o,
      Yamanashi-ken, Japan)
**Higashiarai Site (Ichinomiya-ch-o, Yamanashi-
    ken, Japan)**
  UF Higashiarai Iseki (Ichinomiya-ch-o,
      Yamanashi-ken, Japan)
  BT Japan—Antiquities
Higashiichinose Iseki (Kanazawa-shi, Japan)
  USE Higashiichinose Site (Kanazawa-shi,
      Japan)
Higashiichinose Site (Kanazawa-shi, Japan)
  (Not Subd Geog)
  UF Higashiichinose Iseki (Kanazawa-shi,
      Japan)
  BT Japan—Antiquities
Higashinakane Iseki (Katsuta-shi, Japan)
  USE Higashinakane Site (Katsuta-shi,
      Japan)
Higashinakane Site (Katsuta-shi, Japan)
  (Not Subd Geog)
  UF Higashinakane Iseki (Katsuta-shi,
      Japan)
  BT Japan—Antiquities
Higbe family
  USE Higbee family

Higbee family (Not Subd Geog)
UF Higbe family
Higbey family
Higbie family
Higby family
Higbey family
USE Higbee family
Higbie family
USE Higbee family
Higby family
USE Higbee family
Higden family
USE Higdon family
Higdon family (Not Subd Geog)
UF Higden family
Higenbottam family
USE Higginbotham family
Higens family
USE Higgins family
Higgans family
USE Higgins family
Higgens family
USE Higgins family
Higgin family
USE Higgins family
Higginbotham family (Not Subd Geog)
UF Hickinbotham family
Hickinbottom family
Higenbottam family
Higginbottom family
Higinbotham family
Higinbothom family
Higginbottom family
USE Higginbotham family
Higgins family (Not Subd Geog)
UF Heggins family
Hegins family
Higan family
Higens family
Higgans family
Higgens family
Higgin family
Higginson family
Higgs family
Higings family
Higins family
RT Huggins family
Higginson family
USE Higgins family
Higgs family
USE Higgins family
High (Psychology)
USE Elation
High Altitude Pollution Program
BT Air—Pollution
Aircraft exhaust emissions
High altitude rocket research
USE Atmosphere, Upper—Rocket observations
High-altitude suits
USE Pressure suits
High apartment buildings
USE High-rise apartment buildings
High blood pressure
USE Hypertension
High buildings
USE Tall buildings
High-calcium diet (May Subd Geog)
[RM237.56]
BT Diet therapy
RT Calcium
— Recipes
BT Cookery
High-carbohydrate cookery
USE High-carbohydrate diet—Recipes
High-carbohydrate diet (May Subd Geog)
BT Carbohydrates
Diet
Diet therapy
Food—Carbohydrate content
— Recipes

UF High-carbohydrate cookery
BT Cookery
Cookery for the sick
High Command Trial, Nuremberg, Germany, 1948-1949
UF Subsequent proceedings, Nuremberg War Crime Trials, case no. 12
BT Nuremberg War Crime Trials, 1946-1949
High density lipoproteins
[QP99.3.H53]
UF Alpha lipoproteins
HDL
Lipoproteins, HDL
Lipoproteins, High density
BT Blood lipoproteins
High Eccentric Lunar Occultation Satellite
USE EXOSAT (Artificial satellite)
High energy astronomy observatory (Artificial satellite)
USE HEAO (Artificial satellite)
High energy forming (May Subd Geog)
[TS256]
UF High energy rate metal forming
High velocity forming
Metals—High energy forming
BT Electrohydraulic effect
Forging
Sheet-metal work
NT Bulging (Metalwork)
Explosive forming
Extrusion process
Hydrostatic extrusion
Magnetic forming
Metals—Extrusion
High energy fuels
USE Boron as fuel
High energy physics
USE Particles (Nuclear physics)
High energy radiotherapy
USE Radiotherapy, High energy
High energy rate metal forming
USE High energy forming
High Ercall Manor (Shropshire)
BT Manors—England
High family (Not Subd Geog)
RT Hoch family
Hoeg family
High Fantasy (Game) (May Subd Geog)
[GV1202.H54]
BT Fantasy games
High-fiber diet
[RM237.6]
UF Fiber deficiency diseases—Diet therapy
High-residue diet
BT Diet in disease
Fiber in human nutrition
RT Fiber deficiency diseases
NT Complex carbohydrate diet
Food—Fiber content
— Recipes
BT Cookery
High-fidelity audio equipment
USE High-fidelity sound systems
High-fidelity sound systems
[TK7882.H5]
UF Hi-fi systems
High-fidelity audio equipment
BT Electronic systems
Electronics
Sound—Recording and reproducing
NT Audio equipment industry
Phonograph—High-fidelity systems
Radio—High-fidelity systems
Stereophonic sound systems
— Installation in automobiles
USE Automobiles—Audio equipment
High five (Game)
USE Pedro (Game)

High-frequency induction heating
USE Induction heating
High-frequency radio
USE Radio, Short wave
High Gothic art
USE Art, Gothic—High Gothic
High Holiday sermons
[BM746]
UF High Holy Day sermons
BT Jewish sermons
High Holidays (May Subd Geog)
[BM693.H5]
UF High Holy Days
Holidays, High
BT Fasts and feasts—Judaism
Tishri
NT Rosh ha-Shanah
Shabbat shubah
Synagogue music—High Holiday services
Yom Kippur
High Holy Day sermons
USE High Holiday sermons
High Holy Days
USE High Holidays
High interest-low vocabulary books
[Z1039.S5]
UF Low vocabulary-high interest books
BT Children's literature
High intraocular pressure
USE Glaucoma
High-jacking . . .
USE headings beginning with the term Hijacking . . .
High jumping
USE Jumping
High license
USE License system
Liquor laws
High-line logging
USE Logging, Skyline
High-lysine diet (May Subd Geog)
BT Diet therapy
RT Lysine
— Recipes
BT Cookery
High occupancy vehicle lanes
(May Subd Geog)
[HE336.B8]
UF HOV lanes
Lanes, High occupancy vehicle
BT Roads
NT Bus lanes
High-octane gasoline
USE Gasoline—Anti-knock and anti-knock mixtures
High performance chromatography
USE High performance liquid chromatography
High performance liquid chromatography
UF High performance chromatography
High pressure liquid chromatography
High sensitivity liquid chromatography
High speed liquid chromatography
HPLC
BT High pressure (Science)
Liquid chromatography
High places (Shrines)
UF Places, Sacred
BT Shrines
High Plains (U.S.)
Here are entered works on the tableland in the southern portion of the Great Plains including parts of the panhandles of Texas and Oklahoma, northeastern New Mexico, eastern Colorado, and western Kansas, and extending northward into Nebraska.
BT Great Plains
Plains—United States
High Plains Aquifer (Not Subd Geog)
BT Aquifers—Great Plains

High plains grasshopper
  [QL508.A2]
  UF Dissosteira longipennis
     Long-winged grasshopper of the plains
  BT Dissosteira
High-potassium diet (May Subd Geog)
  [RM237.63]
  BT Diet therapy
     Potassium
  RT Potassium deficiency diseases
  — **Recipes**
       BT Cookery for the sick
High potency (Drugs)
  USE Homeopathy—Attenuations, dilutions,
       and potencies
High power lasers
  BT Lasers
High pressure (Engineering)
  USE High pressure (Technology)
High pressure (Science)
  [QC281]
  BT Pressure
  NT Compressibility
     High performance liquid
        chromatography
     High pressure (Technology)
     Pressure vessels
  — Measurement
       USE High pressure measurements
  — **Research** (May Subd Geog)
       UF High pressure research
High pressure (Technology)
  [TP156.P75]
  UF High pressure (Engineering)
  BT Chemistry, Technical
     High pressure (Science)
  NT Bulging (Metalwork)
     Hydrostatic extrusion
     Isostatic pressing
     Jet cutting
     Materials at high pressures
     Plastics at high pressures
High pressure liquid chromatography
  USE High performance liquid
       chromatography
High pressure measurements
  [QC281]
  UF High pressure (Science)—
       Measurement
     Measurements, High pressure
High pressure research
  USE High pressure (Science)—Research
High-pressure steam
  USE Steam, High-pressure
High-protein diet (May Subd Geog)
  [RM237.65]
  UF Protein deficiency—Diet therapy
  BT Diet in disease
     Diet therapy
High Renaissance art
  USE Art, Renaissance—High Renaissance
High-residue diet
  USE High-fiber diet
High resolution spectroscopy
  [QC454.H618]
  UF Spectroscopy, High resolution
  BT Resolution (Optics)
     Spectrum analysis
High-rise apartment buildings
  (May Subd Geog)
  UF High apartment buildings
     Multistory housing
  BT Apartment houses
     Tall buildings
  — **Access control**
  — **Aerodynamics**
  — **Earthquake effects**
  — **Italy**
       NT Torre Velasca (Milan, Italy)
High-rise buildings
  USE Skyscrapers

Tall buildings
High rise school buildings
  USE School buildings, High rise
High-risk pregnancy
  USE Pregnancy, Complications of
High Rock Lake Wilderness (Nev.)
  (Not Subd Geog)
  UF High Rock Lake Wilderness Study
       Area (Nev.)
  BT National parks and reserves—Nevada
     Wilderness areas—Nevada
High Rock Lake Wilderness Study Area (Nev.)
  USE High Rock Lake Wilderness (Nev.)
High school (Horsemanship)
  USE Haute école (Horsemanship)
High school administration
  USE High schools—Administration
High school attendance
  USE School attendance—High school
High school characteristics index
  UF HSCI
High school dropouts (May Subd Geog)
  [LC146.5]
  UF Secondary school dropouts
  BT Dropouts
     High school students
  — **Employment** (May Subd Geog)
       RT Dropouts—Employment
High school education
  USE Education, Secondary
High school environment (May Subd Geog)
  UF Environment, High school
  BT School environment
High school equivalency certificates
  (May Subd Geog)
  [LB1627.7]
  BT School credits—Outside work
High school equivalency examination
  USE High school equivalency examinations
  NT California High School Proficiency
     Examination
High school equivalency examinations
  (May Subd Geog)
  UF English school certificate examinations
     Equivalency examinations, High school
     High school equivalency examination
     School leaving certificate examinations
  BT Equivalency tests
     General educational development tests
High school facilities (May Subd Geog)
  BT School facilities
  NT High schools—Buildings
     High schools—Furniture, equipment,
        etc.
High school graduates (May Subd Geog)
     Here are entered works on high school graduates
  as a socio-economic group. Works on high school
  graduates in relation to their alma maters are entered
  under High schools—Alumni.
  UF Graduates, High school
  BT High schools—Alumni
  NT Wages—High school graduates
  — **Employment** (May Subd Geog)
       NT High school students—
          Employment
  — Wages
       USE Wages—High school graduates
High school journalism
  USE Journalism, High school
High school libraries (May Subd Geog)
  [Z675.S3]
  UF Libraries, High school
     School libraries (High school)
  BT School libraries
  — **Book lists**
       UF Book lists for high school libraries
       BT Bibliography—Best books
High school personality questionnaire
  BT High school students—Pscyhological
     testing
     Personality questionnaires

High school placement test
  UF Placement test, High school
  BT Educational tests and measurements
High school principals (May Subd Geog)
  [LB2831.9-LB2831.976]
  UF Principals, High school
     Principals, Secondary school
     Principals, Senior high school
     Secondary school principals
     Senior high school principals
  BT School principals
  — **Legal status, laws, etc.**
     (May Subd Geog)
       BT Educational law and legislation
  — **Pensions** (May Subd Geog)
       UF High school principals—Salaries,
          pensions, etc.
  — **Salaries, etc.**
       UF High school principals—Salaries,
          pensions, etc.
  — Salaries, pensions, etc.
       USE High school principals—Pensions
          High school principals—Salaries,
          etc.
High school seniors (May Subd Geog)
  UF Seniors, High school
  BT High school students
High school student journalism
  USE Journalism, High school
High school student newspapers and
  periodicals
  USE Student newspapers and periodicals
High school student publications
  USE Student publications
High school students (May Subd Geog)
  BT Students
  NT High school dropouts
     High school seniors
     Vocational school students
  — **Attitudes**
       BT Attitude (Psychology)
  — **Conduct of life**
       BT Student ethics
  — **Economic conditions**
       UF High school students' socio-
          economic status
  — **Employment** (May Subd Geog)
       BT Children—Employment
          High school graduates—
          Employment
  — **Health and hygiene** (May Subd Geog)
       BT School hygiene
  — **Library orientation**
       [Z675.S3]
       BT Library orientation
  — **Political activity**
       BT Politics, Practical
  — **Pscyhological testing**
       NT High school personality
          questionnaire
  — **Psychological testing**
  — **Social conditions** (May Subd Geog)
       [LC208.4]
       UF High school students' socio-
          economic status
High school students' socio-economic status
  USE High school students—Economic
     conditions
     High school students—Social
     conditions
High school teachers (May Subd Geog)
  UF Secondary school teachers
     Senior high school teachers
     Teachers, High school
     Teachers, Secondary school
     Teachers, Senior high school
  BT Teachers
  — Appointment
       USE High school teachers—Selection
          and appointment
  — **Attitudes**

BT Attitude (Psychology)
— **Certification** *(May Subd Geog)*
 BT High school teachers—Legal status,
 laws, etc.
— **Economic conditions**
 UF High school teachers—
 Socioeconomic status
— **In-service training** *(May Subd Geog)*
— **Leaves of absence**
— **Legal status, laws, etc.**
 (May Subd Geog)
 BT Educational law and legislation
 NT High school teachers—Certification
— **Pensions** *(May Subd Geog)*
 UF High school teachers—Salaries,
 pensions, etc.
— **Political activity**
 BT Politics, Practical
— **Salaries, etc.**
 UF High school teachers—Salaries,
 pensions, etc.
— Salaries, pensions, etc.
 USE High school teachers—Pensions
 High school teachers—Salaries,
 etc.
— **Selection and appointment**
 UF High school teachers—
 Appointment
— **Social conditions**
 UF High school teachers—
 Socioeconomic status
— Socioeconomic status
 USE High school teachers—Economic
 conditions
 High school teachers—Social
 conditions
— **Tenure** *(May Subd Geog)*
 BT Employees, Dismissal of
 Employees, Resignation of
— Work load
 USE High school teachers—Workload
— **Workload**
 UF Faculty workload
 High school teachers—Work load
 Workload of high school teachers
High school teaching *(May Subd Geog)*
 UF Secondary school teaching
 BT Teaching
High school yearbooks
 USE School yearbooks
High schools *(May Subd Geog)*
 ₍LB1603-1694₎
 UF Secondary schools
 BT Public schools
 Schools
 RT Education, Secondary
 NT Catholic high schools
 Comprehensive high schools
— Accounting
 USE Schools—Accounting
— **Accreditation**
— **Administration**
 ₍LB2822₎
 UF High school administration
 BT School management and
 organization
 NT Departmental chairmen (High
 schools)
— **Alumni**
 NT High school graduates
— **Buildings** *(May Subd Geog)*
 BT High school facilities
 School buildings
— **Curricula**
 NT High schools—Honors courses
— **Elective system**
 UF Elective system in high schools
— **Entrance requirements**
 ₍LB1627₎
— Equipment and supplies

USE High schools—Furniture,
 equipment, etc.
— **Furniture, equipment, etc.**
 UF High schools—Equipment and
 supplies
 BT Furniture
 High school facilities
— Graduate work
 USE High schools—Postgraduate work
— **Honors courses**
 UF Honors courses in high schools
 Honors work in high schools
 BT Gifted children—Education
 High schools—Curricula
— **Postgraduate work**
 ₍LB1695₎
 UF High schools—Graduate work
 Post-graduate work in high schools
 Postgraduate work in high schools
 BT Education, Secondary
— Schedules
 USE Schedules, School
— **Great Britain**
— — **Examinations**
 NT General Certificate of Secondary
 Education
High schools, Junior
 USE Junior high schools
High schools, Rural
 USE Rural schools
High seas, Jurisdiction over
 USE Contiguous zones (Maritime law)
 Economic zones (Maritime law)
 Maritime law
 War, Maritime (International law)
High seas fishery management
 USE Fishery management, International
High sensitivity liquid chromatography
 USE High performance liquid
 chromatography
High society
 USE Upper classes
High solids coatings *(May Subd Geog)*
 ₍TP945₎
 BT Coatings
High Sorbian language
 USE Upper Sorbian language
High-speed aerodynamics
 USE Aerodynamics, Supersonic
High-speed aeronautics
 ₍TL551.5₎
 UF Aeronautics, High-speed
 High-speed flight
 Supersonic aeronautics
 BT Aeronautics
 NT Aerodynamics, Supersonic
 Aerodynamics, Transonic
 Aerothermodynamics
 Airplanes—Jet propulsion
 Hypersonic planes
 Rocket planes
 Rockets (Aeronautics)
 Short take-off and landing aircraft—Jet
 propulsion
 Supersonic planes
 Transonic planes
 Vertically rising aircraft—Jet
 propulsion
High-speed cinematography
 USE Cinematography, High-speed
High-speed data processing
 USE Real-time data processing
High-speed flight
 USE High-speed aeronautics
High speed ground transportation
 (May Subd Geog)
 Here are entered general works on intercity
 ground transportation systems differing from the
 conventional ground modes of transportation of the
 1960's both in design and in that they operate at
 speeds upwards of 300 miles per hour.

BT Transportation
 NT High speed trains
 Magnetic levitation vehicles
— **Communication systems**
— **Law and legislation** *(May Subd Geog)*
High speed liquid chromatography
 USE High performance liquid
 chromatography
High-speed machining
 BT Machining
High-speed photography
 USE Photography, High-speed
High-speed radiography
 USE Radiography, High-speed
High speed steel
 USE Tool-steel
High speed trains *(May Subd Geog)*
 UF Bullet trains
 Metroliners
 Trains, High speed
 Turbotrains
 BT High speed ground transportation
 Railroads—Trains
High Steens Wilderness (Or.)
 (Not Subd Geog)
 UF High Steens Wilderness Study Area
 (Or.)
 BT National parks and reserves—Oregon
 Wilderness areas—Oregon
High Steens Wilderness Study Area (Or.)
 USE High Steens Wilderness (Or.)
High strength concrete *(May Subd Geog)*
 UF Concrete, High strength
 BT Concrete
High strength steel
 USE Steel, High strength
High Tatra (Czechoslovakia and Poland)
 USE Tatra Mountains (Czechoslovakia and
 Poland)
High tech
 USE High technology
High technology *(May Subd Geog)*
 Here are entered works on specialized and sophis-
 ticated technology, such as the technology used in
 the manufacture of electronic devices, computers,
 telecommunication systems, aerospace systems, de-
 fense systems, etc.
 UF High tech
 BT Technology
 NT Selling—High technology
High technology and education
 (May Subd Geog)
 ₍LC1087-1087.4₎
 UF Education and high technology
 BT Education
High technology industries
 (May Subd Geog)
— **Employees**
— — Wages
 USE Wages—High technology
 industries employees
High temperature chemistry
 UF Chemistry, High temperature
 BT High temperatures
 Thermochemistry
High temperature materials
 USE Heat resistant materials
High temperature metallurgy
 USE Metals at high temperatures
High temperature metals
 USE Heat resistant alloys
High temperature plasmas
 UF Hot plasmas
 Plasmas, High temperature
 BT Gases at high temperatures
 Plasma (Ionized gases)
 NT Ionizing shock waves
 Plasma confinement
 Plasma heating
 Plasma radiation

High temperature stars
USE Early stars
High temperatures
[QC276]
UF Elevated temperatures
Heat barrier
Ultrahigh temperatures
BT Heat
NT Gases at high temperatures
High temperature chemistry
Materials at high temperatures
Metals at high temperatures
Solar furnaces
— Measurement
USE Pyrometers and pyrometry
— Physiological effect
USE Heat—Physiological effect
High-tension power distribution
USE Electric power distribution—High
tension
High treason
USE Treason
High-tryptophan diet (May Subd Geog)
UF Diet, High-tryptophan
BT Diet therapy
RT Tryptophan
High vacuum technique
USE Vacuum
High Veld (South Africa)
USE Northern Karroo (South Africa)
High Veld Area (South Africa)
USE Highveld Area (South Africa)
High velocity forming
USE High energy forming
High voltage electron microscope
USE Electron microscope, High voltage
High-voltage high-frequency photography
USE Kirlian photography
High voltages
BT Electric engineering
Electricity
High wire performers
USE Aerialists
High wire walking
USE Tightrope walking
High Yielding Varieties Programme
[SB192.I4 (General)]
BT Agricultural innovations—India
Agriculture—India
Agriculture and state—India
Plant introduction—India
Highbarger family
USE Hybarger family
Highberger family
USE Hybarger family
Higher criticism
USE subdivision Criticism, interpretation,
etc. under Bible and under parts
and books of the Bible, e.g. Bible.
N.T.—Criticism, interpretation, etc.;
Bible. O.T. Hexateuch—
Criticism, interpretation, etc.;
Bible. N.T. Matthew—Criticism,
interpretation, etc.
Higher education
USE Education, Higher
Higher education, Employer-supported
USE Employer-supported higher education
Higher education and state
(May Subd Geog)
[LC171-182]
UF State and higher education
BT Education, Higher
Education and state
NT Federal aid to higher education
Medical education policy
Higher education for the physically
handicapped
USE Physically handicapped—Education
(Higher)

Higher education of women
(May Subd Geog)
BT Education, Higher
Women—Education
RT Professional education of women
NT Universities and colleges—Graduate
work of women
Higher law
USE Divine right of kings
Government, Resistance to
Higher nervous activity
[QP395]
UF Cortical function, Higher
Nervous activity, Higher
BT Neurophysiology
NT Neurolinguistics
Higher plane curves
USE Curves, Plane
Highfill family (Not Subd Geog)
Highjacking . . .
USE headings beginning with the term
Hijacking . . .
Highland (Ill.)
— History
— — Civil War, 1861-1865
[F549.H]
Highland clans
USE Clans—Scotland
Highland climate
USE Mountain climate
Highland collie
USE Bearded collie
Highland costume
USE Tartans
Highland fling (Dance)
[GV1796.H]
Highland games (May Subd Geog)
[GV722.5.H54]
UF Scottish Highland games
BT Athletics
Games
Highland Lakes (Tex.)
UF Highland Lakes Country (Tex.)
BT Lakes—Texas
Highland Lakes Country (Tex.)
USE Highland Lakes (Tex.)
Highland Line Cemetery (Dalhousie, Ont.)
BT Cemeteries—Ontario
Highland pony
[SF315.2.H5]
BT Ponies
Highland sheepdog
USE Bearded collie
Highlands (Scotland)
UF Highlands of Scotland (Scotland)
Scottish Highlands (Scotland)
Highlands, Kenya (Kenya)
USE Kenya Highlands (Kenya)
Highlands of Scotland (Scotland)
USE Highlands (Scotland)
Highmore's antrum
USE Maxillary sinus
Highrise buildings
USE Tall buildings
Hight family (Not Subd Geog)
UF Height family
RT Haight family
Hoyt family
Highth family
USE Hite family
Hightower family (Not Subd Geog)
Hightower River (Ga.)
USE Etowah River (Ga.)
Hights family
USE Hite family
Highveld (South Africa)
USE Northern Karroo (South Africa)
Highveld Area (South Africa)
(Not Subd Geog)
UF High Veld Area (South Africa)
Hoëveldgebied (South Africa)

Highway 1 (Calif.)
USE California Highway 1 (Calif.)
Highway 40 (U.S.)
USE United States Highway 40
Highway 64 (U.S.)
USE United States Highway 64
Highway accessories
USE Roads—Accessories
Highway accidents
USE Traffic accidents
Highway beautification
USE Roadside improvement
Highway bridges
USE Bridges
Highway business districts
USE Commercial strips
Highway bypasses (May Subd Geog)
UF Bypasses, Highway
BT Express highways
Roads
Traffic engineering
RT Highway relocation
NT Beltways
Highway capacity (May Subd Geog)
[HE336.H48]
UF Capacity, Highway
Traffic capacity, Highway
BT Traffic engineering
RT Traffic flow
Highway communications (May Subd Geog)
UF Communications, Highway
Road communications
BT Roads
NT Electronic traffic controls
Express highways—Communication
systems
Traffic signs and signals
Highway construction
USE Road construction
Highway construction workers
USE Road construction workers
Highway departments (May Subd Geog)
UF Road departments
BT Highway engineering
Highway law
Roads
— **Employees**
NT Highway engineers
— Malpractice
USE Tort liability of highway
departments
— Tort liability
USE Tort liability of highway
departments
Highway design
USE Roads—Design
Highway drainage
USE Road drainage
Highway drawings
USE Roads—Drawings
Highway driving
USE Automobile driving on highways
Highway engineering (May Subd Geog)
[TE]
UF Road engineering
BT Civil engineering
Transportation engineering
RT Highway planning
Roads
NT Highway departments
Highway relocation
Highway research
Road construction
Roadside improvement
Traffic engineering
Highway engineering, Photography in
USE Photography in highway engineering
Highway engineers (May Subd Geog)
BT Civil engineers
Engineers
Highway departments—Employees

Highway finance
USE Roads—Finance
Highway geometrics
USE Roads—Design
Highway guard fences
USE Roads—Guard fences
Highway law *(May Subd Geog)*
Here are entered works on the law governing the laying out, construction, repair, and use of highways and streets. Works on laws regulating traffic on highways and streets are entered under Traffic regulations.
UF Law, Highway
Road law
Roads—Law and legislation
Traffic safety—Law and legislation
BT Streets
RT Servitudes
NT Automobiles—Law and legislation
Bridges—Law and legislation
Building lines
Corvée
Cycling
Dedication to public use
Driveways—Law and legislation
Express highways—Law and legislation
Ferries—Law and legislation
Highway departments
Private roads
Private roads—Law and legislation
Road construction—Safety regulations
Roads—Finance—Law and legislation
Roads—Right of way
Traffic regulations
Trails—Law and legislation
Highway law (Roman law)
Highway lighting
USE Roads—Lighting
Highway location
USE Roads—Location
Highway noise
USE Traffic noise
Highway patrols
USE Traffic police
Highway planning *(May Subd Geog)*
[TE153]
UF Road planning
Roads—Planning
BT Planning
RT Highway engineering
— **Citizen participation**
Highway post offices
BT Mobile post offices
Postal service
Postal service—Transportation, Automotive
Highway relocation
UF Relocation of highways
BT Express highways
Highway engineering
Roads
Traffic engineering
RT Highway bypasses
Highway research *(May Subd Geog)*
UF Road research
Roads—Research
BT Highway engineering
Research, Industrial
Road materials
Roads
NT Road materials—Testing
Roads, Experimental
— **Information storage and retrieval systems**
USE Information storage and retrieval systems—Highway research
Highway safety
USE Traffic safety
Highway skid resistance
USE Pavements—Skid resistance
Highway taxes
USE Motor fuels—Taxation

Transportation, Automotive—Taxation
Highway traffic noise
USE Traffic noise
Highway transport workers
(May Subd Geog)
UF Automotive transport workers
Road transport workers
Transportation, Automotive—Employees
BT Transport workers
Transportation, Automotive
NT Bus drivers
Collective labor agreements—Trucking industry
Truck drivers
Wages—Highway transport workers
— Collective bargaining
USE Collective bargaining—Highway transport workers
Highway transportation
USE Transportation, Automotive
Highway user taxes
USE Transportation, Automotive—Taxation
Highwaymen
USE Brigands and robbers
Highways
USE Roads
Highways, Elevated
USE Elevated highways
Higi (African people)
USE Kamwe (African people)
Higi language
USE Kamwe language
Higinbotham family
USE Higginbotham family
Higinbothom family
USE Higginbotham family
Higings family
USE Higgins family
Higins family
USE Higgins family
Higley family *(Not Subd Geog)*
UF Higly family
Higly family
USE Higley family
Higrah
USE Muḥammad, Prophet, d. 632—Hijrah
Higuchi family *(Not Subd Geog)*
Hihatl language
USE Chamalal language
Hiin Finiin (Horse)
UF Xiin Finiin (Horse)
BT Horses
Hijacking of aircraft *(May Subd Geog)*
Subdivided by national registry of aircraft.
UF Air piracy
Airlines—Hijacking
Seizure of aircraft in transit
Sky hijacking
Skyjacking
BT Crimes aboard aircraft
RT Aircraft theft
NT Trials (Hijacking of aircraft)
— **France**
NT Entebbe Airport Raid, 1976
— **United States**
NT TWA Flight 847 Hijacking Incident, 1985
Hijacking of ships *(May Subd Geog)*
UF Ships—Hijacking
BT Ships
— **Italy**
NT Achille Lauro Hijacking Incident, 1985
Hijacking of the Achille Lauro, 1985
USE Achille Lauro Hijacking Incident, 1985
Hijacking of trains *(May Subd Geog)*
UF Railroads—Trains—Hijacking
Trains, Hijacking of
BT Railroads—Trains

Hijacking of TWA Flight 847, 1985
USE TWA Flight 847 Hijacking Incident, 1985
Hijacking of yachts *(May Subd Geog)*
UF Yachts and yachting—Hijacking
BT Pirates
Hiji (African people)
USE Kamwe (African people)
Ḥijjat al-wadāʿ
USE Ḥajjat al-wadāʿ
Hijrah
USE Muḥammad, Prophet, d. 632—Hijrah
Hikasa family *(Not Subd Geog)*
Hiking *(May Subd Geog)*
[G504]
UF Tramping
BT Outdoor life
RT Walking
NT Backpacking
Hitchhiking
Mountaineering
Orientation
Trails
Vierdaagse (Hike)
Hiko Mountain (Japan)
UF Hiko-san (Japan)
Hikosan (Japan)
BT Mountains—Japan
Hiko-san (Japan)
USE Hiko Mountain (Japan)
Hikosan (Japan)
USE Hiko Mountain (Japan)
Hilac
USE Heavy ion accelerators
Ḥīlah (Islamic law)
USE Evasion (Islamic law)
Hilara
[QL537.E4]
BT Empididae
Hilara azauensis
[QL537.E4]
Hilara bartaki
[QL537.E4]
Hilara hystricoides
[QL537.E4]
Hilaria mutica
USE Tobosa grass
Hilbert algebras
UF Algebras, Hilbert
BT Functional analysis
Von Neumann algebras
Hilbert family *(Not Subd Geog)*
Hilbert modular surfaces
UF Modular surfaces, Hilbert
BT Forms, Modular
Surfaces
Hilbert-Riemann problems
USE Riemann-Hilbert problems
Hilbert schemes
UF Schemes, Hilbert
BT Schemes (Algebraic geometry)
Hilbert space
[QA322.4]
BT Banach spaces
Hyperspace
RT Inner product spaces
NT Invariant subspaces
Spectral theory (Mathematics)
Von Neumann algebras
Hilbert spaces, Stochastic differential equations in
USE Stochastic partial differential equations
Hild family
USE Hilt family

Hildebrand family *(Not Subd Geog)*
UF Haldebrand family
Heldebrand family
Hellebrant family
Heltebran family
Heltebrand family
Hildebrandt family
Hildebraund family
Hildenbrand family
Hildenbrant family
Hilderbran family
Hilderbrand family
Hildlebrand family
Hillebrand family
Hillebrant family
Hillibrant family
Hiltebrand family
Hilterbrand family
Hildebrandt family
USE Hildebrand family
Hildebraund family
USE Hildebrand family
Hilden (Germany)
— History
— — Revolution, 1848-1849
[DD209.H]
BT Germany—History—Revolution,
1848-1849
Hildenbrand family
USE Hildebrand family
Hildenbrant family
USE Hildebrand family
Hilderbran family
USE Hildebrand family
Hilderbrand family
USE Hildebrand family
Hildereth family
USE Hildreth family
Hildi family
USE Hilty family
Hildie family
USE Hilty family
Hildlebrand family
USE Hildebrand family
Hildoceratidae
[QE807.A5]
BT Ammonoidea
Hildred family
USE Hildreth family
Hildreth family *(Not Subd Geog)*
UF Hedreadge family
Heldreth family
Heldridge family
Hildereth family
Hildred family
Hildrick family
Hildrieth family
Hildrith family
Hilldreath family
Holdreth family
Hydreyth family
Hyldryth family
Hildrick family
USE Hildreth family
Hildrieth family
USE Hildreth family
Hildrith family
USE Hildreth family
Hildrop family
USE Hilldrup family
Hildrope family
USE Hilldrup family
Hildy family
USE Hilty family
Hileman family
USE Heilman family
Hiler family
USE Huyler family
Hiletidae
USE Carabidae

Hilf family *(Not Subd Geog)*
Hilgedick family *(Not Subd Geog)*
UF Hilgedieck family
Hilgedieck family
USE Hilgedick family
Hiligaina language
USE Hiligaynon language
Hiligaynon language *(May Subd Geog)*
[PL5711]
UF Hiligaina language
Ilongo language
Panayan language
BT Bisayan languages
Philippine languages
Hill, The (Washington, D.C.)
USE Capitol Hill (Washington, D.C.)
Hill agriculture
USE Hill farming
Hill arches (Sculpture)
USE Moore, Henry, 1898-   Hill arches
Hill Country (Tex.)
USE Texas Hill Country (Tex.)
Hill Creek Site (Ill.)
BT Illinois—Antiquities
Hill culture
USE Hillside planting
Hill Damaras
[DT709]
UF Damaras
Hill determinant
BT Determinants
Differential equations
Eigenvalues
Periodic functions
Hill family *(Not Subd Geog)*
UF Hilles family
Hills family
Hils family
Hirschland family
RT Hille family
Hiller family
Hillis family
NT Neave-Hill family
Hill farming *(May Subd Geog)*
[S604.3]
UF Alpine agriculture
Alpine farming
Hill agriculture
Hillside farming
Mountain agriculture
Mountain farming
BT Agriculture
RT Crop zones
NT Hillside planting
Hill figures *(May Subd Geog)*
[CC710]
UF Chalk figures
Hillside figures
Turf figures
BT Archaeology
— England
NT Long Man of Wilmington (East
Sussex, England)
Hill-forts
USE Fortification, Prehistoric
Hill gardening
USE Hillside gardening
Hill Grove Cemetery (Connellsville, Pa.)
BT Cemeteries—Pennsylvania
Hill Kachari language
USE Dimasa language
Hill paddy
USE Upland rice
Hill Pandaram (Indic people)
USE Malapandaram (Indic people)
Hill reaction
BT Photosynthesis
Hill star, Andean
USE Andean hillstar
Hill Suk (African people)
USE Suk (African people)

Hill-Tout family *(Not Subd Geog)*
Hillandale (Washington, D.C.)
(Not Subd Geog)
UF Washington (D.C.).   Hillandale
Hillar family
USE Hiller family
Hillbilly music
USE Country music
Hillbilly musicians
USE Country musicians
Hillbrow (Johannesburg, South Africa)
(Not Subd Geog)
UF Johannesburg (South Africa).
Hillbrow
Hillcrest Mine Disaster, Hillcrest, Alta., 1914
BT Mine explosions
Hillculture
USE Hillside planting
Hilldreath family
USE Hildreth family
Hilldrup family *(Not Subd Geog)*
UF Hildrop family
Hildrope family
Hille family *(Not Subd Geog)*
RT Hill family
Hiller family
Hillebrand family
USE Hildebrand family
Hillebrant family
USE Hildebrand family
Hillelites
USE Beth Hillel and Beth Shammai
Hilleman family
USE Hillman family
Hiller family *(Not Subd Geog)*
UF Hillar family
Hillers family
RT Hill family
Hille family
Hillers family
USE Hiller family
Hillersborg family *(Not Subd Geog)*
Hilles family
USE Hill family
Hillhouse family
USE Hillis family
**Hilliard, Nicholas, 1537 (ca.)-1619.
Unknown man clasping a hand issuing from
a cloud**
UF Unknown man clasping a hand issuing
from a cloud (Painting)
Hilliard family *(Not Subd Geog)*
UF Hillyard family
Hillibrant family
USE Hildebrand family
Hilliman family
USE Hillman family
Hillis family *(Not Subd Geog)*
UF Hillhouse family
RT Hill family
Hillman automobile
[TL215.H5]
BT Rootes automobiles
NT Imp automobile
Minx automobile
Hillman family *(Not Subd Geog)*
UF Hilleman family
Hilliman family
Hillmann family
Hillmon family
Hillsman family
Hillsmon family
Hilman family
Hilsman family
Hillmann family
USE Hillman family
Hillmon family
USE Hillman family
Hillotype
[TR510]
BT Color photography

Hills
USE Mountains
Hills, Buried
USE Buried hills
Hill's equation
UF Equation, Hill's
BT Differential equations, Linear
Hills family
USE Hill family
Hillsdale Lake (Kan.)
UF Hillsdale Reservoir (Kan.)
BT Lakes—Kansas
Reservoirs—Kansas
Hillsdale Reservoir (Kan.)
USE Hillsdale Lake (Kan.)
Hillside architecture *(May Subd Geog)*
UF Alpine architecture
Architecture, Hillside
Mountain architecture
BT Architecture
Hillside Cemetery (Silverton, Colo.)
BT Cemeteries—Colorado
Hillside farming
USE Hill farming
Hillside figures
USE Hill figures
Hillside gardening *(May Subd Geog)*
[SB458.95]
UF Hill gardening
BT Gardening
Hillside planting *(May Subd Geog)*
[S627.H5]
UF Hill culture
Hillculture
BT Hill farming
Planting (Plant culture)
Soil-binding
Soil conservation
NT Streambank planting
Hillsman family
USE Hillman family
Hillsmon family
USE Hillman family
Hillstar, Andean
USE Andean hillstar
Hillyard family
USE Hilliard family
Hilman family
USE Hillman family
Hilmand River (Afghanistan)
USE Helmand River (Afghanistan)
Hiloms family
USE Helms family
Hils family
USE Hill family
Hils Ridge (Germany)
BT Mountains—Germany (West)
Hilsch tubes
USE Vortex tubes
Hilsman family
USE Hillman family
Hilt family *(Not Subd Geog)*
UF Hild family
RT Hilts family
Hilty family
Hiltebrand family
USE Hildebrand family
Hilten family
USE Hilton family
Hilterbrand family
USE Hildebrand family
Hiltersried, Battle of, 1433
BT Bavaria (Germany)—History—1180-
1777
Bohemia (Czechoslovakia)—History—
Hussite Wars, 1419-1436—
Campaigns
Hilti family
USE Hilty family

Hilton family *(Not Subd Geog)*
UF Helton family
Hilten family
Hylton family
Hilton Head (S.C.). Sea Pines Plantation
USE Sea Pines Plantation (Hilton Head,
S.C.)
Hilts family *(Not Subd Geog)*
UF Hiltz family
RT Hilt family
Hilty family *(Not Subd Geog)*
UF Hildi family
Hildie family
Hildy family
Hilti family
Hyldi family
RT Hilt family
Hiltz family
USE Hilts family
Hima
USE Bahima (African people)
Himachal
USE Himalaya Mountains
Himachali drama *(May Subd Geog)*
Himachali fiction *(May Subd Geog)*
NT Short stories, Himachali
Himachali folk literature
USE Folk literature, Himachali
Himachali folk-songs
USE Folk-songs, Himachali
Himachali language
[PK2606-2609]
UF Pahadi language
Pahari language, Western
Western Pahari language
BT Pahari languages
NT Bhalesi dialect
Himachali literature *(May Subd Geog)*
NT Folk literature, Himachali
Himachali philology
Himachali poetry *(May Subd Geog)*
Himachali short stories
USE Short stories, Himachali
Himalaya Mountains
UF Himachal
Himalayas
BT Mountains—Asia
NT Annapurna (Nepal)
Changabang Mountain (India)
Chomo Lhari (Bhutan and China)
Dhaulāgiri (Nepal)
Everest, Mount (China and Nepal)
Kānchenjunga (Nepal and India)
Kumaun Himalaya
Lesser Himalaya Mountains
Mahabharat Range (Nepal)
Nanda Devi (India)
Nanga Parbat (India)
Pumori (Nepal)
Zaskar Range (India and China)
Himalayan black bear
USE Selenarctos thibetanus
Himalayan cat
[SF449.H55]
UF Colorpoint cat
Colorpoint longhair cat
Colour-point cat
Colourpoint cat
Colourpoint longhair cat
Himmy cat
Longhair colorpoint cat
Longhair Siamese cat
BT Cat breeds
Longhair cats
Persian cat
Siamese cat
Himalayan golden eagle
[QL696.A2]
UF Aquila chrysaetus daphanea
Berkut eagle
Middle Asian golden eagle

BT Eagles
Golden eagle
Himalayan languages
USE Tibeto-Burman languages
Himalayan pine
USE Pinus griffithii
Himalayan tahr
[QL737.U53]
UF Hemitragus jemlahicus
BT Tahrs
Himalayan white pine
USE Pinus griffithii
Himalayas
USE Himalaya Mountains
Himantoglossum
[QK495.O64]
BT Orchids
Himantoglossum hircinum
[QK495.O64]
UF Loroglossum hircinum
Himantopus
[QL696.C473]
UF Stilts (Birds)
BT Recurvirostridae
Himantopus mexicanus
USE Black-necked stilt
Himantopus nigricollis
USE Black-necked stilt
Himawari (Meteorological satellite)
BT Meteorological satellites
Himba (Bantu people)
[DT709]
UF Cimba (Bantu people)
Shimba (Bantu people)
Simba (Bantu people)
Tjimba (Bantu people)
BT Bantus
Ethnology—Angola
Ethnology—Namibia
Hereros
— Rites and ceremonies
NT Marriage customs and rites, Himba
Himba marriage customs and rites
USE Marriage customs and rites, Himba
Himbeck family
USE Heimlich family
Himeji Peasant Uprising, 1748
Himeji porcelain
USE Tōzan porcelain
Himejijō (Himeji-shi, Japan)
BT Castles—Japan
Himelick family
USE Heimlich family
Himelock family
USE Heimlich family
Himley family
USE Heimlich family
Himmy cat
USE Himalayan cat
Himyaritic inscriptions
USE Inscriptions, Sabaean
Hina family *(Not Subd Geog)*
Hinaray-a language
USE Kinaray-a language
Hinaraya language
USE Kinaray-a language
Hinata Kita Iseki (Higashimurayama-shi,
Japan)
USE Hinata Kita Site (Higashimurayama-
shi, Japan)
**Hinata Kita Site (Higashimurayama-shi,
Japan)** *(Not Subd Geog)*
UF Hinata Kita Iseki (Higashimurayama-
shi, Japan)
BT Japan—Antiquities
Hinayana Buddhism
UF Lesser vehicle (Buddhism)
Little vehicle (Buddhism)
Pali Buddhism
Southern Buddhism
Southern vehicle (Buddhism)

Hinayana Buddhism *(Continued)*
  BT Buddhism
      Buddhist sects
  NT Mahāsāṅghikas
      Sarvāstivādins
      Theravāda Buddhism
  — Essence, genius, nature
  — Relations
  — — Zen Buddhism, ₍etc.₎
Hinchman family *(Not Subd Geog)*
Hinckel family
  USE Hinkle family
Hinckle family
  USE Hinkle family
Hinckley family
  USE Hinkley family
Hind family
  USE Hines family
Hinde family
  USE Hines family
Hindered rotation theory
  USE Molecular rotation
Hindes family
  USE Hines family
Hindi anonyms and pseudonyms
  USE Anonyms and pseudonyms, Hindi
Hindi authors
  USE Authors, Hindi
Hindi children's literature
  USE Children's literature, Hindi
Hindi children's plays
  USE Children's plays, Hindi
Hindi children's poetry
  USE Children's poetry, Hindi
Hindi children's stories
  USE Children's stories, Hindi
Hindi Christian literature
  USE Christian literature, Hindi
Hindi couplets
  USE Couplets, Hindi
Hindi detective and mystery stories
  USE Detective and mystery stories, Hindi
Hindi didactic fiction
  USE Didactic fiction, Hindi
Hindi didactic poetry
  USE Didactic poetry, Hindi
Hindi drama *(May Subd Geog)*
  NT Children's plays, Hindi
      Folk-drama, Hindi
      Hindi farces
      One-act plays, Hindi
      Radio plays, Hindi
      Verse drama, Hindi
Hindi epic poetry
  USE Epic poetry, Hindi
Hindi essays *(May Subd Geog)*
Hindi farces *(May Subd Geog)*
  BT Farces
      Hindi drama
Hindi fiction *(May Subd Geog)*
  NT Children's stories, Hindi
      Detective and mystery stories, Hindi
      Didactic fiction, Hindi
      Historical fiction, Hindi
      Short stories, Hindi
Hindi folk-drama
  USE Folk-drama, Hindi
Hindi folk literature
  USE Folk literature, Hindi
Hindi folk poetry
  USE Folk poetry, Hindi
Hindi folk-songs
  USE Folk-songs, Hindi
Hindi gnomic poetry
  USE Gnomic poetry, Hindi
Hindi historical fiction
  USE Historical fiction, Hindi
Hindi imprints *(May Subd Geog)*
Hindi Jaina poetry
  USE Jaina poetry, Hindi

Hindi language *(May Subd Geog)*
  ₍PK1931-PK1939₎
    Here are entered works on Hindustani in the Devanagari alphabet.
  BT Hindustani language
  RT Urdu language
  NT Awadhi dialect
      Badayuni dialect
      Bagheli dialect
      Bangaru dialect
      Bihari language
      Braj language
      Bundeli dialect
      Chhattisgarhi dialect
      Khari Boli language
— Dialects
— — India
— — — Deccan
      USE Dakhini Hindustani dialect
Hindi language, Eastern
  USE Hindustani language
Hindi language, Western
  USE Hindustani language
Hindi letters *(May Subd Geog)*
  ₍PK2078.L4₎
— 1500-1800
Hindi literature *(May Subd Geog)*
  NT Children's literature, Hindi
      Christian literature, Hindi
      Folk literature, Hindi
      Protest literature, Hindi
      Religious literature, Hindi
      Sufi literature, Hindi
— To 1500
— 1500-1800
— 20th century
  NT Chayavada
— Appreciation *(May Subd Geog)*
— Muslim authors
Hindi love poetry
  USE Love poetry, Hindi
Hindi lullabies
  USE Lullabies, Hindi
Hindi manuscripts
  USE Manuscripts, Hindi
Hindi narrative poetry
  USE Narrative poetry, Hindi
Hindi newspapers *(May Subd Geog)*
  ₍PN5371-PN5380 (History)₎
Hindi one-act plays
  USE One-act plays, Hindi
Hindi patriotic poetry
  USE Patriotic poetry, Hindi
Hindi periodicals
  ₍PN5371-PN5380 (History)₎
Hindi philology
Hindi poetry
  NT Children's poetry, Hindi
      Couplets, Hindi
      Didactic poetry, Hindi
      Epic poetry, Hindi
      Folk poetry, Hindi
      Gnomic poetry, Hindi
      Jaina poetry, Hindi
      Love poetry, Hindi
      Narrative poetry, Hindi
      Patriotic poetry, Hindi
      Protest poetry, Hindi
      Religious poetry, Hindi
      Revolutionary poetry, Hindi
      Sufi poetry, Hindi
      Vaishnava poetry, Hindi
— To 1500
— 1500-1800
— 20th century
  NT Chayavada
Hindi poets
  USE Poets, Hindi
Hindi prose literature *(May Subd Geog)*
Hindi protest literature
  USE Protest literature, Hindi

Hindi protest poetry
  USE Protest poetry, Hindi
Hindi proverbs
  USE Proverbs, Hindi
Hindi radio plays
  USE Radio plays, Hindi
Hindi reference books
  USE Reference books, Hindi
Hindi religious literature
  USE Religious literature, Hindi
Hindi religious poetry
  USE Religious poetry, Hindi
Hindi revolutionary poetry
  USE Revolutionary poetry, Hindi
Hindi riddles
  USE Riddles, Hindi
Hindi satire
  USE Satire, Hindi
Hindi short stories
  USE Short stories, Hindi
Hindi Sufi literature
  USE Sufi literature, Hindi
Hindi Sufi poetry
  USE Sufi poetry, Hindi
Hindi Vaishnava poetry
  USE Vaishnava poetry, Hindi
Hindi verse drama
  USE Verse drama, Hindi
Hindi wit and humor
  BT Indic wit and humor
Hindkō dialect
  ₍PK2269.H5₎
  BT Lahndā language
Hindkō poetry *(May Subd Geog)*
Hindko proverbs
  USE Proverbs, Hindko
Hindlimbs
  USE Extremities, Lower
Hindoos
  USE Hindus
Hindricks family
  USE Hendricks family
Hinds family
  USE Hines family
Hindsgaul (Middelfart, Denmark)
  USE Hindsgavl (Middelfart, Denmark)
Hindsgavl (Middelfart, Denmark)
  UF Hindsgaul (Middelfart, Denmark)
  BT Castles—Denmark
Hindshaw family
  USE Henshaw family
Hindu almanacs
  USE Almanacs, Hindu
Hindu altars
  USE Altars, Hindu
Hindu antiquities *(May Subd Geog)*
  UF Antiquities, Hindu
  BT Antiquities
Hindu architecture
  USE Architecture, Hindu
Hindu art
  USE Art, Hindu
Hindu art objects
  USE Art objects, Hindu
Hindu asceticism
  USE Asceticism—Hinduism
Hindu astrology
  USE Astrology, Hindu
Hindu astronomy
  USE Astronomy, Hindu
Hindu bronzes
  USE Bronzes, Hindu
Hindu calendar
  USE Calendar, Hindu
Hindu chant
  USE Chants (Hindu)
Hindu children *(May Subd Geog)*
  UF Children, Hindu
  BT Children
— Religious life
    ₍BL1228.3.C5₎

UF Children—Religious life
(Hinduism)
BT Religious life (Hinduism)
Hindu civilization
USE Civilization, Hindu
Hindu converts to Buddhism
USE Buddhist converts from Hinduism
Hindu converts to Christianity
USE Converts from Hinduism
Hindu cookery
USE Cookery, Hindu
Hindu cosmogony
USE Cosmogony, Hindu
Hindu cosmology
USE Cosmology, Hindu
Hindu decoration and ornament
USE Decoration and ornament, Hindu
Hindu devotional calendars
UF Devotional calendars—Hinduism
Devotional calendars, Hindu
Hindu drama *(May Subd Geog)*
BT Drama
Religious drama
Hindu embroidery
USE Embroidery, Hindu
Hindu epistemology
USE Knowledge, Theory of (Hinduism)
Hindu eschatology
USE Eschatology, Hindu
Hindu ethics
[BJ121-BJ123]
UF Ethics, Hindu
BT Ethics, Indic
SA *subdivision* Conduct of life *under
special groups of Hindus, e.g.*
Youth, Hindu—Conduct of life
NT Ahiṃsā
Hindu fasts and feasts
USE Fasts and feasts—Hinduism
Hindu funeral rites and ceremonies
USE Funeral rites and ceremonies, Hindu
Hindu giving
[BL1228.5]
UF Giving, Hindu
BT Charity
Hindu goddesses
USE Goddesses, Hindu
Hindu gods
USE Gods, Hindu
Hindu hygiene
USE Hygiene, Hindu
Hindu hymns
[BL1226.3]
UF Hinduism—Hymns
Hymns, Hindu
BT Chants (Hindu)
SA *subdivision* Hymns *under names of
individual Hindu sects, e.g.*
Vaishnavism—Hymns
NT Sivaism—Hymns
Hindu hymns, Bengali, [Marathi, etc.]
Hindu hymns, Dingal *(May Subd Geog)*
[BL1226.3]
UF Dingal Hindu hymns
Hindu hymns, English *(May Subd Geog)*
UF English Hindu hymns
Hindu hymns, French *(May Subd Geog)*
UF French Hindu hymns
Hindu hymns, Kannada *(May Subd Geog)*
UF Kannada Hindu hymns
Hindu hymns, Marathi *(May Subd Geog)*
UF Marathi Hindu hymns
Hindu hymns, Sanskrit *(May Subd Geog)*
UF Sanskrit Hindu hymns
Hindu hymns, Telugu *(May Subd Geog)*
UF Telugu Hindu hymns
**Hindu Kush Mountains (Afghanistan and
Pakistan)**
BT Mountains—Afghanistan
Mountains—Pakistan

Hindu law
UF Law, Hindu
BT Law, Oriental
SA *specific legal headings with* Hindu law
added in parentheses, e.g. Adoption
(Hindu law)
NT Adoption (Hindu law)
Alimony (Hindu law)
Benami transactions
Burmese Buddhist law
Dharma
Domestic relations (Hindu law)
Dowry (Hindu law)
Matrilineal kinship (Hindu law)
Punishment (Hindu law)
Separate maintenance (Hindu law)
Support (Domestic relations law,
Hindu)
— Codification
Hindu legends
USE Legends, Hindu
Hindu literature
[BL1145-7]
BT Religious literature
NT Hinduism—Sacred books
Vaishnava literature
**Hindu literature, Gujarati, [Hindi, Marathi,
etc.]**
Hindu literature, Marathi *(May Subd Geog)*
UF Marathi Hindu literature
BT Marathi literature
Hindu literature, Sanskrit *(May Subd Geog)*
UF Sanskrit Hindu literature
BT Sanskrit literature
Hindu logic
[BC25-6]
UF Logic, Hindu
BT Philosophy, Hindu
Hindu marriage customs and rites
USE Marriage customs and rites, Hindu
Hindu martyrs
BT Hindu saints
Hindus—Biography
Martyrs
Hindu medicine
USE Medicine, Ayurvedic
Hindu meditations
UF Meditations, Hindu
BT Meditation (Hinduism)
Hindu mendicants
USE Sadhus
Hindu monasteries
USE Monasteries, Hindu
Hindu monastic and religious life
USE Monastic and religious life (Hinduism)
Hindu monasticism and religious orders
USE Monasticism and religious orders,
Hindu
Hindu mysticism
USE Mysticism—Hinduism
Hindu painting
USE Painting, Hindu
Hindu parables
USE Parables, Hindu
Hindu pilgrims and pilgrimages
(May Subd Geog)
BT Pilgrims and pilgrimages
NT Hindu shrines
Hindu priests
USE Priests, Hindu
Hindu psychology
USE Hinduism—Psychology
Hindu religious education *(May Subd Geog)*
UF Religious education, Hindu
Hindu saints *(May Subd Geog)*
[BL1171]
BT Hinduism
Saints
NT Alvars
Hindu martyrs

Hindu saints, Tamil
UF Tamil Hindu saints
Tamil saints, Hindu
Hindu scholars
USE Scholars, Hindu
Hindu sculpture
USE Sculpture, Hindu
Hindu sects *(May Subd Geog)*
[BL1245.A1]
UF Hinduism—Sects
Sects, Hindu
BT Brahmanism
Hinduism
NT Alakhiyas
Alekha (Sect)
Bauls
Bāvarī (Sect)
Bhagavatas
Brahmakumari
Chaitanya (Sect)
Dādūpanthīs
Daśnāmīs
Dharmaṭhākura
Gāyatrī Parivāra
Gusains
Kālāmukhas
Kānphaṭas
Kāpālikas
Karthābhajā
Kaulas
Lingayats
Mādhvas
Mahanubhava
Mandala
Meyvaḷi (Sect)
Nagesh sect
Nātha sect
Nimbarka (Sect)
Niranjanis
Palatu sect
Pāñcarātra (Sect)
Radhasoami Satsang
Rādhāvallabha
Rām Sanehīs
Ramakrishna Mission
Rāmānandīs
Sadhs
Sahajiyā
Samartha Sampradaya
Senāpanthīs
Shaktism
Śiva Nārāyanīs
Sivaism
Śrī Vaiṣṇava (Sect)
Swami-Narayanis
Teṅgalai (Sect)
Vaḍagalai (Sect)
Vaikhanasas
Vaishnavism
Vallabhachars
Vārkarī sect
Worship (Hinduism)
Hindu sermons
[BL1226.5]
UF Sermons, Hindu
Hindu sermons, Gujarati, [Marathi, etc.]
Hindu shrines *(May Subd Geog)*
UF Shrines, Hindu
BT Hindu pilgrims and pilgrimages
Hindu sociology
USE Sociology, Hindu
Hindu symbolism
[BL1215.S9]
BT Symbolism
NT Bijas
Yantras
Hindu temples
USE Temples, Hindu
Hindu theological anthropology
USE Man (Hinduism)

Hindu wall hangings
　USE Wall hangings, Hindu
Hindu women
　USE Women, Hindu
Hindu worship
　USE Worship (Hinduism)
Hindu youth
　USE Youth, Hindu
Hinduism *(May Subd Geog)*
　[B130-B133 (Philosophy)]
　[BL1100-BL1270]
　[BL2000-BL2030 (India)]
　BT Religions
　RT Brahmanism
　NT Advaita
　　Arya-Samaj
　　Atonement (Hinduism)
　　Bhakti
　　Brahma-samaj
　　Caste—India
　　Chakra (Hinduism)
　　Civilization, Hindu
　　Classification—Books—Hinduism
　　Deluge (Hinduism)
　　Dev-samaj
　　Dharma
　　Dvaita (Vedanta)
　　Fasts and feasts—Hinduism
　　God (Hinduism)
　　Gods, Hindu
　　Good and evil (Hinduism)
　　Gurus
　　Hindu saints
　　Hindu sects
　　Jains
　　Karma
　　Knowledge, Theory of (Hinduism)
　　Mahima Dharma
　　Man (Hinduism)
　　Maya (Hinduism)
　　Meditation (Hinduism)
　　Mimamsa
　　Miracles (Hinduism)
　　Monasteries, Hindu
　　Monastic and religious life (Hinduism)
　　Mysticism—Hinduism
　　Nyaya
　　Parables, Hindu
　　Prayer (Hinduism)
　　Purity, Ritual (Hinduism)
　　Religious life (Hinduism)
　　Revelation (Hinduism)
　　Salvation (Hinduism)
　　Sankhya
　　Sannyasi
　　Self-worship (Hinduism)
　　Soul (Hinduism)
　　Spiritual life (Hinduism)
　　Śraddhā
　　Tantrism
　　Temples, Hindu
　　Vaiśeṣika
　　Vedanta
　　Vedas
　　Vrata
　　Women in Hinduism
　　Worship (Hinduism)
　　Yoga
　— 20th century
　　USE Hinduism—History—20th
　　　century
　— Asceticism
　　USE Asceticism—Hinduism
　— Biography
　　USE Hindus—Biography
　— **Doctrines**
　　NT Trimūrti
　— **Essence, genius, nature**
　　　[BL1205]
　— **History**
　—— **1765-**

　　　[BL1153.5]
　—— **20th century**
　　　UF Hinduism—20th century
　— Hymns
　　USE Hindu hymns
　— **Missions**
　　　Here are entered works on Hindu missionary
　　activity. Works on Christian missions among
　　Hindus are entered under Missions to Hindus.
　— **Prayer-books and devotions**
　—— **English, [French, German, etc.]**
　— **Psychology**
　　　[BL1215.P8]
　　UF Hindu psychology
　　　Psychology, Hindu
　— **Relations**
　　　[BL1230]
　—— **Buddhism**
　　　[BQ4610.H6]
　　　NT Gautama Buddha—Hindu
　　　　interpretations
　—— **Buddhism, [Christianity, Islam, etc.]**
　—— **Christianity**
　　　NT Missions to Hindus
　— **Rituals**
　　SA *subdivision* Rituals *under names of*
　　　individual Hindu sects, e.g.
　　　Vaishnavism—Rituals
　　NT Agnicayana (Hindu rite)
　　　Agnihotra (Hindu rite)
　　　Bratas
　　　Chants (Hindu)
　　　Funeral rites and ceremonies,
　　　　Hindu
　　　Homa (Rite)
　　　Kirtana
　　　Mahāpradoṣa (Hindu rite)
　　　Marriage customs and rites, Hindu
　　　Marriage service (Hinduism)
　　　Mṛtyuñjaya homa
　　　Mudrās (Hinduism)
　　　Rājasūya
　　　Ṛshipañcamī (Hindu rite)
　　　Sacred thread ceremony
　　　Sandhyā (Hindu rite)
　　　Sivaratri
　　　Temples, Hindu—Dedication
　　　Timiti (Hindu rite)
　　　Vājapeya (Hindu rite)
　　　Vibhūti (Hindu rite)
　— **Sacred books**
　　BT Hindu literature
　　NT Puranas
　— Sects
　　USE Hindu sects
　— **Cambodia**
　　NT Devarāja (Cult)
Hinduism and culture
　　[BL1235.C]
　BT Culture
　　Religion and culture
Hinduism and politics *(May Subd Geog)*
　　[BL1215.P65]
　UF Politics and Hinduism
　BT Hinduism and state
　　Political science
　　Politics, Practical
　　Religion and politics
Hinduism and science
　UF Science and Hinduism
　BT Religion and science
　NT Bhagavadgītā and science
　　Puranas and science
Hinduism and socialism
　USE Socialism and Hinduism
Hinduism and state
　UF State and Hinduism
　BT Religion and state
　NT Hinduism and politics
Hindus *(May Subd Geog)*
　UF Hindoos

　RT East Indians
　NT Brahmans
　　Hare Krishnas
　　Missions to Hindus
　　Youth, Hindu
　— **Biography**
　　UF Hinduism—Biography
　　NT Hindu martyrs
Hindustani drama
　　[PK2041 (History)]
　　[PK2071 (Collections)]
Hindustani language
　　[PK1931-PK1937]
　　Here are entered works on the spoken form of
　Hindi and Urdu.
　UF Hindi language, Eastern
　　Hindi language, Western
　BT Indo-Aryan languages, Modern
　RT Surinam Hindustani language
　NT Dakhini Hindustani dialect
　　Hindi language
　　Urdu language
Hindustani literature
　　[PK2030-2158]
Hindustani music
　USE Music, Hindustani
Hindustani periodicals
　　[PN5371-PN5380 (History)]
Hindustani philology
Hindustani poetry
　　[PK2040 (History)]
　　[PK2057-PK2059 (Collections)]
Hindustani proverbs
　USE Proverbs, Hindustani
Hine family
　USE Hines family
Hiner family
　USE Hayner family
Hines family *(Not Subd Geog)*
　UF Hind family
　　Hinde family
　　Hindes family
　　Hinds family
　　Hine family
　　Hinnes family
　　Hyans family
　　Hynds family
　　Hyne family
　　Hynes family
　　Hynn family
　　Hyns family
　RT Hein family
Hinge axis determination of mandible
　USE Mandible—Hinge axis determination
Hinge moments (Aerodynamics)
　BT Aerodynamics
　　Airplanes—Control surfaces
Hinges
　　[TS400]
　NT Art—Hinging
　　Concrete construction—Hinges
Hinging of works of art
　USE Art—Hinging
Hingley family
　USE Hinkley family
Hining family
　USE Henning family
Hinings family
　USE Henning family
Hinkel family
　USE Hinkle family
Hinkle family *(Not Subd Geog)*
　UF Hinckel family
　　Hinckle family
　　Hinkel family
　　Hinkler family
　RT Henkel family
　　Hinkley family
Hinkler family
　USE Hinkle family

Hinkley family (Not Subd Geog)
　　UF Henkley family
　　　　Hinckley family
　　　　Hingley family
　　　　Hinkly family
　　RT Hinkle family
Hinkly family
　　USE Hinkley family
Hinnes family
　　USE Hines family
Hinnings family
　　USE Henning family
Hino automobile
　　[TL215.H]
　　UF Aichi Hino automobile
Hino Castle (Hino-chō, Shiga-ken, Japan)
　　USE Hinojō (Hino-chō, Shiga-ken, Japan)
Hino family (Not Subd Geog)
Hinojō (Hino-chō, Shiga-ken, Japan)
　　UF Hino Castle (Hino-chō, Shiga-ken,
　　　　　Japan)
　　　　Ōmi Hinojō (Hino-chō, Shiga-ken,
　　　　　Japan)
　　BT Castles—Japan
Hinojosa family (Not Subd Geog)
　　UF Inojosa family
　　　　Ynojosa family
Hinoki cypress
　　USE Chamaecyparis obtusa
Hinoki falsecypress
　　USE Chamaecyparis obtusa
Hinomoto (Sect)
　　[BL2222.H5]
　　BT Shinto sects
Hinsch family
　　USE Hintz family
Hinseley family
　　USE Hensley family
Hinsely family
　　USE Hensley family
Hinshaw family
　　USE Henshaw family
Hinsley family
　　USE Hensley family
Hinsly family
　　USE Hensley family
Hinson family (Not Subd Geog)
Hinterglasmalerei
　　USE Glass underpainting
Hinton family (Not Subd Geog)
　　UF Henton family
　　　　Hynton family
Hintz family (Not Subd Geog)
　　UF Hinsch family
　　　　Hintze family
　　　　Hinz family
　　　　Hinze family
Hintze family
　　USE Hintz family
Hinz family
　　USE Hintz family
Hinze family
　　USE Hintz family
Hinzert (Germany : Concentration camp)
　　BT Concentration camps—Germany
　　　　　(West)
　　　　World War, 1939-1945—
　　　　　Concentration camps—Germany
　　　　　(West)
　　　　World War, 1939-1945—Prisoners and
　　　　　prisons, German
Hiordahlite
　　USE Guarinite
Hip (Rose)
　　USE Rose hips
Hip arch
　　USE Pelvic girdle
Hip dislocation, Congenital
　　USE Hip joint—Dislocation, Congenital
Hip dysplasia, Congenital
　　USE Hip joint—Dislocation, Congenital

Hip dysplasia in dogs
　　USE Canine hip dysplasia
Hip endoprostheses
　　USE Artificial hip joints
Hip joint
　　[QM131]
　　UF Coxa
　　NT Bursae of hip
　—Abnormalities
　　　　NT Canine hip dysplasia
　　　　　　Hip joint—Dislocation, Congenital
　— Congenital dislocation
　　　　USE Hip joint—Dislocation,
　　　　　　Congenital
　— Diseases (May Subd Geog)
　　　　[RD772]
　　　　UF Coxalgia
　　　　NT Hip joint—Radiography
　　　　　　Legg-Calvé-Perthes disease
　— Dislocation (May Subd Geog)
　　　　[RD772]
　　　　NT Canine hip dysplasia
　— Dislocation, Congenital
　　　　(May Subd Geog)
　　　　[RD772]
　　　　UF Congenital dislocation of the hip
　　　　　　Hip dislocation, Congenital
　　　　　　Hip dysplasia, Congenital
　　　　　　Hip joint—Congenital dislocation
　　　　BT Hip joint—Abnormalities
　— Radiography
　　　　BT Hip joint—Diseases
　— Surgery
　　　　UF Excision of hip
　　　　NT Artificial hip joints
Hip joints, Artificial
　　USE Artificial hip joints
Hip prostheses
　　USE Artificial hip joints
Hip replacement, Total
　　USE Artificial hip joints
Hip-ulama (Game)
　　USE Ulama (Game)
HIPO technique
　　UF Hierarchy, plus Input, Process, Output
　　　　technique
　　BT System analysis
Hipparchia
　　[QL561.S3]
　　BT Satyridae
Hipped plate structures
　　USE Folded plate structures
Hippies (May Subd Geog)
　　UF Counter culture
　　BT Bohemianism
　— Religious life
Hippo (Algeria) (Not Subd Geog)
　　UF Hippo Regius (Algeria)
　　BT Algeria—Antiquities
　　　　Cities and towns, Ruined, extinct, etc.
　　　　—Algeria
Hippo Regius (Algeria)
　　USE Hippo (Algeria)
Hippoboscidae
　　USE Louse flies
Hippocampidae
　　USE Syngnathidae
Hippocampus
　　USE Sea horses
Hippocampus (Brain)
　　UF Ammon's horn
　　　　Cornu ammonis
　　BT Cerebral cortex
　　　　Limbic system
Hippocampus zosterae
　　USE Dwarf sea horse
Hippocastanaceae (May Subd Geog)
　　[QK495.H65]
　　UF Aesculaceae
　　BT Sapindales
　　NT Aesculus

Hypoglycin A
Hippocrepis
　　[QK495.L52]
　　BT Leguminosae
Hippodamia
　　[QL596.C65]
　　BT Ladybirds
　　NT Hippodamia quinquesignata
Hippodamia quinquesignata
　　[QL596.C65]
　　BT Hippodamia
Hippodrome (May Subd Geog)
　　UF Theater—Animals
　　RT Circus
Hippoglossoides
　　[QL638.P7]
　　BT Pleuronectidae
Hippoglossoides elassodon
　　USE Flathead sole
Hippoglossoides platessoides
　　USE Plaice, American
Hippoglossus
　　[QL638.P7]
　　BT Pleuronectidae
Hippoglossus hippoglossus
　　USE Atlantic halibut
Hippoglossus stenolepis
　　USE Pacific halibut
Hippology
　　USE Horses
Hippolytos (Greek mythology)
　　USE Hippolytus (Greek mythology)
Hippolytus (Greek mythology)
　　UF Hippolytos (Greek mythology)
　　BT Mythology, Greek
Hippomane
　　[QK495.E9]
　　BT Euphorbiaceae
Hippomane mancinella
　　USE Manchineel
Hippophae
　　USE Sea buckthorn
Hippophae rhamnoides
　　[QK495.E33 (Botany)]
　　[SB386.S4 (Culture)]
　　UF Rhamnus sea buckthorn
　　BT Sea buckthorn
Hippophagy
　　USE Horse meat
Hippopotamus
　　[QL737.U5]
Hippopotamus, Fossil
　　[QE882.U3]
Hippopotamus liberiensis
　　USE Pygmy hippopotamus
Hippotigris
　　USE Equus
Hippotragus leucophaeus
　　USE Blue antelope
Hippotragus niger
　　USE Sable antelope
Hippuric acid
　　[QP211]
　　BT Urine
Hippuritidae
　　[QE812.H57]
　　BT Hippuritoida
Hippuritoida
　　BT Bivalvia, Fossil
　　NT Hippuritidae
　　　　Megalodontacea
　　　　Radiolitidae
Hipsher family (Not Subd Geog)
Hira Mountains (Japan)
　　UF Hira-san (Japan)
　　　　Hira-sanchi (Japan)
　　　　Hira-sankei (Japan)
　　　　Hirasan (Japan)
　　　　Hirasanchi (Japan)
　　　　Hirasankei (Japan)
　　BT Mountains—Japan

Hira-san (Japan)
  USE Hira Mountains (Japan)
Hira-sanchi (Japan)
  USE Hira Mountains (Japan)
Hira-sankei (Japan)
  USE Hira Mountains (Japan)
Hirabaru Nonaka Iseki (Yatsushiro-shi, Japan)
  USE Hirabaru Nonaka Site (Yatsushiro-shi,
       Japan)
Hirabaru Nonaka Site (Yatsushiro-shi, Japan)
  (Not Subd Geog)
  UF Hirabaru Nonaka Iseki (Yatsushiro-shi,
      Japan)
  BT Japan—Antiquities
Hirado porcelain
  [NK4399.H57]
  UF Mikawachi porcelain
  BT Blue and white transfer ware
      Porcelain, Japanese
Hirakiike Iseki (Higashihiroshima-shi, Japan)
  USE Hirakiike Site (Higashihiroshima-shi,
       Japan)
Hirakiike Site (Higashihiroshima-shi, Japan)
  (Not Subd Geog)
  UF Hirakiike Iseki (Higashihiroshima-shi,
      Japan)
  BT Japan—Antiquities
Hiranyakaśipu
Hirao-dai (Japan)
  USE Hirao Plateau (Japan)
Hirao Plateau (Japan)
  UF Hirao-dai (Japan)
  BT Karst—Japan
      Plateaus—Japan
Hiraoka family *(Not Subd Geog)*
Hirasan (Japan)
  USE Hira Mountains (Japan)
Hirasanchi (Japan)
  USE Hira Mountains (Japan)
Hirasankei (Japan)
  USE Hira Mountains (Japan)
Hirawa Kaidō (Japan)
  USE Heiwa Kaidō (Japan)
Hirazakura Kawahigashi Iseki (Oyabe-shi,
    Japan)
  USE Hirazakura Kawahigashi Site (Oyabe-
       shi, Japan)
**Hirazakura Kawahigashi Site (Oyabe-shi,
    Japan)** *(Not Subd Geog)*
  UF Hirazakura Kawahigashi Iseki (Oyabe-
      shi, Japan)
  BT Japan—Antiquities
Hird family
  USE Hurd family
Hire *(May Subd Geog)*
  BT Bailments
      Rent
      Wages
  RT Carriers
      Independent contractors
      Leases
      Mandate (Contract)
      Master and servant
  NT Contracts for work and labor
      Domestics
      Freight forwarders
      Labor contract
Hire (Ancient law)
Hire (Canon law)
  [BX1939.H]
Hire (Jewish law)
Hire (Roman-Dutch law)
Hire (Roman law)
Hire-purchase
  USE Sales, Conditional
Hire-purchase plan
  USE Instalment plan
Hiri Motu language
  [PM7895.H5]
  UF Police Motu language

  BT Languages, Mixed
      Melanesian languages
      Motu language
Hiring halls
  BT Employment agencies
      Trade-unions
Hiritano Highway (Papua New Guinea)
  BT Roads—Papua New Guinea
Hirley family
  USE Hurley family
Hirneola
  USE Auricularia
**Hirohito, Emperor of Japan, 1901-
  — Assassination attempt, 1923**
        UF Toranomon incident, Japan, 1923
Hirono family *(Not Subd Geog)*
Hirosaki Castle (Hirosaki-shi, Japan)
  USE Hirosakijō (Hirosaki-shi, Japan)
Hirosakijō (Hirosaki-shi, Japan)
  UF Hirosaki Castle (Hirosaki-shi, Japan)
      Takaokajō (Hirosaki-shi, Japan)
  BT Castles—Japan
Hirosato 8 Iseki (Kitami-shi, Japan)
  USE Hirosato 8 Site (Kitami-shi, Japan)
Hirosato 8 Site (Kitami-shi, Japan)
  (Not Subd Geog)
  UF Hirosato 8 Iseki (Kitami-shi, Japan)
  BT Japan—Antiquities
Hirosawasan Iseki (Yuzawa-shi, Japan)
  USE Hirosawasan Site (Yuzawa-shi, Japan)
Hirosawasan Site (Yuzawa-shi, Japan)
  (Not Subd Geog)
  UF Hirosawasan Iseki (Yuzawa-shi, Japan)
  BT Japan—Antiquities
Hirpini (Italic people)
  UF Irpini (Italic people)
  BT Ethnology—Italy
      Italic peoples
      Samnites
Hirsch family *(Not Subd Geog)*
  UF Hirsh family
  RT Hershey family
Hirschberg family
  USE Harshbarger family
Hirschberger family
  USE Harshbarger family
Hirschland family
  USE Hill family
Hirschsprung disease
  USE Hirschsprung's disease
Hirschsprung's disease *(May Subd Geog)*
  UF Achalasia, Pelvirectal
      Congenital megacolon
      Hirschsprung disease
      Megacolon, Congenital
      Myà's disease
      Pelvirectal achalasia
  BT Colon (Anatomy)—Abnormalities
      Megacolon
      Pediatric gastroenterology
Hirsh family
  USE Hirsch family
Hirsholmene (Denmark)
  BT Islands—Denmark
Hirst family
  USE Hearst family
Hirsutism
  USE Hypertrichosis
Hirta (Scotland)
  USE Saint Kilda (Scotland)
Hirtshalsbanen
  [HE3150.H (Economics)]
  BT Railroads—Denmark
Hirtzel family
  USE Hartzell family
Hiru Mountain (Japan)
  UF Hiru-sen (Japan)
      Hiru-zen (Japan)
      Hiruzen (Japan)
  BT Mountains—Japan

Hiru-sen (Japan)
  USE Hiru Mountain (Japan)
Hiru-zen (Japan)
  USE Hiru Mountain (Japan)
Hirudinaria
  [QL391.A6]
  BT Hirudinidae
Hirudinaria granulosa
  [QL391.A6]
Hirudinea
  USE Leeches
Hirudinidae
  [QL391.A6]
  BT Leeches
  NT Hirudinaria
Hiruma family *(Not Subd Geog)*
Hirundichthys
  [QL638.E9]
  BT Exocoetidae
  NT Hirundichthys affinis
Hirundichthys affinis
  [QL638.E9]
  UF Flyingfish, Fourwing
      Fourwing flyingfish
  BT Hirundichthys
Hirundinidae
  USE Swallows
Hirundo *(May Subd Geog)*
  [QL696.P247]
  BT Swallows
Hirundo daurica
  USE Red-rumped swallow
Hirundo rustica
  USE Barn swallow
Hiruzen (Japan)
  USE Hiru Mountain (Japan)
Hirzel family
  USE Hartzell family
His bundle
  UF Atrioventricular bundle
      Bundle of His
      Fasciculus atrioventricularis
  BT Heart conduction system
His master's voice (Painting)
  USE Barraud, Francis, 1856-1924. His
       master's voice
Hisamatsu family *(Not Subd Geog)*
Ḥisbah
  USE Muḥtasib
Hise family
  USE Heiss family
Hishiki-shimo Iseki (Sakai-shi, Japan)
  USE Hishiki-shimo Site (Sakai-shi, Japan)
Hishiki-shimo Site (Sakai-shi, Japan)
  (Not Subd Geog)
  UF Hishiki-shimo Iseki (Sakai-shi, Japan)
      Hishikishimo Iseki (Sakai-shi, Japan)
  BT Japan—Antiquities
Hishikishimo Iseki (Sakai-shi, Japan)
  USE Hishiki-shimo Site (Sakai-shi, Japan)
Hishkaryana language
  USE Hixkaryana language
Hisingerite
  BT Silicates
HISKAM (Electronic computer system)
Hislop family
  USE Haislip family
Hispanic American aged *(May Subd Geog)*
  UF Aged, Hispanic American
  BT Minority aged—United States
Hispanic American art *(May Subd Geog)*
  UF Art, Hispanic American
  BT Art, American
Hispanic American arts *(May Subd Geog)*
  UF Arts, Hispanic American
  BT Arts—United States

Hispanic American business enterprises
  (May Subd Geog)
  BT Business enterprises—United States
      Hispanic Americans in business
      Minority business enterprises—United
        States
Hispanic American business people
  USE Hispanic Americans in business
Hispanic American Catholics
  (May Subd Geog)
  UF Catholics, Hispanic American
  BT Catholics—United States
      Hispanic Americans—Religion
  NT Mexican American Catholics
Hispanic American children
  (May Subd Geog)
  UF Children, Hispanic American
  BT Children—United States
  NT Hispanic American youth
      Mexican American children
      Puerto Rican children
Hispanic American communication
  USE Hispanic Americans—Communication
Hispanic American consumers
  USE Hispanic Americans as consumers
Hispanic American decorative arts
  (May Subd Geog)
  UF Decorative arts, Hispanic American
  BT Decorative arts—United States
Hispanic American dentists
  (May Subd Geog)
  UF Dentists, Hispanic American
  BT Dentists—United States
Hispanic American disabled
  USE Hispanic American handicapped
Hispanic American engineers
  (May Subd Geog)
  [TA157]
  UF Engineers, Hispanic American
  BT Engineers—United States
Hispanic American families
  (May Subd Geog)
  [E184.S75]
  UF Families, Hispanic American
  BT Family—United States
Hispanic American handicapped
  (May Subd Geog)
  [HV1569.3.H57]
  UF Disabled, Hispanic American
      Handicapped Hispanic Americans
      Hispanic American disabled
  BT Handicapped—United States
Hispanic American lawyers
  (May Subd Geog)
  UF Lawyers, Hispanic American
  BT Lawyers—United States
Hispanic American leadership
  (May Subd Geog)
  [E184.S75]
  UF Leadership, Hispanic American
  BT Leadership
Hispanic American librarians
  (May Subd Geog)
  UF Librarians, Hispanic American
  BT Librarians—United States
Hispanic American libraries
  USE Hispanic Americans and libraries
Hispanic American literature (English)
  USE American literature—Hispanic
      American authors
Hispanic American mass media
  (May Subd Geog)
  [P94.5.H58]
  UF Hispanic American media
      Mass media, Hispanic American
  BT Ethnic mass media—United States
      Hispanic Americans and mass media
  NT Hispanic American newspapers
      Hispanic American periodicals
Hispanic American media
  USE Hispanic American mass media

Hispanic American medical personnel
  USE Hispanic Americans in medicine
Hispanic American Mennonites
  (May Subd Geog)
  [BX8128.H56]
  UF Mennonites, Hispanic American
  BT Mennonites—United States
Hispanic American mental health personnel
  (May Subd Geog)
  UF Mental health personnel, Hispanic
      American
  BT Mental health personnel—United
      States
Hispanic American military personnel
  USE United States—Armed Forces—
      Hispanic Americans
Hispanic American newspapers
  (May Subd Geog)
  BT American newspapers
      Hispanic American mass media
Hispanic American periodicals
  (May Subd Geog)
  BT American periodicals
      Hispanic American mass media
Hispanic American pharmacists
  (May Subd Geog)
  UF Pharmacists, Hispanic American
  BT Pharmacists—United States
Hispanic American physicians
  (May Subd Geog)
  UF Physicians, Hispanic American
  BT Physicians—United States
Hispanic American politicians
  (May Subd Geog)
  UF Politicians, Hispanic American
  BT Politicians—United States
Hispanic American psychologists
  UF Psychologists, Hispanic American
  BT Psychologists—United States
Hispanic American suffrage
  USE Hispanic Americans—Suffrage
Hispanic American veterans
  (May Subd Geog)
  UF Veterans, Hispanic American
  BT Veterans—United States
Hispanic American women
  (May Subd Geog)
  [E184.S75]
  UF Hispanic Americans—Women
      Women, Hispanic American
  NT Mexican American women
      Puerto Rican women
Hispanic American wood-carvers
  (May Subd Geog)
  UF Wood-carvers, Hispanic American
Hispanic American wood-carving
  (May Subd Geog)
  UF Wood-carving, Hispanic American
  BT Wood-carving—United States
Hispanic American youth *(May Subd Geog)*
  UF Youth, Hispanic American
  BT Hispanic American children
      Youth—United States
Hispanic Americans *(May Subd Geog)*
  [E184.S75]
  Here are entered works on United States citizens
  of Latin American descent. Works on citizens of
  Latin American countries are entered under Latin
  Americans. Works on citizens of Latin American
  countries in the United States are entered under
  Latin Americans—United States.
  UF Latinos (United States)
      Spanish speaking people (United
        States)
      Spanish surnamed people (United
        States)
  BT Ethnology—United States
      Latin Americans—United States
  RT Spanish Americans (Latin America)
  NT Chilean Americans
      Church work with Hispanic Americans

      Cuban Americans
      Mexican Americans
      Missions to Hispanic Americans
      Puerto Ricans—United States
  — Alcohol use
  — Communication
    [P94.5.H58]
    UF Hispanic American communication
    BT Communication
  — Employment
    NT Wages—Hispanic Americans
  — Ethnic identity
  — Food
    BT Food
  — Life skills guides
    [E184.S75]
    BT Life skills—United States
  — Music
    NT Alabados
  — Nutrition
  — Religion
    NT Hispanic American Catholics
  — Services for
    NT Libraries, University and college—
        Services to Hispanic Americans
        Public libraries—Services to
          Hispanic Americans
  — Suffrage
    UF Hispanic American suffrage
    BT Suffrage—United States
  — Women
    USE Hispanic American women
Hispanic Americans, Public library services to
  USE Public libraries—Services to Hispanic
      Americans
Hispanic Americans and libraries
  (May Subd Geog)
  UF Hispanic American libraries
      Libraries, Hispanic American
      Libraries and Hispanic Americans
      Library services to Hispanic
        Americans
  BT Libraries
Hispanic Americans and mass media
  (May Subd Geog)
  BT Mass media
      Mass media and minorities—United
        States
  NT Hispanic American mass media
      Mexican Americans and mass media
Hispanic Americans as consumers
  (May Subd Geog)
  UF Hispanic American consumers
  BT Consumers—United States
Hispanic Americans in business
  (May Subd Geog)
  UF Businessmen, Hispanic American
      Hispanic American business people
  BT Minority business enterprises—United
        States
  NT Hispanic American business
        enterprises
Hispanic Americans in medicine
  (May Subd Geog)
  UF Hispanic American medical personnel
  BT Medical personnel—United States
Hispanic Americans in military service
  USE United States—Armed Forces—
      Hispanic Americans
Hispanic Americans in the Armed Forces
  USE United States—Armed Forces—
      Hispanic Americans
Hispanic Americans in the press
  (May Subd Geog)
  BT Press
Hispanic authors of short stories
  USE Short stories—Hispanic authors
Hispanic civilization
  USE Civilization, Hispanic
Hispanidad
  USE Pan-Hispanism

Hispaniola
UF Haiti (Island)
La Española
Santo Domingo Island
Hispaniola woodpecker
[QL696.P56]
UF Melanerpes striatus
Hispanists *(May Subd Geog)*
BT Civilization, Hispanic
Philologists
Portugal—Study and teaching
Portuguese philology
Scholars
Spain—Study and teaching
Spanish philology
NT Catalanists
Latin Americanists
Hispano-American War, 1898
USE United States—History—War of 1898
Hispano-Islamic architecture
USE Architecture, Islamic—Spain
Hispano-Islamic art
USE Art, Islamic—Spain
Hispano-Moresque architecture
USE Architecture, Islamic—Spain
Hispano-Moresque art
USE Art, Islamic—Spain
Hispano-Moresque luster-ware
USE Luster-ware, Islamic—Spain
Hispano-Moresque majolica
USE Majolica, Islamic—Spain
Hispano-Suiza automobile
[TL215.H]
Hispanoamericanism
USE Pan-Hispanism
Hispanos
USE Mexican Americans
Hispid cotton rat
UF Sigmodon hispidus
BT Cotton rats
Hispidae
USE Chrysomelidae
Hiss (Radio meteorology) *(May Subd Geog)*
[QC973]
UF Auroral hiss
Very-low-frequency hiss
BT Atmospherics
Ionosphere
Radio meteorology
Radio noise
Hiss family *(Not Subd Geog)*
RT Hess family
Hissala language
USE Sisala language
Hissar Parya (Indic people)
USE Parya (Indic people)
Hissar Site (Iran)
USE Hissar Tepe (Iran)
Hissar Tepe (Iran) *(Not Subd Geog)*
UF Hissar Site (Iran)
Tappeh Hissar (Iran)
Tepe Hissar (Iran)
BT Iran—Antiquities
Hissing
USE Applause, demonstrations, etc.
Theater—Applause, demonstrations, etc.
Hissing adders
USE Hognose snakes
Hist family
USE Heiss family
Histaminase
BT Amine oxidase
Histamine
BT Biogenic amines
Imidazole
Inflammation—Mediators
RT Antihistamines
— **Receptors**
UF Histamine receptors
Receptors, Histamine

BT Cell receptors
Chemoreceptors
Histamine cephalgia
USE Cluster headache
Histamine headache
USE Cluster headache
Histamine receptors
USE Histamine—Receptors
Histeridae
[QL596.H5]
BT Beetles
Histiocytic sarcoma
USE Reticulum cell sarcoma
Histiocytosis-X
USE Reticuloendotheliosis
Histiopteridae
USE Pentacerotidae
Histiotus
[QL737.C595]
BT Vespertilionidae
NT Histiotus maculatus
Histiotus maculatus *(May Subd Geog)*
[QL737.C595]
BT Histiotus
Histochemistry
[QH611]
BT Histology
RT Biological chemistry
Cytochemistry
NT Immunohistochemistry
Molecular biology
Plant histochemistry
Histocompatibility
UF Tissue compatibility
RT Immunological tolerance
Transplantation immunology
Histocompatibility antigens
[QR184.3-184.35]
BT Isoantigens
NT H-Y antigen
HLA histocompatibility antigens
Histocompatibility antisera
(May Subd Geog)
[QR184.3]
UF Tissue typing antisera
BT Histocompatibility testing
Immune serums
Histocompatibility complex
USE Major histocompatibility complex
Histocompatibility testing
UF Histocompatibility typing
Tissue typing (Transplantation)
BT Immunological tolerance
Tissues—Analysis
NT Cell-mediated lympholysis
Compatibility testing (Hematology)
Histocompatibility antisera
Lymphocyte culture test, Mixed
— **Law and legislation** *(May Subd Geog)*
BT Medical laws and legislation
Histocompatibility typing
USE Histocompatibility testing
Histoire du Roi (Tapestries)
USE History of the King (Tapestries)
Histological sections, Frozen
USE Frozen tissue sections
Histologists *(May Subd Geog)*
[QM550.5-550.6]
BT Anatomists
Histology
Histology *(May Subd Geog)*
[QM550-QM576]
UF Anatomy, Microscopic
Microscopic anatomy
BT Anatomy
Cells
RT Microscope and microscopy
Tissues

SA *subdivision* Histology *under individual animals and groups of animals, and under individual organs and regions of the body, e.g.* Fishes—Histology; Heart—Histology
NT Cytoarchitectonics
Histochemistry
Histologists
Historadiography
Radioactive tracers in histology
Veterinary histology
— **Technique**
NT Fixation (Histology)
Freeze fracturing
Karyometry
Microtomy
Tissues—Plastic embedment
Histology, Pathological *(May Subd Geog)*
[RB24-RB33]
UF Histopathology
Pathological histology
BT Pathology
RT Pathology, Cellular
SA *subdivision* Histopathology *under organs and regions of the body, e.g.* Heart—Histopathology
Histology, Vegetable
USE Botany—Anatomy
Histology, Veterinary
USE Veterinary histology
Histones
[QP552.H5]
BT Chromatin
Nucleoproteins
NT Globin
Histopathology
USE Histology, Pathological
Histoplasmosis
BT Mycoses
Reticulo-endothelial system—Diseases
Histoplasmosis, Ocular *(May Subd Geog)*
[RE901.H5]
UF Ocular histoplasmosis
Presumed ocular histoplasmosis syndrome
BT Eye—Diseases and defects
Retina—Diseases
Uvea—Diseases
Historadiography
BT Histology
Radiography, Medical
Historia (Liturgy)
USE Rimed offices
Historians *(May Subd Geog)*
[D13-15]
UF Historiographers
BT Historiography
History
NT Antiquarians
Archaeologists
Architectural historians
Art historians
Ballet historians
Church historians
Garden historians
Historians of science
Literary historians
Mathematics historians
Medical historians
Medievalists
Public historians
Religion historians
Women historians
— **Rome**
UF Latin historians
Historians, Afro-American
USE Afro-American historians
Historians, Art
USE Art historians
Historians, Catholic
USE Catholic historians

Historians, Church
  USE Church historians
Historians, Jewish *(May Subd Geog)*
  UF Jewish historians
  BT Scholars, Jewish
Historians of religion
  USE Religion historians
Historians of science *(May Subd Geog)*
  UF Science historians
  BT Historians
      Science—Historiography
Historic American Merchant Marine Survey
  BT Merchant ships—United States
Historic bays (International law)
  USE Territorial waters
Historic bridges *(May Subd Geog)*
  UF Historical bridges
  BT Bridges
      Historic sites
Historic buildings *(May Subd Geog)*
  ₍D-F (History)₎
  ₍NA (Architecture)₎
  UF Historic houses, etc.
  BT Architecture
      Buildings
      Monuments
  RT Historic sites
  SA *types of historic buildings, e.g.*
      Churches; Dwellings; Hotels,
      taverns, etc.
  NT Birthplaces
      Hiding-places (Secret chambers, etc.)
      Historic farms
      Historical markers
      Literary landmarks
      Musical landmarks
  — Access for the physically handicapped
      ₍NA2545.P5₎
      BT Architecture and the physically
          handicapped
  — Conservation and restoration
      ₍NA105-NA112 (Architecture)₎
      ₍TH3301-TH3411 (Technology)₎
      UF Historic preservation
      NT Historic buildings—Remodeling for
          other use
  — Guide-books
  — Law and legislation *(May Subd Geog)*
      BT Building laws
  — Maintenance and repair
      NT Historic buildings—Remodeling for
          other use
  — Remodeling for other use
      UF Historic buildings—Renovation
          Remodeling of historic buildings
          for other use
          Renovation of historic buildings for
          other use
      BT Historic buildings—Conservation
          and restoration
          Historic buildings—Maintenance
          and repair
  — Renovation
      USE Historic buildings—Remodeling
          for other use
  — Visitors
  — Virginia
      NT Pope-Leighey House (Va.)
  — Washington (D.C.)
Historic districts *(May Subd Geog)*
  UF Historic preservation districts
      Historical districts
      Preservation districts
  BT Historic sites
  — Law and legislation *(May Subd Geog)*
  — Florida
      NT Seville Square Historical District
          (Pensacola, Fla.)
  — Micronesia (Federated States)
      NT Tonaachaw Historic Dictrict
          (Moen Island, Micronesia)

— New York (State)
    NT General Electric Realty Plot
        Historic District (Schenectady,
        N.Y.)
— South Dakota
    NT Forest Avenue Historical District
        (Vermillion, S.D.)
— Washington (State)
    NT Washington State Capitol Historic
        District (Olympia, Wash.)
Historic farms *(May Subd Geog)*
  ₍S548-548.6₎
  UF Historical farms
      Living historical farms
  BT Farms
      Historic buildings
      Historic sites
  RT Agricultural museums
Historic gardens *(May Subd Geog)*
  ₍SB451-466₎
  UF Historical gardens
  BT Gardens
      Historic sites
Historic houses, etc.
  USE Historic buildings
Historic peace churches *(May Subd Geog)*
      Here are entered works discussing collectively the
      Mennonites, Society of Friends, and the Church of
      the Brethren, known since 1935 as historic peace
      churches, which have peace as their central doctrine.
  UF Peace churches, Historic
  BT Protestant churches
  RT Peace—Religious aspects—Christianity
Historic preservation
  USE Historic buildings—Conservation and
      restoration
      Historic sites—Conservation and
      restoration
Historic preservation districts
  USE Historic districts
Historic ships *(May Subd Geog)*
  UF Historical ships
      Ships, Historic
  BT Ships
Historic site interpretation
  USE Historic sites—Interpretive programs
Historic sites *(May Subd Geog)*
  UF Historical sites
  BT Archaeology
      History
  RT Historic buildings
      Monuments
  NT Historic bridges
      Historic districts
      Historic farms
      Historic gardens
      Historic trees
      Historical markers
      Memorials
      Military parks
  — Conservation and restoration
      UF Historic preservation
      NT Federal aid to historic sites
  — Interpretive programs
      UF Historic site interpretation
          Interpretation, Historic site
          Interpretive programs of historic
          sites
      BT Public relations—Historic sites
  — Law and legislation *(May Subd Geog)*
      NT Federal aid to historic sites
  — Public relations
      USE Public relations—Historic sites
  — Alberta
      NT Cochrane Ranche Historic Site
          (Alta.)
  — Arizona
      NT Hubbell Trading Post National
          Historic Site (Ganado, Ariz.)
  — California

    NT Hearst-San Simeon State Historical
        Monument (Calif.)
— Colorado
    NT Bent's Old Fort National Historic
        Site (Colo.)
— Czechoslovakia
    NT Spišská Kapitula (Spišské
        Podhradie, Czechoslovakia)
— Florida
— Georgia
    NT Andersonville National Historic
        Site (Ga.)
        Battlefield Park (Savannah, Ga.)
        Martin Luther King, Junior,
        National Historic Site (Atlanta,
        Ga.)
        Savannah Historic District
        (Savannah, Ga.)
— Hawaii
    NT Pu'uhōnua o Honaunau National
        Historical Park (Hawaii)
— Idaho
    NT Nez Perce National Historical Park
        (Idaho)
— Illinois
    NT Illinois and Michigan Canal
        National Heritage Corridor (Ill.)
        Lincoln Home National Historic
        Site (Springfield, Ill.)
— Kansas
    NT Fort Larned National Historic Site
        (Larned, Kan.)
— Kentucky
    NT Cumberland Gap National
        Historical Park
— Korea (South)
    NT Kongsansŏng (Kongju-up, Korea)
— Louisiana
    NT Archbishop Antoine Blanc
        Memorial (New Orleans, La.)
        Jean Lafitte National Historical
        Park and Preserve (La.)
— Maryland
    NT Chesapeake and Ohio Canal
        National Historical Park
        Fort McHenry National
        Monument and Historic Shrine
        (Baltimore, Md.)
        Harpers Ferry National Historical
        Park
— Massachusetts
    NT Adams National Historic Site
        (Quincy, Mass.)
        Boston African American National
        Historic Site (Boston, Mass.)
        Boston National Historical Park
        (Boston, Mass.)
        Frederick Law Olmsted National
        Historic Site (Brookline, Mass.)
        Lowell National Historical Park
        (Mass.)
        Minute Man National Historical
        Park (Mass.)
        Salem Maritime National Historic
        Site (Mass.)
        Saugus Iron Works National
        Historic Site (Saugus, Mass.)
— Michigan
    NT River Raisin Battlefield and
        Massacre Site (Mich.)
— Montana
    NT Grant-Kohrs Ranch National
        Historic Site (Mont.)
— New Hampshire
    NT Governor John Wentworth
        Historic Site (Wolfeboro, N.H.)
— New Jersey
    NT Morristown National Historical
        Park (N.J.)
        Sandy Hook Proving Ground
        (N.J.)

Historic sites *(Continued)*
— **New York (State)**
    NT Eleanor Roosevelt National
         Historic Site (N.Y.)
         Ganondagan State Historic Site
           (N.Y.)
         Hudson-Mohawk Urban Cultural
           Park (N.Y.)
         Sagamore Hill National Historic
           Site (Oyster Bay, N.Y.)
         Saratoga National Historical Park
           (N.Y.)
         Vanderbilt Mansion National
           Historic Site (Hyde Park,
           Dutchess County, N.Y.)
         Women's Rights National
           Historical Park (N.Y.)
— **North Carolina**
    NT Carl Sandburg Home National
         Historic Site (Flat Rock, N.C.)
         Fort Raleigh National Historic Site
           (Roanoke Island, N.C.)
— **Ohio**
    NT James A. Garfield National
         Historic Site (Mentor, Ohio)
         William Howard Taft National
           Historic Site (Cincinnati, Ohio)
— **Pennsylvania**
    NT Allegheny Portage Railroad
         National Historic Site (Pa.)
         Friendship Hill National Historic
           Site (Pa.)
         Hopewell Furnace National
           Historic Site (Pa.)
         Independence National Historical
           Park (Philadelphia, Pa.)
         Washington Crossing Historic Park
           (Pa.)
— **Puerto Rico**
    NT San Juan National Historic Site
         (San Juan, P.R.)
— **South Carolina**
— **Tennessee**
    NT Cumberland Gap National
         Historical Park
— **Texas**
    NT Fort Davis National Historic Site
         (Tex.)
         Landmark Inn State Historic Site
           (Castroville, Tex.)
         Lyndon B. Johnson National
           Historical Park (Tex.)
— **Utah**
    NT Jarvie Historic Site (Utah)
— **Virginia**
    NT Colonial National Historical Park
         (Va.)
         Cumberland Gap National
           Historical Park
         Harpers Ferry National Historical
           Park
— **Washington (D.C.)**
    NT Chesapeake and Ohio Canal
         National Historical Park
— **Washington (State)**
    NT Fort Vancouver National Historic
         Site (Wash.)
— **West Virginia**
    NT Chesapeake and Ohio Canal
         National Historical Park
         Harpers Ferry National Historical
           Park
— **Wyoming**
    NT Fort Laramie National Historic
         Site (Wyo.)
Historic trees *(May Subd Geog)*
  UF Trees, Historic
  BT Historic sites
       Trees
  NT Bodhi Tree
       Liberty trees

— **Venezuela**
    NT Samán de la Trinidad (Caracas,
         Venezuela)
Historic waters (International law)
  USE Territorial waters
Historical archaeology
  USE Archaeology and history
Historical art
  USE History in art
Historical atlases
  USE *subdivision* Historical geography—
       Maps *under names of countries*
       Classical geography—Maps
       Geography, Ancient—Maps
       Geography, Historical—Maps
       Geography, Medieval—Maps
Historical bridges
  USE Historic bridges
Historical charts
  USE Chronology, Historical—Charts,
       diagrams, etc.
Historical chronology
  USE Chronology, Historical
Historical criticism
  USE Historiography
Historical criticism (Literature)
  (May Subd Geog)
  [PN98.H57]
    Here are entered works on methods of criticism
  which consider the literary work in its historical con-
  text, including its relationship to the author's life.
  BT Criticism
       Literature and history
Historical demography
  USE *subdivision* Population—History *under*
       names of countries, cities, etc.
       Demography
       Population—History
Historical dictionaries
  USE History—Dictionaries
Historical districts
  USE Historic districts
Historical drama
  [PN1870-PN1879 (History and
    criticism)]
  UF Chronicle history (Drama)
       Chronicle play
       Docudrama
       Documentary drama
       Drama, Historical
       History—Drama
  BT Drama
       Historiography
       History in literature
       Pageants
  SA *subdivision* History—Drama *or*
       subdivision *History—[period*
       subdivision]—Drama under names
       of countries, cities, etc.; and
       subdivision *Drama* under names of
       historical events and persons
  NT English drama—Early modern and
       Elizabethan, 1500-1600
Historical drama, American
  (May Subd Geog)
  UF American historical drama
  BT American drama
Historical drama, Azerbaijani
  (May Subd Geog)
  UF Azerbaijani historical drama
  BT Azerbaijani drama
Historical drama, Bengali *(May Subd Geog)*
  UF Bengali historical drama
  BT Bengali drama
Historical drama, Chinese *(May Subd Geog)*
  [PL2368.H58 (History)]
  [PL2579.H58 (Collections)]
  UF Chinese historical drama
  BT Chinese drama
Historical drama, English
  BT English drama

Historical drama, French *(May Subd Geog)*
  UF French historical drama
  BT French drama
Historical drama, French, [German, Italian,
  etc.]
Historical drama, German *(May Subd Geog)*
  UF German historical drama
  BT German drama
Historical drama, Greek *(May Subd Geog)*
  UF Greek historical drama
  BT Greek drama
Historical drama, Japanese
  (May Subd Geog)
  UF Japanese historical drama
  BT Japanese drama
Historical drama, Latin American
  (May Subd Geog)
  UF Latin American historical drama
  BT Latin American drama
Historical drama, Oriya *(May Subd Geog)*
  UF Oriya historical drama
  BT Oriya drama
Historical drama, Polish *(May Subd Geog)*
  [PG7090.H (History)]
  [PG7144.H (Collections)]
  UF Polish historical drama
  BT Polish drama
Historical drama, Russian *(May Subd Geog)*
  UF Russian historical drama
  BT Russian drama
Historical drama, Ukrainian
  (May Subd Geog)
  UF Ukrainian historical drama
  BT Ukrainian drama
Historical drama, Vietnamese
  (May Subd Geog)
  UF Vietnamese historical drama
  BT Vietnamese drama
Historical farms
  USE Historic farms
Historical fiction
  [PN3441]
  UF Fiction, Historical
       History—Fiction
  BT Fiction
       History
       History in literature
  SA *subdivision* History—Fiction *or*
       subdivision *History—[period*
       subdivision]—Fiction under names
       of countries, cities, etc.; and
       subdivision *Fiction* under names of
       historical events and persons
Historical fiction, Albanian
  (May Subd Geog)
  UF Albanian historical fiction
  BT Albanian fiction
Historical fiction, American
  (May Subd Geog)
  UF American historical fiction
  BT American fiction
Historical fiction, American, [English,
  German, Spanish, etc.] *(May Subd Geog)*
Historical fiction, Basque *(May Subd Geog)*
  UF Basque historical fiction
  BT Basque fiction
Historical fiction, Bengali *(May Subd Geog)*
  UF Bengali historical fiction
  BT Bengali fiction
Historical fiction, Canadian
  (May Subd Geog)
  UF Canadian historical fiction
  BT Canadian fiction
Historical fiction, Chinese *(May Subd Geog)*
  UF Chinese historical fiction
  BT Chinese fiction
Historical fiction, English *(May Subd Geog)*
  UF English historical fiction
  BT English fiction
Historical fiction, Finnish *(May Subd Geog)*
  UF Finnish historical fiction

BT Finnish fiction
Historical fiction, French *(May Subd Geog)*
UF French historical fiction
BT French fiction
Historical fiction, French-Canadian
(May Subd Geog)
UF French-Canadian historical fiction
BT French-Canadian fiction
Historical fiction, German *(May Subd Geog)*
UF German historical fiction
BT German fiction
Historical fiction, Gujarati
(May Subd Geog)
UF Gujarati historical fiction
BT Gujarati fiction
Historical fiction, Hindi *(May Subd Geog)*
UF Hindi historical fiction
BT Hindi fiction
Historical fiction, Hungarian
(May Subd Geog)
UF Hungarian historical fiction
BT Hungarian fiction
Historical fiction, Italian *(May Subd Geog)*
UF Italian historical fiction
BT Italian fiction
Historical fiction, Japanese
(May Subd Geog)
UF Japanese historical fiction
BT Japanese fiction
Historical fiction, Kazakh *(May Subd Geog)*
UF Kazakh historical fiction
BT Kazakh fiction
Historical fiction, Korean *(May Subd Geog)*
UF Korean historical fiction
BT Korean fiction
Historical fiction, Latin American
(May Subd Geog)
UF Latin American historical fiction
BT Latin American fiction
Historical fiction, Marathi
(May Subd Geog)
UF Marathi historical fiction
BT Marathi fiction
Historical fiction, Mexican
(May Subd Geog)
UF Mexican historical fiction
BT Mexican fiction
Historical fiction, Oriya *(May Subd Geog)*
UF Oriya historical fiction
BT Oriya fiction
Historical fiction, Polish *(May Subd Geog)*
UF Polish historical fiction
BT Polish fiction
Historical fiction, Portuguese
(May Subd Geog)
UF Portuguese historical fiction
BT Portuguese fiction
Historical fiction, Romanian
(May Subd Geog)
UF Romanian historical fiction
BT Romanian fiction
Historical fiction, Russian *(May Subd Geog)*
UF Russian historical fiction
BT Russian fiction
Historical fiction, Scottish
(May Subd Geog)
UF Scottish historical fiction
BT Scottish fiction
Historical fiction, Spanish *(May Subd Geog)*
UF Spanish historical fiction
BT Spanish fiction
Historical fiction, Ukrainian
(May Subd Geog)
UF Ukrainian historical fiction
BT Ukrainian fiction
Historical fiction, Urdu *(May Subd Geog)*
UF Urdu historical fiction
BT Urdu fiction
Historical films *(May Subd Geog)*
BT Feature films
Moving-pictures

RT Moving-pictures and history
Historical gardens
USE Historic gardens
Historical geography
USE Geography, Historical
Historical geology
UF Geology, Historical
BT Geology
RT Geology, Stratigraphic
Paleontology, Stratigraphic
NT Geological time
Historical lexicology *(May Subd Geog)*
[P326]
BT Historical linguistics
Lexicology
NT Language and languages—Etymology
Semantics, Historical
Historical libraries *(May Subd Geog)*
[Z675.H5]
UF History libraries
Libraries, Historical
BT Archives
Humanities libraries
NT Archaeological libraries
Historical linguistics
[P123]
UF Diachronic linguistics
Dynamic linguistics
Evolutionary linguistics
Language and languages—History
BT Language and history
Linguistics
NT Comparative linguistics
Historical lexicology
Linguistic change
Reconstruction (Linguistics)
Historical literature, Bengali
(May Subd Geog)
UF Bengali historical literature
BT Bengali literature
Historical markers *(May Subd Geog)*
UF Markers, Historical
BT Historic buildings
Historic sites
Monuments
Signs and signboards
RT Inscriptions
— **Japan**
NT Yama no Ue no Hi (Takasaki-shi,
Japan)
Historical materialism
Here are entered works on the Marxian theory of
human history. Works on the writing of history from
a historical materialist point of view are entered
under Marxian historiography.
BT Dialectical materialism
History—Philosophy
RT Marxian historiography
Historical models
[D16]
UF History—Models
Models, Historical
BT History—Methodology
Models and modelmaking
NT History—Mathematical models
Historical monuments
USE Monuments
Historical museums *(May Subd Geog)*
UF History—Museums
BT Museums
Historical poetry
UF History—Poetry
BT History in literature
Political ballads and songs
Political poetry
SA *subdivision* History—Poetry *or*
subdivision History—[period
subdivision]—Poetry *under names of*
countries, cities, etc.; and
subdivision Poetry *under names of*
historical events and persons

NT Patriotic poetry
Historical poetry, Albanian
(May Subd Geog)
UF Albanian historical poetry
BT Albanian poetry
Historical poetry, American
(May Subd Geog)
UF American historical poetry
BT American poetry
Historical poetry, Classical
(May Subd Geog)
UF Classical historical poetry
BT Classical poetry
Historical poetry, English *(May Subd Geog)*
UF English historical poetry
BT English poetry
Historical poetry, English, [etc.]
(May Subd Geog)
Historical poetry, Greek *(May Subd Geog)*
UF Greek historical poetry
BT Greek poetry
Historical poetry, Pushto *(May Subd Geog)*
UF Pushto historical poetry
BT Pushto poetry
Historical poetry, Russian *(May Subd Geog)*
UF Russian historical poetry
BT Russian poetry
Historical poetry, Spanish
(May Subd Geog)
UF Spanish historical poetry
BT Spanish poetry
Historical poetry, Telugu *(May Subd Geog)*
UF Telugu historical poetry
BT Telugu poetry
Historical prints *(May Subd Geog)*
UF Prints, Historical
BT Prints
— **18th century** *(May Subd Geog)*
— **19th century** *(May Subd Geog)*
Historical prints, American
(May Subd Geog)
UF American historical prints
Historical prints, Canadian
(May Subd Geog)
UF Canadian historical prints
Historical prints, New Zealand
(May Subd Geog)
UF New Zealand historical prints
Historical prints, Serbian *(May Subd Geog)*
UF Serbian historical prints
Historical programs, Television
USE Historical television programs
Historical publishing
USE History publishing
Historical record preservation
USE Archives
Historical research
USE History—Research
Historical school of economics
[HB97]
BT Economics
Economics—History
Historical ships
USE Historic ships
Historical sites
USE Historic sites
Historical sociology
[HM104]
UF Sociology, Historical
BT Anthropology
History
Social evolution
Sociology
NT Culture
Society, Primitive
Historical source material
USE History—Sources
Historical sources
USE History—Sources
Historical sources, Publishing of
USE History—Sources—Publishing

Historical television programs
  (May Subd Geog)
  UF Historical programs, Television
     Television historical programs
  BT History
     Television programs
Historicism
  ₍D16.9₎
  Here are entered works on the theory that all
  sociocultural phenomena are historically determined,
  that all truths are relative, that there are no absolute
  values, and that the student of the past must enter
  into the mind and attitudes of past periods and avoid
  intrusion of his own standards.
  BT History—Philosophy
Histories of Marie de Médicis (Paintings)
  USE Rubens, Peter Paul, Sir, 1577-1640.
        Histories of Marie de Médicis
Historiographers
  USE Historians
Historiography *(May Subd Geog)*
  ₍D13-D15₎
  Here and with local subdivision are entered works
  on the discipline of historiography. Works on the
  historiography of particular regions, countries, cities,
  etc. are entered under the name of the place subdivid-
  ed by Historiography.
  UF Historical criticism
     History—Authorship
     History—Criticism
     History—Historiography
  BT Authorship
  SA subdivision Historiography *under*
        subjects, e.g. Art—Historiography;
        Catholic Church—Historiography;
        United States—Historiography;
        United States—History—Civil War,
        1861-1865—Historiography
  NT Diplomatics
     Historians
     Historical drama
     History—Methodology
     History—Sources—Publishing
     Local history
     Marxian historiography
     Moving-pictures in historiography
     Photography in historiography
     Psychohistory
     Video tapes in historiography
Historiography, Marxian
  USE Marxian historiography
Historismus (Art)
  USE Eclecticism in art—Germany
History
  ₍B61 (History and philosophy)₎
  ₍D₎
  ₍HM36 (History and sociology)₎
  ₍JA78 (History and political science)₎
  ₍JX1253 (History and international
     law)₎
  ₍PN50 (History and literature)₎
  UF Annals
  RT Auxiliary sciences of history
  SA subdivision History *under specific*
        subjects and under names of
        countries, states, cities, etc.
  NT Anthropo-geography
     Archaeology
     Archaeology and history
     Architecture and history
     Battles
     Biography
     Boundaries
     Chronology
     Church history
     Conspiracies
     Constitutional history
     Coups d'état
     Diplomacy
     Diplomatics
     Diseases and history
     Ethnology

     Folklore and history
     Genealogy
     Geography, Historical
     Heroes
     Historians
     Historic sites
     Historical fiction
     Historical sociology
     Historical television programs
     Kings and rulers
     Language and history
     Man—Migrations
     Massacres
     Medals
     Migrations of nations
     Military history
     Moving-pictures and history
     Naval history
     Numismatics
     Personality and history
     Plants and history
     Political science
     Protohistory
     Public history
     Restorations, Political
     Revolutions
     Riots
     Seals (Numismatics)
     Sex and history
     Sieges
     Social history
     Social sciences and history
     Television and history
     World history
— Atlases
  USE subdivision Historical geography
        —Maps *under names of*
        countries
        Classical geography—Maps
        Geography, Ancient—Maps
        Geography, Historical—Maps
        Geography, Medieval—Maps
— Authorship
  USE Historiography
— Biography
  USE Biography
— Chronology
  USE Chronology, Historical
— Criticism
  USE Historiography
— **Dictionaries**
  ₍D9₎
  UF Historical dictionaries
     World history—Dictionaries
— Drama
  USE Historical drama
— Early works to 1800
  USE World history—Early works to
        1800
— **Errors, inventions, etc.**
  ₍D10₎
  BT Errors, Popular
     Literary forgeries and
        mystifications
  RT Imaginary histories
  SA subdivision History—Errors,
        inventions, etc. *under names of*
        countries, cities, etc.
— **Examinations, questions, etc.**
  ₍D21₎
  UF World history—Examinations,
        questions, etc.
— Fiction
  USE Historical fiction
— Historiography
  USE Historiography
— **Mathematical models**
  BT Historical models
— **Methodology**
  ₍D16₎
  BT Historiography

     NT Historical models
        History—Periodization
        History—Statistical methods
        Oral history
        Prosopography
— **Miscellanea**
  UF World history—Miscellanea
— Models
  USE Historical models
— Museums
  USE Historical museums
— **Outlines, syllabi, etc.**
  UF World history—Outlines, syllabi,
        etc.
— **Periodicals**
  UF History, Modern—Periodicals
— **Periodization**
  UF Periodization in history
  BT History—Methodology
     History—Philosophy
  SA subdivision History—Periodization
        under names of countries, etc.
— **Philosophy**
  ₍D16.7-9₎
  UF History, Modern—Philosophy
     History, Philosophy of
     Philosophy of history
  SA subdivision History—Philosophy
        under names of countries, e.g.
        Great Britain—History—
        Philosophy
  NT Buddhism—History—Philosophy
     Church history—Philosophy
     Frontier thesis
     Historical materialism
     Historicism
     History—Periodization
     History (Theology)
— Pictorial works
  USE World history—Pictorial works
— Poetry
  USE Historical poetry
— **Psychological aspects**
  NT Psychohistory
— Publishing
  USE History publishing
— **Research**
  UF Historical research
— Satire
  USE History, Comic, satirical, etc.
— **Societies, etc.**
— **Sources**
  ₍D5₎
  Here are entered collections of documents,
  records, etc. upon which narrative history is
  based.
  UF Historical source material
     Historical sources
     Source material, Historical
     Sources, Historical
  SA subdivision History—Sources *under*
        specific subjects and under
        names of countries, states, cities,
        etc., e.g. Catholic Church—
        History—Sources; United States
        —History—Sources
  NT Archives
     Charters
     Diplomatics
     Time capsules
— — **Publishing**
  ₍Z286₎
  UF Historical sources, Publishing of
     Publishing of historical sources
  BT Historiography
     History publishing
     Publishers and publishing
— **Statistical methods**
  BT History—Methodology
— **Study and teaching** *(May Subd Geog)*
  UF World history—Study and teaching

— Theology
  USE History (Theology)
— Yearbooks
  NT News recordings
History, Ancient
  [D51-D90]
  UF Ancient history
    World history, Ancient
  BT World history
  SA names of ancient races and peoples,
    e.g. Indo-Europeans; Hittites;
    Mediterranean race; and names of
    countries of antiquity
  NT Archaeology
    Bible
    Chronology
    Civilization, Ancient
    Classical dictionaries
    First century, A.D.
    Inscriptions
    Numismatics
— Biography
  USE Biography—To 500
— **Chronology**
  [D54.5]
  BT Chronology, Historical
History, Biblical
  USE Bible—History of Biblical events
History, Church
  USE Church history
History, Comic, satirical, etc.
  UF History—Satire
    World history, Comic, satirical, etc.
  BT Satire
    Wit and humor
  SA subdivision History, Comic, satirical,
    etc. under names of countries,
    cities, etc., for comprehensive
    humorous histories of those places
History, Constitutional
  USE Constitutional history
History, Ecclesiastical
  USE Church history
History, Economic
  USE Economic history
History, Imaginary
  USE Imaginary histories
History, Juvenile
  USE subdivision History—Juvenile literature
    under names of countries, regions,
    states, cities, etc.
    World history—Juvenile literature
History, Local
  USE Local history
History, Local (Cataloging)
  USE Cataloging of local history
History, Medieval
  USE Middle Ages—History
History, Military
  USE Military history
History, Modern
  [D204-D725]
  UF Modern history
    World history, Modern
  BT World history
  NT Renaissance
— **16th century**
  [D220-234]
— **17th century**
  [D242-280]
— **18th century**
  [D284-309]
— **19th century**
  [D351-D400]
— **20th century**
  [D410-725]
  NT World War, 1914-1918
    World War, 1939-1945
— **1945-**
— Periodicals
  USE History—Periodicals

— Philosophy
  USE History—Philosophy
— **Study and teaching** (May Subd Geog)
  NT Current events
History, Natural
  USE Natural history
History, Naval
  USE Naval history
History, Philosophy of
  USE History—Philosophy
History, Political
  USE subdivision Politics and government
    under the names of regions,
    countries, cities, etc.
    World politics
History, Public
  USE Public history
History, Universal
  USE World history
History (Buddhism)
  [BQ4570.H5]
  BT Buddhism—Doctrines
  NT Buddhism—History—Philosophy
    Saddharma
    Saddharmavipralopa
History (Islamic theology)
  BT History (Theology)
    Islam—Doctrines
— **Koranic teaching**
  [BP134.H57]
History (Theology)
  [BR115.H5]
  UF History—Theology
  BT Church and the world
    History—Philosophy
  NT History (Islamic theology)
    Time (Theology)
— **History of doctrines**
— — **Middle Ages, 600-1500**
  [BR115.H5]
— — **20th century**
History and art
  USE Art and history
History and language
  USE Language and history
History and literature
  USE Literature and history
History and moving-pictures
  USE Moving-pictures and history
History and personality
  USE Personality and history
History and poetry
  USE Literature and history
History and science
  USE Science and civilization
History and sex
  USE Sex and history
History and social sciences
  USE Social sciences and history
History in art
  Here are entered works dealing with the representation of historical events and characters. Works on the relation between art and history are entered under Art and history.
  UF Historical art
  RT Art and history
History in literature
  BT Literature and history
  NT Historical drama
    Historical fiction
    Historical poetry
History libraries
  USE Historical libraries
History of Achilles (Painting)
  USE Rubens, Peter Paul, Sir, 1577-1640.
    History of Achilles
History of Decius Mus (Painting)
  USE Rubens, Peter Paul Sir 1577-1640
    History of Decius Mus

History of matzah (Painting)
  USE Rivers, Larry, 1923-   History of matzah
History of religions school
  USE Religionsgeschichtliche Schule
History of the King (Tapestries)
  UF Histoire du Roi (Tapestries)
    Life of Louis XIV (Tapestries)
    Story of the King (Tapestries)
  BT Tapestry—France
History publishing (May Subd Geog)
  UF Historical publishing
    History—Publishing
  BT Publishers and publishing
  NT History—Sources—Publishing
History teachers (May Subd Geog)
  BT Teachers
Histosols (May Subd Geog)
  [S598 (General)]
  [S599-S599.9 (Local)]
  UF Folisols
    Organic soils
  BT Soils
  NT Humus
    Peat soils
Histrio
  [QL638.A577]
  BT Antennariidae
Histrionics
  USE Acting
    Theater
Hit-and-run drivers (May Subd Geog)
  UF Fleeing from scene of accident
    Leaving the scene of an automobile accident
  BT Automobile drivers
    Traffic accidents
    Traffic violations
Hit family
  USE Hitt family
Hita family (Not Subd Geog)
Hitachiōta Kaidō (Japan)
  USE Mito Kaidō (Japan)
Hitaka Mountain Range (Japan)
  USE Hidaka Mountain Range (Japan)
Hitch-hiking
  USE Hitchhiking
Hitchcock family (Not Subd Geog)
  UF Hichcock family
    Hichcox family
    Hitchcocks family
    Hitchcox family
    Hitchkok family
    Hitcock family
Hitchcocks family
  USE Hitchcock family
Hitchcox family
  USE Hitchcock family
Hitchen family
  USE Hitchings family
Hitchens family
  USE Hitchings family
Hitches
  USE Slings and hitches
Hitchhiking (May Subd Geog)
  UF Hitch-hiking
  BT Hiking
Hitchings family (Not Subd Geog)
  UF Hitchen family
    Hitchens family
    Hitchins family
    Hitchman family
Hitchins family
  USE Hitchings family
Hitchiti language
  [PM1341]
  UF Etcheetee language
    Etchita language
    Ichiti language
  RT Creek language

Hitchkok family
USE Hitchcock family
Hitchman family
USE Hitchings family
Hitchner family (Not Subd Geog)
Hitcock family
USE Hitchcock family
Hite, Isaac, ca. 1757-1836
— Homes and haunts
— — Virginia
NT Belle Grove (Va.)
Hite family (Not Subd Geog)
UF Height family
Heyd family
Heydt family
Highth family
Hights family
Hites family
Hites family
USE Hite family
Hitler, Adolf, 1889-1945
— Assassination attempt, 1944 (July 20)
[DD256.3]
BT Anti-Nazi movement—Germany
— Assassination attempts
Hitler's Putsch, 1923
USE Germany—History—Beer Hall Putsch,
1923
Hitotsubashi family (Not Subd Geog)
Hitt family (Not Subd Geog)
UF Hit family
Hitts family
Hittīn, Battle of, 1187
[D184.8]
BT Jerusalem—History—Latin Kingdom,
1099-1244
Hitting (Baseball)
USE Batting (Baseball)
Hittite art
USE Art, Hittite
Hittite cults (May Subd Geog)
BT Cults
Hittite deeds
USE Deeds, Hittite
Hittite funeral rites and ceremonies
USE Funeral rites and ceremonies, Hittite
Hittite gods
USE Gods, Hittite
Hittite inscriptions
USE Inscriptions, Hittite
Hittite language
[P945]
BT Anatolian languages
NT Luwian language
Palaic language
— Texts
— — Dating
Hittite law
USE Law, Hittite
Hittite literature
[P945]
Hittite medicine
USE Medicine, Hittite
Hittite mythology
USE Mythology, Hittite
Hittite oracles
USE Oracles, Hittite
Hittite relief (Sculpture)
USE Relief (Sculpture), Hittite
Hittite temples
USE Temples, Hittite
Hittites
[DS66]
UF Chatti
Kheta
Khita
BT Indo-Europeans
Syria—History—To 333 B.C.
NT Cypriote syllabary
Kaskans
— Queens

UF Tawananna
— Religion
[BL2370.H5]
NT Gods, Hittite
— Rites and ceremonies
UF Rites and ceremonies—Hittites
NT Funeral rites and ceremonies,
Hittite
Hitts family
USE Hitt family
Hitz family (Not Subd Geog)
HIV (Virus)
USE Human immunodeficiency viruses
HIV antibodies
USE Human immunodeficiency virus
antibodies
Hiva hoa (Marquesas Islands)
USE Hiva Oa (Marquesas Islands)
Hiva Oa (Marquesas Islands)
(Not Subd Geog)
UF Dominica (Marquesas Islands)
Dominique (Marquesas Islands)
Hiva hoa (Marquesas Islands)
Hiva roa (Marquesas Islands)
Hivaoa (Marquesas Islands)
Hiwaoa (Marquesas Islands)
BT Islands—Marquesas Islands
Hiva roa (Marquesas Islands)
USE Hiva Oa (Marquesas Islands)
Hivaoa (Marquesas Islands)
USE Hiva Oa (Marquesas Islands)
Hive bee
USE Honeybee
Hives, Bee
USE Honeybee—Housing
Hivner family
USE Heavener family
Hivon family (Not Subd Geog)
Hiwaoa (Marquesas Islands)
USE Hiva Oa (Marquesas Islands)
Hix family
USE Hicks family
Hixkaryana language
[PM6163]
UF Hishkaryana language
BT Cariban languages
Indians of South America—Languages
Hixon family
USE Hixson family
Hixs family
USE Hicks family
Hixson family (Not Subd Geog)
UF Hickson family
Hixon family
RT Hicks family
Ḥiyal (Islamic law)
USE Evasion (Islamic law)
Hiyoriyamajō (Ishinomaki-shi, Japan)
USE Ishinomakijō (Ishinomaki-shi, Japan)
Hjelmslev planes
UF Planes, Hjelmslev
BT Projective planes
Hjelmsø (Denmark)
BT Manors—Denmark
Hjeltnes family (Not Subd Geog)
Hjort family (Not Subd Geog)
UF Hjorth family
Hjorth family
USE Hjort family
Hjortlund family (Not Subd Geog)
Hka-kaw
USE Kaw people
Hkun language
USE Khün language
HL-A histocompatibility antigens
USE HLA histocompatibility antigens
HLA histocompatibility antigens
[QR184.32]

UF HL-A histocompatibility antigens
HLA transplantation antigens
Human leukocyte antigens
Transplantation antigens, Human
BT Histocompatibility antigens
RT Major histocompatibility complex
HLA transplantation antigens
USE HLA histocompatibility antigens
Hlaðir (Iceland)
BT Farms—Iceland
Hlubi (African people)
UF Amahlubi (African people)
Amahlubi tribe
BT Ethnology—South Africa
— History
NT Langalibalele Rebellion, 1873
Hluboká Castle (Czechoslovakia)
USE Zámek Hluboká (Czechoslovakia)
Hluda family (Not Subd Geog)
Hma Besisi (Malaysian people)
USE Mah-Meri (Malaysian people)
HMAC overlays
USE Pavements—Overlays
Hmar (Hill tribe)
[DS432.H5]
UF Mhar (Hill tribe)
Old Kukis
BT Ethnology—India
Hmar hymns
USE Hymns, Hmar
Hmar language
[PL4001.H55]
UF Hamar language
Mhar language
BT Kuki-Chin languages
Hmar poetry (May Subd Geog)
HMG-Coenzyme A reductases
USE Hydroxymethylglutaryl coenzyme A
reductases
HMO (Chemistry)
USE Hückel molecular orbitals
Hmong (Asian people) (May Subd Geog)
UF Hmu (Asian people)
Hmung (Asian people)
Humung (Asian people)
Meo (Asian people)
Miao (Asian people)
BT Ethnology—Asia
Hmong (Asian people) decorative arts
USE Decorative arts, Hmong (Asian people)
Hmong (Asian people) needlework
USE Needlework, Hmong (Asian people)
Hmong epic poetry
USE Epic poetry, Hmong
Hmong language (May Subd Geog)
UF Hmu language
Hmung language
Humung language
Meo language
Miao language
Mong language
BT Asia, Southeastern—Languages
NT Black Hmong dialect
White Hmong dialect
Hmong literature (May Subd Geog)
Hmong poetry (May Subd Geog)
NT Epic poetry, Hmong
HMOs
USE Health maintenance organizations
HMP (Biochemistry)
USE Pentose phosphate pathway
HMS (Biochemistry)
USE Pentose phosphate pathway
Hmu (Asian people)
USE Hmong (Asian people)
Hmu language
USE Hmong language
Hmung (Asian people)
USE Hmong (Asian people)
Hmung language
USE Hmong language

Ho (Munda tribe)
USE Hos
Hồ Chí Minh, 1890-1969, in motion pictures
BT Moving-pictures
Hồ family *(Not Subd Geog)*
⌐CS1339.H¬
Ho language
⌐PL4547¬
BT Munda languages
Hồ Tây (Vietnam)
USE West Lake (Vietnam)
Hoa Lư (City) *(Not Subd Geog)*
⌐DS559.93.H63¬
BT Cities and towns, Ruined, extinct, etc.
—Vietnam
Vietnam—Antiquities
Hoactzin
⌐QL696.G26¬
UF Hoatzin
Opisthocomi
Opisthocomidae
BT Galliformes
Hoafman family
USE Hoffman family
Hoag family
USE Hogg family
Hoaghan family
USE Hogan family
Hoakes family
USE Hawk family
Hoalt family
USE Holt family
Hoang Ho (China)
USE Yellow River (China)
Hoàng Sa
USE Paracel Islands
Hoar, Depth
USE Depth hoar
Hoar family *(Not Subd Geog)*
UF Hoare family
Hore family
Hoarding of money
UF Money, Hoarding of
BT Currency question
Money
NT Misers
Hoards
USE Coin hoards
Hoare family
USE Hoar family
Hoarseness
BT Symptomatology
Voice disorders
Hoatzin
USE Hoactzin
Hoaxes
USE Impostors and imposture
Hobb family
USE Hobbs family
Hobbes family
USE Hobbs family
Hobbies
⌐GV1201¬
UF Avocations
Recreations
BT Amusements
Collectors and collecting
Handicraft
Leisure
Play
Recreation
NT Beachcombing
Music as recreation
— **Equipment and supplies**
NT Hobby equipment industry
Hobbs family *(Not Subd Geog)*
UF Hobb family
Hobbes family
Hobes family
Hobs family

Hobby equipment industry
(May Subd Geog)
BT Hobbies—Equipment and supplies
Hobby-horses
USE Hobbyhorses
Hobby rooms
USE Recreation rooms
Hobbyhorses *(May Subd Geog)*
UF Hobby-horses
Horses, Hobby
Stick horses
BT Horses—Folklore
Toy horses
**Hobcaw Plantation Site (Mount Pleasant,
S.C.)** *(Not Subd Geog)*
BT Plantations—South Carolina
South Carolina—Antiquities
Hobermill family
USE Hovermale family
Hobes family
USE Hobbs family
Hobgoblins
USE Goblins
Hobkirk's Hill, Battle of, 1781
⌐E241.H¬
BT South Carolina—History—Revolution,
1775-1783
Hoblik (Czechoslovakia)
USE Oblík (Czechoslovakia)
Hobo songs
⌐M1977.H6¬
⌐M1978.H6¬
UF Tramps—Songs and music
Hoboes
USE Tramps
Hobs family
USE Hobbs family
Hobsen family
USE Hobson family
Hobson family *(Not Subd Geog)*
UF Hobsen family
Hobson-jobson
UF Anglo-Indian dialect
BT Languages, Mixed
Hocam family
USE Hocum family
Hoch family *(Not Subd Geog)*
UF Hoche family
RT High family
Hook family
Hochaltar von Sankt Petri
USE Bertram, of Minden, ca. 1340-ca.
1415. Grabow altarpiece
Hochblättern
USE Hypsophylls
Hoche family
USE Hoch family
Hochheimer wine
USE Hock (Wine)
Hochkirch, Battle of, 1758
⌐DD412.6.H7¬
UF Bukec, Battle of, 1758
BT Seven Years' War, 1756-1763
Hochkönig Glacier (Austria)
UF Hochköniggletscher (Austria)
BT Glaciers—Austria
Hochköniggletscher (Austria)
USE Hochkönig Glacier (Austria)
Hochschwab Alps (Austria)
BT Alps
Alps, Austrian (Austria)
Mountains—Austria
Hochstaden family *(Not Subd Geog)*
UF Von Hochstaden family
Höchstädt, Battle of, 1704
USE Blenheim, Battle of, 1704
Hochster family *(Not Subd Geog)*
Hochstetter Foreland (Greenland)
USE Hochstetter Forland (Greenland)

Hochstetter Forland (Greenland)
UF Hochstetter Foreland (Greenland)
Hochstetter Peninsula (Greenland)
Hochstetters Forland (Greenland)
BT Peninsulas—Greenland
Hochstetter Peninsula (Greenland)
USE Hochstetter Forland (Greenland)
Hochstetters Forland (Greenland)
USE Hochstetter Forland (Greenland)
Hochtaunus (Germany)
USE Taunus (Germany)
Hock (Wine)
⌐TP559.G3¬
UF Hochheimer wine
BT Wine and wine making
Hock disease
USE Perosis
Hockett family *(Not Subd Geog)*
UF Hoggatt family
Hockey *(May Subd Geog)*
⌐GV847¬
UF Ice hockey
BT Winter sports
NT Field hockey
Hockey—Offense
Hockey players
Indoor hockey
Lawn hockey
Polo (on skates)
Ring hockey
Roller polo
Roller-skate hockey
Stanley Cup (Hockey)
— **Biography**
— **Clubs**
⌐GV848¬
UF Hockey clubs
BT Athletic clubs
— **Coaches**
UF Hockey coaches
BT Coaches (Athletics)
— **Coaching**
⌐GV848.25¬
UF Hockey coaching
BT Coaching (Athletics)
— **Defense**
UF Defensive hockey
— **Goalkeeping**
— — **Equipment and supplies**
NT Hockey masks
— **Offense**
⌐GV848.7¬
UF Offensive hockey
BT Hockey
— **Rules**
⌐GV847.5¬
— **Training**
⌐GV848.3¬
Hockey clubs
USE Hockey—Clubs
Hockey coaches
USE Hockey—Coaches
Hockey coaching
USE Hockey—Coaching
Hockey in art
Hockey masks *(May Subd Geog)*
⌐GV848.73¬
UF Masks, Hockey
BT Hockey—Goalkeeping—Equipment
and supplies
Hockey players *(May Subd Geog)*
⌐GV848.5¬
BT Hockey
NT Centers (Hockey)
Field hockey players
Hocking Hills State Park and Forest (Ohio)
(Not Subd Geog)
UF Hocking State Park (Ohio)
BT Forest reserves—Ohio
Parks—Ohio

Hocking State Park (Ohio)
    USE Hocking Hills State Park and Forest
        (Ohio)
Hocum family *(Not Subd Geog)*
    UF Hocam family
        Hokam family
        Hokom family
        Hokum family
    RT Holcomb family
Hod Hill Site (England)
    BT England—Antiquities
Hodaka-dake (Japan)
    USE Hotaka Mountain (Japan)
Hodaka motorcycle
    [*TL448.H*]
Hodal family *(Not Subd Geog)*
    UF Haugdahl family
        Haugdal family
Hodari (The Japanese word)
    BT Japanese language—Etymology
Hodge family
    USE Hodges family
Hodge theory
    BT Complex manifolds
        Differentiable manifolds
        Geometry, Algebraic
        Homology theory
Hodgekiss family
    USE Hotchkiss family
Hodges family *(Not Subd Geog)*
    UF Hadges family
        Hodge family
        Hodgis family
Hodgeson family
    USE Hodson family
Hodgin family
    USE Hodgkins family
Hodgins family
    USE Hodgkins family
Hodgis family
    USE Hodges family
Hodgkin family
    USE Hodgkins family
Hodgkings family
    USE Hodgkins family
Hodgkin's disease *(May Subd Geog)*
    [*RC644*]
    UF Lymphadenoma
        Lymphogranuloma
        Lymphogranulomatosis
        Lymphosarcoma
        Pseudoleucemia
    BT Lymphomas
        Lymphoproliferative disorders
Hodgkins family *(Not Subd Geog)*
    UF Hodgin family
        Hodgins family
        Hodgkin family
        Hodgkings family
        Hodgkinson family
        Hodgskin family
        Hodgskins family
        Hodkin family
        Hodkins family
        Hodskin family
        Hodskings family
        Hodskins family
        Hogekins family
        Hogskem family
    RT Hotchkiss family
Hodgkinson family
    USE Hodgkins family
Hodgskin family
    USE Hodgkins family
Hodgskins family
    USE Hodgkins family
Hodgson family
    USE Hodson family
Hodkin family
    USE Hodgkins family

Hodkins family
    USE Hodgkins family
**Hodler, Ferdinand, 1853-1918.   Call from
afar**
    [*ND853.H6*]
    UF Call from afar (Painting)
        Lied aus der Ferne (Painting)
Hodograph
    [*QA841*]
    BT Kinematics
Hodograph equations
    UF Equations, Hodograph
    BT Differential equations, Partial
        Fluid mechanics
Hodotermitidae
    [*QL529.3.H6*]
    UF Dampwood termites
    BT Termites
    NT Zootermopsis
Hodskin family
    USE Hodgkins family
Hodskings family
    USE Hodgkins family
Hodskins family
    USE Hodgkins family
Hodson family *(Not Subd Geog)*
    UF Hodgeson family
        Hodgson family
        Hogson family
        Hogston family
Hodzana River (Alaska) *(Not Subd Geog)*
    BT Rivers—Alaska
Hoefling family
    USE Hofeling family
Hoeft family *(Not Subd Geog)*
Hoeg family *(Not Subd Geog)*
    UF Hyg family
    RT High family
        Hogg family
Hoeing family
    USE Hoing family
Hoeker family *(Not Subd Geog)*
    UF Hoekert family
    RT Hook family
Hoekert family
    USE Hoeker family
Hoelscher family *(Not Subd Geog)*
    UF Holscher family
Höen family
    USE Hüner family
Hoenig family *(Not Subd Geog)*
    UF Hoening family
        Hönig family
Hoening family
    USE Hoenig family
Hoepfner family
    USE Hepner family
Hoepner family
    USE Hepner family
Hoeppener family
    USE Hepner family
Hoeppler family
    USE Hepler family
Hoeppner family
    USE Hepner family
Hoes *(May Subd Geog)*
    [*S683*]
    BT Agricultural implements
        Garden tools
Hoes family *(Not Subd Geog)*
    UF Hoos family
        Hoose family
Hoetzel family
    USE Hutzel family
Hoeve family
    USE Hoeven family
Hoëveldgebied (South Africa)
    USE Highveld Area (South Africa)

Hoeven family *(Not Subd Geog)*
    UF Hoeve family
        Van der Hoeve family
        Van der Hoeven family
Hoey family *(Not Subd Geog)*
    UF Van Hoey family
Hof family
    USE Hoff family
Hofämterspiel (Game)
    [*GV1295.H57*]
Hofburg (Vienna, Austria)
    UF Imperial Palace (Vienna, Austria)
    BT Palaces—Austria
Hofburg Spear
    USE Holy Lance
Hofeli family
    USE Hofeling family
Hofeling family *(Not Subd Geog)*
    UF Hoefling family
        Hofeli family
        Hofling family
Hofeman family
    USE Hoffman family
Hofemen family
    USE Hoffman family
Hoff family *(Not Subd Geog)*
    UF Hof family
        Hoof family
        Hoofes family
        Hooff family
    RT Hoffer family
Hoffar family
    USE Hoffer family
Hoffard family
    USE Hoffer family
Hoffeman family
    USE Hoffman family
Hoffer family *(Not Subd Geog)*
    UF Hoffar family
        Hoffard family
        Hofferd family
        Hoffert family
        Hofford family
    RT Hoff family
Hoffer-Osmond diagnostic test
    [*BF698.8.H53*]
    UF Osmond-Hoffer diagnostic test
    BT Personality tests
        Schizophrenia—Diagnosis
Hofferd family
    USE Hoffer family
Hoffert family
    USE Hoffer family
Hoffman Brook (Chemung County, N.Y.)
    UF Hoffman Creek (N.Y.)
    BT Rivers—New York (State)
Hoffman Creek (N.Y.)
    USE Hoffman Brook (Chemung County,
        N.Y.)
Hoffman family *(Not Subd Geog)*
    UF Hafman family
        Hoafman family
        Hofeman family
        Hofemen family
        Hoffeman family
        Hoffmann family
        Hoffmon family
        Hofman family
        Hoofman family
        Huffman family
        Huffmann family
        Hufman family
Hoffmann family
    USE Hoffman family
Hoffmann kiln
    [*TH842.H7*]
    BT Kilns
Hoffmann-Woodward rule
    USE Conservation of orbital symmetry
Hoffmeier family
    USE Hoffmeyer family

Hoffmeister family (*Not Subd Geog*)
  UF Hofmeister family
      Huffmaster family
Hoffmeyer family (*Not Subd Geog*)
  UF Hoffmeier family
Hoffmon family
  USE Hoffman family
Hofford family
  USE Hoffer family
Hofling family
  USE Hofeling family
Hofman family
  USE Hoffman family
Hofmeister family
  USE Hoffmeister family
Hog Bluff Site (Ill.)
  BT Illinois—Antiquities
Hog cholera (*May Subd Geog*)
  ₍SF973₎
  UF Swine fever
  — **Diagnosis**
  — **Preventive inoculation**
Hog family
  USE Hogg family
Hog houses
  USE Swine—Housing
Hog Island (Va.)
  BT Barrier islands—Virginia
Hog Latin
  USE Pig Latin
Hog lice
  UF Haematopinus suis
  BT Lice
Hog-nosed snakes
  USE Hognose snakes
Hogan, Robert J.
  — **Characters**
  — — **G-8**
      RT G-8 (Fictitious character)
Hogan family (*Not Subd Geog*)
  UF Hoaghan family
      Hogans family
      Hogean family
      Hogen family
Hogans family
  USE Hogan family
**Hogarth, William, 1697-1764. Marriage à la
  mode**
  UF Marriage à la mode (Engravings)
      Marriage à la mode (Paintings)
Hogbacks
  USE Cuestas
Hoge family
  USE Hogg family
Hoge Venen (Belgium and Germany)
  USE Hautes Fagnes (Belgium and
      Germany)
Hogean family
  USE Hogan family
Hogekins family
  USE Hodgkins family
Hogelu Islands (Micronesia)
  USE Truk Islands (Micronesia)
Hogem Batholith (B.C.)
  BT Batholiths—British Columbia
Hōgen Civil War, 1156
  USE Japan—History—Hōgen and Heiji
      Insurrections, 1156-1159
Hogen family
  USE Hogan family
Hōgen monogatari emaki (Paintings)
  ₍ND1059.6.H₎
  BT Scrolls, Japanese
Hōgen Uprising, 1156
  USE Japan—History—Hōgen and Heiji
      Insurrections, 1156-1159
Hoges family
  USE Hogg family
Hogeschoolrijdster (Painting)
  USE Gogh, Vincent van, 1853-1890.
      Hogeschoolrijdster

Hogewood family
  USE Hogwood family
Hogg family (*Not Subd Geog*)
  UF Hoag family
      Hog family
      Hoge family
      Hoges family
      Hogge family
      Hogges family
      Hoggs family
      Hogue family
  RT Hoeg family
Hoggar Mountains (Algeria)
  USE Ahaggar Mountains (Algeria)
Hoggatt family
  USE Hockett family
Hogge family
  USE Hogg family
Hogges family
  USE Hogg family
Hoggs family
  USE Hogg family
Hogni (Medieval literary character)
  USE Hagen (Medieval literary character)
Hognose snakes
  UF Blow vipers
      Blowing adders
      Flatheaded adders
      Hissing adders
      Hog-nosed snakes
      Puffing adders
  NT Eastern hognose snake
      Western hognose snake
Hogolen Islands (Micronesia)
  USE Truk Islands (Micronesia)
Hogoleu Islands (Micronesia)
  USE Truk Islands (Micronesia)
Hogolin Islands (Micronesia)
  USE Truk Islands (Micronesia)
Hogs
  USE Swine
Hogs, Wild
  USE Feral swine
      Wild boar
Hogskem family
  USE Hodgkins family
Hogson family
  USE Hodson family
Hogston family
  USE Hodson family
Hogue, La, Battle of, 1692
  ₍D280.H6₎
  BT Grand Alliance, War of the, 1689-
      1697—Campaigns—France
Hogue family
  USE Hogg family
Hogwood family (*Not Subd Geog*)
  UF Hogewood family
  RT Hagood family
      Hayward family
      Haywood family
Hogy (The Hungarian word)
  BT Hungarian language—Etymology
Hoh River (Wash.)
  BT Rivers—Washington (State)
Hohe Tatra (Czechoslovakia and Poland)
  USE Tatra Mountains (Czechoslovakia and
      Poland)
Hohe Tauern (Austria)
  UF Tauern Mountains (Austria)
      Tauernberg (Austria)
  BT Alps, Eastern
      Mountains—Austria
  RT Nationalpark Hohe Tauern (Austria)
Hohe Tauern, Nationalpark (Austria)
  USE Nationalpark Hohe Tauern (Austria)
Hohe Venn (Belgium and Germany)
  USE Hautes Fagnes (Belgium and
      Germany)
Hohemes family
  USE Holmes family

Hohenfeld family (*Not Subd Geog*)
Hohenfriedberg, Battle of, 1745
  ₍DD407.H7₎
  BT Silesian War, 2d, 1744-1745
Hohenlohe (Germany)
Hohenlohe family (*Not Subd Geog*)
Hohenmeisner (Germany)
  USE Meissner Mountain (Germany)
Hohenstaufen, House of (*Not Subd Geog*)
  BT Germany—Kings and rulers
Hohenstein family (*Not Subd Geog*)
  UF Thun-Hohenstein family
Hohenzollern, House of (*Not Subd Geog*)
  BT Germany—Kings and rulers
Hoher Böhmerwald (Czechoslovakia)
  USE Šumava (Czechoslovakia)
Hoher Dachstein (Austria)
  USE Dachstein Mountains (Austria)
Hoher Fläming (Germany)
  UF Der Hohe Fläming (Germany)
      Fläming, Hoher (Germany)
Hoher Göll (Austria and Germany)
  UF Göll, Hoher (Austria and Germany)
  BT Mountains—Austria
      Mountains—Germany (West)
Hoher Meissner (Germany)
  USE Meissner Mountain (Germany)
Hoher Taunus (Germany)
  USE Taunus (Germany)
Hohes Venn (Belgium and Germany)
  USE Hautes Fagnes (Belgium and
      Germany)
Hohing family
  USE Hoing family
Hohl family (*Not Subd Geog*)
  UF Hohlen family
Hohlen family
  USE Hohl family
Hohmes family
  USE Holmes family
Hohokam culture
Hoiet family
  USE Hoyt family
Hoinck family
  USE Hoing family
Hoing family (*Not Subd Geog*)
  UF Hoeing family
      Hohing family
      Hoinck family
      Hoink family
      Howen family
      Howing family
      Hoying family
      Hoynck family
      Hoyng family
      Hoynk family
      Huinck family
      Huing family
      Hujink family
Hoink family
  USE Hoing family
Hoisting machinery
  ₍TJ1350-1383₎
  UF Lifts
  BT Construction equipment
  RT Conveying machinery
      Mining machinery
  NT Capstan
      Cargo handling—Equipment
      Chains
      Cranes, derricks, etc.
      Elevators
      Fork lift trucks
      Marine railways
      Mine hoisting
      Stacking machines
      Vacuum lifters
      Winches
      Windlasses
      Wire-rope transportation
  — Appraisal

Hoisting machinery
— Appraisal *(Continued)*
   USE Hoisting machinery—Valuation
— **Brakes**
— Drawing
   USE Hoisting machinery—Drawings
— **Drawings**
   UF Hoisting machinery—Drawing
   BT Mechanical drawing
— **Dynamics**
— **Electric driving**
— **Electric equipment**
— **Foundations**
— **Hydraulic equipment**
— **Rigging**
   [TJ1367]
   BT Masts and rigging
      Slings and hitches
— **Transmission devices**
   BT Gearing
— **Valuation**
   UF Hoisting machinery—Appraisal
Hoit family
   USE Hoyt family
Hoitt family
   USE Hoyt family
Hōjō family *(Not Subd Geog)*
Hokaltecan languages
   USE Hokan-Coahuiltecan languages
Hokam family
   USE Hocum family
Hokamish Indians
   USE Skokomish Indians
Hokan-Coahuiltecan languages
   [PM1343]
   UF Hokaltecan languages
   NT Hokan languages
      Pakawan languages
Hokan languages
   BT Hokan-Coahuiltecan languages
   NT Tlapanec language
Hoke family
   USE Hook family
Hoker family
   USE Hook family
Ḥokhmah (Biblical character)
   USE Wisdom (Biblical character)
Hokianga Harbor (N.Z.)
   BT Harbors—New Zealand
Hokkaidō dog
   USE Ainu dog
Hokkaidōchō Kyū Honchōsha (Sapporo-shi, Japan)
   UF Akarenga Chōsha (Sapporo-shi, Japan)
   BT Public buildings—Japan
Hokkedō, Tōdaiji (Nara-shi, Japan)
   USE Tōdaiji (Nara-shi, Japan)—Hokkedō
Hokkerup, Battle of, 1940
   BT World War, 1939-1945—Campaigns—Denmark
Hokku
   USE Haiku
Hoko River Site (Wash.)
   BT Washington (State)—Antiquities
Hōkoku Festival in art
   NT Hōkoku sairei zu (Screen painting)
Hōkoku sairei zu (Screen painting)
   [ND1053.5]
   UF Toyokuni Daimyōjin rinji sairei zu (Screen painting)
   BT Genre painting, Japanese
      Hōkoku Festival in art
      Painting, Japanese—Edo period, 1600-1868
      Screen painting, Japanese
Hokom family
   USE Hocum family
Hokubu-shotō (Japan)
   USE Amami Islands (Japan)
Hokum family
   USE Hocum family

Hokuriku Region (Japan)
Hokusai School
   USE Katsushika School
Hol ha-Moed
   [BM693.H64]
   UF Chol ha-Moed
   BT Fasts and feasts—Judaism
      Passover
      Sukkot
Holacanthodes
   USE Acanthodes
Holacanthus
   [QL638.P768]
   UF Holocanthus
   BT Pomacanthidae
Holahan family
   USE Houlihan family
Holander family
   USE Holland family
Holandesa cattle
   USE Turino cattle
Holando-Argentino cattle
   UF Argentine Friesian cattle
      Dutch Argentine cattle
Holapogon
   [QL638.A7]
   BT Apogonidae
Holapogon maximus
   [QL638.A7]
   UF Apogon maximus
Holbæk Fjord, Denmark
Holbein, Hans, 1497-1543. Ambassadors
   [ND588.H7]
   UF Ambassadors (Painting)
      Gesandten (Painting)
      Scholars (Painting)
Holbein embroidery
   USE Blackwork embroidery
Holben family *(Not Subd Geog)*
Holbert family *(Not Subd Geog)*
   UF Halbert family
      Halbud family
      Hallbert family
      Helbert family
      Hulbert family
      Hulburt family
   RT Hurlburt family
Holbrock family
   USE Holbrook family
Holbrook family *(Not Subd Geog)*
   UF Halbrook family
      Hallbrook family
      Holbrock family
      Holbrooke family
      Holbrooks family
      Holdbrook family
      Holebrook family
      Hollbrook family
      Hoolbrook family
Holbrooke family
   USE Holbrook family
Holbrookia
   [QL666.L25]
   BT Iguanidae
   NT Holbrookia maculata
Holbrookia maculata
   [QL666.L25]
   UF Lesser earless lizard
   BT Holbrookia
Holbrookia proquina
   USE Keeled earless lizard
Holbrooks family
   USE Holbrook family
Holcer family
   USE Holzer family
Holcolmb family
   USE Holcomb family
Holcom family
   USE Holcomb family

Holcomb family *(Not Subd Geog)*
   UF Halcom family
      Halcomb family
      Holcolmb family
      Holcom family
      Holcombe family
   RT Hocum family
Holcombe family
   USE Holcomb family
Holconotus rhodoterus
   USE Redtail surfperch
Holcopasites *(May Subd Geog)*
   [QL568.A4]
   BT Andrenidae
Holcopogonidae
   [QL561.H]
   BT Lepidoptera
      Moths
Holczer family
   USE Holzer family
Hold harmless agreements *(May Subd Geog)*
   UF Exception from liability clauses
      Exclusion from liabiliby clauses
      Exemption from liability clauses
   BT Clauses (Law)
   RT Indemnity against liability
Holdbrook family
   USE Holbrook family
Holden automobile
Holden Mine (Wash.)
   [TN380.H]
   BT Mines and mineral resources—Washington (State)
Holder in due course *(May Subd Geog)*
   BT Banking law
      Bills of exchange
      Negotiable instruments
Holderness (England)
   BT Peninsulas—England
Holders, Pot
   USE Potholders
Holders of speed records
   USE Speed record holders
Holdery family
   USE Holtry family
Holding companies *(May Subd Geog)*
   [HD2709-HD2930 (Corporations)]
   [HD2771-HD2798 (Corporations: United States)]
   [HG4001-HG4280 (Finance)]
   UF Combinations, Industrial
      Companies, Holding
   BT Cartels
      Corporations
   RT Subsidiary corporations
      Trusts, Industrial
   NT Bank holding companies
      Government holding companies
      Insurance holding companies
      Public utility holding companies
— **Accounting**
   NT Financial statements, Consolidated
Holding patterns (Aeronautics) *(May Subd Geog)*
   [TL711.H65]
   Here are entered works on the maneuvers that keep an aircraft within a racetrack-shaped flight pattern anchored at one end to a holding fix while awaiting further clearance from air traffic control.
   UF Aircraft holding patterns
      Patterns, Holding (Aeronautics)
   BT Airplanes—Piloting
Holdree family
   USE Holtry family
Holdreth family
   USE Hildreth family
Holds, Wrestling
   USE Wrestling holds
Hole family
   USE Holl family

Holebrook family
USE Holbrook family
Holen family *(Not Subd Geog)*
Holensworth family
USE Hollingsworth family
Holes
UF Apertures
Cavities
Openings (Holes)
Orifices
Perforations
Pits (Holes)
BT Surfaces
NT Buttonholes
Manholes
Potholes
Potholes (Roads)
Holes (Electron deficiencies)
[QC611.6.H6]
UF Holes (Semiconductors)
Negative ion vacancy
BT Crystals—Defects
Energy-band theory of solids
Semiconductors
RT Excess electrons
NT Electron-hole droplets
Hot carriers
Positrons
Holes (Semiconductors)
USE Holes (Electron deficiencies)
Holestin family
USE Holstein family
Holey dollar *(May Subd Geog)*
UF Colonial dollar
Pierced dollar
Ring dollar
BT Piece of eight
Holgate family *(Not Subd Geog)*
Holī (Hindu festival)
BT Fasts and feasts—Hinduism
Holiday cookery
[TX739]
BT Cookery
Holidays
NT Christmas cookery
Easter cookery
Hanukkah cookery
Passover cookery
Thanksgiving cookery
Holiday decorations
UF Decorations, Holiday
BT Decoration and ornament
NT Christmas decorations
Easter decorations
Halloween decorations
Hanukkah decorations
New Year decorations, etc.
Saint Patrick's Day decorations
Thanksgiving decorations
Holiday family
USE Holliday family
Holiday houses
USE Vacation homes
Holidays *(May Subd Geog)*
[GT3930-GT4995 *(Manners and customs)*]
[HV3167 *(For shop workers)*]
[JK1761 *(National: United States)*]
[PN4305.H7 *(Recitations)*]
UF Legal holidays
National holidays
BT Days
Festivals
Hours of labor
Manners and customs
Memorials
RT Anniversaries
Fasts and feasts
Vacations
NT Arbor Day
Bird Day

Christmas
Columbus Day
Dingaan's Day
Empire Day
Father's Day
Flag Day
Groundhog Day
Holiday cookery
John Marshall Day
John the Baptist's Day
Labor Day
Library Day
May Day
May Day (Labor holiday)
Memorial Day
Mother's Day
New Year
Pan American Day
Patriots' Day
Peace Day
Saint Andrew's Day
Saint David's Day
Saint Joseph's Day
Saint Martin's Day
Saint Patrick's Day
Saint Stephen's Day
Saint Valentine's Day
Saint Vitus Day
Schools—Exercises and recreations
St. George's Day
Thanksgiving Day
Weekly rest-day
World Health Day
— **Exercises, recitations, etc.**
[PN4305.H7 *(English)*]
BT Recitations
— Jews
USE Fasts and feasts—Judaism
— **Law and legislation** *(May Subd Geog)*
RT Sunday legislation
— **Psychological aspects**
— **Songs and music**
SA *subdivision* Songs and music *under special days, e.g.* Fourth of July —Songs and music; Mother's Day—Songs and music
NT Christmas music
Easter music
— **Afghanistan**
NT Independence Day (Afghanistan)
— **Australia**
NT Anzac Day
Australia Day
— **Bahamas**
NT Independence Day (Bahamas)
— **Canada**
NT Dominion Day (Canada)
— **Chile**
NT Independence Day (Chile)
— **Costa Rica**
NT Independence Day (Costa Rica)
— **Djibouti**
NT Independence Day (Djibouti)
— **France**
NT Bastille Day
— **Greece**
NT Hēmera tou Ochi (Greek holiday)
— **India**
NT Independence Day (India)
Republic Day (India)
— **Israel**
NT Independence Day (Israel)
Yom ha-zikaron
— **Japan**
NT Kempō Kinenbi (Japanese holiday)
Kenkoku Kinen no hi
— **Lithuania**
NT Sixteenth of February
— **Malaysia**
NT Independence Day (Malaysia)
— **Mexico**

NT Cinco de Mayo (Mexican holiday)
Independence Day (Mexico)
— **New Zealand**
NT Anzac Day
— **Norway**
NT Independence Day (Norway)
— **Papua New Guinea**
NT Independence Day (Papua New Guinea)
— **Philippines**
NT Independence Day (Philippines)
— **Spain**
NT Onze de setembre (Catalan holiday)
— **Surinam**
NT Independence Day (Surinam)
— **United States**
NT Confederate Memorial Day
Election Day
Fourth of July
Inauguration Day
Lincoln Day
Veterans Day
Washington's Birthday
— **Yugoslavia**
NT Dan Republike (Yugoslavia)
Holidays, High
USE High Holidays
Holidays, Jewish
USE Fasts and feasts—Judaism
Holidays in art
Holidays with pay
USE Vacations, Employee
Holiness
[BT767]
BT Holy, The
Salvation
RT Perfection—Religious aspects
Sanctification
NT Church—Holiness
Consecration
— **Buddhism, [Christianity, etc.]**
Holiness churches *(May Subd Geog)*
Here are entered works dealing with the various modern church bodies stressing the doctrine of holiness.
BT Christian sects—United States
Pentecostal churches
RT Church of God
NT Snake cults (Holiness churches)
Holiness of God
USE God—Holiness
Holingsworth family
USE Hollingsworth family
Holinsworth family
USE Hollingsworth family
Holism
[B818]
UF Wholism
BT Evolution
Whole and parts (Philosophy)
NT Holistic medicine
Holister family
USE Hollis family
Holistic health
USE Holistic medicine
Holistic medicine *(May Subd Geog)*
UF Holistic health
Wholistic medicine
BT Holism
Medicine
Therapeutic systems
RT Health
Mind and body
NT Self-care, Health
— **Religious aspects**
— — **Buddhism, [Christianity, etc.]**
Holl family *(Not Subd Geog)*
UF Hole family
Holla family
USE Hallo family

1711

Hollabrunn (Hollabrunn, Austria), Battle of,
1805
  BT Napoleonic Wars, 1800-1814—
      Campaigns—Austria
Holladay family
  USE Holliday family
Holladays family
  USE Holliday family
Hollam family
  USE Hallam family
Holland
  USE Netherlands
Holland family *(Not Subd Geog)*
  UF Holander family
      Hollander family
Hollandaise (Contract bridge)
  USE Goulasch (Contract bridge)
Hollander family
  USE Holland family
Hollandidae
  USE Cossidae
Hollandsche IJssel River (Netherlands)
  UF Hollandsche Yssel River (Netherlands)
      Hollandse IJssel River (Netherlands)
      Hollandse Yssel River (Netherlands)
      IJssel River (Utrecht Province-South
          Holland, Netherlands)
      Yssel River (Utrecht Province-South
          Holland, Netherlands)
  BT Rivers—Netherlands
Hollandsche Ijzeren Spoorweg
  BT Railroads—Netherlands
Hollandsche Yssel River (Netherlands)
  USE Hollandsche IJssel River (Netherlands)
Hollandse IJssel River (Netherlands)
  USE Hollandsche IJssel River (Netherlands)
Hollandse Yssel River (Netherlands)
  USE Hollandsche IJssel River (Netherlands)
Hollandsworth family
  USE Hollingsworth family
Hollar family *(Not Subd Geog)*
  UF Holler family
  RT Haller family
Hollaway family
  USE Holloway family
Hollawel family
  USE Hallowell family
Hollawell family
  USE Hallowell family
Hollbrook family
  USE Holbrook family
Hollenbeck family *(Not Subd Geog)*
  RT Hallenbeck family
Holler family
  USE Hollar family
Hollevoet family *(Not Subd Geog)*
Holley carburetors
  BT Automobiles—Motors—Carburetors
Holley family *(Not Subd Geog)*
  UF Hollie family
      Holly family
  RT Hawley family
Holliday family *(Not Subd Geog)*
  UF Haliday family
      Halladay family
      Hallade family
      Halliday family
      Holiday family
      Holladay family
      Holladays family
      Hollyday family
**Hollidaysburg Presbyterian Cemetery
(Hollidaysburg, Pa.)**
  BT Cemeteries—Pennsylvania
Hollie family
  USE Holley family
Hollim family
  USE Hallam family

Hollingsworth family *(Not Subd Geog)*
  UF Hallensworth family
      Holensworth family
      Holingsworth family
      Holinsworth family
      Hollandsworth family
      Hollinsworth family
      Hollondsworth family
Hollinsworth family
  USE Hollingsworth family
Hollis family *(Not Subd Geog)*
  UF Holister family
      Hollister family
      Hollistor family
Hollister Adobe (San Luis Obispo, Calif.)
  BT Dwellings—California
Hollister family
  USE Hollis family
Hollistor family
  USE Hollis family
Hollo family
  USE Hallo family
Hollondsworth family
  USE Hollingsworth family
Hollow bricks *(May Subd Geog)*
  BT Bricks
      Tiles
  NT Tile construction
Hollow charges (Explosives)
  USE Shaped charges
Hollow family
  USE Hallo family
Hollow ground saws
  USE Planer saws
Hollow tile construction
  USE Tile construction
Hollow tiles
      Here are entered works on tiles as building materi-
  al. Works on the construction of buildings and other
  engineering structures with tiles are entered under
  the heading Tile construction.
  UF Tiles, Hollow
  BT Tiles
Hollow ware, Silver
  USE Silverware
Holloway family *(Not Subd Geog)*
  UF Hallaway family
      Halloway family
      Hollaway family
      Holway family
Hollowell family
  USE Hallowell family
Hollum family
  USE Hallam family
Hollwell family
  USE Hallowell family
Holly
      ⌈QK495.I3⌉
  NT Ilex vomitoria
  — Varieties
Holly family
  USE Holley family
Hollyburton family
  USE Halliburton family
Hollyday family
  USE Holliday family
Hollywell family
  USE Hallowell family
Hollywood Boulevard (Los Angeles, Calif.)
  (Not Subd Geog)
  BT Streets—California
Hollywood Cemetery (Richmond, Va.)
  BT Cemeteries—Virginia
  BT Cemeteries—Virginia
Holm, Beret (Fictitious character)
  UF Beret Holm (Fictitious character)
  BT Characters and characteristics in
      literature
  RT Rølvaag, O.E. (Ole Edvart), 1876-1931
      —Characters—Beret Holm

Holm family
  USE Holmes family
Holm oak *(May Subd Geog)*
  UF Quercus ilex
  BT Oak
Holman family *(Not Subd Geog)*
  UF Holmans family
      Holmen family
      Holmon family
Holmans Creek (Va.)
  BT Rivers—Virginia
Holmans family
  USE Holman family
Holme family
  USE Holmes family
Holmead's Cemetery (Washington, D.C.)
  UF Western Burial Ground (Washington,
      D.C.)
  BT Cemeteries—Washington (D.C.)
Holmen family
  USE Holman family
Holmes, Sherlock (Fictitious character)
  NT Sherlock Holmes films
Holmes' comet
      ⌈QB723.H7⌉
Holmes family *(Not Subd Geog)*
  UF Hohemes family
      Hohmes family
      Holm family
      Holme family
      Hom family
      Home family
      Hommes family
      Hooms family
  RT Hume family
Holmesella
  USE Acanthodes
Holmgaard family *(Not Subd Geog)*
Holmic oxide
  USE Holmium oxide
Holmium
  — Isotopes
      UF Holmium isotopes
          Isotopic holmium
  — — **Decay**
Holmium isotopes
  USE Holmium—Isotopes
Holmium oxide
  UF Holmic oxide
  BT Oxides
Holmon family
  USE Holman family
Holobomolochus
      ⌈QL444.C73⌉
  BT Bomolochidae
Holocain
      ⌈RE997.H7⌉
  BT Local anesthesia
Holocanthus
  USE Holacanthus
Holocaust, Jewish (1939-1945)
  (May Subd Geog)
      ⌈D810.J4⌉
      ⌈DS135.E83⌉
  UF Destruction of the Jews (1939-1945)
      Extermination, Jewish (1939-1945)
      Jewish holocaust (1939-1945)
  BT Genocide
      Jews—Persecutions
      World War, 1939-1945—Atrocities
  RT World War, 1939-1945—Jews
  NT Children of Holocaust survivors
      Holocaust (Christian theology)
      Holocaust survivors
      Postage-stamps—Topics—Holocaust,
          Jewish (1939-1945)
      Righteous Gentiles in the Holocaust
      World War, 1939-1945—Underground
          movements, Jewish
  — **Causes**
  — **Errors, inventions, etc.**

— Personal narratives
Here are entered works consisting of personal accounts of the Jewish Holocaust. Works on Jews who survived the Jewish Holocaust of 1939-1945, with emphasis on their lives since 1945, are entered under Holocaust survivors.
— Psychological aspects
BT Prison psychology
— Poland
NT Warsaw (Poland)—History—Uprising of 1943
Holocaust, Jewish (1939-1945), in art
Holocaust, Jewish (1939-1945), in literature
BT Jews in literature
Holocaust, Jewish (1939-1945), in motion pictures
[PN1995.9.H53]
BT Moving-pictures
Holocaust (Christian theology)
[BT93]
BT Holocaust, Jewish (1939-1945)
Holocaust (Jewish theology)
BT Good and evil (Judaism)
Theodicy
Holocaust and Jewish law
BT Jewish law
Holocaust survivors *(May Subd Geog)*
Here are entered works on Jews who survived the Jewish Holocaust of 1939-1945, with emphasis on their lives since 1945. Works consisting of personal accounts of the Jewish Holocaust are entered under Holocaust, Jewish (1939-1945)—Personal narratives.
UF Survivors, Holocaust
BT Holocaust, Jewish (1939-1945)
Refugees, Jewish
NT Children of Holocaust survivors
Holocentridae
USE Squirrelfishes
Holocentrus
[QL638.H64]
BT Squirrelfishes
Holocephali
USE Chimaeriformes
Holocystidae
[QE783.C9]
BT Diploporita
NT Holocystites
Holocystites
[QE783.C9]
BT Holocystidae
Hologenidae
USE Helogeneidae
Holographic interferometry
[TA1555]
BT Interferometry
RT Coherence (Optics)
Diffraction patterns
Holography
Holographic radar
USE Coherent radar
Holographic testaments
USE Holographic wills
Holographic testing
[TA417.45]
BT Holography
Non-destructive testing
Holographic wills *(May Subd Geog)*
UF Holographic testaments
Testaments, Holographic
BT Wills
Holography *(May Subd Geog)*
[QC449]
UF Laser photography
Lensless photography
Photography, Lensless
Wavefront reconstruction imaging

BT Diffraction
Interference (Light)
Interferometry
Laser recording
Photonics
Three-dimensional display systems
RT Holographic interferometry
Speckle metrology
NT Acoustic holography
Coherent radar
Holographic testing
Microwave holography
Holography in medicine
[R857.H]
UF Medical holography
BT Lasers in medicine
Medical instruments and apparatus
Holoholo language
UF Horohoro language
BT Bantu languages
Holomorphic functions
UF Functions, Holomorphic
BT Functions of several complex variables
NT Lewy problem
Unit ball
Holomorphic mappings
UF Mappings, Holomorphic
BT Functions of several complex variables
Mappings (Mathematics)
NT Biholomorphic mappings
Kernel functions, Bergman
Holomorphy domains
USE Domains of holomorphy
Holonomy groups
[QA649]
UF Groups, Holonomy
BT Geometry, Differential
Holontalo language
USE Gorontalo language
Holophote
[TC379]
BT Lighthouses—Lighting
Holostraca, Fossil
USE Conchostraca, Fossil
Holothurians *(May Subd Geog)*
[QL384.H7]
UF Holothurioidea
Sea-cucumbers
BT Echinodermata
NT Molpadiida
Holothurians, Fossil
[QE783.H7]
UF Holothurioidea, Fossil
BT Echinodermata, Fossil
Holothurioidea
USE Holothurians
Holothurioidea, Fossil
USE Holothurians, Fossil
Holoubek family *(Not Subd Geog)*
Holquist family *(Not Subd Geog)*
UF Hultqvist family
Holscher family
USE Hoelscher family
Holsinger family *(Not Subd Geog)*
Holson family
USE Holston family
Holst family *(Not Subd Geog)*
UF Holste family
Holste family
USE Holst family
Holstein family *(Not Subd Geog)*
UF Holestin family
RT Holston family
Holstein-Friesian cattle
[SF193.H7 (Herd-books)]
[SF199.H75]
UF Friesian cattle
BT Dairy cattle
Holstein horse
[SF293.H7]

Holstein-Schleswig Canal (Germany)
USE Schleswig-Holstein Canal (Germany)
Holsteiner Schweiz (Germany)
USE Holsteinische Schweiz (Germany)
Holsteiners *(May Subd Geog)*
BT Ethnology—Germany (West)
— Italy
— — Siena
UF Holsteiners in Siena
Holsteiners in Siena
USE Holsteiners—Italy—Siena
Holsteinian Switzerland (Germany)
USE Holsteinische Schweiz (Germany)
Holsteinische Schweiz (Germany)
UF Holsteiner Schweiz (Germany)
Holsteinian Switzerland (Germany)
Holsten family
USE Holston family
Holsters
[TS535.2.H64]
UF Gun holsters
Pistol holsters
BT Firearms
Holston family *(Not Subd Geog)*
UF Holson family
Holsten family
Holstone family
Houlston family
RT Holstein family
Holstone family
USE Holston family
Holt family *(Not Subd Geog)*
UF Hoalt family
Holte family
Holts family
RT Holter family
Holtry family
Holtz family
Holte family
USE Holt family
Holten-Bechtolsheim family
RT Bechtolsheim family
Holten family
USE Holton family
Holter family *(Not Subd Geog)*
RT Holt family
Holter monitor electrocardiography
USE Electrocardiography, Ambulatory
Holtin family
USE Holton family
Holton family *(Not Subd Geog)*
UF Holten family
Holtin family
Holtri family
USE Holtry family
Holtry family *(Not Subd Geog)*
UF Holdery family
Holdree family
Holtri family
RT Holt family
Holtz family
Holts family
USE Holt family
Holtz family *(Not Subd Geog)*
RT Holt family
Holtry family
Holtzele family
USE Hutzel family
Holtzer family
USE Holzer family
Holtzman inkblot technique
[BF698.8.H55]
BT Projective techniques
Holway family
USE Holloway family
Holy, The
UF Numinous, The
Sacred, The
BT God
Religion
NT Holiness

Holy, The, in literature
Holy Alliance
  [D383]
  [JX1349]
  UF Alliance, Holy
  BT Europe—Politics and government—
        1815-1848
Holy ark
  USE Ark of the law
Holy cards (May Subd Geog)
  [BX2310.H6 (Catholic Church)]
  UF Cards, Holy
      Devotional pictures
      Holy pictures
      Pictures, Holy
      Sunday-school cards
  BT Christian art and symbolism
      Devotional objects
Holy Child Current
  USE El Niño Current
Holy Childhood, Devotion to
      Here are entered works on the devotion offered to
      the childhood of Jesus.
  UF Child Jesus, Devotion to
      Childhood, Holy
      Childhood of Jesus, Devotion to
      Holy Infancy
      Infancy, Holy
      Infancy of Jesus, Devotion to
  BT Jesus Christ—Childhood
Holy Coat
  [BT587.C6-7]
  UF Coat, Holy
      Jesus Christ—Holy Coat
  BT Coats
      Jesus Christ—Relics of the Passion
Holy Communion
  USE Lord's Supper
Holy Cross
  [BT465]
  UF Cross
      Jesus Christ—Cross
  BT Jesus Christ—Crucifixion
      Jesus Christ—Relics of the Passion
  NT Cross, Feast of the
  — Legends
  — — Art
      NT Stavelot Triptych
Holy Cross, Feast of the
  USE Cross, Feast of the
Holy Cross Mountains (Poland)
  USE Świętokrzyskie Mountains (Poland)
Holy Crown of Hungary
  UF Crown of Hungary
      Crown of Saint Stephen
      Holy Crown of Saint Stephen
      Hungarian Holy Crown
      Magyar szent korona
      Magyar szentkorona
      Saint Stephen's Crown
      St. Stephen's Crown
      Szentkorona
  BT Crowns
      Regalia (Insignia)—Hungary
Holy Crown of Saint Stephen
  USE Holy Crown of Hungary
Holy days
  USE Fasts and feasts
Holy dog
  USE Tibetan terrier
Holy Family
  USE Jesus Christ—Family
Holy fools (May Subd Geog)
  [BX323 (Orthodox Eastern Church)]
  [BX485 (Russian Orthodox Church)]
  UF Fools for Christ
  BT Christians
Holy Ghost
  USE Holy Spirit
Holy Grail
  USE Grail

Holy Grail, Spear of the
  USE Holy Lance
Holy helpers, Fourteen
  USE Fourteen holy helpers
Holy Hour
  [BX2159.H7]
  BT Jesus Christ—Passion
Holy Infancy
  USE Holy Childhood, Devotion to
Holy Innocents, Feast of the
  [BV50.H6]
  UF Childermas
      Feast of the Holy Innocents
      Innocents, Feast of the Holy
      Innocents' Day
  BT Church year
      Fasts and feasts
  NT Boy-bishop
Holy Innocents, Massacre of the
  [BS2545.H]
  UF Innocents, Massacre of the Holy
      Massacre of the Innocents
  BT Jesus Christ—Nativity
      Magi
Holy Innocents, Massacre of the, in art
  NT Stanzioni, Massimo, 1585-1656.
        Massacre of the Innocents
Holy Lance
  UF Destiny, Spear of
      Hofburg Spear
      Holy Grail, Spear of the
      Lance, Holy
      Longinus, Spear of
      Passion, Spear of the
      Spear of Destiny
      Spear of the Passion
  BT Jesus Christ—Relics of the Passion
Holy League (Venice, Spain, and the Pope)
    1570-1571
  USE Cyprian War, 1570-1571
Holy League against France, 1511-1513
  [DG541]
  NT Anglo-French War, 1512-1513
Holy League against the Turks, 1684
  [DR536]
  BT Turkey—History—1683-1829
Holy mountains
  USE Mountains—Religious aspects
Holy Name, Devotion to
  [BX2159.H75]
  UF Devotion to the Holy Name
  BT God—Name
      Jesus Christ—Name
Holy Office
  USE Inquisition
Holy oils
  UF Oil, Holy
  BT Sacramentals
  RT Unction
  NT Chrism
Holy orders
  USE Clergy—Office
Holy Orthodox Eastern Catholic and Apostolic
    Church
  USE Orthodox Eastern Church
Holy pictures
  USE Holy cards
Holy places
  USE Shrines
Holy places, Christian
  USE Christian shrines
Holy Roman Empire
  BT Church and state—Europe
      Middle Ages—History
  NT Imperial cities (Holy Roman Empire)
  — Civilization
      NT Illumination of books and
            manuscripts, Czech—Ottonian
            influences

      Illumination of books and
        manuscripts, Romanesque—
        Ottonian influences
  — — Byzantine influences
      BT Byzantine Empire—Civilization
  — Constitutional history
      NT Mediatized states
  — History
      [DD125-198.7]
  — — To 1517
  — — 843-1273
      NT Italy—History—Germanic rule,
            962-1268
  — — Saxon House, 919-1024
      UF Ottonian emperors
          Ottonian House
          Saxon emperors
          Saxon House
          Saxony, House of
      RT Germany—History—Saxon
            House, 919-1024
  — — Otto I, 936-973
  — — Otto II, 973-983
  — — Henry II, 1002-1024
  — — Conrad II, 1024-1039
  — — Franconian House, 1024-1125
      UF Franconian emperors
          Salian emperors
      RT Franconian House
          Germany—History—Franconian
            House, 1024-1125
  — — Henry III, 1039-1056
  — — Henry IV, 1056-1106
  — — Henry V, 1106-1125
  — — Lothar III, 1125-1137
  — — Conrad III, 1138-1152
  — — Hohenstaufen, 1138-1254
  — — Frederick I, 1152-1190
      NT Legnano, Battle of, 1176
  — — Henry VI, 1190-1197
  — — Otto IV, 1198-1215
  — — Frederick II, 1215-1250
  — — Interregnum, 1254-1273
  — — 1273-1517
  — — Albert I, 1298-1308
  — — Henry VII, 1308-1313
  — — House of Luxemburg, 1308-1437
  — — Louis IV, 1314-1347
  — — Charles IV, 1347-1378
  — — Rupert, 1400-1410
  — — Sigismund, 1411-1437
  — — Frederick III, 1440-1493
  — — Maximilian I, 1493-1519
  — — 1517-1648
  — — Charles V, 1519-1556
  — — Maximilian II, 1564-1576
  — — Rudolf II, 1576-1612
  — — Matthias, 1612-1619
      [DD187.8]
  — — Ferdinand II, 1619-1637
  — — 1648-1804
  — — Leopold I, 1658-1705
  — — Charles VII, 1742-1745
  — — Francis I, 1745-1765
  — — Joseph II, 1765-1790
  — — Francis II, 1792-1806
  — Kings and rulers
      NT Electors (Kurfürsten)
  — — Election
Holy Saturday
  UF Easter Even
      Great Saturday
      Saturday, Holy
  BT Fasts and feasts
      Holy Week
Holy Saturday music
  [M2149.4.H8 (Catholic liturgical
    music)]
  BT Holy-Week music
Holy Scriptures
  USE Bible

Holy Sea (R.S.F.S.R.)
 USE Baikal Lake (R.S.F.S.R.)
Holy See
 USE Papacy
  Popes
Holy Sepulcher
 ₍DS109.4₎
 UF Jesus Christ—Tomb
  Sepulcher, Holy
 BT Shrines—Palestine
Holy Sepulcher in art
Holy Shroud
 ₍BT587.S4₎
 UF Jesus Christ—Holy Shroud
  Shroud, Holy
  Shroud of Turin
  Turin Shroud
 BT Jesus Christ—Relics of the Passion
Holy Shroud in art
Holy Spirit
 ₍BT120-123₎
 UF Holy Ghost
  Paraclete
  Pneumatology (Theology)
  Spirit, Holy
 BT God
  Theology, Doctrinal
  Trinity
 RT Spirit
 NT Baptism in the Holy Spirit
  Church—Foundation
  Epiclesis
  Inspiration—Religious aspects—
   Christianity
  Pentecost
 — Art
  ₍N8055₎
  BT God—Art
  NT Holy Spirit—Symbolism
 — Name
 — Procession
  UF Filioque
   Procession (in the Trinity)
   Procession of the Holy Spirit
 — Symbolism
  BT Christian art and symbolism
   Holy Spirit—Art
  NT Temple of God
Holy Spirit (Judaism)
 BT God (Judaism)
  Judaism—Doctrines
Holy springs
 USE Springs—Religious aspects
Holy Thursday
 USE Maundy Thursday
Holy war (Islam)
 USE Jihad
Holy water
 ₍BV885 (Practical theology)₎
 ₍BX2307 (Catholic Church)₎
 UF Blessed water
  Water, Blessed
  Water, Holy
 BT Sacramentals
  Water—Religious aspects
 NT Baptismal water
Holy Week *(May Subd Geog)*
 ₍BT414 (Events)₎
 ₍BV90-BV95 (Ceremonial)₎
 ₍GT4930 (Manners and customs)₎
 BT Jesus Christ—Passion
  Lent
 NT Easter
  Good Friday
  Holy Saturday
  Holy Week services
  Maundy Thursday
  Palm Sunday

Holy-Week music
 BT Church music
  Lenten music
  Sacred vocal music
 NT Good Friday music
  Holy Saturday music
  Maundy Thursday music
  Palm Sunday music
  Tenebrae service music
Holy-Week sermons
 ₍BV90₎
 UF Sermons, Holy-Week
 BT Holy Week services
  Jesus Christ—Passion—Sermons
  Lenten sermons
 NT Good Friday sermons
Holy Week services
 UF Services, Holy Week
 BT Holy Week
  Liturgies
  Worship programs
 NT Holy-Week sermons
Holy wells *(May Subd Geog)*
 ₍GR690₎
 UF Wells, Holy
 BT Miracles
  Pilgrims and pilgrimages
  Springs—Folklore
  Springs—Religious aspects
  Water—Religious aspects
Holy Year
 ₍BX961.H6₎
  Here are entered works on the holy or jubilee
 years proclaimed by the popes. For special holy years
 (regular or extraordinary) add date, e.g. Holy Year,
 1925.
 UF Anno santo
  Jubilee Year
  Year, Holy
  Year, Jubilee
 BT Asylum, Right of
  Indulgences
 NT Marian Year
  Year of Faith
Holycross family *(Not Subd Geog)*
Holyoake family
 USE Holyoke family
Holyoke family *(Not Subd Geog)*
 UF Holyoake family
Holyoke Range (Mass.)
 BT Mountains—Massachusetts
Holyoke Range State Park (Mass.)
 BT Parks—Massachusetts
Holzach family *(Not Subd Geog)*
Holzer family *(Not Subd Geog)*
 UF Holcer family
  Holczer family
  Holtzer family
Holzwart family
 USE Holzwarth family
Holzwarth family *(Not Subd Geog)*
 UF Holzwart family
Holzwarth Homestead (Colo.)
 BT Dwellings—Colorado
  Rocky Mountain National Park (Colo.)
Hom family
 USE Holmes family
Hom-idyomo (Artificial language)
 ₍PM8370₎
 BT Languages, Artificial
Homa (Rite)
 ₍BL1226.2₎
 UF Goma (Rite)
 BT Fire—Religious aspects—Buddhism
  Fire—Religious aspects—Hinduism
  Hinduism—Rituals
  Tantric Buddhism—Rituals
Homadaula
 ₍QL561.G65₎
 BT Glyphipterygidae

Homadaula albizziae
 ₍QL561.G65₎
Homage (Feudal law)
 BT Feudal law
  Feudalism
Homage to Goya (Etchings)
 USE Dalí, Salvador, 1904-   Homage to
   Goya
Homage volumes
 USE Festschriften
Homalictus
 ₍QL568.H3₎
 BT Halictidae
Homalobus
 USE Astragalus (Plants)
Homalopsidae
 USE Colubridae
Homalorhagida *(May Subd Geog)*
 ₍QL391.K5₎
 BT Kinorhyncha
 NT Pycnophyidae
Homan family *(Not Subd Geog)*
 UF Homann family
  Homans family
  Hommon family
  Homon family
Homann family
 USE Homan family
Homans family
 USE Homan family
Homaridae *(May Subd Geog)*
 ₍QL444.M33₎
 UF Nephropidae
  Nephropsidae
 BT Decapoda (Crustacea)
  Lobsters
 NT Homarus
Homarus *(May Subd Geog)*
 ₍QL444.M33₎
 BT Homaridae
 NT Homarus vulgaris
Homarus americanus
 USE American lobster
Homarus vulgaris *(May Subd Geog)*
 ₍QL444.M33₎
 BT Homarus
Homathko River (B.C.)
 BT Rivers—British Columbia
Homatropin
 ₍RE997.H8₎
 BT Atropine
  Mydriatics
Hombo language
 USE Ombo language
Hombolo Lake (Tanzania)
 BT Lakes—Tanzania
  Reservoirs—Tanzania
  Wama River (Tanzania)
Home *(May Subd Geog)*
 ₍GT2420 (Manners and customs)₎
 ₍HQ503-HQ743 (Family)₎
 RT Family
  Marriage
 NT Broken homes
  Family life surveys
  Home economics
  Home in literature
 — Sounds
  USE Household sounds
Home accidents *(May Subd Geog)*
 ₍TX150₎
 UF Accidents, Home
 BT Accidents
  Domestic engineering
 — Prevention
  ₍TX150₎
  UF Household safety
  BT Safety education
 — — Equipment and supplies
   NT Home safety equipment industry

Home Accountant (Computer program)
  BT Finance, Personal—Computer
    programs
Home Accountant Plus (Computer program)
  BT Finance, Personal—Computer
    programs
    Home economics—Accounting—
      Computer programs
Home air conditioning
  USE Dwellings—Air conditioning
Home and school *(May Subd Geog)*
  ₍LC225₎
  UF School and home
  BT Education
  RT Parent-teacher relationships
    Parents' and teachers' associations
  NT Parent-student counselor relationships
Home appliances
  USE Household appliances
Home banking services *(May Subd Geog)*
  ₍HG1711₎
  UF Banking services, Home
  BT Banks and banking
  RT Electronic funds transfers
  NT Telephone bill paying services
Home-based businesses *(May Subd Geog)*
    Here are entered works on self-employed persons
  producing and marketing goods or services in their
  homes. Works on industries carried on by persons
  and their families in rural areas producing goods at
  home for an outside employer are entered under Cot-
  tage industries. Works on persons in urban areas pro-
  ducing goods at home for an outside employer are
  entered under Home labor.
  UF Business enterprises, Home
    Businesses, Home
    Home businesses
  BT Self-employed
    Small business
  — **Law and legislation** *(May Subd Geog)*
Home-based education
  USE Domestic education
Home birth
  USE Childbirth at home
Home-built airplanes
  USE Airplanes, Home-built
Home-built automobiles
  USE Automobiles, Home-built
Home-built helicopters
  USE Helicopters, Home-built
Home businesses
  USE Home-based businesses
Home buying
  USE House buying
Home care programs, Hospital-based
  USE Hospitals—Home care programs
Home care services *(May Subd Geog)*
  UF Home health agencies
  BT Community health services
  SA *subdivision* Home care *under classes of
    persons, e.g.* Aged—Home care;
    Cancer—Patients—Home care
  NT Childbirth at home
    Hemodialysis—Home therapy
    Home health aides
    Home nursing
    Hospitals—Home care programs
    Respite care
  — **Accreditation**
  — **Law and legislation** *(May Subd Geog)*
    BT Medical laws and legislation
  — **Utilization**
    UF Home care services use
      Utilization of home care services
Home care services use
  USE Home care services—Utilization
Home childbirth
  USE Childbirth at home
Home computers
  USE Microcomputers
Home conservatories
  USE Garden rooms

Home construction
  USE House construction
Home day care
  USE Family day care
Home decoration
  USE Interior decoration
Home dedication services
  BT Dedication services
  — **Judaism, ₍Hinduism, etc.₎**
Home delivered meals
  USE Meals on wheels programs
Home delivery (Obstetrics)
  USE Childbirth at home
Home delivery of books
  USE Direct delivery of books
Home demonstration work
  (May Subd Geog)
  BT Agricultural extension work
    Home economics extension work
Home design
  USE Architecture, Domestic
Home dialysis
  USE Hemodialysis—Home therapy
Home economics *(May Subd Geog)*
  ₍TX₎
  UF Domestic economy
    Domestic science
    Household management
    Household science
    Housekeeping
    Housework
  BT Family life education
    Home
  RT Consumer education
    Households
  NT Bedmaking
    Classification—Books—Home
      economics
    Cleaning machinery and appliances
    Clothing and dress—Care
    Cookery
    Cost and standard of living
    Domestics
    Entertaining
    Food
    Fuel
    Heating
    Home economists
    House cleaning
    House furnishings
    Household linens
    Househusbands
    Housewives
    Interior decoration
    Laundry
    Marketing (Home economics)
    Mobile home living
    Needlework
    Recipes
    Sewing
    Storage in the home
    Television in home economics
    Visiting housekeepers
  — **Accounting**
    ₍TX326₎
    UF Budgets, Family
      Budgets, Household
      Family budgets
      Household budgets
      Household expenses
    BT Cost and standard of living
      Finance, Personal
      Statistics
  — — **Computer programs**
      NT Home Accountant Plus
        (Computer program)
  — **Bibliography**
      NT Information storage and retrieval
        systems—Home economics
  — **Equipment and supplies**
    ₍TX298-9₎

    UF Home economics, Rural—
      Equipment and supplies
    NT House furnishings
      Household appliances
      Household appliances, Electric
  — **International cooperation**
    UF International cooperation in home
      economics
  — **Study and teaching** *(May Subd Geog)*
    NT Home economics extension work
      Home economics students
  — Subject headings
    USE Subject headings—Home
      economics
  — **Terminology**
    NT English language—Conversation
      and phrase books (for
      domestics)
Home economics, Rural *(May Subd Geog)*
  UF Rural home economics
  BT Country life
    Farm life
  — Equipment and supplies
    USE Home economics—Equipment
      and supplies
Home economics centers
  UF Homemaking centers
    Homemaking departments
  BT School buildings
Home economics extension work
  (May Subd Geog)
  UF Extension work, Home economics
  BT Home economics—Study and teaching
  NT Home demonstration work
    Home economics extension workers
    Nutrition extension work
Home economics extension workers
  (May Subd Geog)
  UF Extension home economists
    Extension workers, Home economics
  BT Home economics extension work
    Home economics teachers
  — **United States**
    NT Afro-American home economics
      extension workers
Home economics extension workers, Afro-
  American
  USE Afro-American home economics
    extension workers
**Home economics for the physically
  handicapped**
  BT Physically handicapped—
    Rehabilitation
    Self-help devices for the disabled
Home economics literature searching
  USE Information storage and retrieval
    systems—Home economics
Home economics students *(May Subd Geog)*
  BT Home economics—Study and teaching
    Students
  — Personality
    USE Home economics students—
      Psychology
  — **Psychology**
    UF Home economics students—
      Personality
Home economics teachers *(May Subd Geog)*
  BT Teachers
  NT Home economics extension workers
Home economists *(May Subd Geog)*
  BT Home economics
Home education
  USE Correspondence schools and courses
    Domestic education
    Self-culture
Home electronics
  USE Household electronics
Home electronics industry
  USE Household electronics industry
Home equity access accounts
  USE Home equity loans

Home equity conversion *(May Subd Geog)*
⌐HG2040.45┐
  UF Conversion of home equity
      Dissaving of home equity
      Equity conversion, Home
      Homeowners' equity conversion
  BT Housing—Finance
      Mortgage loans, Reverse
Home equity line of credit
  USE Home equity loans
Home equity loans *(May Subd Geog)*
⌐HG2040.45┐
  UF Home equity access accounts
      Home equity line of credit
      Homeowners' equity accounts
  BT Bank loans
  — Law and legislation *(May Subd Geog)*
Home evenings (Mormon Church)
  USE Family home evenings (Mormon
       Church)
Home exchanges
  USE Home exchanging
Home exchanging *(May Subd Geog)*
  UF Exchanges, Home
      Exchanges, House
      Exchanging, Home
      Home exchanges
      Home swapping
      House exchanges
      House swapping
      Swapping homes
  BT Barter
Home family
  USE Holmes family
Home freezers *(May Subd Geog)*
  UF Freezers, Home
  BT Refrigeration and refrigerating
       machinery
Home furnishings
  USE House furnishings
Home furnishings industry and trade
  USE House furnishings industry and trade
Home games
  USE Indoor games
Home geography
  USE Local geography
Home health agencies
  USE Home care services
Home health aides *(May Subd Geog)*
⌐RA645.35-645.37┐
  BT Community health aides
      Home care services
  — Supply and demand
Home hemodialysis
  USE Hemodialysis—Home therapy
Home horticulture
  USE House plant industry
Home improvement loans *(May Subd Geog)*
⌐HG2040.4┐
  BT Dwellings—Remodeling—Finance
      Housing—Finance
      Mortgage loans
Home in literature
  BT Home
Home labor *(May Subd Geog)*
⌐HD2331-HD2336┐
    Here are entered works on persons in urban areas
  producing goods at home for an outside employer.
  Works on industries carried on by persons and their
  families in rural areas producing goods at home for an
  outside employer are entered under Cottage indus-
  tries. Works on self-employed persons producing and
  marketing goods or services in their homes are en-
  tered under Home-based businesses.
  UF Homework, Industrial
      Industrial homework
  BT Artisans
      Industry—History
      Labor and laboring classes
      Manufactures
      Women—Employment

  RT Cottage industries
      Sweating system
  NT Telecommuting
  — Law and legislation *(May Subd Geog)*
      BT Labor laws and legislation
Home libraries
  USE Libraries, Private
Home loan banks
  USE Federal home loan banks
Home missions
  USE Missions, Home
Home Money Manager (Computer program)
  BT Computer programs
      Finance, Personal—Computer
        programs
Home movies
  USE Amateur moving-pictures
       Cinematography
Home nursing *(May Subd Geog)*
⌐RT61┐
  BT Home care services
      Nursing
  RT Care of the sick
  NT Visiting nurses
  — Equipment and supplies
      NT Home nursing equipment industry
Home nursing equipment industry
(May Subd Geog)
⌐HD9995.H56┐
  BT Home nursing—Equipment and
       supplies
Home owners
  USE Homeowners
Home owners' associations
  USE Homeowners' associations
Home ownership *(May Subd Geog)*
⌐HD7287┐
  UF Ownership of homes
  BT Housing
      Real estate business
  RT House buying
  NT Farm ownership
      Homeowners' associations
      Urban homesteading
Home purchase
  USE House buying
Home range *(May Subd Geog)*
  BT Animal populations
Home remodeling
  USE Dwellings—Remodeling
Home room guidance *(May Subd Geog)*
⌐LB1620.7┐
  UF Homeroom guidance
  BT Personnel service in secondary
       education
Home room guidance (Elementary)
(May Subd Geog)
⌐LB1027.7┐
  BT Personnel service in elementary
       education
Home rule (District of Columbia)
  BT Municipal home rule
Home rule (Ireland)
⌐DA947-962┐
  BT Ireland—Politics and government
  RT Irish question
  NT Curragh Mutiny, 1914
      Fenians
Home rule (Scotland)
⌐DA765┐
  BT Scotland—Politics and government
Home rule (Wales)
  BT Wales—Politics and government
Home rule for cities
  USE Municipal home rule
Home safety equipment industry
(May Subd Geog)
  BT Home accidents—Prevention—
       Equipment and supplies
      Safety appliances

Home satellite television
  USE Direct broadcast satellite television
Home sharing
  USE Shared housing
Home sites
  USE Homesites
Home sounds
  USE Household sounds
Home storage
  USE Storage in the home
Home study courses
  USE *subdivision* Self-instruction *under
        names of languages; and subdivision*
        Methods—Self-instruction *under
        names of musical instruments*
       Correspondence schools and courses
       Self-culture
       Singing—Methods—Self-instruction
Home swapping
  USE Home exchanging
Home video systems
  BT Television
  NT Camcorders
      Direct broadcast satellite television
      Television cameras
      Television display systems
      Video discs
      Video tape recorders and recording
      Video tapes
Home video systems industry
(May Subd Geog)
Home visiting (Christian education)
  USE Visitations in Christian education
Home visiting (Church work)
  USE Visitations (Church work)
Home visiting (Religious education)
  USE Visitations (Religious education)
Home workshops
  USE Workshops
Homebirth
  USE Childbirth at home
Homebound, Library services for the
  USE Public libraries—Services to shut-ins
Homeland (Theology)
  UF Fatherland (Theology)
      Native land (Theology)
  BT Theology, Doctrinal
Homeland in literature
Homelands (South Africa)
⌐DT763.6┐
  UF Bantoetuislande (South Africa)
      Bantu Homelands (South Africa)
      Bantustans (South Africa)
      Black Homelands (South Africa)
      South African Homelands (South
        Africa)
      Tuislande (South Africa)
Homeless adults
  USE Homeless persons
Homeless persons *(May Subd Geog)*
  UF Homeless adults
      Street people
  BT Persons
  RT Homelessness
  NT Homeless women
      Homeless youth
      Rogues and vagabonds
      Shelters for the homeless
      Tramps
  — Services for *(May Subd Geog)*
  — — Law and legislation
      (May Subd Geog)
Homeless persons shelters
  USE Shelters for the homeless
Homeless women *(May Subd Geog)*
  UF Bag ladies
      Shopping bag ladies
  BT Homeless persons
      Tramps
      Women

Homeless youth *(May Subd Geog)*
　[HV1421-HV1441]
　UF　Youth, Homeless
　BT　Homeless persons
　　　Youth
Homelessness *(May Subd Geog)*
　BT　Housing
　　　Poverty
　RT　Homeless persons
　NT　Domicile in public welfare
　　　Housing—Effect of wars on
　　　Migrant labor
　　　Relief stations (for the poor)
　— **Law and legislation** *(May Subd Geog)*
Homemaker service
　USE　Visiting housekeepers
Homemakers
　USE　Housewives
Homemakers, Displaced
　USE　Displaced homemakers
Homemakers, Men
　USE　Househusbands
Homemaking centers
　USE　Home economics centers
Homemaking departments
　USE　Home economics centers
Homemates
　USE　Roommates
Homeomorphisms
　[QA614 (QA613.7)]
　BT　Manifolds (Mathematics)
　　　Topological spaces
　　　Transformation groups
　NT　Isotopies (Topology)
Homeopathic hospitals
　USE　Homeopathy—Hospitals and
　　　　dispensaries
Homeopathic pharmacy
　USE　Pharmacy, Homeopathic
Homeopathic physicians *(May Subd Geog)*
　UF　Homeopaths
　　　Physicians, Homeopathic
　BT　Homeopathy
　　　Physicians
　— **Biography**
　　　UF　Homeopathy—Biography
Homeopathic research
　USE　Homeopathy—Research
Homeopaths
　USE　Homeopathic physicians
Homeopathy *(May Subd Geog)*
　[RX]
　UF　Homoeopathy
　BT　Medicine
　　　Therapeutic systems
　SA　*subdivision* Homeopathic treatment
　　　　under names of diseases and groups
　　　　of diseases, e.g. Diphtheria—
　　　　Homeopathic treatment; Children—
　　　　Diseases—Homeopathic treatment;
　　　　Nervous system—Diseases—
　　　　Homeopathic treatment
　NT　Electrohomeopathy
　　　Homeopathic physicians
　　　Medicine, Biochemic
　　　Obstetrics, Homeopathic
　　　Pharmacopoeias, Homeopathic
　　　Pharmacy, Homeopathic
　　　Surgery, Homeopathic
　　　Sycosis (Homeopathy)
　　　Veterinary medicine, Homeopathic
　— **Attenuations, dilutions, and potencies**
　　　[RX81]
　　　UF　High potency (Drugs)
　— **Biography**
　　　USE　Homeopathic physicians—
　　　　　Biography
　— **Hospitals and dispensaries**
　　　[RX6]

　　　UF　Dispensaries, Homeopathic
　　　　　Homeopathic hospitals
　　　　　Hospitals, Homeopathic
　　　BT　Hospitals
　— **Law and legislation** *(May Subd Geog)*
　　　BT　Medical laws and legislation
　— **Materia medica and therapeutics**
　　　[RX601-675]
　　　UF　Homeopathy—Therapeutics
　　　BT　Materia medica
　　　　　Therapeutics
　— **Research** *(May Subd Geog)*
　　　UF　Homeopathic research
　— Therapeutics
　　　USE　Homeopathy—Materia medica
　　　　　and therapeutics
Homeostasis
　BT　Biological chemistry
　　　Biological control systems
　　　Body fluids
　　　Physiology
　NT　Water-electrolyte balance (Physiology)
Homeowners *(May Subd Geog)*
　UF　Home owners
　　　Owners, Home
　BT　Persons
Homeowners' associations *(May Subd Geog)*
　[HD7287.8]
　UF　Community associations
　　　Home owners' associations
　BT　Home ownership
　　　Municipal services
　　　Neighborhood government
　— **Law and legislation** *(May Subd Geog)*
Homeowners' equity accounts
　USE　Home equity loans
Homeowners' equity conversion
　USE　Home equity conversion
Homeowners insurance
　USE　Insurance, Homeowners
Homer, Winslow, 1836-1910.　Gulf Stream
　UF　Castaway (Painting)
　　　Gulf Stream (Painting)
　BT　Gulf Stream in art
Homer (Computer program)
　BT　Computer programs
　　　Editing—Computer programs
　　　Rhetoric—Computer programs
Homeric civilization
　USE　Civilization, Homeric
Homerka River (Poland)
　BT　Rivers—Poland
Homeroom guidance
　USE　Home room guidance
Homert, Naturpark (Germany)
　USE　Naturpark Homert (Germany)
Homes
　USE　Dwellings
Homes, Broken
　USE　Broken homes
Homes, Kit
　USE　Prefabricated houses
Homes, Mobile
　USE　Mobile homes
Homes (Institutions)
　USE　Almshouses
　　　Asylums
　　　Blind—Institutional care
　　　Charities
　　　Children—Institutional care
　　　Deaf—Institutional care
　　　Institutional care
　　　Old age homes
　　　Soldiers' homes
Homes for the aged
　USE　Old age homes
Homesickness
　BT　Emotions
　　　Melancholy
　　　Nostalgia

Homesites *(May Subd Geog)*
　UF　Architecture, Domestic—Location
　　　Home sites
　　　Location of homes
　NT　Cluster housing
　　　Zero lot line housing
**Homestake Opera House and Recreation
　Building (Lead, S.D.)**
　BT　Recreation centers—South Dakota
　　　Theaters—South Dakota
Homestead law *(May Subd Geog)*
　[HD197-HD205 (Land law)]
　[HD1337 (Homestead and exemption)]
　UF　Homesteading
　　　Law, Homestead
　　　Scrip
　BT　Exemption (Law)
　　　Land tenure—Law and legislation
　　　Restraints on alienation
　— **United States**
　　　UF　Land scrip (United States)
　　　　　Scrip, Land (United States)
　　　BT　Public lands
　　　NT　Pre-emption rights (United States)
Homestead Strike, 1892
　[HD5325.15 1892.H]
Homesteading
　USE　Agriculture—Handbooks, manuals, etc.
　　　Frontier and pioneer life
　　　Homestead law
Homesteading, Urban
　USE　Urban homesteading
Homework
　[LB1048]
　BT　Study, Method of
Homework, Industrial
　USE　Home labor
Homicide *(May Subd Geog)*
　[HV6499-6535]
　UF　Manslaughter
　BT　Criminal law
　　　Offenses against the person
　　　Violent deaths
　RT　Murder
　NT　Assassination
　　　Crime passionnel
　　　Death by wrongful act
　　　Euthanasia
　　　Filicide
　　　Fratricide
　　　Homicide investigation
　　　Infanticide
　　　Justifiable homicide
　　　Parricide
　　　Poisoning
　　　Prison homicide
　　　Suicide
　　　Trials (Homicide)
　　　Uxoricide
　— **Psychological aspects**
Homicide (Ancient law)
Homicide (Canon law)
Homicide (Greek law)
Homicide (Islamic law) *(May Subd Geog)*
Homicide (Jewish law)
Homicide (Roman law)
Homicide in literature
Homicide investigation *(May Subd Geog)*
　BT　Criminal investigation
　　　Homicide
　NT　Murder—Investigation
Homiculture
　USE　Eugenics
Hōmidō Iseki (Yatsushiro-shi, Japan)
　USE　Hōmidō Site (Yatsushiro-shi, Japan)
Hōmidō Site (Yatsushiro-shi, Japan)
　(Not Subd Geog)
　UF　Hōmidō Iseki (Yatsushiro-shi, Japan)
　BT　Japan—Antiquities
Homiletical illustrations
　[BV4224-BV4230]

Here are entered collections of brief stories intended to be used as illustrations within sermons. Sermons in story form for adults are entered under Story sermons. Sermons for children are entered under Children's sermons.
- UF Catechetical illustrations
  - Illustrations, Homiletical
  - Sermons—Illustrations
- BT Religion—Quotations, maxims, etc.
  - Sermons
- RT Bible—Homiletical use
- NT Allegories
  - Exempla
  - Fables
  - Legends
  - Parables
  - Short stories
  - Tales

Homiletical illustrations, Buddhist
- BT Preaching, Buddhist

Homiletical illustrations, Islamic
- UF Homiletical illustrations, Muslim
  - Islamic homiletical illustrations
  - Muslim homiletical illustrations
- BT Preaching, Islamic
- NT Exempla, Islamic
  - Islamic stories

Homiletical illustrations, Jewish
- UF Jewish homiletical illustrations
- BT Preaching, Jewish

Homiletical illustrations, Muslim
- USE Homiletical illustrations, Islamic

Homiletical stories
- USE Story sermons

Homiletical use of popular music
- USE Popular music—Homiletical use

Homiletics
- USE Preaching

Homilies
- USE Sermons

Homing in animals
- USE Animal homing

Homing pigeons
- ₍SF469 (Animal culture)₎
- ₍UH90 (Military art and science)₎
- UF Carrier pigeons
  - Racing pigeons
- BT Pigeons
- SA subdivision Pigeons under individual wars, e.g. World War, 1939-1945—Pigeons
- NT Pigeon post
  - Pigeon racing
- — Breeding

Homing pigeons in the Bible
- UF Bible—Homing pigeons
- BT Birds in the Bible

Hominidae, Fossil
- USE Fossil man

Hominids, Fossil
- USE Fossil man

Hominy Creek (Okla.)
- BT Rivers—Oklahoma
- NT Skiatook Lake (Okla.)

Hominy grits
- USE Grits

Homma family
- USE Honma family

Hommage à Goya (Etchings)
- USE Dalí, Salvador, 1904-   Homage to Goya

Homme (The French word)
- BT French language—Etymology

Hommel
- USE Noordsche balk

Hommes family
- USE Holmes family

Hommon Butsuryū (Sect)   *(May Subd Geog)*
- ₍BQ8080-8089₎
- UF Hommon Butsuryūkō
  - Hommon Butsuryūshū

BT Buddhist sects
  - Nichiren (Sect)

Hommon Butsuryūkō
- USE Hommon Butsuryū (Sect)

Hommon Butsuryūshū
- USE Hommon Butsuryū (Sect)

Hommon family
- USE Homan family

Homo (The Latin word)
- ₍PA2350.H₎
- BT Latin language—Etymology

Homo capensis
- USE Boskop man

Homo erectus
- USE Pithecanthropus erectus

Homo erectus pekinensis
- USE Peking man

Homo oeconomicus
- USE Economic man

Homo soloensis
- USE Solo man

Homochitto National Forest (Miss.)
- BT Forest reserves—Mississippi
  - National parks and reserves—United States

Homoeopathy
- USE Homeopathy

Homogeneous grouping
- USE Ability grouping in education

Homogeneous spaces
- UF Spaces, Homogeneous
- BT Lie groups

Homogenetic cortex
- USE Neopallium

Homogenized milk
- USE Milk, Homogenized

Homoglossum
- ₍QK495.I75₎
- BT Iridaceae

Homografts
- UF Allogeneic homografts
  - Allografts
  - Homologous transplants
- BT Transplantation of organs, tissues, etc.
- NT Bone-grafting
  - Cadaver homografts
  - Skin-grafting

Homographs
- USE Homonyms

Homological algebra
- USE Algebra, Homological

Homologous serum hepatitis
- USE Hepatitis B

Homologous serum hepatitis virus
- USE Hepatitis B virus

Homologous transplants
- USE Homografts

Homology (Biology)
- ₍QH367.5₎
- BT Anatomy, Comparative
  - Biology—Classification
  - Evolution
  - Morphology
  - Phylogeny

Homology theory
- ₍QA611₎
- UF Cohomology theory
  - Contrahomology theory
- BT Abelian groups
  - Algebraic topology
- RT Sheaves, Theory of
- NT Algebra, Homological
  - Hodge theory
  - K-theory
  - Vanishing theorems
  - Weierstrass points

Homomorphisms (Mathematics)
- BT Functions

Homon family
- USE Homan family

Homonymous authors
- UF Authors, Homonymous
- BT Anonyms and pseudonyms

Homonyms
- UF Homographs
  - Homophones
- BT Semantics
- RT Puns and punning
- SA subdivision Homonyms *under names of languages*

Homophile movement
- USE Gay liberation movement

Homophones
- USE Homonyms

Homophysidae
- USE Pyralidae

Homopolar generators
- ₍TK2665₎
- BT Electric generators—Direct current

Homoptera   *(May Subd Geog)*
- ₍QL525-528.2₎
- BT Hemiptera
- NT Achilidae
  - Adelgidae
  - Aleyrodidae
  - Aphididae
  - Asterolecaniidae
  - Callaphididae
  - Cercopidae
  - Cerococcidae
  - Chaitophoridae
  - Cicadidae
  - Coccidae
  - Dactylopiidae
  - Delphacidae
  - Diaspididae
  - Dictyopharidae
  - Eriococcidae
  - Fulgoridae
  - Issidae
  - Jumping plant-lice
  - Kermesidae
  - Leafhoppers
  - Lecanodiaspididae
  - Margarodidae
  - Mealy bugs
  - Membracidae
  - Phylloxeridae
  - Pseudococcidae
  - Scale-insects
  - Termitococcidae

Homoptera, Fossil
- BT Insects, Fossil
- NT Aphididae, Fossil

Homopteridae
- USE Noctuidae

Homoscedasticity
- BT Analysis of variance
- RT Heteroscedasticity

Homoserine deaminase
- USE Cystathionine gamma-lyase

Homoserine dehydratase
- USE Cystathionine gamma-lyase

Homosexual couples   *(May Subd Geog)*
- UF Couples, Homosexual
  - Gay couples
- BT Homosexuals
  - Unmarried couples
- RT Homosexual parents
- NT Lesbian couples

Homosexual couples, Female
- USE Lesbian couples

Homosexual couples, Male
  (May Subd Geog)
- UF Couples, Male homosexual
  - Male homosexual couples
- BT Homosexuals, Male

Homosexual liberation movement
- USE Gay liberation movement

Homosexual parents   *(May Subd Geog)*
- UF Gay parents

Homosexual parents *(Continued)*
  BT Homosexuals
     Parents
  RT Homosexual couples
  NT Children of homosexual parents
     Lesbian mothers
Homosexuality *(May Subd Geog)*
  ⌈HQ75-HQ76.8 (Sociology)⌉
  ⌈RC558-RC558.5 (Psychiatry)⌉
  BT Sex
  RT Bisexuality
  NT Astrology and homosexuality
     Gay bars
     Gay liberation movement
     Homosexuality, Male
     Homosexuals
     Lesbianism
  — **Law and legislation** *(May Subd Geog)*
       Works on the criminal aspects of homosexu-
     ality are entered under the heading Sodomy.
       UF Homosexuals—Legal status, laws,
          etc.
       BT Sex and law
       RT Sodomy
  — **Mythology**
  — **Religious aspects**
  — — **Baptists, ⌈Catholic Church, etc.⌉**
  — — **Buddhism, ⌈Christianity, etc.⌉**
Homosexuality, Female
  USE Lesbianism
Homosexuality, Male *(May Subd Geog)*
  ⌈HQ75.7-HQ76.2 (Sociology)⌉
  ⌈HQ558.3 (Psychiatry)⌉
  UF Male homosexuality
     Urningism
  BT Homosexuality
     Men—Sexual behavior
Homosexuality and art *(May Subd Geog)*
  · ⌈N72.H64⌉
  UF Art and homosexuality
  BT Art
Homosexuality and employment
  (May Subd Geog)
  UF Employment and homosexuality
Homosexuality and literature
  (May Subd Geog)
  UF Literature and homosexuality
Homosexuality in animals
  ⌈QL761⌉
  BT Sexual behavior in animals
Homosexuality in art
Homosexuality in literature
  BT Sex in literature
Homosexuality in motion pictures
  BT Moving-pictures
Homosexuality in the Bible
  UF Bible—Homosexuality
Homosexuals *(May Subd Geog)*
  UF Gay people
     Gay persons
     Gays
  BT Homosexuality
  NT Church work with homosexuals
     Homosexual couples
     Homosexual parents
     Homosexuals, Male
     Lesbians
     Social work with homosexuals
  — **Attitudes**
       BT Attitude (Psychology)
  — Legal status, laws, etc.
       USE Homosexuality—Law and
          legislation
  — **Travel** *(May Subd Geog)*
  — **United States**
       NT Afro-American homosexuals
Homosexuals, Afro-American
  USE Afro-American homosexuals
Homosexuals, Female
  USE Lesbians

Homosexuals, Male *(May Subd Geog)*
  ⌈HQ75.8⌉
  ⌈HQ75.85⌉
  UF Gays, Male
     Male homosexuals
     Men homosexuals
     Urnings
  BT Homosexuals
  NT Homosexual couples, Male
     Sex instruction for homosexual men
Homosexuals' writings *(May Subd Geog)*
  UF Gays' writings
     Writings of gays
     Writings of homosexuals
  NT Lesbians' writings
Homosexuals' writings, American
  (May Subd Geog)
  UF American homosexuals' writings
  BT American literature
Homosexuals' writings, English
  (May Subd Geog)
  UF English homosexuals' writings
  BT English literature
Homosexuals' writings, Latin American
  (May Subd Geog)
  UF Latin American homosexuals' writings
Homotopy equivalences
  ⌈QA612.72⌉
  UF Equivalences, Homotopy
  BT Homotopy theory
  NT Surgery (Topology)
Homotopy groups
  ⌈QA612.78⌉
  BT Groups, Theory of
     Homotopy theory
Homotopy theory
  ⌈QA611⌉
  UF Deformations, Continuous
  BT Topology
     Transformations (Mathematics)
  NT Cobar construction (Topology)
     Homotopy equivalences
     Homotopy groups
     Localization theory
     Loop spaces
     Shape theory (Topology)
Hōmyō
  USE Buddhist posthumous names
Hon family *(Not Subd Geog)*
  UF Hone family
     Honn family
Honam Line
  USE Honamsŏn
Hon'ami family *(Not Subd Geog)*
Honamsŏn
  ⌈HE3360.5⌉
  UF Honam Line
  BT Railroads—Korea (South)
Honan family *(Not Subd Geog)*
Honda Accord automobile
  ⌈TL215.H⌉
  UF Accord automobile
  BT Honda automobile
Honda ATC (All terrain vehicle)
  BT All terrain vehicles
Honda automobile
  BT Automobiles
  NT Honda Accord automobile
     Honda Civic automobile
     Odyssey (Dune buggy)
     Prelude automobile
Honda Civic automobile
  ⌈TL215.H⌉
  UF Civic automobile
  BT Honda automobile
Honda motor scooters
  ⌈TL453.H⌉
  BT Motor scooters
Honda motorcycle
  ⌈TL448.H6⌉

Hondajō (Suzuka-shi, Japan)
  USE Kanbejō (Suzuka-shi, Japan)
Hondo (Japan)
  USE Honshū (Japan)
Hondo River (Guatemala-Belize)
  (Not Subd Geog)
  UF Azul River (Guatemala-Belize)
     Río Azul (Guatemala-Belize)
     Río Hondo (Guatemala-Belize)
  BT Rivers—Belize
     Rivers—Guatemala
     Rivers—Mexico
Hondschoote, Battle of, 1793
  ⌈DC220.5⌉
  BT First Coalition, War of the, 1792-1797
        —Campaigns—France
Honduran authors
  USE Authors, Honduran
Honduran drama *(May Subd Geog)*
  ⌈PQ7502 (History)⌉
  ⌈PQ7506 (Collections)⌉
Honduran fiction *(May Subd Geog)*
  NT Short stories, Honduran
Honduran literature
  ⌈PQ7500-7509⌉
  BT Spanish American literature
  — **Competitions**
       NT Premio Nacional de Literatura
          Ramón Rosa
Honduran newspapers
Honduran orations
  USE Speeches, addresses, etc., Honduran
Honduran periodicals
Honduran poetry *(May Subd Geog)*
  ⌈PQ7506⌉
Honduran poets
  USE Poets, Honduran
Honduran short stories
  USE Short stories, Honduran
Honduran speeches
  USE Speeches, addresses, etc., Honduran
Honduras
  — **Antiquities**
       NT Copán Site (Honduras)
  — **Description and travel**
  — — **1951-1980**
  — — **1981-**
  — **Economic conditions**
  — — **1918-**
  — — **1918-1980** *(Not Subd Geog)*
  — — **1980-** *(Not Subd Geog)*
  — General Strike, 1954
       USE General Strike, Honduras, 1954
  — **History**
  — — **To 1838**
          ⌈F1507⌉
          NT Trinidad, Battle of, 1827
  — — **1838-1933**
          ⌈F1507.5⌉
  — — **Coup d'état, 1904** *(Not Subd Geog)*
          ⌈F1507.5⌉
          BT Coups d'état—Honduras
  — — **Revolution, 1919**
  — — **1933-**
          ⌈F1508⌉
          NT El Salvador-Honduras Conflict,
             1969
  — **Languages**
       NT Sumo language
  — **Politics and government**
  — — **To 1838**
  — — **1838-1933**
  — — **1933-1982**
  — — **1982-**
Honduras, Gulf of
  UF Bahia de Honduras
     Bay of Honduras
     Golfo de Honduras
     Gulf of Amatique
     Gulf of Honduras

BT Bays—Belize
        Bays—Guatemala
        Bays—Honduras
Honduras-El Salvador Conflict, 1969
    USE El Salvador-Honduras Conflict, 1969
Hone family
    USE Hon family
Hone Heke's Rebellion, 1844-1846
    UF Heke's Rebellion, 1844-1846
    BT New Zealand—History—1843-1870
Hōnen Shōnin eden (Scrolls)
    [ND1053.4]
    UF Hōnen Shōnin gyōjō ezu (Scrolls)
    BT Painting, Japanese—Kamakura-
            Momoyama periods, 1185-1600
        Scrolls, Japanese
Hōnen Shōnin gyōjō ezu (Scrolls)
    USE Hōnen Shōnin eden (Scrolls)
Honesty
    [BF723.H7 (Child psychology)]
    [BJ1533.H7 (Ethics)]
    UF Dishonesty
    BT Reliability
    RT Integrity
        Sincerity
        Truthfulness and falsehood
    NT Cheating (Education)
        Wealth, Ethics of
Honewort
    USE Cryptotaenia canadensis
Honey *(May Subd Geog)*
    [SF539]
    [TX560.H7 (Foods)]
    BT Bee products
        Honeybee
        Natural sweeteners
    RT Nectar
    NT Cookery (Honey)
        Honeydew
        Mead
    — Law and legislation *(May Subd Geog)*
    — Tariff
        USE Tariff on honey
Honey, Comb *(May Subd Geog)*
    [SF521-SF539 (Bee culture)]
    UF Comb honey
        Honey in the comb
    BT Bee culture
        Bee products
        Honeycombs
Honey agaric
    USE Armillaria mellea
Honey-ants
    [QL568.F7]
    UF Myrmecocystus
    BT Ants
        Hymenoptera
Honey as food
    BT Food
Honey-bearing plants
    USE Honey plants
Honey bee
    USE Honeybee
Honey buzzards
    UF Pernis apivorus
    BT Buzzards
Honey cookery
    USE Cookery (Honey)
Honey-creepers
    [QL696.P2]
Honey eaters
    [QL696.P249]
    UF Honeyeaters
        Honeysuckers
        Meliphagidae
    BT Nectarivores
        Passeriformes
    NT Apalopteron
Honey-eating animals
    USE Nectarivores

Honey fungus
    USE Armillaria mellea
Honey-guides
    [QL696.P55]
    UF Indicatoridae
    BT Piciformes
Honey in the comb
    USE Honey, Comb
Honey Lake (Calif.)
    BT Lakes—California
Honey locust
    [SB397]
    UF Gleditsia
        Thorn tree
Honey Locust Ranch (Kan.)
    BT Ranches—Kansas
Honey mesquite *(May Subd Geog)*
    [QK495.L52 (Botany)]
    [SB615.H66 (Weed)]
    UF Prosopis chilensis
        Prosopis glandulosa
    BT Mesquite
Honey mushroom
    USE Armillaria mellea
Honey myrtles
    USE Melaleuca
Honey plants *(May Subd Geog)*
    [SF535]
    UF Honey-bearing plants
        Nectar plants
    BT Bee culture
        Botany, Economic
Honey trade *(May Subd Geog)*
    [HD9120]
Honey tuft
    USE Armillaria mellea
Honeybee *(May Subd Geog)*
    [QL568.A6-Entomology]
    [SF521-SF539 (Culture)]
    UF Apis mellifera
        European honeybee
        Hive bee
        Honey bee
    BT Apis (Insects)
        Bees
    NT Beeswax
        Brazilian honeybee
        Honey
        Honeycombs
        Royal jelly
    — Diseases
        NT Varroa disease
    — Housing *(May Subd Geog)*
        UF Bee hives
            Beehives
            Hives, Bee
    — Parasites
        NT Varroa jacobsoni
Honeybee, Brazilian
    USE Brazilian honeybee
Honeycomb Buttes Wilderness (Wyo.)
    (Not Subd Geog)
    UF Honeycomb Buttes Wilderness Study
            Area (Wyo.)
    BT National parks and reserves—
            Wyoming
        Wilderness areas—Wyoming
Honeycomb Buttes Wilderness Study Area
    (Wyo.)
    USE Honeycomb Buttes Wilderness (Wyo.)
Honeycomb House (Stanford, Calif.)
    USE Paul R. Hanna House (Stanford, Calif.)
Honeycomb stomach (Ruminants)
    USE Reticulum (Ruminants)
Honeycomb structures
    UF Structures, Honeycomb
    BT Laminated materials
        Sandwich construction
Honeycomb weathering *(May Subd Geog)*
    [QE570]

    UF Alveolar weathering
        Cavernous rock surfaces
        Fretting (Geomorphology)
        Fretwork weathering
    BT Weathering
Honeycombs
    BT Bee products
        Honeybee
    NT Beeswax
        Honey, Comb
Honeycombs Wilderness (Or.)
    UF Honeycombs Wilderness Study Area
            (Or.)
    BT National parks and reserves—Oregon
        Wilderness areas—Oregon
Honeycombs Wilderness Study Area (Or.)
    USE Honeycombs Wilderness (Or.)
Honeycreepers, Hawaiian
    USE Drepanididae
Honeycut family
    USE Huneycutt family
Honeydew
    [SF539]
    BT Honey
Honeyeaters
    USE Honey eaters
Honeyfield family *(Not Subd Geog)*
Honeymoon *(May Subd Geog)*
    BT Marriage
Honeymyrtles
    USE Melaleuca
Honeysuckers
    USE Honey eaters
Honeysuckle
    UF Lonicera
        Nintooa
    NT Japanese honeysuckle
Honeysuckle, Australian
    USE Banksia
Honeysuckle clover
    USE White clover
Hong Bang dynasty, 2879-258 B.C.
    (Legendary)
    UF Hung Vuong (Legendary rulers)
    BT Vietnam—History—To 939
Hong family *(Not Subd Geog)*
    [CS1339]
Hong Kong
    — Antiquities
        NT Li-cheng-wu Site (Hong Kong)
            Sham Wan Site (Hong Kong)
Hong Kong atlases
    USE Atlases, Hong Kong
Hong Kong Harbor (Hong Kong)
    USE Victoria Harbor (Hong Kong)
Hong Kong Island (Hong Kong)
    UF Hongkong Island (Hong Kong)
        Hsiang-kang tao (Hong Kong)
    BT Islands—Hong Kong
Hong Kong periodicals *(May Subd Geog)*
Hong Kyŏng-nae Incident, 1811-1812
    BT Korea—History—1637-1864
Høng-Tølløse Jernbane
    BT Railroads—Denmark
Hongalla language
    USE Ngalakan language
Hongkong Island (Hong Kong)
    USE Hong Kong Island (Hong Kong)
Hongō Iseki (Noda-shi, Japan)
    USE Hongō Site (Noda-shi, Japan)
Hongō Site (Noda-shi, Japan)
    (Not Subd Geog)
    UF Hongō Iseki (Noda-shi, Japan)
    BT Japan—Antiquities
Hönig family
    USE Hoenig family
Honing
    BT Grinding and polishing
    NT Honing machines
        Liquid honing

Honing machines
  BT Honing
         Machine-tools
Honiton lace
  USE Bobbin lace
Honky-tonk music *(May Subd Geog)*
  ⌐ML3528⌐
  BT Country music
Honma family *(Not Subd Geog)*
  UF Homma family
Honmiti
  — Doctrines
Honn family
  USE Hon family
Honnōji Incident, 1582 (Japan)
  USE Japan—History—Honnōji Incident,
         1582
Hōno-yama (Japan)
  USE Daisetsu Mountains (Japan)
Honolulu (Hawaii). Kakaako
  USE Kakaako (Honolulu, Hawaii)
Honolulu (Hawaii). McCully
  USE McCully (Honolulu, Hawaii)
Honolulu (Hawaii). Moiliili
  USE Moiliili (Honolulu, Hawaii)
Honolulu Marathon
  ⌐GV1065.22.H⌐
  BT Marathon running—Hawaii
Honor
  ⌐BJ1533.H8 (Ethics)⌐
  BT Chivalry
         Conduct of life
  NT Courts of honor
         Dignity
Honor, Courts of
  USE Courts of honor
Honor, Decorations of
  USE Decorations of honor
Honor in literature
Honor system
  USE Self-government (in education)
Honorary citizenship *(May Subd Geog)*
  BT Citizenship
Honorary degrees
  USE Degrees, Academic
Honorary municipal officials and employees
  USE Municipal officials and employees,
         Honorary
Honorary officials and employees
  USE *subdivision* Officials and employees,
         Honorary *under names of countries*
Honorary titles
  USE Titles of honor and nobility
Honorific
  USE *subdivision* Honorific *under names of*
         languages and groups of languages
         Grammar, Comparative and general—
         Honorific
Honorific unit titles (United States Army)
  USE United States. Army—Honorific unit
         titles
Honoris Crux
  BT South Africa—Armed Forces—Medals,
         badges, decorations, etc.
Honors courses in colleges
  USE Universities and colleges—Honors
         courses
Honors courses in high schools
  USE High schools—Honors courses
Honors work in colleges
  USE Universities and colleges—Honors
         courses
Honors work in high schools
  USE High schools—Honors courses
Honshiu (Japan)
  USE Honshū (Japan)
Honshū (Japan)
  UF Hondo (Japan)
         Honshiu (Japan)
         Honsyū (Japan)
  BT Islands—Japan

Honsyū (Japan)
  USE Honshū (Japan)
Hont (Netherlands)
  USE Westerschelde (Netherlands)
Honzon (Nichiren)
  BT Buddhism—Liturgical objects
         Nichiren (Sect)
Hood, Mount (Or.)
  UF Mount Hood (Or.)
  BT Mountains—Oregon
         Volcanoes—Oregon
Hood, Robin (Legendary character)
  USE Robin Hood (Legendary character)
Hood ornaments on automobiles
  USE Automobiles—Radiator ornaments
Hood River, East Fork (Or.)
  UF East Fork, Hood River (Or.)
  BT Rivers—Oregon
Hood Site (Ont.)
  USE Robin Hood Site (Ont.)
Hooded crow
  UF Corvus corone cornix
  BT Crows
Hooded skunk
  UF Mephitis macroura
  BT Skunks
Hooden horse
  ⌐GT4985⌐
Hoodlums *(May Subd Geog)*
  UF Gangsters
         Hooligans
  BT Crime and criminals
         Juvenile delinquency
  RT Gangs
Hoodoo (Cult) *(May Subd Geog)*
      Here are entered works on a form of cult magic
  practiced primarily in the southern United States.
  Works on the major folk religion practiced primarily
  in Haiti and parts of the southern United States are
  entered under Voodooism.
  BT Afro-Americans—Religion
         Cults—United States
  RT Voodooism
Hoodoo Creek (Idaho)
  BT Rivers—Idaho
Hoodoo Mountains (Idaho)
  (Not Subd Geog)
  BT Mountains—Idaho
Hoodoo Quartzite (Idaho)
  BT Formations (Geology)—Idaho
         Geology, Stratigraphic—Pre-Cambrian
Hoods
  USE Academic costume
Hoof-and-mouth disease
  USE Foot-and-mouth disease
Hoof family
  USE Hoff family
Hoofed animals
  USE Ungulata
Hoofer family
  USE Hoover family
Hoofes family
  USE Hoff family
Hooff family
  USE Hoff family
Hoofman family
  USE Hoffman family
Hoofs
  ⌐QL942⌐
  UF Hooves
  BT Horses
         Horses—Anatomy
Hook family *(Not Subd Geog)*
  UF Hoke family
         Hoker family
         Hooke family
         Hooker family
         Hooks family
  RT Hoch family
         Hoeker family

Hook order
  USE Social hierarchy in animals
Hook-tip moths
  USE Drepanidae
Hooke family
  USE Hook family
Hooked rug industry *(May Subd Geog)*
  ⌐HD9937.3.H66-664⌐
  BT Rugs, Hooked
Hooked rugs
  USE Rugs, Hooked
Hooker family
  USE Hook family
Hookera puchella
  USE Dichelostemma pulchellum
Hookeriaceae
  ⌐QK539.H64⌐
  BT Hookeriales
Hookeriales
  ⌐QK539.H⌐
  BT Mosses
  NT Hookeriaceae
Hookers (Fishing boats) *(May Subd Geog)*
  ⌐VM431⌐
  BT Fishing boats
         Sailboats
Hooke's coupling
  ⌐TJ183⌐
Hookfin dolphin
  USE Pacific whitesided dolphin
Hooking
  BT Fancy work
  NT Rugs, Hooked
Hooking, Locker
  USE Locker hooking
Hooks
  ⌐TA492.H6 (Strength of materials)⌐
  ⌐TS440-TS445⌐
Hooks, Button
  USE Buttonhooks
Hooks and eyes
  ⌐HD9969.H5-HD9969.H53 (Trade)⌐
  ⌐TS2301.H (Manufacture)⌐
  BT Fasteners
Hooks family
  USE Hook family
Hookstep family
  USE Huckstep family
Hooksteppe family
  USE Huckstep family
Hookworm disease *(May Subd Geog)*
  ⌐RC199.95⌐
  UF Ancylostomiasis
         Ankylostomiasis
         Uncinariasis
  BT Anemia
         Helminthiasis
Hookworms
  ⌐QL391.N4⌐
  UF Ancylostomatidae
         Ankylostomatidae
  BT Nematoda
         Worms, Intestinal and parasitic
  NT Ancylostomatidae
         Necator
Hoolbrook family
  USE Holbrook family
Hooligans
  USE Hoodlums
Hooms family
  USE Holmes family
Hoop exercises
  ⌐GV490⌐
  UF Hoops
  BT Callisthenics
Hoop family
  USE Hooper family
Hoop pine
  USE Araucaria cunninghamii
Hoopah Indians
  USE Hupa Indians

Hoope family
  USE Hoopes family
Hooper family *(Not Subd Geog)*
  UF Hoop family
    Hoper family
Hoopes family *(Not Subd Geog)*
  UF Hoope family
    Howpe family
Hoopkins family
  USE Hopkins family
Hoopoes
  [QL696.C7]
  BT Coraciiformes
Hoops
  USE Hoop exercises
Hoops, Baling
  USE Baling hoops
Hoos family
  USE Hoes family
Hoose family
  USE Hoes family
Hooser family
  USE Houser family
Hoosier (Nickname)
  [F257]
Hoosier family *(Not Subd Geog)*
Hoosier National Forest (Ind.)
  BT Forest reserves—Indiana
    National parks and reserves—Indiana
Hooson family
  USE Hewson family
Hoosun family
  USE Hewson family
Hootsill family
  USE Hutzel family
Hootzools
  USE Hutsuls
Hooved animals
  USE Ungulata
Hoovel family *(Not Subd Geog)*
  UF Hovel family
Hoover Dam (Ariz. and Nev.)
  (Not Subd Geog)
  UF Boulder Dam (Ariz. and Nev.)
  BT Dams—Arizona
    Dams—Nevada
Hoover family *(Not Subd Geog)*
  UF Hoofer family
    Houver family
    Hover family
    Hovers family
Hooves
  USE Hoofs
Hop (Plant)
  USE Hops
Hop-aphis
  [SB608.H8]
  BT Hops—Diseases and pests
Hop flea-beetle
  [SB608.H8]
  BT Hops—Diseases and pests
Hop pickers *(May Subd Geog)*
  BT Hops
Hop picking
  USE Hops—Harvesting
Hop, skip, and jump
  USE Triple jump
Hop, step, and jump
  USE Triple jump
HOPDOB (Chemical)
  USE Hexyloxyphenyl decyloxybenzoate
Hope
  [BD216 (Philosophy)]
  BT Emotions
  — Religious aspects
  — — Buddhism, [Christianity, etc.]
  — — Christianity
      UF Hope, Theology of
        Hope (Theology)
      BT Theological virtues

Hope, Theology of
  USE Hope—Religious aspects—Christianity
Hope (Theology)
  USE Hope—Religious aspects—Christianity
Hope diamond
  BT Diamonds
Hope family *(Not Subd Geog)*
  UF Hopes family
Hope in literature
Hope Island (Micronesia)
  USE Kosrae (Micronesia)
Hoper family
  USE Hooper family
Hopes family
  USE Hope family
Hopewell culture *(May Subd Geog)*
  BT Indians of North America—Antiquities
    Mound-builders
  NT Weeden Island culture
Hopewell Furnace National Historic Site (Pa.)
  UF Hopewell Village National Historic
    Site (Pa.)
  BT Historic sites—Pennsylvania
    National parks and reserves—
    Pennsylvania
Hopewell Village National Historic Site (Pa.)
  USE Hopewell Furnace National Historic
    Site (Pa.)
  NT Ironmaster's House (Pa.)
Hopf algebras
  UF Algebras, Hopf
  BT Algebraic topology
Hopf spaces
  USE H-spaces
Hopfian groups
  UF Groups, Hopfian
  BT Automorphisms
    Groups, Theory of
Hopfner aircraft
  [TL686.H]
  BT Airplanes
Hopi Indians
  [E99.H7]
  UF Moki Indians
    Moqui Indians
    Tusayan Indians
  BT Indians of North America
    Shoshonean Indians
  RT Pueblo Indians
  — Art
  — Dances
      NT Snake-dance
  — Land tenure
  — Religion and mythology
  — Rites and ceremonies
      NT Snake-dance
  — Social life and customs
Hopi language
  [PM1351]
  UF Moki language
  RT Shoshonean languages
Hopi poetry *(May Subd Geog)*
Hopkens family
  USE Hopkins family
Hopkin family
  USE Hopkins family
Hopkings family
  USE Hopkins family
Hopkins family *(Not Subd Geog)*
  UF Hoopkins family
    Hopkens family
    Hopkin family
    Hopkings family
    Hopkinson family
Hopkinson family
  USE Hopkins family
Hoplitis
  [QL568.M4]
  BT Megachilidae

Hoplocampa
  [QL568.T3]
  BT Tenthredinidae
Hoplocampa testudinea
  USE Apple sawfly
Hoplolaimidae
  [QL391.N4]
  BT Tylenchida
Hoplomys
  [QL737.R65]
  BT Echimyidae
Hoplonemertea
  [QL391.N6]
  UF Hoplonemertini
  BT Enopla
  NT Ototyphlonemertidae
Hoplonemertini
  USE Hoplonemertea
Hoplophoridae
  USE Glyptodontidae
Hoplopleuridae
  [QL570.3.H68]
  BT Anoplura
Hoplopterygidae
  USE Trachichthyidae
Hoplopteryx
  BT Trachichthyidae, Fossil
  NT Hoplopteryx lewesiensis
Hoplopteryx lewesiensis
  BT Hoplopteryx
Hoppas family
  USE Hoppes family
Hopper family *(Not Subd Geog)*
  UF Hoppers family
Hoppers family
  USE Hopper family
Hoppes family *(Not Subd Geog)*
  UF Happes family
    Haps family
    Hoppas family
Hoppewode family
  USE Hopwood family
Hoppin family *(Not Subd Geog)*
  UF Hopping family
Hopping conduction
  UF Conduction, Hopping
  BT Conduction band
    Percolation (Statistical physics)
  NT Anderson model
Hopping family
  USE Hoppin family
Hops *(May Subd Geog)*
  [QK495.M73 (Botany)]
  [SB317.H64 (Culture)]
  UF Common hop
    European hop
    Hop (Plant)
    Humulus americanus
    Humulus lupulus
  BT Psychotropic plants
  NT Hop pickers
  — Diseases and pests *(May Subd Geog)*
    [SB608.H8]
    NT Hop-aphis
      Hop flea-beetle
  — Harvesting
    UF Hop picking
Hops industry *(May Subd Geog)*
  [HD9019.H7-72]
Hopscotch
  [GV1218.H]
Hopwode family
  USE Hopwood family
Hopwood family *(Not Subd Geog)*
  UF Hoppewode family
    Hopwode family
Hor Abdulla (Kuwait and Iraq)
  USE 'Abd Allāh Inlet (Kuwait and Iraq)
Hora Hoverla (Ukraine)
  USE Goverla, Mount (Ukraine)

Horae (Books of hours)
　　USE Hours, Books of
Ḥorbat Timna (Israel)
　　USE Timna Site (Israel)
Horch automobile
　　[TL215.H]
　　BT Automobiles
Horde
　　USE Nomads
Hordeolum
　　[RE155.H6]
　　UF Sty
　　　　Stye
　　BT Eyelids—Diseases
　　　　Sebaceous glands—Diseases
　— Psychosomatic aspects
Hordeum
　　[QK495.G74 (Botany)]
　　BT Grasses
Hordeum sativum
　　USE Barley
Hordeum vulgare
　　USE Barley
Hore family
　　USE Hoar family
Horeb, Mount (Egypt)
　　USE Sinai, Mount (Egypt)
Ḥorev, Mount (Egypt)
　　USE Sinai, Mount (Egypt)
Hörgárdalur (Iceland)
　　BT Valleys—Iceland
Horgen culture
　　[GN775.5.H6]
　　BT Neolithic period
Horger family (Not Subd Geog)
Hori family (Not Subd Geog)
Hori Iseki (Takatō-machi, Japan)
　　USE Hori Site (Takatō-machi, Japan)
Hori Site (Takatō-machi, Japan)
　　UF Hori Iseki (Takatō-machi, Japan)
　　BT Japan—Antiquities
Horie family (Not Subd Geog)
Horiinidae
　　USE Meloidae
Horikiri family (Not Subd Geog)
Horikiri Iris Gardens (Tokyo, Japan)
　　USE Horikiri Shōbuen (Tokyo, Japan)
Horikiri Shōbuen (Tokyo, Japan)
　　(Not Subd Geog)
　　UF Horikiri Iris Gardens (Tokyo, Japan)
　　　　Iris Gardens of Horikiri (Tokyo,
　　　　　　Japan)
　　BT Gardens—Japan
　　　　Parks—Japan
Horizon, Dip of
　　[VK572]
　　UF Dip of the horizon
Horizon automobile
　　[TL215.H]
　　UF Plymouth Horizon automobile
　　BT Plymouth automobile
Horizon sensors, Infrared
　　USE Infrared horizon sensors
Horizon Spreadsheet (Computer program)
　　BT Computer programs
Horizons, Artificial
　　[VK584.H]
　　UF Artificial horizons
　　BT Geographical positions
　　　　Nautical instruments
Horizontal bar
　　[GV527]
　　UF Bar, Horizontal
　　BT Gymnastics
Horizontal branch stars
　　UF Stars, Horizontal branch
　　BT HR diagrams
　　　　Stars—Globular clusters
Horizontal position (Posture)
　　USE Lying down position

Horizontal price fixing
　　USE Price fixing
Horizontal property
　　USE Condominiums
Hormée, Bordeaux (France), 1652-1653
　　USE Bordeaux (France)—History—
　　　　　Uprising, 1652-1653
Hormogonales
　　USE Oscillatoriales
Hormonal aspects of cancer
　　USE Cancer—Endocrine aspects
Hormonal aspects of fertility
　　USE Fertility—Endocrine aspects
Hormonal aspects of human reproduction
　　USE Human reproduction—Endocrine
　　　　　aspects
Hormonal aspects of immunity
　　USE Immunity—Endocrine aspects
Hormonal aspects of sex differentiation
　　USE Sex differentiation—Endocrine aspects
Hormonal disorders
　　USE Endocrine glands—Diseases
Hormonal peptides
　　USE Peptide hormones
Hormonal polymorphism
　　USE Isohormones
Hormonal steroids
　　USE Steroid hormones
Hormone antagonists
　　UF Antagonists, Hormone
　　　　Antihormones
　　BT Chemical inhibitors
　　　　Immunoglobulins
　　NT Adrenocortical hormones—Antagonists
　　　　Antiandrogens
　　　　Bromocriptine
　　　　Captopril
　　　　Estrogen—Antagonists
　　　　Insulin—Antagonists
　　　　Luteinizing hormone releasing
　　　　　hormone—Antagonists
　　　　Progesterone—Antagonists
　　　　Saralasin
Hormone producing tumors
　　USE Neoplastic endocrine-like syndromes
Hormone receptors
　　UF Receptors, Hormone
　　BT Binding sites (Biochemistry)
　　　　Cell receptors
　　　　Drug receptors
　　　　Endocrinology
　　SA subdivision Receptors under names of
　　　　individual hormones or groups of
　　　　hormones, e.g. Estrogen—
　　　　Receptors; Steroid hormones—
　　　　Receptors
　　NT Chorionic gonadotropins—Receptors
　　　　Endorphins—Receptors
　　　　Hormones, Sex—Receptors
　　　　Insulin—Receptors
　　　　Luteinizing hormone—Receptors
　　　　Neurotransmitter receptors
　　　　Peptide hormones—Receptors
　　　　Pheromones—Receptors
　　　　Progesterone—Receptors
Hormone resistance
　　UF Resistance to hormones
　　BT Drug resistance
Hormone synthesis
　　USE Hormones—Synthesis
Hormone therapy
　　[RM283-298]
　　UF Endocrine therapy
　　　　Hormones—Therapeutic use
　　BT Therapeutics
　　SA subdivision Therapeutic use under
　　　　specific hormones and groups of
　　　　hormones, e.g. Estrogen—
　　　　Therapeutic use; Steroid hormones
　　　　—Therapeutic use

Hormones
　　[QP801.H7]
　　BT Secretion
　　RT Catecholamines
　　　　Endocrine glands
　　　　Endocrinology
　　NT Chalones
　　　　Cortin
　　　　Ecdysone
　　　　Gastrointestinal hormones
　　　　Hormones, Sex
　　　　Hypothalamic hormones
　　　　Insect hormones
　　　　Juvenile hormones
　　　　Metabolism—Regulation
　　　　Peptide hormones
　　　　Pheromones
　　　　Pituitary hormone releasing factors
　　　　Pituitary hormones
　　　　Placental hormones
　　　　Plant hormones
　　　　Steroid hormones
　　　　Sterol hormones
　　　　Sympathin
　　　　Thymic hormones
　　　　Thyroid hormones
　　　　Toxohormone
　— Synthesis
　　　　UF Hormone synthesis
　　　　　　Hormonogenesis
　　　　　　Hormonopoiesis
　— Therapeutic use
　　　　USE Hormone therapy
Hormones, Ectopic
　　UF Ectopic hormones
Hormones, Sex
　　UF Female sex hormone
　　　　Male sex hormone
　　　　Sex hormones
　　BT Androstane
　　　　Endocrinology
　　　　Hormones
　　　　Steroid hormones
　　SA names of hormones, e.g. Androgens,
　　　　Progesterone, Testosterone
　　NT Estrogen
　　　　Inhibin
　　　　Plant sex hormones
　　　　Progestational hormones
　　　　Relaxin
　— Receptors
　　　　BT Hormone receptors
Hormones, Sterol
　　USE Sterol hormones
Hormones (Plants)
　　USE Plant hormones
Hormones in animal nutrition
　　[SF98.H67]
　— Law and legislation (May Subd Geog)
Hormonogenesis
　　USE Hormones—Synthesis
Hormonopoiesis
　　USE Hormones—Synthesis
Hormoz, Strait of
　　USE Hormuz, Strait of
Hormuz, Strait of
　　UF Bāb-e-Hormūz
　　　　Bāb-i-Hormūz
　　　　Būghāz Hormūz
　　　　Hormoz, Strait of
　　　　Hurmuz, Strait of
　　　　Maḍīq Hurmūz
　　　　Ormuz, Strait of
　　　　Strait of Hormuz
　　　　Tangeh Hormoz
　　BT Straits—Oman, Gulf of
　　　　Straits—Persian Gulf
Horn, Cape (Chile)
　　USE Cape Horn (Chile)
Horn (Musical instrument)
　　[ML955-8]

1724

UF French horn
BT Brass instruments
RT Tuba
NT Alpenhorn
  Alto horn
  Lur
  Post horn
  Russian horn
  Shophar
— Orchestra studies
  [MT426]
  BT Horn (Musical instrument)—
    Studies and exercises
— Studies and exercises
  [MT425]
  NT Horn (Musical instrument)—
    Orchestra studies
Horn and bassoon music
USE Bassoon and horn music
Horn and cimbalom music
  [M298]
  UF Cimbalom and horn music
Horn and clarinet music
USE Clarinet and horn music
Horn and flute music
USE Flute and horn music
Horn and guitar music
  [M296-7]
  UF Guitar and horn music
Horn and guitar music, Arranged
  [M296-7]
Horn and harp music
  [M296-297]
  UF Harp and horn music
Horn and harp with orchestra
  [M1040-1041]
  RT Concertos (Horn and harp)
Horn and oboe music
  [M288-9]
  UF Oboe and horn music
Horn and organ music
  [M182-4]
  UF Organ and horn music
  NT Chorale preludes (Horn and organ)
    Suites (Horn and organ)
    Variations (Horn and organ)
Horn and percussion music
  [M298]
  UF Percussion and horn music
Horn and piano music
  [M255-7]
  UF Piano and horn music
  NT Marches (Horn and piano)
    Rondos (Horn and piano)
    Sonatas (Horn and piano)
    Suites (Horn and piano)
    Variations (Horn and piano)
    Waltzes (Horn and piano)
Horn and piano music, Arranged
  [M258-9]
  NT Concertos (Horn)—Solo with piano
    Concertos (Horn with string ensemble)
      —Solo with piano
    Concertos (Horn with string orchestra)
      —Solo with piano
    Horn with band—Solo with piano
    Horn with orchestra—Solo with piano
    Horn with string ensemble—Solo with
      piano
    Horn with string orchestra—Solo with
      piano
    Rondos (Horn with orchestra)—Solo
      with piano
    Variations (Horn with orchestra)—Solo
      with piano
Horn and trombone music
  [M288-M289]
  UF Trombone and horn music
Horn and trombone with orchestra
  [M1040-1041]
  RT Concertos (Horn and trombone)

Horn and trumpet music
  [M288-M289]
  UF Trumpet and horn music
Horn and violin music
  [M290-291]
  UF Violin and horn music
Horn and violoncello music
  [M290-291]
  UF Violoncello and horn music
Horn antennas
USE Antennas, Horn
Horn carving (May Subd Geog)
  [NK6020]
  BT Carving (Decorative arts)
Horn ensembles
  [M955-956]
  [M957.4]
  [M958-959]
  Here are entered compositions for ten or more horns and collections of compositions for a varying number of horns.
  When used in conjunction with specific solo instrument(s), the designation horn ensemble may stand for any number of horns.
  SA Concertos ([Solo instrument(s)] with horn ensemble); [Solo instrument(s)] with horn ensemble; Suites, Variations, Waltzes, and similar headings with specification of instruments which include the specification Horn ensemble
Horn family (Not Subd Geog)
  UF Horne family
    Hornes family
    Hornn family
  RT Van Horn family
Horn fly
  [QL537.M7 (Zoology)]
  [SF810.H6 (Agriculture)]
  UF Haematobia irritans
    Haematobia serrata
    Lyperosia irritans
  BT Flies
Horn Island (Miss.)
  BT Islands—Mississippi
Horn music
  [M80-84]
  SA Concertos, Minuets, Sonatas, Suites, and similar headings with specification of instruments; Brass trios [quartets, etc.], Trios [Quartets, etc.], and Wind trios [quartets, etc.] followed by specifications which include the horn; also Brass ensembles, Wind ensembles, and headings that begin with the words horn or horns
  NT Hunting music
    Recorded accompaniments (Horn)
    Sonatas (Horn)
Horn music (Horns (2))
  [M288-9]
  NT Canons, fugues, etc. (Horns (2))
    Concertos (Horns (2))
    Concertos (Horns (2) with string orchestra)
    Horns (2) with orchestra
    Horns (2) with string orchestra
    Sonatas (Horns (2))
Horn music (Horns (3))
USE Brass trios (Horns (3))
Horn music (Horns (4))
USE Brass quartets (Horns (4))
Horn music (Horns (5))
USE Brass quintets (Horns (5))
Horn music (Horns (6))
USE Brass sextets (Horns (6))
Horn music (Horns (7))
USE Brass septets (Horns (7))
Horn music (Horns (8))
USE Brass octets (Horns (8))

Horn of Africa
USE Africa, Northeast
Horn players
  [ML399]
  [ML419]
Horn shark
  [QL638.95.H4]
  UF California horn shark
    Heterodontus francisci
    Horned shark
    Hornshark
  BT Heterodontus
Horn Sound (Spitsbergen Island, Norway)
  UF Hornsund (Spitsbergen Island, Norway)
  BT Inlets—Norway
Horn, trombone, trumpets (2), tuba with instrumental ensemble
  BT Brass quintets (Horn, trombone, trumpets (2), tuba)
  RT Concertos (Horn, trombone, trumpets (2), tuba with instrumental ensemble)
  NT Variations (Horn, trombone, trumpets (2), tuba with instrumental ensemble)
Horn, trombone, trumpets (2), tuba with orchestra
  [M1040-1041]
  BT Brass quintets (Horn, trombone, trumpets (2), tuba)
  RT Concertos (Horn, trombone, trumpets (2), tuba)
Horn, trombone, trumpets (2), tuba with string orchestra
  [M1140-1141]
  BT Brass quintets (Horn, trombone, trumpets (2), tuba)
  RT Concertos (Horn, trombone, trumpets (2), tuba with string orchestra)
Horn, trombones (2), trumpets (2) with chamber orchestra
  [M1040-1041]
  BT Brass quintets (Horn, trombones (2), trumpets (2))
  RT Concertos (Horn, trombones (2), trumpets (2) with chamber orchestra)
Horn, trombones (2), trumpets (2) with orchestra
  [M1040-1041]
  BT Brass quintets (Horn, trombones (2), trumpets (2))
  RT Concertos (Horn, trombones (2), trumpets (2))
Horn, trombones (2), trumpets (2) with string orchestra
  [M1140-1141]
  BT Brass quintets (Horn, trombones (2), trumpets (2))
  RT Concertos (Horn, trombones (2), trumpets (2) with string orchestra)
Horn with band
  [M1205]
  BT Band music
  RT Concertos (Horn with band)
— Solo with piano
  [M1206]
  BT Horn and piano music, Arranged
Horn with band, Arranged
  [M1257]
— Scores
  [M1257]
Horn with chamber orchestra
  [M1028-9]
  RT Concertos (Horn with chamber orchestra)
Horn with horn ensemble
  RT Concertos (Horn with horn ensemble)

Horn with instrumental ensemble
  RT Concertos (Horn with instrumental
      ensemble)
Horn with orchestra
  [M1028-9]
  BT Orchestral music
  RT Concertos (Horn)
  NT Rondos (Horn with orchestra)
     Variations (Horn with orchestra)
  — Solo with piano
    [M1029]
    BT Horn and piano music, Arranged
Horn with orchestra, Arranged
  [M1028-9]
Horn with percussion ensemble
  RT Concertos (Horn with percussion
      ensemble)
Horn with string ensemble
  RT Concertos (Horn with string ensemble)
  — Solo with piano
    BT Horn and piano music, Arranged
Horn with string orchestra
  [M1105-6]
  RT Concertos (Horn with string orchestra)
  NT Suites (Horn with string orchestra)
  — Solo with piano
    [M1129]
    BT Horn and piano music, Arranged
Horn with string orchestra, Arranged
  [M1105-6]
  — Scores
    [M1105]
Hornabrooke family
  USE Hornbrook family
Hornád River (Czechoslovakia and Hungary)
  USE Hernád River (Czechoslovakia and
     Hungary)
Hornada family
  USE Hornaday family
Hornaday family *(Not Subd Geog)*
  UF Hornada family
    Horniday family
Hornbækbanen
  BT Railroads—Denmark
Hornbeam, European
  USE European hornbeam
Hornberg Castle (Germany)
  USE Burg Hornberg (Germany)
Hornberg family
  USE Hornberger family
Hornberger family *(Not Subd Geog)*
  UF Hornberg family
  RT Hornburg family
Hornbills
  [QL696.C729]
  UF Bucerotidae
  BT Coraciiformes
  NT Bycanistes
    Helmeted hornbill
Hornblende *(May Subd Geog)*
  [QE391.H]
  BT Amphiboles
Hornblow family
  USE Hornblower family
Hornblower family *(Not Subd Geog)*
  UF Hornblow family
Hornbooks
  [Z1033.H8]
  UF Battledores
  BT Primers
Hornbrook family *(Not Subd Geog)*
  UF Hornabrooke family
    Hornbrooke family
    Hornebroke family
Hornbrooke family
  USE Hornbrook family
Hornburg family *(Not Subd Geog)*
  RT Hornberger family
Hornby Island (B.C.)
  BT Islands—British Columbia

Horne family
  USE Horn family
Hornebroke family
  USE Hornbrook family
Horned larks
  USE Larks
Horned lizards
  USE Horned toads
Horned owl
  [QL696.S83]
  UF Bubo virginianus
    Great horned owl
Horned pout
  USE Black bullhead
    Brown bullhead
Horned shark
  USE Horn shark
Horned toads
  [QL666.L25]
  UF Horned lizards
    Lizards, Horned
    Phrynosoma
  BT Iguanidae
  NT Phrynosoma douglassi
    Phrynosoma modestum
    Phrynosoma platyrhinos
Horner family *(Not Subd Geog)*
Horner Site (Wyo.)
  BT Buffalo jump—Wyoming
    Wyoming—Antiquities
Hornero, Pale-legged
  USE Pale-legged hornero
Hornero, Rufous
  USE Furnarius rufus
Hornes family
  USE Horn family
Hornet (Jet fighter plane)
  UF F/A-18 (Jet fighter plane)
  BT Fighter planes
    Jet planes, Military
    McDonnell Douglas airplanes
Hornet automobile
  BT American Motors automobiles
Hornet Bank Station (Qld.)
  BT Sheep ranches—Australia
Hornets
  USE Paper wasps
Horní Slezsko (Poland and Czechoslovakia)
  USE Silesia, Upper (Poland and
    Czechoslovakia)
Hornia
  [QL596.M38]
  BT Meloidae
Horniday family
  USE Hornaday family
Horning family *(Not Subd Geog)*
  UF Hornung family
Hornless loudspeakers
  USE Direct radiator loudspeakers
Hörnli Friedhof (Basel, Switzerland)
  USE Basel-Städtischer Friedhof am Hörnli
    (Basel, Switzerland)
Hornn family
  USE Horn family
Hornpipe (Dance)
Hornpipes
  BT Dance music
Horns
  [QL942]
  NT Antlers
  — Mythology
  — Religious aspects
Horns, Cutaneous
  [RL427]
  UF Cornua cutanea
    Cutaneous horns
  BT Keratosis
  NT Molting
Horns, Removal of
  USE Dehorning

Horns (2), oboes (2) with string orchestra
  [M1140-1141]
  BT Wind quartets (Horns (2), oboes (2))
  RT Concertos (Horns (2), oboes (2) with
    string orchestra)
**Horns (2), trombones (2), trumpets (2), tuba
with orchestra**
  [M1040-1041]
  BT Brass septets (Horns (2), trombones
    (2), trumpets (2), tuba)
  RT Concertos (Horns (2), trombones (2),
    trumpets (2), tuba)
Horns (2) with orchestra
  [M1028-9]
  UF Two horns with orchestra
  BT Horn music (Horns (2))
  RT Concertos (Horns (2))
Horns (2) with string orchestra
  [M1105-6]
  UF Two horns with string orchestra
  BT Horn music (Horns (2))
  RT Concertos (Horns (2) with string
    orchestra)
Horns (3) with band
  [M1205-6]
  BT Brass trios (Horns (3))
  RT Concertos (Horns (3) with band)
Horns (3) with orchestra
  [M1028-9]
  BT Brass trios (Horns (3))
  RT Concertos (Horns (3))
Horns (3) with string orchestra
  [M1128-1129]
  BT Brass trios (Horns (3))
  RT Concertos (Horns (3) with string
    orchestra)
Horns (4) with band
  [M1205-6]
  UF Four horns with band
  BT Brass quartets (Horns (4))
  NT Concertos (Horns (4) with band)
Horns (4) with orchestra
  [M1028-9]
  UF Four horns with orchestra
  BT Brass quartets (Horns (4))
  RT Concertos (Horns (4))
  — Scores
    [M1028]
Hornshark
  USE Horn shark
Hornstone
  USE Chert
Hornsund (Spitsbergen Island, Norway)
  USE Horn Sound (Spitsbergen Island,
    Norway)
Horntail wasps
  USE Siricidae
Hornung, E. W. (Ernest William), 1866-1921
  — Characters
  — — Raffles
    RT Raffles (Fictitious character)
Hornung family
  USE Horning family
Hornworts
  USE Ceratophyllaceae
Horodło, Treaty of, 1413
  BT Lithuania—History
Horohoro language
  USE Holoholo language
Horologion of Andronicus of Cyrrhus (Athens,
  Greece)
  USE Tower of the Winds (Athens, Greece)
Horologium of Andronicus of Cyrrhus (Athens,
  Greece)
  USE Tower of the Winds (Athens, Greece)
Horology
  [TS540-549]
  UF Hours (Time)
  BT Time measurements
  RT Time
  NT Balance springs—Isochronism

Chronometer
Clocks and watches
Days
Pendulum—Isochronism
Horoscopes
 [BF1728.A2]
  BT Astrology
Horoscopy
 USE Astrology
Horrall family
 USE Horrell family
Horrell family (Not Subd Geog)
  UF Horrall family
Horror
   Here are entered works on the expression of
 shock, fear or repulsion caused by an atrocity or a
 danger directed toward oneself or others. Works on
 intense, prolonged fear caused by either recurring
 frightening imageries or imagined or actual present or
 future dangers are entered under Terror.
  BT Emotions
  RT Fear
Horror films (May Subd Geog)
  BT Feature films
     Moving-pictures
  NT Frankenstein films
     Godzilla films
     Vampire films
     Werewolf films
 — Production and direction
Horror in art
 [N8217.H68]
Horror in mass media
 [P96.H65]
  BT Mass media
Horror plays
  BT Drama
Horror plays, American (May Subd Geog)
  UF American horror plays
  BT American drama
Horror radio programs (May Subd Geog)
  BT Radio programs
Horror tales
  UF Terror tales
  BT Detective and mystery stories
     Fiction
  RT Ghost stories
Horror tales, American (May Subd Geog)
  UF American horror tales
  BT American fiction
Horror tales, American, [German, etc.]
 (May Subd Geog)
Horror tales, Canadian (May Subd Geog)
  UF Canadian horror tales
  BT Canadian fiction
Horror tales, Dutch (May Subd Geog)
  UF Dutch horror tales
  BT Dutch fiction
Horror tales, English (May Subd Geog)
  UF English horror tales
  BT English fiction
  NT Penny dreadfuls
Horror tales, Finnish (May Subd Geog)
  UF Finnish horror tales
  BT Finnish fiction
Horror tales, French (May Subd Geog)
  UF French horror tales
  BT French fiction
Horror tales, Hungarian (May Subd Geog)
  UF Hungarian horror tales
  BT Hungarian fiction
Horror tales, Mauritian (English)
 (May Subd Geog)
  UF Mauritian horror tales (English)
  BT Mauritian fiction (English)
Horror tales, Philippine (English)
 (May Subd Geog)
  UF Philippine horror tales (English)
  BT Philippine fiction (English)
Horror tales, Russian (May Subd Geog)
  UF Russian horror tales

  BT Russian fiction
Horror television programs
  BT Television programs
Horrors of war (Painting)
 USE Rubens, Peter Paul, Sir, 1577-1640.
     Horrors of war
Hors d'oeuvres
 USE Cookery (Appetizers)
Horse
 USE Horses
Horse, Vaulting
 USE Vaulting-horse
Horse artists
 USE Equestrian artists
Horse banana
 USE Plantain banana
Horse bean
 USE Faba bean
Horse brasses
 [GT5888]
  BT Brasswork
     Harness
     Metal-work
Horse-breaking
 USE Horses—Training
Horse breeders (May Subd Geog)
  UF Breeders, Horse
     Breeders of horses
  BT Horsemen and horsewomen
     Livestock breeders
Horse breeds (May Subd Geog)
  UF Horses—Breeds
  BT Horses
  SA names of specific breeds, e.g. Arabian
     horse, Clydesdale horse, Tennessee
     walking horse
  NT American saddlebred horse
     Andalusian horse
     Cheju pony
     Hackney horse
     Hungarian horse
     Lipizzaner horse
     Mangalarga horse
     Miniature horses
     Morgan horse
     Nonius horse
     Novokirghiz horse
     Paso fino horse
     Peruvian paso horse
     Pottok
     Shire horse
     Thoroughbred horse
     Turkoman horse
 — Japan
  NT Kiso horse
Horse business
 USE Horse industry
Horse buyers (May Subd Geog)
  UF Buyers, Horse
     Horse purchasers
     Purchasers, Horse
  BT Horsemen and horsewomen
Horse centers
 USE Equestrian centers
Horse chestnut (May Subd Geog)
 [QK495.H65 (Botany)]
  UF Aesculus hippocastanum
     Chestnut, Horse
     Common horse chestnut
     European horse chestnut
Horse chestnut, California
 USE California buckeye
Horse drawn railroads
 USE Horse railroads
Horse-drawn vehicle driving
 USE Driving of horse-drawn vehicles
Horse farms (May Subd Geog)
 [SF290-SF291 (Breeding)]
  UF Farms, Horse
     Farms, Stud
     Stud farms

  BT Farms
Horse flies
 USE Horseflies
Horse-hair worms
 USE Gordiacea
Horse Heaven Hills (Wash.)
  BT Mountains—Washington (State)
Horse industry (May Subd Geog)
 [HD9434]
  UF Horse business
  BT Animal industry
  NT Horse syndication
     Horse trading
Horse mackerel
 USE Trachurus trachurus
Horse mackerel, Mediterranean
 USE Trachurus mediterraneus
Horse meat
 [TX556.H8 (Foods)]
  UF Hippophagy
  BT Meat
  NT Cookery (Horse meat)
Horse mills (May Subd Geog)
  BT Animal-powered engines
     Mills and mill-work
Horse owners (May Subd Geog)
  UF Owners, Horse
  BT Horsemen and horsewomen
 — Taxation (May Subd Geog)
 — — Law and legislation
     (May Subd Geog)
Horse Pasture Cave Site (Or.)
 USE Rigdon's Horse Pasture Cave Site
     (Or.)
Horse players
 USE Horseplayers
Horse processions (May Subd Geog)
  UF Cavalcades
  BT Processions
Horse pulling contests (May Subd Geog)
  UF Pulling contests, Horse
     Weight pulling contests, Horse-drawn
  BT Draft horses
Horse purchasers
 USE Horse buyers
Horse race betting (May Subd Geog)
 [SF331]
  UF Handicapping
     Horseplaying
     Off-track betting
     Playing the horses
  BT Gambling
     Horse-racing
     Sports betting
     Wagers
  NT Book-making (Betting)
     Horseplayers
     Pari-mutuel betting
 — Law and legislation (May Subd Geog)
Horse racetracks
 USE Racetracks (Horse-racing)
Horse-racing (May Subd Geog)
 [SF321-359]
  UF Flat racing
  BT Horse sports
     Racing
  NT Barrel racing
     Chariot racing
     Claiming races
     Doping in horse-racing
     Harness racing
     Horse race betting
     Horses—Paces, gaits, etc.
     Jockeys
     Point-to-point racing
     Quarter racing
     Race horses
     Racetracks (Horse-racing)
     Steeplechasing
     Women in horse racing
 — Employees

Horse-racing
— **Employees** *(Continued)*
  NT Jockeys
— **Law and legislation** *(May Subd Geog)*
— **Records**
  ⌐SF325 (General)⌐
— **Rules**
  ⌐SF329⌐
— **Taxation** *(May Subd Geog)*
  BT Gambling—Taxation
— **England**
  NT Epsom Derby, England (Horse
      race)
    King George VI and Queen
      Elizabeth Diamond Stakes
    Royal Ascot
— **France**
  NT Prix de l'Arc de Triomphe (Horse
      race)
— **Ireland**
  NT Irish Sweeps Derby
— **Kentucky**
  NT Kentucky Derby
— **New York (State)**
  NT Belmont Stakes
— **Ontario**
  NT Canadian International
      Championship Stakes
    Queen's Plate (Horse race)
— **Puerto Rico**
  NT Clásico del Caribe
— **South Africa**
  NT July Handicap (Horse race)
Horse-radish
  ⌐SB307.H⌐
  UF Horseradish
— **Diseases and pests** *(May Subd Geog)*
  NT Horse-radish flea-beetle
    Horse-radish web-worm
Horse-radish flea-beetle
  BT Horse-radish—Diseases and pests
Horse-radish web-worm
  ⌐SB608.H82⌐
  BT Horse-radish—Diseases and pests
Horse railroads *(May Subd Geog)*
  ⌐TF16⌐
  ⌐TF830 (Street railways)⌐
  UF Horse drawn railroads
    Railroads, Horse
    Tramways
  BT Railroads
    Railroads, Local and light
— **Cars**
  ⌐TF830⌐
  UF Cars and car building
    Horsecars
  BT Street-railroads—Rolling-stock
Horse riding
  USE Horsemanship
Horse sense
  USE Common sense
Horse Shoe, Battle of the, 1814
  ⌐E83.813⌐
  UF Horse Shoe Bend, Battle of, 1814
    Horseshoe Bend, Battle of, 1814
    Tohopeka, Battle of, 1814
  BT Creek War, 1813-1814
Horse Shoe Bend, Battle of, 1814
  USE Horse Shoe, Battle of the, 1814
Horse show jumping
  USE Show jumping
Horse-shows *(May Subd Geog)*
  ⌐SF295-7⌐
  UF Horses—Exhibitions
  BT Horsemanship—Competitions
    Horsemanship—Exhibitions
    Livestock exhibitions
  RT Horse sports
    Show horses
  NT Eventing (Horsemanship)
    Gymkhanas (Horsemanship)

Horses—Judging
Horses—Showing
Hunter classes
Hunter seat equitation division
Jockeys
Point-to-point racing
Reining horse class
Rodeos
Saddle seat equitation
Show driving of horse-drawn vehicles
Show jumping
Show riding
Trail horse class
— Driving classes
  USE Show driving of horse-drawn
      vehicles
— Gymkhana division
  USE Gymkhanas (Horsemanship)
— **Halter classes**
  ⌐SF296.H34⌐
  UF Halter horse classes
— **Law and legislation** *(May Subd Geog)*
— **Performance classes**
  UF Performance horse classes
  RT Show jumping
    Show riding
  NT Horse-shows—Western division
      and classes
— Reining classes
  USE Reining horse class
— Trail classes
  USE Trail horse class
— **Western division and classes**
  ⌐SF296.H47⌐
  BT Horse-shows—Performance classes
    Western riding—Competitions
    Western riding—Exhibitions
  NT Reining horse class
    Trail horse class
— — Reining classes
  USE Reining horse class
— — Trail classes
  USE Trail horse class
Horse sports *(May Subd Geog)*
  ⌐SF294.2-359.7⌐
  UF Equestrian sports
    Mounted sports
    Riding sports
  BT Sports
  RT Horse-shows
    Horsemanship
    Tournaments
  NT Buzkashi
    Courses (Horse sports)
    Cross-country (Horsemanship)
    Cutting horse competitions
    Dressage tests
    Eventing (Horsemanship)
    Fox-hunting
    Gymkhanas (Horsemanship)
    Horse-racing
    Horsemen and horsewomen
    Hunt riding
    Polo
    Quintain
    Ride and tie racing
    Rodeos
    Show driving of horse-drawn vehicles
    Show jumping
    Show riding
    Trail riding—Competitions
    Trick riding
    Vaulting (Horsemanship)
    Women in horse sports
— **Australia**
  NT Campdrafting
Horse stealing
  BT Larceny
Horse syndication *(May Subd Geog)*
  UF Syndication, Horse
  BT Horse industry

  RT Race horses as an investment
— **Law and legislation** *(May Subd Geog)*
Horse tick fever
  USE Babesiosis in horses
Horse trading *(May Subd Geog)*
  UF Trading of horses
  BT Horse industry
Horse trails
  USE Trails
Horse trainers *(May Subd Geog)*
  UF Horsetrainers
  BT Animal trainers
    Horsemen and horsewomen
    Horses—Training
  NT Dressage horse trainers
    Racehorse trainers
Horse-training
  USE Horses—Training
Horse trials
  USE Eventing (Horsemanship)
Horse trials horses
  USE Event horses
Horseback camping
  USE Packhorse camping
Horseback riding
  USE Horsemanship
Horseback riding clubs
  USE Riding clubs
Horsebacks (Mining)
  USE Clay veins
Horsecars
  USE Horse railroads—Cars
Horseflesh ore
  USE Bornite
Horseflies
  ⌐QL537.T2⌐
  UF Gadflies
    Horse flies
    Tabanidae
  BT Flies
  NT Dasybasis
    Deerflies
Horseford family
  USE Hosford family
Horsehair
  ⌐TS1747.H6 (Manufactures)⌐
Horsehair worms
  USE Gordiacea
Horseman family
  USE Horsman family
Horsemanship *(May Subd Geog)*
  ⌐SF309 (General)⌐
  ⌐UE470-UE475 (Cavalry)⌐
  UF Eastern horsemanship
    Eastern riding
    English horsemanship
    English riding
    Equestrianism
    Equitation
    Horse riding
    Horseback riding
    Riding
    Riding, Eastern
    Riding, English
  BT Locomotion
  RT Equestrian centers
    Horse sports
  SA *headings beginning with the word
      Riding*
  NT Coaching
    Courses (Horse sports)
    Cross-country (Horsemanship)
    Dressage
    Driving of horse-drawn vehicles
    Endurance riding (Horsemanship)
    Eventing (Horsemanship)
    Gymkhanas (Horsemanship)
    Haute école (Horsemanship)
    Horsemen and horsewomen
    Horses—Paces, gaits, etc.
    Horses—Training

Hunt riding
Hunter seat equitation
Jumping (Horsemanship)
Lungeing (Horsemanship)
Pony trekking
Riding clubs
Riding habit
Show riding
Sidesaddle riding
Trail riding
Trick riding
Vaulting (Horsemanship)
Western riding
— **Competitions**
    NT Horse-shows
         Show riding
— **Etiquette**
    UF Etiquette, Horsemanship
         Etiquette, Riding
         Riding etiquette
    BT Etiquette
— **Exhibitions**
    NT Horse-shows
         Show riding
— **Judging**
    BT Sports officiating
— **Therapeutic use**
    [RM931.H6]
    BT Physical therapy
— **Afghanistan**
    NT Buzkashi
Horsemanship for the handicapped
    (May Subd Geog)
    [SF309.26.H35]
    BT Handicapped—Recreation
Horsemanship in art
Horsemanship in literature
Horsemen and horsewomen
    (May Subd Geog)
    [SF284.4-284.52]
    UF Horsewomen
    BT Horse sports
         Horsemanship
         Horses
    NT Coach drivers
         Cowboys
         Cowgirls
         Dressage riders
         Gauchos
         Harness drivers
         Horse breeders
         Horse buyers
         Horse owners
         Horse trainers
         Jockeys
         Polo players
         Show jumpers (Persons)
         Show riders
         Women in horse sports
         Women jockeys
Horsemen and horsewomen (in numismatics)
    (May Subd Geog)
    [CJ161.H66]
    BT Numismatics
Horsemen and horsewomen in art
    (May Subd Geog)
    NT Equestrian statues
Horsemint
    [QK495.M]
Horseplayers *(May Subd Geog)*
    UF Horse players
    BT Horse race betting
Horseplaying
    USE Horse race betting
Horsepower
    BT Units
         Work (Mechanics)
Horseradish
    USE Horse-radish
Horses *(May Subd Geog)*
    [GR715 (Folk-lore)]

[GT5885 (Manners and customs)]
[HD9434 (Industry)]
[HV4749-4755 (Cruelty to horses)]
[QL737.U6]
[SF277-359 (Horse raising)]
[UF370 (Military service, UC600-695,
    UE460-475)]
UF Farriery
    Hippology
    Horse
BT Domestic animals
    Equus
    Livestock
SA *headings beginning with the word*
    Horse; *and subdivision* Horses
    under individual wars, e.g. World
    War, 1939-1945—Horses
NT Ahlerich (Horse)
    Aldaniti (Race horse)
    Be Fair (Horse)
    Chief of Longview (Horse)
    Chief's Crown (Race horse)
    Clever Hans (Horse)
    Cutting horses
    Dan Patch (Race horse)
    Draft horses
    Dressage horses
    El Paso (Horse)
    Foals
    Harness
    Henry (Horse)
    Hiin Finiin (Horse)
    Hoofs
    Horse breeds
    Horsemen and horsewomen
    Hunters (Horses)
    Justin Morgan (Horse)
    Mares
    Miniature horses
    Mules
    Mustang
    *Naborr (Horse)
    Nijinsky (Race horse)
    Owen Smith (Horse)
    Police horses
    Polo ponies
    Ponies
    Race horses
    *Raseyn (Horse)
    Remount service
    Sefton (Horse)
    Show horses
    Stallions
    Stormy (Horse)
    Toy horses
    Wild horses
    Witez II (Horse)
— **Age**
    [SF869]
— **Anatomy**
    [SF765]
    NT Hoofs
— Breeds
    USE Horse breeds
— Dam-books
    USE Horses—Stud-books
— **Diseases** *(May Subd Geog)*
    [SF951-959]
    NT African horse sickness
         Babesiosis in horses
         Dourine
         Epizootic lymphangitis
         Equine encephalomyelitis
         Equine herpesvirus diseases
         Equine infectious anemia
         Equine influenza
         Glanders
         Lameness in horses
         Laminitis
         Mal de caderas
         Murrina

         Tuberculosis in horses
         Venezuelan equine
           encephalomyelitis
— Exhibitions
    USE Horse-shows
— **Feeding and feeds**
— **Folklore**
    [GR715]
    NT Hobbyhorses
— Gaits
    USE Horses—Paces, gaits, etc.
— **Grooming**
    UF Grooming of horses
— **Growth**
— Infancy
    USE Foals
— **Judging**
    [SF297]
    BT Horse-shows
— Lameness
    USE Lameness in horses
— **Law and legislation** *(May Subd Geog)*
— Locomotion
    USE Horses—Paces, gaits, etc.
— **Mythology**
    NT Hayagrīva
         Pegasus (Greek mythology)
— **Paces, gaits, etc.**
    [SF289]
    UF Gait in horses
         Horses—Gaits
         Horses—Locomotion
    BT Animal locomotion
         Gait in animals
         Horse-racing
         Horsemanship
    NT Dressage
— Photography
    USE Photography of horses
— **Physiology**
— **Psychology**
— **Religious aspects**
    [BL443.H6]
    NT Hayagrīva
— — **Buddhism, [Christianity, etc.]**
— — **Christianity**
    NT Four Horsemen of the
           Apocalypse
— **Showing**
    [SF295]
    BT Horse-shows
    RT Show horses
    NT Show jumping
         Show riding
— **Stud-books**
    [SF293]
    UF Horses—Dam-books
         Stud-books
    NT Ponies—Stud-books
         Race horses—Names
— **Training**
    [GV1831.H8 (Trained animals)]
    [SF287 (Animal culture)]
    UF Horse-breaking
         Horse-training
    BT Animals, Training of
         Horsemanship
    NT Cavalletti
         Dressage
         Haute école (Horsemanship)
         Horse trainers
         Lungeing (Horsemanship)
         Riding aids
Horses, Driving
    USE Driving horses
Horses, Fossil
    [QE882.U6]
    NT Nannippus phlegon
         Pachynolophus
Horses, Hobby
    USE Hobbyhorses

Horses, Rocking
  USE Rocking horses
Horses (in heraldry)
Horses (in numismatics)   *(May Subd Geog)*
  ₍CJ161.H67₎
  BT Numismatics
Horses in art
  ₍N7660₎
  NT Equestrian statues
Horses in literature
  BT Animals in literature
Horses in moving-pictures
  BT Moving-pictures
  NT Henry (Horse)
Horses of San Marco (Venice, Italy)
  USE Cavalli di San Marco (Venice, Italy)
Horseshoe bats
  USE Rhinolophidae
Horseshoe Bend, Battle of, 1814
  USE Horse Shoe, Battle of the, 1814
Horseshoe crab, Atlantic
  USE Limulus polyphemus
Horseshoe Lake (Alexander County, Ill.)
  BT Lakes—Illinois
Horseshoe Lake (Ariz.)   *(Not Subd Geog)*
  BT Lakes—Arizona
Horseshoe pitching   *(May Subd Geog)*
  ₍GV1095₎
  UF Horseshoes (Game)
  RT Quoits
Horseshoeing
  ₍SF907₎
  ₍UC640-UC645 (Military service)₎
  UF Farriery
  BT Blacksmithing
Horseshoers   *(May Subd Geog)*
  BT Blacksmiths
  NT Trade-unions—Horseshoers
Horseshoes (Game)
  USE Horseshoe pitching
Horsetail kelp
  USE Laminaria digitata
Horsetails (Plants)
  USE Equisetum
Horsetooth Reservoir (Colo.)
  (Not Subd Geog)
  BT Reservoirs—Colorado
Horsetrainers
  USE Horse trainers
Horsewomen
  USE Horsemen and horsewomen
Horsfall family   *(Not Subd Geog)*
Horsford family
  USE Hosford family
Horsham and Guildford Direct Railway
  BT Railroads—Great Britain
Horskin family
  USE Hoskins family
Horskins family
  USE Hoskins family
Horsman family   *(Not Subd Geog)*
  UF Horseman family
Horst family   *(Not Subd Geog)*
  UF Horstman family
      Horstmann family
  RT Van der Horst family
Horstman family
  USE Horst family
Horstmann family
  USE Horst family
Horten family
  USE Horton family
Horticultural crops   *(May Subd Geog)*
  ₍SB317.5-319.77₎
  UF Crops, Horticultural
  BT Horticulture
      Plants, Cultivated
  RT Food crops
      Tree crops
  NT Flowers
      Fruit

Greenhouse plants
Nuts
Plants, Ornamental
Vegetables
Horticultural exhibitions   *(May Subd Geog)*
  ₍SB317.7-317.78₎
  UF Garden shows
      Gardening—Exhibitions
  BT Agricultural exhibitions
  NT Flower shows
Horticultural journalism
  USE Journalism, Horticultural
Horticultural journalists
  USE Horticultural writers
Horticultural literature   *(May Subd Geog)*
  ₍SB318.3-SB318.34₎
  UF Garden literature
      Gardening literature
      Literature, Garden
      Literature, Gardening
      Literature, Horticultural
  BT Horticulture—History
  RT Horticulture—Bibliography
Horticultural machinery   *(May Subd Geog)*
  ₍S678.7₎
  BT Agricultural machinery
  NT Gardening—Equipment and supplies
      Nurseries (Horticulture)—Machinery
Horticultural products   *(May Subd Geog)*
  ₍SB318-SB319 (Horticulture)₎
  UF Products, Horticultural
  BT Farm produce
      Horticulture
      Plant products
  NT Cut flowers
      Fruit
      Plants, Ornamental
      Vegetables
— Prices
— — Seasonal variations
— Quality
Horticultural products industry
  (May Subd Geog)
  ₍HD9000-9019₎
Horticultural service industry
  (May Subd Geog)
  ₍SB446-446.6₎
  BT Horticulture
      Ornamental horticulture
  RT Landscape architecture
      Landscape gardening
      Landscape nurseries
      Landscaping industry
  NT Grounds maintenance
Horticultural therapy
  USE Gardening—Therapeutic use
Horticultural writers   *(May Subd Geog)*
  UF Horticultural journalists
      Writers, Horticultural
  BT Journalism, Horticultural
      Journalists
Horticulture   *(May Subd Geog)*
      Here are entered works on the scientific and eco-
  nomic aspects of the cultivation of fruits, vegetables,
  nuts and ornamental plants.
  BT Agriculture
  RT Gardening
  NT Acclimatization (Plants)
      Arboriculture
      Cloche gardening
      Cold-frames
      Electrohorticulture
      Floriculture
      Forcing (Plants)
      Frost protection
      Fruit-culture
      Grafting
      Greenhouse management
      Greenhouse plants
      Greenhouses
      Horticultural crops

Horticultural products
Horticultural service industry
Horticulturists
House plant industry
Hydroponics
Landscape gardening
Mulching
Mushroom culture
Nurseries (Horticulture)
Organic farming
Ornamental horticulture
Plant growing media
Plant propagation
Planting (Plant culture)
Plants—Training
Plants, Potted
Pruning
Puddling (Horticulture)
Seed industry and trade
Truck farming
Vegetable gardening
— **Bibliography**
  RT Horticultural literature
— **History**
  NT Horticultural literature
— **Vocational guidance**
  ₍SB51₎
  BT Horticulturists
Horticulturists   *(May Subd Geog)*
  ₍SB61-63₎
  BT Agriculturists
      Botanists
      Fruit-culture
      Horticulture
  NT Apple growers
      Horticulture—Vocational guidance
      Nursery growers
Hortobágy National Park (Hungary)
  USE Hortobágyi Nemzeti Park (Hungary)
Hortobágyi Nemzeti Park (Hungary)
  UF Hortobágy National Park (Hungary)
  BT National parks and reserves—Hungary
      Parks—Hungary
Horton family   *(Not Subd Geog)*
  UF Horten family
Horton's arteritis
  USE Giant cell arteritis
Horton's syndrome
  USE Cluster headache
Hortus Medicus Amstelodamensis
  (Amsterdam, Netherlands)
  BT Botanical gardens—Netherlands
Horus (Egyptian deity)   *(May Subd Geog)*
  BT Gods, Egyptian
Ḥorvot Metsadah (Israel)
  USE Masada Site (Israel)
Ḥorvot Meẓada (Israel)
  USE Masada Site (Israel)
Hory Rychlebské (Poland and Czechoslovakia)
  USE Złote Mountains (Poland and
      Czechoslovakia)
Hos
  ₍DS432.H6₎
  UF Ho (Munda tribe)
      Larka Kols
  BT Ethnology—India
      Mundas
Hose
  ₍TH9380 (Fire hose)₎
  ₍TS2301.H7₎
  BT Rubber industry and trade
  NT Fire hose
      Sprinklers
Hose (Clothing)
  USE Hosiery
Hose-couplings
  ₍TH9380₎
  ₍TS2301.H7₎
  BT Fire extinction
      Hydrants

Hose industry (May Subd Geog)
 [HD9999.H718-HD9999.H7184]
Hosethaug family (Not Subd Geog)
Hosford family (Not Subd Geog)
 UF Horseford family
    Horsford family
Hoshana Rabba
 UF Hoshana Rabbah
    Hosha'nah raba
    Hoshanah Rabbah
 BT Fasts and feasts—Judaism
    Sukkot
Hoshana Rabbah
 USE Hoshana Rabba
Hosha'nah raba
 USE Hoshana Rabba
Hoshanah Rabbah
 USE Hoshana Rabba
Hoshino Iseki (Tochigi-shi, Japan)
 USE Hoshino Site (Tochigi-shi, Japan)
Hoshino Site (Tochigi-shi, Japan)
 (Not Subd Geog)
 UF Hoshino Iseki (Tochigi-shi, Japan)
 BT Japan—Antiquities
Hōshō school (May Subd Geog)
 [PN2924.5.N6 (Performance)]
 BT Nō
    Utai
Hosiery (May Subd Geog)
 [GT2128 (Manners and customs)]
 [TT679-TT695 (Manufacture)]
 UF Hose (Clothing)
    Stockings
 BT Clothing and dress
 NT Antiembolism stockings
    Socks
 — Advertising
    USE Advertising—Hosiery
 — Dyeing
    USE Dyes and dyeing—Hosiery
Hosiery, Cotton
 [TT681]
 UF Cotton hosiery
Hosiery, Nylon
 [TT681]
 UF Nylon hosiery
Hosiery, Silk
 [TT681]
 UF Silk hosiery
Hosiery dyeing
 USE Dyes and dyeing—Hosiery
Hosiery industry (May Subd Geog)
 [HD9969.H6-HD9969.H8 (Industry)]
 [TT679-TT695 (Manufacture)]
 BT Clothing trade
    Knit goods industry
 — Collective labor agreements
    USE Collective labor agreements—
        Hosiery industry
Hosiery workers (May Subd Geog)
 BT Textile workers
 NT Trade-unions—Hosiery workers
    Wages—Hosiery workers
Hosios (The Greek word)
 BT Greek language—Etymology
Hoskin family
 USE Hoskins family
Hosking family
 USE Hoskins family
Hoskings family
 USE Hoskins family
Hoskins family (Not Subd Geog)
 UF Horskin family
    Horskins family
    Hoskin family
    Hosking family
    Hoskings family
    Hoskinson family
    Hoskison family
 RT Haskins family

Hoskinson family
 USE Hoskins family
Hoskison family
 USE Hoskins family
Hosler family (Not Subd Geog)
 UF Hossler family
 RT Hassler family
    Hostler family
Hosmer family (Not Subd Geog)
 UF Hosmore family
Hosmore family
 USE Hosmer family
Hosoda Iseki (Yokohama-shi, Japan)
 USE Hosoda Site (Yokohama-shi, Japan)
Hosoda Site (Yokohama-shi, Japan)
 (Not Subd Geog)
 UF Hosoda Iseki (Yokohama-shi, Japan)
 BT Japan—Antiquities
Hosokawa family (Not Subd Geog)
Hospice care (May Subd Geog)
 [R726.8 (General)]
 [RT87.T45 (Nursing)]
 BT Hospices (Terminal care)
    Terminal care
 — Law and legislation (May Subd Geog)
    BT Medical laws and legislation
Hospices (Terminal care) (May Subd Geog)
 [R726.8]
 BT Terminal care facilities
 NT Hospice care
Hospital accreditation
 USE Hospitals—Accreditation
Hospital-acquired infections
 USE Nosocomial infections
Hospital administration
 USE Hospitals—Administration
Hospital administrators (May Subd Geog)
 [RA971]
 BT Health services administrators
    Hospitals—Administration
    Hospitals—Staff
 NT Hospitals—Administration—Vocational
    guidance
    Nursing home administrators
Hospital and community (May Subd Geog)
 UF Community and hospital
 BT Community health services
    Community life
 RT Public relations—Hospitals
Hospital attendants
 USE Hospitals—Staff
Hospital attending physicians
 USE Hospitals—Medical staff
Hospital attorneys (May Subd Geog)
 UF Attorneys, Hospital
 BT Hospitals—Staff
    Lawyers
Hospital auxiliaries
 USE Volunteer workers in hospitals
Hospital-based ambulatory care
 USE Hospitals—Outpatient services
Hospital bed capacity
 USE Hospital size
Hospital beds (May Subd Geog)
 BT Beds
    Hospitals—Furniture, equipment, etc.
 NT Hospitals, Rural—Swing beds
Hospital benefactors (May Subd Geog)
 UF Hospital patrons
    Hospital philanthropists
    Patrons, Hospital
 BT Benefactors
    Hospitals—Endowments
 NT Nursing home benefactors
Hospital blood transfusion committees
 USE Hospitals—Transfusion committees
Hospital boards
 USE Hospitals—Trustees
Hospital business management
 USE Hospitals—Business management

Hospital care (May Subd Geog)
 BT Institutional care
    Medical care
 SA subdivision Hospital care under classes
    of persons and ethnic groups
 NT Aged—Hospital care
    Australian aborigines—Hospital care
    Cancer—Patients—Hospital care
    Children—Hospital care
    Handicapped children—Hospital care
    Hospital patients
    Hospital patients—Escort services
    Hospitals—After care
    Hospitals—Case management services
    Hospitals—Complaints against
    Hospitals—Day care
    Hospitals—Diagnostic services
    Hospitals—Hydrotherapy services
    Hospitals—Night care
    Hospitals—Rehabilitation services
    Hospitals—Respiratory services
    Indians of North America—Hospital
       care
    Infants (Newborn)—Hospital care
    Infants (Premature)—Hospital care
    Intensive care units
    Isolation (Hospital care)
    Labor and laboring classes—Hospital
       care
    Partial hospitalization
    Poor—Hospital care
    Psychiatric hospital care
    Youth—Hospital care
 — Contracting out
    BT Contracting out
 — Costs
    USE Hospitals—Cost of operation
        Hospitals—Rates
 — Length of stay
    USE Hospital utilization—Length of
        stay
Hospital care, Cost of
 USE Hospitals—Rates
Hospital case management services
 USE Hospitals—Case management services
Hospital central service department
 USE Hospitals—Central service department
Hospital chaplains
 USE Chaplains, Hospital
Hospital charges
 USE Hospitals—Rates
Hospital communication equipment industry
 (May Subd Geog)
 [HD9696.T44-444]
 BT Hospitals—Communication systems
Hospital consultants (May Subd Geog)
 [RA971]
 UF Hospital management consultants
 BT Business consultants
    Consultants
    Hospital management companies
    Hospitals—Administration
Hospital cooperation in services
 USE Hospitals—Shared services
Hospital dental service (May Subd Geog)
 UF Dental service in hospitals
    Hospital dentistry
    Hospitals—Dental service
 BT Dental care
    Dentistry
    Sick—Dental care
Hospital dentistry
 USE Hospital dental service
Hospital diagnostic services
 USE Hospitals—Diagnostic services
Hospital dietary department
 USE Hospitals—Food service
Hospital drug distribution systems
 USE Hospitals—Drug distribution systems

Hospital emergency equipment industry
(May Subd Geog)
[HD9995.H6]
BT Hospitals—Emergency service—
Equipment and supplies
Hospital emergency service
USE Hospitals—Emergency service
Hospital employees
USE Hospitals—Staff
Hospital engineering departments
USE Hospitals—Engineering departments
Hospital gift shops (May Subd Geog)
BT Gift shops
Hospital house staff
USE Interns (Medicine)
Residents (Medicine)
Hospital housekeeping (May Subd Geog)
[RA975.5.H6]
UF Hospitals—Cleaning
Housekeeping, Hospital
BT Hospitals—Administration
Hospital infections
USE Nosocomial infections
Hospital inpatient units
USE Hospital wards
Hospital interns
USE Interns (Medicine)
Hospital laboratories (May Subd Geog)
UF Hospitals—Laboratories
BT Hospitals—Diagnostic services
Medical laboratories
Hospital laundries
USE Laundries, Hospital
Hospital libraries (May Subd Geog)
[Z675.H7]
UF Libraries, Hospital
BT Institution libraries
Medical libraries
Hospital management
USE Hospitals—Administration
Hospital management companies
(May Subd Geog)
[RA971]
UF Hospital management contract services
Hospitals—Management companies
BT Corporations
Hospitals—Administration
Medical corporations
NT Hospital consultants
Hospital management consultants
USE Hospital consultants
Hospital management contract services
USE Hospital management companies
Hospital materials management
USE Hospitals—Materials management
Hospital medical records
USE Medical records
Hospital medical staff
USE Hospitals—Medical staff
Hospital medication systems
USE Hospitals—Drug distribution systems
Hospital mergers (May Subd Geog)
UF Merger of hospitals
BT Consolidation and merger of
corporations
Hospitals—Administration
Multihospital systems
Hospital multistate alliances
USE Hospitals—Regional alliances
Hospital nurseries
USE Hospitals—Nurseries
Hospital nursing units
USE Hospital wards
Hospital patients (May Subd Geog)
UF Hospitalized patients
Hospitals—Patients
Patients in hospitals
BT Hospital care
Sick
NT Hospitals—Complaints against

Hospitals—Patient representative
services
Nursing home patients
Psychiatric hospital patients
— **Classification**
NT APACHE (Disease classification
system)
Diagnosis related groups
— **Economic conditions**
UF Hospital patients—Socioeconomic
status
— **Escort services**
[RA975.5.P39]
UF Escort services for hospital patients
Hospitals—Escort services for
patients
Hospitals—Patient escort services
BT Hospital care
Hospital patients—Transportation
— **Legal status, laws, etc.**
(May Subd Geog)
UF Patients' rights
— **Psychology**
NT Isolation (Hospital care)—
Psychological aspects
— **Services for** (May Subd Geog)
NT Public libraries—Services to
hospital patients
— **Social conditions**
UF Hospital patients—Socioeconomic
status
— Socioeconomic status
USE Hospital patients—Economic
conditions
Hospital patients—Social
conditions
— **Transportation**
NT Hospital patients—Escort services
Hospital patients, Child
USE Children—Hospital care
Hospital patrons
USE Hospital benefactors
Hospital personnel
USE Hospitals—Staff
Hospital personnel administration
USE Hospitals—Personnel management
Hospital pharmacies (May Subd Geog)
[RA975.5.P5]
UF Hospitals—Pharmaceutical services
Hospitals—Pharmacy departments
BT Drugstores
Hospitals
Pharmaceutical services
Pharmacy
NT Hospitals—Drug distribution systems
— **Inventory control**
— **Law and legislation** (May Subd Geog)
Hospital philanthropists
USE Hospital benefactors
Hospital-physician joint ventures
(May Subd Geog)
[RA410.58]
UF Joint ventures, Hospital-physician
Physician-hospital joint ventures
BT Joint ventures
Medical cooperation
Hospital privileges
USE Hospitals—Medical staff—Clinical
privileges
Hospital prospective payment
USE Hospitals—Prospective payment
Hospital prospective reimbursement
USE Hospitals—Prospective payment
Hospital purchasing
USE Hospitals—Purchasing
Hospital rates
USE Hospitals—Rates
Hospital records (May Subd Geog)
UF Hospitals—Records
NT Medical records
— **United States**

NT System for Hospital Uniform
Reporting
Hospital records on microfilm
(May Subd Geog)
[RA971.6]
BT Microfilms
Hospital regional alliances
USE Hospitals—Regional alliances
Hospital research
USE Hospitals—Research
Hospital risk management
USE Hospitals—Risk management
Hospital schools (May Subd Geog)
UF Preventorium schools
BT Children—Hospitals
Hospitals
Schools
Hospital secretaries (May Subd Geog)
[RA972.55]
BT Hospitals—Staff
Medical secretaries
NT Hospital ward clerks
Hospital service (War)
USE Hospitals, Military
Hospitals, Naval and marine
Red Cross
War—Relief of sick and wounded
Hospital shared services
USE Hospitals—Shared services
Hospital ships (May Subd Geog)
[VG450 (Naval medicine)]
UF Floating hospitals
Hospitals, Floating
Ships, Hospital
BT Hospitals, Mobile
Hospitals, Naval and marine
Ships
SA subdivision Hospital ships under names
of individual military services, e.g.
United States. Navy—Hospital
ships
Hospital size (May Subd Geog)
UF Hospital bed capacity
Hospitals, Size of
Size of hospitals
BT Hospitals
Hospital social work
USE Medical social work
Hospital supplies
USE Hospitals—Furniture, equipment, etc.
Medical supplies
Hospital systems, Multi-institutional
USE Multihospital systems
Hospital training-schools
USE Nursing schools
Hospital trains (May Subd Geog)
UF Ambulance trains
Trains, Hospital
BT Ambulances
Hospitals, Mobile
Railroads—Trains
Transport of sick and wounded
Transportation, Military
Hospital transfusion committees
USE Hospitals—Transfusion committees
Hospital trustees
USE Hospitals—Trustees
Hospital trustees' self-evaluation
USE Hospitals—Trustees—Self-rating of
Hospital use
USE Hospital utilization
Hospital utilization (May Subd Geog)
UF Hospital use
Hospitals—Admission and discharge—
Statistics
Hospitals—Utilization
Utilization of hospitals
BT Health facilities—Utilization
NT Hospitals—Day care
Hospitals—Emergency service—
Utilization

Hospitals—Night care
Hospitals—Outpatient services—
    Utilization
Hospitals, Rural—Swing beds
Hospitals, State—Utilization
Partial hospitalization
Psychiatric hospitals—Utilization
— **Data processing**
    NT ASCS (Computer system)
— **Forecasting**
    BT Forecasting
— **Length of stay**
    UF Hospital care—Length of stay
        Hospitals—Length of stay
        Length of stay in hospitals
— **Reporting** (May Subd Geog)
    [RA971.6]
    UF Reporting of hospital utilization
— — **United States**
      NT System for Hospital Uniform
          Reporting
— **Seasonal variations**
    BT Climatology, Medical
— **Statistical services**
— **United States**
— — **Statistical services**
      NT Professional Activity Study
Hospital violence
  USE Violence in hospitals
Hospital waiting lists
  USE Hospitals—Waiting lists
Hospital ward clerks (May Subd Geog)
  [RA972.55]
  UF Ward clerks, Hospital
      Ward secretaries, Hospital
  BT Clerks
      Hospital secretaries
Hospital wards (May Subd Geog)
  UF Hospital inpatient units
      Hospital nursing units
      Hospitals—Inpatient units
      Hospitals—Nursing units
      Hospitals—Wards
      Wards, Hospital
  BT Hospitals
  NT Hospitals—Nurseries
      Intensive care units
Hospital workers
  USE Hospitals—Staff
**Hospital Workers' Strike, Charleston, S.C.,
1969**
  BT Strikes and lockouts—Hospitals—
      South Carolina
Hospitalers (May Subd Geog)
  [BX2825]
  UF Hospitallers
  BT Hospitals
      Military religious orders
      Monasticism and religious orders
Hospitalet Vell Site (Majorca, Spain)
  BT Spain—Antiquities
Hospitalitermes
  [QL529.3.T4]
  BT Termitidae
Hospitality (May Subd Geog)
  [BJ2021-2028]
  UF Guests
  BT Entertaining
      Etiquette
  — **Religious aspects**
  — — **Buddhism, [Christianity, etc.]**
Hospitalization, Partial
  USE Partial hospitalization
Hospitalization insurance
  USE Insurance, Hospitalization
Hospitalized children
  USE Children—Hospital care
Hospitalized patients
  USE Hospital patients
Hospitallers
  USE Hospitalers

Hospitals (May Subd Geog)
  [RA960-RA996]
  UF Benevolent institutions
      Infirmaries
  BT Charities, Medical
      Health facilities
  RT Medical centers
  SA subdivision Hospitals under classes of
      persons, ethnic groups, and
      individual diseases, e.g. Cancer—
      Hospitals; Tuberculosis—Hospitals;
      and names of individual hospitals
  NT Almshouses
      Care of the sick
      Catholic hospitals
      Clinics
      Homeopathy—Hospitals and
        dispensaries
      Hospital pharmacies
      Hospital schools
      Hospital size
      Hospital wards
      Hospitalers
      Hospitals, Convalescent
      Hospitals, Proprietary
      Medicine, Clinical—Hospital reports
      Multihospital systems
      Nervous system—Diseases—Hospitals
      Nose—Diseases—Hospitals
      Nosocomial infections
      Operating rooms
      Orthopedic hospitals
      Osteopathic hospitals
      Prison hospitals
      Psychiatric hospitals
      Public worship in hospitals
      Terminal care facilities
      Throat—Diseases—Hospitals
      Violence in hospitals
      Volunteer workers in hospitals
  — **Accounting**
    [HF5686.H7]
    BT Hospitals—Business management
  — — **Law and legislation**
    (May Subd Geog)
  — **Accreditation**
    [RA971]
    UF Hospital accreditation
    BT Hospitals—Inspection
  — **Administration**
    UF Hospital administration
      Hospital management
      Hospitals—Management and
        regulation
    BT Health services administration
      Management
    NT GRASP System
      Hospital administrators
      Hospital consultants
      Hospital housekeeping
      Hospital management companies
      Hospital mergers
      Hospitals—Admission and
        discharge
      Hospitals—Business management
      Hospitals—Complaints against
      Hospitals—Materials management
      Hospitals—Risk management
      Hospitals—Shared services
      Hospitals—Transfusion committees
      Hospitals—Trustees
      Medical appointments and
        schedules
      Multihospital systems
  — — **Data processing**
  — — — **Evaluation**
  — — — — **Computer programs**
        NT SEAHIS (Computer
          program)
  — — **Study and teaching**
    (May Subd Geog)

— — **Vocational guidance**
    BT Hospital administrators
— **Admission and discharge**
    [RA971.8]
    UF Hospitals—Discharge
    BT Hospitals—Administration
    NT Hospitals—After care
      Hospitals—Waiting lists
— — **Data processing**
    NT ASCS (Computer system)
— — **Statistics**
    USE Hospital utilization
— **Advertising**
    USE Advertising—Hospitals
— **After care**
    [RA973]
    UF After care (Hospitals)
      Post hospital care
    BT Convalescence
      Hospital care
      Hospitals—Admission and
        discharge
      Medical social work
    NT Long-term care facilities
— **Air conditioning**
    [RA969.4]
— **Ambulatory care**
    USE Hospitals—Outpatient services
— **Anecdotes, facetiae, satire, etc.**
— **Anesthesia services**
    [RA975.5.A5]
    UF Anesthesia services in hospitals
    BT Anesthesia
    NT Hospitals—Respiratory therapy
        services
— **Attendants**
    USE Hospitals—Staff
— **Bathing facilities**
    [RA969.33]
    BT Bathrooms
— **Blood transfusion committees**
    USE Hospitals—Transfusion
        committees
— **Board of trustees**
    USE Hospitals—Trustees
— **Business management**
    [RA971.3]
    UF Hospital business management
    BT Hospitals—Administration
    NT Hospitals—Accounting
— **Cardiovascular services**
    [RA975.5.C3]
    UF Cardiovascular services in hospitals
    NT Coronary care units
— **Case management services**
    [RA975.5.C36]
    UF Case management in hospitals
      Hospital case management services
    BT Hospital care
      Medical social work
— **Central service department**
    UF Central service department
        (Hospitals)
      Hospital central service department
    BT Hospitals—Materials management
    RT Hospitals—Furniture, equipment,
        etc.
— **Chaplains**
    USE Chaplains, Hospital
— **Charges**
    USE Hospitals—Rates
— **Chest services**
    USE Hospitals—Respiratory services
— **Cleaning**
    USE Hospital housekeeping
— **Collective bargaining**
    USE Collective bargaining—Hospitals
— **Collective labor agreements**
    USE Collective labor agreements—
        Hospitals
— **Communication systems**

Hospitals

— **Communication systems** (Continued)
  NT Hospital communication equipment industry
— **Complaints against**
  UF Complaints against hospitals
  BT Hospital care
    Hospital patients
    Hospitals—Administration
    Public relations—Hospitals
  RT Hospitals—Patient representative services
— **Conservation and restoration**
  NT Hospitals—Remodeling for other use
— Cooperative services
  USE Hospitals—Shared services
— **Cost control**
— — **Law and legislation**
    (May Subd Geog)
  BT Medical laws and legislation
— **Cost of construction**
— **Cost of operation**
  UF Hospital care—Costs
    Hospitals—Operating costs
— **Day care**
  [RA974]
  UF Day care in hospitals
    Day hospitals
  BT Hospital care
    Hospital utilization
    Hospitals—Outpatient services
    Partial hospitalization
— Dental service
  USE Hospital dental service
— **Design and construction**
  BT Hospitals—Engineering departments
— **Diagnostic services**
  UF Hospital diagnostic services
  BT Diagnostic services
    Hospital care
  NT Hospital laboratories
    Hospitals—Radiological services
— Dietary departments
  USE Hospitals—Food service
— Discharge
  USE Hospitals—Admission and discharge
— **Disinfection**
  BT Disinfection and disinfectants
— **Drug distribution systems**
  [RA975.5.P5]
  UF Drug delivery systems in hospitals
    Drug distribution systems in hospitals
    Hospital drug distribution systems
    Hospital medication systems
    Hospitals—Medication systems
  BT Hospital pharmacies
  RT Drug utilization
— — **Unit-dose**
  UF Unit-dose drug distribution system
  BT Drugs—Dosage
    Drugs—Packaging
— **Electric equipment**
  BT Hospitals—Furniture, equipment, etc.
— **Emergency service**
  [RA975.5.E5]
  UF Emergency rooms
    Emergency services in hospitals
    Hospital emergency service
  BT Emergency medical services
  NT Ambulance service
    Trauma centers
— — **Equipment and supplies**
    NT Hospital emergency equipment industry
— — **Utilization**

  UF Utilization of hospital emergency service
  BT Hospital utilization
— Employees
  USE Hospitals—Staff
— **Endowments**
  BT Charities, Medical
  NT Hospital benefactors
— **Engineering departments**
  [RA967.8]
  UF Clinical engineering departments in hospitals
    Engineering departments in hospitals
    Hospital engineering departments
  BT Biomedical engineering
  NT Hospitals—Design and construction
    Hospitals—Environmental engineering
    Hospitals—Furniture, equipment, etc.
    Hospitals—Maintenance and repair
— **Environmental engineering**
  [RA967.8]
  BT Environmental engineering
    Hospitals—Engineering departments
— Equipment and supplies
  USE Hospitals—Furniture, equipment, etc.
— Escort services for patients
  USE Hospital patients—Escort services
— **Evacuation**
  UF Evacuation of hospitals
  BT Transport of sick and wounded
— **Extended care units**
  [RA975.5.E9]
  UF Extended care units in hospitals
  BT Long-term care facilities
— Eye, ear, nose, and throat services
  USE Hospitals, Ophthalmic and aural
— Federal aid
  USE Federal aid to hospitals
— **Finance**
  NT Federal aid to hospitals
    State aid to hospitals
— — **Law and legislation**
    (May Subd Geog)
— — **Reporting** (May Subd Geog)
    [RA971.3]
  UF Reporting of hospital finance
— — — **United States**
    NT System for Hospital Uniform Reporting
— **Food service**
  [RA975.5.D5]
  UF Dietary departments of hospitals, etc.
    Hospital dietary department
    Hospitals—Dietary departments
  BT Hospitals—Furniture, equipment, etc.
— **Furniture, equipment, etc.**
  [RA968]
  UF Hospital supplies
    Hospitals—Equipment and supplies
  BT Furniture
    Hospitals—Engineering departments
  RT Hospitals—Central service department
    Hospitals—Purchasing
  NT Hospital beds
    Hospitals—Electric equipment
    Hospitals—Food service
— **Gastroenterology services**
  [RA975.5.G37]
  UF Gastrointestinal services in hospitals
    Hospitals—Gastrointestinal services

  BT Gastroenterology
— Gastrointestinal services
  USE Hospitals—Gastroenterology services
— Governing board
  USE Hospitals—Trustees
— Gynecologic services
  USE Hospitals, Gynecologic and obstetric
— **Health promotion services**
  [RA975.5.H4]
  UF Health promotion services in hospitals
  BT Health promotion
— **Home care programs**
  UF Home care programs, Hospital-based
  BT Home care services
    Hospitals—Outpatient services
— House staff
  USE Interns (Medicine)
    Residents (Medicine)
— **Hydrotherapy services**
  UF Hydrotherapy services in hospitals
  BT Hospital care
— Hygiene
  USE Hospitals—Sanitation
— Inhalation therapy services
  USE Hospitals—Respiratory therapy services
— Inpatient units
  USE Hospital wards
— **Inspection**
  [RA971]
  NT Hospitals—Accreditation
— Laboratories
  USE Hospital laboratories
— **Landscape architecture**
  [RA967.7]
  BT Landscape architecture
— Laundry service
  USE Laundries, Hospital
— **Law and legislation** (May Subd Geog)
  BT Medical laws and legislation
  NT Federal aid to hospitals
    Hospitals (Canon law)
    Tort liability of hospitals
— Length of stay
  USE Hospital utilization—Length of stay
— **Licenses** (May Subd Geog)
  BT Medical laws and legislation
— **Maintenance and repair**
  [RA967.8]
  UF Hospitals—Repairing
  BT Hospitals—Engineering departments
  NT Hospitals—Remodeling for other use
— Management and regulation
  USE Hospitals—Administration
— Management companies
  USE Hospital management companies
— **Materials management**
  [RA971.33]
  UF Hospital materials management
  BT Hospitals—Administration
    Materials management
  NT Hospitals—Central service department
    Hospitals—Purchasing
— Maternity services
  USE Hospitals, Gynecologic and obstetric
— **Medical staff**
  [RA972]
  UF Attending physicians, Hospital
    Hospital attending physicians
    Hospital medical staff
    Medical staff of hospitals

BT Hospitals—Staff
    Physicians
NT Interns (Medicine)
    Residents (Medicine)
— — **Clinical privileges**
    [RA972]
    UF Clinical privileges in hospitals
        Hospital privileges
        Medical staff privileges
        Staff privileges in hospitals
— Medication systems
    USE Hospitals—Drug distribution
           systems
— **Military aspects**
    BT Industrial mobilization
        Military policy
— Multistate alliances
    USE Hospitals—Regional alliances
— **Nephrological services**
    UF Nephrological services in hospitals
    BT Kidneys—Diseases
— **Night care**
    UF Night care in hospitals
    BT Hospital care
        Hospital utilization
        Night work
        Partial hospitalization
    SA *subdivision* Hospitals—Night care
        under names of cities
— **Nurseries** *(May Subd Geog)*
    [RJ27-RJ28]
    UF Hospital nurseries
    BT Hospital wards
        Nurseries
    NT Infants (Newborn)—Hospital care
— Nurses
    USE Hospitals—Staff
— Nursing units
    USE Hospital wards
— Obstetric services
    USE Hospitals, Gynecologic and
           obstetric
— Operating costs
    USE Hospitals—Cost of operation
— Ophthalmic services
    USE Hospitals, Ophthalmic and aural
— Otolaryngological services
    USE Hospitals, Ophthalmic and aural
— **Outpatient services**
    [RA974]
    UF Hospital-based ambulatory care
        Hospitals—Ambulatory care
        Outpatient services in hospitals
    BT Ambulatory medical care
    SA *subdivision* Outpatient services
        under specific types of hospitals,
        e.g. Psychiatric hospitals—
        Outpatient services
    NT Hospitals—Day care
        Hospitals—Home care programs
        Medical emergencies
        Partial hospitalization
        Surgery, Outpatient
— — **Utilization**
    UF Utilization of hospital outpatient
        services
    BT Hospital utilization
— **Parking facilities**
    BT Automobile parking
— Patient escort services
    USE Hospital patients—Escort services
— **Patient representative services**
    [RA965.6]
    UF Patient ombudsmen services in
        hospitals
        Patient representative programs in
        hospitals
        Patient representative services in
        hospitals

    BT Hospital patients
        Patient representatives
        Public relations—Hospitals
    RT Hospitals—Complaints against
— Patients
    USE Hospital patients
— **Personnel management**
    UF Hospital personnel administration
    BT Hospitals—Staff
— Pharmaceutical services
    USE Hospital pharmacies
— Pharmacy departments
    USE Hospital pharmacies
— **Planning**
— — **Law and legislation**
    (May Subd Geog)
— **Prospective payment**
    UF Hospital prospective payment
        Hospital prospective
        reimbursement
        Hospitals—Prospective
        reimbursement
        Medicare hospital prospective
        payment
        Payment, Prospective, Hospital
        PPS (Medical care)
        Prospective payment, Hospital
        Prospective pricing, Hospital
        Prospective reimbursement,
        Hospital
        Reimbursement, Prospective,
        Hospital
    BT Hospitals—Rates
        Insurance, Hospitalization
    RT Diagnosis related groups
— — **Law and legislation**
    (May Subd Geog)
— Prospective reimbursement
    USE Hospitals—Prospective payment
— Psychiatric services
    USE Psychiatric hospitals
— **Psychological aspects**
    [RA965.3]
    BT Medicine and psychology
— **Purchasing**
    [RA971.33]
    UF Hospital purchasing
    BT Hospitals—Materials management
        Purchasing
    RT Hospitals—Furniture, equipment,
        etc.
— **Radiological services**
    UF Radiological services in hospitals
    BT Hospitals—Diagnostic services
        Radiology, Medical
    NT Diagnosis, Radioscopic
        Radiotherapy
— — **Shielding (Radiation)**
— **Rates**
    UF Hospital care—Costs
        Hospital care, Cost of
        Hospital charges
        Hospital rates
        Hospitals—Charges
    BT Medical care, Cost of
    NT Hospitals—Prospective payment
— — **Law and legislation**
    (May Subd Geog)
    BT Medical laws and legislation
— Records
    USE Hospital records
— **Regional alliances**
    Here are entered works on formal arrange-
    ments among hospitals or hospital systems in two
    or more states established for specific purposes
    and functioning under a set of written rules.

    UF Alliances, Hospital regional
        Alliances, Multistate hospital
        Alliances, Regional hospital
        Hospital multistate alliances
        Hospital regional alliances
        Hospitals—Multistate alliances
        Multistate alliances, Hospital
        Multistate hospital alliances
        Regional alliances, Hospital
        Regional hospital alliances
    BT Health facilities—Affiliations
        Regional medical programs
— **Rehabilitation services**
    [RA975.5.R43]
    UF Rehabilitation services in hospitals
    BT Hospital care
    NT Physical therapy services
— **Remodeling for other use**
    UF Hospitals—Renovation
        Remodeling of hospitals for other
        use
        Renovation of hospitals for other
        use
    BT Hospitals—Conservation and
        restoration
        Hospitals—Maintenance and repair
— Renovation
    USE Hospitals—Remodeling for other
        use
— Repairing
    USE Hospitals—Maintenance and
        repair
— **Research**
    UF Hospital research
— **Respiratory services**
    UF Chest services in hospitals
        Hospitals—Chest services
        Respiratory services in hospitals
    BT Hospital care
        Respiratory organs—Diseases
    NT Hospitals—Respiratory therapy
        services
— **Respiratory therapy services**
    [RA975.5.I5]
    UF Hospitals—Inhalation therapy
        services
    BT Hospitals—Anesthesia services
        Hospitals—Respiratory services
        Respiratory therapy
— **Risk management**
    [RA971.38]
    UF Hospital risk management
    BT Hospitals—Administration
        Risk management
— **Sanitation**
    [RA969]
    UF Hospitals—Hygiene
— — **Law and legislation**
    (May Subd Geog)
    BT Public health laws
— **Shared services**
    UF Hospital cooperation in services
        Hospital shared services
        Hospitals—Cooperative services
        Shared services in hospitals
    BT Hospitals—Administration
        Medical cooperation
        Multihospital systems
— **Sociological aspects**
    BT Sociology
— **Space utilization**
    UF Space allocation in hospitals
        Space utilization in hospitals
— **Staff**
    [RA972]

Hospitals
— **Staff** *(Continued)*
    UF Hospital attendants
       Hospital employees
       Hospital personnel
       Hospital workers
       Hospitals—Attendants
       Hospitals—Employees
       Hospitals—Nurses
    BT Medical personnel
    NT Collective bargaining—Hospitals
       Hospital administrators
       Hospital attorneys
       Hospital secretaries
       Hospitals—Medical staff
       Hospitals—Personnel management
       Strikes and lockouts—Hospitals
       Trade-unions—Hospitals
— — **In-service training** *(May Subd Geog)*
       BT Employees, Training of
          Medical education
— — **Incentive awards**
       BT Incentives in industry
— — **Pensions** *(May Subd Geog)*
       UF Hospitals—Staff—Salaries,
          pensions, etc.
— — **Salaries, etc.** *(May Subd Geog)*
       UF Hospitals—Staff—Salaries,
          pensions, etc.
— — — **Law and legislation**
          (May Subd Geog)
— — Salaries, pensions, etc.
       USE Hospitals—Staff—Pensions
          Hospitals—Staff—Salaries, etc.
— State aid
    USE State aid to hospitals
— **Taxation** *(May Subd Geog)*
— — **Law and legislation**
       (May Subd Geog)
— **Toilet facilities**
    [RA969.35]
    BT Toilets
— Tort liability
    USE Tort liability of hospitals
— **Transfusion committees**
    [RM171.3]
    UF Blood transfusion committees,
          Hospital
       Hospital blood transfusion
          committees
       Hospital transfusion committees
       Hospitals—Blood transfusion
          committees
       Transfusion committees, Hospital
    BT Committees
       Hospitals—Administration
    RT Blood—Transfusion
— **Trustees**
    UF Hospital boards
       Hospital trustees
       Hospitals—Board of trustees
       Hospitals—Governing board
       Trustees, Hospital
    BT Hospitals—Administration
— — **Self-rating of**
    UF Hospital trustees' self-evaluation
    BT Self-evaluation
— **Utilization**
    USE Hospital utilization
— **Waiting lists**
    UF Hospital waiting lists
       Lists, Hospital waiting
       Waiting lists for hospitals
    BT Hospitals—Admission and
          discharge
       Medical appointments and
          schedules
— Wards
    USE Hospital wards
— **Waste disposal**

— — **Law and legislation**
       (May Subd Geog)
— **Confederate States of America**
       [E625]
    UF Confederate States of America—
          Hospitals, charities, etc.
— **South Carolina**
— — **Staff**
Hospitals, Ancient *(May Subd Geog)*
    UF Ancient hospitals
    BT Medicine, Ancient
Hospitals, Animal
    USE Veterinary hospitals
Hospitals, Children's
    USE Children—Hospitals
Hospitals, Convalescent *(May Subd Geog)*
    [RA973]
    UF Convalescent hospitals
    BT Hospitals
       Long-term care facilities
    RT Convalescence
Hospitals, County *(May Subd Geog)*
    UF County hospitals
    BT Hospitals, Public
Hospitals, Disaster
    USE Disaster hospitals
Hospitals, Federal
    USE Hospitals, Public
Hospitals, Field
    USE Hospitals, Military
       Medicine, Military
       War—Relief of sick and wounded
Hospitals, Floating
    USE Hospital ships
Hospitals, Government
    USE Hospitals, Public
Hospitals, Gynecologic and obstetric
    (May Subd Geog)
    [RG12-RG16 (Gynecology)]
    [RG500-RG501 (Obstetrics)]
    UF Gynecology—Hospitals
       Hospitals—Gynecologic services
       Hospitals—Maternity services
       Hospitals—Obstetric services
       Hospitals, Maternity
       Hospitals, Obstetric
       Lying-in hospitals
       Maternity hospitals
       Mother and child—Hospital care
       Obstetrics—Hospitals
       Women—Hospitals
    BT Maternal health services
       Women's health services
    NT Maternity homes
— **Utilization**
       UF Utilization of gynecologic and
          obstetric hospitals
Hospitals, Homeopathic
    USE Homeopathy—Hospitals and
          dispensaries
Hospitals, Indian
    USE Indians of North America—Hospitals
Hospitals, Insane
    USE Psychiatric hospitals
Hospitals, Investor-owned
    USE Hospitals, Proprietary
Hospitals, Maternity
    USE Hospitals, Gynecologic and obstetric
Hospitals, Medieval *(May Subd Geog)*
    [RA964]
    BT Medicine, Medieval
Hospitals, Military *(May Subd Geog)*
    [UH460-485]
    UF Field hospitals
       Hospital service (War)
       Hospitals, Field
       Military hospitals

    BT Hospitals, Public
       Medicine, Military
       Military art and science
       Surgery, Military
       War—Relief of sick and wounded
    SA *subdivision* Hospitals *under individual*
       wars, e.g. World War, 1939-1945—
       Hospitals
    NT Hospitals, Veterans'
— **Cardiovascular services**
— Construction
       USE Hospitals, Military—Design and
          construction
— **Design and construction**
       UF Hospitals, Military—Construction
— **Law and legislation** *(May Subd Geog)*
       BT Military law
— **Outpatient services**
— **United States**
       UF United States. Army—Hospitals
Hospitals, Mobile
    UF Mobile hospitals
       Portable hospitals
    NT Hospital ships
       Hospital trains
       Intensive care units, Mobile
Hospitals, National
    USE Hospitals, Public
Hospitals, Naval and marine
    (May Subd Geog)
    [RA980-993 (Marine, RA975)]
    [VG410-450 (Naval)]
    UF Hospital service (War)
       Marine hospitals
       Naval hospitals
    BT Hospitals, Public
       Medicine, Naval
       Naval art and science
       Seamen—Medical care
       Surgery, Naval
       War—Relief of sick and wounded
    NT Hospital ships
Hospitals, Nonprofit private
    USE Hospitals, Voluntary
Hospitals, Obstetric
    USE Hospitals, Gynecologic and obstetric
Hospitals, Ophthalmic and aural
    (May Subd Geog)
    [RE3 (General and ophthalmic)]
    [RF6 (Ear, nose and throat)]
    UF Aural hospitals
       Eye—Hospitals
       Hospitals—Eye, ear, nose, and throat
          services
       Hospitals—Ophthalmic services
       Hospitals—Otolaryngological services
       Ophthalmic and aural hospitals
    BT Ear—Diseases
       Eye—Diseases and defects
Hospitals, Orthopedic
    USE Orthopedic hospitals
Hospitals, Pediatric
    USE Children—Hospitals
Hospitals, Private for profit
    USE Hospitals, Proprietary
Hospitals, Private nonprofit
    USE Hospitals, Voluntary
Hospitals, Proprietary *(May Subd Geog)*
    [RA975.P74]
    UF For profit hospitals
       Hospitals, Investor-owned
       Hospitals, Private for profit
       Investor-owned hospitals
       Private for profit hospitals
       Proprietary hospitals
    BT Health facilities, Proprietary
       Hospitals
Hospitals, Public *(May Subd Geog)*
    [RA960-996]

UF Federal hospitals
     Government hospitals
     Hospitals, Federal
     Hospitals, Government
     Hospitals, National
     National hospitals
     Public hospitals
BT Medicine, State
     Public health
     Public institutions
NT Hospitals, County
     Hospitals, Military
     Hospitals, Naval and marine
     Hospitals, State
— **Medical staff**
    UF Medical staff of public hospitals
    RT Physicians
— **Outpatient services**
    [RA974-974.5]
    UF Outpatient services in public
         hospitals
Hospitals, Public worship in
USE Public worship in hospitals
Hospitals, Rural *(May Subd Geog)*
   [RA975.R87]
  UF Rural hospitals
  BT Rural health services
— **Prospective payment**
    UF Medicare rural hospital prospective
         payment
         Payment, Prospective, Rural
           hospital
         PPS (Medical care)
         Prospective payment, Rural
           hospital
         Prospective reimbursement, Rural
           hospital
         Reimbursement, Prospective, Rural
           hospital
         Rural hospital prospective payment
    BT Hospitals, Rural—Rates
         Insurance, Hospitalization
— **Rates**
    NT Hospitals, Rural—Prospective
         payment
— **Swing beds**
    Here are entered works on beds regularly
    maintained for either short-term or long-term
    use depending upon need.
    UF Swing beds in rural hospitals
    BT Hospital beds
         Hospital utilization
Hospitals, Size of
USE Hospital size
Hospitals, State *(May Subd Geog)*
  UF State hospitals
  BT Hospitals, Public
— **Outpatient services**
    UF Outpatient services in state
         hospitals
    BT Ambulatory medical care
— **Utilization**
    UF Utilization of state hospitals
    BT Hospital utilization
Hospitals, Teaching *(May Subd Geog)*
   [RA975.T43]
  UF Teaching hospitals
  BT Health occupations schools
     Medical centers
  NT Hospitals, University
Hospitals, University *(May Subd Geog)*
   [RA975.U5]
  UF University hospitals
  BT Hospitals, Teaching
     Medical centers
     Medical colleges
     Universities and colleges
Hospitals, Veterans' *(May Subd Geog)*
  UF Veterans' hospitals
  BT Hospitals, Military
     Veterans—Medical care

— **Admission and discharge**
    UF Admission to veterans' hospitals
         Discharge from veterans' hospitals
         Hospitals, Veterans'—Discharge
— **Cardiovascular services**
    UF Cardiovascular services in veterans
         hospitals
— **Discharge**
    USE Hospitals, Veterans'—Admission
         and discharge
— **Law and legislation** *(May Subd Geog)*
— **Medical staff**
    UF Medical staff of veterans' hospitals
    BT Physicians
— **Outpatient services**
    UF Outpatient services in veterans
         hospitals
    BT Ambulatory medical care
Hospitals, Veterinary
USE Veterinary hospitals
Hospitals, Voluntary *(May Subd Geog)*
   [RA960-996]
  UF Hospitals, Nonprofit private
     Hospitals, Private nonprofit
     Non-profit private hospitals
     Nonprofit private hospitals
     Private nonprofit hospitals
     Voluntary hospitals
  BT Voluntary health agencies
  NT Catholic hospitals
Hospitals (Canon law)
  BT Hospitals—Law and legislation
Hospitals in art *(May Subd Geog)*
  BT Medicine and art
Hoss family *(Not Subd Geog)*
Hossēre-Alantīka (Nigeria and Cameroon)
USE Alantika Mountains (Nigeria and
     Cameroon)
Hossler family
USE Hosler family
Hossō (Sect) *(May Subd Geog)*
   [BQ8100-8149]
  UF Fa-hsiang-tsung
     Hosso-shū
  BT Buddhist sects
— **Doctrines**
    [BQ8118]
Hossō (Sect) in art
Hosso-shū
USE Hossō (Sect)
Hosstater family
USE Hostetter family
Host animals to helminths
USE Helminths—Hosts
Host families of foreign students
   (May Subd Geog)
  BT Family
     Students, Foreign
Host mothers
USE Surrogate mothers
Host-organism relationships
USE Host-parasite relationships
Host-parasite relationships
  UF Host-organism relationships
     Host-pathogen relationships
     Parasite-host relationships
     Pathogen-host relationships
  BT Parasitism
  NT Host-virus relationships
     Vector-pathogen relationships
— **Genetic aspects**
Host-pathogen relationships
USE Host-parasite relationships
Host plants *(May Subd Geog)*
  UF Plant parasites—Host plants
  BT Agricultural pests
     Plant diseases
     Weeds
  SA *subdivision* Host plants *under*
     individual organisms
  NT Fishes—Host plants

     Insects—Host plants
     Parasitic plants—Host plants
Host resistance
USE Natural immunity
Host-restriction endonucleases
USE Restriction enzymes, DNA
Host-virus relationships
  UF Virus-host relationships
  BT Host-parasite relationships
     Virus diseases
     Viruses
  NT Virus-vector relationships
Hosta *(May Subd Geog)*
   [QK495.L72 (Botany)]
   [SB413.H73 (Ornamental plants)]
  UF Funkia
  BT Liliaceae
Hostage Crisis, Beirut, Lebanon, 1985
USE TWA Flight 847 Hijacking Incident,
     1985
Hostage negotiations *(May Subd Geog)*
  BT Hostages
     Negotiation
Hostage Trial, Nuremberg, Germany, 1947-
1949
  UF Subsequent proceedings, Nuremberg
     War Crime Trials, case no. 7
  BT Nuremberg War Crime Trials, 1946-
     1949
Hostages *(May Subd Geog)*
   [JX5143 (Law of war)]
  BT Terrorism
     Victims of crimes
     War (International law)
  NT Hostage negotiations
— **Iran**
    NT Iran Hostage Crisis, 1979-1981
— **United States**
    NT Iran Hostage Crisis, 1979-1981
Hostater family
USE Hostetter family
Hostatler family
USE Hostetter family
Hostesses, Airline
USE Flight attendants
Hostesses, Food service
USE Food service hostesses
Hostetler family
USE Hostetter family
Hostetter family *(Not Subd Geog)*
  UF Hosstater family
     Hostater family
     Hostatler family
     Hostetler family
Hostile behavior
USE Hostility (Psychology)
Hostilities
USE War
     War, Declaration of
     War, Maritime (International law)
     War (International law)
Hostility (Psychology)
   [BF575.H6]
  UF Enmity
     Hostile behavior
  BT Aggressiveness (Psychology)
     Psychology
  NT Abrasiveness (Psychology)
     Fighting (Psychology)
Hostler family *(Not Subd Geog)*
  RT Hassler family
     Hosler family
Hosts, Food service
USE Food service hosts
Hot air balloons
   [TL638]
  BT Balloons
— **Launching**
    [TL638]
    UF Launching of hot air balloons

Hot-air baths
USE Baths, Hot-air
Hot-air engines
USE Air-engines
Caloric engines
Hot-air heating
[TH7601-7635]
UF Warm-air heating
BT Heating
— Ducts
USE Air ducts
Hot-air treatment
USE Thermotherapy
Hot-atom chemistry
BT Chemistry
Nuclear chemistry
Hot baths
USE Baths, Hot
Hot-beds
USE Hotbeds
Hot cakes
USE Pancakes, waffles, etc.
Hot carrier conduction
USE Hot carriers
Hot carriers
[QC611.6.H67]
UF Carriers, Hot
Hot carrier conduction
Hot electrons
BT Electrons
Holes (Electron deficiencies)
Semiconductors
Hot dog rolls
BT Baked products
Bread
Hot dogs
USE Frankfurters
Hot electrons
USE Hot carriers
Hot laboratories (Radioactive substances)
(May Subd Geog)
[QD604.8 (Radiochemical laboratories)]
UF Laboratories, Hot (Radioactive substances)
BT Nuclear energy—Research—Laboratories
Nuclear facilities
Radiochemical laboratories
Hot melt adhesives
USE Adhesives, Hot melt
Hot pepper industry *(May Subd Geog)*
[HD9235.P46-462]
Hot pepper sauce industry
(May Subd Geog)
BT Hot pepper sauces
Hot pepper sauces
BT Hot peppers
Sauces
NT Hot pepper sauce industry
Tabasco sauce
Hot peppers *(May Subd Geog)*
[QK495.S7 (Botany)]
[SB307.P4 (Condiment plants)]
UF Chiles (Hot peppers)
Chilies (Hot peppers)
Chillies (Hot peppers)
BT Peppers
NT Capsaicin
Chili powder
Cookery (Hot peppers)
Hot pepper sauces
Tabasco pepper
Hot plasmas
USE High temperature plasmas
Hot pursuit (International law)
BT Search, Right of
Hot reduction of metals
USE Metals—Hot working
Hot rods
[TL236.3]

UF Automobiles, Hot rods
Street machines (Hot rods)
Street rods
BT Automobiles, Racing
Hot shot
BT Munitions
Hot spring ecology *(May Subd Geog)*
BT Spring ecology
NT Hot spring flora
Hydrothermal vent ecology
Hot spring flora *(May Subd Geog)*
[QK108-QK475.5 (Local)]
[QK938.H (Botany, General)]
UF Flora, Hot spring
BT Botany
Botany—Ecology
Hot spring ecology
Hot springs
Spring flora
Hot springs *(May Subd Geog)*
[GB1198-GB1198.4 (Hydrology)]
[QE528 (Geology)]
UF Thermal springs
BT Geothermal resources
Springs
NT Hot spring flora
Hydrothermal vents
— **Arkansas**
NT Hot Springs National Park (Ark.)
Hot Springs National Park (Ark.)
BT Hot springs—Arkansas
National parks and reserves—United States
Parks—Arkansas
Hot stage microscope
BT Microscope and microscopy
Hot stars
USE Early stars
Hot tubbing
USE Hot tubs
Hot tubs *(May Subd Geog)*
UF Hot tubbing
Tubs, Hot
BT Baths, Hot
— **Law and legislation** *(May Subd Geog)*
Hot water
This heading is used only with subdivisions.
— **Therapeutic use**
[RM253]
BT Hydrotherapy
NT Salisbury treatment
Hot-water bags, Tariff on
USE Tariff on hot-water bags
Hot water discharges into rivers, lakes, etc.
USE Thermal pollution of rivers, lakes, etc.
Hot-water heaters
USE Water heaters
Hot-water heating
[TH7511-7549]
BT Heating
— **Regulators**
[TH7541]
BT Heating—Control
Hot-water heating (Jewish law)
Hot water rockets
BT Rockets (Aeronautics)
Hot-water supply *(May Subd Geog)*
[TH6551-TH6568]
BT Plumbing
NT Kitchen-boiler explosions
Solar water heaters
Water heaters
Water heaters, Gas
Hot weather conditions
USE *subdivision* Hot weather conditions *under subjects, e.g.* Energy conservation—Hot weather conditions
Hot-wire anemometer
BT Anemometer

Hot working of metals
USE Metals—Hot working
Hotaka-dake (Japan)
USE Hotaka Mountain (Japan)
Hotaka Mountain (Japan)
UF Hodaka-dake (Japan)
Hotaka-dake (Japan)
BT Mountains—Japan
Hotal (Ancient city)
USE Khotan (Ancient city)
Hotbeds
UF Hot-beds
BT Forcing (Plants)
Plants, Effect of heat on
NT Soil heating
Hotchkin family
USE Hotchkiss family
Hotchkins family
USE Hotchkiss family
Hotchkiss family *(Not Subd Geog)*
UF Hodgekiss family
Hotchkin family
Hotchkins family
RT Hodgkins family
Hotchkiss machine-gun
[UF620.H8]
BT Machine-guns
NT Benet-Mercié machine-gun
Hotchkiss revolving cannon
[UF620.H8]
BT Machine-guns
Hotel administration
USE Hotel management
Hotel bellmen
[TX926]
UF Bellboys, Hotel
Bellhops, Hotel
Bellmen, Hotel
Motel bellmen
BT Hotels, taverns, etc.—Employees
Hôtel Bouctot-Vagniez (Amiens, France)
UF Bouctot-Vagniez House (Amiens, France)
BT Dwellings—France
Hotel communication equipment industry
(May Subd Geog)
[HD9696.T44-444]
BT Hotels, taverns, etc.—Communication systems
Hôtel d'Avelin (Lille, France)
UF Avelin House (Lille, France)
BT Dwellings—France
Hôtel de la Compagnie des notaires de Paris (Paris, France)
UF Compagnie des notaires de Paris hôtel (Paris, France)
BT Buildings—France
Hôtel de La Marck (Paris, France)
UF La Marck House (Paris, France)
Marck House (Paris, France)
BT Dwellings—France
Embassy buildings—France
Hôtel de Salm (Paris, France)
UF Palais de la Légion d'honneur (Paris, France)
Palais de Salm (Paris, France)
Salm Hôtel (Paris, France)
BT Dwellings—France
Hôtel de Ville (Aix-en-Provence, France)
BT City halls—France
Hôtel de Ville (Lausanne, Switzerland)
BT City halls—Switzerland
Hôtel de Ville (Mons, Belgium)
BT City halls—Belgium
Hôtel de ville (Paris, France)
BT City halls—France
Hotel detectives
USE House detectives
Hotel doormen
[TX926]

UF Doormen, Hotel
     Motel doormen
BT Hotels, taverns, etc.—Employees
Hôtel du Parlement (Québec, Québec)
  UF Palais législatif (Québec, Québec)
      Parlement, Hôtel du (Québec, Québec)
      Parliament Building (Québec, Québec)
  BT Québec (Province)—Capital and
      capitol
Hotel housekeeping
   [TX912]
  BT Hotel management
      Hotels, taverns, etc.—Maintenance and
      repair
  NT Hotel laundry service
Hotel keepers
  USE Hotelkeepers
Hôtel Lallemant (Bourges, France)
  UF Allemant House (Bourges, France)
      Lallemant House (Bourges, France)
  BT Dwellings—France
Hotel laundry service
   [TX911.5]
  BT Hotel housekeeping
      Laundry
      Linen supply service
Hotel lobbies *(May Subd Geog)*
  UF Lobbies, Hotel
  BT Entrance halls
      Hotels, taverns, etc.
Hotel maids
   [TX928]
  UF Chambermaids, Hotel
      Maids, Hotel
      Motel maids
  BT Hotels, taverns, etc.—Employees
Hotel management *(May Subd Geog)*
  UF Hotel administration
      Hotels, taverns, etc.—Management
  NT Coffee-house management
      Hotel housekeeping
      Hotelkeepers
      Motel management
      Pullman method
      Stewards
  — Study and teaching *(May Subd Geog)*
    NT Hotel management schools
Hotel management schools
  (May Subd Geog)
  BT Hotel management—Study and
      teaching
Hotel managers
  USE Hotelkeepers
Hotel reservation systems
  USE Hotels, taverns, etc.—Reservations
Hôtel Solvay (Brussels, Belgium)
  UF Solvay House (Brussels, Belgium)
  BT Dwellings—Belgium
Hoteliers
  USE Hotelkeepers
Hotelkeepers *(May Subd Geog)*
  UF Hotel keepers
      Hotel managers
      Hoteliers
      Inn keepers
      Innkeepers
      Tavern keepers
      Tavernkeepers
  BT Hotel management
Hotels, Pet
  USE Pet boarding facilities
Hotels, Single-room occupancy
  USE Single-room occupancy hotels
Hotels, taverns, etc. *(May Subd Geog)*
   [GT3770-GT3899 *(Manners and
     customs)*]
   [NA7800-NA7850 *(Architecture)*]
   [TX901-TX946 *(Home economics)*]

  UF Ale-houses
      Bars (Drinking establishments)
      Boarding-houses
      Cafés
      Dramshops
      Inns
      Public houses
      Pubs
      Rooming houses
      Saloons
      Taverns
  BT Temperance
  RT Restaurants, lunch rooms, etc.
  NT Bartending
      Bed and breakfast accommodations
      Caravansaries
      Casinos
      Coffee-houses
      Convention facilities
      Gay bars
      Hotel lobbies
      House detectives
      Lodging-houses
      Motels
      Music-halls (Variety-theaters, cabarets,
      etc.)
      Pub architecture
      Single-room occupancy hotels
      Tourist camps, hostels, etc.
  — Advertising
    USE Advertising—Hotels, taverns, etc.
  — Collective bargaining
    USE Collective bargaining—Hotels,
       taverns, etc.
  — Collective labor agreements
    USE Collective labor agreements—
       Hotels, taverns, etc.
  — Communication systems
    NT Hotel communication equipment
       industry
  — Conservation and restoration
  — Employees
    UF Motels—Employees
    NT Cocktail waitresses
       Collective bargaining—Hotels,
       taverns, etc.
       English language—Conversation
       and phrase books (for restaurant
       and hotel personnel)
       Hotel bellmen
       Hotel doormen
       Hotel maids
       Hotels, taverns, etc.—Personnel
       management
       Porters
       Restaurants, lunch rooms, etc.—
       Employees
       Trade-unions—Hotels, taverns, etc.
       Wages—Hotels, taverns, etc.
       Waiters
       Waitresses
  — — Supplementary employment
  — Finance
  — — Law and legislation
    (May Subd Geog)
  — Furniture, equipment, etc.
    [TX912]
    NT Bars (Furniture)
  — Law and legislation *(May Subd Geog)*
    UF Innkeeper and guest
    BT Bailments
       Trade regulation
  — Maintenance and repair
    [TX928]
    UF Hotels, taverns, etc.—Repairing
    NT Hotel housekeeping
  — Management
    USE Hotel management
  — Nonsmoking areas

    UF No smoking hotel rooms
       Nonsmoking hotel rooms
       Smoke-free hotel rooms
       Smokeless hotel rooms
    BT Nonsmoking areas
  — Parking facilities
    BT Automobile parking
  — Personnel management
    [TX911.3.P4]
    BT Hotels, taverns, etc.—Employees
  — Repairing
    USE Hotels, taverns, etc.—
       Maintenance and repair
  — Reservations
    UF Hotel reservation systems
    BT Reservation systems
  — Terminology
    NT English language—Conversation
       and phrase books (for restaurant
       and hotel personnel)
  — China
    NT Chung-shan wen ch'üan pin kuan
       (China)
  — Pennsylvania
    NT Lemon House (Pa.)
  — Québec (Province)
    NT Château Montebello (Québec)
  — Texas
    NT Landmark Inn State Historic Site
       (Castroville, Tex.)
  — Washington (D.C.)
    NT Rhodes Tavern (Washington, D.C.)
Hotels, taverns, etc., in literature
Hotfield family
  USE Hatfield family
Hothouses
  USE Greenhouses
Hot'ien (Ancient city)
  USE Khotan (Ancient city)
Hotin, Battle of, 1621
  UF Chocim, Battle of, 1621
      Khotin, Battle of, 1621
  BT Turkey—History—1453-1683
Hotin, Battle of, 1673
  UF Khotin, Battle of, 1673
  BT Poland—History—Michael
      Wisniowiecki, 1669-1673
      Turkey—History—1453-1683
Hotlines (Counseling) *(May Subd Geog)*
  UF Telephone in counseling
  BT Counseling
      Crisis intervention (Psychiatry)
      Information services
  RT Emergency medical services—
      Communication systems
Hotlines (Psychiatry)
  USE Crisis intervention (Psychiatry)
HOTRAN (Computer program)
Hott family
  USE Hatt family
Hottenstein family *(Not Subd Geog)*
Hottentot (Name)
   [DT764.K]
  BT Khoikhoi (African people)—Name
Hottentot language
  USE Khoikhoi language
Hottentots
  USE Khoikhoi (African people)
Hottentots Holland Mountains (South Africa)
  UF Hottentots Hollandsberge (South
      Africa)
  BT Mountains—South Africa
Hottentots Hollandsberge (South Africa)
  USE Hottentots Holland Mountains (South
      Africa)
Hotzenwald (Germany)
  BT Black Forest (Germany)
Hou family *(Not Subd Geog)*
Houailou language
  USE Ajie language

Houar family
  USE Huard family
Houard family
  USE Huard family
Houart family
  USE Huard family
Houbara
  ⌐QL696.L7⌐
  UF Hubara
  BT Bustards
Houchen family
  USE Houchens family
Houchens family *(Not Subd Geog)*
  UF Houchen family
    Houchin family
    Houchins family
    Houtchens family
    Howchin family
  RT Hutchins family
Houchin family
  USE Houchens family
Houchins family
  USE Houchens family
Houck family *(Not Subd Geog)*
  UF Houk family
    Houke family
    Howk family
    Howke family
    Huyck family
    Huycke family
    Huyke family
Houdans (Poultry)
  ⌐SF489.H7⌐
Houel family
  USE Howell family
Houff family *(Not Subd Geog)*
  RT Hoff family
    Huff family
Hough family *(Not Subd Geog)*
  RT Huff family
Hough functions
  UF Functions, Hough
  BT Eigenvalues
Houghton Hall (Norfolk)
  BT Dwellings—England
    Manors—England
Houk family
  USE Houck family
Houke family
  USE Houck family
Houlahan family
  USE Houlihan family
Hould family
  USE Houle family
Houle family *(Not Subd Geog)*
  UF Hould family
Houlette family
  USE Howlett family
Houlihan family *(Not Subd Geog)*
  UF Holahan family
    Houlahan family
Houlston family
  USE Holston family
Houma Indians
  UF Huma Indians
    Ouma Indians
  BT Indians of North America—Louisiana
Hound Dog (Missile)
Hound sharks
  USE Triakidae
Hounds
  ⌐SF429.H6⌐
  SA *particular breeds of hounds, e.g.*
    Foxhounds, Greyhounds
  NT Basset hound
    Coursing
    Irish wolfhound
Houpert family *(Not Subd Geog)*
  UF Houppert family
    Hupert family
    Huppert family

RT Hubbard family
Houppert family
  USE Houpert family
Hour-glass spider
  USE Black widow spider
Hour-glasses
  ⌐QB214⌐
  BT Time measurements
Hour of birth
  USE Birth, Hour of
Hourglass drum
  BT Drum
    Percussion instruments
  NT Changgo
    Kotsuzumi
Houroûffs
  USE Hurufis
Hours, Books of
  ⌐BX2080 (Catholic Church)⌐
  ⌐ND3363 (Art)⌐
  UF Books of hours
    Horae (Books of hours)
  BT Catholic Church—Prayer-books and
    devotions
    Christian art and symbolism
    Decoration and ornament
    Illumination of books and manuscripts
    Illustrated books
    Liturgies
    Prayer-books
    Prayers
  NT Primers (Prayer-books)
Hours (Time)
  USE Chronology
    Days
    Horology
    Sundials
    Time
Hours of labor *(May Subd Geog)*
  ⌐HD5106-5250⌐
  UF Alternative work schedules
    Children—Hours of labor
    Labor, Hours of
    Work schedules
    Working-day
    Working hours
  BT Labor and laboring classes
  RT Weekly rest-day
  NT Absenteeism (Labor)
    Compressed work week
    Daylight saving
    Eight-hour movement
    Four-day week
    Holidays
    Hours of labor, Flexible
    Leave of absence
    Night work
    Overtime
    Rest periods
    Shift systems
    Sunday opening of libraries
    Thirty-five hour week
    Vacations, Employee
  — **Law and legislation** *(May Subd Geog)*
    BT Labor laws and legislation
    NT Sunday legislation
Hours of labor, Flexible *(May Subd Geog)*
  UF Alternative work schedules
    Flexible hours of labor
    Flexible work hours
    Flexitime
    Flextime
  BT Hours of labor
  RT Four-day week
    Shift systems
  — **Law and legislation** *(May Subd Geog)*
    BT Labor laws and legislation
Hours of labor, Staggered *(May Subd Geog)*
  ⌐HD5108⌐
  UF Alternative work schedules
    Staggered working hours

Hous family
  USE House family
Housatonic Indians
  USE Stockbridge Indians
Housatonic River (Mass. and Conn.)
  BT Rivers—Connecticut
    Rivers—Massachusetts
Housatunnuk Indians
  USE Stockbridge Indians
House-boats
  USE Houseboats
House built upon a rock (Parable)
  UF House built upon sand (Parable)
House built upon a rock (Parable) in art
House built upon sand (Parable)
  USE House built upon a rock (Parable)
House buying *(May Subd Geog)*
  UF Home buying
    Home purchase
    House purchasing
  BT Real estate business
  RT Home ownership
    House selling
  — **Costs**
    NT Settlement costs
  — **Law and legislation**
    USE Vendors and purchasers
House churches *(May Subd Geog)*
  ⌐BV601.85⌐
  BT Non-institutional churches
House cleaning
  ⌐TH7692-TH7698 (Vacuum cleaners)⌐
  UF Dwellings—Cleaning
  BT Cleaning
    Home economics
    Sanitation, Household
  NT Bathrooms—Cleaning
House construction *(May Subd Geog)*
  ⌐TH4805-4835⌐
  UF Building, House
    Construction, House
    Home construction
    Residential construction
  BT Architecture, Domestic
    Building
    Dwellings
  SA *special kinds of house construction,*
    e.g. Concrete houses, Prefabricated
    houses
  NT Drainage, House
    Dwellings—Maintenance and repair
    Dwellings—Remodeling
    House framing
    House painting
    Log-end houses
  — **Climatic factors**
  — **Contracts and specifications**
    (May Subd Geog)
    BT Building—Contracts and
      specifications
House decoration
  USE Interior decoration
House detectives *(May Subd Geog)*
  UF Hotel detectives
  BT Detectives
    Hotels, taverns, etc.
    Police, Private
House drainage
  USE Drainage, House
    Plumbing
    Sanitation
    Sewerage
House-dust mite
  UF Dermatophagoides pteronyssinus
House exchanges
  USE Home exchanging
House family *(Not Subd Geog)*
  UF Hous family
    Howse family
    Howze family
  RT Haus family

House fittings
  USE Building fittings
House flags
  USE Steamboat lines—Flags, insignia, etc.
House fly
  USE Housefly
House framing
  ⌜TH2301-2398⌝
  BT Carpentry
      Framing (Building)
      House construction
  NT Half-timbered houses
      Wooden-frame houses
House furnishings *(May Subd Geog)*
  UF Home furnishings
      Household goods
  BT Home economics
      Home economics—Equipment and
        supplies
  RT Interior decoration
  NT Candlesticks
      Carpets
      Chamber pots
      Clocks and watches
      Cushions
      Furniture
      Glassware
      Household appliances
      Kitchen utensils
      Lamps
      Pottery
      Rugs
      Silverwork
      Trivets
  — Fire-testing
      BT Fire-testing
House furnishings industry and trade
  (May Subd Geog)
  UF Home furnishings industry and trade
      Housefurnishings industry and trade
  BT Interior decoration
  — Advertising
      USE Advertising—House furnishings
House husbands
  USE Househusbands
House inscriptions
  USE Architectural inscriptions
      House marks
House journals
  USE House organs
House magazines
  USE House organs
House marks *(May Subd Geog)*
  UF House inscriptions
      Inscriptions, House
      Marks, House
  BT Devices
      Industrial design coordination
      Signs and signboards
      Symbolism
      Tokens
  NT Barn symbols
      Kolam
      Street addresses
House-martin
  ⌜QL396.P2⌝
  UF Martins
  BT Swallows
House mite
  USE Bryobia praetiosa
House mothers
  USE Housemothers
House moving
  USE Moving of buildings, bridges, etc.
House names
  BT Names
House names, Chinese
  UF Chinese house names
House names, German, ⌜etc.⌝
House numbers
  USE Street addresses

House of Augustenborg
  USE Augustenborg, House of
House of Bragança
  USE Bragança, House of
House of Dionysos (New Paphos)
  USE House of Dionysus (New Paphos)
House of Dionysus (New Paphos)
  UF Dionysos, House of (New Paphos)
      Dionysus, House of (New Paphos)
      House of Dionysos (New Paphos)
      Oikos tou Dionysou (New Paphos)
  BT Cyprus—Antiquities
      Dwellings—Cyprus
House of Guelf
  USE Guelf, House of
House of Guelph
  USE Guelf, House of
House of Hanover
  USE Hanover, House of
House of Israel
  USE Falashas
House of Liechtenstein
  USE Liechtenstein, House of
House of Mecklenburg
  USE Mecklenburg, House of
House of Medici
  USE Medici, House of
House of Mengücek
  USE Mengücek, House of
House of Plantagenet
  USE Plantagenet, House of
House of the Governor (Uxmal Site, Mexico)
  USE Governor's Palace (Uxmal Site,
        Mexico)
House of Welf
  USE Guelf, House of
House of Windsor
  USE Windsor, House of
House of Württemberg
  USE Württemberg, House of
House of Yahweh
  USE Temple of God
House on the Klong (Bangkok, Thailand)
  USE 6 Soi Kasemsan II (Bangkok,
        Thailand)
House organs *(May Subd Geog)*
  ⌜HF6121.H6 (Advertising)⌝
  ⌜PN4784.H6 (Journalism)⌝
      Here are entered works treating of the history,
  purpose, etc. of periodical publications published by
  individual business concerns to disseminate informa-
  tion promoting their interests and success. Works on
  periodical publications issued by employees and de-
  voted to their interests are entered under the heading
  Employees' magazines, handbooks, etc.
  UF House journals
      House magazines
      House publications
      Industrial editing
  BT Advertising—Periodicals
      Business—Periodicals
      Business literature
      Journalism, Technical
House organs, Interior
  USE Employees' magazines, handbooks, etc.
House painting
  ⌜TT320-324⌝
  BT House construction
  RT Painting, Industrial
  NT Texture painting
  — **Equipment and supplies**
  — — Drawing
      USE House painting—Equipment
            and supplies—Drawings
  — — **Drawings**
      UF House painting—Equipment and
            supplies—Drawing
      BT Mechanical drawing
  — Tropical conditions
      UF Tropical house painting
House parents
  USE Child care workers

House physicians (Hospitals)
  USE Residents (Medicine)
House plans
  USE Architecture, Domestic—Designs and
        plans
House plant industry *(May Subd Geog)*
  ⌜SB419.3⌝
  UF Home horticulture
  BT Floriculture
      Horticulture
      House plants
  RT Nursery dealers
  NT Garden centers (Retail trade)
House plants
  ⌜SB419-SB419.3⌝
  UF Houseplants
      Indoor plants
  BT Household ecology
      Indoor gardening
      Indoor gardens
      Plants
  RT Garden rooms
      Window-gardening
  NT Artificial light gardening
      Gardens, Miniature
      Hanging plants
      House plant industry
      Plants, Potted
      Potting soils
      Wardian cases
House plants in interior decoration
  (May Subd Geog)
  ⌜SB419.25⌝
  BT Interior decoration
  RT Interior landscaping
  NT House plants in office decoration
House plants in office decoration
  ⌜SB419⌝
  UF Office house plants
  BT House plants in interior decoration
      Office decoration
House publications
  USE House organs
House purchasing
  USE House buying
House-raising parties *(May Subd Geog)*
  UF Houseraising parties
      Parties, House-raising
  RT Dwellings
House rat
  USE Rattus rattus
House sanitation
  USE Sanitation, Household
House selling *(May Subd Geog)*
  BT Real estate business
  RT House buying
  — Law and legislation
      USE Vendors and purchasers
House sparrow
  USE English sparrow
House spirits
  USE Household shrines
House style
  USE Industrial design coordination
House swapping
  USE Home exchanging
House-to-house fighting
  USE Street fighting (Military science)
House trading
  USE Trade-in housing
House trailers
  USE Mobile homes
House-Tree-Person Technique
  ⌜BF698.8.H6 (Psychology)⌝
  ⌜RJ503.7.H68 (Child psychiatry)⌝
  UF H-T-P Technique
  BT Projective techniques
  RT Kinetic-House-Tree-Person Technique
House-tree-person technique
  NT Tree test

Houseboats

    ⌈*GV836 (General)*⌉

    ⌈*VM335 (Naval architecture)*⌉

    UF House-boats

    BT Boats and boating

          Dwellings

    RT Boat living

    NT Shantyboats and shantyboaters

  — **Law and legislation** *(May Subd Geog)*

Housefly

    ⌈*QL537.M7*⌉

    ⌈*RA641.F6*⌉

    UF House fly

          Musca domestica

    BT Flies

  — **Control** *(May Subd Geog)*

      ⌈*RA641.F6 (Public health)*⌉

      UF Housefly—Extermination

           Housefly control

  — **Extermination**

      USE Housefly—Control

  — **Insecticide resistance**

Housefly, Biting

    USE Stomoxys calcitrans

Housefly control

    USE Housefly—Control

Housefurnishings industry and trade

    USE House furnishings industry and trade

Household appliances *(May Subd Geog)*

    UF Domestic appliances

          Home appliances

          Household equipment

          Household goods

    BT Home economics—Equipment and

          supplies

          House furnishings

    NT Irons (Pressing)

          Plastics in household appliances

  — **Efficiency**

  — — **Law and legislation**

      (May Subd Geog)

  — **Maintenance and repair**

Household appliances, Electric

  (May Subd Geog)

    ⌈*HD9697 (Economics)*⌉

    ⌈*TK7018-TK7301 (Technology)*⌉

    UF Domestic electric apparatus

          Electric apparatus and appliances,

          Domestic

          Electric household appliances

    BT Dwellings—Electric equipment

          Electric apparatus and appliances

          Home economics—Equipment and

          supplies

    NT Ceiling fans

          Electric blankets

          Electric household appliances industry

          Electric irons

          Electric water heaters

          Floor polishing machines

          Vacuum cleaners

  — **Advertising**

      USE Advertising—Electric household

           appliances

  — **Amateurs' manuals**

      USE Electric apparatus and appliances

           —Amateurs' manuals

  — **Labeling** *(May Subd Geog)*

  — — **Law and legislation**

      (May Subd Geog)

  — **Maintenance and repair**

      ⌈*TK7018*⌉

      ⌈*TK9901 (Amateurs' manuals)*⌉

Household budgets

    USE Home economics—Accounting

Household ecology *(May Subd Geog)*

    ⌈*QH541.5.H67*⌉

    BT Ecology

    RT Dwellings

    NT House plants

          Household pests

Household electronics

    Here are entered works on electronic equipment in the home, i.e. audio equipment, television, home video systems, etc. Works on electronics for amateurs and hobbyists are entered under Electronics—Amateurs' manuals.

    UF Consumer electronics

          Home electronics

    BT Electronic apparatus and appliances

          Electronics

    NT Electronic toys

          Musical instruments, Electronic

          Radio—Receivers and reception

          Sound—Recording and reproducing—

           Equipment and supplies

          Television—Receivers and reception

          Video tape recorders and recording

  — **Selling**

      USE Selling—Household electronics

Household electronics industry

  (May Subd Geog)

    UF Consumer electronics industry

          Home electronics industry

    BT Electronic industries

Household equipment

    USE Household appliances

Household expenses

    USE Cost and standard of living

          Home economics—Accounting

Household fire prevention equipment industry

  (May Subd Geog)

    ⌈*HD9999.F5*⌉

    BT Dwellings—Fires and fire prevention

Household gods

    USE Household shrines

Household goods

    USE House furnishings

          Household appliances

          Kitchen utensils

Household goods carriers

    USE Storage and moving trade

Household linens

    UF Household textiles

          Linens, Household

          White goods

    BT Home economics

    NT Bedding

          Drapery

          Place mats

          Runners (Household linens)

          Tablecloths

Household linens industry *(May Subd Geog)*

    ⌈*HD9969.H83-833*⌉

    BT Textile industry

Household management

    USE Home economics

Household moving

    USE Moving, Household

Household pests *(May Subd Geog)*

    ⌈*TX325*⌉

    UF Vermin

    BT Household ecology

          Pests

    SA *specific pests, e.g.* Cockroaches; Flies

  — **Control**

      BT Buildings—Pest control

Household repairs

    USE Dwellings—Maintenance and repair—

           Amateurs' manuals

          Repairing—Amateurs' manuals

Household safety

    USE Home accidents—Prevention

Household sanitation

    USE Sanitation, Household

Household science

    USE Home economics

Household shrines

    UF House spirits

          Household gods

    BT Religion, Primitive

          Shrines

    NT Lares

Household shrines, Buddhist

  (May Subd Geog)

    UF Buddhist household shrines

    BT Buddhist shrines

    NT Buddhist household shrines industry

Household sounds

    UF Dwellings—Sounds

          Home—Sounds

          Home sounds

    BT Sounds

Household supplies *(May Subd Geog)*

    UF Domestic supplies

          Supplies, Household

Household surveys *(May Subd Geog)*

    ⌈*HB849.49*⌉

    Here are entered works on the methods and techniques employed in the collection and analysis of information related to selected households within a population, and reports of individual surveys. For household surveys on a special topic, an additional subject entry is made under the special topic, e.g. 1. Family size—United States. 2. Household surveys—United States.

    UF Surveys, Household

    BT Surveys

    RT Census

          Households

  — **Nonresponse**

      USE Household surveys—Response

           rate

  — **Response rate**

      UF Household surveys—Nonresponse

          Response rate of household surveys

Household textiles

    USE Household linens

Household utensils

    USE Implements, utensils, etc.

          Kitchen utensils

Household violence

    USE Family violence

Household workers

    USE Domestics

Households *(May Subd Geog)*

    BT Housing

          Population

    RT Family

          Home economics

          Household surveys

    NT Cost and standard of living

          Living alone

Households, Heads of

    USE Heads of households

Househusbands *(May Subd Geog)*

    UF Homemakers, Men

          House husbands

          Men and homemaking

          Men homemakers

    BT Home economics

    RT Fathers

          Husbands

Housekeepers, Visiting

    USE Visiting housekeepers

Housekeeping

    USE Home economics

Housekeeping, Hospital

    USE Hospital housekeeping

Housekeeping, Industrial

    USE Industrial housekeeping

Housekeeping service (Social work)

    USE Visiting housekeepers

Housemaids

    USE Women domestics

Houseman family

    USE Hausman family

Housemates

    USE Roommates

Housemon family

    USE Hausman family

Housemothers

    UF House mothers

          Matrons of dormitories

BT Children—Institutional care
Dormitories—Staff
NT Residence counselors
Houseplants
USE House plants
Houser family *(Not Subd Geog)*
UF Hawser family
Hooser family
Howser family
Howsor family
RT Hauser family
Houseraising parties
USE House-raising parties
Houses
USE Architecture, Domestic
Dwellings
Houses, Adobe
USE Adobe houses
Houses, Apartment
USE Apartment houses
Houses, Architect-designed
USE Architect-designed houses
Houses, Atrium
USE Courtyard houses
Houses, Brick
USE Brick houses
Houses, Concrete
USE Concrete houses
Houses, Courtyard
USE Courtyard houses
Houses, Demountable
USE Prefabricated houses
Houses, Earth covered
USE Earth sheltered houses
Houses, Earth sheltered
USE Earth sheltered houses
Houses, Fire
USE Fire stations
Houses, Gingerbread
USE Gingerbread houses
Houses, Half-timbered
USE Half-timbered houses
Houses, Log-end
USE Log-end houses
Houses, Model
USE Model houses
Houses, Octagonal
USE Octagonal houses
Houses, Packaged
USE Prefabricated houses
Houses, Patio
USE Courtyard houses
Houses, Pole
USE Pole houses
Houses, Portable
USE Buildings, Portable
Houses, Prefabricated
USE Prefabricated houses
Houses, Single story
USE Single story houses
Houses, Small
USE Small houses
Houses, Sod
USE Sod houses
Houses, Steel
USE Steel houses
Houses, Stone
USE Stone houses
Houses, Underground
USE Earth sheltered houses
Houses, Usonian
USE Usonian houses
Houses of prayer *(May Subd Geog)*
[BX2438.5]
UF Prayer, Houses of
BT Monasteries
Prayer
RT Prayer groups
Housewives *(May Subd Geog)*
UF Homemakers
BT Home economics

RT Mothers
Wives
NT Displaced homemakers
Wages—Housewives
— Legal status, laws, etc.
USE Married women
— **Life skills guides**
— **Time management**
Housewives as authors
BT Authorship
Women authors
Housewives as consumers *(May Subd Geog)*
BT Consumers
Housework
USE Home economics
Housing *(May Subd Geog)*
[HD7285-HD7391]
Here are entered works on the social and econom-
ic aspects of housing. Works on the history and de-
scription of human shelters are entered under Dwell-
ings.
UF Low income housing
Slum clearance
Urban housing
BT City planning
Dwellings—Social aspects
Human settlements
SA *subdivision* Housing *under classes of*
persons and ethnic groups
NT Aged—Dwellings
Agricultural laborers—Housing
Australian aborigines—Housing
Congregate housing
Discrimination in housing
Emergency housing
Handicapped—Housing
Home ownership
Homelessness
Households
Housing, Rural
Housing authorities
Housing management
Housing surveys
Indians of North America—Housing
Industrial housing
Lodging-houses
Minorities—Housing
Mobile homes
Public housing
Real estate management
Relocation (Housing)
Rent—Taxation
Rent strikes
Rental housing
Residential mobility
Self-help housing
Shared housing
Slums
Tenement-houses
Welfare recipients—Housing
Youth—Dwellings
— **Abandonment**
UF Abandonment of housing
BT Abandonment of property
— Accounting
USE Housing management—
Accounting
— **Bibliography**
RT Housing literature
— **Effect of inflation on**
BT Inflation (Finance)
— **Effect of wars on**
[HD7287.5]
UF Effect of wars on housing
BT Homelessness
War
War damage to buildings
— **Finance**
UF Housing finance
BT Mortgages

NT Buildings—Repair and
reconstruction—Finance
Discrimination in mortgage loans
Home equity conversion
Home improvement loans
Housing subsidies
— — **Law and legislation**
(May Subd Geog)
RT Mortgages
NT Deeds of trust
— Health aspects
USE Housing and health
— Information storage and retrieval systems
USE Information storage and retrieval
systems—Housing
— **Law and legislation** *(May Subd Geog)*
BT City planning and redevelopment
law
NT Housing courts
Housing law in mass media
— Management
USE Housing management
— **Religious aspects**
— — **Buddhism, [Christianity, etc.]**
— **Research** *(May Subd Geog)*
UF Housing research
— **Resident satisfaction**
UF Housing satisfaction
Resident satisfaction with housing
Residential satisfaction
BT Satisfaction
— **Great Britain**
NT Immigrants—Great Britain—
Housing
Housing, Afro-American
USE Afro-Americans—Housing
Housing, Animal
USE Animal housing
Housing, Cluster
USE Cluster housing
Housing, Cooperative *(May Subd Geog)*
[HD7287.7]
UF Cooperative housing
Mutual housing
BT Cooperation
RT Communal living
NT Apartment houses, Cooperative
— **Law and legislation** *(May Subd Geog)*
Housing, Discrimination in
USE Discrimination in housing
Housing, Naval
USE United States. Navy—Barracks and
quarters
Housing, Rural *(May Subd Geog)*
UF Rural housing
BT Housing
NT Agricultural laborers—Housing
— **Finance**
UF Housing finance
BT Mortgages
— **Law and legislation**
Housing, Self-help
USE Self-help housing
Housing, Single family *(May Subd Geog)*
UF Single family homes
Single family houses
BT Dwellings
— **Conservation and restoration**
NT Housing, Single family—
Conversion to commercial use
— **Conversion to accessory apartments**
UF Accessory apartments, Conversion
of single family housing to
Conversion of single family
housing to accessory apartments
Single family housing conversion to
accessory apartments
BT Accessory apartments
Buildings—Remodeling for other
use
— **Conversion to commercial use**

Housing, Single family
— Conversion to commercial use
  (Continued)
    UF Conversion of single family
          housing to commercial use
    BT Buildings—Remodeling for other
          use
        Commercial buildings
        Housing, Single family—
          Conservation and restoration
Housing, Student
  USE Student housing
Housing, Zero lot line
  USE Zero lot line housing
Housing allowances
  USE Housing subsidies
        Rent subsidies
Housing and health *(May Subd Geog)*
  [RA770]
  UF Dwellings—Health aspects
      Health and housing
      Housing—Health aspects
  BT Environmental health
      Public health
Housing and state
  USE Housing policy
Housing authorities *(May Subd Geog)*
  BT Housing
      Housing policy
      Public housing
— Law and legislation *(May Subd Geog)*
— Officials and employees
— — Salaries, allowances, etc.
      USE Housing authorities—Officials
           and employees—Salaries,
           etc.
— — Salaries, etc. *(May Subd Geog)*
      UF Housing authorities—Officials
          and employees—Salaries,
          allowances, etc.
Housing courts *(May Subd Geog)*
  UF Landlord-tenant courts
  BT Courts of special jurisdiction
      Housing—Law and legislation
      Landlord and tenant
Housing developers *(May Subd Geog)*
  UF Developers, Housing
  BT Real estate developers
  RT Housing development
  NT Architects and housing developers
Housing developers and architects
  USE Architects and housing developers
Housing development *(May Subd Geog)*
  UF Development, Housing
      Residential development
      Residential subdivisions
  BT Real estate development
  RT Housing developers
Housing finance
  USE Housing—Finance
        Housing, Rural—Finance
        Public housing—Finance
Housing for government employees
  USE *subdivision* Officials and employees—
         Housing *under names of countries,*
         cities, etc.
Housing for the aged
  USE Aged—Dwellings
Housing forecasting *(May Subd Geog)*
  UF Forecasting, Housing
  BT Forecasting
Housing law in mass media
  (May Subd Geog)
  BT Housing—Law and legislation
      Mass media
Housing literature
  UF Literature, Housing
  RT Housing—Bibliography
Housing management *(May Subd Geog)*
  [TX960]
  UF Housing—Management

  BT Apartment houses
      Housing
      Management
      Real estate management
  NT Landlord and tenant
— Accounting
  UF Housing—Accounting
— Law and legislation *(May Subd Geog)*
— United States
  NT Target Projects Program
Housing policy *(May Subd Geog)*
  UF Housing and state
      State and housing
  BT City planning
      Family policy
      Social policy
      Urban policy
  NT Communication in housing policy
      Housing authorities
      Housing rehabilitation
      Inclusionary housing programs
      Public housing
      Urban homesteading
— Citizen participation
Housing programs, Inclusionary
  USE Inclusionary housing programs
Housing projects, Government
  USE Public housing
Housing rehabilitation *(May Subd Geog)*
    Here are entered works on the social and econom-
  ic aspects of renovating homes of older residential
  areas. Works on the technical aspects of home reno-
  vation are entered under Dwellings—Remodeling.
  BT Buildings—Repair and reconstruction
      Housing policy
      Urban renewal
  NT Urban homesteading
— Law and legislation *(May Subd Geog)*
  BT Building laws
Housing research
  USE Housing—Research
Housing satisfaction
  USE Housing—Resident satisfaction
      Public housing—Resident satisfaction
Housing security
  USE Apartment houses—Security measures
      Burglary protection
      Dwellings—Security measures
Housing subsidies *(May Subd Geog)*
  UF Housing allowances
  BT Housing—Finance
      Subsidies
  RT Rent subsidies
— Law and legislation *(May Subd Geog)*
Housing surveys *(May Subd Geog)*
    Here are entered works on the methods and tech-
  niques employed, and reports of individual surveys.
  In the latter case, a subject entry is also made under
  the heading Housing—[local subdivision], e.g. 1.
  Housing—United States. 2. Housing surveys—
  United States.
    For housing surveys on a special topic, the addi-
  tional subject entry is made under the special topic,
  e.g. 1. Apartment houses—United States. 2. Hous-
  ing surveys—United States. For housing surveys of a
  special group of persons, the additional subject entry
  is made under the special group of persons, e.g. 1.
  Handicapped—Housing—United States. 2. Hous-
  ing surveys—United States.
  BT Economic surveys
      Housing
Housley family
  USE Ousley family
Housman family
  USE Hausman family
Housmon family
  USE Hausman family
Houssatonnoc Indians
  USE Stockbridge Indians
Houston, Lake (Tex.)
  UF Lake Houston (Tex.)
  BT Lakes—Texas

Houston family *(Not Subd Geog)*
  UF Houstoun family
      Hueston family
      Husten family
      Hustin family
      Huston family
Houston National Forest (Tex.)
  USE Sam Houston National Forest (Tex.)
Houstoun family
  USE Houston family
Houtchens family
  USE Houchens family
Houthulst, Battle of, 1918
  BT World War, 1914-1918—Campaigns—
      Belgium
Houtland family
  USE Howland family
Houtwijk (Hague, Netherlands)
  (Not Subd Geog)
  UF Hague (Netherlands). Houtwijk
Houver family
  USE Hoover family
Houwart family
  USE Huard family
HOV lanes
  USE High occupancy vehicle lanes
Hova dialect
  USE Malagasy language
Hova rule, 1810-1885
  USE Madagascar—History—Hova rule,
      1810-1885
Hovas
  UF Merina (African people)
Hovden family *(Not Subd Geog)*
Hoved Island (Norway)
  USE Hovedøya (Norway)
Hovedöen (Norway)
  USE Hovedøya (Norway)
Hovedøy (Norway)
  USE Hovedøya (Norway)
Hovedøya (Norway) *(Not Subd Geog)*
  UF Hoved Island (Norway)
      Hovedöen (Norway)
      Hovedøy (Norway)
  BT Islands—Norway
Hovel family
  USE Hoovel family
Hoveland family
  USE Hovland family
Hoven
  USE Bloat in animals
Hovenweep National Monument (Utah and
  Colo.)
  BT Monuments—Colorado
      Monuments—Utah
      National parks and reserves—Colorado
      National parks and reserves—Utah
Hover family
  USE Hoover family
Hover flies
  USE Syrphidae
Hovercraft
  USE Ground-effect machines
Hoverflies
  NT Syrphidae
Hovermail
  [HE6239.H6]
  UF Ground-effect machine mail
  BT Postal service
Hovermale family *(Not Subd Geog)*
  UF Habermehl family
      Hobermill family
      Hovermill family
Hovermill family
  USE Hovermale family
Hovers family
  USE Hoover family
Hovey family *(Not Subd Geog)*
  UF Hovy family
Hovland family *(Not Subd Geog)*
  UF Hoveland family

Hovy family
  USE Hovey family
How family
  USE Howe family
How-to guides
  USE Do-it-yourself work
How to start a business
  USE New business enterprises
Howar (Bahrain)
  USE Ḥawār (Bahrain)
Howard, Robert Ervin, 1906-1936
  (Not Subd Geog)
  — Characters
  — — **Cormac Fitzgeoffrey**
        RT Fitzgeoffrey, Cormac (Fictitious
            character)
Howard family *(Not Subd Geog)*
  UF Howart family
     Howarth family
     Howerd family
     Howert family
     Howerth family
  RT Hayward family
     Hower family
Howard Plan
  BT Education
     Education, Secondary
     Women—Education
Howart family
  USE Howard family
Howarth family
  USE Howard family
Howchin family
  USE Houchens family
Howe family *(Not Subd Geog)*
  UF How family
     Howes family
     Hows family
Howe Sound (B.C.)
  BT Sounds (Geomorphology)—British
     Columbia
Howel family
  USE Howell family
Howell family *(Not Subd Geog)*
  UF Hawel family
     Hawell family
     Houel family
     Howel family
     Howells family
     Howl family
     Howle family
Howells family
  USE Howell family
Howen family
  USE Hoing family
Hower family *(Not Subd Geog)*
  UF Hauer family
     Hauert family
  RT Hauger family
     Howard family
Howerd family
  USE Howard family
Howert family
  USE Howard family
Howerth family
  USE Howard family
Howes family
  USE Howe family
Howett family *(Not Subd Geog)*
Howey family
  USE Howie family
Howgill Fells (England)
  BT Mountains—England
Howie family *(Not Subd Geog)*
  UF Howey family
Howing family
  USE Hoing family
Howitzers *(May Subd Geog)*
  [UF470-UF475]
  [UF560-UF565]
  [VF390-VF395 (Naval)]

  BT Ordnance
Howk family
  USE Houck family
Howke family
  USE Houck family
Howl family
  USE Howell family
Howland family *(Not Subd Geog)*
  UF Houtland family
     Howlind family
     Howling family
     Howlings family
     Howten family
Howle family
  USE Howell family
Howler monkeys
  [QL737.P925]
  UF Alouatta
     Alouattinae
     Howling monkeys
  BT Cebidae
  NT Black howler monkey
     Mantled howler monkey
     Red howler monkey
Howlet family
  USE Howlett family
Howlett family *(Not Subd Geog)*
  UF Houlette family
     Howlet family
     Howlit family
Howlind family
  USE Howland family
Howling Dervishes
  USE Rifaʻīyah
Howling family
  USE Howland family
Howling monkeys
  USE Howler monkeys
Howlings family
  USE Howland family
Howlit family
  USE Howlett family
Howlite
  [QE391.H]
Howpe family
  USE Hoopes family
Hows family
  USE Howe family
Howse family
  USE House family
Howser family
  USE Houser family
Howson family
  USE Hewson family
Howsor family
  USE Houser family
Howten family
  USE Howland family
Howze family
  USE House family
Hoyal family *(Not Subd Geog)*
Hoyet family
  USE Hoyt family
Hoying family
  USE Hoing family
Hoynck family
  USE Hoing family
Hoyng family
  USE Hoing family
Hoynk family
  USE Hoing family
Hoyo Strait (Japan)
  USE Bungo Channel (Japan)
Hoysala architecture
  USE Architecture, Hoysala
Hoysala dynasty, ca. 1006-ca. 1346
  (Not Subd Geog)
  BT India—History—1000-1526
Hoysala sculpture
  USE Sculpture, Hoysala

Hoyt family *(Not Subd Geog)*
  UF Hoiet family
     Hoit family
     Hoitt family
     Hoyet family
     Hoyte family
  BT Haight family
  RT Haught family
     Hight family
Hoyt Street Garden (New York, N.Y.)
  BT Gardens—New York (State)
Hoyte family
  USE Hoyt family
Höytiäinen Lake (Finland)
  UF Lake Höytiäinen (Finland)
  BT Lakes—Finland
Hozameen Range (B.C.)
  BT Cascade Range
     Mountains—British Columbia
Hozdic family *(Not Subd Geog)*
Hozier family *(Not Subd Geog)*
  UF d'Hozier family
HP-12C (Calculator)
  UF Hewlett-Packard HP-12C (Calculator)
  BT Calculators
HP-18C (Calculator)
  UF Hewlett-Packard HP-18C (Calculator)
  BT Hewlett-Packard programmable
     calculators
HP25 (Calculator)
  [QA75]
  BT Hewlett-Packard programmable
     calculators
HP33E (Calculator)
  UF Hewlett-Packard 33E (Calculator)
  BT Hewlett-Packard programmable
     calculators
HP-41 (Calculator)
  UF Hewlett-Packard 41 (Calculator)
  BT Hewlett-Packard programmable
     calculators
HP41C (Calculator)
  UF Hewlett-Packard 41C (Calculator)
  BT Hewlett-Packard programmable
     calculators
HP-41C/CV (Calculator)
  UF Hewlett-Packard 41C/CV (Calculator)
  BT Hewlett-Packard programmable
     calculators
HP-41CV (Calculator)
  UF Hewlett-Packard 41CV (Calculator)
  BT Hewlett-Packard programmable
     calculators
HP-41CX (Calculator)
  UF Hewlett-Packard 41CX (Calculator)
  BT Hewlett-Packard programmable
     calculators
HP-67 (Calculator)
  USE HP-67/97 (Calculator)
HP-67/97 (Calculator)
  UF Hewlett-Packard 67 (Calculator)
     Hewlett-Packard 67/97 (Calculator)
     HP-67 (Calculator)
  BT Hewlett Packard programmable
     calculators
HP-71 (Calculator)
  UF Hewlett-Packard 71 (Calculator)
  BT Hewlett-Packard programmable
     calculators
HP 110 Portable Computer
  [QA76.8.H]
  UF Hewlett-Packard 110 Portable
     Computer
  BT Hewlett-Packard computers
     Portable computers
HP 150 (Computer)
  [QA76.8.H]
  UF Hewlett-Packard 150 (Computer)
     HP 150 Personal Computer
  BT Hewlett-Packard computers
     Microcomputers

HP 150 Personal Computer
USE HP 150 (Computer)
HP/1000 (Computer)
[QA76.8.H]
BT Electronic digital computers
Hewlett-Packard computers
Minicomputers
HP 2000 (Computer)
[QA76.8]
BT Electronic digital computers
Hewlett-Packard computers
— **Programming**
HP 3000 (Computer)
[QA76.8.H]
BT Hewlett-Packard computers
Hp classes
USE Hardy classes
HP computers
USE Hewlett-Packard computers
HP Touchscreen computers
[QA76.8.H]
UF Hewlett-Packard Touchscreen
computers
Touchscreen computers
BT Hewlett-Packard computers
HPB Project
USE Hand-printed Book Project
hPhags-pa alphabet
BT Alphabet
Mongolian language—Alphabet
HPLC
USE High performance liquid
chromatography
HR diagrams
[QB815]
UF H-R diagrams
Hertzsprung-Russell diagrams
Russell diagrams
BT Stars—Charts, diagrams, etc.
NT Horizontal branch stars
HRA (Public health)
USE Health risk assessment
**Hrad Bítov (Bítov, Jihomoravský kraj,
Czechoslovakia)**
UF Bítov Castle (Bítov, Jihomoravský kraj,
Czechoslovakia)
BT Castles—Czechoslovakia
Hrad Týřov (Czechoslovakia)
UF Týřov Castle (Czechoslovakia)
BT Castles—Czechoslovakia
Hradčany (Prague, Czechoslovakia)
(Not Subd Geog)
UF Gradchany (Prague, Czechoslovakia)
Hradschin (Prague, Czechoslovakia)
Prague (Czechoslovakia). Hradčany
Hradschin (Prague, Czechoslovakia)
USE Hradčany (Prague, Czechoslovakia)
Hribar family (Not Subd Geog)
Hron River (Czechoslovakia)
UF Garam River (Czechoslovakia)
Gran River (Czechoslovakia)
BT Rivers—Czechoslovakia
Hruska family (Not Subd Geog)
UF Rushka family
Hruso language
USE Apatani language
Hrussa language
USE Apatani language
Hrvatska krajina (Croatia)
USE Banija (Croatia)
Hrvatsko zagorje (Croatia)
UF Zagorje (Croatia)
Hrway language
USE Haroi language
HSAs (Health planning)
USE Health systems agencies
HSCI
USE High school characteristics index
Hsi-ch'iao Mountains (China)
BT Mountains—China

Hsi ch'ü
USE Chü ch'ü
Hsi Hsia dynasty, 1038-1227
USE China—History—Hsi Hsia dynasty,
1038-1227
Hsi-hsia language
USE Tangut language
Hsi-hsia-pang-ma feng (China)
USE Hsi-hsia-pang-ma Peak (China)
Hsi-hsia-pang-ma Peak (China)
UF Gosainthan (China)
Hsi-hsia-pang-ma feng (China)
Kao-seng-tsan feng (China)
Mount Xixia Bangma (China)
Shisha Pangma (China)
Shishapangma Peak (China)
Sisha Pangma (China)
Xixabangma feng (China)
Xixia Bangma Mount (China)
BT Mountains—China
Hsi-hu (China)
USE West Lake (China)
Hsi Mountain (China)
BT Mountains—China
Hsi Mountains (China)
UF Hsi Shan (China)
BT Mountains—China
Hsi-po language
USE Sibo language
Hsi-sha Islands
USE Paracel Islands
Hsi Shan (China)
USE Hsi Mountains (China)
Hsi-tsang Kao-yüan (China)
USE Tibet, Plateau of (China)
Hsi-tsang t'ai-ti (China)
USE Tibet, Plateau of (China)
Hsi-yüan (Peking, China)
USE Chung-nan-hai (Peking, China)
Hsiang chi (Game)
USE Chinese chess
Hsiang Chiang (China)
USE Hsiang River (China)
Hsiang dialects (May Subd Geog)
[PL1861-1870]
UF Hunanese dialects
BT Chinese language—Dialects
Hsiang-kang tao (Hong Kong)
USE Hong Kong Island (Hong Kong)
Hsiang-kuei Yün-ho (Hsing-an hsien, China)
USE Ling Canal (Hsing-an hsien, China)
Hsiang River (China)
UF Hsiang Chiang (China)
Siang River (China)
BT Rivers—China
Hsiang sheng (May Subd Geog)
[PL2368.H (History)]
[PL2579.H (Collections)]
BT Chinese drama (Comedy)
Chinese wit and humor
Theater—China
Hsiao
[ML980]
BT Flute
Hsiao family (Not Subd Geog)
Hsiao Ho (China)
USE Hsiao River (China)
Hsiao music
[M110.H7]
Hsiao River (China)
UF Ching-hsing Shui (China)
Hsiao Ho (China)
Lu-ch'üan Shui (China)
Ssu-hsiao Shui (China)
T'ung Shui (China)
BT Rivers—China
— **Bridges**
NT Chao-chou ch'iao (Chao-hsien,
China)
Hsien t'ien tao (Cult) (May Subd Geog)
[BL1943.H74]

BT China—Religion
Cults—China
Hsin kang kang chan Bridge (Dairen, China)
USE Hsin kang kang chan ch'iao (Dairen,
China)
Hsin kang kang chan ch'iao (Dairen, China)
UF Hsin kang kang chan Bridge (Dairen,
China)
Hsin kang kang ch'iao (Dairen, China)
BT Bridges—China
Hsin kang kang ch'iao (Dairen, China)
USE Hsin kang kang chan ch'iao (Dairen,
China)
Hsing-an Yün-ho (Hsing-an hsien, China)
USE Ling Canal (Hsing-an hsien, China)
Hsiu-shui Ho (China)
USE Hsiu-shui River (China)
Hsiu-shui River (China)
UF Hsiu-shui Ho (China)
Siao River (China)
Siu River (China)
Xiushui He (China)
BT Rivers—China
Hsiu ting ssu t'a (China)
UF An-yang Hsiu ting ssu t'a (China)
BT Pagodas—China
Hsiung-nu
[DS25]
BT Huns
Turks
Hsiung shih mei shu hsin jen chiang
BT Painting—Taiwan—Awards
Hsüan (Musical instrument)
BT Flute
Musical instruments—China
Wind instruments
Hsüan p'u ch'un shen t'u (Painting)
USE Li, Ssu-hsün, 651-716. Hanging
gardens in spring
Hsüan-yüan (Legendary ruler)
USE Huang-ti (Legendary ruler)
HSX (Vidotex system)
UF Human Sexuality (Videotex system)
BT Sex—Information services—Data
processing
Videotex systems
HTLV (Virus)
USE Human T-cell leukemia lymphoma
virus
HTLV-III (Virus)
USE Human immunodeficiency viruses
HTLV-III antibodies
USE Human immunodeficiency virus
antibodies
HTLV-III/LAV (Virus)
USE Human immunodeficiency viruses
HU-16 (Amphibian planes)
USE Albatross (Amphibian planes)
Hu ch'in
[ML927.H]
UF Ching hu
BT Musical instruments—China
Stringed instruments, Bowed
NT Erh hu
Nan hu
Pan hu
Hu ch'in music
[M175.H8]
Hu ch'in with instrumental ensemble
RT Concertos (Hu ch'in with instrumental
ensemble)
Hu ch'in with orchestra
[M1039.4.H83]
RT Concertos (Hu ch'in)
Hu-kuo yün tung, China, 1915-1916
USE China—History—Revolution, 1915-
1916
!Hū language
USE !Xū language
Hua (Papua New Guinea people)
UF Huva (Papua New Guinea people)

BT Ethnology—Papua New Guinea
Hua-ch'ing ch'ih (China)
  USE Hua-ch'ing Pond (China)
Hua-ch'ing Pond (China)
  UF Hua-ch'ing ch'ih (China)
    Huaching Hot Spring (China)
  BT Ponds—China
    Springs—China
Hua dialect (Papua New Guinea)
  UF Huva dialect
  BT Papua New Guinea—Languages
    Yagaria language
Hua-feng Coal Mine (China)
  BT Coal mines and mining—China
Hua Mountains (China)
  UF Hua Shan (China)
    Hwa Shan (China)
    T'ai-hua Shan (China)
  BT Mountains—China
Hua-owani language
  USE !Xõ language
Hua Shan (China)
  USE Hua Mountains (China)
Hua-yen Buddhism *(May Subd Geog)*
  [BQ8200-8249]
  UF Hwaõn (Sect)
    Kegon (Sect)
  BT Buddhism
    Buddhist sects
    Mahayana Buddhism
Huabi Indians
  USE Huave Indians
Huabi language
  USE Huave language
Huacaloma Site (Peru) *(Not Subd Geog)*
  [F3429.1.C]
  BT Peru—Antiquities
Huacas
  [F1565 (Panaman antiquities)]
  [F3429 (Peruvian antiquities)]
Huaching Hot Spring (China)
  USE Hua-ch'ing Pond (China)
Huachuca Fort (Ariz.)
  USE Fort Huachuca (Ariz.)
Huai Ho (China)
  USE Huai River (China)
Huai Luang River (Thailand)
  UF Luang River (Thailand)
    Mae Nam Luang (Thailand)
    Nam Louang (Thailand)
    Nam Luang (Thailand)
  BT Rivers—Thailand
Huai River (China) *(Not Subd Geog)*
  UF Huai Ho (China)
    Hwai River (China)
  BT Rivers—China
Huaino
  USE Huayno
Hualapai Indians
  UF Hualapi Indians
    Walapai Indians
    Walapi Indians
  BT Indians of North America
    Yuman Indians
Hualapai language
  [PM1356]
  UF Hualpai language
    Jaguallapai language
    Mataveke-paya language
    Walapai language
  BT Arizona—Languages
    Indians of North America—Arizona—
      Languages
    Yuman languages
Hualapi Indians
  USE Hualapai Indians
Huallaga River (Peru)
  UF Huallago River (Peru)
    Río Huallaga (Peru)
    Río Huallago (Peru)
  BT Rivers—Peru

Huallago River (Peru)
  USE Huallaga River (Peru)
Hualpai language
  USE Hualapai language
Huamachuco, Battle of, 1883
  BT War of the Pacific, 1879-1884
Huambisa Indians
  BT Indians of South America
    Jivaro Indians
Huambisa language
  UF Ssimaku language
  BT Indians of South America—Languages
    Jivaran languages
Huana (African people)
  UF Baguana (African people)
    Bahuana (African people)
    Bahuangana (African people)
    Bahungana (African people)
    Hungana (African people)
    Wangana (African people)
  BT Ethnology—Zaire
Huana language
  USE Hungana language
Huanaco
  USE Guanaco
Huanca dialect
  UF Wanka dialect
  BT Quechua language
Huanca Indians
  [F3430.1.H]
  UF Wanka Indians
  BT Indians of South America
Huancavilca Indians
  BT Indians of South America
Huang, Kung-wang, 1269-1358. Dwelling in the Fu-ch'un Mountains *(Not Subd Geog)*
  UF Dwelling in the Fu-ch'un Mountains
    (Scroll)
    Fu-ch'un shan chü t'u (Scroll)
  BT Ink painting, Chinese
    Scrolls, Chinese
Huang Ch'ao Rebellion, China, 874-884
  USE China—History—Huang Ch'ao
    Rebellion, 874-884
Huang chung (Musical instrument)
  [ML990]
  BT Flute
    Musical instruments—China
Huang family
Huang Hai
  USE Yellow Sea
Huang He (China)
  USE Yellow River (China)
Huang Ho (China)
  USE Yellow River (China)
Huang-ho lou (China)
  USE Huang-ho Pavilion (China)
Huang-ho Pavilion (China)
  UF Huang-ho lou (China)
  BT Pavilions—China
Huang Mountains (China)
  UF Huang shan (China)
    Hwang Mountains (China)
    Hwang shan (China)
  BT Mountains—China
Huang shan (China)
  USE Huang Mountains (China)
Huang-ti (Legendary ruler)
  UF Hsüan-yüan (Legendary ruler)
    Yellow Emperor (Legendary ruler)
    Yu-hsiung (Legendary ruler)
  BT China—Kings and rulers
Huanuco coca
  USE Coca
Huánuco Pampa Site (Peru)
  BT Peru—Antiquities
Huao Indians
  [F3722.1.H83]

  UF Auca Indians (Ecuador)
    Huaorani Indians
    Wagrani Indians
    Wao Indians
    Waodãdi Indians
  BT Indians of South America
    Indians of South America—Ecuador
Huao language
  [PM6165]
  BT Ecuador—Languages
    Indians of South America—Ecuador—
      Languages
Huaorani Indians
  USE Huao Indians
Huar family
  USE Huard family
Huarayo Indians (Tacanan)
  USE Ese Ejje Indians
Huarayo language (Tacanan)
  USE Ese Ejja language
Huard family *(Not Subd Geog)*
  UF Houar family
    Houard family
    Houart family
    Houwart family
    Huar family
    Huart family
    Huwart family
Huari Site (Peru)
  [F3429.1.H828]
  UF Wari Site (Peru)
  BT Peru—Antiquities
Huarmey Norte 1 Site (Peru)
  USE Gavilanes Site (Peru)
Huarmey River (Peru)
  UF Río Huarmey (Peru)
  BT Rivers—Peru
Huarpe Indians
  USE Guarpe Indians
Huart family
  USE Huard family
Huasco River (Chile)
  UF Guasco River (Chile)
    Río Huasco (Chile)
  BT Rivers—Chile
Huastec Indians
  [F1221.H]
  UF Guastec Indians
    Huaxtec Indians
  BT Indians of Mexico
    Mayas
Huastec language
  [PM3831]
  UF Guastec language
    Huaxtec language
  BT Mayan languages
Huasteca (Mexico)
  UF La Huasteca (Mexico)
Huatuso Indians
  USE Guatuso Indians
Huave Indians
  [F1221.H]
  UF Huabi Indians
  BT Indians of Mexico
Huave language
  [PM3836]
  UF Huabi language
  BT Indians of Mexico—Languages
Huaxtec Indians
  USE Huastec Indians
Huaxtec language
  USE Huastec language
Huayhuash, Cordillera (Peru)
  UF Cordillera Huayhuash (Peru)
  BT Andes
    Mountains—Peru
Huayno
  UF Guaiño
    Huaino
    Wayñu

Huayno *(Continued)*
    BT Indians of South America—Dances
        Quechua Indians—Dances
Hubald family
    USE Hubbell family
Huball family
    USE Hubbell family
Hubara
    USE Houbara
Hubbard Creek (Tex.)
    UF Big Sandy Creek, West Fork (Tex.)
    BT Rivers—Texas
    NT Hubbard Creek Lake (Tex.)
Hubbard Creek Lake (Tex.)
    UF Hubbard Creek Reservoir (Tex.)
    BT Hubbard Creek (Tex.)
        Lakes—Texas
        Reservoirs—Texas
Hubbard Creek Reservoir (Tex.)
    USE Hubbard Creek Lake (Tex.)
Hubbard family *(Not Subd Geog)*
    UF Hubbart family
        Hubbert family
        Hubberts family
        Hubert family
        Huebert family
    RT Hiebert family
        Houpert family
        Hubert-Valleroux family
Hubbardston, Battle of, 1777
    USE Hubbardton, Battle of, 1777
Hubbardton, Battle of, 1777
    [E241.H8]
    UF Hubbardston, Battle of, 1777
    BT Burgoyne's Invasion, 1777
        United States—History—Revolution,
            1775-1783—Campaigns
        Vermont—History—Revolution, 1775-
            1783
Hubbart family
    USE Hubbard family
Hubbel family
    USE Hubbell family
Hubbell family *(Not Subd Geog)*
    UF Hubald family
        Huball family
        Hubbel family
        Hubble family
        Hubbold family
        Hubel family
        Huble family
Hubbell Trading Post National Historic Site
(Ganado, Ariz.) *(Not Subd Geog)*
    BT Historic sites—Arizona
        Indians of North America—Arizona—
            Trading posts
        National parks and reserves—Arizona
Hubbert family
    USE Hubbard family
Hubberts family
    USE Hubbard family
Hubble family
    USE Hubbell family
Hubble Space Telescope
    [QB500.268]
    UF Large Space Telescope
        Space Telescope
    BT Orbiting astronomical observatories
        Telescope
Hubbold family
    USE Hubbell family
Hubb's beaked whale
    [QL737.C438]
    UF Mesoplodon carlhubbsi
Hubel family
    USE Hubbell family
Huber family *(Not Subd Geog)*
Hubert family
    USE Hubbard family
Hubert-Valleroux family *(Not Subd Geog)*
    RT Hubbard family

Hubertus House (Amsterdam, Netherlands)
    USE Hubertushuis (Amsterdam,
        Netherlands)
Hubertushuis (Amsterdam, Netherlands)
    UF Hubertus House (Amsterdam,
        Netherlands)
    BT Apartment houses—Netherlands
        Single parents—Netherlands—
            Dwellings
Hubinger family *(Not Subd Geog)*
Huble family
    USE Hubbell family
Hubner family
    USE Huebner family
Hubnerite
    USE Huebnerite
Hubrecht family *(Not Subd Geog)*
Hucha de Oro prize
    USE Premio Hucha de Oro
Huchen
    [QL638.S2]
    UF Hucho hucho
Huchingson family
    USE Hutchinson family
Hucho
    [QL638.S2]
    BT Salmonidae
Hucho hucho
    USE Huchen
Huck embroidery
    USE Huckaback darning
Huckaback
    [TS1580]
Huckaback darning
    [TT778.H83]
    UF Darning, Huckaback
        Huck embroidery
    BT Embroidery
Huckabay family
    USE Huckaby family
Huckabee family
    USE Huckaby family
Huckaby family *(Not Subd Geog)*
    UF Huckabay family
        Huckabee family
        Huckerby family
Hückel molecular orbitals
    UF HMO (Chemistry)
    BT Molecular orbitals
Huckerby family
    USE Huckaby family
Huckleberries
    [SB386.H]
Huckstep family *(Not Subd Geog)*
    UF Hookstep family
        Hooksteppe family
        Hucsteppe family
Hucksters
    USE Peddlers and peddling
Hucsteppe family
    USE Huckstep family
Hucul horse
    UF Hutzul horse
        Huzul horse
Huculs
    USE Hutsuls
Huculszczyzna (Ukraine)
    USE Hutsulshchyna (Ukraine)
al-Hudaybiyah, Treaty of, 628
    [DS232]
Huddleson family
    USE Huddleston family
Huddleston family *(Not Subd Geog)*
    UF Huddleson family
        Huddlestone family
        Hudelston family
        Hudleson family
        Hudleston family
        Hudliston family
        Hudlustun family

Huddlestone family
    USE Huddleston family
Hudelston family
    USE Huddleston family
Hudgens family
    USE Hutchins family
Hudgin family
    USE Hutchins family
Hudgins family
    USE Hutchins family
Hudhayl tribe
    UF Banū Hudhayl
    BT Arabs
Hudiburg family
    USE Hudiburgh family
Hudiburgh family *(Not Subd Geog)*
    UF Heudebourg family
        Hudiburg family
Hudleson family
    USE Huddleston family
Hudleston family
    USE Huddleston family
Hudliston family
    USE Huddleston family
Hudlow family *(Not Subd Geog)*
Hudlustun family
    USE Huddleston family
Hudson (Bomber)
    UF A-29 bomber
    BT Bombers
        Lockheed airplanes
Hudson (Locomotive) *(May Subd Geog)*
    UF Baltic (Locomotive)
    BT Locomotives
Hudson automobile
    [TL215.H]
    BT American Motors automobiles
Hudson Bay
    UF Hudson's Bay
    BT Bays—Canada
Hudson County (N.J.)
    — History
    — — Revolution, 1775-1783
Hudson County Courthouse (Jersey City,
N.J.)
    BT Court-houses—New Jersey
Hudson family *(Not Subd Geog)*
    UF Hutsen family
        Hutson family
Hudson-Fulton Celebration, 1909
    [F127.H8]
    BT Steamboats
Hudson Island (Tuvalu)
    USE Nanumanga (Tuvalu)
Hudson-Mohawk Urban Cultural Park (N.Y.)
    BT Historic sites—New York (State)
        Parks—New York (State)
Hudson River (N.Y. and N.J.)
    BT Rivers—New Jersey
        Rivers—New York (State)
    — Bridges
        NT George Washington Bridge (New
            York, N.Y.)
Hudson River School
    USE Hudson River school of landscape
        painting
Hudson River school of landscape painting
    UF Hudson River School
    BT Landscape painting, American
Hudson's Bay
    USE Hudson Bay
Hudspeth family
    USE Hedgpeth family
Huebert family
    USE Hubbard family
Huebner family *(Not Subd Geog)*
    UF Hubner family
    RT Heavener family
Huebnerite
    [QE391.H84]
    UF Hubnerite

BT Tungsten ores
Hueco Mountains (Tex. and N.M.)
  BT Mountains—New Mexico
    Mountains—Texas
Hueco Tanks (Tex.)
  BT Reservoirs—Texas
Huegel family *(Not Subd Geog)*
  UF Hugel family
Huegli family *(Not Subd Geog)*
  UF Hügli family
Huella (Dance)
  ₍GV1796.H75₎
Huen family
  USE Hewins family
Huenemann family *(Not Subd Geog)*
Huener family
  USE Hüner family
Huerkamp family *(Not Subd Geog)*
  UF Hercamp family
    Herekamp family
Huernia
  ₍QK495.A815 (Botany)₎
  BT Asclepiadaceae
Huertas Site (N.M.)
  USE Las Huertas Site (N.M.)
Huerto, Señor del
  ₍BT580.A86₎
  UF Señor del Huerto
  BT Jesus Christ—Cult—Mexico
Huerva River (Spain)
  UF Río Huerva (Spain)
  BT Rivers—Spain
Hues family
  USE Hughes family
Huessy family
  USE Hussey family
Hueston family
  USE Houston family
Huet family
  USE Huyett family
Huetar Indians
  USE Guetar Indians
Huey (Helicopter)
  USE HueyCobra (Helicopter)
HueyCobra (Helicopter)
  UF Cobra (Helicopter)
    Huey (Helicopter)
  BT Helicopters
Huf family
  USE Huff family
Huff family *(Not Subd Geog)*
  UF Huf family
    Huffer family
  RT Houff family
    Hough family
Huffer family
  USE Huff family
Huffman family
  USE Hoffman family
Huffmann family
  USE Hoffman family
Huffmaster family
  USE Hoffmeister family
Hufman family
  USE Hoffman family
Hugans family
  USE Huggins family
Hügel (The German word)
  BT German language—Etymology
Hugel family
  USE Huegel family
Hügel Villa (Essen, Germany)
  USE Villa Hügel (Essen, Germany)
Hugens family
  USE Huggins family
Huggans family
  USE Huggins family
Huggens family
  USE Huggins family
Hugghen family
  USE Huggins family

Hugghens' principle
  USE Huygens' principle
Hugging *(May Subd Geog)*
  ₍BF637.H83 (Psychology)₎
  UF Embracing
    Hugs
  BT Manners and customs
    Nonverbal communication
      (Psychology)
    Touch
Huggins family *(Not Subd Geog)*
  UF Hugans family
    Hugens family
    Huggans family
    Huggens family
    Hugghen family
    Hugins family
  RT Higgins family
Hugh family
  USE Hughes family
Hugh Moore Park (Easton, Pa.)
  UF Moore Park (Easton, Pa.)
  BT Parks—Pennsylvania
Hughbanks family *(Not Subd Geog)*
Hughenden (Melbourne, Vic.)
  BT Dwellings—Australia
Hughes family *(Not Subd Geog)*
  UF Heugh family
    Hewes family
    Hews family
    Hues family
    Hugh family
    Hughs family
    Huse family
    Huws family
  RT Hewson family
Hughes Flying-boat (Seaplane)
  UF Hughes H-4 (Seaplane)
    Spruce Goose (Seaplane)
  BT Seaplanes
Hughes H-4 (Seaplane)
  USE Hughes Flying-boat (Seaplane)
Hughins family
  USE Hewins family
Hughlett family
  USE Hulett family
Hughley family
  USE Huguley family
Hughlin family
  USE Hulen family
Hughs family
  USE Hughes family
Hughson family
  USE Hewson family
Hugins family
  USE Huggins family
Hugley family
  USE Huguley family
Hügli family
  USE Huegli family
Hugo, Victor, 1802-1885 *(Not Subd Geog)*
  — Characters
  —— Hernani *(Not Subd Geog)*
    RT Hernani (Fictitious character)
Hugo family *(Not Subd Geog)*
Hugo Lake (Okla.) *(Not Subd Geog)*
  UF Hugo Reservoir (Okla.)
  BT Lakes—Oklahoma
    Reservoirs—Oklahoma
Hugo Reservoir (Okla.)
  USE Hugo Lake (Okla.)
Hugs
  USE Hugging
Huguelet family
  USE Huguley family
Huguely family
  USE Huguley family
Huguenot decorative arts
  USE Decorative arts, Huguenot

Huguenot Wars
  USE France—History—Wars of the
    Huguenots, 1562-1598
Huguenots *(May Subd Geog)*
  ₍BX9450-9459₎
  UF French Protestants
  BT Christian sects
    Protestants—France
  — Florida
    NT Florida—History—Huguenot
      colony, 1562-1565
  — France
    NT Camisards
      Edict of Nantes
      France—History—Wars of the
        Huguenots, 1562-1598
      St. Germain, Peace of, 1570
Huguley family *(Not Subd Geog)*
  UF Hewgley family
    Hughley family
    Hugley family
    Huguelet family
    Huguely family
Hui-chou school of wood-engraving
  UF Hui p'ai
  BT Wood-engraving, Chinese
Hui Mountains (China)
  UF Hui Shan (China)
  BT Mountains—China
Hui p'ai
  USE Hui-chou school of wood-engraving
Hui Shan (China)
  USE Hui Mountains (China)
Hui wen
  USE Palindromes, Chinese
Huia
  ₍QL696.P224₎
  UF Heteralocha acutirostris
Huichol Indians
  ₍E99.H78₎
  ₍F1221.H (Mexico)₎
  BT Indians of Mexico
    Indians of North America
    Piman Indians
  RT Cora Indians
  — Government relations
  — Religion and mythology
Huichol language
  ₍PM3841₎
  UF Guichola language
  BT Indians of Mexico—Languages
Huiliche Indians
  USE Huilliche Indians
Huilliche Indians
  UF Huiliche Indians
    Hullicos
  BT Araucanian Indians
    Indians of South America
Huinck family
  USE Hoing family
Huing family
  USE Hoing family
Huiras family *(Not Subd Geog)*
Huis der Provincie (Arnhem, Netherlands)
  UF Gelre's Hof (Arnhem, Netherlands)
    Huis der Provincie Gelderland
      (Arnhem, Netherlands)
  BT Gelderland (Netherlands)—Capital and
    capitol
Huis der Provincie Gelderland (Arnhem,
  Netherlands)
  USE Huis der Provincie (Arnhem,
    Netherlands)
Huisache girdler
  ₍SB945.H (Insect pests)₎
Huitoto language
  USE Witoto language
Hujink family
  USE Hoing family
Hul family
  USE Hull family

Hula (Dance)
   [GV1726.H]
Hula language
   [PL6248.H84]
   BT Melanesian languages
Hula teachers *(May Subd Geog)*
   UF Kumu hula
   BT Dance teachers
Hulama (Game)
   USE Ulama (Game)
Hulan family
   USE Hulen family
Hulbert family
   USE Holbert family
Hulburd family
   USE Hurlburt family
Hulburt family
   USE Holbert family
Hulen family *(Not Subd Geog)*
   UF Hewlin family
       Hewlings family
       Hughlin family
       Hulan family
       Hulin family
       Huling family
       Hulings family
       Hullin family
Hulet family
   USE Hulett family
Hulett family *(Not Subd Geog)*
   UF Hewlett family
       Hughlett family
       Hulet family
       Huletts family
Huletts family
   USE Hulett family
Huli (Papua New Guinea people)
   UF Huli (Papuan people)
   BT Ethnology—Papua New Guinea
       Papuans
  — **Agriculture**
      [DU740.42]
      BT Agriculture, Primitive—Papua New
         Guinea
Huli (Papuan people)
   USE Huli (Papua New Guinea people)
Huli language *(May Subd Geog)*
   BT Papua New Guinea—Languages
       Papuan languages
Hulin family
   USE Hulen family
Huling family
   USE Hulen family
Hulings family
   USE Hulen family
Hulks, Aircraft
   USE Aircraft hulks
Hulks, Prison
   USE Prison hulks
Hull family *(Not Subd Geog)*
   UF Hul family
       Hulls family
Hull pottery
   BT Pottery—England
       Pottery, English
Hullicos
   USE Huilliche Indians
Hullin family
   USE Hulen family
Hulling of rice
   USE Rice—Hulling
Hulls, Rice
   USE Rice hulls
Hulls (Naval architecture)
   [VM]
   BT Naval architecture
       Shipfitting
   NT Planing hulls
  — **Welding**
Hulls family
   USE Hull family

Hulmecas
   USE Olmecs
Hulodidae
   USE Noctuidae
Hulsa family
   USE Hulsey family
Hulse family
   USE Hulsey family
Hulsea family
   USE Hulsey family
Hulsey family *(Not Subd Geog)*
   UF Hulsa family
       Hulse family
       Hulsea family
Hulstina
   [QL561.G6]
   BT Geometridae
Hultqvist family
   USE Holquist family
Hulva family
   USE Hulvey family
Hulvey family *(Not Subd Geog)*
   UF Helvey family
       Hulva family
Hulzel family
   USE Hutzel family
Hum (Bosnia and Hercegovina)
   USE Hercegovina (Bosnia and Hercegovina)
Hum family
   USE Hume family
Huma
   USE Bahima (African people)
Huma Indians
   USE Houma Indians
Huma language (Sudan)
   USE Toposa language
Human abnormalities
   USE Abnormalities, Human
Human action
   USE Human behavior
Human acts
   [BV4618]
   UF Acts, Human
   BT Christian ethics
   RT Free will and determinism
   NT Virtue
Human anatomy
   USE Anatomy, Human
Human-animal communication
   [QL776]
   UF Animal communication with humans
       Animal-human communication
       Communication with animals
       Human communication with animals
       Language learning by animals
       Man-animal communication
   BT Animal communication
       Communication
       Human-animal relationships
Human-animal relationships
   (May Subd Geog)
   [QL85]
   UF Animal-human relationships
       Animal-man relationships
       Animals and man
       Man and animals
       Man-animal relationships
       Relationships, Human-animal
   RT Animals
       Man
   NT Animals and civilization
       Bestiality
       Human-animal communication
Human assets
   USE Human capital

Human behavior
   Here are entered general works on the observable
   patterns of human actions and reactions. Works on
   the general science of and explanation of behavior are
   entered under Psychology. Material on particular
   types of behavior are entered under the specific sub-
   ject, e.g. Drinking and traffic accidents; Food habits;
   Leadership.
   UF Action, Human
       Behavior, Human
       Ethology
       Human action
   BT Human biology
       Physical anthropology
       Psychology
       Social sciences
   RT Psychology, Comparative
   NT Behavior evolution
       Behavior modification
       Behavioral embryology
       Biopolitics
       Displacement (Psychology)
       Electronic behavior control
       Health behavior
       Helping behavior
       Life style
       Manipulative behavior
       Nurturing behavior
       Psychobiology
       Self-protective behavior
       Type A behavior
  — **Animal models**
     UF Animal models of human behavior
     BT Animal models in research
  — **Mathematical models**
     [BF39]
     UF Behavioral models
     BT Psychology—Methodology
  — **Nutritional aspects**
     BT Nutrition
Human beings
   USE Man
Human beings on other planets
   USE Life on other planets
Human biology
   BT Biology
       Man
   RT Physical anthropology
   NT Anatomy, Human
       Embryology, Human
       Human behavior
       Human ecology
       Human genetics
       Human physiology
       Medicine
       Psychology
  — **Social aspects** *(May Subd Geog)*
     NT Sociobiology
Human blastogenesis
   BT Blastogenesis (Embryology)
       Embryology, Human
Human body
   USE Body, Human
Human capital *(May Subd Geog)*
   [HB501.5 (Economic theory)]
   UF Human assets
       Human resources
       Man—Economic value
   BT Capital
       Education—Economic aspects
       Labor economics
   RT Labor supply
Human cell culture
   BT Cell culture
Human centrifuge
   BT Acceleration (Physiology)
       Centrifuges
Human chromosome 21
   BT Human chromosomes
   RT Down's syndrome

Human chromosome abnormalities
(May Subd Geog)
[RB155]
  BT Chromosome abnormalities
      Genetic disorders
  NT Down's syndrome
      Fragile X syndrome
      Polycystic kidney disease
      Sex chromosome abnormalities in
        children
  — **Diagnosis**
    UF Genetic diagnosis
       Genetic screening
Human chromosomes
  UF Chromosomes, Human
  BT Chromosomes
      Human genetics
  NT Human chromosome 21
  — **Effect of radiation on**
    UF Human chromosomes—Radiation
       effects
    BT Radiogenetics
  — **Radiation effects**
    USE Human chromosomes—Effect of
       radiation on
Human cold storage
  USE Cryonics
Human combustion, Spontaneous
  USE Combustion, Spontaneous human
Human comfort
    Here are entered works on the balance of physical, physiological, and psychological well-being between humans and the environment.
  UF Comfort, Human
      Creature comfort, Human
  BT Man—Influence of environment
      Senses and sensation
  RT Human engineering
      Quality of life
Human communication with animals
  USE Human-animal communication
Human computers
  USE Mental calculators
Human cytogenetics
[QH431]
  UF Cytogenetics, Human
  BT Cytogenetics
      Human genetics
Human dissection (May Subd Geog)
[QM33.4-QM39]
  UF Anatomy, Practical
      Practical anatomy
  BT Dissection
  SA subdivision Dissection under individual
      organs and regions of the body, e.g.
      Heart—Dissection; Foot—
      Dissection
  NT Autopsy
Human ecology (May Subd Geog)
  UF Ecology—Social aspects
      Ecology, Human
      Ecology, Social
      Environment
      Environment, Human
      Human environment
      Social ecology
      Survival (Human ecology)
  BT Ecology
      Human biology
      Social sciences
  RT Anthropo-geography
      Conservation of natural resources
      Environmental policy
      Sociology
  NT Closed ecological systems
      Community life
      Environmental archaeology
      Environmental health
      Environmental indexes
      Hazardous geographic environments
      Human settlements

      Landscape assessment
      Man—Influence of environment
      Man—Influence on nature
      Population
      Quality of life
      Social psychology
      Survival skills
      War—Environmental aspects
  — **Moral and ethical aspects**
    UF Environmental ethics
  — **Religious aspects**
  — — **Buddhism, [Christianity, etc.]**
  — **Research**
    NT Man and the Biosphere Programme
  — **Study and teaching** (May Subd Geog)
    UF Environmental studies
    NT Nature study
Human ecology in literature
[PN48]
Human ecology in the Bible
  UF Bible—Human ecology
Human embryo
  UF Embryo, Human
  BT Embryology, Human
  — **Effect of drugs on** (May Subd Geog)
    [RG627.6.D79]
    BT Drugs—Physiological effect
       Obstetrical pharmacology
  — **Preservation**
    NT Frozen human embryos
  — **Transplantation**
    UF Human embryo implantation
       Human embryo transfer
       Implantation of human embryo
    BT Embryo transplantation
Human embryo, Frozen
  USE Frozen human embryos
Human embryo implantation
  USE Human embryo—Transplantation
Human embryo transfer
  USE Human embryo—Transplantation
Human embryology
  USE Embryology, Human
Human engineering
    Here are entered works on engineering design with reference to man's anatomical, physiological, and psychological capabilities and limitations. Works in which human engineering is used in the sense of man's relation to his job are entered under the heading Psychology, Applied and other appropriate headings.
  UF Ergonomics
      Human factors in engineering design
  BT Bioengineering
      Design, Industrial
      Environmental engineering
      Industrial engineering
      Machinery—Design
      Psychology, Applied
      Psychology, Physiological
  RT Human comfort
  NT Architecture—Human factors
      Helicopters—Piloting—Human factors
      Human information processing
      Interior decoration—Human factors
      Life support systems (Space
       environment)
      Man-machine systems
      Nuclear power plants—Control rooms
       —Human factors
      Nuclear power plants—Human factors
      Space cabin simulators
      Space vehicles—Piloting—
       Mathematical models
Human environment
  USE Human ecology
Human evolution
[QH368]
  BT Evolution
      Man—Origin
      Physical anthropology
  NT Fossil man

      Genetic psychology
      Sociobiology
      Women—Evolution
  — **Religious aspects**
Human experimentation in medicine
(May Subd Geog)
[R853.H8]
  UF Experimentation on man, Medical
      Medical experimentation on humans
  BT Medical ethics
      Medicine—Research
      Medicine, Experimental
  RT Clinical trials
  NT Self-experimentation in medicine
  — **Law and legislation** (May Subd Geog)
    BT Medical laws and legislation
Human experimentation in psychology
  UF Experimentation on man,
      Psychological
      Psychological experimentation on
      humans
  BT Psychology—Experiments
      Psychology—Research
      Psychology, Experimental
Human factors in aeronautics accidents
  USE Aeronautics—Accidents—Human
      factors
Human factors in architecture
  USE Architecture—Human factors
Human factors in engineering design
  USE Human engineering
Human factors in helicopter piloting
  USE Helicopters—Piloting—Human factors
Human factors in interior decoration
  USE Interior decoration—Human factors
Human females
  USE Women
Human fertility
  USE Fertility, Human
Human fertilization
  USE Conception
Human fertilization in vitro
  USE Fertilization in vitro, Human
Human figure in art
[N7570-N7649]
[NB1930 (Sculpture)]
[NC760-NC775 (Drawing)]
[ND1290-ND1337 (Painting)]
[NK1550 (Design)]
    Here are entered works on the techniques of depicting the human body in art. Works on the representation of human beings in art are entered under Humans in art.
  UF Body, Human, in art
  BT Art
      Composition (Art)
      Figurative art
  RT Anatomy, Artistic
      Figure drawing
      Figure painting
  NT Figure sculpture
      Nude in art
Human figure in literature
[PN56.H]
Human gaits
  USE Gait in humans
Human genetics
  BT Genetics
      Heredity, Human
      Human biology
      Physical anthropology
  NT Dermatoglyphics—Genetic aspects
      Genetic counseling
      Genetic psychology
      Human chromosomes
      Human cytogenetics
      Human population genetics
      Medical genetics
  — **Government policy** (May Subd Geog)

Human genetics
— **Government policy** (Continued)
    UF Human genetics and state
         Human genetics policy
         State and human genetics
    BT Science and state
— **Moral and religious aspects**
    BT Bioethics
— **Variation**
    UF Genetic variation in humans
    BT Variation (Biology)
Human genetics and state
  USE Human genetics—Government policy
Human genetics policy
  USE Human genetics—Government policy
Human geography
  USE Anthropo-geography
Human growth (May Subd Geog)
    [QP84]
    UF Body, Human—Growth
    BT Developmental biology
         Growth
    SA subdivision Growth under classes of
         persons and names of organs and
         regions of the body, e.g. Children—
         Growth; Heart—Growth; Foot—
         Growth
    NT Adolescent girls—Growth
         Adulthood
         Cerebral palsied children—Growth
         Children—Growth
         Infants—Growth
         Infants (Premature)—Growth
         Life cycle, Human
         Youth—Growth
Human habitat
  USE Human settlements
Human immunodeficiency virus antibodies
    UF AIDS virus antibodies
         Antibodies to human
          immunodeficiency virus
         HIV antibodies
         HTLV-III antibodies
         Human immunodeficiency virus-
          associated antibodies
         Human T-cell leukemia virus type III
          antibodies
         Human T-cell lymphotropic virus type
          III antibodies
         LAV antibodies
         Lymphadenopathy-associated virus
          antibodies
    BT Immunoglobulins
Human immunodeficiency virus-associated
  antibodies
  USE Human immunodeficiency virus
        antibodies
Human immunodeficiency viruses
  (May Subd Geog)
    UF AIDS-associated retrovirus
         AIDS virus
         ARV (Virus)
         HIV (Virus)
         HTLV-III (Virus)
         HTLV-III/LAV (Virus)
         Human T-cell lymphotropic virus type
          III
         IDAV (Virus)
         Immunodeficiency-associated virus
         LAV (Virus)
         LAV/HTLV-III (Virus)
         Lymphadenopathy-associated virus
    BT Retroviruses
    RT Human T-cell leukemia lymphoma
         virus
Human in vitro fertilization
  USE Fertilization in vitro, Human
Human information processing
    UF Information processing, Human

    BT Bionics
         Human engineering
         Information theory in psychology
         Perception
    NT Selectivity (Psychology)
Human information processing in children
    [BF723.I63]
    UF Information processing in children
    BT Child psychology
         Cognition in children
Human intelligence
  USE Intellect
Human interaction
  USE Social interaction
Human leopards
  USE Leopard men
Human leukocyte antigens
  USE HLA histocompatibility antigens
Human life cycle
  USE Life cycle, Human
Human locomotion
    BT Human mechanics
         Kinesiology
         Locomotion
    NT Gait in humans
         Locomotion, Disordered
         Man—Attitude and movement
         Running
         Swimming
         Walking
Human magnetism
  USE Animal magnetism
Human males
  USE Men
Human mechanics
    [QP301-QP321]
    UF Body mechanics, Human
         Human movements
         Movements, Human
    BT Animal mechanics
         Human physiology
         Physical anthropology
    RT Kinesiology
    SA subdivision Movements under
         individual parts of the body, e.g.
         Foot—Movements
    NT Human locomotion
         Sitting position
Human movements
  USE Human mechanics
Human operators (Systems engineering)
  USE Man-machine systems
Human paleontology
  USE Fossil man
Human parasitology
  USE Medical parasitology
Human physiology
    [QP34-QP38]
    BT Human biology
         Medical sciences
         Physiology
    RT Body, Human
    SA subdivision Physiology under classes of
         persons and ethnic groups
    NT Acetylator status (Pharmacology)
         Human mechanics
         Human reproduction
         Men—Physiology
         Vital signs
Human population genetics
  (May Subd Geog)
    BT Human genetics
         Population
         Population genetics
Human powered aircraft
    [TL769]
    UF Man powered aircraft
    BT Flying-machines
Human powered vehicles (May Subd Geog)
    UF Vehicles, Human powered
    BT Vehicles

Human records
  USE World records
Human relations
  USE Interpersonal relations
Human reproduction (May Subd Geog)
    [QP251]
    BT Human physiology
         Reproduction
    NT Conception
         Embryology, Human
         Fertility, Human
         Fertilization in vitro, Human
— **Age factors**
    UF Age factors in human reproduction
    BT Aging
— **Endocrine aspects**
    UF Endocrine aspects of human
         reproduction
         Hormonal aspects of human
         reproduction
         Human reproduction—Hormonal
         aspects
         Reproductive endocrinology
    BT Endocrinology
    RT Andrology
         Endocrine gynecology
    NT Obstetrical endocrinology
— Hormonal aspects
    USE Human reproduction—Endocrine
         aspects
— **Immunological aspects**
— **Nutritional aspects**
— **Religious aspects**
— — **Baptists, [Catholic Church, etc.]**
— — **Buddhism, [Christianity, etc.]**
Human resilience
  USE Resilience (Personality trait)
Human resource development
  USE Education
        Manpower policy
Human resource management
  USE Personnel management
Human resources
  USE Human capital
Human rights (May Subd Geog)
    [JC571-JC628 (Political theory)]
    Here are entered works on the rights of persons
  regardless of their legal, socioeconomic or cultural
  status and as recognized by the international com-
  munity. Works on citizens' rights as established by
  law and protected by constitution are entered under
  Civil rights.
    UF Basic rights
         Civil rights (International law)
         Rights, Human
         Rights of man
    NT Children's rights
         Civil rights
         Right to life
         Women's rights
— **Religious aspects**
— — **Baptists, [Catholic Church, etc.]**
— — **Buddhism, [Christianity, etc.]**
— — **Catholic Church**
    UF Civil rights (Canon law)
Human rights activists
  USE Human rights workers
Human rights advocates
  USE Human rights workers
Human rights defenders
  USE Human rights workers
Human rights workers (May Subd Geog)
    UF Activists, Human rights
         Advocates, Human rights
         Defenders of human rights
         Human rights activists
         Human rights advocates
         Human rights defenders
Human risk assessment
  USE Health risk assessment

Human sacrifice
  USE Sacrifice, Human
Human science
  USE Anthroposophy
Human services
  USE Public welfare
     Social service
Human settlements *(May Subd Geog)*
  [GF101-GF127 (Human ecology)]
  [HT51-HT65 (Sociology)]
  UF Habitat, Human
     Human habitat
     Settlements, Human
  BT Anthropo-geography
     Human ecology
     Population
     Sociology
  RT Land settlement
  NT Cities and towns
     Community
     Housing
     Infrastructure (Economics)
     Regional planning
Human Sexuality (Videotex system)
  USE HSX (Vidotex system)
Human skeleton
  [QM101]
  BT Skeleton
  NT Forensic anthropology
     Skeletal maturity
  — **Radiography**
Human spontaneous combustion
  USE Combustion, Spontaneous human
Human subsystems (Systems engineering)
  USE Man-machine systems
Human survival skills
  USE Survival skills
Human T-cell leukemia lymphoma virus
  [QR414.5]
  UF Adult T-cell leukemia lymphoma virus
     HTLV (Virus)
  BT Retroviruses
  RT Human immunodeficiency viruses
Human T-cell leukemia virus type III
  antibodies
  USE Human immunodeficiency virus
     antibodies
Human T-cell lymphotropic virus type III
  USE Human immunodeficiency viruses
Human T-cell lymphotropic virus type III
  antibodies
  USE Human immunodeficiency virus
     antibodies
Human territoriality
  UF Territorial behavior
     Territoriality, Human
  BT Anthropo-geography
     Ethnology
     Spatial behavior
  NT Personal space
Human torpedoes
  USE Kaiten (Torpedoes)
     Midget submarines
Human toxocariasis
  USE Larva migrans, Visceral
Human trapping
  UF Mantrapping
  BT Trapping
Human welfare
  USE Humanitarianism
Humana Building (Louisville, Ky.)
  USE Humana, Inc. Headquarters
     (Louisville, Ky.)
Humana Headquarters (Louisville, Ky.)
  USE Humana, Inc. Headquarters
     (Louisville, Ky.)
Humana, Inc. Headquarters (Louisville, Ky.)
  UF Humana Building (Louisville, Ky.)
     Humana Headquarters (Louisville, Ky.)
  BT Office buildings—Kentucky
     Skyscrapers—Kentucky

Humane education *(May Subd Geog)*
  [HV4712]
  UF Animals, Treatment of—Study and
     teaching
     Education, Humane
  BT Education
     Moral education
Humane societies
  USE Animals, Treatment of—Societies, etc.
     Charities—Societies, etc.
     Child welfare
     Vivisection—Societies, etc.
Humane treatment of animals
  USE Animals, Treatment of
Humanism *(May Subd Geog)*
  [B778 (Renaissance)]
  [B821 (Modern)]
  BT Philosophy
  RT Classical education
     Classical philology
     Learning and scholarship
     Philosophical anthropology
     Renaissance
  NT Ciceronianism
     Devotio moderna
     Humanistic ethics
     Humanities
     Islam and humanism
  — **20th century**
     [B821]
     BT Philosophy, Modern
     NT Lokāyata
Humanism, Religious
  Here are entered works dealing with a movement,
originating in American Unitarianism, which stressed
the idea that man can satisfy all his religious needs
from within himself and discarded in its advanced
thought all theistic concepts.
  UF Religious humanism
  BT Man (Theology)
  NT Christianity and religious humanism
Humanism and the Catholic Church
  USE Catholic Church and humanism
Humanism in art
  BT Art
     Reformation and art
  NT Ut pictura poesis (Aesthetics)
Humanism in literature
Humanist ethics
  USE Humanistic ethics
Humanistic counseling
  [BF637.C6]
  BT Counseling
     Humanistic psychology
Humanistic education
  USE Education, Humanistic
Humanistic ethics
  [BJ1360]
  UF Ethics, Humanistic
     Humanist ethics
  BT Ethics
     Humanism
Humanistic psychology
  [BF204]
  BT Personality
     Psychology
  NT Humanistic counseling
     Humanistic psychotherapy
     Self-actualization (Psychology)
Humanistic psychotherapy
  BT Humanistic psychology
     Psychotherapy
  NT Experiential psychotherapy
Humanistic writing
  USE Writing, Humanistic
Humanists *(May Subd Geog)*
  [PA83-85]
Humanitarian conventions
  USE War victims—Legal status, laws, etc.
Humanitarianism
  [BJ1475.3]

  UF Human welfare
     Philanthropy
     Social welfare
  BT Charities
     Ethics
Humanitarians
  USE Philanthropists
Humanities *(May Subd Geog)*
  Here are entered works on the branches of learn-
ing regarded as having a cultural character, including
literature, the arts, history, philosophy, religion, etc.
  BT Humanism
     Learning and scholarship
  RT Classical education
  NT Arts
     Communication in the humanities
     Education, Humanistic
     Engineering and the humanities
     Medicine and the humanities
     Philosophy
     Psychiatry and the humanities
     Psychology and the humanities
     Religion and the humanities
     Science and the humanities
  — Information storage and retrieval systems
     USE Information storage and retrieval
          systems—Humanities
  — **Study and teaching** *(May Subd Geog)*
  — — **Law and legislation**
      (May Subd Geog)
      BT Educational law and legislation
  — Subject headings
     USE Subject headings—Humanities
Humanities and religion
  USE Religion and the humanities
Humanities and science
  USE Science and the humanities
Humanities libraries *(May Subd Geog)*
  UF Libraries, Humanities
  BT Libraries, Special
  NT Folklore libraries
     Historical libraries
     Linguistics libraries
     Philosophy libraries
Humanity
  [BJ1533.H (Virtues)]
  BT Charity
     Conduct of life
  RT Benevolence
     Kindness
Humanity, Religion of
  USE Positivism
Humanity in art
Humanization of work life
  USE Quality of work life
Humans
  USE Man
Humans in art
  [N7625.5]
  Here are entered works on the representation of
human beings in art. Works on the techniques of
depicting the human body in art are entered under
Human figure in art.
  UF Man in art
     Menschenbild
Humates *(May Subd Geog)*
  BT Humic acid
     Salts
Humba (African people)
  USE Kuanyama (African people)
Humber, River (England)
  UF Abus River (England)
     Humber, River, Estuary (England)
     Humber Estuary (England)
     River Humber (England)
  BT Estuaries—England
     Rivers—England
Humber, River, Estuary (England)
  USE Humber, River (England)
Humber automobile
  BT Rootes automobiles

Humber Estuary (England)
 USE Humber, River (England)
Humber River (Ont.) *(Not Subd Geog)*
 BT Rivers—Ontario
Humberside Audio Visual Catalogue
 USE HAVOC (Information retrieval
  system)
Humbert family *(Not Subd Geog)*
 UF Humbird family
Humbird family
 USE Humbert family
Humblebees
 USE Bumblebees
Humbleflies
 USE Bombyliidae
Humboldt Award
 UF Humboldt-Preis
 BT Engineering—Germany (West)—
  Awards
  Engineering—United States—Awards
  Rewards (Prizes, etc.)—Germany
   (West)
  Rewards (Prizes, etc.)—United States
  Science—Germany (West)—Awards
  Science—United States—Awards
Humboldt Bay (Calif.)
 BT Bays—California
Humboldt Bay Indians
 USE Wiyot Indians
Humboldt coyotillo
 USE Karwinskia humboldtiana
Humboldt Current
 USE Peru Current
Humboldt penguin
 ₍QL696.S5₎
 UF Peruvian penguin
  Spheniscus humboldti
 BT Penguins
Humboldt-Preis
 USE Humboldt Award
Humboldt River (Nev.)
 BT Rivers—Nevada
Humbug
 USE Impostors and imposture
  Swindlers and swindling
Hume family *(Not Subd Geog)*
 UF Hum family
  Humes family
 RT Holmes family
Humectants
 UF Moisture controlling agents
 BT Moisture
Humerus
 ₍QL821 (Comparative anatomy)₎
 ₍QM117 (Human anatomy)₎
 BT Arm
  Bones
 — Dislocation
  USE Shoulder joint—Dislocation
Humes family
 USE Hume family
Humic acid
 ₍QD341.A2₎
 NT Humates
Humidification
 USE Humidity—Control
Humidifiers *(May Subd Geog)*
 BT Humidity—Control
Humidity *(May Subd Geog)*
 ₍QC915-917₎
 UF Air, Moisture of
  Atmospheric humidity
  Relative humidity
 BT Meteorology
  Weather
 RT Moisture
  Water vapor, Atmospheric
 NT Air conditioning—Climatic factors
  Cooling towers—Climatic factors
  Dew point
  Evaporation (Meteorology)

Hygrometers
Hygrometry
Plants, Effect of humidity on
Sultriness
Water vapor transport
— Control
 UF Control of humidity
  Dehumidification
  Humidification
  Humidity control
 BT Air conditioning
  Dampness in buildings
 NT Humidifiers
— Measurement
 USE Hygrometry
— Physiological effect
 NT Plants, Effect of humidity on
Humidity control
 USE Humidity—Control
Humidity meters
 USE Moisture meters
Humiliati
 ₍BX3680.H8₎
 UF Barettini
 RT Waldenses
Humililty (Judaism)
 USE Humility—Judaism
Humility
 RT Meekness
— Buddhism, ₍Christianity, etc.₎
— Judaism
 UF Humililty (Judaism)
Humility in literature
Humin
 ₍S598₎
Ḥummām Ṭubariya (Ancient city)
 USE Ḥamat (Ancient city)
Hummbrella
 ₍QK569.P98₎
 BT Pseudoanemoniaceae
Hummbrella hydra
 ₍QK569.P98₎
Hummel
 USE Noordsche balk
Hummel art *(May Subd Geog)*
  Here are entered works dealing with various types
 of Hummel articles, e.g. prints, cards, dolls, calen-
 dars, plates, bells, music boxes, etc.
 BT Art
  Decorative arts—Germany (West)
 NT Hummel figurines
Hummel family *(Not Subd Geog)*
 UF Hummell family
Hummel figurines
 ₍NK4660₎
 UF "M.I. Hummel" figurines
 BT Figurines—Germany (West)
  Hummel art
  Porcelain, German
Hummel plates *(May Subd Geog)*
 BT Commemorative plates
  Plates (Tableware)
Hummell family
 USE Hummel family
Humming-birds
 USE Hummingbirds
Hummingbirds *(May Subd Geog)*
 ₍QL696.A558₎
 UF Humming-birds
  Trochilidae
 BT Apodiformes
 NT Andean hillstar
  Calypte
  Eulampis
  Lampornis
  Phaethornis
  Purple-throated carib

Humor
 USE American wit and humor, English wit
  and humor *and similar headings;*
  also subdivision History, Comic,
  satirical, etc. *under names of*
  countries, cities, etc; also
  subdivisions Anecdotes *and* Humor
  under individual wars and types of
  animals; and subdivision Anecdotes,
  facetiae, satire, etc. *under subjects*
  Anecdotes
  Wit and humor
Humor in advertising
 UF Advertising, Humor in
  Wit and humor in advertising
 BT Advertising
  Wit and humor
Humor in children *(May Subd Geog)*
 ₍BF723.H85₎
 BT Child psychology
  Wit and humor
Humor in education
 UF Education, Humor in
  Wit and humor in education
 BT Education—Philosophy
  Wit and humor
Humor in medicine
 USE Wit and humor in medicine
Humor in the Bible
 USE Wit and humor in the Bible
Humorists
 ₍PN6147₎
 BT Wit and humor
 NT Satirists
Humorists, American *(May Subd Geog)*
 UF American humorists
Humorists, American, ₍English, French, etc.₎
Humorists, Australian *(May Subd Geog)*
 UF Australian humorists
Humorists, Brazilian *(May Subd Geog)*
 UF Brazilian humorists
Humorists, Canadian *(May Subd Geog)*
 UF Canadian humorists
Humorists, English *(May Subd Geog)*
 UF English humorists
Humorists, Spanish *(May Subd Geog)*
 UF Spanish humorists
Humorous illustrations
 USE Caricatures and cartoons
  Wit and humor, Pictorial
Humorous monologues
 USE Humorous recitations
Humorous photography
 USE Photography, Humorous
Humorous poetry
 UF Humorous verse
  Light verse
 BT Poetry
  Wit and humor
 NT Clerihews
  Doggerel
  Limericks
  Nonsense-verses
Humorous poetry, American
 (May Subd Geog)
 UF American humorous poetry
 BT American poetry
Humorous poetry, Australian
 (May Subd Geog)
 UF Australian humorous poetry
 BT Australian poetry
Humorous poetry, Bolivian
 (May Subd Geog)
 UF Bolivian humorous poetry
 BT Bolivian poetry
Humorous poetry, Canadian
 (May Subd Geog)
 UF Canadian humorous poetry
 BT Canadian poetry

Humorous poetry, Chinese
(May Subd Geog)
UF Chinese humorous poetry
BT Chinese poetry
Humorous poetry, Colombian
(May Subd Geog)
UF Colombian humorous poetry
BT Colombian poetry
Colombian wit and humor
Humorous poetry, English (May Subd Geog)
UF English humorous poetry
BT English poetry
Humorous poetry, English, [etc.]
(May Subd Geog)
Humorous poetry, French (May Subd Geog)
UF French humorous poetry
BT French poetry
Humorous poetry, Japanese
(May Subd Geog)
UF Japanese humorous poetry
BT Japanese poetry
Japanese wit and humor
NT Kyōka
Senryu
Humorous poetry, Norwegian
(May Subd Geog)
UF Norwegian humorous poetry
BT Norwegian poetry
Humorous poetry, Provençal
(May Subd Geog)
UF Provençal humorous poetry
BT Provençal poetry
Humorous poetry, Scottish
(May Subd Geog)
UF Scottish humorous poetry
BT Scottish poetry
Humorous poetry, Swedish
(May Subd Geog)
UF Swedish humorous poetry
BT Swedish poetry
Humorous poetry, Urdu (May Subd Geog)
UF Urdu humorous poetry
BT Urdu poetry
Humorous poetry, Venezuelan
(May Subd Geog)
UF Venezuelan humorous poetry
BT Venezuelan poetry
Venezuelan wit and humor
Humorous recitations
UF Humorous monologues
Monologues, Humorous
Recitations, Humorous
BT Recitations
Wit and humor
Humorous songs
UF Comic songs
Songs, Humorous
BT Songs
Wit and humor, Musical
NT Bawdy songs
Nonsense songs
Humorous stories
UF Comic stories
BT Fiction
Wit and humor
Humorous stories, American
(May Subd Geog)
UF American humorous stories
BT American fiction
American wit and humor
Humorous stories, English
(May Subd Geog)
UF English humorous stories
BT English fiction
English wit and humor
Humorous stories, French (May Subd Geog)
UF French humorous stories
BT French fiction
French wit and humor

Humorous stories, French-Canadian
(May Subd Geog)
UF French-Canadian humorous stories
BT French-Canadian fiction
French-Canadian wit and humor
Humorous stories, Shona (May Subd Geog)
UF Shona humorous stories
BT Shona fiction
Shona wit and humor
Humorous verse
USE Humorous poetry
Humors, Body
USE Body fluids
Hump yards
USE Railroads—Hump yards
Humpback salmon
USE Pink salmon
Humpback sucker
USE Xyrauchen texanus
Humpback whale
[QL737.C424]
UF Megaptera nodosa
Megaptera novaeangliae
BT Whales
NT Humphrey (Whale)
Humpbacked dolphin, Indo-Pacific
USE Chinese white dolphin
Humpbacked dolphins
USE Sousa
Humphrey (Cook Islands)
USE Manihiki Atoll (Cook Islands)
Humphrey (Whale)
BT Humpback whale
Humphrey family (Not Subd Geog)
UF Humphreys family
Humphries family
Humphry family
Humphury family
Humprie family
Umphrey family
Umphries family
Humphreys family
USE Humphrey family
Humphrey's Island (Cook Islands)
USE Manihiki Atoll (Cook Islands)
Humphries family
USE Humphrey family
Humphry family
USE Humphrey family
Humphury family
USE Humphrey family
Humprie family
USE Humphrey family
Humulon
BT Antibacterial agents
Humulus
[QK495.M73 (Botany)]
BT Moraceae
Humulus americanus
USE Hops
Humulus lupulus
USE Hops
Humung (Asian people)
USE Hmong (Asian people)
Humung language
USE Hmong language
Humus (May Subd Geog)
[S592.8 (General)]
[SD390-SD390.3 (Forest soils)]
UF Mold, Vegetable
Mould, Vegetable
Muck
Organic matter in soil
Soil organic matter
Soils—Organic matter
Vegetable mold
BT Histosols
Organic fertilizers
Soils
Soils—Composition
RT Compost

NT Forest litter
Forest soils
Soils—Carbohydrate content
Wood waste as mulch, soil conditioner,
etc.
Hün family
USE Hüner family
Hunan style of Chinese cookery
USE Cookery, Chinese—Hunan style
Hunanese dialects
USE Hsiang dialects
Hundborg family (Not Subd Geog)
Hundertwasser Haus (Vienna, Austria)
UF Hundertwasser House (Vienna,
Austria)
BT Apartment houses—Austria
Hundertwasser House (Vienna, Austria)
USE Hundertwasser Haus (Vienna, Austria)
Hundred (The number)
BT Symbolism of numbers
Hundred Days, 1815
USE Napoleon I, Emperor of the French,
1769-1821—Elba and the Hundred
Days, 1814-1815
Hundred Flowers Campaign, China, 1956
USE China—History—Hundred Flowers
Campaign, 1956
Hundred in the Hands, Battle of the, 1866
USE Fetterman Fight, 1866
Hundred-pace snake
USE Agkistrodon acutus
Hundred Years' War, 1339-1453
[DC96-105]
NT Agincourt, Battle of, 1415
Brétigny, Treaty of, 1360
Crécy, Battle of, 1346
Poitiers, Battle of, 1356
Roosebeke, Battle of, 1382
Troyes, Treaty of, 1420
Hundsberger family
USE Hunsberger family
Hune (African people)
USE Dukawa (African people)
Hüner family (Not Subd Geog)
UF Höen family
Huener family
Hün family
Huneycut family
USE Huneycutt family
Huneycutt family (Not Subd Geog)
UF Honeycut family
Huneycut family
Hunnecut family
Hunneycut family
Hunnicut family
Hung-t'on Hsü (Taiwan)
USE Lan Island (Taiwan)
Hung-t'ou Hsü (Taiwan)
USE Lan Island (Taiwan)
Hung Vuong (Legendary rulers)
USE Hong Bang dynasty, 2879-258 B.C.
(Legendary)
Hungaan language
USE Hungana language
Hungana (African people)
USE Huana (African people)
Hungana language
UF Huana language
Hungaan language
BT Bantu languages
Kongo language
Mbala language (Bandundu region,
Zaire)
Zaire—Languages
Hungarian abbreviations
USE Abbreviations, Hungarian
Hungarian aesthetics
USE Aesthetics, Hungarian
Hungarian Americans (May Subd Geog)
BT Ethnology—United States
Hungarians—United States

Hungarian art
  USE Art, Hungarian
Hungarian arts
  USE Arts, Hungarian
Hungarian atlases
  USE Atlases, Hungarian
Hungarian-Austrian Compromise, 1867
  USE Austro-Hungarian Compromise, 1867
Hungarian authors
  USE Authors, Hungarian
Hungarian ballads
  USE Ballads, Hungarian
Hungarian book-plates
  USE Book-plates, Hungarian
Hungarian Byzantine rite (Catholic Church)
  USE Catholic Church—Byzantine rite,
      Hungarian
Hungarian chamomile
  USE Matricaria chamomilla
Hungarian children's literature
  USE Children's literature, Hungarian
Hungarian children's periodicals
  USE Children's periodicals, Hungarian
Hungarian children's plays
  USE Children's plays, Hungarian
Hungarian children's poetry
  USE Children's poetry, Hungarian
Hungarian children's stories
  USE Children's stories, Hungarian
Hungarian civics
  USE Civics, Hungarian
Hungarian coins
  USE Coins, Hungarian
Hungarian cookery
  USE Cookery, Hungarian
Hungarian-Croatian Compromise, 1868
  USE Croato-Hungarian Compromise, 1868
Hungarian detective and mystery stories
  USE Detective and mystery stories,
      Hungarian
Hungarian drama
  ₍PH3084-PH3096 (History)₎
  ₍PH3165-PH3171 (Collections)₎
  NT Children's plays, Hungarian
      Folk-drama, Hungarian
      Moralities, Hungarian
      Mysteries and miracle-plays,
        Hungarian
      Radio plays, Hungarian
  — To 1800
Hungarian economic assistance
  USE Economic assistance, Hungarian
Hungarian epic poetry
  USE Epic poetry, Hungarian
Hungarian erotic poetry
  USE Erotic poetry, Hungarian
Hungarian fables
  USE Fables, Hungarian
Hungarian fiction *(May Subd Geog)*
  NT Children's stories, Hungarian
      Detective and mystery stories,
        Hungarian
      Historical fiction, Hungarian
      Horror tales, Hungarian
      Science fiction, Hungarian
      Short stories, Hungarian
Hungarian folk-drama
  USE Folk-drama, Hungarian
Hungarian folk literature
  USE Folk literature, Hungarian
Hungarian folk-songs
  USE Folk-songs, Hungarian
Hungarian genre painting
  USE Genre painting, Hungarian
Hungarian historical fiction
  USE Historical fiction, Hungarian
Hungarian Holy Crown
  USE Holy Crown of Hungary
Hungarian horror tales
  USE Horror tales, Hungarian

Hungarian horse
  ₍SF293.H79₎
  UF Hungarian native horse
  BT Horse breeds
Hungarian hymns
  USE Hymns, Hungarian
Hungarian imprints *(May Subd Geog)*
Hungarian Jews
  USE Jews, Hungarian
Hungarian language *(May Subd Geog)*
  ₍PH2001-2800₎
  UF Magyar language
  BT Finno-Ugric languages
  — Abbreviations
      USE Abbreviations, Hungarian
  — **Etymology**
      NT Hogy (The Hungarian word)
  — — Names
        NT Names, Hungarian
  — Names
      USE Names, Hungarian
Hungarian literature *(May Subd Geog)*
  ₍PH3001-3445₎
  UF Magyar literature
  NT Children's literature, Hungarian
      Folk literature, Hungarian
      Hungarian prose literature
  — To 1800
      ₍PH3036 (History)₎
      ₍PH3141 (Collections)₎
  — 20th century
      NT Népi írók mozgalom
  — Foreign countries
      ₍PH3407-3408₎
      UF Hungarian literature in foreign
        countries
Hungarian literature in foreign countries
  USE Hungarian literature—Foreign
      countries
Hungarian love poetry
  USE Love poetry, Hungarian
Hungarian madrigals (Music)
  USE Madrigals (Music), Hungarian
Hungarian manuscripts
  USE Manuscripts, Hungarian
Hungarian miracle-plays
  USE Mysteries and miracle-plays,
      Hungarian
Hungarian moralities
  USE Moralities, Hungarian
Hungarian moving-picture cartoons
  USE Moving-picture cartoons, Hungarian
Hungarian mural painting and decoration
  USE Mural painting and decoration,
      Hungarian
Hungarian mysteries and miracle-plays
  USE Mysteries and miracle-plays,
      Hungarian
Hungarian mythology
  USE Mythology, Finno-Ugrian
Hungarian names
  USE Names, Hungarian
Hungarian national characteristics
  USE National characteristics, Hungarian
Hungarian native horse
  USE Hungarian horse
Hungarian newspapers *(May Subd Geog)*
  ₍PN5355.H8₎
  — Foreign countries
      UF Hungarian newspapers in foreign
        countries
Hungarian newspapers in foreign countries
  USE Hungarian newspapers—Foreign
      countries
Hungarian nursery rhymes
  USE Nursery rhymes, Hungarian
Hungarian panel painting
  USE Panel painting, Hungarian
Hungarian Parliament Building (Budapest,
  Hungary)
  USE Országház (Budapest, Hungary)

Hungarian parodies
  USE Parodies, Hungarian
Hungarian partridge
  USE Perdix perdix
Hungarian patriotic poetry
  USE Patriotic poetry, Hungarian
Hungarian periodicals *(May Subd Geog)*
  ₍PN5355.H8₎
  NT Children's periodicals, Hungarian
  — Circulation
  — Foreign countries
      UF Hungarian periodicals in foreign
        countries
Hungarian periodicals in foreign countries
  USE Hungarian periodicals—Foreign
      countries
Hungarian philology
Hungarian philosophy
  USE Philosophy, Hungarian
Hungarian Plain
  USE Great Alföld
Hungarian poetry
  ₍PH3062-PH3082 (History)₎
  ₍PH3151-PH3164 (Collections)₎
  NT Children's poetry, Hungarian
      Epic poetry, Hungarian
      Erotic poetry, Hungarian
      Love poetry, Hungarian
      Nursery rhymes, Hungarian
      Patriotic poetry, Hungarian
      Religious poetry, Hungarian
      Revolutionary poetry, Hungarian
Hungarian poets
  USE Poets, Hungarian
Hungarian political posters
  USE Political posters, Hungarian
Hungarian posters
  USE Posters, Hungarian
Hungarian pottery
  USE Pottery, Hungarian
Hungarian prints
  USE Prints, Hungarian
Hungarian property *(May Subd Geog)*
  UF Property, Hungarian
  BT Alien property
Hungarian prose literature
  (May Subd Geog)
  BT Hungarian literature
  — To 1800
Hungarian proverbs
  USE Proverbs, Hungarian
Hungarian quotations
  USE Quotations, Hungarian
Hungarian radio plays
  USE Radio plays, Hungarian
Hungarian religious poetry
  USE Religious poetry, Hungarian
Hungarian revolutionary poetry
  USE Revolutionary poetry, Hungarian
Hungarian satire
  USE Satire, Hungarian
Hungarian science fiction
  USE Science fiction, Hungarian
Hungarian sculpture
  USE Sculpture, Hungarian
Hungarian short stories
  USE Short stories, Hungarian
Hungarian shorthand
  USE Shorthand, Hungarian
Hungarian students *(May Subd Geog)*
  BT Students
Hungarian subject headings
  USE Subject headings, Hungarian
Hungarian technical assistance
  USE Technical assistance, Hungarian
Hungarian wit and humor *(May Subd Geog)*
Hungarian wit and humor, Pictorial
  (May Subd Geog)
Hungarian wood-engraving
  USE Wood-engraving, Hungarian

Hungarians *(May Subd Geog)*
  BT Ethnology—Hungary
      Finno-Ugrians
  RT Magyars
  NT Csangos
      Palocs
      Szeklers
  — United States
     NT Hungarian Americans
Hungaroa River (N.Z.)
  USE Hungaroa Stream (N.Z.)
Hungaroa Stream (N.Z.)
  UF Hungaroa River (N.Z.)
  BT Rivers—New Zealand
Hungary
  — Antiquities, Roman
     NT Matrica Site (Hungary)
  — Boundaries
  — — Romania
      NT Vienna award, 1940
  — Capital and capitol
     NT Országház (Budapest, Hungary)
  — Church history
  — — 18th century
      ⌐BR869.55⌐
  — — 20th century
  — Civilization
     NT Civilization—Hungarian influences
       United States—Civilization—
          Hungarian influences
       Venice (Italy)—Civilization—
          Hungarian influences
  — — 1945-   *(Not Subd Geog)*
  — — Italian influences
      BT Italy—Civilization
  — — Turkish influences
      BT Turkey—Civilization
  — — Venetian influences
      BT Venice (Italy)—Civilization
  — Description and travel
  — — 1945-1980
      ⌐DB917⌐
  — — 1981-
      ⌐DB917.3⌐
  — Economic conditions
  — — 18th century
  — — 19th century
  — — 1918-1945
  — — 1945-
  — — 1945-1968
  — — 1968-
  — Economic policy
  — — 1945-
  — — 1945-1968
  — — 1968-
  — Foreign relations
  — — 1849-1867
  — — 1918-1945
  — — 1945-
  — History
      ⌐DB901-975⌐
  — — To 894
  — — 894-1000
      NT Lechfeld, Battle of, 955
  — — 1000-1683
  — — — Juvenile literature
  — — Matthias I, 1458-1490
  — — 1490-1526
      NT Dózsa Uprising, 1514
  — — 1526-1683
      NT Kanisza, Battle of, 1601
          Szöny, Hungary, Peace of, 1642
  — — 1683-1848
  — — Joseph II, 1780-1790
  — — Leopold II, 1790-1792
  — — Uprising of 1848-1849
      UF Revolution of 1848 in Hungary
      BT Austria—History—Revolution,
          1848-1849
      NT Kápolna, Hungary (Heves),
          Battle of, 1849

  — — — Campaigns *(Not Subd Geog)*
      NT Pákozd (Hungary), Battle of,
          1848
  — — — Juvenile literature
  — — — Pictorial works
  — — Francis Joseph, 1848-1916
  — — 1849-1867
  — — 1867-1918
  — — 20th century
  — — Revolution, 1918-1919
  — — 1918-1945
  — — — Juvenile literature
  — — 1945-
  — — Revolution, 1956
  — Intellectual life
  — — 20th century
  — Kings and rulers
     NT Árpád, House of
  — Pictorial works
  — Politics and government
  — — 1683-1848
  — — 19th century
  — — 1849-1867
  — — 1849-1918
  — — 1867-1918
  — — 20th century
  — — 1918-1945
  — — 1945-
  — Social conditions
  — — 1945-
Hungeford family
  USE Hungerford family
Hunger
  ⌐QP141⌐
  RT Appetite
      Fasting
      Starvation
  — Religious aspects
  — — Baptists, ⌐Catholic Church, etc.⌐
  — — Buddhism, ⌐Christianity, etc.⌐
Hunger in art
  ⌐N8217.H8⌐
Hunger strikes *(May Subd Geog)*
  UF Strikes, Hunger
  BT Fasting
      Government, Resistance to
      Nonviolence
      Passive resistance
  — Law and legislation *(May Subd Geog)*
Hungerford family *(Not Subd Geog)*
  UF Hungeford family
Hungersteppe (Kazakh S.S.R.)
  USE Betpak-Dala (Kazakh S.S.R.)
Hungf'ou Hsii (Taiwan)
  USE Lan Island (Taiwan)
Hungtow Island (Taiwan)
  USE Lan Island (Taiwan)
Hunkpapa Indians
  ⌐E99.H795⌐
  BT Dakota Indians
      Indians of North America
      Teton Indians
Hunnecut family
  USE Huneycutt family
Hunneycut family
  USE Huneycutt family
Hunnicut family
  USE Huneycutt family
Huno Indians
  USE Puquina Indians
Huns
  ⌐D141-3⌐
  NT Ephthalites
      Hsiung-nu
Hunsberger family *(Not Subd Geog)*
  UF Hundsberger family
      Hunsberry family
      Huntsberry family
      Huntsbury family
      Huntsperger family
      Huntzberry family

Hunsberry family
  USE Hunsberger family
Hunsdiecker degradation
  USE Hunsdiecker reaction
Hunsdiecker reaction
  UF Hunsdiecker degradation
  BT Chemical reactions
Hunsgi River (India)
  BT Rivers—India
Hunshamar family *(Not Subd Geog)*
Hunsrück (Germany)
  BT Mountains—Germany (West)
Hunt, William Holman, 1827-1910. Finding
  of the Saviour in the Temple
  UF Finding of Christ in the Temple
      (Painting)
      Finding of the Saviour in the Temple
      (Painting)
  BT Jesus Christ—Art
Hunt, William Holman, 1827-1910. Lady of
  Shalott
  UF Lady of Shalott (Painting)
  BT Painting, English
Hunt, William Holman, 1827-1910. Light of
  the world *(Not Subd Geog)*
  UF Light of the world (Painting)
  BT Painting, English
Hunt, William Holman, 1827-1910. Strayed
  sheep
  UF Strayed sheep (Painting)
Hunt family *(Not Subd Geog)*
  UF Hunte family
      Hunts family
  RT Hunter family
Hunt of the unicorn (Tapestries)
  ⌐NK3049.U5⌐
  UF Unicorn tapestries
  BT Tapestry—France
      Tapestry, Gothic—France
Hunt racing
  USE Steeplechasing
Hunt riding *(May Subd Geog)*
  ⌐SF295.65⌐
  UF Riding, Hunt
      Riding to hounds
  BT Horse sports
      Horsemanship
      Hunting
  RT Fox-hunting
      Hunters (Horses)
Hunt roman
  USE Type and type-founding—Hunt roman
Hunt seat equitation
  USE Hunter seat equitation
Hunt terrier, German
  USE German hunt terrier
Huntar family
  USE Hunter family
Hunte family
  USE Hunt family
Hunter (Constellation)
  USE Orion (Constellation)
Hunter (Turbojet fighter planes)
  UF Hawker Hunter (Turbojet fighter
      planes)
  BT Fighter planes
      Jet planes
Hunter classes *(May Subd Geog)*
  ⌐SF296.H86⌐
  BT Horse-shows
  RT Hunters (Horses)
Hunter family *(Not Subd Geog)*
  UF Huntar family
  RT Hunt family
Hunter ponies *(May Subd Geog)*
  BT Ponies
  NT Hunter show ponies
Hunter River (N.S.W.)
  BT Rivers—Australia

Hunter seat equitation *(May Subd Geog)*
  UF Hunt seat equitation
      Hunting seat equitation
  BT Horsemanship
  — Competitions
      USE Hunter seat equitation division
Hunter seat equitation division
  (May Subd Geog)
  ⌈SF296.H87⌉
  UF Hunter seat equitation—Competitions
  BT Horse-shows
Hunter show ponies *(May Subd Geog)*
  BT Hunter ponies
      Show ponies
Hunterellus
  ⌈QL568.E6⌉
  BT Encyrtidae
Hunterellus hookeri
  ⌈QL568.E6⌉
Hunters *(May Subd Geog)*
  UF Huntsmen
  NT Falconers
      Hunting guides
      Trappers
  — **Attitudes**
      BT Attitude (Psychology)
  — **Economic conditions**
      UF Hunters—Socioeconomic status
  — **Social conditions**
      UF Hunters—Socioeconomic status
  — Socioeconomic status
      USE Hunters—Economic conditions
          Hunters—Social conditions
Hunters (Horses)
  UF Point-to-point horses
  BT Fox-hunting
      Horses
  RT Hunt riding
      Hunter classes
Hunter's membrane
  USE Decidua
Hunting *(May Subd Geog)*
  ⌈GT5810-GT5899 (Manners and
      customs)⌉
  ⌈SK (Hunting sports)⌉
  UF Chase, The
      Field sports
      Gunning
  RT Game and game-birds
      Safaris
      Trapping
  SA *headings beginning with names of
      animals and birds hunted, e.g.* Deer
      hunting, Duck shooting, Fox-
      hunting, Moose hunting, Otter
      hunting
  NT Aeronautics in hunting
      Badger hunting
      Beagling
      Bee hunting
      Big game hunting
      Coon hunting
      Coursing
      Decoys (Hunting)
      Falconry
      Ferreting
      Fowling
      Game and game-birds, Dressing of
      Game calling (Hunting)
      Game-preserves
      Hare hunting
      Hunt riding
      Hunting and fishing clubs
      Hunting with bow and arrow
      Kangaroo hunting
      Market hunting (Game hunting)
      Poaching
      Predator hunting
      Pronghorn antelope hunting
      Rabbit hunting
      Tracking and trailing

      Varmint hunting
  — **Accidents and injuries**
      UF Hunting—Injuries
          Hunting accidents
      BT Firearms—Accidents
      NT Hunting—Safety measures
  — **Anecdotes, facetiae, satire, etc.**
      NT Hunting stories
  — Collections
      USE Hunting—Museums and
          collections
  — **Equipment and supplies**
  — — **Taxation** *(May Subd Geog)*
  — — — **Law and legislation**
          (May Subd Geog)
  — Injuries
      USE Hunting—Accidents and injuries
  — Law and legislation
      USE Game-laws
  — Licenses
      USE Fish and game licenses
  — **Museums and collections**
      UF Hunting—Collections
      BT Museums
  — Records
      USE Hunting trophies
  — **Religious aspects**
  — — **Baptists, ⌈Catholic Church, etc.⌉**
  — — **Catholic Church**
          NT Dog Mass
  — **Reporting** *(May Subd Geog)*
  — **Safety measures**
      UF Hunting safety
      BT Hunting—Accidents and injuries
  — **Social aspects** *(May Subd Geog)*
      UF Society and hunting
Hunting, Job
  USE Job hunting
Hunting, Primitive *(May Subd Geog)*
  ⌈GN422⌉
  BT Industries, Primitive
  NT Blowguns
      Indians of Central America—Hunting
      Indians of North America—Hunting
      Indians of South America—Hunting
  — **New Zealand**
      NT Maoris—Hunting
Hunting (in numismatics)
  ⌈CJ161.H⌉
  BT Numismatics
Hunting accidents
  USE Hunting—Accidents and injuries
Hunting and fishing camps
  USE Fishing lodges
      Hunting lodges
Hunting and fishing clubs *(May Subd Geog)*
  ⌈SH403 (Fishing clubs)⌉
  ⌈SK3 (Hunting clubs)⌉
  UF Fishing clubs
  BT Fishing
      Hunting
Hunting and gathering societies
  (May Subd Geog)
  UF Food gathering societies
      Gathering and hunting societies
  BT Society, Primitive
Hunting camps
  USE Hunting lodges
Hunting customs *(May Subd Geog)*
  ⌈GT5810-5850⌉
  BT Manners and customs
Hunting dog, African
  USE Lycaon pictus
Hunting dogs
  ⌈SF428.5⌉
  UF Gun dogs
      Sporting dogs
  BT Working dogs
  SA *particular breeds of hunting dogs*
  NT Bird dogs

Hunting game for sale
  USE Market hunting (Game hunting)
Hunting guides *(May Subd Geog)*
      Here are entered works on persons hired as guides
  for hunters.
  UF Ghillies
      Gillies
      Guides, Hunting
      Guides for hunters, fishermen, etc.
  BT Hunters
Hunting guns *(May Subd Geog)*
  ⌈SK274⌉
  UF Guns, Hunting
  BT Firearms
      Sporting guns
  NT Hunting pouches
      Hunting rifles
      Shotguns
Hunting in art
  ⌈N8250⌉
Hunting in literature
  ⌈PN56.H⌉
Hunting law
  USE Game-laws
Hunting-leopards
  USE Cheetahs
Hunting licenses
  USE Fish and game licenses
Hunting lodges *(May Subd Geog)*
  UF Hunting and fishing camps
      Hunting camps
  BT Architecture, Domestic
      Camps
      Club-houses
      Resorts
  — **Italy**
      NT Castello del Monte (Italy)
Hunting museums *(May Subd Geog)*
  BT Museums
Hunting music
  BT Horn music
      Instrumental music
      Music
  RT Trumpet-calls
  NT Bugle-calls
      Hunting songs
Hunting pouches
  ⌈SK274.45⌉
  UF Shot-pouches
  BT Hunting guns
Hunting records
  USE Hunting trophies
Hunting rifles *(May Subd Geog)*
  ⌈SK274⌉
  UF Sporting rifles
  BT Hunting guns
      Rifles
Hunting safety
  USE Hunting—Safety measures
Hunting seat equitation
  USE Hunter seat equitation
Hunting songs *(May Subd Geog)*
  ⌈M1977.H8⌉
  ⌈ML3780 (History)⌉
  ⌈PR1195.H9 (English poetry)⌉
  BT Hunting music
      Songs
Hunting stories
  BT Fiction
      Hunting—Anecdotes, facetiae, satire,
          etc.
      Sports stories
Hunting stories, American
  (May Subd Geog)
  UF American hunting stories
  BT American fiction
Hunting stories, Bengali *(May Subd Geog)*
  UF Bengali hunting stories
  BT Bengali fiction
Hunting stories, Czech *(May Subd Geog)*
  UF Czech hunting stories

BT   Czech fiction
Hunting stories, English   *(May Subd Geog)*
UF   English hunting stories
BT   English fiction
Hunting stories, Thai   *(May Subd Geog)*
UF   Thai hunting stories
BT   Thai fiction
Hunting surveys   *(May Subd Geog)*
Here are entered works on the methods and techniques employed, and reports of individual surveys. For the latter the heading may be subdivided by place; in such cases a subject entry is also made under the heading Hunting—(local subdivision), e.g. 1. Hunting—United States. 2. Hunting surveys—United States. For hunting surveys on a special topic the additional subject entry is made under the special topic, e.g. 1. Deer hunting—United States. 2. Hunting surveys—United States.
BT   Surveys
Hunting trophies   *(May Subd Geog)*
UF   Hunting—Records
Hunting records
Trophies, Hunting
BT   Records
Hunting with bow and arrow
(May Subd Geog)
[SK36]
UF   Bow hunting
Bowhunting
BT   Bow and arrow
Hunting
— **Law and legislation**   *(May Subd Geog)*
BT   Game-laws
Hunting with ferrets
USE   Ferreting
Huntington (Columbia, Md.)
(Not Subd Geog)
UF   Columbia (Md.).   Huntington
Huntington chorea
USE   Huntington's chorea
Huntington Herb Garden (San Marino, Calif.)
BT   Botanical gardens—California
Herb gardens—California
Knot gardens—California
Huntington's chorea   *(May Subd Geog)*
[RC394.H85]
UF   Chronic progressive chorea
Degenerative chorea
Hereditary chorea
Huntington chorea
Huntington's disease
Lund-Huntington chorea
Microcellular striatal syndrome
BT   Chorea
Genetic disorders
RT   Dementia
Huntington's disease
USE   Huntington's chorea
Huntley family   *(Not Subd Geog)*
UF   Huntly family
Huntly family
USE   Huntley family
Hunts family
USE   Hunt family
Hunts of the Emperor Maximilian (Tapestries)
BT   Tapestry—Belgium—History—16th century
Huntsberry family
USE   Hunsberger family
Huntsbury family
USE   Hunsberger family
Huntsmen
USE   Hunters
Huntsperger family
USE   Hunsberger family
Huntsville Pike (Ala.)
USE   Huntsville Road (Ala.)

Huntsville Road (Ala.)   *(Not Subd Geog)*
UF   Elyton Pike (Ala.)
Frog Level Road (Ala.)
Huntsville Pike (Ala.)
Tuscaloosa Pike (Ala.)
BT   Roads—Alabama
Huntzberry family
USE   Hunsberger family
Hunyani River (Zimbabwe and Mozambique)
UF   Panhame River (Zimbabwe and Mozambique)
Rio Panhame (Zimbabwe and Mozambique)
BT   Rivers—Mozambique
Rivers—Zimbabwe
NT   McIlwaine, Lake (Zimbabwe)
Hunzukuts
USE   Burusho
Huon-Finisterre languages
USE   Finisterre-Huon languages
Hupa Indians
[E99.H8]
UF   Hoopah Indians
BT   Athapascan Indians
Indians of North America
Hupa language
[PM1361-4]
BT   Athapascan languages
Indians of North America—Languages
Hupeh style of Chinese cookery
USE   Cookery, Chinese—Hupeh style
Hupert family
USE   Houpert family
Hupp family   *(Not Subd Geog)*
Huppert family
USE   Houpert family
Hur Rebellion, Sind, Pakistan, 1942-1947
USE   Sind (Pakistan)—History—Hur Rebellion, 1942-1947
Huracán Flora, 1963
USE   Hurricane Flora, 1963
Hurd family   *(Not Subd Geog)*
UF   Heard family
Herd family
Hird family
Hurde family
Hurde family
USE   Hurd family
Hurdle-racing
[GV1067]
BT   Obstacle racing
Racing
Running races
Track-athletics
Hurdle racing (Horse racing)
USE   Steeplechasing
Hurdy-gurdies (2) with instrumental ensemble
RT   Concertos (Hurdy-gurdies (2) with instrumental ensemble)
Hurdy-gurdies (2) with orchestra
[M1039.4.H87]
UF   Two hurdy-gurdies with orchestra
BT   Hurdy-gurdy music (Hurdy-gurdies (2))
RT   Concertos (Hurdy-gurdies (2))
Hurdy-gurdy
[ML1086]
Not to be confused with the barrel and piano organs used chiefly by street musicians.
UF   Vielle
BT   Musical instruments
Hurdy-gurdy and bagpipe music
USE   Bagpipe and hurdy-gurdy music
Hurdy-gurdy and continuo music
UF   Continuo and hurdy-gurdy music
NT   Suites (Hurdy-gurdy and continuo)
Hurdy-gurdy and flute music
USE   Flute and hurdy-gurdy music
Hurdy-gurdy and percussion music
[M298]
UF   Percussion and hurdy-gurdy music

Hurdy-gurdy and viol music
[M990]
UF   Viol and hurdy-gurdy music
Hurdy-gurdy and violin music
UF   Violin and hurdy-gurdy music
Hurdy-gurdy music
[M175.H9]
SA   Concertos, Minuets, Sonatas, Suites, *and similar headings with specification of instruments;* Trios (Quartets, etc.) *followed by specifications which include the hurdy-gurdy; also* Instrumental ensembles *and headings that begin with the words* Hurdy-gurdy *or* Hurdy-gurdies
Hurdy-gurdy music (Hurdy-gurdies (2))
[M298]
NT   Concertos (Hurdy-gurdies (2))
Hurdy-gurdies (2) with orchestra
Suites (Hurdy-gurdies (2))
Hurdy-gurdy with chamber orchestra
[M1039.4.H87]
NT   Concertos (Hurdy-gurdy with chamber orchestra)
Hurdy-gurdy with instrumental ensemble
RT   Concertos (Hurdy-gurdy with instrumental ensemble)
Hurdy-gurdy with orchestra
[M1039.4.H87]
RT   Concertos (Hurdy-gurdy)
Huri (Papuan people)
BT   Ethnology—Papua New Guinea
Hurlbart family
USE   Hurlburt family
Hurlbert family
USE   Hurlburt family
Hurlblatt family
USE   Hurlburt family
Hurlburt family   *(Not Subd Geog)*
UF   Hulburd family
Hurlbart family
Hurlbert family
Hurlblatt family
Hurlbut family
Hurlbutt family
RT   Holbert family
Hurlbut family
USE   Hurlburt family
Hurlbutt family
USE   Hurlburt family
Hurlers
USE   Hurling players
Hurley family   *(Not Subd Geog)*
UF   Herly family
Hirley family
Hurly family
O'Hurley family
Hurling (Game)
[GV1017.H8]
NT   Hurling players
Hurling players   *(May Subd Geog)*
UF   Hurlers
BT   Hurling (Game)
Hurly family
USE   Hurley family
Hurmuz, Strait of
USE   Hormuz, Strait of
Hurn family
USE   Hearn family
Huron, Lake (Mich. and Ont.)
UF   Lake Huron (Mich. and Ont.)
BT   Great Lakes
Lakes—Michigan
Lakes—Ontario
NT   Georgian Bay (Ont.)
North Channel (Huron, Lake, Mich. and Ont.)
Huron Indians
[E99.H9]
UF   Wyandot Indians

Huron Indians *(Continued)*
　BT　Indians of North America
　　　Iroquoian Indians
　— **Antiquities**
　— **Missions**
　— **Religion and mythology**
　— **Wars**
　　　NT　Blue Licks, Battle of the, 1782
　　　　　Champlain-Iroquois Battle, 1615
　　　　　Crawford's Indian Campaign, 1782
Huron language
　[PM1366]
　RT　Iroquoian languages
Huron National Forest (Mich.)
　BT　Forest reserves—Michigan
　　　National parks and reserves—
　　　　Michigan
Huronian epoch
　USE　Geology, Stratigraphic—Huronian
Hurrell family *(Not Subd Geog)*
Hurri
　USE　Hurrians
Hurrian incantations
　USE　Incantations, Hurrian
Hurrian language
　[P948]
　UF　Mitani language
　　　Mitannian language
　　　Subarian language
　BT　Anatolian languages
Hurrians
　[DS59.H]
　UF　Hurri
　　　Kharri
　　　Khurrians
　BT　Mitannians
　RT　Subarians
Hurribomber
　USE　Hurricane (Fighter planes)
Hurricane (Fighter planes)
　UF　Hurribomber
　BT　Fighter planes
Hurricane Amelioration Research Project
　BT　Hurricane modification
　　　Rain-making
Hurricane control
　USE　Hurricane protection
Hurricane Flora, 1963
　UF　Ciclón Flora, 1963
　　　Flora, Hurricane, 1963
　　　Huracán Flora, 1963
　BT　Hurricanes
Hurricane modification *(May Subd Geog)*
　[QC944]
　BT　Hurricanes
　RT　Weather control
　NT　Hurricane Amelioration Research
　　　　Project
Hurricane protection *(May Subd Geog)*
　UF　Hurricane control
　　　Hurricane rehabilitation, Long-range
　BT　Hurricanes
　　　Regional planning
　RT　Disaster relief
　　　Public works
　NT　Afforestation
　　　Flood control
　　　Insurance, Disaster
　　　Zoning
Hurricane rehabilitation, Long-range
　USE　Hurricane protection
Hurricane waves
　USE　Storm surges
Hurricanes *(May Subd Geog)*
　[QC941-959]
　　　Here are entered mainly works on storms in the
　neighborhood of the West Indies. Cf. note under
　Storms.
　BT　Meteorology
　　　Meteorology, Maritime
　　　Winds

　RT　Storms
　　　Typhoons
　NT　Cyclones
　　　Hurricane Flora, 1963
　　　Hurricane modification
　　　Hurricane protection
　　　Storm surges
　— **Kinetic energy**
　　　UF　Kinetic energy of hurricanes
　　　BT　Dynamic meteorology
　— **Tracks** *(May Subd Geog)*
　　　UF　Tracks, Hurricane
Hurst family
　USE　Hearst family
Hurst House (New Orleans, La.)
　BT　Dwellings—Louisiana
Hürtgen, Battle of, 1944
　BT　World War, 1939-1945—Campaigns—
　　　Germany (West)
Hurufis
　UF　Htouroûfîs
　BT　Islamic sects
　　　Shī'ah
Ḥusayn ibn 'Alī, d. 680
　— **Cult**
　　　NT　Tenth of Muḥarram
　— **Death and burial**
　　　NT　Karbalā' (Iraq), Battle of, 680
Husband and wife *(May Subd Geog)*
　UF　Man and wife
　　　Matrimonial regime
　　　Wife and husband
　BT　Domestic relations
　　　Women—Legal status, laws, etc.
　RT　Desertion and non-support
　　　Marriage law
　　　Married women
　NT　Antenuptial contracts
　　　Conjugal violence
　　　Curtesy
　　　Divorce—Law and legislation
　　　Dower
　　　Dowry
　　　Marital property
　　　Runaway husbands
　　　Runaway wives
　　　Separation (Law)
　　　Support (Domestic relations)
　　　Tenancy by the entirety
　— Conflict of laws
　　　USE　Conflict of laws—Husband and
　　　　　wife
　— **Taxation** *(May Subd Geog)*
　　　NT　Community property—Taxation
　　　　　Income tax—Joint returns
Husband and wife (Ancient law)
Husband and wife (Canon law)
Husband and wife (Hindu law)
Husband and wife (Islamic law)
Husband and wife (Jewish law)
Husband and wife (Lübeck law)
Husband and wife (Magdeburg law)
Husband and wife (Roman law)
Husband and wife (Saxon law)
Husband and wife business enterprises
　USE　Couple-owned business enterprises
Husbandmen, Wicked (Parable)
　USE　Wicked husbandmen (Parable)
Husbandry
　USE　Agriculture
Husbandry, Patrons of
　USE　Patrons of Husbandry
Husbands *(May Subd Geog)*
　　　Here are entered works on husbands in general.
　Works on legal relations between husband and wife
　are entered under the heading Husband and wife.
　UF　Married men
　　　Spouses
　BT　Marriage
　RT　Househusbands
　NT　College presidents—Spouses

　　　Mate selection
　　　Runaway husbands
　　　Students, Foreign—Spouses
　　　Wives—Effect of husband's
　　　　employment on
　— **Prayer-books and devotions**
　　　[BV283.H8]
　　　UF　Husbands—Prayer-books and
　　　　　devotions—English
　— — English
　　　　USE　Husbands—Prayer-books and
　　　　　　devotions
　— **Retirement**
　　　NT　Wives—Effect of husband's
　　　　　retirement on
Huse family
　USE　Hughes family
Huseby (Kronobergs län, Sweden)
　BT　Manors—Sweden
Husey family
　USE　Hussey family
Husfloen family *(Not Subd Geog)*
Huske family
　USE　Huskey family
Huskey family *(Not Subd Geog)*
　UF　Huske family
Huskies, Siberian
　USE　Siberian huskies
Husking of corn
　USE　Corn—Husking
Husky, Operation, 1943
　USE　Operation Husky, 1943
Husky, Siberian
　USE　Siberian huskies
Huson family
　USE　Hewson family
Husor
　USE　Bānsurī
Husqvarna firearms
　BT　Firearms
Husqvarna motorcycle
　[TL448.H]
　BT　Motorcycles
Hussey family *(Not Subd Geog)*
　UF　Huessy family
　　　Husey family
　　　Hussy family
　　　Huzey family
　　　Huzzey family
　　　Huzzy family
Hussite Bibles
　USE　Bible—Versions, Hussite
**Hussite Wars, Bohemia, Czechoslovakia, 1419-
1436**
　USE　Bohemia (Czechoslovakia)—History—
　　　　Hussite Wars, 1419-1436
Hussites
　[BX4913-4918]
　NT　Adamites
　　　Bohemia (Czechoslovakia)—History—
　　　　Hussite Wars, 1419-1436
　　　Lord's Supper—Communion in both
　　　　elements
　　　Moravians
　　　Taborites
　　　Utraquists
Hussy family
　USE　Hussey family
Hustad family
　USE　Husted family
Hustead family
　USE　Husted family
Husted family *(Not Subd Geog)*
　UF　Hustad family
　　　Hustead family
　　　Hustedt family
Hustedt family
　USE　Husted family
Husten family
　USE　Houston family

Hustin family
  USE Houston family
Hustle (Dance)
  [GV1796.H88]
  UF Disco hustle
      Latin Hustle
  BT Disco dancing
Hustler (Bombers)
  USE B-58 bomber
Huston family
  USE Houston family
**Husum-Schwesing (Germany : Concentration
  camp)**
  [D805.H]
  BT Concentration camps—Germany
        (West)
      World War, 1939-1945—
        Concentration camps—Germany
        (West)
      World War, 1939-1945—Prisoners and
        prisons, German
Hut family
  USE Hutt family
Hut Point Peninsula (Antarctic regions)
  BT Peninsulas—Antarctic regions
Hutan Maria (Sumbawa, Indonesia)
  USE Maria Forest (Sumbawa, Indonesia)
Hutan Tololai (Sumbawa, Indonesia)
  USE Tololai Forest (Sumbawa, Indonesia)
Hutch (Cartoon character)
  BT Caricatures and cartoons—United
        States
      Comic books, strips, etc.
Hutchens family
  USE Hutchins family
Hutcherson family
  USE Hutchinson family
Hutcheson family
  USE Hutchinson family
Hutchin family
  USE Hutchins family
Hutching family
  USE Hutchins family
Hutchings family
  USE Hutchins family
Hutchingson family
  USE Hutchinson family
Hutchins family *(Not Subd Geog)*
  UF Hudgens family
      Hudgin family
      Hudgins family
      Hutchens family
      Hutchin family
      Hutching family
      Hutchings family
  RT Houchens family
      Hutchinson family
Hutchinson family *(Not Subd Geog)*
  UF Huchingson family
      Hutcherson family
      Hutcheson family
      Hutchingson family
      Hutchison family
      Hutchisson family
  RT Hutchins family
Hutchinson-Gilford disease
  USE Progeria
Hutchinson's syndrome
  USE Neuroblastoma
Hutchison family
  USE Hutchinson family
Hutchisson family
  USE Hutchinson family
Hutens Grab (Switzerland)
  USE Ufenau Island (Switzerland)
Huthmacher family
  USE Hatmaker family
Hutia, Demarest's
  USE Capromys pilorides
Hutia, Dwarf
  USE Capromys nanus

Hutias
  USE Capromyidae
Hutias, Cuban
  USE Capromys
Hutias, Long-tailed
  USE Capromys
Hutmacher family
  USE Hatmaker family
Huton family
  USE Hutton family
Huts *(May Subd Geog)*
  BT Dwellings
  NT Grass huts
      Yurts
Hutsell family
  USE Hutzel family
Hutsen family
  USE Hudson family
Hutsill family
  USE Hutzel family
Hutson family
  USE Hudson family
Hutsul Alps (Ukraine)
  UF Gutsul Alps (Ukraine)
      Gutsul'skie Al'py (Ukraine)
      Gutsul'skiye Al'py (Ukraine)
      Hutsul's'ki Al'py (Ukraine)
      Huzul Alps (Ukraine)
  BT Mountains—Ukraine
Hutsuls *(May Subd Geog)*
  UF Hootzools
      Huculs
      Hutzuls
      Huzule
      Huzuls
  BT Ethnology—Carpathian Mountains
      Ethnology—Ukraine
Hutsulshchyna (Ukraine)
  UF Huculszczyzna (Ukraine)
Hutsul's'ki Al'py (Ukraine)
  USE Hutsul Alps (Ukraine)
Hutt family *(Not Subd Geog)*
  UF Hut family
  RT Hatt family
Hutten family
  USE Hutton family
Hutterian Society of Brothers
  (May Subd Geog)
  [BX8129.B6-BX8129.B68]
  Here are entered works on communities of the
  Hutterian Society of Brothers treated collectively
  and works for which the individual community can-
  not be identified.
  UF Bruderhof Communities
      Society of Brothers
  BT Christian sects
Hutterians
  USE Hutterite Brethren
Hutterite Brethren *(May Subd Geog)*
  [BX8129.H8]
  UF Brethren, Hutterite
      Hutterians
      Hutterites
Hutterite cookery
  USE Cookery, Hutterite
Hutterites
  USE Hutterite Brethren
Hutton family *(Not Subd Geog)*
  UF Huton family
      Hutten family
  RT Hatton family
Hutton Lake National Wildlife Refuge (Wyo.)
  (Not Subd Geog)
  BT National parks and reserves—
        Wyoming
      Wildlife refuges—Wyoming
Hutu
  USE Bahutu

Hutzel family *(Not Subd Geog)*
  UF Heltzel family
      Helzel family
      Hetizel family
      Hoetzel family
      Holtzele family
      Hootsill family
      Hulzel family
      Hutsell family
      Hutsill family
      Hutzell family
      Huzel family
      Jutzel family
Hutzell family
  USE Hutzel family
Hutzul horse
  USE Hucul horse
Hutzuls
  USE Hutsuls
Huus family *(Not Subd Geog)*
Huva (Papua New Guinea people)
  USE Hua (Papua New Guinea people)
Huva dialect
  USE Hua dialect (Papua New Guinea)
Huwart family
  USE Huard family
Ḥuwaytāt (Arab tribe)
  BT Arabs
      Ethnology—Arabian Peninsula
      Ethnology—Jordan
Huws family
  USE Hughes family
Huxtable family *(Not Subd Geog)*
Huyard altarpiece (Sculpture)
  USE Retable de la Passion (Sculpture)
Huyck family
  USE Houck family
Huycke family
  USE Houck family
Huyett family *(Not Subd Geog)*
  UF Huet family
Huygens' principle
  UF Hugghens' principle
  BT Light, Wave theory of
Huyke family
  USE Houck family
Huyler family *(Not Subd Geog)*
  UF Hiler family
      Hyler family
Huyssen family *(Not Subd Geog)*
  UF Huyssens family
Huyssens family
  USE Huyssen family
Huza family
  USE Juza family
Huzel family
  USE Hutzel family
Huzey family
  USE Hussey family
Huzul Alps (Ukraine)
  USE Hutsul Alps (Ukraine)
Huzul horse
  USE Hucul horse
Huzule
  USE Hutsuls
Huzuls
  USE Hutsuls
Huzvaresh
  USE Pahlavi language
Huzzey family
  USE Hussey family
Huzzy family
  USE Hussey family
Hvalsø family *(Not Subd Geog)*
  UF Hvalsøe family
Hvalsøe family
  USE Hvalsø family
Hvas family
  USE Hvass family
Hvass family *(Not Subd Geog)*
  UF Hvas family

Hvidkjær family (Not Subd Geog)
Hvidt family (Not Subd Geog)
Hvoldal family (Not Subd Geog)
Hwa Shan (China)
  USE Hua Mountains (China)
Hwai River (China)
  USE Huai River (China)
Hwang family (Not Subd Geog)
Hwang-hae
  USE Yellow Sea
Hwang Ho (China)
  USE Yellow River (China)
Hwang Mountains (China)
  USE Huang Mountains (China)
Hwang shan (China)
  USE Huang Mountains (China)
Hwaŏn (Sect)
  USE Hua-yen Buddhism
Hwarangdo
    ₍CR6095₎
  BT Chivalry
      Ethics, Korean
      Hand-to-hand fighting, Oriental
      National characteristics, Korean
Hwicce
  BT Ethnology—England
HX-20 (Computer)
  USE Epson HX-20 (Computer)
HY antigen
  USE H-Y antigen
Hyacinth, Water
  USE Water hyacinth
Hyacinth, Wild
  USE Dichelostemma pulchellum
Hyacinths
    ₍SB413.H9₎
Hyaenas
  USE Hyenas
Hyaenodon
    ₍QE882.C9₎
  BT Hyaenodontidae
Hyaenodontidae
    ₍QE882.C9₎
  BT Creodonta
  NT Hyaenodon
Hyakkengawa Haraoshima Iseki (Okayama-shi,
    Japan)
  USE Hyakkengawa Haraoshima Site
      (Okayama-shi, Japan)
Hyakkengawa Haraoshima Site (Okayama-shi,
    Japan)
  UF Hyakkengawa Haraoshima Iseki
      (Okayama-shi, Japan)
  BT Japan—Antiquities
Hyakkengawa Taima Iseki (Okayama-shi,
    Japan)
  USE Hyakkengawa Taima Site (Okayama-
      shi, Japan)
Hyakkengawa Taima Site (Okayama-shi,
    Japan)
  UF Hyakkengawa Taima Iseki (Okayama-
      shi, Japan)
  BT Japan—Antiquities
Hyakunin isshu karuta (Game)
  USE Utagaruta (Game)
Hyaline membrane disease
    (May Subd Geog)
    ₍RJ274₎
  BT Lungs—Diseases
      Pediatric respiratory diseases
      Respiratory distress syndrome
Hyalinization of the periodontal ligament
  USE Periodontal ligament—Hyalinization
Hyalomma (May Subd Geog)
    ₍QL458.2.I9₎
  BT Ixodidae
Hyalophora
    ₍QL561.S2₎
  UF Callosamia
      Eupackardia
      Platysamia

  BT Saturniidae
Hyalopterus
    ₍QL527.A64₎
  BT Aphididae
Hyalopterus arundinus
  USE Mealy plum aphis
Hyalopterus pruni
  USE Mealy plum aphis
Hyaloscyphaceae
  BT Helotiales
Hyalospongea, Fossil
  USE Hexactinellida, Fossil
Hyaluronic acid
    ₍QD321 (Organic chemistry)₎
    ₍QP702.H8 (Biochemistry)₎
    ₍RE992.H88 (Ophthalmology)₎
  BT Acids, Organic
      Mucopolysaccharides
Hyangga
  UF Saenaennorae
      Sanoega
      Sinoega
  BT Korean poetry
Hyans family
  USE Hines family
Hybalicidae
  USE Oehserchestidae
Hybalicus
    ₍QL458.2.L₎
  UF Lordalychus
  BT Lordalycidae
Hybarger family (Not Subd Geog)
  UF Haybarger family
      Highbarger family
      Highberger family
Hybodontidae
    ₍QE852.E6₎
  BT Hybodontoidea
  NT Hybodus
Hybodontoidea
    ₍QE852.E6₎
  BT Chondrichthyes, Fossil
      Sharks, Fossil
  NT Hybodontidae
Hybodus
    ₍QE852.E6₎
  BT Hybodontidae
Hybodus basanus
    ₍QE852.E6₎
Hybognathus
    ₍QL638.C94₎
  BT Cyprinidae
Hybognathus hanksoni
  USE Brassy minnow
Hybognathus stramineus
  USE Sand shiner
Hybopsis
    ₍QL638.C94₎
  BT Cyprinidae
Hybopsis missuriensis
  USE Sand shiner
Hybopsis montana
  USE Sand shiner
Hybopsis scylla
  USE Sand shiner
Hybosoridae
  USE Scarabaeidae
Hybrid computer simulation
  UF Hybrid simulation
  BT Computer simulation
      Electromechanical analogies
      Hybrid computers
      Mathematical models
Hybrid computers
  UF Computers, Hybrid
  BT Computers
  NT Digital-to-analog converters
      Electronic analog computers
      Electronic digital computers
      GVS 100 (Computer)
      Hybrid computer simulation

  — Programming
      BT Programming (Electronic
          computers)
      NT HELP (Computer program)
Hybrid corn (May Subd Geog)
    Here are entered works on cross breeding of corn
    and corn hybrids. General works on corn breeding
    and inbreeding are entered under Corn— Breeding.
  BT Corn—Breeding
      Corn—Varieties
Hybrid Executive Linkage Program
  USE HELP (Computer program)
Hybrid fuel rockets
  USE Hybrid propellant rockets
Hybrid integrated circuits
    ₍TK7874₎
  UF Integrated circuits, Hybrid
  BT Integrated circuits
Hybrid integrated circuits industry
    (May Subd Geog)
    ₍HD9696.I58-584₎
Hybrid languages
  USE Languages, Mixed
      Pidgin languages
Hybrid power plants, Geothermal-coal
  USE Geothermal-coal hybrid power plants
Hybrid propellant rockets
    ₍TL783.45₎
  UF Hybrid fuel rockets
      Rocket motors, Hybrid propellant
  BT Rockets (Aeronautics)
Hybrid rice (May Subd Geog)
    ₍QK495.G74 (Botany)₎
    ₍SB191.R5 (Culture)₎
  UF Rice, Hybrid
  BT Rice—Varieties
Hybrid Sanskrit language, Buddhist
  USE Sanskrit language, Buddhist Hybrid
Hybrid Sanskrit language, Epigraphical
  USE Sanskrit language, Epigraphical Hybrid
Hybrid simulation
  USE Hybrid computer simulation
Hybrid solar energy systems
  USE Solar energy—Hybrid systems
Hybrid sorghum
  BT Sorghum—Varieties
Hybrid tuberous begonias
  USE Tuberous begonias
Hybrid vigor
  USE Heterosis
Hybridism
  USE Hybridization
Hybridity of races
  USE Miscegenation
Hybridization
    ₍QH421-5₎
  UF Hybridism
  BT Biology
      Breeding
      Heredity
  RT Mendel's law
  NT Brazilian honeybee
      Cell hybridization
      Coydogs
      Genetics
      Heterosis
      Leopons
      Nucleic acid hybridization
      Species
      Wolfdogs
Hybridization, Vegetable
    ₍QH423₎
  UF Plants—Hybridization
      Vegetable hybridization
  BT Botany
      Plant-breeding
  NT Triticale
Hybridizers, Plant
  USE Plant breeders
Hybridomas
    ₍QR185.8.H93₎

UF Myeloma-spleen cell hybrids
BT Antibodies, Monoclonal
    Cell culture
    Clone cells
    Lymphocytes
    Plasmacytoma
    Somatic hybrids

Hydantoin
NT Allantoin
    Dantrolene
    Phenytoin

Hydatid cysts
USE Echinococcosis

Hydatid disease
USE Echinococcosis

Hydatidosis
USE Echinococcosis

Hydatids
USE Echinococcosis

Hydatigena taeniaeformis
USE Taenia taeniaeformis

Hyde family (Not Subd Geog)
UF Hide family
    Hides family

Hyde Lake (N.W.T.)
BT Lakes—Northwest Territories

Hyden Coal Mine Disaster, Hyden, Ky., 1970
Hyden family
USE Hayden family

Hydra
   $[QL377.H9]$
BT Hydridae
NT Hydra gangetica

HYDRA/C.mmp (Computer system)
BT C.mmp (Computer)
    Electronic digital computers—
      Programming

Hydra gangetica (May Subd Geog)
   $[QL377.H9]$
BT Hydra

Hydra Island (Greece)
UF Hydrea Island (Greece)
    Idhra Island (Greece)
    Idra Island (Greece)
    Ydra Island (Greece)
BT Islands—Greece

Hydracarina
USE Water mites

Hydrachnellae
USE Water mites

Hydrachnidae
   $[QL458.2.H9]$
BT Mites
    Water mites
NT Hydrodroma
    Nautarachna

Hydrachnidia
USE Water mites

Hydractinia (May Subd Geog)
   $[QL377.H9]$
BT Hydractiniidae
NT Hydractinia echinata

Hydractinia echinata (May Subd Geog)
   $[QL377.H9]$
BT Hydractinia

Hydractiniidae (May Subd Geog)
   $[QL377.H9]$
BT Hydroida
NT Hydractinia

Hydraena
   $[QL596.H79]$
BT Hydraenidae

Hydraenidae
   $[QL596.H79]$
UF Limnebiidae
BT Beetles
NT Hydraena

Hydralazine
BT Cardiovascular agents
    Hypotensive agents

Hydrangea
Hydrants (May Subd Geog)
   $[TH9365$ (Fire prevention)$]$
NT Fire hose
    Hose-couplings
— **Marking**
   UF Marking of hydrants

Hydrate process (Saline water conversion)
USE Saline water conversion—Hydrate
      process

Hydrates
   $[QD181.H1]$
BT Complex compounds
NT Aluminum chloride hexahydrate
    Gas, Natural—Hydrates

Hydration
   $[QD63.H]$
NT Heat of hydration
    Water of hydration

Hydration rind dating
   $[CC78$ (Archaeology)$]$
   $[QE508$ (Geology)$]$
UF Obsidian dating
    Obsidian hydration dating
BT Archaeological dating
    Archaeology—Methodology
    Geological time
    Geology, Stratigraphic—Recent

Hydraulic accumulators
UF Accumulators, Hydraulic
BT Hydraulic machinery

Hydraulic brakes
BT Brakes
    Hydraulic machinery

Hydraulic cement
USE Cement

Hydraulic circuits
UF Circuits, Hydraulic
BT Hydraulic machinery
— **Computer programs**

Hydraulic computers
USE Fluidic computers

Hydraulic conductivity of soils
USE Soil permeability

Hydraulic control
BT Automatic control
    Fluid power technology
    Hydraulic machinery

Hydraulic conveying
   $[TJ898]$
UF Hydraulic transport
BT Conveying machinery
    Materials handling

Hydraulic couplings
UF Fluid couplings
BT Couplings
    Oil hydraulic machinery

Hydraulic cylinders
UF Cylinders, Hydraulic
BT Oil hydraulic machinery

Hydraulic drive
USE subdivision Hydraulic drive under
      subjects, e.g. Diesel locomotives—
      Hydraulic drive; Machine-tools—
      Hydraulic drive

Hydraulic elevators
USE Elevators

Hydraulic engineering (May Subd Geog)
   $[TC]$
UF Engineering, Hydraulic
BT Engineering
    Fluid mechanics
RT Hydraulics
    Shore protection
SA subdivision Power utilization under
      names of individual bodies of water
NT Aerial photography in hydraulic
      engineering
    Asphalt in hydraulic engineering
    Blasting, Submarine
    Boring

    Channels (Hydraulic engineering)
    Drainage
    Dredging
    Hydraulic filling
    Hydraulic fracturing
    Hydraulic machinery
    Hydraulic mining
    Hydraulic structures
    Hydrostatics
    Irrigation engineering
    Offshore structures
    Plastics in hydraulic engineering
    Pontoons
    Pumping machinery
    Retaining walls
    River engineering
    Sediment control
    Tidal power
    Underwater construction
    Underwater drilling
    Water-jet
    Water-supply engineering
    Wells
— **Equipment and supplies**
   UF Hydraulic equipment
   NT Hydraulic engineering—
      Instruments
      Radioisotopes in hydraulic
        engineering
— **Instruments**
   $[TC177]$
   BT Hydraulic engineering—Equipment
      and supplies
   RT Hydraulic measurements
   NT Flow meters
      Liquid level indicators
— **Law and legislation** (May Subd Geog)
— **Research** (May Subd Geog)
   UF Hydraulic research

Hydraulic engineering laboratories
USE Hydraulic laboratories

Hydraulic engineers (May Subd Geog)
BT Engineers
— **Supply and demand**

Hydraulic equipment
USE subdivision Hydraulic equipment under
      subjects, e.g. Ships—Hydraulic
      equipment
    Hydraulic engineering—Equipment
      and supplies
    Hydraulic machinery

Hydraulic fill dams
USE Earth dams

Hydraulic filling
BT Earthwork
    Fills (Earthwork)
    Hydraulic engineering

Hydraulic fluid filters
BT Filters and filtration

Hydraulic fluids
   $[TJ844]$
BT Fluids
RT Petroleum products
— **Contamination**
   BT Contamination (Technology)

Hydraulic fracturing
UF Fracturing, Hydraulic
BT Hydraulic engineering
    Rock mechanics
NT Oil wells—Hydraulic fracturing

Hydraulic gates
UF Gates, Hydraulic
    Water gates
BT Diversion structures (Hydraulic
      engineering)
    Hydraulic structures
NT Sluice gates

Hydraulic jacks
   $[TJ1435]$
UF Jacks, Hydraulic
BT Lifting-jacks

Hydraulic jump
  [TC175]
  BT Hydraulics
Hydraulic laboratories *(May Subd Geog)*
  [TC158]
  UF Hydraulic engineering laboratories
  BT Engineering laboratories
Hydraulic machinery
  [TJ840-890]
  UF Hydraulic equipment
  BT Fluid power technology
     Hydraulic engineering
     Machinery
     Water-power
  SA *subdivision* Hydraulic equipment *under subjects, e.g.* Tractors—Hydraulic equipment
  NT Archimedean screw
     Centrifugal pumps
     Hydraulic accumulators
     Hydraulic brakes
     Hydraulic circuits
     Hydraulic control
     Hydraulic motors
     Hydraulic servomechanisms
     Hydraulic turbines
     Jet pumps
     Oil hydraulic machinery
     Pumping machinery
     Turbines
     Water mills
     Water-wheels
  — **Electric driving**
  — **Vibration**
Hydraulic machinery industry
  (May Subd Geog)
  [HD9705.5.H93-934]
Hydraulic measurements *(May Subd Geog)*
    Here are entered works on scientific and technical measurement of properties and behavior of liquids, including equipment used in measurement. Works on particular measuring instruments are entered under names of instruments, e.g. Flow meters, Hydrometer, Water-meters.
  UF Hydrometry
  BT Hydraulics
  RT Hydraulic engineering—Instruments
  NT Flow meters
     Hydrometer
     Stream measurements
     Water-meters
Hydraulic mining *(May Subd Geog)*
  [TN421 (Gold)]
  UF Placer-mining
  BT Hydraulic engineering
     Mining engineering
  RT Gold mines and mining
     Manganese mines and mining, Submarine
  NT Dredges
Hydraulic models
  [TC163]
  UF Models, Hydraulic
  BT Engineering models
     Hydraulic structures
     Models and modelmaking
  NT Dams—Models
     Hydraulic turbines—Models
     Metallurgical furnaces—Models
Hydraulic motors
  [TJ855-7]
  BT Hydraulic machinery
     Motors
  RT Turbines
  NT Oil hydraulic machinery
     Water-wheels
Hydraulic organ
  [ML553]
  UF Hydraulus
     Water organ
  BT Organ

  NT Barrel organ, Hydraulic
Hydraulic power plants
  USE Water-power
Hydraulic presses
  [TJ1460]
  UF Presses, Hydraulic
  BT Power presses
  — **Numerical control**
      BT Automatic control
Hydraulic propulsion
  USE Jet boat engines
Hydraulic rams
  [TJ905]
  UF Rams, Hydraulic
  BT Pumping machinery
  NT Log splitters (Machines)
Hydraulic research
  USE Hydraulic engineering—Research
Hydraulic servomechanisms
  [TJ857]
  UF Servomechanisms, Hydraulic
  BT Hydraulic machinery
     Oil hydraulic machinery
     Servomechanisms
  — **Dynamics**
Hydraulic structures *(May Subd Geog)*
  BT Hydraulic engineering
     Structural engineering
  NT Aqueducts
     Artesian wells
     Breakwaters
     Bridges—Foundations and piers
     Caissons
     Canals
     Coffer-dams
     Cribwork
     Culverts
     Dams
     Desilting basins
     Dikes (Engineering)
     Diversion structures (Hydraulic engineering)
     Docks
     Draft tubes
     Earthquakes and hydraulic structures
     Embankments
     Fouling organisms
     Fountains
     Groins (Shore protection)
     Harbors
     Hydraulic gates
     Hydraulic models
     Intakes (Hydraulic engineering)
     Jetties
     Levees
     Lighthouses
     Locks (Hydraulic engineering)
     Ocean outfalls
     Piers
     Pipe lines
     Pumping stations
     Railroad bridges—Foundations and piers
     Reservoirs
     Reservoirs, Underground
     Rock traps (Hydraulic engineering)
     Sea-walls
     Sewerage
     Spillways
     Tunnels
     Water tunnels
     Weirs
     Wharves
     Wing walls
  — **Construction**
      USE Hydraulic structures—Design and construction
  — **Design and construction**
      UF Hydraulic structures—Construction
  — **Electric equipment**
  — **Foundations**

    BT Foundations
  — **Ice prevention**
      [TC180]
      BT Ice prevention
  — **Maintenance and repair**
  — **Protection**
  — **Vibration**
Hydraulic torque converters
  UF Torque converters, Hydraulic
  BT Oil hydraulic machinery
     Torque
  NT Automobiles—Transmission devices, Automatic
     Tractors—Transmission devices, Automatic
Hydraulic transients
  BT Hydraulics
     Transients (Dynamics)
  NT Water hammer
Hydraulic transmission
  USE Oil hydraulic machinery
Hydraulic transport
  USE Hydraulic conveying
Hydraulic turbines
  [TJ870-875]
  UF Water turbines
  BT Hydraulic machinery
     Turbines
  NT Draft tubes
     Hydroelectric generators
     Pump turbines
  — **Bearings**
  — **Dynamics**
      [TJ873]
  — **Erecting work**
  — **Fluid dynamics**
  — **Models**
      BT Hydraulic models
  — **Performance**
      UF Performance of hydraulic turbines
  — **Vibration**
Hydraulics
  [TC160-179]
  UF Flow of water
     Water—Flow
  BT Fluid mechanics
     Liquids
     Mechanics
     Physics
  RT Hydraulic engineering
     Jets
     Water—Distribution
  NT Atomization
     Electrohydraulic effect
     Fluids
     Hydraulic jump
     Hydraulic measurements
     Hydraulic transients
     Hydrostatics
     Nozzles
     Seepage
     Surge tanks
     Venturi tubes
     Water—Air entrainment
     Water hammer
     Wave makers
Hydraulus
  USE Hydraulic organ
Hydrazine
  [QD181.N15]
  BT Disinfection and disinfectants
  NT Isoniazid
Hydrazines
  [QD305.A8]
  [QD341.A8]
Hydrazoic acid
  USE Hydronitric acid
Hydrea Island (Greece)
  USE Hydra Island (Greece)
Hydrellia
  [QK537.E7]

1764

BT Ephydridae
Hydreyth family
　USE Hildreth family
Hydriae
　[NK4650.H9]
Hydrick family (Not Subd Geog)
　UF Heydrich family
　　Heydrick family
Hydrictis maculicollis
　USE Lutra maculicollis
Hydridae
　[QL377.H9]
　BT Hydroida
　NT Hydra
Hydrides
　BT Hydrogen
　NT Borane
　　Lithium hydride
　　Sodium dihydrobismethoxyeth
　　　anolatoaluminate
Hydrilla (May Subd Geog)
　[QK495.H86 (Botany)]
　[SB615.H (Weed)]
　BT Aquatic weeds
Hydrilla as feed
　[SF99.H]
　BT Aquatic plants as feed
Hydrindene
　USE Indan
Hydriodic acid
　[QD181.I1]
　UF Iodide of hydrogen
Hydriomena
　[QL561.G6]
　BT Geometridae
Hydriomenidae
　USE Geometridae
Hydro-aeroplanes
　USE Seaplanes
Hydroa vacciniforme
　BT Cutaneous manifestations of general
　　diseases
Hydroacoustics
　USE Underwater acoustics
Hydrobatidae
　[QL696.P64]
　UF Petrels, Storm
　　Storm petrels
　　Stormy petrels
　BT Procellariiformes
　NT Oceanodroma
Hydrobiidae
　NT Marstonia
　　Pyrgulopsis
　　Tryonia
Hydrobiology
　USE Aquatic biology
　　Freshwater biology
　　Marine biology
Hydroboration
　BT Reduction, Chemical
Hydrobotany
　USE Aquatic plants
Hydrobromic acid
　[QD181.B7]
Hydrocal
　BT Cement
Hydrocampidae
　USE Pyralidae
Hydrocarbon-producing plants
　(May Subd Geog)
　[SB291.5-SB291.53]
　UF Plants, Hydrocarbon-producing
　BT Energy crops
　NT Oilseed plants
　　Rubber plants
　　Wax plants
Hydrocarbon research
　USE Hydrocarbons—Research
Hydrocarbons (May Subd Geog)
　[QD305.H5-QD305.H9 (Aliphatic)]

　[QD341.H9 (Aromatic)]
　RT Bitumen
　NT Alkylation
　　Butene
　　Caustobioliths
　　Cracking process
　　Gilsonite
　　Methyl groups
　　Mineral oils
　　Olefins
　　Paraffins
　　Petroleum, Synthetic
　　Petroleum products
　　Polycyclic aromatic hydrocarbons
　— Biodegradation
　— Nomenclature
　— Research (May Subd Geog)
　　UF Hydrocarbon research
　— Spectra
　　[QC463.H9]
Hydrocele (May Subd Geog)
　[RC898]
　BT Spermatic cord—Diseases
　　Testis—Diseases
Hydrocephalus
　[RC391]
　UF Water on the brain
　BT Brain—Diseases
　NT Kleeblattschädel syndrome
Hydrocephalus in children
　(May Subd Geog)
　[RJ496.H9]
　BT Pediatric neurology
Hydrocephalus in infants (May Subd Geog)
　[RJ496.H9]
　UF Infantile hydrocephalus
　BT Infants—Diseases
Hydrocharitaceae
　[QK495.H86]
　BT Helobiae
　NT Lagarosiphon
　　Thalassia
Hydrocharitales
　USE Helobiae
Hydrochidae
　USE Hydrophilidae
Hydrochinone
　USE Hydroquinone
Hydrochloric acid
　[QD181.C5 (Chemistry)]
　[TP217.H8 (Chemical technology)]
　UF Muriatic acid
　BT Biological chemistry
　— Molecular rotation
Hydrochoerus capybara
　USE Capybaras
Hydrocolloid dressings (Surgery)
　USE Hydrocolloid surgical dressings
Hydrocolloid surgical dressings
　(May Subd Geog)
　UF Alginate surgical dressings
　　Hydrocolloid dressings (Surgery)
　　Surgical dressings, Alginate
　　Surgical dressings, Hydrocolloid
　BT Occlusive surgical dressings
Hydrocortisone
　UF Compound F
　　Cortisol
　　Hydrocortone
　BT Glucocorticoids
　NT Cortisone
Hydrocortone
　USE Hydrocortisone
Hydrocotylaceae
　USE Umbelliferae
Hydrocyanic acid
　[QD181.C15 (Chemistry)]
　[RA766.H8 (Disinfectants)]
　UF Prussic acid
　BT Disinfection and disinfectants

Hydrocyanic acid gas
Hydrocyclones
　USE Separators (Machines)
Hydrocynus
　[QL638.C5]
　UF Hydrocyon
　BT Characidae
　NT Tigerfish
Hydrocynus vittatus
　USE Tigerfish
Hydrocyon
　USE Hydrocynus
Hydrodamalis
　[QL737.S62]
　BT Dugongidae
Hydrodamalis, Fossil
　[QE882.S6]
　BT Dugongidae, Fossil
Hydrodamalis gigas
　USE Steller's sea cow
Hydrodamalis stelleri
　USE Steller's sea cow
Hydrodroma
　[QL458.2.H9]
　UF Diplodontus
　BT Hydrachnidae
Hydrodynamic gyroscopes
　USE Fluid rotor gyroscopes
Hydrodynamic impact on seaplanes
　USE Seaplanes—Hydrodynamics
Hydrodynamic short range weather forecasting
　UF Dynamic short range weather
　　forecasting
　　Weather forecasting, Hydrodynamic
　　short range
　BT Hydrodynamic weather forecasting
Hydrodynamic weather forecasting
　UF Dynamic weather forecasting
　　Weather forecasting, Dynamic
　BT Dynamic meteorology
　　Hydrodynamics
　　Meteorology—Mathematical models
　　Weather forecasting
　NT Hydrodynamic short range weather
　　forecasting
　　Numerical weather forecasting
Hydrodynamics
　[QA911-QA930 (Mathematics)]
　[QC150-QC159 (Mechanics)]
　[QC718.5.H9 (Plasma physics)]
　[TC171-TC179 (Hydraulic
　　engineering)]
　Here are entered works on the theory of the mo-
　tion of fluids. Works dealing with the technical ap-
　plication of the science are entered under Hydraulics.
　BT Fluid dynamics
　NT Blades
　　Boundary layer (Meteorology)
　　Buoyant ascent (Hydrodynamics)
　　Cavitation
　　Culverts—Hydrodynamics
　　Cylinders—Hydrodynamics
　　Electrohydrodynamics
　　Frictional resistance (Hydrodynamics)
　　Gravity waves
　　Harbors—Hydrodynamics
　　Hemodynamics
　　Hydrodynamic weather forecasting
　　Hydroelasticity
　　Hydrofoil boats—Hydrodynamics
　　Hydrostatics
　　Jets
　　Krook equation
　　Magnetohydrodynamics
　　Mixing
　　Offshore structures—Hydrodynamics
　　Pipe—Hydrodynamics
　　Pipe lines—Hydrodynamics
　　Rotating masses of fluid
　　Sailboats—Hydrodynamics
　　Seaplanes—Hydrodynamics

Hydrodynamics (Continued)
    Sewage lagoons—Hydrodynamics
    Ship resistance
    Ships—Hydrodynamics
    Siphons
    Sloshing (Hydrodynamics)
    Stratified flow
    Streamflow
    Transition flow
    Turbulence
    Underwater explosions
    Urodynamics
    Viscosity
    Vortex-motion
    Water-pipes—Hydrodynamics
    Water waves
    Wave makers
    Wave resistance (Hydrodynamics)
    Waves
— **Computer programs**
    NT FESWMS-TX (Computer program)
Hydroelasticity
  BT Elastic waves
    Elasticity
    Hydrodynamics
  NT Planing hulls
    Ships—Hydrodynamic impact
    Sloshing (Hydrodynamics)
    Vibration (Marine engineering)
Hydroelectric generators
  UF Generators, Hydroelectric
  BT Electric generators
    Hydraulic turbines
    Hydroelectric power plants
    Turbogenerators
— **Bearings**
    [TK2458.B4]
— **Vibration**
Hydroelectric power plants
  (May Subd Geog)
  [TK1081]
  [TK1421-TK1526 (By plant)]
  UF Power plants, Hydroelectric
    Water-power electric plants
  BT Electric power-plants
    Electric power production
    Water-power
    Water resources development
  NT Hydroelectric generators
    Ocean wave power
    Pumped storage power plants
    Tidal power-plants
— **Combination with steam plants**
    USE Hydrothermal electric power
        systems
— **Finance**
— — **Law and legislation**
    (May Subd Geog)
— **Law and legislation** (May Subd Geog)
— **Surveying**
  BT Surveying
— **Alberta**
  NT Dunvegan Hydro Power Site, Alta.
— **British Columbia**
  NT Revelstoke Project
— **James Bay Region (Ont. and Québec)**
  NT James Bay Hydroelectric Project
— **Papua New Guinea**
  NT Purari River (Wabo) Hydroelectric
      Scheme
— **Saskatchewan**
  NT Poplar River Power Project
— **Turkey**
  NT Berke Hydroelectric Project
Hydrofining
  BT Petroleum—Refining
Hydrofluoric acid
  [QD181.F1]
  RT Hydrogen fluoride
Hydrofoil boats
  [VM362]

  UF Hydrofoils (Vessels)
  BT Boats and boating
— **Hydraulic equipment**
— **Hydrodynamics**
    BT Hydrodynamics
— **Law and legislation** (May Subd Geog)
Hydrofoils
  USE Planing hulls
Hydrofoils (Vessels)
  USE Hydrofoil boats
Hydrogels
  USE Colloids
Hydrogen
  [QD181.H1 (Chemistry)]
  [TP245.H9 (Chemical technology)]
  BT Gases—Liquefaction
    Nonmetals
  NT Hydrides
    Interstellar hydrogen
    Iron—Hydrogen content
    Liquid hydrogen
    Metals—Hydrogen content
    Nonferrous metals—Hydrogen content
    Solid hydrogen
    Steel—Hydrogen content
    Synthesis gas
    Titanium—Hydrogen content
    Water—Electrolysis
    Zirconium alloys—Hydrogen content
— **Analysis**
  NT Hydrogen-ion concentration—
      Measurement
— **Dipole moments**
— **Isotopes**
  UF Heavy hydrogen
    Hydrogen isotopes
  BT Tracers (Chemistry)
  NT Deuterium
    Tritium
— **Spectra**
— **Thermal properties**
Hydrogen as fuel
  BT Fuel
    Synthetic fuels
Hydrogen bomb
  UF H-bomb
    Thermonuclear weapons
  BT Bombs
    Nuclear fusion
    Nuclear weapons
  RT Atomic bomb
  NT Radioactive fallout
Hydrogen bonding
  BT Chemistry, Physical and theoretical
    Molecular association
Hydrogen embrittlement of metals
  USE Metals—Hydrogen embrittlement
Hydrogen fluoride
  UF Anhydrous hydrofluoric acid
  BT Fluorides
    Halides
  RT Hydrofluoric acid
Hydrogen in aluminum alloys
  USE Aluminum alloys—Hydrogen content
Hydrogen in iron
  USE Iron—Hydrogen content
Hydrogen in metals
  USE Metals—Hydrogen content
Hydrogen in steel
  USE Steel—Hydrogen content
Hydrogen in titanium
  USE Titanium—Hydrogen content
Hydrogen industry (May Subd Geog)
  [HD9660.H93-934]
Hydrogen-ion concentration
  [QD561]
  UF pH
  RT Ionization
    Water—Electrolysis
  NT Buffer solutions
    Neutralization (Chemistry)

    Soil acidity
— **Measurement**
    BT Hydrogen—Analysis
Hydrogen ions
  BT Ions
— **Scattering**
Hydrogen isotopes
  USE Hydrogen—Isotopes
Hydrogen nucleus
  USE Protons
Hydrogen peroxide
  [QD181.H1 (Chemistry)]
  [RA766.H9 (Disinfectants)]
  [RM648.H (Therapeutics)]
  BT Disinfection and disinfectants
  NT Hydrogen peroxide rockets
Hydrogen peroxide as a propellant
  USE Hydrogen peroxide rockets
Hydrogen peroxide rockets
  UF Hydrogen peroxide as a propellant
    Rockets, Hydrogen peroxide
  BT Hydrogen peroxide
    Liquid propellant rockets
    Rockets (Aeronautics)
Hydrogen phosphide
  USE Phosphine
Hydrogen stars
  USE A stars
Hydrogen sulphide
  [QD181.S1]
  UF Sulphureted hydrogen
  BT Gases, Asphyxiating and poisonous
    Mine gases
  RT Gas, Natural—Sweetening
— **Spectra**
Hydrogenase
Hydrogenation
  [QD281.H8]
  NT Coal liquefaction
    Fischer-Tropsch process
    Hydrogenolysis
    Methanation
    Petroleum, Synthetic
Hydrogenolysis
  BT Hydrogenation
    Hydrolysis
Hydrogeological surveys
  BT Hydrogeology
    Surveys
Hydrogeology
  Here are entered general works on the study of
  ground water in relation to its geologic environment.
  UF Geohydrology
  BT Geology
    Hydrology
    Water, Underground
  NT Aerial photography in hydrogeology
    Aquifers
    Artesian basins
    Hydrogeological surveys
    Radioactive tracers in hydrogeology
— **Methodology**
  NT Groundwater tracers
Hydrogeton
  USE Aponogeton
Hydrographic charts
  USE Nautical charts
Hydrographic surveying (May Subd Geog)
  [VK591-597]
  UF Maritime surveying
    Nautical surveying
    Surveying, Marine
  BT Surveying
  RT Hydrography
    Navigation
  NT Drags (Hydrography)
    Hydrography—Observers' manuals
    Oceanographic research ships
    Surveyors, Marine
— **Contracting out**
  BT Contracting out

Hydrography (May Subd Geog)
 ₍GB651-GB2597₎
 ₍VK (Marine)₎
  Here are entered works on the results of the investigation of coast waters, rivers, and lakes, primarily with reference to navigation.
  BT Aquatic sciences
     Oceanography
     Physical geography
  RT Hydrographic surveying
     Hydrology
     Rivers
  NT Coastwise navigation
     Drags (Hydrography)
     Hydronymy
     Inland navigation
     Lakes
     Navigation
     Ocean currents
     Sounding and soundings
     Submarine topography
     Tides
— **Graphic methods**
— **Observers' manuals**
     ₍VK593.5₎
  BT Hydrographic surveying
— **Tables**
  UF Hydrography—Tables, etc.
— Tables, etc.
  USE Hydrography—Tables
Hydrohydroxypolyoxyethanediyl
USE Polyethylene oxide
Hydroida
 UF Hydroidea
 BT Hydrozoa
 NT Campanulariidae
    Campanulinidae
    Clathrozoidae
    Clavidae
    Haleciidae
    Hydractiniidae
    Hydridae
    Lafoeidae
    Olindiidae
    Sertulariidae
Hydroida, Fossil
 ₍QE779₎
Hydroidea
 USE Hydroida
     Hydromedusae
     Hydrozoa
Hydrolases
 BT Enzymes
 NT Adenosine deaminase
    Beta lactamases
    Cholinesterases
    Glycosidases
    Nucleases
    Phosphatases
    Phospholipases
    Proteolytic enzymes
    Sulphatases
Hydrologic cycle
 ₍GB848₎
 UF Cycle, Hydrologic
     Water cycle
 BT Cycles
     Energy budget (Geophysics)
     Mass budget (Geophysics)
Hydrologic factors on fisheries
 USE Fisheries—Hydrologic factors
Hydrologic models
 ₍GB665₎
 UF Hydrology—Models
 BT Models and modelmaking
Hydrological diffusion
 USE Diffusion in hydrology
Hydrological forecasting (May Subd Geog)
 ₍GB845₎
 UF Forecasting, Hydrological
 BT Geophysical prediction

 NT Flood forecasting
— **Wales**
  NT Dee Weather Radar and Real Time
     Hydrological Forecasting Project
Hydrological instruments
 UF Instruments, Hydrological
— Appraisal
  USE Hydrological instruments—
       Valuation
— **Valuation**
  UF Hydrological instruments—
       Appraisal
Hydrological research
 USE Hydrology—Research
Hydrological stations (May Subd Geog)
 UF Stations, Hydrological
 BT Hydrology—Research
Hydrologists (May Subd Geog)
 ₍GB659.7₎
 BT Earth scientists
     Hydrology
Hydrology (May Subd Geog)
 ₍GB651-GB2998₎
  Here are entered works on all aspects of water.
 BT Earth sciences
 RT Aquatic sciences
     Hydrography
 SA headings beginning with the words
     Hydrological and Water
 NT Aerial photography in hydrology
     Astronautics in hydrology
     Classification—Books—Hydrology
     Diffusion in hydrology
     Fisheries—Hydrologic factors
     Glaciology
     Hydrogeology
     Hydrologists
     Hydrometeorology
     International Hydrological Decade,
      1965-1974
     International Hydrological Program,
      1975-
     Military hydrology
     Oceanography
     Paleohydrology
     Radar in hydrology
     Radioactive substances in rivers, lakes,
      etc.
     Radioisotopes in hydrology
     Runoff
     Soil piping (Hydrology)
     Urban hydrology
     Water
— **Computer programs**
— Models
  USE Hydrologic models
— **Research** (May Subd Geog)
  UF Hydrological research
  NT Hydrological stations
     Watersheds—Research
Hydrology, Forest (May Subd Geog)
 ₍GB842₎
 UF Forest hydrology
 BT Forest influences
     Forests and forestry
Hydrology, Karst (May Subd Geog)
 ₍GB843₎
 UF Karst hydrology
 BT Karst
     Rocks, Carbonate
     Water, Underground
Hydrology, Rangeland (May Subd Geog)
 ₍GB844₎
 UF Rangeland hydrology
 BT Rangelands
Hydrolysis
 ₍QD281.H (Organic chemistry)₎
 ₍QD501₎
 BT Solvolysis
 NT Hydrogenolysis
     Lysosomes

     Protein hydrolysates
     Sugar—Inversion
Hydromagnetic instabilities
 USE Magnetohydrodynamic instabilities
Hydromagnetic waves
 USE Magnetohydrodynamic waves
Hydromantes
 ₍QL668.C274₎
 BT Plethodontidae
Hydromantes platycephalus
 ₍QL668.C274₎
Hydromechanics
 USE Fluid mechanics
Hydromedusae
 ₍QL377.H9₎
 UF Hydroidea
 BT Coelenterata
     Medusae
 RT Hydrozoa
 NT Discophora (Coelenterata)
     Siphonophora
Hydromel
 ₍GT2920₎
 RT Mead
Hydrometallurgy
 ₍TN688₎
 BT Metallurgy
 NT Metallurgy—Ion exchange process
Hydrometeorological cycles
 USE Hydrometeorology—Periodicity
Hydrometeorological observatories
 USE Hydrometeorological stations
Hydrometeorological periodicity
 USE Hydrometeorology—Periodicity
Hydrometeorological services
 (May Subd Geog)
 BT Meteorological services
Hydrometeorological stations
 (May Subd Geog)
 UF Hydrometeorological observatories
     Observatories, Hydrometeorological
     Stations, Hydrometeorological
 BT Geophysical observatories
Hydrometeorology (May Subd Geog)
 BT Hydrology
     Meteorology
 NT Aeronautics in hydrometeorology
     Depth-area-duration
      (Hydrometeorology)
     Fisheries—Climatic factors
     Moisture index
     Probable maximum precipitation
      (Hydrometeorology)
— **Periodicity**
  UF Hydrometeorological cycles
     Hydrometeorological periodicity
  BT Cycles
Hydrometer
 ₍QC111₎
 UF Areometer
 BT Fluid mechanics
     Hydraulic measurements
     Hydrostatics
     Specific gravity
Hydrometry
 USE Hydraulic measurements
Hydromorphic soils (May Subd Geog)
 ₍S598₎
 BT Soils
     Waterlogging (Soils)
 NT Smonitza
Hydromyine, Red-sided
 USE Paraleptomys rufilatus
Hydromyxales
 BT Hydromyxomycetes
Hydromyxomycetes
 BT Fungi
 NT Hydromyxales
Hydronephrosis
 ₍RC918.H8₎

Hydronephrosis *(Continued)*
  BT Kidneys—Diseases
    Urine—Retention
Hydronephrosis in children
  (May Subd Geog)
  [RJ476.H84]
  BT Pediatric nephrology
Hydronitric acid
  [QD181.N1]
  UF Hydrazoic acid
Hydronium ions
  USE Oxonium ions
Hydronymy
  BT Hydrography
    Names, Geographical
    Toponymy
    Water
Hydropathy
  USE Hydrotherapy
Hydroperitoneum
  USE Ascites
Hydrophidae
  USE Sea snakes
Hydrophiidae
  USE Sea snakes
Hydrophilic contact lenses
  USE Contact lenses, Hydrophilic
Hydrophilidae
  [QL596.H8]
  UF Helopheridae
    Helophoridae
    Hydrochidae
    Palpicornia
    Scavenger beetles, Water
    Spercheidae
    Sphaeridiidae
    Water scavenger beetles
  BT Beetles
  NT Epimetopus
    Helophorus
    Hydrous
Hydrophilus triangularis
  USE Hydrous triangularis
Hydrophobia
  USE Rabies
Hydrophone
  BT Detectors
    Electroacoustic transducers
    Geophone
    Sound—Equipment and supplies
    Underwater acoustics—Instruments
Hydrophyllaceae *(May Subd Geog)*
  [QK495.H88]
  BT Tubiflorae
Hydrophytes
  USE Aquatic plants
Hydropite
  USE Rhodonite
Hydroplanes
  [VM341-VM349]
    Here are entered works dealing with boats that
skim over the surface of the water but do not rise in
the air. Works on planes designed to rise from and
alight on water are entered under the heading Sea-
planes.
  BT Motorboats
  NT Planing hulls
    Seaplanes
Hydroponics
  UF Agriculture, Soilless
    Chemiculture
    Dirtless farming
    Gardening without soil
    Nutriculture gardening
    Plant chemiculture
    Plants—Soilless culture
    Soilless agriculture
    Soilless culture
    Water farming

  BT Horticulture
    Plants—Nutrition
    Plants, Effect of chemicals on
  RT Plant growing media, Artificial
  NT Nutrient film culture
Hydrops
  USE Edema
Hydrops abdominis
  USE Ascites
Hydropsychidae
  [QL518.H94]
  UF Arctopsychidae
    Net-spinning caddisflies
  BT Caddis-flies
  NT Leptonema (Insects)
Hydroptilidae
  [QL518.H95]
  BT Caddis-flies
  NT Ochrotrichia
Hydropus
  [QK629.T73]
  UF Caulorhiza
    Pleurella
  BT Tricholomataceae
Hydroquinone
  UF Benzenediol
    Hydrochinone
    Quinol
  BT Phenols
  — Tariff
    USE Tariff on hydroquinone
Hydrosilyation
  BT Organosilicon compounds
Hydrosme
  USE Amorphophallus
Hydrostatic bearings
  USE Fluid-film bearings
Hydrostatic extrusion
  [TS255]
  BT High energy forming
    High pressure (Technology)
    Metals—Extrusion
Hydrostatic leveling
  BT Level indicators
    Leveling
    Levels (Surveying instruments)
Hydrostatic pressing
  USE Isostatic pressing
Hydrostatic pressure
  UF Underwater pressure
  BT Pressure
  — **Physiological effect**
    [QP82.2.P7]
    NT Underwater explosions—
      Physiological effect
Hydrostatics
  [QA905-QA907 (Analytic)]
  [QC147 (Experimental)]
  BT Capillarity
    Fluid mechanics
    Hydraulic engineering
    Hydraulics
    Hydrodynamics
    Liquids
    Mechanics
    Mechanics, Analytic
    Physics
    Statics
  RT Fluids
  SA *headings beginning with the word*
    Hydrostatic
  NT Compressibility
    Floating bodies
    Gases
    Hydrometer
    Pascal's law
    Rayleigh number
    Rotating masses of fluid
    Saline water conversion—Piezodialysis
      process
    Soil percolation

    Specific gravity
Hydrotherapy
  [RM801-822]
  UF Hydropathy
    Kneipp cure
    Water—Therapeutic use
    Water-cure
  BT Physical therapy
    Therapeutics, Physiological
    Water
  RT Baths
  NT Baths, Moor and mud
    Baths, Partial
    Health resorts, watering-places, etc.
    Hot water—Therapeutic use
    Mineral waters—Therapeutic use
    Spondylotherapy
Hydrotherapy for children
  (May Subd Geog)
  [RJ53.H9]
  BT Physical therapy for children
Hydrotherapy services in hospitals
  USE Hospitals—Hydrotherapy services
Hydrothermal deposits *(May Subd Geog)*
  UF Deposits, Hydrothermal
  BT Mineralogy
    Ore-deposits
Hydrothermal electric power systems
  [TK1005]
  UF Combined hydroelectric and steam
      power systems
    Electric power-plants—Combined
      hydroelectric and steam
    Hydroelectric power plants—
      Combination with steam plants
    Power systems, Hydrothermal electric
  BT Electric power production
    Interconnected electric utility systems
Hydrothermal vent ecology
  (May Subd Geog)
  BT Hot spring ecology
    Hydrothermal vents
    Marine ecology
Hydrothermal vents *(May Subd Geog)*
  UF Black smokers (Oceanography)
    Oceanic hot springs
    Vents, Hydrothermal
  BT Hot springs
    Sea-floor spreading
  NT Hydrothermal vent ecology
Hydrothermic rice treatment
  USE Rice, Parboiled
Hydrothorax
  [RM276]
  BT Pleura—Diseases
Hydrotropism
  BT Growth (Plants)
    Plant-water relationships
    Plants—Irritability and movements
    Tropisms
Hydrous
  [QL596.H8]
  BT Hydrophilidae
  NT Hydrous triangularis
Hydrous triangularis
  [QL596.H8]
  UF Hydrophilus triangularis
  BT Hydrous
Hydroxides
  BT Oxides
  NT Aluminum hydroxide
    Ferric hydroxides
    Sodium hydroxide
Hydroxyacetanilide
  USE Acetaminophen
Hydroxyapatite
  USE Hydroxylapatite
Hydroxychlorosulfamylphenylphthalimidine
  USE Chlorthalidone
Hydroxydimethylarsine oxide
  USE Cacodylic acid

Hydroxyestratrieneone
USE Estrone
Hydroxyethyl starch
⌈RM666.H87⌉
BT Blood plasma substitutes
Starch
Hydroxyethylideneoxooxaazabicycloheptane
carboxylic acid
USE Clavulanic acid
Hydroxyhydroxymethylphenylpropylaminoeth
ylbenzamide
USE Labetalol
Hydroxyhydroxyphenylethylaminoethylbenze
nemethanol
USE Ritodrine
Hydroxyisopropylaminopropoxyacetanilide
USE Practolol
Hydroxylamine
⌈QD181.N15⌉
⌈QD305.A8⌉
— **Spectra**
Hydroxylapatite
UF Calcium phosphate hydroxide
Hydroxyapatite
BT Apatite
Hydroxylase, Cholesterol
USE Cholesterol hydroxylase
Hydroxylation
⌈QD281.H85 (Organic chemistry)⌉
⌈TP156.H85 (Chemical engineering)⌉
BT Chemical reactions
Hydroxymethoxyphenylglycol
USE Methoxyhydroxyphenylglycol
Hydroxymethyl
USE Methanol
Hydroxymethylethylaminopropoxybenzeneace
tamide
USE Atenolol
Hydroxymethylethylaminopropoxytrimethylp
henol acetate
USE Metipranolol
Hydroxymethylglutaryl CoA reductases
USE Hydroxymethylglutaryl coenzyme A
reductases
Hydroxymethylglutaryl coenzyme A
reductases
⌈QP603.H92⌉
UF HMG-Coenzyme A reductases
Hydroxymethylglutaryl CoA
reductases
BT Dehydrogenases
Hydroxymethylpregnenedione
USE Medroxyprogesterone
Hydroxymethylprogesterone
USE Medroxyprogesterone
Hydroxymethylpyridinylbenzothiazinecarbo
xamide dioxide
USE Piroxicam
Hydroxynorpregnenyone
USE Norethindrone
Hydroxyphenyl acetamide
USE Acetaminophen
Hydroxyphenylmethylpropylaminoethylbenze
nediol
USE Dobutamine
Hydroxypregnenedione
USE Hydroxyprogesterone
Hydroxyprogesterone
⌈QP572.H85⌉
UF Hydroxypregnenedione
BT Progesterone
NT Medroxyprogesterone
Hydroxypropylaminopropoxyphenylphenylpro
panone
USE Propafenone
Hydroxypropylaminopropoxyphenylpropiophe
none
USE Propafenone
Hydroxytrimethylphenoxyisopropylaminopro
panol acetate
USE Metipranolol

Hydroxytryptamine
USE Serotonin
Hydroxytryptophan decarboxylase
USE Dopa decarboxylase
Hydroxytyrosine
USE Dopa
Hydrozoa (May Subd Geog)
⌈QL377.H9⌉
UF Hydroidea
BT Coelenterata
RT Hydromedusae
NT Anthomedusae
Hydroida
Siphonophora
Stylasterina
Trachylina
Hydrozoa, Fossil
⌈QE779⌉
BT Invertebrates, Fossil
NT Sphaeractiniida
Hydrozone
⌈RM671⌉
BT Antiseptics
Hydrurga leptonyx
USE Leopard seal
Hydruria
⌈SF871⌉
⌈SF995⌉
Hyena, Painted
USE Lycaon pictus
Hyena dog
USE Lycaon pictus
Hyenas
⌈QL737.C2⌉
UF Hyaenas
NT Spotted hyena
Hyenas, Fossil
⌈QE882.C15⌉
BT Carnivora, Fossil
Hyères Islands (France)
UF Iles d'Hyères (France)
Iles d'Or (France)
Or Islands (France)
BT Islands—France
NT Port-Cros Island (France)
Hyg family
USE Hoeg family
Hygiene
⌈BJ1695 (Ethical aspects)⌉
⌈RA770.5 (Household hygiene)⌉
⌈RA780 (Personal hygiene)⌉
Here are entered works on personal body care and
cleanliness. Works on optimal physical, mental, and
social well-being, as well as how to achieve and pre-
serve it, are entered under Health.
UF Body, Human—Care and hygiene
Body care
Cleanliness
Personal body care
Personal cleanliness
Personal hygiene
BT Medicine, Preventive
RT Health
Sanitation
SA subdivision Care and hygiene under
parts of the body, e.g. Foot—Care
and hygiene; and subdivision Health
and hygiene under classes of
persons and ethnic groups
NT Baths
Beauty, Personal
Boys—Health and hygiene
Breast—Care and hygiene
Exercise
Face—Care and hygiene
Girls—Health and hygiene
Gums—Care and hygiene
Hand washing
Hygiene, Sexual
Local officials and employees—Health
and hygiene

Men—Health and hygiene
Military hygiene
Mouth—Care and hygiene
Naval hygiene
Perineum—Care and hygiene
Political prisoners—Health and
hygiene
Prisoners of war—Health and hygiene
Public health
Relaxation
Rest
School hygiene
Shaving
Solar radiation—Physiological effect
State governments—Officials and
employees—Health and hygiene
Veterinary hygiene
Youth—Health and hygiene
— **Audio-visual aids**
— Authorship
USE Medical writing
— Economic aspects
USE Medical economics
— **Film catalogs**
— Public opinion
USE Health attitudes
— Study and teaching
USE Health education
Hygiene, Dental
USE Teeth—Care and hygiene
Hygiene, Hindu
⌈RA529⌉
⌈RA776⌉
UF Hindu hygiene
BT Health—Religious aspects—Hinduism
Hygiene, Oriental
Hygiene, Industrial
USE Industrial hygiene
Hygiene, Islamic
UF Hygiene, Muslim
Islamic hygiene
Muslim hygiene
BT Health—Religious aspects—Islam
Hygiene, Jewish
⌈RA561⌉
UF Jewish hygiene
Jews—Hygiene
BT Health—Religious aspects—Judaism
Hygiene, Maya
⌈F1435.M4⌉
UF Maya hygiene
Mayas—Hygiene
Hygiene, Military
USE Military hygiene
Hygiene, Mormon
UF Mormon hygiene
BT Health—Religious aspects—Mormon
Church
Mormon Church
Hygiene, Muslim
USE Hygiene, Islamic
Hygiene, Naval
USE Naval hygiene
Hygiene, Oriental
UF Oriental hygiene
BT Medicine, Oriental
NT Hygiene, Hindu
Hygiene, Taoist
Hygiene, Public
USE Public health
Hygiene, Sexual (May Subd Geog)
⌈RA788⌉
UF Hygiene, Social
Sex hygiene
Sexual hygiene
Social hygiene
BT Hygiene
RT Sex instruction
Sexually transmitted diseases
NT Birth control
Contraception

Hygiene, Sexual *(Continued)*
    Promiscuity
    Safe sex in AIDS prevention
Hygiene, Social
  USE Hygiene, Sexual
    Prostitution
    Public health
Hygiene, Taoist
  UF Taoist hygiene
  BT Health—Religious aspects—Taoism
    Hygiene, Oriental
    Taoism
Hygiene, Tropical
  USE Tropical medicine
Hygiene, Veterinary
  USE Veterinary hygiene
Hygiene in literature
Hygienists, Industrial
  USE Industrial hygienists
Hygroamblystegium macroneuron
  USE Donrichardsia macroneuron
Hygrobates
  [QL458.2.H93]
  BT Hygrobatidae
  NT Hygrobates nigromaculatus
Hygrobates nigromaculatus
  [QL458.2.H93]
  BT Hygrobates
Hygrobatidae
  [QL458.2.H93]
  BT Mites
    Water mites
  NT Hygrobates
Hygrobiidae
  [QL596.H9]
  BT Beetles
Hygrometers
  [QC916]
  BT Humidity
    Hygrometry
    Meteorological instruments
  RT Moisture meters
  NT Wet-bulb thermometers
  — **Effect of radiation on**
    UF Hygrometers—Radiation effects
      Hygrometers, Effect of radiation
        on
    BT Radiation
  — Radiation effects
    USE Hygrometers—Effect of radiation
        on
Hygrometers, Effect of radiation on
  USE Hygrometers—Effect of radiation on
Hygrometry
  [QC915-917]
  UF Humidity—Measurement
    Psychrometry
  BT Humidity
    Meteorology
  NT Hygrometers
Hygrothermal effects
  USE Hygrothermoelasticity
Hygrothermoelasticity
  [QA933]
  UF Hygrothermal effects
  BT Thermoelasticity
Hygrotus
  [QL596.D9]
  BT Dytiscidae
Hyh (The Hebrew root)
  BT Hebrew language—Roots
Hyksos
  [DT86]
  UF Shepherd kings
  BT Egypt—History—To 332 B.C.
Hyla
  [QL668.E24]
  BT Hylidae
Hyla albomarginata
  [QL668.E24]

Hyla bistincta
  [QL668.E24]
Hyla boans
  [QL668.E24]
  UF Rana boans
Hyla bogotensis
  [QL668.E24]
Hyla cadaverina
  [QL668.E24]
  UF Canyon tree frog, Western
    Hyla californiae
    Western canyon tree frog
Hyla californiae
  USE Hyla cadaverina
Hyla crepitans
  [QL668.E24]
Hyla crucifer
  [QL668.E24]
Hyla labialis
  [QL668.E24]
Hyla microcephala
  [QL668.E24]
Hyla mykter
  [QL668.E24]
Hyla proboscidea
  [QL668.E24]
Hyla pugnax
  [QL668.E24]
Hyla regilla
  [QL668.E24]
Hyla rosenbergi
  [QL668.E24]
Hyla rubra
  [QL668.E24]
Hyla thysanota
  [QL668.E24]
Hyla trux
  [QL668.E24]
Hyla versicolor
  [QL668.E24]
  UF Chameleon tree frog
Hyla viridis
  [QL668.E24]
Hylaeus
  [QL568.C6]
  BT Colletidae
Hylaeus alocaspidus
  [QL568.C6]
  UF Paraprosopis alocaspidus
Hylambates
  USE Kassina
Hylastes
  [QL596.S35]
  BT Bark beetles
    Conifers—Diseases and pests
    Scolytidae
Hyldi family
  USE Hilty family
Hyldryth family
  USE Hildreth family
Hyleman family
  USE Heilman family
Hylemorphism
  USE Hylomorphism
Hylemya
  [QL537.A5]
  UF Hylemyia
  BT Anthomyiidae
Hylemya brassicae
  USE Cabbage maggot
Hylemya floralis
  — **Insecticide resistance**
Hylemyia
  USE Hylemya
Hylemyia brassicae
  USE Cabbage maggot
Hyler family
  USE Huyler family
Hylesiidae
  USE Saturniidae

Hylesine
  USE Hylesinus
Hylesinus
  [QL596.S35]
  UF Hylesine
  BT Scolytidae
Hylicidae
  USE Leafhoppers
Hylidae
  [QL668.E24]
  UF Tree frogs
    Tree toads
  BT Anura
    Frogs
  NT Allophryne
    Gastrotheca
    Hemiphractus
    Hyla
    Nyctimantis
    Osteocephalus
    Phrynohyas
    Phyllomedusa
    Ptychohyla
    Smilisca
Hylobates
  USE Gibbons
Hylobates lar
  USE Whitehanded gibbon
Hylobates syndactylus
  USE Siamang
Hylobius
  [QL596.C9]
  BT Curculionidae
  NT Hylobius abietis
Hylobius abietis
  [QL596.C9]
  BT Hylobius
    Pine—Diseases and pests
Hylobius pales
  USE Pales weevil
Hylobius radicis
  USE Pine root collar weevil
Hylochoerus
  BT Suidae
Hylocichla *(May Subd Geog)*
  [QL696.P288]
  BT Muscicapidae
Hylocichla mustelina
  USE Wood thrush
Hylodes conspicillatus
  USE Eleutherodactylus conspicillatus
Hylodes peruvianus
  USE Eleutherodactylus conspicillatus
Hyloicus
  USE Sphinx (Insects)
Hylomorphism
  [BD648]
  UF Form and matter
    Hylemorphism
    Matter and form
    Unity of form (Philosophy)
  BT Matter
    Metaphysics
    Peripatetics
    Substance (Philosophy)
Hylophilidae
  USE Euglenidae
Hylophylax
  [QL696.P2455]
  BT Formicariidae
  NT Spotted antbird
Hylophylax naevioides
  USE Spotted antbird
Hylozoism
  Here are entered works dealing with the theory
that all matter has life and that life as such is a proper-
ty of matter.
  BT Philosophy
  RT Animism
    Panpsychism

Hylton family
USE Hilton family
Hylurgidae
USE Scolytidae
Hylurgopinus
[QL596.S35]
BT Scolytidae
NT Hylurgopinus rufipes
Hylurgopinus rufipes
[QL596.S35]
UF Elm bark beetle
BT Elm—Diseases and pests
Hylurgopinus
Hyman family (Not Subd Geog)
UF Hymen family
Hymanella
[QL391.P7]
BT Planariidae
Hymanella retenuova
[QL391.P7]
Hymen (Gynecology)
[QM421 (Anatomy)]
[RG519 (Obstetrics)]
BT Vagina
Hymen family
USE Hyman family
Hymenaea
[QK495.L52 (Botany)]
BT Leguminosae
Hymenocephalus
[QL638.M2]
BT Macrouridae
Hymenocephalus tenuis
[QL638.M2]
Hymenolepididae
[QL391.P7]
BT Cyclophyllidea
NT Hymenolepis
Hymenolepis
[QL391.P7]
BT Hymenolepididae
Hymenolepis diminuta
[QL391.P7]
UF Taenia diminuta
Hymenomycetes
[QK629.H9]
BT Basidiomycetes
NT Agaricales
Aphyllophorales
Hymenopenaeus
[QL444.M33]
BT Penaeidae
Hymenopenaeus mulleri
[QL444.M33]
Hymenophyllaceae
BT Filicales
Hymenoptera (May Subd Geog)
[QL563-9]
BT Insects
NT Agaonidae
Ampulicidae
Anthophoridae
Ants
Bees
Bethylidae
Braconidae
Cephidae
Ceraphronidae
Chalcid wasps
Chalcididae
Chrysididae
Colletidae
Diapriidae
Diprionidae
Encyrtidae
Eucharitidae
Eulophidae
Eumenidae
Eupelmidae
Eurytomidae
Fideliidae

Gallflies
Gasteruptiidae
Halictidae
Heloridae
Honey-ants
Ibaliidae
Ichneumonidae
Leucospididae
Masaridae
Mason-bees
Megachilidae
Melittidae
Mutillidae
Mymaridae
Myrmosidae
Nyssonidae
Orussidae
Oxaeidae
Pamphiliidae
Perilampidae
Philanthidae
Platygastridae
Proctotrupidae
Pteromalidae
Rhopalosomatidae
Roproniidae
Sawflies
Scelionidae
Scoliidae
Siricidae
Solitary wasps
Sphecidae
Spider wasps
Stephanidae
Stingless bees
Symphyta
Tenthredinidae
Tetracampidae
Tiphiidae
Torymidae
Trichogrammatidae
Trigonalidae
Vespidae
Wasps
Xiphydriidae
Xyelidae
Hymenoptera, Fossil
[QE832.H9]
BT Insects, Fossil
NT Bees, Fossil
Hymenosomatidae
[QL444.M33]
BT Decapoda (Crustacea)
Hymenostomatida (May Subd Geog)
[QL368.H87]
BT Ciliata
NT Parameciidae
Hymenoxys chrysanthemoides excurrens
USE Actinea odorata
Hymenoxys cockerellii
USE Actinea odorata
Hymenoxys mearnsii
USE Actinea odorata
Hymenoxys multiflora
USE Actinea odorata
Hymenoxys odorata
USE Actinea odorata
Hymlich family
USE Heimlich family
Hymlick family
USE Heimlich family
Hymn festivals
[BV341]
BT Hymns
Music festivals
Worship programs
Hymn playing
USE Hymns—Accompaniment
Hymn sermons
USE Hymns—Homiletical use

Hymn tunes
Here, with appropriate subdivisions, are entered works about hymn tunes. Collections of hymn tunes (without accompanying text) are entered under the heading Tune-books.
BT Hymns
RT Tune-books
NT Chorale
Old Hundredth (Tune)
Hymn writers (May Subd Geog)
[BV325]
UF Hymnists
BT Hymns—History and criticism
Poets
NT Women hymn writers
Hymnists
USE Hymn writers
Hymnology
USE Hymns
Hymns (May Subd Geog)
[BV301-BV525]
[M2115-M2145 (Hymns with music)]
Here are entered general collections of hymns as well as hymns of a particular Christian denomination, with qualification, when appropriate, by language, e.g. Hymns, English. Duplicate entry is made for the latter under the name of the denomination with subdivision Hymns, e.g. Baptists—Hymns.
UF Christian hymns
Hymnology
BT Church music
Devotional exercises
Liturgies
Poetry
Sacred songs
Sacred vocal music
Theology, Practical
RT Canticles
Christian poetry
Psalmody
Religious poetry
SA names of individual hymns, e.g. Gloria in excelsis Deo
NT Advent hymns
Bible—Use in hymns
Carols
Christmas—Poetry
Easter hymns
Epiphany hymns
Funeral hymns
Hymn festivals
Hymn tunes
Lenten hymns
Revivals—Hymns
Seamen—Hymns
Sequences (Music)
Soldiers—Hymns
Sunday-schools—Hymns
Te Deum laudamus (Music)
Tune-books
— **Accompaniment**
[MT240]
UF Hymn playing
BT Musical accompaniment
RT Chants (Plain, Gregorian, etc.)—Accompaniment
— Concordances
USE Hymns—Indexes
— **Devotional use**
BT Devotional exercises
— **History and criticism**
[BV310-340]
[ML3186 (Music, ML3086)]
NT Hymn writers
— **Homiletical use**
[BV4235.H94]
UF Hymn sermons
BT Preaching
— **Indexes**
UF Hymns—Concordances
— **Metrics and rhythmics**
[BV335]

Hymns
— **Metrics and rhythmics** (*Continued*)
  UF Hymns—Versification
  BT Versification
— **Orchestrations**
— **Versification**
  USE Hymns—Metrics and rhythmics
Hymns, African
 UF Hymns, Black—Africa
Hymns, Afrikaans, ₍Danish, English, etc.₎
Hymns, American
 USE Hymns, English
Hymns, Arikara, ₍Choctaw, Cree, etc.₎
 UF Indians of North America—Hymns
Hymns, Black (*May Subd Geog*)
 UF Black hymns
— **Africa**
  USE Hymns, African
Hymns, Bohemian
 USE Hymns, Czech
Hymns, Buddhist
 USE Buddhist hymns
Hymns, Byzantine
 USE Hymns, Greek
Hymns, Cheyenne
 UF Cheyenne hymns
Hymns, Chinese (*May Subd Geog*)
 UF Chinese hymns
Hymns, Czech
 UF Czech hymns
  Hymns, Bohemian
Hymns, Danish
 RT Hymns, Norwegian
Hymns, Dutch (*May Subd Geog*)
 UF Dutch hymns
Hymns, Early Christian
 ₍BV320₎
 UF Early Christian hymns
 BT Christian literature, Early
Hymns, Egyptian (*May Subd Geog*)
 ₍PJ1565₎
 UF Egyptian hymns
Hymns, English (*May Subd Geog*)
 UF American hymns
  English hymns
  Fuging tunes
  Fuguing tunes
  Hymns, American
— **United States**
  NT Spirituals (Songs)
Hymns, Finnish (*May Subd Geog*)
 UF Finnish hymns
Hymns, French (*May Subd Geog*)
 UF French hymns
Hymns, Georgian (*May Subd Geog*)
 UF Georgian hymns
Hymns, German (*May Subd Geog*)
 UF German hymns
 NT Chorale
  Chorale prelude
  Chorales
  Hymns, Low German
Hymns, Greek
 Here are entered Christian hymns in ancient, By-
 zantine or modern Greek. Pre-Christian classical
 hymns are entered under Hymns, Greek (Classical).
 UF Greek hymns
  Hymns, Byzantine
Hymns, Greek (Classical)
 Here are entered pre-Christian classical hymns.
 Christian hymns in ancient, Byzantine or modern
 Greek are entered under Hymns, Greek.
 UF Greek hymns
Hymns, Guaymi (*May Subd Geog*)
 UF Guaymi hymns
Hymns, Hawaiian (*May Subd Geog*)
 UF Hawaiian hymns
Hymns, Hebrew (*May Subd Geog*)
 UF Hebrew hymns
  Hymns, Jewish
 BT Jewish hymns

 RT Hymns, Yiddish
 NT Piyutim
Hymns, Hindu
 USE Hindu hymns
Hymns, Hmar
 ₍BV510.H₎
 UF Hmar hymns
Hymns, Hungarian (*May Subd Geog*)
 UF Hungarian hymns
Hymns, Irish (*May Subd Geog*)
 UF Irish hymns
Hymns, Islamic
 USE Islamic hymns
Hymns, Jaina
 USE Jaina hymns
Hymns, Jewish
 USE Hymns, Hebrew
  Hymns, Yiddish
  Jewish hymns
  Jewish religious poetry
Hymns, Korean (*May Subd Geog*)
 UF Korean hymns
Hymns, Latin (*May Subd Geog*)
 UF Latin hymns
Hymns, Low German
 UF Low German hymns
 BT Hymns, German
Hymns, Luo
 ₍BV510.L₎
 UF Luo hymns
Hymns, Lushai (*May Subd Geog*)
 UF Lushai hymns
Hymns, Lwo (Sudan) (*May Subd Geog*)
 UF Lwo hymns (Sudan)
Hymns, Mahican
 UF Mahican hymns
Hymns, Malay (*May Subd Geog*)
 ₍BV510.M₎
 UF Malay hymns
Hymns, Muslim
 USE Islamic hymns
Hymns, Norwegian
 UF Norwegian hymns
 RT Hymns, Danish
Hymns, Paite (*May Subd Geog*)
 ₍M2143₎
 UF Paite hymns
Hymns, Ramadan
 USE Ramadan hymns
Hymns, Revival
 USE Revivals—Hymns
Hymns, Romanian (*May Subd Geog*)
 UF Romanian hymns
Hymns, Scandinavian (*May Subd Geog*)
 UF Scandinavian hymns
Hymns, Sikh
 USE Sikh hymns
Hymns, Sindhi (*May Subd Geog*)
 UF Sindhi hymns
Hymns, Sivaite
 USE Sivaism—Hymns
Hymns, Spanish (*May Subd Geog*)
 UF Spanish hymns
 NT Alabados
  Goigs
Hymns, Sumerian (*May Subd Geog*)
 UF Sumerian hymns
Hymns, Swedish (*May Subd Geog*)
Hymns, Tamil (*May Subd Geog*)
 UF Tamil hymns
Hymns, Tswana (*May Subd Geog*)
 UF Tswana hymns
Hymns, Ukrainian (*May Subd Geog*)
 UF Ukrainian hymns
Hymns, Vietnamese (*May Subd Geog*)
 UF Vietnamese hymns
Hymns, Welsh (*May Subd Geog*)
 UF Welsh hymns
Hymns, Xhosa (*May Subd Geog*)
 UF Xhosa hymns

Hymns, Yiddish
 UF Hymns, Jewish
  Yiddish hymns
 BT Jewish hymns
 RT Hymns, Hebrew
Hymns to Apollo
 BT Music, Greek and Roman
Hyn Lake (Sweden)
 BT Lakes—Sweden
Hynds family
 USE Hines family
Hyne family
 USE Hines family
Hyner family
 USE Hayner family
Hynes family
 USE Hines family
Hyning family
 USE Van Hyning family
Hynn family
 USE Hines family
Hynobiidae
 ₍QL668.C25₎
 BT Salamanders
 NT Onychodactylus
Hyns family
 USE Hines family
Hynsley family
 USE Hensley family
Hynton family
 USE Hinton family
Hyōgo kendō kōsoku wangansen (Japan)
 USE Ōsaka fudō kōsoku wangansen (Japan)
Hyoid bone
 UF Lingual bone
 BT Bones
 NT Branchiostegals
Hyon kum
 USE Hyŏn'gŭm
Hyŏndae Group
 BT Conglomerate corporations—Korea
  (South)
Hyŏn'gŭm
 ₍ML1015.H₎
 UF Hyon kum
 BT Musical instruments—Korea
  Zither
Hyŏn'gŭm music
 ₍M142.H9₎
Hyoscyamin
 BT Hyoscyamus niger
Hyoscyamus
 ₍QK495.S7₎
 BT Solanaceae
Hyoscyamus (Drug)
 ₍RS431.H95₎
 UF Oil of henbane
  Oleum hyoscyami
Hyoscyamus niger
 ₍QK495.S7₎
 UF Black henbane
  Henbane, Black
 NT Hyoscyamin
Hypanis River (Ukraine)
 USE I͡Uzhnyĭ Buh River (Ukraine)
Hypenidae
 USE Noctuidae
Hypera
 ₍QL596.C9₎
 UF Phytonomus
 BT Curculionidae
Hypera brunneipennis
 USE Egyptian alfalfa weevil
Hyperabduction syndrome
 USE Thoracic outlet syndrome
Hyperactive child syndrome
 (*May Subd Geog*)
 ₍RJ506.H9₎
 UF Hyperactivity syndrome
  Hyperkinesia in children

BT Behavior disorders in children
   Hyperkinesia
   Minimal brain dysfunction in children
   Syndromes in children

Hyperactive children *(May Subd Geog)*
  UF Hyperkinetic children
     Overactive children
  BT Handicapped children
     Learning disabilities
     Problem children
 — **Education** *(May Subd Geog)*
    [LC4711-4713]
    BT Learning ability

Hyperactivity, Motor
  USE Hyperkinesia

Hyperactivity syndrome
  USE Hyperactive child syndrome

Hyperadrenocorticism
  UF Adrenocortical hyperplasia
     Hypercorticism
  BT Adrenal cortex—Diseases
     Endocrine glands—Diseases
  NT Hyperaldosteronism

Hyperaldosteronism
  UF Aldosteronism
     Conn's disease
  BT Endocrine glands—Diseases
     Hyperadrenocorticism

Hyperalimentation, Enteral
  USE Enteral feeding

Hyperammina
  [QE772]
  BT Foraminifera, Fossil

Hyperammina kentuckyensis
  [QE772]

Hyperaspis
  [QL596.C65]
  BT Ladybirds
  NT Hyperaspis binotata
     Hyperaspis lateralis

Hyperaspis binotata
  [QL596.C65]
  BT Hyperaspis

Hyperaspis lateralis
  [QL596.C65]
  BT Hyperaspis

Hyperbaric oxygenation *(May Subd Geog)*
  UF Oxygenation, Hyperbaric
  BT Compressed air—Therapeutic use
     Oxygen therapy

Hyperbilirubinemia
  BT Bilirubin
     Jaundice

Hyperbilirubinemia, Neonatal
  USE Jaundice, Neonatal

Hyperbola
  [QA485 (Plane geometry)]
  [QA559 (Analytical geometry)]
  BT Conic sections

Hyperbole

Hyperbolic complex manifolds
  USE Hyperbolic spaces

Hyperbolic differential equations
  USE Differential equations, Hyperbolic

Hyperbolic functions
  USE Functions, Exponential

Hyperbolic geometry
  USE Geometry, Hyperbolic

Hyperbolic navigation
  [VK560]
  BT Electronics in aeronautics
     Electronics in navigation
     Navigation
  NT Decca navigation
     Loran
     Loran charts
     Raydist
     Shoran

Hyperbolic spaces
  UF Hyperbolic complex manifolds
     Manifolds, Hyperbolic complex
     Spaces, Hyperbolic
  BT Geometry, Non-Euclidean

Hyperboloid
  [QA561]
  BT Quadrics
     Surfaces

Hyperborean languages
  [PM1-95]
  UF Paleoasiatic languages
     Paleosiberian languages
  NT Aglemiut dialect
     Ainu language
     Aleut language
     Chukchi language
     Eskimo language
     Gilyak language
     Kamchadal language
     Koryak language
     Yeniseian languages
     Yuit language
     Yukaghir language

Hyperboreans
  USE Arctic races

Hyperbrachycephaly
  [GN71]
  BT Brachycephaly
     Craniology

Hypercalcemia
  BT Calcium—Metabolism—Disorders
     Water-electrolyte imbalances

Hypercalciurea *(May Subd Geog)*
  [RC632.C26]
  UF Hypercalciuric states
  BT Calcium—Metabolism—Disorders

Hypercalciuric states
  USE Hypercalciurea

Hypercapnia
  BT Carbon dioxide—Physiological effect

Hypercholesteremia *(May Subd Geog)*
  UF Cholesteremia
  BT Blood cholesterol
     Hyperlipidemia

Hypercholesteremia in children
  (May Subd Geog)
  [RJ399.H94]
  BT Hyperlipidemia in children

Hyperchondroplasia
  USE Marfan syndrome

Hypercinesia
  USE Hyperkinesia

Hypercircle method
  UF Method of the hypercircle
  BT Approximation theory
     Boundary value problems
     Elasticity
     Hyperspace
     Mathematical physics

Hyperconjugation
  [QD471]
  UF No-bond resonance
  BT Mesomerism

Hypercorticism
  USE Hyperadrenocorticism

Hyperdontia
  USE Teeth, Supernumerary

Hyperdulia
  USE Mary, Blessed Virgin, Saint—Cult

Hyperelliptic functions
  USE Integrals, Hyperelliptic

Hyperelliptic integrals
  USE Integrals, Hyperelliptic

Hyperemia
  [RB145]

Hyperemia, Artificial
  [RM184]
  BT Hemospasia

Hyperemia, Cerebral
  USE Brain—Congestion

Hyperergic encephalomyelitis
  USE Allergic encephalomyelitis

Hyperextensibility of joints
  USE Joints—Hypermobility

Hyperfine interactions
  [QC762]
  UF Interactions, Hyperfine
  BT Electron paramagnetic resonance
     Magnetic fields
     Nuclear magnetism
     Nuclear spectroscopy
  RT Hyperfine structure
  NT Isotone shift
     Isotope shift

Hyperfine structure
  [QC173.4.H95]
  UF Structure, Hyperfine
  BT Atomic spectra
     Level-crossing spectroscopy
     Nuclear moments
  RT Atomic structure
     Hyperfine interactions

Hyperfragments
  UF Hypernuclei
  BT Hyperons
     Nuclear structure
 — **Decay**
    [QC793.5.H425]

Hyperfunctions
  [QA324]
  BT Analytic functions
     Distributions, Theory of (Functional
      analysis)

Hypergammaglobulinemia
  [RC647.H9]
  BT Blood hyperviscosity syndrome
     Blood protein disorders
     Gamma globulin
  NT Gammopathies, Monoclonal

Hypergeometric distribution
  [QA273.6]
  BT Distribution (Probability theory)
     Functions, Hypergeometric

Hypergeometric functions
  USE Functions, Hypergeometric

Hypergeometric series
  UF Gaussian hypergeometric series
     Gaussian series
     Gauss's series
  BT Series
  RT Functions, Hypergeometric

Hyperglycemia
  UF Hyperglycosemia
  BT Blood sugar
  NT Obese-hyperglycemic syndrome

Hyperglycemic-obese syndrome
  USE Obese-hyperglycemic syndrome

Hyperglycosemia
  USE Hyperglycemia

Hypergraphs
  BT Graph theory

Hypergroups
  BT Groups, Theory of

Hyperhidrosis
  [RL141]
  UF Excessive perspiration
  BT Perspiration
     Sweat glands—Diseases

Hyperhydration
  USE Water intoxication

Hypericales
  USE Violales

Hypericum
  [QK495.G87]
  UF Saint John's-worts
     Saint Johnsworts
  BT Guttiferae

Hypericum campanulatum
  USE Triadenum virginicum

Hypericum virginicum
  USE Triadenum virginicum

Hyperidae
USE Hyperiidae
Hyperiidae
[QL444.M315]
UF Hyperidae
BT Amphipoda
NT Themisto
Hyperinsulinism
USE Insulin shock
Hyperion (Computer)
[QA76.8.H]
UF Ajile (Computer)
Anderson Jacobson Passport
(Computer)
Bytec Hyperion (Computer)
Passport (Computer)
BT Microcomputers
Portable computers
Hyperkeratosis
USE X disease in cattle
Hyperkinesia
UF Hyperactivity, Motor
Hypercinesia
Hyperkinesis
Overactivity
BT Psychomotor disorders
NT Hyperactive child syndrome
Tardive dyskinesia
Hyperkinesia in children
USE Hyperactive child syndrome
Hyperkinesis
USE Hyperkinesia
Hyperkinetic children
USE Hyperactive children
Hyperlipemia
USE Hyperlipidemia
Hyperlipidemia *(May Subd Geog)*
[RC632.H87]
UF Hyperlipemia
BT Lipids—Metabolism—Disorders
RT Blood lipids
NT Hypercholesteremia
Hyperlipidemia in children
Hyperlipoproteinemia
— **Chemotherapy**
RT Antilipemic agents
Hyperlipidemia in children
(May Subd Geog)
[RJ399.H96]
BT Hyperlipidemia
Metabolic disorders in children
NT Hypercholesteremia in children
Hyperlipoproteinemia in children
Hyperlipoproteinemia *(May Subd Geog)*
[RC632.H88]
BT Blood lipoproteins
Blood lipoproteins—Metabolism—
Disorders
Hyperlipidemia
Hyperlipoproteinemia in children
(May Subd Geog)
[RJ399.H]
BT Hyperlipidemia in children
Hypermobility of joints
USE Joints—Hypermobility
Hypernatremia
BT Sodium—Metabolism—Disorders
Water-electrolyte imbalances
Hypernuclei
USE Hyperfragments
Hyperoartia
USE Lampreys
Hyperoliidae
[QL668.E244]
UF African reed frogs
BT Anura
Frogs
NT Cryptothylax
Hyperolius
Leptopelis
Phlyctimantis

Hyperolius *(May Subd Geog)*
[QL668.E244]
BT Hyperoliidae
Hyperons
UF Y-particles
BT Baryons
Heavy particles (Nuclear physics)
NT Hyperfragments
Hyperoodontidae
USE Beaked whales
Hyperopia
UF Farsightedness
BT Eye—Refractive errors
Hyperoscelidae
USE Canthyloscelidae
Hyperoscelididae
USE Canthyloscelidae
Hyperostosis
USE Exostosis
Hyperostosis corticalis generalisata
(May Subd Geog)
[RC931.H94]
UF Van Buchem's disease
BT Exostosis
Osteosclerosis
Hyperostosis frontalis interna
(May Subd Geog)
[RC936]
UF Calvarial hyperostosis
Cranial hyperostosis
Metabolic craniopathy
Morel's syndrome
Morgagni's syndrome
Stewart-Morel syndrome
BT Exostosis
Skull—Abnormalities
Hyperotreta
USE Hagfishes
Hyperoxide
USE Superoxide
Hyperparathyroidism
BT Endocrine glands—Diseases
Parathyroid glands—Diseases
NT Osteitis fibrosa
Hyperpiesia
USE Essential hypertension
Hyperplasia
[RB140]
BT Pathology, Cellular
NT Gingival hyperplasia
Hyperpyrexia, Malignant
USE Malignant hyperthermia
Hyperrealism
USE Photo-realism
Hypersensitivity, Contact
USE Contact dermatitis
Hypersensitivity, Delayed
USE Delayed hypersensitivity
Hypersensitivity, Immediate
USE Allergy
Hypersomnia *(May Subd Geog)*
BT Sleep disorders
NT Pickwickian syndrome
Hypersonic aerodynamics
USE Aerodynamics, Hypersonic
Hypersonic aircraft
USE Hypersonic planes
Hypersonic planes
UF Hypersonic aircraft
Planes, Hypersonic
BT Aerodynamics, Hypersonic
Airplanes
High-speed aeronautics
Hypersonic speeds
USE Aerodynamics, Hypersonic
Hypersonic wind tunnels
BT Aerodynamics, Hypersonic
Wind tunnels
NT Hypervelocity guns
Hypersonics
USE Aerodynamics, Hypersonic

Hyperspace
[QA691]
Here are entered mathematical works. Philosoph-
ical and imaginative works are entered under Fourth
dimension.
UF Algebraic configurations in hyperspace
Space of more than three dimensions
BT Geometry
Geometry—Foundations
Geometry, Differential
Geometry, Non-Euclidean
Mathematics
RT Space and time
NT Hilbert space
Hypercircle method
Hypersurfaces
Polytopes
Spaces, Generalized
Hypersplenism
[RC645]
BT Spleen—Diseases
Hypersurfaces
BT Hyperspace
Surfaces
Hypersusceptibility
USE Anaphylaxis
Hypertension *(May Subd Geog)*
UF Blood pressure, High
High blood pressure
Vascular hypertension
BT Blood—Circulation, Disorders of
NT Essential hypertension
Hypotensive agents
Intracranial hypertension
Mild hypertension
Nephrosclerosis
Portal hypertension
Pulmonary hypertension
Renal hypertension
— **Diagnosis**
— **Psychosomatic aspects**
Hypertension, Intracranial
USE Intracranial hypertension
Hypertension in children *(May Subd Geog)*
[RJ426.H9]
BT Pediatric cardiology
Hypertension in pregnancy
[RG580.H9]
BT Pregnancy, Complications of
Toxemia of pregnancy
Hyperthermia
USE Fever
Heat—Physiological effect
Hyperthermia, Malignant
USE Malignant hyperthermia
Hyperthyroidism *(May Subd Geog)*
[RC656-RC656.3]
UF Thyrotoxicosis
BT Thyroid gland—Diseases
NT Graves' disease
Hypertonic solutions
UF Solutions, Hypertonic
BT Solution (Chemistry)
Solutions (Pharmacy)
— **Therapeutic use**
BT Fluid therapy
Intravenous therapy
Hypertragulidae
[QE882.U3]
BT Ruminants, Fossil
NT Archaeomeryx
Hypertrichosis
[RL431]
UF Hirsutism
BT Hair—Diseases
Virilism
— **Psychosomatic aspects**
Hypertrophic cardiomyopathy
USE Heart—Hypertrophy
Hypertrophy
[RB140]

SA *subdivision* Hypertrophy *under*
   individual organs and parts of the
   body, e.g. Heart—Hypertrophy
 NT Acromegaly
Hyperuricemia
 [RC632.H8]
 BT Uric acid
 NT Lesch-Nyhan syndrome
Hypervelocity guns
 BT Ballistic ranges
  Hypersonic wind tunnels
  Shock tubes
Hyperventilation
 BT Respiration
 — Psychosomatic aspects
  UF Hyperventilation syndrome
Hyperventilation syndrome
 USE Hyperventilation—Psychosomatic
  aspects
Hyperviscosemia
 USE Blood hyperviscosity syndrome
Hyperviscosity, Blood
 USE Blood hyperviscosity syndrome
Hypervitaminosis
 BT Vitamins
Hyphae of fungi
 USE Fungi—Hyphae
Hyphales
 USE Hyphomycetes
Hyphantria *(May Subd Geog)*
 [QL561.A8]
 BT Arctiidae
 NT Hyphantria cunea
Hyphantria cunea *(May Subd Geog)*
 [QL561.A8]
 UF Fall webworm
 BT Hyphantria
Hyphen
 BT Punctuation
Hyphessobrycon
 [QL638.C5]
 BT Characidae
 NT Hyphessobrycon tortuguerae
Hyphessobrycon tortuguerae
 [QL638.C5]
 BT Hyphessobrycon
Hyphochytridiomycetes
 [QK621.A1]
 UF Hyphochytriomycetes
 BT Phycomycetes
Hyphochytriomycetes
 USE Hyphochytridiomycetes
Hypholoma caerulescene
 USE Psilocybe cubensis
Hyphomycetales
 USE Moniliales
Hyphomycetes
 [QK625.A1]
 UF Hyphales
  Hyphomycetidae
 BT Fungi imperfecti
 NT Agonomycetales
  Hyphomycosis
  Moniliales
  Pyricularia
  Stilbellales
  Tuberculariales
Hyphomycetidae
 USE Hyphomycetes
Hyphomycosis
 BT Hyphomycetes
  Mycoses
  Veterinary mycology
Hyphydrus
 [QL596.D9]
 BT Dytiscidae
Hypnagogia *(May Subd Geog)*
 [QP425]
 UF Hypnagogic state
 BT Consciousness
 RT Sleep

Hypnagogic state
 USE Hypnagogia
Hypno-play therapy *(May Subd Geog)*
 [RC499.H94]
  Here are entered works on the use of play therapy
 with adults in an age-regressed hypnotic state.
 BT Hypnotism—Therapeutic use
  Play therapy
Hypnobryales
 [QK539.H95]
 BT Mosses
 NT Amblystegiaceae
  Brachytheciaceae
  Plagiotheciaceae
Hypnopaedia
 USE Sleep-learning
Hypnosis
 USE Hypnotism
Hypnotherapy
 USE Hypnotism—Therapeutic use
Hypnotic age regression *(May Subd Geog)*
 UF Age regression, Hypnotic
  Hypnotically induced age regression
  Regression, Hypnotic age
 BT Hypnotism
  Regression (Psychology)
Hypnotic susceptibility
 UF Susceptibility, Hypnotic
 BT Hypnotism
 — Testing
  NT Stanford hypnotic susceptibility
   scale
Hypnotically induced age regression
 USE Hypnotic age regression
Hypnotics *(May Subd Geog)*
 [RM325]
 UF Sleep-inducing drugs
  Sleep medication
  Sleeping pills
  Soporifics
 BT Central nervous system depressants
 NT Barbiturates
  Flunitrazepam
  Flurazepam
  Pentobarbital
  Zolpidem
 — Overdosage *(May Subd Geog)*
  UF Overdosage of hypnotics
 — Side effects
  UF Side effects of hypnotics
Hypnotism
 [BF1111-BF1156 (Psychical research)]
 [HV6110 (Hypnotism and crime)]
 [RC490-RC499 (Psychiatry)]
 UF Autosuggestion
  Braidism
  Hypnosis
 BT Psychology, Physiological
  Trance
 RT Animal magnetism
  Mental suggestion
  Mesmerism
  Subconsciousness
 NT Autogenic training
  Forensic hypnotism
  Hypnotic age regression
  Hypnotic susceptibility
  Hypnotism and crime
  Magnetic healing
  Reincarnation therapy
  Rigidity (Psychology)
  Therapeutics, Suggestive
 — Law and legislation *(May Subd Geog)*
  RT Forensic hypnotism
 — Sounds
  BT Sounds
 — Therapeutic use
  UF Hypnotherapy
  BT Therapeutics, Suggestive
  NT Hypno-play therapy

 — — Complications and sequelae
  (May Subd Geog)
Hypnotism and crime
 UF Crime and hypnotism
 BT Crime and criminals
  Criminal psychology
  Hypnotism
Hypnotism in dentistry *(May Subd Geog)*
 [RK512.H95]
 UF Dental hypnosis
 BT Anesthesia in dentistry
  Dentistry
Hypnotism in obstetrics
 BT Anesthesia in obstetrics
  Obstetrics
Hypnotism in ophthalmology
 (May Subd Geog)
 BT Anesthesia in ophthalmology
  Ophthalmology
Hypnotism in surgery
 [RD85.H9]
 BT Anesthesia
  Surgery
Hypoacidity, Gastric
 USE Achlorhydria
Hypoactivity
 USE Hypokinesia
Hypobetalipoproteinemia
 USE Hypolipoproteinemia
Hypocalcemia
 BT Calcium—Metabolism—Disorders
Hypocalidae
 USE Noctuidae
Hypocephalidae
 USE Cerambycidae
Hypochlorinators
 BT Water—Purification
Hypochlorites
 BT Chlorites
 NT Sodium hypochlorite
Hypocholesteremic agents
 USE Anticholesteremic agents
Hypochondria
 [RC552.H8]
 UF Hypochondriasis
 BT Somatoform disorders
 — Early works to 1900
  [BC552.H8]
Hypochondria in literature
 BT Anxiety in literature
  Fear in literature
Hypochondriasis
 USE Hypochondria
Hypochromic anemia *(May Subd Geog)*
 [RC641.7.H9]
 UF Anemia, Microcytic hypochromic
  Microcytic hypochromic anemia
 BT Anemia
 NT Iron deficiency anemia
Hypocreales
 [QK623.P9]
 BT Fungi
Hypocrisy
 [BJ1535.H8 (Ethics)]
 [BV4627.H8 (Theology)]
 BT Truthfulness and falsehood
 — Religious aspects
 — — Buddhism, [**Christianity, etc.**]
Hypocupraemia
 USE Hypocupremia
Hypocupremia
 UF Copper deficiency disease
  Hypocupraemia
  Hypocuprosis
 BT Copper—Metabolism—Disorders
  Copper in the body
  Deficiency diseases in domestic
   animals
Hypocuprosis
 USE Hypocupremia

Hypocycloids
USE Epicycloids and hypocycloids
Hypocyphtus
USE Cypha
Hypocyptus
USE Cypha
Hypoderma bovis
USE Warble-flies
Hypoderma lineatum
USE Warble-flies
Hypodermatidae
USE Oestridae
Hypodermic injections
USE Injections, Hypodermic
Hypodermic jet injectors
UF Injectors, Hypodermic jet
Jet injectors, Hypodermic
BT Injections, Hypodermic
Medical instruments and apparatus
Hypodermic needle industry
(May Subd Geog)
BT Hypodermic needles
Hypodermic needles
BT Injections, Hypodermic
NT Hypodermic needle industry
Hypodermic syringes
Hypodermic syringe industry
(May Subd Geog)
BT Hypodermic syringes
Hypodermic syringes
BT Hypodermic needles
Injections, Hypodermic
Syringes
NT Hypodermic syringe industry
Hypodynerus
[QL568.E84]
BT Eumenidae
Hypodynerus tuberculiventris
[QL568.E84]
Hypoelliptic differential equations
USE Differential equations, Hypoelliptic
Hypoelliptic operators
UF Operators, Hypoelliptic
BT Partial differential operators
Hypoferric anemia
USE Iron deficiency anemia
Hypogaeic acid
[QD305.A2]
[QK866.P3 (Botanical chemistry)]
Hypogammaglobulinemia
USE Agammaglobulinemia
Hypogastric plexus
— Surgery
Hypogastruridae
[QL503.H9]
BT Collembola
NT Anurida
Hypoglossal nerve
UF Nervus hypoglossus
BT Nerves, Cranial
Hypoglycemia
[RC857 (Disease)]
UF Blood sugar, Low
Hypoglycemosis
Low blood sugar
BT Blood sugar
Endocrine glands—Diseases
Hypoglycin A
Insulin
Pancreas—Diseases
RT Hypoglycemic agents
NT Insulin shock
Hypoglycemia, Acute toxic
USE Hypoglycin A—Toxicology
Hypoglycemia in children
[RJ520.H94]
UF Low blood sugar in children
BT Metabolic disorders in children
Hypoglycemic agents
[RC661.A1]
UF Antidiabetics

BT Diabetes
Drugs
RT Hypoglycemia
NT Glibenclamide
Hypoglycemic sulphonylureas
Hypoglycin A
Insulin
Phenformin
Tolbutamide
Hypoglycemic agents industry
(May Subd Geog)
[HD9675.H86-864]
Hypoglycemic sulphonylureas
(May Subd Geog)
[RM666.H]
UF Sulphonylureas, Hypoglycemic
BT Hypoglycemic agents
Sulphonamides
Urea
NT Chlorpropamide
Glibenclamide
Gliclazide
Tolbutamide
Hypoglycemosis
USE Hypoglycemia
Hypoglycin A
UF Aminomethylenecyclop
ropanepropionic acid
BT Aceraceae
Amino acids
Cyclopropane
Hippocastanaceae
Hypoglycemic agents
Poisons
Propionic acid
Sapindaceae
NT Hypoglycemia
— Toxicology
UF Acute toxic hypoglycemia
Akee poisoning
Hypoglycemia, Acute toxic
Jamaican vomiting sickness
Vomiting sickness of Jamaica
Hypogonadism
BT Sexual disorders
NT Klinefelter's syndrome
Hypogrammidae
USE Noctuidae
Hypogymnidae
USE Lymantriidae
Hypoid gearing
USE Gearing, Hypoid
Hypokalaemia
USE Hypokalemia
Hypokalemia (May Subd Geog)
[RC632.P]
UF Hypokalaemia
Hypokaliaemia
Hypokaliemia
Hypopotassemia
BT Potassium—Metabolism—Disorders
Water-electrolyte imbalances
Hypokaliaemia
USE Hypokalemia
Hypokaliemia
USE Hypokalemia
Hypokinesia (May Subd Geog)
UF Hypoactivity
Inactivity, Physical
Physical inactivity
Underactivity
BT Movement disorders
Hypolactasia
USE Lactose intolerance
Hypoleucemia
USE Leucopenia
Hypoleucia
USE Leucopenia
Hypoleucocytosis
USE Leucopenia

Hypolimnas
[QL561.N9]
BT Nymphalidae
Hypolimnas macarthuri
[QL561.N9]
Hypolipaemia
USE Hypolipemia
Hypolipemia (May Subd Geog)
[RC632.H]
UF Hypolipaemia
Hypolipidemia
BT Blood lipids
Lipids—Metabolism—Disorders
Hypolipidemia
USE Hypolipemia
Hypolipoproteinemia (May Subd Geog)
[RC632.H92]
UF Hypobetalipoproteinemia
Lipoprotein deficiency syndromes
Tangier disease
BT Blood lipoproteins—Metabolism—
Disorders
Hypomagnesemia
USE Grass tetany
Hypomania (May Subd Geog)
BT Manic-depressive psychoses
Hypomesus olidus
USE Pond smelt
Hyponatremia
BT Sodium—Metabolism—Disorders
Water-electrolyte imbalances
Hyponomeutidae
USE Yponomeutidae
Hyponormal operators
UF Operators, Hyponormal
BT Linear operators
Hyponotidae
USE Yponomeutidae
Hypopachus
[QL668.E26]
BT Microhylidae
Hypoparathyroidism (May Subd Geog)
UF Parathyroid deficiency
BT Endocrine glands—Diseases
Parathyroid glands—Diseases
NT Tetany
Hypopharynx
[QL861 (Comparative anatomy)]
[QM331 (Human anatomy)]
UF Laryngopharynx
BT Pharynx
NT Pharyngoesophageal sphincter
— Diseases (May Subd Geog)
NT Hypopharynx—Diverticula
— Diverticula
[RF497.H96]
UF Diverticula of the hypopharynx
Pharyngoesophageal diverticula
BT Hypopharynx—Diseases
Hypophosphatasia
BT Phosphorus—Metabolism—Disorders
Hypophosphatemia, Familial
UF Familial hypophosphatemia
BT Familial diseases
Metabolism, Inborn errors of
Renal tubular transport, Disorders of
Hypophosphites
[RM666.H9 (Therapeutics)]
BT Materia medica
Hypophyseal dwarfism
USE Dwarfism, Pituitary
Hypophysectomy (May Subd Geog)
[RD599.5.P58]
UF Pituitary gland—Excision
BT Pituitary gland—Surgery
Hypophysis cerebri
USE Pituitary gland
Hypopituitarism, Postpartum
USE Sheehan's syndrome
Hypopotassemia
USE Hypokalemia

Hypoptidae
USE Cossidae
Hypoptyalism *(May Subd Geog)*
 ₁RC815.5₁
 UF Hyposialosis
 BT Salivary glands—Diseases
Hypopyridae
USE Noctuidae
Hyporhina
 ₁QE862.L2₁
 BT Hyporhinidae
Hyporhina tertia
 ₁QE862.L2₁
Hyporhinidae
 ₁QE862.L2₁
 BT Lizards, Fossil
 NT Hyporhina
Hyposensitization therapy
USE Allergy desensitization
Hyposialosis
USE Hypoptyalism
Hypospadias
 BT Penis
 Urethra
 NT Chordee
Hypostatic union
 ₁BT205₁
 UF Union, Hypostatic
 BT Jesus Christ—Person and offices
 RT Jesus Christ—Natures
 — **History of doctrines**
Hypostomus
 ₁QL638.L785₁
 UF Plecostomus
 BT Loricariidae
Hypostyle Hall, Temple of Amon (Karnak,
 Egypt)
 USE Temple of Amon (Karnak, Egypt)—
 Hypostyle Hall
Hyposulphites
 ₁QD181.S1₁
Hypotension
 UF Blood pressure, Low
 Low blood pressure
 BT Blood—Circulation, Disorders of
 NT Hypotension, Orthostatic
 Hypotension in pregnancy
Hypotension, Controlled
 UF Controlled hypotension
 Hypotension, Induced
 Induced hypotension
 BT Analgesia
 Anesthesia
Hypotension, Induced
 USE Hypotension, Controlled
Hypotension, Orthostatic *(May Subd Geog)*
 ₁RC685.O78₁
 UF Orthostatic hypotension
 Postural hypotension
 BT Hypotension
Hypotension in pregnancy
 ₁RG580.H95₁
 BT Hypotension
 Pregnancy, Complications of
Hypotensive agents
 UF Antihypertensive agents
 BT Cardiovascular agents
 Hypertension
 NT Angiotensin converting enzyme—
 Inhibitors
 Atenolol
 Betaxolol
 Bretylium tosylate
 Captopril
 Clonidine
 Gallopamil
 Hydralazine
 Kinins
 Labetalol
 Metipranolol
 Nitrendipine

Rauwolfia (Drug)
 Saralasin
 Sodium nitroferricyanide
 Timolol maleate
 Vasodilators
Hypothalamic hormones
 ₁QP572.H9₁
 BT Hormones
 Hypothalamus
 Neuropeptides
 NT Neurotensin
 Pituitary hormone releasing factors
 Somatostatin
Hypothalamic hypophysiotropic hormones
 USE Pituitary hormone releasing factors
Hypothalamic substance P
 USE Substance P
Hypothalamo-hypophyseal system
 BT Hypothalamus
 Neuroendocrinology
 Pituitary gland
 NT Pituitary hormone releasing factors
Hypothalamus
 ₁QM455₁
 BT Brain
 Endocrine glands
 Limbic system
 NT Hypothalamic hormones
 Hypothalamo-hypophyseal system
 Infundibulum (Brain)
 Supraoptic nucleus
Hypothecation
 USE Bottomry and respondentia
 Chattel mortgages
 Liens
 Mortgages
 Pledges (Law)
Hypothermia *(May Subd Geog)*
 UF Hypothermy
 Low body temperature
 BT Body temperature
 Cold—Physiological effect
 Cryobiology
 NT Artificial hibernation
Hypothermia, Induced
 UF Induced hypothermia
 BT Anesthesia
 Surgery
 Therapeutics
Hypothermy
 USE Hypothermia
Hypothesis
 ₁BC183 (Logic)₁
 UF Assumption
 Supposition
 BT Logic
 Reasoning
 Science—Methodology
 NT Automatic hypothesis formation
 Statistical hypothesis testing
Hypothesis, Two source (Synoptics criticism)
 USE Two source hypothesis (Synoptics
 criticism)
Hypothesis testing (Statistics)
 USE Statistical hypothesis testing
Hypothetical clauses (Grammar)
 USE Grammar, Comparative and general—
 Conditionals
Hypothetical constructs
 USE Latent variables
Hypothyrea
 USE Hypothyroidism
Hypothyreosis
 USE Hypothyroidism
Hypothyroidism *(May Subd Geog)*
 ₁RC657₁
 UF Hypothyrea
 Hypothyreosis
 Thyroid deficiency
 BT Thyroid gland—Diseases
 NT Cretinism

Myxedema
Hypothyroidism in children
 (May Subd Geog)
 ₁RJ274.7 (Newborn infants)₁
 ₁RJ420.H9 (General)₁
 BT Pediatric endocrinology
Hypotonia, Muscle
 USE Muscle hypotonia
Hypotonia oculi
 USE Ocular hypotony
Hypotony, Ocular
 USE Ocular hypotony
Hypovitaminosis
 USE Avitaminosis
Hypovolemic anemia
 USE Anemia, Hypovolemic
Hypoxanthine-guanine phosphoribosyltransf
 erase deficiency
 USE Lesch-Nyhan syndrome
Hypoxanthine phosphoribosyltransferase
 deficiency
 USE Lesch-Nyhan syndrome
Hypoxemia
 USE Anoxemia
Hypoxia
 USE Anoxemia
Hypoxia cerebral
 USE Cerebral anoxia
Hypoxylon
 BT Xylariaceae
Hypsarrhythmia
 USE Spasms, Infantile
Hypsas River (Sicily)
 USE Belice River (Sicily)
Hypsiglena
 ₁QL666.O636₁
 BT Colubridae
 NT Hypsiglena ochrorhynchus
Hypsiglena ochrorhynchus
 ₁QL666.O636₁
 BT Hypsiglena
Hypsiglena tanzeri
 ₁QL666.O636₁
Hypsilophodon
 ₁QE862.O65₁
 BT Hypsilophodontidae
Hypsilophodontidae
 ₁QE862.O65₁
 BT Ornithischia
 NT Hypsilophodon
Hypsometric colors
 USE Color in cartography
Hypsometry
 USE Altitudes—Measurement
Hypsometry, Barometric
 USE Barometric hypsometry
Hypsophylls
 ₁QK649₁
 UF Hochblättern
 BT Leaves
 — **Anatomy**
Hyptiotes
 ₁QL458.42.U4₁
 BT Uloboridae
Hypurina language
 USE Ipurina language
Hyracoidea
 ₁QL737.H85₁
 BT Mammals
 NT Hyraxes
Hyracoidea, Fossil
 ₁QE882.U8₁
 BT Mammals, Fossil
 NT Pliohyracidae
Hyraxes
 ₁QL737.H9₁
 UF Procaviidae
 BT Hyracoidea
 NT Dendrohyrax

Hyrum Reservoir (Utah)
  BT Little Bear River (Utah)
    Reservoirs—Utah
Hyrynen family *(Not Subd Geog)*
Hyselophidae
  USE Yponomeutidae
Hyslop family
  USE Haislip family
Hyslup family
  USE Haislip family
Hyst family
  USE Heiss family
Hysterectomy *(May Subd Geog)*
  [RG391]
  UF Abdominal hysterectomy
    Hysterectomy, Abdominal
    Uterus—Excision
  BT Sterilization of women
    Uterus—Surgery
  — **Complications and sequelae**
  — **Nursing**
    BT Gynecologic nursing
Hysterectomy, Abdominal
  USE Hysterectomy
Hysterectomy, Vaginal *(May Subd Geog)*
  [RG391]
  UF Colpohysterectomy
    Vaginal hysterectomy
  BT Vagina—Surgery
Hysteresigraph
  [QC755.675.H9]
  BT Hysteresis
    Magnetic instruments
Hysteresis
  [QC761]
  BT Elasticity
    Magnetic induction
  NT Hysteresigraph
    Hysteresis loop
Hysteresis loop
  BT Dielectrics
    Hysteresis
    Magnetic induction
    Magnetic materials
    Magnetism
Hysteresis motors
  USE Electric motors, Hysteresis
Hysteria
  [RC532]
  BT Psychology, Pathological
  RT Ecstasy
  NT Aerophagy
    Astasia and astasia-abasia
    Conversion (Psychoanalysis)
    Paralysis, Hysterical
    Trance
  — **Early works to 1900**
    [RC532]
Hysteria, Epidemic
  [RC532]
  UF Epidemic hysteria
    Epidemics, Mental
    Mental epidemics
  RT Chorea, Epidemic
Hysteria (Social psychology)
  UF Mass hysteria
    National hysteria
  BT Fear
    Social psychology
Hysteria in children *(May Subd Geog)*
  [RJ506.H94]
  BT Child psychiatry
    Child psychopathology
Hysteriaceae
  BT Hysteriales
Hysteriales
  [QK623.H (Botany)]
  BT Loculoascomycetes
  NT Hysteriaceae
    Patellariaceae

Hysterosalpingography *(May Subd Geog)*
  [RG107.5.H97]
  UF Hysterotubography
    Metrosalpingography
    Metrotubography
    Uterosalpingography
    Uterotubography
  BT Fallopian tubes—Radiography
    Uterus—Radiography
Hysteroscopic sterilization
  BT Endoscopic surgery
    Sterilization of women
Hysteroscopy *(May Subd Geog)*
  [RG304.5.H97]
  UF Uteroscopy
  BT Endoscopy
    Uterus—Examination
Hysterotubography
  USE Hysterosalpingography
Hystings family
  USE Hastings family
Hystrichoceras
  USE Schloenbachia
Hystrichopsylla
  [QL599.7.H9]
  BT Hystrichopsyllidae
  NT Hystrichopsylla talpae
Hystrichopsylla talpae
  [QL599.7.H9]
  BT Hystrichopsylla
Hystrichopsyllidae
  [QL599.7.H9]
  BT Fleas
  NT Hystrichopsylla
    Megarthroglossus
Hystriciidae
  USE Tachinidae
Hystricothripidae
  USE Phlaeothripidae
Hyttedalen family *(Not Subd Geog)*
Hyx family
  USE Hicks family
Ḥzh (The Hebrew root)
  BT Hebrew language—Roots
I-66 (Va.)
  USE Interstate 66 (Va.)
I-105 (Calif.)
  USE California Century Freeway (Calif.)
I AM movement
  USE I AM Religious Activity
I AM Religious Activity *(May Subd Geog)*
  [BP605.I18]
  UF I AM movement
  BT Cults
I-beams, Steel
  USE Steel I-beams
I-beams, Steel-wood
  USE Steel-wood I-beams
I.C.I.P.E. Farm (Kenya)
  BT Farms—Kenya
I ching and science
  UF Science and I ching
I.D. cards
  USE Identification cards
I family
  USE Yi family
I.G. Farben Trial, Nuremberg, 1947-1948
  UF Subsequent proceedings, Nuremberg
    War Crime Trials, case no. 6
  BT Nuremberg War Crime Trials, 1946-
    1949
    World War, 1939-1945—Atrocities
I Ho Yüan (Peking, China)
  UF Summer Palace (Peking, China)
  BT Palaces—China
    Parks—China
I-hsing ware
  [NK4367.I35]

  UF Boccaro ware
    Buccaro ware
    Red stoneware
    Yi-hsing ware
    Yi-hsing Yao
  BT Stoneware—China
I-Kiribati language
  USE Gilbertese language
I kuan tao (Cult) *(May Subd Geog)*
  UF Chung-hua tao te tz'u shan hui (Cult)
    Way of Pervading Unity (Cult)
    Yi kuan tao (Cult)
  BT China—Religion
    Cults—China
    Cults—Taiwan
    Taiwan—Religion
I-li-mi (Macao)
  USE Taipa Island (Macao)
I-meng Mountains (China)
  BT Mountains—China
I mille, 1860
  USE Expedition of the Thousand, 1860
I/O equipment (Computers)
  USE Computer input-output equipment
I.O.O.F. Cemetery (Denton, Tex.)
  UF Independent Order of Odd Fellows
    Cemetery (Denton, Tex.)
    IOOF Cemetery (Denton, Tex.)
  BT Cemeteries—Texas
I.O.O.F. Cemetery (Mason City, Iowa)
  USE Mason City Oddfellows Home
    Cemetery (Mason City, Iowa)
I.T.A.
  USE Initial teaching alphabet
I wen chin shih chiang
  BT Painting—Taiwan—Awards
Ia antigens
  [QR184.4]
  UF Immune region antigens
    Immune region associated antigens
  BT Antigens
    Glycoproteins
    Immunogenetics
    Ir genes
IAAF World Cup
  USE World Cup (Track-athletics)
Iaai language
  USE Iai language
Iai language
  [PL6249]
  UF Iaai language
  BT Melanesian languages
Iai language (Papua New Guinea)
  USE Purari language
Iaido
  UF Iainuki
  BT Kendo
    Swordplay
Iainuki
  USE Iaido
Iaka language
  USE Yaka language (Zaire and Angola)
Ĩakutskaĩa A.S.S.R. (R.S.F.S.R.)
  — **History**
  —— **Revolution of 1905**
  —— **Revolution, 1917-1921**
Ialysos (Ancient city) *(Not Subd Geog)*
  UF Ialysus (Ancient city)
  BT Cities and towns, Ruined, extinct, etc.
    —Greece
    Greece—Antiquities
Ialysus (Ancient city)
  USE Ialysos (Ancient city)
Iamalele language
  UF Yamalele language
  BT Melanesian languages
Iambic pentameter
  [PE1531.I24]
  UF Pentameter, Iambic
  BT Versification

Iambic poetry
　BT Poetry
Iambic poetry, Greek *(May Subd Geog)*
　UF Greek iambic poetry
　BT Greek poetry
Iambic tetrameter
Iambic trimeter
　BT Versification
ÍAOS (Computer program language)
　[QA76.73.I]
Iapodes
　USE Iapyges
ÍAponskoe More
　USE Japan, Sea of
Iapudae
　USE Iapyges
Iapudes
　USE Iapyges
Iapudiai
　USE Iapyges
Iapydes
　USE Iapyges
Iapyges *(May Subd Geog)*
　UF Iapodes
　　Iapudae
　　Iapudes
　　Iapudiai
　　Iapydes
　　Iapygians
　　Japodes
　BT Ethnology—Yugoslavia
Iapygian language
　USE Messapian language
Iapygians
　USE Iapyges
Iare language
　USE Purari language
ÍAroslavl' (ÍAroslavskaÍa oblast', R.S.F.S.R.)
　— History
　— — Revolution, 1917-1921
Iasos (Ancient city)
　UF Iassos (Ancient city)
　BT Cities and towns, Ruined, extinct, etc.
　　　—Turkey
　　Turkey—Antiquities
Iassidae
　USE Leafhoppers
Iassos (Ancient city)
　USE Iasos (Ancient city)
Iate Indians
　USE Fulnio Indians
Iate language
　USE Fulnio language
Iatmul folk-songs
　USE Folk-songs, Iatmul
Iatmul language
　UF Big Sepik language
　BT Ndu languages
Iatmul songs
　USE Songs, Iatmul
Iatmul women
　USE Women, Iatmul
Iatmuls
　BT Ethnology—Papua New Guinea
　— Children
　　BT Children—Papua New Guinea
　— Women
　　USE Women, Iatmul
Iato Mountain (Sicily)
　UF Ietas Mountain (Sicily)
　　Jato Mountain (Sicily)
　　Monte Iato (Sicily)
　　Monte Jato (Sicily)
　BT Mountains—Italy
Iatrogenic diseases *(May Subd Geog)*
　[RC90]
　BT Diseases
　　Medical errors
　　Medicine, Psychosomatic
　　Therapeutics—Complications and
　　　sequelae

　NT Drugs—Side effects
　　Iatrogenic diseases in children
　　Tardive dyskinesia
Iatrogenic diseases in children
　(May Subd Geog)
　[RJ520.I28]
　UF Pediatric iatrogenic diseases
　BT Children—Diseases
　　Iatrogenic diseases
Iatromathematical school
　USE Iatrophysical school
Iatrophysical school
　[R148]
　UF Iatromathematical school
　BT Astrology
　　Medicine—15th-18th centuries
　　Therapeutic systems
Ibadites *(May Subd Geog)*
　BT Islamic sects
　　Kharijites
Ibadoy dialect
　USE Nabaloi dialect
IBAL (Computer program language)
　UF Illiac III Basic Assembler Language
　BT Assembler language (Computer
　　program language)
　　Illiac computer—Programming
Ibalia *(May Subd Geog)*
　[QL568.I15]
　BT Ibaliidae
Ibaliidae *(May Subd Geog)*
　[QL568.I15]
　BT Hymenoptera
　NT Ibalia
Ibaloi dialect
　USE Nabaloi dialect
Ibalon, Tierra da (Luzon, Philippines)
　USE Bicol Peninsula (Luzon, Philippines)
Iban (Bornean people) marriage customs and
　rites
　USE Marriage customs and rites, Iban
　　(Bornean people)
Iban (Bornean people) textile fabrics
　USE Textile fabrics, Iban (Bornean people)
Iban folk literature
　USE Folk literature, Iban
Iban folk poetry
　USE Folk poetry, Iban
Iban language
　[PL5333]
　UF Sea Dyak language
　BT Malayan languages
Iban literature *(May Subd Geog)*
　NT Folk literature, Iban
　　Iban poetry
Iban poetry *(May Subd Geog)*
　BT Iban literature
　NT Folk poetry, Iban
Ibanag language
　[PL5721]
　BT Philippine languages
Ibans (Bornean people)
　UF Sea Dyaks (Bornean people)
　BT Dyaks
　　Ethnology—Borneo
　NT Kantu (Indonesian people)
　— Rites and ceremonies
　　NT Marriage customs and rites, Iban
　　　(Bornean people)
Ibaraki Kaidō (Japan)
　USE Mito Kaidō (Japan)
IBAS (Information retrieval system)
　[Z699.4.I13]
　BT Cataloging—Data processing
　　Information storage and retrieval
　　systems
Ibatan language
　USE Batan language
Ibembe language
　USE Bembe language (Lake Tanganyika)

Iberian architecture
　USE Architecture, Iberian
Iberian art
　USE Art, Iberian
Iberian inscriptions
　USE Inscriptions, Iberian
Iberian language
　[P1081]
　— Etymology
　　NT Cules (The Iberian word)
Iberian pottery
　USE Pottery, Iberian
Iberian terra-cotta sculpture
　USE Terra-cotta sculpture, Iberian
Iberians
　[DP53.I2]
　NT Basques
　　Celtiberi
　　Ilergetes
Ibernians
　USE Georgians (Transcaucasians)
Ibero-Insular race
　USE Mediterranean race
Ibex
　USE Bouquetin
Ibex, Spanish
　USE Spanish ibex
Ibibio language *(May Subd Geog)*
　BT Benue-Congo languages
　　Nigeria—Languages
　RT Efik language
Ibibios
　[DT515 (Nigeria)]
　NT Anang (African people)
　　Ubium (African people)
　— Rites and ceremonies
　　NT Marriage customs and rites, Ibibios
Ibibios marriage customs and rites
　USE Marriage customs and rites, Ibibios
Ibibobo (Bolivia), Battle of, 1934
　[F2688.5]
　BT Chaco War, 1932-1935—Campaigns—
　　Bolivia
Ibidium cernuum
　USE Spiranthes cernua
Ibidium incurvum
　USE Spiranthes cernua
Ibis
　[QL696.A7]
　BT Threskiornithidae
Ibiza Island (Spain)
　UF Ebusus Island (Spain)
　　Eivissa Island (Spain)
　　Isla de Ibiza (Spain)
　　Iviza Island (Spain)
　BT Islands—Spain
　　Pityusic Islands (Spain)
Ibla (Ancient city)
　USE Ebla (Ancient city)
Iblīs (Islam)
　USE Devil (Islam)
IBM 360 (Computer)
　BT Electronic digital computers
　— Programming
　　NT AEMOVE (Computer program)
　　MERMAC (Electronic computer
　　　system)
　　MVS (Computer system)
　　POKER 360 (Electronic computer
　　　system)
IBM 370 (Computer)
　BT Electronic digital computers
　— Programming
　　NT MVS (Computer system)
IBM 650 (Computer)
　BT Electronic digital computers
　— Programming
IBM 1130 (Computer)
　BT Electronic digital computers
　— Programming

IBM 1401 (Computer)
  BT Electronic digital computers
  — **Programming**
    ⌜*HF5548 (Business)*⌝
    ⌜*QA76.8.I*⌝
IBM 1440 (Computer)
  BT Electronic digital computers
IBM 1620 (Computer)
  BT Electronic digital computers
  — **Programming**
IBM 1800 (Computer)
  BT Electronic digital computers
  — **Programming**
IBM 3965 (Computer)
  BT Electronic digital computers
  — **Programming**
IBM 5100 (Computer)
  BT IBM microcomputers
    Portable computers
IBM 5150 (Computer)
  USE IBM Personal Computer
IBM 5160 (Computer)
  USE IBM Personal Computer XT
IBM 7030 (Computer)
  UF IBM Stretch computer
    Project Stretch
    Stretch computer
  BT Electronic digital computers
IBM 7040 (Computer)
  BT Electronic digital computers
  — **Programming**
IBM 7044 (Computer)
  BT Electronic digital computers
IBM 7090 (Computer)
  BT Electronic digital computers
  — **Programming**
IBM 7094 (Computer)
  BT Electronic digital computers
  — **Programming**
IBM 9000 (Computer)
  ⌜*QA76.8.I*⌝
  UF CS/9000 (Computer)
    IBM CS/9000 (Computer)
  BT IBM microcomputers
IBM aperture card systems
  USE Microfilm aperture card systems
IBM Assistant Series (Computer programs)
  BT Computer programs
IBM AT (Computer)
  USE IBM Personal Computer AT
IBM Automatic Sequence Controlled
  Calculator
  USE Mark I (Calculator)
IBM computers
  ⌜*QA76.8.I*⌝
  BT Electronic digital computers
  NT IBM microcomputers
    IBM System/34 (Computer)
    IBM System/36 (Computer)
  — **Programming**
    NT IBM Database 2 (Computer
      system)
IBM CS/9000 (Computer)
  USE IBM 9000 (Computer)
IBM Database 2 (Computer system)
  UF DB2 (Computer system)
  BT Data base management
    Electronic digital computers—
      Programming
    IBM computers—Programming
IBM Displaywriter (Word processor)
  ⌜*Z52.5.I24*⌝
  UF Displaywriter (Word processor)
  BT Word processors
IBM microcomputers
  ⌜*QA76.8.I*⌝
  BT IBM computers
    Microcomputers
  NT IBM 5100 (Computer)
    IBM 9000 (Computer)
    IBM PC Convertible (Computer)

IBM PCjr (Computer)
  IBM Personal Computer
  IBM Personal Computer AT
  IBM Personal Computer XT
  IBM Personal System/2 (Computer
    system)
  IBM Portable Personal Computer
IBM PC (Computer)
  USE IBM Personal Computer
IBM PC AT (Computer)
  USE IBM Personal Computer AT
IBM PC Convertible (Computer)
  UF PC Convertible (Computer)
  BT IBM microcomputers
    Portable computers
IBM PC jr (Computer)
  USE IBM PCjr (Computer)
IBM PC junior (Computer)
  USE IBM PCjr (Computer)
IBM PC XT (Computer)
  USE IBM Personal Computer XT
IBM PCjr (Computer)
  ⌜*QA76.8.I*⌝
  UF IBM PC jr (Computer)
    IBM PC junior (Computer)
    IBM Personal Computer jr
    PCjr (Computer)
  BT IBM microcomputers
IBM Personal Computer
  ⌜*QA76.8.I*⌝
  UF IBM 5150 (Computer)
    IBM PC (Computer)
    Personal Computer, IBM
  BT IBM microcomputers
  NT OCLC M300 Workstation
  — **Programming**
    NT SalesCTRL (Computer system)
IBM Personal Computer AT
  ⌜*QA76.8.I*⌝
  UF AT (Computer)
    IBM AT (Computer)
    IBM PC AT (Computer)
  BT IBM microcomputers
IBM Personal Computer jr
  USE IBM PCjr (Computer)
IBM Personal Computer XT
  UF IBM 5160 (Computer)
    IBM PC XT (Computer)
    IBM XT (Computer)
  BT IBM microcomputers
  — **Programming**
    NT SalesCTRL (Computer system)
IBM Personal System/2 (Computer system)
  ⌜*QA76.8.I*⌝
  BT IBM microcomputers
  NT IBM Personal System/2 Model 50
    (Computer)
    IBM Personal System/2 Model 60
    (Computer)
    IBM Personal System/2 Model 80
    (Computer)
**IBM Personal System/2 Model 50
(Computer)**
  ⌜*QA76.8.I*⌝
  BT IBM Personal System/2 (Computer
    system)
**IBM Personal System/2 Model 60
(Computer)**
  ⌜*QA76.8.I*⌝
  BT IBM Personal System/2 (Computer
    system)
**IBM Personal System/2 Model 80
(Computer)**
  ⌜*QA76.8.I*⌝
  BT IBM Personal System/2 (Computer
    system)
IBM Portable (Computer)
  USE IBM Portable Personal Computer
IBM Portable PC (Computer)
  USE IBM Portable Personal Computer

IBM Portable Personal Computer
  ⌜*QA76.8.I*⌝
  UF IBM Portable (Computer)
    IBM Portable PC (Computer)
  BT IBM microcomputers
    Portable computers
IBM Series/1 (Computer)
  ⌜*QA76.8.I*⌝
  BT Electronic digital computers
IBM Stretch computer
  USE IBM 7030 (Computer)
IBM System/3 (Computer)
  BT Electronic digital computers
  — **Programming**
IBM System/32 (Computer)
  BT Electronic digital computers
IBM System/34 (Computer)
  BT IBM computers
IBM System/36 (Computer)
  BT IBM computers
IBM System 38 (Computer)
  BT Electronic digital computers
**IBM Token-Ring Network (Local area
network system)** *(May Subd Geog)*
  ⌜*TK5105.8.I24*⌝
  UF Token-Ring Network (Local area
    network system)
  BT Ring networks (Computer networks)
IBM VSE (Computer operating system)
  UF Disk Operating System/Virtual Storage
    Extended (Computer operating
    system)
    DOS/VSE (Computer operating
    system)
    VSE (Computer operating system)
  BT Operating systems (Computers)
IBM XT (Computer)
  USE IBM Personal Computer XT
Ibo (African people)
  USE Igbo (African people)
Ibo language
  USE Igbo language
Ibsen, Henrik, 1828-1906 *(Not Subd Geog)*
  — **Characters** *(Not Subd Geog)*
  — — **Peer Gynt** *(Not Subd Geog)*
      RT Gynt, Peer (Fictitious character)
Ibsen family *(Not Subd Geog)*
  UF Ibson family
Ibson family
  USE Ibsen family
Iburg Castle (Iburg, Germany)
  USE Schloss Iburg (Iburg, Germany)
Ica language *(May Subd Geog)*
  UF Ijca language
    Ijka language
    Ike language
  BT Chibchan languages
    Colombia—Languages
Ica River (Peru)
  UF Río Ica (Peru)
  BT Rivers—Peru
Icarex camera
Icaria Island (Greece)
  USE Ikaria Island (Greece)
Icarian movement *(May Subd Geog)*
  UF Icarians
  BT Utopian socialism
Icarians
  USE Icarian movement
Icaricia
  USE Plebejus
Icarus (Greek mythology)
  BT Mythology, Greek
ICBM
  USE Intercontinental ballistic missiles
ICCF (Computer system)
  UF Interactive Computing and Control
      Facility (Computer system)
  BT Interactive computer systems
Ice *(May Subd Geog)*
  ⌜*GB2401-2597*⌝

UF Freezing
BT Frost
Physical geography
Water
NT Aufeis
Building, Ice and snow
Dry ice
Glaciers
Glaze (Meteorology)
Ice coring rigs
Ice crystals
Ice on rivers, lakes, etc.
Icebergs
Pingos
Saline water conversion—Freezing
process
Sea ice
Transportation, Military—Cold
weather conditions
— **Bacteriology**
[QR107]
RT Water—Bacteriology
— **Control**
USE Ice prevention
— **Electric properties**
— **Manufacture**
[TP490-495]
UF Ice-machinery
Ice making
BT Ice industry
RT Refrigeration and refrigerating
machinery
— Mechanical properties
USE Ice mechanics
— Prevention
USE Ice prevention
— **Antarctic regions**
UF Ice, Polar
Polar ice
— **Arctic regions**
UF Ice, Polar
Polar ice
— **Greenland**
UF Ice, Polar
Polar ice
— **Newfoundland**
Ice, Frazil
USE Frazil ice
Ice, Lolly
USE Frazil ice
Ice, Needle
USE Frazil ice
Ice, Polar
USE Ice—Antarctic regions
Ice—Arctic regions
Ice—Greenland
Ice accidents
BT Accidents
Ice accretion
USE Icing (Meteorology)
Ice age
USE Glacial epoch
Ice Age National Scientific Reserve (Wis.)
BT Glacial epoch—Wisconsin
National parks and reserves—United
States
Natural areas—Wisconsin
Parks—Wisconsin
Ice and snow building
USE Building, Ice and snow
Ice-boats
[GV843]
BT Boats and boating
Sailing
RT Iceboating
Ice breaking operations *(May Subd Geog)*
[VK1299.5-1299.6]
UF Icebreaking operations
BT Aids to navigation
Ice-breaking vessels

SA *subdivision* Ice breaking operations
under names of individual navies,
e.g. United States. Navy—Ice
breaking operations
Ice-breaking vessels
[VM451]
UF Steamboats, Ice-breaking
BT Ice on rivers, lakes, etc.
Ships
NT Ice breaking operations
Nuclear icebreakers
Ice-breaking vessels, Nuclear
USE Nuclear icebreakers
Ice bridges
USE Ice crossings
Ice caps *(May Subd Geog)*
UF Icecaps
BT Glaciology
Snow
RT Ice sheets
Ice carnivals
USE Winter sports
Ice carving
[NK6030]
BT Carving (Decorative arts)
Sculpture
Ice caves *(May Subd Geog)*
BT Caves
Ice clearing
USE Polynyas
Ice climbing
USE Snow and ice climbing
Ice clouds *(May Subd Geog)*
UF Ice crystal clouds
Ice crystals in clouds
BT Clouds
Ice crystals
— **Optical properties**
Ice control
USE Ice prevention
Ice control (Roads)
USE Roads—Snow and ice control
Ice control on bridges
USE Bridges—Snow and ice control
Ice coring rigs
BT Boring machinery
Ice
Ice covers, Glacial
USE Ice sheets
Ice cream, Soy
USE Soy ice cream
Ice cream dippers
USE Ice cream scoops
Ice cream dishers
USE Ice cream scoops
Ice-cream freezers
BT Refrigeration and refrigerating
machinery
Ice cream, ices, etc.
[TX795]
UF Ices
BT Confectionery
Desserts, Frozen
NT Ice cream industry
Milkshakes
Yogurt, Frozen
— **Law and legislation** *(May Subd Geog)*
BT Dairy laws
Ice cream industry *(May Subd Geog)*
BT Ice cream, ices, etc.
NT Ice cream parlors
Ice cream parlors *(May Subd Geog)*
UF Parlors, Ice cream
Shops, Ice cream
Stores, Ice cream
BT Ice cream industry
Restaurants, lunch rooms, etc.
Ice cream scoops *(May Subd Geog)*
[TX657.124]

UF Dippers, Ice cream
Dishers, Ice cream
Ice cream dippers
Ice cream dishers
Scoops, Ice cream
BT Kitchen utensils
Ice crossings
UF Ice bridges
BT Bridges
Ice on rivers, lakes, etc.
Roads, Ice
Ice crystal clouds
USE Ice clouds
Ice crystal replicators
[QC921.6.C6]
UF Replicators, Ice crystal
BT Ice crystals
Meteorological instruments
Ice crystals
UF Frost mist
Frost snow
Ice needles
Ice prisms
Poudrin
BT Frost
Hail
Ice
RT Ice nuclei
NT Depth hoar
Frazil ice
Ice clouds
Ice crystal replicators
Ice fog
Snow crystals
— **Growth**
[QC929.S7]
— **Spectra**
Ice crystals in clouds
USE Ice clouds
Ice drift
USE Sea ice drift
Ice erosion
USE Glacial erosion
Ice excavation
BT Civil engineering—Cold weather
conditions
Excavation
RT Ice tunneling
Ice field drift
USE Sea ice drift
Ice fishing *(May Subd Geog)*
[SH459]
BT Fishing
Winter sports
Ice fog
[QC929.F7]
UF Air hoar
Frost flakes
Frost fog
Frozen fog
Rime fog
BT Fog
Freezing precipitation
Ice crystals
Ice hockey
USE Hockey
Ice-houses
[NA6360 (Commercial)]
[NA8350 (Private)]
Ice industry *(May Subd Geog)*
[HD9481 (Trade)]
[TP498 (Cutting, storage)]
NT Dry ice
Ice—Manufacture
Wages—Ice industry
Ice islands
UF Islands, Ice
BT Icebergs
Sea ice
RT Drifting ice stations
NT Arlis II (Drifting ice station)

Ice-machinery
  USE Ice—Manufacture
       Refrigeration and refrigerating
         machinery
Ice making
  USE Ice—Manufacture
Ice mantles
  USE Ice sheets
Ice mechanics
    ₍TA714.5₎
  UF Ice—Mechanical properties
  BT Engineering geology
       Frozen ground
       Glaciers
       Glaciology
       Ice on rivers, lakes, etc.
       Mechanics
  RT Snow mechanics
Ice navigation *(May Subd Geog)*
  BT Navigation
       Seamanship
  NT Sea ice
Ice needles
  USE Ice crystals
Ice nuclei *(May Subd Geog)*
  UF Nuclei, Ice
  BT Atmospheric nucleation
  RT Ice crystals
Ice on electric lines
  USE Electric lines—Ice prevention
Ice on rivers, lakes, etc. *(May Subd Geog)*
    ₍GB1201-GB1397 (Rivers)₎
    ₍GB1601-GB1797 (Lakes)₎
  UF Freezing and opening of rivers, lakes,
         etc.
       Lakes, Freezing and opening of
       Rivers, Freezing and opening of
  BT Ice
       Meteorology
  RT Lakes—Temperature
       Rivers—Temperature
  NT Aufeis
       Frazil ice
       Ice-breaking vessels
       Ice crossings
       Ice mechanics
Ice on ships
  USE Ships—Ice prevention
Ice palaces *(May Subd Geog)*
    ₍NA6890₎
  BT Palaces
Ice prevention
    ₍TA197₎
  UF Ice—Control
       Ice—Prevention
       Ice control
  BT Engineering meteorology
       Icing (Meteorology)
  NT Airplanes—Ice prevention
       Docks—Ice prevention
       Electric lines—Ice prevention
       Hydraulic structures—Ice prevention
       Roads—Snow and ice control
       Roofs—Snow and ice control
       Ships—Ice prevention
       Telegraph lines—Ice prevention
       Telephone lines—Ice prevention
Ice prisms
  USE Ice crystals
Ice racing
  USE Speed skating
Ice removing chemicals
  USE Deicing chemicals
Ice rinks
  USE Skating rinks
Ice roads
  USE Roads, Ice
Ice seamanship
  USE Seamanship—Cold weather conditions
Ice sheets *(May Subd Geog)*
    ₍GB2401-GB2598 (Hydrology)₎

    ₍QC981.8.I23 (Climatology)₎
  UF Glacial ice covers
       Ice covers, Glacial
       Ice mantles
       Mantles, Ice
       Sheets, Ice
  BT Glaciers
  RT Ice caps
Ice skates
  USE Skates
Ice skating
  USE Skating
Ice skating races
  USE Skating races
Ice skating racing
  USE Speed skating
Ice sports
  USE Winter sports
Ice stations, Drifting
  USE Drifting ice stations
Ice tunneling
  BT Civil engineering—Cold weather
         conditions
       Tunneling
  RT Ice excavation
Ice-wedge polygons *(May Subd Geog)*
  UF Contraction-crack polygons
  BT Frozen ground
       Patterned ground
Iceberg utilization
  USE Icebergs—Utilization
Icebergs
    ₍GB2401-GB2597₎
    ₍VK1299 (Navigation)₎
  BT Ice
       Physical geography
  RT Sea ice
  SA Ice—₍local subdivision₎, *e.g.* Ice—
         Newfoundland
  NT Ice islands
       International ice patrol
  — Utilization
      UF Iceberg utilization
           Utilization of icebergs
      BT Natural resources
           Water-supply
Icebergs (Painting)
  USE Church, Frederick Edwin, 1826-1900.
       Icebergs
Icebergs in art
  NT Church, Frederick Edwin, 1826-1900.
       Icebergs
Iceboating *(May Subd Geog)*
    ₍GV843₎
  BT Winter sports
  RT Ice-boats
Icebreakers, Nuclear
  USE Nuclear icebreakers
Icebreaking operations
  USE Ice breaking operations
Icecaps
  USE Ice caps
Iceland
  — **Description and travel**
  — — **1945-1980**
  — — **1981-**
  — **Economic conditions**
  — — **1918-1945**
  — — **1945-**
  — **History**
  — — **1918-1945**
  — **Politics and government**
  — — **18th century** *(Not Subd Geog)*
  — — **19th century**
  — — **20th century**
Iceland disease
  USE Myalgic encephalomyelitis
Iceland horse
  USE Iceland pony
Iceland pony
    ₍SF315.2.I3₎

  UF Iceland horse
       Icelandic pony
  BT Ponies
Iceland spar
    ₍QE391.I₎
  BT Polarization (Light)
       Refraction, Double
Icelanders *(May Subd Geog)*
  BT Ethnology—Iceland
       Scandinavians
Icelandic-American literature
    ₍PT7526-7545₎
Icelandic art
  USE Art, Icelandic
Icelandic authors
  USE Authors, Icelandic
Icelandic children's literature
  USE Children's literature, Icelandic
Icelandic disease
  USE Myalgic encephalomyelitis
Icelandic drama
    ₍PT7411 (History)₎
    ₍PT7470-PT7477 (Collections)₎
Icelandic epigrams
  USE Epigrams, Icelandic
Icelandic fiction
    ₍PT7413 (History)₎
    ₍PT7485-PT7487 (Collections)₎
  NT Short stories, Icelandic
Icelandic folk-songs
  USE Folk-songs, Icelandic
Icelandic illumination of books and
    manuscripts
  USE Illumination of books and manuscripts,
       Icelandic
Icelandic language
    ₍PD2401-2447₎
  UF Icelandic language, Modern
  BT Scandinavian languages
  —To 1550
      USE Old Norse language
Icelandic language, Modern
  USE Icelandic language
Icelandic literature *(May Subd Geog)*
    ₍PT7351-PT7438 (History)₎
    ₍PT7451-PT7495 (Collections)₎
  UF Icelandic literature, Modern
  BT Scandinavian literature
  NT Children's literature, Icelandic
       Icelandic prose literature
       Old Norse literature
Icelandic literature, Modern
  USE Icelandic literature
Icelandic newspapers
    ₍PN5355.I3₎
Icelandic painting
  USE Painting, Icelandic
Icelandic periodicals
    ₍PN5355.I3₎
Icelandic poetry
  UF Icelandic poetry, Modern
  NT Religious poetry, Icelandic
Icelandic poetry, Modern
  USE Icelandic poetry
Icelandic poets
  USE Poets, Icelandic
Icelandic pony
  USE Iceland pony
Icelandic prose literature *(May Subd Geog)*
    ₍PT7412-PT7418 (History)₎
    ₍PT7480-PT7495 (Collections)₎
  UF Icelandic prose literature, Modern
  BT Icelandic literature
Icelandic prose literature, Modern
  USE Icelandic prose literature
Icelandic religious poetry
  USE Religious poetry, Icelandic
Icelandic religious poetry, Modern
  USE Religious poetry, Icelandic
Icelandic romances
  USE Romances, Icelandic

Icelandic short stories
    USE Short stories, Icelandic
Icelandic wit and humor, Pictorial
    (May Subd Geog)
Iceni
    BT Britons
        Ethnology—England
Icerya
    ⌐QL527.M37⌐
    BT Margarodidae
Icerya purchasi
    USE Cottony-cushion scale
Ices
    USE Ice cream, ices, etc.
ICES (Electronic computer system)
    ⌐TA345.5.I2⌐
    UF Integrated Civil Engineering System
        (Electronic computer system)
    BT Electronic digital computers—
        Programming
        On-line data processing
    NT STRUDL (Electronic computer
        system)
ICGS (Electronic computer system)
    UF Illinois Computing Graphics System
        (Electronic computer system)
    BT Minicomputers—Programming
Ichang gooseberry
    USE Kiwi fruit
Ichi Iseki (Echigawa-chō, Japan)
    USE Ichi Site (Echigawa-chō, Japan)
Ichi Site (Echigawa-chō, Japan)
    UF Ichi Iseki (Echigawa-chō, Japan)
    BT Japan—Antiquities
Ichigenkin
    ⌐ML1015-1018⌐
    BT Koto
        Musical instruments—Japan
Ichigenkin music
    ⌐M142.I3⌐
Ichijō family *(Not Subd Geog)*
Ichikawa II Iseki (Yūbetsu-chō, Japan)
    USE Ichikawa II Site (Yūbetsu-chō, Japan)
Ichikawa II Site (Yūbetsu-chō, Japan)
    (Not Subd Geog)
    UF Ichikawa II Iseki (Yūbetsu-chō, Japan)
    BT Japan—Antiquities
Ichilala (African people)
    USE Lala (African people)
Ichimaru family *(Not Subd Geog)*
Ichinosaka Dam (Japan) *(Not Subd Geog)*
    BT Dams—Japan
Ichinowatari Iseki (Kuroishi-shi, Japan)
    USE Ichinowatari Site (Kuroishi-shi, Japan)
Ichinowatari Site (Kuroishi-shi, Japan)
    UF Ichinowatari Iseki (Kuroishi-shi, Japan)
    BT Japan—Antiquities
Ichioyo ikebana
    USE Flower arrangement, Japanese—Ichiyo
        school
Ichiti language
    USE Hitchiti language
Ichneumonidae
    ⌐QL568.I2⌐
    BT Hymenoptera
    NT Brachycyrtus
        Cardiochiles
        Cryptanura
        Diadromus
        Eiphosoma
        Epirhyssa
        Exenterus
        Heteropelma
        Megarhyssa
        Pimpla
        Rhyssa
        Temelucha
        Thalessa
        Therion
        Theronia
        Trachysphyrus

Ichnology
    USE Footprints, Fossil
Ichnotropis
    ⌐QL666.L255⌐
    BT Lacertidae
    NT Ichnotropis microlepidota
Ichnotropis microlepidota
    ⌐QL666.L255⌐
    BT Ichnotropis
Ichthyboridae
    USE Distichodontidae
Ichthyborinae
    USE Distichodontidae
Ichthyism
    USE Poisonous fishes—Toxicology
Ichthyobdellidae
    USE Piscicolidae
Ichthyodectiformes
    ⌐QE852.I35⌐
    BT Teleostei, Fossil
Ichthyol
    ⌐QP915.I2 (Physiological effect)⌐
    ⌐RM666.I2 (Therapeutics)⌐
Ichthyological research
    USE Fishes—Research
Ichthyologists *(May Subd Geog)*
    BT Zoologists
    RT Fishery scientists
Ichthyology *(May Subd Geog)*
    BT Zoology
    RT Fishes
    — Research
        USE Fishes—Research
Ichthyomyzon
    ⌐QL638.25.P48⌐
    BT Petromyzonidae
Ichthyomyzon unicuspis
    USE Silver lamprey
Ichthyophiidae
    ⌐QL668.A65⌐
    NT Ichthyophis
        Uraeotyphlus
Ichthyophis
    ⌐QL668.A65⌐
    BT Ichthyophiidae
    NT Ichthyophis glutinosus
        Ichthyophis monochrous
Ichthyophis glutinosus
    ⌐QL668.A65⌐
    BT Ichthyophis
Ichthyophis monochrous
    ⌐QL668.A65⌐
    BT Ichthyophis
Ichthyoplankton
    USE Fishes—Eggs
        Fishes—Larvae
Ichthyosarcotoxism
    USE Poisonous fishes—Toxicology
Ichthyosauria
    ⌐QE862.I2⌐
    BT Reptiles, Fossil
    NT Ichthyosauridae
Ichthyosauridae
    ⌐QE862.I2⌐
    BT Ichthyosauria
    NT Ichthyosaurus
Ichthyosaurus
    ⌐QE862.I2⌐
    BT Ichthyosauridae
Ichthyosis follicularis
    USE Keratosis
Ichthyoxenus
    ⌐QL444.M34⌐
    BT Cymothoidae
Ichthyoxenus geei
    ⌐QL444.M34⌐
Icichthys
    ⌐QL638.S87⌐
    BT Stromateidae

Icila (African dance)
Icing (Meteorology) *(May Subd Geog)*
    ⌐QC929.S7⌐
    UF Accretion, Ice
        Ice accretion
    BT Meteorology
    RT Freezing precipitation
    SA *subdivision* Ice prevention *under
        subjects, e.g.* Airplanes—Ice
        prevention
    NT Aufeis
        Glaze (Meteorology)
        Ice prevention
Icings, Cake
    UF Cake icing
        Frostings, Cake
    RT Cake decorating
Icke family
    USE Ickes family
Ickes family *(Not Subd Geog)*
    UF Icke family
Icknield Street (England)
    USE Icknield Way (England)
Icknield Way (England)
    UF Icknield Street (England)
    BT Roads—England
        Roads, Prehistoric—England
ICL 1900 (Computer)
    ⌐QA76.8.I⌐
    BT Electronic digital computers
    — **Programming**
ICL 2900 (Computer)
    ⌐QA76.8.I⌐
    BT Electronic digital computers
ICL 2903 (Computer)
    ⌐QA76.8.I⌐
    BT Electronic digital computers
    — **Programming**
ICL 2904 (Computer)
    ⌐QA76.8.I⌐
    BT Electronic digital computers
    — **Programming**
Icomkill (Scotland)
    USE Iona (Scotland)
Icon (Computer program language)
    ⌐QA76.73.I⌐
    BT Programming languages (Electronic
        computers)
Icon painters *(May Subd Geog)*
    BT Painters
Icon painting *(May Subd Geog)*
    UF Painting, Icon
    BT Icons
        Miniature painting
        Painting
    — **Byzantine ⌐etc.⌐ influences**
    — **Byzantine influences**
        BT Byzantine Empire—Civilization
    — **Russian S.F.S.R.**
        NT Moscow school of icon painting
Icon veneration
    USE Icons—Cult
ICONDA (Information retrieval system)
    ⌐Z699.5.B8⌐
    UF International Construction Database
    BT Information storage and retrieval
        systems—Building
Iconoclasm
    ⌐BR238 (8th century)⌐
    UF Iconoclasm—History
    BT Idols and images—Worship
    — **History**
        USE Iconoclasm
Iconography
    USE Art
        Idols and images
        Pictures
Iconostases *(May Subd Geog)*
    ⌐NA5082⌐
    BT Screens (Church decoration)

Icons *(May Subd Geog)*
  ₍N7956 (Russian art)₎
  UF Eikons
      Ikons
  BT Christian art and symbolism
      Christian saints in art
      Jesus Christ—Art
      Mary, Blessed Virgin, Saint—Art
  NT Chernigovskaia Chudotvornaia
        Bogomater' (Icon)
      Hagia Eikōn tēs Megalochares Tēnou
        (Icon)
      Icon painting
      Iverskaia Sviataia i Chudotvornaia
        Bogomater' (Icon)
      Thaumatourgos Eikōn tēs Prousiōtissēs
        (Icon)
      Tikhvinskaia Bogomater' (Icon)
  — **Cult** *(May Subd Geog)*
    UF Icon veneration
        Picture veneration
        Veneration of icons
        Veneration of pictures
  — **Private collections** *(May Subd Geog)*
  — **Georgian S.S.R.**
    NT Xaxulius Karedi (Icon)
  — **Greece**
    NT Eikona tēs Panagias tēs
          Chrysovitsas (Icon)
  — **Poland**
    NT Częstochowa, Our Lady of (Icon)
  — **Russian S.F.S.R.**
    NT Bogomater' Donskaia (Icon)
        Umilenie Tsaritsy Nebesnoi (Icon)
        Uspenie (Icon)
  — **Ukraine**
    NT Pochaivs'ka Bohorodytsia (Icon)
        Sambirs'ka Bohorodytsia (Icon)
Icons, Albanian *(May Subd Geog)*
  UF Albanian icons
Icons, Bulgarian *(May Subd Geog)*
  UF Bulgarian icons
Icons, Byzantine *(May Subd Geog)*
  UF Byzantine icons
  BT Christian art and symbolism
Icons, Greek *(May Subd Geog)*
  UF Greek icons
Icons, Polish *(May Subd Geog)*
  UF Polish icons
Icons, Romanian *(May Subd Geog)*
  UF Romanian icons
Icons, Russian *(May Subd Geog)*
  UF Russian icons
  BT Christian art and symbolism
  NT Moscow school of icon painting
      Uspenie (Icon)
Icons, Russian, ₍Serbian, etc.₎
Icosahedra
  ₍QA491₎
  BT Polyhedra
Icosanoic acid
  USE Arachidic acid
Icosanoids
  USE Arachidic acid—Analogs
ICSH (Hormone)
  USE Luteinizing hormone
Ictaluridae
  ₍QL638.I3₎
  UF Ameiuridae
      Amiuridae
  BT Catfishes
  NT Ictalurus
      Noturus
Ictalurus
  ₍QL638.I3₎
  UF Ameiurus
      Bullheads, Freshwater
  BT Ictaluridae
Ictalurus melas
  USE Black bullhead

Ictalurus nebulosus
  USE Brown bullhead
Ictalurus punctatus
  USE Channel catfish
Icteridae
  ₍QL696.P2475₎
  BT Passeriformes
  NT Agelaius
      Blackbirds
      Icterus (Birds)
      Quiscalus
Icterohematuria
  USE Babesiosis in sheep
Icterus (Birds)
  ₍QL696.P2475₎
  UF New World orioles
      Orioles, New World
  BT Icteridae
      Orioles
  NT Northern oriole
Icterus (Pathology)
  USE Jaundice
Icterus abeillei
  USE Northern oriole
Icterus bullockii
  USE Northern oriole
Icterus galbula
  USE Northern oriole
Icterus neonatorum
  USE Jaundice, Neonatal
Icthybotidae
  USE Ephemeridae
Ictinia
  ₍QL696.F32₎
  BT Accipitridae
Ictinia mississippiensis
  USE Mississippi kite
Ictiobus
  USE Buffalo fish
Ictiobus bubalus
  USE Smallmouth buffalo
Ictops acutidens
  USE Leptictis acutidens
Id (Psychology)
  BT Psychoanalysis
      Psychology
'Id al-Adha sermons
  ₍BP183.66₎
  BT Islamic sermons
'Id al-Fiṭr
  ₍BP186.45₎
  UF Bairam
      'Id al-Ṣadaqah
      'Id al-Ṣaghīr
'Id al-Fiṭr sermons
  ₍BP183.645₎
  BT Islamic sermons
'Id al-Ghadīr *(May Subd Geog)*
  ₍BP186.9₎
  UF Ghadīr al-Khumm
  BT Fasts and feasts—Shī'ah
      Ghadīr
'Id al-Ṣadaqah
  USE 'Id al-Fiṭr
'Id al-Ṣaghīr
  USE 'Id al-Fiṭr
IDA (Computer system)
  UF Interactive Data Analysis (Computer
        system)
  BT Electronic digital computers—
        Programming
      Mathematical statistics—Data
        processing
Ida (Indic people)
  USE Idu (Indic people)
Ida Rosen Prize
  BT Music librarianship—Awards
Idaeidae
  USE Geometridae

Idafat
  USE *subdivision* Noun *under names of*
        languages and groups of languages
Idaho
  — **Antiquities**
    NT Wees Bar Site (Idaho)
  — **Description and travel**
  — — **1951-1980**
  — — **1981-**
Idaho Batholith (Idaho and Mont.)
  BT Batholiths—Idaho
      Batholiths—Montana
**Idaho National Engineering Laboratory
  Region (Idaho)**
Idalion (Ancient city)
  ₍DS54.95.I3₎
  UF Idalium (Ancient city)
      Idhalion (Ancient city)
  BT Cities and towns, Ruined, extinct, etc.
        —Cyprus
      Cyprus—Antiquities
Idalium (Ancient city)
  USE Idalion (Ancient city)
Idarnes *(May Subd Geog)*
  ₍QL568.T6₎
  BT Torymidae
IDAV (Virus)
  USE Human immunodeficiency viruses
'Idayd Mountain (Israel)
  USE Karkom Mountain (Israel)
Iddings family
  USE Eddings family
Iddingsite
  ₍QE391.I₎
IDDM
  USE Diabetes
Ide family *(Not Subd Geog)*
  UF Ides family
Ide-san (Japan)
  USE Iide Mountain (Japan)
Idea (Philosophy)
  ₍B398.I3 (Plato)₎
  UF Ideas, Theory of
      Ideas (Philosophy)
      Theory of ideas
  BT Knowledge, Theory of
      Philosophy
  NT Immaterialism (Philosophy)
      Innate ideas (Philosophy)
      One (The One in philosophy)
Idea (Philosophy) in art
Ideal beautiful women
  USE Feminine beauty (Aesthetics)
Ideal gas law
  UF Gas law
      Gas law, Ideal
  BT Chemistry, Physical and theoretical
      Gases
  RT Boyle's law
      Charles' law
Ideal Palace (Hauterives, France)
  USE Palais idéal (Hauterives, France)
Ideal states
  USE Utopias
Idealism
  ₍B823₎
  ₍B851-B4695 (By country)₎
  ₍B941 (United States)₎
  BT Animism
      Monism
      Personalism
      Philosophy
      Positivism
  RT Dualism
      Materialism
      Realism
      Transcendentalism
  NT Form (Philosophy)
      Immanence (Philosophy)
      Immaterialism (Philosophy)
      Neo-Kantianism

Pragmatism
    Vijñaptimātratā
    Yogācāra (Buddhism)
Idealism, American
    UF American idealism
Idealism, American, ⌜English, French, etc.⌝
Idealism, Chinese
    UF Chinese idealism
Idealism, English
    UF English idealism
Idealism, German
    UF German idealism
Idealism, Japanese
    UF Japanese idealism
Idealism in art *(May Subd Geog)*
    BT Aesthetics
        Art
    RT Naturalism in art
        Realism in art
        Romanticism in art
— **England**
        NT Ancients (Group of artists)
Idealism in literature
    ⌜PN56.I4⌝
    BT Aesthetics
    RT Naturalism in literature
        Realism in literature
        Romanticism
Ideals (Aesthetics)
    ⌜BH301.I3⌝
    BT Aesthetics
Ideals (Algebra)
    ⌜QA247⌝
    UF Algebraic ideals
    BT Fields, Algebraic
        Rings (Algebra)
    NT Alexander ideals
        Class groups (Mathematics)
        Divisor theory
        Jacobi sums
        Operator ideals
        Picard groups
        Torsion theory (Algebra)
— **Generators**
        UF Generators of ideals (Algebra)
Ideals (Philosophy)
    ⌜B105.I3⌝
    BT Philosophy
Ideals (Psychology)
    BT Concepts
        Exempla
    RT Example
Ideas, Association of
    USE Association of ideas
Ideas, Flight of
    USE Flight of ideas
Ideas, Reproduction of
    USE Reproduction (Psychology)
Ideas, Theory of
    USE Idea (Philosophy)
Ideas (Philosophy)
    USE Idea (Philosophy)
Ideha (Japan)
    USE Dewa (Japan)
'Ideid Mountain (Israel)
    USE Karkom Mountain (Israel)
Identification *(May Subd Geog)*
    ⌜GN192 (Anthropology)⌝
    ⌜HV8073 (Penology)⌝
    ⌜RA1055 (Medical jurisprudence)⌝
    RT Medical jurisprudence

    SA *subdivision* Identification *under classes
        of persons and subjects, e.g.*
        Adoptees—Identification; Firearms
        —Identification; Legal documents—
        Identification; *and under plants,
        animals, and types of objects as a
        topical subdivision or as a form
        subdivision for works that present
        the characteristics of a group for the
        purpose of determining the names
        of its members, e.g.* Amphibians—
        Identification
    NT Fingerprints
        Footprints
        Forensic anthropology
        Palmprints
        Teeth—Marking
        Voiceprints
— **Equipment and supplies**
        NT Personal identification products
            industry
Identification, Friend or foe (Electronic
    equipment)
    USE Airplanes—IFF equipment
Identification, System
    USE System identification
Identification (Greek law)
Identification (Psychology)
    BT Defense mechanisms (Psychology)
        Internalization
        Psychology
    NT Reference groups
Identification (Psychology) in children
    (May Subd Geog)
    BT Child psychology
Identification (Religion)
    ⌜BV4509.5⌝
    UF Identity (Religion)
        Self-realization (Religion)
    BT Man (Theology)
        Psychology, Religious
Identification cards *(May Subd Geog)*
    UF Cards, Identification
        I.D. cards
        Identity cards
— **Forgeries** *(May Subd Geog)*
— **Law and legislation** *(May Subd Geog)*
Identification marks on airplanes
    USE Airplanes—Identification marks
Identification marks on freight-cars
    USE Railroads—Freight-cars—Markings
Identification marks on military vehicles
    USE Vehicles, Military—Markings
Identification numbers, Personal
    (May Subd Geog)
    UF Person-numbers
        Personal identification numbers
Identification of animals
    USE *subdivision* Identification *under
        particular kinds of animals, e.g.*
        Fishes—Identification
        Animals—Identification
Identification of automobiles
    USE Automobiles—Identification
Identification of biological specimens
    USE Biological specimens—Identification
Identification of criminals
    USE Crime and criminals—Identification
Identification of documents
    USE Legal documents—Identification
Identification of firearms
    USE Firearms—Identification
Identification of handwriting
    USE Writing—Identification
Identification of plants
    USE *subdivision* Identification *under
        particular kinds of plants, e.g.* Fungi
        —Identification
        Plants—Identification
Identification of rocks
    USE Rocks—Identification

Identification of the dead
    USE Dead—Identification
Identification of typewriting
    USE Typewriting—Identification
Identification of wood
    USE Wood—Identification
Identification papers for employees
    USE Labor passports
Identification products industry, Personal
    USE Personal identification products
        industry
Identities, Combinatorial
    USE Combinatorial identities
Identity
    ⌜BC199.I4 (Logic)⌝
    ⌜BD236 (Theory of knowledge)⌝
    BT Comparison (Psychology)
        Individuality
        Knowledge, Theory of
        Logic
        Ontology
        Resemblance (Philosophy)
    NT Mind-brain identity theory
Identity, Collective
    USE Group identity
Identity, Community
    USE Group identity
Identity, Group
    USE Group identity
Identity, Jewish
    USE Jews—Identity
Identity, Loss of
    USE Depersonalization
Identity, Social
    USE Group identity
Identity (Psychology) *(May Subd Geog)*
    BT Personality
        Self
    RT Ego (Psychology)
    NT Gender identity disorders
        Group identity
        Stigma (Social psychology)
— **Testing**
        BT Personality tests
            Psychological tests
Identity (Psychology) in children
    (May Subd Geog)
    ⌜BF723.I56⌝
    BT Child psychology
Identity (Psychology) in motion pictures
    BT Moving-pictures
Identity (Religion)
    USE Identification (Religion)
Identity cards
    USE Identification cards
Ideography
    USE Chinese language—Writing
        Hieroglyphics
        Pasigraphy
        Picture-writing
Idéologues (French philosophers)
    BT Philosophers—France
Ideology
    BT Knowledge, Theory of
        Perception
        Philosophy
        Political science
        Psychology
        Senses and sensation
        Thought and thinking
— **Religious aspects**
— — **Buddhism, ⌜Christianity, etc.⌝**
Ideology and literature
    BT Literature
Ideophone
    USE Grammar, Comparative and general—
        Ideophone
Ides family
    USE Ide family
Idhalion (Ancient city)
    USE Idalion (Ancient city)

Idhra Island (Greece)
USE Hydra Island (Greece)
Idiacanthidae
[QL638.I35]
UF Black dragonfishes
Dragonfishes, Black
Stylophthalmidae
BT Salmoniformes
NT Idiacanthus
Idiacanthus
[QL638.I35]
BT Idiacanthidae
NT Idiacanthus anthrostomus
Idiacanthus anthrostomus
[QL638.I35]
BT Idiacanthus
Idigbo
USE Terminalia ivorensis
Idindji language
USE Yidin language
Idioceridae
USE Leafhoppers
Idiococcidae
USE Eriococcidae
Idiocy *(May Subd Geog)*
[HV891-HV901 (Children)]
[HV3004-HV3008 (Charities)]
[RC571]
UF Idiots
BT Mental retardation
Mentally handicapped
Idiodynamics *(May Subd Geog)*
[BF698.9.I34]
UF Idioverse
BT Environmental psychology
Personality
Idiomatic expressions
USE Idioms
Idiomaticity
USE Idioms
Idioms
UF Idiomatic expressions
Idiomaticity
BT Language and languages—Style
Linguistics
Phraseology
Semantics
SA *subdivision* Idioms *under individual*
languages and groups of languages,
e.g. English language—Idioms
Idiopathic femoral necrosis
(May Subd Geog)
[RC931.I3]
UF Aseptic femoral necrosis
Avascular femoral necrosis
Ischemic femoral necrosis
BT Femur—Diseases
Idiopathic hemorrhagic sarcoma
USE Kaposi's sarcoma
Idiopathic hypermetabolic hypoproteinemia
USE Protein-losing enteropathies
Idiopathic hypertension
USE Essential hypertension
Idiopholis
USE Pseudorabdion
Idiostomidae
USE Scarabaeidae
Idiot savants *(May Subd Geog)*
[RC570]
UF Idiots savants
Savants, Idiot
BT Mental retardation
Idiotopes, Immunoglobulin
USE Immunoglobulin idiotypes
Idiots
USE Idiocy
Idiots savants
USE Idiot savants
Idiotypes, Antibody
USE Immunoglobulin idiotypes

Idiotypes, Immunoglobulin
USE Immunoglobulin idiotypes
Idiotypic antibodies
USE Immunoglobulin idiotypes
Idiotypic immunoglobulins
USE Immunoglobulin idiotypes
Idioverse
USE Idiodynamics
Iditarod National Historic Trail (Alaska)
BT National parks and reserves—Alaska
Trails—Alaska
Iditarod Trail Sled Dog Race
[SF440.15]
UF Anchorage to Nome Sled Dog Race
BT Sled dog racing—Alaska
Idja language
USE Sigi language
Idlers
USE Flaneurs
IDMS (Computer system)
[QA76.9.D3]
UF Integrated Database Management
System (Computer system)
BT Data base management
Electronic digital computers—
Programming
IDMS/R (Computer system)
[QA76.9.D3]
UF Integrated Database Management
System/Relational (Computer
system)
BT Data base management
Ido
[PM8391-4]
BT Languages, Artificial
Ido (African language)
USE Ijo language
Idocrase
USE Vesuvianite
Idoeidae
USE Geometridae
Idolatry *(May Subd Geog)*
Here are entered works on the giving of absolute
religious devotion and ultimate trust to anything that
is not God, such as an idea, way of life, person, or
country. Works on the worship or veneration of a
physical object representing a god or person are en-
tered under Idols and images—Worship.
RT Idols and images—Worship
NT Gods—Biblical teaching
Ten commandments—Other gods
Idolocoris
USE Haematomyzus
Idolothripidae
USE Phlaeothripidae
Idols and images *(May Subd Geog)*
[NB960-NB1113 (Art)]
UF Iconography
Images and idols
Religious art
Statuettes
BT Animism
Art, Primitive
Art and religion
Fetishism
Magic
Religion, Primitive
Sculpture, Primitive
Symbolism
RT Gods in art
NT Golden calf (Bible)
Ming ch'i
Ushabti
— **Biblical teaching**
NT Ten commandments—Images
— **Costume and adornment**
UF Gods—Costume
— **Worship**
[BL485]

Here are entered works on the worship or
veneration of a physical object representing a god
or person. Works on the giving of absolute reli-
gious devotion and ultimate trust to anything
that is not God, such as an idea, way of life,
person or country are entered under Idolatry.
BT Worship
RT Idolatry
NT Gods—Biblical teaching
Gods in rabbinical literature
Iconoclasm
— — **Biblical teaching**
NT Ten commandments—Other
gods
— **Greece**
NT Xoana
Idoma (African people)
UF Agala (African people)
Akpoto (African people)
Igumale (African people)
Ochekwu (African people)
Okwoga (African people)
Oturkpo (African people)
BT Ethnology—Nigeria
— **Rites and ceremonies**
NT Funeral rites and ceremonies,
Idoma (African people)
Idoma (African people) funeral rites and
ceremonies
USE Funeral rites and ceremonies, Idoma
(African people)
Idoma drama *(May Subd Geog)*
Idoma language
[PL8263]
UF Oturkpo dialect
BT Kwa languages
Idongiro (African people)
USE Nyangatom (African people)
Idotea
[QL444.M34]
UF Idothea
BT Idoteidae
Idotea japonica
[QL444.M34]
Idotea metallica
[QL444.M34]
Idoteidae
[QL444.M34]
UF Idotheidae
BT Isopoda
NT Chiridotea
Cleantis
Erichsonella
Glyptonotus
Idotea
Ronalea
Synidotea
Idothea
USE Idotea
Idotheidae
USE Idoteidae
Idra Island (Greece)
USE Hydra Island (Greece)
IDS (Computer program language)
UF Integral Data Store
BT COBOL (Computer program language)
Idu (Indic people)
[DS432.I37]
UF Chilikota (Indic people)
Chulikata Mishmi (Indic people)
Ida (Indic people)
Midhi (Indic people)
Midu (Indic people)
BT Ethnology—India
Idu (Korean language)
USE Korean language—Writing—Idu
Idu language
[PL3801.I38]
UF Chulikata-Mishmi language
BT Tibeto-Burman languages

Iduna language
Idyllic poetry
  USE Pastoral poetry
Idzebu language
  USE Yebu language
Idzo language
  USE Ijo language
Idzumo (Japan)
  USE Izumo Region (Japan)
Iemanjá (Cultus)
  [BL2590.B7]
  UF Yemanjá (Cultus)
  BT Religion, Primitive
Iemoto
  [DS827.I35]
  BT Arts, Japanese
    Japan—Popular culture
    Japan—Social life and customs
    Teachers—Japan
  NT Tea masters
Ieniesī River (R.S.F.S.R.)
  USE Yenisey River (R.S.F.S.R.)
Ieper (Belgium), 1st Battle of, 1914
  USE Ypres, 1st Battle of, 1914
Ieper (Belgium), 2d Battle of, 1915
  USE Ypres, 2d Battle of, 1915
Ieper (Belgium), 3d Battle of, 1917
  USE Ypres, 3d Battle of, 1917
IESS (Electronic computer system)
  USE Interactive Express Statistical System
    (Electronic computer system)
Ietas Mountain (Sicily)
  USE Iato Mountain (Sicily)
Iezer Mountains (Romania)
  UF Munţii Iezer (Romania)
  BT Mountains—Romania
Ifa
  [BF1779.I4]
  BT Divination
    Geomancy
IFA trucks
  [TL230.5.I]
  BT Trucks
IFF systems
  USE Airplanes—IFF equipment
Iffland-Ring
  USE Ifflandring
Ifflandring
  UF Iffland-Ring
  BT Theater—Awards
IFPS (Computer system)
  UF Interactive Financial Planning System
    (Computer system)
  BT Business—Data processing
    Corporations—Finance—Data
      processing
    Electronic digital computers—
      Programming
IFR communications, Bilingual
  USE Air traffic control, Bilingual
Ifugao language
  [PL5725]
  BT Philippine languages
  NT Batad Ifugao dialect
Ifugaos
  [DS666.I15]
IgA
  USE Immunoglobulin A
IgA glomerulonephritis *(May Subd Geog)*
  [RC918.I35]
  UF Berger's disease
    IgA nephropathy
    Nephropathy, IgA
  BT Glomerulonephritis
  RT Immunoglobulin A
IgA nephropathy
  USE IgA glomerulonephritis
Iga pottery *(May Subd Geog)*
  UF Pottery, Iga
  BT Pottery, Japanese

Igabo (African people)
  USE Isoko (African people)
Igala (African people)
  [DT515.42]
  UF Igara (African people)
  BT Ethnology—Nigeria
Igala (African people) wood-carving
  USE Wood-carving, Igala (African people)
Igalikite
Igara (African people)
  USE Igala (African people)
Igbira language
  [PL8273]
  UF Ebira language
  BT Kwa languages
Igbo (African people)
  [DT515.42]
  UF Ibo (African people)
  BT Ethnology—Nigeria
  NT Missions to Igbo (African people)
  — Food
    BT Food
  — Women
    USE Women, Igbo (African people)
Igbo (African people) art
  USE Art, Igbo (African people)
Igbo (African people) arts
  USE Arts, Igbo (African people)
Igbo (African people) folk literature
  USE Folk literature, Igbo (African people)
Igbo (African people) mythology
  USE Mythology, Igbo (African people)
Igbo (African people) philosophy
  USE Philosophy, Igbo (African people)
Igbo (African people) women
  USE Women, Igbo (African people)
Igbo (African people) wood-carving
  USE Wood-carving, Igbo (African people)
Igbo drama *(May Subd Geog)*
  NT Folk-drama, Igbo
    Religious drama, Igbo
Igbo fiction *(May Subd Geog)*
  NT Short stories, Igbo
Igbo folk-drama
  USE Folk-drama, Igbo
Igbo folk poetry
  USE Folk poetry, Igbo
Igbo language
  UF Ibo language
  BT Kwa languages
    Nigeria—Languages
  NT Izi language
    Ngwa dialect
Igbo law
  USE Law, Igbo
Igbo poetry *(May Subd Geog)*
  NT Folk poetry, Igbo
Igbo proverbs
  USE Proverbs, Igbo
Igbo religious drama
  USE Religious drama, Igbo
Igbo short stories
  USE Short stories, Igbo
IgD
  USE Immunoglobulin D
Igdlorssuit (Greenland)
  USE Ubekendt Island (Greenland)
IgE
  USE Immunoglobulin E
Igede language
  BT Kwa languages
Igelites
  [TP986.I]
  BT Vinyl polymers
IgG
  USE Immunoglobulin G
Igilium Island (Italy)
  USE Giglio Island (Italy)
Igle family
  USE Eagle family

Igloolikmiut
  USE Iglulirmiut (Eskimo tribe)
Igloos
  UF Iglus
  BT Building, Ice and snow
    Dwellings
    Eskimos
Igluligmiut
  USE Iglulirmiut (Eskimo tribe)
Iglulingmiut
  USE Iglulirmiut (Eskimo tribe)
Iglulirmiut (Eskimo tribe)
  UF Igloolikmiut
    Igluligmiut
    Iglulingmiut
Iglus
  USE Igloos
IgM
  USE Immunoglobulin M
Ignaciano language
  BT Arawakan languages
    Bolivia—Languages
    Indians of South America—Bolivia—
      Languages
Ignatieff family *(Not Subd Geog)*
  UF Ignatiev family
Ignatiev family
  USE Ignatieff family
Igneous rocks
  USE Rocks, Igneous
Igneous rocks, Alkaline
  USE Alkalic igneous rocks
Igneri language
  USE Island Carib language
Ignimbrite *(May Subd Geog)*
  [QE462.I35]
  UF Welded tuff
  BT Volcanic ash, tuff, etc.
Ignis fatuus
  USE Will-o'-the-wisp
Ignition devices
  USE Automobiles—Ignition
    Internal combustion engines—Ignition
    Internal combustion engines, Spark
      ignition—Ignition
    Magneto
    Spark-plugs
Ignitrons
  BT Gas tubes
    Mercury-arc rectifiers
Ignorance (Canon law)
Ignorance (Law) *(May Subd Geog)*
  BT Criminal liability
    Guilt (Law)
  RT Good faith (Law)
    Mistake (Law)
Ignorance (Theory of knowledge)
  [BD221]
  BT Knowledge, Theory of
    Skepticism
Igo (Game)
  USE Go (Game)
Igorot
  [DS666.I2]
  UF Igorrotes
  NT Bontoks (Philippine people)
    Isneg
Igorot language
  [PL5731-4]
  UF Benguetano language
    Igorrote language
  BT Philippine languages
  NT Kankanay dialect
Igorrote language
  USE Igorot language
Igorrotes
  USE Igorot
Iguaçu National Park (Brazil)
  USE Parque Nacional do Iguaçu (Brazil)

Iguaçu River (Brazil and Argentina)
  (Not Subd Geog)
    UF Iguassú River (Brazil and Argentina)
        Iguazú River (Brazil and Argentina)
        Rio Iguaçu (Brazil and Argentina)
    BT Rivers—Argentina
        Rivers—Brazil
Iguana
  [QL666.L25]
    BT Iguanidae
Iguana, Banded
  USE Banded iguana
Iguana, Common
  USE Iguana iguana
Iguana, Marine
  USE Marine iguana
Iguana iguana
  [QL666.L25]
    UF Common iguana
        Green iguana
        Iguana, Common
Iguanidae
  [QL666.L25]
    BT Lizards
    NT Amblyrhynchus
        Anolis
        Basiliscus
        Brachylophys
        Corythophanes
        Crotaphytus
        Ctenoblepharis
        Ctenosaura
        Cyclura
        Holbrookia
        Horned toads
        Iguana
        Leiocephalus
        Liolaemus
        Norops
        Plica (Lizard)
        Sauromalus
        Sceloporus
        Stenocercus
        Strobilurus
        Tropidurus
        Uma
        Uracentron
        Uta
Iguanodectinae
  USE Characidae
Iguanodon
  [QE862.O65]
    UF Iguanosaurus
        Sphenospondylus
        Therosaurus
    BT Iguanodontidae
Iguanodontidae
  [QE862.O65]
    BT Ornithischia
    NT Iguanodon
Iguanosaurus
  USE Iguanodon
Iguape River (Brazil)
  USE Ribeira de Iguape River (Brazil)
Iguassú River (Brazil and Argentina)
  USE Iguaçu River (Brazil and Argentina)
Iguazú River (Brazil and Argentina)
  USE Iguaçu River (Brazil and Argentina)
Igulua (African people)
  USE Galwa (African people)
Igumale (African people)
  USE Idoma (African people)
Igusa
  USE Juncus effusus
Ih Gobiin barhan zaazpai gazar (Mongolia)
  (Not Subd Geog)
    UF Bol'shoĭ Gobĭĭskiĭ zapovednik
        (Mongolia)
    BT National parks and reserves—
        Mongolia
        Natural areas—Mongolia

Ihansalen
  USE Ahansala
IHC trucks
  [TL230.5.I]
    UF International Harvester trucks
        International trucks
    BT Trucks
    NT Scout automobile
Ihli family
  USE Ely family
Ihnnviertel (Austria)
  USE Innviertel (Austria)
Ihrig family *(Not Subd Geog)*
    RT Arey family
Iḥsā' Oasis (Saudi Arabia)
  USE Hasa Oasis (Saudi Arabia)
Ii family *(Not Subd Geog)*
Iide Mountain (Japan)
    UF Ide-san (Japan)
        Iide-yama (Japan)
        Tidēsan (Japan)
    BT Mountains—Japan
Iide Mountain Range (Japan)
    UF Iide rempō (Japan)
    BT Mountains—Japan
Iide rempō (Japan)
  USE Iide Mountain Range (Japan)
Iide-yama (Japan)
  USE Iide Mountain (Japan)
Iijima Seishi Strike, 1958
IITRAN (Computer program language)
    UF Illinois Institute of Technology
        translator (Computer program
        language)
Iiyama Peasant Uprising, Nagano-ken (Japan),
  1837
  USE Nagano-ken (Japan)—History—Iiyama
        Peasant Uprising, 1837
Ijabu language
  USE Yebu language
Ijaw (African people)
  USE Ijo (African people)
Ijaw language
  USE Ijo language
Ijca Indians
  [F2270.2.I5]
    BT Chibcha Indians
        Indians of South America
Ijca language
  USE Ica language
Ijebu language
  USE Yebu language
Ijiaura (Australian people)
  USE Alyawara (Australian people)
Ijina-shima (Japan)
  USE Izena Island (Japan)
Ijka language
  USE Ica language
Ijmā' (Islam)
  USE Authority (Islam)
        Islamic law—Interpretation and
        construction
Ijo (African people)
    UF Ijaw (African people)
        Kalabari (African people)
    BT Ethnology—Nigeria
Ijo language
  [PL8276]
    UF Bonny language
        Djo language
        Dzo language
        Ejo language
        Ido (African language)
        Idzo language
        Ijaw language
        Ijoh language
        Iyo language
        Ojo language
        Oru language
        Udzo language
    BT Kwa languages

    NT Kalabari dialect
        Kolokuma dialect
        Nembe language
        Okrika dialect
Ijoh language
  USE Ijo language
Ijsel Lake (Netherlands)
  USE IJssel Lake (Netherlands)
Ijsel River (Netherlands)
  USE IJssel River (Netherlands)
IJssel Lake (Netherlands)
    UF Ijsel Lake (Netherlands)
        Issel Lake (Netherlands)
        Ysel Lake (Netherlands)
        Yssel Lake (Netherlands)
        Zuider Zee (Netherlands)
        Zuyder Zee (Netherlands)
    BT Lakes—Netherlands
IJssel River (Netherlands)
    UF Ijsel River (Netherlands)
        Issel River (Netherlands)
        Ysel River (Netherlands)
        Yssel River (Netherlands)
    BT Rivers—Netherlands
IJssel River (Utrecht Province-South Holland,
  Netherlands)
  USE Hollandsche IJssel River (Netherlands)
Ijtihād (Islamic law)
  USE Islamic law—Interpretation and
        construction
Ik (African people)
  [DT433.245.I37]
    UF Teuso (African people)
    BT Ethnology—Kenya
        Ethnology—Sudan
        Ethnology—Uganda
Ikaria Island (Greece)
    UF Icaria Island (Greece)
        Kariot Island (Greece)
        Nicaria Island (Greece)
        Nikaria Island (Greece)
        Nísos Ikaría (Greece)
    BT Aegean Islands (Greece and Turkey)
        Islands—Greece
Ikarigaseki Ōzura Site (Japan)
  USE Ōzura Site (Japan)
Ikat *(May Subd Geog)*
    BT Resist-dyed textiles
Ike family *(Not Subd Geog)*
Ike language
  USE Ica language
Ikebana
  USE Flower arrangement, Japanese
Ikeda family *(Not Subd Geog)*
Ikedaji Ato (Izumi-shi, Japan)
  USE Ikedaji Site (Izumi-shi, Japan)
Ikedaji Site (Izumi-shi, Japan)
  (Not Subd Geog)
    UF Ikedaji Ato (Izumi-shi, Japan)
    BT Japan—Antiquities
Ikeleve language
  USE Kituba language
Ikenobō ikebana
  USE Flower arrangement, Japanese—
        Ikenobō school
Ikeshima Iseki (Japan)
  USE Ikeshima Site (Japan)
Ikeshima Site (Japan) *(Not Subd Geog)*
    UF Ikeshima Iseki (Japan)
    BT Japan—Antiquities
Ikeya-Seki comet
  [QB727]
Ikhshidids
    UF Ikshidids
    BT Egypt—History—640-1250
Ikhwān movement
    BT Saudi Arabia—History
        Wahhābīyah—Saudi Arabia
Iki-kukwe language
  USE Mwamba language

Iki-Zanaki language
USE Zanaki language
Ikikuria (African people)
USE Kuria (African people)
Ikinyi-Kiusa language
USE Ngonde language
IkiZanaki language
USE Zanaki language
Ikkō uprisings *(May Subd Geog)*
Iklig
[ML3730]
Ikoflex camera
[TR263]
BT Zeiss cameras
Ikola family *(Not Subd Geog)*
Ikona Bogomater' Donskaīa
USE Bogomater' Donskaīa (Icon)
Ikona Sviātoĭ i Chudotvornoĭ Iverskoĭ
Bogomateri
USE Iverskaīa Sviātaīa i Chudotvornaīa
Bogomater' (Icon)
Ikona Tikhvinskoĭ Bogomateri
USE Tikhvinskaīa Bogomater' (Icon)
Ikona Umilenīīa TSaritsy Nebesnoĭ
USE Umilenīīe TSaritsy Nebesnoĭ (Icon)
Ikona Uspenie
USE Uspenie (Icon)
Ikons
USE Icons
Ikonta camera
[TR263.I3]
BT Zeiss cameras
Ikounka
BT Berbers
Ethnology—Morocco
Ikposo language
USE Kposo language
Ikposso language
USE Kposo language
Ikshidids
USE Ikhshidids
Ikuhane language
USE Subiya language
Ikumigawa Dam (Japan) *(Not Subd Geog)*
BT Dams—Japan
Ikuno Uprising, 1863
[DS881.3]
BT Japan—History—Restoration, 1853-
1870
Ikuta (Name)
Ikwahani language
USE Subiya language
Ikwo language
BT Kwa languages
Il-76T (Jet transports)
USE Ilīūshin 76T (Jet transports)
Il Gallaratese (Milan, Italy)
USE Quartiere Gallaratese (Milan, Italy)
Il Montello (Italy)
USE Montello (Italy)
Ila (African people)
UF Baila (African people)
Bashukulompo (African people)
Mashukulumbwe (African people)
Shukulumbwe (African people)
Sukulumbwe (African people)
BT Bantus
Ethnology—Zambia
NT Lenje (African people)
Ila (African people) law
USE Law, Ila (African people)
Ila language
[PL8281]
BT Bantu languages
Tonga language (Zambesi)
Ilali language
USE Teke language
Ilamba language
USE Nilamba language
Ilaoquatsh Indians
USE Clayoquot Indians

Ilava dialect
USE Ezhava dialect
Ilavas
USE Ezhavas
Ile aux Coudres (Québec)
USE Coudres Island (Québec)
Ile-aux-Grues (Québec)
USE Crane Island (Québec)
Ile aux Noix (Québec)
UF Isle aux Noix (Québec)
BT Islands—Québec (Province)
Ile d'Anticosti (Québec)
USE Anticosti Island (Québec)
Ile d'Arguin (Mauritania)
USE Arguin Island (Mauritania)
Ile de Bendor (France)
USE Bendor (France)
Ile de Croix (France)
USE Groix Island (France)
Ile de Groix (France)
USE Groix Island (France)
Ile de la Camargue (France)
USE Camargue (France)
Ile de la Cité (Paris, France)
(Not Subd Geog)
UF Cité, Ile de la (Paris, France)
Paris (France). Ile de la Cité
BT Islands—France
Ile de la Recherce (Solomon Islands)
USE Vanikolo (Solomon Islands)
Ile de Montréal (Québec)
USE Montréal Island (Québec)
Ile de Noirmoutier (France)
USE Noirmoutier Island (France)
Île de Port-Cros (France)
USE Port-Cros Island (France)
Ile d'Oléron (France)
USE Oléron, Ile d' (France)
Ile d'Orléans (Québec)
USE Orléans, Isle of (Québec)
Ile d'Ouessant (France)
USE Ouessant Island (France)
Ile du Diable (French Guiana)
USE Devil's Island (French Guiana)
Ile d'Ufenau (Switzerland)
USE Ufenau Island (Switzerland)
Ile d'Yeu (France)
USE Yeu Island (France)
Ile Jésus (Québec)
USE Jesus Island (Québec)
Ile Méralab (Vanuatu)
USE Méré Lava (Vanuatu)
Ile Mururoa
USE Mururoa Atoll
Ile Mwerlav (Vanuatu)
USE Méré Lava (Vanuatu)
Ile Nouka-Hiva (Marquesas Islands)
USE Nuka Hiva (Marquesas Islands)
Ile Nuku-Hiva (Marquesas Islands)
USE Nuka Hiva (Marquesas Islands)
Ile Pic de l'Etoile (Vanuatu)
USE Méré Lava (Vanuatu)
Ile Saint-Louis (Paris, France)
(Not Subd Geog)
[DC752.I]
UF Paris (France). Ile Saint-Louis
Saint-Louis, Ile (Paris, France)
BT Islands—France
Ile Saint-Martin
USE Saint Martin
Ileal conduit surgery
BT Urinary diversion
Ileitis
USE Ileum—Diseases
Ileitis, Regional
USE Enteritis, Regional
Ileostomy
BT Enterostomy
Ileum—Surgery
— **Complications and sequelae**

Ilergetes
BT Iberians
Iles au Diable (French Guiana)
USE Safety Islands (French Guiana)
Iles de Désolation
USE Kerguelen Islands
Iles de Glénan (France)
USE Glénan Islands (France)
Iles de Glénans (France)
USE Glénan Islands (France)
Iles de la Société
USE Society Islands
Iles de Lérins (France)
USE Lérins Islands (France)
Iles d'Hyères (France)
USE Hyères Islands (France)
Iles d'Or (France)
USE Hyères Islands (France)
Iles du Salut (French Guiana)
USE Safety Islands (French Guiana)
Iles Froides
USE Prince Edward Islands
Iles-Glénans (France)
USE Glénan Islands (France)
Iles Kerguélen
USE Kerguelen Islands
Iles Marquises de Mendoça
USE Marquesas Islands
Ileum
BT Intestine, Small
— **Diseases** *(May Subd Geog)*
UF Ileitis
NT Enteritis, Regional
— **Surgery**
NT Ileostomy
Jejunoileal bypass
Ileus
USE Intestines—Obstructions
Ilex caroliniana
USE Ilex vomitoria
Ilex paraguensis
USE Mate (Tea)
Ilex vomitoria
[QK495.A67 (Botany)]
UF Carolina tea plant
Cassena
Cassina
Emetic holly
Ilex caroliniana
Yapa
Yapon
Yaupon
Youpon
BT Holly
NT Black drink
Ilha da Madeira (Madeira Islands)
USE Madeira (Madeira Islands)
Ilha da Taipai (Macao)
USE Taipa Island (Macao)
Ilha de Coloane (Macao)
USE Coloane Island (Macao)
Ilha de Marajó (Brazil)
USE Marajó Island (Brazil)
Ilha de Paquetá (Brazil)
USE Paquetá Island (Brazil)
Ilha de Santa Anna (Brazil)
USE Bananal Island (Brazil)
Ilha de Santa Catarina (Brazil)
USE Santa Catarina Island (Brazil)
Ilha de Santa Maria (Azores)
USE Santa Maria Island (Azores)
Ilha de São Jorge (Azores)
USE São Jorge Island (Azores)
Ilha de São Vicente (Brazil)
USE São Vicente Island (Brazil)
Ilha do Bananal (Brazil)
USE Bananal Island (Brazil)
Ilha Graciosa (Azores)
USE Graciosa Island (Azores)
Ilha Santa Catarina (Brazil)
USE Santa Catarina Island (Brazil)

Ilha Terceira (Azores)
  USE Terceira (Azores)
Ilhas Selvagens (Madeira Islands)
  USE Selvagens Islands (Madeira Islands)
Ili family
  USE Ely family
Il'ia Muromeťs (Bomber)
  UF Illia Mourometz (Bomber)
      Illya Mourometz (Bomber)
      Muromeťs (Bomber)
  BT Bombers
Iliac artery
  BT Arteries
  — Ligature
    BT Ligature (Surgery)
Iliac vein
    ₍QL835 (Anatomy)₎
    ₍QM191 (Human anatomy)₎
  BT Veins
Iliadhromia Island (Greece)
  USE Alónnisos Island (Greece)
Iliaura (Australian people)
  USE Alyawara (Australian people)
Iliaura language
  USE Alyawarra language
iLiku dialect
  USE Leko dialect
Ilimausak Mountain (Greenland)
  USE Ilimaussaq Mountain (Greenland)
Ilímaussak Mountain (Greenland)
  USE Ilimaussaq Mountain (Greenland)
Ilimaussaq Mountain (Greenland)
  UF Ilimausak Mountain (Greenland)
      Ilímaussak Mountain (Greenland)
  BT Mountains—Greenland
Ilimaussite (May Subd Geog)
    ₍QE391.I4₎
Ilindensko vŭstanie, 1903
  USE Macedonia—History—Uprising of
       1903
Iliodhrómia Island (Greece)
  USE Alónnisos Island (Greece)
Iliofemoral joint
  BT Femur
      Ilium
Ilion (Ancient city)
  USE Troy (Ancient city)
Iliopsoas muscle
Ilium (Ancient city)
  USE Troy (Ancient city)
Ilium
  BT Pelvis
  NT Iliofemoral joint
      Sacroiliac joint
  — Fracture
Iliūshin 62 (Jet transports)
  BT Iliūshin airplanes
      Jet transports
Iliūshin 76T (Jet transports)
    ₍TL686.I₎
  UF Il-76T (Jet transports)
  BT Iliūshin airplanes
      Jet transports
Iliūshin airplanes
    ₍TL686.I₎
  UF Ilyushin airplanes
  BT Airplanes
  NT Iliūshin 62 (Jet transports)
      Iliūshin 76T (Jet transports)
Ilkka family (Not Subd Geog)
Illahūn, Pyramid of (Egypt)
  USE Pyramid of Sesostris II (Egypt)
Illawarra District (N.S.W.)
    (Not Subd Geog)
Illegal aliens
  USE Aliens, Illegal
Illegal contracts (May Subd Geog)
  UF Contracts, Illegal
  BT Contracts
      Illegal juristic acts
      Nullity

RT Immoral contracts
Illegal contracts (Jewish law)
Illegal juristic acts (May Subd Geog)
  BT Illegality
      Juristic acts
      Nullity
  NT Illegal contracts
Illegal juristic acts (Roman law)
Illegal libraries (May Subd Geog)
  UF Libraries, Illegal
  BT Libraries
  RT Prohibited books
Illegal literature
  USE Underground literature
Illegal strikes
  USE Wildcat strikes
Illegality (May Subd Geog)
  UF Unlawfulness
  BT Criminal law
      Law
  NT Illegal juristic acts
      Justification (Law)
Illegality (Jewish law)
  BT Jewish law
Illegitimacy (May Subd Geog)
    ₍HB903.I6 (Statistics)₎
    ₍HQ998-HQ999₎
  UF Bastardy
      Legitimacy (Law)
  BT Parent and child (Law)
      Sex and law
  RT Paternity
  NT Acknowledgment of children
      Illegitimate children
      Legitimation of children
      Unmarried fathers
      Unmarried mothers
  — Conflict of laws
    USE Conflict of laws—Illegitimacy
Illegitimacy (Canon law)
Illegitimacy (Germanic law)
Illegitimacy (Islamic law) (May Subd Geog)
Illegitimacy (Jewish law)
  USE Mamzer
Illegitimacy and crime (May Subd Geog)
  UF Crime and illegitimacy
  BT Crime and criminals
Illegitimacy in literature
Illegitimate children (May Subd Geog)
    ₍HQ998-999₎
  UF Bastard children
      Children of unmarried mothers
  BT Children
      Illegitimacy
  RT Unmarried mothers
Iller River (Germany)
  BT Rivers—Germany (West)
Illes Medes (Spain)
  USE Medas Islands (Spain)
Illex
    ₍QL430.3.0₎
  BT Ommastrephidae
  NT Illex illecebrosus
Illex illecebrosus (May Subd Geog)
    ₍QL430.3.O5₎
  UF Ommastrephes argentinus
  BT Illex
Illia Mourometz (Bomber)
  USE Il'ia Muromeťs (Bomber)
Illiac computer
    ₍QA76.8.I5₎
    ₍TK7889.I5 (Engineering)₎
  UF Illinois automatic computer
      MISTIC (Computer)
  BT Electronic digital computers
  — Programming
    ₍QA76.8.I5₎
    NT GLYPNIR (Computer program
        language)
        IBAL (Computer program
        language)

Illiac III Basic Assembler Language
  USE IBAL (Computer program language)
Illiaura language
  USE Alyawarra language
Illiciales
  USE Magnoliales
Illicit coining
  USE Counterfeits and counterfeiting
Illicit distilling
  USE Distilling, Illicit
ILLINET (Local area network system)
    ₍TK5105.8.I44₎
  BT Local area networks (Computer
      networks)
Illing family (Not Subd Geog)
  UF Jiling family
Illinium
  USE Promethium
Illinoia pisi
  USE Pea aphid
Illinois
  — Antiquities
    NT Archie Site (Ill.)
        BBB Motor Site (Ill.)
        Bonnie Creek Site (Ill.)
        Bridges Site (Ill.)
        Campbell Hollow Site (Ill.)
        Carbon Dioxide Site (Ill.)
        Columbia Quarry Site (Ill.)
        Cypress Land Site (Ill.)
        Deer Track Site (Ill.)
        Deere Creek Site (Ill.)
        DeMange Site (Ill.)
        Dickson Camp Site (Ill.)
        Dickson Mounds Site (Ill.)
        Dohack Site (Ill.)
        Dyroff Site (Ill.)
        East Saint Louis Stone Quarry Site
          (Ill.)
        Fish Lake Site (Ill.)
        Florence Street Site (Cahokia, Ill.)
        George Reeves Site (Ill.)
        Go-Kart North Site (Ill.)
        Hill Creek Site (Ill.)
        Hog Bluff Site (Ill.)
        Julien Site (Cahokia, Ill.)
        Kingfish Site (Ill.)
        Koster Site (Ill.)
        Kruse Bluffbase No. 3 Site (Ill.)
        Labras Lake Site (Ill.)
        Levin Site (Ill.)
        Massey Site (Ill.)
        McLean Site (Ill.)
        Milar Site (Ill.)
        Missouri Pacific Number 2 Site
          (Ill.)
        Moss Site (Ill.)
        Mund Site (Ill.)
        Napoleon Hollow Site (Ill.)
        Pond Site (Ill.)
        Range Site (Ill.)
        Riebling Site No. 1 (Ill.)
        Robinson's Lake Site (Ill.)
        Roos Site (Ill.)
        Schild Site (Ill.)
        Smiling Dan Site (Ill.)
        Turner Site (Ill.)
  — Description and travel
  — — To 1865
  — — 1865-1950
  — — 1951-1980
  — — 1981-
  — History
    ₍F536-550₎
  — — To 1778
  — — 1778-1865
  — — War of 1812
  — — Black Hawk War, 1832
        USE Black Hawk War, 1832
  — — Civil War, 1861-1865
    ₍E505₎

— —1865-
— Politics and government
— —To 1865
— —Civil War, 1861-1865
— —1865-1950
— —1951-
— Public buildings
  USE Public buildings—Illinois
— Statistics, Medical
  NT Illinois Cooperative Health
      Information System
Illinois and Michigan Canal (Ill.)
  BT Canals—Illinois
Illinois and Michigan Canal National
  Heritage Corridor (Ill.)
  BT Canals—Illinois
      Historic sites—Illinois
Illinois automatic computer
  USE Illiac computer
Illinois Central Gulf Railroad
  BT Railroads—United States
Illinois Computing Graphics System
  (Electronic computer system)
  USE ICGS (Electronic computer system)
Illinois Cooperative Health Information
  System
  [RA407.4.I3]
  BT Illinois—Statistics, Medical
      Public health—Illinois—Statistical
        services
Illinois Indians
  [E99.I2]
  BT Algonquian Indians
      Indians of North America
  NT Kaskaskia Indians
— Land transfers
    [F542]
— Missions
    [E99.I2]
Illinois Institute of Technology translator
  (Computer program language)
  USE IITRAN (Computer program language)
Illinois language
  [PM1371]
  RT Algonquian languages
Illinois mud turtle
  USE Kinosternon flavescens
Illinois River (Ark. and Okla.)
  BT Rivers—Arkansas
      Rivers—Oklahoma
Illinois River (Ill.)
  BT Rivers—Illinois
Illinois test of psycholinguistic abilities
  UF ITPA
  BT Children—Language—Testing
      Handicapped children—Testing
      Language and languages—Ability
        testing
      Psycholinguistics—Ability testing
Illinois Urban High Crime Reduction Program
  BT Crime prevention—Illinois
      Law enforcement—Illinois
ILLIP (Computer program)
Illite (May Subd Geog)
  BT Clay
      Mica
      Mineralogy
      Silicates
Illiteracy
  USE Literacy
Illiterate, Public library services to the
  USE Public libraries—Services to the
      illiterate
Illness
  USE Diseases
Illness behavior
  USE Sick—Psychology
Illocutionary acts (Linguistics)
  USE Speech acts (Linguistics)

ILLOD-(AND-OR-B) (Computer program)
ILLOD-(ANDOR-B) (Computer program)
ILLOD-(NOR-B) (Computer program)
  BT Switching theory
ILLODIE-AIF (Computer program)
Illuminati (May Subd Geog)
  [HS142]
  BT Mysticism
  NT Alumbrados
      Enlightenment
Illuminating gas
  USE Gas
Illumination
  USE Lighting
Illumination (Buddhism)
  USE Enlightenment (Buddhism)
Illumination of books and manuscripts
  (May Subd Geog)
  [ND2890-3416]
  UF Manuscripts, Illuminated
      Miniatures (Illumination of books and
        manuscripts)
      Ornamental alphabets
  BT Art
      Art, Medieval
      Arts and crafts movement
      Books
      Decoration and ornament
      Illustration of books
      Painting
  RT Alphabets
      Initials
      Manuscripts
      Missals
      Paleography
  NT Exultet rolls
      Hours, Books of
      Miniature painting
      Scriptoria
— Exhibitions
    [ND2893]
    RT Bibliographical exhibitions
— Egypt
    NT Illumination of books and
        manuscripts, Mameluke
Illumination of books and manuscripts,
  Albanian (May Subd Geog)
  UF Albanian illumination of books and
      manuscripts
Illumination of books and manuscripts,
  Ancient
Illumination of books and manuscripts, Anglo-
  Saxon (May Subd Geog)
  UF Anglo-Saxon illumination of books and
      manuscripts
— Byzantine influences
    BT Byzantine Empire—Civilization
Illumination of books and manuscripts, Arabic
  (May Subd Geog)
  UF Arabic illumination of books and
      manuscripts
Illumination of books and manuscripts,
  Armenian (May Subd Geog)
  UF Armenian illumination of books and
      manuscripts
— Syrian influences
    BT Syria—Civilization
Illumination of books and manuscripts,
  Austrian (May Subd Geog)
  UF Austrian illumination of books and
      manuscripts
Illumination of books and manuscripts,
  Bulgarian (May Subd Geog)
  UF Bulgarian illumination of books and
      manuscripts
Illumination of books and manuscripts,
  Byzantine (May Subd Geog)
  UF Byzantine illumination of books and
      manuscripts

Illumination of books and manuscripts,
  Carlovingian (May Subd Geog)
  UF Carlovingian illumination of books and
      manuscripts
Illumination of books and manuscripts, Celtic
  (May Subd Geog)
  UF Celtic illumination of books and
      manuscripts
Illumination of books and manuscripts,
  Cistercian (May Subd Geog)
  UF Cistercian illumination of books and
      manuscripts
Illumination of books and manuscripts, Coptic
  (May Subd Geog)
  UF Coptic illumination of books and
      manuscripts
— Arab influences
    BT Civilization, Arab
— Islamic influences
    BT Civilization, Islamic
Illumination of books and manuscripts, Czech
  (May Subd Geog)
  UF Czech illumination of books and
      manuscripts
— Italian influences
    BT Italy—Civilization
— Ottonian influences
    [ND3399.C]
    BT Holy Roman Empire—Civilization
Illumination of books and manuscripts, Dutch
  (May Subd Geog)
  UF Dutch illumination of books and
      manuscripts
Illumination of books and manuscripts, Early
  Christian (May Subd Geog)
  UF Early Christian illumination of books
      and manuscripts
Illumination of books and manuscripts,
  English, [German, Spanish, etc.]
  (May Subd Geog)
Illumination of books and manuscripts,
  Flemish (May Subd Geog)
  UF Flemish illumination of books and
      manuscripts
Illumination of books and manuscripts, French
  (May Subd Geog)
  UF French illumination of books and
      manuscripts
Illumination of books and manuscripts,
  Georgian
  USE Illumination of books and manuscripts,
      Georgian (Georgian S.S.R.)
Illumination of books and manuscripts,
  Georgian (Georgian S.S.R.)
  (May Subd Geog)
  UF Georgian (Georgian S.S.R.)
      illumination of books and
      manuscripts
      Illumination of books and manuscripts,
      Georgian
Illumination of books and manuscripts,
  German (May Subd Geog)
  UF German illumination of books and
      manuscripts
Illumination of books and manuscripts, Gothic
  (May Subd Geog)
  UF Gothic illumination of books and
      manuscripts
Illumination of books and manuscripts, Hebrew
  USE Illumination of books and manuscripts,
      Jewish
Illumination of books and manuscripts,
  Icelandic (May Subd Geog)
  UF Icelandic illumination of books and
      manuscripts
Illumination of books and manuscripts, Indic
  (May Subd Geog)
  UF Indic illumination of books and
      manuscripts
  NT Deccani painting
— Iranian influences

Illumination of books and manuscripts, Indic
— Iranian influences (Continued)
    BT Iran—Civilization
Illumination of books and manuscripts,
Iranian (May Subd Geog)
  UF Iranian illumination of books and
       manuscripts
Illumination of books and manuscripts,
Islamic (May Subd Geog)
  [ND2955]
  UF Illumination of books and manuscripts,
       Muslim
       Islamic illumination of books and
         manuscripts
       Muslim illumination of books and
         manuscripts
  — Egypt
    NT Illumination of books and
        manuscripts, Mameluke
Illumination of books and manuscripts, Italian
(May Subd Geog)
  UF Italian illumination of books and
       manuscripts
Illumination of books and manuscripts, Jaina
(May Subd Geog)
  UF Jaina illumination of books and
       manuscripts
Illumination of books and manuscripts, Jewish
(May Subd Geog)
  UF Hebrew illumination of books and
       manuscripts
       Illumination of books and manuscripts,
        Hebrew
       Jewish illumination of books and
        manuscripts
Illumination of books and manuscripts,
Mameluke (May Subd Geog)
  UF Mameluke illumination of books and
       manuscripts
  BT Illumination of books and manuscripts
      —Egypt
      Illumination of books and manuscripts,
       Islamic—Egypt
Illumination of books and manuscripts,
Medieval (May Subd Geog)
  BT Painting, Medieval
Illumination of books and manuscripts,
Mennonite (May Subd Geog)
  UF Fraktur art
      Mennonite illumination of books and
       manuscripts
Illumination of books and manuscripts, Mogul
(May Subd Geog)
  UF Mogul illumination of books and
       manuscripts
Illumination of books and manuscripts,
Mozarabic (May Subd Geog)
  UF Mozarabic illumination of books and
       manuscripts
Illumination of books and manuscripts, Muslim
  USE Illumination of books and manuscripts,
       Islamic
Illumination of books and manuscripts,
Norman (May Subd Geog)
  UF Norman illumination of books and
       manuscripts
Illumination of books and manuscripts, Norse
(May Subd Geog)
  UF Norse illumination of books and
       manuscripts
Illumination of books and manuscripts,
Oriental
  UF Oriental illumination of books and
       manuscripts
Illumination of books and manuscripts,
Ottonian (May Subd Geog)
  UF Ottonian illumination of books and
       manuscripts

Illumination of books and manuscripts,
Pennsylvania Dutch (May Subd Geog)
  UF Pennsylvania Dutch illumination of
       books and manuscripts
Illumination of books and manuscripts, Polish
(May Subd Geog)
  UF Polish illumination of books and
       manuscripts
Illumination of books and manuscripts,
Portuguese (May Subd Geog)
  UF Portuguese illumination of books and
       manuscripts
Illumination of books and manuscripts,
Renaissance (May Subd Geog)
  UF Renaissance illumination of books and
       manuscripts
Illumination of books and manuscripts, Roman
(May Subd Geog)
  UF Roman illumination of books and
       manuscripts
Illumination of books and manuscripts,
Romanesque (May Subd Geog)
  UF Romanesque illumination of books and
       manuscripts
  — Byzantine [etc.] influences
  — Italian influences
    BT Italy—Civilization
  — Ottonian influences
    [ND3399.C]
    BT Holy Roman Empire—Civilization
Illumination of books and manuscripts,
Romanian (May Subd Geog)
  UF Romanian illumination of books and
       manuscripts
  — Byzantine influences
    BT Byzantine Empire—Civilization
Illumination of books and manuscripts,
Russian (May Subd Geog)
  UF Russian illumination of books and
       manuscripts
Illumination of books and manuscripts,
Serbian (May Subd Geog)
  UF Serbian illumination of books and
       manuscripts
Illumination of books and manuscripts,
Silesian (May Subd Geog)
  UF Silesian illumination of books and
       manuscripts
Illumination of books and manuscripts,
Southern Slavic (May Subd Geog)
  [ND3215]
  UF Southern Slavic illumination of books
       and manuscripts
  — Byzantine influences
    BT Byzantine Empire—Civilization
Illumination of books and manuscripts, Swiss
(May Subd Geog)
  UF Swiss illumination of books and
       manuscripts
Illumination of books and manuscripts, Syrian
(May Subd Geog)
  UF Syrian illumination of books and
       manuscripts
  — Armenian influences
    BT Armenia—Civilization
Illumination of books and manuscripts, Thai
(May Subd Geog)
  UF Thai illumination of books and
       manuscripts
Illumination of books and manuscripts,
Turkish (May Subd Geog)
  UF Turkish illumination of books and
       manuscripts
  — Iranian influences
    BT Iran—Civilization
Illumination of books and manuscripts,
Visigothic (May Subd Geog)
  UF Visigothic illumination of books and
       manuscripts
Illusion (Philosophy)
  [B105.I44]

  BT Hallucinations and illusions
      Knowledge, Theory of
      Philosophy
Illusion in literature
  BT Aesthetics
      Fictions, Theory of
  RT Reality in literature
  NT Disguise in literature
      Role playing in literature
Illusions
  USE Hallucinations and illusions
Illusions, Optical
  USE Optical illusions
Illusions (Buddhism)
  USE Vice (Buddhism)
Illustrated bookbindings
  USE Bookbinding—Pictorial bindings
Illustrated books (May Subd Geog)
  [Z1023]
  UF Books, Illustrated
  BT Illustration of books
  NT Artists' illustrated books
      Emblem books
      Hours, Books of
      Toy and movable books
  — 15th and 16th centuries
  — 17th century
  — 18th century
  — 19th century
  — 20th century
  — Extra-illustrated
    UF Extra-illustrated books
       Grangerism
    BT Privately printed books
       Rare books
  — Japan
  — — 17th century
      NT Tanrokubon
Illustrated books, Artists'
  USE Artists' illustrated books
Illustrated books, Children's
(May Subd Geog)
  UF Children's books
      Children's illustrated books
      Illustrated children's books
  BT Children's literature
      Children's paraphernalia
  RT Picture-books for children
  NT Caldecott medal books
      Regina medal books
      Toy and movable books
Illustrated children's books
  USE Illustrated books, Children's
Illustrated periodicals (May Subd Geog)
  UF Periodicals, Illustrated
  BT Journalism, Pictorial
      Photography, Journalistic
  RT Newspapers—Illustrations
  NT Magazine illustration
Illustrated periodicals in education
(May Subd Geog)
  [LB1044.9.I44]
  BT Teaching—Aids and devices
      Visual education
Illustration, Biological
  USE Biological illustration
Illustration, Botanical
  USE Botanical illustration
Illustration, Courtroom
  USE Courtroom art
Illustration, Magazine
  USE Magazine illustration
Illustration, Medical
  USE Medical illustration
Illustration, Scientific
  USE Scientific illustration
Illustration, Technical
  USE Technical illustration
Illustration, Zoological
  USE Zoological illustration

Illustration of books *(May Subd Geog)*
⌐NC960-NC996¬
⌐NC975-NC995 (By country)¬
  UF Book illustration
      Books, Illustrated
  BT Art
      Books
      Decoration and ornament
      Pictures
  SA *subdivision* Illustrations *under*
      literatures, literary forms, names of
      individual authors, and individual
      works (author-title or title entries)
      or subjects, e.g. English literature—
      Illustrations; Shakespeare, William,
      1564-1616—Illustrations;
      Shakespeare, William, 1564-1616.
      Hamlet—Illustrations; Beowulf—
      Illustrations; Bible—Illustrations
  NT Archaeological illustration
      Drawing
      Engraving
      Illumination of books and manuscripts
      Illustrated books
      Photomechanical processes
      Scientific illustration
      Technical illustration
  — **15th century** *(May Subd Geog)*
  — **16th century** *(May Subd Geog)*
  — **17th century** *(May Subd Geog)*
  — **18th century** *(May Subd Geog)*
  — **19th century** *(May Subd Geog)*
  — **20th century** *(May Subd Geog)*
  — **Exhibitions**
      ⌐NC15¬
      RT Bibliographical exhibitions
          Book industries and trade—
          Exhibitions
  — Subjects
      USE Illustration of books—Themes,
          motives
  — **Themes, motives**
      UF Illustration of books—Subjects
  — **Japan**
  — — **Edo period, 1600-1868**
Illustrations, Homiletical
  USE Homiletical illustrations
Illustrations, Humorous
  USE Caricatures and cartoons
      Wit and humor, Pictorial
Illustrators *(May Subd Geog)*
  ⌐NC¬
  BT Artists
  NT Fashion illustrators
      Science fiction illustrators
      Scientific illustrators
      Wages—Illustrators
Illustrators, Fashion
  USE Fashion illustrators
Illustrious people
  USE Celebrities
Illya Mourometz (Bomber)
  USE Il'ia Muromets (Bomber)
Illyowra language
  USE Alyawarra language
Illyria
  UF Illyricum
Illyrian antiquities
  UF Antiquities, Illyrian
      Illyrians—Antiquities
  BT Antiquities
Illyrian funeral rites and ceremonies
  USE Funeral rites and ceremonies, Illyrian
Illyrian language (Slavic)
  USE Serbo-Croatian language
Illyrian languages
  ⌐PA2393¬
  BT Indo-European languages
  NT Messapian language
      Venetic language

Illyrian movement
  USE Illyrism
Illyrian wars
  ⌐DG246¬
  BT Rome—History—Republic, 265-30
      B.C.
Illyrians
  ⌐D90.I3¬
  BT Indo-Europeans
  NT Peucetii (Illyrian people)
      Veneti (Italic people)
  — Antiquities
      USE Illyrian antiquities
Illyricum
  USE Illyria
Illyrism
  ⌐DB370.5¬
  UF Illyrian movement
  BT Languages—Political aspects
      Panslavism
Ilmenite *(May Subd Geog)*
  UF Geikielite
      Menacantite
      Menaccanite
      Menachanite
      Titanic iron ore
  BT Gems
      Iron ores
      Titanium ores
  NT Titanium dioxide
Ilocano language
  USE Iloko language
Ilocanos
  USE Ilokanos
Iloco language
  USE Iloko language
Ilokano language
  USE Iloko language
Ilokanos
  ⌐DS666.I6¬
  UF Ilocanos
Iloko fiction *(May Subd Geog)*
Iloko language
  ⌐PL5751-4¬
  UF Ilocano language
      Iloco language
      Ilokano language
  BT Philippine languages
  NT Nabaloi dialect
Iloko literature
  ⌐PL5751¬
  NT Iloko poetry
Iloko poetry *(May Subd Geog)*
  BT Iloko literature
Ilomba
  ⌐SD397.14¬
  UF Akomu
      Boxboard (Tree)
      Cardboard (Tree)
Ilongo language
  USE Hiligaynon language
Ilongot (Philippine tribe)
  ⌐DS666.I4¬
Ilongot language
  ⌐PL5771¬
  BT Philippine languages
Iloprost *(May Subd Geog)*
  UF ZK 36374 (Drug)
  BT Prostacyclin—Derivatives
Ilot n. 6 (Paris, France) *(Not Subd Geog)*
  UF Paris (France). Ilot n. 6
ILS
  USE Instrument landing systems
Ilumbu language
  USE Lumbu language (Gabon)
Ilyarachnidae
  ⌐QL444.M34¬
  BT Isopoda
Ilyauarra (Australian people)
  USE Alyawara (Australian people)

Ilyocryptus *(May Subd Geog)*
  ⌐QL444.B83¬
  BT Macrothricidae
Ilyophidae
  USE Synaphobranchidae
Ilyuarra language
  USE Alyawarra language
Ilyushin airplanes
  USE Iliūshin airplanes
Imafuku Iseki (Kitaarima-chō, Japan)
  USE Imafuku Site (Kitaarima-chō, Japan)
Imafuku Site (Kitaarima-chō, Japan)
  UF Imafuku Iseki (Kitaarima-chō, Japan)
  BT Japan—Antiquities
Imagawa family *(Not Subd Geog)*
Image, Body
  USE Body image
Image (Theology)
  BT Christian art and symbolism
      Communication—Religious aspects—
      Christianity
  NT Image of God
  — **Catholic Church**
      ⌐BX2312¬
IMAGE/3000 (Computer system)
  BT Data base management
      Electronic digital computers—
      Programming
Image converters
  ⌐TK7872.I6¬
  UF Electron image converter tubes
      Image tubes
  BT Electron optics
      Electron tubes
      Image intensifiers
      Imaging systems
      Photoelectronic devices
  NT Infrared image converters
Image converters, Infrared
  USE Infrared image converters
Image furnaces
  UF Arc image furnaces
      Optical furnaces
  BT Furnaces
Image iconoscope
  ⌐TR882¬
  UF Television pick-up tubes
  BT Cathode ray tubes
      Electron optics
      Image intensifiers
      Imaging systems
      Television camera tubes
      Television cameras
Image intensifiers
  BT Electroluminescence
      Electron optics
      Electron tubes
      Imaging systems
      Information display systems
      Phosphorescence
      Photoelectronic devices
  RT Electronography
  NT Electron microscope
      Image converters
      Image iconoscope
      Starlight scopes
      Television camera tubes
      Television picture tubes
Image of God
  UF God—Image
      God, Image of
  BT God
      Image (Theology)
      Man (Theology)
  — **Early works to 1900**
  — **History of doctrines**
Image processing
  UF Pictorial data processing
      Picture processing
      Processing, Image

1793

Image processing *(Continued)*
  BT Imaging systems
      Optical data processing
  NT Computer vision
      Images, Photographic
  — Digital techniques
    UF Digital image processing
    BT Digital electronics
  — Equipment and supplies
    NT Image processing equipment
        industry
Image processing equipment industry
  (May Subd Geog)
  BT Image processing—Equipment and
      supplies
Image quality in imaging systems
  USE Imaging systems—Image quality
Image quality in medical radiography
  USE Radiography, Medical—Image quality
Image quality in radiography
  USE Radiography—Image quality
Image quality in ultrasonic diagnosis
  USE Diagnosis, Ultrasonic—Image quality
Image quality of microfiches
  USE Microfiches—Image quality
Image quality of television cameras
  USE Television cameras—Image quality
Image transmission
  [TK5105.2]
  UF Picture transmission
  BT Imaging systems
      Optical data processing
      Telecommunication
  NT Automatic picture transmission
      Facsimile transmission
      Television—Transmitters and
        transmission
      Video telephone
Image tubes
  USE Image converters
Imagery
  USE Figures of speech
Imagery, Eidetic
  USE Eidetic imagery
Imagery, Mental
  USE Imagery (Psychology)
      Imagination
Imagery (Psychology)
  [BF367]
  UF Imagery, Mental
      Images, Mental
      Mental imagery
      Mental images
  BT Imagination
  RT Visualization
  NT After-images
      Archetype (Psychology)
      Body image
      Eidetic imagery
      Figural aftereffects
Imagery (Psychology) in children
  (May Subd Geog)
  [BF723.I47]
  BT Child psychology
      Cognition in children
Images, Mental
  USE Imagery (Psychology)
      Imagination
Images, Mirror
  USE Mirror images
Images, Optical
  UF Optical images
  BT Optics, Geometrical
      Optics, Physiological
      Visual perception
  NT Images, Photographic
      Mirror images
      Photoferroelectric effect
Images, Photographic
  [TR222]
  UF Photographic images

  BT Image processing
      Images, Optical
      Imaging systems
      Photography
  NT Microfiches—Image quality
Images and idols
  USE Idols and images
Imaginal buds
  USE Imaginal disks
Imaginal cells
  USE Imaginal disks
Imaginal communication
  USE Visual communication
Imaginal dialogues
  USE Imaginary conversations
Imaginal disks
  [QL494.5]
  UF Cells, Imaginal
      Disks, Imaginal
      Imaginal buds
      Imaginal cells
  BT Insects—Larvae
      Insects—Metamorphosis
Imaginary animals
  USE Animals, Mythical
Imaginary battles
  USE Imaginary wars and battles
Imaginary book-plates
  USE Book-plates, Imaginary
Imaginary books and libraries
  [Z1024]
  UF Books, Imaginary
      Imaginary libraries
      Libraries, Imaginary
      Libraries and imaginary books
  BT Libraries
  RT Literary forgeries and mystifications
Imaginary cities
  USE Geographical myths
Imaginary conversations
  UF Conversation, Imaginal
      Conversation, Imaginary
      Dialogues, Imaginal
      Imaginal dialogues
  BT Conversation
      Dialogues
  NT Imaginary conversations in children
Imaginary conversations in children
  (May Subd Geog)
  [BF723.I49 (Child psychology)]
  BT Fantasy in children
      Imaginary conversations
Imaginary forensic orations
  USE Forensic orations, Imaginary
Imaginary histories
  UF History, Imaginary
  RT History—Errors, inventions, etc.
Imaginary imprints
  USE Imprints (in books), Fictitious
Imaginary islands
  USE Geographical myths
Imaginary languages
  UF English language—Imaginary histories
      Language, Imaginary
      Language and languages—Errors,
        inventions, etc.
      Languages, Imaginary
  BT Language and languages
      Languages, Artificial
Imaginary languages in literature
  BT Language and languages
Imaginary letters
  UF Letters, Imaginary
  BT Letters
  NT Heroid
Imaginary libraries
  USE Imaginary books and libraries
Imaginary places
  USE Geographical myths
Imaginary quantities
  USE Numbers, Complex

Imaginary revolutions
  UF Revolutions, Imaginary
  BT Imaginary wars and battles
      Revolutions
Imaginary societies
  UF Fictitious societies
      Societies, Imaginary
  BT Societies
Imaginary travels
  USE Voyages, Imaginary
Imaginary voyages
  USE Voyages, Imaginary
Imaginary wars and battles
  [D445 (World politics)]
  [JX1964 (Peace literature)]
  [U313]
  [UA (Military situation in special
      countries)]
  [V253 (Naval)]
  UF Imaginary battles
      Wars and battles, Imaginary
  BT Battles
      Military art and science
      Naval art and science
      War
  NT Dropshot Plan
      Imaginary revolutions
      Prophecies
Imagination
  [BF408]
  [N61-N79 (Artistic)]
  UF Imagery, Mental
      Images, Mental
      Mental imagery
      Mental images
  BT Educational psychology
      Intellect
      Psychology
  RT Reproduction (Psychology)
  NT Creation (Literary, artistic, etc.)
      Fantasy
      Imagery (Psychology)
      Originality
      Originality (in literature)
      Visualization
  — Religious aspects
  — — Buddhism, [Christianity, etc.]
Imagination (Philosophy)
  [BH301.I53]
  BT Philosophy
Imagination in children
  [BF723.I5]
  BT Child psychology
Imaging, Acoustic
  USE Acoustic imaging
Imaging, Diagnostic
  USE Diagnostic imaging
Imaging, Magnetic resonance
  USE Magnetic resonance imaging
Imaging, Microwave
  USE Microwave imaging
Imaging, Ultrasonic
  USE Ultrasonic imaging
Imaging of the heart
  USE Heart—Imaging
Imaging systems
  BT Optics
      Optoelectronic devices
      Photoelectronic devices
      Remote sensing—Equipment and
        supplies
  RT Scanning systems
  NT Acoustic imaging
      Catadioptric systems
      Electron bombardment conductivity
      Hadamard transform spectroscopy
      Image converters
      Image iconoscope
      Image intensifiers
      Image processing
      Image transmission

Images, Photographic
Infrared imaging
Laser recording
Microwave imaging
Photoferroelectric effect
Synthetic aperture radar
Synthetic apertures
— Image quality
UF Image quality in imaging systems
Imaging systems in astronomy
UF Astronomical imaging systems
BT Astronomical instruments
Imaging systems in biology
(May Subd Geog)
UF Biological imaging systems
BT Biology
Imaging systems in genetics
UF Genetical imaging systems
BT Genetics—Instruments
Genetics—Technique
Imaging systems in medicine
[R857.O6]
UF Medical imaging systems
BT Medical instruments and apparatus
NT Diagnostic imaging
Photography, Medical
— Equipment and supplies
NT Medical imaging equipment
industry
Imaging systems in meteorology
UF Meteorological imaging systems
BT Meteorological instruments
Imaging systems in seismology
UF Seismological imaging systems
BT Seismology—Instruments
Imagism
USE Imagist poetry
Imagist poetry
UF Imagism
BT Poetry
RT Free verse
Imajuku Higashi Iseki (Yamaguchi-shi, Japan)
USE Imajuku Higashi Site (Yamaguchi-shi,
Japan)
Imajuku Higashi Site (Yamaguchi-shi, Japan)
(Not Subd Geog)
UF Imajuku Higashi Iseki (Yamaguchi-shi,
Japan)
BT Japan—Antiquities
Imajuku Takada Iseki (Fukuoka-shi, Japan)
USE Takada Site (Fukuoka-shi, Japan)
Imajukunishi Iseki (Yamaguchi-shi, Japan)
USE Imajukunishi Site (Yamaguchi-shi,
Japan)
Imajukunishi Site (Yamaguchi-shi, Japan)
UF Imajukunishi Iseki (Yamaguchi-shi,
Japan)
BT Japan—Antiquities
Imamate
[BP166.94]
BT Islam
Shi'ah—Doctrines
NT 'Alī ibn Abī Ṭālib, Caliph, 600 (ca.)-
661—Imamate
Imams
Imamites
USE Shi'ah
Imams
BT Imamate
NT Hadith (Shiites)
— Hadith
USE Hadith (Shiites)
— Tombs
USE Shiite shrines
— Traditions
USE Hadith (Shiites)
Imams as teachers
BT Teachers
Iman (Australian people)
USE Jiman (Australian people)

Imana (Rundi deity)
BT Gods, Rundi
Imanan (Niger)
UF Imannan (Niger)
Imandra, Lake (R.S.F.S.R.)
UF Lake Imandra (R.S.F.S.R.)
Ozero Imandra (R.S.F.S.R.)
BT Lakes—Russian S.F.S.R.
Imannan (Niger)
USE Imanan (Niger)
Imantodes
[QL666.O636]
BT Colubridae
Imantodes cenchoa
[QL666.O636]
UF Blunt-headed tree snake
Tree snake, Blunt-headed
Imari (Finland)
USE Inari Lake (Finland)
Imari porcelain *(May Subd Geog)*
[NK4399.I4]
UF Porcelain, Imari
BT Arita porcelain
Imazawa family *(Not Subd Geog)*
Ĭmbabu, Ethiopia, Battle of, 1882
[DT386.7]
BT Ethiopia—History—1490-1889
Imbalances, Acid-base
USE Acid-base imbalances
Imbalances, Regional economic
USE Regional economic disparities
Imbalances, Water-electrolyte
USE Water-electrolyte imbalances
Imbecility
USE Mentally handicapped
Imbedding theorems
USE Embedding theorems
Imbeddings, Topological
USE Topological imbeddings
Imbeddings (Mathematics)
USE Embeddings (Mathematics)
Imbrasia
[QL51.S2]
UF Nudaurelia
BT Saturniidae
Imbrasia cytherea
[QL561.S2]
UF Pine emperor moth
Pine tree emperor moth
Imeretian dialect *(May Subd Geog)*
UF Imeritian dialect
BT Georgian language
Georgian S.S.R.—Languages
Imeritian dialect
USE Imeretian dialect
Imerson family *(Not Subd Geog)*
UF Imeson family
Imeson family
USE Imerson family
Imidazole
NT Cimetidine
Clonidine
Histamine
Levamisole
Miconazole
Nitroimidazoles
Tioconazole
Imidazoline
NT Phentolamine
Imidazolinylmethyltoluidinophenol
USE Phentolamine
Imidazopyridines
BT Amides
Azo compounds
Pyridine
NT Zolpidem
Imides
BT Amines
NT Polyimides
Imidoesters
[QD305.I6]

Imidogen derivatives
USE Nitrenes
Imines
BT Organonitrogen compounds
NT Imino compounds
Polyamines
Sulphilimines
Sulphoximines
Imino acids
UF Secondary amino acids
BT Imino compounds
RT Amino acids
Imino compounds
BT Imines
Organonitrogen compounds
NT Imino acids
Iminourea
USE Guanidine
Imint
[BL2450.I44]
BT Anubis (Egyptian deity)
Imipramine
— Side effects
BT Drugs—Side effects
Imitation
[BF357]
UF Mimicry
BT Psychology
RT Influence (Psychology)
NT Example
Impersonation
Imitation (in art)
BT Art
Art—Reproduction
Influence (Literary, artistic, etc.)
Pictures—Copying
SA *subdivision* Parodies, imitations, etc.
under names of individual artists
Imitation (in literature)
[PN166]
BT Arts—Reproduction
Authorship
Influence (Literary, artistic, etc.)
Literature
Quotation
RT Mimesis in literature
Originality (in literature)
Parody
Plagiarism
SA *subdivision* Parodies, imitations, etc.
*under names of individual literary
authors and individual literary
works entered under title, e.g.
Shakespeare, William, 1564-1616—
Parodies, imitations, etc.; Beowulf—
Parodies, imitations, etc.*
Imitation (in music)
[ML430]
UF Music, Imitation in
BT Composition (Music)
Imitation in children
[BF723.I53]
BT Child psychology
Imitation of Jesus Christ
USE Jesus Christ—Example
Imitation wood
USE Simulated wood
Imjin-gang, Battle of, 1951
BT Korean War, 1950-1953
Imlĭhĭyah, Tall (Egypt)
[DT73.I46]
UF Imlihiye, Tell (Egypt)
Tall Imlĭhĭyah (Egypt)
Tell Imlihiye (Egypt)
BT Egypt—Antiquities
Imlihiye, Tell (Egypt)
USE Imlĭhĭyah, Tall (Egypt)
Immaculate Conception
[BT620]
BT Conception—Religious aspects—
Catholic Church

Immaculate Conception *(Continued)*
RT Mary, Blessed Virgin, Saint—
    Sinlessness
— **History of doctrines**
— **Sermons**
    UF Immaculate Conception, Feast of
        the—Sermons
Immaculate Conception, Feast of the
    [BV50.16]
    UF Feast of the Immaculate Conception
    BT Church year
        Fasts and feasts
— **Sermons**
    USE Immaculate Conception—
        Sermons
Immaculate Heart of Mary
    USE Sacred Heart of Mary, Devotion to
Immanence (Philosophy)
    BT Consciousness
        Experience
        Idealism
        Knowledge, Theory of
        Metaphysics
        Transcendentalism
Immanence of God
    [BT124]
    UF Divine immanence
        God—Immanence
        God, Immanence of
    BT God
    NT Mystical union
— **History of doctrines**
Immaterialism (Philosophy)
    [B105.I52]
    UF Immateriality (Philosophy)
    BT Concepts
        Idea (Philosophy)
        Idealism
        Philosophy
        Spiritualism (Philosophy)
        Substance (Philosophy)
        Universals (Philosophy)
Immateriality (Philosophy)
    USE Immaterialism (Philosophy)
Immediate allergy
    USE Allergy
Immediate dentures
    USE Dentures, Immediate
Immediate hypersensitivity
    USE Allergy
Immediate insertion dentures
    USE Dentures, Immediate
Immediate memory
    USE Short-term memory
Immemorial usage
    USE Prescription (Law)
        Time immemorial (Law)
Immersion, Baptismal
    USE Baptism
Immersion, Heat of
    USE Heat of wetting
Immersion (Judaism)
    USE Purity, Ritual (Judaism)
Immersion method (Refractive index of
    minerals)
    USE Refractive index of minerals—
        Immersion method
Immersion technique (Education)
    USE Concentrated study
Immersions (Mathematics)
    BT Manifolds (Mathematics)
        Mappings (Mathematics)
    RT Embeddings (Mathematics)
Immidae
    [QL561.I45]
    BT Lepidoptera
Immigrant folklore
    USE Ethnic folklore
Immigrant labor
    USE Alien labor

Immigrant remittances
    USE Emigrant remittances
Immigrant species
    USE Animal introduction
        Plant introduction
Immigrants *(May Subd Geog)*
    Here are entered works on foreign-born persons
who enter a country intending to become permanent
residents or citizens. This heading may be locally
subdivided by names of places where immigrants set-
tle. For works discussing emigrants from a particular
place, an additional heading is assigned to designate
the nationality of origin of the emigrant group and the
place to which they have immigrated, e.g. Chinese—
United States; Americans—Foreign countries.
    UF Emigrants
        Foreign population
        Foreigners
    BT Persons
    RT Aliens
    NT Children of immigrants
        Church work with immigrants
        Libraries and immigrants
        Social work with immigrants
        Women immigrants
— Legal status, laws, etc.
    USE Emigration and immigration law
— **Medical examinations**
    (May Subd Geog)
— — **United States**
    [JV6485]
    UF United States—Emigration and
        immigration—Medical
        inspection
— **Confederate States of America**
    [E487]
    UF Confederate States of America—
        Foreign population
— **Great Britain**
    UF Great Britain—Foreign population
— — **Housing**
    UF Great Britain—Foreign
        population—Housing
    BT Housing—Great Britain
— **United States**
    UF United States—Foreign population
— — **Juvenile literature**
    UF United States—Foreign
        population—Juvenile
        literature
Immigrants and libraries
    USE Libraries and immigrants
Immigrants' children
    USE Children of immigrants
Immigrants in art
Immigrants in literature
Immigration
    USE Emigration and immigration
Immigration consultants *(May Subd Geog)*
    BT Consultants
        Emigration and immigration
— **Legal status, laws, etc.**
    (May Subd Geog)
    BT Emigration and immigration law
    NT Immigration consultants—
        Malpractice
— **Malpractice** *(May Subd Geog)*
    UF Tort liability of immigration
        consultants
    BT Emigration and immigration law
        Immigration consultants—Legal
        status, laws, etc.
        Malpractice
Immigration law
    USE Emigration and immigration law
Immobilization of animals
    USE Animal immobilization
Immobilized cell organelles
    [QH585.5.I45]
    BT Cell culture
        Cell organelles

Immobilized cells
    [QH585.5.I45]
    BT Cell culture
        Cells
Immobilized enzymes
    [QP601]
    UF Insoluble enzymes
        Localized enzymes
        Water-insoluble enzymes
    BT Enzymes
        Immobilized proteins
Immobilized micro-organisms
    USE Micro-organisms, Immobilized
Immobilized proteins
    UF Insolubilized proteins
        Localized proteins
        Proteins, Immobilized
        Proteins, Insolubilized
        Proteins, Localized
    BT Proteins
        Proteins—Denaturation
    NT Immobilized enzymes
Immoral conditions (Law) *(May Subd Geog)*
    UF Conditions, Immoral (Law)
    BT Conditions (Law)
Immoral consideration
    USE Immoral contracts
Immoral contracts *(May Subd Geog)*
    UF Contracts, Immoral
        Contracts contra bonos mores
        Immoral consideration
    BT Contracts
        Lesion (Law)
    RT Illegal contracts
        Undue influence
    NT Usury laws
Immoral literature
    USE Literature, Immoral
Immoralism
    USE Immorality
Immorality
    [BJ1410-1418]
    UF Immoralism
    BT Ethics
    RT Right and wrong
Immortalism
    Here are entered works on the concept of living
indefinitely in the flesh. For works on the concept of
the survival of the soul after death see Immortality.
    UF Prolongation of life span
    BT Aging
        Death—Religious aspects
        Longevity
    RT Immortality
    NT Cryonics
Immortality
    [BL530 (Comparative religion)]
    [BL2450.I5 (Egyptian religion)]
    [BT919-BT925 (Theology)]
    Here are entered works on the concept of the
survival of the soul after death. For works on the
concept of living indefinitely in the flesh see Immor-
talism.
    UF Life after death
    BT Eschatology
    RT Future life
        Immortalism
    NT Annihilationism
        Conditional immortality
        Tree of life
— **Buddhism, [Judaism, etc.]**
Immortality, Conditional
    USE Conditional immortality
Immortality, Conditioned
    USE Conditional immortality
Immortality (Philosophy)
    [BD419-423]
    BT Philosophy
Immortelles
    USE Everlasting flowers
Immune complex diseases
    BT Immunologic diseases

NT Allergy
    Glomerulonephritis
    Serum sickness
Immune complex removal
  USE Immune complexes—Removal
Immune complexes
  UF Antibody-antigen complexes
    Antigen-antibody complexes
  BT Antigens
    Immunoglobulins
  — Removal
    UF Immune complex removal
      Immune complexes, Removal of
    BT Immunotherapy
Immune complexes, Removal of
  USE Immune complexes—Removal
Immune deficiency syndromes
  USE Immunological deficiency syndromes
Immune depression
  USE Immunosuppression
Immune disorders
  USE Immunologic diseases
Immune memory
  USE Immunologic memory
Immune region antigens
  USE Ia antigens
Immune region associated antigens
  USE Ia antigens
Immune response
  [QR186]
    Here are entered general works on the total response of the body to invasion by micro-organisms, organ transplants or any antigenic substance. General works on various types of immunity, e.g. natural immunity, cellular immunity, etc. are entered under Immunity.
  BT Immunology
  NT Allergy
    Antigen-antibody reactions
    Cellular immunity
    Delayed hypersensitivity
    Immunological tolerance
    Inflammation—Immunological aspects
    Phagocytosis
  — Regulation
    UF Immunity—Regulation
      Regulation of immunity
      Regulation of the immune response
    BT Biological control systems
    RT Biological response modifiers
      Interferon inducers
      Ir genes
    NT Cytokines
      Immunosuppression
      Interleukins
      Lymphokines
      Monokines
Immune response genes
  USE Ir genes
Immune serum globulin
  USE Immunoglobulins
Immune serums
  [RM279]
  UF Antisera
  BT Biological products
    Immunology
  NT Histocompatibility antisera
Immune suppression
  USE Immunosuppression
Immune system
  [QR180-QR188.9]
  UF Immunological system
  BT Anatomy
    Immunology
  NT Bone marrow
    Immunocompetent cells
    Lymphoid tissue
  — Diseases
    USE Immunologic diseases
Immune tolerance
  USE Immunological tolerance

Immunities and privileges
  USE Privileges and immunities
Immunities of foreign sovereigns
  USE Immunities of foreign states
Immunities of foreign states
  (May Subd Geog)
  UF Immunities of foreign sovereigns
    Jurisdictional immunities of foreign states
    Sovereign immunity (International law)
    State immunities (International law)
  BT Government liability (International law)
    Jurisdiction (International law)
    Privileges and immunities
    Sovereignty
  NT Diplomatic privileges and immunities
    Exterritoriality
    Government vessels
Immunity
  [QR181-QR185]
    Here are entered general works on various types of immunity, e.g. natural immunity, cellular immunity, etc. General works on the total response of the body to invasion by micro-organisms, organ transplants or any antigenic substance are entered under Immune response.
  BT Immunology
    Medicine, Preventive
    Pathology
  RT Communicable diseases
    Serumtherapy
    Vaccination
  SA subdivision Preventive inoculation under names of certain diseases, e.g. Plague—Preventive inoculation; Typhoid fever—Preventive inoculation
  NT Agglutination
    Allergy
    Antigens
    B cells
    Cellular immunity
    Clonal selection theory
    Conglutination
    Hemagglutinin
    Hemolysis and hemolysins
    Immunization
    Immunochemistry
    Immunologic memory
    Maternally acquired immunity
    Natural immunity
    T cells
    Tuftsin
  — Endocrine aspects
    UF Endocrine aspects of immunity
      Hormonal aspects of immunity
      Immunity—Hormonal aspects
    BT Endocrinology
  — Genetic aspects
    USE Immunogenetics
  — Hormonal aspects
    USE Immunity—Endocrine aspects
  — Nutritional aspects
  — Regulation
    USE Immune response—Regulation
Immunity, Ecclesiastical
  USE Privileges and immunities, Ecclesiastical
Immunity, Maternally acquired
  USE Maternally acquired immunity
Immunity, Parliamentary
  USE Legislative bodies—Privileges and immunities
Immunity, Political
  USE Legislative bodies—Privileges and immunities
Immunity (Canon law)
  USE Privileges and immunities, Ecclesiastical

Immunity (Exemption)
  USE Privileges and immunities
Immunity (Feudalism)
  [JC116.I3]
  BT Feudalism
Immunity (Plants)
  USE Plants—Disease and pest resistance
Immunity from self-incrimination
  USE Self-incrimination
Immunization (May Subd Geog)
    Here are entered works on any process, active or passive, that leads to increased immunity. Works on active immunization with a vaccine are entered under Vaccination.
  BT Immunity
    Immunotherapy
  NT Allergy desensitization
    Contraception, Immunological
    Volunteer workers in immunization
Immunization centers
  USE Vaccination centers
Immunization of children (May Subd Geog)
  [RJ240]
  BT Child health services
    Communicable diseases in children— Prevention
    Pediatrics—Immunological aspects
  NT Vaccination of children
  — Religious aspects
Immunoadsorption
  [QR187.I44]
  BT Adsorption
    Antigens
    Immunochemistry
    Immunoglobulins
Immunoassay
  [QP519.9.I42]
  BT Antigens
    Immunoglobulins
    Immunology
  RT Immunodiagnosis
  NT Hemagglutination tests
    Immunoblotting
    Immunoenzyme technique
    Radioimmunoassay
Immunoassay, Enzyme
  USE Enzyme-linked immunosorbent assay
Immunoblastomas
  USE Lymphomas
Immunoblotting
  [QP519.9.I43]
  UF Western blot analysis
    Western blotting
  BT Antigens—Analysis
    Immunoassay
Immunochemistry
  BT Biological chemistry
    Chemistry
    Immunity
  NT Immunoadsorption
    Immunocytochemistry
    Immunohistochemistry
    Plant immunochemistry
Immunocompetent cells
  UF Immunologically competent cells
  BT Cells
    Immune system
  NT Cell-mediated lympholysis
    Killer cells
    Plasma cells
Immunocontraception
  USE Contraception, Immunological
Immunocytochemistry
  [QR187.I45 (General)]
  [RC270.3.I44 (Cancer diagnosis)]
  BT Cytochemistry
    Immunochemistry
  RT Immunofluorescence
Immunodeficiency-associated virus
  USE Human immunodeficiency viruses

Immunodeficiency syndromes
  USE Immunological deficiency syndromes
Immunodepression
  USE Immunosuppression
Immunodermatology
  USE Skin—Diseases—Immunological
        aspects
Immunodiagnosis
  [RB46.5]
  UF Diagnosis, Immunological
        Immunological diagnosis
  BT Diagnosis, Laboratory
        Immunology
  RT Immunoassay
  NT Autoantibodies—Analysis
        Complement fixation
        Immunoelectrophoresis
        Leucocyte adherence inhibition test
        Radioallergosorbent test
        Radioimmunoassay
        Radioimmunoimaging
  — Equipment and supplies
        NT Immunodiagnostic equipment
              industry
Immunodiagnostic equipment industry
  (May Subd Geog)
  [HD9995.I45-454]
  BT Immunodiagnosis—Equipment and
        supplies
Immunodiffusion
  UF Gel diffusion tests
  BT Antigen-antibody reactions
        Immunology
Immunoelectrophoresis
  [QR187.I47]
  BT Electrophoresis
        Immunodiagnosis
  NT Crossed immunoelectrophoresis
        Sepharose
Immunoenzyme technique
  [QP519.9.I44]
  UF Antibody enzyme techniques,
        Unlabeled
        Immunoperoxidase technique
        Peroxidase labeled antibody technique
  BT Enzymatic analysis
        Immunoassay
        Immunology—Technique
        Protein binding
  NT Enzyme-linked immunosorbent assay
Immunoenzymometric assay
  USE Enzyme-linked immunosorbent assay
Immunofluorescence
  BT Fluorescence
        Immunoglobulins
        Immunology—Technique
  RT Immunocytochemistry
  NT Fluorescence microscopy
        Fluorescent antibody technique
        Fluorescent antigen technique
Immunogenetics
  UF Genetics—Immunological aspects
        Immunity—Genetic aspects
        Immunology—Genetic aspects
  BT Genetics
        Immunology
        Serology
  NT Antibody diversity
        Carcinoembryonic antigens
        H-2 locus
        H-Y antigen
        Ia antigens
        Immunoglobulin allotypes
        Immunoglobulin idiotypes
        Ir genes
        Major histocompatibility complex
        Plants—Disease and pest resistance—
              Genetic aspects
        Rheumatoid factor
Immunoglobulin A
  [QR186.8.A2]

UF IgA
BT Immunoglobulins
RT IgA glomerulonephritis
Immunoglobulin allotypes
  [GN265 (Physical anthropology)]
  UF Allotypes, Immunoglobulin
        Allotypic antibodies
        Antibodies, Allotypic
  BT Genetic polymorphisms
        Immunogenetics
  RT Blood groups
Immunoglobulin D
  [QR186.8.D2]
  UF IgD
  BT Immunoglobulins
Immunoglobulin diversity
  USE Antibody diversity
Immunoglobulin E
  [QR186.8.E2]
  UF IgE
  BT Immunoglobulins
  RT Allergy
Immunoglobulin G
  [QR186.8.G2]
  UF IgG
  BT Immunoglobulins
Immunoglobulin idiotypes
  [QR186.7]
  UF Antibodies, Idiotypic
        Antibody idiotypes
        Idiotopes, Immunoglobulin
        Idiotypes, Antibody
        Idiotypes, Immunoglobulin
        Idiotypic antibodies
        Idiotypic immunoglobulins
  BT Genetic polymorphisms
        Immunogenetics
        Immunoglobulins
        Immunospecificity
        Myeloma proteins
  RT Binding sites (Biochemistry)
Immunoglobulin M
  [QR186.8.M2]
  UF IgM
  BT Immunoglobulins
        Macroglobulins
Immunoglobulinopathies, Monoclonal
  USE Gammopathies, Monoclonal
Immunoglobulins
  [QR186.7-QR186.8]
  UF Antibodies
        Immune serum globulin
  BT Blood proteins
        Globulin
        Plasma cells
  RT Antibody diversity
        Antigens
  NT Adjuvants, Immunological
        Anti-antibodies
        Antibodies, Monoclonal
        Antigen-antibody reactions
        Autoantibodies
        Blood coagulation factor VIII
              antibodies
        Clonal selection theory
        Fluorescent antibody technique
        Gammopathies, Monoclonal
        Hormone antagonists
        Human immunodeficiency virus
              antibodies
        Immune complexes
        Immunoadsorption
        Immunoassay
        Immunofluorescence
        Immunoglobulin A
        Immunoglobulin D
        Immunoglobulin E
        Immunoglobulin G
        Immunoglobulin idiotypes
        Immunoglobulin M
        Insulin antibodies

        Lectins
        Lipoprotein antibodies
        Precipitin reaction
        Rho(D) immune globulin
Immunohematology
  UF Blood groups—Immunological aspects
  BT Hematology
        Immunology
  NT Compatibility testing (Hematology)
Immunohistochemistry *(May Subd Geog)*
  UF Immunohistology
  BT Histochemistry
        Immunochemistry
Immunohistology
  USE Immunohistochemistry
Immunologic deficiency syndromes
  USE Immunological deficiency syndromes
Immunologic diseases *(May Subd Geog)*
  [RC581-RC607]
  UF Immune disorders
        Immune system—Diseases
        Immunological diseases
  BT Diseases
        Immunology
  RT Immunopathology
  NT Allergy
        Autoimmune diseases
        Collagen diseases
        Graft versus host reaction
        Immune complex diseases
        Immunological deficiency syndromes
        Mast cell disease
        Plasma cell diseases
Immunologic diseases in children
  (May Subd Geog)
  [RJ385-386]
  UF Pediatric immunopathology
  BT Children—Diseases
  NT AIDS (Disease) in children
        Erythroblastosis fetalis
        Immunological deficiency syndromes
              in children
        Pediatric allergy
Immunologic memory
  [QR185.35]
  UF Immune memory
        Immunological memory
        Memory, Immune
        Memory, Immunologic
  BT Immunity
Immunologic toxicology
  USE Immunotoxicology
Immunological adjuvants
  USE Adjuvants, Immunological
Immunological contraception
  USE Contraception, Immunological
Immunological deficiency syndromes
  (May Subd Geog)
  [RC606]
  UF Immune deficiency syndromes
        Immunodeficiency syndromes
        Immunologic deficiency syndromes
  BT Immunologic diseases
        Syndromes
  RT Immunosuppression
  NT Agammaglobulinemia
        AIDS (Disease)
        AIDS-related complex
        Ataxia telangiectasia
        Complement deficiency (Immunology)
        Lymphoproliferative disorders
  — Complications and sequelae
        NT Interstitial plasma cell pneumonia
Immunological deficiency syndromes in
  children *(May Subd Geog)*
  [RJ387.D42]
  BT Immunologic diseases in children
  NT Ataxia telangiectasia in children
        Chronic granulomatous disease
Immunological diagnosis
  USE Immunodiagnosis

1798

Immunological diseases
   USE Immunologic diseases
Immunological memory
   USE Immunologic memory
Immunological phylogeny
   USE Immunotaxonomy
Immunological specifics
   USE Immunospecificity
Immunological system
   USE Immune system
Immunological taxonomy
   USE Immunotaxonomy
Immunological tolerance
   UF Immune tolerance
      Tolerance, Immunological
   BT Immune response
      Immunology
      Transplantation of organs, tissues, etc.
   RT Histocompatibility
      Transplantation immunology
   SA *subdivision* Trypanotolerance *under*
      individual animals, e.g. Cattle—
      Trypanotolerance
   NT Antilymphocytic serum
      Histocompatibility testing
      Immunosuppression
      Livestock—Trypanotolerance
Immunologically competent cells
   USE Immunocompetent cells
Immunologists *(May Subd Geog)*
   BT Immunology
      Medical scientists
   NT Allergists
Immunology *(May Subd Geog)*
   ₍QR180-QR189.5₎
   RT Serology
   SA *subdivision* Immunological aspects
      under physiological topics and
      individual diseases, e.g. Aging—
      Immunological aspects; Cancer—
      Immunological aspects; *and*
      subdivision Immunology *under*
      individual animals and groups of
      animals and chemical substances,
      e.g. Fishes—Immunology; Insulin—
      Immunology
   NT Antigen-antibody reactions
      Cellular immunity
      Cellular recognition
      Complement (Immunology)
      Immune response
      Immune serums
      Immune system
      Immunity
      Immunoassay
      Immunodiagnosis
      Immunodiffusion
      Immunogenetics
      Immunohematology
      Immunologic diseases
      Immunological tolerance
      Immunologists
      Immunology, Experimental
      Immunopathology
      Immunopharmacology
      Immunotaxonomy
      Neuroimmunology
      Phagocytosis
      Phytohemagglutinins
      Plant immunology
      Radiation immunology
      Transplantation immunology
      Veterinary immunology
   — **Awards**
      ₍QR182.5₎
      BT Rewards (Prizes, etc.)
   — Genetic aspects
      USE Immunogenetics
   — **Technique**
      NT Flow cytometry
         Immunoenzyme technique

Immunofluorescence
   Radioactive tracers in immunology
Immunology, Comparative
   UF Comparative immunology
Immunology, Developmental
   ₍QR184.5₎
   UF Developmental immunology
   NT H-Y antigen
Immunology, Experimental
   ₍QR180-183.5₎
   UF Experimental immunology
   BT Biology, Experimental
      Immunology
Immunology, Plant
   USE Plant immunology
Immunology of inflammation
   USE Inflammation—Immunological aspects
Immunomodulators
   USE Biological response modifiers
Immunoparasitology, Veterinary
   USE Veterinary parasitology—
      Immunological aspects
Immunopathology
   BT Immunology
      Pathology
   RT Immunologic diseases
   NT Delayed hypersensitivity
      Immunotoxicology
Immunoperoxidase technique
   USE Immunoenzyme technique
Immunopharmacology *(May Subd Geog)*
   ₍RM370₎
   BT Immunology
      Pharmacology
   RT Immunotoxicology
   NT Adjuvants, Immunological
      Antiallergic agents
      Biological response modifiers
      Immunosuppressive agents
Immunophylogeny
   USE Immunotaxonomy
Immunopotentiation
   USE Adjuvants, Immunological
Immunoproliferative disorders
   USE Lymphoproliferative disorders
Immunospecificity
   ₍QR186.9₎
   UF Immunological specifics
      Serological specificity
      Specificity (Immunology)
   RT Antibody diversity
      Binding sites (Biochemistry)
   NT Immunoglobulin idiotypes
      Tissue specific antigens
Immunostimulants
   USE Adjuvants, Immunological
Immunosuppression
   UF Immune depression
      Immune suppression
      Immunodepression
   BT Immune response—Regulation
      Immunological tolerance
      Therapeutics
   RT Immunological deficiency syndromes
   NT Antilymphocytic serum
      Suppressor cells
Immunosuppressive agents
   (May Subd Geog)
   UF Immunosuppressive drugs
   BT Drugs
      Immunopharmacology
   NT Bleomycin
      Cyclosporin A
      Methotrexate
      Mitomycin C
      Streptozotocin
      Thiamphenicol
Immunosuppressive drugs
   USE Immunosuppressive agents
Immunosympathectomy
   BT Sympathectomy

Immunotaxonomy
   ₍QR185.153₎
   UF Immunological phylogeny
      Immunological taxonomy
      Immunophylogeny
      Taxonomy, Immunological
   BT Biology—Classification
      Immunology
      Phylogeny
Immunotherapy *(May Subd Geog)*
   ₍RM270-RM282₎
   BT Therapeutics
   SA *subdivision* Immunotherapy *under*
      individual diseases, e.g. Cancer—
      Immunotherapy; Heart—Diseases—
      Immunotherapy; *etc.*
   NT Immune complexes—Removal
      Immunization
      Interferon inducers
      Levamisole
      Radioimmunotherapy
      Serumtherapy
      Thymosin
   — **Complications and sequelae**
      (May Subd Geog)
Immunotoxicity
   USE Immunotoxicology
Immunotoxicology *(May Subd Geog)*
   ₍RC582.17₎
   UF Immunologic toxicology
      Immunotoxicity
   BT Immunopathology
      Toxicology
   RT Immunopharmacology
Imo Incident, Korea, 1882
   BT Korea—History—1864-1910
Imona (African people)
   USE Mbole (African people)
IMP (Artificial satellite)
   UF Interplanetary monitoring platform
      (Artificial satellite)
   BT Artificial satellites
      Explorer (Artificial satellite)
      Scientific satellites
Imp automobile
   ₍TL215.I4₎
   BT Hillman automobile
Impact
   ₍QA935₎
   ₍QC131₎
   BT Collisions (Physics)
      Materials—Dynamic testing
   RT Blast effect
      Shock (Mechanics)
   NT Elasticity
      Metals—Impact testing
      Penetration mechanics
      Splashes
      Structural dynamics
   — **Physiological effect**
      NT Crash injuries
         Falls (Accidents)
Impact, Ion
   USE Ion bombardment
Impact analysis, Environmental
   USE Environmental impact analysis
Impact analysis, Urban
   USE Urban impact analysis
Impact attenuation systems on roads
   USE Roads—Crash cushions
Impact avalanche and transit time diodes
   USE Diodes, IMPATT
Impact fees *(May Subd Geog)*
      Here are entered works on fees imposed by local
   governments on new construction projects in order to
   provide revenue to finance the extra services neces-
   sitated by the new development.
   UF Development fees
      Fees, Development
      Fees, Impact
   BT Fees, Administrative

1799

Impact limiter
  USE Cushioning materials
Impact of legislation on courts, Statements of
  USE Judicial impact statements
Impact phenomena (Nuclear physics)
  USE Collisions (Nuclear physics)
IMPACT Program
  USE Increasing Membership, Participation,
      Activities, Communication and
      Trust Program
Impact statements, Arms control
  USE Arms control impact statements
Impact statements, Environmental
  USE Environmental impact statements
Impact statements, Judicial
  USE Judicial impact statements
Impact tubes
  USE Pitot tubes
Impaction of feces
  USE Feces—Impaction
Impaction of teeth
  USE Teeth—Impaction
Impactless printing
  USE Nonimpact printing
Impactometers, Cascade (Meteorological
    instruments)
  USE Cascade impactors (Meteorological
      instruments)
Impactors, Cascade (Meteorological
    instruments)
  USE Cascade impactors (Meteorological
      instruments)
Impaired vision
  USE Vision disorders
Impala
  ⌈QL737.U53⌉
  UF Aepyceros melampus
  BT Aepyceros
Impala automobile
  ⌈TL215.I⌉
  BT Chevrolet automobile
Imparales
  ⌈QL638.P6⌉
  BT Pimelodidae
  NT Imparales panamensis
Imparales panamensis
  ⌈QL638.P6⌉
  BT Imparales
Impartiality
  USE Fairness
Impartiality of God
  USE God—Impartiality
Impasse (Psychotherapy)
  ⌈RC489.I45⌉
  UF Psychotherapeutic impasse
      Therapeutic impasse in psychotherapy
      Treatment impasse in psychotherapy
  BT Psychotherapy
Impassibility of God
  USE Suffering of God
Impassivity
  USE Apathy
Impatiens
  ⌈QK495.B25 (Botany)⌉
  BT Balsaminaceae
IMPATT diodes
  USE Diodes, IMPATT
Impeachments *(May Subd Geog)*
  ⌈JF295 (Executive)⌉
  ⌈JF475 (Procedure)⌉
  ⌈JK446 (Impeachable offenses)⌉
  ⌈JK593-5 (President)⌉
  ⌈JK751-2 (United States: Civil service)⌉
  ⌈JK1268 (Powers and procedure of
      Congress, JK1079)⌉
  ⌈JK1595 (Judiciary)⌉
  ⌈JK2700-9599 (States)⌉

  BT Administrative responsibility
      Criminal justice, Administration of
      Legislative bodies as courts
      Political crimes and offenses
      Public administration
  RT Privileges and immunities
  SA *subdivision* Impeachment *under names
      of individual persons*
  NT Recall
      Trials (Impeachment)
Impeachments (Greek law)
  BT Law, Greek
Impedance, Acoustic
  USE Acoustic impedance
Impedance, Bioelectric
  ⌈QP341⌉
  UF Bioelectric impedance
  BT Electrophysiology
      Impedance (Electricity)
  NT Audiometry, Impedance
      Impedance plethysmography
Impedance, Mechanical
  USE Mechanical impedance
Impedance (Electricity)
  BT Electric currents, Alternating
      Electricity
  RT Electric resistance
      Reactance (Electricity)
  NT Impedance, Bioelectric
      Impedance matching
      Transfer impedance
Impedance audiometry
  USE Audiometry, Impedance
Impedance matching
  BT Electric lines
      Impedance (Electricity)
Impedance plethysmography
  UF Electric impedance plethysmography
  BT Impedance, Bioelectric
      Plethysmography
Impedance spectroscopy
  ⌈QD116.I57⌉
  UF IS (Electrochemical analysis)
      Spectroscopy, Impedance
  BT Electrochemical analysis
Impediments (Canon law)
  USE Impediments to marriage (Canon law)
      Irregularities (Canon law)
Impediments to marriage *(May Subd Geog)*
  UF Marriage—Impediments
  BT Marriage law
  NT Abduction
      Adultery
      Affinity (Law)
      Age (Law)
      Banns
      Bigamy
      Consanguinity (Law)
      Marriage—Dispensations
      Marriage with deceased wife's sister
Impediments to marriage (Canon law)
  UF Impediments (Canon law)
  BT Marriage (Canon law)
**Impediments to marriage (Canon law,
    Oriental)**
  BT Canon law, Oriental
**Impediments to marriage (Canon law,
    Orthodox Eastern)**
  BT Canon law, Orthodox Eastern
Impediments to marriage (Jewish law)
Impediments to marriage (Roman law)
  BT Roman law
Impellers
  ⌈TJ267.I6⌉
  UF Turbomachines—Impellers
      Turbomachines—Rotors
  BT Turbomachines
 — Dynamics
      ⌈TJ267.5.I6⌉
Impennes
  USE Penguins

Imperative (Grammar)
  USE Grammar, Comparative and general—
      Imperative
Imperatives (Logic)
  USE Commands (Logic)
Imperator (Roman title)
  ⌈DG83.5.I6⌉
Imperfect competition
  USE Competition, Imperfect
Imperfect fungi
  USE Fungi imperfecti
Imperfect gases
  USE Gases, Real
Imperial automobile
  ⌈TL215.I⌉
  BT Chrysler automobile
Imperial Canal (Spain)
  UF Canal Imperial de Aragón (Spain)
  BT Canals—Spain
Imperial cities (Holy Roman Empire)
  UF Imperial towns
  BT Holy Roman Empire
Imperial federation
  ⌈DA18 (History)⌉
  ⌈JN276⌉
  UF Federation, Imperial
  BT Federal government
      Great Britain—Colonies
      Imperialism
      Persons (International law)
Imperial inspection tour of the South (Scroll)
  USE Wang, Hui, 1632-1717. Imperial
      inspection tour of the South
Imperial Japanese morning glory
  USE Japanese morning glory
Imperial Palace (Peking, China)
  USE Forbidden City (Peking, China)
Imperial Palace (Shen-yang shih, China)
  USE Shen-yang ku kung (Shen-yang shih,
      China)
Imperial Palace (Tokyo, Japan)
  USE Kōkyo (Tokyo, Japan)
Imperial Palace (Vienna, Austria)
  USE Hofburg (Vienna, Austria)
Imperial Poetry Contest (Japan)
  USE Utakaihajime
Imperial preference
Imperial procession departing from and
    returning to the palace (Scroll)
  USE Ch'u-ching T'u (Scroll)
      Ju-pi T'u (Scroll)
Imperial towns
  USE Imperial cities (Holy Roman Empire)
**Imperial Trans-Antarctic Expedition, 1914-
1917**
  ⌈G850 1914⌉
Imperial Treasures of Japan, Three
  USE Sanshu no Jingi
Imperial Valley (Calif. and Mexico)
  BT Valleys—California
      Valleys—Mexico
Imperial Villa (Piazza Armerina, Sicily)
  USE Roman Villa of Casale (Piazza
      Armerina, Sicily)
Imperialism
  ⌈E713 (Diplomatic history: United
      States)⌉
  ⌈JC359 (Political theory)⌉
  ⌈JK304 (Constitutional history: United
      States)⌉
  ⌈JN276 (Constitutional history: Great
      Britain)⌉
  UF Colonialism
      Expansion (United States politics)
      Neocolonialism
  BT Political science
  RT Anti-imperialist movements
      Caesarism
      Chauvinism and jingoism
      Militarism

SA *subdivision* Foreign relations *under*
    names of countries
NT Colonies
    Colonization
    Decolonization
    Dependency
    Drang nach Osten
    Imperial federation

Imperium (Roman law)
  BT Jurisdiction (Roman law)

Impermanence (Buddhism)
    ⌐BQ4261┐
  UF Anicca (Buddhism)
    Anitya (Buddhism)
  BT Buddhism—Doctrines

Impero Road (Rome, Italy)
  USE Via dei Fori Imperiali (Rome, Italy)

Impersonal constructions (Grammar)
  USE Grammar, Comparative and general—
      Subjectless constructions

Impersonal judgment
  USE Judgment (Logic)

Impersonating an officer *(May Subd Geog)*
  BT False personation

Impersonation
  BT Acting
    Comedy
    Imitation
  NT False personation
    Impersonators, Female
    Impersonators, Male
    Transvestism

Impersonation (Law)
  USE False personation

Impersonation in literature
  BT Disguise in literature

Impersonators, Female *(May Subd Geog)*
    Here are entered works on men impersonating
women. Works on women impersonating men are
entered under Impersonators, Male. Works on the
practice of wearing clothing appropriate to the opposite sex are entered under Transvestism.
  UF Drag queens
    Female impersonators
    Impersonators of women
    Queens, Drag
  BT Actresses
    Impersonation

Impersonators, Female, in motion pictures
  BT Moving-pictures

Impersonators, Male
    Here are entered works on women impersonating
men. Works on the practice of wearing clothing appropriate to the opposite sex are entered under
Transvestism. Works on men impersonating women
are entered under Impersonators, Female.
  UF Impersonators of men
    Male impersonators
  BT Actors
    Impersonation

Impersonators, Male, in motion pictures
  BT Moving-pictures

Impersonators of men
  USE Impersonators, Male

Impersonators of women
  USE Impersonators, Female

Impetigo
    ⌐RL283┐
  BT Pyoderma

Impetus theory
  BT Motion

Imphal, Battle of, 1944
  BT World War, 1939-1945—Campaigns—
      India

Imphee
  USE Sorgo

Implant dentures
    ⌐RK667.I45┐
  UF Dental implantation
    Dental prosthesis, Surgical
    Oral implantology
    Surgical dental prosthesis

  BT Dentures
    Implants, Artificial
    Mouth—Surgery
— **Complications and sequelae**
    (May Subd Geog)

Implant dentures, Endosseous
    ⌐RK667.I45┐
  UF Endosseous implant dentures
    Endosteal implant dentures
    Implant dentures, Endosteal

Implant dentures, Endosteal
  USE Implant dentures, Endosseous

Implant lenses
  USE Intraocular lenses

Implant radiotherapy
  USE Radioisotope brachytherapy

Implantable contraceptive drugs
  USE Contraceptive drug implants

Implantation, Intracochlear electrode
  USE Cochlear implants

Implantation, Ion
  USE Ion implantation

Implantation of growth promoting substances
  USE Growth promoting substances—
      Implantation

Implantation of human embryo
  USE Human embryo—Transplantation

Implantation of ovum
  USE Ovum implantation

Implanted cardiovascular instruments
  USE Cardiovascular instruments, Implanted

Implants, Artificial *(May Subd Geog)*
    ⌐RD132┐
  UF Artificial implants
    Implants, Surgical
    Surgical implants
  BT Biomedical materials
    Surgery
  RT Prosthesis
  NT Cardiovascular instruments, Implanted
    Cochlear implants
    Implant dentures
    Intraocular lenses
    Orthopedic implants
    Penile prostheses
    Radioisotope brachytherapy

Implants, Cochlear
  USE Cochlear implants

Implants, Contraceptive drug
  USE Contraceptive drug implants

Implants, Orthopedic
  USE Orthopedic implants

Implants, Penile
  USE Penile prostheses

Implants, Surgical
  USE Implants, Artificial

Implement seats, Cast-iron
  USE Cast-iron implement seats

Implements, utensils, etc. *(May Subd Geog)*
    ⌐GN446-GN447 (Primitive)┐
  UF Gadgets
    Household utensils
    Utensils
    Vessels (Utensils)
  BT Furniture
  RT Tools
  SA *subdivision* Implements *under* Indians,
    Mound-builders, *and similar*
    headings; and names of particular
    implements, utensils, etc., e.g.
    Knives, Mortars, Scythes
  NT Agricultural implements
    Agricultural machinery
    Artists' tools
    Bone implements
    Bronze implements
    Copper implements
    Corkscrews
    Handles
    Kashering of utensils
    Kitchen utensils

    Man, Prehistoric—Tools
    Openers (Implements)
    Stone implements
    Stoppers (Implements)

Impletol
  UF Procaine hydrochloride
  BT Local anesthesia
    Novocaine

Implication (Linguistics)
  USE Connotation (Linguistics)

Implication (Logic)
    ⌐BC199.I43┐
  BT Logic

Implicit functions
  USE Functions, Implicit

Implied powers (Constitutional law)
  (May Subd Geog)
  BT Constitutional law—Interpretation and
      construction
  RT Executive power
    Judicial power
    Legislative power
  NT War and emergency powers

Import and export controls
  USE Foreign trade regulation

Import controls
  USE Import quotas
    Tariff

Import credit *(May Subd Geog)*
    ⌐HG3753-3754.5┐
  BT Commerce
    Commercial policy
    Credit
    Letters of credit
  RT Export credit
— **Law and legislation** *(May Subd Geog)*
    BT Commercial law

Import fees
  USE Tariff

Import licenses
  USE Import quotas

Import quotas *(May Subd Geog)*
    ⌐HF1401-1650┐
  UF Import controls
    Import licenses
    Import restrictions
    Quotas, Import
  BT Foreign trade regulation
    Free trade and protection
    Nontariff trade barriers
    Trade adjustment assistance

Import restrictions
  USE Foreign trade regulation
    Import quotas

Import substitution *(May Subd Geog)*
    ⌐HF1420┐
  BT Commerce
    Commercial policy
    Foreign trade promotion
    Industrial promotion

Imported fire ant, Black
  USE Solenopsis richteri

Imported fire ant, Red
  USE Solenopsis invicta

Imported willow leaf beetle
  USE Plagiodera versicolora

Imports
  USE Commerce
    Tariff

Importunate widow (Parable)
  USE Unjust judge (Parable)

Imposition (Typography)
  USE Printing, Practical—Imposition, etc.

Imposition of hands
    ⌐BM715 (Jewish sacrifices)┐
    ⌐BV873.L3 (Christian sacraments)┐
  UF Hands, Imposition of
    Hands, Laying on of
    Laying on of hands
  BT Ordination
    Rites and ceremonies

Impossibility of performance
(May Subd Geog)
  UF Frustration of contracts
      Supervening impossibility
  BT Contracts
      Discharge of contracts
      Liability (Law)
      Performance (Law)
  RT Rebus sic stantibus clause
  NT Accident (Casus fortuitus)
      Vis major (Civil law)
Impossibility of performance (International law)
  BT International law
Impossibility of performance (Islamic law)
Imposter phenomenon
  USE Impostor phenomenon
Imposters
  USE Impostors and imposture
Impostor phenomenon
      ₜBF637.I46 (Psychology)₎
      Here are entered works on feeling like a fake or
  fraud although one is successful. Works on impostors
  in the legal sense are entered under Impostors and
  imposture.
  UF Imposter phenomenon
      IP
      Phenomenon, Impostor
  BT Fear of success
      Self-perception
Impostors and imposture (May Subd Geog)
      ₜCT9980-CT9981₎
      ₜHV6751-HV6761 (Criminal)₎
      Here are entered works on impostors in the legal
  sense. Works on feeling like a fake or fraud although
  one is successful are entered under Impostor phe-
  nomenon.
  UF Charlatans
      Delusions
      Hoaxes
      Humbug
      Imposters
      Pretenders
  BT Crime and criminals
  RT Fraud
  NT Quacks and quackery
      Trials (Impostors and imposture)
Impotence (May Subd Geog)
      ₜRC560.I45 (Psychiatry)₎
      ₜRC889 (Medicine)₎
  BT Psychosexual disorders
      Sexual disorders
Impotence (Canon law)
Impotence (Jewish law)
Impotence (Roman law)
Impoundment of appropriated funds, Executive
  USE Executive impoundment of
       appropriated funds
Impoverished people
  USE Poor
Imprecation
  USE Blessing and cursing
Impregnation, Artificial
  USE Artificial insemination
Impresarios (May Subd Geog)
      ₜML429₎
  BT Opera
      Performing arts sponsorship
  RT Concert agents
  NT Theatrical agencies
      Theatrical agents
Impression materials, Dental
  USE Dental impression materials
Impressionism
      ₜBH301.I6 (Aesthetics)₎
  BT Style, Literary
Impressionism (Art) (May Subd Geog)
      ₜND1265₎
  BT Aesthetics
      Art, Modern—19th century
      Modernism (Art)
      Painting

  RT Post-impressionism (Art)
  NT Abstract impressionism
      Luminism (Art)
      Neo-impressionism (Art)
  — **Australia**
      NT Heidelberg school
  — **Japan**
  — — **French influences**
          BT France—Civilization
Impressionism (Music)
      ₜML197₎
  UF Music, Impressionism in
  BT Music
      Music—Philosophy and aesthetics
      Style, Musical
Impressionism in motion pictures
      ₜPN1995.9.I45₎
  BT Moving-pictures
Impressions, Dental
  USE Dental impressions
Impressions in paste
  USE Prints in paste
Impressment
      ₜE357.2-E357.3 (War of 1812)₎
  UF Press-gangs
  BT Naval history
      Seamen
      Ships—Manning
  NT Chesapeake-Leopard Affair, 1807
      Shanghaiing
Imprint catalogs
  USE Catalogs, Imprint
Imprinting (Psychology)
  BT Attachment behavior
      Birds—Behavior
      Child psychology
      Critical periods (Biology)
      Education—Experimental methods
Imprints, Imaginary
  USE Imprints (in books), Fictitious
Imprints (in books)
      ₜZ242.I3₎
  UF Printers' imprints
      Publishers' imprints
  BT Book industries and trade
      Books
      Cataloging
      Printing—History
      Title-page
  RT Colophons
Imprints (in books), Fictitious
  UF Imaginary imprints
      Imprints, Imaginary
  BT Anonyms and pseudonyms
  RT Literary forgeries and mystifications
Imprints (Publications)
  USE English imprints; French imprints; and
       similar headings; and subdivision
       Imprints under names of countries,
       cities, etc.
       English imprints
       French imprints
Imprisonment (May Subd Geog)
  UF Confinement
      Incarceration
  BT Corrections
      Criminal justice, Administration of
      Detention of persons
      Punishment
  RT Prisons
  SA subdivision Biography—Imprisonment
      under names of individual literary
      authors; and subdivision
      Imprisonment, ₜdates₎ under
      names of other individual persons
  NT Arrest
      Debt, Imprisonment for
      False imprisonment
      Preventive detention
Imprisonment, False
  USE False imprisonment

Imprisonment for debt
  USE Debt, Imprisonment for
Impromptu speaking
  USE Extemporaneous speaking
Impromptu theater
  USE Improvisation (Acting)
Improper integrals
  USE Integrals, Improper
Improperly posed problems (Boundary value
  problems)
  USE Boundary value problems—Improperly
       posed problems
Improperly posed problems (Integro-differential
  equations)
  USE Integro-differential equations—
       Improperly posed problems
Improperly posed problems (Partial differential
  equations)
  USE Differential equations, Partial—
       Improperly posed problems
Improperly posed problems in numerical
  analysis
  USE Numerical analysis—Improperly posed
       problems
Impropriation
  USE Secularization
Improvement, Civic
  USE Civic improvement
Improvement, Roadside
  USE Roadside improvement
Improvement programs, School
  USE School improvement programs
Improvements (Law) (May Subd Geog)
      Here are entered works on amelioration of real
  and personal property.
  BT Negotiorum gestio
      Property
  NT Betterments
      Mechanics' liens
Improvements (Real property)
  USE Betterments
Improvisation (Acting)
      ₜPN2071.I5₎
  UF Impromptu theater
      Theater, Impromptu
  BT Acting
      Amateur theater
  RT Commedia dell'arte
Improvisation (Music)
      ₜMT68₎
  UF Extemporization (Music)
  BT Music
      Music—Performance
  NT Chance composition
      Harmony, Keyboard
      Rapping (Music)
Improvisation in dance (May Subd Geog)
      ₜGV1781.2₎
  UF Dance improvisation
      Dancing improvisation
      Improvisational dance
  BT Dancing
Improvisational dance
  USE Improvisation in dance
Impulse
      ₜBF575.I46 (Psychology)₎
  BT Emotions
      Instinct
      Psychology
      Will
  RT Impulsive personality
      Inhibition
  NT Compulsive behavior
Impulse-ridden personality
  USE Impulsive personality
Impulsive personality
      ₜRC569.5.I46₎
  UF Impulse-ridden personality
  BT Personality
      Personality, Disorders of
  RT Impulse

Impurities (Technology)
  USE Contamination (Technology)
Impurities in metals
  USE Metals—Inclusions
Impurity centers
  UF Centers, Impurity
  BT Crystals—Defects
  RT Electron donor-acceptor complexes
      Point defects
  NT Color centers
Impurity distribution in semiconductors
  USE Semiconductors—Impurity distribution
Imputation, Multiple (Statistics)
  USE Multiple imputation (Statistics)
Imry family
  USE Emery family
IMS (DL/I) (Computer system)
  UF Information Management Systems
      (Data Language/I) (Computer
      system)
  BT Data base management
      Electronic digital computers—
      Programming
IMS/VS (Computer system)
  UF Information Management
      Systems/Virtual Storage (Computer
      system)
  BT Data base management
      Virtual storage (Computer science)
Imsdahl family *(Not Subd Geog)*
Imus family *(Not Subd Geog)*
In
  USE Jen
In-and-out surgery
  USE Surgery, Outpatient
In-beam gamma ray spectroscopy
  ₍QC793.5.G327₎
  BT Gamma ray spectrometry
In-bond industry
  USE Offshore assembly industry
In Coena Domini bulls
  UF Bulls, In Coena Domini
      Coena Domini bulls
  BT Bulls, Papal
      Heresies, Christian
      Maundy Thursday
In convertendo (Music)
  USE Psalms (Music)—126th Psalm
In exitu Israel (Music)
  USE Psalms (Music)—114th Psalm
In-flight feeding (Space flight)
  USE Menus for space flight
In-flight monitoring of turbojet engines
  USE Airplanes—Turbojet engines—In-flight
      monitoring
In forma pauperis *(May Subd Geog)*
  UF Forma pauperis
      Pauperis, In forma
      Poor persons procedure
  BT Costs (Law)
  RT Legal aid
  NT Appeals in forma pauperis
      Public defenders
In fraudem legis
  USE Evasion (Law)
In-ko-pah/Jacumba Wilderness (Calif.)
  USE Jacumba/In-ko-pah Wilderness (Calif.)
In-law apartments
  USE Accessory apartments
In-laws
  USE Parents-in-law
In-line data processing
  USE On-line data processing
In nomine (Music)
In-pile loops of materials testing reactors
  USE Materials testing reactors—In-pile
      loops
In-plant data collection systems, Automatic
  USE Automatic data collection systems
In pleno parliamento (The phrase)
  BT Latin language—Terms and phrases

In rem actions
  USE Actions in rem
In-Search (Computer program)
  BT Information retrieval—Computer
      programs
In-service training
  USE *subdivision* In-service training *under
      occupational groups and types of
      employees for works on their
      continuing professional education
      during service to increase their
      effectiveness on the job, e.g.*
      Teachers—In-service training
      Employees, Training of
In situ extraction
  USE In situ processing (Mining)
In situ processing (Mining)
  (May Subd Geog)
  ₍TN278.3₎
  UF In situ extraction
      In situ recovery
  BT Mining engineering
  NT Coal gasification, Underground
      Leaching
      Solution mining
In situ recovery
  USE In situ processing (Mining)
In Storage Information System (Computer
  system)
  USE ISIS (Computer system)
In te, Domine, speravi, non confundar in
  aeternum, in justitia tua libera me, Inclina
  (Music)
  USE Psalms (Music)—31st Psalm
In vitro fertilization
  USE Fertilization in vitro
In vitro plant propagation
  USE Plant propagation—In vitro
In vitro propagation of corn
  USE Corn—Propagation—In vitro
In vitro storage of plant germplasm resources
  USE Germplasm resources, Plant—Storage
      —In vitro
In vitro toxicity testing
  USE Toxicity testing—In vitro
INA (Information retrieval system)
  ₍R864₎
  UF Informationssystem für
      Niedergelassene Ärzte
  BT Information storage and retrieval
      systems—Medicine
Ina family *(Not Subd Geog)*
Inabaknon language
  USE Abaknon language
INAC (Computer)
  BT Electronic digital computers
Inachus (Greek deity)
  BT Gods, Greek
      Mythology, Greek
Inactivated oil adjuvant vaccines
  (May Subd Geog)
  UF Inactivated oil emulsion vaccines
      Inactivated vaccines in oil emulsion
      Oil adjuvant vaccines, Inactivated
      Oil emulsion vaccines, Inactivated
  BT Emulsions (Pharmacy)
      Vaccines
Inactivated oil emulsion vaccines
  USE Inactivated oil adjuvant vaccines
Inactivated vaccines in oil emulsion
  USE Inactivated oil adjuvant vaccines
Inactivity, Physical
  USE Hypokinesia
Inadequate corpus luteum
  USE Luteal phase defects
Inadequate luteal phase
  USE Luteal phase defects
Inama family *(Not Subd Geog)*
Inambari River (Peru)
  UF Río Inambari (Peru)
  BT Rivers—Peru

Inamura Castle (Tateyama-shi, Japan)
  USE Inamurajō (Tateyama-shi, Japan)
Inamurajō (Tateyama-shi, Japan)
  UF Inamura Castle (Tateyama-shi, Japan)
  BT Castles—Japan
Inanda Dam (South Africa)
  UF Inandadam (South Africa)
  BT Dams—South Africa
Inandadam (South Africa)
  USE Inanda Dam (South Africa)
Inaniwa Kaidō (Japan)
  USE Oyasu Kaidō (Japan)
Inanna (Sumerian deity)
  ₍BL1616.I5₎
  BT Gods, Sumerian
      Mythology, Sumerian
      Venus deities
Inari
  ₍BL2211.I5₎
  BT Cults—Japan
      Foxes—Religious aspects
Inari Lake (Finland)
  UF Enareträsk (Finland)
      Imari (Finland)
      Lake Enare (Finland)
      Ozero Inari (Finland)
  BT Lakes—Finland
Inarizakai Iseki (Japan)
  USE Inarizakai Site (Japan)
Inarizakai Site (Japan) *(Not Subd Geog)*
  UF Inarizakai Iseki (Japan)
  BT Japan—Antiquities
Inarticulata, Fossil
Inaudible sound
  USE Ultrasonics
Inaugural addresses of presidents (United
  States)
  USE Presidents—United States—Inaugural
      addresses
Inauguration
  USE *subdivision* Inauguration, ₍date₎
      under names of individual persons
Inauguration Day
  ₍JK536-550₎
  BT Holidays—United States
  RT Presidents—United States—
      Inauguration
Inauguration of United States presidents
  USE Presidents—United States—
      Inauguration
Inazuka family *(Not Subd Geog)*
Inboard-outboard engines
  UF Inboard-outdrives
      Outboard drives
      Stern drives
      Transom drives
  BT Motorboats—Motors
Inboard-outdrives
  USE Inboard-outboard engines
Inborn errors of metabolism
  USE Metabolism, Inborn errors of
Inbreeding
  ₍HV4981 (Inbreeding and
      degeneration)₎
  ₍S494 (Principles of breeding)₎
  ₍SF105 (Animal breeding)₎
  RT Breeding
      Consanguinity
Inca Indians
  USE Incas
Inca language
  USE Quechua language
Inca law
  USE Law, Inca
Inca music
  USE Incas—Music
Incahuasi Site (Peru)
  USE Inkawasi Site (Peru)
Incallajta Site (Bolivia)
  USE Inkallajta Site (Bolivia)

Incan language
  USE Callahuaya language
Incandescent electric lighting
  USE Electric lighting, Incandescent
Incandescent gas-lighting
  ₍TH7953-5₎
  UF Incandescent mantles
  BT Gas-lighting
    Lighting
  — Fixtures
    ₍TH7953-5₎
    BT Gas light fixtures
Incandescent lamps
  USE Electric lamps, Incandescent
Incandescent lamps, Iodine
  USE Iodine incandescent lamps
Incandescent lighting
  USE Electric lighting, Incandescent
Incandescent mantles
  USE Incandescent gas-lighting
Incantations
  ₍BF1558 (Occultism)₎
  ₍GR540 (Folklore)₎
  UF Spells
  BT Magic
    Rites and ceremonies
  NT Blessing and cursing
    Mantras
Incantations, Aramaic, ₍Finnish, Latin, etc.₎
Incantations, Bonpo
  USE Bonpo incantations
Incantations, Brazilian *(May Subd Geog)*
  UF Brazilian incantations
Incantations, Buddhist
  USE Buddhist incantations
Incantations, Croatian *(May Subd Geog)*
  UF Croatian incantations
Incantations, English *(May Subd Geog)*
  UF English incantations
Incantations, Georgian *(May Subd Geog)*
  UF Georgian incantations
Incantations, Hebrew
  UF Hebrew incantations
Incantations, Hurrian
  UF Hurrian incantations
Incantations, Jaina
  USE Jaina incantations
Incantations, Javanese *(May Subd Geog)*
  UF Javanese incantations
Incantations, Korean *(May Subd Geog)*
  UF Korean incantations
Incantations, Serbian *(May Subd Geog)*
  UF Serbian incantations
Incantations, Shamanist *(May Subd Geog)*
  UF Shamanist incantations
Incantations, Sumerian *(May Subd Geog)*
  UF Sumerian incantations
Incantations, Thai *(May Subd Geog)*
  UF Thai incantations
Incapacity, Estimation of
  USE Disability evaluation
Incapacity (Law)
  USE Capacity and disability
Incarceration
  USE Imprisonment
Incardination (Canon law)
  ₍BX1939.I44₎
  BT Benefices, Ecclesiastical (Canon law)
    Clergy (Canon law)
    Ordination (Canon law)
  RT Excardination (Canon law)
Incarnation
  ₍BL510₎
  ₍BT220 (Christology)₎
  UF Jesus Christ—Incarnation
    Kenosis (Theology)
  BT Avatars
    Jesus Christ
  RT Theophanies
Incas
  ₍F3429₎

₍F3442₎
  UF Inca Indians
  BT Indians of South America
  NT Peru—History—To 1548
    Peru—History—Insurrection of Tupac
      Amaru, 1780-1781
    Yanaconas
— Antiquities
— Law
  USE Law, Inca
— Mathematics
  ₍F3429.3.M36₎
  UF Mathematics, Inca
— Music
  ₍ML3575₎
  UF Inca music
    Music, Inca
— Religion and mythology
  ₍F3429.3.R38₎
Incendiaries (Military science)
  USE Incendiary weapons
Incendiarism
  USE Arson
    Pyromania
Incendiary bombs
  UF Bombs, Incendiary
    Fire bombs
  BT Bombs
    Incendiary weapons
Incendiary weapons
  ₍UG447.65₎
  UF Incendiaries (Military science)
  BT Chemical warfare
    Military fireworks
  NT Flame throwers
    Incendiary bombs
    Napalm
Incense
  ₍BV197.I6 (Christian worship)₎
  BT Essences and essential oils
    Odors
Incense burners and containers
  (May Subd Geog)
  ₍NK6078₎
  UF Burners, Incense
    Incense containers
  BT Containers
Incense-burning parties, Japanese
  USE Japanese incense ceremony
Incense cedar
  UF California incense cedar
    California white cedar
    Calocedrus decurrens
    White cedar
  BT Cedar
    Libocedrus
Incense cedar, Taiwan
  USE Calocedrus formosana
Incense ceremonies, Japanese
  USE Japanese incense ceremony
Incense containers
  USE Incense burners and containers
Incense industry *(May Subd Geog)*
  ₍HD9769.I53-533₎
Incense-smelling parties, Japanese
  USE Japanese incense ceremony
Incentive (Psychology)
  BT Motivation (Psychology)
  NT Reinforcement (Psychology)
    Rewards and punishments in education
Incentives, Tax
  USE Tax incentives
Incentives in education
  USE Rewards and punishments in education
Incentives in industry *(May Subd Geog)*
  ₍HF5549.5.I5₎
  UF Employee incentives
    Labor incentives
  BT Employee morale
    Employee motivation
    Personnel management

  RT Employee competitive behavior
    Goal setting in personnel management
  NT Bonus system
    Employee ownership
    Gain sharing
    Hospitals—Staff—Incentive awards
    Performance awards
    Profit-sharing
    Rewards (Prizes, etc.)
    Wages
  — Law and legislation *(May Subd Geog)*
    BT Labor laws and legislation
Incest *(May Subd Geog)*
  ₍GN480.3 (Anthropology)₎
  ₍HQ71 (Sociology)₎
  BT Consanguinity
    Crimes without victims
    Sex crimes
  RT Child molesting
  — Mythology
    ₍BL325.I48₎
  — Religious aspects
  — — Buddhism, ₍Christianity, etc.₎
Incest (Roman law)
  BT Roman law
Incest in literature
  ₍PN56.I55₎
  BT Sex in literature
Incest in popular culture *(May Subd Geog)*
    Here are entered works which discuss the repre-
    sentation of incest in popular culture.
  BT Popular culture
Incest victims *(May Subd Geog)*
  BT Victims of crimes
  RT Sexually abused children
Inchoate offenses *(May Subd Geog)*
  BT Criminal law
  NT Conspiracy
    Criminal attempt
Incidence, Grazing
  USE Grazing incidence
Incidence algebras
  UF Algebras, Incidence
  BT Commutative algebra
Incidence functions
  UF Functions, Incidence
  BT Arithmetic functions
Incidence of taxation
  USE Tax incidence
Incidental music
  USE Music, Incidental
Incidental questions (Conflict of laws)
  USE Preliminary questions (Conflict of
    laws)
Incineration *(May Subd Geog)*
  BT Refuse and refuse disposal
  NT Cremation
    Hazardous wastes—Incineration
    Incinerators
    Leaves—Burning
    Organic wastes—Burning
    Sewage sludge—Incineration
    Wood waste—Burning
Incinerators *(May Subd Geog)*
  UF Destructors, Refuse
    Refuse destructors
    Refuse incinerators
    Teepee burners
  BT Incineration
    Refuse disposal facilities
    Smoke prevention
    Waste disposal sites
  NT Crematoriums
Incipits
  BT Colophons
    Incunabula
    Manuscripts
    Titles of books
Incisalia
  USE Callophrys

Incised effigial slabs
  USE Sepulchral slabs
Incised monumental slabs
  USE Sepulchral slabs
Incised sepulchral slabs
  USE Sepulchral slabs
Incised stone slabs
  USE Sepulchral slabs
Incisors
  UF Anterior teeth
  BT Teeth
Incitement to war
  USE Crimes against peace
Inclina Domine (Music)
  USE Psalms (Music)—86th Psalm
Inclined passenger lifts
  USE Elevators, Private residence
Inclined planes
  UF Ramps
  BT Machinery
      Power transmission
      Simple machines
  NT Wedges
Inclinometer
  [TL89 (Aeronautical instruments)]
  BT Aeronautical instruments
      Oil wells—Equipment and supplies
Inclosures (May Subd Geog)
  [HD594 (Great Britain)]
  UF Enclosures
  BT Land tenure—Law and legislation
      Real property
Inclusion bodies in erythrocytes
  USE Erythrocytes—Inclusions
Inclusion bodies in liver cells
  USE Liver cells—Inclusions
Inclusion bodies in plant cells and tissues
  USE Plant cells and tissues—Inclusions
Inclusion disease, Cytomegalic
  USE Cytomegalic inclusion disease
Inclusionary housing programs
  (May Subd Geog)
    Here are entered works on programs which oblige
  or encourage developers of upper income housing to
  include a number of low or moderate income units.
  UF Housing programs, Inclusionary
  BT Housing policy
  RT Poor—Housing
      Zoning
Inclusions, Differential
  USE Differential inclusions
Inclusions, Fluid
  USE Fluid inclusions
Inclusions in basalt
  USE Basalt—Inclusions
Inclusions in fluorspar
  USE Fluorspar—Inclusions
Inclusions in granite
  USE Granite—Inclusions
Inclusions in gypsum
  USE Gypsum—Inclusions
Inclusions in igneous rocks
  USE Rocks, Igneous—Inclusions
Inclusions in iron
  USE Iron—Inclusions
Inclusions in kimberlite
  USE Kimberlite—Inclusions
Inclusions in metals
  USE Metals—Inclusions
Inclusions in metamorphic rocks
  USE Rocks, Metamorphic—Inclusions
Inclusions in porphyry
  USE Porphyry—Inclusions
Inclusions in precious stones
  USE Precious stones—Inclusions
Inclusions in quartz
  USE Quartz—Inclusions
Inclusions in steel
  USE Steel—Inclusions
Inclusions of minerals in coal
  USE Coal—Mineral inclusions

Inclusive processes (Nuclear physics)
  [QC794.8.I52]
  BT Nuclear reactions
Inclusive reactions (Nuclear physics)
  [QC794.8.S8]
  BT Nuclear reactions
Inco Metals Company Strike, Sudbury, Ont.,
  1978-1979
  [HD5329.N53]
  BT Nickel industry—Ontario—Employees
      Strikes and lockouts—Nickel industry
        —Ontario
      Strikes and lockouts—Ontario
Incoherent scatter radar
  BT Radar
Income (May Subd Geog)
  [HB601 (Theory)]
  [HC (National income)]
  UF Fortunes
      Personal income
  BT Economics
      Finance
      Property
      Wealth
  RT Gross national product
      Profit
      Purchasing power
  NT Capital
      Consumption (Economics)
      Discretionary income
      Engel's law
      Farm income
      Guaranteed annual income
      Income maintenance programs
      Interest
      Migrant remittances
      Multiplier (Economics)
      National income
      Negative income tax
      Permanent income theory
      Retirement income
      Wages
  — Accounting
      USE Income accounting
  — Effect of inflation on
      UF Inflation (Finance) and income
      BT Inflation (Finance)
  — Regional disparities
      BT Regional economic disparities
Income accounting
  UF Income—Accounting
  BT Accounting
  NT National income—Accounting
Income averaging (May Subd Geog)
  BT Income tax—Accounting
  — Law and legislation (May Subd Geog)
Income distribution (May Subd Geog)
  UF Distribution of income
      Inequality of income
  BT Distribution (Economic theory)
  NT Collective farms—Income distribution
      State farms—Income distribution
      Transfer payments
  — Effect of inflation on
      BT Inflation (Finance)
  — Mathematical models
      NT Gini coefficient
          Lorenz curve
  — China
      NT Communes (China)—Income
          distribution
Income forecasting (May Subd Geog)
  UF Forecasting, Income
  BT Economic forecasting
Income maintenance programs
  (May Subd Geog)
  UF Annual income guarantee
      Income transfer programs
      Minimum income

  BT Income
      Public welfare
      Transfer payments
  RT Family allowances
      Social security
  NT Guaranteed annual income
      Insurance, Unemployment
      Labor supply—Effect of income
        maintenance programs on
      Negative income tax
      Supplemental security income program
  — Computer programs
      NT MAPSIT (Computer program)
Income statements
  USE Financial statements
Income tax (May Subd Geog)
  [HJ4621-HJ4831 (General)]
  [HJ4651-HJ4655 (United States)]
  UF Direct taxation
      Personal income tax
      Taxation of income
  BT Internal revenue
      Taxation
      Taxation, Progressive
      Wealth
  RT Tithes
      Wages—Taxation
  NT Capital gains tax
      Commuters—Taxation
      Copyright—Royalties—Taxation
      Damages—Taxation
      Deferred compensation—Taxation
      Dividends—Taxation
      Earned income tax credit
      Excess profits tax
      Flat-rate income tax
      Interstate commerce—Taxation
      Old age pensions—Taxation
      Profit-sharing—Taxation
      Real property and taxation
      Rent—Taxation
      Undistributed profits tax
      Unjust enrichment tax
      Usufruct—Taxation
      Withholding tax
  — Accounting
      NT Income averaging
          Volunteer workers in income tax
            return preparation
  — — Law and legislation
        (May Subd Geog)
  — Auditing
      USE Tax auditing
  — Consolidated returns
      USE Corporations—Taxation—
          Consolidated returns
  — Deductions
  — — Charitable contributions
        UF Charitable contributions as tax
            deductions
            Charities—Taxation
  — — Educational expenses
        USE Income tax—Deductions—
            Expenses
  — — Expenses
        UF Expenses as tax deductions
            Income tax—Deductions—
              Educational expenses
            Income tax—Deductions—
              Medical expenses
            Income tax—Deductions—
              Repairs
        BT Expense accounts
        NT Expense accounts and taxation
  — — Interest
        UF Interest as tax deductions
  — — Losses
        UF Business losses as tax deductions
            Carry-back of business losses
            Carry-over of business losses
            Losses as tax deductions

Income tax
— **Deductions**
— — **Losses** *(Continued)*
    NT Commodity tax straddles
— — Medical expenses
    USE Income tax—Deductions—
        Expenses
— — **Political contributions**
    UF Political contributions as tax
        deductions
— — Repairs
    USE Income tax—Deductions—
        Expenses
— — **Retirement contributions**
    UF Retirement contributions as tax
        deductions
— — **Taxes**
    UF Taxes as tax deductions
— **Effect of inflation on**
    [HJ4645]
    BT Inflation (Finance)
— **Foreign income**
    UF Foreign income, Taxation of
        Taxation of foreign income
    NT Corporations, Foreign—Taxation
        Foreign tax credit
        Investments, Foreign—Taxation
        Taxation, Double
— **Joint returns** *(May Subd Geog)*
    UF Joint returns (Income tax)
    BT Husband and wife—Taxation
        Tax returns
— **Law and legislation** *(May Subd Geog)*
— **Rates and tables**
— Treaties
    USE Taxation, Double—Treaties
— Withholding
    USE Withholding tax
— **United States**
— — **Foreign income**
    NT Domestic international sales
        corporations
Income tax, Flat-rate
  USE Flat-rate income tax
Income tax, Municipal *(May Subd Geog)*
  Here are entered general works on municipal in-
come taxes and works limited to such taxes in re-
gions, countries, states, etc. Works on the municipal
income tax of individual cities are entered under In-
come tax with local subdivision.
  UF City income tax
      Municipal income tax
  BT Local taxation
Income transfer programs
  USE Income maintenance programs
Incomes policy
  USE Wage-price policy
Incommunicants
  USE Louisets
Incomparability of God
  USE God—Incomparability
Incompatibility of offices *(May Subd Geog)*
  BT Constitutional law
      Separation of powers
Incompatibility of offices (Canon law)
Incompatibles (Pharmacy)
  [RM143]
  UF Drug incompatibility
  BT Chemistry, Pharmaceutical
      Drugs—Prescribing
      Pharmacy
Incompetence, Mitral
  USE Mitral valve insufficiency
Incompetency to stand trial
  USE Competency to stand trial
Incomplete block designs
  [QA166.3 (Combinatorial analysis)]
  [QA279 (Experimental design)]
  BT Block designs
Incomplete books
  USE Unfinished books

Incomplete man test
  USE Gesell incomplete man test
Incomplete sentence test
  USE Sentence completion test
Incomplete works of art
  USE Unfinished works of art
Incompleteness theorems
  UF Theorems, Incompleteness
  BT Constructive mathematics
      Proof theory
  NT Gödel's theorem
Inconel
  BT Chromium-iron-nickel alloys
Inconfidencia mineira, Minas Gerais (Brazil),
1789
  USE Minas Gerais (Brazil)—History—
      Revolution, 1789
Inconnu (Fish)
  [QL638.S2]
  UF Sheefish
      Stenodus leucichthys
  BT Stenodus
Inconsistency (Logic)
  [BC199.I45]
  BT Logic
Incontinence
  USE Feces—Incontinence
      Urine—Incontinence
Incontinence, Urinary stress
  USE Urinary stress incontinence
Inconvenient forum
  USE Forum non conveniens
Incoronazione della Vergine (Mural painting)
  USE Nelli, Ottaviano, ca. 1370-ca. 1446.
      Incoronazione della Vergine
Incorporated bar
  USE Integrated bar
Incorporated farms
  USE Farm corporations
Incorporation *(May Subd Geog)*
  UF Federal incorporation
      Formation of corporations
  BT Corporation law
  NT Articles of incorporation
      Certificates of incorporation
      Charters
      De facto corporations
      Municipal incorporation
      Promoters
Incorporation, Certificates of
  USE Certificates of incorporation
Incorporation, Municipal
  USE Municipal incorporation
Incorporation (Feudal law)
  BT Feudal law
Incorporeal property
  USE Intangible property
Incorrigibles (Juvenile delinquency)
  BT Delinquents
      Juvenile delinquency
Incran language
  USE Gã language
**Increasing Membership, Participation,
Activities, Communication and Trust
Program**
  UF IMPACT Program
  BT Science—Study and teaching—United
      States
Increasing returns
  USE Economies of scale
Incredulity of Thomas (Painting)
  USE Christus en de ongelovige Thomas
      (Painting)
Increment, Unearned
  USE Unearned increment
Incremental control
  USE Incremental motion control
Incremental costing
  USE Direct costing

Incremental motion control
  UF Control, Incremental
      Incremental control
      Motion control, Incremental
  BT Automatic control
      Servomechanisms
      Stepping motors
Incremental motion control industry
Incremental System Programming Language
(Electronic computer system)
  USE ISPL (Electronic computer system)
Incrustation removal
  USE Descaling
Incrustations
  UF Deposits, Scale
      Encrustations
      Scale deposits
      Water-formed scale deposits
  BT Fouling
  SA *subdivision* Incrustations *under*
      subjects, e.g. Saline water
      conversion plants—Incrustations;
      Steam-boilers—Incrustations
  NT Pipes, Deposits in
      Pulp mills—Incrustations
Incrustations (Saline water conversion plants)
  USE Saline water conversion plants—
      Incrustations
Incrustations (Steam-boilers)
  USE Steam-boilers—Incrustations
Incrusted cameos
  USE Sulphides (Art)
Incubation (Religion)
  [BL325.I5]
  BT Medicine, Magic, mystic, and spagiric
      Religion
      Religion, Primitive
      Revelation
      Spiritual healing
Incubation of eggs
  USE Eggs—Incubation
Incubation of fish eggs
  USE Fishes—Eggs—Incubation
Incubators
  [SF495-7]
  UF Brooders
  BT Chickens—Hatcheries
      Eggs—Incubation
      Poultry—Hatcheries
  NT Fishes—Eggs—Incubation
Incubators (Pediatrics)
  BT Infants (Premature)
      Infants' supplies
      Neonatal intensive care
Incubi
  [BF1556]
  BT Demonology
      Spirits
Incumbrances (Law)
  USE Encumbrances (Law)
Incunabula
  [Z240-241]
  UF Bibliography—Early printed books—
      15th century
      Early printed books
  BT Bibliography
      Books—History—1400-1600
      Printing
      Rare books
  RT Printing—History
  NT Block-books
      Colophons
      Incipits
      Printers' marks
      Registers (in early printed books)
— **Bibliography**
    [Z240-241]
— Cataloging
    USE Cataloging of incunabula
— **Facsimiles**
    [Z241]

BT Block-books—Facsimiles
Printing—Specimens
— **Music**
_[ML112]_
UF Music—Incunabula
Incurable diseases _(May Subd Geog)_
BT Diseases
— **Hospitals** _(May Subd Geog)_
UF Incurables—Hospitals and asylums
Incurables
BT Sick
— Hospitals and asylums
USE Incurable diseases—Hospitals
Incursions (Military science)
USE Raids (Military science)
Incurvariidae
_[QL561.I5]_
UF Adelidae
Crinopterygidae
Lamproniidae
Nemophoridae
BT Lepidoptera
Moths
NT Yucca moths
Indan
UF Dihydroindene
Hydrindene
BT Indene
NT Indandione
Metindione
Indandione
BT Drugs
Indan
NT Arylindandiones
Indanyl carbenicillin
USE Carbenicillin
Indebtedness
USE Debt
Indecent assault _(May Subd Geog)_
UF Indecent liberties
BT Assault and battery
Sex crimes
Indecent exposure _(May Subd Geog)_
Here are entered works on exhibitionism as an
unlawful act. Works on attaining sexual gratification
by exhibiting and attracting attention to the genitals
are entered under Exhibitionism.
UF Exposure of person
BT Exhibitionism
Sex crimes
Indecent liberties
USE Indecent assault
Indeclinable words
USE _subdivision_ Indeclinable words _under_
individual languages or groups of
languages, e.g. English language—
Indeclinable words
Indefinite inner product spaces
USE Inner product spaces, Indefinite
Indefinite scalar product spaces
USE Inner product spaces, Indefinite
Indefinite sentence
USE Indeterminate sentence
Indefiniteness (Linguistics)
USE Definiteness (Linguistics)
Indemnification claims (1933-   )
USE Restitution and indemnification claims
(1933-   )
Indemnity
_[JX5326]_
BT Compensation (Law)
Damages
International law
NT Alien property—Valuation
Reparations
Requisitions, Military
Indemnity (Unification Church)
USE Restoration through indemnity
(Unification Church)

Indemnity against liability
(May Subd Geog)
BT Conditions (Law)
Liability (Law)
RT Hold harmless agreements
Insurance, Liability
Indemnity insurance
USE Insurance, Liability
Indene
UF Indonapthene
NT Indan
Sulindac
Indene resins
_[TP1180.I5]_
BT Gums and resins, Synthetic
Indenes
BT Polycyclic aromatic hydrocarbons
Indents of brasses
USE Brasses—Indents
Indentured servants _(May Subd Geog)_
[HD4871-HD4875 (General)]
[HD4875.U5 (United States)]
UF Servants, Indentured
BT Contract labor
Redemptioners
Slave labor
Indentures
USE Deeds
Trust indentures
Independence (Tuvalu)
USE Niulakita (Tuvalu)
Independence
USE Autonomy
Independence (Mathematics)
BT Logic, Symbolic and mathematical
Independence (Psychology)
USE Autonomy (Psychology)
Independence Day (Afghanistan)
UF Jeshan
Salgre Jeshyn-i-Estiqlal
BT Afghanistan—Anniversaries, etc.
Holidays—Afghanistan
Independence Day (Bahamas)
BT Bahamas—Anniversaries, etc.
Holidays—Bahamas
Independence Day (Chile)
BT Chile—Anniversaries, etc.
Holidays—Chile
Independence Day (Costa Rica)
BT Costa Rica—Anniversaries, etc.
Holidays—Costa Rica
Independence Day (Djibouti)
BT Djibouti—Anniversaries, etc.
Holidays—Djibouti
Independence Day (India)
BT Holidays—India
India—Anniversaries, etc.
Independence Day (Israel)
BT Holidays—Israel
Israel—Anniversaries, etc.
Independence Day (Malaysia)
UF Hari Kebangsaan Malaysia
BT Holidays—Malaysia
Malaysia—Anniversaries, etc.
Independence Day (Mexico)
BT Holidays—Mexico
Mexico—Anniversaries, etc.
Independence Day (Mexico) orations
BT Speeches, addresses, etc., Mexican
Independence Day (Norway)
BT Holidays—Norway
Norway—Anniversaries, etc.
Independence Day (Papua New Guinea)
BT Holidays—Papua New Guinea
Papua New Guinea—Anniversaries,
etc.
Independence Day (Philippines)
UF Philippine Independence Day
BT Holidays—Philippines
Philippines—Anniversaries, etc.

Independence Day (Surinam)
BT Holidays—Surinam
Surinam—Anniversaries, etc.
Independence Day (United States)
USE Fourth of July
Independence movements
USE _subdivision_ History—Autonomy and
independence movements _under_
names of countries, etc.
Independence National Historical Park (Pa.)
USE Independence National Historical Park
(Philadelphia, Pa.)
Independence National Historical Park
(Philadelphia, Pa.) _(Not Subd Geog)_
UF Independence National Historical Park
(Pa.)
BT Historic sites—Pennsylvania
National parks and reserves—
Pennsylvania
RT Carpenters' Hall (Philadelphia, Pa.)
Independence Operation (Project)
USE Operation Independence (Project)
Independency (Church polity)
USE Congregationalism
Independent administrative agencies
USE Independent regulatory commissions
Independent agencies
USE Independent regulatory commissions
Independent Catholic churches
(May Subd Geog)
_[BX4793.5-BX4795]_
Here are entered works on churches that are
Catholic or Orthodox by self-designation but are not
part of or recognized by the Catholic Church, the
Eastern churches, the Anglican Communion, or the
Old Catholic Church. Works on churches which se-
ceded from the Anglican Communion over issues of
the ordination of women, Prayer Book revision, and
modernizing theology are entered under Traditional-
ist Anglican churches.
UF Catholic independent churches
BT Christian sects
Independent churches _(May Subd Geog)_
UF Churches, Nondenominational
Churches, Undenominational
Nondenominational churches
Undenominational churches
BT Christian sects
RT Community churches
NT Non-institutional churches
Independent contractors _(May Subd Geog)_
UF Contractors, Independent
Vicarious liability
RT Agency (Law)
Contracts for work and labor
Employers' liability
Hire
Labor contract
Liability (Law)
Master and servant
Independent contractors (Roman law)
Independent counsels
USE Special prosecutors
Independent insurance agents
(May Subd Geog)
_[HG8091]_
UF Insurance agents, Independent
BT Insurance—Agents
Independent ocean freight forwarders
USE Ocean freight forwarders
Independent Order of Odd Fellows
(May Subd Geog)
_[HS951-HS1179]_
UF Odd-Fellows, Independent Order of
— **Charities**
— **Constitution**
UF Independent Order of Odd Fellows
—Laws, decisions, etc.
— **Costumes, supplies, etc.**
USE Independent Order of Odd
Fellows—Equipment and
supplies

Independent Order of Odd Fellows
— Costumes, supplies, etc. *(Continued)*
    Independent Order of Odd
      Fellows—Uniforms
— **Equipment and supplies**
    [HS1025-HS1026]
    UF Independent Order of Odd Fellows
        —Costumes, supplies, etc.
— Laws, decisions, etc.
    USE Independent Order of Odd
        Fellows—Constitution
— **Rituals**
    [HS1019-HS1021]
— **Songs and music**
    [M1905.O3 (Collections)]
    [M1906.O3 (Separate works)]
— **Uniforms**
    UF Independent Order of Odd Fellows
        —Costumes, supplies, etc.
Independent Order of Odd Fellows Cemetery
(Denton, Tex.)
USE I.O.O.F. Cemetery (Denton, Tex.)
Independent Party
USE National Greenback Party
Independent regulatory commissions
(May Subd Geog)
  UF Commissions, Independent regulatory
      Commissions of the federal
        government
      Independent administrative agencies
      Independent agencies
      Quasi-judicial agencies
      Regulatory agencies
      Regulatory commissions
  BT Administrative agencies
      Administrative law
  NT Public service commissions
Independent school trustees
USE Private school trustees
Independent schools
USE Private schools
Independent study
  [LB1049]
  UF Modular approach in education
      Study, Independent
  BT Study, Method of
      Tutors and tutoring
      Universities and colleges—Honors
        courses
Independent telephone companies
USE Telephone—United States
Independent treasury
  [HG2535-HG2539 (United States)]
  UF Subtreasury bill, 1840
      Subtreasury system
      Treasury, Independent
Independent unions *(May Subd Geog)*
  UF Local independent unions
  BT Trade-unions
Indeterminacy, Places of (Literature)
USE Places of indeterminacy (Literature)
Indeterminancy principle
USE Heisenberg uncertainty principle
Indeterminate analysis
USE Diophantine analysis
Indeterminate sentence *(May Subd Geog)*
  [HV8715]
  UF Indefinite sentence
      Sentence, Indeterminate
  BT Criminal law
      Criminal procedure
      Judgments
      Judgments, Criminal
      Juvenile courts
      Prison sentences
      Punishment
      Sentences (Criminal procedure)
  RT Probation
Indeterminism
USE Free will and determinism

Index, Maslov
USE Maslov index
Index, Site (Forestry)
USE Site index (Forestry)
Index expurgatorius
USE Index librorum prohibitorum
Index librorum prohibitorum
  [Z1020]
  UF Index expurgatorius
  BT Catholic Church—Bibliography
      Catholic Church—Discipline
      Catholic literature
      Condemned books
      Expurgated books
      Prohibited books (Canon law)
  RT Censorship
Index linking (Economics)
USE Indexation (Economics)
Index maps
  BT Maps
  SA *subdivision* Index maps *under names*
      of countries, regions, cities, etc.
Index numbers (Economics)
  [HB225]
    Here are entered general works on the construc-
  tion and use of index numbers. Specific types or the
  index numbers themselves are entered under their
  subjects.
  UF Numbers, Index
  BT Economics
      Prices
  RT Economic indicators
      Indexation (Economics)
  NT Price indexes
Index of refraction
USE Refractive index
Index of Work Satisfaction
  BT Job satisfaction—Testing
Index theorems
  [QA614.92]
  BT Differential operators
      Global analysis (Mathematics)
      Index theory (Mathematics)
      Manifolds (Mathematics)
Index theory (Mathematics)
  BT Mathematics
  NT Index theorems
Indexation (Economics) *(May Subd Geog)*
  UF Index linking (Economics)
      Indexing (Economics)
      Monetary correction
  BT Deflation (Finance)
      Economics
      Inflation (Finance)
  RT Escalator clause
      Index numbers (Economics)
— **Law and legislation** *(May Subd Geog)*
  NT Revalorization of debts
Indexers *(May Subd Geog)*
  BT Abstracting and indexing services
      Indexing
Indexes
  [AI]
  UF Indices
  BT Bibliography
      Concordances
  SA *subdivision* Dictionaries, indexes, etc.
      under names of individual persons;
      and subdivision Indexes *under*
      names of individual works (author-
      title or title entries) and under
      topical subjects
  NT Abstracting and indexing services
      Citation indexes
      Periodicals—Indexes
      Permutation indexes
      Reverse indexes
— **Use studies**
    BT Information services—Use studies
        Library use studies

Indexes, Card
USE Card system in business
      Catalogs, Card
Indexes, Environmental
USE Environmental indexes
Indexes, Geomagnetic
USE Geomagnetic indexes
Indexes, Health status
USE Health status indicators
Indexes, Stock
USE Stock price indexes
Indexing
  [HF5735-HF5746 (Business filing and
    indexing)]
  [Z695.9]
  UF Books—Indexing
  BT Abstracting
      Bibliography
      Cataloging
      Documentation
      Information retrieval
  RT Filing systems
      Thesauri
  SA *subdivision* Abstracting and indexing
      under specific subjects, e.g.
      Chemistry—Abstracting and
      indexing
  NT Automatic indexing
      Chain indexing
      Coordinate indexing
      Cross references (Cataloging)
      Indexers
      Municipal government—Records and
        correspondence—Indexing
      Newspapers—Abstracting and indexing
      Punched card systems
      Subject cataloging
      Transportation—Records and
        correspondence—Indexing
Indexing, Automatic
USE Automatic indexing
Indexing (Economics)
USE Indexation (Economics)
Indexing (Machine-shop practice)
  [TJ1167]
  BT Gages
      Gearing
      Machine-shop practice
      Machine-tools
Indexing and abstracting services
USE Abstracting and indexing services
Indexing vocabularies
USE Subject headings
      Thesauri
India
— **Anniversaries, etc.**
  NT Independence Day (India)
— **Antiquities**
  NT Ahicchatra (City)
      Atranjīkherā Site (India)
      Burzahom Site (India)
      Daimabad Site (India)
      Durkadi Nala Site (India)
      Kesarisingh's Khetar Site (India)
      Nālandā Site (India)
      Podouké (Ancient city)
      Ratnagiri Site (India)
      Rudramahālaya Site (India)
      Sahasraliṅga Site (India)
      Sai no Tekro Site (India)
      Sānchi Site (India)
      Satanikota Site (India)
      Vaiśālī (Ancient city)
      Vájra (Weapons)
      Veerapuram Site (India)
— **Civilization**
  NT Africa, Sub-Saharan—Civilization—
      Indic influences
      Architecture—Europe—Indic
      influences
      Art, Asian—Indic influences

Art, European—Indic influences
Art, Khmer—Indic influences
Asia—Civilization—Indic
  influences
Bronzes, Javanese—Indic
  influences
Cambodia—Civilization—Indic
  influences
Civilization—Indic influences
English literature—Indic influences
Europe—Civilization—Indic
  influences
Germany—Civilization—Indic
  influences
Greece—Civilization—Indic
  influences
Japan—Civilization—Indic
  influences
Laos—Civilization—Indic
  influences
Laos—Intellectual life—Indic
  influences
Mauritius—Civilization—Indic
  influences
Meroe (Sudan)—Civilization—
  Indic influences
Shawls—France—Indic influences
Silverwork—Portugal—Indic
  influences
Temples—Nepal—Indic influences
Thailand—Civilization—Indic
  influences
Vietnam—Civilization—Indic
  influences
— —To 1200
    [DS425]
— —1200-1765
    [DS427]
— —1765-1947
    [DS428]
— —1947-
    [DS428.2]
— —American influences
    BT United States—Civilization
— —Arab influences   (Not Subd Geog)
    BT Civilization, Arab
— —European influences
    BT Europe—Civilization
— —Greek influences
    BT Greece—Civilization
— —Iranian influences
    BT Iran—Civilization
— —Jaina influences
    BT Civilization, Jaina
— Climate
— Denotified tribes
    UF Criminal tribes (India)
       Denotified tribes (India)
    BT Caste—India
       Crime and criminals—India
       Ethnology—India
    SA subdivision Denotified tribes under
       names of states, regions, cities,
       etc. of India
    NT Koravas
       Lodhas
       Sansis
— Description and travel
— —To 1000
— —1001-1497
— —1498-1761
— —1762-1858
— —1859-1900
— —1901-1946
— —1947-1980
— —1981-
— Economic conditions
— —To 1000
— —1918-1947
— —1947-
— Economic policy

— —1947-
    [HC435.2]
— —1951-1956
— —1956-1961
— —1961-1966
— —1966-
— —1966-1974
    [HC435.2]
— —1974-1980
— —1980-
— Foreign relations
— —1984-
— Government publications (State
  governments)
    [Z3205]
— Governors
— —Dwellings
    NT Raj Bhavan (Calcutta, India)
— History
    [DS401-498]
— —To 324 B.C.
— — —Juvenile literature
— —324 B.C.-1000 A.D.
    NT Bhanja dynasty
       Chalukyas
       Chandela dynasty
       Cheras
       Cholas
       Gangas
       Gupta dynasty
       Gurjara-Pratihara dynasty
       Indo-Greeks
       Indo-Scythians
       Kalabhras
       Kalinga, Battle of, 260 B.C.
       Kushans
       Maitrakas
       Maukhari dynasty
       Pala dynasty
       Pallavas
       Pandyas
       Pāradas
       Paramaras
       Pushyabhūti dynasty, ca. 550-
         647
       Rashtrakutas
       Śailodbhava dynasty, ca. 550-
         736
       Satavahana dynasty
       Shāhi dynasty, ca. 865-1026
       Śuṅga dynasty, ca. 185 B.C.-ca.
         73 B.C.
       Vakataka dynasty
       Vishṇukuṇḍin dynasty, ca. 375-
         612
       Yadava dynasty
— — —Juvenile literature
— —Maurya dynasty, ca. 322 B.C.-ca. 185
  B.C.
— —1000-1526
    NT Bahmani dynasty, 1347-ca. 1527
       Bhanja dynasty
       Chalukya-Chola dynasty
       Chauhan dynasties
       Gangas
       Hoysala dynasty, ca. 1006-ca.
         1346
       Kakatiya dynasty
       Khilji dynasty
       Pala dynasty
       Pandyas
       Paramaras
       Sayyid dynasty, 1414-1451
       Sharqi dynasty
       Tughlug dynasty, 1320-1413
       Yadava dynasty
— —1000-1765
    NT Sūryavaṁśi Gajapati dynasty,
       1435-1550
— —1500-1765
    NT Ahmadnagar (Kingdom)

       Marathas
       Mogul Empire
       Panipat, Battle of, 1526
       Panipat, Battle of, 1556
— —18th century
    NT Buxar, Battle of, 1764
       Panipat, Battle of, 1761
       Plassey, Battle of, 1757
       Sindhia dynasty, 1726-1947
— —British occupation, 1765-1947
    NT Chota Nāgpur (India)—History
       —Insurrection, 1831-1832
       Maratha War, 1775-1782
       Maratha War, 1803
       Maratha War, 1816-1818
       Nepalese War, 1814-1816
       Pakistan movement
       Sindhia dynasty, 1726-1947
— — —Juvenile literature
— —Rohilla War, 1774
    USE Rohilla War, 1774
— —Mysore War, 1790-1792
    [DS474.1]
    UF Mysore War, 1790-1792
— —Mysore War, 1799
    [DS475.3]
    UF Mysore War, 1799
    NT Periyapatna, India, Battle of,
       1799
— —19th century
— —Mutiny, 1809
— —Afghan Wars, 1838-1919
    USE Afghan Wars
— —Sikh Wars, 1845-1849
    USE Sikh War, 1845-1846
       Sikh War, 1848-1849
— —Sepoy Rebellion, 1857-1858
    UF Indian Mutiny, 1857-1858
       Sepoy Rebellion
— — —Atrocities
    [DS478]
— — —Personal narratives
— —Sikkim Expedition, 1861
    USE Sikkim Expedition, 1861
— —Sikkim Expedition, 1888
    USE Sikkim Expedition, 1888
— —Chitral Campaign, 1895
— —Tirah Campaign, 1897-1898
    UF Tirah Campaign, 1897-1898
— —20th century
— — —Anecdotes, facetiae, satire, etc.
— — —Pictorial works
— —Amritsar Massacre, 1919
    UF Amritsar Massacre, India, 1919
       Jallianwala Bagh Massacre,
         India, 1919
       Jallianwalla Bāgh Massacre,
         India, 1919
    BT Massacres—India
— —Waziristan Campaign, 1919-1920
    UF Waziristan Campaign, 1919-
       1920
— —Quit India Movement, 1942
    [DS480.82]
    UF Quit India Movement, India,
       1942
— —1947-
    NT India-Pakistan Conflict, 1947-
       1949
       India-Pakistan Conflict, 1965
       India-Pakistan Conflict, 1971
       Sino-Indian Border Dispute,
         1957-
— —Golden Temple (Amritsar) Assault,
  1984
    UF Golden Temple Assault,
       Amritsar, India, 1984
       Operation Blue Star, Amritsar,
         India, 1984
— —Burmese Wars
    USE Burmese War, 1824-1826

India
— **History**
— — **Burmese Wars** *(Continued)*
      Burmese War, 1852
      Burmese War, 1885
— **Kings and rulers**
   UF Maharajahs
— — **Art patronage**
      BT Art patronage
— **Languages**
   NT Abor language
      Abujhmaria dialect
      Agri dialect
      Andamanese language
      Bajjika language
      Bhalesi dialect
      Bishnupuriya dialect
      Brokpa dialect
      Danuwar Rai language
      Ezhava dialect
      Gadaba language (Dravidian)
      Gujuri language
      Halari dialect
      Havyaka dialect
      Kamma dialect
      Koshti dialect (Marathi)
      Kotia dialect
      Ladakhi language
      Lahuli language
      Lambadi language
      Lushai language
      Manipravalam language
         (Malayalam)
      Marari dialect
      Mewari dialect
      Mewati dialect
      Miji language
      Miju dialect
      Milang language
      Mishmi language
      Moklum dialect
      Muduva dialect
      Nimadi dialect
      Padam language
      Pahari languages, Central
      Parengi language
      Parsi-Gujarati dialect
      Pattani dialect (India)
      Pawari dialect
      Rajasthani language
      Rajbangsi dialect
      Rongmei dialect
      Sadan dialect
      Sambalpuri dialect
      Sherpa language
      Soliga dialect
      Tagin language
      Zou dialect
— **Literatures** *(Not Subd Geog)*
   USE Indic literature
   NT Dakhini Hindustani literature
      Manipravalam literature
         (Malayalam)
— **Officials and employees**
— — **Discipline**
— **Politics and government**
— — **To 997**
— — **997-1765**
— — **1765-1947**
— — **19th century**
— — **1857-1919**
   NT Ghadr movement
— — **20th century**
— — **1919-1947**
— — **1947-**
   NT Razakars
— — **1975-1977**
— — **1977-**
— **Religion**
   NT Ḍerā Saccā Saudā
      Gods, Indic

— — **To 1200**
— — **1200-1765**
      ₍BL2006₎
— **Scheduled tribes**
   UF Scheduled tribes (India)
   BT Ethnology—India
      Tribes—India
   RT Untouchables
   SA *subdivision* Scheduled tribes *under*
      names of states, regions, cities,
      etc. of India
   NT Asurs
      Grasia (Indic people)
      Halams (Indic people)
      Koras
      Noatia (Indic people)
— **Social conditions**
— — **To 1200**
— — **1947-**
— **Social life and customs**
— — **To 1200**
— **Study and teaching** *(May Subd Geog)*
   NT Indologists
India. Army
— **Madras regiments**
      ₍UA844.M₎
India, Northeastern
   UF Northeast India
      Northeastern India
India, South
   UF India, Southern
      South India
      Southern India
India, Southern
   USE India, South
India in motion pictures
   BT Moving-pictures
India ink
      ₍TP948.I6₎
   BT Artists' materials
      Ink
India-Pakistan Conflict, 1947-1949
   (May Subd Geog)
      ₍DS385.9₎
   UF Indo-Pakistan Conflict, 1947-1949
      Kashmir War, 1947-1949
      Pakistan-India Conflict, 1947-1949
   BT India—History—1947-
      Pakistan—History
India-Pakistan Conflict, 1965
   UF Indian-Pakistan Conflict, 1965
      Indo-Pakistan Conflict, 1965
      Pakistan-Indian Conflict, 1965
   BT India—History—1947-
India-Pakistan Conflict, 1971
   UF Indo-Pakistan Conflict, 1971
      Pakistan-Indian Conflict, 1971
   BT India—History—1947-
      Pakistan—History
   RT Bangladesh—History—Revolution,
      1971
India rubber
   USE Rubber
India rubber industry
   USE Rubber industry and trade
Indiamen *(May Subd Geog)*
      ₍VM393.I64₎
   UF East Indiamen
      Indiamen, East
   BT Cargo ships
      Sailing ships
Indiamen, East
   USE Indiamen
Indian-Afro-American relations
   USE Afro-Americans—Relations with
      Indians
Indian agents *(May Subd Geog)*
      ₍E93 (United States)₎
   UF Agents, Indian

   BT Indians—Government relations
      Indians of North America—
         Government relations
      Indians of North America—
         Reservations
Indian almond myrobalan
   USE Terminalia catappa
Indian aloe
   USE Aloe barbadensis
Indian antelope
   USE Antilope cervicapra
Indian appropriations
   USE Indians of North America—
      Appropriations
Indian art, Modern
   USE Art, Indian
Indian arts
   USE Indians of North America—Arts
Indian athletes
   USE Athletes, Indian
Indian authors
   USE Authors, Indian
Indian bael tree
   USE Bael (Tree)
Indian baskets
   USE *subdivision* Basket making *under*
      Indians of North America; Indians
      of South America; *and similar*
      headings
      Basketwork
Indian belts
   USE Wampum belts
Indian blackbuck antelope
   USE Antilope cervicapra
Indian blankets
   USE Indians—Textile industry and fabrics
Indian blue pine
   USE Pinus griffithii
Indian bread
   USE Poria cocos
Indian broad-beaked dolphin
   USE Lagenorhynchus electra
Indian buffalo
   USE Water buffalo
Indian captivities
   USE *subdivision* Captivities *under individual*
      Indian tribes and groups of Indians,
      e.g. Indians of North America—
         Captivities
Indian-Chinese Border Dispute, 1957-
   USE Sino-Indian Border Dispute, 1957-
Indian clubs
      ₍GV491-GV493 (Exercises)₎
   BT Gymnastics
   RT Callisthenics
Indian Coast (Africa)
   BT Coasts—Africa
   NT Indian Coast (Kenya)
      Indian Coast (South Africa)
      Indian Coast (Tanzania)
Indian Coast (India)
   BT Coasts—India
Indian Coast (Kenya)
   BT Coasts—Kenya
      Indian Coast (Africa)
Indian Coast (South Africa)
   BT Coasts—South Africa
      Indian Coast (Africa)
Indian Coast (Tanzania)
   BT Coasts—Tanzania
      Indian Coast (Africa)
Indian cookery
   USE Cookery, Indian
Indian corn
   USE Corn
Indian-corn paper
   USE Paper, Maize
Indian craft
      ₍TT21-54₎

Here are entered works giving instruction and examples for duplicating Indian crafts. Works on the crafts as practiced by the Indians themselves are entered under headings such as Indians—Art; Indians of Central America—Industries; Indians of North America—Costume and adornment; Indians of South America—Pottery; etc.; and names of specific items, e.g. Moccasins; Totem poles; Wampum belts; etc.
  BT Handicraft
  NT Eskimo craft
      Ojo de Dios (Talisman)
Indian crape myrtle
  USE Crape myrtle, Common
Indian Creek (Chesapeake, Va.)
  BT Rivers—Virginia
Indian Creek (Ritchie County, W. Va.)
  BT Rivers—West Virginia
Indian Creek, Big (Iowa)
  USE Big Indian Creek (Iowa)
Indian danio
  USE Zebra danio
Indian Desert (India and Pakistan)
  USE Thar Desert (India and Pakistan)
Indian dhole
  USE Cuon alpinus
Indian drama *(May Subd Geog)*
  BT Drama
Indian elephant
  UF Elephas indicus
      Elephas maximus
  BT Elephants
  NT Siri (Elephant)
  — **Pictorial works**
Indian ethics
  USE Indians of North America—Ethics
Indian fiction (American)
  USE American fiction—Indian authors
Indian garden lizard
  USE Calotes versicolor
Indian hemp, Brown
  USE Sunn hemp
Indian hospitals
  USE Indians of North America—Hospitals
Indian incantations
  USE Indians of North America—
      Incantations
Indian Lake (Indian Lake, N.Y.)
  BT Lakes—New York (State)
Indian Lake (Man.)
  USE Southern Indian Lake (Man.)
Indian Lake (Ohio)
  BT Lakes—Ohio
Indian languages
  USE Indians—Languages
Indian libraries
  USE Libraries and Indians
Indian literature *(May Subd Geog)*
      Here are entered collections of works by Indian authors in Indian languages. Collections of works in a specific Indian language are entered under the corresponding heading for the literature, e.g. Aztec literature. Collections of works by Indian authors in non-Indian languages are entered under the specific non-Indian literature with the subdivision Indian authors, e.g. Canadian literature—Indian authors.
  UF Indian literature (American Indian)
      Indians—Literature
  BT Literature—Indian authors
  NT Yuman literature
  — **United States**
      BT United States—Literatures
Indian literature (American)
  USE American literature—Indian authors
Indian literature (American Indian)
  USE Indian literature
Indian literature (Canadian)
  USE Canadian literature—Indian authors
Indian literature (East Indian)
  USE Indic literature
Indian lotus
  USE Lotus, East Indian
Indian love poetry
  USE Love poetry, Indian

Indian mackerel
  USE Rastrelliger kanagurta
Indian meal
  USE Corn meal
Indian medical personnel
  USE Indians in medicine
Indian millet
  USE Durra
Indian mirror embroidery
  USE Shisha mirror embroidery
Indian motorcycles
  ₜTL448.Iₜ
Indian music (American Indian)
  USE Indians—Music
Indian Mutiny, 1857-1858
  USE India—History—Sepoy Rebellion,
      1857-1858
Indian mythology (American Indian)
  USE Indians—Religion and mythology
Indian Neck Ossuary (Mass.)
  (Not Subd Geog)
  UF Indian Neck Site (Mass.)
  BT Massachusetts—Antiquities
Indian Neck Site (Mass.)
  USE Indian Neck Ossuary (Mass.)
Indian newspapers *(May Subd Geog)*
  ₜPN4883 (United States)ₜ
  UF Indians—Newspapers
Indian numeration
  USE Numeration, Indian
Indian occupation of Wounded Knee, S.D.,
1973
  USE Wounded Knee (S.D.)—History—
      Indian occupation, 1973
Indian Ocean
  NT Arabian Sea
      Indo-Pacific Region
      Timor Sea
  — **Strategic aspects**
      BT Military geography
          Strategy
Indian Ocean Islands
  USE Islands of the Indian Ocean
Indian Ocean Region
  — **Civilization**
  — — **French influences**
          BT France—Civilization
Indian oil sardine
  USE Sardinella longiceps
Indian orations
  USE Indians of North America—Oratory
Indian paint fungus
  UF Echinodontium tinctorium
  BT Wood-decaying fungi
Indian paintbrush (Plant)
  USE Castilleja
Indian painting, Modern
  USE Painting, Indian
Indian painting, Traditional
  USE Indians—Painting
Indian-Pakistan Conflict, 1965
  USE India-Pakistan Conflict, 1965
Indian Pass Wilderness (Calif.)
  (Not Subd Geog)
  UF Indian Pass Wilderness Study Area
      (Calif.)
  BT National parks and reserves—
      California
      Wilderness areas—California
Indian Pass Wilderness Study Area (Calif.)
  USE Indian Pass Wilderness (Calif.)
Indian Peaks Wilderness (Colo.)
  BT Wilderness areas—Colorado
Indian periodicals *(May Subd Geog)*
  ₜPN4883 (United States)ₜ
Indian physicians *(May Subd Geog)*
  ₜR696ₜ
  UF Physicians, Indian
  BT Indians in medicine
      Physicians

Indian pilot whale
  USE Globicephala macrorhynchus
Indian podophyllum
  USE Podophyllum emodi
Indian poetry *(May Subd Geog)*
      Here are entered collections of poetry written by Indians in Indian languages. Collections of poetry about Indians are entered under Indians—Poetry.
  BT Folk poetry
      Poetry
  SA Cherokee poetry; Chippewa poetry;
      Dakota poetry; *and similar headings*
  NT Cherokee poetry
      Chippewa poetry
      Dakota poetry
      Love poetry, Indian
      Yaqui poetry
Indian poetry (American)
  USE American poetry—Indian authors
Indian poetry (Canadian)
  USE Canadian poetry—Indian authors
Indian poetry (Peruvian)
  USE Peruvian poetry—Indian authors
Indian Point Nuclear Power Plant (N.Y.)
  BT Nuclear power plants—New York
      (State)
Indian ponies
  ₜE98.H55 (Indians of North America)ₜ
  ₜSF315 (Animal culture)ₜ
  UF Indians of North America—Ponies
  BT Indians of North America—Domestic
      animals
      Indians of North America—
      Transportation
      Mustang
      Ponies
      Wild horses
  NT Appaloosa horse
Indian prints
  USE Prints, Indian
Indian python
  ₜQL666.O63ₜ
  UF Python molurus
Indian removal
  USE Indians of North America—Removal
Indian reservations
  USE *names of reservations*
      Indians of North America—
      Reservations
Indian rhinoceros beetle
  USE Oryctes rhinoceros
Indian rice
  USE Wild rice
Indian River (Fla.)
  BT Rivers—Florida
Indian rosewood
  USE Dalbergia latifolia
Indian rupee
  USE Rupee, Indian
Indian saffron
  USE Turmeric
Indian sandalwood
  USE Sandalwood
Indian scholarships
  USE Indians of North America—
      Scholarships, fellowships, etc.
Indian studies
  USE Indians—Study and teaching
Indian studies, North American
  USE Indians of North America—Study and
      teaching
Indian sub-continent
  USE South Asia
Indian sumac
  USE Rhus cotinus
Indian trade factories
  USE Indians of North America—Trading
      posts
Indian trails *(May Subd Geog)*
  ₜE98.T7ₜ

Indian trails (Continued)
   UF Indians of North America—Trails
        Trails, Indian
   BT Roads
        Trails
   RT Indians of North America—Roads
        Portages

Indian warfare
   [E98.W2]
   [U240]
   Here are entered treatises on the Indian method of fighting and instructions for campaigns against the Indians. Works on Indian wars are entered under Indians of Mexico [North America, South America, etc.]—Wars and under names of specific Indian wars.
   UF Indians of North America—Military capacity and organization
        Warfare, Indian
   BT Indians of North America—Wars
   NT Indians of North America as soldiers
        Scalping

Indian willow tree
   USE Salix tetrasperma

Indian wrestling
   USE Arm wrestling

Indian youth (North America)
   USE Indians of North America—Youth

Indiana
   — **Antiquities**
       NT Leonard Haag Site (Ind.)
   — **Description and travel**
   — — **1951-1980**
   — — **1981-**
   — **History**
       [F521-535]
   — — **To 1787**
   — — **Revolution, 1775-1783**
       [E263.I5]
   — — **War of 1812**
       NT Mississinewa, Battle of, 1812
   — — **War with Mexico, 1845-1848**
       [E409.5.I7]
   — — **Civil War, 1861-1865**
       [E506]
   — **Politics and government**
   — — **Civil War, 1861-1865**

Indiana bat
   USE Myotis sodalis

Indiana Dunes National Lakeshore (Ind.)
   BT National parks and reserves—United States
        Parks—Indiana
        Sand-dunes—Indiana

Indiana Dunes State Park (Ind.)
   BT Parks—Indiana
        Sand-dunes—Indiana

Indiana myotis
   USE Myotis sodalis

Indiana Railroad
   BT Railroads—United States

Indiana Toll Road (Ind.)
   BT Express highways—Indiana
        Interstate 80
        Interstate 90
        Toll roads—Indiana

Indianapolis (Ind.)
   — **History**
   — — **Civil War, 1861-1865**

Indianapolis Speedway Race
   UF Indy 500
   BT Automobile racing—Indiana

Indianists (May Subd Geog)
   [E57]
   BT Anthropologists
        Indians—Historiography

Indians
   [E51-E99]
   Here are entered works on the aboriginal peoples of the Western Hemisphere, including Eskimos. Works on the inhabitants of India in general are entered under East Indians.

For convenience, the Western Hemisphere has been divided into five basic geographical regions: North America, Mexico, Central America, West Indies and South America. Works pertaining to Indian groups located within the confines of one of these regions are entered under Indians of the pertinent region, e.g. Indians of North America; Indians of Mexico.

Names of Indian linguistic families are distinguished as such (and from the names of single languages or tribes) by the termination an or ian.
   UF American aborigines
        American Indians
        Amerinds
        Indians—Ethnology
        Pre-Columbian Indians
        Precolumbian Indians
        Stone age—America
   BT Indians—Metal-work
        Man, Prehistoric—America
   SA headings beginning with the word Indian; and subdivision Indians under individual wars, e.g. World War, 1939-1945—Indians
   NT Civilization—Indian influences
        Jesus Christ—Indian interpretations
        Libraries and Indians
        Paleo-Indians
   — **Agriculture**
       [E59.A]
   — **Antiquities**
       [E58]
       [E59.A63]
       [E61]
       BT America—Antiquities
          Archaeology
       NT Indians—Pottery
          Man, Prehistoric—America
          Paleo-Indians
   — **Architecture**
       [E59.A67]
       BT Architecture
   — **Arms and armor**
       BT Arms and armor, Primitive
   — **Art**
       [E59.A7]
       UF Pre-Columbian art
          Precolumbian art
       BT Art, Primitive
       RT Art, Indian
       NT Indians—Metal-work
          Indians—Painting
          Indians—Sculpture
          Painting, Indian
          Prints, Indian
   — **Basket making**
       BT Basket making
          Indians—Industries
   — **Boats**
       [E59.C2]
       BT Navigation, Primitive
   — **Calendar**
   — **Cartography**
       [E59.C25]
       BT Cartography, Primitive
   — **City planning**
       BT City planning
   — **Civilization**
       NT Christian art and symbolism—Mexico—Indian influences
   — **Color**
       [E59.C]
       BT Color of man
   — **Costume and adornment**
       [E98.C8]
   — **Dwellings**
       [E59.D9]
       BT Dwellings
   — **Education**
       [E57.E4]
   — Ethnology

       USE Indians; Indians of North America; Indians of South America; and similar headings
          Indians
          Indians of North America
          Indians of South America
   — **Food**
       [E59.F]
       NT Cookery, Indian
   — **Games**
       [E59.G3]
   — **Government relations**
       [E59.G]
       RT Indians, Treatment of
       NT Corregidores de indios
          Indian agents
   — **Historiography**
       NT Indianists
   — **History**
       [E58]
   — **Implements**
       [E59.I4]
       BT Industries, Primitive
   — **Industries**
       NT Indians—Basket making
          Indians—Metal-work
   — **Land tenure**
       UF Indians—Land titles
          Indians—Real property
   — Land titles
       USE Indians—Land tenure
   — **Languages**
       [PM1-7356]
       UF Indian languages
       NT Penutian languages
   — **Legal status, laws, etc.**
       Here are entered works containing, or treating of legislation enacted by Western colonial powers or national governments, governing the status of, and relations to Indian tribes and individuals in general. Laws governing the Indians of individual regions or individual tribes are entered under pertinent headings followed by the subdivision Legal status, laws, etc., e.g. Indians of North America—Oklahoma—Legal status, laws, etc.; Cherokee Indians—Legal status, laws, etc. Works on the native law of Indian tribes are entered under a heading appropriate for the respective legal system, e.g. Law, Cheyenne.
       SA subdivision Legal status, laws, etc. under names of groups of Indians and names of individual Indian tribes, e.g. Indians of North America—Legal status, laws, etc.; Cherokee Indians—Legal status, laws, etc.
       NT Legal assistance to Indians
   — **Legends**
       [E59.F6]
   — Literature
       USE Indian literature
   — **Marriage customs and rites**
       UF Marriage customs and rites, Indian
       BT Indians—Social life and customs
   — **Mathematics**
       UF Mathematics, Indian
   — **Medicine**
       BT Medicine, Primitive
   — **Metal-work**
       BT Art metal-work
          Indians—Art
          Indians—Industries
          Metal-work
       NT Indians
   — **Missions**
       [E59.M65]
       UF Missions, Indian
   — **Mixed bloods**
       UF Half-breed Indians
          Mixed bloods (American Indians)
       BT Miscegenation
   — **Money**

Indians of Central America
— **Dances** *(Continued)*
  BT Indians of Central America—
     Religion and mythology
     Indians of Central America—Social
     life and customs
  NT Moros y Cristianos (Dance)
— **Dwellings**
  BT Dwellings
     Indians of Central America—
     Architecture
— **Ethnology**
  USE Ethnology—Central America
     Indians of Central America
— **Games**
  UF Indians of Central America—
     Amusements
     Indians of Central America—
     Recreations
     Indians of Central America—
     Sports
  BT Games, Primitive
     Indians of Central America—Social
     life and customs
— **Health and hygiene** *(May Subd Geog)*
  BT Medical anthropology
— **Hunting**
  BT Hunting, Primitive
— **Industries**
  NT Indians of Central America—
     Metal-work
— **Labor service**
  BT Labor service
— **Languages**
  [PM3001-4566]
  NT Black Carib language
     Boruca language
     Bribri dialect
     Cakchikel language
     Chorti language
     Doraskean languages
     Guaymi language
     Island Carib language
     Ixil language
     Jacalteca language
     Jicaque language
     Kekchi language
     Lenca language
     Maya language
     Mayan languages
     Mopan language
     Otomanguean languages
     Otomi language
     Pipil language
     Pokomam language
     Pokonchi language
     Quiché language
     Quichean languages
     Talamanca language
     Terraba language
     Tlascalteca language
     Xinca language
— **Magic**
  UF Magic, Indian
  BT Indians of Central America—
     Religion and mythology
— **Marriage customs and rites**
  BT Indians of Central America—Social
     life and customs
     Marriage customs and rites
— **Masks**
— **Metal-work**
  [F1434.2.M4]
  BT Art metal-work
     Indians of Central America—Art
     Indians of Central America—
     Industries
     Metal-work
— **Missions**
  [F1434.2.M6]
— **Mixed bloods**

  NT Black Carib Indians
— **Mortuary customs**
— **Music**
  [ML3572]
— **Pottery**
  [F1434.2.P6]
  BT Indians of Central America—
     Antiquities
  NT Plumbate ware
— **Recreations**
  USE Indians of Central America—
     Games
— **Religion and mythology**
  [F1434.2.R3]
  NT Indians of Central America—
     Dances
     Indians of Central America—
     Magic
     Kukulcan
— **Rites and ceremonies**
— **Sculpture**
  UF Indians of Central America—
     Stone-sculpture
  BT Indians of Central America—Art
     Sculpture
     Sculpture, Primitive
— **Social life and customs**
  UF Indians of Central America—
     Amusements
     Indians of Central America—
     Customs
  NT Indians of Central America—
     Dances
     Indians of Central America—
     Games
     Indians of Central America—
     Marriage customs and rites
— **Sports**
  USE Indians of Central America—
     Games
— **Stone-sculpture**
  USE Indians of Central America—
     Sculpture
— **Textile industry and fabrics**
  UF Indians of Central America—
     Weaving
— **Trading posts**
  UF Trading posts (Central American
     Indian)
  BT Indians of Central America—
     Commerce
— **Transportation**
  NT Indians of Central America—Boats
— **Weaving**
  USE Indians of Central America—
     Textile industry and fabrics
— **Women**
— **Wood-carving**
  BT Indians of Central America—Art
     Wood-carving
— **Writing**
  NT Mayas—Writing
— **Belize**
  NT Carib Indians
     Mayas
— — **Languages**
  NT Maya language
— **Costa Rica**
  NT Guatuso Indians
— **El Salvador**
  NT Lenca Indians
— **Guatemala**
  NT Tzutuhil Indians
— — **Antiquities**
— — **Languages**
  NT Aguacatec language
     Chuj language
     Cubulco Achi language
     Kanjobal language
     Rabinal Achi language
— **Honduras**

  NT Lenca Indians
— — **Languages**
  NT Jicaque language
— **Panama**
— — **Art**
  NT Molas
Indians of Mexico
  [F1219-F1220]
  Subdivided by regions or states of Mexico.
  The names of individual tribes provided as NT
  references under this heading constitute a complete
  list of all tribes of Mexico included in LCSH.
  UF Indians of Mexico—Ethnology
     Meso-America
     Meso-American Indians
     Mesoamerica
     Mesoamerican Indians
     Pre-Columbian Indians
     Precolumbian Indians
  NT Acaxee Indians
     Akwa'ala Indians
     Amuzgo Indians
     Azteco-Tanoan Indians
     Aztecs
     Basket-Maker Indians
     Cahita Indians
     Cazcan Indians
     Chañabal Indians
     Chatino Indians
     Chiapanec Indians
     Chichimeca-Jonaz Indians
     Chichimecs
     Chinantec Indians
     Chol Indians
     Chontal Indians
     Coahuiltecan Indians
     Coca Indians
     Cocopa Indians
     Cora Indians
     Cuicatec Indians
     Guachichile Indians
     Huastec Indians
     Huave Indians
     Huichol Indians
     Kickapoo Indians
     Kiliwa Indians
     Lacandon Indians
     Mam Indians
     Matlatzinca Indians
     Mayas
     Mayo Indians
     Mazahua Indians
     Mazatec Indians
     Mixe Indians
     Mixtec Indians
     Nahuas
     Olmecs
     Opata Indians
     Otomi Indians
     Pame Indians
     Papago Indians
     Pipil Indians
     Popoloca Indians
     Popoluca Indians (Vera Cruz)
     Seri Indians
     Tarahumare Indians
     Tarasco Indians
     Teco Indians
     Tecuexe Indians
     Tepanecas
     Tepecano Indians
     Tepehua Indians
     Tepehuane Indians
     Tezcucan Indians
     Tlahuica Indians
     Tlapanec Indians
     Tlaxcalan Indians
     Toltecs
     Totonacos
     Trique Indians
     Tzeltal Indians

Tzotzil Indians
Uto-Aztecan Indians
Yaqui Indians
Zacateca Indians
Zapotec Indians
Zoque Indians
— **Agriculture**
  [F1219.3.A]
— Amusements
  USE Indians of Mexico—Games
— **Anthropometry**
  [F1219.3.A]
— **Antiquities**
  [F1219]
  NT Indians of Mexico—Implements
     Indians of Mexico—Pottery
     Indians of Mexico—Pyramids
     Indians of Mexico—Seals
        (Numismatics)
— **Architecture**
  [F1219.3.A6]
  UF Architecture, Aztec
     Aztec architecture
— **Arms and armor**
  [F1219.3.A]
  NT Throwing-sticks
— **Art**
  [F1219.3.A7]
  UF Pre-Columbian art
     Precolumbian art
  SA subdivision Art under names of
     tribes
  NT Indians of Mexico—Bone carving
     Indians of Mexico—Metal-work
     Indians of Mexico—Sculpture
     Indians of Mexico—Wood-carving
     Tarasco Indians—Art
— **Astronomy**
  UF Astronomy, Mexican Indian
  BT Astronomy
— **Bone carving**
  BT Bone carving
     Indians of Mexico—Art
— **Children**
  BT Children
— **Costume and adornment**
  [F1219.3.C]
— **Craniology**
  [F1219.3.C8]
— **Dances**
  [F1219.3.D2]
  NT Matachines (Dance)
     Moros y Cristianos (Dance)
— **Dentistry**
  BT Dentistry
     Indians of Mexico—Medicine
— **Diseases** (May Subd Geog)
  BT Indians of Mexico—Health and
     hygiene
— **Education** (May Subd Geog)
  UF Indians of Mexico—Schools
— Ethnology
  USE Ethnology—Mexico
     Indians of Mexico
— **Fishing**
— **Games**
  UF Indians of Mexico—Amusements
     Indians of Mexico—Recreations
     Indians of Mexico—Sports
  BT Games, Primitive
     Indians of Mexico—Social life and
        customs
  NT Ulama (Game)
— **Government relations**
  RT Indians, Treatment of—Mexico
  NT Indians of Mexico—Taxation
— **Health and hygiene** (May Subd Geog)
  NT Indians of Mexico—Diseases
— **Implements**
  UF Indians of Mexico—Stone
     implements

BT Indians of Mexico—Antiquities
NT Metates
— **Industries**
  NT Indians of Mexico—Metal-work
— **Kinship**
  BT Indians of Mexico—Social life and
     customs
     Kinship
— **Labor service**
  BT Labor service
— **Land tenure**
  SA subdivision Land tenure under
     names of tribes
— **Languages**
  [PM3001-4566]
  NT Aztec language
     Cahita language
     Chañabal language
     Chinantecan languages
     Chiricahua language
     Chocho language
     Chontal language
     Coca language
     Cochimi language
     Cocopa language
     Cuicatec language
     Cuitlateco language
     Huave language
     Huichol language
     Ixcateco language
     Kiliwa language
     Lacandon language
     Matlatzinca language
     Maya language
     Mayo language (Piman)
     Mazahua language
     Mazateco language
     Mixe language
     Mixtec language
     Ocuiltec language
     Otomanguean languages
     Otomian languages
     Papabuco language
     Papago language
     Piman languages
     Pokomam language
     Pokonchi language
     Popoloca language
     Popolocan languages
     Popoluca language (Vera Cruz)
     Proto-Chinantec language
     Proto-Popotecan language
     Proto-Yuman language
     Seri language
     Tarahumare language
     Tarascan language
     Tepehua language
     Tepehuan language
     Tlapanec language
     Trique language
     Uspanteca language
     Uto-Aztecan languages
     Yaqui language
     Yuma language
     Yuman languages
     Zapotec language
— **Legends**
  SA subdivision Legends under names
     of tribes
— **Marriage customs and rites**
  UF Marriage customs and rites, Indian
  BT Indians of Mexico—Social life and
     customs
— **Masks**
  [F1219.3.M4]
— **Medicine**
  [F1219.3.M5]
  NT Indians of Mexico—Dentistry
— **Metal-work**
  [F1219.3.M52]

BT Art metal-work
     Indians of Mexico—Art
     Indians of Mexico—Industries
     Metal-work
— **Missions**
— **Mixed bloods**
— **Mortuary customs**
  [F1219.3.M]
— **Museums**
  BT Archaeological museums and
     collections
     Ethnological museums and
     collections
— **Music**
  [F1219.3.M]
  [ML3570]
— **Pottery**
  [F1219.3.P8]
  BT Indians of Mexico—Antiquities
  NT Plumbate ware
— **Pyramids**
  BT Indians of Mexico—Antiquities
— Recreations
  USE Indians of Mexico—Games
— **Religion and mythology**
  [F1219.3.R38]
  NT Aztecs—Religion and mythology
     Coyolxauhqui (Aztec deity)
     Kukulcan
     Mayas—Religion and mythology
     Nagualism
     Nahuas—Religion and mythology
— **Rites and ceremonies**
  SA names of special ceremonies, e.g.
     Mushroom ceremony; and
     subdivision Rites and
     ceremonies under names of
     Indian tribes
— Schools
  USE Indians of Mexico—Education
— **Sculpture**
  UF Indians of Mexico—Stone-
     sculpture
  BT Indians of Mexico—Art
     Sculpture
     Sculpture, Primitive
— **Seals (Numismatics)**
  BT Indians of Mexico—Antiquities
     Seals (Numismatics)
— **Social life and customs**
  [F1219]
  NT Indians of Mexico—Games
     Indians of Mexico—Kinship
     Indians of Mexico—Marriage
        customs and rites
— Sports
  USE Indians of Mexico—Games
— Stone implements
  USE Indians of Mexico—Implements
— Stone-sculpture
  USE Indians of Mexico—Sculpture
— **Taxation**
  [F1219.3.T]
  BT Indians, Treatment of—Mexico
     Indians of Mexico—Government
     relations
— **Textile industry and fabrics**
  [F1219.3.T35]
  NT Ojo de Dios (Talisman)
— **Wars**
  NT Champotón, Battle of, 1517
     Mixton War, 1541-1542
— **Women**
  [F1219.3.W]
— **Wood-carving**
  BT Indians of Mexico—Art
     Wood-carving
— **Writing**
  [F1219.3.W94]

Indians of Mexico
  — Writing *(Continued)*
    UF Hieroglyphics, Mexican
       Inscriptions, Mexican
       Mexican hieroglyphics
       Picture-writing, Mexican
    NT Aztecs—Writing
       Mayas—Writing
       Mixtec Indians—Writing
       Zapotec Indians—Writing
  — Chiapas
    NT Harvard Chiapas Project
Indians of North America
    [E77-E99]
    Subdivided by states, provinces, regions, etc., e.g.
    Indians of North America—Massachusetts; Indians
    of North America—British Columbia; Indians of
    North America—Mississippi Valley.
    The names of individual tribes provided as NT
    references under this heading, or under this heading
    with local subdivision, constitute a complete list of all
    North American tribes included in LCSH.
    UF American aborigines
       American Indians
       Indians—Ethnology
       Indians of North America—Culture
       Indians of North America—Ethnology
       Indians of North America—United
         States
       Indians of the United States
       Native Americans
       North American Indians
    NT Abitibi Indians
       Abnaki Indians
       Achomawi Indians
       Acoma Indians
       Agua Caliente Indians
       Ahtena Indians
       Aleuts
       Algonkin Indians
       Algonquian Indians
       Alibamu Indians
       Alsea Indians
       Apache Indians
       Apalachee Indians
       Apalachicola Indians
       Arapaho Indians
       Arikara Indians
       Arosaguntacook Indians
       Assateague Indians
       Assiniboin Indians
       Athapascan Indians
       Atsina Indians
       Atsugewi Indians
       Azteco-Tanoan Indians
       Bannock Indians
       Basket-Maker Indians
       Bella Coola Indians
       Bellabella Indians
       Beothuk Indians
       Biloxi Indians
       Bocootawwonauke Indians
       Brotherton Indians
       Brulé Indians
       Caddo Indians
       Caddoan Indians
       Cahuilla Indians
       Calusa Indians
       Capote Indians
       Carrier Indians
       Catawba Indians
       Caughnawaga Indians
       Cayuga Indians
       Cayuse Indians
       Chasta Indians
       Chehalis Indians
       Cheraw Indians
       Cherokee Indians
       Chetco Indians
       Cheyenne Indians
       Chickasaw Indians
       Chilkat Indians

Chilliwack Indians
Chilula Indians
Chimariko Indians
Chimmesyan Indians
Chinook Indians
Chinookan Indians
Chipewyan Indians
Chippewa Indians
Chitimacha Indians
Choctaw Indians
Choptank Indians
Chumashan Indians
Clackamas Indians
Clallam Indians
Clayoquot Indians
Cliff-dwellers
Coahuiltecan Indians
Coast Salish Indians
Cochiti Indians
Cocopa Indians
Colville Indians
Comanche Indians
Comox Indians
Conestoga Indians
Conoy Indians
Coos Indians
Costanoan Indians
Cowichan Indians
Cowlitz Indians
Cree Indians
Creek Indians
Crow Indians
Cupeño Indians
Dakota Indians
Delaware Indians
Dhegiha Indians
Diegueño Indians
Dudley Indians
Dwamish Indians
Erie Indians
Eskimos
Esopus Indians
Eyak Indians
Fox Indians
Gabrieleño Indians
Gay Head Indians
Gosiute Indians
Hackensack Indians
Haida Indians
Haisla Indians
Hasinai Indians
Havasupai Indians
Hidatsa Indians
Hopi Indians
Hualapai Indians
Huichol Indians
Hunkpapa Indians
Hupa Indians
Huron Indians
Illinois Indians
Ingalik Indians
Iowa Indians
Iroquoian Indians
Iroquois Indians
Isleta Indians
Jemez Indians
Jicarilla Indians
Juaneño Indians
Jumano Indians
Kainah Indians
Kalapuyan Indians
Kalispel Indians
Kamia Indians
Kaniagmiut (Eskimo tribe)
Kansa Indians
Karankawa Indians
Karok Indians
Kashaya Indians
Kaska Indians
Kaskaskia Indians
Kato Indians

Kawaiisu Indians
Kawchottine Indians
Keeche Indians
Keresan Indians
Keyauwee Indians
Kickapoo Indians
Kiowa Apache Indians
Kiowa Indians
Kitksan Indians
Kitwancool Indians
Kiyuksa Indians
Klamath Indians
Klikitat Indians
Koasati Indians
Koyukon Indians
Kuitsh Indians
Kusso Indians
Kutchin Indians
Kutenai Indians
Kuuvanmiit Eskimos
Kwakiutl Indians
Laguna Indians
Lillooet Indians
Lipan Indians
Luiseño Indians
Lumbee Indians
Lummi Indians
Lutuamian Indians
Madehsi Indians
Mahican Indians
Maidu Indians
Makah Indians
Malecite Indians
Manahoac Indians
Mandan Indians
Manhattan Indians
Maricopa Indians
Mascouten Indians
Mashpee Indians
Massachuset Indians
Massapequa Indians
Mdewakanton Indians
Menominee Indians
Mescalero Indians
Miami Indians
Micmac Indians
Mikasuki Indians
Mill Creek Indians
Mimbreño Indians
Mingo Indians
Miniconjou Indians
Minisink Indians
Missisauga Indians
Missouri Indians
Mistassin Indians
Miwok Indians
Moache Indians
Mobile Indians
Modoc Indians
Mogollon Indians
Mohave Indians
Mohawk Indians
Mohegan Indians
Molala Indians
Monacan Indians
Mono Indians
Montagnais Indians
Montauk Indians
Moquelumnan Indians
Moravian Indians
Mound-builders
Muckleshoot Indians
Multnomah Indians
Munsee Indians
Muskhogean Indians
Nahane Indians
Nanticoke Indians
Narraganset Indians
Nascapee Indians
Natchesan Indians
Natchez Indians

Natsitkutchin Indians
Nauset Indians
Navajo Indians
Nehalem Indians
Nespelim Indians
Neutral Nation Indians
Nez Percé Indians
Nicoleño Indians
Nipissing Indians
Nipmuc Indians
Niska Indians
Nisqualli Indians
Nomlaki Indians
Nooksack Indians
Nootka Indians
Norridgewock Indians
Ntlakyapamuk Indians
Numic Indians
Occoneechee Indians
Oglala Indians
Oka Indians
Okinagan Indians
Omaha Indians
Oneida Indians
Oneota Indians (Great Plains)
Onondaga Indians
Oohenonpa Indians
Osage Indians
Oto Indians
Ottawa Indians
Paiute Indians
Palaihnihan Indians
Paloos Indians
Pamunkey Indians
Papago Indians
Pascagoula Indians
Passamaquoddy Indians
Patwin Indians
Paugusset Indians
Pawnee Indians
Pennacook Indians
Penobscot Indians
Peoria Indians
Pequawket Indians
Pequot Indians
Piankashaw Indians
Piegan Indians
Pima Indians
Piman Indians
Piro Pueblo Indians
Pocasset Indians
Pomo Indians
Ponca Indians
Potawatomi Indians
Potomac Indians
Powhatan Indians
Pueblo Indians
Puyallup Indians
Quapaw Indians
Quileute Indians
Quinault Indians
Quinnipiac Indians
Rappahannock Indians
Saclan Indians
Salinan Indians
Salish Indians
Salishan Indians
Samish Indians
Sanpoil Indians
Sans Arc Indians
Santee Indians
Saone Indians
Sarsi Indians
Sauk Indians
Scaticook Indians (Conn.)
Scaticook Indians (N.Y.)
Seminole Indians
Seneca Indians
Serrano Indians
Sewee Indians
Shahaptian Indians

Shastan Indians
Shawnee Indians
Shinnecock Indians
Shoshonean Indians
Shoshoni Indians
Shoto Indians
Shuswap Indians
Sia Indians
Sihasapa Indians
Siksika Indians
Siletz Indians
Sinkiuse-Columbia Indians
Sinkyone Indians
Siouan Indians
Sisseton Indians
Siuslaw Indians
Siwanoy Indians
Skagit Indians
Skitswish Indians
Skokomish Indians
Slave Indians
Sobaipuri Indians
Sokoki Indians
Spokan Indians
Squawmish Indians
St. Regis Indians
Stalo Indians
Stillaquamish Indians
Stockbridge Indians
Suquamish Indians
Susquehanna Indians
Swinomish Indians
Tabeguache Indians
Taensa Indians
Tahltan Indians
Takelma Indians
Tanaina Indians
Tanana Indians
Tanoan Indians
Taos Indians
Tawakoni Indians
Tepehuane Indians
Têtes de Boule Indians
Teton Indians
Tewa Indians
Thlingchadinne Indians
Tigua Indians
Tillamook Indians
Timiskaming Indians
Timucua Indians
Tinne Indians
Tionontati Indians
Tlakluit Indians
Tlingit Indians
Tolowa Indians
Tonikan Indians
Tonkawa Indians
Tsattine Indians
Tsilkotin Indians
Tsimshian Indians
Tubatulabal Indians
Tukkuthkutchin Indians
Tukuarika Indians
Tulalip Indians
Tunica Indians
Tunxis Indians
Tuscarora Indians
Tutelo Indians
Tututni Indians
Twana Indians
Ugalakmiut Indians
Uinta Indians
Umatilla Indians
Umpqua Indians
United States—Civilization—Indian
    influences
Ute Indians
Uto-Aztecan Indians
Vuntakutchin Indians
Wachuset Indians
Waco Indians

Wahpekute Indians
Wahpeton Indians
Wailaki Indians
Wakashan Indians
Walla Walla Indians
Walpapi Indians
Wamesit Indians
Wampanoag Indians
Wanapum Indians
Wappinger Indians
Wappo Indians
Warm Spring Apache Indians
Wasco Indians
Washo Indians
Wawenock Indians
Wea Indians
Welsh Indians
Wenatchi Indians
Wenrohronon Indians
Wichita Indians
Wiminuche Indians
Winnebago Indians
Wintun Indians
Wiyot Indians
Woodland Indians
Wyam Indians
Yahuskin Indians
Yakima Indians
Yakonan Indians
Yamassee Indians
Yampa Indians
Yana Indians
Yankton Indians
Yanktonai Indians
Yavapai Indians
Yokayo Indians
Yokuts Indians
Yoncalla Indians
Yuchi Indians
Yukian Indians
Yuma Indians
Yuman Indians
Yurok Indians
Zuñi Indians
— Adoption
    BT Adoption
— Aesthetics
    [E98]
    BT Aesthetics
— African influences
    BT Africa—Civilization
— Aged
    [E98.A27]
    BT Aged
— — Mental health
— Agriculture
    [E98.A3]
    BT Agriculture, Primitive
    NT Indians of North America—
        Domestic animals
        Indians of North America—
        Irrigation
— Alcohol use
    [E98.L7]
    UF Indians of North America—Liquor
        problem
    BT Indians of North America—
        Beverages
— Amusements
    USE Indians of North America—
        Recreation
— Anecdotes, facetiae, satire, etc.
— Animals, Domestic
    USE Indians of North America—
        Domestic animals
— Anthropometry
    [E98.A55]
    BT Anthropometry
        Indians of North America—
        Physical characteristics

Indians of North America
 — **Anthropometry** *(Continued)*
   RT Indians of North America—
      Craniology
 — **Antiquities**
   [E98.A6]
   Antiquities of a particular tribe are entered
   under name of tribe; antiquities of a locality,
   under name of locality.
   BT Indians of North America—
      Industries
      United States—Antiquities
   NT Adena culture
      Arrow-heads
      Blackduck culture
      Hopewell culture
      Indians of North America—
        Implements
      Indians of North America—Pottery
      Kitchen-middens
      Mississippian culture
      Mound-builders
      Mounds
 — — **Collection and preservation**
 — — **Collectors and collecting**
      (May Subd Geog)
 — — **Private collections** *(May Subd Geog)*
 — **Appellate courts**
   BT Appellate courts
      Indians of North America—Courts
 — **Appropriations**
   [E91-93]
   UF Appropriations, Indian
      Indian appropriations
   BT Indians of North America—
      Government relations
 — **Arbitration and award**
   BT Arbitration and award
      Indians of North America—Legal
        status, laws, etc.
 — **Architecture**
   [E98.A65]
   RT Indians of North America—
        Dwellings
   NT Kivas
 — **Archives**
   [E97.9]
   BT Archives
 — **Arms and armor**
   [E98.A65]
   BT Arms and armor, Primitive
   NT Bow and arrow
      Slings
      Throwing-sticks
      Tomahawks
 — **Art**
   [E98.A7]
   BT Art, Primitive
      Ethnic art—United States
   SA *subdivision* Art *under names of*
        Indian tribes, e.g. Hopi Indians
        —Art
   NT Indians of North America—
        Embroidery
      Indians of North America—
        Feather-work
      Indians of North America—Metal-
        work
      Indians of North America—
        Painting
      Indians of North America—
        Sculpture
      Indians of North America—Shell
        engraving
      Indians of North America—Wood-
        carving
      Mound-builders—Art
      Quillwork
      Sandpaintings
 — — **Endowments**
      [E98.A7]

 — — **Exhibitions**
 — **Arts**
   [E98.A73]
   UF Arts, Indian
      Indian arts
 — **Astrology**
   BT Astrology
 — **Astronomy**
 — **Basket making**
   [E98.B3]
   BT Basket making
      Indians of North America—
        Industries
 — **Beadwork**
   USE Beadwork
      Indians of North America—
        Costume and adornment
      Wampum belts
 — **Beverages**
   BT Beverages
   NT Indians of North America—
        Alcohol use
 — **Bibliography**
   [Z1209-1210]
 — **Biography**
   [E89-90]
 — **Boats**
   [E98.C2]
   UF Birch-bark canoes
   BT Boats, Primitive
      Canoes and canoeing
      Indians of North America—
        Transportation
      Navigation, Primitive
   NT Eskimos—Boats
 — **Boxing**
   BT Boxing
      Indians of North America—Games
 — Burial
   USE Indians of North America—
        Mortuary customs
 — **Business enterprises**
   BT Indians of North America—
        Commerce
      Indians of North America—
        Economic conditions
      Minority business enterprises
 — **Calendar**
   [E98.C14]
 — **Captivities**
   [E85-87]
   BT Frontier and pioneer life
   SA *subdivision* Captivity, [dates]
        under names of individual
        persons
 — **Census**
   [E98.C3]
   NT Indians of North America—
        Population
 — **Census, [date]**
 — **Child welfare**
   [E98.C5]
   BT Child welfare
      Indians of North America—
        Children
      Indians of North America—Public
        welfare
   NT Indians of North America—
        Children—Day care
      Indians of North America—
        Orphanages
 — **Children**
   [E98.C5]
   BT Children—United States
   NT Indians of North America—Child
        welfare
      Indians of North America—
        Handicapped children
      Indians of North America—
        Orphanages
      Indians of North America—Youth

 — — **Day care**
   BT Day care centers
      Indians of North America—
        Child welfare
 — — **Legal status, laws, etc.**
   BT Indians of North America—
        Domestic relations
      Indians of North America—
        Legal status, laws, etc.
 — **Chinese influences**
 — **Chronology**
   BT Chronology
 — **Citizenship**
   [E91-E93]
   Here are entered works on United States citi-
   zenship of American Indians. Works on tribal
   citizenship of American Indians are entered
   under Indians of North America—Tribal citizen-
   ship.
   BT Citizenship
 — **Civil rights**
   BT Civil rights
   NT Indians of North America—
        Freedom of religion
 — Civilization
   USE Indians of North America—
        Cultural assimilation
 — **Claims**
   [E98.C6]
   BT Indians of North America—Legal
        status, laws, etc.
 — **Claims (against the Indians)**
   [E98.C62]
   UF United States—Claims against
        Indians of North America
 — **Colonization** *(May Subd Geog)*
 — **Commerce**
   [E98.C7]
   BT Commerce
   NT Indians of North America—
        Business enterprises
      Indians of North America—
        Trading posts
 — **Constitutional law**
   BT Constitutional law
      Indians of North America—Legal
        status, laws, etc.
 — **Costume and adornment**
   [E98.C8]
   UF Indians of North America—
        Beadwork
      Indians of North America—
        Footwear
   BT Costume
   RT Wampum
   NT Moccasins
      Wampum belts
 — **Councils**
   [E98.C]
 — **Courts**
   [E93]
   BT Courts
      Indians of North America—Legal
        status, laws, etc.
   NT Indians of North America—
        Appellate courts
 — Cradleboards
   USE Indians of North America—
        Cradles
 — **Cradles**
   UF Indians of North America—
        Cradleboards
   BT Cradles
 — **Craniology**
   [E98.C85]
   BT Craniology
      Indians of North America—
        Physical characteristics
   RT Indians of North America—
        Anthropometry
 — **Crime**

[E98.C87]
  BT Crime and criminals
       Indians of North America—Social
          conditions
  NT Indians of North America—
       Juvenile delinquency
       Indians of North America—Wife
         abuse

— Criminal justice system
  [E98.C87]
  BT Criminal justice, Administration of
       —Canada
       Criminal justice, Administration of
        —United States
       Indians of North America—
        Government relations

— Cultural assimilation
  UF Indians of North America—
       Civilization
       Indians of North America,
        Civilization of
  BT Indians, Treatment of—North
       America
       Indians of North America—
        Government relations

— Culture
  USE *subdivision* Chinese, [Egyptian,
      Transpacific, etc.] *influences*
      under Indians of North
      America *for specific foreign*
      influences on the culture of
      Indians of North America
      Indians of North America
      Indians of North America—
       Foreign influences

— Customs
  USE Indians of North America—
      Social life and customs

— Dances
  [E98.D2]
  BT Indians of North America—
       Religion and mythology
       Indians of North America—Social
        life and customs
  NT Butterfly dance
       Calumet dance
       Corn maidens' dance
       Eagle dance
       Ghost dance
       O-kee-pa (Religious ceremony)
       Snake-dance
       Sun-dance
       Sunflower dance
       Urine dance
       Wolf ritual

— Dental care

— Dentistry
  BT Indians of North America—
       Medicine

— Dentition
  USE Indians of North America—Teeth

— Dictionaries and encyclopedias

— Diseases *(May Subd Geog)*
  [E98.D6]
  NT Indians of North America—
       Hospitals

— Dolls
  [E98.D65]
  UF Dolls, Indian
  BT Indians of North America—Games
  NT Katcinas

— Domestic animals
  UF Indians of North America—
       Animals, Domestic
  BT Domestic animals
       Indians of North America—
        Agriculture
  NT Indian ponies

— Domestic relations

  BT Domestic relations
       Indians of North America—Legal
        status, laws, etc.
  NT Indians of North America—
       Children—Legal status, laws,
        etc.

— Drama

— Drug use
  [E98.N5]
  UF Indians of North America—
       Narcotics

— Dwellings
  [E98.D9]
  Here are entered works on dwellings from the
  standpoint of architecture, construction, eth-
  nology, etc. Works on the social or economic
  aspects of housing problems are entered under
  Indians of North America—Housing.
  UF Teepees
       Tepees
       Tipis
       Wigwams
  BT Dwellings
  RT Indians of North America—
       Architecture
  NT Pueblos

— Economic conditions
  [E98.E2]
  NT Indians of North America—
       Business enterprises
       Indians of North America—
        Employment
       Indians of North America—Public
        welfare

— Education
  [E97 (United States)]
  [LC2629 (Canada)]
  Here are entered works on the education of
  Indians of North America. Works on courses of
  study, research, etc. about North American Indi-
  ans are entered under Indians of North America
  —Study and teaching.
  UF Indians of North America—
       Schools
  SA *names of individual schools*
  NT Indians of North America—
       Scholarships, fellowships, etc.

— — Law and legislation

— Egyptian influences
  [E99.C9]
  BT Egypt—Civilization

— Embroidery
  [E98.E5]
  UF Embroidery, Indian
  BT Indians of North America—Art
       Indians of North America—Textile
        industry and fabrics

— Employment
  [E59.E3]
  BT Indians of North America—
       Economic conditions

— — Law and legislation
  BT Labor laws and legislation

— Ethics
  UF Ethics, Indian
       Indian ethics

— Ethnic identity

— Ethnobotany
  BT Ethnobotany

— Ethnology
  USE Ethnology—North America
       Indians of North America

— Ethnozoology
  BT Ethnozoology

— Exhibitions

— Extraterrestrial influences
  UF Extraterrestrial influences on
       Indians of North America
  BT Interplanetary voyages

— Factory system
  USE Indians of North America—
      Trading posts

— Feather-work
  BT Feather-work
       Indians of North America—Art
       Indians of North America—
        Industries

— Fiction
  SA *subdivision* Fiction *under names of*
      Indian tribes, e.g. Iroquois
      Indians—Fiction

— Financial affairs
  [E98.F3]
  BT Indians of North America—
       Property
  SA *subdivision* Financial affairs *under*
      names of tribes

— — Law and legislation

— Fire use
  UF Fire use by Indians of North
       America
       Use of fire by Indians of North
        America
  BT Fire

— First contact with Occidental civilization
  UF Contact, First, of the Indians of
       North America with Occidental
       civilization
  BT Acculturation
       America—Discovery and
        exploration
       Civilization, Occidental
       Man, Primitive—First contact with
        Occidental civilization

— Fishing
  [E98.F]
  BT Fishing, Primitive

— — Law and legislation
  BT Fishery law and legislation

— Five Civilized Tribes
  USE Five Civilized Tribes

— Folklore
  UF Indians of North America—
       Mythology
  NT Indians of North America—
       Legends

— Food
  [E98.F7]
  NT Indians of North America—Salt

— Footwear
  USE Indians of North America—
      Costume and adornment
      Moccasins

— Forced removal
  USE Indians of North America—
      Removal

— Foreign influences
  UF Indians of North America—Culture

— Freedom of religion
  UF Indians of North America—
       Religious liberty
  BT Freedom of religion
       Indians of North America—Civil
        rights

— Gambling
  BT Gambling

— Games
  [E98.G2]
  UF Indians of North America—Sports
  BT Games, Primitive
       Indians of North America—
        Recreation
       Indians of North America—Social
        life and customs
  NT Indians of North America—Boxing
       Indians of North America—Dolls

— Genealogy
  BT Genealogy

— Gifts

Indians of North America
  — **Gifts** *(Continued)*
    BT Gifts
      Indians of North America—
        Government relations
      Indians of North America—Social
        life and customs
    NT Potlatch
  — **Goldwork**
    BT Goldwork
  — **Government relations**
    [E91]
    [E93 (United States)]
    Here are entered works on the Indian policy
    and relations with the Indians of the United
    States Government.
    Works on government relations with Indians
    of a particular state have a secondary subject
    entry under Indians of North America subdivid-
    ed by name of the state, e.g. Indians of North
    America—California.
    BT Indians, Treatment of
      Indians of North America—Land
        transfers
      Indians of North America—
        Treaties
    RT Indians, Treatment of—United
      States
    SA *subdivision* Government relations
      under names of tribes, e.g.
      Dakota Indians—Government
      relations; *and names of agencies,*
      e.g. Red Cloud Indian Agency
    NT Indian agents
      Indians of North America—
        Appropriations
      Indians of North America—
        Criminal justice system
      Indians of North America—
        Cultural assimilation
      Indians of North America—Gifts
      Indians of North America—
        Removal
      Indians of North America—Canada
        —Government relations
  — — **To 1789**
  — — **1789-1869**
  — — **1869-1934**
  — — **1934-**
    NT Wounded Knee (S.D.)—History
        —Indian occupation, 1973
  — **Handicapped children**
    BT Handicapped children
      Indians of North America—
        Children
  — Handicraft
    USE Indians of North America—
      Industries
  — **Health and hygiene**
    BT Medical anthropology
    NT Indians of North America—
      Hospitals
      Indians of North America—Mental
        health services
  — — **Law and legislation**
  — **Hindu influences**
  — **Historiography**
  — **History**
    [E77]
    NT Indians of North America—Wars
  — — **Colonial period, ca. 1600-1775**
    [E77]
  — — **Civil War, 1861-1865**
    [E540.I3]
  — — **Study and teaching**
    (May Subd Geog)
  — — — **Text-books**
  — **Hospital care**
    BT Hospital care
      Indians of North America—
        Medical care
  — **Hospitals**

    [RA981.A35]
    UF Hospitals, Indian
      Indian hospitals
    BT Indians of North America—
      Diseases
      Indians of North America—Health
        and hygiene
  — **Housing**
    Here are entered works on the social or eco-
    nomic aspects of housing problems. Works on
    dwellings from the standpoint of architecture,
    construction, ethnology, etc. are entered under
    Indians of North America—Dwellings.
    BT Housing
  — — — **Finance**
  — — — — **Law and legislation**
  — — — **Law and legislation**
  — **Hunting**
    [E98.H]
    BT Hunting, Primitive
      Indians of North America—
        Industries
      Indians of North America—Social
        life and customs
    NT Buffalo jump
  — — **Law and legislation**
    BT Game-laws
  — Hymns
    USE Hymns, Arikara, [Choctaw,
      Cree, etc.]
  — **Implements**
    [E98.I4]
    BT Indians of North America—
      Antiquities
      Indians of North America—
        Quarries
    NT Folsom points
      Harpoons
      Indians of North America—Knives
      Scottsbluff points
      Throwing-sticks
      Tomahawks
  — **Incantations**
    [E98.M2]
    UF Indian incantations
    BT Indians of North America—Magic
  — **Industries**
    [E98.I5]
    UF Indians of North America—
      Handicraft
      Indians of North America—
        Manufactures
    BT Handicraft
      Indians of North America—
        Material culture
      Industries, Primitive
    SA *subdivisions* Basket making;
      Hunting; Metal-work; Pottery;
      Quarries; Textile industry and
      fabrics; Trading posts; Trapping;
      etc. *under* Indians of North
      America
    NT Indians of North America—
      Antiquities
      Indians of North America—Basket
        making
      Indians of North America—
        Feather-work
      Indians of North America—
        Hunting
      Indians of North America—Metal-
        work
      Indians of North America—Pottery
      Indians of North America—
        Quarries
      Indians of North America—Salt
      Indians of North America—Textile
        industry and fabrics
      Indians of North America—
        Trading posts

    Indians of North America—
      Trapping
      Quillwork
  — **Inheritance and succession**
    BT Indians of North America—
      Property
    RT Indians of North America—
      Probate law and practice
    NT Indians of North America—Wills
  — **Irrigation**
    BT Indians of North America—
      Agriculture
      Irrigation
  — **Joking**
    BT Joking
  — **Juvenile delinquency**
    [E98.C87]
    BT Indians of North America—Crime
      Juvenile delinquency
  — **Kings and rulers**
    BT Kings and rulers, Primitive
  — **Kinship**
    BT Indians of North America—Social
      life and customs
      Kinship
  — **Knives**
    [E98.K54]
    BT Indians of North America—
      Implements
      Knives
  — **Land tenure**
    [E98.L3]
    UF Indians of North America—Land
      titles
      Indians of North America—Real
        property
    BT Indians of North America—Legal
      status, laws, etc.
      Indians of North America—
        Property
    SA *subdivision* Land tenure *under*
      names of tribes, e.g. Ute Indians
      —Land tenure
  — Land titles
    USE Indians of North America—Land
      tenure
  — **Land transfers**
    [E91-93]
    BT Indians of North America—Legal
      status, laws, etc.
    RT Indians of North America—
      Treaties
    SA *subdivisions* Government relations,
      Property, Treaties *under* Indians
      of North America; *and*
      subdivision Land transfers *under*
      names of Indian tribes, e.g.
      Dakota Indians—Land transfers
    NT Indians of North America—
      Government relations
      Indians of North America—
        Property
      Indians of North America—
        Removal
  — **Languages**
    [PM1-7356]
    SA *names of languages, e.g.*
      Algonquian languages, Chippewa
      language, Hupa language
    NT Alabama language
      Carrier language
      Chippewa language
      Chiricahua language
      Hupa language
      Mahican language
      Michif language
      Mobilian trade language
      Na-Dene languages
      Navajo language
      Puget Sound Salish languages
  — — **Imprints**

[Z7118]
— **Leather work**
    BT Leather work
    NT Parfleches
— **Legal status, laws, etc.**
    SA *subdivisions* Claims, Courts, Land
        tenure, Land transfers, Pensions,
        Property, Suffrage, Treaties,
        Wills *under* Indians of North
        America; *and subdivision* Legal
        status, laws, etc. *under names of*
        tribes, e.g. Cherokee Indians—
        Legal status, laws, etc.
    NT Indians of North America—
        Arbitration and award
        Indians of North America—
        Children—Legal status, laws,
        etc.
        Indians of North America—Claims
        Indians of North America—
        Constitutional law
        Indians of North America—Courts
        Indians of North America—
        Domestic relations
        Indians of North America—Land
        tenure
        Indians of North America—Land
        transfers
        Indians of North America—
        Mediation
        Indians of North America—
        Pensions
        Indians of North America—
        Probate law and practice
        Indians of North America—
        Property
        Indians of North America—
        Suffrage
        Indians of North America—
        Treaties
        Indians of North America—Water
        rights
        Indians of North America—Wills
— **Legends**
    [E98.F6]
    BT Indians of North America—
        Folklore
    SA *subdivision* Legends *under names*
        of Indian tribes, e.g. Iroquois
        Indians—Legends
    NT Coyote (Legendary character)
— **Library resources** *(May Subd Geog)*
— Liquor problem
    USE Indians of North America—
        Alcohol use
— **Magic**
    [E98.M2]
    UF Magic, Indian
    BT Indians of North America—
        Religion and mythology
    NT Indians of North America—
        Incantations
— Manufactures
    USE Indians of North America—
        Industries
— **Maps**
— **Marriage customs and rites**
    UF Marriage customs and rites, Indian
— **Masks**
    [E98.M3]
— **Mass media**
    BT Mass media
— **Material culture**
    BT Material culture
    NT Indians of North America—
        Industries
— **Mathematics**
    BT Mathematics
— **Medals**
— **Mediation**

    BT Indians of North America—Legal
        status, laws, etc.
        Mediation
— **Medical care**
    NT Indians of North America—
        Hospital care
— — **Law and legislation**
— **Medicine**
    [E98.M4]
    BT Medicine, Primitive
    NT Indians of North America—
        Dentistry
— — **Formulae, receipts, prescriptions**
    [E98.M4]
— **Mental health**
— **Mental health services**
    BT Indians of North America—Health
        and hygiene
— **Metal-work**
    BT Art metal-work
        Indians of North America—Art
        Indians of North America—
        Industries
        Metal-work
— Military capacity and organization
    USE Indian warfare
        Indians of North America as
        soldiers
— Mineral resources
    USE Indians of North America—
        Mines and mining
— **Mines and mining**
    UF Indians of North America—
        Mineral resources
— — **Law and legislation**
    BT Mining law
— **Missions**
    [E98.M6]
    UF Missions to Indians of North
        America
    BT Missions
    SA *subdivision* Missions *under names*
        of Indian tribes, e.g. Illinois
        Indians—Missions
    NT Jesuits—Missions
— **Mixed bloods**
    [E99.M693]
    NT Melungeons
        Ramapo Mountain people
        Wesorts
— **Money**
    [E98.M7]
    BT Money
        Shell money
    RT Wampum
— **Mortality**
— **Mortuary customs**
    [E98.M8]
    UF Indians of North America—Burial
        Mortuary customs
    BT Burial
        Funeral rites and ceremonies
— **Museums**
    [E56]
    BT Archaeological museums and
        collections
        Ethnological museums and
        collections
— **Music**
    [E98.M9]
    [ML3557]
    The music or works about the music of a par-
    ticular tribe are entered under Indians of North
    America—[local subdivision]—Music, and
    under the name of the tribe with the subdivision
    Music.
— Mythology
    USE Indians of North America—
        Folklore
        Indians of North America—
        Religion and mythology

— **Names**
    [E98.N2]
    UF Names, Geographical—Indians of
        North America
        Names, North American Indian
    SA *subdivision* Names *under particular*
        tribes, e.g. Delaware Indians—
        Names
— Narcotics
    USE Indians of North America—Drug
        use
— **Nutrition**
— **Oratory**
    [E98.O7]
    Here are entered collections of orations in
    Indian languages as well as works about Indian
    orations. Collections of orations by American In-
    dians belonging to a specific tribe and in an in-
    dividual Indian language receive additional sub-
    ject entries under the name of the tribe subdivid-
    ed by Oratory and the heading for orations in
    that language, e.g. Pima Indians—Oratory and
    Speeches, addresses, etc., Pima. Collections of
    orations by American Indians in an individual
    non-Indian language are entered under the ap-
    propriate heading for orations in that language
    with the subdivision Indian authors, e.g.
    Speeches, addresses, etc., American—Indian
    authors.
    UF Indian orations
    BT Oratory
        Oratory, Primitive
    NT Speeches, addresses, etc., American
        —Indian authors
        Speeches, addresses, etc., Papago
        Speeches, addresses, etc., Pima
— **Orphanages**
    BT Indians of North America—Child
        welfare
        Indians of North America—
        Children
— Ownership of slaves
    USE Indians of North America—
        Slaves, Ownership of
— **Painting**
    BT Indians of North America—Art
— **Papermaking**
    BT Papermaking
— **Pensions**
    [E98.P3]
    BT Indians of North America—Legal
        status, laws, etc.
        Indians of North America—Public
        welfare
— **Philosophy**
    BT Ethnophilosophy
— **Physical characteristics**
    [E98.P53]
    UF Indians of North America—
        Somatology
    NT Indians of North America—
        Anthropometry
        Indians of North America—
        Craniology
— **Pictorial works**
    [E77.5]
    SA *subdivision* Pictorial works *under*
        names of tribes
— — **Exhibitions**
— **Poetry**
    BT Indians in literature
    SA *subdivision* Poetry *under names of*
        Indian tribes, e.g. Dakota
        Indians—Poetry
— Ponies
    USE Indian ponies
— **Population**
    BT Indians of North America—Census
        North America—Population
    NT Indians of North America—
        Statistics, Vital
— **Portraits**

Indians of North America
  — Portraits *(Continued)*
    ₍E89₎
      This heading covers general collections of portraits of Indians and also works containing portraits of Indians of a particular tribe or of the tribes of a specific locality. The latter are entered also under the name of the tribe or under the local subdivision, e.g. a work which deals with portraits of Indians of Oregon will appear under: 1. Indians of North America—Portraits. 2. Indians of North America—Oregon.
  — Pottery
    ₍E98.P8₎
    BT Indians of North America—
      Antiquities
      Indians of North America—
      Industries
  — Probate law and practice
    BT Indians of North America—Legal
      status, laws, etc.
    RT Indians of North America—
      Inheritance and succession
  — Property
    ₍E98.P9₎
    BT Indians of North America—Land
      transfers
      Indians of North America—Legal
      status, laws, etc.
    NT Indians of North America—
      Financial affairs
      Indians of North America—
      Inheritance and succession
      Indians of North America—Land
      tenure
  — Psychology
    ₍E98.P95₎
    NT Indians of North America—
      Suicidal behavior
  — Public contracts
  — Public opinion
  — Public welfare
    BT Indians of North America—
      Economic conditions
      Public welfare
    NT Indians of North America—Child
      welfare
      Indians of North America—
      Pensions
  — Quarries
    ₍E98.I5₎
    BT Indians of North America—
      Industries
      Quarries and quarrying
      Quarries and quarrying, Prehistoric
    NT Indians of North America—
      Implements
  — Real property
    USE Indians of North America—Land
      tenure
  — Recreation
    ₍E99.G2₎
    UF Indians of North America—
      Amusements
    BT Indians of North America—Social
      life and customs
    NT Indians of North America—Games
  — Relations with Afro-Americans
    USE Afro-Americans—Relations with
      Indians
  — Religion and mythology
    ₍E98.R3₎
    UF Indians of North America—
      Mythology
    SA *subdivision* Religion and
      mythology *under names of
      tribes*
    NT Corn maidens' dance
      Indians of North America—Dances
      Indians of North America—Magic
      Indians of North America—Rites
      and ceremonies

      Katcinas
      Peyotism
      Totems
      Vision quests
  — Religious liberty
    USE Indians of North America—
      Freedom of religion
  — Removal
    ₍E93 (United States)₎
    UF Forced removal of Indians
      Indian removal
      Indians of North America—Forced
      removal
      Removal of Indians
    BT Indians, Treatment of—United
      States
      Indians of North America—
      Government relations
      Indians of North America—Land
      transfers
    NT Cherokee Removal, 1838
  — Research *(May Subd Geog)*
  — Reservations
    ₍E78₎
    ₍E91-E93₎
    ₍E99₎
    UF Indian reservations
      Reservations, Indian
    SA *names of reservations*
    NT Indian agents
      Navajo Indian Reservation
      Papago Indian Reservation (Ariz.)
  — Rites and ceremonies
    BT Indians of North America—
      Religion and mythology
    SA *names of special ceremonies, e.g.
      O-kee-pa (Religious ceremony);
      and subdivision* Rites and
      ceremonies *under names of
      tribes*
    NT Ajilee (Navajo rite)
      Butterfly dance
      Peyotism
  — Roads
    BT Roads
    RT Indian trails
  — Rugs
    USE Indians of North America—
      Textile industry and fabrics
  — Salt
    ₍E98.S26₎
    BT Indians of North America—Food
      Indians of North America—
      Industries
      Salt
  — Sanatoriums
  — Scholarships, fellowships, etc.
    (May Subd Geog)
    UF Indian scholarships
    BT Indians of North America—
      Education
  — Schools
    USE *names of individual schools*
      Indians of North America—
      Education
  — Sculpture
    UF Indians of North America—Stone-
      sculpture
    BT Indians of North America—Art
      Sculpture
      Sculpture, Primitive
  — Secret societies
    ₍E98.S75₎
    BT Secret societies
  — Semitic influences
    BT Civilization, Semitic
  — Sexual behavior
    BT Sex customs
  — Shell engraving
    BT Indians of North America—Art
      Shell engraving

  — Sign language
    ₍E98.S5₎
    UF Gesture language
    BT Sign language
  — Silverwork
    BT Silverwork
  — Slaves, Ownership of
    UF Indians of North America—
      Ownership of slaves
      Ownership of slaves
    BT Slavery—United States
  — Smoking
    USE Indians of North America—
      Tobacco use
  — Social conditions
    NT Indians of North America—Crime
      Indians of North America—Urban
      residence
  — Social life and customs
    UF Indians of North America—
      Customs
    SA *subdivisions* Dances, Games,
      Hunting *under* Indians of North
      America; *and subdivision* Social
      life and customs *under names of
      Indian tribes, e.g.* Omaha
      Indians—Social life and customs
    NT Indians of North America—Dances
      Indians of North America—Games
      Indians of North America—Gifts
      Indians of North America—
      Hunting
      Indians of North America—
      Kinship
      Indians of North America—
      Recreation
      Potlatch
  — Societies, etc.
  — Somatology
    USE Indians of North America—
      Physical characteristics
  — Sports
    USE Indians of North America—
      Games
  — Statistics
    SA *subdivision* Statistics *under names
      of Indian tribes*
  — Statistics, Vital
    BT Indians of North America—
      Population
      Vital statistics
  — Stone-sculpture
    USE Indians of North America—
      Sculpture
  — Study and teaching *(May Subd Geog)*
      Here are entered works on courses of study, research, etc. about Indians of North America. Works on the education of the Indians themselves are entered under Indians of North America—Education.
    UF Indian studies, North American
  — Suffrage
    BT Indians of North America—Legal
      status, laws, etc.
  — Suicidal behavior
    BT Indians of North America—
      Psychology
      Suicide
  — Taxation
    SA *subdivision* Taxation *under names
      of individual Indian tribes, e.g.*
      Cherokee Indians—Taxation
  — — Law and legislation
  — Teeth
    UF Indians of North America—
      Dentition
    BT Dental anthropology
      Teeth
  — Textile industry and fabrics
    ₍E98.T35₎
    UF Indians of North America—Rugs

BT Blankets
Indians of North America—
Industries
Textile fabrics
Textile industry
NT Indians of North America—
Embroidery
— Tobacco-pipes
[E98.T6]
UF Calumets
Pipes, Indian
BT Indians of North America—
Tobacco use
Tobacco-pipes
— Tobacco use
UF Indians of North America—
Smoking
BT Smoking
Tobacco
NT Indians of North America—
Tobacco-pipes
— Trading posts
[E98.C7]
UF Indian trade factories
Indians of North America—
Factory system
Trading posts (North American
Indian)
BT Indians of North America—
Commerce
Indians of North America—
Industries
— Trails
USE Indian trails
— Transpacific influences
UF Transpacific influences on Indians
BT America—Discovery and
exploration—Pre-Columbian
Indians—Origin
Man—Migrations
— Transportation
NT Indian ponies
Indians of North America—Boats
— Trapping
[E98.T75]
BT Indians of North America—
Industries
Trapping
— Treaties
[E95]
BT Indians of North America—Legal
status, laws, etc.
Treaties
RT Indians of North America—Land
transfers
SA names of specific treaties, e.g.
Penn's treaty with the Indians,
1682; and subdivision Treaties
under names of Indian tribes,
e.g. Iroquois Indians—Treaties
NT Indians of North America—
Government relations
— Treaties, [date]
— Treatment
USE Indians, Treatment of—North
America
— Tribal citizenship
Here are entered works on tribal citizenship
of American Indians. Works on United States
citizenship of American Indians are entered
under Indians of North America—Citizenship.
SA subdivision Tribal citizenship under
individual Indian tribes, e.g.
Chickasaw Indians—Tribal
citizenship
— Tribal government
SA subdivision Tribal government
under names of Indian tribes,
e.g. Iroquois Indians—Tribal
government
— Urban residence

BT City and town life
Indians of North America—Social
conditions
Urbanization
SA subdivision Urban residence under
names of tribes
— Wars
[E81-83]
BT Indians of North America—
History
SA subdivision Wars under names of
Indian tribes, e.g. Dakota
Indians—Wars
NT Indian warfare
Indians of North America as
seamen
Indians of North America as
soldiers
— — 1600-1750
[E82]
NT Ackia, Battle of, 1736
Chickasaw Indians—Wars,
1739-1740
Eastern Indians, Wars with,
1722-1726
Esopus Indians—Wars, 1655-
1660
Esopus Indians—Wars, 1663-
1664
King Philip's War, 1675-1676
Natchez Indians—Wars, 1716
Pequot War, 1636-1638
Tuscarora Indians—Wars, 1711-
1713
United States—History—King
William's War, 1689-1697
United States—History—Queen
Anne's War, 1702-1713
United States—History—King
George's War, 1744-1748
Wappinger Indians—Wars,
1655-1660
— — 1750-1815
[E81]
NT Cherokee Indians—Wars, 1759-
1761
Dunmore's Expedition, 1774
Pontiac's Conspiracy, 1763-1765
Tippecanoe, Battle of, 1811
United States—History—French
and Indian War, 1755-1763
— — 1775-1783
[E83.775]
BT United States—History—
Revolution, 1775-1783
NT Blue Licks, Battle of the, 1782
Crawford's Indian Campaign,
1782
Shawnee Indians—Wars, 1775-
1783
Sullivan's Indian Campaign,
1779
Yuma Indians—Wars, 1781-
1782
— — 1790-1794
[E83.79]
BT Delaware Indians
NT Harmar's Expedition, 1790
St. Clair's Campaign, 1791
Wayne's Campaign, 1794
— — 1812-1815
[E83.812]
NT Creek War, 1813-1814
Harrison, Fort, Battle of, 1812
— — 1815-1875
[E81]
NT Black Hawk War, 1832
Comanche Indians—Wars, 1840
Creek War, 1836
Mill Creek Indians—Wars,
1857-1865

Pacific Coast Indians, Wars
with, 1847-1865
Paiute Indians—Wars, 1860
Rogue River Indian War, 1855-
1856
Seminole War, 1st, 1817-1818
Seminole War, 2d, 1835-1842
Seminole War, 3d, 1855-1858
— — 1862-1865
[E83.863]
NT Birch Coulee, Battle of, 1862
Dakota Indians—Wars, 1862-
1865
Platte Bridge, Battle of, 1865
Sand Creek, Battle of, 1864
Shoshoni Indians—Wars, 1863-
1865
— — 1866-1895
[E83.866]
NT Apache Indians—Wars, 1883-
1886
Bannock Indians—Wars, 1878
Black Hawk War (Utah), 1865-
1872
Butte, Battle of the, 1877
Cheyenne Indians—Wars, 1876
Dakota Indians—Wars, 1876
Dakota Indians—Wars, 1890-
1891
Fetterman Fight, 1866
Modoc Indians—Wars, 1873
Nez Percé Indians—Wars, 1877
Red River War, 1874-1875
Tukuarika Indians—Wars, 1879
Ute Indians—Wars, 1879
— — 1868-1869
[E83.866]
UF Washita Campaign, 1868-1869
NT Beecher Island, Battle of, 1868
— Water rights
BT Indians of North America—Legal
status, laws, etc.
Water-rights—North America
— Weights and measures
BT Weights and measures
— Wife abuse
BT Indians of North America—Crime
Wife abuse
— Wills
[E98.W5]
BT Indians of North America—
Inheritance and succession
Indians of North America—Legal
status, laws, etc.
— Women
[E98.W8]
— Wood-carving
[E98.W85]
BT Indians of North America—Art
Wood-carving
— Writing
[E98.W9]
SA subdivision Writing under names of
Indian tribes
— Youth
UF Indian youth (North America)
Youth, Indian (North America)
BT Indians of North America—
Children
— Alabama
NT Mobile Indians
— — Antiquities
— Alaska
BT Arctic races
NT Tanaina Indians
Tsetsaut Indians
— — Antiquities
— — Languages
NT Ahtena language
Eyak language
Tanaina language

Indians of North America *(Continued)*
 —**Alberta**
 ——**Antiquities**
 ——**Reservations**
   NT Blood Indian Reserve (Alta.)
 —**Arizona**
 ——**Antiquities**
   NT Antelope House Site (Ariz.)
 ——**Languages**
   NT Cocopa language
       Hualapai language
       White Mountain Apache
         language
 ——**Music**
   NT Chicken scratch music
 ——**Reservations**
   NT Colorado River Indian
         Reservation (Ariz. and Calif.)
       Fort Apache Indian Reservation
         (Ariz.)
       Salt River Indian Reservation
         (Ariz.)
 ——**Trading posts**
   NT Hubbell Trading Post National
         Historic Site (Ganado, Ariz.)
 ——**Wars**
   NT Maricopa Wells (Ariz.), Battle
         of, 1857
 —**Arkansas**
 ——**Antiquities**
   NT Cedar Grove Site (Lafayette
         County, Ark.)
 —**British Columbia**
   NT Chilliwack Indians
       Coast Salish Indians
       Comox Indians
 ——**Antiquities**
 ——**Languages**
   NT Bella Coola language
 —**California**
   UF Mission Indians of California
   NT Agua Caliente Indians
       Kawaiisu Indians
       Nisenan Indians
       Saclan Indians
 ——**Antiquities**
 ——**Languages**
   NT Chemehuevi language
       Wikchamni dialect
       Wintun language
       Yuki language
 ——**Reservations**
   NT Colorado River Indian
         Reservation (Ariz. and Calif.)
 —**Canada**
   UF Indians of Canada
 ——**Government relations**
   BT Indians of North America—
         Government relations
   NT Indians, Treatment of—Canada
 ——**Mixed bloods**
   UF Métis (Canadian people)
 —**Colorado**
 ——**Antiquities**
 —**Connecticut**
 ——**Reservations**
   NT Golden Hill Reservation (Conn.)
 —**Florida**
 ——**Antiquities**
 —**Georgia**
 ——**Antiquities**
   NT Cemochechobee Archaeological
         District (Ga.)
 —**Great Plains**
   NT American Indian Research Project
 ——**Antiquities**
   NT Mill Creek culture
 —**Idaho**
 ——**Antiquities**
 ——**Reservations**

 NT Duck Valley Indian Reservation
       (Idaho and Nev.)
     Lemhi Indian Reservation
       (Idaho)
 —**Illinois**
 ——**Antiquities**
 —**Indian Territory**
   NT Five Civilized Tribes
 —**Indiana**
 ——**Antiquities**
 —**Iowa**
 ——**Antiquities**
   NT Mill Creek culture
 —[local subdivision]
 ——**Music**
 —**Louisiana**
   NT Houma Indians
 ——**Antiquities**
   NT Tchefuncte culture
 —**Maine**
 ——**Antiquities**
 —**Manitoba**
 ——**Antiquities**
 —**Massachusetts**
 ——**Antiquities**
 —**Michigan**
 ——**Antiquities**
 —**Minnesota**
 ——**Reservations**
   NT Mille Lacs Indian Reservation
       (Minn.)
 —**Mississippi**
 ——**Antiquities**
 —**Missouri**
 ——**Antiquities**
 —**Montana**
 ——**Antiquities**
 ——**Reservations**
   NT Blackfeet Indian Reservation
       (Mont.)
     Crow Indian Reservation
       (Mont.)
     Flathead Indian Reservation
       (Mont.)
     Fort Belknap Indian Reservation
       (Mont.)
 —**Nevada**
 ——**Antiquities**
 ——**Reservations**
   NT Duck Valley Indian Reservation
       (Idaho and Nev.)
     Pyramid Lake Indian
       Reservation (Nev.)
 —**New Mexico**
 ——**Antiquities**
 ——**Languages**
   NT Mescalero language
 —**New York (State)**
 ——**Reservations**
   NT Allegany Indian Reservation
       (N.Y.)
 —**North Carolina**
 ——**Reservations**
   NT Cherokee Indian Reservation
       (N.C.)
 —**North Dakota**
 ——**Antiquities**
 ——**Reservations**
   NT Fort Berthold Indian
       Reservation (N.D.)
     Lake Traverse Indian
       Reservation (N.D. and S.D.)
 —**Northwest Territories**
 ——**Antiquities**
 —**Ohio**
 ——**Antiquities**
 —**Oklahoma**
   NT Five Civilized Tribes
 ——**Antiquities**
   NT Edwards I Site (Okla.)
       Panhandle culture

 ——**Legal status, laws, etc.**
 —**Ontario**
 ——**Antiquities**
 ——**Reservations**
   NT Fort Hope Indian Reserve
         (Ont.)
       Grassy Narrows Indian
         Reservation (Ont.)
       Whitefish Lake Indian
         Reservation No. 6 (Ont.)
 —**Oregon**
   NT Coquille Indians
 ——**Antiquities**
 ——**Reservations**
   NT Warm Springs Indian
         Reservation (Or.)
 —**Rhode Island**
   NT Sakonnet Indians
 —**Saskatchewan**
 ——**Antiquities**
 —**South Carolina**
   NT Kusso Indians
 —**South Dakota**
 ——**Reservations**
   NT Cheyenne River Indian
         Reservation (S.D.)
       Lake Traverse Indian
         Reservation (N.D. and S.D.)
       Rosebud Indian Reservation
         (S.D.)
 ——**Trading posts**
   NT Fort Manuel (S.D.)
 —**Southern States**
   NT Pascagoula Indians
 ——**Antiquities**
   NT Poverty Point culture
 ——**Beverages**
   NT Black drink
 —**Southwest, New**
 ——**Antiquities**
   NT Mogollon culture
       Panhandle culture
 ——**Dances**
   NT Matachines (Dance)
 ——**Languages**
   NT Apache languages
 ——**Textile industry and fabrics**
   NT Ojo de Dios (Talisman)
 —**Tennessee**
 ——**Antiquities**
   NT Normandy Archaeological
         Project
 —**Texas**
   NT Coahuiltecan Indians
 ——**Antiquities**
   NT Panhandle culture
 ——**Wars**
   NT Adobe Walls, Battle of, Tex.,
         1874
 —**United States**
   USE Indians of North America
 —**Utah**
 ——**Antiquities**
 —**Washington (State)**
   NT Coast Salish Indians
       Muckleshoot Indians
       Samish Indians
       Skokomish Indians
       Wenatchi Indians
 ——**Reservations**
   NT Colville Indian Reservation
         (Wash.)
       Shoalwater Bay Indian
         Reservation (Wash.)
 —**Wyoming**
 ——**Antiquities**
   NT Colby Mammoth Site (Wyo.)
 —**Yukon Territory**
 ——**Antiquities**

Indians of North America, Civilization of
  USE Indians of North America—Cultural
        assimilation
Indians of North America, Treatment of
  USE Indians, Treatment of—North America
Indians of North America as seamen
  BT Indians of North America—Wars
  SA *subdivision* Participation, Indian *under*
      individual wars
  NT United States. Navy—Indians
Indians of North America as soldiers
  [E98.M5]
  UF Indians of North America—Military
      capacity and organization
  BT Indian warfare
      Indians of North America—Wars
      Soldiers
  SA *subdivision* Participation, Indian *under*
      individual wars
  NT United States. Army—Indian troops
Indians of South America
  [F2229-F2230]
    Subdivided by countries or regions, e.g. Indians of
South America—Chile; Indians of South America—
Amazon Valley.
    The names of individual tribes provided as NT
references under this heading, or under this heading
with local subdivision, constitute a complete list of all
South American tribes included in LCSH.
  UF American aborigines
      American Indians
      Indians—Ethnology
      Indians of South America—Ethnology
  BT Indians of the West Indies
  NT Abipone Indians
      Accawai Indians
      Achagua Indians
      Achuale Indians
      Aguaruna Indians
      Akwĕ-Shavante Indians
      Alacaluf Indians
      Amahuaca Indians
      Amuesha Indians
      Andaqui Indians
      Anserma Indians
      Apalai Indians
      Apalakiri Indians
      Apapocuva Indians
      Apiacá Indians
      Apinagé Indians
      Araona Indians
      Arara Indians
      Araucanian Indians
      Arawak Indians
      Arawakan Indians
      Arecuna Indians
      Arekena Indians
      Arhuaco Indians
      Ashluslay Indians
      Asto Indians
      Asurini Indians
      Atacameño Indians
      Aváchiripá Indians
      Aymara Indians
      Bakairi Indians
      Baniva Indians
      Barasana Indians
      Boro Indians
      Bororo Indians
      Botocudo Indians
      Cadioéo Indians
      Caingua Indians
      Calchaqui Indians
      Callahuaya Indians
      Campa Indians
      Cañari Indians
      Canella Indians
      Canelo Indians
      Canoeiro Indians
      Capanahua Indians
      Cara Indians
      Caraja Indians

Carib Indians
Carijona Indians
Cashibo Indians
Cashinawa Indians
Catio Indians
Catoquina Indians
Cayapa Indians
Cayapo Indians
Chacobo Indians
Chamacoco Indians
Chamí Indians
Chanca Indians
Chané Indians
Charrua Indians
Chibcha Indians
Chicous Indians
Chimane Indians
Chimu Indians
Chiquito Indians
Chiriguano Indians
Chiripá Indians
Choco Indians
Chono Indians
Choroti Indians
Chupacho Indians
Cinta Larga Indians
Cobaría Indians
Cocama Indians
Cofán Indians
Colla Indians
Colorado Indians (Ecuador)
Comechingone Indians
Craho Indians
Crao Indians
Crichaná Indians
Cubeo Indians
Cuiva Indians
Cumana Indians
Cupisnique Indians
Desana Indians
Diaguita Indians
Ese Ejje Indians
Fuegians
Fulnio Indians
Galibi Indians
Gaviões Indians
Gê Indians
Goajiro Indians
Guaharibo Indians
Guahibo Indians
Guana Indians
Guarani Indians
Guarayo Indians
Guarino Indians
Guarpe Indians
Guato Indians
Guayana Indians
Guayaqui Indians
Guaycuru Indians
Héta Indians
Huambisa Indians
Huanca Indians
Huancavilca Indians
Huao Indians
Huilliche Indians
Ijca Indians
Incas
Ipurucotó Indians
Iranxe Indians
Irapa Indians
Iscaycinca Indians
Itenez Indians
Jivaro Indians
Juruna Indians
Kagaba Indians
Kaingangue Indians
Kamaiurá Indians
Kariri Indians
Kreen-Akrore Indians
Kuikuru Indians
Lengua Indians

Lule Indians
Macá Indians
Machiganga Indians
Macú Indians (Papury River
  watershed)
Macuna Indians
Macusi Indians
Mamaindê Indians
Manacica Indians
Manta Indians
Maruba Indians
Masacali Indians
Mataco Indians
Maue Indians
Mayna Indians
Mayoruna Indians
Mbaya Indians
Mbya Indians
Mehinacu Indians
Mekranoti Indians
Mochica Indians
Mocobi Indians
Moguex Indians
Moro Indians
Morochucan Indians
Motilon Indians
Moxo Indians
Mundurucu Indians
Muzo Indians
Nambicuara Indians
Ona Indians
Otavalo Indians
Otuquis Indians
Oyampi Indians
Oyana Indians
Oyaricoulet Indians
Paez Indians
Palenque Indians
Pampean Indians
Panare Indians
Pancararu Indians
Parintintin Indians
Pasto Indians
Patamona Indians
Pauishana Indians
Pauserna Indians
Payagua Indians
Pehuenche Indians
Piaroa Indians
Pilaga Indians
Piro Indians (Peru)
Pocra Indians
Puelche Indians
Puquina Indians
Purí Indians
Puruha Indians
Quechua Indians
Querandi Indians
Quijo Indians
Quillacinga Indians
Quimbaya Indians
Ranqueles Indians
Sanavirona Indians
Secoya Indians
Shapra Indians
Sharanahua Indians
Sherente Indians
Shokleng Indians
Sipibo Indians
Siriono Indians
Surui Indians
Suya Indians
Tacana Indians
Tairona Indians
Tamanac Indians
Tapajó Indians
Tapirapé Indians
Tapuya Indians
Tenetehara Indians
Teque Indians
Tereno Indians

Indians of South America *(Continued)*
    Timbira Indians
    Toba Indians
    Tonocote Indians
    Trio Indians
    Tucano Indians
    Tucuna Indians
    Tunebo Indians
    Tupari Indians
    Tupi Indians
    Tupinamba Indians
    Txicaos Indians
    Tzoneca Indians
    Uaboi Indians
    Umotina Indians
    Urubu Indians
    Vilela Indians
    Waica Indians
    Waiwai Indians
    Wapisiana Indians
    Warrau Indians
    Witoto Indians
    Xikrin Indians
    Yabarana Indians
    Yagua Indians
    Yahgan Indians
    Yakalamarure Indians
    Yanaconas
    Yanoama Indians
    Yaruro Indians
    Yecuana Indians
    Yuko Indians
    Yunca Indians
    Yupa Indians
    Yurucari Indians
    Zamucoan Indians
— **Agriculture**
    [F2230.1.A3]
    BT Agriculture, Primitive
— **Amusements**
    USE Indians of South America—
        Games
        Indians of South America—Social
        life and customs
— **Anthropometry**
    [F2230.1.A]
— **Antiquities**
    [F2229]
    BT Indians of South America—
        Industries
    NT Indians of South America—
        Implements
        Indians of South America—Pottery
— **Architecture**
    [F2230.1.A]
— **Arms and armor**
    BT Arms and armor, Primitive
    NT Throwing-sticks
— **Art**
    [F2230.1.A7]
    NT Indians of South America—Metal-
        work
        Indians of South America—
        Sculpture
— **Astronomy**
    UF Astronomy, South American
        Indian
    BT Astronomy
— **Basket making**
    [F2230.1.B]
    BT Basket making
        Indians of South America—
        Industries
— **Blankets**
    USE Indians of South America—
          Textile industry and fabrics
— **Boats**
    [F2230.1.B6]

    BT Canoes and canoeing
        Indians of South America—
        Transportation
        Navigation, Primitive
— Burial
    USE Indians of South America—
        Mortuary customs
— **Calendar**
    [F2230.1.C2]
— **Census**
— **Children**
    [F2230.1.C5]
— **Costume and adornment**
    [F2230.1.C8]
— **Craniology**
    [F2230.1.C85]
— Customs
    USE Indians of South America—Social
        life and customs
— **Dances**
    NT Huayno
— Ethnology
    USE Ethnology—South America
        Indians of South America
— **Food**
    [F2230.1.F]
— **Games**
    [F2230.1.G2]
    UF Indians of South America—
        Amusements
        Indians of South America—
        Recreations
        Indians of South America—Sports
    BT Games, Primitive
        Indians of South America—Social
        life and customs
— **Health and hygiene** *(May Subd Geog)*
    BT Medical anthropology
— **Hunting**
    BT Hunting, Primitive
        Indians of South America—
        Industries
        Indians of South America—Social
        life and customs
— **Implements**
    [F2230.1.I4]
    UF Indians of South America—Stone
        implements
    BT Indians of South America—
        Antiquities
— **Industries**
    BT Industries, Primitive
    SA *subdivisions* Basket making, Metal-
        work, Pottery, Textile industry
        and fabrics *under* Indians of
        South America
    NT Indians of South America—
        Antiquities
        Indians of South America—Basket
        making
        Indians of South America—
        Hunting
        Indians of South America—Metal-
        work
        Indians of South America—Pottery
        Indians of South America—Textile
        industry and fabrics
— **Kinship**
    [F2230.1.K5]
    BT Indians of South America—Social
        life and customs
        Kinship
— **Land tenure**
    UF Indians of South America—Land
        titles
        Indians of South America—Real
        property
    BT Indians of South America—
        Property

    SA *subdivision* Land tenure *under*
        names of tribes, e.g. Aymara
        Indians—Land tenure
— Land titles
    USE Indians of South America—Land
        tenure
— **Languages**
    [PM5001-7356]
    NT Abipone language
        Accawai language
        Achagua language
        Achuale language
        Aguaruna dialect
        Akwē-Shavante language
        Alacaluf language
        Allentiac language
        Amahuaca language
        Araona language
        Arasa language
        Araucanian language
        Arawak language
        Arawakan languages
        Arecuna language
        Aymara language
        Bakairi language
        Barasana del Norte language
        Barasana del Sur language
        Bauré language
        Bora language
        Bororo language
        Cacán language
        Cacua language
        Callahuaya language
        Campa language
        Campa languages
        Cañarian language
        Canella language
        Canichana language
        Capanahua language
        Carib language
        Cariban languages
        Catio language
        Cavineño language
        Cayapo language
        Chacobo language
        Chayahuita language
        Chechehet language
        Chibcha language
        Chibchan languages
        Chimu language
        Chiquito language
        Chuntaquiro language
        Cocama language
        Cofán language
        Cuaiquer language
        Cubeo language
        Culina language
        Cumana language
        Ese Ejja language
        Fulnio language
        Galibi language
        Goajiro language
        Guahibo language
        Guana language
        Guarani language
        Guaraúna language
        Guarayo language
        Guaycuruan languages
        Güenoa language
        Hixkaryana language
        Huambisa language
        Ingano language
        Ipurina language
        Iranxe language
        Itonama language
        Jaminaua language
        Jupda language
        Kagaba language
        Kaingangue language
        Kamarakoto language
        Kariri language

Lorenzan language
Machiganga language
Macú language
Macuna language
Macusi language
Masacali language
Mashco language
Mataco language
Mayoruna language
Mbaya language
Mbya language
Motilon language
Movima language
Muinane language
Mundurucu language
Murui language
Nomatsiguenga language
Ocaina language
Ona language
Otomaco language
Oyampi language
Oyana language
Palicur language
Parentintim language
Pasto language
Patamona language
Pauserna language
Pemón dialects
Pilaga language
Puquina language
Quechua language
Sabela language
Saliva language
Sharanahua language
Siriono language
Tacanan languages
Taparita language
Tapuyan languages
Taurepan language
Tereno language
Toba language (Indian)
Trumai language
Tucano language
Tucuna language
Tupi language
Tupi languages
Tzoneca language
Uaiuai language
Urubu language
Vejoz language
Witoto language
Yagua language
Yanoama language
Yaruro language
Yecuana language
Yunca language
Yupa language
Yurucarean language
Zamucoan languages
— **Legends**
  ⌈*F2230.1.F6*⌉
  SA *subdivision* Legends *under names*
      of Indian tribes, e.g. Tupi
      Indians—Legends
— **Magic**
  ⌈*F2230.1.M3*⌉
  BT Indians of South America—
      Religion and mythology
— **Marriage customs and rites**
  UF Marriage customs and rites, Indian
  BT Indians of South America—Social
      life and customs
— **Masks**
— **Medicine**
  ⌈*F2230.1.M4*⌉
— **Metal-work**
  BT Art metal-work
      Indians of South America—Art
      Indians of South America—
      Industries
      Metal-work

— **Missions**
  ⌈*F2230-3799*⌉
  SA *subdivision* Missions *under names*
      of Indian tribes, e.g. Moro
      Indians—Missions
  NT Missions of Piritu
— **Mixed bloods**
  ⌈*F2230.1.M*⌉
— **Mortuary customs**
  ⌈*F2230.1.M*⌉
  UF Indians of South America—Burial
  BT Burial
      Funeral rites and ceremonies
— **Music**
  ⌈*F2230.1.M9*⌉
  ⌈*ML3575*⌉
  This heading covers general works on the
  music of the South American Indians and also
  works dealing with the music of a particular tribe.
  The latter are entered also under name of tribe.
— **Philosophy**
— **Plant lore**
— **Pottery**
  ⌈*F2230.1.P8*⌉
  BT Indians of South America—
      Antiquities
      Indians of South America—
      Industries
— **Property**
  NT Indians of South America—Land
      tenure
— Real property
  USE Indians of South America—Land
       tenure
— Recreations
  USE Indians of South America—
       Games
— **Religion and mythology**
  ⌈*F2230.1.R3*⌉
  SA *subdivision* Religion and
      mythology *under names of*
      tribes
  NT Indians of South America—Magic
— **Rites and ceremonies**
  SA *subdivision* Rites and ceremonies
      under names of tribes
— **Sculpture**
  UF Indians of South America—Stone-
      sculpture
  BT Indians of South America—Art
      Sculpture
      Sculpture, Primitive
— **Social life and customs**
  ⌈*F2230.1.S7*⌉
  UF Indians of South America—
      Amusements
      Indians of South America—
      Customs
  NT Indians of South America—Games
      Indians of South America—
      Hunting
      Indians of South America—Kinship
      Indians of South America—
      Marriage customs and rites
— Sports
  USE Indians of South America—
       Games
— **Statistics**
  SA *subdivision* Statistics *under names*
      of Indian tribes
— Stone implements
  USE Indians of South America—
       Implements
— Stone-sculpture
  USE Indians of South America—
       Sculpture
— **Textile industry and fabrics**
  ⌈*F2230.1.T3*⌉

  UF Indians of South America—
      Blankets
      Indians of South America—
      Weaving
  BT Indians of South America—
      Industries
— **Transportation**
  NT Indians of South America—Boats
— **Wars**
— **Weaving**
  USE Indians of South America—
       Textile industry and fabrics
— **Weights and measures**
  BT Weights and measures
— **Women**
— **Writing**
  ⌈*F2301.W*⌉
— **Andes Region**
— — **Religion and mythology**
  NT Pacamama (Goddess)
— **Argentina**
— — **Antiquities**
— **Bolivia**
  NT Araona Indians
      Chimane Indians
      Ese Ejje Indians
— — **Antiquities**
— — **Languages**
  NT Chimane language
      Ignaciano language
      Moro language (South America)
      Tacana language (Bolivia)
— **Brazil**
  NT Apapocuva Indians
      Araona Indians
      Araweté Indians
      Asurini Indians
      Aváchiripá Indians
      Capanahua Indians
      Chicous Indians
      Cinta Larga Indians
      Culina Indians
      Gê Indians
      Héta Indians
      Iranxe Indians
      Macú Indians (Papury River
      watershed)
      Macuna Indians
      Mamaindê Indians
      Maruba Indians
      Mayoruna Indians
      Mehinacu Indians
      Parintintin Indians
      Patashó Indians
      Potiguara Indians
      Purí Indians
      Sherente Indians
      Shocó Indians
      Surui Indians
      Suya Indians
      Tariana Indians
      Teremembé Indians
— — **Languages**
  NT Apalai language
      Caingua language
      Cashinawa language
      Mamaindê dialect
      Maue language
      Nambicuara language
      Paressi language
      Purupuru language
      Rikbaktsa language
      Tapirapé language
      Tenetehara language
      Yahuna language
— — **Reservations**
  NT Parque Nacional do Xingu
      (Brazil)
— **Colombia**
  NT Carijona Indians
      Cofán Indians

Indians of South America
  — **Colombia** *(Continued)*
        Cuaiquer Indians
        Irapa Indians
        Macú Indians (Papury River
          watershed)
        Macuna Indians
        Pijao Indians
  — — **Antiquities**
      NT Calima culture
          San Agustín culture (Colombia)
  — — **Languages**
      NT Andoke language
          Barasana del Sur language
          Camsa language
          Carapana language (Tucanan)
          Correguaje language
          Guayabero language
          Malayo language
          Moguex language
          Paez language
          Pamoa language
          Resigero language
          Tucanoan languages
          Tunebo language
          Yahuna language
          Yucuna language
  — — **Mixed bloods**
      NT Guarino Indians
  — **Ecuador**
      NT Achuale Indians
          Cofán Indians
          Cuaiquer Indians
          Huao Indians
          Secoya Indians
          Tallán Indians
  — — **Antiquities**
  — — **Languages**
      NT Huao language
          Jivaro language
  — **Guyana**
  — — **Languages**
      NT Patamona language
  — **Paraguay**
      NT Aváchiripá Indians
  — — **Colonization**
      NT Paraguayan Chaco Indian
          Colony (Paraguay)
  — — **Languages**
      NT Lengua-Mascoi language
          Maca language
  — — **Missions**
      NT Paraguayan Chaco Indian
          Colony (Paraguay)
  — **Peru**
      NT Achuale Indians
          Candoshi Indians
          Capanahua Indians
          Conibo Indians
          Culina Indians
          Ese Ejje Indians
          Mashco Indians
          Mayoruna Indians
  — — **Antiquities**
      NT Chavín culture
  — — **Languages**
      NT Arabela language
          Candoshi language
          Cashibo language
          Cashinawa language
          Coto language (Tucanoan)
          Ese Ejja language
          Resigero language
          Urarina language
  — **Surinam**
      NT Akurio Indians
  — **Tierra del Fuego**
      USE Fuegians
  — **Venezuela**
      NT Arekena Indians
          Ayaman Indians

        Irapa Indians
  — — **Antiquities**
  — — **Languages**
      NT Arekena language
          Panare language
Indians of the United States
  USE Indians of North America
Indians of the West Indies
  [F1619]
  Subdivided by names of islands, e.g. Indians of the
  West Indies—Cuba.
      NT Arawak Indians
          Black Carib Indians
          Carib Indians
          Ciboney Indians
          Indians of South America
          Lucayan Indians
          Quisqueyano Indians
          Taino Indians
  — **Agriculture**
  — **Anthropometry**
      [F1619]
  — **Antiquities**
      NT Elbow-stones
  — **Commerce**
      BT Commerce
  — **Implements**
  — **Languages**
      [PM5071-9]
      NT Island Carib language
          Taino language
  — **Pottery**
  — **Religion and mythology**
      [F1619]
  — **Wars**
      NT Saint Vincent—History—Carib
          War, 1795-1796
  — **Dominica**
  — — **Reservations**
        NT Carib Reserve (Dominica)
Indic aesthetics
  USE Aesthetics, Indic
Indic art
  USE Art, Indic
Indic arts
  USE Arts, Indic
Indic astrology
  USE Astrology, Indic
Indic atlases
  USE Atlases, Indic
Indic authors
  USE Authors, Indic
Indic bronze sculpture
  USE Bronze sculpture, Indic
Indic bronzes
  USE Bronzes, Indic
Indic children's literature
  USE Children's literature, Indic
Indic children's literature (English)
  USE Children's literature, Indic (English)
Indic children's periodicals
  USE Children's periodicals, Indic
Indic children's poetry
  USE Children's poetry, Indic
Indic coins
  USE Coins, Indic
Indic cookery
  USE Cookery, Indic
Indic drama
      [PK5421 (Modern history)]
      [PK5437-PK5438 (Modern collections)]
      NT Folk-drama, Indic
          Yakṣagāna plays
  — **1500-1800** *(May Subd Geog)*
Indic drama, Christian (English)
  (May Subd Geog)
      UF Christian drama, English—Indic
          authors
          Christian drama, Indic (English)
      BT Indic drama (English)

Indic drama (English)
      UF English drama—Indic authors
      NT Indic drama, Christian (English)
          One-act plays, Indic (English)
Indic drawing
  USE Drawing, Indic
Indic encyclopedias and dictionaries
  USE Encyclopedias and dictionaries, Indic
Indic epic poetry
  USE Epic poetry, Indic
Indic erotic painting
  USE Erotic painting, Indic
Indic ethics
  USE Ethics, Indic
Indic fables
  USE Fables, Indic
Indic fantastic fiction (English)
  USE Fantastic fiction, Indic (English)
Indic fiction
      NT Short stories, Indic
Indic fiction (English) *(May Subd Geog)*
      [PR9492.2-PR9492.6 (History)]
      [PR9497.3-PR9497.35 (Collections)]
      UF English fiction—Indic authors
          Indo-English fiction
      NT Fantastic fiction, Indic (English)
          Love stories, Indic (English)
          Short stories, Indic (English)
  — **British influences**
      BT Great Britain—Civilization
Indic folk-drama
  USE Folk-drama, Indic
Indic folk literature
  USE Folk literature, Indic
Indic folk-songs
  USE Folk-songs, Indic
Indic gods
  USE Gods, Indic
Indic illumination of books and manuscripts
  USE Illumination of books and manuscripts,
      Indic
Indic languages
  Here are entered works on the languages of India
  in general, and works not confined to the Indo-Aryan
  languages, or to any other special group or language.
      NT Dravidian languages
          Indo-Aryan languages
          Indo-Aryan languages, Modern
          Iranian languages
          Mon-Khmer languages
          Munda languages
          Pisacha languages
          Tibeto-Burman languages
  — **Alphabet**
      NT Devanagari alphabet
Indic letter-writing
  USE Letter-writing, Indic
Indic literature *(May Subd Geog)*
  Here are entered works dealing with the literature
  of India in general, works on Indo-Aryan literature,
  and other works not confined to the literature of a
  single language.
      UF East Indian literature
          India—Literatures
          Indian literature (East Indian)
          Indo-Aryan literature
      BT Iranian literature
      NT Children's literature, Indic
          Folk literature, Indic
          Paite literature
          Religious literature, Indic
          Sambalpuri literature
  — **To 1500**
Indic literature (English) *(May Subd Geog)*
      [PR9480-PR9489.6 (History)]
      [PR9494-PR9494.9 (Collections)]
  Here are entered collections of literary works in
  English by native residents of India. Collections of
  literary works in English by British residents of India
  are entered under Anglo-Indian literature.
      UF English literature—Indic authors
          Indo-English literature

NT Children's literature, Indic (English)
Indic literature (Portuguese)
  (May Subd Geog)
  UF Portuguese literature—Indic authors
Indic love poetry
  USE Love poetry, Indic
Indic love stories (English)
  USE Love stories, Indic (English)
Indic manuscripts
  USE Manuscripts, Indic
Indic miniature painting
  USE Miniature painting, Indic
Indic missions
  USE Missions, Indic
Indic mural painting and decoration
  USE Mural painting and decoration, Indic
Indic national characteristics
  USE National characteristics, East Indian
Indic newspapers *(May Subd Geog)*
  NT Malayalam newspapers
      Tamil newspapers
Indic novelists
  USE Novelists, Indic
Indic one-act plays (English)
  USE One-act plays, Indic (English)
Indic orations (English)
  USE Speeches, addresses, etc., Indic
      (English)
Indic patriotic poetry
  USE Patriotic poetry, Indic
Indic periodicals
  NT Children's periodicals, Indic
      Tamil periodicals
Indic philology
Indic philosophy
  USE Philosophy, Indic
Indic poetry *(May Subd Geog)*
  NT Children's poetry, Indic
      Epic poetry, Indic
      Love poetry, Indic
      Patriotic poetry, Indic
      Protest poetry, Indic
      Religious poetry, Indic
      Sufi poetry, Indic
  — To 1500
  — 1500-1800
  — **Women authors**
      [PK2916 (History)]
      [PK5434 (Collections)]
Indic poetry (English) *(May Subd Geog)*
  [PR9490.2-PR9490.9 (History)]
  [PR9495.1-PR9495.95 (Collections)]
  UF English poetry—Indic authors
      Indo-English poetry
  NT Protest poetry, Indic (English)
  — **Women authors**
      [PR9495.3 (Collections)]
Indic poets
  USE Poets, Indic
Indic portrait miniatures
  USE Portrait miniatures, Indic
Indic prints
  USE Prints, Indic
Indic prose literature *(May Subd Geog)*
Indic prose literature (English)
  (May Subd Geog)
  UF English prose literature—Indic authors
      Indo-English prose literature
Indic protest poetry
  USE Protest poetry, Indic
Indic protest poetry (English)
  USE Protest poetry, Indic (English)
Indic publications, Acquisition of
  USE Acquisition of Indic publications
Indic relief (Sculpture)
  USE Relief (Sculpture), Indic
Indic religious literature
  USE Religious literature, Indic
Indic religious poetry
  USE Religious poetry, Indic

Indic short stories
  USE Short stories, Indic
Indic short stories (English)
  USE Short stories, Indic (English)
Indic songs
  USE Songs, Indic
Indic speeches (English)
  USE Speeches, addresses, etc., Indic
      (English)
Indic Sufi poetry
  USE Sufi poetry, Indic
Indic terra-cotta sculpture
  USE Terra-cotta sculpture, Indic
Indic vases
  USE Vases, Indic
Indic watercolor painting
  USE Watercolor painting, Indic
Indic wit and humor
  NT Assamese wit and humor
      Bengali wit and humor
      Gujarati wit and humor
      Hindi wit and humor
      Kannada wit and humor
      Malayalam wit and humor
      Manipuri wit and humor
      Marathi wit and humor
      Panjabi wit and humor
      Rajasthani wit and humor
      Sanskrit wit and humor
      Sindhi wit and humor
      Tamil wit and humor
      Telugu wit and humor
      Urdu wit and humor
Indic wit and humor, Pictorial
  (May Subd Geog)
Indican
  [QP211 (Secretions)]
  [QP801.I4 (Physiological chemistry)]
  [SF771 (Veterinary medicine)]
  BT Indole
      Urine—Analysis
Indicating instruments
  USE Recording instruments
Indications, Clinical
  USE Clinical indications
Indications, Medical
  USE Clinical indications
Indications, Surgical
  USE Surgical indications
Indicative mood
  USE Grammar, Comparative and general—
      Indicative
Indicator dilution
  UF Indicator dilution technics
  BT Heart function tests
Indicator dilution technics
  USE Indicator dilution
Indicator plants
  USE Plant indicators
Indicatoridae
  USE Honey-guides
Indicators, Health status
  USE Health status indicators
Indicators, Political
  USE Political indicators
Indicators, Science
  USE Science indicators
Indicators (Biology) *(May Subd Geog)*
  UF Biological indicators
      Sentinel organisms
  BT Ecology
  RT Biological monitoring
      Biological reagents
  NT Biochemical markers
      Plant indicators
      Water quality bioassay
Indicators and test-papers
  [QD77 (Analytic chemistry)]
  UF Chemical indicators
      Test-papers, Chemical

  BT Chemistry—Laboratory manuals
      Chemistry, Analytic
      Volumetric analysis
  RT Chemical tests and reagents
  NT Biological reagents
      Chromogenic compounds
      Methylene blue
      Resazurin
Indicators for internal combustion engines
  USE Internal combustion engines—
      Indicators
Indicators for steam-engines
  [TJ478]
  UF Steam-engine indicators
  BT Steam-engines
Indices
  USE Indexes
Indictments *(May Subd Geog)*
  UF Accusation
  BT Criminal procedure
      Prosecution
  RT Grand jury
      Informations
  NT Joinder of offenses
Indies, East
  USE East Indies
Indifference
  USE Apathy
Indifference, Religious
  USE Indifferentism (Religion)
Indifference curves
  BT Consumption (Economics)
      Utility theory
Indifferentism (Ethics)
  [BJ1535.I]
  BT Ethics
Indifferentism (Ethics) in literature
Indifferentism (Religion)
  [BT33]
  UF Indifference, Religious
      Religious indifference
  BT Religion
  NT Communicatio in sacris
      Liberalism (Religion)
      Unionism (Lutheranism)
Indigenous architecture
  USE Vernacular architecture
Indigenous church administration
  (May Subd Geog)
    Here are entered works dealing with the transfer
  of church administration in the mission field from
  missionaries to native Christians.
  UF Church administration, Indigenous
      Church management, Indigenous
      Missions—Devolution
      Native church administration
  BT Church management
Indigenous clergy
  USE Clergy
Indigenous labor
  USE Native labor
Indigestion *(May Subd Geog)*
  [RC827]
  UF Dyspepsia
  BT Gastrointestinal system—Diseases
  RT Digestion
  NT Heartburn
  — **Homeopathic treatment**
      [RX336.D9]
Indigestion in children *(May Subd Geog)*
  [RJ456.D94]
  UF Dyspepsia in children
  BT Pediatric gastroenterology
Indigirka River (R.S.F.S.R.)
  UF Indigirko River (R.S.F.S.R.)
      Reka Indigirka (R.S.F.S.R.)
  BT Rivers—Russian S.F.S.R.
Indigirko River (R.S.F.S.R.)
  USE Indigirka River (R.S.F.S.R.)
Indignation
  USE Anger

Indignitas
    USE Unworthiness of heirs (Roman law)
Indigo *(May Subd Geog)*
    ⌈*HD9019 (Economics)*⌉
    ⌈*SB287.I4 (Agriculture)*⌉
    ⌈*TB923-TB924 (Technology)*⌉
    BT Anil
        Dyes and dyeing
        Polygonum tinctorium
Indigo copper
    USE Covellite
Indigo industry *(May Subd Geog)*
    ⌈*HD9019.I3-32*⌉
Indigofera anil
    USE Anil
Indigofera suffruticosa
    USE Anil
Indigofera sufructicosa
    USE Anil
INDIOS (Computer system)
    UF Integrierte Dialog-Orientierte Statistik
        System (Computer system)
    BT Electronic digital computers—
        Programming
        Statistics—Data processing
Indirect costs
    USE Overhead costs
Indirect discourse (Grammar)
    USE Grammar, Comparative and general—
        Indirect discourse
Indirect discourse in literature
    UF Discourse, Indirect, in literature
    BT Quotation
        Style, Literary
    RT Direct discourse in literature
        Free indirect speech
Indirect quotation (Grammar)
    USE Grammar, Comparative and general—
        Indirect discourse
Indirect speech, Free
    USE Free indirect speech
Indirect speech (Grammar)
    USE Grammar, Comparative and general—
        Indirect discourse
Indirect taxation
    USE Internal revenue
        Tariff
        Taxation
Indium
    ⌈*QD181.I5 (Chemistry)*⌉
    — Isotopes
    — Metallurgy
    — Spectra
Indium alloys
    NT Indium-thallium alloys
Indium antimonide crystals
Indium compounds
    ⌈*QD181.I5*⌉
    NT Organoindium compounds
Indium deposits
    USE Indium ores
Indium halides
    BT Metal halides
Indium ores *(May Subd Geog)*
    UF Indium deposits
Indium organic compounds
    USE Organoindium compounds
Indium-thallium alloys
    UF Thallium-indium alloys
    BT Indium alloys
        Thallium alloys
Individual instruction
    USE Individualized instruction
Individual judgment (Theology)
    USE Particular judgment (Theology)
Individual medley (Swimming)
    USE Swimming, Medley

Individual retirement accounts
    (May Subd Geog)
    UF Accounts, Individual retirement
        IRA's
        Retirement accounts, Individual
    BT Pension trusts
        Tax planning
    NT Keogh plans
        Self-directed individual retirement
        accounts
    — Law and legislation *(May Subd Geog)*
    — Taxation *(May Subd Geog)*
    — — Law and legislation
        (May Subd Geog)
Individual retirement accounts, Self-directed
    USE Self-directed individual retirement
        accounts
Individual sports
    USE Sports for individuals
Individualism
    ⌈*B824 (Philosophy)*⌉
    ⌈*HM136 (Sociology)*⌉
    ⌈*JC571 (Political theory)*⌉
    BT Economics
        Equality
        Political science
        Self-interest
        Sociology
    RT Libertarianism
        Personalism
        Persons
    NT Communism and individualism
        Laissez-faire
    — Religious aspects
    — — Buddhism, ⌈Christianity, etc.⌉
Individualist school of economics
    USE Classical school of economics
Individuality
    ⌈*BF697*⌉
    BT Consciousness
        Psychology
    RT Conformity
        Personality
        Self
    NT Identity
Individuality in children *(May Subd Geog)*
    ⌈*BF720.I55 (Infant psychology)*⌉
    ⌈*BF723.I56 (Child psychology)*⌉
    BT Child psychology
Individualized instruction
    UF Individual instruction
    BT Slow learning children
        Tutors and tutoring
    RT Open plan schools
Individualized reading instruction
    UF Reading instruction, Individualized
    BT Reading
Individuals (Philosophy)
    USE Individuation
Individuals in art
Individuation
    UF Individuals (Philosophy)
        Particulars (Philosophy)
    BT Philosophy
        Scholasticism
        Universals (Philosophy)
        Whole and parts (Philosophy)
    NT Ahankāra
        Self (Philosophy)
Indivisibles (Philosophy)
    ⌈*B105.I53*⌉
    BT Philosophy
    RT Continuity
Indjibandi language
    USE Jindjibandji language
Indo-Aryan languages
    ⌈*PK101-2899*⌉
    BT Indic languages
        Indo-Iranian languages
    NT Pali language
        Pisacha languages

        Prakrit languages
        Sanskrit language
        Saurashtra language
        Vedic language
    — Writing
        NT Brahmi alphabet
            Kharosthi alphabet
Indo-Aryan languages, Middle
    UF Middle Indo-Aryan languages
    NT Prakrit languages
        Sanskrit language, Buddhist Hybrid
        Sanskrit language, Epigraphical Hybrid
Indo-Aryan languages, Modern
    ⌈*PK1501-2845*⌉
    UF Gaudian languages
    BT Indic languages
    NT Assamese language
        Bengali language
        Bhili language
        Bihari language
        Chakma language
        Changari language
        Danuwar Rai language
        Darai language
        Dingal language
        Dumaki language
        Gujarati language
        Halbi language
        Hindustani language
        Kashmiri language
        Khari Boli language
        Konkani language
        Kupia language
        Lahndā language
        Maldivian language
        Marathi language
        Nepali language
        Oriya language
        Panjabi language
        Parya language
        Pisacha languages
        Rajasthani language
        Sindhi language
        Sinhalese language
        Vaagri Boli language
Indo-Aryan literature
    USE Indic literature
Indo-Aryan manuscripts
    USE Manuscripts, Indic
Indo-Aryan paleography
    USE Paleography, Indo-Aryan
Indo-Aryan philology
    ⌈*PK101-119*⌉
    UF Philology, Indic
    RT Pali philology
    NT Indo-Iranian philology
        Iranian philology
        Sanskrit philology
        Sirāikī Hindkī philology
Indo-Aryans
    ⌈*DS425*⌉
    UF Aryans
    BT Ethnology—South Asia
        Indo-Iranians
    NT Parya (Indic people)
Indo-Australian Region
    BT Australia
        Indonesia
Indo-English fiction
    USE Indic fiction (English)
Indo-English literature
    USE Indic literature (English)
Indo-English poetry
    USE Indic poetry (English)
Indo-English prose literature
    USE Indic prose literature (English)
Indo-European antiquities
    ⌈*DS15 (History)*⌉
    UF Antiquities, Indo-European

Indo-European funeral rites and ceremonies
USE Funeral rites and ceremonies, Indo-
European
Indo-European languages
[P501-769]
UF Aryan languages
Indo-Germanic languages
NT Albanian language
Anatolian languages
Armenian language
Baltic languages
Celtic languages
Germanic languages
Greek language
Illyrian languages
Indo-Iranian languages
Italic languages and dialects
Macedonian language (Ancient)
Phrygian language
Proto-Indo-European language
Slavic languages
Thracian language
Tokharian language
Venetic language
— Periodicals
USE Indo-European philology—
Periodicals
— **Phonology**
UF Sievers' law
Verner's law
Indo-European law
USE Law, Indo-European
Indo-European mythology
USE Mythology, Indo-European
Indo-European names
USE Names, Indo-European
Indo-European philology
[P501-769]
SA *names of languages and literatures*
belonging to the Indo-European
group
— **Periodicals**
UF Indo-European languages—
Periodicals
Indo-Europeans
[CB201-CB231 (History of
civilization)]
[DS15 (History)]
[GN539 (Ethnology)]
UF Aryans
Civilization, Indo-European
Indo-Germanic peoples
BT Caucasian race
Ethnology—Eurasia
NT Albanians
Armenians
Balts (Indo-European people)
Celts
Germanic tribes
Greeks
Hittites
Illyrians
Indo-Iranians
Latin peoples
Luwians
Slavs
Thracians
Tokhari
Indo-Germanic languages
USE Indo-European languages
Indo-Germanic peoples
USE Indo-Europeans
Indo-Greeks
BT India—History—324 B.C.-1000 A.D.
Indo-Iranian languages
[PK1-9201]
BT Indo-European languages
NT Indo-Aryan languages
Iranian languages
Pisacha languages

Indo-Iranian literature *(May Subd Geog)*
Indo-Iranian philology
[PK1-PK17]
BT Indo-Aryan philology
Indo-Iranians
UF Aryans
BT Ethnology—Middle East
Indo-Europeans
RT Iranians
NT Indo-Aryans
— **Religion**
NT Haoma
Indo-Muslim architecture
USE Architecture, Mogul
Indo-Pacific humpbacked dolphin
USE Chinese white dolphin
Indo-Pacific Region
Here are entered works on the combined regions
of the Indian and Pacific Oceans, including the is-
lands of the Indian Ocean, South India, Sri Lanka,
the Malay Peninsula, Indonesia, the Philippines, and
the Southwest Pacific islands.
BT Indian Ocean
Pacific Ocean
Indo-Pakistan Conflict, 1947-1949
USE India-Pakistan Conflict, 1947-1949
Indo-Pakistan Conflict, 1965
USE India-Pakistan Conflict, 1965
Indo-Pakistan Conflict, 1971
USE India-Pakistan Conflict, 1971
Indo-Russian Treaty, 1971
USE Indo-Soviet Treaty of Peace,
Friendship, and Cooperation, 1971
Indo-Scythians
BT India—History—324 B.C.-1000 A.D.
Iranians
Scythians
NT Saka
Yüeh-chih
Indo-Soviet Treaty of Peace, Friendship, and
Cooperation, 1971
UF Indo-Russian Treaty, 1971
Russo-Indian Treaty, 1971
Soviet-Indian Treaty, 1971
Indochina *(Not Subd Geog)*
Here are entered works on the area comprising
Laos, Cambodia and Vietnam.
UF French Indochina
BT Asia, Southeastern
— **History**
— — **1945-**
[DS550]
NT Cambodian-Vietnamese Conflict,
1977-
Indochinese War, 1946-1954
Indochina War, 1946-1954
USE Indochinese War, 1946-1954
Indochinese *(May Subd Geog)*
BT Ethnology—Indochina
— **United States**
NT Indochinese Americans
Indochinese alien labor
USE Alien labor, Indochinese
Indochinese American business enterprises
(May Subd Geog)
UF Business enterprises, Indochinese
American
BT Minority business enterprises—United
States
Indochinese Americans *(May Subd Geog)*
[E184.I43]
UF Indochinese Americans—United States
BT Ethnology—United States
Indochinese—United States
— **United States**
USE Indochinese Americans
Indochinese art
USE Art, Indochinese
Indochinese languages
USE Sino-Tibetan languages

Indochinese philology
Indochinese War, 1946-1954
(May Subd Geog)
[DS553-557]
UF Indochina War, 1946-1954
BT Indochina—History—1945-
Vietnam—History—1945-1975
NT Điện Biên Phủ (Vietnam), Battle of,
1954
Indoctrination, Forced
USE Brainwashing
Indocyanine green
[QP801.I43]
UF Anhydrotetramethylbi
ssulfobutyldibenzoin
dotricarbocyanine hydroxide inner
salt sodium salt
Dihydrodimethylsulfo
butylbenzeindolinyl
deneheptatrienyldime
thylsulfobutylbenzeindolium
hydroxide inner salt sodium salt
BT Dyes and dyeing
Heterocyclic compounds
Polycyclic compounds
Indolacetic acid
USE Indoleacetic acid
Indole
NT Carbolines
Indican
Isoindole
Mitomycin C
Indole acetic acid
USE Indoleacetic acid
Indole alkaloids
BT Alkaloids
— **Spectra**
[QC463.I5]
— **Synthesis**
Indoleacetic acid
UF Heteroauxin
Indolacetic acid
Indole acetic acid
BT Acetic acid
Growth promoting substances
Plant hormones
Indolence
USE Laziness
Indologists *(May Subd Geog)*
[DS435.5-435.7]
BT India—Study and teaching
Indomethacin
BT Antiarthritic agents
Antirheumatic agents
Nonsteroidal anti-inflammatory agents
Indonapthene
USE Indene
Indonesia
NT Indo-Australian Region
— **Antiquities**
NT Pasar Ikan Site (Jakarta, Indonesia)
— **Civilization**
NT Africa, Sub-Saharan—Civilization—
Indonesian influences
— — **Portuguese influences**
(Not Subd Geog)
BT Portugal—Civilization
— **Description and travel**
— — **To 1800**
— — **1800-1945**
— — **1945-**
— **Economic conditions**
— — **1945-**
— **History**
— — **To 1478**
[DS641]
— — **1478-1798**
[DS642]
— — **1798-1942**
[DS643]
— — **British occupation, 1811-1816**

Indonesia
— History *(Continued)*
— — **Java War, 1825-1830**
    UF Dipanegara's War, Indonesia,
        1825-1830
        Dipo Negoro's War, Indonesia,
        1825-1830
        Java War, Indonesia, 1825-1830
— — **Achinese War, 1873-1904**
    [DS643]
    UF Achinese War, Indonesia, 1873-
        1904
— — **20th century**
— — **Japanese occupation, 1942-1945**
    [DS643.5]
— — **1945-**
— — **Revolution, 1945-1949**
— — — **Personal narratives**
— — **1950-1966**
— — **Coup d'etat, 1965**
    [DS644.32]
    UF Gerakan Tigapuluh September
        September 30 Movement
— — **1966-**
    [DS644.4]
— **Kings and rulers**
    NT Mangkunegara, House of
— **Languages**
    NT Achinese language
        Alas dialect
        Atinggola language
        Bajau language
        Bakumpai dialect
        Balaesang language
        Barangas language
        Bauzi language
        Berik language
        Besemah dialect
        Biak language
        Bolaang Mongondow language
        Bukar Sadong language
        Buol language
        Dairi Pakpak dialect
        Deli dialect
        Dusun Deyah dialect
        East Makian language
        Eipo language
        Kambera dialect
        Kamtuk language
        Katingan language
        Kayan language
        Kemak language
        Kendayan language
        Kerinci language
        Komering dialect
        Kubu language
        Kubuang Tigo Baleh dialect
        Kwerba language
        Lembak Bilide dialect
        Mentawai language
        Mori language
        Muna language
        Musi dialect
        Napu language
        Ngaju language
        Osing dialect
        Pasir dialect
        Rawas dialect
        Rejang language (Sumatra,
          Indonesia)
        Saberi language
        Sangen language
        Sasak language
        Sawu language
        Semendo dialect
        Serawai language
        Sigi language
        Siladang dialect
        Sokop language
        Sumba language
        Sumbawa language

        Suwawa language
        Talaud language
        Tanahmerah language (Northeast
          Irian Jaya)
        Tepera dialect
        Ternate language
        Tobelo language
        Tolaki language
        Tondano language
        Toradja language
        Toradja languages
        Toraja Sa'dan language
        Wandamen language
        West Makian language
        Wewewa dialect
        Woisika language
        Wolio language
        Yamdena language
— **Literatures** *(Not Subd Geog)*
    NT Buginese literature
        Makasar literature
        Minangkabau literature
        Ogan literature
        Simelungun literature
        Toba-Batak literature
        Wolio literature
— **Politics and government**
— — **1478-1798**
— — **1798-1942**
— — **20th century**
    NT Darul Islam Movement
— — **1942-1949**
— — **1950-1966**
— — **1966-**
    NT Sawito Affair, Indonesia, 1976
— **Readers**
    USE Readers—Indonesia
Indonesian art
  USE Art, Indonesian
Indonesian arts
  USE Arts, Indonesian
Indonesian atlases
  USE Atlases, Indonesian
Indonesian authors
  USE Authors, Indonesian
Indonesian Borneo (Indonesia)
  USE Kalimantan (Indonesia)
Indonesian children's literature
  USE Children's literature, Indonesian
Indonesian children's stories
  USE Children's stories, Indonesian
Indonesian children's writings
  USE Children's writings, Indonesian
Indonesian civics
  USE Civics, Indonesian
Indonesian coins
  USE Coins, Indonesian
Indonesian drama *(May Subd Geog)*
  BT Indonesian literature
  NT Folk-drama, Indonesian
Indonesian drama (Comedy)
Indonesian encyclopedias and dictionaries
  USE Encyclopedias and dictionaries,
      Indonesian
Indonesian fiction *(May Subd Geog)*
  NT Children's stories, Indonesian
      Islamic stories, Indonesian
      Short stories, Indonesian
Indonesian folk-drama
  USE Folk-drama, Indonesian
Indonesian imprints *(May Subd Geog)*
Indonesian Islamic sermons
  USE Islamic sermons, Indonesian
Indonesian Islamic stories
  USE Islamic stories, Indonesian
Indonesian language
  [PL5071-9]
  UF Bahasa Indonesia
  BT Malayan languages
  RT Malay language

Indonesian languages
  USE Malayan languages
Indonesian literature *(May Subd Geog)*
  NT Children's literature, Indonesian
      Indonesian drama
      Revolutionary literature, Indonesian
      Sufi literature, Indonesian
— **20th century**
Indonesian manuscripts
  USE Manuscripts, Indonesian
Indonesian mythology
  USE Mythology, Indonesian
Indonesian national characteristics
  USE National characteristics, Indonesian
Indonesian newspapers *(May Subd Geog)*
— Circulation
Indonesian novelists
  USE Novelists, Indonesian
Indonesian painting
  USE Painting, Indonesian
Indonesian patriotic poetry
  USE Patriotic poetry, Indonesian
Indonesian periodicals *(May Subd Geog)*
— Circulation
Indonesian philology
Indonesian philosophy
  USE Philosophy, Indonesian
Indonesian poetry *(May Subd Geog)*
  NT Patriotic poetry, Indonesian
Indonesian pottery
  USE Pottery, Indonesian
Indonesian prose literature
  (May Subd Geog)
Indonesian prose literature (Dutch)
  UF Dutch prose literature—Indonesian
      authors
Indonesian proverbs
  USE Proverbs, Indonesian
Indonesian quotations
  USE Quotations, Indonesian
Indonesian reference books
  USE Reference books, Indonesian
Indonesian revolutionary literature
  USE Revolutionary literature, Indonesian
Indonesian short stories
  USE Short stories, Indonesian
Indonesian songs
  USE Songs, Indonesian
Indonesian students *(May Subd Geog)*
  BT Students
Indonesian subject headings
  USE Subject headings, Indonesian
Indonesian Sufi literature
  USE Sufi literature, Indonesian
Indonesian watercolor painting
  USE Watercolor painting, Indonesian
Indonesian wit and humor, Pictorial
  (May Subd Geog)
Indonesians *(May Subd Geog)*
  BT Ethnology—Indonesia
Indoor air pollution
  USE Air—Pollution, Indoor
Indoor baseball
  [GV881]
  BT Baseball
  RT Softball
Indoor games
  [GV1221-9]
  UF Home games
      Rainy day games
  BT Games
  RT Amusements
  NT Psychic games
Indoor gardening *(May Subd Geog)*
  [SB324.5 (Vegetables)]
  [SB419 (General)]
  BT Gardening
      Window-gardening
  RT Container gardening
      House plants
      Indoor gardens

NT Aquariums
    Artificial light gardening
    Gardens, Miniature
    Glass gardens
    Greenhouse gardening
    House plants
    Interior landscaping
    Terrariums
    Vivariums
Indoor gardens *(May Subd Geog)*
   [SB419-SB419.25]
  UF Gardens, Indoor
  BT Gardens
  RT Indoor gardening
  NT Glass gardens
    House plants
Indoor hockey *(May Subd Geog)*
   [GV1017.I53]
  UF Floor hockey
  BT Hockey
Indoor photography
  USE Photography, Indoor
Indoor plants
  USE House plants
Indoor process
  USE Compost
Indoor soccer
   [GV943.9.I6]
  UF Salon soccer
  BT Soccer
Indoor track-athletics *(May Subd Geog)*
  BT Track-athletics
Indopacetus
   [QL737.C438]
  BT Beaked whales
Indopacetus pacificus
   [QL737.C438]
  UF Longman's beaked whale
    Mesoplodon pacificus
Indophenol
  BT Phenols
Indophenol oxidase
  USE Cytochrome oxidase
Indophenolase
  USE Cytochrome oxidase
Indorsements *(May Subd Geog)*
  UF Endorsements
  BT Negotiable instruments
  NT Accommodation indorsements
Indorsements, Accommodation
  USE Accommodation indorsements
Indosteiformes
  USE Indostomidae
Indostomidae
   [QL638.I4]
  UF Indosteiformes
  BT Gasterosteiformes
  NT Indostomus
Indostomus
   [QL638.I4]
  BT Indostomidae
Indra (Hindu deity)
  BT Gods, Hindu
Indrajit
Indre River (France)
  BT Rivers—France
Indridae
  UF Lemurs, Atypical
  NT Sifakas
Induba
   [QL561.N8]
  BT Notodontidae
Indubitability
  USE Certainty
INDUCE-1 (Computer program)
  BT Many-valued logic
    PASCAL (Computer program
      language)
    VL21 system
Induced abortion
  USE Abortion

Induced cardiac arrest
  USE Cardiac arrest, Induced
Induced hypotension
  USE Hypotension, Controlled
Induced hypothermia
  USE Hypothermia, Induced
Induced labor (Obstetrics)
  USE Labor, Induced (Obstetrics)
Induced magnetism
  USE Magnetic induction
Induced mutations in breeding
  USE Mutation breeding
Induced ovulation
  USE Ovulation—Induction
Induced polarization
  BT Dielectrics
    Polarization (Electricity)
Induced radioactivity
   [QC795]
  UF Artificial radioactivity
  BT Nuclear reactions
    Radioactivity
Induced spawning of fishes
  USE Fishes—Spawning, Induced
Inducers, Interferon
  USE Interferon inducers
Inducing catalysts
  USE Catalyst supports
Inductance
   [QC638]
    Here are entered works relating to the constants
of coils (mutual and self-inductance), their calcula-
tion or measurement.
  BT Electric measurements
    Electrodynamics
    Electromagnetism
  NT Electric inductors
    Mutual inductance
    Reactance (Electricity)
    Self-inductance
Induction, Ampliative
  USE Inference
Induction, Electromagnetic
   [QC638]
  UF Electromagnetic induction
  BT Electromagnetism
  RT Induction, Electrostatic
    Magnetic induction
Induction, Electrostatic
   [QC581.I5]
  UF Electrostatic induction
  BT Electrostatics
  RT Induction, Electromagnetic
Induction, Enzyme
  USE Enzyme induction
Induction, Menstrual
  USE Menstrual regulation
Induction (Logic)
  UF Inductive logic
    Logic, Inductive
  BT Logic
    Reasoning
  NT Induction (Mathematics)
Induction (Magnetism)
  USE Magnetic induction
Induction (Mathematics)
  UF Mathematical induction
  BT Induction (Logic)
    Mathematics
  NT AQVAL programs (Computer
      programs)
    Automatic hypothesis formation
  — Computer programs
    NT AQ7UNI (Computer program)
Induction accelerators
  USE Betatrons
Induction coils
   [QC645]
  BT Electric apparatus and appliances
  NT Mutual inductance
    Resistance-coils

    Self-inductance
    Tesla coils
Induction furnaces
   [TK4661 (General)]
   [TN687 (Electric metallurgy)]
  BT Electric furnaces
    Induction heating
Induction hardening
   [TN672]
   [TN752.I5]
  BT Induction heating
    Metals—Heat treatment
    Surface hardening
Induction heating
   [TK4601]
  UF High-frequency induction heating
  BT Electric heating
  NT Induction furnaces
    Induction hardening
  — Regulators
    BT Heating—Control
Induction machinery
  USE Electric machinery, Induction
Induction motors
  USE Electric motors, Induction
Induction of labor (Obstetrics)
  USE Labor, Induced (Obstetrics)
Induction of ovulation
  USE Ovulation—Induction
Induction pumps
  USE Electromagnetic pumps
Inductive logic
  USE Induction (Logic)
Inductors, Electric
  USE Electric inductors
Indulgences *(May Subd Geog)*
   [BX2279-2283]
  UF Jubilee indulgences
  BT Church discipline
  RT Catholic Church—Discipline
  NT Absolution
    Crusade bulls
    Holy Year
    Marian Year
    Scapulars
Indulgences (Canon law)
   [BX1939.I45]
Induline
  BT Dyes and dyeing
Indumatī (Character)
Induration, Penile
  USE Penile induration
Indus civilization
   [DS425]
  UF Harappa culture
    Indus Valley civilization
    Indus Valley culture
  — Writing
    USE Indus script
Indus dolphin
   [QL737.C436]
  UF Platanista indi
    Platanista minor
  BT Platanista
Indus River
  UF Sindhu River
  BT Rivers—China
    Rivers—India
    Rivers—Pakistan
Indus script
   [PK119]
  UF Indus civilization—Writing
    Script, Indus
  BT Inscriptions, Indic
Indus Valley civilization
  USE Indus civilization
Indus Valley culture
  USE Indus civilization
Industrial accident investigation
  USE Industrial accidents—Investigation

Industrial accidents *(May Subd Geog)*
  [HD7262-HD7262.5]
  UF Accidents, Industrial
      Accidents, Occupational
      Industrial injuries
      Labor and laboring classes—Accidents
      Occupational accidents
  BT Accidents
      Factory inspection
      Factory laws and legislation
      Industrial hygiene
      Industrial safety
      Insurance, Accident
      Insurance, Employers' liability
      Personal injuries
  RT Disability evaluation
      Employers' liability
      Occupations, Dangerous
  SA *subdivision* Accidents *under types of*
      industries, structures, equipment,
      and processes, e.g. Construction
      industry—Accidents; Coal mines
      and mining—Accidents
  NT Dust explosion
      Mine accidents
      Workers' compensation
  — **Investigation**
      [HD7262.25]
      UF Industrial accident investigation
  — Prevention
      USE Industrial safety
  — **Reporting** *(May Subd Geog)*
      UF Reporting of industrial accidents
  — Study and teaching
      USE Safety education, Industrial
Industrial administration
  USE Industrial management
Industrial advertising
  USE Advertising, Industrial
Industrial alcohol
  USE Alcohol, Denatured
Industrial allocations
  USE Priorities, Industrial
Industrial applications
  USE *subdivision* Industrial applications
      under scientific phenomena or
      substances, e.g. Ultrasonic waves—
      Industrial applications
Industrial arbitration
  USE Arbitration, Industrial
Industrial arbitrators
  USE Arbitrators, Industrial
Industrial archaeology *(May Subd Geog)*
  [T37]
      Here are entered works on the organized study of
  the physical remains of industries of the 18th and
  19th centuries, including industrial buildings, ma-
  chinery, tools, etc.
  UF Antiquities, Industrial
  BT Archaeology
      Industrial buildings—History
      Industrial equipment—History
  NT Aerial photography in industrial
      archaeology
Industrial architecture
  USE Architecture, Industrial
Industrial art libraries
  [Z675.T3]
  UF Libraries, Industrial art
  BT Technical libraries
Industrial arts *(May Subd Geog)*
  [T-TX]
  UF Arts, Useful
      Discoveries (in science)
      Mechanic arts
      Trades
      Useful arts
  BT Handicraft
      Manufactures
  RT Technical education
      Technology

  NT Agriculture
      Artisans
      Arts and crafts movement
      Classification—Books—Technology
      Do-it-yourself work
      Engineering
      Industries, Primitive
      Inventions
      Machinery
      Manual training
      Manufacturing processes
      Mechanical engineering
      Mills and mill-work
      Occupations, Dangerous
      Patents
      Research, Industrial
      Women artisans
  — **Awards**
      BT Rewards (Prizes, etc.)
  — **Biography**
      [T39-40]
  — Exhibitions
      USE Exhibitions
  — Film catalogs
      USE Technology—Film catalogs
  — **History**
      [T15-35]
      RT Lost arts
      NT Industries, Primitive
          Inventions
  — Museums
      USE Industrial museums
  — **Study and teaching** *(May Subd Geog)*
      NT Area vocational-technical centers
          Television in vocational education
  — **Terminology**
      [T9-10]
      BT Technology—Terminology
  — **Vocational guidance**
      UF Factories—Vocational guidance
Industrial arts shops
  USE School shops
Industrial arts teachers *(May Subd Geog)*
  BT Teachers
  — **Supply and demand** *(May Subd Geog)*
Industrial buildings *(May Subd Geog)*
  [NA6400-NA6589 (Architecture)]
  UF Buildings, Industrial
  BT Buildings
  NT Employees' buildings and facilities
      Factories
      Nuclear reactors—Containment
      Office buildings
  — **Design and construction**
  — **Details**
  — — **Drawings**
        [TH4516]
        BT Structural drawing
  — **Floors**
      BT Floors
  — **Foundations**
      BT Foundations
  — **Heating and ventilation**
      UF Industrial buildings—Ventilation
  — **History**
      NT Industrial archaeology
  — **Landscape architecture**
      BT Landscape architecture
  — **Maintenance and repair**
  — Ventilation
      USE Industrial buildings—Heating and
          ventilation
Industrial buying
  USE Industrial procurement
Industrial cafeterias
  USE Industrial feeding
Industrial canteens
  USE Industrial feeding
Industrial capacity *(May Subd Geog)*
  UF Capacity, Industrial
      Manufacturing capacity

  BT Industry
      Manufactures
  SA *subdivision* Industrial capacity *under*
      types of industries, e.g.
      Construction industry—Industrial
      capacity
Industrial ceramics
  USE Ceramics
Industrial chaplains
  USE Chaplains, Industrial
Industrial chemistry
  USE Chemical engineering
      Chemistry, Technical
Industrial cinematography
  USE Cinematography, Industrial
Industrial clothing
  USE Work clothes
Industrial combinations
  USE Cartels
      Trusts, Industrial
Industrial communication
  USE Business communication
Industrial concentration *(May Subd Geog)*
  UF Combinations, Industrial
      Concentration, Industrial
      Economic concentration
  BT Big business
      Duopolies
      Industries, Size of
      Oligopolies
      Trusts, Industrial
  RT Competition
      Consolidation and merger of
          corporations
      Industrial organization
  NT Barriers to entry (Industrial
          organization)
      Cartels
      Conglomerate corporations
      Countervailing power
      Interlocking directorates
      Monopsonies
      Vertical integration
  — **Government policy** *(May Subd Geog)*
      [HD2757-2930.7]
Industrial conciliation
  USE Mediation and conciliation, Industrial
Industrial contamination
  USE Contamination (Technology)
Industrial costs
  USE Costs, Industrial
Industrial councils
  USE Works councils
Industrial counseling
  USE Employee counseling
Industrial courts
  USE Labor courts
Industrial Cromotex Strike, Lima, Peru, 1979
  [HD5361.T4]
  UF Cromotex Strike, Lima, Peru, 1979
  BT Strikes and lockouts—Textile industry
      —Peru
Industrial democracy
  USE Management—Employee participation
Industrial dentistry
  BT Dentistry
      Medicine, Industrial
Industrial dermatitis
  USE Occupational dermatitis
Industrial design
  USE Design, Industrial
Industrial design coordination
  (May Subd Geog)
  [T324]

UF Coordination of industrial designs
Corporate design coordination
Corporate image and design
Corporate style
Design coordination, Industrial
Designs (Industrial publicity)
House style
Visual designs (Industrial publicity)
BT Design, Industrial
Emblems
Industrial property
Industrial publicity
NT Advertising cards
Design protection
House marks
Letterheads
Railroads—Freight-cars—Markings
Service marks
Industrial design departments
USE Design, Industrial—Management
Industrial designers *(May Subd Geog)*
BT Design, Industrial
Designers
NT Design, Industrial—Vocational
guidance
Industrial development
USE Industrialization
Industrial development bonds
(May Subd Geog)
UF Industrial revenue bonds
BT Bonds
Industrial promotion
Municipal bonds
— **Law and legislation** *(May Subd Geog)*
— **Ratings** *(May Subd Geog)*
UF Rating of industrial development
bonds
— **Taxation** *(May Subd Geog)*
— — **Law and legislation**
(May Subd Geog)
Industrial development centers
USE Industrial productivity centers
Industrial development projects
(May Subd Geog)
UF Projects, Industrial development
BT Economic development projects
RT Industrial promotion
Industrial diamonds
USE Diamonds, Industrial
Industrial discipline
USE Labor discipline
Industrial diseases
USE Occupational diseases
Industrial disputes
USE Labor disputes
Industrial districts *(May Subd Geog)*
[HC (Economic history)]
[HD1393.5 (Real estate)]
Here are entered works on self-contained indus-
trial areas within which utilities, transportation, and
other general services are offered to a group of in-
dividual companies.
UF Districts, Industrial
Industrial estates
Industrial parks
BT Industrial sites
NT Export processing zones
Research parks
— **Law and legislation** *(May Subd Geog)*
BT Real property
— Water-supply
USE Water-supply, Industrial
— **Florida**
NT Cape Coral Industrial Park (Cape
Coral, Fla.)
North Cape Coral Industrial Park
(Cape Coral, Fla.)
— **New York (State)**
NT Bathgate Industrial Park (New
York, N.Y.)

Industrial doctors
USE Occupational physicians
Industrial drawing
USE Mechanical drawing
Industrial economics
USE Industrial organization (Economic
theory)
Industrial editing
USE House organs
Industrial education
USE Manual training
Technical education
Industrial efficiency
USE Efficiency, Industrial
Industrial effluent
USE Sewage
Industrial effluents
USE Factory and trade waste
Industrial electric tractors
USE Industrial electric trucks
Industrial electric trucks
UF Electric industrial trucks
Electric tractors, Industrial
Electric trucks, Industrial
Industrial electric tractors
BT Conveying machinery
Electric motors
Electric vehicles
Industrial power trucks
Materials handling
Trucks
RT Automated guided vehicle systems
NT Fork lift trucks
— **Batteries**
Industrial electrochemistry
USE Electrochemistry, Industrial
Industrial electronics
[TK7881]
UF Electronics in industry
Factories—Electronic equipment
BT Electronic apparatus and appliances
Electronics
Factories—Electric equipment
NT Electronic control
Electronic instruments
Industrial television
Industrial energy conservation
USE Industry—Energy conservation
Industrial engineering *(May Subd Geog)*
Here are entered works on the application of engi-
neering principles and techniques to the design, in-
stallation and improvement of integrated systems
employing men, materials, and equipment for a high
level of productivity at an optimum cost. Works deal-
ing with the planning and control of the mechanical
means of changing the shape, condition, and relation-
ship of materials toward greater effectiveness and
value are entered under Production engineering.
UF Engineering, Industrial
Management engineering
BT Efficiency, Industrial
Engineering
Factory management
Industrial management
Simplification in industry
NT Automation
Computer integrated manufacturing
systems
Costs, Industrial
Engineering economy
Human engineering
Industrial project management
Industrial statistics
Methods engineering
Operations research
Plant layout
Production control
Production engineering
Psychology, Industrial
Quality control
Standardization
Systems engineering

Wages and labor productivity
Work environment
Work measurement
— **Mathematics**
BT Engineering mathematics
— **Notation**
UF Industrial engineering symbols
— **Statistical methods**
[T57.35]
BT Industrial statistics
Industrial engineering symbols
USE Industrial engineering—Notation
Industrial engineers *(May Subd Geog)*
BT Engineers
Industrial enzymology
USE Enzymes—Industrial applications
Industrial equipment *(May Subd Geog)*
UF Capital equipment
Capital goods
Equipment, Capital
Equipment, Industrial
BT Industry
SA *subdivision* Equipment and supplies
under names of industries, e.g.
Petroleum industry and trade—
Equipment and supplies
NT Factories—Equipment and supplies
Industrial equipment leases
Installation of industrial equipment
Office equipment and supplies
Pollution control equipment
Replacement of industrial equipment
Selling—Industrial equipment
Semiconductor industrial equipment
industry
Surplus industrial property
— **History**
NT Industrial archaeology
— **Law and legislation** *(May Subd Geog)*
BT Industrial laws and legislation
— **Maintenance and repair**
BT Plant maintenance
— Performance
USE Plant performance
— **Taxation** *(May Subd Geog)*
— — **Law and legislation**
(May Subd Geog)
— **Utilization**
UF Utilization of industrial equipment
Industrial equipment, Replacement of
USE Replacement of industrial equipment
Industrial equipment in interior decoration
[NK2115.I5]
Here are entered works on the use of industrial
equipment as household furnishings and decoration.
BT Interior decoration
Industrial equipment industry
(May Subd Geog)
— **Agents**
BT Commercial agents
Industrial equipment leases
(May Subd Geog)
UF Equipment leasing
Leases, Industrial equipment
BT Industrial equipment
Lease and rental services
Leases
NT Computer leases
Office equipment leases
Industrial espionage
USE Business intelligence
Industrial estates
USE Industrial districts
Industrial exhibitions
USE Exhibitions
Industrial fabrics
UF Fabrics, Industrial
Industrial textiles
Textiles, Industrial
BT Textile fabrics

Industrial fabrics *(Continued)*
  SA *individual industrial fabrics, e.g.*
    Papermaking machinery felts
Industrial fabrics industry *(May Subd Geog)*
Industrial feeding *(May Subd Geog)*
  UF Canteens (Industrial)
    Employee food service
    Factory canteens
    Industrial cafeterias
    Industrial canteens
    Industrial lunchrooms
    Industry—Food service
  BT Food service
    Restaurants, lunch rooms, etc.
Industrial films
  USE Moving-pictures in industry
Industrial Free Zone of Paraguaná (Venezuela)
  USE Paraguaná Industrial Free Zone
    (Venezuela)
Industrial gaming
  USE Management games
Industrial health engineering
  USE Industrial hygiene
Industrial homework
  USE Home labor
Industrial housekeeping
  UF Factory housekeeping
    Housekeeping, Industrial
  BT Buildings—Cleaning
    Factory sanitation
    Plant maintenance
Industrial housing *(May Subd Geog)*
  [HD7289.5]
  Here are entered works on housing provided by an industry to its employees. Works on communities in which all or the major portion of the property and businesses are owned by one industry are entered under Company towns.
  UF Employee housing
  BT Housing
    Labor and laboring classes—Dwellings
    Welfare work in industry
— **Law and legislation** *(May Subd Geog)*
Industrial hygiene *(May Subd Geog)*
  [HD7260-HD7780.5 (Administration)]
  [RC967 (Industrial medicine)]
  UF Health of workers
    Hygiene, Industrial
    Industrial health engineering
    Occupational health and safety
    Occupational safety and health
    Occupations—Health aspects
    Work environment—Health aspects
  BT Environmental health
    Industrial management
    Medicine, Industrial
  SA *subdivision* Health and hygiene *under occupational groups, e.g.* Printers—Health and hygiene; *also subdivision* Employees—Health and hygiene *under types of industries, e.g.* Construction industry—Employees—Health and hygiene; *and subdivision* Health aspects *under types of industries, structures, and processes, e.g.* Construction industry—Health aspects; Welding—Health aspects
  NT Employee assistance programs
    Factories—Safety measures
    Factory sanitation
    Industrial accidents
    Mine sanitation
— **Law and legislation** *(May Subd Geog)*
  UF Factory sanitation—Law and legislation
  BT Labor laws and legislation
  RT Factory laws and legislation
  NT Medicine, Industrial—Law and legislation

Painting, Industrial—Law and legislation
— — **Criminal provisions**
Industrial hygiene libraries
  USE Occupational health libraries
Industrial hygienists *(May Subd Geog)*
  [RC963]
  UF Hygienists, Industrial
  BT Allied health personnel
Industrial injuries
  USE Industrial accidents
Industrial installation
  USE Installation of industrial equipment
Industrial insurance
  USE Insurance, Industrial
Industrial laboratories
  USE Engineering laboratories
    Research, Industrial—Laboratories
Industrial laboratory equipment industry *(May Subd Geog)*
  RT Research, Industrial—Laboratories—Equipment and supplies
Industrial laws and legislation *(May Subd Geog)*
  [HD3621-7]
  Here are entered works of a comprehensive character which deal with laws and legislation regulating industry. Works on the theory of state regulation of industry are entered under Industry and state; Laissez-faire.
  UF Government regulation of commerce
    Law, Industrial
  BT Economic policy
    Industry and state
  NT Business relocation—Law and legislation
    Factory laws and legislation
    Freedom of movement
    Industrial equipment—Law and legislation
    Industrial management—Employee participation—Law and legislation
    Industrial mobilization—Law and legislation
    Industrial promotion—Law and legislation
    Labor laws and legislation
    Occupations, Dangerous
    Patent laws and legislation
    Priorities, Industrial—Law and legislation
    Privatization—Law and legislation
    Rationing, Consumer—Law and legislation
    Standardization—Law and legislation
— Conflict of laws
  USE Conflict of laws—Industrial laws and legislation
Industrial libraries
  USE Corporate libraries
Industrial lighting
  USE Factories—Lighting
Industrial loan associations *(May Subd Geog)*
  BT Banks and banking
    Credit
    Instalment plan
    Loans, Personal
Industrial location
  USE Industry—Location
Industrial lunchrooms
  USE Industrial feeding
Industrial maintenance
  USE Plant maintenance
Industrial management *(May Subd Geog)*
  Here are entered works on the application of the principles of management to industrial enterprises, including, in addition to the production aspects, office management, marketing, financial controls, etc.
  Works limited to technical control of manufacturing processes are entered under the heading Factory management.

  UF Business administration
    Business enterprises—Management
    Corporations—Management
    Industrial administration
    Management, Industrial
    Rationalization of industry
    Scientific management
  BT Management
  RT Business
    Industrial organization
  SA *subdivision* Management *under types of industries, industrial plants and processes, e.g.* Construction industry—Management; *and under names of individual corporate bodies*
  NT Assembly-line methods
    Big business
    Break-even analysis
    Business intelligence
    Business logistics
    Classification—Books—Industrial management
    Communication in management
    Controllership
    Corporate planning
    Delegation of authority
    Efficiency, Industrial
    Employment stabilization
    Factory management
    Industrial engineering
    Industrial hygiene
    Industrial procurement
    Industrial productivity
    Industrial relations
    Industrial sociology
    Industries, Size of
    Industry—Location
    Management audit
    Management by exception
    Management committees
    Management games
    Management rights
    Managerial economics
    Marketing
    Materials management
    Matrix organization
    Physical distribution of goods—Management
    Production control
    Production management
    Production standards
    Ratio analysis
    Sales management
    Service industries—Management
    Shift systems
    Shipment of goods
    Simplification in industry
    Small business—Management
    Technological innovations
    Welfare work in industry
— **Audio-visual aids**
— **Effect of inflation on**
  UF Industrial management and inflation
  BT Inflation (Finance)
— **Employee participation**
  [HD5650-5660]
— — **Law and legislation**
  (May Subd Geog)
  BT Industrial laws and legislation
    Labor laws and legislation
— **Mathematical models**
  UF Quantitative business analysis
  BT Business mathematics
  NT DYNAMO (Computer program language)
— **Japan**
  UF Japanese management
— **Soviet Union**
  NT Socialist competition
    Stakhanov movement

Industrial management and inflation
  USE Industrial management—Effect of
        inflation on
Industrial management games
  USE Management games
Industrial marketing *(May Subd Geog)*
    Here are entered works on the marketing of goods
    and services to business enterprises, governmental
    units and nonprofit institutions for use by them in
    their operations or for reprocessing into other pro-
    ducts.
  BT Marketing
Industrial materials
  USE Materials
Industrial mechanics
  USE Millwrights
Industrial mediation
  USE Mediation and conciliation, Industrial
Industrial medicine
  USE Medicine, Industrial
Industrial melanism
  BT Melanism
Industrial mental health
  USE Industrial psychiatry
Industrial meteorology
  USE Industry and weather
Industrial microbiology *(May Subd Geog)*
    ₁QR53₁
  UF Microbiology—Industrial applications
        Microbiology, Industrial
  BT Biotechnology
        Microbiology
  SA *subdivision* Microbiology *under*
        subjects, e.g. Petroleum—
        Microbiology; Textile fibers—
        Microbiology
  NT Bacterial starter cultures
        Fermentation
        Micro-organisms, Immobilized
        Microbial mutation breeding
        Microbiological synthesis
        Pharmaceutical microbiology
        Sanitary microbiology
Industrial microscopy
  UF Microscopy, Industrial
  BT Microscope and microscopy
  SA *subdivision* Microscopy *under*
        individual products, e.g. Concrete—
        Microscopy
  NT Metallography
Industrial minerals *(May Subd Geog)*
    Here are entered works on nonmetallic minerals,
    exclusive of fuels.
  UF Minerals, Industrial
  BT Mines and mineral resources
        Nonfuel minerals
        Nonmetallic minerals
Industrial missions
  USE Missions—Industrial work
Industrial mobilization *(May Subd Geog)*
    ₁UA18₁
  UF Defenses
        Mobilization, Industrial
  BT Armaments
        Economic policy
        Military art and science
        War—Economic aspects
  SA *subdivision* Military aspects *under*
        types of industries, e.g.
        Construction industry—Military
        aspects
  NT Aircraft industry—Military aspects
        Hospitals—Military aspects
        Military supplies
        Munitions
  — **Law and legislation** *(May Subd Geog)*
      BT Industrial laws and legislation
Industrial morale
  USE Employee morale
Industrial museums *(May Subd Geog)*
    ₁T179-183₁

UF Industrial arts—Museums
      Technological museums
      Technology—Museums
  BT Museums
Industrial mycology
  USE Fungi—Industrial applications
Industrial noise *(May Subd Geog)*
    ₁TA365₁
  UF Factories—Noise
        Factory noise
        Industry—Noise
  BT Noise
  SA *subdivision* Noise *under industrial*
        subjects, e.g. Construction industry
        —Noise
Industrial nursing
    ₁RC966₁
  UF Occupational health nursing
  BT Medicine, Industrial
        Nursing
  RT Public health nursing
Industrial ophthalmology
    ₁RE825₁
  UF Ophthalmology, Industrial
  BT Medicine, Industrial
Industrial organization *(May Subd Geog)*
  UF Industry—Organization
        Organization, Industrial
  BT Industry
        Organization
  RT Industrial concentration
        Industrial management
        Industrial sociology
  NT Matrix organization
        Span of control
        Vertical integration
        Work groups
Industrial organization (Economic theory)
  UF Industrial economics
        Market structure
  BT Industry
        Microeconomics
  NT Barriers to entry (Industrial
        organization)
Industrial painters
  USE Painters, Industrial
Industrial painting
  USE Painting, Industrial
Industrial parks
  USE Industrial districts
Industrial photochemistry
  USE Photochemistry—Industrial
        applications
Industrial photography
  USE Photography, Industrial
Industrial physicians
  USE Occupational physicians
Industrial plant protection
  USE *subdivision* Defense measures *under*
        industries and plants, e.g. Gas
        industry—Defense measures;
        Petroleum industry and trade—
        Defense measures
        Factories—Protection
Industrial plants
  USE Factories
Industrial plasma chemistry
  USE Plasma chemistry—Industrial
        applications
Industrial poisoning
  USE Industrial toxicology
Industrial poisons
  USE Industrial toxicology
Industrial police
  USE Police, Private
Industrial policy
  USE Industry and state
Industrial power trucks
    ₁TL296 (Manufacture)₁
    ₁TS155 (Material handling)₁

UF Industrial tractors
      Industrial trucks
      Power trucks, Industrial
  BT Materials handling
        Trucks
  NT Fork lift trucks
        Industrial electric trucks
        Straddle trucks
  — **Hydraulic drive**
  — **Parts**
Industrial priorities
  USE Priorities, Industrial
Industrial process control
  USE Process control
Industrial processing
  USE Manufacturing processes
Industrial procurement *(May Subd Geog)*
  UF Buying, Industrial
        Industrial buying
        Industrial purchasing
        Procurement, Industrial
        Purchasing, Industrial
  BT Industrial management
        Purchasing
  SA *subdivision* Purchasing *under specific*
        products, e.g. Minicomputers—
        Purchasing
  NT Make-or-buy decisions
        Priorities, Industrial
        Purchasing agents
        Purchasing departments
        Small orders
Industrial production
  USE Industry
        Overproduction
        Supply and demand
Industrial productivity *(May Subd Geog)*
  UF Productivity, Industrial
  BT Efficiency, Industrial
        Industrial management
        Industry
        Production (Economic theory)
  NT Capital productivity
        Inflation (Finance)—Effect of
          productivity on
        Labor productivity
        Productivity accounting
        Technological innovations
  — **Effect of inflation on**
      BT Inflation (Finance)
  — **Measurement**
  — **Regional disparities**
      BT Regional economic disparities
Industrial productivity centers
    (May Subd Geog)
  UF Industrial development centers
        Productivity centers
  BT Economic development
        Research, Industrial
        Technical assistance
Industrial project management
  UF Project management
        Project management, Industrial
  BT Factory management
        Industrial engineering
        Management
  NT Economic development projects
        Matrix organization
        Network analysis (Planning)
  — **Computer programs**
      NT SuperProject Plus (Computer
            program)
Industrial promotion *(May Subd Geog)*
  BT Boards of trade
        Industry
        Industry and state
        Small business
  RT Industrial development projects
  NT Enterprise zones
        Enterprise zones, Rural
        Import substitution

Industrial promotion (Continued)
    Industrial development bonds
  — **Law and legislation** (May Subd Geog)
    BT Industrial laws and legislation
Industrial property (May Subd Geog)
    Here are entered works dealing collectively with several categories of intangible property rights connected with industry, commerce, and agriculture, as, ownership of patents, trade-marks, business names, etc.
    UF Proprietary rights
    BT Intellectual property
    NT Business names
        Competition, Unfair
        Design protection
        Good-will (in business, etc.)
        Industrial design coordination
        License agreements
        Marks of origin
        Models (Patents)
        Patent laws and legislation
        Service marks
        Surplus industrial property
        Technology transfer—Law and legislation
        Trademarks
  — **Criminal provisions**
Industrial property (International law)
    BT International law
Industrial psychiatry (May Subd Geog)
    [RC967.5]
    UF Industrial mental health
        Psychiatry, Industrial
    BT Medicine, Industrial
        Psychiatry
        Psychology, Industrial
    NT Employee assistance programs
Industrial psychology
  USE Psychology, Industrial
Industrial publicity
    UF Publicity, Industrial
    BT Industry
        Mass media and business
        Publicity
    RT Public relations
    NT Advertising
        Advertising departments
        Industrial design coordination
Industrial purchasing
  USE Industrial procurement
Industrial radiochemistry
  USE Radiochemistry—Industrial applications
Industrial radiography
  USE Radiography, Industrial
Industrial railroads
  USE Railroads, Industrial
Industrial rationing
  USE Priorities, Industrial
Industrial recreation (May Subd Geog)
    [HD7395.R4]
    UF Employee recreation
        Recreation, Industrial
    BT Recreation
        Welfare work in industry
Industrial relations (May Subd Geog)
    [HD6958.5-HD6976]
    Here are entered works dealing with employer-employee relations in general. Works on that field of management which has the fundamental responsibility for recruiting, hiring, training, compensating, developing and caring for the general welfare of employees are entered under Personnel management. Works on the managing of employees by their supervisors so that their duties are performed according to instructions are entered under Supervision of employees.

    UF Capital and labor
        Employee-employer relations
        Employer-employee relations
        Labor and capital
        Labor-management relations
        Labor relations
    BT Industrial management
        Labor and laboring classes
    NT Arbitration, Industrial
        Collective bargaining
        Communication in industrial relations
        Company towns
        Electronic data processing and industrial relations
        Employee-management relations in government
        Employee rights
        Employees, Reporting to
        Employees' magazines, handbooks, etc.
        Industrial sociology
        Labor contract
        Labor disputes
        Labor-management committees
        Management rights
        Mediation and conciliation, Industrial
        Personnel directors
        Restrictive practices in industrial relations
        Trade-unions
        Trade-unions—Recognition
        Unfair labor practices
        Works councils
  — **Audio-visual aids**
  — **Bibliography**
    RT Industrial relations literature
  — **Effect of technological innovations on**
    BT Technological innovations
  — **Research** (May Subd Geog)
    UF Industrial relations research
    BT Research, Industrial
Industrial relations councils
  USE Works councils
Industrial relations libraries
  (May Subd Geog)
    UF Libraries, Industrial relations
    BT Libraries, Special
Industrial relations literature
  (May Subd Geog)
    UF Literature, Industrial relations
    RT Industrial relations—Bibliography
Industrial relations research
  USE Industrial relations—Research
Industrial research
  USE Research, Industrial
Industrial revenue bonds
  USE Industrial development bonds
Industrial revolution
  USE subdivisions Economic conditions and Industries under names of countries
        Industry—History
Industrial robots
  USE Robots, Industrial
Industrial safety (May Subd Geog)
    [T55]
    UF Industrial accidents—Prevention
        Job safety
        Occupational health and safety
        Occupational safety and health
        Safety, Industrial
        Safety engineering
        Safety measures
        Safety of workers
    BT Accidents—Prevention
    RT System safety
    SA subdivisions Safety appliances and Safety measures under subjects, e.g. Cotton machinery—Safety appliances; Construction industry—Safety measures
    NT Clothing, Protective
        Communication in industrial safety

        Dam safety
        Hazardous substances
        Industrial accidents
        Mine safety
        Redundancy (Engineering)
        Safety appliances
        Safety education, Industrial
        Safety engineers
        Safety signs
  — **Law and legislation** (May Subd Geog)
    BT Accident law
        Employers' liability
    RT Factory laws and legislation
        Safety regulations
    SA subdivision Safety regulations under subjects, e.g. Construction industry—Safety regulations; Machinery—Safety regulations
    NT Mine safety—Law and legislation
  — — **Criminal provisions**
  — **Psychological aspects**
    BT Psychology, Industrial
  — Study and teaching
    USE Safety education, Industrial
Industrial safety committees
  (May Subd Geog)
    BT Committees
Industrial safety consultants
  USE Safety consultants
Industrial safety education
  USE Safety education, Industrial
Industrial safety engineers
  USE Safety engineers
Industrial safety equipment industry
  (May Subd Geog)
    [HD9999.I43-434]
    BT Safety appliances
Industrial safety libraries
  USE Occupational health libraries
Industrial salvage
  USE Salvage (Waste, etc.)
Industrial scale removal
  USE Descaling
Industrial schools
  USE Manual training
        Reformatories
        Trade schools
Industrial security measures
  USE Industry—Security measures
Industrial security program (United States)
    BT Labor and laboring classes—United States—1914-
        Loyalty-security program, 1947-
Industrial sites (May Subd Geog)
    UF Factory sites
    BT Factories—Location
        Industry—Location
        Plant engineering
        Real property
    NT Business parks
        Industrial districts
  — **Law and legislation** (May Subd Geog)
Industrial sociologists (May Subd Geog)
    BT Industrial sociology
        Sociologists
Industrial sociology (May Subd Geog)
    [HD6971-6974]
    Here are entered works on social relations within industry, as distinguished from labor-management relations. Works about the impact of industry on culture and societal changes, and works about the social responsibilities of businessmen are entered under Industry—Social aspects.
    UF Sociology, Industrial
    BT Industrial management
        Industrial relations
        Personnel management
        Psychology, Industrial
        Sociology
        Work

RT Industrial organization
    Industry—Social aspects
NT Industrial sociologists
    Managing your boss
    Office politics
    Sex role in the work environment
— **Research** *(May Subd Geog)*
Industrial statistics
    [HB137 (Methodology)]
    [HC (General data)]
    [HD9000-HD9999 (Special industries)]
  UF Industry—Statistical methods
    Industry—Statistics
  BT Industrial engineering
    Statistics
  SA *subdivision* Industries—Statistics *under*
    names of countries, cities, etc.
  NT Industrial engineering—Statistical
    methods
Industrial storage racks
  USE Storage racks
Industrial stores
  USE Company stores
Industrial supervisors
  USE Supervisors, Industrial
Industrial supply houses
  UF Industry—Equipment and supplies
Industrial surveys *(May Subd Geog)*
    Here are entered works on the methods and techniques employed in conducting industrial surveys, and reports of individual surveys. For the latter the heading may be subdivided by place; in such cases an additional subject entry is made under the heading [local subdivision]—Industries, e.g. 1. Industrial surveys—[United States]. 2. [United States]—Industries.
  UF Industry—Surveys
  BT Economic surveys
Industrial technicians
  USE Technicians in industry
Industrial television
  UF Television—Industrial applications
    Television, Industrial
    Television in industry
  BT Closed-circuit television
    Industrial electronics
    Microwave communication systems
  RT Television in management
Industrial textiles
  USE Industrial fabrics
Industrial tours *(May Subd Geog)*
  UF Factory tours
    Plant tours
  BT Business education
    Employees, Training of
    Field work (Educational method)
    School excursions
    Technical education
Industrial toxicology *(May Subd Geog)*
    [HD7263 (Industrial hygiene)]
    [RA1229 (Toxicology)]
  UF Industrial poisoning
    Industrial poisons
    Occupational poisoning
    Occupational toxicology
    Poisoning, Industrial
    Poisoning, Occupational
    Poisons, Industrial
  BT Occupational diseases
    Toxicology
  NT Biological limit values (Industrial
    toxicology)
    Threshold limit values (Industrial
    toxicology)
— **Diagnosis**
  BT Diagnosis
Industrial tractors
  USE Industrial power trucks
Industrial traffic management
  USE Shipment of goods
Industrial trucks
  USE Industrial power trucks

Industrial trusts
  USE Trusts, Industrial
Industrial unions
  USE Trade-unions
Industrial uses of space
  USE Space industrialization
Industrial vacuum
  USE Vacuum technology
Industrial waste treatment facilities, Centralized
  USE Centralized industrial waste treatment
    facilities
Industrial wastes
  USE Factory and trade waste
    Waste products
Industrial water-supply
  USE Water-supply, Industrial
Industrial welfare work
  USE Welfare work in industry
Industrialists *(May Subd Geog)*
  UF Manufacturers
  BT Businessmen
    Industry
Industrialization *(Not Subd Geog)*
    Works on the industrialization of individual countries or regions are entered under the name of the area followed by the subdivision Industries.
  UF Industrial development
  BT Economic development
    Economic policy
    Industry
  RT Technical assistance
  SA *subdivision* Industries *under names of*
    countries, cities, etc.
  NT Developing countries
    Space industrialization
    Territorial production complexes
    United Nations—Economic assistance
    United Nations—Technical assistance
Industrialization, Rural
  USE Rural industry
Industrialized building *(May Subd Geog)*
    [TH1000]
  UF Building, Industrialized
    Construction, Industrialized
    Industrialized construction
    System building
    Systems building
  BT Building
    Construction industry—Management
  NT Buildings, Prefabricated
    Modular construction
    Precast concrete construction
Industrialized construction
  USE Industrialized building
Industries
  USE Industry
Industries, Location of
  USE Industry—Location
Industries, Primitive *(May Subd Geog)*
    [GN429-GN434]
    Here are entered works limited to the techniques of production of pre-literate and folk cultures. Works on the objects made or used by people, especially the folk artifacts produced by traditional methods, as well as techniques of their production, are entered under Material culture. Works on the industries of particular ethnic groups are entered under the name of the group with the subdivision Industries, e.g. Indians of North America—Industries. Works on the material culture of particular ethnic groups are entered under the name of the group with the subdivision Material culture, e.g. Indians of North America—Material culture.
    When this heading is divided by place an additional subject entry is made under the name of the place with the subdivision Industries.
  UF Primitive technology
    Technology, Primitive

  BT Archaeology
    Ethnology
    Industrial arts
    Industrial arts—History
    Material culture
    Society, Primitive
  SA *subdivision* Industries *under names of*
    particular ethnic groups, e.g.
    Australian aborigines—Industries
  NT Agriculture, Primitive
    Arms and armor, Primitive
    Bone implements
    Bow and arrow
    Cordage, Prehistoric
    Fishing, Primitive
    Fortification, Primitive
    Hunting, Primitive
    Indians—Implements
    Indians of North America—Industries
    Indians of South America—Industries
    Man, Prehistoric
    Man, Prehistoric—Tools
    Matting
    Nets
    Pottery, Prehistoric
    Pottery, Primitive
    Stone implements
    Technological complexity
    Weaving
Industries, Rural
  USE Rural industry
Industries, Size of *(May Subd Geog)*
  UF Size of industries
  BT Industrial management
    Industry
  RT Big business
    Small business
  NT Economies of scale
    Industrial concentration
Industry
    [HC]
    [HD]
  UF Industrial production
    Industries
  BT Economics
  RT Technology
  SA *subdivision* Industries *under names of*
    countries, cities, etc.; also under
    names of preliterate groups for the
    crafts and technologies of those
    groups, e.g. Australian aborigines—
    Industries; *and headings for*
    individual types of industries, e.g.
    Construction industry
  NT Big business
    Business losses
    Color in industry
    Costs, Industrial
    Day care centers and industry
    Efficiency, Industrial
    Floor space, Industrial
    Industrial capacity
    Industrial equipment
    Industrial organization
    Industrial organization (Economic
    theory)
    Industrial productivity
    Industrial promotion
    Industrial publicity
    Industrialists
    Industrialization
    Industries, Size of
    Input-output analysis
    Libraries and industry
    Machinery in industry
    Moving-pictures in industry
    New business enterprises
    Prison industries
    Production (Economic theory)
    Research, Industrial
    Rural industry

Industry *(Continued)*
    Science and industry
    Seasonal industries
    Seasonal variations (Economics)
    Service industries
    Substitution (Economics)
    Turnover (Business)
    Water-supply, Industrial
— **Classification**
    SA *subdivision* Industries—
        Classification *under names of*
        countries, e.g. United States—
        Industries—Classification
— Costs
    USE Costs, Industrial
— **Defense measures** *(May Subd Geog)*
    BT Civil defense
    SA *subdivision* Defense measures
        under types of industries, e.g.
        Construction industry—Defense
        measures
— Deregulation
    USE Deregulation
— **Energy conservation**
    UF Industrial energy conservation
    SA *subdivision* Industries—Energy
        conservation *under names of*
        countries, cities, etc., e.g. South
        Carolina—Industries—Energy
        conservation
— — **Law and legislation**
    SA *subdivision* Industries—Energy
        conservation—Law and
        legislation *under names of*
        countries, cities, etc.
— **Environmental aspects**
    SA *subdivision* Industries—
        Environmental aspects *under*
        names of countries, cities, etc.
— Equipment and supplies
    USE Industrial supply houses
— Food service
    USE Industrial feeding
— Government policy
    USE Industry and state
— **History**
    [HD2321]
    UF Industrial revolution
    BT Economic history
    NT Commerce—History
        Factory system
        Home labor
— **Information services**
    SA *subdivision* Industries—Information
        services *under names of*
        countries, cities, etc., e.g.
        Europe—Industries—
        Information services
— Information storage and retrieval systems
    USE Information storage and retrieval
        systems—Industry
— **Location**
    UF Industrial location
        Industries, Location of
        Location in business
        Location of industries
        Plant location
    BT Industrial management
        Regional planning
        Space in economics
    SA *subdivision* Industries—Location
        under names of countries, cities,
        etc.; and subdivision Location
        under types of industries, e.g.
        Construction industry—Location
    NT Business relocation
        Industrial sites
        Store location
        Territorial production complexes
— — **Environmental aspects**

    SA *subdivision* Industries—Location
        —Environmental aspects
        under names of countries,
        cities, etc.
— Noise
    USE Industrial noise
— Organization
    USE Industrial organization
— **Power supply**
    UF Energy sources for industry
    BT Power resources
    SA *subdivision* Industries—Power
        supply *under names of*
        countries, e.g. United States—
        Industries—Power supply
    NT Energy parks
— **Security measures** *(May Subd Geog)*
    [HV8290]
    [UB249 (Protection of classified
    information)]
    UF Industrial security measures
        Security measures, Industrial
        Security measures (Military
        information)
    BT Factories—Protection
— **Social aspects** *(May Subd Geog)*
    [HD60-HD60.5]
    Here are entered works about the impact of
    industry on culture and societal changes, and
    works about the social responsibilities of busi-
    nessmen. Works on social relations within indus-
    try, as distinguished from labor-management re-
    lations, are entered under Industrial sociology
    UF Business—Social aspects
        Business—Social responsibility
        Business and social problems
        Corporate social responsibility
        Corporations—Social responsiblity
        Social responsibility, Corporate
        Social responsibility of business
        Social responsiblity of industry
    BT Social change
    RT Corporations—Charitable
        contributions
        Industrial sociology
        Issues management
        Social accounting
    NT Architecture—Conservation and
        restoration—Business
        community participation
        Medical policy—Business
        community participation
— Statistical methods
    USE Industrial statistics
— Statistics
    USE *subdivision* Industries—Statistics
        under names of countries,
        cities, etc.
        Industrial statistics
— Subject headings
    USE Subject headings—Industry
— Surveys
    USE *subdivision* Industries *under*
        name of city or district
        concerned
        Industrial surveys
— Vertical integration
    USE Vertical integration
Industry, Public library services to
    USE Public libraries—Services to business
        and industry
Industry, Rural
    USE Rural industry
Industry (Psychology)
    USE Work
Industry and art
    USE Art and industry
Industry and climate
    USE Industry and weather
Industry and colleges
    USE Industry and education

Industry and education *(May Subd Geog)*
    UF Education and industry
        Industry and colleges
    BT Universities and colleges
    NT Education, Cooperative
Industry and libraries
    USE Libraries and industry
Industry and literature *(May Subd Geog)*
    BT Literature
Industry and music
    USE Music in industry
Industry and state *(May Subd Geog)*
    [HD3611-3790]
    UF Business and government
        Government and business
        Government regulation of commerce
        Industrial policy
        Industry—Government policy
        Law, Industrial
        State and industry
    BT Socialism
        Technology and state
    RT Economic policy
        Laissez-faire
    SA *subdivision* Government policy *under*
        types of industries and topical
        headings, e.g. Construction industry
        —Government policy; Industrial
        concentration—Government policy
    NT Agriculture and state
        Commercial policy
        Concessions
        Corporate state
        Deregulation
        Fishery policy
        Foreign trade promotion
        Forest policy
        Full employment policies
        Government business enterprises
        Government competition
        Government lending
        Government ownership
        Government questionnaires
        Industrial laws and legislation
        Industrial promotion
        Insurance—State supervision
        Labor policy
        Mercantile system
        Priorities, Industrial
        Public interest
        Public service commissions
        Railroads and state
        Right to labor
        Subsidies
        Trade adjustment assistance
        Transportation and state
Industry and the church
    USE Church and industry
Industry and war
    USE War—Economic aspects
Industry and weather
    UF Industrial meteorology
        Industry and climate
        Weather and industry
    BT Man—Influence of climate
        Weather
    RT Engineering meteorology
    NT Degree days
        Unemployment, Seasonal
Industry in art
    [N8218]
    BT Art and industry
Industry in literature
    [PN56.I]
    BT Economics in literature
Industry in space
    USE Space industrialization
Industry-sponsored education
    USE Employer-supported education
Industry-sponsored higher education
    USE Employer-supported higher education

Indwelling of God
USE Mystical union
Indy 500
USE Indianapolis Speedway Race
Inebriates
USE Alcoholics
Inebriety
USE Alcoholism
Drunkenness (Criminal law)
Ineffable, The
UF Unutterable, The
BT Languages—Philosophy
Philosophy
RT Taboo, Linguistic
Inefficiency, Intellectual
[BF435-7]
UF Intellectual inefficiency
Stupidity
BT Ability
Education
Intellect
Intellect—Deterioration
Psychology, Pathological
Thought and thinking
RT Fatigue, Mental
NT Intelligence tests
Mentally handicapped children
Ineko family (Not Subd Geog)
Inelastic collisions, Damp
USE Deep inelastic collisions
Inelastic collisions, Deep
USE Deep inelastic collisions
Inelastic cross sections
[QC173]
UF Cross sections, Inelastic
BT Collisions (Nuclear physics)
Cross sections (Nuclear physics)
Fission cross sections
RT Elastic cross sections
Inequalities, Gronwall
USE Gronwall inequalities
Inequalities, Variational (Mathematics)
USE Variational inequalities (Mathematics)
Inequalities (Mathematics)
[QA295]
BT Processes, Infinite
NT Differential inequalities
Integral inequalities
Isoperimetric inequalities
Inequality
USE Equality
Inequality of income
USE Income distribution
Inequality of leg length
USE Leg length inequality
Inert elements
USE Gases, Rare
Inert gas narcosis
UF Narcosis, Inert gas
BT Atmospheric pressure—Physiological
effect
Diving, Submarine—Physiological
aspects
Loss of consciousness
Occupational diseases
Submarine medicine
Inert gas solids
USE Solid rare gases
Inert gas systems (Ships)
USE Ships—Inert gas systems
Inertia, Moments of
USE Moments of inertia
Inertia, Products of
USE Moments of inertia
Inertia (Mechanics)
BT Acceleration (Mechanics)
Mechanics
RT Mass (Physics)
NT Momentum (Mechanics)
Inertial confinement fusion
USE Pellet fusion

Inertial guidance
USE Inertial navigation systems
Inertial guidance sensors
USE Inertial navigation systems
Inertial impaction (Dust removal)
USE Dust—Removal—Inertial separation
Inertial mass
USE Mass (Physics)
Inertial navigation
UF Navigation, Inertial
BT Dead reckoning (Navigation)
Nautical instruments
Navigation
Inertial navigation (Aeronautics)
[TL588.5]
UF Navigation, Inertial (Aeronautics)
BT Aeronautical instruments
Dead reckoning (Navigation)
Navigation (Aeronautics)
Inertial navigation (Astronautics)
UF Navigation, Inertial (Astronautics)
BT Astrodynamics
Navigation (Astronautics)
Space vehicles—Guidance systems
NT Stellar inertial navigation systems
Inertial navigation systems
UF Inertial guidance
Inertial guidance sensors
BT Nautical instruments
Inertial separation (Dust removal)
USE Dust—Removal—Inertial separation
INF (Computer program language)
[QA76.73.I]
Infallibility (Philosophy)
[BD234]
BT Knowledge, Theory of
Philosophy
NT Popes—Infallibility
Infallibility of the church
USE Catholic Church—Infallibility
Church—Infallibility
Infallibility of the Pope
USE Popes—Infallibility
Infamy (Canon law)
Infamy (Law)
BT Civil law
Criminal law
Punishment
RT Civil death
Political rights, Loss of
Infamy (Roman law)
Infancy, Holy
USE Holy Childhood, Devotion to
Infancy of animals
USE Animals—Infancy
Infancy of apes
USE Apes—Infancy
Infancy of domestic animals
USE Domestic animals—Infancy
Infancy of fishes
USE Fishes—Infancy
Infancy of Jesus, Devotion to
USE Holy Childhood, Devotion to
Infant and mother
USE Mother and infant
Infant animals
USE Animals—Infancy
Infant apes
USE Apes—Infancy
Infant baptism
[BV813]
UF Pedobaptism
BT Baptism
NT Children—Conversion to Christianity
Predestination
— **History**
— — **Early church, ca. 30-600**
Infant care
USE Infants—Care
Infant care leave
USE Parental leave

Infant communion
[BV828]
UF Communion, Infant
Lord's Supper—Infant communion
BT Lord's Supper
Lord's Supper—Child participation
Infant CPR
USE CPR (First aid) for infants
Infant development
USE Infants—Development
Infant domestic animals
USE Domestic animals—Infancy
Infant education
USE Education, Preschool
Infant foods
USE Baby foods
Infant formulas
UF Baby formulas
Formulas, Infant
BT Baby foods
Infants—Nutrition
RT Bottle feeding
— **Contamination**
UF Contamination of infant formulas
BT Food contamination
— **Law and legislation** (May Subd Geog)
BT Food law and legislation
— **Sterilization**
Infant health services (May Subd Geog)
[RJ101-RJ103]
UF Infants—Medical care
Maternal and infant health services
BT Child health services
Maternal and infant welfare
NT Neonatal intensive care
— Federal aid
USE Federal aid to infant health
services
— **Finance**
NT Federal aid to infant health
services
— **Utilization**
UF Utilization of infant health services
Infant Jesus of Prague (Sculpture)
UF Infant of Prague (Sculpture)
Little King (Sculpture)
Prague, Infant Jesus of (Sculpture)
BT Sculpture, Medieval
Infant mortality
USE Infants—Mortality
Infant nutrition disorders
USE Nutrition disorders in infants
Infant of Prague (Sculpture)
USE Infant Jesus of Prague (Sculpture)
Infant psychiatry (May Subd Geog)
[RJ502.5]
UF Psychiatry, Infant
BT Child psychiatry
Infant psychology
NT Depression in infants
Infant psychology (May Subd Geog)
[BF719-720]
Here are entered works on the psychological
growth and characteristics of infants. Works on the
physical, psychological and social growth of infants
are entered under Infants—Development.
UF Infants—Psychology
BT Child psychology
Infants—Development
NT Emotions in infants
Infant psychiatry
Infants—Intelligence testing
Infants (Newborn)—Diseases—
Psychological aspects
Perception in infants
Separation-individuation
Infant salvation
[BT758]
BT Salvation
RT Children—Death—Religious aspects
Limbo

Infant salvation *(Continued)*
  NT Children—Conversion to Christianity
        Predestination
Infant sudden death
  USE Sudden death in infants
Infant welfare
  USE Maternal and infant welfare
Infantes of Lara
  UF Lara, Infantes of
  BT Legends—Spain
Infanticide *(May Subd Geog)*
  ⌐HV6537-6541⌐
  BT Criminal law
        Homicide
        Murder
        Offenses against the person
  NT Filicide
        Trials (Infanticide)
  — Religious aspects
  — — Buddhism, ⌐Christianity, etc.⌐
Infanticide (Roman law)
Infanticide in animals *(May Subd Geog)*
  ⌐QL762.5⌐
  UF Animals, Infanticide in
  BT Familial behavior in animals
        Parental behavior in animals
        Social behavior in animals
  RT Animals—Infancy
Infanticide in literature
Infantile atrophy
  USE Marasmus
Infantile conjunctivitis
  USE Conjunctivitis, Infantile
Infantile diarrhea
  USE Diarrhea, Infantile
Infantile hydrocephalus
  USE Hydrocephalus in infants
Infantile myoclonic epilepsy
  USE Spasms, Infantile
Infantile paralysis
  USE Poliomyelitis
Infantile scurvy
  USE Scurvy, Infantile
Infantile spasms
  USE Spasms, Infantile
Infantilism
  ⌐RJ135⌐
  RT Childishness
Infantry
  ⌐UD⌐
  UF Foot soldiers
  SA *names of individual infantries and*
        subdivision Militia *under states of*
        the United States
  NT Commando troops
  — Equipment
    ⌐UD370-375⌐
Infantry drill and tactics
  ⌐UD157-302⌐
    Here are entered general works only. Works on
  the army of any particular country are entered under
  the name of the country, with subheading Army. In-
  fantry—Drill and tactics.
  BT Drill and minor tactics
        Military art and science
        Tactics
  NT Night fighting (Military science)
        Skirmishing
        Target practice
Infantry landing craft
  USE Landing craft
Infants *(May Subd Geog)*
  ⌐HQ774 (Social groups)⌐
  UF Babies
  BT Life cycle, Human
  RT Children
  NT Children, First-born
        Crawling and creeping
        Diet therapy for infants
        Infants' supplies
        Swimming for infants

— Anatomy
  ⌐QM24.5⌐
  BT Anatomy, Human
— Anthropometry
  NT Infants—Weight
— Bathing
  BT Baths
— Books and reading
  ⌐Z1037-1038⌐
— Care *(May Subd Geog)*
  ⌐RJ61 (Popular works)⌐
  ⌐RJ101-RJ103 (General works)⌐
  UF Baby care
        Infant care
        Infants—Care and hygiene
— Care and hygiene
  USE Infants—Care
        Infants—Health and hygiene
— Charities, protection, etc.
  USE Maternal and infant welfare
— Clothing
  ⌐TT635-645⌐
  UF Baby clothes
  BT Children's clothing
        Infants' supplies
  NT Diapers
        Layettes
— — Fires and fire prevention
  BT Fireproofing of fabrics
        Inflammable textiles
— — Tariff
  USE Tariff on infants' clothing
— Crying
  USE Crying
— Death
  ⌐RJ59-RJ60⌐
    Here are entered works on the death of in-
  fants. Works on infant death rates and causes are
  entered under Infants—Mortality.
  BT Death
— Development
  ⌐HQ774 (Social)⌐
  ⌐RJ134 (Pediatrics)⌐
    Here are entered works on the physical, psy-
  chological and social growth of normal infants.
  Works on the psychological growth and charac-
  teristics of infants are entered under Infant psy-
  chology.
  UF Development, Infant
        Infant development
  BT Child development
  NT Infant psychology
        Infants—Growth
— Discipline
  USE Discipline of infants
— Diseases *(May Subd Geog)*
  ⌐RJ⌐
  UF Diseases of children
  BT Children—Diseases
  NT Conjunctivitis, Infantile
        Craniotabes
        Dehydration in infants
        Diarrhea, Infantile
        Failure to thrive syndrome
        Hydrocephalus in infants
        Marasmus
        Nutrition disorders in infants
        Scurvy, Infantile
        Spasms, Infantile
— — Diagnosis
  ⌐RJ50⌐
  BT Diagnosis
— — Diet therapy
  USE Diet therapy for infants
— — Homeopathic treatment
  ⌐RX501-531⌐
— Effect of drugs on
  UF Drugs and infants
  BT Drugs—Physiological effect
        Pediatric pharmacology
— Equipment and supplies
  USE Infants' supplies

— Food
  USE Baby foods
— Growth
  ⌐RJ134⌐
  BT Human growth
        Infants—Development
— Health and hygiene *(May Subd Geog)*
  ⌐RJ61 (Popular works)⌐
  ⌐RJ101-RJ103 (General works)⌐
  UF Infants—Care and hygiene
— Insurance
  USE Insurance, Child
— Intelligence testing
  BT Infant psychology
        Intelligence tests
— Medical care
  USE Infant health services
— Mortality
  ⌐HB1323.I4 (Vital statistics)⌐
  ⌐RJ59-RJ60 (Pediatrics)⌐
    Here are entered works on infant death rates
  and causes. Works on the death of infants are
  entered under Infants—Death.
  UF Infant mortality
  NT Insurance, Child
        Perinatal mortality
        Sudden death in infants
— Nutrition
  ⌐RJ216⌐
  UF Infants, Food for
        Nutrition of children
  BT Children—Nutrition
        Milk, Human
  NT Baby foods
        Bottle feeding
        Breast feeding
        Cookery (Baby foods)
        Infant formulas
        Infants—Weaning
        Lactated food
        Marasmus
        Milk depots
        Wet-nurses
— — Immunological aspects
— — Requirements
  ⌐RJ216⌐
— Photography
  USE Photography of infants
— Physiology
  ⌐RJ125-RJ133⌐
— Psychology
  USE Infant psychology
— Surgery
  ⌐RD137-139⌐
— Weaning
  ⌐RJ216⌐
  UF Weaning of infants
  BT Infants—Nutrition
— Weight
  ⌐GN63⌐
  UF Weight in infancy
  BT Body weight
        Infants—Anthropometry
— Wounds and injuries *(May Subd Geog)*
— United States
— — Nutrition
Infants, Food for
  USE Infants—Nutrition
Infants, Photography of
  USE Photography of infants
Infants, Sale of
  USE Adoption—Corrupt practices
Infants (Newborn) *(May Subd Geog)*
  UF Neonates
        Newborn infants
  RT Neonatology
  NT Birth injuries
        Birth size
        Birth weight
        Infants (Premature)

Respiratory therapy for newborn
infants
— Anatomy
[QM24.5]
UF Neonatal anatomy
BT Anatomy, Human
— Bathing
UF Bathing of newborn infants
BT Baths
— Care (May Subd Geog)
[RJ253-RJ253.5]
UF Infants (Newborn)—Care and
hygiene
Perinatal care
— Care and hygiene
USE Infants (Newborn)—Care
Infants (Newborn)—Health and
hygiene
— Death
[RJ59-RJ60]
Here are entered works on the death of new-
born infants. Works on newborn infant death
rates and causes are entered under Infants (New-
born)—Mortality.
UF Neonatal death
BT Death
— Diseases (May Subd Geog)
BT Neonatology
SA names of special diseases, e.g.
Asphyxia neonatorum;
Erythroblastosis fetalis
NT Hepatitis, Neonatal
Retrolental fibroplasia
Syphilis, Congenital, hereditary,
and infantile
Tuberculosis, Congenital,
hereditary, and infantile
— — Diagnosis
— — Psychological aspects
BT Infant psychology
— Drug effects
USE Infants (Newborn)—Effect of
drugs on
— Effect of drugs on
UF Infants (Newborn)—Drug effects
Neonatal pharmacology
BT Drugs—Physiological effect
Obstetrical pharmacology
Pediatric pharmacology
— Health and hygiene (May Subd Geog)
UF Infants (Newborn)—Care and
hygiene
— Hospital care (May Subd Geog)
[RJ253]
BT Hospital care
Hospitals—Nurseries
NT Neonatal intensive care
— Medical examinations
NT Apgar score
Brazelton Neonatal Behavioral
Assessment Scale
— Metabolism
BT Infants (Newborn)—Physiology
Metabolism
— Mortality
[HB1323.I4 (Vital statistics)]
[RJ59-RJ60 (Pediatrics)]
Here are entered works on newborn infant
death rates and causes. Works on the death of
newborn infants are entered under Infants (New-
born)—Death.
UF Neonatal mortality
BT Perinatal mortality
— Nutrition
— Physiology
[RJ252]
NT Infants (Newborn)—Metabolism
— Psychology
NT Brazelton Neonatal Behavioral
Assessment Scale
— Surgery (May Subd Geog)
[RD137.5]

UF Neonatal surgery
Surgery, Neonatal
— Wounds and injuries (May Subd Geog)
BT Wounds and injuries
Infants (Premature) (May Subd Geog)
[RJ250]
UF Birth, Premature
Premature infants
Preterm infants
BT Infants (Newborn)
Labor, Premature
NT Birth weight, Low
Gestational age
Incubators (Pediatrics)
— Development (May Subd Geog)
[RJ250.3]
BT Child development
— Diseases (May Subd Geog)
NT Retrolental fibroplasia
— Growth
BT Human growth
— Home care (May Subd Geog)
— Hospital care (May Subd Geog)
BT Hospital care
— Nutrition
[RJ216]
— — Requirements
— Physiology
Infants (Still-born)
USE Still-birth
Infants' goods
USE Infants' supplies
Infants in the Bible
[BS576]
UF Bible—Infants
Infants' supplies (May Subd Geog)
UF Infants—Equipment and supplies
Infants' goods
Supplies, Infants'
BT Children's paraphernalia
Infants
RT Nurseries—Equipment and supplies
NT Baby books
Incubators (Pediatrics)
Infants—Clothing
Layettes
Pacifiers (Infant care)
Toys
Infants' supplies industry (May Subd Geog)
[HD9970.5.I54-544]
Infarction
[RB144]
BT Embolism
Hemorrhage
Thrombosis
SA subdivision Infarction under names of
organs of the body, e.g. Heart—
Infarction
Infection
UF Infectious diseases
BT Diseases—Causes and theories of
causation
Medical microbiology
SA subdivision Infections under names of
organs and regions of the body, e.g.
Heart—Infections; Foot—Infections
NT Abortion, Septic
Airborne infection
Carrier state (Communicable diseases)
Communicable diseases
Cross infection
Focal infection
Laboratory infections
Nosocomial infections
Opportunistic infections
Soilborne infection
Surgical wound infections
Urinary tract infections
Waterborne infection
Wounds and injuries—Infections

Infection, Airborne
USE Airborne infection
Infection, Focal
USE Focal infection
Infection, Soil-borne
USE Soilborne infection
Infection in children (May Subd Geog)
[RJ401]
BT Children—Diseases
Pediatric pathology
NT Bacterial diseases in children
Communicable diseases in children
Larva migrans, Visceral, in children
Meningitis in children
Oxyuriasis in children
Urinary tract infections in children
Infectious abortion
USE Brucellosis in cattle
Infectious anemia
UF Anemia, Infectious
Swamp fever
BT Anemia
NT Equine infectious anemia
Infectious arthritis
UF Arthritis, Infectious
BT Arthritis
Collagen diseases
Infectious avian encephalomyelitis
USE Avian encephalomyelitis
Infectious bovine rhinotracheitis
(May Subd Geog)
[SF967.I48]
UF Bovine rhinotracheitis, Infectious
Red nose
Rhinotracheitis, Infectious bovine
BT Herpesvirus diseases in animals
Mucosal diseases of cattle
Infectious bronchitis in poultry
UF Chick bronchitis, Infectious
Poultry bronchitis, Infectious
BT Bronchitis
Poultry—Diseases
Infectious diseases
USE Communicable diseases
Infection
Infectious endocarditis
USE Endocarditis, Bacterial
Infectious enteritis in pigs
USE Necrotic enteritis
Infectious enterotoxemia
USE Enterotoxemia
Infectious equine encephalomyelitis
USE Equine encephalomyelitis
Infectious hepatitis
USE Hepatitis A
Infectious jaundice
USE Hepatitis A
Infectious mononucleosis
USE Mononucleosis
Infectious mononucleosis virus
USE Epstein-Barr virus
Infectious necrotic hepatitis
USE Braxy
Infectious polyneuritis
USE Polyradiculoneuritis
Infectious protein particles
USE Prions
Infectious ribonucleic acid
USE Viroids
Infective endocarditis
USE Endocarditis, Bacterial
Inference
UF Ampliative induction
Induction, Ampliative
Inference (Logic)
BT Reasoning
Inference (Logic)
USE Inference
Inferior carotid triangle
USE Carotid triangle, Inferior

1843

Inferior colliculus
  BT Mesencephalon
Inferior olivary body
  USE Olivary nucleus
Inferior olivary nucleus
  USE Olivary nucleus
Inferior vena cava
  USE Vena cava, Inferior
Inferiority complex
  BT Complexes (Psychology)
     Neuroses
  NT Attention-seeking
Inferno Crater Lake (N.Z.)
  BT Lakes—New Zealand
Infertility *(May Subd Geog)*
  [RC889]
  UF Sterility in humans
  BT Childlessness
     Generative organs—Diseases
  RT Fertility, Human
     Sterilization (Birth control)
  — **Religious aspects**
  — — **Baptists,** [**Catholic Church, etc.**]
  — — **Buddhism,** [**Christianity, etc.**]
Infertility, Female *(May Subd Geog)*
  [RG201]
  UF Female infertility
     Female sterility
  BT Generative organs, Female—Diseases
  RT Sterilization of women
  NT Luteal phase defects
Infertility, Male *(May Subd Geog)*
  [RC889]
  UF Male infertility
     Male sterility
  BT Generative organs, Male—Diseases
  NT Oligospermia
Infertility in animals *(May Subd Geog)*
  [SF871]
  UF Animal infertility
     Animal sterility
     Domestic animals—Infertility
     Sterility in animals
  RT Fertility
  SA *subdivision* Infertility *under individual*
     animals and groups of animals, e.g.
     Cattle—Infertility; Livestock—
     Infertility
Infibulation
  [GN481]
  BT Circumcision
     Vagina
Infidelity, Marital
  USE Adultery
Infield (Baseball)
  USE Fielding (Baseball)
Infielders (Baseball) *(May Subd Geog)*
  [GV865]
  BT Baseball players
Infiltration
  USE Seepage
Infiltration (Military science)
  BT Military art and science
Infiltrometer
  BT Soil percolation
Infinitary languages
  UF Languages, Infinitary
  BT Logic, Symbolic and mathematical
Infinite
  [BD411 (Metaphysics)]
  [QA9 (Mathematics)]
  UF Infinity
  RT Finite, The
  NT Eternity
     Space and time
Infinite-dimensional manifolds
  UF Manifolds, Infinite-dimensional
  BT Global analysis (Mathematics)
     Topological manifolds
Infinite groups
  [QA171]

  UF Groups, Infinite
  BT Groups, Theory of
  NT Discrete groups
     Existentially closed groups
     FC-groups
     Orderable groups
     Polycyclic groups
Infinite integrals
  USE Integrals, Infinite
Infinite matrices
  USE Matrices, Infinite
Infinite processes
  USE Processes, Infinite
Infinite products
  USE Products, Infinite
Infinite series
  USE Series, Infinite
Infinitesimal calculus
  USE Calculus
Infinitesimal geometry
  USE Geometry, Infinitesimal
Infinitesimal transformations
  USE Transformations, Infinitesimal
Infinitive
  USE *subdivision* Infinitive *under names of*
     languages and groups of languages
     Grammar, Comparative and general—
     Infinitive
Infinity
  USE Infinite
Infirmaries
  USE Hospitals
Infixes
  USE Grammar, Comparative and general—
     Infixes
Inflammable liquids
  [HD3623-HD3624 (Dangerous
  industries)]
  UF Combustible liquids
     Liquids, Inflammable
  BT Gasoline
     Inflammable materials
     Petroleum
  RT Oil inspection
  SA *names of inflammable liquids, e.g.*
     Gasoline, Petroleum
  — **Law and legislation** *(May Subd Geog)*
Inflammable materials
  [TA407]
  UF Flammable materials
  BT Hazardous substances
  NT Inflammable liquids
  — **Law and legislation** *(May Subd Geog)*
Inflammable textiles *(May Subd Geog)*
  UF Flammable textiles
  BT Textile fabrics
  NT Children's clothing—Fires and fire
     prevention
     Clothing and dress—Fires and fire
     prevention
     Infants—Clothing—Fires and fire
     prevention
  — **Law and legislation** *(May Subd Geog)*
Inflammation
  [RB131 (Pathology)]
  BT Pathology
  SA *particular inflammations, e.g.*
     Appendicitis; Bursitis; *and*
     subdivision Inflammation *under*
     regions of the body, e.g. Eye—
     Inflammation
  NT Adnexitis
     Anti-inflammatory agents
     C-reactive protein
     Granuloma
     Keratitis
     Myositis
     Orchitis
     Otitis externa
     Periodontitis
     Pulpitis

     Rhinitis
     Suppuration
     Urethritis
     Vasculitis
  — **Immunological aspects**
     [RB131]
     UF Immunology of inflammation
        Inflammation—Immunology
     BT Immune response
  — **Immunology**
     USE Inflammation—Immunological
        aspects
  — **Mediators**
     [RB131]
     UF Inflammatory mediators
        Mediators of inflammation
     BT Biomolecules
     NT Histamine
        Leukotrienes
        Platelet activating factor
        Prostaglandins
        Substance P
Inflammatory bowel disease
  USE Enteritis, Regional
     Ulcerative colitis
Inflammatory disease, Pelvic
  USE Adnexitis
Inflammatory mediators
  USE Inflammation—Mediators
Inflatable boats
  [VM360]
  BT Boats and boating
  NT Inflatable canoes
Inflatable canoes *(May Subd Geog)*
  [GV790.3]
  BT Canoes and canoeing
     Inflatable boats
Inflatable penis
  USE Penile prostheses
Inflatable restraint systems
  USE Air bag restraint systems
Inflatable space structures
  USE Expandable space structures
Inflatable structures
  USE Air-supported structures
Inflation (Finance) *(May Subd Geog)*
  BT Circular velocity of money
     Economic policy
     Finance
     Money
  RT Currency question
  NT Accounting—Effect of inflation on
     Banks and banking—Effect of inflation
        on
     Consumer credit—Effect of inflation
        on
     Corporate profits—Effect of inflation
        on
     Escalator clause
     Expenditures, Public—Effect of
        inflation on
     Government securities—Effect of
        inflation on
     Housing—Effect of inflation on
     Income—Effect of inflation on
     Income distribution—Effect of
        inflation on
     Income tax—Effect of inflation on
     Indexation (Economics)
     Industrial management—Effect of
        inflation on
     Industrial productivity—Effect of
        inflation on
     Insurance—Effect of inflation on
     Insurance, Life—Effect of inflation on
     Interest rates—Effect of inflation on
     Investments—Effect of inflation on
     Labor productivity—Effect of inflation
        on
     National income—Accounting—Effect
        of inflation on

Old age pensions—Effect of inflation on
Paper money
Pension trusts—Investments—Effect of inflation on
Pensions—Effect of inflation on
Public contracts—Effect of inflation on
Rehabilitation—Effect of inflation on
Retirement income—Effect of inflation on
Saving and investment—Effect of inflation on
Taxation—Effect of inflation on
Transportation—Effect of inflation on
Unemployment—Effect of inflation on
Wage-price policy
Wages—Effect of inflation on
— **Effect of energy costs on**
   BT Power resources—Costs
— **Effect of government paperwork on**
   BT Government paperwork
— **Effect of productivity on**
   BT Industrial productivity
— **Effect of taxation on**
   BT Fiscal policy
     Taxation
— **Mathematical models**
   NT Phillips curve
— **France**
   NT Assignats
— **United States**
   NT Greenbacks
Inflation (Finance) and accounting
  USE Accounting—Effect of inflation on
Inflation (Finance) and income
  USE Income—Effect of inflation on
Inflation (Finance) and public expenditures
  USE Expenditures, Public—Effect of inflation on
Inflation (Finance) and taxation
  USE Taxation—Effect of inflation on
Inflation accounting
  USE Accounting—Effect of inflation on
Inflation pressure of automobile tires
  USE Automobiles—Tires—Inflation pressure
Inflection
  USE *subdivision* Inflection *under names of languages and groups of languages*
     Grammar, Comparative and general—Inflection
     Languages, Modern—Inflection
Inflectional morphology
  USE Grammar, Comparative and general—Inflection
Inflexibility (Psychology)
  USE Rigidity (Psychology)
Inflexible words
  USE English language—Indeclinable words
Inflorescence
  [QK652]
  [QK691]
  BT Botany—Anatomy
  NT Flowers
     Involucre
Influence, Undue
  USE Undue influence
Influence (Literary, artistic, etc.)
  UF Artistic influence
     Literary influence
     Literary tradition
     Tradition (Literature)
  BT Art
     Influence (Psychology)
     Literature
     Originality (in literature)
  NT Imitation (in art)
     Imitation (in literature)
Influence (Psychology)
  BT Psychology

  RT Conformity
     Example
     Imitation
     Persuasion (Psychology)
  NT Influence (Literary, artistic, etc.)
     Social facilitation
Influence fields
  USE Influence surfaces
Influence lines
  [TG270]
  BT Bridges
     Girders
     Girders, Continuous
     Graphic statics
     Strains and stresses
     Structural frames
     Trusses
  RT Influence surfaces
Influence machines
  USE Electric machines
Influence of English on foreign languages
  USE English language—Influence on foreign languages
Influence of war
  USE *subdivision* Influence *under individual wars, e.g.* World War, 1939-1945—Influence
Influence surfaces
  UF Influence fields
     Surfaces, Influence
  BT Plates (Engineering)
     Structures, Theory of
  RT Influence lines
Influenza *(May Subd Geog)*
  [RA644.I6 (Public health)]
  [RC150-RC150.9 (Internal medicine)]
  UF Flu
     Grippe
  BT Cold (Disease)
     Virus diseases
  NT Asian flu
     Avian influenza
     Equine influenza
     Swine influenza
— **Complications and sequelae**
— **Homeopathic treatment**
  [RX326.I]
— **Prevention**
  NT Influenza vaccines
— **Research** *(May Subd Geog)*
  UF Influenza research
Influenza, Avian
  USE Avian influenza
Influenza D virus
  USE Sendai virus
Influenza research
  USE Influenza—Research
Influenza vaccines *(May Subd Geog)*
  [QR189.5.I]
  UF Influenza virus vaccines
  BT Influenza—Prevention
     Influenza viruses
  NT Equine influenza vaccines
Influenza virus vaccines
  USE Influenza vaccines
Influenza viruses
  [QR201.I6]
  BT Myxoviruses
  NT Influenza vaccines
— **Variation**
  BT Variation (Biology)
INFOPLAN (Information retrieval system)
  BT Information storage and retrieval systems—Latin America—Economic conditions
     Information storage and retrieval systems—Latin America—Social conditions
Informal sector (Economics)
  (May Subd Geog)
  [HD2340.8-2346]

  UF Hidden economy
     Parallel economy
     Subterranean economy
     Underground economy
  BT Artisans
     Economics
     Small business
— **Law and legislation** *(May Subd Geog)*
  BT Trade regulation
— **Taxation** *(May Subd Geog)*
— — **Law and legislation**
  (May Subd Geog)
Informants, Linguistic
  USE Linguistic informants
INFORMAP (Information retrieval system)
  [SD421.45.D3]
  UF Information Necessary for Optimum Resource Management and Protection
  BT Forest fires—Prevention and control—Data processing
     Information storage and retrieval systems—Forest fires
Informatics Teaching System Project
  USE ITS Project
Information, Freedom of
  USE Freedom of information
Information, Government
  USE Government information
Information centers
  USE Information services
Information consultants *(May Subd Geog)*
  BT Consultants
     Information science
     Information scientists
Information display systems
  UF Data display systems
     Display systems, Information
     Dynamic display systems
     Electronic displays
  BT Computer input-output equipment
     Computers—Optical equipment
     Optical data processing
     Optoelectronic devices
     Photoelectronic devices
     Recording instruments
     Teaching—Aids and devices
  NT Aeronautical instruments—Display systems
     Airports—Traffic control—Display systems
     Astronautical instruments—Display systems
     Automatic checkout equipment—Display systems
     Automobiles—Instruments—Display systems
     Cathode ray tubes
     DMS/VS (Computer system)
     Electroluminescent display systems
     Image intensifiers
     Radar indicators
     Television display systems
     Three-dimensional display systems
     Video display terminals
— **Formatting**
  UF Formatting of information display systems
— **Psychological aspects**
  BT Reading, Psychology of
     Recognition (Psychology)
     Visual discrimination
Information display systems industry
  (May Subd Geog)
Information dissemination, Selective
  USE Selective dissemination of information
Information libraries
  USE Overseas information libraries
Information Management Systems (Data Language/I) (Computer system)
  USE IMS (DL/I) (Computer system)

Information Management Systems/Virtual
  Storage (Computer system)
  USE IMS/VS (Computer system)
Information measurement
  UF Information measures (Information
      theory)
      Informational measure
      Measure of information
      Shannon-Wiener information measure
      Signals (Information theory)
  BT Information theory
  NT Signal processing
      Uncertainty (Information theory)
Information measures (Information theory)
  USE Information measurement
Information Necessary for Optimum Resource
  Management and Protection
  USE INFORMAP (Information retrieval
      system)
Information networks *(May Subd Geog)*
  UF Automated information networks
      Networks, Information
  BT Data transmission systems
      Exchanges, Literary and scientific
      Information services
      Information storage and retrieval
      systems
      Intellectual cooperation
  NT Classification, Broad System of
      Ordering
      Command and control systems
      Computer networks
      Document delivery
      Library information networks
      Meteorological Rocket Network
      Referral centers (Information services)
  — Law and legislation *(May Subd Geog)*
Information networks, Library
  USE Library information networks
Information processing, Human
  USE Human information processing
Information processing in children
  USE Human information processing in
      children
Information processing language (Computer
  program language)
  USE IPL (Computer program language)
Information processing systems
  USE Information storage and retrieval
      systems
Information referral centers
  USE Referral centers (Information services)
Information resource management
  USE Information resources management
Information resources management
  [T58.64]
  Here are entered works on the coordination of
information gathering and dissemination respon-
sibilities within an organization. The concept com-
bines under one management such traditional organi-
zational functions as: ADP management, communi-
cation technology management, procurement, for-
mulation of regulations standards, paperwork
management, security, information systems
development, data base management, and library and
information services.
  UF Information resource management
      Information systems management
      IRM
  BT Management
  RT Management information systems
Information retrieval
  UF Data retrieval
      Data storage
      Information storage
      Information storage and retrieval
      Retrieval of information
  BT Documentation
      Information science
  NT Abstracting
      Cataloging
      Data base searching

      Filing systems
      Indexing
      Information services
      Information storage and retrieval
      systems
  — Computer programs
    NT In-Search (Computer program)
Information retrieval systems
  USE Information storage and retrieval
      systems
Information science *(May Subd Geog)*
  BT Communication
  NT Communication in information science
      Documentation
      Electronic data processing
      Information consultants
      Information retrieval
      Information services
      Information storage and retrieval
      systems
      Library science
      Women in information science
  — Bibliography
    RT Information science literature
  — History
    NT Information science literature
  — Study and teaching *(May Subd Geog)*
    NT Information services—User
      education
Information science libraries
  (May Subd Geog)
  UF Libraries, Information science
  BT Libraries, Special
  NT Library science libraries
Information science literature
  UF Literature, Information science
  BT Communication in information science
      Communication in science
      Information science—History
  RT Information science—Bibliography
      Library science—Lexicography
      Library science literature
Information scientists *(May Subd Geog)*
  Here are entered works on individuals who organ-
ize information and provide services for its use.
  BT Scientists
  NT Bibliographers
      Classificationists
      Information consultants
      Librarians
      Women information scientists
Information services *(May Subd Geog)*
  [AG500-551]
  UF Data collection services
      Information centers
  BT Information retrieval
      Information science
  RT Documentation
      Reference services (Libraries)
      Research
  SA *subdivision* Information services *under*
      special subjects or organizations,
      e.g. Child welfare—Information
      services; United Nations—
      Information services
  NT Archives
      Bibliographical services
      Community information services
      Current awareness services
      Exchange of bibliographic information
      Hotlines (Counseling)
      Information networks
      Information services and state
      Information storage and retrieval
      systems
      Preprints
      Referral centers (Information services)
      Selective dissemination of information
      Statistical services
  — Advertising
    USE Advertising—Information services

  — State aid
    USE Information services and state
  — Use studies
    NT Indexes—Use studies
      Library use studies
      Subject headings—Use studies
  — User education
    UF Information services instruction
      Orientation (Information services)
      User education (Information
      science)
    BT Information science—Study and
      teaching
    RT Library orientation
  — United States
    NT Neighborhood Information Center
      Project
Information services, Community
  USE Community information services
Information services, Government
  USE Government publicity
Information services and state
  (May Subd Geog)
  UF Information services—State aid
      State aid to information services
      State and information services
  BT Information services
  RT Libraries and state
Information services employees
  (May Subd Geog)
  NT Wages—Information services
      employees
Information services instruction
  USE Information services—User education
Information storage
  USE Information retrieval
Information storage and retrieval
  USE Information retrieval
Information storage and retrieval systems
  UF Automatic data storage
      Automatic information retrieval
      Automation in documentation
      Computer-based information systems
      Data processing
      Data storage and retrieval systems
      Information processing systems
      Information retrieval systems
      Machine data storage and retrieval
      Mechanized information storage and
      retrieval systems
  BT Abstracting and indexing services
      Bibliography
      Classification
      Documentation
      Information retrieval
      Information science
      Information services
      Library science
  RT Computers
      Data libraries
      Libraries—Automation
  NT 3RIP (Information retrieval system)
      ADLIB (Information retrieval system)
      AIS (Information retrieval system)
      Automatic abstracting
      Automatic classification
      Automatic indexing
      Ballots Project
      BASIS-E (Information retrieval
      system)
      BIBLIOS (Information retrieval
      system)
      BLAISE (Information retrieval system)
      C I S S (Information retrieval system)
      Catalogs, On-line—Subject access
      CLAP (Information retrieval system)
      Codat (Information retrieval system)
      Computer output microfilm devices—
      Library applications
      Data base management
      DAVID (Information retrieval system)

DOBIS (Computer system)
DRL (Computer program language)
Electronic data processing
ELIAS (Information retrieval system)
EUREKA (Information retrieval
  system)
Expert systems (Computer science)
FAMULUS (Information retrieval
  system)
FAUST (Information retrieval system)
File organization (Computer science)
GIPSY (Information retrieval system)
GOLEM (Information retrieval
  system)
GUIDE-O (Information retrieval
  system)
Harmonie (Information retrieval
  system)
IBAS (Information retrieval system)
Information networks
ISORID (Information retrieval system)
KAMA (Information retrieval system)
KONKAT (Information retrieval
  system)
LCS (Information retrieval system)
LIBRIS (Information retrieval system)
LITMAS (Computer program)
LITSYS (Information retrieval system)
MADOK (Information retrieval
  system)
Magnacard data processing system
Management information systems
MELVYL (Information retrieval
  system)
Microcomputers—Library applications
Microfilm aperture card systems
MIND (Computer system)
MINSK-ARDIS (Information retrieval
  system)
Multi-State Information System
Omnidata (Computer system)
ORBIT (Information retrieval system)
Permutation indexes
PIS (Information retrieval system)
Project Spires
Punched card systems
QUERY (Information retrieval system)
REMARC (Information retrieval
  system)
RESI (Information retrieval system)
RLIN (Information retrieval system)
RLIN II (Information retrieval system)
SAMKAT (Information retrieval
  system)
SAOL (Computer system)
SATIN 1 (Information retrieval
  system)
SCARABÉE (Information retrieval
  system)
Selective dissemination of information
Selling—Information storage and
  retrieval systems
SESAM (Information retrieval system)
SISMAKOM (Information retrieval
  system)
SMART (Information retrieval system)
SOURCE (Information retrieval
  system)
STAIRS (Information retrieval system)
STATUS (Information retrieval
  system)
SYNTOL (Information storage and
  retrieval system)
TAUBIPE (Information retrieval
  system)
Text processing (Computer science)
TRAMPS (Information retrieval
  system)
UNDIS (Information retrieval system)
— **Accounting**

UF Accounting—Information storage
  and retrieval systems
NT FMS (Information retrieval system)
— **Accounting, ₜChina, Electronics, Korea,
  etc.₎**
— **Advertising**
NT MARS (Information retrieval
  system)
— **Aeronautics**
UF Aeronautical literature searching
— **Agriculture**
UF Agricultural literature searching
BT Agriculture—Documentation
NT AGREP (Information retrieval
  system)
  AGRINTER (Information retrieval
  system)
  AGRIS (Information retrieval
  system)
  CAIN (Information retrieval
  system)
  CARIS (Information retrieval
  system)
  Moisture Utilization in Semi-Arid
  Tropics: Summer Rainfall
  Agriculture Project
  Punched card systems—Agriculture
  Sistema Nacional de Informação
  Rural
— American studies
USE Information storage and retrieval
  systems—United States—
  Study and teaching
— **Architectural drawing**
UF Architectural drawing—
  Information storage and
  retrieval systems
— **Architecture**
— — **Contracts and specifications**
UF Architecture—Contracts and
  specifications—Information
  storage and retrieval systems
— **Archival material**
  ₜZ699.5.A₎
UF Archives—Information storage and
  retrieval systems
NT CDS/ISIS (Information retrieval
  system)
  MINISIS (Information retrieval
  system)
  SPINDEX (Information retrieval
  system)
  TEKLA (Information retrieval
  system)
— **Arts**
UF Arts—Information storage and
  retrieval systems
— **Astronomy**
UF Astronomy—Information storage
  and retrieval systems
NT Punched card systems—Astronomy
— **Audio-visual materials**
NT HAVOC (Information retrieval
  system)
  SLIDEX (Information retrieval
  system)
— **Bacteriology**
— **Biology**
UF Biological literature searching
BT Biological libraries
  Biology—Bibliography
NT Punched card systems—Biology
— **Building**
NT BRD/SfB (Information retrieval
  system)
  ICONDA (Information retrieval
  system)
— **Business**
UF Business—Information storage and
  retrieval systems

NT Dow Jones News/Retrieval
  (Information retrieval system)
  Predicasts Terminal System
  (Information retrieval system)
— Cancer
USE Information storage and retrieval
  systems—Oncology
— **Carcinogens**
UF Carcinogens—Information storage
  and retrieval systems
— **Chemistry**
  ₜZ699.5.C5₎
UF Chemical literature searching
NT Punched card systems—Chemistry
— **Child welfare**
NT CYCIS (Information retrieval
  system)
— **Cities and towns**
— **City planning**
NT SIGET (Information retrieval
  system)
— **Code numbers**
UF Code numbers (Information storage
  and retrieval)
SA *subdivision* Code words *under*
  Information storage and
  retrieval systems—ₜtopic₎
— **Code words**
UF Code words (Information storage
  and retrieval)
SA *subdivision* Code words *under*
  topical subdivisions, e.g.
  Information storage and
  retrieval systems—Engineering
  —Code words
— **Commercial statistics**
NT COMTAP (Information retrieval
  system)
— **Community health services**
  (May Subd Geog)
UF Community health services—
  Information storage and
  retrieval systems
— **Complex litigation** *(May Subd Geog)*
— **Corporations**
— — **Finance**
NT Codat (Information retrieval
  system)
  DRI-SEC (Information retrieval
  system)
— **Corrections**
NT OBSCIS (Information retrieval
  system)
— **Cost accounting**
UF Cost accounting—Information
  storage and retrieval systems
— **Court administration** *(May Subd Geog)*
UF Court administration—Information
  storage and retrieval systems
— **Criminal justice, Administration of**
  (May Subd Geog)
— **Crops and climate**
UF Crops and climate—Information
  storage and retrieval systems
— **Ecology**
NT Enviroline (Information retrieval
  system)
— **Economic indicators**
NT DRICEI (Information retrieval
  system)
— — **Canada**
NT DBCAND (Information
  retrieval system)
  DBCANM (Information
  retrieval system)
— **Education**
NT PROBE Project
— **Electronics**
  ₜZ699.5.E5₎
UF Electronics literature searching

Information storage and retrieval systems
— **Electronics** *(Continued)*
   NT INSPEC (Information retrieval system)
— **Engineering**
   UF Engineering literature searching
   NT ENGINE (Information retrieval system)
       INSPEC (Information retrieval system)
       Project SHARP
— — **Code words**
— **Environmental chemistry**
   UF Environmental chemistry—Information storage and retrieval systems
— **Environmental engineering**
   NT ELIAS (Information retrieval system)
— **Environmental policy**
   NT SIGET (Information retrieval system)
— **Environmental protection**
   UF Environmental protection—Information storage and retrieval systems
   NT Enviroline (Information retrieval system)
       UMPLIS (Information retrieval system)
— **Finance**
   NT FMS (Information retrieval system)
— **Forest fires**
   NT INFORMAP (Information retrieval system)
— **Forest products**
   UF Forest products—Information storage and retrieval systems
— **Forestry**
   UF Forests and forestry—Information storage and retrieval systems
— **Freight and freightage**
   NT SITRAM (Information retrieval system)
— **Geochemistry**
   UF Geochemistry—Information storage and retrieval systems
— **Geology**
   UF Geological literature searching
   BT Geology—Bibliography
— **Government publications**
   NT PARLIS (Information retrieval system)
— **Highway research**
   UF Highway research—Information storage and retrieval systems
— **Home economics**
   UF Home economics literature searching
   BT Home economics—Bibliography
— **Hospitals**
   NT KIEL KIS (Information retrieval system)
— — **Evaluation**
— — — **Computer programs**
     NT SEAHIS (Computer program)
— — **United States**
     NT Professional Activity Study
— **Housing**
   UF Housing—Information storage and retrieval systems
— **Humanities**
   UF Humanities—Information storage and retrieval systems
   NT FRANCIS (Information retrieval system)
— **Industrial statistics**
   NT COMTAP (Information retrieval system)
— **Industry**
   [Z699.5.I52]

   UF Industry—Information storage and retrieval systems
— **International business enterprises**
   UF International business enterprises—Information storage and retrieval systems
— **Juvenile justice, Administration of**
   (May Subd Geog)
— **Labor supply**
   UF Labor supply—Information storage and retrieval systems
— **Land use**
   NT SIGET (Information retrieval system)
— **Law** *(May Subd Geog)*
   UF Legal literature searching
   BT Law—Bibliography
   NT LEXIS (Information retrieval system)
       PARLIS (Information retrieval system)
       Statutes—Word frequency
       WESTLAW (Information retrieval system)
— **Management**
   NT ABI/INFORM (Information retrieval system)
— **Marine biology**
   [Z699.5.M28]
   UF Marine biology—Information storage and retrieval systems
— **Marketing**
   NT MARS (Information retrieval system)
— **Materials**
   UF Materials literature searching
— **Mathematical models**
   BT Mathematical models—Bibliography
— **Medical care** *(May Subd Geog)*
   UF Medical care—Information storage and retrieval systems
— **Medical instruments and apparatus**
— **Medical personnel** *(May Subd Geog)*
   UF Medical personnel—Information storage and retrieval systems
— **Medical statistics** *(May Subd Geog)*
   [RA409.5]
   UF Medical statistics—Information storage and retrieval systems
— **Medical supplies**
— **Medicine**
   UF Medical literature searching
   BT Medicine—Bibliography
   NT INA (Information retrieval system)
       MEDLARS
       SICSG (Information retrieval system)
— **Metallurgy**
   [Z699.5.M4]
   UF Metallurgical literature searching
— **Metals**
   NT METADEX (Information retrieval system)
— **Meteorology**
   UF Meteorological literature searching
   BT Meteorology—Bibliography
— **Mines and mineral resources**
   NT CANMINDEX (Information retrieval system)
       MANIFILE (Information retrieval system)
       MILS (Information retrieval system)
       MRDS (Information retrieval system)
       Pohjois-Suomen malmitiedostoprojekti
— **Motion pictures**
   NT APPARAT (Information retrieval system)

— **Names, Geographical**
   UF Names, Geographical—Information storage and retrieval systems
— **Natural disasters**
   UF Natural disasters—Information storage and retrieval systems
— **Naval art and science**
   UF Naval literature searching
   NT Project SHARP
— **Newspapers**
   [Z699.5.N47]
   UF Newspapers—Information storage and retrieval systems
— **Nucleotide sequence**
   UF Nucleotide sequence—Information storage and retrieval systems
— **Nursing**
   UF Nursing literature searching
— **Ocean temperature**
— — **Baltic Sea**
     NT BASIS (Information retrieval system)
— **Oncology**
   UF Cancer—Information storage and retrieval systems
       Information storage and retrieval systems—Cancer
       Information storage and retrieval systems—Tumors
       Oncology—Information storage and retrieval systems
       Tumors—Information storage and retrieval systems
— **Patent documentation**
   [Z699.5.P3]
   BT Patent searching
— **Personnel management**
   UF Personnel management—Information storage and retrieval systems
— **Photographs**
— — **Conservation and restoration**
     NT PHOCUS (Information retrieval system)
— **Physics**
   NT INSPEC (Information retrieval system)
— **Political science**
   NT LOGOS (Information retrieval system)
— **Polymers and polymerization**
   NT PLASDOC (Information retrieval system)
— **Power resources**
   UF Power resources—Information storage and retrieval systems
— **Psychology**
   NT SURVEY.UNC75 (Information retrieval system)
— **Public health** *(May Subd Geog)*
   UF Public health—Information storage and retrieval systems
— **Rehabilitation**
   [Z699.5.R43]
— **Research**
   [Z699.5.R47]
   UF Research—Information storage and retrieval systems
— **Roads**
— — **Location**
     UF Roads—Location—Information storage and retrieval systems
     NT GCARS II (Information retrieval system)
— **Science**
   [Z699.5.S3]
   UF Scientific literature searching
   NT ALPHA (Information retrieval system)
       APIN (Information retrieval system)

CAN/OLE (Information retrieval system)
CSIRO SDI (Information retrieval system)
DIALOG (Information retrieval system)
ISTIS (Information retrieval system)
LIBRA (Information retrieval system)
— Science and state
  NT SPINES (Information retrieval system)
— Sea ice
— — Baltic Sea
  NT BASIS (Information retrieval system)
— Securities
  UF Securities—Information storage and retrieval systems
  NT DRI-SEC (Information retrieval system)
      EDGAR (Information retrieval system)
— Seismology
  UF Seismology—Information storage and retrieval systems
— Serial publications
  UF Periodicals—Information storage and retrieval systems
— Siouan languages
  UF Siouan languages—Information storage and retrieval systems
  NT Siouan Languages Archive (Information retrieval system)
— Slavic literature
  [Z699.5.S6]
  UF Slavic literature searching
  BT Slavic literature—Bibliography
— Small business
  NT PASS (Information retrieval system)
— Social sciences
  NT DARE (Information retrieval system)
      FRANCIS (Information retrieval system)
— Social service
  UF Social service—Information storage and retrieval systems
  NT SIMS (Information retrieval system)
— Soil science
  NT British Columbia Soil Information System
— Soybean as food
  NT SOYA (Information retrieval system)
— Statistics
  NT CANSIM (Information retrieval system)
— Technology
  [Z699.5.T4]
  UF Technical literature searching
  BT Technology—Bibliography
  NT ALPHA (Information retrieval system)
      APIN (Information retrieval system)
      CAN/OLE (Information retrieval system)
      DIALOG (Information retrieval system)
      ISTIS (Information retrieval system)
      LIBRA (Information retrieval system)
— Technology and state
  NT SPINES (Information retrieval system)
— Telecommunication

  UF Telecommunication—Information storage and retrieval systems
— Traffic accidents
  UF Traffic accidents—Information storage and retrieval systems
— Transportation
  NT JPTRS (Information retrieval system)
— Tumors
  USE Information storage and retrieval systems—Oncology
— United Nations
  NT UNBIS (Information retrieval system)
— User education
— Veterans
  UF Veterans—Information storage and retrieval systems
— Vocational guidance
  NT CHOICES (Information retrieval system)
— Water quality
  UF Water quality—Information storage and retrieval systems
— Water resources development
  UF Water resources development—Information storage and retrieval systems
— Water-supply
  [Z699.5.W3]
  UF Water-supply literature searching
— Youth services
  NT CYCIS (Information retrieval system)
— Africa
  UF Africa—Information storage and retrieval systems
  BT Africa—Bibliography
  NT PADIS (Information retrieval system)
— China
  UF China—Information storage and retrieval systems
  BT China—Bibliography
— Latin America
— — Economic conditions
    NT INFOPLAN (Information retrieval system)
— — Social conditions
    NT INFOPLAN (Information retrieval system)
— United States
— — Study and teaching
    [Z699.5.U5]
    UF Information storage and retrieval systems—American studies
       United States—Study and teaching—Information storage and retrieval systems

Information structures (Computer science)
  USE Data structures (Computer science)
Information systems management
  USE Information resources management
Information technology (May Subd Geog)
  Here are entered works on the acquisition, processing, storage and dissemination of vocal, pictorial, textual and numeric information by microelectronics, computers and telecommunication.
  UF Technology, Information
  BT Technology
Information theory
  UF Communication theory
  BT Communication
      Cybernetics
  NT Automatic control
      Coding theory
      Communication models
      Data transmission systems
      Entropy (Information theory)

      Error-correcting codes (Information theory)
      Frames (Information theory)
      Information measurement
      Language and languages
      Machine translating
      Mathematical linguistics
      Modulation theory
      Punched card systems
      Rate distortion theory
      Redundancy (Linguistics)
      Semantics
      Signal theory (Telecommunication)
      Speech processing systems
      Statistical communication theory
      Switching theory
      Telecommunication
Information theory in aesthetics
  BT Aesthetics
      Cybernetics
      Perception
      Psychology
  NT Information theory in music
Information theory in biology
  BT Biology
      Biomathematics
Information theory in chemistry
  BT Chemistry
Information theory in economics
  UF Economic cybernetics
  BT Econometrics
Information theory in education (May Subd Geog)
  UF Education—Information theory
  BT Education
Information theory in geophysics
  [QC806]
  BT Geophysics
Information theory in mathematics
  [QA10.4]
  BT Mathematics
Information theory in music
  BT Information theory in aesthetics
      Music
Information theory in optics
  [QC370]
  BT Optics
Information theory in physics
  [QC28]
  BT Physics
Information theory in psychology
  BT Cybernetics
      Perception
      Psychology
      Psychology, Physiological
  NT Human information processing
Information theory in research
  BT Research
Information theory in sociology
  BT Sociology
Information theory in the social sciences
  BT Social sciences
Information theory in translating
  BT Translating and interpreting
Informational measure
  USE Information measurement
Informations (May Subd Geog)
  UF Accusation
  BT Criminal procedure
      Lay prosecutors
      Prosecution
      Public prosecutors
  RT Grand jury
      Indictments
      Quo warranto
  NT Joinder of offenses
Informationssystem für Niedergelassene Ärzte
  USE INA (Information retrieval system)

Informed consent (Medical law)
(*May Subd Geog*)
UF Consent, Informed
    Consent to treatment
    Disclosure, Medical
    Medical disclosure
    Treatment, Consent to
BT Consent (Law)
    Medical ethics
    Medical personnel—Malpractice
    Patient education
NT Right to die—Law and legislation
Informers (*May Subd Geog*)
UF Police informers
    Stool pigeons
BT Complaints (Criminal procedure)
    Crime prevention
    Criminal investigation
    Prosecution
INFORMIX-4GL (Computer program language)
UF INFORMIX-Fourth Generation
      Language (Computer program
      language)
BT Programming languages (Electronic
      computers)
INFORMIX-Fourth Generation Language
   (Computer program language)
USE INFORMIX-4GL (Computer program
      language)
InfoStar (Computer program)
BT Data base management—Computer
      programs
Infra-red . . .
USE *subject headings beginning with the*
      word Infrared
Infrabony pockets
USE Periodontal pockets
Infrared albedo
UF Albedo, Infrared
BT Infrared radiation
    Terrestrial radiation
NT Greenhouse effect, Atmospheric
— **Diurnal variation**
    UF Diurnal infrared albedo variations
        Diurnal variation of infrared albedo
— **Measurement**
    NT Heat Capacity Mapping Mission
        Program
Infrared antenna array detectors
USE Infrared array detectors
Infrared apparatus and appliances
USE Infrared equipment
Infrared array detectors (*May Subd Geog*)
UF Antenna array detectors, Infrared
    Array detectors, Infrared
    Infrared antenna array detectors
BT Infrared detectors
Infrared astronomy
   [QB470]
BT Astronomy
    Infrared radiation
Infrared detectors (*May Subd Geog*)
BT Detectors
    Infrared equipment
NT Bolometer
    Infrared array detectors
    Infrared horizon sensors
    Photoelectric cells
Infrared drying equipment
(*May Subd Geog*)
   [TP363]
BT Drying apparatus
    Infrared equipment
Infrared equipment (*May Subd Geog*)
UF Infrared apparatus and appliances
BT Infrared technology
    Optoelectronic devices
NT Infrared detectors
    Infrared drying equipment
    Infrared image converters

Infrared telescope
Infrared heating (*May Subd Geog*)
   [TK4635 (Electric engineering)]
   [TP363 (Chemical engineering)]
UF Heating, Infrared
BT Electric heating
    Infrared technology
Infrared horizon scanners
USE Infrared horizon sensors
Infrared horizon sensors
UF Horizon sensors, Infrared
    Infrared horizon scanners
BT Infrared detectors
    Remote sensing—Equipment and
      supplies
    Scanning systems
Infrared image converters
UF Image converters, Infrared
BT Image converters
    Infrared equipment
Infrared imaging
BT Imaging systems
    Infrared technology
Infrared photography (*May Subd Geog*)
   [TR755]
UF Photography, Infrared
BT Infrared technology
    Photography
NT Thermography
Infrared radiation (*May Subd Geog*)
UF Infrared rays
    Radiation, Infrared
    Rays, Infrared
BT Electromagnetic waves
RT Atmospheric radiation
    Infrared spectra
    Terrestrial radiation
NT Infrared albedo
    Infrared astronomy
    Infrared technology
— **Atmospheric effects**
    UF Atmospheric effects on infrared
        radiation
    BT Meteorological optics
— **Industrial applications**
    BT Infrared technology
— **Military applications**
    BT Infrared technology
        Military engineering
Infrared radiation in medicine
(*May Subd Geog*)
   [RM857]
BT Infrared technology
    Radiology, Medical
Infrared rays
USE Infrared radiation
Infrared sources
   [TA1570]
UF Sources, Infrared
BT Infrared technology
    Light sources
NT Far infrared lasers
    Lasers
    Masers
Infrared spectra
   [QC457]
UF Spectrum, Infrared
RT Infrared radiation
    Infrared spectroscopy
Infrared spectrometry
USE Infrared spectroscopy
Infrared spectroscopy
   [QC457 (Light)]
   [QD96.I5 (Qualitative analysis)]
UF Infrared spectrometry
    Spectrometry, Infrared
    Spectroscopy, Infrared
BT Molecular spectroscopy
    Spectrum analysis
RT Infrared spectra

Infrared technology (*May Subd Geog*)
   [TA1570]
UF Technology, Infrared
BT Infrared radiation
NT Infrared equipment
    Infrared heating
    Infrared imaging
    Infrared photography
    Infrared radiation—Industrial
      applications
    Infrared radiation—Military
      applications
    Infrared radiation in medicine
    Infrared sources
Infrared telescope
BT Infrared equipment
    Telescope
Infraroentgen rays
USE Grenz rays
Infrasonic waves
   [QC243.5]
UF Waves, Infrasonic
BT Sound-waves
Infrastructure (Economics)
(*May Subd Geog*)
   [HC79.C3]
    Here are entered works on the underlying capital
of a society embodied in roads and other transporta-
tion and communication systems as well as water
supplies, electric power, and other public services.
UF Economic infrastructure
    Social capital
    Social infrastructure
    Social overhead capital
BT Economic development
    Human settlements
    Public goods
    Public works
RT Capital
Infringement of copyright
USE Copyright infringement
Infundibulum (Brain)
   [QL938.H (Comparative anatomy)]
   [QM455 (Human anatomy)]
   [QP383.7 (Physiology)]
BT Hypothalamus
Infurcitinea
   [QL561.T55]
BT Tineidae
Infused virtue
USE Virtue, Infused
Infusion of water in coal mine dust control
USE Coal mines and mining—Dust control
      —Water infusion
Infusion pumps, Drug
USE Drug infusion pumps
Infusion therapy (*May Subd Geog*)
   [RM170-RM180]
UF Infusions (Therapeutics)
BT Parenteral therapy
— **Equipment and supplies**
    NT Drug infusion pumps
Infusions, Intravenous
USE Intravenous therapy
Infusions (Therapeutics)
USE Infusion therapy
Infusoria
   [QL365 (Early works)]
   [QL368-QL369]
BT Animalcules
    Protozoa
NT Ciliata
    Flagellata
Infusorial earth
USE Diatomaceous earth
Infusors (Therapeutics)
USE Drug infusion pumps
Ing family
USE Inge family
Inga (Plants)
   [QK495.L52 (Botany)]

BT Leguminosae
Inga language (Colombia)
  USE Ingano language
Ingal bone
  USE Cheek-bone
Ingal family
  USE Ingalls family
Ingalik Indians
  [E99.I5]
  UF Inkalik Indians
    Ten'a Indians
  BT Athapascan Indians
    Indians of North America
    Tinne Indians
Ingalik language
  [PM1373]
  UF Inkalik language
    Ten'a language
  BT Athapascan languages
    Tinne languages
  NT Tanaina language
Ingall family
  USE Ingalls family
Ingalls family *(Not Subd Geog)*
  UF Ingal family
    Ingall family
    Ingals family
    Ingeles family
    Ingels family
    Ingills family
    Ingle family
    Ingles family
    Ingolls family
    Ingols family
    Ingulls family
  RT Engel family
Ingals family
  USE Ingalls family
Ingano language
  [PM6221]
  UF Inga language (Colombia)
  BT Indians of South America—Languages
    Quechua language
Ingapirca Site (Ecuador) *(Not Subd Geog)*
  BT Ecuador—Antiquities
Ingard family
  USE Enyart family
Ingassana language
  [PL8282.I55]
  UF Ingessana language
    Tabi language
  BT Nilo-Saharan languages
    Sudan—Languages
Ingavi, Battle of, 1841
  [F3324]
  BT Bolivia—History—1825-1879
    Peru—History—1829-1919
Ingavi, Battle of, 1935
  [F2688.5]
  BT Chaco War, 1932-1935
Inge family *(Not Subd Geog)*
  UF Ing family
Ingeborg-Bachmann-Preis
  [PT110.I53]
  BT Literary prizes—Germany (West)
Ingeles family
  USE Ingalls family
Ingelheim dooms
  USE Ingelheim law
Ingelheim law
  UF Ingelheim dooms
  BT Law—Germany
Ingels family
  USE Ingalls family
Ingemar (Name)
  UF Ingmar (Name)
  BT Names, Personal
Ingermanland (R.S.F.S.R.)
  USE Ingria (R.S.F.S.R.)
Ingermans
  USE Ingrians

Ingers
  USE Ingrians
Ingessana language
  USE Ingassana language
Ingestion
  UF Eating
    Food intake
    Nutrient intake
  BT Absorption (Physiology)
    Phagocytosis
  NT Deglutition
    Drinking (Physiology)
  — Regulation
    UF Regulation of ingestion
    BT Biological control systems
Ingestion disorders *(May Subd Geog)*
  [RC815.2]
  UF Disorders of ingestion
    Feeding disorders
  BT Mouth—Diseases
    Neuromuscular diseases
    Nutrition disorders
  NT Deglutition disorders
    Mastication disorders
Ingham family *(Not Subd Geog)*
Ingibandi language
  USE Jindjibandji language
Ingilby family *(Not Subd Geog)*
Ingills family
  USE Ingalls family
Ingland family
  USE England family
Ingle family
  USE Ingalls family
Ingles family
  USE Ingalls family
Inglish family
  USE English family
Inglisia
  [QL527.C6]
  BT Coccidae
Ingmar (Name)
  USE Ingemar (Name)
Ingolls family
  USE Ingalls family
Ingols family
  USE Ingalls family
Ingot molds
Ingots, Aluminum
  USE Aluminum ingots
Ingots, Brass
  USE Brass ingots
Ingots, Bronze
  USE Bronze ingots
Ingots, Copper
  USE Copper ingots
Ingots, Lead
  USE Lead ingots
Ingots, Nonferrous
  USE Nonferrous ingots
Ingots, Silver
  USE Silver ingots
Ingots, Steel
  USE Steel ingots
Ingots, Zinc alloy
  USE Zinc alloy ingots
Ingraham family
  USE Ingram family
Ingrahm family
  USE Ingram family
Ingram family *(Not Subd Geog)*
  UF Engram family
    Engrim family
    Ingraham family
    Ingrahm family
    Ingrim family
    Ingrime family
    Ingrom family
    Ingrum family
Ingram's Rebellion (Virginia)
  USE Bacon's Rebellion, 1676

Ingratitude
  UF Thanklessness
    Ungratefulness
    Unthankfulness
  BT Conduct of life
Ingres, Jean-Auguste-Dominique, 1780-1867.
  Comtesse d'Haussonville
  [ND1329.I]
  UF Comtesse d'Haussonville (Portrait
    painting)
    Madame d'Haussonville (Portrait
    painting)
  BT Portrait painting, French
Ingres, Jean-Auguste-Dominique, 1780-1867.
  Madame Moitessier
  [ND1329.I]
  UF Madame Moitessier (Portrait painting)
INGRES (Computer system)
  BT Data base management
    Electronic data processing—
    Programming
Ingria (R.S.F.S.R.)
  UF Ingermanland (R.S.F.S.R.)
    Inkeri (R.S.F.S.R.)
    Izhora (R.S.F.S.R.)
Ingrian language
  UF Izhorskiĭ language
  BT Baltic-Finnic languages
Ingrians *(May Subd Geog)*
  UF Ingermans
    Ingers
    Izhortsy
  BT Ethnology—Soviet Union
Ingrim family
  USE Ingram family
Ingrime family
  USE Ingram family
Ingrom family
  USE Ingram family
Ingrowing nails
  USE Nails, Ingrowing
Ingrum family
  USE Ingram family
Ingstad family *(Not Subd Geog)*
Inguanez family *(Not Subd Geog)*
Inguen
  USE Groin
Inguinal hernia
  BT Hernia
Inguinal region
  USE Groin
Ingulls family
  USE Ingalls family
Ingush
  [DK34.I]
  UF Galga
  BT Ethnology—Caucasus
Ingush epic literature
  USE Epic literature, Ingush
Ingush folk-songs
  USE Folk-songs, Ingush
Ingush language
  [PK9201.I6]
  BT Caucasian languages
    Nakh languages
Ingush literature *(May Subd Geog)*
  BT Daghestan literature
  NT Epic literature, Ingush
Ingush philology *(May Subd Geog)*
Ingush poetry *(May Subd Geog)*
Ingush songs
  USE Songs, Ingush
INH (Drug)
  USE Isoniazid
Inhalation abuse of solvents
  USE Solvent abuse
Inhalation anesthesia *(May Subd Geog)*
  [RD85.I48]
  UF Anesthesia, Inhalation
  BT Anesthesia
  — **Complications and sequelae**

Inhalation provocation tests
  USE Bronchial provocation tests
Inhalation therapists
  USE Respiratory therapists
Inhalation therapy
  USE Respiratory therapy
Inhalation toxicology
  USE Gases, Asphyxiating and poisonous—
      Toxicology
Inheritance (Biology)
  USE Heredity
Inheritance (Christian theology)
  BT Salvation
Inheritance and succession
  (May Subd Geog)
    ⌜*HB715 (Economics)*⌝
  UF Bequests
      Descent and distribution
      Descents
      Heirs
      Hereditary succession
      Intestacy
      Intestate succession
      Law of succession
      Succession, Intestate
  BT Real property
      Universal succession
  NT Ademption
      Benefit of inventory
      Charitable bequests
      Claims against decedents' estates
      Co-heirs
      Contracts to make wills
      Curtesy
      Decedents' estates
      Decedents' family maintenance
      Disinheritance
      Distribution of decedents' estates
      Dower
      Droit d'aubaine
      Election (Wills)
      Entail
      Escheat
      Estate settlement costs
      Estates, Unclaimed
      Estates (Law)
      Fideicommissum
      Freedom of testation
      Heir apparent
      Heirlooms
      Inheritance and transfer tax—Law and
        legislation
      Inquisitiones post mortem
      Kings and rulers—Succession
      Land tenure
      Legacies
      Legitime
      Marriage settlements
      Mejora
      Primogeniture
      Probate law and practice
      Renunciation of inheritance
      Restraints on alienation
      Reversion
      Separation of patrimony
      Substitution of heirs
      Testamentary trusts
      Trusts and trustees
      Unborn children (Law)
      Unworthiness of heirs
      Widow's allowance
      Widow's share
      Wills
      Worthier title
  — Conflict of laws
      USE Conflict of laws—Inheritance and
          succession
  — Criminal provisions

Inheritance and succession (Adat law)
  (May Subd Geog)
Inheritance and succession (Angoni law)
  USE Inheritance and succession (Ngoni
      law)
Inheritance and succession (Bafokeng law)
Inheritance and succession (Canon law)
    ⌜*BX1939.I*⌝
**Inheritance and succession (Canon law,
  Eastern)**
Inheritance and succession (Frankish law)
Inheritance and succession (Germanic law)
Inheritance and succession (Greek law)
Inheritance and succession (Hindu law)
Inheritance and succession (Islamic law)
  (May Subd Geog)
Inheritance and succession (Jewish law)
  (May Subd Geog)
  NT Primogeniture (Jewish law)
Inheritance and succession (Kgatla law)
  BT Law, Kgatla
Inheritance and succession (Lübeck law)
Inheritance and succession (Magdeburg law)
Inheritance and succession (Maori law)
Inheritance and succession (Ngoni law)
  UF Inheritance and succession (Angoni
      law)
  BT Law, Ngoni (African people)
Inheritance and succession (Oriental law)
Inheritance and succession (Primitive law)
  (May Subd Geog)
Inheritance and succession (Roman law)
Inheritance and succession (Samaritan law)
Inheritance and succession (Saxon law)
Inheritance and succession (Toka law)
  BT Law, Toka (African people)
Inheritance and transfer tax
  (May Subd Geog)
    ⌜*HJ5801-HJ5823*⌝
  UF Death-duties
      Estate tax
      Estates (Law)—Taxation
      Inheritance tax
      Legacies, Taxation of
      Succession taxes
      Taxable transfers
      Taxation of legacies
      Transfer tax
  BT Internal revenue
      Taxation
      Taxation, Progressive
      Wealth tax
  NT Decedents' estates—Taxation
      Gifts—Taxation
      Real property and taxation
  — Deductions
      NT Marital deduction
  — — Law and legislation
        (May Subd Geog)
  — Law and legislation *(May Subd Geog)*
      BT Estate planning
          Inheritance and succession
          Internal revenue law
          Probate law and practice
  — Rates and tables
  — Treaties
      USE Taxation, Double—Treaties
Inheritance of acquired characters
  UF Acquired characters, Heredity of
      Acquired characters, Inheritance of
      Heredity of acquired characters
  BT Heredity
Inheritance tax
  USE Inheritance and transfer tax
Inherited diseases
  USE Genetic disorders
Inherited polyendocrine syndrome
  USE Adenomatosis, Familial endocrine
Inhibin
    ⌜*QP572.I47*⌝

  BT Hormones, Sex
      Ovaries
      Peptide hormones
      Testis
Inhibition
    ⌜*BF335-BF337 (Psychology)*⌝
  BT Free will and determinism
      Habit
      Neurology
      Psychology
      Will
  RT Impulse
  NT Writer's block
Inhibition, Contact (Biology)
  USE Contact inhibition (Biology)
Inhibition (Writ)
  USE Prohibition (Writ)
Inhibitors, Adenylate cyclase
  USE Adenylate cyclase—Inhibitors
Inhibitors, Amylase
  USE Amylases—Inhibitors
Inhibitors, Angiotensin converting enzyme
  USE Angiotensin converting enzyme—
      Inhibitors
Inhibitors, Aspartic proteinase
  USE Aspartic proteinases—Inhibitors
Inhibitors, Chemical
  USE Chemical inhibitors
Inhibitors, Enkephalinase
  USE Enkephalinase—Inhibitors
Inhibitors, Enzyme
  USE Enzyme inhibitors
Inhibitors, Glucosidase
  USE Glucosidase inhibitors
Inhibitors, Monoamine oxidase
  USE Monoamine oxidase—Inhibitors
Inhibitors, Nitrification
  USE Nitrification inhibitors
Inhibitors, Subtilisin
  USE Subtilisins—Inhibitors
Inhibitors, Trypsin
  USE Trypsin inhibitors
Inhibitors of aromatic amino acid
    decarboxylase
  USE Aromatic amino acid decarboxylases—
      Inhibitors
Inhibitors of bacterial cell wall synthesis
  USE Bacterial cell walls—Synthesis—
      Inhibitors
Inhibitors of factor VIII
  USE Blood coagulation factor VIII
      antibodies
Inhibitors of insulin synthesis
  USE Insulin—Synthesis—Inhibitors
Inholdings *(May Subd Geog)*
  BT Land tenure
      National parks and reserves
Inhomogeneous materials
    ⌜*QC173.4.I53 (Physics)*⌝
  UF Inhomogeneous media
      Media, Inhomogeneous
  BT Materials
      Matter
Inhomogeneous media
  USE Inhomogeneous materials
Inhuman treatment (Divorce)
  USE Legal cruelty
Inia
    ⌜*QL737.C436*⌝
  BT River dolphins
  NT Inia geoffrensis
Inia geoffrensis
    ⌜*QL737.C436*⌝
  UF Amazon dolphin
      Boutu
      Geoffroy's dolphin
  BT Inia
INIAZAL (Computer program language)
    ⌜*QA76.73.I*⌝
  UF Inzhinernyĭ ﬁazyk algoritmi

Inibaloi dialect
USE Nabaloi dialect
Iniet (Cult)
BT Cults—Papua New Guinea
Religion, Primitive—Papua New
Guinea
Inimicitia (The Latin word)
BT Latin language—Etymology
Iniomi
USE Myctophiformes
INIS (Information retrieval system)
[Z699.5.A85]
UF International Nuclear Information
System
— **Format**
Inis Beag (Ireland)
USE Inishbeg (Ireland)
Inis Eoghain (Ireland)
USE Inishowen Peninsula (Ireland)
Inishbeg (Ireland)
UF Inis Beag (Ireland)
BT Islands—Ireland
Inishmurray (Ireland)
[DA990.I54]
BT Islands—Ireland
Inishowen Peninsula (Ireland)
UF Inis Eoghain (Ireland)
BT Peninsulas—Ireland
Initial mass function of stars
USE Stars—Initial mass function
Initial teaching alphabet
[LB1181]
UF Alphabet, Initial teaching
I.T.A.
BT English language—Alphabet
Reading—Code emphasis approaches
Reading (Elementary)
Initial value problems
[QA378]
UF Problems, Initial value
BT Differential equations
RT Boundary value problems
— **Numerical solutions**
BT Numerical analysis
Initialisms
USE Acronyms
Initials
[ND3335 (Illumination)]
[NK3600-NK3640]
BT Printers' ornaments
Type ornaments
RT Alphabets
Illumination of books and manuscripts
Lettering
Monograms
Type and type-founding
NT Artists' marks
Printing—Specimens
Initials on trees
USE Names carved on trees
Initiation rites *(May Subd Geog)*
UF Initiations
BT Rites and ceremonies
NT Circumcision
Puberty rites
— **Mythology**
— **Religious aspects**
[BL615]
BT Religion, Primitive
NT Baptism
— — **Baptists, [Catholic Church, etc.]**
— — **Buddhism, [Christianity, etc.]**
— — **Catholic Church**
UF Christian initiation of adults
(Catholic Church)
RCIA (Catholic Church)
Rite of Christian initiation of
adults (Catholic Church)
— — **Christianity**
NT Confirmation
First communion

Installation (Clergy)
— — **Judaism**
NT Installation (Rabbis)
Initiations
USE Initiation rites
Initiations (into trades, societies, etc.)
Initiations (into trades, societies, etc.)
[HD4889 (Labor)]
UF Fraternities
Initiations
Trades, Initiations into
Youth dedication
BT Rites and ceremonies
RT Greek letter societies
Hazing
Secret societies
Initiations in literature
Initiative, Right of *(May Subd Geog)*
BT Administrative law
Executive power
Legislation
Political science
Public law
Initiative and referendum
USE Referendum
Iniuria (Roman law)
UF Injuria (Roman law)
Injart family
USE Enyart family
Injectable contraceptives
USE Contraceptive drugs, Injectable
Injection-gneiss
USE Migmatite
Injection lasers
[TA1700]
UF Junction lasers, Semiconductor
BT Lasers
Semiconductor lasers
Injection molding of plastics
[TP1150]
BT Plastics—Molding
Injection molding of rubber
UF Rubber—Injection molding
Rubber, Injection molding of
Injection of plasma
USE Plasma injection
Injection wells *(May Subd Geog)*
UF Wells, Injection
BT Wells
— **Law and legislation** *(May Subd Geog)*
Injections
[RM163-RM176 (Therapeutics)]
UF Inoculation
BT Drugs—Administration
NT Ampuls
Contraceptive drugs, Injectable
Microinjections
Parenteral therapy
— **Microbiology**
Injections, Anatomical
[QH324 (Biology)]
[QL812 (Comparative anatomy)]
[QM39 (Human anatomy)]
NT Anatomical specimens
Injections, Bronchial
UF Bronchial injections
BT Lungs—Diseases
Injections, Hypodermic
[RM169]
UF Hypodermic injections
Injections, Subcutaneous
BT Therapeutics
NT Hypodermic jet injectors
Hypodermic needles
Hypodermic syringes
Injections, Intra-arterial
UF Intra-arterial injections
NT Arterial catheterization
Injections, Intra-articular
UF Intra-articular injections
BT Therapeutics

NT Injections, Intradiscal
Injections, Intradermal
UF Intradermal injections
Injections, Intradiscal *(May Subd Geog)*
UF Intradiscal injections
BT Injections, Intra-articular
Injections, Spinal
Intervertebral disk
Injections, Intramuscular
UF Intramuscular injections
— **Complications and sequelae**
[RM69]
Injections, Intraperitoneal
[RM180]
UF Intraperitoneal injections
BT Peritoneum
Injections, Intravenous *(May Subd Geog)*
UF Intravenous injections
IV injections
BT Intravenous therapy
Injections, Saline
[RM178]
UF Saline injections
Injections, Sclerosing
UF Sclerosing injections
Sclerotherapy
BT Irritation
Injections, Spinal
UF Intraspinal injections
Spinal injections
NT Injections, Intradiscal
Injections, Subcutaneous
USE Injections, Hypodermic
Injective modules (Algebra)
BT Modules (Algebra)
Injectors
[TJ387 (Steam-boilers)]
UF Steam-injectors
BT Boilers
Jet pumps
Pumping machinery
Steam-boilers
Injectors, Hypodermic jet
USE Hypodermic jet injectors
Injibandi language
USE Jindjibandji language
Injunctions *(May Subd Geog)*
[HD7819 (Labor law)]
[JF721 (Theory)]
[JK1542 (United States judiciary)]
UF Anti-injunction law
BT Actions and defenses
Civil procedure
Constitutional law
Equitable remedies
Extraordinary remedies
Provisional remedies
RT Interdict (Civil law)
NT Labor injunctions
Injunctions, Labor
USE Labor injunctions
Injuria (Roman law)
USE Iniuria (Roman law)
Injuries
USE *subdivision* Accidents *under subjects;
also subdivision* Accidents and
injuries *under sports and games;
and subdivision* Wounds and
injuries *under individual regions and
organs of the body*
Accidents
First aid in illness and injury
Traumatology
Wounds and injuries
Injuries, Birth
USE Birth injuries
Injuries, Crash
USE Crash injuries
Injuries, Overuse
USE Overuse injuries

Injuries, Whiplash
USE Whiplash injuries
Injuries (Law)
USE Accident law
Damages
Employers' liability
Medical jurisprudence
Personal injuries
Torts
Injuries and wounds of plants
USE Plants—Wounds and injuries
Injuries from electricity
USE Electricity, Injuries from
Injuries from sports
USE Sports—Accidents and injuries
Injurious and beneficial animals
USE Zoology, Economic
Injurious birds
USE Bird pests
Injurious insects
USE Insect pests
Injurious occupations
USE Occupations, Dangerous
Injustice
USE Justice
Ink
  ⸢TP946-TP950 (Technology)⸣
  ⸢Z112 (Paleography)⸣
  BT Writing—Materials and instruments
  NT India ink
  Inkstands
  Printing-ink
Ink bottles (May Subd Geog)
  BT Bottles
Ink brushwork
  USE Ink painting
Ink drawing
  USE Pen drawing
Ink droplet printing
  USE Printing, Ink jet
Ink drying
  USE Printing-ink—Drying
Ink jet printing
  USE Printing, Ink jet
Ink painting (May Subd Geog)
  UF Brush painting, Oriental
  Ink brushwork
  Oriental brush painting
  BT Brush drawing
  Painting, Oriental
  — 20th century (May Subd Geog)
Ink painting, American (May Subd Geog)
  UF American ink painting
Ink painting, Chinese (May Subd Geog)
  UF Chinese ink painting
  NT Huang, Kung-wang, 1269-1358.
    Dwelling in the Fu-ch'un Mountains
  — Sung-Yüan dynasties, 960-1368
  — Ming-Ch'ing dynasties, 1368-1912
  — 20th century (May Subd Geog)
Ink painting, Japanese (May Subd Geog)
  UF Japanese ink painting
  NT Sumie
  — Kamakura-Momoyama period, 1185-1600
  — Edo period, 1600-1868
  — 19th century (May Subd Geog)
  — Meiji period, 1868-1912
  — 20th century
  — Chinese influences
    BT China—Civilization
  — Zen influences
    BT Zen Buddhism
Ink painting, Ōbaku (May Subd Geog)
  UF Ōbaku ink painting
Ink slabs
  USE Ink-stones
Ink sticks
  USE Inksticks
Ink-stones (May Subd Geog)
  ⸢Z45⸣
  UF Ink slabs

BT Seals (Numismatics)
  Writing—Materials and instruments
Inkalik Indians
  USE Ingalik Indians
Inkalik language
  USE Ingalik language
Inkallajta Site (Bolivia)
  UF Incallajta Site (Bolivia)
  BT Bolivia—Antiquities
Inkawasi Site (Peru)
  UF Incahuasi Site (Peru)
  BT Peru—Antiquities
Inkberry
  USE Pokeweed
Inkblot test, Harrower psychodiagnostic
  USE Harrower psychodiagnostic inkblot test
Inkblot test, Rorschach
  USE Rorschach test
Inkeri (R.S.F.S.R.)
  USE Ingria (R.S.F.S.R.)
Inkermann, Battle of, 1854
  ⸢DK215.5⸣
  BT Crimean War, 1853-1856
Inkle loom weaving
  USE Inkle weaving
Inkle weaving
  ⸢TT848⸣
  UF Inkle loom weaving
  BT Hand weaving
Inklings (Group of writers)
  ⸢PR478.I54⸣
  BT English literature—Societies, etc.
Inks Lake (Tex.)
  BT Lakes—Texas
  RT Reservoirs—Texas
Inkstands (May Subd Geog)
  BT Ink
Inksticks
  UF Ink sticks
  BT Art objects, Oriental
Inkundo (African people)
  USE Nkundu (African people)
Inkwells
  ⸢NK6035⸣
Inland marine insurance
  USE Insurance, Inland marine
Inland navigation (May Subd Geog)
  ⸢HE617-HE720 (Transportation)⸣
  ⸢TC601-TC791 (Engineering)⸣
  UF Interior navigation
  Navigation, Inland
  BT Commerce
  Communication and traffic
  Hydrography
  Navigation
  Shipping
  Transportation
  Water resources development
  RT Inland water transportation
  Intracoastal waterways
  SA subdivision Navigation under names of
    canals, rivers, etc.
  NT Bridges—Navigation clearances
  Canals
  Lakes
  Rivers
  Towing
  Work boats
  — Collective labor agreements
    USE Collective labor agreements—
      Inland water transportation
  — Communication systems
    ⸢TC753⸣
  — Employees
    USE Inland water transportation—
      Employees
  — Law and legislation (May Subd Geog)

UF Inland rules of the road
  Navigation—Law and legislation
  Navigation laws
  Rule of the road, Inland
  Rules of the road, Inland
  SA subdivision Navigation—Law and
    legislation under names of
    waterways
  NT International lakes
  International rivers
  — Maps
    USE Nautical charts
  — United States
    UF United States—Inland navigation
Inland Passage
  USE Inside Passage
Inland revenue
  USE Internal revenue
Inland rules of the road
  USE Inland navigation—Law and legislation
Inland Sea (Japan)
  ⸢DS894.79.I54⸣
  UF Seto-naikai (Japan)
  Seto uchi (Japan)
Inland shipping
  USE Inland water transportation
Inland transportation insurance
  USE Insurance, Inland marine
Inland water transportation
  (May Subd Geog)
    Works on shipping on individual lakes, rivers, etc.
  are entered under the heading Shipping subdivided
  by the name of the lake, river, etc.
  UF Inland shipping
  Shipping, Inland water
  Water transportation, Inland
  BT Commerce
  Shipping
  Transportation
  RT Inland navigation
  NT Wages—Inland water transportation
  — Collective labor agreements
    USE Collective labor agreements—
      Inland water transportation
  — Communication systems
    ⸢VM479⸣
  — Employees
    UF Inland navigation—Employees
    Inland water transportation
      workers
    BT Boatmen
    Merchant marine—Officers
    Merchant seamen
    Transport workers
    NT Collective labor agreements—
      Inland water transportation
  — Freight traffic
    BT Freight and freightage
  — Law and legislation (May Subd Geog)
  — Passenger traffic
  — Time-tables
    UF Time-tables (Transportation)
  — Transit charges
    BT Tolls
Inland water transportation workers
  USE Inland water transportation—
    Employees
Inland waterway vessels (May Subd Geog)
  BT Ships
  Work boats
  NT Canal-boats
  Lake steamers
  River boats
  — Appraisal
    USE Inland waterway vessels—
      Valuation
  — Cargo
    BT Stowage
  — Handling
  — Registration and transfer
    (May Subd Geog)

UF Registration of inland waterway
vessels
BT Recording and registration
Ship registers
— Valuation
UF Inland waterway vessels—Appraisal
Inlaying in wood
USE Marquetry
Inlays (Dentistry)
BT Dentistry, Operative
Fillings (Dentistry)
Prosthodontics
Inlet boxes (Naval architecture)
USE Sea chests (Naval architecture)
Inlets *(May Subd Geog)*
[GB450-460]
BT Coasts
Geomorphology
RT Bays
— **Alaska**
NT Cook Inlet (Alaska)
Knik Arm (Alaska)
— **Australia**
NT Peel Inlet (W.A.)
— **British Columbia**
NT False Creek (B.C.)
— **Ecuador**
NT Salado Inlet (Ecuador)
— **Germany (West)**
NT Helgoland Bight (Germany)
— **Greenland**
NT Kangerlussuaq (Greenland)
— **Netherlands**
NT Haringvliet (Netherlands)
Oosterschelde (Netherlands)
Westerschelde (Netherlands)
— **New Jersey**
NT Barnegat Inlet (N.J.)
Little Egg Harbor (N.J.)
— **New Zealand**
NT Doubtful Sound (N.Z.)
Pauatahanui Inlet (N.Z.)
Porirua Inlet (N.Z.)
Preservation Inlet (N.Z.)
— **North Carolina**
NT Oregon Inlet (N.C.)
— **Northwest Territories**
NT Bathurst Inlet (N.W.T.)
Lyon Inlet (N.W.T.)
Pond Inlet (N.W.T.)
Rankin Inlet (N.W.T. : Inlet)
— **Norway**
NT Horn Sound (Spitsbergen Island,
Norway)
— **Persian Gulf**
NT 'Abd Allāh Inlet (Kuwait and Iraq)
— **Washington (State)**
NT Grays Harbor (Wash.)
Inmate classification
USE Prisoners—Classification
Inmate guards *(May Subd Geog)*
UF Guards, Inmate
Prisoners as guards
BT Correctional personnel
Prisoners
Inmates of institutions *(May Subd Geog)*
UF Institutionalized persons
Institutions, Inmates of
Public institutions—Inmates
BT Institutional care
NT Mental retardation facilities patients
— **Attitudes**
BT Attitude (Psychology)
— **Sexual behavior**
Inmeas language
USE Isinay language
Inn keepers
USE Hotelkeepers
Innate ideas (Philosophy)
[B105.I54]

UF Innateness (Philosophy)
Innatism (Philosophy)
BT Idea (Philosophy)
Philosophy
Innate immunity
USE Natural immunity
Innate resistance
USE Natural immunity
Innateness (Philosophy)
USE Innate ideas (Philosophy)
Innateness hypothesis (Linguistics)
USE Cartesian linguistics
Innatism (Philosophy)
USE Innate ideas (Philosophy)
Inner ear
USE Labyrinth (Ear)
Inner Hebrides (Scotland)
BT Hebrides (Scotland)
Islands—Scotland
NT Canna (Scotland)
Iona (Scotland)
Mull, Island of (Scotland)
Inner Himalaya Mountains
USE Lesser Himalaya Mountains
Inner Light
[BX7748.I6]
UF Light, Inner
BT Authority (Religion)
Experience (Religion)
Revelation
Society of Friends—Doctrines
Inner missions *(May Subd Geog)*
[BV2950 (Germany)]
UF Missions, Inner
BT Missions, Home
Inner peace
USE Peace of mind
Inner product spaces
UF Hermitian inner product spaces
Scalar product spaces
Spaces, Inner product
Spaces, Scalar product
BT Forms, Bilinear
Vector spaces
RT Hilbert space
— **Witt classification**
UF Witt classification of inner product
spaces
Inner product spaces, Indefinite
[QA322.5]
UF Indefinite inner product spaces
Indefinite scalar product spaces
Scalar product spaces, Indefinite
Inner-shell ionization
BT Ionization
Nuclear shell theory
Nuclear spectroscopy
Inner tube industry *(May Subd Geog)*
BT Inner tubes
Inner tube rafting
USE Tubing (Aquatic sports)
Inner tubes
[TS1920]
UF Tire tubes
BT Tires, Rubber
Tubes
NT Inner tube industry
— **Tariff**
USE Tariff on inner tubes
Innerebner family *(Not Subd Geog)*
Innerland (Art object)
BT Engraved glass—United States
Steuben Glass, inc.
Innerste River (Germany) *(Not Subd Geog)*
BT Rivers—Germany (West)
Innes family *(Not Subd Geog)*
UF Inness family
Innis family
Inniss family
Inness family
USE Innes family

Innis family
USE Innes family
Inniss family
USE Innes family
Innkeeper and guest
USE Hotels, taverns, etc.—Law and
legislation
Innkeepers
USE Hotelkeepers
Innocence, Presumption of
USE Presumption of innocence
Innocence (Psychology)
[BF575.I48]
UF Naïveté
BT Emotions
Personality
Innocence (Theology)
BT Man (Christian theology)
Innocents, Feast of the Holy
USE Holy Innocents, Feast of the
Innocents, Massacre of the Holy
USE Holy Innocents, Massacre of the
Innocents' Day
USE Holy Innocents, Feast of the
**Innokentiĭ, Saint, Metropolitan of Moscow
and Kolomna, 1797-1879**
— **Homes and haunts**
— — **Alaska**
NT Russian Bishop's House (Sitka,
Alaska)
Innoko River (Alaska)
BT Rivers—Alaska
Innovar
BT Anesthetics
Innovations, Agricultural
USE Agricultural innovations
Innovations, Diffusion of
USE Diffusion of innovations
Innovations, Educational
USE Educational innovations
Innovations, Fishery
USE Fishery innovations
Innovations, Forestry
USE Forestry innovations
Innovations, Industrial
USE Technological innovations
Innovations, Medical
USE Medical innovations
Innovations, Technological
USE Technological innovations
Inns
USE Hotels, taverns, etc.
Inns of Chancery
UF Chancery, Inns of
BT Bar associations—Great Britain
Inns of court
UF Court, Inns of
BT Bar associations—Great Britain
Innuit
USE Eskimos
Innuit language
USE Eskimo language
Innviertel (Austria)
UF Ihnnviertel (Austria)
Quarter of the Inn (Austria)
INO (Artificial language)
[PM8396]
BT Languages, Artificial
Pasigraphy
Inoceramidae
[QE812.I5]
BT Mollusks, Fossil
NT Inoceramus
Inoceramus
[QE812.I5]
BT Inoceramidae
Inoculation
USE *subdivision* Preventive inoculation
under names of diseases, e.g.
Anthrax—Preventive inoculation;
Smallpox—Preventive inoculation

Inoculation *(Continued)*
    Injections
    Vaccination
Inoculation (Founding)
  BT Founding
Inoculation of legumes
  USE Legume inoculation
Inoculation of plants
  USE Plant inoculation
Inoculation of soils
  USE Soil inoculation
Inogashira Kōen (Tokyo, Japan)
  USE Inokashira Kōen (Tokyo, Japan)
Inojosa family
  USE Hinojosa family
Inokashira Kōen (Tokyo, Japan)
  UF Inogashira Kōen (Tokyo, Japan)
    Inokashira Park (Tokyo, Japan)
  BT Parks—Japan
Inokashira Park (Tokyo, Japan)
  USE Inokashira Kōen (Tokyo, Japan)
İnönü, Battle of, 1921
  BT Greco-Turkish War, 1921-1922
    Turkey—History—Revolution, 1918-1923
Inoperculates
  USE Discomycetes
Inorganic acids
  USE Acids, Inorganic
Inorganic biochemistry
  USE Bioinorganic chemistry
Inorganic chemicals
  USE Inorganic compounds
Inorganic chemistry
  USE Chemistry, Inorganic
Inorganic compounds
  UF Compounds, Inorganic
    Inorganic chemicals
  BT Chemicals
  RT Chemistry, Inorganic
  SA *groups and classes of inorganic*
    compounds, and individual
    inorganic substances
  NT Acids, Inorganic
    Inorganic polymers
Inorganic fibers
  UF Fibers, Inorganic
  BT Textile fibers
  NT Asbestos fibers
    Carbon fibers
    Ceramic fibers
    Graphite fibers
Inorganic ion exchange materials
  UF Inorganic ion exchangers
    Ion exchange materials, Inorganic
  BT Chemistry, Inorganic
    Materials
Inorganic ion exchangers
  USE Inorganic ion exchange materials
Inorganic polymers
  [QD196]
  BT Inorganic compounds
    Polymers and polymerization
Inosite
  [QD321]
Inositol
  [QP772.I5]
  UF Cyclohexanehexol
    Mesoinositol
    Myoinositol
  BT Alcohols
    Sugars
    Vitamin B complex
  RT Phosphoinositides
Inotropic agents, Negative cardiac
  USE Myocardial depressants
Inotropic agents, Positive cardiac
  USE Cardiotonic agents
Inpatient Admissions Scheduling and Control
  System (Computer system)
  USE ASCS (Computer system)

Input design, Computer
  [QA76.9.I55]
  UF Computer input design
    Data entry design
    Data input design
    Design of computer inputs
    Entry design, Data
    Input design, Data
    Input design, Keyed
    Keyed input design
  BT Coding theory
    Computer input-output equipment
    Data base management
    Data structures (Computer science)
    Electronic data processing—Data entry
  RT Electronic data processing—Data
    preparation
Input design, Data
  USE Input design, Computer
Input design, Keyed
  USE Input design, Computer
Input equipment (Computers)
  USE Computer input-output equipment
Input-output analysis *(May Subd Geog)*
  [HB142]
  Here are entered works on studying the quantitative interdependence of the various economic sectors through coefficients derived from the solution of a system of linear equations.
  UF Interindustry economics
  BT Economics, Mathematical
    Industry
    National income—Accounting
  RT Input-output tables
  NT Diversification in industry
    Production functions (Economic
    theory)
  — **Computer programs**
    NT PASSION (Computer program)
Input-output equipment (Computers)
  USE Computer input-output equipment
Input-output tables *(May Subd Geog)*
  [HC79.I57]
  RT Input-output analysis
Inquests, Coroners'
  USE Coroners
Inquiry, Courts of
  USE Courts-martial and courts of inquiry
Inquiry (Theory of knowledge)
  [BD183]
  BT Knowledge, Theory of
Inquisition *(May Subd Geog)*
  [BX1700-1745]
  UF Holy Office
  BT Catholic Church—Discipline
  NT Auto-da-fe sermons
  — **Spain**
    UF Spanish inquisition
Inquisition, Islamic
  USE Miḥna
Inquisition, Motazilite
  USE Miḥna
Inquisitiones post mortem
  [CS434-CS436 (English genealogical
    records)]
  [DA25 (English records)]
  [DA670 (English counties)]
  UF Post-mortem inquisitions
    Postmortem inquisitions
  BT Inheritance and succession
    Registers of births, etc.
Inquisitiveness
  USE Curiosity
Inro *(May Subd Geog)*
  [NK6080]
  NT Netsukes
    Ojime
Insall family *(Not Subd Geog)*
Insane
  This heading is used only with legal subdivisions.
  Other material is entered under Mentally ill.

— Care
  USE Mentally ill—Care
— **Commitment and detention**
  (May Subd Geog)
  UF Civil commitment of the insane
    Commitment of the insane
    Detention of the insane
    Mentally ill—Commitment and
    detention
  BT Insanity—Jurisprudence
    Mental health laws
  RT Psychiatric hospitals—Admission
    and discharge
— Legal status, laws, etc.
  USE Insanity—Jurisprudence
    Mental health laws
Insane, Criminal and dangerous
  (May Subd Geog)
  [HV6133 (Insanity and crime)]
  [HV8741-HV8742 (Prisons)]
  UF Crime and insanity
    Criminal insane
    Insanity and crime
  BT Crime and criminals
  RT Forensic psychiatry
    Insanity—Jurisprudence
    Insanity, Moral
  NT Criminal liability
Insane, Killing of the
  UF Killing of the insane
  BT Euthanasia
Insane artists
  USE Artists, Mentally handicapped
Insanity *(May Subd Geog)*
  [BF423 (Insanity and genius)]
  [HV4977 (Insanity and degeneration)]
  [HV6133 (Insanity and crime)]
  Here are entered works on the legal aspects of mental disorders. Popular works and works on regional or social aspects of mental disorders are entered under Mental illness. Systematic descriptions of mental disorders are entered under Psychology, Pathological. Works on clinical aspects of mental disorders, including therapy, are entered under Psychiatry.
  UF Lunacy
    Madness
    Mental illness—Law and legislation
  BT Hallucinations and illusions
    Mental illness
  RT Psychiatry
    Psychology, Pathological
    Psychoses
— Genetic aspects
  USE Mental illness—Genetic aspects
— **Jurisprudence** *(May Subd Geog)*
  [RA1151]
  Here are entered works on the legal status of persons of unsound mind. Works on the law affecting the welfare of the insane are entered under the heading Mental health laws. Works on psychiatry as applied in courts of law are entered under the heading Forensic psychiatry
  UF Insane—Legal status, laws, etc.
    Law and mental illness
    Mental illness and law
    Mentally ill—Legal status, laws,
    etc.
  BT Status (Law)
  RT Insane, Criminal and dangerous
    Insanity, Moral
  NT Capacity and disability
    Competency to stand trial
    Criminal liability
    Forensic psychiatry
    Insane—Commitment and
    detention
    Interdiction (Civil law)
    Legal assistance to the mentally
    handicapped
    Liability (Law)
    Litigious paranoia

Psychosurgery—Law and
legislation
— **Jurisprudence (Canon Law)**
— **Jurisprudence (Jewish law)**
— **Jurisprudence (Roman law)**
Insanity, Moral
UF Moral insanity
BT Crime and criminals
Psychology, Pathological
RT Insane, Criminal and dangerous
Insanity—Jurisprudence
Insanity, Periodic and transitory
UF Insanity, Transitory
Insanity, Religious
UF Religious insanity
BT Psychology, Religious
Insanity, Transitory
USE Insanity, Periodic and transitory
Insanity and art
USE Art and mental illness
Insanity and crime
USE Insane, Criminal and dangerous
Insanity and genius
USE Genius and mental illness
Insanity in literature
USE Mental illness in literature
Inscribed rugs
USE Inscription rugs
Inscription rugs   *(May Subd Geog)*
UF Inscribed rugs
Rugs, Inscribed
Rugs, Inscription
BT Rugs, Oriental
Inscriptions   *(May Subd Geog)*
⌈CN⌉
UF Epigraphy
BT Archaeology
Auxiliary sciences of history
History, Ancient
Paleography
RT Extinct languages
Historical markers
NT Architectural inscriptions
Brasses
Brick stamps
Calligraphy, Chinese—Inscriptions
Chronograms
Cuneiform writing
Epigraphists
Epitaphs
Graffiti
Hieroglyphics
Lacquer and lacquering—Inscriptions
Monograms
Mural painting and decoration, Italian
—Inscriptions
Mural painting and decoration,
Renaissance—Inscriptions
Painting, Chinese—Inscriptions
Painting, Japanese—Inscriptions
Painting, Korean—Inscriptions
Panel painting, Italian—Inscriptions
Panel painting, Renaissance—
Inscriptions
Petroglyphs
Picture-writing
Runes
Sculpture, Buddhist—Inscriptions
Sculpture, Japanese—Inscriptions
Seals (Numismatics)
Signatures (Writing)
Tablets (Paleography)
— Forgeries
USE Forgery of inscriptions
— **Private collections**   *(May Subd Geog)*
⌈CN30⌉
— **Greece**
NT Inscriptions, Eteocretan
— — **Crete**
UF Inscriptions, Minoan
Minoan writing

BT Inscriptions, Linear B
NT Phaistos Disk
— — **Mycenae (Ancient city)**
UF Inscriptions, Mycenaean
BT Inscriptions, Linear B
— **Japan**
NT Yama no Ue no Hi (Takasaki-shi,
Japan)
Inscriptions, Achaemenian
USE Achaemenian inscriptions
Inscriptions, Ancient   *(May Subd Geog)*
UF Ancient inscriptions
Inscriptions, Anglo-Saxon
USE Inscriptions, English (Old)
Inscriptions, Arabic   *(May Subd Geog)*
UF Arabic inscriptions
NT Inscriptions, Lihyanic
Inscriptions, Safaitic
Inscriptions, Thamudic
Inscriptions, Aramaic   *(May Subd Geog)*
UF Aramaic inscriptions
NT Inscriptions, Nabataean
Inscriptions, Architectural
USE Architectural inscriptions
Inscriptions, Armenian   *(May Subd Geog)*
UF Armenian inscriptions
Inscriptions, Aztec
USE Aztecs—Writing
Inscriptions, Balinese   *(May Subd Geog)*
UF Balinese inscriptions
Inscriptions, Behistun
USE Achaemenian inscriptions
Old Persian inscriptions
Inscriptions, Buddhist   *(May Subd Geog)*
UF Buddhist inscriptions
Inscriptions, Bulgaro-Turkic
(May Subd Geog)
⌈PL378-380⌉
UF Bulgaro-Turkic inscriptions
Inscriptions, Burmese   *(May Subd Geog)*
UF Burmese inscriptions
Inscriptions, Byzantine   *(May Subd Geog)*
⌈CN455⌉
UF Byzantine inscriptions
Inscriptions, Celtiberian
BT Celtic languages, Continental
Inscriptions, Iberian
Inscriptions, Chinese   *(May Subd Geog)*
UF Chinese inscriptions
NT Oracle bones
Inscriptions, Cuneiform
USE Cuneiform inscriptions
Inscriptions, Cypro-Minoan
(May Subd Geog)
⌈P1035⌉
UF Cypro-Minoan inscriptions
Cypro-Minoan script
BT Inscriptions, Linear A
Inscriptions, Linear B
Inscriptions, Cyrillic   *(May Subd Geog)*
UF Cyrillic inscriptions
Inscriptions, Demotic
USE Egyptian language—Inscriptions
Inscriptions, Egyptian
USE Egyptian language—Inscriptions
Inscriptions, Elamite
USE Cuneiform inscriptions, Elamite
Inscriptions, English   *(May Subd Geog)*
UF English inscriptions
Inscriptions, English, ⌈**Aramaic, etc.**⌉
(May Subd Geog)
Inscriptions, English (Old)
UF Anglo-Saxon inscriptions
English inscriptions, Old
Inscriptions, Anglo-Saxon
Inscriptions, Old English
Old English inscriptions
Inscriptions, Eteocretan   *(May Subd Geog)*
UF Eteocretan inscriptions
BT Crete—Antiquities
Inscriptions—Greece

Inscriptions, Etruscan   *(May Subd Geog)*
⌈CN479⌉
UF Etruscan inscriptions
Inscriptions, Gaulish   *(May Subd Geog)*
UF Gaulish inscriptions
Inscriptions, Glagolitic   *(May Subd Geog)*
UF Glagolitic inscriptions
Inscriptions, Greek   *(May Subd Geog)*
UF Greek inscriptions
BT Greek language
Greek philology
NT Heraclean tablets
Inscriptions, Linear A
Inscriptions, Linear B
Stoichedon inscriptions
Inscriptions, Hadrami
⌈PJ6971⌉
UF Hadhrami inscriptions
Hadrami inscriptions
Inscriptions, Hebrew   *(May Subd Geog)*
⌈PJ5034.4-5034.9⌉
UF Hebrew inscriptions
Inscriptions, Hieratic
USE Egyptian language—Inscriptions
Inscriptions, Hieroglyphic
UF Hieroglyphic inscriptions
NT Egyptian language—Inscriptions
Inscriptions, Linear A
Inscriptions, Linear B
Inscriptions, Meroitic
Inscriptions, Himyaritic
USE Inscriptions, Sabaean
Inscriptions, Hittite   *(May Subd Geog)*
UF Hittite inscriptions
NT Inscriptions, Luwian
Inscriptions, House
USE House marks
Inscriptions, Iberian   *(May Subd Geog)*
⌈P1081⌉
UF Iberian inscriptions
NT Inscriptions, Celtiberian
Inscriptions, Indic
NT Indus script
Sanskrit language, Epigraphical Hybrid
Inscriptions, Irish   *(May Subd Geog)*
UF Irish inscriptions
NT Ogham alphabet
Inscriptions, Islamic   *(May Subd Geog)*
⌈CN1153⌉
UF Inscriptions, Muslim
Islamic inscriptions
Muslim inscriptions
BT Islamic antiquities
Inscriptions, Italic
UF Italic inscriptions
NT Inscriptions, Picenian
Inscriptions, Jaina   *(May Subd Geog)*
UF Jaina inscriptions
Inscriptions, Japanese   *(May Subd Geog)*
UF Japanese inscriptions
Inscriptions, Jewish   *(May Subd Geog)*
UF Jewish inscriptions
BT Jews—Antiquities
Inscriptions, Kannada   *(May Subd Geog)*
UF Kannada inscriptions
Inscriptions, Kawi   *(May Subd Geog)*
UF Kawi inscriptions
Inscriptions, Korean   *(May Subd Geog)*
UF Korean inscriptions
Inscriptions, Köturk
USE Inscriptions, Old Turkic
Inscriptions, Latin   *(May Subd Geog)*
UF Latin inscriptions
BT Latin language
Latin philology
NT Fasti consulares
— **France**
UF Inscriptions, Latin—Gaul
— Gaul
USE Inscriptions, Latin—France
— **Italy**

Inscriptions, Latin
— **Italy** *(Continued)*
    NT Tabula Alimentaria Ligurum
          Baebianorum
Inscriptions, Lihyanic
    UF Lihyanic inscriptions
    BT Inscriptions, Arabic
Inscriptions, Linear A *(May Subd Geog)*
    UF Linear A inscriptions
        Minoan writing
        Picture-writing, Cretan
    BT Alphabet
        Inscriptions, Greek
        Inscriptions, Hieroglyphic
    NT Inscriptions, Cypro-Minoan
Inscriptions, Linear B *(May Subd Geog)*
    UF Linear B inscriptions
        Minoan writing
    BT Greek language—Alphabet
        Inscriptions, Greek
        Inscriptions, Hieroglyphic
    NT Inscriptions—Greece—Crete
        Inscriptions—Greece—Mycenae
          (Ancient city)
        Inscriptions, Cypro-Minoan
Inscriptions, Luwian *(May Subd Geog)*
    UF Luwian inscriptions
    BT Inscriptions, Hittite
Inscriptions, Maya
    USE Mayas—Writing
Inscriptions, Meroitic
    UF Meroitic inscriptions
    BT Inscriptions, Hieroglyphic
Inscriptions, Messapian *(May Subd Geog)*
    UF Messapian inscriptions
Inscriptions, Mexican
    USE Indians of Mexico—Writing
Inscriptions, Minoan
    USE Inscriptions—Greece—Crete
Inscriptions, Moabitic
    USE Moabite stone
Inscriptions, Mongolian *(May Subd Geog)*
    UF Mongolian inscriptions
Inscriptions, Muslim
    USE Inscriptions, Islamic
Inscriptions, Mycenaean
    USE Inscriptions—Greece—Mycenae
        (Ancient city)
Inscriptions, Nabataean
    [PJ5239]
    UF Nabataean inscriptions
    BT Inscriptions, Aramaic
Inscriptions, Nepali *(May Subd Geog)*
    UF Nepali inscriptions
Inscriptions, Norse
    UF Norse inscriptions
    RT Inscriptions, Runic
Inscriptions, Old English
    USE Inscriptions, English (Old)
Inscriptions, Old Russian
    USE Inscriptions, Russian (Old)
Inscriptions, Old Turkic *(May Subd Geog)*
    [PL31]
    UF Inscriptions, Köturk
        Inscriptions, Turkic (Old)
        Kökturk inscriptions
        Köturk inscriptions
        Old Turkic inscriptions
        Orkhon inscriptions (Turkic)
        Yenisei inscriptions (Turkic)
    NT Old Turkic language
Inscriptions, Oriental
    UF Oriental inscriptions
Inscriptions, Oscan-Umbrian
    (May Subd Geog)
    UF Inscriptions, Umbrian
        Oscan-Umbrian inscriptions
    NT Eugubine tables
Inscriptions, Pahlavi *(May Subd Geog)*
    [PK6193]
    UF Pahlavi inscriptions

Inscriptions, Palm-leaf
    USE Palm-leaf inscriptions
Inscriptions, Parthian *(May Subd Geog)*
    UF Parthian inscriptions
Inscriptions, Persian (Old)
    USE Old Persian inscriptions
Inscriptions, Phoenician *(May Subd Geog)*
    UF Phoenician inscriptions
    NT Inscriptions, Punic
— **Relation to the Old Testament**
        UF Bible. O.T.—Relation to
            Phoenician inscriptions
Inscriptions, Picenian *(May Subd Geog)*
    UF Picene inscriptions
        Picenian inscriptions
    BT Inscriptions, Italic
Inscriptions, Polish *(May Subd Geog)*
    UF Polish inscriptions
Inscriptions, Prakrit *(May Subd Geog)*
    UF Prakrit inscriptions
Inscriptions, Proto-Sinaitic
    [PJ4160]
    UF Proto-Sinaitic inscriptions
    BT Inscriptions, Semitic
Inscriptions, Punic
    BT Inscriptions, Phoenician
Inscriptions, Runic *(May Subd Geog)*
    UF Runic inscriptions
    RT Inscriptions, Norse
        Runes
    NT Rök stone inscription
— **Minnesota**
    NT Kensington Rune Stone
— **Norway**
    NT Tune Rune Stone
Inscriptions, Russian (Old)
    (May Subd Geog)
    UF Inscriptions, Old Russian
        Old Russian inscriptions
        Russian inscriptions (Old)
Inscriptions, Sabaean
    UF Hamyaritic inscriptions
        Himyaritic inscriptions
        Inscriptions, Himyaritic
        Sabaean inscriptions
Inscriptions, Safaitic
    UF Safaitic inscriptions
    BT Inscriptions, Arabic
Inscriptions, Sanskrit *(May Subd Geog)*
    UF Sanskrit inscriptions
Inscriptions, Semitic *(May Subd Geog)*
    UF Semitic inscriptions
    BT Semitic philology
    NT Inscriptions, Proto-Sinaitic
Inscriptions, Slavic *(May Subd Geog)*
    UF Slavic inscriptions
Inscriptions, South Arabic
    (May Subd Geog)
    UF South Arabic inscriptions
Inscriptions, Stoichedon
    USE Stoichedon inscriptions
Inscriptions, Sundanese *(May Subd Geog)*
    UF Sundanese inscriptions
Inscriptions, Tamil *(May Subd Geog)*
    UF Tamil inscriptions
Inscriptions, Telugu *(May Subd Geog)*
    UF Telugu inscriptions
Inscriptions, Thamudic
    UF Thamudic inscriptions
    BT Inscriptions, Arabic
Inscriptions, Turkic (Old)
    USE Inscriptions, Old Turkic
Inscriptions, Umbrian
    USE Inscriptions, Oscan-Umbrian
Inscriptions, Venetic *(May Subd Geog)*
    [CN473]
    UF Venetic inscriptions
Inscriptions (Philately)
    USE Overprints and surcharges (Philately)
Inscriptions on bark
    USE Bark inscriptions

Inscriptions on bells
    USE Bells—Inscriptions
Inscriptions on Buddhist sculpture
    USE Sculpture, Buddhist—Inscriptions
Inscriptions on Chinese calligraphy
    USE Calligraphy, Chinese—Inscriptions
Inscriptions on Chinese paintings
    USE Painting, Chinese—Inscriptions
Inscriptions on dōtaku
    USE Dōtaku—Inscriptions
Inscriptions on Italian mural painting
    USE Mural painting and decoration, Italian
          —Inscriptions
Inscriptions on Italian panel painting
    USE Panel painting, Italian—Inscriptions
Inscriptions on Japanese paintings
    USE Painting, Japanese—Inscriptions
Inscriptions on Japanese sculpture
    USE Sculpture, Japanese—Inscriptions
Inscriptions on Korean paintings
    USE Painting, Korean—Inscriptions
Inscriptions on lacquer and lacquering
    USE Lacquer and lacquering—Inscriptions
Inscriptions on Renaissance mural painting
    USE Mural painting and decoration,
        Renaissance—Inscriptions
Inscriptions on Renaissance panel painting
    USE Panel painting, Renaissance—
        Inscriptions
Insect antifeedants *(May Subd Geog)*
    UF Anti-feeding compounds, Insect
        Anti-feeding substances, Insect
        Antifeedants, Insect
        Antifeeding compounds, Insect
        Antifeeding substances, Insect
        Insect antifeeding compounds
        Insect antifeeding substances
    BT Insecticides
    RT Insect baits and repellents
Insect antifeeding compounds
    USE Insect antifeedants
Insect antifeeding substances
    USE Insect antifeedants
Insect attractants
    USE Insect baits and repellents
Insect baits and repellents
    [SB951]
    UF Insect attractants
        Insect repellents
        Insects—Baits
        Insects—Repellents
    BT Insect pests—Control
        Insecticides
        Repellents
    RT Insect antifeedants
    NT Insect sex attractants
Insect behavior
    USE Insects—Behavior
Insect cages
    UF Insects—Cages
    BT Entomology—Research
        Insect traps
Insect calls
    USE Insect sounds
Insect chemosterilization
    UF Chemical sterilization of insects
        Chemosterilization of insects
    BT Agricultural chemistry
        Insect sterilization
Insect control
    USE Insect pests—Control
Insect culture
    USE Insect rearing
Insect-eating insects
    USE Entomophagous insects
Insect epizootiology
    USE Insects—Diseases—Epidemiology
Insect flight
    USE Insects—Flight
Insect flowers, Dalmatian
    USE Pyrethrum

Pyrethrum (Insecticide)
Insect forms in art and archaeology
  UF Decoration and ornament—Insect
       forms
  BT Archaeology
  NT Scarabs
Insect galls
  USE Galls (Botany)
Insect hormones
  BT Hormones
  RT Natural pesticides
  NT Ecdysone
      Juvenile hormones
      Pheromones
Insect metamorphosis
  USE Insects—Metamorphosis
Insect pests *(May Subd Geog)*
  [SB818-SB945 (Agriculture)]
  UF Destructive insects
      Economic entomology
      Entomology, Economic
      Injurious insects
      Insects, Injurious and beneficial
  BT Arthropod pests
      Insects
      Zoology, Economic
  RT Galls (Botany)
      Veterinary entomology
  SA *individual insects and groups of*
      insects, e.g. Desert locust;
      Mosquitoes
  NT Insects as carriers of disease
  — **Biological control** *(May Subd Geog)*
    [SB932]
    UF Biological control of insects
       Insects—Biological control
    BT Insect pests—Control
    SA *subdivision* Biological control
       under individual and groups of
       insect pests, e.g. Oriental fruit
       fly—Biological control
    NT Insect sterilization
       Microbial insecticides
  — **Control** *(May Subd Geog)*
    [SB931]
    UF Insect control
       Insects—Control
       Insects—Extermination
    BT Pests—Control
    RT Insecticides
    SA *subdivision* Control *under*
       individual and groups of insect
       pests, e.g. Oriental fruit fly—
       Control
    NT Insect baits and repellents
       Insect pests—Biological control
  — — **Law and legislation**
       (May Subd Geog)
  — **Law and legislation** *(May Subd Geog)*
Insect-plant relationships *(May Subd Geog)*
  UF Plant-insect relationships
  BT Insects
  RT Plant parasites
  NT Fertilization of plants by insects
      Insects—Food
      Insects—Host plants
      Insects as carriers of plant disease
Insect pollenizers
  USE Pollination by insects
Insect populations *(May Subd Geog)*
  UF Populations, Insect
  BT Arthropod populations
      Insect societies
      Insects—Geographical distribution
      Invertebrate populations
Insect powder, Dalmatian
  USE Pyrethrum (Insecticide)
Insect-proof packaging
  USE Insect-resistant packaging
Insect radiosterilization *(May Subd Geog)*
  [SB933.6]

  UF Radiation sterilization of insects
      Radiosterilization of insects
  BT Insect sterilization
      Insects—Effect of radiation on
Insect rearing *(May Subd Geog)*
  [SF518]
  UF Entomology—Cultures and culture
      media
      Insect culture
      Insects—Cultures and culture media
      Insects—Rearing
      Mass rearing of insects
      Rearing of insects
  BT Animal culture
  NT Butterfly farming
      Insects—Feeding and feeds
      Moths—Cultures and culture media
Insect repellents
  USE Insect baits and repellents
Insect-resistant packaging
  [TS198.I58]
  UF Insect-proof packaging
  BT Packaging
Insect sex attractants
  [SB933.5]
  UF Insects—Sex attractants
      Sex attractants, Insect
  BT Insect baits and repellents
      Pheromones
  — **Controlled release**
    [SB933.5]
    BT Controlled release preparations
Insect societies *(May Subd Geog)*
  UF Insects, Social
      Social insects
  BT Animal behavior
      Animal societies
      Insects
      Insects—Behavior
  NT Ants
      Bees
      Insect populations
      Termites
      Wasps
Insect song
  USE Insect sounds
Insect sounds
  UF Insect calls
      Insect song
  BT Animal sounds
      Insects
      Nature sounds
  RT Sound production by insects
Insect sterilization
  [SB933.6]
  UF Sterile-male technique (Insect control)
      Sterilization of insects
  BT Agricultural chemistry
      Insect pests—Biological control
  NT Insect chemosterilization
      Insect radiosterilization
Insect traps
  [SB959]
  UF Light traps
  BT Animal traps
  NT Insect cages
Insect venom
  USE Insects—Venom
Insect viruses *(May Subd Geog)*
  [QR327 (Virology)]
  [SB942 (Insect control)]
  BT Viruses
  RT Viral insecticides
      Virus diseases of insects
  NT Baculoviruses
      Cytoplasmic polyhedrosis virus
Insecticidal plants
  USE Plants, Insecticidal
Insecticide research
  USE Insecticides—Research

Insecticide resistance *(May Subd Geog)*
  [SB951.5]
  UF Insects—Insecticide resistance
      Insects—Resistance to insecticides
      Resistance to insecticides
  BT Pesticide resistance
  SA *subdivision* Insecticide resistance *under*
      individual insects and groups of
      insects, e.g. Housefly—Insecticide
      resistance; Aphididae—Insecticide
      resistance
Insecticides *(May Subd Geog)*
  [SB951]
  BT Agricultural chemicals
      Pesticides
      Trees—Diseases and pests
      Wood preservatives
  RT Insect pests—Control
  SA *particular insecticides and groups of*
      insecticides, e.g. Pyrethrum
      (Insecticide); Sheep-dip
  NT Benzoylphenyl ureas
      Carbaryl
      DDT (Insecticide)
      Endosulfan
      Ethylene oxide
      Heptachlor
      Insect antifeedants
      Insect baits and repellents
      Kelevan
      Microbial insecticides
      Mothproofing
      Plants, Effect of insecticides on
      Plants, Insecticidal
      Pyrethroids
      Systemic insecticides
      Temephos
  — **Biodegradation**
    UF Insecticides—Biodeterioration
  — Biodeterioration
    USE Insecticides—Biodegradation
  — Law and legislation
    USE Pesticides—Law and legislation
  — **Research**
    UF Insecticide research
  — **Toxicology**
    UF Wildlife, Effect of insecticides on
Insecticides, Microbial
  USE Microbial insecticides
Insecticides, Systemic
  USE Systemic insecticides
Insecticides, Viral
  USE Viral insecticides
Insectivora *(May Subd Geog)*
  [QL737.I5]
  BT Mammals
  NT Erinaceidae
      Moles (Animals)
      Shrews
      Tenrecs
Insectivora, Fossil
  [QE882.I5]
  NT Adapisoricidae
      Deltatheridia
      Geolabididae
      Hedgehogs, Fossil
      Leptictidae
      Nyctitheriidae, Fossil
      Taeniodonta
Insectivorous plants *(May Subd Geog)*
  [QK917 (Botany)]
  [SB432.7 (Culture)]
  UF Carnivorous plants
  BT Botany
      Botany—Ecology
      Plants
      Plants—Irritability and movements
  RT Sarraceniales
  NT Pitcher plants
Insects *(May Subd Geog)*
  [GR750 (Folk-lore)]

Insects *(Continued)*
  ₍QL461-QL599₎
  UF Hexapoda
      Pterygota
  BT Arthropoda
      Invertebrates
  RT Entomology
  SA Ants, Butterflies, Moths, Wasps, *and*
        similar headings
  NT Anoplura
      Ants
      Aphidophagous insects
      Apterygota
      Beetles
      Beneficial insects
      Butterflies
      Caddis-flies
      Cockroaches
      Collembola
      Dermaptera
      Diplura
      Diptera
      Electric organs in insects
      Embioptera
      Entomophagous insects
      Fertilization of plants by insects
      Fleas
      Forest insects
      Hemiptera
      Hymenoptera
      Insect pests
      Insect-plant relationships
      Insect societies
      Insect sounds
      Lac-insects
      Lepidoptera
      Lice
      Mallophaga
      Mayflies
      Mecoptera
      Moths
      Neuroptera
      Odonata
      Orthoptera
      Protura
      Psocoptera
      Scale-insects
      Stoneflies
      Strepsiptera
      Thrips
      Thysanura
      Wasps
— **Anatomy**
    ₍QL494₎
    SA *subdivision* Insects *under* Digestive
          organs, Nervous system, Sense-
          organs
    NT Aedeagus
        Furca
        Head capsule
        Prothorax
        Spermatheca
— Baits
    USE Insect baits and repellents
— **Behavior**
    UF Insect behavior
    SA *subdivision* Behavior *under*
          particular insects, e.g. Ants—
          Behavior
    NT Insect societies
        Parasitic insects
        Pheromones
— Biological control
    USE Insect pests—Biological control
— Cages
    USE Insect cages
— Collected works
    USE Entomology—Collected works
— **Collection and preservation**
    ₍QL465₎
— Congresses

    USE Entomology—Congresses
— Control
    USE Insect pests—Control
— Cultures and culture media
    USE Insect rearing
— **Cytology**
— **Development**
    ₍QL494.5₎
    NT Cocoons
        Ecdysis
        Insects—Larvae
        Insects—Metamorphosis
        Molting
        Pupae
— **Diseases** *(May Subd Geog)*
    NT Virus diseases of insects
— — **Epidemiology**
      UF Epizootiology, Insect
          Insect epizootiology
— **Dispersal**
    UF Dispersal of insects
— — **Climatic factors**
— **Effect of radiation on**
    UF Insects, Effect of radiation on
    NT Insect radiosterilization
— **Eggs**
— **Evolution**
— Extermination
    USE Insect pests—Control
— **Feeding and feeds**
    BT Insect rearing
— **Flight**
    ₍QL496.7₎
    UF Insect flight
    BT Animal flight
— — **Climatic factors**
— **Food**
    BT Insect-plant relationships
— **Geographical distribution**
    ₍QL469-491₎
    NT Insect populations
— **Host plants**
    ₍SB818-SB935 (Economic
      entomology)₎
    BT Host plants
        Insect-plant relationships
— Insecticide resistance
    USE Insecticide resistance
— Laboratory manuals
    USE Entomology—Laboratory
          manuals
— **Larvae**
    UF Larvae—Insects
    BT Insects—Development
    NT Caterpillars
        Imaginal disks
        Nymphs (Insects)
— **Metamorphosis**
    ₍QL494.5₎
    UF Insect metamorphosis
    BT Insects—Development
        Metamorphosis
    NT Diapause
        Imaginal disks
— **Microbiology**
— **Migration**
    ₍QL496₎
    UF Migration of insects
— — **Climatic factors**
      BT Bioclimatology
          Phenology
— **Morphology**
— **Nomenclature**
    ₍QL353-4₎
— **Nomenclature (Popular)**
    ₍QL355₎
— Periodicals
    USE Entomology—Periodicals
— **Physiology**
    ₍QL495₎
    NT Dormancy in insects

      Pheromones
— Rearing
    USE Insect rearing
— Repellents
    USE Insect baits and repellents
— **Reproduction**
    NT Aedeagus
        Spermatheca
— Resistance to insecticides
    USE Insecticide resistance
— Sex attractants
    USE Insect sex attractants
— Societies, etc.
    USE Entomology—Societies, etc.
— Study and teaching
    USE Entomology—Study and teaching
— **Symbolic aspects**
    BT Symbolism
— **Venom**
    UF Insect venom
Insects, Aphidophagous
  USE Aphidophagous insects
Insects, Aquatic *(May Subd Geog)*
  ₍QL496₎
  UF Aquatic insects
      Water flies
  BT Aquatic animals
      Aquatic invertebrates
  NT Corixidae
      Insects, Marine
Insects, Beneficial
  USE Beneficial insects
Insects, Effect of radiation on
  USE Insects—Effect of radiation on
Insects, Fossil
  ₍QE831-2₎
  NT Beetles, Fossil
      Butterflies, Fossil
      Heteroptera, Fossil
      Homoptera, Fossil
      Hymenoptera, Fossil
      Orthoptera, Fossil
      Stoneflies, Fossil
      Thrips, Fossil
Insects, Injurious and beneficial
  USE Beneficial insects
      Insect pests
Insects, Insect-eating
  USE Entomophagous insects
Insects, Marine *(May Subd Geog)*
  ₍QL461-497₎
  UF Marine insects
  BT Insects, Aquatic
      Marine fauna
Insects, Parasitic
  USE Parasitic insects
Insects, Social
  USE Insect societies
Insects, Sound production by
  USE Sound production by insects
Insects, Wingless
  USE Apterygota
Insects and plant diseases
  USE Insects as carriers of plant disease
Insects as carriers of disease
  ₍RA639-641₎
  UF Medical entomology
  BT Arthropod vectors
      Insect pests
  NT Cockroaches as carriers of disease
      Fleas as carriers of disease
      Flies as carriers of disease
      Insects as carriers of plant disease
      Lice as carriers of disease
      Mosquitoes as carriers of disease
      Veterinary entomology
Insects as carriers of plant disease
  (May Subd Geog)
  ₍SB931₎
  UF Insects and plant diseases

BT Insect-plant relationships
    Insects as carriers of disease
    Invertebrates as carriers of plant
      disease
    Plant diseases
NT Aphididae as carriers of disease
Insects as food
BT Beneficial insects
    Food
NT Cookery (Insects)
Insects as pets
   [SF459.I5]
Insects in art
Insecurity (Psychology)
USE Security (Psychology)
Insel Amrum (Germany)
USE Amrum Island (Germany)
Insel Fehmarn (Germany)
USE Fehmarn (Germany)
Insel Föhr (Germany)
USE Föhr (Germany)
Insel Ponape (Micronesia)
USE Ponape Island (Micronesia)
Insel Rügen (Germany)
USE Rügen Island (Germany)
Insel Usedom (Germany)
USE Usedom Island (Germany)
Insel Wollin (Poland)
USE Wolin Island (Poland)
Inselbergs *(May Subd Geog)*
BT Mountains
NT Bornhardts (Geomorphology)
Insemination, Artificial
USE Artificial insemination
Insensibility
USE Loss of consciousness
Insensibility to pleasure
USE Anhedonia
Insertion elements, DNA
   [QH462.I48]
UF Deoxyribonucleic acid insertion
     elements
    DNA insertion elements
    Insertion sequence elements
    Transposable elements
BT Molecular genetics
    Recombinant DNA
    Translocation (Genetics)
NT Episomes
    Tn elements
Insertion sequence elements
USE Insertion elements, DNA
Inserts, Concrete
USE Concrete inserts
Inside Passage
UF Inland Passage
BT Intracoastal waterways—Alaska
    Intracoastal waterways—British
      Columbia
    Intracoastal waterways—Washington
      (State)
Insider trading in securities
(May Subd Geog)
BT Directors of corporations
    Securities
— **Law and legislation** *(May Subd Geog)*
BT Securities
Insight
BT Problem solving
    Thought and thinking
RT Intuition
Insight (Buddhism)
USE Vipaśyanā (Buddhism)
Insight (Psychotherapy)
USE Insight in psychotherapy
Insight in psychotherapy
UF Insight (Psychotherapy)
BT Psychoanalysis
    Psychotherapy
Insignia *(May Subd Geog)*
   [CR4480 (Royalty)]

[HS159-HS160 (Secret societies)]
[NK7400-NK7419 (Jeweled)]
[UC530-UC535 (Military)]
[VC345 (Naval)]
   Here are entered works on the paraphernalia of
offices, institutions, orders, etc. Works on the em-
blems and symbols of royalty, including coronation
regalia, are entered under Regalia (Insignia).
UF Badges of honor
    Jewels
BT Emblems
    Heraldry
RT Decorations of honor
    Devices
    Emblems, National
SA *subdivision* Insignia *under names of*
    individual corporate bodies and
    under types of organizations, e.g.
    Harvard University—Insignia;
    Universities and colleges—Insignia
NT American Revolution Bicentennial,
     1776-1976—Insignia
    Armed Forces—Insignia
    Armies—Insignia
    Badges
    Baseball insignia
    Buttons
    Campaign insignia
    Fishing boats—Flags, insignia, etc.
    Ju-i (Scepters)
    Maces, Ceremonial
    Military religious orders—Insignia
    Orders of knighthood and chivalry—
     Insignia
    Patriotic societies—Insignia
    Regalia (Insignia)
    Sashes (Costume)
    Schools—Insignia
    Steamboat lines—Flags, insignia, etc.
Insignia, Municipal
USE Municipal insignia
Insignia, Royal
USE Regalia (Insignia)
Insinuation (Civil law) *(May Subd Geog)*
BT Formalities (Law)
    Gifts
    Wills
Insolation
USE Solar radiation
Insolubilia (Logic)
   [BC21.I64]
UF Insolubles (Logic)
BT Liar paradox
    Logic, Medieval
Insolubilized proteins
USE Immobilized proteins
Insoluble enzymes
USE Immobilized enzymes
Insolubles (Logic)
USE Insolubilia (Logic)
Insolvency
USE Bankruptcy
Insomnia
   [RC548]
UF Abnormal wakefulness
    Sleeplessness
BT Sleep deprivation
    Sleep disorders
    Wakefulness
INSPEC (Information retrieval system)
BT Information storage and retrieval
     systems—Electronics
    Information storage and retrieval
     systems—Engineering
    Information storage and retrieval
     systems—Physics
INSPEC classification
USE Classification, INSPEC

Inspection
USE *subdivision* Inspection *under topical*
    headings and names of individual
    military services, e.g. Automobiles—
    Inspection; United States. Army—
    Inspection; *and phrase headings for*
    particular types of inspection
Inspection, Engineering
USE Engineering inspection
Inspection by sampling
USE Sampling
Inspection for disarmament
USE Disarmament—Inspection
Inspection of buildings
USE Building inspection
Inspection of disarmament
USE Disarmament—Inspection
Inspection of factories
USE Factory inspection
Inspection of fish
USE Fish inspection
Inspection of food
USE Food adulteration and inspection
Inspection of meat
USE Meat inspection
Inspection of mines
USE Mine inspection
Inspection of oil
USE Oil inspection
Inspection of schools
USE School management and organization
Inspection of steam-boilers
USE Steam-boiler inspection
Inspectors, Electric wiring
USE Electric wiring inspectors
Inspectors general, Military
USE Military inspectors general
Inspiration
   [BF410 (Psychology)]
   [BT125 (Theology)]
BT Creative ability
NT Creation (Literary, artistic, etc.)
    Revelation
— **Religious aspects**
BT Supernatural
NT Bible—Inspiration
    Sacred books—Inspiration
— — **Buddhism, [Christianity, etc.]**
— — **Christianity**
BT Holy Spirit
Inspirationists
   [HX656.A4]
Instabilities, Magnetohydrodynamic
USE Magnetohydrodynamic instabilities
Instabilities, Trapped-particle
USE Trapped-particle instabilities
Instabilities, Valence
USE Valence fluctuations
Instability, Spinal
USE Spine—Instability
Instability lines (Meteorology)
USE Squall lines
Instability of joints
USE Joints—Hypermobility
Installation (Clergy)
   [BV4290]
   Here are entered works dealing with the installa-
tion of a clergyman as the pastor of a church. Works
dealing with the ordination of a clergyman (i.e. his
first entrance into the clerical office) are entered
under the heading Ordination. Whenever ordination
and installation are simultaneous, preference is given
to the heading Ordination.
UF Clergy—Installation
BT Initiation rites—Religious aspects—
     Christianity
RT Installation sermons
NT Catholic Church—Clergy—Installation
    Installation (Rabbis)
    Priests, Zen—Installation
— **Anniversary sermons**
   [BV4290]

Installation (Rabbis)
  UF Rabbis—Installation
  BT Initiation rites—Religious aspects—
         Judaism
      Installation (Clergy)
  — **Anniversary sermons**
Installation of carpets
  USE Carpet laying
Installation of electric apparatus and appliances
  USE Electric apparatus and appliances—
         Installation
Installation of industrial electric equipment
  USE Factories—Electric equipment—
         Installation
Installation of industrial equipment
  ₍TS191.3₎
  UF Industrial installation
      Installing of industrial equipment
  BT Industrial equipment
      Plant engineering
  SA subdivision Erecting work under
         special machines or equipment, e.g.
         Gas-turbines—Erecting work;
         Electronic industries—Equipment
         and supplies—Erecting work
  NT Electric machinery—Erecting work
      Gas-turbines—Erecting work
Installation of telegraph equipment
  USE Telegraph—Equipment and supplies—
         Installation
Installation sermons
  ₍BV4290₎
  BT Sermons
  RT Installation (Clergy)
Installation service (Church officers)
  ₍BV199.I5₎
  BT Church officers
      Liturgies
      Worship programs
Installations (Art) (May Subd Geog)
  BT Art, Modern—20th century
      Environment (Art)
  — **United States**
      NT Conwill, Houston, 1947-
             Passion of Saint Matthew
           Yarde, Richard, 1939-   Savoy
Installing of industrial equipment
  USE Installation of industrial equipment
Installment . . .
  USE headings beginning with the word
         Instalment
Instalment contracts (May Subd Geog)
      Here are entered works on contracts where, by the
    terms of the contract, a partial delivery is contemplat-
    ed, or where a thing is delivered periodically or con-
    tinuously. Works on the law of sale of consumer
    goods purchased on the instalment plan are entered
    under Sales, Conditional.
  UF Instalment sales
  BT Contracts
Instalment credit companies
  USE Commercial finance companies
      Instalment plan
Instalment land contracts (May Subd Geog)
  UF Land contracts
  BT Sales, Conditional
      Vendors and purchasers
Instalment plan (May Subd Geog)
  ₍HF5681.I5 (Accounting)₎
  ₍HG3755.5 (Consumer credit)₎
  UF Accounts receivable finance companies
      Commercial credit companies
      Credit companies
      Finance companies, Commercial
      Hire-purchase plan
      Instalment credit companies
      Sales-finance companies
  BT Consumer credit
      Purchasing
  RT Layaway plan
  NT Commercial finance companies

      Industrial loan associations
      Insurance, Group creditors
  — Law and legislation
      USE Sales, Conditional
Instalment sales
  USE Instalment contracts
      Sales, Conditional
Instamatic camera
  ₍TR263.I₎
  UF Pocket instamatic camera
  BT Cameras
      Kodak camera
Instant camera, Kodak
  USE Kodak instant camera
Instant coffee
  USE Coffee, Instant
Instant photography
  ₍TR269₎
      Here are entered works on photography using a
    photographic system which yields a finished picture
    immediately after the exposure.
  UF Photography, Instant
  NT Kodak instant camera
      Polaroid Land camera
  — **Films**
      UF Films, Instant photography
Instant printing
  USE Printing, Instant
Instant rice
  USE Rice, Quick-cooking
Instant sweet potatoes
  USE Sweet potato flakes
Instant tea
  USE Soluble tea
Instantaneous photography
  USE Photography, Instantaneous
Instantaneous radiography
  USE Flash radiography
Instantons
  BT Field theory (Physics)
      Gauge fields (Physics)
      Renormalization (Physics)
      Wave equation
Instinct
  ₍BF685 (Psychology)₎
  ₍QL781 (Zoology)₎
  UF Animal instinct
      Intelligence of animals
  BT Habit
      Psychology
  RT Animal intelligence
      Psychology, Comparative
  NT Death instinct
      Herding behavior in animals
      Impulse
      Orientation (Physiology)
      Orientation (Psychology)
      Self-preservation
      Sublimation
Instinct (Philosophy)
  ₍B824.14₎
  BT Philosophy
Institutes, Farmers'
  USE Farmers' institutes
Institutes, Research
  USE Research institutes
Institutes, Teachers'
  USE Teachers' institutes
Institutes and workshops, Archival
  USE Archival institutes and workshops
Institutes and workshops, Library
  USE Library institutes and workshops
Institution building
  BT Social change
      Social institutions
      Social policy
Institution farms, State-owned
  USE State farms
Institution libraries (May Subd Geog)
  ₍Z675.I6₎

      UF Learned institutions and societies—
             Libraries
           Libraries, Institution
      BT Libraries, Special
      RT Public libraries—Services to
             institutions
      NT Hospital libraries
           Prison libraries
           Reformatory libraries
Institution management
  ₍HV40 (Charities)₎
  ₍TX147 (Home economics)₎
  UF Management, Institution
  BT Management
  SA subdivision Accounting under types of
         institutions, e.g. Hospitals—
         Accounting
  NT Church management
Institutional care (May Subd Geog)
  UF Benevolent institutions
      Care, Institutional
      Charitable institutions
      Homes (Institutions)
  BT Charities
      Public institutions
      Public welfare
  RT Deinstitutionalization
  SA subdivision Institutional care under
         classes of persons and ethnic groups
  NT Almshouses
      Group homes
      Hospital care
      Inmates of institutions
      Nursing home care
  — **Law and legislation** (May Subd Geog)
Institutional church
  USE Church work
Institutional economics
  ₍HB99.5₎
  BT Economics
  NT Chicago school of economics
Institutional investments (May Subd Geog)
  BT Investments
  NT Endowments—Program-related
         investments
  — **Law and legislation** (May Subd Geog)
Institutional linguistics
  USE Language policy
Institutional market (May Subd Geog)
  BT Marketing
Institutional missions (May Subd Geog)
  ₍BV2000-3705₎
  UF Missions, Institutional
  BT Church work
      City missions
      Evangelistic work
      Missions, Home
Institutional research (Education)
  USE Education, Higher—Research
Institutionalism (Religion)
  BT Polity (Religion)
Institutionalized persons
  USE Inmates of institutions
Institutions, Catholic
  USE Catholic institutions
Institutions, Charitable and philanthropic
  USE Charities
Institutions, Ecclesiastical
  USE Religious and ecclesiastical institutions
Institutions, Inmates of
  USE Inmates of institutions
Institutions, International
  USE special international congresses,
         societies, etc.
      International agencies
      International cooperation
Institutions, Open-air
  USE Open-air institutions
Institutions, Public
  USE Public institutions

1862

Institutions, Public library services to
USE Public libraries—Services to
institutions
Institutions, Religious
USE Religious and ecclesiastical institutions
Institutions, Social
USE Social institutions
Institutions, State
USE Public institutions
Institutions, associations, etc.
USE Associations, institutions, etc.
Institutions, associations, etc., Foreign
USE Associations, institutions, etc., Foreign
Instruction
USE subdivision Instruction and study
under Music and under names of
musical instruments
Education
Teaching
Instruction, Camps of
USE Military training camps
Instruction Set Processors (Computer program
language)
USE ISP (Computer program language)
Instructional change
USE Curriculum change
Instructional improvement programs
USE School improvement programs
Instructional materials
USE Teaching—Aids and devices
Instructional materials centers
(May Subd Geog)
UF Audio-visual materials centers
Curriculum laboratories
Educational media centers
Laboratories, Curriculum
Learning resource centers
Media centers (Education)
School media centers
BT Schools
RT Audio-visual library service
School libraries
NT Instructional materials personnel
Selection of non-book materials
— **Acquisitions**
BT Acquisitions (Libraries)
— **Book selection**
BT Book selection
— **Services to minorities**
BT Minorities
RT Libraries and minorities
— **Services to the handicapped**
RT Libraries and the handicapped
— **User education**
UF User education (Instructional
materials centers)
RT Library orientation
Instructional materials industry
(May Subd Geog)
[HD9999.I57-574]
UF Audio-visual materials industry
Educational materials industry
BT Audio-visual materials
Teaching—Aids and devices
Instructional materials personnel
(May Subd Geog)
UF Audio-visual materials personnel
Audio-visual specialists
Educational media personnel
Media service personnel in education
BT Instructional materials centers
School management and organization
RT Audio-visual education
— Collective bargaining
USE Collective bargaining—
Instructional materials
personnel
Instructional materials programs
USE Media programs (Education)
Instructional objectives
USE Education—Aims and objectives

Instructional supervision
USE School supervision
Instructional systems *(May Subd Geog)*
[LB1028.35]
Here are entered works on comprehensive formal
programs of teaching and learning, comprising
courses of study, teaching methods and personnel,
facilities, equipment, and other supportive services.
UF Learning systems
BT Education
RT Teaching
NT Education—Curricula
Educational technology
School facilities
— **Design**
NT Curriculum planning
Instructional systems analysis
USE Educational evaluation
Instructional technology
USE Educational technology
Instructions to juries *(May Subd Geog)*
UF Prayers and instructions
BT Civil procedure
Criminal procedure
Jury
Trial practice
NT Special issues
Verdicts
Instructive games
USE Educational games
Instructive toys
USE Educational toys
Instructors
USE College teachers
Instructors, Genealogical
USE Genealogy teachers
Instrument approach systems
USE Instrument landing systems
Instrument display systems in automobiles
USE Automobiles—Instruments—Display
systems
Instrument flight
USE Instrument flying
Instrument flying
[TL711.B6]
UF Blind flying
Instrument flight
BT Aeronautical instruments
Airplanes—Piloting
NT Instrument landing systems
Link trainers
Microwave landing systems
Night flying
Omnirange system
Runway localizing beacons
Tacan
Instrument industry *(May Subd Geog)*
BT Engineering instruments
RT Scientific apparatus and instruments
SA names of categories of instruments,
e.g. Chemical apparatus; Optical
instruments
NT Optical industry
Wages—Instrument industry
— Automation
USE Instrument manufacture—
Automation
— **Employees** *(May Subd Geog)*
UF Instrument manufacture—
Employees
Instrument landing systems
[TL696.L33]
Here are entered general works on systems of
landing aeroplanes by instruments when visibility is
low or practically nonexistent, and also works on the
specific system known as ILS (instrument landing
system) Works on other individual systems are en-
tered under specific headings, e.g. Ground controlled
approach.
UF Blind landing
ILS
Instrument approach systems

BT Airplanes—Landing
Electronics in aeronautics
Instrument flying
Landing aids (Aeronautics)
NT Distance measuring equipment
(Aircraft to ground station)
Glide path systems
Ground controlled approach
Runway localizing beacons
Surveillance radar
— **Charts, diagrams, etc.**
BT Aeronautical charts
Instrument-making
USE Instrument manufacture
Instrument manufacture *(May Subd Geog)*
[TS500]
UF Instrument-making
Physical instruments—Trade and
manufacture
BT Engineering instruments
Measuring instruments
Scientific apparatus and instruments
NT Lens mounts
— **Automation**
UF Instrument industry—Automation
— Employees
USE Instrument industry—Employees
Instrument panel padding in automobiles
USE Automobiles—Instrument panels—
Padding
Instrument platforms, Floating
USE Oceanographic buoys
Instrument transformers, Electric
USE Electric instrument transformers
Instrumental analysis
[QD73]
BT Chemistry, Analytic
Chemistry, Physical and theoretical
Physical instruments
Physical measurements
NT Chemical detectors
Instrumental behavior
USE Operant behavior
Instrumental conditioning
USE Operant conditioning
Instrumental ensembles
[M900-M949]
[M960-M985]
Here are entered compositions for ten or more
solo instruments belonging to various families.
Compositions for ten or more like solo instru-
ments are entered under Recorder ensembles, Viol
ensembles, and similar headings.
Compositions for ten or more different solo in-
struments of the same family are entered as follows:
bowed stringed instruments under String ensembles;
wind instruments under Wind ensembles; brass instruments under Brass ensembles; woodwind instruments under Woodwind ensembles; plectral instruments under Plectral ensembles; and percussion instruments under Percussion ensembles.
The qualifier Instrumental ensemble stands for
two or more different solo instruments when used in
conjunction with specific solo instrument(s) or voi-
ce(s), in headings for choruses, and in other headings
as specified, e.g. Monologues with music.
UF Brass choir music
Ensembles (Music)
BT Organ with instrumental ensemble
SA Concertos ([Solo instrument(s)] with
instrumental ensemble); [Solo
instrument(s)] with instrumental
ensemble; Suites, Variations,
Waltzes, and similar headings with
specification of instruments which
include the specification
Instrumental ensemble
NT Canons, fugues, etc. (Instrumental
ensemble)
Chorale preludes (Instrumental
ensemble)
Overtures (Instrumental ensemble)
Polkas (Instrumental ensemble)

Instrumental ensembles *(Continued)*
  Polonaises (Instrumental ensemble)
  Suites (Instrumental ensemble)
  Suites (Pianos (2) with instrumental
      ensemble)
  Symphonies (Instrumental ensemble)
  Variations (Instrumental ensemble)
  Violin and piano with instrumental
      ensemble
  Vocal ensembles with instrumental
      ensemble
Instrumental ensembles, Arranged
Instrumental masses
  USE Organ masses
Instrumental music *(May Subd Geog)*
  [M5-1459]
  UF Music, Instrumental
  BT Music
  SA Piano music, Violoncello and
      harpsichord music, *and similar*
      headings
  NT Accordion ensembles
      Band music
      Chamber music
      Chamber-orchestra music
      Concertina ensembles
      Dance music
      Dance-orchestra music
      Hunting music
      Jazz nonets
      Jazz quartets
      Jazz quintets
      Jazz septets
      Jazz sextets
      Jazz trios
      Military music
      Orchestral music
      Percussion music
      Piano music
      Plectral ensembles
      Popular instrumental music
      Salon-orchestra music
      Solo instrument music
      String instrument music
      String-orchestra music
      Violoncello and harpsichord music
— Bibliography
— — Graded lists
      [ML132.I5]
      UF Instrumental music—Graded
          lists
— Graded lists
      USE Instrumental music—Bibliography
          —Graded lists
— History and criticism
      [ML460-547]
      RT Musical instruments
      SA *various forms of instrumental*
          music, e.g. Sonata, Symphony
      NT Bands (Music)
          Orchestra
— Instruction and study
      [MT170]
      BT Music—Instruction and study
      SA *subdivision* Instruction and study
          under names of musical
          instruments, e.g. Piano—
          Instruction and study
Instrumental settings
  USE *subdivision* Instrumental settings *under*
      headings for vocal music, e.g. Folk-
      songs—Instrumental settings;
      Operas—Instrumental settings;
      Spirituals (Songs)—Instrumental
      settings
Instrumental variables (Statistics)
  UF Variables, Instrumental (Statistics)
  BT Econometrics
      Estimation theory
      Variables (Mathematics)

  RT Correlation (Statistics)
      Error analysis (Mathematics)
Instrumentalism (Philosophy)
  BT Philosophy
      Pragmatism
Instrumentalisten
  USE Stadtpfeifer
Instrumentation and orchestration
  [ML455 (History)]
  [MT70 (Instruction)]
  UF Orchestration
  BT Chamber orchestra
      Composition (Music)
      Music
      Music—Instruction and study
      Music—Theory
      Orchestra
  RT Arrangement (Music)
      Musical instruments
Instrumentation and orchestration (Band)
  [ML455]
  [MT73]
  BT Bands (Music)
      Military music—History and criticism
      Wind instruments
  NT Instrumentation and orchestration
      (Brass band)
**Instrumentation and orchestration (Brass
band)**
  [ML455 (History and criticism)]
  [MT73 (Instruction and study)]
  BT Brass bands
      Brass instruments
      Instrumentation and orchestration
      (Band)
**Instrumentation and orchestration (Dance
orchestra)**
  [MT86]
  BT Dance music—History and criticism
      Dance orchestras
      Jazz music
Instrumentmen, Naval
  USE United States.   Navy—Instrumentmen
Instruments, Acoustic impedance
  USE Acoustic impedance—Instruments
Instruments, Aeronautical
  USE Aeronautical instruments
Instruments, Agricultural
  USE Agricultural instruments
Instruments, Astronautical
  USE Astronautical instruments
Instruments, Astronomical
  USE Astronomical instruments
Instruments, Atomic absorption spectroscopy
  USE Atomic absorption spectroscopy—
      Instruments
Instruments, Audiology
  USE Audiology—Instruments
Instruments, Automobile
  USE Automobiles—Instruments
Instruments, Ballistic
  USE Ballistic instruments
Instruments, Computerized
  USE Computerized instruments
Instruments, Dental
  USE Dental instruments and apparatus
Instruments, Drawing
  USE Drawing instruments
Instruments, Earth science
  USE Earth science instruments
Instruments, Electric
  USE Electric apparatus and appliances
Instruments, Electronic
  USE Electronic instruments
Instruments, Engineering
  USE Engineering instruments
Instruments, Engineering geology
  USE Engineering geology—Instruments
Instruments, Floating rate
  USE Floating rate notes

Instruments, Geomorphological
  USE Geomorphology—Instruments
Instruments, Geophysical
  USE Geophysical instruments
Instruments, Heat engineering
  USE Heat engineering—Instruments
Instruments, Heat transfer
  USE Heat—Transmission—Instruments
Instruments, Hydrological
  USE Hydrological instruments
Instruments, Internal friction
  USE Internal friction—Instruments
Instruments, Magnetic
  USE Magnetic instruments
Instruments, Marine
  USE Nautical instruments
Instruments, Mathematical
  USE Mathematical instruments
Instruments, Measuring
  USE Measuring instruments
Instruments, Medical
  USE Medical instruments and apparatus
Instruments, Meteorological
  USE Meteorological instruments
Instruments, Military topography
  USE Military topography—Instruments
Instruments, Musical
  USE Musical instruments
Instruments, Nautical
  USE Nautical instruments
Instruments, Negotiable
  USE Negotiable instruments
Instruments, Nuclear power plant
  USE Nuclear power plants—Instruments
Instruments, Oceanographic
  USE Oceanographic instruments
Instruments, Ophthalmological
  USE Eye, Instruments and apparatus for
Instruments, Optical
  USE Optical instruments
Instruments, Percussion
  USE Percussion instruments
Instruments, Physical
  USE Physical instruments
Instruments, Portable computerized
  USE Portable computerized instruments
Instruments, Printing
  USE Printing, Practical—Instruments
Instruments, Radiochemical
  USE Radiochemistry—Instruments
Instruments, Rectifier
  USE Rectifier instruments
Instruments, Scientific
  USE Scientific apparatus and instruments
Instruments, Speech therapy
  USE Speech therapy—Instruments
Instruments, Surface discharge (Electricity)
  USE Surface discharges (Electricity)—
      Instruments
Instruments, Surgical
  USE Surgical instruments and apparatus
Instruments, Surveying
  USE Surveying—Instruments
Instruments, Suturing
  USE Suturing—Instruments
Instruments, Ultrasonic diagnosis
  USE Diagnosis, Ultrasonic—Instruments
Instruments, Underwater acoustics
  USE Underwater acoustics—Instruments
Instruments, Veterinary
  USE Veterinary instruments and apparatus
Instruments for suturing
  USE Suturing—Instruments
Instruments of war
  USE Munitions
Insubordination *(May Subd Geog)*
  [UB789 (Military)]
  [VB880 (Naval)]
  BT Military offenses
      Naval offenses
  NT Mutiny

Insubordination (Canon law)
Insufficiency, Vertebrobasilar
    USE Vertebrobasilar insufficiency
Insulae Pontiae (Italy)
    USE Pontine Islands (Italy)
Insular fauna
    USE Island fauna
Insular flora
    USE Island flora
Insular possessions of the United States
    USE United States—Insular possessions
Insulating board
    USE Fiberboard
Insulating materials
    BT Building materials
    NT Cellular glass
        Electric insulators and insulation
    — Advertising
        USE Advertising—Insulating materials
    — Labeling
    — — Law and legislation
        (May Subd Geog)
Insulating materials industry
    (May Subd Geog)
    [HD9715]
Insulating oils
    USE Electric insulators and insulation—Oils
Insulating paper
    UF Paper, Insulating
    BT Paper
    NT Electric insulators and insulation—
        Paper
Insulating varnish
    USE Electric insulators and insulation
        Electric insulators and insulation—
        Varnish
Insulation (Electric)
    USE Electric insulators and insulation
Insulation (Heat)
    [TH1715]
    UF Heat insulating materials
        Thermal insulation
    BT Heating
    RT Exterior walls—Thermal properties
    NT Aircraft cabins—Insulation
        Cattle—Housing—Insulation
        Clothing, Cold weather
        Cold storage—Insulation
        Doors—Thermal properties
        Dwellings—Insulation
        Mineral wool
        Mobile homes—Insulation
        Oil storage tanks—Insulation
        Petroleum—Pipe lines—Insulation
        Railroads—Cars—Insulation
        Shielding (Heat)
        Ships—Insulation
        Steam-pipe coverings
        Storm doors
        Storm windows
        Windows—Thermal properties
        Wooden-frame houses—Insulation
Insulation (Sound)
    USE Soundproofing
Insulin
    [QP951]
    BT Diabetes
        Hypoglycemic agents
        Pancreas—Secretions
    RT Proinsulin
    NT Hypoglycemia
        Insulin shock
    — Agonists
        UF Agonists, Insulin
    — Analogs
        USE Insulin—Derivatives
    — Antagonists
        UF Antagonists, Insulin
        BT Hormone antagonists
    — Biodegradation
    — Biotechnology

— Congeners
    USE Insulin—Derivatives
— Decontamination
— Derivatives
    UF Analogs of insulin
        Congeners of insulin
        Derivatives of insulin
        Insulin—Analogs
        Insulin—Congeners
— Immunology
— Receptors
    UF Receptors, Insulin
    BT Hormone receptors
— Separation
— Structure
— Synthesis
— — Inhibitors
    UF Inhibitors of insulin synthesis
    BT Chemical inhibitors
— Therapeutic use
— — Evaluation
    USE Insulin—Therapeutic use—
        Testing
— — Testing
    UF Insulin—Therapeutic use—
        Evaluation
Insulin antibodies
    UF Anti-insulin antibodies
        Antibodies against insulin
    BT Immunoglobulins
    RT Insulin resistance
Insulin-dependent diabetes
    USE Diabetes
Insulin hypoglycemia
    USE Insulin shock
Insulin-like growth factor
    USE Somatomedin
Insulin resistance (May Subd Geog)
    [RC662.4]
    UF Insulin tolerance
        Resistant diabetes
    BT Diabetes—Complications and sequelae
        Drug resistance
    RT Insulin antibodies
Insulin shock
    UF Hyperinsulinism
        Insulin hypoglycemia
    BT Diabetes
        Hypoglycemia
        Insulin
        Shock
    NT Insulin shock therapy
Insulin shock therapy
    BT Insulin shock
        Shock therapy
Insulin tolerance
    USE Insulin resistance
Insulinoma
    USE Islands of Langerhans—Tumors
Insuloma
    USE Islands of Langerhans—Tumors
Insults
    USE Invective
Insults, Verbal
    USE Invective
Insurance (May Subd Geog)
    [HG8011-HG9970]
    UF Assurance (Insurance)
        Insurance, Mutual
        Mutual insurance
        Underwriting
    BT Estate planning
        Finance
        Finance, Personal
    SA subdivision Insurance under individual
        industries; and subdivision
        Insurance requirements under
        classes of persons
    NT Banks and banking—Insurance
        business
        Coinsurance

        Collective farms—Insurance
        Corporations, Nonprofit—Insurance
        Discrimination in insurance
        Insurance companies
        Insurance departments
        Insurance policies
        Libraries—Insurance
        Reinsurance
        Revalorization of insurance
        Risk management
        Saving and thrift
        Self-insurance
— Accounting
    [HG8077]
    UF Insurance companies—Accounting
— — Law and legislation
    (May Subd Geog)
— Adjustment of claims
    UF Adjustment of claims
        Claims, Adjustment of
    SA subdivision Adjustment of claims
        under types of insurance
— Agents
    [HG8091-8102]
    UF Insurance—Employees
        Insurance—Salesmanship
        Insurance agents
    BT Insurance companies—Employees
    NT Independent insurance agents
        Insurance—Vocational guidance
— — Directories
    USE Insurance—Directories
— — Legal status, laws, etc.
    NT Insurance—Agents—Malpractice
— — Malpractice (May Subd Geog)
    UF Tort liability of insurance agents
    BT Insurance—Agents—Legal
        status, laws, etc.
        Insurance law
        Malpractice
— — Professional ethics
    (May Subd Geog)
    UF Insurance ethics
    BT Ethics
        Professional ethics
— Caricatures and cartoons
    UF Insurance—Cartoons
— Cartoons
    USE Insurance—Caricatures and
        cartoons
— Confidential communications
    USE Confidential communications—
        Insurance
— Directories
    [HG8021]
    UF Insurance—Agents—Directories
        Insurance companies—Directories
— Effect of inflation on
    UF Insurance and inflation
    BT Inflation (Finance)
— Employees
    USE Insurance—Agents
        Insurance companies—Employees
— Experience rating
    Here are entered works on the rating or rate
    making based on an individual or specific com-
    pany's record for the purpose of determining the
    rate to be charged for that specific risk.
    UF Experience rating (Insurance)
    BT Insurance—Rates and tables
— Finance
    [HG8076-8]
    NT Insurance—Reserves
        Insurance companies—Investments
— Government ownership
    (May Subd Geog)
    UF Government ownership of
        insurance companies
    BT Insurance, Government
— Management

1865

Insurance
— Management *(Continued)*
    USE Insurance companies—
        Management
— **Mathematics**
    ⌐HG8781-2⌐
    UF Actuarial science
    BT Business mathematics
    NT Actuaries
       Insurance—Rates and tables
       Insurance—Statistical methods
— **Plans**
    ⌐HG8051⌐
— Policies
    USE Insurance policies
— Premiums
    USE Insurance—Rates and tables
— **Rates and tables**
    ⌐HG8065-HG8067⌐
       Here are entered works on the theory and
    computation of premiums, as well as lists of rates
    in force.
    UF Actuarial statistics
       Insurance—Premiums
       Insurance rates
       Insurance statistics
       Rates, Insurance
    BT Insurance—Mathematics
    SA *subdivision* Rates and tables *under*
        particular branches of insurance
    NT Insurance—Experience rating
— **Reserves**
    UF Insurance reserves
       Premium reserves
       Reserves (Insurance)
    BT Corporation reserves
       Insurance—Finance
       Insurance law
       Reserves (Accounting)
— Risk
    USE Risk (Insurance)
— Salesmanship
    USE Insurance—Agents
— Self-insurance
    USE Self-insurance
— **Social aspects** *(May Subd Geog)*
    UF Society and insurance
— **State supervision**
    ⌐HG8111-8117⌐
    UF Insurance and state
       State and insurance
    BT Consumer protection
       Industry and state
    RT Insurance law
— **Statistical methods**
    UF Actuarial statistics
       Insurance statistics
    BT Insurance—Mathematics
— **Statistics**
    ⌐HG8045⌐
    UF Actuarial statistics
       Insurance statistics
— **Taxation** *(May Subd Geog)*
    ⌐HG8119-8123⌐
    UF Insurance companies—Taxation
— — **Law and legislation**
    (May Subd Geog)
— **Vocational guidance**
    ⌐HG8091⌐
    BT Insurance—Agents
— **War risks**
    ⌐HG8055⌐
    UF Insurance, War
       Risks (Insurance)
       War insurance
       War risks (Insurance)
Insurance, Accident *(May Subd Geog)*
    ⌐HD7101-HD7102 (Industrial)⌐
    ⌐HG9301-HG9343⌐
    Cf. note under Insurance, Employers' liability.

    UF Accident insurance
       Labor and laboring classes—Insurance
    BT Insurance, Casualty
    RT Disability evaluation
       Insurance, Liability
    NT Industrial accidents
       Insurance, Athletic accident
       Insurance, Employers' liability
       Insurance, Life—Disability benefits
       Insurance, Travelers'
       Workers' compensation
— **Adjustment of claims**
    ⌐HG9323.A3⌐
— **Agents**
— **Medical examinations**
    ⌐HG8886-8891⌐
    UF Insurance, Employers' liability—
        Medical examinations
— **Policies**
— **Rates and tables**
    ⌐HG9323.R3⌐
— **War risks**
Insurance, Aeronautical
    USE Insurance, Aviation
Insurance, Agricultural *(May Subd Geog)*
    ⌐HG9966-9⌐
    UF Agricultural insurance
    BT Insurance, Casualty
    NT Farm risks
       Insurance, Food supply
       Insurance, Forest
       Insurance, Windstorm
— **Crops** *(May Subd Geog)*
    ⌐HG9968.C6-8⌐
    UF Crop insurance
       Insurance, Crop
    RT Crop losses
— — **Law and legislation**
    (May Subd Geog)
— Hail
    USE Insurance, Hail
— **Law and legislation** *(May Subd Geog)*
    BT Insurance law
— Lightning
    USE Insurance, Lightning
— **Livestock** *(May Subd Geog)*
    ⌐HG9968.L5-8⌐
    UF Cattle insurance
       Insurance, Livestock
       Livestock—Insurance
    RT Livestock—Losses
— Windstorm
    USE Insurance, Windstorm
Insurance, Aircraft mortgage
(May Subd Geog)
    UF Aircraft mortgage guaranty
    BT Aircraft mortgages
       Insurance, Credit
       Insurance, Mortgage guaranty
Insurance, Architects'
    USE Architects—Insurance requirements
Insurance, Architects' liability
(May Subd Geog)
    UF Architects' liability insurance
       Architects' malpractice insurance
       Insurance, Architects' malpractice
       Malpractice insurance, Architects'
    BT Insurance, Liability
       Insurance, Malpractice
    RT Architects—Malpractice
Insurance, Architects' malpractice
    USE Insurance, Architects' liability
Insurance, Art
    ⌐HG9970.A⌐
    UF Art insurance
    NT Art—Protection
Insurance, Assessment *(May Subd Geog)*
    ⌐HG8826⌐
    ⌐HG9201-HG9245⌐
    UF Assessment insurance
    BT Insurance, Life

    RT Friendly societies
— **Rates and tables**
    ⌐HG9221.R3⌐
Insurance, Athletic accident
    UF Athletic accident insurance
    BT Athletics
       Insurance, Accident
Insurance, Atomic hazards
    USE Insurance, Nuclear hazards
Insurance, Automobile *(May Subd Geog)*
    ⌐HG9970.A4-68⌐
    UF Automobile insurance
       Automobiles—Insurance
    BT Insurance, Casualty
       Insurance, Liability
    NT Insurance, No-fault automobile
       Insurance, Uninsured motorist
— **Adjustment of claims**
— **Law and legislation** *(May Subd Geog)*
    BT Insurance law
    NT Unsatisfied judgment funds (Traffic
        accidents)
— **Policies**
— **Premiums**
    USE Insurance, Automobile—Rates
        and tables
— **Rates and tables**
    ⌐HG9970.2⌐
    UF Insurance, Automobile—Premiums
— **Risks**
— **Self-insurance**
— — **Law and legislation**
    (May Subd Geog)
Insurance, Aviation *(May Subd Geog)*
    ⌐HG9972⌐
    UF Aeronautics—Insurance
       Airplanes—Insurance
       Airships—Insurance
       Aviation insurance
       Insurance, Aeronautical
       Insurance, Transportation
    BT Insurance, Travelers'
    NT Insurance, Life—Aviation risks
       Insurance, Satellite
— **Law and legislation** *(May Subd Geog)*
    BT Insurance law
— **War risks**
— — **Law and legislation**
    (May Subd Geog)
Insurance, Bank *(May Subd Geog)*
    ⌐HG9970.B36-364⌐
       Here are entered works on the insurance coverage
    of general banking activities. Works on the insurance
    business activities conducted by banks are entered
    under Banks and banking—Insurance business.
    UF Bank insurance
       Banks and banking—Insurance
    BT Insurance, Business
— **Law and legislation** *(May Subd Geog)*
    BT Insurance law
Insurance, Bank deposit
    USE Insurance, Deposit
Insurance, Bicycle
    UF Bicycle insurance
    BT Insurance, Casualty
       Insurance, Liability
Insurance, Boiler *(May Subd Geog)*
    ⌐HG9963⌐
    UF Boiler insurance
    BT Insurance, Casualty
       Steam-boilers
Insurance, Burglary *(May Subd Geog)*
    ⌐HG9970.B8⌐
       Here are entered works on insurance against rob-
    bery and theft, as well as burglary in the legal sense.
    (This conforms to insurance usage)
    UF Burglary insurance
       Insurance, Robbery
       Insurance, Theft
       Robbery insurance
       Theft insurance

BT Burglary protection
    Insurance, Casualty
Insurance, Burial *(May Subd Geog)*
    [HG9466-9479]
    UF Burial clubs
        Burial insurance
        Clubs, Burial
    BT Insurance, Industrial
   — Law and legislation *(May Subd Geog)*
      BT Insurance law
Insurance, Business *(May Subd Geog)*
    [HG8059]
    UF Business insurance
        Company insurance
        Corporate insurance
        Insurance, Corporate
    NT Construction industry—Insurance
        Insurance, Bank
   — Law and legislation *(May Subd Geog)*
      BT Insurance law
   — Self-insurance
   — — Law and legislation
      (May Subd Geog)
Insurance, Business interruption
    (May Subd Geog)
    [HG8060]
    UF Business interruption insurance
        Insurance, Profits
        Insurance, Use and occupancy
        Profits insurance
        Use and occupancy insurance
    BT Insurance, Casualty
    NT Insurance, Strike
   — Law and legislation *(May Subd Geog)*
      BT Insurance law
Insurance, Business life *(May Subd Geog)*
    [HG8937 (Economics)]
    UF Business insurance
        Business life insurance
        Insurance, Partnership
        Partnership insurance
    BT Insurance, Life
    NT Stock purchase agreements (Close
        corporations)
   — Law and legislation *(May Subd Geog)*
      BT Insurance law
Insurance, Cancer *(May Subd Geog)*
    UF Cancer insurance
    BT Cancer—Economic aspects
        Insurance, Health
Insurance, Casualty *(May Subd Geog)*
    [HG9956-9970]
    UF Casualty insurance
    RT Insurance, Property
    NT Insurance, Accident
        Insurance, Agricultural
        Insurance, Automobile
        Insurance, Bicycle
        Insurance, Boiler
        Insurance, Burglary
        Insurance, Business interruption
        Insurance, Computer
        Insurance, Disaster
        Insurance, Earthquake
        Insurance, Employers' liability
        Insurance, Explosion
        Insurance, Flood
        Insurance, Government risks
        Insurance, Hail
        Insurance, Landslide
        Insurance, Liability
        Insurance, Lightning
        Insurance, Machinery
        Insurance, Plate-glass
        Insurance, Strike
        Insurance, Surety and fidelity
        Insurance, Title
        Insurance, Windstorm
   — Adjustment of claims
      [HG9956]
   — Agents

   — Inspectors
   — Law and legislation *(May Subd Geog)*
      BT Insurance law
   — Premiums
      USE Insurance, Casualty—Rates and
         tables
   — Rates and tables
      UF Insurance, Casualty—Premiums
   — Taxation *(May Subd Geog)*
   — — Law and legislation
      (May Subd Geog)
Insurance, Child *(May Subd Geog)*
    [HG9271-9277]
    UF Child insurance
        Infants—Insurance
        Insurance, Infant
    BT Children—Mortality
        Infants—Mortality
        Insurance, Life
Insurance, Computer *(May Subd Geog)*
    UF Computer insurance
        Computer software insurance
    BT Insurance, Casualty
        Insurance, Property
Insurance, Consumer credit
    USE Insurance, Credit
Insurance, Contractors'
    USE Contractors—Insurance requirements
Insurance, Cooperative *(May Subd Geog)*
    [HG8059.C6]
    UF Cooperative insurance
Insurance, Corporate
    USE Insurance, Business
Insurance, Credit *(May Subd Geog)*
    [HG9970.C6-89]
    UF Credit insurance
        Insurance, Consumer credit
        Insurance, Loan
        Loan insurance
    BT Credit
    NT Insurance, Aircraft mortgage
        Insurance, Credit disability
        Insurance, Credit life
        Insurance, Export credit
        Insurance, Foreign loan
        Insurance, Investment guaranty
        Insurance, Mortgage guaranty
        Insurance, Ship mortgage
   — Premiums
      USE Insurance, Credit—Rates and
         tables
   — Rates and tables
      UF Insurance, Credit—Premiums
Insurance, Credit accident and health
    USE Insurance, Credit disability
Insurance, Credit disability
    (May Subd Geog)
    UF Credit accident and health insurance
        Credit disability insurance
        Insurance, Credit accident and health
    BT Insurance, Credit
        Insurance, Disability
Insurance, Credit life *(May Subd Geog)*
    Here are entered works on term life insurance
    purchased in conjunction with a consumer credit
    transaction, excluding first mortgage loans, which
    provides for a death benefit sufficient to pay off the
    credit obligation in the event of an insured's death
    during the term of the coverage.
    UF Credit life insurance
    BT Insurance, Credit
        Insurance, Life
Insurance, Creditors group
    USE Insurance, Group creditors
Insurance, Crop
    USE Insurance, Agricultural—Crops
Insurance, Dental *(May Subd Geog)*
    UF Dental care, Prepaid
        Dental insurance
        Socialized dentistry

    BT Dental care
        Insurance, Health
    NT Insurance, Government employees'
        dental
   — Law and legislation *(May Subd Geog)*
      BT Insurance law
Insurance, Deposit
    [HG1662]
    Here are entered works on private insurance of
    bank deposits. Works on government insurance of
    bank deposits are entered under Banks and banking
    —Government guaranty of deposits.
    UF Bank deposit insurance
        Deposit insurance
        Insurance, Bank deposit
        Insurance, Savings
        Savings insurance
    BT Bank deposits
        Insurance, Property
    NT Banks and banking—Government
        guaranty of deposits
   — Law and legislation *(May Subd Geog)*
      BT Insurance law
Insurance, Depreciation
    USE Insurance, Replacement cost
Insurance, Directors and officers liability
    USE Insurance, Executives' liability
Insurance, Disability *(May Subd Geog)*
    UF Disability insurance
        Insurance, Invalidity
        Invalidity insurance
        Old age, survivors and disability
         insurance
    BT Social security
    RT Disability retirement
    NT Disability evaluation
        Insurance, Credit disability
        Insurance, Government employees'
         disability
   — Law and legislation *(May Subd Geog)*
      BT Insurance law
Insurance, Disaster *(May Subd Geog)*
    UF Disaster insurance
    BT Disaster relief
        Hurricane protection
        Insurance, Casualty
    NT Insurance, Earthquake
        Insurance, Explosion
        Insurance, Fire
        Insurance, Flood
        Insurance, Hail
        Insurance, Landslide
        Insurance, Lightning
        Insurance, Windstorm
Insurance, Dowry
    USE Insurance, Marriage endowment
Insurance, Drug
    USE Insurance, Pharmaceutical services
Insurance, Earthquake *(May Subd Geog)*
    [HG9981]
    UF Earthquake insurance
    BT Insurance, Casualty
        Insurance, Disaster
Insurance, Employers' liability
    (May Subd Geog)
    [HG9964.E4-7]
    Here are entered works on the insurance of an
    employer's liability for compensation to his em-
    ployees in case of accident.
    UF Employers' liability insurance
    BT Employers' liability
        Insurance, Accident
        Insurance, Casualty
        Insurance, Liability
        Workers' compensation
    NT Disability evaluation
        Industrial accidents
   — Adjustment of claims
   — Experience rating
   — Medical examinations
      USE Insurance, Accident—Medical
         examinations

Insurance, Employers' liability
(Continued)
— **Rates and tables**
Insurance, Endowment
  USE Insurance, Life—Endowment policies
Insurance, Engineers' liability
  (May Subd Geog)
  UF Engineers' liability insurance
     Engineers' malpractice insurance
     Insurance, Engineers' malpractice
     Malpractice insurance, Engineers'
  BT Insurance, Liability
     Insurance, Malpractice
  RT Engineers—Malpractice
Insurance, Engineers' malpractice
  USE Insurance, Engineers' liability
Insurance, Executives' liability
  (May Subd Geog)
  [HG8053.8]
  UF Directors and officers liability
      insurance
     Executives' liability insurance
     Insurance, Directors and officers
      liability
     Malpractice insurance, Executive
  BT Insurance, Malpractice
Insurance, Explosion
  UF Explosion insurance
  BT Explosions
     Insurance, Casualty
     Insurance, Disaster
     Insurance, Fire
Insurance, Export
  USE Insurance, Inland marine
Insurance, Export control *(May Subd Geog)*
  UF Export control insurance
  BT Export controls
Insurance, Export credit *(May Subd Geog)*
  UF Export credit guarantees
     Export credit insurance
  BT Export credit
     Foreign trade promotion
     Insurance, Credit
— **Law and legislation** *(May Subd Geog)*
  BT Insurance law
Insurance, Fidelity
  USE Insurance, Surety and fidelity
Insurance, Fire *(May Subd Geog)*
  [HG9651-9899]
  UF Fire insurance
     Fire losses
  BT Building, Fireproof
     Insurance, Disaster
     Insurance, Property
  RT Insurance, Lightning
  NT Fire-marks
     Fireproofing
     Insurance, Explosion
     Insurance engineering
— **Adjustment of claims**
  [HG9721-7]
— **Agents**
  [HG9706-9]
    Manuals of individual companies are entered
  under the company alone.
— **Classification of risks**
  [HG9687]
  UF Classification of risks
— **Inspectors**
  [HG9711-9717]
— **Law and legislation** *(May Subd Geog)*
  BT Insurance law
— **Maps and surveys**
  [HG9771]
  UF Insurance, Fire—Surveys
  BT Surveys
— **Office marks**
  USE Fire-marks
— **Plans**
  [HG9665]
  [HG9882]

— **Policies**
  [HG9695-9]
— **Premiums**
  USE Insurance, Fire—Rates and tables
— **Rates and tables**
  [HG9685-9691]
    Includes works on the theory and computa-
  tion of premiums, as well as lists of rates in force.
  Rates of a particular district are entered here
  and also under Insurance, Fire—[local subdivi-
  sion]
  UF Insurance, Fire—Premiums
— **Risks**
  [HG9731.A-Z]
  UF Risks (Insurance)
  NT Electric engineering—Insurance
      requirements
— **Self-insurance**
— **State supervision**
  [HG9739]
  UF Insurance and state
— **Statistics**
  [HG9663]
  BT Fires
— Surveys
  USE Insurance, Fire—Maps and
      surveys
— **War risks**
  [HG9731.W3]
Insurance, Flood *(May Subd Geog)*
  [HG9970.F55-554]
  UF Flood insurance
  BT Insurance, Casualty
     Insurance, Disaster
     Insurance, Property
— **Law and legislation** *(May Subd Geog)*
  BT Insurance law
Insurance, Food supply *(May Subd Geog)*
  UF Food insurance
     Food supply insurance
  BT Food supply—International
      cooperation
     Insurance, Agricultural
Insurance, Foreign loan *(May Subd Geog)*
  [HG9977]
  UF Foreign loan insurance
  BT Insurance, Credit
  RT Loans, Foreign
Insurance, Forest *(May Subd Geog)*
  [HG9970.F]
  UF Forest fire insurance
     Forest insurance
     Insurance, Timber
     Timber insurance
  BT Forest fires
     Forests and forestry
     Insurance, Agricultural
Insurance, Fraternal *(May Subd Geog)*
  UF Fraternal insurance
  BT Friendly societies
— **Law and legislation** *(May Subd Geog)*
  BT Insurance law
Insurance, Freight *(May Subd Geog)*
  UF Freight insurance
     Insurance, Transportation
  BT Freight and freightage
     Insurance, Liability
— **Policies**
Insurance, Government *(May Subd Geog)*
  UF Government insurance
  BT Government lending
  SA *other types of insurance underwritten*
     by government authorities, e.g.
     Banks and banking—Government
     guaranty of deposits; Insurance,
     Agricultural—Crops; Insurance, War
     risk
  NT Building and loan associations—
     Government guaranty of deposits
     Insurance—Government ownership

     Savings-banks—Government guaranty
      of deposits
Insurance, Government employees' dental
  (May Subd Geog)
  UF Government employees' dental
      insurance
  BT Insurance, Dental
     Insurance, Government employees'
     health
Insurance, Government employees' disability
  (May Subd Geog)
  BT Insurance, Disability
Insurance, Government employees' health
  (May Subd Geog)
  UF Government employees' health
      insurance
  BT Insurance, Health
  NT Insurance, Government employees'
     dental
— **Law and legislation**
  BT Insurance law
— **United States**
  UF United States—Officials and
      employees—Health insurance
Insurance, Government employees' life
  (May Subd Geog)
  UF Government employees' life insurance
  BT Insurance, Government life
     Insurance, Life
— **Law and legislation** *(May Subd Geog)*
  BT Insurance law
— **United States**
  UF Federal employees group life
      insurance program
     United States—Officials and
      employees—Life insurance
Insurance, Government liability
  USE Insurance, Government risks
Insurance, Government life
  (May Subd Geog)
  UF Government life insurance
     Veterans' insurance
  BT Insurance, Life
  NT Insurance, Government employees' life
— **Law and legislation** *(May Subd Geog)*
  BT Insurance law
Insurance, Government risks
  (May Subd Geog)
  [HG8059.G6]
    Here are entered works on insurance protection
  against risks involving government agencies, espe-
  cially losses and claims connected with government-
  owned property or resulting from wrongful actions of
  government officials and employees. Works on insur-
  ance underwritten by government authorities are en-
  tered under Insurance, Government.
  UF Government liability insurance
     Government risks insurance
     Insurance, Government liability
  BT Government liability
     Insurance, Casualty
Insurance, Group *(May Subd Geog)*
  [HG8058]
    Here are entered works on group insurance in
  general and on group life insurance. Works on group
  insurance in other specific fields are entered under
  Insurance, Casualty; Insurance, Hospitalization; etc.
  UF Group insurance
  BT Insurance, Life
  NT Insurance, Group creditors
— **Law and legislation** *(May Subd Geog)*
  BT Insurance law
— **Taxation** *(May Subd Geog)*
— — **Law and legislation**
    (May Subd Geog)
Insurance, Group creditors
  UF Creditors group insurance
     Group creditors insurance
     Insurance, Creditors group

BT Consumer credit
   Instalment plan
   Insurance, Group
   Insurance, Life
Insurance, Guaranty
  USE Insurance, Surety and fidelity
Insurance, Hail *(May Subd Geog)*
   [HG9968.H2-5]
  UF Hail insurance
    Insurance, Agricultural—Hail
    Storm insurance
  BT Insurance, Casualty
    Insurance, Disaster
Insurance, Health *(May Subd Geog)*
   [HD7101-HD7102 (Industrial)]
   [HG9383-HG9399]
  UF Health insurance
    Health plans, Prepaid
    Insurance, Sickness
    Labor and laboring classes—Insurance
    Medical care, Prepaid
    Medical service, Prepaid
    Prepaid health plans
    Prepaid medical care
    Sickness insurance
    Socialized medicine
  BT Social security
  RT Medical care
  NT Compulsory health insurance
    Health maintenance organizations
    Insurance, Cancer
    Insurance, Dental
    Insurance, Government employees'
      health
    Insurance, Hospitalization
    Insurance, Life—Disability benefits
    Insurance, Mental health
    Insurance, Optometric services
    Insurance, Pharmaceutical services
    Preferred provider organizations
      (Medical care)
    Voluntary employees' beneficiary
      associations
    Workers' compensation
  — **Adjustment of claims**
  — **Agents**
  — **Coinsurance**
    BT Coinsurance
  — **Finance**
  — — **Law and legislation**
     (May Subd Geog)
  — **Law and legislation** *(May Subd Geog)*
    BT Insurance law
  — — **Conflict of laws**
     USE Conflict of laws—Insurance,
      Health
  — **Rates and tables**
    [HG9389.R3]
  — **Self-insurance**
  — **Taxation**
  — — **Law and legislation**
     (May Subd Geog)
  — **United States**
    NT Medicaid
      Medicare
      Medigap
Insurance, Homeowners *(May Subd Geog)*
   [HG9970.H6-64]
  UF Homeowners insurance
  BT Insurance, Multiple-line
Insurance, Hospitalization
  (May Subd Geog)
  UF Group hospitalization
    Hospitalization insurance
  BT Insurance, Health
  NT Hospitals—Prospective payment
    Hospitals, Rural—Prospective payment
    Nursing homes—Prospective payment
Insurance, Indemnity
  USE Insurance, Liability

Insurance, Industrial *(May Subd Geog)*
   [HD7090-HD7250 (Labor)]
   [HG9251-HG9262 (Finance)]
  UF Industrial insurance
  BT Insurance, Life
  NT Insurance, Burial
  — **Adjustment of claims**
    [HG9257.A3]
  — **Agents**
    [HG9255]
  — **Law and legislation** *(May Subd Geog)*
    BT Insurance law
  — **Policies**
  — **Rates and tables**
    [HG9257.R3]
Insurance, Infant
  USE Insurance, Child
Insurance, Inland marine *(May Subd Geog)*
   [HG9903]
  UF Export insurance
    Inland marine insurance
    Inland transportation insurance
    Insurance, Export
    Insurance, Transportation
    Transportation insurance
  BT Insurance, Marine
    Insurance, Property
  — **Policies**
Insurance, Invalidity
  USE Insurance, Disability
Insurance, Investment guaranty
  (May Subd Geog)
   [HG4538]
  UF Investment guaranty insurance
    Investment insurance
  BT Insurance, Credit
    Insurance, Property
    Investments, Foreign
Insurance, Landslide *(May Subd Geog)*
  UF Landslide insurance
  BT Insurance, Casualty
    Insurance, Disaster
Insurance, Lawyers'
  USE Lawyers—Insurance requirements
Insurance, Legal costs
  USE Insurance, Litigation
Insurance, Legal services
  USE Prepaid legal services
Insurance, Liability *(May Subd Geog)*
   [HG9990]
  UF Indemnity insurance
    Insurance, Indemnity
    Liability insurance
  BT Insurance, Casualty
    Liability (Law)
  RT Indemnity against liability
    Insurance, Accident
  NT Insurance, Architects' liability
    Insurance, Automobile
    Insurance, Bicycle
    Insurance, Employers' liability
    Insurance, Engineers' liability
    Insurance, Freight
    Insurance, Malpractice
    Insurance, Nuclear hazards
    Insurance, Physicians' liability
    Insurance, Police liability
    Insurance, Pollution liability
    Insurance, Products liability
    Insurance, Travel agents' liability
  — **Adjustment of claims**
  — **Policies**
  — **Rate of return**
    UF Insurance, Liability—Return
      Return of liability insurance
    BT Rate of return
  — **Rates and tables**
  — **Return**
    USE Insurance, Liability—Rate of
      return

Insurance, Life *(May Subd Geog)*
   [HG8751-9200]
  UF Actuarial science
    Insurance, Postal life
    Life insurance
    Postal life insurance
  NT Annuities
    Death—Proof and certification
    Insurance, Assessment
    Insurance, Business life
    Insurance, Child
    Insurance, Credit life
    Insurance, Government employees' life
    Insurance, Government life
    Insurance, Group
    Insurance, Group creditors
    Insurance, Industrial
    Insurance, Mortgage life
    Insurance, Savings-bank life
    Life insurance trusts
    Mortality, Law of
    Survivors' benefits
    Voluntary employees' beneficiary
      associations
  — **Accounting**
    [HG8848]
  — **Adjustment of claims**
  — **Agents** *(May Subd Geog)*
    [HG8876-8883]
  — **Aviation risks**
    UF Risks (Insurance)
    BT Insurance, Aviation
  — **Corrupt practices**
    NT Insurance, Life—Twisting
  — **Directories**
    [HG8758]
    UF Insurance companies—Directories
  — **Disability benefits**
    [HG8811.D6]
    BT Insurance, Accident
      Insurance, Health
  — **Effect of inflation on**
    BT Inflation (Finance)
  — **Endowment policies**
    [HG8818]
    UF Endowment insurance
      Insurance, Endowment
    BT Insurance, Life—Policies
    NT Insurance, Marriage endowment
  — **Finance**
  — — **Law and legislation**
     (May Subd Geog)
  — **Law and legislation** *(May Subd Geog)*
    BT Insurance law
  — **Mathematics**
    [HG8781-8793]
    UF Actuarial science
    BT Mortality
      Vital statistics
    NT Insurance, Life—Rates and tables
  — **Plans**
    [HG8816-8830]
  — **Policies**
    [HG8861-6]
    NT Insurance, Life—Endowment
      policies
      Insurance, Life—Split dollar
      policies
      Insurance, Life—Tontine policies
  — **Premiums**
    USE Insurance, Life—Rates and tables
  — **Rates and tables**
    [HG8851-3]
    Includes works on the theory and computation of premiums, as well as general tables of rates in force. Rates and tables of particular companies are entered under the company alone.
    UF Insurance, Life—Premiums
      Present-value tables
    BT Insurance, Life—Mathematics
  — **Sales letters**

Insurance, Life *(Continued)*
— **Split dollar policies**
  ₍HG8824₎
    UF Split dollar life insurance policies
    BT Insurance, Life—Policies
— **State supervision**
  ₍HG8916-8919₎
    UF Insurance and state
— **Taxation** *(May Subd Geog)*
  ₍HG8910-8914₎
    UF Insurance companies—Taxation
— — **Law and legislation**
    (May Subd Geog)
— **Tontine policies**
  ₍HG8817₎
    UF Tontine policies
    BT Insurance, Life—Policies
— **Twisting**
    Here are entered works on the use of misrep-
    resentation or deception to induce a policyholder
    to lapse or cancel a life insurance policy and
    purchase another.
    UF Twisting (Life insurance)
    BT Insurance, Life—Corrupt practices
— **Variable policies**
  ₍HG8823₎
    UF Equity-linked life insurance
        Variable life insurance
    BT Variable annuities
— — **Law and legislation**
    (May Subd Geog)
— **War risks**
  ₍HG8811.W2₎
    Here are entered works on the war risk in
    private life insurance policies. Works on life in-
    surance written by the government for members
    of the Armed Forces are entered under the head-
    ing Insurance, War risk.
    UF Insurance, War
        Risks (Insurance)
        War insurance
        War risks (Insurance)
    BT Veterans
    RT Insurance, War risk
— — **Law and legislation**
    (May Subd Geog)
Insurance, Lightning *(May Subd Geog)*
    UF Insurance, Agricultural—Lightning
        Lightning insurance
        Storm insurance
    BT Insurance, Casualty
        Insurance, Disaster
    RT Insurance, Fire
Insurance, Litigation *(May Subd Geog)*
  ₍HG9970.L6₎
    UF Insurance, Legal costs
        Litigation insurance
    BT Costs (Law)
Insurance, Livestock
    USE Insurance, Agricultural—Livestock
Insurance, Loan
    USE Insurance, Credit
Insurance, Machinery
  ₍HG9963.M₎
    UF Machinery insurance
    BT Insurance, Casualty
        Insurance, Property
Insurance, Malpractice *(May Subd Geog)*
    UF Insurance, Professional liability
        Malpractice insurance
        Professional liability insurance
    BT Insurance, Liability
    NT Insurance, Architects' liability
        Insurance, Engineers' liability
        Insurance, Executives' liability
        Insurance, Physicians' liability
        Insurance, Police liability
— **Policies**
Insurance, Manufacturers' liability
    USE Insurance, Products liability
Insurance, Marine *(May Subd Geog)*
  ₍HE961-971₎

    UF Abandonment (Marine insurance)
        Insurance, Transportation
        Marine insurance
        Transportation insurance
    BT Commerce
        Contracts, Maritime
        Insurance, Property
        Maritime law
        Merchant marine
        Shipping
    NT Average (Maritime law)
        Bottomry and respondentia
        Insurance, Inland marine
        Salvage
        Seaworthiness, Warranty of
— **Adjustment of claims**
  ₍HE965-7₎
— **Policies**
  ₍HE967₎
— **War risks**
  ₍HE966₎
    UF Insurance, War
        Risks (Insurance)
        War insurance
        War risks (Insurance)
Insurance, Marine (Jewish law)
Insurance, Marriage endowment
  ₍HG9281-7₎
    UF Dowry insurance
        Insurance, Dowry
        Marriage endowment insurance
    BT Insurance, Life—Endowment policies
Insurance, Maternity *(May Subd Geog)*
  ₍HG9291-5₎
    UF Maternity insurance
        Motherhood insurance
    BT Maternal and infant welfare
        Social security
— **Law and legislation** *(May Subd Geog)*
    BT Insurance law
Insurance, Medical malpractice
    USE Insurance, Physicians' liability
Insurance, Medicare supplemental health
    USE Medigap
Insurance, Mental health *(May Subd Geog)*
    UF Insurance, Psychiatric
        Mental health insurance
        Mental illness insurance
        Psychiatric insurance
    BT Insurance, Health
Insurance, Military
    USE Insurance, War risk
Insurance, Mortgage guaranty
    (May Subd Geog)
  ₍HG9970.M6₎
    UF Mortgage guaranty insurance
    BT Insurance, Credit
        Insurance, Property
        Insurance, Title
        Mortgages
    NT Insurance, Aircraft mortgage
        Insurance, Ship mortgage
— **Law and legislation** *(May Subd Geog)*
    BT Insurance law
Insurance, Mortgage life
    BT Insurance, Life
        Mortgages
Insurance, Moving-picture *(May Subd Geog)*
    UF Moving-picture insurance
        Moving-pictures—Insurance
Insurance, Multiple-line *(May Subd Geog)*
    UF Insurance companies—Multiple-line
        underwriting
        Multiple-line insurance
    NT Insurance, Homeowners
        Insurance, School
Insurance, Mutual
    USE Insurance
Insurance, No-fault automobile
    (May Subd Geog)
  ₍HG9970.A4-68₎

    UF No-fault automobile insurance
    BT Insurance, Automobile
— **Law and legislation** *(May Subd Geog)*
    BT Insurance law
Insurance, Nuclear hazards
    (May Subd Geog)
    UF Atomic hazards insurance
        Insurance, Atomic hazards
        Nuclear hazards insurance
        Nuclear insurance
    BT Insurance, Liability
— **Law and legislation** *(May Subd Geog)*
    BT Insurance law
Insurance, Optometric services
    (May Subd Geog)
    UF Optometric services insurance
    BT Insurance, Health
        Optometry—Economic aspects
— **Law and legislation** *(May Subd Geog)*
    BT Insurance law
Insurance, Partnership
    USE Insurance, Business life
Insurance, Pension trust guaranty
    (May Subd Geog)
    UF Pension trust guaranty insurance
    BT Pension trusts
Insurance, Pharmaceutical services
    (May Subd Geog)
    UF Drug benefit plans
        Drug insurance
        Insurance, Drug
        Insurance, Prescription
        Pharmaceutical insurance
        Pharmaceutical services insurance
        Prepaid prescription drug plans
        Prescription insurance
    BT Insurance, Health
    NT Aged—Pharmaceutical assistance
— **Law and legislation** *(May Subd Geog)*
    BT Insurance law
Insurance, Physicians'
    USE Physicians—Insurance requirements
Insurance, Physicians' liability
    (May Subd Geog)
  ₍HG8054₎
    UF Insurance, Medical malpractice
        Malpractice insurance, Medical
        Medical malpractice insurance
        Physicians' liability insurance
    BT Insurance, Liability
        Insurance, Malpractice
        Physicians—Insurance requirements
        Physicians—Malpractice
    NT Insurance, Psychiatrists' liability
Insurance, Plate-glass
  ₍HG9963.P6₎
    UF Plate-glass insurance
    BT Insurance, Casualty
Insurance, Police liability *(May Subd Geog)*
  ₍HG8054.P63₎
    UF Insurance, Police malpractice
        Malpractice insurance, Police
        Police malpractice insurance
    BT Insurance, Liability
        Insurance, Malpractice
        Police—Malpractice
Insurance, Police malpractice
    USE Insurance, Police liability
Insurance, Pollution liability
    (May Subd Geog)
    UF Environmental impairment liability
        insurance
        Pollution liability insurance
    BT Insurance, Liability
Insurance, Postal life
    USE Insurance, Life
Insurance, Prescription
    USE Insurance, Pharmaceutical services

Insurance, Products liability
(May Subd Geog)
  UF Insurance, Manufacturers' liability
      Manufacturers' liability insurance
      Products liability insurance
  BT Insurance, Liability
      Products liability
Insurance, Professional liability
  USE Insurance, Malpractice
Insurance, Profits
  USE Insurance, Business interruption
Insurance, Property (May Subd Geog)
  UF Property insurance
  RT Insurance, Casualty
  NT Insurance, Computer
      Insurance, Deposit
      Insurance, Fire
      Insurance, Flood
      Insurance, Inland marine
      Insurance, Investment guaranty
      Insurance, Machinery
      Insurance, Marine
      Insurance, Mortgage guaranty
      Insurance, Windstorm
— **Adjustment of claims**
— **Agents**
— **Law and legislation** (May Subd Geog)
    BT Insurance law
— **Policies**
— **Rate of return**
    UF Insurance, Property—Return
        Return of property insurance
    BT Rate of return
— **Rates and tables**
— **Return**
    USE Insurance, Property—Rate of
        return
— **Taxation** (May Subd Geog)
— — **Law and legislation**
      (May Subd Geog)
Insurance, Psychiatric
  USE Insurance, Mental health
Insurance, Psychiatrists' liability
(May Subd Geog)
[HG8054.4]
  UF Insurance, Psychiatrists' malpractice
      Malpractice insurance, Psychiatrists'
      Psychiatrists' malpractice insurance
  BT Insurance, Physicians' liability
      Psychiatrists—Malpractice
Insurance, Psychiatrists' malpractice
  USE Insurance, Psychiatrists' liability
Insurance, Replacement cost
(May Subd Geog)
  UF Actual cash value insurance
      Insurance, Depreciation
      Replacement cost insurance
  NT Revalorization of insurance
Insurance, Robbery
  USE Insurance, Burglary
Insurance, Satellite (May Subd Geog)
[HG9972]
  UF Artificial satellite insurance
      Satellite insurance
  BT Insurance, Aviation
Insurance, Savings
  USE Insurance, Deposit
Insurance, Savings-bank life
(May Subd Geog)
  UF Savings-bank insurance
      Savings-bank life insurance
  BT Insurance, Life
      Savings-banks
Insurance, School (May Subd Geog)
  UF School insurance
  BT Insurance, Multiple-line
      School plant management
— **Self-insurance**
Insurance, Self
  USE Self-insurance

Insurance, Sex discrimination in
  USE Sex discrimination in insurance
Insurance, Ship mortgage (May Subd Geog)
[VM299.5-7]
  UF Ship mortgage insurance
  BT Insurance, Credit
      Insurance, Mortgage guaranty
Insurance, Sickness
  USE Insurance, Health
Insurance, Social
  USE Social security
Insurance, State and compulsory
  USE Social security
Insurance, Strike (May Subd Geog)
[HG9964.S6]
  UF Strike insurance
  BT Insurance, Business interruption
      Insurance, Casualty
  RT Insurance, Unemployment
      Strikes and lockouts
Insurance, Surety and fidelity
(May Subd Geog)
[HG9970.S4-HG9970.S8 (Economics)]
  UF Bonding of employees
      Bonds, Fidelity
      Bonds, Surety
      Fidelity bonds
      Fidelity insurance
      Guaranty insurance
      Insurance, Fidelity
      Insurance, Guaranty
      Surety and fidelity insurance
      Surety bonds
      Surety companies
  BT Insurance, Casualty
      Judicial bonds
      Suretyship and guaranty
  SA *subdivision* Bonding *under*
      occupational groups and types of
      employees; and subdivision Officials
      and employees—Bonding under
      names of countries, cities, etc.
— **Self-insurance**
Insurance, Survivors
  USE Survivors' benefits
Insurance, Theft
  USE Insurance, Burglary
Insurance, Timber
  USE Insurance, Forest
Insurance, Title (May Subd Geog)
[HG9970.T4-68]
  UF Real estate title insurance
      Title guaranty
      Title insurance
  BT Insurance, Casualty
      Land titles
      Real property
  NT Insurance, Mortgage guaranty
      Title companies
Insurance, Tornado
  USE Insurance, Windstorm
Insurance, Transportation
  USE Insurance, Aviation
      Insurance, Freight
      Insurance, Inland marine
      Insurance, Marine
      Insurance, Travelers'
Insurance, Travel agents' liability
(May Subd Geog)
[HG8054.45]
  UF Travel agents' liability insurance
  BT Insurance, Liability
Insurance, Travelers' (May Subd Geog)
  UF Insurance, Transportation
  BT Insurance, Accident
  NT Insurance, Aviation
Insurance, Unemployment (May Subd Geog)
[HD7095-7096]

  UF Labor and laboring classes—Insurance
      Unemployment benefits
      Unemployment compensation
      Unemployment insurance
  BT Income maintenance programs
      Social security
      Unemployed
      Unemployment
  RT Insurance, Strike
  NT Supplemental unemployment benefits
      Unemployment—Effect of
        unemployment insurance on
      Unemployment, Seasonal
— **Case studies**
— **Claimants**
    UF Claimants of unemployment
        insurance
    BT Social security beneficiaries
        Unemployed
— **Experience rating**
— **Finance**
— — **Law and legislation**
      (May Subd Geog)
— **Law and legislation** (May Subd Geog)
    BT Insurance law
Insurance, Uninsured motorist
(May Subd Geog)
  UF Uninsured motorist insurance
  BT Insurance, Automobile
Insurance, Use and occupancy
  USE Insurance, Business interruption
Insurance, War
  USE Insurance—War risks
      Insurance, Life—War risks
      Insurance, Marine—War risks
      Insurance, War risk
Insurance, War damage
  USE War damage compensation
Insurance, War risk (May Subd Geog)
[UB370-375]
  Here are entered works on life and disability in-
surance written by the government for members of
the Armed Forces. Works on government insurance
of property against damage from enemy action are
entered under the heading War damage compensa-
tion. Works on war risk in private insurance policies
are entered under Insurance and under the names of
certain types of insurance, with subdivision War
risks.
  UF Insurance, Military
      Insurance, War
      Risks (Insurance)
      War insurance
      War risk insurance
      War risks (Insurance)
  BT Pensions, Military
  RT Insurance, Life—War risks
— **Law and legislation** (May Subd Geog)
    BT Insurance law
Insurance, Windstorm (May Subd Geog)
  UF Insurance, Agricultural—Windstorm
      Insurance, Tornado
      Storm insurance
      Tornado insurance
      Windstorm insurance
  BT Insurance, Agricultural
      Insurance, Casualty
      Insurance, Disaster
      Insurance, Property
Insurance, Workers' compensation
  USE Workers' compensation
Insurance, Working-men's
  USE Social security
Insurance agents
  USE Insurance—Agents
Insurance agents, Independent
  USE Independent insurance agents
Insurance and inflation
  USE Insurance—Effect of inflation on
Insurance and state
  USE Insurance—State supervision
      Insurance, Fire—State supervision

Insurance and state   *(Continued)*
        Insurance, Life—State supervision
Insurance business activities of banks
    USE Banks and banking—Insurance
         business
Insurance companies   *(May Subd Geog)*
    UF Companies, Insurance
    BT Financial institutions
        Insurance
    NT Insurance holding companies
        Insurance stocks
        Lloyds associations
  — Accounting
    USE Insurance—Accounting
  — **Captive companies**
    UF Captive insurance companies
  — Collective bargaining
    USE Collective bargaining—Insurance
         companies
  — Collective labor agreements
    USE Collective labor agreements—
         Insurance companies
  — Directories
    USE Insurance—Directories;
         Insurance, Life—Directories;
         and similar headings
         Insurance—Directories
         Insurance, Life—Directories
  — **Employees**
    UF Insurance—Employees
    NT Collective bargaining—Insurance
         companies
        Collective labor agreements—
         Insurance companies
        Insurance—Agents
        Trade-unions—Insurance
         companies
        Wages—Insurance companies
  — **Investments**
    UF Insurance company investments
    BT Insurance—Finance
        Investments
  — — **Law and legislation**
      (May Subd Geog)
  — **Management**
    UF Insurance—Management
  — Multiple-line underwriting
    USE Insurance, Multiple-line
  — Taxation
    USE Insurance—Taxation; Insurance,
         Life—Taxation; *and similar*
         headings
         Insurance—Taxation
         Insurance, Life—Taxation
  — Tort liability
    USE Tort liability of insurance
         companies
Insurance companies, American, [British, etc.]
  (May Subd Geog)
Insurance companies, British
  (May Subd Geog)
    UF British insurance companies
Insurance companies, Foreign
  (May Subd Geog)
    UF Foreign insurance companies
    BT Corporations, Foreign
Insurance company investments
    USE Insurance companies—Investments
Insurance contracts
    USE Insurance policies
Insurance crimes   *(May Subd Geog)*
    UF Crimes, Insurance
    BT Criminal law
        Fraud
        Insurance law
Insurance departments   *(May Subd Geog)*
    UF Corporate insurance departments
        Corporations—Insurance departments
    BT Insurance
Insurance engineering
    [TH9201-9237]

  BT Insurance, Fire
      Safety appliances
  RT Building, Fireproof
      Fire extinction
      Fire prevention
Insurance ethics
    USE Insurance—Agents—Professional
        ethics
Insurance holding companies
  (May Subd Geog)
    BT Holding companies
        Insurance companies
Insurance law   *(May Subd Geog)*
    [HG8115]
    [HG8906-HG8909 (Life)]
    [HG9393 (Health)]
    [HG9471 (Burial)]
    [HG9734 (Fire)]
    UF Law, Insurance
    BT Commercial law
        Contracts, Aleatory
    RT Insurance—State supervision
    NT Banks and banking—Insurance
         business—Law and legislation
        Discrimination in insurance—Law and
         legislation
        Insurance—Agents—Malpractice
        Insurance—Reserves
        Insurance, Agricultural—Law and
         legislation
        Insurance, Automobile—Law and
         legislation
        Insurance, Aviation—Law and
         legislation
        Insurance, Bank—Law and legislation
        Insurance, Burial—Law and legislation
        Insurance, Business—Law and
         legislation
        Insurance, Business interruption—Law
         and legislation
        Insurance, Business life—Law and
         legislation
        Insurance, Casualty—Law and
         legislation
        Insurance, Dental—Law and legislation
        Insurance, Deposit—Law and
         legislation
        Insurance, Disability—Law and
         legislation
        Insurance, Export credit—Law and
         legislation
        Insurance, Fire—Law and legislation
        Insurance, Flood—Law and legislation
        Insurance, Fraternal—Law and
         legislation
        Insurance, Government employees'
         health—Law and legislation
        Insurance, Government employees' life
         —Law and legislation
        Insurance, Government life—Law and
         legislation
        Insurance, Group—Law and legislation
        Insurance, Health—Law and legislation
        Insurance, Industrial—Law and
         legislation
        Insurance, Life—Law and legislation
        Insurance, Maternity—Law and
         legislation
        Insurance, Mortgage guaranty—Law
         and legislation
        Insurance, No-fault automobile—Law
         and legislation
        Insurance, Nuclear hazards—Law and
         legislation
        Insurance, Optometric services—Law
         and legislation
        Insurance, Pharmaceutical services—
         Law and legislation
        Insurance, Property—Law and
         legislation

        Insurance, Unemployment—Law and
         legislation
        Insurance, War risk—Law and
         legislation
        Insurance crimes
        Insurance policies
        Reinsurance—Law and legislation
        Revalorization of insurance
        Sex discrimination in insurance—Law
         and legislation
        Warranty
  — Conflict of laws
    USE Conflict of laws—Insurance
  — **United States**
    NT Medigap—Law and legislation
Insurance law, International
    Here are entered works dealing with insurance
    laws adopted or proposed by international conven-
    tion or treaty.
    UF International insurance law
    BT International law
    RT Conflict of laws—Insurance
Insurance law (Islamic law)
Insurance libraries
    [Z675.I7]
    UF Libraries, Insurance
    BT Business libraries
Insurance policies   *(May Subd Geog)*
    UF Contracts, Insurance
        Insurance—Policies
        Insurance contracts
        Policies of insurance
        Policy of insurance
    BT Contracts
        Insurance
        Insurance law
    SA *subdivision* Policies *under various*
        kinds of insurance, e.g. Insurance,
        Fire—Policies
Insurance policies (Islamic law)
  (May Subd Geog)
    BT Islamic law
Insurance rates
    USE Insurance—Rates and tables
Insurance reserves
    USE Insurance—Reserves
Insurance statistics
    USE Insurance—Rates and tables
        Insurance—Statistical methods
        Insurance—Statistics
Insurance stocks   *(May Subd Geog)*
    BT Insurance companies
        Stocks
    NT Life insurance stocks
Insurance surveys   *(May Subd Geog)*
    UF Surveys, Insurance
    BT Surveys
Insurance trusts
    USE Life insurance trusts
Insured mail   *(May Subd Geog)*
    UF Postal service—Insurance
Insurgency   *(May Subd Geog)*
    [JC328.5]
    UF Rebellions
    BT Civil war
        Political crimes and offenses
        Revolutions
    RT Government, Resistance to
        Internal security
    NT Counterinsurgency
        Guerrilla warfare
        Peasant uprisings
        Subversive activities
        Terrorism
  — **Japan**
    NT Japan—History—March and
        October Incidents, 1931
Insurrection of Mamadou Lamine, 1885-1887
    USE Mamadou Lamine, Rebellion of, 1885-
        1887

Insurrections
  USE *particular insurrections, e.g.* Whiskey
      Insurrection, 1794
      Revolutions
Intaglio printing
  UF Gravure printing
  BT Printing
      Prints—Technique
  NT Autotype process printing
      Collagraph printing
Intaglios *(May Subd Geog)*
  ₍NK5730₎
  UF Sealings (Intaglios)
  BT Glyptics
  RT Gems
  NT Seals (Numismatics)
— **China**
— — **History**
— — — **Ch'in-Han dynasties, 221 B.C.-220
      A.D.**
Intakes (Hydraulic engineering)
  (May Subd Geog)
  BT Hydraulic structures
INTAL (Artificial language)
  USE International auxiliari linguo (Artificial
      language)
Intangible assets
  USE Intangible property
Intangible property *(May Subd Geog)*
  UF Incorporeal property
      Intangible assets
      Intangibles
  BT Property
  NT Business names
      Choses in action
      Copyright
      Good-will (in business, etc.)
      Intellectual property
      License agreements
      Licenses
      Patents
      Trademarks
— **Taxation** *(May Subd Geog)*
      UF Taxation of intangible property
      BT Property tax
      NT Taxation of bonds, securities, etc.
Intangible property (Canon law)
Intangibles
  USE Intangible property
Intarsia
  USE Marquetry
Integer programming
  BT Programming (Mathematics)
Integers, Rings of
  USE Rings of integers
Integral, Pettis
  USE Pettis integral
Integral, Riemann
  USE Riemann integral
INTEGRAL (Network analysis)
  BT Network analysis (Planning)
Integral calculus
  USE Calculus, Integral
Integral closure
  UF Closure, Integral
  BT Commutative rings
      Ring extensions (Algebra)
Integral Data Store
  USE IDS (Computer program language)
Integral equations
  ₍QA431 (Mathematics)₎
  ₍TA347.I5 (Engineering)₎
  UF Equations, Integral
  BT Functional equations
  RT Functional analysis
  NT Calculus, Operational
      Fredholm equations
      Integral transforms
      Integro-differential equations
      Stochastic integral equations
      Volterra equations

      Wiener-Hopf equations
— **Asymptotic theory**
      UF Asymptotic theory in integral
          equations
      BT Asymptotic expansions
— **Numerical solutions**
      BT Numerical calculations
      NT Collocation methods
          Eigenfunctions
Integral equations, Dual
  ₍QC20.7.I58₎
  UF Dual integral equations
Integral equations, Nonlinear
  UF Nonlinear integral equations
  BT Nonlinear theories
— **Numerical solutions**
      ₍QA372₎
      BT Numerical analysis
Integral error function
  USE Error functions
Integral formula, Poisson
  USE Poisson integral formula
Integral functions
  USE Functions, Entire
Integral geometry
  USE Geometry, Integral
Integral inequalities
  BT Inequalities (Mathematics)
  NT Gronwall inequalities
Integral operators
  UF Operators, Integral
  BT Integrals
      Operator theory
  NT Fourier integral operators
      Hankel operators
      Integrals, Singular
Integral representations
  UF Representations, Integral
  BT Algebraic number theory
      Crystallography, Mathematical
      Representations of groups
Integral theorems
  UF Theorems, Integral
  BT Integrals
Integral transforms
  UF Transform calculus
      Transforms, Integral
  BT Integral equations
      Transformations (Mathematics)
  NT Integrals, Singular
      Mellin transform
      Radon transforms
      Stieltjes transform
Integralismo
  USE Fascism—Brazil
Integralist Revolt, Brazil, 1938
  USE Brazil—History—Revolution, 1938
Integrals
  ₍QA308-311₎
  BT Calculus, Integral
  NT Bernstein polynomials
      Calculus of residues
      Convolutions (Mathematics)
      Dilogarithms
      Integral operators
      Integral theorems
      Integrals, Fractional
      Integrals, Fresnel
      Integrals, Logarithmic
      Integrals, Path
      Integrals, Stieltjes
      Overlap integral
      Pettis integral
      Poisson integral formula
      Resonance integral
      Stokes' theorem
Integrals, Abelian
  USE Functions, Abelian
Integrals, Bochner
  UF Bochner integrals

  BT Banach spaces
      Convergence
      Integrals, Generalized
      Vector valued functions
Integrals, Collision
  USE Collision integrals
Integrals, Definite
  ₍QA311₎
  NT Error functions
      Numerical integration
      Riemann integral
Integrals, Denjoy
  UF Denjoy integrals
  BT Functions of real variables
      Integrals, Singular
Integrals, Dirichlet
  UF Dirichlet integrals
  BT Fourier series
  NT Dirichlet principle
Integrals, Double
  USE Integrals, Multiple
Integrals, Elliptic
  USE Functions, Elliptic
Integrals, Feynman
  USE Feynman integrals
Integrals, Fractional
  UF Fractional integrals
  BT Integrals
Integrals, Fresnel
  UF Fresnel integrals
  BT Integrals
Integrals, Generalized
  ₍QA312₎
  BT Calculus, Integral
  NT Integrals, Bochner
      Integrals, Haar
      Integration, Functional
      Measure theory
      Wiener integrals
Integrals, Haar
  UF Haar integral
      Haar measure
      Haar's measure
  BT Integrals, Generalized
      Invariants
      Measure theory
Integrals, Henstock
  USE Henstock integrals
Integrals, Hyperelliptic
  UF Functions, Hyperelliptic
      Hyperelliptic functions
      Hyperelliptic integrals
  RT Functions, Elliptic
Integrals, Improper
  UF Improper integrals
  NT Integrals, Infinite
Integrals, Infinite
  UF Infinite integrals
  BT Integrals, Improper
Integrals, Iterated
  USE Integrals, Multiple
Integrals, Logarithmic
  UF Logarithmic integrals
  BT Integrals
Integrals, Multiple
  ₍QA311₎
  UF Double integrals
      Integrals, Double
      Integrals, Iterated
      Iterated integrals
      Multiple integrals
      Triple integrals
  BT Probabilities
  NT Collision integrals
      Feynman integrals
Integrals, Path
  ₍QC174.17.P27 (Quantum theory)₎
  ₍QC174.52.P37 (Quantum field
      theory)₎
  UF Path integrals

Integrals, Path *(Continued)*
  BT Integrals
      Probabilities
      Quantum theory
      Statistical physics
Integrals, Singular
  UF Singular integrals
  BT Integral operators
      Integral transforms
  NT Integrals, Denjoy
Integrals, Stieltjes
  UF Stieltjes integrals
  BT Integrals
Integrals, Stochastic
  [QA274.22]
  UF Stochastic integrals
  BT Stochastic analysis
Integrals, Wiener
  USE Wiener integrals
Integrated bar *(May Subd Geog)*
      Here are entered works on state or local bar as-
      sociations, membership in which is compulsory as a
      condition to practice law in the area.
  UF Bar integration
      Incorporated bar
      State bar
      Unified bar
  BT Bar associations
      Lawyers
      Practice of law
Integrated circuit cards
  USE Smart cards
Integrated circuits
  UF Chips (Electronics)
      Circuits, Integrated
      Microchips
  BT Electronic circuits
      Microelectronics
  NT Bipolar integrated circuits
      Charge coupled devices
      Digital integrated circuits
      Emitter-coupled logic circuits
      Gate array circuits
      Hybrid integrated circuits
      Integrated optics
      Line drivers (Integrated circuits)
      Line receivers (Integrated circuits)
      Linear integrated circuits
      Magnetic bubble devices
      Microwave integrated circuits
      Thick-film circuits
      Thin-film circuits
 — **Design and construction**
 — — **Data processing**
 — **Effect of radiation on**
  UF Integrated circuits, Effect of
      radiation on
  BT Radiation
 — **Large scale integration**
  [TK7874]
  UF Large scale integration
  NT Integrated injection logic
 — **Masks**
  BT Masks (Electronics)
 — **Medium scale integration**
  UF Medium scale integration of
      circuits
 — **Passivation**
  UF Passivation of integrated circuits
  BT Passivity (Chemistry)
      Protective coatings
 — **Very large scale integration**
  UF Very large scale integration of
      circuits
      VLSI circuits
  NT Very high speed integrated circuits
Integrated circuits, Effect of radiation on
  USE Integrated circuits—Effect of radiation
      on
Integrated circuits, Hybrid
  USE Hybrid integrated circuits

Integrated circuits industry
  (May Subd Geog)
  [HD9696.I58-584]
Integrated Civil Engineering System
  (Electronic computer system)
  USE ICES (Electronic computer system)
Integrated control of agricultural pests
  USE Agricultural pests—Integrated control
Integrated control of pests
  USE Pests—Integrated control
Integrated curriculum
  USE Interdisciplinary approach in education
Integrated data processing
  USE Electronic data processing
Integrated Database Management System
  (Computer system)
  USE IDMS (Computer system)
Integrated Database Management
  System/Relational (Computer system)
  USE IDMS/R (Computer system)
Integrated development of water resources
  USE Integrated water development
Integrated injection logic
  UF Merged transistor logic
  BT Integrated circuits—Large scale
      integration
      Logic circuits
      Transistor circuits
Integrated logistic support
  [U168]
  UF Logistic support, Integrated
  BT Logistics
Integrated optical circuits
  USE Integrated optics
Integrated optics
  [TA1660]
  UF Integrated optical circuits
  BT Integrated circuits
      Photonics
      Thin films
  NT Acoustooptical devices
      Electrooptical devices
      Fiber optics
      Laser communication systems
      Optical data processing
      Optical wave guides
Integrated pest control
  USE Pests—Integrated control
Integrated pest management
  USE Pests—Integrated control
Integrated Scientific Information System
  USE ISIS (Information retrieval system)
Integrated services digital networks
  UF ISDN (Digital networks)
  BT Data transmission systems
      Digital communications
Integrated utility systems, Modular
  USE Modular integrated utility systems
Integrated water development
  (May Subd Geog)
  UF Integrated development of water
      resources
      Water development, Integrated
  BT Water conservation
      Water resources development
      Water use
Integration, Faculty
  USE Faculty integration
Integration, Functional
  [QC20.7.F85]
  UF Functional integration
  BT Functional analysis
      Integrals, Generalized
Integration, Numerical
  USE Numerical integration
Integration, Racial
  USE Race relations
Integration, Sensorimotor
  USE Sensorimotor integration
Integration, Social
  USE Social integration

Integration, Vertical
  USE Vertical integration
Integration (Theory of knowledge)
  BT Knowledge, Theory of
Integration in education
  USE Articulation (Education)
      School integration
Integration in higher education
  USE College integration
      Segregation in higher education
Integration in sports
  USE Discrimination in sports
Integrators
  [QA75]
  BT Analog computers
  NT Planimeter
Integrierte Dialog-Orientierte Statistik System
  (Computer system)
  USE INDIOS (Computer system)
Integrity
  BT Reliability
  RT Honesty
Integro-differential equations
  UF Integrodifferential equations
  BT Differential equations
      Integral equations
 — **Asymptotic theory**
  UF Asymptotic theory in integro-
      differential equations
  BT Asymptotic expansions
 — **Improperly posed problems**
  UF Improperly posed problems
      (Integro-differential equations)
 — **Numerical solutions**
  BT Numerical analysis
Integrodifferential equations
  USE Integro-differential equations
Integument (Skin)
  USE Skin
Intel 286 (Microprocessor)
  USE Intel 80286 (Microprocessor)
Intel 287 (Microprocessor)
  USE Intel 80287 (Microprocessor)
Intel 432 (Computer)
  [QA76.8.I]
  BT Electronic digital computers
 — **Programming**
Intel 8048 (Computer)
  [QA76.8.I]
  UF 8048 (Computer)
  BT Microcomputers
INTEL 8051 (Computer)
  [QA76.8.I]
  BT Electronic digital computers
 — **Programming**
Intel 8080 (Microprocessor)
  [QA76.8.I]
  UF 8080 (Microprocessor)
  BT Microprocessors
 — **Programming**
  NT DBUG (Computer program)
      Monitor Command System
      (Computer program)
INTEL 8080A (Computer)
  [QA76.8.I]
  BT Electronic digital computers
 — **Programming**
Intel 8085 (Microprocessor)
  [QA76.8.I]
  BT Microprocessors
Intel 8085A (Microprocessor)
  [QA76.8.I]
  UF 8085A (Microprocessor)
  BT Microprocessors
Intel 8086 (Microprocessor)
  UF 8086 (Microprocessor)
  BT Microprocessors
Intel 8087 (Microprocessor)
  [QA76.8.I]
  UF 8087 (Microprocessor)
  BT Microprocessors

Intel 8088 (Microprocessor)
  UF 8088 (Microprocessor)
  BT Microprocessors
Intel 8089 (Microprocessor)
  UF 8089 (Microprocessor)
  BT Computer input-output equipment
      Microprocessors
Intel 8096 (Microprocessor)
  UF 8096 (Microprocessor)
  BT Microprocessors
Intel 80286 (Microprocessor)
  UF 80286 (Microprocessor)
      Intel 286 (Microprocessor)
  BT Microprocessors
Intel 80287 (Microprocessor)
  UF 80287 (Microprocessor)
      Intel 287 (Microprocessor)
  BT Microprocessors
Intel 80386 (Microprocessor)
  ⌐QA76.8.I⌐
  UF 80386 (Microprocessor)
  BT Microprocessors
Intel 80387 (Microprocessor)
  ⌐QA76.8.I⌐
  UF 80387 (Microprocessor)
  BT Microprocessors
Intel SDK-85 (Microprocessor)
  UF SDK-85 (Microprocessor)
  BT Microprocessors
Intel SDK-86 (Microprocessor)
  UF SDK-86 (Microprocessor)
  BT Microprocessors
Intellect
  ⌐BF431-BF433 (Psychology)⌐
  UF Human intelligence
      Intelligence
      Mind
  BT Ability
      Psychology
  RT Knowledge, Theory of
      Mental retardation
      Reasoning (Psychology)
      Thought and thinking
  SA *subdivision* Intelligence levels *under*
      classes of persons and ethnic groups
  NT Age and intelligence
      Cognitive styles
      Creation (Literary, artistic, etc.)
      Imagination
      Inefficiency, Intellectual
      Intelligence tests
      Logic
      Memory
      Motor ability and intelligence
      Perception
      Reason
      Self-organizing systems
      Social intelligence
      Wisdom
  — Deterioration
      ⌐BF431⌐
      NT Inefficiency, Intellectual
  — Genetic aspects
      ⌐BF431⌐
  — Nutritional aspects
      ⌐QP398⌐
      BT Psychology, Physiological
  — Religious aspects
  —— Buddhism, ⌐Christianity, etc.⌐
Intellect and age
  USE Age and intelligence
Intellect and personality
  USE Personality and intelligence
Intellect of animals
  USE Animal intelligence
Intellectronics
  USE Artificial intelligence
      Bionics
Intellectual activity
  USE Mental work

Intellectual cooperation
  ⌐AS4⌐
  ⌐JC362 (Political theory)⌐
  ⌐JX1975 (League of Nations)⌐
  UF Cooperation, Intellectual
      Cultural exchange programs
  BT International cooperation
  RT International education
      Library cooperation
  SA *subdivision* Relations *under names of*
      countries, cities, etc.
  NT Authorship—Collaboration
      Cataloging, Cooperative
      Congresses and conventions
      Cultural relations
      Educational exchanges
      Endowment of research
      Exchange of persons programs
      Exchanges, Literary and scientific
      Information networks
      International correspondence
      International Education Year, 1970
      International Geophysical Year, 1957-
      1958
      International Years of the Quiet Sun,
      1964-1965
      Internationalism
      University cooperation
Intellectual freedom
  USE Academic freedom
      Censorship
      Freedom of information
      Freedom of speech
      Teaching, Freedom of
Intellectual history
  USE *subdivision* Intellectual life *under*
      particular classes of people and
      under names of countries, cities,
      etc., e.g. French-Canadians—
      Intellectual life; Jews—Intellectual
      life; France—Intellectual life
      Intellectual life—History
Intellectual inefficiency
  USE Inefficiency, Intellectual
Intellectual life
      Here are entered general works on learning and
  scholarship, literature, the arts, etc. Works on litera-
  ture, art, music, motion pictures, etc. produced for a
  mass audience are entered under Popular culture.
  BT Culture
  SA *subdivision* Intellectual life *under*
      names of countries, cities, etc.; and
      under individual ethnic or religious
      groups
  NT Cultural policy
      Learning and scholarship
      Popular culture
      Salons
  — Government policy
      USE Cultural policy
  — History
      UF Intellectual history
Intellectual property *(May Subd Geog)*
  UF Proprietary rights
  BT Intangible property
  NT Copyright
      Industrial property
Intellectual property (International law)
  BT International law
Intellectuals *(May Subd Geog)*
  ⌐HM213⌐
  UF Intelligentsia
  RT Professions
  SA *subdivision* Intellectual life *under*
      particular classes of people and
      under names of countries, cities,
      etc., e.g. French-Canadians—
      Intellectual life; Jews—Intellectual
      life; United States—Intellectual life
  NT Libraries and intellectuals
      Women intellectuals

  — Books and reading
Intellectuals and communism
  USE Communism and intellectuals
Intellectuals in literature
  BT Characters and characteristics in
      literature
  SA *subdivision* Characters—Intellectuals
      under names of individual literary
      authors, e.g. Shakespeare, William,
      1564-1616—Characters—
      Intellectuals
Intellektueller (The German word)
  BT German language—Etymology
Intelligence
  USE Intellect
Intelligence, Artificial
  USE Artificial intelligence
Intelligence, Business
  USE Business intelligence
Intelligence, Electronic
  USE Electronic intelligence
Intelligence, Social
  USE Social intelligence
Intelligence, Verbal
  USE Verbal ability
Intelligence and age
  USE Age and intelligence
Intelligence and motor ability
  USE Motor ability and intelligence
Intelligence community
  USE Intelligence service
Intelligence levels *(May Subd Geog)*
  UF Intelligence quotient
      IQ
  BT Educational psychology
      Genetic psychology
  SA *subdivision* Intelligence levels *under*
      classes of persons and ethnic groups
  NT Intelligence tests
      Mental age
  — Testing
      USE Intelligence tests
Intelligence of animals
  USE Animal intelligence
      Instinct
      Psychology, Comparative
Intelligence officers *(May Subd Geog)*
  BT Intelligence service
Intelligence quotient
  USE Intelligence levels
Intelligence service *(May Subd Geog)*
  UF Counterespionage
      Counterintelligence
      Intelligence community
  BT Public administration
      Research
  RT Disinformation
      Secret service
  NT Electronic intelligence
      Espionage
      Intelligence officers
      Military intelligence
  — Finance
  —— Law and legislation
      (May Subd Geog)
  — Law and legislation *(May Subd Geog)*
  — United States
      NT Jennifer Project
Intelligence specialists (United States Navy)
  USE United States. Navy—Intelligence
      specialists
Intelligence testing
  USE Intelligence tests
Intelligence tests *(May Subd Geog)*
  ⌐BF431.5⌐
  UF Intelligence levels—Testing
      Intelligence testing
      Mental tests

Intelligence tests *(Continued)*
  BT Ability—Testing
      Inefficiency, Intellectual
      Intellect
      Intelligence levels
      Psychological tests
  NT Binet-Simon test
      Canadian intelligence test
      Children—Intelligence testing
      Goodenough draw-a-man test
      Goodenough-Harris drawing test
      Group intelligence tests
      Infants—Intelligence testing
      Intelligence tests for pre-literates
      Kohs block design test
      Kuhlmann-Anderson test
      Learning Potential Assessment Device
      Multidimensional Aptitude Battery
      Non-verbal intelligence tests
      Otis quick-scoring mental ability tests
      Peabody picture vocabulary test
      Purdue non-language adaptability test
      Stanford-Binet test
      Stanford-Ohwaki-Kohs tactile block
        design intelligence test for the blind
      Wechsler adult intelligence scale
      Wechsler intelligence scale for children
      Woodcock-Johnson Tests of Cognitive
        Ability

Intelligence tests for pre-literates
  (May Subd Geog)
  BT Intelligence tests
      Literacy
Intelligent machines
  USE Artificial intelligence
      Conscious automata
      Logic machines
Intelligent terminals
  USE Computer terminals—Intelligent
      terminals
Intelligentsia
  USE Intellectuals
Intelligibility of related languages
  USE Languages, Modern—Mutual
      intelligibility
Intelligibility of speech
  USE Speech, Intelligibility of
Intemperance
  USE Alcoholism
      Temperance
Intendants *(May Subd Geog)*
  BT Local officials and employees
Intension (Philosophy)
  USE Semantics (Philosophy)
Intensity, Earthquake
  USE Earthquake intensity
Intensity correlation spectroscopy
  USE Quasielastic light scattering
Intensity variations of the sun
  USE Solar oscillations
Intensive Agricultural Area Programme
  BT Agriculture—India
      Agriculture and state—India
  RT Intensive Agricultural District
      Programme
Intensive Agricultural District Programme
  [S471.13 (General)]
  BT Agriculture—India
      Agriculture and state—India
  RT Intensive Agricultural Area
      Programme
Intensive care, Neonatal
  USE Neonatal intensive care
Intensive care, Pediatric
  USE Pediatric intensive care
Intensive care nursing *(May Subd Geog)*
  [RT120.15]
  BT Critical care medicine
      Intensive care units
      Nursing

Intensive care of the newborn
  USE Neonatal intensive care
Intensive care units *(May Subd Geog)*
  [RA975.5.I56]
  UF Critical care units
  BT Hospital care
      Hospital wards
  RT Critical care medicine
  NT Burn care units
      Coronary care units
      Intensive care nursing
      Intensive care units, Mobile
      Recovery room (Surgery)
  — **Law and legislation** *(May Subd Geog)*
      BT Medical laws and legislation
Intensive care units, Mobile
  (May Subd Geog)
  UF Mobile intensive care units
  BT Ambulances
      Hospitals, Mobile
      Intensive care units
  NT Coronary care units, Mobile
Intensive Cattle Development Programme
  BT Agriculture and state—India
      Cattle—India
Intensive medicine
  USE Critical care medicine
Intensive programs in education
  USE Concentrated study
      Educational acceleration
Intensive veterinary medicine
  USE Veterinary critical care
Intent, Criminal
  USE Criminal intent
Intent, Letters of
  USE Letters of intent
Intention
  BT Attitude (Psychology)
  — **Religious aspects**
      UF Purity of intention
  — — **Buddhism, [Christianity, etc.]**
Intention, Declaration of
  USE Declaration of intention
Intention (Logic)
  [BC199.I5]
  BT Logic
      Reasoning
Intentionalism
  [BF619.5]
  UF Act psychology
      Action psychology
  BT Psychology
Intentionality (Philosophy)
  [B105.I56]
  BT Act (Philosophy)
      Mind and body
      Philosophy
Inter-American conferences
  UF International American conferences
      Pan American conferences
  BT Latin America—Politics and
      government
      Pan-Americanism
  SA *particular conferences and congresses*
Inter-American conventions
  USE Pan-American treaties and conventions
Inter-American cooperation
  USE Pan-Americanism
Inter-American relations
  USE Pan-Americanism
Inter-American treaties
  USE Pan-American treaties and conventions
Inter-college cooperation
  USE University cooperation
Inter-cultural studies
  USE Cross-cultural studies
Inter-library loans *(May Subd Geog)*
  [Z713]
  UF Book lending
      Books, Lending of
      Loans, Inter-library

  BT Libraries—Circulation, loans
      Library cooperation
  RT Exchanges, Literary and scientific
  NT Document delivery
  — **Law and legislation** *(May Subd Geog)*
      BT Library legislation
  — **Florida**
      NT Florida Interlibrary Loan
        Improvement Project
  — **Texas**
  — **United States**
      NT OCLC Interlibrary Loan Subsystem
        SILC (Library information
        network)
Inter-male aggression *(May Subd Geog)*
  Here are entered works on aggression among
males which is directed solely toward members of
their own species, and which is triggered by specific
events in the environment.
  UF Aggression, Inter-male
  BT Aggressiveness (Psychology)
Inter vivos trusts
  USE Living trusts
INTERACT (Computer program)
Interaction, Social
  USE Social interaction
Interaction (Philosophy)
  [B824.1]
  BT Philosophy
Interaction analysis in education
  UF Analysis, Interaction (Education)
      Interaction process analysis in
       education
      Teacher-pupil interaction
  BT Observation (Educational method)
      Social interaction
      Teacher-student relationships
      Verbal behavior
  NT Communication in education
      Microteaching
Interaction of atmosphere and ocean
  USE Ocean-atmosphere interaction
Interaction of snow and wind
  USE Wind-snow interaction
Interaction process analysis in education
  USE Interaction analysis in education
Interactions, Deuteron
  USE Deuteron reactions
Interactions, Effective
  USE Effective interactions (Nuclear
      physics)
Interactions, Electromagnetic
  USE Electromagnetic interactions
Interactions, Electron-electron
  USE Electron-electron interactions
Interactions, Electron-phonon
  USE Electron-phonon interactions
Interactions, Electron-positron
  USE Electron-positron interactions
Interactions, Electroweak
  USE Electroweak interactions
Interactions, Gamma-gamma
  USE Photon-photon interactions
Interactions, Hadron
  USE Hadron interactions
Interactions, Hyperfine
  USE Hyperfine interactions
Interactions, Laser-plasma
  USE Laser-plasma interactions
Interactions, Meson-nucleon
  USE Meson-nucleon interactions
Interactions, Neutron-proton
  USE Neutron-proton interactions
Interactions, Nucleon-antinucleon
  USE Nucleon-antinucleon interactions
Interactions, Nucleon-nucleon
  USE Nucleon-nucleon interactions
Interactions, Photon-photon
  USE Photon-photon interactions
Interactions, Pion-pion
  USE Pion-pion interactions

Interactions, Plasma-wall
USE Plasma-wall interactions
Interactions, Proton-antiproton
USE Proton-antiproton interactions
Interactions, Proton-neutron
USE Neutron-proton interactions
Interactions, Quark-gluon
USE Quark-gluon interactions
Interactive computer systems
[QA76.9.I58]
UF Computer systems, Interactive
BT Electronic data processing
Man-machine systems
On-line data processing
Question-answering systems
NT BIOMOD (Computer system)
Computer terminals—Interactive
terminals
CRJE (Computer program)
GIML (Computer program language)
GOLEM (Information retrieval
system)
ICCF (Computer system)
ISPF Dialog Manager (Computer
program)
MUSIC (Computer system)
Omnidata (Computer system)
PISA (Computer system)
S (Computer system)
SalesCTRL (Computer system)
SURVIS (Computer program language)
TICCIT (Computer system)
Interactive Computing and Control Facility
(Computer system)
USE ICCF (Computer system)
Interactive cooperativity (Biochemistry)
USE Cooperative binding (Biochemistry)
Interactive Data Analysis (Computer system)
USE IDA (Computer system)
**Interactive Express Statistical System
(Electronic computer system)**
[QA278.2]
UF IESS (Electronic computer system)
Interactive Financial Planning System
(Computer system)
USE IFPS (Computer system)
**Interactive Statistical Programs (Computer
programs)**
UF ISP (Computer programs)
BT Computer programs
Mathematical statistics—Computer
programs
Statistics—Computer programs
Interactive System Productivity Facility Dialog
Manager (Computer program)
USE ISPF Dialog Manager (Computer
program)
Interactive terminals
USE Computer terminals—Interactive
terminals
Interactive video (May Subd Geog)
[LB1028.75 (Computer-assisted
instruction)]
UF Video systems, Interactive
BT Video recordings
RT Computer-assisted instruction
NT Videotex systems
Interanimal memory transfer
USE Memory transfer
Intercalation compounds
USE Clathrate compounds
Intercarotid body
USE Carotid body
Intercellular matrix
USE Extracellular matrix
Intercept method
USE Saint Hilaire method
Intercept systems, Automatic telephone
USE Telephone—Automatic intercept
system

Interception of communications, Unauthorized
USE Eavesdropping
Interceptive orthodontics
USE Orthodontics, Interceptive
Intercession between God and man
USE Mediation between God and man
Interchange of bibliographic information
USE Exchange of bibliographic information
Interchange of librarians
USE Librarians, Interchange of
Interchange of library students
USE Librarians, Interchange of
Interchange of patents and technical
information
USE Exchanges of patents and technical
information
Interchange of persons
USE Exchange of persons programs
Interchange of population
USE Population transfers
Interchange of students
USE Students, Interchange of
Interchange of teachers
USE Teachers, Interchange of
Interchange of visitors
USE Exchange of persons programs
Interchangeable mechanisms
[TJ233]
[TJ1180]
UF Mechanisms, Interchangeable
BT Machine parts
Machinery
Unit construction
Interchanges (Highway engineering)
USE Roads—Interchanges and intersections
Interchurch cooperation
USE Interdenominational cooperation
Intercoastal shipping (May Subd Geog)
[HE751]
BT Shipping
RT Coastwise shipping
— **Law and legislation** (May Subd Geog)
BT Maritime law
Intercommunication systems
UF Intercoms
Interoffice communication systems
BT Electro-acoustics
Electronic apparatus and appliances
Electronic systems
Sound—Recording and reproducing
Telecommunication systems
RT Public address systems
SA subdivision Communication systems
under subjects, e.g. Railroads—
Communication systems
NT Closed-circuit television
Microwave communication systems
Police communication systems
Intercommunion
[BX9.5.I5]
BT Close and open communion
NT Communicatio in sacris
Unionism (Lutheranism)
Intercoms
USE Intercommunication systems
Interconnected electric utility systems
(May Subd Geog)
UF Electric power pooling
Electric utility systems, Interconnected
System interconnection, Electric power
BT Electric power distribution
Electric power-plants
Electric power systems
Electric utilities
NT Hydrothermal electric power systems
International interconnected electric
utility systems
— **Automation**
UF Automatic load dispatching
(Electric power)

BT Automatic control
Electric power distribution
Electric power-plants—Load
Interconnection (Plumbing)
USE Cross-connections (Plumbing)
Intercontinental ballistic missile bases
(May Subd Geog)
BT Astronautics, Military
Intercontinental ballistic missiles
Weapons systems
RT Air bases
NT Bombing and gunnery ranges
Intercontinental ballistic missiles
UF ICBM
BT Ballistic missiles
Strategic forces
SA names of specific intercontinental
ballistic missiles, e.g. Atlas
(Missile); Minuteman (Missile)
NT Intercontinental ballistic missile bases
MX (Weapons system)
— **Trajectories**
UF Trajectories of intercontinental
ballistic missiles
— — **Computer programs**
NT COMET (Computer program)
Intercontinental bombers
USE Supersonic bombers
Intercorrelation of traits
USE Trait intercorrelations
Intercostal muscles
BT Muscles
Intercountry adoption (May Subd Geog)
[HV875.2]
UF International adoption
Trans-national adoption
BT Adoption
RT Interracial adoption
Intercourse, Anal
USE Anal intercourse
Intercourse, Oral
USE Oral intercourse
Intercourse, Sexual
USE Sexual intercourse
Intercropping (May Subd Geog)
[S603.5]
Here are entered works on the growing of two or
more crops simultaneously in the same field or gar-
den. Works on the growing of certain selected inter-
planting combinations in order to achieve a specific
benefit such as pest control or enhanced growth are
entered under Companion planting.
BT Cropping systems
RT Agroforestry
Catch crops
Companion crops
NT Companion planting
Intercrops
USE Catch crops
Intercultural communication
(May Subd Geog)
[GN496 (Anthropology)]
[HM258 (Social psychology)]
UF Communication, Intercultural
Cross-cultural communication
BT Communication
Culture
East and West
RT Cross-cultural orientation
Technical assistance—Anthropological
aspects
NT Cross-cultural orientation
Culture shock
Intercultural education (May Subd Geog)
[LC1099]
UF Education, Intercultural
BT Acculturation
Assimilation (Sociology)
Comparative education
Ethnic relations
Race relations

Intercultural education *(Continued)*
  RT Cross-cultural orientation
  NT Cross-cultural orientation
       Education, Bilingual
       Race awareness
Intercultural relations
  USE Cultural relations
Intercultural studies
  USE Cross-cultural studies
Interdenominational cooperation
  [BV625]
      Here are entered works on religious activities planned and conducted cooperatively by two or more Christian sects. Works on the unification of Christian sects are entered under Christian union. Works on movements whose goal is the world-wide unification of the church are entered under Ecumenical movement. Works on unity as one of the "marks" of the church are entered under Church—Unity.
  UF Cooperation, Interchurch
      Cooperation, Interdenominational
      Interchurch cooperation
      Simultaneum
  BT Christian sects
      Church work
  NT Churches—Interdenominational use
      Federated churches
      Local church councils
      Missions—Interdenominational
        cooperation
Interdependence of nations
  USE International cooperation
      International economic relations
      International organization
      International relations
Interdict (Canon law)
  [BX1939.I5]
  BT Catholic Church—Discipline
      Censures, Ecclesiastical
      Excommunication
      Punishment (Canon law)
  NT Venice (Italy)—History—Papal
        Interdict, 1606-1607
Interdict (Civil law) *(May Subd Geog)*
  UF Uti possidetis (Civil law)
  BT Possession (Law)
  RT Injunctions
  NT Possessory actions
Interdict (Roman-Dutch law)
Interdict (Roman law)
Interdiction, Air
  USE Air interdiction
Interdiction (Civil law) *(May Subd Geog)*
  BT Insanity—Jurisprudence
      Persons (Law)
  RT Capacity and disability
      Guardian and ward
      Prodigals (Law)
Interdiction (Islamic law)
  RT Guardian and ward (Islamic law)
Interdigital transducers
  USE Transducers, Interdigital
Interdisciplinarity in education
  USE Interdisciplinary approach in education
Interdisciplinary approach in education
  (May Subd Geog)
  UF Integrated curriculum
      Interdisciplinarity in education
      Interdisciplinary studies
  BT Curriculum planning
      Universities and colleges—Curricula
  NT Language arts—Correlation with
        content subjects
Interdisciplinary approach to knowledge
  [BD255]
  BT Knowledge, Theory of
      Methodology
      Science and the humanities
Interdisciplinary studies
  USE Interdisciplinary approach in education
Interdivisional transfer pricing
  USE Transfer pricing

Interdominion Championship
  [SF345.I58]
  BT Harness racing—New Zealand
Interest *(May Subd Geog)*
  [HB531-HB549 (Economic theory)]
  [HG1621-HG1623 (Banking practice)]
  BT Banks and banking
      Credit
      Finance charges
      Income
      Loans
  NT Interest rates
      NOW accounts
      Roll-over credits
      Usury
  — **Law and legislation** *(May Subd Geog)*
    BT Banking law
       Commercial law
    RT Usury laws
  — **Taxation** *(May Subd Geog)*
  — — **Law and legislation**
      (May Subd Geog)
Interest (Islamic law) *(May Subd Geog)*
  BT Islamic law
Interest (Jewish law)
  [BM523.5.I5]
  BT Jewish law
Interest (Law) *(May Subd Geog)*
  BT Civil law
  NT Damages
Interest (Philosophy)
  [B105.I57]
  BT Philosophy
Interest (Psychology)
  [BF321]
  UF Interests (Psychology)
  BT Educational psychology
      Psychology
  RT Attention
  NT Attention-seeking
      Curiosity
      Interest inventories
      Personality-interest test
Interest arbitration *(May Subd Geog)*
  UF Arbitration, Interest
  BT Arbitration, Industrial
  NT Final offer arbitration
Interest as tax deductions
  USE Income tax—Deductions—Interest
Interest centers approach to teaching
  USE Classroom learning centers
      Open plan schools
Interest groups
  USE Pressure groups
Interest inventories
  [LB1027.5]
  UF Interest measures
  BT Interest (Psychology)
      Personnel service in education
Interest measures
  USE Interest inventories
Interest rate futures *(May Subd Geog)*
  [HG6043]
  UF Futures, Interest rate
  BT Financial futures
      Interest rates
      Money market
      Speculation
  — **Law and legislation** *(May Subd Geog)*
    BT Usury laws
Interest rates *(May Subd Geog)*
  [HB531-HB549 (Economic theory)]
  [HG1621-HG1623 (Banking practice)]
  UF Rate of interest
      Rates, Interest
  BT Interest
  NT Discount
      Gibson paradox
      Interest rate futures
      Prime rate
      Usury

  — **Effect of inflation on**
    BT Inflation (Finance)
Interests, Conflict of
  USE Conflict of interests
Interests, Reading
  USE Reading interests
Interests (Psychology)
  USE Interest (Psychology)
Interethnic relations
  USE Ethnic relations
Interface circuits
  [TK7868.I58]
  UF Circuits, Interface
  BT Electronic circuits
  RT Logic circuits
  NT Computer interfaces
Interfaces, Biological
  USE Biological interfaces
Interfaces, Chemistry of
  USE Surface chemistry
Interfaces, Computer
  USE Computer interfaces
**Interfaces, Programmable peripheral
  microcomputer**
  USE Microcomputers—Programmable
        peripheral interfaces
Interfacings, Fusible
  USE Fusible materials in sewing
Interfacings (Clothing)
  BT Clothing and dress
      Sewing
  NT Fusible materials in sewing
Interfaith marriage *(May Subd Geog)*
  [HQ1031]
  UF Intermarriage, Religious
      Interreligious marriage
      Marriage, Interfaith
      Marriage, Mixed
      Mixed marriage
      Religious intermarriage
  BT Intermarriage
  NT Children of interfaith marriage
Interfaith marriage (Canon law)
  UF Marriage, Mixed (Canon law)
  BT Canon law
Interfaith marriage (Islamic law)
  UF Marriage, Mixed (Islamic law)
  BT Islamic law
Interfaith marriage (Jewish law)
  UF Marriage, Mixed (Jewish law)
  BT Jewish law
Interfaith marriage (Roman law)
  UF Marriage, Mixed (Roman law)
  BT Roman law
Interfaith marriage in literature
  UF Marriage, Mixed, in literature
Interfaith worship *(May Subd Geog)*
  BT Worship
Interference, Electromagnetic
  USE Electromagnetic interference
Interference, Gearing
  USE Gearing—Interference
Interference (Aerodynamics)
  BT Aerodynamics
Interference (Electricity)
  USE Electric interference
Interference (Light)
  [QC411]
  UF Newton's rings
  BT Light
      Optics
      Wave-motion, Theory of
  NT Electric waves
      Holography
      Interferometry
      Iridescence
Interference (Linguistics)
  [P53 (Language study)]
  [P115 (Bilingualism)]
  [P130.5 (Languages in contact)]
  UF Linguistic interference

BT Bilingualism
    Language transfer (Language learning)
Interference (Sound)
    [QC233]
  NT Acoustic holography
Interference microscope
    [QH212.I5]
  BT Microscope and microscopy
Interference spectrometry
  USE Fourier transform spectroscopy
Interferometer
    [QC411]
  RT Interferometry
  NT Fourier transform spectroscopy
    Laser interferometer
    Polarization interferometer
    Radio interferometers
Interferometry
  BT Interference (Light)
    Optical measurements
  RT Interferometer
  NT Acoustic holography
    Diffraction patterns
    Holographic interferometry
    Holography
    Meteorological optics
    Spectrum analysis
Interferometry, Neutron
    [QC793.5.N4627]
  UF Neutron interferometry
  BT Neutrons—Spectra
  NT Neutron capture gamma ray
     spectroscopy
Interferometry, Very long baseline
  USE Very long baseline interferometry
Interferon
    [QR187.5 (Immunology)]
    [RC271.I46 (Cancer therapy)]
  BT Antineoplastic agents
    Antiviral agents
    Glycoproteins
    Lymphokines
Interferon inducers
    [QR187.5]
  UF Inducers, Interferon
    Interferonogens
  BT Antiviral agents
    Immunotherapy
    Nucleotides
  RT Immune response—Regulation
  NT Adamantane
Interferon industry *(May Subd Geog)*
    [HD9675.I48-484]
Interferonogens
  USE Interferon inducers
Intergenerational Christian education
    [BV1579]
  BT Christian education
Intergenerational relations
    (May Subd Geog)
  UF Relations, Intergenerational
  BT Interpersonal relations
  NT Children and adults
    Conflict of generations
Interglossa (Artificial language)
    [PM8398]
  BT Languages, Artificial
Intergovernmental fiscal relations
    (May Subd Geog)
  UF Federal-state fiscal relations
    Fiscal relations, Intergovernmental
    Fiscal relations, International
    International fiscal relations
    State-local fiscal relations
  BT Federal government
    Finance, Public
    International cooperation
    International relations
    Local finance—Law and legislation
  NT Grants-in-aid
    Intergovernmental tax relations

    Revenue sharing
Intergovernmental personnel programs
    (May Subd Geog)
  UF Personnel programs, Intergovernmental
  BT Civil service
  — Law and legislation *(May Subd Geog)*
Intergovernmental tax relations
    (May Subd Geog)
  UF Federal-state tax relations
    State-local tax relations
    Tax relations, Intergovernmental
    Tax sharing
  BT Federal government
    Intergovernmental fiscal relations
    Taxation
  NT Revenue sharing
    Taxation, Double
    Taxation and government property
Intergroup conflict
  USE Intergroup relations
Intergroup relations *(May Subd Geog)*
  UF Conflict, Intergroup
    Intergroup conflict
    Relations, Intergroup
  BT Social interaction
  NT Interorganizational relations
Interieur van de St. Bavo kerk te Haarlem
  (1648) (Painting)
  USE Saenredam, Pieter Jansz, 1597-1665.
     Sint Bavo-kerk te Haarlem (1648)
Interim certificates *(May Subd Geog)*
  BT Commercial documents
    Securities
  RT Stock certificates
Interim clergy *(May Subd Geog)*
  UF Clergy, Interim
    Locum tenens clergy
  BT Clergy
  — Baptists, [Catholic Church, etc.]
Interim financial statements
  USE Financial statements, Interim
Interim statements, Financial
  USE Financial statements, Interim
Interindustry economics
  USE Input-output analysis
Interior architecture *(May Subd Geog)*
    [NA2850]
  UF Architectural interiors
    Architecture, Interior
    Interior space (Architecture)
    Interiors
  BT Space (Architecture)
  NT Floor space, Industrial
    Office layout
    Room layout (Dwellings)
  — Japan
  — — Edo period, 1600-1868
Interior ballistics
  USE Ballistics, Interior
Interior Building (Washington, D.C.)
  USE Department of the Interior Building
    (Washington, D.C.)
Interior communications electricians (United
  States Navy)
  USE United States. Navy—Interior
    communications electricians
Interior decoration *(May Subd Geog)*
    [NK1700-NK3505 (Art)]
    [TX311-TX317 (Home economics)]
  UF Arts, Decorative
    Decoration, Interior
    Home decoration
    House decoration
    Interior design
  BT Art
    Buildings—Environmental engineering
    Decoration and ornament
    Home economics
  RT Furniture
    House furnishings
    Upholstery

  NT Americana in interior decoration
    Antiques in interior decoration
    Bank buildings—Decoration
    Chandeliers
    Church decoration and ornament
    Color in architecture
    Color in interior decoration
    Coverlets
    Drapery in interior decoration
    Floor coverings
    Found objects (Art) in interior
     decoration
    House furnishings industry and trade
    House plants in interior decoration
    Industrial equipment in interior
     decoration
    Interior decorators
    Interior landscaping
    Library decoration
    Lighting, Architectural and decorative
    Mural painting and decoration
    Office decoration
    Paper-hanging
    Photographs in interior decoration
    Plastics in interior decoration
    Rugs in interior decoration
    School decoration
    Screens
    Staircases
    Store decoration
    Stove-plates
    Tapestry
    Textile fabrics in interior decoration
    Texture painting
    Tiles in interior decoration
    Victoriana in interior decoration
    Wall coverings
    White in interior decoration
    Windows—Valances
    Windows in interior decoration
  — Amateurs' manuals
    Here are entered works on the practical, technical aspects of interior decoration. Works on the planning and art work are entered under the heading Interior decoration.
  — English influences
    BT England—Civilization
  — Human factors
    UF Human factors in interior
     decoration
    BT Anthropometry
     Human engineering
     Space (Architecture)
  — England
    NT Brettingham, Matthew, 1699-1769.
     Norfolk House Music Room
  — Japan
  — — History
  — — — Edo period, 1600-1868
Interior decoration accessories
    (May Subd Geog)
    [NK2115.5.A25]
  UF Accessories in interior decoration
Interior decoration in art
Interior decorators *(May Subd Geog)*
  UF Decorators, Interior
    Interior designers
  BT Designers
    Interior decoration
  NT Interior landscape contractors
    Paperhangers
Interior Department Building (Washington,
  D.C.)
  USE Department of the Interior Building
    (Washington, D.C.)
Interior design
  USE Interior decoration
Interior designers
  USE Interior decorators
Interior electric wiring
  USE Electric wiring, Interior

Interior landscape contractors
  (May Subd Geog)
    [SB419.25]
    BT Interior decorators
         Interior landscaping
         Landscape contractors
Interior landscaping *(May Subd Geog)*
    [SB419.25]
    UF Interior plantscaping
         Landscaping, Interior
         Plantscaping, Interior
    BT Indoor gardening
         Interior decoration
         Landscaping industry
    RT House plants in interior decoration
    NT Interior landscape contractors
Interior lighting
    UF Buildings—Lighting
    BT Buildings—Environmental engineering
         Lighting
    SA *subdivision* Lighting *under types of*
         buildings, e.g. Factories—Lighting;
         Office buildings—Lighting
    NT Lighting, Architectural and decorative
Interior navigation
    USE Inland navigation
Interior of St. Bavo's Church (1648) (Painting)
    USE Saenredam, Pieter Jansz, 1597-1665.
         Sint Bavo-kerk te Haarlem (1648)
Interior plantscaping
    USE Interior landscaping
Interior space (Architecture)
    USE Interior architecture
Interior valleys
    USE Polje (Geomorphology)
Interior walls
    [TH2239]
    BT Walls
    NT Dry wall
         Paneling
         Paper-hanging
         Partitions (Building)
Interiors
    USE Interior architecture
Interlace (Computer program)
    BT Data base management—Computer
         programs
Interlacing fishing rods
    USE Fishing rods—Wrapping
Interlake Region (Man.)
    BT Lakes—Manitoba
Interlanguage (Language learning)
    [P53]
    BT Language acquisition
         Language and languages—Study and
         teaching
         Languages, Mixed
Interleukins
    BT Cellular immunity
         Immune response—Regulation
         Lymphocytes
Interlingua (International Auxiliary Language
Association)
    Cf. note under Interlingua (Latin without inflec-
    tions)
    BT Languages, Artificial
Interlingua (Latin without inflections)
    Here are entered works on the artificial language
    evolved by Giuseppe Peano through a simplification
    of classical Latin. Works dealing with the artificial
    language promoted by the International Auxiliary
    Language Association are entered under Interlingua
    (International Auxiliary Language Association).
    BT Languages, Artificial
         Latin language—Glossaries,
         vocabularies, etc.
Interlinguistics
    USE Language, Universal
         Languages, Artificial
Interlinings, Tariff on
    USE Tariff on interlinings

Interlinings (Sewing)
    BT Linings (Sewing)
Interlocking directorates *(May Subd Geog)*
    Here are entered works on the holding by one
    individual of directorships in two or more separate
    corporations.
    UF Combinations, Industrial
         Combinations in restraint of trade
         Directorates, Interlocking
    BT Directors of corporations
         Industrial concentration
    RT Cartels
Interlocking signals
    USE Railroads—Signaling—Interlocking
         systems
Interlocutory decisions *(May Subd Geog)*
    UF Interlocutory decrees
         Interlocutory judgments
         Interlocutory orders
    BT Judgments
Interlocutory decisions (Canon law)
Interlocutory decrees
    USE Interlocutory decisions
Interlocutory judgments
    USE Interlocutory decisions
Interlocutory orders
    USE Interlocutory decisions
Interludes
    [PN1934 (Drama)]
    BT Drama
Interludes, English, [German, etc.]
Interludes, Spanish
    NT Entremés
         Sainetes
Intermarriage *(May Subd Geog)*
    [HQ1031]
    Here are entered works which discuss collectively
    marriage between persons of different religions, reli-
    gious denominations, races, and ethnic groups.
    UF Marriage, Mixed
         Mixed marriage
    BT Marriage
    USE Consanguinity
    NT Interfaith marriage
         Interracial marriage
Intermarriage, Racial
    USE Interracial marriage
Intermarriage, Religious
    USE Interfaith marriage
Intermaxillary bones
    [QL821 (Comparative anatomy)]
    [QM105 (Human anatomy)]
Intermediaries in public contracts, etc.
    USE Brokers in public contracts, etc.
Intermediate bosons
    [QC793.5.B62-629]
    UF Bosons, Intermediate
         Intermediate vector bosons
    BT Bosons
Intermediate filament proteins
    UF Fibroblast intermediate filament
         proteins
    BT Cytoplasmic filaments
         Proteins
Intermediate filaments
    USE Cytoplasmic filaments
Intermediate frequency amplifiers
    BT Tuned amplifiers
Intermediate goods *(May Subd Geog)*
    Here are entered works on goods that are in
    course of manufacture and not yet finished.
    UF Goods, Intermediate
         Intermediate products
         Semi-finished products
    BT Commercial products
         Manufactures
Intermediate products
    USE Intermediate goods
Intermediate-range ballistic missiles
    UF IRBM
    BT Ballistic missiles

    SA *names of specific intermediate-range*
         ballistic missiles, e.g. Jupiter missile
Intermediate school districts
    USE School districts
Intermediate schools
    USE Junior high schools
         Middle schools
Intermediate service units (Education)
    [LB2813]
    UF Regional service agencies (Education)
    BT County school systems
  — Law and legislation *(May Subd Geog)*
    BT Educational law and legislation
Intermediate state
    [BT830]
    BT Eschatology
         Future life
         Heaven
         Hell
         Purgatory
         Soul
    RT Death—Religious aspects
  — Buddhism, [Islam, etc.]
Intermediate vector bosons
    USE Intermediate bosons
Intermediation (Finance) *(May Subd Geog)*
    [HG3891.5 (International finance)]
    Here are entered works on the process whereby a
    financial institution interposes its name and trustwor-
    thiness between a lender and a borrower.
    UF Financial intermediation
    BT Finance
Intermedin
    UF Melanocyte stimulating hormone
         Melanotropin
    BT Pituitary hormones
Interment
    USE Burial
Intermetallic compounds
    BT Metals
  — Magnetic properties
  — Thermal properties
Intermittent claudication *(May Subd Geog)*
    UF Angina cruris
         Angiosclerotica intermittens
         Charcot's syndrome
         Claudication, Intermittent
         Dysbasia intermittens angiosclerotica
         Myasthenia angiosclerotica
    BT Arteriosclerosis
         Extremities, Lower—Diseases
         Thromboangiitis obliterans
Intermittent fever
    USE Malaria
Intermittent-motion mechanisms
    [TJ181.6]
    UF Mechanisms for intermittent motion
    BT Mechanical movements
    NT Clocks and watches—Escapements
Intermittent positive pressure breathing
  (May Subd Geog)
    BT Pressure breathing
Intermodal transportation
    USE Containerization
Intermolecular forces
    UF Forces, Intermolecular
    BT Chemical bonds
         Molecules
Intermontane region
    USE Great Basin
Intermunicipal law
    USE Conflict of laws
Internal acoustic meatus
    USE Auditory meatus, Internal
Internal auditing
    USE Auditing, Internal
Internal auditory meatus
    USE Auditory meatus, Internal
Internal combustion engine industry
  (May Subd Geog)
    BT Internal combustion engines

Internal combustion engines
(May Subd Geog)
[TJ751-805]
UF Gas and oil engines
Gas engines
BT Engines
Gas producers
Heat-engines
Motors
NT Air cooled engines
Alcohol motors
Automobiles—Motors
Diesel motor
Free piston engines
Fuel pumps
Internal combustion engine industry
Jet propulsion
Motorboats—Motors
Satz engine
Stratified charge engines
Two-stroke cycle engines
Wankel engine
— Bearings
— Carburetors
USE Carburetors
— Combustion
— Cooling
NT Automobiles—Motors—Cooling
Marine engines—Cooling
— Cylinder blocks
[TJ762.C94]
BT Cylinders
— Cylinder heads
BT Cylinders
— Cylinders
— Dynamics
— Fluid dynamics
— Fuel systems
RT Fuel pumps
— Ignition
UF Ignition devices
NT Magneto
— Indicators
UF Indicators for internal combustion engines
BT Internal combustion engines—Testing
— Lubrication
— Mufflers
UF Mufflers (Internal combustion engines)
— Oil filters
— Starting devices
UF Starting devices for internal combustion engines
— Superchargers
USE Superchargers
— Tariff
USE Tariff on internal combustion engines
— Testing
NT Internal combustion engines—Indicators
— — Equipment
USE Internal combustion engines—Testing equipment
— Testing equipment
UF Internal combustion engines—Testing—Equipment
BT Testing-machines
— — Tariff
USE Tariff on internal combustion engine testing equipment
— Tropical conditions
— Valve-gears
UF Valve-gears
— Valves
BT Valves
NT Automobiles—Motors—Valves

Internal combustion engines, Spark ignition
(May Subd Geog)
UF Engines, Spark ignition
Gasoline engines
Gasoline motors
Otto-cycle engines
Petroleum engines
Spark ignition engines
BT Motors
NT Spark-plugs
— Alternate fuels
UF Alternate fuels for spark ignition internal combustion engines
Alternative fuels for spark ignition internal combustion engines
BT Fuel
Motor fuels
Synthetic fuels
— Combustion
— Fuel consumption
— Fuel systems
— Ignition
UF Ignition devices
— Valve-gears
UF Valve-gears
Internal conversion (Nuclear physics)
BT Decay schemes (Radioactivity)
Electromagnetic theory
Electrons
Nuclear physics
Quantum theory
NT Auger effect
Beta rays
Electrons—Emission
X-rays
— Tables
UF Internal conversion (Nuclear physics)—Tables, etc.
— Tables, etc.
USE Internal conversion (Nuclear physics)—Tables
Internal ear
USE Labyrinth (Ear)
Internal fixation in fractures
[RD103.I5]
UF Fracture fixation, Internal
Internal fracture fixation
Internal skeletal fixation (Surgery)
Osteosynthesis
Skeletal fixation, Internal (Surgery)
BT Fracture fixation
Orthopedic implants
RT Bone screws (Orthopedics)
NT Bone nails (Orthopedics)
Bone plates (Orthopedics)
Intramedullary fracture fixation
Internal fracture fixation
USE Internal fixation in fractures
Internal friction
[QC191]
UF Anelasticity
BT Damping (Mechanics)
Elastic solids
Elastic waves
Friction
Vibration
— Instruments
[QC191]
UF Instruments, Internal friction
Internal friction (Liquids)
USE Viscosity
Internal grinding
UF Grinding, Internal
BT Grinding and polishing
Internal improvement movement
USE Public works
Internal medicine (May Subd Geog)
UF Medicine, Internal
BT Medicine
Medicine—Practice
NT Cardiology

Endocrinology
Gastroenterology
Hematology
Internists
Nephrology
Internal migration
USE Migration, Internal
Internal reconstruction (Linguistics)
USE Reconstruction (Linguistics)
Internal reflection, Total (Optics)
USE Total internal reflection (Optics)
Internal reflection spectroscopy
UF Spectroscopy, Internal reflection
BT Absorption spectra
Reflection (Optics)
Internal revenue (May Subd Geog)
[HJ5001-5231]
UF Excise
Fee system (Taxation)
Indirect taxation
Inland revenue
Revenue, Internal
BT Finance, Public
Taxation
NT Bonded warehouses and goods
Distillery warehouses
Excise tax
Income tax
Inheritance and transfer tax
Licenses
Octroi
Revenue-stamps
Stamp-duties
Tolls
— United States
UF United States—Internal revenue
United States—Revenue
Internal revenue law (May Subd Geog)
[HJ3251 (United States)]
UF Excise
Law, Internal revenue
Revenue law
NT Government monopolies—Law and legislation
Inheritance and transfer tax—Law and legislation
Internal Revenue Service Taxpayer Service
USE Taxpayer Assistance Program
Internal revenue stamps
USE Revenue-stamps
Internal rotation (Molecular)
USE Molecular rotation
Internal security (May Subd Geog)
UF Security, Internal
RT Insurgency
Subversive activities
NT Loyalty oaths
— United States
NT Loyalty-security program, 1947-
Internal skeletal fixation (Surgery)
USE Internal fixation in fractures
Internal transfer pricing
USE Transfer pricing
Internal waves
UF Boundary waves (Oceanography)
Waves, Internal
BT Ocean waves
Internalization
BT Psychoanalysis
Social learning
NT Identification (Psychology)
International administration
USE International agencies
International organization
International administrative courts
UF Administrative courts, International
Administrative international courts
BT Administrative courts
International courts
International adoption
USE Intercountry adoption

International affairs and Christianity
USE Christianity and international affairs
International affairs and religion
USE Religion and international affairs
International affairs and technology
USE Technology and international affairs
International agencies *(May Subd Geog)*
Here are entered works on public international organizations and agencies of international government. Particular organizations are entered under their respective names.
UF Associations, International
Institutions, International
International administration
International associations
International institutions
International organizations
International unions
Organizations, International
Specialized agencies of the United Nations
United Nations—Specialized agencies
BT International cooperation
Interorganizational relations
RT International organization
NT International officials and employees
Medicine—International cooperation
Non-governmental organizations
Public health—International cooperation
United Nations—Economic assistance
United Nations—Technical assistance
— **Language policy**
BT Language policy
— **Privileges and immunities**
UF International officials and employees—Privileges and immunities
BT Diplomatic privileges and immunities
Privileges and immunities
SA *subdivision* Privileges and immunities *under names of individual international organizations, e.g.* International Labor Office—Privileges and immunities
— **Rules and practice**
— **Tort liability**
USE Tort liability of international agencies
— **Voting**
BT Voting
International agency libraries
(May Subd Geog)
UF Libraries, International agency
BT Libraries, Governmental, administrative, etc.
International agreements
USE International obligations
Treaties
International agricultural cooperation
USE Agriculture—International cooperation
International air traffic rules
USE Air traffic rules, International
International airport charges
USE International airports—Landing fees
International airports *(May Subd Geog)*
[TL726.15]
UF Airports of entry
BT Airports
Ports of entry
SA *names of individual international airports*
— **Landing fees**
UF International airport charges
International airports—Port charges
Port charges
BT Airports—Landing fees
— **Port charges**

USE International airports—Landing fees
— **England**
NT Birmingham International Airport (Birmingham, West Midlands, England)
International alphabet
USE Phonetic alphabet
Transliteration
International American conferences
USE Inter-American conferences
International and municipal law
(May Subd Geog)
[JK-JQ]
[JX1248]
Here are entered works on the relation of international law to the internal or national law of a country or countries.
UF Municipal and international law
BT International law
NT Contracts (International law)
Treaties—Accession
Treaties—Ratification
Treaties—Reservations
International Antarctic Expedition, 1901-1903
[Q115 (Scientific results)]
International arbitration
USE Arbitration, International
International arbitration and award
USE Arbitration and award, International
International architectural practice
USE Architectural practice, International
International Association of the Congo
USE Zaire
International associations
USE *particular international agencies, congresses, societies, etc.*
International agencies
International cooperation—Societies, etc.
International auxiliari linguo (Artificial language)
UF INTAL (Artificial language)
BT Languages, Artificial
International baccalaureate
UF Baccalaureate, International
BT Examinations—Questions
International education
Universities and colleges—Entrance requirements
International banking
USE Banks and banking, International
International bibliography
USE Bibliography, International
International bimetallism
USE Bimetallism
International boundaries
USE Boundaries
International brigades in the Spanish Civil War, 1936-1939
USE *names of individual brigades*
Spain—History—Civil War, 1936-1939 —Participation, Foreign
International broadcasting
(May Subd Geog)
UF Broadcasting, International
BT Radio broadcasting
International buffer stocks
USE Buffer stocks
International business enterprises
(May Subd Geog)
UF Business enterprises, International
Corporations, International
International corporations
Multinational corporations
Transnational corporations
BT Business enterprises
Commerce
Corporations
International economic relations
RT Joint ventures

NT Corporations, Foreign
Foreign licensing agreements
— Collective bargaining
USE Collective bargaining—International business enterprises
— **Employees**
NT Collective bargaining—International business enterprises
— — **Training of** *(May Subd Geog)*
BT Employees, Training of
— Information storage and retrieval systems
USE Information storage and retrieval systems—International business enterprises
— **Law and legislation** *(May Subd Geog)*
BT Corporation law
— **Religious aspects**
— — **Baptists, [Catholic Church, etc.]**
— — **Buddhism, [Christianity, etc.]**
— **Social aspects** *(May Subd Geog)*
UF Society and international business enterprises
— **Subcontracting**
BT Subcontracting
— **Taxation** *(May Subd Geog)*
— — **Law and legislation**
(May Subd Geog)
International civil service
USE International officials and employees
International claims
USE Claims
Government liability (International law)
International clearing *(May Subd Geog)*
UF Clearing, International
Clearing agreements
BT Balance of payments
Foreign exchange
Foreign trade regulation
International finance
— Conflict of laws
USE Conflict of laws—International clearing
International coinage
USE Coinage, International
International commissions of inquiry
USE Commissions of inquiry, International
International communication
USE Communication, International
International competition
USE Competition, International
International conciliation
USE Mediation, International
International conferences, congresses and conventions
USE Congresses and conventions
International Construction Database
USE ICONDA (Information retrieval system)
International cookery
USE Cookery, International
International cooperation
[JC362]
[JX1995 (International bureaus)]
Here are entered general works on international cooperative activities with or without the participation of governments.
UF Cooperation, International
Institutions, International
Interdependence of nations
International institutions
World order
BT Competition, International
Cooperation
International law
International relations
RT International organization
Reconstruction (1939-1951)

SA *subdivision* International cooperation
under subjects which do not lend
themselves to the phrase form of
heading, e.g. Public health—
International cooperation
NT African cooperation
Arbitration, International
Asian cooperation
Congresses and conventions
Economic assistance
European cooperation
European Economic Community—
Economic assistance
Intellectual cooperation
Intergovernmental fiscal relations
International agencies
International education
International Hydrological Decade,
1965-1974
International librarianship
International museums
International police
Internationalism
League of Nations
Pacific Area cooperation
Pan-Americanism
Scandinavian cooperation
South Asian cooperation
Technical assistance
United Nations—Economic assistance
United Nations—Technical assistance
World Mental Health Year, 1960
World Refugee Year, 1959-1960
— Societies, etc.
UF Associations, International
International associations
International cooperation in documentary
moving-pictures
USE Moving-pictures, Documentary—
International cooperation
International cooperation in home economics
USE Home economics—International
cooperation
International cooperation in science
USE Science—International cooperation
International cooperation in telecommunication
USE Telecommunication—International
cooperation
International copyright
USE Copyright, International
International corporations
USE International business enterprises
International correspondence
[LB3614 (Students)]
UF Correspondence
Friendship letters
BT Intellectual cooperation
International education
Letter-writing
RT Pen pals
International courtesy
USE Comity of nations
International courts
UF Courts, International
International tribunals
Tribunals, International
BT Arbitration, International
International law
International relations
Pacific settlement of international
disputes
Peaceful change (International
relations)
RT Jurisdiction (International law)
SA *names of individual international*
courts
NT Arbitration and award, International
International administrative courts
International criminal law
USE Criminal jurisdiction
International offenses

International customary law
USE Customary law, International
International date line
UF Date line, International
BT Meridian lines
Time—Systems and standards
International debts
USE Debts, External
International Decade for Women, 1976-1985
USE International Women's Decade, 1976-
1985
International Decade of Ocean Exploration,
1970-1980
BT Oceanography—Research
International disputes, Pacific settlement of
USE Pacific settlement of international
disputes
International division of labor
Here are entered works on the theory and practice
of international planning and agreements whereby
countries specialize in or participate in a phase of the
production of those products for which they have the
greatest comparative advantage.
BT Commerce
Division of labor
International economic relations
RT Comparative advantage (Commerce)
International Dressage Championship,
Goodwood, West Sussex
UF Goodwood (West Sussex) International
Dressage Championship
BT Dressage—Competitions—England
International Drinking Water Supply and
Sanitation Decade, 1981-1990
(May Subd Geog)
BT Drinking water—International
cooperation
Sanitation—International cooperation
Water-supply—International
cooperation
International economic integration
UF Economic integration, International
Economic union
BT International economic relations
SA *subdivision* Economic integration
under continents and regions for
works discussing the integration of
the economies of a group of
countries, e.g. Europe—Economic
integration; *and names of*
international organizations
established to integrate the
economies of various countries, e.g.
European Economic Community
NT Customs unions
International economic policy
USE International economic relations
International economic relations
Here are entered works on economic relations
among the nations of the world. Works on the international economic relations of an individual region or
country are entered under the name of the region or
country with the subdivision Foreign economic rela-
tions, further subdivided by the name of a region or
country, if appropriate. If so subdivided, a second
heading is assigned with the place names in reverse
position, e.g. 1. United States—Foreign economic re-
lations—France. 2. France—Foreign economic re-
lations—United States.
UF Economic policy, Foreign
Economic relations, Foreign
Economics, International
Foreign economic policy
Foreign economic relations
Interdependence of nations
International economic policy
International economics
New international economic order
BT Economic policy
International relations
RT Economic sanctions
SA *subdivision* Foreign economic relations
under names of countries

NT Balance of payments
Commercial policy
East-West trade (1945-   )
Economic assistance
Foreign licensing agreements
International business enterprises
International division of labor
International economic integration
International finance
Technical assistance
— Religious aspects
— — Buddhism, [Christianity, etc.]
International economic relations and youth
(May Subd Geog)
BT Youth
International economics
USE International economic relations
International education *(May Subd Geog)*
Here are entered works on education for interna-
tional understanding, world citizenship, etc.
UF Education, International
BT Education
International cooperation
Peace
RT Intellectual cooperation
Internationalism
NT Comparative librarianship
Cross-cultural orientation
International baccalaureate
International correspondence
Students, Interchange of
— Law and legislation *(May Subd Geog)*
BT Educational law and legislation
International Education Year, 1970
(May Subd Geog)
UF Education Year, 1970
BT Education—1965-
Intellectual cooperation
International educational exchanges
USE Educational exchanges
International environmental law
USE Environmental law, International
International exchange
USE Foreign exchange
International exchange of librarians
USE Librarians, Interchange of
International exchange of literary and scientific
publications
USE Exchanges, Literary and scientific
International exchange of persons programs
USE Exchange of persons programs
International exchange of students
USE Students, Interchange of
International exchange of teachers
USE Teachers, Interchange of
International exhibitions
USE *names of individual exhibitions*
Exhibitions
International farm youth exchange project
UF Farm youth exchange project,
International
BT 4-H clubs
Agriculture—International cooperation
Educational exchanges
Exchange of persons programs
International federation
USE International organization
International Festival of Jazz
BT Jazz festivals—Belgium
International finance
UF Finance, International
International monetary system
International money
BT Finance
International economic relations
NT Asian dollar market
Balance of payments
Banks and banking, International
Capital movements
Debts, External
Euro-bond market

International finance *(Continued)*
    Euro-dollar market
    Financial institutions, International
    Foreign exchange
    International clearing
    International liquidity
    Roll-over credits
    Special drawing rights
  — Law and legislation *(May Subd Geog)*
International financial institutions
  USE Financial institutions, International
International fiscal relations
  USE Intergovernmental fiscal relations
International fishery management
  USE Fishery management, International
International flow of news
  USE Communication—International
      cooperation
    Foreign news
International forwarding agents
  USE Ocean freight forwarders
International Geophysical Year, 1957-1958
  (May Subd Geog)
  ₜQC801.3₎
  BT Geophysics—International cooperation
    Intellectual cooperation
  NT Project Vanguard
International grants-in-aid
  USE Economic assistance
    International relief
International Harvester trucks
  USE IHC trucks
International health
  USE World health
International Hydrological Decade, 1965-1974
  (May Subd Geog)
  BT Hydrology
    International cooperation
International Hydrological Program, 1975-
  (May Subd Geog)
  BT Hydrology
International ice patrol
  BT Icebergs
International Information System for the
  Agricultural Sciences and Technology
  USE AGRIS (Information retrieval system)
International Information System on Research
  in Documentation
  USE ISORID (Information retrieval system)
International institutions
  USE *particular international congresses,*
     societies, etc.
    International agencies
    International cooperation
International insurance law
  USE Insurance law, International
International interconnected electric utility
  systems *(May Subd Geog)*
  BT Interconnected electric utility systems
International inventory of musical sources
  BT Music—Bibliography
International investment
  USE Investments, Foreign
International jurisdiction
  USE Jurisdiction (International law)
International Kalinga Prize
  USE Kalinga Prize
International labor activities
  UF Labor activities, International
    Trade-unions—International
      cooperation
  BT Trade-unions
  SA *names of individual labor organizations*
International Labor Day
  USE May Day (Labor holiday)
International labor laws and legislation
  USE Labor laws and legislation,
    International
International Labor Office
  — Privileges and immunities

International lakes *(May Subd Geog)*
  UF Lakes, Right of navigation on
  BT Inland navigation—Law and legislation
    International law
    Lakes
    Water—Law and legislation
International language
  USE Diplomacy—Language
    Language, Universal
International law *(May Subd Geog)*
  UF Law, International
    Law of nations
    Nations, Law of
  BT International relations
    Public law
  RT International organization
    Natural law
    Space law
  SA *subdivision* Law and legislation *under*
    topics of international concern; and
    subdivision International status
    under names of countries, cities,
    etc.
  NT Acquiescence (International law)
    Act of state
    Aggression (International law)
    Air traffic rules, International
    Airspace (International law)
    Alien property
    Angary, Right of
    Annexation (International law)
    Antitrust law (International law)
    Arbitration, International
    Archipelagoes—Law and legislation
    Asylum, Right of
    Autonomy
    Bills of exchange (International law)
    Boundaries
    Chicanery (International law)
    Children (International law)
    Citizenship (International law)
    Civil defense (International law)
    Civil procedure (International law)
    Civil war
    Claims
    Colonies (International law)
    Comity of nations
    Concordats
    Condominium (International law)
    Conquest, Right of
    Consular law
    Consuls
    Criminal liability (International law)
    Criminal procedure (International law)
    Customary law, International
    Denial of justice
    Design protection (International law)
    Diplomatic and consular service
    Diplomatic documents
    Diplomatic protection
    Diplomatic protests
    Diplomats
    Dismemberment of nations
    Domestic relations (International law)
    Drago doctrine
    Duress (International law)
    Effectiveness and validity of law
    Embargo
    Eminent domain (International law)
    Environmental law, International
    Equality of states
    Equity (International law)
    Estoppel (International law)
    Exclaves
    Executions (International law)
    Executive agreements
    Exhaustion of local remedies
      (International law)
    Exhibitions (International law)
    Expatriation
    Exterritoriality

    Extradition
    Fishery law and legislation
    Forced labor (International law)
    Foreign offices
    Freedom of information (International
      law)
    Freedom of movement (International
      law)
    Freedom of religion (International law)
    Freedom of the seas
    Good faith (International law)
    Government liability (International
      law)
    Governments in exile
    Great powers
    Habeas corpus (International law)
    Impossibility of performance
      (International law)
    Indemnity
    Industrial property (International law)
    Insurance law, International
    Intellectual property (International
      law)
    International and municipal law
    International cooperation
    International courts
    International lakes
    International obligations
    International offenses
    Intervention (International law)
    Investments, Foreign (International
      law)
    Judicial assistance
    Jurisdiction (International law)
    Jurisdiction over ships at sea
    Labor laws and legislation,
      International
    Lis pendens (International law)
    Maritime law
    Medical laws and legislation,
      International
    Military law
    Missing persons (International law)
    Naturalization
    Naval law
    Necessity (International law)
    Neutrality
    Notification (International relations)
    Nuclear ships (International law)
    Nuisances (International law)
    Occupancy (International law)
    Ocean bottom (Maritime law)
    Pacta sunt servanda (International law)
    Papacy (International law)
    Passports
    Persons (International law)
    Pirates
    Political crimes and offenses
    Postliminy
    Prescription (International law)
    Presumptions (International law)
    Prior consultation (International law)
    Promissory notes (International law)
    Property (International law)
    Protective signs (International law)
    Protectorates
    Public health laws, International
    Public policy (International law)
    Radioactive substances—
      Transportation (International law)
    Radioactive waste disposal
      (International law)
    Radioactive waste disposal in the
      ocean (International law)
    Recognition (International law)
    Refugees, Political—Legal status, laws,
      etc.
    Repatriation
    Salvage
    Sanctions (International law)
    Self-defense (International law)

Servitudes (International law)
Ships—Nationality
Slave-trade
Slavery (International law)
Social security (International law)
Sovereignty
State bankruptcy
State succession
Tax evasion (International law)
Territorial waters
Territory, National
Third parties (International law)
Time (International law)
Torture (International law)
Trademarks (International law)
Transit by land (International law)
Treaties
Ultimatums
Unilateral acts (International law)
Unjust enrichment (International law)
Uti possidetis (International law)
Vis major (International law)
War, Maritime (International law)
War (International law)
Warships—Visits to foreign ports
Water-rights (International law)
Women (International law)
— **Classification**
   UF Classification—International law
— **Codification**
   [JX1261-1283]
— **Interpretation and construction**
— **Philosophy**
   UF Philosophy of international law
   BT Jurisprudence
      Natural law
— **Sources**
   [JX63-91]
   NT Treaties
International law, Private
   USE Conflict of laws
International law (Islamic law)
   UF Islamic international law
International law and communism
   USE International law and socialism
International law and socialism
   UF Communism and international law
      International law and communism
   BT Socialism
International lawn tennis championship
   USE Davis cup
International librarianship
   [Z672]
   Here are entered works on the activities, cooperation, exchange, etc., in librarianship at the international level. Works on the study and analysis of the libraries and library systems of different countries are entered under Comparative librarianship.
   UF Librarianship, International
   BT International cooperation
      Library science
   RT Comparative librarianship
      Library cooperation
   NT Bibliography, International
      Bibliography, Universal
International libraries
   USE Libraries, International
International liquidity
   BT International finance
      Liquidity (Economics)
   RT Balance of payments
   NT Foreign exchange problem
      Gold standard
      Special drawing rights
International loans
   USE Loans, Foreign
International marketing
   USE Export marketing
International marriages
   USE Marriages, International

International mediation
   USE Mediation, International
International medical laws and legislation
   USE Medical laws and legislation, International
International metric system
   USE Metric system
International migration
   USE Emigration and immigration
International monetary system
   USE International finance
International money
   USE Coinage, International
       International finance
International museums
   [AM]
   BT International cooperation
      Museums
International news
   USE Foreign news
International Nuclear Information System
   USE INIS (Information retrieval system)
International obligations
   [JX4171.O3]
   Here are entered works on obligations between states. Works on the public international law dealing with private contractual obligations are entered under Contracts (International law).
   UF International agreements
   BT International law
   RT Treaties
   NT Pacta sunt servanda (International law)
International offenses
   Here are entered works on the criminal law aspects of violations of international law. Works on exterritorial crimes and on the conflict of jurisdictions in the administration of criminal law are entered under the heading Criminal jurisdiction.
   UF Criminal law, International
      International criminal law
   BT Criminal law
      International law
   NT Aggression (International law)
      Assaulting a foreign official
      Crimes against humanity
      Crimes against peace
      Criminal liability (International law)
      Criminal procedure (International law)
      Genocide
      Sovereignty, Violation of
      Terrorism
      War crimes
International officials and employees
   [JX1995]
   UF Civil service, International
      International civil service
      Officials and employees, International
   BT International agencies
      International organization
      Public officers
   SA *subdivision* Officials and employees *under names of international agencies, e.g.* International Telecommunication Union—Officials and employees
— **Privileges and immunities**
   USE *subdivision* Privileges and immunities *under names of individual international agencies*
      International agencies—Privileges and immunities
International organization
   Here are entered works on theories and efforts leading toward world-wide or regional political organization of nations.

   UF Federation, International
      Interdependence of nations
      International administration
      International federation
      Organization, International
      World federation
      World government
      World order
      World organization
   BT Congresses and conventions
      International relations
      Peace
      Political science
   RT International agencies
      International cooperation
      International law
      Security, International
      World politics
   SA *names of specific organizations, e.g.* League of Nations, Pan American Union
   NT Church and international organization
      Concert of Europe
      International officials and employees
      International police
      International trusteeships
      Latin American federation
      Mandates
      Reconstruction (1914-1939)
      Reconstruction (1939-1951)
      Regionalism (International organization)
International organization and the church
   USE Church and international organization
International organizations
   USE International agencies
International payments, Balance of
   USE Balance of payments
International Polar Expedition, 1882-1883
   [G670]
International police
   [JX1981.P7]
   UF Peacekeeping forces
      Police, International
   BT International cooperation
      International organization
      International relations
      Sanctions (International law)
      Security, International
   RT United Nations—Armed Forces
International politics
   USE World politics
International press law
   USE Press law, International
International private law
   USE Conflict of laws
International propaganda
   USE Propaganda, International
International public health laws
   USE Public health laws, International
International railroad law
   USE Railroad law, International
International relations
   Here are entered theoretical works on the relations among the nations of the world. Works on general political history and historical accounts of relations among nations are entered under World politics. Works on the foreign relations of an individual country are entered under the name of the country with the subdivision Foreign relations.
   UF Coexistence
      Foreign affairs
      Foreign policy
      Foreign relations
      Interdependence of nations
      Peaceful coexistence
      World order
   RT National security
      World politics

International relations (Continued)
SA *subdivisions* Foreign relations *and*
Foreign relations administration
under names of countries; and
names of international alliances,
congresses, treaties, etc.
NT Alliances
Ambassadors
Arbitration, International
Balance of power
Boundaries
Catholic Church—Relations
(diplomatic)
Comity of nations
Commissions of inquiry, International
Communism and international
relations
Competition, International
Concordats
Congresses and conventions
Consuls
Cultural relations
Detente
Diplomacy
Diplomatic and consular service
Diplomatic documents
Diplomatic negotiations in
international disputes
Diplomatic protection
Diplomats
Disarmament
Executive agreements
Foreign offices
Geography, Political
Geopolitics
Government missions
Governments in exile
Great powers
Guaranty, Treaties of
Intergovernmental fiscal relations
International cooperation
International courts
International economic relations
International law
International organization
International police
Jihad
Mediation, International
Middle powers
Military missions
Monroe doctrine
Nationalism
Neutrality, Armed
Nonalignment
Notification (International relations)
Nuclear crisis control
Orders in council
Pacific settlement of international
disputes
Pan-Pacific relations
Peace
Peaceful change (International
relations)
Plebiscite
Prior consultation (International law)
Propaganda, International
Reconstruction (1914-1939)
Reconstruction (1939-1951)
Religion and international affairs
Security, International
Technology and international affairs
Treaties
Ultimatums
Warships—Visits to foreign ports
— Bibliography
RT International relations literature
— Forecasting
BT Forecasting
— Psychological aspects
BT Political psychology

International relations and communism
USE Communism and international
relations
International relations and culture
(May Subd Geog)
BT Culture
International relations literature
(May Subd Geog)
UF Literature, International relations
RT International relations—Bibliography
International relations specialists
(May Subd Geog)
UF Foreign relations specialists
BT Area specialists
Policy scientists
NT United States foreign relations
specialists
Women international relations
specialists
International relief *(May Subd Geog)*
UF Grants-in-aid, International
International grants-in-aid
Relief, International
Relief (Aid)
BT Charities
Economic assistance
Public welfare
SA *subdivision* Civilian relief *under*
individual wars, e.g. World War,
1939-1945—Civilian relief
NT Disaster relief
Duty-free importation of relief supplies
International rivers *(May Subd Geog)*
[JX4150]
UF Rivers, Right of navigation of
BT Inland navigation—Law and legislation
Rivers
International Sail Training Races
BT Naval education
Sailing ships
Yacht racing
NT Tall Ships Pacific, 1978
International sales
USE Export sales
International sales corporations, Domestic
USE Domestic international sales
corporations
International sanitary regulations
USE Public health laws, International
International Satellite for Ionospheric Studies
USE ISIS-II (Artificial satellite)
International Scientific and Technical
Information System
USE ISTIS (Information retrieval system)
International security
USE Security, International
International Serials Data System
International Settlements, Bank for
USE Bank for International Settlements
International shorthand
USE Shorthand—International
International Simón Bolívar Prize
UF Simón Bolívar Prize, International
BT Rewards (Prizes, etc.)
International Six Days Trial
[GV1060]
BT Motorcycle racing
International Society for Krishna
Consciousness
— Biography
USE Hare Krishnas—Biography
International space cooperation
USE Astronautics—International
cooperation
International Standard Bibliographic
Description for Non-Book Materials
[Z695.66]
BT Cataloging of non-book materials

International Standard Bibliographic
Description for Older Monographic
Publications (Antiquarian)
[Z695.3]
UF ISBD(A)
BT Cataloging of early printed books
International Standard Book Numbers
(May Subd Geog)
UF ISBN
BT Publishers' standard book numbers
RT International Standard Serial Numbers
International Standard Serial Numbers
(May Subd Geog)
UF ISSN
BT Publishers' standard book numbers
RT International Standard Book Numbers
International students
USE Students, Foreign
International style (Architecture)
(May Subd Geog)
BT Architecture, Modern—20th century
NT Functionalism (Architecture)
— **Europe**
— — **American influences**
BT United States—Civilization
International style (Decoration and ornament)
USE Decoration and ornament—
International style
International system of units
USE Metric system
International teaching positions
USE Teachers, Foreign—Employment
International Telecommunication Union
— **Officials and employees**
International territories
USE Internationalized territories
International trade
USE Commerce
International trade control
USE Foreign trade regulation
International trade regulation
USE Foreign trade regulation
International transit
USE Transit, International
International travel regulations
UF Frontier formalities
Travel regulations, International
BT Customs administration—Law and
legislation
Travel
NT Admission of nonimmigrants
Customs administration and tourists
Emigration and immigration law
Foreign exchange—Law and legislation
Passports
Travel restrictions
Travel restrictions, Diplomatic
International tribunals
USE International courts
International trucks
USE IHC trucks
International trusteeships *(May Subd Geog)*
UF Nonselfgoverning territories
Trust territories
Trusteeships, International
United Nations—International
trusteeships
BT International organization
Internationalized territories
Protectorates
RT Mandates
State succession
International Ultraviolet Explorer (Artificial
satellite)
USE IUE (Artificial satellite)
International unification of civil law
USE Civil law—International unification

International unification of law
  USE Law—International unification; *and* subdivision International unification *under particular branches of the law, e.g.* Civil law—International unification
    Law—International unification
International unification of private law
  USE Civil law—International unification
International unions
  USE International agencies
International upper mantle project
  USE Upper mantle project
International visitors
  USE Visitors, Foreign
International voluntary work camps
  USE Work camps
International Women's Decade, 1976-1985
  (May Subd Geog)
  UF Decade for Women, 1976-1985
    International Decade for Women, 1976-1985
    U.N. Decade for Women, 1976-1985
    United Nations Decade for Women, 1976-1985
    Women's Decade, 1976-1985
  BT Feminism
    Women
International Women's Year, 1975
  (May Subd Geog)
  UF Women's Year, International
  BT Feminism
    Women
    Women—Congresses
International words
  USE Language and languages—Foreign words and phrases
International Year of Disabled Persons, 1981
  (May Subd Geog)
  BT Handicapped
International Year of the Child, 1979
  (May Subd Geog)
  BT Child welfare
    Children's rights
    Education of children
International Years of the Quiet Sun, 1964-1965
  ₍QC801.4₎
  UF IQSY
  BT Geophysics—International cooperation
    Intellectual cooperation
    Solar activity
International Youth Year, 1985
  (May Subd Geog)
  BT Youth
Internationale Karlspreis der Stadt Aachen
  USE Karlspreis
Internationalism
  ₍JC361₎
    Here are entered works on internationalism as an attitude, in contrast to extreme nationalism; also works on cosmopolitanism as opposed to provincialism.
    Works on measures advocated by internationalists are entered under International cooperation; International organization; etc.
  UF Cosmopolitanism
  BT Intellectual cooperation
    International cooperation
  RT International education
    Nationalism
  NT Internationalists
Internationalism in literature
Internationalists *(May Subd Geog)*
  BT Internationalism
Internationalized territories
  ₍JX4068.I6₎
  UF Free cities
    International territories
    Territories, International
  BT Sovereignty
  NT International trusteeships

Mandates
Internists *(May Subd Geog)*
  BT Internal medicine
    Medicine—Specialties and specialists
    Physicians
  NT Allergists
    Endocrinologists
    Gastroenterologists
    Nephrologists
    Rheumatologists
Internment camps
  USE Concentration camps
Internment of Japanese Americans, 1942-1945
  USE Japanese Americans—Evacuation and relocation, 1942-1945
Internment of Japanese in Canada, 1942-1945
  USE Japanese—Canada—Evacuation and relocation, 1942-1945
Internment of warships
  USE Warships, Internment of
Interns *(May Subd Geog)*
  ₍LC1051-LC1064₎
  BT Professional education
  NT Accounting—Study and teaching (Internship)
    Business education (Internship)
    City planning—Study and teaching (Internship)
    Civil service—Study and teaching (Internship)
    Criminal justice, Administration of—Study and teaching (Internship)
Interns (Clinical psychology)
  BT Clinical psychology
Interns (Education) *(May Subd Geog)*
  UF Teaching internship
  BT Student teachers
  NT Student teaching
Interns (Geography)
  UF Student trainee program (Geography)
  BT Geography—Vocational guidance
Interns (Landscape architecture)
  USE Landscape architecture—Study and teaching (Internship)
Interns (Legislation) *(May Subd Geog)*
  UF Government interns (Legislation)
    Legislative interns
  BT Legislation
    Legislative bodies—Officials and employees
Interns (Library science)
  UF Internships (Library science)
    Library interns
  BT Library education
Interns (Medicine) *(May Subd Geog)*
  ₍RA972₎
  UF Hospital house staff
    Hospital interns
    Hospitals—House staff
    Medical interns
  BT Hospitals—Medical staff
Interns (Meteorology)
  UF Student trainee program (Meteorology)
  BT Meteorology—Study and teaching
Interns (Psychiatry)
  BT Psychiatric hospitals
    Psychiatrists
    Psychiatry—Study and teaching
Internship programs *(May Subd Geog)*
  UF Internships
    Programs, Internship
  BT Employees, Training of
  SA *subdivision* Study and teaching (Internship) *under subjects*
Internships
  USE Internship programs
Internships (Library science)
  USE Interns (Library science)
Interoceanic canals
  USE Canals, Interoceanic

Interoceanic ship-railroads
  USE Ship-railroads
Interoception
  BT Perception
    Reflexes
Interoffice communication systems
  USE Intercommunication systems
Interorganizational relations
  (May Subd Geog)
  BT Intergroup relations
    Organization
  NT Bureaucracy
    Community organization
    International agencies
    Multihospital systems
    Oligopolies
Interpedare (The Latin word)
  BT Latin language—Etymology
Interpellation *(May Subd Geog)*
  UF Questions (Parliamentary practice)
  BT Ministerial responsibility
    Parliamentary practice
Interpersonal attraction
  UF Attraction, Interpersonal
  BT Interpersonal relations
Interpersonal communication
  (May Subd Geog)
  ₍BF637.C45₎
  BT Communication—Psychological aspects
    Interpersonal relations
  NT Communication in small groups
    Double bind (Psychology)
    Nonverbal communication (Psychology)
    Self-disclosure
Interpersonal communication in children
  (May Subd Geog)
  ₍BF723.C57₎
  BT Child psychology
  NT Children—Language
    Language acquisition
    Nonverbal communication in children
Interpersonal competence
  USE Social skills
Interpersonal conflict *(May Subd Geog)*
  ₍BF637.I48 (Psychology)₎
  UF Conflict, Interpersonal
  BT Conflict (Psychology)
    Interpersonal relations
  RT Social conflict
Interpersonal perception
  USE Social perception
Interpersonal relations
  ₍HM132₎
  UF Human relations
    Personal relations
    Relations, Interpersonal
    Social behavior
  BT Social psychology
  RT Object relations (Psychoanalysis)
  SA *subdivision* Relations with ₍specific class of persons or ethnic group₎ *under names of individual persons*
  NT Assertiveness training
    Communication—Psychological aspects
    Communication in organizations
    Competition (Psychology)
    Compliments
    Counselor and client
    Criticism, Personal
    Dependency (Psychology)
    Friendship
    Grandparent and child
    Group relations training
    Help-seeking behavior
    Helping behavior
    Intergenerational relations
    Interpersonal attraction
    Interpersonal communication
    Interpersonal conflict
    Interpersonal relations in children

Interpersonal relations *(Continued)*
    Intimacy (Psychology)
    Joking relationships
    Life skills
    Machiavellianism (Psychology)
    Medical personnel and patient
    Nurse and physician
    Parent and child
    Personal space
    Separation (Psychology)
    Social exchange
    Social perception
    Social skills
    Symbiosis (Psychology)
    Teacher-student relationships
    Verbal self-defense
    Veterinarian and client
— **Religious aspects**
— — **Buddhism, ₍Christianity, etc.₎**
Interpersonal relations in children
(May Subd Geog)
   ₍BF723.I646₎
  BT Child psychology
      Interpersonal relations
Interphotoreceptor matrix
  UF Interstitial matrix
      Interstitial mucoid
      Matrix, Interphotoreceptor
      Matrix, Interstitial
      Mucoid, Interstitial
  BT Extracellular matrix
      Retina
  RT Photoreceptors
  NT Interphotoreceptor retinoid-binding
      protein
Interphotoreceptor retinoid-binding protein
   ₍QP552.I56₎
  UF Interphotoreceptor retinol-binding
      protein
      Interstitial retinoid-binding protein
      Interstitial retinol-binding protein
      Protein, Interphotoreceptor retinoid-
        binding
      Protein, Interstitial retinoid-binding
      Protein, Interstitial retinol-binding
  BT Glycoproteins
      Interphotoreceptor matrix
  RT Retinoids
Interphotoreceptor retinol-binding protein
  USE Interphotoreceptor retinoid-binding
      protein
Interplanetary communication
  USE Interstellar communication
Interplanetary magnetic field
  USE Interplanetary magnetic fields
Interplanetary magnetic fields
  UF Interplanetary magnetic field
  BT Magnetic fields (Cosmic physics)
Interplanetary monitoring platform (Artificial
satellite)
  USE IMP (Artificial satellite)
Interplanetary propulsion
  USE Space vehicles—Propulsion systems
Interplanetary voyages
   ₍TL789-790₎
    Here are entered general works and imaginary
accounts on travel to the planets. Works on the phy-
sics and technical details of flight beyond the earth's
atmosphere are entered under Space flight.
  UF Moon, Voyages to
      Space travel
      Voyages, Interplanetary
      Voyages to the moon
  BT Aeronautics
      Astronautics
      Science fiction
      Voyages, Imaginary
  RT Rockets (Aeronautics)
      Space flight
  NT Art—Extraterrestrial influences

    Civilization, Ancient—Extraterrestrial
      influences
    Extraterrestrial anthropology
    Indians of North America—
      Extraterrestrial influences
    Outer space—Exploration
    Space flight in literature
    Space flight to Jupiter
    Space flight to Mars
    Space flight to Mercury
Interplanetary warfare
  USE Space warfare
Interpleader
  USE Actions and defenses
Interpolation
   ₍QA281₎
  BT Algebra
      Mathematics
      Numerical analysis
  RT Approximation theory
  NT Numerical integration
      Spline theory
Interpolation spaces
  UF Spaces, Interpolation
  BT Function spaces
  NT Lorentz spaces
Interpretation
  USE Hermeneutics
Interpretation, Biblical
  USE Bible—Criticism, interpretation, etc.
Interpretation, City
  USE Cities and towns—Interpretive
      programs
Interpretation, Historic site
  USE Historic sites—Interpretive programs
Interpretation, Literary
  USE *subdivision* Explication *under specific*
      literatures, e.g. English literature—
      Explication; English poetry—
      Explication
Interpretation, Musical
  USE Music—Interpretation (Phrasing,
      dynamics, etc.)
Interpretation, Park
  USE National parks and reserves—
      Interpretive programs
      Parks—Interpretive programs
Interpretation, Photographic
  USE Photographic interpretation
Interpretation, Recreation area
  USE Recreation areas—Interpretive
      programs
Interpretation (Philosophy)
   ₍B824.12₎
  BT Philosophy
Interpretation and construction (Law)
  USE Law—Interpretation and construction
Interpretation in psychoanalysis
  USE Psychoanalytic interpretation
Interpretation of examinations
  USE Examinations—Interpretation
Interpretation of pictures
  USE Picture interpretation
Interpretative reading
  USE Oral interpretation
Interpretative speech
  USE Oral interpretation
Interpreters
  USE Translators
Interpreters (Computer programs)
   ₍QA76.6₎
  UF Interpretive programs (Computer
      programs)
  BT Automatic programming (Computer
      science)
      Computer programs
  NT MOPI (Computer system)
      RUN/C (Computer program)
      UNIX C Shell (Computer program)
      UNIX Shells (Computer programs)

Interpreters for the deaf *(May Subd Geog)*
   ₍HV2402₎
  UF Deaf—Translating services
      Deaf, Interpreters for
      Sign language interpreters
  BT Deaf—Means of communication
      Translators
Interpreting and translating
  USE Translating and interpreting
Interpretive dancing
  USE Modern dance
Interpretive programs (Computer programs)
  USE Interpreters (Computer programs)
Interpretive programs for cities
  USE Cities and towns—Interpretive
      programs
Interpretive programs of historic sites
  USE Historic sites—Interpretive programs
Interpretive programs of national parks and
reserves
  USE National parks and reserves—
      Interpretive programs
Interpretive programs of parks
  USE Parks—Interpretive programs
Interpretive programs of recreation areas
  USE Recreation areas—Interpretive
      programs
Interracial adoption *(May Subd Geog)*
  UF Mixed race adoption
      Trans-racial adoption
  BT Adoption
      Race relations
  RT Intercountry adoption
Interracial marriage *(May Subd Geog)*
   ₍HQ1031₎
  UF Intermarriage, Racial
      Marriage, Interracial
  BT Intermarriage
  NT Children of interracial marriage
Interracial marriage, Children of
  USE Children of interracial marriage
Interreligious marriage
  USE Interfaith marriage
Interreligious relations
  USE Religions—Relations
Interrenal body
  USE Interrenal gland
Interrenal gland
  UF Interrenal body
  BT Endocrine glands
      Fishes—Anatomy
      Kidneys
Interrogation
  USE Questioning
Interrogative (Grammar)
  USE *subdivision* Interrogative *under names*
      of languages and groups of
      languages
      Grammar, Comparative and general—
      Interrogative
Interrogator-transpondor systems
  USE Airplanes—IFF equipment
      Distance measuring equipment
      (Aircraft to ground station)
Interrogatories *(May Subd Geog)*
  BT Discovery (Law)
      Forms (Law)
      Pre-trial procedure
      Questionnaires
      Witnesses
Interrogatories (Criminal procedure)
  USE Preliminary examinations (Criminal
      procedure)
Interruption (Psychology)
   ₍BF378.I65₎
  UF Zeigarnik effect
  BT Memory
      Motivation (Psychology)
Interscholastic athletics
  USE School sports

Intersection theory
BT Geometry, Algebraic
Intersections, Rotary
USE Traffic circles
Intersections (Highway engineering)
USE Roads—Interchanges and intersections
Intersensory effects
UF Heteromodal effects
BT Perception
Senses and sensation
NT Synesthesia
Intersexuality
USE Hermaphroditism
Interspecific competition
USE Competition (Biology)
Interstate 66 (Va.)
UF I-66 (Va.)
BT Express highways—Virginia
Interstate 69 *(May Subd Geog)*
BT Express highways—United States
Interstate 70 *(May Subd Geog)*
⌐TE25.5.I⌐
BT Express highways—United States
Interstate 77 *(May Subd Geog)*
⌐TE25.5.I⌐
BT Express highways—United States
Interstate 80
BT Express highways—United States
NT Indiana Toll Road (Ind.)
Interstate 87 (N.Y.)
BT Express highways—New York (State)
Interstate 90
BT Express highways—United States
NT Indiana Toll Road (Ind.)
Interstate 95
BT Express highways—United States
Interstate 105 (Calif.)
USE California Century Freeway (Calif.)
Interstate 478 (New York, N.Y.)
USE Westway (New York, N.Y.)
Interstate agencies *(May Subd Geog)*
UF Agencies, Interstate
BT Administrative agencies
Interstate agreements *(May Subd Geog)*
⌐JK2441⌐
UF Agreements, Interstate
Compacts, Interstate
Cooperation, Interstate
Interstate compacts
Interstate cooperation
BT Interstate relations
State governments
Uniform state laws
Interstate banking *(May Subd Geog)*
UF Banking, Interstate
Banks and banking, Interstate
BT Banks and banking
Interstate commerce
RT Banks and banking—Branch banks
— **Law and legislation** *(May Subd Geog)*
BT Banking law
Interstate commerce *(May Subd Geog)*
Works dealing with interstate commerce in countries organized on a federal basis are entered under Interstate commerce—⌐local subdivision⌐, e.g. Interstate commerce—Australia.
UF Commerce clause (United States. Constitution)
Government regulation of commerce
Government regulation of railroads
BT Commerce
Railroads—Rates
Railroads and state
Trusts, Industrial
RT Carriers
NT Bills of lading
Employers' liability—United States
Interstate banking
Interstate land sales
Railroad law—United States
Railroads and state—United States

Use tax
— **Taxation** *(May Subd Geog)*
BT Income tax
— **Australia**
Interstate compacts
USE Interstate agreements
Interstate controversies *(May Subd Geog)*
UF Controversies, Interstate
Interstate disputes
BT Constitutional law
Federal government
Interstate relations
State governments
Interstate cooperation
USE Interstate agreements
Interstate disputes
USE Interstate controversies
Interstate H-3 (Hawaii)
BT Express highways—Hawaii
Interstate Highway System
(May Subd Geog)
UF Interstate Highway System—United States
National System of Interstate and Defense Highways
BT Express highways—United States
— United States
USE Interstate Highway System
Interstate land sales *(May Subd Geog)*
UF Land sales, Interstate
Sales, Interstate land
BT Interstate commerce
Real estate business
— **Law and legislation** *(May Subd Geog)*
BT Vendors and purchasers
Interstate relations *(May Subd Geog)*
BT Federal government
State governments
NT Interstate agreements
Interstate controversies
Interstate rendition
USE Extradition
Interstellar communication
UF Interplanetary communication
Outer space communication
Space communication
Space telecommunication
BT Life on other planets
Telecommunication
RT Radio astronomy
NT Astronautics—Communication systems
Interstellar extinction
USE Interstellar reddening
Interstellar hydrogen
BT Hydrogen
Interstellar matter
Radio astronomy
NT H II regions (Astrophysics)
Interstellar magnetic fields
⌐QB791.7⌐
UF Galactic magnetic fields
BT Magnetic fields (Cosmic physics)
Interstellar matter
⌐QB500⌐
BT Astrophysics
Cosmogony
Ether (of space)
Light—Scattering
Matter
Space environment
RT Interstellar reddening
NT Circumstellar matter
Cosmic dust
Interstellar hydrogen
Interstellar molecules
Masers, Celestial
Oort cloud
Planetary nebulae
— **Optical properties**
Interstellar molecules
UF Molecules, Interstellar

BT Cosmochemistry
Interstellar matter
Molecular astrophysics
Molecules
Interstellar reddening
UF Extinction, Interstellar
Interstellar extinction
Reddening, Interstellar
BT Absorption of light
RT Interstellar matter
Interstellar travel
Here are entered general works and imaginary accounts on travel to the stars. Works on the physics and technical details of flight beyond the earth's atmosphere are entered under Space flight.
BT Astronautics
Science fiction
Space flight
Travel
Interstellar warfare
USE Space warfare
Interstitial cell-stimulating hormone
USE Luteinizing hormone
Interstitial cells of Leydig
USE Leydig cells
Interstitial fauna *(May Subd Geog)*
BT Marine fauna
Seashore biology
Interstitial fluid
USE Extracellular fluid
Interstitial lung diseases *(May Subd Geog)*
UF Lungs—Diseases, Interstitial
Lungs—Interstitial diseases
BT Lungs—Diseases
Interstitial lung diseases in children
(May Subd Geog)
⌐RJ436.I56⌐
BT Pediatric respiratory diseases
Interstitial matrix
USE Interphotoreceptor matrix
Interstitial mucoid
USE Interphotoreceptor matrix
Interstitial nephritis
USE Nephritis, Interstitial
Interstitial plasma cell pneumonia
(May Subd Geog)
⌐RC772.I56⌐
UF Pneumocystis carinii pneumonitis
Pneumocystis pneumonia
Pneumocystis pneumonitis
BT Immunological deficiency syndromes—Complications and sequelae
Parasitic diseases
Plasma cell diseases
Pneumonia
Interstitial radiotherapy
USE Radioisotope brachytherapy
Interstitial retinoid-binding protein
USE Interphotoreceptor retinoid-binding protein
Interstitial retinol-binding protein
USE Interphotoreceptor retinoid-binding protein
Interstitial substance
USE Extracellular matrix
Intersubjectivity
⌐B824.18⌐
BT Ontology
Phenomenology
Social psychology
Subjectivity
Intertemporal law
USE Retroactive judicial decisions
Retroactive laws
Intertidal animals
USE Intertidal fauna
Intertidal ecology *(May Subd Geog)*
BT Seashore ecology
Intertidal fauna *(May Subd Geog)*
⌐QL121⌐
UF Intertidal animals

Intertidal fauna *(Continued)*
 BT Intertidal zonation
  Seashore biology
  Tide pool ecology
Intertidal zonation *(May Subd Geog)*
 UF Eulittoral zonation
  Littoral zonation, Intertidal
  Tidal zonation
  Zonation, Intertidal
 BT Seashore biology
 NT Intertidal fauna
Intertropical convergence zone
 UF Doldrums
  Equatorial convergence zone
 BT Atmospheric circulation
  Fronts (Meteorology)
  Trade-winds
  Tropics
Intertype
 BT Printing machinery and supplies
  Type-setting machines
Interurban railroads
 USE Street-railroads
Interval analysis (Mathematics)
 [QA297.75]
 UF Analysis, Interval
  Arithmetic, Interval
  Interval arithmetic
  Interval mathematics
  Mathematics, Interval
 BT Mathematics
  Numerical analysis
Interval arithmetic
 USE Interval analysis (Mathematics)
Interval mathematics
 USE Interval analysis (Mathematics)
Intervals, Confidence
 USE Confidence intervals
Intervals (Music)
 USE Musical intervals and scales
Intervention (Civil procedure)
 (May Subd Geog)
 UF Third parties (Civil procedure)
 BT Civil procedure
  Parties to actions
  Third parties (Law)
 RT Joinder of parties
Intervention (Criminal procedure)
 (May Subd Geog)
 BT Criminal procedure
 RT Reparation
Intervention (Federal government)
 (May Subd Geog)
 UF Federal intervention
 BT Federal government
  Intervention (International law)
Intervention (International law)
 [JX4481]
 UF Military intervention
 BT Diplomatic protection
  International law
  War (International law)
 RT Neutrality
 NT Drago doctrine
  Intervention (Federal government)
  Jurisdiction (International law)
  Monroe doctrine
Intervention (Psychology)
 USE Operant behavior
Interventional radiology
 USE Radiology, Interventional
Interventricular heart block
 USE Bundle-branch block
Intervertebral disc
 USE Intervertebral disk
Intervertebral disk
 UF Disc, Intervertebral
  Disk, Intervertebral
  Intervertebral disc
 BT Cartilage
  Vertebrae

 NT Injections, Intradiscal
— **Diseases** *(May Subd Geog)*
  NT Intervertebral disk displacement
— **Hernia**
  RT Intervertebral disk displacement
— **Radiography**
— **Surgery**
  NT Discectomy
Intervertebral disk displacement
 [RD771.I6]
 UF Slipped disk
 BT Intervertebral disk—Diseases
 RT Intervertebral disk—Hernia
Interviewing
 [BF761-BF768 (Evidence)]
 [HV43 (Charities)]
 UF Social psychotechnics
 BT Applications for positions
  Evidence
  Personnel management
  Psychology, Applied
  Social psychology
 RT Counseling
  Social case work
 NT Employment interviewing
  Interviewing in psychiatry
  Interviews
  Medical history taking
  Questioning
Interviewing, Radio
 USE Interviewing in radio
Interviewing, Television
 USE Interviewing in television
Interviewing (Journalism)
 USE Interviewing in journalism
Interviewing in auditing *(May Subd Geog)*
 BT Auditing
Interviewing in child abuse
 BT Child abuse
Interviewing in child psychiatry
 (May Subd Geog)
 [RJ503.6]
 UF Child psychiatric interviewing
 BT Child psychiatry
Interviewing in corrections
 BT Corrections
Interviewing in ethnology
 BT Ethnology—Methodology
Interviewing in genealogy *(May Subd Geog)*
 BT Genealogy
Interviewing in journalism
 [PN4784.I6]
 UF Interviewing (Journalism)
 BT Journalism
Interviewing in law enforcement
 BT Law enforcement
 RT Police questioning
 NT Police patrol—Field interrogation
Interviewing in law practice
 (May Subd Geog)
 UF Legal interviewing
 BT Attorney and client
  Practice of law
Interviewing in marketing research
 BT Marketing research
Interviewing in mass media
 [P96.I]
 BT Mass media—Methodology
Interviewing in mental health
 [RC480.7]
 BT Mental health
 NT Interviewing in psychiatry
Interviewing in psychiatry
 [RC480.7]
 UF Psychiatric interviewing
 BT Interviewing
  Interviewing in mental health
  Medical history taking
  Psychotherapist and patient
  Psychotherapy

Interviewing in radio
 UF Interviewing, Radio
  Radio interviewing
 BT Radio broadcasting
 RT Talk shows
Interviewing in rehabilitation counseling
 BT Rehabilitation counseling
Interviewing in sociolinguistics
 BT Sociolinguistics
Interviewing in sociology
 BT Sociology—Methodology
Interviewing in television
 [PN1992.8.I68]
 UF Interviewing, Television
  Television interviewing
 BT Television broadcasting
 RT Talk shows
Interviewing in urban sociology
 BT Sociology, Urban
Interviews *(May Subd Geog)*
 BT Conversation
  Interviewing
 SA *subdivision* Interviews *under classes of*
   persons and ethnic groups and
   under names of individual persons
 NT Art—Interviews
  Theater—Interviews
Interviews, Parent-teacher
 USE Parent-teacher conferences
Intestacy
 USE Inheritance and succession
Intestate succession
 USE Inheritance and succession
Intestinal absorption
 UF Absorption, Intestinal
 BT Absorption (Physiology)
 RT Enterohepatic circulation
  Malabsorption syndromes
Intestinal and parasitic worms
 USE Worms, Intestinal and parasitic
Intestinal angina
 USE Intestinal ischemia
Intestinal fistula
 USE Fistula, Intestinal
Intestinal gas
 USE Gastrointestinal gas
Intestinal granulomatosis, Lipophagic
 USE Whipple's disease
Intestinal infections
 USE Intestines—Infections
Intestinal intoxication
 USE Auto-intoxication
Intestinal irrigation
 USE Enema
Intestinal ischemia
 [RC862.I8]
 UF Intestinal angina
  Ischemic bowel disease
 BT Ischemia
 RT Intestines—Infarction
 NT Ischemic colitis
Intestinal lipodystrophy
 USE Whipple's disease
Intestinal neurosis
 USE Irritable colon
Intestinal obstructions
 USE Intestines—Obstructions
Intestinal ostomy
 USE Enterostomy
Intestinal peptides, Vasoactive
 USE Vasoactive intestinal peptides
Intestinal polyps
 BT Intestines—Diseases
  Polyps (Pathology)
 NT Peutz-Teghers syndrome
Intestinal secretion
 USE Intestines—Secretions
Intestinal stoma
 USE Enterostomy

Intestine, Large
  UF Bowel, Large
      Large bowel
      Large intestine
  BT Intestines
  NT Cecum
      Colon (Anatomy)
      Rectum
  — Cancer
  — Radiography
  — Surgery
Intestine, Small
  UF Small intestine
  BT Intestines
  NT Duodenum
      Enterohepatic circulation
      Ileum
      Jejunum
  — Innervation
  — Radiography
  — Surgery
  —— Complications and sequelae
  — Ulcers
      ⌐RC862.U5¬
Intestines
    ⌐QL863 (Comparative anatomy)¬
    ⌐QM345 (Human anatomy)¬
    ⌐QP156 (Physiology)¬
  BT Abdomen
      Gastrointestinal system
  NT Appendix (Anatomy)
      Brush border membrane
      Defecation
      Intestine, Large
      Intestine, Small
      Mesentery
      Myenteric plexus
      Omentum
      Peritoneum
      Viscera
  — Bacteriology
      ⌐QR171¬
      BT Intestines—Microbiology
      NT Escherichia coli infections
  — Biopsy
  — Blood-vessels
  — Cancer
  — Diseases (May Subd Geog)
      ⌐RC860-862¬
      UF Enteropathy
      NT Constipation
          Diarrhea
          Digestive organs—Diseases
          Diverticulosis
          Dysentery
          Enteritis
          Enteritis, Regional
          Enteroptosis
          Intestinal polyps
          Intestines—Radiography
          Intestines—Tuberculosis
          Malabsorption syndromes
          Melaena
  —— Diagnosis
      ⌐RC803-5¬
  —— Psychosomatic aspects
  — Indigitation
      USE Intestines—Intussusception
  — Infarction
      RT Intestinal ischemia
  — Infections
      UF Enteric infections
          Intestinal infections
  — Inflammation
      NT Diverticulitis
  — Innervation
  — Intubation
  — Intussusception
      UF Intestines—Indigitation
          Intestines—Invagination
          Intussusception, Intestinal

      NT Intussusception in children
  — Invagination
      USE Intestines—Intussusception
  — Micro-organisms
      USE Intestines—Microbiology
  — Microbiology
      ⌐QR171.I6¬
      UF Intestines—Micro-organisms
      NT Intestines—Bacteriology
  — Obstructions
      UF Ileus
          Intestinal obstructions
          Obstructions, Intestinal
      BT Intestines—Surgery
      NT Feces—Impaction
          Volvulus
  — Parasites
      NT Helminths
  — Radiography
      BT Intestines—Diseases
  — Secretions
      UF Intestinal secretion
  — Surgery
      ⌐RD540-544¬
      NT Enterostomy
          Hernia
          Intestines—Obstructions
          Intestines—Wounds and injuries
  — Tuberculosis
      ⌐RC312.5.T7¬
      BT Intestines—Diseases
  — Wounds and injuries
      BT Intestines—Surgery
Intestines, Gases in
  USE Gastrointestinal gas
Intimacy (Psychology)
  BT Emotions
      Interpersonal relations
  RT Love
  NT Separation (Psychology)
  — Religious aspects
  —— Buddhism, ⌐Christianity, etc.¬
Intimidation
  BT Fear
      Motivation (Psychology)
      Threat (Psychology)
Intocostrin
  USE Curare
Intolerance
  USE Fanaticism
       Freedom of religion
       Liberty of conscience
       Toleration
Intonarium
  USE Tonarius
Intonation (Phonetics)
    ⌐P222¬
  UF Grammar, Comparative and general—
          Intonation
      Language and languages—Intonation
      Linguistics—Intonation
  BT Phonetics
      Prosodic analysis (Linguistics)
      Tone (Phonetics)
  RT Oral interpretation
  SA subdivision Intonation under names of
          languages and groups of languages
  NT Whistle speech
Intoxicants
  USE Alcohol
       Alcoholic beverages
       Liquors
       Stimulants
Intoxication
  USE Alcoholism
       Drunkenness (Criminal law)
       Narcotic habit
       Temperance
Intoxication, Intestinal
  USE Auto-intoxication

Intoxication, Water
  USE Water intoxication
Intra-airport transportation
    ⌐TL725.3.I6¬
  BT Airports
      Transportation
Intra-aortic balloon counterpulsation
    ⌐RD598¬
  UF Aortic balloon counterpulsation
      Aortic balloon pumping
      Balloon counterpulsation, Intra-aortic
      Balloon pumping, Intra-aortic
      Counterpulsation, Intra-aortic balloon
      Intra-aortic balloon pumping
      Pumping, Intra-aortic balloon
  BT Arterial catheterization
      Blood—Circulation, Artificial
      Heart, Mechanical
Intra-aortic balloon pumping
  USE Intra-aortic balloon counterpulsation
Intra-arterial injections
  USE Injections, Intra-arterial
Intra-articular injections
  USE Injections, Intra-articular
Intra-aural reflex
  USE Acoustic reflex
Intrabony pockets
  USE Periodontal pockets
Intracoastal navigation
  USE Intracoastal waterways
Intracoastal Waterway, Atlantic Section
  USE Atlantic Intracoastal Waterway
Intracoastal Waterway, Gulf Section
  USE Gulf Intracoastal Waterway
Intracoastal waterways (May Subd Geog)
    ⌐TC623.4-TC624 (United States)¬
      Here are entered works on inland waterways,
    natural, artificial, or both closely following a coast-
    line, improved or constructed for the purpose of con-
    necting points on the same coast. Works on the eco-
    nomic aspects are entered under the heading Coast-
    wise shipping.
  UF Coastal waterways
      Intracoastal navigation
      Waterways, Intracoastal
  BT Coastwise navigation
      Waterways
  RT Canals
      Inland navigation
  — Alaska
      NT Inside Passage
  — Atlantic States
      NT Atlantic Intracoastal Waterway
  — British Columbia
      NT Inside Passage
  — Gulf States
      NT Gulf Intracoastal Waterway
  — Washington (State)
      NT Inside Passage
Intracochlear electrode implantation
  USE Cochlear implants
Intracorporeal artificial heart
  USE Heart, Artificial
Intracostal muscles
  BT Respiratory muscles
Intracranial aneurysms
    ⌐RC693¬
  UF Cerebral aneurysms
  BT Aneurysms
      Cerebrovascular disease
Intracranial hypertension
  UF Benign intracranial hypertension
      Hypertension, Intracranial
      Otitic hydrocephalus
      Pseudotumor cerebri
      Serous meningitis
  BT Hypertension
      Intracranial pressure
Intracranial pressure
  UF Pressure, Intracranial

Intracranial pressure *(Continued)*
  BT Brain—Diseases
      Cerebrospinal fluid pressure
  NT Intracranial hypertension
Intracranial stimulation
  USE Brain stimulation
Intracranial tumors
  BT Tumors
Intracranial tumors in children
  (May Subd Geog)
  BT Pediatric neurology
      Tumors in children
Intractable pain *(May Subd Geog)*
  UF Chronic pain
  BT Pain
Intradermal injections
  USE Injections, Intradermal
Intradiscal injections
  USE Injections, Intradiscal
Intrafamily violence
  USE Family violence
Intramedullary fracture fixation
  (May Subd Geog)
  [RD103.I53]
  UF Fracture fixation, Intramedullary
      Intramedullary nailing
      Intramedullary osteosynthesis
      Medullary nailing
      Nailing, Intramedullary
      Nailing, Medullary
      Osteosynthesis, Intramedullary
  BT Internal fixation in fractures
Intramedullary nailing
  USE Intramedullary fracture fixation
Intramedullary osteosynthesis
  USE Intramedullary fracture fixation
Intramercurial planets
  USE Planets, Intramercurial
Intramural soccer
  USE Soccer—Intramural games
Intramural sports *(May Subd Geog)*
  [GV710]
  UF Sports, Intramural
  BT College sports
      School sports
  NT Soccer—Intramural games
Intramuscular injections
  USE Injections, Intramuscular
Intranasal drugs
  USE Intranasal medication
Intranasal medication *(May Subd Geog)*
  [RM160]
  UF Drugs, Intranasal
      Intranasal drugs
      Medication, Intranasal
      Nasal medication
      Pernasal medication
      Transnasal medication
  BT Drugs—Administration
  RT Respiratory therapy
Intraocular implant lenses
  USE Intraocular lenses
Intraocular lenses
  [RE988]
  UF Crystalline lens prosthesis
      Implant lenses
      Intraocular implant lenses
      Lens implantation
  BT Aphakia
      Implants, Artificial
      Ophthalmic lenses
  — **Complications and sequelae**
Intraocular pressure
  UF Ocular tension
      Pressure, Intraocular
  BT Body fluids—Pressure
      Eye
Intraocular pressure, High
  USE Glaucoma
Intraocular pressure, Low
  USE Ocular hypotony

Intraosseous anesthesia
  USE Anesthesia, Intraosseous
Intraperitoneal injections
  USE Injections, Intraperitoneal
Intrapreneur
  USE Entrepreneurship
Intrapsychic conflict
  USE Conflict (Psychology)
Intrapulpal anesthesia
  USE Anesthesia, Intrapulpal
Intraspecific competition
  USE Competition (Biology)
Intraspinal injections
  USE Injections, Spinal
Intratracheal anesthesia
  [RD85.I]
  UF Anesthesia, Endotracheal
      Anesthesia, Intratracheal
      Endotracheal anesthesia
Intrauterine blood transfusion
  USE Blood—Transfusion, Intrauterine
Intrauterine contraceptives
  (May Subd Geog)
  [RG137.3]
  UF Intrauterine devices
      IUD (Contraceptive)
  BT Contraceptives
  RT Intrauterine contraceptives industry
  NT Dalkon Shield (Intrauterine
      contraceptive)
  — **Complications and sequelae**
Intrauterine contraceptives, Medicated
  (May Subd Geog)
  [RG137.3]
  UF Medicated intrauterine contraceptives
  BT Contraceptive drugs
      Drugs—Dosage forms
Intrauterine contraceptives industry
  (May Subd Geog)
  [HD9995.C6-64]
  RT Intrauterine contraceptives
Intrauterine devices
  USE Intrauterine contraceptives
Intrauterine diagnosis
  USE Prenatal diagnosis
Intrauterine growth
  USE Fetus—Growth
Intrauterine growth retardation
  USE Fetus—Growth retardation
Intrauterine visualization, Direct
  USE Fetoscopy
Intravaginal contraceptives
  USE Contraceptives, Vaginal
Intravascular coagulation, Diffuse
  USE Disseminated intravascular coagulation
Intravenous anesthesia *(May Subd Geog)*
  [RD85.I6]
  UF Anesthesia, Intravenous
      IV anesthesia
  BT Anesthesia
  — **Complications and sequelae**
Intravenous catheterization
  (May Subd Geog)
  [RC683.5.I5]
  UF Access, Vascular
      Angioaccess
      Catheterization, Intravenous
      Vascular access
      Venous catheterization
  BT Catheters
      Intravenous therapy
  — **Complications and sequelae**
Intravenous fat emulsions
  USE Fat emulsions, Intravenous
Intravenous feeding
  USE Parenteral feeding
Intravenous infusions
  USE Intravenous therapy
Intravenous injections
  USE Injections, Intravenous

Intravenous lipid emulsions
  USE Fat emulsions, Intravenous
Intravenous therapy *(May Subd Geog)*
  [RM170-RM178]
  UF Infusions, Intravenous
      Intravenous infusions
      IV therapy
  BT Parenteral therapy
  NT Hypertonic solutions—Therapeutic use
      Injections, Intravenous
      Intravenous catheterization
  — **Complications and sequelae**
  — **Equipment and supplies**
      NT Intravenous therapy equipment
          industry
Intravenous therapy equipment industry
  (May Subd Geog)
  [HD9995.I58-584]
  BT Intravenous therapy—Equipment and
      supplies
Intravenous therapy for children
  (May Subd Geog)
  BT Parenteral therapy for children
Intravesical pressure, Measurement of
  USE Cystometry
Intrenching tools
  [UG380]
  BT Tools
Intrenchments
  [UG403 (Field fortification)]
  [UG446 (Trenches and trench warfare)]
  UF Entrenchments
      Foxholes
      Trench warfare
  BT Camps (Military)
      Fortification
      Military art and science
      Military engineering
      Military field engineering
      Obstacles (Military science)
  SA *subdivision* Trench warfare *under*
      individual wars, e.g. World War,
      1939-1945—Trench warfare
  NT Attack and defense (Military science)
      Fortification, Field
      Mines, Military
      Sapping
Intrinsic factor (Physiology)
Intrinsic motivation
  UF Motivation, Intrinsic
  BT Motivation (Psychology)
Introduction of animals
  USE Animal introduction
Introduction of pests
  USE Pest introduction
Introduction of plants
  USE Plant introduction
Introduction of speakers
  BT After-dinner speeches
      Lectures and lecturing
      Oratory
      Public speaking
      Speeches, addresses, etc.
Introduction of trees
  USE Tree introduction
Introits
  BT Propers (Liturgy)
Introits (Music)
  BT Propers (Music)
      Psalms (Music)
INTROSOFTWARE (Computer programs)
  BT Computer programs
Introspection
  UF Self-observation
  BT Observation (Psychology)
      Psychology
  — **Religious aspects**
  — — **Buddhism, [Christianity, etc.]**
Introspection (Theory of knowledge)
  USE Self-knowledge, Theory of

Introversion
　[BF175]
　　BT　Personality
　　RT　Extraversion
　　NT　Maudsley personality inventory
Intruder (Bombers)
　[UG1242.B6]
　　UF　A-6 (Bomber)
　　BT　Bombers
　　　　Jet planes, Military
　　NT　EA-6 (Electronic warfare aircraft)
Intruder (Electronic warfare aircraft)
　　USE　EA-6 (Electronic warfare aircraft)
Intrusion, Saltwater
　　USE　Saltwater encroachment
Intrusion alarm systems
　　USE　Electronic alarm systems
Intrusions (Geology)　*(May Subd Geog)*
　　UF　Intrusive bodies
　　　　Pluton
　　BT　Geology, Structural
　　　　Rocks, Igneous
　　NT　Batholiths
　　　　Dikes (Geology)
　　　　Laccoliths
　　　　Necks (Geology)
　　　　Sills (Geology)
　　　　Stocks (Geology)
Intrusive bodies
　　USE　Intrusions (Geology)
Intubation
　　USE　*subdivision* Intubation *under subjects,*
　　　　　e.g. Larynx—Intubation; Trachea—
　　　　　Intubation
Intuition
　[BD181]
　　UF　Intuitionalism
　　BT　Consciousness
　　　　Knowledge, Theory of
　　　　Philosophy
　　　　Rationalism
　　RT　Insight
Intuition (Computer system)
　　BT　Amiga (Computer)—Programming
Intuition (Psychology)
　[BF311]
　　BT　Consciousness
　　　　Psychology
　　　　Senses and sensation
　　RT　Perception
Intuition of duration
　　USE　Time perception
Intuitionalism
　　USE　Intuition
Intuitionistic mathematics
　　BT　Constructive mathematics
　　　　Mathematics
　　NT　Brouwerian algebras
Intumescences (Botany)
　[SB732 (Plant pathology)]
Intussusception, Intestinal
　　USE　Intestines—Intussusception
Intussusception in children
　　BT　Intestines—Intussusception
Inuit
　　USE　Eskimos
Inuit language
　　USE　Eskimo language
Inulase
　[QK896 (Plant physiology)]
Inulin
　[QD321]
Inundations
　　USE　Floods
Inupiaq language
　　USE　Eskimo language
Inupiat language
　　USE　Eskimo language
Inupik language
　　USE　Eskimo language

Invalid cookery
　　USE　Cookery for the sick
Invalidity insurance
　　USE　Insurance, Disability
Invalids　*(May Subd Geog)*
　　BT　Sick
　　RT　Convalescence
　　　　Handicapped
　　NT　Self-help devices for the disabled
　— **Occupations**
　　　BT　Occupations
　　　RT　Occupational therapy
　— **Recreation**
　　　USE　Aged—Recreation
　　　　　　Handicapped—Recreation
　　　　　　Sick—Recreation
Invariance, Gauge
　　USE　Gauge invariance
Invariance principles (Physics)
　　USE　Symmetry (Physics)
Invariant imbedding
　[QA431]
　　BT　Functional equations
　　　　Invariants
　　　　Mathematical physics
　　　　Radiation
Invariant subspaces
　　UF　Subspaces, Invariant
　　BT　Functional analysis
　　　　Hilbert space
Invariant wave equations
　　USE　Wave equations, Invariant
Invariants
　[QA201]
　[QA244 (Theory of numbers)]
　　NT　Adiabatic invariants
　　　　Integrals, Haar
　　　　Invariant imbedding
Invariants, Conformal
　　USE　Conformal invariants
Invariants, Differential
　　USE　Differential invariants
Invasion of privacy
　　USE　Privacy, Right of
Invasion of Timur, Turkey, 1402
　　USE　Turkey—History—Invasion of Timur,
　　　　　1402
Invasions of China
　　USE　China—History—Invasions
Invasions of France
　　USE　France—History—Invasions
Invasions of Great Britain
　　USE　Great Britain—History—Invasions
Invasions of Minorca (Spain)
　　USE　Minorca (Spain)—History—Invasions
Invasions of Rome, Germanic
　　USE　Rome—History—Germanic Invasions,
　　　　　3d-6th centuries
Invasiveness (Oncology)
　　USE　Cancer invasiveness
Invective　*(May Subd Geog)*
　[PR1111.I65 (English literature)]
　　UF　Abuse, Verbal
　　　　Insults
　　　　Insults, Verbal
　　　　Verbal abuse
　　　　Vituperation
　　RT　Satire
　　NT　Hate mail
Invention (Rhetoric)
　[PN221]
　　BT　Rhetoric
Inventions　*(May Subd Geog)*
　[T15-T35 (History)]
　[T201T-T339 (Patents)]
　　UF　Discoveries (in science)

　　BT　Civilization
　　　　Creative ability in technology
　　　　Industrial arts
　　　　Industrial arts—History
　　　　Machinery
　　　　Technology
　　RT　Patents
　　　　Research, Industrial
　　NT　Agricultural inventions
　　　　Exchanges of patents and technical
　　　　　information
　　　　Inventors
　　　　Musical inventions and patents
　　　　Patents and government-developed
　　　　　inventions
　　　　Technological innovations
　　　　Technology transfer
Inventions, Employees'　*(May Subd Geog)*
　　UF　Employees' inventions
　　　　Inventions of employees
　　　　Shop rights (Patent law)
　　BT　Master and servant
　　　　Patent laws and legislation
　　RT　Technological innovations—Employee
　　　　　participation
　　NT　Patents and government-developed
　　　　　inventions
Inventions of employees
　　USE　Inventions, Employees'
Inventories　*(May Subd Geog)*
　[HF5681.S8]
　　Here are entered works about, or consisting of,
　lists of raw materials, supplies, finished goods, etc.,
　on hand at a particular time.
　　UF　Stock in trade
　　　　Stock-taking
　　RT　Inventory control
　　SA　*subdivision* Inventories *under types of*
　　　　　industries, institutions, and subjects,
　　　　　e.g. Construction industry—
　　　　　Inventories; Libraries—Inventories;
　　　　　Materials—Inventories
　　NT　Commercial finance companies
　　　　Inventories, Retail
　　　　Inventory shortages
　— **Accounting**
　— — **Computer programs**
　　　　NT　Inventory Accounting
　　　　　　(Computer program)
　— **Taxation**
　— — **Law and legislation**
　　　　(May Subd Geog)
Inventories, Retail　*(May Subd Geog)*
　　UF　Retail inventories
　　　　Retail trade—Inventories
　　BT　Inventories
　　　　Product management
　　　　Retail trade
Inventories as collateral
　　USE　Inventory loans
Inventories in libraries
　　USE　Libraries—Inventories
Inventories of decedents' estates
　　(May Subd Geog)
　　BT　Decedents' estates
　　　　Liquidation
　　　　Registers of births, etc.
　　RT　Collation (Law)
Inventors　*(May Subd Geog)*
　[T39-40]
　　BT　Inventions
　　RT　Engineers
　　NT　Women inventors
Inventors, Afro-American
　　USE　Afro-American inventors
Inventory Accounting (Computer program)
　　BT　Inventories—Accounting—Computer
　　　　programs

Inventory control
UF Control, Inventory
      Inventory management
      Stock control
BT Business logistics
      Physical distribution of goods
      Production control
RT Inventories
SA *subdivision* Inventory control *under
      names of individual military services
      and types of industries, e.g.* United
      States. Army—Inventory control;
      Construction industry—Inventory
      control
NT Economic lot size
      Material accountability
      Materials management
      Stores or stock-room keeping
      Warehouses
Inventory financing
USE Inventory loans
Inventory lending
USE Inventory loans
Inventory loans *(May Subd Geog)*
UF Inventories as collateral
      Inventory financing
      Inventory lending
BT Business enterprises—Finance
      Loans
Inventory management
USE Inventory control
Inventory shortages *(May Subd Geog)*
UF Shortages, Inventory
BT Inventories
      Retail trade
      Retail trade—Security measures
RT Shoplifting
NT Employee theft
Inverarden (Cornwall, Ont.)
BT Dwellings—Ontario
Inverewe Garden (Scotland)
    (Not Subd Geog)
BT Gardens—Scotland
Invergordon Mutiny, 1931
    [DA89]
Inversaria
    [QL398.C5]
BT Onychocellidae
Inverse functions
USE Functions, Inverse
Inverse matrices
USE Matrix inversion
Inverse of a matrix
USE Matrix inversion
Inverse problems (Differential equations)
BT Differential equations
— **Numerical solutions**
    BT Numerical analysis
Inverse scattering transform
UF Scattering transform, Inverse
      Transform, Inverse scattering
BT Scattering (Mathematics)
      Transformations (Mathematics)
Inverse semigroups
BT Semigroups
Inverses of linear operators, Generalized
USE Linear operators—Generalized inverses
Inversion, Matrix
USE Matrix inversion
Inversion, Symbolic
USE Symbolic inversion
Inversion, Symmetrical
USE Symmetrical inversion (Music)
Inversion geometry
USE Inversions (Geometry)
Inversion of atmospheric temperature
USE Temperature inversions
Inversion of sugar
USE Sugar—Inversion
Inversions (Geometry)
    [QA473]

UF Inversion geometry
BT Circle
      Geometry, Modern
      Sphere
      Transformations (Mathematics)
NT Involutes (Mathematics)
Invertase
    [QD321 (Organic chemistry)]
    [QP601 (Physiological chemistry)]
UF Fructofuranosidase
NT Sugar—Inversion
Invertebrate populations *(May Subd Geog)*
BT Animal populations
NT Arthropod populations
      Insect populations
      Plankton populations
      Starfish populations
Invertebrate vectors
USE Invertebrates as carriers of disease
Invertebrates *(May Subd Geog)*
    [QL362-599]
BT Animals
NT Animal colonies
      Aquatic invertebrates
      Arachnida
      Arthropoda
      Aschelminthes
      Brachiopoda
      Bryozoa
      Coelenterata
      Crustacea
      Cryptozoa
      Ctenophora
      Echinodermata
      Echiura
      Freshwater invertebrates
      Insects
      Invertebrates as carriers of disease
      Marine invertebrates
      Mesozoa
      Mollusks
      Phoronidea
      Protozoa
      Pseudocoelomata
      Sipuncula
      Soil invertebrates
      Sponges
      Worms
— **Anatomy**
    [QL363]
    NT Cement glands
         Trichobothrium
— **Behavior**
    SA *subdivision* Behavior *under names
         of particular invertebrates, e.g.*
         Sea-urchins—Behavior
— **Cultures and culture media**
    BT Laboratory animals
         Small animal culture
    NT Invertebrates as laboratory animals
— **Physiology**
    [QL364]
— **Research** *(May Subd Geog)*
Invertebrates, Fossil
    [QE770-832]
SA *names of individual fossil phyla,
      classes, orders, etc., e.g.*
      Coelenterata, Fossil
NT Hydrozoa, Fossil
— **Type specimens**
    [QE770]
    UF Type specimens (Invertebrates,
         Fossil)
    BT Paleontology—Catalogs and
         collections
         Type specimens (Natural history)
Invertebrates as carriers of disease
    (May Subd Geog)
UF Invertebrate vectors
BT Animals as carriers of disease
      Invertebrates

NT Arthropod vectors
      Invertebrates as carriers of plant
         disease
      Mollusks as carriers of disease
      Shellfish as carriers of disease
      Worms as carriers of disease
Invertebrates as carriers of plant disease
    (May Subd Geog)
BT Invertebrates as carriers of disease
      Plant diseases
NT Insects as carriers of plant disease
      Plant mites as carriers of disease
      Plant nematodes as carriers of disease
Invertebrates as laboratory animals
BT Invertebrates—Cultures and culture
      media
Invertebrates as pets
NT Marine invertebrates as pets
Inverted posture
USE Posture, Inverted
Inverters, Electric
USE Electric inverters
Investigation, Welfare fraud
USE Welfare fraud investigation
Investigation of computer crimes
USE Computer crimes—Investigation
Investigation of employee theft
USE Employee theft—Investigation
Investigations
    Here are entered works on the technique of inves-
tigations in general. Works dealing with investiga-
tions in a specific field are entered under specific
subject headings, e.g. Criminal investigation; Struc-
tural failures—Investigation.
NT Accidents—Investigation
      Building failures—Investigation
      Criminal investigation
      Dam failures—Investigation
      Fire investigation
      Governmental investigations
      Missing persons—Investigation
      Structural failures—Investigation
Investigations, Governmental
USE Governmental investigations
Investigative reporting *(May Subd Geog)*
UF Reporting, Investigative
BT Reporters and reporting
— **Awards**
    NT Drew Pearson Prize for
         Investigative Reporting
Investiture
    [BX1198 (Church history)]
BT Bishops
      Catholic Church—Government
      Church and state
      Church polity
RT Consecration of bishops
NT Simony
Investiture (Canon law)
BT Canon law
Investment advisers *(May Subd Geog)*
UF Investment counselors
BT Investments
RT Financial planners
NT Investment analysis
— **Marketing**
Investment analysis
UF Security analysis
BT Investment advisers
      Investments
      Securities
NT Portfolio management
— **Computer programs**
    NT Dow Jones Market Analyzer PLUS
         (Computer program)
Investment and saving
USE Saving and investment
Investment banking *(May Subd Geog)*
UF Banks and banking, Investment
      Investment banks

BT Banks and banking
      Investments
      Securities
RT Merchant banks
NT Development banks
      Over-the-counter markets
      Syndicates (Finance)
Investment banks
  USE Investment banking
Investment casting
  USE Precision casting
Investment clubs *(May Subd Geog)*
  [HG4530]
  RT Mutual funds
Investment companies
  USE Mutual funds
      Small business investment companies
Investment counselors
  USE Investment advisers
Investment guaranty insurance
  USE Insurance, Investment guaranty
Investment in real estate
  USE Real estate investment
Investment insurance
  USE Insurance, Investment guaranty
Investment of public funds
  (May Subd Geog)
    Here are entered works on investments or pur-
chases of securities by governments to earn a return.
Works on the expenditure of public funds for projects
in the various sectors of the economy, such as agricul-
ture, transportation, health, etc., in order to achieve
economic and social development are entered under
Public investments.
  UF Public funds, Investment of
  BT Finance, Public
      Investments
      Legal investments
  RT Public investments
— **Law and legislation** *(May Subd Geog)*
Investment recovery in industrial property
  USE Surplus industrial property
Investment tax credit *(May Subd Geog)*
  BT Capital investments
      Depreciation allowances
      Tax credits
— **Law and legislation** *(May Subd Geog)*
Investment trusts
  USE Mutual funds
Investments *(May Subd Geog)*
  [HG4501-HG5900]
  UF Portfolio
  BT Finance
  RT Disinvestment
      Loans
      Saving and investment
      Saving and thrift
      Speculation
  NT Annuities
      Art as an investment
      Art objects as an investment
      Bank investments
      Bonds
      Building and loan associations
      Capital investments
      Coins as an investment
      Collectibles as an investment
      Diamonds as an investment
      Financial institutions—Investments
      Gems as an investment
      Glassware as an investment
      Institutional investments
      Insurance companies—Investments
      Investment advisers
      Investment analysis
      Investment banking
      Investment of public funds
      Investments, Foreign
      Jewelry as an investment
      Jouissance shares
      Legal investments
      Metals as an investment

      Mortgages
      Mutual funds
      Pension trusts—Investments
      Pewter as an investment
      Porcelain as an investment
      Portfolio management
      Postage-stamps as an investment
      Pottery as an investment
      Prints as an investment
      Prospectus writing
      Public investments
      Race horses as an investment
      Real estate investment
      Religious and ecclesiastical institutions
        —Investments
      Rugs, Oriental, as an investment
      Securities
      Stock-exchange
      Stocks
      University investments
      Venture capital
      Wine as an investment
— **Effect of inflation on**
  BT Inflation (Finance)
— **Law and legislation** *(May Subd Geog)*
— **Mathematical models**
  NT Capital assets pricing model
— **Mathematics**
  UF Mathematics of investment
  BT Business mathematics
— **Taxation** *(May Subd Geog)*
  NT Capital gains tax
      Investments, American, [French,
        etc.]—Taxation
      Tax shelters
— — **Law and legislation**
    (May Subd Geog)
Investments, American *(May Subd Geog)*
  UF American investments
— **Law and legislation** *(May Subd Geog)*
— **Taxation** *(May Subd Geog)*
— — **Law and legislation**
    (May Subd Geog)
Investments, American, [French, etc.]
  (May Subd Geog)
    Here are entered works on foreign investments
originating in individual countries and made in the
country, if any, indicated by the subdivision. Works
on investments originating in several countries are
entered under Investments, Foreign.
— **Taxation** *(May Subd Geog)*
  BT Investments—Taxation
Investments, Arab *(May Subd Geog)*
  UF Arab investments
Investments, Argentine *(May Subd Geog)*
  UF Argentine investments
Investments, Australian *(May Subd Geog)*
  UF Australian investments
Investments, Austrian *(May Subd Geog)*
  UF Austrian investments
Investments, Bank
  USE Bank investments
Investments, Brazilian *(May Subd Geog)*
  UF Brazilian investments
Investments, British *(May Subd Geog)*
  UF British investments
Investments, Canadian *(May Subd Geog)*
  UF Canadian investments
Investments, Danish *(May Subd Geog)*
  UF Danish investments
Investments, Developing country
  (May Subd Geog)
  UF Developing country investments
Investments, Dutch *(May Subd Geog)*
  UF Dutch investments
Investments, East European
  (May Subd Geog)
  UF East European investments
Investments, East Indian *(May Subd Geog)*
  UF East Indian investments

Investments, European *(May Subd Geog)*
  UF European investments
Investments, Foreign *(May Subd Geog)*
  [HG4538]
    Here are entered works on investments originat-
ing in several countries. Works on foreign invest-
ments originating in individual countries and made in
the country, if any, indicated by the subdivision are
entered under Investments, American, [French,
etc.].
  UF Capital exports
      Capital imports
      Foreign investments
      International investment
  BT Capital movements
      Investments
  RT Technical assistance
  NT Absorptive capacity (Economics)
      Construction industry—Foreign
        ownership
      Corporations, Foreign
      Debts, External
      Export processing zones
      Farms—Foreign ownership
      Foreign licensing agreements
      Insurance, Investment guaranty
      Investments, Foreign, and employment
      Real property—Foreign ownership
— **Law and legislation** *(May Subd Geog)*
— **Taxation** *(May Subd Geog)*
  UF Taxation of foreign investments
  BT Income tax—Foreign income
— — **Law and legislation**
    (May Subd Geog)
Investments, Foreign, and employment
  (May Subd Geog)
  UF Employment and foreign investments
  BT Investments, Foreign
      Labor supply
  RT Foreign trade and employment
Investments, Foreign (International law)
  BT International law
  NT Calvo doctrine and clause
      Drago doctrine
Investments, French *(May Subd Geog)*
  UF French investments
— **Law and legislation** *(May Subd Geog)*
— **Taxation** *(May Subd Geog)*
— — **Law and legislation**
    (May Subd Geog)
Investments, German *(May Subd Geog)*
  UF German investments
— **Palestine**
  NT Haavara
Investments, Italian *(May Subd Geog)*
  UF Italian investments
Investments, Japanese *(May Subd Geog)*
  UF Japanese investments
Investments, Libyan *(May Subd Geog)*
  UF Libyan investments
Investments, New Zealand
  (May Subd Geog)
  UF New Zealand investments
Investments, Norwegian *(May Subd Geog)*
  UF Norwegian investments
Investments, Pakistani *(May Subd Geog)*
  UF Pakistani investments
Investments, Public
  USE Public investments
Investments, Russian *(May Subd Geog)*
  UF Russian investments
Investments, Scottish *(May Subd Geog)*
  UF Scottish investments
Investments, South African
  (May Subd Geog)
  UF South African investments
Investments, South Korean
  (May Subd Geog)
  UF South Korean investments
Investments, Spanish *(May Subd Geog)*
  UF Spanish investments

Investments, Swedish *(May Subd Geog)*
  UF Swedish investments
Investments, Swiss *(May Subd Geog)*
  UF Swiss investments
Investments, West German
  (May Subd Geog)
Investments (Canon law)
  BT Catholic Church—Finance
Investor-owned health facilities
  USE Health facilities, Proprietary
Investor-owned hospitals
  USE Hospitals, Proprietary
Investor-owned nursing homes
  USE Nursing homes, Proprietary
Investor relations (Corporations)
  USE Corporations—Investor relations
Investors
  USE Capitalists and financiers
Invisible deposits
  USE Disseminated deposits
Invisible exports
  USE Invisible items of trade
Invisible imports
  USE Invisible items of trade
Invisible items of trade *(May Subd Geog)*
  UF Invisible exports
     Invisible imports
  BT Balance of payments
Invisible military airplanes
  USE Stealth aircraft
Invisible reweaving
  USE Reweaving
Invisible world
  USE Powers (Christian theology)
     Spirits
Invisible writing
  USE Writing, Invisible
Invitation cards *(May Subd Geog)*
  UF Invitations (Cards)
  BT Cards
     Social stationery
Invitations (Cards)
  USE Invitation cards
Invitations (Evangelistic work)
  USE Evangelistic invitations
Invocation
  BT Prayer
Invocation of angels
  USE Angels—Cult
Invocation of Christian martyrs
  USE Christian martyrs—Cult
Invocation of Christian saints
  USE Christian saints—Cult
Invocation of martyrs
  USE Martyrs—Cult
Invocation of saints
  USE Saints—Cult
Invoices *(May Subd Geog)*
  UF Billing
     Bills (Invoices)
  BT Bookkeeping
     Commercial documents
     Commercial law
     Sales
     Shipment of goods
  NT Billing machines
     Consular invoices
Invoices, Consular
  USE Consular invoices
Involucre
  BT Botany—Morphology
     Inflorescence
Involuntary smoking
  USE Passive smoking
Involuntary sterilization
  USE Sterilization, Eugenic
Involutes (Mathematics)
  [QA557]
  BT Curves
     Inversions (Geometry)

Involvement (Philosophy)
  USE Engagement (Philosophy)
Inyart family
  USE Enyart family
Inyo Mountains (Calif.)
  BT Mountains—California
Inzhinernyĭ i͡azyk algoritmi
  USE INI͡AZAL (Computer program
     language)
Io (Greek mythology)
  UF Callithyia (Greek mythology)
  BT Mythology, Greek
Iōanna (Legendary Pope)
  USE Joan (Legendary Pope)
Ioannina, Lake (Greece)
  UF Ioanninon Limni (Greece)
     Janina, Lake (Greece)
     Lake Ioannina (Greece)
     Limnē Iōanninōn (Greece)
     Pambotis, Lake (Greece)
     Pamvótis, Lake (Greece)
     Yannina, Lake (Greece)
  BT Lakes—Greece
Iōannina Island (Greece) *(Not Subd Geog)*
  UF Island of Iōannina (Greece)
     Nísos tōn Iōanninōn (Greece)
  BT Islands—Greece
Ioanninon Limni (Greece)
  USE Ioannina, Lake (Greece)
Iodates
  [QD181.I1]
  NT Lithium iodate
Ioder family
  USE Yoder family
Iodide incandescent lamps
  USE Iodine incandescent lamps
Iodide of hydrogen
  USE Hydriodic acid
Iodides
  [QD181.I1]
  BT Halides
  NT Cuprous iodide
     Zirconium iodide
Iodimetry
  USE Iodometry
Iodinated salt
  USE Salt, Iodized
Iodination of blood proteins
  USE Blood proteins—Radioiodination
Iodine
  [QD181.I1 (Chemistry)]
  [TP245.I6 (Chemical technology)]
  BT Halogens
  NT Iodine compounds
     Povidone-iodine
     Sandell-Kolthoff reaction
  — **Analysis**
  — **Isotopes**
     UF Radioactive iodine
        Radioiodine
     NT Blood proteins—Radioiodination
  — — **Decay**
  — — **Half-life**
  — — **Therapeutic use**
        BT Iodine—Therapeutic use
           Radioisotopes—Therapeutic use
  — **Spectra**
  — **Therapeutic use**
     [RM666.I6]
     NT Iodine—Isotopes—Therapeutic use
        Iodine compounds—Therapeutic
        use
Iodine compounds
  BT Iodine
  NT Organoiodine compounds
     Salt, Iodized
  — **Therapeutic use**
     BT Iodine—Therapeutic use
Iodine deficiency diseases *(May Subd Geog)*
  [RC627.I63]
  UF Iodine deficiency disorders

  BT Trace element deficiency diseases
  NT Cretinism
     Goiter
Iodine deficiency disorders
  USE Iodine deficiency diseases
Iodine in soils
  USE Soils—Iodine content
Iodine in the blood
  USE Iodine in the body
Iodine in the body
  UF Iodine in the blood
Iodine incandescent lamps
  UF Incandescent lamps, Iodine
     Iodide incandescent lamps
  BT Electric lamps, Incandescent
     Lamps
Iodine lasers
  UF Lasers, Iodine
  BT Chemical lasers
Iodine organic compounds
  USE Organoiodine compounds
Iodized salt
  USE Salt, Iodized
Iodobenzene
  NT Metrizamide
Iodochlorhydroxyquin
  BT Antiparasitic agents
  — **Toxicology**
     NT Subacute myelooptic neuropathy
Iodocrase
  USE Vesuvianite
Iodoform
Iodometry
  UF Iodimetry
  BT Chemistry, Analytic
Iodopsin
  BT Retina
Iolite
  USE Cordierite
Iomud horse
  USE Yomud horse
Ion (Greek mythology)
  BT Mythology, Greek
Ion accelerators
  [QC787.L5]
  UF Accelerators, Ion
  BT Linear accelerators
     Particle accelerators
  NT Heavy ion accelerators
Ion acoustic waves
  UF Ion plasma waves
     Ion waves
     Ionic waves
  BT Electrons
     Ions
     Plasma waves
Ion-atom collisions
  [QC794.6.C6]
  UF Atom-ion collisions
     Ion-atom interactions
  BT Atoms
     Collisions (Nuclear physics)
     Ions
Ion-atom interactions
  USE Ion-atom collisions
Ion beam lithography
  BT Ion bombardment—Industrial
     applications
     Lithography
Ion beams
  USE Ion bombardment
Ion bombardment
  UF Beams, Ion
     Bombardment, Ion
     Impact, Ion
     Ion beams
     Ion impact
     Ionic bombardment
  BT Collisions (Nuclear physics)
     Ions

RT Heavy ion collisions
    Sputtering (Physics)
NT Ion implantation
    Particle range (Nuclear physics)
  — **Industrial applications**
    NT Ion beam lithography
Ion carriers
  USE Ionophores
Ion channels
  UF Channels, Ion
  BT Biological transport, Active
    Ion-permeable membranes
  NT Calcium channels
    Sodium channels
Ion columns
  USE Meteor trails
Ion cyclotron resonance spectrometry
    $_{[}QD96.I54_{]}$
  UF Spectrometry, Ion cyclotron resonance
  BT Cyclotron resonance
    Mass spectrometry
Ion-electron collisions
  USE Electron-ion collisions
Ion-electron interactions
  USE Electron-ion collisions
Ion emission, Secondary
  USE Secondary ion emission
Ion exchange
    $_{[}QD561$ (Chemistry)$_{]}$
    $_{[}TP156.I6$ (Chemical engineering)$_{]}$
  UF Base-exchange
    Exchange adsorption
  BT Adsorption
    Ionization
  NT Charge transfer
    Ion-permeable membranes
    Metallurgy—Ion exchange process
    Saline water conversion—Ion exchange
      process
    Sephadex
    Sewage—Purification—Ion exchange
      process
    Water—Purification—Ion exchange
      process
Ion exchange chromatography
  BT Chromatographic analysis
Ion exchange materials, Inorganic
  USE Inorganic ion exchange materials
Ion exchange membranes
  USE Ion-permeable membranes
Ion exchange resins
  BT Gums and resins
Ion exchange resins, Effect of temperature on
Ion flow dynamics
    $_{[}QC717_{]}$
  UF Ionic flows
  BT Electrodynamics
    Electron optics
    Fluid dynamics
    Gases, Ionized
  RT Magnetohydrodynamics
  NT Ion swarms
    Plasma (Ionized gases)
Ion impact
  USE Ion bombardment
Ion implantation
  UF Implantation, Ion
    Solids—Ion implantation
  BT Ion bombardment
    Solids—Effect of radiation on
  RT Ion plating
    Semiconductor doping
Ion-ion collisions
  UF Ion-ion interactions
  BT Collisions (Nuclear physics)
    Ions
  RT Electron-ion collisions
Ion-ion interactions
  USE Ion-ion collisions
Ion microscope
  USE Field ion microscope

Ion-permeable membranes
  UF Ion exchange membranes
    Permeable membranes (Electrodialysis)
    Permselective membranes
  BT Ion exchange
    Membranes (Technology)
  RT Electrodes, Ion selective
    Electrodialysis
  NT Ion channels
Ion plasma waves
  USE Ion acoustic waves
Ion plating
    $_{[}TS695.2_{]}$
  BT Metals—Finishing
    Plating
    Thin films
  RT Cathode sputtering (Plating process)
    Ion implantation
    Vapor-plating
Ion power
  USE Ion rockets
Ion propulsion
  USE Ion rockets
Ion pumps
  UF Getter-ion pumps
    Penning pumps
    Pumps, Ion
    Sputter-ion pumps
  BT Getters
    Pumping machinery
    Vacuum-pumps
Ion rockets
    $_{[}TL783.63_{]}$
  UF Electrostatic propulsion systems
    Ion power
    Ion propulsion
    Ionic propulsion
  BT Direct energy conversion
    Electric rocket engines
    Ions
    Rockets (Aeronautics)—Ionization
      phenomena
  — **Propellant feed systems**
    UF Propellant feed systems of ion
      rockets
Ion selective electrodes
  USE Electrodes, Ion selective
Ion sensitive electrodes
  USE Electrodes, Ion selective
Ion sources
    $_{[}QC702.3_{]}$
  UF Sources, Ion
  BT Ions
    Nuclear physics—Instruments
Ion swarms
    $_{[}QC702.7.IS7_{]}$
  UF Swarms of ions
  BT Ion flow dynamics
    Ionic mobility
    Transport theory
Ion waves
  USE Ion acoustic waves
Iona (Scotland)
  UF Icomkill (Scotland)
  BT Inner Hebrides (Scotland)
    Islands—Scotland
Ionian Islands (Greece)
  UF Iónioi Nísoi (Greece)
  BT Islands—Greece
  NT Cephalonia Island (Greece)
    Corfu Island (Greece)
    Ithaca Island (Greece)
    Levkás Island (Greece)
    Paxos Island (Greece)
    Zakynthos Island (Greece)
  — **Description and travel**
  — — **1981-**
  — **History**
    NT Greece—History—Ionian Revolt,
      499-494 B.C.
  — — **1797-1815**

    $_{[}DF901.I642_{]}$
  — — **1815-1864**
Ionian Revolt, Greece, 499-494 B.C.
  USE Greece—History—Ionian Revolt, 499-
    494 B.C.
Ionians (May Subd Geog)
  BT Ethnology—Greece
  NT Architecture, Greek—Ukraine—Black
    Sea Lowland—Ionian influences
    Art, Greek—Ionian influences
Ionic bombardment
  USE Ion bombardment
Ionic capitals (Architecture)
  USE Capitals (Architecture), Ionic
Ionic columns
  USE Columns, Ionic
Ionic crystals
  NT Polarons
  — **Spectra**
Ionic equilibrium
  UF Equilibrium, Ionic
  BT Ionization
Ionic flows
  USE Ion flow dynamics
Ionic Greek dialect (May Subd Geog)
    $_{[}PA510-PA519_{]}$
  UF Greek dialect, Ionic
  BT Greece—Languages
    Greek language
Ionic mobility
  UF Mobility of ions
  BT Ions—Migration and velocity
  NT Ion swarms
Ionic polymerization
  USE Addition polymerization
Ionic propulsion
  USE Ion rockets
Ionic solutions
  UF Solutions, Ionic
  BT Ions
    Solution (Chemistry)
  NT Buffer solutions
Ionic therapy
  USE Iontophoresis
Ionic waves
  USE Ion acoustic waves
Iónioi Nísoi (Greece)
  USE Ionian Islands (Greece)
Ionization
    $_{[}QC702_{]}$
  RT Collisions (Nuclear physics)
    Hydrogen-ion concentration
  NT Auger effect
    Cosmic ray showers
    Electron impact ionization
    Inner-shell ionization
    Ion exchange
    Ionic equilibrium
    Ionization chambers
    Photoionization
    Radio auroras
    Rockets (Aeronautics)—Ionization
      phenomena
    Scintillation counters
    Scintillators
    Sporadic E (Ionosphere)
    Stopping power (Nuclear physics)
Ionization by electron impact
  USE Electron impact ionization
Ionization chambers
  UF Counting tubes
  BT Electronic measurements
    Ionization
    Radiation
    Radioactivity
    Radioactivity—Instruments
    Radioactivity—Measurement
  RT Nuclear counters
  NT Bubble chamber
    Cloud chamber
    Geiger-Müller counters

Ionization chambers *(Continued)*
    Spark chamber
Ionization constants
    [QD561]
    UF Constants, Ionization
    BT Constants, Physical
  — Measurement
      [QD561]
Ionization in rocketry
  USE Rockets (Aeronautics)—Ionization
        phenomena
Ionization of gases
    [QC702-QC721]
    [QC918 (Atmosphere)]
    UF Gases—Ionization
        Gases, Ionization of
    BT Atmospheric electricity
        Atmospheric nucleation
        Electric discharges through gases
        Radioactivity
    NT Active nitrogen
        Active oxygen
        Air, Ionized
        Breakdown voltage
        Gases, Ionized
        Ionizing shock waves
        Meteor trails
        Photoionization of gases
Ionized air
  USE Air, Ionized
Ionized gases
  USE Gases, Ionized
Ionizing radiation
    [QC794.95-QC795.55 (Physics)]
    [QH652 (Biology)]
    [QP82.2.I53 (Physiology)]
    [RA1231.R2 (Toxicology)]
    UF Radiation, Ionizing
    BT Radiation
        Radioactivity
    NT Alpha rays
        Beta rays
        Cosmic rays
        Gamma rays
        Ultraviolet radiation
        X-rays
  — Dosage
      UF Dosage of ionizing radiation
      BT Ionizing radiation—Measurement
  — Dose-effect relationship
      USE Ionizing radiation—Dose-
          response relationship
  — Dose-response relationship
      UF Dose-effect relationship
         (Radiology)
        Dose-response relationship
         (Radiology)
        Ionizing radiation—Dose-effect
         relationship
  — Measurement
      NT Ionizing radiation—Dosage
Ionizing shock waves
    [QC718.5.H5]
    BT High temperature plasmas
        Ionization of gases
        Shock waves
Ionomers
    [QD382.I45]
    BT Chemical bonds
        Ions
        Polymers and polymerization
Ionones
    [QD305.A6]
Ionophores
    [QP801.I55]
    UF Ion carriers
    BT Biological transport
        Cations—Metabolism
        Cells—Permeability
        Organic compounds
    NT Amphotericin B

    Dinitrophenol
    Gramicidins
Ionophoresis
  USE Iontophoresis
Ionosphere
    UF Heaviside layer
        Kennelly-Heaviside layer
    BT Air, Ionized
        Atmosphere, Upper
    RT Thermosphere
    NT Dawn chorus (Radio meteorology)
        F region
        Heliosphere
        Hiss (Radio meteorology)
        Ionospheric electron density
        Ionospheric forecasting
        Lower ionosphere
        Outer planets—Ionospheres
        Planets—Ionospheres
        Polar ionosphere
        Radio auroras
        Sudden ionospheric disturbances
        Whistlers (Radio meteorology)
  — Research *(May Subd Geog)*
      UF Ionospheric research
      NT Ariel (Artificial satellite)
         ISIS-II (Artificial satellite)
         ISS-b (Artificial satellite)
Ionospheres, Outer planetary
  USE Outer planets—Ionospheres
Ionospheres, Planetary
  USE Planets—Ionospheres
Ionospheric critical frequencies
    UF Critical frequencies, Ionospheric
        Penetration frequencies, Ionospheric
    BT F region
        Ionospheric radio wave propagation
        Radio frequency
Ionospheric disturbances, Sudden
  USE Sudden ionospheric disturbances
Ionospheric drift
    UF Drift, Ionospheric
    BT Magnetism, Terrestrial
        Radio meteorology
    NT Equatorial electrojet
        Geomagnetic micropulsations
        Van Allen radiation belts
Ionospheric electron density
    UF Electron density, Ionospheric
    BT Electrons
        Ionosphere
        Upper air temperature distribution
Ionospheric forecasting *(May Subd Geog)*
    [QC879]
    UF Forecasting, Ionospheric
    BT Ionosphere
        Weather forecasting
    RT Ionospheric radio wave propagation
    NT SOTAS (Artificial satellite)
Ionospheric radio wave absorption
  (May Subd Geog)
    UF Radio wave absorption in the
        ionosphere
    BT Radio meteorology
        Radio waves
Ionospheric radio wave propagation
    UF Radio wave propagation in the
        ionosphere
    BT Radio meteorology
        Radio wave propagation
        Radio waves
        VLF radio wave propagation
    RT Ionospheric forecasting
        Magneto-ionic theory
        Sporadic E (Ionosphere)
    NT Ionospheric critical frequencies
        Maximum usable frequency (Radio)
        VLF emissions
Ionospheric research
  USE Ionosphere—Research

Ionospheric Sounding Satellite-b
  USE ISS-b (Artificial satellite)
Ionospheric sounds
Ions
    [QC702-QC721 (Physics)]
    [QD561 (Electrochemistry)]
    BT Matter—Properties
        Physics
        Solution (Chemistry)
    RT Electrolysis
        Electrons
    NT Ammonium ions
        Anions
        Bromide ions
        Calcium ions
        Carbanions
        Carbonium ions
        Cations
        Charge exchange
        Chromium ions
        Cloud chamber
        Complex ions
        Copper ions
        Crystalline electric field
        Deuterium ions
        Electric discharges through gases
        Electron-ion collisions
        Heavy ions
        Helium ions
        Hydrogen ions
        Ion acoustic waves
        Ion-atom collisions
        Ion bombardment
        Ion-ion collisions
        Ion rockets
        Ion sources
        Ionic solutions
        Ionomers
        Iron ions
        Magnetic ions
        Metal ions
        Molybdenum ions
        Oxonium ions
        Plasma (Ionized gases)
        Rare earth ions
        Secondary ion emission
        Silver ions
        Space charge
        Thermionic emission
        Tungsten ions
        Ylides
  — Migration and velocity
      [QD561]
      UF Migration of ions
      BT Chemistry, Physical and theoretical
      NT Activity coefficients
         Ionic mobility
         Superionic conductors
  — Scattering
  — Spectra
      NT Beam-foil spectroscopy
Iontherapy
  USE Iontophoresis
Iontophoresis
    [RK320.I5 (Dental therapeutics)]
    [RM884 (Therapeutics)]
    UF Electroionic therapy
        Galvanoionization
        Ionic therapy
        Ionophoresis
        Iontherapy
    BT Electrophoresis
        Electrotherapeutics
IOOF Cemetery (Denton, Tex.)
  USE I.O.O.F. Cemetery (Denton, Tex.)
IOOF Cemetery (Mason City, Iowa)
  USE Mason City Oddfellows Home
        Cemetery (Mason City, Iowa)

Ios Island (Greece)   (Not Subd Geog)
　　UF　Nio Island (Greece)
　　　　Nios Island (Greece)
　　　　Nísos Íos (Greece)
　　BT　Cyclades (Greece)
　　　　Islands—Greece
Iosegun Lake (Alta.)
　　BT　Lakes—Alberta
Iowa
　— Antiquities
　　　NT　Brewster Site (Iowa)
　　　　　Chan-ya-ta Site (Iowa)
　　　　　Cherokee Sewer Site (Iowa)
　　　　　Mill Creek culture
　— Description and travel
　—　— To 1846
　—　— 1846-1950
　—　— 1951-1980
　—　— 1981-　　(Not Subd Geog)
　—　— Poetry
　— History
　　　[F616-630]
　—　— War with Mexico, 1845-1848
　—　— Civil War, 1861-1865
　　　　[E507]
Iowa Indians
　　[E99.I6]
　　BT　Indians of North America
　　　　Siouan Indians
Iowa language
　　[PM1376]
　　RT　Siouan languages
Iowa picture interpretation test
　　UF　Picture interpretation test, Iowa
　　BT　Picture interpretation tests
　　　　Projective techniques
Iowa tests of educational development
　　BT　Educational tests and measurements
Iōzan Funbogun (Kaminokuni-chō, Japan)
　　USE　Iōzan Site (Kaminokuni-chō, Japan)
Iōzan Site (Kaminokuni-chō, Japan)
　　UF　Iōzan Funbogun (Kaminokuni-chō,
　　　　　Japan)
　　BT　Japan—Antiquities
IP
　　USE　Impostor phenomenon
IPAT anxiety scale
　　[RC531]
　　BT　Anxiety—Testing
　　　　Psychiatric rating scales
IPAT depression scale
　　[RC537]
　　BT　Depression, Mental—Diagnosis
　　　　Psychiatric rating scales
Ipecac (Drug)
　　[RM666.I7]
　　UF　Brazilian ipecac (Drug)
　　　　Ipecacuanha (Drug)
　　BT　Alkaloids
　　　　Cephaelis ipecacuanha
　　　　Emetics
　　　　Expectorants
　　NT　Emetine
Ipecac (Plant)
　　USE　Cephaelis ipecacuanha
Ipecacuanha (Drug)
　　USE　Ipecac (Drug)
Ipecacuanha (Plant)
　　USE　Cephaelis ipecacuanha
Ipeľ River (Czechoslovakia and Hungary)
　　UF　Eipel River (Czechoslovakia and
　　　　　Hungary)
　　　　Ipoly River (Czechoslovakia and
　　　　　Hungary)
　　BT　Rivers—Czechoslovakia
　　　　Rivers—Hungary
Iphigeneia (Greek mythology)
　　BT　Mythology, Greek
Ipidae
　　USE　Scolytidae

Ipil-ipil
　　USE　Lead tree
Ipiranga, Grito de, Brazil, 1822
　　USE　Brazil—History—Revolution, 1822
Ípiros (Greece and Albania)
　　USE　Epirus (Greece and Albania)
Ipitinere Indians
　　USE　Amahuaca Indians
IPL (Computer program language)
　　UF　Information processing language
　　　　　(Computer program language)
　　BT　List processing (Electronic computers)
　　　　Mathematical linguistics
Ipoly River (Czechoslovakia and Hungary)
　　USE　Ipeľ River (Czechoslovakia and
　　　　　Hungary)
Ipomea
　　USE　Ipomoea
Ipomoea
　　[QK495.C78 (Botany)]
　　UF　Batates
　　　　Bonanox
　　　　Calonyction
　　　　Ipomea
　　　　Pharbitis
　　　　Quamoclit
　　BT　Convolvulaceae
　　NT　Japanese morning glory
　　　　Morning glories
　　　　Sweet potatoes
Ipomoea batatas
　　USE　Sweet potatoes
Ipomoea imperialis
　　USE　Japanese morning glory
Ipomoea nil
　　USE　Japanese morning glory
Iponemus
　　[QL458.2.T3]
　　UF　Moseria
　　BT　Tarsonemidae
Ippen Hijiri e (Scrolls)
　　USE　Ippen Shōnin eden (Scrolls)
Ippen Shōnin eden (Scrolls)
　　[ND1053.4]
　　UF　Ippen Hijiri e (Scrolls)
　　BT　Painting, Japanese—Kamakura-
　　　　　Momoyama periods, 1185-1600
　　　　Pure Land Buddhism in art
　　　　Scrolls, Japanese
Ippen Shōnin engi (Scrolls)
　　USE　Sōshun, fl. 1299-1303.　Ippen Shōnin
　　　　　engi
Ips　(May Subd Geog)
　　[QL596.S35]
　　BT　Bark beetles
　　　　Scolytidae
　　NT　Ips avulsus
　　　　Ips calligraphus
　　　　Ips confusus
　　　　Ips curvidens
　　　　Ips grandicollis
　　　　Ips radiatae
　　　　Ips typographus
Ips avulsus　(May Subd Geog)
　　[QL596.S35 (Zoology)]
　　UF　Pine engraver, Small southern
　　　　Small southern pine engraver
　　　　Southern pine engraver, Small
　　BT　Ips
Ips calligraphus　(May Subd Geog)
　　[QL596.S35 (Zoology)]
　　UF　Bostrichus chloroticus
　　　　Bostrichus conformis
　　　　Bostrichus exesus
　　　　Ips ponderosae
　　　　Six-spined engraver
　　　　Tomicus calligraphus
　　　　Tomicus interstitialis
　　　　Tomicus praemorsus
　　BT　Ips

Ips chagnoni
　　USE　Ips grandicollis
Ips confusus
　　[QL596.S35]
　　UF　California five-spined engraver
　　　　Five-spined engraver
　　BT　Ips
　　　　Pine—Diseases and pests
Ips curvidens
　　[QL596.S35]
　　BT　Ips
Ips grandicollis　(May Subd Geog)
　　[QL596.S35 (Zoology)]
　　UF　Bostrichus pini
　　　　Ips chagnoni
　　　　Pine engraver, Southern
　　　　Southern pine engraver
　　　　Tomicus cacographus
　　BT　Ips
Ips ponderosae
　　USE　Ips calligraphus
Ips radiatae
　　[QL596.S35]
　　UF　Monterey pine engraver
　　BT　Ips
Ips typographus
　　[QL596.S35]
　　BT　Ips
Ipsara (Greece)
　　USE　Psara (Greece)
Ipswich sparrow
　　USE　Savannah sparrow
Ipurina language
　　UF　Apurina language
　　　　Hypurina language
　　　　Jupurina language
　　　　Kangütü language
　　　　Kankiti language
　　BT　Arawakan languages
　　　　Indians of South America—Languages
Ipurucotó Indians
　　[F2520.1.I (Brazil)]
　　UF　Purigotos
　　BT　Carib Indians
　　　　Indians of South America
IQ
　　USE　Intelligence levels
Iqar'iyen (Berber people)　(May Subd Geog)
　　[DT313.3.I]
　　UF　Guelaia (Berber people)
　　BT　Berbers
　　　　Ethnology—Morocco
IQSY
　　USE　International Years of the Quiet Sun,
　　　　　1964-1965
Iquique (Chile), Battle of, 1879
　　[F3097]
　　BT　War of the Pacific, 1879-1884—
　　　　　Campaigns—Chile
Iqwaye (Papua New Guinea people)
　　USE　Yagwoia (Papua New Guinea people)
'Ir (The Hebrew word)
　　BT　Hebrew language—Etymology
'Ir Dayid (Jerusalem)
　　USE　City of David (Jerusalem)
Ir genes
　　[QR184.4]
　　UF　Immune response genes
　　BT　Chromosomes
　　　　Immunogenetics
　　RT　Immune response—Regulation
　　NT　Ia antigens
Irahqkiah (Papua New Guinea people)
　　USE　Awa (Papua New Guinea people)
Irakov (African people)
　　USE　Iraqw (African people)
Iramba language
　　USE　Nilamba language
Iran
　　UF　Northern Tier
　— Antiquities

Iran
— Antiquities (Continued)
    NT Architecture, Safavid
        Farrokhabad, Tepe (Iran)
        Hajji Firuz Tepe (Iran)
        Hissar Tepe (Iran)
        Kara Tepe (Iran)
        Marlik Site (Iran)
        Qaṣr-i Abū Naṣr Site (Iran)
        Susa (Ancient city)
        Tāq-e Bostān Site (Iran)
        Yahya, Tepe (Iran)
— Civilization
    NT Arts, Pakistani—Iranian influences
        Asia—Civilization—Iranian
          influences
        English literature—Iranian
          influences
        Gujarati literature—Iranian
          influences
        Illumination of books and
          manuscripts, Indic—Iranian
          influences
        Illumination of books and
          manuscripts, Turkish—Iranian
          influences
        India—Civilization—Iranian
          influences
        Japan—Civilization—Iranian
          influences
— — To 640
— — Greek influences
    BT Greece—Civilization
— — Occidental influences
    BT Civilization, Occidental
— Description and travel
— — 1979-
    [DS259.2]
— Economic conditions
— — 1918-
— — 1945-
— Foreign relations
— — To 640 (Not Subd Geog)
— — 1941-1979
    [DS316.8]
— — 1979-
    [DS318.83]
— — United States
    NT Iran Hostage Crisis, 1979-1981
— History
    [DS270-318]
— — To 640
    NT Achaemenid dynasty, 559-330
        B.C.
        Eurymedon, Battle of the, ca.
          469 B.C.
        Greece—History—Persian Wars,
          500-449 B.C.
        Greece—History—Expedition of
          Cyrus, 401 B.C.
        Mazdakism
        Plataea, Battle of, 479 B.C.
        Qādisīyah, Battle of, 637
— — Macedonian Conquest, 334-325 B.C.
    UF Macedonian Conquest, Iran,
        334-325 B.C.
    NT Gaugamela, Battle of, 331 B.C.
        Granicus, Battle of the, 334 B.C.
— — Medieval and modern, 640-
    NT Ṭāhirids
— — 640-1500
    NT Buwayhids
        Jalāyirids
        Muzaffarids
        Nahāvand, Iran, Battle of, 642
        Seljuks
        Timurids
— — 16th-18th centuries
— — Qajar dynasty, 1779-1925
    [DS298-316]
— — 19th century

— — War with Great Britain, 1856-1857
    [DS307.5]
— — 20th century
— — 1905-1911
— — Pahlavi dynasty, 1925-1979
    [DS316.2-316.9]
— — Mohammed Reza Pahlavi, 1941-1979
    [DS318]
— — 1979-
    [DS318.8]
— — Revolution, 1979
    UF Iranian Revolution, Iran, 1979
        Islamic Revolution, Iran, 1979
— — 1979-
    NT Iraqi-Iranian Conflict, 1980-
— Languages
    NT Gilaki language
        Turkmen language
        Uighur language
— Politics and government
— — 20th century
— — 1925-1979
— — 1941-1979
    [DS318]
— — 1979-
    NT Iran Hostage Crisis, 1979-1981
— Public buildings
    USE Public buildings—Iran
— Religion
    NT Mazdakism
— Study and teaching (May Subd Geog)
    NT Iranologists
Iran-Contra Affair, 1985-
    [E876]
    UF Contra-Iran Affair, 1985-
        Contragate, 1985-
        Iran-Contra Arms Scandal, 1985-
        Irangate, 1985-
    BT Corruption (in politics)—United States
        Military assistance, American—Iran
        Military assistance, American—
          Nicaragua
        United States—Politics and
          government—1981-
Iran-Contra Arms Scandal, 1985-
    USE Iran-Contra Affair, 1985-
Iran Hostage Crisis, 1979-1981
    BT Hostages—Iran
        Hostages—United States
        Iran—Foreign relations—United States
        Iran—Politics and government—1979-
        United States—Foreign relations—Iran
        United States—Politics and
          government—1977-1981
Iran in the Hadith
    BT Hadith
Iran in the Koran
    [BP134.I72]
    UF Koran—Iran
Iran-Iraq War, 1980-
    USE Iraqi-Iranian Conflict, 1980-
Iran specialists
    USE Iranologists
Iranche Indians
    USE Iranxe Indians
Iranche language
    USE Iranxe language
Irangate, 1985-
    USE Iran-Contra Affair, 1985-
Irangi (African people)
    USE Rangi (African people)
Iranian Americans (May Subd Geog)
    UF Iranian Americans—United States
    BT Ethnology—United States
        Iranians—United States
    NT Missions to Iranian Americans
— United States
    USE Iranian Americans
Iranian art
    USE Art, Iranian

Iranian authors
    USE Authors, Iranian
Iranian bronzes
    USE Bronzes, Iranian
Iranian calendar
    USE Calendar, Iranian
Iranian epic literature
    USE Epic literature, Iranian
Iranian illumination of books and manuscripts
    USE Illumination of books and manuscripts,
        Iranian
Iranian-Iraqi Conflict, 1980-
    USE Iraqi-Iranian Conflict, 1980-
Iranian Jews
    USE Jews, Iranian
Iranian languages (May Subd Geog)
    [PK6001-6996]
    UF Eranian languages
    BT Indic languages
        Indo-Iranian languages
    NT Avesta language
        Baluchi language
        Dari language
        Ephthalite language
        Gilaki language
        Hazara language
        Kurdish language
        Median language
        Old Persian language
        Ormuri language
        Ossetic language
        Pamir languages
        Persian language
        Pushto language
        Tajik language
        Talysh language
        Tat language
        Wakhi language
        Yaghnobi language
        Yüeh-chih language
Iranian languages, Middle
    [PK6135]
    UF Middle Iranian languages
    NT Khorezmi language
        Khotanese language
        Pahlavi language
        Parthian language
        Sogdian language
Iranian literature
    [PK6001-6996]
    UF Eranian literature
    BT Pahlavi literature
    NT Epic literature, Iranian
        Indic literature
Iranian mythology
    USE Mythology, Iranian
Iranian newspapers (May Subd Geog)
Iranian periodicals (May Subd Geog)
Iranian philology
    [PK6001-6996]
    UF Eranian philology
    BT Indo-Aryan philology
Iranian poets
    USE Poets, Iranian
Iranian property (May Subd Geog)
    UF Property, Iranian
    BT Alien property
Iranian Revolution, Iran, 1979
    USE Iran—History—Revolution, 1979
Iranian schools
    USE Schools, Iranian
Iranian wit and humor, Pictorial
Iranians (May Subd Geog)
    UF Persians
    BT Ethnology—Iran
    RT Indo-Iranians
    NT Alani
        Bakhtiari
        Baluchis
        Indo-Scythians
        Kurds

Missions to Iranians
Ossetes
Parthians
Pushtuns
Saka
Sarmatians
Scythians
Tajiks
Yaghnobi
— United States
    NT Iranian Americans
Iranologists
   [DS271.6-271.7]
   UF Iran specialists
   BT Iran—Study and teaching
Irantxe Indians
   USE Iranxe Indians
Iranxe Indians
   [F2520.1.I7]
   UF Iranche Indians
      Irantxe Indians
      Münkü Indians
   BT Indians of South America
      Indians of South America—Brazil
Iranxe language
   UF Iranche language
   BT Indians of South America—Languages
Irapa Indians
   [F2319.2.I7]
   BT Indians of South America
      Indians of South America—Colombia
      Indians of South America—Venezuela
      Yupa Indians
Iraq
   UF Mesopotamia
— Antiquities
    NT Ashur (Ancient city)
      Babylon (Ancient city)
      Calah (Ancient city)
      Dur Sharrukin (Ancient city)
      Erech (Ancient city)
      Eridu (Ancient city)
      Girsu (Ancient city)
      Isin (Ancient city)
      Jarmo Site (Iraq)
      Karana (Ancient city)
      Lagash (Ancient city)
      Larsa (Ancient city)
      Nineveh (Ancient city)
      Nippur (Ancient city)
      Nuzi (Ancient city)
      Oueili, Tall al- (Iraq)
      Shanidar Cave (Iraq)
      Umma (Ancient city)
      Ur (Ancient city)
      Yarim Tepe (Iraq)
      Zawi Chemi Shanidar Site (Iraq)
— Civilization
— — To 634
    NT Civilization, Assyro-Babylonian
— — 634-1921
— — 1921-
— History
— — To 634
— — 634-1534
    NT Abbasids
      Buwayhids
      Camel, Battle of the, 656
      Hamdanids
      Jalāyirids
      Mazyadids
      Qādisīyah, Battle of, 637
      Seljuks
— — Zanj Rebellion, 868-883
    [DS76.4]
    UF Zanj Revolt, 868-883
    BT Blacks—Iraq
— — 1534-1921
    NT Musha'sha'ids
— — Revolt of 1920
— — 1921-

— — Hashemite Kingdom, 1921-1958
    [DS79-79.6]
    UF Hashemite Kingdom, 1921-1958
— — Revolution, 1958
— — 1958-
    [DS79.65-79.66]
    NT Iraqi-Iranian Conflict, 1980-
— — Revolution, 1958
— — — Anniversaries, etc.
— — — Pictorial works
— — Revolution, 1963
— Antiquities
    NT Northwest Palace (Calah)
Iraq-Iran War, 1980-
   USE Iraqi-Iranian Conflict, 1980-
Iraqi art
   USE Art, Iraqi
Iraqi arts
   USE Arts, Iraqi
Iraqi children's periodicals
   USE Children's periodicals, Iraqi
Iraqi-Iranian Conflict, 1980-
   (May Subd Geog)
   UF Iran-Iraq War, 1980-
      Iranian-Iraqi Conflict, 1980-
      Iraq-Iran War, 1980-
      Persian Gulf War, 1980-
   BT Iran—History—1979-
      Iraq—History—1958-
Iraqi Jews
   USE Jews, Iraqi
Iraqi newspapers *(May Subd Geog)*
Iraqi painting
   USE Painting, Iraqi
Iraqi periodicals *(May Subd Geog)*
   BT Arabic periodicals
   NT Children's periodicals, Iraqi
Iraqi sculpture
   USE Sculpture, Iraqi
Iraqi wit and humor, Pictorial
   (May Subd Geog)
Iraqis *(May Subd Geog)*
   BT Ethnology—Iraq
Iraqw (African people)
   UF Erokh (African people)
      Irakov (African people)
      Mbulu (African people)
      Wambulu (African tribe)
   BT Ethnology—Tanzania
   NT Missions to Iraqw (African people)
Iraqw language
   BT Cushitic languages, Southern
IRA's
   USE Individual retirement accounts
IRAs, Self-directed
   USE Self-directed individual retirement
      accounts
Irawadi River (Burma)
   USE Irrawaddy River (Burma)
Iraya language
   USE Mangyan language
Irazú Volcano (Costa Rica)
   UF Monte Irazú (Costa Rica)
      Volcán Irazú (Costa Rica)
   BT Mountains—Costa Rica
      Volcanoes—Costa Rica
— Eruption, 1963
IRBM
   USE Intermediate-range ballistic missiles
Irbore language
   USE Arbore language
Ire (The French word)
   BT French language—Etymology
Iregua River (Spain)
   BT Rivers—Spain

Ireland
   Here are entered works on the Republic of Ireland and on the island of the British Isles called Ireland. Works on the United Kingdom of Great Britain and Northern Ireland, which comprises England, Northern Ireland, Scotland, and Wales, as well as works on the island of Great Britain, are entered under Great Britain. Works on the non-jurisdictional island group comprising the islands of Great Britain, Ireland, and smaller adjacent islands are entered under British Isles.
— Antiquities
    NT Derrynaflan Site (Ireland)
      Knowth Site (Ireland)
      Newgrange Site (Ireland)
      Wood Quay Site (Dublin, Dublin)
— Church history
— — To 1172
— — Medieval period, 600-1500
— — 19th century
— — 20th century
— Civilization
    NT England—Civilization—Irish
      influences
      Europe—Civilization—Irish
      influences
— — To 1172
— — 17th century
— — 20th century
    [DA959.1]
— — African influences *(Not Subd Geog)*
    BT Africa—Civilization
— — Greek influences
    BT Greece—Civilization
— — Middle Eastern influences
    (Not Subd Geog)
    BT Middle East—Civilization
— — Roman influences
    BT Rome—Civilization
— Description and travel
— — To 1700
— — 1701-1800
— — 1801-1900
— — 1901-1950
— — 1951-1980
— — 1981-
— Economic conditions
— — 1918-1949
— — 1949-
— Foreign relations
— — 1922-
— History
    [DA900-995]
— — To 1172
    NT Clontarf, Battle of, 1014
      Magh Rath, Battle of, 637
— — To 1603
— — — Juvenile literature
— — English Conquest, 1166-1186
— — 1172-
— — 1172-1603
— — 16th century
— — 1558-1603
— — 1595-1612
    NT Tyrone's Rebellion, 1597-1603
— — 17th century
— — 1603-1625
— — 1625-1649
— — Rebellion of 1641
— — 1649-1660
— — 1649-1775
— — 1660-1688
— — 1660-1690
— — James II, 1685-1688
— — 1688-1689
— — War of 1689-1691
— — — Campaigns *(Not Subd Geog)*
    NT Boyne, Battle of the, 1690
— — 1691-
— — 18th century
— — 1760-1820

Irish bulls
   USE Bulls, Colloquial
        Irish wit and humor
Irish calligraphy
   USE Calligraphy, Irish
Irish children's poetry
   USE Children's poetry, Irish
Irish Christian poetry
   USE Christian poetry, Irish
Irish Confederation, 1642-1648
   [DA943]
   UF Kilkenny Confederation
Irish cookery
   USE Cookery, Irish
Irish crochet lace
   [TT805]
   BT Lace and lace making
Irish Derby
   USE Irish Sweeps Derby
Irish Derby Sweepstakes
   USE Irish Sweeps Derby
Irish diaries
   BT Diaries
Irish diaries (English)
   USE English diaries—Irish authors
Irish drama
Irish drama (English)
   USE English drama—Irish authors
Irish economic assistance
   USE Economic assistance, Irish
Irish Elk
   USE Megaloceros
Irish epic literature
   USE Epic literature, Irish
Irish fiction *(May Subd Geog)*
   NT Short stories, Irish
Irish fiction (English)
   USE English fiction—Irish authors
Irish folk literature
   USE Folk literature, Irish
Irish folk poetry
   USE Folk poetry, Irish
Irish folk-songs
   USE Folk-songs, Irish
Irish harp
   USE Harp
Irish heath
   USE Daboecia
Irish hymns
   USE Hymns, Irish
Irish imprints *(May Subd Geog)*
Irish in literature
   [PR151.I (English literature)]
Irish inscriptions
   USE Inscriptions, Irish
Irish Land League
   [DA951 (History of Ireland)]
   [HD625 (Economic history)]
   UF Land League, Irish
Irish land question
   USE Land tenure—Ireland
Irish language
   [PB1201-1299]
   UF Erse
        Gaelic language (Irish)
   BT Celtic languages
        Goidelic languages
   RT Gaelic language
   NT Shelta
   — **To 1100**
        [PB1218]
        UF Irish language—Old Irish
   — **Middle Irish, 1100-1550**
        [PB1218]
   — **Alphabet**
        NT Ogham alphabet
   — **Names**
        USE Names, Irish
   — **Old Irish**
        USE Irish language—To 1100
   — **Revival**

Irish literature
   [PB1306-PB1449]
   BT British literature
        Celtic literature
   NT Epic literature, Irish
        Irish-American literature
   — **To 1100**
        [PB1321 (History)]
        [PB1347-PB1351 (Collections)]
   — **Middle Irish, 1100-1550**
        [PB1322 (History)]
        [PB1347-PB1351 (Collections)]
   — **Early modern, 1550-1700**
   — American authors
        USE Irish-American literature
Irish literature (English)
   USE English literature—Irish authors
Irish love poetry
   USE Love poetry, Irish
Irish manuscripts
   USE Manuscripts, Irish
Irish missions
   USE Missions, Irish
Irish names
   USE Names, Irish
Irish national characteristics
   USE National characteristics, Irish
Irish newspapers
   [PN5141-PN5149 (History)]
        Here are entered works on newspapers published
     in Ireland, and on newspapers in the Irish language,
     or devoted to Irish interests, published outside of
     Ireland.
   UF British newspapers
   NT Irish-American newspapers
Irish paleography
   USE Paleography, Irish
Irish periodicals
   [PN5141-PN5150 (History)]
        Cf. note under Irish newspapers.
   UF British periodicals
Irish philology
Irish poetry *(May Subd Geog)*
   [PB1331-PB1333 (History)]
   UF British poetry
   NT Children's poetry, Irish
        Christian poetry, Irish
        Fili (Irish poets)
        Folk poetry, Irish
        Love poetry, Irish
        Religious poetry, Irish
        Triads (Literature)
   — **To 1100**
        UF Irish poetry—Old Irish
   — **Middle Irish, 1100-1550**
   — Old Irish
        USE Irish poetry—To 1100
Irish poetry (English)
   USE English poetry—Irish authors
Irish porcelain
   USE Porcelain, Irish
Irish portraits
   USE Portraits, Irish
Irish potatoes
   USE Potatoes
Irish pottery
   USE Pottery, Irish
Irish prose literature *(May Subd Geog)*
   [PB379 (Collections)]
   [PB1336 (History)]
Irish question
   [DA947-965]
   RT Home rule (Ireland)
   NT Fenians
        Land tenure—Ireland
        Phoenix Park Assassination, 1882
Irish quotations
   USE Quotations, Irish
Irish regiments
   USE France. Armée—Irish regiments
        Spain. Ejército—Irish regiments

Irish religious poetry
   USE Religious poetry, Irish
Irish satirists
   USE Satirists, Irish
Irish sculpture
   USE Sculpture, Irish
Irish Sea
   BT North Atlantic Ocean
Irish setters
   [SF429.I7]
   BT Setters (Dogs)
Irish short stories
   USE Short stories, Irish
Irish songs
   USE Songs, Irish
Irish Sweeps Derby
   [SF357.I74]
   UF Irish Derby
        Irish Derby Sweepstakes
   BT Horse-racing—Ireland
Irish terriers
   [SF429.I8]
   BT Terriers
Irish type
   USE Type and type-founding—Irish type
Irish unification question
   UF Ireland—Unification
        Unification of Ireland
   BT Ireland—Politics and government—
        1922-
Irish university question
   USE Education—Ireland
        Universities and colleges—Ireland
Irish water spaniel
   [SF429.I83]
   BT Spaniels
Irish watercolor painting
   USE Watercolor painting, Irish
Irish wit and humor
   [PN6178.I6]
        Here are entered collections from several authors
     and individual authors who have not written in other
     literary forms.
   UF Bulls, Irish
        Irish bulls
   NT Bulls, Colloquial
        Irish-American wit and humor
Irish wit and humor, Pictorial
   [NC1470-1479]
Irish wolf-hound
   USE Irish wolfhound
Irish wolfhound
   [SF429.I85]
   UF Irish wolf-hound
        Wolf-hound, Irish
        Wolfhound, Irish
   BT Dog breeds
        Gazehounds
        Hounds
Iritis
   [RE352]
   UF Iris (Eye)—Inflammation
   BT Iris (Eye)—Diseases
        Uveitis
   NT Iridocyclitis
Irland family
   USE Ireland family
IRM
   USE Information resources management
Irminsul
   BT Germanic tribes—Religion
        Tree worship
Irmtraut family
   USE Armentrout family
Irō Cape (Japan)
   UF Irō-saki (Japan)
        Irō-zaki (Japan)
        Irōsaki (Japan)
        Irōzaki (Japan)
   BT Capes (Coasts)—Japan

Irō-saki (Japan)
USE Irō Cape (Japan)
Irō-zaki (Japan)
USE Irō Cape (Japan)
Iroha karuta
[GV1299.I7]
Irohauta
BT Japanese poetry
Iron
[QD181.F4 (Chemistry)]
[TA464-TA479 (Properties, testing)]
[TN693.I7 (Metallography)]
[TS300-TS445 (Manufactures)]
RT Siderophores
NT Building, Iron and steel
Cast-iron
Clay minerals—Iron content
Electrolytic iron
Iron—Hydrogen content
Iron, Sponge
Iron ores
Ironwork
Meteorites, Iron
Soils—Iron content
Steel
Wrought-iron
— **Analysis**
[QD133]
RT Steel—Analysis
NT Cast-iron—Analysis
Iron ores—Analysis
— **Brittleness**
— **Corrosion**
UF Rust
— **Electrometallurgy**
[TN706]
— **Fatigue**
— **Heat treatment**
NT Iron—Quenching
— **Hydrogen content**
[TN707]
UF Hydrogen in iron
Iron, Hydrogen in
BT Gases in metals
Hydrogen
Iron
— **Inclusions**
UF Inclusions in iron
— **Isotopes**
UF Iron isotopes
Isotopic iron
— **Magnetic properties**
— **Metabolism**
[QP535.F4]
UF Iron metabolism
BT Iron in the body
— — **Disorders** (May Subd Geog)
[RC632.I7]
UF Iron metabolism disorders
NT Hemosiderosis
— **Metallography**
[TN693.I7]
— **Metallurgy**
[TN703-757]
NT Puddling
Sintering
— **Physiological effect**
[QP913.F4]
[RM666.I8 (Therapeutics)]
NT Plants, Effect of iron on
— **Quenching**
[TN752.Q4]
BT Cooling
Iron—Heat treatment
— **Radiography**
— **Spectra**
Iron, Galvanized
[TS660]
UF Galvanized iron

BT Galvanizing
Metal coating
Sheet-iron
Iron, Hydrogen in
USE Iron—Hydrogen content
Iron, Nodular
UF Ductile cast iron
Nodular iron
Spheroidal graphite cast iron
BT Cast-iron
Iron, Phosphoric salts of
[RM666.I8]
UF Pyrophosphate of iron
Iron, Sponge
[TN727]
UF Sponge iron
BT Iron
Porous materials
Iron, Structural
[TA684-TA685 (Engineering)]
[TS350 (Manufacture)]
UF Structural iron
BT Building materials
RT Bridges, Iron and steel
Building, Iron and steel
Steel, Structural
NT Columns, Iron and steel
Plates, Iron and steel
Ships, Iron and steel
Iron, Wrought
USE Wrought-iron
Iron 3-chloride
USE Ferric chloride
Iron age (May Subd Geog)
[GN779-780]
RT Archaeology
Bronze age
NT Hallstatt period
La Téne period
— **England**
— **Europe, Eastern**
NT Cherniakhiv culture
Wielbark culture
— **Germany (West)**
— **Pakistan**
— **Poland**
NT Przeworsk culture
— **Spain**
— **Wales**
— **Yugoslavia**
Iron alloy industry (May Subd Geog)
[HD9529.A48-5]
RT Iron alloys
Iron alloys
[TN756-7]
RT Iron alloy industry
SA specific iron alloys, e.g. Iron-cobalt
alloys, Iron-nickel alloys
NT Iron-molybdenum-aluminum alloys
Iron-rhodium alloys
Meehanite metal
Rare earth-silicon-iron-aluminum
alloys
— **Electrometallurgy**
— **Metallography**
[TN693.I7]
— **Metallurgy**
Iron-aluminum alloys
[TA479.A4]
UF Aluminum-iron alloys
Iron-aluminum-molybdenum alloys
USE Iron-molybdenum-aluminum alloys
Iron and steel bridges
USE Bridges, Iron and steel
Iron and steel building
USE Building, Iron and steel
Iron and steel columns
USE Columns, Iron and steel
Iron and steel plates
USE Plates, Iron and steel

Iron and steel ships
USE Ships, Iron and steel
Iron and steel workers (May Subd Geog)
UF Iron workers
Steel workers
BT Iron industry and trade
Metal-workers
Steel industry and trade
NT Collective bargaining—Iron industry
Collective bargaining—Steel industry
Collective labor agreements—Iron
industry
Collective labor agreements—Steel
industry
Strikes and lockouts—Iron industry
Strikes and lockouts—Steel industry
Trade-unions—Iron and steel workers
Wages—Iron and steel workers
Women iron and steel workers
— **Diseases** (May Subd Geog)
UF Iron and steel workers—Diseases
and hygiene
— Diseases and hygiene
USE Iron and steel workers—Diseases
Iron and steel workers—Health
and hygiene
— **Effect of technological innovations on**
— **Health and hygiene** (May Subd Geog)
UF Iron and steel workers—Diseases
and hygiene
— **Medical examinations**
UF Physical examination of iron and
steel workers
BT Medicine, Industrial
— **Mortality**
— **Political activity**
BT Politics, Practical
— **France**
NT Metal-Workers' Strike, France,
1905
— **Great Britain**
NT British Steel Corporation Strike,
1980
— **Mexico**
NT Truchas (Firm) Strike, 1979
— **United States**
NT Afro-American iron and steel
workers
Iron and steel workers, Afro-American
USE Afro-American iron and steel workers
Iron bacteria
[QR84]
BT Bacteria
Iron casting
USE Iron-founding
Iron catalysts
BT Catalysts
Iron chelates
[RM666.I82 (Therapeutics)]
UF Chelators, Iron
Iron chelators
BT Chelates
— **Therapeutic use**
BT Chelation therapy
Iron chelators
USE Iron chelates
Iron chloride
USE Ferric chloride
Iron-chromium alloys
USE Chromium-iron alloys
Iron-clad vessels
USE Armored vessels
Iron-cobalt alloys
UF Cobalt-iron alloys
BT Cobalt alloys
NT Vanadium permendur
Iron compounds
BT Rock-forming minerals
Iron construction
USE Building, Iron and steel

Iron-copper alloys
UF Copper-iron alloys
BT Copper alloys
Iron Cross
  ⌜CR5351⌝
Iron Crown of Italy
  USE Order of the Crown of Italy
Iron Crown of Lombardy
  ⌜CR5511⌝
BT Crowns
Iron crystals
Iron curtain lands
  USE Communist countries
Iron deficiency anemia *(May Subd Geog)*
  ⌜RA645.I75 (Public health)⌝
  ⌜RC641.7.I7 (Internal medicine)⌝
UF Hypoferric anemia
BT Hypochromic anemia
  Iron deficiency diseases
— **Diagnosis**
Iron deficiency anemia in children
  (May Subd Geog)
  ⌜RJ416.I75⌝
BT Anemia in children
Iron deficiency diseases *(May Subd Geog)*
  ⌜RC627.I75⌝
BT Trace element deficiency diseases
NT Iron deficiency anemia
Iron dynasty, China
  USE Khitan Mongols
Iron electrodes
  USE Electrodes, Iron
Iron electroplating
  USE Iron plating
Iron-founding
  ⌜TS228.99-TS240⌝
UF Casting
  Iron casting
BT Founding
  Iron industry and trade
RT Cast-iron
NT Cupola-furnaces
  Pattern-making
  Stove industry and trade
Iron foundries *(May Subd Geog)*
BT Foundries
  Iron-works
— **Massachusetts**
  NT Saugus Iron Works National
    Historic Site (Saugus, Mass.)
Iron fronts (Architecture)
  USE Cast-iron fronts (Architecture)
Iron Gate (Romania and Serbia)
  USE Iron Gates (Romania and Serbia)
Iron Gates (Romania and Serbia)
UF Đerdap (Romania and Serbia)
  Eisernes Tor (Romania and Serbia)
  Gvozdena vrata (Romania and Serbia)
  Iron Gate (Romania and Serbia)
  Porţile de Fier (Romania and Serbia)
BT Gorges—Romania
  Gorges—Yugoslavia
Iron geology
  USE Iron ores—Geology
Iron group
  ⌜QD172.F4⌝
Iron horse (Sculpture)
BT Sculpture, American
Iron in soils
  USE Soils—Iron content
Iron in the body *(May Subd Geog)*
  ⌜QP535.F4⌝
BT Biological chemistry
RT Transferrin
NT Ferritin
  Iron—Metabolism
Iron industry and trade *(May Subd Geog)*
  ⌜HD9510-9529⌝
UF Ferrous metal industries
BT Metal trade
RT Steel industry and trade

NT Cast-iron
  Enameled ware
  Forging industry
  Hardware
  Iron and steel workers
  Iron-founding
  Ironwork
  Rolling-mills
  Strikes and lockouts—Iron industry
  Wrought-iron
— Collective bargaining
  USE Collective bargaining—Iron
    industry
— Collective labor agreements
  USE Collective labor agreements—Iron
    industry
— **Health aspects** *(May Subd Geog)*
  UF Iron industry and trade—Hygienic
    aspects
— Hygienic aspects
  USE Iron industry and trade—Health
    aspects
— **Prices**
Iron ions
UF Ferric ions
  Ferrous ions
BT Ions
Iron isotopes
  USE Iron—Isotopes
Iron lung
UF Drinker respirator
BT Artificial respiration
  Poliomyelitis
Iron-manganese alloys
UF Manganese-iron alloys
BT Manganese alloys
NT Ferromanganese
Iron metabolism
  USE Iron—Metabolism
Iron metabolism disorders
  USE Iron—Metabolism—Disorders
Iron meteorites
  USE Meteorites, Iron
Iron miners *(May Subd Geog)*
BT Iron mines and mining
  Miners
Iron mines and mining *(May Subd Geog)*
  ⌜TN400-TN409 (Mining)⌝
NT Iron miners
  Strikes and lockouts—Iron mining
  Trade-unions—Iron miners
— **Law and legislation** *(May Subd Geog)*
  BT Mining law
— **Taxation** *(May Subd Geog)*
— — **Law and legislation**
  (May Subd Geog)
— **Michigan**
  NT Mather Mine (Mich.)
— **Minnesota**
  NT Cuyuna Range (Minn.)
Iron molders *(May Subd Geog)*
  ⌜HD4966.F8 (Founders' wages)⌝
  ⌜HD6350.I7 (Trade-union periodicals)⌝
BT Foundries
RT Coremakers
NT Trade-unions—Iron molders
Iron-molybdenum alloys
UF Molybdenum-iron alloys
  Molybdenum-steel alloys
BT Molybdenum alloys
Iron-molybdenum-aluminum alloys
UF Iron-aluminum-molybdenum alloys
BT Aluminum alloys
  Iron alloys
  Molybdenum alloys
Iron-nickel alloys
  ⌜TA479.N (Testing)⌝
  ⌜TN757.N (Metallurgy)⌝
BT Nickel alloys
NT Iron-nickel-phosphorus alloys

Iron-nickel-cobalt alloys
UF Fernico
  Kovar
BT Cobalt alloys
  Nickel alloys
Iron-nickel-copper alloys
Iron-nickel-phosphorus alloys
BT Iron-nickel alloys
  Nickel alloys
  Phosphorus compounds
Iron-nickel-silicon alloys
Iron-on bonding materials
  USE Fusible materials in sewing
Iron-on decals
  USE Iron-on transfers
Iron-on transfers
  ⌜TT852.7⌝
UF Decals, Iron-on
  Iron-on decals
  Transfers, Iron-on
BT Decalcomania
  Textile printing
  Transfer-printing
Iron ore geology
  USE Iron ores—Geology
Iron ores *(May Subd Geog)*
  ⌜TN400-409⌝
BT Iron
NT Hematite
  Ilmenite
  Maghemite
  Magnetite
  Pyrites
  Pyrrhotite
  Sand, Iron
  Taconite
— **Analysis**
  ⌜TN580.I8⌝
  BT Iron—Analysis
— **Geology** *(May Subd Geog)*
  ⌜QE390.2.I76⌝
  UF Iron geology
    Iron ore geology
  BT Geology
Iron organic compounds
  USE Organoiron compounds
Iron oxides
  ⌜QD181.F4⌝
NT Goethite
— **Magnetic properties**
— **Metabolism**
Iron-palladium alloys
UF Palladium-iron alloys
BT Palladium alloys
— **Magnetic properties**
Iron perchloride
  USE Ferric chloride
Iron pipe
  USE Pipe, Iron
Iron plating
UF Iron electroplating
BT Electroplating
Iron porcelain
  USE Böttger ware
Iron powder
  ⌜TN697.I7⌝
BT Metal powders
Iron proteins
  ⌜QP552.I67⌝
UF Ferroproteins
BT Metalloproteins
  Organoiron compounds
NT Ferritin
  Hemosiderin
  Iron sulphur proteins
  Lactoferrins
  Transferrin
Iron quartermaster
  USE Automatic pilot (Ships)
Iron removal (Water purification)
  USE Water—Purification—Iron removal

1905

Iron-rhodium alloys
    UF Rhodium-iron alloys
    BT Iron alloys
        Rhodium alloys
Iron roofing
    USE Roofing, Iron and steel
Iron salts
    ⌈QD181.F4⌉
    NT Ferrinatrite
        Sideronatrite
Iron sand
    USE Sand, Iron
Iron sculpture *(May Subd Geog)*
    ⌈NB1240.I75⌉
    BT Ironwork
        Metal sculpture
        Sculpture
Iron sculpture, Buddhist *(May Subd Geog)*
    ⌈NB1240.I75⌉
    UF Buddhist iron sculpture
    BT Sculpture, Buddhist
Iron sculpture, Japanese *(May Subd Geog)*
    ⌈NB1240.I75⌉
    UF Japanese iron sculpture
Iron-silicon alloys
    ⌈TA479.S5⌉
    UF Silicon-iron alloys
    BT Silicon alloys
    NT Ferrosilicon
        Silicon steel
    — **Magnetic properties**
Iron storage disease
    USE Hemochromatosis
Iron sulphate
    USE Ferrous sulphate
Iron sulphur proteins
    ⌈QP552.I7⌉
    UF Sulphur iron proteins
    BT Iron proteins
        Organosulphur compounds
Iron Theatre (New Orleans, La.)
    USE Faranta's Iron Theatre (New Orleans, La.)
Iron-tin alloys
    UF Tin-iron alloys
    BT Tin alloys
Iron-titanium alloys
    USE Titanium-iron alloys
Iron trees
    USE Metrosideros
Iron trichloride
    USE Ferric chloride
Iron-tungsten alloys
    UF Tungsten-iron alloys
    BT Tungsten alloys
    NT Ferrotungsten
Iron workers
    USE Iron and steel workers
Iron-works *(May Subd Geog)*
    ⌈TS330-360⌉
    NT Iron foundries
    — **Pilot plants**
    — **Japan**
Ironbark eucalyptus, Narrowleaf
    USE Eucalyptus creba
Ironbark trees
    USE Eucalyptus
Ironclads
    USE Armored vessels
Ironic chloride
    USE Ferric chloride
Ironing
    USE Laundry
Ironmaster's House (Pa.)
    BT Dwellings—Pennsylvania
        Hopewell Village National Historic Site (Pa.)
Ironmongers Piece Site (Marshfield, Avon)
    BT England—Antiquities
Irons, Angle
    USE Angles (Structural members)

Irons, Electric
    USE Electric irons
Irons, Waffle
    USE Waffle irons
Irons (Meteorites)
    USE Meteorites, Iron
Irons (Pressing)
    UF Box irons
        Flatirons
        Hand irons
        Pressing irons
        Sadirons
    BT Household appliances
        Pressing of garments
    NT Electric irons
Irons family *(Not Subd Geog)*
Ironstone
    USE Tiger's eye
Ironstone china
    ⌈NK4367.I7 (Decorative arts)⌉
    UF Flint china
        Opaque porcelain
        White granite
    BT Stoneware—England
        Stoneware—United States
Ironwood, Borneo
    USE Borneo ironwood
Ironwork *(May Subd Geog)*
    ⌈NK8200-NK8299 (Ornamental ironwork)⌉
    ⌈TA890-TA891 (Engineering construction)⌉
    ⌈TT215-TT240 (Mechanic trades)⌉
    BT Art metal-work
        Arts and crafts movement
        Decoration and ornament
        Iron
        Iron industry and trade
        Metal-work
        Wrought-iron
    RT Blacksmithing
        Forging
    NT Architectural ironwork
        Decorative cast-ironwork
        Firebacks
        Grilles
        Iron sculpture
        Welding
    — **Private collections**
    — **Russian S.F.S.R.**
        NT Kaslinskiĭ chugunnyĭ pavil'on (Ironwork)
Ironwork, Baroque *(May Subd Geog)*
    UF Baroque ironwork
Ironwork, Colonial *(May Subd Geog)*
    UF Colonial ironwork
Ironwork, Medieval *(May Subd Geog)*
    UF Medieval ironwork
Ironwork, Renaissance *(May Subd Geog)*
    UF Renaissance ironwork
Ironwork, Rococo *(May Subd Geog)*
    UF Rococo ironwork
Ironworkers (Construction)
    USE Structural steel workers
Irony
    ⌈BH301.I7 (Aesthetics)⌉
    ⌈PN1680 (Drama)⌉
    UF Sarcasm
    BT Cynicism
        Rhetoric
        Satire
        Tragic, The
    RT Understatement
Irony in art
Irony in literature
Irony in the Bible
    UF Bible—Irony
Iroquoian Indians
    ⌈E99.I69⌉
    BT Indians of North America
    NT Caughnawaga Indians

        Cayuga Indians
        Cherokee Indians
        Conestoga Indians
        Huron Indians
        Iroquois Indians
        Mohawk Indians
        Neutral Nation Indians
        Oka Indians
        Oneida Indians
        Onondaga Indians
        Seneca Indians
        St. Regis Indians
        Tuscarora Indians
Iroquoian languages
    ⌈PM1381-4⌉
    RT Cherokee language
        Huron language
        Iroquois language
        Mohawk language
        Oneida language
        Onondaga language
        Seneca language
    NT Tuscarora language
Iroquois Indians
    ⌈E99.I7⌉
    UF Agoneaseah Indians
        Five Nations
        Massawomeke Indians
        Mengwe Indians
        Six Nations
    BT Indians of North America
        Iroquoian Indians
        Mingo Indians
    NT Caughnawaga Indians
        Cayuga Indians
        Mohawk Indians
        Oka Indians
        Oneida Indians
        Onondaga Indians
        Seneca Indians
        Tuscarora Indians
    — **Antiquities**
    — **Fiction**
    — **Government relations**
    — **Land transfers**
    — **Law and legislation**
    — **Legends**
    — **Missions**
    — **Religion and mythology**
    — **Social life and customs**
    — **Treaties**
    — **Tribal government**
    — **Wars**
        NT Champlain-Iroquois Battle, 1615
            Sullivan's Indian Campaign, 1779
Iroquois language
    ⌈PM1381-4⌉
    RT Iroquoian languages
Iroquois law
    USE Law, Iroquois
Iroquois poetry
Iroquois River (Ind. and Ill.)
    BT Rivers—Illinois
        Rivers—Indiana
Irōsaki (Japan)
    USE Irō Cape (Japan)
Irōzaki (Japan)
    USE Irō Cape (Japan)
Irpini (Italic people)
    USE Hirpini (Italic people)
Irpinia (Italy)
Irradiated blood
    USE Blood irradiation
Irradiated ergosterol
    USE Ergocalciferol
Irradiated fish
    USE Fish, Irradiated
Irradiated foods
    USE Food, Irradiated
Irradiated seafood
    USE Seafood, Irradiated

Irradiated shrimps
  USE Shrimps, Irradiated
Irradiation
  BT Radiation
  NT Neutron irradiation
      Sewage—Purification—Irradiation
Irradiation of sewage sludge
  USE Sewage sludge—Irradiation
Irrational numbers
  USE Numbers, Irrational
Irrationalism (Philosophy)
  ₍B824.2₎
  BT Belief and doubt
      Philosophy
      Rationalism
  RT Absurd (Philosophy)
Irrawaddy River (Burma) (Not Subd Geog)
  UF Erāvatī Mrac' (Burma)
      Irawadi River (Burma)
      Iyawadi River (Burma)
  BT Rivers—Burma
Irregular heart beats
  USE Arrhythmia
Irregularities (Canon law)
  UF Impediments (Canon law)
  BT Clergy (Canon law)
      Ordination (Canon law)
Irreligion (May Subd Geog)
      Here are entered works dealing with a condition
  of complete absence of religion.
  UF Non-belief
      Unbelief
  BT Religion
  RT Atheism
  NT Non church-affiliated people
      Secularism
Irreligion and society
  USE Irreligion and sociology
Irreligion and sociology
  UF Irreligion and society
      Society and irreligion
      Sociology and irreligion
  BT Religion and sociology
Irreversible coma
  USE Brain death
Irreversible processes
  UF Processes, Irreversible
  BT Dynamics
      Equilibrium
      Molecular dynamics
      Statistical mechanics
      Thermodynamics
  RT Nonequilibrium thermodynamics
  NT Open systems (Physics)
Irreversible thermodynamics
  USE Nonequilibrium thermodynamics
Irrigated agriculture
  USE Irrigation farming
Irrigated farming
  USE Irrigation farming
Irrigated forestry
  USE Forests and forestry—Irrigation
Irrigated soils
  USE Soils, Irrigated
Irrigated tree farms
  USE Tree farms—Irrigation
Irrigation (May Subd Geog)
  ₍HD1711-HD1741 (Economic history)₎
  ₍S613-S615 (Agriculture)₎
  ₍TC801-TC937 (Irrigation engineering)₎
  BT Agriculture
      Engineering
      Reclamation of land
      Soils
      Waste lands
      Water in agriculture
      Water resources development
      Water-supply
  RT Reservoirs
      Water-storage

  SA subdivision Irrigation under names of
      crops, e.g. Cotton—Irrigation
  NT Alkali lands
      Corn—Irrigation
      Forests and forestry—Irrigation
      Indians of North America—Irrigation
      Irrigation farming
      Irrigation water
      Lift irrigation
      Plants—Water requirements
      Radioisotopes in irrigation
      Rain and rainfall—Effect of irrigation
      on
      Saline irrigation
      Sewage irrigation
      Soils, Irrigated
      Sprinkler irrigation
      Tree farms—Irrigation
      Trickle irrigation
  — **Equipment and supplies**
      NT Irrigation equipment industry
  — **Management**
      ₍TC812₎
      NT Irrigation scheduling
  — **Research** (May Subd Geog)
      ₍S612.5-S612.55 (Agriculture)₎
      UF Irrigation research
  — **Social aspects** (May Subd Geog)
      UF Society and irrigation
  — **Tailwater recovery systems**
      UF Flow, Irrigation return
          Irrigation return flow
          Irrigation runoff recovery systems
          Return flow, Irrigation
          Runoff recovery systems, Irrigation
          Tailwater recovery systems,
          Irrigation
      BT Irrigation water
          Water reuse
  — **India**
      NT Cauvery-Mettur Project
          Malampuzha Project
Irrigation, Forest
  USE Forests and forestry—Irrigation
Irrigation, Furrow (May Subd Geog)
  ₍S619.F87₎
  UF Furrow irrigation
Irrigation, Overhead
  USE Sprinkler irrigation
Irrigation, Sewage
  USE Sewage irrigation
Irrigation, Tree farm
  USE Tree farms—Irrigation
Irrigation (Medicine)
  UF Lavage
  BT Asepsis and antisepsis
      Therapeutics
  NT Enema
      Gastric lavage
Irrigation agriculture
  USE Irrigation farming
Irrigation canals and flumes
  (May Subd Geog)
  ₍TC930-TC933₎
  BT Canals
      Diversion structures (Hydraulic
      engineering)
      Flumes
  NT Desilting basins
  — **Linings**
      UF Linings of irrigation canals
  — — **Frost damage**
      BT Frost
Irrigation districts (May Subd Geog)
  BT Special districts
Irrigation efficiency (May Subd Geog)
  ₍S619.E34₎
  UF Efficiency, Irrigation
  BT Irrigation farming
      Irrigation scheduling
      Irrigation water

Irrigation engineering (May Subd Geog)
  ₍TC801-937₎
  UF Engineering, Irrigation
  BT Agricultural engineering
      Hydraulic engineering
  NT Plastics in irrigation
      Qanat
Irrigation equipment industry
  (May Subd Geog)
  ₍HD9486₎
  BT Irrigation—Equipment and supplies
Irrigation farming (May Subd Geog)
  ₍S612-S619 (General)₎
  ₍SB112 (Manuals)₎
  UF Irrigated agriculture
      Irrigated farming
      Irrigation agriculture
      Paddy field culture
  BT Agriculture
      Arid regions agriculture
      Field crops
      Irrigation
  RT Crops and water
  SA subdivision Irrigation under crops, e.g.
      Corn—Irrigation; Cotton—Irrigation
  NT Irrigation efficiency
      Irrigation scheduling
      Soils, Irrigated
  — **Climatic factors**
      ₍S619.C55₎
      BT Crops and climate
          Meteorology, Agricultural
  — **Economic aspects** (May Subd Geog)
Irrigation laws (May Subd Geog)
  ₍HD1727-HD1729 (United States)₎
  ₍HD1741 (Other countries)₎
  UF Law, Irrigation
  BT Reclamation of land—Law and
      legislation
      Water—Law and legislation
      Water-rights
  NT Arid regions—Law and legislation
  — Colonies
      USE Irrigation laws, Colonial
Irrigation laws, Colonial
      Here are entered general and comparative works
  only. Works on irrigation laws of the colonies of an
  individual country are entered under the heading Irri-
  gation laws with subdivision ₍country₎—Colonies.
  Works dealing with a specific colony are entered
  under the same heading, subdivided by the name of
  the colony.
  UF Colonial irrigation laws
      Colonies—Irrigation laws
      Irrigation laws—Colonies
Irrigation pumps (May Subd Geog)
  UF Pumps, Irrigation
  BT Pumping machinery
Irrigation research
  USE Irrigation—Research
Irrigation return flow
  USE Irrigation—Tailwater recovery systems
      Irrigation water—Return flow
Irrigation runoff recovery systems
  USE Irrigation—Tailwater recovery systems
Irrigation scheduling (May Subd Geog)
  ₍S619.S33₎
  UF Scheduling, Irrigation
  BT Irrigation—Management
      Irrigation farming
  NT Irrigation efficiency
Irrigation water (May Subd Geog)
  BT Irrigation
      Water
      Water-supply
  NT Irrigation—Tailwater recovery systems
      Irrigation efficiency
      San Joaquin Valley Drainage
      Monitoring Program
  — **Boron content**
      ₍S618.6.B₎
      UF Boron in irrigation water

Irrigation water
  — **Boron content** *(Continued)*
    BT Boron
  — **Carbonate content**
    UF Carbonates in irrigation water
    BT Carbonates
  — **Pollution**
    [S618.47]
    BT Pollution
  — **Quality**
    [S618.45]
    BT Water quality
  — **Return flow**
    UF Irrigation return flow
        Return flow of irrigation water
        Surface return flows of irrigation
          water
  — **Pakistan**
    NT Bela Plain Groundwater
        Development Project
Irrigators, Oral
  USE Oral irrigators
Irritability
  [QH647 (Cells)]
  UF Animals, Irritability of
      Animals, Movements of
      Compensatory motion
      Motion, Compensatory
      Movements of animals
  BT Biology
      Cells
  NT Excitation (Physiology)
      Geotropism
      Phototropism
      Plants—Irritability and movements
      Taxes (Biology)
Irritable bowel syndrome
  USE Irritable colon
Irritable colon *(May Subd Geog)*
  [RC862.I77]
  UF Adaptive colitis
      Colic myxoneurosis
      Colon, Irritable
      Colonic diseases, Functional
      Functional bowel disease
      Intestinal neurosis
      Irritable bowel syndrome
      Irritable colon syndrome
      Mucous colitis
      Myxomembranous colitis
      Spastic colon
      Unstable colon
  BT Colon (Anatomy)—Diseases
Irritable colon syndrome
  USE Irritable colon
Irritation
  NT Counter-irritants
      Injections, Sclerosing
IRS Taxpayer Service
  USE Taxpayer Assistance Program
Irtish River (Kazakh S.S.R. and R.S.F.S.R.)
  USE Irtysh River (Kazakh S.S.R. and
      R.S.F.S.R.)
Irtysh River (Kazakh S.S.R. and R.S.F.S.R.)
  UF Irtish River (Kazakh S.S.R. and
      R.S.F.S.R.)
  BT Rivers—Kazakh S.S.R.
      Rivers—Russian S.F.S.R.
Irula language
  [PL4636]
  BT Dravidian languages
Irulas (Indic people)
  [DS432.I78]
  BT Ethnology—India
Irvin family
  USE Irwin family
Irvine family
  USE Irwin family
IRVING (Library information network)
  BT Library information networks—
      Colorado

Irving (Night fighter plane)
  [UG1242.F5]
  UF Gekkō (Night fighter plane)
      J1N1-S (Night fighter plane)
      Nakajima J1N1-S (Night fighter plane)
  BT Night fighter planes
Irving family
  USE Irwin family
Irwin family *(Not Subd Geog)*
  UF Ervin family
      Ervine family
      Erving family
      Erwin family
      Irvin family
      Irvine family
      Irving family
  RT Arvin family
Irwin Maurice Fletcher (Fictitious character)
  USE Fletch (Fictitious character)
IS (Electrochemical analysis)
  USE Impedance spectroscopy
IS-LM model (Macroeconomics)
  BT Macroeconomics
'Īsā (Koranic character)
  USE Jesus Christ in the Koran
Isaac (Biblical patriarch)
  — **Sacrifice**
    UF Akedah
        'Aḳedat Yitsḥaḳ
        'Aqedah
        Binding of Isaac
        Sacrifice of Isaac
Isaac (Biblical patriarch) in rabbinical literature
  UF Isaac (Biblical patriarch) in the
      Midrash
  BT Rabbinical literature
Isaac (Biblical patriarch) in the Midrash
  USE Isaac (Biblical patriarch) in rabbinical
      literature
Isaac family
  USE Isaacson family
Isaacs family
  USE Isaacson family
Isaacson family *(Not Subd Geog)*
  UF Isaac family
      Isaacs family
      Isacson family
  RT Isacksson family
Isachsen Peninsula (Ellef Ringnes Island, N.W.T.)
  BT Peninsulas—Northwest Territories
Isackson family
  USE Isacksson family
Isacksson family *(Not Subd Geog)*
  UF Isackson family
      Isaksen family
      Isakson family
  RT Isaacson family
Isacson family
  USE Isaacson family
Isadora (Ballet)
  BT Ballets
Ísafjörður (Iceland)
  BT Fjords—Iceland
Isaksen family
  USE Isacksson family
Isakson family
  USE Isacksson family
Isala (African people)
  USE Sisala (African people)
Isamurang language
  USE Batan language
Isan (Thailand)
  USE Thailand, Northeastern
Isandlwana (South Africa), Battle of, 1879
  BT Zulu War, 1879—Campaigns
Isano oil
  UF Boleko oil
      Isano seed oil

Isano seed oil
  USE Isano oil
Isar automobile
  USE Glas automobile
Isar River (Germany)
  BT Rivers—Germany (West)
Isarco River (Italy)
  UF Eisack River (Italy)
      Fiume Isarco (Italy)
  BT Rivers—Italy
Isatan
  USE Woad (Plant)
Isatis
  [QK495.C9 (Botany)]
  BT Cruciferae
Isatis tinctoria
  USE Woad (Plant)
Isaurian dynasty, Byzantine Empire, 717-811
  USE Byzantine Empire—History—Isaurian
      dynasty, 717-811
Isazai
  BT Ethnology—India
ISBD(A)
  USE International Standard Bibliographic
      Description for Older Monographic
      Publications (Antiquarian)
Isbister Site (Scotland) *(Not Subd Geog)*
  BT Scotland—Antiquities
ISBN
  USE International Standard Book Numbers
Iscaycinca Indians
  [F3430.1.I]
  BT Indians of South America
Ischaemia
  USE Ischemia
Ischemia *(May Subd Geog)*
  [RB144]
  UF Ischaemia
  BT Blood—Circulation, Disorders of
  NT Compartment syndrome
      Intestinal ischemia
Ischemia, Cerebral
  USE Cerebral ischemia
Ischemic bowel disease
  USE Intestinal ischemia
Ischemic colitis *(May Subd Geog)*
  [RC862.I82]
  BT Colitis
      Intestinal ischemia
Ischemic femoral necrosis
  USE Idiopathic femoral necrosis
Ischemic heart disease
  USE Coronary heart disease
Ischia Island (Italy)
  UF Isola d'Ischia (Italy)
  BT Islands—Italy
Ischias
  USE Sciatica
Ischnochiton *(May Subd Geog)*
  [QL430.1]
  BT Ischnochitonidae
  NT Ischnochiton abyssicola
Ischnochiton abyssicola *(May Subd Geog)*
  [QL430.1]
  BT Ischnochiton
Ischnochitonidae *(May Subd Geog)*
  [QL430.1]
  BT Chitons
  NT Ischnochiton
Ischnodemus
  [QL523.L9]
  BT Lygaeidae
Ischnopsyllidae
  [QL599.7.I3]
  BT Fleas
  NT Ischnopsyllus
      Nycteridopsylla
Ischnopsyllus
  [QL599.7.I3]
  BT Ischnopsyllidae

Ischyromyidae
  NT Microparamys
Ischyrosmilus
  ⌈QE882.C15⌉
  BT Felidae, Fossil
Isdell family (Not Subd Geog)
  UF Esdall family
     Esdell family
ISDN (Digital networks)
  USE Integrated services digital networks
Ise Bay (Japan)
  UF Atsuta Bay (Japan)
     Ise-kai (Japan)
     Ise no Umi (Japan)
     Ise Wan (Japan)
     Isewan (Japan)
     Owari Bay (Japan)
  BT Bays—Japan
Ise Honkaidō (Japan)
  BT Roads—Japan
Ise-kai (Japan)
  USE Ise Bay (Japan)
Ise no Umi (Japan)
  USE Ise Bay (Japan)
Ise Shintō
  ⌈BL2221.9.I8⌉
  UF Gekū Shintō
     Outer Shrine Shinto
     Watarai Shintō
  BT Shinto
Ise Wan (Japan)
  USE Ise Bay (Japan)
Isectolophidae
  BT Perissodactyla, Fossil
  NT Isectolophus
Isectolophus
  BT Isectolophidae
  NT Isectolophus radinskyi
Isectolophus radinskyi
  BT Isectolophus
Isei family (Not Subd Geog)
  UF Iseo family
Iseksawan
  USE Seksawa (Berber tribe)
Isel Mountain, Battle of, 1809
  BT Tyrol (Austria)—History—Uprising of
     1809
Iseley family (Not Subd Geog)
  UF Isley family
  RT Easley family
Isen family
  USE Isom family
Isenberg family (Not Subd Geog)
  UF Isenberger family
     Isenburg family
     Isenburger family
     Ysenburg family
Isenberger family
  USE Isenberg family
Isenburg family
  USE Isenberg family
Isenburger family
  USE Isenberg family
Isenman family
  USE Isenmann family
Isenmann family (Not Subd Geog)
  UF Isenman family
Iseo, Lake (Italy)
  UF Lacus Sebinus (Italy)
     Lago di Sebino (Italy)
     Lago d'Iseo (Italy)
     Lake Iseo (Italy)
     Lake Sebino (Italy)
     Sebino, Lake (Italy)
     Sebinus, Lake (Italy)
  BT Lakes—Italy
Iseo family
  USE Isei family
Isergebirge (Poland and Czechoslovakia)
  USE Izerskie Mountains (Poland and
     Czechoslovakia)

Iseult (Legendary character)
  UF Essylt (Legendary character)
     Isolde (Legendary character)
     Isolt (Legendary character)
     Ysolt (Legendary character)
  BT Folklore—Europe
Isewan (Japan)
  USE Ise Bay (Japan)
Isezakijō (Ueda-shi, Japan)
  USE Uedajō (Ueda-shi, Japan)
Isfendiyar Mountains (Turkey)
  USE Kure Mountains (Turkey)
İshak Paşa family (Not Subd Geog)
İshak Paşa Sarayı (Doğubayazıt, Turkey)
  UF İshak Paşa's Palace (Doğubayazıt,
     Turkey)
  BT Palaces—Turkey
İshak Paşa's Palace (Doğubayazıt, Turkey)
  USE İshak Paşa Sarayı (Doğubayazıt,
     Turkey)
Isham family
  USE Isom family
Ishi-kawa (Osaka, Japan)
  USE Ishi River (Osaka, Japan)
Ishi River (Osaka, Japan) (Not Subd Geog)
  UF Ishi-kawa (Osaka, Japan)
  BT Rivers—Japan
Ishiba family (Not Subd Geog)
Ishiba-ke Jūtaku (Hirosaki-shi, Japan)
  BT Dwellings—Japan
Ishibashiyama, Battle of, 1180
  BT Japan—History—Heian period, 794-
     1185
     Japan—History—Gempei Wars, 1180-
     1185
Ishigakibaru, Battle of, 1600
  ⌈DS894.965⌉
  UF Bungo Ishigakibaru, Battle of, 1600
Ishii family (Not Subd Geog)
Ishikawa family (Not Subd Geog)
Ishimoda family (Not Subd Geog)
Ishinadate Iseki (Sennan-mura, Japan)
  USE Ishinadate Site (Sennan-mura, Japan)
Ishinadate Site (Sennan-mura, Japan)
  (Not Subd Geog)
  UF Ishinadate Iseki (Sennan-mura, Japan)
  BT Japan—Antiquities
Ishinomakijō (Ishinomaki-shi, Japan)
  UF Hiyoriyamajō (Ishinomaki-shi, Japan)
  BT Castles—Japan
     Fortification—Japan
Ishitani family (Not Subd Geog)
Ishiyama, Battle of, 1570-1580
  BT Japan—History—Azuchi-Momoyama
     period, 1568-1603
     Shin (Sect)—History
Ishiyamadera engi (Scrolls)
  ⌈ND1053.4⌉
  UF Ishiyamadera engi emaki (Scrolls)
  BT Ishiyamadera, Ōtsu, Japan, in art
     Painting, Japanese—Kamakura-
     Momoyama periods, 1185-1600
     Painting, Japanese—Edo period, 1600-
     1868
     Scrolls, Japanese
Ishiyamadera engi emaki (Scrolls)
  USE Ishiyamadera engi (Scrolls)
Ishiyamadera, Ōtsu, Japan, in art
  NT Ishiyamadera engi (Scrolls)
Ishiyamajō (Okayama-shi, Japan)
  USE Okayamajō (Okayama-shi, Japan)
Ishizaki Magarida Iseki (Nijō-machi, Japan)
  USE Ishizaki Magarida Site (Nijō-machi,
     Japan)
Ishizaki Magarida Site (Nijō-machi, Japan)
  (Not Subd Geog)
  UF Ishizaki Magarida Iseki (Nijō-machi,
     Japan)
  BT Japan—Antiquities

Ishizuchi, Mount (Japan)
  UF Ishizuchi-san (Japan)
     Ishizuchi-yama (Japan)
     Ishizuchino (Japan)
     Mount Ishizuchi (Japan)
  BT Mountains—Japan
Ishizuchi Gongen Kofungun (Fukuyama-shi,
     Japan)
  USE Ishizuchi Gongen Site (Fukuyama-shi,
     Japan)
Ishizuchi Gongen Site (Fukuyama-shi, Japan)
  (Not Subd Geog)
  UF Ishizuchi Gongen Kofungun
     (Fukuyama-shi, Japan)
  BT Japan—Antiquities
Ishizuchi-san (Japan)
  USE Ishizuchi, Mount (Japan)
Ishizuchi-yama (Japan)
  USE Ishizuchi, Mount (Japan)
Ishizuchino (Japan)
  USE Ishizuchi, Mount (Japan)
Ishkashmi dialect
  ⌈PK6996.I7⌉
  BT Pamir languages
  RT Zebaki dialect
Ishmaelites
  Not to be confused with the Mohammedan sect,
  Ismailites.
Ishtar Gate (Babylon)
  BT Gates—Iraq
Isi-Lololo
  USE Fanakalo
Isi-Piki
  USE Fanakalo
Isiac tablet
  ⌈BL2450.I7⌉
  UF Bembine table of Isis
     Mensa Isiaca
     Table of Isis
     Tablet of Isis
  BT Isis
Isidae
  USE Isididae
Isididae
  ⌈QL377.C6⌉
  UF Isidae
  BT Gorgonacea
Isin (Ancient city) (Not Subd Geog)
  UF Issin (Ancient city)
  BT Cities and towns, Ruined, extinct, etc.
     —Iraq
     Iraq—Antiquities
Isinai dialect
  USE Isinay language
Isinay language
  ⌈PL5801⌉
  UF Inmeas language
     Isinai dialect
  BT Philippine languages
     Philippines—Languages
IsiNdebele language
  USE Ndebele language (Zimbabwe)
Ising model
  ⌈QC174.85.I8⌉
  UF Lenz-Ising model
  BT Ferromagnetism
     Phase transformations (Statistical
     physics)
Isinglass
  ⌈TS2301.I8⌉
Isirawa language
  USE Saberi language
Isis
  NT Isiac tablet
ISIS (Computer system)
  UF In Storage Information System
     (Computer system)
Isis (Egyptian deity)
  BT Gods, Egyptian
ISIS (Information retrieval system)
  ⌈Z699.5.E25⌉

ISIS (Information retrieval system)
    (Continued)
    UF Integrated Scientific Information
          System
Isis (Sculpture)
    USE Di Suvero, Mark, 1933-   Isis
ISIS-II (Artificial satellite)
    UF International Satellite for Ionospheric
          Studies
    BT Artificial satellites
          Astronautics—International
            cooperation
          Ionosphere—Research
          Meteorological satellites
Isiswazi (African people)
    USE Swazi (African people)
isiXhosa language
    USE Xhosa language
Iskanwaya Site (Bolivia)
    BT Bolivia—Antiquities
Iskar River (Bulgaria)
    USE Iskŭr River (Bulgaria)
Isker River (Bulgaria)
    USE Iskŭr River (Bulgaria)
Iskoot River (B.C.)
    USE Iskut River (B.C.)
Iskr River (Bulgaria)
    USE Iskŭr River (Bulgaria)
Iskra (Training planes)
    BT Training planes
Iskra-555 (Calculator)
    [HF5679]
    BT Programmable calculators
Iskra computer
    [QA76.8.I78]
  — Programming
      [QA76.8.I78]
Iskŭr River (Bulgaria)
    UF Golem Iskar River (Bulgaria)
          Golyem Iskŭr River (Bulgaria)
          Iskar River (Bulgaria)
          Isker River (Bulgaria)
          Iskr River (Bulgaria)
          Oescus River (Bulgaria)
    BT Rivers—Bulgaria
Iskut River (B.C.)
    UF Iskoot River (B.C.)
          Skoot River (B.C.)
    BT Rivers—British Columbia
Isla Barro Colorado (Panama)
    USE Barro Colorado Island (Panama)
Isla Cozumel (Mexico)
    USE Cozumel Island (Mexico)
Isla Cubagua (Venezuela)
    USE Cubagua Island (Venezuela)
Isla de Aves (Venezuela)
    USE Aves Island (Venezuela)
Isla de Bioco (Equatorial Guinea)
    USE Fernando Po (Equatorial Guinea)
Isla de Bioko (Equatorial Guinea)
    USE Fernando Po (Equatorial Guinea)
Isla de Chiloé (Chile)
    USE Chiloé Island (Chile)
Isla de Formentera (Spain)
    USE Formentera (Spain)
Isla de Guadalupe (Mexico)
    USE Guadalupe Island (Mexico)
Isla de Ibiza (Spain)
    USE Ibiza Island (Spain)
Isla de la Gomera (Canary Islands)
    USE Gomera (Canary Islands)
Isla de la Palma (Canary Islands)
    USE Palma (Canary Islands)
Isla de Lanzarote (Canary Islands)
    USE Lanzarote (Canary Islands)
Isla de Mallorca (Spain)
    USE Majorca (Spain)
Isla de Margarita (Venezuela)
    USE Margarita Island (Venezuela)
Isla de Menorca (Spain)
    USE Minorca (Spain)

Isla de Pascua
    USE Easter Island
Isla de Pinos, Battle of, 1596
    [F1799.I8]
    UF Pines, Isle of, Battle of, 1596
Isla de San Antonio (Spain)
    USE Peñón de Vélez de la Gomera (Spain)
Isla de San Miguel de la Palma (Canary
    Islands)
    USE Palma (Canary Islands)
Isla de Taquili (Peru)
    USE Taquili (Peru)
Isla del Coco (Costa Rica)
    USE Cocos Island (Costa Rica)
Isla Guadalupe (Mexico)
    USE Guadalupe Island (Mexico)
Isla Manzanillo (Panama)
    USE Manzanillo Island (Panama)
Isla Ons (Spain)
    USE Ons Island (Spain)
Isla Quinchao (Chile)
    USE Quinchao Island (Chile)
Isla Santa María (Galapagos Islands)
    USE Santa María Island (Galapagos Islands)
Isla Taboga (Panama)
    USE Taboga Island (Panama)
Isla Taquili (Peru)
    USE Taquili (Peru)
Isla Tiburon (Mexico)
    USE Tiburon Island (Mexico)
Islam *(May Subd Geog)*
    [BP1-223]
    Here are entered works on the religion of which
Muḥammad is the prophet. Works on the community
of believers in this religion are entered under Mus-
lims. Works on the cultural system or civilization
erected on the foundations of this religion are entered
under Civilization, Islamic. Works on the group of
countries in which the majority of the people are
Muslims or in which Islam is the established religion
are entered under Islamic countries.
    UF Islamism
          Mohammedanism
          Muhammadanism
          Muslimism
          Mussulmanism
    BT Religions
    SA *special headings with* Islam *added in
          parentheses, e.g.* Angels (Islam);
          and subdivision Islam *under special
          topics, e.g.* Mysticism—Islam; *also
          headings beginning with the words*
          Islamic *and* Muslim
    NT Arabs and Islam
          Caliphate
          Dervishes
          Imamate
          Jerusalem in Islam
          Koran
          Mahdism
          Miḥna
          Muslim saints
          Muslims
          Palestine in Islam
          Prophets, Pre-Islamic
          Slavery and Islam
          Temperance and Islam
  — 1800-
  — 20th century
      [BP163]
  — Apologetic works
      [BP170]
      UF Apologetics, Islamic
            Apologetics, Muslim
            Islamic apologetics
            Muslim apologetics
  — Appreciation
      [BP163]
  — Arab influences
      USE Arabs and Islam
  — Asceticism
      USE Asceticism—Islam

  — Charities
      UF Alms and almsgiving (Islam)
            Waqf
      NT Zakat
  — Clergy
      USE Islam—Functionaries
  — Doctrines
      [BP165.5-166.94]
      UF Islamic theology
            Kalam
            Muslim theology
            Theology, Islamic
            Theology, Muslim
      NT Authority (Islam)
            Bareilly School (Islam)
            Basmalah
            Deoband School (Islam)
            Eschatology, Islamic
            Faith (Islam)
            Faith and reason (Islam)
            Forgiveness of sin (Islam)
            Free will and determinism (Islam)
            God (Islam)
            Good and evil (Islam)
            Heresies, Islamic
            History (Islamic theology)
            Islam and reason
            Koran—Theology
            Kufr (Islam)
            Man (Islam)
            Merit (Islam)
            Miracles (Islam)
            Mysticism—Islam
            Predestination (Islam)
            Revelation (Islam)
            Salvation (Islam)
            Spirits (Islam)
            Taqlīd
  — — Early works to 1800
  — Education *(May Subd Geog)*
      [BP1-223]
      UF Education, Islamic
            Education, Muslim
            Islamic education
            Muslim education
            Muslims—Education
      RT Islamic religious education
      NT Islamic universities and colleges
            Muslim teachers
            Students, Muslim
            Women, Muslim—Education
  — Essence, genius, nature
  — Evangelistic work
      USE Da'wah (Islam)
  — Five pillars
      USE Pillars of Islam
  — Functionaries
      [BP185]
      UF Islam—Clergy
            Islamic religious functionaries
            Muslim religious functionaries
      BT Pastoral theology (Islam)
      NT Hafiz
            Shaykh al-Islām
            Ulama
  — Government
      [BP185]
      NT Mosques—Organization and
            administration
            Shaykh al-Islām
  — Historiography
      [BP49]
      BT Islamic research
  — History
      NT Badr, Battle of, 624
            Ditch, Battle of the, 627
            Uḥud, Battle of, 625
  — Hymns
      USE Islamic hymns
  — Liturgical objects
      NT Islamic rosary

— **Missions** (May Subd Geog)
  ₍BP170.3₎
    Here are entered works on Islamic missionary activity. Works on Christian missions among Muslims are entered under Missions to Muslims.
    UF Islamic missions
        Missions, Islamic
        Missions, Muslim
        Muslim missions
    NT Da'wah (Islam)
— Pillars
    USE Pillars of Islam
— Poetry
    USE Islamic poetry
— **Prayer-books and devotions**
  ₍BP183.3₎
    Subdivided by language.
— **Psychology**
    UF Islamic psychology
        Muslim psychology
        Psychology, Islamic
        Psychology, Muslim
    NT Faith (Islam)—Psychology
— **Relations**
  ₍BP171₎
— — **Christianity**
  ₍BP172₎
    NT Bible—Islamic interpretations
        Islam—Relations—Coptic
          Church
        Islamic literature—Christian
          interpretations
        Jesus Christ—Islamic
          interpretations
        Mary, Blessed Virgin, Saint—
          Islamic interpretations
        Missions to Muslims
— — **Coptic Church**
  ₍BP172.5.C6₎
    BT Islam—Relations—Christianity
— — **Judaism**
    Here are entered works on relations between the religions of Islam and Judaism. When this heading is assigned, duplicate entry is made under Judaism—Relations—Islam. Works on the conflicts between the Arab countries and Israel are entered under Israel-Arab conflicts. Works that discuss collectively the relations between Arabs and Jews, including religious, ethnic, and ideological relations, are entered under Jewish-Arab relations, subdivided further by dates, if appropriate.
— **Research** (May Subd Geog)
  ₍BP42-BP43 (Religion)₎
    UF Islamic research
        Muslim research
        Research, Islamic
        Research, Muslim
— Rites and ceremonies
    USE Islamic religious practice
— Sects
    USE Islamic sects
— **Study and teaching** (May Subd Geog)
    UF Islamic studies
— **Unity**
  ₍BP170.82₎
— **Universality**
  ₍BP170.8₎
— **India**
    NT Bareilly School (Islam)
        Deoband School (Islam)
Islam and Arabs
  USE Arabs and Islam
Islam and art
  ₍BP190.5.A7₎
  UF Art and Islam
  BT Art, Islamic
      Art and religion
  NT Islam and the performing arts
Islam and astronautics
  ₍BP190.5.A8₎
  UF Astronautics and Islam

  BT Cosmology, Islamic
      Islam and science
      Religion and astronautics
Islam and communism
  USE Communism and Islam
Islam and humanism
  ₍BP190.5.H78₎
  BT Humanism
Islam and humor
  USE Wit and humor—Religious aspects—
        Islam
Islam and justice
  ₍BP173.43₎
  BT Justice
      Religion and justice
      Religion and law
Islam and labor (May Subd Geog)
  ₍HD6338.4₎
  UF Labor and Islam
  BT Religion and labor
Islam and literature
  UF Literature and Islam
  BT Religion and literature
Islam and music
  USE Music—Religious aspects—Islam
Islam and philosophy
  UF Philosophy and Islam
  BT Philosophy, Islamic
      Philosophy and religion
  NT Koran and philosophy
Islam and poetry
  UF Poetry and Islam
  BT Religion and poetry
Islam and politics (May Subd Geog)
  ₍BP173.7₎
  UF Politics and Islam
  BT Islam and state
— **India**
    NT Razakars
— **Indonesia**
    NT Darul Islam Movement
Islam and reason
  ₍BP190.5.R4₎
  UF 'Aql (Islam)
      Reason (Islam)
  BT Islam—Doctrines
      Philosophy, Islamic
      Reason
Islam and science
  ₍BP190.5.S₎
  UF Science and Islam
  BT Religion and science
  NT Islam and astronautics
      Koran and science
Islam and slavery
  USE Slavery and Islam
Islam and social problems (May Subd Geog)
  ₍HN40.I₎
  UF Religion and social problems
      Social problems and Islam
  BT Sociology, Islamic
  NT Temperance and Islam
Islam and socialism
  USE Socialism and Islam
Islam and state (May Subd Geog)
  ₍BP173.6₎
  UF State and Islam
  BT Religion and state
  NT Islam and politics
      Jihad
— **Koranic teaching**
    BT Koran—Political science
— **Indonesia**
    NT Darul Islam Movement
Islam and the performing arts
  ₍BP190.5.P4₎
  UF Performing arts and Islam
  BT Islam and art
Islam and world politics
  ₍BP173.5₎
  UF World politics and Islam

Islam in literature
Islamic angelology
  USE Angels (Islam)
Islamic antiquities (May Subd Geog)
  UF Antiquities, Islamic
      Antiquities, Muslim
      Muslim antiquities
  BT Antiquities
  NT Inscriptions, Islamic
— **Spain**
Islamic apologetics
  USE Islam—Apologetic works
Islamic architects
  USE Architects, Muslim
Islamic architecture
  USE Architecture, Islamic
Islamic arms and armor
  USE Arms and armor, Islamic
Islamic art
  USE Art, Islamic
Islamic art and symbolism
  (May Subd Geog)
  ₍BP182.5-BP182.6 (Religion)₎
  ₍N6260-N6271 (Art, general works)₎
  ₍N6501-N7413 (Special countries)₎
  UF Islamic symbolism
      Symbolism, Islamic
  BT Art, Islamic
      Arts, Islamic
      Symbolism
      Symbolism in art
Islamic art metal-work
  USE Art metal-work, Islamic
Islamic art objects
  USE Art objects, Islamic
Islamic arts
  USE Arts, Islamic
Islamic asceticism
  USE Asceticism—Islam
Islamic authors
  USE Muslim authors
Islamic banks and banking
  USE Banks and banking—Islamic countries
Islamic Bareilly School
  USE Bareilly School (Islam)
Islamic beads
  USE Islamic rosary
Islamic bookbinding
  USE Bookbinding, Islamic
Islamic bronzes
  USE Bronzes, Islamic
Islamic calendar
  USE Calendar, Islamic
Islamic calligraphy
  USE Calligraphy, Islamic
Islamic children
  USE Muslim children
Islamic chronology
  USE Chronology, Islamic
Islamic cities and towns
  USE Cities and towns, Islamic
Islamic civilization
  USE Civilization, Islamic
Islamic coins
  USE Coins, Islamic
Islamic converts
  USE Muslim converts
Islamic converts to Christianity
  USE Converts from Islam
Islamic cosmology
  USE Cosmology, Islamic
Islamic costume
  USE Costume, Islamic
Islamic countries
  ₍DS36-DS40₎
  UF Muslim countries
  NT Arab countries
— **Civilization**

Islamic countries
— **Civilization** *(Continued)*
Here are entered works on the civilization of
the Islamic countries in general, or during the
pre-Islamic and modern periods only, as well as
non-Islamic culture during the medieval period.
Works on the Islamic civilization of the medieval
period in the Islamic countries, or the Near East,
North Africa and Arab Spain collectively are en-
tered under Civilization, Islamic.
— **History, Naval**
— **Study and teaching** *(May Subd Geog)*
[DS35.7]
UF Islamic studies
Islamic courts
USE Courts, Islamic
Islamic decoration and ornament
USE Decoration and ornament, Islamic
Islamic decorative arts
USE Decorative arts, Islamic
Islamic demonology
USE Demonology, Islamic
Islamic Deoband School
USE Deoband School (Islam)
Islamic devotional calendars
UF Devotional calendars—Islam
Devotional calendars, Islamic
Devotional calendars, Muslim
Muslim devotional calendars
NT Shiite devotional calendars
Islamic domes
USE Domes, Islamic
Islamic drama *(May Subd Geog)*
BT Drama
Islamic literature
Religious drama
NT Ta'ziyah
Islamic drama, Arabic, [etc.]
(May Subd Geog)
Islamic drama, Javanese *(May Subd Geog)*
UF Javanese Islamic drama
BT Javanese drama
Islamic education
USE Islam—Education
Islamic educators
USE Educators, Muslim
Islamic Empire
Here are entered works dealing with the Middle
East alone, or the Middle East, North Africa and
Islamic Spain as a whole, during the period 622-1517,
i.e., from the rise and expansion of Islam to the crea-
tion of the Ottoman Empire.
UF Arab countries—History—622-1516
Arab Empire
Arabs—History—622-1517
Empire, Islamic
Futuḥ
Middle East—History—622-1517
Muslim Empire
Saracens
NT Abbasids
Almohades
Mamelukes
Omayyads
Songhai Empire
— **Biography**
— **History**
— — **622-661**
[DS38.1]
NT Camel, Battle of the, 656
Dhāt al-Ṣawārī, Battle of, 655
Nahāvand, Iran, Battle of, 642
Qādisīyah, Battle of, 637
Yarmuk River, Battle of the,
636
— — **661-750**
[DS38.5]
— — **750-1258**
[DS38.6]
NT Crusades
Latin Orient
Shu'-ub-iyah

— — **1258-1517**
[DS38.7]
NT 'Ayn Jālūt, Battle of, 1260
Islamic enamel and enameling
USE Enamel and enameling, Islamic
Islamic enameled glass bottles
USE Enameled glass bottles, Islamic
Islamic enameled glass lamps
USE Enameled glass lamps, Islamic
Islamic epistemology
USE Knowledge, Theory of (Islam)
Islamic eschatology
USE Eschatology, Islamic
Islamic ethics
[BJ1291]
UF Ethics, Islamic
Ethics, Muslim
Muslim ethics
BT Philosophy, Islamic
Religion and ethics
SA *subdivision* Conduct of life *under*
special groups of Muslims, e.g.
Women, Muslim—Conduct of life
NT Blasphemy (Islam)
Free will and determinism (Islam)
Good and evil (Islam)
Islamic etiquette
Koran—Ethics
Pillars of Islam
Sin (Islam)
Truthfulness and falsehood (Islam)
Islamic etiquette
[BJ2020]
UF Etiquette, Islamic
Etiquette, Muslim
Muslim etiquette
BT Islamic ethics
NT Mosque etiquette
Islamic exempla
USE Exempla, Islamic
Islamic fasts and feasts
USE Fasts and feasts—Islam
Islamic funeral rites and ceremonies
USE Funeral rites and ceremonies, Islamic
Islamic gardens
USE Gardens, Islamic
Islamic glass painting and staining
USE Glass painting and staining, Islamic
Islamic glassware
USE Glassware, Islamic
Islamic heresies
USE Heresies, Islamic
Islamic heretics
USE Heretics, Muslim
Islamic holy war
USE Jihad
Islamic homiletical illustrations
USE Homiletical illustrations, Islamic
Islamic homiletics
USE Preaching, Islamic
Islamic hygiene
USE Hygiene, Islamic
Islamic hymns
[BP183.5]
UF Hymns, Islamic
Hymns, Muslim
Islam—Hymns
Muslim hymns
NT Ramadan hymns
Islamic illumination of books and manuscripts
USE Illumination of books and manuscripts,
Islamic
Islamic inscriptions
USE Inscriptions, Islamic
Islamic international law
USE International law (Islamic law)
Islamic ivories
USE Ivories, Islamic
Islamic jewelry
USE Jewelry, Islamic

Islamic law *(May Subd Geog)*
UF Civil law (Islamic law)
Koran—Law
Law, Arab
Law, Islamic
Law in the Koran
Sharia (Islamic law)
BT Law, Oriental
Law, Semitic
SA *special legal headings and subdivisions*
with Islamic law *added in*
parentheses, e.g. Aliens (Islamic
law); Guardian and ward (Islamic
law); Wills (Islamic law)
NT Absence and presumption of death
(Islamic law)
Acquisition of property (Islamic law)
Actions and defenses (Islamic law)
Adultery (Islamic law)
Advisory opinions (Islamic law)
Agricultural laws and legislation
(Islamic law)
Aliens (Islamic law)
Antenuptial contracts (Islamic law)
Apostasy (Islamic law)
Artificial insemination, Human
(Islamic law)
Bank deposits (Islamic law)
Birth control (Islamic law)
Breach of contract (Islamic law)
Civil service (Islamic law)
Conditions (Islamic law)
Consumer protection (Islamic law)
Criminal intent (Islamic law)
Dower (Islamic law)
Fertilization in vitro, Human (Islamic
law)
Finance, Public (Islamic law)
Gifts (Islamic law)
Hanafis
Hanbalites
Insurance policies (Islamic law)
Interest (Islamic law)
Interfaith marriage (Islamic law)
Justification (Islamic law)
Land trusts (Islamic law)
Legislation (Islamic law)
Liability for animals (Islamic law)
Limited partnership (Islamic law)
Loans (Islamic law)
Malikis
Narcotic laws (Islamic law)
Payment (Islamic law)
Product safety (Islamic law)
Products liability (Islamic law)
Professions (Islamic law)
Public interest (Islamic law)
Recidivists (Islamic law)
Referendum (Islamic law)
Retroactive laws (Islamic law)
Reward (Islamic law)
Rif law
Right of property (Islamic law)
Self-defense (Islamic law)
Sex crimes (Islamic law)
Shafiites
Smoking (Islamic law)
Stoning (Islamic law)
Sunnites
Taqlīd
Torts (Islamic law)
Transplantation of organs, tissues, etc.
(Islamic law)
Wages (Islamic law)
— **Interpretation and construction**

UF Analogy (Islamic law)
    Consensus (Islam)
    Ijmā' (Islam)
    Ijtihād (Islamic law)
    Islamic law—Uṣūl al-Fiqh
    Qiyās (Islamic law)
    Uṣūl al-fiqh (Islamic law)
 — **Roman influences**
  UF Roman law—Influence—Islamic
      law
  BT Rome—Civilization
 — **Sources**
  NT Fatwās
     Hadith
     Koran
 — **Uṣūl al-Fiqh**
  USE Islamic law—Interpretation and
      construction
Islamic learning and scholarship
  (May Subd Geog)
  UF Learning and scholarship—Muslims
     Muslim learning and scholarship
     Muslims—Learning and scholarship
  RT Muslims—Intellectual life
  NT Scholars, Muslim
 — **Philosophy**
Islamic legends
  USE Legends, Islamic
Islamic libraries
  UF Libraries, Islamic
     Libraries, Muslim
     Muslim libraries
  BT Religious libraries
  NT Mosque libraries
Islamic literature
  [BP87-89]
  UF Muslim literature
  BT Religious literature
  NT Hadith
     Islamic drama
     Ismaili literature
     Koran
     Muslim authors
     Shiite literature
     Sufi literature
     Sunna
 — **Christian interpretations**
   [BP172]
    Here are entered works about Christian inter-
    pretations of Islamic literature. Studies by Chris-
    tian authors on Islamic literature are entered
    under Islamic literature—History and criticism.
   BT Christianity and other religions—
      Islam
     Islam—Relations—Christianity
 — **History and criticism**
Islamic literature, Arabic (May Subd Geog)
  UF Arabic Islamic literature
  BT Arabic literature
Islamic literature, Arabic, [English, etc.]
  (May Subd Geog)
Islamic logicians
  USE Logicians, Muslim
Islamic luster-ware
  USE Luster-ware, Islamic
Islamic magic
  USE Magic, Islamic
Islamic majolica
  USE Majolica, Islamic
Islamic marriage customs and rites
  USE Marriage customs and rites, Islamic
Islamic martyrs
  USE Muslim martyrs
Islamic meditations
  UF Meditations, Islamic
     Meditations, Muslim
     Muslim meditations
Islamic metal-work
  USE Metal-work, Islamic
Islamic miniature painting
  USE Miniature painting, Islamic

Islamic missions
  USE Islam—Missions
Islamic monasticism and religious orders
  USE Monasticism and religious orders,
      Islamic
Islamic mosaics
  USE Mosaics, Islamic
Islamic mural painting and decoration
  USE Mural painting and decoration, Islamic
Islamic mysticism
  USE Mysticism—Islam
Islamic names
  USE Names, Personal—Islamic
Islamic New Year
  [BP186.2]
  UF Muslim New Year
     New Year, Islamic
     New Year, Muslim
Islamic numismatics
  USE Numismatics, Islamic
Islamic occultism
  USE Occultism, Islamic
Islamic orders of knighthood and chivalry
  USE Orders of knighthood and chivalry,
      Islamic
Islamic painting
  USE Painting, Islamic
Islamic pastoral theology
  USE Pastoral theology (Islam)
Islamic personal names
  USE Names, Personal—Islamic
Islamic philosophers
  USE Philosophers, Muslim
Islamic philosophy
  USE Philosophy, Islamic
Islamic physicians
  USE Physicians, Muslim
Islamic pilgrims and pilgrimages
  USE Muslim pilgrims and pilgrimages
Islamic poetry (May Subd Geog)
  UF Islam—Poetry
  BT Religious poetry
  NT Shiite poetry
     Sufi poetry
Islamic poetry, Arabic, [Urdu, etc.]
  (May Subd Geog)
Islamic poetry, Baluchi (May Subd Geog)
  UF Baluchi Islamic poetry
  BT Baluchi poetry
Islamic poetry, Gayo (May Subd Geog)
  UF Gayo Islamic poetry
  BT Gayo poetry
Islamic poetry, Javanese (May Subd Geog)
  UF Javanese Islamic poetry
  BT Javanese poetry
Islamic poetry, Panjabi (May Subd Geog)
  UF Panjabi Islamic poetry
  BT Panjabi poetry
Islamic poetry, Sindhi (May Subd Geog)
  UF Sindhi Islamic poetry
  BT Sindhi poetry
Islamic pottery
  USE Pottery, Islamic
Islamic preaching
  USE Preaching, Islamic
Islamic press
  USE Press, Islamic
Islamic psychology
  USE Islam—Psychology
Islamic public finance
  USE Finance, Public—Islamic countries
Islamic relics and reliquaries
  USE Relics and reliquaries, Islamic
Islamic religious education
  (May Subd Geog)
  [BP42-48]
  UF Education, Islamic
     Muslim religious education
     Religious education, Islamic

  BT Education
     Moral education
     Religious education
     Religious life (Islam)
  RT Islam—Education
  NT Koran—Study
 — **Text-books for children**
   [BP45]
   BT Islamic religious education of
      children
Islamic religious education of children
  [BP44-48]
  BT Children
  NT Islamic religious education—Text-
      books for children
Islamic religious functionaries
  USE Islam—Functionaries
Islamic religious practice
  [BP174]
  UF Islam—Rites and ceremonies
     Muslim religious practice
     Theology, Practical (Islam)
  BT Rites and ceremonies
  NT Fasts and feasts—Islam
     Funeral rites and ceremonies, Islamic
     Mysticism—Islam
     Pastoral theology (Islam)
     Pillars of Islam
     Purity, Ritual (Islam)
     Religious life (Islam)
     Sharia (Islamic religious practice)
     Worship (Islam)
 — **Shiites**
   USE Shiite religious practice
Islamic research
  USE Islam—Research
  NT Islam—Historiography
Islamic Revolution, Iran, 1979
  USE Iran—History—Revolution, 1979
Islamic rosary
  [BP184.96.R66]
  UF Beads, Islamic
     Islamic beads
     Rosary, Islamic
  BT Beads—Religious aspects—Islam
     Islam—Liturgical objects
Islamic rugs
  USE Rugs, Islamic
Islamic saints
  USE Muslim saints
Islamic scholars
  USE Scholars, Muslim
Islamic scientists
  USE Scientists, Muslim
Islamic sculpture
  USE Sculpture, Islamic
Islamic sects (May Subd Geog)
  [BP191-BP223]
  UF Islam—Sects
     Muslim sects
  BT Sects
  NT Ahl-i Hadīth
     Ahmadiyya
     al-Jahmīyah
     Assassins (Ismailites)
     Azraqites
     Badawiyah
     Batinites
     Bektashi
     Dīn-i Ilāhī
     Druzes
     Hanafis
     Hanbalites
     Ḥashwīya
     Heresies, Islamic
     Hurufis
     Ibadites
     Ismailites
     Karramites
     Kaysānıyah
     Kharijites

Islamic sects *(Continued)*
    Khojahs
    Malikis
    Motazilites
    Mu'aṭṭilah
    Murīdīyah
    Nosairians
    Sālimīyah
    Shabak
    Shafiites
    Shī'ah
    Sunnites
    Wahhābīyah
    Zaidites
Islamic sermons
    [BP183.6]
  UF Muslim sermons
    Sermons, Islamic
    Sermons, Muslim
  BT Jum'ah
    Preaching, Islamic
  NT 'Īd al-Aḍḥā sermons
    'Īd al-Fiṭr sermons
    Laylat al-Mi'rāj sermons
    Ramadan sermons
    Shiite sermons
    Wedding sermons, Islamic
Islamic sermons, Arabic, [**Indonesian, Turkish, etc.**]
    [BP183.6]
Islamic sermons, Indonesian
  UF Indonesian Islamic sermons
Islamic sermons, Javanese
  UF Javanese Islamic sermons
Islamic sermons, Sundanese
    (May Subd Geog)
    [BP183.6]
  UF Sundanese Islamic sermons
Islamic sermons, Turkish *(May Subd Geog)*
  UF Turkish Islamic sermons
Islamic sermons, Urdu *(May Subd Geog)*
  UF Urdu Islamic sermons
Islamic shrines *(May Subd Geog)*
    [BP187]
  UF Muslim shrines
    Shrines, Islamic
    Shrines, Muslim
  BT Muslim pilgrims and pilgrimages
  NT Shiite shrines
Islamic silver jewelry
  USE Silver jewelry, Islamic
Islamic silverwork
  USE Silverwork, Islamic
Islamic sociology
  USE Sociology, Islamic
Islamic stories *(May Subd Geog)*
    [BP87-89]
  UF Religious life (Islam)—Stories
    Stories, Islamic
  BT Fiction
    Homiletical illustrations, Islamic
Islamic stories, Arabic, [**etc.**]
    (May Subd Geog)
Islamic stories, Indonesian
  UF Indonesian Islamic stories
  BT Indonesian fiction
Islamic students
  USE Students, Muslim
Islamic studies
  USE Islam—Study and teaching
    Islamic countries—Study and teaching
Islamic swords
  USE Swords, Islamic
Islamic symbolism
  USE Islamic art and symbolism
Islamic taxation
  USE Taxation—Islamic countries
Islamic textile fabrics
  USE Textile fabrics, Islamic
Islamic theologians
  USE Theologians, Muslim

Islamic theological anthropology
  USE Man (Islam)
Islamic theology
  USE Islam—Doctrines
Islamic tiles
  USE Tiles, Islamic
Islamic universities and colleges
    (May Subd Geog)
  BT Islam—Education
    Universities and colleges
Islamic wedding sermons
  USE Wedding sermons, Islamic
Islamic women
  USE Women, Muslim
Islamic women saints
  USE Muslim saints, Women
Islamic wood-carving
  USE Wood-carving, Islamic
Islamic youth
  USE Youth, Muslim
Islamism
  USE Islam
Island arcs *(May Subd Geog)*
    [QE511.2]
  UF Volcanic arcs
  BT Geology, Structural
    Islands
    Plate tectonics
Island Beach (N.J. : Beach)
  BT Beaches—New Jersey
Island Carib language
    [PM6239]
  UF Carib language (Island)
    Igneri language
  BT Arawakan languages
    Indians of Central America—
      Languages
    Indians of the West Indies—Languages
  RT Black Carib language
Island chains
  USE Archipelagoes
Island ecology *(May Subd Geog)*
  BT Ecology
Island fauna *(May Subd Geog)*
  UF Insular fauna
  BT Islands
    Isolating mechanisms
    Zoogeography
    Zoology
Island flora *(May Subd Geog)*
  UF Insular flora
  BT Botany—Ecology
    Botany—Variation
    Islands
    Isolating mechanisms
Island groups
  USE Archipelagoes
Island of Arran (Scotland)
  USE Arran, Island of (Scotland)
Island of Galveston (Tex.)
  USE Galveston Island (Tex.)
Island of Iōannina (Greece)
  USE Iōannina Island (Greece)
Islands, Bay of (N.Z.) *(Not Subd Geog)*
  UF Bay of Islands (N.Z.)
  BT Bays—New Zealand
Islands *(May Subd Geog)*
    [G555 (Lost islands)]
    [GB471-GB478]
    [GR675 (Folk-lore)]
  UF Isles
  BT Landforms
  NT Archipelagoes
    Barrier islands
    Coral reefs and islands
    Island arcs
    Island fauna
    Island flora
  — **Law and legislation** *(May Subd Geog)*
    BT Jurisdiction, Territorial
      Maritime law

    NT Offshore structures (International
        law)
  — **Adriatic Sea**
    USE Islands of the Adriatic
  — **Aegean Sea**
    USE Aegean Islands (Greece and
        Turkey)
  — **Alaska**
    NT Admiralty Island (Alaska)
    Afognak Island (Alaska)
    Aleutian Islands (Alaska)
    Atka Island (Alaska)
    Attu Island (Alaska)
    Augustine Island (Alaska)
    Baranof Island (Alaska)
    Blashke Islands (Alaska)
    Buldir Island (Alaska)
    Fox Islands (Alaska)
    Kiska Island (Alaska)
    Kodiak Island (Alaska)
    Nelson Island (Alaska)
    Pribilof Islands (Alaska)
    Renard Island (Alaska)
    Saint Lawrence Island (Alaska)
    Sergief Island (Alaska)
    Sitkinak Island (Alaska)
    Spruce Island (Alaska)
    Summit Island (Alaska)
  — **Antarctic regions**
    UF Islands of the Antarctic
    NT Brabant Island (Antarctic regions)
    Flatvaer Islands (Antarctic regions)
    Seymour Island (Antarctic regions)
    South Shetland Islands
  — **Antigua and Barbuda**
    NT Redonda (Antigua and Barbuda)
  — **Arctic regions**
    USE Islands of the Arctic
  — **Atlantic Ocean**
    USE Islands of the Atlantic
  — **Australia**
    NT Bribie Island (Qld.)
    Bruny Island (Tas.)
    Cockatoo Island (N.S.W.)
    Dunk Island (Qld.)
    Flinders Island (Tas.)
    Fraser Island (Qld.)
    Furneaux Islands (Tas.)
    Gabo Island (Vic.)
    Garden Island (W.A.)
    Goat Island (N.S.W.)
    Groote Eylandt (N.T.)
    Kangaroo Island (S. Aust.)
    Lord Howe Island (N.S.W.)
    Macquarie Island (Tas.)
    Moreton Island (Qld.)
    One Tree Island (Qld.)
    Phillip Island (Vic.)
    Rottnest Island (W.A.)
    Torres Strait Islands (Qld.)
    Tuin (Qld.)
    Whitsunday Group (Qld.)
  — **Bahamas**
    NT Bimini Islands (Bahamas)
    Grand Bahama (Bahamas)
    Green Turtle Cay (Bahamas :
      Island)
    Mayaguana Island (Bahamas)
    New Providence Island (Bahamas)
    Ragged Island Range (Bahamas)
  — **Bahrain**
    NT Ḥawār (Bahrain)
  — **Belize**
    NT Albion Island (Belize)
    Ambergris Cay (Belize)
    Carry Bow Cay (Belize)
    Caulker Cay (Belize : Island)
  — **Bermuda Islands**
    NT Bermuda Island (Bermuda Islands)
    Nonsuch Island (Bermuda Islands)
  — **Brazil**

NT Bananal Island (Brazil)
   Marajó Island (Brazil)
   Paquetá Island (Brazil)
   Santa Catarina Island (Brazil)
   São Vicente Island (Brazil)
— **British Columbia**
NT Calvert Island (B.C.)
   Gabriola Island (B.C.)
   Galiano Island (B.C.)
   Hornby Island (B.C.)
   Mayne Island (B.C.)
   Moresby Island (B.C.)
   North Pender Island (B.C.)
   Prevost Island (B.C.)
   Queen Charlotte Islands (B.C.)
   Saturna Island (B.C.)
   South Pender Island (B.C.)
   Texada Island (B.C.)
   Vancouver Island (B.C.)
— **British Virgin Islands**
NT Virgin Gorda Island (V.I.)
— **California**
NT Alcatraz Island (Calif.)
   Anacapa Island (Calif.)
   Año Nuevo Island (Calif.)
   Balboa Island (Calif.)
   Channel Islands (Calif.)
   Channel Islands National Park
     (Calif.)
   Farallon Islands (Calif.)
   Santa Catalina Island (Calif.)
   Santa Cruz Island (Calif.)
— **Canary Islands**
NT Gomera (Canary Islands)
   Hierro (Canary Islands)
   Lanzarote (Canary Islands)
   Palma (Canary Islands)
— Caribbean Area
   USE West Indies
— **Chile**
NT Chiloé Island (Chile)
   Quinchao Island (Chile)
— **China**
NT Hainan Island (China)
   P'u-t'o Shan Island (China)
   Tung-yin Island (China)
— **Connecticut**
NT Leetes Island (Conn.)
— **Cook Islands**
NT Aitutaki Atoll (Cook Islands)
   Mangaia (Cook Islands)
   Manihiki Atoll (Cook Islands)
   Mitiaro (Cook Islands)
   Nassau Island (Cook Islands)
   Penrhyn Atoll (Cook Islands)
   Pukapuka Atoll (Cook Islands)
   Rakahanga Atoll (Cook Islands)
— **Costa Rica**
NT Cocos Island (Costa Rica)
— **Czechoslovakia**
NT Žitný Island (Czechoslovakia)
— **Denmark**
NT Als Island (Denmark)
   Amager (Denmark)
   Anholt (Denmark)
   Bornholm (Denmark)
   Christiansø (Denmark)
   Falster (Denmark)
   Farø (Denmark)
   Frisian Islands
   Fyn (Denmark)
   Hirsholmene (Denmark)
   Læsø (Denmark)
   Langeland (Denmark)
   Lolland (Denmark)
   Lyø (Denmark)
   Moen (Denmark)
   North Frisian Islands (Denmark
     and Germany)
   Rømø (Denmark)
   Samsø (Denmark)

Sprogø (Denmark)
   Vejrø (Denmark)
— **Ecuador**
NT Santa María Island (Galapagos
     Islands)
— **Egypt**
NT Elephantine (Egypt)
   Philae (Egypt)
— **England**
NT Lundy Island (England)
   Scilly, Isles of (England)
   Thorney Island (England)
   Tresco (England)
— **Equatorial Guinea**
NT Fernando Po (Equatorial Guinea)
— **Estonia**
NT Aegna Island (Estonia)
   Naissaar Island (Estonia)
— **Fiji**
NT Lakemba Island (Fiji)
   Mothe Island (Fiji)
   Taveuni (Fiji)
   Vanua Levu (Fiji)
   Viti Levu (Fiji)
— **Finland**
NT Åland Islands (Finland)
   Haapasaari (Finland : Island)
   Hailuoto Island (Finland)
— **Florida**
NT Amelia Island (Fla.)
   Anna Maria Island (Fla.)
   Captiva Island (Fla.)
   Dry Tortugas (Fla.)
   Florida Keys (Fla.)
   Gulf Islands National Seashore
     (Fla. and Miss.)
   Lido Key (Fla.)
   Marco Island (Fla. : Island)
   Pine Island (Fla.)
   Saint Armands Key (Fla.)
   Saint George Island (Fla.)
   Sanibel Island (Fla.)
   Sea Islands
— **France**
NT Belle-Ile-en-Mer (France)
   Bendor (France)
   Camargue (France)
   Glénan Islands (France)
   Groix Island (France)
   Hyères Islands (France)
   Ile de la Cité (Paris, France)
   Ile Saint-Louis (Paris, France)
   Lérins Islands (France)
   Noirmoutier Island (France)
   Oléron, Ile d' (France)
   Ouessant Island (France)
   Port-Cros Island (France)
   Yeu Island (France)
— **French Guiana**
NT Devil's Island (French Guiana)
   Safety Islands (French Guiana)
— **French Polynesia**
NT Marquesas Islands
— **Georgia**
NT Cumberland Island (Ga.)
   Golden Isles (Ga.)
   Saint Catherine Island (Ga.)
   Saint Simon's Island (Ga.)
   Sapelo Island (Ga.)
   Sea Island (Ga.)
   Sea Islands
   Tybee Island (Ga. : Island)
— **Germany (East)**
NT Hiddensee (Germany)
   Rügen Island (Germany)
   Usedom Island (Germany)
— **Germany (West)**
NT Amrum Island (Germany)
   East Frisian Islands (Germany)
   Fehmarn (Germany)
   Föhr (Germany)

Frisian Islands
   North Frisian Islands (Denmark
     and Germany)
   Spiekeroog Island (Germany)
   Sylt (Germany)
— **Greece**
NT Aegean Islands (Greece and
     Turkey)
   Aegina Island (Greece)
   Alónnisos Island (Greece)
   Amorgos Island (Greece)
   Andros Island (Greece)
   Antiparos Island (Greece)
   Cephalonia Island (Greece)
   Chios Island (Greece)
   Corfu Island (Greece)
   Cyclades (Greece)
   Delos Island (Greece)
   Dodecanese
   Euboea Island (Greece)
   Giali Island (Greece)
   Gyaros Island (Greece)
   Hydra Island (Greece)
   Ikaria Island (Greece)
   Iōannina Island (Greece)
   Ionian Islands (Greece)
   Ios Island (Greece)
   Ithaca Island (Greece)
   Karpathos Island (Greece)
   Kasos Island (Greece)
   Kastellorizo Island (Greece)
   Kea Island (Greece)
   Khalki Island (Greece)
   Kos Island (Greece)
   Kythēra Island (Greece)
   Lemnos Island (Greece)
   Lesbos Island (Greece)
   Levkás Island (Greece)
   Makronēsos (Greece)
   Melos Island (Greece)
   Mykonos Island (Greece)
   Naxos Island (Greece)
   Nisyros Island (Greece)
   Paros Island (Greece)
   Patmos Island (Greece)
   Paxos Island (Greece)
   Pelagonesi (Greece)
   Peristera Island (Greece)
   Psara (Greece)
   Rhodes (Greece : Island)
   Samos Island (Greece)
   Samothrace Island (Greece)
   Saria Island (Greece)
   Sím.i Island (Greece)
   Siphnos Island (Greece)
   Skiathos Island (Greece)
   Skopelos Island (Greece)
   Skyros Island (Greece)
   Syros Island (Greece)
   Telos Island (Greece)
   Thasos Island (Greece)
   Thera Island (Greece)
   Tinos Island (Greece)
   Zakynthos Island (Greece)
— **Greenland**
NT Disko Island (Greenland)
   Milne Land (Greenland)
   Ubekendt Island (Greenland)
— **Guadeloupe**
NT Basse-Terre Island (Guadeloupe)
   Désirade (Guadeloupe)
— **Hawaii**
NT Hawaii Island (Hawaii)
   Kauai (Hawaii)
   Lanai (Hawaii)
   Maui (Hawaii)
   Molokai (Hawaii)
   Niihau (Hawaii)
   Oahu (Hawaii)
— **Hong Kong**
NT Hong Kong Island (Hong Kong)

Islands
— **Hong Kong** *(Continued)*
    Lantau (Hong Kong)
    Po Toi Island (Hong Kong)
    Wang Lang Island (Hong Kong)
— **Hungary**
    NT Csepel Island (Hungary)
    Szigetköz (Hungary)
— **India**
    NT Elephanta Island (India)
— **Indian Ocean**
    USE Islands of the Indian Ocean
— **Indonesia**
    NT Ambon Island (Indonesia)
    Bali Island (Indonesia)
    Batam Island (Indonesia)
    Biak Island (Indonesia)
    Celebes (Indonesia)
    Ceram Island (Indonesia)
    Flores Island (Indonesia)
    Halmahera (Indonesia)
    Java (Indonesia)
    Komodo Island (Indonesia)
    Lombok (Indonesia)
    Madura Island (Indonesia)
    Mentawai Islands (Indonesia)
    Nias Island (Indonesia)
    Pabbiring Archipelago (Indonesia)
    Raja Ampat Islands (Indonesia)
    Roti Island (Indonesia)
    Samosir Island (Indonesia)
    Schouten Islands (Indonesia)
    Siberut (Indonesia)
    Sumatra (Indonesia)
    Sumba Island (Indonesia)
    Sumbawa (Indonesia)
    Sunda Islands, Lesser (Indonesia)
    Tarakan Island (Indonesia)
    Timor Island (Indonesia)
    Togian Islands (Indonesia)
— **Iran**
    NT Abu Musa
    Khark Island (Iran)
    Tunb Islands
— **Ireland**
    NT Achill Island (Ireland)
    Blasket Islands (Ireland)
    Inishbeg (Ireland)
    Inishmurray (Ireland)
    Tory Island (Ireland)
— **Italy**
    NT Capri Island (Italy)
    Elba (Italy)
    Giglio Island (Italy)
    Ischia Island (Italy)
    Lipari Island (Italy)
    Lipari Islands (Italy)
    Pantelleria Island (Italy)
    Pontine Islands (Italy)
    Procida Island (Italy)
    San Clemente Island (Italy)
    San Giorgio Maggiore Island
      (Italy)
    San Pietro Island (Italy)
    Sant'Antioco Island (Italy)
    Santo Stefano Island (Italy)
    Stromboli (Italy)
    Ventotene Island (Italy)
— **Japan**
    NT Amakusa-Shimo Island (Japan)
    Amami Islands (Japan)
    Amami Ōshima (Japan)
    Aoga Island (Japan)
    Awa Island (Japan)
    Awaji Island (Japan)
    Bonin Islands (Japan)
    Chichi Island (Japan)
    Eno Island (Kanagawa-ken, Japan)
    Geiyo Islands (Japan)
    Gotō Islands (Japan)
    Hachijō Island (Japan)

Honshū (Japan)
Iriomote Island (Japan)
Izena Island (Japan)
Izu Islands (Japan)
Jōga Island (Kanagawa-ken, Japan)
Kikai Island (Japan)
Kō Island (Miyazaki-ken, Japan)
Koshiki Islands (Japan)
Kōzu Island (Japan)
Kudaka Island (Japan)
Kume Island (Japan)
Miyake Island (Japan)
Miyako Island (Japan)
Nii Island (Japan)
Oki Islands (Japan)
Okinawa Island (Japan)
Okinoerabu Island (Japan)
Okushiri Island (Japan)
Ōsumi Islands (Japan)
Rebun Island (Japan)
Rishiri Island (Japan)
Sado Island (Japan)
Sakura Island (Japan)
Satsunan Islands (Japan)
Shishi Island (Takuma-chō, Japan)
Tanegashima (Japan)
Tokara Islands (Japan)
Tokuno Island (Japan)
Tsushima Island (Japan)
Volcano Islands (Japan)
Yaeyama Islands (Japan)
Yaku Island (Japan)
Yashiro Island (Japan)
Yonaguni Island (Japan)
Yoron Island (Japan)
— **Kenya**
    NT Manda Island (Kenya)
— **Kiribati**
    NT Kiritimati (Kiribati)
— **Korea (South)**
    NT Amt'ae Island (Korea)
    Tok Island (Korea)
— **Kuwait**
    NT Failaka Island (Kuwait)
— **Louisiana**
    NT Avery Island (La.)
    Belle Isle (Saint Mary Parish, La.)
    Five Islands (La.)
— **Lousiana**
    NT Grand Terre Island (La.)
— **Macao**
    NT Coloane Island (Macao)
    Taipa Island (Macao)
— **Madeira Islands**
    NT Madeira (Madeira Islands)
    Selvagens Islands (Madeira Islands)
— **Maine**
    NT Appledore Island (Me.)
    Arrowsic Island (Me.)
    Bartlett Island (Me.)
    Isles of Shoals (Me. and N.H.)
    Islesboro Island (Me.)
    Matinicus Rock (Me.)
    Mount Desert Island (Me.)
    Sears Island (Me.)
— **Malaysia**
    NT Pinang Island (Pinang)
    Si Amil Island (Sabah)
— **Malta**
    NT Gozo Island (Malta)
— **Marquesas Islands**
    NT Hiva Oa (Marquesas Islands)
    Nuka Hiva (Marquesas Islands)
— **Maryland**
    NT Assateague Island (Md. and Va.)
    Kent Island (Md.)
    Poplar Island (Talbot County, Md.)
    Smith Island (Md. and Va.)
— **Massachusetts**
    NT Boston Harbor Islands (Mass.)
    Chappaquiddick Island (Mass.)

Choate Island (Mass.)
Cuttyhunk Island (Mass.)
Elizabeth Islands (Mass.)
Martha's Vineyard (Mass.)
Nantucket Island (Mass.)
Naushon Island (Mass.)
Thacher Island (Mass.)
— **Mauritania**
    NT Arguin Island (Mauritania)
— **Mauritius**
    NT Rodrigues Island (Mauritius)
— **Mexico**
    NT Cedros Island (Mexico)
    Cozumel Island (Mexico)
    Guadalupe Island (Mexico)
    San Juan de Ulúa Island (Mexico)
    Tiburon Island (Mexico)
— **Michigan**
    NT Beaver Island (Mich.)
    Drummond Island (Mich.)
    Isle Royale (Mich.)
    Les Cheneaux Islands (Mich.)
    Mackinac Island (Mich. : Island)
— **Micronesia (Federated States)**
    NT Moen Island (Micronesia)
    Ponape Island (Micronesia)
— **Minnesota**
    NT Magnusons Island (Minn.)
— **Mississippi**
    NT Gulf Islands National Seashore
      (Fla. and Miss.)
    Horn Island (Miss.)
    Ship Island (Miss.)
— **Netherlands**
    NT Ameland Island (Netherlands)
    Frisian Islands
    Terschelling (Netherlands)
    Walcheren (Netherlands)
    West Frisian Islands (Netherlands)
— **Netherlands Antilles**
    NT Saba Bank (Netherlands Antilles)
— **New Caledonia**
    NT Maré Island (New Caledonia)
— **New Hampshire**
    NT Isles of Shoals (Me. and N.H.)
    Welch Island (N.H.)
— **New Jersey**
    NT Long Beach Island (N.J.)
— **New York (State)**
    NT Fire Island (N.Y.)
    Fishers Island (N.Y. : Island)
    Grand Island (N.Y. : Island)
    Long Island (N.Y.)
    Robins Island (N.Y.)
    Tea Island (N.Y.)
    Thousand Islands (N.Y. and Ont.)
— **New Zealand**
    NT Bounty Islands (N.Z.)
    Campbell Island (N.Z.)
    Chatham Islands (N.Z.)
    Kapiti Island (N.Z.)
    Kawau Island (N.Z. : Island)
    Mayor Island (N.Z.)
    North Island (N.Z.)
    Raoul Island (Kermadec Islands)
    Snares Islands (N.Z.)
    South Island (N.Z.)
    Stewart Island (N.Z.)
    Waiheke Island (N.Z.)
— **Newfoundland**
    NT Bonne Espérance (Nfld.)
    New World Island (Nfld.)
    Random Island (Nfld.)
— **Nicaragua**
    NT Ometepe Island (Nicaragua)
— **North Atlantic Ocean**
    USE Islands of the Atlantic
— **North Carolina**
    NT Bald Head Island (N.C.)
    Outer Banks (N.C.)
    Roanoke Island (N.C.)

Smith Island (N.C.)
— **Northern Mariana Islands**
   NT Agrihan Island (Northern Mariana
       Islands)
     Tinian (Northern Mariana Islands)
— **Northwest Territories**
   NT Amund Ringnes Island (N.W.T.)
     Arctic Archipelago (N.W.T.)
     Baffin Island (N.W.T.)
     Banks Island (N.W.T.)
     Bathurst Island (N.W.T.)
     Byam Martin Island (N.W.T.)
     Coburg Island (N.W.T.)
     Cornwall Island (N.W.T.)
     Devon Island (N.W.T.)
     Ellef Ringnes Island (N.W.T.)
     Ellesmere Island (N.W.T.)
     Haig-Thomas Island (N.W.T.)
     Lougheed Island (N.W.T.)
     Melville Island (N.W.T.)
     Parry Islands (N.W.T.)
     Prince Leopold Island (N.W.T.)
     Queen Elizabeth Islands (N.W.T.)
     Somerset Island (N.W.T.)
     Southampton Island (N.W.T.)
— **Norway**
   NT Andøya (Norway)
     Arnøya (Norway)
     Bear Island (Norway)
     Eigerøy (Norway)
     Hovedøya (Norway)
     Jeløya (Norway)
     Lofoten (Norway)
     Magerøy Island (Norway)
     Skogsøy (Vest-Agder fylke,
       Norway)
     Smøla (Norway)
     Spitsbergen Island (Norway)
     Tjøtta Island (Norway)
     Værlandet Island, Norway
     Vesterålen (Norway)
— **Nova Scotia**
   NT Cape Sable Island (N.S.)
     Sable Island (N.S.)
— **Ohio**
   NT Bass Islands (Ohio)
— **Oman**
   NT Masirah Island (Oman)
— **Ontario**
   NT Manitoulin Island (Ont.)
     Thousand Islands (N.Y. and Ont.)
     Toronto Islands (Ont.)
     Wolfe Island (Ont.)
— **Oregon**
   NT Sauvie Island (Or.)
— **Pacific Islands (Trust Territory)**
— Pacific Ocean
   USE Islands of the Pacific
— **Palau**
   NT Peleliu Island (Palau)
— **Panama**
   NT Barro Colorado Island (Panama)
     Caimito Island (Panama)
     Carti Keys (Panama)
     Mandinga Keys (Panama)
     Manzanillo Island (Panama)
     Robeson Islands (Panama)
     Taboga Island (Panama)
— **Papua New Guinea**
   NT Bismarck Archipelago (Papua New
      Guinea)
     Bougainville Island (Papua New
      Guinea)
     D'Entrecasteaux Islands (Papua
      New Guinea)
     Goodenough Island (Papua New
      Guinea)
     New Britain Island (Papua New
      Guinea)
     Siassi Islands (Papua New Guinea)

     Trobriand Islands (Papua New
      Guinea)
     Woodlark Island (Papua New
      Guinea)
     Woodlark Islands (Papua New
      Guinea)
— **Peru**
   NT Taquili (Peru)
— **Philippines**
   NT Cabra Island (Philippines)
     Cebu Island (Philippines)
     Corregidor Island (Philippines)
     Leyte Island (Philippines)
     Luzon (Philippines)
     Mindanao Island (Philippines)
     Mindoro (Philippines)
     Negros Island (Philippines)
     Panay Island (Philippines)
     Pata Island (Philippines)
     Samar (Philippines)
     Visayan Islands (Philippines)
     Volcano Island (Philippines)
— **Poland**
   NT Wolin Island (Poland)
— **Puerto Rico**
   NT Mona Island (P.R.)
     Santiago Cay (P.R.)
     Vieques Island (P.R.)
— **Québec (Province)**
   NT Anticosti Island (Québec)
     Coudres Island (Québec)
     Crane Island (Québec)
     Grosse Ile (Québec)
     Ile aux Noix (Québec)
     Jesus Island (Québec)
     Mingan Islands (Québec)
     Montréal Island (Québec)
     Orléans, Isle of (Québec)
— **Russian S.F.S.R.**
   NT Commander Islands (R.S.F.S.R.)
     Dolgiĭ Island (R.S.F.S.R.)
     Franz Josef Land (R.S.F.S.R.)
     Kizhi Island (R.S.F.S.R.)
     Kuril Islands (R.S.F.S.R.)
     Moneron Island (R.S.F.S.R.)
     Sakhalin (R.S.F.S.R.)
     Severnaĭa Zemlĭa (R.S.F.S.R.)
     Solovetski Islands (R.S.F.S.R.)
     Vaigach Island (R.S.F.S.R.)
     Valaam Island (R.S.F.S.R.)
     Wrangel Island (R.S.F.S.R.)
— **Scotland**
   NT Arran, Island of (Scotland)
     Barra Island (Scotland)
     Brough of Birsay (Scotland)
     Canna (Scotland)
     Egilsay (Scotland)
     Fair Isle (Scotland)
     Foula Island (Scotland)
     Hebrides (Scotland)
     Inner Hebrides (Scotland)
     Iona (Scotland)
     Lewis with Harris Island (Scotland)
     May, Isle of (Scotland)
     Mull, Island of (Scotland)
     North Ronaldsay (Scotland)
     Papa Stour (Scotland)
     Papa Westray (Scotland)
     Rum, Isle of (Scotland)
     Saint Kilda (Scotland)
     Saint Ninian's Island (Scotland)
     Sanday (Scotland)
     Shona Island (Scotland)
     South Uist (Scotland)
     Western Isles (Scotland)
     Westray (Scotland)
— **Seychelles**
   NT Aldabra Island (Seychelles)
     La Digue Island (Seychelles)
— **Solomon Islands**
   NT Anuta Island (Solomon Islands)

     Choiseul (Solomon Islands)
     Duff Islands (Solomon Islands)
     Florida Islands (Solomon Islands)
     Malaita (Solomon Islands)
     Nendö (Solomon Islands)
     Reef Islands (Solomon Islands)
     Rennell Island (Solomon Islands)
     San Cristobal (Solomon Islands)
     Santa Cruz Islands (Solomon
      Islands)
     Shortland Islands (Solomon
      Islands)
     Utupua (Solomon Islands)
     Vanikolo (Solomon Islands)
— **South Africa**
   NT Robben Island (South Africa)
— South Atlantic Ocean
   USE Islands of the Atlantic
— **South Carolina**
   NT Daufuskie Island (S.C.)
     Edisto Island (S.C.)
     Pinkney Island (S.C.)
     Saint Helena Island (S.C.)
     Sea Islands
     Sol Legare Island (S.C.)
— **South Orkney Islands**
   NT Signy Island (South Orkney
      Islands)
— **Spain**
   NT Formentera (Spain)
     Ibiza Island (Spain)
     Majorca (Spain)
     Medas Islands (Spain)
     Minorca (Spain)
     Ons Island (Spain)
     Peñón de Vélez de la Gomera
      (Spain)
     Pityusic Islands (Spain)
— **Sweden**
   NT Alnö (Sweden)
     Andersön (Sweden)
     Furusund (Sweden)
     Gotland (Sweden)
     Helgeandsholmen (Stockholm,
      Sweden)
     Karlsöarna (Sweden)
     Lillön (Sweden)
     Lovö (Sweden)
     Öland (Sweden)
     Reimersholme (Stockholm,
      Sweden)
— **Switzerland**
   NT Ufenau Island (Switzerland)
— **Taiwan**
   NT Lan Island (Taiwan)
— **Texas**
   NT Galveston Island (Tex.)
     Padre Island (Tex.)
     South Padre Island (Tex. : Island)
— **Thailand**
   NT Kradad Island (Thailand)
     Si Chang Island (Thailand)
— **Tokelau Islands**
   NT Fakaofo (Tokelau Islands)
— **Tonga**
   NT Eua Island (Tonga)
     Ha'apai Group (Tonga)
     Late Island (Tonga)
     Vava'u Island (Tonga)
— **Tunisia**
   NT Jarbah Island (Tunisia)
— **Turkey**
   NT Aegean Islands (Greece and
      Turkey)
     Yassi Island (Turkey)
— **United Arab Emirates**
   NT Abu Musa
     Das Island (United Arab Emirates)
     Tunb Islands
— **United States**
   NT United States—Insular possessions

Islands   (Continued)
  — Vanuatu
      NT Banks Islands (Vanuatu)
          Eromanga (Vanuatu)
          Espíritu Santo Island (Vanuatu)
          Malekula (Vanuatu)
          Méré Lava (Vanuatu)
          Pentecost Island (Vanuatu)
  — Venezuela
      NT Aves Island (Venezuela)
          Cubagua Island (Venezuela)
          Margarita Island (Venezuela)
          Monjes Islands (Venezuela)
  — Virgin Islands
      NT Tortola (V.I.)
  — Virgin Islands of the United States
      NT Saint John (V.I.)
  — Virginia
      NT Assateague Island (Md. and Va.)
          Chincoteague Island (Va.)
          Gwynn Island (Va.)
          Smith Island (Md. and Va.)
          Tangier Island (Va.)
  — Wales
      NT Caldey Island (Wales)
  — Washington (State)
      NT Protection Island (Wash.)
          San Juan Island (Wash.)
          San Juan Islands (Wash.)
          Waldron Island (Wash.)
          Whidbey Island (Wash.)
  — West Virginia
      NT Virginius Island (W. Va.)
  — Yemen (People's Democratic Republic)
      NT Socotra (Yemen)
  — Yugoslavia
      NT Cres Island (Croatia)
          Korčula Island (Croatia)
          Lošinj Island (Croatia)
          Zlarin Island (Croatia)
Islands, Ice
  USE Ice islands
Islands, Imaginary
  USE Geographical myths
Islands in literature
Islands of Langerhans
  UF Endocrine pancreas
      Islet cells
      Langerhans, Islands of
  BT Endocrine glands
      Pancreas
  NT Somatostatin
  — Tumors
      UF Insulinoma
          Insuloma
          Islet cell tumors
      BT Chromaffin cells—Tumors
      NT Glucagonoma
Islands of the Adriatic
      As a geographic subdivision, this heading is used
      directly.
  UF Adriatic Islands
      Islands—Adriatic Sea
Islands of the Aegean
  USE Aegean Islands (Greece and Turkey)
Islands of the Antarctic
  USE Islands—Antarctic regions
Islands of the Arctic
  UF Islands—Arctic regions
  BT Arctic regions
  NT Arctic Archipelago (N.W.T.)
      Franz Josef Land (R.S.F.S.R.)
      Jan Mayen Island
      Novaīa Zemlīa (R.S.F.S.R.)
      Severnaīa Zemlīa (R.S.F.S.R.)
Islands of the Atlantic
  UF Atlantic Islands
      Islands—Atlantic Ocean
      Islands—North Atlantic Ocean
      Islands—South Atlantic Ocean
  NT Bermuda Islands

British Isles
      Santa Maria Island (Azores)
      Signy Island (South Orkney Islands)
      South Georgia Island
      Terceira (Azores)
      Tristan da Cunha Islands
      West Indies
Islands of the Caribbean
  USE West Indies
Islands of the Indian Ocean
  UF Indian Ocean Islands
      Islands—Indian Ocean
  NT Comoros
      Diego Garcia
      Kerguelen Islands
      Maldives
      Marion Island (Prince Edward Islands)
      Mascarene Islands
      Mauritius
      Praslin Island (Seychelles)
      Prince Edward Island (Prince Edward
        Islands)
      Prince Edward Islands
      Réunion
      Seychelles
  — Civilization
  — — Oriental influences
        BT Civilization, Oriental
  — Description and travel
  — — 1981-
Islands of the Pacific
      Here are entered comprehensive works on all of
      the islands of the Pacific Ocean. Comprehensive
      works on the islands of the Pacific Ocean belonging
      to the island groups of Melanesia, Micronesia, and
      Polynesia are entered under Oceania.
  UF Islands—Pacific Ocean
      Pacific Islands
      Pacific Ocean Islands
  NT Bora-Bora (Society Islands)
      Borneo
      Caroline Islands
      Easter Island
      Guadalcanal Island (Solomon Islands)
      Juan Fernández Islands
      Kwajalein Island (Marshall Islands)
      Melanesia
      Midway Islands
      Oceania
      Paracel Islands
      Rotuma Island (Fiji)
      Samoan Islands
      Senkaku Islands
      Society Islands
      Spratly Islands
Islas Juan Fernández
  USE Juan Fernández Islands
Islas Marquesas de Mendoza
  USE Marquesas Islands
Islas Medas (Spain)
  USE Medas Islands (Spain)
Islas Robeson (Panama)
  USE Robeson Islands (Panama)
Islas Salvajes (Madeira Islands)
  USE Selvagens Islands (Madeira Islands)
Isle aux Noix (Québec)
  USE Ile aux Noix (Québec)
Isle de Salute (French Guiana)
  USE Safety Islands (French Guiana)
Isle of Arran (Scotland)
  USE Arran, Island of (Scotland)
Isle of Capri (Italy)
  USE Capri Island (Italy)
Isle of Lewis (Scotland)
  USE Lewis with Harris Island (Scotland)
Isle of May (Scotland)
  USE May, Isle of (Scotland)
Isle of Mull (Scotland)
  USE Mull, Island of (Scotland)
Isle of Rhum (Scotland)
  USE Rum, Isle of (Scotland)

Isle of Rum (Scotland)
  USE Rum, Isle of (Scotland)
Isle of Syme (Greece)
  USE Sími Island (Greece)
Isle of Symi (Greece)
  USE Sími Island (Greece)
Isle River (France)
  UF L'Isle River (France)
  BT Rivers—France
Isle Royale (Mich.)
  BT Islands—Michigan
Isle Royale National Park (Mich.)
  BT Game-preserves—Michigan
      National parks and reserves—United
        States
      Parks—Michigan
Isler family
  USE Eilers family
Islers family
  USE Eilers family
Isles
  USE Islands
Isles de Mingan (Québec)
  USE Mingan Islands (Québec)
Isles de Pierres Indians
  USE Sinkiuse-Columbia Indians
Isles of Scilly (England)
  USE Scilly, Isles of (England)
Isles of Shoals (Me. and N.H.)
  UF Shoals, Isles of (Me. and N.H.)
  BT Islands—Maine
      Islands—New Hampshire
  NT Appledore Island (Me.)
Islesboro Island (Me.)
  BT Islands—Maine
Islet cell tumor, Ulcerogenic
  USE Zollinger-Ellison syndrome
Islet cell tumors
  USE Islands of Langerhans—Tumors
Islet cells
  USE Islands of Langerhans
Isleta (Panama)
  USE Manzanillo Island (Panama)
Isleta Indians
      [E99.I8]
  BT Indians of North America
      Pueblo Indians
      Tanoan Indians
Isleta language
      [PM1387]
  BT Tanoan languages
Isley family
  USE Iseley family
Ismael Pérez Pazmiño prize
  USE Premio Ismael Pérez Pazmiño
Ismaili
  USE Ismailites
Ismaili literature
      [PJ891.I55]
  BT Arabic literature
      Islamic literature
      Persian literature
Ismailians
  USE Ismailites
Ismailites   (May Subd Geog)
      [BP195.I8]
  UF Ismaili
      Ismailians
  BT Islamic sects
      Shīʻah
  RT Assassins (Ismailites)
  NT Batinites
      Fatimites
      Nosairians
  — India
      UF Bohras
Ismelia
  USE Chrysanthemums
Isneg
      [DS666.I7]

UF Apayao
Apoyao
BT Igorot
Isneg language
[PL5805]
UF Apayao language
BT Philippine languages
Isoagglutination
USE Blood—Agglutination
Isoantigens
BT Antigens
NT Blood group antigens
Histocompatibility antigens
Isobaric spin
UF Isospin
Isotopic spin
Spin, Isobaric
BT Nuclear physics
Quantum theory
Isobars
USE Atmospheric pressure
Isobars, Nuclear
USE Nuclear isobars
Isobryales
[QK539.I]
BT Mosses
NT Orthotrichaceae
Isocardia
USE Glossus
Isocephaly (Craniology)
USE Brachycephaly
Isochromatic photography
USE Photography, Orthochromatic
Isochronism of balance springs
USE Balance springs—Isochronism
Isocortex
USE Neopallium
Isocyanates
[TP248.I8]
UF Carbimides
BT Isocyanic acid
NT Methyl isocyanate
Isocyanatomethane
USE Methyl isocyanate
Isocyanic acid
BT Cyanic acid
NT Isocyanates
Isodermidae
USE Aradidae
Isoelectric focusing
[QP519.9.I8 (Biological chemistry)]
UF Electrofocusing
Focusing, Isoelectric
BT Biological chemistry—Technique
Chemistry, Analytic—Qualitative
Chemistry, Organic
Electrophoresis
Isoenzymes
UF Isozymes
BT Enzymes
Isoferritin
BT Carrier proteins
RT Ferritin
Isoflurane
[RD86.I84]
UF Chlorodifluoromethoxytrifluoroethane
BT Anesthetics
Fluorocarbons
Methyl ether
Isogo (African people)
USE Mitsogho (African people)
Isogonic lines
USE Magnetism, Terrestrial
Isohemagglutination
USE Blood—Agglutination
Isohormones
UF Hormonal polymorphism
Multiple molecular forms of hormones
Polymorphism, Hormonal
BT Peptide hormones

Isohypse
USE Contours (Cartography)
Isoindole
UF Benzazole
BT Indole
Isoko (African people)
[DT515.42]
UF Biotu (African people)
Igabo (African people)
BT Ethnology—Nigeria
Sobo (African people)
Isokontae
USE Green algae
Isola del Giglio (Italy)
USE Giglio Island (Italy)
Isola d'Elba (Italy)
USE Elba (Italy)
Isola di Capri (Italy)
USE Capri Island (Italy)
Isola di Lipari (Italy)
USE Lipari Island (Italy)
Isola di Procida (Italy)
USE Procida Island (Italy)
Isola di San Clemente (Italy)
USE San Clemente Island (Italy)
Isola di San Giorgio Maggiore (Italy)
USE San Giorgio Maggiore Island (Italy)
Isola di San Pietro (Italy)
USE San Pietro Island (Italy)
Isola di Sant'Antioco (Italy)
USE Sant'Antioco Island (Italy)
Isola di Stromboli (Italy)
USE Stromboli (Italy)
Isola d'Ischia (Italy)
USE Ischia Island (Italy)
Isola Lipari (Italy)
USE Lipari Island (Italy)
Isolani family (Not Subd Geog)
Isolated organ perfusion (Physiology)
USE Isolation perfusion (Physiology)
Isolating mechanisms (May Subd Geog)
UF Isolation, Biotic
BT Evolution
Reproduction
Species
NT Island fauna
Island flora
Isolation, Biotic
USE Isolating mechanisms
Isolation, Fear of
USE Agoraphobia
Isolation, Perceptual
USE Sensory deprivation
Isolation, Social
USE Social isolation
Isolation (Hospital care)
[RA975]
UF Isolation techniques in hospitals
BT Asepsis and antisepsis
Communicable diseases—Hospitals
Communicable diseases—Prevention
Hospital care
Quarantine
— Psychological aspects
BT Hospital patients—Psychology
Medicine and psychology
Isolation (Philosophy)
[B824.3]
BT Alienation (Philosophy)
Philosophy
Isolation hospitals
USE Communicable diseases—Hospitals
Isolation of viruses
USE Viruses—Isolation
Isolation perfusion (Physiology)
UF Isolated organ perfusion (Physiology)
Organs (Anatomy)—Perfusion
Perfusion, Isolation (Physiology)
Regional perfusion

BT Biology—Technique
Perfusion (Physiology)
Preservation of organs, tissues, etc.
Isolation techniques in hospitals
USE Isolation (Hospital care)
Isolationism
USE subdivision Neutrality under names of
countries, e.g. United States—
Neutrality
Neutrality
Isolators, Ferrite
USE Ferrite isolators
Isolde (Legendary character)
USE Iseult (Legendary character)
Isole di Ponza (Italy)
USE Pontine Islands (Italy)
Isole Eolie (Italy)
USE Lipari Islands (Italy)
Isole Lipari (Italy)
USE Lipari Islands (Italy)
Isole Ponziane (Italy)
USE Pontine Islands (Italy)
Isolone del Mincio Site (Italy)
UF Isolone della Prevaldesca Site (Italy)
Isolone delle Moradelle Site (Italy)
RT Italy—Antiquities
Isolone della Prevaldesca Site (Italy)
USE Isolone del Mincio Site (Italy)
Isolone delle Moradelle Site (Italy)
USE Isolone del Mincio Site (Italy)
Isols
BT Recursion theory
Isolt (Legendary character)
USE Iseult (Legendary character)
Isom family (Not Subd Geog)
UF Isen family
Isham family
Ison family
Izen family
Izon family
Isomaltase
USE Dextranase
Isomerase
USE Isomerases
Isomerases
[QP615-616]
UF Isomerase
BT Enzymes
Isomerism
[QD471]
BT Chemistry, Physical and theoretical
Molecular rotation
RT Stereochemistry
NT Isomerization
Mesomerism
Stereoisomers
Tautomerism
Isomerism (Nuclear physics)
USE Nuclear isomers
Isomerization
BT Isomerism
Petroleum—Refining
Rearrangements (Chemistry)
Isomers, Mirror-image
USE Enantiomers
Isomers, Nuclear
USE Nuclear isomers
Isomers, Optical
USE Optical isomers
Isomers, Optically active
USE Optical isomers
Isomers (Nuclear physics)
USE Nuclear isomers
Isometopidae
USE Miridae
Isometric drawing
USE Isometric projection
Isometric exercise
[RA781.2]

1919

Isometric exercise *(Continued)*
  UF Isometrics (Exercise)
      Resistance exercise
      Resistive exercise
  BT Exercise
Isometric projection
  ⌜QA505 (Mathematics)⌝
  ⌜T365 (Mechanical drawing)⌝
  UF Isometric drawing
      Projection, Isometric
  BT Axonometric projection
      Geometry, Descriptive
      Mechanical drawing
      Projection
Isometrics (Exercise)
  USE Isometric exercise
Isometrics (Mathematics)
  BT Transformations (Mathematics)
Isomonodromic deformation method
  UF Deformation, Monodromy preserving
      Deformation method, Isomonodromic
      Monodromy preserving deformation
  BT Differential equations—Numerical
      solutions
Isomorphines
  NT Azidomorphines
Isomorphism (Crystallography)
  ⌜QD951⌝
  BT Crystallography
Isomorphisms (Mathematics)
  ⌜QA169 (Category theory)⌝
  ⌜QA171 (Group theory)⌝
  BT Categories (Mathematics)
      Groups, Theory of
      Morphisms (Mathematics)
      Set theory
Isomyia *(May Subd Geog)*
  ⌜QL537.C24⌝
  BT Blowflies
Ison family
  USE Isom family
Isongo (African people)
  USE Mbati (Central African Republic
      people)
Isoniazid
  UF INH (Drug)
      Isonicotinic acid hydrazide
      Pyridinecarboxylic acid hydrazide
  BT Antitubercular agents
      Hydrazine
      Isonicotinic acid
Isonicotinic acid
  UF Carboxypyridine
      Pyridinecarboxylic acid
  BT Carboxylic acids
      Pyridine
  RT Niacin
  NT Isoniazid
Isonicotinic acid hydrazide
  USE Isoniazid
Isonipecaine
  UF Demerol
      Dolantin
      Eudolat
  BT Narcotics
Isonychiidae
  USE Siphlonuridae
Isonzo, Battles of the, 1915-1917
  ⌜D569.I7⌝
  BT World War, 1914-1918—Campaigns—
      Italy
      World War, 1914-1918—Campaigns—
      Yugoslavia
  NT Gorizia, Battle of, 1916
Isonzo River (Slovenia and Italy)
  UF Fiume Isonzo (Slovenia and Italy)
      Soča River (Slovenia and Italy)
      Sontius River (Slovenia and Italy)
  BT Rivers—Italy
      Rivers—Yugoslavia

Isopentenoids
  ⌜QK898.I76 (Botanical chemistry)⌝
  BT Olefins
Isoperimetric inequalities
  BT Geometry, Plane
      Inequalities (Mathematics)
Isoperimetrical problems
  USE Calculus of variations
Isoperla
  ⌜QL530.3.P48⌝
  BT Perlodidae
Isopoda *(May Subd Geog)*
  ⌜QL444.M34⌝
  UF Oniscoidea
      Pill bugs
      Sow bugs
      Wood lice, Isopod
  BT Arthrostraca
      Crustacea
      Malacostraca
  NT Aegidae
      Amphisopidae
      Anthuridae
      Apseudidae
      Arcturidae
      Armadillidae
      Armadillididae
      Asellidae
      Bopyridae
      Cirolanidae
      Cymothoidae
      Desmosomatidae
      Eurycopidae
      Idoteidae
      Ilyarachnidae
      Ligiidae
      Limnoriidae
      Oniscidae
      Paranthuridae
      Phreatoicidae
      Porcellionidae
      Protallocoxidae
      Pudeoniscidae
      Sphaeromidae
      Stenetriidae
Isopoliteia (The Greek word)
  BT Greek language—Etymology
Isopotential mapping (Electrophysiology)
  USE Body surface mapping
Isoprenalene
  USE Isoproterenol
Isoprene
  NT Isoprenoid compounds
Isoprenoid compounds
  ⌜QD305.H7 (Organic chemistry)⌝
  ⌜QP801.I76 (Biochemistry)⌝
  BT Isoprene
  NT Cholesterol
      Terpenes
      Ubiquinones
      Vitamin E
      Vitamin K
  — Synthesis
      BT Biosynthesis
Isopropylamine
  NT Betaxolol
      Glyphosate
      Isoproterenol
Isopropylaminomethoxyethylphenoxypropanol
  USE Metoprolol
Isopropylarterenol
  USE Isoproterenol
Isopropylidenedithiobisditertbutylphenol
  USE Probucol
Isoproterenol *(May Subd Geog)*
  ⌜RM666.I⌝
  UF Dihydroxyisopropylaminomethylbenzyl
      alcohol
      Isoprenalene
      Isopropylarterenol

  BT Aminobenzyl alcohol
      Antispasmodics
      Bronchodilator agents
      Cardiovascular agents
      Isopropylamine
      Sympathomimetic agents
Isoptera
  USE Termites
Isoquinoline
  BT Quinoline
  NT Emetine
      Nomifensine
      Tetrahydroisoquinolines
ISORID (Information retrieval system)
  UF International Information System on
      Research in Documentation
  BT Information storage and retrieval
      systems
Isorno River (Italy) *(Not Subd Geog)*
  UF Torrente Isorno (Italy)
  BT Rivers—Italy
Isosoma
  USE Harmolita
Isospin
  USE Isobaric spin
Isostasy
  ⌜QB283⌝
  ⌜QB331 (Gravity)⌝
  ⌜QE511 (Geology)⌝
  BT Earth—Figure
      Geodesy
Isostatic anomalies
  USE Gravity anomalies
Isostatic pressing
  UF Hydrostatic pressing
      Pressing, Isostatic
  BT High pressure (Technology)
      Powder metallurgy
  RT Compacting
      Sintering
Isotachophoresis
  BT Electrophoresis
Isothermal transformation diagrams
  ⌜TN690⌝
  UF S curves (Metallurgy)
      Time-temperature-transformation
      curves (Metallurgy)
      TTT curves (Metallurgy)
  BT Phase diagrams
      Physical metallurgy
  RT Cooling curves
Isothermic curves
  USE Curves, Isothermic
Isothermic surfaces
  USE Surfaces, Isothermic
Isotherms
  USE Atmospheric temperature
Isotomidae
  ⌜QL503.I8⌝
  BT Collembola
  NT Anurophorus
      Isotomodes
Isotomodes
  ⌜QL503.I8⌝
  BT Isotomidae
Isotone shift
  ⌜QC794⌝
  UF Shift, Isotone
  BT Hyperfine interactions
      Nuclear spectroscopy
  RT Isotope shift
Isotonic solutions
  USE Physiologic salines
Isotope dilution analysis
  ⌜QD608⌝
  UF Isotopic dilution analysis
  BT Radiochemical analysis
      Radioisotopes
Isotope enrichment
  USE Isotope separation

Isotope geochemistry
  USE Isotope geology
Isotope geology *(May Subd Geog)*
  ₍QE501.4.N9₎
  UF Isotope geochemistry
      Nuclear geochemistry
      Nuclear geology
      Nuclear geophysics
      Stable isotope geology
  BT Physical geology
  NT Radioisotopes in geology
Isotope separation
  ₍QD466 (General)₎
  ₍TK9350-TK9360 (Engineering)₎
  UF Isotope enrichment
      Separation of isotopes
  BT Isotopes
      Radiochemistry
      Separation (Technology)
  NT Calutron
      Gaseous diffusion plants
      Lasers in isotope separation
      Nuclear fuels
      Uranium enrichment
Isotope shift
  ₍QC794₎
  BT Atomic spectra
      Hyperfine interactions
  RT Isotone shift
Isotope tracers, Stable
  USE Stable isotope tracers
Isotopes
  ₍QD466₎
  BT Nuclides
  SA *subdivision* Isotopes *under names of*
      elements or groups of elements, e.g.
      Carbon—Isotopes; Uranium—
      Isotopes
  NT Calutron
      Isotope separation
      Isotopic power generators
      Nuclear isobars
      Packing fractions
      Radioisotopes
      Stable isotopes
  — Mass
Isotopic actinium
  USE Actinium—Isotopes
Isotopic antimony
  USE Antimony—Isotopes
Isotopic beryllium
  USE Beryllium—Isotopes
Isotopic boron
  USE Boron—Isotopes
Isotopic bromine
  USE Bromine—Isotopes
Isotopic cadmium
  USE Cadmium—Isotopes
Isotopic carbon
  USE Carbon—Isotopes
Isotopic cerium
  USE Cerium—Isotopes
Isotopic cesium
  USE Cesium—Isotopes
Isotopic dilution analysis
  USE Isotope dilution analysis
Isotopic europium
  USE Europium—Isotopes
Isotopic germanium
  USE Germanium—Isotopes
Isotopic helium
  USE Helium—Isotopes
Isotopic holmium
  USE Holmium—Isotopes
Isotopic indicators, Radioactive
  USE Radioactive tracers
Isotopic indicators, Stable
  USE Stable isotope tracers
Isotopic iron
  USE Iron—Isotopes

Isotopic lanthanum
  USE Lanthanum—Isotopes
Isotopic lutetium
  USE Lutetium—Isotopes
Isotopic manganese
  USE Manganese—Isotopes
Isotopic mercury
  USE Mercury—Isotopes
Isotopic milking systems
  USE Radionuclide generators
Isotopic platinum
  USE Platinum—Isotopes
Isotopic polonium
  USE Polonium—Isotopes
Isotopic power generators
  UF Radioisotopic power generators
  BT Isotopes
      Radioisotopes—Decay
  SA *subdivision* Isotopic power generators
      under subjects, e.g. Automatic
      meteorological stations—Isotopic
      power generators; Space vehicles—
      Isotopic power generators
  NT Nuclear batteries
Isotopic praseodymium
  USE Praseodymium—Isotopes
Isotopic protactinium
  USE Protactinium—Isotopes
Isotopic radon
  USE Radon—Isotopes
Isotopic rubidium
  USE Rubidium—Isotopes
Isotopic silicon
  USE Silicon—Isotopes
Isotopic spin
  USE Isobaric spin
Isotopic sulphur
  USE Sulphur—Isotopes
Isotopic tellurium
  USE Tellurium—Isotopes
Isotopic thallium
  USE Thallium—Isotopes
Isotopic thorium
  USE Thorium—Isotopes
Isotopic thulium
  USE Thulium—Isotopes
Isotopic uranium
  USE Uranium—Isotopes
Isotopic vanadium
  USE Vanadium—Isotopes
Isotopic xenon
  USE Xenon—Isotopes
Isotopies (Topology)
  BT Homeomorphisms
      Piecewise linear topology
      Topological imbeddings
  RT Concordances (Topology)
Isotretinoin
  UF Cis-retinoic acid
      Dimethyltrimethylcyc
          lohexenylnonatetraenoic acid
      Retinoic acid, Cis-
  BT Dermatologic agents
      Retinoids
Isotta automobile
Isotype (Picture language)
  ₍PM8999₎
  BT Language, Universal
      Languages, Artificial
      Pasigraphy
Isozymes
  USE Isoenzymes
ISP (Computer program language)
  ₍QA76.73.I₎
  UF Instruction Set Processors (Computer
      program language)
  BT Programming languages (Electronic
      computers)
ISP (Computer programs)
  USE Interactive Statistical Programs
      (Computer programs)

ISPF Dialog Manager (Computer program)
  UF Dialog Manager (Computer program)
      Interactive System Productivity
          Facility Dialog Manager (Computer
          program)
  BT Computer programs
      Interactive computer systems
ISPL (Electronic computer system)
  UF Incremental System Programming
      Language (Electronic computer
      system)
Isrāʾ
  USE Muḥammad, Prophet, d. 632—Isrāʾ
      and Miʿrāj
Israel *(Not Subd Geog)*
  BT Palestine
  — **Anniversaries, etc.**
      NT Independence Day (Israel)
  — **Antiquities**
      NT Gerisah Site (Israel)
          Ḥamat (Ancient city)
          Jalamat al-Asafna Site (Israel)
          Masada Site (Israel)
          Megiddo (Ancient city)
          Sepphoris (Ancient city)
          Timna Site (Israel)
  — **Civilization**
      NT Canaanites (Movement)
  — **Foreign relations**
  — — **Treaties**
  — — **Uganda**
          NT Entebbe Airport Raid, 1976
  — **History**
      NT Israel-Arab conflicts
  — — **1948-1949**
  — — Suez Campaign, 1956
          USE Sinai Campaign, 1956
  — **Name**
      BT Jews—Name
          Names in the Bible
  — **Politics and government**
      NT Canaanites (Movement)
Israel, Ancient
  USE *subdivision* History—₍ancient period
      subdivisions₎ *under the heading*
      Jews
Israel, Beta
  USE Falashas
Israel, Election of
  USE Jews—Election, Doctrine of
Israel, House of
  USE Falashas
Israel, Ten lost tribes
  USE Lost tribes of Israel
Israel, Twelve tribes of
  USE Twelve tribes of Israel
Israel (Christian theology)
  ₍BM535₎
  BT Judaism (Christian theology)
Israel and the Diaspora
  UF Diaspora
  BT Jews—Diaspora
      Zionism
  NT Jews—Attitudes toward Israel
Israel-Arab Border Conflicts, 1949-
  (May Subd Geog)
  UF Arab-Israel Border Conflicts, 1949-
      Israeli-Arab Border Conflicts, 1949-
  BT Israel-Arab conflicts
  NT Fedayeen
  — **Lebanon**
      NT Lebanon—History—Israeli
          intervention, 1982-

Israel-Arab conflicts *(May Subd Geog)*
Here are entered works on the conflicts between the Arab countries and Israel. Works that discuss collectively the relations between Arabs and Jews, including religious, ethnic, and ideological relations, are entered under Jewish-Arab relations, subdivided further by dates, if appropriate. Works on relations between the religions of Judaism and Islam are entered under Judaism—Relations—Islam. When this heading is assigned, duplicate entry is made under Islam—Relations—Judaism.
- UF Arab-Israel conflicts
      Arab-Israeli conflicts
      Israeli-Arab conflicts
- BT Arab countries—History—20th century
      Israel—History
- RT Jewish-Arab relations—1949-
- NT Israel-Arab Border Conflicts, 1949-
      Israel-Arab War, 1948-1949
      Israel-Arab War, 1967
      Israel-Arab War, 1973
— **Uganda**
  - NT Entebbe Airport Raid, 1976

Israel-Arab War, 1948-1949
(May Subd Geog)
[DS126.9-DS126.99]
- UF Arab-Israel War, 1948-1949
      Jewish-Arab War, 1948-1949
- BT Israel-Arab conflicts
- NT Jerusalem—Siege, 1948
— **Aerial operations**
— **Armistices**
— Charities
  - USE Israel-Arab War, 1948-1949—Civilian relief
— **Civilian relief**
  - UF Israel-Arab War, 1948-1949—Charities
        Israel-Arab War, 1948-1949—Social work
— **Destruction and pillage**
  - UF Israel-Arab War, 1948-1949—Pillage
— **Diplomatic history**
— **Naval operations**
— **Pictorial works**
— Pillage
  - USE Israel-Arab War, 1948-1949—Destruction and pillage
— **Propaganda**
— Social work
  - USE Israel-Arab War, 1948-1949—Civilian relief

Israel-Arab War, 1956
- USE Egypt—History—Intervention, 1956
       Sinai Campaign, 1956

Israel-Arab War, 1967 *(May Subd Geog)*
- UF Arab-Israel War, 1967
      Six Day War, 1967
- BT Israel-Arab conflicts
— **Aerial operations**
— **Campaigns**
  - NT Jerusalem, Battle of, 1967
— — **Syria**
  - NT Faher, Tel (Syria), Battle of, 1967
— **Causes**
— **Diplomatic history**
— **Naval operations**
— **Occupied territories**
  - BT Military occupation
— **Regimental histories** *(May Subd Geog)*
— **Religious aspects**
— **Territorial questions** *(May Subd Geog)*
— **Campaigns**
— **Syria**

Israel-Arab War, 1973
- UF Arab-Israel War, 1973
      October Middle East War, 1973
      Yom Kippur War, 1973
- BT Israel-Arab conflicts

— Prisoners and prisons
— Prisoners and prisons, Syrian, [etc.]
Israel-Arab War, 1973, in motion pictures
[DS128.16.M65]
- BT Moving-pictures
Israel family *(Not Subd Geog)*
- UF Israelson family
Israel prize
- UF Peras Yisrael
Israeli-Arab Border Conflicts, 1949-
- USE Israel-Arab Border Conflicts, 1949-
Israeli-Arab conflicts
- USE Israel-Arab conflicts
Israeli art
- USE Art, Israeli
Israeli authors
- USE Authors, Israeli
Israeli children's writings
- USE Children's writings, Israeli
Israeli cookery
- USE Cookery, Israeli
Israeli drama
Here are entered collections of drama originating in Israel in Hebrew or in several languages collectively. Such collections in Arabic are entered under Arabic drama—Israel; in Yiddish under Yiddish drama—Israel. Collections of such drama in other individual languages are entered under Israeli drama (name of language)
- UF Hebrew drama—Israel
      Israeli drama (Hebrew)
- RT Hebrew drama
Israeli drama (Arabic)
- USE Arabic drama—Israel
Israeli drama (Hebrew)
- USE Israeli drama
Israeli drama (Yiddish)
- USE Yiddish drama—Israel
Israeli espionage
- USE Espionage, Israeli
Israeli etching
- USE Etching, Israeli
Israeli fiction *(May Subd Geog)*
[PJ5045]
Here are entered collections of fiction originating in Israel in Hebrew or in several languages collectively. Such collections in Arabic are entered under Arabic fiction—Israel; in Yiddish under Yiddish fiction—Israel. Collections of such fiction in other individual languages are entered under Israeli fiction (name of language)
- UF Hebrew fiction—Israel
      Israeli fiction (Hebrew)
- NT Short stories, Israeli
      War stories, Israeli
Israeli fiction (Arabic)
- USE Arabic fiction—Israel
Israeli fiction (Hebrew)
- USE Israeli fiction
Israeli fiction (Yiddish)
- USE Yiddish fiction—Israel
Israeli folk literature
- USE Folk literature, Israeli
Israeli intervention in Lebanon, 1982-
- USE Lebanon—History—Israeli intervention, 1982-
Israeli Jewish religious poetry (English)
- USE Jewish religious poetry, Israeli (English)
Israeli literature *(May Subd Geog)*
Here are entered collections of literature originating in Israel in Hebrew or in several languages collectively. Such collections in Arabic are entered under Arabic literature—Israel; in Yiddish under Yiddish literature—Israel. Collections of such literature in other individual languages are entered under Israeli literature (name of language)
- UF Hebrew literature, Modern—Israel
      Israeli literature (Hebrew)
- NT Children's writings, Israeli
      Folk literature, Israeli
Israeli literature (Arabic)
- USE Arabic literature—Israel

Israeli literature (English)
- UF English literature—Israeli authors
Israeli literature (Hebrew)
- USE Israeli literature
Israeli literature (Yiddish)
- USE Yiddish literature—Israel
Israeli military assistance
- USE Military assistance, Israeli
Israeli national characteristics
- USE National characteristics, Israeli
Israeli newspapers
Israeli painting
- USE Painting, Israeli
Israeli patriotic poetry
- USE Patriotic poetry, Israeli
Israeli periodicals
Israeli philosophy
- USE Philosophy, Israeli
Israeli poetry *(May Subd Geog)*
Here are entered collections of poetry originating in Israel in Hebrew or in several languages collectively. Such collections in Arabic are entered under Arabic poetry—Israel; in Yiddish under Yiddish poetry—Israel. Collections of such poetry in other individual languages are entered under Israeli poetry (name of language)
- UF Hebrew poetry, Modern—Israel
      Israeli poetry (Hebrew)
- NT Patriotic poetry, Israeli
      War poetry, Israeli
Israeli poetry (Arabic)
- USE Arabic poetry—Israel
Israeli poetry (English) *(May Subd Geog)*
- UF English poetry—Israeli authors
- NT Jewish religious poetry, Israeli (English)
Israeli poetry (Hebrew)
- USE Israeli poetry
Israeli poetry (Yiddish)
- USE Yiddish poetry—Israel
Israeli poets
- USE Poets, Israeli
Israeli posters
- USE Posters, Israeli
Israeli pound
- USE Pound, Israeli
Israeli prints
- USE Prints, Israeli
Israeli propaganda
- USE Propaganda, Israeli
Israeli sculpture
- USE Sculpture, Israeli
Israeli short stories
- USE Short stories, Israeli
Israeli students *(May Subd Geog)*
- BT Students
Israeli technical assistance
- USE Technical assistance, Israeli
Israeli war poetry
- USE War poetry, Israeli
Israeli war stories
- USE War stories, Israeli
Israeli wit and humor *(May Subd Geog)*
[PN6222.I8]
- BT Hebrew wit and humor
      Jewish wit and humor
Israeli wit and humor, Pictorial
Israelis *(May Subd Geog)*
- BT Ethnology—Israel
      Jews
Israelites
- USE Jews
Israelites (Bohemia)
- USE Abrahamites (Bohemia)
Israelson family
- USE Israel family
ISS 714 (Computer)
- BT Electronic digital computers
ISS-b (Artificial satellite)
- UF Ionospheric Sounding Satellite-b

BT Artificial satellites
    Ionosphere—Research
    Meteorological satellites
Issala language
  USE Sisala language
Issel Lake (Netherlands)
  USE IJssel Lake (Netherlands)
Issel River (Netherlands)
  USE IJssel River (Netherlands)
Issidae
  [QL527.I8]
  BT Homoptera
    Planthoppers
Issin (Ancient city)
  USE Isin (Ancient city)
ISSN
  USE International Standard Serial Numbers
Issök-Kul' (Kirghiz S.S.R.)
  USE Issyk-Kul' (Kirghiz S.S.R.)
Isson Kyōdai (Sect)
  USE Nyoraikyō (Sect)
Issues management *(May Subd Geog)*
  [HD59.5]
  UF Management, Issues
  BT Public relations—Corporations
  RT Industry—Social aspects
Issus, Battle of, 333 B.C.
  BT Greece—History—To 146 B.C.
Issus, Battle of, 333 B.C., in art
  NT Altdorfer, Albrecht, (ca.) 1480-1538.
    Battle of Alexander and Darius at
    Issus
Issyk-Kul' (Kirghiz S.S.R.)
  UF Issök-Kul' (Kirghiz S.S.R.)
    Lake Issyk (Kirghiz S.S.R.)
    Ozero Issyk-Kul' (Kirghiz S.S.R.)
  BT Lakes—Kirghiz S.S.R.
Istanbul (Turkey)
  UF Constantinople (Turkey)
  — History *(Not Subd Geog)*
  ——To 1453 *(Not Subd Geog)*
    [DR729]
  — Siege, 1203-1204
    BT Latin Empire, 1204-1261
    RT Crusades—Fourth, 1202-1204
  — Siege, 1453
    BT Byzantine Empire—History
      Turkey—History—1288-1453
Istanbul (Turkey). Çamlıca
  USE Çamlıca (Istanbul, Turkey)
İstanbul Boğazı (Turkey)
  USE Bosporus (Turkey)
İstanköy (Greece)
  USE Kos Island (Greece)
Istanpittas
  USE Estampies
Isthme de l'Acadie (N.B. and N.S.)
  USE Chignecto Isthmus (N.B. and N.S.)
Isthmian canals
  USE Canals, Interoceanic
Isthmocoris
  [QL523.L9]
  BT Lygaeidae
Isthmus of Chignecto (N.B. and N.S.)
  USE Chignecto Isthmus (N.B. and N.S.)
Isthmus of Darien (Panama)
  USE Panama, Isthmus of (Panama)
Isthmus of Panama (Panama)
  USE Panama, Isthmus of (Panama)
Isthmus of Tehuantepec (Mexico)
  USE Tehuantepec, Isthmus of (Mexico)
Isthmuses *(May Subd Geog)*
  — Mexico
    NT Tehuantepec, Isthmus of (Mexico)
  — New Brunswick
    NT Chignecto Isthmus (N.B. and N.S.)
  — Nova Scotia
    NT Chignecto Isthmus (N.B. and N.S.)
  — Panama
    NT Panama, Isthmus of (Panama)
  — Russian S.F.S.R.

  NT Karelian Isthmus (R.S.F.S.R.)
Istina (The Slavic word)
  BT Slavic languages—Etymology
Istiophoridae
  [QL638.I88]
  BT Billfishes
    Perciformes
  NT Marlin
    Sailfish
    Spearfishes
Istiophorus
  USE Sailfish
Istiophorus americanus
  USE Sailfish
Istiophorus greyi
  USE Sailfish
Istiophorus orientalis
  USE Sailfish
Istiophorus platypterus
  USE Sailfish
ISTIS (Information retrieval system)
  [Z699.5.S3]
  UF International Scientific and Technical
    Information System
  BT Information storage and retrieval
    systems—Science
    Information storage and retrieval
    systems—Technology
Istmo de Panama (Panama)
  USE Panama, Isthmus of (Panama)
Istmo de Tehuantepec (Mexico)
  USE Tehuantepec, Isthmus of (Mexico)
Istmo Panameno (Panama)
  USE Panama, Isthmus of (Panama)
Istra (Croatia and Slovenia)
  USE Istria (Croatia and Slovenia)
Istranca Mountains (Turkey and Bulgaria)
  UF Strandzha Mountains (Turkey and
    Bulgaria)
    Yıldız dağları (Turkey and Bulgaria)
  BT Mountains—Bulgaria
    Mountains—Turkey
Istria (Croatia and Slovenia)
  UF Istra (Croatia and Slovenia)
    Istrian Peninsula (Croatia and
    Slovenia)
  BT Peninsulas—Yugoslavia
Istrian Peninsula (Croatia and Slovenia)
  USE Istria (Croatia and Slovenia)
Istrio-Romanian dialect
  USE Istro-Romanian dialect
Istro-Romanian dialect *(May Subd Geog)*
  [PC798]
  UF Istrio-Romanian dialect
  BT Aromanian dialect
Isumi-gawa (Japan)
  USE Isumi River (Japan)
Isumi River (Japan)
  UF Isumi-gawa (Japan)
  BT Rivers—Japan
Isurus
  [QL638.95.L3]
  BT Lamnidae
Isurus paucus
  [QL638.95.L3]
  UF Lamna punctata
Isyiyamadera, Ōtsu, Japan, in art
Ita (Philippine people)
  USE Aeta (Philippine people)
Itaboca Falls (Brazil)
  UF Cachoeira Itaboca (Brazil)
  BT Waterfalls—Brazil
Itacaiunas River (Brazil)
  UF Itacayuna River (Brazil)
    Itacayunas River (Brazil)
    Rio Itacaiunas (Brazil)
    Rio Itacayunas (Brazil)
  BT Rivers—Brazil
Itacayuna River (Brazil)
  USE Itacaiunas River (Brazil)

Itacayunas River (Brazil)
  USE Itacaiunas River (Brazil)
Italian aesthetics
  USE Aesthetics, Italian
Italian alien labor
  USE Alien labor, Italian
Italian almanacs
  USE Almanacs, Italian
Italian Alps (Italy)
  USE Alps, Italian (Italy)
Italian American children *(May Subd Geog)*
  UF Children, Italian American
  BT Children—United States
Italian American criminals
  (May Subd Geog)
  UF Criminals, Italian American
  BT Crime and criminals—United States
    Organized crime—United States
  NT Black Hand (United States)
    Mafia
Italian American families *(May Subd Geog)*
  UF Families, Italian American
  BT Family—United States
Italian-American literature
  (May Subd Geog)
  UF American literature (Italian)
    Italian literature—American authors
  BT Italian literature
Italian American literature (English)
  USE American literature—Italian American
    authors
Italian-American newspapers
  [PN4885.I (History)]
  BT American newspapers
    Italian newspapers
Italian American painters *(May Subd Geog)*
  UF Painters, Italian American
  BT Painters—United States
Italian-American periodicals
  [PN4885.I (History)]
  BT American periodicals
    Italian periodicals
Italian-American poetry *(May Subd Geog)*
  UF American poetry (Italian)
    Italian poetry—American authors
  BT Italian poetry
Italian American women *(May Subd Geog)*
  UF Women, Italian American
  — Economic conditions
    NT Italian American women—
      Employment
  — Employment *(May Subd Geog)*
    BT Italian American women—
      Economic conditions
Italian Americans *(May Subd Geog)*
  BT Ethnology—United States
    Italians—United States
  — New York (State)
    NT San Gennaro Festival (New York,
      N.Y.)
Italian Americans in motion pictures
  [PN1995.9.I73]
  BT Moving-pictures
Italian architecture
  USE Architecture, Italian
Italian art
  USE Art, Italian
Italian arts
  USE Arts, Italian
Italian atlases
  USE Atlases, Italian
Italian authors
  USE Authors, Italian
Italian autobiographical fiction
  USE Autobiographical fiction, Italian
Italian ballads
  USE Ballads, Italian
Italian book-plates
  USE Book-plates, Italian
Italian broccoli
  USE Calabrese (Vegetable)

Italian bronze figurines
USE Bronze figurines, Italian
Italian bronze sculpture
USE Bronze sculpture, Italian
Italian bronzes
USE Bronzes, Italian
Italian chestnut
USE Chestnut
Italian children's encyclopedias and dictionaries
USE Children's encyclopedias and
dictionaries, Italian
Italian children's literature
USE Children's literature, Italian
Italian children's plays
USE Children's plays, Italian
Italian children's stories
USE Children's stories, Italian
Italian Christian literature
USE Christian literature, Italian
Italian clergymen's writings
USE Clergymen's writings, Italian
Italian coins
USE Coins, Italian
Italian college and school drama
USE College and school drama, Italian
Italian commercial correspondence
USE Commercial correspondence, Italian
Italian cookery
USE Cookery, Italian
Italian corporations
USE Corporations, Italian
Italian cypress
[QK494.5.C975]
UF Cupressus sempervirens
BT Cypress
Italian detective stories
USE Detective and mystery stories, Italian
Italian devotional literature
USE Devotional literature, Italian
Italian dialect literature
USE Dialect literature, Italian
Italian dialogues
USE Dialogues, Italian
Italian drama (May Subd Geog)
[PQ4133-PQ4160 (History)]
[PQ4227-PQ4245 (Collections)]
NT Children's plays, Italian
College and school drama, Italian
Mysteries and miracle-plays, Italian
Pastoral drama, Italian
Radio plays, Italian
— **To 1700**
[PQ4137-9]
— **18th century**
[PQ4141]
— **19th century**
[PQ4143]
— **20th century**
[PQ4145]
Italian drama (Comedy)
[PQ4149]
BT Comedy
NT Commedia dell'arte
Italian drama (Tragedy)
[PQ4147]
BT Tragedy
Italian dramatists
USE Dramatists, Italian
Italian drawing
USE Drawing, Italian
Italian economic assistance
USE Economic assistance, Italian
Italian elegiac poetry
USE Elegiac poetry, Italian
Italian encyclopedias and dictionaries
USE Encyclopedias and dictionaries, Italian
Italian engraving
USE Engraving, Italian
Italian epic literature
USE Epic literature, Italian

Italian epic poetry
USE Epic poetry, Italian
Italian epigrams
USE Epigrams, Italian
Italian erotic literature
USE Erotic literature, Italian
Italian erotic painting
USE Erotic painting, Italian
Italian erotic poetry
USE Erotic poetry, Italian
Italian erotic stories
USE Erotic stories, Italian
Italian espionage
USE Espionage, Italian
Italian essays
[PQ4183.E8 (History)]
[PQ4260 (Collections)]
Here are entered collections of essays by several
authors.
Italian etching
USE Etching, Italian
Italian fables
USE Fables, Italian
Italian fan painting
USE Fan painting, Italian
Italian fantastic fiction
USE Fantastic fiction, Italian
Italian farces (May Subd Geog)
[PQ4155-PQ4159 (History)]
[PQ4236-PQ4238 (Collections)]
Italian feminist poetry
USE Feminist poetry, Italian
Italian fiction (May Subd Geog)
[PQ4169-PQ4181 (History)]
[PQ4251-PQ4257 (Collections)]
NT Autobiographical fiction, Italian
Children's stories, Italian
Detective and mystery stories, Italian
Erotic stories, Italian
Fantastic fiction, Italian
Historical fiction, Italian
Short stories, Italian
— **To 1400**
[PQ4171]
— **15th century**
[PQ4171-2]
— **16th century**
[PQ4172]
— **17th century**
[PQ4172]
— **18th century**
[PQ4173]
— **19th century**
[PQ4173]
— **20th century**
[PQ4174]
Italian film posters
USE Film posters, Italian
Italian folk literature
USE Folk literature, Italian
Italian folk poetry
USE Folk poetry, Italian
Italian folk-songs
USE Folk-songs, Italian
Italian food relief
USE Food relief, Italian
Italian Garden (Richmond, Va.)
(Not Subd Geog)
BT Gardens—Virginia
Maymont Park (Richmond, Va.)
Italian gardens
USE Gardens, Italian
Italian Grand Prix Race
[GV1034.51.I]
BT Automobile racing
Grand Prix racing
Italian graphic arts
USE Graphic arts, Italian
Italian greyhound
[SF429.I89]

BT Dog breeds
Greyhounds
Toy dogs
Italian historical fiction
USE Historical fiction, Italian
Italian illumination of books and manuscripts
USE Illumination of books and manuscripts,
Italian
Italian imprints (May Subd Geog)
Italian investments
USE Investments, Italian
Italian Jews
USE Jews, Italian
Italian landscape painting
USE Landscape painting, Italian
Italian language (May Subd Geog)
[PC1001-1977]
— **To 1300**
[PC1715]
— **1300-1500**
[PC1077-1079]
— **Dialects**
— — **Judeo-Italian**
[PC1784]
UF Jewish-Italian dialect
Judeo-Italian dialect
BT Hebrew language
Jews—Languages
— **Dictionaries**
NT Picture dictionaries, Italian
— **Etymology**
NT Ananasso (The Italian word)
Come (The Italian word)
Diligenza (The Italian word)
Ecco (The Italian word)
Fare (The Italian word)
Granturco (The Italian word)
Patata (The Italian word)
Pittoresco (The Italian word)
Tranvai (The Italian word)
— — **Names**
NT Names, Italian
— **Euphemism**
— Names
USE Names, Italian
— Scientific Italian
USE Italian language—Technical
Italian
— **Technical Italian**
UF Italian language—Scientific Italian
Scientific Italian
Technical Italian
BT Technical writing
Technology—Language
Italian letters
[PQ4183.L4 (History)]
[PQ4259 (Collections)]
Italian literature (May Subd Geog)
[PQ4001-PQ4199 (History)]
[PQ4201-PQ4263 (Collections)]
NT Children's literature, Italian
Christian literature, Italian
Dialect literature, Italian
Epic literature, Italian
Erotic literature, Italian
Folk literature, Italian
Italian-American literature
Mentally ill, Writings of the, Italian
Romances, Italian
Sardinian literature
Young adult literature, Italian
— **To 1400**
— **15th century**
[PQ4075]
— **16th century**
[PQ4079-4080]
— **17th century**
[PQ4081-2]
— **18th century**
[PQ4083-4]
— **19th century**

[PQ4085-6]
—— **History and criticism**
　　NT　Positivism (Italian literature)
　　　　Verism (Italian literature)
— **20th century**
　　[PQ4087]
— **American authors**
　　USE　Italian-American literature
— **Bibliography**
　　[Z2341-2369]
—— **Early**
　　　[Z2342]
　　　[Z2352]
— **Catholic authors**
— **Competitions**
　　NT　Premio Antico Fattore
　　　　Premio di narrativa fantastica
　　　　　"J.R.R. Tolkien"
　　　　Premio letterario "Libera Stampa"
　　　　Premio letterario "Mario Pettenon"
　　　　Premio letterario Massarosa
　　　　Premio Strega
　　　　Premio Viareggio
— **History and criticism**
　　NT　Marinism
— **Jewish authors**
　　　Duplicate entry is made under Jewish litera-
　　　ture (Italian)
— **France**
—— **Corsica**
　　　NT　Corsican literature
— **Italy**
—— **Calabria**
　　　UF　Calabrian literature
—— **Liguria**
　　　UF　Ligurian literature
—— **Sicily**
　　　UF　Sicilian literature
— **Switzerland**
　　BT　Swiss literature
Italian literature (English)
　USE　English literature—Italian authors
Italian love poetry
　USE　Love poetry, Italian
Italian lullabies
　USE　Lullabies, Italian
Italian madrigals (Music)
　USE　Madrigals (Music), Italian
Italian majolica
　USE　Majolica, Italian
Italian manuscripts
　USE　Manuscripts, Italian
Italian marble sculpture
　USE　Marble sculpture, Italian
Italian mastiff
　USE　Neapolitan mastiff
Italian metal sculpture
　USE　Metal sculpture, Italian
Italian miracle-plays
　USE　Mysteries and miracle-plays, Italian
Italian missions
　USE　Missions, Italian
Italian mosaics
　USE　Mosaics, Italian
Italian mural painting and decoration
　USE　Mural painting and decoration, Italian
Italian mysteries and miracle-plays
　USE　Mysteries and miracle-plays, Italian
Italian mystery stories
　USE　Detective and mystery stories, Italian
Italian names
　USE　Names, Italian
Italian narrative art
　USE　Narrative art, Italian
Italian narrative painting
　USE　Narrative painting, Italian
Italian national characteristics
　USE　National characteristics, Italian
Italian newspapers　*(May Subd Geog)*
　[PN5241-PN5249 (History)]
　NT　Italian-American newspapers

Italian novelists
　USE　Novelists, Italian
Italian occupation, Albania, 1939-1943
　USE　Albania—History—Axis occupation,
　　　　1939-1944
Italian orations
　USE　Speeches, addresses, etc., Italian
Italian painting
　USE　Painting, Italian
Italian paleography
　USE　Paleography, Italian
Italian panel painting
　USE　Panel painting, Italian
Italian paste
　USE　Macaroni products
Italian pastoral drama
　USE　Pastoral drama, Italian
Italian pastoral poetry
　USE　Pastoral poetry, Italian
Italian patriotic poetry
　USE　Patriotic poetry, Italian
Italian periodicals　*(May Subd Geog)*
　[PN5241-PN5250 (History)]
　NT　Italian-American periodicals
Italian philology
　[PC1001-1977]
Italian picture dictionaries
　USE　Picture dictionaries, Italian
Italian poetry　*(May Subd Geog)*
　[PQ4091-PQ4131 (History)]
　[PQ4207-PQ4225 (Collections)]
　BT　Poetry
　NT　Elegiac poetry, Italian
　　　Epic poetry, Italian
　　　Erotic poetry, Italian
　　　Feminist poetry, Italian
　　　Folk poetry, Italian
　　　Italian-American poetry
　　　Love poetry, Italian
　　　Pastoral poetry, Italian
　　　Patriotic poetry, Italian
　　　Political poetry, Italian
　　　Religious poetry, Italian
　　　Revolutionary poetry, Italian
　　　Sonnets, Italian
　　　Verse satire, Italian
　　　Visual poetry, Italian
— **To 1400**
　　[PQ4094-9]
　　UF　Dolce stil nuovo
　　　　Sicilian poetry
　　　　Stile nuovo (Italian poetry)
— **15th century**
　　[PQ4101]
　　NT　Strambotto
— **16th century**
　　[PQ4103]
— **17th century**
　　[PQ4105]
— **18th century**
　　[PQ4107]
— **19th century**
　　[PQ4109]
— **20th century**
　　[PQ4113]
—— **History and criticism**
　　　NT　Ermetismo (Italian literature)
— **American authors**
　　USE　Italian-American poetry
Italian poets
　USE　Poets, Italian
Italian pointer
　USE　Spinone
Italian political poetry
　USE　Political poetry, Italian
Italian political posters
　USE　Political posters, Italian
Italian porcelain
　USE　Porcelain, Italian
Italian portrait drawing
　USE　Portrait drawing, Italian

Italian portrait painting
　USE　Portrait painting, Italian
Italian portraits
　USE　Portraits, Italian
Italian posters
　USE　Posters, Italian
Italian pottery
　USE　Pottery, Italian
Italian prints
　USE　Prints, Italian
Italian propaganda
　USE　Propaganda, Italian
Italian property　*(May Subd Geog)*
　UF　Property, Italian
　BT　Alien property
Italian prose literature　*(May Subd Geog)*
　[PQ4161-PQ4185 (History)]
　[PQ4247-PQ4263 (Collections)]
— **To 1700**
— **18th century**
— **19th century**
— **20th century**
Italian proverbs
　USE　Proverbs, Italian
Italian question, 1849-1870
　USE　Italy—History—1849-1870
Italian quilting
　USE　Trapunto
Italian quotations
　USE　Quotations, Italian
Italian radio plays
　USE　Radio plays, Italian
Italian reference books
　USE　Reference books, Italian
Italian relief (Sculpture)
　USE　Relief (Sculpture), Italian
Italian religious poetry
　USE　Religious poetry, Italian
Italian revolutionary poetry
　USE　Revolutionary poetry, Italian
Italian riddles
　USE　Riddles, Italian
Italian Riviera (Italy)
　USE　Riviera (Italy)
Italian romances
　USE　Romances, Italian
Italian satire
　USE　Satire, Italian
Italian school drama
　USE　College and school drama, Italian
Italian schools
　USE　Schools—Italy
Italian sermons
　USE　Sermons, Italian
Italian short stories
　USE　Short stories, Italian
Italian songs
　USE　Songs, Italian
Italian sonnets
　USE　Sonnets, Italian
Italian-speaking Switzerland
　USE　Switzerland, Italian-speaking
Italian speeches
　USE　Speeches, addresses, etc., Italian
Italian spinone
　USE　Spinone
Italian still-life painting
　USE　Still-life painting, Italian
Italian students　*(May Subd Geog)*
　BT　Students
Italian technical assistance
　USE　Technical assistance, Italian
Italian verse satire
　USE　Verse satire, Italian
Italian visual poetry
　USE　Visual poetry, Italian
Italian watercolor painting
　USE　Watercolor painting, Italian
Italian wit and humor　*(May Subd Geog)*
　[PN6203-6205]

Italian wit and humor *(Continued)*
Here are entered collections from several authors and individual authors who have not written in other literary forms.
Italian wit and humor, Pictorial
(May Subd Geog)
Italian women authors
USE Women authors, Italian
Italian writings of the mentally ill
USE Mentally ill, Writings of the, Italian
Italian young adult literature
USE Young adult literature, Italian
Italianists *(May Subd Geog)*
BT Italy—Study and teaching
Italians *(May Subd Geog)*
BT Ethnology—Italy
NT Missions to Italians
— **Ethnic identity**
— **United States**
NT Italian Americans
Italic art
USE Art, Italic
Italic bronze figurines
USE Bronze figurines, Italic
Italic bronzes
USE Bronzes, Italic
Italic inscriptions
USE Inscriptions, Italic
Italic languages and dialects
₍PA2420-2550₎
UF Dialects
BT Indo-European languages
RT Latin language
NT Faliscan language
Venetic language
— **Etymology**
NT Dōnom (The Italic word)
Italic numismatics
USE Numismatics, Italic
Italic peoples *(May Subd Geog)*
BT Ethnology—Italy
RT Etruscans
NT Art, Classical—Italic influences
Art, Roman—Italic influences
Aurunci
Bruttii (Italic people)
Daunii
Faliscans (Italic people)
Frentani (Italic people)
Hirpini (Italic people)
Latini (Italic people)
Ligurians
Lucani (Italic people)
Marsi
Oscans
Picenes (Italic people)
Romans
Rutuli (Italic people)
Sabines
Samnites
Siculi
Umbrians (Italic people)
Veneti (Italic people)
Vestini
Vittimuli (Italic people)
Volsci (Italic people)
— **Cultural assimilation**
BT Acculturation
Italic pottery
USE Pottery, Italic
Italic type
USE Type and type-founding—Italic type
Italic writing
USE Writing, Italic
Italica (Ancient city) *(Not Subd Geog)*
₍DP402.185₎
BT Cities and towns, Ruined, extinct, etc.
—Spain
Spain—Antiquities, Roman
Italics
RT Type and type-founding—Italic type

Italo-Ethiopian War, 1895-1896
₍DT387.3₎
UF Abyssino-Italian War, 1895-1896
Ethiopian-Italian War, 1895-1896
Italy—History—War with Ethiopia, 1895-1896
BT Ethiopia—History—1889-1974
NT Adowa, Battle of, 1896
Italo-Ethiopian War, 1935-1936
₍DT387.8₎
UF Ethiopian-Italian War, 1935-1936
Italy—History—War with Ethiopia, 1935-1936
BT Ethiopia—History—1889-1974
— **Aerial operations**
— **Causes**
— **Diplomatic history**
— **Naval operations**
Italo-Turkish War, 1911-1912
USE Turco-Italian War, 1911-1912
Italy
— **Antiquities**
NT Acquarossa (Ancient city)
Alba Fucens (Ancient city)
Ardea (Ancient city)
Arpi (Ancient city)
Broglio di Trebisacce Site (Italy)
Brucato (City)
Caelia (Bari, Italy : Ancient city)
Cales (Ancient city)
Camarina (Ancient city)
Colosseum (Rome, Italy)
Cornus (Ancient city)
Cosa (Ancient city)
Crustumerium (Italy)
Cumae (City)
Ficana (Ancient city)
Fiorentino (City)
Fregellae (Ancient city)
Gabii (Ancient city)
Graviscae (Ancient city)
Herculaneum (Ancient city)
Laurentum (Ancient city)
Lavinium (Ancient city)
Locri Epizephyrii (Ancient city)
Lucus Feroniae (Italy : Ancient sanctuary)
Martanum (Ancient city)
Matauros (Ancient city)
Medma (Ancient city)
Megara Hyblaea (Ancient city)
Metapontum (Ancient city)
Motya (Ancient city)
Nora (Ancient city)
Norba (Puglia, Italy : Ancient city)
Nuraghi
Ostia (Ancient city)
Paestum (Ancient city)
Passo di Corvo Site (Italy)
Poggio Civitate Site (Italy)
Poggio Pinci Site (Italy)
Pompeii (Ancient city)
Porto Badisco Cave (Italy)
Pyrgi (Ancient city)
Sabucina (Ancient city)
San Giorgio di Angarano Site (Italy)
San Giovanni di Ruoti Site (Italy)
Satricum (Lazio, Italy : Ancient city)
Segesta (Ancient city)
Sorgenti della Nova Site (Italy)
Stabiae (Ancient city)
Sulcis (City)
Tabula Alimentaria Ligurum Baebianorum
Taurianum (Ancient city)
Tharros (Ancient city)
Vases, Apulian
Veii (Ancient city)
Villa di Settefinestre Site (Italy)

Villa of the Papyri (Herculaneum)
Voghenza Site (Italy)
Volsinii (Viterbo, Italy : Ancient city)
Vulci (Ancient city)
— **Antiquities, Roman**
NT Hadrian's Villa (Tivoli, Italy)
Laurentine Villa (Laurentum)
Trajan's Column (Rome, Italy)
Villa of the Volusii Saturnini (Lucus Feroniae, Italy)
— **Church history**
— — **476-1400**
— — **15th century**
— — **16th century**
— — **Modern period, 1559-**
— — **18th century**
— — **19th century**
— — **20th century**
₍BR876-876.3₎
— **Civilization**
NT America—Civilization—Italian influences
Architecture, Domestic—Italian influences
Argentina—Civilization—Italian influences
Art, Dutch—Italian influences
Art, French—Italian influences
Art, Hungarian—Italian influences
Art, Japanese—Italian influences
Art, Polish—Italian influences
Arts, Baroque—Italian influences
Arts, Polish—Italian influences
Arts, Yugoslav—Italian influences
Church architecture—Sweden—Italian influences
Decoration and ornament, Architectural—Italian influences
Drawing, Spanish—Italian influences
England—Civilization—Italian influences
English literature—Italian influences
English poetry—Italian influences
France—Civilization—Italian influences
Gardens, English—Italian influences
Germany—Civilization—Italian influences
Hungary—Civilization—Italian influences
Illumination of books and manuscripts, Czech—Italian influences
Illumination of books and manuscripts, Romanesque—Italian influences
Japan—Civilization—Italian influences
Maltese literature—Italian influences
Mural painting and decoration, Gothic—Italian influences
Painting, Dutch—Italian influences
Painting, Japanese—Italian influences
Scotland—Civilization—Italian influences
Sculpture, American—Italian influences
Sculpture, Gothic—Italian influences
Sculpture, Spanish—Italian influences
— — **476-1268**
₍DG443₎
— — **1268-1559**
₍DG445₎

— — 1559-1789
— — 18th century
    [DG447]
— — 1789-1900
— — 20th century
— — 1945-
    [DG451]
— — Aegean influences
    BT Civilization, Aegean
— — American influences
    BT United States—Civilization
— — Byzantine influences
    BT Byzantine Empire—Civilization
— — Celtic influences
    BT Celts
— — Egyptian influences
    BT Egypt—Civilization
— — Etruscan influences
    BT Etruscans
— — French influences
    BT France—Civilization
— — German influences
    BT Germany—Civilization
    RT Italy—Civilization—Germanic
       influences
— — Germanic influences
    UF Italy—Civilization—Gothic
       influences
    BT Civilization, Germanic
       Goths
    RT Italy—Civilization—German
       influences
— — Gothic influences
    USE Italy—Civilization—Germanic
       influences
— — Islamic influences
    BT Civilization, Islamic
— — Latin American influences
    BT Latin America—Civilization
— — Oriental influences
    BT Civilization, Oriental
— — Roman influences
    BT Rome—Civilization
— Commercial policy
— Description and travel
— — To 1500
— — 1501-1800
— — 1801-1860
— — 1861-1900
— — 1901-1944
— — 1945-1974
— — 1975-
— Diplomatic and consular service
— — United States
— Economic conditions
— — 1849-1870
— — 1870-1918
— — 1918-1945
— — 1945-
— — 1945-1976
— — 1976-
— Foreign relations
— — 476-1268
— — 1492-1559
— — 1559-1789
— — 1815-1870
— — 1849-1870
— — 1870-1915
— — 20th century
— — 1914-1945
— — 1922-1945
— — 1945-1976
— — 1976-
— History
    [DG]
— — To 476
    RT Rome—History—Germanic
       Invasions, 3d-6th centuries
    NT Aurunci
       Goths—Italy
       Samnites

Veneti (Italic people)
— — Austro-Italian War, 1866
    USE Austro-Italian War, 1866
— — 476-774
    [DG503-514.5]
    BT Goths—Italy
       Lombards—Italy
    RT Rome—History—Germanic
       Invasions, 3d-6th centuries
— — 476-1268
    NT Tagliacozzo, Battle of, 1268
       Verdun, Treaty of, 843
— — — Historiography
— — 476-1492
— — Gothic War, 535-555
    [DG509]
    UF Byzantine invasion, Italy, 535-
       555
       Gothic War, Italy, 535-555
    BT Byzantine Empire—History—
       Justinian I, 527-565
       Goths—Italy
— — Carlovingian rule, 774-887
    [DG515-517]
    BT Carlovingians
       France—History—To 987
— — Period of the Italian Kings, 887-962
— — Germanic rule, 962-1268
    [DG520-529]
    BT Holy Roman Empire—History—
       843-1273
       Naples (Kingdom)—History—
       1016-1268
— — 13th century
— — 1268-1492
— — 15th century
    NT Lodi, Peace of, 1454
— — — Pictorial works
— — 1492-1559
    NT Cérisoles, Battle of, 1544
       Novara, Battle of, 1513
       Pavia, Battle of, 1525
       Ravenna, Battle of, 1512
— — 1492-1870
— — Expedition of Charles VIII, 1494-1496
    UF Caroline War, 1494-1496
    NT Fornovo, Battle of, 1495
— — 16th century
— — 1559-1789
— — 17th century
— — 18th century
— — 1789-1815
    NT Civita Castellana, Italy, Battle
       of, 1798
       Naples (Kingdom)—History—
       War of 1815
— — 1789-1870
— — 19th century
— — 1815-1870
    NT Carbonari
— — Uprising, 1831
    [DG551]
    BT Austria—History—1815-1848
— — Revolution of 1848
    UF Revolution of 1848 in Italy
    BT Austria—History—Revolution,
       1848-1849
       Rome (Italy)—History—1798-
       1870
— — 1849-1870
    UF Italian question, 1849-1870
       Risorgimento (Italian history)
— — — Historiography
— — — Juvenile literature
— — — Pictorial works
— — War of 1859
    UF Austria—History—Italian
       Campaign, 1859
       France—History—Italian
       Campaign, 1859
    NT San Martino, Battle of, 1859

— — — Campaigns (Not Subd Geog)
    NT Magenta, Battle of, 1859
       Solferino, Battle of, 1859
— — War of 1860-1861
    NT Volturno, Battle of the, 1860-
       1861
— — — Campaigns (Not Subd Geog)
    NT Expedition of the Thousand,
       1860
— — 1870-1915
— — War with Ethiopia, 1895-1896
    USE Italo-Ethiopian War, 1895-
       1896
— — 20th century
— — War with Turkey, 1911-1912
    USE Turco-Italian War, 1911-1912
— — 1914-1945
— — — Caricatures and cartoons
— — — Historiography
— — 1915-1922
— — March on Rome, 1922
    [DG571.75]
    UF March on Rome, Italy, 1922
       Mussolini's March on Rome,
       Italy, 1922
— — 1922-1945
    NT World War, 1939-1945—
       Deportations from Italy
— — War with Ethiopia, 1935-1936
    USE Italo-Ethiopian War, 1935-
       1936
— — Grand Council, 1943
    [DG572]
    UF Grand Council, Italy, 1943
    BT Italy—History—German
       occupation, 1943-1945
       Verona Trial, 1943-1944
— — German occupation, 1943-1945
    [DG572]
    NT Italy—History—Grand Council,
       1943
       Monticchiello (Italy), Battle of,
       1943
— — Allied occupation, 1943-1947
— — — Pictorial works
— — — Posters
— — 1945-
— — 1945-1976
    [DG577.5-579]
— — 1976-
    [DG581-583]
— Intellectual life
— — To 1268
— — 1268-1559
— — 1559-1789
— — 1789-1900
— — 20th century
— Kings and rulers
    NT Medici, House of
       Savoy, House of
— Languages
    NT Friulian dialect
       Ladin dialect
— — Pre-Italic
    NT Etruscan language
— Literatures
    NT Friulian literature
       Ladin literature
— Neutrality
    NT Italy—Politics and government—
       1915-1922
— Nobility
    NT Bourbon, House of
— Politics and government
— — 476-1268
— — 1268-1559
— — 1559-1789
— — 18th century
— — 1789-1815
— — 1789-1900
— — 1815-1870

Italy
— **Politics and government**   *(Continued)*
— — **1849-1870**
— — **1870-**
— — **1870-1915**
— — **20th century**
— — **1914-1945**
— — **1915-1922**
       BT Italy—Neutrality
— — **1922-1945**
— — **1943-1947**
— — **1945-**
       NT Fascism—Italy—1945-
— — **1945-**
— — — **Posters**   *(Not Subd Geog)*
— — **1945-1976**
— — **1976-**
       ₍DG579.2₎
— **Social conditions**
— — **1268-1559**
— — **1849-1870**
— — **1870-1918**
— — **1918-1945**
— — **1945-1976**
— — **1976-**
— **Social life and customs**
— — **1914-1945**
— — **1945-**
— **Statistics, Vital**
— **Study and teaching**   *(May Subd Geog)*
       NT Italianists
Italy. Esercito
    BT Armies
— **Medals, badges, decorations, etc.**
       NT Medaglia d'Oro
Italy, Central
    UF Central Italy
Italy, Northern
    UF Northern Italy
Italy, Southern
    UF Southern Italy
    BT Naples (Kingdom)
— **Civilization**
— — **Greek influences**
       BT Greece—Civilization
— **Economic conditions**
— — **1945-**
— **History**
— — **535-1268**
       ₍DG827₎
— — **1848-1861**
       ₍DG828₎
— — **1861-1945**
— — **1945-**
— **Politics and government**
— — **1848-1861**
— — **1861-1922**
— — **1922-1945**
— **Social conditions**
— — **1945-**
Italy-Algeria Natural Gas Pipeline
    USE Algeria-Italy Natural Gas Pipeline
Italy in art
Itami family   *(Not Subd Geog)*
Itasca, Lake (Minn.)
    UF Lake Itasca (Minn.)
    BT Lakes—Minnesota
Itatiaia National Park (Brazil)
    UF Parque Itatiáia (Brazil)
       Parque Nacional de Itatiáia (Brazil)
       Parque Nacional do Itatiáia (Brazil)
    BT National parks and reserves—Brazil
       Parks—Brazil
Itawes (Philippine people)
    USE Itawis (Philippine people)
Itawes language
    USE Itawis language
Itawi language
    USE Itawis language
Itawis (Philippine people)
    ₍DS666.I77₎

    UF Itawes (Philippine people)
    BT Ethnology—Philippines
Itawis language
    ₍PL5815₎
    UF Itawes language
       Itawi language
    BT Philippine languages
Itbayat language
    USE Batan language
Itch
    USE Pruritus
Itch (Disease)
    USE Scabies
Itchen Lake (N.W.T.)
    BT Lakes—Northwest Territories
Itching
    USE Pruritus
Ite Indians
    USE Itenez Indians
Itelmes language
    USE Kamchadal language
Item response theory
    BT Educational tests and measurements
       Psychological tests
       Psychometrics
Item veto   *(May Subd Geog)*
    UF Line-item veto
       Veto, Item
    BT Veto
Itenes Indians
    USE Itenez Indians
Itenez Indians
    UF Guniam Indians
       Ite Indians
       Itenes Indians
       Moré Indians
    BT Indians of South America
Iterated integrals
    USE Integrals, Multiple
Iteration (Mathematics)
    USE Iterative methods (Mathematics)
Iterative circuit computers
    USE Cellular automata
Iterative methods (Mathematics)
    ₍QA297.8₎
    UF Iteration (Mathematics)
    BT Numerical analysis
    NT Conjugate gradient methods
Iteso
    USE Teso tribe
Iteso language
    USE Teso language
Itezhi-Tezhi Dam (Zambia)
    (Not Subd Geog)
    UF Itezhitezhi Dam (Zambia)
    BT Dams—Zambia
Itezhitezhi Dam (Zambia)
    USE Itezhi-Tezhi Dam (Zambia)
Ith Ridge (Germany)
    UF Der Ith (Germany)
    BT Mountains—Germany (West)
Ithaca Island (Greece)
    UF Ithak-e Island (Greece)
       Itháki Island (Greece)
       Nísos Itháki (Greece)
    BT Ionian Islands (Greece)
       Islands—Greece
Ithaginis
    USE Blood pheasants
Ithak-e Island (Greece)
    USE Ithaca Island (Greece)
Itháki Island (Greece)
    USE Ithaca Island (Greece)
Ithe-wa-Gathoni Farm (Kenya)
    BT Farms—Kenya
Itinerancy (Church polity)
    ₍BV664₎
    May be subdivided by denomination.
    UF Circuit riding
    NT Circuit riders
— **Methodist Church**

    ₍BX8345₎
    BT Methodism
Itinerant clergy
    USE Circuit riders
Itinerant-electron magnetism
    USE Magnetism, Band theory of
Itio language
    USE Teke language
Itneg language
    USE Tinggian language
Itō family   *(Not Subd Geog)*
Itō-ke Jūtaku (Kawasaki-shi, Japan)
    BT Dwellings—Japan
Itonama language
    ₍PM6241₎
    BT Indians of South America—Languages
Itonididae
    USE Gall midges
ITPA
    USE Illinois test of psycholinguistic abilities
ITS Project
    UF Informatics Teaching System Project
    BT Electronic data processing—Study and
       teaching (Higher)—Europe
Itsekiri (African people)
    USE Jekri (African people)
Itsuki no miko
    USE Saiō
Itsukinomiko
    USE Saiō
Itsukushima, Battle of, 1555
    BT Japan—History—Period of civil wars,
       1480-1603
Ittōen
    ₍BP605.I8₎
— **Missions**
Ittu dialect
    USE Qottu dialect
Itucale language
    USE Urarina language
Iturbide Palace (Mexico City, Mexico)
    USE Palacio de Iturbide (Mexico City,
       Mexico)
Ituri forest pygmies
    USE Bambute
Ituzaingó, Battle of, 1827
    ₍F2726₎
    BT Argentine-Brazilian War, 1825-1828
Itz River (Germany)
    BT Rivers—Germany (West)
Itza Indians
IUD (Contraceptive)
    USE Intrauterine contraceptives
IUE (Artificial satellite)
    UF International Ultraviolet Explorer
       (Artificial satellite)
    BT Artificial satellites
       Explorer (Artificial satellite)
       Scientific satellites
IUgo-Osetinskaia avtonomnaia oblast'
(Georgian S.S.R.)
— **History**
— — **Revolution of 1905**
       ₍DK264.2.I₎
— — **Revolution, 1917-1921**
IUkagir
    USE Yukaghir
Iunu (Ancient city)
    USE Heliopolis (Ancient city)
Iuridae
    ₍QL458.72.I95₎
    BT Scorpions
    NT Hadrurus
Ius . . .
    USE *subject headings beginning with the*
       word Jus

ĪUzhnyĭ Bug River (Ukraine)
   (Not Subd Geog)
   UF Boh River (Ukraine)
       Bug River (Ukraine)
       Buh River (Ukraine)
       Hypanis River (Ukraine)
       Pivdennyĭ Buh River (Ukraine)
       Southern Bug River (Ukraine)
       Yuzhnyy Bug River (Ukraine)
   BT Rivers—Ukraine
IV anesthesia
   USE Intravenous anesthesia
IV injections
   USE Injections, Intravenous
IV therapy
   USE Intravenous therapy
Ivaiojoki (Finland)
   USE Ivalo River (Finland)
Ivalo River (Finland)
   UF Ivaiojoki (Finland)
       Ivalojoki (Finland)
   BT Rivers—Finland
Ivalojoki (Finland)
   USE Ivalo River (Finland)
Ivankovac (Serbia), Battle of, 1805
   ₍DR2015.7₎
   BT Serbia—History—Insurrection, 1804-
       1813—Campaigns
Ivan′kovo Reservoir (R.S.F.S.R.)
   UF Ivan′kovskoe vodokhranilishche
       (R.S.F.S.R.)
       Ivan′kovskoye vodokhranilishche
       (R.S.F.S.R.)
       Moscow Sea (R.S.F.S.R.)
       Moskovskoe more (R.S.F.S.R.)
       Moskovskoye more (R.S.F.S.R.)
       Velikoe Reservoir (R.S.F.S.R.)
       Velikoye Reservoir (R.S.F.S.R.)
       Volga Reservoir (R.S.F.S.R.)
       Volzhskoe Reservoir (R.S.F.S.R.)
       Volzhskoye Reservoir (R.S.F.S.R.)
   BT Reservoirs—Russian S.F.S.R.
Ivan′kovskoe vodokhranilishche (R.S.F.S.R.)
   USE Ivan′kovo Reservoir (R.S.F.S.R.)
Ivan′kovskoye vodokhranilishche (R.S.F.S.R.)
   USE Ivan′kovo Reservoir (R.S.F.S.R.)
Ivanov reaction
   BT Chemical reactions
Ivaparé Indians
   USE Héta Indians
Ivatan language
   USE Batan language
Ivermectin
   BT Heterocyclic compounds
       Veterinary drugs
       Veterinary parasitology
Iverskaîa Svîataîa i Chudotvornaîa Bogomater′
   (Icon)
   UF Ikona Svîatoĭ i Chudotvornoĭ Iverskoĭ
       Bogomateri
   BT Icons
       Mary, Blessed Virgin, Saint—Art
Ives family *(Not Subd Geog)*
   UF Ivey family
       Ivie family
       Ivy family
   RT Eaves family
Ivey family
   USE Ives family
IVF
   USE Fertilization in vitro
Ivie family
   USE Ives family
Ivies
   USE Ivy
Ivisaartoq (Greenland)
   UF Ivisartok (Greenland)
       Ivisârtoq (Greenland)
Ivisartok (Greenland)
   USE Ivisaartoq (Greenland)

Ivisârtoq (Greenland)
   USE Ivisaartoq (Greenland)
Iviza Island (Spain)
   USE Ibiza Island (Spain)
Ivories *(May Subd Geog)*
   ₍NK5800-NK5998 (Art industries)₎
   ₍TS1050 (Manufacture)₎
   UF Statuettes
   RT Ivory carving
   NT Netsukes
  — Private collections
     ₍NK5815₎
  — England
     NT Bury Saint Edmunds Cross
  — Italy
     NT Avori salernitani
  — Philippines
  —— Spanish influences
       BT Spain—Civilization
Ivories, American, ₍Greek, etc.₎
   (May Subd Geog)
Ivories, Ancient *(May Subd Geog)*
   UF Ancient ivories
Ivories, Assyro-Babylonian
   UF Nimrud ivories
Ivories, Baroque *(May Subd Geog)*
   UF Baroque ivories
Ivories, Byzantine *(May Subd Geog)*
   UF Byzantine ivories
Ivories, Carlovingian *(May Subd Geog)*
   UF Carlovingian ivories
Ivories, Gothic *(May Subd Geog)*
   UF Gothic ivories
Ivories, Islamic *(May Subd Geog)*
   UF Islamic ivories
       Ivories, Muslim
       Muslim ivories
Ivories, Medieval *(May Subd Geog)*
  — Italy
     NT Avori salernitani
Ivories, Muslim
   USE Ivories, Islamic
Ivories, Ottonian *(May Subd Geog)*
   UF Ottonian ivories
Ivories, Phoenician *(May Subd Geog)*
   UF Phoenician ivories
Ivories, Primitive *(May Subd Geog)*
   UF Primitive ivories
Ivories, Renaissance *(May Subd Geog)*
   UF Renaissance ivories
Ivories, Romanesque *(May Subd Geog)*
   UF Romanesque ivories
  — England
     NT Bury Saint Edmunds Cross
Ivory *(May Subd Geog)*
  — Staining
     USE Stains and staining
Ivory bookbindings
   USE Bookbinding—Ivory bindings
Ivory carving
   ₍NK5800-5998₎
   BT Carving (Decorative arts)
       Sculpture
   RT Ivories
   NT Scrimshaws
       Sculpture, Chryselephantine
Ivory Coast
  — Civilization
  —— Occidental influences
       BT Civilization, Occidental
  — Description and travel
  —— 1981-
  — Economic conditions
  —— To 1960
  —— 1960-
  — History
     NT Denkyira (Kingdom)
  — Languages
     NT Abidji language
       Abure language
       Adyukru language

       Attie language
       Bete language
       Dan language
       Dida dialect
       Gagu language
       Godye dialect
       Kru languages
       Kulango language
       Kweni language
       Mau dialect (Ivory Coast)
       Mo language (Ghana and Ivory
         Coast)
       Muana language
       Nyabwa language
       Southern Mande languages
       Tagbana language
       Tepo language
       Tura language
       Vige language
       Wobe language
  — Politics and government
  —— To 1960
  —— 1960-
  — Social conditions
  —— To 1960
  —— 1960-
Ivory Coast fiction (French)
   (May Subd Geog)
   UF French fiction—Ivory Coast authors
Ivory Coast literature (French)
   (May Subd Geog)
   ₍PQ3988.5.I₎
   UF French literature—Ivory Coast authors
Ivory Coast proverbs
   USE Proverbs, Ivory Coast
Ivory Coast terminalia
   USE Terminalia ivorensis
Ivory industry *(May Subd Geog)*
   ₍HD9429.I86-HD9429.I864₎
Ivory-nut
   ₍SB317.I (Vegetable ivory)₎
   UF Vegetable ivory
Ivory nut palms
   USE Metroxylon
Ivory palms
   USE Metroxylon
Ivorynutpalms
   USE Metroxylon
'Ivri (The Hebrew word)
   UF Ha 'Ivri (The Hebrew word)
   BT Hebrew language—Etymology
       Jews—Name
Ivy
   ₍SB413.I84₎
   UF Ivies
Ivy family
   USE Ives family
Ivy Hill Cemetery (Alexandria, Va.)
   BT Cemeteries—Virginia
Iwai no Ran, Japan, 527-528
   USE Japan—History—Iwai Rebellion, 527-
       528
Iwai Rebellion, Japan, 527-528
   USE Japan—History—Iwai Rebellion, 527-
       528
Iwaidja language
   USE Iwaidji language
Iwaidji language
   ₍PL7101.I93₎
   UF Eaewandja language
       Eiwaja language
       Iwaidja language
       Jiwadja language
       Limbakaraja language
       Unalla language
       Uwadja language
       Yiwadja language
   BT Australia—Languages
       Australian languages
Iwaki Kaidō (Japan) *(Not Subd Geog)*
   BT Roads—Japan

Iwaki Mountain (Japan)
  UF Iwaki-san (Japan)
      Iwaki-yama (Japan)
      Iwakisan (Japan)
      Iwakiyama (Japan)
  BT Mountains—Japan
Iwaki-san (Japan)
  USE Iwaki Mountain (Japan)
Iwaki-yama (Japan)
  USE Iwaki Mountain (Japan)
Iwakisan (Japan)
  USE Iwaki Mountain (Japan)
Iwakiyama (Japan)
  USE Iwaki Mountain (Japan)
Iwam language
  BT Papuan languages
Iwami Unomarujō (Yunotsu-machi, Japan)
  USE Unomarujō (Yunotsu-machi, Japan)
Iwamuroike Kofun (Tenri-shi, Japan)
  USE Iwamuroike Site (Tenri-shi, Japan)
Iwamuroike Site (Tenri-shi, Japan)
  UF Iwamuroike Kofun (Tenri-shi, Japan)
  BT Japan—Antiquities
Iwasaki family *(Not Subd Geog)*
Iwayoshi Iseki (Miyakonojō-shi, Japan)
  USE Iwayoshi Site (Miyakonojō-shi, Japan)
Iwayoshi Site (Miyakonojō-shi, Japan)
  (Not Subd Geog)
  UF Iwayoshi Iseki (Miyakonojō-shi, Japan)
  BT Japan—Antiquities
Iwo Jima, Battle of, 1945
  [D767.99.I9]
  BT World War, 1939-1945—Campaigns—
      Japan
Iwo Retto (Japan)
  USE Volcano Islands (Japan)
Ixcateco language
  [PM3876]
  BT Indians of Mexico—Languages
      Mixtec language
      Popolocan languages
Ixil Indians
  BT Indians of Central America
      Mayas
Ixil language
  [PM3881]
  BT Indians of Central America—
      Languages
      Mayan languages
Ixil orations
  USE Speeches, addresses, etc., Ixil
Ixil poetry
  [PM3881.Z77]
Ixil speeches
  USE Speeches, addresses, etc., Ixil
Ixion (Greek mythology)
  BT Mythology, Greek
Ixodes
  [QL458.2.I9]
  BT Ixodidae
  NT Ixodes capromydis
      Ixodes scapularis
      Ixodes sculptus
Ixodes capromydis
  [QL458.2.I9]
  BT Ixodes
Ixodes ricinus
  USE Castor bean tick
Ixodes scapularis
  [QL458.2.I9]
  BT Ixodes
Ixodes sculptus
  [QL458.2.I9]
  BT Ixodes
Ixodida
  USE Ticks
Ixodidae
  [QL458.2.I9]
  UF Hard ticks
      Wood ticks

  BT Mites
      Ticks
  NT Amblyomma
      Aponomma
      Boophilus
      Dermacentor
      Haemaphysalis
      Hyalomma
      Ixodes
      Rhipicephalus
Ixodides
  USE Ticks
Ixodoidea
  USE Ticks
Ixtaccihuatl (Mexico)
  USE Iztaccihuatl (Mexico)
Ixtacihuatl (Mexico)
  USE Iztaccihuatl (Mexico)
Ixtlahuaca Valley (Mexico)
  UF Valle de Ixtlahuaca (Mexico)
  BT Valleys—Mexico
Iyagbe
  USE Ayo (Game)
iYans language
  USE Yanzi language
iYanzi language
  USE Yanzi language
Iyasakataira Iseki (Rokkasho-mura, Japan)
  USE Iyasakataira Site (Rokkasho-mura,
      Japan)
Iyasakataira Site (Rokkasho-mura, Japan)
  (Not Subd Geog)
  UF Iyasakataira Iseki (Rokkasho-mura,
      Japan)
  BT Japan—Antiquities
Iyawadi River (Burma)
  USE Irrawaddy River (Burma)
Iyekhee language
  USE Etsako language
Iyo language
  USE Ijo language
Izafat
  USE *subdivision* Noun *under names of*
      languages and groups of languages
Izapa Site (Mexico) *(Not Subd Geog)*
  BT Mexico—Antiquities
Izen family
  USE Isom family
Izena Island (Japan)
  UF Ijina-shima (Japan)
      Izena-jima (Japan)
      Izena-shima (Japan)
  BT Islands—Japan
      Ryukyu Islands
Izena-jima (Japan)
  USE Izena Island (Japan)
Izena-shima (Japan)
  USE Izena Island (Japan)
Izerskie Mountains (Poland and
Czechoslovakia)
  UF Góry Izerskie (Poland and
      Czechoslovakia)
      Isergebirge (Poland and
      Czechoslovakia)
      Jizera Mountains (Poland and
      Czechoslovakia)
      Jizerské hory (Poland and
      Czechoslovakia)
  BT Mountains—Czechoslovakia
      Mountains—Poland
Izhora (R.S.F.S.R.)
  USE Ingria (R.S.F.S.R.)
Izhorskiĭ language
  USE Ingrian language
Izhortsy
  USE Ingrians
Izi language
  UF Izzi language
  BT Igbo language
      Kwa languages

İznik pottery
  [NK4340.I9]
  UF Pottery, İznik
  BT Pottery, Turkish
Izon family
  USE Isom family
Iztaccihuatl (Mexico)
  UF Ixtaccihuatl (Mexico)
      Ixtacihuatl (Mexico)
      Sleeping Woman (Mexico)
  BT Mountains—Mexico
      Volcanoes—Mexico
Izu-hantō (Japan)
  USE Izu Peninsula (Japan)
Izu Islands (Japan)
  UF Izu shichitō (Japan)
      Seven Islands of Izu (Japan)
  BT Islands—Japan
  NT Aoga Island (Japan)
      Hachijō Island (Japan)
      Kōzu Island (Japan)
      Nii Island (Japan)
Izu-numa (Japan)
  USE Izu Pond (Japan)
Izu Peninsula (Japan)
  UF Izu-hantō (Japan)
  BT Peninsulas—Japan
Izu Pond (Japan)
  UF Izu-numa (Japan)
  BT Ponds—Japan
Izu shichitō (Japan)
  USE Izu Islands (Japan)
Izumi Nada (Japan)
  USE Osaka Bay (Japan)
Izumiya family *(Not Subd Geog)*
Izumo (Japan : Region)
  USE Izumo Region (Japan)
Izumo no Kuni (Japan)
  USE Izumo Region (Japan)
Izumo pottery *(May Subd Geog)*
  [NK4168.S]
  UF Pottery, Izumo
  BT Pottery, Japanese
Izumo Region (Japan) *(Not Subd Geog)*
  UF Idzumo (Japan)
      Izumo (Japan : Region)
      Izumo no Kuni (Japan)
Izumo Taisha (Sect)
  UF Taishakyo
  BT Shinto sects
Izzi language
  USE Izi language
J1N1-S (Night fighter plane)
  USE Irving (Night fighter plane)
J2M (Fighter plane)
  USE Raiden (Fighter plane)
J-cars
  USE General Motors J-cars
J document (Biblical criticism)
  [BS1181.4]
  UF Jahwist document
      Yahwist document
  BT Bible. O.T.—Criticism, interpretation,
      etc.
J.G.L. Collection (Australia)
  BT Painting—Private collections—
      Australia
J. Paul Getty Museum Herb Garden (Malibu,
Calif.)
  UF Getty Museum Herb Garden (Malibu,
      Calif.)
  BT Herb gardens—California
Ja (The German word)
  BT German language—Etymology
Jaawambe (African people)
  BT Ethnology—Africa, French-speaking
      West
      Fulahs
Jabal al-Akhḍar (Libya)
  USE Akhḍar Mountains (Libya)

Jabal 'Āmil (Lebanon)
  USE 'Āmil Mountains (Lebanon)
Jabal 'Atāqah (Egypt)
  USE Ataqa Mountains (Egypt)
Jabal Mūsā (Egypt)
  USE Sinai, Mount (Egypt)
Jabal Nafusah language
  USE Jebel Nefusa language
Jabal Ṣa'id (Saudi Arabia)
  USE Ṣa'id Mountain (Saudi Arabia)
Jabal Sayid (Saudi Arabia)
  USE Ṣa'id Mountain (Saudi Arabia)
Jabāli
Jabalinas
  USE Peccaries
Jabêm language
  USE Jabim language
Jabim language
  ₋PL6251₎
  UF Jabêm language
    Yabim language
  BT Melanesian languages
Jābir family *(Not Subd Geog)*
Jablonczay family *(Not Subd Geog)*
Jabo (African people)
  ₋DT630.5.J3₎
Jabo language
  ₋PL8287₎
  UF Gweabo language
  BT Kru languages
    Liberia—Languages
Jaborandi
  ₋RM666.J15 (Therapeutics)₎
  ₋RS165.J2 (Pharmacy)₎
Jabu (Australian people)
  USE Pitjantjatjara (Australian people)
Jaca (Spain)
  — History
Jaca (African people)
  USE Bayaka (African people)
Jacal (Mexico)
  UF El Jacal (Mexico)
  BT Ejidos—Mexico
Jacalteca Indians
  ₋F1221.J3 (Mexico)₎
  ₋F1465.2.J3 (Guatemala)₎
  BT Indians of Central America
    Mayas
Jacalteca language
  ₋PM3889₎
  BT Indians of Central America—
    Languages
    Mayan languages
Jacamars
  ₋QL696.P54₎
  UF Galbulidae
  BT Piciformes
Jacaranda wax scale
  UF Ceroplastes helichrysi sinoiae
    Ceroplastes sinoiae
    Wax scale, Jacaranda
Jacby family
  USE Jacoby family
Jack (Fighter plane)
  USE Raiden (Fighter plane)
Jack Cade's Rebellion
  USE Cade's Rebellion, 1450
Jack family *(Not Subd Geog)*
  UF Jacks family
    Jakes family
  RT Jackson family
    Jaques family
Jack-in-the-box
  BT Toys
Jack-Jack (African people)
  USE Alagya (African people)
Jack-knife dive
  USE Diving—Jackknife dive
Jack mackerel
  USE Trachurus symmetricus

Jack mackerel, Australian
  USE Trachurus declivis
Jack-o'-lantern (Will-o'-the-wisp)
  USE Will-o'-the-wisp
Jack-o-lanterns
  BT Halloween
    Pumpkin
Jack-pine
  ₋SD397.P575₎
  UF Gray pine
    Pinus banksiana
  — **Diseases and pests** *(May Subd Geog)*
    NT Jack-pine budworm
Jack pine (Painting)
  USE Thomson, Tom, 1877-1917. Jack
    pine
Jack-pine budworm
  UF Budworm, Jack-pine
    Choristoneura pinus
  BT Choristoneura
    Jack-pine—Diseases and pests
Jack-pine warbler
  USE Kirtland's warbler
Jack-rabbits
  USE Jackrabbits
Jack Russell terrier
  ₋SF429.J27₎
  UF Parson Jack Russell terrier
    Russell terrier
  BT Terriers
Jack Smith Lake (Vic.) *(Not Subd Geog)*
  BT Lakes—Australia
Jackal buzzard
  USE Buteo rufofuscus
Jackals
  ₋QL737.C2₎
  NT Black-backed jackal
    Canis aureus
Jackass penguin
  ₋QL696.S5₎
  UF Blackfooted penguin
    Cape penguin
    Spheniscus demersus
  BT Penguins
Jackdaw
Jackeroos *(May Subd Geog)*
  BT Apprentices—Australia
    Herders—Australia
    Ranches—Australia—Employees
    Sheep ranches—Australia—Employees
Jackets, Leather
  USE Leather jackets
Jackets, Record
  USE Sound recordings—Album covers
Jackets (Clothing)
  USE Coats
Jackets for bottles, vases, etc.
  ₋TT879.J3₎
  BT Containers
    Handicraft
Jackfork Creek (Okla.)
  BT Rivers—Oklahoma
  NT Clayton Lake (Okla.)
Jackknife dive
  USE Diving—Jackknife dive
Jackknives
  USE Pocketknives
Jackman family *(Not Subd Geog)*
  UF Jackmon family
Jackmon family
  USE Jackman family
Jackpot (Dog)
  BT Dogs
Jackrabbits
  ₋QL737.L32₎
  UF Jack-rabbits
  NT Black-tailed jackrabbit
Jackrabbits as pets
  ₋SF455.J33₎
Jacks
  USE Lifting-jacks

Jacks, Hydraulic
  USE Hydraulic jacks
Jacks (Fishes)
  USE Carangidae
Jacks (Game)
Jacks family
  USE Jack family
Jacks Fork (Mo.)
  BT Rivers—Missouri
  NT Ozark National Scenic Riverways
    (Mo.)
Jackson, Harry, 1924-   Sacagawea
  UF Sacagawea (Statue)
Jackson (Miss.)
  — History
  — — Civil War, 1861-1865
    NT Jackson (Miss.), Battle of, 1863
Jackson (Miss.), Battle of, 1863
  ₋E475.29₎
  BT Jackson (Miss.)—History—Civil War,
    1861-1865
    United States—History—Civil War,
    1861-1865—Campaigns
Jackson-Dickinson Duel
  UF Dickinson-Jackson Duel
Jackson family *(Not Subd Geog)*
  UF Jackston family
    Jacson family
    Jaxon family
    Jaxson family
  RT Jack family
Jackson Hole (Wyo.)
  BT Grand Teton National Park (Wyo.)
    Valleys—Wyoming
Jackson-Hope Medal
  BT Rewards (Prizes, etc.)—Virginia
Jackson Purchase (Ky.) *(Not Subd Geog)*
  Here are entered works on that area of Western
  Kentucky ceded by the Chickasaw Indians in 1818.
Jackson Square (Weymouth, Mass.)
  BT Plazas—Massachusetts
Jackson structured programming
  UF JSP technique
    Structured programming, Jackson
  BT Structured programming
Jackson system development method
  UF JSD method
  BT Electronic data processing—Structured
    techniques
    System design
Jackson Whites
  USE Ramapo Mountain people
Jacksonville (Fla.).   Maxville
  USE Maxville (Jacksonville, Fla.)
Jacksonville (Fla.).   Mayport
  USE Mayport (Jacksonville, Fla.)
Jackston family
  USE Jackson family
Jackstraws (Game)
  ₋GV1511.J3₎
Jacob altar
  USE Jakobialtar
Jacob family
  USE Jacobs family
Jacob Wolf House (Norfork, Ark.)
  UF Wolf House (Norfork, Ark.)
  BT Dwellings—Arkansas
Jacobean architecture
  USE Architecture, Jacobean
Jacobean art
  USE Art, Jacobean
Jacobean decoration and ornament
  USE Decoration and ornament, Jacobean
Jacobi family
  USE Jacoby family
Jacobi forms
  UF Forms, Jacobi
  BT Forms, Modular
    Functions, Elliptic
    Series, Theta

1931

Jacobi-Hamilton equations
  USE Hamilton-Jacobi equations
Jacobi method
  BT Eigenvalues
    Matrices
Jacobi polynomials
  UF Polynomials, Jacobi
  BT Orthogonal polynomials
Jacobi series
  [QA404.5]
  UF Series, Jacobi
  BT Harmonic analysis
    Series
Jacobi sums
  UF Sums, Jacobi
  BT Fields, Algebraic
    Ideals (Algebra)
    Series
Jacobi varieties
  [QA333]
  UF Varieties, Jacobi
  BT Riemann surfaces
Jacobian determinants
  USE Jacobians
Jacobians
  UF Functional determinants
    Jacobian determinants
  BT Curves, Algebraic
    Determinants
    Functions of real variables
    Functions of several complex variables
    Geometry, Algebraic
    Matrices
  NT Torelli theorem
Jacobie family
  USE Jacoby family
Jacobin Conspiracy, Naples, 1794
  USE Naples (Kingdom)—History—Jacobin
    Conspiracy, 1794
Jacobins (Dominicans)
  USE Dominicans
Jacobins *(May Subd Geog)*
  [DC178]
  UF Breton Club
  BT France—History—Revolution, 1789-
    1799
    France—History—Revolution, 1789-
    1799—Clubs
  NT Naples (Kingdom)—History—Jacobin
    Conspiracy, 1794
Jacobite ballads and songs
  USE Jacobites—Poetry
Jacobite Expedition, 1707
  [DA814.2]
Jacobite Rebellion, 1715
  [DA814.3]
  UF Scotland—History—Jacobite Rebellion,
    1715
  — Campaigns
    NT Sheriffmuir, Battle of, 1715
Jacobite Rebellion, 1719
  [DA814.4]
  UF Scotland—History—Jacobite Rebellion,
    1719
Jacobite Rebellion, 1745-1746
  [DA814.5]
  UF Scotland—History—Jacobite Rebellion,
    1745-1746
  — Campaigns
    NT Culloden, Battle of, 1746
Jacobites
  [DA813-814]
  NT Lancashire Plot, 1689-1694
    Nonjurors
  — Poetry
    [PR1195.H5 (English poetry)]
    [PR8661.J3 (Scottish poetry)]
    UF Jacobite ballads and songs
Jacobites (Syrian Christians)
  (May Subd Geog)
  [DS59.J25]

  UF Syrian Orthodox
  BT Christian sects—Middle East
    Monophysites
    Syriac Christians
  NT Catholic Church—Antiochene rite
    St. Thomas Christians
Jacobs family *(Not Subd Geog)*
  UF Jacob family
    Jacobsen family
    Jacobson family
    Jacobsson family
  RT Jacoby family
Jacobsen family
  USE Jacobs family
Jacobsen reaction
  UF Jacobsen rearrangement
  BT Chemical reactions
Jacobsen rearrangement
  USE Jacobsen reaction
Jacobson family
  USE Jacobs family
Jacobson radical
  UF Jacobson's radical
    Radical, Jacobson
  BT Radical theory
Jacobson's organ
  [QL947]
  BT Nose
Jacobson's radical
  USE Jacobson radical
Jacobsson family
  USE Jacobs family
Jacoby family
  UF Jacby family
    Jacobi family
    Jacobie family
    Jcoby family
  RT Jacobs family
Jacquard knitting machines
  [TT685]
  BT Knitting-machines
Jacquard weaving
  [TS1500]
  BT Looms
    Weaving
Jacquemarts
  USE Jaquemarts
Jacquerie, 1358
  [DC99.3]
  NT Peasantry—France
Jacques Cartier Park (Québec)
  USE Parc de la Jacques-Cartier (Québec)
Jacques family
  USE Jaques family
Jacquess family
  USE Jaques family
Jacqueth family
  USE Jaquith family
Jacquett family
  USE Jaquith family
Jacson family
  USE Jackson family
Jactitation of title *(May Subd Geog)*
  BT Land titles
    Possessory actions
Jacuhype River (Brazil)
  USE Jacuípe River (Brazil)
Jacuípe River (Brazil)
  UF Jacuhype River (Brazil)
    Rio Jacuhype (Brazil)
    Rio Jacuípe (Brazil)
  BT Rivers—Brazil
Jacumba/In-ko-pah Wilderness (Calif.)
  (Not Subd Geog)
  UF In-ko-pah/Jacumba Wilderness (Calif.)
    Jacumba/In-ko-pah Wilderness Study
    Area (Calif.)
  BT National parks and reserves—
    California
    Wilderness areas—California

Jacumba/In-ko-pah Wilderness Study Area
    (Calif.)
  USE Jacumba/In-ko-pah Wilderness (Calif.)
Jaćwież *(May Subd Geog)*
  [DK4121.5.J32]
  UF Getwezi
    Gotwezi
    Jatvingi
    Sudovians
    Yadzvings
    Yatvyags
    Yotvingians
  BT Balts (Indo-European people)
    Ethnology—Lithuania
    Ethnology—Poland
Jacwith family
  USE Jaquith family
Jade *(May Subd Geog)*
  [NK5750-NK5750.2 (Decorative arts)]
  [QE394.J3 (Mineralogy)]
  UF Nephrite
    Statuettes
Jade art objects *(May Subd Geog)*
  UF Art objects, Jade
    Jades
  NT Jade carvers
  — Expertising
Jade Bay (Germany) *(Not Subd Geog)*
  UF Jadebusen (Germany)
  BT Bays—Germany (West)
Jade carvers *(May Subd Geog)*
  BT Jade art objects
Jadebusen (Germany)
  USE Jade Bay (Germany)
Jadeite (Petrology) *(May Subd Geog)*
  [QE475.J27]
  BT Rocks, Metamorphic
Jades
  USE Jade art objects
Jadransko More
  USE Adriatic Sea
Jaeger, Parasitic
  USE Stercorarius parasiticus
Jaegers (Birds)
  USE Stercorarius
Jæren (Norway)
Jærkysten, Norway
Jaffa Riot, 1921
  [DS126]
Jafijufa language
  USE Yabiyufa language
Jagane language
  USE Yahgan language
Jagannath (Hindu deity)
  USE Jagannātha (Hindu deity)
Jagannātha (Hindu deity) *(May Subd Geog)*
  [BL1225.J3]
  UF Jagannath (Hindu deity)
    Juggernaut (Hindu deity)
  BT Gods, Hindu
    Krishna (Hindu deity)
Jagataic language
  USE Chagatai language
Jagdpanther (Tank destroyer)
  [UG446.5]
  UF Jagdpanzer V (Tank destroyer)
  BT Tank destroyers
Jagdpanzer IV (Tank destroyer)
  [UG446.5]
  UF Panzerjäger 39 (Tank destroyer)
  BT Tank destroyers
Jagdpanzer V (Tank destroyer)
  USE Jagdpanther (Tank destroyer)
Jagellon dynasty *(Not Subd Geog)*
  UF Yagello dynasty
  RT Poland—History—Jagellons, 1386-
    1572
Jager family *(Not Subd Geog)*
  UF Jaggar family
    Jagger family
  RT Gager family

Jagga (African people)
    USE Chaga (African people)
Jagga language
    USE Chaga language
Jaggar family
    USE Jager family
Jagger family
    USE Jager family
Jaggers (Tattoo artists)
    USE Tattoo artists
Jagli family
    USE Yeakley family
Jaguallapai language
    USE Hualapai language
Jaguar (Jet attack plane)
    [UG1242.A]
    BT Jet planes, Military
Jaguar automobile
    [TL215.J]
Jaguar hunting (May Subd Geog)
    [SK305.J3]
    BT Big game hunting
Jaguars
    [QL737.C23]
    UF Leo onca
        Panthera onca
    BT Panthera
Jaguars, Fossil
Jah Hut (Malaysian people)
    BT Ethnology—Malaysia
        Senoi (Malaysian people)
Jahad
    USE Jihad
Jahn-Teller effect
    UF Teller-Jahn effect
    BT Coupled mode theory
        Crystal field theory
        Energy levels (Quantum mechanics)
Jahnson family
    USE Johnson family
Jahre prize
    UF Anders Jahre prize
Jahwist document
    USE J document (Biblical criticism)
Jai alai
    USE Pelota (Game)
Jai alai players
    USE Pelota players
Jaihun River
    USE Amu Darya
Jail Accounting Microcomputer System
    USE JAMS (Computer system)
Jail-fever
    USE Typhus fever
Jailjadshik Mountains (Bulgaria)
    USE Eledzhik Mountains (Bulgaria)
Jails (May Subd Geog)
    UF Gaols
    BT Correctional institutions
        Prisons
Jaina almsgiving
    USE Jaina giving
Jaina architecture
    USE Architecture, Jaina
Jaina art
    USE Art, Jaina
Jaina civilization
    USE Civilization, Jaina
Jaina converts
    UF Converts, Jaina
        Converts to Jainism
Jaina cosmology
    USE Cosmology, Jaina
Jaina cults (May Subd Geog)
    BT Cults
Jaina epistomology
    USE Knowledge, Theory of (Jainism)
Jaina ethics
    [BJ1290]
    UF Ethics, Jaina
    NT Ahiṃsā

Jaina fasts and feasts
    USE Fasts and feasts—Jainism
Jaina giving
    [BL1375.G58]
    UF Almsgiving, Jaina
        Dāna (Jainism)
        Giving, Jaina
        Jaina almsgiving
    BT Religious life (Jainism)
Jaina gods
    USE Gods, Jaina
Jaina hymns
    [BL1377.3]
    UF Hymns, Jaina
        Jainism—Hymns
Jaina hymns, Gujarati (May Subd Geog)
    [BL1377.3]
    UF Gujarati Jaina hymns
Jaina illumination of books and manuscripts
    USE Illumination of books and manuscripts,
        Jaina
Jaina incantations
    [BL1377.4]
    UF Incantations, Jaina
    NT Sri Namaskara Mahaamantra
Jaina inscriptions
    USE Inscriptions, Jaina
Jaina legends
    USE Legends, Jaina
Jaina literature (May Subd Geog)
    [BL1315-1317]
Jaina literature, Kannada (May Subd Geog)
    UF Kannada Jaina literature
    BT Kannada literature
Jaina literature, Prakrit (May Subd Geog)
    UF Prakrit Jaina literature
    BT Prakrit literature
Jaina literature, Tamil (May Subd Geog)
    UF Tamil Jaina literature
    BT Tamil literature
Jaina logic
    [B162.5]
    [BC25-26 (Ancient)]
    UF Logic, Jaina
    BT Jainism
        Nyaya
        Philosophy, Jaina
Jaina meditations
    UF Meditations, Jaina
Jaina miniature painting
    USE Miniature painting, Jaina
Jaina monasteries
    USE Monasteries, Jaina
Jaina monasticism and religious orders
    USE Monasticism and religious orders,
        Jaina
Jaina mural painting and decoration
    USE Mural painting and decoration, Jaina
Jaina mysticism
    USE Mysticism—Jainism
Jaina philosophy
    USE Philosophy, Jaina
Jaina pilgrims and pilgrimages
    (May Subd Geog)
    UF Pilgrims and pilgrimages, Jaina
    BT Pilgrims and pilgrimages
    NT Jaina shrines
Jaina poetry
    UF Jainism—Poetry
    BT Religious poetry
Jaina poetry, Apabhraṃśa (May Subd Geog)
    UF Apabhraṃśa Jaina poetry
    BT Apabhraṃśa poetry
Jaina poetry, Gujarati
    UF Gujarati Jaina poetry
    BT Gujarati poetry
Jaina poetry, Hindi
    UF Hindi Jaina poetry
    BT Hindi poetry
Jaina poetry, Kannada (May Subd Geog)
    UF Kannada Jaina poetry

    BT Kannada poetry
Jaina poetry, Prakrit
    UF Prakrit Jaina poetry
    BT Prakrit poetry
Jaina poetry, Rajasthani (May Subd Geog)
    UF Rajasthani Jaina poetry
    BT Rajasthani poetry
Jaina religious practice
    [BL1376]
    UF Theology, Practical (Jainism)
    BT Jainism
    NT Religious life (Jainism)
Jaina saints
    BT Jainism
        Saints
Jaina sculpture
    USE Sculpture, Jaina
Jaina sects
    UF Sects, Jaina
    BT Jainism
    NT Añcalagaccha (Jaina sect)
        Digambara (Jaina sect)
        Śvetāmbara (Jaina sect)
        Terehpanth (Jaina sect)
Jaina sermons
    [BL1377.5]
    UF Sermons, Jaina
Jaina sermons, Gujarati
    [BL1377.5]
Jaina shrines (May Subd Geog)
    UF Shrines, Jaina
    BT Jaina pilgrims and pilgrimages
Jaina symbolism
    UF Symbolism, Jaina
    BT Jainism
        Symbolism
Jaina temples
    USE Temples, Jaina
Jaina women
    USE Women, Jaina
Jaina worship
    USE Worship (Jainism)
Jainas
    USE Jains
Jainism (May Subd Geog)
    [BL1300-BL1365]
    BT Religions
    NT Ajivikas
        Aṇuvrata
        Architecture, Jaina
        Atonement (Jainism)
        Civilization, Jaina
        Fasts and feasts—Jainism
        God (Jainism)
        Gods, Jaina
        Jaina logic
        Jaina religious practice
        Jaina saints
        Jaina sects
        Jaina symbolism
        Knowledge, Theory of (Jainism)
        Meditation (Jainism)
        Monasteries, Jaina
        Monastic and religious life (Jainism)
        Monasticism and religious orders,
            Jaina
        Mysticism—Jainism
        Penance (Jainism)
        Prayer (Jainism)
        Sallekhanā
        Salvation (Jainism)
        Soul (Jainism)
        Spiritual life (Jainism)
        Women in Jainism
        Worship (Jainism)
        Yoga (Jainism)
    — Hymns
        USE Jaina hymns
    — Poetry
        USE Jaina poetry
    — Relations

1933

Jainism
— **Relations** *(Continued)*
— — **Buddhism,** ₍etc.₎
— **Rituals**
    NT Benediction—Jainism
— **Sacred books**
Jainism in literature
Jains *(May Subd Geog)*
   ₍BL1300-1365₎
    UF Jainas
    BT Brahmanism
        Hinduism
        Religions
    NT Poravālas
        Saraks
— **Dietary laws**
    ₍BL1375.D53₎
    UF Dietary laws, Jaina
    BT Diet
        Food—Religious aspects—Jainism
        Nutrition—Religious aspects—
          Jainism
Jaintia (Indic people)
   ₍DS432.J225₎
    BT Ethnology—India
        Khasis
Jaintia Hills (India)
    BT Mountains—India
Jaipurī dialect
   ₍PK2215-2218₎
    UF Dhundhari dialect
    BT Rajasthani language
Jairus' daughter, Raising of (Miracle)
    USE Raising of Jairus' daughter (Miracle)
Jairus' daughter (Biblical character)
    USE Daughter of Jairus (Biblical character)
Jajoba
    USE Jojoba
Jakarta (Indonesia). Tanahabang
    USE Tanahabang (Jakarta, Indonesia)
Jakarta Bay (Indonesia)
    UF Baai van Batavia (Indonesia)
        Teluk Djakarta (Indonesia)
        Teluk Jakarta (Indonesia)
    BT Bays—Indonesia
Jakes family
    USE Jack family
Jakob-Creutzfeldt disease *(May Subd Geog)*
   ₍RC394.J34₎
    UF Creutzfeldt-Jakob disease
        Heidenhain syndrome
        Spastic pseudosclerosis
        Subacute spongiform encephalopathy
    BT Central nervous system—Diseases
        Presenile dementia
        Virus diseases, Slow
Jakobi-Altar
    USE Jakobialtar
Jakobialtar
    UF Jacob altar
        Jakobi-Altar
        Jakobus Altar
        Saint James altar
    BT Altarpieces, German
Jakobus Altar
    USE Jakobialtar
Jakri (African people)
    USE Jekri (African people)
Jakun (Malayan people)
    BT Ethnology—Malaysia
    NT Orang Hulu (Malayan people)
        Temuan (Malayan people)
Jakut language
    USE Yakut language
Jalama Beach Park (Calif.)
    (Not Subd Geog)
    BT Parks—California
Jalamat al-Asafna Site (Israel)
   ₍DS110.J34₎
    UF Jalame Site (Israel)
        Jalamet el-Asafna Site (Israel)

    BT Israel—Antiquities
Jalame Site (Israel)
    USE Jalamat al-Asafna Site (Israel)
Jalamet el-Asafna Site (Israel)
    USE Jalamat al-Asafna Site (Israel)
Jalandhara (Hindu mythology)
    BT Mythology, Hindu
Jalandji language
    USE Gugu Yalanji language
Jalap
   ₍RM666.J (Therapeutics)₎
   ₍RS165.J (Pharmacy)₎
    UF Convolvulin
        Jalapin
Jalapin
    USE Jalap
Jalāyirids
   ₍DS289.5₎
    UF Āl Jalāyir
    BT Iran—History—640-1500
        Iraq—History—634-1534
Jalčen
    USE Solons (Tungusic tribe)
Jalé (Papuan people)
   ₍DU744.35.J28₎
    UF Yali (Indonesian people)
    BT Ethnology—Indonesia
        Papuans
    NT Missions to Jalé (Papuan people)
Jallianwala Bagh Massacre, India, 1919
    USE India—History—Amritsar Massacre,
        1919
Jallianwalla Bāgh Massacre, India, 1919
    USE India—History—Amritsar Massacre,
        1919
Jaloof language
    USE Wolof language
Jalpa Hacienda (Mexico)
    UF Hacienda de Jalpa (Mexico)
        La Hacienda de Jalpa (Mexico)
    BT Haciendas—Mexico
Jaluo (African people)
    USE Luo (African people)
Jam *(May Subd Geog)*
   ₍TX612.J3₎
    BT Cookery (Fruit)
    NT Cookery (Jam)
        Marmalade
Jama Mapun language *(May Subd Geog)*
    UF Cagayan de Sulu language
        Cagayanon language
        Mapun language
        Pullon Mapun language
        Sama Mapun language
    BT Philippine languages
        Philippines—Languages
Jamaa Movement
    BT Bantus—Religion
        Catholic Church—Zaire
Jamaica
— **Civilization** *(Not Subd Geog)*
— — **African influences** *(Not Subd Geog)*
    ₍F1874₎
    BT Africa—Civilization
— **Description and travel**
— — **1951-**
— — **1951-1980**
— — **1981-**
— **History**
    ₍F1861-1895₎
— — **To 1962**
    ₍F1884-1886₎
— — **Maroon War, 1795-1796**
    BT Maroons
— — **Slave Insurrection, 1831**
— — **Insurrection, 1865**
— — **1962-**
    ₍F1887₎
— **Politics and government**
— — **To 1962**
— — **1962-**

— **Public buildings**
    USE Public buildings—Jamaica
— **Religion**
    NT Kumina (Cult)
Jamaica pepper
    USE Allspice
Jamaican alien labor
    USE Alien labor, Jamaican
Jamaican art
    USE Art, Jamaican
Jamaican atlases
    USE Atlases, Jamaican
Jamaican authors
    USE Authors, Jamaican
Jamaican children's poetry
    USE Children's poetry, Jamaican
Jamaican children's stories
    USE Children's stories, Jamaican
Jamaican cookery
    USE Cookery, Jamaican
Jamaican fiction *(May Subd Geog)*
    BT Jamaican literature
    NT Children's stories, Jamaican
Jamaican folk literature
    USE Folk literature, Jamaican
Jamaican fruit-eating bat
    USE Artibeus jamaicensis
Jamaican literature *(May Subd Geog)*
   ₍PR9265₎
    UF English literature—Jamaican authors
    NT Folk literature, Jamaican
        Jamaican fiction
Jamaican poetry *(May Subd Geog)*
   ₍PR9265₎
    UF English poetry—Jamaican authors
    NT Children's poetry, Jamaican
Jamaican vomiting sickness
    USE Hypoglycin A—Toxicology
Jamaican wit and humor, Pictorial
    (May Subd Geog)
Jamaican woodpecker
   ₍QL696.P65₎
    UF Melanerpes radiolatus
Jamaicans *(May Subd Geog)*
    BT Ethnology—Jamaica
Jamatia (Indic people)
    USE Tipura (Indic people)
Jamatiya (Indic people)
    USE Tipura (Indic people)
Jāmbavatī
Jambos
    USE Anuaks
Jamden language
    USE Yamdena language
Jamdena language
    USE Yamdena language
Jamerson family
    USE Jameson family
James, P. D. *(Not Subd Geog)*
— **Characters**
— — **Adam Dalgliesh**
    RT Dalgliesh, Adam (Fictitious
        character)
James A. FitzPatrick/Nine Mile Point
Nuclear Power Plant (N.Y.)
    UF James A. FitzPatrick Nuclear Power
        Plant (N.Y.)
        Nine Mile Point Nuclear Power Plant
        (N.Y.)
    BT Nuclear power plants—New York
        (State)
James A. FitzPatrick Nuclear Power Plant
(N.Y.)
    USE James A. FitzPatrick/Nine Mile Point
        Nuclear Power Plant (N.Y.)
James A. Garfield Home (Mentor, Ohio)
    UF Dickey Farm (Mentor, Ohio)
        Garfield Home (Mentor, Ohio)
        Lawnfield (Mentor, Ohio)
        Mentor Farm (Mentor, Ohio)
    BT Dwellings—Ohio

James A. Garfield National Historic Site
(Mentor, Ohio)
  BT Historic sites—Ohio
      National parks and reserves—Ohio
James Bay (Ont. and Québec)
  BT Bays—Ontario
      Bays—Québec (Province)
James Bay Hydroelectric Project
  BT Hydroelectric power plants—James
      Bay Region (Ont. and Québec)
James Bond (Fictitious character)
  USE Bond, James (Fictitious character)
James Bond films
  BT Bond, James (Fictitious character)
      Characters and characteristics in
        moving-pictures
      Moving-pictures
James family *(Not Subd Geog)*
  UF Jams family
      Jeames family
      Jemes family
  RT Jameson family
James G. Blaine House (Augusta, Me.)
  USE Blaine House (Augusta, Me.)
James Madison Memorial Building
(Washington, D.C.)
  USE Library of Congress James Madison
      Memorial Building (Washington,
      D.C.)
James River (Va.)
  BT Rivers—Virginia
James W. Ellsworth Land (Antarctic regions)
  USE Ellsworth Land (Antarctic regions)
James-York Peninsula (Va.)
  USE Virginia Peninsula (Va.)
Jamesianthus
  [QK495.C74]
  BT Compositae
Jameson family *(Not Subd Geog)*
  UF Jamerson family
      Jamieson family
      Jamison family
      Jamson family
      Jemerson family
      Jeminson family
      Jemison family
      Jimerson family
  RT James family
Jameson Land (Greenland)
Jameson's Raid, 1895-1896
  [DT929]
  BT South African War, 1899-1902
      Transvaal (South Africa)—History—
      1880-1910
Jamestown weed
  USE Datura
      Datura stramonium
Jamieson family
  USE Jameson family
Jaminaua language
  UF Nishinahua language
      Yaminahua language
      Yaminawa language
  BT Brazil—Languages
      Indians of South America—Languages
      Panoan languages
      Peru—Languages
Jamison family
  USE Jameson family
Jamming (Radio)
  USE Radio—Interference
Jammu and Kashmir (India) in Ahmadiyya
  [BP195.A5-6]
  BT Ahmadiyya
      Jesus Christ—Islamic interpretations
JAMS (Computer system)
  UF Jail Accounting Microcomputer
      System
Jams family
  USE James family

Jamson family
  USE Jameson family
Jamuna River (Bangladesh)
  BT Rivers—Bangladesh
Jamunda Indians
  USE Uaboi Indians
Jamundá River (Brazil)
  USE Nhamundá River (Brazil)
Jan de Beur family
  USE Jandebeur family
Jan Mayen Island *(Not Subd Geog)*
  BT Islands of the Arctic
Jandebeur family *(Not Subd Geog)*
  UF De Schandenburg family
      Debeur family
      Jan de Beur family
      Janderbeur family
      Jean de Beur family
      Jean de Beurre family
      Jeandebeur family
      Jeandipeur family
      Schandebar family
      Schandebehr family
      Schandeber family
      Schandebeur family
      Schandenberger family
Janderbeur family
  USE Jandebeur family
Jandjinung language
  USE Djinang language
Jane family
  USE Janes family
Jane Marple (Fictitious character)
  USE Marple, Jane (Fictitious character)
Janes family *(Not Subd Geog)*
  UF Jane family
      Jayn family
      Jayne family
      Jaynes family
      Jean family
      Jeans family
Janetiella
  [QL537.C33]
  BT Gall-gnats
Janetiella oenophila
  [QL537.C33 (General)]
  [SB945.J27 (Pest)]
  BT Grapes—Diseases and pests
Jang (African people)
  USE Dinka (African people)
Jangadas *(May Subd Geog)*
  BT Sailboats
Janggun Mine (Korea)
  BT Manganese mines and mining—Korea
Jangstēn language
  USE Thādo language
Janina, Lake (Greece)
  USE Ioannina, Lake (Greece)
Janissaries
  USE Janizaries
Janitors *(May Subd Geog)*
  [TX339]
  UF Building superintendents
      Custodian-engineers
      Custodians
      Superintendents of buildings and
        grounds
  BT Building-service employees
  RT Charwomen and cleaners
  NT School custodians
      Sextons
  — Collective labor agreements
      USE Collective labor agreements—
        Janitors
Janizaries
  [DR448 (Turkish history)]
  [UA816 (Turkish army)]
  UF Janissaries
Jankau, Battle of, 1645
  [D267.J]
  BT Thirty Years' War, 1618-1648

Janko groups
  [QA171]
  UF Groups, Janko
  BT Chevalley groups
Janney family *(Not Subd Geog)*
  UF Janny family
Janny family
  USE Janney family
Jans family *(Not Subd Geog)*
  RT Janzen family
      Jensen family
Janse family
  USE Jensen family
Jansen family
  USE Jensen family
Jansenists *(May Subd Geog)*
  [BX4720-4735]
  BT Christian sects
  NT Convulsionaries
      Fareinistes
      Old Catholic Church
Jansky-Bielschowsky disease
  USE Neuronal ceroid-lipofuscinosis
Janson family
  USE Jensen family
Jansonists
  [BX7990.J3]
  BT Collective settlements
      Communism
Janssen family
  USE Jensen family
Jansson family
  USE Jensen family
Jansz family
  USE Janzen family
Jantz family
  USE Janzen family
Jantzen family
  USE Janzen family
Janz family
  USE Janzen family
Janzen family *(Not Subd Geog)*
  UF Jansz family
      Jantz family
      Jantzen family
      Janz family
  RT Jans family
      Jensen family
Japan
  — Antiquities
     NT Abokke Site (Mito-shi, Japan)
        Ainohara Site (Chikushino-shi,
          Japan)
        Akaide Site (Japan)
        Akami Maeda Site (Jōnan-machi,
          Japan)
        Amako Minami Site (Kōra-chō,
          Japan)
        Amidadō Site (Chino-shi, Japan)
        Amidahara Site (Miyata-mura,
          Nagano-ken, Japan)
        Ayaragi Gōdaichi Site
          (Shimonoseki-shi, Japan)
        Ayaragigō Site (Shimonoseki-shi,
          Japan)
        Azami Site (Kasakake-mura, Japan)
        Babase Site (Nangō-mura, Aomori-
          ken, Japan)
        Bungō Hatsusaki Site
          (Kitatachibana-mura, Japan)
        Byōdōbō Iwamuro Site (Tenri-shi,
          Japan)
        Chiamigaido Site (Kiryū-shi, Japan)
        Chikamori Site (Kanazawa-shi,
          Japan)
        Chikaoka Nakashima Site
          (Kanazawa-shi, Japan)
        Chōjabara Site (Minamikata-machi,
          Japan)
        Chokushikan Site (Kaga-shi, Japan)

Miharada Site (Akagi-mura, Japan)

Mikumo Site (Maebaru-machi, Japan)

Minamihanada Site (Sakai-shi, Japan)

Minamishinbo Sanmaida Site (Kanazawa-shi, Japan)

Minamishinpo Site (Kanazawa-shi, Japan)

Mine Site (Yasu-machi, Fukuoka-ken, Japan)

Misayama Daini Site (Minowa-machi, Nagano-ken, Japan)

Mishirosugō Site (Shingū-machi, Fukuoka-ken, Japan)

Misu Haiji Site (Tanabe-shi, Japan)

Mitama Ōtsuka Site (Kisa-chō, Japan)

Mitoko Matsubara Site (Shima-machi, Japan)

Mitsuwa Site (Hatogaya-shi, Japan)

Miyako-machi Kita Site (Kudamatsu-shi, Japan)

Miyanohara Site (Ajimu-machi, Japan)

Miyanosako Site (Japan)

Miyauchi Kita Site (Oyama-shi, Japan)

Mizuho Site (Fukuoka-shi, Japan)

Monomizuka Site (Kushigata-machi, Japan)

Motojuku Site (Japan)

Mujinaoka Site (Kushigata-machi, Japan)

Mukaihara Site (Hiratsuka-shi, Japan)

Mukaiyama Site (Hamamatsu-shi, Japan)

Muryōji B Site (Kanazawa-shi, Japan)

Muryōji Site (Kanazawa-shi, Japan)

Musashigaoka Site (Machida-shi, Japan)

Myōmae Site (Japan)

Nagano Site (Ikarigaseki-mura, Japan)

Nagaoka-kyō Site (Kyoto, Japan)

Nagasako Site (Fukuyama-shi, Japan)

Nagase B Site (Ninohe-shi, Japan)

Nagase C Site (Japan)

Nagase D Site (Japan)

Nagino Site (Setaka-machi, Japan)

Naitō Site (Shari-chō, Japan)

Nakabyō Kōshinzuka Site (Abiko-shi, Japan)

Nakano Site (Neba-mura, Japan)

Nakasai Site (Mishima-machi, Fukushima-ken, Japan)

Nakasuji Site (Nose-chō, Japan)

Nakatomi Site (Kyoto, Japan)

Nakaya Site (Kanazawa-shi, Japan)

Nakazato Maehara Site (Japan)

Nakiri Site (Gōnoura-chō, Japan)

Nanaita Site (Yasu-machi, Fukuoka-ken, Japan)

Naniwa Kyū (Osaka, Japan)

Narikawa Site (Japan)

Natsushima Shell Mounds (Yokosuka-shi, Japan)

Nihongi Site (Ōno-machi, Ōita-ken, Japan)

Niihama Site (Shiogama-shi, Japan)

Niken'ya Site (Japan)

Nishi Miyayama Tomb (Tatsuno-shi, Japan)

Nishigōchi Kami Site (Ochiai-chō, Japan)

Nishikiori Site (Tondabayashi-shi, Japan)

Nishioku Site (Mitsu-chō, Okayama-ken, Japan)

Nishisaigyō Site (Azuchi-chō, Japan)

Nishiyama Site (Suwa-shi, Japan)

NN-278 Koyō Site (Japan)

NN-314 Koyō Site (Japan)

Nodai Site (Nagaizumi-chō, Japan)

Noji Onoyama Site (Kusatsu-shi, Japan)

Nōso Site (Japan)

Nukazuka Site (Takayama-shi, Japan)

Ōba Kita Site (Moriguchi-shi, Japan)

Obamayama Site (Nagato-shi, Japan)

Ōdate Cave (Takahata-machi, Japan)

Ōgiyama Site (Tokyo, Japan)

Ogōshibaru Site (Nishigōshi-machi, Japan)

Ōishidaira Site (Rokkasho-mura, Japan)

Okamura Site (Japan)

Okisuga Site (Tamano-shi, Japan)

Okitsuke Site (Rokkasho-mura, Japan)

Okusaka Site (Okayama-shi, Japan)

Okushōgonji Site (Hōfu-shi, Japan)

Ōmori Shell Mounds (Tokyo, Japan)

Omotedate Site (Rokkasho-mura, Japan)

Onji Site (Japan)

Ono Site (Isahaya-shi, Japan)

Ōnogō Site (Mitsukaidō-shi, Japan)

Orimoto Nishihara Site (Yokohama-shi, Japan)

Ōsaki Maeyama Site (Yachiyo-machi, Ibaraki-ken, Japan)

Osaki Site (Tokyo, Japan)

Ōsato Site (Nose-chō, Japan)

Ōta Site (Maebaru-machi, Japan)

Ōtani Site (Kasuga-shi, Japan)

Ōtohara Site (Japan)

Otome Fudōhara Kitaura Site (Oyama-shi, Japan)

Ōtomo Site (Ōtsu-shi, Japan)

Otosazuka Site (Ushimado-chō, Japan)

Ōtsubo Site (Okagaki-machi, Japan)

Ōtsuka Site (Matsubara-shi, Japan)

Ōtsuka Site (Tachibana-machi, Japan)

Ōtsuka Site (Yamaguchi-shi, Japan)

Ōuchihikami Site (Yamaguchi-shi, Japan)

Oyanagawa Site (Shichigashuku-machi, Japan)

Ōzura Site (Japan)

Rōkaida Site (Matsuura-shi, Japan)

Roppaiuchi Site (Shōnan-machi, Japan)

Ryokugan Site (Miyoshi-shi, Japan)

Sakaeura daiichi Site (Tokoro-chō, Japan)

Sakai Site (Machida-shi, Japan)

Sakuno Site (Murayama-shi, Japan)

Sakuradai Site (Noda-shi, Japan)

Sakuragaoka Site (Maebashi-shi, Japan)

Sannō Site (Tokyo, Japan)

San'oi Site (Ichihasama-chō, Japan)

Sanrizuka Baba Site (Narita-shi, Japan)

Sarukoba Site (Japan)

Sawadanosawa Site (Higashikagura-chō, Japan)

Seinen Site (Kanazawa-shi, Japan)

Shichinotsubo Site (Izumiōtsu-shi, Japan)

Shimada Site (Kaminokawa-machi, Japan)

Shimegi Site (Kushigata-machi, Japan)

Shimobaru Site (Amagi-shi, Japan)

Shimofuda Site (Chōfu-shi, Japan)

Shimogō Site (Japan)

Shimohondani Site (Miyoshi-shi, Japan)

Shimotakabora Site (Ōshima-machi, Tokyo, Japan)

Shinke Site (Tondabayashi-shi, Japan)

Shinmei Site (Shōwa-machi, Saitama-ken, Japan)

Shinnabe Site (Kumamoto-shi, Japan)

Shinnaya Site (2) (Rokkasho-mura, Japan)

Shinohara Shingō Site (Kaga-shi, Japan)

Shin'yama Site (Japan)

Shin'yashiki Site (Hayashima-chō, Japan)

Shiraiwa Yabunoue Site (Tateyama-machi, Japan)

Shirasu Tatara Seitetsu Site (Abu-chō, Japan)

Shiroyama Site (Kami-mura, Shizuoka-ken, Japan)

Shiroyama Site (Osaka, Japan)

Shiroyama Site (Toyoura-chō, Yamaguchi-ken, Japan)

Shiroyamadaira 2 Site (Hachinohe-shi, Japan)

Sōbara Site (Atō-chō, Japan)

Sorimaru Site (Ōta-shi, Japan)

Sudō Site (Shari-chō, Japan)

Sugigadō Kofun Site (Seki-shi, Japan)

Sunagawa A Site (Asahi-mura, Yamagata-ken, Japan)

Suwano Site (Ōkuchi-shi, Japan)

Suwanoki Site (Japan)

Suzenji Ōtoshi Site (Yamaguchi-shi, Japan)

Suzu no Miya Site (Sakai-shi, Japan)

Tabata Site (Kikugawa-chō, Yamaguchi-ken, Japan)

Tachibana Site (Toshima-mura, Kagoshima-ken, Japan)

Tagara Shell Mounds (Kesennuma-shi, Japan)

Takada A Site (Tsuruoka-shi, Japan)

Takada Site (Fukuoka-shi, Japan)

Takada Site (Nagahama-shi, Japan)

Takahachi Site (Miyoshi-shi, Japan)

Takahata Site (Heki-chō, Japan)

Takahoko Site (Rokkasho-mura, Japan)

Takamori Site (Takefu-shi, Japan)

Takano Site (Rittō-chō, Japan)

Takasaki Mizuiri Site (Tagajō-shi, Japan)

Takaseyama Site (Sagae-shi, Japan)

Takō Minamihara Site (Kaminokawa-machi, Japan)

Tamanoi B Site (Kiyama-chō, Saga-ken, Japan)

Tamonjimae Site (Higashikurume-shi, Japan)

Tanabe Site (Kashiwara-shi, Japan)

Tanjiri Site (Hokubō-chō, Japan)

Tannowa Site (Misaki-chō, Japan)

Tareyanagi Site (Inakadate-mura, Japan)

Japanese atlases
USE Atlases, Japanese
Japanese authors
USE Authors, Japanese
Japanese autobiographical fiction
USE Autobiographical fiction, Japanese
Japanese ballads
USE Ballads, Japanese
Japanese banks and banking
USE Banks and banking, Japanese
Japanese beetle
[QL596.S3]
[SB945.J3 (Insect pests)]
UF Popillia japonica
BT Beetles
Japanese book-plates
USE Book-plates, Japanese
Japanese Buddhist hymns
USE Buddhist hymns, Japanese
Japanese Buddhist literature
USE Buddhist literature, Japanese
Japanese calendar
USE Calendar, Japanese
Japanese Canadian poetry
USE Japanese poetry—Canadian authors
Japanese character sets (Data processing)
(May Subd Geog)
UF REACC (Character set)
RLIN East Asian Character Code
BT Character sets (Data processing)
Japanese language—Data processing
— **Data bases**
NT CJK thesaurus (Data base)
Japanese cherry
USE Japanese flowering cherry
Japanese chess
USE Shogi
Japanese children's encyclopedias and
dictionaries
USE Children's encyclopedias and
dictionaries, Japanese
Japanese children's literature
USE Children's literature, Japanese
Japanese children's periodicals
USE Children's periodicals, Japanese
Japanese children's poetry
USE Children's poetry, Japanese
Japanese children's stories
USE Children's stories, Japanese
Japanese children's writings
USE Children's writings, Japanese
Japanese-Chinese Conflict, 1937-1945
USE Sino-Japanese Conflict, 1937-1945
Japanese-Chinese War, 1894-1895
USE Chinese-Japanese War, 1894-1895
Japanese chins (Dogs)
USE Japanese spaniels
Japanese chipmunk
USE Siberian chipmunk
Japanese Christian drama
USE Christian drama, Japanese
Japanese Christian literature
USE Christian literature, Japanese
Japanese Christian poetry
USE Christian poetry, Japanese
Japanese civics
USE Civics, Japanese
Japanese clethra
USE Pepperbush
Japanese code and cipher stories
USE Code and cipher stories, Japanese
Japanese coins
USE Coins, Japanese
Japanese college and school drama
USE College and school drama, Japanese
Japanese college verse
USE College verse, Japanese
Japanese colored carp
USE Ornamental carp
Japanese commercial correspondence
USE Commercial correspondence, Japanese

Japanese crane (May Subd Geog)
[QL696.G84]
UF Grus japonensis
Red-crowned crane
Tanchō crane
Tanchōzuru
BT Grus
Japanese crested ibis
USE Nipponia nippon
Japanese decimal classification
USE Classification, Japanese decimal
Japanese deer
USE Sika deer
Japanese diaries
[PL771 (Collections)]
BT Diaries
— **To 1868**
[PL741.1-PL741.112 (History)]
[PL771.1-PL771.112 (Collections)]
— **Heian period, 794-1185**
[PL741.2 (History)]
[PL771.2 (Collections)]
— **1185-1600**
[PL741.3-741.33 (History)]
[PL771.3-771.33 (Collections)]
— **Edo period, 1600-1868**
[PL741.35-PL741.53 (History)]
[PL771.35-PL771.53 (Collections)]
— **Meiji period, 1868-1912**
[PL741.6-PL741.63 (History)]
[PL771.6-PL771.63 (Collections)]
Japanese diplomatics
USE Diplomatics, Japanese
Japanese drama
[PL771-7 (Japanese, PL734-5)]
[PL871 (History in European
languages)]
[PL887-8 (Collections in European
languages)]
NT Christian drama, Japanese
College and school drama, Japanese
Ghost plays, Japanese
Historical drama, Japanese
Jōruri
Kabuki plays
Kōwaka plays
Kyōgen plays
Nō plays
Political plays, Japanese
— **1185-1600**
[PL739.3 (History)]
[PL769.3 (Collections)]
— **Edo period, 1600-1868**
[PL739.35-PL739.5 (History)]
[PL769.35-PL769.5 (Collections)]
NT Sekkyō jōruri
— **Meiji period, 1868-1912**
[PL739.6 (History)]
[PL769.6 (Collections)]
— **Women authors**
Japanese drama (Comedy)
NT Manzai (Comedy)
Japanese dramatists
USE Dramatists, Japanese
Japanese economic assistance
USE Economic assistance, Japanese
Japanese eel
USE Anguilla japonica
Japanese emperor worship
USE Emperor worship, Japanese
Japanese emperors
USE Japan—Emperors
Japanese empresses
USE Japan—Empresses
Japanese encephalitis
UF Encephalitis Type B
BT Encephalitis, Epidemic
Japanese encephalitis vaccine
[QR189.5.E5]

Japanese encyclopedias and dictionaries
USE Encyclopedias and dictionaries,
Japanese
Japanese epic poetry
USE Epic poetry, Japanese
Japanese erotic literature
USE Erotic literature, Japanese
Japanese erotic poetry
USE Erotic poetry, Japanese
Japanese erotic stories
USE Erotic stories, Japanese
Japanese espionage
USE Espionage, Japanese
Japanese espionage stories
USE Spy stories, Japanese
Japanese essays (May Subd Geog)
[PL742-PL742.83 (History)]
[PL772-PL772.83 (Collections)]
— **To 1600**
[PL742.115-PL742.118 (History)]
[PL772.115-PL772.118
(Collections)]
— **To 1868**
[PL742.1 (History)]
[PL772.1 (Collections)]
— **1185-1600**
[PL742.3-PL742.33 (History)]
[PL772.3-PL772.33 (Collection)]
Japanese exchange of persons programs
USE Exchange of persons programs,
Japanese
Japanese fantastic fiction
USE Fantastic fiction, Japanese
Japanese fencing
USE Kendo
Japanese fiction
[PL781-2 (Japanese, PL736-740)]
[PL873 (History in European
languages)]
[PL890 (Collections in European
languages)]
NT Autobiographical fiction, Japanese
Children's stories, Japanese
Code and cipher stories, Japanese
Erotic stories, Japanese
Fantastic fiction, Japanese
Ghost stories, Japanese
Historical fiction, Japanese
Nonfiction novel, Japanese
Ryukyu fiction
Short stories, Japanese
Sports stories, Japanese
Spy stories, Japanese
— **To 1600**
[PL747.115 (History)]
[PL777.115 (Collections)]
— **To 1868**
[PL747.1 (History)]
[PL777.1 (Collections)]
— **Heian period, 794-1185**
— **1185-1600**
[PL747.3-PL747.33 (History)]
[PL777.3-PL777.33 (Collections)]
— **Edo period, 1600-1868**
NT Kibyoshi-bon
— **19th century**
— **1868-**
— **Meiji period, 1868-1912**
[PL747.6 (History)]
[PL777.6 (Collections)]
— **Taishō period, 1912-1926**
[PL747.6 (History)]
[PL777.6 (Collections)]
— **Competitions**
— — **Japan**
NT Naoki shō
Japanese film posters
USE Film posters, Japanese
Japanese five-needle pine
[QK494.5.P66 (Botany)]
[SB413.P54 (Ornamental plants)]

Japanese five-needle pine *(Continued)*
  UF Five-needle pine, Japanese
      Japanese white pine
      Pinus parviflora
      White pine, Japanese
Japanese flower arrangement
  USE Flower arrangement, Japanese
Japanese flowering cherry *(May Subd Geog)*
  [SB413.C5 (Culture)]
  UF Cherry, Japanese
      Japanese cherry
      Potomac cherry
      Prunus yedoensis
      Yoshino cherry
  BT Flowering cherries
Japanese folk dancing
  USE Folk dancing, Japanese
Japanese folk literature
  USE Folk literature, Japanese
Japanese folk poetry
  USE Folk poetry, Japanese
Japanese folk-songs
  USE Folk-songs, Japanese
Japanese ghost plays
  USE Ghost plays, Japanese
Japanese ghost stories
  USE Ghost stories, Japanese
Japanese gilt bronzes
  USE Gilt bronzes, Japanese
Japanese gods
  USE Gods, Japanese
Japanese historical drama
  USE Historical drama, Japanese
Japanese historical fiction
  USE Historical fiction, Japanese
Japanese honeysuckle
  [QK495.C199 (Botany)]
  UF Lonicera japonica
  BT Honeysuckle
Japanese humorous poetry
  USE Humorous poetry, Japanese
Japanese idealism
  USE Idealism, Japanese
Japanese imprints *(May Subd Geog)*
  — Cataloging
      USE Cataloging of Japanese imprints
Japanese incense ceremony
  [GT3032]
  UF Incense-burning parties, Japanese
      Incense ceremonies, Japanese
      Incense-smelling parties, Japanese
  BT Aromatic plants—Folklore
Japanese indigo
  USE Polygonum tinctorium
Japanese ink painting
  USE Ink painting, Japanese
Japanese inscriptions
  USE Inscriptions, Japanese
Japanese invasion, Shanghai, China, 1932
  USE Shanghai (China)—History—Japanese
      invasion, 1932
Japanese investments
  USE Investments, Japanese
Japanese iron sculpture
  USE Iron sculpture, Japanese
Japanese juvenile delinquents' writings
  USE Juvenile delinquents' writings,
      Japanese
Japanese laboring class writings
  USE Laboring class writings, Japanese
Japanese lacquer tree
  USE Rhus verniciflua
Japanese landscape painting
  USE Landscape painting, Japanese
Japanese language
  [PL501-700]
  NT Ryukyu language
  — **To 794**
      [PL525.2]
      UF Japanese language—Old Japanese
  — **To 1868**

— **Heian period, 794-1185**
      [PL525.3]
— **Middle Japanese, 1185-1600**
      [PL525.4]
— **Edo period, 1600-1868**
      [PL525.5]
— **Meiji period, 1868-1912**
      [PL525.6]
— Classical grammar
      USE Japanese language—Grammar,
         Classical
— **Data processing**
      NT Japanese character sets (Data
         processing)
— **Dialects**
— — **Japan**
— — — Ryukyu Islands
         USE Ryukyu language
— **Dictionaries**
      NT Picture dictionaries, Japanese
— — **Early works to 1867**
— **Epithets**
      [PL659]
      UF Makurakotoba
— **Etymology**
      NT Aware (The Japanese word)
         Desu (The Japanese word)
         E (The Japanese word)
         Eiyō (The Japanese word)
         Haberu (The Japanese word)
         Hodari (The Japanese word)
         Kiyoshi (The Japanese word)
         Masu (The Japanese word)
         Omoshiroshi (The Japanese word)
         Shizen (The Japanese word)
         Utsukushi (The Japanese word)
— Final particle
      USE Japanese language—Sentence
         particles
— **Grammar, Classical**
      [PL531.3]
      UF Classical Japanese grammar
         Japanese language—Classical
         grammar
— Names
      USE Names, Japanese
— Old Japanese
      USE Japanese language—To 794
— **Particles**
      NT Japanese language—Sentence
         particles
— **Punctuation**
      NT Kunten
— **Sentence particles**
      UF Japanese language—Final particle
      BT Japanese language—Particles
         Japanese language—Spoken
         Japanese
— **Spoken Japanese**
      NT Japanese language—Sentence
         particles
— **Writing**
— — **Kana**
      NT Japanese language—Writing—
         Man'yōgana
— — **Man'yōgana**
      [PL525.2]
      BT Japanese language—Writing—
         Kana
— **Writing, Cursive**
      UF Cursive writing of Japanese
         Sōsho
      BT Writing
— **Writing, Seal style**
      UF Seal style writing of Japanese
         Writing, Seal style, of Japanese
      BT Writing
Japanese larch
  UF Larix leptolepis
  BT Larch

Japanese lepers writings
  USE Lepers' writings, Japanese
Japanese letter-writing
  USE Letter-writing, Japanese
Japanese letters *(May Subd Geog)*
— **Edo period, 1600-1868**
      [PL743.35-PL743.53 (History)]
      [PL773.35-PL773.53 (Collections)]
Japanese literature *(May Subd Geog)*
  [PL701-898]
  NT Buddhist literature, Japanese
      Children's literature, Japanese
      Children's writings, Japanese
      Christian literature, Japanese
      Erotic literature, Japanese
      Folk literature, Japanese
      Haikai
      Laboring class writings, Japanese
— **To 794**
      [PL726.12 (History)]
      [PL755.12 (Collections)]
— **To 1185**
      [PL726.1185-PL726.1186 (History)]
      [PL755.1185-PL755.1186
        (Collections)]
— **To 1600**
— **To 1868**
— — **Modernized versions**
      [PL755.1 (Collections)]
— **Heian period, 794-1185**
— **1185-1600**
— **Edo period, 1600-1868**
— **1868-**
— **Meiji period, 1868-1912**
      NT Negishi School
— **20th century**
      NT Shirakaba School
— **Taishō period, 1912-1926**
— Cataloging
      USE Cataloging of Japanese literature
— **Japanese American authors**
— **Korean authors**
— **Women authors**
— **Zen authors**
      UF Gozan literature
      BT Zen literature
Japanese literature (Chinese)
  USE Chinese literature—Japanese authors
Japanese literature (English)
  USE English literature—Japanese authors
Japanese lithography
  USE Lithography, Japanese
Japanese loans
  USE Loans, Japanese
Japanese love poetry
  USE Love poetry, Japanese
Japanese lullabies
  USE Lullabies, Japanese
Japanese macaque
  [QL737.P93]
  UF Macaca fuscata
      Snow monkeys
  BT Macaques
Japanese management
  USE Industrial management—Japan
      Management—Japan
      Quality circles
Japanese manuscripts
  USE Manuscripts, Japanese
Japanese maple
  [QK495.A17 (Botany)]
  [SB413.J34 (Ornamental plant)]
  UF Acer palmatum
  BT Maple
      Ornamental shrubs
      Ornamental trees
  NT Fullmoon maple
Japanese maxims
  USE Maxims, Japanese
Japanese medlar
  USE Loquat

Japanese metal sculpture
  USE Metal sculpture, Japanese
Japanese military bases
  USE Military bases, Japanese
Japanese missions
  USE Missions, Japanese
Japanese morning glory *(May Subd Geog)*
  ₍QK495.C78 (Botany)₎
  ₍SB413.M67 (Ornamental plant)₎
  UF Imperial Japanese morning glory
      Ipomoea imperialis
      Ipomoea nil
      Pharbitis nil
      White-edge morning glory
  BT Ipomoea
      Morning glories
Japanese names
  USE Names, Japanese
Japanese narrative painting
  USE Narrative painting, Japanese
Japanese newspapers *(May Subd Geog)*
  ₍PN5401-5409₎
  — Circulation
Japanese newspapers in foreign countries
Japanese nonfiction novel
  USE Nonfiction novel, Japanese
Japanese novelists
  USE Novelists, Japanese
Japanese nursery rhymes
  USE Nursery rhymes, Japanese
Japanese oak silkworm moth
  USE Yamamai
Japanese occupation of Malaya, 1942-1945
  USE Malaya—History—Japanese
       occupation, 1942-1945
Japanese oyster
  USE Crassostrea gigas
Japanese painting
  USE Painting, Japanese
Japanese paleography
  USE Paleography, Japanese
Japanese paper *(May Subd Geog)*
  ₍TS1130₎
  UF Japan paper
  BT Paper
Japanese paper folding
  USE Origami
Japanese parodies
  USE Parodies, Japanese
Japanese patriotic poetry
  USE Patriotic poetry, Japanese
Japanese penmanship
  USE Penmanship, Japanese
Japanese periodicals
  ₍PN5401-5410₎
  NT Children's periodicals, Japanese
      Women's periodicals, Japanese
Japanese persimmon
  USE Kaki persimmon
Japanese philology
  ₍PL501-699₎
Japanese physically handicapped, Writings of
  the
  USE Physically handicapped, Writings of
       the, Japanese
Japanese physically handicapped children's
  writings
  USE Physically handicapped children's
       writings, Japanese
Japanese picture dictionaries
  USE Picture dictionaries, Japanese
Japanese poetry *(May Subd Geog)*
  ₍PL756-770 (Japanese, PL717-720)₎
  ₍PL867-870 (History in European
   languages)₎
  ₍PL884-6 (Collections in European
   languages)₎
  NT Children's poetry, Japanese
      Christian poetry, Japanese
      College verse, Japanese
      Epic poetry, Japanese

Erotic poetry, Japanese
Folk poetry, Japanese
Haikai
Haiku
Humorous poetry, Japanese
Irohauta
Kaiawase (Game)
Love poetry, Japanese
Nursery rhymes, Japanese
Patriotic poetry, Japanese
Protest poetry, Japanese
Renku
Ryukyu poetry
School verse, Japanese
Sea poetry, Japanese
Senryu
Shigin
Visual poetry, Japanese
Waka
Zen poetry, Japanese
— To 794
    ₍PL733.12 (History)₎
    ₍PL763.12 (Collections)₎
— To 1185
    ₍PL733.1185-PL733.1186 (History)₎
    ₍PL763.1185-PL763.1186
     (Collections)₎
— To 1600
— To 1868
    ₍PL733.1 (History)₎
    ₍PL763.1 (Collections)₎
— Heian period, 794-1185
    ₍PL733.2 (History)₎
    ₍PL763.2 (Collections)₎
    NT Sandaishū
        Sanjūrokkasen'e (Scrolls)
— 1185-1600
    ₍PL733.3 (History)₎
    ₍PL763.3 (Collections)₎
— Edo period, 1600-1868
    ₍PL733.35-PL733.5 (History)₎
    ₍PL763.35-PL763.5 (Collections)₎
    NT Bashō school
        Danrin School
        Keien school
— 1868-
    ₍PL733.55-PL733.58 (History)₎
    ₍PL763.55-PL763.58 (Collections)₎
— Meiji period, 1868-1912
    ₍PL733.6 (History)₎
    ₍PL763.6 (Collections)₎
— Taishō period, 1912-1926
    ₍PL733.6 (History)₎
    ₍PL763.6 (Collections)₎
— Canadian authors
    UF Canadian poetry (Japanese)
        Japanese Canadian poetry
— Emperors' writings
— Japanese American authors
    UF American poetry (Japanese)
        Japanese American poetry
        (Japanese)
— Women authors
Japanese poetry (Chinese)
  USE Chinese poetry—Japanese authors
Japanese poets
  USE Poets, Japanese
Japanese political plays
  USE Political plays, Japanese
Japanese polo
  USE Polo, Japanese
Japanese portraits
  USE Portraits, Japanese
Japanese posters
  USE Posters, Japanese
Japanese prints
  USE Prints, Japanese
Japanese propaganda
  USE Propaganda, Japanese
Japanese property *(May Subd Geog)*
  UF Property, Japanese

  BT Alien property
  — Foreign countries
Japanese prose literature *(May Subd Geog)*
  NT Nonfiction novel, Japanese
  — Heian period, 794-1185
      ₍PL747.2-PL747.25 (History)₎
      ₍PL777.2-PL777.25 (Collections)₎
  — 1185-1600
      ₍PL747.3 (History)₎
      ₍PL777.3 (Collections)₎
  — Edo period, 1600-1868
  — 1868-
      ₍PL747.55 (History)₎
      ₍PL777.55 (Collections)₎
  — Meiji period, 1868-1912
      ₍PL747.6 (History)₎
      ₍PL777.6 (Collections)₎
Japanese protest poetry
  USE Protest poetry, Japanese
Japanese proverbs
  USE Proverbs, Japanese
Japanese quail
  UF Coturnix coturnix japonica
  BT Quails
  — Anatomy
Japanese quail as laboratory animals
  ₍SF407.J3₎
  BT Birds as laboratory animals
Japanese quotations
  USE Quotations, Japanese
Japanese red pine
  ₍QK494.5.P66₎
  UF Pinus densiflora
  BT Pine
Japanese reference books
  USE Reference books, Japanese
Japanese riddles
  USE Riddles, Japanese
Japanese river fever
  USE Tsutsugamushi disease
Japanese rock gardens
  USE Rock gardens, Japanese
Japanese-Russian Border Conflicts, 1932-1941
  USE Russo-Japanese Border Conflicts,
       1932-1941
Japanese-Russian War, 1904-1905
  USE Russo-Japanese War, 1904-1905
Japanese sailors' writings
  USE Sailors' writings, Japanese
Japanese sardine
  USE Sardinops melanosticta
Japanese satire
  USE Satire, Japanese
Japanese school prose
  USE School prose, Japanese
Japanese school verse
  USE School verse, Japanese
Japanese schools
  USE Schools, Japanese
Japanese scrolls
  USE Scrolls, Japanese
Japanese sculpture
  USE Sculpture, Japanese
Japanese sea poetry
  USE Sea poetry, Japanese
Japanese sermons
  USE Sermons, Japanese
Japanese serow *(May Subd Geog)*
  ₍QL737.U53₎
  UF Capricornis crispus
      Formosa serow
Japanese short stories
  USE Short stories, Japanese
Japanese shorthand
  USE Shorthand, Japanese
Japanese soldiers' writings
  USE Soldiers' writings, Japanese
Japanese songs
  USE Songs, Japanese

Japanese spaniels
   UF Chins, Japanese (Dogs)
         Japanese chins (Dogs)
   BT Spaniels
         Toy dogs
Japanese sports stories
   USE Sports stories, Japanese
Japanese spy stories
   USE Spy stories, Japanese
Japanese stone gardens
   USE Rock gardens, Japanese
Japanese stone pine
   USE Pinus pumila
Japanese students *(May Subd Geog)*
   BT Students
   — Foreign countries
      UF Japanese students in foreign
            countries
      BT Students, Foreign
Japanese students in foreign countries
   USE Japanese students—Foreign countries
Japanese-style painting
   USE Yamatoe
Japanese subject headings
   USE Subject headings, Japanese
Japanese tamarisk
   USE Tamarix chinensis
Japanese tea ceremony *(May Subd Geog)*
   [GT2910-2916]
   UF Cha-no-yu
         Tea ceremony, Japanese
   BT Drinking customs
         Tea
   NT Chashitsu (Japanese tearooms)
         Japanese tea masters
         Tea masters
   — Edo Sen-ke school
      USE Japanese tea ceremony—Edo
           Senke school
   — Edo Senke school
      [GT2912.E35]
      UF Edo Sen-ke school of Japanese tea
           ceremony
         Edo Senke school of Japanese tea
           ceremony
         Japanese tea ceremony—Edo Sen-
           ke school
   — Enshū school *(May Subd Geog)*
      [GT2912.E57]
      UF Enshū school of Japanese tea
           ceremony
   — History
   — Kankyūan school
      USE Japanese tea ceremony—
           Mushanokōji Senke school
   — Mushakoji Senke school
      USE Japanese tea ceremony—
           Mushanokōji Senke school
   — Mushanokōji Senke school
      [GT2912.M8]
      UF Japanese tea ceremony—Kankyūan
           school
         Japanese tea ceremony—Mushakoji
           Senke school
         Kankyūan school of Japanese tea
           ceremony
         Mushakōji Senke school of
           Japanese tea ceremony
         Mushanokōji Senke school of
           Japanese tea ceremony
   — Oribe school *(May Subd Geog)*
      [GT2912.O73]
      UF Japanese tea ceremony—Oriberyū
           school
         Oribe school of Japanese tea
           ceremony
   — Oriberyū school
      USE Japanese tea ceremony—Oribe
           school
   — Sekishū school
      [GT2912.S42]

      UF Japanese tea ceremony—
           Sekishūryū school
         Sekishū school of Japanese tea
           ceremony
   — Sekishūryū school
      USE Japanese tea ceremony—Sekishū
           school
   — Sōhen school
      [GT2912.S55]
      UF Japanese tea ceremony—Sōhenryū
           school
         Sōhen school of Japanese tea
           ceremony
   — Sōhenryū school
      USE Japanese tea ceremony—Sōhen
           school
   — Ura Senke school
      [GT2912.U7]
      UF Ura Senke school of Japanese tea
           ceremony
   — Utensils
      [GT2915]
      BT Pottery, Japanese
      NT Raku pottery
Japanese tea masters *(May Subd Geog)*
   [GT2911]
   BT Japanese tea ceremony
Japanese technical assistance
   USE Technical assistance, Japanese
Japanese terra-cotta sculpture
   USE Terra-cotta sculpture, Japanese
Japanese theatrical posters
   USE Theatrical posters, Japanese
Japanese tuberculosis patients' writings
   USE Tuberculosis patients' writings,
         Japanese
Japanese varnish tree
   USE Rhus verniciflua
Japanese veterans' writings
   USE Veterans' writings, Japanese
Japanese visual poetry
   USE Visual poetry, Japanese
Japanese watercolor painting
   USE Watercolor painting, Japanese
Japanese white pine
   USE Japanese five-needle pine
Japanese widows' writings
   USE Widows' writings, Japanese
Japanese wit and humor *(May Subd Geog)*
   Here are entered collections from several authors
   and individual authors who have not written in other
   literary forms.
   NT Humorous poetry, Japanese
         Manzai (Comedy)
         Rakugo
   — Edo period, 1600-1868
      [PL746 (History)]
      [PL776.81-PL776.883 (Collections)]
Japanese wit and humor, Pictorial
Japanese women authors
   USE Women authors, Japanese
Japanese women poets
   USE Women poets, Japanese
Japanese women's periodicals
   USE Women's periodicals, Japanese
Japanese wood-engraving
   USE Wood-engraving, Japanese
Japanese wrestling
   USE Sumo
Japanese Zen poetry
   USE Zen poetry, Japanese
Japanning
   [TP942]
   BT Lacquer and lacquering
   RT Varnish and varnishing
   NT Metals—Finishing
         Tole painting
Japanologists *(May Subd Geog)*
   BT Scholars
Japodes
   USE Iapyges

Japp-Klingemann reaction
   BT Chemical reactions
Jappe family
   USE Joppe family
Japu (The Panjabi word)
   BT Panjabi language—Etymology
Japygidae
   [QL503.4.J3]
   BT Diplura
   NT Japyx
Japyx
   [QL503.4.J3]
   BT Japygidae
Jaqai
   BT Ethnology—New Guinea
Jaqaru language
   USE Cauqui dialect
Jaqua family
   USE Jaques family
Jaquays family
   USE Jaques family
Jaquemarts
   UF Jacquemarts
   BT Bells
         Church architecture
         Tower-clocks
Jaques family *(Not Subd Geog)*
   UF Jacques family
         Jacquess family
         Jaqua family
         Jaquays family
         Jaquess family
         Jaquis family
         Jaquish family
   RT Jack family
Jaquess family
   USE Jaques family
Jaquet family
   USE Jaquith family
Jaqueth family
   USE Jaquith family
Jaquette family
   USE Jaquith family
Jaquis family
   USE Jaques family
Jaquish family
   USE Jaques family
Jaquith family *(Not Subd Geog)*
   UF Jacqueth family
         Jacquett family
         Jacwith family
         Jaquet family
         Jaqueth family
         Jaquette family
Jar with decoration of the "three friends" (Art object)
   USE Jar with "three friends of winter"
         decoration (Art object)
Jar with "three friends of winter" decoration (Art object)
   UF Jar with decoration of the "three
         friends" (Art object)
   BT Porcelain, Chinese
Jarabe (Dance)
   [GV1796.J]
   UF Jarave (Dance)
Jarai
   UF Djarai
         Jrai (Indochinese people)
   BT Ethnology—Vietnam
Jarai language
   [PL4498.J3]
   BT Chamic languages
         Mon-Khmer languages
Jarāi Maṭh (Barwā Sāgar, India)
   UF Jarāi Temple (Barwā Sāgar, India)
   BT Temples, Hindu—India
Jarāi Temple (Barwā Sāgar, India)
   USE Jarāi Maṭh (Barwā Sāgar, India)
Jarāsandha (Hindu mythology)
   BT Mythology, Hindu

Jarat family
    USE Jarrett family
Jarave (Dance)
    USE Jarabe (Dance)
Jarbah Island (Tunisia)
    UF Djarbah Island (Tunisia)
        Djerba Island (Tunisia)
        Djerbah Island (Tunisia)
        Gerbah Island (Tunisia)
        Jazīrat Jarbah (Tunisia)
        Jerbah Island (Tunisia)
    BT Islands—Tunisia
Jarchas
    USE Muwashshah
Jardin de Monceau (Paris, France)
    USE Parc Monceau (Paris, France)
Jardin d'émail (Environment (Art))
    USE Dubuffet, Jean, 1901-   Jardin
        d'émail
Jardins du Château de Versailles (Versailles,
        France)
    USE Parc de Versailles (Versailles, France)
Jarecoune Indians
    USE Arecuna Indians
Jaredites (Mormon Church)
    ₍BX8627₎
    BT Book of Mormon
        Mormon Church—Doctrines
Jargon (Terminology)
    ₍P409₎
    UF Gobbledygook
    BT Slang
        Terms and phrases
    SA *subdivision* Jargon *under names of*
        languages and groups of languages,
        e.g. English language—Jargon; *and*
        specific types of jargon, e.g. English
        language—Government jargon
Jargons
    USE Languages, Mixed
        Pidgin languages
Jari River (Amapá and Pará, Brazil)
    UF Jary River (Amapá and Pará, Brazil)
        Rio Jary (Amapá and Pará, Brazil)
    BT Rivers—Brazil
Jaricuna Indians
    USE Arecuna Indians
Jarishe, Tell (Israel)
    USE Gerisah Site (Israel)
Jarīzat Fīlah (Egypt)
    USE Philae (Egypt)
Jarkon River (Israel)
    USE Yarḳon River (Israel)
Jarmo Site (Iraq)   *(Not Subd Geog)*
    BT Iraq—Antiquities
Jarnagin family
    USE Jernigan family
Jarnigan family
    USE Jernigan family
Jaroo language
    USE Djaru language
Jarosławice, Battle of, 1914
    BT World War, 1914-1918—Campaigns—
        Poland
Jarot language
    USE Jarut language
Jarrah eucalyptus
    USE Eucalyptus marginata
Jarral family
    USE Jarrell family
Jarrat family
    USE Jarrett family
Jarrate family
    USE Jarrett family
Jarratt family
    USE Jarrett family
Jarrel family
    USE Jarrell family

Jarrell family   *(Not Subd Geog)*
    UF Garell family
        Garrald family
        Garreld family
        Gerald family
        Gerrauld family
        Jarral family
        Jarrel family
        Jerols family
        Jerould family
        Jerrald family
        Jerrall family
        Jerrel family
        Jerrold family
        Jerulld family
Jarrell Plantation (Ga.)   *(Not Subd Geog)*
    BT Plantations—Georgia
Jarres Plain (Laos)
    USE Jars, Plain of (Laos)
Jarret family
    USE Jarrett family
Jarrett family   *(Not Subd Geog)*
    UF Garred family
        Jarat family
        Jarrat family
        Jarrate family
        Jarratt family
        Jarret family
        Jarrot family
        Jarrott family
        Jerret family
        Jerrett family
        Jerrit family
    RT Garrett family
Jarrot family
    USE Jarrett family
Jarrott family
    USE Jarrett family
Jarry, Alfred, 1873-1907   *(Not Subd Geog)*
    — Characters
    — — Ubu
        RT Ubu (Fictitious character)
Jars, Plain of (Laos)
    UF Haihin Plain (Laos)
        Jarres Plain (Laos)
        Plain of Jars (Laos)
        Plaine des Jarres (Laos)
        Thông Haihin (Laos)
    BT Plains—Laos
Jars, Apothecary
    USE Apothecary jars
Jars, Canopic
    USE Canopic jars
Jars, Cookie
    USE Cookie jars
Jars, Storage
    USE Storage jars
Jaruru language
    USE Djaru language
Jarut language
    UF Jarot language
    BT Mongolian languages
Jarvais family
    USE Jarvis family
Jarves family
    USE Jarvis family
Jarvie Historic Site (Utah)
    (Not Subd Geog)
    UF Jarvie Ranch (Utah)
    BT Historic sites—Utah
        Ranches—Utah
Jarvie Ranch (Utah)
    USE Jarvie Historic Site (Utah)

Jarvis family   *(Not Subd Geog)*
    UF Garvis family
        Gervais family
        Gervase family
        Gervis family
        Jarvais family
        Jarves family
        Jarviss family
        Jervis family
Jarvis Street (Toronto, Ont.)
    BT Streets—Ontario
Jarviss family
    USE Jarvis family
Jary River (Amapá and Pará, Brazil)
    USE Jari River (Amapá and Pará, Brazil)
Jaryas
    USE Muwashshah
Jasenovac (Croatia : Concentration camp)
    BT World War, 1939-1945—
        Concentration camps—Yugoslavia
Jasirat Bades (Spain)
    USE Peñón de Vélez de la Gomera (Spain)
Jasmine   *(May Subd Geog)*
    ₍QK495.O44 (Botany)₎
    ₍SB303.J (Aromatic plant)₎
    ₍SB413.J (Ornamental plant)₎
    UF Jasminum
        Jessamine
    BT Aromatic plants
        Oleaceae
        Tea
Jasminum
    USE Jasmine
Jason (Greek mythology)
    ₍BL820.A8₎
    BT Mythology, Greek
    RT Argonauts (Greek mythology)
Jasper
    ₍QE391.J₎
Jasper National Park (Alta.)
    UF Parc national de Jasper (Alta.)
        Parc national Jasper (Alta.)
    BT National parks and reserves—Alberta
Jasperoid   *(May Subd Geog)*
    ₍QE475.J3₎
    UF Limestone quartzite
        Silicified limestone
    BT Limestone
        Quartz
Jaspis Porzellan
    USE Böttger ware
Jass (Game)
    ₍GV1295.J3₎
    UF Klaberjass
Jassen
    USE Jazyge
Jassidae
    USE Leafhoppers
Jassy, Battle of, 1944
    UF Kishinev, Battle of, 1944
    BT World War, 1939-1945—Campaigns—
        Romania
Jasus
    ₍QL444.M33₎
    BT Spiny lobsters
Jasus edwardsii
    ₍QL444.D3₎
Jasus lalandii
    ₍QL444.D3₎
    UF Cape crawfish
Jasus tristani
    ₍QL444.M33₎
Jaszság (Hungary)
    UF Jazygia (Hungary)
Jat caste
    USE Jats
Jataka stories
    BT Buddhist stories
Jataka stories, English
Jatapu (Indic people)
    ₍DS432.J23₎

Jatapu (Indic people) *(Continued)*
  BT Ethnology—India
Jatavs
      [DS432.J25]
  BT Caste—India
      Untouchables
Jaṭkī language
  USE Lahndā language
JATO
  USE Airplanes—Assisted take-off
Jato Mountain (Sicily)
  USE Iato Mountain (Sicily)
Jatropha
      [QK495.E9]
  BT Euphorbiaceae
Jatropha gossypiifolia
      [QK495.E9 (Botany)]
  UF Bellyache nettlespurge
      Nettlespurge, Bellyache
  BT Medicinal plants
Jatropha manihot
  USE Cassava
Jats
  UF Jat caste
  BT Caste—India
      Ethnology—India
Jatu dialect
  USE Bangaru dialect
Jatvingi
  USE Jaćwież
Ja'udi language
  USE Ya'udi language
Jaudon family
  USE Jordan family
Jaulān Region
  USE Golan Heights
Jaunde (African people)
  USE Ewondo (African people)
Jaunde language
  USE Ewondo language
Jaundice
      [RC851]
      [RJ276 (Infants)]
  UF Icterus (Pathology)
  BT Biliary tract—Diseases
  NT Hyperbilirubinemia
      Jaundice, Obstructive
      Kernicterus
Jaundice, Neonatal
      [RJ276]
  UF Buhl's disease
      Hyperbilirubinemia, Neonatal
      Icterus neonatorum
      Neonatal jaundice
      Ritter's disease
      Wickel's disease
Jaundice, Obstructive
  UF Obstructive jaundice
  BT Bile-ducts—Obstructions
      Jaundice
  NT Cholestasis
Jaundice, Spirochaetal
  USE Weil's disease
Java (Indonesia)
  UF Jawa (Indonesia)
      Pulau Jawa (Indonesia)
  BT Islands—Indonesia
Java devilpepper
  USE Rauvolfia serpentina
Java gum disease
  USE Sugarcane leaf scald
Java jute
  USE Kenaf
Java Sea
  UF Laut Djawa
      Laut Jawa
Java Sea, Battle of the, 1942
      [D774.J]
  BT World War, 1939-1945—Naval
      operations

Java War, Indonesia, 1825-1830
  USE Indonesia—History—Java War, 1825-
      1830
Javalambre Mountains (Spain)
  UF Sierra de Javalambre (Spain)
  BT Mountains—Spain
Javanese *(May Subd Geog)*
  BT Ethnology—Indonesia
  — **Rites and ceremonies**
      NT Marriage customs and rites,
          Javanese
Javanese aesthetics
  USE Aesthetics, Javanese
Javanese art
  USE Art, Javanese
Javanese astrology
  USE Astrology, Javanese
Javanese authors
  USE Authors, Javanese
Javanese bronzes
  USE Bronzes, Javanese
Javanese didactic poetry
  USE Didactic poetry, Javanese
Javanese drama
      [PL5173 (History)]
      [PL5177 (Collections)]
  NT Islamic drama, Javanese
      Ludruk plays
      Wayang plays
Javanese ethics
  USE Ethics, Javanese
Javanese fiction *(May Subd Geog)*
  NT Short stories, Javanese
Javanese folk-songs
  USE Folk-songs, Javanese
Javanese imprints *(May Subd Geog)*
Javanese incantations
  USE Incantations, Javanese
Javanese Islamic drama
  USE Islamic drama, Javanese
Javanese Islamic poetry
  USE Islamic poetry, Javanese
Javanese Islamic sermons
  USE Islamic sermons, Javanese
Javanese language
      [PL5161-PL5169]
  BT Malayan languages
  NT Osing dialect
  — **Old Javanese**
      USE Kawi language
Javanese literature
      [PL5170-5179]
Javanese manuscripts
  USE Manuscripts, Javanese
Javanese marriage customs and rites
  USE Marriage customs and rites, Javanese
Javanese newspapers
Javanese poetry *(May Subd Geog)*
  NT Didactic poetry, Javanese
      Islamic poetry, Javanese
Javanese proverbs
  USE Proverbs, Javanese
Javanese short stories
  USE Short stories, Javanese
Javanese terra-cotta sculpture
  USE Terra-cotta sculpture, Javanese
Javanthropus soloensis
  USE Solo man
Javelin (Computer program)
      [HF5548.4.J37]
  BT Computer programs
Javelin (Jet fighter plane)
  BT Fighter planes
      Gloster aircraft
      Jet planes, Military
Javelin automobile
  BT American Motors automobiles
Javelin throwing
      [GV1093]
  BT Track-athletics

Javelinas
  USE Peccaries
Javiyufa language
  USE Yabiyufa language
Jaw, Lower
  USE Mandible
Jaw, Upper
  USE Maxilla
Jaw bone, Musical
      [ML1040]
  UF Musical jaw bone
  BT Percussion instruments
Jaw harp
  USE Jew's harp
Jaw joint
  USE Temporomandibular joint
Jaw relation records *(May Subd Geog)*
      [RK522]
  UF Bite registration (Dentistry)
      Maxillomandibular records
  BT Dental records
      Jaws
      Occlusion (Dentistry)
  NT Mandible—Hinge axis determination
Jawa (Indonesia)
  USE Java (Indonesia)
Jāwā (Jordan) *(Not Subd Geog)*
  BT Cities and towns, Ruined, extinct, etc.
      —Jordan
      Jordan—Antiquities
Jawa motorcycle
Jawboning
  USE Wage-price policy
Jawfishes
  USE Opisthognathidae
Jawi alphabet
      [PL5052]
  UF Malay alphabet
  BT Alphabet
      Arabic alphabet
      Malayan languages—Alphabet
Jawlān Region
  USE Golan Heights
Jaws
      [QL821 (Comparative anatomy)]
      [QM105 (Human anatomy)]
      [QP311 (Physiology)]
  UF Masticatory apparatus
  BT Craniology
      Facial bones
      Head
      Mouth
  NT Jaw relation records
      Mandible
      Mandibular condyle
      Mastication
      Maxilla
      Micrognathia
      Rhynchokinesis
      Temporomandibular joint
      Urohyal
  — **Abnormalities** *(May Subd Geog)*
      BT Orthodontics
      NT Cleft palate
          Hemifacial microsomia
          Prognathism
  — **Biopsy**
  — **Cancer**
  — **Cysts**
      NT Basal cell nevus syndrome
  — **Diseases** *(May Subd Geog)*
      [RC936]
      NT Jaws—Radiography
          Mastication disorders
          Trismus
  — **Necrosis**
      *[RA1231.P5 (Phosphorus
      poisoning)]*
      UF Phossy jaw
      BT Phosphorus—Toxicology
  — **Radiography**

1946

BT Jaws—Diseases
— Surgery
[RD526]
— Tumors
[RC280.J]
[RD661]
NT Odontogenic cysts
Odontogenic tumors
— Wounds and injuries
Jaw's-harp
USE Jew's harp
Jaxartes River
USE Syrdar'ia River
Jaxon family
USE Jackson family
Jaxson family
USE Jackson family
Jay family (Not Subd Geog)
UF Jaye family
Jaye family
USE Jay family
Jayhawk
[GR830]
Jayhun River
USE Amu Darya
Jayn family
USE Janes family
Jayne family
USE Janes family
Jaynes family
USE Janes family
Jays
[QL696.P2]
NT Blue jay
Cyanocitta
Cyanocorax
Garrulus
Scrub jay
Steller's jay
Jay's treaty, 1794
[E314]
Jaywick, Operation
USE Operation Jaywick
Jazira (Iraq and Syria) (Not Subd Geog)
UF al-Jazira (Iraq and Syria)
el-Jezire (Iraq and Syria)
Jazirah Doberai (Indonesia)
USE Doberai Peninsula (Indonesia)
Jazīrah Kharg (Iran)
USE Khark Island (Iran)
Jazīrah Khārj (Iran)
USE Khark Island (Iran)
Jazīrah-ya Khark (Iran)
USE Khark Island (Iran)
Jazīrat al Masīrah (Oman)
USE Masirah Island (Oman)
Jazīrat Aswān (Egypt)
USE Elephantine (Egypt)
Jazīrat Bādis (Spain)
USE Peñón de Vélez de la Gomera (Spain)
Jazīrat Dās (United Arab Emirates)
USE Das Island (United Arab Emirates)
Jazīrat Jarbah (Tunisia)
USE Jarbah Island (Tunisia)
Jazīrat Kharg (Iran)
USE Khark Island (Iran)
Jazīrat Khārj (Iran)
USE Khark Island (Iran)
Jazīrat Masīrah (Oman)
USE Masirah Island (Oman)
Jazīrat Sharīk (Tunisia)
USE Sharīk Peninsula (Tunisia)
Jazīreh-ye Abū Mūsá
USE Abu Musa
Jazīreh-ye Khark (Iran)
USE Khark Island (Iran)
Jazyge
UF Jassen
BT Alani
Ethnology—Hungary

Jazygia (Hungary)
USE Jaszság (Hungary)
Jazz (Computer program)
BT Computer programs
Jazz audiences (May Subd Geog)
[ML3505.8-ML3509]
BT Music audiences
Jazz band music
USE Big band music
Jazz bands
USE Big bands
Jazz dance
BT Dancing
Jazz duets
[M1366]
BT Duets
Jazz ensemble with chamber orchestra
[M1040-1041]
BT Jazz ensembles
RT Concertos (Jazz ensemble with
chamber orchestra)
NT Monologues with music (Jazz
ensemble with chamber orchestra)
— Scores
[M1040]
Jazz ensemble with orchestra
[M1040-1041]
BT Jazz ensembles
RT Concertos (Jazz ensemble)
NT Suites (Jazz ensemble with orchestra)
Jazz ensemble with string orchestra
[M1140-1141]
BT Jazz ensembles
RT Concertos (Jazz ensemble with string
orchestra)
Jazz ensembles
[M900-M949]
[M960-M985]
Here are entered single jazz compositions for ten
or more solo instruments, also collections of jazz
compositions for any number or combination of solo
instruments.
When used in conjunction with specific solo in-
strument(s), the qualifier jazz ensemble may stand for
any number or combination of solo instruments.
UF Ensembles (Music)
RT Dance-orchestra music
SA Concertos (Solo instrument(s)) with
jazz ensemble; [Solo
instrument(s)] with jazz ensemble
NT Big band music
Choruses, Sacred (Mixed voices) with
jazz ensemble
Concertos (Jazz ensemble)
Concertos (Jazz ensemble with
chamber orchestra)
Concertos (Jazz ensemble with string
orchestra)
Dixieland music
Jazz ensemble with chamber orchestra
Jazz ensemble with orchestra
Jazz ensemble with string orchestra
Jazz vocals
Percussion with jazz ensemble
Saxophone with jazz ensemble
Suites (Jazz ensemble)
Vocalises (High voice) with jazz
ensemble
Jazz festivals (May Subd Geog)
BT Music festivals
— Belgium
NT International Festival of Jazz
— California
NT Concord Summer Jazz Festival
Jazz music (May Subd Geog)
[ML3561]
UF Be bop music
Bebop music
Swing music
BT Afro-Americans—Music
Dance music—History and criticism
Music

SA Jazz quintets, Jazz septets, and similar
headings; and various headings for
instrumental music followed by the
qualifying adjective (Jazz), e.g.
Piano music (Jazz); also
subdivisions Methods (Jazz) and
Studies and exercises (Jazz) under
names of instruments or groups of
instruments, e.g. Saxophone—
Studies and exercises (Jazz); Wind
instruments—Methods (Jazz)
NT Big band music
Big bands
Dixieland music
Fakebooks (Music)
Instrumentation and orchestration
(Dance orchestra)
Jazz quintets
Jazz septets
Jazz vocals
Ragtime music
Western swing (Music)
— Interpretation (Phrasing, dynamics, etc.)
[MT75]
Jazz musicians (May Subd Geog)
BT Musicians
NT Women jazz musicians
Jazz nonets
BT Instrumental music
Jazz octet with orchestra
[M1040-1041]
RT Concertos (Jazz octet)
Jazz octets
Jazz octets
RT Concertos (Jazz octet)
Jazz octet with orchestra
Jazz quartet with chamber orchestra
[M1040-1041]
BT Chamber-orchestra music
Jazz quartets
Jazz quartet with orchestra
[M1040-1041]
BT Jazz quartets
RT Concertos (Jazz quartet)
Jazz quartets
BT Instrumental music
Quartets (Piano, percussion,
vibraphone, double bass)
NT Concertos (Jazz quartet)
Jazz quartet with chamber orchestra
Jazz quartet with orchestra
Suites (Jazz quartet)
Jazz quintet with band
[M1205-1206]
RT Concertos (Jazz quintet with band)
NT Suites (Jazz quintet with band)
Jazz quintet with orchestra
[M1040-1041]
BT Jazz quintets
RT Concertos (Jazz quintet)
Jazz quintet with string orchestra
[M1140-1141]
BT Jazz quintets
RT Concertos (Jazz quintet with string
orchestra)
Jazz quintets
BT Instrumental music
Jazz music
NT Concertos (Jazz quintet)
Concertos (Jazz quintet with string
orchestra)
Jazz quintet with orchestra
Jazz quintet with string orchestra
Monologues with music (Jazz quintet)
Jazz septets
BT Instrumental music
Jazz music
Jazz sextet with band
[M1205-M1206]
NT Suites (Jazz sextet with band)

Jazz sextet with orchestra
　[M1040-M1041]
Jazz sextets
　BT　Instrumental music
Jazz songs
　USE　Jazz vocals
Jazz trio with chamber orchestra
　[M1040-1041]
　RT　Concertos (Jazz trio with chamber
　　　orchestra)
　NT　Suites (Jazz trio with chamber
　　　orchestra)
Jazz trio with orchestra
　[M1040-1041]
　BT　Jazz trios
　RT　Concertos (Jazz trio)
Jazz trios
　BT　Instrumental music
　NT　Concertos (Jazz trio)
　　　Jazz trio with orchestra
　　　Suites (Jazz trio)
Jazz vocals
　　　Here are entered songs performed in jazz style by
　　a vocalist, vocal ensemble, or chorus, generally ac-
　　companied by a solo instrument, jazz ensemble, or
　　big band.
　UF　Jazz songs
　　　Scat singing
　　　Songs, Jazz
　　　Vocals, Jazz
　BT　Big band music
　　　Jazz ensembles
　　　Jazz music
　　　Popular music
　　　Songs
JCD Library Public Relations Award
　USE　John Cotton Dana Library Public
　　　Relations Award
JCL (Computer program language)
　USE　Job Control Language (Computer
　　　program language)
Jcoby family
　USE　Jacoby family
Je (New Guinea people)
　USE　Yei (New Guinea people)
Jealousy
　[BF575.J4 (Psychology)]
　BT　Emotions
　RT　Envy
　NT　Jealousy in children
　— **Religious aspects**
　　　NT　God—Jealousy
　— — **Buddhism, [Christianity, etc.]**
Jealousy (Child psychology)
　USE　Jealousy in children
Jealousy in children
　[BF723.J4 (Psychology)]
　UF　Jealousy (Child psychology)
　BT　Emotions in children
　　　Jealousy
　RT　Sibling rivalry
Jealousy of God
　USE　God—Jealousy
Jeames family
　USE　James family
Jean de Beur family
　USE　Jandebeur family
Jean de Beurre family
　USE　Jandebeur family
Jean family
　USE　Janes family
Jean Lafitte National Historical Park and
　Preserve (La.)　(Not Subd Geog)
　BT　Historic sites—Louisiana
　　　National parks and reserves—
　　　Louisiana
　NT　Chalmette Unit, Jean Lafitte National
　　　Historical Park and Preserve (La.)
Jeandebeur family
　USE　Jandebeur family

Jeandipeur family
　USE　Jandebeur family
Jeanne (Legendary Pope)
　USE　Joan (Legendary Pope)
Jeanne d'Arc malade est interrogée dans sa
　prison par le cardinal de Winchester
　(Painting)
　USE　Delaroche, Paul, 1797-1856.　Joan of
　　　Arc in prison
Jeanneret family　(Not Subd Geog)
Jeans (Clothing)
　UF　Blue jeans
　　　Levis
　BT　Trousers
Jeans family
　USE　Janes family
Jebel 'Idayd (Israel)
　USE　Karkom Mountain (Israel)
Jebel 'Ideid (Israel)
　USE　Karkom Mountain (Israel)
Jebel Mūsa (Syria), Defense of, 1915
　BT　World War, 1914-1918—Campaigns—
　　　Syria
Jebel Nefusa language
　[PJ2395.J43]
　UF　Jabal Nafusah language
　BT　Berber languages
Jeep automobile
　UF　Jeep vehicle
　　　Willys jeep
　BT　American Motors automobiles
　　　Automobiles, Military
　　　Tractors
　　　Trucks
　NT　Cherokee automobile
　　　Commando automobile
　　　Wagoneer automobile
Jeep vehicle
　USE　Jeep automobile
Jeepster automobile
　USE　Commando automobile
Jeepster Commando automobile
　USE　Commando automobile
Jefers family
　USE　Jeffers family
Jefferds family　(Not Subd Geog)
Jeffereys family
　USE　Jeffries family
Jefferie family
　USE　Jeffries family
Jefferies family
　USE　Jeffries family
Jefferis family
　USE　Jeffries family
Jeffers family　(Not Subd Geog)
　UF　Jefers family
　RT　Jefferson family
　　　Jeffries family
Jefferson, Thomas, 1743-1826
　— **Museums, relics, etc.**
　　　NT　Declaration of Independence desk
Jefferson, Fort (Dry Tortugas, Fla.)
　USE　Fort Jefferson (Dry Tortugas, Fla.)
Jefferson Building, Library of Congress
　(Washington, D.C.)
　USE　Library of Congress Thomas Jefferson
　　　Building (Washington, D.C.)
Jefferson desk
　USE　Declaration of Independence desk
Jefferson family　(Not Subd Geog)
　UF　Jeffison family
　RT　Jeffers family
Jefferson lap desk
　USE　Declaration of Independence desk
Jefferson Memorial (Washington, D.C.)
　USE　Thomas Jefferson Memorial
　　　(Washington, D.C.)
Jefferson salamander
　USE　Ambystoma jeffersonianum
Jeffery family
　USE　Jeffries family

Jefferyes family
　USE　Jeffries family
Jefferys family
　USE　Jeffries family
Jeffison family
　USE　Jefferson family
Jeffray family
　USE　Jeffries family
Jeffres family
　USE　Jeffries family
Jeffress family
　USE　Jeffries family
Jeffrey family
　USE　Jeffries family
Jeffrey pine
　UF　Pinus jeffreyi
Jeffreys family
　USE　Jeffries family
Jeffries family　(Not Subd Geog)
　UF　Geffereys family
　　　Gefries family
　　　Jeffereys family
　　　Jefferie family
　　　Jefferies family
　　　Jefferis family
　　　Jeffery family
　　　Jefferyes family
　　　Jefferys family
　　　Jeffray family
　　　Jeffres family
　　　Jeffress family
　　　Jeffrey family
　　　Jeffreys family
　　　Jeffryes family
　　　Jeffrys family
　RT　Jeffers family
Jeffryes family
　USE　Jeffries family
Jeffrys family
　USE　Jeffries family
Jeh language
　[PL4351.J45]
　UF　Die language
　　　Yeh language
　BT　Mon-Khmer languages
Jehad
　USE　Jihad
Jehan (Name)
　USE　John (Name)
Jehovah
　USE　God—Name—Biblical teaching
　　　God (Judaism)—Name
Jehovah, Day of
　USE　Day of Jehovah
Jehovah, Servant of
　USE　Servant of Jehovah
Jehovah's Witnesses　(May Subd Geog)
　[BX8525-BX8528]
　　　Here are entered works on members of the Watch
　Tower Bible and Tract Society.
　BT　Christians
Jei (New Guinea people)
　USE　Yei (New Guinea people)
Jeinnings family
　USE　Jennings family
Jeji dialect
　USE　Fon dialect
Jeju Strait (Korea)
　USE　Cheju Strait (Korea)
Jejunal bypass
　USE　Jejunoileal bypass
Jejunal ileal bypass
　USE　Jejunoileal bypass
Jejunectomy
　USE　Jejunoileal bypass
Jejunoileal bypass　(May Subd Geog)
　[RD540.85]

UF Jejunal bypass
Jejunal ileal bypass
Jejunectomy
Jejunoileal shunt
Jejunoileostomy
BT Ileum—Surgery
Jejunum—Surgery
Jejunoileal shunt
USE Jejunoileal bypass
Jejunoileostomy
USE Jejunoileal bypass
Jejunostomy
BT Enterostomy
Jejunum—Surgery
NT Esophagojejunostomy
Jejunum
BT Intestine, Small
— **Surgery**
NT Jejunoileal bypass
Jejunostomy
Jekri (African people)
UF Itsekiri (African people)
Jakri (African people)
BT Ethnology—Nigeria
Jekri (African people) law
USE Law, Jekri (African people)
Jelbeng (Malaysian people)
USE Chewong (Malaysian people)
Jelecote pine
USE Pinus patula
Jellet family
USE Gillette family
Jellinek's disease
USE Alcoholism
Jelly
⌈TX612.J4⌉
BT Cookery
Cookery (Fruit)
NT Cookery (Jelly)
Marmalade
Jellyfish
USE Medusae
Jellyfish, Box
USE Cubomedusae
Jellyfish, Four-sided
USE Cubomedusae
Jeløya (Norway)
BT Islands—Norway
Jemappes (Belgium), Battle of, 1792
⌈DC222.J4⌉
UF Jemmappes, Battle of, 1792
BT France—History—Revolution, 1792—
Campaigns
Jemerson family
USE Jameson family
Jemes family
USE James family
Jemez Indians
⌈E99.J4⌉
BT Indians of North America
Pueblo Indians
Tanoan Indians
Jemima Shore (Fictitious character)
USE Shore, Jemima (Fictitious character)
Jeminson family
USE Jameson family
Jemison family
USE Jameson family
Jemmappes, Battle of, 1792
USE Jemappes (Belgium), Battle of, 1792
Jen
⌈B127.J4⌉
UF In
Jin
BT Philosophy, Confucian
Jen-ching-lu (Mei-chou shih, China)
BT Dwellings—China
Jen family *(Not Subd Geog)*
**Jen min ying hsiung chi nien pei (Peking,
China)**
⌈DS795.5⌉

UF Monument to the People's Heroes
(Peking, China)
BT Monuments—China
Jen wang po je ching
BT Buddhism—Sacred books
Mahayana Buddhism—Sacred books
Jena, Battle of, 1806
⌈DC230.J4⌉
BT Napoleonic Wars, 1800-1814—
Campaigns—Germany (East)
Jena glass
⌈QC375⌉
BT Glass
Jena plan
⌈LB1029.J⌉
BT Education—Experimental methods
Vocational education
Jenana
USE Chesiadodes
Jencken family
USE Jenkins family
Jenckes family
USE Jenkins family
Jenckins family
USE Jenkins family
Jencks family
USE Jenkins family
Jenings family
USE Jennings family
Jenissei River (R.S.F.S.R.)
USE Yenisey River (R.S.F.S.R.)
Jenken family
USE Jenkins family
Jenkens family
USE Jenkins family
Jenkes family
USE Jenkins family
Jenkin family
USE Jenkins family
Jenkins' Ear, War of
USE Anglo-Spanish War, 1739-1748
Jenkins family *(Not Subd Geog)*
UF Ginks family
Jencken family
Jenckes family
Jenckins family
Jencks family
Jenken family
Jenkens family
Jenkes family
Jenkin family
Jenks family
Jincks family
Jinkens family
Jinkins family
Jinks family
Junken family
Junkin family
Junkins family
McJunkin family
Jenkins process
USE Front-screen projection
Jenkinsia
⌈QL638.C64⌉
BT Clupeidae
Jenks family
USE Jenkins family
Jenne family
USE Jenny family
Jennens family
USE Jennings family
Jenney family
USE Jenny family
Jenni family
USE Jenny family
Jennifer Project
UF Azorian Project
Project Azorian
Project Jennifer

BT Intelligence service—United States
Military intelligence
Salvage
Submarine disasters
Jenning family
USE Jennings family
Jennings family *(Not Subd Geog)*
UF Gennings family
Ginnings family
Jeinnings family
Jenings family
Jennens family
Jenning family
Jennins family
Jinings family
Jinnings family
Jinnins family
Jennins family
USE Jennings family
Jenny (Training planes)
USE JN-4D (Training planes)
Jenny family *(Not Subd Geog)*
UF Jenne family
Jenney family
Jenni family
Jensen automobile
Jensen-Daugaard Land (Greenland)
USE Daugaard-Jensen Land (Greenland)
Jensen family *(Not Subd Geog)*
UF Janse family
Jansen family
Janson family
Janssen family
Jansson family
Jenson family
Jenssen family
Jenzen family
RT Genson family
Jans family
Janzen family
Johnson family
Jensen-Healey automobile
Jenson family
USE Jensen family
Jenssen family
USE Jensen family
Jentinkia
USE Bassariscus
Jentzer family
USE Yenzer family
Jenzen family
USE Jensen family
Jenzer family
USE Yenzer family
Jeopardy, Double
USE Double jeopardy
Jephson family
USE Jepson family
Jeppesen family
USE Jepson family
Jeppson family
USE Jepson family
Jepsen family
USE Jepson family
Jepson family *(Not Subd Geog)*
UF Jephson family
Jeppesen family
Jeppson family
Jepsen family
Jequetepeque River (Peru)
UF Río Jequetepeque (Peru)
BT Rivers—Peru
Jequirity
⌈RH666.J (Therapeutics)⌉
⌈RS165.J (Pharmacy)⌉
Jequitinhonha River (Brazil)
(Not Subd Geog)
UF Rio Jequitinhonha (Brazil)
BT Rivers—Brazil
Jerash (Ancient city)
USE Gerasa (Ancient city)

Jerbah Island (Tunisia)
USE Jarbah Island (Tunisia)
Jerboas
 [QL737.R648]
 UF Dipodidae
 BT Rodents
Jerdee family
 USE Gjerde family
Jeremiads *(May Subd Geog)*
 BT Laments
 Sermons
Jericho Bridge (Va.), Battle of, 1864
 USE North Anna River (Va.), Battle of,
 1864
Jericho Ford (Va.), Battle of, 1864
 USE North Anna River (Va.), Battle of,
 1864
Jericho Mills (Va.), Battle of, 1864
 USE North Anna River (Va.), Battle of,
 1864
Jericho Operation
 USE Operation Jericho
Jerin-Jerin
 USE Ayo (Game)
Jerishe, Tell (Israel)
 USE Gerisah Site (Israel)
Jerky
 USE Beef, Dried
Jernagan family
 USE Jernigan family
Jernegan family
 USE Jernigan family
Jerne's plaque technique
 USE Hemolytic plaque technique
Jernian family
 USE Jernigan family
Jernigan family *(Not Subd Geog)*
 UF Jarnagin family
 Jarnigan family
 Jernagan family
 Jernegan family
 Jernian family
 Jerningham family
 Jernogan family
 Jernorgan family
Jernigan II Site (Tenn.) *(Not Subd Geog)*
 BT Normandy Reservoir Region (Tenn.)—
 Antiquities
 Tennessee—Antiquities
Jerningham family
 USE Jernigan family
Jernogan family
 USE Jernigan family
Jernorgan family
 USE Jernigan family
Jerols family
 USE Jarrell family
Jerould family
 USE Jarrell family
Jerrald family
 USE Jarrell family
Jerrall family
 USE Jarrell family
Jerrel family
 USE Jarrell family
Jerret family
 USE Jarrett family
Jerrett family
 USE Jarrett family
Jerrit family
 USE Jarrett family
Jerrold family
 USE Jarrell family
Jersey
 As a geographic subdivision, this heading is used
 indirectly through Channel Islands.
 — History
 NT Jersey, Battle of, 1781
Jersey, Battle of, 1781
 [DA670.J5]
 UF French Expedition to Jersey, 1781

 BT France—History, Military—1774-1793
 Great Britain—History—Invasions
 Great Britain—History, Military—18th
 century
 Jersey—History
Jersey cattle
 [SF193.J5 (Herd-books)]
 [SF199.J5]
 BT Dairy cattle
Jersey pine
 USE Scrub-pine
Jerulld family
 USE Jarrell family
Jerusalem
 As a geographic subdivision, this heading is used
 directly.
 — History
 — — Latin Kingdom, 1099-1244
 UF Latin Kingdom of Jerusalem
 BT Crusades
 Latin Orient
 Palestine—History—638-1917
 NT Ḥiṭṭīn, Battle of, 1187
 — Plazas
 NT Temple Mount (Jerusalem)
 — Siege, 70 A.D.
 [DS122.8]
 NT Jews—History—Rebellion, 66-73
 — — Religious aspects
 — Siege, 586 B.C.
 BT Jews—History—953-586 B.C.
 — Siege, 701 B.C.
 BT Jews—History—953-586 B.C.
 — Siege, 1948
 BT Israel-Arab War, 1948-1949
 Palestine—History—1929-1948
 — Temples
 NT Temple of Jerusalem (Jerusalem)
 — Walls
 NT Western Wall (Jerusalem)
Jerusalem. Armenian Quarter
 USE Armenian Quarter (Jerusalem)
Jerusalem. City of David
 USE City of David (Jerusalem)
Jerusalem. Mea Shearim
 USE Mea Shearim (Jerusalem)
Jerusalem. Me'ah She'arim
 USE Mea Shearim (Jerusalem)
Jerusalem. Ohel Moshe
 USE Ohel Moshe (Jerusalem)
Jerusalem. Ohel Mosheh
 USE Ohel Moshe (Jerusalem)
Jerusalem. Rova' armeni
 USE Armenian Quarter (Jerusalem)
Jerusalem. Shekhunat Ohel Mosheh
 USE Ohel Moshe (Jerusalem)
Jerusalem. Yemin Moshe
 USE Yemin Moshe (Jerusalem)
Jerusalem, Battle of, 1967
 BT Israel-Arab War, 1967—Campaigns
Jerusalem artichoke
 [QK495.C74 (Botany)]
 [SB211.J4 (Culture)]
 UF Artichoke, Jerusalem
 Helianthus tuberosus
 Topinambur
 BT Root-crops
Jerusalem in Christianity
 [BT93.5]
 BT Judaism (Christian theology)
 Theology, Doctrinal
Jerusalem in Islam
 BT Islam
 Palestine in Islam
Jerusalem in Judaism
 BT Jews—Restoration
 Judaism
 Palestine in Judaism
 Zionism
Jerusalem in rabbinical literature
 [BM518.J4]

 UF Jerusalem in the Midrash
 BT Rabbinical literature
Jerusalem in the Bible
 BT Bible—Theology
 Religion and geography
Jerusalem in the Midrash
 USE Jerusalem in rabbinical literature
Jerusalem stabile (Sculpture)
 USE Calder, Alexander, 1898-1976.
 Jerusalem stabile
Jervis Bay (N.S.W. and A.C.T.)
 (Not Subd Geog)
 BT Bays—Australia
Jervis family
 USE Jarvis family
Jeseníky Mountains (Czechoslovakia)
 UF Altvater Gebirge (Czechoslovakia)
 Gesenke Mountains (Czechoslovakia)
 BT Mountains—Czechoslovakia
 Sudeten
Jeshan
 USE Independence Day (Afghanistan)
Jeshimmon
 USE Judaea, Wilderness of
Jesness inventory
 BT Criminal behavior, Prediction of
 Personality tests
Jespersen family *(Not Subd Geog)*
 UF Jesperson family
 Jespersson family
Jesperson family
 USE Jespersen family
Jespersson family
 USE Jespersen family
Jessamine
 USE Jasmine
Jessen family *(Not Subd Geog)*
Jessenia
 [QK495.P17 (Botany)]
 UF Jessiana
 BT Palms
Jessenia bataua
 USE Oenocarpus bataua
Jessiana
 USE Jessenia
Jessop family
 USE Jessup family
Jessopp family
 USE Jessup family
Jessup family *(Not Subd Geog)*
 UF Jessop family
 Jessopp family
 Jesup family
Jest-books
 USE Chap-books
 Wit and humor
Jesters
 USE Fools and jesters
Jests
 USE Wit and humor
Jesuats
 [BX3760.J]
Jesuit architecture
 USE Architecture, Jesuit
Jesuit art
 USE Art, Jesuit
Jesuit artists
 USE Artists, Jesuit
Jesuit drama
 BT Drama
Jesuit drama, English *(May Subd Geog)*
 UF English Jesuit drama
 BT English drama
Jesuit drama, French, [etc.]
 (May Subd Geog)
Jesuit drama, German *(May Subd Geog)*
 UF German Jesuit drama
 BT German drama

Jesuit drama, Latin (Medieval and modern)
  (May Subd Geog)
    UF Latin Jesuit drama, Medieval and
          modern
    BT Latin drama, Medieval and modern
Jesuit theater *(May Subd Geog)*
    ₍PN3178.J46₎
    UF Theater, Jesuit
    BT Theater—Religious aspects—Catholic
          Church
Jesuit War, 1754-1756 (South America)
    USE Seven Reductions, War of the, 1754-
          1756
Jesuits *(May Subd Geog)*
    ₍BX3701-BX3755 (Men)₎
    ₍BX4371-BX4374 (Women)₎
    UF Jesus, Society of
          Society of Jesus
    BT Counter-Reformation
          Monasticism and religious orders
    NT Bollandists
  — Bibliography
  — Bio-bibliography
      ₍Z7840.J5₎
  — Biography
      ₍BX3755₎
  — — Dictionaries
  — Controversial literature
  — Dictionaries
  — Education *(May Subd Geog)*
      ₍LC493₎
  — Heraldry
  — History
      ₍BX3706-3749₎
  — — 16th century
  — — 17th century
  — — 18th century
  — — 19th century
  — — 20th century
  — Missions *(May Subd Geog)*
      ₍BV2290₎
      BT Indians of North America—
            Missions
  — — Brazil
  — Necrology
  — Occupations
  — Portraits
  — Prayer-books and devotions
        Individual texts are always further subdivided
      by the language of the text.
  — — English, ₍French, German, etc.₎
  — — History and criticism
  — Rules
      ₍BX3704₎
  — Spiritual life
      ₍BX3703₎
  — Theology
  — England
      NT Archpriest controversy, 1598-1602
            Popish Plot, 1678
  — Paraguay
      NT Seven Reductions, War of the,
            1754-1756
Jesuits' bark
    USE Cinchona
Jesuits in literature
Jesup family
    USE Jessup family
Jesus Christ
    ₍BT198-590₎
    UF Christ
          Christology
    BT God
          Theology, Doctrinal
          Trinity
    RT Christianity
    NT Antichrist
          Crosses
          Incarnation
          Logos
          Messiah

          Paschal mystery
          Second Advent
Jesus Christ.   Sermon on the mount
    USE Sermon on the mount
Jesus Christ
— **Adversaries**
      ₍BT361₎
      UF Adversaries of Jesus Christ
— **Afro-American interpretations**
      BT Afro-Americans—Religion
— Agrapha
      USE Jesus Christ—Words—Extra-
            canonical parallels
— **Anointing at Bethany**
— **Anthroposophical interpretations**
— **Apparitions and miracles (Modern)**
      ₍BT580₎
      BT Apparitions
— Appearance
      USE Jesus Christ—Physical
            appearance
— **Appearances**
      ₍BT490₎
        Here are entered works on the appearances of
      Jesus Christ after His resurrection.
      BT Jesus Christ—Forty days
            Jesus Christ—Resurrection
— **Appreciation**
— **Art**
      ₍N8050-8054₎
      UF Jesus Christ—Pictures, illustrations,
            etc.
            Jesus Christ in art
      BT God—Art
      NT Bailey, Jackson, 1927-   Life of
            Christ
            Bible—Picture Bibles
            Botticelli, Sandro, 1444 or 5-1510.
              Nativity
            Christus en de ongelovige Thomas
              (Painting)
            Fazzini, Pericle, 1913-
              Resurrection
            Giorgione, 1477-1511.   Nativity
            Goes, Hugo van der, 1435?-1482.
              Adoration of the shepherds
            Grünewald, Matthias, 16th cent.
              Mocking of Christ
            Hunt, William Holman, 1827-1910.
              Finding of the Saviour in the
              Temple
            Icons
            Jesus Christ—Iconography
            Leonardo, da Vinci, 1452-1519.
              Savior of the World
            Magi—Art
            Michelangelo Buonarroti, 1475-
              1564. Pietà
            Raphael, 1483-1520.   Madonna of
              Loretto
            Second Advent in art
            Steiner, Rudolf, 1861-1925.
              Group of Three Figures
            Taufe Christi (Tapestry)
            Titian, ca. 1488-1576.
              Resurrection altarpiece
            Veit, Philipp, 1793-1877.   Mainz
              Cathedral frescoes
— **Ascension**
      ₍BT500₎
      UF Ascension of Christ
      NT Ascension Day
— — **History of doctrines**
      ₍BT500₎
— Atonement
      USE Atonement
— Attitude towards Jewish dietary laws,
      ₍Attitude towards Jewish law, etc.₎
      USE Jesus Christ—Views on Jewish
            dietary laws, ₍Views on
            Jewish law, etc.₎

— Attitude towards politics
      USE Jesus Christ—Political and social
            views
— Attitude towards society
      USE Jesus Christ—Political and social
            views
— **Baptism**
      ₍BT350₎
— — **Art**
      NT Francesca, Piero della, 1416?-
            1492. Baptism
— Beatitudes
      USE Beatitudes
— **Betrayal**
      ₍BT435₎
      UF Betrayal of Christ
            Jesus Christ—Garden of
              Gethsemane
      BT Jesus Christ—Biography—Passion
            Week
            Jesus Christ—Passion
— **Biography**
      ₍BT298-500₎
      UF Jesus Christ—Life
      NT Mysteries of the Rosary
— — **Apocryphal and legendary literature**
      ₍BT520₎
      BT Christian literature, Early
— — — **Juvenile literature**
— — **Devotional literature**
      ₍BT306.28-5₎
      BT Devotional literature
— — Drama
      USE Jesus Christ—Drama
— — **Early life**
      ₍BT310-330₎
      NT Jesus Christ—Childhood
            Jesus Christ—Flight into Egypt
— — — Juvenile literature
      USE Jesus Christ—Childhood—
            Juvenile literature
— — **Early works to 1800**
      ₍BT300₎
— — **History and criticism**
      ₍BT303₎
— — **Juvenile literature**
      ₍BT302₎
— — **Meditations**
— — Ministry
      USE Jesus Christ—Biography—
            Public life
— — **Passion Week**
      ₍BT414₎
      RT Jesus Christ—Passion
      NT Jesus Christ—Betrayal
— — — **Juvenile literature**
— — **Public life**
      ₍BT340-500₎
      UF Jesus Christ—Biography—
            Ministry
— — Sources
      RT Jesus Christ—Historicity
— — **Sources, Biblical**
      ₍BT298-9₎
        Here are entered works purporting to give
      a life of Jesus Christ in the words of the four
      Gospels, harmonized into a continuous narra-
      tive.
— — **Sources, Jewish**
      ₍BT305₎
      BT Christianity and other religions
            —Judaism
— Birth
      USE Jesus Christ—Nativity
            Virgin birth
— Birth date
      USE Jesus Christ—Date of birth
— **Birthplace**
— **Blessing of children**
— — **Art**

Jesus Christ
— Blessing of children
— — Art   (Continued)
      NT Van Dyck, Anthony, Sir, 1599-
          1641. Suffer little children
          to come unto Me
— Brethren
   [BT313]
   UF Brethren of Jesus
       Brothers of Jesus
       Jesus Christ—Brothers
   BT Apostles
   RT Jesus Christ—Family
       Mary, Blessed Virgin, Saint—
         Virginity
— Brothers
   USE Jesus Christ—Brethren
— Buddhist interpretations
   UF Jesus Christ—Interpretations,
       Buddhist
       Jesus Christ in Buddhism
   BT Christianity and other religions—
       Buddhism
— Burial
   [BT460]
   UF Jesus Christ—Descent from the
       cross
   RT Jesus Christ—Three days in the
       tomb
— Calling of the twelve
   [BT360]
   UF Calling of the twelve apostles
       Calling of the twelve disciples
   BT Apostles
— Caricatures and cartoons
   UF Jesus Christ—Cartoons, satire, etc.
— Cartoons, satire, etc.
   USE Jesus Christ—Caricatures and
       cartoons
— Character
   [BT304]
   UF Jesus Christ—Personality
— — Juvenile literature
— Childhood
   [BT320-325]
   BT Jesus Christ—Biography—Early
       life
   NT Holy Childhood, Devotion to
       Jesus Christ—Temple visit at age
        twelve
— — Juvenile literature
   UF Jesus Christ—Biography—Early
       life—Juvenile literature
       Jesus Christ—Juvenile literature
— — Meditations
   [BT320]
— Chronology
   [BT303]
   NT Jesus Christ—Date of birth
       Jesus Christ—Date of death
— Cleansing of the Temple
— Commandments
   USE Summary of the Law (Theology)
— Conflicts
   [BT303]
   Here are entered works dealing with the con-
   troversies which Jesus Christ had with His oppo-
   nents.
— Conversations
   [BT306]
   BT Jesus Christ—Words
— Counseling methods
   [BT590.C78]
   UF Counseling methods of Jesus Christ
   BT Pastoral counseling
— Cross
   USE Holy Cross
       Jesus Christ—Crucifixion
— — Crucifixion
   [BT450-455]

   UF Crucifixion of Christ
       Jesus Christ—Cross
   RT Good Friday
       Stigmatization
   NT Five Sacred Wounds
       Holy Cross
       Jesus Christ—Date of death
— — Art
   NT Erasmus, Desiderius, d. 1536.
       Christ on the Cross
       Velázquez, Diego, 1599-1660.
        Crucifixion
— — Role of Jews
   USE Jesus Christ—Passion—Role of
       Jews
— — Role of Romans
   USE Jesus Christ—Passion—Role of
       Romans
— — Songs and music
   USE Passion-music
— Crucifixion date
   USE Jesus Christ—Date of death
— Cult   (May Subd Geog)
   NT Precious Blood, Devotion to
       Sacred Heart, Devotion to
       Scourging of Christ, Devotion to
— — Mexico
   NT Huerto, Señor del
— — Peru
   NT Milagros, Señor de los
— Date of birth
   [BT318]
   UF Jesus Christ—Birth date
   BT Jesus Christ—Chronology
       Jesus Christ—Nativity
— Date of crucifixion
   USE Jesus Christ—Date of death
— Date of death
   UF Jesus Christ—Crucifixion date
       Jesus Christ—Date of crucifixion
       Jesus Christ—Death date
   BT Jesus Christ—Chronology
       Jesus Christ—Crucifixion
   RT Passover in the New Testament
— Death date
   USE Jesus Christ—Date of death
— Descent from the cross
   USE Jesus Christ—Burial
— Descent into hell
   [BT470]
   RT Jesus Christ—Three days in the
       tomb
— Devotional literature
   BT Devotional literature
— Divinity
   [BT214-215]
   UF Divinity of Christ
   BT Arianism
       Jesus Christ—Natures
   RT Socinianism
       Unitarianism
— Drama
   [BT555]
   UF Jesus Christ—Biography—Drama
       Jesus Christ—Nativity—Drama
       Jesus Christ—Passion—Drama
   NT Christmas plays
       Easter—Drama
       Passion-plays
— Education
   [BT330]
— Entry into Jerusalem
   [BT415]
   RT Palm Sunday
— Ethics
   [BS2417.E8]
   BT Christian ethics
   NT Summary of the Law (Theology)
— Evangelistic methods
   [BT590.E8]
   BT Evangelistic work

— Exaltation
   [BT200-201]
— Example
   [BT304.2]
   Here are entered works dealing with Jesus
   Christ as an example or pattern to be followed.
   UF Imitation of Jesus Christ
— — Biblical teaching
— Face
   [BT590.P45]
   UF Face of Jesus Christ
   BT Jesus Christ—Physical appearance
— Family
   [BT313]
   UF Family, Holy
       Holy Family
   RT Jesus Christ—Brethren
— Fiction
   [BT560]
— Filiation
   USE Jesus Christ—Procession
— Flight into Egypt
   [BP315]
   UF Flight into Egypt
   BT Jesus Christ—Biography—Early
       life
— Forty days
   [BT485]
   Here are entered works descriptive of the
   forty days between the resurrection and the as-
   cension.
   NT Jesus Christ—Appearances
— Forty days in the wilderness
   USE Jesus Christ—Temptation
— Foundation of the church
   USE Church—Foundation
— Friends and associates
   [BS2430-2520]
— Garden of Gethsemane
   USE Jesus Christ—Betrayal
       Jesus Christ—Prayer in
        Gethsemane
— Genealogy
   [BT314]
   BT Genealogy
       Genealogy in the Bible
— Hindu interpretations
   UF Jesus Christ—Interpretations,
       Hindu
       Jesus Christ in Hinduism
   BT Christianity and other religions—
       Hinduism
— Historicity
   [BT303]
   RT Jesus Christ—Biography—Sources
— History of doctrines
   [BT198]
   UF Jesus Christ—Person and offices—
       History of doctrines
— — Early church, ca. 30-600
   UF Jesus Christ—Interpretations,
       New Testament
       Jesus Christ—New Testament
        interpretations
   NT Monothelitism
       Three chapters (Christological
        controversy)
— — Middle Ages, 600-1500
— — Modern period, 1500-
— — 16th century
— — 17th century
— — 18th century
— — 19th century
— — 20th century
   [BT198]
— Holy Coat
   USE Holy Coat
— Holy Shroud
   USE Holy Shroud
— Humanity
   [BT218]

BT Jesus Christ—Natures
NT Scourging of Christ, Devotion to
— **Humiliation**
[BT220]
— **Humor**
UF Jesus Christ—Wit and humor
BT Wit and humor—Religious aspects
—Christianity
— **Iconography**
[BT590.I]
BT Jesus Christ—Art
— Incarnation
USE Incarnation
— **Indian interpretations**
BT Indians
— **Influence**
[BT303]
— **Intellectual life**
[BT590.I6]
— **Intercession**
[BT255]
BT Mediation between God and man
—Christianity
— Interpretations, Buddhist
USE Jesus Christ—Buddhist
interpretations
— Interpretations, Hindu
USE Jesus Christ—Hindu
interpretations
— Interpretations, Islamic
USE Jesus Christ—Islamic
interpretations
— Interpretations, Jewish
USE Jesus Christ—Jewish
interpretations
— Interpretations, New Testament
USE Jesus Christ—History of
doctrines—Early church, ca.
30-600
— **Islamic interpretations**
[BP172]
UF Jesus Christ—Interpretations,
Islamic
Jesus Christ—Mohammedan
interpretations
Jesus Christ—Muslim
interpretations
Jesus Christ in Islam
BT Christianity and other religions—
Islam
Islam—Relations—Christianity
NT Jammu and Kashmir (India) in
Ahmadiyya
Jesus Christ in the Koran
— — **Juvenile literature**
— **Jewish interpretations**
[BM620]
UF Jesus Christ—Interpretations,
Jewish
BT Judaism
NT Jesus Christ—Passion—Role of
Jews
— **Journeys**
[BT590.J7]
— Juvenile literature
USE Jesus Christ—Childhood—
Juvenile literature
— **Kingdom**
[BT94]
Here are entered works on the Christian be-
lief that the followers of Jesus compose his king-
dom. Works on the kingship of Jesus are entered
under Jesus Christ—Royal office. Works on the
Christian doctrine of the spiritual reign of God
are entered under Kingdom of God.
BT Kingdom of God
— Kingship
USE Jesus Christ—Royal office
— **Knowableness**
[BT205]

UF Jesus Christ, Knowledge of
Knowableness of Jesus Christ
Knowledge of Jesus Christ
BT Knowledge, Theory of (Religion)
— **Knowledge and learning**
[BT590.K6]
— **Language**
[BT590.L3]
Here are entered works dealing with the prob-
lem of the language used by Jesus Christ, specifi-
cally whether He spoke Hebrew, Aramaic, or
Greek.
— Last Supper
USE Last Supper
— Last words
USE Jesus Christ—Seven last words
— Life
USE Jesus Christ—Biography
— Logos doctrine
USE Logos
— Lord's prayer
USE Lord's prayer
— Lord's Supper
USE Lord's Supper
— **Meditations**
— **Messiahship**
[BT230-240]
NT Messiah
Messianic secret (Bible)
— **Miracles**
[BT364-BT365]
UF Bible—Miracles
BT Miracles
NT Feeding of the five thousand
(Miracle)
Healing of Peter's mother-in-law
(Miracle)
Healing of the epileptic boy
(Miracle)
Healing of the Gerasene demoniac
(Miracle)
Healing of the lame man (Miracle)
Healing of the man born blind
(Miracle)
Healing of the man sick of the
palsy (Miracle)
Healing of the nobleman's son
(Miracle)
Jesus walking on the water
(Miracle)
Marriage in Cana (Miracle)
Miraculous draught of fishes
(Miracle)
Opening of the eyes of one blind at
Bethsaida (Miracle)
Raising of Jairus' daughter
(Miracle)
Raising of Lazarus (Miracle)
Stilling of the storm (Miracle)
— **Miscellanea**
[BT295]
[BT308 (Occult)]
— Mohammedan interpretations
USE Jesus Christ—Islamic
interpretations
— **Mormon interpretations**
BT Mormon Church
— Muslim interpretations
USE Jesus Christ—Islamic
interpretations
— **Mystical body**
Here are entered works on the Christian doc-
trine that the church is the mystical body of
Christ. Works on the relationship between God
and the individual Christian at the highest level
of mystical experience are entered under Mysti-
cal union.
UF Mystical body of Christ
BT Church
NT Communion of saints
— **Name**
[BT590.N2]

UF Jesus Christ—Titles
BT Names in the Bible
NT Holy Name, Devotion to
Servant of Jehovah
Son of God
Son of Man
— — **Biblical teaching**
— — **Juvenile literature**
— — **Meditations**
— — **Sermons**
— — — **Outlines**
— **Nativity**
[BT315]
UF Jesus Christ—Birth
Nativity of Christ
RT Christmas
NT Epiphany
Holy Innocents, Massacre of the
Jesus Christ—Date of birth
Jesus Christ—Relics of the
Nativity
Star of Bethlehem
Virgin birth
— — Drama
USE Jesus Christ—Drama
— — Sermons
USE Christmas sermons
— **Natures**
RT Hypostatic union
NT Jesus Christ—Divinity
Jesus Christ—Humanity
— New Testament interpretations
USE Jesus Christ—History of
doctrines—Early church, ca.
30-600
— **New Thought interpretations**
[BT304.92]
BT New Thought
— **Oriental interpretations**
[BT304.94]
— **Parables**
[BT373-8]
UF Parables, Biblical
Parables, Christian
BT Bible—Parables
Parables
SA names of parables, e.g. Good
Samaritan (Parable)
NT Mustard seed (Parable)
Pearl of great price (Parable)
Pharisee and the publican (Parable)
Prodigal son (Parable)
Sower (Parable)
Ten virgins (Parable)
Unjust judge (Parable)
Unjust steward (Parable)
Wicked husbandmen (Parable)
— — **Meditations**
— **Passion**
[BT430-465]
BT Lent
Suffering of God
RT Jesus Christ—Biography—Passion
Week
Passion narratives (Gospels)
NT Holy Hour
Holy Week
Jesus Christ—Betrayal
Jesus Christ—Relics of the Passion
Scourging of Christ, Devotion to
Stations of the Cross
— — Drama
USE Jesus Christ—Drama
Passion-plays
— — **History of doctrines**
— — **Juvenile literature**
— — **Manuscripts**
— — **Meditations**
— — Music
USE Passion-music
— — Poetry

Jesus Christ
  — **Passion**
    — — Poetry *(Continued)*
        USE Jesus Christ—Poetry
    — — **Role of Jews**
        UF Jesus Christ—Crucifixion—Role
            of Jews
        BT Jesus Christ—Jewish
            interpretations
    — — **Role of Romans**
        [BT431.6]
        UF Jesus Christ—Crucifixion—Role
            of Romans
            Roman role in the Passion of
            Jesus Christ
        BT Romans—Palestine
    — — **Sermons**
            Here are entered sermons dealing exclu-
        sively with the passion of Jesus Christ.
        NT Good Friday sermons
            Holy-Week sermons
    — — Songs and music
        USE Passion-music
  — **Person and offices**
        [BT200-BT201]
        [BT304]
        NT Hypostatic union
            Oneness doctrine (Pentecostalism)
            Sanctuary doctrine (Seventh-Day
            Adventists)
            Shut door (Seventh-Day
            Adventists)
    — — **Early works to 1800**
    — — History of doctrines
        USE Jesus Christ—History of
            doctrines
    — — **Juvenile literature**
    — — **Sermons**
    — — **Study** *(May Subd Geog)*
        [BT203]
  — Personality
        USE Jesus Christ—Character
  — **Physical appearance**
        [BT590.P45]
        UF Jesus Christ—Appearance
        NT Jesus Christ—Face
  — Pictures, illustrations, etc.
        USE Jesus Christ—Art
  — **Poetry**
        [BT550]
        UF Jesus Christ—Passion—Poetry
        BT Christian poetry
  — **Political and social views**
        UF Jesus Christ—Attitude towards
            politics
            Jesus Christ—Attitude towards
            society
            Jesus Christ—Views on politics
            Jesus Christ—Views on society
  — **Popular works**
  — **Prayer in Gethsemane**
        [BV234]
        UF Gethsemane, Prayer of
            Jesus Christ—Garden of
            Gethsemane
            Prayer in Gethsemane
        BT Bible—Prayers
  — **Prayers**
        [BV229-234]
        BT Bible—Prayers
  — **Pre-existence**
        [BT200-201]
        BT Logos
  — **Preaching**
        [BT590.P7]
  — **Preaching at Nazareth**
        UF Jesus Christ—Rejection at
            Nazareth
  — Precious Blood
        USE Precious Blood, Relics of the
  — **Presence**

        [BT590.P75]
        UF Presence of Jesus Christ
        RT God—Omnipresence
            Presence of God
        NT Lord's Supper—Real presence
  — **Presentation**
        RT Candlemas
    — — **Sermons**
  — **Priesthood**
        [BT260]
        BT Atonement
            Priesthood
  — **Primacy**
        UF Primacy of Jesus Christ
        BT Creation
        NT Logos
  — **Procession**
        [BT114]
            Here are entered works on the eternal proces-
        sion of God the Son from God the Father.
        UF Jesus Christ—Filiation
            Procession (in the Trinity)
            Trinity—Procession
  — **Promises**
        UF Promises of Jesus Christ
        BT Jesus Christ—Words
            Promises—Religious aspects—
            Christianity
  — **Prophecies**
        [BT370]
            Here are entered works dealing with prophe-
        cies made by Jesus Christ. Works dealing with
        prophecies concerning Jesus Christ are entered
        under the heading Messiah—Prophecies.
        BT Bible—Prophecies
  — **Prophetic office**
        [BT252]
  — **Psychology**
        [BT590.P9]
            Here are entered works on modern psycho-
        logical and/or psychiatric methods of investigat-
        ing Jesus Christ.
  — **Rationalistic interpretations**
        [BT304.95]
        BT Christianity—Controversial
            literature
  — Rejection at Nazareth
        USE Jesus Christ—Preaching at
            Nazareth
  — **Relics of the Nativity**
        BT Jesus Christ—Nativity
            Relics and reliquaries
  — **Relics of the Passion**
        [BT465]
        BT Jesus Christ—Passion
            Relics and reliquaries
        NT Holy Coat
            Holy Cross
            Holy Lance
            Holy Shroud
            Precious Blood, Relics of the
  — **Resurrection**
        [BT480-490]
        UF Resurrection of Christ
        BT Resurrection
        RT Easter
        NT Jesus Christ—Appearances
    — — **Biblical teaching**
    — — **Juvenile literature**
    — — **Meditations**
        [BT481]
    — — **Sermons**
  — **Rosicrucian interpretations**
        [BF1623.R7]
        BT Rosicrucians
  — **Royal office**
        [BT270]

        Here are entered works on the kingship of
    Jesus. Works on the Christian belief that the fol-
    lowers of Jesus compose his kingdom are entered
    under Jesus Christ—Kingdom. Works on the
    Christian doctrine of the spiritual reign of God
    are entered under Kingdom of God.
        UF Jesus Christ—Kingship
    — — **History of doctrines**
  — Sacred Heart, Devotion to
        USE Sacred Heart, Devotion to
  — Sayings
        USE Jesus Christ—Words
  — Second Advent
        USE Second Advent
  — **Sending of the twelve**
        [BT360]
        UF Mission of the twelve apostles
            Sending of the twelve apostles
        BT Apostles
  — **Servanthood**
        [BT257]
        UF Jesus Christ—Slavery
            Servanthood of Jesus Christ
            Slavery of Jesus Christ
        RT Servant of Jehovah
  — **Seven last words**
        [BT455-6]
        UF Jesus Christ—Last words
            Seven last words
        BT Jesus Christ—Words
    — — **Drama**
    — — **Sermons**
        BT Good Friday sermons
    — — Songs and music
        USE Passion-music
  — **Significance**
  — **Similitudes**
        [BT590.S5]
  — **Sinlessness**
  — Slavery
        USE Jesus Christ—Servanthood
  — **Spiritual life**
  — **Spiritualistic interpretations**
        [BT304.96]
        BT Bible and spiritualism
  — Summary of the Law
        USE Summary of the Law (Theology)
  — **Teaching methods**
        [BT590.T5]
        BT Christian education
  — **Teachings**
        [BS2415-2417]
        UF Teachings of Jesus
    — — **Meditations**
        [BS2415]
  — **Temple visit at age twelve**
        [BT320]
        UF Jesus Christ—Visit to the temple at
            age twelve
        BT Jesus Christ—Childhood
  — **Temptation**
        [BT355]
        UF Jesus Christ—Forty days in the
            wilderness
    — — **History of doctrines**
  — **Theosophical interpretations**
        [BT304.97]
        BT Bible and theosophy
            Theosophy
  — Three days between burial and
    resurrection
        USE Jesus Christ—Three days in the
            tomb
  — **Three days in the tomb**
        [BT468]
        UF Jesus Christ—Three days between
            burial and resurrection
        RT Jesus Christ—Burial
            Jesus Christ—Descent into hell
  — Titles
        USE Jesus Christ—Name

— Tomb
  USE Holy Sepulcher
— **Transfiguration**
  [BT410]
  UF Transfiguration of Christ
— **Trial**
  [BT440-445]
— — **Apocryphal and legendary literature**
    BT Christian literature, Early
— Typology
  USE Typology (Theology)
— **Unitarian interpretations**
  BT Unitarianism
— **Views on Jewish dietary laws, [Views on Jewish law, etc.]**
  UF Jesus Christ—Attitude towards
      Jewish dietary laws, [Attitude
      towards Jewish law, etc.]
— Views on politics
  USE Jesus Christ—Political and social
      views
— Views on society
  USE Jesus Christ—Political and social
      views
— Visit to the temple at age twelve
  USE Jesus Christ—Temple visit at age
      twelve
— Wit and humor
  USE Jesus Christ—Humor
— **Words**
  [BT306]
  UF Jesus Christ—Sayings
  NT Jesus Christ—Conversations
      Jesus Christ—Promises
      Jesus Christ—Seven last words
      Q hypothesis (Synoptics criticism)
— — **Extra-canonical parallels**
    [BT306]
    UF Jesus Christ—Agrapha
Jesus Christ in fiction, drama, poetry, etc.
  UF Jesus Christ in literature
Jesus Christ in literature
  USE Jesus Christ in fiction, drama, poetry,
      etc.
Jesus Christ
— **Art**
  NT Christian art and symbolism
Jesus Christ, Knowledge of
  USE Jesus Christ—Knowableness
Jesus Christ in art
  USE Jesus Christ—Art
Jesus Christ in Buddhism
  USE Jesus Christ—Buddhist interpretations
Jesus Christ in Hinduism
  USE Jesus Christ—Hindu interpretations
Jesus Christ in Islam
  USE Jesus Christ—Islamic interpretations
Jesus Christ in moving-pictures
  BT Moving-pictures
Jesus Christ in the Koran
  [BP134.J37]
  UF 'Īsā (Koranic character)
  BT Jesus Christ—Islamic interpretations
      Koran—Theology
Jesus Christ in the liturgy
  [BT575]
Jesus Christ the King, Feast of
  [BV64.J4]
  UF Christ the King, Feast of
      Feast of Jesus Christ the King
  BT Church year
      Fasts and feasts
Jesus Freaks
  USE Jesus People
Jesus Island (Québec)
  UF Ile Jésus (Québec)
  BT Islands—Québec (Province)
Jesus Maria Jesuit Mission Site (Brazil)
  USE Redução Jesuítica de Jesus Maria Site
      (Brazil)

Jesus Movement
  USE Jesus People
Jesus music
  USE Contemporary Christian music
Jesús Nazareno Plantation (Cuba)
  BT Plantations—Cuba
Jesus only doctrine (Pentecostalism)
  USE Oneness doctrine (Pentecostalism)
Jesus People *(May Subd Geog)*
  [BV3793]
  UF Jesus Freaks
      Jesus Movement
      Street Christians
  BT Pentecostalism
      Revivals
      Youth—Religious life
  NT Children of God (Movement)
Jesus prayer
  [BT590.J28]
  UF Prayer of Jesus
  BT Prayers
Jesus rock music
  USE Christian rock music
Jesus, Society of
  USE Jesuits
Jesus walking on the sea (Miracle)
  USE Jesus walking on the water (Miracle)
Jesus walking on the water (Miracle)
  [BT367.W]
  UF Jesus walking on the sea (Miracle)
      Walking on the sea (Miracle)
      Walking on the water (Miracle)
  BT Jesus Christ—Miracles
Jet (Precious stone) *(May Subd Geog)*
  BT Gems
Jet airplanes
  USE Jet planes
Jet-assisted take-off (Aircraft)
  USE Airplanes—Assisted take-off
Jet boat engines
  UF Cone propulsion (Boats)
      Hydraulic propulsion
      Marine jet engines
      Marine jet propellers
      Marine jet propulsion
      Water-jet engines
  BT Jet propulsion
      Jet pumps
      Motorboats—Motors
Jet boats
  [VM348.5]
  UF Boats, Jet-propelled
      Jet-propelled boats
  BT Motorboats
Jet bundles (Mathematics)
  [QA614]
  BT Global analysis (Mathematics)
      Manifolds (Mathematics)
      Vector bundles
Jet cutting
    Here are entered works on the use of fluid under
  pressure released through a nozzle to wash, erode,
  break, pierce and cut materials. Applications of fluid
  jets in a particular field are entered under the appro-
  priate heading, e.g. Hydraulic mining.
  UF Fluid jet cutting
  BT Cutting
      Fluid power technology
      High pressure (Technology)
  NT Fusion piercing drilling
Jet engine noise
  USE Jet planes—Noise
Jet engine sounds
  USE Jet plane sounds
Jet flaps (Airplanes)
  BT Air jets
      Flaps (Airplanes)
Jet flow
  USE Jets—Fluid dynamics
Jet fuel
  USE Jet planes—Fuel

Jet helicopters
  BT Helicopters
  NT Helicopters—Turbojet engines
— **Identification marks**
Jet injectors, Hypodermic
  USE Hypodermic jet injectors
Jet lag
  [RC1076.J48 (Aviation medicine)]
  UF Lag, Jet
  BT Aviation medicine
      Biological rhythms
      Flight—Physiological aspects
      Travel—Physiological aspects
Jet mills
  UF Fluid energy mills
  BT Milling machinery
Jet nacelles (Airplane)
  USE Airplanes—Nacelles
Jet nozzles
  BT Nozzles
Jet plane noise
  USE Jet planes—Noise
Jet plane sounds
  UF Jet engine sounds
      Jet planes, Military—Sounds
  BT Airplane sounds
      Sounds
Jet planes
  UF Jet airplanes
      Jet propelled airplanes
  BT Airplanes
  NT Aermacchi MB326 (Jet fighter plane)
      Alpha Jet (Training plane)
      Avro 707 (Jet planes)
      BAC Lightning (Fighter plane)
      BAC TSR 2 (Turbojet fighter planes)
      Delfin (Training planes)
      Delta wing airplanes
      Fairey Delta (Jet planes)
      Grumman X-29A (Jet plane)
      Handley Page 115 (Jet planes)
      Harrier (Jet fighter plane)
      Heinkel 162 (Jet fighter planes)
      Hunter (Turbojet fighter planes)
      Jet transports
      Lear jet aircraft
      Messerschmitt 262 (Fighter planes)
      Meteor (Fighter planes)
      Provost (Training planes)
      T2J (Training planes)
      Tomcat (Jet fighter plane)
      Vampire (Turbojet fighter planes)
      Victor (Jet planes)
— **Flight testing**
— **Fuel**
    UF Jet fuel
        Jet propellants
    BT Airplanes—Fuel
        Motor fuels
    NT Boron as fuel
— **Motors**
    USE Airplanes—Jet propulsion
        Airplanes—Ramjet engines
        Airplanes—Turbofan engines
        Airplanes—Turbojet engines
— **Noise**
    UF Aircraft noise
        Jet engine noise
        Jet plane noise
    BT Aerodynamic noise
    NT Airplanes—Turbojet engines—
        Mufflers
— **Piloting**
— **Radar equipment**
    BT Radar in aeronautics
— **Thrust reversers**
    [TL709.5.T5]
    UF Thrust reversers (Jet plane)
    BT Airplanes—Landing
Jet planes, Military *(May Subd Geog)*
  UF Military jets

Jet planes, Military *(Continued)*
  BT Airplanes, Military
  NT A-10 (Jet attack plane)
     Ar 234 bomber
     Avro Arrow (Turbojet fighter plane)
     B-1 bomber
     B-47 bomber
     B-52 Bomber
     B-58 bomber
     Banshee (Jet fighter plane)
     Canuck (Jet fighter plane)
     Corsair II (Jet attack plane)
     Cougar (Jet fighter plane)
     Crusader (Jet fighter plane)
     Cutlass (Jet fighter plane)
     Eagle (Jet fighter plane)
     F-5 (Jet fighter plane)
     F-16 (Fighter planes)
     Hornet (Jet fighter plane)
     Intruder (Bombers)
     Jaguar (Jet attack plane)
     Javelin (Jet fighter plane)
     Junkers Ju 287 (Jet bomber)
     KC-135 (Tanker aircraft)
     Kikka (Jet fighter plane)
     MIG-25 (Jet fighter plane)
     Panther (Jet fighter plane)
     Shooting Star (Jet fighter plane)
     Skyknight (Jet fighter plane)
     SR-71 (Jet reconnaissance plane)
     Starfire (Jet fighter plane)
     Stealth aircraft
     Tiger (Jet fighter plane)
     Tornado (Jet fighter plane)
     Valiant (Jet bomber)
     Viggen (Jet fighter plane)
     Voodoo (Jet fighter plane)
     Vulcan (Jet bomber)
  — Sounds
     USE Jet plane sounds
Jet propellants
  USE Jet planes—Fuel
Jet propelled airplanes
  USE Jet planes
Jet-propelled boats
  USE Jet boats
Jet propelled short take-off and landing aircraft
  USE Short take-off and landing aircraft—Jet
     propulsion
Jet propelled vertically rising aircraft
  USE Vertically rising aircraft—Jet
     propulsion
Jet propulsion
  BT Internal combustion engines
  RT Rockets (Aeronautics)
  NT Airplanes—Jet propulsion
     Jet boat engines
     Rockets (Ordnance)
     Short take-off and landing aircraft—Jet
      propulsion
     Vertically rising aircraft—Jet
      propulsion
Jet pumps
  [TJ901]
  UF Momentum pumps
  BT Hydraulic machinery
     Pumping machinery
  NT Ejector pumps
     Injectors
     Jet boat engines
     Short take-off and landing aircraft—Jet
      propulsion—Ejectors
     Vertically rising aircraft—Jet
      propulsion—Ejectors
Jet stream
  [QC935]
  BT Atmosphere, Upper
     Atmospheric circulation
     Meteorology
     Winds
     Winds aloft

  NT Clear air turbulence
Jet transports
  [TL685.7]
  UF Jetliners
     Turbine-powered transports
     Turbojet transports
  BT Airplanes
     Jet planes
     Transport planes
  RT Supersonic transport planes
  NT Airbus (Jet transport)
     Avro C. 102 Jetliner (Jet transport)
     Boeing 707 (Jet transports)
     Boeing 720 (Jet transports)
     Boeing 727 (Jet transports)
     Boeing 747 (Jet transports)
     Boeing 757 (Jet transport)
     C-5A (Jet transports)
     C-17 (Jet transport)
     Canadair Challenger (Jet transport)
     Caravelle (Jet transports)
     Comet (Jet transports)
     Convair 990 (Jet transport)
     Dassault Falcon (Jet transport)
     Electra (Turboprop transports)
     Hercules (Turboprop transports)
     Ilíushin 62 (Jet transports)
     Ilíushin 76T (Jet transports)
     Jetstream (Turboprop transport)
     KC-135 (Tanker aircraft)
     McDonnell Douglas DC-9 Super 80
      (Jet transport)
     McDonnell Douglas DC-10 (Jet
      transport)
     TriStar (Jet transport)
     Tupolev 134 (Jet transport)
     Tupolev 154 (Jet transport)
  — Identification marks
  — Landing
  — Piloting
  — Take-off
     [TL711.T3]
Jeter family *(Not Subd Geog)*
  UF Jetter family
     Jetters family
Jethro Coffin House (Nantucket, Mass.)
  UF Coffin House (Nantucket, Mass.)
  BT Dwellings—Massachusetts
Jetliners
  USE Jet transports
Jetons
  USE Jettons
Jets
  [TC173 (Hydraulic engineering)]
  BT Capillarity
     Fluids
     Hydrodynamics
     Liquids
  RT Atomization
     Hydraulics
  NT Air jets
     Astrophysical jets
     Density currents
     Plasma jets
     Spinnerets (Textile machinery)
     Wall jets
  — Fluid dynamics
     [QA911]
     UF Jet flow
     BT Gas dynamics
     NT Coanda effect
Jets, Plasma
  USE Plasma jets
Jets (Nuclear physics)
  BT Nuclear reactions
     Scattering (Physics)
Jets (Topology)
  [QA614.4]
  BT Differentiable manifolds
     Topology

Jetstream (Turboprop transport)
  [TL685.7]
  BT Jet transports
     Turboprop transports
Jett family *(Not Subd Geog)*
  UF Jette family
Jetta automobile
  [TL215.J]
  BT Volkswagen automobile
Jette family
  USE Jett family
Jetter family
  USE Jeter family
Jetters family
  USE Jeter family
Jetties
  [TC535]
  BT Harbors
     Hydraulic structures
  SA *subdivision* Jetties *under names of*
     rivers, e.g. Mississippi River—Jetties
Jettison
  BT Contracts, Maritime
  RT Average (Maritime law)
     Salvage
     Ships—Cargo
     Wreck
  NT Airplanes—Fuel—Jettisoning
Jettisoning of airplane fuel
  USE Airplanes—Fuel—Jettisoning
Jettons *(May Subd Geog)*
  [CJ5450]
  UF Counting coins
     Jetons
  BT Numismatics
  RT Tokens
Jeu de paume
  USE Court tennis
Jeu de paume, Serment du
  USE Tennis Court Oath, June 20, 1789
Jeupen family
  USE Joppe family
Jeux Canada
  USE Canada Games
Jeux floraux
  USE Floral games
Jeux-partis
  [PQ1323.J4 (Old French verse)]
  UF Partimen
  BT Debate poetry
     Provençal poetry
     Troubadours
Jeverland cattle
  [SF193.J6 (Herd-books)]
  BT Dairy cattle
Jew family *(Not Subd Geog)*
Jewel bearings
  [TJ1073.J4]
  BT Bearings (Machinery)
     Nonmetallic bearings
     Precious stones
  RT Clocks and watches—Jewels
Jewel family
  USE Jewell family
Jewel thieves *(May Subd Geog)*
  BT Jewelry
     Thieves
Jeweled bindings
  USE Bookbinding—Jeweled bindings
Jeweled lacerta
  USE Lacerta lepida
Jewelers *(May Subd Geog)*
  [HD9747 (Trade)]
  [NK7100-NK7695 (Art)]
  [TS720-TS770 (Manufactures)]
  BT Art metal-workers
  NT Clock and watch makers
     Trade-unions—Jewelers
Jewelers' supplies
  [TS760]

Jewell family (*Not Subd Geog*)
  UF Jewel family
    Jewill family
Jewelry (*May Subd Geog*)
    [GT2250-GT2280 (Manners and
      customs)]
    [HJ5783 (Taxation)]
    [NK7100-NK7695 (Art industries)]
    [TS720-TS770 (Manufacture)]
  UF Jewels
  BT Art
    Art metal-work
    Arts and crafts movement
    Costume
    Decoration and ornament
    Decorative arts
    Silverwork
  RT Gems
  NT Anklets (Ornaments)
    Architect-designed jewelry
    Bracelets
    Bridal crowns
    Brooches
    Cameos
    Chains (Jewelry)
    Coral jewelry
    Costume jewelry
    Crown jewels
    Earrings
    Ethnic jewelry
    Fibula (Archaeology)
    Garnet jewelry
    Gold jewelry
    Hatpins
    Jewel thieves
    Necklaces
    Nose ornaments
    Paste jewelry
    Pendants (Jewelry)
    Pins and needles
    Rings
    Silver jewelry
    Stickpins
  — Collectors and collecting
    NT Jewelry as an investment
  — Finishing
    BT Finishes and finishing
  — History
  — — 18th century
  — — 19th century
      [NK7309.8]
    NT Jewelry, Victorian
  — — 20th century
      [NK7310]
  — Labeling
  — Law and legislation
      (*May Subd Geog*)
  — Oriental influences
    BT Civilization, Oriental
  — Prices (*May Subd Geog*)
    NT Jewelry as an investment
  — Private collections (*May Subd Geog*)
      [NK7303]
  — Purchasing
  — Religious aspects
  — — Baptists, [Catholic Church, etc.]
  — — Buddhism, [Christianity, etc.]
  — Repairing
      [TS740]
    BT Jewelry making
  — Taxation (*May Subd Geog*)
    BT Luxuries—Taxation
  — India
  — — Greek influences
      BT Greece—Civilization
Jewelry, Ancient (*May Subd Geog*)
    [NK7307]
  — Oriental influences
    BT Civilization, Oriental
Jewelry, Bedouin (*May Subd Geog*)
  UF Bedouin jewelry

Jewelry, Black (*May Subd Geog*)
  UF Black jewelry
Jewelry, Byzantine, [Gallo-Roman, etc.]
  (*May Subd Geog*)
Jewelry, Classical (*May Subd Geog*)
  UF Classical jewelry
Jewelry, Finno-Ugrian (*May Subd Geog*)
  UF Finno-Ugrian jewelry
Jewelry, Garnet
  USE Garnet jewelry
Jewelry, Germanic (*May Subd Geog*)
  UF Germanic jewelry
Jewelry, Islamic (*May Subd Geog*)
  UF Islamic jewelry
Jewelry, Medieval (*May Subd Geog*)
Jewelry, Phoenician (*May Subd Geog*)
  UF Phoenician jewelry
Jewelry, Prehistoric (*May Subd Geog*)
  UF Prehistoric jewelry
Jewelry, Primitive (*May Subd Geog*)
    [GN418.4]
  UF Primitive jewelry
Jewelry, Rhinestone
  USE Rhinestone jewelry
Jewelry, Rustic (*May Subd Geog*)
  UF Rustic jewelry
  BT Folk art
Jewelry, Silver
  USE Silver jewelry
Jewelry, Tuareg (*May Subd Geog*)
  UF Tuareg jewelry
Jewelry, Victorian (*May Subd Geog*)
  UF Victorian jewelry
  BT Jewelry—History—19th century
Jewelry as an investment
  BT Investments
    Jewelry—Collectors and collecting
    Jewelry—Prices
Jewelry engraving
  BT Engraving
Jewelry making
    [TS740-761]
  BT Handicraft
  RT Goldwork
    Silverwork
  NT Enamel and enameling
    Engraving (Metal-work)
    Jewelry—Repairing
Jewelry mountings
  USE Jewelry settings
Jewelry settings
  UF Jewelry mountings
    Mountings, Jewelry
    Settings, Jewelry
  BT Mounts (Decorative arts)
    Precious stones
Jewelry shops
  USE Jewelry stores
Jewelry stores (*May Subd Geog*)
    [NA6227.J4 (Architecture)]
  UF Jewelry shops
  BT Specialty stores
Jewelry trade (*May Subd Geog*)
    [HD9747]
  — Advertising
    USE Advertising—Jewelry trade
  — Credit guides
      [HF5585.J4]
  — Vocational guidance
Jewels
  USE Crown jewels
    Gems
    Insignia
    Jewelry
    Precious stones
Jewet family
  USE Jewett family

Jewett family (*Not Subd Geog*)
  UF Jewet family
    Jewit family
    Jewitt family
    Jouett family
    Juett family
    Juwet family
Jewill family
  USE Jewell family
Jewish actors
  USE Actors, Jewish
Jewish aesthetics (*May Subd Geog*)
  UF Aesthetics, Jewish
Jewish-Afro-American relations
  USE Afro-Americans—Relations with Jews
Jewish aged (*May Subd Geog*)
  UF Aged, Jewish
  BT Minority aged
Jewish almanacs
  USE Almanacs, Jewish
Jewish anarchists (*May Subd Geog*)
  UF Anarchists, Jewish
  BT Anarchists
Jewish apologetics
  USE Judaism—Apologetic works
Jewish-Arab relations
    Here are entered works that discuss collectively
  the relations between Arabs and Jews, including reli-
  gious, ethnic, and ideological relations, subdivided
  further by dates, if appropriate. Works on relations
  between the religions of Judaism and Islam are en-
  tered under Judaism—Relations—Islam. When this
  heading is assigned, duplicate entry is made under
  Islam—Relations—Judaism. Works on the conflicts
  between the Arab countries and Israel are entered
  under Israel-Arab conflicts.
  UF Arab-Jewish relations
    Palestine problem
  BT Arab countries—History—20th
      century
    Palestinian Arabs
  NT Propaganda, Anti-Israeli
    Propaganda, Zionist
  — To 1917
  — 1917-
  — 1917-1949
    NT Palestine—History—Arab riots,
        1920
      Palestine—History—Arab riots,
        1929
      Palestine—History—Arab rebellion,
        1936-1939
      Palestine—History—Partition, 1947
  — 1949-
      [DS119.7]
    RT Israel-Arab conflicts
      Palestine—Politics and government
        —1948-
    NT Fedayeen
  — 1949-1967
  — 1967-1973
  — 1973-
    NT Lebanon—History—Israeli
        intervention, 1982-
  — Religious aspects
Jewish-Arab relations in literature
    [PJ7519.J4 (Arabic literature)]
Jewish-Arab relations in motion pictures
  BT Moving-pictures
Jewish-Arab War, 1948-1949
  USE Israel-Arab War, 1948-1949
Jewish architecture
  USE Architecture, Jewish
Jewish archives (*May Subd Geog*)
  UF Jews—Archives
  BT Archives
Jewish art
  USE Art, Jewish
Jewish art and symbolism (*May Subd Geog*)
  UF Jewish symbolism and art

1957

Jewish art and symbolism *(Continued)*
  BT Art, Jewish
       Arts, Jewish
       Christian art and symbolism
       Symbolism
       Symbolism in art
  NT Bible—Illustrations
       Folk art, Jewish
       Jewish crafts
       Judaism—Liturgical objects
       Magen David
       Menorah
       Symbolism in the Bible
       Synagogue art
       Tallith bags
       Tefillin bags
       Temple of God
       Torah ornaments
       Torah wrappers

Jewish artisans *(May Subd Geog)*
  UF Artisans, Jewish
  BT Artisans

Jewish artists
  USE Artists, Jewish

Jewish arts
  USE Arts, Jewish

Jewish asceticism
  USE Asceticism—Judaism

Jewish astrology
  USE Astrology, Jewish

Jewish astronomy
  USE Astronomy, Jewish

Jewish athletes *(May Subd Geog)*
  BT Athletes

Jewish authors *(May Subd Geog)*
  UF Authors, Jewish
  BT Jewish literature
  SA *subdivision* Jewish authors *under*
      names of literatures, e.g. American
      literature—Jewish authors
  NT Authors, Hebrew
       Sephardic authors

Jewish authors, Oriental *(May Subd Geog)*
  UF Authors, Oriental Jewish
       Oriental Jewish authors
  BT Jews, Oriental

Jewish bankers *(May Subd Geog)*
  BT Bankers

Jewish Bibles
  USE Bible. O.T.—Versions, Jewish

Jewish Biblical criticism
  USE Bible. O.T.—Criticism, interpretation,
      etc., Jewish

Jewish-Black relations
  USE Blacks—Relations with Jews

Jewish book-plates
  USE Book-plates, Jewish

Jewish businessmen *(May Subd Geog)*
  UF Businessmen, Jewish
  BT Businessmen

Jewish calendar
  USE Calendar, Jewish

Jewish camps *(May Subd Geog)*
  [BM135]
  UF Jewish religious camps
  BT Camps
       Jewish children
       Religious camps

Jewish cantors
  USE Cantors, Jewish

Jewish capitalists and financiers
(May Subd Geog)
  UF Capitalists and financiers—Jews
       Capitalists and financiers, Jewish
       Jewish financiers
  — **Europe**
      NT Court Jews

Jewish Cemetery in Warsaw (Warsaw, Poland)
  USE Cmentarz żydowski w Warszawie
      (Warsaw, Poland)

Jewish chant
  USE Chants (Jewish)

Jewish charities
  USE Jews—Charities

Jewish chess players *(May Subd Geog)*
  UF Chess players, Jewish
  BT Chess players

Jewish children *(May Subd Geog)*
  UF Children, Jewish
       Jews—Children
  BT Children
  NT Jewish camps
  — **Prayer-books and devotions**
      [BM666]
      UF Children—Prayer-books and
         devotions, Jewish
         Jewish children—Prayer-books and
         devotions—English
  — — **English**
        USE Jewish children—Prayer-books
          and devotions
  — — **French, [German, Italian, etc.]**

Jewish children's sermons
  USE Children's sermons, Jewish

Jewish Christian Science
  USE Jewish Science

Jewish Christians *(May Subd Geog)*
  [BR158]
  Here are entered works dealing with Christians of
  Jewish antecedence.
  UF Christians, Hebrew
       Christians, Jewish
       Hebrew Christians
       Messianic Jews
  BT Christians
  NT Converts from Judaism
       Marranos
  — **History**
  — — **Early church, ca. 30-600**
      NT Ebionism
         Elkesaites

Jewish chronology
  USE Chronology, Jewish

Jewish civilization
  USE Jews—Civilization

Jewish college teachers *(May Subd Geog)*
  UF Jewish university teachers
  BT College teachers
       Jewish teachers

Jewish communists *(May Subd Geog)*
  UF Communism—Jews
       Communists, Jewish

Jewish community centers
  USE Community centers, Jewish

Jewish composers
  USE Composers, Jewish

Jewish converts
  USE Proselytes and proselyting, Jewish

Jewish converts to Christianity
  USE Converts from Judaism

Jewish converts to Islam
  USE Muslim converts from Judaism

Jewish cosmology
  USE Cosmology, Jewish

Jewish costume
  USE Costume, Jewish

Jewish councils and synods
  UF Councils and synods, Jewish
       Jewish synods
       Synods, Jewish
  BT Jews—Politics and government
  NT Sanhedrin

Jewish courts
  USE Courts, Jewish

Jewish crafts
  [BM729.H35]
  UF Jewish handicrafts
  BT Creative activities and seat work
       Handicraft
       Jewish art and symbolism
  NT Hanukkah decorations

Jewish creeds
  USE Creeds, Jewish

Jewish criminals *(May Subd Geog)*
  UF Jews—Crime
       Jews as criminals
  BT Crime and criminals

Jewish Day of Atonement
  USE Yom Kippur

Jewish day schools *(May Subd Geog)*
  Here are entered works dealing with elementary
  and secondary schools whose pupils receive their entire education under Jewish auspices, control, or support. Works dealing with schools teaching Jewish
  subject matter only are entered under Jewish religious schools.
  UF Hebrew day schools
       Jewish schools
       Schools—Jews
       Schools, Jewish
  BT Jewish religious education
       Jews—Education
  RT Jewish religious schools
  NT Heder

Jewish deeds
  USE Deeds, Jewish

Jewish demonology
  USE Demonology, Jewish

Jewish devotional calendars
  UF Devotional calendars—Judaism
       Devotional calendars, Jewish

Jewish drama
  NT Hebrew drama
       Ladino drama
       Yiddish drama

Jewish educators *(May Subd Geog)*
  [LB75]
  UF Educators, Jewish
  BT Jews—Education

Jewish emancipation
  USE Jews—Emancipation

Jewish embroidery
  USE Embroidery, Jewish

Jewish engraving
  USE Engraving, Jewish

Jewish entertainers *(May Subd Geog)*
  [PN1583]
  UF Entertainers, Jewish
  BT Entertainers
  RT Jewish theater

Jewish epitaphs *(May Subd Geog)*
  BT Epitaphs

Jewish ethics
  USE Ethics, Jewish

Jewish etiquette
  UF Etiquette, Jewish
  BT Etiquette
  NT Bar mitzvah etiquette
       Synagogue etiquette
       Table etiquette, Jewish

Jewish exempla
  USE Exempla, Jewish

Jewish families *(May Subd Geog)*
  UF Families, Jewish
  BT Family

Jewish farmers
  USE Farmers, Jewish

Jewish festival-day sermons
  USE Festival-day sermons, Jewish

Jewish fiction
  BT Religious fiction
  NT Jewish religious fiction
       Short stories, Jewish

Jewish fiction (American)
  USE American fiction—Jewish authors

Jewish financiers
  USE Jewish capitalists and financiers

Jewish folk art
  USE Folk art, Jewish

Jewish folk literature *(May Subd Geog)*
  UF Folk literature, Jewish
  BT Jewish literature

Jewish funeral rites and ceremonies
  USE Funeral rites and ceremonies, Jewish
Jewish guilds *(May Subd Geog)*
  UF Guilds, Jewish
  BT Guilds
Jewish handicrafts
  USE Jewish crafts
Jewish heresies
  USE Heresies, Jewish
Jewish heretics
  USE Heretics, Jewish
Jewish historians
  USE Historians, Jewish
Jewish holidays
  USE Fasts and feasts—Judaism
Jewish holocaust (1939-1945)
  USE Holocaust, Jewish (1939-1945)
Jewish homiletical illustrations
  USE Homiletical illustrations, Jewish
Jewish homiletics
  USE Preaching, Jewish
Jewish hygiene
  USE Hygiene, Jewish
Jewish hymns
  UF Hymns, Jewish
     Jews—Hymns
  BT Synagogue music
  RT Jewish religious poetry
  NT Hymns, Hebrew
     Hymns, Yiddish
     Piyutim
Jewish identity
  USE Jews—Identity
Jewish illumination of books and manuscripts
  USE Illumination of books and manuscripts,
       Jewish
Jewish inscriptions
  USE Inscriptions, Jewish
Jewish-Italian dialect
  USE Italian language—Dialects—Judeo-
       Italian
Jewish journalists *(May Subd Geog)*
  UF Journalists, Jewish
  BT Journalists
Jewish judges *(May Subd Geog)*
  BT Judges
Jewish labor unions
  USE Jewish trade-unions
Jewish lamps
  USE Lamps, Jewish
Jewish language
  USE Hebrew language
     Yiddish language
Jewish law
    Here are entered works on Jewish law, including
  law in the Bible. Works on the influence of the Bible
  upon secular law are entered under Bible and law.
  UF Bible—Law
     Biblical law
     Civil law (Jewish law)
     Halacha
     Halakha
     Hebrew law
     Jews—Law
     Law, Hebrew
     Law, Jewish
     Law, Mosaic
     Law in the Bible
     Mosaic law
  BT Law, Semitic
  SA *special legal headings with Jewish law*
     added in parentheses, e.g. Aliens
     (Jewish law); Contracts (Jewish
     law); Larceny (Jewish law); Torts
     (Jewish law)
  NT Abortion (Jewish law)
     Absence and presumption of death
       (Jewish law)
     Acquisition of property (Jewish law)
     Admissions (Jewish law)
     Adoption (Jewish law)

Adultery (Jewish law)
Agency (Jewish law)
Agricultural laws and legislation
  (Jewish law)
Antenuptial contracts (Jewish law)
Artificial insemination, Human (Jewish
  law)
Autopsy (Jewish law)
Children (Jewish law)
Commandments, Six hundred and
  thirteen
Commandments (Judaism)
Cookery in Jewish law
Courts, Jewish
Credit (Jewish law)
Equality before the law—Biblical
  teaching
Euthanasia (Jewish law)
Evidence, Documentary (Jewish law)
Exiles (Jewish law)
Gelatin (Jewish law)
Ḥazaḳah
Holocaust and Jewish law
Illegality (Jewish law)
Interest (Jewish law)
Interfaith marriage (Jewish law)
Jews—Dietary laws
Jews—Identity
Karaite law
Legal instruments (Jewish law)
Lifting and carrying (Jewish law)
Mamzer
Mourning customs, Jewish
Noahide Laws
Passover—Customs and practices
Personal injuries (Jewish law)
Polygamy (Jewish law)
Prohibited books (Jewish law)
Public domain (Jewish law)
Responsa
Revelation on Sinai
Sabbath legislation
Sabbatical year (Judaism)
Summer (Jewish law)
Torah scrolls (Jewish law)
Transfer (Jewish law)
Weaving (Jewish law)
Writing (Jewish law)
— **Interpretation and construction**
    NT Eruv
— **Language**
    BT Law—Language
— **Literary history**
— **Reform Judaism**
    BT Reform Judaism
— **Palestine**
      Here are entered works dealing with that part
  of Jewish law operative only in Palestine.
— — **Cases**
Jewish law and technology
  USE Technology and Jewish law
Jewish lawyers
  USE Lawyers, Jewish
Jewish leadership *(May Subd Geog)*
  BT Leadership
Jewish learning and scholarship
  (May Subd Geog)
  ₍DS113₎
  UF Jews—Learning and scholarship
     Learning and scholarship—Jews
  RT Jews—Intellectual life
  NT Kallah
     Scientists, Jewish
     Talmud Torah (Judaism)
Jewish legends
  USE Legends, Jewish
Jewish Legion
  ₍D568.7₎
  BT World War, 1914-1918—Participation,
     Jewish

Jewish letters
Jewish librarians *(May Subd Geog)*
  UF Librarians, Jewish
  BT Librarians
Jewish libraries *(May Subd Geog)*
  ₍Z675.J4₎
  UF Hebrew libraries
     Libraries, Hebrew
     Libraries, Jewish
  BT Religious libraries
  NT Rabbinical seminary libraries
     Synagogue libraries
Jewish life
  USE Jewish way of life
     Jews—Social life and customs
     Judaism—Customs and practices
Jewish literature *(May Subd Geog)*
  UF Jews—Literature
     Judaica
  RT Hebrew literature
  NT Bible
     Cabala
     Classification—Books—Jewish
       literature
     Folk literature, Hebrew
     Geonic literature
     Jewish authors
     Jewish folk literature
     Jewish religious literature
     Judeo-Arabic literature
     Midrash
     Proverbs, Jewish
     Rabbinical literature
     Talmud
     Yiddish literature
  — Cataloging
     USE Cataloging of Jewish literature
  — **Publication and distribution**
     BT Booksellers and bookselling—
        Colportage, subscription trade,
        etc.
Jewish literature (American)
  USE American literature—Jewish authors
Jewish literature (Arabic)
  USE Arabic literature—Jewish authors
Jewish literature (Dutch)
  USE Dutch literature—Jewish authors
Jewish literature (English)
    Duplicate entry is made under English literature
  —Jewish authors.
Jewish literature (Ethiopic)
Jewish literature (French)
  USE French literature—Jewish authors
Jewish literature (German)
  USE German literature—Jewish authors
Jewish literature (Hellenistic)
  USE Greek literature—Jewish authors
Jewish literature (Italian)
    Duplicate entry is made under Italian literature—
  Jewish authors.
Jewish literature (Portuguese)
  USE Portuguese literature—Jewish authors
Jewish literature (Russian)
  USE Russian literature—Jewish authors
Jewish literature (Spanish)
  ₍PQ6056₎
    Duplicate entry is made under Spanish literature
  —Jewish authors.
Jewish liturgical music
  USE Synagogue music
Jewish magic
  USE Magic, Jewish
Jewish marriage customs and rites
  USE Marriage customs and rites, Jewish
Jewish martyrs *(May Subd Geog)*
  UF Martyrs, Jewish
Jewish medalists
  USE Medalists, Jewish
Jewish medals
  USE Medals, Jewish

Jewish medicine
USE Medicine, Jewish
Jewish meditations
UF Meditations, Jewish
BT Meditation (Judaism)
Jewish merchants
USE Merchants, Jewish
Jewish migrations
USE Jews—Migrations
Jewish minters
USE Minters, Jewish
Jewish mourning customs
USE Mourning customs, Jewish
Jewish museums *(May Subd Geog)*
BT Museums
Jewish music
USE Jews—Music
Jewish musicians
USE Musicians, Jewish
Jewish names
USE Names, Personal—Jewish
Jewish nationalism
UF Jews—Nationalism
Nationalism—Jews
Nationalism, Jewish
RT Zionism
NT Jews—Identity
Jewish needlework
USE Needlework, Jewish
Jewish New Year
USE Rosh ha-Shanah
Jewish newspapers *(May Subd Geog)*
UF Jews—Newspapers
NT Hebrew newspapers
Ladino newspapers
Yiddish newspapers
Jewish numismatics
USE Numismatics, Jewish
Jewish old age homes
USE Old age homes, Jewish
Jewish orphanages *(May Subd Geog)*
UF Orphanages, Jewish
BT Jews—Charities
Jewish orphans *(May Subd Geog)*
UF Orphans, Jewish
BT Jews—Charities
Jewish parables
USE Parables, Jewish
Jewish Pentecost
USE Shavuot
Jewish periodicals *(May Subd Geog)*
BT Jews—Periodicals
NT Synagogue bulletins
Jewish personal names
USE Names, Personal—Jewish
Jewish philosophers
USE Philosophers, Jewish
Jewish philosophy
USE Philosophy, Jewish
Jewish physicians
USE Physicians, Jewish
Jewish pilgrims and pilgrimages
(May Subd Geog)
BT Pilgrims and pilgrimages
RT Pilgrimage Festivals (Judaism)
Jewish poetry *(May Subd Geog)*
NT Badḥanim
Hebrew poetry
Jewish religious poetry
Jewish poetry (American)
USE American poetry—Jewish authors
Jewish poetry (Arabic)
USE Arabic poetry—Jewish authors
Jewish poetry (Spanish)
USE Spanish poetry—Jewish authors
Jewish portraits
USE Portraits, Jewish
Jewish prayers for rain
USE Prayers for rain, Jewish
Jewish preaching
USE Preaching, Jewish

Jewish property *(May Subd Geog)*
UF Property, Jewish
BT Alien property
Restitution and indemnification claims
(1933-   )
— **Germany**
NT Haavara
Jewish proselytes and proselyting
USE Proselytes and proselyting, Jewish
Jewish proverbs
USE Proverbs, Jewish
Jewish proverbs (Judeo-Arabic)
USE Proverbs, Judeo-Arabic
Jewish proverbs (Ladino)
USE Proverbs, Ladino
Jewish question
USE Jews—[place], *other subdivisions
under the heading* Jews, *and related
topics*
Jewish quotations
USE Quotations, Jewish
Jewish rabbis
USE Rabbis
Jewish radicals *(May Subd Geog)*
UF Jews—Radicalism
Radicalism—Jews
Radicalism, Jewish
BT Radicals
Jewish refugees
USE Refugees, Jewish
Jewish religious camps
USE Jewish camps
Jewish religious education *(May Subd Geog)*
UF Education, Jewish
Jews—Religious education
BT Jews—Education
Judaism—Study and teaching
Moral education
Religious education
NT Drama in Jewish religious education
Games in Jewish religious education
Jewish day schools
Jewish religious schools
Puppets and puppet-plays in Jewish
religious education
Rabbinical seminaries
Talmud Torah (Judaism)
— **Home training**
— **Teaching methods**
— **Text-books for adolescents** [adults, etc.]
Jewish religious education of adolescents
BT Youth
Jewish religious education of adults
(May Subd Geog)
BT Religious education of adults
Jewish religious education of children
(May Subd Geog)
BT Children
NT Jewish religious education of girls
Jewish religious education of girls
(May Subd Geog)
BT Jewish religious education of children
Religious education of girls
**Jewish religious education of preschool
children**
BT Children
Jewish religious education of young people
BT Youth
Jewish religious fiction *(May Subd Geog)*
BT Jewish fiction
Jewish religious literature
Religious fiction
Jewish religious functionaries
USE Judaism—Functionaries
Jewish religious literature *(May Subd Geog)*
UF Religious literature, Jewish
BT Jewish literature
Religious literature
NT Jewish religious fiction
Jewish religious poetry

Jewish religious poetry
UF Hymns, Jewish
Judaism—Poetry
BT Jewish poetry
Jewish religious literature
Religious poetry
RT Jewish hymns
Jewish religious poetry, American
(May Subd Geog)
UF American Jewish religious poetry
BT American poetry
Jewish religious poetry, Arabic
(May Subd Geog)
BT Arabic poetry—Jewish authors
Jewish religious poetry, Canadian
(May Subd Geog)
UF Canadian Jewish religious poetry
BT Canadian poetry
Jewish religious poetry, English, [etc.]
Jewish religious poetry, German
(May Subd Geog)
UF German Jewish religious poetry
BT German poetry
Jewish religious poetry, Hebrew
(May Subd Geog)
BT Hebrew poetry
RT Piyutim
NT Azharot
Jewish religious poetry, Israeli (English)
(May Subd Geog)
UF Israeli Jewish religious poetry
(English)
BT Israeli poetry (English)
Jewish religious poetry, Judeo-Arabic
(May Subd Geog)
UF Judeo-Arabic Jewish religious poetry
BT Judeo-Arabic poetry
Jewish religious schools *(May Subd Geog)*
Here are entered works dealing with elementary
and secondary schools teaching Jewish subject mat-
ter only. Works dealing with schools whose pupils
receive their entire education under Jewish auspices,
control, or support are entered under Jewish day
schools.
UF Jewish schools
Schools—Jews
Schools, Jewish
Talmud Torahs (Schools)
BT Jewish religious education
Jews—Education
RT Jewish day schools
Jewish resistance movements
USE *subdivision* Underground movements,
Jewish *under individual wars, e.g.*
World War, 1939-1945—
Underground movements, Jewish
Jewish-Roman War, 66-73
USE Jews—History—Rebellion, 66-73
Jewish saints *(May Subd Geog)*
UF Saints, Jewish
BT Saints
NT Zaddikim
Jewish scholarships
USE Jews—Scholarships, fellowships, etc.
Jewish schools
USE Jewish day schools
Jewish religious schools
Jewish Science
[BM729.J4]
Here are entered works dealing with a movement
that, negatively, seeks to counteract Christian
Science with a Jewish counterpart and, positively,
reveals to the Jew the sources of health, serenity, and
peace of mind within his own faith.
UF Christian Science, Jewish
Jewish Christian Science
Science, Jewish
BT Christian Science
Mental healing
Spiritual healing
Jewish scientists
USE Scientists, Jewish

Jewish sculpture
  USE Sculpture, Jewish
Jewish seals (Numismatics)
  (May Subd Geog)
    BT Seals (Law)
       Seals (Numismatics)
Jewish seamen
  USE Seamen, Jewish
Jewish sects
  ₍BM175₎
    UF Jews—Sects
       Sects, Jewish
    BT Judaism
       Sects
    NT Conservative Judaism
       Essenes
       Hasidism
       Heresies, Jewish
       Karaites
       Orthodox Judaism
       Pharisees
       Qumran community
       Rechabites
       Reconstructionist Judaism
       Reform Judaism
       Sabbathaians
       Sadducees
       Zadokites
       Zealots (Jewish party)
Jewish sermons *(May Subd Geog)*
  ₍BM735-747₎
    UF Sermons, Jewish
    BT Preaching, Jewish
    NT Bar mitzvah sermons
       Bat mitzvah sermons
       Children's sermons, Jewish
       Festival-day sermons, Jewish
       Funeral sermons, Jewish
       Hadran
       High Holiday sermons
       Midrash
       Passover sermons
       Rosh ha-Shanah sermons
       Shabbat ha-gadol sermons
       Shabbat shubah sermons
       Synagogue dedication sermons
       Wedding sermons, Jewish
  — United States
       NT Sermons, American—Jewish
          authors
Jewish sermons for children
  USE Children's sermons, Jewish
Jewish short stories
  USE Short stories, Jewish
Jewish shrines
    BT Shrines
Jewish singers
  USE Singers, Jewish
Jewish socialists *(May Subd Geog)*
    UF Socialists, Jewish
    BT Socialists
Jewish sociology
  USE Sociology, Jewish
Jewish soldiers *(May Subd Geog)*
    UF Jews as soldiers
    BT Soldiers
    SA *subdivision* Participation, Jewish *under
       individual wars, e.g.* World War,
       1939-1945—Participation, Jewish
    NT Cantonists
  — Prayer-books and devotions
       BT Armed Forces—Prayer-books and
          devotions
          Judaism—Prayer-books and
          devotions
    — — English, ₍French, German, etc.₎
  — Religious life
       USE Soldiers—Religious life (Judaism)
Jewish statesmen *(May Subd Geog)*
    UF Statesmen, Jewish
    BT Jews in public life

Jewish students
  USE Students, Jewish
Jewish symbolism and art
  USE Jewish art and symbolism
Jewish synods
  USE Jewish councils and synods
Jewish table etiquette
  USE Table etiquette, Jewish
Jewish teachers *(May Subd Geog)*
    UF Teachers, Jewish
    NT Jewish college teachers
Jewish teachers colleges *(May Subd Geog)*
    BT Teachers colleges
Jewish theater *(May Subd Geog)*
  ₍PN3035₎
    Here are entered works on the theater under Jew-
    ish auspices outside of Israel. Works on the theater in
    Israel are entered under Theater—Israel. Works on
    Yiddish drama as acted upon the stage are entered
    under Theater, Yiddish.
    UF Theater—Jews
       Theater, Hebrew
       Theater, Jewish
    RT Jewish entertainers
    NT Theater, Yiddish
Jewish theological seminaries
  USE Rabbinical seminaries
Jewish theology
  USE Judaism—Doctrines
Jewish trade-unions *(May Subd Geog)*
    UF Jewish labor unions
       Trade-unions, Jewish
    BT Trade-unions
Jewish travelers *(May Subd Geog)*
    UF Travelers, Jewish
Jewish underground movements
  USE *subdivision* Underground movements,
       Jewish *under individual wars, e.g.*
       World War, 1939-1945—
       Underground movements, Jewish
Jewish university teachers
  USE Jewish college teachers
Jewish war resistance movements
  USE *subdivision* Underground movements,
       Jewish *under individual wars, e.g.*
       World War, 1939-1945—
       Underground movements, Jewish
Jewish way of life
  ₍BM723₎
    UF Jewish life
       Life, Jewish way of
       Religious life (Judaism)
       Way of life, Jewish
    BT Ethics, Jewish
       Jews—Social life and customs
       Judaism—Customs and practices
       Sociology, Jewish
    NT Asceticism—Judaism
       Family—Religious life (Judaism)
       Students, Jewish—Religious life
       Women, Jewish—Religious life
Jewish way of life in art
  USE Jews in art
Jewish wedding sermons
  USE Wedding sermons, Jewish
Jewish wit and humor
  ₍PN6231.J5₎
    RT Hebrew wit and humor
    NT Israeli wit and humor
       Purim parodies
       Schlemiel in literature
       Yiddish wit and humor
Jewish wit and humor, Pictorial
Jewish women
  USE Women, Jewish
Jewish youth
  USE Youth, Jewish
Jewit family
  USE Jewett family
Jewitt family
  USE Jewett family

Jews. Liturgy and ritual
  USE Judaism—Liturgy
Jews *(May Subd Geog)*
  ₍DS101-DS151₎
  ₍GN547 (Anthropology)₎
    UF Hebrews
       Israelites
       Judaica
    BT Christianity
       Ethnology—Israel
       Judaism
    SA *subdivision* Jews *under individual
       wars, e.g.* World War, 1939-1945—
       Jews; *and headings beginning with
       the word* Jewish
    NT Anglo-Israelism
       Ashkenazim
       Benjamin (Tribe of Israel)
       Classification—Books—Jewish
          literature
       Falashas
       Hasidim
       Israelis
       Kemants
       Missions to Jews
       Naphtali (Tribe of Israel)
       Patriarchs (Bible)
       Postage-stamps—Topics—Jews
       Prophets
       Romaniots
       Samaritans
       Sephardim
       Youth, Jewish
  — Alcohol use
    ₍HV5185₎
  — Anecdotes, facetiae, satire, etc.
       NT Rabbis—Anecdotes, facetiae, satire,
          etc.
  — Anthropometry
  — Antiquities
    ₍DS111₎
       RT Bible—Antiquities
       NT Ark of the Covenant
          Brazen serpent
          Breastplate of the High Priest
          Ephod
          Hanukkah lamp
          Inscriptions, Jewish
          Menorah
          Numismatics, Jewish
          Priests, Jewish—Vestments
          Tabernacle
          Tefillin
  — Apologetic works
       USE Judaism—Apologetic works
  — Archives
       USE Jewish archives
  — Attitudes toward Israel
       BT Israel and the Diaspora
  — Autographs
  — Bio-bibliography
    ₍Z7070 (Hebrew and Yiddish)₎
  — Biography
    ₍DS115 (Collective)₎
       UF Judaism—Biography
       RT Rabbis
       NT Actors, Jewish
          Pseudo-Messiahs
          Women, Jewish
  — Cabala
       USE Cabala
  — Charities
    ₍HV3191-HV3192₎
       UF Jewish charities
       NT Jewish orphanages
          Jewish orphans
          Old age homes, Jewish
  — Children
       USE Jewish children
  — Chosen people
       USE Jews—Election, Doctrine of

Jews *(Continued)*
— Civil rights
   USE Jews—Legal status, laws, etc.
— **Civilization**
   [DS112-DS113]
   UF Civilization, Jewish
       Jewish civilization
   BT Civilization, Semitic
   NT Africa—Civilization—Jewish
       influences
       Brazil—Civilization—Jewish
       influences
       Civilization, Medieval—Jewish
       influences
       Civilization, Modern—Jewish
       influences
       Czechoslovakia—Civilization—
       Jewish influences
       Germany—Civilization—Jewish
       influences
       Soviet Union—Civilization—Jewish
       influences
       United States—Civilization—
       Jewish influences
— — **To 70 A.D.**
— — **Arab influences**
   BT Civilization, Arab
— — **Greek influences**
   UF Hellenistic Judaism
       Judaism, Hellenistic
— Clothing and dress
   USE Costume, Jewish
— **Colonization** *(May Subd Geog)*
   BT Agricultural colonies
— **Commerce**
   [HF369 (Ancient)]
— Conquest of Canaan
   USE Jews—History—To 1200 B.C.
— **Conversion to Christianity**
   [BV4922]
   Here are entered works dealing theoretically
   with the conversion of Jews to Christianity.
   BT Conversion
— Converts to Christianity
   USE Converts from Judaism
— Courts
   USE Courts, Jewish
       Rabbinical courts
— **Craniology**
   [GN130.J4]
   UF Craniology—Jews
— Crime
   USE Jewish criminals
— **Cultural assimilation**
   [DS148]
— Customs
   USE Jews—Social life and customs
— Dancing
   USE Dancing—Jews
— **Diaspora**
   Here are entered works dealing with the dis-
   persion of the Jewish people beyond the confines
   of Palestine, together with a description of life,
   attitude and outlook in their new surroundings.
   UF Diaspora of the Jews
       Dispersion of the Jews
       Galuth
       Jews—Dispersion
       Jews in foreign countries
   BT Jews—Restoration
       Man—Migrations
       Minorities
   RT Jews—Migrations
   NT Israel and the Diaspora
       Proselytes and proselyting, Jewish
— **Dictionaries and encyclopedias**
   [DS102.8]
   RT Judaism—Dictionaries
— — **Juvenile literature**
— **Dietary laws**
   [BM710]

   UF Dietary laws, Jewish
       Kashruth, Laws of
   BT Cookery, Jewish
       Diet
       Food—Religious aspects—Judaism
       Jewish law
       Nutrition—Religious aspects—
       Judaism
   RT Kosher food
   NT Gelatin (Jewish law)
       Kashering of utensils
       Kosher food industry
       Kosher restaurants
       Meat inspection (Jewish law)
       Passover—Customs and practices
       Shehitah
       Wine and wine making (Judaism)
— — **Biblical teaching**
   BT Bible—Theology
— **Directories**
— Dispersion
   USE Jews—Diaspora
— Divorce
   USE Divorce (Jewish law)
— Doctrine of election
   USE Jews—Election, Doctrine of
— **Economic conditions**
   NT Occupational training for Jews
— **Education** *(May Subd Geog)*
   [LA47 (Ancient)]
   [LC701-LC775 (Modern)]
   UF Education, Jewish
       Judaism—Education
   NT Education in the Talmud
       Heder
       Jewish day schools
       Jewish educators
       Jewish religious education
       Jewish religious schools
       Jews—Scholarships, fellowships,
       etc.
       Students, Jewish
— **Election, Doctrine of**
   [BM613]
   UF Chosen people (Jews)
       Election of Israel
       Israel, Election of
       Jews—Chosen people
       Jews—Doctrine of election
       Jews—Mission
   BT Election (Theology)
       Judaism—Relations
       People of God
— **Emancipation**
   [DS147]
   UF Disabilities, Political
       Emancipation of Jews
       Jewish emancipation
       Political disabilities
   BT Jews—History—1789-1945
— Emigration and immigration
   USE Jews—Migrations
— **Employment**
   UF Labor and laboring classes—Jews
— Ethics
   USE Ethics, Jewish
— Exodus
   USE Exodus, The
— Fasts and feasts
   USE Fasts and feasts—Judaism
— Festivals
   USE Fasts and feasts—Judaism
— Folk art
   USE Folk art, Jewish
— **Folklore**
   [GR97-GR98]
   Here are entered works on post-Biblical Jew-
   ish folklore and Jews as a theme in folklore.
   NT Wandering Jew
— Funeral rites and ceremonies

   USE Funeral rites and ceremonies,
       Jewish
— **Genealogy**
   [CS3010]
   BT Genealogy
— **History**
   [DS101-DS135]
— — **To 1200 B.C.**
   UF Jews—Conquest of Canaan
       Jews—Settlement in Canaan
       Jews—Wanderings in the
       wilderness
   NT Exodus, The
       Pharaoh's army (in religion,
       folk-lore, etc.)
— — **To 953 B.C.**
— — **To 586 B.C.**
   NT Treaties in the Bible
       Twelve tribes of Israel
— — **To 70 A.D.**
   BT Judaism—History—To 70 A.D.
       Palestine—History—To 70 A.D.
— — — **Juvenile literature**
— — **1200-953 B.C.**
   [DS121.55]
— — **953-586 B.C.**
   [DS121]
   NT Jerusalem—Siege, 586 B.C.
       Jerusalem—Siege, 701 B.C.
       Omri dynasty, 9th century B.C.
— — **Babylonian captivity, 598-515 B.C.**
   UF Babylonian captivity, Jewish
       Babylonian exile, Jewish
   BT Jews—Iraq—Babylonia
— — **586 B.C.-70 A.D.**
   NT Maccabees
— — **168 B.C.-135 A.D.**
   [DS122]
   NT Am Haarez
       Zealots (Jewish party)
— — — **Miscellanea**
— — **Rebellion, 66-73**
   UF Jewish-Roman War, 66-73
       Roman-Jewish War, 66-73
   BT Jerusalem—Siege, 70 A.D.
       Rome—History—Empire, 30
       B.C.-284 A.D.
   NT Masada Site (Israel)—Siege, 72-
       73
— — — **Juvenile literature**
— — **70-**
— — **70-638**
   [DS123.5]
— — **70-1789**
   [DS124]
— — **Rebellion, 115-117**
— — **Bar Kokhba Rebellion, 132-135**
   [DS122.9]
   UF Bar Kokhba Rebellion, 132-135
   BT Palestine—History—70-638
       Rome—History—Hadrian, 117-
       138
— — **1789-1945**
   NT Jews—Emancipation
— — **1945-**
— — **Book reviews**
— — **Chronology**
   RT Chronology, Jewish
— — **Juvenile literature**
   UF Jews—History, Juvenile
— — **Pictorial works**
— — **Study and teaching**
   (May Subd Geog)
— History, Juvenile
   USE Jews—History—Juvenile
       literature
— Hygiene
   USE Hygiene, Jewish
— Hymns
   USE Jewish hymns
— **Identity**

UF Identity, Jewish
    Jewish identity
BT Jewish law
    Jewish nationalism
    Jews—Legal status, laws, etc.
— **Intellectual life**
  RT Jewish learning and scholarship
  NT Jews—Publishing
— **Kings and rulers**
  NT Kings and rulers—Biblical teaching
      Omri dynasty, 9th century B.C.
— **Languages**
  NT Hebrew language
      Italian language—Dialects—Judeo-
        Italian
      Judeo-Arabic language
      Judeo-Persian language
      Karaim language
      Yiddish language
— Law
  USE Jewish law
       Jews—Legal status, laws, etc.
— Learning and scholarship
  USE Jewish learning and scholarship
— **Legal status, laws, etc.**
    (*May Subd Geog*)
  UF Jews—Civil rights
      Jews—Law
      Law—Jews
      Refugees, Jewish—Legal status,
        laws, etc.
  BT Jews—Persecutions
  NT Jews—Identity
      Oaths—Jews
      Restitution and indemnification
        claims (1933-   )
— — **Germany**
  UF Nuremberg laws
— **Legal status, laws, etc. (Canon law)**
— Legends
  USE Legends, Jewish
— Literature
  USE Hebrew literature
       Jewish literature
— Lost tribes
  USE Lost tribes of Israel
— Medicine
  USE Medicine, Jewish
       Physicians, Jewish
— **Migrations**
  UF Jewish migrations
      Jews—Emigration and immigration
      Migrations, Jewish
  BT Migrations of nations
  RT Jews—Diaspora
      Refugees, Jewish
— Mission
  USE Jews—Election, Doctrine of
— Missions
  USE Proselytes and proselyting,
         Jewish
— **Music**
  UF Hebrew music
      Jewish music
      Music, Hebrew
      Music, Jewish
  NT Cantillation
      Chants (Jewish)
      Klezmer music
      Music in synagogues
      Music in the Bible
      Synagogue music
— **Name**
    ₍BM729.N3₎
  BT Names in the Bible
  NT Israel—Name
      'Ivri (The Hebrew word)
— Nationalism
  USE Jewish nationalism
— Newspapers
  USE Jewish newspapers

— Nobility
— Origin
    ₍GN547₎
  NT Habiru
— **Periodicals**
    ₍DS101 (General)₎
    ₍DS133 (Jews outside of Israel)₎
    ₍E184.J5 (United States)₎
  UF Jews—Yearbooks
  NT Jewish periodicals
— **Persecutions**
  BT Antisemitism
      Persecution
      Political atrocities
  NT Blood accusation
      Holocaust, Jewish (1939-1945)
      Jews—Legal status, laws, etc.
      Refugees, Jewish
      World War, 1939-1945—Jews—
        Rescue
— — **Public opinion**
— Philosophy
  USE Philosophy, Jewish
— **Politics and government**
    ₍JC67 (Ancient)₎
  BT Zionism
  NT Jewish councils and synods
      Judaism and politics
      Sanhedrin
      Zealots (Jewish party)
— — **To 70 A.D.**
    ₍DS112₎
— — **1948-**
— Priests
  USE Priests, Jewish
— **Psychology**
— **Public opinion**
      Here are entered works dealing with public
    opinion about Jews. Works on public opinion of
    Jews are entered under Public opinion—Jews.
  UF Judaism—Public opinion
— **Publishing**
  BT Jews—Intellectual life
— Radicalism
  USE Jewish radicals
— **Recreation**
— Relations with Afro-Americans
  USE Afro-Americans—Relations with
         Jews
— Relations with Blacks
  USE Blacks—Relations with Jews
— Religion
  USE Judaism
— Religious education
  USE Jewish religious education
— Rescue, 1939-1945
  USE World War, 1939-1945—Jews—
         Rescue
— **Restoration**
    ₍BS649.J5₎
      Here are entered works dealing with the be-
    lief—whether held by Jews or by Christians—
    that, in fulfillment of Biblical prophecy, the Jews
    would some day return to Palestine, and thereby
    also meet a requirement for the realization of
    eschatological expectations.
  RT Zionism
  NT Christian Zionism
      Jerusalem in Judaism
      Jews—Diaspora
      Messianic era (Judaism)
— — **History of doctrines**
— **Return to Orthodox Judaism**
  UF Return to Orthodox Judaism
      Revival (Religion)
  BT Orthodox Judaism
— Rites and ceremonies
  USE Judaism—Customs and practices
— Ritual
  USE Jews—Social life and customs
       Judaism—Liturgy

— **Scholarships, fellowships, etc.**
    (*May Subd Geog*)
  UF Jewish scholarships
  BT Jews—Education
— Sects
  USE Jewish sects
— **Segregation**
  UF Ghettos
  BT Antisemitism
      Discrimination in housing
— Settlement in Canaan
  USE Jews—History—To 1200 B.C.
— **Social life and customs**
    ₍DS112-DS113₎
  UF Customs, Social
      Jewish life
      Jews—Customs
      Jews—Ritual
  BT Manners and customs
  NT Community centers, Jewish
      Excommunication (Jewish law)
      Jewish way of life
— — **To 70 A.D.**
— — **Juvenile literature**
— **Societies, etc.**
    ₍DS101₎
    ₍E184.J5 (United States)₎
    ₍HS2226-HS2230₎
  NT Young Men's Hebrew Associations
— **Statistics, Vital**
  BT Vital statistics
— **Study and teaching**   (*May Subd Geog*)
— Ten lost tribes
  USE Lost tribes of Israel
— **Territorialism**
  UF Territorialism (Jewish movement)
  RT Zionism
— Tithes
  USE Tithes—Jews
— Wanderings in the wilderness
  USE Jews—History—To 1200 B.C.
— Women
  USE Women, Jewish
— Yearbooks
  USE Jews—Periodicals
— Zionism
  USE Zionism
— **Afghanistan**
  NT Jews, Afghan
— **Africa, North**
  NT Jews, North African
— **Caucasus**
  NT Jews, Caucasian
— **Czechoslovakia**
  NT Czechoslovakia—Civilization—
        Jewish influences
— **Egypt**
  RT Jews, Egyptian
— **Europe, Eastern**
  NT Jews, East European
— **Germany**
  NT Jews, German
— — **History**
— — — **To 1096**
— — — **1096-1147**
— — — **1096-1800**
— — — **1800-1933**
— — — **1933-1945**
      UF Jews—Germany—
            Persecutions—1933-1945
      NT Crystal Night, 1938
— — — **1945-**
— — **Persecutions**
— — — **1933-1945**
      USE Jews—Germany—History—
             1933-1945
— **Great Britain**
  NT Jews, British
— **Hungary**
  NT Jews, Hungarian
— **India**

Jews

— India *(Continued)*
  NT Bene-Israel
       Jews, East Indian
— Iran
  NT Jews, Iranian
— Iraq
  NT Jews, Iraqi
— — Babylonia
    NT Exilarchate
        Jews—History—Babylonian
          captivity, 598-515 B.C.
— Islamic countries
  NT Exilarchate
       Nagid
— Italy
  NT Jews, Italian
— Kurdistan
— Latin America
  NT Jews, Latin American
— Lithuania
  NT Jews, Lithuanian
— Morocco
  UF Mellahs
  NT Jews, Moroccan
— — Languages
    NT Ḥakétia language
— Netherlands
  NT Jews, Dutch
— Palestine
— — Charities
    NT Halukkah
— Poland
  NT Jews, Polish
       Warsaw (Poland)—History—
         Uprising of 1943
— Soviet Union
  NT Cantonists
       Jews, Russian
       Khazars
       Refuseniks
— — History
— — — Pogroms, 1881-1882
      [*DS135.R9*]
      UF Pogroms against the Jews,
          Soviet Union, 1881-1882
      BT Jews—Soviet Union—
          Persecutions
— — — 1917-
      [*DS135.R92*]
— — Persecutions
    NT Jews—Soviet Union—History—
        Pogroms, 1881-1882
— Ukraine
— — History
— — — Pogroms, 1919-1920
      UF Pogroms against the Jews,
         Ukraine, 1919-1920
      BT Jews—Ukraine—Persecutions
— — Persecutions
    NT Jews—Ukraine—History—
        Pogroms, 1919-1920
— United States
  NT Afro-American Jews
       Jews, American
       United States—History—Civil War,
        1861-1865—Jews
— Yemen
  NT Jews, Yemenite
Jews, Afghan *(May Subd Geog)*
  UF Afghan Jews
  BT Jews—Afghanistan
Jews, Afro-American
  USE Afro-American Jews
Jews, Afro-Asian
  USE Jews, Oriental
Jews, American *(May Subd Geog)*
  BT Jews—United States

Jews, British *(May Subd Geog)*
  UF British Jews
      English Jews
      Jews, English
  BT Jews—Great Britain
Jews, Caucasian *(May Subd Geog)*
    Here are entered works dealing with Jews from
the Caucasus Region.
  UF Caucasian Jews
  BT Jews—Caucasus
Jews, Dutch *(May Subd Geog)*
  UF Dutch Jews
  BT Jews—Netherlands
Jews, East European *(May Subd Geog)*
  UF East European Jews
  BT Jews—Europe, Eastern
Jews, East Indian *(May Subd Geog)*
  UF East Indian Jews
  BT Jews—India
Jews, Egyptian *(May Subd Geog)*
  UF Egyptian Jews
  RT Jews—Egypt
Jews, English
  USE Jews, British
Jews, Ethiopian
  USE Falashas
Jews, German
  UF German Jews
  BT Jews—Germany
Jews, Hungarian *(May Subd Geog)*
  UF Hungarian Jews
  BT Jews—Hungary
Jews, Iranian *(May Subd Geog)*
  UF Iranian Jews
  BT Jews—Iran
Jews, Iraqi *(May Subd Geog)*
  UF Iraqi Jews
  BT Jews—Iraq
Jews, Italian *(May Subd Geog)*
  UF Italian Jews
  BT Jews—Italy
Jews, Kurdish *(May Subd Geog)*
  UF Kurdish Jews
  RT Jews—Kurdistan
Jews, Kurdish, [**Yemenite, etc.**]
Jews, Latin American *(May Subd Geog)*
  UF Latin American Jews
  BT Jews—Latin America
Jews, Lithuanian *(May Subd Geog)*
  UF Lithuanian Jews
  BT Jews—Lithuania
Jews, Moroccan *(May Subd Geog)*
  UF Moroccan Jews
  BT Jews—Morocco
  NT Maimuna
  — Israel
    NT Maimuna
Jews, North African *(May Subd Geog)*
  UF North African Jews
  BT Jews—Africa, North
Jews, Oriental *(May Subd Geog)*
  UF Afro-Asian Jews
      Jews, Afro-Asian
      Oriental Jews
  NT Jewish authors, Oriental
Jews, Polish *(May Subd Geog)*
  UF Polish Jews
  BT Jews—Poland
Jews, Russian *(May Subd Geog)*
  UF Russian Jews
  BT Jews—Soviet Union
Jews, Sephardic
  USE Sephardim
Jews, Yemenite *(May Subd Geog)*
  UF Yemenite Jews
  BT Jews—Yemen
Jews as criminals
  USE Jewish criminals
Jews as engineers
  USE Engineers, Jewish

Jews as farmers
  USE Farmers, Jewish
Jews as lawyers
  USE Lawyers, Jewish
Jews as scientists
  USE Scientists, Jewish
Jews as seamen
  USE Seamen, Jewish
Jews as soldiers
  USE Jewish soldiers
Jew's ear
  USE Auricularia auricula-judae
Jew's harp
  [*ML1087*]
  UF Jaw harp
      Jaw's-harp
      Trump
  BT Musical instruments
Jew's harp music
  [*M175.J4*]
  SA Concertos, Minuets, Sonatas, Suites,
      *and similar headings with
      specification of instruments;* Trios
      [Quartets, etc.] *followed by
      specifications which include the
      Jew's harp; also Percussion
      ensembles and headings that begin
      with the words* Jew's harp *or* Jew's
      harps
Jews in art
  [*N7415*]
  UF Jewish way of life in art
  NT Antisemitism in art
Jews in foreign countries
  USE Jews—Diaspora
Jews in literature
  [*PR151.J5 (English literature)*]
  [*PT149.J4 (German literature)*]
  BT Characters and characteristics in
      literature
  SA *subdivision* Characters—Jews *under
      names of authors, e.g.* Shakespeare,
      William, 1564-1616—Characters—
      Jews
  NT Folklore in rabbinical literature
      Holocaust, Jewish (1939-1945), in
        literature
      Jews in rabbinical literature
      Judaism in literature
      Schlemiel in literature
Jews in motion pictures
  [*PN1995.9.J46*]
  BT Moving-pictures
  NT Antisemitism in motion pictures
Jews in public life *(May Subd Geog)*
  NT Jewish statesmen
Jews in rabbinical literature
  [*BM509.J48*]
  BT Jews in literature
      Rabbinical literature
Jews in the Hadith
  BT Hadith
Jews in the Koran
  [*BP134.J4*]
  UF Koran—Jews
Jews in the New Testament
  UF Bible. N.T.—Jews
Jews in the professions *(May Subd Geog)*
  BT Professions
Jezides
  USE Yezidis
Jezioro Mamry (Poland)
  USE Mamry Lake (Poland)
Jezioro Raduńskie (Poland)
  USE Radunia Lake (Poland)
Jezioro Śniardwy (Poland)
  USE Śniardwy Lake (Poland)
Jezioro Wdzydze (Poland)
  USE Wdzydze Lake (Poland)
Jezioro Wigry (Poland)
  USE Wigry, Lake (Poland)

Jezreeli family
USE Yizre'eli family
Język maszynowe rozmowy
USE MARO (Computer program language)
Jharkhand (India)
Ji (Sect)
    [BQ8550-8559]
    UF Jishū
    BT Buddhist sects
Jibāl an Nūba (Sudan)
    USE Nuba Mountains (Sudan)
Jibuti-Addis Ababa Railroad
    BT Railroads—Africa, Northeast
Jicaque Indians
    USE Xicaque Indians
Jicaque language
    UF Tol language
        Tolpan language
        Torrupan language
        Xicaque language
    BT Indians of Central America—
        Languages
        Indians of Central America—Honduras
        —Languages
Jicarilla Apache Indians
    USE Jicarilla Indians
Jicarilla Indians
    [E99.J]
    UF Jicarilla Apache Indians
    BT Apache Indians
        Athapascan Indians
        Indians of North America
Jicarilla language
    [PM1389]
    BT Athapascan languages
Jie (African people)
    UF Jie (African tribe)
    BT Ethnology—Uganda
        Nilo-Hamitic tribes
Jie (African tribe)
    USE Jie (African people)
Jig (Dance)
    [GV1796.J5]
        Here are entered works on the jig. Music for the
    dance is entered under the heading Jigs followed by
    specification of medium.
Jig borers
    UF Borers, Jig
    BT Machine-tools
Jig saws
    UF Scroll saws
    BT Saws
Jiggermen
    USE Potters
Jiggers (Mites)
    USE Chiggers (Mites)
Jigging
    USE Ore-dressing
Jigs
    UF Gigues
    BT Dance music
Jigs (Fishing lures)   (May Subd Geog)
    [SH449]
    BT Fishing lures
Jigs (Mechanical devices)
    USE Jigs and fixtures
Jigs and fixtures
    [TJ1185]
    UF Fixtures (Mechanical devices)
        Jigs (Mechanical devices)
    BT Machine-tools
    NT Collets
    — **Design and construction**
    —— **Computer programs**
        [TJ1187]
    — Drawing
        USE Jigs and fixtures—Drawings
    — **Drawings**
        UF Jigs and fixtures—Drawing
        BT Mechanical drawing

Jigsaw puzzles
    BT Puzzles
Jigüe (Cuba), Battle of, 1958
    USE El Jigüe (Cuba), Battle of, 1958
Jihad
    [BP182]
    UF Holy war (Islam)
        Islamic holy war
        Jahad
        Jehad
        Muslim holy war
    BT International relations
        Islam and state
        Pillars of Islam
        War
        War—Religious aspects—Islam
Jihei Iseki (Iijima-machi, Japan)
    USE Jihei Site (Iijima-machi, Japan)
Jihei Site (Iijima-machi, Japan)
    (Not Subd Geog)
    UF Jihei Iseki (Iijima-machi, Japan)
    BT Japan—Antiquities
Jihi
    USE Compassion (Buddhism)
Jikai language
    USE Burera language
Jike Iseki (Hakui-shi, Japan)
    USE Jike Site (Hakui-shi, Japan)
Jike Site (Hakui-shi, Japan)
    (Not Subd Geog)
    UF Jike Iseki (Hakui-shi, Japan)
    BT Japan—Antiquities
Jiles family
    USE Giles family
Jiling family
    USE Illing family
Jillet family
    USE Gillette family
Jillitt family
    USE Gillette family
Jiloca River (Spain)
    UF Giloca River (Spain)
        Río Giloca (Spain)
        Río Jiloca (Spain)
    BT Rivers—Spain
Jiman (Australian people)
    [DU125.J55]
    UF Emon (Australian people)
        Iman (Australian people)
        Jimun (Australian people)
        Yeeman (Australian people)
    BT Australian aborigines
        Ethnology—Australia
Jimenez family   (Not Subd Geog)
    UF Jiminez family
Jimerson family
    USE Jameson family
Jiminez family
    USE Jimenez family
Jimini (African people)
    USE Djimini (African people)
Jimmy Christopher (Fictitious character)
    USE Operator 5 (Fictitious character)
Jimmy truck
    USE GMC Jimmy truck
Jimomys
    [QE882.R6]
    BT Rodents, Fossil
Jimomys labaughi
    [QE882.R6]
Jimpson weed
    USE Datura stramonium
Jimpsonweed
    USE Datura stramonium
Jimun (Australian people)
    USE Jiman (Australian people)
Jin
    USE Jen
Jinbochō (Tokyo, Japan)   (Not Subd Geog)
    UF Tokyo (Japan). Jinbochō

Jincks family
    USE Jenkins family
Jindjibandji language
    [PL7101.J55]
    UF Indjibandi language
        Ingibandi language
        Injibandi language
        Jindjiparndi language
        Yindjibarndi language
        Yingiebandie language
        Yintjipanti language
        Yinytyipanti language
    BT Australia—Languages
        Australian languages
Jindjiparndi language
    USE Jindjibandji language
Jines family
    USE Joines family
Jingali language
    USE Djingili language
Jingan gum   (May Subd Geog)
    [SB291.L35 (Gum plant)]
    BT Lannea coromandelica
Jinghpaw language
    USE Kachin language
Jingju
    USE Operas, Chinese
Jingoism
    USE Chauvinism and jingoism
Jinings family
    USE Jennings family
Jinja (African people)
    USE Zinza (African people)
Jinkens family
    USE Jenkins family
Jinkins family
    USE Jenkins family
Jinks family
    USE Jenkins family
Jinn
    [GR582]
    UF Genii
        Jinni
        Jinns
    BT Demonology
        Spirits (Islam)
    RT Genius (Companion spirit)
    — **Koranic teaching**
Jinni
    USE Jinn
Jinnings family
    USE Jennings family
Jinnins family
    USE Jennings family
Jinns
    USE Jinn
Jinrikimen
    USE Rickshaw men
Jinseiza (Tokyo, Japan)
    BT Moving-picture theaters—Japan
Jinshin Revolt, 672
    BT Japan—Emperors
        Japan—History—645-794
Jionji Iseki (Azuchi-chō, Japan)
    USE Jionji Site (Azuchi-chō, Japan)
Jionji Site (Azuchi-chō, Japan)
    UF Jionji Iseki (Azuchi-chō, Japan)
    BT Japan—Antiquities
Jirel language
    [PL3801.J55]
    BT Tibeto-Burman languages
Jishō no nairan, 1180-1185
    USE Japan—History—Gempei Wars, 1180-
        1185
Jishū
    USE Ji (Sect)
Jita language
    UF Kijita language
    BT Bantu languages
Jitney buses
    USE Buses

Jitterbug dancing
  [GV1796.J]
  UF Swing dancing
  BT Dancing
  NT Country swing (Dance)
Jiu-jitsu
  [GV1114]
  Here are entered works on the various Japanese schools on the art of self-defense prior to their unification by Chigorō Kanō in 1882.
  UF Jujitsu
  BT Athletics
    Hand-to-hand fighting, Oriental
    Physical education and training
    Self-defense
    Wrestling
  NT Judo
    San-jitsu
Jiu River (Romania)
  UF Jiul (Romania)
    Schyl (Romania)
  BT Rivers—Romania
Jiuhua Shan (China)
  USE Chiu-hua Mountains (China)
Jiul (Romania)
  USE Jiu River (Romania)
Jiul River, Battle of, 1916
  BT Romania—History—1914-1918
    World War, 1914-1918—Campaigns—Romania
Jiva
  [B132.J58]
  BT Life
    Philosophy, Indic
    Soul
Jivaran languages
  [PM6273]
  UF Jivaroan languages
  RT Aguaruna dialect
  NT Achuale language
    Candoshi language
    Huambisa language
    Jivaro language
Jivaro Indians
  [F3722.1.J5]
  UF Givaro Indians
    Shuara Indians
    Xivaro Indians
  BT Indians of South America
  NT Achuale Indians
    Aguaruna Indians
    Huambisa Indians
  — Religion and mythology
Jivaro language
  [PM6273]
  UF Chiwaro language
    Shiwora language
    Shuar language
    Shuara language
    Xivaro language
  BT Ecuador—Languages
    Indians of South America—Ecuador—Languages
    Jivaran languages
Jivaro poetry (May Subd Geog)
Jivaroan languages
  USE Jivaran languages
Jiw language
  USE Guayabero language
Jiwadja language
  USE Iwaidji language
Jizera Mountains (Poland and Czechoslovakia)
  USE Izerskie Mountains (Poland and Czechoslovakia)
Jizerské hory (Poland and Czechoslovakia)
  USE Izerskie Mountains (Poland and Czechoslovakia)
Jizō (Buddhist deity)
  USE Kṣitigarbha (Buddhist deity)
Jizyah (Islamic law)
  USE Poll-tax (Islamic law)

JKDIGIT (Computer program)
  UF John Kork Digitizing (Computer program)
  BT Geology—Computer programs
Jmetic Lubton Site (Mexico)
  BT Mexico—Antiquities
JN-4D (Training planes)
  UF Jenny (Training planes)
  BT Airplanes, Military
    Training planes
Jñāna yoga
  USE Yoga, Jñāna
Jŏ (Secret language)
  BT Languages, Secret
Jo-Ben (Malaysian people)
  USE Chewong (Malaysian people)
Jo-jotte (Game)
  [GV1295.J6]
Jo Luo (African people)
  USE Luo (African people)
Jo Luo language
  USE Luo language (Kenya and Tanzania)
Jo Lwo language
  USE Lwo language (Sudan)
Jo-nań-pa (Sect) (May Subd Geog)
  [BQ7674]
  UF Jonań-pa (Sect)
  BT Buddhist sects
    Sa-skya-pa (Sect)
Jō-numa (Japan)
  USE Jō Pond (Japan)
Jō Pond (Japan)
  UF Jō-numa (Japan)
  BT Ponds—Japan
Joan, of Arc, Saint, 1412-1431
  — Portraits
      UF Joan, of Arc, Saint, 1412-1431—Portraits, etc.
  — Portraits, etc.
      USE Joan, of Arc, Saint, 1412-1431—Portraits
Joan (Legendary Pope)
  UF Giovanna (Legendary Pope)
    Iōanna (Legendary Pope)
    Jeanne (Legendary Pope)
    Joana (Legendary Pope)
    Joannes VIII, Anglicus, (Legendary Pope)
    Johanna (Legendary Pope)
    John VIII (Legendary Pope)
  BT Folklore—Europe
Joan Crexells Prize
  USE Premi Joan Crexells
Joan of Arc in prison (Painting)
  USE Delaroche, Paul, 1797-1856. Joan of Arc in prison
Joana (Legendary Pope)
  USE Joan (Legendary Pope)
Joanna Reservoir (Mo.)
  USE Clarence Cannon Reservoir (Mo.)
Joannes VIII, Anglicus, (Legendary Pope)
  USE Joan (Legendary Pope)
João do Vale Hills (Brazil)
  UF Serra João do Vale (Brazil)
  BT Mountains—Brazil
Joaquim Francisco de Assis Brasil, Parque Florestal (Brazil)
  USE Floresta Nacional de São Francisco de Paula (Brazil)
Joaquim Vanda
  USE Vanda Miss Joaquim
Joaquin Miller Park (Oakland, Calif.)
  BT Parks—California
Job analysis
  [HF5549.5.J6]

Here are entered works on the process of making a detailed study of a job to determine the duties, facilities required, conditions of work, and the qualifications needed for its performance. Works on the appraisal of the relative value of individual jobs in an organization for wage determination, promotions, etc., are entered under Job evaluation. Works on the process of identifying all the things that must be done to complete an activity satisfactorily are entered under Task analysis.
  UF Analysis, Job
  BT Personnel management
  RT Job evaluation
  NT Critical incident technique
    Job descriptions
    Medical personnel—Classification
Job applications
  USE Applications for positions
Job bias
  USE Discrimination in employment
Job Control Language (Computer program language)
  UF JCL (Computer program language)
  BT Programming languages (Electronic computers)
Job descriptions
  Here are entered works about, or consisting of, summaries of the essential activities involved in the performance of jobs.
  UF Assignment specifications
  BT Job analysis
    Occupations
  SA subdivision Job descriptions under names of individual corporate bodies, types of industries, and occupational groups, e.g. United States. Navy—Job descriptions; Construction industry—Job descriptions; Librarians—Job descriptions
Job design
  USE Work design
Job discrimination
  USE Discrimination in employment
Job enlargement
  USE Job enrichment
Job enrichment (May Subd Geog)
  [HF5549.5.J616]
  UF Job enlargement
    Job restructuring
  BT Division of labor
    Employee morale
    Motivation (Psychology)
    Organizational change
    Personnel management
    Work—Psychological aspects
  RT Job satisfaction
Job evaluation (May Subd Geog)
  [HF5549.5.J62]
  Here are entered works on the appraisal of the relative value of individual jobs in an organization for wage determination, promotions, etc. Works on the process of making a detailed study of a job to determine the duties, facilities required, conditions of work, and the qualifications needed for its performance are entered under Job analysis.
  UF Evaluation, Job
    Job rating
    Rating, Job
  BT Evaluation
    Occupations
    Personnel management
  RT Job analysis
  NT Civil service positions—Classification
  — Law and legislation (May Subd Geog)
    BT Labor laws and legislation
Job hunting (May Subd Geog)
  [HF5382.7-5382.75]
  UF Hunting, Job
    Job searching
  BT Employment agencies
    Vocational guidance
  NT Applications for positions

Help-wanted advertising
Résumés (Employment)
Job interviews
USE Employment interviewing
Job mobility
USE Occupational mobility
Job offers (May Subd Geog)
UF Offers, Job
BT Employee selection
Job openings
USE Job vacancies
Job performance standards
USE Performance standards
Job postings (May Subd Geog)
UF Postings, Job
BT Applications for positions
Job vacancies
Personnel management
Job promotions
USE Promotions
Job rating
USE Job evaluation
Job restructuring
USE Job enrichment
Job résumés
USE Résumés (Employment)
Job safety
USE Industrial safety
Job satisfaction (May Subd Geog)
BT Attitude (Psychology)
Employee morale
Labor and laboring classes
Personnel management
Quality of work life
Satisfaction
Work
RT Job enrichment
NT Burn out (Psychology)
Nurses—Job satisfaction
Residents (Medicine)—Job satisfaction
Teachers—Job satisfaction
Teaching satisfaction
— **Bibliography**
RT Job satisfaction literature
— **Testing**
NT Index of Work Satisfaction
Schaffer job satisfaction test
Job satisfaction literature (May Subd Geog)
[HF5549.5.J63]
UF Literature, Job satisfaction
RT Job satisfaction—Bibliography
Job searching
USE Job hunting
Job security (May Subd Geog)
UF Employment security
Security, Job
BT Economic security
Personnel management
RT Layoff systems
— **Law and legislation** (May Subd Geog)
BT Labor laws and legislation
Job sharing (May Subd Geog)
Here are entered works on the sharing of one full-time job or position by two or more persons as an alternative to the traditional work week. Works on the spreading of available work among members of a working group to avoid redundancy or layoff, or to equalize the distribution of income among them, are entered under Work sharing.
UF Sharing of jobs
BT Part-time employment
RT Work sharing
— **Law and legislation** (May Subd Geog)
BT Labor laws and legislation
Job stress (May Subd Geog)
[HF5548.85]
UF Occupational stress
On-the-job stress
Organizational stress
Work stress

BT Psychology, Industrial
Stress (Physiology)
Stress (Psychology)
Work—Physiological aspects
Work—Psychological aspects
SA subdivision Job stress under classes of persons and ethnic groups; and subdivision Officials and employees —Job stress under names of countries, cities, etc. and names of individual government agencies
NT Burn out (Psychology)
— **Bibliography**
RT Job stress literature
Job stress literature (May Subd Geog)
[HF5548.85]
UF Literature, Job stress
RT Job stress—Bibliography
Job training
USE Occupational training
Job vacancies (May Subd Geog)
UF Employment opportunities
Job openings
BT Employment (Economic theory)
Employment agencies
Labor supply
Unemployed
NT Job postings
Jōban Region (Japan)
UF Jōban Tanden (Japan)
Jōban Tanden (Japan)
USE Jōban Region (Japan)
Jobless people
USE Unemployed
Joblessness
USE Unemployment
Jobs
USE Occupations
Professions
Job's syndrome
USE Chronic granulomatous disease
Jobs tax credit
USE New jobs tax credit
JOBSHOP (Computer program)
Jocelin family
USE Josselyn family
Jocelyn family
USE Josselyn family
Jockeys (May Subd Geog)
BT Horse-racing
Horse-racing—Employees
Horse-shows
Horsemen and horsewomen
NT Women jockeys
Joconde (Game)
UF Mona Lisa (Game)
Jocteur family (Not Subd Geog)
Jodel
USE Yodel and yodeling
Joder family
USE Yoder family
Jodo-shin-shu
USE Shin (Sect)
Jōdoshū Buddhists (May Subd Geog)
BT Buddhists
NT Priests, Jōdoshū
Jōdoshū priests
USE Priests, Jōdoshū
Jody calls
UF Cadence calls
Cadences (Soldiers' songs)
Calls, Cadence
Calls, Jody
Chants, Jody
Jody chants
BT War-songs
Jody chants
USE Jody calls
Joe Magarac (Legendary character)
USE Magarac, Joe (Legendary character)

Joepen family
USE Joppe family
Joergensen family
USE Jorgensen family
Joes Valley Reservoir (Utah)
BT Cottonwood Creek (Utah)
Reservoirs—Utah
Jōga Island (Kanagawa-ken, Japan)
(Not Subd Geog)
UF Jōga-shima (Kanagawa-ken, Japan)
Jōgashima (Kanagawa-ken, Japan)
BT Islands—Japan
Jōga-shima (Kanagawa-ken, Japan)
USE Jōga Island (Kanagawa-ken, Japan)
Jōgashima (Kanagawa-ken, Japan)
USE Jōga Island (Kanagawa-ken, Japan)
Jogging (May Subd Geog)
[GV494]
BT Running
Joghurt
USE Yogurt
Jogurt
USE Yogurt
Johann family
USE Johannes family
Johanna (Legendary Pope)
USE Joan (Legendary Pope)
Johannes, Presbyter (Legendary character)
USE Prester John (Legendary character)
Johannes (Name)
USE John (Name)
Johannes family (Not Subd Geog)
UF Johann family
Johannis family
Johannes V. Jensen Land (Greenland)
Johannesburg (South Africa). Hillbrow
USE Hillbrow (Johannesburg, South Africa)
Johannesburg (South Africa). Pageview
USE Pageview (Johannesburg, South Africa)
Johannine circle
USE Johannine school
Johannine school
[BS2615-BS2615.2]
UF Johannine circle
School of John (Biblical criticism)
BT Bible. N.T. John—Criticism, interpretation, etc.
Johannis family
USE Johannes family
Johannisburg Castle (Aschaffenburg, Germany)
USE Schloss Johannisburg (Aschaffenburg, Germany)
Johannisson family
USE Johansson family
Johannsen family
USE Johansson family
Johansen family
USE Johansson family
Johansson family (Not Subd Geog)
UF Johannisson family
Johannsen family
Johansen family
NT Johnson family
Lohff-Johansen family
John, the Baptist, Saint
— **Art**
NT Michelangelo Buonarroti, 1475-1564. Saint John
John, Prester (Legendary character)
USE Prester John (Legendary character)
John (Name)
UF Giovanni (Name)
Jehan (Name)
Johannes (Name)
BT Names, Personal
John A. Roebling Statue (Trenton, N.J.)
UF Couper, William. John A. Roebling Statue
Roebling Memorial (Trenton, N.J.)
Roebling Monument (Trenton, N.J.)
BT Statues—New Jersey

John Alden House (Duxbury, Mass.)
  UF Alden House (Duxbury, Mass.)
  BT Dwellings—Massachusetts
John B. Putnam, Jr., Memorial Collection (Princeton, N.J.)
  UF Putnam Collection (Princeton, N.J.)
      Putnam Memorial Collection (Princeton, N.J.)
  BT Sculpture—New Jersey
John Balch House (Beverly, Mass.)
  UF Balch House (Beverly, Mass.)
  BT Dwellings—Massachusetts
John Brown series (Gouache painting)
  USE Lawrence, Jacob, 1917-   John Brown series
John Brown's Raid, Harpers Ferry, W. Va., 1859
  USE Harpers Ferry (W. Va.)—History—John Brown's Raid, 1859
John Carlyle House (Alexandria, Va.)
  USE Carlyle House (Alexandria, Va.)
John Charles Frémont House (Tucson, Ariz.)
  USE Frémont House (Tucson, Ariz.)
John Cotton Dana Award
  USE John Cotton Dana Library Public Relations Award
John Cotton Dana Library Public Relations Award
  UF American Library Association John Cotton Dana Library Public Relations Award
      Dana Library Public Relations Award
      JCD Library Public Relations Award
      John Cotton Dana Award
      John Cotton Dana Public Relations Award
  BT Library science—Awards
      Public relations—Libraries—Awards
      Rewards (Prizes, etc.)—United States
John Cotton Dana Public Relations Award
  USE John Cotton Dana Library Public Relations Award
John Deere tractors *(May Subd Geog)*
  UF Deere tractors
  BT Tractors
John-dory
  USE Dory (Fish)
John family
  USE Johns family
John H. Kerr Reservoir (Va. and N.C.)
  UF Kerr, Lake (Va. and N.C.)
      Kerr Reservoir (Va. and N.C.)
      Lake Kerr (Va. and N.C.)
  BT Lakes—North Carolina
      Lakes—Virginia
      Reservoirs—North Carolina
      Reservoirs—Virginia
      Roanoke River (Va. and N.C.)
John Henry (Legendary character)
  BT Afro-Americans—Folklore
      Folklore—United States
John Kork Digitizing (Computer program)
  USE JKDIGIT (Computer program)
John Marshall Day
  [E302.6.M4]
  UF Marshall Day
  BT Holidays
John Martin Dam (Colo.)
  BT Dams—Colorado
John Martin Reservoir (Colo.)
  BT Reservoirs—Colorado
John Muir Trail (Calif.)
  BT Trails—California
John Newbery medal books
  USE Newbery medal books
John Peter Zenger award
  BT Journalism—Awards
John Redmond Reservoir (Kan.)
  BT Reservoirs—Kansas
John, the Baptist, Saint, in the Koran
  [BP133.7.J65]

UF Yaḥyá (Koranic character)
  BT Koran—Biography
John the Baptist's Day *(May Subd Geog)*
  [BV70.J]
  UF St. John the Baptist's Day
      St. John's Day
  BT Holidays
John the Elder (Legendary character)
  USE Prester John (Legendary character)
John VIII (Legendary Pope)
  USE Joan (Legendary Pope)
Johnboats *(May Subd Geog)*
  BT Boats and boating
      River life
Johne's disease
  [SF810.J6]
  UF Paratuberculosis of cattle
      Paratuberculous enteritis
      Pseudotubercular enteritis
  BT Cattle—Diseases
      Pseudotuberculosis
Johnes family
  USE Johns family
JOHNNIAC computer
  BT Electronic digital computers
Johnniac open shop system (Electronic computer system)
  USE JOSS (Electronic computer system)
Johnns family
  USE Johns family
Johns family *(Not Subd Geog)*
  UF John family
      Johnes family
      Johnns family
Johnsen family
  USE Johnson family
Johnsin family
  USE Johnson family
Johnsom family
  USE Johnson family
Johnson Canyon (Colo.)
  BT Canyons—Colorado
Johnson County Cattle War, 1892
  USE Johnson County War, 1892
Johnson County Invasion, 1892
  USE Johnson County War, 1892
Johnson County War, 1892
  UF Johnson County Cattle War, 1892
      Johnson County Invasion, 1892
      Powder River Invasion, 1892
      Rustler War, 1892
  BT Wyoming—History
Johnson family *(Not Subd Geog)*
  UF Jahnson family
      Johnsen family
      Johnsin family
      Johnsom family
      Johnsson family
      Jonson family
      Jonsson family
  BT Johansson family
  RT Jensen family
      Johnston family
Johnson grass *(May Subd Geog)*
  [SB201.J5]
Johnson light machine-gun
  BT Machine-guns
Johnson semiautomatic rifle
  BT Rifles
Johnson's Island Confederate Cemetery (Ohio)
  BT Cemeteries—Ohio
Johnsonville Campaign, 1864
  BT United States—History—Civil War, 1861-1865—Campaigns
Johnsson family
  USE Johnson family
Johnston family *(Not Subd Geog)*
  UF Johnstone family
      Jonston family
  RT Johnson family

Johnstone, Will B.   You know me Al (Comic strip)
  USE You know me Al (Comic strip)
Johnstone family
  USE Johnston family
Johnstown Flood National Memorial (Pa.)
  BT Memorials—Pennsylvania
      National parks and reserves—Pennsylvania
Jōhōji Iseki (Yao-shi, Japan)
  USE Jōhōji Site (Yao-shi, Japan)
Jōhōji Site (Yao-shi, Japan)
  (Not Subd Geog)
  UF Jōhōji Iseki (Yao-shi, Japan)
  BT Japan—Antiquities
Join spaces
  UF Spaces, Join
  BT Convex sets
      Topological spaces
      Vector spaces
Joinder in issue
  USE Joinder of issue
Joinder of actions *(May Subd Geog)*
  BT Actions and defenses
  RT Separate actions
Joinder of issue *(May Subd Geog)*
  UF Joinder in issue
      Joining of issue
      Litis contestatio
      Litiscontestation
      Similiter (Pleading)
  BT Civil procedure
      Pleading
Joinder of issue (Canon law)
Joinder of issue (Roman law)
Joinder of offenses *(May Subd Geog)*
  BT Criminal procedure
      Indictments
      Informations
  RT Compound offenses
Joinder of parties *(May Subd Geog)*
  UF Third parties (Civil procedure)
      Third party practice
  BT Parties to actions
  RT Intervention (Civil procedure)
Joinder of parties (Roman law)
Joiner family
  USE Joyner family
Joiners *(May Subd Geog)*
  BT Carpenters
      Woodworkers
  NT Cabinet-workers
Joinery *(May Subd Geog)*
  [TH5662-TH5663]
  RT Carpentry
      Woodwork
  NT Cabinet-work
      Furniture making
      Gluing
Joines family *(Not Subd Geog)*
  UF Gines family
      Jines family
      Joins family
Joining of issue
  USE Joinder of issue
Joinor family
  USE Joyner family
Joins family
  USE Joines family
Joint adventures
  USE Joint ventures
"Joint and several"
  USE Correality and solidarity
Joint and several contracts
  USE Contracts, Joint and several
Joint authors
  USE Authorship—Collaboration

Joint custody of children (May Subd Geog)
  UF Co-parenting
      Concurrent custody of children
      Parenting, Shared
      Shared custody of children
      Shared parenting
  BT Custody of children
      Parenting
  NT Children of divorced parents
      Parenting, Part-time
Joint disease, Degenerative
  USE Osteoarthritis
Joint family (May Subd Geog)
  UF Joint household
      Undivided family
  BT Domestic relations
      Family
Joint Français Strike, 1972
  [HD5375.R91972]
Joint heirs
  USE Co-heirs
Joint household
  USE Joint family
Joint occupancy of buildings
  (May Subd Geog)
  UF Mixed use of buildings
      Multiple use of buildings
      Multipurpose buildings
      Occupancy of buildings, Joint
  BT Buildings
  NT Megastructures
Joint operations (Military science)
  USE Amphibious warfare
      Landing operations
      Unified operations (Military science)
Joint ownership of personal property
  (May Subd Geog)
  UF Co-ownership of personal property
  BT Personal property
Joint practice of nurses and physicians
  USE Nurse-physician joint practice
Joint production committees
  USE Works councils
Joint Program in Transportation Retrieval
  System
  USE JPTRS (Information retrieval system)
Joint returns (Income tax)
  USE Income tax—Joint returns
Joint-stock companies
  USE Stock companies
Joint tenancy (May Subd Geog)
  UF Co-ownership
      Cotenancy
  BT Land tenure—Law and legislation
      Property
      Real property
  NT Apartment houses, Cooperative
      Condominiums
      Copyright (Joint tenancy)
      Partition
      Patents (Joint tenancy)
      Tenancy by the entirety
Joint tenancy (Roman law)
Joint testaments
  USE Joint wills
Joint tortfeasors (May Subd Geog)
  UF Joint torts
  BT Correality and solidarity
      Torts
Joint torts
  USE Joint tortfeasors
Joint undertakings
  USE Joint ventures
Joint-venture agreements
  USE Foreign licensing agreements
      License agreements

Joint ventures (May Subd Geog)
  UF Adventures, Joint
      Joint adventures
      Joint undertakings
      Joint ventures—Law and legislation
      Ventures, Joint
  BT Partnership
  RT International business enterprises
  NT Hospital-physician joint ventures
  — Law and legislation
      USE Joint ventures
Joint ventures, Hospital-physician
  USE Hospital-physician joint ventures
Joint wills (May Subd Geog)
  UF Joint testaments
  BT Wills
Joint wiping
  [TH6295 (Plumbing)]
  BT Plumbing
Joint-worms
  USE Harmolita
Jointer (Woodworking machine)
  BT Planing-machines
Jointless rails (Railroads)
  USE Railroads—Continuous rails
Joints
  [QL825 (Comparative anatomy)]
  [QM131 (Human anatomy)]
  UF Articulations
  BT Bones
      Skeleton
  SA *names of anatomical joints, e.g.* Elbow,
      Knee, Wrist
  NT Articular cartilage
      Atlanto-occipital joint
      Bursae mucosae
      Ligaments
      Pseudarthrosis
      Synovia
      Synovial membranes
  — Aging
  — Diseases (May Subd Geog)
      [RC932-933]
      UF Arthropathy
      NT Ankylosis
          Arthritis
          Arthrogryposis
          Charcot joints
          Hemarthrosis
          Joints—Hypermobility
          Joints—Radiography
  — Dislocation
      USE Dislocations
  — Examination
      NT Arthroscopy
          Joints—Range of motion—
             Measurement
  — Flexibility
      USE Joints—Range of motion
  — Hyperextensibility
      USE Joints—Hypermobility
  — Hypermobility
      UF Hyperextensibility of joints
          Hypermobility of joints
          Instability of joints
          Joints—Hyperextensibility
          Joints—Instability
          Joints—Laxity
          Laxity of joints
      BT Joints—Diseases
          Joints—Range of motion
          Movement disorders
  — Instability
      USE Joints—Hypermobility
  — Laxity
      USE Joints—Hypermobility
  — Motion, Range of
      USE Joints—Range of motion
  — Paracentesis
      USE Arthrocentesis
  — Puncture

      USE Arthrocentesis
  — Radiography
      BT Joints—Diseases
  — Range of motion
      UF Flexibility of joints
          Joints—Flexibility
          Joints—Motion, Range of
          Range of motion of joints
      BT Biomechanics
      NT Joints—Hypermobility
  — — Measurement
      BT Joints—Examination
  — Surgery
      [RD551]
      [RD684]
      [RD686]
      NT Arthrodesis
          Arthroplasty
  — Tuberculosis
      [RC312.5.J]
  — Tumors
  — Wounds and injuries
      NT Sprains
Joints, Artificial
  USE Artificial joints
Joints, Riveted
  USE Riveted joints
Joints (Engineering)
  BT Engineering
  NT Adhesive joints
      Bolted joints
      Bolts and nuts
      Boring machinery—Joints
      Brackets
      Brazed joints
      Bridges—Floors—Joints
      Bridges, Concrete—Floors—Joints
      Bridges, Concrete—Joints
      Building, Iron and steel—Joints
      Buildings—Joints
      Buildings, Prefabricated—Joints
      Clamps (Engineering)
      Concrete construction—Joints
      Drill pipe—Joints
      Electric cables—Joints
      Expansion joints
      Exterior walls—Joints
      Fasteners
      Fiber reinforced plastics—Joints
      Gas, Natural—Pipe lines—Joints
      Offshore structures—Joints
      Optical fibers—Joints
      Pavements, Bituminous—Joints
      Pavements, Concrete—Joints
      Pipe, Lead—Joints
      Pipe joints
      Precast concrete construction—Joints
      Press fits
      Pressure vessels—Joints
      Prestressed concrete construction—
          Joints
      Riveted joints
      Roads—Shoulders—Joints
      Roofing, Concrete—Joints
      Sewer-pipe—Joints
      Shrink fitting
      Splines
      Tables—Joints
      Timber joints
      Universal joints
      Welded joints
  — Drawing
      USE Joints (Engineering)—Drawings
  — Drawings
      UF Joints (Engineering)—Drawing
      BT Mechanical drawing
Joints (Geology) (May Subd Geog)
  [QE605]
  BT Geology, Structural
Joists, Steel
  USE Steel joists

Jojoba (May Subd Geog)
  [QK495.B85 (Botany)]
  [SB299.J6 (Oilseed plant)]
  UF Buxus chinensis
      Goat nut
      Jajoba
      Simmondsia californica
      Simmondsia chinensis
  BT Oilseed plants
Jojoba products (May Subd Geog)
  BT Plant products
Jok language
  USE Chokwe language
Jokes
  USE American wit and humor, English wit
       and humor, and similar headings;
       also subdivision Humor under
       individual wars and types of
       animals; and subdivision Anecdotes,
       facetiae, satire, etc. under subjects
       Wit and humor
Jokha, Tell (Iraq)
  USE Umma (Ancient city)
Joking (May Subd Geog)
  RT Wit and humor
  NT Fools and jesters
      Indians of North America—Joking
      Practical jokes
Joking relationships
  UF Teasing relationships
  BT Interpersonal relations
      Kinship
Jökulsá á Fjöllum (Iceland)
  UF Fjöllum (Iceland)
  BT Rivers—Iceland
Jōkyū no Hen, 1221
  USE Japan—History—Jōkyū Revolt, 1221
Jōkyū Revolt, 1221
  USE Japan—History—Jōkyū Revolt, 1221
Jolie family
  USE Jolly family
Jolley family
  USE Jolly family
Jollie family
  USE Jolly family
Jolliff family
  USE Jolliffe family
Jolliffe family (Not Subd Geog)
  UF Jolliff family
Jolly family (Not Subd Geog)
  UF Jolie family
      Jolley family
      Jollie family
      Jollys family
      Joly family
Jollys family
  USE Jolly family
Joloano language
  USE Sulu language
Jolof language
  USE Wolof language
Joly family
  USE Jolly family
Jomanes River (India)
  USE Yamuna River (India)
Jomolhari (Bhutan and China)
  USE Chomo Lhari (Bhutan and China)
Jōmon culture (May Subd Geog)
  [GN776.3.J6]
  UF Jōmonshiki culture
  BT Neolithic period
  NT Pottery, Jōmon
      Shimotakabora Site (Ōshima-machi,
        Tokyo, Japan)
  — Japan
Jōmon pottery
  USE Pottery, Jōmon
Jōmonshiki culture
  USE Jōmon culture
Jonacatepec (Mexico)
  — Antiquities

    NT Pilas Site (Jonacatepec, Mexico)
Jonah, Sign of
  USE Sign of Jonah
Jonan-pa (Sect)
  USE Jo-nan-pa (Sect)
Jonas family (Not Subd Geog)
  RT Jones family
Jonathan, Brother (Nickname)
  USE Brother Jonathan (Nickname)
Jonathan Operation, 1976
  USE Entebbe Airport Raid, 1976
Jonaz-Chichimeca Indians
  USE Chichimeca-Jonaz Indians
Jones family (Not Subd Geog)
  RT Jonas family
Jones Mountain (Va.)
  BT Blue Ridge Mountains
      Mountains—Virginia
Jonglei Canal (Sudan)
  BT Canals—Sudan
Jongleurs
  USE Minstrels
      Troubadours
      Trouvères
Jongor language (May Subd Geog)
  UF Dionkor language
      Djongor language
      Djonkor language
  BT Chad—Languages
      Chadic languages
Jonson family
  USE Johnson family
Jonsson family
  USE Johnson family
Jonston family
  USE Johnston family
Joodse begraafplaats (Overveen, Netherlands)
  UF Joodse begraafplaats te Overveen
        (Overveen, Netherlands)
  BT Cemeteries—Netherlands
Joodse begraafplaats te Overveen (Overveen,
  Netherlands)
  USE Joodse begraafplaats (Overveen,
        Netherlands)
Joost-van-den-Vondel-Preis
Joplin family (Not Subd Geog)
  UF Jopling family
Jopling family
  USE Joplin family
Joppas family
  USE Joppe family
Joppe family (Not Subd Geog)
  UF Jappe family
      Jeupen family
      Joepen family
      Joppas family
      Joppey family
      Joppy family
Joppey family
  USE Joppe family
Joppy family
  USE Joppe family
Jorat Mountains (Switzerland)
  UF Massif du Jorat (Switzerland)
  BT Mountains—Switzerland
Jordain family
  USE Jordan family
Jordan
  — Antiquities
      NT Amman Airport Site (Jordan)
          Araq el-Emir Site (Jordan)
          Dayr 'Allā, Tall (Jordan)
          Fūl, Tall
          Gerasa (Ancient city)
          Ghassul Site (Jordan)
          Jāwā (Jordan)
          Mazar, Tall al- (Jordan)
          Petra (Ancient city)
          Sa'īdīyah, Tall (Jordan)
  — History
      NT Karāmah (Jordan), Battle of, 1968

————Intervention, 1958
  — Languages
      NT Ammonite language
Jordan algebras
  UF Algebras, Jordan
  BT Algebra, Abstract
      Algebras, Linear
  NT Universal enveloping algebras
Jordan curves
  USE Curves, Jordan
Jordan family (Not Subd Geog)
  UF Jaudon family
      Jordain family
      Jordeen family
      Jorden family
      Jordin family
      Jordon family
      Jordone family
      Jourdain family
      Jourdan family
      Jourden family
      Jourdin family
      Jurdan family
      Jurden family
      Jurdon family
Jordan form
  USE Jordan matrix
Jordan Lake (N.C.)
  USE B. Everett Jordan Lake (N.C.)
Jordan matrix
  [QA188]
  UF Form, Jordan
      Form, Jordan normal
      Jordan form
      Jordan normal form
      Matrix, Jordan
  BT Matrices
Jordan normal form
  USE Jordan matrix
Jordan River
  UF ash-Sharī'ah
      Aulon
      ha-Yarden
      Nahr al-Urdunn
  BT Rivers—Middle East
Jordanian coins
  USE Coins, Jordanian
Jordanian periodicals (May Subd Geog)
Jordanichthys
  [QL638.L9]
  BT Lutjanidae
  NT Jordanichthys holei
Jordanichthys holei
  [QL638.L9]
  BT Jordanichthys
Jordans
  USE Chamber pots
Jordansmühl culture
  USE Lengyel-Jordansmühl complex
Jordeen family
  USE Jordan family
Jorden family
  USE Jordan family
Jordin family
  USE Jordan family
Jordon family
  USE Jordan family
Jordone family
  USE Jordan family
Jorge family
  USE George family
Jorgensen family (Not Subd Geog)
  UF Joergensen family
      Jorgenson family
Jorgenson family
  USE Jorgensen family
Jorkanden Peak (India)
  USE Kinner Kailash (India)

Jornada del Muerto Wilderness (N.M.)
 (Not Subd Geog)
  UF Jornada del Muerto Wilderness Study
    Area (N.M.)
  BT National parks and reserves—New
    Mexico
    Wilderness areas—New Mexico
Jornada del Muerto Wilderness Study Area
 (N.M.)
 USE Jornada del Muerto Wilderness (N.M.)
Jorns family *(Not Subd Geog)*
Joropo (Dance)
  [GV1796.J7]
  BT Tango (Dance)
Jōruri
  UF Gidayū
  BT Japanese drama
    Monologue
    Monologues with music (Shamisen)
  NT Katōbushi
    Sekkyō jōruri
    Shinnai
  — Texts
    UF Bunraku plays
Jōruri, Emaki (Scrolls)
 USE Emaki Jōruri (Scrolls)
Jōruri puppet plays
 USE Bunraku
Jos Plateau (Nigeria)
  UF Bauchi Plateau (Nigeria)
  BT Plateaus—Nigeria
Jōsan-kei (Japan)
 USE Jōzan Valley (Japan)
Josef (Computer program language)
  [QA76.73.J]
  BT Programming languages (Electronic
    computers)
Joselane family
 USE Josselyn family
Joseph (Son of Jacob) in the Koran
  [BP133.7.J67]
  UF Y-usuf (Koranic character)
  BT Koran—Biography
Joseph E. Drexel Preis
  BT Journalism—Awards
Joseph family *(Not Subd Geog)*
  UF Josephs family
    Josephson family
Joseph Legende (Ballet)
 USE Legend of Joseph (Ballet)
Joseph Wharton Estate (N.J.)
 USE Wharton State Forest (N.J.)
Josephinism
  [BR815]
  Here are entered works on the ecclesiastical re-
  forms of Joseph II, Holy Roman Emperor, including
  religious toleration, the right of the state to regulate
  ecclesiastical affairs, and restrictions on the rights
  and powers of the Pope.
  UF Josephism
  BT Catholic Church—Austria—
    Government
    Church and state—Austria—History—
    18th century
Josephism
 USE Josephinism
Josephlegende (Ballet)
 USE Legend of Joseph (Ballet)
Joseph's Day
 USE Saint Joseph's Day
Josephs family
 USE Joseph family
Josephson effect
  [QC176.8.T8]
  BT Superconductors
    Tunneling (Physics)
  NT Josephson junctions
Josephson family
 USE Joseph family
Josephson junctions
  UF Junctions, Josephson

BT Josephson effect
  Superconductors
Josephthal family *(Not Subd Geog)*
Joseylin family
 USE Josselyn family
Joshi effect
 USE Glow discharges
Joshi family *(Not Subd Geog)*
  UF Jośī family
Jōshin'etsu Highland National Park (Japan)
 USE Jōshin'etsu Kōgen Kokuritsu Kōen
   (Japan)
Jōshin'etsu Kōgen Kokuritsu Kōen (Japan)
  UF Jōshin'etsu Highland National Park
    (Japan)
    Jōshin'etsu Plateau National Park
    (Japan)
  BT National parks and reserves—Japan
    Parks—Japan
Jōshin'etsu Plateau National Park (Japan)
 USE Jōshin'etsu Kōgen Kokuritsu Kōen
   (Japan)
Joshua (Lion)
  BT Lions
    Zoo animals
Joshua tree *(May Subd Geog)*
  [QK495.A26]
  UF Clistoyucca brevifolia
    Yucca arborescens
    Yucca brevifolia
  — California
Joshua Tree National Monument (Calif.)
  BT National monuments—California
Jośī family
 USE Joshi family
Joslen family
 USE Josselyn family
Joslin family
 USE Josselyn family
Josling family
 USE Josselyn family
Joslun family
 USE Josselyn family
Joslyn family
 USE Josselyn family
JOSS (Electronic computer system)
  UF Johnniac open shop system (Electronic
    computer system)
  BT On-line data processing
Jössehärad polska (Dance)
Josselin family
 USE Josselyn family
Josselyn family *(Not Subd Geog)*
  UF Jocelin family
    Jocelyn family
    Joselane family
    Joseylin family
    Joslen family
    Joslin family
    Josling family
    Joslun family
    Joslyn family
    Josselin family
    Josslyn family
    Josylin family
Josslyn family
 USE Josselyn family
Josslyn Island Mound (Fla.)
  BT Florida—Antiquities
Josylin family
 USE Josselyn family
Jota
  [GV1796.J (Dancing)]
  [ML3447 (Musical history)]
Jota (The Serbo-Croatian letter)
  BT Serbo-Croatian language—Alphabet
    Serbo-Croatian language—Consonants
Jotas
  BT Dance music
Jou-jan (Tatar tribe)
  [DS25]

BT Tatars
Joubiniteuthidae *(May Subd Geog)*
  [QL430.3.J68]
  BT Squids
Jouett family
 USE Jewett family
Jouissance shares *(May Subd Geog)*
  Here are entered works on legal instruments giving owner a right in net profits or dissolution of a
  corporation, but not in management or stockholders'
  voting. Such instruments do not necessarily embody
  a share in capital stock. They are known in various
  legal systems by such terms as "bon de participa-
  tion," "buono di godimento," "Genussschein," "part
  bénéficiaire," "part de fondateur," "Partizipations-
  schein," etc. for which an adequate English equiva-
  lent is wanting.
  UF Profit sharing certificates
  BT Corporation law
    Investments
    Securities
Joule-Thomson effect
  [QC286]
  UF Joule-Thomson expansion
    Thomson-Joule effect
  BT Gases, Kinetic theory of
Joule-Thomson expansion
 USE Joule-Thomson effect
Jourdain family
 USE Jordan family
Jourdan family
 USE Jordan family
Jourden family
 USE Jordan family
Jourdin family
 USE Jordan family
**Journal Square Transportation Center (Jersey
 City, N.J.)**
  UF PATH Journal Square Transportation
    Center (Jersey City, N.J.)
  BT Terminals (Transportation)—New
    Jersey
Journal writing
 USE Diaries—Authorship
Journalism *(May Subd Geog)*
  [PN4700-5650]
  UF Writing (Authorship)
  BT Literature
    Publicity
  NT Amateur journalism
    Broadcast journalism
    Broadsides
    Canards (Journalism)
    City planning and the press
    Copy-reading
    Copyright—Newspaper articles
    Crime and the press
    Editorials
    Family in the press
    Feuilletons
    Foreign news
    Freedom of the press
    Government and the press
    Interviewing in journalism
    Journalists
    Local government and the press
    Minorities in the press
    Moving-picture journalism
    Musical criticism
    Newsletters
    Newspaper court reporting
    Newspaper layout and typography
    Newspaper publishing
    Newspaper reading
    Newspapers
    Nuclear industry in the press
    Periodicals
    Periodicals, Publishing of
    Press
    Press and propaganda
    Press conferences
    Press councils

Journalism *(Continued)*
    Race relations and the press
    Reporters and reporting
    Science news
    Sensationalism in journalism
    Sports journalism
    Syndicates (Journalism)
    Women and journalism
— Agriculture
    USE Journalism, Agricultural
— Authorship
    BT Authorship
    NT Feature writing
— Automobile industry and trade
    USE Journalism, Automotive
— Automobiles
    USE Journalism, Automotive
— Awards
    BT Rewards (Prizes, etc.)
    NT Ernst Schneider Preis
       Hadiah Adinegoro
       John Peter Zenger award
       Joseph E. Drexel Preis
       Sigma Delta Chi Awards for
          Distinguished Service in
          Journalism
— Commerce
    USE Journalism, Commercial
— Continuing education
    USE Journalism—Study and teaching
          (Continuing education)
— Editing
    [PN4778]
    UF Magazine editing
       News editing
       Newspapers—Editing
       Periodicals—Editing
    BT Editing
    NT Copy-reading
       Editorials
       Newspaper layout and typography
— Education
    USE Journalism, Educational
— Educational aspects
    USE Journalism and education
— Exhibitions and museums
— Fellowships
    USE Journalism—Scholarships,
          fellowships, etc.
— Forestry
    USE Journalism, Forestry
— Handbooks, manuals, etc.
— Horticulture
    USE Journalism, Horticultural
— Labor
    USE Journalism, Labor
— Medicine
    USE Journalism, Medical
— Merchant marine
    USE Journalism, Maritime
— Mineral industries
    USE Journalism, Mining
— Objectivity
    UF Slanted news
    BT Journalistic ethics
       Objectivity
    RT Press and propaganda
    NT Canards (Journalism)
— Outdoor life
    USE Journalism, Outdoor
— Political aspects *(May Subd Geog)*
    [PN4751]
    RT Press and politics
— Religion
    USE Journalism, Religious
— Scholarships, fellowships, etc.
    (May Subd Geog)
    UF Journalism—Fellowships
    BT Journalism—Study and teaching
— Social aspects *(May Subd Geog)*
    [PN4749]

    UF Press—Social aspects
— Societies, etc.
    UF Newspapers—Societies, etc.
       Press—Societies, etc.
       Press associations
       Press clubs
— Sports
    USE Sports journalism
— Study and teaching *(May Subd Geog)*
    NT Journalism—Scholarships,
          fellowships, etc.
**— Study and teaching (Continuing
    education)** *(May Subd Geog)*
    UF Journalism—Continuing education
— Style manuals
    [PN4783]
    UF Newspaper style
       Style books (Journalism)
       Style manuals (Journalism)
       Stylebooks (Journalism)
— Vocational guidance
    [PN4797]
    BT Journalists
— Austria
— — Awards
       NT René-Marcic-Preis
— United States
    UF New journalism
Journalism, Aeronautical
    UF Aeronautical journalism
    BT Journalism, Technical
Journalism, Afro-American
    USE Afro-American press
Journalism, Agricultural *(May Subd Geog)*
    UF Agricultural journalism
       Dairy journalism
       Journalism—Agriculture
       Journalism, Dairy
    RT Journalism, Rural
    NT Journalism, Forestry
       Journalism, Horticultural
— Biography
    [S415-417]
    BT Agriculturists—Biography
       Journalists—Biography
Journalism, Automotive *(May Subd Geog)*
    UF Automotive journalism
       Journalism—Automobile industry and
          trade
       Journalism—Automobiles
Journalism, College *(May Subd Geog)*
    [LB3621.6]
    UF College journalism
       College student journalism
    BT Journalism, School
    NT College student newspapers and
       periodicals
Journalism, Commercial *(May Subd Geog)*
    [PN4784.C7]
    UF Business journalism
       Commercial journalism
       Economic journalism
       Financial journalism
       Financial news
       Journalism—Commerce
       Journalism, Economic
       Trade journalism
Journalism, Communist *(May Subd Geog)*
    UF Communist journalism
    NT Press, Communist
Journalism, Consumer *(May Subd Geog)*
    UF Consumer journalism
    BT Consumer education
Journalism, Dairy
    USE Journalism, Agricultural
Journalism, Dental *(May Subd Geog)*
    UF Dental journalism
    BT Journalism, Medical
Journalism, Economic
    USE Journalism, Commercial

Journalism, Educational
    UF Educational journalism
       Journalism—Education
    BT Journalism and education
Journalism, Elementary school
    (May Subd Geog)
    [LB3621.3]
    UF Elementary school journalism
       Elementary school student journalism
    BT Journalism, School
Journalism, Ethnic
    USE Ethnic press
Journalism, Forestry *(May Subd Geog)*
    UF Forestry journalism
       Journalism—Forestry
    BT Journalism, Agricultural
Journalism, High school *(May Subd Geog)*
    [LB3621.5]
    UF High school journalism
       High school student journalism
    BT Journalism, School
Journalism, Horticultural *(May Subd Geog)*
    UF Horticultural journalism
       Journalism—Horticulture
    BT Journalism, Agricultural
    NT Horticultural writers
Journalism, Industrial
    USE Journalism, Technical
Journalism, Junior high school
    (May Subd Geog)
    [LB3621.4]
    UF Junior high school journalism
       Junior high school student journalism
    BT Journalism, School
Journalism, Labor *(May Subd Geog)*
    UF Journalism—Labor
       Journalism, Trade-union
       Labor journalism
       Trade-union journalism
    NT Press, Labor
Journalism, Legal *(May Subd Geog)*
    UF Legal journalism
    NT Newspaper court reporting
Journalism, Maritime *(May Subd Geog)*
    UF Journalism—Merchant marine
       Maritime journalism
Journalism, Medical *(May Subd Geog)*
    [PN4784.M4]
    UF Journalism—Medicine
       Medical journalism
    NT Journalism, Dental
Journalism, Military *(May Subd Geog)*
    UF Armed Forces—Journalism
       Armed Forces newspapers
       Army newspapers
       Military journalism
    BT War correspondents
    SA *subdivision* Journalism, Military *under
       individual wars, e.g.* World War,
       1939-1945—Journalism, Military
Journalism, Mining *(May Subd Geog)*
    [PN4784.M]
    UF Journalism—Mineral industries
       Mining journalism
    BT Journalism, Technical
Journalism, Outdoor *(May Subd Geog)*
    [PN4784.O9]
    UF Journalism—Outdoor life
       Outdoor journalism
Journalism, Pictorial
    UF Photojournalism
       Pictorial journalism
    BT Magazine illustration
    NT Illustrated periodicals
       Newspapers—Illustrations
       Photography, Journalistic
Journalism, Prison *(May Subd Geog)*
    UF Prison journalism
    NT Prison periodicals
Journalism, Provincial
    USE Journalism, Regional

Journalism, Regional *(May Subd Geog)*
　UF　Journalism, Provincial
　　　Provincial journalism
　　　Regional journalism
Journalism, Religious *(May Subd Geog)*
　UF　Catholic journalism
　　　Journalism—Religion
　　　Religious journalism
　BT　Advertising—Churches
　　　Mass media in religion
　　　Religious literature—Authorship
　RT　Church and the press
　　　Press, Catholic
　　　Religion and the press
　　　Religious newspapers and periodicals
　NT　Press, Baptist
　　　Press, Lutheran
　　　Press, Protestant
Journalism, Rural *(May Subd Geog)*
　UF　Country journalism
　　　Country newspapers
　　　Rural journalism
　RT　Community newspapers
　　　Journalism, Agricultural
Journalism, School *(May Subd Geog)*
　[LB3620]
　UF　School journalism
　　　Student journalism
　BT　Amateur journalism
　　　Student activities
　RT　Journalism and education
　NT　Journalism, College
　　　Journalism, Elementary school
　　　Journalism, High school
　　　Journalism, Junior high school
　　　Student newspapers and periodicals
　　　Student publications
Journalism, Scientific *(May Subd Geog)*
　UF　Scientific journalism
Journalism, Socialist *(May Subd Geog)*
　UF　Socialist journalism
　NT　Press, Socialist
Journalism, Technical *(May Subd Geog)*
　[PN4784.T3]
　UF　Journalism, Industrial
　　　Technical journalism
　NT　Employees' magazines, handbooks, etc.
　　　House organs
　　　Journalism, Aeronautical
　　　Journalism, Mining
Journalism, Trade-union
　USE　Journalism, Labor
Journalism and education *(May Subd Geog)*
　UF　Education and journalism
　　　Journalism—Educational aspects
　RT　Journalism, School
　NT　Journalism, Educational
　　　Newspapers in education
Journalism and literature *(May Subd Geog)*
　UF　Literature and journalism
　NT　Newspapers—Sections, columns, etc.—
　　　　Reviews
Journalism and moving-pictures
　UF　Moving-pictures and journalism
　NT　Moving-picture journalism
Journalism in literature
　USE　Press and journalism in literature
Journalistic ethics *(May Subd Geog)*
　[PN4756 (General)]
　UF　Ethics, Journalistic
　　　Journalists—Professional ethics
　BT　Professional ethics
　NT　Attribution of news
　　　Confidential communications—Press
　　　Free press and fair trial
　　　Journalism—Objectivity
　　　Newspapers—Objectivity
Journalistic libraries
　USE　Newspaper office libraries
Journalistic novel
　USE　Nonfiction novel

Journalistic photography
　USE　Photography, Journalistic
Journalists *(May Subd Geog)*
　[PN4871-PN4874 (United States)]
　[PN5122-PN5123 (Great Britain)]
　[PR4820-PR4823 (General)]
　UF　Columnists
　　　Commentators
　　　Editors (Journalism)
　　　Radio journalists
　BT　Journalism
　SA　*subdivision* Journalists *under names of
　　　wars, e.g.* United States—History—
　　　Civil War, 1861-1865—Journalists
　NT　Broadcast journalism—Vocational
　　　　guidance
　　　Fashion editors
　　　Horticultural writers
　　　Jewish journalists
　　　Journalism—Vocational guidance
　　　Minority journalists
　　　News photographers
　　　Pamphleteers
　　　Sportswriters
　　　Strikes and lockouts—Journalists
　　　Trade-unions—Journalists
　　　War correspondents
　　　Women journalists
　— Biography
　　　NT　Journalism, Agricultural—
　　　　　Biography
　— Collective bargaining
　　　USE　Collective bargaining—Journalists
　— Collective labor agreements
　　　USE　Collective labor agreements—
　　　　　Journalists
　— Job stress
　— Legal status, laws, etc.
　　　(May Subd Geog)
　　　BT　Press law
　— Professional ethics
　　　USE　Journalistic ethics
Journalists, Afro-American
　USE　Afro-American journalists
Journalists, Jewish
　USE　Jewish journalists
Journalists, Minority
　USE　Minority journalists
Journalists, Slavic
　[PN5355.S53]
　UF　Slavic journalists
Journalists (United States Armed Forces)
　USE　United States—Armed Forces—
　　　Journalists
Journalists as artists *(May Subd Geog)*
　BT　Artists
Journalists in government *(May Subd Geog)*
Journalists in motion-pictures
　BT　Moving-pictures
Journals, Scholarly
　USE　Scholarly periodicals
Journals (Diaries)
　USE　Diaries
Journals (Machinery)
　USE　Bearings (Machinery)
Journee family
　USE　Journey family
Journey family *(Not Subd Geog)*
　UF　Journee family
Journey workers *(May Subd Geog)*
　UF　Journeymen
　BT　Artisans
　　　Skilled labor
　— Societies, etc.
　　　UF　Journey workers' fraternities
　　　　Journey workers' guilds
　　　　Journeymen's societies
　　　　Yeomanry guilds
　　　BT　Guilds
　　　NT　Compagnonnages
　— Strikes and lockouts

　　　USE　Strikes and lockouts—Journey
　　　　　workers
Journey workers' fraternities
　USE　Journey workers—Societies, etc.
Journey workers' guilds
　USE　Journey workers—Societies, etc.
Journeymen
　USE　Journey workers
Journeymen's societies
　USE　Journey workers—Societies, etc.
Journeys
　USE　*subdivision* Description and travel
　　　　*under names of countries, regions,
　　　　etc.*
　　　Voyages and travels
　　　Voyages around the world
Jousting, Ring
　USE　Ring jousting
Joux Valley (Switzerland)
　UF　Vallée de Joux (Switzerland)
　BT　Valleys—Switzerland
Jova family *(Not Subd Geog)*
　UF　Jovas family
　　　Jove family
Jovas family
　USE　Jova family
Jove family
　USE　Jova family
Jovian atmosphere
　USE　Jupiter (Planet)—Atmosphere
Jowar
　USE　Durra
Jowett Jupiter automobile
　USE　Jupiter automobile
Joy
　BT　Emotions
　RT　Happiness
　— Religious aspects
　— — Buddhism, [Christianity, etc.]
Joy family *(Not Subd Geog)*
　UF　Joye family
　　　Joys family
Joy in art
Joy in literature
Joyce, James, 1882-1941
　— Characters
　— — Leopold Bloom
　　　RT　Bloom, Leopold (Fictitious
　　　　　character)
Joye family
　USE　Joy family
Joyner family *(Not Subd Geog)*
　UF　Joiner family
　　　Joinor family
Joys family
　USE　Joy family
Jōzan-kei (Japan)
　USE　Jōzan Valley (Japan)
Jōzan Valley (Japan)
　UF　Jōsan-kei (Japan)
　　　Jōzan-kei (Japan)
　BT　Valleys—Japan
Jozaria
　[QE882.P8]
　BT　Anthracobunidae
Jozaria palustris
　[QE882.P8]
JPTRS (Information retrieval system)
　[Z699.4.J18]
　UF　Joint Program in Transportation
　　　Retrieval System
　BT　Information storage and retrieval
　　　systems—Transportation
Jrai (Indochinese people)
　USE　Jarai
JSD method
　USE　Jackson system development method
JSP technique
　USE　Jackson structured programming
Ju 87 (Bombers)
　USE　Stuka (Bombers)

Ju 287 (Jet bomber)
USE Junkers Ju 287 (Jet bomber)
Ju-chen (Manchurian people)
BT Ethnology—China
Tunguses
Ju-chen language
[PL481.J8]
UF Jucen language
Juchen language
Jurchi language
Nü-chen language
BT Manchu language
Manchuria (China)—Languages
Tungus-Manchu languages
Ju chou porcelain
USE Ju ware
Ju-i (Scepters)
[NK6100]
BT Insignia
Ju language (Benue-Congo)
USE Kaje language
Ju-pi T'u (Scroll)
[ND1049.6.J]
UF Emperor's procession (Scroll)
Imperial procession departing from
and returning to the palace (Scroll)
BT Painting, Chinese—Ming-Ch'ing
dynasties, 1368-1912
Scrolls, Chinese
Ju ware
UF Ju chou porcelain
BT Porcelain, Chinese—Sung-Yuan
dynasties, 960-1368
Jŭ/wăsi (African people)
USE !Kung (African people)
Jualjai language
USE Yualyai language
Juan, Don (Legendary character)
USE Don Juan (Legendary character)
Juan Bobo (Legendary character)
[GR121.P8]
BT Folklore—Puerto Rico
Juan de Fuca Strait (B.C. and Wash.)
UF Fuca, Strait of (B.C. and Wash.)
Strait of Fuca (B.C. and Wash.)
Strait of Juan de Fuca (B.C. and
Wash.)
BT Straits—British Columbia
Straits—Washington (State)
Juan de Herrera (Portrait drawing)
USE Maea, José, 1759-1826.   Portrait of
Juan de Herrera
Juan family   *(Not Subd Geog)*
Juan Fernandez fur seal
USE Guadalupe fur seal
Juan Fernández Islands
UF Islas Juan Fernández
BT Islands of the Pacific
Juana River (Java, Indonesia)
BT Rivers—Indonesia
Juanambú River, Battle of the, 1814
BT Colombia—History—War of
Independence, 1810-1822—
Campaigns
Juaneño Indians
[E99.J]
UF Acagchemin Indians
BT Indians of North America
Shoshonean Indians
— **Religion and mythology**
Juang (Indic people)
BT Ethnology—India
Mundas
Juar
USE Durra
Juares family
USE Juarez family
Juarez family   *(Not Subd Geog)*
UF Juares family

Juba River (Ethiopia and Somalia)
UF Ganana River (Ehtiopia and Somalia)
Giuba River (Ethiopia and Somalia)
BT Rivers—Ethiopia
Rivers—Somalia
Jubes
USE Screens (Church decoration)
Jubilate Deo omnis terra, Servite Domino
(Music)
USE Psalms (Music)—100th Psalm
Jubilate Deo omnis terra, psalmum dicite
(Music)
USE Psalms (Music)—66th Psalm
Jubilee (Judaism)
UF Year of Jubilee (Judaism)
BT Agricultural laws and legislation
(Jewish law)
Sabbatical year (Judaism)
Jubilee indulgences
USE Indulgences
Jubilee singers
[ML400]
Jubilee volumes
USE Festschriften
Jubilee Year
USE Holy Year
Juč (Serbia)
USE Ključ (Serbia)
Júcar River (Spain)
UF Río Júcar (Spain)
BT Rivers—Spain
Jucen language
USE Ju-chen language
Juchen language
USE Ju-chen language
Juchitán, Battle of, 1866
BT Mexico—History—European
intervention, 1861-1867
Jud family
USE Judd family
Judaea, Wilderness of
UF Barrīyat al Yahūdīyah
Jeshimmon
Judea, Wilderness of
Midbar Yehuda
Midbar Yehudah
Wilderness of Judaea
Wilderness of Judah
Wilderness of Judea
Yeshimon
Judaea and Samaria
USE West Bank
Judaica
USE Jewish literature
Jews
Judaism   *(May Subd Geog)*
Polemic works limited to any one of the sects,
schisms, or cleavages within Judaism are entered
under the name of such a movement, e.g. Hasidism,
Jewish Science, Reform Judaism.
UF Jews—Religion
BT Religions
Semites—Religion
SA *subdivision* Judaism *under religious*
headings; also subdivision Religious
aspects—Judaism under subjects;
and headings beginning with the
word Jewish
NT Baptism—Judaism
Chief Rabbinate
Classification—Books—Jewish
literature
Cohanim
Commandments, Six hundred and
thirteen
Communism and Judaism
Confession—Judaism
Conservative Judaism
Fasts and feasts—Judaism
Haskalah
Jerusalem in Judaism

Jesus Christ—Jewish interpretations
Jewish sects
Jews
Messiah
Mysticism—Judaism
Mythology, Jewish
Orthodox Judaism
Parables, Jewish
Printing, Hebrew—Religious aspects
Proselytes and proselyting, Jewish
Purity, Ritual (Judaism)
Reconstructionist Judaism
Reform Judaism
Religious Zionism
Synagogues
Urim and Thummim
Worship (Judaism)
Zionism and Judaism
— **20th century**
[BM565]
— **Apologetic works**
[BM648]
Here are entered works defending the Jewish
religion and Judaism in general.
UF Apologetics, Jewish
Jewish apologetics
Jews—Apologetic works
— **Ari rite**
UF Ari rite of Judaism
Judaism—Minhag Ari
Judaism—Nusaḥ Ari
Minhag Ari
Nusaḥ Ari
BT Judaism—Customs and practices
— Asceticism
USE Asceticism—Judaism
— Biography
USE Jews—Biography
— Clergy
USE Judaism—Functionaries
— **Controversial literature**
[BM585]
[BT173.J8 (Mohammedan
apologetics)]
[BT1120 (Christian apologetics)]
Here are entered works against the Jewish
religion.
— **Customs and practices**
[BM700]
UF Jewish life
Jews—Rites and ceremonies
Minhagim
NT Bar mitzvah
Bat mitzvah
Berit milah
Confirmation (Jewish rite)
Funeral rites and ceremonies,
Jewish
Hakafoth
Hand washing (Jewish rite)
Jewish way of life
Judaism—Ari rite
Judaism—Frankfurt rite
Judaism—Romaniot rite
Judaism—Sephardic rite
Marriage customs and rites, Jewish
Purity, Ritual (Judaism)
Redemption of the first-born
Seder
Shehitah
Tashlikh
Zizith
— **Dictionaries**
RT Jews—Dictionaries and
encyclopedias
— **Discipline**
NT Freedom of speech in Judaism
— **Doctrines**
[BM600-603]
UF Jewish theology
Theology, Jewish

SA *special headings with Jewish
theology added in parentheses,
e.g.* Freedom (Jewish theology)
NT Bible. O.T.—Criticism,
interpretation, etc., Jewish
Creeds, Jewish
Faith (Judaism)
God (Judaism)
Good and evil (Judaism)
Heresies, Jewish
Holy Spirit (Judaism)
Revelation on Sinai
Talmud—Theology
— Early works to 1900
USE Judaism—Works to 1900
— Education
USE Jews—Education
— **Frankfurt rite**
UF Frankfurt rite of Judaism
Judaism—Minhag Frankfurt
Judaism—Nusaḥ Frankfurt
Minhag Frankfurt
Nusaḥ Frankfurt
BT Judaism—Customs and practices
Judaism—Germany (West)
— **Functionaries**
⌐BM652⌐
UF Jewish religious functionaries
Judaism—Clergy
NT Cantors, Jewish
Marbits Torah
Rabbis
Scribes, Jewish
— **Hasidic rite**
UF Hasidic rite
Judaism—Minhag Ḥasidim
Judaism—Nusaḥ Ḥasidim
Minhag Ḥasidim
Nusaḥ Ḥasidim
BT Hasidism
— **History**
— — To 140 B.C.
USE Judaism—History—To 70
A.D.
— — **To 70 A.D.**
⌐BM165⌐
Here are entered works dealing with Juda-
ism on a developmental or evolutionary basis
from its beginnings to the downfall of the
Jewish state in 70 A.D.
UF Judaism—History—To 140 B.C.
BT Palestine—History—To 70 A.D.
NT Jews—History—To 70 A.D.
— — Inter-testamental period, 140 B.C.-30
A.D.
USE Judaism—History—Post-exilic
period, 586 B.C.-210 A.D.
— — Greco-Roman period, 332 B.C.-210
A.D.
USE Judaism—History—Post-exilic
period, 586 B.C.-210 A.D.
— — **Post-exilic period, 586 B.C.-210 A.D.**
⌐BM176⌐
Here are entered works dealing with the
history of Judaism from the exile to the down-
fall of the Jewish state and the earliest redac-
tion of Jewish law in the Mishnah.
UF Bible—History of inter-
testamental events
Hellenistic Judaism
Judaism—History—Inter-
testamental period, 140 B.C.-
30 A.D.
Judaism—History—Greco-
Roman period, 332 B.C.-210
A.D.
Judaism—History—Pre-
Talmudic period, 586 B.C.-10
A.D.
Judaism, Hellenistic
BT Palestine—History—To 70 A.D.
— — Pre-Talmudic period, 586 B.C.-10 A.D.

USE Judaism—History—Post-exilic
period, 586 B.C.-210 A.D.
— — Tannaitic period, 10-220
USE Tannaim
— — **Talmudic period, 10-425**
⌐BM177⌐
Here are entered works dealing with the
history of Judaism during the redaction of the
Jewish law, approximately the first five centu-
ries of the Christian era.
NT Am Haarez
Talmud—Theology
Tannaim
— — **Medieval and early modern period,
425-1789**
Here are entered works dealing with the
history of Judaism from the completion of the
Talmud in the fifth century of the Christian
era to the time of the emancipation of the
Jews in the eighteenth century.
— — **Modern period, 1750-**
⌐BM195⌐
Here are entered works dealing with the
history of Judaism from the time of the eman-
cipation of the Jews in the eighteenth century
of the Christian era down to present times.
— **History of doctrines**
Here are entered works dealing with two or
more individual tenets of Jewish faith. Works
dealing with a single tenet are entered under the
specific heading, e.g. Atonement (Judaism).
Works limited to a particular period of history
are entered under the specific heading, e.g. Juda-
ism—History—Talmudic period, 10-425.
— **Liturgical objects**
⌐BM657.A1⌐
BT Jewish art and symbolism
NT Ark of the law
Candles and lights (Judaism)
Etrog
Hanukkah lamp
Lulav
Menorah
Mezuzah
Myrtle (Sukkot)
Spice boxes (Jewish liturgical
objects)
Tallith
Tefillin
Torah scrolls
Willow (Sukkot)
Zizith
— **Liturgy**
UF Jews. Liturgy and ritual
Jews—Ritual
BT Worship (Judaism)
NT Mahzorim
Piyutim
Siddurim
Synagogue dedication services
Synagogue music
— — **Texts**
NT Piyutim
— Minhag Ari
USE Judaism—Ari rite
— Minhag Frankfurt
USE Judaism—Frankfurt rite
— Minhag ha-Romanyoṭim
USE Judaism—Romaniot rite
— Minhag Ḥasidim
USE Judaism—Hasidic rite
— Minhag Sefarad
USE Judaism—Sephardic rite
— Nusaḥ Ari
USE Judaism—Ari rite
— Nusaḥ Frankfurt
USE Judaism—Frankfurt rite
— Nusaḥ ha-Romanyoṭim
USE Judaism—Romaniot rite
— Nusaḥ Ḥasidim
USE Judaism—Hasidic rite
— Nusaḥ Sefarad
USE Judaism—Sephardic rite

— Poetry
USE Jewish religious poetry
— **Prayer-books and devotions**
NT Jewish soldiers—Prayer-books and
devotions
Sick—Prayer-books and devotions,
Jewish
Tehinnot
— Public opinion
USE Jews—Public opinion
— **Quotations, maxims, etc.**
BT Quotations, Jewish
NT Quotations, Talmudic
— Reconstructionist movement
USE Reconstructionist Judaism
— Reform movement
USE Reform Judaism
— **Relations**
NT Jews—Election, Doctrine of
— — **Buddhism, ⌐Christianity, Islam, etc.⌐**
— — **Christianity**
NT Barcelona Disputation, 1263
Brotherhood Week
Cabala and Christianity
Mary, Blessed Virgin, Saint—
Jewish interpretations
— — — **1945-**
— — **Evangelicalism**
⌐BR1641.J83⌐
— — **Mormon Church, ⌐Catholic Church,
etc.⌐**
— — **Islam**
Here are entered works on relations be-
tween the religions of Judaism and Islam.
When this heading is assigned, duplicate
entry is made under Islam—Relations—Juda-
ism. Works on the conflicts between the Arab
countries and Israel are entered under Israel-
Arab conflicts. Works that discuss collective-
ly the relations between Arabs and Jews, in-
cluding religious, ethnic, and ideological rela-
tions, are entered under Jewish-Arab
relations, subdivided further by dates, if
appropriate.
— **Romaniot rite**
UF Judaism—Minhag ha-Romanyoṭim
Judaism—Nusaḥ ha-Romanyoṭim
Minhag ha-Romanyoṭim
Nusaḥ ha-Romanyoṭim
Romaniot rite of Judaism
BT Judaism—Customs and practices
Romaniots
— **Sephardic rite**
UF Judaism—Minhag Sefarad
Judaism—Nusaḥ Sefarad
Minhag Sefarad
Nusaḥ Sefarad
Sephardic rite
BT Judaism—Customs and practices
Sephardim
— **Study and teaching** *(May Subd Geog)*
NT Jewish religious education
Talmud Torah (Judaism)
— **Works to 1900**
Here are entered general works on Judaism
written before 1900. For specific aspects see the
specific subdivision.
UF Judaism—Early works to 1900
— **Germany**
NT Hasidism, Medieval
— **Germany (West)**
NT Judaism—Frankfurt rite
Judaism, Conservative
USE Conservative Judaism
Judaism, Hellenistic
USE Jews—Civilization—Greek influences
Judaism—History—Post-exilic period,
586 B.C.-210 A.D.
Judaism, Orthodox
USE Orthodox Judaism
Judaism, Reconstructionist
USE Reconstructionist Judaism

Judaism, Reform
    USE Reform Judaism
Judaism (Christian theology)
    BT Christianity and other religions—
        Judaism
    NT Israel (Christian theology)
        Jerusalem in Christianity
Judaism and art
    ₍BM538.A7₎
    UF Art and Judaism
    BT Art and religion
    RT Art, Jewish
Judaism and astronautics
    ₍BM538.A75₎
    BT Astronautics
        Cosmology, Jewish
        Judaism and science
        Religion and astronautics
    NT Moon—Exploration (Jewish theology)
Judaism and communism
    USE Communism and Judaism
Judaism and democracy
    BT Democracy
Judaism and economics
    USE Economics—Religious aspects—
        Judaism
Judaism and labor
    UF Labor and Judaism
    BT Church and labor
    NT Labor laws and legislation (Jewish law)
Judaism and literature (May Subd Geog)
    UF Literature and Judaism
    BT Literature
Judaism and parapsychology
    UF Parapsychology and Judaism
    BT Psychical research
Judaism and philosophy
    UF Philosophy and Judaism
    BT Philosophy, Jewish
        Philosophy and religion
Judaism and politics
    ₍BM645.P64₎
    UF Politics and Judaism
    BT Jews—Politics and government
        Judaism and state
Judaism and psychoanalysis
    (May Subd Geog)
    ₍BM538.P68₎
    BT Psychoanalysis
        Psychoanalysis and religion
Judaism and psychology
    UF Psychology and Judaism
Judaism and science
    ₍BM538.S3₎
    UF Science and Judaism
    BT Religion and science
    NT Judaism and astronautics
Judaism and social problems
    ₍HN40.J5₎
    UF Religion and social problems
        Social problems and Judaism
    BT Church and social problems
        Social problems
        Sociology, Jewish
Judaism and socialism
    USE Socialism and Judaism
Judaism and state
    ₍BM538.S7₎
    UF State and Judaism
    BT Religion and state
    NT Judaism and politics
        Zionism
Judaism and Zionism
    USE Zionism and Judaism
Judaism in literature
    BT Jews in literature
        Religion in literature

Judd family (Not Subd Geog)
    UF Jud family
        Jude family
        Judkin family
        Judkins family
        Judkyn family
    RT Judson family
Jude family
    USE Judd family
Judea, Wilderness of
    USE Judaea, Wilderness of
Judea and Samaria
    USE West Bank
Judean sibyl
    USE Babylonian sibyl
Judenburg Mutiny, 1918
Judengasse (Worms, Germany)
    BT Streets—Germany (West)
Judeo-Arabic folk literature
    USE Folk literature, Judeo-Arabic
Judeo-Arabic imprints (May Subd Geog)
Judeo-Arabic Jewish religious poetry
    USE Jewish religious poetry, Judeo-Arabic
Judeo-Arabic language (May Subd Geog)
    ₍PJ5071-PJ5079₎
    BT Arab countries—Languages
        Arabic language
        Jews—Languages
Judeo-Arabic literature (May Subd Geog)
    ₍PJ5078₎
    BT Arabic literature
        Jewish literature
    NT Folk literature, Judeo-Arabic
Judeo-Arabic manuscripts
    USE Manuscripts, Judeo-Arabic
Judeo-Arabic poetry (May Subd Geog)
    BT Arabic poetry
    NT Jewish religious poetry, Judeo-Arabic
Judeo-Arabic proverbs
    USE Proverbs, Judeo-Arabic
Judeo-Catalan poetry
    USE Catalan poetry—Jewish authors
Judeo-German language
    USE Yiddish language
Judeo-Italian dialect
    USE Italian language—Dialects—Judeo-
        Italian
Judeo-Persian language
    UF Persian language—Dialects—Judeo-
        Persian
    BT Jews—Languages
Judeo-Persian literature (May Subd Geog)
Judeo-Persian manuscripts
    USE Manuscripts, Judeo-Persian
Judeo-Persian poetry (May Subd Geog)
Judeo-Spanish language
    USE Ladino language
Judesmo
    USE Ladino language
Judey family
    USE Judy family
Judge advocates (May Subd Geog)
    BT Government attorneys
Judge-made law (May Subd Geog)
    UF Judicial law
        Judicial legislation
        Law, Judge-made
    BT Common law
        Judicial power
        Judicial process
        Lacunae in law
        Law—Interpretation and construction
        Legislation
        Legislative power
Judges (May Subd Geog)
    UF Chief justices
        Magistrates
    BT Courts—Officials and employees
    RT Courts
        Justice, Administration of
    NT Disqualification of judges

        Jewish judges
        Judgments
        Judicial corruption
        Judicial discretion
        Judicial ethics
        Judicial process
        Justices of the peace
        Law officers (Courts-martial)
        Lay judges
        Police magistrates
        Women judges
    — Appointment, qualifications, tenure, etc.
        USE Judges—Selection and
            appointment
    — **Attitudes**
        BT Attitude (Psychology)
    — **Costume**
        ₍GT6230-6280₎
        UF Legal dress
    — **Discipline**
        BT Judicial ethics
    — Disqualification
        USE Disqualification of judges
    — **Education** (May Subd Geog)
        UF Judicial education
        BT Law—Study and teaching
    — **Election**
        UF Judicial elections
    — **Pensions** (May Subd Geog)
        UF Judges—Salaries, pensions, etc.
    — **Retirement**
    — **Salaries, etc.** (May Subd Geog)
        UF Judges—Salaries, pensions, etc.
            Judicial compensation
    — Salaries, pensions, etc.
        USE Judges—Pensions
            Judges—Salaries, etc.
    — **Selection and appointment**
        UF Judges—Appointment,
            qualifications, tenure, etc.
            Judicial tenure
    — **Travel regulations**
Judges, Afro-American
    USE Afro-American judges
Judges (Canon law)
    NT Disqualification of judges (Canon law)
Judges (Germanic law)
Judges (Islamic law)
    NT Cadis
Judges (Jewish law)
Judges (Roman law)
Judges' clerks
    USE Law clerks
Judges' wives (May Subd Geog)
    BT Wives
Judging (Sports)
    USE Sports officiating
Judging counted thread embroidery
    USE Counted thread embroidery—
        Exhibitions—Judging
Judging debates and debating
    USE Debates and debating—Judging
Judging embroidery
    USE Embroidery—Exhibitions—Judging
Judging hooked rugs
    USE Rugs, Hooked—Exhibitions—Judging
Judging radio competitions
    USE Radio—Competitions—Judging
Judgment
    BT Knowledge, Theory of
        Language and languages
        Psychology
        Thought and thinking
        Wisdom
    NT Attitude change
        Common sense
        Conservation (Psychology)
        Discretion
        Similarity judgment
        Size judgment
        Weight judgment

1976

— Religious aspects
Judgment, Last
  USE Judgment Day
Judgment, Practical
  USE Practical judgment
Judgment (Aesthetics)
Judgment (Ethics)
  UF Moral judgment
  BT Ethics
Judgment (Logic)
  [BC181]
  UF Impersonal judgment
  BT Logic
  RT Reasoning
  NT Fallacies (Logic)
     Negation (Logic)
     Prediction (Logic)
Judgment Day
  [BT880-881]
  UF Day of Judgment
     Doomsday
     General judgment
     Judgment, Last
     Last Judgment
  BT End of the world
     Judgment of God
  RT Second Advent
  — Biblical teaching
     NT Day of Jehovah
Judgment Day (Egyptian religion)
Judgment Day (Islam)
  [BP166.85]
  BT End of the world (Islam)
     Eschatology, Islamic
  — Koranic teaching
     [BP134.E7]
Judgment Day in art
  BT Christian art and symbolism
  NT Michelangelo Buonarroti, 1475-1564.
     Last judgment
     Miroglio, Valerio. Last judgment
Judgment Day in literature
Judgment notes *(May Subd Geog)*
  BT Promissory notes
Judgment of Cambyses (Panel painting)
  USE David, Gérard, ca. 1460-1523.
     Judgment of Cambyses
Judgment of God
  UF God—Judgment
  BT God
  NT Judgment Day
Judgment of the soul (Theology)
  USE Particular judgment (Theology)
Judgments *(May Subd Geog)*
  BT Civil procedure
     Courts
     Criminal procedure
     Estoppel
     Judges
     Judicial process
  RT Jurisdiction
     Stare decisis
  NT Alternative convictions
     Arrest of judgment
     Confession of judgment
     Conflict of judicial decisions
     Dismissal and nonsuit
     Executions (Law)
     Indeterminate sentence
     Interlocutory decisions
     Judgments by default
     Judicial opinions
     Res judicata
     Retroactive judicial decisions
     Scire facias
     Speaking orders (Law)
     Supplementary proceedings
Judgments, Criminal *(May Subd Geog)*
  UF Criminal judgments
     Judgments of conviction

BT Criminal courts
   Criminal procedure
NT Acquittals
   Indeterminate sentence
   Sentences (Criminal procedure)
Judgments, Declaratory *(May Subd Geog)*
  UF Declaratory judgments
  BT Declaratory acts
Judgments, Foreign *(May Subd Geog)*
  [JX6607]
  Here are entered works dealing with the legal
  status in one country or state of the judicial decisions
  of other countries or states in general.
  Works relating to the enforcement by one state or
  country of the judicial acts of another are entered
  under the heading Judicial assistance.
  UF Foreign judgments
  BT Civil procedure (International law)
     Conflict of laws
  RT Judicial assistance
Judgments (Canon law)
  [BX1939.J8]
Judgments (Roman law)
Judgments by default *(May Subd Geog)*
  UF Default judgments
  BT Contumacy
     Default (Law)
     Judgments
Judgments by default (Roman law)
Judgments by peers
  USE Jury
Judgments of conviction
  USE Judgments, Criminal
Judica me, Deus (Music)
  USE Psalms (Music)—43d Psalm
Judicable arbitration
  USE Grievance arbitration
Judicare
  USE Legal assistance to the poor
Judicial activism
  USE Political questions and judicial power
Judicial assistance *(May Subd Geog)*
  Here are entered works relating to the enforce-
  ment by one state or country of judicial acts of anoth-
  er state or country.
  To be distinguished from the French "assistance
  judiciare" for which "legal aid" is the English equiva-
  lent.
  Works dealing with the treatment of nationals of
  one country in the civil courts of another are entered
  under the heading Civil procedure (International
  law)
  BT Civil procedure
     Civil procedure (International law)
     Criminal procedure
     International law
  RT Judgments, Foreign
  NT Extradition
     Legalization
     Letters rogatory
Judicial assistance (Canon law)
Judicial assistance (Jewish law)
Judicial behavior
  USE Judicial process
Judicial bonds *(May Subd Geog)*
  UF Court bonds
  BT Security (Law)
     Suretyship and guaranty
  NT Insurance, Surety and fidelity
     Security for costs
Judicial compensation
  USE Judges—Salaries, etc.
Judicial corruption *(May Subd Geog)*
  UF Corrupt practices
     Corruption, Judicial
  BT Bribery
     Judges
     Judicial ethics
     Misconduct in office
  NT Corruption investigation
Judicial councils *(May Subd Geog)*
  BT Courts
     Justice, Administration of

— Public meetings
  BT Public meetings
Judicial decision-making
  USE Judicial process
Judicial decisions, Conflict of
  USE Conflict of judicial decisions
Judicial decisions, Recall of
  USE Recall of judicial decisions
Judicial discretion *(May Subd Geog)*
  UF Discretion, Judicial
     Discretion (Law)
     Discretion of court
  BT Judges
  RT Administrative discretion
     Law—Interpretation and construction
Judicial discretion (Canon law)
Judicial discretion (Roman law)
Judicial disqualification
  USE Disqualification of judges
Judicial districts *(May Subd Geog)*
  BT Administrative and political divisions
     Justice, Administration of
  NT Courts
Judicial education
  USE Judges—Education
Judicial elections
  USE Judges—Election
Judicial error *(May Subd Geog)*
  UF Criminal justice, Errors of
     Errors of criminal justice
     Justice, Miscarriage of
     Miscarriage of justice
  BT Criminal justice, Administration of
     Justice, Administration of
     Trials
  NT Compensation for judicial error
Judicial error (Canon law)
Judicial error (Roman law)
Judicial error in literature
Judicial ethics *(May Subd Geog)*
  UF Ethics, Judicial
  BT Judges
     Law and ethics
     Legal ethics
     Professional ethics
  NT Judges—Discipline
     Judicial corruption
Judicial functions of legislative bodies
  USE Legislative bodies as courts
Judicial impact statements
  (May Subd Geog)
  UF Impact of legislation on courts,
     Statements of
     Impact statements, Judicial
     Legislative impact on courts,
     Statements of
  BT Courts
     Legislation
Judicial investigations
  USE Governmental investigations
Judicial law
  USE Judge-made law
Judicial legislation
  USE Judge-made law
Judicial notice *(May Subd Geog)*
  UF Notice, Judicial
     Notoriety (Law)
  BT Evidence (Law)
  NT Foreign law, Pleading and proof of
Judicial notice (Canon law)
Judicial officers
  USE Courts—Officials and employees
Judicial opinions *(May Subd Geog)*
  UF Opinions, Judicial
  BT Judgments
     Law reports, digests, etc.
  NT Advisory opinions
     Dissenting opinions

1977

Judicial opinions (Islamic law)
   (May Subd Geog)
Judicial power *(May Subd Geog)*
   UF Judiciary
       Power, Judicial
   BT Constitutional law
   RT Courts
       Implied powers (Constitutional law)
   NT Delegation of powers
       Judge-made law
       Judicial review
       Legislative bodies as courts
       Separation of powers
Judicial power (Canon law)
Judicial power (Islamic law)
   (May Subd Geog)
Judicial power and political questions
   USE Political questions and judicial power
Judicial process *(May Subd Geog)*
   UF Decision-making, Judicial
       Judicial behavior
       Judicial decision-making
   BT Judges
       Law—Psychology
       Procedure (Law)
   RT Law—Interpretation and construction
   NT Evidence (Law)
       Judge-made law
       Judgments
       Stare decisis
Judicial process (Islamic law)
   (May Subd Geog)
Judicial process (Primitive law)
   (May Subd Geog)
Judicial process (Roman law)
Judicial review *(May Subd Geog)*
   ₍JF711₎
   ₍JK1541 (United States)₎
   UF Review, Judicial
   BT Constitutional law
       Courts
       Delegation of powers
       Executive power
       Judicial power
       Legislation
       Rule of law
   RT Legislative power
       Separation of powers
   NT Amparo (Writ)
       Political questions and judicial power
Judicial review of administrative acts
   (May Subd Geog)
   BT Administrative acts
       Administrative courts
       Administrative law
       Administrative procedure
       Appellate procedure
       Rule of law
   NT Abuse of administrative power
       Actions and defenses (Administrative
          law)
       Administrative remedies
       Equitable remedies
       Exhaustion of administrative remedies
       Extraordinary remedies
Judicial sales *(May Subd Geog)*
   UF Sales, Judicial
   BT Executions (Law)
       Sales
   RT Tax-sales
   NT Foreclosure
Judicial sales (Roman law)
Judicial separation
   USE Separation (Law)
Judicial statistics *(May Subd Geog)*
   UF Courts—Statistics
       Justice, Administration of—Statistics
       Law—Statistics
       Legal statistics
   BT Statistics
   NT Criminal statistics

Judicial tenure
   USE Judges—Selection and appointment
Judiciary
   USE Courts
       Judicial power
Judiciary, State
   USE Courts—United States—States
Jüdische Friedhof in Fulda (Fulda, Germany)
   BT Cemeteries—Germany (West)
Judkin family
   USE Judd family
Judkins family
   USE Judd family
Judkyn family
   USE Judd family
Judo *(May Subd Geog)*
   ₍GV1114₎
      Here are entered works on the art of self-defense
   as unified by Chigorō Kanō in 1882.
   BT Hand-to-hand fighting, Oriental
       Jiu-jitsu
       Self-defense
   NT Karate
   — Accidents and injuries
       UF Judo—Injuries
   — History
   — Injuries
       USE Judo—Accidents and injuries
   — Rules
       ₍GV475₎
Judo participants
   USE Martial artists
Judoists
   USE Martial artists
Judoka
   USE Martial artists
Judson family *(Not Subd Geog)*
   UF Jutson family
   RT Judd family
Judy family *(Not Subd Geog)*
   UF Judey family
   RT De Lajudie family
       Tschudi family
Juegel family *(Not Subd Geog)*
   UF Jügel family
Juei no nairan, Japan, 1182-1185
   USE Japan—History—Gempei Wars, 1180-
       1185
Juelsberg (Denmark)
   UF Raschenberg (Denmark)
   BT Manors—Denmark
Juerres family
   USE Jurries family
Juerries family
   USE Jurries family
Juessen family
   USE Jussen family
Juett family
   USE Jewett family
Jugambe dialect
   USE Jugumbir dialect
Jūgatsu jiken, 1931
   USE Japan—History—March and October
       Incidents, 1931
Jügel family
   USE Juegel family
Jugendstil
   USE Art nouveau
Juggernaut (Hindu deity)
   USE Jagannātha (Hindu deity)
Jugglers *(May Subd Geog)*
   UF Jugglers and juggling
   BT Entertainers
Jugglers and juggling
   USE Jugglers
       Juggling
Juggling *(May Subd Geog)*
   UF Jugglers and juggling
       Legerdemain
       Sleight of hand

   BT Amusements
       Tricks
   RT Conjuring
Juglandaceae
   ₍QK495.J85₎
   BT Juglandales
   NT Hickories
       Walnut
Juglandales
   ₍QK495.A12₎
   BT Dicotyledons
   NT Juglandaceae
       Myricaceae
Juglans
   USE Walnut
Juglans nigra
   USE Eastern black walnut
Juglans orientis
   USE Walnut, English
Juglans regia
   USE Walnut, English
Jugoslav . . .
   USE *subject headings beginning with the
       word* Yugoslav
Jugoslav Americans
   USE Yugoslav Americans
Jugoslavs
   USE Yugoslavs
Jugs
   USE Pitchers
Jugs, Character
   USE Character jugs
Jugs, Relief-decorated
   USE Relief-decorated jugs
Jugs, Toby
   USE Toby jugs
Jugs, Whiskey
   USE Whiskey jugs
Jugtown pottery
   ₍NK4340.J7₎
Jugular body
   USE Glomus jugulare
Jugular paraganglia
   USE Glomus jugulare
Jugular vein
Jugumbir dialect
   UF Jugambe dialect
       Yugumbir dialect
       Yukambe dialect
   BT Australia—Languages
       Bandjalang language
Jugurthine War, 111-105 B.C.
   ₍DG255₎
   BT Rome—History—Republic, 265-30
       B.C.
Juhani (Arab tribe)
   USE Juhaynah (Arab tribe)
Juhaynah (Arab tribe)
   UF Juhani (Arab tribe)
   BT Arabs
Juices, Fruit
   USE Fruit juices
Juices, Vegetable
   USE Vegetable juices
Jujitsu
   USE Jiu-jitsu
Jujube (Plant) *(May Subd Geog)*
   ₍QK495.R45 (Botany)₎
   ₍SB379.J8 (Culture)₎
   UF Ziziphus
       Zizyphus
       Zizyphys
   BT Rhamnaceae
   NT Zizyphus joazeiro
Jukado
   BT Self-defense
Jukaghir language
   USE Yukaghir language
Juke boxes
   USE Jukeboxes

Jukeboxes
UF Juke boxes
BT Coin operated machines
Musical instruments (Mechanical)
Phonograph
— **Law and legislation** (May Subd Geog)
Jukon language
USE Jukun language
Juku language
USE Jukun language
Jukun language
[PL8301]
UF Jukon language
Juku language
Kurorofa language
BT Jukunoid languages
Jukunoid languages
[PL8302]
BT Benue-Congo languages
Cameroon—Languages
Nigeria—Languages
NT Jukun language
Jula language
USE Dyula language
Julan Region
USE Golan Heights
Julian Alps (Slovenia and Italy)
(Not Subd Geog)
UF Alpes Juliae (Slovenia and Italy)
Alpi Giulie (Slovenia and Italy)
Julijske Alpe (Slovenia and Italy)
Julische Alpen (Slovenia and Italy)
BT Alps, Eastern
Mountains—Italy
Mountains—Yugoslavia
Julian calendar
USE Calendar, Julian
Julian March (Yugoslavia and Italy)
UF Beneska-Slovenija (Yugoslavia and Italy)
Julian Venice (Yugoslavia and Italy)
Julijska krajina (Yugoslavia and Italy)
Küstenland (Yugoslavia and Italy)
Primorje (Yugoslavia and Italy)
Venezia Giulia (Yugoslavia and Italy)
Julian Venice (Yugoslavia and Italy)
USE Julian March (Yugoslavia and Italy)
Julien Site (Cahokia, Ill.) (Not Subd Geog)
BT Illinois—Antiquities
Julii family (Not Subd Geog)
UF Gens Julia
Julijska krajina (Yugoslavia and Italy)
USE Julian March (Yugoslavia and Italy)
Julijske Alpe (Slovenia and Italy)
USE Julian Alps (Slovenia and Italy)
Julische Alpen (Slovenia and Italy)
USE Julian Alps (Slovenia and Italy)
Jullundur Mutiny, 1920
July
July fourteenth
USE Bastille Day
July Fourth
USE Fourth of July
July Handicap (Horse race)
[SF357.J8]
UF Rothmans July Handicap (Horse race)
BT Horse-racing—South Africa
July Revolution, 1830
USE France—History—July Revolution, 1830
Jum'ah
[BP186.15]
UF Friday prayer (Islam)
Sabbath (Islam)
Yawm al-Jum'ah
BT Fasts and feasts—Islam
Prayer (Islam)
NT Islamic sermons
Jumano Indians
[E99.J9]

BT Indians of North America
Pueblo Indians
Jumaring
USE Prusiking
Jumble sales
USE Rummage sales
Jumis (Latvian deity)
[BL945]
BT Gods, Latvian
Jumna River (India)
USE Yamuna River (India)
Jump processes
[QA274.755]
UF Processes, Jump
BT Markov processes
Jump rope
USE Rope skipping
Jump rope rhymes (May Subd Geog)
[PZ8.3]
UF Rope skipping rhymes
Skipping rhymes
BT Nursery rhymes
Jumpers, Show (Horses)
USE Show jumpers (Horses)
Jumpers, Show (Persons)
USE Show jumpers (Persons)
Jumping
[GV529]
UF High jumping
BT Athletics
College sports
Sports
Track-athletics
NT Animal jumping
Barrel jumping
Broad jump
Ski jumping
Triple jump
Jumping (Horsemanship)
BT Animal jumping
Horsemanship
NT Cavalletti
Show jumping
— **Competitions**
USE Show jumping
— **Exhibitions**
USE Show jumping
Jumping bail
USE Bail
Jumping cholla (Sculpture)
USE Christie, Keith. Jumping cholla
Jumping jacks
BT Toys
Jumping mice
USE Zapodidae
Jumping plant-lice
[QL523.P8]
UF Plant-lice, Jumping
Psyllidae
Psyllids
Psylloidea
BT Homoptera
NT Ctenarytaina
Paratrioza
Phytolyma
Psylla
Trioza
Jumping spiders (May Subd Geog)
[QL458.42.S24]
UF Attidae
Salticidae
BT Spiders
NT Darwinneon
Habronattus
Lyssomanes
Myrmarachne
Portia
Sarinda
Jūn al Kuwayt (Kuwait)
USE Kuwait Bay (Kuwait)

Juna language
USE Pamoa language
Juncaceae
[QK495.J87 (Botany)]
BT Juncales
NT Juncus
Luzula
Juncales
[QK495.A14 (Botany)]
BT Monocotyledons
NT Juncaceae
Juncoides
USE Luzula
Junction (Toronto, Ont.)
USE West Toronto (Toronto, Ont.)
Junction, Esophagogastric
USE Esophagogastric junction
Junction lasers, Semiconductor
USE Injection lasers
Junction transistors
[TK7872.T73]
UF Transistors, Junction
BT Bipolar transistors
Electric current rectifiers
Semiconductors—Junctions
Transistors
Triodes
RT Tunnel diodes
NT Planar transistors
Power transistors
Junctional complexes (Epithelium)
[QP88.4]
UF Complexes, Junctional (Epithelium)
BT Cell junctions
Epithelial cells
RT Cell adhesion
Junctions, Josephson
USE Josephson junctions
Junctions, Semiconductor
USE Semiconductors—Junctions
Junctions, Wave-guide
[TK7871.65]
UF Wave-guide junctions
Waveguide junctions
BT Wave guides
Juncture (Linguistics)
[P218.5]
UF Pause (Linguistics)
Transition (Linguistics)
BT Grammar, Comparative and general—Phonology
Linguistics
Prosodic analysis (Linguistics)
NT Caesura in versification
Juncus
[QK495.J87 (Botany)]
BT Juncaceae
NT Juncus triformis
Juncus communis
USE Juncus effusus
Juncus effusus
[QK495.J87 (Botany)]
[SB283.J86 (Culture)]
UF Igusa
Juncus communis
Soft rush
BT Matwork plants
Juncus triformis
[QK495.J87 (Botany)]
BT Juncus
June beetle, Green
USE Green June beetle
June Days, Paris, France, 1848
USE Paris (France)—History—June Days, 1848
June devotions
USE Sacred Heart, Devotion to
June grass
USE Kentucky bluegrass

June Uprising, Bulgaria, 1923
  USE Bulgaria—History—Uprising, 1923
      (June)
Juneberries
  USE Amelanchier
Jungblut family
  USE Youngblood family
Jungbluth family
  USE Youngblood family
Jungermaniales
  USE Jungermanniales
Jungermanniaceae
  BT Jungermanniales
Jungermanniales
  UF Jungermaniales
  BT Liverworts
  NT Adelanthaceae
      Bryopteris
      Frullaniaceae
      Geocalycaceae
      Jungermanniaceae
      Lejeuneaceae
      Lepidoziaceae
      Lophocoleaceae
Jungfrau (Switzerland)
  BT Alps, Swiss (Switzerland)
      Mountains—Switzerland
Junggrammatiker
  USE Neogrammarians
Jungle ecology *(May Subd Geog)*
  [QH541.5.J8]
  BT Ecology
      Forest ecology
Jungle fauna
  BT Forest fauna
      Zoology
      Zoology—Tropics
Jungle fowl
  UF Gallus
      Junglefowl
  BT Pheasants
  NT Red junglefowl
Jungle warfare
  [U167.5.J]
  BT Military art and science
      Strategy
      Tactics
      War
  NT World War, 1939-1945—Jungle
      warfare
Jungle zoos
  USE Open-air zoos
Junglefowl
  USE Jungle fowl
Jüngste Gericht (Panel painting)
  USE Cranach, Lucas, 1472-1553. Last
      judgment
Juniata River (Pa.)
  BT Rivers—Pennsylvania
Junin, Battle of, 1824
  [F3446]
  BT Peru—History—War of Independence,
      1820-1829—Campaigns
Junior class (High school)
  USE Eleventh grade (Education)
Junior college libraries *(May Subd Geog)*
  [Z675.J8]
  UF Libraries, Junior college
  BT Libraries, University and college
Junior college students *(May Subd Geog)*
  UF Students, Junior college
  BT College students
  NT Community college students
Junior college trustees
  UF Junior colleges—Trustees
      Trustees, Junior college
  BT College trustees
      Junior colleges—Administration
Junior colleges *(May Subd Geog)*
  [LB2328]
  UF Two-year colleges

  BT Universities and colleges
  NT Community colleges
      Nursing—Study and teaching
      (Associate degree)
  — **Administration**
      NT Junior college trustees
  — **Faculty**
      UF Faculty (Education)
      BT College teachers
  — **Finance**
      UF Tuition
  — **Law and legislation** *(May Subd Geog)*
  — **Statistics**
  — **Trustees**
      USE Junior college trustees
Junior high school facilities
  (May Subd Geog)
  BT School facilities
  NT Junior high schools—Furniture,
      equipment, etc.
  — **Planning** *(May Subd Geog)*
      BT Educational planning
Junior high school graduates
  (May Subd Geog)
  UF Graduates, Junior high school
Junior high school journalism
  USE Journalism, Junior high school
Junior high school libraries
  (May Subd Geog)
  UF Libraries, Junior high school
  BT School libraries
Junior high school principals
  (May Subd Geog)
  [LB2831.9-LB2831.976]
  UF Principals, Junior high school
  BT School principals
  — **Legal status, laws, etc.**
      (May Subd Geog)
      BT Educational law and legislation
Junior high school student journalism
  USE Journalism, Junior high school
Junior high school student newspapers and
      periodicals
  USE Student newspapers and periodicals
Junior high school student publications
  USE Student publications
Junior high school students
  (May Subd Geog)
  UF Junior high schools—Students
  BT Students
  — **Books and reading**
  — **Economic conditions**
      UF Junior high school students—
          Socioeconomic status
  — **Social conditions**
      UF Junior high school students—
          Socioeconomic status
  — Socioeconomic status
      USE Junior high school students—
          Economic conditions
          Junior high school students—
          Social conditions
Junior high school teachers
  (May Subd Geog)
  BT Teachers
Junior high schools *(May Subd Geog)*
  [LB1623]
  UF High schools, Junior
      Intermediate schools
  BT Education, Secondary
  NT Middle schools
  — **Accreditation**
  — **Administration**
      BT School management and
          organization
  — Equipment and supplies
      USE Junior high schools—Furniture,
          equipment, etc.
  — **Furniture, equipment, etc.**
      UF Junior high schools—Equipment
          and supplies

  BT Furniture
      Junior high school facilities
  — Students
      USE Junior high school students
Junior police
  USE School safety patrols
Junior republics
  [HV876]
  UF George junior republics
  BT Children—Institutional care
      Self-government (in education)
  NT School city, state, etc.
Junior showmanship classes (Dog shows)
  USE Dog shows—Junior showmanship
      classes
Juniorate
  [BX903]
  BT Monasticism and religious orders—
      Education
Juniper *(May Subd Geog)*
  [QK494.5.C975]
  UF Juniperus
  BT Cupressaceae
  NT Juniperus communis
Juniper, Common
  USE Juniperus communis
Juniper Creek Wilderness (Idaho)
  UF Juniper Creek Wilderness Study Area
      (Idaho)
  BT National parks and reserves—Idaho
      Wilderness areas—Idaho
Juniper Creek Wilderness Study Area (Idaho)
  USE Juniper Creek Wilderness (Idaho)
Juniperus
  USE Juniper
Juniperus communis
  [QK494.5.C975 (Botany)]
  UF Common juniper
      Ground cedar
      Hackmatack
      Juniper, Common
  BT Juniper
Juniperus virginiana
  UF Redcedar, Eastern
Jūniten gazō (Painting)
  USE Jūnitenzō (Painting)
Jūnitenzō (Painting)
  UF Jūniten gazō (Painting)
      Twelve Devas (Painting)
  BT Gods, Buddhist, in art
      Painting, Buddhist—Japan
      Painting, Japanese—Heian period, 794-
      1185
Junk
  USE Waste products
Junk bonds *(May Subd Geog)*
  UF Bonds, Junk
  BT Bonds
Junk family *(Not Subd Geog)*
Junk food
  USE Food, Junk
Junk in space
  USE Space debris
Junk mail
  USE Advertising, Direct-mail
Junk trade *(May Subd Geog)*
  UF Waste trade
  RT Secondhand trade
  NT Flea markets
      Rummage sales
  — **Sounds**
      BT Sounds
Junkandadjara (Australian people)
  USE Junkandjara (Australian people)
Junkandjara (Australian people)
  UF Junkandadjara (Australian people)
  BT Australian aborigines
Junken family
  USE Jenkins family
Junkers 290 (Transport plane)
  [UG1242.T7]

BT Airplanes, Military
      Transport planes
Junkers airplanes
  NT Junkers Ju-52 (Transport plane)
      Junkers Ju 287 (Jet bomber)
Junkers Ju-52 (Transport plane)
  BT Junkers airplanes
      Transport planes
Junkers Ju 87 (Bombers)
  USE Stuka (Bombers)
Junkers Ju-88 (Bomber)
  BT Bombers
Junkers Ju 287 (Jet bomber)
  UF Ju 287 (Jet bomber)
  BT Bombers
      Jet planes, Military
      Junkers airplanes
Junkin family
  USE Jenkins family
Junkins family
  USE Jenkins family
Junks
  [VM101]
  UF Chinese junks
  BT Ships
  — **Motors**
    BT Marine engines
Juno (Roman deity)
  BT Gods, Roman
      Mythology, Roman
  RT Hera (Greek deity)
Junonia (Insect)
  [QL561.N9]
  UF Buckeyes (Insect)
      Pansies (Insect)
  BT Nymphalidae
Junot family *(Not Subd Geog)*
Junqueira family *(Not Subd Geog)*
  UF Junquera family
Junqueira horse
  USE Mangalarga horse
Junquera family
  USE Junqueira family
Jupda language
  UF Macú de tucano language
  BT Indians of South America—Languages
      Macú language
Jupe family *(Not Subd Geog)*
  UF Juppe family
Jupiter (Planet)
  [QB384 (Theoretical astronomy)]
  [QB661 (Descriptive astronomy)]
  BT Outer planets
  NT Jupiter probes
      Space flight to Jupiter
  — **Atmosphere**
    [QB661]
    UF Jovian atmosphere
  — **Ephemerides**
    BT Ephemerides
  — **Juvenile literature**
    [QB661]
  — **Mass**
    [QB661]
  — **Observations**
    [QB661]
  — **Orbit**
  — **Radiation**
    [QB661]
    UF Radiation, Jovian
Jupiter (Roman deity)
  [BL820.J8]
  BT Gods, Roman
      Mythology, Roman
  RT Zeus (Greek deity)
Jupiter automobile
  [TL215.J]
  UF Jowett Jupiter automobile
  BT Sports cars
Jupiter missile
  UF Jupiter rocket

Jupiter probes
  BT Jupiter (Planet)
      Outer space—Exploration
  NT Galileo Project
      Project Voyager
Jupiter rocket
  USE Jupiter missile
Juppe family
  USE Jupe family
Jupurina language
  USE Ipurina language
Jur language
  USE Lwo language (Sudan)
Jura horse
  BT Draft horses
Jura Krakowska (Poland)
  USE Kraków-Częstochowa Highland
      (Poland)
Jura Krakowska-Wieluńska (Poland)
  USE Kraków-Częstochowa Highland
      (Poland)
Jura Mountains (France and Switzerland)
  UF Monts du Jura (France and
      Switzerland)
      Monts Jura (France and Switzerland)
  BT Mountains—France
      Mountains—Switzerland
  NT Revermont (France)
Jurak language
  USE Nenets language
Jurakuyaki
  USE Raku pottery
Jurassic period
  USE Geology, Stratigraphic—Jurassic
      Paleobotany—Jurassic
      Paleontology—Jurassic
Jurchi language
  USE Ju-chen language
Jurdan family
  USE Jordan family
Jurden family
  USE Jordan family
Jurdon family
  USE Jordan family
Juridical psychology
  USE Law—Psychology
      Psychology, Forensic
Juries
  USE Jury
Jurisdiction *(May Subd Geog)*
  [JX4173-4195]
  BT Competent authority
      Law
  RT Conflict of judicial decisions
      Courts
      Judgments
      Venue
  NT Appeal as from an abuse
      Conflict of laws
      Courts of special jurisdiction
      Criminal jurisdiction
      Denial of justice
      Forum non conveniens
      Lex loci delicti
      Political questions and judicial power
      Privileges and immunities
      Prohibition (Writ)
      Prorogated jurisdiction
  — Conflict of laws
    USE Conflict of laws—Jurisdiction
  — Rome
    USE Jurisdiction (Roman law)
  — **United States**
    NT Removal of causes
Jurisdiction, Consular
  USE Consular jurisdiction
Jurisdiction, Domestic
  USE Jurisdiction (International law)
Jurisdiction, Exterritorial
  USE Exterritoriality

Jurisdiction, International
  USE Jurisdiction (International law)
Jurisdiction, Non-contentious
  USE Non-contentious jurisdiction
Jurisdiction, Territorial
  UF Territorial jurisdiction
  BT Territory, National
  NT Archipelagoes—Law and legislation
      Islands—Law and legislation
      Leased territories
      Offshore structures (International law)
      Territorial waters
Jurisdiction, Voluntary
  USE Non-contentious jurisdiction
Jurisdiction (Canon law)
  [BX1939.J85]
  RT Bishops (Canon law)
  NT Appeal as from an abuse
      Delegation of powers (Canon law)
      Privilegium fori
Jurisdiction (Ecclesiastical law)
  (May Subd Geog)
  BT Ecclesiastical law
Jurisdiction (Germanic law)
Jurisdiction (International law)
  UF Domestic jurisdiction
      International jurisdiction
      Jurisdiction, Domestic
      Jurisdiction, International
  BT International law
      Intervention (International law)
      Sovereignty
  RT Arbitration, International
      Conflict of laws—Jurisdiction
      International courts
  NT Immunities of foreign states
  — **Cases**
    NT Sabbatino case
Jurisdiction (Roman law)
  UF Jurisdiction—Rome
  NT Imperium (Roman law)
Jurisdiction over aircraft *(May Subd Geog)*
  BT Aeronautics—Law and legislation
      Airplanes—Nationality
      Airspace (International law)
Jurisdiction over ships at sea
  BT Freedom of the seas
      International law
      Maritime law
      Ships—Nationality
      War, Maritime (International law)
  NT Contraband of war
      Search, Right of
      Seizure of vessels and cargoes
Jurisdictional disputes (Trade-unions)
  USE Trade-unions—Jurisdictional disputes
Jurisdictional immunities of foreign states
  USE Immunities of foreign states
Jurisprudence *(May Subd Geog)*
    Here and with local subdivision are entered works
  on the science of law. Works on the law or legal
  system of particular regions, countries, cities, etc. are
  entered under Law—[place].
  BT Natural law
      Political science
  RT Law
      Law—Philosophy
  NT Effectiveness and validity of law
      International law—Philosophy
      Law—Methodology
      Law and politics
      Legal certainty
      Legal positivism
      Public law
      Sociological jurisprudence
      Strict law
  — **History**
    UF Law—Literary history

Jurisprudence
— **History** *(Continued)*
    SA *subdivision* Literary history *under particular legal systems, branches of law, and legal subjects, e.g. Jewish law—Literary history*
Jurisprudence, Comparative
    USE Comparative law
Jurisprudence, Dental
    USE Dental jurisprudence
Jurisprudence, Doctor of
    USE Doctor of laws degree
Jurisprudence, Ethnological
    USE Ethnological jurisprudence
Jurisprudence, Medical
    USE Medical jurisprudence
Jurisprudence, Veterinary
    USE Veterinary jurisprudence
Juristic acts *(May Subd Geog)*
    UF Acts, Juristic
        Juristic transactions
        Transactions, Juristic
    RT Contracts
    NT Administrative acts
        Capacity and disability
        Declaration of intention
        Declaratory acts
        Illegal juristic acts
        Rescission (Law)
        Simulation (Civil law)
    — **Interpretation and construction**
Juristic acts (Canon law)
Juristic acts (Roman law)
Juristic persons *(May Subd Geog)*
    UF Artificial persons
        Conventional persons
        Legal persons
        Persons, Artificial
        Persons, Conventional
        Persons, Juristic
        Persons, Legal
    BT Persons (Law)
    NT Charitable uses, trusts, and foundations
        Corporation law
        Corporations, Government
        Corporations, Nonprofit
        Criminal liability of juristic persons
        Unincorporated societies
    — Conflict of laws
        USE Conflict of laws—Juristic persons
    — Criminal liability
        USE Criminal liability of juristic persons
    — Nationality
        USE Corporations—Nationality
    — France
        NT Groupement d'intérêt economique
Juristic persons, Foreign
    USE Corporations, Foreign
Juristic persons (Canon law)
Juristic persons (Hindu law)
Juristic persons (International law)
    USE Persons (International law)
Juristic persons (Roman law)
    NT Universitates (Civil law)
Juristic psychology
    USE Law—Psychology
        Psychology, Forensic
Juristic transactions
    USE Juristic acts
Jurists
    USE Lawyers
Jurors
    USE Jury
Jurres family
    USE Jurries family
Jurries family *(Not Subd Geog)*
    UF Juerres family
        Juerries family
        Jurres family

Juruks (Turkic people)
    USE Yuruks (Turkic people)
Juruna Indians
    [F2520.1.J]
    UF Yuruna Indians
    BT Indians of South America
Jury *(May Subd Geog)*
    UF Judgments by peers
        Juries
        Jurors
        Trial by jury
        Trial by peers
    BT Trials
    RT Law and fact
        Lay judges
    NT Grand jury
        Instructions to juries
        Jury commissioners
        Nisi prius
        Summation (Law)
        Verdicts
        Women jurors
Jury (Germanic law)
Jury (Roman law)
Jury commissioners *(May Subd Geog)*
    BT Jury
Jury selection *(May Subd Geog)*
    UF Selection of jury
        Voir dire
Jus ad rem *(May Subd Geog)*
    BT Obligations (Law)
Jus ad rem (Canon law)
Jus exclusivae
    USE Exclusion, Right of
Jus gentium (Roman law)
    BT Aliens (Roman law)
Jus primae noctis
    UF Droit du seigneur
    BT Defloration
        Feudalism
        Marriage customs and rites
        Virginity
Jus primariarum precum
    BT Benefices, Ecclesiastical
Jus reformandi
    UF Cuius regio eius religio
    BT Church and state—Germany
        Ecclesiastical law—Germany
Jus strictum
    USE Strict law
Jushi
    UF Shushi
    BT Sarugaku
Jussari family *(Not Subd Geog)*
Jussen family *(Not Subd Geog)*
    UF Juessen family
Jussila family *(Not Subd Geog)*
Jussive (Grammar)
    USE Grammar, Comparative and general—Imperative
Just family *(Not Subd Geog)*
    RT Justice family
Just war doctrine
    UF War—Moral aspects
    BT War—Moral and ethical aspects
        War—Religious aspects
        War (Philosophy)
Justes family
    USE Justice family
Justese family
    USE Justice family
Justesen family *(Not Subd Geog)*
Justice
    [GN493 (Primitive)]
    [JC578 (Political theory)]
    UF Injustice
    BT Conduct of life
        Ethics
        Law
    RT Common good
        Fairness

    NT Christianity and justice
        Distributive justice
        Equality before the law
        Islam and justice
        Religion and justice
        Social justice
    — **Biblical teaching**
        BT Bible—Theology
Justice, Administration of *(May Subd Geog)*
    UF Administration of justice
    BT Law
    RT Courts
        Judges
    NT Adversary system (Law)
        Court congestion and delay
        Criminal justice, Administration of
        Denial of justice
        Dispute resolution (Law)
        Due process of law
        Governmental investigations
        Judicial councils
        Judicial districts
        Judicial error
        Justice and politics
        Neighborhood justice centers
        Public defenders
        Speedy trial
    — **History**
    — — Sources
        USE Justice, Administration of—Sources
    — **Sources**
        UF Justice, Administration of—History—Sources
    — Statistics
        USE Judicial statistics
    — **France**
Justice, Administration of (Adat law)
Justice, Administration of (Canon law)
Justice, Administration of (Frankish law)
Justice, Administration of (Greek law)
Justice, Administration of (Hindu law)
Justice, Administration of, in motion pictures
    BT Moving-pictures
Justice, Administration of, in the Bible
    UF Bible—Justice, Administration of
Justice, Administration of (Islamic law) *(May Subd Geog)*
Justice, Administration of (Jewish law)
Justice, Administration of (Roman law)
Justice, Denial of
    USE Denial of justice
Justice, Miscarriage of
    USE Judicial error
Justice, Poetic
    USE Poetic justice
Justice (Jewish theology)
    UF Righteousness (Jewish theology)
    BT Religion and justice
Justice (Philosophy)
    [B105.J]
    BT Philosophy
Justice (Virtue)
    [BV4647.J]
Justice and politics *(May Subd Geog)*
    UF Politics and justice
    BT Justice, Administration of
        Trials
Justice family *(Not Subd Geog)*
    UF Justes family
        Justese family
        Justis family
        Justiss family
        Justus family
    RT Just family
Justice in art
Justice in literature
Justice of Cambyses (Panel painting)
    USE David, Gérard, ca. 1460-1523. Judgment of Cambyses

1982

Justice Palace (Bogotá, Colombia)
　USE　Palacio de Justicia (Bogotá, Colombia)
Justice Palace (Dijon, France)
　USE　Palais de justice (Dijon, France)
Justice panels (Panel painting)
　USE　David, Gérard, ca. 1460-1523.
　　　　Judgment of Cambyses
Justice Society of America (Comic strip
**　characters)**
　BT　Comic books, strips, etc.
Justice Trial, Nuremberg, Germany, 1947
　UF　Subsequent proceedings, Nuremberg
　　　　War Crime Trials, case no. 3
　BT　Nuremberg War Crime Trials, 1946-
　　　　1949
Justices' clerks
　USE　Clerks of court
Justices of the peace　(May Subd Geog)
　UF　Magistrates
　BT　Acknowledgments
　　　Courts of first instance
　　　Criminal courts
　　　Criminal procedure
　　　Judges
　RT　Notaries
　　　Police magistrates
　NT　Mayors' courts
Justicia
　　[QK495.A1655 (Botany)]
　BT　Acanthaceae
Justicia americana
　　[QK495.A1655 (Botany)]
　UF　Water willow
Justicia, Palacio de (Bogotá, Colombia)
　USE　Palacio de Justicia (Bogotá, Colombia)
Justicialism
　USE　Peronism
Justiciars (England)
　　[JN389.J8]
　UF　Capitalis justiciarius
Justifiable homicide　(May Subd Geog)
　BT　Homicide
　　　Necessity (Law)
　　　Self-defense (Law)
Justification
　　[BT763-4]
　UF　Faith and justification
　　　Justification by faith
　BT　Salvation
Justification (Islamic law)　(May Subd Geog)
　BT　Islamic law
Justification (Law)　(May Subd Geog)
　BT　Criminal law
　　　Illegality
　NT　Consent (Law)
　　　Necessity (Law)
　　　Self-defense (Law)
　　　Superior orders (Criminal law)
　— Conflict of laws
　　　USE　Conflict of laws—Justification
Justification (Theory of knowledge)
　BT　Knowledge, Theory of
Justification by faith
　USE　Justification
Justin Morgan (Horse)
　UF　Figure (Horse)
　　　Little Bub (Horse)
　　　Morgan, Justin (Horse)
　BT　Horses
Justiniana Prima (City)　(Not Subd Geog)
　UF　Caričin Grad (City)
　　　Prima Justinana (City)
　BT　Cities and towns, Ruined, extinct, etc.
　　　—Yugoslavia
　　　Yugoslavia—Antiquities, Byzantine
Justis family
　USE　Justice family
Justiss family
　USE　Justice family
Justum pretium
　USE　Prices

Justus family
　USE　Justice family
Jute　(May Subd Geog)
　　[HD9156.J8 (Industry)]
　　[QK495.T5 (Botany)]
　　[SB257 (Culture)]
　　[TS1735 (Manufacture)]
　BT　Hemp
　　　Plant fibers
　NT　Bagging
　　　Kenaf
　　　Twine
　— Breeding
　　　USE　Jute breeding
　— **Chemistry**
　　　BT　Chemistry, Technical
Jute bag industry
　USE　Burlap bag industry
Jute breeding
　UF　Jute—Breeding
　BT　Plant-breeding
Jute industry　(May Subd Geog)
　　[HD9156.J7-8]
　NT　Strikes and lockouts—Jute industry
Jute industry workers　(May Subd Geog)
　　[HD8039.J8]
　NT　Strikes and lockouts—Jute industry
　　　Trade-unions—Jute industry workers
　　　Wages—Jute industry workers
Jute manufacture　(May Subd Geog)
　　[TS1735]
　BT　Textile industry
Jute spinning
　　[TS1735]
　BT　Spinning
Jutes
　BT　Anglo-Saxons
　　　Germanic tribes
Jutland (Denmark)
　UF　Jylland (Denmark)
Jutland, Battle of, 1916
　　[D582.J8]
　　[DA122.J8 (English history)]
　UF　Skagerrak, Battle of, 1916
　BT　World War, 1914-1918—Naval
　　　operations
Jutson family
　USE　Judson family
Jutte
　USE　Sai
Jutzel family
　USE　Hutzel family
Juve family　(Not Subd Geog)
Juvenellidae
　USE　Carangidae
Juvenile arthritis deformans
　USE　Rheumatoid arthritis in children
Juvenile automobile drivers
　(May Subd Geog)
　　[HE5620.J8]
　UF　Juvenile drivers
　　　Teen-age drivers
　BT　Automobile drivers
Juvenile book-plates
　USE　Book-plates, Children's
Juvenile Christian saints
　USE　Christian saints, Juvenile
Juvenile corrections　(May Subd Geog)
　　[HV9051-9230.7]
　BT　Corrections
　　　Juvenile justice, Administration of
　RT　Juvenile delinquency
　NT　Juvenile detention homes
　　　Juvenile parole
　　　Juvenile probation
　　　Rehabilitation of juvenile delinquents
　— **England**
　　　NT　Hammersmith Teenage Project
Juvenile courts　(May Subd Geog)
　UF　Children's courts
　　　Family courts

　BT　Courts of special jurisdiction
　　　Criminal courts
　　　Juvenile justice, Administration of
　SA　names of individual juvenile courts
　NT　Domestic relations courts
　　　Indeterminate sentence
　　　Probation
Juvenile delinquency　(May Subd Geog)
　　[HV9051-HV9230.7]
　UF　Delinquency, Juvenile
　　　Youth crime
　BT　Behavior disorders in children
　　　Crime and age
　　　Crime and criminals
　RT　Juvenile corrections
　　　Reformatories
　NT　Children, Vagrant
　　　Delinquent girls
　　　Gangs
　　　Hoodlums
　　　Incorrigibles (Juvenile delinquency)
　　　Indians of North America—Juvenile
　　　　delinquency
　　　Juvenile delinquents
　　　Juvenile detention homes
　　　Legal assistance to juvenile delinquents
　　　Prostitution, Juvenile
　　　Rehabilitation of juvenile delinquents
　　　School violence
　— **Case studies**
　— **Prevention**
　　　UF　Prevention of juvenile delinquency
　　　BT　Crime prevention
　— **Sex differences**
　— **California**
　— — **Prevention**
　　　　NT　Youth Development and
　　　　　　Delinquency Prevention
　　　　　　Project
　— **Washington (State)**
　　　　NT　Community and State Diagnostic
　　　　　　Services Project
Juvenile delinquency and recreation
　USE　Recreation and juvenile delinquency
Juvenile delinquency films　(May Subd Geog)
　　[PN1995.9.J87]
　BT　Feature films
　　　Moving-pictures
Juvenile delinquents　(May Subd Geog)
　　[HV9051-9230.7]
　UF　Delinquents, Juvenile
　BT　Juvenile delinquency
　NT　Church work with juvenile delinquents
　— **Mental health services**
　　　(May Subd Geog)
　　　[RJ506.J88]
　　　BT　Child mental health services
　　　　Juvenile delinquents—Services for
　— **Services for**
　　　NT　Juvenile delinquents—Mental
　　　　health services
Juvenile delinquents' writings
　(May Subd Geog)
　UF　Writings of juvenile delinquents
　BT　Children's writings
Juvenile delinquents' writings, Japanese
　(May Subd Geog)
　UF　Japanese juvenile delinquents' writings
Juvenile detention homes　(May Subd Geog)
　UF　Borstal system
　　　Detention homes, Juvenile
　　　Remand homes
　BT　Correctional institutions
　　　Juvenile corrections
　　　Juvenile delinquency
　　　Juvenile justice, Administration of
　　　Reformatories
Juvenile diabetes
　USE　Diabetes in children
　　　Diabetes in youth

Juvenile dictionaries
 USE Children's encyclopedias and
  dictionaries
Juvenile diseases
 USE Children—Diseases
Juvenile drivers
 USE Juvenile automobile drivers
Juvenile encyclopedias
 USE Children's encyclopedias and
  dictionaries
Juvenile fiction
 USE *subdivision* Juvenile fiction *under
  historical events and characters, etc.*
Juvenile films
 USE Children's films
Juvenile hormones
 UF Neotenin
 BT Hormones
  Insect hormones
Juvenile justice, Administration of
 (May Subd Geog)
 UF Administration of juvenile justice
 BT Criminal justice, Administration of
 NT Juvenile corrections
  Juvenile courts
  Juvenile detention homes
  Juvenile parole
  Juvenile probation
  Rehabilitation of juvenile delinquents
  Status offenders
 — Washington (State)
  NT Community and State Diagnostic
   Services Project
Juvenile kyphosis
 USE Scheuermann's disease
Juvenile limericks
 USE Limericks, Juvenile
Juvenile literature
 USE *subdivision* Juvenile literature *under
  specific subjects*
  Children's literature
Juvenile music
 USE Music—Juvenile
Juvenile opera
 USE Opera—Juvenile
Juvenile parole *(May Subd Geog)*
 BT Juvenile corrections
  Juvenile justice, Administration of
  Parole
  Rehabilitation of juvenile delinquents
 RT Juvenile probation
Juvenile phonorecords
 USE *subdivision* Juvenile sound recordings
  under subjects
Juvenile poetry
 USE *and subdivision* Juvenile poetry *under
  specific subjects*
  Children's poetry
Juvenile press
 USE Press, Juvenile
Juvenile probation *(May Subd Geog)*
 BT Juvenile corrections
  Juvenile justice, Administration of
  Probation
  Rehabilitation of juvenile delinquents
 RT Juvenile parole
Juvenile prostitution
 USE Prostitution, Juvenile
Juvenile reference books
 USE Children's reference books
Juvenile rheumatoid arthritis
 USE Rheumatoid arthritis in children
Juvenile riddles
 USE Riddles, Juvenile
Juvenile saints
 USE Saints, Juvenile
Juvenile saints, Christian
 USE Christian saints, Juvenile
Juvenile series (Publications)
 USE Children's literature in series

Juvenile sound recordings
 USE *subdivision* Juvenile sound recordings
  under subjects
Juvenile status offenders
 USE Status offenders
Juvenile wit and humor
 USE Wit and humor, Juvenile
Juwalarai language
 USE Yualyai language
Juwang San (Korea)
 USE Chuwang Mountain (Korea)
Juwet family
 USE Jewett family
Juxtaglomerular apparatus
  ⌜Ql873 (Comparative anatomy)⌝
  ⌜QM404 (Human anatomy)⌝
  ⌜QP249 (Physiology)⌝
 UF Apparatus, Juxtaglomerular
 BT Kidneys
 NT Renin
Juxtaoral organ
 USE Chievitz's organ
Juza family *(Not Subd Geog)*
 UF Huza family
  Yusa family
  Yuza family
Juzu
 USE Buddhist rosary
Jyeshṭhimalla
  ⌜DS432.J94⌝
 BT Brahmans
  Caste—India
  Ethnology—India
  Wrestlers—India
Jylland (Denmark)
 USE Jutland (Denmark)
Jyngidae
 USE Jynx
Jynx
  ⌜QL696.P56⌝
 UF Jyngidae
  Wrynecks (Birds)
 BT Picidae
 NT Jynx torquilla
Jynx torquilla
  ⌜QL696.P56⌝
 UF Eurasian wryneck
  Wryneck (Bird)
 BT Jynx
Jyotibā (Hindu deity)
  ⌜BL1225.J⌝
 BT Gods, Hindu
K2 (Pakistan : Mountain)
 UF Dapsang (Pakistan)
  Godwin Austen, Mount (Pakistan)
  Gogir Feng (Pakistan)
  Mount Godwin Austen (Pakistan)
 BT Karakoram Range
  Mountains—Pakistan
K.A.L. Flight 007 Incident, 1983
 USE Korean Air Lines Incident, 1983
K-cars
 USE Chrysler K-cars
K cells
 USE Killer cells
K-H-T-P Technique
 USE Kinetic-House-Tree-Person Technique
K mesons
 USE Kaons
K stars
 BT Cool stars
 — Absolute magnitude
  USE K stars—Magnitudes
 — Galactic orbits
  USE K stars—Orbits
 — Magnitudes
  UF K stars—Absolute magnitude
 — Motion in line of sight
  UF K stars—Radial velocity
 — Orbits

 UF Galactic orbits of K stars
  K stars—Galactic orbits
 BT Orbits
 — Radial velocity
  USE K stars—Motion in line of sight
 — Spectra
K-theory
 BT Algebraic topology
  Homology theory
 NT Whitehead groups
Ka (Egyptian religion)
 BT Personality
Ka-26 (Helicopter)
 BT Helicopters
Ka-La-Bre-Osh (Game)
 USE Belote (Game)
Ka Tawng Luang (Southeast Asian people)
 USE Phi Tong Luang (Southeast Asian
  people)
Ka-Tu
 USE Kha Tahoi
Kaae family *(Not Subd Geog)*
 RT Coe family
  Koe family
Kaagan language
 USE Tagakaolo language
Kaapor Indians
 USE Urubu Indians
Kaapsedrifrivier (South Africa)
 UF Klasies River (South Africa)
 BT Rivers—South Africa
Kaapsedrifrivier Valley (South Africa)
 UF Klasies Valley (South Africa)
 BT Valleys—South Africa
Kaara family *(Not Subd Geog)*
 RT Carr family
Kaarta (Mali)
 UF Kaarta Massif (Mali)
  Massif du Kaarta (Mali)
 BT Plateaus—Mali
Kaarta Massif (Mali)
 USE Kaarta (Mali)
Ka'b (Arab people)
 BT Arabs
  Ethnology—Iran
Kababish
 BT Ethnology—Sudan
Kabaddi (Game)
Kabah Site (Mexico) *(Not Subd Geog)*
  ⌜F1435.1.K⌝
 BT Mexico—Antiquities
Kabail
 USE Kabyles
Kabail language
 USE Kabyle language
Kabana River (Ethiopia)
 BT Rivers—Ethiopia
Kabaphēs family
 USE Kavaphēs family
Kabardian drama *(May Subd Geog)*
Kabardian fiction *(May Subd Geog)*
Kabardian language
  ⌜PK9201.K3⌝
 UF Cabardan language
  East Circassian language
  Kabardino-Cherkes language
  Qabardian language
  Upper Circassian language
 BT Circassian languages
 RT Adyghe language
Kabardian literature *(May Subd Geog)*
Kabardian philology
  ⌜PK9201.K3⌝
Kabardian prose literature
 (May Subd Geog)
Kabardian songs
 USE Songs, Kabardian
Kabardians
  ⌜DK34.K⌝
 BT Ethnology—Caucasus

Kabardino-Cherkes language
    USE Kabardian language
Kabasan Uprising, 1884
    BT Japan—History—Meiji period, 1868-1912
Kabba Laka dialect
    USE Gambai dialect
Kabbala
    USE Cabala
Kabeirion (Voiōtia, Greece)
    USE Sanctuary of the Kabeiroi (Voiōtia, Greece)
Kabeiroi, Sanctuary of the (Voiōtia, Greece)
    USE Sanctuary of the Kabeiroi (Voiōtia, Greece)
Kabi tribe
    ₍DU274 (History)₎
    ₍GN667.Q8 (Anthropology)₎
    BT Australian aborigines
Kabile (Ancient city) *(Not Subd Geog)*
    UF Cabyle (Ancient city)
        Kabyle (Ancient city)
    BT Bulgaria—Antiquities
        Cities and towns, Ruined, extinct, etc.
            —Bulgaria
Kabin (African people)
    USE Gaanda (African people)
Kabiye (African people)
    USE Kabre (African people)
Kabobs
    USE Skewer cookery
Kabre (African people)
    UF Cabrais
        Kabiye (African people)
        Kabure
        Kabye (African people)
    —Women
        USE Women, Kabre
Kabre women
    USE Women, Kabre
Kabui language
    ₍PL4001.K2₎
    UF Kapwī language
    BT Naga languages
    NT Rongmei dialect
Kabuki *(May Subd Geog)*
    ₍PN2924.5.K3₎
        Here are entered general works and those that deal solely with the presentation of Kabuki plays on the stage. The texts of the Kabuki plays and works treating of them from a literary point of view are entered under Kabuki plays.
    BT Theater—Japan
    — **Stage-setting and scenery**
Kabuki in art
    NT Torii School
Kabuki kyōgen
    USE Kyōgen
Kabuki kyōgen plays
    USE Kyōgen plays
Kabuki music
    UF Kabuki plays—Incidental music
    BT Music—Japan
Kabuki plays
    ₍PL737₎
    ₍PL767 (Collections)₎
        Here are entered the texts of the Kabuki plays and works treating of them from a literary point of view. General works and those that deal solely with the presentation of Kabuki plays on the stage are entered under Kabuki.
    BT Japanese drama
    — Incidental music
        USE Kabuki music
    — **Stories, plots, etc.**
Kabuli language
    USE Dari language
Kabuli-Persian imprints *(May Subd Geog)*
Kabuli-Persian language
    USE Dari language
Kabundji (Legendary character)
    BT Folklore—Zaire

Kabure
    USE Kabre (African people)
Kabuto family *(Not Subd Geog)*
Kabye (African people)
    USE Kabre (African people)
Kabyle (Ancient city)
    USE Kabile (Ancient city)
Kabyle language
    ₍PJ2373₎
    UF Kabail language
    BT Berber languages
    NT Zouave dialect
Kabyle law
    USE Law, Kabyle
Kabyle poetry *(May Subd Geog)*
Kabyle pottery
    USE Pottery, Kabyle
Kabyle women
    USE Women, Kabyle
Kabyles
    ₍DT298.K2₎
    UF Kabail
    RT Berbers
    —Women
        USE Women, Kabyle
Kabylia (Algeria)
    UF Kabylie (Algeria)
Kabylie (Algeria)
    USE Kabylia (Algeria)
Kaca
    UF Kacha
Kacchī dialect
    USE Kachchhi dialect
Kacchiquel Indians
    USE Cakchikel Indians
Kacchiquel language
    USE Cakchikel language
Kacha
    USE Kaca
Kachari language
    USE Bara language
        Dimasa language
Kacharis
    ₍DS432.K15₎
    UF Cachari (Indic people)
        Dimasa (Indic people)
    BT Bodos
        Ethnology—India
Kachchhi dialect
    ₍PK2790.K3₎
    UF Kacchī dialect
    BT Sindhi language
Kachchhi proverbs
    USE Proverbs, Kachchhi
Kachchwahas
    USE Kachhwahas
Kachemak Bay (Alaska)
    BT Bays—Alaska
    NT China Poot Bay (Alaska)
Kachhawahas
    USE Kachhwahas
Kachhwahas
    ₍DS485.J25₎
    UF Kachchwahas
        Kachhawahas
        Kachwahas
    BT Rajputs
Kachin (Asian people)
    ₍DS528.2.K3₎
    UF Chingpa (Asian people)
        Chingpaw (Asian people)
        Kachin tribes
        Singpho (Asian people)
    BT Ethnology—Asia
    NT Missions to Kachin (Asian people)
Kachin (Chinese people)
    USE Ching-p'o (Chinese people)
Kachin dialects
    ₍PL3901-4₎

        A number of cognate dialects grouped together under the general name of Kachin or Singpho, spoken by the wild Kachin tribes, east of Assam, in the north of Upper Burma. The group comprises: Kachin or Singpho, Lashi, Maingtha, Maru, Szi Lepai.
    RT Tibeto-Burman languages
    NT A-ch'ang language
        Kachin language
        Nung language
Kachin language
    ₍PL4001.K3₎
    UF Chingpaw language
        Jinghpaw language
        Singpho language
    BT Kachin dialects
Kachin tribes
    USE Kachin (Asian people)
Kachinas
    USE Katcinas
Kachwahas
    USE Kachhwahas
Kackler family
    USE Cackler family
Käcko family *(Not Subd Geog)*
    UF Kecko family
Kaczawa Mountains (Poland)
    UF Góry Kaczawskie (Poland)
        Karzbach-Gebirge (Poland)
        Katzbachgebirge (Poland)
    BT Mountains—Poland
Kadagas
    USE Coorgs
Kadambas
    ₍DS485.K17₎
Kadampa (Sect)
    USE Bka'-gdams-pa (Sect)
Kadang-kadang
    USE Cadang-cadang
Kadara (African people)
    ₍DT515.42₎
    UF Adara (African people)
        Kedara (African people)
    BT Ethnology—Nigeria
Kadars
    ₍DS432.K₎
    BT Ethnology—India
Kadazan language
    USE Dusun language
Kadesh, Battle of, 1300 B.C.(?)
    ₍DT88₎
Kadiak (Eskimo tribe)
    USE Kaniagmiut (Eskimo tribe)
Kadiak language
    USE Kaniagmiut language
Kadieuéu Indians
    USE Cadioéo Indians
Kadıköy Site (Turkey)
    USE Chalcedon (Turkey)
Kadiriyya
    USE Qādirīyah
Kadis
    USE Cadis
Ḳādisīya, Battle of, 637
    USE Qādisīyah, Battle of, 637
Kadjeroen (Australian people)
    USE Gadjerong (Australian people)
Kadjerong (Australian people)
    USE Gadjerong (Australian people)
Kadomt͡sev family *(Not Subd Geog)*
Ḳadr, Lailat
    USE Laylat al-Qadr
Kadumodi language
    USE Krongo language
Kaelin family *(Not Subd Geog)*
Kaemmel family
    USE Kemmerer family
Kaemmer family
    USE Kemmerer family
Kaempfer family
    USE Kemp family

Kaen

    [M1089.K]

    UF Khen

    BT Mouth organs

          Musical instruments—Laos

          Musical instruments—Thailand

Kaenel family *(Not Subd Geog)*

    UF Von Kaenel family

Kaeppel family

    USE Keppel family

Kaeter family

    USE Karter family

Kafe language

    USE Kamano language

Kaffa

    [DT380]

Kaffa language

    [PJ2578]

    BT Omotic languages

Kaffer language

    USE Xhosa language

Kaffir (Islam)

    USE Kufr (Islam)

Kaffir corn

    USE Kafir corn

Kaffir language

    USE Xhosa language

Kaffir Wars, 1811-1878

    USE South Africa—History—Frontier Wars,

          1811-1878

Kaffirs

    USE Kafirs (Kafiristan)

Kaffirs (African people)

    USE Xhosa (African people)

Kāfir (Islam)

    USE Kufr (Islam)

Kafir corn

    [SB191.S7]

    UF Kaffir corn

    BT Forage plants

          Sorghum

Kafir language

    USE Xhosa language

Kafir languages (Kafiristan)

    USE Pisacha languages

Kafir Wars, 1811-1878

    USE South Africa—History—Frontier Wars,

          1811-1878

Kafirs (African people)

    USE Pondos

          Xhosa (African people)

          Zulus

Kafirs (Kafiristan)

    [DS374.K2]

    UF Cafirs

          Kaffirs

    NT Kalashum (Afghanistan people)

Kafue Flats (Zambia)

    BT Floodplains—Zambia

          Kafue River Valley (Zambia)

Kafue River (Zambia)

    BT Rivers—Zambia

Kafue River Valley (Zambia)

    BT Valleys—Zambia

    NT Kafue Flats (Zambia)

Kafukai Iseki (Japan)

    USE Kafukai Site (Japan)

Kafukai Site (Japan) *(Not Subd Geog)*

    UF Kafukai Iseki (Japan)

    BT Japan—Antiquities

Kagaba Indians

    UF Arhouaques-Kaggaba

          Ca Gaba Indians

          Cagaba Indians

          Cogui Indians

          Kagabas

          Kaggaba

          Koggaba

          Köggabas

          Kogi Indians

    BT Indians of South America

Kagaba language

    [PM6321]

    UF Cagaba language

    BT Chibchan languages

          Indians of South America—Languages

Kagabas

    USE Kagaba Indians

Kagan language

    USE Tagakaolo language

Kagarice family *(Not Subd Geog)*

    UF Kagarise family

          Kegerreis family

Kagarise family

    USE Kagarice family

Kagata family *(Not Subd Geog)*

Kagate dialect

    [PL3651.K3]

    BT Tibetan language

Kagawa family *(Not Subd Geog)*

Kagayanen language *(May Subd Geog)*

    UF Cagayano Cillo language

    BT Philippine languages

          Philippines—Languages

Kagel family

    USE Kegel family

Kagera River

    UF Akagera River

          Alexandra Nile River

    BT Rivers—Africa, East

Kaggaba

    USE Kagaba Indians

Kagohashi family *(Not Subd Geog)*

Kagok

    BT Sijo

          Songs, Korean

Kagoro (African people)

    UF Kagoro (African tribe)

    BT Ethnology—Nigeria

    NT Missions to Kagoro (African people)

Kagoro (African tribe)

    USE Kagoro (African people)

Kagoshimajō (Kagoshima-shi, Japan)

    USE Tsurumarujō (Kagoshima-shi, Japan)

Kagou (African people)

    USE Gagou (African people)

Kagura *(May Subd Geog)*

    BT Dancing—Religious aspects—Shinto

          Shinto—Rituals

Kagura Jinja Shimoiwakage (Tanabe-shi, Japan)

    USE Kikyōgan Iwakage II Site (Tanabe-shi,

          Japan)

Kaguru (African people)

    UF Wakaguru (African people)

    BT Ethnology—Tanzania

    NT Missions to Kaguru (African people)

Kaguru (African people) philosophy

    USE Philosophy, Kaguru (African people)

Kaguru language

    [PL8341]

Kaguyama Kofun (Ōuda-chō, Japan)

    USE Kaguyama Site (Ōuda-chō, Japan)

Kaguyama Site (Ōuda-chō, Japan)

    UF Kaguyama Kofun (Ōuda-chō, Japan)

    BT Japan—Antiquities

Kagwahiv Indians

    USE Parintintin Indians

Kahl family

    USE Kahler family

Kahlamba

    USE Drakensberg Mountains

Kahle family

    USE Kahler family

Kahler family *(Not Subd Geog)*

    UF Caler family

          Callar family

          Caller family

          Calor family

          Caylor family

          Kahl family

          Kahle family

          Kailer family

          Kaler family

          Kalor family

          Kayler family

          Kaylor family

Kählerian manifolds

    BT Geometry, Differential

          Kählerian structures

          Manifolds (Mathematics)

Kählerian structures

    UF Structures, Kählerian

    BT Complex manifolds

          Geometry, Differential

    RT Hermitian structures

    NT Kählerian manifolds

Kahler's disease

    USE Multiple myeloma

Kahlgrund-Eisenbahn

    BT Railroads—Germany (West)

Kahn test of symbol arrangement

    [BF698.8.K3]

    BT Personality tests

          Projective techniques

          Symbolism (Psychology)

Kahonde (African people)

    USE Kaonde (African people)

Kahumamahon (Indonesian people)

    BT Ethnology—Indonesia

Kahun (Ancient city)

    [DT73.K28]

    UF Hetep Senwosret (Ancient city)

    BT Cities and towns, Ruined, extinct, etc.

          —Egypt

          Egypt—Antiquities

Kahuna

    [BL2630.H38]

    BT Priests

          Shamans—Hawaii

Kai (The Greek word)

    BT Greek language—Etymology

Kai (Tribe)

    USE Kaia-kaias

Kai Klong (Macao)

    USE Taipa Island (Macao)

Kaia-kaias

    [DU740]

    UF Kai (Tribe)

          Kaja-kajas

Kaiapo language

    USE Cayapo language

Kaiawase (Game)

    UF Kaiōi (Game)

    BT Japanese poetry

          Shells—Japan

Kaiba-to (R.S.F.S.R.)

    USE Moneron Island (R.S.F.S.R.)

Kaibab squirrel

    [QL737.R68]

    UF Sciurus kaibabensis

          Tassel-eared squirrels

Kaibalian dialect

    USE Koibalian dialect

Kaibate, Battle of, 1756

    USE Caibate, Battle of, 1756

Kaign family

    USE Cain family

Kaihōgyō

    [BQ8824 (Shugen)]

    [BQ9139-BQ9139.5 (Tendai)]

    BT Shugen (Sect)—Rituals

          Spiritual life (Buddhism)

          Tendai (Sect)—Rituals

Kaikalar
USE Kaikōlar
Kaike language
[PL3801.K15]
BT Tibeto-Burman languages
Kaikeyī (Hindu mythology)
BT Mythology, Hindu
Kaikkoolars
USE Kaikōlar
Kaikōlan
USE Kaikōlar
Kaikōlar
[DS432.K17]
UF Kaikalar
Kaikkoolars
Kaikōlan
BT Caste—India
Ethnology—India
Weavers—India
Kaikomas
USE Sinkyone Indians
KAIL (Computer program language)
BT PLATO (Electronic computer system)
Kaila
USE Falashas
Kailas Mountain (China)
UF Gangdisê Shan (China)
Kang-ti-ssu Shan (China)
Nyenchen Tanglha (China)
BT Mountains—China
Kailer family
USE Kahler family
Kailinon (Bari, Italy : Ancient city)
USE Caelia (Bari, Italy : Ancient city)
Kaimai-Mamaku Forest Park (N.Z.)
USE Kaimai-Mamaku State Forest Park
(N.Z.)
Kaimai-Mamaku State Forest Park (N.Z.)
UF Kaimai-Mamaku Forest Park (N.Z.)
BT Forest reserves—New Zealand
Parks—New Zealand
Kaimanawa State Forest (N.Z.)
UF Kaimanawa State Forest Park (N.Z.)
BT Forest reserves—New Zealand
Parks—New Zealand
Kaimanawa State Forest Park (N.Z.)
USE Kaimanawa State Forest (N.Z.)
Kaimare language
USE Purari language
Kaimyō
USE Buddhist posthumous names
Kain family
USE Cain family
Kainah Indians
[E99.K15]
UF Blood Indians
BT Indians of North America
Siksika Indians
— Reservations
NT Blood Indian Reserve (Alta.)
Kaindl family (Not Subd Geog)
Kaingangue Indians
[F2520.1.K (Brazil)]
[F2823.K3 (Argentine Republic)]
UF Caingangue Indians
BT Indians of South America
NT Botocudo Indians
Kaingangue language
[PM6276]
UF Caingangue language
BT Indians of South America—Languages
Tapuyan languages
Kaingaroa Plateau (N.Z.)
BT Plateaus—New Zealand
Kaingua Indians
USE Caingua Indians
Kaingua language
USE Caingua language
Kainic acid
[QP563.K33]

UF Carboxyisopropenylpyrrolidineacetic
acid
BT Algae—Toxicology
Amino acids
Anthelmintics
Neurotoxic agents
Pyrrolidine
Kainji Lake (Nigeria)
USE Kainji Reservoir (Nigeria)
Kainji Reservoir (Nigeria)
UF Kainji Lake (Nigeria)
BT Lakes—Nigeria
Niger River
Reservoirs—Nigeria
Kainuu (Finland : Region)
Kainyao language
USE Gumatj language
Kaiōi (Game)
USE Kaiawase (Game)
Kaiparowits Coal Basin (Utah)
USE Kaiparowits Plateau (Utah)
Kaiparowits Plateau (Utah)
UF Kaiparowits Coal Basin (Utah)
BT Plateaus—Utah
Kaipengs (Indic people)
USE Halams (Indic people)
Kaira
[QL458.42.A7]
BT Araneidae
Kairakuen (Mito-shi, Japan)
UF Tokiwa Kōen (Mito-shi, Japan)
BT Gardens—Japan
Parks—Japan
Kairós (The Greek word)
BT Greek language—Etymology
Kaisaks
USE Kirghiz
Kaisānıyah
USE Kaysānıyah
Kaisei 6 Iseki (Kitami-shi, Japan)
USE Kaisei 6 Site (Kitami-shi, Japan)
Kaisei 6 Site (Kitami-shi, Japan)
(Not Subd Geog)
UF Kaisei 6 Iseki (Kitami-shi, Japan)
BT Japan—Antiquities
Kaiser automobile
Kaiser family (Not Subd Geog)
UF Kaisor family
Kayser family
Keiser family
Keysar family
Keyser family
Kiaser family
Kiesser family
Kioser family
Kisear family
Kiser family
Kisor family
Kizer family
Kizier family
Kizor family
Kysar family
Kyser family
Kysor family
Kyzer family
Kaiser Wilhelm Kanal (Germany)
USE Kiel Canal (Germany)
Kaiserin Augusta River (New Guinea)
USE Sepik River (New Guinea)
Kaisersaal, Frankfurter Römer (Frankfurt am
Main, Germany)
USE Frankfurter Römer (Frankfurt am
Main, Germany)—Kaisersaal
Kaisersage
[PN687.K3]
Kaiserstuhl (Germany)
Kaisor family
USE Kaiser family
Kaissaks
USE Kirghiz

Kaiten (Torpedoes)
UF Human torpedoes
Kaiten torpedoes
Manned torpedoes
BT Midget submarines
Submarine warfare
Torpedoes
World War, 1939-1945—Naval
operations—Submarine
Kaiten torpedoes
USE Kaiten (Torpedoes)
Kaiwa language
USE Caingua language
Kaja-kajas
USE Kaia-kaias
Kajan language
USE Kayan language
Kajans
USE Kayans
Kaje language
UF Ju language (Benue-Congo)
BT Plateau languages (Nigeria)
Kajkavian dialect
[PG1395]
BT Serbo-Croatian language
Yugoslavia—Languages
Kajkavian literature (May Subd Geog)
[PG1395]
BT Croatian literature
Kaka (African people)
USE Mfumte (African people)
Yamba (African people)
Kaka language
USE Cacán language
Kaka language (Grasslands Bantu)
USE Yamba language (Cameroon and
Nigeria)
Kakaako (Honolulu, Hawaii)
(Not Subd Geog)
UF Honolulu (Hawaii). Kakaako
Kakadu National Park (N.T.)
BT National parks and reserves—Australia
Parks—Australia
Kakamega Forest Reserve (Kenya)
(Not Subd Geog)
BT Forest reserves—Kenya
National parks and reserves—Kenya
Kakan language
USE Cacán language
Kakana language
USE Cacán language
Kakapo
[QL696.P7]
UF Owl parrot
Strigops habroptilus
BT Strigops
Kakatiya dynasty (Not Subd Geog)
BT India—History—1000-1526
Kaki
USE Kaki persimmon
Kaki persimmon (May Subd Geog)
[QK495.E25 (Botany)]
[SB379.P4 (Culture)]
UF Chinese persimmon
Diospyros kaki
Japanese persimmon
Kaki
Oriental persimmon
Persimmon, Chinese
Persimmon, Japanese
Persimmon, Kaki
Persimmon, Oriental
Yamagaki
Kakibaru Kofungun (Amagi-shi, Japan)
USE Kakibaru Site (Amagi-shi, Japan)
Kakibaru Site (Amagi-shi, Japan)
UF Kakibaru Kofungun (Amagi-shi, Japan)
BT Japan—Antiquities
Kakiemon porcelain (May Subd Geog)
[NK4399.K3]
UF Porcelain, Kakiemon

Kakiemon porcelain (Continued)
  BT Arita porcelain
Kakké
  USE Beri-beri
Kako genzai ingakyō emaki (Scrolls)
  USE E Ingakyō (Scrolls)
Kakongo dialect
  USE Koongo dialect (Western Kongo)
Kakoongo dialect
  USE Koongo dialect (Western Kongo)
Kakua dialect
  USE Kakwa dialect
Kakunodate Kaidō (Japan) (Not Subd Geog)
  BT Roads—Japan
Kakure Nembutsu
  USE Kakushi Nembutsu
Kakushi Nembutsu (May Subd Geog)
  UF Kakure Nembutsu
      Kayakabe
  BT Heresies, Buddhist
      Shin (Sect)
Kakutstha (Hindu mythology)
  BT Mahābhārata—Biography
      Mythology, Hindu
Kakwa dialect
  [PL8061.95.K]
  UF Kakua dialect
  BT Bari language
      Sudan—Languages
      Uganda—Languages
      Zaire—Languages
KAL Flight 007 Incident, 1983
  USE Korean Air Lines Incident, 1983
Kála-azár
  [RC152]
  UF Leishmaniasis, Visceral
      Visceral leishmaniasis
  NT Leishman-Donovan bodies
Kalabari (African people)
  USE Ijo (African people)
Kalabari dialect
  [PL8276.95.K]
  BT Ijo language
Kalabhras
  BT India—History—324 B.C.-1000 A.D.
Kalachuri art
  USE Art, Kalachuri
Kalachuri dynasty (Not Subd Geog)
  [DS441]
  UF Chedi era
Kalacuri art
  USE Art, Kalachuri
Kalagan language
  USE Tagakaolo language
Kalah
  USE Kallah
Kalahari Desert
  BT Deserts—Africa, Southern
Kalakaua, House of (Not Subd Geog)
  BT Hawaii—Kings and rulers
Kalakh (Ancient city)
  USE Calah (Ancient city)
Kalam
  USE Islam—Doctrines
Kalamalka Lake (B.C.)
  BT Lakes—British Columbia
Kalamian language
  [PL5841]
  UF Calamian language
      Calamiano language
  BT Philippine languages
  RT Tagbanua language
Kālāmukhas
  [BL1245.S5]
  BT Hindu sects
      Sivaism
Kalandarānis (Pakistani people)
  USE Qalandar (Pakistani people)
Kalang (Indonesian people)
  [DS632.K28]
  BT Ethnology—Indonesia

Kalanga (African people)
  USE Karanga (African people)
Kalapalo Indians
  USE Apalakiri Indians
Kalapooian Indians
  USE Kalapuyan Indians
Kalapuyan Indians
  [E99.K]
  UF Calapooyan Indians
      Kalapooian Indians
  BT Indians of North America
  NT Yoncalla Indians
Kalapuyan language
  [PM1421]
Kalasa (Pakistani people)
  USE Kalash (Pakistani people)
Kalash (Pakistani people)
  UF Kalasa (Pakistani people)
  BT Ethnology—Pakistan
Kalashnikov automatic rifle
  USE AK-47 rifle
Kalashnikov machine-gun
  BT Machine-guns
Kalashum (Afghanistan people)
  BT Ethnology—Afghanistan
      Kafirs (Kafiristan)
Kalauna (Papua New Guinea people)
  BT Ethnology—Papua New Guinea
      Melanesians
Kalavryta (Greece : Eparchy)
Kalaway family
  USE Callaway family
Kalb family
  USE Kolb family
Kalber family
  USE Kolb family
KALDAS (Computer program language)
  BT ALGOL (Computer program language)
Kale (May Subd Geog)
  [SB351.K3]
  UF Brassica oleracea acephala
  BT Brassica
      Cole crops
Kalebwe language (Luba-Lulua)
  USE Luba-Lulua language
Kalebwe language (Songe)
  USE Songe language
Kaledor family
  USE Calder family
Kaleidoscope
  [QC373.K3]
  BT Design
      Symmetry
Kalela (African dance)
Kalemegdan Fortress (Belgrade, Serbia)
  USE Belgrade Fortress (Belgrade, Serbia)
Kalenjin language
  BT Kenya—Languages
      Nandi languages
      Tanzania—Languages
      Uganda—Languages
  NT Nandi language
      Suk language
  — Tone
      BT Tone (Phonetics)
Kalenjin riddles
  USE Riddles, Kalenjin
Kaler family
  USE Kahler family
Kaleri tribe
  BT Ethnology—Nigeria
Kalhu (Ancient city)
  USE Calah (Ancient city)
Kali Brantas (Java, Indonesia)
  USE Brantas River (Java, Indonesia)
Kali Putih River (Java, Indonesia)
  BT Rivers—Indonesia
Kali Serang (Java, Indonesia)
  USE Serang River (Java, Indonesia)
Kaliai language
  USE Lusi language

Kalimantan (Indonesia)
  UF Dutch Borneo (Indonesia)
      Indonesian Borneo (Indonesia)
Kalimantan Island
  USE Borneo
Kalimanten Island
  USE Borneo
Kalinga, Battle of, 260 B.C.
  BT India—History—324 B.C.-1000 A.D.
Kalinga ballads
  USE Ballads, Kalinga
Kalinga language
  [PL5851]
  BT Philippine languages
Kalinga law
  USE Law, Kalinga
Kalinga Prize (May Subd Geog)
  UF International Kalinga Prize
  BT Science news—Awards
      Technology—Awards
Kalingas
  BT Ethnology—Philippines
Kalinin, Battle of, 1941
  [D764]
  BT World War, 1939-1945—Campaigns—
      Russian S.F.S.R.
Kalios
  USE Behosys
Kalis (Indonesian people)
  USE Maloh (Indonesian people)
Kalispel Indians
  [E99.K]
  UF Pend d'Oreille Indians
  BT Indians of North America
      Salish Indians
Kalispel language
  [PM1431]
  UF Pend d'Oreille language
  BT Salishan languages
Kalitās
  [DS432.K177]
  BT Caste—India
      Ethnology—India
Kaliuresis (May Subd Geog)
  UF Kaluresis
  BT Diuresis
      Potassium—Metabolism
      Urination
      Water-electrolyte balance (Physiology)
Kalka dialect
  USE Khalkha dialect
Kalkadun language
  USE Kalkatungu language
Kalkas
  USE Khalkhas
Kalkatungu language
  [PL7101.K3]
  UF Galgadung language
      Kalkadun language
  BT Australia—Languages
      Australian languages
Kallah
  UF Kalah
  BT Jewish learning and scholarship
      Talmudic academies
Kallan caste
  USE Kallans
Kallan dialect
  UF Kallar dialect
      Mukkulattor dialect
  BT Tamil language
Kallans
  [DS432.K18]
  UF Cullar
      Kallan caste
      Kallar
  BT Caste—India
      Ethnology—India
  NT Pramalai Kallans
Kallar
  USE Kallans

Kallar dialect
USE Kallan dialect
Kallaway family
USE Callaway family
Kallawaya Indians
USE Callahuaya Indians
Kallenberg family
USE Kellenberger family
Kallenberger family
USE Kellenberger family
Kalley family
USE Kelley family
Kallidin
BT Oligopeptides
Kallidin-9
USE Bradykinin
Kallikrein
UF Padutin
Vascormone
BT Pancreas—Secretions
Kallitype
[TR400]
UF Callitype
BT Photography—Printing processes—
Silver
Kalloway family
USE Callaway family
Kallsall family
USE Kelsall family
Kalman filtering
UF Filtering, Kalman
BT Control theory
Estimation theory
Prediction theory
Stochastic processes
Kalmar, Union of, 1397
[DL179 (Denmark)]
[DL485 (Norway)]
[DL694 (Sweden)]
UF Calmar, Union of, 1397
BT Denmark—History—1397-1448
Norway—History—1397-1814
Sweden—History—1397-1523
Kalmar War, 1611-1613
[DL710]
UF Calmar War, 1611-1613
BT Denmark—History—Christian IV,
1588-1648
Sweden—History—Gustavus II
Adolphus, 1611-1632
NT Knäred, Peace of, 1613
Vittsjö, Battle of, 1612
Kalmia
[QK495.E68 (Botany)]
[SB413.K3 (Culture)]
BT Ericaceae
Laurel
Kalmia latifolia
USE Mountain laurel
Kalmuck language
USE Kalmyk language
Kalmucks
USE Kalmyks
Kalmuk language
USE Kalmyk language
Kalmyk art
USE Art, Kalmyk
Kalmyk artists laureate
USE Artists laureate, Kalmyk
Kalmyk arts
USE Arts, Kalmyk
Kalmyk drama (May Subd Geog)
[PL430]
Kalmyk folk dancing
USE Folk dancing, Kalmyk
Kalmyk folk-songs
USE Folk-songs, Kalmyk
Kalmyk language
[PL429]

UF Calmuck language
Kalmuck language
Kalmuk language
Kalmytž language
BT Mongolian languages
RT Oirat language
NT Torgut dialect
Kalmyk literature (May Subd Geog)
[PL430]
Kalmyk philology
[PL429]
Kalmyk poetry
[PL430]
Kalmyk prose literature (May Subd Geog)
[PL430]
Kalmyk proverbs
USE Proverbs, Kalmyk
Kalmyk riddles
USE Riddles, Kalmyk
Kalmyks (May Subd Geog)
[DK34.K14]
UF Calmucks
Kalmucks
BT Ethnology—Russian S.F.S.R.
Mongols
Oirats
Kalmytž language
USE Kalmyk language
Kalničko Gorje (Croatia)
USE Kalnik Mountain (Croatia)
Kalnik Mountain (Croatia)
UF Kalničko Gorje (Croatia)
BT Mountains—Yugoslavia
Kalo
USE Taro
Kalogeros
Kalokairinos family (Not Subd Geog)
UF Kalokerinos family
Kalokerinos family
USE Kalokairinos family
Kaloosas Indians
USE Calusa Indians
Kalor family
USE Kahler family
Kalorama (Washington, D.C.)
(Not Subd Geog)
UF Kalorama Triangle (Washington, D.C.)
Washington (D.C.). Kalorama
Kalorama Triangle (Washington, D.C.)
USE Kalorama (Washington, D.C.)
Kalos kagathos (The Greek phrase)
BT Greek language—Terms and phrases
Kalotermes
[QL529.3.K35]
BT Kalotermitidae
NT Kalotermes flavicollis
Kalotermes minor
Kalotermes simplicicornis
Kalotermes flavicollis
[QL529.3.K35]
BT Kalotermes
Kalotermes minor
[QL529.3.K35]
BT Kalotermes
Kalotermes simplicicornis
[QL529.3.K35]
UF Paraneotermes simplicicornis
BT Kalotermes
Kalotermitidae
[QL529.3.K35]
UF Calotermitidae
BT Termites
NT Cryptotermes
Kalotermes
Kaloway family
USE Callaway family
Kalsomining
USE Calcimining
Kalton family
USE Kelton family

Kaluli (Papua New Guinea people)
[DU740.42]
BT Bosavi (Papua New Guinea people)
Ethnology—Papua New Guinea
Kalunda (African people)
USE Lunda, Northern (African people)
Kaluresis
USE Kaliuresis
Kalusa Indians
USE Calusa Indians
Kaluszite
USE Syngenite
Kaluza-Klein theories
UF Kaluza-Klein theory
Kaluza theory
Klein-Kaluza theory
BT Unified field theories
Kaluza-Klein theory
USE Kaluza-Klein theories
Kaluza theory
USE Kaluza-Klein theories
Kálvária-oltár (Panel painting)
USE Kolozsvári, Tamás, fl. 1427. Calvary
altarpiece
Kam (Chinese people)
USE Tung (Chinese people)
Kam language
USE T'ung language
Kam Tai (Indic people)
USE Ahoms (Indic people)
Kāma (Hindu deity)
UF Kāmadeva (Hindu deity)
Maṇmataṇ (Hindu deity)
BT Gods, Hindu
Mahābhārata—Biography
KAMA (Information retrieval system)
BT Information storage and retrieval
systems
Kama no kami
USE Kamagami
Kama River (R.S.F.S.R.)
BT Rivers—Russian S.F.S.R.
Kāmadeva (Hindu deity)
USE Kāma (Hindu deity)
Kamagami (May Subd Geog)
[BL2211.K35]
UF Kama no kami
BT Gods, Japanese
Religion, Primitive
Kamai Iseki (Chino-shi, Japan)
USE Kamai Site (Chino-shi, Japan)
Kamai Site (Chino-shi, Japan)
(Not Subd Geog)
UF Kamai Iseki (Chino-shi, Japan)
BT Japan—Antiquities
Kamaishi Bay (Japan) (Not Subd Geog)
UF Kamaishi ko (Japan)
Kamaishi-oki (Japan)
Kamaishi-wan (Japan)
BT Bays—Japan
Kamaishi ko (Japan)
USE Kamaishi Bay (Japan)
Kamaishi-oki (Japan)
USE Kamaishi Bay (Japan)
Kamaishi-wan (Japan)
USE Kamaishi Bay (Japan)
Kamaiurá Indians
UF Camayura Indians
BT Indians of South America
Tupi Indians
Kamakura shogunate
USE Japan—History—Kamakura period,
1185-1333
Kamala
UF Kamela
Kamila
BT Dyes and dyeing
Kamano language
UF Kafe language
BT Papuan languages

Kamant language
    USE Kemant language
Kamapua'a (Hawaiian deity)
    (May Subd Geog)
    BT Gods, Hawaiian
Kamarakoto language
    BT Cariban languages
        Indians of South America—Languages
    NT Pemón dialects
Kamarer family
    USE Kemmerer family
Kamars
    ⌐DS432.K187⌐
    BT Ethnology—India
Kamassin language
    ⌐PL16.K3⌐
    UF Sayan-Samoyedic language
        South Samoyedic language
    BT Samoyedic languages
Kamba (African people)
    UF Akamba (African people)
        Wakamba (African people)
    BT Bantus
        Ethnology—Kenya
Kamba (African people) women
    USE Women, Kamba (African people)
Kamba folk-songs
    USE Folk-songs, Kamba
Kamba language
    ⌐PL8351⌐
    UF Kikamba language
    BT Bantu languages
    NT Kikuyu language
Kamba law
    USE Law, Kamba
Kambe family *(Not Subd Geog)*
Kamber family
    USE Kammer family
Kambera dialect
    BT Indonesia—Languages
        Sumba language
Kambfer family
    USE Kemp family
Kambilombilo State Farm (Zambia)
    BT State farms—Zambia
Kambonsenga (Zambian people)
    USE Ambo (Zambian people)
Kamchadal language
    ⌐PM70⌐
    UF Itelmes language
    BT Hyperborean languages
Kamchadals
    BT Ethnology—Soviet Union
Kamchatka Basin
    USE Komandorskie Basin
Kamchatka Peninsula (R.S.F.S.R.)
    UF Poluostrov Kamchatka (R.S.F.S.R.)
    BT Peninsulas—Russian S.F.S.R.
Kame Hills Site (Man.) *(Not Subd Geog)*
    BT Manitoba—Antiquities
Kame.ntzá language
    USE Camsa language
Kameda-hantō (Japan)
    USE Kameda Peninsula (Japan)
Kameda Peninsula (Japan)
    UF Kameda-hantō (Japan)
    BT Peninsulas—Japan
Kamegawa Iseki (Kainan-shi, Japan)
    USE Kamegawa Site (Kainan-shi, Japan)
Kamegawa Site (Kainan-shi, Japan)
    (Not Subd Geog)
    UF Kamegawa Iseki (Kainan-shi, Japan)
    BT Japan—Antiquities
Kamehameha, House of *(Not Subd Geog)*
    BT Hawaii—Kings and rulers
Kamei family *(Not Subd Geog)*
Kamei Iseki (Yao-shi, Japan)
    USE Kamei Site (Yao-shi, Japan)
Kamei Site (Yao-shi, Japan)
    UF Kamei Iseki (Yao-shi, Japan)
    BT Japan—Antiquities

Kameiros (Ancient city) *(Not Subd Geog)*
    UF Camirus (Ancient city)
        Kamiros (Ancient city)
    BT Cities and towns, Ruined, extinct, etc.
        —Greece
        Greece—Antiquities
Kamela
    USE Kamala
Kamelaukions
    BT Head-gear—Religious aspects
Kamenets-Podol'skiy, Battle of, 1944
    UF Podol'skiy, Battle of, 1944
    BT World War, 1939-1945—Campaigns—
        Ukraine
Kamer family
    USE Kammer family
Kamera family
    USE Kemmerer family
Kameralism
    USE Mercantile system
Kamerer family
    USE Kemmerer family
Kamerun
    USE Cameroon
Kames
    USE Eskar
Kamhau dialect
    USE Tiddim Chin dialect
Kamhmu (Southeast Asian people)
    USE Khmu' (Southeast Asian people)
Kamhmu language
    USE Khmu' language
Kami (Burmese tribe)
    USE Khumis
Kami language (Papua New Guinea)
    USE Yagaria language
Kamia Indians
    ⌐E99.K18⌐
    UF Comeya Indians
        Kumeyaay Indians
    BT Diegueño Indians
        Indians of North America
Kāmid al-Lawz Site (Lebanon)
    (Not Subd Geog)
    ⌐DS89.K27⌐
    UF Kāmid el-Lōz (Lebanon)
    BT Cities and towns, Ruined, extinct, etc.
        —Lebanon
        Lebanon—Antiquities
Kāmid el-Lōz (Lebanon)
    USE Kāmid al-Lawz Site (Lebanon)
Kamienne Mountains (Poland)
    UF Góry Kamienne (Poland)
    BT Mountains—Poland
Kamik-ochi Region (Japan)
Kamikaji family *(Not Subd Geog)*
Kamikaze airplanes
    UF Suicide airplanes
    BT Bombers
Kamikurata Iseki (Yokohama-shi, Japan)
    USE Kamikurata Site (Yokohama-shi,
        Japan)
Kamikurata Site (Yokohama-shi, Japan)
    (Not Subd Geog)
    UF Kamikurata Iseki (Yokohama-shi,
        Japan)
    BT Japan—Antiquities
Kamila
    USE Kamala
Kamilaroi (Australian people)
    ⌐DU125.K26⌐
    UF Koomil-Roi (Australian people)
    BT Australian aborigines
        Ethnology—Australia
Kamimoriyadan Site (Japan)
    (Not Subd Geog)
    BT Japan—Antiquities
Kaminagao Iseki (Japan)
    USE Kaminagao Site (Japan)
Kaminagao Site (Japan) *(Not Subd Geog)*
    UF Kaminagao Iseki (Japan)

    BT Japan—Antiquities
Kaminal-Juyú Site (Guatemala)
    USE Kaminaljuyu Site (Guatemala)
Kaminaljuyu Site (Guatemala)
    ⌐F1435.1.K3 (Mayas)⌐
    UF Kaminal-Juyú Site (Guatemala)
    BT Guatemala—Antiquities
Kaminishihara Iseki (Kumamoto-shi, Japan)
    USE Shinnabe Site (Kumamoto-shi, Japan)
Kaminoyama Peasant Uprising, 1747
Kamiros (Ancient city)
    USE Kameiros (Ancient city)
Kamishibai
    ⌐PN1979.K3⌐
    Here are entered general works and those that
    deal solely with the presentation of Kamishibai plays.
    The texts of Kamishibai plays and works treating
    them from a textual point of view are entered under
    Kamishibai plays.
    BT Children's plays—Presentation, etc.
        Street theater
Kamishibai, Educational
    USE Kamishibai in education
Kamishibai in education
    UF Educational kamishibai
        Kamishibai, Educational
    BT Audio-visual education
Kamishibai plays
    ⌐PN1979.K3⌐
    Here are entered the texts of Kamishibai plays and
    works treating them from a textual point of view.
    General works and those that deal solely with the
    presentation of Kamishibai plays are entered under
    Kamishibai.
    BT Children's plays
Kamishinden Iseki (Shikama-chō, Japan)
    USE Kamishinden Site (Shikama-chō,
        Japan)
Kamishinden Site (Shikama-chō, Japan)
    (Not Subd Geog)
    UF Kamishinden Iseki (Shikama-chō,
        Japan)
    BT Japan—Antiquities
Kamishirane Iseki (Yokohama-shi, Japan)
    USE Kamishirane Omote Site (Yokohama-
        shi, Japan)
**Kamishirane Omote Site (Yokohama-shi,
Japan)** *(Not Subd Geog)*
    UF Kamishirane Iseki (Yokohama-shi,
        Japan)
    BT Japan—Antiquities
Kamishitada Iseki (Mie-machi, Japan)
    USE Kamishitada Site (Mie-machi, Japan)
Kamishitada Site (Mie-machi, Japan)
    (Not Subd Geog)
    UF Kamishitada Iseki (Mie-machi, Japan)
    BT Japan—Antiquities
Kamitajino Kofun (Tomioka-shi, Japan)
    USE Kamitajino Site (Tomioka-shi, Japan)
Kamitajino Site (Tomioka-shi, Japan)
    UF Kamitajino Kofun (Tomioka-shi,
        Japan)
    BT Japan—Antiquities
Kamitoyoura Sōendō Iseki (Azuchi-chō, Japan)
    USE Kamitoyoura Sōendō Site (Azuchi-chō,
        Japan)
Kamitoyoura Sōendō Site (Azuchi-chō, Japan)
    UF Kamitoyoura Sōendō Iseki (Azuchi-
        chō, Japan)
    BT Japan—Antiquities
Kamitsuji Iseki (Yamaguchi-shi, Japan)
    USE Kamitsuji Site (Yamaguchi-shi, Japan)
Kamitsuji Site (Yamaguchi-shi, Japan)
    UF Kamitsuji Iseki (Yamaguchi-shi, Japan)
    BT Japan—Antiquities
Kamitsurugashira Iseki (Shichijō-machi, Japan)
    USE Kamitsurugashira Site (Shichijō-machi,
        Japan)
Kamitsurugashira Site (Shichijō-machi, Japan)
    (Not Subd Geog)
    UF Kamitsurugashira Iseki (Shichijō-
        machi, Japan)

BT Japan—Antiquities
Kamiyama family *(Not Subd Geog)*
Kamiyamajō (Kōbe-shi, Japan)
USE Ōgojō (Kōbe-shi, Japan)
Kamiyamajō (Miki-shi, Japan)
USE Mikijō (Miki-shi, Japan)
Kamler family
USE Kemmerer family
Kamloops Forest Region (B.C.)
BT Forest districts—British Columbia
Kamloops trout
[QL638.S2]
BT Rainbow trout
Kamm family
USE Kemmerer family
Kamma dialect
BT India—Languages
Telugu language
Kammas
BT Caste—India
Kammer family *(Not Subd Geog)*
UF Cambray family
Cambre family
Cammare family
Camper family
Campert family
Camrar family
Carmer family
Commere family
Kamber family
Kamer family
Kampur family
RT Kemmerer family
Kammerer family
USE Kemmerer family
Kämmererite
USE Stichtite
Kammu (Southeast Asian people)
USE Khmu' (Southeast Asian people)
Kammu language
USE Khmu' language
Kammyang language
USE Northern Thai language
Kamoro language
BT Papuan languages
Kamotai (1) Iseki (Aomori-shi, Japan)
USE Kamotai (1) Site (Aomori-shi, Japan)
Kamotai (1) Site (Aomori-shi, Japan)
(Not Subd Geog)
UF Kamotai (1) Iseki (Aomori-shi, Japan)
BT Japan—Antiquities
Kamotai (2) Iseki (Aomori-shi, Japan)
USE Kamotai (2) Site (Aomori-shi, Japan)
Kamotai (2) Site (Aomori-shi, Japan)
(Not Subd Geog)
UF Kamotai (2) Iseki (Aomori-shi, Japan)
BT Japan—Antiquities
Kamp family
USE Kemp family
Kampe family
USE Kemp family
Kampen (Oslo, Norway) *(Not Subd Geog)*
UF Oslo (Norway). Kampen
Kamper family
USE Kemp family
Kampf family
USE Kemp family
Kampfer family
USE Kemp family
Kampinos National Park (Poland)
USE Kampinoski Park Narodowy (Poland)
Kampinoska Forest (Poland)
UF Puszcza Kampinoska (Poland)
BT Forests and forestry—Poland
Kampinoski Park Narodowy (Poland)
UF Kampinos National Park (Poland)
BT National parks and reserves—Poland
Kampman family
USE Kampmann family
Kampmann family *(Not Subd Geog)*
UF Kampman family

Kampometer
[QC912]
Kamps family
USE Kemp family
Kampton family
USE Compton family
Kamptozoa
USE Entoprocta
Kampuchea
USE Cambodia
Kampuchean Civil War, 1970-1975
USE Cambodia—History—Civil War, 1970-
1975
Kampuchean-Vietnamese Conflict, 1977-
USE Cambodian-Vietnamese Conflict, 1977-
Kampur family
USE Kammer family
Kāmrūpī dialect
[PK1559.K36]
BT Assamese language
Kamsa
Kamsa language
USE Camsa language
Kamtuk language *(May Subd Geog)*
UF Kemtuik language
Kemtuk language
BT Indonesia—Languages
Papuan languages
Kamu (Southeast Asian people)
USE Khmu' (Southeast Asian people)
Kamun (African people)
USE Kamwe (African people)
Kamuti
USE Bonsai
Kamwe (African people)
UF Higi (African people)
Hiji (African people)
Kamun (African people)
Kamwes (African people)
Kapsiki (African people)
Vacamwe (African people)
BT Ethnology—Cameroon
Ethnology—Nigeria
NT Missions to Kamwe (African people)
Kamwe language *(May Subd Geog)*
UF Higi language
BT Cameroon—Languages
Chadic languages
Nigeria—Languages
Kamwes (African people)
USE Kamwe (African people)
Kan dialects *(May Subd Geog)*
[PL1871-1880]
UF Kiangsi dialects
BT Chinese language—Dialects
Kana language
UF Khana language
Ogoni language
BT Benue-Congo languages
Kanab Creek (Utah and Ariz.)
BT Rivers—Arizona
Rivers—Utah
Kanada family
USE Kennedy family
Kanada language
USE Kannada language
Kanaday family
USE Kennedy family
Kanadey family
USE Kennedy family
Kanadori Iseki (Taiwa-chō, Japan)
USE Kanadori Site (Taiwa-chō, Japan)
Kanadori Site (Taiwa-chō, Japan)
(Not Subd Geog)
UF Kanadori Iseki (Taiwa-chō, Japan)
BT Japan—Antiquities
Kanady family
USE Kennedy family
Kanaf
USE Kenaf

Kanagawa, Japan (Prefecture), in art
Kanagawa-eki (Yokohama-shi, Japan)
USE Yokohama-eki (Yokohama-shi, Japan)
Kanagy family *(Not Subd Geog)*
Kanak (Malaysian people)
USE Kanaq (Malaysian people)
Kanaka (New Caledonian people)
UF Canaque (New Caledonian people)
BT Ethnology—New Caledonia
Kanakhoe language
USE G//ana language
Kanakuru language
[PL8358]
UF Dera language
Deru language
BT Bolewa languages
Kanał Elbląski (Poland)
USE Elbląg Canal (Poland)
Kanal imeni Moskvy (R.S.F.S.R.)
USE Moscow Canal (R.S.F.S.R.)
Kanal Moskva-Volga (R.S.F.S.R.)
USE Moscow Canal (R.S.F.S.R.)
Kanalu (Papua New Guinea people)
USE Barok (Papua New Guinea people)
Kanamori family *(Not Subd Geog)*
Kanamuro family *(Not Subd Geog)*
Kananaskis Country (Alta.)
(Not Subd Geog)
BT Recreation areas—Alberta
Kananaskis Provincial Park (Alta.)
USE Peter Lougheed Provincial Park (Alta.)
Kanapit (Papua New Guinea people)
USE Barok (Papua New Guinea people)
Kanaq (Malaysian people)
[DS595.2.K35]
UF Kanak (Malaysian people)
BT Ethnology—Malaysia
Kanarese (Indic people)
UF Canarese (Indic people)
BT Ethnology—India
Kanarese language
USE Kannada language
Kanât
USE Qanat
Kanaura (Indic people)
[DS432.K191]
UF Kanauri (Indic people)
Kanawari (Indic people)
Kanawi (Indic people)
Khunu (Indic people)
BT Ethnology—India
Kanauri (Indic people)
USE Kanaura (Indic people)
Kanauri language
[PL3801.K3]
UF Kanawari language
Thebörskad language
Tibarskad language
BT Tibeto-Burman languages
Kanawari (Indic people)
USE Kanaura (Indic people)
Kanawari language
USE Kanauri language
Kanawha River (W. Va.)
BT Rivers—West Virginia
Kanawi (Indic people)
USE Kanaura (Indic people)
Kanazawa-shi Muryōji B Iseki (Kanazawa-shi,
Japan)
USE Muryōji B Site (Kanazawa-shi, Japan)
Kanbe Castle (Suzuka-shi, Japan)
USE Kanbejō (Suzuka-shi, Japan)
Kanbejō (Suzuka-shi, Japan)
UF Hondajō (Suzuka-shi, Japan)
Kanbe Castle (Suzuka-shi, Japan)
BT Castles—Japan
Kanbis
USE Patidars

Kānchenjunga (Nepal and India)
  UF Khangchendzonga (Nepal and India)
      Kinchinjunga (Nepal and India)
      Kumbhkaran Lungur (Nepal and
        India)
  BT Himalaya Mountains
      Mountains—India
      Mountains—Nepal
Kanda (African people)
  USE Gaanda (African people)
Kanda family *(Not Subd Geog)*
Kanda-gawa (Japan)
  USE Kanda River (Japan)
Kanda Iseki (Ōtsu-shi, Japan)
  USE Kanda Site (Ōtsu-shi, Japan)
Kanda River (Japan)
  UF Kanda-gawa (Japan)
  BT Rivers—Japan
Kanda Site (Ōtsu-shi, Japan)
  UF Kanda Iseki (Ōtsu-shi, Japan)
  BT Japan—Antiquities
Kandalakshskiĭ gosudarstvennyĭ zapovednik
  (R.S.F.S.R.)
  USE Kandalakshskiĭ zapovednik
      (R.S.F.S.R.)
Kandalakshskiĭ Preserve (R.S.F.S.R.)
  USE Kandalakshskiĭ zapovednik
      (R.S.F.S.R.)
Kandalakshskiĭ zapovednik (R.S.F.S.R.)
  (Not Subd Geog)
  UF Kandalakshskiĭ gosudarstvennyĭ
      zapovednik (R.S.F.S.R.)
      Kandalakshskiĭ Preserve (R.S.F.S.R.)
      Kandalakshsky Preserve (R.S.F.S.R.)
  BT National parks and reserves—Russian
      S.F.S.R.
      Natural areas—Russian S.F.S.R.
Kandalakshsky Preserve (R.S.F.S.R.)
  USE Kandalakshskiĭ zapovednik
      (R.S.F.S.R.)
Kandawo language
  USE Narak language
Kandeevka Uprising, 1861
  USE Soviet Union—History—Kandiyevka
      Uprising, 1861
Kandh language
  USE Kui language
Kandhs
  [DS432.K192]
  UF Khonds
      Kondh (Indic people)
      Konds
      Kuis
  BT Ethnology—India
  NT Missions to Kandhs
Kandiyevka Uprising, 1861
  USE Soviet Union—History—Kandiyevka
      Uprising, 1861
Kandoshi Indians
  USE Candoshi Indians
Kandoshi language
  USE Candoshi language
Kandyan law
  USE Law, Kandyan
Kane family
  USE Cain family
Kanedajō (Mitsushima-chō, Japan)
  USE Kaneta no ki (Mitsushima-chō, Japan)
Kanegamori Nishi Iseki (Moriyama-shi, Japan)
  USE Kanegamori Nishi Site (Moriyama-shi,
      Japan)
Kanegamori Nishi Site (Moriyama-shi, Japan)
  UF Kanegamori Nishi Iseki (Moriyama-
      shi, Japan)
  BT Japan—Antiquities
Kaneko family *(Not Subd Geog)*
Kanela Indians
  USE Canelo Indians
Kanematsu family *(Not Subd Geog)*
Kanembu (African people)
  [DT546.445.K36]

  BT Ethnology—Chad
      Ethnology—Niger
      Ethnology—Nigeria
Kaneta Castle (Mitsushima-chō, Japan)
  USE Kaneta no ki (Mitsushima-chō, Japan)
Kaneta no ki (Mitsushima-chō, Japan)
  UF Kanedajō (Mitsushima-chō, Japan)
      Kaneta Castle (Mitsushima-chō, Japan)
      Kurosejō (Mitsushima-chō, Japan)
  BT Castles—Japan
      Fortification—Japan
Kang (Game)
  [GV1017.K3]
Kang family *(Not Subd Geog)*
  [CS1339.K]
K'ang-hsi nan hsün t'u (Scroll)
  USE Wang, Hui, 1632-1717. Imperial
      inspection tour of the South
Kang-ti-ssu Shan (China)
  USE Kailas Mountain (China)
Kangable (African people)
  USE Tagbana (African people)
Kangar
  USE Pechenegs
Kangari dialect
  USE Kangri dialect
Kangaroo hunting *(May Subd Geog)*
  [SK305.K3]
  BT Hunting
Kangaroo Island (S. Aust.)
  BT Islands—Australia
Kangaroo rats
  [QL737.R66]
  UF Dipodomyinae
      Dipodomys
  BT Heteromyidae
  NT Dipodomys agilis
      Dipodomys microps
      Dipodomys ordii
      Dipodomys spectabilis
      Merriam's kangaroo rat
Kangaroos
  [QL737.M35 (General)]
  [QL795.K3 (Stories)]
  UF Macropodidae
  NT Bettongia
      Grey kangaroo
      Macropus
      Red kangaroo
      Tree kangaroos
      Wallabies
Kangerdlugssuaq (Greenland)
  USE Kangerlussuaq (Greenland)
Kangerlussuaq (Greenland)
  UF Kangerdlugssuaq (Greenland)
  BT Inlets—Greenland
Kangra dialect
  USE Kangri dialect
Kangri dialect
  [PK2649.K4]
  UF Kangari dialect
      Kangra dialect
  BT Dogri dialect
      Panjabi language
Kangri folk-songs
  USE Folk-songs, Kangri
Kangütü language
  USE Ipurina language
Kanhobal language
  USE Kanjobal language
Kaniagmiut (Eskimo tribe)
  [E99.E7]
  UF Kadiak (Eskimo tribe)
      Koniagi Indians
      Konjagen Indians
  BT Eskimos
      Indians of North America
Kaniagmiut language
  [PM72]
  UF Kadiak language

Kanichana language
  USE Canichana language
Kanikars
  USE Kanis
Kaniksu National Forest *(Not Subd Geog)*
  BT Forest reserves—Idaho
      Forest reserves—Montana
      Forest reserves—Washington (State)
      National parks and reserves—Idaho
      National parks and reserves—Montana
      National parks and reserves—
        Washington (State)
Kanis
  [DS432.K]
  UF Kanikars
  BT Ethnology—India
Kanisza, Battle of, 1601
  [DR521]
  BT Hungary—History—1526-1683
Kanite language
  UF Kemiju Jate language
  BT Papuan languages
Kanjaga (African people)
  USE Builsa (African people)
Kanjobal language
  UF Conob language
      Kanhobal language
  BT Guatemala—Languages
      Indians of Central America—
        Guatemala—Languages
      Mayan languages
Kankakee River (Ind. and Ill.)
  BT Rivers—Illinois
      Rivers—Indiana
Kankanay dialect
  [PL5865]
  UF Cancanai dialect
      Lepanto-Igorot dialect
  BT Igorot language
      Philippine languages
Kankhā (Buddhism)
  USE Doubt (Buddhism)
Kankiti language
  USE Ipurina language
Kanklės
  [ML509 (Lithuanian)]
  BT Gusli
      Kantele (Musical instrument)
      Musical instruments—Lithuania
Kankomo Clay Deposit (Zambia)
  UF Kankomo dambo (Zambia)
  BT Clay—Zambia
Kankomo dambo (Zambia)
  USE Kankomo Clay Deposit (Zambia)
Kankyūan school of Japanese tea ceremony
  USE Japanese tea ceremony—Mushanokōji
      Senke school
Kanmel family
  USE Kemmerer family
Kann family *(Not Subd Geog)*
  UF Kanne family
Kannabe Goryō Iseki (Kannabe-chō, Japan)
  USE Kannabe Goryō Site (Kannabe-chō,
      Japan)
Kannabe Goryō Site (Kannabe-chō, Japan)
  (Not Subd Geog)
  UF Kannabe Goryō Iseki (Kannabe-chō,
      Japan)
  BT Japan—Antiquities
Kannada authors
  USE Authors, Kannada
Kannada ballads
  USE Ballads, Kannada
Kannada Christian literature
  USE Christian literature, Kannada
Kannada drama *(May Subd Geog)*
  RT Dramatists, Kannada
  NT Folk-drama, Kannada
      Radio plays, Kannada
Kannada dramatists
  USE Dramatists, Kannada

Kannada encyclopedias and dictionaries
  USE Encyclopedias and dictionaries,
      Kannada
Kannada epigrams
  USE Epigrams, Kannada
Kannada erotic poetry
  USE Erotic poetry, Kannada
Kannada essays *(May Subd Geog)*
Kannada fiction *(May Subd Geog)*
  NT Short stories, Kannada
Kannada folk-drama
  USE Folk-drama, Kannada
Kannada folk literature
  USE Folk literature, Kannada
Kannada folk poetry
  USE Folk poetry, Kannada
Kannada folk-songs
  USE Folk-songs, Kannada
Kannada Hindu hymns
  USE Hindu hymns, Kannada
Kannada imprints *(May Subd Geog)*
Kannada inscriptions
  USE Inscriptions, Kannada
Kannada Jaina literature
  USE Jaina literature, Kannada
Kannada Jaina poetry
  USE Jaina poetry, Kannada
Kannada language
  ₁PL4641-9₁
  UF Canarese language
      Carnataca language
      Kanada language
      Kanarese language
  BT Dravidian languages
  NT Havyaka dialect
      Soliga dialect
  — **Dialects**
  — — **Gowda**
      UF Gowda dialect
  — — Havyaka
      USE Havyaka dialect
Kannada Lingayat poetry
  USE Lingayat poetry, Kannada
Kannada literature
  ₁PL4650-4659₁
  NT Christian literature, Kannada
      Folk literature, Kannada
      Jaina literature, Kannada
  — To 1500
  — 1500-1800
  — 19th century
  — 20th century
Kannada manuscripts
  USE Manuscripts, Kannada
Kannada newspapers *(May Subd Geog)*
Kannada novelists
  USE Novelists, Kannada
Kannada nursery rhymes
  USE Nursery rhymes, Kannada
Kannada paleography
  USE Paleography, Kannada
Kannada periodicals *(May Subd Geog)*
Kannada philology
Kannada poetry
  NT Erotic poetry, Kannada
      Folk poetry, Kannada
      Jaina poetry, Kannada
      Lingayat poetry, Kannada
      Nursery rhymes, Kannada
      Religious poetry, Kannada
  — To 1500
  — 1500-1800
  — 20th century
Kannada poets
  USE Poets, Kannada
Kannada prose literature *(May Subd Geog)*
Kannada proverbs
  USE Proverbs, Kannada
Kannada radio plays
  USE Radio plays, Kannada

Kannada religious poetry
  USE Religious poetry, Kannada
Kannada riddles
  USE Riddles, Kannada
Kannada short stories
  USE Short stories, Kannada
Kannada Virasivaite poetry
  USE Lingayat poetry, Kannada
Kannada wit and humor
  BT Indic wit and humor
Kannada women authors
  USE Women authors, Kannada
Ḳanna'im
  USE Zealots (Jewish party)
Kaṇṇaki (Hindu deity)
  UF Cīrmma (Hindu deity)
      Śrīkurumba (Hindu deity)
  BT Gods, Hindu
Kannawarf family
  USE Kannewurf family
Kannawurf family
  USE Kannewurf family
Kanne family
  USE Kann family
Kannedy family
  USE Kennedy family
Kanneworff family
  USE Kannewurf family
Kannewurf family *(Not Subd Geog)*
  UF Canneworff family
      Kannawarf family
      Kannawurf family
      Kanneworff family
Kannon (Buddhist deity)
  USE Avalokiteśvara (Buddhist deity)
Kannon family
  USE Cannon family
Kannonchiku
  USE Rhapis excelsa
Kano-gawa (Japan)
  USE Kano River (Japan)
Kano Kawa (Japan)
  USE Kano River (Japan)
Kano River (Japan)
  UF Kano-gawa (Japan)
      Kano Kawa (Japan)
      Kanogawa (Japan)
  BT Rivers—Japan
Kanō School
  BT Painting, Japanese—Kamakura-
      Momoyama periods, 1185-1600
      Painting, Japanese—Edo period, 1600-
      1868
Kanogawa (Japan)
  USE Kano River (Japan)
Kanoko C Iseki (Japan)
  USE Kanoko C Site (Japan)
Kanoko C Site (Japan) *(Not Subd Geog)*
  UF Kanoko C Iseki (Japan)
  BT Japan—Antiquities
Kanop language
  USE Mandjak language
Kānphaṭas *(May Subd Geog)*
  BT Hindu sects
      Sivaism
      Yoga, Haṭha
Kanra-san (Korea)
  USE Halla Mountain (Korea)
Kansa Indians
  ₁E99.K2₁
  UF Kaw Indians
  BT Dhegiha Indians
      Indians of North America
      Siouan Indians
  — **Land transfers**
  ₁E99.K2₁
Kansai-chihō (Japan)
  USE Kansai Region (Japan)
Kansai Region (Japan)
  UF Kansai-chihō (Japan)

Kansas
  — **Description and travel**
  — — **To 1861**
  — — **1861-1950**
  — — **1951-1980**
  — — **1981-**
  — **History**
      ₁F676-690₁
  — — **1854-1861**
      NT Osawatomie, Battle of, 1856
  — — — **Juvenile literature**
  — — **Civil War, 1861-1865**
      ₁E508₁
      NT Big Blue, Battle of the, 1864
          Price's Missouri Expedition,
          1864
  — — — **Juvenile literature**
  — **Politics and government**
  — — **1854-1861**
  — — **Civil War, 1861-1865**
  — — **1865-1950**
  — — **1951-**
Kansas City (Kan.). Strawberry Hill
  USE Strawberry Hill (Kansas City, Kan.)
Kansas-Nebraska bill
  ₁E433₁
  BT Missouri compromise
      Slavery—United States
Kansas River (Kan.)
  UF Kaw River (Kan.)
  BT Rivers—Kansas
Kansk-Achinsk Basin (R.S.F.S.R.)
  UF Kansko-Achinskiĭ basseĭn (R.S.F.S.R.)
      Kansko-Achinskiĭ ugol'nyĭ basseĭn
      (R.S.F.S.R.)
  BT Geology—Russian S.F.S.R.
Kansko-Achinskiĭ basseĭn (R.S.F.S.R.)
  USE Kansk-Achinsk Basin (R.S.F.S.R.)
Kansko-Achinskiĭ ugol'nyĭ basseĭn (R.S.F.S.R.)
  USE Kansk-Achinsk Basin (R.S.F.S.R.)
Kantele (Musical instrument)
  ₁ML509 (Finnish)₁
  BT Dulcimer
      Gusli
      Harp
  NT Kanklės
Kantele music
  ₁M142.K₁
Kanter family
  USE Canter family
Kantishna Hills (Alaska)
  BT Mountains—Alaska
Kantō Region (Japan)
Kantor family
  USE Canter family
Kantrowitz family *(Not Subd Geog)*
Kantu (Indonesian people)
  ₁DS646.32.K36₁
  BT Ethnology—Indonesia
      Ibans (Bornean people)
Kanuri
  BT Ethnology—Nigeria
Kanuri language
  ₁PL8361₁
  UF Bornu language
  BT Nigeria—Languages
      Nilo-Saharan languages
  NT Teda language
Kanuti River (Alaska) *(Not Subd Geog)*
  BT Rivers—Alaska
Kanyak language
  USE Konyak language
Kanyakāpāramēśvari (Hindu deity)
  BT Gods, Hindu
Kanze family *(Not Subd Geog)*
  UF Kwanze family
Kanze school *(May Subd Geog)*
  ₁PN2924.5.N6 (Performance)₁
  BT Nō
      Utai
  NT Umewaka school

Kanzler family *(Not Subd Geog)*
Kao language
  USE Katu language
Kao-seng-tsan feng (China)
  USE Hsi-hsia-pang-ma Peak (China)
Kaokogecko
  ₍QL666.L245₎
  BT Geckos
Kaokogecko vanzyli
  ₍QL666.L245₎
Kaokoveld Coast (Namibia)
  USE Skeleton Coast (Namibia)
Kaoku monkyō (Bronze mirror)
  BT Bronze mirrors—Japan
    Bronzes, Japanese—To 794
Kaoliang *(May Subd Geog)*
  ₍QK495.G74 (Botany)₎
  ₍SB191.S7 (Culture)₎
  UF Sorghum nervosum
  BT Sorghum
Kaoliang liquor
Kaolin *(May Subd Geog)*
  ₍QE391.K (Mineralogy)₎
  ₍TN941-TN943 (Mineral resources)₎
  ₍TP811 (Pottery)₎
  UF China-clay
  BT Aluminum silicates
    Clay
Kaolinite
  ₍QE391.K₎
Kaonde (African people)
  ₍DT963.42₎
  UF Bakahonde (African people)
    Bakaonde (African people)
    Kahonde (African people)
    Kaunde (African people)
  BT Bantus
    Ethnology—Zambia
    Luba (African people)
Kaonde language
  UF Luba-Kaonde language
  BT Bantu languages
Kaons
  ₍QC793.5.M42-429₎
  UF K mesons
    Kappa mesons
    Tau mesons
  BT Heavy particles (Nuclear physics)
    Mesons
    Particles (Nuclear physics)
    Strange particles
  RT Muons
    Pions
  — Decay
    ₍QC793.5.M425₎
  — Scattering
    ₍QC793.5.M428₎
  — Spectra
Kaouar (Niger)
  UF Kawar (Niger)
  BT Oases—Niger
Kaoussan, Rebellion of, 1916-1918
  USE Senussite Rebellion, 1916-1918
Kaowerawédj (Papuan tribe)
  BT Ethnology—Indonesia
Kap Stosch (Greenland)
  USE Stosch Cape (Greenland)
Kapa
  USE Tapa
Kapala language
  USE Kresh language
Kāpālikas
  ₍BL1245.S5₎
  BT Hindu sects
    Sivaism
Kapampangan language
  USE Pampanga language
Kapanci
  USE Kapantsi
Kapantsi
  ₍DR64.2.K37₎

UF Kapanci
  Kapantsy
BT Ethnology—Bulgaria
Kapantsy
  USE Kapantsi
Kapaonik Mountains (Serbia)
  USE Kopaonik Mountains (Serbia)
Kapau language
  BT Kukukuku languages
Kapauku (Papuan people)
  UF Capaukoos (Papuan people)
    Ekari (Papuan people)
    Kepaukoe (Papuan people)
  BT Ethnology—Indonesia
    Papuans
Kapauku language
  UF Ekagi language
    Ekari language
  BT Papuan languages
Kapauku law
  USE Law, Kapauku
Kapeenos family
  USE Kapinos family
Kapel family
  USE Keppel family
Kapikapi language
  USE Mukawa language
Kapilavastu (Ancient city) *(Not Subd Geog)*
  ₍DS495.8.K267₎
  BT Cities and towns, Ruined, extinct, etc.
    —Nepal
    Nepal—Antiquities
Kapingamarangi Atoll (Caroline Islands)
  UF Greenwich Island (Caroline Islands)
  BT Coral reefs and islands—Caroline
    Islands
Kapingamarangi language
  ₍PL6452₎
  BT Micronesian languages
Kapinos family *(Not Subd Geog)*
  UF Kapeenos family
    Kapinus family
Kapinus family
  USE Kapinos family
Kapiśa (Afghanistan : Region)
  (Not Subd Geog)
Kapiti Island (N.Z.)
  UF Entry Island (N.Z.)
  BT Islands—New Zealand
Kapok
  ₍SB261.K3 (Culture)₎
  UF Silk-cotton tree
Kápolna, Hungary (Heves), Battle of, 1849
  ₍DB936₎
  BT Hungary—History—Uprising of 1848-
    1849
Kapone language
  BT Melanesian languages
Kaposi's disease
  USE Xeroderma pigmentosum
Kaposi's sarcoma
  UF Idiopathic hemorrhagic sarcoma
    Multiple hemorrhagic sarcoma
  BT Cancer
    Sarcoma
Kapp family
  USE Capps family
Kapp Putsch
  USE Germany—History—Kapp Putsch,
    1920
Kappa (Japanese water goblin)
  BT Folklore—Japan
Kappa (Japanese water goblin) in art
Kappa mesons
  USE Kaons
Kappe family
  USE Capps family
Kappel family
  USE Keppel family
Kappelgaard family *(Not Subd Geog)*
  UF Kappelgård family

Kappelgård family
  USE Kappelgaard family
Kappes family
  USE Capps family
Kapron
  USE Nylon
Kapsiki (African people)
  USE Kamwe (African people)
Kapsin Incident, 1884
  BT Korea—History—1864-1910
Kapsner family *(Not Subd Geog)*
Kapul language
  USE Abaknon language
Kapwī language
  USE Kabui language
Kar formation
  ₍GB601-8₎
Kar-gyu (Sect)
  USE Bka'-rgyud-pa (Sect)
Kar-ma-pa (Sect) *(May Subd Geog)*
  ₍BQ7682₎
  UF Black hats (Sect)
    Karma (Sect)
    Karma-pa (Sect)
    Red hats (Sect)
  BT Bka'-rgyud-pa (Sect)
    Buddhist sects
  NT Kar-ma-pa lamas
Kar-ma-pa lamas *(May Subd Geog)*
  ₍BQ7682₎
  UF Lamas, Kar-ma-pa
    Priests, Kar-ma-pa
  BT Kar-ma-pa (Sect)
    Lamas
    Priests, Buddhist
Kara (Gbayan people)
  ₍DT474.5₎
  BT Ethnology—Africa, West
    Gbaya (African people)
Kara Balkan Mountains (Bulgaria)
  USE Chernatitsa Mountains (Bulgaria)
Kara Dag Mountains (Bulgaria)
  USE Chernatitsa Mountains (Bulgaria)
Kara-Kalpak embroidery
  USE Embroidery, Kara-Kalpak
Kara-Kalpak fiction *(May Subd Geog)*
Kara-Kalpak language
  ₍PL55.K₎
  UF Qaraqalpaq language
  BT Turkic languages
    Turkic languages, Northwest
Kara-Kalpak literature *(May Subd Geog)*
Kara-Kalpak poetry *(May Subd Geog)*
Kara-Kalpaks
  ₍DK855.4₎
  BT Ethnology—Soviet Central Asia
Kara-Kirghiz language
  USE Kirghiz language
Kara Kitai
  USE Khitan Mongols
Kara Kum (Turkmen S.S.R.)
  UF Karakumy (Turkmen S.S.R.)
    Qara Qum (Turkmen S.S.R.)
    Qaraqum (Turkmen S.S.R.)
  BT Deserts—Turkmen S.S.R.
Kara language
  BT Bongo-Bagirmi languages
    Sudan—Languages
Kara Sea
  UF Karskoe more
    Karskoye more
  BT Arctic Ocean
Kara Site (Iran)
  USE Kara Tepe (Iran)
Kara-Su River (Bulgaria and Greece)
  USE Struma River (Bulgaria and Greece)
Kara-Tau (Kazakh S.S.R.)
  UF Karatau (Kazakh S.S.R.)
  BT Mountains—Kazakh S.S.R.
Kara Tepe (Iran) *(Not Subd Geog)*
  UF Kara Site (Iran)

BT Iran—Antiquities
Karachaevs
    [DK34.K]
    BT Ethnology—Caucasus
Karachai language
    USE Karachay-Balkar language
Karachay-Balkar language
    UF Balkar language
        Karachai language
        Karatchai language
    BT Soviet Union—Languages
        Turkic languages
        Turkic languages, Northwest
Karachay literature *(May Subd Geog)*
Karadeniz Boğazı (Turkey)
    USE Bosporus (Turkey)
Karadžić family *(Not Subd Geog)*
Karafuto dogs
    UF Sakhalin dogs
    BT Dog breeds
        Sled dogs
Karagas language
    USE Tofa language
Karagasi
    USE Karagasses
Karagasses
    UF Karagasi
    BT Ethnology—Russian S.F.S.R.
Karagassian language
    USE Tofa language
Karageōrgiadēs family *(Not Subd Geog)*
Karaiai language
    USE Anem language
Karaim language
    UF Karaitic language
    BT Jews—Languages
        Soviet Union—Languages
        Turkic languages
        Turkic languages, Northwest
Karaite law
    UF Law, Karaite
    BT Jewish law
    NT Divorce (Karaite law)
        Marriage (Karaite law)
Karaite manuscripts
    USE Manuscripts, Karaite
Karaites *(May Subd Geog)*
    [BM185]
    BT Jewish sects
    NT Commandments, Six hundred and
        thirteen (Karaites)
Karaites (Jewish law)
Karaitic language
    USE Karaim language
Karaitic literature
    [BM185]
Karajá Indians
    USE Caraja Indians
Karak (Kingdom)
    [DS911.78]
    UF Kaya (Kingdom)
    BT Korea—History—To 935
Karakachani
    USE Sarakatsans
Karakoram Range
    UF Karakorum Range
        Muztagh-Karakoram
    BT Mountains—Asia
    NT Gasherbrum I (Pakistan)
        Haramosh (Pakistan)
        K2 (Pakistan : Mountain)
        Mango Gusor Range (Pakistan)
        Masherbrum Peak (Pakistan)
        Saser Kangri (India)
Karakorum Range
    USE Karakoram Range
Karakoyunlus
    UF Qara Qoyunlus
    BT Turks
Karakul sheep *(May Subd Geog)*
    [SF373.K3]

Karakumy (Turkmen S.S.R.)
    USE Kara Kum (Turkmen S.S.R.)
Karāmah (Jordan), Battle of, 1968
    BT Fedayeen
        Jordan—History
Karamojong (African people)
    UF Karimojong (African people)
    BT Ethnology—Uganda
Karamojong folk-songs
    USE Folk-songs, Karamojong
Karamojong language
    UF Akarimojong language
        Karimojong language
    BT Nilo-Hamitic languages
        Teso language
        Uganda—Languages
Karan Kayasths
    USE Karana Kayasths
Karaṅ language
    USE Angas language
Karana (Ancient city) *(Not Subd Geog)*
    UF Rimah, Tall al- (Iraq)
        Tall al-Rimah (Iraq)
        Tell el-Rimah (Iraq)
    BT Cities and towns, Ruined, extinct, etc.
        —Iraq
        Iraq—Antiquities
Karana Kayasths
    [DS432.K198]
    UF Karan Kayasths
    BT Caste—India
        Ethnology—India
        Kayasths
Karang (African people)
    USE Angas (African people)
Karanga (African people)
    UF Kalanga (African people)
        Wakaranga (African people)
    BT Ethnology—Zimbabwe
        Mashona
    — **Kings and rulers**
Karanis (Egypt) *(Not Subd Geog)*
    [DT73.K33]
    BT Cities and towns, Ruined, extinct, etc.
        —Egypt
        Egypt—Antiquities
Karankawa Indians
    [E99.K26]
    UF Carancahua Indians
        Clamcoët Indians
        Karankawan Indians
    BT Indians of North America
Karankawan Indians
    USE Karankawa Indians
Karapana language (Tucanan)
    USE Carapana language (Tucanan)
Karapapaks (Turkic people)
    [DS27.54]
    BT Turks
Kāṟāra (Bangladesh people)
    [DS393.83.K37]
    BT Ethnology—Bangladesh
Karasawa Site (Japan) *(Not Subd Geog)*
    BT Japan—Antiquities
Karastoīanov family *(Not Subd Geog)*
Karasujō (Okayama-shi, Japan)
    USE Okayamajō (Okayama-shi, Japan)
Karat camera
    [TR263.K]
Karata language
    BT Avaric language
Karatau (Kazakh S.S.R.)
    USE Kara-Tau (Kazakh S.S.R.)
Karatchai language
    USE Karachay-Balkar language
Karate
    [GV1114.3]
    UF Feet Kune Do
        Soo bahk do
        Tae kwon do
        Tang soo do

    BT Hand-to-hand fighting, Oriental
        Judo
        Kung fu
    NT Sai
    — **Accidents and injuries**
        UF Karate—Injuries
    — Injuries
        USE Karate—Accidents and injuries
    — **Rules**
        [GV1114.3]
Karate for children *(May Subd Geog)*
    [GV1114.32]
    BT Sports for children
Karate in motion-pictures
    BT Moving-pictures
Karate weapons
    USE Martial arts weapons
Karateists
    USE Martial artists
Karateka
    USE Martial artists
Karatsu pottery
    UF Kokaratsu pottery
        Pottery, Karatsu
    BT Pottery, Japanese
    NT Agano pottery
        Takatori pottery
Karavanke (Austia and Slovenia)
    USE Karawanken (Austria and Slovenia)
Karavas
    BT Caste—Sri Lanka
Karawa language (Australia)
    USE Garawa language
Karawanken (Austria and Slovenia)
    UF Caravanca Mons (Austria and
        Slovenia)
        Caravanche (Austria and Slovenia)
        Karavanke (Austia and Slovenia)
        Karawanken Mountains (Austria and
        Slovenia)
    BT Alps, Eastern
        Mountains—Austria
        Mountains—Yugoslavia
Karawanken Mountains (Austria and Slovenia)
    USE Karawanken (Austria and Slovenia)
Karay-a language
    USE Kinaray-a language
Karbalā', Iraq, Battle of, 680, in literature
Karbalā' (Iraq), Battle of, 680
    BT Ḥusayn ibn 'Alī, d. 680—Death and
        burial
    — **Anniversaries, etc.**
        NT Tenth of Muḥarram
Karbi language
    USE Mikir language
Karbis (Indic people)
    [DS432.K198]
    BT Ethnology—India
Karcher family
    USE Karriker family
Karchi Island (Greece)
    USE Khalki Island (Greece)
Kardon camera
    [TR263.K]
    BT Leica camera
Kare language
    [PL8374.K33]
    UF Akare language
        Bakare language
        Kari language
    BT Bantu languages
Kare language (Sudan)
    USE Toposa language
Kareius
    [QL638.P7]
    BT Pleuronectidae
Kareius bicoloratus
    [QL638.P7]
Karek family
    USE Carrick family

Karelian arts
  USE Arts, Karelian
Karelian authors
  USE Authors, Karelian
Karelian epic poetry
  USE Epic poetry, Karelian
Karelian folk dancing
  USE Folk dancing, Karelian
Karelian folk literature
  USE Folk literature, Karelian
Karelian folk poetry
  USE Folk poetry, Karelian
Karelian folk-songs
  USE Folk-songs, Karelian
Karelian Isthmus (R.S.F.S.R.)
  UF Karelskanäset (R.S.F.S.R.)
      Karel'skiĭ peresheek (R.S.F.S.R.)
      Karel'skiy peresheyek (R.S.F.S.R.)
      Karjalankannas (R.S.F.S.R.)
  BT Isthmuses—Russian S.F.S.R.
Karelian language
  ₍PH501-9₎
  UF Carelian language
  BT Baltic-Finnic languages
  NT Ludic dialect
      Olonets dialect
Karelian literature *(May Subd Geog)*
  ₍PH508.5-PH508.9 (Collections)₎
  ₍PH508 (History)₎
  NT Folk literature, Karelian
Karelian poetry *(May Subd Geog)*
  NT Epic poetry, Karelian
      Folk poetry, Karelian
Karelian proverbs
  USE Proverbs, Karelian
Karelian riddles
  USE Riddles, Karelian
Karelians *(May Subd Geog)*
  ₍DK34.K3 (Soviet Union)₎
  ₍DK511.K18 (Karelian A.S.S.R.)₎
  BT Ethnology—Soviet Union
      Finno-Ugrians
Karell family
  USE Carroll family
Karel'skaiā A.S.S.R. (R.S.F.S.R.)
  — History
  — —Revolution of 1905
  — —Revolution, 1917-1921
Karelskanäset (R.S.F.S.R.)
  USE Karelian Isthmus (R.S.F.S.R.)
Karel'skiĭ peresheek (R.S.F.S.R.)
  USE Karelian Isthmus (R.S.F.S.R.)
Karel'skiy peresheyek (R.S.F.S.R.)
  USE Karelian Isthmus (R.S.F.S.R.)
Karen language
  ₍PL4051-4₎
  UF Pgho dialect
      Pwo dialect
      Sho dialect
  NT Pwo Karen dialect
      Sgaw Karen dialect
Karens
  ₍DS432.K2₎
  BT Ethnology—Asia, Southeastern
  RT Lamet (Tribe)
  NT Kayah (Southeast Asian people)
      Missions to Karens
  — Ethnic identity
Kareol (Aerdenhout, Netherlands)
  BT Dwellings—Netherlands
Karez
  USE Qanat
Kargyudpa
  USE Bka'-rgyud-pa (Sect)
Karhade Vainyas
  ₍DS432.K25₎
  UF Vainyas, Karhade
  BT Brahmans
      Caste—India
      Ethnology—India

Kari language
  USE Kare language
Karich family
  USE Carrick family
Karick family
  USE Carrick family
Karicofe family
  USE Kiracofe family
Karigites
  USE Kharijites
Karijona Indians
  USE Carijona Indians
Karik family
  USE Carrick family
Kariker family
  USE Karriker family
Karimojong (African people)
  USE Karamojong (African people)
Karimojong language
  USE Karamojong language
Karimui language
  USE Daribi language
Karinya Indians
  USE Carib Indians
Kariot Island (Greece)
  USE Ikaria Island (Greece)
Karipuna Creole dialect *(May Subd Geog)*
  BT Brazil—Languages
      Creole dialects, French—Brazil
Kariri (Brazil)
  UF Cariri (Brazil)
      Vale do Cariri (Brazil)
Kariri Indians
  ₍F2520.1.K (Brazil)₎
  UF Cariri Indians
      Kiriri Indians
  BT Indians of South America
Kariri language
  ₍PM6286-9₎
  UF Cariri language
      Kiriri language
  BT Indians of South America—Languages
Käris
  USE Qanat
Kariwano Kaidō (Japan) *(Not Subd Geog)*
  BT Roads—Japan
Kariyajō (Akō-shi, Japan)
  USE Akōjō (Akō-shi, Japan)
Kariz
  USE Qanat
Karjalankannas (R.S.F.S.R.)
  USE Karelian Isthmus (R.S.F.S.R.)
Karkaker family
  USE Karriker family
Karker family
  USE Karriker family
Karkinorhynchidae
  ₍QL391.P7₎
  BT Neorhabdocoela
  NT Karkinorhynchus
Karkinorhynchus
  ₍QL391.P7₎
  BT Karkinorhynchidae
Karkinorhynchus tetragnathus
  ₍QL391.P7₎
Karkom Mountain (Israel) *(Not Subd Geog)*
  UF Geshur Mountain (Israel)
      Har Geshur (Israel)
      Har Karkom (Israel)
      'Idayd Mountain (Israel)
      'Ideid Mountain (Israel)
      Jebel 'Idayd (Israel)
      Jebel 'Ideid (Israel)
  BT Mountains—Israel
Karkonoski National Park (Poland)
  USE Karkonoski Park Narodowy (Poland)
Karkonoski Park Narodowy (Poland)
  UF Karkonoski National Park (Poland)
      Karkonosze National Park (Poland)
  BT National parks and reserves—Poland

Karkonosze (Czechoslovakia and Poland)
  USE Krkonoše (Czechoslovakia and Poland)
Karkonosze National Park (Poland)
  USE Karkonoski Park Narodowy (Poland)
Karl-Ernst-Osthaus-Preis
  ₍N396₎
  BT Art—Competitions
Karl family
  USE Carl family
Karl Fischer technique
  UF Karl Fischer titration
      Titration, Karl Fischer
  BT Volumetric analysis
      Water—Analysis
Karl Fischer titration
  USE Karl Fischer technique
Karl-Hofer-Preis
  BT Arts—Competitions
      Rewards (Prizes, etc.)—Germany
        (West)
Karl-Theodor-Strasse (Hamburg, Germany)
  BT Streets—Germany (West)
Karlburg (Bratislava, Czechoslovakia)
  USE Rusovce (Bratislava, Czechoslovakia)
Karle family
  USE Carl family
Karlfeldt family *(Not Subd Geog)*
Karlidag (Cyprus)
  USE Troodos Mountains (Cyprus)
Karlö (Finland)
  USE Hailuoto Island (Finland)
Karlowitz, Peace of, 1699
  USE Sremski Karlovci, Peace of, 1699
Karls-Platz (Vienna, Austria)
  USE Karlsplatz (Vienna, Austria)
Karlsbad salt
  ₍RK858.K2₎
Karlsöarna (Sweden)
  BT Islands—Sweden
Karlsplatz (Vienna, Austria)
  UF Karls-Platz (Vienna, Austria)
  BT Plazas—Austria
Karlspreis
  UF Internationale Karlspreis der Stadt
        Aachen
      Premio Carlomagno
  BT Rewards (Prizes, etc.)—Germany
        (West)
Karlsruhe Castle (Karlsruhe, Germany)
  USE Schloss Karlsruhe (Karlsruhe,
        Germany)
Karlström family *(Not Subd Geog)*
  UF Carlström family
Karlugh
  USE Karluks
Karluk Turkic languages
  USE Turkic languages, Southeast
Karluks
  UF Karlugh
      Khallukh
      Kharlukh
      Ko-lo-lu
      Uzbegs-Karluks
  BT Ethnology—Asia, Central
      Turks
Karma
  ₍BL2015.K3₎
  BT Hinduism
      Reincarnation
      Theosophy
  RT Anthroposophy
  NT Pretas (Buddhism)
Karma (Sect)
  USE Kar-ma-pa (Sect)
Karma-pa (Sect)
  USE Kar-ma-pa (Sect)
Karma yoga
  USE Yoga, Karma
Kármán equations
  USE Von Kármán equations

Karmann Ghia automobile
  BT Volkswagen automobile
Karmathians
  ₍BP195.K3₎
  UF Carmathians
      Qarmathians
Karmer family
  USE Kerner family
Ḳarmi family
  USE Carmi family
Karṇa (Hindu mythology)
  BT Mythology, Hindu
Karnata dynasty, ca. 1570-ca. 1646
  USE Āravīḍu dynasty, ca. 1570-ca. 1646
Karnata dynasty of Mithila and Nepal, ca. 1097-1325 *(Not Subd Geog)*
  UF Karnatas of Mithila and Nepal, ca. 1097-1325
  BT Nepal—History—To 1768
Karnatak (India)
  USE Carnatic (India)
Karnatas of Mithila and Nepal, ca. 1097-1325
  USE Karnata dynasty of Mithila and Nepal, ca. 1097-1325
Karnatic (India)
  USE Carnatic (India)
Karnatic music
  USE Music, Karnatic
Karnatik (India)
  USE Carnatic (India)
Karner family
  USE Kerner family
Karnische Alpen (Italy and Austria)
  USE Carnic Alps (Italy and Austria)
Karns family
  USE Carnes family
Karo-Batak
  BT Batak
      Ethnology—Indonesia
  NT Missions to Karo-Batak
Karo-Batak decoration and ornament
  USE Decoration and ornament, Karo-Batak
Karo-Batak dialect
  ₍PL5334₎
  UF Karo dialect (Sumatra)
  BT Batak language
  NT Alas dialect
Karo-Batak folk-songs
  USE Folk-songs, Karo-Batak
Karo-Batak literature *(May Subd Geog)*
Karo-Batak poetry *(May Subd Geog)*
Karo dialect (Sumatra)
  USE Karo-Batak dialect
Karok Indians
  ₍E99.K25₎
  BT Indians of North America
Karok language
  ₍PM1461₎
Karoo, Great (South Africa)
  USE Great Karroo (South Africa)
Karoo, Northern (South Africa)
  USE Northern Karroo (South Africa)
Karoo, Upper (South Africa)
  USE Northern Karroo (South Africa)
Karpas Peninsula (Cyprus)
  USE Karpass Peninsula (Cyprus)
Karpass Peninsula (Cyprus)
  (Not Subd Geog)
  UF Carpas Peninsula (Cyprus)
      Karpas Peninsula (Cyprus)
  BT Peninsulas—Cyprus
Karpathos Island (Greece)
  UF Carpathos Island (Greece)
      Carpathus Island (Greece)
      Nísos Kárpathos (Greece)
      Scarpanto Island (Greece)
  BT Dodecanese
      Islands—Greece
Karr family
  USE Carr family

Karramites
  UF Karrāmīyah
  BT Islamic sects
Karrāmīyah
  USE Karramites
Karrawar language
  USE Garawa language
Karre family
  USE Carr family
Karré language
  BT Adamawa languages
      Chad—Languages
Karrebæk Fjord, Denmark
Karri eucalyptus
  USE Eucalyptus diversicolor
Karri tree
  USE Paulownia tomentosa
Karrick family
  USE Carrick family
Karriker family *(Not Subd Geog)*
  UF Caraker family
      Cariker family
      Carkar family
      Carker family
      Carriker family
      Karcher family
      Kariker family
      Karkaker family
      Karker family
      Kearker family
      Kerker family
      Kiker family
Karroo, Great (South Africa)
  USE Great Karroo (South Africa)
Karroo, Northern (South Africa)
  USE Northern Karroo (South Africa)
Karskoe more
  USE Kara Sea
Karskoye more
  USE Kara Sea
Karst (Yugoslavia and Italy)
  UF Carso (Yugoslavia and Italy)
      Dinaric Karst (Yugoslavia and Italy)
      Kras (Yugoslavia and Italy)
  BT Karst—Italy
      Karst—Yugoslavia
      Plateaus—Italy
      Plateaus—Yugoslavia
Karst *(May Subd Geog)*
  ₍GB601-8₎
  BT Erosion
  NT Hydrology, Karst
      Polje (Geomorphology)
      Sinkholes
  — Czechoslovakia
      NT Český kras (Czechoslovakia)
  — Italy
      NT Karst (Yugoslavia and Italy)
  — Japan
      NT Akiyoshi Plateau (Japan)
          Hirao Plateau (Japan)
  — Yugoslavia
      NT Karst (Yugoslavia and Italy)
Karst bridge
  USE Natural bridges
Karst hydrology
  USE Hydrology, Karst
Kart Hadasht (Ancient city)
  USE Carthage (Ancient city)
Kart racing
  USE Karting
Kartangarurru (Australian people)
  BT Australian aborigines
      Ethnology—Australia
Kartause Cella Salutis in art
  NT Votivbild Kartause Cella Salutis zu Tückelhausen (Panel painting)
Karteia (Ancient city)
  USE Carteia (Ancient city)

Karter family *(Not Subd Geog)*
  UF Kaeter family
      Käter family
  RT Carter family
Karthābhajā
  ₍BL1245.K29₎
  BT Hindu sects
Karthveli
  USE Georgians (Transcaucasians)
Karting *(May Subd Geog)*
  ₍GV1029.5₎
  UF Go-cart racing
      Go-Kart racing
      Gocart racing
      Kart racing
  BT Automobile racing
  NT Karts (Midget cars)
Kartneer family
  USE Kerner family
Kartner family
  USE Kerner family
Karts (Midget cars)
  ₍TL236.5₎
  UF Automobiles, Midget
      Go-Karts (Midget cars)
      Midget cars
  BT Automobiles, Racing
      Karting
Kārttikeya (Hindu deity) *(May Subd Geog)*
  ₍BL1225.K38₎
  UF Kumāra (Hindu deity)
      Skanda (Hindu deity)
  BT Gods, Hindu
Kartvelian languages
  UF South Caucasian languages
  BT Caucasian languages
  NT Georgian language
      Laz language
      Mingrelian language
      Svan language
Karubeike Nishi Iseki (Kishiwada-shi, Japan)
  USE Karubeike Nishi Site (Kishiwada-shi, Japan)
Karubeike Nishi Site (Kishiwada-shi, Japan) *(Not Subd Geog)*
  UF Karubeike Nishi Iseki (Kishiwada-shi, Japan)
  BT Japan—Antiquities
Karumāri (Hindu deity)
  ₍BL1225.K39₎
  BT Gods, Hindu
Karumari Amman (Hindu deity)
  BT Gods, Hindu
      Parvati (Hindu deity)
Karun (Ancient city)
  USE Susa (Ancient city)
Karunā
  USE Compassion (Buddhism)
Karuta (Game)
  USE Utagaruta (Game)
Karutana Indians
  USE Baniva Indians
Karwa language
  USE Garawa language
Karwinskia
  ₍QK495.R45 (Botany)₎
  UF Coyotillo
  BT Rhamnaceae
Karwinskia humboldtiana
  ₍QK495.R45 (Botany)₎
  ₍QP981.K37 (Experimental pharmacology)₎
  UF Humboldt coyotillo
  BT Poisonous plants
Karya Pudja Pantja Wali Krama
Karyokinesis
  ₍QH605₎
  UF Caryocinesis
      Nuclear division (Cytology)
  BT Biology
      Cell division

Karyokinesis *(Continued)*
  RT Chromosomes
       Meiosis
  NT Centrosomes
       Mitosis
Karyometry
  ₍QH595₎
  UF Nuclear size measurements
  BT Cell nuclei
       Cytology—Technique
       Histology—Technique
Karyotypes *(May Subd Geog)*
  BT Chromosomes
       Cytotaxonomy
       Genetics
  RT Chromosome abnormalities
  NT Medical genetics—Technique
       Plant karyotypes
Karzbach-Gebirge (Poland)
  USE Kaczawa Mountains (Poland)
Kasa *(May Subd Geog)*
  BT Korean poetry
  — **Women authors**
Kasaba dialect
  UF Kasava dialect
  BT Tamil language
Kasahara family *(Not Subd Geog)*
Kasai family *(Not Subd Geog)*
Kasai River (Angola and Zaire)
  UF Cassai River (Angola and Zaire)
       Kassai River (Angola and Zaire)
  BT Rivers—Angola
       Rivers—Zaire
Kasamai Iseki (Kanazawa-shi, Japan)
  USE Kasamai Site (Kanazawa-shi, Japan)
Kasamai Site (Kanazawa-shi, Japan)
  (Not Subd Geog)
  UF Kasamai Iseki (Kanazawa-shi, Japan)
  BT Japan—Antiquities
Kasava dialect
  USE Kasaba dialect
Kasem dialect
  USE Kasena dialect
Kasena (African people)
  ₍DT510.42₎
  BT Ethnology—Ghana
Kasena dialect
  ₍PL8223.G995K₎
  UF Kasem dialect
       Kassena dialect
  BT Gurunsi dialects
  NT Nunuma dialect
Käsermann family
  USE Kasserman family
Kashaya Indians
  BT Indians of North America
       Pomo Indians
Kashaya language
  ₍PM1463₎
Kasher food
  USE Kosher food
Kasher food industry
  USE Kosher food industry
Kasher restaurants
  USE Kosher restaurants
Kashering of utensils
  ₍BM710₎
  UF Koshering of utensils
       Utensils, Kashering of
  BT Implements, utensils, etc.
       Jews—Dietary laws
Kashgar-Yarkend dialect
  USE Uighur language
Kashimamae Iseki (Abiko-shi, Japan)
  USE Kashimamae Site (Abiko-shi, Japan)
Kashimamae Site (Abiko-shi, Japan)
  (Not Subd Geog)
  UF Kashimamae Iseki (Abiko-shi, Japan)
  BT Japan—Antiquities
Kashinaua Indians
  USE Cashinawa Indians

Kashinaua language
  USE Cashinawa language
Kashinawa language
  USE Cashinawa language
Kashkai tribe
  UF Qashqai tribe
  BT Ethnology—Iran
       Oghuz
Kashmir, Vale of (India) *(Not Subd Geog)*
  UF Kashmir Valley (India)
       Vale of Kashmir (India)
  BT Valleys—India
Kashmir Śaivism *(May Subd Geog)*
  ₍BL1281.15-BL1281.1592₎
  UF Kashmir Shaivism
       Kashmir Shivaism
       Kashmir Sivaism
       Kasmir Saivism
       Kasmir Shaivism
       Śaivism, Kashmir
       Trika school
  BT Sivaism
Kashmir Shaivism
  USE Kashmir Śaivism
Kashmir Shivaism
  USE Kashmir Śaivism
Kashmir Sivaism
  USE Kashmir Śaivism
Kashmir Valley (India)
  USE Kashmir, Vale of (India)
Kashmir War, 1947-1949
  USE India-Pakistan Conflict, 1947-1949
Kashmiri drama *(May Subd Geog)*
  NT One-act plays, Kashmiri
Kashmiri language
  ₍PK7021-9₎
  BT Indo-Aryan languages, Modern
  — **Alphabet**
       NT Sarada alphabet
Kashmiri literature
  ₍PK7031-7₎
Kashmiri one-act plays
  USE One-act plays, Kashmiri
Kashmiri philology
Kashmiri poetry *(May Subd Geog)*
Kashmiri poets
  USE Poets, Kashmiri
Kashmiri proverbs
  USE Proverbs, Kashmiri
Kashruth, Laws of
  USE Jews—Dietary laws
Kashubes *(May Subd Geog)*
  ₍DK4600.K34₎
  UF Kassubes
  BT Ethnology—Poland
Kashubian folk-songs
  USE Folk-songs, Kashubian
Kashubian language
  ₍PG7901-5₎
  UF Cashubian language
       Kašube language
  BT Lechitic languages
       Slavic languages, Western
  NT Slovincian dialect
Kashubian literature *(May Subd Geog)*
  ₍PG7901-7904₎
  UF Cassubian literature
       Casubian literature
       Kassubian literature
       Kasubian literature
       Kaszubian literature
  BT Slavic literature, Western
Kashubian philology *(May Subd Geog)*
  ₍PG7901₎
Kashubian poetry *(May Subd Geog)*
Kashubian poets
  USE Poets, Kashubian
Kasidas
  USE Qasidas
Kasidoridae
  USE Gibberichthyidae

Kasidoroidae
  USE Gibberichthyidae
Kaska Indians
  ₍E99.K₎
  BT Athapascan Indians
       Indians of North America
       Nahane Indians
Kaskans
  ₍DS59.K3₎
  BT Ethnology—Turkey
       Hittites
Kaskaskia Indians
  ₍E99.K264₎
  BT Illinois Indians
       Indians of North America
  — **Antiquities**
  — **Missions**
Kaskaskia River (Ill.)
  BT Rivers—Illinois
  NT Shelbyville, Lake (Ill.)
Kasli cast-iron pavilion (Ironwork)
  USE Kaslinskiĭ chugunnyĭ pavil'on
       (Ironwork)
Kaslinskiĭ chugunnyĭ pavil'on (Ironwork)
  UF Kasli cast-iron pavilion (Ironwork)
  BT Ironwork—Russian S.F.S.R.
Kasmere Lake (Man.)
  BT Lakes—Manitoba
Kasmir Saivism
  USE Kashmir Śaivism
Kasmir Shaivism
  USE Kashmir Śaivism
Kasos Island (Greece)
  UF Caso Island (Greece)
       Casus Island (Greece)
       Nísos Kásos (Greece)
  BT Dodecanese
       Islands—Greece
Kaspar family
  USE Casper family
Kasper family
  USE Casper family
Kaspiĭskoe more
  USE Caspian Sea
Kaspiyskoye more
  USE Caspian Sea
Kassai River (Angola and Zaire)
  USE Kasai River (Angola and Zaire)
Kassena dialect
  USE Kasena dialect
Kassener family
  USE Kastner family
Kasserman family *(Not Subd Geog)*
  UF Käsermann family
Kassina *(May Subd Geog)*
  ₍QL668.E274₎
  UF Cassina (Amphibians)
       Hylambates
       Rothschildia
  BT Rhacophoridae
  NT Kassina ingeri
Kassina ingeri
  ₍QL668.E274₎
  BT Kassina
Kassiope (Mythical queen)
  USE Cassiope (Mythical queen)
Kassiopeia (Mythical queen)
  USE Cassiope (Mythical queen)
Kassites
  ₍DS73.4₎
Kassner family
  USE Kastner family
Kassr-el-Kebir, Battle of, 1578
  ₍DP614₎
  ₍DT322₎
  BT Morocco—History—1516-1830
Kassubes
  USE Kashubes
Kassubia (Poland)
  USE Kaszuby (Poland)

Kassubian literature
USE Kashubian literature
Kastanas Site (Greece) *(Not Subd Geog)*
UF Kastania Site (Greece)
BT Greece—Antiquities
Kastania Site (Greece)
USE Kastanas Site (Greece)
Kastbierg family *(Not Subd Geog)*
Kaštela Bay (Croatia)
BT Bays—Yugoslavia
Kastellholmen (Stockholm, Sweden)
(Not Subd Geog)
UF Stockholm (Sweden). Kastellholmen
Kastellorizo Island (Greece)
[DF901.K29]
UF Castellorizo Island (Greece)
Castelrosso Island (Greece)
Kastellorizon Island (Greece)
Megísti (Greece)
Nísos Megisti (Greece)
BT Dodecanese
Islands—Greece
Kastellorizon Island (Greece)
USE Kastellorizo Island (Greece)
Kasten family
USE Kastner family
Kaster family
USE Kastner family
Kastl family *(Not Subd Geog)*
Kastner family *(Not Subd Geog)*
UF Casner family
Cassner family
Castner family
Chostner family
Costner family
Kassener family
Kassner family
Kasten family
Kaster family
Kestner family
RT Castor family
Kástro (Antiparos Island, Greece)
BT Castles—Greece
Kastron Island (Greece)
USE Chios Island (Greece)
Kastron Khostion (Ancient city)
USE Chorsiai (Ancient city)
Kašube language
USE Kashubian language
Kasubian literature
USE Kashubian literature
Kasuga Valley (Japan)
UF Kasugadani (Japan)
BT Valleys—Japan
Kasugadani (Japan)
USE Kasuga Valley (Japan)
Kasugayama Castle (Jōetsu-shi, Japan)
USE Kasugayamajō (Jōetsu-shi, Japan)
Kasugayama Yōgai (Jōetsu-shi, Japan)
USE Kasugayamajō (Jōetsu-shi, Japan)
Kasugayamajō (Jōetsu-shi, Japan)
UF Hachigaminejō (Jōetsu-shi, Japan)
Kasugayama Castle (Jōetsu-shi, Japan)
Kasugayama Yōgai (Jōetsu-shi, Japan)
BT Castles—Japan
Kasumidai Iseki (Ōme-shi, Japan)
USE Kasumidai Site (Ōme-shi, Japan)
Kasumidai Site (Ōme-shi, Japan)
UF Kasumidai Iseki (Ōme-shi, Japan)
BT Japan—Antiquities
Kasumiga Bay (Japan)
USE Kasumigaura (Japan)
Kasumigajō (Yamagata-shi, Japan)
USE Yamagatajō (Yamagata-shi, Japan)
Kasumigaura (Japan)
UF Kasumiga Bay (Japan)
Nishi-ura (Japan)
BT Lakes—Japan
Kaszubian literature
USE Kashubian literature

Kaszuby (Poland)
UF Kassubia (Poland)
Pojezierze Kaszubskie (Poland)
Kat
USE Qat
Kataba Indians
USE Catawba Indians
Katabiramine Iseki (Yokohama-shi, Japan)
USE Katabiramine Site (Yokohama-shi, Japan)
Katabiramine Site (Yokohama-shi, Japan)
(Not Subd Geog)
UF Katabiramine Iseki (Yokohama-shi, Japan)
BT Japan—Antiquities
Katabu
USE Killekyatha
Katahdin, Mount (Me.)
UF Mount Katahdin (Me.)
Mount Ktaadn (Me.)
BT Mountains—Maine
Kataka Indians
USE Kiowa Apache Indians
Katal (Indic people)
USE Noatia (Indic people)
Katanga (Secessionist government, 1960-1963)
USE Shaba (Zaire)
Katanga (Zaire)
USE Shaba (Zaire)
Katanga language
USE Luba-Katanga language
Katanganese Invasion, Zaire, 1977
USE Zaire—History—Shaba Invasion, 1977
Katans
USE Ulladans
Kataribe *(May Subd Geog)*
BT Oral tradition—Japan
Katarimono
BT Monologues with music
Music—Japan
NT Sekkyō jōruri
Katathermometer
BT Thermometers and thermometry
Katatonia
USE Catatonia
Katayama disease
USE Schistosomiasis
Katchokue language
USE Chokwe language
Katchung, Oil of
USE Peanut oil
Katcinas
[E99.K]
UF Kachinas
BT Dolls—Religious aspects
Indians of North America—Dolls
Indians of North America—Religion and mythology
Kate family
USE Cates family
Kate language
BT Finisterre-Huon languages
Katekelayi Hill (Zaire) *(Not Subd Geog)*
BT Mountains—Zaire
Katelin family
USE Catlin family
Käter family
USE Karter family
Kates family
USE Cates family
Kathak (Dance)
[GV1796.K38]
BT Dancing—India
Kathakali
[PN2884.5.K36]
Kathakali plays *(May Subd Geog)*
BT Malayalam drama
Katharine (Name)
USE Katherine (Name)
Katharyn (Name)
USE Katherine (Name)

Kathcart family
USE Cathcart family
Käthe-Kollwitz-Preis
BT Art—Germany (East)—Awards
Katherine (Name)
UF Catharine (Name)
Catherine (Name)
Katharine (Name)
Katharyn (Name)
Kathryn (Name)
Katherman family
USE Ketterman family
Kathlamet dialect
USE Cathlamet dialect
Kathmandu Valley (Nepal)
(Not Subd Geog)
UF Central Nepal Valley (Nepal)
Central Valley (Nepal)
Katmandu Valley (Nepal)
Nepal Valley (Nepal)
BT Valleys—Nepal
Kathryn (Name)
USE Katherine (Name)
Kati language
USE Bashgali language
Katie Woodencloak (Legendary character)
USE Cinderella (Legendary character)
Katingan language *(May Subd Geog)*
BT Indonesia—Languages
Malayan languages
Katio Indians
USE Catio Indians
Katio language
USE Catio language
Katlun family
USE Catlin family
Katlyn family
USE Catlin family
Katmai National Monument (Alaska)
USE Katmai National Park and Preserve (Alaska)
Katmai National Park and Preserve (Alaska)
(Not Subd Geog)
UF Katmai National Monument (Alaska)
BT National parks and reserves—Alaska
Katmandu Valley (Nepal)
USE Kathmandu Valley (Nepal)
Katō family *(Not Subd Geog)*
Kato Indians
[E99.K]
BT Athapascan Indians
Indians of North America
Kato language
[PM1481]
RT Athapascan languages
Katōbushi
BT Jōruri
Monologues with music (Shamisen)
Katori family *(Not Subd Geog)*
Kats family
USE Katz family
Katsch family *(Not Subd Geog)*
UF Von Katsch family
RT Katz family
Katsukawa School
BT Color prints, Japanese—Edo period, 1600-1868
Painting, Japanese—Edo period, 1600-1868
Ukiyoe
Katsura Imperial Villa (Kyoto, Japan)
USE Katsura Rikyū (Kyoto, Japan)
Katsura Rikyū (Kyoto, Japan)
UF Katsura Imperial Villa (Kyoto, Japan)
BT Palaces—Japan
Suburban homes—Japan
Katsusaka Iseki (Sagamihara-shi, Japan)
USE Katsusaka Site (Sagamihara-shi, Japan)

Katsusaka Site (Sagamihara-shi, Japan)
(Not Subd Geog)
UF Katsusaka Iseki (Sagamihara-shi, Japan)
BT Japan—Antiquities

Katsushika School
UF Hokusai School
BT Color prints, Japanese—Edo period, 1600-1868
Painting, Japanese—Edo period, 1600-1868
Ukiyoe

Katsuwonidae
USE Scombridae

Katsuwonus pelamis
USE Skipjack tuna

Katsuyamatate Ato (Kaminokuni-ch-o, Japan)
USE Katsuyamatate Site (Kaminokuni-ch-o, Japan)

Katsuyamatate Site (Kaminokuni-ch-o, Japan)
UF Katsuyamatate Ato (Kaminokuni-ch-o, Japan)
Wakitate Ato (Kaminokuni-ch-o, Japan)
BT Japan—Antiquities

Katt family
USE Katz family

Kattalans
USE Ulladans

Kattang language
[PL7101.K]
UF Kutthung language
BT Australia—Languages
Australian languages

Kattegat (Denmark and Sweden)
UF Cattegat (Denmark and Sweden)
BT Straits—Denmark
Straits—Sweden

Kattermann family
USE Ketterman family

Katts family
USE Katz family

Katu language
[PL4351.K38]
UF Attouat language
Kao language
Khat language
Ta River Van Kieu language
Teu language
Thap language
BT Mon-Khmer languages

Katydids
[QL508.L8]
BT Orthoptera
NT Scudderia

Katyn Forest Massacre, 1940
[D804.S65]
BT World War, 1939-1945—Atrocities

Katz family (Not Subd Geog)
UF Catt family
Catts family
Kats family
Katt family
Katts family
RT Katsch family

Katzbachgebirge (Poland)
USE Kaczawa Mountains (Poland)

Kauai (Hawaii)
BT Hawaii
Islands—Hawaii

Kauffman family (Not Subd Geog)
UF Cauffman family
Caufman family
Caughman family
Coafman family
Coffman family
Coffmon family
Cofman family
Coufman family
Coughman family
Cowfman family
Kauffmann family
Kaufman family
Kaufmann family

Kauffmann family
USE Kauffman family

Kaufman family
USE Kauffman family

Kaufmann family
USE Kauffman family

Kaufmann House (Pa.)
USE Fallingwater (Pa.)

Kaugel language
USE Gawigl language

Kauil language
USE Gawigl language

Kaulas
[BL1245.K3]
UF Kaulikas
Kulinas
BT Hindu sects

Kaulbach family (Not Subd Geog)
UF Kaulback family

Kaulback family
USE Kaulbach family

Kaulikas
USE Kaulas

Kaulu (Indic people)
USE Kulu (Indic people)

Kaunde (African people)
USE Kaonde (African people)

Kaupang Site (Norway)
BT Norway—Antiquities

Kaupichthys
[QL638.X45]
BT Xenocongridae

Kaupichthys diodontus
[QL638.X45]

Kaura language
USE Kaurna language

Kaura language (Papua New Guinea)
USE Purari language

Kauri
UF New Zealand kauri

Kauri gum
[RS165.K2 (Pharmacy)]

Kauri pines
USE Agathis

Kaurna (Australian people)
BT Australian aborigines

Kaurna language
[PL7101.K38]
UF Coorna language
Gauna language
Gaurna language
Gawurna language
Kaura language
Kawurna language
BT Australia—Languages
Australian languages

Kaus language
USE Coos language

Kausambi (City)
[DS486.K37]
UF Kaushambi (City)
Kosambi (City)
BT Cities and towns, Ruined, extinct, etc.—India

Kaushambi (City)
USE Kausambi (City)

Kautsa (Hindu mythology)
BT Mahābhārata—Biography
Mythology, Hindu

Kautunigan Lake (Man.)
BT Lakes—Manitoba

Kautz-Wilson Raid, Va., 1864
USE Wilson-Kautz Raid, Va., 1864

Kauya Iseki (Kisakata-machi, Japan)
USE Kauya Site (Kisakata-machi, Japan)

Kauya Site (Kisakata-machi, Japan)
(Not Subd Geog)
UF Kauya Iseki (Kisakata-machi, Japan)
BT Japan—Antiquities

Kavafis family
USE Kavaphēs family

Kavanagh family
USE Cavanaugh family

Kavanaugh family
USE Cavanaugh family

Kavaphēs family (Not Subd Geog)
UF Cavafis family
Cavafy family
Kabaphēs family
Kavafis family

Kaveri River (India)
USE Cauvery River (India)

Kavi language
USE Kawi language

Kavirondo (African people)
[DT429]
[DT434.E2 (East Africa Protectorate)]
UF Kavirondo (Bantu people)
BT Bantus
NT Gisu (African people)

Kavirondo (Bantu people)
USE Kavirondo (African people)

Kavirondo (Nilotic people)
USE Luo (African people)

Kavirondo language, Nilotic
USE Luo language (Kenya and Tanzania)

Kavkazskiĭ gosudarstvennyĭ zapovednik (R.S.F.S.R.)
USE Kavkazskiĭ zapovednik (R.S.F.S.R.)

Kavkazskiĭ zapovednik (R.S.F.S.R.)
UF Caucasian Preserve (R.S.F.S.R.)
Kavkazskiĭ gosudarstvennyĭ zapovednik (R.S.F.S.R.)
Kavkazskiy gosudarstvennyy zapovednik (R.S.F.S.R.)
Kavkazskiy zapovednik (R.S.F.S.R.)
BT National parks and reserves—Russian S.F.S.R.

Kavkazskiy gosudarstvennyy zapovednik (R.S.F.S.R.)
USE Kavkazskiĭ zapovednik (R.S.F.S.R.)

Kavkazskiy zapovednik (R.S.F.S.R.)
USE Kavkazskiĭ zapovednik (R.S.F.S.R.)

Kaw Indians
USE Kansa Indians

Kaw Lake (Okla.)
BT Lakes—Oklahoma
Reservoirs—Oklahoma

Kaw language
[PL4001.K35]
UF Akha language
Ekaw language

Kaw people
UF Akha people
Hka-kaw

Kaw River (Kan.)
USE Kansas River (Kan.)

Kawabata family (Not Subd Geog)

Kawagoe Castle (Kawagoe-shi, Japan)
USE Kawagoejō (Kawagoe-shi, Japan)

Kawagoe family (Not Subd Geog)

Kawagoejō (Kawagoe-shi, Japan)
UF Hatsukarijō (Kawagoe-shi, Japan)
Kawagoe Castle (Kawagoe-shi, Japan)
Kirikakujō (Kawagoe-shi, Japan)
BT Castles—Japan

Kawaguchi family (Not Subd Geog)
Kawaguchi-ko (Japan)
  USE Kawaguchi Lake (Japan)
Kawaguchi Lake (Japan)
  UF Kawaguchi-ko (Japan)
  BT Lakes—Japan
Kawaiisu Indians
  [E99.K269]
  BT Indians of North America
    Indians of North America—California
    Numic Indians
Kawaiisu language
  [PM1487]
  BT Numic languages
Kawakami Iseki (Minakami-machi, Japan)
  USE Kawakami Site (Minakami-machi, Japan)
Kawakami Site (Minakami-machi, Japan)
  UF Kawakami Iseki (Minakami-machi, Japan)
  BT Japan—Antiquities
Kawakatsu family (Not Subd Geog)
Kawamura family (Not Subd Geog)
Kawanakajima kassen zu (Screen painting)
  [ND1059.6]
  BT Painting, Japanese—Edo period, 1600-1868
    Screen painting, Japanese
Kawanakajima War, 1553-1564
  [DS868]
  BT Japan—History—Period of civil wars, 1480-1603
  — Art and the war
    UF Kawanakajima War, 1553-1564, in art
Kawanakajima War, 1553-1564, in art
  USE Kawanakajima War, 1553-1564—Art and the war
Kawananakoa, House of (Not Subd Geog)
  BT Hawaii—Kings and rulers
Kawanga dialect
  USE Hanga dialect (Kenya)
Kawar (Niger)
  USE Kaouar (Niger)
Kawasaki airplanes
  BT Airplanes
  NT Hien (Fighter planes)
    Toryū (Fighter plane)
Kawasaki disease
  USE Mucocutaneous lymph node syndrome
Kawasaki family (Not Subd Geog)
Kawasaki Ki-45 (Fighter plane)
  USE Toryū (Fighter plane)
Kawasaki Ki 61 (Fighter planes)
  USE Hien (Fighter planes)
Kawasaki Ki 100 (Fighter planes)
  USE Hien (Fighter planes)
Kawasaki motorcycle
  [TL448.K]
Kawasaki's disease
  USE Mucocutaneous lymph node syndrome
Kawashima family (Not Subd Geog)
Kawatiri (N.Z.)
  USE Buller River (N.Z.)
Kawau Island (N.Z. : Island)
  BT Islands—New Zealand
Kawauchi Iseki (Yoshii-machi, Gunma-ken, Japan)
  USE Kawauchi Site (Yoshii-machi, Gunma-ken, Japan)
Kawauchi Site (Yoshii-machi, Gunma-ken, Japan) (Not Subd Geog)
  UF Kawauchi Iseki (Yoshii-machi, Gunma-ken, Japan)
  BT Japan—Antiquities
Kawchodinne Indians
  USE Kawchottine Indians
Kawchottine Indians
  UF Hare Indians
    Kawchodinne Indians
    Peaux-de-Lièvres Indians

  BT Athapascan Indians
    Indians of North America
Kawchottine language
  [PM1489]
  UF Hare language
    Peaux-de-Lièvre language
  BT Athapascan languages
Kaweka State Forest Park (N.Z.)
  BT Forest reserves—New Zealand
    Parks—New Zealand
Kawelka (New Guinea people)
  BT Ethnology—Papua New Guinea
    Medlpa (Papua New Guinea people)
Kawesqar language
  USE Alacaluf language
Kawi gnomic poetry
  USE Gnomic poetry, Kawi
Kawi inscriptions
  USE Inscriptions, Kawi
Kawi language
  [PL5151-PL5159]
  UF Javanese language—Old Javanese
    Kavi language
  BT Malayan languages
Kawi literature (May Subd Geog)
  [PL5158.5 (Collections)]
  [PL5158 (History)]
  NT Kawi poetry
Kawi philology
Kawi poetry (May Subd Geog)
  BT Kawi literature
  NT Gnomic poetry, Kawi
Kawia Indians (Shoshoneans)
  USE Cahuilla Indians
Kawia language (Shoshone)
  USE Cahuilla language
Kawm Madīnat Wāṭifah (Egypt)
  USE Madīnat Wāṭifah, Kawm (Egypt)
Kawurna language
  USE Kaurna language
Kaxinawa language
  USE Cashinawa language
Kay family (Not Subd Geog)
  UF Cay family
    Caye family
    Kaye family
    Kayes family
    Kays family
Kaya (Kingdom)
  USE Karak (Kingdom)
Kayafuri Iseki (Yao-shi, Japan)
  USE Kayafuri Site (Yao-shi, Japan)
Kayafuri Site (Yao-shi, Japan) (Not Subd Geog)
  UF Kayafuri Iseki (Yao-shi, Japan)
  BT Japan—Antiquities
Kayagŭm
  USE Kayakeum
Kayah (Southeast Asian people)
  [DS528.2.K38]
  BT Ethnology—Burma
    Ethnology—Thailand
    Karens
Kayak touring (May Subd Geog)
  [GV789]
  BT Kayaks
Kayakabe
  USE Kakushi Nembutsu
Kayakeum
  [ML1015.K39]
  [ML1018.K39]
  UF Kayagŭm
    Kayakko
  BT Musical instruments—Korea
    Zither
Kayakeum music
  [M142.K39]
Kayakeum players (May Subd Geog)
  BT Musicians—Korea
Kayaking
  USE Canoes and canoeing

Kayaking, Sea
  USE Sea kayaking
Kayakko
  USE Kayakeum
Kayaks (May Subd Geog)
  BT Canoes and canoeing
  NT Kayak touring
Kayan language (May Subd Geog)
  [PL5336]
  UF Kajan language
  BT Indonesia—Languages
    Malayan languages
    Malaysia—Languages
Kayans
  [DS646.3 (Borneo)]
  UF Kajans
Kayapo Indians
  USE Cayapo Indians
Kayapo language
  USE Cayapo language
Kayasthas
  USE Kayasths
Kayasths
  [DS432.K29]
  UF Kayasthas
  BT Caste—India
    Ethnology—India
  NT Karana Kayasths
Kaye family
  USE Kay family
Kayes family
  USE Kay family
Kayford family
  USE Cayford family
Kaykendall family
  USE Kuykendall family
Kayler family
  USE Kahler family
Kaylor family
  USE Kahler family
Kayowe language
  USE Kiowa language
Kaypro 10 (Computer)
  [QA76.8.K]
  BT Kaypro computers
    Microcomputers
    Portable computers
  — Programming
Kaypro computers
  [QA76.8.K]
  BT Electronic digital computers
  NT Kaypro 10 (Computer)
    Kaypro II (Computer)
  — Programming
Kaypro II (Computer)
  [QA76.8.K]
  BT Kaypro computers
    Microcomputers
    Portable computers
  — Programming
Kays family
  USE Kay family
Kaysānīyah
  UF Kaisānīyah
  BT Islamic sects
    Shīʻah
Kayser family
  USE Kaiser family
Kayuá Indians
  USE Caingua Indians
Kazak-Kirghiz language
  USE Kazakh language
Kazakh art
  USE Art, Kazakh
Kazakh arts
  USE Arts, Kazakh
Kazakh drama (May Subd Geog)
Kazakh encyclopedias and dictionaries
  USE Encyclopedias and dictionaries, Kazakh

Kazakh fiction
  NT Historical fiction, Kazakh
      Short stories, Kazakh
Kazakh folk literature
  USE Folk literature, Kazakh
Kazakh folk poetry
  USE Folk poetry, Kazakh
Kazakh folk-songs
  USE Folk-songs, Kazakh
Kazakh historical fiction
  USE Historical fiction, Kazakh
Kazakh language
  [PL65.K4-44]
  UF Kazak-Kirghiz language
      Kirghiz-Kaissak language
  BT Turkic languages
      Turkic languages, Northwest
  — Etymology
  — — Names
      NT Names, Kazakh
  — Names
      USE Names, Kazakh
Kazakh literature *(May Subd Geog)*
  [PL65.K45 (History)]
  [PL65.K46-PL65.K48 (Collections)]
  NT Folk literature, Kazakh
Kazakh motion picture cartoons
  USE Moving-picture cartoons, Kazakh
Kazakh names
  USE Names, Kazakh
Kazakh philology
Kazakh poetry *(May Subd Geog)*
  [PL65.K45 (History)]
  [PL65.K47 (Collections)]
  NT Folk poetry, Kazakh
Kazakh prose literature *(May Subd Geog)*
Kazakh proverbs
  USE Proverbs, Kazakh
Kazakh S.S.R.
  UF Kazakhstan
  — History
  — — Revolution, 1917-1921
Kazakh short stories
  USE Short stories, Kazakh
Kazakh wit and humor *(May Subd Geog)*
Kazakhs *(May Subd Geog)*
  UF Kazaks
      Kirghiz-Kaissacks
      Kirghiz-Kazaks
  BT Ethnology—Kazakh S.S.R.
  RT Kirghiz
Kazakhskaïa zhelezaïa dorogo
  BT Railroads—Soviet Union
Kazakhstan
  USE Kazakh S.S.R.
Kazaks
  USE Kazakhs
Kazan Rettō (Japan)
  USE Volcano Islands (Japan)
Kazan Tatars
  BT Ethnology—Russian S.F.S.R.
      Tatars
Kazennyĭ ravvin
  USE Crown Rabbinate
Kazhdan-Lusztig polynomials
  UF Lusztig-Kazhdan polynomials
  BT Polynomials
Kazimierz (Kraków, Poland)
  (Not Subd Geog)
  UF Kraków (Poland). Kazimierz
Kazoo
  [MT533.K36 (Instruction)]
  UF Bazoo
      Eunuch flute
      Gazoo
      Tommy talker
      Zarah
  BT Mirliton
Kazuno Kaid-o (Japan)
  BT Roads—Japan

Kazyonny ravvin
  USE Crown Rabbinate
KC-135 (Tanker aircraft)
  UF Boeing Stratotanker
  BT Boeing airplanes
      Jet planes, Military
      Jet transports
Ke-Ney
  USE Kenney
Kea
  [QL696.P688]
  UF Mountain parrot
      Nestor notabilis
  BT Parrots
Kea Island (Greece)
  UF Cea Island (Greece)
      Ceos Island (Greece)
      Keos Island (Greece)
      Tzia Island (Greece)
      Zea Island (Greece)
      Zia Island (Greece)
  BT Cyclades (Greece)
      Islands—Greece
Keachen family
  USE Kitchen family
Keafer family
  USE Keefer family
Keahey family *(Not Subd Geog)*
Keal family
  USE Keel family
Kealakekua Bay (Hawaii)
  BT Bays—Hawaii
Kealer family
  USE Keeler family
Kealey family
  USE Keeley family
Kealley family
  USE Keeley family
Kealy family
  USE Keeley family
Kean family
  USE Keane family
Keane family *(Not Subd Geog)*
  UF Kean family
      Keen family
      Keene family
      Keens family
      Keign family
      Kein family
      Keine family
      Kene family
Keaney family
  USE Kenney family
Kear family
  UF Cears family
Kearker family
  USE Karriker family
Kearn family
  USE Kern family
Kearney family
  USE Carney family
Kearns family
  USE Kern family
Kearny (N.J.). Arlington
  USE Arlington (Kearny, N.J.)
Kearny Expedition, 1845
  UF Kearny's Expedition, 1845
  BT West (U.S.)—History—To 1848
Kearny family
  USE Carney family
Kearny's Expedition, 1845
  USE Kearny Expedition, 1845
Kearny's Expedition, 1846
  [E405.2]
  BT California—History—1846-1850
Kearsey family
  USE Kersey family
Keats prizes
Keawee Indians
  USE Keyauwee Indians

Keban Barajı (Turkey)
  USE Keban Reservoir (Turkey)
Keban Reservoir (Turkey) *(Not Subd Geog)*
  UF Keban Barajı (Turkey)
  BT Reservoirs—Turkey
Kebbi River (Nigeria)
  USE Sokoto River (Nigeria)
Kebeirka (African people)
  USE Uduk (African people)
Kebir Wadi (Spain)
  USE Guadalquivir River (Spain)
Kebler family
  USE Kiebler family
Kebobs
  USE Skewer cookery
Kechruk
  USE Angklung
Kechua Indians
  USE Quechua Indians
Kechua language
  USE Quechua language
Keck family *(Not Subd Geog)*
  UF Kecker family
Kecker family
  USE Keck family
Keckler family
  USE Cackler family
Kecko family
  USE Käcko family
Kedara (African people)
  USE Kadara (African people)
Keddeman family
  USE Kitterman family
Kediri River (Java, Indonesia)
  USE Brantas River (Java, Indonesia)
Kedleston Hall (Derbyshire)
  BT Manors—England
Kedrovaïa pad' (R.S.F.S.R.)
  (Not Subd Geog)
  UF Kedrovaja pad' (R.S.F.S.R.)
      Kedrovaya pad' (R.S.F.S.R.)
  BT National parks and reserves—Russian
      S.F.S.R.
      Natural areas—Russian S.F.S.R.
Kedrovaja pad' (R.S.F.S.R.)
  USE Kedrovaïa pad' (R.S.F.S.R.)
Kedrovaya pad' (R.S.F.S.R.)
  USE Kedrovaïa pad' (R.S.F.S.R.)
Kee family *(Not Subd Geog)*
  RT Keys family
Keeawawe Indians
  USE Keyauwee Indians
Keebaugh family *(Not Subd Geog)*
  UF Kibach family
      Kiebach family
      Kuhbach family
      Kuhbauch family
Keeche Indians
  [E99.K]
  BT Indians of North America
Keederman family
  USE Kitterman family
Keedman family
  USE Kitterman family
Keefer family *(Not Subd Geog)*
  UF Keafer family
      Kefer family
      Keffer family
      Keifer family
      Keiffer family
      Kiefer family
      Kieffer family
Keegan family *(Not Subd Geog)*
  UF Keegin family
Keegin family
  USE Keegan family
Keel family *(Not Subd Geog)*
  UF Keal family
      Keele family
  RT Kiel family

Keele family
  USE Keel family
Keeled earless lizard
  [QL666.L25]
  UF Holbrookia proquina
Keeler family *(Not Subd Geog)*
  UF Kealer family
    Keelor family
    Kehler family
    Keler family
    Keyler family
    Keylor family
Keeley cure
  USE Alcoholism—Treatment
Keeley family *(Not Subd Geog)*
  UF Kealey family
    Kealley family
    Kealy family
    Keelley family
    Keely family
Keelley family
  USE Keeley family
Keelogg family
  USE Kellogg family
Keelor family
  USE Keeler family
Keels
  BT Naval architecture
Keely family
  USE Keeley family
Keely motor
  [TJ220]
Keen family
  USE Keane family
Keenamer family
  USE Kennamer family
Keene family
  USE Keane family
Keene Valley (N.Y. : Valley)
  BT Valleys—New York (State)
Keeneland (Lexington, Ky.)
  BT Racetracks (Horse-racing)—Kentucky
Keeney family
  USE Kenney family
Keens family
  USE Keane family
Keeny family
  USE Kenney family
Keeowee Indians
  USE Keyauwee Indians
Keep family *(Not Subd Geog)*
Keep Plain (N.T.)
  BT Plains—Australia
Keep River National Park (N.T.)
  (Not Subd Geog)
  BT National parks and reserves—Australia
Keepers, Zoo
  USE Zoo keepers
Keeping notes
  USE Note-taking
Keepsakes (Books)
  USE Gift-books (Annuals, etc.)
Keepsakes (Souvenirs)
  USE Souvenirs (Keepsakes)
KeepTrack (Computer program)
  BT Computer programs
    Electronic filing systems—Computer
      programs
Keern family
  USE Kern family
Keersey family
  USE Kersey family
Keeshonds
  [SF429.K4]
  BT Dog breeds
    Spitz dogs
Keeth family
  USE Keith family
Keevil family *(Not Subd Geog)*
Kefallinía Island (Greece)
  USE Cephalonia Island (Greece)

Kefer family
  USE Keefer family
Keffer family
  USE Keefer family
Kegel family *(Not Subd Geog)*
  UF Kagel family
  RT Cagle family
Kegerreis family
  USE Kagarice family
Kegon (Sect)
  USE Hua-yen Buddhism
Kegon engi (Scrolls)
  [ND1053.4]
  UF Gishō Gengyō e (Scrolls)
    Kegon engi emaki (Scrolls)
  BT Painting, Buddhist—Japan
    Painting, Japanese—Kamakura-
      Momoyama periods, 1185-1600
    Scrolls, Japanese
Kegon engi emaki (Scrolls)
  USE Kegon engi (Scrolls)
Kehal Yahveh
  USE People of God
Kehl family
  USE Kiel family
Kehler family
  USE Keeler family
Kehly family
  USE Kelley family
Kei
  BT Musical instruments—Japan
    Percussion instruments
Keichō Peasant Uprising, 1614-1615
  USE Japan—History—Keichō Peasant
    Uprising, 1614-1615
Keien-ha
  USE Keien school
Keien school
  UF Keien-ha
    Keienha
  BT Japanese poetry—Edo period, 1600-
    1868
    Waka
Keienha
  USE Keien school
Keifer family
  USE Keefer family
Keiferia
  [QL561.G4]
  BT Gelechiidae
Keiferia lycopersicella
  USE Tomato pinworm
Keiffer family
  USE Keefer family
Keifling family *(Not Subd Geog)*
Keig family *(Not Subd Geog)*
Keign family
  USE Keane family
Keihan Denki Tetsudō
  BT Railroads—Japan
    Street-railroads—Japan
Keihin Kyūkō Dentetsu
  BT Railroads—Japan
    Street-railroads—Japan
Keikaku, Sanshain
  USE Sanshain Keikaku
Keil family
  USE Kiel family
Keilberg (Czechoslovakia)
  USE Klínovec Mountain (Czechoslovakia)
Keilen family *(Not Subd Geog)*
  RT Kiel family
Keiley family
  USE Kelley family
Keiltz family
  USE Kilts family
Keim family
  USE Kimes family
Kein family
  USE Keane family

Keinapel family
  USE Kinnapel family
Keine family
  USE Keane family
Keinicke family *(Not Subd Geog)*
Keiningham family *(Not Subd Geog)*
  UF Keningham family
    Kiningham family
    Kinningham family
Keiō Teito Dentetsu
  BT Railroads—Japan
    Street-railroads—Japan
Keirns family
  USE Kern family
Keirsey family
  USE Kersey family
Keisei Dentetsu
  BT Railroads—Japan
    Street-railroads—Japan
Keiser family
  USE Kaiser family
Keitele Lake (Finland)
  UF Keytele Lake (Finland)
    Ozero Keĭtele (Finland)
    Ozero Keytele (Finland)
  BT Lakes—Finland
Keith and Flack's node
  USE Sinoatrial node
Keith family *(Not Subd Geog)*
  UF Keeth family
    Kieth family
Keithcart family
  USE Cathcart family
Keithcirt family
  USE Cathcart family
Keith's node
  USE Sinoatrial node
Keiyo (African people)
  USE Elgeyo (African people)
Kejimkujik Lake (N.S.)
  BT Lakes—Nova Scotia
Kekchi Indians
  [F1465.2.K5]
  UF Cacchi Indians
    Cakchi Indians
    Quekchi Indians
  BT Indians of Central America
Kekchi language
  [PM3913]
  UF Cacchi language
    Cakchi language
    Ghec-chi language
    Quekchi language
  BT Indians of Central America—
    Languages
Kekkonens nationalpark, Urho (Finland)
  USE Urho Kekkosen kansallispuisto
    (Finland)
Kekkosen kansallispuisto, Urho (Finland)
  USE Urho Kekkosen kansallispuisto
    (Finland)
Kel Azdjer (African people)
  USE Ajjer (African people)
Kela language
  [PL8376.K45]
  UF Lemba language
    Okela language
  BT Bantu languages
Kelabit (Malaysian people)
  [DS597.367.K44]
  BT Dyaks
    Ethnology—Malaysia
    Muruts
Kelasa Strait (Indonesia)
  USE Gelasa Strait (Indonesia)
Kelce family
  USE Kelsey family
Kelcy family
  USE Kelsey family
Kele family
  USE Kelley family

Kele language
  [PL8377]
  UF Bakele language
      Di-kele language
  BT Bantu languages
Kelechin River (Pakistan)
  USE Muztāgh River (Pakistan)
Keleher family
  USE Kelleher family
Kelelwa Farm (Kenya) *(Not Subd Geog)*
  BT Farms—Kenya
Kelep
  [QL568.F7 (Zoology)]
  [SB945.C8 (Boll weevil control)]
  UF Ectatomma tuberculatum
      Guatemalan cotton boll weevil ant
  BT Ants
      Boll-weevil
      Parasitic ants
Keler family
  USE Keeler family
Kelevan
  BT Esters
      Insecticides
      Organochlorine compounds
Keley family
  USE Kelley family
Keli Range (Georgian S.S.R.)
  UF Kel'skoe nagor'e (Georgian S.S.R.)
  BT Caucasus
      Mountains—Georgian S.S.R.
Kelims
  USE Kilims
Kelita
  [QL568.A53]
  BT Anthophoridae
Kell family *(Not Subd Geog)*
  UF Kells family
  RT Kilts family
Kellam family *(Not Subd Geog)*
  UF Kellams family
      Kellamus family
      Kellems family
      Kellum family
Kellams family
  USE Kellam family
Kellamus family
  USE Kellam family
Kellar Cemetery (Ill.)
  UF Keller Cemetery (Ill.)
      Lovington Cemetery (Ill.)
  BT Cemeteries—Illinois
Kellar family
  USE Keller family
Kelleg family
  USE Kellogg family
Kellegg family
  USE Kellogg family
Kellegher family
  USE Kelleher family
Kelleham family
  USE Callahan family
Kelleher family *(Not Subd Geog)*
  UF Keleher family
      Kellegher family
      Kelliher family
Kellems family
  USE Kellam family
Kellenbarger family
  USE Kellenberger family
Kellenberger family *(Not Subd Geog)*
  UF Kallenberg family
      Kallenberger family
      Kellenbarger family
Keller Cemetery (Ill.)
  USE Kellar Cemetery (Ill.)

Keller family *(Not Subd Geog)*
  UF Kellar family
      Kellere family
      Kelloe family
      Kellough family
      Kellow family
      Kelugh family
      Killar family
      Killer family
Kellere family
  USE Keller family
Kelley family *(Not Subd Geog)*
  UF Kalley family
      Kehly family
      Keiley family
      Kele family
      Keley family
      Kelly family
      Kely family
      Kiely family
      Killey family
      Killy family
      O'Kelia family
      O'Kelley family
      O'Kelly family
      O'Killey family
      O'Killia family
Kellia Site (Egypt)
  [DT73.K47]
  UF Kelya Site (Egypt)
  BT Egypt—Antiquities
Kelliellidae, Fossil
  BT Veneroida, Fossil
  NT Lutetia
Kelliher family
  USE Kelleher family
Kellman family
  USE Kelman family
Kellmann family
  USE Kelman family
Kelloch family
  USE Kellogg family
Kellock family
  USE Kellogg family
Kelloe family
  USE Keller family
Kellog family
  USE Kellogg family
Kellogg Community College Roll Building
    (Battle Creek, Mich.)
  USE Roll Building (Battle Creek, Mich.)
Kellogg family *(Not Subd Geog)*
  UF Keelogg family
      Kelleg family
      Kellegg family
      Kelloch family
      Kellock family
      Kellog family
      Kelogg family
Kellogg Terrace (Great Barrington, Mass.)
  USE Searles Castle (Great Barrington,
      Mass.)
Kelloggella
  [QL638.G7]
  BT Gobiidae
Kelloggella centralis
  [QL638.G7]
Kellogg's oak
  USE California black oak
Kellough family
  USE Keller family
Kellow family
  USE Keller family
Kells family
  USE Kell family
Kellsall family
  USE Kelsall family
Kellsey family
  USE Kelsey family
Kellshall family
  USE Kelsall family

Kellum family
  USE Kellam family
Kelly, Walt. Pogo (Comic strip)
  USE Pogo (Comic strip)
Kelly family
  USE Kelley family
Kellyham family
  USE Callahan family
Kellyhan family
  USE Callahan family
Kelly's Ford (Va.)
  BT Fords (Stream crossings)—Virginia
Kelly's Ford (Va.), Battle of, 1863
  [E475.3]
  BT United States—History—Civil War,
      1861-1865—Campaigns
      Virginia—History—Civil War, 1861-
      1865
Kelm family *(Not Subd Geog)*
  UF Kelmer family
Kelman family *(Not Subd Geog)*
  UF Kellman family
      Kellmann family
Kelmer family
  USE Kelm family
Kelogg family
  USE Kellogg family
Kelp
  USE Kelps
Kelp, Giant
  USE Giant kelp
Kelp, Horsetail
  USE Laminaria digitata
Kelp bass
  UF Paralabrax clathratus
  BT Bass
Kelp bed ecology *(May Subd Geog)*
  [QH541.5.K4]
  UF Kelp forest ecology
  BT Marine ecology
Kelp forest ecology
  USE Kelp bed ecology
Kelpatrick family
  USE Kilpatrick family
Kelpie (Dogs)
  [SF429.K45]
  BT Sheep dogs
Kelps *(May Subd Geog)*
  [SH391.K44 (Fisheries)]
  UF Kelp
  BT Brown algae
  NT Fucales
      Laminariales
  — Therapeutic use
Kelsall family *(Not Subd Geog)*
  UF Calsol family
      Cocle family
      Culsha family
      Culshaw family
      Culshew family
      Kallsall family
      Kellsall family
      Kellshall family
      Kelsel family
      Kelsell family
      Kelshall family
      Kelshaw family
      Kelsoll family
      Kilsal family
      Kilshall family
      Kilshaw family
      Kilshawe family
      Kulshaw family
      Kylshawe family
  RT Kelso family
Kelsel family
  USE Kelsall family
Kelsell family
  USE Kelsall family

Kelsey family (Not Subd Geog)
 UF Kelce family
    Kelcy family
    Kellsey family
    Kelsy family
Kelshall family
 USE Kelsall family
Kelshaw family
 USE Kelsall family
Kel'skoe nagor'e (Georgian S.S.R.)
 USE Keli Range (Georgian S.S.R.)
Kelso Cemetery (Kaukauna, Wis.)
 BT Cemeteries—Wisconsin
Kelso family (Not Subd Geog)
 UF Calco family
    Kelsoe family
 RT Kelsall family
Kelsoe family
 USE Kelso family
Kelsoll family
 USE Kelsall family
Kelsy family
 USE Kelsey family
Keltic . . .
 USE subject headings beginning with the
     word Celtic
Kelton family (Not Subd Geog)
 UF Kalton family
    Kilton family
Kelts family
 USE Kilts family
Keltz family
 USE Kilts family
Kelugh family
 USE Keller family
Kely family
 USE Kelley family
Kelya Site (Egypt)
 USE Kellia Site (Egypt)
Kemak (Indonesian people)
 UF Ema (Indonesian people)
 BT Ethnology—Indonesia
Kemak folk-songs
 USE Folk-songs, Kemak
Kemak language
 UF Ema language
 BT Indonesia—Languages
    Malayan languages
Kemalism
  [DR590]
   Here are entered works on the political, economic
 and social principles advocated by Kemal Ataturk
 designed to create a modern republican secular Turk-
 ish state.
 UF Ataturkism
    Kemalist policies
 BT Turkey—Politics and government—
    1918-1960
Kemalist policies
 USE Kemalism
Kemanak
  [ML1040.K4]
 BT Percussion instruments
Kemant language
  [PJ2438]
 UF Gamant language
    Kamant language
    Komant language
    Qomant language
 BT Agau language
    Cushitic languages
Kemants
  [DT380]
 BT Ethnology—Ethiopia
    Jews
Kemari
  [GV960.K]
 UF Shūkiku
 BT Football
Kemel family
 USE Campbell family

Kemerer family
 USE Kemmerer family
Kemering dialect
 USE Komering dialect
Kemi River (Finland)
 UF Kemijoki (Finland)
 BT Rivers—Finland
Kemijoki (Finland)
 USE Kemi River (Finland)
Kemiju Jate language
 USE Kanite language
Kemler family
 USE Kemmerer family
Kemm family
 USE Kemmerer family
Kemmel, Battles of, 1918
 BT World War, 1914-1918—Campaigns—
    Belgium
Kemmell family
 USE Campbell family
Kemmer family
 USE Kemmerer family
Kemmerer family (Not Subd Geog)
 UF Kaemmer family
    Kamarer family
    Kamera family
    Kamerer family
    Kamler family
    Kamm family
    Kammerer family
    Kanmel family
    Kemerer family
    Kemler family
    Kemm family
    Kemmer family
    Kemmler family
 RT Kammer family
Kemmler family
 USE Kemmerer family
Kemnade Reservoir (Germany)
 UF Kemnade See (Germany)
    Kemnade Stausee (Germany)
    Kemnadesee (Germany)
    Kemnadestau See (Germany)
    Stausee Kemnade (Germany)
 BT Kemnade River (Germany)
    Reservoirs—Germany (West)
Kemnade River (Germany)
 BT Rivers—Germany (West)
 NT Kemnade Reservoir (Germany)
Kemnade See (Germany)
 USE Kemnade Reservoir (Germany)
Kemnade Stausee (Germany)
 USE Kemnade Reservoir (Germany)
Kemnader See (Germany) (Not Subd Geog)
 BT Lakes—Germany (West)
Kemnadesee (Germany)
 USE Kemnade Reservoir (Germany)
Kemnadestau See (Germany)
 USE Kemnade Reservoir (Germany)
Kemp family (Not Subd Geog)
 UF Kaempfer family
    Kambfer family
    Kamp family
    Kampe family
    Kamper family
    Kampf family
    Kampfer family
    Kamps family
    Kempe family
    Kemper family
    Kempf family
    Kempfer family
    Kemph family
    Kemps family
    Kimp family
 RT Camp family
    Kempton family
Kempe family
 USE Kemp family

Kemper family
 USE Kemp family
Kempf family
 USE Kemp family
Kempfer family
 USE Kemp family
Kemph family
 USE Kemp family
Kempo
 USE Kung fu
Kempō Kinenbi (Japanese holiday)
 UF Constitution Day (Japan)
    Constitution Memorial Day (Japan)
    May 3 (Japanese holiday)
 BT Holidays—Japan
Kemps family
 USE Kemp family
Kempton family (Not Subd Geog)
 UF Kimpton family
 RT Kemp family
Kemsley family (Not Subd Geog)
Kemtuik language
 USE Kamtuk language
Kemtuk language
 USE Kamtuk language
Ken-Ey
 USE Kenney
K'en-ting kuo chia kung yüan (Taiwan)
 UF K'en-ting National Park (Taiwan)
 BT National parks and reserves—Taiwan
K'en-ting National Park (Taiwan)
 USE K'en-ting kuo chia kung yüan (Taiwan)
Kenada family
 USE Kennedy family
Kenaf (May Subd Geog)
  [QK495.M27 (Botany)]
  [SB261.A5 (Fiber plant)]
  [TS1544.A5 (Fiber)]
 UF Ambari hemp
    Ambary hemp
    Bimli hemp
    Bimlipatam hemp
    Bombay hemp
    Deccan hemp
    Gambo hemp
    Hibiscus cannabinus
    Java jute
    Kanaf
    Mesta
 BT Fibers
    Hemp
    Jute
Kenaf industry (May Subd Geog)
  [HD9156.K66-HD9156.K663]
Kenai Fjords (Alaska)
 BT Fjords—Alaska
 RT Kenai Fjords National Park (Alaska)
Kenai Fjords National Park (Alaska)
 BT National parks and reserves—Alaska
 RT Kenai Fjords (Alaska)
Kenai Peninsula (Alaska)
 BT Peninsulas—Alaska
Kenai River (Alaska)
 BT Rivers—Alaska
Kenama family
 USE Kennamer family
Kenchikugyō Kyōkai shō
 BT Architecture—Competitions
Kendal, Eng., in art
Kendal family
 USE Kendall family

Kendall family *(Not Subd Geog)*
  UF Kendal family
      Kendel family
      Kendele family
      Kendell family
      Kendle family
      Kenndall family
      Kindal family
      Kindall family
      Kindel family
      Kindell family
      Kindle family
      Kindol family
      Kinnel family
      Kinnell family
  RT Kindley family
Kendari language
  USE Tolaki language
Kendayan language *(May Subd Geog)*
  [PL5338]
  UF Bideyu language
      Dayak Kendayan language
      Land Dayak language
  BT Indonesia—Languages
      Malayan languages
Kendel family
  USE Kendall family
Kendele family
  USE Kendall family
Kendell family
  USE Kendall family
Kendle family
  USE Kendall family
Kendo
  UF Japanese fencing
  BT Fencing
      Hand-to-hand fighting, Oriental
      Stick fighting
      Swordplay—Japan
  NT Iaido
  — Tournaments
Kendrick family *(Not Subd Geog)*
  UF Kendricks family
Kendricks family
  USE Kendrick family
Kendy family
  USE Kennedy family
Kene family
  USE Keane family
Keneday family
  USE Kennedy family
Kenedy family
  USE Kennedy family
Kenemore family
  USE Kennamer family
Kenerdy family
  USE Kennedy family
Kenerson family
  USE Kennison family
Keneson family
  USE Kennison family
Keney family
  USE Kenney family
Kenga language
  BT Bongo-Bagirmi languages
      Chad—Languages
      Sara languages
Kenga proverbs
  USE Proverbs, Kenga
Kenilworth Castle (Kenilworth, Warwickshire)
  BT Castles—England
Keningham family
  USE Keiningham family
Kenison family
  USE Kennison family
Keniston family
  USE Kennison family
Kenistone family
  USE Kennison family
Kenjas
  USE Kenyas

Kenkade family
  USE Kincaid family
Kenkead family
  USE Kincaid family
Kenkiidae
  [QL391.P7]
  BT Tricladida
  NT Sphalloplana
Kenkoku Kinen no hi
  UF Empire Day (Japan)
      February 11 (Holiday)
      Kigensetsu
      National Foundation Day
  BT Holidays—Japan
Kenman family
  USE Kinsman family
Kenmin Forest (Japan)
  USE Kenminno Forest (Japan)
Kenmin no Forest (Japan)
  USE Kenminno Forest (Japan)
Kenminno Forest (Japan) *(Not Subd Geog)*
  UF Kenmin Forest (Japan)
      Kenmin no Forest (Japan)
  BT Forest reserves—Japan
Kenmu Restoration, Japan, 1333-1336
  USE Japan—History—Kenmu Restoration,
      1333-1336
Kennaday family
  USE Kennedy family
Kennady family
  USE Kennedy family
Kennamer family *(Not Subd Geog)*
  UF Canamore family
      Gannemer family
      Keenamer family
      Kenama family
      Kenemore family
      Kennamour family
      Kennemar family
      Kennemer family
      Kennemere family
      Kennemore family
      Kennemur family
      Kennemure family
      Kennimer family
      Kinmore family
      Kinnemore family
Kennamour family
  USE Kennamer family
Kenndall family
  USE Kendall family
Kenndy family
  USE Kennedy family
Kenne
  USE Kenney
Kennebec claims
  USE Kennebec Patent
Kennebec Indians
  USE Abnaki Indians
      Norridgewock Indians
Kennebec Patent
  [F27.K3]
  UF Kennebec claims
      New Plymouth Purchase, Maine
Kennebec River (Me.)
  BT Rivers—Maine
Kennebrew family
  USE Killebrew family
Kenneday family
  USE Kennedy family

Kennedy family *(Not Subd Geog)*
  UF Canada family
      Canaday family
      Canadey family
      Canady family
      Caneday family
      Canedy family
      Caniday family
      Cannada family
      Cannaday family
      Cannady family
      Canneday family
      Canniday family
      Cenedy family
      Ceniday family
      Kanada family
      Kanaday family
      Kanadey family
      Kanady family
      Kannedy family
      Kenada family
      Kendy family
      Keneday family
      Kenedy family
      Kenerdy family
      Kennaday family
      Kennady family
      Kenndy family
      Kenneday family
      Kennerday family
      Kennidy family
Kennedy Stadium (Washington, D.C.)
  USE Robert F. Kennedy Memorial Stadium
      (Washington, D.C.)
Kennel management
  [SF428]
  BT Kennels
      Management
Kennel owners *(May Subd Geog)*
  UF Kennel proprietors
      Owners, Kennel
      Proprietors, Kennel
  BT Kennels
Kennel proprietors
  USE Kennel owners
Kennelly-Heaviside layer
  USE Ionosphere
Kennels *(May Subd Geog)*
  [SF428]
  BT Dogs—Housing
      Pet boarding facilities
  NT Kennel management
      Kennel owners
  — Law and legislation *(May Subd Geog)*
Kennemar family
  USE Kennamer family
Kennemer family
  USE Kennamer family
Kennemere family
  USE Kennamer family
Kennemerland (Netherlands)
Kennemore family
  USE Kennamer family
Kennemur family
  USE Kennamer family
Kennemure family
  USE Kennamer family
Kennerday family
  USE Kennedy family
Kennesaw Mountain, Battle of, 1864
  [E476.7]
  BT United States—History—Civil War,
      1861-1865—Campaigns
Kenneston family
  USE Kennison family
Kennet, River (England)
  UF River Kennet (England)
  BT Rivers—England
Kennet and Avon Canal (England)
  UF Kennet-Avon Canal (England)
  BT Canals—England

Kennet-Avon Canal (England)
  USE Kennet and Avon Canal (England)
Kenney
  UF Ke-Ney
      Ken-Ey
      Kenne
      Kön-Öy
      Kun-Uy
      Queney
  BT Ethnology—Philippines
Kenney family   (Not Subd Geog)
  UF Keaney family
      Keeney family
      Keeny family
      Keney family
      Kenny family
      Kinne family
      Kinney family
Kennidy family
  USE Kennedy family
Kennimer family
  USE Kennamer family
Kennison family   (Not Subd Geog)
  UF Kenerson family
      Keneson family
      Kenison family
      Keniston family
      Kenistone family
      Kenneston family
      Kenniston family
      Kineson family
      Kiniston family
      Kinistone family
      Kinneston family
      Kinnison family
Kenniston family
  USE Kennison family
Kenny family
  USE Kenney family
Kennywood Park (Pa.)
  BT Amusement parks—Pennsylvania
      Parks—Pennsylvania
Keno (Game)
  USE Bingo
Kenosis (Theology)
  USE Incarnation
Kenoska (Imaginary place)
  BT Geographical myths
Kenotrons
  ₁TK7871.79.K4₁
  BT Diodes, Electron-tube
      Electric current rectifiers
Kenpon Hokke (Sect)
  USE Kenpon Hokkeshū
Kenpon Hokke-shū
  USE Kenpon Hokkeshū
Kenpon Hokkeshū   (May Subd Geog)
  ₁BQ8449.5.K45₁
  UF Kenpon Hokke (Sect)
      Kenpon Hokke-shū
  BT Nichiren (Sect)
Kense family
  USE Kinsey family
Kensington (Game)
  ₁GV1469.K45₁
  BT Board games
Kensington Rune Stone
  ₁E105₁
  BT America—Discovery and exploration—
      Norse
      Forgery of antiquities
      Inscriptions, Runic—Minnesota
      Minnesota—Antiquities
      Runes
Kensy family
  USE Kinsey family
Kent (Conn.)
  — History
  — — Revolution, 1775-1783
        ₁F104.K₁

Kent, River (England)
  UF River Kent (England)
  BT Rivers—England
Kent family   (Not Subd Geog)
Kent Island (Md.)
  BT Islands—Maryland
Kent River (W.A. : River)
  BT Rivers—Australia
Kentish Weald (England)
  USE Weald of Kent (England)
Kentrolite   (May Subd Geog)
  BT Silicates
Kentrophyta
  USE Astragalus (Plants)
Kentucky
  — Antiquities
      NT Dameron Rockshelter (Ky.)
          Slone Site (Ky.)
  — Description and travel
  — — 1951-1980
  — — 1981-
  — Governors
  — — Dwellings
        NT Kentucky Governor's Mansion
           (Frankfort, Ky.)
  — History
      ₁F446-460₁
  — — To 1792
  — — Revolution, 1775-1783
        ₁E263.K₁
        NT Blue Licks, Battle of the, 1782
  — — 1792-1865
  — — Resolutions of 1798
        USE Kentucky and Virginia
            resolutions of 1798
  — — War of 1812
  — — War with Mexico, 1845-1848
        ₁E409.5.K₁
  — — Civil War, 1861-1865
        ₁E509₁
        ₁E564₁
        NT Perryville (Ky.), Battle of, 1862
  — — 1865-
  — — War of 1898
        ₁E726.K37₁
  — Politics and government
  — — To 1792
  — — 1792-1865
  — — Civil War, 1861-1865
  — — 1865-1950
  — — 1951-
  — Public buildings
      USE Public buildings—Kentucky
Kentucky and Virginia resolutions of 1798
  ₁E328₁
  ₁JK176 (Constitutional history)₁
  UF Kentucky—History—Resolutions of
      1798
      Virginia resolutions, 1798
  BT State rights
  RT Alien and Sedition laws, 1798
     Nullification
Kentucky bluegrass
  ₁QK495.G74 (Botany)₁
  ₁SB201.K4 (Culture)₁
  UF June grass
      Poa pratensis
  BT Blue-grass
Kentucky coffeetree
  ₁QK495.L52₁
  UF American coffee bean
      Gymnocladus canadensis
      Gymnocladus dioicus
  — Seed
Kentucky Derby
  ₁SF357.K4₁
  BT Horse-racing—Kentucky
**Kentucky Governor's Mansion (Frankfort,
Ky.)**
  UF Governor's Mansion (Frankfort, Ky.)

  BT Dwellings—Kentucky
     Kentucky—Governors—Dwellings
Kentucky Lake (Ky. and Tenn.)
  (Not Subd Geog)
  UF Kentucky Reservoir (Ky. and Tenn.)
  BT Lakes—Kentucky
     Lakes—Tennessee
     Reservoirs—Kentucky
     Reservoirs—Tennessee
Kentucky movement
  BT Moral education
Kentucky Reservoir (Ky. and Tenn.)
  USE Kentucky Lake (Ky. and Tenn.)
Kentucky rifle
  UF American long rifle
      Long rifle
      Pennsylvania rifle
  BT Muzzle-loading firearms
     Rifles
Kentucky saddle horse
  USE American saddlebred horse
Kentucky saddler
  USE American saddlebred horse
Kentucky West Lakes Area (Ky. and Tenn.)
  USE Land Between the Lakes (Ky. and
      Tenn.)
Kentucky's Western Waterland (Ky. and
  Tenn.)
  USE Land Between the Lakes (Ky. and
      Tenn.)
Kenu (African people)
  USE Kenuz (African people)
Kenuz (African people)
  UF Kenu (African people)
      Mattokki (African people)
  BT Ethnology—Egypt
Kenuz dialect
  UF Kunuzi dialect
  BT Egypt—Languages
     Nubian language
Kenya
  UF East Africa Protectorate
  — Antiquities
      NT Lopoy Site (Kenya)
          Lothagam Site (Kenya)
          Mtongwe Site (Kenya)
  — Description and travel
  — — 1981-
        ₁DT433.527₁
  — Economic conditions
  — — To 1963
  — — 1963-
  — History
  — — To 1895
        ₁DT433.565₁
  — — To 1963
        ₁DT433.565-575₁
  — — 1895-1963
        ₁DT433.57-576₁
  — — 1963-
        ₁DT433.58₁
  — Languages
      NT Boni language
          Burji language
          Cushitic languages, Southern
          Dahalo language
          Hanga dialect (Kenya)
          Kalenjin language
          Kipsikis dialect
          Luo language (Kenya and
             Tanzania)
          Masai language
          Nandi language
          Nandi languages
          Nubi language
          Oromo language
          Rendile language
          Somali languages
          Suk language
          Teso language
          Turkana language

Kenya *(Continued)*
— Politics and government
— — To 1963
— — 1963-1978
— — 1978-
— Social conditions
— — 1963-
— Social life and customs
— — 1895-1963
Kenya, Mount (Kenya)
    UF Kilinyaga (Kenya)
        Kirinyaga (Kenya)
        Mount Kenya (Kenya)
    BT Mountains—Kenya
        Volcanoes—Kenya
Kenya Highlands (Kenya) *(Not Subd Geog)*
    UF Highlands, Kenya (Kenya)
        White Highlands (Kenya)
    BT Mountains—Kenya
        Plateaus—Kenya
Kenyan art
    USE Art, Kenyan
Kenyan atlases
    USE Atlases, Kenyan
Kenyan authors
    USE Authors, Kenyan
Kenyan children's poetry (English)
    USE Children's poetry, Kenyan (English)
Kenyan children's stories (English)
    USE Children's stories, Kenyan (English)
Kenyan college and school drama (English)
    USE College and school drama, Kenyan
        (English)
Kenyan cookery
    USE Cookery, Kenyan
Kenyan drama (English)
    UF English drama—Kenyan authors
    NT College and school drama, Kenyan
        (English)
Kenyan fiction (English)
    UF English fiction—Kenyan authors
    NT Children's stories, Kenyan (English)
Kenyan literature (English)
    (May Subd Geog)
    UF English literature—Kenyan authors
Kenyan periodicals *(May Subd Geog)*
Kenyan poetry (English)
    UF English poetry—Kenyan authors
    NT Children's poetry, Kenyan (English)
Kenyan prisoners' writings
    USE Prisoners' writings, Kenyan
Kenyan wit and humor *(May Subd Geog)*
Kenyan wit and humor, Pictorial
Kenyas
    [DS646.3 (Borneo)]
    UF Kenjas
Kenyon family *(Not Subd Geog)*
Keogh plans *(May Subd Geog)*
    UF H.R. 10 plans
    BT Individual retirement accounts
        Pension trusts
        Self-employed—Pensions
    — Law and legislation *(May Subd Geog)*
    — Taxation *(May Subd Geog)*
    — — Law and legislation
        (May Subd Geog)
Keopu Burial Site (Hawaii)
    (Not Subd Geog)
    BT Hawaii—Antiquities
Keos Island (Greece)
    USE Kea Island (Greece)
Kępa Oksywska (Poland)
    USE Oksywie Hill (Poland)
Kepaukoe (Papuan people)
    USE Kapauku (Papuan people)
Kepele family
    USE Keppel family
Kephallēnia Island (Greece)
    USE Cephalonia Island (Greece)
Kephart family
    USE Gebhardt family

Kephir
    [RM257.K4 (Therapeutics)]
    [TP565 (Beverages)]
    BT Milk
        Milk, Fermented
Keple family
    USE Keppel family
Kepler family *(Not Subd Geog)*
    UF Kepner family
        Keppler family
        Keppner family
Kepler's equation
    USE Orbits
Kepler's laws
    USE Orbits
Kepley family
    USE Keppel family
Keply family
    USE Keppel family
Kepner family
    USE Kepler family
Kepone
    USE Chlordecone
Keppel family *(Not Subd Geog)*
    UF Capel family
        Capell family
        Capelle family
        Capely family
        Caplay family
        Caple family
        Capley family
        Caply family
        Cople family
        Copley family
        Coppel family
        Copple family
        Kaeppel family
        Kapel family
        Kappel family
        Kepele family
        Keple family
        Kepley family
        Keply family
        Keppelay family
        Keppele family
        Keppell family
        Keppelle family
        Keppely family
        Kepplay family
        Kepple family
        Keppley family
        Kepply family
        Kiple family
        Kipple family
        Koeppel family
    RT Caples family
Keppelay family
    USE Keppel family
Keppele family
    USE Keppel family
Keppell family
    USE Keppel family
Keppelle family
    USE Keppel family
Keppely family
    USE Keppel family
Kepplay family
    USE Keppel family
Kepple family
    USE Keppel family
Keppler family
    USE Kepler family
Keppley family
    USE Keppel family
Kepply family
    USE Keppel family
Keppner family
    USE Kepler family
Kepulauan Mentawai (Indonesia)
    USE Mentawai Islands (Indonesia)

Kepulauan Pabbiring (Indonesia)
    USE Pabbiring Archipelago (Indonesia)
Kepulauan Sangkarang (Indonesia)
    USE Pabbiring Archipelago (Indonesia)
Kepulauan Togian (Indonesia)
    USE Togian Islands (Indonesia)
Ker family
    USE Kerr family
Kera (African people)
    BT Ethnology—Chad
Kera language
Kerala (India)
    — History
        NT Mūshaka dynasty
Keramics
    USE Ceramics
Keramos (Ancient city) *(Not Subd Geog)*
    UF Gereme (Ancient city)
        Kerme (Ancient city)
    BT Cities and towns, Ruined extinct, etc.
        —Turkey
        Turkey—Antiquities
Kerang (African people)
    USE Angas (African people)
Keratin
    [QL942]
    UF Neurokeratin
Keratinization
    BT Epidermis
Keratinocytes
    BT Cells
Keratitis *(May Subd Geog)*
    [RE338]
    UF Cornea—Inflammation
    BT Cornea—Diseases
        Inflammation
    RT Keratoconjunctivitis
Keratoacanthoma
    BT Tumors
Keratoconjunctivitis
    BT Conjunctivitis
        Cornea—Diseases
    RT Keratitis
Keratoconjunctivitis sicca
    [RE201]
    NT Sjogren's syndrome
Keratomalacia
    USE Cornea—Diseases
Keratophyre *(May Subd Geog)*
    [QE462.K44]
    UF Soda trachyte
    BT Lava
        Trachyte
        Volcanic ash, tuff, etc.
Keratoplasty
    USE Cornea—Surgery
Keratoplasty, Refractive
    USE Refractive keratoplasty
Keratoprostheses
    USE Artificial corneas
Keratosis
    [RL435]
    UF Ichthyosis follicularis
    NT Acanthosis nigricans
        Horns, Cutaneous
Keratosis follicularis
    [RL435]
    UF Darier's disease
        Hereditary dyskeratosis follicularis
    BT Skin—Diseases—Genetic aspects
Keratosis nigricans
    USE Acanthosis nigricans
Keratotomy, Radial *(May Subd Geog)*
    [RE336]
    UF Radial keratotomy
    BT Cornea—Surgery
Kerbey family
    USE Kirby family
Kerby family
    USE Kirby family

Kerch family
  USE Kirch family
Kerch Strait (Ukraine and R.S.F.S.R.)
  UF Bosporous Cimmerius (Ukraine and
        R.S.F.S.R.)
      Enikale Strait (Ukraine and
        R.S.F.S.R.)
      Kerchenskiĭ proliv (Ukraine and
        R.S.F.S.R.)
      Yenikali Strait (Ukraine and
        R.S.F.S.R.)
  BT Straits—Russian S.F.S.R.
      Straits—Ukraine
Kerchal family *(Not Subd Geog)*
  UF Krchal family
Kerchenskiĭ proliv (Ukraine and R.S.F.S.R.)
  USE Kerch Strait (Ukraine and R.S.F.S.R.)
Kerchiefs *(May Subd Geog)*
  ⌈TT657⌉
  BT Head-gear
      Scarves
  NT Bandannas
Kerebe (Bantu people)
  ⌈DT443⌉
  BT Bantus
      Ethnology—Tanzania
Kerebe language
  UF eciKerebe language
      ekiKerebe language
      Kerewe language
  BT Bantu languages
      Tanzania—Languages
Kereks
  ⌈DK759.K37⌉
  BT Ethnology—Soviet Union
Keren, Battle of, 1941
  USE Cheren, Battle of, 1941
Keres language
  ⌈PM1511⌉
  NT Acoma dialect
Keresan Indians
  ⌈E99.K39⌉
  BT Indians of North America
  RT Pueblo Indians
  NT Cochiti Indians
      Laguna Indians
      Sia Indians
Keresey family
  USE Kersey family
Kerewe language
  USE Kerebe language
Kerguelen Islands
  UF Desolation Islands
      Iles de Désolation
      Iles Kerguélen
  BT Islands of the Indian Ocean
Kerich family
  USE Carrick family
Kerin family *(Not Subd Geog)*
Kerinchi language
  USE Kerinci language
Kerinci Lake (Sumatra, Indonesia)
  UF Danau Kerinci (Sumatra, Indonesia)
      Kerintji Lake (Sumatra, Indonesia)
      Korintji Lake (Sumatra, Indonesia)
  BT Lakes—Indonesia
Kerinci language *(May Subd Geog)*
  UF Kerinchi language
      Kerintji language
      Kinchai language
      Korintje language
  BT Indonesia—Languages
      Malayan languages
Kerintji Lake (Sumatra, Indonesia)
  USE Kerinci Lake (Sumatra, Indonesia)
Kerintji language
  USE Kerinci language
Kerio River (Kenya)
  UF Endo River (Kenya)
      Ndo River (Kenya)
  BT Rivers—Kenya

Kerk family
  USE Kirk family
Kerka River (Hungary) *(Not Subd Geog)*
  BT Rivers—Hungary
Kerker family
  USE Karriker family
Kérkira Island (Greece)
  USE Corfu Island (Greece)
Kerkouane (Ancient city)
  ⌈DT269.K37⌉
  BT Cities and towns, Ruined, extinct, etc.
        —Tunisia
      Tunisia—Antiquities
Kermadec Islands
  NT Raoul Island (Kermadec Islands)
Kerme (Ancient city)
  USE Keramos (Ancient city)
Kermes (Insect)
  ⌈QL527.K4⌉
  UF Kermococcus
  BT Kermesidae
Kermesidae
  ⌈QL527.K4⌉
  UF Hemicoccidae
      Kermidae
  BT Homoptera
      Scale-insects
  NT Kermes (Insect)
Kermichael family
  USE Carmichael family
Kermicus graminis
  USE Rhodes grass scale
Kermidae
  USE Kermesidae
Kermococcus
  USE Kermes (Insect)
Kern family *(Not Subd Geog)*
  UF Kearn family
      Kearns family
      Keern family
      Keirns family
      Kerne family
      Kernes family
      Kerns family
      Kirn family
  RT Carnes family
Kern River (Calif.) *(Not Subd Geog)*
  BT Rivers—California
Kernal (Computer operating system)
  BT Operating systems (Computers)
Kernar family
  USE Kerner family
Kerne family
  USE Kern family
Kernel functions
  UF Functions, Kernel
  BT Functions of complex variables
      Geometric function theory
  NT Kernel functions, Bergman
Kernel functions, Bergman
  UF Bergman kernel functions
  BT Holomorphic mappings
      Kernel functions
Kerner family *(Not Subd Geog)*
  UF Karmer family
      Karner family
      Kartneer family
      Kartner family
      Kernar family
Kernes family
  USE Kern family
Kerney family
  USE Carney family
Kernicterus
  UF Bilirubin encephalopathy
      Nuclear jaundice
  BT Central nervous system—Diseases
      Jaundice
  — Complications and sequelae
Kerns family
  USE Kern family

Kernstown, Battle of, 1862
  ⌈E473.72⌉
  UF Winchester, Battle of, Mar. 23, 1862
  BT Shenandoah Valley Campaign, 1862
      United States—History—Civil War,
        1861-1865—Campaigns
Kerny family
  USE Carney family
Kerogen
  BT Oil-shales
Keroplatidae
  USE Mycetophilidae
Kerosene
  ⌈TP692.4.K4⌉
  UF Coal-oil
Kerosene heaters *(May Subd Geog)*
  ⌈TH7450.5⌉
  UF Heaters, Kerosene
  BT Space heaters
Kerosene lamps
  ⌈TP746⌉
  BT Lamps
  NT Glass kerosene lamps
Kerosene lamps, Glass
  USE Glass kerosene lamps
Kerr, Lake (Va. and N.C.)
  USE John H. Kerr Reservoir (Va. and N.C.)
Kerr cell shutters
  ⌈QC463⌉
  UF Electro-optical shutters
      Kerr cells
  BT Kerr effect
      Liquid crystal devices
  NT Geodimeter
Kerr cells
  USE Kerr cell shutters
Kerr effect
  ⌈QC463⌉
  UF Kerr electro-optical effect
  BT Dielectrics
      Electrooptics
      Electrostatics
      Optics
      Polarization (Light)
  NT Kerr cell shutters
Kerr electro-optical effect
  USE Kerr effect
Kerr family *(Not Subd Geog)*
  UF Ker family
  RT Carr family
Kerr Reservoir (Va. and N.C.)
  USE John H. Kerr Reservoir (Va. and N.C.)
Kerria
  USE Kerria japonica
Kerria japonica
  ⌈QK495.R78 (Botany)⌉
  UF Corchorus japonicus
      Kerria
  BT Rosaceae
Kerrick family
  USE Carrick family
Kerridae
  USE Lac-insects
Kerriher family
  USE Corriher family
Kerriidae
  USE Lac-insects
Kerril family
  USE Carroll family
Kerrol family
  USE Carroll family
Kerry blue terriers
  ⌈SF429.K5⌉
  BT Terriers
Kersantite
  ⌈QE461⌉
Kerscher family
  USE Kershner family

Kersey family (Not Subd Geog)
UF Carsey family
Kearsey family
Keersey family
Keirsey family
Keresey family
Kersy family
Kiersey family
Kirsey family
Kursey family
Kersh family (Not Subd Geog)
Kershner family (Not Subd Geog)
UF Kerscher family
Kersner family
Kirschner family
Kirsener family
Kirshner family
Kersner family
USE Kershner family
Kersnic family
USE Kosnick family
Kersy family
USE Kersey family
Kerves family
USE Kirves family
Kerygma
BT Missions—Biblical teaching
Preaching—History—Early church, ca.
30-600
Kesarisingh's Khetar Site (India)
BT India—Antiquities
Kesem River (Ethiopia)
UF Kessem River (Ethiopia)
BT Rivers—Ethiopia
Keski-Pohjanmaa (Finland)
USE Pohjanmaa (Finland)
Kesler family
USE Kessler family
Kesseler family
USE Kessler family
Kesselring family (Not Subd Geog)
Kesselsdorf, Battle of, 1745
[DD407.K4]
BT Silesian War, 2d, 1744-1745
Kessem River (Ethiopia)
USE Kesem River (Ethiopia)
Kessler family (Not Subd Geog)
UF Kesler family
Kesseler family
Kestler family
Kesterson National Wildlife Refuge (Calif.)
BT National parks and reserves—United
States
Wildlife refuges—California
Kesterson Reservoir (Calif.)
BT Reservoirs—California
Kestler family
USE Kessler family
Kestner family
USE Kastner family
Kestrels
[QL696.F34]
BT Falco
Falconidae
Keswick Convention movement
USE Keswick movement
Keswick movement
[BV4487.K5]
UF Keswick Convention movement
BT Evangelicalism—Church of England
Keswick River (N.B.) (Not Subd Geog)
UF Rivière Keswick (N.B.)
BT Rivers—New Brunswick
Keszthely Mountains (Hungary)
UF Keszthelyi-hegység (Hungary)
BT Mountains—Hungary
Keszthelyi-hegység (Hungary)
USE Keszthely Mountains (Hungary)
Ket
USE Kets

Ket language
UF Ketika language
Kety language
Yenisei-Ostiak language
BT Yeniseian languages
Ketcham, Hank, 1920-   Dennis the
Menace (Cartoon character)
USE Dennis the Menace (Cartoon
character)
Ketchem Dome (Alaska) (Not Subd Geog)
BT Mountains—Alaska
Ketchen family
USE Kitchen family
Ketchun family
USE Kitchen family
Kete language
[PL8378.K45]
UF KiKete language
LuKete language
BT Bantu languages
Zaire—Languages
Ketenes
NT Polyketides
Kethubah
USE Ketubah
Ketika language
USE Ket language
Ketine
[QD305.K2]
Keto acids
USE Ketonic acids
Ketoacetic acid
USE Pyruvic acid
Ketoacidosis (May Subd Geog)
BT Acetonemia
Acidosis
RT Ketones
NT Diabetic acidosis
Ketoacids
USE Ketonic acids
Ketogenic diet
BT Acetonemia
Diet in disease
Ketones
Metabolism
Ketohydroxyestrin
USE Estrone
Ketohydroxyestrone
USE Estrone
Ketone acids
USE Ketonic acids
Ketone body metabolism
BT Metabolism
Ketonemia
USE Acetonemia
Ketones
[QD305.K2]
[QD341.K2]
UF Diketones
BT Oxo compounds
RT Ketoacidosis
Ketonuria
NT Amiodarone
Ketogenic diet
Menthenone
Ketonic acids
UF Keto acids
Ketoacids
Ketone acids
BT Acids, Organic
NT Pyruvates
Ketonuria (May Subd Geog)
[RC905]
RT Ketones
Ketopropionic acid
USE Pyruvic acid
Ketopyrazoline
USE Pyrazolone
Ketosis
USE Acetonemia

Ketosis prone diabetes
USE Diabetes
Ketosis resistant diabetes
USE Non-insulin-dependent diabetes
Ketosulfamylchlorophenylhydroxyisoindoline
USE Chlorthalidone
Ketotifen
UF Dihydromethylpiperid
inylidenebenzocycloh
eptathiophenone
Dihydromethylpiperid
ylidenebenzocycloheptathiophenone
BT Antiasthmatic agents
Antihistamines
Benzene
Piperidine
Thiophene
Kets
[DK759.K4]
UF Ket
Ostiaks of the Yenisei
Yenisei Ostyak
Yeniseians
Yenisey-Ostyaks
BT Ethnology—Russian S.F.S.R.
Ket's Rebellion, 1549
USE Kett's Rebellion, 1549
Ketshuck family
USE Kitshoff family
Ketteman family
USE Kitterman family
Ketterman family (Not Subd Geog)
UF Catherman family
Cotherman family
Cotterman family
Katherman family
Kattermann family
RT Kitterman family
Kettle bottoms (Mining)
USE Kettlebottoms (Mining)
Kettle River (B.C. and Wash.)
BT Rivers—British Columbia
Rivers—Washington (State)
Kettlebottoms (Mining)
UF Bells (Mining)
Caldron bottoms (Mining)
Camelbacks (Mining)
Kettle bottoms (Mining)
Pot bottoms (Mining)
Tortoises (Mining)
BT Coal mines and mining
Ground control (Mining)
Mine roof control
Rock mechanics
Kettledrum
USE Timpani
Kettleman family
USE Kitterman family
Kettles
[TX657.K4]
Kett's Rebellion, 1549
[DA345]
UF Ket's Rebellion, 1549
BT Great Britain—History—Edward VI,
1547-1553
Ketuba
USE Ketubah
Ketubah
UF Kethubah
Ketuba
Ketubba
Ketubbah
BT Antenuptial contracts (Jewish law)
Marriage (Jewish law)
Ketubba
USE Ketubah
Ketubbah
USE Ketubah
Ketupa
[QL696.S83]
BT Strigidae

Ketupa blakistoni
  USE Blakiston's fish-owl
Kety language
  USE Ket language
Keuka Lake (N.Y.)
  UF Crooked Lake (N.Y.)
  BT Finger Lakes (N.Y.)
     Lakes—New York (State)
Keura
  USE Pandanus
Keurva
  USE Pandanus
Kevill family *(Not Subd Geog)*
  UF Keville family
Keville family
  USE Kevill family
Kewa (Papua New Guinea people)
  UF Kewabe (Papua New Guinea people)
     Kewapi (Papua New Guinea people)
  BT Ethnology—Papua New Guinea
Kewa (Papua New Guinea people) women
  USE Women, Kewa (Papua New Guinea
     people)
Kewa language
  ₍PL6621.K4₎
  UF Kewapi language
  BT Papuan languages
Kewabe (Papua New Guinea people)
  USE Kewa (Papua New Guinea people)
Kewapi (Papua New Guinea people)
  USE Kewa (Papua New Guinea people)
Kewapi language
  USE Kewa language
Kewari Iseki (Yamaguchi-shi, Japan)
  USE Kewari Site (Yamaguchi-shi, Japan)
Kewari Site (Yamaguchi-shi, Japan)
  (Not Subd Geog)
  UF Kewari Iseki (Yamaguchi-shi, Japan)
  BT Japan—Antiquities
KEWB
  USE Water boiler reactors
Keweenaw Peninsula (Mich.)
  BT Peninsulas—Michigan
Keweenaw Waterway (Mich.)
  BT Canals—Michigan
Key accounts in marketing
  USE Marketing—Key accounts
Key accounts in selling
  USE Selling—Key accounts
Key deer
  USE White-tailed deer
Key fiddle
  USE Keyed fiddle
Key Marco (Fla.)
  USE Marco Island (Fla. : Island)
Key punches
  USE Keypunches
Key stones
  USE Keystones
Key System Transit
  BT Railroads—United States
Key West Cemetery (Key West, Fla.)
  BT Cemeteries—Florida
Key Word and Context
  USE KWAC (Indexing system)
Key Word Augmented in Context
  USE KWAC (Indexing system)
Keyauwee Indians
  UF Keawee Indians
     Keeawawe Indians
     Keeowee Indians
  BT Indians of North America
     Siouan Indians
Keyblock theory (Rock mechanics)
  USE Block theory (Rock mechanics)
Keyboard, Electronic (Synthesizer)
  USE Electronic keyboard (Synthesizer)
Keyboard harmony
  USE Harmony, Keyboard
Keyboard instrument and flute music
  USE Flute and keyboard instrument music

Keyboard instrument and oboe music
  USE Oboe and keyboard instrument music
Keyboard instrument and recorder music
  USE Recorder and keyboard instrument
     music
Keyboard instrument and violin music
  USE Violin and keyboard instrument music
Keyboard instrument music
  UF Keyboard music
  SA Concertos, Minuets, Sonatas, Suites,
     *and similar headings with
     specification of instruments;* Trios
     ₍Quartets, etc.₎ *followed by
     specifications which include
     keyboard instrument(s); also
     headings that begin with the words*
     Keyboard instrument *or* Keyboard
     instruments
  NT Clavichord music
     Harpsichord music
     Organ music
     Piano music
**Keyboard instrument music (Keyboard
instruments (2))**
Keyboard instruments
  ₍ML549₎
  NT Celesta
     Clavi-harp
     Organ
     Piano
  — Tuning
Keyboard music
  USE Keyboard instrument music
Keyboarding in electronic data processing
  USE Electronic data processing—
     Keyboarding
Keyboards
  ₍ML549-697₎
  BT Harpsichord
     Organ
     Piano
     Reed-organ
Keyboards (Electronics)
  BT Computer input-output equipment
     Electric switchgear
  RT Electronic data processing—
     Keyboarding
Keyboards (Electronics) industry
  (May Subd Geog)
Keyed fiddle
  ₍ML760₎
  UF Key fiddle
     Nyckelgiga
     Nyckelharpa
     Schlüsselfidel
     Schlüsselfiedel
  BT Musical instruments—Sweden
     Stringed instruments, Bowed
Keyed fiddle music
  ₍M59₎
  SA Concertos, Minuets, Sonatas, Suites,
     *and similar headings with
     specification of instruments;* String
     trios ₍Quartets, etc.₎ *and* Trios
     ₍Quartets, etc.₎ *followed by
     specifications which include the
     keyed fiddle; also headings that
     begin with the words* Keyed fiddle
     or Keyed fiddles
Keyed fiddle music (Keyed fiddles (2))
  ₍M286-287₎
Keyed fiddle with orchestra
  ₍M1019.K₎
  NT Concertos (Keyed fiddle)
Keyed harp
  USE Clavi-harp
Keyed input design
  USE Input design, Computer
Keyes family
  USE Keys family

Keyford family
  USE Cayford family
Keying, Phase shift
  USE Phase shift keying
Keykendall family
  USE Kuykendall family
Keyler family
  USE Keeler family
Keylor family
  USE Keeler family
Keynesian economics
  BT Economics
     Supply-side economics
Keypunches
  UF Key punches
  BT Computer input-output equipment
     Punched card systems
Keys, Florida (Fla.)
  USE Florida Keys (Fla.)
Keys
  USE Locks and keys
Keys, Power of the
  USE Power of the keys
Keys (Machinery)
  USE Keys and keyways (Machinery)
Keys (Music theory)
  USE Tonality
Keys (Musical instruments)
  USE *subdivision* Keys *under names of
     individual instruments, e.g.* Piano—
     Keys
Keys and keyways (Machinery)
  ₍TJ1329₎
  UF Keys (Machinery)
  BT Fasteners
     Shafting
Keys, etc., Mailing of
  BT Postal service
Keys family *(Not Subd Geog)*
  UF Keyes family
  RT Kee family
Keys-Willmer cells
  USE Chloride cells
Keysar family
  USE Kaiser family
Keyser family
  USE Kaiser family
KEYSTAT (Computer programs)
  BT Computer programs
     Statistics—Computer programs
Keystone Lake (Okla.)
  UF Keystone Reservoir (Okla.)
  BT Lakes—Oklahoma
     Reservoirs—Oklahoma
Keystone moving-picture camera
Keystone Reservoir (Okla.)
  USE Keystone Lake (Okla.)
Keystones *(May Subd Geog)*
  UF Key stones
  BT Arches
     Architecture—Details
Keystroke timing authentication in computer
     access control
  USE Computers—Access control—
     Keystroke timing authentication
Keytele Lake (Finland)
  USE Keitele Lake (Finland)
Keyword and Context
  USE KWAC (Indexing system)
Keyword Augmented in Context
  USE KWAC (Indexing system)
Kezha language
  USE Khezha language
Kezhama language
  USE Khezha language
Kfr (The Hebrew root)
  USE Kpr (The Hebrew root)
Kfr (The Semitic root)
  USE Kpr (The Semitic root)
Kgaga (African people)
  ₍DT764.K42₎

Kgaga (African people) *(Continued)*
  UF Bakhaha (African people)
      Khaha (African people)
      Kxaxa (African people)
  BT Ethnology—South Africa
      Sotho (African people)
Kgaga (African people) philosophy
  USE Philosophy, Kgaga (African people)
Kgalagadi (African people)
  ⌐DT797.K⌐
  UF Bakalahadi
      Bakgalagadi
      Balala
Kgalagadi dialect
  ⌐PL8747.95.K⌐
  UF Khalahadi dialect
      Kxhalaxadi dialect
  BT Botswana—Languages
      Tswana language
Kgatla (African people)
  UF Ba-Katlha (African people)
      Bakatla (African people)
      Bakgatla (African people)
      Bakhatla (African people)
  BT Ethnology—Botswana
      Ethnology—South Africa
      Ethnology—Zimbabwe
      Tswana (African people)
  NT Missions to Kgatla (African people)
Kgatla law
  USE Law, Kgatla
Kha (Southeast-Asiatic people)
  USE Moi (Southeast-Asiatic people)
Kha Mou (Southeast Asian people)
  USE Khmu' (Southeast Asian people)
Kha Tahoi
  ⌐DS539.K5⌐
  UF Ka-Tu
Kha Tong Luong (Southeast Asian people)
  USE Phi Tong Luang (Southeast Asian
      people)
Khabiri
  USE Habiru
Khadzhitoshev family *(Not Subd Geog)*
Khaha (African people)
  USE Kgaga (African people)
Khaiass language
  USE Khayasa language
Khaiduti
  USE Haiduks
Khajuna language
  USE Burushaski language
Khakass folk-songs
  USE Folk-songs, Khakass
Khakass language
  ⌐PL391-4⌐
  BT Turkic languages
      Turkic languages, Northeast
  NT Koibalian dialect
Khakass literature *(May Subd Geog)*
  ⌐PL393.5 (History)⌐
  ⌐PL394.A2 (Collections)⌐
Khakass philology
Khakassians
  ⌐DK759.K5⌐
  BT Ethnology—Russian S.F.S.R.
Khakhuli Triptych (Icon)
  USE Xaxulius Karedi (Icon)
Khakhul'skiĭ Triptikh (Icon)
  USE Xaxulius Karedi (Icon)
Khaki
  ⌐TP907⌐
  BT Cotton
      Dyes and dyeing
      Textile fabrics
Khaksar Movement
  BT Muslims—India
Khalahadi dialect
  USE Kgalagadi dialect
Khalaj language
  BT Turkic languages

Khaldian language
  USE Urartian language
Khalifat
  USE Caliphate
Khalifs
  USE Caliphs
Khalīj al-ʿAqabah
  USE Aqaba, Gulf of
Khalij as Suways
  USE Suez, Gulf of
Khalij Surt, Battle of, 1942
  USE Sidra, Gulf of, Battle of, 1942
Khalīj ʿUmān
  USE Oman, Gulf of
Khaling language
  ⌐PL3801.K4⌐
  BT Tibeto-Burman languages
Khalji dynasty
  USE Khilji dynasty
Khalkē Island (Greece)
  USE Khalki Island (Greece)
Khalkha dialect
  ⌐PL421⌐
  UF Kalka dialect
      Khalkha language
  BT Mongolian language
Khalkha language
  USE Khalkha dialect
Khalkhas
  ⌐DS793.M7 (Mongolia)⌐
  UF Kalkas
Khalkhasian Plain (Mongolia)
  BT Plains—Mongolia
Khalki Island (Greece)
  UF Calchi Island (Greece)
      Chalke Island (Greece)
      Charki Island (Greece)
      Karchi Island (Greece)
      Khalkē Island (Greece)
      Nísos Chálkē (Greece)
  BT Dodecanese
      Islands—Greece
Khalkidhikí Peninsula (Greece)
  USE Chalcidice Peninsula (Greece)
Khalkidikē Peninsula (Greece)
  USE Chalcidice Peninsula (Greece)
Khalkidiki Peninsula (Greece)
  USE Chalcidice Peninsula (Greece)
Khallukh
  USE Karluks
Kham language
  BT San languages
      South Africa—Languages
Kham language (Nepal)
  ⌐PL3801.K497⌐
  BT Tibeto-Burman languages
Khamlāṃba (Hindu deity)
  ⌐BL1225.K48⌐
  BT Gods, Hindu
Khamou language
  USE Khmu' language
Khamti language
  ⌐PL4251.K4⌐
  BT Tai languages
Khamtis
  ⌐DS432.K44⌐
  UF Tai Khamtis
  BT Ethnology—Burma
      Ethnology—India
      Tai (Southeast Asian people)
Khamu (Southeast Asian people)
  USE Khmu' (Southeast Asian people)
Khamuk (Southeast Asian people)
  USE Khmu' (Southeast Asian people)
Khamuk language
  USE Khmu' language
Khān Maysalūn, Battle of, 1920
  UF Maysalūn, Battle of, 1920
  BT Syria—History—20th century
Khan Omurtag Fort (Bulgaria)
  USE Aulŭt na Khan Omurtag (Bulgaria)

Khana language
  USE Kana language
Khanal family
  USE Khanāla family
Khanāla family *(Not Subd Geog)*
  UF Khanal family
Khand language
  USE Kui language
Khandelwals
  ⌐DS432.K46⌐
  BT Caste—India
      Ethnology—India
      Vaisyas
Khangai Mountains (Mongolia)
  UF Hangay Mountains (Mongolia)
      Hangayn Nuruu (Mongolia)
  BT Mountains—Mongolia
Khangchendzonga (Nepal and India)
  USE Kānchenjunga (Nepal and India)
Khanka, Battle of, 1936
  UF Hanka, Battle of, 1936
  BT Russo-Japanese Border Conflicts,
      1932-1941
Khanty
  ⌐DK759.K53⌐
  UF Ostiaks
      Ostyaks
  BT Ethnology—Russian S.F.S.R.
      Finno-Ugrians
Khanty decoration and ornament
  USE Decoration and ornament, Khanty
Khanty epic poetry
  USE Epic poetry, Khanty
Khanty folk literature
  USE Folk literature, Khanty
Khanty folk-songs
  USE Folk-songs, Khanty
Khanty language
  ⌐PH1401-1409⌐
  UF Ostiak language
      Ostyak language
  BT Ob-Ugric languages
      Russian S.F.S.R.—Languages
Khanty literature *(May Subd Geog)*
  ⌐PH1408-1409⌐
  NT Folk literature, Khanty
Khanty poetry *(May Subd Geog)*
  NT Epic poetry, Khanty
Khapra beetle
  ⌐QL596.D4 (Entomology)⌐
  ⌐SB945.K45 (Pest)⌐
  UF Trogoderma granarium
  BT Beetles
      Grain—Storage—Diseases and injuries
Kharāna (Jordan)
  USE Qaṣr Kharāna (Jordan)
Kharejites
  USE Kharijites
Kharg Island (Iran)
  USE Khark Island (Iran)
Khari Boli language
  ⌐PK1969.3⌐
  UF Kharībolī language
  BT Hindi language
      Indo-Aryan languages, Modern
Khari Boli philology
Khari Boli poetry *(May Subd Geog)*
Kharia language
  ⌐PL4579⌐
  BT Munda languages
Kharias
  ⌐DS432.K48⌐
  UF Kharrias
      Kherias
  BT Mundas
Kharībolī language
  USE Khari Boli language
Kharijites *(May Subd Geog)*
  ⌐BP195.K4-42⌐

UF Karigites
    Kharejites
    Khawarijs
BT Islamic sects
NT Azraqites
    Ibadites
Kharj Island (Iran)
  USE Khark Island (Iran)
Kharjas
  USE Muwashshah
Khark Island (Iran)
  UF Jazīrah Kharg (Iran)
    Jazīrah Khārj (Iran)
    Jazīrah-ya Khark (Iran)
    Jazīrat Kharg (Iran)
    Jazīrat Khārj (Iran)
    Jazīreh-ye Khark (Iran)
    Kharg Island (Iran)
    Kharj Island (Iran)
  BT Islands—Iran
Kharkov, Battle of, 1942
  BT World War, 1939-1945—Campaigns—
    Ukraine
Kharkov, Battle of, 1943
    [D764]
  BT World War, 1939-1945—Campaigns—
    Ukraine
Kharlukh
  USE Karluks
Kharosthi alphabet
    [PK119]
  BT Alphabet
    Indo-Aryan languages—Writing
Kharri
  USE Hurrians
Kharrias
  USE Kharias
Khas (Indic people)
  USE Khasa (Indic people)
Khas language
  USE Nepali language
Khas tribe
  USE Khasa (Indic people)
Khasa (Indic people)
  UF Khas (Indic people)
    Khas tribe
    Khasias (Indic people)
    Khasyas (Indic people)
  BT Ethnology—India
    Ethnology—Nepal
Khasa (Indic people) law
  USE Law, Khasa (Indic people)
Khasan Incident, 1938
  USE Changkufeng Incident, 1938
Khasi authors
  USE Authors, Khasi
Khasi ethics
  USE Ethics, Khasi
Khasi imprints *(May Subd Geog)*
Khasi language
    [PL4451]
  UF Khassi language
  BT Austroasiatic languages
  NT War dialect
Khasi law
  USE Law, Khasi
Khasi literature *(May Subd Geog)*
Khasi marriage customs and rites
  USE Marriage customs and rites, Khasi
Khasi nursery rhymes
  USE Nursery rhymes, Khasi
Khasi philology
Khasi poetry *(May Subd Geog)*
  NT Nursery rhymes, Khasi
Khasia pine
    [QK494.5.P66 (Botany)]
    [SD397.P576 (Forestry)]
  UF Pinus kesiya
    Pinus khasya
  BT Pine

Khasias (Indic people)
  USE Khasa (Indic people)
Khasis
    [DS432.K5]
  BT Ethnology—India
  NT Jaintia (Indic people)
    Missions to Khasis
Khassi language
  USE Khasi language
Khasyas (Indic people)
  USE Khasa (Indic people)
Khat language
  USE Katu language
Khatanga River (R.S.F.S.R.)
  UF Reka Khatanga (R.S.F.S.R.)
  BT Rivers—Russian S.F.S.R.
Khatmīyah members *(May Subd Geog)*
Khattaks
    [DS432.K53]
  BT Ethnology—Pakistan
Khattili language
  USE Hattic language
Khattish language
  USE Hattic language
Khatyn' Memorial Complex (Byelorussian
  S.S.R.)
  USE Khatyn' War Memorial (Byelorussian
    S.S.R.)
Khatyn' War Memorial (Byelorussian S.S.R.)
  UF Khatyn' Memorial Complex
    (Byelorussian S.S.R.)
    Memorial "Khatyn'" (Byelorussian
    S.S.R.)
    Memorial'nyĭ kompleks "Khatyn'"
    (Byelorussian S.S.R.)
  BT War memorials—Byelorussian S.S.R.
    World War, 1939-1945—Byelorussian
    S.S.R.
Khawarijs
  USE Kharijites
Khawr 'Abd Allāh (Kuwait and Iraq)
  USE 'Abd Allāh Inlet (Kuwait and Iraq)
Khaya
    [QK495.M52]
  BT Meliaceae
Khaya anthotheca
    [QK495.M52 (Botany)]
    [SD397.K (Forestry)]
  UF Mahogany, White
    White mahogany
Khayāl
  USE Khyāl (Musical form)
Khayasa language
  UF Hayasa language
    Khaiass language
  BT Armenian language
Khaybar, Battle of, 628
Khazā'il (Arab people)
  BT Arabs
    Ethnology—Iraq
Khazara language
  USE Hazara language
Khazars *(May Subd Geog)*
  UF Akatziroi
    Chazars
    Chozars
    Khazirs
    Khwalisses
  BT Ethnology—Soviet Union
    Jews—Soviet Union
    Soviet Union—History—To 1533
Khazirs
  USE Khazars
Khe Sanh, Battle of, 1968
    [DS557.8.K5]
  BT Vietnamese Conflict, 1961-1975—
    Campaigns—Vietnam
Kheja language
  USE Khezha language
Kheliodromia Island (Greece)
  USE Alónnisos Island (Greece)

Khen
  USE Kaen
Khephongs (Indic people)
  USE Halams (Indic people)
Kherias
  USE Kharias
Khersones Tavricheskiĭ (City)
  USE Chersonese (City)
Kherwari language
    [PL4511-4519]
  BT Santali language
  RT Munda languages
Kheta
  USE Hittites
Khevsurs
  USE Khevzurs
Khevzurs
  UF Khevsurs
Khezare language
  USE Hazara language
Khezha language
    [PL4001.K54]
  UF Kezha language
    Kezhama language
    Kheja language
  BT Naga languages
Khibinskaya tundra (R.S.F.S.R.)
  USE Khibiny Mountains (R.S.F.S.R.)
Khibinskie gory (R.S.F.S.R.)
  USE Khibiny Mountains (R.S.F.S.R.)
Khibiny Mountains (R.S.F.S.R.)
  UF Khibinskaya tundra (R.S.F.S.R.)
    Khibinskie gory (R.S.F.S.R.)
    Umptek Mountains (R.S.F.S.R.)
  BT Mountains—Russian S.F.S.R.
Khil-khuur
  USE Morin khuur
Khilafat
  USE Caliphate
Khilafat Movement
  BT Caliphate
    Muslims—India
    Panislamism
Khiliodhrómia Island (Greece)
  USE Alónnisos Island (Greece)
Khilji dynasty *(Not Subd Geog)*
    [DS459.2]
  UF Khalji dynasty
  BT India—History—1000-1526
Khinalugh language
    [PK9201.K51]
  BT Daghestan languages
Khíos Island (Greece)
  USE Chios Island (Greece)
Khipu
  USE Quipu
Khirbat al-Marī (Syria)
  USE Mari (Ancient city)
Khirbat Firdaws
  USE Herodium
Khirbat Qumrān
  USE Qumran Site
Khirbat Tall al-Fāri'ah
  USE Fāri'ah, Tall al-
Khirbet Qumrān
  USE Qumran Site
Khirokitia Site (Cyprus) *(Not Subd Geog)*
  BT Cyprus—Antiquities
Khita
  USE Hittites
Khitan language
    [PL3311.K45]
  BT China—Languages
    Mongolian languages
Khitan Mongols *(Not Subd Geog)*
  UF Ch'itan
    Iron dynasty, China
    Kara Kitai
    Kitai

Khitan Mongols *(Continued)*
  BT China—History—Sung dynasty, 960-
        1279
      Mongols
  NT China—History—Liao dynasty, 947-
        1125
Khjai Mendung (Gamelan)
  UF Venerable Dark Cloud
  BT Gamelan
Khlysty
  UF Chlysty
  BT Christian sects—Soviet Union
Khmer art
  USE Art, Khmer
Khmer astronomy
  USE Astronomy, Khmer
Khmer Empire
  USE Cambodia—History—800-1444
Khmer fiction *(May Subd Geog)*
Khmer language
  ₍PL4321-9₎
  UF Cambodian language
  BT Cambodia—Languages
      Mon-Khmer languages
Khmer literature
  ₍PL4328₎
Khmer manuscripts
  USE Manuscripts, Khmer
Khmer mural painting and decoration
  USE Mural painting and decoration, Khmer
Khmer pottery
  USE Pottery, Khmer
Khmer temples
  USE Temples, Khmer
Khmers *(May Subd Geog)*
  UF Cambodians
  BT Cambodia
      Ethnology—Cambodia
Khmou language
  USE Khmu' language
Khmu' (Southeast Asian people)
  (May Subd Geog)
  UF Kamhmu (Southeast Asian people)
      Kammu (Southeast Asian people)
      Kamu (Southeast Asian people)
      Kha Mou (Southeast Asian people)
      Khamu (Southeast Asian people)
      Khamuk (Southeast Asian people)
      Mou (Southeast Asian people)
      Pouteng (Southeast Asian people)
  BT Ethnology—Asia, Southeastern
Khmu' language
  UF Kamhmu language
      Kammu language
      Khamou language
      Khamuk language
      Khmou language
      Phouteng language
  BT Mon-Khmer languages
Khmun (City)
  USE Hermopolis Magna (City)
Khmunu (City)
  USE Hermopolis Magna (City)
Khnum, Temple of (Elephantine, Egypt)
  USE Temple of Khnum (Elephantine,
        Egypt)
Kho kho (Game)
  ₍GV1099₎
Khōḍiyāra Mātā (Hindu deity)
  (May Subd Geog)
  ₍BL1225.K53₎
  BT Gods, Hindu
Khoikhoi (African people)
  ₍DT737 (General)₎
  ₍DT764.H6 (South Africa)₎
  UF Hottentots
  BT Ethnology—Africa, Southern
  NT Bondelswarts (African people)
      Griquas
      Heikum (African people)
      Korana (African people)

Missions to Khoikhoi
      Nama (African people)
      Tannekwe (African people)
— **Anthropometry**
— **Name**
  NT Hottentot (Name)
Khoikhoi language
  ₍PL8251₎
  UF Hottentot language
  BT Africa, Southern—Languages
      Khoisan languages
  NT Korana language
      Nama language
— **Names**
  USE Names, Khoikhoi
Khoikhoi names
  USE Names, Khoikhoi
Khoisan languages
  UF Click languages, Non-Bantu
  BT Africa, Southern—Languages
      African languages
  NT G//ana language
      G/wi language
      Khoikhoi language
      San languages
      Sandawe language
— **Clicks**
  BT Clicks (Phonetics)
Khojahs
  ₍BP195.K45₎
  BT Islamic sects
Khond language
  USE Kui language
Khonds
  USE Kandhs
Khōr 'Abdullah (Kuwait and Iraq)
  USE 'Abd Allāh Inlet (Kuwait and Iraq)
Khora
  USE Korana (African people)
Khorat Plateau (Thailand)
  UF Korat Plateau (Thailand)
  BT Plateaus—Thailand
Khorezmi language
  ₍P918₎
  UF Choresmian language
      Khwarezmian language
  BT Iranian languages, Middle
      Turkic languages
      Turkic languages, Southeast
Khorsiai (Ancient city)
  USE Chorsiai (Ancient city)
Khotan (Ancient city) *(Not Subd Geog)*
  UF Hotal (Ancient city)
      Hot'ien (Ancient city)
  BT China—Antiquities
      Cities and towns, Ruined, extinct, etc.
        —China
Khotan-Saka language
  USE Khotanese language
Khotana Indians
  USE Koyukon Indians
Khotanese language
  ₍PK6199.8₎
  UF Khotan-Saka language
      Khotani language
      Khotansaka language
      Middle Khotanese language
      North Aryan language
      Old Khotanese language
      Saka language
  BT Iranian languages, Middle
Khotanese philology *(May Subd Geog)*
Khotani language
  USE Khotanese language
Khotansaka language
  USE Khotanese language
Khotin, Battle of, 1621
  USE Hotin, Battle of, 1621
Khotin, Battle of, 1673
  USE Hotin, Battle of, 1673

Khowar language
  ₍PK7070₎
  BT Pisacha languages
Khrebet Cherskogo (R.S.F.S.R.)
  USE Cherskiĭ Range (R.S.F.S.R.)
Khrebet Chingiztau (Kazakh S.S.R.)
  USE Chingiztau (Kazakh S.S.R.)
Khrebet Gissarskiy (Tajik S.S.R. and Uzbek
    S.S.R.)
  USE Gissar Range (Tajik S.S.R. and Uzbek
        S.S.R.)
Khrebet Koryatskiy (R.S.F.S.R.)
  USE Koryak Range (R.S.F.S.R.)
Khrebet Kuryatskiy (R.S.F.S.R.)
  USE Koryak Range (R.S.F.S.R.)
Khrebet Kuznetskiĭ Alatau (R.S.F.S.R.)
  USE Kuznetsk Alatau (R.S.F.S.R.)
Khrebet Paĭ-Khoĭ (R.S.F.S.R.)
  USE Paĭ-Khoĭ Range (R.S.F.S.R.)
Khrebet Pay-Khoy (R.S.F.S.R.)
  USE Paĭ-Khoĭ Range (R.S.F.S.R.)
Khrebet Putorana (R.S.F.S.R.)
  USE Putorana Plateau (R.S.F.S.R.)
Khrebet Sette-Daban (R.S.F.S.R.)
  USE Sette-Daban Range (R.S.F.S.R.)
Khrebet Sikhota Alin' (R.S.F.S.R.)
  USE Sikhote-Alin' Range (R.S.F.S.R.)
Khrebet Tarbagataĭ (Kazakh S.S.R. and China)
  USE Tarbagataĭ Range (Kazakh S.S.R. and
        China)
Khrebet Trialeti (Georgian S.S.R.)
  USE Trialet Range (Georgian S.S.R.)
Khrebet Turkestanski
  USE Turkestan Range
Khrebet Udokan (R.S.F.S.R.)
  USE Udokan Range (R.S.F.S.R.)
Khuf dialect
  ₍PK6996.K₎
  UF Chuf dialect
  BT Pamir languages
Khufu, Pyramid of (Egypt)
  USE Great Pyramid (Egypt)
Khumana family *(Not Subd Geog)*
Khumbu Valley (Nepal)
  BT Valleys—Nepal
Khumi language (Sudan)
  USE Toposa language
Khumis
  UF Kami (Burmese tribe)
      Kwemi
Khün language *(May Subd Geog)*
  ₍PL4251.K5₎
  UF Hkun language
  BT Burma—Languages
      Tai languages
      Thailand—Languages
!Khung (African people)
  USE !Kung (African people)
!Khung language
  USE !Xũ language
Khunu (Indic people)
  USE Kanaura (Indic people)
Khunung language
  USE Nung language
Khūr 'Abdullah (Kuwait and Iraq)
  USE 'Abd Allāh Inlet (Kuwait and Iraq)
Khurrians
  USE Hurrians
Khuwārizmī (Computer program language)
  ₍QA76.73.K₎
  BT Programming languages (Electronic
        computers)
Khwae Yai River (Thailand)
  USE Mae Klong River (Thailand)
Khwakhwa (African people)
  ₍DT786.5₎
  BT Ethnology—Lesotho
Khwalisses
  USE Khazars
Khwara language
  USE Quara language

Khwarezmian language
USE Khorezmi language
Khyāl (Musical form)
UF Khayāl
BT Music, Hindustani
Vocal music—India
Khyang language
⌜PL4001.K6⌝
UF Khyeng language
RT Chin languages
Khyeng language
USE Khyang language
Ki (Chinese philosophy)
USE Ch'i (Chinese philosophy)
Ki (The Hebrew particle)
BT Hebrew language—Particles
Ki-45 (Fighter plane)
USE Toryū (Fighter plane)
Ki 61 (Fighter plane)
USE Hien (Fighter planes)
Ki 84 (Fighter planes)
USE Hayate (Fighter planes)
K'i-lien-schan (China)
USE Ch'i-lien Mountains (China)
Ki River (Japan)
UF Kinokawa (Japan)
BT Rivers—Japan
Ki-vili language
USE Vili language
Ki-vumbu language
USE Vili language
Kiaerulf family
USE Kjaerulf family
Kiaerulff family
USE Kjaerulf family
Kiakh language
USE Adyghe language
Kiang
USE Equus hemionus
Kiangsi dialects
USE Kan dialects
Kiangsu style of Chinese cookery
USE Cookery, Chinese—Kiangsu style
Kiaser family
USE Kaiser family
Kibach family
USE Keebaugh family
Kibale Forest Reserve (Uganda)
BT Forest reserves—Uganda
National parks and reserves—Uganda
Kibbutz Haggadot
USE Haggadot, Kibbutz
Kibbutzim *(May Subd Geog)*
⌜HX742.2⌝
UF Collective settlements—Israel
Ḳibutsim
RT Moshav shitufi
NT Youth volunteers in kibbutzim
KiBeembe language
USE Bembe language (Congo (Brazzaville))
KiBembe language
USE Bembe language (Congo (Brazzaville))
Kibi Daijin nittō ekotoba (Scrolls)
UF Kibi's adventures scroll
BT Painting, Japanese—Kamakura-
Momoyama periods, 1185-1600
Scrolls, Japanese
Kibi Region (Japan)
Kibi's adventures scroll
USE Kibi Daijin nittō ekotoba (Scrolls)
Kiblah
USE Qiblah
Kiboma (African people)
USE Boma (African people)
Kiboma language
USE Boma language
Kibulamatadi language
USE Kituba language
Ḳibutsim
USE Kibbutzim

Kibyoshi-bon
BT Japanese fiction—Edo period, 1600-1868
Kīcaka (Hindu mythology)
UF Kichaka (Hindu mythology)
BT Mythology, Hindu
Kichaka (Hindu mythology)
USE Kīcaka (Hindu mythology)
Kiché language
USE Quiché language
Kichean languages
USE Quichean languages
Kichik Site (Alaska)
USE Kijik Site (Alaska)
Kicho Indians
USE Quijo Indians
Kick (Swimming)
USE Swimming—Kick
Kick sorters
USE Pulse height analyzers
Kickapoo, Battle of, 1838
BT Texas—History—Republic, 1836-1846
Kickapoo Indians
⌜E99.K4⌝
UF Kikapoo Indians
BT Algonquian Indians
Indians of Mexico
Indians of North America
Kickapoo language
⌜PM1526⌝
BT Algonquian languages
Kickers (Football)
USE Placekickers (Football)
Kicking (Football)
⌜GV951.7⌝
UF Placekicking (Football)
Punting (Football)
BT Football
NT Placekickers (Football)
Kicking (Swimming)
USE Swimming—Kick
Kicking in soccer
USE Soccer—Kicking
Kicksorters
USE Pulse height analyzers
Kid family
USE Kidd family
Kida family *(Not Subd Geog)*
Kidawida dialect
USE Dabida dialect
Kidd family *(Not Subd Geog)*
UF Kid family
Kidde family
Kiddall family
USE Kidwell family
Kidde family
USE Kidd family
Kiddell family
USE Kidwell family
Kiddeman family
USE Kitterman family
Kidder Point (Me.)
BT Peninsulas—Maine
Kiddie porn
USE Children in pornography
Kiddle family
USE Kidwell family
Kiddoo family *(Not Subd Geog)*
KiDigo language
USE Digo language
Kidnapping *(May Subd Geog)*
⌜HV6595-6604⌝
BT Criminal law
Offenses against the person
RT Abduction
SA *subdivision* Kidnapping, ⌜date⌝ *under
names of individual persons*
NT Ransom
— Italy

Kidnapping, Parental *(May Subd Geog)*
UF Child snatching by parents
Parental kidnapping
BT Custody of children
Kidnapping (Roman law)
USE Plagium
Kidney, Artificial
USE Artificial kidney
Kidney, Cystic
UF Cystic disease of the kidney
Cystic kidney
Kidneys—Cysts
Renal cystic disease
BT Kidneys—Diseases
Kidney, Polycystic
USE Polycystic kidney disease
Kidney bean *(May Subd Geog)*
UF Navy bean
Phaseolus vulgaris
Pinto bean
Snap bean
String bean
BT Beans
Kidney calculi
USE Kidneys—Calculi
Kidney dialysis
USE Hemodialysis
Kidney disease, Polycystic
USE Polycystic kidney disease
Kidney failure
USE Renal insufficiency
Kidney function tests
UF Renography
BT Function tests (Medicine)
Kidneys—Diseases—Diagnosis
NT Glomerular filtration rate
Kidney glomerulus
UF Glomeruli renis
Glomerulus, Kidney
Malpighian glomerulus
Renal glomerulus
Ruysch's glomeruli
BT Kidneys—Blood-vessels
NT Glomerular filtration rate
— **Diseases** *(May Subd Geog)*
NT Glomerulonephritis
Kidney hypertrophy
USE Kidneys—Hypertrophy
Kidney pelvis
UF Pelvis, Kidney
BT Kidneys
Kidney stones
USE Kidneys—Calculi
Kidney tubular transport
USE Renal tubular transport
Kidney tubules
UF Nephron
Renal tubules
Tubules, Kidney
BT Kidneys
NT Brush border membrane
Renal tubular transport
Kidney worms
USE Stephanurus
Kidneys
⌜QL872 (Comparative anatomy)⌝
⌜QM404 (Human anatomy)⌝
⌜QP211 (Physiology)⌝
BT Abdomen
Urinary organs
RT Nephrology
SA *headings beginning with the word
Renal*
NT Adrenal glands
Diuresis
Gerota's fascia
Interrenal gland
Juxtaglomerular apparatus
Kidney pelvis
Kidney tubules
Renal papilla

Kidneys *(Continued)*
    Somatomedin
    Urine
    Wolffian body
— **Biopsy**
    UF Renal biopsy
— **Blood-vessels**
    NT Kidney glomerulus
         Renal artery
— — **Radiography**
— — **Surgery**
    NT Splenorenal shunt, Surgical
— **Calculi**
    [RC916]
    UF Kidney calculi
         Kidney stones
         Nephritic calculi
         Nephrolithiasis
         Renal calculi
         Renal lithiasis
         Renal stones
         Stones, Kidney
    BT Calculi, Urinary
         Kidneys—Diseases
— **Cancer**
    [RC280.K5]
    NT Nephroblastoma
— **Cysts**
    USE Kidney, Cystic
— **Diseases** *(May Subd Geog)*
    [RC902-918]
    UF Nephritis
         Nephropathy
         Renal diseases
    NT Adrenal glands—Diseases
         Albuminuria
         Alport's syndrome
         Bright's disease
         Diabetic nephropathies
         Hospitals—Nephrological services
         Hydronephrosis
         Kidney, Cystic
         Kidneys—Calculi
         Nephritis, Interstitial
         Nephrologists
         Nephrosclerosis
         Nephrotic syndrome
         Polycystic kidney disease
         Proteinuria
         Pyelonephritis
         Renal artery obstruction
         Renal hypertension
         Renal insufficiency
         Renal manifestations of general
           diseases
         Renal osteodystrophy
         Renal tubular transport, Disorders
           of
         Uremia
— — **Diagnosis**
    NT Kidney function tests
         Kidneys—Radiography
         Urine—Analysis
         Urine—Examination
— — **Homeopathic treatment**
    [RX351-6]
— — **Nutritional aspects**
— **Displacement**
    UF Nephroptosis
— **Drug effects**
    USE Renal pharmacology
— **Effect of drugs on**
    USE Renal pharmacology
— **Hydatids**
    [RC184.T6]
— **Hypertrophy**
    UF Kidney hypertrophy
         Renal hypertrophy
— **Innervation**
— **Necrosis**
— **Preservation**

— **Radiography**
    UF Pyelography
         Renography
    BT Kidneys—Diseases—Diagnosis
— **Surgery**
    [RD575]
    UF Nephrotomy
    NT Kidneys, Movable
         Nephrostomy
— **Transplantation**
— **Tuberculosis**
    [RC312.5.K5]
— **Tumors**
    [RC280.K5]
Kidneys, Effect of drugs on
    USE Renal pharmacology
Kidneys, Movable
    [RC918.M8]
    BT Kidneys—Surgery
Kids (Goats) *(May Subd Geog)*
    BT Domestic animals—Infancy
         Goats
Kidwell family *(Not Subd Geog)*
    UF Kiddall family
         Kiddell family
         Kiddle family
Kidzhil Site (Alaska)
    USE Kijik Site (Alaska)
Kiebach family
    USE Keebaugh family
Kiebler family *(Not Subd Geog)*
    UF Kebler family
         Kubler family
         Kuebler family
Kiefer family
    USE Keefer family
Kieffer family
    USE Keefer family
Kiehl family
    USE Kiel family
Kiel Bay (Germany) *(Not Subd Geog)*
    UF Kiel Bight (Germany)
         Kiel Firth (Germany)
         Kieler Bucht (Germany)
    BT Bays—Germany (West)
Kiel Bight (Germany)
    USE Kiel Bay (Germany)
Kiel Canal (Germany)
    UF Kaiser Wilhelm Kanal (Germany)
         Kieler Kanal (Germany)
         Nord-Ostsee Kanal (Germany)
         North Sea-Baltic Canal (Germany)
    BT Canals—Germany (West)
Kiel Castle (Kiel, Germany)
    USE Schloss Kiel (Kiel, Germany)
Kiel family *(Not Subd Geog)*
    UF Kehl family
         Keil family
         Kiehl family
    RT Keel family
         Keilen family
Kiel Fiord (Germany)
    USE Kiel Fjord (Germany)
Kiel Firth (Germany)
    USE Kiel Bay (Germany)
         Kiel Fjord (Germany)
Kiel Fjord (Germany)
    UF Kiel Fiord (Germany)
         Kiel Firth (Germany)
         Kieler Fiord (Germany)
         Kieler Föhrde (Germany)
         Kieler Förde (Germany)
    BT Fjords—Germany (West)
Kiel House (Zurich, Switzerland)
    USE Haus zum Kiel (Zurich, Switzerland)
KIEL KIS (Information retrieval system)
    [RA971.6]
    UF Kieler Klinik-Informationssystem
    BT Information storage and retrieval
         systems—Hospitals

Kiel pottery
    UF Pottery, Kiel
    BT Pottery—Germany (West)
Kiel Regatta, 1907
    [GV827]
Kiel Regatta, 1914
    [GV827]
Kiel, Treaty of, 1814
    [DL500-501]
Kielce Palace (Kielce, Poland)
    USE Pałac w Kielcach (Kielce, Poland)
Kieler Bucht (Germany)
    USE Kiel Bay (Germany)
Kieler Burg (Kiel, Germany)
    USE Schloss Kiel (Kiel, Germany)
Kieler Fiord (Germany)
    USE Kiel Fjord (Germany)
Kieler Föhrde (Germany)
    USE Kiel Fjord (Germany)
Kieler Förde (Germany)
    USE Kiel Fjord (Germany)
Kieler Kanal (Germany)
    USE Kiel Canal (Germany)
Kieler Klinik-Informationssystem
    USE KIEL KIS (Information retrieval
        system)
Kieler Rathaus (Kiel, Germany)
    BT City halls—Germany (West)
Kieler Schloss (Kiel, Germany)
    USE Schloss Kiel (Kiel, Germany)
Kieltz family
    USE Kilts family
Kiely family
    USE Kelley family
Kien language
    USE Tchien language
Kienapel family
    USE Kinnapel family
Kierkegaard family *(Not Subd Geog)*
Kierkendall family
    USE Kuykendall family
Kierrulf family
    USE Kjaerulf family
Kiersey family
    USE Kersey family
Kierulf family
    USE Kjaerulf family
Kierulff family
    USE Kjaerulf family
Kiesel family *(Not Subd Geog)*
    UF Kiesler family
         Kiessel family
         Kisel family
         Kissel family
Kieselguhr
    USE Diatomaceous earth
Kieselmangan
    USE Rhodonite
Kiesler family
    USE Kiesel family
Kiessel family
    USE Kiesel family
Kiesser family
    USE Kaiser family
Kieth family
    USE Keith family
Kiev (Ukraine)
— **History**
— — **Revolution, 1917-1921**
Kiev (Ukraine). Podil
    USE Podol (Kiev, Ukraine)
Kiev (Ukraine). Podol
    USE Podol (Kiev, Ukraine)
Kiev, Battle of, 1943
    USE World War, 1939-1945—Campaigns—
        Dnieper River
Kiev camera
    [TR263.K]
Kiev computer
    BT Electronic digital computers

Kievan Russia
  USE Soviet Union—History—Kievan
       period, 862-1237
Kievit family
  USE Kiewit family
Kiewit family *(Not Subd Geog)*
  UF Kievit family
     Kiewitt family
Kiewitt family
  USE Kiewit family
Kieżgajło family *(Not Subd Geog)*
  UF Kieżgajłowie family
Kieżgajłowie family
  USE Kieżgajło family
Kiga (African people)
  USE Chiga (African people)
Kiga language
  UF Chiga language
     Ciga language
     Lukiga language
     Rukiga language
  BT Bantu languages
  RT Nyankore-Kiga language
Kigensetsu
  USE Kenkoku Kinen no hi
Kight family *(Not Subd Geog)*
  UF Kite family
Kigiriama (African people)
  USE Giryama (African people)
Kigiryama language
  USE Giryama language
Kii Channel (Japan)
  USE Kii Strait (Japan)
Kii Strait (Japan) *(Not Subd Geog)*
  UF Kii Channel (Japan)
     Kii-suidō (Japan)
  BT Straits—Japan
Kii-suidō (Japan)
  USE Kii Strait (Japan)
Kiil family *(Not Subd Geog)*
Kijik Site (Alaska) *(Not Subd Geog)*
  UF Kichik Site (Alaska)
     Kidzhil Site (Alaska)
     Kilchich Site (Alaska)
     Klichikh Site (Alaska)
     Kyzzhakh Site (Alaska)
     Nikhak Site (Alaska)
     Nikhkak Site (Alaska)
     Qizhjeh Site (Alaska)
  BT Alaska—Antiquities
Kijita language
  USE Jita language
Kijkuit (N.Y.)
  BT Dwellings—New York (State)
Kijkuit Gardens (N.Y.)
  BT Gardens—New York (State)
Kikai Island (Japan)
  UF Kikai-jima (Japan)
     Kikaiga-shima (Japan)
  BT Islands—Japan
     Ryukyu Islands
Kikai-jima (Japan)
  USE Kikai Island (Japan)
Kikaiga-shima (Japan)
  USE Kikai Island (Japan)
Kikamba language
  USE Kamba language
Kikapoo Indians
  USE Kickapoo Indians
Kikar ha-Yarden (Jordan)
  USE Ghawr (Jordan)
Kikendall family
  USE Kuykendall family
Kiker family
  USE Karriker family
KiKete language
  USE Kete language
Kikka (Jet fighter plane)
  UF Nakajima kikka

  BT Airplanes, Military
     Fighter planes
     Jet planes, Military
Kikkar ha-Yarden (Jordan)
  USE Ghawr (Jordan)
Kikkawa Shintō
  USE Yoshikawa Shintō
Kiklades (Greece)
  USE Cyclades (Greece)
Kikládhes Nísoi (Greece)
  USE Cyclades (Greece)
Kikon
  USE Man (Buddhism)
Kikongo language
  USE Kongo language
Kikongo ya Leta language
  USE Kituba language
Kikoria language
  USE Kuria language
Kikouria language
  USE Kuria language
Kikuchi family *(Not Subd Geog)*
Kikuchijō (Kikuka-machi, Japan)
  USE Kukuchijō (Kikuka-machi, Japan)
Kikuria language
  USE Kuria language
Kikuyu (African people)
  [DT433.545.K55]
  UF Akikuyu (African people)
     Gikuyu (African people)
     Wakikuyu (African people)
  BT Bantus
     Ethnology—Kenya
  NT Missions to Kikuyu (African people)
  — Food
     BT Food
  — Rites and ceremonies
     NT Marriage customs and rites,
        Kikuyu
  — Women
     USE Women, Kikuyu (African people)
Kikuyu (African people) women
  USE Women, Kikuyu (African people)
Kikuyu folk-songs
  USE Folk-songs, Kikuyu
Kikuyu grass *(May Subd Geog)*
  [QK495.G74 (Botany)]
  [SB201.K (Culture)]
  UF Pennisetum clandestinum
  BT Forage plants
Kikuyu language
  [PL8379]
  UF Gikuyu language
  BT Bantu languages
     Kamba language
Kikuyu marriage customs and rites
  USE Marriage customs and rites, Kikuyu
Kikwango language
  USE Kituba language
KiKwese language
  USE Kwese language
Kikyōgan Iwakage II Iseki (Tanabe-shi, Japan)
  USE Kikyōgan Iwakage II Site (Tanabe-shi,
       Japan)
Kikyōgan Iwakage II Site (Tanabe-shi, Japan)
  (Not Subd Geog)
  UF Kagura Jinja Shimoiwakage (Tanabe-
       shi, Japan)
     Kikyōgan Iwakage II Iseki (Tanabe-shi,
       Japan)
  BT Japan—Antiquities
Kilari dialect
  USE Laadi dialect
Kilauea Volcano (Hawaii)
  BT Volcanoes—Hawaii
Kilbraith family
  USE Galbraith family
Kilbreath family
  USE Galbraith family

Kilby family *(Not Subd Geog)*
Kilchich Site (Alaska)
  USE Kijik Site (Alaska)
Kilcoyne family
  USE Coyne family
Kilega language
  [PL8380.K5]
  UF Balega language
     Lega language
  BT Bantu languages
Kilenge (Melanesian people)
  [DU553.N35]
  BT Ethnology—Papua New Guinea
Kilesa (Buddhism)
  USE Vice (Buddhism)
Kileta language
  USE Kituba language
Kilgerril (Ireland)
  UF Kilgerrill (Ireland)
Kilgerrill (Ireland)
  USE Kilgerril (Ireland)
Kilgo family
  USE Kilgore family
Kilgore family *(Not Subd Geog)*
  UF Kilgo family
     Kilgour family
     Killgo family
     Killgore family
     Killgour family
     Killgow family
Kilgour family
  USE Kilgore family
Kilian family
  USE Killian family
Kiliket
  USE Killekyatha
Kilimandjaro, Mount (Tanzania)
  USE Kilimanjaro, Mount (Tanzania)
Kilimandscharo, Mount (Tanzania)
  USE Kilimanjaro, Mount (Tanzania)
Kilimanjaro, Mount (Tanzania)
  UF Kilimandjaro, Mount (Tanzania)
     Kilimandscharo, Mount (Tanzania)
     Mount Kilimanjaro (Tanzania)
  BT Mountains—Tanzania
     Volcanoes—Tanzania
Kilims *(May Subd Geog)*
  [NK2775-2896]
  UF Kelims
  BT Carpets
     Rugs, Oriental
  NT Rugs, Baluchi
     Rugs, Nomadic
     Soumaks
  — Middle East
     UF Kilims—Near East
     NT Rugs, Yuruk
  — Near East
     USE Kilims—Middle East
  — Turkey
     NT Rugs, Yuruk
Kilindi (African people)
  UF Wakilindi (African people)
  BT Ethnology—Tanzania
Kilinyaga (Kenya)
  USE Kenya, Mount (Kenya)
Kiliu Indians
  USE Trio Indians
Kilivila language
  USE Kiriwinian language
Kiliwa Indians
  [F1221.K5]
  BT Indians of Mexico
     Yuman Indians
Kiliwa language
  [PM3914]
  UF Kiliwee language
     Kiliwi language
     Yukaliwa language

Kiliwa language *(Continued)*
    BT Indians of Mexico—Languages
          Mexico—Languages
          Yuman languages
Kiliwee language
    USE Kiliwa language
Kiliwi language
    USE Kiliwa language
Kilkenny Confederation
    USE Irish Confederation, 1642-1648
Kill River (Germany)
    USE Kyll River (Germany)
Kill Van Coll (N.J. and N.Y.)
    USE Kill Van Kull (N.J. and N.Y.)
Kill Van Kuhl (N.J. and N.Y.)
    USE Kill Van Kull (N.J. and N.Y.)
Kill Van Kull (N.J. and N.Y.)
    UF Kill Van Coll (N.J. and N.Y.)
          Kill Van Kuhl (N.J. and N.Y.)
    BT Rivers—New Jersey
          Rivers—New York (State)
Killala Lake (Ont.)
    BT Lakes—Ontario
Killar family
    USE Keller family
Killarney Provincial Park (Ont.)
    BT Parks—Ontario
Killdeer
    UF Aegialitis vocifera
    BT Plovers
Killebrew family *(Not Subd Geog)*
    UF Kennebrew family
          Killigrew family
          Kinebrew family
Killekyatha
    [DS432.K54]
    UF Chhatri
          Gombe Rama
          Katabu
          Kiliket
          Killikyatha
          Sillekyatha
    BT Artists—India
          Caste—India
          Ethnology—India
Killer bee
    USE Brazilian honeybee
Killer cells
    [QR185.8.K54]
    UF Cells, Killer
          K cells
          Natural killer cells
          NK cells
    BT Immunocompetent cells
    RT Cell-mediated cytotoxicity
    NT Antibody-dependent cell cytotoxicity
          Leucocytes
          Macrophages
Killer family
    USE Keller family
Killer whale
    [QL737.C432]
    UF Grampus orca
          Orca orca
          Orcinus orca
    BT Delphinidae
          Whales
    NT Namu (Whale)
Killer whale, False
    USE False killer whale
Killer whale, Pygmy
    USE Pygmy killer whale
Killey family
    USE Kelley family
Killgo family
    USE Kilgore family
Killgore family
    USE Kilgore family
Killgour family
    USE Kilgore family

Killgow family
    USE Kilgore family
Killian family *(Not Subd Geog)*
    UF Kilian family
          Killion family
Killifishes *(May Subd Geog)*
    [QL637.9.A8]
    UF Cyprinodontoidea
          Toothcarps
          Topminnows
    BT Atheriniformes
    NT Cyprinodontidae
          Goodeidae
          Poeciliidae
Killigrew family
    USE Killebrew family
Killikyatha
    USE Killekyatha
Killing, Mercy
    USE Euthanasia
Killing of police
    USE Police murders
Killing of the aged
    USE Aged, Killing of the
Killing of the insane
    USE Insane, Killing of the
Killingsworth family *(Not Subd Geog)*
    UF Chillingsworth family
          Killingworth family
Killingworth family
    USE Killingsworth family
Killion family
    USE Killian family
Killmer family
    USE Kilmer family
Killmor family
    USE Kilmer family
Killmore family
    USE Kilmer family
Killoran family
    USE Killoren family
Killoren family *(Not Subd Geog)*
    UF Killoran family
          Killorin family
Killorin family
    USE Killoren family
Killough Massacre, 1838
    BT Texas—History—Republic, 1836-1846
Killpatrick family
    USE Kilpatrick family
Kills family
    USE Kilts family
Killsz family
    USE Kilts family
Killure (Ireland)
Killy family
    USE Kelley family
Kilmer family *(Not Subd Geog)*
    UF Killmer family
          Killmor family
          Killmore family
          Kilmor family
          Kilmore family
    RT Kuhlman family
Kilmor family
    USE Kilmer family
Kilmore family
    USE Kilmer family
Kilns *(May Subd Geog)*
    [TP841-842]
    RT Brickmaking
          Drying apparatus
          Furnaces
    NT Cement kilns
          Chamber kilns
          Charcoal kilns
          Electric kilns
          Hoffmann kiln
          Lime-kilns
          Tunnel kilns

Kilns, Electric
    USE Electric kilns
Kilns, Rotary
    [TP841-TP842]
    [TP881 (Cement)]
    UF Rotary kilns
    RT Cement kilns
  — **Foundations**
        BT Foundations
Kilogram
    USE Standards of mass
Kilpartrick family
    USE Kilpatrick family
Kilpatric family
    USE Kilpatrick family
Kilpatrick-Dahlgren Raid, 1864
    [E476.27]
    UF Dahlgren's Raid
          Kilpatrick's Raid
          Richmond (Va.)—Raid, 1864
    BT Richmond (Va.)—History—Civil War,
          1861-1865
          United States—History—Civil War,
          1861-1865—Campaigns
Kilpatrick family *(Not Subd Geog)*
    UF Kelpatrick family
          Killpatrick family
          Kilpartrick family
          Kilpatric family
          Kilpatrieck family
Kilpatrick's Raid
    USE Kilpatrick-Dahlgren Raid, 1864
Kilpatrieck family
    USE Kilpatrick family
Kilpis Lake (Finland and Sweden)
    USE Kilpisjärvi (Finland and Sweden)
Kilpisjärvi (Finland and Sweden)
  (Not Subd Geog)
    UF Kilpis Lake (Finland and Sweden)
    BT Lakes—Finland
          Lakes—Sweden
Kils family
    USE Kilts family
Kilsal family
    USE Kelsall family
Kilshall family
    USE Kelsall family
Kilshaw family
    USE Kelsall family
Kilshawe family
    USE Kelsall family
Kilston's comet
Kilton family
    USE Kelton family
Kilts *(May Subd Geog)*
    BT Plaid
          Skirts
          Tartans
Kilts family *(Not Subd Geog)*
    UF Gieltz family
          Giltz family
          Keiltz family
          Kelts family
          Keltz family
          Kieltz family
          Kills family
          Killsz family
          Kils family
          Kiltz family
          Kultz family
    RT Kell family
Kiltz family
    USE Kilts family
Kiluba language
    USE Luba-Katanga language
Kiluba-Sanga language
    USE Sanga language
Kim
    USE Nori
KIM-1 (Computer)
    [QA76.8.K]

BT Electronic digital computers
— **Programming**
Kim Ssi Chip (Chŏngŭp-gun, Korea)
BT Dwellings—Korea (South)
Kimbala language
USE Mbala language (Bandundu region, Zaire)
Kimball family (Not Subd Geog)
UF Kimble family
RT Kimbrel family
Kimpel family
Kimball organ
 ⌐ML597⌐
BT Electronic organ
Organ
Kimberland family
USE Kimberlin family
Kimberlane family
USE Kimberlin family
Kimberley languages, Northern
USE Wororan languages
Kimberley Region (W.A.)
UF Kimberleys (W.A.)
Kimberleys (W.A.)
USE Kimberley Region (W.A.)
Kimberlin family (Not Subd Geog)
UF Cimberline family
Kimberland family
Kimberlane family
Kimberling family
Kimberling family
USE Kimberlin family
Kimberlite (May Subd Geog)
BT Peridotite
— **Inclusions**
 ⌐QE462.K5⌐
UF Enclaves in kimberlite
Inclusions in kimberlite
Kimble family
USE Kimball family
Kimboro family
USE Kimbrough family
Kimborough family
USE Kimbrough family
Kimborrow family
USE Kimbrough family
Kimbrel family (Not Subd Geog)
UF Kimbrell family
Kimbril family
RT Kimball family
Kimbrell family
USE Kimbrel family
Kimbril family
USE Kimbrel family
Kimbro family
USE Kimbrough family
Kimbrough family (Not Subd Geog)
UF Cymbrough family
Kimboro family
Kimborough family
Kimborrow family
Kimbro family
Kimbrow family
Kymborough family
Kimbrow family
USE Kimbrough family
Kimbu (Bantu people)
UF Akimbu (Bantu people)
Ukimbu (Bantu people)
BT Bantus
Ethnology—Tanzania
Kimbunda language
USE Mbunda language (Zambia)
Kimbundu folk-songs
USE Folk-songs, Kimbundu
Kimbundu language
 ⌐PL8381⌐
UF Angola language
Bunda language
Mbundu language
BT Bantu languages

Kimbundu proverbs
USE Proverbs, Kimbundu
Kimbusen Shugen Honshu
USE Shugen (Sect)
Kimch'i
 ⌐TX806⌐
BT Food, Pickled
Kimch'i industry (May Subd Geog)
Kime family
USE Kimes family
Kimegi language
USE Sagara language
Kimeru language
USE Meru language
Kimes family (Not Subd Geog)
UF Keim family
Kime family
Kimonos (May Subd Geog)
 ⌐GT1560⌐
NT Obi
— **Pattern design**
 ⌐TT560⌐
BT Dressmaking—Pattern design
Kimp family
USE Kemp family
Kimpel family (Not Subd Geog)
UF Kimple family
RT Kimball family
Kimple family
USE Kimpel family
Kimpton family
USE Kempton family
Kimsey family
USE Kimzey family
Kimzey family (Not Subd Geog)
UF Kimsey family
Kin recognition in animals
 (May Subd Geog)
 ⌐QL761.5⌐
UF Recognition of kin in animals
BT Familial behavior in animals
Kin selection (Evolution)
BT Familial behavior in animals
Natural selection
Kinagase Iseki (Gokashō-chō, Japan)
USE Kinagase Site (Gokashō-chō, Japan)
Kinagase Site (Gokashō-chō, Japan)
 (Not Subd Geog)
UF Kinagase Iseki (Gokashō-chō, Japan)
BT Japan—Antiquities
Kinai Region (Japan)
 ⌐DS894.69.K5⌐
UF Go Kinai (Japan)
Kinapel family
USE Kinnapel family
Kinaray-a language (May Subd Geog)
UF Antiqueno language
Binukidnon language
Hamtiknon language
Hinaray-a language
Hinaraya language
Karay-a language
Kinaraya language
BT Philippine languages
Philippines—Languages
Kinaraya language
USE Kinaray-a language
Kinard family (Not Subd Geog)
UF Kinerd family
Kinnard family
Kynard family
Kynerd family
Kincade family
USE Kincaid family

Kincaid family (Not Subd Geog)
UF Kenkade family
Kenkead family
Kincade family
Kincaide family
Kinkad family
Kinkade family
Kinkaid family
Kinkead family
Kincaide family
USE Kincaid family
Kincannon family (Not Subd Geog)
UF Concannon family
Kincanon family
Kincanon family
USE Kincannon family
Kincey family
USE Kinsey family
Kinchai language
USE Kerinci language
Kinchinjunga (Nepal and India)
USE Kānchenjunga (Nepal and India)
Kind family (Not Subd Geog)
UF Kinn family
Kindal family
USE Kendall family
Kindall family
USE Kendall family
Kindel family
USE Kendall family
Kindell family
USE Kendall family
Kinder-Angst-Test
 ⌐BF698.8.K5⌐
BT Anxiety in children—Testing
Projective techniques for children
Kinder Scout (England)
UF Kinderscout (England)
Peak, The (England)
BT Mountains—England
Peak District (England)
Pennine Chain (England)
Kindergarten (May Subd Geog)
 ⌐HV1643 (Blind)⌐
 ⌐HV2443 (Deaf)⌐
 ⌐LB1141-LB1499⌐
UF Froebel system of education
BT Schools
RT Education, Preschool
Nursery schools
NT Creative activities and seat work
Full-day kindergarten
Montessori method of education
Object-teaching
Reading (Kindergarten)
School supervision, Primary
— **Activity programs**
UF Activity programs in kindergarten
BT Activity programs in education
— **Gifts**
USE Kindergarten—Methods and manuals
— **Methods and manuals**
 ⌐LB1169-LB1188⌐
UF Gifts (Kindergarten)
Kindergarten—Gifts
— **Music**
 ⌐M1990⌐
 ⌐MT920-MT925 (Instruction and study)⌐
UF Music—Kindergarten
BT Children's songs
Music
Music—Instruction and study
NT Nursery schools—Music
Kindergarten facilities (May Subd Geog)
 ⌐LB3325.K5⌐
UF Kindergartens
BT School facilities
Kindergarten teachers (May Subd Geog)
BT Teachers

Kindergarten teachers *(Continued)*
  NT Women kindergarten teachers
  — **Training of** *(May Subd Geog)*
      UF Kindergarten teachers, Training of
Kindergarten teachers, Training of
  USE Kindergarten teachers—Training of
Kindergartens
  USE Kindergarten facilities
Kinderscout (England)
  USE Kinder Scout (England)
Kinderspelen (Painting)
  USE Bruegel, Pieter, ca. 1525-1569.
      Children's games
Kindig family *(Not Subd Geog)*
Kindiga (African people)
  USE Tindiga (African people)
Kindle family
  USE Kendall family
Kindley family *(Not Subd Geog)*
  RT Kendall family
Kindling (Neurology)
  [RC372.5]
  BT Brain stimulation
      Convulsions
      Epilepsy
      Stimulus compounding
Kindness
  [BJ1533.K5]
  UF Affection
  BT Charity
      Conduct of life
  RT Benevolence
      Humanity
  NT Mercy
  — **Religious aspects**
  — — **Buddhism,** *[Christianity, etc.]*
Kindness to animals
  USE Animals, Treatment of
Kindol family
  USE Kendall family
Kindred family *(Not Subd Geog)*
Kinebrew family
  USE Killebrew family
Kinematic experiment water boiler
  USE Water boiler reactors
Kinematic geometry
  [QA623]
  UF Geometry, Kinematic
  NT Cyclodes
Kinematic relativity
  BT Cosmology
      Relativity (Physics)
Kinematics
  [QA841]
  [QA913 (Fluids)]
  [QC231 (Vibrations)]
  BT Dynamics
      Mathematics
      Mechanics, Analytic
      Physics
  RT Mechanics
      Motion
  NT Hodograph
      Mechanical movements
      Quaternions
      Relativistic kinematics
      Screws, Theory of
Kinematics of machinery
  USE Machinery, Kinematics of
Kinematocardiography
  [RC683.5.K5]
  UF Kinetocardiography
  BT Cardiography
Kinerd family
  USE Kinard family
Kineret, Yam (Israel)
  USE Tiberias Lake (Israel)
Kinescope recording
  USE Television film recording

Kinesics
  USE Nonverbal communication
      (Psychology)
Kinesiology *(May Subd Geog)*
  [QP303]
  UF Cinesiology
  RT Human mechanics
      Motor ability
  NT Human locomotion
      Movement education
      Sleep movements
Kinesiotherapy
  USE Exercise therapy
Kinesitherapy
  USE Mechanotherapy
Kineson family
  USE Kennison family
Kinesthesia
  USE Muscular sense
Kinetic art *(May Subd Geog)*
  [N6494.K5]
  UF Art, Kinetic
      Art in motion
  BT Art, Modern—20th century
  NT Kinetic sculpture
      Optical art
Kinetic energy of hurricanes
  USE Hurricanes—Kinetic energy
Kinetic energy of particles (Nuclear physics)
  USE Stopping power (Nuclear physics)
Kinetic family drawing test
  (May Subd Geog)
  [BF698.8.K53]
  UF Family drawing test
  BT Drawing, Psychology of
      Family
      Projective techniques
      Psychological tests for children
  RT Draw-a-family test
Kinetic-House-Tree-Person Technique
  [BF698.8.K55]
  UF K-H-T-P Technique
  BT Projective techniques
  RT House-Tree-Person-Technique
Kinetic sculpture
  [NB1272]
  UF Sculpture, Kinetic
      Sculpture in motion
  BT Art, Abstract
      Futurism (Art)
      Kinetic art
      Sound sculpture
  RT Mobiles (Sculpture)
Kinetic sculpture, American
  (May Subd Geog)
  UF American kinetic sculpture
Kinetic theory, Nuclear reactor
  USE Nuclear reactor kinetics
Kinetic theory of gases
  USE Gases, Kinetic theory of
Kinetic theory of liquids
  USE Liquids, Kinetic theory of
Kinetic theory of matter
  USE Matter, Kinetic theory of
Kinetics
  USE Dynamics
      Mechanics, Analytic
      Motion
Kinetics, Enzyme
  USE Enzyme kinetics
Kineto-phonograph
  [TR885]
  BT Cinematography
      Phonograph
Kinetocardiography
  USE Kinematocardiography
Kinetograph
  [TR885]
  BT Cinematography
      Moving-picture cameras

Kinetography
  USE Movement notation
Kinetophone
  USE Moving-pictures, Talking
Kinetoplastida
  [QL368.K5]
  BT Flagellata
  NT Trypanosomidae
Kinetoscope
  [TR870]
  BT Cinematography
King, Martin Luther
  USE King, Martin Luther, Jr., 1929-1968
King, Martin Luther, Jr., 1929-1968
  UF King, Martin Luther
  — **Monuments** *(May Subd Geog)*
  — — **Georgia**
King (Chess)
  BT Chess
      Chessmen
King cobra
  UF Hamadryad
      Naja hannah
      Ophiophagus hannah
  BT Cobras
King crab, Alaskan
  USE Alaskan king crab
King crab, Atlantic
  USE Limulus polyphemus
King family *(Not Subd Geog)*
  UF Kings family
  RT Koenig family
**King George VI and Queen Elizabeth
  Diamond Stakes**
  [SF357.K5]
  UF King George VI and Queen Elizabeth
      Festival of Britain Stakes
      Queen Elizabeth and King George VI
      Diamond Stakes
      Queen Elizabeth and King George VI
      Festival of Britain Stakes
  BT Horse-racing—England
King George VI and Queen Elizabeth Festival
  of Britain Stakes
  USE King George VI and Queen Elizabeth
      Diamond Stakes
King George's War, 1744-1748
  USE United States—History—King
      George's War, 1744-1748
King Hill Creek Wilderness (Idaho)
  (Not Subd Geog)
  UF King Hill Creek Wilderness Study
      Area (Idaho)
  BT National parks and reserves—Idaho
      Wilderness areas—Idaho
King Hill Creek Wilderness Study Area
  (Idaho)
  USE King Hill Creek Wilderness (Idaho)
**King John's Hunting Lodge Site (Writtle,
  Essex)**
  UF King John's Palace Site (Writtle,
      Essex)
  BT England—Antiquities
King John's Palace Site (Writtle, Essex)
  USE King John's Hunting Lodge Site
      (Writtle, Essex)
King Lear (Legendary character)
  USE Lear, King (Legendary character)
King mackerel
  [QL638.S35]
  UF Scomberomorus cavalla
King National Historic Site (Atlanta, Ga.)
  USE Martin Luther King, Junior, National
      Historic Site (Atlanta, Ga.)
King of Rome Palace at Chaillot (Paris,
  France)
  USE Palais du Roi de Rome (Paris, France)
King of the Confessors Cross
  USE Bury Saint Edmunds Cross

King penguin
UF Aptenodytes longirostris
Aptenodytes patagonica
BT Penguins
King Philip's War, 1675-1676
[E83.67]
UF United States—History—King Philip's
War, 1675-1676
BT Indians of North America—Wars—
1600-1750
Massachusetts—History—Colonial
period, ca. 1600-1775
New England—History—Colonial
period, ca. 1600-1775
Wampanoag Indians
NT Bloody Brook, Battle of, 1675
Falls Fight, 1676
Pierce Fight, Central Falls, R.I., 1676
King pigeons
[SF470.K56]
BT Pigeon breeds
King prawn
USE Penaeus plebejus
King rail
[QL696.G876]
UF Rallus elegans
BT Rallus
King Ranch (Tex.)
[F392.K47]
BT Ranches—Texas
King salmon
USE Chinook salmon
King snake, Common
USE Lampropeltis getulus
King snakes
USE Lampropeltis
King whitings
USE Menticirrhus
King William's War, 1689-1697
USE United States—History—King
William's War, 1689-1697
Kingala language
USE Kituba language
Kingbird, Eastern
USE Eastern kingbird
Kingbirds
USE Tyrannus
Kingcobra (Fighter plane)
UF P-63 (Fighter plane)
BT Fighter planes
Kingdom of God
[BT94]
Here are entered works on the Christian
doctrine of the spiritual reign of God. Works
on the Christian belief that the followers of
Jesus compose his kingdom are entered under
Jesus Christ—Kingdom. Works on the
kingship of Jesus are entered under
Jesus Christ—Royal office.
UF God, Kingdom of
BT Eschatology
God
NT God—Fatherhood
Jesus Christ—Kingdom
People of God
Realized eschatology
Two kingdoms (Lutheran theology)
— **Biblical teaching**
NT Day of Jehovah
— **History of doctrines**
Kingdom of God (Mormon theology)
BT Church and state—Mormon Church
Mormon Church
Kingery family *(Not Subd Geog)*
UF Kingrea family
Kingrey family
Kingrick family
Kingry family
RT Gingrich family
Kingfish Site (Ill.) *(Not Subd Geog)*
BT Illinois—Antiquities

Kingfisher, Common
USE Alcedo atthis
Kingfishers
[QL696.C72]
UF Alcedinidae
BT Coraciiformes
NT Alcedo
Belted kingfisher
Kookaburra
Kingfishes
USE Menticirrhus
Kinghunter
USE Kookaburra
Kinglet, Golden-crested
USE Regulus regulus
Kinglet, Ruby-crowned
USE Ruby-crowned kinglet
Kinglets (Birds)
USE Regulus
Kingley family
USE Kingsley family
Kingrea family
USE Kingery family
Kingrey family
USE Kingery family
Kingrick family
USE Kingery family
Kingry family
USE Kingery family
Kings, Divine right of
USE Divine right of kings
Kings and rulers
[D107 (Biography: comprehensive)]
[D352.1 (19th century)]
[D399.7 (1871-1900)]
[D412.7 (20th century)]
[JC374-JC408 (Political theory)]
[JF253 (Constitutional history)]
UF Kings and rulers, Modern
Monarchs
Royalty
Rulers
Sovereigns
Sultans
BT Heads of state
History
Political science
RT Despotism
Queens
Regency
SA *subdivisions* Kings and rulers *and*
Queens *under names of geographic
areas and ethnic groups, e.g.* Egypt
—Kings and rulers; Great Britain—
Queens; Aztecs—Kings and rulers
NT Caliphate
Caliphs
Civil list
Command performances
Coronations
Courts and courtiers
Dei gratia (in royal titles)
Dictators
Divine right of kings
Emperors
Governors
Philosopher-kings
Postage-stamps—Topics—Kings and
rulers
Prerogative, Royal
Presidents
Regents
Roman emperors
Royal houses
Royal touch
Sultanate
Temporal power of religious rulers
Thrones
Viceroys
— **Abdication**
UF Abdication of kings and rulers

SA *subdivision* Abdication, [date]
under names of rulers, e.g.
Napoleon I, Emperor of the
French, 1769-1821—Abdication,
1814
— **Biblical teaching**
BT Jews—Kings and rulers
— **Children**
BT Children
SA *subdivision* Kings and rulers—
Children *under names of
regions, countries and ethnic
groups*
— Cultus
USE Kings and rulers—Religious
aspects
— **Death and burial**
SA *subdivision* Kings and rulers—
Death and burial *under names
of countries, etc.*
— Divinity
USE Kings and rulers—Religious
aspects
— **Duties**
[JC381]
NT Education of princes
— **Dwellings**
BT Dwellings
SA *subdivision* Kings and rulers—
Dwellings *under names of
individual countries*
— Education
USE Education of princes
— **Folklore**
SA *subdivision* Kings and rulers—
Folklore *under names of
regions, countries and ethnic
groups, e.g.* Egypt—Kings and
rulers—Folklore; Aztecs—Kings
and rulers—Folklore
NT Royal touch
— **Genealogy**
[CS27]
BT Genealogy
NT Royal descent, Families of
— **Heraldry**
[CR4480-4485]
BT Heraldry
SA *subdivision* Kings and rulers—
Heraldry *under names of
countries, etc.*
— **Journeys** *(May Subd Geog)*
This heading is subdivided locally by the
name of the place visited.
SA *subdivision* Kings and rulers—
Journeys *under names of
countries, etc.*
— **Mistresses**
BT Favorites, Royal
Mistresses
SA *subdivision* Kings and rulers—
Mistresses *under names of
countries, etc.*
— **Mothers**
BT Mothers
SA *subdivision* Kings and rulers—
Mothers *under names of
regions, countries, etc.*
— **Mythology**
BT Apotheosis
Cults
SA *subdivision* Kings and rulers—
Mythology *under names of
regions, countries and ethnic
groups, e.g.* Egypt—Kings and
rulers—Mythology; Aztecs—
Kings and rulers—Mythology
NT Kings and rulers, Primitive
— **Nicknames**
— **Portraits**
[N7575-7639]

Kings and rulers
— **Portraits** *(Continued)*
  BT Kings and rulers in art
— **Religious aspects**
  UF Kings and rulers—Cultus
     Kings and rulers—Divinity
  BT Apotheosis
     Divine right of kings
     Gods
     Religion, Primitive
     Theocracy
  SA *subdivision* Kings and rulers—
     Religious aspects *under names
     of regions, countries and ethnic
     groups, e.g.* Japan—Kings and
     rulers—Religious aspects; Aztecs
     —Kings and rulers—Religious
     aspects
  NT Emperor worship
     Kings and rulers, Primitive
— **Religious life (Islam)**
— **Sisters**
  SA *subdivision* Kings and rulers—
     Sisters *under names of regions,
     countries, etc.*
— **Succession**
     ₍JF285 (Constitutional history)₎
  UF Law of succession
     Succession to the crown
  BT Inheritance and succession
     Monarchy
  NT Divine right of kings
     Marriages of royalty and nobility
     Primogeniture
     Salic law
— **Tombs**
  SA *subdivision* Kings and rulers—
     Tombs *under names of
     countries, etc.*
Kings and rulers, Ancient
Kings and rulers, Medieval
— **Succession**
Kings and rulers, Modern
  USE Kings and rulers
Kings and rulers, Primitive
  ₍GN495.5₎
  BT Kings and rulers—Mythology
     Kings and rulers—Religious aspects
  NT Indians of North America—Kings and
     rulers
Kings and rulers (in numismatics)
  (May Subd Geog)
  ₍CJ161.K54₎
  BT Numismatics
Kings and rulers as poets *(May Subd Geog)*
  UF Emperors as poets
  BT Poets
Kings and rulers in art
  ₍N8219.K5₎
  UF Kings in art
     Queens in art
  NT Kings and rulers—Portraits
Kings and rulers in literature
  NT Shakespeare, William, 1564-1616—
     Characters—Kings and rulers
Kings and rulers in rabbinical literature
  ₍BM496.9.K5₎
  BT Rabbinical literature
  UF Kings and rulers in the Midrash
  BT Rabbinical literature
Kings and rulers in the Midrash
  USE Kings and rulers in rabbinical literature
Kings' and rulers' writings
  (May Subd Geog)
  UF Writings of kings and rulers
  BT Literature
Kings' and rulers' writings, Chinese
  (May Subd Geog)
  UF Chinese kings' and rulers' writings
  BT Chinese literature

Kings Bay (Ga.)
  BT Bays—Georgia
Kings Canyon National Park (Calif.)
  BT National parks and reserves—United
     States
     Parks—California
Kings County (Calif.)
— **History**
  NT Mussel Slough Tragedy, 1880
King's Creek Plantation (Va.)
  (Not Subd Geog)
  UF Utimaria (Va.)
  BT Dwellings—Virginia
     Plantations—Virginia
Kings Cross (Sydney, N.S.W.)
  (Not Subd Geog)
  UF Cross (Sydney, N.S.W.)
     Sydney (N.S.W.). Kings Cross
King's evil
  USE Scrofula
Kings family
  USE King family
Kings in art
  USE Kings and rulers in art
King's Mountain, Battle of, 1780
  ₍E241.K5₎
  BT South Carolina—History—Revolution,
     1775-1783
     United States—History—Revolution,
     1775-1783—Campaigns
Kings Park (Perth, W.A.)
  BT Parks—Australia
King's peace
  UF Queen's peace
King's Plate (Horse race)
  USE Queen's Plate (Horse race)
King's Retreat Plantation (Ga.)
  USE Retreat Plantation (Ga.)
King's son, Marriage of (Parable)
  USE Great supper (Parable)
King's touch
  USE Royal touch
Kingsbury Place (Saint Louis, Mo.)
  (Not Subd Geog)
  UF Saint Louis (Mo.). Kingsbury Place
Kingsley family *(Not Subd Geog)*
  UF Kingley family
     Kingsly family
     Kinsley family
     Kinsly family
  RT Kinsey family
Kingsly family
  USE Kingsley family
Kingsmill Plantation Site (Va.)
  (Not Subd Geog)
  BT Plantations—Virginia
     Virginia—Antiquities
Kingsnake, Common
  USE Lampropeltis getulus
Kingsnakes
  USE Lampropeltis
Kingsolver family
  USE Kinsolving family
Kingsport Press Strike, 1963-
Kingston (N.Y.)
— **Burning by the British, 1777**
  BT United States—History—
     Revolution, 1775-1783—
     Campaigns
Kingston Peninsula (N.B.)
  BT Peninsulas—New Brunswick
Kingston Range (Calif.)
  BT Mountains—California
Kingston Range Wilderness (Calif.)
  UF Kingston Range Wilderness Study
     Area (Calif.)
  BT National parks and reserves—
     California
     Wilderness areas—California
Kingston Range Wilderness Study Area (Calif.)
  USE Kingston Range Wilderness (Calif.)

Kingwana language
  ₍PL8387₎
  BT Swahili language
     Zaire—Languages
Kiniassa language
  USE Nyanja language
Kininase II
  USE Angiotensin converting enzyme
Kiningham family
  USE Keiningham family
Kininmont family
  USE Kinnaman family
Kinins
  BT Hypotensive agents
     Vasodilators
  NT Bradykinin
     Cytokinins
     Tachykinins
Kiniramba language
  USE Nilamba language
Kiniston family
  USE Kennison family
Kinistone family
  USE Kennison family
Kinkad family
  USE Kincaid family
Kinkade family
  USE Kincaid family
Kinkaid family
  USE Kincaid family
Kinkajou
  ₍QL737.C26₎
  UF Cercoleptes caudivolvulus
     Potos caudivolvulus
     Potos flarus
Kinkajou as pets
  BT Pets
Kinkead family
  USE Kincaid family
Kinkell Castle (Scotland)
  BT Castles—Scotland
Kinkerbuurt (Amsterdam, Netherlands)
  (Not Subd Geog)
  UF Amsterdam (Netherlands).
     Kinkerbuurt
Kinki chihō (Japan)
  USE Kinki Region (Japan)
Kinki kakumei jiken, 1931
  USE Japan—History—March and October
     Incidents, 1931
Kinki Region (Japan)
  ₍DS894.6-DS894.685 (History)₎
  UF Kinki chihō (Japan)
Kinman family
  USE Kinsman family
Kinmore family
  USE Kennamer family
Kinn family
  USE Kind family
Kinnaman family *(Not Subd Geog)*
  UF Kininmont family
     Kinnamon family
     Kinnamont family
     Kinneman family
     Kuehnemann family
Kinnamon family
  USE Kinnaman family
Kinnamont family
  USE Kinnaman family
Kinnapel family *(Not Subd Geog)*
  UF Keinapel family
     Kienapel family
     Kinapel family
Kinnard family
  USE Kinard family
Kinne family
  USE Kenney family
Kinnel family
  USE Kendall family
Kinnell family
  USE Kendall family

Kinneman family
    USE Kinnaman family
        Kinsman family
Kinnemore family
    USE Kennamer family
Kinner Kailash (India)
    UF Jorkanden Peak (India)
    BT Mountains—India
Kinneret, Sea of (Israel)
    USE Tiberias Lake (Israel)
Kinnereth Lake (Israel)
    USE Tiberias Lake (Israel)
Kinnerød family *(Not Subd Geog)*
Kinneston family
    USE Kennison family
Kinney family
    USE Kenney family
Kinnikinic
    USE Arctostaphylos uva-ursi
Kinnikinnick
    USE Arctostaphylos uva-ursi
Kinningham family
    USE Keiningham family
Kinnison family
    USE Kennison family
Kino
    [*RM666.K (Therapeutics)*]
    [*RS165.K5 (Pharmacy)*]
    BT Astringents
        Hemostatics
        Tannins
    NT Catechin
Kino Bay (Mexico)
    UF Bahía Kino (Mexico)
    BT Bays—Mexico
Kinokawa (Japan)
    USE Ki River (Japan)
Kinorhyncha
    [*QL391.K5*]
    UF Echinodera
    BT Marine invertebrates
        Worms
    NT Cyclorhagida
        Homalorhagida
Kinosternidae
    [*QL666.C55*]
    UF Mud turtles
        Musk turtles
    BT Turtles
    NT Kinosternon
        Sternotherus
Kinosternon
    [*QL666.C55*]
    BT Kinosternidae
    NT Kinosternon angustipons
        Kinosternon dunni
        Kinosternon flavescens
        Kinosternon scorpioides
Kinosternon albogulare
    USE Kinosternon scorpioides
Kinosternon angustipons
    [*QL666.C55*]
    BT Kinosternon
Kinosternon dunni
    [*QL666.C55*]
    BT Kinosternon
Kinosternon flavescens
    [*QL666.C55*]
    UF Illinois mud turtle
        Kinosternon spooneri
        Kinosternon stejnegeri
        Platythyra flavescens
        Southwestern mud turtle
        Yellow mud turtle
    BT Kinosternon
Kinosternon integrum
    USE Kinosternon scorpioides
Kinosternon pachyrum
    USE Kinosternon scorpioides
Kinosternon panamense
    USE Kinosternon scorpioides

Kinosternon scorpioides
    [*QL666.C55*]
    UF Kinosternon albogulare
        Kinosternon integrum
        Kinosternon pachyrum
        Kinosternon panamense
        Kinosternon seriei
    BT Kinosternon
Kinosternon seriei
    USE Kinosternon scorpioides
Kinosternon spooneri
    USE Kinosternon flavescens
Kinosternon stejnegeri
    USE Kinosternon flavescens
Kinsay family
    USE Kinsey family
Kinsey family *(Not Subd Geog)*
    UF Kense family
        Kensy family
        Kincey family
        Kinsay family
        Kinsy family
        Kintzy family
        Kinzee family
        Kinzey family
    RT Kingsley family
Kinship *(May Subd Geog)*
    [*GN480*]
    BT Ethnology
    RT Clans
        Consanguinity
        Family
        Tribes
    SA *subdivision* Kinship *under individual*
        ethnic groups
    NT Double descent (Kinship)
        Indians of Mexico—Kinship
        Indians of North America—Kinship
        Indians of South America—Kinship
        Joking relationships
        Matrilineal kinship
        Postnuptial residence (Ethnology)
        Tuaregs—Kinship
    — Terminology
        UF Family—Terminology
Kinship (Frankish law)
    BT Law, Frankish
Kinship (Germanic law)
    BT Law, Germanic
Kinship (Law) *(May Subd Geog)*
    BT Domestic relations
Kinship (Roman law)
    BT Roman law
Kinship behavior in animals
    USE Familial behavior in animals
Kinshō Mountain (Japan)
    UF Kinshō-zan (Japan)
    BT Mountains—Japan
Kinshō-zan (Japan)
    USE Kinshō Mountain (Japan)
Kinsley family
    USE Kingsley family
Kinsly family
    USE Kingsley family
Kinsman family *(Not Subd Geog)*
    UF Kenman family
        Kinman family
        Kinneman family
Kinsolving family *(Not Subd Geog)*
    UF Kingsolver family
    RT Consolver family
Kinsy family
    USE Kinsey family
Kintaandu dialect
    USE Ntaandu dialect
Kintandu dialect
    USE Ntaandu dialect
Kinte family *(Not Subd Geog)*
Kintyre (Scotland)
    UF Cantyre (Scotland)
    BT Peninsulas—Scotland

Kintzy family
    USE Kinsey family
Kinu-gawa (Japan)
    USE Kinu River (Japan)
Kinu River (Japan)
    UF Kinu-gawa (Japan)
        Kinugawa (Japan)
    BT Rivers—Japan
KiNubi language
    USE Nubi language
Kinugawa (Japan)
    USE Kinu River (Japan)
KiNyanga language
    USE Nyanga language
Kinyaruanda language
    USE Ruanda language
Kinzee family
    USE Kinsey family
Kinzey family
    USE Kinsey family
Kinzig River (Hesse, Germany)
    BT Rivers—Germany (West)
Kioko (African people)
    USE Chokwe (African people)
Kioko language
    USE Chokwe language
Kiokwe language
    USE Chokwe language
Kiøller family
    USE Koehler family
Kiombe (African people)
    USE Yombe (African people)
Kiombe language
    USE Yombe language
Kiørem family *(Not Subd Geog)*
Kioser family
    USE Kaiser family
Kiosks
    USE Pavilions
Kiosques
    USE Pavilions
Kioumen River (Finland)
    USE Kymi River (Finland)
Kiowa Apache Indians
    [*E99.K52*]
    UF Kataka Indians
    BT Indians of North America
        Kiowa Indians
Kiowa Cemetery (Okla.) *(Not Subd Geog)*
    BT Cemeteries—Oklahoma
Kiowa Indians
    [*E99.K5*]
    UF Kiowan Indians
    BT Indians of North America
    NT Kiowa Apache Indians
    — Missions
Kiowa language
    [*PM1531*]
    UF Kayowe language
Kiowa National Grassland (N.M.)
    BT Grasslands—New Mexico
        National parks and reserves—New
            Mexico
Kiowan Indians
    USE Kiowa Indians
Kip family
    USE Kipp family
Kipaia language
    USE Purari language
Kipchak
    UF Comans
        Cumans
        Kumans
        Polovtsi
    BT Turks
Kipchak (Khanate)
    USE Golden Horde
Kipchak language
    [*PL318*]

Kipchak language *(Continued)*
  UF Coman language
      Cuman language
      Falven language
      Kiptchak language
      Kuman language
      Polovtsi language
      Walwen language
  BT Turkic languages
      Turkic languages, Northwest
Kipchak Turkic languages
  USE Turkic languages, Northwest
Kipende language
  USE Pende language
Kiple family
  USE Keppel family
Kipp family *(Not Subd Geog)*
  UF Kip family
      Kippes family
      Kipps family
      Kips family
Kippes family
  USE Kipp family
Kipple family
  USE Gibble family
      Keppel family
Kipps family
  USE Kipp family
Kips family
  USE Kipp family
Kipsigis
  USE Kipsigis (African people)
Kipsigis (African people)
  [DT433.545.K57]
  UF Kipsigis
      Kipsikis (African people)
      Lumbwa (African people)
      Sikisi (African people)
  BT Ethnology—Kenya
      Nilo-Hamitic tribes
Kipsigis dialect
  USE Kipsikis dialect
Kipsigis law
  USE Law, Kipsigis (African people)
Kipsikis (African people)
  USE Kipsigis (African people)
Kipsikis dialect
  [PL8545.95.K]
  UF Kipsigis dialect
  BT Kenya—Languages
      Nandi language
Kiptchak (Khanate)
  USE Golden Horde
Kiptchak language
  USE Kipchak language
Kipu
  USE Quipu
Kira language
  USE Vagala language
Kiracofe family *(Not Subd Geog)*
  UF Caracofe family
      Caricofe family
      Karicofe family
      Kirkhove family
      Kirshof family
Kiranti (Tribe)
  USE Kirati (Tribe)
Kirati (Tribe)
  [DS432.K]
  UF Kiranti (Tribe)
Kirbey family
  USE Kirby family
Kirby, Jack. Captain America (Comic strip)
  USE Captain America (Comic strip)

Kirby family *(Not Subd Geog)*
  UF Curbey family
      Curbie family
      Curby family
      Kerbey family
      Kerby family
      Kirbey family
      Kirbye family
      Kirkby family
      Kurbee family
Kirbye family
  USE Kirby family
Kirch family *(Not Subd Geog)*
  UF Kerch family
      Kirchen family
  RT Carrick family
      Kirk family
Kirchen family
  USE Kirch family
Kirchgater family
  USE Kirchgatter family
Kirchgatter family *(Not Subd Geog)*
  UF Kirchgater family
Kirchherr family *(Not Subd Geog)*
Kirchholm, Battle of, 1605
  BT Poland—History—Sigismund III, 1587-
      1632
      Sweden—History—Charles IX, 1604-
      1611
Kirchmayer family
  USE Kirchmeyer family
Kirchmayr family
  USE Kirchmeyer family
Kirchmeier family
  USE Kirchmeyer family
Kirchmeir family
  USE Kirchmeyer family
Kirchmeyer family *(Not Subd Geog)*
  UF Kirchmayer family
      Kirchmayr family
      Kirchmeier family
      Kirchmeir family
      Kirchmeyr family
Kirchmeyr family
  USE Kirchmeyer family
Kirchner, Ernst Ludwig, 1880-1938. Absalom
  UF Absalom (Wood-engraving)
  BT Wood-engraving—20th century—
      Germany
      Wood-engraving, German
Kirchner, Ernst Ludwig, 1880-1938. Peter Schlemihl
  UF Peter Schlemihl (Wood-engraving)
  BT Wood-engraving—20th century—
      Germany
      Wood-engraving, German
Kirchner, Ernst Ludwig, 1880-1938. Triumph of Love
  UF Triumph der Liebe (Wood-engraving)
      Triumph of Love (Wood-engraving)
  BT Wood-engraving—20th century—
      Germany
      Wood-engraving, German
Kirckpatrick family
  USE Kirkpatrick family
Kirdiwat language
  USE Ngizim language
Kirghese
  USE Kirghiz
Kirghiz *(May Subd Geog)*
  UF Kaisaks
      Kaissaks
      Kirghese
      Kirguis
  RT Kazakhs
Kirghiz art
  USE Art, Kirghiz
Kirghiz arts
  USE Arts, Kirghiz
Kirghiz authors
  USE Authors, Kirghiz

Kirghiz book-plates
  USE Book-plates, Kirghiz
Kirghiz cookery
  USE Cookery, Kirghiz
Kirghiz drama *(May Subd Geog)*
Kirghiz fiction *(May Subd Geog)*
  NT Short stories, Kirghiz
Kirghiz horse, New
  USE Novokirghiz horse
Kirghiz-Kaissacks
  USE Kazakhs
Kirghiz-Kaissak language
  USE Kazakh language
Kirghiz-Kazaks
  USE Kazakhs
Kirghiz landscape painting
  USE Landscape painting, Kirghiz
Kirghiz language
  [PL65.K5]
  UF Kara-Kirghiz language
  BT Turkic languages
      Turkic languages, Northwest
Kirghiz literature *(May Subd Geog)*
Kirghiz literature (English)
  USE English literature—Kirghiz authors
Kirghiz painting
  USE Painting, Kirghiz
Kirghiz philology
  [PL65.K5]
Kirghiz prints
  USE Prints, Kirghiz
Kirghiz prose literature *(May Subd Geog)*
Kirghiz S.S.R.
  UF Kirghizistan
  — History
  —— Revolution, 1917-1921
Kirghiz sculpture
  USE Sculpture, Kirghiz
Kirghiz short stories
  USE Short stories, Kirghiz
Kirghizistan
  USE Kirghiz S.S.R.
Kirgizskiĭ Alatau Mountains (Kirghiz S.S.R. and Kazakh S.S.R.)
  USE Kirgizskiĭ Range (Kirghiz S.S.R. and
      Kazakh S.S.R.)
Kirgizskiĭ Khrebet (Kirghiz S.S.R. and Kazakh S.S.R.)
  USE Kirgizskiĭ Range (Kirghiz S.S.R. and
      Kazakh S.S.R.)
Kirgizskiĭ Range (Kirghiz S.S.R. and Kazakh S.S.R.)
  UF Aleksandrovskiĭ Kirgiz Range (Kirghiz
      S.S.R. and Kazakh S.S.R.)
      Aleksandrovskiĭ Mountains (Kirghiz
      S.S.R. and Kazakh S.S.R.)
      Kirgizskiĭ Alatau Mountains (Kirghiz
      S.S.R. and Kazakh S.S.R.)
      Kirgizskiĭ Khrebet (Kirghiz S.S.R. and
      Kazakh S.S.R.)
  BT Mountains—Kazakh S.S.R.
      Mountains—Kirghiz S.S.R.
Kirguis
  USE Kirghiz
Kiri
  USE Paulownia tomentosa
Kiri-ga-mine (Japan)
  USE Kiriga Plateau (Japan)
Kiribatese language
  USE Gilbertese language
Kiribati
  UF Gilbert Islands
Kiribati language
  USE Gilbertese language
Kiriga Plateau (Japan) *(Not Subd Geog)*
  UF Kiri-ga-mine (Japan)
      Kirigamine (Japan)
  BT Plateaus—Japan
Kirigamine (Japan)
  USE Kiriga Plateau (Japan)

Kirikakujō (Kawagoe-shi, Japan)
  USE Kawagoejō (Kawagoe-shi, Japan)
Kirikōbe pottery
  USE Kirikomi pottery
Kirikomi pottery
  ₍NK4168.M₎
  UF Kirikōbe pottery
      Pottery, Kirikōbe
      Pottery, Kirikomi
  BT Pottery, Japanese
Kirinyaga (Kenya)
  USE Kenya, Mount (Kenya)
Kiriri Indians
  USE Kariri Indians
Kiriri language
  USE Kariri language
Kirishitan Uprising in Shimabara, 1637-1638
  USE Shimabara Uprising, 1637-1638
Kiritimati (Kiribati)
  UF Christmas Island (Kiribati)
      Christmas Island (Pacific Ocean)
  BT Islands—Kiribati
Kiriwinian language
  ₍PL6252.K5₎
  UF Kilivila language
      Trobriand language
  BT Melanesian languages
Kirk family *(Not Subd Geog)*
  UF Kerk family
      Kirke family
      Kirkes family
      Kirks family
  RT Kirch family
      Kirkland family
Kirkby family
  USE Kirby family
Kirke family
  USE Kirk family
Kirkendahl family
  USE Kuykendall family
Kirkendale family
  USE Kuykendall family
Kirkendall effect
  ₍QC176.8.D5₎
  UF Bulk diffusion
      Diffusion in solids
      Grain boundary diffusion
      Lattice diffusion
      Pipe diffusion
      Solids—Diffusion
      Volume diffusion
  BT Diffusion
      Solids
Kirkendall family
  USE Kuykendall family
Kirkendawl family
  USE Kuykendall family
Kirkendoll family
  USE Kuykendall family
Kirkenstall family
  USE Kuykendall family
Kirkenthall family
  USE Kuykendall family
Kirkes family
  USE Kirk family
Kirkhove family
  USE Kiracofe family
Kirkland family *(Not Subd Geog)*
  UF Kirtland family
  RT Kirk family
Kirkor family *(Not Subd Geog)*
Kirkpatrick family *(Not Subd Geog)*
  UF Kirckpatrick family
      Kirkpattrick family
      Kirkpetreck family
      Kirkpetrick family
Kirkpattrick family
  USE Kirkpatrick family
Kirkpetreck family
  USE Kirkpatrick family

Kirkpetrick family
  USE Kirkpatrick family
Kirk's dik-dik
  USE Madoqua kirki
Kirks family
  USE Kirk family
Kirksey family *(Not Subd Geog)*
Kirku language
  USE Kurku language
Kirkwood Formation (N.J. and Pa.)
  BT Formations (Geology)—New Jersey
      Formations (Geology)—Pennsylvania
      Geology, Stratigraphic—Miocene
Kirlian photography
  ₍TR760₎
  UF Corona discharge photography
      Electrography
      High-voltage high-frequency
        photography
      Photography, Kirlian
      Photopsychography
      Radiation field photography
  BT Aura
      Corona (Electricity)
      Photograms
      Photography
Kirn family
  USE Kern family
Kirneck family
  USE Kürneck family
Kirnegk family
  USE Kürneck family
Kirschner family
  USE Kershner family
Kirsener family
  USE Kershner family
Kirsey family
  USE Kersey family
Kirshner family
  USE Kershner family
Kirshof family
  USE Kiracofe family
Kirtana
  ₍BL1226₎
  BT Hinduism—Rituals
      Worship (Hinduism)
Kirtland family
  USE Kirkland family
Kirtland's warbler
  UF Dendroica kirtlandii
      Jack-pine warbler
      Sylvicola kirtlandii
  BT Wood warblers
Kirundi language
  USE Rundi language
Kirves family *(Not Subd Geog)*
  UF Kerves family
Kiryat Haim (Haifa, Israel)
  USE Ḳiryat Ḥayim (Haifa, Israel)
Kiryat Haiyim (Haifa, Israel)
  USE Ḳiryat Ḥayim (Haifa, Israel)
Ḳiryat Ḥayim (Haifa, Israel)
  (Not Subd Geog)
  UF Haifa (Israel). Kiryat Haim
      Haifa (Israel). Kiryat Haiyim
      Haifa (Israel). Ḳiryat Ḥayim
      Haifa (Israel). Ḳiryat Ḥayyim
      Haifa (Israel). Qiryat Haim
      Haifa (Israel). Qiryat Haiyim
      Haifa (Israel). Qiryat Ḥayim
      Haifa (Israel). Qiryat Ḥayyim
      Kiryat Haim (Haifa, Israel)
      Kiryat Haiyim (Haifa, Israel)
      Kiryat Ḥayyim (Haifa, Israel)
      Qiryat Haim (Haifa, Israel)
      Qiryat Haiyim (Haifa, Israel)
      Qiryat Ḥayim (Haifa, Israel)
      Qiryat Ḥayyim (Haifa, Israel)
Kiryat Ḥayyim (Haifa, Israel)
  USE Ḳiryat Ḥayim (Haifa, Israel)

Kisa dialect
  ₍PL8474.L895K57₎
  UF LuKisa dialect
      Lushisa dialect
      Olushisa dialect
  BT Luyia language
Kisaengs
  UF Kisangs
  BT Entertainers
Kisakata language
  USE Sakata language
Kisan (Indic people)
  USE Nagesia (Indic people)
Kisangs
  USE Kisaengs
Kisantu dialect
  USE Ntaandu dialect
Kisear family
  USE Kaiser family
Kisel family
  USE Kiesel family
Kiser family
  USE Kaiser family
Kishacoquillas Creek (Pa.)
  BT Rivers—Pennsylvania
Kishambala language
  USE Shambala language
Kishinev, Battle of, 1944
  USE Jassy, Battle of, 1944
Kishira family *(Not Subd Geog)*
Kishiwada Bōseki Kabushiki Kaisha Strike,
  Kishiwada, Japan, 1930
  UF Kishiwada Bōseki Sōgi, Kishiwada,
        Japan, 1930
  BT Strikes and lockouts—Textile industry
        —Japan
      Strikes and lockouts—Japan
      Textile workers—Japan
Kishiwada Bōseki Sōgi, Kishiwada, Japan, 1930
  USE Kishiwada Bōseki Kabushiki Kaisha
        Strike, Kishiwada, Japan, 1930
Kisi language
  USE Kissi language
Kisii (African people)
  USE Gusii (African people)
Kisii language
  USE Gusii language
Kiska Island (Alaska)
  BT Aleutian Islands (Alaska)
      Islands—Alaska
Kisköre Reservoir (Hungary)
  UF Kiskörei-víztároló (Hungary)
      Kiskörei-víztározó (Hungary)
      Wasserspeicher Kisköre (Hungary)
  BT Reservoirs—Hungary
Kiskörei-víztároló (Hungary)
  USE Kisköre Reservoir (Hungary)
Kiskörei-víztározó (Hungary)
  USE Kisköre Reservoir (Hungary)
Kiso-gawa (Japan)
  USE Kiso River (Japan)
Kiso horse
  ₍SF293.K47₎
  BT Horse breeds—Japan
Kiso-kaidō (Japan)
  USE Nakasendō (Japan)
Kiso Kawa (Japan)
  USE Kiso River (Japan)
Kiso River (Japan)
  UF Kiso-gawa (Japan)
      Kiso Kawa (Japan)
  BT Rivers—Japan
Kisōgo language
  USE Kwafi language
Kisoji (Japan)
  USE Nakasendō (Japan)
Kisolongo dialect
  USE Solongo dialect
Kisonge language
  USE Songe language

Kisor family
  USE Kaiser family
Kispest (Budapest, Hungary)
  (Not Subd Geog)
  UF Budapest (Hungary). Kispest
Kiss (Sculpture)
  USE Brancusi, Constantin, 1876-1957.
       The kiss
Kissandaui language
  USE Sandawe language
Kissel family
  USE Kiesel family
Kissi (African people)
  UF Kissi (African tribe)
  BT Ethnology—Guinea
     Ethnology—Liberia
     Ethnology—Sierra Leone
Kissi (African tribe)
  USE Kissi (African people)
Kissi language
  UF Dei language
     Gihi language
     Gii language
     Gisi language
     Gizi language
     Gizima language
     Kisi language
     Kissien language
  BT Guinea—Languages
     Liberia—Languages
     Niger-Congo languages
     Sierra Leone—Languages
Kissien language
  USE Kissi language
Kissimmee River (Fla.)
  BT Rivers—Florida
Kissing
  ⌜GT2640⌝
  BT Manners and customs
  — Religious aspects
Kissing-bug
  ⌜QL523.R⌝
Kissing bugs
  USE Triatominae
Kissing in art
Kissing in literature
Kissow family *(Not Subd Geog)*
Kist family *(Not Subd Geog)*
  UF Kister family
Kist languages
  USE Nakh languages
Kister family
  USE Kist family
Kistna River (India)
  USE Krishna River (India)
Kisuku language
  USE Suku language (Zaire)
Kiswah
  ⌜BP187.4⌝
Kiswahili language
  USE Swahili language
Kit (Musical instrument)
  USE Pochette
Kit bag frames
  UF Tool bag frames
Kit fox
  UF Swift fox
     Vulpes velox
  BT Foxes
Kit homes
  USE Prefabricated houses
Kitabatake family *(Not Subd Geog)*
Kitabul dialect
  USE Gidabal dialect
Kitabwa language
  ⌜PL8391⌝
  BT Bantu languages
Kitagami-gawa (Japan)
  USE Kitakami River (Japan)
Kitagamigawa (Japan)
  USE Kitakami River (Japan)

Kitagata iseki (Kitakyūshū-shi, Japan)
  USE Kitagata Site (Kitakyūshū-shi, Japan)
Kitagata Site (Kitakyūshū-shi, Japan)
  (Not Subd Geog)
  UF Kitagata iseki (Kitakyūshū-shi, Japan)
  BT Japan—Antiquities
Kitahama (Osaka, Japan) *(Not Subd Geog)*
  UF Osaka (Japan). Kitahama
Kitai
  USE Khitan Mongols
Kitakaito Iseki (Minakami-machi, Japan)
  USE Kitakaito Site (Minakami-machi,
       Japan)
Kitakaito Site (Minakami-machi, Japan)
  UF Kitakaito Iseki (Minakami-machi,
       Japan)
  BT Japan—Antiquities
Kitakami-gawa (Japan)
  USE Kitakami River (Japan)
Kitakami Region (Japan)
Kitakami River (Japan) *(Not Subd Geog)*
  UF Kitagami-gawa (Japan)
     Kitagamigawa (Japan)
     Kitakami-gawa (Japan)
     Kitakamigawa (Japan)
  BT Rivers—Japan
Kitakamigawa (Japan)
  USE Kitakami River (Japan)
Kitamat Indians
  USE Haisla Indians
Kitamat language
  USE Haisla language
Kitamura family *(Not Subd Geog)*
Kitara
  USE Banyoro
Kitayama Peasant Uprising, 1614-1615
  USE Japan—History—Keichō Peasant
       Uprising, 1614-1615
Kitcars
  USE Automobiles, Home-built
Kitchel family *(Not Subd Geog)*
  UF Kitchell family
Kitchell family
  USE Kitchel family
Kitchen-boiler explosions
  ⌜TH6565⌝
  UF Boiler explosions
  BT Explosions
     Hot-water supply
     Steam-boiler explosions
Kitchen cabinet industry *(May Subd Geog)*
  ⌜HD9773⌝
  BT Furniture industry and trade
     Kitchen cabinets
  — Employees
Kitchen cabinets
  BT Cabinet-work
     Kitchens
  NT Kitchen cabinet industry
Kitchen family *(Not Subd Geog)*
  UF Keachen family
     Ketchen family
     Ketchun family
     Kitchener family
     Kitchens family
     Kitchin family
     Kitching family
Kitchen-gardens
  USE Vegetable gardening
Kitchen Kaffir
  USE Fanakalo
Kitchen-middens *(May Subd Geog)*
  ⌜GN787-GN788⌝
  UF Middens, Kitchen
     Sambaquis
     Shell heaps
     Shell middens
     Shell mounds

  BT Animal remains (Archaeology)
     Archaeology
     Indians of North America—Antiquities
     Terremare
  RT Mounds
  NT Soil science in archaeology
  — Australia
     NT Wombah Site (N.S.W.)
  — Japan
     NT Chōjabara Site (Minamikata-machi,
          Japan)
        Natsushima Shell Mounds
          (Yokosuka-shi, Japan)
        Ōmori Shell Mounds (Tokyo,
          Japan)
        Shinmei Site (Shōwa-machi,
          Saitama-ken, Japan)
        Tagara Shell Mounds (Kesennuma-
          shi, Japan)
  — Maryland
     NT Hallowing Point Site (Md.)
  — Massachusetts
     NT Wheeler's Site (Mass.)
  — Mississippi
     NT F. L. Brinkley Midden (Miss.)
Kitchen utensils *(May Subd Geog)*
  ⌜TX656-8⌝
  UF Cooking utensils
     Household goods
     Household utensils
  BT Cookery
     House furnishings
     Implements, utensils, etc.
  NT Blenders (Cookery)
     Cookware
     Cutlery
     Dishwashing machines
     Eggbeaters
     Food processor cookery
     Fryers, Deep fat
     Gas toasters
     Ice cream scoops
     Ladles (Utensils)
     Mixers (Cookery)
     Nutmeg graters
     Potato peeling machines
     Potholders
     Slicing machines (Cookery)
     Waffle irons
Kitchen utensils industry *(May Subd Geog)*
  ⌜HD9971.5.K58-584⌝
Kitchener family
  USE Kitchen family
**Kitchener Mount Hope Cemetery (Kitchener,
Ont.)**
  UF Mount Hope Cemetery (Kitchener,
       Ont.)
  BT Cemeteries—Ontario
Kitchens *(May Subd Geog)*
  ⌜NA8330 (Architecture)⌝
  ⌜TX653-TX655 (Arrangement)⌝
  NT Galleys (Ship kitchens)
     Kitchen cabinets
  — Remodeling
     UF Remodeling of kitchens
     BT Dwellings—Remodeling
Kitchens family
  USE Kitchen family
Kitchin family
  USE Kitchen family
Kitching family
  USE Kitchen family
K'itdlarssuák family *(Not Subd Geog)*
Kite, White-tailed
  USE White-tailed kite
Kite balloons
  USE Balloons, Kite
Kite family
  USE Kight family
Kiteenjärvi (Finland)
  UF Ktteenjärvi (Finland)

BT Lakes—Finland
Kiteke language
 USE Teke language
KiTembo language
 USE Tembo language (Kivu, Zaire)
Kites *(May Subd Geog)*
 ₍TL800-830₎
 BT Aeronautics
 NT Balloons, Kite
Kites (Meteorology)
 ₍QC879₎
 BT Meteorological instruments
 NT Atmosphere, Upper
Kites (Military and naval reconnaissance)
 ₍UG670₎
 BT Aeronautics, Military
 Naval reconnaissance
 Submarine warfare
Kithara
 USE Cithara
Kitharaka (African people)
 USE Tharaka (African people)
Kithira Island (Greece)
 USE Kythēra Island (Greece)
Kitimaat language
 USE Haisla language
Kitimat Indians
 USE Haisla Indians
Kitimat language
 USE Haisla language
Kition (Ancient city) *(Not Subd Geog)*
 ₍DS54.95.K58₎
 UF Chittim (Ancient city)
 Citium (Ancient city)
 Kitium (Ancient city)
 Kittim (Ancient city)
 BT Cities and towns, Ruined, extinct, etc.
 —Cyprus
 Cyprus—Antiquities
Kition-Bamboula Site (Cyprus)
 USE Bamboula Site (Kition)
Kitium (Ancient city)
 USE Kition (Ancient city)
Kitksan Indians
 UF Gitksan Indians
 Gyitkshan Indians
 BT Indians of North America
 NT Kitwancool Indians
Kitlope Indians
 USE Haisla Indians
Kitonaqa language
 USE Kutenai language
Kits, Diagnostic reagents and test
 USE Diagnostic reagents and test kits
Kitsch *(May Subd Geog)*
 ₍BH301.K5₎
 BT Aesthetics
Kitschuck family
 USE Kitshoff family
Kitshoff family *(Not Subd Geog)*
 UF Ketshuck family
 Kitschuck family
 Kitzhoff family
Kitsos Cave (Greece) *(Not Subd Geog)*
 BT Caves—Greece
 Greece—Antiquities
Kitsukura family *(Not Subd Geog)*
Kitsuregawa family *(Not Subd Geog)*
Kitswa language
 USE Tswa language
Kittens
 BT Cats
 Domestic animals—Infancy
Kitterman family *(Not Subd Geog)*
 UF Keddeman family
 Keederman family
 Keedman family
 Ketteman family
 Kettleman family
 Kiddeman family
 RT Ketterman family

Kittim (Ancient city)
 USE Kition (Ancient city)
Kittiwake
 UF Rissa
 BT Charadriiformes
Kittleson family *(Not Subd Geog)*
Kittrell family *(Not Subd Geog)*
Kitty Hawk (Airplane)
 USE Wright Flyer (Airplane)
Kittyhawk (Fighter planes)
 USE P-40 (Fighter planes)
Kituba language
 UF Fiote language
 Ikeleve language
 Kibulamatadi language
 Kikongo ya Leta language
 Kikwango language
 Kileta language
 Kingala language
 Kizabave language
 Monokutuba language
 Munukutuba language
 BT Congo (Brazzaville)—Languages
 Kongo language
 Lingua francas
 Zaire—Languages
Kitunahan Indians
 USE Kutenai Indians
Kitunahan languages
 USE Kutenai language
Kitwancool Indians
 ₍E99.K56₎
 UF Kitwinskole Indians
 BT Indians of North America
 Kitksan Indians
Kitwinskole Indians
 USE Kitwancool Indians
Kitzhoff family
 USE Kitshoff family
Kiuchi family *(Not Subd Geog)*
Kiuch'üan Basin (China)
 USE Chiu-ch'üan Basin (China)
Kiuch'üan p'en ti (China)
 USE Chiu-ch'üan Basin (China)
Kiūmi-łoki (Finland)
 USE Kymi River (Finland)
Kiūmin-łoki (Finland)
 USE Kymi River (Finland)
Kiusa language
 USE Ngonde language
Kivas
 BT Indians of North America—
 Architecture
 Pueblos
Kivett family *(Not Subd Geog)*
 UF Kivette family
Kivette family
 USE Kivett family
Kivili language
 USE Vili language
Kivu, Lake (Rwanda and Zaire)
 UF Lac Kivu (Rwanda and Zaire)
 Lake Kivu (Rwanda and Zaire)
 BT Lakes—Rwanda
 Lakes—Zaire
Kivumbu language
 USE Vili language
Kiwai (Papuan people)
 ₍DU740₎
 BT Ethnology—Papua New Guinea
Kiwai languages
 ₍PL6621.K5₎
 BT Papuan languages
 NT Bamu River language
Kiwi berry
 USE Kiwi fruit
Kiwi fruit *(May Subd Geog)*
 ₍QK495.A177 (Botany)₎

 UF Actinidia chinensis
 Chinese gooseberry
 Gooseberry, Chinese
 Gooseberry, Ichang
 Ichang gooseberry
 Kiwi berry
 Kiwifruit
 Monkey peach
 Peach, Monkey
 Yang tao
 Yangtao
 NT Cookery (Kiwi fruit)
Kiwi fruit industry
Kiwifruit
 USE Kiwi fruit
Kiwis
 ₍QL696.A6₎
 UF Apterygidae
 Apterygiformes
 Apteryxes
Kiyaka language
 USE Yaka language (Zaire and Angola)
KiYanzi language
 USE Yanzi language
Kiyombe language
 USE Yombe language
Kiyomizu Mountain (Japan)
 (Not Subd Geog)
 UF Kiyomizu-san (Japan)
 Kiyomizu-yama (Japan)
 Kiyomizuyama (Japan)
 BT Mountains—Japan
Kiyomizu pottery *(May Subd Geog)*
 ₍NK4168.K₎
 UF Ko Kiyomizu pottery
 Kokiyomizu pottery
 Pottery, Kiyomizu
 BT Kyō pottery
 Pottery, Japanese
Kiyomizu-san (Japan)
 USE Kiyomizu Mountain (Japan)
Kiyomizu-yama (Japan)
 USE Kiyomizu Mountain (Japan)
Kiyomizuyama (Japan)
 USE Kiyomizu Mountain (Japan)
Kiyoshi (The Japanese word)
 BT Japanese language—Etymology
Kiyosumi Garden (Tokyo, Japan)
 USE Kiyosumi Teien (Tokyo, Japan)
Kiyosumi Teien (Tokyo, Japan)
 UF Fukagawa Shimbokuen (Tokyo, Japan)
 Kiyosumi Garden (Tokyo, Japan)
 BT Gardens—Japan
 Parks—Japan
Kiyuksa Indians
 ₍E99.K59₎
 UF Wa-ha-shaw Indians
 BT Dakota Indians
 Indians of North America
 Mdewakanton Indians
Kizabave language
 USE Kituba language
Kizawa Kaidō Kan Iseki (Oyama-shi, Japan)
 USE Kizawa Kaidō Kan Site (Oyama-shi,
 Japan)
Kizawa Kaidō Kan Site (Oyama-shi, Japan)
 (Not Subd Geog)
 UF Kizawa Kaidō Kan Iseki (Oyama-shi,
 Japan)
 BT Japan—Antiquities
Kizer family
 USE Kaiser family
Kizh Indians
 USE Gabrieleño Indians
Kizhi Island (R.S.F.S.R.)
 UF Kizhi ostrov (R.S.F.S.R.)
 BT Islands—Russian S.F.S.R.
Kizhi ostrov (R.S.F.S.R.)
 USE Kizhi Island (R.S.F.S.R.)
Kiziba (African people)
 USE Haya (African people)

Kizier family
　　USE　Kaiser family
Kizil Irmak (Turkey)
　　USE　Kizil River (Turkey)
Kizil-Kum (Kazakh S.S.R. and Uzbek S.S.R.)
　　USE　Kyzyl-Kum (Kazakh S.S.R. and Uzbek S.S.R.)
Kizil River (Turkey)
　　UF　Halys River (Turkey)
　　　　Kizil Irmak (Turkey)
　　　　Kizilirmak (Turkey)
　　BT　Rivers—Turkey
Kizil Tatars
　　USE　Kyzyl Tatars
Kizilirmak (Turkey)
　　USE　Kizil River (Turkey)
Kizombo dialect
　　USE　Zoombo dialect
Kizoombo dialect
　　USE　Zoombo dialect
Kizor family
　　USE　Kaiser family
Kizoro Omote Iseki (Kawaguchi-shi, Japan)
　　USE　Kizoroomote Site (Kawaguchi-shi, Japan)
Kizoroomote Iseki (Kawaguchi-shi, Japan)
　　USE　Kizoroomote Site (Kawaguchi-shi, Japan)
Kizoroomote Site (Kawaguchi-shi, Japan)
　　(Not Subd Geog)
　　UF　Kizoro Omote Iseki (Kawaguchi-shi, Japan)
　　　　Kizoroomote Iseki (Kawaguchi-shi, Japan)
　　BT　Japan—Antiquities
Kjaergaard family
　　USE　Kjaersgaard family
Kjaersgaard family　(Not Subd Geog)
　　UF　Kjaergaard family
Kjaerulf family　(Not Subd Geog)
　　UF　Kiaerulf family
　　　　Kiaerulff family
　　　　Kierrulf family
　　　　Kierulf family
　　　　Kierulff family
　　　　Kjaerulff family
　　　　Kjarulff family
Kjaerulff family
　　USE　Kjaerulf family
Kjarulff family
　　USE　Kjaerulf family
Kjax language
　　USE　Adyghe language
Kjeåsen (Norway)　(Not Subd Geog)
　　BT　Farms—Norway
Kjeldsen family　(Not Subd Geog)
Kjelgaard family　(Not Subd Geog)
Kjelstrup family　(Not Subd Geog)
Kjerkreit family　(Not Subd Geog)
Kjøbenhavn-Slangerup Banen
　　BT　Railroads—Denmark
Kjöge Bay (Denmark)
　　USE　Køge Bay (Denmark)
Kjølen Mountains (Sweden and Norway)
　　USE　Kölen Mountains (Sweden and Norway)
Kjøller family
　　USE　Koehler family
Kjos family　(Not Subd Geog)
　　UF　Kjoss family
Kjoss family
　　USE　Kjos family
Klaar family　(Not Subd Geog)
　　RT　Clare family
Klaberjass
　　USE　Jass (Game)
Kladrub horse
　　[SF293.K]
Klagefrauensarkophag (Sidon, Lebanon)
　　USE　Mourners Sarcophagus (Sidon, Lebanon)

Klahoquaht Indians
　　USE　Clayoquot Indians
Klaiber family　(Not Subd Geog)
　　UF　Kleiber family
Klallam Indians
　　USE　Clallam Indians
Klamath Indians
　　[E99.K7]
　　UF　Muckaluck Indians
　　BT　Indians of North America
　　　　Lutuamian Indians
Klamath language
　　[PM1551]
　　RT　Lutuamian languages
Klamath Mountains (Calif. and Or.)
　　BT　Mountains—California
　　　　Mountains—Oregon
Klamath River (Or. and Calif.)
　　BT　Rivers—California
　　　　Rivers—Oregon
Klao language
　　USE　Kru language
Klapp family
　　USE　Clapp family
Klapper family
　　USE　Clapper family
Klappert family
　　USE　Clapper family
Klasies River (South Africa)
　　USE　Kaapsedrifrivier (South Africa)
Klasies Valley (South Africa)
　　USE　Kaapsedrifrivier Valley (South Africa)
Klasmura
　　[QE783.O6]
　　BT　Klasmuridae
Klasmuridae
　　[QE783.O6]
　　BT　Stenurida
　　NT　Antiquaster
　　　　Klasmura
Klassiker (The German word)
　　BT　German language—Etymology
Klaudiu Polis (Ancient city)
　　USE　Claudiopolis (Ancient city)
Klaus family
　　USE　Claus family
Klause family
　　USE　Claus family
Klaw family
　　USE　Claus family
Klazomenai (Ancient city)
　　USE　Clazomenae (Ancient city)
Klaztimen (Ancient city)
　　USE　Clazomenae (Ancient city)
Kleb (Malaysian people)
　　USE　Batek (Malaysian people)
　　　　Chewong (Malaysian people)
Kleberg family　(Not Subd Geog)
Kleck family　(Not Subd Geog)
Kleeblattschädel syndrome
　　(May Subd Geog)
　　[RD763]
　　UF　Cloverleaf skull
　　　　Trilobular skull
　　BT　Face—Abnormalities
　　　　Hydrocephalus
　　　　Mental retardation
　　　　Skull—Abnormalities
　　　　Syndromes
Kleiber family
　　USE　Klaiber family
Klein family　(Not Subd Geog)
　　UF　Cline family
　　　　Kleine family
　　　　Kline family
Klein-Kaluza theory
　　USE　Kaluza-Klein theories
Klein-Waardenburg syndrome
　　(May Subd Geog)
　　UF　Waardenburg syndrome

　　BT　Deafness
　　　　Genetic disorders
　　　　Pigmentation disorders
　　　　Syndromes
Kleine, George
　— Film collections
　　　　USE　George Kleine Film Collection
Kleine family
　　USE　Klein family
Kleiner family
　　USE　Clinard family
Kleiner Morgen (Painting)
　　USE　Runge, Philipp Otto, 1777-1810. Small morning
Kleinert family
　　USE　Clinard family
Kleinian groups
　　[QA331]
　　UF　Groups, Kleinian
　　BT　Discontinuous groups
Kleinmeister
　　USE　Little masters (Artists)
Kleist prize
　　BT　Literary prizes
Klem family
　　USE　Clem family
Klemm family
　　USE　Clem family
Klephts
　　[DF801]
　　BT　Brigands and robbers
Klepinger family
　　USE　Kleppinger family
Klepper family　(Not Subd Geog)
　　UF　Clepper family
Klepping family
　　USE　Kleppinger family
Kleppinger family　(Not Subd Geog)
　　UF　Clippinger family
　　　　Klepinger family
　　　　Klepping family
　　　　Klöppinger family
Kleptomania
　　[BF173]
　　UF　Cleptomania
　　BT　Crime and criminals
　　　　Psychology, Pathological
　　　　Stealing
　　　　Thieves
Kleśa (Buddhism)
　　USE　Vice (Buddhism)
Klezmer music　(May Subd Geog)
　　BT　Jews—Music
　　　　Popular music
Kli͡az'ma Reservoir (R.S.F.S.R.)
　　UF　Kli͡az'minskoe vodokhranilishche (R.S.F.S.R.)
　　　　Klyaz'ma Reservoir (R.S.F.S.R.)
　　　　Klyaz'minskoye vodokhranilishche (R.S.F.S.R.)
　　BT　Reservoirs—Russian S.F.S.R.
Kli͡az'ma River (R.S.F.S.R.)
　　UF　Klyaz'ma River (R.S.F.S.R.)
　　　　Reka Kli͡az'ma (R.S.F.S.R.)
　　BT　Rivers—Russian S.F.S.R.
Kli͡az'minskoe vodokhranilishche (R.S.F.S.R.)
　　USE　Kli͡az'ma Reservoir (R.S.F.S.R.)
Klichikh Site (Alaska)
　　USE　Kijik Site (Alaska)
Klikitat Indians
　　[E99.K76]
　　BT　Indians of North America
　　　　Shahaptian Indians
Klimpel family　(Not Subd Geog)
Klimt, Gustav, 1862-1918.　Beethoven frieze
Klinck family
　　USE　Klink family
Kline family
　　USE　Klein family
Klinefelter's syndrome
　　[RC882]

BT Hypogonadism
　Sex chromosome abnormalities
　Sex differentiation disorders
　Sexual disorders
　Syndromes
Klingaman family *(Not Subd Geog)*
UF Klingeman family
　Klingemann family
　Klingman family
Klingelschmidt family
USE Klingensmith family
Klingelsmith family
USE Klingensmith family
Klingeman family
USE Klingaman family
Klingemann family
USE Klingaman family
Klingensmith family *(Not Subd Geog)*
UF Clingingsmith family
　Klingelschmidt family
　Klingelsmith family
　Klinginsmith family
　Klingonsmith family
Klinger, Max, 1857-1920.   Salome
UF Neue Salome (Sculpture)
　Salome (Sculpture)
BT Marble sculpture, German
　Salome (Biblical figure)—Art
　Sculpture, Modern—20th century—
　　Germany
Klinginsmith family
USE Klingensmith family
Klingman family
USE Klingaman family
Klingonsmith family
USE Klingensmith family
Klingshirn family *(Not Subd Geog)*
Kliningan
USE Gender (Musical instrument)
Klink family *(Not Subd Geog)*
UF Clink family
　Klinck family
　Klinke family
Klinke family
USE Klink family
Klínovec Mountain (Czechoslovakia)
UF Keilberg (Czechoslovakia)
BT Mountains—Czechoslovakia
Kliopsyllus
　[QL444.C74]
BT Paramesochridae
Kliopsyllus spiniger
　[QL444.C74]
Klipfish
BT Codfish
　Fishery products
Klitzman family *(Not Subd Geog)*
UF Kluetzman family
Ključ (Serbia)
UF Juč (Serbia)
　Kojuč (Serbia)
Klondike gold fields
USE Klondike River Valley (Yukon)—Gold
　　discoveries
Klondike River (Yukon)
BT Rivers—Yukon Territory
Klondike River Valley (Yukon)
— Gold discoveries
　UF Klondike gold fields
Klong River (Thailand)
USE Mae Klong River (Thailand)
Klopper family
USE Clapper family
Klöppinger family
USE Kleppinger family
Klopsch family *(Not Subd Geog)*
Klos (Albania : Concentration camp)
BT World War, 1939-1945—
　　Concentration camps—Albania

Klos family *(Not Subd Geog)*
UF Klose family
　Kloss family
RT Claus family
　Close family
Klose family
USE Klos family
Kloss family
USE Klos family
Klosterkamp, Battle of, 1760
BT Seven Years' War, 1756-1763
Kloute family
USE Cloudt family
Kluane National Park (Yukon)
UF Parc National de Kluane (Yukon)
BT National parks and reserves—Canada
　Parks—Yukon Territory
Kluch family
USE Kluck family
Kluck family *(Not Subd Geog)*
UF Kluch family
Kluckhohn family *(Not Subd Geog)*
UF Kluckhuhn family
Kluckhuhn family
USE Kluckhohn family
Kluetzman family
USE Klitzman family
Klug family
USE Kluge family
Kluge family *(Not Subd Geog)*
UF Klug family
　Klugman family
　Klugmann family
Kluge Hans (Horse)
USE Clever Hans (Horse)
Klugman family
USE Kluge family
Klugmann family
USE Kluge family
Kluken family
USE Klukken family
Klukken family *(Not Subd Geog)*
UF Kluken family
Klukwalle
USE Wolf ritual
Klukwana
USE Wolf ritual
Klum family
USE Clum family
Klunk family *(Not Subd Geog)*
UF Clunk family
Klyaz'ma Reservoir (R.S.F.S.R.)
USE Kliaz'ma Reservoir (R.S.F.S.R.)
Klyaz'ma River (R.S.F.S.R.)
USE Kliaz'ma River (R.S.F.S.R.)
Klyaz'minskoye vodokhranilishche (R.S.F.S.R.)
USE Kliaz'ma Reservoir (R.S.F.S.R.)
Klystrons
BT Electric current converters
　Microwave tubes
　Vacuum-tubes
NT Klystrons, Reflex
Klystrons, Reflex
　[TK7871.74]
UF Reflex klystrons
BT Klystrons
Kmiotek family *(Not Subd Geog)*
Knaiakhotana Indians
USE Tanaina Indians
Knaiakhotana language
USE Tanaina language
Knap family
USE Knapp family
Knapheide family *(Not Subd Geog)*
Knapp family *(Not Subd Geog)*
UF Knap family
　Knappe family
　Nap family
　Napp family
　Nappe family
RT Napper family

Knapp Site (Ark.)
USE Toltec Mounds Site (Ark.)
Knappe family
USE Knapp family
Knapper family
USE Napper family
Knapping of flint
USE Flintknapping
Knapweed, Diffuse
USE Diffuse knapweed
Knapweed, Russian
USE Russian knapweed
Knapweed, Spotted
USE Spotted knapweed
Knapweeds *(May Subd Geog)*
　[QK495.C74 (Botany)]
　[SB615.K55 (Weeds)]
BT Centaurea
　Weeds
NT Diffuse knapweed
　Russian knapweed
　Spotted knapweed
Knäred, Peace of, 1613
BT Kalmar War, 1611-1613
Knarr family
USE Knorr family
Knauer family *(Not Subd Geog)*
Kneading machinery
USE Mixing machinery
Knee
　[QL825 (Comparative anatomy)]
　[QM131 (Human anatomy)]
UF Knee joint
BT Leg
NT Anterior cruciate ligament
　Artificial knee
　Meniscus (Anatomy)
　Patella
　Popliteal fossa
　Stifle joint
— Amputation
　USE Amputations of leg
— **Ankylosis**
— **Diseases** *(May Subd Geog)*
　NT Knee—Radiography
— **Fracture**
— **Radiography**
　BT Knee—Diseases
— **Surgery**
　UF Excision of knee
— **Tuberculosis**
— **Wounds and injuries**
Knee hollow
USE Popliteal fossa
Knee jerk
UF Knee reflex
　Patellar reflex
　Quadriceps reflex
BT Patella
　Reflex, Tendon
Knee joint
USE Knee
Knee prosthesis
USE Artificial knee
Knee reflex
USE Knee jerk
Kneecap
USE Patella
Kneelers (Church furniture)
　(May Subd Geog)
UF Church kneelers (Furniture)
BT Church furniture
Kneeling (Posture in worship)
USE Posture in worship
Kneely family
USE Neely family
Kneipp cure
USE Hydrotherapy
Kner, family of printers *(Not Subd Geog)*
　[Z232.K]

Kneriidae
  ₍QL638.K5₎
  UF Cromeriidae
    Grasseichthyidae
  BT Gonorynchiformes
  NT Parakneria
Knerr family
  USE Knorr family
Knew family
  USE New family
Kniazev family (Not Subd Geog)
Knidos (Ancient city)
  USE Cnidus (Ancient city)
Knife coins (May Subd Geog)
  ₍CJ1367₎
  BT Coins, Chinese
Knife fighting
  UF Fighting, Knife
  BT Knives
    Self-defense
Knife rests (May Subd Geog)
  BT Tableware
Knife throwing
  ₍GV1096₎
  UF Throwing, Knife
  BT Knives
Knifemakers
  USE Knifesmiths
Knifesmiths (May Subd Geog)
  UF Knifemakers
  BT Cutlers
Knight (Chess)
  ₍GV1451.5.K6₎
  BT Chess
    Chessmen
Knight family (Not Subd Geog)
  UF Knights family
Knight of the swan
  USE Swan-knight
Knight shift
  UF Shift, Knight
  BT Nuclear magnetic resonance
  RT Nuclear magnetic resonance
    spectroscopy
Knighthood
  USE Knights and knighthood
Knighthood, Orders of
  USE Military religious orders
    Orders of knighthood and chivalry
Knightia
  BT Clupeidae, Fossil
Knights, Athenian
  USE Equestrian order (Athens)
Knights, Roman
  USE Equestrian order (Rome)
Knights and knighthood (May Subd Geog)
  ₍CR₎
  UF Knighthood
  BT Middle Ages—History
    Nobility
  RT Chivalry
    Heraldry
    Orders of knighthood and chivalry
    Tournaments
  NT Ministerials
    Pages, Medieval
    Templars
    Teutonic Knights
Knights and knighthood in art
Knights and knighthood in literature
Knight's Cross (Germany)
  USE Ritterkreuz (Germany)
Knights family
  USE Knight family
Knights in book-plates
  BT Book-plates
Knights of Malta (May Subd Geog)
  BT Orders of knighthood and chivalry
Knights Templars (Monastic and military
  order)
  USE Templars

Knik Arm (Alaska)
  BT Cook Inlet (Alaska)
    Inlets—Alaska
Knippers family (Not Subd Geog)
Knistenaux language
  USE Cree language
Knisteneux language
  USE Cree language
Knit goods
  ₍TT679-695₎
  BT Knitting
    Textile fabrics
  NT Sweaters
  — Dyeing
    USE Dyes and dyeing—Knit goods
  — Finishing
    ₍TT690₎
    BT Textile finishing
    NT Dyes and dyeing—Knit goods
  — Quality control
    UF Knit goods industry—Quality
      control
  — Repairing
    BT Clothing and dress—Care
  — Shrinkage
    UF Shrinkage of knit goods
Knit goods industry (May Subd Geog)
  BT Textile industry
  NT Hosiery industry
  — Collective labor agreements
    USE Collective labor agreements—
      Knit goods industry
  — Electric equipment
  — Quality control
    USE Knit goods—Quality control
Knitted lace (May Subd Geog)
  ₍TT805₎
  BT Knitting
    Lace and lace making
  — Patterns
Knitting (May Subd Geog)
  ₍TT820-829₎
  BT Fancy work
  NT Afghans (Coverlets)
    Beadwork
    Knit goods
    Knitted lace
    Sweaters
  — Patterns
  — Therapeutic use
    ₍RM735.7.K54₎
    BT Occupational therapy
      Therapeutics
Knitting, Machine
  ₍TT679-695₎
  UF Machine knitting
Knitting-machines
  ₍TT685-7₎
  NT Jacquard knitting machines
    Raschel knitting machines
  — Electric driving
    ₍TK4059.K55₎
  — Needles
    BT Pins and needles
Knitting shops
  UF Yarn shops
  BT Specialty stores
Knives (May Subd Geog)
  ₍HD9745 (Trade)₎
  ₍TS380 (Manufacture)₎
  BT Cutlery
    Flatware
    Hardware
    Silverware
  NT Bowie knife
    Glass knives
    Indians of North America—Knives
    Knife fighting
    Knife throwing
    Machetes
    Painting knives

    Palette knives
    Pocketknives
    Switchblade knives
Knives, Prehistoric (May Subd Geog)
  UF Prehistoric knives
  BT Man, Prehistoric—Tools
Kniveton family (Not Subd Geog)
Knoblauch family
  USE Knoblock family
Knobloch family
  USE Knoblock family
Knoblock family (Not Subd Geog)
  UF Knoblauch family
    Knobloch family
Knobs, Door
  USE Door knobs
Knock family
  USE Knox family
Knock in automobile motors
  USE Automobiles—Motors—Knock
Knock-knock jokes
  ₍PN6231.K55₎
  BT Wit and humor
Knockers, Door
  USE Door knockers
Knoff family (Not Subd Geog)
Knold family (Not Subd Geog)
Knoles family
  USE Knowles family
Knoll family (Not Subd Geog)
  RT Noll family
Knolton family
  USE Knowlton family
Knor family
  USE Knorr family
Knorr family (Not Subd Geog)
  UF Canair family
    Knarr family
    Knerr family
    Knor family
Knosós (Ancient city)
  USE Knossos (Ancient city)
Knossos (Ancient city) (Not Subd Geog)
  UF Cnossos (Ancient city)
    Cnossus (Ancient city)
    Gnossus (Ancient city)
    Knosós (Ancient city)
  BT Cities and towns, Ruined, extinct, etc.
    —Greece
    Crete—Antiquities
    Greece—Antiquities
Knossos Palace (Knossos)
  USE Palace of Knossos (Knossos)
Knot family
  USE Knott family
Knot gardens (May Subd Geog)
  ₍SB475₎
  UF Rope-knot gardens
  BT Gardens
    Landscape gardening
  — California
    NT Huntington Herb Garden (San
      Marino, Calif.)
Knot theory
  UF Knots (Topology)
  BT Low-dimensional topology
  NT Alexander ideals
    Braid theory
Knotless netting
  USE Sprang
Knots (Birds)
  USE Calidris
Knots (Topology)
  USE Knot theory
Knots and splices
  ₍VM533₎
  UF Knotting and splicing
    Splicing

BT Cordage
    Marline spike seamanship
    Navigation
    Rope
    Seamanship
RT Ropework
NT Fishing knots
    Macramé
    Slings and hitches
Knott family *(Not Subd Geog)*
UF Knot family
    Knotts family
    Knut family
    Knutt family
    Not family
    Nut family
    Nute family
    Nutt family
    Nutter family
    Nutts family
RT McNutt family
Knotted curves
  USE Curves of double curvature
Knotting and splicing
  USE Knots and splices
Knotts family
  USE Knott family
Knotweeds
  USE Polygonum
Knoulton family
  USE Knowlton family
Knoviz culture *(May Subd Geog)*
BT Czechoslovakia—Antiquities
    Lausitz culture
Know-how assistance agreements
  USE Foreign licensing agreements
Know-it-all persons
BT Characters and characteristics
Knowableness of God
  USE God—Knowableness
Knowableness of Jesus Christ
  USE Jesus Christ—Knowableness
Knowland family
  USE Nolan family
Knowledge, Books of
  USE Encyclopedias and dictionaries
Knowledge, Classification of
  USE Classification
    Classification of sciences
Knowledge, Reflexive
  USE Self-knowledge, Theory of
Knowledge, Sociology of
  [BD175]
UF Knowledge, Theory of (Sociology)
    Sociology of knowledge
BT Communication
    Knowledge, Theory of
    Public opinion
    Sociology
Knowledge, Theory of
  [BD150-241]
UF Epistemology
    Mind
BT Consciousness
    Logic
    Metaphysics
    Philosophy
    Psychology
RT Apperception
    Cognition
    Intellect
    Reality
    Truth
SA *subdivision* Knowledge, Theory of
    under names of philosophers
NT A priori
    Analogy
    Ataraxia
    Belief and doubt
    Categories (Philosophy)
    Certainty

    Common sense
    Comparison (Psychology)
    Comprehension (Theory of knowledge)
    Concepts
    Criterion (Theory of knowledge)
    Ding an sich
    Ejection (Psychology)
    Empiricism
    Epistemics
    Error
    Experience
    Explanation (Philosophy)
    Fictions, Theory of
    Formalization (Philosophy)
    Gestalt psychology
    Idea (Philosophy)
    Identity
    Ideology
    Ignorance (Theory of knowledge)
    Illusion (Philosophy)
    Immanence (Philosophy)
    Infallibility (Philosophy)
    Inquiry (Theory of knowledge)
    Integration (Theory of knowledge)
    Interdisciplinary approach to
      knowledge
    Intuition
    Judgment
    Justification (Theory of knowledge)
    Knowledge, Sociology of
    Modality (Theory of knowledge)
    Objectivity
    Observation (Psychology)
    Omniscience (Theory of knowledge)
    Other minds (Theory of knowledge)
    Paradigm (Theory of knowledge)
    Perception
    Personality (Theory of knowledge)
    Phenomenalism
    Pragmatism
    Rationalism
    Relativity
    Resemblance (Philosophy)
    Scientism
    Self-knowledge, Theory of
    Sense data
    Senses and sensation
    Solipsism
    Subjectivity
    Sufficient reason
    Uniformity of nature
    Universals (Philosophy)
    Values
Knowledge, Theory of (Buddhism)
  [BQ4440]
UF Buddhist epistemology
    Theory of knowledge (Buddhism)
BT Buddhism—Doctrines
    Buddhist logic
    Knowledge, Theory of (Religion)
    Philosophy, Buddhist
Knowledge, Theory of (Hinduism)
  [B132.K6]
UF Hindu epistemology
BT Hinduism
    Philosophy, Hindu
Knowledge, Theory of (Islam)
UF Islamic epistemology
BT Philosophy, Islamic
— **Koranic teaching**
Knowledge, Theory of (Jainism)
UF Jaina epistomology
BT Jainism
    Philosophy, Jaina
Knowledge, Theory of (Religion)
  [BL51]
UF Religious knowledge, Theory of
BT Religion—Philosophy
    Theology, Doctrinal
NT Analogy (Religion)
    God—Knowableness

    Jesus Christ—Knowableness
    Knowledge, Theory of (Buddhism)
    Truth (Christian theology)
Knowledge, Theory of (Sociology)
  USE Knowledge, Sociology of
Knowledge, Tree of
  USE Tree of life
Knowledge and learning
  USE *subdivision* Knowledge and learning
     under names of persons for works
     about their formal or informal
     learning or scholarship and
     subdivision Knowledge—[topic]
     under names of persons for works
     on their knowledge of, or
     educational background in, a
     specific topic
Knowledge-based systems (Computer science)
  USE Expert systems (Computer science)
Knowledge of God
  USE God—Knowableness
    God—Omniscience
Knowledge of Jesus Christ
  USE Jesus Christ—Knowableness
Knowledge of self, Theory of
  USE Self-knowledge, Theory of
Knowles family *(Not Subd Geog)*
UF Knoles family
    Knowls family
Knowlon family
  USE Nolan family
Knowls family
  USE Knowles family
Knowlton family *(Not Subd Geog)*
UF Knolton family
    Knoulton family
    Nolten family
    Nolton family
    Noulton family
Knows family
  USE Knox family
Knowth Mound (Ireland)
  USE Knowth Site (Ireland)
Knowth Site (Ireland) *(Not Subd Geog)*
UF Knowth Mound (Ireland)
BT Ireland—Antiquities
Knox family *(Not Subd Geog)*
UF Knock family
    Knows family
    Noc family
    Noch family
    Nock family
    Nocks family
    Nox family
Knox Island (Kiribati)
  USE Tarawa Atoll (Kiribati)
Knoxville Zoo (Knoxville, Tenn.)
  USE Knoxville Zoological Park (Knoxville,
    Tenn.)
Knoxville Zoological Park (Knoxville, Tenn.)
UF Knoxville Zoo (Knoxville, Tenn.)
BT Zoos—Tennessee
Knoy Island (Kiribati)
  USE Tarawa Atoll (Kiribati)
Knudsen family *(Not Subd Geog)*
UF Knudson family
    Knudssøn family
    Knudtsen family
    Knudtson family
    Knudtzon family
    Knutsen family
    Knutson family
RT Knuth family
Knudson family
  USE Knudsen family
Knudssøn family
  USE Knudsen family
Knudtsen family
  USE Knudsen family
Knudtson family
  USE Knudsen family

Knudtzon family
　USE Knudsen family
Knurling
　BT Metal-cutting
　　Turning
Knut family
　USE Knott family
Knuth family *(Not Subd Geog)*
　RT Knudsen family
Knutsen family
　USE Knudsen family
Knutson family
　USE Knudsen family
Knutt family
　USE Knott family
Ko-chou Dam (China)
　BT Dams—China
Ko family *(Not Subd Geog)*
Ko Ho Island (Macao)
　USE Coloane Island (Macao)
Kō Island (Miyazaki-ken, Japan)
　UF Kō-jima (Miyazaki-ken, Japan)
　BT Islands—Japan
Kō-jima (Miyazaki-ken, Japan)
　USE Kō Island (Miyazaki-ken, Japan)
Ko Kiyomizu pottery
　USE Kiyomizu pottery
Ko Kradad (Thailand)
　USE Kradad Island (Thailand)
Kö language
　USE Yakö language
!Kō language (Botswana and Namibia)
　USE !Xō language
Ko-lo-lu
　USE Karluks
Ko Satsuma pottery
　USE Satsuma pottery
Ko Si Chang (Thailand)
　USE Si Chang Island (Thailand)
Ko Sichang (Thailand)
　USE Si Chang Island (Thailand)
Ko tsuzumi
　USE Kotsuzumi
Koa *(May Subd Geog)*
　[QK495.L52 (Botany)]
　[SD397 (Forestry)]
　UF Acacia koa
　NT Furniture, Koa
Koa haole
　USE Lead tree
Koaiker Indians
　USE Cuaiquer Indians
Koaiker language
　USE Cuaiquer language
Koala bear
　USE Koalas
Koalas
　[QL737.M384]
　UF Coala
　　Koala bear
　　Koolah
　BT Marsupialia
Koan
　BT Meditation (Zen Buddhism)
　　Monasticism and religious orders,
　　　Buddhist
　　Zen Buddhism
Koasati Indians
　[E99.K77]
　UF Coshatta Indians
　　Coushatta Indians
　BT Indians of North America
　　Muskhogean Indians
Kob, White-eared
　USE White-eared kob
Koba family *(Not Subd Geog)*
KOBAS System
　[Z699.4.K14]
　BT Libraries—Automation

Kobayashi (Name)
Kōbe Daigaku
Kōbe Denki Tetsudō
　UF Kōbe Dentetsu
　BT Railroads—Japan
　　Street-railroads—Japan
Kōbe Dentetsu
　USE Kōbe Denki Tetsudō
Kobe family *(Not Subd Geog)*
Kobena Indians
　USE Cubeo Indians
Kober family *(Not Subd Geog)*
　UF Koeber family
　RT Cover family
Koberlein family
　USE Koeberlein family
Kobizen pottery
　USE Bizen pottery
Köbner's disease
　USE Epidermolysis bullosa
Kobon language
　BT Papuan languages
Kobsa
　USE Kobza
Kobuk River (Alaska)
　BT Rivers—Alaska
Kobus
　[QL737.U53]
　BT Antelopes
　　Bovidae
Kobus defassa
　USE Kobus ellipsiprymnus
Kobus ellipsiprymnus
　[QL737.U53]
　UF Kobus defassa
　　Waterbucks
Kobza
　[ML1015.K6]
　UF Kobsa
　BT Lute
　　Musical instruments—Ukraine
Kobza music
　[M142.K55]
Kobzari *(May Subd Geog)*
　BT Musicians
Koccikkaṇēcaiyar family *(Not Subd Geog)*
Koch (Asian people)
　USE Rajbansi
Koch family *(Not Subd Geog)*
　UF Koche family
　RT Cocke family
　　Cook family
Koch Palace (Rome, Italy)
　USE Palazzo Koch (Rome, Italy)
Kochanowski family *(Not Subd Geog)*
Koche family
　USE Koch family
Kochersberg (France)
Kochert family *(Not Subd Geog)*
Kochinor family
　USE Coughenour family
Koch's lymph
　USE Tuberculin
Kochuvelans
　USE Ulladans
Kociewie (Poland) *(Not Subd Geog)*
Kočina krajina, 1788
　USE Serbia—History—Insurrection, 1788
Kock, Battle of, 1939
　BT World War, 1939-1945—Campaigns—
　　Poland
Kōda Minami Iseki (Tondabayashi-shi, Japan)
　USE Kōda Minami Site (Tondabayashi-shi,
　　Japan)
Kōda Minami Site (Tondabayashi-shi, Japan)
　(Not Subd Geog)
　UF Kōda Minami Iseki (Tondabayashi-shi,
　　Japan)
　BT Japan—Antiquities
Kodagas
　USE Coorgs

Kodagu folk-songs
　USE Folk-songs, Kodagu
Kodagu language
　[PL4671]
　UF Coorg language
　　Kurg language
　BT Dravidian languages
Kodagus
　USE Coorgs
Kodak camera
　NT Brownie camera
　　Instamatic camera
　　Kodak instant camera
　　Retina camera
Kodak instant camera
　UF Instant camera, Kodak
　BT Instant photography
　　Kodak camera
Kodak moving-picture camera
Kodavas
　USE Coorgs
Koder family
　USE Coder family
Kodesh (The Hebrew word)
　UF Qdš (The Hebrew word)
　BT Hebrew language—Etymology
Kodiak bear
　[QL737.C27]
　UF Alaskan brown bear
　　Brown bear, Alaskan
　　Ursus arctos middendorffi
　　Ursus middendorffi
　BT Bears
　　Brown bear
Kodiak Island (Alaska)
　BT Islands—Alaska
Koe family *(Not Subd Geog)*
　RT Coe family
　　Kaae family
Koebeliidae
　USE Leafhoppers
Koeber family
　USE Kober family
Koeberlein family *(Not Subd Geog)*
　UF Koberlein family
Koefoed family
　USE Kofoed family
Koehler family
　UF Culler family
　　Kiøller family
　　Kjøller family
　　Koeller family
　　Kohler family
　　Koller family
Koeller family
　USE Koehler family
Koeneke family *(Not Subd Geog)*
Koenig family *(Not Subd Geog)*
　UF Konig family
　RT King family
Koenitzer family
　USE Konitzer family
Koepfli family *(Not Subd Geog)*
Koeppel family
　USE Keppel family
Koetai-rivier (Kalimantan Timur, Indonesia)
　USE Mahakam River (Kalimantan Timur,
　　Indonesia)
Koetei River (Kalimantan Timur, Indonesia)
　USE Mahakam River (Kalimantan Timur,
　　Indonesia)
Koetenay Indians
　USE Kutenai Indians
Koetenay language
　USE Kutenai language
Kofán Indians
　USE Cofán Indians
Kofán language
　USE Cofán language
Kofane language
　USE Cofán language

Koffel family *(Not Subd Geog)*
UF Coffel family
RT Kuffel family
Kofod family
USE Kofoed family
Kofoed family *(Not Subd Geog)*
UF Koefoed family
Kofod family
Kofoid family
Kofoid family
USE Kofoed family
Koga family *(Not Subd Geog)*
Kogai language
[*PL7101.K6*]
BT Australia—Languages
Australian languages
Kogai tribes
[*DU274 (Queensland)*]
BT Australian aborigines
Koganei family *(Not Subd Geog)*
Koganei Kōen (Tokyo, Japan)
UF Koganei Park (Tokyo, Japan)
BT Parks—Japan
Koganei Park (Tokyo, Japan)
USE Koganei Kōen (Tokyo, Japan)
Køge Bay (Denmark)
UF Kjöge Bay (Denmark)
BT Bays—Denmark
Køge Bay (Denmark), Battle of, 1677
BT Scanian War, 1675-1679—Campaigns
—Denmark
Koggaba
USE Kagaba Indians
Köggabas
USE Kagaba Indians
Kogi Indians
USE Kagaba Indians
Kogia
[*QL737.C435*]
BT Physeteridae
Kogia breviceps
USE Pygmy sperm whale
Kogiidae
USE Physeteridae
Koguryŏ (Kingdom)
[*DS911.74*]
BT Korea—History—To 935
Koh-i-noor (Diamond)
BT Crown jewels—Great Britain
Diamonds—India
Koh-i-nuh (Turkey)
USE Ararat, Mount (Turkey)
Koh Kradad (Thailand)
USE Kradad Island (Thailand)
Koh Si Chang (Thailand)
USE Si Chang Island (Thailand)
Koh Sichang (Thailand)
USE Si Chang Island (Thailand)
Kohanim
USE Cohanim
Kohathites
USE Korahites
Kohder family
USE Coder family
Kohemp
USE Kudzu
Kohen (Cohanim)
USE Cohanim
Kohen family
USE Cohen family
Kohl family
USE Cole family
Kohl language
USE Mundari language
Kohler family
USE Koehler family
Kohn family
USE Cohen family
Kohnen family
USE Cohen family

Kōho language
USE Srê language
Kohoutek comet *(Not Subd Geog)*
[*QB723.K63*]
BT Comets
Kohs block design test
BT Intelligence tests
Non-verbal intelligence tests
Kohunlich Site (Mexico)
[*F1435.1.K64*]
BT Mexico—Antiquities
Koi
USE Carp
Koiali language, Mountain
USE Mountain Koiari language
Koiari language, Mountain
USE Mountain Koiari language
Koibalian dialect
UF Kaibalian dialect
BT Khakass language
Russian S.F.S.R.—Languages
Koide Iseki (Kikugawa-chō, Yamaguchi-ken,
Japan)
USE Koide Site (Kikugawa-chō, Yamaguchi-
ken, Japan)
**Koide Site (Kikugawa-chō, Yamaguchi-ken,
Japan)** *(Not Subd Geog)*
UF Koide Iseki (Kikugawa-chō,
Yamaguchi-ken, Japan)
BT Japan—Antiquities
Koikendal family
USE Kuykendall family
Koil family
USE Coyle family
Koils family
USE Coyle family
Koinē (Greek language)
USE Greek language, Hellenistic (300 B.C.-
600 A.D.)
Koiner family
USE Coiner family
Koio language
USE Kwaio language
Koishikawa Kōrakuen (Tokyo, Japan)
UF Kōrakuen Park (Tokyo, Japan)
BT Gardens—Japan
Parks—Japan
Koiva River (Latvia and Estonia)
USE Gauja River (Latvia and Estonia)
Koizumi family *(Not Subd Geog)*
Kojedal family *(Not Subd Geog)*
Kojima Bay (Japan) *(Not Subd Geog)*
UF Kojima-wan (Japan)
Kojimawan (Japan)
BT Bays—Japan
Kojima family *(Not Subd Geog)*
Kojima-wan (Japan)
USE Kojima Bay (Japan)
Kojimawan (Japan)
USE Kojima Bay (Japan)
Kojōjō (Ueda-shi, Japan)
USE Shiodajō (Ueda-shi, Japan)
Kojonen family *(Not Subd Geog)*
Kojuč (Serbia)
USE Ključ (Serbia)
Kok-saghyz
[*SB291.K (Culture)*]
UF Taraxacum kok-saghyz
BT Dandelions
Latex
Rubber
Rubber plants
Kök-Türk language
USE Old Turkic language
Kokama Indians
USE Cocama Indians
Kokaratsu pottery
USE Karatsu pottery
Kokawadera engi (Scrolls)
[*ND1053.4*]

BT Kokawadera in art
Painting, Japanese—Kamakura-
Momoyama periods, 1185-1600
Scrolls, Japanese
Kokawadera in art
NT Kokawadera engi (Scrolls)
Kokborok language
BT Bodo languages
Kokburi
USE Buzkashi
Kokemäenjoki (Finland)
USE Kokemäki River (Finland)
Kokemäki River (Finland)
UF Kokemäenjoki (Finland)
Kumo River (Finland)
BT Rivers—Finland
Kokenge family *(Not Subd Geog)*
Kokeshi dolls *(May Subd Geog)*
UF Dolls, Kokeshi
— Awards
[*NK4894.J3*]
BT Rewards (Prizes, etc.)
Kokiyomizu pottery
USE Kiyomizu pottery
Kokkai Gijidō (Tokyo, Japan)
UF Gijidō, Kokkai (Tokyo, Japan)
BT Japan—Capital and capitol
Koklas pheasant
USE Pucrasia macrolopha
Koklass pheasant
USE Pucrasia macrolopha
Kokle
[*ML1015.K64*]
BT Dulcimer
Harp
Musical instruments—Latvia
Kokna (Indic people)
USE Konkans (Indic people)
Koknas (Indic people)
UF Koknis (Indic people)
Kuknas (Indic people)
BT Ethnology—India
Koknese (Indic people)
USE Konkans (Indic people)
Koknis (Indic people)
USE Koknas (Indic people)
Koko (Gorilla)
BT Gorillas
Koko Jelandji language
USE Gugu Yalanji language
Koko Nor (China)
USE Ch'ing-hai Lake (China)
Koko Yalanji language
USE Gugu Yalanji language
Kokomish Indians
USE Skokomish Indians
Kokořín (Czechoslovakia)
UF Kokořínsko (Czechoslovakia)
Kokořínsko (Czechoslovakia)
USE Kokořín (Czechoslovakia)
Kökturk inscriptions
USE Inscriptions, Old Turkic
Kokubugahara (Japan)
USE Miyagi Plain (Japan)
Kokufu Iseki (Fujiidera-shi, Japan)
USE Kokufu Site (Fujiidera-shi, Japan)
Kokufu Site (Fujiidera-shi, Japan)
(Not Subd Geog)
UF Kokufu Iseki (Fujiidera-shi, Japan)
BT Japan—Antiquities
Kokugaku
UF National Learning Movement
Wagaku
BT Philosophy, Japanese
Kokusen byōbu
USE Namban screen painting
Kokutai
BT Japan—Emperors
Japan—Kings and rulers—Religious
aspects

Kokutani porcelain
  USE Kutani porcelain
Kokutani pottery
  USE Kutani pottery
Kōkyo (Tokyo, Japan)
  UF Imperial Palace (Tokyo, Japan)
  BT Palaces—Japan
  NT Fukiage Gyoen (Tokyo, Japan)
        Kōkyo gaien (Tokyo, Japan)
Kōkyo gaien (Tokyo, Japan)
  BT Gardens—Japan
        Kōkyo (Tokyo, Japan)
        Parks—Japan
Kol Insurrection, Chota Nāgpur, India, 1831-1832
  USE Chota Nāgpur (India)—History—
        Insurrection, 1831-1832
Kol language
  USE Mundari language
Kol language (Papua New Guinea)
  USE Narak language
Kola (R.S.F.S.R.)
  USE Kola Peninsula (R.S.F.S.R.)
Kola nut industry *(May Subd Geog)*
  ₁HD9259.K64-643₁
  BT Kola nuts
Kola nuts *(May Subd Geog)*
  UF Cola nuts
        Kolanuts
  BT Cola acuminata
        Kola tree
  NT Kola nut industry
Kola Peninsula (R.S.F.S.R.)
  UF Kola (R.S.F.S.R.)
        Kol'skiĭ Poluostrov (R.S.F.S.R.)
        Lapland Peninsula (R.S.F.S.R.)
        Murmansk Peninsula (R.S.F.S.R.)
  BT Peninsulas—Russian S.F.S.R.
Kola tree
  ₁QK495.S8 (Botany)₁
  ₁SB279.K64 (Crop)₁
  UF Cola nitida
        Cola vera
        Gbanja kola tree
        Sterculia nitida
  NT Kola nuts
Kolam
  UF Rāngoļí
  BT House marks
Kolami language
  ₁PL4681₁
  BT Dravidian languages
Kolams
  ₁DS432.K58₁
  BT Ethnology—India
        Gonds
Kolango language
  USE Kulango language
Kolanko (African people)
  USE Kuranko (African people)
Kolanuts
  USE Kola nuts
Kolarian languages
  USE Munda languages
Kolb family *(Not Subd Geog)*
  UF Kalb family
        Kalber family
        Kolbe family
Kolbe family
  USE Kolb family
Kolbe reaction
  UF Kolbe synthesis
  BT Chemical reactions
        Chemistry, Organic—Synthesis
        Electrolysis
Kolbe synthesis
  USE Kolbe reaction

Kölen Mountains (Sweden and Norway)
  (Not Subd Geog)
  UF Kjølen Mountains (Sweden and
        Norway)
        Scandes (Sweden and Norway)
  BT Mountains—Norway
        Mountains—Sweden
Kolhaṭakara family *(Not Subd Geog)*
  UF Kolhatkar family
Kolhatkar family
  USE Kolhaṭakara family
Kolima River (R.S.F.S.R.)
  USE Kolyma River (R.S.F.S.R.)
Kolín (Czechoslovakia), Battle of, 1757
  BT Seven Years' War, 1756-1763—
        Campaigns—Czechoslovakia
Kolina Indians
  USE Culina Indians
Kolindsund (Denmark) *(Not Subd Geog)*
Kolintang
  ₁ML1040₁
  BT Musical instruments—Indonesia
        Percussion instruments
Kolis
  ₁DS432.K585₁
  BT Ethnology—India
Koliumbe River (R.S.F.S.R.)
  USE Kuliūmbe River (R.S.F.S.R.)
Kolka Glacier (R.S.F.S.R.)
  UF Lednik Kolka (R.S.F.S.R.)
  BT Glaciers—Russian S.F.S.R.
Kolkotta language
  USE Baria language
Kolla Indians
  USE Colla Indians
Koller family
  USE Koehler family
Kolmakovskiy Redoubt (Alaska)
  BT Fortification—Alaska
        Russians—Alaska
Kolo (Dance)
  ₁GV1796.K6₁
K'olo-ch'ung Ho (Pakistan)
  USE Muztāgh River (Pakistan)
Koloa-maoli
  USE Hawaiian duck
Kołobrzeg, Battle of, 1945
  ₁D765.2.K₁
  BT World War, 1939-1945—Campaigns—
        Poland
Kolokuma dialect
  ₁PL8276.95.K₁
  UF Patani dialect (Nigeria)
  BT Ijo language
Kololo language
  USE Lozi language
Kolomyĭky
  BT Folk-songs, Ukrainian
Kolos
  BT Dance music
Kolossi Castle (Kolossi, Cyprus)
  UF Phrourio tou Kolossiou (Kolossi,
        Cyprus)
  BT Castles—Cyprus
**Kolozsvári, Tamás, fl. 1427. Calvary
altarpiece**
  UF Calvary altarpiece (Panel painting)
        Garamszentbenedek altarpiece (Panel
        painting)
        Kálvária-oltár (Panel painting)
  BT Panel painting, Hungarian
Kolping societies
  BT Catholic Church—Societies, etc.
        Church and social problems—Catholic
        Church
Kolposaurus
  USE Nothosaurus
Kols
  USE Mundas
Kol'skiĭ Poluostrov (R.S.F.S.R.)
  USE Kola Peninsula (R.S.F.S.R.)

Koltas (Indic people)
  ₁DS432.K588₁
  BT Ethnology—India
Koltes family *(Not Subd Geog)*
Kolthoff-Sandell reaction
  USE Sandell-Kolthoff reaction
Kolubara River (Serbia)
  BT Rivers—Yugoslavia
Kolube (Papua New Guinea people)
  USE Barok (Papua New Guinea people)
Koluschan Indians
  USE Tlingit Indians
Koluschan language
  USE Tlingit language
Kolyivshchyna, 1768
  USE Ukraine—History—Uprising, 1768
Kolyma River (R.S.F.S.R.)
  UF Kolima River (R.S.F.S.R.)
        Reka Kolyma (R.S.F.S.R.)
  BT Rivers—Russian S.F.S.R.
Kolyumbe River (R.S.F.S.R.)
  USE Kuliūmbe River (R.S.F.S.R.)
Kom (African people)
  ₁DT570₁
  UF Bamekon (African people)
        Bekom (African people)
        Bikom (African people)
        Nkom (African people)
  BT Ethnology—Cameroon
Kom (African people) art
  USE Art, Kom (African people)
Kom language
  ₁PL4001.K73₁
  UF Kom Rem language
  BT Kuki-Chin languages
Kom Madi (Egypt)
  USE Madīnat Wāṭifah, Kawm (Egypt)
Kom Rem language
  USE Kom language
Koma Iseki (Higashiōsaka-shi, Japan)
  USE Koma Site (Higashiōsaka-shi, Japan)
Koma Site (Higashiōsaka-shi, Japan)
  UF Koma Iseki (Higashiōsaka-shi, Japan)
  BT Japan—Antiquities
Komagata Iseki (Minano-machi, Japan)
  USE Komagata Site (Minano-machi, Japan)
Komagata Site (Minano-machi, Japan)
  (Not Subd Geog)
  UF Chichibu Komagata Iseki (Minano-
        machi, Japan)
        Komagata Iseki (Minano-machi, Japan)
  BT Japan—Antiquities
Komaits language
  USE Gumatj language
Komaki Nagakute, Battle of, Japan, 1584
  UF Komaki Nagakute no tatakai, Japan,
        1584
  BT Japan—History—Azuchi-Momoyama
        period, 1568-1603
**Komaki Nagakute, Battle of, Japan, 1584, in
art**
  NT Komaki Nagakute kassen zu (Screen
        painting)
Komaki Nagakute kassen zu (Screen painting)
  ₁ND1059.6₁
  BT Komaki Nagakute, Battle of, Japan,
        1584, in art
        Painting, Japanese—Edo period, 1600-
        1868
        Screen painting, Japanese
Komaki Nagakute no tatakai, Japan, 1584
  USE Komaki Nagakute, Battle of, Japan,
        1584
Komalu (Papua New Guinea people)
  USE Barok (Papua New Guinea people)
Komandorski Basin
  USE Komandorskie Basin
Komandorski Islands (R.S.F.S.R.)
  USE Commander Islands (R.S.F.S.R.)

Komandorskie Basin
  UF Commander Basin
      Kamchatka Basin
      Komandorski Basin
      Komandorskiye Basin
      Zapadnaia Kotlovina
  BT Bering Sea
Komandorskie ostrova (R.S.F.S.R.)
  USE Commander Islands (R.S.F.S.R.)
Komandorskiye Basin
  USE Komandorskie Basin
Komandorskiye ostrova (R.S.F.S.R.)
  USE Commander Islands (R.S.F.S.R.)
Komant language
  USE Kemant language
Komarekiona
  [QL391.A6]
  BT Komarekionidae
Komarekiona eatoni
  [QL391.A6]
Komarekionidae
  [QL391.A6]
  BT Oligochaeta
  NT Komarekiona
Komarów, Battle of, 1914
  UF Zamosc-Komarov, Battle of, 1914
  BT World War, 1914-1918—Campaigns—
      Czechoslovakia
Komatiite
  [QE462.K66]
  BT Rocks, Igneous
Komatsukawa Kaidō (Japan)
  USE Heiwa Kaidō (Japan)
Komazawa Olympic Park (Tokyo, Japan)
  USE Komazawa Orimpikku Kōen (Tokyo,
      Japan)
Komazawa Orimpikku Kōen (Tokyo, Japan)
  (Not Subd Geog)
  UF Komazawa Olympic Park (Tokyo,
      Japan)
  BT Parks—Japan
      Sports facilities—Japan
Komba language *(May Subd Geog)*
  BT Finisterre-Huon languages
      Papua New Guinea—Languages
Kombawats
  USE Kumbavats
Kombe language
  [PL8396]
  BT Bantu languages
Komering dialect *(May Subd Geog)*
  [PL5341.95.K]
  UF Kemering dialect
  BT Indonesia—Languages
      Lampung language
Komet (Fighter planes)
  USE Messerschmitt 163 (Fighter planes)
Komi
  [DK34.K65]
  UF Syryenians
      Zyrians
      Zyryans
  BT Ethnology—Russian S.F.S.R.
      Finno-Ugrians
Komi A.S.S.R. (R.S.F.S.R.)
  (Not Subd Geog)
  — History *(Not Subd Geog)*
  — — Revolution, 1917-1921
      (Not Subd Geog)
      [DK265.8.K]
Komi children's literature
  USE Children's literature, Komi
Komi drama *(May Subd Geog)*
Komi folk poetry
  USE Folk poetry, Komi
Komi-iāzvinski dialect
  USE Komi-Yaz'va dialect
Komi language
  [PH1051-1059]

UF Syryenian language
    Zyrian language
    Zyryen language
BT Permic languages
    Russian S.F.S.R.—Languages
NT Komi-Permyak dialect
Komi literature *(May Subd Geog)*
  [PH1058-9]
  NT Children's literature, Komi
Komi-Permyak dialect
  [PH1071-1079]
  UF Permiak dialect
      Permyak dialect
  BT Komi language
      Russian S.F.S.R.—Languages
Komi-Permyak literature *(May Subd Geog)*
  [PH1078-1079]
Komi-Permyak prose literature
  (May Subd Geog)
Komi philology
Komi poetry *(May Subd Geog)*
  NT Folk poetry, Komi
Komi riddles
  USE Riddles, Komi
Komi-Yaz'va dialect
  UF Komi-iāzvinski dialect
Komisang Island (Japan)
  USE Kume Island (Japan)
Komkani language
  USE Konkani language
Kommerer family
  USE Komro family
Kommos Site (Crete) *(Not Subd Geog)*
  [DF221.C8]
  BT Greece—Antiquities
Kommunisticheskaiā partiiā Sovetskogo Soiūza
  (May Subd Geog)
  — Elections
      [JN6598]
  — Finance
  — History
  — — Pictorial works
  — Membership
      NT Kommunisticheskaiā partiiā
          Sovetskogo Soiūza—Purges
  — Party work
      RT Propaganda, Russian
  — Purges
      BT Kommunisticheskaiā partiiā
          Sovetskogo
          Soiūza—Membership
Komo (Secret order)
  BT Ethnology—Africa, French-speaking
      West
Komo (Zairian people)
  USE Kumu (Zairian people)
Komodo Island (Indonesia)
  UF Pulau Komodo (Indonesia)
  BT Islands—Indonesia
Komondors
  [SF429.K65]
Komoro Castle (Komoro-shi, Japan)
  USE Komorojō (Komoro-shi, Japan)
Komorojō (Komoro-shi, Japan)
  UF Komoro Castle (Komoro-shi, Japan)
  BT Castles—Japan
KOMPAS (Computer system)
  BT Data base management
      Electronic digital computers—
      Programming
Kompleksnyĭ ėnergeticheskiĭ ėksperiment
  BT Atmosphere
      Dynamic meteorology
Komro family *(Not Subd Geog)*
  UF Comero family
      Kommerer family
Komton family
  USE Compton family
Komunko
  [ML1015-1018]
  UF Kum

BT Musical instruments—Korea
    Zither
Komunko music
  [M42.K58]
Komushū
  USE Fuke (Sect)
Kon' (The Russian word)
  BT Russian language—Etymology
Kön-Öy
  USE Kenney
Kona (Hawaii Island, Hawaii)
Konaka Iseki (Azuchi-chō, Japan)
  USE Konaka Site (Azuchi-chō, Japan)
Konaka Site (Azuchi-chō, Japan)
  UF Konaka Iseki (Azuchi-chō, Japan)
  BT Japan—Antiquities
Konarka (Konārak, India : Temple)
  USE Sun Temple (Konārak, India)
Konavle (Croatia)
  USE Konavli (Croatia)
Konavli (Croatia)
  UF Konavle (Croatia)
      Konavlje (Croatia)
Konavlje (Croatia)
  USE Konavli (Croatia)
Konbaung dynasty, Burma, 1752-1885
  USE Burma—History—Konbaung dynasty,
      1752-1885
Konda Hakuchō Iseki (Habikino-shi, Japan)
  USE Konda Hakuchō Site (Habikino-shi,
      Japan)
Konda Hakuchō Site (Habikino-shi, Japan)
  (Not Subd Geog)
  UF Konda Hakuchō Iseki (Habikino-shi,
      Japan)
  BT Japan—Antiquities
Konda language
  UF Kūbi language
  BT Dravidian languages
Konde (African people)
  USE Makonde (African people)
      Ngonde (African people)
Konde language
  USE Makonde language
      Ngonde language
Kondh (Indic people)
  USE Kandhs
Kondjo dialect
  BT Makasar language
Kondo effect
  BT Electric resistance
      Magnetic materials
      Solids—Electric properties
Kondō family *(Not Subd Geog)*
Kondratieff cycles (Economics)
  USE Long waves (Economics)
Konds
  USE Kandhs
Koņekor Gadaba language
  USE Gadaba language (Dravidian)
Konga-desa (India)
  USE Kongu Region (India)
Kongabula language
  USE Gungabula language
**Kongelige Porcelainsfabrik & Fajancefabriken
  Aluminia a/s Strike, Copenhagen, 1972-
  1973**
  BT Porcelain industry—Denmark—
      Employees
      Strikes and lockouts—Porcelain
      industry—Denmark
      Strikes and lockouts—Denmark
Konger Mount (China)
  UF Kongur (China)
      Kung-ko-erh (China)
      Kungur (China)
      Mount Kongur (China)
      Qungar (China)
      Qungur (China)
  BT Mountains—China

Kongju Sansŏng (Kongju-up, Korea)
  USE Kongsansŏng (Kongju-up, Korea)
Kongo imprints *(May Subd Geog)*
  [Z7108.K65]
Kongo Kingdom
  UF Congo (Kingdom)
Kongo language
  UF Congo language
     Fiote language
     Kikongo language
  BT Angola—Languages
     Bantu languages
     Congo (Brazzaville)—Languages
     Zaire—Languages
  NT Bembe language (Congo (Brazzaville))
     Hungana language
     Kituba language
     Koongo dialect (Western Kongo)
     Kwese language
     Laadi dialect
     Mbala language (Bandundu region,
       Zaire)
     Ntaandu dialect
     Pende language
     Solongo dialect
     Suku language (Zaire)
     Yaka language (Zaire and Angola)
     Zoombo dialect
Kongo proverbs
  USE Proverbs, Kongo
Kongō Rikishi (Buddhist deity)
  USE Vajradhara (Buddhist deity)
Kongō-zan (Korea)
  USE Diamond Mountains (Korea)
Kongōji Iseki (Ōmihachiman-shi, Japan)
  USE Kongōji Site (Ōmihachiman-shi, Japan)
Kongōji Site (Ōmihachiman-shi, Japan)
  (Not Subd Geog)
  UF Kongōji Iseki (Ōmihachiman-shi,
       Japan)
  BT Japan—Antiquities
Kongsan Sansŏng (Kongju-up, Korea)
  USE Kongsansŏng (Kongju-up, Korea)
Kongsansŏng (Kongju-up, Korea)
  [DS925.K]
  UF Kongju Sansŏng (Kongju-up, Korea)
     Kongsan Sansŏng (Kongju-up, Korea)
  BT Fortification—Korea (South)
     Historic sites—Korea (South)
Kongu-desa (India)
  USE Kongu Region (India)
Kongu Nadu (India)
  USE Kongu Region (India)
Kongu Region (India)
  UF Konga-desa (India)
     Kongu-desa (India)
     Kongu Nadu (India)
     Koṅku Region (India)
Kongur (China)
  USE Konger Mount (China)
Koniagi Indians
  USE Kaniagmiut (Eskimo tribe)
Koniagui (African people)
  [DT530]
  UF Coniagui (African people)
Konica camera
Konig family
  USE Koenig family
König See (Germany)
  USE Königssee (Germany)
Königgrätz, Battle of, 1866
  [DD439.K7]
  UF Sadowa, Battle of, 1866
  BT Austro-Prussian War, 1866
**Königlich Württembergischen
  Staatseisenbahnen**
  BT Railroads—Germany (West)
Königs See (Germany)
  USE Königssee (Germany)
Königsberg, Battle of, 1945
  [D764]

  BT World War, 1939-1945—Campaigns—
     Russian S.F.S.R.
Königsee (Germany)
  USE Königssee (Germany)
Königssee (Germany)
  UF Bartholomäussee (Germany)
     König See (Germany)
     Königs See (Germany)
     Königsee (Germany)
     Lake of Saint Bartholomew (Germany)
     Saint Bartholomew's Lake (Germany)
  BT Lakes—Germany (West)
Koninklijk Paleis (Amsterdam, Netherlands)
  UF Old Town Hall (Amsterdam,
       Netherlands)
     Oude Stadthuis (Amsterdam,
       Netherlands)
     Paleis (Amsterdam, Netherlands)
     Paleis op de Dam (Amsterdam,
       Netherlands)
     Royal Palace (Amsterdam,
       Netherlands)
  BT City halls—Netherlands
     Palaces—Netherlands
Konishi family *(Not Subd Geog)*
Konita Iseki (Minakami-machi, Japan)
  USE Konita Site (Minakami-machi, Japan)
Konita Site (Minakami-machi, Japan)
  UF Konita Iseki (Minakami-machi, Japan)
  BT Japan—Antiquities
Konitzer family *(Not Subd Geog)*
  UF Koenitzer family
Konjac
  USE Konjak
Konjagen Indians
  USE Kaniagmiut (Eskimo tribe)
Konjak
  [QK495.A685 (Botany)]
  [SB211.K (Culture)]
  UF Devil's tongue
     Konjac
  NT Konnyaku
Konjaku
  USE Konnyaku
Konjo (Zairian people)
  USE Nande (Zairian people)
Konkan (India)
Konkani fiction *(May Subd Geog)*
  NT Short stories, Konkani
Konkani folk-songs
  USE Folk-songs, Konkani
Konkani language
  [PK2231-7]
  UF Concani language
     Komkani language
  BT Indo-Aryan languages, Modern
  RT Marathi language
  NT Agri dialect
     Kudali dialect
Konkani poetry *(May Subd Geog)*
Konkani short stories
  USE Short stories, Konkani
Konkans (Indic people)
  UF Concorinum (Indic people)
     Cugani (Indic people)
     Kokna (Indic people)
     Koknese (Indic people)
  BT Ethnology—India
KONKAT (Information retrieval system)
  [Z699.4.K2]
  UF Konvertering af Katalogoplysninger
  BT Catalogs, Book
     Information storage and retrieval
       systems
Konkōkyō members *(May Subd Geog)*
Konkomba (African people)
  UF Konkomba (African tribe)
  BT Ethnology—Ghana
     Ethnology—Togo
Konkomba (African tribe)
  USE Konkomba (African people)

Konkomba language
  [PL8405.K65]
  BT Gur languages
Koṅku Region (India)
  USE Kongu Region (India)
Konniaku
  USE Konnyaku
Konnyaku
  UF Konjaku
     Konniaku
  BT Konjak
Kono (African people)
  UF Kono (African tribe)
  BT Ethnology—Guinea
     Ethnology—Sierra Leone
Kono (African tribe)
  USE Kono (African people)
Kōno family *(Not Subd Geog)*
Kono language
  [PL8406]
  BT Guinea—Languages
     Liberia—Languages
     Mande languages
     Sierra Leone—Languages
     Vai language
Konoe family *(Not Subd Geog)*
Kōnoike family *(Not Subd Geog)*
Konomihu language
  [PM1585]
  RT Shastan languages
Konosarola language
  USE Vagala language
Konrad family
  USE Conrad family
Konrad von Soest-Preis
  BT Art—Competitions
Konsen Daichi (Japan)
  USE Konsen Plateau (Japan)
Konsen Genya (Japan)
  USE Konsen Plateau (Japan)
Konsen Heiya (Japan)
  USE Konsen Plateau (Japan)
Konsen Plateau (Japan)
  UF Konsen Daichi (Japan)
     Konsen Genya (Japan)
     Konsen Heiya (Japan)
     Konsen Taichi (Japan)
  BT Plateaus—Japan
Konsen Taichi (Japan)
  USE Konsen Plateau (Japan)
Konso (African people)
  BT Cushites
     Ethnology—Ethiopia
KONSTA (Computer programs)
  BT Sampling (Statistics)—Computer
     programs
Kontić family *(Not Subd Geog)*
Konventikelplakatet, 1726
  UF Conventicle act, 1726
  BT Church and state—Sweden
Konvertering af Katalogoplysninger
  USE KONKAT (Information retrieval
     system)
Konyak language
  [PL4001.K75]
  UF Kanyak language
  BT Naga languages
Konza Prairie Research Natural Area (Kan.)
  (Not Subd Geog)
  BT Research natural areas—Kansas
Koocanusa, Lake (B.C. and Mont.)
  UF Koocanusa Reservoir (B.C. and Mont.)
     Lake Koocanusa (B.C. and Mont.)
  BT Kootenai River
     Lakes—British Columbia
     Lakes—Montana
     Reservoirs—British Columbia
     Reservoirs—Montana
Koocanusa Reservoir (B.C. and Mont.)
  USE Koocanusa, Lake (B.C. and Mont.)

Kooder family
    USE Coder family
Koodoo
    USE Greater kudu
Køoge Bugt, Battle of, 1677
Kookaburra
    UF Dacelo gigas
        Dacelo novaguineae
        Kinghunter
        Laughing jackass
    BT Kingfishers
Kookendall family
    USE Kuykendall family
Kool family *(Not Subd Geog)*
    RT Cole family
        Cool family
Koolah
    USE Koalas
Koomil-Roi (Australian people)
    USE Kamilaroi (Australian people)
Koomis
    USE Kumiss
Koon family
    USE Kuhn family
Koon language
    USE !Xõ language
Koone family
    USE Kuhn family
Koones family
    USE Kuhn family
Koongo dialect (Western Kongo)
    UF Fiote language
        Kakongo dialect
        Kakoongo dialect
        Western Kongo dialect
    BT Congo (Brazzaville)—Languages
        Kongo language
Koonjan dialects
    USE Gundjun dialects
Koonrod family
    USE Conrad family
Koons family
    USE Kuhn family
Koonts family
    USE Koontz family
Koontz family *(Not Subd Geog)*
    UF Coontz family
        Koonts family
        Koonz family
        Kumze family
        Kunce family
        Kunts family
        Kuntz family
        Kuntze family
        Kuntzi family
        Kunz family
        Kunze family
    RT Counts family
        Kuhn family
Koonz family
    USE Koontz family
Koorungo (Australian people)
    USE Gunwinggu (Australian people)
Koosa (African people)
    USE Xhosa (African people)
Koose dialect (Bakossi)
    USE Bakossi dialect
Kootanie Lake (B.C.)
    USE Kootenay Lake (B.C.)
Kootanie River
    USE Kootenai River
Kootenai Indians
    USE Kutenai Indians
Kootenai Lake (B.C.)
    USE Kootenay Lake (B.C.)
Kootenai language
    USE Kutenai language

Kootenai River
    UF Kootanie River
        Kootenay River
        Kootenie River
        Kootienay River
        Kutenai River
        Swan River
    BT Rivers—British Columbia
        Rivers—Idaho
        Rivers—Montana
    NT Koocanusa, Lake (B.C. and Mont.)
Kootenay Lake (B.C.)
    UF Kootanie Lake (B.C.)
        Kootenai Lake (B.C.)
    BT Lakes—British Columbia
Kootenay National Park (B.C.)
    (Not Subd Geog)
    UF Parc national Kootenay (B.C.)
    BT National parks and reserves—British
        Columbia
Kootenay River
    USE Kootenai River
Kootenie River
    USE Kootenai River
Kootienay River
    USE Kootenai River
Kop Dağı (Turkey)
    USE Kop Mountains (Turkey)
Kop Dağları (Turkey)
    USE Kop Mountains (Turkey)
Kop Mountains (Turkey)
    UF Kop Dağı (Turkey)
        Kop Dağları (Turkey)
        Kopdağ (Turkey)
        Kopdağı (Turkey)
    BT Mountains—Turkey
Kopagmiut language
    [PM73]
    UF Chiglit language
Kopais Lake (Greece)
    USE Copais Lake (Greece)
Kopaonik Mountains (Serbia)
    UF Kapaonik Mountains (Serbia)
    BT Mountains—Yugoslavia
Kopasz Hegy (Hungary)
    USE Tokaj, Mount (Hungary)
Kopdağ (Turkey)
    USE Kop Mountains (Turkey)
Kopdağı (Turkey)
    USE Kop Mountains (Turkey)
Kopeck
    UF Copeck
Kopenhaver family
    USE Copenhaver family
Kopenhofer family
    USE Copenhaver family
Kopet Dag (Turkmen S.S.R. and Iran)
    UF Kopet-Dag (Turkmen S.S.R. and Iran)
        Kopet Dagh (Turkmen S.S.R. and
        Iran)
        Koppeh Dagh (Turkmen S.S.R. and
        Iran)
    BT Mountains—Iran
        Mountains—Turkmen S.S.R.
Kopet-Dag (Turkmen S.S.R. and Iran)
    USE Kopet Dag (Turkmen S.S.R. and Iran)
Kopet Dagh (Turkmen S.S.R. and Iran)
    USE Kopet Dag (Turkmen S.S.R. and Iran)
Kopka family *(Not Subd Geog)*
Kopp family *(Not Subd Geog)*
    UF Koppe family
Koppe family
    USE Kopp family
Koppeh Dagh (Turkmen S.S.R. and Iran)
    USE Kopet Dag (Turkmen S.S.R. and Iran)
Koppenhaver family
    USE Copenhaver family
Koppenhoefer family
    USE Copenhaver family
Koppenhofer family
    USE Copenhaver family

Kopp's asthma
    USE Laryngismus stridulus
Koprino River (Vancouver Island, B.C.)
    BT Rivers—British Columbia
Kor language
    USE Cua language
KOR MARC
    USE MARC System—Korea (South)
Kora (Musical instrument)
    [ML1015-1018]
    UF Harp-lute
    BT Musical instruments—Africa
Kora language
    USE Korana language
Kora music
    [M142.K595]
Korafe language
    USE Korape language
Korafi language
    USE Korape language
Koraga language
    BT Dravidian languages
        Tulu language
Koragas (Indic people)
    [DS432.K59]
    BT Ethnology—India
Korah, Sons of
    USE Korahites
Korahites
    UF Kohathites
        Korah, Sons of
        Kore, Sons of
        Korhites
        Sons of Korah
    BT Levites
Korai statues
    USE Kore statues
Korakan
    USE Ragi
Kōrakuen Park (Tokyo, Japan)
    USE Koishikawa Kōrakuen (Tokyo, Japan)
Koran
    [BP100-130]
    UF Alcoran
        Alkoran
    BT Islam
        Islamic law—Sources
        Islamic literature
    NT Basmalah
        Egypt in the Koran
        Nature in the Koran
        Prophets in the Koran
        Women in the Koran
    — **Abrogator and abrogated verses**
        [BP130.3]
    — **Animals**
        USE Koran—Natural history
    — **Appreciation**
    — **Astronomy**
        [BP134.A8]
        BT Astronomy
    — **Biography**
        NT John, the Baptist, Saint, in the
            Koran
            Joseph (Son of Jacob) in the Koran
            Mary, Blessed Virgin, Saint, in the
            Koran
    — **Birds**
        USE Koran—Natural history
    — **Botany**
        USE Koran—Natural history
    — **Chanting**
        USE Koran—Recitation
    — **Colportage**
        USE Koran—Publication and
            distribution
    — **Comparative studies**
    — **Criticism, interpretation, etc.**
        NT Koran as literature
    — — **Biography**
    — — **History**

Koran
— **Criticism, interpretation, etc.**
— — **History** *(Continued)*
    NT Koranic scholars
— — Theory, methods, etc.
    USE Koran—Hermeneutics
— **Criticism, Textual**
    NT Koran—Readings
— **Ethics**
    ⌐BP134.E84⌐
    BT Islamic ethics
— **Ethnology**
    UF Ethnology, Koranic
    BT Man (Islam)—Koranic teaching
— **Evidences, authority, etc.**
    UF Koran—Inimitability
    RT Koran—Language, style
— Exegesis
    USE Koran—Hermeneutics
— Food
    USE Food in the Koran
— Gardens
    USE Koran—Natural history
— **Geography**
    UF Geography, Islamic
— **Hermeneutics**
    ⌐BP130.2⌐
    UF Koran—Criticism, interpretation,
        etc.—Theory, methods, etc.
        Koran—Exegesis
        Koran—Interpretation
— **Historiography**
    ⌐BP134.H5⌐
    Here are entered works on the representation
    of historical events in the Koran.
— **Indexes, First line**
— Inimitability
    USE Koran—Evidences, authority, etc.
— Interpretation
    USE Koran—Hermeneutics
— Jews
    USE Jews in the Koran
— **Juvenile literature**
— **Language, style**
    RT Koran—Evidences, authority, etc.
    NT Koran as literature
— Law
    USE Islamic law
— **Manuscripts**
— Mathematics
    USE Mathematics in the Koran
— Medicine
    USE Medicine in the Koran
— Melodic reading
    USE Koran—Recitation
— **Memorizing**
    NT Hafiz
— Military art and science
    USE Military art and science in the
        Koran
— Musical declamation
    USE Koran—Recitation
— **Natural history**
    UF Botany of the Koran
        Koran—Animals
        Koran—Birds
        Koran—Botany
        Koran—Gardens
        Koran—Zoology
        Natural history, Koranic
        Zoology of the Koran
— Oaths
    USE Oaths in the Koran
— **Orthography**
    ⌐PJ6696.Z5A4⌐
    UF Arabic language—Writing, Koranic
        Koran—Spelling
    BT Writing, Arabic
— **Political science**
    UF Koran and political science
        Political science and the Koran

BT Political science
    NT Islam and state—Koranic teaching
— **Prayers**
— Printing
    USE Koran—Publication and
        distribution
— **Prophecies**
    ⌐BP134.P74⌐
— **Psychology**
    ⌐BP134.P747⌐
    UF Koranic psychology
        Psychology, Koranic
— **Publication and distribution**
    (May Subd Geog)
    UF Koran—Colportage
        Koran—Printing
— Qirā'āt
    USE Koran—Readings
— **Quotations**
— **Reading**
— **Readings**
    ⌐BP131.5⌐
    Here are entered works on the Koranic
    science known as the "science of the readings"
    (Arabic: qirā'āt) which deals with various rendi-
    tions of the text of the Koran according to differ-
    ent oral traditions.
    UF Koran—Qirā'āt
        Qirā'āt
    BT Koran—Criticism, Textual
— **Recitation**
    ⌐BP131.6⌐
    UF Chanting
        Koran—Chanting
        Koran—Melodic reading
        Koran—Musical declamation
    BT Music, Islamic
        Oral interpretation
    NT Hafiz
— **Relation to the Bible**
    ⌐BP134.B4⌐
    UF Bible—Relation to the Koran
        Bible and the Koran
    BT Christianity and other religions—
        Islam
— Science
    USE Koran and science
— **Sociology**
    ⌐BP134.S6⌐
    BT Sociology, Islamic
— Spelling
    USE Koran—Orthography
— **Study** *(May Subd Geog)*
    ⌐BP130.8-86⌐
    BT Islamic religious education
— **Theology**
    ⌐BP132⌐
    BT Islam—Doctrines
    SA *subdivision* Koranic teaching *under*
        subjects, e.g. Religious life
        (Islam)—Koranic teaching
    NT Jesus Christ in the Koran
        Mary, Blessed Virgin, Saint, in the
        Koran
— **Translating**
    ⌐BP131.13⌐
— **Use**
    ⌐BP130.7⌐
— Zoology
    USE Koran—Natural history
— Iran
    USE Iran in the Koran
Koran and philosophy
    ⌐BP134.P5⌐
    UF Philosophy and the Koran
    BT Islam and philosophy
Koran and political science
    USE Koran—Political science
Koran and science
    ⌐BP134.S3⌐

    UF Koran—Science
        Science and the Koran
    BT Islam and science
Koran as literature
    ⌐BP131.8⌐
    BT Arabic literature
        Koran—Criticism, interpretation, etc.
        Koran—Language, style
        Religious literature
Koran holders
    USE Koran stands
Koran reading desks
    USE Koran stands
Koran stands *(May Subd Geog)*
    UF Koran holders
        Koran reading desks
    BT Stands (Furniture)
Koran stories
    ⌐BP130.58⌐
Koran stories, Chinese *(May Subd Geog)*
    UF Chinese Koran stories
Koran stories, Korean ⌐etc.⌐
    (May Subd Geog)
Korana (African people)
    ⌐DT764.K6⌐
    UF Corannas
        Gorona
        Khora
    BT Khoikhoi (African people)
    NT Korana War, 1st, 1868-1870
        Korana War, 2nd, 1878-1879
Korana language
    ⌐PL8407⌐
    UF Coranna language
        Kora language
    BT Khoikhoi language
        South Africa—Languages
Korana War, 1st, 1868-1870
    UF Northern Border War, 1st, South
        Africa, 1868-1870
        South Africa—History—Korana War,
        1868-1870
    BT Korana (African people)
        South Africa—History—Frontier Wars,
        1811-1878
Korana War, 2nd, 1878-1879
    UF Northern Border War, 2nd, South
        Africa, 1878-1879
        South Africa—History—Korana War,
        1878-1879
    BT Korana (African people)
        South Africa—History—Frontier Wars,
        1811-1878
Koranic psychology
    USE Koran—Psychology
Koranic scholars *(May Subd Geog)*
    UF Scholars, Koranic
    BT Koran—Criticism, interpretation, etc.
        —History
        Scholars, Muslim
Korape language *(May Subd Geog)*
    UF Korafe language
        Korafi language
        Kwarafe language
        Okeina language
    BT Papua New Guinea—Languages
        Papuan languages
Koras
    BT Ethnology—India
        India—Scheduled tribes
Korat Plateau (Thailand)
    USE Khorat Plateau (Thailand)
Koravas
    ⌐DS432.K6⌐
    UF Kuravers
        Yerukulas
    BT Ethnology—India
        India—Denotified tribes

Korčula Island (Croatia)
  UF Corcyra Molaina (Croatia)
      Corcyra Nigra (Croatia)
      Curzola Island (Croatia)
      Kótkyra Mélaina (Croatia)
      Ostrvo Korčula (Croatia)
      Otok Korčula (Croatia)
  BT Islands—Yugoslavia
Kordall family
  USE Cordell family
Kordell family
  USE Cordell family
Kordes family
  USE Cordes family
Kordestān
  USE Kurdistan
Kordofanian languages
  BT African languages
      Sudan—Languages
  NT Krongo language
      Tagoi language
Kore, Sons of
  USE Korahites
Kore statues *(May Subd Geog)*
  [NB1210.M3]
  UF Korai statues
  BT Greece—Antiquities
      Marble sculpture, Greek
      Women in art
Kore statues in art
  [NX652.K65]
Korea
    Here are entered works on Korea as a whole for the pre-1948 period.
  NT Korea (North)
      Korea (South)
  — **Church history**
  — — **20th century**
  — **Civilization**
    NT Architecture—Japan—Korean influences
      Japan—Civilization—Korean influences
      Pottery, Japanese—Korean influences
      Ryukyu Islands—Civilization—Korean influences
  — — **To 935**
  — — **935-1392**
  — — **20th century**
  — — **American influences**
    BT United States—Civilization
  — — **Buddhist influences**
    BT Civilization, Buddhist
  — — **Chinese influences**
    BT China—Civilization
  — — **Occidental influences**
    (Not Subd Geog)
    BT Civilization, Occidental
  — — **Shamanistic influences**
    BT Shamanism—Korea
  — **Description and travel**
  — — **To 1900**
  — — **1901-1947**
    [DS902.3]
  — **Economic conditions**
  — — **1910-1945** *(Not Subd Geog)*
    [HC467]
  — — **1945-**
  — **Foreign relations**
  — — **1864-1910**
    [DS915.37]
  — — **1945-**
    [DS917.37]
  — **History**
  — — **To 935**
    NT Karak (Kingdom)
      Koguryŏ (Kingdom)
      Paekche (Kingdom)
      Silla (Kingdom)
  — — **Koryŏ period, 935-1392**

— — **Mongolian invasions, 1231-1270**
— — **Yi dynasty, 1392-1910**
— — **Japanese invasions, 1592-1598**
    BT Japan—History—To 1868
— — **Manchu invasions, 1627-1637**
    [DS913.6]
— — **1637-1864**
— — **1864-**
— — **1864-1910**
    NT Hong Kyŏng-nae Incident, 1811-1812
    NT Imo Incident, Korea, 1882
      Kapsin Incident, 1884
      Tonghak Incident, 1894
— — — **Anecdotes, facetiae, satire, etc.**
— — **20th century**
    [DS916]
— — **Japanese occupation, 1910-1945**
    [DS916.525-916.58]
    BT Japan—History—20th century
    NT Korean resistance movements, 1905-1945
— — **Independence movement, 1919**
    UF Korean declaration of independence, 1919
      Mansei movement, 1919
    BT Korean resistance movements, 1905-1945
— — **1945-**
— — **Partition, 1945**
    RT Korean reunification question (1945-   )
— — **1945-**
    NT Korean reunification question (1945-   )
— — — **Pictorial works**
— — **Allied occupation, 1945-1948**
— — War and intervention, 1950-1953
    USE Korean War, 1950-1953
— **Industries**
— — **1945-**
— **Politics and government**
— — **1392-1910**
— — **1864-1910**
— — **1905-**
— — **1910-1945**
— — **1945-1948**
— **Religion**
    NT Taejonggyo
— **Social conditions**
— — **1945-**
    [HN730.5]
Korea (Democratic People's Republic)
  USE Korea (North)
Korea (North)
    Here are entered works on the Democratic People's Republic of Korea, established in 1948.
  UF Korea (Democratic People's Republic)
      North Korea
  BT Korea
Korea (Republic)
  USE Korea (South)
Korea (South)
    Here are entered works on the Republic of Korea, established in 1948.
  UF Korea (Republic)
      South Korea
  BT Korea
— **Economic conditions**
— — **1948-1960**
— — **1960-**
— **Economic policy**
— — **1960-**
— **History**
— — **1948-1960**
— — **1960-**
— — **April Revolution, 1960**
    UF April Revolution, Korea (South), 1960
    BT Korea (South)—History—1960-
— — **1960-**

    NT Korea (South)—History—April Revolution, 1960
      Korea (South)—History—May Revolution, 1961
      Kwangju Uprising, Korea (South), 1980
— — **May Revolution, 1961**
    UF May Revolution, Korea (South), 1961
    BT Korea (South)—History—1960-
— — Kwangju Uprising, 1980
    USE Kwangju Uprising, Korea (South), 1980
— **Industries**
— — **1960-**
— **Politics and government**
— — **1948-1960**
— — **1960-**
Korean aesthetics
  USE Aesthetics, Korean
Korean Air Lines Flight 007 Incident, 1983
  USE Korean Air Lines Incident, 1983
Korean Air Lines Incident, 1983
  UF Downing of Korean Air Lines Flight 007, 1983
      Flight 007 Incident, 1983
      K.A.L. Flight 007 Incident, 1983
      KAL Flight 007 Incident, 1983
      Korean Air Lines Flight 007 Incident, 1983
      Korean Airliner Incident, 1983
      Shooting Down of Korean Air Lines Flight 007, 1983
      South Korean Airliner Incident, 1983
  BT Aeronautics—Accidents—1983
      World politics—1975-1985
Korean Airliner Incident, 1983
  USE Korean Air Lines Incident, 1983
Korean alien labor
  USE Alien labor, Korean
Korean American business enterprises
  (May Subd Geog)
  BT Minority business enterprises—United States
Korean American engineers
  (May Subd Geog)
  UF Engineers, Korean American
  BT Engineers—United States
Korean-American poetry
  BT Korean poetry
Korean American scientists
  (May Subd Geog)
  UF Scientists, Korean American
  BT Scientists—United States
Korean American women *(May Subd Geog)*
  UF Women, Korean American
  BT Women—United States
Korean Americans *(May Subd Geog)*
  BT Ethnology—United States
      Koreans—United States
  NT Church work with Korean Americans
Korean anonyms and pseudonyms
  USE Anonyms and pseudonyms, Korean
Korean art
  USE Art, Korean
Korean art objects
  USE Art objects, Korean
Korean artists' literary writings
  USE Artists' literary writings, Korean
Korean arts
  USE Arts, Korean
Korean astrology
  USE Astrology, Korean
Korean atlases
  USE Atlases, Korean
Korean authors
  USE Authors, Korean
Korean ballads
  USE Ballads, Korean
Korean Bible plays
  USE Bible plays, Korean

Korean Bible stories
  USE Bible stories, Korean
Korean Buddhist hymns
  USE Buddhist hymns, Korean
Korean Buddhist literature
  USE Buddhist literature, Korean
Korean Buddhist sermons
  USE Buddhist sermons, Korean
Korean Buddhist stories
  USE Buddhist stories, Korean
Korean calendar
  USE Calendar, Korean
Korean calligraphy
  USE Calligraphy, Korean
Korean character sets (Data processing)
  (May Subd Geog)
  UF REACC (Character set)
      RLIN East Asian Character Code
  BT Character sets (Data processing)
      Korean language—Data processing
  — Data bases
      NT CJK thesaurus (Data base)
Korean children's encyclopedias and
    dictionaries
  USE Children's encyclopedias and
      dictionaries, Korean
Korean children's literature
  USE Children's literature, Korean
Korean children's plays
  USE Children's plays, Korean
Korean children's poetry
  USE Children's poetry, Korean
Korean children's stories
  USE Children's stories, Korean
Korean children's writings
  USE Children's writings, Korean
Korean Christian literature
  USE Christian literature, Korean
Korean Christian poetry
  USE Christian poetry, Korean
Korean civics
  USE Civics, Korean
Korean coins
  USE Coins, Korean
Korean college verse
  USE College verse, Korean
Korean color prints
  USE Color prints, Korean
Korean cookery
  USE Cookery, Korean
Korean corporations
  USE Corporations, Korean
Korean decimal classification
  USE Classification, Korean decimal
Korean declaration of independence, 1919
  USE Korea—History—Independence
      movement, 1919
Korean Demilitarized Zone (Korea)
  [DS921.7]
  UF Demilitarized Zone, Korean (Korea)
      DMZ (Korea)
      Korean War, 1950-1953—
          Demilitarized Zone
      Neutral Buffer Zone, Korean (Korea)
  BT Korean War, 1950-1953—Armistices
Korean detective and mystery stories
  USE Detective and mystery stories, Korean
Korean drama *(May Subd Geog)*
  NT Bible plays, Korean
      Children's plays, Korean
      Folk-drama, Korean
      Sandae plays
Korean dramatists
  USE Dramatists, Korean
Korean encyclopedias and dictionaries
  USE Encyclopedias and dictionaries,
      Korean
Korean epic literature
  USE Epic literature, Korean
Korean essays
  — Women authors

Korean fables
  USE Fables, Korean
Korean fiction *(May Subd Geog)*
  NT Buddhist stories, Korean
      Children's stories, Korean
      Detective and mystery stories, Korean
      Historical fiction, Korean
      Love stories, Korean
      Short stories, Korean
      War stories, Korean
  — To 1900
  — 1894-1919
      [PL967.5 (History)]
      [PL981.5 (Collections)]
  — 20th century
Korean fiction (Chinese)
  USE Chinese fiction—Korean authors
Korean flower arrangement
  USE Flower arrangement, Korean
Korean folk dancing
  USE Folk dancing, Korean
Korean folk-drama
  USE Folk-drama, Korean
Korean folk literature
  USE Folk literature, Korean
Korean folk poetry
  USE Folk poetry, Korean
Korean folk-songs
  USE Folk-songs, Korean
Korean genre painting
  USE Genre painting, Korean
Korean historical fiction
  USE Historical fiction, Korean
Korean hymns
  USE Hymns, Korean
Korean imprints *(May Subd Geog)*
  — Cataloging
      USE Cataloging of Korean imprints
Korean incantations
  USE Incantations, Korean
Korean inscriptions
  USE Inscriptions, Korean
Korean laboring class writings
  USE Laboring class writings, Korean
Korean landscape painting
  USE Landscape painting, Korean
Korean language
  [PL901-949]
  — To 935
      [PL909.2]
      UF Korean language—Old Korean
          Old Korean
      NT Korean language—Writing—Idu
  — Middle Korean, 935-1500
      NT Korean language—Writing—Idu
  — Data processing
      NT Korean character sets (Data
          processing)
  — Etymology
  — — Names
      NT Names, Korean
  — Names
      USE Names, Korean
  — Old Korean
      USE Korean language—To 935
  — Orthography and spelling
      NT Korean language—Writing—Idu
  — Writing
  — — Idu
      UF Idu (Korean language)
      BT Korean language—To 935
          Korean language—Middle
              Korean, 935-1500
          Korean language—Orthography
              and spelling
Korean letter-writing
  USE Letter-writing, Korean
Korean letters
Korean literature
  [PL950-988]
  NT Buddhist literature, Korean

Children's literature, Korean
Christian literature, Korean
Epic literature, Korean
Folk literature, Korean
Laboring class writings, Korean
Religious literature, Korean
  — To 1900
      [PL958 (History)]
      [PL972 (Collections)]
  — Koryŏ period, 935-1392
      [PL958.12 (History)]
      [PL972.12 (Collections)]
  — Middle Korean, 935-1500
      UF Middle Korean literature
  — 1598-1800
      [PL958.26 (History)]
      [PL972.26 (Collections)]
  — 19th century
      [PL958.3 (History)]
      [PL972.3 (Collections)]
  — 1894-1919
      [PL972.5 (Collections)]
      [PL985.5 (History and criticism)]
  — 20th century
Korean literature (Chinese)
  USE Chinese literature—Korean authors
Korean literature (English)
  USE English literature—Korean authors
Korean love poetry
  USE Love poetry, Korean
Korean love stories
  USE Love stories, Korean
Korean medicine
  USE Medicine, Korean
Korean mural painting and decoration
  USE Mural painting and decoration, Korean
Korean mythology
  USE Mythology, Korean
Korean names
  USE Names, Korean
Korean newspapers *(May Subd Geog)*
Korean orations
  USE Speeches, addresses, etc., Korean
Korean patriotic poetry
  USE Patriotic poetry, Korean
Korean periodicals *(May Subd Geog)*
  NT Women's periodicals, Korean
Korean philosophy
  USE Philosophy, Korean
Korean pine
  USE Pinus koraiensis
Korean poetry *(May Subd Geog)*
  NT Changga
      Children's poetry, Korean
      Christian poetry, Korean
      College verse, Korean
      Folk poetry, Korean
      Hyangga
      Kasa
      Korean-American poetry
      Love poetry, Korean
      Patriotic poetry, Korean
      Political poetry, Korean
      School verse, Korean
      Sijo
  — Middle Korean, 935-1500
  — 20th century
      [PL961.4 (History)]
      [PL976.4 (Collections)]
  — Women authors
Korean poetry (Chinese)
  USE Chinese poetry—Korean authors
Korean poets
  USE Poets, Korean
Korean political poetry
  USE Political poetry, Korean
Korean portrait painting
  USE Portrait painting, Korean
Korean property *(May Subd Geog)*
  UF Property, Korean
  BT Alien property

Korean prose literature (May Subd Geog)
  NT Reportage literature, Korean
     School prose, Korean
Korean proverbs
  USE Proverbs, Korean
Korean quotations
  USE Quotations, Korean
Korean religious literature
  USE Religious literature, Korean
Korean reportage literature
  USE Reportage literature, Korean
Korean resistance movements, 1905-1945
  UF Anti-Japanese movements, Korean
  BT Korea—History—Japanese occupation,
     1910-1945
  NT Korea—History—Independence
     movement, 1919
  — Registers, lists, etc.
Korean resistance movements, 1905-1945, in
  literature
Korean reunification question (1945-   )
  UF Korean unification question (1945-
)
     Reunification of Korea (1945-   )
     Unification of Korea (1945-   )
  BT Korea—History—1945-
  RT Korea—History—Partition, 1945
Korean riddles
  USE Riddles, Korean
Korean school prose
  USE School prose, Korean
Korean school verse
  USE School verse, Korean
Korean screen painting
  USE Screen painting, Korean
Korean sermons
  USE Sermons, Korean
Korean short stories
  USE Short stories, Korean
Korean shorthand
  USE Shorthand, Korean
Korean songs
  USE Songs, Korean
Korean speeches
  USE Speeches, addresses, etc., Korean
Korean students (May Subd Geog)
Korean typewriters
  USE Typewriters, Korean
Korean unification question (1945-   )
  USE Korean reunification question (1945-
)
Korean War, 1950-1953 (May Subd Geog)
  [DS918]
  UF Korea—History—War and
     intervention, 1950-1953
  NT Chip'yŏng-ni, Battle of, 1951
     Ch'ŏngch'ŏn-gang, Battle of, 1950
     Imjin-gang, Battle of, 1951
     Tabuwŏn (Korea), Battle of, 1950
  — Aerial operations
  — Armistices
     NT Korean Demilitarized Zone
        (Korea)
  — Battles, sieges, etc.
     USE Korean War, 1950-1953—
        Campaigns
  — Campaigns (May Subd Geog)
     UF Korean War, 1950-1953—Battles,
        sieges, etc.
        Korean War, 1950-1953—Military
        operations
     NT Naktong River (Korea), Battle of,
        1950
  — Casualties (Statistics, etc.)
  — Causes
  — Charities
     USE Korean War, 1950-1953—War
        work
  — Civilian relief
     [DS921.3]

     NT Korean War, 1950-1953—War
        work
  — Collaborationists
  — Destruction and pillage
     [DS921.5.D4]
  — Diplomatic history
     BT Korean War, 1950-1953—Sources
  — Manpower
  — Military operations
     USE Korean War, 1950-1953—
        Campaigns
  — Naval operations
  — Personal narratives, American, [British,
     Chinese, etc.]
  — Postal service
  — Prisoners and prisons
  — Railroad transportation
     BT Korean War, 1950-1953—
        Transportation
  — Refugees
  — Regimental histories (May Subd Geog)
  — Religious aspects
  — Secret service (May Subd Geog)
     [DS921.5.S7-8]
  — Social work
     USE Korean War, 1950-1953—War
        work
  — Sources
     [DS918.A2-55]
     NT Korean War, 1950-1953—
        Diplomatic history
  — Transportation
     NT Korean War, 1950-1953—Railroad
        transportation
  — War work (May Subd Geog)
     UF Korean War, 1950-1953—Charities
        Korean War, 1950-1953—Social
        work
     BT Korean War, 1950-1953—Civilian
        relief
  — — Boy scouts
  — Demilitarized Zone
     USE Korean Demilitarized Zone
        (Korea)
Korean war stories
  USE War stories, Korean
Korean watercolor painting
  USE Watercolor painting, Korean
Korean wit and humor (May Subd Geog)
Korean wit and humor, Pictorial
  (May Subd Geog)
Korean women authors
  USE Women authors, Korean
Korean women's periodicals
  USE Women's periodicals, Korean
Koreans (May Subd Geog)
  BT Ethnology—Korea
  — United States
     NT Korean Americans
Koreher family
  USE Corriher family
Korelle camera
  [TR263.K]
Koren family (Not Subd Geog)
Koreshanity
  [BP605.K6]
  BT Religions
Koretaru Indians
  USE Baniva Indians
Korfball
  [GV889.5]
  BT Basketball
  — Training
Korhites
  USE Korahites
Koria language
  USE Kuria language
Koriaks
  USE Koryaks
Koriākskiĭ khrebet (R.S.F.S.R.)
  USE Koryak Range (R.S.F.S.R.)

Koriākskoe nagor'e (R.S.F.S.R.)
  USE Koryak Range (R.S.F.S.R.)
Koriaques
  USE Koryaks
Koriki language
  USE Purari language
Kōrin School
  USE Sōtatsu-Kōrin School
Korina
  USE Terminalia superba
Korintje language
  USE Kerinci language
Korintji Lake (Sumatra, Indonesia)
  USE Kerinci Lake (Sumatra, Indonesia)
Korku language
  USE Kurku language
Kórkyra Mélaina (Croatia)
  USE Korčula Island (Croatia)
Korman family
  USE Corman family
Kormann family
  USE Corman family
Korn family
  USE Corn family
Kornbau family
  USE Cornbower family
Korner family
  USE Corn family
Kornerup family (Not Subd Geog)
Kornfeld family (Not Subd Geog)
  UF Kornfield family
Kornfield family
  USE Kornfeld family
Kórnik (Poland). Bnin
  USE Bnin (Kórnik, Poland)
Kórnik Castle (Kórnik, Poland)
  USE Zamek Kórnicki (Kórnik, Poland)
Kornwerderzand, Battle of, 1940
  BT World War, 1939-1945—Campaigns—
     Netherlands
Koro (African people)
  UF Koro (African tribe)
     Korofawa (African people)
  BT Ethnology—Nigeria
Koro (African tribe)
  USE Koro (African people)
Koro Lafia language
  USE Migili language
Korofawa (African people)
  USE Koro (African people)
Koroko language
  USE Valman language
Koromfe language
  USE Kurumba language
Koromo Castle (Toyota-shi, Japan)
  USE Koromojō (Toyota-shi, Japan)
Koromojō (Toyota-shi, Japan)
  UF Hichishūjō (Toyota-shi, Japan)
     Koromo Castle (Toyota-shi, Japan)
  BT Castles—Japan
Korongo language
  USE Krongo language
Korps (Estonia)
  BT Manors—Estonia
Korrawa language
  USE Garawa language
Korreher family
  USE Corriher family
Korsakoff's syndrome
  [RC394.K6]
  UF Amnestic confabulatory syndrome
     Cerebropathia psychica toxaemica
     Chronic alcoholic delirium
     Polyneuritic neurosis
  BT Alcoholic psychoses
     Alcoholism
     Brain—Diseases
     Syndromes

Korsakov Harbor (R.S.F.S.R.)
(Not Subd Geog)
  UF Odomari Harbor (R.S.F.S.R.)
      Otomari Harbor (R.S.F.S.R.)
  BT Harbors—Russian S.F.S.R.

Korslien family *(Not Subd Geog)*

Korsun (City)
  USE Chersonese (City)

Korsun'-Shevchenkovskiy, Battle of, 1944
  [D764]
  BT World War, 1939-1945—Campaigns—
      Ukraine

Kortright family
  USE Cartwright family

Kortwright family
  USE Cartwright family

Korwa (Indic people)
  [DS432.K63]
  BT Ethnology—India

Korwars (Sculpture)
  BT Sculpture

Korwin family
  USE Corwin family

Koryak language
  [PM75]
  BT Hyperborean languages
  NT Palan dialect

Koryak Mountains (R.S.F.S.R.)
  USE Koryak Range (R.S.F.S.R.)

Koryak Range (R.S.F.S.R.)
  UF Khrebet Koryatskiy (R.S.F.S.R.)
      Khrebet Kuryatskiy (R.S.F.S.R.)
      Koriākskiĭ khrebet (R.S.F.S.R.)
      Koriākskoe nagor'e (R.S.F.S.R.)
      Koryak Mountains (R.S.F.S.R.)
      Koryakskiy khrebet (R.S.F.S.R.)
      Koryakskoye nagor'ye (R.S.F.S.R.)
      Kuriātskiĭ khrebet (R.S.F.S.R.)
      Kuryatskiy khrebet (R.S.F.S.R.)
  BT Mountains—Russian S.F.S.R.

Koryaks
  [DK759.K6]
  UF Koriaks
      Koriaques

Koryakskiy khrebet (R.S.F.S.R.)
  USE Koryak Range (R.S.F.S.R.)

Koryakskoye nagor'ye (R.S.F.S.R.)
  USE Koryak Range (R.S.F.S.R.)

Korynetidae
  USE Cleridae

Koryŏ kayo
  USE Changga

Koryta family *(Not Subd Geog)*

Koryū ikebana
  USE Flower arrangement, Japanese—Koryū
      school

Koryū Sōkenryū ikebana
  USE Flower arrangement, Japanese—Koryū
      Sōkenryū school

Kos Island (Greece)
  UF Coo Island (Greece)
      Cos Island (Greece)
      İstanköy (Greece)
      Nísos Kos (Greece)
  BT Dodecanese
      Islands—Greece

Kosambi (City)
  USE Kausambi (City)

Kościół O.O. Karmelitów na Piasku w Krakowie
  — Kaplica Matki Boskiej Piaskowej
    USE Kościół O.O. Karmelitów na
      Piasku w Krakowie—
      Sanktuarium Maryjne
  — **Sanktuarium Maryjne**
    UF Kościół O.O. Karmelitów na
      Piasku w Krakowie—Kaplica
      Matki Boskiej Piaskowej
      Sanktuarium Maryjne, Kościół
      O.O. Karmelitów na Piasku w
      Krakowie

  BT Chapels—Poland
      Christian shrines—Poland

Kosciusko National Park (N.S.W.)
  BT National parks and reserves—Australia
      Parks—Australia

Kosena (Papua New Guinea people)
  USE Auyana (Papua New Guinea people)

Kosena dialect
  BT Auyana language

Koseto pottery
  USE Seto pottery

Kosher cookery
  USE Cookery, Jewish

Kosher food *(May Subd Geog)*
  UF Food, Kasher
      Food, Kosher
      Kasher food
  BT Food
  RT Jews—Dietary laws

Kosher food industry *(May Subd Geog)*
  UF Kasher food industry
  BT Food industry and trade
      Jews—Dietary laws
      Meat industry and trade

Kosher restaurants *(May Subd Geog)*
  UF Kasher restaurants
  BT Jews—Dietary laws
      Restaurants, lunch rooms, etc.

Koshering of utensils
  USE Kashering of utensils

Koshiki Archipelago (Japan)
  USE Koshiki Islands (Japan)

Koshiki Islands (Japan)
  UF Koshiki Archipelago (Japan)
      Koshiki-jima (Japan)
      Koshiki Rettō (Japan)
      Koshikijima (Japan)
  BT Islands—Japan

Koshiki-jima (Japan)
  USE Koshiki Islands (Japan)

Koshiki Rettō (Japan)
  USE Koshiki Islands (Japan)

Koshikijima (Japan)
  USE Koshiki Islands (Japan)

Kōshin *(May Subd Geog)*
  [BL2211.K6]
  BT Cults—Japan
      Gods, Japanese
      Monkeys—Religious aspects
      Religion, Primitive

Koshok family *(Not Subd Geog)*

Koshti dialect (Marathi) *(May Subd Geog)*
  [PK2378.K67]
  UF Kosti dialect (Marathi)
  BT India—Languages
      Marathi language

Kōshū Dōchū (Japan)
  USE Kōshū Kaidō (Japan)

Kōshū Kaidō (Japan) *(Not Subd Geog)*
  UF Kōshū Dōchū (Japan)
  BT Roads—Japan

Kōshū ondo (Dance)

Kōshun'en (Tokyo, Japan)
  USE Roka Kōshun'en (Tokyo, Japan)

Kosi Plain (India)
  BT Plains—India

Kosman family
  USE Kuzma family

Kosmann family
  USE Kuzma family

Kosmian family
  USE Kuzma family

Kosmiany family
  USE Kuzma family

Kosmoceratidae
  BT Ammonoidea

Kosmos (Artificial satellite)
  USE Cosmos (Artificial satellite)

Kosnick family *(Not Subd Geog)*
  UF Kersnic family

Kōsoku wangansen (Japan)
  USE Ōsaka fudō kōsoku wangansen (Japan)

Kosova (African people)
  USE Gusii (African people)

Kosovo (Serbia)
  — History
    — — 1945-

Kosovo, Battle of, 1389
  [DR337]
  BT Serbia—History—To 1456
      Turkey—History—1288-1453

Kosovo, Battle of, 1448
  [DR498]
  BT Serbia—History—To 1456
      Turkey—History—1288-1453

Kosovo Polje, Battle of, 1944
  BT World War, 1939-1945—Campaigns—
      Yugoslavia

Kosrae (Micronesia)
  UF Arao (Micronesia)
      Armstrong Island (Micronesia)
      Experiment Island (Micronesia)
      Hope Island (Micronesia)
      Kusae (Micronesia)
      Kusai-to (Micronesia)
      Kusaie (Micronesia)
      Kusie (Micronesia)
      Kussai (Micronesia)
      Kussiu (Micronesia)
      Kuthiu (Micronesia)
      Oualan (Micronesia)
      Quollen (Micronesia)
      Strong Island (Micronesia)
      Teyoa (Micronesia)
      Ualan (Micronesia)
      Ualang (Micronesia)
      Walan (Micronesia)
      Walang (Micronesia)
  BT Caroline Islands
      Micronesia (Federated States)

Kossebau family
  USE Kotzebue family

Kossebu family
  USE Kotzebue family

Kosseir el-Kadim (Ancient city)
  USE Qusayr al-Qadīm (Ancient city)

Kossi (Bantu people)
  USE Bakossi (Bantu people)

Kōstakē family *(Not Subd Geog)*

Koster family
  USE Custer family

Koster Site (Ill.) *(Not Subd Geog)*
  BT Illinois—Antiquities

Kosti dialect (Marathi)
  USE Koshti dialect (Marathi)

Kostroma (Kostromskaīa oblast', R.S.F.S.R.)
  — History
    — — **Revolution of 1905**
      [DK264.2.K]

Kostroma cattle

Kosugi Maruyama Iseki (Japan)
  USE Kosugi Maruyama Site (Japan)

Kosugi Maruyama Site (Japan)
(Not Subd Geog)
  UF Kosugi Maruyama Iseki (Japan)
  BT Japan—Antiquities

Kot Massacre, 1846

Kota (African people)
  UF Bakota (African people)
      Mahongwe (African people)
      Shake (African people)
  BT Ethnology—Congo (Brazzaville)
      Ethnology—Gabon

Kota (African people) relics and reliquaries
  USE Relics and reliquaries, Kota (African
      people)

Kota (African people) sculpture
  USE Sculpture, Kota (African people)

Kota language
  [PL4691]
  BT Dravidian languages

Kotaro Takamura Grand Prize
USE Takamura Kōtarō Taishō
Koter family
USE Coder family
Kothsebu family
USE Kotzebue family
Kotia dialect
[PK2579.5.K68]
UF Desia dialect
BT India—Languages
Oriya language
Kotiria language
USE Guanano language
Koto
[ML1015-1018]
BT Musical instruments—Japan
Zither
NT Ichigenkin
Koto and clarinet music
USE Clarinet and koto music
Koto and flute music
USE Flute and koto music
Koto and shakuhachi music
USE Shakuhachi and koto music
Koto Island (Taiwan)
USE Lan Island (Taiwan)
Koto music
[M142.K6]
NT Concertos (Koto)
Koto with orchestra
Quartets (Shakuhachi, kotos (2),
shamisen)
Quartets (Shakuhachi, kotos (3))
Sextets (Shakuhachi, biwa, kotos (2),
shamisen, percussion)
Sextets (Shakuhachi, guitar, kotos (2),
percussion, double bass)
Sonatas (Koto)
Suites (Kotos (6))
Koto with orchestra
[M1037.4.K68]
BT Koto music
RT Concertos (Koto)
Kotodeshi Plain, Albania, Battle of, 1444
[DR960.3]
BT Albania—History—Turkish Wars, 15th
century
Kotoko (African people)
BT Ethnology—Cameroon
Ethnology—Chad
Ethnology—Nigeria
RT São (Chad people)
Kotoko (African people) art
USE Art, Kotoko (African people)
Kotoko dialects
BT Chadic languages
NT Afade dialect
Kotokoli (African people)
USE Tem (African people)
Kotor, Gulf of (Montenegro)
UF Bocche di Cattaro (Montenegro)
Boka kotorska (Montenegro)
Gulf of Kotor (Montenegro)
Kotorski zaliv (Montenegro)
BT Bays—Yugoslavia
Kotor Mutiny, 1918
[DB86.7]
Kotorski zaliv (Montenegro)
USE Kotor, Gulf of (Montenegro)
Kotosho Island (Taiwan)
USE Lan Island (Taiwan)
Kotsuka Iseki (Nakamura-shi, Japan)
USE Kotsuka Site (Nakamura-shi, Japan)
Kotsuka Site (Nakamura-shi, Japan)
UF Kotsuka Iseki (Nakamura-shi, Japan)
BT Japan—Antiquities
Kotsuzumi
[ML1038.K7]
UF Ko tsuzumi
BT Hourglass drum
Musical instruments—Japan

Kottenforst-Ville, Naturpark (Germany)
USE Naturpark Kottenforst-Ville (Germany)
Kottmeier family *(Not Subd Geog)*
UF Cottmeyer family
Kottmeyer family
Kottmeyer family
USE Kottmeier family
Kotuĭ River (R.S.F.S.R.)
UF Kotuy River (R.S.F.S.R.)
Reka Kotuĭ (R.S.F.S.R.)
BT Rivers—Russian S.F.S.R.
Kōturk inscriptions
USE Inscriptions, Old Turkic
Kotuy River (R.S.F.S.R.)
USE Kotuĭ River (R.S.F.S.R.)
Kotzé family *(Not Subd Geog)*
UF Kotzee family
Kotzebau family
USE Kotzebue family
Kotzebode family
USE Kotzebue family
Kotzebowes family
USE Kotzebue family
Kotzebu family
USE Kotzebue family
Kotzebue family *(Not Subd Geog)*
UF Cossebade family
Cossebau family
Cossebu family
Kossebau family
Kossebu family
Kothsebu family
Kotzebau family
Kotzebode family
Kotzebowes family
Kotzebu family
Kotzebue Sound (Alaska)
BT Sounds (Geomorphology)—Alaska
Kotzee family
USE Kotzé family
Kouchibouguac National Park (N.B.)
(Not Subd Geog)
UF Parc national de Kouchibouguac (N.B.)
BT National parks and reserves—New
Brunswick
Koudou
USE Greater kudu
Koui language
USE Kui language (Mon-Khmer)
Koulango language
USE Kulango language
Koumys
USE Kumiss
Kountz family
USE Counts family
Kountze family
USE Counts family
Kourfey (African people)
USE Kurtey (African people)
Kourion (Ancient city) *(Not Subd Geog)*
[DS54.95.K68]
UF Curium (Ancient city)
Kurion (Ancient city)
Kurium (Ancient city)
BT Cities and towns, Ruined, extinct, etc.
—Cyprus
Cyprus—Antiquities
Kouroumba language
USE Kurumba language
Kouroumbs
USE Kurumbas
Kourtey (African people)
USE Kurtey (African people)
Koustrup family *(Not Subd Geog)*
Kouta
[PL732.K6 (History)]
[PL762.K6 (Collections)]
BT Ballads, Japanese
Songs, Japanese
Kouwenhoven family
USE Conover family

Kovalsky family
USE Kowalski family
Kovar
USE Iron-nickel-cobalt alloys
Kovrovets motorcycle
Kōwaka
[PN2924.5.K6]
Here are entered general works and those that
deal solely with the presentation of the Kōwaka
plays on the stage. The texts of the Kōwaka plays and
works treating of them from a literary point of view
are entered under Kōwaka plays.
UF Kōwakamai
Kusemai
BT Theater—Japan
Kōwaka plays
[PL738]
[PL768.K (Collections)]
Here are entered texts of the Kōwaka plays and
works treating of them from a literary point of view.
General works and those that deal solely with the
presentation of the Kōwaka plays on the stage are
entered under Kōwaka.
BT Japanese drama
Kōwakamai
USE Kōwaka
Kowalski family *(Not Subd Geog)*
UF Kovalsky family
Kowm, Tall (Syria) *(Not Subd Geog)*
UF Kowm Site (Syria)
Tell el-Kowm (Syria)
BT Syria—Antiquities
Kowm Site (Syria)
USE Kowm, Tall (Syria)
Koya language
[PL4693]
BT Dravidian languages
Kōyasan Monasteries (Japan)
[BQ6353.K]
BT Monasteries, Buddhist—Japan
Temples, Buddhist—Japan
Koyatsu family *(Not Subd Geog)*
Koyl family
USE Coyle family
Koyle family
USE Coyle family
Koyukon Indians
[E99.K79]
UF Khotana Indians
Koyukukkhotana Indians
BT Athapascan Indians
Indians of North America
Koyukon language
UF Koyukukhotana language
BT Athapascan languages
Koyukuk River (Alaska)
BT Rivers—Alaska
Koyukukhotana language
USE Koyukon language
Koyukukkhotana Indians
USE Koyukon Indians
Kozakewich family *(Not Subd Geog)*
Kozaki
USE Cosaques
Kozara, Battle of, 1942
BT World War, 1939-1945—Campaigns—
Yugoslavia
Kozara Mountains (Bosnia and Hercegovina)
UF Kozara Planina (Bosnia and
Hercegovina)
Zozara Mountains (Bosnia and
Hercegovina)
BT Mountains—Yugoslavia
Kozara Planina (Bosnia and Hercegovina)
USE Kozara Mountains (Bosnia and
Hercegovina)
Koźmian family *(Not Subd Geog)*
Kozo
USE Paper mulberry
Kōzu Island (Japan)
UF Kōzu-shima (Japan)

Kōzu Island (Japan) *(Continued)*
  BT Islands—Japan
      Izu Islands (Japan)
Kōzu-shima (Japan)
  USE Kōzu Island (Japan)
Kōzu Shimogō Isekugun (Kōriyama-shi, Japan)
  USE Kōzu Shimogō Site (Kōriyama-shi, Japan)
Kōzu Shimogō Site (Kōriyama-shi, Japan)
  UF Kōzu Shimogō Isekugun (Kōriyama-shi, Japan)
  BT Japan—Antiquities
Kozukatajō (Morioka-shi, Japan)
  USE Moriokajō (Morioka-shi, Japan)
Kpa (African people)
  USE Bafia (African people)
Kpa language
  USE Bafia language
Kpala language
  USE Kresh language
Kpara language
  USE Kresh language
Kpe
  USE Bakwiri (African people)
Kpelego language
  USE Kulango language
Kpelle
  USE Kpelle (African people)
  — **Rites and ceremonies**
      NT Marriage customs and rites, Kpelle
Kpelle (African people)
  UF Guerze (African people)
      Kpelle
      Kpwélé (African people)
  BT Ethnology—Liberia
  NT Missions to Kpelle (African people)
  — **Children**
      BT Children
  — **Rites and ceremonies**
Kpelle folk-songs
  USE Folk-songs, Kpelle
Kpelle language
  ₁PL8411₁
  UF Guerzé language
      Kpwélé language
  BT Guinea—Languages
      Liberia—Languages
      Mande languages
Kpelle marriage customs and rites
  USE Marriage customs and rites, Kpelle
Kposo (African people)
  UF Akposo (African people)
      Akposso (African people)
  BT Ethnology—Togo
Kposo language *(May Subd Geog)*
  UF Akposo language
      Akposso language
      Ikposo language
      Ikposso language
  BT Kwa languages
      Togo—Languages
Kpr (The Hebrew root)
  UF Kfr (The Hebrew root)
  BT Hebrew language—Roots
Kpr (The Semitic root)
  UF Kfr (The Semitic root)
  BT Semitic languages—Roots
Kpwélé (African people)
  USE Kpelle (African people)
Kpwélé language
  USE Kpelle language
Kra
  ₁QL737.P93₁
  UF Crab-eating macaque
      Croo monkey
      Cynomolgus monkey
      Long-tailed macaque
      Macaca fascicularis
      Macaca irus
      Macacus cynomolgus
      Philippine macaque

  BT Macaques
Krabat (Tale)
  BT Tales
Krabbe's disease
  USE Leukodystrophy, Globoid cell
Krachi (African people)
  ₁DT510.43.K72₁
  BT Ethnology—Ghana
  — **Religion**
      NT Dente (African deity)
Kradad Island (Thailand) *(Not Subd Geog)*
  UF Ko Kradad (Thailand)
      Koh Kradad (Thailand)
  BT Islands—Thailand
Kraemer family
  USE Cramer family
Kraft dissolving tank explosions
  USE Smelt-water explosions (Wood-pulping)
Kraft process
  USE Sulphate pulping process
Kraft waste liquor
  USE Sulphate waste liquor
Krag family
  USE Kragh family
Krag-Jörgensen rifle
  ₁UD395.K9₁
  BT Rifles
Kragelund family *(Not Subd Geog)*
Kragh family *(Not Subd Geog)*
  UF Krag family
Kragujevac (Serbia)
  — **History**
  — — **Soldiers' Uprising, 1918**
      UF Kragujevac Soldiers' Uprising, Serbia, 1918
          Soldiers' Uprising, Kragujevac, Serbia, 1918
Kragujevac Soldiers' Uprising, Serbia, 1918
  USE Kragujevac (Serbia)—History— Soldiers' Uprising, 1918
Krahn family
  USE Craun family
Kraho Indians
  USE Craho Indians
Kraho language
  USE Canella language
Kraichgau (Germany)
Kraig family
  USE Craig family
Kraimer family
  USE Cramer family
Kraĭniĭ Sever
  USE Soviet Union, Northern
Kraisinger family *(Not Subd Geog)*
  UF Krajzinger family
      Kreising family
      Kreisinger family
      Krisinger family
Krajewski family
  USE Krajewsky family
Krajewsky family *(Not Subd Geog)*
  UF Krajewski family
Krajina (Bosnia and Hercegovina)
  UF Bosanska Krajina (Bosnia and Hercegovina)
Krajzinger family
  USE Kraisinger family
Krakatao (Indonesia)
  USE Krakatoa (Indonesia)
Krakatau (Indonesia)
  USE Krakatoa (Indonesia)
Krakatoa (Indonesia) *(Not Subd Geog)*
  UF Krakatao (Indonesia)
      Krakatau (Indonesia)
      Rakata (Indonesia)
  BT Volcanoes—Indonesia
Kraków (Poland). Kazimierz
  USE Kazimierz (Kraków, Poland)
Kraków (Poland). Wawel
  USE Wawel (Kraków, Poland)

Kraków-Częstochowa Highland (Poland)
  UF Cracow-Czestochowa Highland (Poland)
      Cracow Jura (Poland)
      Jura Krakowska (Poland)
      Jura Krakowska-Wieluńska (Poland)
      Krakowska Jura (Poland)
      Wyżyna Krakowska (Poland)
      Wyżyna Krakowsko-Częstochowska (Poland)
  BT Mountains—Poland
Kraków-Olszanica Site (Poland)
  USE Olszanica Site (Poland)
Krakowiak (Dance)
Krakowiaks
  BT Dance music
      Folk dance music—Poland
Krakowska Jura (Poland)
  USE Kraków-Częstochowa Highland (Poland)
Králóv stól (Czechoslovakia)
  USE Králův stůl (Czechoslovakia)
Králův stůl (Czechoslovakia)
  UF Králóv stól (Czechoslovakia)
Kram family *(Not Subd Geog)*
  UF Kramm family
Krama *(May Subd Geog)*
  ₁BL1245.K7₁
  BT Philosophy, Indic
      Sivaism
      Tantrism
Kramer family
  USE Cramer family
Kramer Village Site (Ohio)
  BT Ohio—Antiquities
Krameria
  USE Ratany
Krameriaceae
  USE Ratany
Kramers family
  USE Cramer family
Kramm family
  USE Kram family
Krammer family
  USE Cramer family
Krao (African people)
  USE Kru (African people)
Krao language
  USE Kru language
Krapf family
  USE Krapfl family
Krapfel family
  USE Krapfl family
Krapfl family *(Not Subd Geog)*
  UF Krapf family
      Krapfel family
Kras (Yugoslavia and Italy)
  USE Karst (Yugoslavia and Italy)
Krasnaĭa ploshchad' (Moscow, R.S.F.S.R.)
  USE Red Square (Moscow, R.S.F.S.R.)
Krasnodar Trial, Krasnodar, R.S.F.S.R., 1943
  UF Krasnodar Trial, 1943
  BT War crime trials—Russian S.F.S.R.
Krasnodar Trial, 1943
  USE Krasnodar Trial, Krasnodar, R.S.F.S.R., 1943
Krasnoe Znamĭa (Medal)
Krasnozems
  USE Ferralsols
Kraters *(May Subd Geog)*
  UF Craters (Pottery)
  — **Great Britain**
      NT Colossus Vase
Kratz family *(Not Subd Geog)*
Kratzer family *(Not Subd Geog)*
Kraull (Indic people)
  USE Anal (Indic people)
Kraun family
  USE Craun family
Kraunhia
  USE Wisteria

Kraus family
    USE Krause family
Krause family *(Not Subd Geog)*
    UF Kraus family
        Krauser family
        Krauss family
        Krausse family
        Krausz family
        Krauz family
        Krauze family
    RT Crouse family
Krauser family
    USE Krause family
Krauss family
    USE Krause family
Krausse family
    USE Krause family
Krausz family
    USE Krause family
Krauthausen family *(Not Subd Geog)*
Krautwurst family *(Not Subd Geog)*
Krauz family
    USE Krause family
Krauze family
    USE Krause family
Krawi language
    USE Kru language
Krawn family
    USE Craun family
Kraybill family
    USE Graybill family
KrAZ trucks
    BT Trucks—Soviet Union
Krchal family
    USE Kerchal family
Kreachbaum family
    USE Kriechbaum family
Kreamer family
    USE Cramer family
Kreashbaum family
    USE Kriechbaum family
Kreatine
    USE Creatine
Krebiozen
    BT Antineoplastic agents
Krebo (African people)
    USE Grebo (African people)
Krebo language
    USE Grebo language
Krebs cycle
    UF Citric acid cycle
        Tricarboxylic acid cycle
    BT Metabolism
        Oxidation
Kreckel family
    USE Krekel family
Kredj language
    USE Kresh language
Kreen-Akrore Indians
    BT Indians of South America
**Kreenholmi Puuvillasaaduste Manufaktuur
    Strike, 1872**
    BT Strikes and lockouts—Cotton
        manufacture—Estonia
        Strikes and lockouts—Estonia
Kregel family *(Not Subd Geog)*
Krehbiel family *(Not Subd Geog)*
    RT Graybill family
Kreider family
    USE Crider family
Kreidler family
    USE Crider family
Kreienheder family *(Not Subd Geog)*
Kreig family
    USE Craig family
Kreighbaum family
    USE Kriechbaum family
Kreiman family
    USE Kreymann family
Kreimann family
    USE Kreymann family

Kreinsdorff family
    USE Grenzdörfer family
Kreish language
    USE Kresh language
Kreising family
    USE Kraisinger family
Kreisinger family
    USE Kraisinger family
Kreisler family
    USE Chrysler family
Kreiter family
    USE Grider family
Krej language
    USE Kresh language
Krekel family *(Not Subd Geog)*
    UF Kreckel family
        Krekeler family
    RT Crecelius family
Krekeler family
    USE Krekel family
Kremer family
    USE Cramer family
Kreml' (Moscow, R.S.F.S.R.)
    USE Kremlin (Moscow, R.S.F.S.R.)
Kreml' (Novgorod, R.S.F.S.R.)
    USE Kremlin (Novgorod, R.S.F.S.R.)
Kremlin (Moscow, R.S.F.S.R.)
    UF Kreml' (Moscow, R.S.F.S.R.)
    BT Fortification—Russian S.F.S.R.
Kremlin (Novgorod, R.S.F.S.R.)
    UF Kreml' (Novgorod, R.S.F.S.R.)
    BT Fortification—Russian S.F.S.R.
Kremlinologists
    USE Sovietologists
Krenek family *(Not Subd Geog)*
    UF Krenka family
        Krzenek family
        Krzenka family
Krenides (City)
    USE Philippi (City)
Krenka family
    USE Krenek family
Krenkerup (Denmark)
    BT Manors—Denmark
Krensky family *(Not Subd Geog)*
Krenzdörffer family
    USE Grenzdörfer family
Kreosote
    USE Creosote
Kresh language
    ₍PL8413₎
    UF Kapala language
        Kpala language
        Kpara language
        Kredj language
        Kreish language
        Krej language
    BT Bongo-Bagirmi languages
        Sudan—Languages
Kresna Uprising, 1878
    USE Kresnensko Uprising, 1878
Kresnensko-Razlozhkoto Uprising, 1878
    USE Kresnensko Uprising, 1878
Kresnensko Uprising, 1878
    UF Kresna Uprising, 1878
        Kresnensko-Razlozhkoto Uprising,
        1878
    BT Bulgaria—History—1878-1944
        Macedonia—History—1389-1912
Kresol
    USE Cresol
Kress family *(Not Subd Geog)*
    UF Cress family
        Kresse family
Kresse family
    USE Kress family
Kressman family
    USE Crossman family
Kretchmar family
    USE Kretchmer family

Kretchmer family *(Not Subd Geog)*
    UF Kretchmar family
    RT Kretschmer family
Kretschmar family
    USE Kretschmer family
Kretschmer family *(Not Subd Geog)*
    UF Cretschmer family
        Kretschmar family
        Kretzmer family
        Kretzschmar family
    RT Kretchmer family
Kretzmer family
    USE Kretschmer family
Kretzschmar family
    USE Kretschmer family
Kreuger family *(Not Subd Geog)*
    UF Krieger family
        Krueger family
        Kruger family
Kreussen pottery
    USE Creussen pottery
Kreutter family *(Not Subd Geog)*
Kreutzer family *(Not Subd Geog)*
    UF Kreuz family
        Kreuzer family
Kreuz family
    USE Kreutzer family
Kreuzenstein Castle (Austria)
    USE Burg Kreuzenstein (Austria)
Kreuzer family
    USE Kreutzer family
Kreuzigung Christi (Painting)
    USE Erasmus, Desiderius, d. 1536. Christ
        on the Cross
Kreuztafel mit hölzener Scheibe (Sculpture)
    USE Soester Scheibenkreuz (Sculpture)
Kreymann family *(Not Subd Geog)*
    UF Kreiman family
        Kreimann family
Krichbaum family
    USE Kriechbaum family
Krickbaum family
    USE Kriechbaum family
Krider family
    USE Crider family
Kriechbaum family *(Not Subd Geog)*
    UF Creebaum family
        Creekbaum family
        Creighbaum family
        Kreachbaum family
        Kreashbaum family
        Kreighbaum family
        Krichbaum family
        Krickbaum family
        Kriegbaum family
        Krigbaum family
        Krishbaum family
Kriegbaum family
    USE Kriechbaum family
Krieger family
    USE Kreuger family
**Krieghoff, Cornelius, 1815-1872. Habitant
    farm**
    UF Habitant farm (Painting)
Kriegsspiel
    USE War games
Kriehn family
    USE Kroehn family
Krien family
    USE Kroehn family
Krigbaum family
    USE Kriechbaum family
Krill *(May Subd Geog)*
    BT Euphausiacea
    NT Euphausia superba
Krill fisheries *(May Subd Geog)*
    ₍SH380.7-380.72₎
    BT Fisheries
        Shellfish fisheries
Krimpenerwaard (Netherlands)
    BT Polders—Netherlands

Kring family (Not Subd Geog)
Kringel family
    USE Kringle family
Kringle family (Not Subd Geog)
    UF Kringel family
Krio (African people)
    USE Creoles (Sierra Leone)
Krio drama (May Subd Geog)
Krio folk literature
    USE Folk literature, Krio
Krio language
    [PM7875.K73]
    UF Aku language (Creole)
    BT Creole dialects, English
Krio literature (May Subd Geog)
    [PM7875.K73]
    NT Folk literature, Krio
Krio proverbs
    USE Proverbs, Krio
Krises
    USE Daggers, Malay
Krishbaum family
    USE Kriechbaum family
Krishman family
    USE Chrisman family
Krishna (Hindu deity)
    UF Christna (Hindu deity)
        Gopal (Hindu deity)
        Kṛṣṇa (Hindu deity)
    BT Gods, Hindu
    NT Jagannātha (Hindu deity)
Krishna (Hindu deity) in the performing arts
    BT Performing arts
Krishna in literature
Krishna River (India)
    UF Kistna River (India)
    BT Rivers—India
Krisinger family
    USE Kraisinger family
Krisler family
    USE Chrysler family
Krisman family
    USE Chrisman family
Kristallnacht, 1938
    USE Crystal Night, 1938
Kristensen family
    USE Christensen family
Kristiansen family
    USE Christensen family
Kristiansson family
    USE Christensen family
Kristman family
    USE Chrisman family
Kristmann family
    USE Chrisman family
Kristophel family (Not Subd Geog)
Kritsman family
    USE Chrisman family
Krivichi (Slavic people)
    [DK34.K7]
    BT Ethnology—Soviet Union
        Slavs, Eastern
Krivoĭ Rog Basin (Ukraine)
    UF Krivorozhskiĭ zhelezorudnyĭ basseĭn
            (Ukraine)
        Krivoy Rog Basin (Ukraine)
    BT Geology—Ukraine
Krivorozhskiĭ zhelezorudnyĭ basseĭn (Ukraine)
    USE Krivoĭ Rog Basin (Ukraine)
Krivošije (Montenegro) (Not Subd Geog)
    UF Krivošite (Montenegro)
Krivošite (Montenegro)
    USE Krivošije (Montenegro)
Krivoy Rog Basin (Ukraine)
    USE Krivoĭ Rog Basin (Ukraine)
Kriya yoga
    USE Yoga, Kriya

Krkonoše (Czechoslovakia and Poland)
    UF Karkonosze (Czechoslovakia and
            Poland)
        Riesengebirge (Czechoslovakia and
            Poland)
    BT Mountains—Czechoslovakia
        Mountains—Poland
Kroan family
    USE Craun family
Krobo (African people)
    UF Crobo (African people)
        Krobo (African tribe)
    BT Ethnology—Ghana
Krobo (African tribe)
    USE Krobo (African people)
Kroehn family (Not Subd Geog)
    UF Kriehn family
        Krien family
        Kroehne family
Kroehne family
    USE Kroehn family
Krogness family (Not Subd Geog)
Krogsdal family (Not Subd Geog)
Kroh family (Not Subd Geog)
Krohn family
    USE Craun family
Krohnitta
    [QL391.C6]
    BT Sagittoidea
Krohnittidae (May Subd Geog)
    [QL391.C6]
    BT Aphragmophora
Krol family
    USE Kroll family
Kroll family (Not Subd Geog)
    UF Krol family
    RT Crull family
Krollig family (Not Subd Geog)
Krom family
    USE Crump family
Krome family
    USE Crump family
Krompir (The Slovenian word)
    BT Slovenian language—Etymology
Kron family
    USE Craun family
Kronan family
    USE Cronin family
Kronborg family (Not Subd Geog)
Kronecker products
    UF Products, Kronecker
    BT Matrices
        Tensor products
Kronenscheldt family
    USE Crowninshield family
Krongo language (May Subd Geog)
    [PL8414.K76]
    UF Kadumodi language
        Korongo language
        Kurungu language
    BT Kordofanian languages
        Sudan—Languages
Kronin family
    USE Cronin family
Kronos (Greek deity)
    USE Cronus (Greek deity)
Kronshtadt (R.S.F.S.R.)
— History
— — 1917-1921
Krook equation
    BT Gases, Kinetic theory of
        Hydrodynamics
Kroomen (African people)
    USE Kru (African people)
Kropf family
    USE Krupp family
Kropp family
    USE Krupp family
Krosch family (Not Subd Geog)
Krosman family
    USE Crossman family

Krou (African people)
    USE Kru (African people)
Kroumen language
    USE Tepo language
Krouse family
    USE Crouse family
KRS4201 (Computer)
    BT Electronic digital computers
— Programming
Kṛṣṇa (Hindu deity)
    USE Krishna (Hindu deity)
Kṛṣṇā (Hindu mythology)
    USE Draupadī (Hindu mythology)
Kru (African people)
    UF Crau (African people)
        Krao (African people)
        Kroomen (African people)
        Krou (African people)
        Krumen (African people)
    BT Ethnology—Africa, West
    NT Grebo (African people)
Kru language
    [PL8415]
    UF Klao language
        Krao language
        Krawi language
    BT Kru languages
        Liberia—Languages
Kru languages
    [PL8416]
    BT Ivory Coast—Languages
        Kwa languages
        Liberia—Languages
    NT Bassa language (Liberia)
        Bete language
        Grebo language
        Jabo language
        Kru language
        Nyabwa language
        Tchien language
        Tepo language
        Wobe language
Krueger family
    USE Kreuger family
Kruger family
    USE Kreuger family
Kruger National Park (South Africa)
    UF Nasionale Kruger Wildtuin (South
            Africa)
    BT National parks and reserves—South
            Africa
        Parks—South Africa
Krugerrand (Coin) (May Subd Geog)
    [CJ3948]
    BT Coins, South African
        Gold coins—South Africa
Krull rings
    [QA251.3]
    UF Rings, Krull
    BT Commutative rings
Krum family
    USE Crump family
Krumen (African people)
    USE Kru (African people)
Krummhorn
    USE Crumhorn
Krupina Mountains (Czechoslovakia)
    USE Krupina Plateau (Czechoslovakia)
Krupina Plateau (Czechoslovakia)
    UF Krupina Mountains (Czechoslovakia)
        Krupinská výšina (Czechoslovakia)
    BT Mountains—Czechoslovakia
        Plateaus—Czechoslovakia
Krupinská výšina (Czechoslovakia)
    USE Krupina Plateau (Czechoslovakia)
Krupinski family (Not Subd Geog)
Krupnicza Street (Kraków, Poland)
    USE Ulica Krupnicza (Kraków, Poland)
Krupp family (Not Subd Geog)
    UF Kropf family
        Kropp family

Krupp Trial, Nuremberg, 1947-1948
   USE Krupp Trial, Nuremberg, Germany,
        1947-1948
Krupp Trial, Nuremberg, Germany, 1947-1948
   UF Krupp Trial, Nuremberg, 1947-1948
        Subsequent proceedings, Nuremberg
        War Crime Trials, case no. 10
   BT Nuremberg War Crime Trials,
        Nuremberg, Germany, 1946-1949
Kruse Bluffbase No. 3 Site (Ill.)
   UF Kruse Site (Ill.)
   BT Illinois—Antiquities
Kruse family *(Not Subd Geog)*
Kruse Site (Ill.)
   USE Kruse Bluffbase No. 3 Site (Ill.)
Krusenstern, Cape (Alaska)
   (Not Subd Geog)
   UF Cape Krusenstern (Alaska)
   BT Capes (Coasts)—Alaska
   RT Cape Krusenstern National Monument
        (Alaska)
Krusenstjerna family *(Not Subd Geog)*
   UF Von Krusenstjerna family
Krušné hory (Czechoslovakia and Germany)
   USE Erzgebirge (Czechoslovakia and
        Germany)
Krušnohoří (Czechoslovakia and Germany)
   USE Erzgebirge (Czechoslovakia and
        Germany)
Kruty, Battle of, 1918
   BT Ukraine—History—Revolution, 1917-
        1921
Kryder family
   USE Crider family
Krypton
   [QD181.K6]
   BT Auroras
        Gases, Rare
   RT Argon
   — Isotopes
        BT Fission gases
   — — Decay
   — Spectra
Krzenek family
   USE Krenek family
Krzenka family
   USE Krenek family
Krzesławice Fort (Kraków, Poland)
   USE Fort Krzesławicki (Kraków, Poland)
Krzyż Kawalerski Orderu Odrodzenia Polski
   BT Decorations of honor—Poland
Ksanka language
   USE Kutenai language
Ksar Pharaoun (City)
   USE Volubilis (City)
Kṣatriyas
   USE Kshatriyas
Kṣattṛ (The Sanskrit word)
   BT Sanskrit language—Etymology
Kshatriyas
   [DS432.K7]
   UF Kṣatriyas
   BT Caste—India
   NT Pal Kshatriyas
        Somavāśī Kshatriyas
Kṣitigarbha (Buddhist deity)
   (May Subd Geog)
   [BQ4710.K7]
   UF Jizō (Buddhist deity)
        Ti-ts'ang (Buddhist deity)
   BT Bodhisattvas
        Gods, Buddhist
Ktteenjärvi (Finland)
   USE Kiteenjärvi (Finland)
Ku Kien San (Japan)
   USE Iriomote Island (Japan)
Ku-Klux Klan
   [E668]
   BT Reconstruction

Ku Klux Klan (1915-   )
   (May Subd Geog)
   [HS2330.K6-63]
   BT Nativism
Ku-kung (Peking, China)
   USE Forbidden City (Peking, China)
!Kũ language
   USE !Xũ language
Ku Mountain (China)
   UF Gu Mountain (China)
        Gu-shan (China)
        Ku-shan (China)
   BT Mountains—China
Ku-pi Sha-mo (Mongolia and China)
   USE Gobi Desert (Mongolia and China)
Ku-ring-gai Chase National Park (N.S.W.)
   UF Kuring-gai Chase (N.S.W.)
   BT National parks and reserves—Australia
Ku-shan (China)
   USE Ku Mountain (China)
Ku tz'u
   [PL2367 (History)]
   [PL2576 (Collections)]
   UF Northern song-tales (Chinese drama)
   BT Chinese drama
Ku-yang Basin (China)
   UF Ku yang p'en ti (China)
   BT Geology—China
Ku yang p'en ti (China)
   USE Ku-yang Basin (China)
K'uai shu
   [PL2368.K77 (History)]
   [PL2579.K83 (Collections)]
   [PN2874.5.K83 (Theater)]
   UF Kuaishu
        Shantung Kuai shu
        Tzu ti shu
   BT Chinese drama
Kuaishu
   USE K'uai shu
Kuan family *(Not Subd Geog)*
Kuan mu chi ch'in t'u (Scroll)
   USE Lin, Liang, ca. 1416-ca. 1480.   Trees
        and birds
Kuan P'u-hsien p'u sa hsing fa ching
   BT Buddhism—Sacred books
        Mahayana Buddhism—Sacred books
Kuan-tung Pan-tao (China)
   USE Kuan-tung Peninsula (China)
Kuan-tung Peninsula (China)
   (Not Subd Geog)
   UF Kuan-tung Pan-tao (China)
        Kwangtung Peninsula (China)
        Kwantung Peninsula (China)
   BT Peninsulas—China
Kuan wu liang shou ching
   BT Buddhism—Sacred books
        Mahayana Buddhism—Sacred books
Kuan-yin (Buddhist deity)
   USE Avalokiteśvara (Buddhist deity)
Kuanua (Melanesian people)
   USE Tolai (Melanesian people)
Kuanua folk-songs
   USE Folk-songs, Kuanua
Kuanua language
   UF Blanche Bay language
        Gunantuna language
        Neu Pommern language
        New Britain language
        Raluana language
        Tinata tuna language
        Tolai language
        Tuna language
   BT Melanesian languages
        Papua New Guinea—Languages

Kuanyama (African people)
   UF Cuanhama (African people)
        Humba (African people)
        Kwanyama (African people)
        Oshikuanjame (African people)
        Osikuanyame (African people)
        Oswidonga (African people)
        Ovaguanyama (African people)
        Ovakuanyama (African people)
        Vakuanyama (African people)
   BT Ethnology—Angola
        Ethnology—Namibia
        Ovambo (African people)
Kuanyama language
   [PL8417]
   UF Ambo language (Southwest Africa and
        Angola)
        Cuanhama language
        Kwanyama language
        Ovambo language
   BT Bantu languages
Kuanyama proverbs
   USE Proverbs, Kuanyama
Kuba (African people)
   [DT650.K83]
   UF Bakuba (African people)
        Bushongo (African people)
        Tukubba (African people)
   BT Bantus
        Ethnology—Zaire
   NT Shoowa (African people)
Kubachi dialect
   BT Daghestan languages
        Dargwa language
Kubaenk family
   USE Kubank family
Kuban River (R.S.F.S.R.) *(Not Subd Geog)*
   BT Rivers—Russian S.F.S.R.
Kubango River
   USE Okavango River
Kubank family *(Not Subd Geog)*
   UF Kubaenk family
        Kubeck family
        Kubeng family
        Kubengke family
        Kubenk family
        Kubing family
        Kuhbank family
        Kuhbenk family
Kubbaniya, Wadi (Egypt)
   UF Wadi Kubbaniya (Egypt)
   BT Wadis—Egypt
Kubeck family
   USE Kubank family
Kubeng family
   USE Kubank family
Kubengke family
   USE Kubank family
Kubenk family
   USE Kubank family
Kubeno Lake (R.S.F.S.R.)
   USE Kubenskoe Lake (R.S.F.S.R.)
Kubenskoe Lake (R.S.F.S.R.)
   (Not Subd Geog)
   UF Kubeno Lake (R.S.F.S.R.)
        Kubenskoye Lake (R.S.F.S.R.)
        Kubino Lake (R.S.F.S.R.)
        Ozero Kubenskoe (R.S.F.S.R.)
        Ozero Kubenskoye (R.S.F.S.R.)
   BT Lakes—Russian S.F.S.R.
Kubenskoye Lake (R.S.F.S.R.)
   USE Kubenskoe Lake (R.S.F.S.R.)
Kūbi language
   USE Konda language
Kubing family
   USE Kubank family
Kubino Lake (R.S.F.S.R.)
   USE Kubenskoe Lake (R.S.F.S.R.)
Kubler family
   USE Kiebler family

Kubo family (Not Subd Geog)
Kubu (Indonesian people)
[DS632.K78]
  UF Suku Anak Dalam (Indonesian people)
  BT Ethnology—Indonesia
Kubu language (May Subd Geog)
[PL5339]
  BT Indonesia—Languages
      Malayan languages
Kubuang Tigo Baleh dialect
(May Subd Geog)
[PL5415.95.K]
  BT Indonesia—Languages
      Minangkabau language
Kubung (African people)
  USE Ghoya (African people)
Kubus Hannover (Hannover, Germany)
  UF Hannover Kubus (Hannover,
      Germany)
  BT Exhibition buildings—Germany (West)
      Municipal buildings—Germany (West)
Kuce (African people)
  USE Rukuba (African people)
Kucera family (Not Subd Geog)
Kuchean language
  USE Tokharian language
Kuchin language
  USE Kutchakutchin language
Kuchuk Kainarji, Treaty of, 1774
[DR553]
  UF Küçükkaynarca, Treaty of, 1774
  BT Russo-Turkish War, 1768-1774
Kuči family (Not Subd Geog)
Kuckenheim family (Not Subd Geog)
  RT Cookingham family
Küçükkaynarca, Treaty of, 1774
  USE Kuchuk Kainarji, Treaty of, 1774
Kudaka Island (Japan)
  UF Kudaka-shima (Japan)
      Kutaka-jima (Japan)
      Kutaka-shima (Japan)
  BT Islands—Japan
Kudaka-shima (Japan)
  USE Kudaka Island (Japan)
Kudali dialect
  UF Malvani dialect
  BT Konkani language
Kuder preference record
[HF5381.5]
  BT Vocational interests
Kudoa
[QL368.M8]
  UF Neochloromyxum
  BT Chloromyxidae
Kudoa peruvianus
[QL368.M8]
Kudu, Greater
  USE Greater kudu
Kudurru inscriptions
  USE Boundary stones, Babylonian
Kudzu (May Subd Geog)
[QK495.L52 (Botany)]
[SB205.K8 (Forage crop)]
[SB615.K (Weed)]
  UF Kohemp
  BT Climbing plants
      Forage plants
  NT Cookery (Kudzu)
Kuebler family
  USE Kiebler family
Kuehn family
  USE Kuhn family
Kuehne family
  USE Kuhn family
Kuehnemann family
  USE Kinnaman family
Kuei-lin, China, Battle of, 1944
  BT Sino-Japanese Conflict, 1937-1945
Kuejerin-to (Marshall Islands)
  USE Kwajalein Island (Marshall Islands)

Kuejierin To (Marshall Islands)
  USE Kwajalein Island (Marshall Islands)
Kuenburg family (Not Subd Geog)
Kuenringer family (Not Subd Geog)
  UF Kunringer family
Kuerkendol family
  USE Kuykendall family
Kuezyerin-to (Marshall Islands)
  USE Kwajalein Island (Marshall Islands)
Kuffel family (Not Subd Geog)
  UF Cuffel family
  RT Koffel family
Kufic coins
  USE Coins, Cufic
Kufic paleography
  USE Paleography, Arabic (Cufic)
Kufr (Islam)
[BP166.785]
  UF Caffer (Islam)
      Kaffir (Islam)
      Kāfir (Islam)
      Mukaffirat (Islam)
      Unbelief (Islam)
  BT Faith (Islam)
      Islam—Doctrines
  RT Sin (Islam)
  NT Apostasy—Islam
      Heresies, Islamic
Kufs disease
  USE Neuronal ceroid-lipofuscinosis
Kuga family (Not Subd Geog)
Kugbo dialect
  USE Abua-Ogbia languages
Kughkendall family
  USE Kuykendall family
Kugikas (New Guinea tribe)
  USE Kumas (New Guinea tribe)
Kuh-e-Bozqūsh (Iran)
  USE Bozqūsh Mountains (Iran)
Kuhbach family
  USE Keebaugh family
Kuhbank family
  USE Kubank family
Kuhbauch family
  USE Keebaugh family
Kuhbenk family
  USE Kubank family
Kūhhā-ye Ṭavālesh (Azerbaijan S.S.R. and
  Iran)
  USE Talish Mountains (Azerbaijan S.S.R.
      and Iran)
Kūhhā-ye Zagros (Iran)
  USE Zagros Mountains (Iran)
Kuhland cattle
[SF199.K9]
Kuhlia
[QL638.K8]
  BT Kuhliidae
  NT Kuhlia sandvicensis
Kuhlia sandvicensis
[QL638.K8]
  UF Aholehole
  BT Kuhlia
Kuhlidae
  USE Kuhliidae
Kuhliidae
[QL638.K8]
  UF Kuhlidae
  BT Perciformes
  NT Kuhlia
Kuhlman family (Not Subd Geog)
  UF Kuhlmann family
      Kuhlmer family
  RT Kilmer family
Kuhlmann-Anderson test
  BT Intelligence tests
Kuhlmann family
  USE Kuhlman family
Kuhlmer family
  USE Kuhlman family

Kuhn family (Not Subd Geog)
  UF Coon family
      Coone family
      Coones family
      Coons family
      Koon family
      Koone family
      Koones family
      Koons family
      Kuehn family
      Kuehne family
      Kuhne family
      Kuhns family
  RT Gohn family
      Koontz family
Kuhne family
  USE Kuhn family
Kuhnhausen family (Not Subd Geog)
Kuhnle family (Not Subd Geog)
Kuhns family
  USE Kuhn family
Kui language
[PL4695]
  UF Kandh language
      Khand language
      Khond language
  BT Dravidian languages
  NT Kuvi language
Kui language (Mon-Khmer)
[PL4351.K8]
  UF Koui language
      Kuy language
      Suai language
  BT Cambodia—Languages
      Laos—Languages
      Mon-Khmer languages
      Thailand—Languages
Kuikendall family
  USE Kuykendall family
Kuikuru Indians
  UF Cuicurús
  BT Indians of South America
Kuis
  USE Kandhs
Kuitsh Indians
[E99.K]
  BT Athapascan Indians
      Indians of North America
      Yakonan Indians
Kuitsh language
[PM1598]
  UF Lower Umpqua language
      Umpqua (Lower) language
  BT Athapascan languages
Kujawy (Poland)
  UF Pojezierze Kujawskie (Poland)
      Ziemie Kujawskie (Poland)
Kujō family (Not Subd Geog)
Kuju, Mount (Japan)
  UF Kujū-san (Japan)
      Kujū-zan (Japan)
      Kujusan (Japan)
      Kujuzan (Japan)
      Mount Kuju (Japan)
  BT Mountains—Japan
Kujū-san (Japan)
  USE Kuju, Mount (Japan)
Kujū-zan (Japan)
  USE Kuju, Mount (Japan)
Kujusan (Japan)
  USE Kuju, Mount (Japan)
Kujuzan (Japan)
  USE Kuju, Mount (Japan)
Kukas
  USE Namdharis
Kuki-Chin languages
[PL3891-4]
  RT Chin languages
      Tibeto-Burman languages
  NT Anal language
      Hmar language

Kom language
Kuki language
Lushai language
Paite language
Thādo language
Vaiphei language

Kuki language
  [PL4001.K8]
  BT Kuki-Chin languages

Kukis
  [DS432.K8 (India)]
  BT Chin tribes
  NT Thados

Kuknas (Indic people)
  USE Koknas (Indic people)

Kukota dialect
  USE Gugada dialect

Kuku Yalanji language
  USE Gugu Yalanji language

Kukuchi Castle (Kikuka-machi, Japan)
  USE Kukuchijō (Kikuka-machi, Japan)

Kukuchi no Ki (Kikuka-machi, Japan)
  USE Kukuchijō (Kikuka-machi, Japan)

Kukuchijō (Kikuka-machi, Japan)
  UF Kikuchijō (Kikuka-machi, Japan)
    Kukuchi Castle (Kikuka-machi, Japan)
    Kukuchi no Ki (Kikuka-machi, Japan)
  BT Castles—Japan
    Fortification—Japan

Kukui
  USE Candlenut tree

Kukukuku (Papuan people)
  UF Anga (Papuan people)
  BT Ethnology—New Guinea
    Papuans
  NT Baruya (Papuan people)

Kukukuku languages
  [PL6621.K78]
  UF Anga languages (Papua New Guinea)
    Angan languages (Papua New Guinea)
  BT Papua New Guinea—Languages
    Papuan languages
  NT Ampale language
    Baruya language
    Kapau language

Kukulcan
  BT Indians of Central America—Religion
    and mythology
    Indians of Mexico—Religion and
    mythology
    Mayas—Religion and mythology
  RT Quetzalcoatl

Kukuruku language
  USE Etsako language

Kukus
  BT Ethnology—Sudan (Region)

Kukuya (African people)
  USE Kukwa (African people)

Kukuya language
  USE Kukwa language

Kukwa (African people)
  UF Kukuya (African people)
  BT Ethnology—Congo (Brazzaville)

Kukwa language
  [PL8418.K84]
  UF Cikuya language
    Kukuya language
  BT Bantu languages

Kukwa proverbs
  USE Proverbs, Kukwa

Kula exchange
  [DU740.42]
  UF Kula ring

  BT Ceremonial exchange
    Commerce, Primitive—Papua New
    Guinea
    Massim (Melanesian people)—
    Commerce
    Massim (Melanesian people)—Rites
    and ceremonies
    Rites and ceremonies—Papua New
    Guinea

Kula ring
  USE Kula exchange

Kùláál language
  UF Gula language (Lake Iro, Chad)
  BT Bua languages
    Chad—Languages

Kulal, Mount (Kenya)
  UF Mount Kulal (Kenya)
  BT Mountains—Kenya

Kulalars
  [DS432.K758]
  BT Caste—India
    Ethnology—India

Kulan
  USE Equus hemionus

Kulanapan Indians
  USE Pomo Indians

Kulanapan language (Eastern)
  USE Pomo language (Eastern)

Kulanapan language (Southeastern)
  USE Pomo language (Southeastern)

Kulanapan languages
  USE Pomo languages

Kulango language
  UF Kolango language
    Koulango language
    Kpelego language
    Nabe language
    Nambai language
    Ngwala language
    Nkurange language
    Zazere language
  BT Gur languages
    Ivory Coast—Languages

Kulanko (African people)
  USE Kuranko (African people)

Kulawi (Indonesian people)
  [DS632.K785]
  BT Ethnology—Indonesia
    Toradjas

Kulebele (African people)
  [DT545.42]
  UF Dalebele (African people)
    Daleo (African people)
    Guleo (African people)
  BT Ethnology—Ivory Coast
    Ethnology—Mali
    Senufo (African people)

Kulembe River (R.S.F.S.R.)
  USE Kulũmbe River (R.S.F.S.R.)

Kuliak languages
  USE Teuso languages

Kulikovo, Battle of, 1380
  BT Soviet Union—History—1237-1480

Kulin
  USE Kulins

Kulina Indians
  USE Culina Indians

Kulinas
  USE Kaulas

Kulinism
  USE Kulins

Kulins
  [DS432.K76]
  UF Kulin
    Kulinism
  BT Caste—India
    Ethnology—India

Kulũmbe River (R.S.F.S.R.)
  UF Kolũmbe River (R.S.F.S.R.)
    Kolyumbe River (R.S.F.S.R.)
    Kulembe River (R.S.F.S.R.)
    Kulyumbe River (R.S.F.S.R.)
  BT Rivers—Russian S.F.S.R.

Kulkyne State Forest (Vic.)
  BT Forest reserves—Australia

Kulla family *(Not Subd Geog)*
  RT Vuolle family

Kullen (Sweden)
  BT Capes (Coasts)—Sweden

Kulshaw family
  USE Kelsall family

Kulturabgabe
  USE Domaine public payant

Kulturkampf *(May Subd Geog)*
  [DD118]
  BT Church and state—Germany—History
    —19th century

Kulturpfennig
  USE Domaine public payant

Kultz family
  USE Kilts family

Kulu (Indic people)
  [DS432.K77]
  UF Kaulu (Indic people)
    Kulu Bali (Indic people)
    Kulu Pahari (Indic people)
    Kului (Indic people)
    Kulvi (Indic people)
    Kulwali (Indic people)
    Manali (Indic people)
    Phari Kulu (Indic people)
  BT Ethnology—India

Kulu Bali (Indic people)
  USE Kulu (Indic people)

Kulu language
  USE Kului language

Kulu Pahari (Indic people)
  USE Kulu (Indic people)

Kulu Valley (India)
  BT Valleys—India

Kulubi (Papua New Guinea people)
  USE Barok (Papua New Guinea people)

Kuluhi language
  USE Kului language

Kului (Indic people)
  USE Kulu (Indic people)

Kului folk-songs
  USE Folk-songs, Kului

Kului language
  [PK2610.K8]
  UF Kulu language
    Kuluhi language
  BT Pahari languages

Kulung language
  [PL3801.K8]
  BT Tibeto-Burman languages
  NT Sotang Kura dialect

Kulunglutji (Australian people)
  USE Gunwinggu (Australian people)

Kulvi (Indic people)
  USE Kulu (Indic people)

Kulwali (Indic people)
  USE Kulu (Indic people)

Kulyumbe River (R.S.F.S.R.)
  USE Kulũmbe River (R.S.F.S.R.)

Kum
  USE Komunko

Kum Island (Japan)
  USE Kume Island (Japan)

Kuma-gawa (Japan)
  USE Kuma River (Japan)

Kuma River (Japan)
  UF Kuma-gawa (Japan)
    Kumagawa (Japan)
  BT Rivers—Japan

Kumabito (Japanese people)
  BT Ethnology—Japan

Kumagai family *(Not Subd Geog)*
Kumagawa (Japan)
  USE Kuma River (Japan)
Kumait language
  USE Gumatj language
Kumamoto Band
  BT Protestants—Japan
Kuman (New Guinea people)
  USE Chimbu (New Guinea people)
Kuman language
  USE Kipchak language
Kuman language (New Guinea)
  USE Chimbu language
Kumano Region (Japan)
Kumans
  USE Kipchak
Kumanugu language
  USE Chimbu language
Kumaon Himalaya
  USE Kumaun Himalaya
Kumaoni (Indic people)
  USE Kumauni (Indic people)
Kumaoni dialect
  USE Kumauni dialect
Kumāra (Hindu deity)
  USE Kārttikeya (Hindu deity)
Kumars
  USE Kumhars
Kumas (New Guinea tribe)
  UF Kugikas (New Guinea tribe)
  BT Ethnology—New Guinea
Kumasaki Castle (Yoshiwa-mura, Japan)
  USE Kumasakijō (Yoshiwa-mura, Japan)
Kumasakijō (Yoshiwa-mura, Japan)
  UF Kumasaki Castle (Yoshiwa-mura,
        Japan)
  BT Castles—Japan
Kumasi, Ghana, Battle of, 1874
  BT Ashanti War, 1873-1874
Kumatj language
  USE Gumatj language
Kumaun Himalaya *(Not Subd Geog)*
  UF Kumaon Himalaya
  BT Himalaya Mountains
        Mountains—Asia
Kumauni (Indic people)
  UF Kumaoni (Indic people)
  BT Ethnology—India
Kumauni dialect
  UF Kumaoni dialect
  BT Pahari languages
Kumauni folk literature
  USE Folk literature, Kumauni
Kumauni literature *(May Subd Geog)*
  NT Folk literature, Kumauni
Kumauni poetry *(May Subd Geog)*
Kumbainggeri language
  USE Gumbáingar language
Kumbars, Maru
  USE Maru-Kumbars
Kumbavats
  ₍DS432.K78₎
  UF Kombawats
  BT Caste—India
        Ethnology—India
Kumbh Melā (Hindu festival)
  USE Kumbha Melā (Hindu festival)
Kumbha Melā (Hindu festival)
  ₍BL1239.82.K85₎
  UF Kumbh Melā (Hindu festival)
  BT Fasts and feasts—Hinduism
Kumbhakar
  USE Kumhars
Kumbhars
  USE Kumhars
Kumbhars, Maru
  USE Maru-Kumbars
Kumbhkaran Lungur (Nepal and India)
  USE Kānchenjunga (Nepal and India)

Kume Island (Japan)
  UF Komisang Island (Japan)
        Kum Island (Japan)
        Kume-shima (Japan)
  BT Islands—Japan
        Ryukyu Islands
Kume-shima (Japan)
  USE Kume Island (Japan)
Kumeyaay Indians
  USE Kamia Indians
Kŭmgang Mountains (Korea)
  USE Diamond Mountains (Korea)
Kŭmgang-san (Korea)
  USE Diamond Mountains (Korea)
Kumhars
  ₍DS432.K785₎
  UF Kumars
        Kumbhakar
        Kumbhars
        Kurāḷas
  BT Caste—India
        Ethnology—India
        Potters—India
Kumi Island (Japan)
  USE Yonaguni Island (Japan)
Kumina (Cult) *(May Subd Geog)*
  ₍BL2532.K85₎
  BT Cults—Jamaica
        Jamaica—Religion
Kumiss
  ₍RM257.K8 (Therapeutics)₎
  ₍TP565 (Manufacture)₎
  UF Koomis
        Koumys
  BT Milk
        Milk, Fermented
Kumiuta
  BT Songs, Japanese
        Songs with koto
        Songs with shamisen
Kumlien family *(Not Subd Geog)*
Kumo (Zairian people)
  USE Kumu (Zairian people)
Kumo River (Finland)
  USE Kokemäki River (Finland)
Kumon family *(Not Subd Geog)*
Kumran community
  USE Qumran community
Kumu (Zairian people)
  ₍DT650.K86₎
  UF Bakumbu (Zairian people)
        Komo (Zairian people)
        Kumo (Zairian people)
        Kuumu (Zairian people)
        Wakumu (Zairian people)
  BT Ethnology—Zaire
  — Rites and ceremonies
    NT Funeral rites and ceremonies,
          Kumu (Zairian people)
Kumu (Zairian people) funeral rites and
    ceremonies
  USE Funeral rites and ceremonies, Kumu
        (Zairian people)
Kumu hula
  USE Hula teachers
Kumyk language
  ₍PL65.K₎
  BT Turkic languages
        Turkic languages, Northwest
Kumyk literature
Kumyks
  ₍DK34.K₎
  BT Ethnology—Caucasus
Kumze family
  USE Koontz family
Kun-dga'-gźon-nu (Buddhist deity)
  ₍BQ4890.K₎
  BT Gods, Buddhist
Kun-Uy
  USE Kenney

Kunabi dialect
  BT Marathi language
Kunama language
  ₍PL8421₎
  UF Baden language
        Bāza language
        Bāzen language
        Cunama language
  BT Chadic languages
        Ethiopia—Languages
        Nilo-Saharan languages
        Sudan—Languages
Kunamas
  ₍DT393.5₎
  UF Cunamas
  BT Ethnology—Ethiopia
Kunana (Australian people)
  USE Lardil (Australian people)
Kunce family
  USE Koontz family
Kunckel family
  USE Kunkel family
Kuṇḍalinī
  ₍BL1238.56.K86₎
  UF Kuṇḍalinī yoga
        Yoga, Kuṇḍalinī
  BT Occultism
        Yoga, Haṭha
Kuṇḍalinī yoga
  USE Kuṇḍalinī
Kunde family *(Not Subd Geog)*
Kundoku
  BT Kunten
Kundu (African people)
  USE Nkundu (African people)
Kundu language
  USE Bakundu language
Kunersdorf, Battle of, 1759
  ₍DD412.6.K8₎
  BT Seven Years' War, 1756-1763
!Kung (African people)
  UF Auen (African people)
        Jū/wăsi (African people)
        !Khung (African people)
        !Kuong (African people)
        Makaukau (African people)
        Qhung (African people)
        !Xũ (African people)
        Zhũ/twăsi (African people)
  BT Ethnology—Africa, Southern
        San (African people)
Kung family *(Not Subd Geog)*
Kung fu
  ₍GV1114.7₎
  UF Gung fu
        Kempo
  BT Hand-to-hand fighting, Oriental
  NT Karate
Kung-ka Mountains (China)
  USE Minya Konka (China)
Kung-ko-erh (China)
  USE Konger Mount (China)
!Kung language
  USE !Xũ language
Kungnakchŏn, Muwisa (Wŏrha-ri, Sŏngjŏn-
    myŏn, Korea)
  USE Muwisa (Wŏrha-ri, Sŏngjŏn-myŏn,
        Korea)—Kungnakchŏn
Kungsholmen (Stockholm, Sweden)
  (Not Subd Geog)
  UF Stockholm (Sweden). Kungsholmen
Kungur (China)
  USE Konger Mount (China)
Kūṇi (Legendary character)
  USE Mantharā (Legendary character)
Kunimaipa language
  BT Papuan languages
  NT Hazili dialect

Kunimatsu family *(Not Subd Geog)*
Kunimi family *(Not Subd Geog)*
Kuningham family
  USE Cunningham family
Kunisaki-hantō (Japan)
  USE Kunisaki Peninsula (Japan)
Kunisaki Peninsula (Japan)
  UF Kunisaki-hantō (Japan)
     Kunizaki-hantō (Japan)
  BT Peninsulas—Japan
Kunizaki-hantō (Japan)
  USE Kunisaki Peninsula (Japan)
Kunjen dialects
  USE Gundjun dialects
Kunkel family *(Not Subd Geog)*
  UF Conkel family
     Conkle family
     Cunkel family
     Cunkle family
     Gunkel family
     Gunkle family
     Kunckel family
     Kunkle family
Kunkle family
  USE Kunkel family
Kunningham family
  USE Cunningham family
Kunringer family
  USE Kuenringer family
Kunsthalle Waaghaus (Winterthur, Switzerland)
  UF Waaghaus Kunsthalle (Winterthur, Switzerland)
  BT Exhibition buildings—Switzerland
Künstlerhaus (Graz, Austria)
  UF Graz Künstlerhaus (Graz, Austria)
  BT Exhibition buildings—Austria
     Municipal buildings—Austria
Kunstpfeifer
  USE Stadtpfeifer
Kunstpreis Villa Romana
  [N396]
  UF Premio d'arte tedesco Villa Romana
     Villa Romana Prize
  BT Art—Competitions
     Rewards (Prizes, etc.)—Germany (West)
     Rewards (Prizes, etc.)—Italy
Kunte family *(Not Subd Geog)*
Kunten
  [PL627]
  UF Okototen
  BT Chinese language—Translating
     Japanese language—Punctuation
  NT Kundoku
Kunts family
  USE Koontz family
Kuntz family
  USE Koontz family
Kuntze family
  USE Koontz family
Kuntzelmann family
  USE Gunzelman family
Kuntzi family
  USE Koontz family
Kunugi family *(Not Subd Geog)*
Kunuzi dialect
  USE Kenuz dialect
Kunz family
  USE Koontz family
Kunze family
  USE Koontz family
Kunzia (Plant)
  USE Purshia
Kuo min tang
  [DS775]
!Kuong (African people)
  USE !Kung (African people)
Kuparuk River (Alaska)
  BT Rivers—Alaska

Kupe family
  USE Coop family
Kupffer cells
  UF Pyramidal liver cells
     Stellate liver cells
  BT Liver cells
     Macrophages
Kupia language
  [PK2246]
  UF Valmiki language
  BT Indo-Aryan languages, Modern
Kurai (Indonesian people)
  BT Ethnology—Indonesia
Kuraish (Arab tribe)
  USE Quraysh (Arab tribe)
Kurāḷas
  USE Kumhars
Kurama Range (Uzbek S.S.R. and Tajik S.S.R.)
  UF Kuraminskiĭ khrebet (Uzbek S.S.R. and Tajik S.S.R.)
  BT Mountains—Tajik S.S.R.
     Mountains—Uzbek S.S.R.
Kuraminskiĭ khrebet (Uzbek S.S.R. and Tajik S.S.R.)
  USE Kurama Range (Uzbek S.S.R. and Tajik S.S.R.)
Kuranko (African people)
  [DT516.42 (Sierra Leone)]
  [DT543.42 (Guinea)]
  UF Kolanko (African people)
     Kulanko (African people)
  BT Ethnology—Guinea
     Ethnology—Sierra Leone
     Mandingo (African people)
Kurasaki family *(Not Subd Geog)*
Kurasawa family *(Not Subd Geog)*
Kuṟavañci plays *(May Subd Geog)*
  BT Tamil drama
Kuravers
  USE Koravas
Kurawa Iseki (Hachijō-machi, Japan)
  USE Kurawa Site (Hachijō-machi, Japan)
Kurawa Site (Hachijō-machi, Japan)
  (Not Subd Geog)
  UF Kurawa Iseki (Hachijō-machi, Japan)
  BT Japan—Antiquities
Kurbee family
  USE Kirby family
Kurdish folk poetry
  USE Folk poetry, Kurdish
Kurdish folk-songs
  USE Folk-songs, Kurdish
Kurdish Jews
  USE Jews, Kurdish
Kurdish language
  [PK6901-9]
  UF Kurmanji language
  BT Iranian languages
  NT Mukri dialect
Kurdish literature
  [PK6908]
Kurdish poetry
  [PK6908]
  NT Folk poetry, Kurdish
Kurdish rugs
  USE Rugs, Kurdish
Kurdistan
  UF Kordestān
  — History *(Not Subd Geog)*
     NT Banī Ardalān dynasty
Kurds *(May Subd Geog)*
  BT Iranians
Kure Mountains (Turkey) *(Not Subd Geog)*
  UF Isfendiyar Mountains (Turkey)
  BT Mountains—Turkey
Kurelek, William, 1927-   Ukrainian pioneer
  UF Ukrainian pioneer (Mural painting)
  BT Ukrainians—Canada—Portraits

Kurfei (African people)
  USE Kurtey (African people)
Kurfürstendamm (Berlin, Germany)
  UF Kurfürstendamm Avenue (Berlin, Germany)
  BT Streets—Germany (West)
Kurfürstendamm Avenue (Berlin, Germany)
  USE Kurfürstendamm (Berlin, Germany)
Kurg language
  USE Kodagu language
Kuri language
  USE Lezghian language
Kuria (African people) *(May Subd Geog)*
  UF Abakuria (African people)
     Bakulia (African people)
     Bakuria (African people)
     Batende (African people)
     Ikikuria (African people)
     Kurya (African people)
  BT Ethnology—Kenya
     Ethnology—Tanzania
Kuria (African people) law
  USE Law, Kuria (African people)
Kuria (African people) women
  USE Women, Kuria (African people)
Kuria language
  UF Kikoria language
     Kikouria language
     Kikuria language
     Koria language
     Kurya language
     Tende language
  BT Bantu languages
Kuriatskiĭ khrebet (R.S.F.S.R.)
  USE Koryak Range (R.S.F.S.R.)
Kuriel family
  USE Coryell family
Kurihara Nakamaru Iseki (Zama-shi, Japan)
  USE Kurihara Nakamaru Site (Zama-shi, Japan)
Kurihara Nakamaru Site (Zama-shi, Japan)
  (Not Subd Geog)
  UF Kurihara Nakamaru Iseki (Zama-shi, Japan)
  BT Japan—Antiquities
Kuril Islands (R.S.F.S.R.)
  UF Chishima-retto (R.S.F.S.R.)
     Kurile Islands (R.S.F.S.R.)
     Kuril'skie Ostrova (R.S.F.S.R.)
  BT Islands—Russian S.F.S.R.
Kurile Islands (R.S.F.S.R.)
  USE Kuril Islands (R.S.F.S.R.)
Kuril'skie Ostrova (R.S.F.S.R.)
  USE Kuril Islands (R.S.F.S.R.)
Kurina Indians
  USE Culina Indians
Kuring-gai Chase (N.S.W.)
  USE Ku-ring-gai Chase National Park (N.S.W.)
Kurintji (Australian people)
  USE Gurindji (Australian people)
Kurion (Ancient city)
  USE Kourion (Ancient city)
Kurium (Ancient city)
  USE Kourion (Ancient city)
Kurku language
  [PL4583]
  UF Kirku language
     Korku language
  RT Munda languages
Kurland Spit (Lithuania and R.S.F.S.R.)
  USE Courland Spit (Lithuania and R.S.F.S.R.)
Kurmanji language
  USE Kurdish language
Kurmis
  [DS432.K787]
  BT Caste—India
     Ethnology—India
Kurnai (Australian people)
  [DU125.K77]

Kurnai (Australian people) *(Continued)*
  BT Australian aborigines
      Ethnology—Australia
Kürneck family *(Not Subd Geog)*
  UF Kirneck family
      Kirnegk family
      Kürnege family
      Kürnegg family
      Kürnegge family
      Kürnegk family
Kürnege family
  USE Kürneck family
Kürnegg family
  USE Kürneck family
Kürnegge family
  USE Kürneck family
Kürnegk family
  USE Kürneck family
Kuro Siwo
  USE Kuroshio
Kuroba (African people)
  USE Attie (African people)
Kurobe Gorge (Japan)
  USE Kurobe River Gorge (Japan)
Kurobe Kyōkoku (Japan)
  USE Kurobe River Gorge (Japan)
Kurobe River Gorge (Japan)
    (Not Subd Geog)
  UF Kurobe Gorge (Japan)
      Kurobe Kyōkoku (Japan)
  BT Gorges—Japan
Kurobu language
  USE Attie language
Kuroda family *(Not Subd Geog)*
Kurokawa Castle (Aizuwakamatsu-shi, Japan)
  USE Wakamatsujō (Aizuwakamatsu-shi,
      Japan)
Kurokawajō (Aizuwakamatsu-shi, Japan)
  USE Wakamatsujō (Aizuwakamatsu-shi,
      Japan)
Kurokoma Iseki (Yoshii-machi, Gunma-ken,
    Japan)
  USE Kurokuma Site (Yoshii-machi, Gunma-
      ken, Japan)
**Kurokuma Site (Yoshii-machi, Gunma-ken,
    Japan)** *(Not Subd Geog)*
  UF Kurokoma Iseki (Yoshii-machi,
      Gunma-ken, Japan)
  BT Japan—Antiquities
Kuronezumia
  USE Nezumia
Kurorofa language
  USE Jukun language
Kurosejō (Mitsushima-chō, Japan)
  USE Kaneta no ki (Mitsushima-chō, Japan)
Kuroshio
    ₍GC296.K85₎
  UF Gulf Stream of Japan
      Japan Current
      Kuro Siwo
  BT Ocean currents
Kurozumi (Sect)
    ₍BL2222.K8₎
  BT Shinto sects
  — Sermons
      BT Shinto sermons
Kurpie
    ₍DK4121.5.K87₎
  UF Kurps
  BT Ethnology—Poland
Kurpiowska Forest (Poland)
  UF Kurpiowszczyzna (Poland)
      Myszyniecka Puszcza (Poland)
      Puszcza Kurpiowska (Poland)
      Puszcza Myszyniecka (Poland)
      Puszcza Zielona (Poland)
      Zielona Puszcza Kurpiowska (Poland)
  BT Forest reserves—Poland
      Forests and forestry—Poland
Kurpiowszczyzna (Poland)
  USE Kurpiowska Forest (Poland)

Kurps
  USE Kurpie
Kurrawar language
  USE Garawa language
Kurrichane thrush
  UF Turdus libonyana
      Turdus libonyanus
  BT Thrushes
Kursa language
  USE Maba language
Kursaal-Cirque (Besançon, France)
  BT Municipal buildings—France
Kursey family
  USE Kersey family
Kurshskaīa kosa (Lithuania and R.S.F.S.R.)
  USE Courland Spit (Lithuania and
      R.S.F.S.R.)
Kurshskaya kosa (Lithuania and R.S.F.S.R.)
  USE Courland Spit (Lithuania and
      R.S.F.S.R.)
Kuršių nerija (Lithuania and R.S.F.S.R.)
  USE Courland Spit (Lithuania and
      R.S.F.S.R.)
Kuršių neringa (Lithuania and R.S.F.S.R.)
  USE Courland Spit (Lithuania and
      R.S.F.S.R.)
Kursk, Battle of, 1943
  UF Prokhorovka, Battle of, 1943
  BT World War, 1939-1945—Campaigns—
      Russian S.F.S.R.
  NT Operation Citadel
Kurskaīa kosa (Lithuania and R.S.F.S.R.)
  USE Courland Spit (Lithuania and
      R.S.F.S.R.)
Kurskaja kosa (Lithuania and R.S.F.S.R.)
  USE Courland Spit (Lithuania and
      R.S.F.S.R.)
Kurskaya kosa (Lithuania and R.S.F.S.R.)
  USE Courland Spit (Lithuania and
      R.S.F.S.R.)
Kurtey (African people)
    ₍DT547.42₎
  UF Kourfey (African people)
      Kourtey (African people)
      Kurfei (African people)
  BT Ethnology—Niger
Kurtner family
  USE Curtner family
Kuru *(May Subd Geog)*
    ₍RC394.K8₎
  BT Central nervous system—Diseases
      Virus diseases, Slow
Kurukh folk literature
  USE Folk literature, Kurukh
Kurukh folk-songs
  USE Folk-songs, Kurukh
Kurukh language
    ₍PL4701-4₎
  UF Oraon language
      Uraon language
  BT Dravidian languages
Kurukh literature *(May Subd Geog)*
    ₍PL4703.5-4704₎
  NT Folk literature, Kurukh
Kurukh poetry
    ₍PL4704₎
  UF Oraon poetry
  NT Religious poetry, Kurukh
Kurukh religious poetry
  USE Religious poetry, Kurukh
Kurukh songs
  USE Songs, Oraon
Kurukullā (Buddhist deity)
    ₍BQ4890.K96₎
  BT Gods, Buddhist
      Tārā (Goddess)
Kurumba (African people)
    ₍DT555.45.K88₎
  UF Kurumba (African tribe)
  BT Ethnology—Burkina Faso

Kurumba (African tribe)
  USE Kurumba (African people)
Kurumba language *(May Subd Geog)*
  UF Deforo language
      Foulse language
      Fulse language
      Koromfe language
      Kouroumba language
      Kurumfe language
      Lilse language
  BT Burkina Faso—Languages
      Gur languages
Kurumbas
    ₍DS432.K8₎
  UF Kouroumbs
Kurumfe language
  USE Kurumba language
Kurungu language
  USE Krongo language
Kurupa Lake (Alaska)
  BT Lakes—Alaska
Kurya (African people)
  USE Kuria (African people)
Kurya language
  USE Kuria language
Kuryatskiy khrebet (R.S.F.S.R.)
  USE Koryak Range (R.S.F.S.R.)
Kurzweil family *(Not Subd Geog)*
Kuśa (Hindu mythology)
  BT Mythology, Hindu
Kusa language
  USE Kussassi language
Kusae (Micronesia)
  USE Kosrae (Micronesia)
Kusae language
  USE Kussassi language
Kusai-to (Micronesia)
  USE Kosrae (Micronesia)
Kusaie (Micronesia)
  USE Kosrae (Micronesia)
Kusaie language
    ₍PL6252.K86₎
  BT Micronesian languages
Kusair el-Kadim (Ancient city)
  USE Qusayr al-Qadīm (Ancient city)
Kusal language
  USE Kussassi language
Kusan Indians
  USE Coos Indians
Kusan languages
    ₍PM1611₎
  NT Coos language
Kuṣāṇa
  USE Kushans
Kusasi language
  USE Kussassi language
Kusatsu Shirane (Gunma-ken, Japan)
  USE Shirane Mountain (Gunma-ken, Japan)
Kusatsu Shirane-san (Gunma-ken, Japan)
  USE Shirane Mountain (Gunma-ken, Japan)
Kusayama B iseki (Kosugi-machi, Japan)
  USE Kusayama B Site (Kosugi-machi,
      Japan)
Kusayama B Site (Kosugi-machi, Japan)
    (Not Subd Geog)
  UF Kusayama B iseki (Kosugi-machi,
      Japan)
  BT Japan—Antiquities
Kusbas (R.S.F.S.R.)
  USE Kuznetsk Basin (R.S.F.S.R.)
Kusemai
  USE Kōwaka
Kush family
  USE Kutsch family
Kushan art
  USE Art, Kushan
Kushanas
  USE Kushans
Kushans *(May Subd Geog)*
  UF Kuṣāṇa
      Kushanas

2052

BT Ethnology—South Asia
India—History—324 B.C.-1000 A.D.
Yüeh-chih
Kushi-jima (Japan)
USE Awa Island (Japan)
Kushimoto family *(Not Subd Geog)*
Kŭshta na Dimitŭr Georgiadi (Plovdiv, Bulgaria)
UF Dimitŭr Georgiadi House (Plovdiv, Bulgaria)
BT Dwellings—Bulgaria
Georgiadi, Dimitŭr—Homes and haunts—Bulgaria
Kusie (Micronesia)
USE Kosrae (Micronesia)
Kuskokwim River (Alaska)
BT Rivers—Alaska
Kuskus
USE Couscous
Kussai (Micronesia)
USE Kosrae (Micronesia)
Kussassi language
[PL8423]
UF Kusa language
Kusae language
Kusal language
Kusasi language
BT Mossi languages
Kussiu (Micronesia)
USE Kosrae (Micronesia)
Kusso Indians
[E99.K83]
BT Indians of North America
Indians of North America—South Carolina
Küstenland (Yugoslavia and Italy)
USE Julian March (Yugoslavia and Italy)
Kuster family
USE Custer family
Kusterer family
USE Custer family
Kusunda language
[PL3801.K9]
BT Tibeto-Burman languages
Kusunoki family *(Not Subd Geog)*
Kŭtahya pottery
UF Pottery, Kŭtahya
BT Pottery, Turkish
Kutaka-jima (Japan)
USE Kudaka Island (Japan)
Kutaka-shima (Japan)
USE Kudaka Island (Japan)
Kutandji (Australian people)
USE Gurindji (Australian people)
Kutani porcelain *(May Subd Geog)*
[NK4399.K87]
UF Kokutani porcelain
Kutani ware
Porcelain, Kutani
BT Porcelain, Japanese
Kutani pottery
UF Kokutani pottery
Pottery, Kutani
BT Pottery, Japanese
Kutani ware
USE Kutani porcelain
Kutch family
USE Kutsch family
Kutchakutchin language
[PM1615]
UF Gwich'in language
Kuchin language
BT Kutchin languages
RT Athapascan languages
Kutchin Indians
[E99.K]
UF Loucheux Indians
BT Athapascan Indians
Indians of North America
NT Natsitkutchin Indians
Tukkuthkutchin Indians

Vuntakutchin Indians
Kutchin languages
[PM1621]
NT Athapascan languages
Kutchakutchin language
Tukkuthkutchin language
Kutei River (Kalimantan Timur, Indonesia)
USE Mahakam River (Kalimantan Timur, Indonesia)
Kutenai Indians
[E99.K85]
UF Cootenai Indians
Kitunahan Indians
Koetenay Indians
Kootenai Indians
Skalzi Indians
BT Indians of North America
— **Antiquities**
— **Reservations**
NT Flathead Indian Reservation (Mont.)
Kutenai language
[PM1631]
UF Cootenai language
Kitonaqa language
Kitunahan languages
Koetenay language
Kootenai language
Ksanka language
Kutenai River
USE Kootenai River
Kuthiu (Micronesia)
USE Kosrae (Micronesia)
Kutno, Battle of, 1939
BT World War, 1939-1945—Campaigns—Poland
Kutsch family *(Not Subd Geog)*
UF Gutsch family
Kush family
Kutch family
Kutso-Vlachs
USE Aromanians
Kutsuki family *(Not Subd Geog)*
Kutthung language
USE Kattang language
Kutz family *(Not Subd Geog)*
Kuu language
USE Fe'fe' language
Kuumu (Zairian people)
USE Kumu (Zairian people)
Kuuvanmiit Eskimos
BT Eskimos
Indians of North America
Kuvasz
[SF429.K]
BT Dog breeds
Kuvi language
[PL4706]
BT Dravidian languages
Kui language
Kuwait *(Not Subd Geog)*
— **History** *(Not Subd Geog)*
NT Sabah dynasty, 1752-
Kuwait (Kuwait). Shuwaykh
USE Shuwaykh (Kuwait, Kuwait)
Kuwait Bay (Kuwait)
UF Jūn al Kuwayt (Kuwait)
BT Bays—Kuwait
Kuwaiti cookery
USE Cookery, Kuwaiti
Kuwaiti economic assistance
USE Economic assistance, Kuwaiti
Kuwamizu Iseki (Kumamoto-shi, Japan)
USE Kuwamizu Site (Kumamoto-shi, Japan)
Kuwamizu Site (Kumamoto-shi, Japan)
UF Kuwamizu Iseki (Kumamoto-shi, Japan)
BT Japan—Antiquities
Kuwe (African people)
USE We (African people)

Kuy language
USE Kui language (Mon-Khmer)
Kuyckendal family
USE Kuykendall family
Kuykendaal family
USE Kuykendall family
Kuykendall family *(Not Subd Geog)*
UF Coikendall family
Cookendall family
Coukendall family
Coykendall family
Cuickendall family
Cuirkendal family
Curkendall family
Cuykendall family
Cyrkendall family
Kaykendall family
Keykendall family
Kierkendall family
Kikendall family
Kirkendahl family
Kirkendale family
Kirkendall family
Kirkendawl family
Kirkendoll family
Kirkenstall family
Kirkenthall family
Koikendal family
Kookendall family
Kuerkendol family
Kuikendall family
Kuyckendal family
Kuykendaal family
Kuykendoll family
Kuyrkendal family
Kuykendoll family
USE Kuykendall family
Kuyonon language
USE Cuyunon language
Kuyrkendal family
USE Kuykendall family
Kuzbass (R.S.F.S.R.)
USE Kuznetsk Basin (R.S.F.S.R.)
Kuzma family *(Not Subd Geog)*
UF Kosman family
Kosmann family
Kosmian family
Kosmiany family
Kuzman family
Kuzmanić family
Kuzmanni family
Kuzmanovski family
Kuzmany family
Kuzman family
USE Kuzma family
Kuzmanić family
USE Kuzma family
Kuzmanni family
USE Kuzma family
Kuzmanovski family
USE Kuzma family
Kuzmany family
USE Kuzma family
Kuznetsk Alatau (R.S.F.S.R.)
UF Alatau, Kuznetskiĭ (R.S.F.S.R.)
Khrebet Kuznetskiĭ Alatau (R.S.F.S.R.)
Kuznetskiĭ Alatau (R.S.F.S.R.)
BT Mountains—Russian S.F.S.R.
Kuznetsk Basin (R.S.F.S.R.)
UF Kusbas (R.S.F.S.R.)
Kuzbass (R.S.F.S.R.)
Kuznetskiĭ basseĭn (R.S.F.S.R.)
BT Geology—Russian S.F.S.R.
Kuznetskiĭ Alatau (R.S.F.S.R.)
USE Kuznetsk Alatau (R.S.F.S.R.)
Kuznetskiĭ basseĭn (R.S.F.S.R.)
USE Kuznetsk Basin (R.S.F.S.R.)
Kuzukawa Iseki (Kanda-machi, Japan)
USE Kuzukawa Site (Kanda-machi, Japan)

Kuzukawa Site (Kanda-machi, Japan)
  UF Kuzukawa Iseki (Kanda-machi, Japan)
  BT Japan—Antiquities
Kvanada language
  USE Bagulal language
Kvanadin language
  USE Bagulal language
Kvas
  USE Kvass
Kvass
  UF Kvas
      Quas
      Quass
  BT Beer
Kvebæk family sculpture technique
  [BF698.8.K83]
  BT Family—Testing
      Family psychotherapy
      Psychological tests
Kvist family (Not Subd Geog)
  UF Qvist family
Kvistgaard family
  USE Qvistgaard family
Kwa languages (May Subd Geog)
  BT Niger-Congo languages
  NT Abe language
      Adangme language
      Akan language
      Aladian language
      Anufo dialect
      Anyi language
      Atisa language
      Bini language
      Degema language
      Ekpeye language
      Engenni language
      Etsako language
      Ewe language
      Ezaa language
      Gã language
      Gbagyi language
      Gonja language
      Gwa dialect (Ghana)
      Gwari language
      Idoma language
      Igbira language
      Igbo language
      Igede language
      Ijo language
      Ikwo language
      Izi language
      Kposo language
      Kru languages
      Lagoon languages
      Lefana language
      Nupe language
      Nzima language
      Okpe language
      Yebu language
      Yoruba language
Kwaaymi Indians
  USE Diegueño Indians
KWAC (Indexing system)
  UF Key Word and Context
      Key Word Augmented in Context
      Keyword and Context
      Keyword Augmented in Context
  BT Automatic indexing
Kwadjelinn (Marshall Islands)
  USE Kwajalein Island (Marshall Islands)
Kwafi language
  [PL8425]
  UF Kisõgo language
      Kwapi language
      Kwavi language
      Loygob language
      Loykop language
Kwahu (African people)
  [DT510.42]
  UF Okouahou (African people)
  BT Ethnology—Ghana

Kwaiker Indians
  USE Cuaiquer Indians
Kwaiker language
  USE Cuaiquer language
Kwaio (Melanesian people)
  [DV850]
  BT Ethnology—Solomon Islands
      Melanesians
Kwaio language
  [PL6252.K88]
  UF Fataia language
      Koio language
      Uru language (Malaita, Solomon
        Islands)
      Welakau language
  BT Melanesian languages
Kwajalein Atoll (Marshall Islands)
  BT Coral reefs and islands—Marshall
      Islands
Kwajalein Atoll, Battle of, 1944
  BT World War, 1939-1945—Campaigns—
      Marshall Islands
Kwajalein Island (Marshall Islands)
  UF Kuejerin-to (Marshall Islands)
      Kuejierin To (Marshall Islands)
      Kuezyerin-to (Marshall Islands)
      Kwadjelinn (Marshall Islands)
      Kwajelinn (Marshall Islands)
  BT Coral reefs and islands—Marshall
      Islands
      Islands of the Pacific
      Marshall Islands
Kwajelinn (Marshall Islands)
  USE Kwajalein Island (Marshall Islands)
Kwak family (Not Subd Geog)
Kwakiutl Indians
  [E99.K9]
  BT Indians of North America
      Wakashan Indians
  NT Bellabella Indians
      Haisla Indians
Kwakiutl language
  [PM1641]
  RT Wakashan languages
Kwandara language
  USE Gwandara language
Kwandoh family
  USE Quander family
Kwang Sea
  USE Yellow Sea
Kwangali language
  UF Kwangari language
  BT Bantu languages
Kwangari language
  USE Kwangali language
Kwangju (Korea)
  — History
      NT Kwangju Uprising, Korea (South),
          1980
Kwangju Incident, Korea (South), 1980
  USE Kwangju Uprising, Korea (South),
      1980
Kwangju Uprising, Korea (South), 1980
  UF Korea (South)—History—Kwangju
      Uprising, 1980
      Kwangju Incident, Korea (South),
        1980
  BT Korea (South)—History—1960-
      Kwangju (Korea)—History
Kwangtung Peninsula (China)
  USE Kuan-tung Peninsula (China)
Kwangwa (Bantu people)
  UF Makwangwa (Bantu people)
  BT Ethnology—Zambia
Kwanim pas (African people)
  USE Uduk (African people)
Kwantung Peninsula (China)
  USE Kuan-tung Peninsula (China)
Kwanyama (African people)
  USE Kuanyama (African people)

Kwanyama language
  USE Kuanyama language
Kwanze family
  USE Kanze family
Kwapi language
  USE Kwafi language
Kwara language
  USE Quara language
Kwarafe language
  USE Korape language
Kwashiorkor (May Subd Geog)
  [RJ399.K9]
  BT Malnutrition in children
      Protein deficiency
Kwathlamba
  USE Drakensberg Mountains
Kwavi language
  USE Kwafi language
Kwaya (African people)
  UF Kwaya (African tribe)
  BT Ethnology—Tanzania
  — Rites and ceremonies
      NT Marriage customs and rites, Kwaya
          (African people)
Kwaya (African people) marriage customs and
    rites
  USE Marriage customs and rites, Kwaya
      (African people)
Kwaya (African tribe)
  USE Kwaya (African people)
Kwedi language
  USE Bakwiri language
Kwegi (African people)
  USE Kwegu (African people)
Kwegu (African people)
  UF Bacha (African people)
      Kwegi (African people)
      Menja (African people)
      Nyidi (African people)
      Yidi (African people)
  BT Ethnology—Ethiopia
Kweli
  USE Bakwiri (African people)
Kweli language
  USE Bakwiri language
Kwemi
  USE Khumis
Kweni (African people)
  USE Guro (African people)
Kweni language
  UF Gouro language
      Guro language
  BT Ivory Coast—Languages
      Southern Mande languages
  NT Gagu language
      Tura language
Kwerba language (May Subd Geog)
  BT Indonesia—Languages
      Papuan languages
Kwese (African people)
  UF Bakwese (African people)
  BT Ethnology—Zaire
Kwese language
  [PL8430.K84]
  UF Gikwezo language
      KiKwese language
      Kwezo language
      Pindi language (Kwese)
      Ukwese language
  BT Bantu languages
      Kongo language
      Zaire—Languages
Kwezo language
  USE Kwese language
Kwichan Indians
  USE Yuma Indians
Kwik Print process
  UF Kwik Proof process
  BT Photography—Printing processes—
      Pigment
  RT Color-printing

2054

Kwik Proof process
　　USE Kwik Print process
Kwili
　　USE Bakwiri (African people)
Kwili language
　　USE Bakwiri language
Kwinaiult Indians
　　USE Quinault Indians
Kwinti people
　　USE Djuka people
Kwiri
　　USE Bakwiri (African people)
Kwiri language
　　USE Bakwiri language
Kwokwoos language
　　USE Coos language
Kwoma (Papua New Guinea people)
　　UF Kwoma tribe
　　BT Ethnology—Papua New Guinea
Kwoma language
　　USE Washkuk language
Kwoma tribe
　　USE Kwoma (Papua New Guinea people)
Kwongan *(May Subd Geog)*
　　[QK461]
　　BT Shrublands
Kwottu dialect
　　USE Qottu dialect
Kxaxa (African people)
　　USE Kgaga (African people)
Kxhalaxadi dialect
　　USE Kgalagadi dialect
Kyanizing
　　USE Wood—Preservation
Kyi Chhu (China)
　　USE Lhasa River (China)
Kyi Chu (China)
　　USE Lhasa River (China)
Kyi River (China)
　　USE Lhasa River (China)
Kyichu River (China)
　　USE Lhasa River (China)
Kyklades (Greece)
　　USE Cyclades (Greece)
Kykladon (Greece)
　　USE Cyclades (Greece)
Kyle family *(Not Subd Geog)*
　　UF Kyles family
Kyles family
　　USE Kyle family
Kyll River (Germany)
　　UF Kill River (Germany)
　　BT Rivers—Germany (West)
Kylshawe family
　　USE Kelsall family
Kymborough family
　　USE Kimbrough family
Kymenjoki (Finland)
　　USE Kymi River (Finland)
Kymenne River (Finland)
　　USE Kymi River (Finland)
Kymi River (Finland)
　　UF Kioumen River (Finland)
　　　 Kīūmi-ĺoki (Finland)
　　　 Kīūmin-ĺoki (Finland)
　　　 Kymenjoki (Finland)
　　　 Kymenne River (Finland)
　　　 Kymijoki (Finland)
　　　 Kyminjoki (Finland)
　　　 Kymmene Älv (Finland)
　　　 Kymu Joki (Finland)
　　　 Kyumin-yoki (Finland)
　　BT Rivers—Finland
Kymijoki (Finland)
　　USE Kymi River (Finland)
Kyminjoki (Finland)
　　USE Kymi River (Finland)
Kymmene Älv (Finland)
　　USE Kymi River (Finland)
Kymograph
　　UF Cymograph

BT Aeronautical instruments
Kymu Joki (Finland)
　　USE Kymi River (Finland)
Kynard family
　　USE Kinard family
Kynerd family
　　USE Kinard family
Kyō porcelain *(May Subd Geog)*
　　[NK4568.K]
　　UF Kyoto wares
　　　 Porcelain, Kyō
　　BT Porcelain, Japanese
Kyō pottery *(May Subd Geog)*
　　[NK4168.K]
　　UF Kyoto wares
　　　 Porcelain, Kyō
　　BT Pottery, Japanese
　　NT Kiyomizu pottery
Kyōgen *(May Subd Geog)*
　　　Here are entered general works and those that
　　deal solely with the presentation of Kyōgen plays on
　　the stage. The texts of the Kyōgen plays and works
　　treating of them from a literary point of view are
　　entered under Kyōgen plays.
　　UF Kabuki kyōgen
　　　 Nō kyōgen
　　BT Nō
　　— Costume
　　　 BT Costume—Japan
　　— Masks
　　　 BT Masks—Japan
　　— Stage-setting and scenery
Kyōgen plays
　　[PL736]
　　[PL766 (Collections)]
　　　Here are entered the texts of the Kyōgen plays
　　and works treating of them from a literary point of
　　view. General works and those that deal solely with
　　the presentation of Kyōgen plays on the stage are
　　entered under Kyōgen.
　　UF Kabuki kyōgen plays
　　　 Nō kyōgen plays
　　BT Japanese drama
　　— Stories, plots, etc.
Kyōgoku family *(Not Subd Geog)*
Kyōka
　　[PL762.K9]
　　BT Humorous poetry, Japanese
　　　 Waka
Kyŏngbokkung Palace (Seoul, Korea)
　　USE Kyŏngbokkung (Seoul, Korea)
Kyŏngbokkung (Seoul, Korea)
　　UF Kyŏngbokgung Palace (Seoul, Korea)
　　BT Palaces—Korea (South)
　　— Chibokchae
　　　 UF Chibokchae, Kyŏngbokkung (Seoul,
　　　　　 Korea)
Kyonggich'ega
　　USE Changga
Kyŏnggiyŏhaga
　　USE Changga
Kyoto (Japan)
　　— Civilization
　　— — 1600-1868
　　— History
　　　 [DS897.K857]
　　— — 1600-1868
　　— Social life and customs
　　— — 1600-1868
　　— — 1868-1912
Kyoto (Japan). Sagano
　　USE Sagano (Kyoto, Japan)
Kyōto Mishōryū ikebana
　　USE Flower arrangement, Japanese—
　　　　 Mishōryū school
Kyoto wares
　　USE Kyō porcelain
　　　 Kyō pottery
Kyōzuka *(May Subd Geog)*
　　UF Kyōzuka—Japan
　　　 Mainōkyō
　　　 Sūtra mounds

BT Buddhism—Sacred books—
　　　 Preservation
　　NT Kyōzutsu
　　— Japan
　　　 USE Kyōzuka
Kyōzutsu *(May Subd Geog)*
　　[BQ1128-9]
　　UF Sūtra cases
　　BT Buddhism—Sacred books—
　　　 Preservation
　　　 Buddhist antiquities
　　　 Kyōzuka
Kyphosidae
　　[QL638.K9]
　　UF Sea chubs (Fishes)
　　BT Perciformes
　　NT Kyphosus
Kyphosis
　　BT Spine—Abnormalities
　　NT Scheuermann's disease
Kyphosus
　　[QL638.K9]
　　UF Cyphosus
　　BT Kyphosidae
Kyra Panagia Island (Greece)
　　USE Pelagonesi (Greece)
Kyra Panyia Island (Greece)
　　USE Pelagonesi (Greece)
Kyra Pélagos (Greece)
　　USE Pelagonesi (Greece)
Kyrene (Ancient city)
　　USE Cyrene (Ancient city)
Kyrie eleison
　　BT Liturgies
Kyrie eleison (Music)
　　BT Masses
Kysar family
　　USE Kaiser family
Kyser family
　　USE Kaiser family
Kysor family
　　USE Kaiser family
Kythēra Island (Greece)
　　UF Cerigo Island (Greece)
　　　 Cythera Island (Greece)
　　　 Kithira Island (Greece)
　　　 Kythira Island (Greece)
　　　 Nisos Kithira (Greece)
　　　 Tsirigo Island (Greece)
　　BT Islands—Greece
Kythira Island (Greece)
　　USE Kythēra Island (Greece)
Kyū Ringā (Otōto) Jūtaku (Nagasaki-shi,
　　Japan)
　　UF Frederick Ringer House (Nagasaki-shi,
　　　　 Japan)
　　　 Ringā (Otōto) Jūtaku (Nagasaki-shi,
　　　　 Japan)
　　　 Ringer House (Nagaskai-shi, Japan)
　　BT Dwellings—Japan
Kyumin-yoki (Finland)
　　USE Kymi River (Finland)
Kyuri language
　　USE Lezghian language
Kyūshōjō (Tottori-shi, Japan)
　　USE Tottorijō (Tottori-shi, Japan)
Kyūshū Region (Japan)
Kyusyu Zhelob
　　USE Nankai Trough
Kyzer family
　　USE Kaiser family
Kyzyl-Kum (Kazakh S.S.R. and Uzbek S.S.R.)
　　(Not Subd Geog)
　　UF Kizil-Kum (Kazakh S.S.R. and Uzbek
　　　　 S.S.R.)
　　　 Kyzylkum (Kazakh S.S.R. and Uzbek
　　　　 S.S.R.)
　　　 Qizil-Kum (Kazakh S.S.R. and Uzbek
　　　　 S.S.R.)
　　BT Deserts—Kazakh S.S.R.
　　　 Deserts—Uzbek S.S.R.

Kyzyl Tatars
  UF Kizil Tatars
  BT Ethnology—Russian S.F.S.R.
      Tatars
Kyzylkum (Kazakh S.S.R. and Uzbek S.S.R.)
  USE Kyzyl-Kum (Kazakh S.S.R. and Uzbek
       S.S.R.)
Kyzzhakh Site (Alaska)
  USE Kijik Site (Alaska)
L1 algebras
  UF Algebras, L1
  BT Harmonic analysis
      Locally compact groups
L-29 (Training planes)
  USE Delfin (Training planes)
L.C. Smith shotgun
  UF Smith shotgun
  BT Shotguns
L developmental languages
  USE L systems
L-Dopa
  USE Dopa
L-form bacteria
  UF Cell-wall-deficient bacteria
      L-phase variants
      Pleomorphic bacteria
  BT Bacteria
      Bacterial cell walls
L-functions
  UF Functions, L-
  BT Numbers, Theory of
  NT Stark's conjectures
L-phase variants
  USE L-form bacteria
L systems
    ₍QH491 (Biology)₎
  UF L developmental languages
      Lindenmayer developmental languages
      Lindenmayer systems
  BT Developmental biology—Mathematical
      models
      Formal languages
      Machine theory
La Alcarria Plateau (Spain)
  USE Alcarria Plateau (Spain)
La Beauce (France)
  USE Beauce (France)
La Bisten River (Germany and France)
  USE Bist River (Germany and France)
La Brea Pits (Calif.)
  UF La Brea Tar Pits (Calif.)
      Rancho La Brea (Calif.)
  BT Bitumen—California
La Brea Tar Pits (Calif.)
  USE La Brea Pits (Calif.)
La Brea y Pariñas (Peru)
  USE Brea y Pariñas (Peru)
La Bresse (France : Region)
  USE Bresse (France : Region)
La Camargue (France)
  USE Camargue (France)
La Chaîne des Vosges (France)
  USE Vosges Mountains (France)
La Concha Hacienda (Mexico)
  USE Concha Hacienda (Mexico)
La Cordillera Maritima (Peru)
  USE Cordillera Occidental (Peru)
La Coste Castle (Lacoste, Vaucluse, France)
  USE Château de la Coste (Lacoste,
       Vaucluse, France)
La Cotte de Saint-Brelade Site (Jersey)
  USE Cotte de Saint-Brelade Site (Jersey)
La Croix family
  USE Lacroix family
La Croix Rousse (Lyon, France)
  USE Croix Rousse (Lyon, France)
La Cueva Pintada Site (Calif.)
    (Not Subd Geog)
  BT California—Antiquities

La Culebra Site (Guatemala, Guatemala)
  USE Culebra, Gran Monticulo de la
       (Guatemala, Guatemala)
La Cygne Lake (Kan.)
  UF La Cygnes Lake (Kan.)
      LaCygne Lake (Kan.)
      LaCygnes Lake (Kan.)
  BT Lakes—Kansas
      Reservoirs—Kansas
La Cygnes Lake (Kan.)
  USE La Cygne Lake (Kan.)
La Défense (Paris, France)
  USE Défense (Paris, France)
La Désirade (Guadeloupe)
  USE Désirade (Guadeloupe)
La Digue Island (Seychelles)
  UF Digue Island (Seychelles)
  BT Islands—Seychelles
La Dombes (France)
  USE Dombes (France)
La Durance (France)
  USE Durance River (France)
La Española
  USE Hispaniola
La Estación Site (Colombia)
  USE Estación Site (Colombia)
La Fargue family (Not Subd Geog)
  UF Laffargue family
La Fayette family (Not Subd Geog)
  UF Lafayette family
La Ferradura Site (Spain)
  USE Ferradura Site (Spain)
La Ferrassie Rock-shelter (France)
  USE Ferrassie Rock-shelter (France)
La Follette family (Not Subd Geog)
  UF Lafollette family
  RT Follett family
La Fontaine family
  USE Fontaine family
La Franchini family
  USE Lafranchini family
La Franchino family
  USE Lafranchini family
La Francini family
  USE Lafranchini family
La Fumée Mountain (French Guiana)
  USE Fumée Mountain (French Guiana)
La Garonne Fleuve (Spain and France)
  USE Garonne River (Spain and France)
La Gomera (Canary Islands)
  USE Gomera (Canary Islands)
La Grande Soufrière (Basse-Terre Island,
    Guadeloupe)
  USE Soufrière (Basse-Terre Island,
       Guadeloupe)
La Graufesenque Site (Millau, France)
  USE Graufesenque Site (Millau, France)
La Hacienda de Jalpa (Mexico)
  USE Jalpa Hacienda (Mexico)
La Hacienda de La Concha (Mexico)
  USE Concha Hacienda (Mexico)
La Hacienda de San Antonio Tochatlaco
    (Mexico)
  USE San Antonio Tochatlaco Hacienda
       (Mexico)
La Hacienda de San Juan de los Otates
    (Mexico)
  USE San Juan de los Otates Hacienda
       (Mexico)
La Harpe family (Not Subd Geog)
  RT Harp family
La Hougue, Battle of, 1692
La Huasteca (Mexico)
  USE Huasteca (Mexico)
La Isleta (Panama)
  USE Manzanillo Island (Panama)
La Laguna (Mexico)
  USE Laguna Region (Mexico)
La Laouza Rock Shelter (France)
  USE Laouza Rock Shelter (France)

La Léopolda (Villefranche-sur-Mer, France)
  UF Léopolda (Villefranche-sur-Mer,
       France)
      Villa La Léopolda (Villefranche-sur-
       Mer, France)
  BT Codman, Ogden—Homes and haunts
       —France
      Dwellings—France
La Liquière Site (France)
  USE Liquière Site (France)
La Luz (Puebla, Mexico)
  USE Luz (Puebla, Mexico)
La Madre Mountains Wilderness (Nev.)
  UF La Madre Mountains Wilderness
       Study Area (Nev.)
  BT National parks and reserves—Nevada
      Wilderness areas—Nevada
La Madre Mountains Wilderness Study Area
    (Nev.)
  USE La Madre Mountains Wilderness
       (Nev.)
La Mancha (Spain)
  USE Mancha (Spain)
La Manche
  USE English Channel
La Manna family
  USE Lamonna family
La Marck family
  USE Marck family
La Marck House (Paris, France)
  USE Hôtel de La Marck (Paris, France)
La Morandière family
  USE Morandière family
La Moselle Rivière
  USE Moselle River
La Mussara Site (Spain)
  USE Mussara Site (Spain)
La Noguera (Spain)
  USE Noguera (Spain)
La Noire River (France and Belgium)
  USE Eau Noire River (France and Belgium)
La Noue family
  USE Lanneau family
La Noya River (Spain)
  USE Noya River (Spain)
La Omaña (Spain)
  USE Omaña (Spain)
La-oop language
  USE Lawa language (Thailand)
La pa
  USE So na
La Padania (Italy)
  USE Po River Plain (Italy)
La Palma (Canary Islands)
  USE Palma (Canary Islands)
La Paz (Bolivia)
  — History
  — — **Revolution, 1809**
        UF Revolución paceña de 1809
             (Bolivia)
        BT Bolivia—History—Wars of
             Independence, 1809-1825
La Perla (Córdoba, Argentina : Concentration
    camp)
  USE Perla (Córdoba, Argentina :
       Concentration camp)
La Perla Theater (Ponce, P.R.)
  USE Teatro La Perla (Ponce, P.R.)
La Pérouse (Solomon Islands)
  USE Vanikolo (Solomon Islands)
La Petite Église
  USE Louisets
La Plante family
  USE Laplante family
La Plata dolphin
    ₍QL737.C436₎
  UF Franciscana dolphin
      Pontoporia blainvillei
      Stenodelphis blainvillei
  BT Pontoporia
      River dolphins

La Plata River (Colombia)
  USE Plata River (Colombia)
La Pole family
  USE De la Pole family
La Ponga Site (Ecuador)
  USE Ponga Site (Ecuador)
La Puna (Bolivia and Peru)
  USE Altiplano (Bolivia and Peru)
La Región Oriental (Ecuador)
  USE Oriente (Ecuador)
La Rieu family
  USE Larue family
La Roche-l'Abeille, Battle of, 1569
  [DC117]
  BT France—History—Wars of the
        Huguenots, 1562-1598
La-sa Ho (China)
  USE Lhasa River (China)
La Safor (Spain)
  USE Safor (Spain)
La Salle automobile
  [TL215.L]
  UF LaSalle automobile
  BT General Motors automobiles
La Sals (Utah and Colo.)
  USE Manti La Sal National Forest (Utah
        and Colo.)
La Segarra Region (Spain)
  USE Segarra Region (Spain)
La Selva Region (Spain)
  UF Comarca de La Selva (Spain)
        Selva Region (Spain)
La Sologne (France)
  USE Sologne (France)
La Soufrière de Guadeloupe (Basse-Terre
    Island, Gaudeloupe)
  USE Soufrière (Basse-Terre Island,
        Guadeloupe)
La Taille family
  USE Taille family
La Téne period (May Subd Geog)
  [GN779-780]
  BT Iron age
        Man, Prehistoric
  NT Mounds—Rhine River Valley
  — Switzerland
La Tour, Georges du Mesnil de, 1593-1652.
  Fortune teller
  [ND553.L28]
  UF Bonne aventure (Painting)
        Fortune teller (Painting)
La Trobe Collection (Melbourne, Vic.)
  BT Victoria—History—Library resources—
        Australia
La Trobe Valley (Vic.)
  USE Latrobe Valley (Vic.)
La Vallée family
  USE Vallée family
Laadi (African people) (May Subd Geog)
  UF Laali (African people)
        Lali (African people)
  BT Ethnology—Congo (Brazzaville)
Laadi dialect
  UF Kilari dialect
        Ladi dialect
        Lari dialect (Kongo)
  BT Congo (Brazzaville)—Languages
        Kongo language
        Zaire—Languages
Laadi folk literature
  USE Folk literature, Laadi
Laal language (May Subd Geog)
  UF Gori language
  BT African languages
        Chad—Languages
Laali (African people)
  USE Laadi (African people)
Laamanen family (Not Subd Geog)
Laamang language
  UF Lamang language

  BT Cameroon—Languages
        Chadic languages
        Nigeria—Languages
Laan, Die (Stellenbosch, South Africa)
  USE Avenue, The (Stellenbosch, South
        Africa)
Laaschet family
  USE Lawshe family
Laashett family
  USE Lawshe family
Laatokka Lake (R.S.F.S.R.)
  USE Ladoga Lake (R.S.F.S.R.)
Laatste oordeel (Panel painting)
  USE Bosch, Hieronymus, d. 1516. Last
        judgment
Labadists (May Subd Geog)
  [BX7990.L2]
  BT Protestants
  — Maryland
      [BX7990.L2]
      UF Labadists in Maryland
Labadists in Maryland
  USE Labadists—Maryland
Labbe family (Not Subd Geog)
  UF Labbee family
Labbee family
  USE Labbe family
Labe River
  USE Elbe River
Label, Union
  USE Union label
Label industry (May Subd Geog)
  [HD9999.L17-174]
  BT Labels
Labeling deviant behavior
  USE Deviant behavior—Labeling theory
Labeling laws
  USE Labels—Law and legislation
Labeling-machines
  [TP659 (Bottling)]
  BT Marking devices
Labels (May Subd Geog)
  [HF5773.L3 (Shipment of goods)]
  [NC1002.L3 (Commercial art)]
  UF Etiquettes
        Grade labeling
        Price labels
  BT Grading
        Packaging
        Standardization
        Testing
  SA subdivision Labeling under names of
        products, e.g. Food, Canned—
        Labeling; Hardwoods—Labeling
  NT Beer labels
        Cigar bands and labels
        Cigarette package labels
        Label industry
        Matchbox labels
        Museum labels
        Orange box labels
        Poster stamps
        Seals and labels (Philately)
        Sound recordings—Labels
        Tobacco package labels
        Union label
        Violin—Labels
        Wine labels
  — Law and legislation (May Subd Geog)
      UF Labeling laws
      BT Consumer protection—Law and
            legislation
Labels, Affinity
  USE Proteins—Affinity labeling
Labels, Record
  USE Sound recordings—Labels
Labels, Spin
  USE Spin labels
Labels (Philately)
  USE Seals and labels (Philately)

Labels (Trade-union)
  USE Union label
Labeo
  [QL638.C94]
  BT Cyprinidae
Labeo horai
  USE Rohu
Labeo rohita
  USE Rohu
Labetalol (May Subd Geog)
  UF Hydroxyhydroxymethyl
        phenylpropylaminoethylbenzamide
  BT Adrenergic alpha blockers
        Adrenergic beta blockers
        Ethanolamines
        Hypotensive agents
Labhani language
  USE Lambadi language
Labhart-Willi-Prader syndrome
  USE Prader-Willi syndrome
Labia Palace (Venice, Italy)
  USE Palazzo Labia (Venice, Italy)
Labial frenulum
  UF Frenulum labii
  BT Lips
Labial sounds (Phonetics)
  USE Labiality (Phonetics)
Labiality (Phonetics)
  [P238]
  UF Labial sounds (Phonetics)
        Labialization (Phonetics)
  BT Grammar, Comparative and general—
        Phonology
        Lips
        Phonetics
  SA subdivision Labiality under names of
        languages and groups of languages,
        e.g. English language—Labiality
Labialization (Phonetics)
  USE Labiality (Phonetics)
Labiatae
  USE Lamiaceae
Labidocarpidae
  BT Mites
Labile hypertension
  USE Mild hypertension
Labná Site (Mexico) (Not Subd Geog)
  [F1435.1.L2]
  BT Mexico—Antiquities
Labonte family (Not Subd Geog)
Labor, Casual
  USE Casual labor
Labor, Complicated (May Subd Geog)
  [RG701-721]
  UF Complicated labor (Obstetrics)
        Labor (Obstetrics)—Complications and
          sequelae
  BT Obstetrical emergencies
  NT Anesthesia in obstetrics
        Birth injuries
        Breech delivery
        Episiotomy
        Hemorrhage, Uterine
        Obstetrical extraction
        Placenta praevia
        Still-birth
        Umbilical cord—Prolapse
        Version (Obstetrics)
Labor, Compulsory
  USE Forced labor
Labor, Conscription of
  USE Service, Compulsory non-military
Labor, Division of
  USE Division of labor
Labor, Forced
  USE Forced labor
Labor, Hours of
  USE Hours of labor
Labor, Induced (Obstetrics)
  (May Subd Geog)
  [RG734]

Labor, Induced (Obstetrics)
    (Continued)
    UF Induced labor (Obstetrics)
          Induction of labor (Obstetrics)
          Labor (Obstetrics)—Induction
    BT Obstetrics—Surgery
Labor, Migrant
    USE Migrant labor
Labor, Organized
    USE Trade-unions
Labor, Painless (Obstetrics)
    USE Natural childbirth
Labor, Physiology of
    USE Work—Physiological aspects
Labor, Premature
    [RG649]
    UF Labor, Preterm
          Premature labor
          Preterm labor
    BT Pregnancy—Duration
    NT Infants (Premature)
Labor, Preterm
    USE Labor, Premature
Labor, Right to
    USE Right to labor
Labor, Seasonal
    USE Seasonal labor
Labor, Skilled
    USE Skilled labor
Labor, Unskilled
    USE Unskilled labor
Labor (Obstetrics)
    [RG651-791]
    UF Birth
    BT Obstetrics
          Pregnancy
    RT Childbirth
          Delivery (Obstetrics)
    NT Electrohysterography
          Natural childbirth
          Puerperium
    — Complications and sequelae
        USE Labor, Complicated
    — Induction
        USE Labor, Induced (Obstetrics)
    — Regulation
        [RG655]
        UF Regulation of labor (Obstetrics)
        BT Biological control systems
Labor (The Latin word)
    [PA2350]
    BT Latin language—Etymology
Labor absenteeism
    USE Absenteeism (Labor)
Labor activities, International
    USE International labor activities
Labor agreements
    USE Collective labor agreements
Labor and capital
    USE Industrial relations
Labor and Islam
    USE Islam and labor
Labor and Judaism
    USE Judaism and labor
Labor and laboring classes
    (May Subd Geog)
    [HD4801-HD8942]
    UF Blue collar workers
          Commons (Social order)
          Laborers
          Navvies
          Workers
          Working-classes
          Workingmen
    BT Economics
          Labor economics
          Work
    RT Poor
          Proletariat
          Socialism

    SA *classes of laborers, e.g.* Agricultural
          laborers; Coal miners; Railroads—
          Employees; *and other headings*
          beginning with the word Labor
    NT Alien labor
          Apprentices
          Artisans
          Blacklisting, Labor
          Capital
          Casual labor
          Children—Employment
          Church and labor
          Church work with laboring classes
          Compagnonnages
          Consumers' leagues
          Contract labor
          Convict labor
          Division of labor
          Domestics
          Employee rights
          Employees, Probationary
          Employees, Rating of
          Employees, Temporary
          Employment of men
          Factory system
          Forced labor
          Friendly societies
          Guilds
          Home labor
          Hours of labor
          Industrial relations
          Job satisfaction
          Labor bureaus
          Labor classification
          Libraries and labor
          Manual labor
          Migrant labor
          Native labor
          Occupations
          Occupations, Dangerous
          Padrone system
          Part-time employment
          Peasantry
          Peonage
          Quality of work life
          Religion and labor
          Right to labor
          Seasonal labor
          Serfdom
          Skilled labor
          Slave labor
          Slavery
          Sweating system
          Syndicalism
          Textile workers
          Trade-unions
          Unskilled labor
          Veterans—Employment
          Welfare work in industry
          Women—Employment
          Women artisans
          Work ethic
          Workaholics
          Workers' monuments
          Workers' theater
          Working class whites
          Working class women
          Working-men's clubs
          Working-men's gardens
          Working-women's clubs
          Youth—Employment
    — 1914-
    — 1970-
    — Accidents
        USE Industrial accidents
    — Authors
        USE Authors, Laboring class
    — Books and reading
        [Z1039.L3]
    — Charitable contributions
    — Child labor

        USE Children—Employment
    — Congresses
        [HD4813]
        UF Labor congresses
    — Discipline
        USE Labor discipline
    — Dwellings *(May Subd Geog)*
        Here are entered works on the architecture,
        construction, equipment, etc. of dwellings for the
        working classes.
        UF Working-men's dwellings
        BT Architecture, Domestic
             Dwellings
        NT Agricultural laborers—Housing
             Industrial housing
             Labor camps
             Lodging-houses
             Slums
    — Education *(May Subd Geog)*
        [LC5001-LC5060]
        UF Education of workers
        NT Labor and laboring classes—
             Scholarships, fellowships, etc.
             Workers' travel programs
    — Education (Higher) *(May Subd Geog)*
    — Family relationships
    — Hospital care *(May Subd Geog)*
        BT Hospital care
    — Insurance
        USE Insurance, Accident
              Insurance, Health
              Insurance, Unemployment
              Old age pensions
    — Jews
        USE Jews—Employment
    — Life skills guides
    — Medical care *(May Subd Geog)*
        [RC963]
        BT Employee fringe benefits
        RT Welfare work in industry
    — Medical examinations
        [HD7261]
        RT Medicine, Industrial
    — Nutrition
        [TX361.W6]
    — Periodicals
        NT Employees' magazines, handbooks,
             etc.
    — Physical training
    — Political activity
        BT Politics, Practical
    — Religious life
        [BV4593]
        NT Priest workers
    — Research *(May Subd Geog)*
        UF Labor research
    — Scholarships, fellowships, etc.
        (May Subd Geog)
        UF Labor scholarships
        BT Labor and laboring classes—
             Education
    — Songs and music
        [M1664-M1665.L3 (Political
          songs)]
        [M1977.L3 (Collections)]
        [M1978.L3 (Single songs)]
        [ML3780 (History and criticism)]
        RT Work-songs
        SA Lumbermen—Songs and music;
             Miners—Songs and music; *and*
             similar headings
        NT Lumbermen—Songs and music
             Miners—Songs and music
    — Statistics
        UF Labor statistics
    — Wages
        USE Wages
    — England
        NT Luddites
    — France
        NT Priest workers

— Great Britain
— — History
— — — 19th century
    NT Chartism
— United States
— — 1914-
    [HD8072]
    NT Industrial security program
        (United States)
— — 1970-
Labor and laboring classes, Writings of the
  USE Laboring class writings
Labor and laboring classes in art
  [N8219.L2]
  UF Work and workers in art
Labor and laboring classes in literature
  BT Economics in literature
    Social problems in literature
  RT Authors, Laboring class
  NT Domestic drama
    Proletariat in literature
Labor and laboring classes in motion pictures
  [PN1995.9.L28]
  BT Moving-pictures
Labor and laboring classes in television
  UF Labor and laboring classes on
    television
  BT Television
Labor and laboring classes on television
  USE Labor and laboring classes in television
Labor and libraries
  USE Libraries and labor
Labor and religion
  USE Religion and labor
Labor and state
  USE Labor policy
Labor and the church
  USE Church and labor
Labor arbitration
  USE Arbitration, Industrial
Labor attachés *(May Subd Geog)*
  UF Attachés
  BT Diplomatic and consular service
Labor attachés, American, [etc.]
  (May Subd Geog)
Labor bank movement
  USE Banks and banking, Trade-union
Labor banks
  USE Banks and banking, Trade-union
Labor bureaus *(May Subd Geog)*
  [HD4831-5]
  UF Labor departments
    Labor ministries
  BT Labor and laboring classes
Labor camps *(May Subd Geog)*
  [HD7290]
  Here are entered works on camps constructed by
  public or private agencies for the housing of non-
  compulsory laborers.
  UF Construction camps
  BT Camps
    Labor and laboring classes—Dwellings
  NT Agricultural laborers—Housing
Labor classification
  Here are entered books on the rationale of labor
  categories, e.g. skilled, semi-skilled, unskilled, etc.
  BT Labor and laboring classes
Labor colonies
  USE Agricultural colonies
Labor congresses
  USE Labor and laboring classes—
    Congresses
Labor conscription
  USE Service, Compulsory non-military
Labor contract *(May Subd Geog)*
  UF Employment contract
  BT Contracts
    Hire
    Industrial relations
    Labor laws and legislation
  RT Independent contractors

  NT Absenteeism (Labor)—Law and
    legislation
    Collective labor agreements
    Contract system (Labor)
    Employees, Dismissal of—Law and
    legislation
    Employees, Probationary
    Employees, Reinstatement of—Law
    and legislation
    Employees, Relocation of—Law and
    legislation
    Employees, Resignation of
    Employees, Resignation of—Law and
    legislation
    Employees, Suspension of—Law and
    legislation
    Employees, Transfer of—Law and
    legislation
    Temporary employment—Law and
    legislation
    Wages—Law and legislation
    Yellow dog contract
— Conflict of laws
  USE Conflict of laws—Labor contract
Labor contractors *(May Subd Geog)*
  UF Contractors, Labor
  BT Contractors
    Employment agencies
Labor costs *(May Subd Geog)*
  UF Costs, Labor
  BT Costs, Industrial
  NT Employee fringe benefits
    Wages
Labor courts *(May Subd Geog)*
  Here are entered works on permanent courts deal-
  ing with litigations in labor questions, including
  procedure before such courts.
  UF Courts, Industrial
    Courts, Labor
    Industrial courts
  BT Administrative courts
    Courts of special jurisdiction
    Labor disputes
    Labor laws and legislation
  RT Arbitration, Industrial
  NT Limitation of actions (Labor law)
Labor Day *(May Subd Geog)*
  [HD7791]
  BT Holidays
  RT May Day (Labor holiday)
  NT Labor Day Mass
Labor Day Mass
  [BX2015.9.J6]
  BT Church and labor
    Labor Day
Labor departments
  USE Labor bureaus
Labor discipline *(May Subd Geog)*
  UF Discipline, Industrial
    Discipline, Labor
    Industrial discipline
    Labor and laboring classes—Discipline
  BT Discipline
    Personnel management
  NT Employee rules
    Trade-unions—Discipline
— **Law and legislation** *(May Subd Geog)*
  BT Labor laws and legislation
Labor disputes *(May Subd Geog)*
  UF Disputes, Labor
    Industrial disputes
  BT Industrial relations
    Labor laws and legislation
  NT Boycott
    Labor courts
    Labor injunctions
    Picketing—Law and legislation
    Strikes and lockouts
    Strikes and lockouts—Law and
    legislation
    Trade-unions—Jurisdictional disputes

— **Criminal provisions**
— **Wales**
  NT Newport Uprising, Wales, 1839
Labor economics *(May Subd Geog)*
  BT Economics
  NT Human capital
    Labor and laboring classes
Labor exchanges
  USE Employment agencies
Labor force
  USE Labor supply
Labor force participation
  USE Labor supply
Labor grievances
  USE Grievance procedures
Labor incentives
  USE Incentives in industry
Labor injunctions *(May Subd Geog)*
  UF Injunctions, Labor
  BT Injunctions
    Labor disputes
    Labor laws and legislation
Labor inspection *(May Subd Geog)*
  BT Labor laws and legislation
  RT Factory inspection
— **Law and legislation** *(May Subd Geog)*
  BT Labor laws and legislation
Labor journalism
  USE Journalism, Labor
Labor law, Maritime
  USE Merchant seamen—Legal status, laws,
    etc.
Labor laws and legislation *(May Subd Geog)*
  UF Law, Industrial
    Law, Labor
  BT Industrial laws and legislation
    Social legislation
  SA *subdivision* Legal status, laws, etc.
    under categories of professionals
    and employees, e.g. Actors—Legal
    status, laws, etc.; Aircraft industry
    workers—Legal status, laws, etc.;
    Construction industry—Employees
    —Legal status, laws, etc.
  NT Alien labor
    Americans—Employment—Foreign
      countries—Law and legislation
    Blacks—Employment—Law and
      legislation
    Boycott—Law and legislation
    Children—Employment—Law and
      legislation
    Confidential communications—
      Personnel records
    Criminal syndicalism
    Discrimination in employment—Law
      and legislation
    Employee assistance programs—Law
      and legislation
    Employee-management relations in
      government—Law and legislation
    Employee rules
    Employee selection—Law and
      legislation
    Employees, Dismissal of—Law and
      legislation
    Employees, Rating of—Law and
      legislation
    Employment interviewing—Law and
      legislation
    Employment stabilization—Law and
      legislation
    Employment tests—Law and
      legislation
    Equal pay for equal work—Law and
      legislation
    Four-day week—Law and legislation
    Freedom of movement
    Handicapped—Employment—Law and
      legislation
    Home labor—Law and legislation

Labor laws and legislation (Continued)
    Hours of labor—Law and legislation
    Hours of labor, Flexible—Law and legislation
    Incentives in industry—Law and legislation
    Indians of North America—Employment—Law and legislation
    Industrial hygiene—Law and legislation
    Industrial management—Employee participation—Law and legislation
    Job evaluation—Law and legislation
    Job security—Law and legislation
    Job sharing—Law and legislation
    Labor contract
    Labor courts
    Labor discipline—Law and legislation
    Labor disputes
    Labor injunctions
    Labor inspection
    Labor inspection—Law and legislation
    Layoff systems—Law and legislation
    Leave of absence—Law and legislation
    Limitation of actions (Labor law)
    Management—Employee participation—Law and legislation
    Maternal and infant welfare—Law and legislation
    Maternity leave—Law and legislation
    Military unions—Law and legislation
    Mining law
    Mothers—Employment—Law and legislation
    Open and closed shop—Law and legislation
    Palestinian Arabs—Employment—Law and legislation
    Part-time employment—Law and legislation
    Pension trusts—Law and legislation
    Performance awards—Law and legislation
    Pregnant women—Employment—Law and legislation
    Production standards—Law and legislation
    Public service employment—Law and legislation
    Recruiting of employees—Law and legislation
    Retirement, Mandatory—Law and legislation
    Reverse discrimination in employment—Law and legislation
    Seniority, Employee—Law and legislation
    Sex discrimination in employment—Law and legislation
    Sheltered workshops—Law and legislation
    Sick leave—Law and legislation
    Summer employment—Law and legislation
    Sunday legislation
    Supervisors, Dismissal of—Law and legislation
    Supplementary employment—Law and legislation
    Temporary employment—Law and legislation
    Trade adjustment assistance—Law and legislation
    Trade-unions—Law and legislation
    Truck system
    Unfair labor practices
    Vacations, Employee—Law and legislation
    Wages—Law and legislation
    Welfare recipients—Employment—Law and legislation

    Women—Employment—Law and legislation
    Workers' compensation—Law and legislation
    Works councils—Law and legislation
    Youth—Employment—Law and legislation
  — **Cases**
  — **Codification**
  — Colonies
    USE Labor laws and legislation, Colonial
  — **Compliance costs**
  — Conflict of laws
    USE Conflict of laws—Labor laws and legislation
  — **Criminal provisions**
  — **Digests**
  — **Forms**
  — **Interpretation and construction**
  — **Language**
  — **Legal research**
  — **Popular works**
  — **Research** (May Subd Geog)
  — **Terms and phrases**
  — **Trial practice**
  — ₍country₎
  — — Colonies
  — **United States**
    NT Work Incentive Program—Law and legislation

Labor laws and legislation, Colonial
    Here are entered general and comparative works only. Works on labor laws and legislation of the colonies of an individual country are entered under the heading Labor laws and legislation with subdivision ₍country₎—Colonies. Works dealing with a specific colony are entered under the same heading subdivided by the name of the colony.
    UF Colonial labor laws and legislation
        Colonies—Labor laws and legislation
        Labor laws and legislation—Colonies
    RT Native labor
    NT Contract labor

Labor laws and legislation, International
    ₍HD7801-HD7809₎
    Here are entered works on labor laws adopted or proposed by two or more countries jointly by convention or treaty.
    UF International labor laws and legislation
    BT International law

Labor laws and legislation (Canon law)
Labor laws and legislation (Islamic law)
Labor laws and legislation (Jewish law)
    BT Judaism and labor

Labor laws and legislation (Roman law)
    BT Roman law
    NT Colonatus (Roman law)

Labor literature (May Subd Geog)
    Here are entered works on publications about labor and laboring classes including the labor movement in general.
    UF Literature, Labor
        Literature on labor and laboring classes
    BT Press, Labor
        Social science literature
        Trade-unions

Labor-management committees
    (May Subd Geog)
    ₍HD6490.L33₎
    UF Union-management committees
    BT Committees
        Industrial relations
        Management—Employee participation
    RT Management committees
        Works councils

Labor-management relations
    USE Industrial relations

Labor market
    USE Labor supply

Labor market research
    USE Labor supply—Research

Labor ministries
    USE Labor bureaus

Labor mobility (May Subd Geog)
    UF Mobility
    BT Migrant labor
        Migration, Internal
    RT Labor supply
        Labor turnover
    NT Employees, Relocation of
        Employees, Resignation of
        Unemployment, Frictional
        Wages—Effect of labor mobility on

Labor negotiations
    USE Arbitration, Industrial
        Collective bargaining

Labor organizations
    USE Guilds
        Trade-unions

Labor organizing
    USE Trade-unions—Organizing

Labor output
    USE Labor productivity

Labor participation in management
    USE Management—Employee participation

Labor passports (May Subd Geog)
    Here are entered works on identification papers, such as the German Arbeitsbuch, that contain training and employment information on workers, are a condition for employment, and facilitate state control of the labor supply.
    UF Employees, Identification of
        Identification papers for employees
    BT Personnel records

Labor policy (May Subd Geog)
    UF Labor and state
        Public labor policy
        State and labor
    BT Economic policy
        Industry and state
    NT Export processing zones
        Manpower policy

Labor presentation (Obstetrics)
    USE Fetal presentation

Labor press
    USE Press, Labor

Labor productivity (May Subd Geog)
    Here are entered works on the units produced by a worker in relation to a given effort or unit of time expended.
    UF Labor output
        Productivity of labor
    BT Industrial productivity
    RT Capital productivity
        Machinery in industry
        Productivity bargaining
    SA subdivision Labor productivity under types of industries, occupations, and processes, e.g. Construction industry—Labor productivity; Coal mines and mining—Labor productivity
    NT Learning curve (Industrial engineering)
        Paydays
        Production standards
        Wages and labor productivity
  — Accounting
    USE Productivity accounting
  — **Effect of inflation on**
    BT Inflation (Finance)
  — **Nutritional aspects**

Labor productivity and wages
    USE Wages and labor productivity

Labor relations
    USE Industrial relations

Labor research
    USE Labor and laboring classes—Research

Labor rest homes (May Subd Geog)
    UF Rest homes, Labor

BT Health resorts, watering-places, etc.
    Rest homes
    Trade-unions
    Vacations, Employee
    Welfare work in industry
Labor scholarships
  USE Labor and laboring classes—
        Scholarships, fellowships, etc.
Labor service *(May Subd Geog)*
    Here are entered works on national or community
organized voluntary labor. Works on compulsory
labor service are entered under Service, Compulsory
non-military.
  UF Service, Labor
  BT Service, Compulsory non-military
    Unemployed
  SA *names of individual agencies*
      responsible for voluntary labor
      service
  NT Indians of Central America—Labor
      service
    Indians of Mexico—Labor service
Labor statistics
  USE Labor and laboring classes—Statistics
    Labor supply—Statistics
Labor supply *(May Subd Geog)*
  [HD5701-HD5852]
  UF Labor force
    Labor force participation
    Labor market
  BT Employment (Economic theory)
    Full employment policies
    Supply-side economics
  RT Human capital
    Labor mobility
    Manpower
    Manpower policy
  SA *subdivision* Supply and demand *under*
      classes of professional persons, e.g.
      Allied health personnel—Supply
      and demand; Teachers—Supply and
      demand
  NT Foreign trade and employment
    Free choice of employment
    Hard-core unemployed
    Investments, Foreign, and employment
    Job vacancies
    Public service employment
    Shift-share analysis
    Underemployment
    Unemployed
    Unemployment
    Work sharing
    Youth—Employment
— **Effect of automation on**
  [HD6331]
  BT Automation
— **Effect of education on**
  BT Education
— **Effect of energy costs on**
  BT Power resources—Costs
— **Effect of income maintenance programs on**
  BT Income maintenance programs
— **Effect of taxation on**
  BT Taxation
— **Effect of technological innovations on**
  [HD6331]
  BT Technological innovations
  RT Unemployment, Technological
— Forecasting
  USE Employment forecasting
— Information storage and retrieval systems
  USE Information storage and retrieval
      systems—Labor supply
— **Regional disparities**
  BT Regional economic disparities
    Shift-share analysis
— **Religious aspects** *(May Subd Geog)*
  BT Church and labor
    Religion and labor

— **Research** *(May Subd Geog)*
  UF Labor market research
— **Statistics**
  UF Labor statistics
Labor theater
  USE Workers' theater
Labor theory of value *(May Subd Geog)*
  [HB206]
  BT Marxian economics
    Value
  RT Surplus value
Labor turnover *(May Subd Geog)*
  [HF5549]
  UF Employee turnover
    Turnover of labor
  BT Personnel management
  RT Labor mobility
  SA *subdivision* Officials and employees—
      Turnover *under names of countries,*
      cities, etc., and under individual
      government departments, agencies,
      etc.
  NT Employees, Resignation of
    Employment stabilization
    Recruiting of employees
    United States—Officials and
      employees—Turnover
Labor-unions
  USE Trade-unions
Labor unions, Catholic
  USE Trade-unions, Catholic
Labor Zionism *(May Subd Geog)*
  UF Socialist Zionism
  BT Zionism
Labor Zionists *(May Subd Geog)*
  BT Zionists
Laboratories *(May Subd Geog)*
  [Q183]
  UF Laboratories, Scientific
    Research buildings
    Science laboratories
    Scientific laboratories
  NT Fishery research stations
    Forestry laboratories
    Printing laboratories
    Robotics laboratories
— Construction
  USE Laboratories—Design and
      construction
— **Design and construction**
  UF Laboratories—Construction
— **Furniture, equipment, etc.**
  [Q183]
— **Law and legislation** *(May Subd Geog)*
— **Maintenance and repair**
— **Management**
  NT Supervisors, Laboratory
— **Michigan**
  NT Roll Building (Battle Creek, Mich.)
Laboratories, Aerodynamical
  USE Aeronautical laboratories
Laboratories, Aeronautical
  USE Aeronautical laboratories
Laboratories, Agricultural
  USE Agricultural laboratories
Laboratories, Agricultural chemistry
  USE Agricultural chemistry laboratories
Laboratories, Anatomical
  USE Anatomical laboratories
Laboratories, Bacteriological
  USE Bacteriological laboratories
Laboratories, Biological
  USE Biological laboratories
Laboratories, Botanical
  USE Botanical laboratories
Laboratories, Chemical
  USE Chemical laboratories
Laboratories, Chemical engineering
  USE Chemical engineering laboratories
Laboratories, Crime
  USE Crime laboratories

Laboratories, Curriculum
  USE Instructional materials centers
Laboratories, Dental
  USE Dental laboratories
Laboratories, Electric
  USE Electric laboratories
Laboratories, Electronics
  USE Electronics laboratories
Laboratories, Engineering
  USE Engineering laboratories
Laboratories, Environmental
  USE Environmental laboratories
Laboratories, Forestry
  USE Forestry laboratories
Laboratories, Hot (Radioactive substances)
  USE Hot laboratories (Radioactive
      substances)
Laboratories, Industrial
  USE Engineering laboratories
    Research, Industrial—Laboratories
Laboratories, Industrial research
  USE Research, Industrial—Laboratories
Laboratories, Language
  USE Language laboratories
Laboratories, Mathematics
  USE Mathematics laboratories
Laboratories, Mechanical
  USE Engineering laboratories
Laboratories, Medical
  USE Medical laboratories
Laboratories, Metallurgical
  USE Metallurgical laboratories
Laboratories, Microbiological
  USE Microbiological laboratories
Laboratories, Nuclear energy research
  USE Nuclear energy—Research—
      Laboratories
Laboratories, Optical
  USE Optical laboratories
Laboratories, Pathological
  USE Pathological laboratories
Laboratories, Physical
  USE Physical laboratories
Laboratories, Physiological
  USE Physiological laboratories
Laboratories, Radiochemical
  USE Radiochemical laboratories
Laboratories, Robotics
  USE Robotics laboratories
Laboratories, Scientific
  USE Laboratories
Laboratories, Sensory evaluation
  USE Sensory evaluation—Laboratories
Laboratories, Sound
  USE Sound laboratories
Laboratories, Technical
  USE Engineering laboratories
    Research, Industrial—Laboratories
Laboratories, Testing
  USE Testing laboratories
Laboratories, Textile
  USE Textile laboratories
Laboratories, Veterinary
  USE Veterinary laboratories
Laboratory-acquired infection
  USE Laboratory infections
Laboratory animal technicians
  UF Animal technicians
    Technicians, Animal
    Technicians, Laboratory animal
  BT Biomedical technicians
    Laboratory technicians
Laboratory animals *(May Subd Geog)*
  [QL55]
  [SF77]
  UF Animals, Experimental
    Animals, Laboratory
    Animals in research
    Experimental animals

Laboratory animals *(Continued)*
    BT Animal culture
          Physiology, Comparative
          Vivisection
          Working animals
          Zoology
    RT Animal experimentation
    SA Dogs as laboratory animals; Hamsters
          as laboratory animals; *and similar*
          headings
    NT Animal models in research
          Brattleboro rat
          Diseases—Animal models
          Dogs as laboratory animals
          Guinea pigs as laboratory animals
          Hamsters as laboratory animals
          Invertebrates—Cultures and culture
            media
          Nude mouse
  — Feeding and feeds
  — Housing
      BT Animal housing
  — Law and legislation *(May Subd Geog)*
Laboratory diagnosis
  USE Diagnosis, Laboratory
Laboratory fertilization
  USE Fertilization in vitro
Laboratory infections *(May Subd Geog)*
    UF Laboratory-acquired infection
    BT Infection
          Occupational diseases
Laboratory manuals
  USE *subdivision* Laboratory manuals *under*
          scientific and technical headings for
          workbooks containing concise
          background information and
          directions for performing work,
          including experiments, in the
          laboratory, e.g. Cancer—Diagnosis
          —Laboratory manuals; Radio—
          Laboratory manuals
Laboratory medicine
  USE Diagnosis, Laboratory
Laboratory notebooks *(May Subd Geog)*
    [Q180.58]
    UF Notebooks, Laboratory
    BT Notebooks
Laboratory schools *(May Subd Geog)*
    [LB2153-LB2155]
    UF Campus schools
          Demonstration schools
          Model schools
          Schools, Demonstration
          Schools, Laboratory
          Schools, Model
    BT Schools
    RT Demonstration centers in education
  — Evaluation
      BT Educational surveys
Laboratory supervisors
  USE Supervisors, Laboratory
Laboratory technicians *(May Subd Geog)*
    UF Technicians, Laboratory
    BT Technologists
    NT Chemical laboratory technicians
          Dental technicians
          Laboratory animal technicians
          Medical technologists
Labored breathing
  USE Dyspnea
Laborers
  USE *classes of laborers, e.g.* Agricultural
          laborers; Coal miners; Railroads—
          Employees
          Labor and laboring classes
          Unskilled labor
Laborers in the vineyard (Parable)
    [BT378.L3]
Laboring class authors
  USE Authors, Laboring class

Laboring class whites
  USE Working class whites
Laboring class women
  USE Working class women
Laboring class writings *(May Subd Geog)*
    UF Labor and laboring classes, Writings of
          the
          Workers' writings
    BT Authors, Laboring class
          Literature
  — Awards
      NT Schweizer Arbeiterliteraturpreis
Laboring class writings, American
  (May Subd Geog)
    UF American laboring class writings
    BT American literature
Laboring class writings, Bulgarian
  (May Subd Geog)
    UF Bulgarian laboring class writings
    BT Bulgarian literature
Laboring class writings, Canadian
  (May Subd Geog)
    UF Canadian laboring class writings
    BT Canadian literature
Laboring class writings, Chinese
  (May Subd Geog)
    [PL2278.5.L33 (History)]
    [PL2515.5.L33 (Collections)]
    UF Chinese laboring class writings
    BT Chinese literature
Laboring class writings, Cuban
  (May Subd Geog)
    UF Cuban laboring class writings
    BT Cuban literature
Laboring class writings, Czech
  (May Subd Geog)
    UF Czech laboring class writings
    BT Czech literature
Laboring class writings, Danish
  (May Subd Geog)
    UF Danish laboring class writings
    BT Danish literature
Laboring class writings, English
  (May Subd Geog)
    UF English laboring class writings
    BT English literature
Laboring class writings, Finnish
  (May Subd Geog)
    UF Finnish laboring class writings
    BT Finnish literature
Laboring class writings, French
  (May Subd Geog)
    UF French laboring class writings
    BT French literature
Laboring class writings, German
  (May Subd Geog)
    UF German laboring class writings
    BT German literature
  — Swiss authors
      USE Laboring class writings, Swiss
          (German)
Laboring class writings, Japanese
  (May Subd Geog)
    UF Japanese laboring class writings
    BT Japanese literature
Laboring class writings, Korean
  (May Subd Geog)
    UF Korean laboring class writings
    BT Korean literature
Laboring class writings, Norwegian
  (May Subd Geog)
    UF Norwegian laboring class writings
    BT Norwegian literature
Laboring class writings, Polish
  (May Subd Geog)
    UF Polish laboring class writings
    BT Polish literature
Laboring class writings, Portuguese
  (May Subd Geog)
    UF Portuguese laboring class writings
    BT Portuguese literature

Laboring class writings, Scandinavian
  (May Subd Geog)
    UF Scandinavian laboring class writings
    BT Scandinavian literature
Laboring class writings, Slavic
  (May Subd Geog)
    UF Slavic laboring class writings
    BT Slavic literature
Laboring class writings, Swedish
  (May Subd Geog)
    UF Swedish laboring class writings
    BT Swedish literature
Laboring class writings, Swiss (German)
  (May Subd Geog)
    UF Laboring class writings, German—
          Swiss authors
    BT Swiss literature (German)
Laboring class writings, Venezuelan
  (May Subd Geog)
    UF Venezuelan laboring class writings
    BT Venezuelan literature
Laboulbeniales
    [QK623.L3]
    BT Ascomycetes
Labour . . .
  USE *subject headings beginning with the*
          word Labor
Labrador (Nfld.)
Labrador dog
  USE Labrador retriever
Labrador duck
    UF Camptorhynchus labradorius
    BT Ducks
Labrador retriever
    [SF429.L3]
    UF Black Labrador retriever
          Labrador dog
          Yellow Labrador retriever
    BT Dog breeds
          Retrievers
    NT Greff (Dog)
Labrador Sea
    BT North Atlantic Ocean
Labranche family *(Not Subd Geog)*
Labranda (Ancient city) *(Not Subd Geog)*
    UF Labraunda (Ancient city)
          Labraynda (Ancient city)
    BT Cities and towns, Ruined, extinct, etc.
          —Turkey
          Turkey—Antiquities
Labras Lake Site (Ill.)
    BT Illinois—Antiquities
Labraunda (Ancient city)
  USE Labranda (Ancient city)
Labraynda (Ancient city)
  USE Labranda (Ancient city)
Labrets
    [GN419.L]
Labridae
  USE Wrasses
Labrisomidae *(May Subd Geog)*
    BT Perciformes
Labritermes
    [QL529.3.T4]
    BT Termitidae
Labrosaurus
  USE Allosaurus
Labrus
    [QL638.L12]
    BT Wrasses
Labrus auratus
  USE Pagrosomus auratus
Labrus berggylta
  USE Ballan wrasse
Labrus bergylta
  USE Ballan wrasse
Labské pískovce (Czechoslovakia and
  Germany)
  USE Elbe Sandstone Rocks (Czechoslovakia
          and Germany)

Laburnine
  USE Cytisine
Labuscagne family
  USE Labuschagne family
Labuschagne family *(Not Subd Geog)*
  UF De La Buscagne family
      Labuscagne family
Labwor (African people)
  ⌐DT433.245.L3⌐
  BT Ethnology—Uganda
Labyrinth (Ear)
  ⌐QL948 (Comparative anatomy)⌐
  ⌐QM507 (Human anatomy)⌐
  ⌐QP461 (Physiology)⌐
  UF Inner ear
      Internal ear
  BT Ear
      Hearing
  NT Auditory meatus, Internal
      Cochlea
      Fistula, Labyrinthine
      Vestibular apparatus
  — Blood-vessels
  — Diseases *(May Subd Geog)*
    NT Ménière's disease
        Otosclerosis
        Vertigo
  — Wounds and injuries
Labyrinth fishes *(May Subd Geog)*
  ⌐SF458.L26 (Aquarium fishes)⌐
  UF Anabantoidei
      Labyrinthici
  BT Perciformes
  NT Anabantidae
      Belontiidae
Labyrinth gardens
  USE Maze gardens
Labyrinthici
  USE Labyrinth fishes
Labyrinthine fistula
  USE Fistula, Labyrinthine
Labyrinthine fluids
  BT Body fluids
  NT Perilymph
Labyrinthine hydrops
  USE Ménière's disease
Labyrinths
  NT Hiding-places (Secret chambers, etc.)
      Maze gardens
      Maze puzzles
      Maze tests
Labyrinths in art
Lac
  ⌐HD9769.L3-HD9769.L33 (Trade)⌐
  ⌐SF561 (Animal culture)⌐
  ⌐TP938 (Varnishes)⌐
  RT Shellac
  NT Lac industry
      Laccol
Lac de Bienne (Switzerland)
  USE Biel, Lake of (Switzerland)
Lac de Constance
  USE Constance, Lake of
Lac de Genève (Switzerland and France)
  USE Geneva, Lake (Switzerland and
      France)
Lac de Locarno (Italy and Switzerland)
  USE Maggiore, Lake (Italy and
      Switzerland)
Lac de Morat (Switzerland)
  USE Morat, Lake of (Switzerland)
Lac de Neuchâtel (Switzerland)
  USE Neuchâtel, Lake of (Switzerland)
Lac de Vassivière (France)
  USE Vassivière Lake (France)
Lac des quatre cantons (Switzerland)
  USE Lucerne Lake (Switzerland)
Lac d'Hallwil (Switzerland)
  USE Hallwil, Lake (Switzerland)
Lac Domène (Switzerland)
  USE Schwarzsee (Switzerland : Lake)

Lac industry *(May Subd Geog)*
  ⌐HD9769.L3-33⌐
  BT Lac
Lac-insects
  ⌐QL527.K44⌐
  UF Kerridae
      Kerriidae
      Lac scales
      Lacciferidae
      Tachardiidae
  BT Insects
      Scale-insects
Lac Kivu (Rwanda and Zaire)
  USE Kivu, Lake (Rwanda and Zaire)
Lac Laflamme (Québec)
  USE Laflamme Lake (Québec)
Lac Léman (Switzerland and France)
  USE Geneva, Lake (Switzerland and
      France)
Lac Léopold II (Zaire)
  USE Mai-Ndombe, Lake (Zaire)
Lac Mai-Ndombe (Zaire)
  USE Mai-Ndombe, Lake (Zaire)
Lac Majeur (Italy and Switzerland)
  USE Maggiore, Lake (Italy and
      Switzerland)
Lac Mégantic (Québec)
  USE Mégantic, Lake (Québec)
Lac Mistassini (Québec)
  USE Mistassini Lake (Québec)
Lac Noir (Switzerland)
  USE Schwarzsee (Switzerland : Lake)
Lac-Saint-Jean (Québec)
  USE Saint John, Lake (Québec)
Lac scales
  USE Lac-insects
Lac Tanganika
  USE Tanganyika, Lake
Lac Tchad
  USE Chad, Lake
Lacandon Indians
  ⌐F1221.L2 (Mexico)⌐
  ⌐F1465.2.L2 (Guatemala)⌐
  UF Xoquinoe Indians
  BT Indians of Central America
      Indians of Mexico
      Mayas
Lacandon language
  ⌐PM3916⌐
  UF Lakandon language
  BT Indians of Mexico—Languages
      Mayan languages
LACAP
  USE Latin American Cooperative
      Acquisitions Program
Laccase
  ⌐QK898.L23 (Botanical chemistry)⌐
  UF Diphenol oxidase
  BT Oxidoreductases
Lacciferidae
  USE Lac-insects
Laccol
  ⌐HD9679.L3-HD9679.L33 (Trade)⌐
  ⌐SF561 (Animal culture)⌐
  BT Lac
Laccoliths
  ⌐QE611⌐
  BT Intrusions (Geology)
Lace and lace making *(May Subd Geog)*
  ⌐HD9933 (Trade)⌐
  ⌐NK9400-NK9499 (Fine arts)⌐
  ⌐TS1782 (Manufacture)⌐
  ⌐TT800-TT805 (Needlework)⌐
    Here are entered works on lace or the making of
  lace. Works on the use of lace as a material of handi-
  craft are entered under Lace craft.
  UF Tulle embroidery

  BT Arts and crafts movement
      Crocheting
      Fancy work
      Needlework
      Textile industry
      Weaving
  NT Battenberg lace
      Bobbin lace
      Doilies
      Hairpin lace
      Irish crochet lace
      Knitted lace
      Lace makers
      Macramé
      Needlepoint lace
      Raschel knitting machines
      Tatting
  — Patterns
  — Private collections
Lace and lace making, Baroque
  (May Subd Geog)
  UF Baroque lace and lace making
Lace and lace making, Victorian
  (May Subd Geog)
  UF Victorian lace and lace making
Lace bobbins *(May Subd Geog)*
  ⌐TT800⌐
  UF Bobbins (Lace)
  BT Bobbin lace
Lace bugs *(May Subd Geog)*
  ⌐QL523.T5⌐
  UF Tingidae
      Tingididae
      Tingitidae
  BT Hemiptera
  USE Alloeoderes
  NT Corythuca
Lace craft *(May Subd Geog)*
  ⌐TT810⌐
    Here are entered works on the use of lace as a
  material of handicraft. Works on lace or the making
  of lace are entered under Lace and lace making.
  UF Lacecraft
  BT Handicraft
Lace industry *(May Subd Geog)*
  ⌐HD9933⌐
Lace makers *(May Subd Geog)*
  BT Lace and lace making
  NT Wages—Lace makers
      Women lace makers
Lace makers, Women
  USE Women lace makers
Lacecraft
  USE Lace craft
Lacedaemon (Ancient city)
  USE Sparta (Ancient city)
Lacerta
  ⌐QL666.L255⌐
  BT Lacertidae
  NT Lacerta agilis
      Lacerta lepida
      Lacerta sicula
      Lacerta vivipara
Lacerta agilis
  ⌐QL666.L255⌐
  UF European fence lizard
      Fence lizard, European
  BT Lacerta
Lacerta lepida
  ⌐QL666.L255⌐
  UF Jeweled lacerta
  BT Lacerta
Lacerta monticola
  ⌐QL666.L255⌐
Lacerta sicula
  ⌐QL666.L255⌐
  BT Lacerta
Lacerta viridis
  ⌐QL666.L255⌐
Lacerta vivipara
  ⌐QL666.L255⌐

Lacerta vivipara *(Continued)*
  UF Viviparous lacerta
  BT Lacerta
Lacertidae
  ⌈QL666.L255⌉
  BT Lizards
  NT Algyroides
      Eremias
      Ichnotropis
      Lacerta
      Nucras
      Psammodromus
      Zootoco
Lacertilia
  USE Lizards
Lacewing flies
  ⌈QL513⌉
  BT Neuroptera
  NT Chrysopidae
      Hemerobiidae
Lacey family
  USE Lacy family
Lach (Legendary character)
  USE Lech (Legendary character)
Lachance family *(Not Subd Geog)*
Lachesilla
  ⌈QL515.2.P73⌉
  BT Pseudocaeciliidae
Lachesis
  ⌈QL666.O69⌉
  BT Pit-vipers
      Viperidae
Lachesis (Greek deity)
  BT Goddesses, Greek
Lachesis muta
  ⌈QL666.O69⌉
  UF Bushmaster
      Mapepire
      Sirocucu
Lachine Canal (Québec)
  UF Canal de Lachine (Québec)
  BT Canals—Québec (Province)
Lachine Canal Strike, Québec, 1843
  UF Canal de Lachine, Grève de, Québec, 1843
  BT Canal construction workers—Québec (Province)
      Strikes and lockouts—Canal construction workers—Québec (Province)
      Strikes and lockouts—Québec (Province)
Lachlan River (N.S.W.)
  BT Rivers—Australia
Lachneidae
  USE Lasiocampidae
Lachnidae
  USE Aphididae
Lachnosterna
  USE Phyllophaga
Lachnosterna fusca
  USE Phyllophaga fusca
Lachnus
  ⌈QL527.A64⌉
  BT Aphididae
  NT Lachnus persicae
Lachnus persicae
  ⌈QL527.A64⌉
  BT Lachnus
Lachrymal organs
  USE Lacrimal organs
Lack family *(Not Subd Geog)*
Lack of self (Psychology)
  USE Selflessness (Psychology)
Lackawanna River (Pa.)
  BT Rivers—Pennsylvania
Lackwood family
  USE Lockwood family
Lacock family *(Not Subd Geog)*
  RT Laycock family

Lacoma River (Haiti)
  USE Dispute River (Haiti)
Lacomat River (Haiti)
  USE Dispute River (Haiti)
Lacosomidae
  USE Mimallonidae
Lacoste Castle (Lacoste, Vaucluse, France)
  USE Château de la Coste (Lacoste, Vaucluse, France)
Lacquer and lacquering *(May Subd Geog)*
  ⌈NK9900 (Fine arts)⌉
  ⌈TP939 (Chemical technology)⌉
  ⌈TS710 (Lacquering of metals)⌉
  BT Arts and crafts movement
      Coatings
      Decorative arts
      Finishes and finishing
      Paint materials
      Protective coatings
      Wood finishing
  RT Varnish and varnishing
  NT Crackle
      Japanning
      Lacquer boxes
      Lacquerers
      Metals—Finishing
  — Awards
      BT Rewards (Prizes, etc.)
  — Inscriptions
      UF Inscriptions on lacquer and lacquering
      BT Inscriptions
  — Private collections *(May Subd Geog)*
  — Testing
  — China
  — — History
  — — — Ch'in-Han dynasties, 221 B.C.-220 A.D.
  — — — Sung-Yüan dynasties, 960-1368
  — — — Ming-Ch'ing dynasties, 1368-1912
  — Japan
  — — History
  — — — Kamakura-Momoyama periods, 1185-1600
  — — — Edo period, 1600-1868
  — — — 1868-
  — Korea
  — — History
  — — — Koryŏ period, 935-1392
Lacquer boxes *(May Subd Geog)*
  UF Boxes, Lacquer
      Lacquered boxes
  BT Boxes, Ornamental
      Lacquer and lacquering
Lacquer tree, Chinese
  USE Rhus verniciflua
Lacquer tree, Japanese
  USE Rhus verniciflua
Lacquered boxes
  USE Lacquer boxes
Lacquerers *(May Subd Geog)*
  BT Lacquer and lacquering
Lacramarca River (Peru)
  UF Río Lacramarca (Peru)
  BT Rivers—Peru
Lacrimal canal
  USE Lacrimal organs
Lacrimal fistula
  USE Fistula, Lacrimal
Lacrimal organs
  ⌈QL949 (Comparative anatomy)⌉
  ⌈QM511 (Human anatomy)⌉
  ⌈QP231 (Physiology)⌉
  UF Glands, Lacrimal
      Lachrymal organs
      Lacrimal canal
      Lacrymal organs
      Tear sacs
  BT Adnexa oculi
      Exocrine glands
      Eye

  NT Aqueous humor
  — Diseases *(May Subd Geog)*
      ⌈RE201-216⌉
      NT Dacryocystitis
          Fistula, Lacrimal
  — Surgery
  — Transplantation
Lacrimators
  USE Tear gas
Lacroix family *(Not Subd Geog)*
  UF La Croix family
Lacrompe family *(Not Subd Geog)*
Lacrosse *(May Subd Geog)*
  ⌈GV989⌉
  — Coaching
      UF Lacrosse coaching
      BT Coaching (Athletics)
Lacrosse coaching
  USE Lacrosse—Coaching
Lacrosse for women *(May Subd Geog)*
  ⌈GV989.15⌉
  BT Sports for women
Lacrosse players *(May Subd Geog)*
Lacrymal organs
  USE Lacrimal organs
Lactam antibiotics
  USE Beta lactam antibiotics
Lactamases, Beta
  USE Beta lactamases
Lactaminic acid
  USE Sialic acids
Lactams *(May Subd Geog)*
  UF Azetidinones
      Lactan
  BT Amides
      Heterocyclic compounds
  NT Aztreonam
      Beta lactam antibiotics
Lactan
  USE Lactams
Lactariella
  USE Lactarius
Lactariopsis
  USE Lactarius
Lactarius
  ⌈QK629.R87⌉
  UF Lactariella
      Lactariopsis
  BT Russulaceae
Lactase
  BT Sugars
Lactase deficiency
  USE Lactose intolerance
Lactate dehydrogenase
  ⌈QP603.L33⌉
  UF Lactic acid dehydrogenase
      Lactic dehydrogenase
      LD (Enzyme)
      LDH (Enzyme)
  BT Oxidoreductases
  RT Lactic acid
Lactated food
  ⌈RJ231⌉
  BT Infants—Nutrition
Lactation
  ⌈QP246 (Physiology)⌉
  ⌈RJ216⌉
  UF Milk—Secretion
      Milk secretion
  BT Milk production
      Physiology
  RT Breast feeding
      Milk, Human
      Prolactin
  NT Amenorrhea, Lactation
      Milk fever
  — Regulation
      UF Regulation of lactation
      BT Biological control systems
Lactation disorders
  ⌈RC861⌉

UF Galactorrhea
BT Breast—Diseases
Puerperal disorders
Lactic acid
  [QD305.A2 (Chemistry)]
  [RM666.L18 (Therapeutics)]
  RT Lactate dehydrogenase
Milk, Fermented
Lactic acid bacteria
  [QR121]
  NT Streptococcus lactis
Lactic acid dehydrogenase
  USE Lactate dehydrogenase
Lactic dehydrogenase
  USE Lactate dehydrogenase
Lactic dehydrogenase virus
  [QR303]
  UF Riley's lactic dehydrogenase elevating
virus
  BT Arthropod-borne viruses
Togaviruses
Lactic starter cultures
  USE Bacterial starter cultures
Lactococcus dextranicus
  USE Leuconostoc dextranicum
Lactoferrins
  [QP552.L345]
  BT Iron proteins
Proteins
Lactoflavin
  USE Vitamin B2
Lactogenic hormones
  USE Prolactin
Lactones
  [QD305.A2]
  BT Cyclic compounds
  NT Macrolide antibiotics
Uzarigenin
Lactose
  [QD321]
  [RM666.L2 (Therapeutics)]
  UF Milk sugar
Sugar of milk
Lactose in the body
  [QP701]
  NT Lactose intolerance
Lactose intolerance *(May Subd Geog)*
  [RC632.L33]
  UF Hypolactasia
Lactase deficiency
Lactose malabsorption
  BT Carbohydrates—Metabolism—
Disorders
Lactose in the body
Malabsorption syndromes
  NT Milk-free diet
Lactose intolerance in children
  (May Subd Geog)
  [RJ399.L33]
  BT Metabolic disorders in children
Pediatric gastroenterology
Lactose malabsorption
  USE Lactose intolerance
Lactuca
  [QK495.C74 (Botany)]
  BT Compositae
Lactuca sativa
  USE Lettuce
Lactucarium
  [RM666.L]
  UF Lettuce opium
  BT Narcotics
Lacunae in law *(May Subd Geog)*
  UF Law, Lacunae in
  BT Law—Interpretation and construction
Legislation
  RT Evasion (Law)
  NT Judge-made law
Lacus Asphaltites (Israel and Jordan)
  USE Dead Sea (Israel and Jordan)

Lacus Larius (Italy)
  USE Como, Lake (Italy)
Lacus Sebinus (Italy)
  USE Iseo, Lake (Italy)
Lacy family *(Not Subd Geog)*
  UF Lacey family
Laicey family
Lasey family
Leacy family
LaCygne Lake (Kan.)
  USE La Cygne Lake (Kan.)
LaCygnes Lake (Kan.)
  USE La Cygne Lake (Kan.)
LAD (Statistics)
  USE Least absolute deviations (Statistics)
Lad family
  USE Ladd family
Lada automobile
  USE Zhiguli automobile
Ladakhi (South Asian people)
  (May Subd Geog)
  UF Ladaki (South Asian people)
  BT Ethnology—China
Ethnology—India
Ladakhi folk-songs
  USE Folk-songs, Ladakhi
Ladakhi language
  [PL3651.L3]
  BT India—Languages
Pakistan—Languages
Tibetan language
Ladaki (South Asian people)
  USE Ladakhi (South Asian people)
Ladd family *(Not Subd Geog)*
  UF Lad family
Ladds family
Lads family
Ladder-backed woodpecker
  [QL696.P56]
  UF Picoides scalaris
  BT Picoides
Ladder networks
  [TK7872.F5]
  BT Electric filters
Electric networks
Ladders
  [TS903]
Ladders, Aerial
  [TH9383]
  UF Aerial ladders
  BT Fire-departments—Equipment and
supplies
Ladds family
  USE Ladd family
Ladefoged family *(Not Subd Geog)*
Lademan family
  USE Lademann family
Lademann family *(Not Subd Geog)*
  UF Lademan family
Laderach family
  USE Ladrach family
Laderer family *(Not Subd Geog)*
Ladi dialect
  USE Laadi dialect
Ladies' book-plates
  USE Book-plates, Women's
Ladies-in-waiting *(May Subd Geog)*
  BT Courts and courtiers
Queens
Ladies of fashion dolls
  USE Fashion dolls
Ladin dialect *(May Subd Geog)*
  [PC945]
  UF Rhaetian dialects
  BT Italy—Languages
Raeto-Romance language
Switzerland—Languages
Ladin language
  USE Raeto-Romance language
Ladin literature *(May Subd Geog)*
  [PC945.5 (History)]

  [PC945.6 (Collections)]
  BT Italy—Literatures
Switzerland—Literatures
  NT Ladin poetry
Ladin poetry *(May Subd Geog)*
  [PC945.5 (History)]
  [PC945.7 (Collections)]
  BT Ladin literature
Lading, Bills of
  USE Bills of lading
Ladino ballads
  USE Ballads, Ladino
Ladino clover
  BT White clover
Ladino drama *(May Subd Geog)*
  BT Jewish drama
Ladino folk literature
  USE Folk literature, Ladino
Ladino folk-songs
  USE Folk-songs, Ladino
Ladino imprints *(May Subd Geog)*
Ladino language *(May Subd Geog)*
  [PC4813]
  UF Judeo-Spanish language
Judesmo
Spaniol language
  BT Hebrew language
Spanish language
— **Dialects**
— — **Morocco**
      NT Ḥakétia language
Ladino literature *(May Subd Geog)*
  NT Folk literature, Ladino
Ladino newspapers *(May Subd Geog)*
  [PN5650]
  BT Jewish newspapers
Ladino philology
Ladino poetry *(May Subd Geog)*
Ladino proverbs
  USE Proverbs, Ladino
Ladinos (Spanish Jews)
  USE Sephardim
Ladins
  [DG457.L3]
  BT Ethnology—Italy
Ladles, Foundry
  USE Foundry ladles
Ladles (Utensils) *(May Subd Geog)*
  BT Kitchen utensils
Spoons
Ladner family *(Not Subd Geog)*
  UF Ladnier family
Ladnier family
  USE Ladner family
Ladoga Lake (R.S.F.S.R.)
  UF Laatokka Lake (R.S.F.S.R.)
Ladozhskoe Ozero (R.S.F.S.R.)
  BT Lakes—Russian S.F.S.R.
Ladozhskoe Ozero (R.S.F.S.R.)
  USE Ladoga Lake (R.S.F.S.R.)
Ladrach family *(Not Subd Geog)*
  UF Laderach family
Laederach family
Lads family
  USE Ladd family
LaDuke family *(Not Subd Geog)*
Lady and the Unicorn (Tapestries)
  [NK3049.U5]
  UF Dame à la Licorne (Tapestries)
Unicorn tapestries
  BT Tapestry—France
Tapestry, Gothic—France
Unicorns in art
Lady Be Good (Airplane)
  BT Airplanes
Lady-beetles
  USE Ladybirds
Lady Dudley Challenge Cup
  [SF359.7.L33]
  UF Dudley Cup
Lady Dudley Cup

Lady Dudley Challenge Cup *(Continued)*
  BT Point-to-point racing—England
Lady Dudley Cup
  USE Lady Dudley Challenge Cup
Lady of Shalott (Painting)
  USE Hunt, William Holman, 1827-1910.
        Lady of Shalott
Lady palms
    [QK495.P17 (Botany)]
  UF Ladypalms
      Rhapis
  BT Palms
  NT Rhapis excelsa
      Rhapis humilis
Lady Rapids Site (Ont.) *(Not Subd Geog)*
  BT Ontario—Antiquities
Lady Southern Cross (Airplane)
Lady Wen-chi's return to China (Painting)
  USE Chang, Yü, 12th/13th cent.   Lady
          Wen-chi's return to China
Ladybird beetles
  USE Ladybirds
Ladybirds
    [QL596.C65]
  UF Cerasommatidiidae
      Coccinellidae
      Epilachnidae
      Lady-beetles
      Ladybird beetles
      Ladybugs
  BT Beetles
  NT Anatis
      Diomus
      Epilachna
      Hippodamia
      Hyperaspis
      Mexican bean beetle
      Nephus
      Scymnus
      Zenoria
  — Religious aspects
  —— Buddhism, [Christianity, etc.]
  —— Christianity
        NT Mary, Blessed Virgin, Saint
Ladybugs
  USE Ladybirds
Ladyfish
  USE Elops saurus
Ladyfish (Albula)
  USE Bonefish
Ladypalms
  USE Lady palms
Ladysthumb, Water
  USE Polygonum amphibium
Laederach family
  USE Ladrach family
Laedza Batanani, Botswana
  BT Education, Rural—Botswana
      Folk festivals—Botswana
Laelapidae
    [QL458.2.L33]
  UF Laelaptidae
  BT Mites
  NT Haemolaelaps
      Laelaps
      Tropilaelaps
Laelaps
    [QL458.2.L33]
  BT Laelapidae
Laelaptidae
  USE Laelapidae
Laemophloeidae
  USE Cucujidae
Laemophloeus
    [QL596.C8]
  BT Cucujidae
Laemopsylla
  USE Xenopsylla
Laennec's disease
  USE Dissecting aortic aneurysms

Laeonereis
    [QL391.A6]
  BT Nereidae
Laesa majestas
  USE Lese majesty
Laesio enormis
  USE Lesion (Law)
Læsø (Denmark)
  BT Islands—Denmark
Laestadians *(May Subd Geog)*
  BT Christian sects—Finland
Laetare festivals
  USE Vernal equinox festivals
Laetatus sum (Music)
  USE Psalms (Music)—122d Psalm
Laethem-Saint-Martin (Group of artists)
  USE Sint-Martens-Latem (Group of artists)
Laethem-Saint-Martin school
  USE Sint-Martens-Latem (Group of artists)
Laetinaevia
    [QK623.D47]
  UF Myridium
  BT Dermateaceae
Laetoli Site (Tanzania)
  UF Garusi Site (Tanzania)
      Laetolil Site (Tanzania)
  BT Tanzania—Antiquities
Laetolil Site (Tanzania)
  USE Laetoli Site (Tanzania)
Laetrile *(May Subd Geog)*
    [RC271.L3]
  UF Amygdalin
      Cyanophenylmethylglu
        copyranosiduronic acid
      Mandelonitrile glucuronoside
      Nitriloside
      Vitamin B17
  BT Antineoplastic agents
      Glucuronic acid
Laevulose
  USE Levulose
Laewamba (New Guinea people)
  USE Wampar (New Guinea people)
Lafayette family
  USE La Fayette family
Laferrière family *(Not Subd Geog)*
Laffargue family
  USE La Fargue family
Lafflin family
  USE Laughlin family
Laflamme Lake (Québec)
  UF Lac Laflamme (Québec)
  BT Lakes—Québec (Province)
Laflin family
  USE Laughlin family
Lafoeidae
    [QL377.H9]
  BT Hydroida
Lafollette family
  USE La Follette family
Lafond family
  USE Fontaine family
Lafont family
  USE Fontaine family
Lafontant family
  USE Fontaine family
Lafors family
  USE Lefors family
Lafourche, Bayou (La.)
  UF Bayou Lafourche (La.)
  BT Bayous—Louisiana
Lafranchini family *(Not Subd Geog)*
  UF La Franchini family
      La Franchino family
      La Francini family
Lag, Cultural
  USE Cultural lag
Lag, Economic
  USE Economic lag
Lag, Jet
  USE Jet lag

Lag b'Omer
  BT Sefirah period
Lagan Canal (Northern Ireland)
  UF Lagan Navigation (Northern Ireland)
  BT Canals—Northern Ireland
Lagan Navigation (Northern Ireland)
  USE Lagan Canal (Northern Ireland)
Lagarde, Battle of, 1940
    [D756.5.L3]
  BT World War, 1939-1945—Campaigns—
        France
Lagarosiphon
    [QK495.H86]
  BT Hydrocharitaceae
Lagarosiphon major
    [QK495.H86 (Botany)]
    [SB615.L24 (Weed)]
  BT Aquatic weeds
Lagascea
    [QK495.C74 (Botany)]
  BT Compositae
Lagash (Ancient city)
  UF Hiba, Tall (Iraq)
      Shirpurla (Ancient city)
      Tall al-Hiba (Iraq)
      Tell al-Hiba (Iraq)
  BT Cities and towns, Ruined, extinct, etc.
      —Iraq
      Iraq—Antiquities
Lagenaria
    [QK495.C96]
  BT Cucurbitaceae
      Gourds
Lagenaria leucantha
  USE Lagenaria siceraria
Lagenaria siceraria
    [QK495.C96]
  UF Bottle gourd
      Calabash gourd
      Cucurbita lagenaria
      Gourd, Bottle
      Gourd, Calabash
      Gourd, White-flowered
      Lagenaria leucantha
      Lagenaria vulgaris
      White-flowered gourd
Lagenaria vulgaris
  USE Lagenaria siceraria
Lagenidiaceae
    [QK621.L]
  BT Lagenidiales
  NT Lagenidium
Lagenidiales
    [QL621.L]
  BT Oomycetes
  NT Lagenidiaceae
Lagenidium
    [QK621.L]
  BT Lagenidiaceae
Lagenidium callinectes
    [QL621.L]
Lagenodelphis
    [QL737.C432]
  BT Delphinidae
      Dolphins
  NT Lagenodelphis hosei
Lagenodelphis hosei
    [QL737.C432]
  UF Bornean dolphin
      Fraser's dolphin
      Sarawak dolphin
  BT Lagenodelphis
Lagenorhynchus
    [QL737.C432]
  BT Delphinidae
      Dolphins
  NT Atlantic white-sided dolphin
      Lagenorhynchus electra
      Pacific whitesided dolphin
Lagenorhynchus acutus
  USE Atlantic white-sided dolphin

Lagenorhynchus electra
　[QL737.C432]
　UF　Broad-beaked dolphin
　　　Electra dolphin
　　　Indian broad-beaked dolphin
　　　Little blackfish
　　　Melon-headed whale
　　　Peponocephala electra
　BT　Lagenorhynchus
Lagenorhynchus obliquidens
　USE　Pacific whitesided dolphin
Lagerstroemia
　[QK495.L9 (Botany)]
　[SB413.L34 (Ornamental plants)]
　BT　Lythraceae
Lagerstroemia indica
　USE　Crape myrtle, Common
Lagimodiere family　(Not Subd Geog)
Lagle family
　USE　Lail family
Lago Alajuela (Panama)
　USE　Madden Lake (Panama)
Lago Benaco (Italy)
　USE　Garda, Lake (Italy)
Lago Chapala (Mexico)
　USE　Chapala, Lake (Mexico)
Lago de Atitlán (Guatemala)
　USE　Atitlán, Lake (Guatemala)
Lago de Chapala (Mexico)
　USE　Chapala, Lake (Mexico)
Lago de Maracaibo (Venezuela)
　USE　Maracaibo Lake (Venezuela)
Lago de Miraflores (Panama)
　USE　Miraflores Lake (Panama)
Lago di Brienz (Switzerland)
　USE　Brienz, Lake of (Switzerland)
Lago di Como (Italy)
　USE　Como, Lake (Italy)
Lago di Costanza
　USE　Constance, Lake of
Lago di Garda (Italy)
　USE　Garda, Lake (Italy)
Lago di Neuchâtel (Switzerland)
　USE　Neuchâtel, Lake of (Switzerland)
Lago di Sebino (Italy)
　USE　Iseo, Lake (Italy)
Lago di Thun (Switzerland)
　USE　Thun, Lake of (Switzerland)
Lago d'Iseo (Italy)
　USE　Iseo, Lake (Italy)
Lago d'Orta (Italy)
　USE　Orta, Lake (Italy)
Lago Gatún (Panama)
　USE　Gatun Lake (Panama)
Lago Madden (Panama)
　USE　Madden Lake (Panama)
Lago Maggiore (Italy and Switzerland)
　USE　Maggiore, Lake (Italy and
　　　Switzerland)
Lago Titicaca (Peru and Bolivia)
　USE　Titicaca Lake (Peru and Bolivia)
Lagoa Mirim (Brazil and Uruguay)
　USE　Mirim Lake (Brazil and Uruguay)
Lagocephalidae
　USE　Tetraodontidae
Lagodon
　[QL638.S74]
　BT　Sparidae
　NT　Lagodon rhomboides
Lagodon rhomboides
　[QL638.S74]
　UF　Pinfish
　　　Sailor's choice
　BT　Lagodon
Lagomorpha　(May Subd Geog)
　[QL737.L3]
　UF　Duplicidentata
　BT　Mammals
　NT　Leporidae
　　　Ochotonidae

Lagomorpha, Fossil
　[QE882.L3]
　BT　Mammals, Fossil
Lagonda automobile
　[TL215.L]
　BT　Sports cars
Lagoon ecology　(May Subd Geog)
　[QH541.5.L27]
　BT　Ecology
Lagoon languages
　[PL8430.L33]
　BT　Kwa languages
　NT　Abe language
　　　Abidji language
　　　Abure language
　　　Adyukru language
　　　Ahizi language
　　　Aladian language
　　　Attie language
Lagoon of Venice (Italy)
　USE　Venice, Lagoon of (Italy)
Lagoon Site (Banks Island, N.W.T.)
　(Not Subd Geog)
　BT　Banks Island (N.W.T.)—Antiquities
　　　Northwest Territories—Antiquities
Lagoons　(May Subd Geog)
　[GB2201-2397]
　— **Australia**
　　　NT　Harvey Estuary (W.A.)
　　　　　Peel Inlet (W.A.)
　— **Bermuda Islands**
　　　NT　Harrington Sound (Bermuda
　　　　　Islands)
　— **California**
　　　NT　Mugu Lagoon (Calif.)
　— **Colombia**
　　　NT　Tesca Lagoon (Colombia)
　— **England**
　　　NT　Broads, The (England)
　— **Germany (East)**
　　　NT　Szczeciński Lagoon (Poland and
　　　　　Germany)
　— **India**
　　　NT　Chilka Lake (India)
　— **Italy**
　　　NT　Grado Lagoon (Italy)
　　　　　Marano Lagoon (Italy)
　　　　　Venice, Lagoon of (Italy)
　— **Mexico**
　　　NT　Terminos Lagoon (Mexico)
　— **Micronesia**
　　　NT　Truk Lagoon (Truk, Micronesia)
　— **Poland**
　　　NT　Szczeciński Lagoon (Poland and
　　　　　Germany)
　— **Spain**
　　　NT　Mar Menor (Spain)
Lagoons, Sewage
　USE　Sewage lagoons
Lagopus
　USE　Ptarmigans
Lagopus lagopus
　USE　Willow ptarmigan
Lagopus leucurus
　USE　White-tailed ptarmigan
Lagopus mutus
　USE　Rock ptarmigan
Lagopus rupestris
　USE　Rock ptarmigan
Lagopus scoticus
　USE　Willow ptarmigan
Lagrange equations
　UF　D'Alembert equation
　　　Equations, Euler-Lagrange
　　　Equations, Lagrange
　　　Euler-Lagrange equations
　　　Lagrangian equations
　BT　Differential equations
　RT　Equations of motion
　— **Numerical solutions**
　　　BT　Numerical analysis

Lagrange's series (Mathematics)
　USE　Series, Lagrange's
Lagrangian equations
　USE　Lagrange equations
Lagrangian functions
　UF　Functions, Lagrangian
　BT　Calculus of variations
　　　Dynamics
　　　Mathematical optimization
　NT　Maslov index
Lagrangian points
　UF　Libration points
　　　Points, Lagrangian
　BT　Gravitation
　　　Mechanics, Celestial
　　　Orbits
　　　Three-body problem
Lagrenée family　(Not Subd Geog)
Lagubi language
　USE　Mambila language
Laguerre geometry
　UF　Geometry, Laguerre
　BT　Geometry, Analytic
Laguerre polynomials
　UF　Polynomials, Laguerre
　BT　Orthogonal polynomials
Laguiche family　(Not Subd Geog)
　UF　De Laguiche family
Laguna Bay (Luzon, Philippines)
　USE　Laguna de Bay (Luzon, Philippines)
Laguna Chichoj (Guatemala)
　USE　Chichoj Lake (Guatemala)
Laguna de Bay (Luzon, Philippines)
　UF　Bay, Laguna de (Luzon, Philippines)
　　　Laguna Bay (Luzon, Philippines)
　　　Laguna Lake (Luzon, Philippines)
　BT　Lakes—Philippines
Laguna de Términos (Mexico)
　USE　Terminos Lagoon (Mexico)
Laguna di Grado (Italy)
　USE　Grado Lagoon (Italy)
Laguna di Marano (Italy)
　USE　Marano Lagoon (Italy)
Laguna Francesa Site (Mexico)
　(Not Subd Geog)
　BT　Mexico—Antiquities
Laguna Indians
　[E99.L2]
　BT　Indians of North America
　　　Keresan Indians
Laguna Lake (Luzon, Philippines)
　USE　Laguna de Bay (Luzon, Philippines)
Laguna language
　[PM1645]
Laguna Madre (Tex.)
　UF　Madre, Laguna (Tex.)
　BT　Estuaries—Texas
Laguna Mar Chiquita (Córdoba, Argentina :
　Province)
　USE　Mar Chiquita Lake (Córdoba,
　　　Argentina : Province)
Laguna Merín (Brazil and Uruguay)
　USE　Mirim Lake (Brazil and Uruguay)
Laguna Mirim (Brazil and Uruguay)
　USE　Mirim Lake (Brazil and Uruguay)
Laguna Mountains (Mexico)
　UF　Sierra de la Laguna (Mexico)
　BT　Mountains—Mexico
Laguna Region (Mexico)
　UF　Comarca Lagunera (Mexico)
　　　La Laguna (Mexico)
Laguna Veneta (Italy)
　USE　Venice, Lagoon of (Italy)
Laguneta Chichoj (Guatemala)
　USE　Chichoj Lake (Guatemala)
Lagurostemon
　USE　Saussurea
Lagurus
　[QL737.R638]
　UF　Steppe lemmings

Lagurus *(Continued)*
  BT Cricetidae
      Voles
Lagurus curtatus
  USE Sagebrush vole
Lahars *(May Subd Geog)*
  [GB481-8]
  UF Mudflows, Volcanic
      Volcanic mudflows
  BT Mudflows
      Volcanism
Lahauli language
  USE Lahuli language
Lahemaa National Park (Estonia)
  USE Lahemaa Rahvuspark (Estonia)
Lahemaa Rahvuspark (Estonia)
  UF Lahemaa National Park (Estonia)
      Lakhemaaskiĭ natsional'nyĭ park
      (Estonia)
  BT National parks and reserves—Soviet
      Union
      Parks—Estonia
Lahn River (Germany)
  BT Rivers—Germany (West)
Lahndā language
  [PK2261-2274]
  UF Jaṭkī language
      Lahndi language
      Panjabi language, Western
  BT Indo-Aryan languages, Modern
  NT Hindkō dialect
      Pōṭhwārī dialect
      Sirāikī Hindkī dialect
Lahndā poetry *(May Subd Geog)*
Lahndi language
  USE Lahndā language
Lahners family
  USE Lehnert family
Lahnert family
  USE Lehnert family
Lahouli language
  USE Lahuli language
Lahu (Asian people)
  [DS523.4.L33]
  UF Lohei (Asian people)
      Musso (Asian people)
  BT Ethnology—Asia
Lahu language
  [PL3311.L35]
  UF Muhso language
  BT Loloish languages
Lahugh family
  USE Lehew family
Lahuli language *(May Subd Geog)*
  [PL3651.L4]
  UF Lahauli language
      Lahouli language
  BT India—Languages
      Tibeto-Burman languages
  NT Pattani dialect (India)
Lahun, Pyramid of (Egypt)
  USE Pyramid of Sesostris II (Egypt)
Lai family *(Not Subd Geog)*
Lai language
  [PL4001.L2]
  UF Baungshè dialect
      Haka dialect
  BT Chin languages
      Tibeto-Burman languages
Laicey family
  USE Lacy family
Laicism *(May Subd Geog)*
  BT Laity—Catholic Church
      Secularism
Laidet family
  USE Ledet family
Laidlaw family *(Not Subd Geog)*
Laierdila (Australian people)
  USE Lardil (Australian people)
Laigle Forest (France)
  USE Laigue Forest (France)

Laigue Forest (France)
  UF Forêt de Laigle (France)
      Forêt de Laigue (France)
      Laigle Forest (France)
  BT Forests and forestry—France
Laika, East Siberian
  USE East Siberian laika
Lail family *(Not Subd Geog)*
  UF Lagle family
      Laile family
      Lale family
      Layle family
Lailat . . .
  USE *subject headings beginning with the*
      word Laylat
Laile family
  USE Lail family
Lain family
  USE Lane family
L'Ain Rivière (France)
  USE Ain River (France)
Laine family
  USE Lane family
Lains family
  USE Lane family
Laird family *(Not Subd Geog)*
  UF Lard family
      Larde family
      Leaird family
      Leard family
      Leird family
Lairy family
  USE Lary family
Laisné family *(Not Subd Geog)*
Laissez-faire
  [HB95]
  UF Free enterprise
  BT Economic policy
      Economics
      Free trade and protection
      Individualism
      Liberalism
  RT Competition
      Industry and state
      Privatization
  NT Manchester school of economics
Laity *(May Subd Geog)*
  [BV687]
  UF Laymen
  BT Church polity
  RT Lay ministry
  NT Buddhist laymen
      Fish movement (Christianity)
      Men in church work
  — **Baptists, [Catholic Church, etc.]**
  — **Catholic Church**
      [BX1920]
      BT Catholic action
      NT Laicism
          Lay teachers
  — **Catholic Church, [etc.]**
Laity (Canon law)
Lak language
  [PK9201.L3]
  BT Daghestan languages
Lak literature
  USE Lakh literature
Lak poets
  USE Poets, Lak
Lakalai (Melanesian people)
  UF Bileki (Melanesian people)
      Muku (Melanesian people)
      Nakanais (Melanesian people)
  BT Ethnology—Papua New Guinea
      Melanesians
Lakalai language
  USE Nakanai language
Lakandon language
  USE Lacandon language
Lakavishki Hills (Bulgaria)
  UF Lakavishki rid (Bulgaria)

  BT Mountains—Bulgaria
Lakavishki rid (Bulgaria)
  USE Lakavishki Hills (Bulgaria)
Lake . . .
    Lakes in English speaking countries whose names
    begin with the word "lake" are established in inverted
    form under the word following "lake," e.g. Lake Erie
    is established as Erie, Lake.
Lake Abert (Or.)
  USE Abert, Lake (Or.)
Lake Agassiz
  USE Agassiz, Lake
Lake Algonquin
  USE Algonquin, Lake
Lake Allatoona (Ga.)
  USE Allatoona Lake (Ga.)
Lake Almanor (Calif.)
  USE Almanor, Lake (Calif.)
Lake Almanor Project, Calif.
  UF Almanor Project, Calif.
      Project Lake Almanor, Calif.
  BT Water resources development—
      California
Lake and Clarke Company Site (Arrowsic
  Island, Me.)
  USE Clarke and Lake Company Site
      (Arrowsic Island, Me.)
Lake Anna (Va.)
  USE Anna, Lake (Va.)
Lake Aral (Uzbek S.S.R. and Kazakh S.S.R.)
  USE Aral Sea (Uzbek S.S.R. and Kazakh
      S.S.R.)
Lake Argyle (W.A.)
  USE Argyle, Lake (W.A.)
Lake Athabasca (Sask. and Alta.)
  USE Athabasca, Lake (Sask. and Alta.)
Lake Atitlán (Guatemala)
  USE Atitlán, Lake (Guatemala)
Lake Attitash (Mass.)
  USE Attitash, Lake (Mass.)
Lake Baikal (R.S.F.S.R.)
  USE Baikal Lake (R.S.F.S.R.)
Lake Balaton (Hungary)
  USE Balaton, Lake (Hungary)
Lake Barkley (Ky. and Tenn.)
  USE Barkley, Lake (Ky. and Tenn.)
Lake Berryessa (Calif.)
  USE Berryessa, Lake (Calif.)
Lake Bonneville
  USE Bonneville, Lake
Lake Borgne (La.)
  USE Borgne, Lake (La.)
Lake Borovoe (Kazakh S.S.R.)
  USE Borovoe Lake (Kazakh S.S.R.)
Lake Borovoye (Kazakh S.S.R.)
  USE Borovoe Lake (Kazakh S.S.R.)
Lake Bridgeport (Tex.)
  USE Bridgeport, Lake (Tex.)
Lake Brienz (Switzerland)
  USE Brienz, Lake of (Switzerland)
Lake Brownwood (Tex.)
  USE Brownwood, Lake (Tex.)
Lake Buchanan (Tex.)
  USE Buchanan, Lake (Tex.)
Lake Burragorang (N.S.W.)
  USE Burragorang, Lake (N.S.W.)
Lake Chad
  USE Chad, Lake
Lake Champlain
  USE Champlain, Lake
Lake Champlain Tercentenary Celebration,
  1909
  USE Champlain tercentenary celebrations
Lake Chapala (Mexico)
  USE Chapala, Lake (Mexico)
Lake Charm (Vic.)
  USE Charm, Lake (Vic.)

Lake Chelan National Recreation Area
   (Wash.)   (Not Subd Geog)
      BT   National parks and reserves—
            Washington (State)
         Recreation areas—Washington (State)
Lake Chesdin (Va.)
   USE   Chesdin, Lake (Va.)
Lake Chiem (Germany)
   USE   Chiem, Lake (Germany)
Lake circulation
   USE   Lakes—Circulation
Lake Claiborne (La.)
   USE   Claiborne, Lake (La.)
Lake Claire (Alta.)
   USE   Claire, Lake (Alta.)
Lake Cochituate (Mass.)
   USE   Cochituate, Lake (Mass.)
Lake Como (Italy)
   USE   Como, Lake (Italy)
Lake Copais (Greece)
   USE   Copais Lake (Greece)
Lake Corpus Christi (Tex.)
   USE   Corpus Christi, Lake (Tex.)
Lake Creek (Lincoln County, Mont.)
   BT   Rivers—Montana
Lake D'Arbonne (La.)
   USE   Bayou D'Arbonne Lake (La.)
Lake Dardanelle (Ark.)
   USE   Dardanelle Lake (Ark.)
Lake Dauphin (Man.)
   USE   Dauphin Lake (Man.)
Lake deposits
   USE   Lake sediments
Lake Diefenbaker (Sask.)
   USE   Diefenbaker, Lake (Sask.)
Lake Dillon (Colo.)
   USE   Dillon Reservoir (Colo.)
Lake disposal of radioactive wastes
   USE   Radioactive waste disposal in rivers,
            lakes, etc.
Lake District (England)
   UF   Lakeland (England)
         Lakes (England)
   RT   Lake District National Park (England)
Lake District National Park (England)
   BT   National parks and reserves—Great
            Britain
         Parks—England
   RT   Lake District (England)
Lake-dwellers and lake-dwellings
      (May Subd Geog)
      ₍GN785-6₎
   UF   Pile-dwellings
   BT   Dwellings
         Man, Prehistoric
   RT   Terremare
   — Ireland
      UF   Crannogs
   — Switzerland
      NT   Pfyn culture
Lake ecology   (May Subd Geog)
      ₍QH541.5.L3₎
   BT   Ecology
         Freshwater ecology
         Lakes
         Limnology
   NT   Lake flora
         Saline lake ecology
Lake Eleanor (Calif.)
   USE   Eleanor, Lake (Calif.)
Lake Ellyn (Ill.)
   USE   Ellyn, Lake (Ill.)
Lake Enare (Finland)
   USE   Inari Lake (Finland)
Lake Erie
   USE   Erie, Lake
Lake Eufaula (Ala. and Ga.)
   USE   Walter F. George Reservoir (Ala. and
            Ga.)
Lake Eyasi (Tanzania)
   USE   Eyasi, Lake (Tanzania)

Lake Eyre (S. Aust.)
   USE   Eyre, Lake (S. Aust.)
Lake family   (Not Subd Geog)
   UF   Laker family
         Llake family
Lake fauna   (May Subd Geog)
      ₍QL146₎
   UF   Fauna, Lake
   BT   Freshwater fauna
         Zoology
Lake flora   (May Subd Geog)
      ₍QK108-QK474.5 (Local)₎
   BT   Botany
         Botany—Ecology
         Freshwater flora
         Lake ecology
Lake Fork Creek (Tex.)
   BT   Rivers—Texas
   NT   Lake Fork Reservoir (Tex.)
Lake Fork Reservoir (Tex.)
   BT   Lake Fork Creek (Tex.)
         Lakes—Texas
         Reservoirs—Texas
Lake Francis Case (S.D.)
   USE   Francis Case, Lake (S.D.)
Lake frontage development
   USE   Lakeshore development
Lake Gairdner (S. Aust.)
   USE   Gairdner, Lake (S. Aust.)
Lake Garda (Italy)
   USE   Garda, Lake (Italy)
Lake Gaston (N.C. and Va.)
   USE   Gaston, Lake (N.C. and Va.)
Lake Geneva (Switzerland and France)
   USE   Geneva, Lake (Switzerland and
            France)
Lake George (N.Y.)
   USE   George, Lake (N.Y.)
Lake George Site (Miss.)
   BT   Mississippi—Antiquities
         Mounds—Mississippi
Lake Glubokoe (R.S.F.S.R.)
   USE   Glubokoe Lake (R.S.F.S.R.)
Lake Gordon (Tas.)
   USE   Gordon, Lake (Tas.)
Lake Hallwil (Switzerland)
   USE   Hallwil, Lake (Switzerland)
Lake Hawea (N.Z.)
   USE   Hawea, Lake (N.Z.)
Lake Hazen (Ellesmere Island, N.W.T.)
   USE   Hazen, Lake (Ellesmere Island,
            N.W.T.)
Lake herring
      ₍QL638.S2₎
   UF   Cisco, Great Lakes
         Coregonus artedii
         Great Lakes cisco
         Herring, Lake
         Leucichthys artedi
Lake Houston (Tex.)
   USE   Houston, Lake (Tex.)
Lake Höytiäinen (Finland)
   USE   Höytiäinen Lake (Finland)
Lake Huron (Mich. and Ont.)
   USE   Huron, Lake (Mich. and Ont.)
Lake Imandra (R.S.F.S.R.)
   USE   Imandra, Lake (R.S.F.S.R.)
Lake Ioannina (Greece)
   USE   Ioannina, Lake (Greece)
Lake Iseo (Italy)
   USE   Iseo, Lake (Italy)
Lake Issyk (Kirghiz S.S.R.)
   USE   Issyk-Kul' (Kirghiz S.S.R.)
Lake Itasca (Minn.)
   USE   Itasca, Lake (Minn.)
Lake Kerr (Va. and N.C.)
   USE   John H. Kerr Reservoir (Va. and N.C.)
Lake Kivu (Rwanda and Zaire)
   USE   Kivu, Lake (Rwanda and Zaire)
Lake Koocanusa (B.C. and Mont.)
   USE   Koocanusa, Lake (B.C. and Mont.)

Lake Lanier (Ga.)
   USE   Sidney Lanier, Lake (Ga.)
Lake Lavon (Tex.)
   USE   Lavon Lake (Tex.)
Lake Leopold II (Zaire)
   USE   Mai-Ndombe, Lake (Zaire)
Lake Lewisville (Tex.)
   USE   Garza-Little Elm Reservoir (Tex.)
Lake Louise (Alta.)
   USE   Louise, Lake (Alta.)
Lake Lucerne (Switzerland)
   USE   Lucerne Lake (Switzerland)
Lake Macquarie (N.S.W.)
   USE   Macquarie, Lake (N.S.W.)
Lake Maggiore (Italy and Switzerland)
   USE   Maggiore, Lake (Italy and
            Switzerland)
Lake Mai-Ndombe (Zaire)
   USE   Mai-Ndombe, Lake (Zaire)
Lake Malawi
   USE   Nyasa, Lake
Lake Maracaibo (Venezuela)
   USE   Maracaibo Lake (Venezuela)
Lake Maracaibo, Battle of, 1823
   USE   Maracaibo Lake (Venezuela), Battle of,
            1823
Lake Marburg (Pa.)
   USE   Marburg, Lake (Pa.)
Lake Martin (Ala.)
   USE   Martin, Lake (Ala.)
Lake Maryūt (Egypt)
   USE   Maryūt, Lake (Egypt)
Lake Mason National Wildlife Refuge (Mont.)
      (Not Subd Geog)
      BT   National parks and reserves—Montana
         Wildlife refuges—Montana
Lake Mattoon (Ill.)
   USE   Mattoon, Lake (Ill.)
Lake McIlwaine (Zimbabwe)
   USE   McIlwaine, Lake (Zimbabwe)
Lake Mead (Ariz. and Nev.)
   USE   Mead, Lake (Ariz. and Nev.)
Lake Mead National Recreation Area (Ariz.
      and Nev.)
      BT   National parks and reserves—United
            States
         Recreation areas—Arizona
         Recreation areas—Nevada
      NT   Mead, Lake (Ariz. and Nev.)
Lake Mégantic (Québec)
   USE   Mégantic, Lake (Québec)
Lake Melville (Nfld.)
   USE   Melville, Lake (Nfld.)
Lake Mendota (Wis.)
   USE   Mendota, Lake (Wis.)
Lake Menteith (Scotland)
   USE   Menteith, Lake (Scotland)
Lake Michigan
   USE   Michigan, Lake
Lake Minnetonka (Minn.)
   USE   Minnetonka, Lake (Minn.)
Lake Mirim (Brazil and Uruguay)
   USE   Mirim Lake (Brazil and Uruguay)
Lake Missoula
   USE   Missoula, Lake
Lake Mistassini (Québec)
   USE   Mistassini Lake (Québec)
Lake Mistassinie (Québec)
   USE   Mistassini Lake (Québec)
Lake Moeris (Egypt)
   USE   Moeris, Lake (Egypt)
Lake Mohave (Nev.)
   USE   Mohave, Lake (Nev.)
Lake Nasser (Egypt and Sudan)
   USE   Nasser, Lake (Egypt and Sudan)
Lake New Found (N.H.)
   USE   Newfound Lake (N.H.)
Lake Newfound (N.H.)
   USE   Newfound Lake (N.H.)
Lake Nipissing (Ont.)
   USE   Nipissing, Lake (Ont.)

Lake Njarasa (Tanzania)
USE Eyasi, Lake (Tanzania)
Lake Nockamixon (Pa.)
USE Nockamixon, Lake (Pa.)
Lake Norman (N.C.)
USE Norman, Lake (N.C.)
Lake Nyasa
USE Nyasa, Lake
Lake Nyassa
USE Nyasa, Lake
Lake of Biel (Switzerland)
USE Biel, Lake of (Switzerland)
Lake of Bienne (Switzerland)
USE Biel, Lake of (Switzerland)
Lake of Brienz (Switzerland)
USE Brienz, Lake of (Switzerland)
Lake of Constance
USE Constance, Lake of
Lake of Morat (Switzerland)
USE Morat, Lake of (Switzerland)
Lake of Neuchâtel (Switzerland)
USE Neuchâtel, Lake of (Switzerland)
Lake of Saint Bartholomew (Germany)
USE Königssee (Germany)
Lake of Starnberg (Germany)
USE Starnberger See (Germany)
Lake of the Ozarks (Mo.)
USE Ozarks, Lake of the (Mo.)
Lake of the Woods Massacre, 1736
  ⌜F1030⌝
BT Dakota Indians—Wars
Lake of Thoune (Switzerland)
USE Thun, Lake of (Switzerland)
Lake of Thun (Switzerland)
USE Thun, Lake of (Switzerland)
Lake of Zurich (Switzerland)
USE Zurich, Lake of (Switzerland)
Lake Okeechobee (Fla.)
USE Okeechobee, Lake (Fla.)
Lake Onega (R.S.F.S.R.)
USE Onega Lake (R.S.F.S.R.)
Lake Ontario (N.Y. and Ont.)
USE Ontario, Lake (N.Y. and Ont.)
Lake Oroville (Calif.)
USE Oroville, Lake (Calif.)
Lake Oswego (Or. : Lake)
USE Oswego, Lake (Or.)
Lake Oswego Dam (Or.)
BT Dams—Oregon
Oswego, Lake (Or.)
Lake Ouachita (Ark.)
USE Ouachita, Lake (Ark.)
Lake Panache (Ont.)
USE Panache, Lake (Ont.)
Lake Pedder (Tas.)
USE Pedder, Lake (Tas.)
Lake Peipus (Estonia and R.S.F.S.R.)
USE Peipus, Lake (Estonia and R.S.F.S.R.)
Lake Pleasant (Ariz.)
USE Pleasant, Lake (Ariz.)
Lake poets
  ⌜PR590⌝
UF Lake school
Lakists
BT Poets, English—19th century
Lake Pontchartrain (La.)
USE Pontchartrain, Lake (La.)
Lake Powell (Utah and Ariz.)
USE Powell, Lake (Utah and Ariz.)
Lake Pskov (Estonia and R.S.F.S.R.)
USE Pskov, Lake (Estonia and R.S.F.S.R.)
Lake Redstone (Wis.)
USE Redstone, Lake (Wis.)
Lake Redstone Reservoir (Wis.)
USE Redstone, Lake (Wis.)
Lake rehabilitation
USE Lake renewal
Lake renewal *(May Subd Geog)*
UF Lake rehabilitation
BT Lakes
RT Eutrophication

Lake Rotorua (N.Z.)
USE Rotorua, Lake (N.Z.)
Lake Rudolf (Kenya and Ethiopia)
USE Rudolf, Lake (Kenya and Ethiopia)
Lake Russell Wildlife Management Area (Ga.)
BT Shooting preserves—Georgia
Wildlife management areas—Georgia
Lake Saint Clair (Mich. and Ont.)
USE Saint Clair, Lake (Mich. and Ont.)
Lake Saint Clair National Park (Tas.)
USE Cradle Mountain-Lake Saint Clair
National Park (Tas.)
Lake Saint John (Québec)
USE Saint John, Lake (Québec)
Lake Sam Rayburn (Tex.)
USE Sam Rayburn Reservoir (Tex.)
Lake Sara (Ill.)
USE Sara, Lake (Ill.)
Lake school
USE Lake poets
Lake Sebino (Italy)
USE Iseo, Lake (Italy)
Lake sediments *(May Subd Geog)*
UF Bottom deposits in lakes
Lake deposits
Sediments, Lake
BT Sediments (Geology)
Lake Seliger (R.S.F.S.R.)
USE Seliger, Lake (R.S.F.S.R.)
Lake Sharpe (S.D.)
USE Sharpe, Lake (S.D.)
Lake Shelbyville (Ill.)
USE Shelbyville, Lake (Ill.)
Lake Shinji (Japan)
USE Shinji Lake (Japan)
Lake Shinji-ko (Japan)
USE Shinji Lake (Japan)
Lake Shore Electric Railway
BT Railroads—United States
Lake side architecture
USE Lakeside architecture
Lake Sidney Lanier (Ga.)
USE Sidney Lanier, Lake (Ga.)
Lake Sonoma (Calif.)
USE Sonoma, Lake (Calif.)
Lake States
Here are entered works discussing collectively the
states bordering the Great Lakes, i.e. New York,
Pennsylvania, Ohio, Michigan, Indiana, Illinois, Wis-
consin, and Minnesota.
UF Great Lakes States
BT Middle West
RT Great Lakes
Lake steamers *(May Subd Geog)*
BT Inland waterway vessels
Steamboats
NT Paddle steamers
Lake Stechlin (Germany)
USE Stechlin Lake (Germany)
Lake Stor (Sweden)
USE Storsjön (Sweden)
Lake sturgeon
  ⌜QL638.A25⌝
UF Acipenser fulvescens
Lake Sumner State Forest Park (N.Z.)
BT Forest reserves—New Zealand
Parks—New Zealand
Lake Superior
USE Superior, Lake
Lake Superior Provincial Park (Ont.)
  (Not Subd Geog)
BT Parks—Ontario
Lake Tahoe (Calif. and Nev.)
USE Tahoe, Lake (Calif. and Nev.)
Lake T'ai (China)
USE T'ai Lake (China)
Lake Talquin (Fla.)
USE Talquin, Lake (Fla.)
Lake Tana (Ethiopia)
USE Tana, Lake (Ethiopia)

Lake Tanganyika
USE Tanganyika, Lake
Lake Taupo (N.Z.)
USE Taupo, Lake (N.Z.)
Lake Taupo region, N.Z., in art
Lake Tawakoni (Tex.)
USE Tawakoni, Lake (Tex.)
Lake Texoma (Okla. and Tex.)
USE Texoma, Lake (Okla. and Tex.)
**Lake Thibadeau National Wildlife Refuge
(Mont.)** *(Not Subd Geog)*
BT National parks and reserves—Montana
Wildlife refuges—Montana
Lake Thun (Switzerland)
USE Thun, Lake of (Switzerland)
Lake Thunderbird (Okla.)
USE Thunderbird, Lake (Okla.)
Lake Tiberias (Israel)
USE Tiberias Lake (Israel)
Lake Titicaca (Peru and Bolivia)
USE Titicaca Lake (Peru and Bolivia)
**Lake Traverse Indian Reservation (N.D. and
S.D.)**
UF Sisseton Indian Reservation (N.D. and
S.D.)
BT Indians of North America—North
Dakota—Reservations
Indians of North America—South
Dakota—Reservations
Sisseton Indians—Reservations
Wahpeton Indians—Reservations
Lake Travis (Tex.)
USE Travis, Lake (Tex.)
Lake Trichonis (Greece)
USE Trichonis, Lake (Greece)
Lake Trikhonis (Greece)
USE Trichonis, Lake (Greece)
Lake trout
UF Cristivomer namaycush
Mackinaw trout
Salvelinus namaycush
BT Trout
Lake Turkana (Kenya and Ethiopia)
USE Rudolf, Lake (Kenya and Ethiopia)
Lake Vechten (Netherlands)
USE Vechten, Lake (Netherlands)
Lake Waikare Moana (N.Z.)
USE Waikaremoana, Lake (N.Z.)
Lake Waikaremoana (N.Z.)
USE Waikaremoana, Lake (N.Z.)
Lake Wallenpaupack (Pa.)
USE Wallenpaupack, Lake (Pa.)
Lake Walter F. George (Ala. and Ga.)
USE Walter F. George Reservoir (Ala. and
Ga.)
Lake Wanaka (N.Z.)
USE Wanaka, Lake (N.Z.)
Lake Webster (Mass.)
USE Webster Lake (Mass.)
Lake Wedowee (Ala.)
USE Wedowee, Lake (Ala.)
Lake Wentworth (N.H.)
USE Wentworth, Lake (N.H.)
Lake whitefish
  ⌜QL638.S2⌝
UF Coregonus clupeaformis
Whitefish, Lake
Lake Wigry (Poland)
USE Wigry, Lake (Poland)
Lake Wilhelm (Pa.)
USE Wilhelm, Lake (Pa.)
Lake Windermere (England)
USE Windermere, Lake (England)
Lake Winnebago (Wis.)
USE Winnebago, Lake (Wis.)
Lake Winnekeening (Mass.)
USE Winthrop, Lake (Mass.)
Lake Winnipeg (Man.)
USE Winnipeg, Lake (Man.)
Lake Winnipesaukee (N.H.)
USE Winnipesaukee, Lake (N.H.)

Lake Winthrop (Mass.)
  USE Winthrop, Lake (Mass.)
Lake Worth (Tex. : Lake)
  USE Worth, Lake (Tex. : Lake)
Lake Wylie (N.C. and S.C.)
  USE Wylie, Lake (N.C. and S.C.)
Lakeba Island (Fiji)
  USE Lakemba Island (Fiji)
Lakedaímon (Ancient city)
  USE Sparta (Ancient city)
Lakeland (England)
  USE Lake District (England)
Lakeland terriers
  [SF429.L35]
  BT Terriers
Lakemba Island (Fiji)
  UF Lakeba Island (Fiji)
     Laquemba Island (Fiji)
  BT Islands—Fiji
Laker family
  USE Lake family
Lakes (England)
  USE Lake District (England)
Lakes *(May Subd Geog)*
  [GB1601-GB1797]
  [TD392 (Water-supply)]
  BT Channels (Hydraulic engineering)
    Hydrography
    Inland navigation
    Physical geography
    Water
  NT Eutrophication
    Glacial lakes
    International lakes
    Lake ecology
    Lake renewal
    Lakes—Circulation
    Limnology
    Playas
    Pluvial lakes
    Salt pans (Geology)
  — Aeration
    [TD458]
    UF Aeration of lakes
    BT Water—Aeration
  — Circulation *(May Subd Geog)*
    UF Circulation in lakes
      Lake circulation
    BT Lakes
  — Destratification
    UF Destratification of lakes
    BT Eutrophication
  — Fertilization
    UF Fertilization of lakes
    BT Aquaculture
      Eutrophication
      Fertilizers
  — Pollution
    USE Water—Pollution
  — Recreational use
    BT Outdoor recreation
    SA *subdivision* Recreational use *under names of specific lakes*
  — Regulation
    UF Regulation of lakes
    BT Flood control
    SA *subdivision* Regulation *under names of individual lakes*
  — Shorelines
    NT Lakeshore development
  — Temperature
    [GB1798.6-1798.9]
    BT Meteorology
      Temperature
    RT Ice on rivers, lakes, etc.
    SA *subdivision* Temperature *under particular lakes and groups of lakes, e.g.* Michigan, Lake—Temperature; Great Lakes—Temperature

    NT Thermal pollution of rivers, lakes, etc.
— Africa, East
  NT Tanganyika, Lake
— Africa, West
  NT Chad, Lake
— Alabama
  NT Gainesville Lake (Ala.)
    Guntersville Lake (Ala. and Tenn.)
    Martin, Lake (Ala.)
    Walter F. George Reservoir (Ala. and Ga.)
    Wedowee, Lake (Ala.)
    Weiss Lake (Ala.)
    West Point Lake (Ga. and Ala.)
— Alaska
  NT Beluga Lake (Alaska)
    Kurupa Lake (Alaska)
— Alberta
  NT Alexander Lake (Alta.)
    Athabasca, Lake (Sask. and Alta.)
    Bistcho Lake (Alta.)
    Calling Lake (Alta. : Lake)
    Claire, Lake (Alta.)
    Cold Lake (Alta. : Lake)
    Gift Lake (Alta.)
    Iosegun Lake (Alta.)
    Lesser Slave Lake (Alta.)
    Louise, Lake (Alta.)
    Wolf Lake (Alta.)
    Wylie Lake (Alta.)
    Zama Lake (Alta.)
— Argentina
  NT Mar Chiquita Lake (Córdoba, Argentina : Province)
— Arizona
  NT Apache Lake (Ariz.)
    Bartlett Reservoir (Ariz.)
    Canyon Lake (Ariz.)
    Horseshoe Lake (Ariz.)
    Mead, Lake (Ariz. and Nev.)
    Pleasant, Lake (Ariz.)
    Powell, Lake (Utah and Ariz.)
    Saguaro Lake (Ariz.)
    Theodore Roosevelt Lake (Ariz.)
— Arkansas
  NT Beaver Lake (Ark.)
    Bull Shoals Lake (Ark. and Mo.)
    Calion Navigation Pool (Ark.)
    Dardanelle Lake (Ark.)
    Greers Ferry Lake (Ark.)
    Lomond, Loch (Ark.)
    Millwood Lake (Ark.)
    Nimrod Lake (Ark.)
    Ouachita, Lake (Ark.)
    Table Rock Lake (Mo. and Ark.)
— Australia
  NT Argyle, Lake (W.A.)
    Burragorang, Lake (N.S.W.)
    Charm, Lake (Vic.)
    Eyre, Lake (S. Aust.)
    Gairdner, Lake (S. Aust.)
    Gippsland Lakes (Vic.)
    Gordon, Lake (Tas.)
    Great Lake (Tas.)
    Jack Smith Lake (Vic.)
    Macquarie, Lake (N.S.W.)
    Pedder, Lake (Tas.)
— Austria
  NT Achensee (Austria)
    Constance, Lake of
    Neusiedler Lake (Austria and Hungary)
    Wallersee (Austria)
    Wolfgangsee (Austria)
— Bolivia
  NT Titicaca Lake (Peru and Bolivia)
— Brazil
  NT Mirim Lake (Brazil and Uruguay)
    Três Marias Reservoir (Brazil)
— British Columbia

  NT Deka Lake (B.C.)
    Kalamalka Lake (B.C.)
    Koocanusa, Lake (B.C. and Mont.)
    Kootenay Lake (B.C.)
    Quinsam Lake (Vancouver Island, B.C.)
    Tahtsa Lake (B.C.)
    Tatlayoko Lake (B.C.)
    Windermere Lake (B.C.)
    Wood Lake (B.C.)
— California
  NT Almanor, Lake (Calif.)
    Berryessa, Lake (Calif.)
    Crane Valley Lake (Calif.)
    Eleanor, Lake (Calif.)
    Goose Lake (Calif. and Or.)
    Honey Lake (Calif.)
    Mono Lake (Calif.)
    Oroville, Lake (Calif.)
    Pyramid Lake (Calif.)
    Salton Sea (Calif.)
    Searles Lake (Calif.)
    Shasta Lake (Calif.)
    Sonoma, Lake (Calif.)
    Tahoe, Lake (Calif. and Nev.)
    Tulare Lake (Calif.)
— China
  NT Ch'ing-hai Lake (China)
    Ching-po Lake (China)
    Lop Nor (China)
    Manasarowar Lake (China)
    Pai-yang Lake (China)
    T'ai Lake (China)
    T'ien-ch'ih (China and Korea)
    Tung-t'ing Lake (China)
    West Lake (China)
— Colorado
  NT Boyd Lake (Colo.)
    Dillon Reservoir (Colo.)
    East Delaney Lake (Colo.)
    Hack Lake (Colo.)
    North Delaney Lake (Colo.)
    Shadow Mountain Lake (Colo.)
    South Delaney Lake (Colo.)
    Steamboat Lake (Colo.)
    Turquois Lake (Colo.)
— Egypt
  NT Birket Habu (Egypt)
    Maryūt, Lake (Egypt)
    Moeris, Lake (Egypt)
    Nasser, Lake (Egypt and Sudan)
— England
  NT Chew Valley Lake (England)
    Windermere, Lake (England)
— Estonia
  NT Peipus, Lake (Estonia and R.S.F.S.R.)
    Pskov, Lake (Estonia and R.S.F.S.R.)
— Ethiopia
  NT Rudolf, Lake (Kenya and Ethiopia)
    Tana, Lake (Ethiopia)
— Finland
  NT Eräjärvi (Finland)
    Höytiäinen Lake (Finland)
    Inari Lake (Finland)
    Keitele Lake (Finland)
    Kilpisjärvi (Finland and Sweden)
    Kiteenjärvi (Finland)
    Oulujärvi (Finland)
    Päijänne Lake (Finland)
    Pielinen Lake (Finland)
    Puula Lake (Finland)
    Saimaa Lake (Finland)
— Florida
  NT Deer Point Lake (Fla.)
    Okeechobee, Lake (Fla.)
    Talquin, Lake (Fla.)
— France
  NT Geneva, Lake (Switzerland and France)

Lakes
— **France** *(Continued)*
  Vassivière Lake (France)
— **Georgia**
  NT Allatoona Lake (Ga.)
   Carters Lake (Ga.)
   Hartwell Lake (S.C. and Ga.)
   Richard B. Russell Lake (Ga. and S.C.)
   Sidney Lanier, Lake (Ga.)
   Walter F. George Reservoir (Ala. and Ga.)
   West Point Lake (Ga. and Ala.)
— **Germany (East)**
  NT Havel Lake (Germany)
   Parsteiner See (Germany)
   Stechlin Lake (Germany)
   Tollense Lake (Germany)
   Werbellinsee (Frankfurt an der Oder, Germany)
— **Germany (West)**
  NT Ammer Lake (Germany)
   Chiem, Lake (Germany)
   Constance, Lake of
   Dümmer Lake (Germany)
   Eder Reservoir (Germany)
   Federsee (Germany)
   Kemnader See (Germany)
   Königssee (Germany)
   Masch Lake (Germany)
   Naturpark Lauenburgische Seen (Germany)
   Starnberger See (Germany)
   Steinhuder Lake (Germany)
— **Greece**
  NT Copais Lake (Greece)
   Ioannina, Lake (Greece)
   Trichonis, Lake (Greece)
— **Guatemala**
  NT Atitlán, Lake (Guatemala)
   Chichoj Lake (Guatemala)
— **Hungary**
  NT Balaton, Lake (Hungary)
   Neusiedler Lake (Austria and Hungary)
   Velence Lake (Hungary)
— **Iceland**
  NT Hagavatn (Iceland)
— **Idaho**
— **Illinois**
  NT Ellyn, Lake (Ill.)
   Horseshoe Lake (Alexander County, Ill.)
   Mattoon, Lake (Ill.)
   Sara, Lake (Ill.)
   Shelbyville, Lake (Ill.)
— **India**
  NT Chilka Lake (India)
— **Indonesia**
  NT Kerinci Lake (Sumatra, Indonesia)
   Tondano Lake (Celebes, Indonesia)
— **Iran**
  NT Caspian Sea
— **Ireland**
  NT Corrib, Lough (Ireland)
— **Israel**
  NT Dead Sea (Israel and Jordan)
   Tiberias Lake (Israel)
— **Italy**
  NT Como, Lake (Italy)
   Garda, Lake (Italy)
   Iseo, Lake (Italy)
   Maggiore, Lake (Italy and Switzerland)
   Orta, Lake (Italy)
— **Japan**
  NT Biwa Lake (Japan)
   Hamana Lake (Japan)
   Kasumigaura (Japan)
   Kawaguchi Lake (Japan)
   Mashū Lake (Japan)

Nojiri Lake (Japan)
Okutadami Lake (Japan)
Okutama Lake (Japan)
Oze Lake (Japan)
Shikotsu Lake (Japan)
Shinji Lake (Japan)
Tazawa Lake (Japan)
Towada Lake (Japan)
Toya Lake (Japan)
Utonai Lake (Japan)
Yamanaka Lake (Japan)
— **Jordan**
  NT Dead Sea (Israel and Jordan)
— **Kansas**
  NT Big Hill Lake (Kan.)
   Copan Lake (Okla. and Kan.)
   El Dorado Lake (Kan.)
   Hillsdale Lake (Kan.)
   La Cygne Lake (Kan.)
   Timber Creek Lake (Kan.)
   Wilson Lake (Kan.)
— **Kazakh S.S.R.**
  NT Aral Sea (Uzbek S.S.R. and Kazakh S.S.R.)
   Borovoe Lake (Kazakh S.S.R.)
   Zaisan Lake (Kazakh S.S.R.)
— **Kentucky**
  NT Barkley, Lake (Ky. and Tenn.)
   Barren River Lake (Ky.)
   Dale Hollow Lake (Tenn. and Ky.)
   Green River Lake (Ky.)
   Herrington Lake (Ky.)
   Kentucky Lake (Ky. and Tenn.)
   Nolin Lake (Ky.)
   Rough River Lake (Ky.)
   Taylorsville Lake (Ky.)
— **Kenya**
  NT Rudolf, Lake (Kenya and Ethiopia)
— **Kirghiz S.S.R.**
  NT Issyk-Kul' (Kirghiz S.S.R.)
— **Korea (North)**
  NT Changjin Reservoir (Korea)
   T'ien-ch'ih (China and Korea)
— **Louisiana**
  NT Bayou D'Arbonne Lake (La.)
   Borgne, Lake (La.)
   Caddo Lake (La. and Tex.)
   Claiborne, Lake (La.)
   Pontchartrain, Lake (La.)
   Toledo Bend Reservoir (La. and Tex.)
— **Maine**
  NT China Lake (Me.)
   Moosehead Lake (Me.)
   Rangeley Lakes (Me. and N.H.)
   Sebago Lake (Me. : Lake)
   Sebasticook Lake (Me.)
— **Malawi**
  NT Nyasa, Lake
— **Malaysia**
  NT Bera Lake (Pahang)
— **Manitoba**
  NT Dauphin Lake (Man.)
   Interlake Region (Man.)
   Kasmere Lake (Man.)
   Kautunigan Lake (Man.)
   Reindeer Lake (Sask. and Man.)
   Southern Indian Lake (Man.)
   West Hawk Lake (Man.)
   Winnipeg, Lake (Man.)
— **Maryland**
  NT Bloomington Lake (Md. and W. Va.)
   Deep Creek Lake (Md.)
   Liberty Lake (Md.)
   Piney Run Reservoir (Md.)
   Youghiogheny River Lake (Pa. and Md.)
— **Massachusetts**
  NT Attitash, Lake (Mass.)
   Cochituate, Lake (Mass.)

October Mountain Lake (Mass.)
Quabbin Reservoir (Mass.)
Queen Lake (Mass.)
Schoolhouse Lake (Mass.)
Webster Lake (Mass.)
White Island Pond (Mass.)
Winthrop, Lake (Mass.)
— **Mexico**
  NT Chapala, Lake (Mexico)
— **Michigan**
  NT Crystal Lake (Mich. : Lake)
   Huron, Lake (Mich. and Ont.)
   Saint Clair, Lake (Mich. and Ont.)
   Walloon Lake (Mich.)
— **Minnesota**
  NT Itasca, Lake (Minn.)
   Minnetonka, Lake (Minn.)
   Pelican Lake (Otter Tail County, Minn.)
   Pelican Lake (Saint Louis County, Minn.)
   Rainy Lake (Minn. and Ont.)
   Saganaga Lake (Minn. and Ont.)
   Side Lake (Minn. : Lake)
— **Mississippi**
  NT Okatibbee Lake (Miss.)
— **Missouri**
  NT Bull Shoals Lake (Ark. and Mo.)
   Harry S. Truman Reservoir (Mo.)
   Long Branch Lake (Mo.)
   Ozarks, Lake of the (Mo.)
   Pine Ford Reservoir (Mo.)
   Smithville Lake (Mo.)
   Swan Lake (Mo.)
   Table Rock Lake (Mo. and Ark.)
— **Montana**
  NT Clearwater Lakes (Mont.)
   Koocanusa, Lake (B.C. and Mont.)
   Placid Lake (Mont.)
— **Mozambique**
  NT Nyasa, Lake
— **Nebraska**
  NT Swan Lake (Saline County, Neb.)
— **Netherlands**
  NT IJssel Lake (Netherlands)
   Randmeren (Netherlands)
   Tjeukemeer (Netherlands)
   Vechten, Lake (Netherlands)
— **Nevada**
  NT Mead, Lake (Ariz. and Nev.)
   Mohave, Lake (Nev.)
   Pyramid Lake (Nev.)
   Tahoe, Lake (Calif. and Nev.)
— **New Hampshire**
  NT Crescent Lake (N.H.)
   Mirror Lake (Grafton County, N.H.)
   Newfound Lake (N.H.)
   Ossipee Lake (N.H.)
   Rangeley Lakes (Me. and N.H.)
   Sunapee Lake (N.H.)
   Wentworth, Lake (N.H.)
   Winnipesaukee, Lake (N.H.)
— **New Jersey**
  NT Greenwood Lake (N.J. and N.Y.)
— **New Mexico**
  NT Cochiti Reservoir (N.M.)
   Star Lake (McKinley County, N.M.)
— **New York (State)**
  NT Cayuga Lake (N.Y.)
   Champlain, Lake
   Finger Lakes (N.Y.)
   George, Lake (N.Y.)
   Great Sacandaga Lake (N.Y.)
   Greenwood Lake (N.J. and N.Y.)
   Indian Lake (Indian Lake, N.Y.)
   Keuka Lake (N.Y.)
   Ontario, Lake (N.Y. and Ont.)
   Skaneateles Lake (N.Y.)
— **New Zealand**

NT Frying Pan Lake (N.Z.)
   Hawea, Lake (N.Z.)
   Inferno Crater Lake (N.Z.)
   Rotorua, Lake (N.Z.)
   Taupo, Lake (N.Z.)
   Waikaremoana, Lake (N.Z.)
   Wanaka, Lake (N.Z.)
— Newfoundland
NT Buchans Lake (Nfld.)
   Dead Wolf Pond (Nfld.)
   Double Mer (Nfld.)
   Melville, Lake (Nfld.)
   Seal Lake (Nfld.)
— Nigeria
NT Kainji Reservoir (Nigeria)
— North Carolina
NT B. Everett Jordan Lake (N.C.)
   Gaston, Lake (N.C. and Va.)
   John H. Kerr Reservoir (Va. and
   N.C.)
   Mountain Island Lake (N.C.)
   Norman, Lake (N.C.)
   Wylie, Lake (N.C. and S.C.)
— North Dakota
NT Cottonwood Lake (Stutsman
   County, N.D.)
   Sheyenne Lake (N.D.)
— Northern Ireland
NT Erne, Lower Lough (Northern
   Ireland)
— Northwest Territories
NT Baker Lake (N.W.T. : Lake)
   Great Bear Lake (N.W.T.)
   Hazen, Lake (Ellesmere Island,
   N.W.T.)
   Hyde Lake (N.W.T.)
   Itchen Lake (N.W.T.)
   Laughland Lake (N.W.T.)
   Nonacho Lake (N.W.T.)
   Nose Lake (N.W.T.)
   Rainy Lake (N.W.T.)
   Walker Lake (N.W.T.)
   Watterson Lake (N.W.T.)
— Norway
NT Engeren (Norway)
   Gjende (Norway)
   Mjøsa Lake (Norway)
   Nordåsvannet (Norway)
— Nova Scotia
NT Kejimkujik Lake (N.S.)
— Ohio
NT Indian Lake (Ohio)
— Oklahoma
NT Broken Bow Lake (Okla.)
   Clayton Lake (Okla.)
   Copan Lake (Okla. and Kan.)
   Fort Gibson Lake (Okla.)
   Hugo Lake (Okla.)
   Kaw Lake (Okla.)
   Keystone Lake (Okla.)
   Oologah Lake (Okla.)
   Skiatook Lake (Okla.)
   Texoma, Lake (Okla. and Tex.)
   Thunderbird, Lake (Okla.)
— Ontario
NT Erie, Lake
   Huron, Lake (Mich. and Ont.)
   Killala Lake (Ont.)
   Lower Manitou Lake (Ont.)
   Midlothian Lake (Ont.)
   Natal Lake (Ont.)
   Nipissing, Lake (Ont.)
   Ontario, Lake (N.Y. and Ont.)
   Panache, Lake (Ont.)
   Prairie Lake (Ont.)
   Rainy Lake (Minn. and Ont.)
   Saganaga Lake (Minn. and Ont.)
   Saint Clair, Lake (Mich. and Ont.)
   Superior, Lake
— Oregon
NT Abert, Lake (Or.)

   Crater Lake (Or.)
   Goose Lake (Calif. and Or.)
   Oswego, Lake (Or.)
— Panama
NT Gatun Lake (Panama)
   Madden Lake (Panama)
   Miraflores Lake (Panama)
— Pennsylvania
NT Blue Marsh Lake (Pa.)
   East Branch Lake (Pa.)
   Glendale Lake (Pa.)
   Marburg, Lake (Pa.)
   Nockamixon, Lake (Pa.)
   Quaker Lake (Pa.)
   Raystown Lake (Pa.)
   Wallenpaupack, Lake (Pa.)
   Wilhelm, Lake (Pa.)
   Youghiogheny River Lake (Pa. and
   Md.)
— Peru
NT Titicaca Lake (Peru and Bolivia)
— Philippines
NT Laguna de Bay (Luzon,
   Philippines)
— Poland
NT Mamry Lake (Poland)
   Morskie Oko (Poland)
   Pojezierze Suwalskie (Poland)
   Radunia Lake (Poland)
   Śniardwy Lake (Poland)
   Wdzydze Lake (Poland)
   Wigry, Lake (Poland)
— Québec (Province)
NT Champlain, Lake
   Laflamme Lake (Québec)
   Meech Lake (Québec)
   Mégantic, Lake (Québec)
   Mistassini Lake (Québec)
   Saint John, Lake (Québec)
— Russian S.F.S.R.
NT Baikal Lake (R.S.F.S.R.)
   Beloe Lake (R.S.F.S.R.)
   Chany Lake (R.S.F.S.R.)
   Glubokoe Lake (R.S.F.S.R.)
   Imandra, Lake (R.S.F.S.R.)
   Kubenskoe Lake (R.S.F.S.R.)
   Ladoga Lake (R.S.F.S.R.)
   Onega Lake (R.S.F.S.R.)
   Peipus, Lake (Estonia and
   R.S.F.S.R.)
   Pskov, Lake (Estonia and
   R.S.F.S.R.)
   Seliger, Lake (R.S.F.S.R.)
   Siverskoe Lake (R.S.F.S.R.)
— Rwanda
NT Kivu, Lake (Rwanda and Zaire)
— Saskatchewan
NT Amisk Lake (Sask.)
   Athabasca, Lake (Sask. and Alta.)
   Chaplin Lake (Sask.)
   Cree Lake (Sask.)
   Diefenbaker, Lake (Sask.)
   Last Mountain Lake (Sask.)
   Nelson Lake (Sask.)
   Parker Lake (Sask.)
   Reindeer Lake (Sask. and Man.)
   Rottenstone Lake (Sask.)
   Spalding Lake (Sask.)
   Wollaston Lake (Sask.)
— Scotland
NT Lomond, Loch (Scotland)
   Menteith, Lake (Scotland)
   Ness, Loch (Scotland)
— South Carolina
NT Back River Reservoir (S.C.)
   Fishing Creek Reservoir (S.C.)
   Hartwell Lake (S.C. and Ga.)
   Richard B. Russell Lake (Ga. and
   S.C.)
   Wateree Lake (S.C.)
   Wylie, Lake (N.C. and S.C.)

— South Dakota
NT Francis Case, Lake (S.D.)
   Sharpe, Lake (S.D.)
— Soviet Union
NT Caspian Sea
— Spain
NT Albufera Lake (Spain)
— Sudan
NT Nasser, Lake (Egypt and Sudan)
— Sweden
NT Frykensjöarna (Sweden)
   Gardiken Reservoir (Sweden)
   Hyn Lake (Sweden)
   Kilpisjärvi (Finland and Sweden)
   Mälar Lake (Sweden)
   Siljan (Sweden)
   Storsjön (Sweden)
   Vänern (Sweden)
— Switzerland
NT Biel, Lake of (Switzerland)
   Constance, Lake of
   Geneva, Lake (Switzerland and
   France)
   Hallwil, Lake (Switzerland)
   Lucerne Lake (Switzerland)
   Maggiore, Lake (Italy and
   Switzerland)
   Morat, Lake of (Switzerland)
   Neuchâtel, Lake of (Switzerland)
   Schwarzsee (Switzerland : Lake)
   Thun, Lake of (Switzerland)
   Zurich, Lake of (Switzerland)
— Tanzania
NT Eyasi, Lake (Tanzania)
   Hombolo Lake (Tanzania)
   Nyasa, Lake
— Tennessee
NT Barkley, Lake (Ky. and Tenn.)
   Dale Hollow Lake (Tenn. and Ky.)
   Guntersville Lake (Ala. and Tenn.)
   Kentucky Lake (Ky. and Tenn.)
   Normandy Reservoir (Tenn.)
   Norris Lake (Tenn.)
   Reelfoot Lake (Tenn.)
   Tellico Lake (Tenn.)
— Texas
NT Benbrook Lake (Tex.)
   Braunig Lake (Tex.)
   Bridgeport, Lake (Tex.)
   Brownwood, Lake (Tex.)
   Buchanan, Lake (Tex.)
   Caddo Lake (La. and Tex.)
   Canyon Lake (Tex.)
   Cedar Creek Reservoir (Tex.)
   Corpus Christi, Lake (Tex.)
   Eagle Mountain Lake (Tex.)
   Fairfield Lake (Tex.)
   Garza-Little Elm Reservoir (Tex.)
   Highland Lakes (Tex.)
   Houston, Lake (Tex.)
   Hubbard Creek Lake (Tex.)
   Inks Lake (Tex.)
   Lake Fork Reservoir (Tex.)
   Lavon Lake (Tex.)
   Sam Rayburn Reservoir (Tex.)
   Tawakoni, Lake (Tex.)
   Texoma, Lake (Okla. and Tex.)
   Toledo Bend Reservoir (La. and
   Tex.)
   Travis, Lake (Tex.)
   Worth, Lake (Tex. : Lake)
— Thailand
NT Songkhla Lake (Thailand)
— United States
NT Erie, Lake
   Michigan, Lake
   Superior, Lake
— Uruguay
NT Mirim Lake (Brazil and Uruguay)
— Utah
NT Great Salt Lake (Utah)

Lakes

— **Utah** *(Continued)*
  Powell, Lake (Utah and Ariz.)
  Utah Lake (Utah)
— **Uzbek S.S.R.**
  NT Aral Sea (Uzbek S.S.R. and Kazakh S.S.R.)
— **Venezuela**
  NT Maracaibo Lake (Venezuela)
— **Vermont**
  NT Champlain, Lake
  Shelburne Pond (Vt.)
— **Vietnam**
  NT West Lake (Vietnam)
— **Virginia**
  NT Anna, Lake (Va.)
  Chesdin, Lake (Va.)
  Gaston, Lake (N.C. and Va.)
  John H. Kerr Reservoir (Va. and N.C.)
  Moomaw Lake (Va.)
  Smith Mountain Lake (Va.)
— **Washington (State)**
— **West Virginia**
  NT Bloomington Lake (Md. and W. Va.)
  Summersville Lake (W. Va.)
— **Wisconsin**
  NT Castle Rock Flowage (Wis.)
  Mendota, Lake (Wis.)
  Petenwell Lake (Wis.)
  Redstone, Lake (Wis.)
  Whitewater Lake (Wis.)
  Winnebago, Lake (Wis.)
— **Zaire**
  NT Kivu, Lake (Rwanda and Zaire)
  Mai-Ndombe, Lake (Zaire)
— **Zimbabwe**
  NT McIlwaine, Lake (Zimbabwe)
Lakes, Freezing and opening of
  USE Ice on rivers, lakes, etc.
Lakes, Right of navigation on
  USE International lakes
Lakes in art
Lakeshore development *(May Subd Geog)*
  UF Development, Lakeshore
  Lake frontage development
  Shoreline development of lakes
  BT Lakes—Shorelines
  Real estate development
Lakeside and Haverthwaite Railway
  BT Railroads—Great Britain
Lakeside architecture *(May Subd Geog)*
  UF Lake side architecture
  BT Architecture
Lakeview (S.D.)
  BT Rosebud Indian Reservation (S.D.)
Lakeview Cemetery (Howell, Mich.)
  UF Oak Grove Cemetery (Howell, Mich.)
  BT Cemeteries—Michigan
Lakh literature
  UF Lak literature
Lakhemaaskiĭ natsional'nyĭ park (Estonia)
  USE Lahemaa Rahvuspark (Estonia)
Lakher language
  [PL4001.L28]
  UF Mara language (India and Burma)
  BT Tibeto-Burman languages
Lakhers
  [DS485.A86]
  UF Mărās
  Shendus
Lakhǫn chātrī *(May Subd Geog)*
  Here are entered general works and those that deal solely with the presentation of Lakhǫn chātrī on the stage. The texts of Lakhǫn chātrī plays and works about them from a literary point of view are entered under Lakhǫn chātri plays.
  UF Lakon jatri
  BT Theater—Thailand

Lakhǫn chātrī plays *(May Subd Geog)*
  Here are entered the texts of Lakhǫn chātrī plays and works about them from a literary point of view. General works and those that deal solely with the presentation of Lakhǫn chātrī plays on the stage are entered under Lakhǫn chātrī.
  BT Thai drama
Lakhs (Daghestan people)
  UF Lakks (Daghestan people)
  Laks (Daghestan people)
  BT Ethnology—Daghestan
Laki-Lorand factor
  USE Blood coagulation factor XIII
Lakists
  USE Lake poets
Lakks (Daghestan people)
  USE Lakhs (Daghestan people)
Lakon jatri
  USE Lakhǫn chātrī
Lakota dialect
  UF Teton dialect
  BT Dakota language
Lakota Indians
  USE Teton Indians
Lakota language
  USE Dakota language
Lakota songs
  USE Songs, Lakota
Laks (Daghestan people)
  USE Lakhs (Daghestan people)
Lakshmana (Hindu deity)
  USE Lakṣmaṇa (Hindu deity)
Lakshmi (Hindu deity)
  BT Gods, Hindu
Lakṣmaṇa (Hindu deity)
  UF Lakshmana (Hindu deity)
  BT Gods, Hindu
Lala (African people)
  UF Balala (African people)
  Bukanda (African people)
  Ichilala (African people)
  Walala (African people)
  BT Ethnology—Zaire
  Ethnology—Zambia
  NT Ambo (Zambian people)
Lala language
  BT Bantu languages
  NT Ambo dialect (Zambia)
Lale family
  USE Lail family
Lali (African people)
  USE Laadi (African people)
Lali language
  USE Teke language
Lallans language
  USE Scots language
Lallemant House (Bourges, France)
  USE Hôtel Lallemant (Bourges, France)
Lalor family *(Not Subd Geog)*
Lalungs (Indic people)
  [DS432.L26]
  UF Tiwas (Indic people)
  BT Bodos
  Ethnology—India
  NT Missions to Lalungs (Indic people)
Lam-'bras (Sa-skya-pa)
  [BQ7672.4]
  BT Sa-skya-pa (Sect)—Doctrines
  Sa-skya-pa (Sect)—Rituals
Lam family
  USE Lamb family
Lam Gods-retabel (Panel painting)
  USE Eyck, Jan van, 1390-1440. Ghent altarpiece
Lam-rim
  [BQ7645.L35]
  BT Dge-lugs-pa (Sect)—Doctrines
Lam-rim (Bonpo)
  [BQ7980.5]
  BT Bonpo (Sect)—Doctrines

Lam Sơn Uprising, Vietnam, 1418-1428
  USE Vietnam—History—Lam Sơn Uprising, 1418-1428
Lama (Genus)
  [QL737.U54]
  UF Lamoids
  BT Camelidae
  NT Alpaca
  Guanaco
  Llamas
Lama glama
  USE Llamas
Lama guanicoe
  USE Guanaco
Lamaholot (Indonesian people)
  BT Ethnology—Indonesia
Lamaholot (Indonesian people) marriage customs and rites
  USE Marriage customs and rites, Lamaholot (Indonesian people)
Lamaism
  USE Buddhism
  Dge-lugs-pa (Sect)
Laman family
  USE Lamonna family
Lamang language
  USE Laamang language
Lamani language
  USE Lambadi language
Lamanites (Mormon Church)
  [BX8627.A3-BX8627.Z]
  BT Book of Mormon
  Mormon Church—Doctrines
Lamanna family
  USE Lamonna family
Lamap language
  USE Port Sandwich language
Lamar family *(Not Subd Geog)*
  UF De La Mare family
  De Lamar family
  Lamare family
  Lamarr family
  Lamarre family
  Lemar family
  Lemare family
Lamarck family
  USE Marck family
Lamare family
  USE Lamar family
Lamarr family
  USE Lamar family
Lamarre family
  USE Lamar family
Lamartine family *(Not Subd Geog)*
Lamas *(May Subd Geog)*
  BT Priests, Buddhist
  NT Bka'-gdams-pa lamas
  Bka'-rgyud-pa lamas
  Bonpo lamas
  'Bri-guṅ-pa lamas
  'Brug-pa lamas
  Dalai lamas
  Kar-ma-pa lamas
  Panchen lamas
  Rñiṅ-ma-pa lamas
  Sa-skya-pa lamas
  Śaṅs-pa lamas
— **Lineage**
  UF Lineage of lamas
Lamas, Bka'-gdams-pa
  USE Bka'-gdams-pa lamas
Lamas, Bka'-rgyud-pa
  USE Bka'-rgyud-pa lamas
Lamas, Kar-ma-pa
  USE Kar-ma-pa lamas
Lamas, Rñiṅ-ma-pa
  USE Rñiṅ-ma-pa lamas
Lamas, Sa-skya-pa
  USE Sa-skya-pa lamas
Lamas, 'Bri-guṅ-pa
  USE 'Bri-guṅ-pa lamas

Lamas, 'Brug-pa
  USE 'Brug-pa lamas
Lamas, Śaṅs-pa
  USE Śaṅs-pa lamas
Lamaze method of childbirth
  USE Natural childbirth
Lamb (Meat) *(May Subd Geog)*
  BT Lambs
     Meat
  RT Mutton
  NT Cookery (Lamb and mutton)
     Lamb meat industry
Lamb family *(Not Subd Geog)*
  UF Lam family
     Lambe family
     Lambs family
  RT Lamm family
     Lamson family
Lamb meat industry *(May Subd Geog)*
  ₁HD9436₁
  BT Lamb (Meat)
Lamb waves
  ₁QC244 (Physics)₁
  ₁TA417.4 (Engineering)₁
  UF Plate waves
     Waves, Lamb
     Waves, Plate
  BT Ultrasonic waves
Lamba language
  ₁PL8431₁
  BT Bantu languages
Lambadi language
  ₁PK2251₁
  UF Banjara language
     Labhani language
     Lamani language
     Lambani language
  BT India—Languages
     Rajasthani language
Lambadi proverbs
  USE Proverbs, Lambadi
Lambani language
  USE Lambadi language
Lambart family
  USE Lambert family
Lambas
  ₁DT955₁
  UF Balamba
  BT Bantus
     Ethnology—Zambia
  NT Missions to Lambas
Lambda algebra
  UF Algebra, Lambda
  BT Algebra, Homological
Lambda bacteriophage
  USE Bacteriophage lambda
Lambda calculus
  ₁QA9.5₁
  UF Calculus, Lambda
  BT Logic, Symbolic and mathematical
Lambda phage
  USE Bacteriophage lambda
Lambdina
  ₁QL561.G6₁
  BT Geometridae
Lambdina fiscellaria
  USE Hemlock looper
Lambe family
  USE Lamb family
Lambers family *(Not Subd Geog)*
  UF Lomars family
     Lumbus family
Lambert conformal conic projection
  (Cartography)
  BT Conical projection (Cartography)
     Map-projection

Lambert family *(Not Subd Geog)*
  UF Lambart family
     Lamberth family
     Lamberts family
     Lambertsen family
     Lambertson family
     Lamberty family
     Lambertz family
     Lampert family
Lamberth family
  USE Lambert family
Lamberts family
  USE Lambert family
Lambertsen family
  USE Lambert family
Lambertson family
  USE Lambert family
Lamberty family
  USE Lambert family
Lambertz family
  USE Lambert family
Lambeth Conference
  NT Lambeth Quadrilateral
Lambeth Quadrilateral
  UF Chicago-Lambeth Quadrilateral
  BT Anglican Communion—Relations
     Christian union
     Lambeth Conference
Lambi Bar cattle
  USE Sahiwal cattle
Lamblia intestinalis
  USE Giardia lamblia
Lambliasis
  USE Giardiasis
Lamborghini automobile
  ₁TL215.L₁
Lambrachton family
  USE Lambrochton family
Lambretta motor scooter
Lambrianides family *(Not Subd Geog)*
Lambroch family
  USE Lambrochton family
Lambrochton family *(Not Subd Geog)*
  UF Lambrachton family
     Lambroch family
     Lambroughton family
     Lamroch family
     Lamrock family
Lambroughton family
  USE Lambrochton family
Lambs *(May Subd Geog)*
  ₁SF376.5₁
  BT Domestic animals—Infancy
     Sheep
  NT Lamb (Meat)
  — **Feeding and feeds**
  — **Physiology**
Lambs family
  USE Lamb family
Lamb's-quarters
  USE Chenopodium album
Lambsen family
  USE Lamson family
Lambshead Ranch (Tex.) *(Not Subd Geog)*
  BT Ranches—Texas
Lambson family
  USE Lamson family
Lambsquarters
  USE Chenopodium album
Lambsquarters goosefoot
  USE Chenopodium album
Lamé
  USE Metal cloth
Lamé differential equation
  USE Lamé polynomials
Lamé language (Cameroon)
  (May Subd Geog)
  ₁PL8433₁
  UF Djibao language
     Dzepao language

     BT Cameroon—Languages
        Chadic languages
Lame man (Miracle)
  USE Healing of the lame man (Miracle)
Lamé polynomials
  UF Lamé differential equation
     Polynomials, Lamé
  BT Differential equations—Numerical
     solutions
Lamellibranchia
  USE Bivalvia
Lamellibranchia, Fossil
  USE Bivalvia, Fossil
Lamellibranchiata
  USE Bivalvia
Lamellibranchiata, Fossil
  USE Bivalvia, Fossil
Lamellorthoceratidae
  ₁QE807.L3₁
  BT Orthocerida
Lameness in cattle
  ₁SF967.L3₁
  UF Cattle—Lameness
  BT Cattle—Diseases
Lameness in horses
  ₁SF959.L25₁
  UF Horses—Lameness
  BT Horses—Diseases
Lameness in literature
Lameness in swine *(May Subd Geog)*
  ₁SF977.L₁
  UF Swine—Lameness
  BT Swine—Diseases
Lamentations
  USE Elegiac poetry
     Laments
Lamentations of Jeremiah (Music)
  BT Laments
     Tenebrae service music
Laments *(May Subd Geog)*
  UF Complancha
     Lamentations
  BT Elegiac poetry
     Mourning customs
  NT Dirges
     Jeremiads
     Lamentations of Jeremiah (Music)
Laments in the Bible
  UF Bible—Laments
Lamé's functions
  ₁QA409₁
  UF Ellipsoidal harmonics
     Functions, Lamé's
  BT Harmonic analysis
  RT Harmonic functions
Lameson family
  USE Lamson family
Lamesteer National Wildlife Refuge (Mont.)
  (Not Subd Geog)
  BT National parks and reserves—Montana
     Wildlife refuges—Montana
Lamet (Tribe)
  UF Lemet (Tribe)
  RT Karens
Lamey family *(Not Subd Geog)*
Lamiaceae
  ₁QK495.L25 (Botany)₁
  UF Labiatae
     Menthaceae
     Nepetaceae
  BT Lamiales
  NT Agastache
     Basil
     Bystropogon
     Eplingia
     Germander
     Leonurus
     Marrubium
     Mentha
     Nepeta
     Origanum

Lamiaceae (Continued)
    Otostegia
    Pogogyne
    Prunella
    Rosmarinus
    Salvia
    Stachys
    Thymbra
    Thymes
Lamiales
    [QK495.A12]
  BT Dicotyledons
  NT Lamiaceae
      Verbenaceae
Lamian War, 323-322 B.C.
    [DF235.5]
  BT Greece—History—Macedonian
       Expansion, 359-323 B.C.
Lamiidae
  USE Cerambycidae
Lamina epithelialis
  BT Epithelium
Lamina terminalis, Vascular organ of
  USE Organon vasculosum laminae
       terminalis
Laminagraphy
  USE Tomography
Laminar flow
    [QA929 (Theory)]
    [TL574.L (Aerodynamics)]
  BT Boundary layer
      Fluid dynamics
      Turbulent boundary layer
Laminar flow biological safety cabinets
  UF Safety cabinets, Laminar flow
  BT Biological apparatus and supplies
      Biological safety cabinets
Laminar flow clean rooms (May Subd Geog)
    [R857.C6 (Medicine)]
    [RA969.43 (Hospitals)]
  UF Filtered laminar airflow systems
  BT Clean rooms
Laminaria (May Subd Geog)
    [QK569.L2]
  BT Laminariaceae
  NT Laminaria digitata
Laminaria digitata
    [QK569.L2 (Algology)]
    [SH391.L33 (Fisheries)]
  UF Fucus digitatus
      Horsetail kelp
      Kelp, Horsetail
      Red ware (Marine algae)
      Redware (Marine algae)
      Sea girdle (Marine algae)
      Sea staff (Marine algae)
      Sea wand (Marine algae)
      Seastaff (Marine algae)
      Ulva digitata
  BT Laminaria
Laminariaceae
    [QK569.L2 (Algology)]
  BT Laminariales
  NT Laminaria
Laminariales (May Subd Geog)
    [QK569.L34]
  BT Brown algae
      Kelps
  NT Laminariaceae
      Lessoniaceae
Laminated cortex
  USE Neopallium
Laminated fabrics
  UF Fabrics, Laminated
  BT Laminated materials
      Textile fabrics
  — **Bonding**
Laminated fabrics industry
  (May Subd Geog)
    [HD9869.L]

Laminated glass
  USE Glass, Safety
Laminated materials
    [TA418.9.L3]
  BT Coating processes
      Composite materials
      Plates (Engineering)
  NT Glass, Safety
      Honeycomb structures
      Laminated fabrics
      Laminated plastics
      Laminated wood
      Sandwich construction
Laminated metals
  UF Bimetal
  BT Metals
  NT Thermostat
  — **Founding**
  — **Welding**
Laminated plastics
  UF Plastic laminates
      Plastics—Lamination
  BT Laminated materials
      Plastics
  NT Flake-glass laminates
Laminated wood
    [TS869]
  BT Laminated materials
      Wood products
  RT Veneers and veneering
  NT Plywood
  — **Testing**
  — — **Computer programs**
Laminectomy
  BT Spine—Surgery
  — **Complications and sequelae**
Laminitis
    [SF959.L]
  BT Horses—Diseases
Laminograph
  USE Tomograph
Laminography
  USE Tomography
Lamm family (Not Subd Geog)
  UF Lamme family
  RT Lamb family
Lamme family
  USE Lamm family
Lammen family
  USE Lemmen family
Lammer River (Austria)
  BT Rivers—Austria
Lammergeier
  UF Gypaetus barbatus
  BT Eagles
      Vultures
Lammers family (Not Subd Geog)
Lammert family (Not Subd Geog)
Lamna
    [QL638.95.L3]
  BT Lamnidae
Lamna punctata
  USE Isurus paucus
Lamnidae
    [QL638.95.L3]
  UF Mackerel sharks
  BT Lamniformes
  NT Carcharodon
      Isurus
      Lamna
Lamniformes
    [QL638.9]
  BT Chondrichthyes
      Sharks
  NT Alopiidae
      Cetorhinidae
      Lamnidae
      Mitsukurinidae
      Odontaspididae
Lamnso (African people)
  USE Nso (African people)

Lamoids
  USE Lama (Genus)
Lamonna family (Not Subd Geog)
  UF La Manna family
      Laman family
      Lamanna family
Lamoreaux family (Not Subd Geog)
  UF Lamoreux family
Lamoreux family
  USE Lamoreaux family
Lamourouxia
    [QK495.S43]
  BT Scrophulariaceae
Lamp-chimneys, globes, etc.
    [TP868]
  BT Glassware
  NT Lampshades
Lamp family
  USE Lampe family
Lamp shades
  USE Lampshades
Lampadena
    [QL638.M9]
  BT Lantern-fishes
Lampadena notialis
    [QL638.M9]
Lampanyctus
    [QL638.M9]
  BT Lantern-fishes
Lampblack
    [TP951]
Lampbrush chromosomes
    [QH600.6]
  UF Chromosomes, Lampbrush
  BT Giant chromosomes
Lampe family (Not Subd Geog)
  UF Lamp family
Lamperina
  USE Pacific hagfish
Lampern
  USE Lampetra fluviatilis
Lampert family
  USE Lambert family
Lampeter Brethren
  USE Church of the Agapemone
Lampetians
  USE Messalians
Lampetra
    [QL638.15.P4]
  BT Lampreys
Lampetra aepyptera
  USE Least brook lamprey
Lampetra fluviatilis
    [QL638.25.P]
  UF Lampern
      Petromyzon fluviatilis
      River lamprey
Lampman family (Not Subd Geog)
  UF Lampmann family
Lampmann family
  USE Lampman family
Lampoon
    [PN6149.L35]
  BT Polemics
      Satire
Lampornis
    [QL696.A558]
  BT Hummingbirds
  NT Lampornis viridipallens
Lampornis viridipallens
    [QL696.A558]
  UF Green-throated mountain gem
      Mountain gem, Green-throated
  BT Lampornis
Lamport family (Not Subd Geog)
Lamprey, Gulf brook
  USE Gulf brook lamprey
Lamprey, Least brook
  USE Least brook lamprey
Lampreys
    [QL638.1]

UF Hyperoartia
  Petromyzontiformes
BT Agnatha
NT Ammocoetes
  Lampetra
  Lethenteron
  Petromyzonidae
  Sea lamprey
— Anatomy
Lampridae
  [QL638.L24]
UF Lamprididae
BT Lampriformes
NT Lampris
Lamprididae
USE Lampridae
Lampridiformes
USE Lampriformes
Lampriformes
  [QL638.L24]
UF Allotriognathi
  Lampridiformes
  Selenichthyes
BT Osteichthyes
NT Lampridae
  Trachipteridae
Lampris
  [QL638.L24]
BT Lampridae
NT Opah
Lampris guttatus
USE Opah
Lampris luna
USE Opah
Lampris regius
USE Opah
Lamproite *(May Subd Geog)*
  [QE462.L35]
BT Basalt
Lamproniidae
USE Incurvariidae
Lampropeltis
  [QL666.O636]
UF King snakes
  Kingsnakes
  Milk snakes
  Ophibolus
BT Colubridae
Lampropeltis doliata triangulum
USE Lampropeltis triangulum
Lampropeltis getulus
  [QL666.O636]
UF King snake, Common
  Kingsnake, Common
Lampropeltis triangulum
  [QL666.O636]
UF American milk snake
  Lampropeltis doliata triangulum
  Milk snake, Common
  Osceola doliata
Lampropholis
  [QL666.L28]
Lampropholis tetradactyla
  [QL666.L28]
Lamprophyres
  [QE461]
BT Basalt
Lamproscatella
  [QL537.E7]
BT Ephydridae
Lamprosomatidae
USE Chrysomelidae
Lamps *(May Subd Geog)*
  [GR950.L3 (Folk-lore)]
  [GT445 (Manners and customs)]
BT House furnishings
  Light sources
  Lighting
NT Acetylene lamps
  Electric lamps
  Enameled glass lamps

Fairy lamps
  Flashlights
  Gas street lamps
  Iodine incandescent lamps
  Kerosene lamps
  Lampshades
  Miniature lamps
  Night lamps
  Safety-lamp
  Solar radiation simulation
Lamps, Ancient *(May Subd Geog)*
UF Ancient lamps
Lamps, Classical *(May Subd Geog)*
UF Classical lamps
BT Classical antiquities
NT Lamps, Hellenistic
  Lamps, Roman
Lamps, Enameled glass
USE Enameled glass lamps
Lamps, Hellenistic *(May Subd Geog)*
UF Hellenistic lamps
BT Lamps, Classical
Lamps, Jewish *(May Subd Geog)*
UF Jewish lamps
Lamps, Resonance
USE Resonance lamps
Lamps, Roman *(May Subd Geog)*
UF Roman lamps
BT Lamps, Classical
Lamps, Xenon
USE Xenon lamps
Lampsen family
USE Lamson family
Lampshades
UF Lamp shades
BT Lamp-chimneys, globes, etc.
  Lamps
NT Painted lampshades
Lampshades, Glass *(May Subd Geog)*
  [NK5440.L3]
UF Art glass lampshades
  Glass lampshades
BT Glassware
Lampson family
USE Lamson family
Lampton family *(Not Subd Geog)*
Lampugnani family *(Not Subd Geog)*
Lampung language
  [PL5341]
BT Malayan languages
NT Komering dialect
Lampwork (Paperweights)
  (May Subd Geog)
  [NK5440.P3]
BT Paperweights
Lampyridae
USE Fireflies
Lamroch family
USE Lambrochton family
Lamrock family
USE Lambrochton family
Lamso (African people)
USE Nso (African people)
Lamson family *(Not Subd Geog)*
UF Lambsen family
  Lambson family
  Lameson family
  Lampsen family
  Lampson family
RT Lamb family
Lamut language
USE Even language
Lamutski
USE Okhotsk, Sea of
Lan family *(Not Subd Geog)*
Lan Hsü (Taiwan)
USE Lan Island (Taiwan)

Lan Island (Taiwan)
UF Botel Tobago Island (Taiwan)
  Hung-t'on Hsü (Taiwan)
  Hung-t'ou Hsü (Taiwan)
  Hungf'ou Hsii (Taiwan)
  Hungtow Island (Taiwan)
  Koto Island (Taiwan)
  Kotosho Island (Taiwan)
  Lan Hsü (Taiwan)
  Lan Yü (Taiwan)
  Orchid Island (Taiwan)
BT Islands—Taiwan
Lan Tao (Hong Kong)
USE Lantau (Hong Kong)
Lan Tau (Hong Kong)
USE Lantau (Hong Kong)
Lan-ts'ang Chiang
USE Mekong River
Lan Yü (Taiwan)
USE Lan Island (Taiwan)
Lanai (Hawaii)
BT Hawaii
  Islands—Hawaii
Lanao Moro dialect
  [PL5884]
UF Moro languages
Lancang Jiang
USE Mekong River
Lancashire Plot, 1689-1694
  [DA461]
BT Great Britain—History—William and
  Mary, 1689-1702
  Jacobites
Lancaster, House of *(Not Subd Geog)*
BT Great Britain—Kings and rulers
Lancaster, Pa., Massacre at, 1763
USE Conestoga Massacre, Pa., 1763
Lancaster (Bombers)
BT Bombers
Lancaster County (Pa.)
NT Amish Country (Pa.)
Lancaster family *(Not Subd Geog)*
UF Lancastor family
  Lancester family
  Lancestor family
  Lanchester family
  Langcaster family
  Lankester family
  Lankister family
Lancaster Sound (N.W.T.)
BT Sounds (Geomorphology)—Northwest
  Territories
Lancasterian system
USE Monitorial system of education
Lancastor family
USE Lancaster family
Lance, Holy
USE Holy Lance
Lance (Missile)
Lancelets
USE Cephalochordata
Lancelot (Legendary character)
UF Lancelot du Lac (Legendary character)
  Launcelot (Legendary character)
BT Arthurian romances
Lancelot du Lac (Legendary character)
USE Lancelot (Legendary character)
Lances
  [U872]
Lancester family
USE Lancaster family
Lancestor family
USE Lancaster family
Lancha
  [QL523.C67]
BT Coreidae
Lanchester family
USE Lancaster family
Lancia automobile
Land
USE Land use

2077

Land, Allotment of
  USE Allotment of land
Land, Burning of
  USE Burning of land
Land, Condemnation of
  USE Eminent domain
Land, Liability for condition and use of
  USE Liability for condition and use of land
Land, Nationalization of *(May Subd Geog)*
  [HD1301-1315]
  UF Nationalization of land
     Socialization of land
  BT Communism
     Government ownership
     Single tax
     Socialism
  RT Land tenure
     Real property
  NT Collectivization of agriculture
Land, Reclamation of
  USE Reclamation of land
Land application of wastewater
  USE Land treatment of wastewater
Land art
  USE Earthworks (Art)
Land banks *(May Subd Geog)*
  BT Banks and banking
Land Between the Lakes (Ky. and Tenn.)
  UF Between-the-Rivers National
     Recreation Area (Ky. and Tenn.)
     Kentucky West Lakes Area (Ky. and
     Tenn.)
     Kentucky's Western Waterland (Ky.
     and Tenn.)
     Land Between the Lakes National
     Recreation Area (Ky. and Tenn.)
  BT National parks and reserves—
     Kentucky
     National parks and reserves—
     Tennessee
     Recreation areas—Kentucky
     Recreation areas—Tennessee
Land Between the Lakes National Recreation
Area (Ky. and Tenn.)
  USE Land Between the Lakes (Ky. and
     Tenn.)
Land breeze *(May Subd Geog)*
  BT Ocean-atmosphere interaction
     Winds
Land burning
  USE Burning of land
Land capability for agriculture
(May Subd Geog)
  [HD101-HD1131 (Economics)]
  [S590-S599.9 (Agriculture)]
  UF Agricultural capability of land
     Land suitability for agriculture
  BT Agriculture
     Land use
     Physical geography
  RT Soils
Land charges (Great Britain)
Land claim associations
  [HD226]
  UF Claim associations
  BT Frontier and pioneer life
Land clearing
  USE Clearing of land
Land companies *(May Subd Geog)*
  BT Land grants
     Land use, Rural
     Public lands
     Real property
Land consolidation
  USE Consolidation of land holdings
Land contracts
  USE Instalment land contracts
Land crabs, Burrowing
  USE Gecarcinidae
     Grapsidae

Land Dayak language
  USE Kendayan language
Land development
  USE Real estate development
Land drainage
  USE Drainage
Land family *(Not Subd Geog)*
  UF Lande family
     Lands family
Land fills
  USE Fills (Earthwork)
Land forms
  USE Landforms
Land-grant colleges
  USE State universities and colleges
Land grants *(May Subd Geog)*
  UF Grants, Land
     Land patents
  BT Colonization
     Public lands
  SA *subdivision* Public lands *under names*
     of countries, e.g. United States—
     Public lands
  NT Church lands
     Land companies
     Railroad land grants
     Ranches
     School lands
  — **Law and legislation** *(May Subd Geog)*
  — **Colorado**
     NT Maxwell Land Grant (N.M. and
       Colo.)
  — **New Mexico**
     NT Maxwell Land Grant (N.M. and
       Colo.)
Land grants for education
  USE School lands
Land hermit crabs
  USE Coenobitidae
Land laws
  USE Land reform—Law and legislation
     Land tenure—Law and legislation
Land League, Irish
  USE Irish Land League
Land-locked states
  USE Landlocked states
Land melioration
  USE Reclamation of land
Land of Bliss (Buddhism)
  USE Western Paradise (Buddhism)
Land patents
  USE Land grants
Land question
  USE Land tenure
Land rail, European
  USE Corncrake
Land reclamation
  USE Reclamation of land
Land reform *(May Subd Geog)*
  Here are entered works on land distribution com-
  bined with the socio-economic policy relating to the
  population of that area of distribution.
  UF Agrarian reform
  BT Economic policy
     Land use, Rural
     Social policy
  RT Agriculture and state
  NT Aerial photography in land reform
     Land reform beneficiaries
     Land tenure
  — **Finance**
  — **Law and legislation** *(May Subd Geog)*
     UF Land laws
     BT Agricultural laws and legislation
Land reform beneficiaries *(May Subd Geog)*
  UF Beneficiaries, Land reform
  BT Land reform
Land research *(May Subd Geog)*
  BT Research
Land Rover automobile
  USE Rover automobile

Land-Rover truck
  [TL230.5.L]
  BT Rover automobile
     Trucks
Land Rush, Oklahoma, 1889
  USE Oklahoma—History—Land Rush, 1889
Land sales, Interstate
  USE Interstate land sales
Land scrip (United States)
  USE Bounties, Military—United States
     Homestead law—United States
Land settlement *(May Subd Geog)*
  Here are entered general works on occupation of
  the land. Works on settlement of the land by organ-
  ized groups of colonists are entered under Agricultur-
  al colonies.
  UF Resettlement
     Settlement of land
  BT Colonies
     Land use, Rural
  RT Human settlements
  NT Agricultural colonies
     Colonization
     Land settlement patterns
  — **Law and legislation** *(May Subd Geog)*
Land settlement patterns *(May Subd Geog)*
  UF Patterns, Land settlement
     Settlement patterns
  BT Anthropo-geography
     Land settlement
Land settlement patterns, Prehistoric
(May Subd Geog)
  UF Prehistoric land settlement patterns
  BT Archaeology
     Man, Prehistoric
Land slides
  USE Landslides
Land subdivision *(May Subd Geog)*
  UF Real estate subdivision
     Subdivision of land
  BT Cities and towns—Growth
     City planning
     Land use, Rural
     Real estate business
     Real property
  RT Development rights transfer
     Real estate development
  NT Cluster housing
     Planned unit developments
  — **Law and legislation** *(May Subd Geog)*
     BT City planning and redevelopment
       law
     RT Zoning law
Land subsidences
  USE Subsidences (Earth movements)
Land suitability for agriculture
  USE Land capability for agriculture
Land surveying
  USE Surveying
Land tax
  USE Land value taxation
     Real property tax
Land tenure *(May Subd Geog)*
  [HD101-1395]
  UF Agrarian question
     Feudal tenure
     Freehold
     Land question
     Tenure of land
  BT Agriculture
     Agriculture—Economic aspects
     Inheritance and succession
     Land reform
     Land use, Rural
     Real property
     Single tax
  RT Land, Nationalization of
     Landowners
     Peasantry
     Serfdom

SA *subdivision* Land tenure *under* Indians,
    Indians of Mexico, [North
    America, etc.]
NT Absenteeism
    Allotment of land
    Australian aborigines—Land tenure
    Church lands
    Commons
    Consolidation of land holdings
    Entail
    Farm management
    Farm ownership
    Farm tenancy—Economic aspects
    Farms—Foreign ownership
    Feudalism
    Haciendas
    Inholdings
    Lapps—Land tenure
    Latifundio
    Maoris—Land tenure
    Mark
    Mbere (African people)—Land tenure
    Métayer system
    Mir
    Murngin (Australian people)—Land
      tenure
    Pre-emption
    Real property—Foreign ownership
    Rent
    School lands
    Shrine lands
    Temple lands
    Udal system
    Unearned increment
    Village communities
    Zadruga
— **Law and legislation** *(May Subd Geog)*
  UF Land laws
  NT Allodium
     Borough-English (Law)
     Contracts, Agricultural
     Conveyancing
     Copyhold
     Farm tenancy
     Feudal law
     Homestead law
     Inclosures
     Joint tenancy
     Land titles
     Landlord and tenant
     Leases
     Mortmain
     Ousiakē gē (The Greek phrase)
     Real property
     Riparian rights
— — **Germany**
    NT Anerbengerichte (Germany)
— **Religious aspects**
— — **Baptists, [Catholic Church, etc.]**
— — **Buddhism, [Christianity, etc.]**
— **Ireland**
  UF Irish land question
  BT Irish question
— **Latin America**
  NT Haciendas
— **Nepal**
  NT Sherpas—Land tenure
— **Turkey**
  NT Timar
Land tenure (Adat law)
Land tenure (Byzantine law)
  BT Law, Byzantine
Land tenure (Germanic law)
Land tenure (Greek law)
Land tenure (Hindu law)
Land tenure (Islamic law) *(May Subd Geog)*
Land tenure (Jekri law)
  BT Law, Jekri (African people)

Land tenure (Jewish law)
Land tenure (Kipsigis law)
  (May Subd Geog)
  BT Law, Kipsigis (African people)
Land tenure (Maori law)
  BT Law, Maori
Land tenure (Maya law)
  BT Law, Maya
Land tenure (Murngin law)
  BT Law, Murngin (Australian people)
Land tenure (Primitive law)
  (May Subd Geog)
Land tenure (Roman law)
Land tenure (Saxon law)
Land tenure (Yoruba law)
Land terracing
  USE Terracing
Land title examinations
  USE Title examinations
Land titles *(May Subd Geog)*
  UF Land-warrants
     Titles, Land
  BT Land tenure—Law and legislation
  RT Conveyancing
     Deeds
     Ejectment
     Prescription (Law)
     Real property
     Vendors and purchasers
  NT Abstracts of title
     Adverse possession
     Contracts for deeds
     Insurance, Title
     Jactitation of title
     Leases
     Mortgages
     Quiet title actions
     Tax-sales
     Title companies
     Title examinations
— **Examinations**
  USE Title examinations
— **Registration and transfer**
  (May Subd Geog)
    [HD1188-1208]
  UF Land transfer
     Registration of title
  BT Non-contentious jurisdiction
     Publicity (Law)
     Recording and registration
     Transfer (Law)
  RT Priorities of claims and liens
  NT Cadasters
     Manorial extents
     Real covenants
     Torrens system
— — **Cases**
— — — **Digests**
    USE Land titles—Registration
      and transfer—Digests
— — **Digests**
    UF Land titles—Registration and
      transfer—Cases—Digests
— — **Punched card systems**
    USE Punched card systems—Land
      titles
— **Registration and transfer (Frankish law)**
— **Registration and transfer (Germanic law)**
— **Registration and transfer (Roman law)**
Land transfer
  USE Land titles—Registration and transfer
Land treatment of wastewater
  (May Subd Geog)
  UF Land application of wastewater
     Soil treatment of wastewater
     Wastewater land treatment
     Wastewater renovation by land
      treatment
  BT Sewage—Purification
  RT Sewage disposal in the ground
  NT Sewage irrigation

Land trusts *(May Subd Geog)*
  BT Land use, Rural
     Real property
     Trusts and trustees
Land trusts (Islamic law) *(May Subd Geog)*
  UF Waqf
  BT Islamic law
Land use *(May Subd Geog)*
  [HD101-1395]
  UF Land
     Use of land
     Utilization of land
  BT Economics
  RT Landscape assessment
  NT Aerial photography in land use
     Cadasters
     Cemeteries—Multiple use
     Church lands
     Eminent domain
     Feudalism
     Land capability for agriculture
     Open spaces
     Public lands
     Real estate business
     Real estate development
     Real property
     Reclamation of land
     Rent
     Rent (Economic theory)
     Sanitary landfills
     School lands
     Temple lands
     Underground areas
     Waste lands
     Zoning
— **Effect of taxation on**
  BT Land value taxation
     Real property and taxation
     Real property tax
     Taxation
— **Law and legislation** *(May Subd Geog)*
  NT Zoning law
— **Planning**
  NT City planning
     Regional planning
     Women and land use planning
— — **Citizen participation**
— **Study and teaching** *(May Subd Geog)*
— — **Law and legislation**
    (May Subd Geog)
    BT Educational law and legislation
— **Taxation**
  USE Land value taxation
     Real property tax
Land use, Rural *(May Subd Geog)*
  UF Rural land use
  RT Agriculture
  NT Agricultural conservation
     Agriculture—Economic aspects
     Agroforestry
     Burning of land
     Consolidation of land holdings
     Farms
     Feudalism
     Land companies
     Land reform
     Land settlement
     Land subdivision
     Land tenure
     Land trusts
     Rangelands
     Wetlands
— **Law and legislation** *(May Subd Geog)*
  BT Agricultural laws and legislation
— **United States**
  NT Agricultural Conservation Program
Land use, Urban *(May Subd Geog)*
  UF Urban land use
  BT Cities and towns
     Urban economics
     Urban policy

Land use, Urban *(Continued)*
- RT Urban renewal
- NT Urban agriculture
- — Law and legislation
  - USE City planning and redevelopment law
  - Zoning law
- — Management
  - USE City planning
- — Planning
  - USE City planning

Land use and energy conservation
(May Subd Geog)
[HD108.2]
- BT Energy conservation

Land use surveys *(May Subd Geog)*
  Here are entered works on the methods and techniques employed in conducting land use surveys, and reports of individual surveys. For the latter the heading may be subdivided by place; in such cases an additional subject entry is made under the heading Land use—[local subdivision], e.g. 1. Land use—Florida. 2. Land use surveys—Florida. For land use surveys on a special topic, the additional subject entry is made under the special topic, e.g. 1. Real estate development—Florida. 2. Land use surveys—Florida.
- BT Surveys

Land valuation
- USE Farms—Valuation
  - Real property—Valuation

Land value taxation *(May Subd Geog)*
  Here are entered works on the taxation of the value of land exclusive of buildings and other improvements. Works dealing with land value taxation as the sole source of a government's tax revenue are entered under Single tax. Works on the taxation of real property, including land and all property attached to the land are entered under Real property tax.
- UF Land tax
  - Land use—Taxation
  - Taxation of land values
- BT Real property tax
  - Unearned increment
- RT Single tax
- NT Land use—Effect of taxation on
- **— Law and legislation** *(May Subd Geog)*
- **— Great Britain**
  - NT Hidage

Land value taxation (Islamic law)
(May Subd Geog)
Land-warrants
- USE subdivision Public lands under names of countries, e.g. United States—Public lands
  - Land titles

Land Wursten (Germany)
- USE Wursten (Germany)

Land-yachts
- USE Sand-yachts

Landa family
- USE Landers family

Landau damping
[QC718]
- UF Damping, Landau
- BT Plasma waves

Landau family *(Not Subd Geog)*
- UF Landauer family

Landauer family
- USE Landau family

Lande family
- USE Land family

Landed gentry
- USE Gentry

Landeiro family *(Not Subd Geog)*
Landen family
- USE Langston family

Lander family
- USE Landers family

Landers family *(Not Subd Geog)*
- UF Landa family
  - Lander family
  - Landor family

Landes (France)
- UF Les Landes (France)

Landesfoerderungspreis fuer Fotografie
- USE Landesförderungspreis für Fotografie

Landesförderungspreis für Fotografie
- UF Landesfoerderungspreis fuer Fotografie
- BT Photography—Competitions—Austria

Landesförderungspreis für Fotografie in der Steiermark
- BT Photography—Competitions—Austria

Landespavillon (Stuttgart, Germany)
- BT Exhibition buildings—Germany (West)

Landfills
- USE Fills (Earthwork)

Landfills, Coal ash
- USE Coal ash sites

Landfills, Sanitary
- USE Sanitary landfills

Landford family
- USE Langford family

Landforms *(May Subd Geog)*
[GB423-445]
- UF Land forms
- BT Geomorphology
  - Physical geography
- SA names of topographical features, e.g. Mountains; Plains; Valleys; also subdivision Maps, Physical under names of countries, regions, etc.
- NT Cliffs
  - Glacial landforms
  - Islands
  - Natural bridges
  - Pans (Geomorphology)
  - Reefs
  - Valleys

Landfriede
[DD165.5 (German history, DD137.5)]
[JN3259]
- UF Landpeace
  - Public peace (Landfriede)
- BT Feudal law
- RT Truce of God

Landholders
- USE Landowners

Landi family *(Not Subd Geog)*
- UF Lando family

Landim language
- USE Ronga language

Landing aids (Aeronautics)
[TL725.3.L2]
- UF Aircraft landing aids
  - Airports—Landing aids
- BT Aeronautics
  - Airplanes—Electric equipment
  - Airplanes—Electronic equipment
  - Airplanes—Landing
  - Airports
  - Navigation (Aeronautics)
  - Transportation markings
- RT Electronics in aeronautics
- NT Airports—Lighting
  - Ground controlled approach
  - Instrument landing systems
  - Landing mats
  - Microwave landing systems

Landing barges
- USE Landing craft

Landing craft *(May Subd Geog)*
- UF Infantry landing craft
  - Landing barges
  - Landing ships
  - Tank landing ships
- BT Motor vehicles, Amphibious
  - Ships
  - Transportation, Military
- NT United States. Navy—Boats

Landing family
- USE Langston family

Landing fees (Airports)
- USE Airports—Landing fees

Landing gear
- USE subdivision Landing gear under types of aircraft, e.g. Airplanes, Military—Landing gear

Landing lights, Aircraft
- USE Airplanes—Lighting

Landing mats
- UF Airfield landing mats
  - Airplane landing mats
- BT Air bases—Runways
  - Landing aids (Aeronautics)

Landing of aircraft
- USE subdivision Landing under particular types of aircraft, e.g. Airplanes—Landing; Seaplanes—Landing

Landing of space shuttles
- USE Space shuttles—Landing

Landing of space vehicles
- USE Space vehicles—Landing

Landing operations
  Here are entered general works on the landing of waterborne or airborne troops on hostile territory, including the tactics of transporting, landing and establishing such troops and their supplies, and combat during the landing phase. Works on the joint operation of air, land, and sea forces to establish troops on shore, as developed in World War II, are entered under Amphibious warfare.
- UF Disembarkation
  - Joint operations (Military science)
  - Troops, Landing of
- BT Transportation, Military
  - Unified operations (Military science)

Landing path
- USE Glide path systems

Landing ships
- USE Landing craft

Landing strips
- USE Air bases—Runways
  - Airports—Runways

Landing systems, Microwave
- USE Microwave landing systems

Landing vehicles, Tracked
- USE Tracked landing vehicles

Landings at Fort Myers (Fort Myers, Fla.)
(Not Subd Geog)
- UF Fort Myers (Fla.). Landings at Fort Myers

Ländler
- BT Dance music
  - Waltzes
- NT Schuhplattler

Landlocked Atlantic salmon
- USE Ouananiche

Landlocked states
- UF Land-locked states
  - States, Landlocked
- RT Access to the sea (International law)

Landlocked tide pool ecology
- USE Tide pool ecology, Landlocked

Landlord and tenant *(May Subd Geog)*
- UF Tenants
- BT Apartment houses
  - Commercial law
  - Housing management
  - Land tenure—Law and legislation
  - Possessory interests in land
  - Real property
- RT Distress (Law)
  - Farm tenancy
  - Leases
  - Rent
  - Waste (Law)
- NT Commercial leases
  - Crofters
  - Dilapidations
  - Eviction
  - Fixtures (Law)

Forcible entry and detainer
Housing courts
Landlords
Real covenants
Rent control
Rent strikes
Rental housing—Law and legislation
Subtenants
— **Cases**
— — **Digests**
  USE Landlord and tenant—Digests
— **Digests**
  UF Landlord and tenant—Cases—
    Digests
Landlord and tenant (Jewish law)
Landlord and tenant (Roman law)
Landlord-tenant courts
  USE Housing courts
Landlords *(May Subd Geog)*
  BT Landlord and tenant
Landman family *(Not Subd Geog)*
  UF Landmann family
Landmann family
  USE Landman family
Landmark Inn Complex (Castroville, Tex.)
  USE Landmark Inn State Historic Site
    (Castroville, Tex.)
Landmark Inn State Historic Site
  (Castroville, Tex.) *(Not Subd Geog)*
  UF Landmark Inn Complex (Castroville,
    Tex.)
  BT Historic sites—Texas
    Hotels, taverns, etc.—Texas
Landmark Movement
  USE Landmarkism
Landmark shorthand
  USE Shorthand—Landmark
Landmarkers
  USE Landmarkism
Landmarkism
  ₍BX6237₎
  UF Landmark Movement
    Landmarkers
  BT Baptists—United States—History
Landmarks, Literary
  USE Literary landmarks
Landmarks, Preservation of
  USE Natural monuments
Landmarks (Boundaries)
  USE Boundaries (Estates)
Lando family
  USE Landi family
Landon family
  USE Langston family
Landor family
  USE Landers family
Landown family
  USE Langston family
Landowners *(May Subd Geog)*
  UF Landholders
    Owners of land
  RT Land tenure
  NT Adjoining landowners
    Forest landowners
    Plantation owners
Landowners, Adjoining
  USE Adjoining landowners
Landowners, Forest
  USE Forest landowners
Landpeace
  USE Landfriede
Landrace swine
Landrey family
  USE Landry family
Landri family
  USE Landry family
Landro family
  USE Landry family
Landrückentunnel (Germany)
  BT Railroad tunnels—Germany (West)

Landry family *(Not Subd Geog)*
  UF Landrey family
    Landri family
    Landro family
Landry-Guillain-Barré syndrome
  USE Polyradiculoneuritis
Lands, Mineral
  USE Mineral lands
Lands, Shrine
  USE Shrine lands
Lands beneath navigable waters
  USE Submerged lands
Land's End (England)
Lands family
  USE Land family
Lands under the marginal sea
  USE Submerged lands
Lands with mineral deposits
  USE Mineral lands
Landsat satellites
  UF Satellites, Landsat
  BT Artificial satellites in remote sensing
    Astronautics in earth sciences
    Natural resources
    Scientific satellites
— **Law and legislation** *(May Subd Geog)*
  BT Space law
**Landsberg am Lech (Germany : Refugee
  camp)** *(Not Subd Geog)*
  UF Landsberg Displaced Persons Camp
    (Germany)
  BT Refugees—Germany (West)
    World War, 1939-1945—Refugees
Landsberg Displaced Persons Camp (Germany)
  USE Landsberg am Lech (Germany :
    Refugee camp)
Landsberg family *(Not Subd Geog)*
  UF Landsborough family
    Landsburg family
Landsborough family
  USE Landsberg family
Landsburg family
  USE Landsberg family
Landscape *(May Subd Geog)*
  ₍BH301.L3 (Aesthetics)₎
  ₍QH75 (Natural history)₎
  UF Natural scenery
    Scenery
    Scenic beauty
  BT Nature
  RT Nature (Aesthetics)
  NT Mountains in literature
    Natural monuments
    Nature in literature
    Sea in literature
Landscape architects *(May Subd Geog)*
  BT Architects
  NT Landscape architectural firms
    Landscape architecture—Vocational
      guidance
    Women landscape architects
Landscape architectural drawing
  (May Subd Geog)
  ₍SB476.4₎
  UF Drawing, Landscape architectural
  BT Architectural drawing
— **Tilt-up technique**
  UF Tilt-up technique in landscape
    architectural drawing
Landscape architectural firms
  (May Subd Geog)
  UF Landscape architecture firms
  BT Architectural firms
    Business enterprises
    Landscape architects
    Landscaping industry
Landscape architectural services
  (May Subd Geog)
  ₍SB472.5-472.565₎
  BT Design services
    Landscape architecture

Landscape architecture *(May Subd Geog)*
  ₍SB469-476.4₎
  UF Landscape design
  RT Horticultural service industry
    Landscape gardening
    Landscape nurseries
    Landscape protection
    Landscaping industry
  NT Airports—Landscape architecture
    Apartment houses—Landscape
      architecture
    Cemeteries—Landscape architecture
    Decks (Architecture, Domestic)
    Garden borders
    Garden lighting
    Garden ornaments and furniture
    Garden structures
    Garden walks
    Gardens—Design
    Gardens, English
    Hedges
    Hospitals—Landscape architecture
    Industrial buildings—Landscape
      architecture
    Landscape architectural services
    Parking lots—Landscape architecture
    Parks
    Patios
    Perennials
    Pergolas
    Plants, Ornamental
    Roadside improvement
    Schools—Landscape architecture
    Shrubs
    Topiary work
    Trees
    Urban beautification
    Water in landscape architecture
    Women in landscape architecture
    Woody plants
— **Study and teaching (Internship)**
  (May Subd Geog)
  UF Interns (Landscape architecture)
— **Vocational guidance**
  BT Landscape architects
— **Great Britain**
— — **Competitions**
— — **Exhibitions**
**Landscape architecture and energy
  conservation** *(May Subd Geog)*
  ₍SB475.9.E53₎
  BT Architecture and energy conservation
    Energy conservation
Landscape architecture firms
  USE Landscape architectural firms
**Landscape architecture for the physically
  handicapped** *(May Subd Geog)*
  ₍SB476₎
  BT Physically handicapped
Landscape architecture in water conservation
  (May Subd Geog)
  ₍SB475.83₎
  BT Water conservation
  RT Water in landscape architecture
Landscape assessment *(May Subd Geog)*
  ₍GF90-91₎
  UF Assessment, Landscape
    Environmental perception
    Landscape evaluation
    Landscape perception
    Perception, Landscape
  BT Human ecology
  RT Land use
    Landscape protection
Landscape changes *(May Subd Geog)*
  UF Change, Landscape
  BT Physical geography
Landscape contracting *(May Subd Geog)*
  ₍SB472.55₎
  BT Landscaping industry
  NT Landscape contractors

Landscape contractors *(May Subd Geog)*
  BT Contractors
      Landscape contracting
  NT Interior landscape contractors
Landscape design
  USE Landscape architecture
Landscape drawing *(May Subd Geog)*
  [NC790-800]
  BT Drawing
  —**16th century** *(May Subd Geog)*
  —**17th century** *(May Subd Geog)*
  —**18th century** *(May Subd Geog)*
  —**19th century** *(May Subd Geog)*
Landscape drawing, American
  (May Subd Geog)
  UF American landscape drawing
Landscape drawing, British
  (May Subd Geog)
  UF British landscape drawing
Landscape drawing, Chinese
  (May Subd Geog)
  UF Chinese landscape drawing
Landscape drawing, Dutch
  (May Subd Geog)
  UF Dutch landscape drawing
Landscape drawing, Dutch, [English, French, etc.]
Landscape drawing, Flemish
  (May Subd Geog)
  UF Flemish landscape drawing
Landscape evaluation
  USE Landscape assessment
Landscape gardening *(May Subd Geog)*
  [SB469-479]
  BT Forests and forestry
      Gardening
      Hedges
      Horticulture
      Parks
      Trees
  RT Gardens—Design
      Horticultural service industry
      Landscape architecture
      Landscaping industry
      Ornamental horticulture
  NT Autumn gardening
      Bedding plants
      Church gardens
      Espaliers
      Gardens, English
      Grounds maintenance
      Knot gardens
      Landscape nurseries
      Maze gardens
      Meadow gardening
      Turf management
  —**Contracts and specifications**
    (May Subd Geog)
    UF Garden contracting
  —**History**
    NT Garden historians
Landscape gardens, English
  USE Gardens, English
Landscape in art
  [N8213]
Landscape nurseries *(May Subd Geog)*
  BT Landscape gardening
      Landscaping industry
      Nurseries (Horticulture)
      Ornamental horticulture
  RT Grounds maintenance
      Horticultural service industry
      Landscape architecture
Landscape on porcelain *(May Subd Geog)*
  BT Porcelain
Landscape painters *(May Subd Geog)*
  [ND1340-1367]
  BT Painters
  NT Barbizon school
Landscape painting *(May Subd Geog)*
  [ND1340-1367]

  BT Painting
  —**16th century** *(May Subd Geog)*
    NT Landscape painting, Renaissance
  —**17th century** *(May Subd Geog)*
  —**18th century** *(May Subd Geog)*
  —**19th century** *(May Subd Geog)*
    NT Luminism (Art)
  ——**England**
    NT Norwich school of painting
  ——**France**
    NT Barbizon school
        Saint-Siméon school of painting
  ——**United States**
  —**20th century** *(May Subd Geog)*
Landscape painting, American
  (May Subd Geog)
  UF American landscape painting
  NT Hudson River school of landscape
      painting
      Luminism (Art)
      Pennsylvania school of landscape
      painting
  —**British influences**
    BT Great Britain—Civilization
Landscape painting, Asian *(May Subd Geog)*
  [ND1365]
  UF Asian landscape painting
Landscape painting, Australian
  (May Subd Geog)
  UF Australian landscape painting
Landscape painting, Austrian
  (May Subd Geog)
  UF Austrian landscape painting
Landscape painting, Brazilian
  (May Subd Geog)
  UF Brazilian landscape painting
  NT Grupo Grimm (Group of artists)
Landscape painting, British
  (May Subd Geog)
  UF British landscape painting
Landscape painting, Bulgarian
  (May Subd Geog)
  UF Bulgarian landscape painting
Landscape painting, Byelorussian
  (May Subd Geog)
  UF Byelorussian landscape painting
Landscape painting, Canadian
  (May Subd Geog)
  UF Canadian landscape painting
Landscape painting, Chinese
  (May Subd Geog)
  —**Three kingdoms-Sui dynasty, 220-618**
    UF Landscape painting, Chinese—
        Three kingdoms, six dynasties-
        Sui dynasty, 220-618
  —Three kingdoms, six dynasties-Sui
    dynasty, 220-618
    USE Landscape painting, Chinese—
        Three kingdoms-Sui dynasty,
        220-618
  —**Sung-Yüan dynasties, 960-1368**
  —**Ming-Ch'ing dynasties, 1368-1912**
  —**20th century**
Landscape painting, Czech
  (May Subd Geog)
  UF Czech landscape painting
Landscape painting, Danish
  (May Subd Geog)
  UF Danish landscape painting
  UF Danish landscape painting
Landscape painting, Dutch, [Flemish, etc.]
  (May Subd Geog)
  —**Italian [etc.] influences**
Landscape painting, English
  (May Subd Geog)
  UF English landscape painting
  NT Norwich school of painting
Landscape painting, European
  (May Subd Geog)
  UF European landscape painting

Landscape painting, French
  NT Saint-Siméon school of painting
Landscape painting, German
  (May Subd Geog)
  UF German landscape painting
Landscape painting, Greek (Modern)
  UF Greek landscape painting (Modern)
      Modern Greek landscape painting
Landscape painting, Guatemalan
  (May Subd Geog)
  UF Guatemalan landscape painting
Landscape painting, Italian
  (May Subd Geog)
  UF Italian landscape painting
Landscape painting, Japanese
  (May Subd Geog)
  UF Japanese landscape painting
  —**To 1868**
  —**1868-**
Landscape painting, Kirghiz
  (May Subd Geog)
  UF Kirghiz landscape painting
Landscape painting, Korean
  (May Subd Geog)
  UF Korean landscape painting
Landscape painting, Latvian
  (May Subd Geog)
  UF Latvian landscape painting
Landscape painting, Medieval
  (May Subd Geog)
  UF Medieval landscape painting
Landscape painting, New Zealand
  (May Subd Geog)
  UF New Zealand landscape painting
Landscape painting, Norwegian
  (May Subd Geog)
  UF Norwegian landscape painting
Landscape painting, Renaissance
  (May Subd Geog)
  UF Renaissance landscape painting
  BT Landscape painting—16th century
Landscape painting, Russian
  (May Subd Geog)
  UF Russian landscape painting
Landscape painting, Spanish
  (May Subd Geog)
  UF Spanish landscape painting
Landscape painting, Swiss *(May Subd Geog)*
  UF Swiss landscape painting
Landscape painting, Venezuelan
  (May Subd Geog)
  UF Venezuelan landscape painting
Landscape perception
  USE Landscape assessment
Landscape photography
  USE Photography—Landscapes
Landscape prints *(May Subd Geog)*
  [NE954-NE954.3 (General)]
  [NE2143 (Etching)]
  [NE2454 (Lithography)]
  BT Prints
  —**17th century** *(May Subd Geog)*
  —**19th century** *(May Subd Geog)*
  —**20th century** *(May Subd Geog)*
Landscape prints, Canadian
  (May Subd Geog)
  UF Canadian landscape prints
Landscape prints, Dutch *(May Subd Geog)*
  UF Dutch landscape prints
Landscape prints, European
  UF European landscape prints
Landscape prints, French *(May Subd Geog)*
  UF French landscape prints
Landscape prints, German *(May Subd Geog)*
  UF German landscape prints
Landscape protection *(May Subd Geog)*
  [QH75]

UF Beautification of the landscape
 Conservation of scenic beauty
 Natural beauty conservation
 Preservation of natural scenery
 Protection of scenic beauty
 Scenery preservation
BT Environmental protection
 Nature conservation
RT Landscape architecture
 Landscape assessment
 Regional planning
NT Natural monuments
 Stream conservation
— **Law and legislation** *(May Subd Geog)*
Landscaping, Interior
USE Interior landscaping
Landscaping industry *(May Subd Geog)*
 [SB472.5-472.565]
RT Horticultural service industry
 Landscape architecture
 Landscape gardening
 Ornamental horticulture
NT Grounds maintenance
 Interior landscaping
 Landscape architectural firms
 Landscape contracting
 Landscape nurseries
 Turf management
 Turfgrasses industry
Landsknechte
USE German mercenaries
Landslide damages, Liability for
USE Liability for landslide damages
Landslide dams *(May Subd Geog)*
 [TC543]
UF Dams, Landslide
BT Earth dams
Landslide insurance
USE Insurance, Landslide
Landslides *(May Subd Geog)*
 [QE599]
UF Land slides
BT Avalanches
 Mass-wasting
 Physical geography
 Slopes (Soil mechanics)
NT Earthflows
 Rockslides
— **Law and legislation** *(May Subd Geog)*
BT Real property
Landsmaal
USE Norwegian language (Nynorsk)
Landsmaal literature
USE Norwegian literature (Nynorsk)
Landsmaal poetry
USE Norwegian poetry (Nynorsk)
LANDUSE (Computer program)
Lane Bryant annual awards
BT Volunteer workers in social service
Lane family *(Not Subd Geog)*
UF Lain family
 Laine family
 Lains family
 Lanes family
 Layn family
 Layne family
Lane snapper
UF Lutjanus synagris
 Snapper, Lane
Lanels family
USE Linnell family
Lanes, Bowling
USE Bowling alleys
Lanes, Bus
USE Bus lanes
Lanes, High occupancy vehicle
USE High occupancy vehicle lanes
Lanes, Truck
USE Truck lanes
Lanes family
USE Lane family

Lanestosa family *(Not Subd Geog)*
Lanford family
USE Langford family
Lang family *(Not Subd Geog)*
UF Lange family
RT Langer family
 Long family
LANG-PACK (Electronic computer system)
 [QA76.7]
Langa (Italy)
USE Langhe (Italy)
Langalibalele Rebellion, 1873
 [DT875]
BT Hlubi (African people)—History
 Natal (South Africa)—History—1843-
 1893
Lang'ata Region (Kenya)
Langbas (African people)
 [GN652.L3 (Ethnology)]
UF Langbase
 Langbwasse
 Languassi
 Langwasi
BT Banda (African people)
 Ethnology—Central African Republic
Langbase
USE Langbas (African people)
Langbwasse
USE Langbas (African people)
Langcaster family
USE Lancaster family
Langdale Fell (England)
BT Mountains—England
Langdalen family *(Not Subd Geog)*
Langdan River (N.T.)
USE Daly River (N.T.)
Langdell family *(Not Subd Geog)*
Langdin family
USE Langston family
Langdon family
USE Langston family
Langdon House (Modesto, Calif.)
USE McHenry Mansion (Modesto, Calif.)
Lange family
USE Lang family
Lange/Ferguson Locality (S.D.)
USE Lange/Ferguson Site (S.D.)
Lange/Ferguson Site (S.D.)
UF Lange/Ferguson Locality (S.D.)
BT South Dakota—Antiquities
Langedon family
USE Langston family
Langel family *(Not Subd Geog)*
Langeland (Denmark)
BT Islands—Denmark
L'Angelier family *(Not Subd Geog)*
UF Angelier family
 Langelier family
Langelier family
USE L'Angelier family
Langemarck, Battle of, 1914
 [D542.L]
BT World War, 1914-1918—Campaigns—
 Belgium
 Ypres, 1st Battle of, 1914
Langendörfer family *(Not Subd Geog)*
Langer family *(Not Subd Geog)*
RT Lang family
Langerhans, Islands of
USE Islands of Langerhans
Langeteig family
USE Longeteig family
Langevin family
USE Angevine family
Langford family *(Not Subd Geog)*
UF Landford family
 Lanford family
 Langsford family
 Lansford family
 Lantford family

Langhe (Italy)
UF Langa (Italy)
Langhorn family
USE Langhorne family
Langhorne family *(Not Subd Geog)*
UF Langhorn family
Langi (African people)
USE Rangi (African people)
Langi Ghiran 1 Site (Vic.) *(Not Subd Geog)*
BT Australia—Antiquities
Langill family
USE Langille family
Langille family *(Not Subd Geog)*
UF Langill family
 Languilles family
Langjökull Glacier (Iceland)
BT Glaciers—Iceland
Langlard family
USE Lenglart family
Langleik
USE Noordsche balk
Langley family *(Not Subd Geog)*
UF Langlie family
 Lengley family
 Longley family
 Longly family
Langlie family
USE Langley family
Langlo family *(Not Subd Geog)*
Langmuir-Blodgett films
USE Thin films, Multilayered
Langmuir frequencies
USE Plasma frequencies
Langmuir plasma frequencies
USE Plasma frequencies
Lango (African people)
UF Lango (African tribe)
BT Ethnology—Uganda
 Luo (African people)
Lango (African people) women
USE Women, Lango (African people)
Lango (African tribe)
USE Lango (African people)
Lango language
 [PL8437]
BT Latuka language
 Nilotic languages
 Uganda—Languages
Langobards
USE Lombards
Langsam family *(Not Subd Geog)*
Langsdon family
USE Langston family
Langsdown family
USE Langston family
Langsford family
USE Langford family
Langslet family *(Not Subd Geog)*
Langstaff family *(Not Subd Geog)*
UF Longstaff family
 Longstaffe family
Langston family *(Not Subd Geog)*
UF Landen family
 Landing family
 Landon family
 Landown family
 Langdin family
 Langdon family
 Langedon family
 Langsdon family
 Langsdown family
 Langton family
Langton family
USE Langston family
Language, Imaginary
USE Imaginary languages
Language, International
USE Diplomacy—Language
 Language, Universal
Language, Legal
USE Law—Language

Language, Liturgical
  USE Liturgical language
Language, Philosophy of
  USE Languages—Philosophy
Language, Psychology of
  USE Psycholinguistics
Language, Universal
  [PM8008]
  UF Interlinguistics
     International language
     Language, International
     Language, World
     Universal language
     World language
  NT Diplomacy—Language
     Isotype (Picture language)
     Languages, Artificial
     Lingua italiana infinitiva
     Neoglify (Picture language)
     Pasigraphy
     Translingua script
  — Alphabet
Language, World
  USE Language, Universal
Language acquisition
  [P118]
  Here are entered works which discuss from the
  linguistic or psycholinguistic viewpoint the process of
  the acquisition of the native language in children.
  Works which discuss child language in general or
  within an educational framework, including general
  characteristics and usage, are entered under the head-
  ing Children—Language.
  UF Acquisition of language
     Developmental linguistics
     Developmental psycholinguistics
     Language and languages—Acquisition
     Language development in children
     Psycholinguistics, Developmental
  BT Interpersonal communication in
        children
     Psycholinguistics
  SA subdivision Acquisition under names
        of individual languages, e.g. English
        language—Acquisition
  NT Interlanguage (Language learning)
     Language awareness in children
     Language transfer (Language learning)
     Second language acquisition
  — Age factors
     UF Age factors in language acquisition
     BT Ability, Influence of age on
  — Testing
     NT Miller-Yoder Language
           Comprehension Test
        Rhode Island Test of Language
           Structure
Language and culture *(May Subd Geog)*
  [P35]
  BT Culture
  NT Anthropological linguistics
     Sociolinguistics
Language and education *(May Subd Geog)*
  UF Educational linguistics
  BT Education
     Language and languages
  NT Education, Bilingual
     Language and languages—Study and
        teaching
     Languages, Modern—Study and
        teaching
     Native language—Study and teaching
     Native language and education
Language and ethics
  [BJ44]
  BT Ethics
Language and history *(May Subd Geog)*
  [P41]
  UF History and language
     Linguistics and history
  BT History
  NT Historical linguistics

Language and languages
  [P1-P410]
  Here are entered works on language in general,
  works on the origin and history of language, and sur-
  veys of languages. Works dealing with the scientific
  study of human speech, including phonetics, pho-
  nemics, morphology and syntax, are entered under
  Linguistics. Works on the philosophy and psychology
  of language are entered under Languages—Philoso-
  phy, and Psycholinguistics, respectively.
  UF Foreign languages
  BT Anthropology
     Communication
     Ethnology
     Grammar, Comparative and general
     Information theory
     Meaning (Psychology)
  RT Philology
     Speech
  SA individual languages and groups of
        languages, e.g. English language;
        Semitic languages; also subdivision
        Language under names of individual
        corporate bodies, names of
        individual persons, and under
        classes of persons; and subdivision
        Languages under names of
        countries, cities, etc., and under
        ethnic groups
  NT Alien labor—Language
     Bilingualism
     Children—Language
     Children, Deaf—Language
     Christian education and language
     Christian union—Language question
     Classification—Books—Language and
        languages
     Colloquial language
     Confusion of tongues
     Courts and courtiers—Language
     Elocution
     Executives—Language
     Extinct languages
     Formal languages
     Imaginary languages
     Imaginary languages in literature
     Judgment
     Language and education
     Language and logic
     Language disorders
     Languages—Philosophy
     Languages—Religious aspects
     Linguistic change
     Linguistics
     Literature
     Mass media and language
     Mentally handicapped—Language
     Metal, Words for
     Multilingualism
     Music and language
     Native language
     Onomatopoeia
     Oratory
     Phonetic spelling
     Physically handicapped children—
        Language
     Programming languages (Electronic
        computers)
     Psycholinguistics
     Racism in language
     Rhetoric
     Schizophrenics—Language
     Semantics
     Semantics (Philosophy)
     Shepherds—Language
     Sign language
     Sociolinguistics
     Space and time in language
     Standard language
     Statesmen—Language
     Teachers—Language
     Tramps—Language

     Translating and interpreting
     Translingua script
     Voice
     Women—Language
     Writing
     Written communication
  — Ability testing
     UF Language assessment
     BT Language and languages—Study
           and teaching
     NT Bankson language screening test
        Children—Language—Testing
        Illinois test of psycholinguistic
           abilities
        Rhode Island Test of Language
           Structure
  — Accents and accentuation
     USE Accents and accentuation
  — Acquisition
     USE Language acquisition
  — Analogy
     USE Analogy (Linguistics)
  — Classification
     [P203]
     SA subdivision Classification under
           names of linguistic groups, e.g.
           Bantu languages—Classification
     NT Nostratic hypothesis
        Typology (Linguistics)
  — Clicks
     USE Clicks (Phonetics)
  — Cognate words
     USE Cognate words
  — Composition and exercises
  — Data processing
     USE Linguistics—Data processing
  — Dialects
     USE Dialectology
  — Dictionaries
     UF Language and languages—
           Terminology
     NT Dictionaries, Polyglot
  — Diffusion
     USE Language spread
  — Duration
     USE Duration (Phonetics)
  — Errors, inventions, etc.
     USE Imaginary languages
  — Etymology
     [P321]
     UF Etymology
        Grammar, Comparative and
           general—Derivation
        Word history
     BT Historical lexicology
     SA subdivision Etymology under
           names of languages
     NT Cognate words
        Hand—Words for
        Linguistic paleontology
        Names
        Onomastics
  — Foreign elements
     SA subdivisions Foreign elements and
           Influence on foreign languages
           under names of individual
           languages, e.g. English language
           —Foreign elements; English
           language—Influence on foreign
           languages
     NT Calques
        Language and languages—Foreign
           words and phrases
  — Foreign words and phrases
     UF International words
        Loanwords
     BT Language and languages—Foreign
           elements
  — Glossaries, vocabularies, etc.
     [P331-P347]
     BT Dictionaries, Polyglot

SA *subdivision* Language—Glossaries,
etc. *under names of individual
literary authors for listings of
the words used by those
authors, e.g.* Shakespeare,
William, 1564-1616—Language
—Glossaries, etc.
— Grammar, Comparative
USE Grammar, Comparative and
general
— **Grammars**
[P207]
UF Grammar
Grammar, Polyglot
Polyglot grammar
— History
USE Historical linguistics
— Inflection
USE *subdivision* Inflection *under
names of languages and groups
of languages*
Grammar, Comparative and
general—Inflection
Languages, Modern—Inflection
— Intonation
USE Intonation (Phonetics)
— Law and legislation
USE Languages—Law and legislation
— Lexicology
USE Lexicology
— **Origin**
[P116]
UF Languages—Origin
Origin of languages
Speech—Origin
— **Orthography and spelling**
Here are entered works on orthography,
spelling, and spelling reform in languages in gen-
eral. Works dealing with the effort to reform
English orthography are entered under Spelling
reform. Works dealing with orthography, spell-
ing, and spelling reform in specific languages or
groups of languages are entered under the name
of the language with subdivision Orthography
and spelling, e.g. French language—Orthogra-
phy and spelling.
UF Language and languages—Spelling
reform
Orthography
Spelling
BT Writing
SA *subdivision* Orthography and
spelling *under names of
languages or groups of
languages, e.g.,* English language
—Orthography and spelling
NT Phonetic alphabet
Phonetic spelling
Spelling errors
— Philosophy
USE Languages—Philosophy
— **Phonetic transcriptions**
UF Phonetic transcriptions
Transcriptions, Phonetic
BT Phonetics
Transcription
SA *subdivision* Phonetic transcriptions
*under linguistic groups,
particular languages, and
dialects.*
— Phraseology
USE Phraseology
— **Physiological aspects**
[QP399]
UF Languages—Physiological aspects
BT Biolinguistics
Neurophysiology
NT Language disorders
Neurolinguistics
— Political aspects
USE Languages—Political aspects
— Printing

USE Printing, Practical—Style manuals
— **Programmed instruction**
UF Language and languages—Study
and teaching—Programmed
instruction
— Psychology
USE Psycholinguistics
— Public relations
USE Public relations—Language and
languages
— Quantifiers
USE Grammar, Comparative and
general—Quantifiers
— Religious aspects
USE Language question in the church
Languages—Religious aspects
Liturgical language
— **Rhythm**
BT Prosodic analysis (Linguistics)
Rhythm
NT Caesura in versification
— Sentences
USE Grammar, Comparative and
general—Sentences
— **Sex differences**
[P120.S48]
UF Language and sex
Sex and language
RT Sexism in language
SA *subdivision* Sex differences *under
names of languages and groups
of languages, e.g.* English
language—Sex differences
NT Grammar, Comparative and
general—Gender
Women—Language
— Spelling reform
USE Language and languages—
Orthography and spelling
— Spread
USE Language spread
— Statistical methods
USE Linguistics—Statistical methods
Mathematical linguistics
— Stress
USE Accents and accentuation
— **Study and teaching** (May Subd Geog)
[P51-P59]
Here are entered works which discuss the
study and teaching of a second or foreign lan-
guage. Works which discuss the social and psy-
chological processes involved in learning a sec-
ond language are entered under the heading Sec-
ond language acquisition.
UF Foreign language study
BT Language and education
NT Audio-lingual method (Language
teaching)
Communication in foreign language
education
Interlanguage (Language learning)
Language and languages—Ability
testing
Language and languages—
Vocational guidance
Language teachers
Language transfer (Language
learning)
— — **Bilingual method**
UF Bilingual method (Language
teaching)
BT Education, Bilingual
Languages, Modern—Study and
teaching
SA *subdivision* Study and teaching
—Bilingual method *under
names of languages or groups
of languages, e.g.* English
language—Study and teaching
—Bilingual method
— — **Error analysis**

[P53]
UF Error analysis in language
teaching
BT Errors
SA *subdivision* Errors of usage
*under names of languages
and groups of languages, e.g.*
English language—Errors of
usage
— — **Law and legislation**
(May Subd Geog)
BT Educational law and legislation
— — Programmed instruction
USE Language and languages—
Programmed instruction
— — Public relations
USE Public relations—Language
and languages—Study and
teaching
— **Style**
[P301]
UF Linguostylistics
Stylistics
RT Style, Literary
NT Foregrounding
Idioms
Parallelism (Linguistics)
— Syllable
USE Grammar, Comparative and
general—Syllable
— Syntax
USE Grammar, Comparative and
general—Syntax
— Terminology
USE Language and languages—
Dictionaries
— Texts
USE Polyglot texts, selections,
quotations, etc.
— Tone
USE Tone (Phonetics)
— Transcription
USE Transcription
— Typology
USE Typology (Linguistics)
— Universals
USE Universals (Linguistics)
— **Variation**
UF Characterology of speech
Language subsystems
Variation in language
SA *subdivision* Variation *under names
of individual languages, e.g.*
English language—Variation
NT Register (Linguistics)
Sublanguage
Urban dialects
— **Vocational guidance** (May Subd Geog)
[P60]
UF Languages—Vocational guidance
BT Language and languages—Study
and teaching
Languages, Modern—Study and
teaching
— **Word frequency**
UF Frequency counts of words
Frequency word lists
Word counts
Word frequency
BT Linguistics—Statistical methods
Vocabulary
SA *subdivision* Word frequency *under
names of languages and groups
of languages, e.g.* English
language—Word frequency; *and
subdivision* Language—Word
frequency *under individual
authors, e.g.* Shakespeare,
William, 1564-1616—Language
—Word frequency
NT Zipf's law

Language and languages *(Continued)*
— Word order
    USE *subdivision* Word order *under*
        particular languages, e.g.
        English language—Word order
        Grammar, Comparative and
          general—Word order
        Languages, Modern—Word order
Language and logic
    [BC57 (Logic)]
    [P39 (Linguistics)]
  UF Linguistics and logic
    Logic in language
  BT Language and languages
    Languages—Philosophy
    Logic
    Semantics
  NT Logical positivism
    Montague grammar
    Predicate (Logic)
    Presupposition (Logic)
    Proposition (Logic)
Language and music
  USE Music and language
Language and racism
  USE Racism in language
Language and sex
  USE Language and languages—Sex
      differences
    Sexism in language
Language and society
  USE Sociolinguistics
Language and state
  USE Language policy
Language art (Fine arts)
  USE Conceptual art
Language arts *(May Subd Geog)*
  UF Communication arts
    Language arts—Study and teaching
  BT Communication
  NT Literature—Study and teaching
    Penmanship
    Reading
    Speech
— **Correlation with content subjects**
  (May Subd Geog)
  UF Content area language arts
      instruction
    Correlation of language arts with
      content subjects
  BT Interdisciplinary approach in
      education
  NT Content area reading
— **Psychological aspects**
  BT Educational psychology
— **Remedial teaching**
  BT Remedial teaching
— Study and teaching
  USE Language arts
Language arts (Elementary)
  (May Subd Geog)
  [LB1576]
  NT Reading (Elementary)—Language
      experience approach
Language arts (Higher) *(May Subd Geog)*
Language arts (Preschool) *(May Subd Geog)*
  [LB1140]
Language arts (Primary) *(May Subd Geog)*
  NT Reading (Primary)—Language
      experience approach
Language arts (Secondary)
  (May Subd Geog)
Language assessment
  USE Language and languages—Ability
      testing
Language awareness *(May Subd Geog)*
  UF Linguistic awareness
    Metalinguistic knowledge
  BT Awareness
    Psycholinguistics

Language awareness in children
  (May Subd Geog)
  [P118]
  BT Children—Language
    Language acquisition
Language camps *(May Subd Geog)*
  UF Foreign language camps
    Language immersion events
    Language live-ins
    Language villages
    Summer camps, Language
    Weekend camps, Language
  BT Camps
    Languages, Modern—Study and
      teaching
Language data processing
  USE Linguistics—Data processing
Language development in children
  USE Children—Language
    Language acquisition
Language diffusion
  USE Language spread
Language disorders *(May Subd Geog)*
  Here are entered works on disorders of the central
  neurological functions affecting the reception, proc-
  essing, or expression of language. Works on disorders
  of the physiological mechanisms required for the ar-
  ticulation, patterning, or production of speech are
  entered under Speech, Disorders of.
  UF Dysphasia
  BT Communicative disorders
    Language and languages
    Language and languages—
      Physiological aspects
    Psycholinguistics
  RT Speech, Disorders of
  NT Agraphia
    Aphasia
    Dyslexia
Language disorders in children
  (May Subd Geog)
  [RJ496.L35]
  BT Children—Language
    Communicative disorders in children
  RT Speech disorders in children
  NT Aphasic children
— **Diagnosis**
  NT Screening Kit of Language
      Development
    Temple University Short Syntax
      Inventory
Language disorders in the aged
  (May Subd Geog)
  BT Communicative disorders in the aged
Language experience approach to teaching
  reading
  USE Reading (Elementary)—Language
      experience approach
    Reading (Primary)—Language
      experience approach
Language for editing and formating text
  USE LEFT (Computer program language)
Language for special purposes
  USE Sublanguage
Language games
  USE Literary recreations
Language geography
  USE Linguistic geography
Language immersion events
  USE Language camps
Language in missionary work
  [BV2082.L3]
  BT Missions
Language laboratories
  UF Foreign language laboratories
    Laboratories, Language
  RT Languages, Modern—Study and
      teaching—Audio-visual aids
Language learning by animals
  USE Animal communication
    Human-animal communication

Language live-ins
  USE Language camps
Language of flowers
  USE Flower language
Language planning *(May Subd Geog)*
  [P40.5.L35]
  UF Languages—Planning
    Planned language change
  BT Sociolinguistics
  RT Languages—Political aspects
    Languages—Revival
  NT Language policy
    Languages, Artificial
    Standard language
Language policy *(May Subd Geog)*
  [P119.3]
  UF Glottopolitics
    Institutional linguistics
    Language and state
    Languages—Government policy
    Languages, National
    Languages, Official
    State and language
  BT Communication policy
    Language planning
  NT International agencies—Language
      policy
    United Nations—Language policy
Language problem, Private
  USE Private language problem
Language question in literature
  USE Questione della lingua
Language question in the church
  (May Subd Geog)
  UF Language and languages—Religious
      aspects
  BT Church
  NT Bible—Versions
    Christian union—Language question
    Latin language—Church Latin
Language reform
  USE *subdivision* Reform *under names of*
    languages, e.g. Chinese language—
    Reform
Language revival
  USE Languages—Revival
Language services *(May Subd Geog)*
  [P40.5.L36]
  Here are entered works that deal collectively with
  the various services provided by government agen-
  cies, corporations, etc., relating to language, such as
  translating, setting standards for terminology, main-
  taining data bases of terminology, providing sign lan-
  guage interpretations, etc.
  UF Linguistic services
  BT Applied linguistics
  NT Translating services
Language shift
  USE Code switching (Linguistics)
    Diglossia (Linguistics)
Language spread *(May Subd Geog)*
  [P40.5.L37]
  UF Diffusion of language
    Language and languages—Diffusion
    Language and languages—Spread
    Language diffusion
    Spread of language
  BT Sociolinguistics
Language standardization
  USE Standard language
Language subsystems
  USE Language and languages—Variation

Language surveys *(May Subd Geog)*
  Here are entered works on the methods and techniques employed in conducting language surveys, and reports of individual surveys. For the latter the heading may be subdivided by place; in such cases an additional subject entry is made under the heading [place]—Languages, e.g. 1.United States—Languages. 2. Language surveys—United States. For language surveys on a special topic, the additional subject entry is made under the special topic, e.g. 1. Speech and social status—United States. 2. Language surveys—United States.
  UF Languages—Surveys
      Linguistic surveys
  BT Linguistic geography
      Linguistics
      Surveys
Language teachers *(May Subd Geog)*
  BT Language and languages—Study and teaching
      Teachers
Language testing
  USE *subdivision* Examinations *under names of languages or groups of languages, e.g.* English language—Examinations; Languages, Modern—Examinations
Language transfer (Language learning)
  UF Transfer, Language (Language learning)
  BT Language acquisition
      Language and languages—Study and teaching
  NT Interference (Linguistics)
Language villages
  USE Language camps
Languages
  This heading is used only with subdivisions.
  — Geography
      USE Linguistic geography
  — Government policy
      USE Language policy
  — **Law and legislation**
      UF Language and languages—Law and legislation
      SA *subdivision* Languages—Law and legislation *under names of countries, cities, etc.*
  — Origin
      USE Language and languages—Origin
  — **Philosophy**
      [P101-5]
      UF Language, Philosophy of
          Language and languages—Philosophy
          Philosophy of language
      BT Language and languages
      NT Analysis (Philosophy)
          Cartesian linguistics
          Ineffable, The
          Language and logic
          Ordinary-language philosophy
          Performative (Philosophy)
          Pragmatics
          Private language problem
          Speech acts (Linguistics)
  — Physiological aspects
      USE Language and languages—Physiological aspects
  — Planning
      USE Language planning
  — **Political aspects** *(Not Subd Geog)*
      [P119.3]
      Here are entered general works on the political aspects of languages. Works on the political aspects of the languages of a particular place are entered under [place]—Languages—Political aspects. Works on the political aspects of a particular language are entered under [name of language]—Political aspects—[place].
      UF Language and languages—Political aspects
      BT Nationalism

  RT Language planning
      Languages—Revival
  SA *subdivision* Languages—Political aspects *under names of regions, countries, cities, etc., and* subdivision Political aspects *under names of languages and groups of languages, e.g.* English language—Political aspects
  NT Diplomacy—Language
      Illyrism
      Linguistic minorities
      Treaties—Language
  — Psychoanalysis
      USE Psycholinguistics
  — Psychology
      USE Psycholinguistics
  — **Religious aspects**
      UF Biblical languages
          Ecclesiastical languages
          Language and languages—Religious aspects
          Languages, Biblical
          Languages, Ecclesiastical
          Religion and language
      BT Language and languages
      SA *subdivision* Religious aspects *under individual languages and groups of languages, e.g.* English language—Religious aspects
      NT Aramaic language
          Bible—Language, style
          Bible—Versions
          Christian union—Language question
          Greek language, Biblical
          Hebrew language
          Latin language—Church Latin
          Liturgical language
  — — **Baptists, [Catholic Church, etc.]**
  — — **Buddhism, [Christianity, etc.]**
  — — **Christianity**
      UF Christianity and language
      NT Christian education and language
  — Restoration
      USE Languages—Revival
  — **Revival**
      UF Language revival
          Languages—Restoration
          Revival of languages
      RT Language planning
          Languages—Political aspects
      SA *subdivision* Revival *under names of languages and groups of languages, e.g.* English language—Revival
  — Sociological aspects
      USE Sociolinguistics
  — Surveys
      USE Language surveys
  — Vocational guidance
      USE Language and languages—Vocational guidance
          Languages, Modern—Vocational guidance
Languages, Artificial
  [PM8001-9021]
  UF Artificial languages
      Interlinguistics
  BT Language, Universal
      Language planning
  NT Afrihili (Artificial language)
      American (Artificial language)
      Ande (Artificial language)
      Antélangue (Artificial language)
      Antibabele (Artificial language)
      Arulo (Artificial language)
      Babm
      Berendt (Artificial language)
      Bolak

      Cesges de damis (Artificial language)
      Chabé (Artificial language)
      Code Ari (Artificial language)
      Esperanto
      Eurolengo
      Gab (Artificial language)
      Glosa (Artificial language)
      Hom-idyomo (Artificial language)
      Ido
      Imaginary languages
      INO (Artificial language)
      Interglossa (Artificial language)
      Interlingua (International Auxiliary Language Association)
      Interlingua (Latin without inflections)
      International auxiliari linguo (Artificial language)
      Isotype (Picture language)
      Langue internationale néo-latine (Artificial language)
      Leno gi-nasu (Artificial language)
      Lincos (Artificial language)
      Ling (Artificial language)
      Lingua philosophica (Artificial language)
      Loglan (Artificial language)
      Manavabhasha (Artificial language)
      Mondi linguo (Artificial language)
      Mondial (Artificial language)
      Mundal (Artificial language)
      Neo (Artificial language)
      Neoglify (Picture language)
      Neoispano (Artificial language)
      Neolatinus (Artificial language)
      North American language
      Novial (Artificial language)
      Novolingua
      Nula (Artificial language)
      NUMAUDO (Computer program language)
      Occidental (Artificial language)
      Olingo (Artificial language)
      Oz (Artificial language)
      Panamane (Artificial language)
      Pasigraphy
      Pasilingua
      Pikto
      Programming languages (Electronic computers)
      Qôsmiani (Artificial language)
      Ro (Artificial language)
      Romanal (Artificial language)
      Romanid (Artificial language)
      Rosicrucian language
      Sona (Artificial language)
      Spelin (Artificial language)
      SPL (Artificial language)
      Spokil (Artificial language)
      Suma (Artificial language)
      Teutonish
      Tsolyáni (Artificial language)
      Unilingua
      Universal-Latein (Artificial language)
      Universala (Artificial language)
      Veltlang (Artificial language)
      Volapük
      Voldu (Artificial language)
      Wede (Artificial language)
Languages, Biblical
  USE Languages—Religious aspects
Languages, Classical
  USE Classical languages
Languages, Ecclesiastical
  USE Languages—Religious aspects
Languages, Extinct
  USE Extinct languages
Languages, Foreign
  USE Languages, Modern
Languages, Imaginary
  USE Imaginary languages

Languages, Infinitary
  USE Infinitary languages
Languages, Living
  USE Languages, Modern
Languages, Mixed
  [PM7801-PM7895]
    Here are entered works discussing langugages resulting from the intermingling of phonological, grammatical and/or lexical elements from different languages in areas of intensive language contact. Works discussing auxiliary, sometimes mixed, languages used among groups having no other language in common are entered under the heading Lingua francas. Works discussing lingua francas which are native to none of those using them and are characterized by a simplified grammar and often mixed vocabulary are entered under the heading Pidgin languages. Works discussing pidgin languages that have become established as the native language of a speech community are entered under the heading Creole dialects.
    UF Dialects
       Gobbledygook
       Hybrid languages
       Jargons
       Mixed languages
    BT Languages in contact
    RT Pidgin languages
    NT Arabic-Afrikaans dialect
       Creole dialects
       Dilpok language
       Hiri Motu language
       Hobson-jobson
       Interlanguage (Language learning)
       Manipravalam language (Malayalam)
       Ngadju language (Australia)
       Pitcairnese language
       Substratum (Linguistics)
Languages, Modern
  [PB1-PB431]
    Here are entered works which deal collectively with all modern living languages.
    UF Foreign languages
       Languages, Foreign
       Languages, Living
       Living languages
       Modern languages
    SA names of particular modern, living languages or groups of languages, e.g. Indo-European languages, African languages, Oriental langauges; and subdivision Languages under names of continents, countries, cities, etc., e.g. Europe—Languages; Africa—Languages; Asia—Languages
  — **Conversation and phrase books**
    [PB73]
    UF Phrase books
  — **Dictionaries**
  — — Polyglot
       USE Dictionaries, Polyglot
  — **Etymology**
  — **Examinations**
  — Fellowships
       USE Languages, Modern—Scholarships, fellowships, etc.
  — **Idioms, corrections, errors**
    [PB260]
  — **Inflection**
    [PB101]
    UF Inflection
       Language and languages—Inflection
  — **Mutual intelligibility**
       Here are entered works on the ability of speakers of one language to understand and be understood by speakers of a related language.
    UF Intelligibility of related languages
       Mutual intelligibility of related languages

    SA subdivision Mutual intelligibility under names of individual groups of languages, e.g. Romance languages—Mutual intelligibility
  — **Phonetics**
    [PB77]
  — **Phonology**
    [PB76-82]
  — **Phonotape catalogs**
    BT Languages, Modern—Study and teaching—Audio-visual aids
  — **Pronunciation**
    [PB79]
  — **Punctuation**
  — **Scholarships, fellowships, etc.** (May Subd Geog)
    UF Languages, Modern—Fellowships
       Modern language fellowships
       Modern language scholarships
    BT Languages, Modern—Study and teaching
  — **Semantics**
  — **Spoken language**
  — **Study and teaching** (May Subd Geog)
    [PB35-39]
    BT Language and education
    SA subdivision Officials and employees in foreign countries—Foreign language competency under names of countries
    NT Audio-lingual method (Language teaching)
       Communication in foreign language education
       Language and languages—Study and teaching—Bilingual method
       Language and languages—Vocational guidance
       Language camps
       Languages, Modern—Scholarships, fellowships, etc.
       Languages, Modern—Vocational guidance
  — — **Audio-visual aids**
    RT Language laboratories
    NT Languages, Modern—Phonotape catalogs
  — **Syntax**
    [PB201-225]
  — **Transliteration into Chinese, [Japanese, etc.]**
  — **Vocational guidance** (May Subd Geog)
    UF Languages—Vocational guidance
    BT Languages, Modern—Study and teaching
  — **Word order**
    [PB213]
    UF Language and languages—Word order
       Word order
    BT Grammar, Comparative and general—Word order
Languages, National
  USE Language policy
Languages, Non procedural (Programming languages)
  USE Nonprocedural languages (Programming languages)
Languages, Nonprocedural (Programming languages)
  USE Nonprocedural languages (Programming languages)
Languages, Official
  USE Language policy
Languages, Oriental
  USE Oriental languages
Languages, Secret
  [PM9001-9021]
  UF Secret languages
  NT Enochian language

       Jŏ (Secret language)
       Pig Latin
       Shelta
Languages in contact (May Subd Geog)
    BT Areal linguistics
    NT Bilingualism
       Languages, Mixed
       Lingua francas
       Substratum (Linguistics)
       Urban dialects
Languassi
  USE Langbas (African people)
Langue bleue (Artificial language)
  USE Bolak
Langue d'oc (May Subd Geog)
    Here are entered works about the speech or dialects of the Midi (the South) of France after 1500. Works about the language of that region before 1500 are entered under the heading Provençal language.
    UF Languedoc
       Occitan language
       Provençal language, Modern
    BT France—Languages
       Romance languages
    NT Béarnais dialect
       Gascon dialect
  — Names
       USE Names, Langue d'oc
Langue d'oc anonyms and pseudonyms
  USE Anonyms and pseudonyms, Langue d'oc
Langue d'oc authors
  USE Authors, Langue d'oc
Langue d'oc children's plays
  USE Children's plays, Langue d'oc
Langue d'oc children's writings
  USE Children's writings, Langue d'oc
Langue d'oc drama (May Subd Geog)
    [PC3386 (History)]
    [PC3395-PC3398 (Collections)]
    NT Children's plays, Langue d'oc
Langue d'oc folk-songs
  USE Folk-songs, Langue d'oc
Langue d'oc imprints (May Subd Geog)
Langue d'oc literature (May Subd Geog)
    [PC3381-PC3382 (History)]
    [PC3395-PC3398 (Collections)]
    Here are entered collections of work written after 1500 in the modern Provençal language called "langue d'oc." Collections of works written in the medieval Provençal language before 1500 are entered under the heading Provençal literature.
Langue d'oc names
  USE Names, Langue d'oc
Langue d'oc philology (May Subd Geog)
    [PC3201-PC3213]
Langue d'oc poetry (May Subd Geog)
    [PC3385 (History)]
    [PC3395-PC3398 (Collections)]
Langue d'oc poets
  USE Poets, Langue d'oc
Langue d'oc prose literature (May Subd Geog)
    [PC3387 (History)]
    [PC3395-PC3398 (Collections)]
Langue d'oc proverbs
  USE Proverbs, Langue d'oc
Langue d'oïl
  USE French language
Langue internationale naturelle
  USE Chabé (Artificial language)
Langue internationale néo-latine (Artificial language)
    [PM8457]
    UF Néo-latine, Langue internationale
    BT Languages, Artificial
Languedoc
  USE Langue d'oc
Languilles family
  USE Langille family
Languriitae
  USE Erotylidae

2088

Langurs
  USE Presbytis
Langwasi
  USE Langbas (African people)
Laniarius
  [QL696.P248]
  BT Shrikes
  NT Laniarius fulleborni
Laniarius fulleborni
  [QL696.P248]
  UF Boubou, Fulleborn's black
      Fulleborn's black boubou
  BT Laniarius
Lanier, Lake (Ga.)
  USE Sidney Lanier, Lake (Ga.)
Lanier family (Not Subd Geog)
  UF Laniere family
      Lennier family
Lanier word processors
  USE AES word processors
Laniere family
  USE Lanier family
Laniidae
  USE Shrikes
Lanius
  [QL696.P248]
  BT Shrikes
  NT Red-backed shrike
Lanius collurio
  USE Red-backed shrike
Lanius family (Not Subd Geog)
Lankester family
  USE Lancaster family
Lankister family
  USE Lancaster family
Lanna Thai language
  USE Northern Thai language
Lännaskärgården (Sweden)
  BT Archipelagoes—Sweden
Lannate (Insecticide)
  USE Methomyl
Lannea
  [QK495.A498 (Botany)]
  UF Odina
  BT Anacardiaceae
Lannea coromandelica
  [QK495.A498 (Botany)]
  [SB291.L35 (Gum plant)]
  UF Lannea grandis
      Lannea wodier
  NT Jingan gum
Lannea grandis
  USE Lannea coromandelica
Lannea wodier
  USE Lannea coromandelica
Lanneau family (Not Subd Geog)
  UF La Noue family
Lanolin
  [TP676]
  RT Wool-fat
Lanphear family (Not Subd Geog)
  UF Lanpher family
      Lanphere family
      Lanphier family
Lanpher family
  USE Lanphear family
Lanphere family
  USE Lanphear family
Lanphier family
  USE Lanphear family
LAN's
  USE Local area networks (Computer
      networks)
Lansdown family (Not Subd Geog)
  UF Lansdowne family
Lansdowne family
  USE Lansdown family
Lansford family
  USE Langford family

**Lansing, Alma, Mt. Pleasant and Northern
    Railroad**
  BT Railroads—United States
Lantana
  [QK495.V48 (Botany)]
  BT Verbenaceae
Lantao (Hong Kong)
  USE Lantau (Hong Kong)
Lantau (Hong Kong)
  UF Lan Tao (Hong Kong)
      Lan Tau (Hong Kong)
      Lantao (Hong Kong)
      Ta-hsü Tao (Hong Kong)
      Tai Yu Shan (Hong Kong)
      Taiyu Shan (Hong Kong)
  BT Islands—Hong Kong
Lanter family (Not Subd Geog)
  UF Lantor family
Lantern-fishes
  [QL638.M9]
  UF Lanternfishes
      Myctophidae
  BT Myctophiformes
  NT Diaphus
      Dorsadena
      Lampadena
      Lampanyctus
      Lobianchia
Lantern projection
  [Q186 (Science)]
  [TR505 (Photography)]
  UF Projection, Lantern
  RT Projectors
  NT Front-screen projection
      Microprojection
      Moving-picture projection
      Overhead projection
      Tachistoscope
Lantern slides
  USE Slides (Photography)
Lanternfishes
  USE Lantern-fishes
Lanterns (May Subd Geog)
  [GR950.L4 (Folk-lore)]
  [GT445 (Manners and customs)]
  NT Stone lanterns
Lanterns of the dead
  [NB1420]
  UF Dead, Lanterns of the
  BT Cemeteries
      Dead
      Funeral rites and ceremonies
      Sepulchral monuments
      Towers
Lantford family
  USE Langford family
Lanthanide NMR shift reagents
  USE Lanthanide shift reagents
Lanthanide shift reagents
  [QD77]
  UF Lanthanide NMR shift reagents
      LSR (Chemical reagents)
      NMR shift reagents, Lanthanide
  BT Chemical tests and reagents
      Rare earth metals
Lanthanides
  USE Rare earth metals
Lanthanons
  USE Rare earth metals
Lanthanotidae
  [QL666.L2556]
  BT Lizards
  NT Lanthanotus
Lanthanotus
  [QL666.L2556]
  BT Lanthanotidae
Lanthanum
  [QD181.L2]
  BT Bastnaesite
  — Isotopes

  UF Isotopic lanthanum
      Lanthanum isotopes
  — — Decay
  — — Spectra
  — Spectra
Lanthanum isotopes
  USE Lanthanum—Isotopes
Lantor family
  USE Lanter family
Lanx of Parabiago
  UF Patera of Parabiago
  BT Silverware—Italy
      Silverwork—Italy
Lanza family (Not Subd Geog)
  UF Lanzi family
      Lanzo family
Lanzarote (Canary Islands)
  UF Isla de Lanzarote (Canary Islands)
  BT Islands—Canary Islands
Lanzi family
  USE Lanza family
Lanzo family
  USE Lanza family
Lanzo River (Italy)
  UF Fosso Lanzo (Italy)
  BT Rivers—Italy
Lao (Tai people)
  USE Laos (Tai people)
Lao art
  USE Art, Lao
Lao cookery
  USE Cookery, Lao
Lao fiction (May Subd Geog)
  NT Short stories, Lao
Lao folk-songs
  USE Folk-songs, Lao
Lao language
  [PL4251.L3]
  BT Tai languages
Lao Mountain (China)
  BT Mountains—China
Lao poetry (May Subd Geog)
Lao short stories
  USE Short stories, Lao
Laoag River (Luzon, Philippines)
  BT Rivers—Philippines
Laocoön (Legendary character)
  UF Laokoon (Legendary character)
  BT Folklore—Greece
Laocoön (Sculpture)
  USE Agesander. Laocoön group
Laocoön and his sons assailed by serpents
    (Sculpture)
  USE Agesander. Laocoön group
Laokoon (Legendary character)
  USE Laocoön (Legendary character)
Laos
  — Civilization
  — — Indic influences
        BT India—Civilization
  — Description and travel
  — — 1975-
        [DS555.382]
  — History
  — — 1975-
        [DS555.84-555.86]
  — Intellectual life
  — — Indic influences
        BT India—Civilization
  — Languages
        NT Kui language (Mon-Khmer)
            Northern Thai language
            Phu Thai language
Laos (Tai people) (May Subd Geog)
  [DS560 (Indochina)]
  UF Lao (Tai people)
      Laotians
Laotian . . .
  USE subject headings beginning with the
      word Lao

Laotians
    USE Laos (Tai people)
Laouza Rock Shelter (France)
    (Not Subd Geog)
    UF La Laouza Rock Shelter (France)
        Lausa Rock Shelter (France)
        Lauso Rock Shelter (France)
    BT Caves—France
        France—Antiquities
Lap family
    USE Lapp family
Lapak Site (Mexico)
    USE Xlapak Site (Mexico)
Lapara
    ₍QL561.S7₎
    BT Sphingidae
Laparoscopes *(May Subd Geog)*
    UF Peritoneoscopes
    BT Endoscopes
Laparoscopy *(May Subd Geog)*
    ₍RG107.5.L34 (Gynecologic
        examination)₎
    UF Celioscopy
        Peritoneoscopy
    BT Abdomen—Examination
        Endoscopy
    — **Complications and sequelae**
        (May Subd Geog)
Laparotomy
    USE Abdomen—Surgery
Lape family
    USE Lapp family
Lapeirousia
    ₍QK495.I75₎
    UF Lapeyrousia
    BT Iridaceae
Lapels
    BT Clothing and dress
        Coats
        Collars
        Facings (Clothing)
Lapeyrousia
    USE Lapeirousia
Laph family
    USE Lapp family
Lapham family *(Not Subd Geog)*
Lapidaries (Medieval literature)
    ₍PN682.L₎
    ₍PQ1327.L3 (Old French)₎
    BT Gems
Lapidary art
    USE Gem cutting
Lapierre family
    USE Pierre family
Lapis niger (Rome, Italy)
    ₍DG69₎
    UF Black Stone (Rome, Italy)
        Niger lapis (Rome, Italy)
    BT Sepulchral slabs—Italy
Laplace transformation
    ₍QA432₎
    UF Transformation, Laplace
    BT Calculus, Operational
        Differential equations
        Transformations (Mathematics)
    NT Z transformation
Laplace's equations
    USE Harmonic functions
Laplacian operator
    UF Operator, Laplacian
    BT Differential equations, Partial
Lapland
        As a geographic subdivision, this heading is used
        directly.
Lapland Peninsula (R.S.F.S.R.)
    USE Kola Peninsula (R.S.F.S.R.)
Laplanders
    USE Lapps
Laplandskiĭ gosudarstvennyĭ zapovednik
    (R.S.F.S.R.)
    USE Laplandskiĭ zapovednik (R.S.F.S.R.)

Laplandskiĭ Preserve (R.S.F.S.R.)
    USE Laplandskiĭ zapovednik (R.S.F.S.R.)
Laplandskiĭ zapovednik (R.S.F.S.R.)
    (Not Subd Geog)
    UF Laplandskiĭ gosudarstvennyĭ
        zapovednik (R.S.F.S.R.)
        Laplandskiĭ Preserve (R.S.F.S.R.)
        Laplandskiy zapovednik (R.S.F.S.R.)
    BT National parks and reserves—Russian
        S.F.S.R.
        Natural areas—Russian S.F.S.R.
Laplandskiy zapovednik (R.S.F.S.R.)
    USE Laplandskiĭ zapovednik (R.S.F.S.R.)
Laplante family *(Not Subd Geog)*
    UF La Plante family
    RT Plant family
Lapp family *(Not Subd Geog)*
    UF Lap family
        Lape family
        Laph family
        Lappe family
Lapp folk art
    USE Folk art, Lapp
Lapp gods
    USE Gods, Lapp
Lapp language
    ₍PH701-729₎
    UF Lappish language
        Saam language
    BT Finno-Ugric languages
        Russian S.F.S.R.—Languages
        Scandinavia—Languages
    — **Etymology**
        NT Sájva (The Lapp word)
Lapp literature *(May Subd Geog)*
    ₍PH731-735₎
    BT Europe, Northern—Literatures
Lapp poetry *(May Subd Geog)*
Lappe family
    USE Lapp family
Lapphund
    UF Swedish Lapland dog
Lapping
    USE Grinding and polishing
Lappish funeral rites and ceremonies
    USE Funeral rites and ceremonies, Lappish
Lappish language
    USE Lapp language
Lappish mythology
    USE Mythology, Finno-Ugrian
Lapps *(May Subd Geog)*
    ₍DL971.L2 (Sweden)₎
    ₍GN585.L2 (Anthropology)₎
    UF Laplanders
        Saams
        Samis (European people)
    BT Arctic races
        Finno-Ugrians
    — **Anthropometry**
    — **Children**
        BT Children
    — **Craniology**
    — **Land tenure**
        BT Land tenure
    — **Finland**
        NT Suenjelsijd (Lapp community)
    — **Russian S.F.S.R.**
        NT Suenjelsijd (Lapp community)
Lapse (Law) *(May Subd Geog)*
    UF Expiration of rights
    BT Forfeiture
Lapsley family *(Not Subd Geog)*
    UF Lapsly family
Lapsly family
    USE Lapsley family
Lapsus linguae
    USE Speech errors
Lapta (Game)
    ₍GV1017.L3₎
Lapuyan Subanen dialect
    USE Southern Subanen dialect

Lapwings
    ₍QL696.L7₎
    UF Green plovers
        Peewits
        Vanellus vanellus
    BT Charadriiformes
        Plovers
Laquemba Island (Fiji)
    USE Lakemba Island (Fiji)
Lar gibbon
    USE Whitehanded gibbon
Lara, Infantes of
    USE Infantes of Lara
Lara (Indonesian people)
    UF Luru (Indonesian people)
    BT Dyaks
        Ethnology—Indonesia
Laramare family
    USE Larrimore family
Laramie, Fort (Wyo. : Fort)
    USE Fort Laramie (Wyo. : Fort)
Laramie Basin (Wyo.)
    UF Laramie Plains (Wyo.)
    BT Geology—Wyoming
Laramie formation
    USE Geology, Stratigraphic—Cretaceous
        Paleobotany—Cretaceous
        Paleontology—Cretaceous
Laramie Mountains (Wyo. and Colo.)
    UF Laramie Range (Wyo. and Colo.)
    BT Front Range (Colo. and Wyo.)
        Mountains—Colorado
        Mountains—Wyoming
Laramie Plains (Wyo.)
    USE Laramie Basin (Wyo.)
Laramie Range (Wyo. and Colo.)
    USE Laramie Mountains (Wyo. and Colo.)
Larance family
    USE Lawrence family
Larceny *(May Subd Geog)*
    UF Petit larceny
        Petty larceny
        Theft
    BT Criminal law
        Offenses against property
    RT Stealing
    NT Aircraft theft
        Art thefts
        Automobile theft
        Bicycle theft
        Brigands and robbers
        Burglary
        Cargo theft
        Cattle stealing
        Embezzlement
        Firearms theft
        Horse stealing
        Motorcycle theft
        Receiving stolen goods
        Robbery
        Securities theft
        Shoplifting
        Theft from motor vehicles
        Thieves
        Trials (Larceny)
        Unauthorized use
    — **Biblical teaching**
        NT Ten commandments—Theft
Larceny (Germanic law)
Larceny (Greek law)
Larceny (Islamic law)
Larceny (Jewish law)
Larceny (Roman-Dutch law)
Larceny (Roman law)
Larch *(May Subd Geog)*
    ₍QK494.5.P66 (Botany)₎
    ₍SD397.L3 (Forestry)₎
    UF Larix
    BT Pinaceae
    NT Dahurian larch
        European larch

Japanese larch
Siberian larch
— **Diseases and pests** *(May Subd Geog)*
SA *particular diseases and pests, e.g.*
Larch case-bearer, Larch leaf-roller
NT Tetropium gabriele
Zeiraphera diniana
Larch bud moth, Grey
USE Zeiraphera diniana
Larch case-bearer
[QL561.C58]
UF Coleophora laricella
BT Beetles
Larch leaf-roller
[SB608.L3]
Larch sawfly
UF Lygaeonematus erichsonii
Nematus erichsonii
Pristiphora erichsonii
Lard
[HD9441 (Economics)]
[TS1980 (Technology)]
NT Rendering apparatus
Rendering works
Lard family
USE Laird family
Lard-oil
[TP676]
Larde family
USE Laird family
Lardeau River (B.C.)
BT Rivers—British Columbia
Larderel family *(Not Subd Geog)*
RT Viviani della Robbia family
Lardil (Australian people)
[DU125.L37]
UF Kunana (Australian people)
Laierdila (Australian people)
Lardill (Australian people)
BT Australian aborigines
Ethnology—Australia
Lardill (Australian people)
USE Lardil (Australian people)
Lardner, Ring, 1885-1933. You know me Al
(Comic strip)
USE You know me Al (Comic strip)
Lardner family *(Not Subd Geog)*
Lardworm
USE Swine kidney worm
Lardworms
USE Stephanurus
Lareau family *(Not Subd Geog)*
Laremore family
USE Larrimore family
Larence family
USE Lawrence family
Larentia
USE Oporinia
Larentidae
USE Geometridae
Larentiidae
USE Geometridae
Lares
BT Cults—Rome
Household shrines
Lareu family
USE Larue family
Larew family
USE Larue family
Larey family
USE Lary family
Larga Street (Buenos Aires, Argentina)
USE Avenida Montes de Oca (Buenos
Aires, Argentina)
Large American opossum
USE Virginia opossum
Large bowel
USE Intestine, Large
Large cell auditory nucleus
USE Lateral vestibular nucleus

Large churches
USE Big churches
Large cranberry
USE Cranberries
Large deviations
UF Deviations, Large
BT Limit theorems (Probability theory)
Statistics
Large farms
USE Farms, Large
Large glass (Assemblage)
USE Duchamp, Marcel, 1887-1968. Bride
stripped bare by her bachelors, even
Large Hadron Collider *(May Subd Geog)*
UF Collider, Large Hadron
BT Proton-antiproton colliders
Large intestine
USE Intestine, Large
Large lemurs
USE Lemuridae
Large Magellanic Cloud
USE Magellanic Clouds
Large numbers, Law of
USE Law of large numbers
Large print books
USE Large type books
Large scale integration
USE Integrated circuits—Large scale
integration
Large scale systems
UF Systems, Large scale
BT System analysis
Systems engineering
Large space structures (Astronautics)
UF Structures, Large space (Astronautics)
RT Space stations
NT Antenna arrays
Satellite solar power stations
Space colonies
— **Propulsion systems**
UF Propulsion of large space structures
Large Space Telescope
USE Hubble Space Telescope
Large-spotted genet
USE Genetta tigrina
Large stature
USE Stature, Tall
Large-tailed nightjar
USE Long-tailed nightjar
Large-toothed aspen
USE Populus grandidentata
Large two forms (Sculpture)
USE Moore, Henry, 1898-   Large two
forms
Large type books
UF Books, Large type
Large print books
Sight-saving books
BT Blind—Books and reading
Visually handicapped
Large white cabbage butterfly
USE Pieris brassicae
Largemouth bass
UF Micropterus salmoides
BT Black bass
Largemouth bass fishing
[SH681]
UF Big-mouth bass fishing
BT Black bass fishing
Fishing
Largent family *(Not Subd Geog)*
Larger grain borer
USE Dinoderus truncatus
Larger parishes
[BV638.4]
UF Parishes, Larger
BT Churches
— **Baptists, [Catholic Church, etc.]**
Larger wax moth
USE Galleria mellonella

Largetooth aspen
USE Populus grandidentata
Lari dialect (Kongo)
USE Laadi dialect
Lari language
USE Teke language
Laria
USE Bruchus
Laridae
[QL696.C46]
UF Gaviae
BT Charadriiformes
NT Larus
Sterna
Terns
Lariidae
USE Bruchidae
Larimer family
USE Larrimore family
Larimer Street (Denver, Colo.)
(Not Subd Geog)
BT Streets—Colorado
Larimore family
USE Larrimore family
Larince family
USE Lawrence family
Larinia
[QL458.42.A7]
BT Araneidae
Lario (Italy)
USE Como, Lake (Italy)
Larix
USE Larch
Larix dahurica
USE Dahurian larch
Larix decidua
USE European larch
Larix europea
USE European larch
Larix gmelini
USE Dahurian larch
Larix leptolepis
USE Japanese larch
Larix sibirica
USE Siberian larch
Larix sukaczewii
USE Siberian larch
Lark family *(Not Subd Geog)*
UF Larke family
Larka Kols
USE Hos
Larke family
USE Lark family
Larken family
USE Larkin family
Larkin Administration Building (Buffalo, N.Y.)
USE Larkin Building (Buffalo, N.Y.)
Larkin Building (Buffalo, N.Y.)
UF Larkin Administration Building
(Buffalo, N.Y.)
Larkin Company Administration
Building (Buffalo, N.Y.)
BT Office buildings—New York (State)
Larkin Company Administration Building
(Buffalo, N.Y.)
USE Larkin Building (Buffalo, N.Y.)
Larkin family *(Not Subd Geog)*
UF Larken family
Larking family
Larkins family
Learkin family
Larking family
USE Larkin family
Larkins family
USE Larkin family
Larks
[QL696.P2]
UF Alaudidae
Horned larks
Otocorys
NT Alauda

Larks *(Continued)*
    Crested lark
    Short-toed lark
    Wood lark
Larkspur
  USE Delphinium
Larkwood family
  USE Lockwood family
Larmer family
  USE Larrimore family
Larmore family
  USE Larrimore family
Larmour family
  USE Larrimore family
Larnakes
  UF Larnax
  BT Pottery, Greek
Larnax
  USE Larnakes
Larned, Fort (Larned, Kan.)
  USE Fort Larned (Larned, Kan.)
Larraín family *(Not Subd Geog)*
Larrance family
  USE Lawrence family
Larrea
    [QK495.Z9 (Botany)]
  UF Covillea
  BT Zygophyllaceae
Larrea divaricata
    [QK495.Z9 (Botany)]
  UF Creosote bush, Spreading
     Spreading creosotebush
Larree family
  USE Lary family
Larrence family
  USE Lawrence family
Larrey family
  USE Lary family
Larridae
  USE Sphecidae
Larrimer family
  USE Larrimore family
Larrimore family *(Not Subd Geog)*
  UF Laramare family
    Laremore family
    Larimer family
    Larimore family
    Larmer family
    Larmore family
    Larmour family
    Larrimer family
    Laurimer family
    Lawremare family
    Lawrimor family
    Lawrimore family
    Loramore family
    Lorimer family
    Lorimor family
    Lorumor family
Larry family
  USE Lary family
Larsa (Ancient city) *(Not Subd Geog)*
  UF Ellasar (Ancient city)
    Sankarah (Iraq)
    Senkerah (Iraq)
    Tall Sankarah (Iraq)
  BT Cities and towns, Ruined, extinct, etc.
    —Iraq
    Iraq—Antiquities
Larsen family *(Not Subd Geog)*
  UF Larson family
    Larsson family
Larsen's syndrome *(May Subd Geog)*
  BT Abnormalities, Human
    Cleft palate
    Dislocations
    Face—Abnormalities
    Foot—Abnormalities
    Syndromes
Larson family
  USE Larsen family

Larsson family
  USE Larsen family
Larue family *(Not Subd Geog)*
  UF De La Rüe family
    De Larue family
    Delarue family
    La Rieu family
    Lareu family
    Larew family
    Lereaux family
    Lerew family
    Leru family
    Lerue family
    Lurue family
  RT Rue family
Larus
    [QL696.C46]
  BT Gulls
    Laridae
Larus atricilla
  USE Laughing gull
Larus californicus
  USE California gull
Larus canus
    [QL696.C46]
  UF Common gull
    Mew gull
    Short-billed gull
Larus crassirostris
  USE Black-tailed gull
Larus delawarensis
  USE Ring-billed gull
Larus fuscus
  USE Lesser black-backed gull
Larus glaucescens
  USE Glaucous-winged gull
Larus modestus
  USE Gray gull
Larus pipixan
  USE Franklin's gull
Larus ridibundus
  USE Black-headed gull
Larva migrans, Visceral *(May Subd Geog)*
  UF Human toxocariasis
    Toxocariasis, Human
    Visceral larva migrans
  BT Ascariasis
Larva migrans, Visceral, in children
  (May Subd Geog)
    [RJ406.L37]
  BT Infection in children
Larvae
  BT Developmental biology
  SA *subdivision Larvae under names of*
    animals or groups of animals, e.g.
    Fishes—Larvae; Insects—Larvae
  NT Paedogenesis
    Trochophore
    Wireworms
  — Fishes
    USE Fishes—Larvae
  — Insects
    USE Insects—Larvae
Larvaevoridae
  USE Tachinidae
Lary family *(Not Subd Geog)*
  UF Lairy family
    Larey family
    Larree family
    Larrey family
    Larry family
Laryngeal nerve
    [QL939]
    [QM471]
    [QP366]
Laryngeal prosthesis
  USE Artificial larynx
Laryngectomees *(May Subd Geog)*
    [RF540 (Rehabilitation)]

  UF Laryngectomized persons
    Laryngectomy—Patients
    Patients, Laryngectomy
  BT Physically handicapped
  — Clothing
    UF Clothing for laryngectomees
    BT Clothing and dress
Laryngectomized persons
  USE Laryngectomees
Laryngectomy
  BT Larynx—Surgery
  NT Speech, Alaryngeal
  — Patients
    USE Laryngectomees
Laryngismus stridulus
    [RC794]
  UF Glottis—Spasm
    Kopp's asthma
    Millar's asthma
    Thymic asthma
  BT Larynx—Diseases
Laryngopharynx
  USE Hypopharynx
Laryngoplasty *(May Subd Geog)*
    [RF516]
  BT Larynx—Surgery
    Surgery, Plastic
Laryngoscope and laryngoscopy
  USE Laryngoscopes
    Laryngoscopy
Laryngoscopes *(May Subd Geog)*
  UF Laryngoscope and laryngoscopy
  BT Endoscopes
Laryngoscopy *(May Subd Geog)*
    [RF514]
  UF Laryngoscope and laryngoscopy
  BT Larynx—Examination
    Rhinolaryngoscopy
Laryngostenosis
  USE Larynx—Stenosis
Laryngostroboscope
  BT Larynx
Laryngotomy, Inferior
  USE Cricothyrotomy
Laryngotracheobronchitis
  USE Croup
Larynx
    [QL853 (Comparative anatomy)]
    [QM255 (Human anatomy)]
    [QP306 (Physiology)]
  BT Respiratory organs
    Throat
  RT Trachea
    Voice
  NT Artificial larynx
    Epiglottis
    Glottis
    Laryngostroboscope
    Vocal cords
  — Cancer *(May Subd Geog)*
    [RC280.T5]
  — Diseases *(May Subd Geog)*
    [RF510-547]
    NT Laryngismus stridulus
     Larynx—Radiography
     Larynx—Stenosis
     Voice disorders
  — — Homeopathic treatment
    [RX456]
  — Examination
    NT Laryngoscopy
  — Fracture
    [RD533]
  — Innervation
  — Intubation
    [RF517]
  — Muscles
    BT Muscles
    NT Vocalis muscle
  — Radiography
    BT Larynx—Diseases

— Stenosis
  UF Laryngostenosis
      Stenosis of the larynx
  BT Larynx—Diseases
— Surgery
  [RF516-517]
  BT Otolaryngology, Operative
  NT Arytenoidectomy
      Cricothyrotomy
      Laryngectomy
      Laryngoplasty
— Tumors
  [RC280.T]
  [RF516]
— Ulcers
— Wounds and injuries

Larynx, Lower
  USE Syrinx (of birds)
Larzac, Causse du (France)
  USE Causse du Larzac (France)
Las Alpujarras (Spain)
  USE Alpujarras (Spain)
Las Cañadas (Tenerife, Canary Islands)
  USE Cañadas del Teide (Tenerife, Canary
      Islands)
Las Carreras, Battle of, 1849
  UF Carreras, Las, Battle of
  BT Dominican Republic—History—1844-
      1930
      Haiti—History—1844-1915
Las Colinas Site (Phoenix, Ariz.)
  [E99.H68 (Hohokam culture)]
  BT Arizona—Antiquities
Las Cruces Trail (Panama)
  USE Cruces Trail (Panama)
Las Esplanadas (Panama, Panama)
  USE Esplanade (Panama, Panama)
Las Huertas Site (N.M.) *(Not Subd Geog)*
  UF Huertas Site (N.M.)
  BT New Mexico—Antiquities
**Las Piedras (Canelones, Uruguay), Battle of,
1811**
  [F2725]
  BT Uruguay—History—1810-1830
Las Pilas Site (Jonacatepec, Mexico)
  USE Pilas Site (Jonacatepec, Mexico)
Las Salinas, Battle of, 1538
  [F3442]
  BT Peru—History—Conquest, 1522-1548
Las Vegas Valley (Nev.)
  BT Valleys—Nevada
LaSalle automobile
  USE La Salle automobile
Lascaux Cave (France) *(Not Subd Geog)*
  UF Grotte de Lascaux (France)
  BT Caves—France
      France—Antiquities
Lascelles family *(Not Subd Geog)*
  RT Lashells family
Laschet family
  USE Lawshe family
Lasciviousness
  USE Lust
Lascomb family
  USE Lipscomb family
Lascome family
  USE Lipscomb family
Lascosomatidae
  USE Mimallonidae
Lascurain family *(Not Subd Geog)*
Laser anemometer
  USE Laser Doppler velocimeter
Laser automobile
  [TL215.L]
  BT Plymouth automobile
Laser beam cutting
  UF Cutting, Laser beam
  BT Cutting
      Machining
      Metal-cutting

Laser-beam recording
  USE Laser recording
Laser beams
  UF Beams, Laser
      Laser radiation
  NT Laser fusion
      Laser-plasma interactions
      Laser plasmas
      Laser pulses, Ultrashort
— Atmospheric effects
  [QC976.L]
  UF Atmospheric effects on laser beams
  BT Meteorological optics
— Diffraction
  [QC446.2]
— Scattering
  NT Laser speckle
Laser cell counting
  USE Flow cytometry
Laser cell separation
  USE Flow cytometry
Laser cell sorting
  USE Flow cytometry
Laser coagulation
  UF Laser photocoagulation
  BT Light coagulation
  RT Lasers in surgery
Laser communication systems
  UF Coherent light communication systems
      Communication systems, Optical
        (Laser-based)
      Light communication systems, Laser-
        based
      Optical communication systems, Laser-
        based
  BT Integrated optics
      Optical communications
      Telecommunication systems
  NT Astronautics—Optical communication
        systems
      Optical radar
Laser communication systems industry
(May Subd Geog)
Laser Doppler velocimeter
  [TA357]
  UF Anemometer, Laser
      Doppler velocimeter, Laser
      Flowmeter, Laser
      Laser anemometer
      Laser flowmeter
      Velocimeter, Laser Doppler
  BT Fluid dynamic measurements
Laser flowmeter
  USE Laser Doppler velocimeter
Laser fusion
  [QC791-791.77]
  UF Fusion, Laser
  BT Controlled fusion
      Laser beams
Laser gyroscopes
  USE Optical gyroscopes
Laser industry *(May Subd Geog)*
  [HD9999.L3 (Economics)]
  UF Laser-using industries
  BT Lasers
      Optical industry
Laser interferometer
  [TA1677]
  BT Interferometer
      Lasers
Laser mapping
  USE Cartography—Laser use in
Laser materials
  [QC374 (Physics)]
  [TK871.3 (Engineering)]
  RT Optical materials
Laser mirrors
  USE Lasers—Mirrors
Laser photocoagulation
  USE Laser coagulation

Laser photography
  USE Holography
Laser-plasma interactions
  UF Interactions, Laser-plasma
  BT Laser beams
      Plasma (Ionized gases)
Laser plasmas
  [QC718.5.L3]
  UF Laser-produced plasmas
      Plasmas, Laser
      Plasmas, Laser-produced
  BT Laser beams
      Plasma (Ionized gases)
Laser printing
  USE Printing, Practical—Laser use in
Laser-produced plasmas
  USE Laser plasmas
Laser pulses, Picosecond
  USE Laser pulses, Ultrashort
Laser pulses, Ultrashort
  [QC689.5.L37]
  UF Laser pulses, Picosecond
      Light pulses, Picosecond
      Light pulses, Ultrashort
      Picosecond laser pulses
      Picosecond light pulses
      Ultrashort laser pulses
      Ultrashort light pulses
  BT Laser beams
      Pulse generators
  RT Picosecond pulses
Laser radar
  USE Optical radar
Laser radiation
  USE Laser beams
Laser ranging, Lunar
  USE Lunar laser ranging
Laser recording
  UF Laser-beam recording
      Recording, Laser
  BT Imaging systems
      Lasers
      Optical data processing
  RT Optical storage devices
  NT Holography
      Optical scanners
Laser resonators
  USE Lasers—Resonators
Laser speckle
  UF Speckle, Laser
  BT Laser beams—Scattering
      Speckle
Laser spectroscopy
  UF Spectroscopy, Laser
  BT Lasers in chemistry
      Spectrum analysis
  NT Light beating spectroscopy
      Optoacoustic spectroscopy
Laser transitions
  UF Transitions, Laser
  BT Lasers
Laser-using industries
  USE Laser industry
Laser welding
  BT Welding
Laser windows
  USE Lasers—Windows
Laser Writer (Printer)
  USE LaserWriter (Printer)
Lasers *(May Subd Geog)*
  UF Light amplification by stimulated
        emission of radiation
      Masers, Optical
      Optical masers

Lasers *(Continued)*
  BT Infrared sources
      Light
      Light amplifiers
      Light sources
      Optical pumping
      Optoelectronic devices
      Photoelectronic devices
      Photonics
      Photons
  RT Astronautics—Optical communication
        systems
      Nonlinear optics
  SA *headings beginning with the word*
        Laser
  NT Atmosphere—Laser observations
      Carbon monoxide lasers
      Cartography—Laser use in
      Chemical lasers
      Dye lasers
      Far infrared lasers
      Fingerprints—Laser use in
      Free electron lasers
      Gamma ray lasers
      Gas lasers
      High power lasers
      Injection lasers
      Laser industry
      Laser interferometer
      Laser recording
      Laser transitions
      Lasers in controlled fusion
      Lasers in plasma diagnostics
      Lasers in plasma research
      Metallurgy—Laser use in
      Mode-locked lasers
      Molecular gas lasers
      Negative temperature
      Neodymium glass lasers
      Nuclear-pumped lasers
      Plasma lasers
      Precipitation (Meteorology)—Laser
        observations
      Printing, Practical—Laser use in
      Rare earth lasers
      Ruby lasers
      Semiconductor industry—Laser use in
      Semiconductor lasers
      Solid-state lasers
      Tunable lasers
  — Diagnostic use
      BT Diagnosis
          Lasers in medicine
  — Effect of radiation on
      UF Lasers, Effect of radiation on
      BT Radiation
  — Military applications
        ⌈*UG486*⌉
      BT Military engineering
          Weapons systems
  — Mirrors
      UF Laser mirrors
      BT Mirrors
  — Resonators
      UF Laser resonators
      BT Resonators
  — Windows
      UF Laser windows
          Windows, Laser
Lasers, Argon
  USE Argon lasers
Lasers, Effect of radiation on
  USE Lasers—Effect of radiation on
Lasers, Excimer
  USE Excimer lasers
Lasers, Gasdynamic
  USE Gasdynamic lasers
Lasers, Helium-mercury
  USE Helium-mercury lasers
Lasers, Helium-neon
  USE Helium-neon lasers

Lasers, Iodine
  USE Iodine lasers
Lasers, X-ray
  USE X-ray lasers
Lasers (Sailboats)
  BT Sailboats
Lasers in aeronautics
    ⌈*TL697.L34*⌉
  BT Aeronautics
Lasers in art
    ⌈*N6494.L3*⌉
  BT Art
Lasers in biochemistry
  BT Biological chemistry—Technique
      Lasers in biology
      Lasers in chemistry
Lasers in biology
  BT Biological apparatus and supplies
  NT Lasers in biochemistry
Lasers in biophysics
  BT Biophysics
Lasers in chemistry
  BT Chemical apparatus
      Photochemistry
  NT Laser spectroscopy
      Lasers in biochemistry
      Multiphoton processes
Lasers in controlled fusion
  BT Controlled fusion
      Lasers
Lasers in engineering
  BT Engineering
Lasers in isotope separation
  BT Isotope separation
Lasers in medicine
    ⌈*R857.L37*⌉
  BT Medical instruments and apparatus
  NT Holography in medicine
      Lasers—Diagnostic use
      Lasers in surgery
Lasers in mining
    ⌈*TN292*⌉
  BT Mining engineering
Lasers in ophthalmology *(May Subd Geog)*
    ⌈*RE86*⌉
  UF Ophthalmic lasers
  BT Ophthalmology
Lasers in physics
  BT Physics
Lasers in plasma diagnostics
  BT Lasers
      Plasma diagnostics
Lasers in plasma research
  BT Lasers
      Plasma (Ionized gases)—Research
Lasers in surgery
    ⌈*RD73.L3*⌉
  BT Lasers in medicine
      Surgical instruments and apparatus
  RT Laser coagulation
  — Complications and sequelae
      (May Subd Geog)
Lasers in surveying
  BT Surveying—Instruments
Lasers in the graphic arts
  BT Graphic arts
LaserWriter (Printer)
  UF Apple LaserWriter (Printer)
      Laser Writer (Printer)
  BT Printers (Data processing systems)
Lasey family
  USE Lacy family
LASH ships
  USE Barge-carrying ships
Lashbrook family *(Not Subd Geog)*
  UF Lashbrooke family
      Lashbrooks family
Lashbrooke family
  USE Lashbrook family
Lashbrooks family
  USE Lashbrook family

LaShell family
  USE Lashells family
LaShelle family
  USE Lashells family
Lashells family *(Not Subd Geog)*
  UF LaShell family
      LaShelle family
      Latshell family
  RT Lascelles family
Lasher family *(Not Subd Geog)*
  RT Le Sueur family
      Lesher family
      Lozier family
Lashet family
  USE Lawshe family
Lashis
  USE Moso (Tribe)
Lasianthaea
    ⌈*QK495.C74 (Botany)*⌉
  BT Compositae
Lasiocampidae
    ⌈*QL561.L3*⌉
  UF Lachneidae
  BT Lepidoptera
      Moths
  NT Dendrolimus
      Tent-caterpillars
Lasioderma
    ⌈*QL596.A5*⌉
  BT Anobiidae
Lasioglossum
    ⌈*QL568.H3*⌉
  BT Halictidae
Lasiopyga
  USE Cercopithecus
Lasius *(May Subd Geog)*
    ⌈*QL568.F7*⌉
  BT Ants
Lasker Awards
  USE Albert Lasker Awards
Lasley family
  USE Leslie family
Laslie family
  USE Leslie family
Lasowiacy
  BT Ethnology—Poland
Laspeyresia
    ⌈*QL561.T8*⌉
  BT Tortricidae
Laspeyresia woeberiana
  USE Grapholitha woeberiana
Lassa fever *(May Subd Geog)*
    ⌈*RC152.5*⌉
  BT Arbovirus diseases
      Arenavirus diseases
      Fever
Lassa fever virus
    ⌈*QR201.L*⌉
  BT Arenaviruses
Lassen Peak (Calif.)
  UF Mount Lassen (Calif.)
  BT Cascade Range
      Lassen Volcanic National Park (Calif.)
      Mountains—California
      Volcanoes—California
Lassen Volcanic National Park (Calif.)
  BT National parks and reserves—United
        States
      Parks—California
      Volcanoes—California
  NT Lassen Peak (Calif.)
Lassley family
  USE Leslie family
Lasso
    ⌈*F596 (Cowboys)*⌉
    ⌈*GV1559 (Sports and games)*⌉
  RT Bolas
L'Assomption River (Québec)
  UF Assomption River (Québec)
  BT Rivers—Québec (Province)

Last best offer arbitration
USE Final offer arbitration
Last clear chance *(May Subd Geog)*
BT Negligence, Contributory
Last Judgment
USE Judgment Day
Last judgment (Painting)
USE Michelangelo Buonarroti, 1475-1564.
Last judgment
Miroglio, Valerio. Last judgment
Last judgment (Panel painting)
USE Bosch, Hieronymus, d. 1516. Last
judgment
Cranach, Lucas, 1472-1553. Last
judgment
Last letters before death
UF Death, Last letters before
BT Farewells
Letters
Last meal before execution
UF Henkersmahl
BT Capital punishment
Executions and executioners
Rites and ceremonies
Last Mountain Lake (Sask.)
UF Long Lake (Sask.)
BT Lakes—Saskatchewan
Last resort, Courts of
USE Courts of last resort
Last resort, Lenders of
USE Lenders of last resort
Last rites (Sacraments)
USE Extreme unction
Viaticum
Last sacraments
USE Extreme unction
Last Supper
[BT420]
Here are entered works on the final meal of Christ
with his apostles when the sacrament of the Lord's
Supper was instituted.
UF Jesus Christ—Last Supper
BT Dinners and dining in the Bible
RT Lord's Supper
Maundy Thursday
Passover in the New Testament
Last Supper (Mural)
USE Leonardo, da Vinci, 1452-1519. Last
Supper
Last Supper in art
NT Leonardo, da Vinci, 1452-1519. Last
Supper
Last theorem, Fermat's
USE Fermat's last theorem
Last things (Theology)
USE Eschatology
Last words
UF Deathbed words
Dying words
BT Anecdotes
Farewells
Quotations
NT Dying declarations
Last years
USE *subdivision* Biography—Last years and
death *under names of individual
literary authors; and subdivision*
Last years *under names of other
individual persons*
Lastenausgleich (1949-   )
Here are entered works on emergency legislation
passed in the Federal Republic of Germany since
1949 to distribute the burdens of the last war and its
consequences equitably among those who retained
their property and gained by the revalorization of
debts on the one hand and those who suffered war
damages and other injuries, including German refugees and former prisoners of war, on the other hand.
BT Capital levy—Germany (West)
Lasthenia
[QK495.C74]
BT Compositae

**Lastman, Pieter, 1583-1633. Susanna and
the elders**
[ND653.L]
UF Susanna and the elders (Painting)
Susanna and the two elders (Painting)
Suzanna en de ouderlingen (Painting)
BT Susanna (Biblical character)—Art
Latabár family *(Not Subd Geog)*
Latamore family
USE Latimer family
Latchkey children *(May Subd Geog)*
[HQ777.65]
BT Children of working parents
— **Life skills guides**
Late blight of potato
UF Potato late blight
RT Phytophthora infestans
Late fetal death
USE Still-birth
Late Gothic art
USE Art, Gothic—Late Gothic
Late Island (Tonga)
BT Islands—Tonga
Volcanoes—Tonga
Late-type stars
USE Cool stars
Lateens
USE Dhows
Latem Saint-Martin (Group of artists)
USE Sint-Martens-Latem (Group of artists)
Latemore family
USE Latimer family
Latent heat of evaporation
USE Evaporation, Latent heat of
Latent heat of fusion
USE Fusion, Latent heat of
Latent heat release in the atmosphere
USE Atmosphere—Latent heat release
Latent life
USE Cryptobiosis
Latent structure analysis
[QA278.6]
BT Correlation (Statistics)
Multivariate analysis
RT Latent variables
Latent variables
UF Constructs, Hypothetical
Hypothetical constructs
Variables, Latent
BT Multivariate analysis
Variables (Mathematics)
RT Latent structure analysis
Later Le dynasty
USE Vietnam—History—Later Le dynasty,
1428-1787
Lateral cervical nucleus
BT Spinal cord
Lateral dominance
USE Laterality
Lateral line organs
BT Sense-organs—Amphibians
Sense-organs—Fishes
NT Ampulla of Lorenzini
Lateral sclerosis
USE Amyotrophic lateral sclerosis
Lateral stability of airplanes
USE Stability of airplanes, Lateral
Lateral vestibular nucleus
[QP366]
UF Deiter's nucleus
Large cell auditory nucleus
Nucleus magnocellularis
BT Vestibular nuclei
Lateral waves
USE Head waves
Laterality
UF Lateral dominance
BT Cerebral hemispheres
Psychology, Physiological
RT Cerebral dominance
NT Left and right (Psychology)

Left- and right-handedness
Lateralization (Brain)
USE Cerebral dominance
Laterallus *(May Subd Geog)*
[QL696.G876]
BT Rallidae
Lateran Councils
BT Councils and synods
Laterellus jamaicensis
USE Black rail
Laterite *(May Subd Geog)*
[QE495]
Laternser Valley (Austria)
UF Laternsertal (Austria)
BT Valleys—Austria
Laternsertal (Austria)
USE Laternser Valley (Austria)
Lates
[QL638.C34]
BT Centropomidae
NT Barramundi
Lates calcarifer
USE Barramundi
Lates niloticus
USE Nile perch
Latex
BT Plant exudates
NT Kok-saghyz
Latex sculpture
Rubber
Latex, Artificial
USE Latex, Synthetic
Latex, Synthetic
UF Latex, Artificial
Synthetic latex
BT Polymers and polymerization
Rubber, Artificial
LaTeX (Computer system)
[Z253.4.L38]
BT Computerized typesetting
Latex asphalt
USE Asphalt-rubber
Latex paint *(May Subd Geog)*
UF Latex water paint
BT Emulsion paint
Latex sculpture *(May Subd Geog)*
UF Sculpture, Latex
BT Latex
Plastic sculpture
Sculpture
Latex water paint
USE Latex paint
Latgale (Latvia)
— **History**
— — **Revolution of 1905**
Latham family *(Not Subd Geog)*
UF Lathem family
Lathim family
Lathom family
Lathrom family
Lathrum family
Lathum family
Lathbury family
USE Leatherbury family
Lathe work
USE Lathes
Turning
Lathem family
USE Latham family
Lathers (Building trades) *(May Subd Geog)*
BT Lathing
NT Trade-unions—Lathers (Building
trades)
Lathes
[TJ1218-TJ1222]
[TS546 (Watchmakers' lathes)]
UF Lathe work
BT Carpentry—Tools
RT Turning
NT Screw-cutting machines
Screw machines, Automatic

2095

Lathes *(Continued)*
— Drawing
    USE Lathes—Drawings
— **Drawings**
    UF Lathes—Drawing
    BT Mechanical drawing
— **Electric driving**
— **Maintenance and repair**
— **Numerical control**
    BT Automatic control
    NT MELTS (Computer system)
— — **Data processing**
      NT DERO (Computer system)
— **Vibration**
Latheticomyia
   [QL537.C7]
   BT Cryptochaetidae
Latheticus
   [QL596.B5]
   BT Bostrichidae
Lathim family
   USE Latham family
Lathing
   [TH1675 (Metal)]
   [TH8132 (Plastering)]
   UF Laths
   BT Building
      Plastering
   NT Lathers (Building trades)
Lathom family
   USE Latham family
Lathouresa Site (Greece)
   [DF261.L34]
   UF Lathuresa Site (Greece)
   BT Greece—Antiquities
Lathridiidae
   [QL596.L3]
   UF Aculognathidae
      Melanophthalmidae
      Merophysiidae
   BT Beetles
Lathrom family
   USE Latham family
Lathrop family
   USE Lothrop family
Lathrope family
   USE Lothrop family
Lathrum family
   USE Latham family
Laths
   USE Lathing
Lathum family
   USE Latham family
Lathuresa Site (Greece)
   USE Lathouresa Site (Greece)
Lathyrism
   [RA1242.L35]
Lathyrus
   [QK495.152]
   BT Leguminosae
— **Composition**
    NT Aminoacetonitrile
Lathyrus odorata
   USE Sweet peas
Laticauda
   [QL666.O645]
   BT Elapidae
      Sea snakes
   NT Laticauda schistorhynchus
      Laticauda semifasciata
Laticauda schistorhynchus
   [QL666.O64]
   BT Laticauda
Laticauda semifasciata
   [QL666.O64]
   BT Laticauda
Latidae
   USE Centropomidae
Latifundio *(May Subd Geog)*
   UF Latifundium
   BT Land tenure

RT Haciendas
Latifundium
   USE Latifundio
Latimer family *(Not Subd Geog)*
   UF Latamore family
      Latemore family
      Latimor family
      Latimore family
      Latiner family
      Lattamore family
      Lattemer family
      Lattemore family
      Lattimer family
      Lattimore family
      Lettimore family
Latimeria chalumnae
   USE Coelacanth
Latimeriidae
   [QL638.L26]
   BT Coelacanthiformes
   NT Coelacanth
Latimor family
   USE Latimer family
Latimore family
   USE Latimer family
Latin, Max (Fictitious character)
   UF Max Latin (Fictitious character)
   BT Characters and characteristics in
      literature
   RT Davis, Norbert—Characters—Max
      Latin
Latin abbreviations
   USE Abbreviations, Latin
Latin America *(Not Subd Geog)*
   UF Spanish America
— **Boundaries**
— **Civilization**
    UF Civilization, American
    BT Civilization, Hispanic
    NT Italy—Civilization—Latin
       American influences
— — **1948-**
     [F1414.2]
— — **African influences**
    BT Africa—Civilization
— — **European influences**
    BT Europe—Civilization
— **Description and travel**
— — **1951-1980**
— — **1981-**
— **Economic conditions**
— — **1918-**
— — **1918-1945**
— — **1945-**
— **Foreign relations** *(May Subd Geog)*
— — **1948-**
— — **United States**
    UF Good neighbor policy
    NT Monroe doctrine
— **History**
   [F1409.6-1419]
— — **To 1600**
— — — **Juvenile literature**
— — **To 1830**
— — — **Juvenile literature**
— — **Wars of Independence, 1806-1830**
— — — **Causes**
     [F1412]
— — — **Foreign public opinion**
— — **1830-**
     [F1413]
— — **1830-1898**
— — **1898-1948**
— — **20th century**
— — **1948-**
— **Intellectual life**
— — **19th century**
— — **20th century**
— **Politics and government**
    NT Inter-American conferences
      Latin American federation

— — **To 1830**
— — **1806-1830**
— — **1830-1948**
— — **1948-**
— — **1980-** *(Not Subd Geog)*
— **Social conditions**
— — **1945-**
— **Subject headings**
    USE Subject headings—Latin America
Latin America in motion pictures
   BT Moving-pictures
Latin America specialists
   USE Latin Americanists
Latin American alien labor
   USE Alien labor, Latin American
Latin American art
   USE Art, Latin American
Latin American arts
   USE Arts, Latin American
Latin American authors
   USE Authors, Latin American
Latin American autobiographical fiction
   USE Autobiographical fiction, Latin
      American
Latin American children's literature
   USE Children's literature, Latin American
Latin American coins
   USE Coins, Latin American
Latin American cookery
   USE Cookery, Latin American
Latin American Cooperative Acquisitions Program
   UF LACAP
   BT Acquisitions, Cooperative (Libraries)
      Acquisitions (Libraries)
Latin American drama
   NT Historical drama, Latin American
      Spanish American drama
Latin American engraving
   USE Engraving, Latin American
Latin American essays
   NT Spanish American essays
Latin American exchange of persons programs
   USE Exchange of persons programs, Latin
      American
Latin American fantastic fiction
   USE Fantastic fiction, Latin American
Latin American federation
   UF Federation of Latin America
      Latin American integration
      Latin American union
   BT Federal government
      International organization
      Latin America—Politics and
       government
      Pan-Americanism
      Pan-Hispanism
Latin American fiction
   NT Autobiographical fiction, Latin
      American
      Fantastic fiction, Latin American
      Historical fiction, Latin American
      Short stories, Latin American
      Spanish American fiction
Latin American historical drama
   USE Historical drama, Latin American
Latin American historical fiction
   USE Historical fiction, Latin American
Latin American homosexuals' writings
   USE Homosexuals' writings, Latin
      American
Latin American integration
   USE Latin American federation
Latin American Jews
   USE Jews, Latin American
Latin American literature
   [PQ7081-8560]
   NT Children's literature, Latin American
      Latin American prose literature
      Revolutionary literature, Latin
      American

Spanish American literature
— 20th century
Latin American literature (English)
  USE American literature—Latin American
      authors
Latin American love poetry
  USE Love poetry, Latin American
Latin American loyalists
  USE Royalists—Latin America
Latin American missions
  USE Missions, Latin American
Latin American national characteristics
  USE National characteristics, Latin
      American
Latin American newspapers
  NT Brazilian newspapers
     Puerto Rican newspapers
Latin American painting
  USE Painting, Latin American
Latin American periodicals
  NT Brazilian periodicals
     South American periodicals
Latin American philosophy
  USE Philosophy, Latin American
Latin American poetry *(May Subd Geog)*
  NT Love poetry, Latin American
     Protest poetry, Latin American
     Spanish American poetry
Latin American poetry (English)
  USE American poetry—Latin American
      authors
Latin American political posters
  USE Political posters, Latin American
Latin American prints
  USE Prints, Latin American
Latin American prose literature
  (May Subd Geog)
  BT Latin American literature
Latin American protest poetry
  USE Protest poetry, Latin American
Latin American publications, Acquisition of
  USE Acquisition of Latin American
     publications
Latin American revolutionary literature
  USE Revolutionary literature, Latin
     American
Latin American short stories
  USE Short stories, Latin American
Latin American students *(May Subd Geog)*
  BT Students
Latin American technical assistance
  USE Technical assistance, Latin American
Latin American union
  USE Latin American federation
Latin American wit and humor, Pictorial
Latin Americanists *(May Subd Geog)*
  UF Latin America specialists
  BT Hispanists
Latin Americans *(May Subd Geog)*
  Here are entered works on citizens of Latin
  American countries. Works on citizens of Latin
  American countries in the United States are entered
  under Latin Americans—United States. Works on
  United States citizens of Latin American descent are
  entered under Hispanic Americans.
  BT Ethnology—Latin America
  NT Spanish Americans (Latin America)
  — **Mental health** *(May Subd Geog)*
  — **United States**
     NT Hispanic Americans
Latin anapestic poetry
  USE Anapestic poetry, Latin
Latin authors
  USE Authors, Latin
Latin authors (Medieval and modern)
  USE Authors, Latin (Medieval and modern)
Latin Christian drama, Medieval and modern
  USE Christian drama, Latin (Medieval and
     modern)

Latin Christian literature, Medieval and
  modern
  USE Christian literature, Latin (Medieval
     and modern)
Latin Christian poetry
  USE Christian poetry, Latin
Latin Christian poetry, Medieval and modern
  USE Christian poetry, Latin (Medieval and
     modern)
Latin civilization
  USE Civilization, Latin
Latin college and school drama, Medieval and
  modern
  USE College and school drama, Latin
     (Medieval and modern)
Latin dialogues
  USE Dialogues, Latin
Latin dialogues, Medieval and modern
  USE Dialogues, Latin (Medieval and
     modern)
Latin didactic poetry
  USE Didactic poetry, Latin
Latin didactic poetry, Medieval and modern
  USE Didactic poetry, Latin (Medieval and
     modern)
Latin diplomatics
  USE Diplomatics, Latin
Latin drama
  [PA6067-PA6071 (History)]
  [PA6137 (Collections)]
  BT Classical drama
  NT Religious drama, Latin
Latin drama, Medieval and modern
  (May Subd Geog)
  [PA8073-PA8079 (History)]
  [PA8135-PA8140 (Collections)]
  NT Christian drama, Latin (Medieval and
     modern)
     College and school drama, Latin
      (Medieval and modern)
     Jesuit drama, Latin (Medieval and
      modern)
Latin drama (Comedy)
  [PA6069]
  NT Atellanae
Latin drama (Tragedy)
  [PA6068]
Latin dramatists (Medieval and modern)
  USE Dramatists, Latin (Medieval and
     modern)
Latin East
  USE Latin Orient
Latin elegiac poetry
  USE Elegiac poetry, Latin
Latin Empire, 1204-1261
  [DF610-629]
  BT France—History—Capetians, 987-1328
  RT Latin Orient
  NT Crusades—Fourth, 1202-1204
     Istanbul (Turkey)—Siege, 1203-1204
Latin epic poetry
  USE Epic poetry, Latin
Latin epic poetry, Medieval and modern
  USE Epic poetry, Latin (Medieval and
     modern)
Latin epigrams
  USE Epigrams, Latin
Latin epistolary poetry
  USE Epistolary poetry, Latin
Latin erotic poetry
  USE Erotic poetry, Latin
Latin erotic poetry, Medieval and modern
  USE Erotic poetry, Latin (Medieval and
     modern)
Latin essays *(May Subd Geog)*
Latin fables, Medieval and modern
  USE Fables, Latin (Medieval and modern)
Latin fiction
  [PA6091 (Ancient)]
  *[PA8150-8155 (Medieval and modern,
    PA8091, PA8145)]*

  BT Classical fiction
Latin gardens
  USE Gardens, Latin
Latin historians
  USE Historians—Rome
Latin Hustle
  USE Hustle (Dance)
Latin hymns
  USE Hymns, Latin
Latin imprints *(May Subd Geog)*
Latin inscriptions
  USE Inscriptions, Latin
Latin Jesuit drama, Medieval and modern
  USE Jesuit drama, Latin (Medieval and
     modern)
Latin Kingdom of Jerusalem
  USE Jerusalem—History—Latin Kingdom,
     1099-1244
Latin language
  [PA2001-2995]
  BT Classical languages
  RT Classical philology
     Italic languages and dialects
     Latin philology
  NT Inscriptions, Latin
     Manuscripts, Latin
     Romance languages
  — Abbreviations
     USE Abbreviations, Latin
  — **Church Latin**
     UF Church Latin
      Liturgical Latin
     BT Language question in the church
      Languages—Religious aspects
     RT Liturgical language—Latin
  — — **Etymology**
     NT Epulum (The Latin word)
  — **Epithets**
  — **Etymology**
     NT Belua (The Latin word)
     Bestia (The Latin word)
     Cupidus (The Latin word)
     Fas (The Latin word)
     Grex (The Latin word)
     Homo (The Latin word)
     Inimicitia (The Latin word)
     Interpedare (The Latin word)
     Labor (The Latin word)
     Mora (The Latin word)
     Mysterium (The Latin word)
     Nefas (The Latin word)
     Opulus (The Latin word)
     Profundus (The Latin word)
     Quidem (The Latin word)
     Rumpus (The Latin word)
     Sacramentum (The Latin word)
     Scurra (The Latin word)
     Talentum (The Latin word)
     Templum (The Latin word)
     Virtus (The Latin word)
  — **Glossaries, vocabularies, etc.**
     NT Interlingua (Latin without
      inflections)
  — **Grammar**
  — — **1870-1975**
     [PA2087]
  — — **1976-**
     [PA2087.5]
  — — **Early works to 1500**
  — **Law Latin**
     UF Law Latin
  — Liturgical use
     USE Liturgical language—Latin
  — **Medical Latin**
     UF Medical Latin
     BT Medicine—Language
      Medicine—Terminology
  — **Metrics and rhythmics**
  — Names
     USE Names, Latin
  — **Saturnian verse**

Latin language
— Saturnian verse *(Continued)*
   USE Saturnian verse
— **Study and teaching** *(May Subd Geog)*
— **Terms and phrases**
   NT In pleno parliamento (The phrase)
Latin language, Colloquial
  UF Colloquial Latin
  BT Colloquial language
  RT Latin language, Vulgar
Latin language, Medieval and modern
  (May Subd Geog)
  [PA2801-2915]
— **Grammar**
   NT Speculative grammar
— **History**
   NT Questione della lingua
Latin language, Popular
  USE Latin language, Vulgar
Latin language, Postclassical
  [PA2300-2309]
Latin language, Preclassical to ca. 100 B.C.
  [PA2510-2519]
Latin language, Vulgar
  [PA2600-2748]
  UF Latin language, Popular
  RT Latin language, Colloquial
  NT Romance languages
Latin laudatory poetry
  USE Laudatory poetry, Latin
Latin letter-writing
  USE Letter-writing, Latin
Latin letters
  [PA6089 (History)]
  [PA6139.E7 (Collections)]
  BT Classical letters
    Letters
Latin letters, Medieval and modern
  (May Subd Geog)
  [PA8089 (History)]
  [PA8147 (Collections)]
Latin literature *(May Subd Geog)*
  [PA6001-PA6098 (History)]
  [PA6101-PA6139 (Collections)]
  UF Roman literature
  RT Classical literature
    Classical philology
    Latin philology
  NT Pastoral literature, Latin
— **Study and teaching** *(May Subd Geog)*
Latin literature, Medieval and modern
  (May Subd Geog)
  [PA8001-PA8595]
  NT Christian literature, Latin (Medieval
    and modern)
    Dialogues, Latin (Medieval and
    modern)
    Pastoral literature, Latin
Latin love poetry
  USE Love poetry, Latin
Latin love poetry, Medieval and modern
  USE Love poetry, Latin (Medieval and
    modern)
Latin manuscripts
  USE Manuscripts, Latin
Latin names
  USE Names, Latin
Latin occasional verse, Medieval and modern
  USE Occasional verse, Latin (Medieval and
    modern)
Latin orations
  USE Speeches, addresses, etc., Latin
Latin orations, Medieval and modern
  USE Speeches, addresses, etc., Latin
    (Medieval and modern)
Latin Orient *(Not Subd Geog)*
  [D175-D195]

Here are entered works which treat of the Levant
(i.e., the Mediterranean countries east of the Adriat-
ic: Greece, Asia Minor, Armenia, Syria, Palestine,
Egypt, Cyprus, Rhodes, Malta, etc.) from the 11th to
the 13th century, with special reference to the influ-
ence of the Crusaders.
  UF East, Latin
    Latin East
    Orient, Latin
  BT Islamic Empire—History—750-1258
    Middle East
    Orient
  RT Crusades
    Crusades—Fourth, 1202-1204
    Latin Empire, 1204-1261
  NT Jerusalem—History—Latin Kingdom,
    1099-1244
    Templars
Latin papyri
  USE Manuscripts, Latin (Papyri)
Latin part-songs
  USE Part-songs, Latin
Latin pastoral literature
  USE Pastoral literature, Latin
Latin pastoral poetry
  USE Pastoral poetry, Latin
Latin pastoral poetry, Medieval and modern
  USE Pastoral poetry, Latin (Medieval and
    modern)
Latin patriotic poetry
  USE Patriotic poetry, Latin
Latin peoples *(May Subd Geog)*
  UF Latin races
  BT Indo-Europeans
  RT Mediterranean race
    Panlatinism
Latin philology
  [PA2001-2067]
  RT Classical philology
    Latin language
    Latin literature
  NT Inscriptions, Latin
    Manuscripts, Latin
Latin philology, Medieval and modern
  (May Subd Geog)
Latin poetry *(May Subd Geog)*
  [PA6047-PA6066 (History)]
  [PA6121-PA6135 (Collections)]
  NT Anapestic poetry, Latin
    Christian poetry, Latin
    Didactic poetry, Latin
    Elegiac poetry, Latin
    Epic poetry, Latin
    Epistolary poetry, Latin
    Erotic poetry, Latin
    Laudatory poetry, Latin
    Love poetry, Latin
    Pastoral poetry, Latin
    Patriotic poetry, Latin
    Political poetry, Latin
    Religious poetry, Latin
Latin poetry, Medieval and modern
  (May Subd Geog)
  [PA8050-PA8065 (History)]
  [PA8120-PA8133 (Collections)]
  NT Christian poetry, Latin (Medieval and
    modern)
    Didactic poetry, Latin (Medieval and
    modern)
    Epic poetry, Latin (Medieval and
    modern)
    Erotic poetry, Latin (Medieval and
    modern)
    Love poetry, Latin (Medieval and
    modern)
    Occasional verse, Latin (Medieval and
    modern)
    Pastoral poetry, Latin (Medieval and
    modern)
    Political poetry, Latin (Medieval and
    modern)

    Romances, Latin (Medieval and
    modern)
Latin poets
  USE Poets, Latin
Latin poets (Medieval and modern)
  USE Poets, Latin (Medieval and modern)
Latin political poetry
  USE Political poetry, Latin
Latin political poetry, Medieval and modern
  USE Political poetry, Latin (Medieval and
    modern)
Latin prose literature
  [PA6081-PA6097 (History)]
  [PA6138-PA6139 (Collections)]
Latin prose literature, Medieval and modern
  (May Subd Geog)
  [PA8081-PA8096 (History)]
  [PA8145-PA8149 (Collections)]
Latin proverbs
  USE Proverbs, Latin
Latin Quarter (Paris, France)
  (Not Subd Geog)
  [DC752.Q4]
  UF Paris (France). Latin Quarter
    Paris (France). Quartier latin
    Quartier latin (Paris, France)
Latin races
  USE Latin peoples
Latin religious drama
  USE Religious drama, Latin
Latin religious poetry
  USE Religious poetry, Latin
Latin rhetoric
  USE Rhetoric, Ancient
Latin romances, Medieval and modern
  USE Romances, Latin (Medieval and
    modern)
Latin satire
  USE Satire, Latin
Latin satire, Medieval and modern
  USE Satire, Latin (Medieval and modern)
Latin sermons
  USE Sermons, Latin
Latin shorthand
  USE Shorthand, Latin
Latin songs, Medieval and modern
  USE Songs, Latin (Medieval and modern)
Latin speeches
  USE Speeches, addresses, etc., Latin
Latin speeches, Medieval and modern
  USE Speeches, addresses, etc., Latin
    (Medieval and modern)
Latin squares and rectangles
  USE Magic squares
Latin wit and humor
  [PA6095 (History)]
  [PA6137.5.W5 (Collections)]
  BT Classical wit and humor
Latiner family
  USE Latimer family
Latini (Italic people) *(May Subd Geog)*
  UF Latins (Italic people)
  BT Ethnology—Italy
    Italic peoples
  RT Romans
Latinists
  USE Classicists
Latinos (United States)
  USE Hispanic Americans
Latins (Italic people)
  USE Latini (Italic people)
Latite *(May Subd Geog)*
  UF Rhyodactite
  BT Lava
    Volcanic ash, tuff, etc.
Latitude
  [QB231-QB235]
  [VK565 (Navigation)]
  UF Degrees of latitude and longitude

BT Astronomical geography
Astronomy, Spherical and practical
Earth
Geodesy
Geodetic astronomy
Geography, Mathematical
Nautical astronomy
Navigation
RT Geographical positions

Latitude variation
[QB237]
UF Variation of latitude

Latobici (Celtic people)
BT Celts

Latooka (African people)
USE Latuka (African people)

Latosols
USE Ferralsols

Latouka language
USE Latuka language

Latrines
USE Privies
Toilets

Latrobe Valley (Vic.)
UF La Trobe Valley (Vic.)
BT Valleys—Australia

Latrodectus
[QL458.42.T54]
UF Widow spiders
BT Theridiidae
NT Latrodectus geometricus

Latrodectus geometricus
[QL458.42.T54]
UF Brown widow spider
Gray widow spider
BT Latrodectus

Latrodectus mactans
USE Black widow spider

Latshell family
USE Lashells family

Lattamore family
USE Latimer family

Lattemer family
USE Latimer family

Lattemore family
USE Latimer family

Latter-Day Saints
USE Mormons

Latter Rain movement
USE Pentecostalism

Lattice defects
USE Crystals—Defects

Lattice diffusion
USE Kirkendall effect

Lattice dynamics
UF Dynamics, Lattice
BT Crystal lattices
Solids
RT Phonons
NT Long range order (Solid state physics)

Lattice gas
UF Gas, Lattice
BT Crystal lattices

Lattice ordered groups
UF Ordered groups, Lattice
BT Groups, Theory of

Lattice ordered rings
UF Ordered rings, Lattice
BT Rings (Algebra)

Lattice paths
UF Paths, Lattice
BT Combinatorial probabilities
Graph theory
Lattice theory

Lattice theory
[QA171.5]
[QD911-QD915 (Crystallography)]
UF Lattices (Mathematics)
Space lattice (Mathematics)
Structural analysis (Mathematics)

BT Algebra, Abstract
Algebra, Boolean
Groups, Theory of
Set theory
Topology
Transformations (Mathematics)
RT Crystallography, Mathematical
NT Banach lattices
Closure operators
Congruence lattices
Crystal lattices
Deformation potential
Lattice paths
Lattices, Continuous
Lattices, Distributive
Modular lattices
Orlicz lattices
Percolation (Statistical physics)
Riesz spaces
Semilattices
Vector lattices, Archimedian

Lattice windows *(May Subd Geog)*
BT Decoration and ornament
Decoration and ornament,
Architectural
Windows

Lattices, Banach
USE Banach lattices

Lattices, Continuous
UF Continuous lattices
BT Functions, Continuous
Lattice theory
Topological spaces

Lattices, Distributive
[QA171.5]
UF Distributive lattices
BT Distributive law (Mathematics)
Lattice theory
NT Brouwerian algebras

Lattices, Garden
USE Trellises

Lattices, Orlicz
USE Orlicz lattices

Lattices, Orthomodular
USE Orthomodular lattices

Lattices (Gardening)
USE Trellises

Lattices (Mathematics)
USE Lattice theory

Latticework *(May Subd Geog)*
[NK1570]
BT Decoration and ornament

Lattimer family
USE Latimer family

Lattimo
USE Milk glass

Lattimore family
USE Latimer family

Lattin family
USE Latting family

Latting family *(Not Subd Geog)*
UF Lattin family
Lettin family

Latuka (African people)
UF Latooka (African people)
Latuka (African tribe)
Latuko (African people)
Lotuka (African people)
Lotuko (African people)
BT Ethnology—Sudan

Latuka (African tribe)
USE Latuka (African people)

Latuka language
UF Latouka language
Lotuho language
Lotuko language
BT Nilo-Hamitic languages
Sudan—Languages
NT Lango language

Latuko (African people)
USE Latuka (African people)

Latvia
— **Economic conditions** *(Not Subd Geog)*
—— 1918-1940 *(Not Subd Geog)*
—— 1940- *(Not Subd Geog)*
— **History**
—— To 1562
—— 1562-1918
—— **Revolution of 1905**
[DK511.L176]
—— 1914-1918
—— 1918-1940
—— 1940-
NT World War, 1939-1945—
Deportations from Latvia
—— **Russian occupation, 1940-1941**

Latvian-American children's poetry
USE Children's poetry, Latvian-American

Latvian-American children's stories
USE Children's stories, Latvian-American

Latvian Americans *(May Subd Geog)*
BT Ethnology—United States
Latvians—United States

Latvian art
USE Art, Latvian

Latvian authors
USE Authors, Latvian

Latvian book-plates
USE Book-plates, Latvian

Latvian Catholics
USE Catholics, Latvian

Latvian children's literature
USE Children's literature, Latvian

Latvian children's poetry
USE Children's poetry, Latvian

Latvian drama *(May Subd Geog)*
[PG9010 (History)]
[PG9037 (Collections)]

Latvian dramatists
USE Dramatists, Latvian

Latvian encyclopedias and dictionaries
USE Encyclopedias and dictionaries,
Latvian

Latvian fiction *(May Subd Geog)*
[PG9000-PG9011 (History)]
[PG9039 (Collections)]
NT Love stories, Latvian
Short stories, Latvian

Latvian folk dancing
USE Folk dancing, Latvian

Latvian folk poetry
USE Folk poetry, Latvian

Latvian folk-songs
USE Folk-songs, Latvian

Latvian imprints *(May Subd Geog)*

Latvian landscape painting
USE Landscape painting, Latvian

Latvian language
[PG8801-8993]
BT Baltic languages

Latvian literature *(May Subd Geog)*
[PG9000-PG9011 (History)]
[PG9031-PG9146 (Collections)]
BT Baltic literature
NT Children's literature, Latvian
— 20th century
— Foreign countries
UF Latvian literature in foreign
countries

Latvian literature in foreign countries
USE Latvian literature—Foreign countries

Latvian love stories
USE Love stories, Latvian

Latvian mythology
USE Mythology, Baltic

Latvian narrative poetry
USE Narrative poetry, Latvian

Latvian newspapers *(May Subd Geog)*

Latvian painting
USE Painting, Latvian

Latvian periodicals (May Subd Geog)
Latvian philology
  ₍PG8801-8993₎
Latvian philosophy
  USE Philosophy, Latvian
Latvian poetry (May Subd Geog)
  ₍PG9009 (History)₎
  ₍PG9034 (Collections)₎
  NT Children's poetry, Latvian
      Folk poetry, Latvian
      Narrative poetry, Latvian
  — 20th century
  — Foreign countries
      UF Latvian poetry in foreign countries
Latvian poetry in foreign countries
  USE Latvian poetry—Foreign countries
Latvian poets
  USE Poets, Latvian
Latvian political posters
  USE Political posters, Latvian
Latvian porcelain
  USE Porcelain, Latvian
Latvian portrait sculpture
  USE Portrait sculpture, Latvian
Latvian posters
  USE Posters, Latvian
Latvian prints
  USE Prints, Latvian
Latvian prose literature (May Subd Geog)
  ₍PG9011 (History)₎
  ₍PG9039 (Collections)₎
Latvian proverbs
  USE Proverbs, Latvian
Latvian sculpture
  USE Sculpture, Latvian
Latvian short stories
  USE Short stories, Latvian
Latvian Song Festival
  ₍ML36₎
  UF Vispārējie latviešu dziesmu svētki
  BT Music festivals—Canada
      Music festivals—United States
Latvian songs
  USE Songs, Latvian
Latvian watercolor painting
  USE Watercolor painting, Latvian
Latvian wit and humor (May Subd Geog)
  ₍PG9011 (History)₎
  ₍PN6222 (Collections)₎
    Here are entered collections from several authors
    and individual authors who have not written in other
    literary forms.
Latvian wit and humor, Pictorial
  (May Subd Geog)
Latvians (May Subd Geog)
  UF Letts
  BT Balts (Indo-European people)
      Ethnology—Latvia
  — United States
      NT Latvian Americans
Lau language
  ₍PL6253.L38₎
Laub family (Not Subd Geog)
  UF Lauber family
Lauber family
  USE Laub family
Lauch family
  USE Lausch family
Laud family
  USE Lord family
Lauda, anima mea (Music)
  USE Psalms (Music)—146th Psalm
Lauda Jerusalem Dominum (Music)
  USE Psalms (Music)—147th Psalm
Laudate Dominum de caelis (Music)
  USE Psalms (Music)—148th Psalm
Laudate Dominum in sanctis eius (Music)
  USE Psalms (Music)—150th Psalm
Laudate Dominum omnes gentes (Music)
  USE Psalms (Music)—117th Psalm

Laudate Dominum quoniam bonus (Music)
  USE Psalms (Music)—147th Psalm
Laudate nomen Domini (Music)
  USE Psalms (Music)—135th Psalm
Laudate, pueri, Dominum (Music)
  USE Psalms (Music)—113th Psalm
Laudatory poetry
  UF Encomiums
      Epideictic poetry
      Eulogistic poetry
      Panegyrics
      Praise poems
  BT Poetry
  NT Qasidas
Laudatory poetry, African
  UF African laudatory poetry
  BT African poetry
Laudatory poetry, Classical
  (May Subd Geog)
  UF Classical laudatory poetry
  BT Classical poetry
Laudatory poetry, English (May Subd Geog)
  UF English laudatory poetry
  BT English poetry
Laudatory poetry, English, ₍Urdu, etc.₎
  (May Subd Geog)
Laudatory poetry, Greek (May Subd Geog)
  UF Greek laudatory poetry
  BT Greek poetry
Laudatory poetry, Latin (May Subd Geog)
  ₍PA6138.P3₎
  UF Latin laudatory poetry
  BT Latin poetry
Laudatory poetry, Tswana (May Subd Geog)
  UF Tswana laudatory poetry
  BT Tswana poetry
Laudatory poetry, Urdu (May Subd Geog)
  UF Urdu laudatory poetry
  BT Urdu poetry
Lauder family (Not Subd Geog)
  UF Lauter family
      Lawder family
      Lawter family
      Lawther family
  RT DeLawder family
Laudermilch family
  USE Lowdermilk family
Laudermilk family
  USE Lowdermilk family
Lauds
  ₍BX2000.62₎
  BT Divine office
Lauds (Music)
  BT Morning-service music
Lauenburgische Seen, Naturpark (Germany)
  USE Naturpark Lauenburgische Seen
        (Germany)
Lauer family (Not Subd Geog)
Laufer family (Not Subd Geog)
  UF Lauffer family
Lauffer family
  USE Laufer family
Laufwerk
  USE Musical clock
Laughing frog
  USE Rana ridibunda
Laughing-gas
  USE Nitrous oxide
Laughing gull
  UF Larus atricilla
  BT Gulls
Laughing jackass
  USE Kookaburra
Laughingthrushes
  USE Garrulax
Laughland Lake (N.W.T.)
  BT Lakes—Northwest Territories

Laughlin family
  UF Lafflin family
      Laflin family
      Laughling family
      Lofland family
      Loflin family
      Loughlin family
Laughling family
  USE Laughlin family
Laughter
  ₍BF575.L3 (Psychology)₎
  ₍PN6149.P5 (Literature)₎
  BT Emotions
      Wit and humor
  NT Smile
  — Religious aspects
  — — Baptists, ₍Catholic Church, etc.₎
  — — Buddhism, ₍Christianity, etc.₎
Laughter in art
Laughter in literature
Laughton family
  USE Lawton family
Lauhala weaving (May Subd Geog)
  ₍TT877.5₎
  UF Hala leaf weaving
  BT Fiberwork
      Hala tree
      Hand weaving
Laumiss family
  USE Loomis family
Launcelot (Legendary character)
  USE Lancelot (Legendary character)
Launch complexes (Astronautics)
  (May Subd Geog)
  ₍TL4020-4027₎
  UF Launch sites (Astronautics)
      Launching sites (Astronautics)
  BT Astronautics
      Ground support systems (Astronautics)
  NT Satellite launching ships
  — Location
      UF Location of launch complexes
Launch sites (Astronautics)
  USE Launch complexes (Astronautics)
Launch vehicles (Astronautics)
  UF Space launch vehicles
  BT Artificial satellites—Launching
      Rockets (Aeronautics)
  NT Ariane rocket
      Blue Streak rocket
      Delta launch vehicle
  — Law and legislation (May Subd Geog)
      BT Space law
Launch windows (Astronautics)
  UF Windows, Launch (Astronautics)
  BT Rockets (Aeronautics)—Launching
  — Computer programs
      ₍TL1078₎
Launches
  ₍GV835 (Boating)₎
  ₍VM341-VM349 (Construction)₎
  BT Boats and boating
      Motorboats
      Ships
  NT Naphtha-launches
Launching equipment on aircraft carriers
  USE Aircraft carriers—Aircraft launching
        and recovery equipment
Launching of artificial satellites
  USE Artificial satellites—Launching
Launching of hot air balloons
  USE Hot air balloons—Launching
Launching of rockets
  USE Rockets (Aeronautics)—Launching
Launching of ships
  USE Ships—Launching
Launching sites (Astronautics)
  USE Launch complexes (Astronautics)
Launderettes
  USE Laundries, Self-service

Laundering of money
  USE Money laundering
Laundresses *(May Subd Geog)*
  UF Laundry women
      Washerwomen
Laundresses in art
  ₜN8219.L27₎
Laundries
  ₜTT980-999₎
  BT Laundry industry
  NT Laundries, Public
Laundries, Hospital
  ₜRA975.5.L3₎
  UF Hospital laundries
      Hospitals—Laundry service
Laundries, Military
  ₜUC440₎
  UF Laundries, Naval
      Military laundries
      Naval laundries
Laundries, Naval
  USE Laundries, Military
Laundries, Public *(May Subd Geog)*
  ₜTD1015₎
  UF Municipal laundries
      Public laundries
      Public wash-houses
      Wash-houses, Public
  BT Laundries
Laundries, Self-service *(May Subd Geog)*
  UF Coin operated laundries
      Launderettes
      Laundromats
      Self-service laundries
      Washeterias
  BT Coin operated machines
      Laundry industry
Laundromats
  USE Laundries, Self-service
Laundry *(May Subd Geog)*
  ₜTT980-999₎
  UF Clothing and dress—Cleaning
      Ironing
      Washing
  BT Cleaning
      Home economics
      Laundry industry
  NT Bleaching materials
      Hotel laundry service
  — Equipment and supplies
    NT Clothespins
        Washboards
Laundry, Steam
  ₜTT990₎
  UF Steam laundry
  BT Laundry industry
Laundry in art
Laundry industry *(May Subd Geog)*
  NT Diaper service
      Laundries
      Laundries, Self-service
      Laundry
      Laundry, Steam
      Laundry workers
      Linen supply service
  — Collective labor agreements
    USE Collective labor agreements—
        Laundry industry
  — **Law and legislation** *(May Subd Geog)*
  — **Vocational guidance**
    BT Laundry workers
Laundry machinery
  ₜTT997-9₎
  NT Washing-machines
  — Appraisal
    USE Laundry machinery—Valuation
  — **Electric driving**
  — **Valuation**
    UF Laundry machinery—Appraisal
Laundry women
  USE Laundresses

Laundry workers *(May Subd Geog)*
  ₜHD5119.L3 (Hours)₎
  ₜHD6073.L3 (Women)₎
  BT Laundry industry
  NT Laundry industry—Vocational
      guidance
      Trade-unions—Laundry workers
      Wages—Laundry workers
Laune (The German word)
  BT German language—Etymology
Lauraceae
  ₜQK495.L375₎
  NT Aiouea
      Aniba
      Cinnamomum
      Eusideroxylon
      Laurel
      Persea
Laurales
  USE Magnoliales
Laurance family
  USE Lawrence family
Laure family
  USE Lowry family
L'Aure River (France)
  USE Aure River (France)
Laureates, Artist
  USE Artists laureate
Laureates, Poet
  USE Poets laureate
Laurel
  ₜQK495.L375 (Botany)₎
  UF Laurus
  BT Lauraceae
  NT Kalmia
Laurel Hill Farm (Pa.)
  USE Slateford Farm (Pa.)
Laurence-Biedl syndrome
  USE Laurence-Moon-Biedl syndrome
Laurence family
  USE Lawrence family
Laurence-Moon-Biedl-Bardet syndrome
  USE Laurence-Moon-Biedl syndrome
Laurence-Moon-Biedl syndrome
  (May Subd Geog)
  ₜRC665₎
  UF Bardet-Biedl syndrome
      Biedl's syndrome
      Biemond's syndrome
      Laurence-Biedl syndrome
      Laurence-Moon-Biedl-Bardet
      syndrome
  BT Abnormalities, Human
      Endocrine glands—Diseases
      Generative organs—Abnormalities
      Genetic disorders
      Mental retardation
      Syndromes
Laurens family
  USE Lawrence family
Laurent series
  UF Series, Laurent
  BT Functions of complex variables
      Series, Taylor's
Laurentian Channel (Nfld. and N.S.)
  BT Saint Lawrence, Gulf of
      Straits—Newfoundland
      Straits—Nova Scotia
Laurentian Hills (Québec)
  USE Laurentian Mountains (Québec)
Laurentian Mountains (Québec)
  UF Laurentian Hills (Québec)
      Laurentide Hills (Québec)
      Laurentide Mountains (Québec)
      Laurentides (Québec)
  BT Mountains—Québec (Province)
Laurentian Plateau
  USE Canadian Shield
Laurentian Shield
  USE Canadian Shield

Laurentian Upland
  USE Canadian Shield
Laurentide Hills (Québec)
  USE Laurentian Mountains (Québec)
Laurentide Mountains (Québec)
  USE Laurentian Mountains (Québec)
Laurentides (Québec)
  USE Laurentian Mountains (Québec)
Laurentides Provincial Park (Québec)
  USE Parc provincial des Laurentides
      (Québec)
Laurentine Villa (Laurentum)
  UF Villa Laurentina (Laurentum)
  BT Dwellings—Italy
      Italy—Antiquities, Roman
Laurentum (Ancient city) *(Not Subd Geog)*
  ₜDG70.L37₎
  BT Cities and towns, Ruined, extinct, etc.
      —Italy
      Italy—Antiquities
Laurentze-Hansen family *(Not Subd Geog)*
  RT Hansen family
Lauric acid
  ₜQD305.A2₎
Lauridae
  NT Baccalaureus
Lauridsen family
  USE Lauritsen family
Laurie family *(Not Subd Geog)*
Laurier Park (Hull, Québec)
  USE Parc Laurier (Hull, Québec)
Laurimer family
  USE Larrimore family
Lauritsen family *(Not Subd Geog)*
  UF Lauridsen family
      Lauritson family
      Lauritzen family
Lauritson family
  USE Lauritsen family
Lauritzen family
  USE Lauritsen family
Laurus
  USE Laurel
Laurus cinnamomum
  USE Cinnamon tree
Laury family
  USE Lowry family
Lausa Rock Shelter (France)
  USE Laouza Rock Shelter (France)
Lausanne disputation, 1536
  BT Disputations, Religious
Lausavísur
  BT Old Norse poetry
      Poetry
Lausch family *(Not Subd Geog)*
  UF Lauch family
      Lausche family
Lausche family
  USE Lausch family
Lausitz (Germany)
  USE Lusatia (Germany)
Lausitz culture *(May Subd Geog)*
  UF Lusatian culture
  BT Bronze age
      Man, Prehistoric
      Urnfield culture
  NT Knoviz culture
Lausitzer Neisse River
  USE Neisse River
Lauso Rock Shelter (France)
  USE Laouza Rock Shelter (France)
Lauson family
  USE Lawson family
Laustsen family *(Not Subd Geog)*
Laut Alifuru
  USE Arafura Sea
Laut Arafuru
  USE Arafura Sea
Laut Cina Selatan
  USE South China Sea

Laut Djawa
  USE Java Sea
Laut Harafura
  USE Arafura Sea
Laut Jawa
  USE Java Sea
Laut Tjina
  USE South China Sea
Lauter family
  USE Lauder family
Lautermilch family
  USE Lowdermilk family
Lautermilche family
  USE Lowdermilk family
Lautermilk family
  USE Lowdermilk family
Lauth family (Not Subd Geog)
Lautner family (Not Subd Geog)
Lauton family
  USE Lawton family
Lauttermilch family
  USE Lowdermilk family
LAV (Virus)
  USE Human immunodeficiency viruses
LAV antibodies
  USE Human immunodeficiency virus
       antibodies
LAV/HTLV-III (Virus)
  USE Human immunodeficiency viruses
Lava (May Subd Geog)
  ⌐QE461 (Igneous rocks)¬
  ⌐QE522 (Volcanoes)¬
  BT Volcanoes
  RT Volcanic soils
  NT Keratophyre
       Latite
       Perlite
       Pumice
Lava (Hindu mythology)
  BT Mythology, Hindu
Lava Beds National Monument (Calif.)
  BT National monuments—California
Lava language
  USE Lawa language (Thailand)
Lava tubes (May Subd Geog)
  ⌐GB649.L3¬
  UF Lava tunnel
       Tubes, Lava
  BT Caves
       Volcanism
Lava tunnel
  USE Lava tubes
Lavabos (Architecture) (May Subd Geog)
  BT Architecture
Lavaca Bay (Tex.)
  BT Bays—Texas
Lavaca River (Tex.)
  BT Rivers—Texas
Lavage
  USE Irrigation (Medicine)
Lavage, Peritoneal
  USE Peritoneal dialysis
Lavaison family
  USE Lavison family
Laval family
  USE Lavalle family
Lavalette family (Not Subd Geog)
  UF De Lavalette family
Lavalle family (Not Subd Geog)
  UF Laval family
Lavalle Plaza (Buenos Aires, Argentina)
  USE Plaza Lavalle (Buenos Aires,
       Argentina)
Lavandula
  USE Lavender (Plant)
Lavant River (Austria)
  BT Rivers—Austria
Lavashian family (Not Subd Geog)
Lavatera
  ⌐QK495.M27 (Botany)¬
  BT Malvaceae

Laveison family
  USE Lavison family
Laveline family (Not Subd Geog)
Lavell family
  USE Leavell family
Lavender (Plant)
  ⌐SB303.L¬
  UF Lavandula
  BT Aromatic plants
       Herbs
       Perfumes
Lavender family (Not Subd Geog)
Lavender oil
  UF Oil of lavender
Laves phases (Metallurgy)
  BT Phase rule and equilibrium
       Physical metallurgy
Lavesen family
  USE Lavison family
Laveson family
  USE Lavison family
Lavesoun family
  USE Lavison family
Laveysan family
  USE Lavison family
Lavingston family
  USE Livingston family
Lavinio (Ancient city)
  USE Lavinium (Ancient city)
Lavinium (Ancient city) (Not Subd Geog)
  ⌐DG70.L373¬
  UF Lavinio (Ancient city)
  BT Cities and towns, Ruined, extinct, etc.
       —Italy
       Italy—Antiquities
Lavison family (Not Subd Geog)
  UF Lavaison family
       Laveison family
       Lavesen family
       Laveson family
       Lavesoun family
       Laveysan family
Lavon Lake (Tex.)
  UF Lake Lavon (Tex.)
       Lavon Reservoir (Tex.)
  BT Lakes—Texas
       Reservoirs—Texas
Lavon Reservoir (Tex.)
  USE Lavon Lake (Tex.)
LaVoy family (Not Subd Geog)
Lavua language
  USE Lawa language (Thailand)
Law (May Subd Geog)
  RT Jurisprudence
       Legislation
  SA names of legal systems, e.g. Canon
       law, Common law, Roman law;
       special branches of law, e.g.
       Constitutional law, Criminal law,
       Maritime law; specific legal topics,
       e.g. Contracts, Mortgages;
       subdivision Law and legislation
       under topics, e.g.
       Telecommunication—Law and
       legislation; also subdivision Legal
       status, laws, etc. under headings for
       groups of people, e.g. Teachers—
       Legal status, laws, etc.
  NT Bible and law
       Christianity and law
       Commercial law
       Courts
       Illegality
       Jurisdiction
       Justice
       Justice, Administration of
       Legal ethics
       Natural law
       Statutes
  — Abbreviations

      UF Abbreviations, Legal
           Legal abbreviations
  — Abridgments
      USE Law—Digests
  — **Anecdotes, facetiae, satire, etc.**
      ⌐PN6231.L4 (Wit and humor)¬
      ⌐PN6268.L4 (Anecdotes)¬
      UF Anecdotes, Legal
           Law, Wit and humor of
           Lawyers—Anecdotes, facetiae,
           satire, etc.
           Legal anecdotes
  — **Antiquities**
      UF Antiquities, Legal
           Legal antiquities
      BT Law—History and criticism
      NT Gallows
           Pillories
           Roman law—Antiquities
           Stocks (Punishment)
  — Authorship
      USE Legal composition
  — Aztecs
      USE Law, Aztec
  — **Bibliography**
      ⌐Z6451-6466¬
      UF Law books
           Lawbooks
           Legal bibliography
      RT Legal literature
      NT Information storage and retrieval
           systems—Law
           Law—United States—Indexes
  — **Biography**
      Here are entered collective biographies of the
      professions identified with the law.
      SA subdivision Biography under
           individual legal professions
  — Burgundians
      USE Law, Burgundian
  — **Cases**
      BT Law reports, digests, etc.
  — Cataloging
      USE Cataloging of legal literature
  — Cheyenne Indians
      USE Law, Cheyenne
  — **Classification**
      UF Classification—Law
      NT Classification—Books—Law
           Classification (Conflict of laws)
  — **Codification**
      UF Codification of law
      BT Common law
  — Commonplace-books
      USE Lawyers—Handbooks, manuals,
           etc.
  — **Congresses**
      UF Lawyers—Congresses
  — Construction
      USE Law—Interpretation and
           construction
  — Continuing education
      USE Law—Study and teaching
           (Continuing education)
  — **Dictionaries**
      SA subdivision Dictionaries under Law
           —⌐country subdivision¬, e.g.
           Law—Denmark—Dictionaries
  — **Digests**
      UF Law—Abridgments
  — Examinations
      USE Bar examinations
           Law examinations
  — **Examinations, questions, etc.**
      SA subdivision Examinations,
           questions, etc. under particular
           branches of law and under legal
           subjects
  — Fiction
      USE Legal novels
  — Franks

2102

USE Law, Frankish
— Handbooks, manuals, etc.
    USE Lawyers—Handbooks, manuals,
        etc.
— **History and criticism**
    UF Legal history
    RT Comparative law
    NT Law—Antiquities
        Law and socialism
— Hittites
    USE Law, Hittite
— **International unification**
    UF Harmonization of law
        International unification of law
        Unification of law
        Uniform law, International
— **Interpretation and construction**
    Here are entered works on the interpretation
of law, including statutory interpretation. Works
on the theory or practice of statute making are
entered under Legislation. Works on statute law,
as a source of law, as distinguished from constitutional law and from the law arising from judicial
or administrative decisions are entered under
Statutes.
    UF Analogy (Law)
        Construction and interpretation
          (Law)
        Construction and interpretation of
          statutes
        Interpretation and construction
          (Law)
        Law—Construction
        Statutes—Interpretation and
          construction
        Statutory construction
    RT Judicial discretion
        Judicial process
        Legal certainty
    SA *subdivision* Interpretation and
        construction *under names of*
        legal systems, special branches
        of law and specific legal topics,
        e.g. Canon law—Interpretation
        and construction; Criminal law
        —Interpretation and
        construction; Juristic acts—
        Interpretation and construction
    NT Cy pres doctrine
        Free-law movement
        Judge-made law
        Lacunae in law
        Stare decisis
        Strict law
— Jews
    USE Jews—Legal status, laws, etc.
— **Language**
    UF Language, Legal
        Legal language
        Legal style
        Style, Legal
    RT Bill drafting
    SA *subdivision* Language *under*
        specific legal topics, e.g. Labor
        laws and legislation—Language
    NT Administrative regulation drafting
        Canon law—Language
        Jewish law—Language
        Roman law—Language
        Semantics (Law)
— Literary history
    USE Jurisprudence—History
— Mayas
    USE Law, Maya
— **Methodology**
    BT Jurisprudence
— **Periodicals** *(May Subd Geog)*

    This heading is locally subdivided by country
of publication (or first order political subdivision
in the case of Canada, Great Britain, the Soviet
Union, and the United States). Periodicals limit-
ed in subject coverage to the law of a particular
jurisdiction are assigned the additional heading
Law—[place]—Periodicals.
— **Philosophy**
    [B65]
    UF Philosophy of law
    BT Natural law
    RT Jurisprudence
    NT Adversary system (Law)
        Free-law movement
        Free will and determinism
        Law and ethics
        Law and socialism
        Legal positivism
— **Popular works**
    SA *subdivision* Popular works *under*
        specific legal topics
— Practice
    USE Procedure (Law)
— Procedure
    USE Procedure (Law)
— **Psychology**
    UF Juridical psychology
        Juristic psychology
        Legal psychology
        Psychology, Juridical
        Psychology, Juristic
        Psychology, Legal
    BT Psychology, Applied
    NT Criminal psychology
        Judicial process
        Psychology, Forensic
— **Quotations**
    UF Legal quotations
    BT Quotations
    RT Legal maxims
— Religious aspects
    USE *subdivision* Religious aspects
        under the law of different
        jurisdictions, e.g. Law—Great
        Britain—Religious aspects
        Religion and law
— Sanction
    USE Sanctions (Law)
— Sociology
    USE Sociological jurisprudence
— **Sources**
    NT Custumals
— Statistics
    USE Judicial statistics
— **Study and teaching** *(May Subd Geog)*
    UF Legal education
    NT Judges—Education
        Law examinations
        Law students
        Law teachers
        Moot courts
        Public prosecutors—Education
        Student bar associations
— **Study and teaching (Clinical education)**
    (May Subd Geog)
    UF Clinical education, Legal
        Clinical legal education
— **Study and teaching (Continuing**
    education) *(May Subd Geog)*
    UF Law—Continuing education
        Post-admission legal education
    BT Practice of law
— **Terms and phrases**
    NT English language—Conversation
        and phrase books (for police)
— **Translating**
    UF Law translating
        Legal translating
— Zuñi Indians
    USE Law, Zuñi
— **Assyria**
    UF Assyro-Babylonian law

— **Babylonia**
    UF Assyro-Babylonian law
— **Brazil**
— — **Roman influences**
    UF Roman law—Influence—Brazil
    BT Rome—Civilization
— **Chile**
— — **Roman influences**
    UF Roman law—Influence—Chile
    BT Rome—Civilization
— **Europe**
— — **Roman influences**
    UF Roman law—Influence—Europe
    BT Rome—Civilization
— **Europe, Eastern**
— — **Roman influences**
    UF Roman law—Influence—Europe,
        Eastern
    BT Rome—Civilization
— **France**
— — **Roman influences**
    UF Roman law—Influence—France
    BT Rome—Civilization
— **Germany**
    BT Law, Germanic
    NT Ingelheim law
        Lübeck law
        Magdeburg law
— **Great Britain**
    UF Anglo-American law
        Law, Anglo-American
— — **History and criticism**
    BT Common law
— — **Religious aspects**
— — **Roman influences**
    UF Roman law—Influence—Great
        Britain
    BT Rome—Civilization
— **Greece**
    Here are entered works on modern Greek
law. Works on ancient Greek law are entered
under Law, Greek.
— — Sparta (Ancient city)
    USE Law, Spartan
— **Hungary**
— — **Roman influences**
    UF Roman law—Influence—
        Hungary
    BT Rome—Civilization
— **Iran**
    NT Law, Sassanid
— **Ireland**
    UF Brehon laws
— **Italy**
— — **Roman influences**
    UF Roman law—Influence—Italy
    BT Rome—Civilization
— **Latin America**
— — **American influences**
    BT United States—Civilization
— — **Roman influences**
    UF Roman law—Influence—Latin
        America
    BT Rome—Civilization
— **Netherlands**
— — **Roman influences**
    UF Roman law—Influence—
        Netherlands
    BT Rome—Civilization
— **Poland**
— — **Roman influences**
    UF Roman law—Influence—Poland
    BT Rome—Civilization
— **Portugal**
— — **Roman influences**
    UF Roman law—Influence—
        Portugal
    BT Rome—Civilization
— **Scandinavia**
— — **Roman influences**

Law
— Scandinavia
— — Roman influences *(Continued)*
UF Roman law—Influence—
Scandinavia
BT Rome—Civilization
— Scotland
UF Scots law
— Soviet Union
— — Roman influences
UF Roman law—Influence—Soviet
Union
BT Rome—Civilization
— Spain
— — Autonomous communities
— — Roman influences
UF Roman law—Influence—Spain
BT Rome—Civilization
— Switzerland
— — Roman influences
UF Roman law—Influence—
Switzerland
BT Rome—Civilization
— United States
UF Anglo-American law
Law, Anglo-American
United States—Law
— — Examinations, questions, etc.
— — History and criticism
BT Common law
— — Indexes
BT Law—Bibliography
— — Roman influences
UF Roman law—Influence—United
States
BT Rome—Civilization
— — Territories and possessions
UF United States—Territories and
possessions—Law
Law, Accident
USE Accident law
Law, Administrative
USE Administrative law
Law, Advertising
USE Advertising laws
Law, Agricultural
USE Agricultural laws and legislation
Law, Ancient
SA *special legal headings with* Ancient
law *added in parentheses, e.g.*
Divorce (Ancient law); Marriage
(Ancient law)
NT Exiles (Ancient law)
Law, Greek
Law, Hittite
Law, Sumerian
Law, Anglo-American
USE Common law
Law—Great Britain
Law—United States
Law, Anglo-Saxon
UF Anglo-Saxon law
BT Law, Germanic
NT Wergild
Law, Angoni
USE Law, Ngoni (African people)
Law, Ao (Indic people)
UF Ao (Indic people) law
BT Customary law—India
Law, Arab
USE Islamic law
Law, Arusha
UF Arusha law
Law, Aryan
USE Law, Indo-European
Law, Ashanti
UF Ashanti law
NT Real property (Ashanti law)
Law, Automobile
USE Automobiles—Law and legislation

Law, Aztec
UF Aztec law
Aztecs—Law
Law—Aztecs
BT Law, Nahua
NT Adultery (Aztec law)
Marriage (Aztec law)
Law, Bafokeng
UF Bafokeng law
BT Law, Bantu
Law, Bahnar *(May Subd Geog)*
UF Bahnar law
Law, Banjal (African people)
UF Banjal (African people) law
Law, Banking
USE Banking law
Law, Bantu
UF Bantu law
NT Civil procedure (Bantu law)
Courts, Bantu
Law, Bafokeng
Law, Ila (African people)
Law, Basuto
USE Law, Sotho
Law, Bedouin
UF Bedouin law
Law, Berber
UF Berber law
Law, Building
USE Building laws
Law, Burgundian
UF Burgundian law
Law—Burgundians
BT Law, Germanic
SA *special legal headings with* Burgundian
law *added in parentheses, e.g.*
Criminal law (Burgundian law)
Law, Burial
USE Burial laws
Law, Burmese Buddhist
USE Burmese Buddhist law
Law, Business
USE Business law
Law, Byzantine
UF Byzantine law
Graeco-Roman law
Greco-Roman law
Law, Greco-Roman
BT Roman law
SA *special legal headings with* Byzantine
law *added in parentheses, e.g.*
Guardian and ward (Byzantine law);
Possession (Byzantine law)
NT Adultery (Byzantine law)
Land tenure (Byzantine law)
— History
NT Law, Byzantine—Reception
— Reception *(May Subd Geog)*
UF Reception of Byzantine law
BT Law, Byzantine—History
Law, Celtic
UF Brehon laws
Celtic law
Law, Chaga (African people)
UF Chaga (African people) law
BT Customary law—Tanzania
Law, Charity
USE Charity laws and legislation
Law, Chemehuevi
UF Chemehuevi Indians—Law
Chemehuevi law
Law, Cherokee
UF Cherokee Indians—Law
Cherokee law
Law, Cheyenne
UF Cheyenne law
Law—Cheyenne Indians
Law, Chickasaw
UF Chickasaw Indians—Law
Chickasaw law
NT Chickasaw Indians—Tribal citizenship

Law, Chin
UF Chin law
Law, Choctaw
UF Choctaw Indians—Law
Choctaw law
NT Choctaw Indians—Tribal citizenship
Law, Civil
USE Civil law
Law, Colonial
USE Colonies—Law and legislation
Law, Commercial
USE Commercial law
Law, Comparative
USE Comparative law
Law, Constitutional
USE Constitutional law
Law, Consular
USE Consular law
Law, Corporation
USE Corporation law
Law, Creek
UF Creek Indians—Law
Creek law
Law, Criminal
USE Criminal law
Law, Dairy
USE Dairy laws
Law, Dakota
UF Dakota Indians—Law
Dakota law
Law, Dental
USE Dental laws and legislation
Law, Dinka
USE Law, Dinka (African people)
Law, Dinka (African people)
UF Dinka (African people) law
Law, Dinka
NT Bride price (Dinka law)
Law, Doctor of
USE Doctor of laws degree
Law, Drainage
USE Drainage laws
Law, Dusun
UF Dusun law
Law, Ecclesiastical
USE Ecclesiastical law
Law, Educational
USE Educational law and legislation
Law, Election
USE Election law
Law, Emigration
USE Emigration and immigration law
Law, Engineering
USE Engineering law
Law, Ewe
UF Ewe law
SA *special legal headings with* Ewe law
added in parentheses, e.g. Property
(Ewe law)
Law, Factory
USE Factory laws and legislation
Law, Farm
USE Farm law
Law, Feudal
USE Feudal law
Law, Fishery
USE Fishery law and legislation
Law, Food
USE Food law and legislation
Law, Forestry
USE Forestry law and legislation
Law, Franconian
USE Law, Frankish
Law, Frankish
UF Franconian law
Frankish law
Law—Franks
Law, Franconian
BT Law, Germanic

SA *special legal headings with* Frankish
　　law *added in parentheses, e.g.*
　　Contracts (Frankish law); Marriage
　　(Frankish law)
NT Adoption (Frankish law)
　　Kinship (Frankish law)
　　Ripuarian law
　　Salic law
Law, Friesian
UF Friesian law
BT Law, Germanic
Law, Fulah
UF Fulah law
Law, Garo
UF Garo law
Law, Germanic
UF Germanic law
SA *special legal headings with* Germanic
　　law *added in parentheses, e.g.*
　　Domestic relations (Germanic law);
　　Larceny (Germanic law)
NT Actions in rem (Germanic law)
　　Adultery (Germanic law)
　　Constituent power (Germanic law)
　　Kinship (Germanic law)
　　Law—Germany
　　Law, Anglo-Saxon
　　Law, Burgundian
　　Law, Frankish
　　Law, Friesian
　　Law, Lombard
　　Law, Saxon
　　Law, Scandinavian
　　Law, Visigothic
　　Wergild
— **Roman influences**
　　UF Roman law—Influence—Law,
　　　　Germanic
　　BT Rome—Civilization
Law, Gothic
UF Gothic law
Law, Greco-Roman
USE Law, Byzantine
Law, Greek
　　Here are entered works on ancient Greek law.
Works on modern Greek law are entered under Law
—Greece.
UF Greek law
BT Law, Ancient
SA *special legal headings with* Greek law
　　added in parentheses, e.g. Domestic
　　relations (Greek law)
NT Actions and defenses (Greek law)
　　Affinity (Greek law)
　　Agency (Greek law)
　　Agricultural laws and legislation
　　　　(Greek law)
　　Alien property (Greek law)
　　Aliens (Greek law)
　　Contracts, Maritime (Greek law)
　　Evidence (Greek law)
　　Exiles (Greek law)
　　Impeachments (Greek law)
　　Law, Spartan
　　Loans (Greek law)
　　Maritime law (Greek law)
　　Military law (Greek law)
　　Slavery (Greek law)
　　Torture (Greek law)
　　War (Greek law)
　　Women—Legal status, laws, etc.
　　　　(Greek law)
Law, Guahibo *(May Subd Geog)*
UF Guahibo law
Law, Haya
UF Haya law
Law, Hebrew
USE Jewish law
Law, Hehe
USE Law, Wahehe

Law, Highway
USE Highway law
Law, Hindu
USE Hindu law
Law, Hittite
UF Hittite law
　　Law—Hittites
BT Law, Ancient
NT Deeds, Hittite
Law, Homestead
USE Homestead law
Law, Igbo
UF Igbo law
NT Marriage (Igbo law)
　　Property (Igbo law)
Law, Ila (African people)
UF Ila (African people) law
BT Law, Bantu
NT Married women (Ila law)
Law, Immigration
USE Emigration and immigration law
Law, Inca
UF Inca law
　　Incas—Law
NT Adultery (Inca law)
　　Criminal law (Inca law)
Law, Indo-European
UF Aryan law
　　Indo-European law
　　Law, Aryan
Law, Industrial
USE Factory laws and legislation
　　Industrial laws and legislation
　　Industry and state
　　Labor laws and legislation
Law, Insurance
USE Insurance law
Law, Internal revenue
USE Internal revenue law
Law, International
USE International law
Law, Iroquois
UF Iroquois law
Law, Irrigation
USE Irrigation laws
Law, Islamic
USE Islamic law
Law, Jekri (African people)
UF Jekri (African people) law
BT Customary law—Nigeria
NT Land tenure (Jekri law)
Law, Jewish
USE Jewish law
Law, Judge-made
USE Judge-made law
Law, Kabyle
UF Kabyle law
Law, Kalinga
UF Kalinga law
Law, Kamba *(May Subd Geog)*
UF Kamba law
Law, Kandyan
UF Kandyan law
Law, Kapauku
UF Kapauku law
Law, Karaite
USE Karaite law
Law, Kgatla
UF Kgatla law
BT Law, Tswana
SA *special legal headings with* Kgatla law
　　added in parentheses, e.g. Domestic
　　relations (Kgatla law)
NT Inheritance and succession (Kgatla
　　　　law)
Law, Khasa (Indic people)
UF Khasa (Indic people) law
BT Customary law—India
　　Customary law—Nepal
Law, Khasi
UF Khasi law

Law, Kipsigis
USE Law, Kipsigis (African people)
Law, Kipsigis (African people)
(May Subd Geog)
UF Kipsigis law
　　Law, Kipsigis
NT Land tenure (Kipsigis law)
Law, Kuria (African people)
(May Subd Geog)
UF Kuria (African people) law
BT Customary law—Kenya
　　Customary law—Tanzania
NT Domestic relations (Kuria law)
Law, Labor
USE Labor laws and legislation
Law, Lacunae in
USE Lacunae in law
Law, Library
USE Library legislation
Law, Liquor
USE Liquor laws
Law, Local
USE Local laws
Law, Lombard
UF Lombard law
BT Law, Germanic
NT Criminal law (Lombard law)
　　Evidence (Lombard law)
Law, Lozi
UF Lozi law
Law, Lubish
USE Lübeck law
Law, Luo
UF Luo law
NT Marriage (Luo law)
Law, Maori
UF Maori law
NT Land tenure (Maori law)
Law, Maritime
USE Maritime law
Law, Marriage
USE Marriage law
Law, Martial
USE Martial law
Law, Mashona
UF Mashona law
Law, Maya
UF Law—Mayas
　　Maya law
　　Mayas—Law
NT Land tenure (Maya law)
　　Marriage (Maya law)
Law, Medical
USE Medical laws and legislation
Law, Medieval
Law, Meos (Indic people)
UF Meos (Indic people) law
Law, Military
USE Military law
Law, Mining
USE Mining law
Law, Mohave
UF Mohave Indians—Law
　　Mohave law
Law, Mongolian
UF Mongolian law
Law, Mosaic
USE Jewish law
Law, Mossi
UF Mossi law
Law, Murngin (Australian people)
UF Murngin (Australian people) law
BT Customary law—Australia
NT Land tenure (Murngin law)
Law, Nahua
UF Nahua law
NT Law, Aztec
Law, Nandi
UF Nandi law
Law, Natural
USE Natural law

Law, Navajo
  UF Navajo Indians—Law
       Navajo law
Law, Naval
  USE Naval law
Law, Ngoni (African people)
  UF Law, Angoni
       Ngoni (African people) law
  BT Customary law—Africa, Eastern
  NT Inheritance and succession (Ngoni
       law)
       Property (Ngoni law)
Law, Nuer
  USE Law, Nuer (African people)
Law, Nuer (African people)
  UF Law, Nuer
       Nuer (African people) law
       Nuer law
Law, Oriental
  UF Oriental law
  SA *special legal headings with* Oriental
       law *added in parentheses, e.g.*
       Dowry (Oriental law)
  NT Burmese Buddhist law
       Hindu law
       Islamic law
       Law, Semitic
Law, Patent
  USE Patent laws and legislation
Law, Poverty
  USE Legal assistance to the poor
       Public welfare—Law and legislation
Law, Practice of
  USE Practice of law
Law, Press
  USE Press law
Law, Primitive *(May Subd Geog)*
  [GN493]
  BT Society, Primitive
  RT Ethnological jurisprudence
  SA *special legal headings with* Primitive
       law *added in parentheses, e.g.*
       Domestic relations (Primitive law)
Law, Probate
  USE Probate law and practice
Law, Public
  USE Public law
Law, Public interest
  USE Public interest law
Law, Railroad
  USE Railroad law
Law, Roman
  USE Roman law
Law, Roman-Dutch
  USE Roman-Dutch law
Law, Samaritan *(May Subd Geog)*
  UF Samaritan law
Law, Santali
  UF Santali law
Law, Sassanid
  UF Sassanid law
  BT Law—Iran
Law, Saxon
  UF Saxon law
  BT Law, Germanic
  SA *special legal headings with* Saxon law
       added in parentheses, e.g.
       Inheritance and succession (Saxon
       law); Land tenure (Saxon law)
  NT Magdeburg law
Law, Scandinavian
  UF Scandinavian law
  BT Law, Germanic
Law, Scroll of the
  USE Torah scrolls
Law, Sebei
  UF Sebei law
Law, Semitic
  BT Law, Oriental

  SA *special legal headings with* Semitic law
       added in parentheses, e.g. Marriage
       (Semitic law)
  NT Islamic law
       Jewish law
       Law, Sumerian
Law, Siksika
  UF Siksika Indians—Law
       Siksika law
Law, Slavic
  UF Slavic law
Law, Sotho
  UF Basuto law
       Law, Basuto
       Sotho law
  NT Domestic relations (Sotho law)
Law, Spartan
  UF Law—Greece—Sparta (Ancient city)
       Spartan law
  BT Law, Greek
Law, Sugar
  USE Sugar laws and legislation
Law, Suku
  USE Law, Sukuma (African people)
Law, Sukuma (African people)
  UF Law, Suku
       Sukuma (African people) law
Law, Sumerian
  UF Sumerian law
  BT Law, Ancient
       Law, Semitic
Law, Sumptuary
  USE Sumptuary laws
Law, Sunday
  USE Sunday legislation
Law, Tiruray
  UF Tiruray law
Law, Tivi
  UF Tivi law
Law, Toka (African people)
  UF Toka (African people) law
  BT Customary law—Zambia
  NT Inheritance and succession (Toka law)
Law, Townsite
  USE Townsite law
Law, Tswana
  UF Tswana law
  NT Civil procedure (Tswana law)
       Law, Kgatla
Law, Usury
  USE Usury laws
Law, Venda *(May Subd Geog)*
  UF Venda law
Law, Visigothic
  UF Visigothic law
  BT Law, Germanic
  SA *special legal headings with* Visigothic
       law *added in parentheses, e.g.*
       Marriage (Visigothic law)
  NT Administrative law (Visigothic law)
       Suretyship and guaranty (Visigothic
       law)
Law, Wager of
  USE Wager of law
Law, Wahehe
  UF Hehe law
       Law, Hehe
       Wahehe law
Law, Wit and humor of
  USE Law—Anecdotes, facetiae, satire, etc.
Law, Yanzi (African people)
  UF Yanzi (African people) law
  BT Customary law—Zaire
  NT Adultery (Yanzi law)
       Reparation (Yanzi law)
Law, Yoruba
  UF Yoruba law
  SA *special legal headings with* Yoruba law
       added in parentheses, e.g. Land
       tenure (Yoruba law)

Law, Zande
  UF Zande law
Law, Zapotec
  UF Zapotec Indians—Law
       Zapotec law
Law, Zoroastrian
  USE Zoroastrian law
Law, Zuñi
  UF Law—Zuñi Indians
       Zuñi law
Law (Philosophy)
  [B105.L3]
  BT Philosophy
Law (Theology)
  [BT95-BT96]
  Here are entered works on law as a theological
concept.
  BT Providence and government of God
  RT Christianity and law
  NT Law and gospel
       Neonomianism
  — **Biblical teaching**
    UF Bible—Law
Law and anthropology
  BT Anthropology
       Ethnological jurisprudence
  NT Forensic anthropology
Law and art
  UF Art and law
  NT Art—Protection
       Artists—Legal status, laws, etc.
       Artists' contracts
       Copyright—Art
       Performing arts—Law and legislation
       Theater—Law and legislation
Law and communism
  USE Law and socialism
Law and ethics
  UF Ethics and law
       Law and morals
       Morals and law
  BT Law—Philosophy
  NT Abuse of rights
       Judicial ethics
       Legal ethics
Law and fact *(May Subd Geog)*
  UF Fact and law
       Questions of fact
       Questions of law
  BT Appellate procedure
       Civil procedure
       Criminal procedure
       Evidence (Law)
  RT Jury
  NT Material facts (Law)
Law and gospel
  [BT85]
  Here are entered works dealing with the theologi-
cal concept of law in its relation to the gospel.
  UF Gospel and law
  BT Law (Theology)
  RT Grace (Theology)
  NT Antinomianism
       Freedom (Theology)
       Neonomianism
Law and literature
  UF Literature and law
  NT Copyright
       Law in literature
       Lawyers as authors
       Obscenity (Law)
Law and mental illness
  USE Insanity—Jurisprudence
       Mental health laws
Law and morals
  USE Law and ethics
Law and politics
  UF Politics and law
  BT Jurisprudence
       Power (Social sciences)
       State, The

NT Political questions and judicial power
Law and public relations
  USE Public relations and law
Law and religion
  USE Religion and law
Law and science
  USE Science and law
Law and sex
  USE Sex and law
Law and socialism
  UF Communism and law
    Law and communism
    Socialism and law
  BT Law—History and criticism
    Law—Philosophy
Law and society
  USE Sociological jurisprudence
Law and sociobiology
  BT Sociobiology
Law and technology
  USE Technology and law
Law and the Bible
  USE Bible and law
Law books
  USE Law—Bibliography
    Legal literature
Law clerks *(May Subd Geog)*
    Here are entered works on law school graduates
  or lawyers who serve as staff assistants to individual
  judges.
  UF Clerks, Law
    Clerkship (Law)
    Judges' clerks
  BT Courts—Officials and employees
    Lawyers
Law departments, Corporate
  USE Corporate legal departments
Law enforcement *(May Subd Geog)*
  UF Enforcement of law
  BT Criminal justice, Administration of
  NT Crime analysis
    Federal aid to law enforcement
      agencies
    Interviewing in law enforcement
    Narcotic enforcement agents
    Peace officers
    Sanctions, Administrative
    Vice control
    Volunteer workers in law enforcement
  — **Optical equipment**
    BT Optical instruments
  — **Illinois**
    NT Illinois Urban High Crime
      Reduction Program
Law enforcement officers
  USE Police
Law examinations *(May Subd Geog)*
  UF Law—Examinations
  BT Law—Study and teaching
  NT Bar examinations
    Law schools—Entrance examinations
Law family *(Not Subd Geog)*
  UF Lawe family
    Laws family
Law firms *(May Subd Geog)*
  UF Firms, Law
  BT Lawyers
    Practice of law
  NT Law partnership
Law in art
Law in literature
  [PN56.L]
  BT Law and literature
  NT Legal novels
Law in the Bible
  USE Jewish law
Law in the Koran
  USE Islamic law
Law Latin
  USE Latin language—Law Latin

Law librarians *(May Subd Geog)*
  [Z675.L2]
  UF Librarians, Law
  BT Special librarians
Law libraries *(May Subd Geog)*
  [Z675.L2]
  UF Law school libraries
    Libraries, Law
    Libraries, Law school
  BT Libraries, Special
  — **Acquisitions**
    BT Acquisitions (Libraries)
  — **Book lists**
    UF Book lists for law libraries
    BT Bibliography—Best books
  — **Special collections**
  — — **Rare books**
      BT Rare books
Law lists
  USE Lawyers—Directories
Law merchant *(May Subd Geog)*
  BT Customary law
  RT Commercial law
  NT Usages of trade
Law of areas (Mechanics)
  UF Areas, Law of (Mechanics)
  BT Dynamics of a particle
Law of diffusion, Graham's
  USE Graham's law
Law of diminishing returns
  USE Diminishing returns
Law of large numbers
  UF Large numbers, Law of
    Numbers, Large
  BT Convergence
    Mathematical statistics
    Probabilities
Law of mortality
  USE Mortality, Law of
Law of nations
  USE International law
Law of nature
  USE Natural law
Law of negation of negation (Dialectical
    materialism)
  USE Negation of negation (Dialectical
      materialism)
Law of partial pressures, Dalton's
  USE Dalton's law
Law of persons
  USE Persons (Law)
Law of succession
  USE Inheritance and succession
    Kings and rulers—Succession
Law of supply and demand
  USE Supply and demand
Law of the sea
  USE Maritime law
Law officers (Courts-martial)
  (May Subd Geog)
  UF Courts-martial and courts of inquiry—
      Law officers
  BT Courts-martial and courts of inquiry
    Judges
Law offices *(May Subd Geog)*
  UF Legal offices
  BT Lawyers
    Offices
    Practice of law
  RT Legal secretaries
  NT Corporate legal departments
    Legal assistants
Law partnership *(May Subd Geog)*
  UF Partnership of attorneys
  BT Law firms
    Lawyers
    Partnership
    Practice of law
Law printing
  BT Printing
    Printing, Legislative

Law professors
  USE Law teachers
Law reform *(May Subd Geog)*
  UF Legal reform
Law reporters *(May Subd Geog)*
  UF Court reporters
  BT Courts—Officials and employees
    Law reporting
    Reporters and reporting
Law reporters (Publications)
  USE Law reports, digests, etc.
Law reporting *(May Subd Geog)*
  UF Court reporting
    Verbatim reporting
  BT Reporters and reporting
  NT Law reporters
    Video tapes in courtroom proceedings
Law reports, digests, etc. *(May Subd Geog)*
  UF Court reports
    Digests of cases (Law)
    Law reporters (Publications)
  RT Annotations and citations (Law)
  SA *subdivisions* Cases *or* Digests *under
      legal subjects*
  NT Advisory opinions
    Attorneys general's opinions
    Dissenting opinions
    Judicial opinions
    Law—Cases
Law school libraries
  USE Law libraries
Law schools *(May Subd Geog)*
  [LC1101-1261]
  NT Law students
    Law teachers
    Student bar associations
  — **Accreditation**
  — **Admission**
      BT Universities and colleges—
        Admission
      NT Law schools—Entrance
        examinations
  — **Entrance examinations**
      BT Law examinations
        Law schools—Admission
  — **Entrance requirements**
      BT Universities and colleges—
        Entrance requirements
Law student associations
  USE Student bar associations
Law students *(May Subd Geog)*
  BT Law—Study and teaching
    Law schools
    Students
  NT Student bar associations
    Women law students
Law teachers *(May Subd Geog)*
  UF Law professors
    Professors of law
    Teachers, Law
  BT Law—Study and teaching
    Law schools
    Teachers
Law translating
  USE Law—Translating
Lawa (Mon-Khmer tribe)
  UF Lua' (Mon-Khmer tribe)
  BT Ethnology—Thailand
Lawa language (Thailand) *(May Subd Geog)*
  UF La-oop language
    Lava language
    Lavua language
    Luwa language
    L'wa language
  BT Mon Khmer languages
    Thailand—Languages
Lawbooks
  USE Law—Bibliography
    Legal literature
Lawd family
  USE Lord family

Lawder family
USE Lauder family
Lawe family
USE Law family
Lawed family
USE Lord family
Lawler family (Not Subd Geog)
UF Lawlor family
Lawlor family
USE Lawler family
Lawmakers
USE Legislators
Lawn bowls
USE Bowling on the green
Lawn hockey
[GV1017.L]
BT Hockey
Lawn Lake Dam (Colo.)
BT Dams—Colorado
Lawn mowers, Power
USE Power lawn mowers
Lawn sprinklers
USE Sprinklers
Lawn tempest (Game)
[GV1017.L48]
Lawn tennis
USE Tennis
Lawn tractors (May Subd Geog)
BT Tractors
NT Used lawn tractors
Lawn tractors, Used
USE Used lawn tractors
Lawnfield (Mentor, Ohio)
USE James A. Garfield Home (Mentor, Ohio)
Lawnmowers, Power
USE Power lawn mowers
Lawns (May Subd Geog)
[SB433]
BT Turf management
RT Turfgrasses
NT Bowling greens
Grasses
Ground cover plants
— Irrigation
[SB433]
— Weed control (May Subd Geog)
BT Weeds—Control
Lawrance family
USE Lawrence family
Lawremare family
USE Larrimore family
Lawrence, Jacob, 1917- John Brown series
UF John Brown series (Gouache painting)
Lawrence, Sandra. Overlord embroidery
UF Overlord embroidery (Tapestry)
BT Tapestry—England—History—20th century
Lawrence family (Not Subd Geog)
UF Larance family
Larence family
Larince family
Larrance family
Larrence family
Laurance family
Laurence family
Laurens family
Lawrance family
Lawrens family
Lawrrance family
Lieurance family
Lorance family
Lorrentz family
Lowrance family
RT Lawrenz family
Lorenz family
Lawrencium
Lawrens family
USE Lawrence family

Lawrenz family (Not Subd Geog)
RT Lawrence family
Lorenz family
Lawrey family
USE Lowry family
Lawrimor family
USE Larrimore family
Lawrimore family
USE Larrimore family
Lawrrance family
USE Lawrence family
Lawry family
USE Lowry family
Laws, Local
USE Local laws
Laws, Session
USE Session laws
Laws family
USE Law family
Lawson family
Laws of dialectical materialism
USE Dialectical materialism, Laws of
Laws of the mean (Calculus)
USE Mean value theorems (Calculus)
Lawshe family (Not Subd Geog)
UF Laaschet family
Laashett family
Laschet family
Lashet family
Van Laaschet family
Lawson cypress
USE Port Orford cedar
Lawson family (Not Subd Geog)
UF Lauson family
Laws family
Lawsonite
[QE391.L]
Lawsuits
USE Actions and defenses
Lawter family
USE Lauder family
Lawther family
USE Lauder family
Lawton family (Not Subd Geog)
UF Laughton family
Lauton family
RT Layton family
Lawyer-client privilege
USE Confidential communications—Lawyers
Lawyer reference plan
USE Lawyer referral service
Lawyer referral service (May Subd Geog)
UF Lawyer reference plan
Legal referral service
BT Lawyers
Practice of law
NT Ambulance chasing
Lawyers (May Subd Geog)
UF Advocates
Attorneys
Bar
Barristers
Jurists
Legal profession
Solicitors
RT Representation in administrative proceedings
NT Admission to the bar
Attorney and client
Bar associations
Canonists
City attorneys
Corporate legal departments
County attorneys
Government attorneys
Hospital attorneys
Integrated bar
Law clerks
Law firms
Law offices

Law partnership
Lawyer referral service
Legal assistants
Legal ethics
Maintenance and champerty
Minority lawyers
Patent lawyers
Practice of law
Right to counsel
Tax consultants
Trade-unions—Lawyers
Unauthorized practice of law
Women lawyers
— Advertising
USE Advertising—Lawyers
— Anecdotes, facetiae, satire, etc.
USE Law—Anecdotes, facetiae, satire, etc.
— Collective labor agreements
USE Collective labor agreements—Lawyers
— Confidential communications
USE Confidential communications—Lawyers
— Congresses
USE Law—Congresses
— Costume
UF Legal dress
— Directories
UF Law lists
Legal directories
— Disbarment, disqualification, etc.
UF Disbarment of lawyers
Disqualification of lawyers
BT Lawyers—Discipline
— Discipline
BT Legal ethics
NT Lawyers—Disbarment, disqualification, etc.
— Fees
UF Contingent fees
Fees, Legal
Fees (Law)
Legal fees
BT Costs (Law)
NT Executors and administrators—Fees
Prepaid legal services
— Handbooks, manuals, etc.
UF Commonplace-books (Law)
Law—Commonplace-books
Law—Handbooks, manuals, etc.
— Insurance requirements
UF Insurance, Lawyers'
Lawyers' insurance
— Malpractice (May Subd Geog)
UF Lawyers—Tort liability
Tort liability of lawyers
BT Attorney and client
Legal ethics
Practice of law
— Marketing
UF Marketing of legal services
— Pensions (May Subd Geog)
— Portraits
— Residence requirements
UF Residence requirements for lawyers
BT Admission to the bar
— Specialties and specialists
(May Subd Geog)
UF Specialization among lawyers
— Tort liability
USE Lawyers—Malpractice
— Austria
— — Fees
— Scotland
UF Lord advocates
— United States
NT Hispanic American lawyers
Lawyers, Afro-American
USE Afro-American lawyers

Lawyers, Blind *(May Subd Geog)*
  BT Blind
      Minority lawyers
Lawyers, Foreign *(May Subd Geog)*
  UF Foreign lawyers
      Foreign-trained lawyers
Lawyers, Government
  USE Government attorneys
Lawyers, Hispanic American
  USE Hispanic American lawyers
Lawyers, Jewish *(May Subd Geog)*
  UF Jewish lawyers
      Jews as lawyers
Lawyers, Military
  USE *subdivision* Lawyers *under particular*
       branches of the armed forces, e.g.
       United States. Army—Lawyers
Lawyers (Canon law)
  ₍BX1939.L25₎
Lawyers (Islamic law)
Lawyers (Roman law)
Lawyers as authors
  BT Authors
      Law and literature
Lawyers' corporations
  USE Legal service corporations
Lawyers in literature
  BT Characters and characteristics in
      literature
      Occupations in literature
  SA *subdivision* Characters—Lawyers
      under names of authors, e.g.
      Shakespeare, William, 1564-1616—
      Characters—Lawyers
  NT Notaries in literature
Lawyers in politics *(May Subd Geog)*
  ₍JA75₎
  BT Political participation
      Politics, Practical
Lawyers' insurance
  USE Lawyers—Insurance requirements
Lawyers' wives *(May Subd Geog)*
  BT Wives
Laxatives
  USE Purgatives
Laxism
  USE Probabilism
Laxity of joints
  USE Joints—Hypermobility
Lay administration of the Lord's Supper
  USE Lord's Supper—Lay administration
Lay apostolate
  USE Catholic action
Lay brothers
  ₍BX2835₎
  UF Brothers, Lay
      Monasticism and religious orders—Lay
      brothers
      Religious brothers
  BT Brothers (in religious orders,
      congregations, etc.)
Lay Buddhists
  USE Buddhist laymen
Lay celebration of the Lord's Supper
  USE Lord's Supper—Lay celebration
Lay days *(May Subd Geog)*
  UF Lay time
  BT Charter-parties
      Loading and unloading
  RT Demurrage
Lay family *(Not Subd Geog)*
  UF Lays family
Lay Franciscans
  USE Secular Franciscans
Lay judges *(May Subd Geog)*
  BT Judges
  RT Jury
  — Europe
      NT Boni homines
Lay lawyers
  USE Pro se representation

Lay leadership
  USE Christian leadership
Lay ministry *(May Subd Geog)*
  UF Ministry, Lay
      Volunteers in church work
  BT Church work
  RT Laity
      Priesthood, Universal
  NT Lay readers
      Lord's Supper—Lay administration
      Lord's Supper—Lay celebration
      Preaching, Lay
  — Catholic Church, ₍etc.₎
  — Recruiting
      UF Recruiting of lay ministers
Lay missionaries
  USE Missionaries, Lay
Lay-off compensation
  USE Wages—Dismissal wage
Lay preaching
  USE Preaching, Lay
Lay prosecutors *(May Subd Geog)*
  UF Prosecutors, Lay
  BT Criminal justice, Administration of
      Criminal procedure
      Prosecution
      Public prosecutors
  NT Informations
Lay readers *(May Subd Geog)*
  ₍BV677₎
  UF Lectors
      Parish clerks
  BT Lay ministry
  — Anglican Communion, ₍Catholic Church,
  etc.₎
Lay teachers *(May Subd Geog)*
  UF Teachers, Lay
  BT Catholic Church—Education
      Laity—Catholic Church
      Teachers
Lay time
  USE Lay days
Laya yoga
  USE Yoga, Laya
Layaway plan *(May Subd Geog)*
  UF Will-call sales
  BT Sales, Conditional
  RT Instalment plan
Laybourn family *(Not Subd Geog)*
  UF Laybourne family
      Layburn family
Laybourne family
  USE Laybourn family
Layburn family
  USE Laybourn family
Laycock family *(Not Subd Geog)*
  RT Lacock family
Laydet family
  USE Ledet family
Layer structure (Solids)
  ₍QD921₎
  UF Layered structure (Solids)
  BT Crystallography
      Solids
Layered structure (Solids)
  USE Layer structure (Solids)
Layering of plants
  USE Air layering
Layettes
  ₍TT637₎
  BT Infants—Clothing
      Infants' supplies
Laying down (Shipbuilding)
  USE Laying off (Shipbuilding)
Laying of carpets
  USE Carpet laying
Laying of corner stones
  USE Corner stones, Laying of
Laying off (Shipbuilding) *(May Subd Geog)*
  ₍VM297.5₎

  UF Laying down (Shipbuilding)
      Lofting (Shipbuilding)
  BT Shipbuilding
Laying on of hands
  USE Imposition of hands
Laying-out (Machine-shop practice)
  UF Marking-out
  BT Machine-shop practice
      Pattern-making
Laying-out (Woodwork)
  UF Marking-out (Woodwork)
  BT Pattern-making
      Woodwork
Laylat al-Barā'ah
  ₍BP186.38₎
  UF Barā'ah, Laylat
      Berat gecesi
      Laylat niṣf al-Sha'bān
      Night of mid-Sha'bān
      Night of the barā'ah
      Shab-i barāt
Laylat al-Mi'rāj
  ₍BP186.36₎
  UF Mi'rāj, Laylat
Laylat al-Mi'rāj sermons
  ₍BP183.636₎
  BT Islamic sermons
Laylat al-Qadr
  ₍BP186.43₎
  UF Ḳadr, Lailat
      Qadr, Laylat
Laylat niṣf al-Sha'bān
  USE Laylat al-Barā'ah
Layle family
  USE Lail family
Layman family *(Not Subd Geog)*
  UF Laymon family
      Leaman family
      Leamon family
  RT Lehman family
Laymen
  USE Laity
Laymon family
  USE Layman family
Layn family
  USE Lane family
Layne family
  USE Lane family
Layoff systems *(May Subd Geog)*
  BT Employees, Dismissal of
      Personnel management
  RT Job security
  NT Civil service—Furloughs
      Work sharing
  — Law and legislation *(May Subd Geog)*
      BT Labor laws and legislation
Layout, Building
  USE Building layout
Layout, Factory
  USE Plant layout
Layout, Office
  USE Office layout
Layout, Plant
  USE Plant layout
Layout, Room (Dwellings)
  USE Room layout (Dwellings)
Layout (Typography)
  USE Printing, Practical—Layout
Layout and typography, Advertising
  USE Advertising layout and typography
Layout and typography, Newspaper
  USE Newspaper layout and typography
Lays
  ₍PN691 (Medieval)₎
  ₍PN1351-1525₎
  ₍PQ1323.L3 (French, PQ1317)₎
  BT Folk-songs
      French poetry
      Poetry
      Tales

Lays family
  USE Lay family
Laysan albatross
  UF Diomedea immutabilis
  BT Albatrosses
Layton family *(Not Subd Geog)*
  UF Leighton family
  RT Lawton family
Layzon Site (Peru)
  BT Peru—Antiquities
Laz
  BT Ethnology—Caucasus
Laz language
  [PK9151]
  UF Lazian language
  BT Kartvelian languages
Lazaretto Creek (Va.)
  BT Rivers—Virginia
Lazarettos
  USE Communicable diseases—Hospitals
         Leprosy—Hospitals
         Quarantine
Lazarus, Raising of (Miracle)
  USE Raising of Lazarus (Miracle)
Lazarus (Dog)
  BT Dogs
Lazian language
  USE Laz language
Łazienki (Warsaw, Poland)
  UF Łazienki Park (Warsaw, Poland)
         Łazienki Warszawskie (Warsaw,
           Poland)
         Łazienkowski Park (Warsaw, Poland)
  BT Parks—Poland
Łazienki Park (Warsaw, Poland)
  USE Łazienki (Warsaw, Poland)
Łazienki Warszawskie (Warsaw, Poland)
  USE Łazienki (Warsaw, Poland)
Łazienkowski Park (Warsaw, Poland)
  USE Łazienki (Warsaw, Poland)
Laziness
  [BF485]
  UF Indolence
         Sloth
  BT Deadly sins
         Personality
  NT Procrastination
Lazzu Mountain (Corsica)
  UF Monte Lazzu (Corsica)
  BT Mountains—France
LBJ Ranch House (Tex.)
  [E847.2 (History)]
  UF Lyndon B. Johnson Ranch House
           (Tex.)
         Texas White House (Tex.)
  BT Presidents—United States—Dwellings
  RT Lyndon B. Johnson National Historical
           Park (Tex.)
LC subject headings
  USE Subject headings, Library of Congress
LCS (Information retrieval system)
  [Z699.4.L15]
  UF Library Control System (Information
           retrieval system)
  BT Information storage and retrieval
           systems
LD (Enzyme)
  USE Lactate dehydrogenase
LDC's
  USE Developing countries
LDEF (Artificial satellite)
  UF Long-Duration Exposure Facility
           (Artificial satellite)
  BT Reusable space vehicles
         Scientific satellites
LDH (Enzyme)
  USE Lactate dehydrogenase
LDOS (Computer operating system)
  UF Logical Disk Operating System
           (Computer operating system)
  BT Operating systems (Computers)

Le Baril family
  USE Baril family
Le Beau family
  USE Lebeau family
Le Bel family
  USE Lebel family
Le Bon's rays
  [QC485]
Le Boulengé chronograph
  [UF830.L4-5]
  BT Chronograph
Le Boutillier family
  USE Boutillier family
Le Carré, John, 1931-
1931-
  — Characters
  —— George Smiley
         RT Smiley, George (Fictitious
                 character)
Le Cateau, Battle of, 1914
  [D545.L3]
  BT World War, 1914-1918—Campaigns—
           France
Le Conte, Mount (Tenn.)
  USE LeConte, Mount (Tenn.)
Le dynasty, Later
  USE Vietnam—History—Later Le dynasty,
           1428-1787
Le Fanu family
  USE LeFanu family
Le Flageolet Rockshelter (France)
  USE Flageolet Rockshelter (France)
Le Flau family
  USE Leflore family
Le Gois (France)
  USE Gois Causeway (France)
Le Mans, Battle of, 1871
  [DC305.5]
  BT Franco-German War, 1870-1871
Le Mans 24-Hour Race, France
  USE Le Mans Endurance Race, France
Le Mans automobile
  [TL215.L]
  BT Pontiac automobile
Le Mans Endurance Race, France
  UF Grand Prix d'endurance, France
         Le Mans 24-Hour Race, France
         Le Mans Race, France
  BT Automobile racing—France
Le Mans Race, France
  USE Le Mans Endurance Race, France
Le May family
  USE Lemay family
Le Moignan family *(Not Subd Geog)*
Le Paradis Massacre, 1940
  BT World War, 1939-1945—Atrocities
Le Poittevain family *(Not Subd Geog)*
  UF Poidevain family
         Poittevain, Le, family
Le Saicherre family *(Not Subd Geog)*
  UF Lesaicherre family
Le Salat (France)
  USE Salat River (France)
Le Salaves (France)
  USE Salaves (France)
Le Strange family *(Not Subd Geog)*
  RT Strange family
Le Sueur family *(Not Subd Geog)*
  UF Le Sure family
         Lesueur family
         Lesure family
  RT Lasher family
         Lesher family
         Lozier family
Le Sure family
  USE Le Sueur family
Le Tonnellier de Breteuil family
  USE Breteuil family
Le Trièves (France)
  USE Trièves (France)

Le Tullier family
  USE Tullier family
Le Velay (France)
  USE Velay (France)
Le Verrier family *(Not Subd Geog)*
Lea family
  USE Lee family
Lea-Francis automobile
  [TL215.L]
  BT Automobiles—Great Britain
Leach Cemetery (Lake City, Tenn.)
  UF Clear Branch Cemetery (Lake City,
           Tenn.)
  BT Cemeteries—Tennessee
Leach family *(Not Subd Geog)*
  UF Leache family
         Leech family
         Leitch family
Leach petrel
  USE Oceanodroma leucorhoa
Leachate
  UF Lixivium
  BT Leaching
         Pollutants
  NT Hazardous waste sites—Leaching
         Sanitary landfills—Leaching
Leache family
  USE Leach family
Leaching
  [TP156.L]
  BT Chemical engineering
         In situ processing (Mining)
         Ore-dressing
  RT Solution mining
  NT Factory and trade waste—Leaching
         Hazardous waste sites—Leaching
         Leachate
         Sanitary landfills—Leaching
         Spoil banks—Leaching
Leaching of soils
  USE Soils—Leaching
Leachman family *(Not Subd Geog)*
  UF Leechman family
Leach's storm-petrel
  USE Oceanodroma leucorhoa
Leack family
  USE Leak family
Leacy family
  USE Lacy family
Lead
  [QD181.P3 (Chemistry)]
  NT Copper—Lead content
         Drinking water—Lead content
         Lead-work
         Sheet-lead
         Soils—Lead content
         White lead
  — Electrometallurgy
         [TN785]
  — Isotopes
  —— Decay
  — Metallurgy
         [TN785]
  — Physiological effect
         NT Plants, Effect of lead on
  — Toxicology
         USE Lead-poisoning
  — Welding
Lead-acid batteries
  USE Storage batteries
Lead alloys
  NT Babbitt metal
         Copper-lead alloys
         Lead-antimony alloys
         Lead-bismuth alloys
         Lead bronze
         Lead-silver alloys
         Lead-sodium alloys
         Lead-tin alloys
         Lead-zinc-cadmium-tin alloys
         Lithium-lead alloys

2110

Lead-antimony alloys
　UF　Antimony-lead alloys
　BT　Antimony alloys
　　　Lead alloys
Lead arsenate
　　[SB951-SB953 (Insecticides)]
　　[TN245.A8 (Technology)]
　UF　Arsenate of lead
Lead based paint　(May Subd Geog)
　UF　Lead paint
　BT　Paint
　RT　White lead
　— **Law and legislation**　(May Subd Geog)
　　　BT　Poisons—Law and legislation
　— **Removal**
　　　UF　Removal of lead based paint
　　　BT　Paint removers
Lead-bismuth alloys
　UF　Bismuth-lead alloys
　BT　Bismuth alloys
　　　Lead alloys
Lead bronze
　BT　Bronze
　　　Copper alloys
　　　Lead alloys
Lead burning
　　[TH6691]
　BT　Plumbing
Lead chloride
　BT　Chlorides
Lead compounds
　　[QD181.P3]
Lead contamination in copper
　USE　Copper—Lead content
Lead content in copper
　USE　Copper—Lead content
Lead-copper alloys
　USE　Copper-lead alloys
Lead crystals
Lead figurines　(May Subd Geog)
　BT　Figurines
Lead glance
　USE　Galena
Lead in the body
Lead industry and trade　(May Subd Geog)
　　[HD9539.L38-43]
Lead ingots
　UF　Ingots, Lead
Lead-lithium alloys
　USE　Lithium-lead alloys
Lead miners　(May Subd Geog)
　BT　Miners
Lead mines and mining　(May Subd Geog)
　　[TN450-459]
　— **Northwest Territories**
　　　NT　Strathcona Sound Mining Project
Lead ores　(May Subd Geog)
　　[TN450-459]
　NT　Galena
Lead organic compounds
　USE　Organolead compounds
Lead paint
　USE　Lead based paint
Lead pipe
　USE　Pipe, Lead
Lead plating
　BT　Electroplating
Lead-poisoning　(May Subd Geog)
　　[RA1231.L4]
　UF　Lead—Toxicology
　　　Plumbism
　　　Saturnism
　BT　Occupational diseases
　　　Poisoning
　— **Law and legislation**　(May Subd Geog)
　　　BT　Poisons—Law and legislation
Lead-poisoning in animals　(May Subd Geog)
　BT　Veterinary toxicology
Lead-poisoning in children
　(May Subd Geog)
　　[RA1231.L4]

　BT　Pediatric toxicology
Lead selenide crystals
Lead silicates
　BT　Silicates
Lead-silver alloys
　UF　Silver-lead alloys
　BT　Lead alloys
　　　Silver alloys
Lead-sodium alloys
　　[TN785]
　UF　Sodium-lead alloys
　BT　Lead alloys
　　　Sodium alloys
Lead sulfide
　USE　Lead sulphide
Lead sulphide　(May Subd Geog)
　　[QD181.P3]
　UF　Lead sulfide
　　　Plumbous sulphide
　BT　Sulphides
Lead sulphide crystals
Lead telluride crystals
Lead-tin alloys
　UF　Tin-lead alloys
　BT　Lead alloys
　　　Tin alloys
Lead tin telluride
　BT　Tellurides
Lead tin telluride crystals
　BT　Crystals
Lead tree　(May Subd Geog)
　　[QK495.L52 (Botany)]
　　[SB317.L4 (Culture)]
　UF　Haole koa
　　　Ipil-ipil
　　　Koa haole
　　　Leadtree
　　　Leucaena glauca
　　　Leucaena leucocephala
　　　Mimosa glauca
　　　Popinac, White
　　　White popinac
　　　Whitepopinac
　BT　Legumes
　NT　Mimosine
Lead-uranium dating
　USE　Uranium-lead dating
Lead-work　(May Subd Geog)
　　[NK835 (Ornamental)]
　　[TT265 (Handicraft)]
　BT　Art metal-work
　　　Decoration and ornament
　　　Lead
　　　Metal-work
Lead-zinc-cadmium-tin alloys
　BT　Cadmium alloys
　　　Lead alloys
　　　Tin alloys
　　　Zinc alloys
Leadbeater family
　USE　Ledbetter family
Leadbetter family
　USE　Ledbetter family
Leader family　(Not Subd Geog)
Leaders, Recreation
　USE　Recreation leaders
Leadership
　　[BF637.L4 (Applied psychology)]
　　[BF723.L4 (Child psychology)]
　　[HM141 (Sociology)]
　　[UB210 (Military science)]
　　Here are entered works on the quality, power, or ability to lead others founded upon the prestige of position or upon ability and qualities of character. Works on the exercise of military leadership and power of decision by a commander over his subordinates by virtue of authority, rank, and responsibility are entered under Command of troops.

　BT　Ability
　　　Executive ability
　　　Psychology, Military
　　　Social groups
　　　Social psychology
　　　Sociology
　RT　Command of troops
　　　Meetings
　NT　Christian leadership
　　　Communism and leadership
　　　Communist leadership
　　　Community leadership
　　　Discussion
　　　Elite (Social sciences)
　　　Hispanic American leadership
　　　Jewish leadership
　　　Mexican American leadership
　　　Political leadership
　　　Recreation leadership
　— **Religious aspects**
　　　NT　Leadership in the Bible
Leadership, Afro-American
　USE　Afro-American leadership
Leadership, Hispanic American
　USE　Hispanic American leadership
Leadership, Mexican American
　USE　Mexican American leadership
Leadership, Military
　USE　Command of troops
Leadership and communism
　USE　Communism and leadership
Leadership in the Bible
　UF　Bible—Leadership
　BT　Leadership—Religious aspects
Leadford family
　USE　Ledford family
Leading Edge Nutshell (Computer program)
　UF　Nutshell (Computer program)
　BT　Data base management—Computer
　　　　programs
Leading edges (Aerodynamics)
　　[TL574.L4]
　BT　Aerodynamics
　　　Aerofoils
　　　Airplanes—Wings
Leadtree
　USE　Lead tree
Leaf analysis
　USE　Foliar diagnosis
Leaf application of agricultural chemicals
　USE　Agricultural chemicals—Foliar
　　　　application
Leaf application of plant regulators
　USE　Plant regulators—Foliar application
Leaf beetles
　USE　Chrysomelidae
Leaf blotch miners
　USE　Gracillariidae
Leaf burning
　USE　Leaves—Burning
Leaf catalogs
　USE　Catalogs, Sheaf
Leaf-cutter ants
　USE　Leaf-cutting ants
Leaf-cutting ants
　　[QL568.F7]
　UF　Leaf-cutter ants
　　　Parasol ants
　BT　Ants
Leaf-eating animals
　USE　Folivores
Leaf-eating monkeys
　USE　Presbytis
Leaf feeding
　USE　Foliar feeding
Leaf hoppers
　USE　Leafhoppers
Leaf impressions
　USE　Leaf prints
Leaf-miners
　　[SB945.L55]

Leaf-miners *(Continued)*

    NT Chrysanthemum leaf miner

        Coffee leaf-miner

        Locust leaf-miner

        Serpentine leaf-miner

Leaf-mold
    [S598]

    BT Leaves
        Soils

    NT Forest litter

Leaf monkeys
    USE Presbytis

Leaf-nosed bats, American
    USE Phyllostomatidae

Leaf-nosed flies
    USE Therevidae

Leaf plants
    USE Foliage plants

Leaf prints
    UF Leaf impressions

    BT Leaves—Collection and preservation
        Plant prints

Leaf-rollers
    [SB945.L]

    SA *names of leaf-rollers, e.g.* Canna leaf-roller, Cotton leaf-roller

    NT Sugarcane leafroller

Leaf rust, Coffee
    USE Coffee leaf rust

Leaf rust of wheat
    BT Wheat rusts

Leaf scald of sugarcane
    USE Sugarcane leaf scald

Leaf scorch of sugarcane
    USE Sugarcane leaf scald

Leaf-spot
    [SB741.L45]

Leaf spot disease of barley
    USE Barley net-spot blotch disease

Leaf springs
    UF Flat springs

    BT Springs (Mechanism)

Leaf stalks
    USE Petioles

Leaf stripe disease of barley
    USE Barley leaf stripe disease

Leaf temperature
    USE Leaves—Temperature

Leafblotch miners
    USE Gracillariidae

Leafcutter-bee, Alfalfa
    USE Alfalfa leafcutter-bee

Leafcutting-bee, Alfalfa
    USE Alfalfa leafcutter-bee

Leafcutting bees
    USE Megachilidae

Leafhoppers
    [QL527.C49]

    UF Agalliidae
        Aphrodidae
        Bythoscopidae
        Cicadellidae
        Coelidiidae
        Deltocephalidae
        Euacanthidae
        Eurymelidae
        Euscelidae
        Evacanthidae
        Gyponidae
        Hecalidae
        Hylicidae
        Iassidae
        Idioceridae
        Jassidae
        Koebeliidae
        Leaf hoppers
        Ledridae
        Macropsidae
        Megophthalmidae
        Neobalidae
        Neocoelidiidae
        Nirvanidae
        Paropiidae
        Penthimiidae
        Proconiidae
        Pythamidae
        Signoretiidae
        Stenocotidae
        Tettigellidae
        Tettigoniellidae
        Thaumastoscopidae
        Typhlocybidae
        Ulopidae
    BT Homoptera
        Homoptera
    NT Batracomorphus
        Cicadula
        Cicadulina
        Circulifer
        Colladonus
        Cuerna
        Dikraneura
        Draeculacephala
        Empoasca
        Erythroneura
        Eutettix
        Exitianus
        Flexamia
        Gypona
        Macropsis
        Macrosteles
        Scaphoideus
        Spartopyge
        Typhlocyba

Leaflets
    USE Leaflets dropped from aircraft
          Pamphlets

Leaflets dropped from aircraft
    [HE9739]
    UF Leaflets
    BT Communication
        Propaganda

Leafminer flies
    USE Agromyzidae

Leafmining moths
    USE Gracillariidae

Leafroll virus of potatoes
    USE Potato leafroll virus

Leafrolling sawflies
    USE Pamphiliidae

Leafstalks
    USE Petioles

Leafy salad vegetables
    USE Salad greens

Leafy vegetables
    USE Greens, Edible

Leagh family
    USE Lee family

League, Lombard
    USE Lombard League

League of Augsburg, War of the, 1689-1697
    USE Grand Alliance, War of the, 1689-1697

League of Cambrai, 1508
    USE Cambrai, League of, 1508

League of Chalcidic Cities
    USE Chalcidic League

League of Nations *(May Subd Geog)*
    [JX1975]
    BT International cooperation
        Peace
        World War, 1914-1918—Peace
    — Buildings
    — Caricatures and cartoons
    — Exhibitions
    — Finance
    — Mandatory system
        USE Mandates
    — Membership
    — Officials and employees
    — — Privileges and immunities
        USE League of Nations—Privileges and immunities
    — Postal service
        UF Postal service—League of Nations
    — Privileges and immunities
        UF League of Nations—Officials and employees—Privileges and immunities
    — Publicity
    — Sanctions
        [JX1975.6]

League of Rhine Cities
    USE Rhine Cities, League of, 1254

League of the Three Emperors, 1872
    USE Three Emperors' League, 1872

League of the Three Emperors, 1881
    USE Three Emperors' League, 1881

League, Swabian, 1488-1533
    USE Schwäbischer Bund

Leagues of armed neutrality
    USE Neutrality, Armed

Leah family
    USE Lee family

Leaird family
    USE Laird family

Leak detectors
    BT Detectors
        Engineering instruments
        Vacuum technology
    NT Gas-detectors

Leak family *(Not Subd Geog)*
    UF Leack family
        Leake family
        Leakes family
        Leek family
        Leeke family
        Leeks family
        Lekes family
        Lieke family

Leakage, Gas
    USE Gas leakage

Leakage of air in concrete stoppings (Mining)
    USE Concrete stoppings (Mining)—Airtightness

Leake family
    USE Leak family

Leakes family
    USE Leak family

Leaman family
    USE Layman family

Leamer family *(Not Subd Geog)*
    UF Lehmer family

Leaming family *(Not Subd Geog)*
    UF Leamyng family
        Leeming family

Leamon family
    USE Layman family

Leamyng family
USE Leaming family
Leanard family
USE Leonard family
Leander
BT Mythology, Greek
RT Hero
— **Art**
NT Hero and Leander (Tapestries)
Leanhart family
USE Leonard family
Leanira
[QL391.A6]
BT Sigalionidae
Leanness (May Subd Geog)
UF Emaciation
Thinness
BT Body weight
Leanness in children (May Subd Geog)
BT Children
Leanord family
USE Leonard family
Leão family (Not Subd Geog)
Leap year
BT Calendar
Days
Leaphart family
USE Lippert family
Lear, King
USE Lear, King (Legendary character)
Lear, King (Legendary character)
UF King Lear (Legendary character)
Lear, King
Leir, King (Legendary character)
Ler, King (Legendary character)
Llyr, King (Legendary character)
BT Folklore—Great Britain
Lear jet aircraft
[TL686.G]
UF Gates Learjet aircraft
Learjet aircraft
BT Airplanes, Company
Airplanes, Private
Jet planes
Leard Cemetery (Fort Smith, Ark.)
(Not Subd Geog)
BT Cemeteries—Arkansas
Leard family
USE Laird family
Learjet aircraft
USE Lear jet aircraft
Learkin family
USE Larkin family
Learnard family
USE Leonard family
Learned family
USE Leonard family
Learned institutions and societies
[AS]
UF Academies (Learned societies)
BT Learning and scholarship
RT Societies
SA subdivision Learned institutions and
societies under names of countries,
cities, etc.; and subdivision
Societies, etc. under topics, e.g.
Botany—Societies, etc.
NT Decorations of honor, Academic
United Nations and learned
institutions, societies, etc.
— **Libraries**
USE Institution libraries
Society libraries
— **Publishing** (May Subd Geog)
BT Scholarly publishing
Learned periodicals
USE Scholarly periodicals
Learners, Industrial (May Subd Geog)
BT Employees, Training of
Technical education
Vocational education

RT Apprentices
— **Attitudes**
BT Attitude (Psychology)
— **Political activity**
BT Political participation
Learnhart family
USE Leonard family
Learning
[LB1060]
UF Learning process
BT Comprehension
Education
NT Experiential learning
Visual learning
— **Effect of drugs on**
BT Drugs—Physiological effect
Psychopharmacology
— **Mathematical models**
NT Learning models (Stochastic
processes)
— **Physiological aspects**
[QP408]
UF Physiological aspects of learning
BT Neuropsychology
NT Memory transfer
— Psychological aspects
USE Learning, Psychology of
— **Religious aspects**
— — **Buddhism, [Christianity, etc.]**
Learning, Art of
USE Study, Method of
Learning, Experiential
USE Experiential learning
Learning, Machine
USE Machine learning
Learning, Psychology of
[BF318 (Psychology)]
[LB1051 (Educational psychology)]
UF Learning—Psychological aspects
Psychology of learning
BT Animal intelligence
Child psychology
Education
Educational psychology
Memory
RT Comprehension
Learning ability
NT Behavior modification
Concept learning
Conditioned response
Educability
Feedback (Psychology)
Learning by discovery
Maze tests
Memory transfer
Motivation in education
Motor learning
Paired-association learning
Perceptual learning
Perceptual-motor learning
Praise
Probability learning
Programmed instruction
Sleep-learning
Social learning
Transfer of training
Verbal learning
Learning, Social
USE Social learning
Learning, Verbal
USE Verbal learning
Learning, Visual
USE Visual learning
Learning ability
[LB1134]
BT Ability
RT Learning, Psychology of
NT Hyperactive children—Education
Self-organizing systems
Underachievers
— **Testing**

NT Detroit tests of learning aptitude
Early Learning Skills Analysis
Learning activities in Christian education
USE Activity programs in Christian
education
Learning and scholarship (May Subd Geog)
[AZ (History of learning)]
UF Erudition
Scholarship
BT Civilization
Intellectual life
RT Culture
Education
Humanism
Research
NT Catholic learning and scholarship
Ciceronianism
Humanities
Learned institutions and societies
Pedantry
Professional education
Scholarly publishing
Scholars
Wisdom
— Catholics
USE Catholic learning and scholarship
— **History**
— — **Medieval, 500-1500**
UF Medieval learning and
scholarship
RT Education, Medieval
— **Introductions**
— Jews
USE Jewish learning and scholarship
— Muslims
USE Islamic learning and scholarship
— **Religious aspects**
— — **Baptists, [Catholic Church, etc.]**
— — **Buddhism, [Christianity, etc.]**
Learning by discovery
UF Discovery, Learning by
BT Learning, Psychology of
Learning center approach to teaching
USE Classroom learning centers
Open plan schools
Learning centers, Classroom
USE Classroom learning centers
Learning curve (Industrial engineering)
BT Labor productivity
Time study
Learning disabilities (May Subd Geog)
[LC4704-LC4706 (Education)]
[RC394.L37 (Neurology)]
[RJ496.L4 (Pediatric neurology)]
[RJ506.L4 (Child psychopathology)]
UF Learning disorders
BT Cognition disorders
RT Minimal brain dysfunction in children
NT Hyperactive children
Reading disability
— **Nutritional aspects**
— **Treatment** (May Subd Geog)
[RJ506.L4]
Learning disabled children
(May Subd Geog)
[LC4704]
BT Handicapped children
Learning disabled teenagers
USE Learning disabled youth
Learning disabled youth (May Subd Geog)
UF Learning disabled teenagers
BT Handicapped youth
Learning disorders
USE Learning disabilities
Learning in animals
[QL785]
UF Animal learning
BT Animal intelligence
Learning models (Stochastic processes)
[QA274.6]

2113

Learning models (Stochastic processes)
(Continued)
  UF Mathematical learning models
     (Stochastic processes)
    Models, Learning (Stochastic
     processes)
    Stochastic learning models (Stochastic
     processes)
  BT Learning—Mathematical models
    Sequential analysis
    Stochastic processes
Learning Potential Assessment Device
  ⌜BF432.5.L4 (Psychology)⌝
  UF LPAD (Psychological test)
  BT Intelligence tests
Learning process
  USE Learning
Learning resource centers
  USE Instructional materials centers
Learning systems
  USE Instructional systems
Learning systems (Automatic control)
  USE Self-organizing systems
Learning teams
  USE Team learning approach in education
Leary family (Not Subd Geog)
  UF Lerry family
  RT O'Leary family
Leas family
  USE Lease family
Lease and rental services (May Subd Geog)
  ⌜HD9999.L436⌝
  UF Lease services
    Leasing services
    Rental industries
    Rental services
  BT Leases
    Rent
  NT Art rental and lending services
    Automobiles, Rental
    Industrial equipment leases
    Office equipment leases
    Sailboats—Chartering
    Stage props leasing services
    Television, Rental
    Trucks, Rental
  — **Law and legislation** (May Subd Geog)
  — **Taxation** (May Subd Geog)
  — — **Law and legislation**
      (May Subd Geog)
Lease family (Not Subd Geog)
  UF Leas family
    Leece family
    Lees family
    Leese family
    Leeser family
Lease-lend operations
  USE Lend-lease operations (1941-1945)
Lease or buy decisions
  UF Buy or lease decisions
    Lease-purchase decisions
    Purchase or lease decisions
  BT Finance
  RT Leases
    Purchasing
Lease-purchase decisions
  USE Lease or buy decisions
Lease services
  USE Lease and rental services
Lease system
  USE Convict labor
Leased departments, concessions, etc.
  (May Subd Geog)
  UF Concessions, Leased
  BT Commercial leases
    Retail trade
Leased territories
  UF Leases of territory
    Territories, Leased

  BT Jurisdiction, Territorial
    Protectorates
    Territory, National
Leases (May Subd Geog)
  BT Commercial law
    Contracts
    Conveyancing
    Land tenure—Law and legislation
    Land titles
    Possessory interests in land
    Real property
  RT Hire
    Landlord and tenant
    Lease or buy decisions
  NT Building leases
    Commercial leases
    Computer leases
    Emphyteusis
    Eviction
    Geothermal leases
    Industrial equipment leases
    Lease and rental services
    Mining leases
    Office leases
    Superficies
    Telecommunication equipment leases
  — **Cases**
  — — Digests
      USE Leases—Digests
  — **Digests**
     UF Leases—Cases—Digests
  — **Taxation** (May Subd Geog)
     UF Safe-harbor leasing
Leases, Industrial equipment
  USE Industrial equipment leases
Leases, Office equipment
  USE Office equipment leases
Leases, Usufructuary
  USE Farm tenancy
Leases (Greek law)
Leases (Islamic law) (May Subd Geog)
Leases (Roman-Dutch law)
Leases (Roman law)
Leases of territory
  USE Leased territories
Leasing services
  USE Lease and rental services
Leasowes (Halesowen, Worcestershire)
  BT Dwellings—England
    Shenstone, William, 1714-1763—
      Homes and haunts
Leasowes Garden (Halesowen, Worcestershire)
  (Not Subd Geog)
  BT Gardens—England
Least absolute deviations (Statistics)
  UF Absolute deviations, Least (Statistics)
    Absolute values, Least (Statistics)
    Deviations, Least absolute (Statistics)
    LAD (Statistics)
    Least absolute values (Statistics)
    Values, Least absolute (Statistics)
  BT Least squares
Least absolute values (Statistics)
  USE Least absolute deviations (Statistics)
Least action
  ⌜QA871⌝
  BT Mechanics
    Variational principles
Least brook lamprey
  ⌜QL638.15.P4⌝
  UF Brook lamprey, Least
    Lampetra aepyptera
    Lamprey, Least brook
    Maryland brook lamprey
Least cisco
  ⌜QL638.S2⌝
  UF Coregonus sardinella
Least developed countries
  USE Developing countries
Least shrew
  ⌜QL737.I56⌝

  UF Cryptotis parva
  BT Cryptotis
Least Siberian shrew
  ⌜QL737.I56⌝
  UF Sorex minutissimus
Least squares
  ⌜QA275⌝
  UF Method of least squares
    Squares, Least
  BT Astronomy—Observations
    Geodesy
    Mathematical statistics
    Mathematics
    Triangulation
  RT Curve fitting
    Probabilities
  NT Correlation (Statistics)
    Estimation theory
    Graphic methods
    Heteroscedasticity
    Least absolute deviations (Statistics)
  — **Computer programs**
Least tern
  ⌜QL696.C46⌝
  UF Sterna albifrons
Least-time ship routing
  USE Optimum ship routing
Least weasel
  USE Mustela nivalis
Leat family
  USE Leet family
Leather
  ⌜TS940-1043⌝
  RT Hides and skins
    Tanning
  NT Buckskin
    Leather painting
    Morocco leather
    Russia leather
  — **Bonding**
    UF Leather bonding
    BT Adhesives
      Sealing (Technology)
  — By-products
    USE Leather industry and trade—By-
      products
  — **Defects**
    RT Hides and skins—Defects
  — **Machinery**
    ⌜TS1043⌝
  — **Research** (May Subd Geog)
    UF Leather research
Leather, Artificial
  ⌜TS1045-7⌝
  UF Artificial leather
  BT Leather substitutes
  — **Welding**
Leather, Cordovan
  USE Leather work
Leather, Russia
  USE Russia leather
Leather auxiliaries
  USE Leather chemicals
Leather bergenia
  ⌜SB315.L4 (Tannin plants)⌝
  UF Bergenia crassifolia
    Saxifraga crassifolia
  BT Tannin plants
Leather bonding
  USE Leather—Bonding
Leather bookbindings
  USE Bookbinding—Leather bindings
Leather by-products
  USE Leather industry and trade—By-
    products
Leather carving
  BT Carving (Decorative arts)
    Leather work
Leather chemicals
  UF Chemicals, Leather
    Leather auxiliaries

BT Chemicals
Leather District (Boston, Mass.)
(Not Subd Geog)
UF Boston (Mass.). Leather District
Leather dyeing
USE Dyes and dyeing—Leather
Leather embroidery *(May Subd Geog)*
BT Embroidery
Leather work
Leather embroidery, Romanian, [etc.]
(May Subd Geog)
Leather-flower
[QK495.C]
Leather garments *(May Subd Geog)*
UF Clothing, Leather
Garments, Leather
Skin garments
BT Clothing and dress
NT Leather jackets
Lederhosen
— Tariff
USE Tariff on leather garments
Leather garments industry
(May Subd Geog)
[HD9780]
Leather goods *(May Subd Geog)*
BT Leather industry and trade
Leather work
SA *specific articles made of leather*
Leather industry and trade
(May Subd Geog)
[HD9780 (Economics)]
[TS940-TS1043 (Technology)]
NT Bookbinding
Dyes and dyeing—Leather
Harness making and trade
Leather goods
Leather workers
Luggage
— **By-products**
UF Leather—By-products
Leather by-products
— Collective labor agreements
USE Collective labor agreements—
Leather industry
— **Electric equipment**
— **Equipment and supplies**
Leather jackets *(May Subd Geog)*
UF Jackets, Leather
BT Coats
Leather garments
NT Black leather jackets
Leather jackets, Black
USE Black leather jackets
Leather painting *(May Subd Geog)*
UF Painting, Leather
Painting on leather
BT Leather
Painting
Leather research
USE Leather—Research
Leather substitutes
BT Substitute products
NT Leather, Artificial
Leather work *(May Subd Geog)*
[NK6200 (Art industries)]
[TT290 (Mechanic trades)]
UF Cordovan leather
Leather, Cordovan
Leathercraft
Leatherwork
BT Arts and crafts movement
Decorative arts
Handicraft
NT Embossing (Leather work)
Indians of North America—Leather
work
Leather carving
Leather embroidery
Leather goods
Saddlery

— **Conservation and restoration**
UF Conservation of leather work
Preservation of leather work
Restoration of leather work
Leather workers *(May Subd Geog)*
BT Leather industry and trade
NT Collective labor agreements—Leather
industry
Trade-unions—Leather workers
Wages—Leather workers
Leatherback turtle
[QL666.C546]
UF Chelonias lutaria
Chelyra coriacea
Coriudo coriacea
Dermatochelys porcata
Dermochelidae
Dermochelis atlantica
Dermochelydidae
Dermochelys
Dermochelys coriacea
Leathery turtle
Luth
Seytina coriacea
Sphargis angusta
Sphargis coriacea
Sphargis mercurialis
Testudo arcuata
Testudo coriacea
Testudo lyra
Testudo tuberculata
Trunk turtle
BT Sea turtles
Turtles
Leatherbarrow family
USE Leatherbury family
Leatherberry family
USE Leatherbury family
Leatherbury family *(Not Subd Geog)*
UF Lathbury family
Leatherbarrow family
Leatherberry family
Letherberry family
Letherbury family
Leathercraft
USE Leather work
Leatherwork
USE Leather work
Leathery turtle
USE Leatherback turtle
Leaton, Fort (Tex.)
USE Fort Leaton (Tex.)
Leatt family
USE Leet family
Leave for parenting
USE Parental leave
Leave of absence *(May Subd Geog)*
UF Absence, Leave of
BT Hours of labor
RT Vacations, Employee
SA *subdivision* Officials and employees—
Leave regulations *under names of
countries, cities, etc; and under
names of individual government
departments, agencies, etc.*
NT Educational leave
Parental leave
Postal service—Employees—Leave
regulations
Sick leave
Teachers—Leaves of absence
— **Law and legislation** *(May Subd Geog)*
BT Labor laws and legislation
Leave-takings
USE Farewells
Leave with pay
USE Vacations, Employee
Leavell family *(Not Subd Geog)*
UF Lavell family
Leavens family *(Not Subd Geog)*
UF Levens family

Leavenworth, Kansas and Western Railway
BT Railroads—United States
Leaves *(May Subd Geog)*
[QK649]
UF Foliage
BT Botany
Shoots (Botany)
Trees
NT Cut foliage
Defoliation
Hypsophylls
Leaf-mold
Petioles
Phyllocladia
Pseudostipules
Stipules (Botany)
— Analysis
USE Foliar diagnosis
— **Anatomy**
[QK649]
[QK689]
BT Botany—Anatomy
NT Stomata
— **Burning**
UF Burning of leaves
Leaf burning
BT Incineration
— **Collection and preservation**
BT Plants—Collection and
preservation
NT Leaf prints
— **Color**
UF Color of leaves
NT Fall foliage
— **Development**
BT Plants—Development
— Fertilization
USE Foliar feeding
— **Growth**
— **Microbiology**
— **Morphology**
[QK649]
— Photography
USE Photography of leaves
— Shedding
USE Defoliation
— **Temperature**
UF Leaf temperature
BT Temperature
Leaves, Artificial
USE Artificial leaves
Leaves, Feeding of
USE Foliar feeding
Leaves, Fossil
BT Paleobotany
Leaves, Shedding of
USE Defoliation
Leavetakings
USE Farewells
Leaving the scene of an automobile accident
USE Hit-and-run drivers
Lebanese *(May Subd Geog)*
BT Ethnology—Lebanon
— **United States**
NT Lebanese Americans
Lebanese Americans *(May Subd Geog)*
BT Ethnology—United States
Lebanese—United States
Lebanese art
USE Art, Lebanese
Lebanese atlases
USE Atlases, Lebanese
Lebanese cookery
USE Cookery, Lebanese
Lebanese literature (Arabic)
USE Arabic literature—Lebanon
Lebanese literature (French)
(May Subd Geog)
[PQ3977.L39]
UF French literature—Lebanese authors

Lebanese maxims (French)
USE Maxims, Lebanese (French)
Lebanese newspapers
Lebanese periodicals *(May Subd Geog)*
Lebanese wit and humor *(May Subd Geog)*
Lebanon
— **Antiquities**
NT Kāmid al-Lawz Site (Lebanon)
Tyre (City)
— **Antiquities, Phoenician**
NT Mourners Sarcophagus (Sidon, Lebanon)
— **History**
— — **635-1516**
[DS83]
— — **1516-**
— — **1516-1918**
[DS84]
— — **French occupation, 1918-1946**
— — **1946-**
— — **1946-1975**
— — **Intervention, 1958**
— — **1975-**
— — **Civil War, 1975-1976**
[DS87.5]
NT Mukhayyam Tall az Za'tar, Battle of, 1976
— — **Israeli intervention, 1982-**
[DS87.53]
UF Israeli intervention in Lebanon, 1982-
BT Israel-Arab Border Conflicts, 1949- —Lebanon
Jewish-Arab relations—1973-
— **Politics and government**
— — **1946-**
— — **1946-1975**
— — **1975-**
Lebanon (N.H.). West Lebanon
USE West Lebanon (Lebanon, N.H.)
Lebanon cedar
USE Cedar of Lebanon
Lebanon in art
LeBaron family *(Not Subd Geog)*
RT Barron family
Lebbe family *(Not Subd Geog)*
Lebbeck
USE Lebbek tree
Lebbek tree
[QK495.L52 (Botany)]
[RM666.L39 (Therapeutics)]
[SD397.L (Forestry)]
UF Albizzia lebbeck
Lebbeck
Siris tree
Lebby family
USE Libby family
Lebeau family *(Not Subd Geog)*
UF Le Beau family
Lebeaux family
Lebo family
Lebeaux family
USE Lebeau family
Lebegood family
USE Levengood family
Lebel family *(Not Subd Geog)*
UF Le Bel family
Lebell family
Lebelle family
Lebell family
USE Lebel family
Lebelle family
USE Lebel family
Leberger family
USE Lybarger family
Lébéron (France)
USE Lubéron Mountains (France)
Lebertia
[QL458.2.L42]
BT Lebertiidae
NT Lebertia groenlandica

Lebertia groenlandica
[QL458.2.L42]
UF Pseudolebertia groenlandica
BT Lebertia
Lebertiidae
[QL458.2.L42]
BT Mites
NT Lebertia
Lebesgue measure
USE Measure theory
Lebesgue-Nikodym theorems
USE Lebesgue-Radon-Nikodym theorems
Lebesgue-Radon-Nikodym theorems
[QA312]
UF Lebesgue-Nikodym theorems
Radon-Nikodym theorems
BT Measure theory
Lebiidae
USE Carabidae
Lebistes reticulatus
USE Guppies
Leblanc family *(Not Subd Geog)*
LeBleu family *(Not Subd Geog)*
UF Lebleue family
Lebleue family
USE LeBleu family
Lebo family
USE Lebeau family
Lebou (African people)
BT Ethnology—Senegal
Wolofs
Lebou (African people) women
USE Women, Lebou (African people)
Lebrija River (Colombia) *(Not Subd Geog)*
UF Río Lebrija (Colombia)
BT Rivers—Colombia
Lecaniidae
USE Coccidae
Lecanium
[QL527.C6]
BT Coccidae
Lecanodiaspididae
[QL527.L43]
BT Homoptera
Scale-insects
NT Lecanodiaspis
Lecanodiaspis
[QL527.L43]
BT Lecanodiaspididae
Lecanora
BT Lecanoraceae
Lecanoraceae
[QK585.L (Botany)]
BT Lecanorales
NT Lecanora
Ochrolechia
Lecanorales
[QK585.L (Botany)]
BT Ascolichens
NT Cladoniaceae
Collemataceae
Lecanoraceae
Megalosporaceae
Pannariaceae
Parmeliaceae
Peltigeraceae
Pertusariaceae
Physciaceae
Stereocaulaceae
Teloschistaceae
Umbilicariaceae
Lech (Legendary character)
UF Lach (Legendary character)
BT Folklore—Poland
Lech languages
USE Lechitic languages
Lech River (Austria and Germany)
BT Rivers—Austria
Rivers—Germany (West)
Lechery
USE Lust

Lechfeld, Battle of, 955
[DD801.B4583]
BT Germany—History—Otto I, 936-973
Hungary—History—894-1000
Lechitic languages
UF Lech languages
Lekhitic languages
BT Slavic languages, Western
NT Kashubian language
Polabian language
Polish language
Slovincian dialect
Lechleiter family
USE Leckliter family
Lechliter family
USE Leckliter family
Lecithin
[RM666.L4 (Therapeutics)]
UF Phosphatidylcholine
BT Phospholipids
NT Lysolecithin
Lecithinase
Lecithoceridae
[QL561.L]
UF Timyridae
BT Lepidoptera
Moths
Leckenton family *(Not Subd Geog)*
UF Leckonton family
Lecklider family
USE Leckliter family
Leckliter family *(Not Subd Geog)*
UF Lechleiter family
Lechliter family
Lecklider family
Leichleiter family
Lichlyter family
Licklider family
Lickliter family
Leckonton family
USE Leckenton family
LeConte, Mount (Tenn.)
UF Le Conte, Mount (Tenn.)
Mount Le Conte (Tenn.)
Mount LeConte (Tenn.)
Mt. Le Conte (Tenn.)
Mt. LeConte (Tenn.)
BT Mountains—Tennessee
Leconte family *(Not Subd Geog)*
Leconte's sawfly
USE Redheaded pine sawfly
Lectins
[QP552.L42]
UF Protectins
Receptor-specific proteins
BT Hemagglutinin
Immunoglobulins
NT Mitogens
Plant lectins
Lectionaries
[BX2003 (Catholic Church)]
[BX5147.L4 (Church of England)]
[BX5947 (Protestant Episcopal Church)]
[BX8067.L4 (Lutheran Church)]
UF Pericopes
NT Epistolaries
Evangeliaries
Lectors
USE Lay readers
Lecture halls
USE Auditoriums
Lecture method in teaching
[LB2393]
BT Lectures and lecturing
Teaching
Lecture theaters
USE Auditoriums
Lecturers *(May Subd Geog)*
[PN4058]
UF Speakers

Lectures and lecturing *(May Subd Geog)*
  [*LC6501-LC6560.4 (Lyceums and*
    lecture courses)]
  [*PN4193.L4 (Oratory)*]
  UF Addresses
      Discourses
      Lecturing
      Speaking
  BT Elocution
      Public speaking
      Rhetoric
  RT Lyceums
      Oratory
      Speeches, addresses, etc.
  NT Chautauquas
      Introduction of speakers
      Lecture method in teaching
      Radio addresses, debates, etc.
  — Copyright
      USE Copyright—Lectures, sermons,
          etc.
Lecturing
  USE Lectures and lecturing
Lecythi
  [*NK4650.L5*]
  UF Lekythoi
Lecythidaceae *(May Subd Geog)*
  [*QK495.L42*]
  BT Myrtales
Leda (Greek mythology)
  BT Mythology, Greek
Ledai family
  USE Ledet family
Ledais family
  USE Ledet family
Ledait family
  USE Ledet family
Leday family
  USE Ledet family
Ledbeater family
  USE Ledbetter family
Ledbetter family *(Not Subd Geog)*
  UF Leadbeater family
      Leadbetter family
      Ledbeater family
      Letbetter family
Lede family
  USE Ledet family
Ledeboer family
  USE Ledebur family
Ledebour family
  USE Ledebur family
Ledebur family *(Not Subd Geog)*
  UF Ledeboer family
      Ledebour family
Ledee family
  USE Ledet family
Lederhosen *(May Subd Geog)*
  [*GT2350*]
  BT Leather garments
      Trousers
Ledet family *(Not Subd Geog)*
  UF Laidet family
      Laydet family
      Ledai family
      Ledais family
      Ledait family
      Leday family
      Lede family
      Ledee family
Ledford family *(Not Subd Geog)*
  UF Leadford family
Ledgering (Fishing)
  USE Bait fishing
Ledgers (Accounting)
  USE Accounting—Books of account
Ledgerwood family *(Not Subd Geog)*
Ledgewood (Falmouth, Me.)
  (Not Subd Geog)
  UF Falmouth (Me.). Ledgewood

Lednik Kolka (R.S.F.S.R.)
  USE Kolka Glacier (R.S.F.S.R.)
Ledo family *(Not Subd Geog)*
Ledocar family
  USE Ledogar family
Ledocart family
  USE Ledogar family
Ledogar family *(Not Subd Geog)*
  UF Ledocar family
      Ledocart family
      Lestocart family
      Lestoquart family
      Letocard family
      Letocart family
      Letogart family
Ledridae
  USE Leafhoppers
Ledson family
  USE Lett family
Ledyard family *(Not Subd Geog)*
Lee, Stan. Captain America (Comic strip)
  USE Captain America (Comic strip)
Lee, Stan. Doctor Strange (Comic strip)
  USE Doctor Strange (Comic strip)
Lee Creek Mine (N.C.)
  BT Mines and mineral resources—North
      Carolina
Lee-Enfield rifle
  [*UD395.L*]
  BT Rifles
Lee family *(Not Subd Geog)*
  UF Lea family
      Leagh family
      Leah family
      Leigh family
      Ley family
  RT Lie family
Lee Mansion (Va.)
  USE Arlington House, the Robert E. Lee
      Memorial (Va.)
Lee Metcalf Management Area (Mont.)
  UF Metcalf Management Area (Mont.)
  BT National parks and reserves—United
      States
      Wildlife management areas—Montana
Lee Metcalf National Wildlife Refuge (Mont.)
  (Not Subd Geog)
  BT National parks and reserves—Montana
      Wildlife refuges—Montana
Lee Metcalf Wilderness (Mont.)
  UF Metcalf Wilderness (Mont.)
  BT National parks and reserves—United
      States
      Wilderness areas—Montana
Lee-Metford rifle
  BT Rifles
Lee waves
  USE Mountain wave
Leearrawa language
  USE Garawa language
Leeb family
  USE Leib family
Leece family
  USE Lease family
Leech family
  USE Leach family
Leechee
  USE Litchi
      Litchi chinensis
Leeches *(May Subd Geog)*
  [*QL391.H6*]
  [*RM182 (Blood-letting)*]
  UF Clitellata
      Hirudinea
  BT Annelida
      Bloodletting
      Worms
  NT Acanthobdellidae
      Erpobdellidae
      Glossiphoniidae
      Hirudinidae

      Piscicolidae
Leechman family
  USE Leachman family
LEED (Solids)
  USE Low energy electron diffraction
Leedam family
  USE Leedom family
Leedham family
  USE Leedom family
Leedom family *(Not Subd Geog)*
  UF Leedam family
      Leedham family
Leeds pottery
  UF Pottery, Leeds
  BT Pottery, English
Leedy family *(Not Subd Geog)*
  UF Lidi family
  RT Luthi family
Leegaard family *(Not Subd Geog)*
Leek family
  USE Leak family
Leeke family
  USE Leak family
Leeks
  [*QK495.L72 (Botany)*]
  [*SB351.L5 (Vegetables)*]
  UF Allium porrum
      Allium tuberosum (Allium odorum)
  BT Onions
  NT Cookery (Leeks)
Leeks family
  USE Leak family
Leela (Game)
  [*GV1469.L44*]
  UF Chutes and ladders (Game)
      Gyan chaupar (Game)
      Līla (Game)
      Snakes and ladders (Game)
Leelalwarra language
  USE Mara language (Australia)
Leelawarra language
  USE Mara language (Australia)
Leeming family
  USE Leaming family
Leenderts family
  USE Lehnert family
Leeners family
  USE Lehnert family
Leersia calycina
  USE Veld grass
Lee's 1st Northern Invasion
  USE Maryland Campaign, 1862
Lee's 2d Northern Invasion
  USE Gettysburg Campaign, 1863
Lees family
  USE Lease family
Leese family
  USE Lease family
Leeser family
  USE Lease family
Leet family *(Not Subd Geog)*
  UF Leat family
      Leatt family
      Leete family
      Leets family
Leete family
  USE Leet family
Leetes Island (Conn.)
  BT Islands—Connecticut
Leets family
  USE Leet family
Leeuwenhoekiidae
  [*QL458.2.L*]
  BT Mites
Leeward Islands (West Indies)
  As a geographic subdivision, this heading is used
  directly.
  BT Antilles, Lesser
  NT Saba (Netherlands Antilles)
      Saint Eustatius (Netherlands Antilles)
      Saint Martin

Lefaivre family
USE Lefevre family

Lefana language
UF Bouem language
Buem language
Bwem language
Lelemi language
BT Kwa languages

LeFanu family *(Not Subd Geog)*
UF Le Fanu family

Lefavour family
USE Lefevre family

Lefeber family
USE Lefevre family

Lefebre family
USE Lefevre family

Lefébure family
USE Lefevre family

Lefever family
USE Lefevre family

Lefevere family
USE Lefevre family

Lefevour family
USE Lefevre family

Lefevre family *(Not Subd Geog)*
UF Lefaivre family
Lefavour family
Lefeber family
Lefebre family
Lefébure family
Lefever family
Lefevere family
Lefevour family

Leffler family *(Not Subd Geog)*
UF Lefler family
RT Loeffler family

Lefler family
USE Leffler family

Leflore family *(Not Subd Geog)*
UF Le Flau family

Lefors family *(Not Subd Geog)*
UF Lafors family

LEFT (Computer program language)
UF Language for editing and formating text
BT Computerized typesetting
Editing

Left (Philosophy)
USE Right and left (Philosophy)

Left (Political science)
USE Right and left (Political science)

Left and right (Psychology)
BT Laterality
Psychology
NT Left- and right-handedness

Left and right (Symbolism)
UF Right and left (Symbolism)
BT Symbolism
RT Left- and right-handedness

Left- and right-handedness
⌈GN233 (Anthropology)⌉
⌈QP385 (Physiological psychology)⌉
UF Handedness
Right- and left-handedness
BT Laterality
Left and right (Psychology)
Psychology, Physiological
RT Hand
Left and right (Symbolism)
NT Mirror-writing

Left Bank (Paris, France) *(Not Subd Geog)*
UF Paris (France). Left Bank
Paris (France). Rive gauche
Rive gauche (Paris, France)

Left colectomy
USE Left hemicolectomy

Left-eyed flounders
USE Bothidae

Left-hand piano music
USE Piano music (1 hand)

Left-handed penmanship
USE Penmanship, Left-handed

Left hemicolectomy *(May Subd Geog)*
⌈RD543.C57⌉
UF Colectomy, Left
Hemicolectomy, Left
Left colectomy
BT Hemicolectomy

Leftovers cookery
USE Cookery (Leftovers)

Leftwich family *(Not Subd Geog)*

Lefty Feep (Fictitious character)
USE Feep, Lefty (Fictitious character)

Leg
⌈QL821 (muscles)⌉
⌈QL950.7 (Comparative anatomy: general)⌉
⌈QM117 (skeleton)⌉
⌈QM165 (Human anatomy: muscles)⌉
⌈QM549 (Surgical and topographical anatomy)⌉
BT Extremities, Lower
NT Ankle
Femur
Fibula
Knee
Scarpa's triangle
Tarsus
Thigh
Tibia
— **Abnormalities**
NT Leg length inequality
— Amputation
USE Amputations of leg
— **Blood-vessels**
NT Peroneal artery
Saphenous vein
— Discrepancy of length
USE Leg length inequality
— Inequality of length
USE Leg length inequality
— **Innervation**
— Prosthesis
USE Artificial legs
— **Ulcers**
⌈RC951⌉

Leg family
USE Legg family

Leg length inequality *(May Subd Geog)*
⌈RD779.3⌉
UF Discrepancy of leg length
Inequality of leg length
Leg—Discrepancy of length
Leg—Inequality of length
BT Leg—Abnormalities

Leg length inequality in children *(May Subd Geog)*
BT Pediatric orthopedia

Lega language
USE Kilega language

Legacies *(May Subd Geog)*
UF Bequests
BT Inheritance and succession
Probate law and practice
RT Wills
NT Charitable bequests
Libraries—Gifts, legacies
Mejora

Legacies, Taxation of
USE Inheritance and transfer tax

Legacies (Roman-Dutch law)

Legacies (Roman law)

Legal abbreviations
USE Law—Abbreviations

Legal advertising *(May Subd Geog)*
Here are entered works on the law of public notice. Works on the legal aspects of advertising in general are entered under Advertising laws. Works on the legal aspects of advertising a particular product or in connection with a particular activity or industry are entered under headings of the type Advertising—⌈product, activity or industry⌉—Law and legislation, e.g. Advertising—Optical trade—Law and legislation. Works on the advertising of legal services are entered under Advertising—Lawyers.
UF Advertising, Legal
Public notice
BT Notice (Law)

Legal advisors, Police
USE Police legal advisors

Legal-aged children
USE Adult children

Legal aid *(May Subd Geog)*
⌈HV680-HV685⌉
Here are entered works on organized programs for providing legal assistance to the poor, usually under the sponsorship of local bar associations or governmental units. General works on legal services to the poor are entered under Legal assistance to the poor.
UF Legal charities
BT Legal assistance to the poor
RT In forma pauperis
Public defenders

Legal anecdotes
USE Law—Anecdotes, facetiae, satire, etc.

Legal antiquities
USE Law—Antiquities

Legal arguments
USE Forensic orations

Legal assistance to abused wives *(May Subd Geog)*
UF Legal representation of abused wives
BT Abused wives—Legal status, laws, etc.
Legal services

Legal assistance to children *(May Subd Geog)*
UF Child advocacy (Law)
Legal representation of children
BT Children—Legal status, laws, etc.
Legal services
NT Legal assistance to juvenile delinquents

Legal assistance to Indians *(May Subd Geog)*
UF Legal representation of Indians
Legal services for Indians
BT Indians—Legal status, laws, etc.
Legal services

Legal assistance to juvenile delinquents *(May Subd Geog)*
UF Legal representation of juvenile delinquents
BT Juvenile delinquency
Legal assistance to children
Legal services

Legal assistance to prisoners *(May Subd Geog)*
UF Legal representation of prisoners
Legal services for prisoners
BT Legal services
Prisoners—Legal status, laws, etc.

Legal assistance to refugees *(May Subd Geog)*
UF Legal representation of refugees
Legal services for refugees
BT Legal services
Refugees—Legal status, laws, etc.

Legal assistance to servicemen *(May Subd Geog)*
UF Military legal assistance
BT Legal services
Soldiers—Civil status

Legal assistance to the aged *(May Subd Geog)*
UF Legal representation of the aged
Legal services for the aged

BT Aged—Legal status, laws, etc.
   Legal services

Legal assistance to the handicapped
(May Subd Geog)
   UF Legal representation of the
      handicapped
      Legal services for the handicapped
   BT Handicapped—Legal status, laws, etc.
      Legal services
   NT Legal assistance to the mentally
      handicapped

Legal assistance to the mentally handicapped
(May Subd Geog)
   UF Legal representation of the mentally
      handicapped
      Legal services for the mentally
      handicapped
      Mentally handicapped, Legal
      assistance to the
   BT Insanity—Jurisprudence
      Legal assistance to the handicapped
      Mental health laws

Legal assistance to the poor
(May Subd Geog)
   Here are entered general works on legal services
to the poor. Works on organized programs for provid-
ing legal assistance to the poor, usually under the
sponsorship of local bar associations or governmental
units, are entered under Legal aid.
   UF Judicare
      Law, Poverty
      Legal representation of the poor
      Legal services for the poor
      Poverty law
      Pro bono publico legal services
   BT Legal services
      Public welfare
   NT Legal aid
      Public defenders

Legal assistants *(May Subd Geog)*
   UF Paralegal personnel
   BT Law offices
      Lawyers
      Practice of law
   NT United States. Navy—Legalmen

Legal authorities *(May Subd Geog)*
   UF Authorities, Legal
      Authority in law
      Primary authorities (Law)
      Secondary authorities (Law)
   BT Legal research
   SA *different types of legal authorities, e.g.*
      Law reports, digests, etc.; Statutes
   NT Citation of legal authorities
Legal bibliography
   USE Law—Bibliography
      Legal research
Legal bonds
   USE Legal investments
Legal certainty
   UF Certainty of law
   BT Jurisprudence
   RT Law—Interpretation and construction
   NT Stare decisis
Legal charities
   USE Legal aid
Legal chemistry
   USE Chemistry, Forensic
Legal citations
   USE Annotations and citations (Law)
      Citation of legal authorities
Legal composition
   UF Law—Authorship
   BT Practice of law
   RT Forms (Law)
   NT Briefs
      Clauses (Law)
      Conveyancing
      Legal correspondence

Legal consultants *(May Subd Geog)*
   BT Consultants
      Practice of law
Legal correspondence
   UF Correspondence
      Correspondence, Legal
      Legal correspondence, English
   BT Forms (Law)
      Legal composition
      Letter-writing
Legal correspondence, Chinese
   UF Chinese legal correspondence
Legal correspondence, English
   USE Legal correspondence
**Legal correspondence, French, [German,
Spanish, etc.]**
Legal counseling
   USE Attorney and client
Legal cruelty *(May Subd Geog)*
   Here are entered works on cruelty as a grounds for
the granting of a divorce to the injured party.
   UF Abusive treatment (Divorce)
      Cruelty, Legal
      Cruelty, Matrimonial
      Inhuman treatment (Divorce)
      Matrimonial cruelty
   BT Divorce—Law and legislation
Legal decorum
   USE Conduct of court proceedings
Legal departments, Corporate
   USE Corporate legal departments
Legal deposit (of books, etc.)
   (May Subd Geog)
   UF Copyright—Depository copies
      Copyright deposit
      Deposit of books
      Depository copies
   BT Copyright
      Press law
   RT Libraries, Depository
Legal directories
   USE Lawyers—Directories
Legal documents *(May Subd Geog)*
   Here are entered works on documents having
legal relevance in general. Works on documents writ-
ten in order to give expression to a legal act or agree-
ment for the purpose of creating, securing, modifying,
or terminating a right, or for the purpose of furnishing
evidence of a right, are entered under the heading
Legal instruments.
   UF Documents
      Documents, Legal
   RT Authentication
      Commercial documents
      Legal instruments
      Legalization
   NT Blanks in legal documents
      Evidence, Documentary
      False certification
      Receipts (Acknowledgments)
      Reproduction of money, documents,
      etc.
   — **Cancellation** *(May Subd Geog)*
      UF Cancellation of legal documents
      BT Discharge of contracts
   — **Destruction and reconstruction**
      (May Subd Geog)
      UF Destruction of legal documents
         Legal documents—Reconstruction
         Reconstruction of legal documents
      BT Evidence, Documentary
   — **Identification**
      [HV8074]
      UF Documents, Identification of
         Identification of documents
      BT Criminal investigation
         Evidence, Documentary
      NT Typewriting—Identification
         Writing—Identification
   — **Interpretation and construction**
      (May Subd Geog)
   — Reconstruction

   USE Legal documents—Destruction
      and reconstruction
Legal documents (Roman-Dutch law)
Legal dress
   USE Judges—Costume
      Lawyers—Costume
Legal drinking age
   USE Drinking age—Law and legislation
Legal ecclesiastical acts
   USE Legitimate ecclesiastical acts
Legal education
   USE Law—Study and teaching
Legal ethics *(May Subd Geog)*
   UF Ethics, Legal
   BT Ethics
      Law
      Law and ethics
      Lawyers
      Practice of law
      Professional ethics
   NT Ambulance chasing
      Attorney and client
      Confidential communications—
      Lawyers
      Confidential communications—
      Notaries
      Courts of honor
      Judicial ethics
      Lawyers—Discipline
      Lawyers—Malpractice
      Legal etiquette
      Maintenance and champerty
      Prevarication (Law)
      Unauthorized practice of law
Legal ethics, Catholic
Legal etiquette *(May Subd Geog)*
   UF Etiquette, Legal
   BT Legal ethics
      Practice of law
      Procedure (Law)
      Trial practice
   NT Conduct of court proceedings
Legal fees
   USE Costs (Law)
      Lawyers—Fees
Legal fictions
   USE Fictions (Law)
Legal forms
   USE Forms (Law)
Legal history
   USE Law—History and criticism
Legal holidays
   USE Holidays
Legal instruments *(May Subd Geog)*
   Here are entered works on documents written in
order to give expression to a legal act or agreement,
for the purpose of creating, securing, modifying, or
terminating a right, or for the purpose of furnishing
evidence of a right. Works on documents having legal
relevance in general are entered under the heading
Legal documents.
   RT Legal documents
   NT Clauses (Law)
      Contracts
      Escrows
      Negotiable instruments
      Recording and registration
      Reformation of instruments
      Trust receipts
      Wills
Legal instruments (Canon law)
Legal instruments (Greek law)
Legal instruments (Islamic law)
Legal instruments (Jewish law)
   BT Jewish law
Legal instruments (Roman law)
Legal interviewing
   USE Interviewing in law practice
Legal investments *(May Subd Geog)*
   Here are entered works on investments permitted
by law for certain fiduciary institutions.

Legal investments (Continued)
UF Legal bonds
Legal investments for trust funds,
savings-banks, etc.
Legal securities
BT Investments
Trusts and trustees
NT Investment of public funds
Pension trusts—Investments—Law and
legislation
Legal investments for trust funds, savings-
banks, etc.
USE Legal investments
Legal journalism
USE Journalism, Legal
Legal language
USE Law—Language
Legal literature (May Subd Geog)
UF Law books
Lawbooks
Literature, Legal
RT Law—Bibliography
NT Loose-leaf publications, Legal
— **History and criticism**
SA subdivision Literary history under
particular legal systems,
branches of law, and legal
subjects, e.g. Jewish law—
Literary history
Legal literature searching
USE Information storage and retrieval
systems—Law
Legal maxims (May Subd Geog)
UF Legal proverbs
Maxims, Legal
Proverbs, Legal
BT Maxims
RT Law—Quotations
SA subdivision Terms and phrases under
particular branches of law, e.g.
Constitutional law—Terms and
phrases
Legal maxims (Canon law)
Legal maxims (Feudal law)
Legal maxims (Roman law)
Legal medicine
USE Medical jurisprudence
Legal neopositivism
USE Legal positivism
Legal novels
UF Law—Fiction
BT Fiction
Law in literature
Legal officers, Military
USE subdivision Lawyers under particular
branches of the armed forces, e.g.
United States. Army—Lawyers
Legal offices
USE Law offices
Legal persons
USE Juristic persons
Legal photography
USE Photography, Legal
Legal positivism
UF Legal neopositivism
Neopositivism in law
BT Jurisprudence
Law—Philosophy
Positivism
Legal procedure
USE Procedure (Law)
Legal profession
USE Lawyers
Legal proverbs
USE Legal maxims
Legal psychology
USE Law—Psychology
Psychology, Forensic
Legal quotations
USE Law—Quotations

Legal referral service
USE Lawyer referral service
Legal reform
USE Law reform
Legal representation of abused wives
USE Legal assistance to abused wives
Legal representation of children
USE Legal assistance to children
Legal representation of Indians
USE Legal assistance to Indians
Legal representation of juvenile delinquents
USE Legal assistance to juvenile delinquents
Legal representation of prisoners
USE Legal assistance to prisoners
Legal representation of refugees
USE Legal assistance to refugees
Legal representation of the aged
USE Legal assistance to the aged
Legal representation of the handicapped
USE Legal assistance to the handicapped
Legal representation of the mentally
handicapped
USE Legal assistance to the mentally
handicapped
Legal representation of the poor
USE Legal assistance to the poor
Legal research (May Subd Geog)
UF Legal bibliography
Research, Legal
BT Research
SA subdivision Legal research under
headings for legal topics
NT Citation of legal authorities
Educational law and legislation—Legal
research
Legal authorities
Legal responsibility
USE Liability (Law)
Legal secretaries (May Subd Geog)
BT Practice of law
Secretaries
RT Law offices
— **Wages**
USE Wages—Legal secretaries
Legal securities
USE Legal investments
Legal service corporations (May Subd Geog)
UF Corporate practice of law
Lawyers' corporations
BT Practice of law
Professional corporations
Legal services (May Subd Geog)
Here are entered works on the adequacy of, and
provision of, legal services generally. Works on legal
services to particular groups are entered under specif-
ic headings, e.g. Legal assistance to the poor; Legal
assistance to the aged.
UF Services, Legal
BT Practice of law
RT Public interest law
NT Legal assistance to abused wives
Legal assistance to children
Legal assistance to Indians
Legal assistance to juvenile delinquents
Legal assistance to prisoners
Legal assistance to refugees
Legal assistance to servicemen
Legal assistance to the aged
Legal assistance to the handicapped
Legal assistance to the poor
Legal services, Group
USE Prepaid legal services
Legal services, Prepaid
USE Prepaid legal services
Legal services for Indians
USE Legal assistance to Indians
Legal services for prisoners
USE Legal assistance to prisoners
Legal services for refugees
USE Legal assistance to refugees

Legal services for the aged
USE Legal assistance to the aged
Legal services for the handicapped
USE Legal assistance to the handicapped
Legal services for the mentally handicapped
USE Legal assistance to the mentally
handicapped
Legal services for the poor
USE Legal assistance to the poor
Legal services insurance
USE Prepaid legal services
Legal statistics
USE Judicial statistics
Legal status of women
USE Women—Legal status, laws, etc.
Legal style
USE Law—Language
Legal symbolism
USE Symbolism in law
Legal tender (May Subd Geog)
[HG361-363]
UF Fiat money
Specie
Tender, Legal
BT Coinage
RT Bank-notes
Currency question
Money
NT Greenbacks
Legal translating
USE Law—Translating
Legalism (Chinese philosophy)
(May Subd Geog)
[B127.L43]
UF Legalist school of Chinese philosophy
BT Philosophy, Chinese
Legalist school of Chinese philosophy
USE Legalism (Chinese philosophy)
Legalization (May Subd Geog)
BT Contracts
Judicial assistance
Non-contentious jurisdiction
RT Authentication
Legal documents
Legalmen (United States Navy)
USE United States. Navy—Legalmen
Legarth family (Not Subd Geog)
Legas
USE Waregas
Legates, Papal (May Subd Geog)
[BX1908]
UF Papal legates
BT Ambassadors
Catholic Church—Diplomatic service
Catholic Church—Government
Diplomatic and consular service
Diplomats
RT Nuncios, Papal
Legates (Rome)
BT Rome—Officials and employees
Legations
USE Diplomatic and consular service
Legend of Joseph (Ballet)
UF Joseph Legende (Ballet)
Josephlegende (Ballet)
BT Ballets
Legendre's coefficients
USE Legendre's functions
Legendre's equation
USE Legendre's functions
Legendre's functions
[QA406]
UF Functions, Legendre's
Legendre's coefficients
Legendre's equation
BT Spherical harmonics
Legendre's polynomials
UF Polynomials, Legendre's
BT Orthogonal polynomials
Legends (May Subd Geog)
[N7760 (Iconography)]

[PN683-PN687 (Medieval literature)]
[PZ8.1 (Juvenile)]
  UF Folk-tales
       Traditions
  BT Exempla
       Fiction
       Folk literature
       Homiletical illustrations
       Literature
       Tales
  SA *subdivision* Legends *under subjects,*
       e.g. Martyrs—Legends; Mary,
       Blessed Virgin, Saint—Legends
  NT Chansons de geste
       Fables
       Fairy tales
       Heldensage
       Mythology
       Romances
— Jews
    USE Legends, Jewish
— Canary Islands
    NT San Borondon (Imaginary place)
— Egypt
    NT Eudoxia (Legendary character)
— Europe
    NT Milon d'Angers
— Greece
— Ireland
    NT Blarney Castle (Blarney, Cork)—
       Blarney Stone
— Middle East
    NT Sindbad the Sailor (Legendary
       character)
— Spain
    NT Infantes of Lara
       Lovers of Teruel (Legend)
Legends, Aztec
USE Aztecs—Legends
Legends, Buddhist *(May Subd Geog)*
  UF Buddhist legends
  NT Miao-shan (Legendary character)
Legends, Christian *(May Subd Geog)*
  UF Christian legends
Legends, Hasidic
USE Hasidim—Legends
Legends, Hindu *(May Subd Geog)*
  UF Hindu legends
Legends, Indian
USE *subdivision* Legends *under* Indians;
     Indians of Mexico; Indians of North
     America; *and similar headings; and*
     under names of Indian tribes
Legends, Islamic
  [BP137-7.5]
  UF Islamic legends
       Legends, Muslim
       Muslim legends
Legends, Jaina *(May Subd Geog)*
  UF Jaina legends
  NT Meghakumāra (Legendary character)
Legends, Jewish
  Here are entered collections of and works about
Jewish legends, including comprehensive works cov-
ering both Old Testament legends and post-Biblical
Jewish legends. Works on legends in the Bible and on
extra-Biblical legends about Biblical characters and
events are entered under Bible—Legends. Works lim-
ited to legends in or about the Old or New Testament
are entered under Bible. O.T.—Legends or Bible.
N.T.—Legends.
  UF Jewish legends
       Jews—Legends
       Legends—Jews
  RT Bible. O.T.—Legends
  NT Aggada
       Golem
       Hasidim—Legends
       Midrash—Legends
       Talmud—Legends
Legends, Muslim
USE Legends, Islamic

Legends, Shinto *(May Subd Geog)*
  UF Shinto legends
Legends, Toltec
USE Toltecs—Legends
Legends, Zapotec
USE Zapotec Indians—Legends
Legenne family *(Not Subd Geog)*
Leger family *(Not Subd Geog)*
Legerdemain
USE Conjuring
      Juggling
Legg-Calvé-Perthes disease
  [RJ482.O8]
  UF Calvé-Legg-Perthes syndrome
       Coxa plana
       Legg-Perthes disease
       Osteochondritis deformans juvenilis
       Perthes-Calvé-Legg-Waldenström
        syndrome
       Perthes disease
       Pseudocoxalgia
       Waldenström's syndrome
  BT Hip joint—Diseases
       Osteochondrosis
       Pediatric orthopedia
Legg family *(Not Subd Geog)*
  UF Leg family
       Legge family
       Leggs family
Legg-Perthes disease
USE Legg-Calvé-Perthes disease
Legge family
USE Legg family
Leggon family
USE Ligon family
Leggs family
USE Legg family
Leghorns (Poultry)
  [SF489.L5]
Leghoya (African people)
USE Ghoya (African people)
Legibility (Printing)
  [Z250.A4]
  UF Readability (Printing)
  BT Printing, Practical
       Reading, Psychology of
       Type and type-founding
  NT Show-through (Printing)
Legionary ants
USE Eciton
Legionella pneumophila
  [QR201.L44]
  UF Legionnaires' disease bacterium
  BT Bacteria, Pathogenic
       Gram negative bacteria
  RT Legionnaires' disease
Legionnaires' disease *(May Subd Geog)*
  UF Broad street disease
       Respiratory disease of Philadelphia
  BT Bacterial diseases
       Respiratory organs—Diseases
  RT Legionella pneumophila
Legionnaires' disease bacterium
USE Legionella pneumophila
Legislation *(May Subd Geog)*
  [JF401-JF637]
  Here are entered works on the theory or practice
of statute making. Works on statute law, as a source
of law, as distinguished from constitutional law and
from the law arising from judicial or administrative
decisions are entered under Statutes. Works on the
interpretation of law, including statutory interpreta-
tion, are entered under Law—Interpretation and con-
struction.
  UF Legislative process
  RT Law
       Legislative power
  SA *legislation on particular subjects, e.g.*
       Factory laws and legislation;
       Forestry law and legislation; Sunday
       legislation
  NT Bills, Legislative

       Bills, Private
       Delegated legislation
       Derogation (Law)
       Disallowance of legislation
       Exclusive and concurrent legislative
        powers
       Governmental investigations
       Initiative, Right of
       Interns (Legislation)
       Judge-made law
       Judicial impact statements
       Judicial review
       Lacunae in law
       Legislative histories
       Legislative reference bureaus
       Parliamentary practice
       Promulgation (Law)
       Repeal of legislation
— Compliance costs
    UF Compliance with legislation, Costs
      of
Legislation, Comparative
USE Comparative law
Legislation, Direct
USE Referendum
Legislation, Local
USE Local laws
Legislation, Private
USE Bills, Private
Legislation (Canon law)
  NT Promulgation (Canon law)
Legislation (Islamic law) *(May Subd Geog)*
  BT Islamic law
Legislation (Roman law)
  BT Roman law
Legislation by reference
USE Reference legislation
Legislation drafting
USE Bill drafting
Legislative advocates
USE Lobbyists
Legislative amendments
USE Amendments (Parliamentary practice)
Legislative auditing *(May Subd Geog)*
  UF Auditing, Legislative
  BT Auditing
       Budget
       Finance, Public—Accounting
       Legislative oversight
Legislative bills
USE Bills, Legislative
Legislative bodies *(May Subd Geog)*
  [JF501-JF637]
  UF Bicameralism
       Legislatures
       Parliaments
       Unicameral legislatures
  BT Constitutional law
       Estates (Social orders)
       Representative government and
        representation
  RT Legislative power
  SA *names of individual legislative bodies,*
       e.g. United States. Congress
  NT Caucus
       City councils
       Gerrymander
       Legislative calendars
       Legislative councils
       Legislative journals
       Legislators
       Ministerial responsibility
       Parliamentary practice
       Pre-legislative conferences
       Resolutions, Legislative
       Right and left (Political science)
— Chaplains' prayers
    [BV280]
    UF Chaplains' prayers
    BT Prayers
— Cloture

Legislative bodies
— Cloture *(Continued)*
   USE Cloture
— **Committees**
   [JK2495 (United States, JK1029)]
   [JN605 (Great Britain)]
   [JN2815 (France)]
   BT Committees
   SA *subdivision* Committees *under
       names of individual legislative
       bodies, e.g.* United States.
       Congress—Committees
   NT Governmental investigations
       Legislative conference committees
       Legislative hearings
— Conference committees
   USE Legislative conference
        committees
— **Dissolution**
   UF Dissolution of legislative bodies
   SA *subdivision* Dissolution *under
       names of individual legislative
       bodies, e.g.* Germany.
       Reichstag—Dissolution
— **Ethics**
   UF Ethics, Legislative
       Legislative ethics
   BT Political ethics
   SA *subdivision* Ethics *under names of
       individual legislative bodies*
— **Freedom of debate**
   UF Freedom of debate (Legislative
       bodies)
       Gag rule
       Limitation of debate
   BT Freedom of speech
       Legislative bodies—Privileges and
       immunities
   SA *subdivision* Freedom of debate
       *under names of individual
       legislative bodies, e.g.* United
       States. Congress—Freedom of
       debate
   NT Cloture
— **Leadership**
   BT Political leadership
   SA *subdivision* Leadership *under
       names of individual legislative
       bodies*
— **Lower chambers**
   [JF601-637]
— **Officials and employees**
   UF Legislative clerks
       Legislative secretaries
   SA *subdivision* Officials and employees
       *under names of individual
       legislative bodies, e.g.* United
       States. Congress—Officials and
       employees
   NT Interns (Legislation)
— — Literary writings
      USE Legislative employees' literary
           writings
— — **Pensions** *(May Subd Geog)*
      SA *subdivision* Officials and
          employees—Pensions *under
          names of individual legislative
          bodies, e.g.* United States.
          Congress—Officials and
          employees—Pensions
— — **Salaries, etc.** *(May Subd Geog)*
      SA *subdivision* Officials and
          employees—Salaries, etc.
          *under names of individual
          legislative bodies, e.g.* United
          States. Congress—Officials
          and employees—Salaries, etc.
— **Presiding officer**
   UF Presiding officer of legislative
       bodies

   SA *subdivision* Presiding officer *under
       names of individual legislative
       bodies, e.g.* United States.
       Congress. Senate—Presiding
       officer
— **Privileges and immunities**
   UF Immunity, Parliamentary
       Immunity, Political
       Parliamentary immunity
       Parliamentary privileges
       Political immunity
       Privileges, Parliamentary
   BT Privileges and immunities
   SA *subdivision* Privileges and
       immunities *under names of
       individual legislative bodies*
   NT Legislative bodies—Freedom of
       debate
— **Public meetings**
   UF Government in the sunshine
       Open meetings of legislative bodies
       Public meetings of legislative
       bodies
       Sunshine, Government in the
   BT Public meetings
— **Publication of proceedings**
— **Qualifications**
   SA *subdivision* Qualifications *under
       names of individual legislative
       bodies, e.g.* United States.
       Congress—Qualifications
— **Reform**
   UF Legislative reorganization
       Parliamentary reform
       Reform, Parliamentary
       Reform of legislative bodies
       Reorganization of legislative bodies
   SA *subdivision* Reform *under names of
       individual legislative bodies*
— Reporters and reporting
   USE Legislative reporting
— Rules and practice
   USE Parliamentary practice
— Salaries, pensions, etc.
   USE Legislators—Pensions
        Legislators—Salaries, etc.
— **Upper chambers**
   [JF541-567]
   UF Upper chambers
— **Voting**
   UF Legislative record votes
       Legislative roll calls
       Legislative voting
       Voting, Legislative
   BT Voting
   SA *subdivision* Voting *under names of
       individual legislative bodies, e.g.*
       United States. Congress—
       Voting
   NT Confidence voting
— **United States**
   UF United States—Legislative bodies
Legislative bodies (Canon law)
Legislative bodies as courts
   UF Judicial functions of legislative bodies
   BT Courts
       Judicial power
   NT Impeachments
Legislative calendars *(May Subd Geog)*
   UF Calendars, Legislative
   BT Bills, Legislative
       Legislative bodies
       Resolutions, Legislative
   SA *subdivision* Calendars *under names of
       individual legislative bodies*
Legislative clerks
   USE Legislative bodies—Officials and
        employees

Legislative conference committees
   (May Subd Geog)
   UF Conference committees, Legislative
       Legislative bodies—Conference
       committees
   BT Legislative bodies—Committees
   SA *subdivision* Conference committees
       *under names of individual legislative
       bodies, e.g.* United States.
       Congress—Conference committees
Legislative councils
   Here are entered works on interim legislative
   committees, composed of legislators with other offi-
   cials sometimes added, whose function it is to con-
   duct a continuous study of state problems and pre-
   pare programs of legislation for each legislative ses-
   sion.
   BT Legislative bodies
   NT Legislative reference bureaus
Legislative districts
   USE Election districts
Legislative documents
   USE Legislative hearings
        Legislative journals
Legislative employees' literary writings
   UF Legislative bodies—Officials and
       employees—Literary writings
   BT Literature
**Legislative employees' literary writings,
   Brazilian** *(May Subd Geog)*
   UF Brazilian legislative employees' literary
       writings
   BT Brazilian literature
Legislative ethics
   USE Legislative bodies—Ethics
Legislative, executive, and judicial
   appropriation bills
   USE United States—Appropriations and
        expenditures
Legislative hearings *(May Subd Geog)*
   UF Hearings, Legislative
       Legislative documents
   BT Governmental investigations
       Legislative bodies—Committees
       Legislative histories
— **United States**
   UF Congressional hearings
Legislative histories *(May Subd Geog)*
   BT Legislation
   NT Bills, Legislative
       Legislative hearings
Legislative impact on courts, Statements of
   USE Judicial impact statements
Legislative interns
   USE Interns (Legislation)
Legislative investigations
   USE Governmental investigations
Legislative journals *(May Subd Geog)*
   UF Legislative documents
   BT Legislative bodies
Legislative libraries
   USE Libraries, Governmental,
        administrative, etc.
Legislative oversight *(May Subd Geog)*
   UF Oversight, Legislative
   BT Legislative power
       Separation of powers
   NT Governmental investigations
       Legislative auditing
       Legislative veto
       Sunset reviews of government
       programs
— **United States**
   UF Congressional oversight
       Oversight, Congressional
Legislative power *(May Subd Geog)*
   [JF441-JF483]
   UF Power, Legislative
   BT Constitutional law

RT Federal government
Implied powers (Constitutional law)
Judicial review
Legislation
Legislative bodies
State governments
SA *subdivision* Powers and duties *under
names of individual legislative
bodies, e.g.* United States.
Congress—Powers and duties
NT Civil supremacy over the military
Constituent power
Delegated legislation
Delegation of powers
Exclusive and concurrent legislative
powers
Executive impoundment of
appropriated funds
Judge-made law
Legislative oversight
Repeal of legislation
Separation of powers
Treaty-making power
War and emergency powers
— United States
NT United States. Congress—Powers
and duties
Legislative powers, Exclusive and concurrent
USE Exclusive and concurrent legislative
powers
Legislative printing
USE Printing, Legislative
Legislative procedure
USE *subdivision* Rules and practice *under
names of individual legislative
bodies, e.g.* United States.
Congress—Rules and practice
Parliamentary practice
Legislative process
USE Legislation
Legislative record votes
USE Legislative bodies—Voting
Legislative reference bureaus
(May Subd Geog)
[JF527 (Public administration)]
[JK1108 (United States)]
BT Legislation
Legislative councils
Legislative reorganization
USE Legislative bodies—Reform
Legislative reporting
UF Legislative bodies—Reporters and
reporting
Parliamentary reporting
Verbatim reporting
BT Reporters and reporting
SA *subdivision* Reporters and reporting
*under names of individual legislative
bodies, e.g.* United States.
Congress—Reporters and reporting
Legislative resolutions
USE Resolutions, Legislative
Legislative right to information from executive
agencies
USE Executive privilege (Government
information)
Legislative roll calls
USE Legislative bodies—Voting
Legislative secretaries
USE Legislative bodies—Officials and
employees
Legislative service organizations
USE *subdivision* Caucuses *under names of
individual legislative bodies, e.g.*
United States. Congress—
Caucuses
Legislative veto *(May Subd Geog)*
BT Administrative procedure
Legislative oversight
Separation of powers
Veto

— **United States**
UF Congressional veto
Legislative voting
USE Legislative bodies—Voting
Legislators *(May Subd Geog)*
UF Lawmakers
BT Legislative bodies
NT Pre-legislative conferences
Women legislators
— **Attitudes**
BT Attitude (Psychology)
— **Pensions** *(May Subd Geog)*
UF Legislative bodies—Salaries,
pensions, etc.
SA *subdivision* Pensions *under names
of individual legislative bodies,
e.g.* United States. Congress—
Pensions
— **Salaries, etc.** *(May Subd Geog)*
UF Legislative bodies—Salaries,
pensions, etc.
SA *subdivision* Salaries, etc. *under
names of individual legislative
bodies, e.g.* United States.
Congress—Salaries, etc.
— **Taxation** *(May Subd Geog)*
— — **Law and legislation**
(May Subd Geog)
— **United States**
UF Congressmen
Members of Congress (United
States)
Members of Congress (United
States House of Representatives)
Members of Congress (United
States Senate)
Representatives in Congress
(United States)
Senators (United States)
NT Afro-American legislators
— — Term of office
USE United States. Congress—
Term of office
Legislators, Afro-American
USE Afro-American legislators
Legislators' literary writings
BT Literature
Legislators' literary writings, Brazilian
(May Subd Geog)
UF Brazilian legislators' literary writings
BT Brazilian literature
Legislators' wives *(May Subd Geog)*
BT Wives
Women in politics
Legislatures
USE Legislative bodies
Legitim
USE Legitime
Legitimacy (Constitutional law)
USE Legitimacy of governments
Legitimacy (Law)
USE Illegitimacy
Legitimacy of governments
(May Subd Geog)
UF Governments, Legitimacy of
Legitimacy (Constitutional law)
BT Consensus (Social sciences)
Revolutions
Sovereignty
State, The
RT General will
Political stability
Legitimate ecclesiastical acts
(May Subd Geog)
UF Actus legitimi ecclesiastici
Authorized ecclesiastical acts
Ecclesiastical acts, Legitimate
Legal ecclesiastical acts
BT Canon law

Legitimation of children *(May Subd Geog)*
BT Illegitimacy
Parent and child (Law)
— Conflict of laws
USE Conflict of laws—Legitimation of
children
Legitimation of children (Canon law)
Legitimation of children (Germanic law)
Legitimation of children (Roman law)
Legitime *(May Subd Geog)*
UF Falcidian law
Family provision
Forced heirs
Legitim
Lex Falcidia
BT Disinheritance
Freedom of testation
Inheritance and succession
Wills
RT Dower
NT Decedents' family maintenance
Mejora
Widow's share
Legitime (Canon law)
Legitime (Roman-Dutch law)
Legitime (Roman law)
UF Querela inofficiosi testamenti
Legless lizards
USE Anniellidae
Legnano, Battle of, 1176
[DG657.45]
BT Holy Roman Empire—History—
Frederick I, 1152-1190
Lombardy (Italy)—History—To 1535
Legnica, Battle of, 1241
BT Mongols—History
Poland—History—Mongol Invasion,
1241
**Legnicko-Głogowski Okręg Miedziowy
(Poland)**
BT Copper mines and mining—Poland
LEGO toys
BT Toys
Legon family
USE Ligon family
Leguerrier family *(Not Subd Geog)*
Legume industry *(May Subd Geog)*
[HD9235.L37-374]
BT Legumes
Legume inoculation
UF Inoculation of legumes
BT Soil inoculation
Legume mite
UF Petrobia apicalis
Tetranychina apicalis
BT Legumes—Diseases and pests
Legumes *(May Subd Geog)*
[SB177.L45 (Food plants)]
[SB203-SB205 (Forage plants)]
[SB317.L43 (General)]
Here are entered comprehensive works on plants,
belonging to the family Leguminosae, with pods or
seeds edible for man or domestic animals. Botanical
works on this family are entered under Leguminosae.
UF Pulse crops
BT Food crops
Forage plants
RT Cover crops
Leguminosae
NT Bambarra groundnut
Bur clover
Chickpea
Cowpea
Guar
Lead tree
Legume industry
— **Diseases and pests** *(May Subd Geog)*
[SB608.L4]
NT Ascochyta
Bean yellow mosaic disease
Cowpea curculio

Legumes
— **Diseases and pests** *(Continued)*
    Cowpea weevil
    Legume mite
    Pea aphid
    Red clover vein mosaic virus
— **Harvesting**
— **Varieties**
Legumes as feed *(May Subd Geog)*
  BT Feeds
Legumes as food *(May Subd Geog)*
  BT Food
  NT Porridge
Legumin
  ⌈QD431 (Chemistry)⌉
Leguminosae *(May Subd Geog)*
  ⌈QK495.L52⌉
  Here are entered botanical works on the family
Leguminosae. Comprehensive works on plants, be-
longing to this family, with pods or seeds edible for
man or domestic animals are entered under Legumes.
  UF Pulse family
  BT Rosales
  RT Legumes
  SA *names of leguminous plants, e.g.*
     Beans; Clover; Peas
  NT Acacia
     Andira
     Aspalathus
     Astragalus (Plants)
     Bauhinia
     Cajanus
     Calliandra
     Cassia
     Centrosema
     Cercidium
     Cercis
     Chamaecrista
     Cicer
     Dalbergia
     Desmodium
     Eriosema
     Erythrina
     Hippocrepis
     Hymenaea
     Inga (Plants)
     Lathyrus
     Leucaena
     Locust trees
     Lotus
     Lupines
     Mesquite
     Mimosa
     Mucuna
     Pisum
     Ratany
     Rhynchosia
     Robinia
     Senna
     Sesbania
     Silk tree
     Sophora
     Stylosanthes
     Sweet clover
     Ulex
     Vetch
     Vigna
     Voandzeia
     Wisteria
Lehenbauer family *(Not Subd Geog)*
Lehew family *(Not Subd Geog)*
  UF Lahugh family
     Lehue family
     Lehugh family
Lehi (Book of Mormon character)
  ⌈BX8627.A3-Z⌉
  BT Book of Mormon—Biography
Lehigh Canal (Pa.)
  BT Canals—Pennsylvania
Lehigh River (Pa.)
  BT Rivers—Pennsylvania

Lehman family *(Not Subd Geog)*
  UF Lehmann family
     Lehmans family
     Lemann family
  RT Layman family
Lehmann family
  USE Lehman family
Lehmans family
  USE Lehman family
Lehmer family
  USE Leamer family
Lehmkuhl family *(Not Subd Geog)*
Lehn family
  USE Lehnert family
Lehner family
  USE Lehnert family
Lehners family
  USE Lehnert family
Lehnert family *(Not Subd Geog)*
  UF Lahners family
     Lahnert family
     Leenderts family
     Leeners family
     Lehn family
     Lehner family
     Lehners family
     Lehnerts family
     Lehnertz family
     Lenarts family
     Leners family
Lehnerts family
  USE Lehnert family
Lehnertz family
  USE Lehnert family
Lehnhart family
  USE Leonard family
Lehr family *(Not Subd Geog)*
  RT Lohr family
Lehua tree
  USE Ohia-lehua
Lehue family
  USE Lehew family
Lehugh family
  USE Lehew family
Lei-chou Peninsula (China)
  USE Luichow Peninsula (China)
Leib family *(Not Subd Geog)*
  UF Leeb family
     Leibe family
  RT Lipe family
Leibe family
  USE Leib family
Leibenguth family
  USE Levengood family
Leibert family
  USE Lippert family
Leibl Circle
  USE Leibl-Kreis
Leibl-Kreis
  ⌈ND567.5⌉
  UF Leibl Circle
  BT Munich school of painting
     Painting, German
     Painting, Modern—19th century—
      Germany
Leica camera
  NT Kardon camera
     Leicaflex camera
Leicaflex camera
  BT Leica camera
     Single-lens reflex cameras
Leichleiter family
  USE Leckliter family
Leichti family
  USE Leighty family
Leichty family
  USE Leighty family
Leidenfrost effect
  USE Film boiling
Leidy family
  USE Lyda family

Leidya
  ⌈QL444.M34⌉
  BT Bopyridae
Leidya distorta
  ⌈QL444.M34⌉
Leidyosuchus
  ⌈QE862.C8⌉
  BT Crocodiles, Fossil
Leidyosuchus formidabilis
  ⌈QE862.C8⌉
Leifeste family *(Not Subd Geog)*
  UF Leifester family
     Leiweste family
Leifester family
  USE Leifeste family
Leigeber family *(Not Subd Geog)*
Leigh family
  USE Lee family
Leighton family
  USE Layton family
Leighty family *(Not Subd Geog)*
  UF Leichti family
     Leichty family
     Lichdi family
     Lichty family
     Liechti family
     Liechty family
Leilat . . .
  USE *subject headings beginning with the*
     word Laylat
Leiman family
  USE Lyman family
Leinan family *(Not Subd Geog)*
  UF Leinum family
  RT Lennon family
Leinbach family *(Not Subd Geog)*
  UF Leinbaugh family
     Lineback family
     Linebah family
     Linebaugh family
Leinbaugh family
  USE Leinbach family
Leinebergland (Germany) *(Not Subd Geog)*
  UF Weser-Leinebergland (Germany)
Leiningen, Counts of *(Not Subd Geog)*
  UF Counts of Leiningen
  BT Germany—Nobility
Leininger family *(Not Subd Geog)*
Leinster, Dukes of *(Not Subd Geog)*
  BT Ireland—Nobility
Leinster House (Dublin, Dublin)
  UF Teach Laighean (Dublin, Dublin)
     Tigh Laighean (Dublin, Dublin)
  BT Dwellings—Ireland
Leinum family
  USE Leinan family
Leiocephalus
  ⌈QL666.L25⌉
  UF Liocephalus
  BT Iguanidae
Leiocephalus macropus
  ⌈QL666.L25⌉
Leiocephalus raviceps
  ⌈QL666.L25⌉
Leiocephalus stictigaster
  ⌈QL666.L25⌉
Leiochrini
  USE Tenebrionidae
Leiodidae
  ⌈QL596.L35⌉
  UF Agathidiidae
     Agnathidiidae
     Anisotomidae
     Camiaridae
     Catopidae
     Chloevidae
     Cholevidae
     Colonidae
     Liodesidae
     Liodidae
  BT Beetles

Leiomyoma uteri *(May Subd Geog)*
  [RC280.U8]
    UF Fibroid tumor
         Fibroids
         Fibromyoma uteri
         Myoma previum
         Uterine fibroids
         Uterine leiomyoma
    BT Myometrium—Tumors
         Smooth muscle—Tumors
Leiomyomas
    USE Smooth muscle—Tumors
Leiomyomata
    USE Smooth muscle—Tumors
Leiopelmatidae
    [QL668.E255]
    UF Ascaphidae
         Ribbed frogs
    BT Anura
         Frogs
    NT Ascaphus
Leiostomus
    [QL638.S34]
    BT Sciaenidae
Leiostomus xanthurus
    USE Spot (Fish)
Leipert family
    USE Lippert family
Leiphardt family
    USE Lippert family
Leiphart family
    USE Lippert family
Leipoa
    [QL696.G25]
    BT Megapodiidae
    NT Leipoa ocellata
Leipoa ocellata
    [QL696.G25]
    UF Mallee fowl
    BT Leipoa
Leipzig, Battle of, 1631
    [D267.L3]
    UF Breitenfeld, Battle of, 1631
    BT Thirty Years' War, 1618-1648—
         Campaigns—Germany (East)
Leipzig, Battle of, 1813
    [DC236.5-68]
    BT Napoleonic Wars, 1800-1814—
         Campaigns—Germany (East)
Leipzig disputation, 1519
    [BR355.L5]
    BT Disputations, Religious
Leipzig School (Linguistics)
    USE Neogrammarians
Leipzig Trials, Leipzig, Germany, 1921
    UF Leipzig Trials, 1921
         Leipzig War Crime Trials, Leipzig,
           Germany, 1921
    BT War crime trials—Germany (East)
Leipzig Trials, 1921
    USE Leipzig Trials, Leipzig, Germany, 1921
Leipzig War Crime Trials, Leipzig, Germany,
    1921
    USE Leipzig Trials, Leipzig, Germany, 1921
Leir, King (Legendary character)
    USE Lear, King (Legendary character)
Leird family
    USE Laird family
Leis *(May Subd Geog)*
    BT Wreaths
    NT Flower leis
Leishman-Donovan bodies
    [RC152]
    UF Leishmania forms
    BT Kála-azár
Leishmania
    [QL368.K5]
    BT Trypanosomidae
Leishmania forms
    USE Leishman-Donovan bodies

Leishmaniasis *(May Subd Geog)*
    [RA644.L25 (Public health)]
    [RC153-RC153.5 (Internal medicine)]
    BT Medical protozoology
Leishmaniasis, Cutaneous
    UF Cutaneous leishmaniasis
         Delhi boil
         Oriental sore
Leishmaniasis, Mucocutaneous
    [RC153.5]
    UF American leishmaniasis
         Leishmaniasis americana
         Mucocutaneous leishmaniasis
    BT Otolaryngology
Leishmaniasis, Visceral
    USE Kála-azár
Leishmaniasis americana
    USE Leishmaniasis, Mucocutaneous
Leisure *(May Subd Geog)*
    [BJ1498]
    [GV1-GV200]
    UF Free time (Leisure)
         Leisure time
    RT Recreation
    NT Amateurism
         Hobbies
         Retirement
         Time management
    — **Religious aspects**
    — — **Buddhism,** [Christianity, etc.]
    — — **Christianity** *(May Subd Geog)*
         UF Church and leisure
Leisure and architecture
    USE Architecture and recreation
Leisure class
    [HB831 (Economic theory)]
    BT Economics
         Sociology
         Wealth
    RT Luxury
Leisure counseling *(May Subd Geog)*
    [GV181.42]
    UF Recreation counseling
         Recreational counseling
    BT Counseling
         Recreation leadership
Leisure in literature
Leisure industry *(May Subd Geog)*
    [GV188-188.3]
    UF Commercial leisure services
         Leisure services
Leisure services
    USE Leisure industry
Leisure time
    USE Leisure
Leisure wear industry
    USE Sport clothes industry
Leitch family
    USE Leach family
Leite family *(Not Subd Geog)*
    UF Leites family
Leiter International Performance Scale
    (May Subd Geog)
    [BF432.5.L44]
    BT Non-verbal intelligence tests
Leites family
    USE Leite family
Leitmotiv
    [MT90]
    [MT100.W2 (Wagner)]
    BT Music
         Opera
         Program music
Leitsch family
    USE Litz family
Leitz family
    USE Litz family
Leiweste family
    USE Leifeste family
Leizhou Peninsula (China)
    USE Luichow Peninsula (China)

Lejeuneaceae
    [QK555.L37 (Botany)]
    BT Jungermanniales
    NT Acrolejeunea
Lek behavior
    BT Courtship of animals
         Display behavior in animals
Lekachmacher family *(Not Subd Geog)*
Lekes family
    USE Leak family
Lekhitic languages
    USE Lechitic languages
Leko dialect *(May Subd Geog)*
    UF Eleko dialect
         Eleku dialect
         iLiku dialect
         loLeku dialect
    BT Losengo language
         Zaire—Languages
LEKTOR (Computer system)
    BT Computer-assisted instruction
         Electronic digital computers—
           Programming
Lekve family *(Not Subd Geog)*
Lekythoi
    USE Lecythi
Lela dialect
    USE Lele dialect
Lele (African people)
    UF Bachilele (African people)
         Bashi-Lele (African people)
         Bashilele (African people)
         Lele (Bantu tribe)
         Lyela (African people)
    BT Bantus
         Ethnology—Zaire
    — **Children**
         BT Children
Lele (Bantu tribe)
    USE Lele (African people)
Lelê (Dance)
    [GV1796.L44]
    UF Dança do Lelê
    BT Folk dancing—Brazil
Lele dialect
    [PL8452]
    UF Élé dialect
         Lela dialect
         Lere dialect
         Lyele dialect
    BT Gur languages
Lelemi language
    USE Lefana language
LEM
    USE Lunar excursion module
Lemaignan family
    USE Lemaignen family
Lemaignen family *(Not Subd Geog)*
    UF Lemaignan family
Lemaistre family
    USE Lemaitre family
Lemaitre family *(Not Subd Geog)*
    UF Lemaistre family
Lemaky
    USE Lemky
Léman Lake (Switzerland and France)
    USE Geneva, Lake (Switzerland and
           France)
Lemann family
    USE Lehman family
Lemannus (Switzerland and France)
    USE Geneva, Lake (Switzerland and
           France)
Lemanus (Switzerland and France)
    USE Geneva, Lake (Switzerland and
           France)
Lemar family
    USE Lamar family
Lemare family
    USE Lamar family

Lemay family *(Not Subd Geog)*
  UF Le May family
Lemba (Cult)
  BT Cults—Congo (Brazzaville)
    Cults—Zaire
Lemba language
  USE Kela language
Lembak Bilide dialect *(May Subd Geog)*
    ₜPL5128.Lꜜ
  UF Lembak Bliti dialect
  BT Indonesia—Languages
    Malay language
Lembak Bliti dialect
  USE Lembak Bilide dialect
Lemberg, Battle of, 1914
  UF Lvov, Battle of, 1914
  BT World War, 1914-1918—Campaigns—
    Ukraine
Lemche family *(Not Subd Geog)*
Lemelin family *(Not Subd Geog)*
Lemet (Tribe)
  USE Lamet (Tribe)
Lemhi Indian Agency (Idaho)
  USE Lemhi Indian Reservation (Idaho)
Lemhi Indian Reservation (Idaho)
  UF Lemhi Indian Agency (Idaho)
  BT Bannock Indians—Reservations
    Indians of North America—Idaho—
      Reservations
    Shoshoni Indians—Reservations
    Tukuarika Indians—Reservations
Lemieux family *(Not Subd Geog)*
Leming language
  USE Valman language
Lemki
  USE Lemky
Lemkian Region (Poland and Czechoslovakia)
  USE Lemkivshchyna (Poland and
    Czechoslovakia)
Lemkians
  USE Lemky
Lemkivshchyna (Poland and Czechoslovakia)
  UF Lemkian Region (Poland and
      Czechoslovakia)
    Lemko Region (Poland and
      Czechoslovakia)
    Lemkovina (Poland and
      Czechoslovakia)
Lemko Region (Poland and Czechoslovakia)
  USE Lemkivshchyna (Poland and
    Czechoslovakia)
Lemkos
  USE Lemky
Lemkovina (Poland and Czechoslovakia)
  USE Lemkivshchyna (Poland and
    Czechoslovakia)
Lemkowie
  USE Lemky
Lemky
  UF Lemaky
    Lemki
    Lemkians
    Lemkos
    Lemkowie
  BT Ethnology—Carpathian Mountains
    Ethnology—Czechoslovakia
    Ethnology—Poland
    Ukrainians
Lemm family *(Not Subd Geog)*
Lemme River (Italy) *(Not Subd Geog)*
  UF Lemmo River (Italy)
    Torrente Lemme (Italy)
  BT Rivers—Italy

Lemmen family *(Not Subd Geog)*
  UF Lammen family
    Lemmon family
    Lemmond family
    Lemmonds family
    Lemmons family
    Lemon family
    Lemond family
    Lemonds family
    Lemons family
Lemmings
    ₜQL737.R6ꜜ
  UF Microtinae
  BT Cricetidae
  NT Brown lemming
    Collared lemming
    Norway lemming
    Synaptomys
Lemmo River (Italy)
  USE Lemme River (Italy)
Lemmon, Mount (Ariz.) *(Not Subd Geog)*
  UF Lemon, Mount (Ariz.)
    Mount Lemmon (Ariz.)
    Mount Lemon (Ariz.)
  BT Mountains—Arizona
  RT Coronado National Forest (Ariz. and
    N.M.)
Lemmon family
  USE Lemmen family
Lemmond family
  USE Lemmen family
Lemmonds family
  USE Lemmen family
Lemmons family
  USE Lemmen family
Lemmus lemmus
  USE Norway lemming
Lemmus trimucronatus
  USE Brown lemming
Lemna
    ₜQK495.L527 (Botany)ꜜ
  BT Lemnaceae
Lemna minor
    ₜQK495.L527 (Botany)ꜜ
  UF Duckweed, Common
Lemnaceae
    ₜQK495.L527 (Botany)ꜜ
  UF Duckweeds
  BT Spathiflorae
  NT Lemna
    Spirodela
Lemnos Island (Greece)
  UF Limnos Island (Greece)
  BT Islands—Greece
LeMoine family
  USE Monet family
Lemon, Mount (Ariz.)
  USE Lemmon, Mount (Ariz.)
Lemon *(May Subd Geog)*
    ₜSB370.L4ꜜ
  UF Lemon tree
  BT Citrus fruits
  NT Cookery (Lemons)
  — **Packaging**
      NT Lemon wrappers
Lemon dab
  USE Microstomus kitt
Lemon Fair River (Vt.)
  BT Rivers—Vermont
Lemon family
  USE Lemmen family
Lemon flounder
  USE Parophrys vetulus
Lemon-grass oil
  USE Lemongrass oil
Lemon House (Pa.)
  UF Lemon Inn (Pa.)
  BT Allegheny Portage Railroad National
    Historic Site (Pa.)
    Dwellings—Pennsylvania
    Hotels, taverns, etc.—Pennsylvania

Lemon Inn (Pa.)
  USE Lemon House (Pa.)
Lemon juice
  BT Citrus juices
    Fruit juices
  RT Lemon juice industry
Lemon juice industry *(May Subd Geog)*
  RT Lemon juice
Lemon-scented gum tree
  USE Eucalyptus citriodora
Lemon sole
  USE Microstomus kitt
Lemon sole, New Zealand
  USE Pelotretis flavilatus
Lemon trade *(May Subd Geog)*
Lemon tree
  USE Lemon
Lemon wrappers *(May Subd Geog)*
    ₜNC1002.W72 (Commercial art)ꜜ
  BT Lemon—Packaging
    Wrappers
Lemonade *(May Subd Geog)*
  BT Beverages
Lemond family
  USE Lemmen family
Lemonds family
  USE Lemmen family
Lemongrass oil *(May Subd Geog)*
  UF Lemon-grass oil
  BT Essences and essential oils
Lemongrass oil industry *(May Subd Geog)*
    ₜHD9166.L45-454ꜜ
Lemons family
  USE Lemmen family
Lemur
    ₜQL737.P95ꜜ
  BT Lemurs
  NT Black lemur
    Brown lemur
    Mongoose lemur
Lemur fulvus
  USE Brown lemur
Lemur macaco
  USE Black lemur
Lemur mongoz
  USE Mongoose lemur
Lemuria
  BT Geographical myths
    Lost continents
Lemuridae
    ₜQL737.P95ꜜ
  UF Large lemurs
  BT Lemurs
    Primates
Lemurs
    ₜQL737.P95ꜜ
  UF Lemurs, Typical
  BT Primates
  NT Cheirogaleidae
    Lemur
    Lemuridae
  — **Anatomy**
Lemurs, Atypical
  USE Aye-aye
    Indridae
Lemurs, Typical
  USE Lemurs
Lena River (R.S.F.S.R.)
  BT Rivers—Russian S.F.S.R.
Lenakel dialect
  BT Tanna language
Lenamon family
  USE Lindeman family
Lenamond family
  USE Lindeman family
Lenape Indians
  USE Delaware Indians
Lenape language
  USE Delaware language
Lenard family
  USE Leonard family

Lenarts family
    USE Lehnert family
Lenca Indians
    [F1505.2.L4]
    BT Indians of Central America
        Indians of Central America—El
            Salvador
        Indians of Central America—Honduras
Lenca language
    [PM3921]
    BT Indians of Central America—
        Languages
Lend-lease operations (1941-1945)
    [D753.2]
    UF Lease-lend operations
        World War, 1939-1945—Lend-lease
            operations
    BT Economic assistance
        World War, 1939-1945—Economic
            aspects
        World War, 1939-1945—Equipment
            and supplies
        World War, 1939-1945—Finance
Lendeman family
    USE Lindeman family
Lenderman family
    USE Lindeman family
Lenders of last resort *(May Subd Geog)*
        Here are entered works on central banks or finan-
    cial institutions that will extend credit to banks ex-
    periencing difficulties when other banks or financial
    institutions are no longer willing to do so.
    UF Last resort, Lenders of
    BT Banks and banking, Central
        Financial institutions
Lending
    USE Loans
Lending of library materials
    USE Libraries—Circulation, loans
Lending rights (Copyright law)
    USE Public lending rights (of authors)
Lenel family
    USE Linnell family
Leners family
    USE Lehnert family
Lenge language
    USE Chopi language
Lengel family *(Not Subd Geog)*
    UF Lengl family
        Lengle family
        Lingel family
Lengl family
    USE Lengel family
Lenglart family *(Not Subd Geog)*
    UF Englars family
        Englart family
        Englelars family
        Langlard family
Lengle family
    USE Lengel family
Lengley family
    USE Langley family
Length, Scattering (Nuclear physics)
    USE Scattering length (Nuclear physics)
Length, Standards of
    USE Standards of length
Length (Phonetics)
    USE Duration (Phonetics)
Length measurement *(May Subd Geog)*
    [QC102]
    UF Linear measurement
        Measurement of length
    BT Dimensions
        Mensuration
        Standards of length
    RT Area measurement
        Thickness measurement
    NT Cartometry
        Meter (Unit)
Length of classes
    USE Class periods

Length of pregnancy
    USE Pregnancy—Duration
Length of school day
    USE School day
Length of stay in hospitals
    USE Hospital utilization—Length of stay
Lengua Indians
    [F2679]
    BT Indians of South America
Lengua-Mascoi language
    [PM6351]
    UF Ençlĩt language
        Enenslet language
        Machicui language
        Mascoi language
    BT Indians of South America—Paraguay—
        Languages
        Paraguay—Languages
Lengyel culture
    USE Lengyel-Jordansmühl complex
Lengyel-Jordansmühl complex
    (May Subd Geog)
    [GN776.2.L4]
    UF Jordansmühl culture
        Lengyel culture
Lenhart family
    USE Leonard family
Lenhert family
    USE Leonard family
**Lenin, Vladimir Ilích, 1870-1924, in motion
pictures**
    [PN19195.9.L46]
    BT Moving-pictures
Lenin Prize for Literature
    USE Leninskaia premiia v oblasti literatury
Lenin prizes
    RT Stalin prizes
Lenin Shipyard Strike, Gdańsk, Poland, 1980
    USE Stocznia Gdańska im. Lenina Strike,
        Gdańsk, Poland, 1980
Leningrad (R.S.F.S.R.)
— History
— — To 1917
— — **Revolution of 1905**
— — 1917-
— — **Revolution, 1917-1921**
        (Not Subd Geog)
Leninism
    USE Communism
Lenino, Battle of, 1943
    BT World War, 1939-1945—Campaigns—
        Byelorussian S.S.R.
Leninskaia premiia v oblasti literatury
    UF Lenin Prize for Literature
    BT Literary prizes
        Russian literature—Competitions
Lenition (Phonetics)
    USE Mutation (Phonetics)
Leniwka River (Poland)
    USE Vistula River (Poland)
Lenje (African people)
    UF Balenje (African people)
        Benimukuni (African people)
        Ciina Mukuna (African people)
    BT Ethnology—Zambia
        Ila (African people)
Lenje language
    [PL8453]
    UF Bwine-Mukuni language
        Ci-Renje language
    BT Bantu languages
        Tonga language (Zambesi)
Lennard family
    USE Leonard family
Lennartz family
    USE Lennarz family
Lennarz family *(Not Subd Geog)*
    UF Lennartz family
Lennerd family
    USE Leonard family

Lenni Lenape
    USE Delaware Indians
Lenni Lenape language
    USE Delaware language
Lennier family
    USE Lanier family
Lennoaceae
    [QK495.L528 (Botany)]
    BT Tubiflorae
Lennon family *(Not Subd Geog)*
    UF Lenon family
    RT Leinan family
Lennox, Bill (Fictitious character)
    UF Bill Lennox (Fictitious character)
    BT Characters and characteristics in
        literature
    RT Ballard, Todhunter, 1903-   —
        Characters—Bill Lennox
Leno gi-nasu (Artificial language)
    BT Languages, Artificial
Lenon family
    USE Lennon family
Lenord family
    USE Leonard family
Lenormand family *(Not Subd Geog)*
Lenothrix
    USE Rattus
Lens, Crystalline
    USE Crystalline lens
Lens antennas
    [TK7871.6]
    BT Antennas (Electronics)
    NT Microwave lenses
Lens implantation
    USE Intraocular lenses
Lens mechanisms
    USE Lens mounts
Lens mounts
    UF Lens mechanisms
        Mounts, Lens
    BT Instrument manufacture
Lenses
    [QB85-QB135 (Astronomical
        instruments)]
    [QC385 (Optics)]
    UF Aberration, Chromatic and spherical
        Chromatic aberration (Optics)
    BT Optical instruments
    NT Achromatism
        Acoustic lenses
        Aspherical lenses
        Catadioptric systems
        Converging lenses
        Electromagnetic lenses
        Electrostatic lenses
        Fresnel lenses
        Gas lenses
        Glass, Optical
        Gravitational lenses
        Hand lenses
        Magnetic lenses
        Ophthalmic lenses
        Plastic lenses
Lenses, Contact
    USE Contact lenses
Lenses, Hand
    USE Hand lenses
Lenses, Microwave
    USE Microwave lenses
Lenses, Photographic
    [TR270]
    UF Camera lenses
        Photographic lenses
        Photography—Lenses
    BT Photographic optics
        Photography
        Photography—Apparatus and supplies
    NT Telephoto lenses
        Zoom lenses
Lenses, Pocket
    USE Hand lenses

Lenses, Zoom
USE Zoom lenses
Lensink family (Not Subd Geog)
UF Van Buren Lensink family
Lensless photography
USE Holography
Lent (May Subd Geog)
  ⌈BV85-95⌉
BT Church year
Fasts and feasts
NT Ash Wednesday
Easter
Holy Week
Jesus Christ—Passion
Lenten sermons
— Hymns
USE Lenten hymns
— **Prayer-books and devotions**
  ⌈BV85⌉
  ⌈BX2170.L4 (Catholic)⌉
— — **French, ⌈German, Italian, etc.⌉**
— Songs and music
USE Lenten music
Lenten hymns
UF Lent—Hymns
BT Hymns
RT Lenten music
Lenten menus
  ⌈TX739⌉
  ⌈TX837 (With recipes)⌉
UF Ember-day menus
Fast-day menus
Friday menus
Meatless meals
BT Cookery
Cookery (Fish)
Menus
Lenten music
  ⌈M2088.L5⌉
  ⌈M2098.L5⌉
UF Lent—Songs and music
BT Church music
Sacred vocal music
RT Lenten hymns
NT Good Friday music
Holy-Week music
Passion-music
Lenten sermons
  ⌈BV4277⌉
    Here are entered sermons on any subject
preached during the season of Lent. Sermons limited
to the passion of Christ are entered under Jesus
Christ—Passion—Sermons.
UF Sermons, Lenten
BT Church year sermons
Lent
NT Holy-Week sermons
Lentibulariaceae
  ⌈QK495.L53⌉
UF Utriculariaceae
BT Tubiflorae
NT Utricularia
Lenticels
  ⌈QK648⌉
BT Botany—Anatomy
Botany—Morphology
RT Bark
Lenticular degeneration
USE Hepatolenticular degeneration
Lentils (May Subd Geog)
  ⌈QK495.L52 (Botany)⌉
  ⌈SB351.L55 (Vegetable)⌉
NT Cookery (Lentils)
Lentinus
  ⌈QK629.A4⌉
BT Agaricaceae
Lentinus edodes
  ⌈SB353.5.L46 (Culture)⌉
UF Cortinellus shiitake
Shanku
Shiitake

BT Mushrooms, Edible
Lentz family (Not Subd Geog)
UF Lenz family
Lenz family
USE Lentz family
Lenz-Ising model
USE Ising model
LEO (Computer)
USE Leo computer
Leo computer
UF LEO (Computer)
Lyons Electronic Office computer
BT Electronic digital computers
Leo leo
USE Lions
Leo onca
USE Jaguars
Leo pardalis
USE Leopards
Leo tigris
USE Tigers
Leo uncia
USE Snow leopard
Leochilus
  ⌈QK495.O64 (Botany)⌉
BT Orchids
Leod family
USE Loud family
Leominster State Forest (Mass.)
  (Not Subd Geog)
BT Forest reserves—Massachusetts
Léon (France)
    Here are entered works on the region of Brittany
corresponding to the northwestern part of the dé-
partement of Finistère.
UF Pays de Léon (France)
Leon (Kingdom)
— History
— — **Ordoño III, 951-956**
  ⌈DP151.8⌉
León River (Colombia)
UF Río León (Colombia)
BT Rivers—Colombia
Leonard family (Not Subd Geog)
UF Leanard family
Leanhart family
Leanord family
Learnard family
Learned family
Learnhart family
Lehnhart family
Lenard family
Lenhart family
Lenhert family
Lennard family
Lennerd family
Lenord family
Leonerd family
Leonard Haag Site (Ind.) (Not Subd Geog)
UF Haag Site (Ind.)
BT Indiana—Antiquities
Leonardo, da Vinci, 1452-1519. Last Supper
UF Cenacolo (Mural)
Last Supper (Mural)
BT Last Supper in art
**Leonardo, da Vinci, 1452-1519. Savior of the
World**
UF Salvator Mundi (Painting)
Savior of the World (Painting)
Saviour of the World (Painting)
BT Jesus Christ—Art
**Leonardo, da Vinci, 1452-1519. Virgin with
the yarn winder** (Not Subd Geog)
UF Madonna dei fusi (Painting)
Virgin with Child (Painting)
Virgin with the yarn winder (Painting)
BT Painting, Italian
Leonardo da Vinci school
BT Art, Italian
Art, Renaissance—Italy
Artists' studios—Italy

Leonberg (Germany : Concentration camp)
  (Not Subd Geog)
  ⌈D805.G3⌉
BT Concentration camps—Germany
(West)
World War, 1939-1945—
Concentration camps
World War, 1939-1945—Prisoners and
prisons, German
Léonberg dog
USE Leonberger dog
Leonberger dog
  ⌈SF429.L45⌉
UF Léonberg dog
BT Dog breeds
Leonerd family
USE Leonard family
Leoni Montanari Palace (Vicenza, Italy)
USE Palazzo Leoni Montanari (Vicenza,
Italy)
Leontice leontopetaloides
USE Tacca leontopetaloides
Leontideus rosalia
USE Leontopithecus rosalia
Leontopithecus
  ⌈QL737.P92⌉
BT Callitrichidae
Leontopithecus rosalia
  ⌈QL737.P92⌉
UF Golden lion tamarin
Leontideus rosalia
Lion tamarin
Leontopodium
  ⌈QK495.C74⌉
BT Compositae
Leontopodium alpinum
USE Edelweiss
Leonurus
  ⌈QK495.L25⌉
BT Lamiaceae
NT Leonurus cardiaca
Leonurus cardiaca
  ⌈QK495.L25⌉
UF Motherwort
BT Leonurus
Leonza, María (Legendary character)
USE Lionza, María (Legendary character)
Leopard (Tank)
  ⌈UG446.5⌉
BT Mechanization, Military—Germany
(West)
Tanks (Military science)
Leopard 2 (Tank)
  ⌈UG446.5⌉
BT Tanks (Military science)
Leopard frog, Northern
USE Rana pipiens
Leopard frog, Plains
USE Plains leopard frog
Leopard hunting (May Subd Geog)
  ⌈SK305.L4⌉
BT Leopards
Leopard men
  ⌈GN495.2⌉
UF Human leopards
Leopard societies
Wereleopards
Werleopards
BT Metamorphosis—Folklore
Secret societies
Werewolves
Leopard moth
  ⌈QL561.C6⌉
UF Zeuzera pyrina
Leopard seal
UF Hydrurga leptonyx
Sea leopard
BT Seals (Animals)
Leopard societies
USE Leopard men

Leopardi family *(Not Subd Geog)*
　UF　Leopardo family
Leopardo family
　USE　Leopardi family
Leopards
　[QL737.C23]
　UF　Leo pardalis
　　　Panthera pardalis
　BT　Panthera
　NT　Clouded leopard
　　　Leopard hunting
　　　Leopons
Leopards as pets
　[SF459.L4]
Leopards in art
Leopold Bloom (Fictitious character)
　USE　Bloom, Leopold (Fictitious character)
Leopold II, Lake (Zaire)
　USE　Mai-Ndombe, Lake (Zaire)
Leopold-Lucas-Preis
　USE　Dr. Leopold-Lucas-Preis
Léopolda (Villefranche-sur-Mer, France)
　USE　La Léopolda (Villefranche-sur-Mer,
　　　　France)
Leopons
　BT　Hybridization
　　　Leopards
　　　Lions
Leotiaceae
　[QK623.L39]
　BT　Helotiales
　NT　Crocicreas
　　　Phaeofabraea
Lepadogaster
　[QL638.G6]
　UF　Lepadogasterus
　　　Lepidogaster
　BT　Clingfishes
Lepadogasterus
　USE　Lepadogaster
Lepanto, Battle of, 1571
　[DR516]
　UF　Cursolari, Battle of, 1571
　BT　Cyprian War, 1570-1571
　　　Turkey—History—1453-1683
Lepanto-Igorot dialect
　USE　Kankanay dialect
Lepcha Bible stories
　USE　Bible stories, Lepcha
Lepcha folk-songs
　USE　Folk-songs, Lepcha
Lepcha language
　[PL3801.L4]
　UF　Rong language
Lepcha poetry *(May Subd Geog)*
Lepchas
　[DS432.L4]
　UF　Rongs
Lepenski Vir Site (Serbia) *(Not Subd Geog)*
　BT　Yugoslavia—Antiquities
Leperditicopida
　[QE817.O8]
　BT　Ostracoda, Fossil
Lepers *(May Subd Geog)*
　BT　Chronically ill
　RT　Leprosy
　— Economic conditions
　　UF　Lepers—Socioeconomic status
　— Psychiatric care
　　BT　Leprosy
　　　　Psychiatry
　— Social conditions
　　UF　Lepers—Socioeconomic status
　— Socioeconomic status
　　USE　Lepers—Economic conditions
　　　　Lepers—Social conditions
Lepers' writings *(May Subd Geog)*
　UF　Writings of lepers
Lepers' writings, Japanese
　(May Subd Geog)
　UF　Japanese lepers writings

Lepibema chrysops
　USE　White bass
Lepidarbelidae
　USE　Cossidae
Lepidion
　[QL638.M67]
　UF　Haloporphyrus
　BT　Moridae
Lepidocephalus
　[QL638.C647]
　BT　Loaches
　NT　Lepidocephalus hasselti
Lepidocephalus hasselti
　[QL638.C647]
　BT　Lepidocephalus
Lepidochelys
　[QL666.C536]
　UF　Ridley sea turtles
　　　Ridley turtles
　BT　Cheloniidae
　NT　Lepidochelys olivacea
Lepidochelys olivacea
　[QL666.C536]
　UF　Olive loggerhead turtle
　　　Pacific ridley turtle
　　　Ridley turtle, Pacific
　BT　Lepidochelys
Lepidocybium
　[QL638.G4]
　BT　Gempylidae
Lepidocybium flavobrunneum
　[QL638.G4]
　UF　Escolar
　BT　Gempylidae
Lepidodactylus
　[QL666.L245]
　BT　Geckos
Lepidogaster
　USE　Lepadogaster
Lepidolite
　BT　Mica
Lepidophyma
　[QL666.L293]
　BT　Xantusiidae
Lepidophyma mayae
　[QL666.L293]
Lepidopidae
　USE　Trichiuridae
Lepidopsetta
　[QL638.P7]
　BT　Pleuronectidae
Lepidopsetta bilineata
　USE　Rock sole
Lepidoptera *(May Subd Geog)*
　[QL541-562]
　UF　Macrolepidoptera
　　　Microlepidoptera
　BT　Insects
　NT　Acanthopteroctetidae
　　　Acraeidae
　　　Acrolepiidae
　　　Agaristidae
　　　Alucitidae
　　　Anomologidae
　　　Argyresthiidae
　　　Bombycidae
　　　Brachodidae
　　　Butterflies
　　　Carposinidae
　　　Castniidae
　　　Caterpillars
　　　Choreutidae
　　　Clearwing moths
　　　Cochylidae
　　　Coleophoridae
　　　Cosmopterigidae
　　　Cossidae
　　　Ctenuchidae
　　　Dioptidae
　　　Drepanidae
　　　Elachistidae

　　　Epipyropidae
　　　Eriocraniidae
　　　Ethmiidae
　　　Gelechiidae
　　　Glyphipterygidae
　　　Gracillariidae
　　　Hepialidae
　　　Hesperiidae
　　　Holcopogonidae
　　　Immidae
　　　Incurvariidae
　　　Lasiocampidae
　　　Lecithoceridae
　　　Limacodidae
　　　Lycaenidae
　　　Lymantriidae
　　　Lyonetiidae
　　　Megathymidae
　　　Milkweed butterflies
　　　Mimallonidae
　　　Moths
　　　Neopseustidae
　　　Nepticulidae
　　　Notodontidae
　　　Nymphalidae
　　　Ochsenheimeriidae
　　　Oecophoridae
　　　Palaephatidae
　　　Papilionidae
　　　Pieridae
　　　Plutellidae
　　　Psychidae
　　　Pterophoridae
　　　Pyralidae
　　　Riodinidae
　　　Saturniidae
　　　Satyridae
　　　Scythridae
　　　Sphingidae
　　　Stenomidae
　　　Symmocidae
　　　Thyrididae
　　　Tineidae
　　　Tortricidae
　　　Uraniidae
　　　Xylorictidae
　　　Yponomeutidae
　　　Zygaenidae
　— Anatomy
　— Host plants
　— Larvae
　　USE　Caterpillars
Lepidoptera, Fossil
　[QE832.L5]
Lepidoptera diurna
　USE　Butterflies
Lepidoptera nocturna
　USE　Moths
Lepidosaphes
　[QL527.D5]
　UF　Lepidosaphis
　　　Mytilaspis
　BT　Diaspididae
Lepidosaphis
　USE　Lepidosaphes
Lepidosirenidae
　[QE852.D5]
　BT　Lung-fishes, Fossil
　NT　Monongahela (Fish)
Lepidosphaeria
　USE　Zopfia
Lepidospora
　[QL503.8.N5]
　BT　Nicoletiidae
Lepidosteiformes
　USE　Semionotiformes
Lepidotidae
　USE　Bramidae
Lepidozia grossiseta
　USE　Telaranea grossiseta

Lepidoziaceae
[QK555.L4]
 BT Jungermanniales
 NT Telaranea
Lepini Mountains (Italy)
 UF Monti Lepini (Italy)
 BT Mountains—Italy
Lepisma
[QL503.8.L4]
 BT Lepismatidae
 NT Silverfish (Insect)
Lepisma saccharina
 USE Silverfish (Insect)
Lepismatidae
[QL503.8.L4]
 BT Thysanura
 NT Lepisma
  Thermobia
Lepisosteiformes
 USE Semionotiformes
Lepisosteus
 USE Garpikes
Lepodidae
 USE Bramidae
Lepomis
[QL638.C3]
 BT Centrarchidae
Lepomis cyanellus
 USE Green sunfish
Lepomis gibbosus
 USE Pumpkinseed (Fish)
Lepomis gulosus
 USE Warmouth
Lepomis humilis
 USE Orangespotted sunfish
Lepomis macrochirus
 USE Bluegill
Lepomis microlophus
 USE Redear sunfish
Leporidae
[QL737.L32]
 Here are entered works on the family of rabbits. Works on the domestic rabbit are entered under Rabbits.
 BT Lagomorpha
 NT Hares
  Lepus
  Oryctolagus
  Pentalagus
  Rabbits
  Sylvilagus
Leposoma
[QL666.L285]
 BT Teiidae
Leposoma ioanna
[QL666.L285]
Leposoma percarinatum
[QL666.L285]
Leppard family
 USE Lippert family
Leppert family
 USE Lippert family
Leprechauns
 BT Fairies
Leprosariums
 USE Leprosy—Hospitals
Leprosy (May Subd Geog)
[QR201.L5 (Bacteriology)]
[RC154]
 UF Hansen's disease
 BT Mycobacterial diseases
 RT Lepers
 NT Lepers—Psychiatric care
  Missions to lepers
— **Diagnosis**
[RC154]
— **Hospitals** (May Subd Geog)
[RC154]
 UF Lazarettos
  Leprosariums
 BT Charities, Medical

— **Research** (May Subd Geog)
 UF Leprosy research
Leprosy in children (May Subd Geog)
[RJ406.L4]
 BT Bacterial diseases in children
Leprosy in the Bible
 UF Bible—Leprosy
 NT Healing of the ten lepers (Miracle)
Leprosy research
 USE Leprosy—Research
Lepscomb family
 USE Lipscomb family
Leptasea
 USE Saxifraga
Leptictidae
[QE882.I5]
 BT Insectivora, Fossil
 NT Leptictis
Leptictis
[QE882.I5]
 BT Leptictidae
Leptictis acutidens
[QE882.I5]
 UF Ictops acutidens
Leptidae
 USE Rhagionidae
Leptinidae
[QL596.L4]
 BT Beetles
 NT Leptinus
Leptinotarsa
[QL596.C5]
 BT Chrysomelidae
Leptinotarsa decemlineata
 USE Colorado potato beetle
Leptinus
[QL596.L4]
 BT Leptinidae
Leptinus testaceus
[QL596.L4]
Leptite
 USE Granulite
Leptobarbus
[QL638.C94]
 BT Cyprinidae
Leptobarbus hoeveni
[QL638.C94]
Leptocardia
 USE Cephalochordata
Leptocephali (Larvae)
 USE Leptocephalous larvae
Leptocephalidae
 USE Congridae
Leptocephalidae, Fossil
 USE Eels, Fossil
Leptocephalous larvae
[QL639.25]
 UF Leptocephali (Larvae)
 BT Fishes—Larvae
Leptocera
[QL537.S7]
 UF Limosina
 BT Sphaeroceridae
Leptocereus
 USE Cereus
Leptoceridae
[QL518.L48]
 BT Caddis-flies
 NT Setodes
Leptochela
[QL444.M33]
 BT Pasiphaeidae
Leptochilus
[QL568.E84]
 BT Eumenidae
Leptoclinum macdonaldi
 USE Diplosoma macdonaldi
Leptoconopidae
 USE Ceratopogonidae
Leptocoris
[QL523.C67]

 BT Coreidae
 NT Leptocoris trivittatus
Leptocoris trivittatus (May Subd Geog)
[QL523.C67]
 UF Box-elder bug
  Boxelder bug
 BT Leptocoris
Leptocottus
[QL638.C8]
 BT Cottidae
Leptocottus armatus
 USE Pacific staghorn sculpin
Leptocucares
 USE Neuromuscular depolarizing agents
Leptodactylidae
[QL668.E257]
 UF Southern frogs
 BT Anura
  Frogs
 NT Amblyphrynus
  Calyptocephalus
  Cyclorana
  Dischiodactylus
  Eleutherodactylus
  Leptodactylus
  Macrogenioglottus
  Niceforonia
  Phrynopus
  Pleurodema
  Syrrhophus
  Telmatobius
  Telmatobufo
  Trachyphrynus
Leptodactylus
[QL668.E257]
 BT Leptodactylidae
Leptodactylus hylaedactylus
[QL668.E257]
Leptodactylus knudseni
[QL668.E257]
Leptodactylus marmoratus
[QL668.E257]
Leptodactylus pentadactylus
[QL668.E257]
Leptodactylus pumilio
 USE Eleutherodactylus parvus
Leptodeira
[QL666.O636]
 UF Leptodira
 BT Colubridae
Leptodira
 USE Leptodeira
Leptodiridae
 NT Glacicavicola
Leptofoenidae
 USE Pteromalidae
Leptogastrinae
 USE Robber flies
Leptohylemia
[QL537.M8]
 BT Muscidae
Leptohylemia coarctata
 USE Wheat bulb fly
Leptolepiformes
[QE852.L45]
 BT Teleostei, Fossil
Leptology
 USE Crystallography
Leptolophus hollandicus
 USE Cockatiel
Leptome
 USE Phloem
Leptomeningitis
 USE Meningitis
Leptomerycidae
[QE882.U3]
 BT Artiodactyla, Fossil
 NT Leptomeryx
Leptomeryx
 BT Leptomerycidae

Leptomitaceae
  BT Leptomitales
Leptomitales
  ₍QK621.L44 (Botany)₎
  BT Oomycetes
  NT Leptomitaceae
Lepton interactions
  BT Leptons (Nuclear physics)
    Nuclear reactions
  NT Electron-electron interactions
    Electron-positron interactions
Lepton-nucleon scattering
  UF Nucleon-lepton scattering
  BT Collisions (Nuclear physics)
    Leptons (Nuclear physics)
    Particles (Nuclear physics)
    Scattering (Physics)
Lepton pair production
  USE Dilepton production
Lepton production
  USE Dilepton production
Leptonema (Insects) *(May Subd Geog)*
  ₍QL518.H94₎
  BT Hydropsychidae
Leptonereis
  ₍QL391.A6₎
  BT Nereidae
Leptonia
  ₍QK629.A4 (Botany)₎
  UF Leptoniella
  BT Agaricaceae
Leptoniella
  USE Leptonia
Leptons (Nuclear physics)
  ₍QC793.5.L42-429₎
  RT Fermions
  NT Dilepton production
    Electrons
    Lepton interactions
    Lepton-nucleon scattering
    Muons
    Neutrinos
    Positrons
    Quantum flavor dynamics
  — Decay
    ₍QC793.5.L425₎
  — Polarization
Leptonychotes
  ₍QL737.P64₎
  BT Seals (Animals)
Leptonychotes weddelli
  USE Weddell seal
Leptopanorpa
  ₍QL598.7.P3₎
  BT Panorpidae
Leptopelis
  ₍QL668.E244₎
  BT Hyperoliidae
Leptophis
  ₍QL666.O636₎
  BT Colubridae
Leptophlebiidae
  ₍QL505.3.L4₎
  BT Mayflies
  NT Choroterpes
    Thraulodes
Leptopodidae
  ₍QL523.L46₎
  BT Hemiptera
  NT Saldolepta
Leptosomatidae
  ₍QL391.N4₎
  BT Enoplida
  NT Deontostoma
Leptospirosis *(May Subd Geog)*
  BT Spirochaetosis
  NT Blackwater fever
    Weil's disease
Leptospirosis in animals *(May Subd Geog)*
  ₍SF809.L4₎
  BT Veterinary bacteriology

Leptostraca
  ₍QL444.L6₎
  UF Phyllocarida
  BT Crustacea
    Malacostraca
Leptostraca, Fossil
  ₍QE817.L5₎
Leptotaenia
  ₍QK495.U48₎
  BT Umbelliferae
Leptotaenia multifida
  ₍QK495.U48₎
Leptotila
  ₍QL696.C63₎
  BT Columbidae
  NT Gray-headed dove
Leptotila plumbeiceps
  USE Gray-headed dove
Leptotrombidium
  ₍QL458.2.T75₎
  BT Trombiculidae
Leptotyphlopidae
  ₍QL666.O65₎
  UF Blind snakes, Slender
    Glauconiidae
    Slender blind snakes
  BT Snakes
  NT Anomalepis
    Leptotyphlops
Leptotyphlops
  ₍QL666.O65₎
  BT Leptotyphlopidae
Leptotyphlops humilis
  ₍QL666.O65₎
Leptozancla
  ₍QL561.T55₎
  UF Philagrias
  BT Tineidae
Lepturidae
  USE Cerambycidae
Leptusa
  ₍QL596.S75₎
  BT Staphylinidae
Lepus
  ₍QL737.L32₎
  BT Leporidae
  NT Black-tailed jackrabbit
Lepus californicus
  USE Black-tailed jackrabbit
Lepus europaeus
  USE European hare
Lequier family
  USE Quier family
Ler, King (Legendary character)
  USE Lear, King (Legendary character)
Lerberg family
  USE Lerberghe family
Lerberghe family *(Not Subd Geog)*
  UF Lerberg family
    Van Lerberghe family
Lerchenborg (Denmark)
  BT Manors—Denmark
Lere dialect
  USE Lele dialect
Lereaux family
  USE Larue family
Lerentz family
  USE Lorenz family
Lerew family
  USE Larue family
Lérins Islands (France)
  UF Iles de Lérins (France)
  BT Islands—France
Lerm Castle (Lerm-et-Musset, France)
  USE Château de Lerm (Lerm-et-Musset,
    France)
Lernaeidae
  NT Peniculus
    Peroderma
Lernen (The German word)
  BT German language—Etymology

Leros, Battle of, 1943
  BT World War, 1939-1945—Campaigns—
    Greece
Lerry family
  USE Leary family
Leru family
  USE Larue family
Lerue family
  USE Larue family
Les Calanques (France)
  USE Calanques (France)
Les Cévennes (France)
  USE Cévennes Mountains (France)
Les Chenaux (Québec)
  USE Saint Maurice River (Québec)
Les Cheneaux Islands (Mich.)
  UF Cheneaux Islands (Mich.)
  BT Islands—Michigan
Les Garrigues Region (Spain)
  USE Garrigues Region (Spain)
Les Glénans (France)
  USE Glénan Islands (France)
Les Landes (France)
  USE Landes (France)
Les Voirons (France)
  USE Voirons (France)
Les Vosges (France)
  USE Vosges Mountains (France)
Lesaicherre family
  USE Le Saicherre family
Lesbian couples *(May Subd Geog)*
  UF Couples, Lesbian
    Homosexual couples, Female
  BT Homosexual couples
    Lesbians
Lesbian love
  USE Lesbianism
Lesbian mothers *(May Subd Geog)*
  ₍HQ75.53₎
  BT Homosexual parents
    Lesbians
    Mothers
Lesbian nuns *(May Subd Geog)*
  UF Nuns, Lesbian
  BT Lesbians
    Nuns
Lesbianism *(May Subd Geog)*
  UF Homosexuality, Female
    Lesbian love
  BT Homosexuality
    Sex
    Women—Sexual behavior
  NT Lesbians
  — History
  — — To 500
  — Religious aspects
  — — Baptists, ₍Catholic Church, etc.₎
  — — Buddhism, ₍Christianity, etc.₎
Lesbians *(May Subd Geog)*
  ₍HQ75.2₎
  ₍HQ75.5₎
  UF Female homosexuals
    Gays, Female
    Homosexuals, Female
    Women homosexuals
  BT Homosexuals
    Lesbianism
  NT Abused lesbians
    Aged lesbians
    Lesbian couples
    Lesbian mothers
    Lesbian nuns
    Sex instruction for lesbians
    Social work with lesbians
  — Travel *(May Subd Geog)*
Lesbians, Afro-American
  USE Afro-American lesbians
Lesbians' writings *(May Subd Geog)*
  UF Writings of lesbians
  BT Homosexuals' writings

Lesbians' writings, American
(May Subd Geog)
UF American lesbians' writings
BT American literature
Lesbos Island (Greece)
UF Lésvos Island (Greece)
Metelino Island (Greece)
Midilli Island (Greece)
Midillu Island (Greece)
Mitilini Island (Greece)
Mytilēnē Island (Greece)
Mytilini Island (Greece)
Nísos Lésvos (Greece)
BT Aegean Islands (Greece and Turkey)
Islands—Greece
Lešće Springs (Croatia)
UF Lešće Toplice (Croatia)
Toplo Kupalište Lešće (Croatia)
BT Springs—Yugoslavia
Lešće Toplice (Croatia)
USE Lešće Springs (Croatia)
Lesch family
USE Lesh family
Lesch-Nyhan syndrome (May Subd Geog)
[RJ399.L47]
UF Hypoxanthine-guanine
phosphoribosyltransferase deficiency
Hypoxanthine phosphoribosyltransf
erase deficiency
BT Brain—Diseases
Hyperuricemia
Mental retardation
Metabolism, Inborn errors of
Syndromes in children
Lesche (Delphi)
USE Cnidian Lesche (Delphi)
Lesche family
USE Lesh family
Leschenault Peninsula (W.A.)
BT Peninsulas—Australia
Lescher family
USE Lesher family
Leschi (Seattle, Wash.) (Not Subd Geog)
UF Seattle (Wash.). Leschi
Lescum family
USE Lipscomb family
Lese language
USE Balese language
Lese majesty (May Subd Geog)
UF Crimen laesae majestatis
Laesa majestas
Leze majesty
BT Political crimes and offenses
Leser family (Not Subd Geog)
Lesghian language
USE Lezghian language
Lesghians
USE Lezghians
Lesh family (Not Subd Geog)
UF Lesch family
Lesche family
Loesch family
Loesche family
Leshenotsky family (Not Subd Geog)
Lesher family (Not Subd Geog)
UF Lescher family
RT Lasher family
Le Sueur family
Lozier family
Lesion (Canon law)
Lesion (Law) (May Subd Geog)
UF Laesio enormis
BT Contracts
Rescission (Law)
NT Immoral contracts
Undue influence
Lesion (Roman law)
Lesions, Precancerous
USE Precancerous conditions
Leslee family
USE Leslie family

Lesley family
USE Leslie family
Leslie family (Not Subd Geog)
UF Lasley family
Laslie family
Lassley family
Leslee family
Lesley family
Lesly family
Lessle family
Lessley family
Lessly family
Leslie's Retreat, 1775
[E216]
BT United States—History—Revolution,
1775-1783—Campaigns
Lesly family
USE Leslie family
Lesotho
UF Basutoland
— **Economic conditions**
— — **To 1966**
— — **1966-**
— **History**
— — **To 1966**
NT Sotho-Free State War, 1865-
1866
— — **1966-**
— **Politics and government**
— — **To 1966**
— — **1966-**
— **Social conditions**
— — **1966-**
Lesothosuchus
[QE862.C8]
BT Protosuchidae
Lesothosuchus charigi
[QE862.C8]
Lespedeza
UF Bush clover
Japan clover
BT Forage plants
Lespedeza as feed
Less developed countries
USE Developing countries
Lesseps family (Not Subd Geog)
Lesser anteaters
USE Tamandua
Lesser Antilles
USE Antilles, Lesser
Lesser black-backed gull
UF Larus fuscus
BT Gulls
Lesser bud moth
USE Recurvaria nanella
Lesser bushbaby
[QL737.P955]
UF Bushbaby, Lesser
Galago senegalensis
Senegal bushbaby
Lesser earless lizard
USE Holbrookia maculata
Lesser Eastern Orthodox churches
USE Oriental Orthodox churches
Lesser Himalaya Mountains
UF Inner Himalaya Mountains
Lower Himalaya Mountains
Middle Himalaya Mountains
BT Himalaya Mountains
Mountains—Asia
Lesser kestrel
[QL696.A2]
UF Falco naumanni
BT Falcons
Lesser mouse lemur
USE Microcebus murinus
Lesser purple emperor butterfly
[QL561.N9]
UF Apatura ilia
Purple emperor butterfly, Lesser

Lesser Slave Lake (Alta.)
BT Lakes—Alberta
Lesser spotted dogfish
USE Scyliorhinus canicula
Lesser Sunda Islands (Indonesia)
USE Sunda Islands, Lesser (Indonesia)
Lesser vehicle (Buddhism)
USE Hinayana Buddhism
Lesser whitethroat
[QL696.P279]
UF Sylvia curruca
Whitethroat, Lesser
BT Sylvia (Bird)
Lesser yellowlegs
[QL696.C48]
UF Totanus flavipes
Tringa flavipes
Yellowlegs, Lesser
Lessin family (Not Subd Geog)
Lessini Mountains (Italy)
UF Monti Lessini (Italy)
BT Mountains—Italy
Lessle family
USE Leslie family
Lessley family
USE Leslie family
Lessly family
USE Leslie family
Lesson planning (May Subd Geog)
BT Education—Curricula
Planning
Teaching
Lessoniaceae (May Subd Geog)
[QK569.L53 (Algology)]
BT Laminariales
NT Macrocystis
Nereocystis
Lessor rorqual
USE Balaenoptera acutorostrata
Lestevenon family (Not Subd Geog)
Lestocart family
USE Ledogar family
Lestodon
BT Sloths, Fossil
Lestoquart family
USE Ledogar family
Lesueur family
USE Le Sueur family
Lesure family
USE Le Sueur family
Lésvos Island (Greece)
USE Lesbos Island (Greece)
Letbetter family
USE Ledbetter family
Letchworth State Park (N.Y.)
(Not Subd Geog)
BT Parks—New York (State)
Lethal gene
USE Lethal mutation
Lethal mutation
UF Gene, Lethal
Lethal gene
BT Mutation (Biology)
Lethenteron
[QL638.25.P48]
BT Lampreys
Petromyzonidae
Lethenteron alaskense
[QL638.25.P48]
Lethenteron meridionale
USE Gulf brook lamprey
Letherberry family
USE Leatherbury family
Letherbury family
USE Leatherbury family
Lethocerus
[QL523.B4]
BT Belostomatidae
NT Lethocerus indicus
Lethocerus indicus (May Subd Geog)
[QL523.B4]

BT Lethocerus
Lethrinidae
   [QL638.L48]
   UF Monotaxidae
        Neolethrinidae
   BT Perciformes
   NT Lethrinus
Lethrinops
   [QL638.C55]
   BT Cichlidae
Lethrinus
   [QL638.L48]
   BT Lethrinidae
Lethrinus rubriopercalatus
   [QL638.L48]
Leticia Dispute, 1932-1934
   BT Colombia—Boundaries—Peru
        Colombia—Foreign relations—Peru
        Peru—Boundaries—Colombia
        Peru—Foreign relations—Colombia
   NT Puca-Urco, Peru, Battle of, 1933
Leto (Genre painting)
   USE Plastov, Arkadiĭ Aleksandrovich, 1893-
         1972. Summer
Letocard family
   USE Ledogar family
Letocart family
   USE Ledogar family
Letogart family
   USE Ledogar family
Letoum (Ancient city) *(Not Subd Geog)*
   BT Cities and towns, Ruined, extinct, etc.
         —Turkey
        Turkey—Antiquities
Letourneau family *(Not Subd Geog)*
Letson family
   USE Lett family
Lett family *(Not Subd Geog)*
   UF Ledson family
        Letson family
        Letteson family
        Letts family
        Lettsom family
        Lettson family
        Liddeson family
        Lidson family
        Litsen family
        Litson family
Letter carriers
   USE Postal service—Letter carriers
Letter mail handling
   UF Mail handling, Letter
   BT Postal service
   NT Mail sorting
Letter men's clubs, Varsity
   USE Varsity lettermen's clubs
Letter-pictures
   UF Calligraphic paintings
        Peinture lettriste
   BT Art, Modern—20th century
        Dadaism
        Futurism (Art)
        Lettrism
        Typewriter art
        Visual literature
        Visual poetry
   NT Concrete poetry
Letter services
   UF Addressing services
        Duplicating services
        Letter shops
        Mailing services
   BT Advertising
        Commercial correspondence
        Office management
   RT Mail preparation
   NT Copying processes
        Envelopes, Addressing of
        Mail receiving and forwarding services
Letter sheets, Air
   USE Aerogrammes

Letter shops
   USE Letter services
Letter-sound association
   USE Reading (Elementary)—Phonetic
         method
Letter spacing
   UF Letterspacing
        Spacing, Letter
   BT Lettering
        Printing, Practical—Make-up
        Type-setting
Letter-writing
   [BJ2100-BJ2115 (Etiquette)]
   [PE1481-PE1497 (English rhetoric)]
   Here are entered general works and works on
English letter-writing.
   UF Composition (Rhetoric)
        Correspondence
        Letter-writing, English
        Writing of letters
   BT Etiquette
        Rhetoric
        Sytle, Literary
   RT Letters
   NT Buddhist temple correspondence
        Church correspondence
        Circular letters
        Commercial correspondence
        Form letters
        Forms of address
        Genealogical correspondence
        Government correspondence
        International correspondence
        Legal correspondence
        Love-letters
        Pen pals
        Technical correspondence
   — **Religious aspects**
   — — **Buddhism,** *[Christianity, etc.]*
Letter-writing, Arabic
   UF Arabic letter-writing
Letter-writing, Chinese *(May Subd Geog)*
   [PL1275]
   UF Chinese letter-writing
Letter-writing, Classical
   UF Classical letter-writing
Letter-writing, English
   USE Letter-writing
Letter-writing, French *(May Subd Geog)*
   UF French letter-writing
Letter-writing, French, *[German, Italian, etc.]*
Letter-writing, German *(May Subd Geog)*
   UF German letter-writing
Letter-writing, Greek *(May Subd Geog)*
   UF Greek letter-writing
Letter-writing, Indic *(May Subd Geog)*
   UF Indic letter-writing
Letter-writing, Japanese *(May Subd Geog)*
   UF Japanese letter-writing
Letter-writing, Korean
   [PL927]
   UF Korean letter-writing
Letter-writing, Latin *(May Subd Geog)*
   [PA2317]
   UF Latin letter-writing
Letter-writing, Persian
   [PK6349]
   UF Persian letter-writing
Letter-writing, Political
   USE Political letter-writing
Letter-writing, Romanian *(May Subd Geog)*
   UF Romanian letter-writing
Letter-writing, Russian *(May Subd Geog)*
   [PG2483]
   UF Russian letter-writing
Letter-writing, Sindhi
   UF Sindhi letter-writing
Letter-writing, Tibetan *(May Subd Geog)*
   UF Tibetan letter-writing
Letter-writing, Turkish *(May Subd Geog)*
   UF Turkish letter-writing

Letter-writing, Urdu *(May Subd Geog)*
   UF Urdu letter-writing
Letter writing recreations *(May Subd Geog)*
   [GV1488]
   UF Mail recreations
        Postal games
        Postal recreations
   BT Amusements
        Creative activities and seat work
        Games
        Postal service
Letterer-Siwe disease
   UF Nonlipid histiocytosis
   BT Reticuloendotheliosis
Letterheads
   BT Business—Forms
        Commercial correspondence
        Industrial design coordination
        Stationery
Lettering *(May Subd Geog)*
   [NK3600-NK3640 (Art industries)]
   [T371 (Mechanical drawing)]
   [TT360 (Signs and show-cards)]
   UF Ornamental alphabets
   BT Decoration and ornament
        Mechanical drawing
        Painting, Industrial
   RT Alphabets
        Initials
        Sign painting
   NT Architectural inscriptions
        Filigree lettering
        Letter spacing
        Logotype
        Monograms
        Roman capitals (Lettering)
        Sepulchral monuments—Lettering
        Signs and signboards—Lettering
        Street names—Lettering
Lettering plans of freight-cars
   USE Railroads—Freight-cars—Markings
Lettermen's clubs, Varsity
   USE Varsity lettermen's clubs
Letters
   [PN4400 (History and criticism)]
   [PN6130-PN6140 (Collections)]
   UF Correspondence
   BT Biography
        Literature
        Privacy, Right of
   RT Letter-writing
   SA English letters; French letters; Latin
        letters; *and similar headings*
   NT Anonymous letters
        Canadian letters
        Colombian letters
        Cover letters
        English letters
        Epistolary fiction
        Epistolary poetry
        French-Canadian letters
        French letters
        Hate mail
        Imaginary letters
        Last letters before death
        Latin letters
        Love-letters
        Queries (Authorship)
        Thank-you notes
Letters, Cover
   USE Cover letters
Letters, Imaginary
   USE Imaginary letters
Letters, Papal
   [BX863]
   UF Papal letters
   BT Papal documents
Letters, Unclaimed
   USE Postal service—Unclaimed mail
Letters as a theme in literature
   USE Letters in literature

Letters in art
[L8219.L43]
Letters in literature
UF Letters as a theme in literature
Letters in manuscript
USE Autographs
Letters of credit (May Subd Geog)
[HG3745]
UF Bills of credit
Credit, Letters of
Letters of credit—Law and legislation
BT Drafts
Negotiable instruments
NT Documentary credit
Import credit
Money orders
Traveler's checks
— Conflict of laws
USE Conflict of laws—Letters of credit
— Law and legislation
USE Letters of credit
Letters of intent (May Subd Geog)
UF Intent, Letters of
BT Contracts, Preliminary
Letters of marque
USE Privateering
Reprisals
Letters of recommendation
USE Employment references
Letters of the alphabet
USE subdivisions Consonants and Vowels under names of languages
Alphabet
Letters patent (May Subd Geog)
BT Forms (Law)
Formularies (Diplomatics)
Letters rogatory (May Subd Geog)
[JX6608]
UF Rogatory letters
BT Evidence (Law)
Judicial assistance
Letters to the editor
USE Newspapers—Sections, columns, etc.—Letters to the editor
Letterspacing
USE Letter spacing
Letteson family
USE Lett family
Lettimore family
USE Latimer family
Lettin family
USE Latting family
Letting of contracts
USE Contracts, Letting of
Lettish . . .
USE subject headings beginning with the word Latvian
Lettow family (Not Subd Geog)
Lettres de cachet
[HV8204]
BT Arrest—France
Lettrism
[BH301.L4 (Aesthetics)]
BT Aesthetics
Art
Literature
Typewriter art
Visual poetry
RT Visual literature
NT Letter-pictures
Letts
USE Latvians
Letts family
USE Lett family
Lettsom family
USE Lett family
Lettson family
USE Lett family
Lettuce (May Subd Geog)
[SB351.L6]

UF Lactuca sativa
— **Diseases and pests** (May Subd Geog)
NT Downy mildew of lettuce
Lettuce mosaic disease
— **Fertilizers**
[S667.L4]
UF Lettuce—Fertilizers and manures
— Fertilizers and manures
USE Lettuce—Fertilizers
— **Varieties**
Lettuce, Effect of temperature on
Lettuce cabbage
USE Bok choy
Lettuce industry (May Subd Geog)
[HD9235.L4-42]
Lettuce mosaic disease
BT Lettuce—Diseases and pests
Lettuce opium
USE Lactucarium
Letuana language
USE Yahuna language
Leuangiua language
[PL6459]
UF Leueneuwa language
Luangiua language
Luaniua language
BT Polynesian languages
Leuca Cape (Italy)
USE Santa Maria di Leuca, Cape (Italy)
Leucadia Island (Greece)
USE Levkás Island (Greece)
Leucaena
[QK495.L52 (Botany)]
[SB317.L48 (Economic plants)]
BT Leguminosae
Leucaena glauca
USE Lead tree
Leucaena leucocephala
USE Lead tree
Leucapheresis
USE Leukapheresis
Leucas Island (Greece)
USE Levkás Island (Greece)
Leucaspoidae
USE Leucospididae
Leucemia
USE Leukemia
Leucenine
USE Mimosine
Leucenol
USE Mimosine
Leuch's anhydrides
USE Amino acid anhydrides
Leuchtenberg, Dukes of (Not Subd Geog)
UF Dukes of Leuchtenberg
BT Germany—Nobility
RT Beauharnais family
Leucichthys artedi
USE Lake herring
Leucine
BT Amino acids
Amino acids, Branched chain
NT Bestatin
Leucine aminopeptidase
BT Aminopeptidases
Leucinodes (May Subd Geog)
[QL561.P9]
BT Pyralidae
Leuciscus
[QL638.C94]
BT Cyprinidae
Leuciscus bergi
[QL638.C94]
Leuciscus cephalus
USE Chub, European
Leuciscus leuciscus
USE European dace
Leucite (May Subd Geog)
[QE391.L4 (Mineralogy)]
UF Amphigene

BT Feldspathoid
Silicates
Leuckart reaction
UF Leuckart thiophenol reaction
BT Chemical reactions
Leuckart thiophenol reaction
USE Leuckart reaction
Leucoagglutinins
UF Leuko-agglutinins
BT Agglutinins
Leucocasia
USE Colocasia
Leucocirca leucophrys
USE Willie wagtail
Leucocirca tricolor
USE Willie wagtail
Leucocyte adherence inhibition test
[QR187.L47]
UF Adherence inhibition test, Leucocyte
BT Cell adhesion
Immunodiagnosis
Leucocytes
Leucocyte culture test, Mixed
USE Lymphocyte culture test, Mixed
Leucocyte disorders
BT Blood—Diseases
Leucocytes
NT Chronic granulomatous disease
Leucocytosis
Leucopenia
Leucocyte locomotion
USE Leucocytes—Motility
Leucocyte motility
USE Leucocytes—Motility
Leucocyte transfer factor
USE Transfer factor (Immunology)
Leucocytes
[QP95]
UF Leukocytes
White blood cells
White cells
BT Blood cells
Killer cells
NT Basophil leucocytes
Eosinophiles
Granulocytes
Leucocyte adherence inhibition test
Leucocyte disorders
Leukapheresis
Leukolysins
Lymphocytes
Monocytes
Neutrophils
Radiolabeled leucocytes
— **Motility**
UF Leucocyte locomotion
Leucocyte motility
Locomotion of leucocytes
Motility of leucocytes
Leucocytes, Granular
USE Granulocytes
Leucocytes, Nongranular
USE Lymphocytes
Monocytes
Leucocythemia
USE Leukemia
Leucocytosis
[RB145]
BT Leucocyte disorders
Suppuration
NT Eosinophilia
Leukemia
Monocytosis
Mononucleosis
Leucoderma
USE Albinos and albinism
Vitiligo
Leucodystrophy, Globoid cell
USE Leukodystrophy, Globoid cell
Leucodystrophy, Metachromatic
USE Leukodystrophy, Metachromatic

Leucoma salicis
  USE Satin moth
Leucomaines
  [QP801.P7]
Leucomidae
  USE Lymantriidae
Leuconostoc
  [QR82.S78]
  UF Betacoccus
  BT Streptococcaceae
Leuconostoc dextranicum
  [QR82.S78]
  UF Lactococcus dextranicus
     Streptococcus paracitrovorus
Leucopathy
  USE Albinos and albinism
Leucopenia
  [RC640]
  UF Hypoleucemia
     Hypoleucia
     Hypoleucocytosis
  BT Leucocyte disorders
  NT Agranulocytosis
     Preleukemia
Leucopenia, Malignant
  USE Agranulocytosis
Leucopheresis
  USE Leukapheresis
Leucopis
  BT Chamaemyiidae
Leucoplakia
  USE Leukoplakia
Leucopsar
  [QL696.P278]
  BT Mynahs
     Sturnidae
Leucopsidae
  USE Leucospididae
Leucoptera
  [QL561.L95]
  BT Lyonetiidae
Leucopterygidae
  USE Lyonetiidae
Leucorrhea
  [RG190]
  — Homeopathic treatment
     [RX471]
Leucosis
  USE Leukemia
Leucospidae
  USE Leucospididae
Leucospididae
  [QL568.L49]
  UF Leucaspoidae
     Leucopsidae
     Leucospidae
  BT Hymenoptera
Leucotermes flavipes
  USE Reticulitermes flavipes
Leucotomy
  USE Frontal lobotomy
Leucovorin
  USE Folinic acid
Leucoxene
  BT Titanium ores
Leuctra, Battle of, 371 B.C.
  [DF231.8]
  BT Greece—History—Spartan and Theban
     Supremacies, 404-362 B.C.
Leueneuwa language
  USE Leuangiua language
Leukádhia Island (Greece)
  USE Levkás Island (Greece)
Leukapheresis
  UF Leucapheresis
     Leucopheresis
     Leukopheresis
  BT Cell separation
     Hemapheresis
     Leucocytes

Leukas Island (Greece)
  USE Levkás Island (Greece)
Leukemia *(May Subd Geog)*
  [RC643]
  UF Leucemia
     Leucocythemia
     Leucosis
     Leukosis
  BT Anemia
     Cancer
     Leucocytosis
  RT Preleukemia
  NT Acute leukemia
     Leukemia, Hairy cell
     Lymphocytic leukemia
     Nonlymphoid leukemia
     Plasmacytic leukemia
  — Chemotherapy
  — Complications and sequelae
  — Diagnosis
  — Etiology
     UF Leukemogenesis
  — Genetic aspects
  — Immunological aspects
  — Psychological aspects
     BT Sick—Psychology
Leukemia, Acute
  USE Acute leukemia
Leukemia, Chronic lymphatic
  USE Chronic lymphocytic leukemia
Leukemia, Chronic lymphocytic
  USE Chronic lymphocytic leukemia
Leukemia, Chronic lymphoid
  USE Chronic lymphocytic leukemia
Leukemia, Experimental
  UF Experimental leukemia
  BT Oncology, Experimental
Leukemia, Feline
  USE Feline leukemia
Leukemia, Hairy cell *(May Subd Geog)*
  [RC643]
  UF Hairy cell leukemia
     Leukemic reticuloendotheliosis
  BT Leukemia
     Lymphoproliferative disorders
  RT Reticuloendotheliosis
Leukemia, Lymphoblastic
  USE Lymphoblastic leukemia
Leukemia, Lymphocytic
  USE Lymphocytic leukemia
Leukemia, Nonlymphoid
  USE Nonlymphoid leukemia
Leukemia, Plasmacytic
  USE Plasmacytic leukemia
Leukemia, Radiation-induced
  (May Subd Geog)
  UF Radiation-induced leukemia
  BT Radiation injuries
Leukemia in animals *(May Subd Geog)*
  [SF910.L4]
  NT Avian leukosis
     Bovine leukosis
     Feline leukemia
     Mouse leukemia complex
Leukemia in children *(May Subd Geog)*
  [RJ416.L4]
  BT Pediatric hematology
     Tumors in children
  NT Lymphoblastic leukemia in children
     Nonlymphoid leukemia in children
Leukemia in poultry
  USE Avian leukosis
Leukemia virus, Bovine
  USE Bovine leukemia virus
Leukemia virus, Feline
  USE Feline leukemia virus
Leukemic reticuloendotheliosis
  USE Leukemia, Hairy cell
Leukemogenesis
  USE Leukemia—Etiology

Leukemogenic viruses
  USE Retroviruses
Leuko-agglutinins
  USE Leucoagglutinins
Leukocytes
  USE Leucocytes
Leukoderma
  USE Vitiligo
Leukodystrophy, Globoid cell
  (May Subd Geog)
  UF Globoid cell leukodystrophy
     Globoid leukodystrophy
     Krabbe's disease
     Leucodystrophy, Globoid cell
  BT Cerebral sclerosis, Diffuse
     Mental retardation
     Sphingolipidoses
Leukodystrophy, Metachromatic
  (May Subd Geog)
  UF Leucodystrophy, Metachromatic
     Metachromatic leukodystrophy
     Sulfatide lipidosis
     Sulfatidosis
     Sulphatide lipidosis
     Sulphatidosis
  BT Cerebral sclerosis, Diffuse
     Mental retardation
     Sphingolipidoses
Leukoerythroblastic anemia
  USE Myeloid metaplasia
Leukokeratosis
  USE Leukoplakia
Leukolysins
  [QR185.8.L49]
  BT Cytokines
     Leucocytes
Leukopheresis
  USE Leukapheresis
Leukoplakia
  UF Leucoplakia
     Leukokeratosis
  BT Mucous membrane—Diseases
     Precancerous conditions
Leukoplakia, Oral
  UF Leukoplakia buccalis
     Leukoplakia lingualis
     Leukoplakia oris
     Oral leukoplakia
     Smokers' tongue
  BT Oral mucosa—Diseases
Leukoplakia buccalis
  USE Leukoplakia, Oral
Leukoplakia lingualis
  USE Leukoplakia, Oral
Leukoplakia oris
  USE Leukoplakia, Oral
Leukosis
  USE Leukemia
Leukosis, Avian
  USE Avian leukosis
Leukosis, Bovine
  USE Bovine leukosis
Leukosis, Mouse
  USE Mouse leukemia complex
Leukosis virus, Bovine
  USE Bovine leukemia virus
Leukotomy
  USE Frontal lobotomy
Leukotrienes
  [QP801.L47]
  UF Slow reacting substance of anaphylaxis
     SRS-A
  BT Arachidonic acid
     Inflammation—Mediators
     Unsaturated fatty acids
  — Synthesis
Leukoviruses
  USE Retroviruses
Leuresthes tenuis
  USE Grunion

Leurognathus
  [QL668.C274]
  BT Plethodontidae
Leuthen, Battle of, 1757
  [DD412.6.L6]
  BT Seven Years' War, 1756-1763
Leuthold family *(Not Subd Geog)*
Leutwiler family
  USE Leutwyler family
Leutwyler family *(Not Subd Geog)*
  UF Leutwiler family
Leutze, Emanuel, 1816-1868. Washington
  crossing the Delaware
  [ND237.L6]
  UF Washington crossing the Delaware
      (Painting)
  BT Painting, American
Lev (The Hebrew word)
  BT Hebrew language—Etymology
Levamisole
  [RM666.L]
  UF Tetrahydrophenylimidazothiazole
  BT Adjuvants, Immunological
      Anthelmintics
      Imidazole
      Immunotherapy
      Thiazoles
LeVan family *(Not Subd Geog)*
Levant
  USE Middle East
Levant vole
  USE Microtus guentheri
Levante Coast (Spain)
  USE Maresme (Spain)
Levavi oculos (Music)
  USE Psalms (Music)—121st Psalm
Levee districts *(May Subd Geog)*
  UF Dike districts
  BT Flood control
      Flood dams and reservoirs
      Special districts
Levees *(May Subd Geog)*
  [TC337 (Coast protection)]
  [TC533 (Rivers)]
  BT Embankments
      Hydraulic structures
  SA *subdivision* Levees *under names of*
      rivers
  NT Dikes (Engineering)
Levegood family
  USE Levengood family
Level-crossing spectroscopy
  [QC454.L58]
  BT Energy levels (Quantum mechanics)
      Spectrum analysis
      Zeeman effect
  NT Hyperfine structure
Level gages
  USE Level indicators
Level indicators
  UF Level gages
  BT Gages
  NT Hydrostatic leveling
      Liquid level indicators
Level nets
  USE Nets (Geodesy)
Level of aspiration
  UF Aspiration level
  BT Achievement motivation
  NT Student aspirations
Leveling *(May Subd Geog)*
  [TA606-610]
  UF Spirit leveling
  BT Altitudes—Measurement
      Barometric hypsometry
  RT Surveying
  NT Bench-marks
      Hydrostatic leveling
      Levels (Surveying instruments)
      Nets (Geodesy)

Levellers
  [DA405]
  UF Diggers
Levels (Surveying instruments)
  BT Leveling
  NT Boning rod
      Hydrostatic leveling
Levengood family *(Not Subd Geog)*
  UF Lebegood family
      Leibenguth family
      Levegood family
      Levingood family
      Liebenguth family
      Lovinggood family
      Lovingood family
Levens family
  USE Leavens family
Levensohn family
  USE Levinson family
Levenson family
  USE Levinson family
Leveque family
  USE Levesque family
Lever action rifles
  USE Leveraction rifles
Leveraction rifles
  [TS536.6.L48]
  UF Lever action rifles
      Rifles, Leveraction
  BT Rifles
Leveraged buyouts
  UF Buyouts, Leveraged
  BT Consolidation and merger of
      corporations
  NT Management buyouts
  — **Law and legislation** *(May Subd Geog)*
  — **Taxation** *(May Subd Geog)*
  — — **Law and legislation**
      (May Subd Geog)
Leverrierite
  [QE391.L]
  BT Silicates
Levers
  BT Power transmission
      Simple machines
Leveson-Gower family
  USE Gower family
Levesque family *(Not Subd Geog)*
  UF Leveque family
Lévezou (France)
  UF Lévezou Range (France)
  BT Mountains—France
Lévezou Range (France)
  USE Lévezou (France)
Levi-Lorian dwarfism
  USE Dwarfism, Pituitary
Leviathan
  BT Dragons in the Bible
Levies en masse
  UF Levy en masse
  BT Combatants and noncombatants
      (International law)
      War (International law)
Levin Site (Ill.) *(Not Subd Geog)*
  BT Illinois—Antiquities
Levingood family
  USE Levengood family
Levinsen family
  USE Levinson family
Levinson family *(Not Subd Geog)*
  UF Levensohn family
      Levenson family
      Levinsen family
Levirate
  BT Marriage (Hindu law)
      Marriage (Jewish law)
  NT Ḥalitsah
Levis
  USE Jeans (Clothing)
Levitation
  [BF1385]

  BT Psychokinesis
      Spiritualism
Levites
  NT Korahites
Levkás Island (Greece)
  UF Amaxíkhi Island (Greece)
      Leucadia Island (Greece)
      Leucas Island (Greece)
      Leukádhia Island (Greece)
      Leukas Island (Greece)
      Nísos Levkás (Greece)
      Santa Maura Island (Greece)
  BT Ionian Islands (Greece)
      Islands—Greece
Levodopa
  USE Dopa
Levon family *(Not Subd Geog)*
Levu (Fiji)
  USE Viti Levu (Fiji)
Levulose
  [QD321]
  UF Laevulose
Levy en masse
  USE Levies en masse
Levy on capital
  USE Capital levy
Lewallen family
  USE Llewellyn family
Lewellen family
  USE Llewellyn family
Lewellin family
  USE Llewellyn family
Lewelling family
  USE Llewellyn family
Lewellyn family
  USE Llewellyn family
Lewes, Eng., Battle of, 1264
  USE Lewes (East Sussex), Battle of, 1264
Lewes (East Sussex), Battle of, 1264
  UF Lewes, Eng., Battle of, 1264
  BT Great Britain—History—Barons' War,
      1263-1267—Campaigns
Lewes family
  USE Lewis family
Lewis, Lesley
  — **Homes and haunts**
      NT Pilgrims' Hall (Essex)
Lewis, Isle of (Scotland)
  USE Lewis with Harris Island (Scotland)
Lewis blood group system
  USE Blood groups—Lewis system
Lewis Cass Expedition, 1820
  BT Northwest, Old—History—1775-1865
Lewis Creek (Vt.)
  BT Rivers—Vermont
Lewis family *(Not Subd Geog)*
  UF Lewes family
      Louis family
Lewis machine-gun
  [UF620.L5]
  BT Machine-guns
Lewis Pass Highway (N.Z.)
  (Not Subd Geog)
  BT Roads—New Zealand
Lewis-Weber Site (Tucson, Ariz.)
  (Not Subd Geog)
  UF Weber-Lewis Site (Tucson, Ariz.)
  BT Arizona—Antiquities
      Ranch houses—Arizona
Lewis with Harris Island (Scotland)
  (Not Subd Geog)
  UF Harris Island (Scotland)
      Isle of Lewis (Scotland)
      Lewis, Isle of (Scotland)
  BT Islands—Scotland
      Western Isles (Scotland)
Lewis woodpecker
  [QL696.P5]
  UF Asyndesmus lewis
      Melanerpes lewis
  BT Woodpeckers

Lewisite (Poison gas)
  [QD412.A7 (Chemistry)]
  [UG447.5.L (Military science)]
  BT Gases, Asphyxiating and poisonous
Lewiston Railroad
  BT Railroads—United States
Lewisville, Lake (Tex.)
  USE Garza-Little Elm Reservoir (Tex.)
Lewy problem
  BT Differential equations, Partial
      Holomorphic functions
Lex Aquilia
  USE Torts (Roman law)
Lex commissoria (Foreclosure of pledge)
  USE Pledges (Law)
Lex commissoria (Rescission)
  USE Rescission (Law)
      Resolution (Civil law)
      Sales, Conditional
Lex Fabia
  USE Plagium
Lex Falcidia
  USE Legitime
Lex fori
  BT Conflict of laws—Jurisdiction
Lex Iulia peculatus
  USE Embezzlement (Roman law)
Lex Licinia
  USE Licinian laws
Lex loci delicti (May Subd Geog)
  BT Jurisdiction
  — Conflict of laws
      USE Conflict of laws—Lex loci delicti
Lex ribuaria
  USE Ripuarian law
Lex ripuaria
  USE Ripuarian law
Lex salica
  USE Salic law
Lex talionis
  UF Retaliation (Law)
  BT Revenge
  RT Vendetta
Lex talionis (Islamic law)
Lexden Tumulus Site (Colchester, Essex)
  (Not Subd Geog)
  BT England—Antiquities
Lexell's comet
  [QB723.L6]
Lexhy Castle (Lexhy, Belgium)
  USE Château de Lexhy (Lexhy, Belgium)
Lexical-functional grammar
  BT Generative grammar
Lexical grammar
  [P326]
  BT Generative grammar
      Grammar, Comparative and general
      Lexicology
Lexical tone (Phonetics)
  USE Tone (Phonetics)
Lexicographers (May Subd Geog)
  BT Lexicography
      Linguists
Lexicography (May Subd Geog)
  BT Encyclopedias and dictionaries
  SA subdivision Lexicography under names
      of languages and disciplines, e.g.
      English language—Lexicography;
      Science—Lexicography
  NT Encyclopedias and dictionaries—
      History and criticism
      Lexicographers
      Library science—Lexicography
      Mathematics—Lexicography
      Toponymy
      Translating and interpreting—
      Lexicography
  — Data processing
      BT Linguistics—Data processing

Lexicology
    Here are entered general works and works on
English lexicology. Works dealing with the lexicolo-
gy of other languages are entered under names of
specific languages, with subdivision Lexicology, e.g.
French language—Lexicology.
  UF English language—Lexicology
      Language and languages—Lexicology
  NT Calques
      Glottochronology
      Hapax legomenon
      Heteronyms
      Historical lexicology
      Lexical grammar
      Lexicostatistics
      Semantics
      Vocabulary
  — Data processing
      BT Linguistics—Data processing
  — Statistical methods
      USE Lexicostatistics
Lexicostatistics
  [P143.3 (Comparative linguistics)]
  [P326 (General)]
  UF Lexicology—Statistical methods
  BT Glottochronology
      Lexicology
      Linguistics—Statistical methods
Lexington, Battle of, 1775
  [E241.L6]
  BT Massachusetts—History—Revolution,
      1775-1783
      United States—History—Revolution,
      1775-1783—Campaigns
  — Anniversaries, etc.
LEXIS (Information retrieval system)
  BT Information storage and retrieval
      systems—Law
Lexow family (Not Subd Geog)
Ley family
  USE Lee family
Leydig cells
  UF Interstitial cells of Leydig
      Leydig's cells
      Testicular interstitial cells
  BT Cells
      Testis
Leydig's cells
  USE Leydig cells
Leydig's organ
  USE Eye, Parietal
Leyen family (Not Subd Geog)
  UF Von der Leyen family
Leyerla family
  USE Lyerly family
Leyland Atlantean bus
  USE Atlantean bus
Leyland buses
  UF Buses, Leyland
  BT Buses
  NT Atlantean bus
Leyland trucks
  [TL230.5.L]
  BT Trucks
Leylet . . .
  USE subject headings beginning with the
      word Laylat
Leys (May Subd Geog)
  UF Alignment of sites, Prehistoric
      Straight tracks, Prehistoric
      Trackways, Prehistoric
  BT Antiquities
Leyte Gulf (Philippines)
  BT Bays—Philippines
Leyte Gulf, Battle of, 1944
  USE Philippine Sea, Battles of the, 1944
Leyte Island (Philippines)
  BT Islands—Philippines
Leyte-Samar language
  USE Waray language

Leytean language
  USE Waray language
Leza River (Spain) (Not Subd Geog)
  UF Río Leza (Spain)
  BT Rivers—Spain
Lézay-Marnésia family (Not Subd Geog)
  UF Marnésia-Lézay family
Leze majesty
  USE Lese majesty
Lezghian language
  [PK9201.L5]
  UF Kuri language
      Kyuri language
      Lesghian language
      Lezgian language
      Lezgin language
  BT Daghestan languages
Lezghian literature (May Subd Geog)
Lezghian poetry (May Subd Geog)
Lezghians
  [DK34.L4]
  UF Lesghians
      Lezgins
  BT Ethnology—Caucasus
Lezgian language
  USE Lezghian language
Lezgin language
  USE Lezghian language
Lezgins
  USE Lezghians
LeZotte family (Not Subd Geog)
LFP System
  [Z699.4.L17]
  UF Library File Processing System
  BT Libraries—Automation
LH (Hormone)
  USE Luteinizing hormone
LH-releasing factor
  USE Luteinizing hormone releasing
      hormone
LH-RH
  USE Luteinizing hormone releasing
      hormone
Lhasa apsos
  [SF429.L5]
  UF Lhasa terrier
      Terrier, Lhasa
  BT Dog breeds
Lhasa He (China)
  USE Lhasa River (China)
Lhasa River (China) (Not Subd Geog)
  UF Kyi Chhu (China)
      Kyi Chu (China)
      Kyi River (China)
      Kyichu River (China)
      La-sa Ho (China)
      Lhasa He (China)
  BT Rivers—China
Lhasa terrier
  USE Lhasa apsos
      Tibetan terrier
Lherzolite
  [QE461]
Lhomi language (May Subd Geog)
  [PL3801.L54]
  BT Nepal—Languages
      Tibeto-Burman languages
Lhota language
  [PL4001.L5]
  UF Lotha language
      Tsöntsü language
  BT Naga languages
Lhotse (China and Nepal)
  UF E1 (Mountain) (China and Nepal)
      Lhotse II (China and Nepal)
      Lhotse Shar (China and Nepal)
      Lo-tzu-sha Feng (China and Nepal)
  BT Everest, Mount (China and Nepal)
      Mountains—China
      Mountains—Nepal

Lhotse II (China and Nepal)
USE Lhotse (China and Nepal)
Lhotse Shar (China and Nepal)
USE Lhotse (China and Nepal)
Li, Kung-lin, 1049-1106. Wei Mo-ch'i (Vimalakirti) in conversation with Wen Shu (Manjusri)
UF Wei Mo-ch'i (Vimalakirti) in conversation with Wen Shu (Manjusri) (Painting)
Wei Mo yen chiao t'u (Painting)
BT Mañjuśrī (Buddhist deity)—Art
Vimalakirti—Art
Li, Ssu-hsün, 651-716. Hanging gardens in spring
UF Hanging gardens in spring (Painting)
Hsüan p'u ch'un shen t'u (Painting)
BT Painting, Chinese
Li, Yü, 937-978
— Art
NT Chou, Wen-chü, 10th cent.
Emperor Li Yü of the Southern T'ang dynasty playing wei-ch'i
Li
[B127.L5]
BT Confucian ethics
Ethics, Chinese
Philosophy, Confucian
Li (Hainan people)
UF Loi (Hainan people)
Sheng-Li (Hainan people)
Shu-Li (Hainan people)
Li-cheng-wu Site (Hong Kong)
BT Hong Kong—Antiquities
Li-Ch'i-t'o-fan Shan (China)
USE Ch'i-lien Mountains (China)
Li language
[PL4251.L5]
UF Bê language
Org Bê language
BT Tai languages
Li River (China)
BT Rivers—China
Li Shan (China)
USE Lu Mountains (China)
Li-shu
USE Chinese language—Writing, Li style
Li Tzu ch'eng Rebellion, China, 1628-1645
USE China—History—Li Tzu ch'eng Rebellion, 1628-1645
Li-yü-t'an Dam (Taiwan)
BT Dams—Taiwan
Lia Fail
USE Stone of Scone
Liabilities (Accounting)
BT Accounting
NT Deferred credit
Deferred tax
Liability, Criminal
USE Criminal liability
Liability, Employers'
USE Employers' liability
Liability, Government
USE Government liability
Liability, Limited
USE Limited liability
Liability, Professional
USE Malpractice
Liability, Public
USE Government liability
Liability (Canon law)
Liability (Greek law)
Liability (Islamic law)
Liability (Jewish law)
Liability (Law) *(May Subd Geog)*
UF Accountability
Legal responsibility
Responsibility, Legal
Responsibility (Law)

BT Civil law
Contracts
Insanity—Jurisprudence
Obligations (Law)
RT Independent contractors
NT Abandonment (Maritime law)
Accident (Casus fortuitus)
Administrative responsibility
Criminal liability
Culpa in contrahendo
Dolus (Civil law)
Employers' liability
Government liability
Impossibility of performance
Indemnity against liability
Insurance, Liability
Liability for aircraft accidents
Liability for environmental damages
Liability for hazardous substances pollution damages
Liability for oil pollution damages
Liability for railroad accidents
Liability for school accidents
Liability for slip and fall accidents
Liability for traffic accidents
Liability for water pollution damages
Limited liability
Malpractice
Necessity (Law)
Negligence
Products liability
Proximate cause (Law)
Respondeat superior
Strict liability
Suretyship and guaranty
Tort liability of charitable organizations
Tort liability of corporations
Tort liability of highway departments
Tort liability of hospitals
Tort liability of insurance companies
Tort liability of parks
Tort liability of partnerships
Tort liability of recreation agencies
Tort liability of social service agencies
Tort liability of trade-unions
Tort liability of unincorporated societies
Tort liability of universities and colleges
Tort liability of works councils
Torts
Vis major (Civil law)
Warranty
— Conflict of laws
USE Conflict of laws—Liability
Liability (Roman-Dutch law)
Liability (Roman law)
Liability for aircraft accidents
(May Subd Geog)
UF Aircraft accidents, Liability for
Airplane accidents, Liability for
BT Accident law
Aeronautics—Accidents
Aeronautics—Law and legislation
Aeronautics, Commercial—Law and legislation
Liability (Law)
Strict liability
Torts
— Conflict of laws
USE Conflict of laws—Liability for aircraft accidents
Liability for animals *(May Subd Geog)*
BT Domestic animals—Law and legislation
Pets—Law and legislation
Strict liability
Torts

Liability for animals (Islamic law)
(May Subd Geog)
BT Islamic law
Liability for atomic damages
USE Liability for nuclear damages
Liability for building accidents
(May Subd Geog)
UF Building accidents, Liability for
Liability for unsafe buildings
BT Accident law
Liability for condition and use of land
Negligence
Torts
RT Architects—Malpractice
Engineers—Malpractice
Liability for condition and use of land
(May Subd Geog)
UF Land, Liability for condition and use of
Tort liability of landowners
Tort liability of possessors of land
BT Negligence
Torts
NT Attractive nuisance
Liability for building accidents
Premises liability
Liability for credit information
(May Subd Geog)
UF Credit information, Liability for
BT Business—Information services
Credit bureaus—Law and legislation
Libel and slander
Liability for environmental damages
(May Subd Geog)
UF Environmental damages, Liability for
BT Environmental law
Liability (Law)
Torts
NT Liability for flood damages
Liability for hazardous substances pollution damages
Liability for noise pollution damages
Liability for oil pollution damages
Liability for water pollution damages
— Conflict of laws
USE Conflict of laws—Liability for environmental damages
Liability for fire damages *(May Subd Geog)*
UF Fire damages, Liability for
Fire liability law
BT Arson
Fires
Negligence
Torts
Liability for flood damages
(May Subd Geog)
UF Flood damages, Liability for
BT Liability for environmental damages
Liability for hazardous substances damages
USE Toxic torts
Liability for hazardous substances pollution damages *(May Subd Geog)*
UF Hazardous substances pollution damages, Liability for
Liability for toxic substances pollution damages
Toxic substances pollution damages, Liability for
BT Accident law
Hazardous substances—Law and legislation
Liability (Law)
Liability for environmental damages
Liability for water pollution damages
Toxic torts
Liability for landslide damages
(May Subd Geog)
UF Landslide damages, Liability for
BT Negligence
Torts

Liability for marine accidents
(May Subd Geog)
  UF Marine accidents—Liability
  BT Accident law
      Admiralty
      Collisions at sea
  — Conflict of laws
      USE Conflict of laws—Liability for
           marine accidents
Liability for mine accidents
(May Subd Geog)
  UF Mine accidents—Liability
  BT Accident law
      Mining law
      Torts
Liability for noise pollution damages
(May Subd Geog)
  UF Noise pollution damages, Liability for
  BT Liability for environmental damages
Liability for nuclear damages
(May Subd Geog)
  UF Atomic damages, Liability for
      Liability for atomic damages
      Nuclear damages, Liability for
  BT Accident law
      Nuclear energy—Law and legislation
      Torts
Liability for oil pollution damages
(May Subd Geog)
  UF Liability for oil spill damages
      Oil pollution damages, Liability for
      Oil spill damages, Liability for
  BT Liability (Law)
      Liability for environmental damages
      Oil pollution of rivers, harbors, etc.—
        Law and legislation
      Oil pollution of the sea—Law and
        legislation
      Oil spills—Law and legislation
      Torts
  RT Oil spills—Claims
Liability for oil spill damages
  USE Liability for oil pollution damages
Liability for personal injuries
  USE Personal injuries
Liability for railroad accidents
(May Subd Geog)
  UF Railroads—Accidents—Liability
  BT Accident law
      Liability (Law)
      Railroad law
      Strict liability
      Torts
Liability for school accidents
(May Subd Geog)
  UF School accidents—Liability
  BT Accident law
      Educational law and legislation
      Government liability
      Liability (Law)
      Teachers—Legal status, laws, etc.
      Torts
  RT Tort liability of school districts
Liability for skiing accidents
(May Subd Geog)
  UF Skiing accidents, Liability for
  BT Accident law
      Liability for sports accidents
      Skis and skiing—Law and legislation
      Torts
Liability for slip and fall accidents
(May Subd Geog)
  UF Slip and fall accidents, Liability for
  BT Accident law
      Falls (Accidents)
      Liability (Law)
      Negligence
      Torts
Liability for space vehicle accidents
(May Subd Geog)
  UF Space vehicle accidents, Liability for

  BT Accident law
      Space law
      Torts
Liability for sports accidents
(May Subd Geog)
  BT Accident law
      Sports—Law and legislation
      Torts
  NT Liability for skiing accidents
Liability for toxic substances damages
  USE Toxic torts
Liability for toxic substances pollution damages
  USE Liability for hazardous substances
       pollution damages
Liability for traffic accidents
(May Subd Geog)
  UF Traffic accidents—Law and legislation
      Traffic accidents—Liability
  BT Accident law
      Liability (Law)
      Strict liability
      Torts
  RT Traffic violations
  NT Tort liability of highway departments
      Unsatisfied judgment funds (Traffic
        accidents)
  — Cases
      Here are entered civil cases. Criminal cases
      are entered under Traffic violations—Cases.
  — Conflict of laws
      USE Conflict of laws—Liability for
           traffic accidents
Liability for unsafe buildings
  USE Liability for building accidents
Liability for water pollution damages
(May Subd Geog)
  UF Water pollution damages, Liability for
  BT Liability (Law)
      Liability for environmental damages
      Torts
      Water—Pollution—Law and legislation
  NT Liability for hazardous substances
        pollution damages
Liability insurance
  USE Insurance, Liability
Liability of the state
  USE Government liability
Liability without fault
  USE Strict liability
Liadhrómia Island (Greece)
  USE Alónnisos Island (Greece)
Liaison psychiatry
  USE Consultation-liaison psychiatry
Liambliasis
  USE Giardiasis
Liang dynasty, 502-557
  USE China—History—Liang dynasty, 502-
       557
Liang language
  USE Liyang language
Liang Mountains (China)
  BT Mountains—China
Liangmai language
  USE Liyang language
Liao dynasty, 947-1125
  USE China—History—Liao dynasty, 947-
       1125
Liao He (China)
  USE Liao River (China)
Liao Ho (China)
  USE Liao River (China)
Liao River (China)
  UF Liao He (China)
      Liao Ho (China)
      Liao-whang-ho (China)
      Ta-liao-ho (China)
  BT Rivers—China
Liao-whang-ho (China)
  USE Liao River (China)
Liao-yang, Battle of, 1904
  [DS517]

  BT Russo-Japanese War, 1904-1905
LÍAPAS (Computer program language)
Liapunov functions
  UF Functions, Liapunov
      Lyapunov functions
  BT Differential equations
      Motion
      Stability
Liar antinomy
  USE Liar paradox
Liar paradox
  [BC199.P2]
  UF Antinomy of the liar
      Epimenidean paradox
      Liar antinomy
      Paradox of Epimenides
      Paradox of Russell
      Paradox of the liar
      Russell's paradox
  BT Logic
      Paradox
      Semantics (Philosophy)
  NT Insolubilia (Logic)
Liard River
  UF Mountain River
      River of the Mountains
  BT Rivers—British Columbia
      Rivers—Northwest Territories
      Rivers—Yukon Territory
Lias
  USE Geology, Stratigraphic—Jurassic
       Paleobotany—Jurassic
       Paleontology—Jurassic
Libations
  UF Drink offerings
  BT Drinking customs
      Religion, Primitive
      Sacrifice
Libbe family
  USE Libby family
Libbee family
  USE Libby family
Libbey family
  USE Libby family
Libbie family
  USE Libby family
Libby family (Not Subd Geog)
  UF Lebby family
      Libbe family
      Libbee family
      Libbey family
      Libbie family
Libel and slander (May Subd Geog)
  UF Calumny
      Defamation
      Slander (Law)
  BT Criminal law
      Freedom of speech
      Freedom of the press
      Personality (Law)
      Publicity (Law)
      Torts
  RT Press law
  NT Blasphemy
      Liability for credit information
      Privacy, Right of
      Privileged communications (Libel and
        slander)
      Right of reply
      Seditious libel
      Trials (Libel)
      Trials (Slander)
Libel and slander (Canon law)
Libel and slander (Ethics)
  USE Slander
Libel and slander (Roman-Dutch law)
Libel and slander (Roman law)
Libel and slander in art
  NT Apelles. Calumny
Libellulidae
  [QL520.3.L6]

2139

Libellulidae *(Continued)*
  UF Macrodiplactidae
  BT Dragonflies
    Odonata
  NT Diastatops
    Plathemis
    Sympetrum
    Trithemis
Libelluloidea
  USE Odonata
Libenge language
  USE Benge language
"Liber in deum" bottle
  USE Vaso borraccia di Salò
Liber Pater (Roman deity)
  BT Gods, Roman
    Mythology, Roman
  RT Dionysus (Greek deity)
Liber promissionum
  USE Profession (in religious orders,
    congregations, etc.)
Liberal (The German word)
  BT German language—Etymology
Liberal education
  USE Education, Humanistic
Liberal Judaism
  USE Reform Judaism
Liberal Party
  [JK2391.L (United States)]
Liberal Republican Party
  [JK2391.L78-82]
Liberal studies, Bachelor of
  USE Bachelor of liberal studies
Liberal theology
  USE Liberalism (Religion)
Liberalism *(May Subd Geog)*
  [HM276]
  BT Liberty
    Political science
    Social sciences
  NT Laissez-faire
    Libertines (French philosophers)
Liberalism (Religion) *(May Subd Geog)*
  [BR1615-BR1617 (Christianity)]
  UF Liberal theology
  BT Indifferentism (Religion)
  NT Haskalah
  **— Anglican Communion, [Catholic Church,
    Lutheran Church, etc.]**
  — Protestant churches
Liberate rolls
  [DA25]
Liberation
  USE Liberty
Liberation, Wars of, 1813-1814
  USE Wars of Liberation, 1813-1814
Liberation movements, National
  USE National liberation movements
Liberation movements (Civil rights)
  USE Civil rights movements
Liberation theology
  [BT83.57]
  UF Theology of liberation
  BT Freedom (Theology)
    Theology, Doctrinal
  NT Civil rights—Religious aspects—
    Christianity
Liberator, Statue of the (Caracas, Venezuela)
  USE Estatua del Libertador (Caracas,
    Venezuela)
Liberator (Bombers)
  USE B-24 bomber
Liberator pistol
  [UD413]
  UF Flare projector pistol
    FP-45 pistol
  BT Pistols
Liberia
  — Civilization
  —— American influences
      BT United States—Civilization

— Economic conditions
—— 1971-1980
—— 1980-
— History
—— To 1847
    [DT633]
—— 1847-1944
    [DT634]
—— 1944-1971
    [DT635]
—— 1971-1980
    [DT636.2]
—— Coup d'état, 1980
    [DT636.5]
    BT Coups d'état—Liberia
—— 1980-
— Languages
  NT Bassa language (Liberia)
    Dan language
    Gbandi language
    Gola language
    Grebo language
    Jabo language
    Kissi language
    Kono language
    Kpelle language
    Kru language
    Kru languages
    Loma language
    Mano language
    Southern Mande languages
    Tchien language
    Vai language
— Politics and government
—— To 1944
    [DT633-DT634.2 (History)]
    [JQ3920-JQ3929 (Political
     science)]
—— 1944-1971
    [DT635]
    [History]
    [JQ3920-3929 (Political science)]
—— 1971-1980
—— 1980-
— Social conditions
—— 1971-1980
—— 1980-
Liberian art
  USE Art, Liberian
Liberian fiction (English) *(May Subd Geog)*
  [PR9384]
  UF English fiction—Liberian authors
  NT Short stories, Liberian (English)
Liberian literature *(May Subd Geog)*
Liberian literature (English)
  (May Subd Geog)
  UF English literature—Liberian authors
Liberian poetry (English) *(May Subd Geog)*
  UF English poetry—Liberian authors
Liberian short stories (English)
  USE Short stories, Liberian (English)
Libertador, Estatua del (Caracas, Venezuela)
  USE Estatua del Libertador (Caracas,
    Venezuela)
Libertarian literature *(May Subd Geog)*
  BT Libertarianism
Libertarianism *(May Subd Geog)*
  RT Anarchism
    Individualism
    Liberty
  NT Libertarian literature
Liberté guidant le peuple (Painting)
  USE Delacroix, Eugène, 1798-1863
    Liberty leading the people
Libertinage
  USE Libertinism
Libertines (French philosophers)
  UF Libertins

  BT Free will and determinism
    Liberalism
    Philosophy, French
    Rationalism
Libertines (Spirituals)
  UF Spirituals (Libertines)
  BT Antinomianism
    Brethren of the Free Spirit
    Pantheism
Libertines in literature
  UF Dissolute persons in literature
    Licentious persons in literature
    Profligates in literature
    Rakes in literature
  BT Characters and characteristics in
    literature
Libertinism *(May Subd Geog)*
  UF Libertinage
Libertins
  USE Libertines (French philosophers)
Liberty
  [HM271 (Sociology)]
  [JC585-JC599 (Political theory)]
  UF Civil liberty
    Emancipation
    Freedom
    Liberation
    Personal liberty
  BT Democracy
    Natural law
    Political science
  RT Equality
    Libertarianism
    Social control
  NT Academic freedom
    Assembly, Right of
    Communism and liberty
    Conformity
    Freedom of association
    Freedom of movement
    Freedom of religion
    Liberalism
    Liberty of contract
    Life and death, Power over
    Socialism and liberty
Liberty (Islam)
  USE Freedom (Islam)
Liberty (Theology)
  USE Freedom (Theology)
Liberty as a theme in literature
  USE Liberty in literature
Liberty as a topic in art
  USE Liberty in art
Liberty at the barricade (Painting)
  USE Delacroix, Eugène, 1798-1863
    Liberty leading the people
Liberty diebreak errors
  USE Cent—Errors
Liberty enlightening the world (Statue)
  USE Statue of Liberty (New York, N.Y.)
Liberty in art
  UF Liberty as a topic in art
Liberty in literature
  UF Liberty as a theme in literature
Liberty Lake (Md.) *(Not Subd Geog)*
  UF Liberty Reservoir (Md.)
  BT Lakes—Maryland
    Reservoirs—Maryland
Liberty leading the people (Painting)
  USE Delacroix, Eugène, 1798-1863
    Liberty leading the people
Liberty of association
  USE Freedom of association
Liberty of conscience *(May Subd Geog)*
  [BV741]
  UF Intolerance
  BT Conscience
    Toleration
  NT Conscientious objectors
    Dissenters, Religious
    Public opinion

Liberty of conscience (Islam)
  [BP173.65]
Liberty of contract *(May Subd Geog)*
  UF Contract, Freedom of
      Contract, Liberty of
      Freedom of contract
  BT Liberty
  RT Contracts
  NT Prorogated jurisdiction
Liberty of employment
  USE Free choice of employment
Liberty of information
  USE Freedom of information
Liberty of occupation
  USE Free choice of employment
Liberty of religion
  USE Freedom of religion
Liberty of speech
  USE Freedom of speech
Liberty of speech in Judaism
  USE Freedom of speech in Judaism
Liberty of speech in the church
  USE Freedom of speech in the church
Liberty of testation
  USE Freedom of testation
Liberty of the press
  USE Freedom of the press
Liberty of the will
  USE Free will and determinism
Liberty on the barricade (Painting)
  USE Delacroix, Eugène, 1798-1863
        Liberty leading the people
Liberty Reservoir (Md.)
  USE Liberty Lake (Md.)
Liberty ships *(May Subd Geog)*
  UF EC-2 vessels (Ships)
      Ships, Liberty
  BT Cargo ships
Liberty trees
  UF Trees of liberty
  BT Historic trees
      Trees—Folklore
Libhart family
  USE Lippert family
Libinston family
  USE Livingston family
LIBMAINT (Computer program)
  [QA76.6]
  BT Electronic data processing—Batch
        processing
      Programmer Productivity System
        (Computer system)
Libman-Sacks disease
  USE Lupus erythematosus, Systemic
Libo (Indic people)
  USE Pailibo (Indic people)
Libocedrus
  [QK494.5.C975]
  BT Cupressaceae
  NT Incense cedar
LIBRA (Information retrieval system)
  [Z699.5.S3]
  BT Information storage and retrieval
        systems—Science
      Information storage and retrieval
        systems—Technology
Librarians *(May Subd Geog)*
  [Z682 (Personnel)]
  [Z720 (Biography)]
  BT Information scientists
      Library employees
  RT Libraries
  NT Afro-American librarians
      Catalogers
      Children's librarians
      College librarians
      Jewish librarians
      Librarians, Part-time
      Librarians, Physically handicapped
      Public librarians
      Reference librarians

School librarians
      Special librarians
      Women librarians
— **Certification** *(May Subd Geog)*
    [Z677]
    UF Certification of librarians
— Collective bargaining
    USE Collective bargaining—Librarians
— Congresses
    USE Library science—Congresses
— **Job descriptions**
    [Z682]
    UF Libraries—Job descriptions
— Personality
    USE Librarians—Psychology
— Personnel management
    USE Library personnel management
— **Professional ethics** *(May Subd Geog)*
    UF Library ethics
    BT Professional ethics
— **Psychology**
    UF Librarians—Personality
— **Recruiting**
— **United States**
    NT Asian American librarians
        Hispanic American librarians
        Oceanian American librarians
Librarians, Academic
  USE College librarians
Librarians, Afro-American
  USE Afro-American librarians
Librarians, Agricultural
  USE Agricultural librarians
Librarians, Area specialist
  USE Area specialist librarians
Librarians, Asian American
  USE Asian American librarians
Librarians, Business
  USE Business librarians
Librarians, Children's
  USE Children's librarians
Librarians, College
  USE College librarians
Librarians, Documents
  USE Documents librarians
Librarians, Education of
  USE Library education
Librarians, Government
  USE Government librarians
Librarians, Handicapped
  USE Librarians, Physically handicapped
Librarians, Hispanic American
  USE Hispanic American librarians
Librarians, Interchange of
  UF Interchange of librarians
      Interchange of library students
      International exchange of librarians
      Library students, Interchange of
  BT Exchange of persons programs
Librarians, Jewish
  USE Jewish librarians
Librarians, Law
  USE Law librarians
Librarians, Medical
  USE Medical librarians
Librarians, Oceanian American
  USE Oceanian American librarians
Librarians, Part-time *(May Subd Geog)*
  UF Part-time librarians
  BT Librarians
      Part-time library employees
Librarians, Physically handicapped
  (May Subd Geog)
  UF Handicapped librarians
      Librarians, Handicapped
      Physically handicapped librarians
  BT Librarians
      Physically handicapped
Librarians, Public
  USE Public librarians

Librarians, Reference
  USE Reference librarians
Librarians, School
  USE School librarians
Librarians, Special
  USE Special librarians
Librarians, Training of
  USE Library education
Librarians, University
  USE College librarians
Librarians, Volunteer
  USE Volunteer workers in libraries
Librarians in literature
Librarians' unions *(May Subd Geog)*
  BT Trade-unions
      Trade-unions—Library employees
Librarianship
  USE Library science
Librarianship, Comparative
  USE Comparative librarianship
Librarianship, International
  USE International librarianship
Libraries *(May Subd Geog)*
  [Z665-997]
  BT Documentation
      Public institutions
  RT Librarians
  SA *subdivision* Library *under names of*
        individual persons, families, and
        corporate bodies; also subdivision
        Libraries under names of individual
        corporate bodies; also headings
        beginnning with the word Library;
        and names of individual libraries
  NT Afro-Americans and libraries
      Audio-visual library service
      Bibliographical libraries
      Fiction in libraries
      Hispanic Americans and libraries
      Illegal libraries
      Imaginary books and libraries
      Libraries, International
      Libraries, Private
      Libraries, Proprietary
      Libraries, Rental
      Libraries, Special
      Libraries, Subscription
      Libraries, Traveling
      Libraries, University and college
      Public libraries
      Reference services (Libraries)
      Research libraries
      School libraries
      Small libraries
— Accession department
    USE Acquisitions (Libraries)
— Accounting
    USE Library finance
— Administration
    USE Library administration
        Library science
— Advertising
    USE Advertising—Libraries
— **Aims and objectives**
    BT Library administration
— Arrangement of books on shelves
    USE Classification—Books
        Shelf-listing (Library science)
— **Automation**
    [Z678.9]
    UF Library automation
        Mechanization of library processes
    RT Information storage and retrieval
          systems
    NT Geac (Computer system)
        KOBAS System
        LFP System
        MARC System
        MINICS project
        MONOCLE project
        SOKRATUS System

Libraries
— **Automation** (Continued)
        URICA (Computer system)
        UTLAS System
— Bibliographical searching
        USE Searching, Bibliographical
— Boards
        USE Libraries—Trustees
— Bookkeeping
        USE Bookkeeping, Library
— **Branches, delivery stations, etc.**
        [Z686]
        UF Branch libraries
             Libraries, Branch
        NT Bookmobiles
— Buildings
        USE Library buildings
— Catalogs
        USE Library catalogs
— **Censorship**
        UF Censorship in libraries
             Library censorship
        BT Censorship
— **Centralization**
        [Z678]
        UF Centralization of libraries
             Unified libraries
        NT Centralized processing (Libraries)
— Charging systems
        USE Charging systems (Libraries)
— Children's rooms
        USE Libraries, Children's
— **Circulation analysis**
        UF Circulation analysis in libraries
             Library circulation analysis
        BT Library use studies
— **Circulation, loans**
        [Z712]
        UF Book lending
             Books, Lending of
             Circulation of library materials
             Lending of library materials
             Library circulation
        RT Document delivery
        NT Book drops
             Charging systems (Libraries)
             Direct delivery of books
             Inter-library loans
             SLICE Project
— Classification
        USE Classification—Books
— Collection development
        USE Collection development
             (Libraries)
— Congresses
        USE Library science—Congresses
— **Cultural programs**
        [Z716]
        UF Cultural activities of libraries
             Cultural programs in libraries
             Library cultural programs
        BT Libraries and community
             Libraries and society
— Decoration
        USE Library decoration
— Duplicate books
        USE Duplicates in libraries
— Employees
        USE Library employees
— Exhibitions
        USE Library exhibits
— Federal aid
        USE Federal aid to libraries
— Finance
        USE Library finance
— Fines and fees
        USE Library fines and fees
— **Gifts, legacies**
        [Z689]

        BT Acquisitions (Libraries)
             Endowments
             Legacies
— **History**
        [Z721]
— — To 400
— — 400-1400
— — 1400-1600
— — 17th-18th centuries
— — 19th century
— — 20th century
— Information networks
        USE Library information networks
— **Insurance**
        [Z683.5]
        UF Library insurance
        BT Insurance
— **Inventories**
        UF Inventories in libraries
             Library inventories
        BT Libraries—Shelf department
        NT Discarding of books, periodicals,
             etc.
— Job descriptions
        USE Librarians—Job descriptions
— Law and legislation
        USE Library legislation
— Location
        USE Library sites
— **Mechanical aids**
        BT Library fittings and supplies
        NT Photography—Library applications
— Order department
        USE Acquisitions (Libraries)
— Organization
        USE Library administration
             Library science
— **Periodicals**
        UF Library bulletins
        BT Library publications
— Personnel management
        USE Library personnel management
— Programmed instruction
        USE Library orientation
— Public relations
        USE Public relations—Libraries
— **Publishing**
        UF Library publishing
             Publishing by libraries
        BT Publishers and publishing
        NT Library publications
— Punched card systems
        USE Punched card systems—Libraries
— Reclassification
        USE Reclassification (Libraries)
— Records
        USE Library records
— Reference books
        USE Reference books
— Reference department
        USE Reference services (Libraries)
— Searching, Bibliographical
        USE Searching, Bibliographical
— **Security measures**
        [Z679.6]
        BT Security systems
        RT Book thefts
             Books—Mutilation, defacement,
             etc.
— **Self-evaluation** (May Subd Geog)
        [Z678.85]
        UF Library self-evaluation
        BT Self-evaluation
— **Shelf department**
        [Z703.5]
        UF Shelf department (Library science)
        BT Shelf-listing (Library science)
        NT Libraries—Inventories
— Shelving
        USE Shelving (for books)
             Shelving (for non-book materials)

        Shelving (for periodicals)
— Signs
        USE Library signs
— **Societies, etc.**
        NT Friends of the library
— **Space utilization**
        [Z679.55]
        UF Library space utilization
             Space problems in libraries
             Space utilization in libraries
        BT Library architecture
             Library planning
— **Special collections**
        [Z688]
        Subdivided by subject or form, e.g. Libraries
        —Special collections—Chinese literature; Li-
        braries—Special collections—Slides (Photogra-
        phy)
        UF Library special collections,
             Administration of
             Special collections in libraries,
             Administration of
        BT Collection development (Libraries)
        NT Cataloging of special collections in
             libraries
— — **Audio-visual materials**
        NT Acquisition of audio-visual
             materials
— — **Chinese literature, [Slides
        (Photography), etc.]**
— — Directories
        USE Libraries, Special—Directories
             Library resources—Directories
— — **Foreign publications**
        NT Acquisition of foreign
             publications
— — **Microforms**
        BT Microforms
        NT Acquisition of microforms
— — **Non-book materials**
        UF Non-book materials, Library
             collections of
        BT Library materials
— — Periodical collections
        USE Serials control systems
— — **Reports**
        [Z692.R45]
        NT Cataloging of technical reports
— — **Video tapes**
        [Z716.8]
        BT Video tape recorders and
             recording—Library
             applications
— — **Africa**
        NT Cataloging of African literature
— **Staff manuals**
        UF Library staff manuals
             Staff manuals (Library)
        BT Library administration
             Library rules and regulations
— State aid
        USE Libraries and state
— Statistical methods
        USE Library statistics
— Statistics
        USE Library statistics
— Sunday opening
        USE Sunday opening of libraries
— Supplies
        USE Library fittings and supplies
— **Taxation** (May Subd Geog)
— — **Law and legislation**
        (May Subd Geog)
— Teletype systems
        USE Teletype in libraries
— **Trustees**
        [Z682]
        UF Libraries—Boards
             Library boards
             Library trustees
             Trustees, Library

BT Library administration
— Use studies
    USE Library use studies
— **United States**
— — **Code numbers**
    NT Standard Address Number
— **Wisconsin**
— — **Statistics**
Libraries, Administrative
    USE Libraries, Governmental,
        administrative, etc.
Libraries, Administrative agency
    USE Libraries, Governmental,
        administrative, etc.
Libraries, Aeronautical
    USE Aeronautical libraries
Libraries, Afro-American
    USE Afro-Americans and libraries
Libraries, Afro-American university and college
    USE Afro-American university and college
        libraries
Libraries, Agricultural
    USE Agricultural libraries
Libraries, American overseas information
    USE Overseas information libraries,
        American
Libraries, Anthropological
    USE Anthropological libraries
Libraries, Aquarium
    USE Aquarium libraries
Libraries, Arabic
    USE Arabic libraries
Libraries, Archaeological
    USE Archaeological libraries
Libraries, Architectural
    USE Architectural libraries
Libraries, Art
    USE Art libraries
Libraries, Bible college *(May Subd Geog)*
    UF Bible college libraries
    BT Libraries, University and college
        Religious libraries
Libraries, Bibliographical
    USE Bibliographical libraries
Libraries, Black
    USE Libraries and Blacks
Libraries, Botanical
    USE Botanical libraries
Libraries, Branch
    USE Libraries—Branches, delivery stations,
        etc.
Libraries, British overseas information
    USE Overseas information libraries, British
Libraries, Broadcasting
    UF Broadcasting libraries
    BT Libraries, Special
Libraries, Business
    USE Business libraries
Libraries, Business school
    USE Business libraries
Libraries, Camp
    USE Soldiers' libraries
Libraries, Cathedral
    USE Cathedral libraries
Libraries, Catholic *(May Subd Geog)*
    UF Catholic libraries
    BT Religious libraries
Libraries, Chapter-house
    USE Fraternity libraries
Libraries, Chemical
    USE Chemical libraries
Libraries, Children's *(May Subd Geog)*
    [Z718.1]
    UF Children's libraries
        Libraries—Children's rooms
    BT Libraries, Special
    RT Libraries and handicapped children
        Libraries and schools
        Public libraries—Services to preschool
            children
— **Acquisitions**

BT Acquisitions (Libraries)
— **Administration**
— **Book selection**
    BT Book selection
— **Use studies**
    BT Library use studies
Libraries, Church *(May Subd Geog)*
    [Z675.C5]
    UF Church libraries
        Churches—Libraries
        Libraries, Parish
        Libraries, Parochial
        Parish libraries
        Parochial libraries
    BT Religious libraries
    NT Cathedral libraries
— **Book lists**
    UF Book lists for church libraries
    BT Bibliography—Best books
Libraries, City planning
    USE City planning libraries
Libraries, Club-house
    USE Fraternity libraries
Libraries, College
    USE Libraries, University and college
Libraries, Combined public-school
    USE Libraries, Community-school
Libraries, Commercial
    USE Corporate libraries
Libraries, Community college
    (May Subd Geog)
    [Z675.J8]
    UF Community college libraries
    BT Libraries, University and college
Libraries, Community development
    USE Community development libraries
Libraries, Community-school
    (May Subd Geog)
    [Z675.S3]
    UF Combined public-school libraries
        Community-school libraries
        Libraries, Combined public-school
        Libraries, Public school
        Libraries, School-public
        Public school libraries
        School-public libraries
    BT Public libraries
        School libraries
    RT Libraries and schools
Libraries, Company
    USE Corporate libraries
Libraries, Cooperative society
    (May Subd Geog)
    [Z675.C77]
    UF Cooperative society libraries
    BT Libraries, Special
Libraries, Corporate
    USE Corporate libraries
Libraries, Costume design
    USE Costume design libraries
Libraries, County *(May Subd Geog)*
    [Z675.C8]
    Here are entered works on public libraries serving
    part of or an entire county.
    UF County libraries
    BT Public libraries
Libraries, Criminal justice
    USE Criminal justice libraries
Libraries, Dance
    USE Dance libraries
Libraries, Data
    USE Data libraries
Libraries, Demographic
    USE Demographic libraries
Libraries, Dental
    USE Dental libraries
Libraries, Deposit
    USE Libraries, Storage
Libraries, Depository *(May Subd Geog)*
    [Z675.D4]
    UF Depository libraries

BT Documents libraries
    RT Legal deposit (of books, etc.)
Libraries, District
    USE Libraries, Regional
Libraries, Documents
    USE Documents libraries
Libraries, Ecological
    USE Environmental libraries
Libraries, Economics
    USE Economics libraries
Libraries, Education
    USE Education libraries
Libraries, Electronics
    USE Electronics libraries
Libraries, Elementary school
    USE Elementary school libraries
Libraries, Engineering
    USE Engineering libraries
Libraries, Environmental
    USE Environmental libraries
Libraries, Factory
    USE Factory libraries
Libraries, Fashion design
    USE Costume design libraries
Libraries, Fiction in
    USE Fiction in libraries
Libraries, Film
    USE Moving-picture film collections
Libraries, Filmstrip
    USE Filmstrip collections
Libraries, Financial
    USE Financial libraries
Libraries, Fishery
    USE Fishery libraries
Libraries, Folklore
    USE Folklore libraries
Libraries, Forestry
    USE Forestry libraries
Libraries, Fraternity
    USE Fraternity libraries
Libraries, Governmental, administrative, etc.
    (May Subd Geog)
    [Z675.G7]
    UF Administrative agency libraries
        Administrative libraries
        Federal libraries
        Government libraries
        Legislative libraries
        Libraries, Administrative
        Libraries, Administrative agency
        Libraries, Legislative
        Libraries, Official
        Libraries, Parliamentary
        Official libraries
        Parliamentary libraries
    BT Libraries, Special
    RT Libraries and state
    NT International agency libraries
        Libraries, National
        Municipal reference libraries
        Overseas information libraries
        State libraries
Libraries, Greek letter society
    USE Fraternity libraries
Libraries, Health sciences
    USE Medical libraries
Libraries, Hebrew
    USE Jewish libraries
Libraries, High school
    USE High school libraries
Libraries, Hispanic American
    USE Hispanic Americans and libraries
Libraries, Historical
    USE Historical libraries
Libraries, Home
    USE Libraries, Private
Libraries, Hospital
    USE Hospital libraries
Libraries, Humanities
    USE Humanities libraries

2143

Libraries, Illegal
USE Illegal libraries
Libraries, Imaginary
USE Imaginary books and libraries
Libraries, Indian
USE Libraries and Indians
Libraries, Industrial
USE Corporate libraries
Libraries, Industrial art
USE Industrial art libraries
Libraries, Industrial hygiene
USE Occupational health libraries
Libraries, Industrial relations
USE Industrial relations libraries
Libraries, Industrial safety
USE Occupational health libraries
Libraries, Information science
USE Information science libraries
Libraries, Institution
USE Institution libraries
Libraries, Insurance
USE Insurance libraries
Libraries, International *(May Subd Geog)*
UF International libraries
BT Libraries
Libraries, International agency
USE International agency libraries
Libraries, Islamic
USE Islamic libraries
Libraries, Jewish
USE Jewish libraries
Libraries, Journalistic
USE Newspaper office libraries
Libraries, Junior college
USE Junior college libraries
Libraries, Junior high school
USE Junior high school libraries
Libraries, Law
USE Law libraries
Libraries, Law school
USE Law libraries
Libraries, Legislative
USE Libraries, Governmental,
administrative, etc.
Libraries, Library science
USE Library science libraries
Libraries, Life sciences
USE Life sciences libraries
Libraries, Linguistics
USE Linguistics libraries
Libraries, Literary
USE Literary libraries
Libraries, Map
USE Map collections
Libraries, Marine science
USE Marine science libraries
Libraries, Maritime
USE Libraries, Naval
Libraries, Masonic
USE Masonic libraries
Libraries, Medical
USE Medical libraries
Libraries, Medical college
USE Medical libraries
Libraries, Mental health
USE Mental health libraries
Libraries, Meteorological
USE Meteorological libraries
Libraries, Mexican-American
USE Mexican Americans and libraries
Libraries, Military
USE Military libraries
Libraries, Mining
USE Mining libraries
Libraries, Monastic
USE Monastic libraries
Libraries, Mosque
USE Mosque libraries
Libraries, Motion picture
USE Moving-picture film collections

Libraries, Municipal reference
USE Municipal reference libraries
Libraries, Municipal university and college
USE Municipal university and college
libraries
Libraries, Museum
USE Museum libraries
Libraries, Music
USE Music libraries
Libraries, Muslim
USE Islamic libraries
Libraries, National *(May Subd Geog)*
[Z675.N2]
UF National libraries
BT Libraries, Governmental,
administrative, etc.
SA *names of individual national libraries*
Libraries, Natural history
USE Natural history libraries
Libraries, Naval *(May Subd Geog)*
[Z675.N3]
Here are entered works on libraries whose collec-
tions focus on naval art and science. Works on library
collections for personal use by naval personnel, espe-
cially during wars, are entered under Soldiers' librar-
ies. Works on libraries located within naval institu-
tions or the naval branch of the military service are
entered under Libraries, Naval and/or Soldiers' li-
braries, depending on their purpose and subject focus.
UF Libraries, Maritime
Maritime libraries
Naval libraries
BT Military libraries
Libraries, Newspaper
USE Newspaper and periodical libraries
Libraries, Newspaper office
USE Newspaper office libraries
Libraries, Numismatic
USE Numismatic libraries
Libraries, Nursing
USE Nursing libraries
Libraries, Nursing school
USE Nursing school libraries
Libraries, Occupational health
USE Occupational health libraries
Libraries, Occupational safety
USE Occupational health libraries
Libraries, Oceanographic
USE Oceanographic libraries
Libraries, Official
USE Libraries, Governmental,
administrative, etc.
Libraries, Overseas information
USE Overseas information libraries
Libraries, Package
[Z716.1]
UF Package libraries
BT Libraries, Traveling
Libraries, Parish
USE Libraries, Church
Libraries, Parliamentary
USE Libraries, Governmental,
administrative, etc.
Libraries, Parochial
USE Libraries, Church
Libraries, Pedagogical
USE Education libraries
Libraries, Performing arts
USE Performing arts libraries
Libraries, Periodical
USE Newspaper and periodical libraries
Libraries, Personnel management
USE Personnel management libraries
Libraries, Pharmaceutical
USE Pharmaceutical libraries
Libraries, Pharmacy school
(May Subd Geog)
[Z675.P48]
UF Pharmacy school libraries
BT Libraries, University and college
Pharmaceutical libraries

Libraries, Philanthropy
USE Philanthropy libraries
Libraries, Philosophy
USE Philosophy libraries
Libraries, Physical education
USE Physical education libraries
Libraries, Physics
USE Physics libraries
Libraries, Political science
USE Political science libraries
Libraries, Polytechnic
USE Libraries, Technical college
Libraries, Postal
USE Postal libraries
Libraries, Presidential
USE Presidents—United States—Archives
Libraries, Printing
USE Printing libraries
Libraries, Prison
USE Prison libraries
Libraries, Private *(May Subd Geog)*
[Z987-997]
UF Home libraries
Libraries, Home
Private libraries
BT Libraries
RT Book collectors
SA *subdivision* Library *under names of
individuals*
Libraries, Private school *(May Subd Geog)*
[Z675.S3]
UF Private school libraries
BT Libraries, University and college
School libraries
Libraries, Proprietary *(May Subd Geog)*
[Z675.P85]
Here are entered works on libraries funded by
joint stock issues, i.e., libraries owned by stockhold-
ers.
UF Proprietary libraries
BT Libraries
Libraries, Public
USE Public libraries
Libraries, Public health *(May Subd Geog)*
UF Public health libraries
BT Medical libraries
NT Occupational health libraries
Libraries, Public school
USE Libraries, Community-school
School libraries
Libraries, Publishers'
USE Publishers' libraries
Libraries, Rabbinical seminary
USE Rabbinical seminary libraries
Libraries, Railroad Y.M.C.A.
[Z675.Y7]
UF Railroad Y.M.C.A. libraries
BT Libraries, Special
Libraries, Rare book
USE Rare book libraries
Libraries, Real estate *(May Subd Geog)*
[Z675.R33]
UF Real estate libraries
BT Business libraries
Libraries, Reformatory
USE Reformatory libraries
Libraries, Regional *(May Subd Geog)*
[Z675.R35]
Here are entered works on public libraries serving
a group of communities, several counties, or other
regions.
UF District libraries
Libraries, District
Regional libraries
BT Public libraries
RT Library districts
Libraries, Religious
USE Religious libraries
Libraries, Rental *(May Subd Geog)*
[Z675.R4]

Here are entered works on libraries that circulate some or all of their materials to the public for a small fee per item, and works on collections circulated in this manner.
  UF Rental libraries
  BT Libraries
Libraries, Repository
  USE Libraries, Storage
Libraries, Research
  USE Research libraries
Libraries, Rural
  USE Rural libraries
Libraries, School
  USE School libraries
Libraries, School-public
  USE Libraries, Community-school
Libraries, Scientific
  USE Scientific libraries
Libraries, Seamen's
  USE Soldiers' libraries
Libraries, Ships'
  USE Soldiers' libraries
Libraries, Shore
  USE Soldiers' libraries
Libraries, Shorthand
  USE Shorthand libraries
Libraries, Small
  USE Small libraries
Libraries, Social science
  USE Social science libraries
Libraries, Society
  USE Society libraries
Libraries, Soldiers'
  USE Soldiers' libraries
Libraries, Sorority
  USE Fraternity libraries
Libraries, Sound recording
  USE Sound recording libraries
Libraries, Special (May Subd Geog)
  [Z675.A2]
  Here are entered works on libraries covering specialized subjects, containing special format materials, or serving a specialized clientele.
  UF Special libraries
  BT Libraries
  NT Aquarium libraries
      Arabic libraries
      Architectural libraries
      Art libraries
      Bibliographical libraries
      City planning libraries
      Corporate libraries
      Costume design libraries
      Dance libraries
      Documents libraries
      Economics libraries
      Filmstrip collections
      Humanities libraries
      Industrial relations libraries
      Information science libraries
      Institution libraries
      Law libraries
      Libraries, Broadcasting
      Libraries, Children's
      Libraries, Cooperative society
      Libraries, Governmental,
         administrative, etc.
      Libraries, Railroad Y.M.C.A.
      Libraries, Trade-union
      Libraries, Working-men's
      Libraries, Y.M.C.A.
      Libraries, Young people's
      Library resources
      Literary libraries
      Map collections
      Masonic libraries
      Military libraries
      Moving-picture film collections
      Museum libraries
      Music libraries
      Newspaper and periodical libraries
      Newspaper office libraries

      Numismatic libraries
      Performing arts libraries
      Philanthropy libraries
      Physical education libraries
      Political science libraries
      Postal libraries
      Presidents—United States—Archives
      Printing libraries
      Publishers' libraries
      Rare book libraries
      Religious libraries
      Scientific libraries
      Shorthand libraries
      Social science libraries
      Society libraries
      Statistical libraries
      Technical libraries
      Toy lending libraries
      Ukrainian libraries
      Wine libraries
  — Directories
      Here are entered directories of special libraries or of special collections in other libraries. Directories of resources on special subjects are entered under Library resources—Directories, and under special headings, e.g. Asia, Southeastern—Library resources—Directories.
      UF Libraries—Special collections—
            Directories
          Special library directories
Libraries, State
  USE State libraries
Libraries, Statistical
  USE Statistical libraries
Libraries, Stenography
  USE Shorthand libraries
Libraries, Storage (May Subd Geog)
      Here are entered works on facilities in which a library or cooperating libraries store little-used library materials.
  UF Deposit libraries
      Libraries, Deposit
      Libraries, Repository
      Repository libraries
      Storage libraries
  BT Library buildings
  RT Library cooperation
Libraries, Subscription (May Subd Geog)
  [Z675.S8]
      Here are entered works on libraries whose members pay annual dues entitling them to library services.
  UF Subscription libraries
  BT Libraries
Libraries, Sunday-school
  [Z675.S9]
  UF Sunday-school libraries
  BT Religious libraries
Libraries, Synagogue
  USE Synagogue libraries
Libraries, Teachers college
  (May Subd Geog)
  UF Teachers college libraries
  BT Libraries, University and college
Libraries, Technical
  USE Technical libraries
Libraries, Technical college
  (May Subd Geog)
  UF Libraries, Polytechnic
      Polytechnic libraries
      Technical college libraries
  BT Libraries, University and college
  — Use studies
      BT Library use studies
Libraries, Telecommunications
  USE Telecommunications libraries
Libraries, Theatrical (May Subd Geog)
  [Z675.T]
  UF Theater libraries
      Theatrical libraries
  BT Performing arts libraries

Libraries, Thefts from
  USE Book thefts
Libraries, Theological
  USE Theological libraries
Libraries, Theological seminary
  USE Theological seminary libraries
Libraries, Toy lending
  USE Toy lending libraries
Libraries, Trade-union (May Subd Geog)
  UF Trade-union libraries
  BT Libraries, Special
  RT Libraries and trade-unions
Libraries, Transportation
  USE Transportation libraries
Libraries, Traveling (May Subd Geog)
  [Z716]
  [Z732]
  UF Traveling libraries
  BT Libraries
  RT Bookmobiles
  NT Libraries, Package
Libraries, Typographic
  USE Printing libraries
Libraries, Ukrainian
  USE Ukrainian libraries
Libraries, Undergraduate
  USE Libraries, University and college—
         Undergraduate libraries
Libraries, University and college
  (May Subd Geog)
  [Z675.U5]
      Works on departmental libraries or school libraries in special fields, such as law school libraries, are entered under headings for special libraries, e.g. Law libraries; Business libraries; etc.
  UF College libraries
      Libraries, College
      University libraries
  BT Libraries
  RT Public libraries—Services to colleges
         and universities
  SA subdivision Libraries under names of
         individual universities, colleges, etc.
  NT Afro-American university and college
         libraries
      Fraternity libraries
      Junior college libraries
      Libraries, Bible college
      Libraries, Community college
      Libraries, Pharmacy school
      Libraries, Private school
      Libraries, Teachers college
      Libraries, Technical college
      Municipal university and college
         libraries
      Nursing school libraries
      Rabbinical seminary libraries
      Theological seminary libraries
  — Acquisitions
      BT Acquisitions (Libraries)
  — Administration
  — — Staff participation
        BT Management—Employee
              participation
  — Aims and objectives
  — Book lists
      [Z1039.C65]
      UF Book lists for university and
            college libraries
      BT Bibliography—Best books
  — Circulation analysis
      UF Circulation analysis of university
            and college libraries
  — Collection development
  — Departmental libraries
      UF College departmental libraries
          Departmental libraries in
            universities and colleges
          Libraries, University and college—
            Divisional libraries
          University departmental libraries

Libraries, University and college
(Continued)
— Divisional libraries
   USE Libraries, University and college
      —Departmental libraries
— **Reference services**
   BT Reference services (Libraries)
— **Relations with faculty and curriculum**
   BT Universities and colleges—
      Curricula
     Universities and colleges—Faculty
   RT College librarians—Faculty status
— **Reserve collections**
   BT Reserve collections in libraries
— **Services to Hispanic Americans**
   BT Hispanic Americans—Services for
     Libraries and minorities
— **Space utilization**
   [Z679.55]
   UF Space utilization in university and
     college libraries
— **Statistics**
— **Undergraduate libraries**
   UF Libraries, Undergraduate
     Undergraduate libraries
— **Use studies**
   BT Library use studies
— **Massachusetts**
   NT Harvard University—Libraries
Libraries, Veterinary
USE Veterinary libraries
Libraries, Village
USE Rural libraries
Libraries, Vocational school
(May Subd Geog)
[Z675.V8]
UF Vocational school libraries
BT School libraries
Libraries, War
USE Soldiers' libraries
Libraries, Wine
USE Wine libraries
Libraries, Working-men's *(May Subd Geog)*
[Z675.W]
UF Working-men's libraries
BT Libraries, Special
Libraries, Y.M.C.A.
[Z675.Y7]
UF Young Men's Christian Association
   libraries
BT Libraries, Special
Libraries, Young people's *(May Subd Geog)*
[Z718.5]
UF Young people's libraries
BT Libraries, Special
— **Book selection**
   BT Book selection
— **Use studies**
   BT Library use studies
Libraries and adult education
(May Subd Geog)
[Z711.2]
UF Adult education and libraries
   Library adult education
   Public libraries and adult education
BT Libraries and community
   Libraries and education
   Library extension
RT Public libraries—Services to adults
NT Libraries and continuing education
— **United States**
   NT Adult Independent Learning
     Project
Libraries and Afro-Americans
USE Afro-Americans and libraries
Libraries and Blacks *(May Subd Geog)*
UF Black libraries
   Blacks and libraries
   Libraries, Black
   Library services to Blacks
BT Blacks

Libraries and booksellers
[Z716.6]
BT Booksellers and bookselling
Libraries and communism
UF Communism and libraries
Libraries and community *(May Subd Geog)*
UF Community and libraries
BT Community life
   Libraries and state
NT Libraries—Cultural programs
   Libraries and adult education
   Public libraries—Administration—
     Citizen participation
   Public relations—Libraries
**Libraries and computer output microfilm
devices**
USE Computer output microfilm devices—
   Library applications
Libraries and continuing education
(May Subd Geog)
[Z718.8]
BT Continuing education
   Libraries and adult education
Libraries and data tapes
USE Data tapes—Library applications
Libraries and education *(May Subd Geog)*
UF Education and libraries
NT Libraries and adult education
   Libraries and students
Libraries and electronic publishing
(May Subd Geog)
[Z678.93.E]
BT Electronic publishing
Libraries and families *(May Subd Geog)*
[Z711.92.F34]
UF Families and libraries
BT Family
Libraries and foreign population
USE Libraries and immigrants
Libraries and handicapped children
(May Subd Geog)
[Z711.92.H3]
UF Handicapped children and libraries
   Library services to handicapped
     children
BT Handicapped children
RT Libraries, Children's
Libraries and Hispanic Americans
USE Hispanic Americans and libraries
Libraries and imaginary books
USE Imaginary books and libraries
Libraries and immigrants *(May Subd Geog)*
[Z711.8]
UF Immigrants and libraries
   Libraries and foreign population
   Library services to foreign population
   Library services to immigrants
BT Immigrants
Libraries and Indians *(May Subd Geog)*
UF Indian libraries
   Indians and libraries
   Libraries, Indian
   Libraries for Indians
   Library services to Indians
BT Indians
Libraries and industry *(May Subd Geog)*
UF Industry and libraries
   Library services to industry
BT Industry
RT Corporate libraries
NT Public libraries—Services to business
   and industry
Libraries and intellectuals *(May Subd Geog)*
[Z711.92.I58]
UF Library service to intellectuals
BT Intellectuals
Libraries and labor *(May Subd Geog)*
[Z711.85]
UF Labor and libraries
   Library services to labor and laboring
     classes

BT Labor and laboring classes
NT Libraries and trade-unions
Libraries and magnetic disks
USE Magnetic disks—Library applications
Libraries and magnetic tapes
USE Magnetic tapes—Library applications
Libraries and mass media
BT Mass media
NT Libraries and moving-pictures
   Libraries and radio
   Libraries and television
Libraries and mentally handicapped children
(May Subd Geog)
[Z711.92.M4]
UF Library services to mentally
   handicapped children
   Mentally handicapped children and
     libraries
BT Mentally handicapped children
Libraries and metropolitan areas
(May Subd Geog)
UF Library service to metropolitan areas
   Metropolitan areas and libraries
Libraries and Mexican Americans
USE Mexican Americans and libraries
Libraries and microcomputers
USE Microcomputers—Library applications
Libraries and microfilms
USE Microfilms—Library applications
Libraries and micrographics
USE Micrographics—Library applications
Libraries and minicomputers
USE Minicomputers—Library applications
Libraries and minorities *(May Subd Geog)*
[Z711.8]
UF Library services to minorities
   Minorities and libraries
BT Minorities
RT Instructional materials centers—
   Services to minorities
NT Afro-Americans and libraries
   Libraries, University and college—
     Services to Hispanic Americans
   Mexican Americans and libraries
   Public libraries—Services to Hispanic
     Americans
   Public libraries—Services to minorities
   School libraries—Services to minorities
Libraries and moving-pictures
UF Moving-pictures and libraries
   Moving-pictures in libraries
BT Audio-visual library service
   Libraries and mass media
   Libraries and pictures
   Moving-pictures
   Moving-pictures in education
RT Moving-picture film collections
   Moving-pictures, Documentary—
     Distribution
Libraries and museums *(May Subd Geog)*
  Here are entered works on cooperative relation-
ships or programs between libraries and museums.
BT Museums
RT Museum libraries
Libraries and national socialism
BT National socialism
Libraries and new literates
UF New literates and libraries
BT Literacy
NT Public libraries—Services to the
   illiterate
**Libraries and optical character recognition
devices**
USE Optical character recognition devices
   —Library applications
Libraries and optical disks
USE Optical disks—Library applications
Libraries and optical storage devices
USE Optical storage devices—Library
   applications

Libraries and photography
  USE Photography—Library applications
Libraries and pictures
  ⌐Z717⌐
  UF Pictures in libraries
  BT Audio-visual library service
     Pictures
  NT Libraries and moving-pictures
Libraries and printers (Data processing
  systems)
  USE Printers (Data processing systems)—
       Library applications
Libraries and publishing *(May Subd Geog)*
  ⌐Z716.6⌐
  UF Publishing and libraries
  BT Publishers and publishing
  RT Publishers' libraries
Libraries and puppets
  UF Puppets and libraries
  BT Puppets and puppet-plays
Libraries and radio
  ⌐Z716.7⌐
  UF Radio and libraries
  BT Advertising—Libraries
     Audio-visual library service
     Libraries and mass media
     Radio broadcasting
Libraries and readers
  ⌐Z704⌐
  ⌐Z711⌐
  Works on services for specific types of library
  users or on services for users involved in specific
  activities are entered under specific headings, e.g.
  Libraries and the aged; Public libraries—Services to
  minorities; Libraries and adult education.
  UF Library services to readers
     Public services (Libraries)
     Readers and libraries
     Reading public
  NT Library catalogs and readers
     Library rules and regulations
     Reader guidance
  — Programmed instruction
     USE Library orientation
Libraries and schools *(May Subd Geog)*
  ⌐Z718⌐
  UF Schools and libraries
  BT Schools
  RT Libraries, Children's
     Libraries, Community-school
     School libraries
  NT Libraries and students
     Library Day
     Public libraries—Services to colleges
       and universities
  — France
Libraries and society *(May Subd Geog)*
  UF Society and libraries
  NT Libraries—Cultural programs
Libraries and state *(May Subd Geog)*
  UF Libraries—State aid
     State aid to libraries
     State and libraries
  BT Cultural policy
  RT Information services and state
     Libraries, Governmental,
       administrative, etc.
     Library legislation
  NT Federal aid to libraries
     Libraries and community
     Public libraries—Political aspects
Libraries and students *(May Subd Geog)*
  ⌐Z718.7⌐
  UF Students and libraries
  BT Libraries and education
     Libraries and schools
  NT College students—Library orientation
     Public libraries—Services to students
     Reserve collections in libraries
     School children—Library orientation

Libraries and teachers *(May Subd Geog)*
  UF Library service to teachers
  BT Teachers
Libraries and teletext systems
  USE Teletext systems—Library applications
Libraries and television *(May Subd Geog)*
  ⌐Z716.8⌐
  UF Television and libraries
  BT Audio-visual library service
     Libraries and mass media
     Television
  NT Video tape recorders and recording—
       Library applications
Libraries and the aged *(May Subd Geog)*
  UF Aged—Library service
  BT Aged
  NT Public libraries—Services to shut-ins
     Public libraries—Services to the aged
Libraries and the blind *(May Subd Geog)*
  ⌐Z675.B6⌐
  UF Blind, Libraries for the
     Blind and libraries
     Libraries for the blind
     Library services to the blind
  BT Blind
Libraries and the deaf *(May Subd Geog)*
  ⌐Z711.92.D4⌐
  UF Deaf, Libraries for the
     Deaf and libraries
     Libraries for the deaf
     Library services to the deaf
  BT Deaf
Libraries and the handicapped
  (May Subd Geog)
  ⌐Z711.92.H3⌐
  UF Handicapped and libraries
     Library services to the handicapped
  BT Handicapped
  RT Instructional materials centers—
       Services to the handicapped
  NT Public libraries—Services to shut-ins
     School libraries—Services to the
       handicapped
Libraries and the hearing impaired
  (May Subd Geog)
  ⌐Z11.92.D4⌐
  UF Hearing impaired, Libraries for the
     Hearing impaired and libraries
     Libraries for the hearing impaired
     Library services to the hearing
       impaired
  BT Hearing impaired
Libraries and the mentally handicapped
  (May Subd Geog)
  ⌐Z711.92.M4⌐
  UF Library services to the mentally
       handicapped
     Mentally handicapped and libraries
  BT Mentally handicapped
Libraries and the physically handicapped
  (May Subd Geog)
  ⌐Z711.92.P5⌐
  UF Library services to the physically
       handicapped
     Physically handicapped and libraries
  BT Physically handicapped
  NT Library architecture and the physically
       handicapped
Libraries and the socially handicapped
  (May Subd Geog)
  ⌐Z711.92.S6⌐
  UF Library services to the socially
       handicapped
     Socially handicapped and libraries
  BT Socially handicapped
Libraries and the unemployed
  (May Subd Geog)
  ⌐Z711.92.U53⌐
  UF Library service to the unemployed
     Unemployed and libraries
  BT Unemployed

  SA *subdivision* Services to the
       unemployed *under individual types
       of libraries, e.g.* Public libraries—
       Services to the unemployed
Libraries and the visually handicapped
  (May Subd Geog)
  ⌐Z711.92.V57⌐
  UF Libraries for the visually handicapped
     Library services to the visually
       handicapped
     Visually handicapped, Libraries for the
     Visually handicapped and libraries
  BT Visually handicapped
Libraries and trade-unions *(May Subd Geog)*
  BT Libraries and labor
     Trade-unions
  RT Libraries, Trade-union
  NT Public libraries—Services to trade-
       unions
Libraries and video discs
  USE Video discs—Library applications
Libraries and video tape recorders and
  recording
  USE Video tape recorders and recording—
       Library applications
Libraries and videotex systems
  USE Videotex systems—Library applications
Libraries and women *(May Subd Geog)*
  UF Library service to women
     Women—Library service
     Women and libraries
  BT Women
  NT Public libraries—Services to women
Libraries for Indians
  USE Libraries and Indians
Libraries for the blind
  USE Libraries and the blind
Libraries for the deaf
  USE Libraries and the deaf
Libraries for the hearing impaired
  USE Libraries and the hearing impaired
Libraries for the visually handicapped
  USE Libraries and the visually handicapped
Library acquisitions
  USE Acquisitions (Libraries)
Library administration *(May Subd Geog)*
  ⌐Z678⌐
  UF Libraries—Administration
     Libraries—Organization
  SA *subdivision* Administration *under types
       of libraries, e.g.* Libraries, Children's
       —Administration
  NT ALMS (Library management system)
     Communication in library
       administration
     Libraries—Aims and objectives
     Libraries—Staff manuals
     Libraries—Trustees
     Library administrators
     Library personnel management
     Public libraries—Trustees
  — **Research**
  — — **United States**
       NT Management Review and
            Analysis Program
  — **Staff participation**
     UF Staff participation in library
          administration
     BT Library employees
        Management—Employee
          participation
  — **Study and teaching** *(May Subd Geog)*
Library administrators *(May Subd Geog)*
  UF Administrators, Library
  BT Executives
     Library administration
     Library employees
Library adult education
  USE Libraries and adult education
Library advertising
  USE Advertising—Libraries

Library agencies, School
    USE School library agencies
Library agencies, State
    USE State library agencies
Library applications of computer output
    microfilm devices
    USE Computer output microfilm devices—
          Library applications
Library applications of data tapes
    USE Data tapes—Library applications
Library applications of magnetic disks
    USE Magnetic disks—Library applications
Library applications of magnetic tapes
    USE Magnetic tapes—Library applications
Library applications of microcomputers
    USE Microcomputers—Library applications
Library applications of microfilms
    USE Microfilms—Library applications
Library applications of micrographics
    USE Micrographics—Library applications
Library applications of minicomputers
    USE Minicomputers—Library applications
Library applications of optical character
    recognition devices
    USE Optical character recognition devices
          —Library applications
Library applications of optical disks
    USE Optical disks—Library applications
Library applications of optical storage devices
    USE Optical storage devices—Library
          applications
Library applications of printers (Data
    processing systems)
    USE Printers (Data processing systems)—
          Library applications
Library applications of teletext systems
    USE Teletext systems—Library applications
Library applications of video discs
    USE Video discs—Library applications
Library applications of video tape recorders
    and recording
    USE Video tape recorders and recording—
          Library applications
Library applications of videotex systems
    USE Videotex systems—Library applications
Library architecture *(May Subd Geog)*
    [Z679]
    UF Architecture, Library
    NT Libraries—Space utilization
          Library buildings
          Library decoration
**Library architecture and the physically
handicapped** *(May Subd Geog)*
    BT Architecture and the physically
          handicapped
          Libraries and the physically
          handicapped
          Physically handicapped
Library assistants
    USE Library technicians
Library assistants, Student
    USE Student library assistants
Library Association Carnegie Medal
    UF Carnegie Medal
    BT Children's literature
          Literary prizes
Library associations
    USE Library science—Societies, etc.
Library authority files
    USE Authority files (Cataloging)
Library automation
    USE Libraries—Automation
Library bindings, Books in
    USE Bibliography—Library editions
Library boards
    USE Libraries—Trustees
Library bonds *(May Subd Geog)*
    UF Bonds, Library
    BT Library finance
          Municipal bonds
    RT Public libraries—Finance

Library book-plates
    USE Book-plates, Library
Library bookkeeping
    USE Bookkeeping, Library
Library buildings *(May Subd Geog)*
    UF Buildings, Library
          Libraries—Buildings
    BT Library architecture
          Public buildings
    NT Libraries, Storage
          Reading rooms
  — Maryland
      NT Library of Congress Mass Book
            Deacidification Facility (Md.)
  — Washington (D.C.)
      NT Library of Congress James
            Madison Memorial Building
            (Washington, D.C.)
           Library of Congress Thomas
            Jefferson Building (Washington,
            D.C.)
Library bulletins
    USE Libraries—Periodicals
Library catalog analytical entries
    USE Cataloging—Analytical entry
Library catalogers
    USE Catalogers
Library catalogs *(May Subd Geog)*
    [Z710]
    UF Catalogs, Library
          Finding lists
          Libraries—Catalogs
    BT Catalogs
          Library publications
    NT Author catalogs
          Catalogs, Book
          Catalogs, Card
          Catalogs, Classified
          Catalogs, Dictionary
          Catalogs, Divided
          Catalogs, Imprint
          Catalogs, Sheaf
          Catalogs, Subject
          Catalogs, Union
  — Automation
      NT Catalogs, On-line
  — Union catalogs
      USE Catalogs, Union
  — Use studies
      BT Library use studies
Library catalogs and readers
  (May Subd Geog)
    [Z710-Z711.4]
    UF Catalog use
          Readers and library catalogs
    BT Libraries and readers
    NT Library catalogs on microfilm—Use
          studies
Library catalogs on microfiche
    BT Microfiches
Library catalogs on microfilm
    BT Microfilms
  — Use studies
      BT Library catalogs and readers
          Library use studies
Library censorship
    USE Libraries—Censorship
Library charging systems
    USE Charging systems (Libraries)
Library circulation
    USE Libraries—Circulation, loans
Library circulation analysis
    USE Libraries—Circulation analysis
Library classification
    USE Classification—Books
Library clubs *(May Subd Geog)*
    BT Clubs
          Societies
Library collection development
    USE Collection development (Libraries)

Library commissions *(May Subd Geog)*
    [Z716]
    [Z732 (State library commission
        reports)]
    UF Commissions, Library
          State library commissions
    BT Library extension
    RT State library agencies
Library conferences
    USE Library science—Congresses
Library consortia
    USE Library cooperation
Library consultants
    BT Consultants
          Library service agencies
Library Control System (Information retrieval
    system)
    USE LCS (Information retrieval system)
Library cooperation *(May Subd Geog)*
    UF Cooperation, Library
          Library consortia
    RT Cataloging, Cooperative
          Intellectual cooperation
          International librarianship
          Libraries, Storage
    NT Acquisitions, Cooperative (Libraries)
          Bibliographical centers
          Catalogs, Union
          Centralized processing (Libraries)
          Exchange of bibliographic information
          Farmington plan
          Inter-library loans
          Library information networks
          National Program for Acquisitions and
            Cataloging
          Periodicals—Bibliography—Union lists
          Teletype in libraries
  — England
      NT Local Library Cooperation Project
  — Scandinavia
      NT Scandia Plan
Library cultural programs
    USE Libraries—Cultural programs
Library Day
    [Z718]
    BT Holidays
          Libraries and schools
    RT National Library Week
Library decoration
    [Z679]
    UF Libraries—Decoration
    BT Decoration and ornament
          Interior decoration
          Library architecture
    NT Library fittings and supplies
Library displays
    USE Library exhibits
Library districts *(May Subd Geog)*
    BT Special districts
    RT Libraries, Regional
Library duplicates
    USE Duplicates in libraries
Library economy
    USE Library science
Library editions
    USE Bibliography—Library editions
Library education *(May Subd Geog)*
    [Z668-Z669]
    Here are entered works on the education of li-
    brarians. Works dealing with the instruction of read-
    ers in library use are entered under the heading Li-
    brary orientation.
    UF Education for librarianship
          Librarians, Education of
          Librarians, Training of
          Library school education
          Library science—Study and teaching
    BT Education, Higher
          Professional education
    RT Library schools

SA *subdivision* Study and teaching *under*
     special subjects, e.g. Book selection
     —Study and teaching
NT Interns (Library science)
    Library education (Continuing
     education)
    Library institutes and workshops
Library education (Continuing education)
  (May Subd Geog)
  BT Continuing education
    Library education
Library employees *(May Subd Geog)*
  UF Libraries—Employees
    Library personnel
  NT Librarians
    Library administration—Staff
     participation
    Library administrators
    Library pages
    Library personnel management
    Library technicians
    Part-time library employees
    School library supervisors
    Student library assistants
    Trade-unions—Library employees
    Volunteer workers in libraries
  — Collective bargaining
    USE Collective bargaining—Library
     employees
Library employees, Part-time
  USE Part-time library employees
Library ethics
  USE Librarians—Professional ethics
Library exhibits *(May Subd Geog)*
  ⌐Z673.5¬
  UF Libraries—Exhibitions
    Library displays
  BT Advertising—Libraries
    Public relations—Libraries
  RT Bibliographical exhibitions
Library extension *(May Subd Geog)*
  ⌐Z716¬
    Here, without subdivision, are entered general
  works and works on library extension in the United
  States. Applied to works on library extension in par-
  ticular states or in foreign countries, the heading is
  subdivided by state or country.
  UF Extension education
  NT Advertising—Libraries
    Bookmobiles
    Direct delivery of books
    Libraries and adult education
    Library commissions
Library fees
  USE Library fines and fees
Library File Processing System
  USE LFP System
Library filing rules
  ⌐Z695.95¬
  UF Filing rules, Library
  BT Filing systems
Library finance *(May Subd Geog)*
  ⌐Z683¬
  UF Libraries—Accounting
    Libraries—Finance
  NT ALMS (Library management system)
    Federal aid to libraries
    Library bonds
    Library fines and fees
    Library fund raising
    Public libraries—Finance
    School library finance
    Taxation, Exemption from
Library fines and fees *(May Subd Geog)*
  ⌐Z683¬
  UF Libraries—Fines and fees
    Library fees
  BT Library finance
Library fittings and supplies
  (May Subd Geog)
  ⌐Z684-685¬

  UF Libraries—Supplies
    Library supplies
  BT Furniture
    Library decoration
  NT Book drops
    Bookmobiles
    Libraries—Mechanical aids
    Library service agencies
    Shelving (for books)
  — Advertising
    USE Advertising—Library fittings and
     supplies
Library fund raising *(May Subd Geog)*
  ⌐Z683¬
  BT Fund raising
    Library finance
Library handwriting
  ⌐Z695¬
  BT Penmanship
    Writing
  RT Penmanship, Vertical
Library humor
  USE Library science—Anecdotes, facetiae,
    satire, etc.
Library information networks
  (May Subd Geog)
  ⌐Z680.3¬
  UF Information networks, Library
    Libraries—Information networks
    Library networks
    Networks of libraries
  BT Data transmission systems
    Information networks
    Library cooperation
  NT MEDLINE
  — **Australia**
    NT BIBDATA (Library information
     network)
  — **Colorado**
    NT IRVING (Library information
     network)
  — **England**
    NT COLA Project
  — **Florida**
    NT Florida Library Information
     Network
  — **Texas**
    NT Texas State Library
     Communications Network
  — **United States**
    NT SILC (Library information
     network)
Library Information System
  USE LIBRIS (Information retrieval system)
Library institutes and workshops
  (May Subd Geog)
  UF Institutes and workshops, Library
    Workshops and institutes, Library
  BT Communication in library science
    Library education
Library instruction
  USE Library orientation
Library insurance
  USE Libraries—Insurance
Library interns
  USE Interns (Library science)
Library inventories
  USE Libraries—Inventories
Library law
  USE Library legislation
Library legislation *(May Subd Geog)*
  ⌐Z677¬
  UF Law, Library
    Libraries—Law and legislation
    Library law
  BT Educational law and legislation
    Public institutions—Law and
     legislation
  RT Libraries and state
  NT Federal aid to libraries

    Inter-library loans—Law and
     legislation
    Public lending rights (of authors)
    School libraries—Law and legislation
Library locations
  USE Library sites
Library materials
  UF Materials, Library
  SA *heading* Libraries—Special collections
    further subdivided by topic, e.g.
    Libraries—Special collections—
    Video tapes
  NT Audio-visual materials
    Books
    Clippings (Books, newspapers, etc.)
    Collectanea files
    Government publications
    Libraries—Special collections—Non-
    book materials
    Manuscripts
    Maps
    Newspapers
    Periodicals
    Series (Publications)
    Vertical files (Libraries)
  — Reproduction
    ⌐Z681-Z681.3¬
    UF Reproduction of library materials
    BT Copying
Library moving
  ⌐Z703.5¬
Library networks
  USE Library information networks
Library of Congress. Thomas Jefferson
  Building (Washington, D.C.)
  USE Library of Congress Thomas Jefferson
    Building (Washington, D.C.)
Library of Congress Building (Washington,
  D.C.)
  USE Library of Congress Thomas Jefferson
    Building (Washington, D.C.)
Library of Congress classification
  USE Classification, Library of Congress
Library of Congress George Kleine Film
  Collection
  USE George Kleine Film Collection
Library of Congress James Madison Memorial
  Building (Washington, D.C.)
  UF James Madison Memorial Building
    (Washington, D.C.)
    Library of Congress Madison Building
    (Washington, D.C.)
    Madison Building, Library of Congress
    (Washington, D.C.)
  BT Library buildings—Washington (D.C.)
Library of Congress Madison Building
  (Washington, D.C.)
  USE Library of Congress James Madison
    Memorial Building (Washington,
    D.C.)
Library of Congress Mass Book
  Deacidification Facility (Md.)
  UF Deacidification Facility, Library of
    Congress Mass Book (Md.)
    Mass Book Deacidification Facility
    (Md.)
  BT Library buildings—Maryland
Library of Congress subject headings
  USE Subject headings, Library of Congress

Library of Congress Thomas Jefferson Building (Washington, D.C.)
- UF Jefferson Building, Library of Congress (Washington, D.C.)
  - Library of Congress. Thomas Jefferson Building (Washington, D.C.)
  - Library of Congress Building (Washington, D.C.)
  - Main Building, Library of Congress (Washington, D.C.)
  - Thomas Jefferson Building, Library of Congress (Washington, D.C.)
- BT Library buildings—Washington (D.C.)

Library of Congress World War II Recorded History Collection
- USE World War II Recorded History Collection

Library orientation *(May Subd Geog)*
  ₍Z710 (Library guides)₎
  ₍Z711.2 (Use of books)₎
  Here are entered works dealing with the instruction of readers in library use. Works on the education of librarians are entered under the heading Library education.
- UF Libraries—Programmed instruction
  - Libraries and readers—Programmed instruction
  - Library instruction
  - Library skills
  - Library user orientation
  - Orientation (Library use)
- RT Information services—User education
  - Instructional materials centers—User education
- SA *subdivision* Library orientation *under groups of persons, e.g.* College students—Library orientation; School children—Library orientation
- NT Business students—Library orientation
  - Catalogs, On-line—User education
  - College students—Library orientation
  - Engineering students—Library orientation
  - High school students—Library orientation
  - School children—Library orientation
— **Aids and devices**

Library pages *(May Subd Geog)*
- UF Pages, Library
  - Stack attendants
- BT Library employees

Library paraprofessionals
- USE Library technicians

Library personnel
- USE Library employees

Library personnel management *(May Subd Geog)*
  ₍Z682₎
- UF Librarians—Personnel management
  - Libraries—Personnel management
- BT Library administration
  - Library employees
  - Personnel management

Library planning *(May Subd Geog)*
  ₍Z679.5₎
- BT Planning
- NT Libraries—Space utilization
  - Library service agencies

Library processing
- USE Processing (Libraries)

Library publications *(May Subd Geog)*
  ₍Z719 (Bibliography)₎
- UF Publications, Library
- BT Communication in library science
  - Libraries—Publishing
  - Library science literature
- NT Libraries—Periodicals
  - Library catalogs
  - Library reports

Library publicity
- USE Public relations—Libraries

Library publishing
- USE Libraries—Publishing

Library reclassification
- USE Reclassification (Libraries)

Library records
- UF Libraries—Records
- BT Files (Records)
- NT Exchange of bibliographic information

Library reference services
- USE Reference services (Libraries)

Library reports
  Here are entered works on the preparation of reports. Reports themselves are entered under Libraries—₍local subdivision₎, or under names of individual libraries.
- BT Library publications
  - Report writing

Library research
- USE Library science—Research

Library resources *(May Subd Geog)*
  Here are entered works describing the resources and special collections in libraries which are available for research in various fields. Works describing the resources and special collections in a particular field are entered under the subject with subdivision Library resources, e.g. Biology—Library resources; United States—Library resources. Works on the methods used to acquire, process, and maintain special collections in libraries are entered under Libraries—Special collections.
- UF Library special collections
  - Special collections in libraries
- BT Libraries, Special
- NT Reserve collections in libraries
  - Shakespeare, William, 1564-1616—Library resources
— **Directories**
  Here are entered directories of resources on special subjects. Directories of special libraries or of special collections in other libraries are entered under Libraries, Special—Directories.
  - UF Libraries—Special collections—Directories

Library rules and regulations
  ₍Z704₎
  ₍Z731-Z880₎
- BT Libraries and readers
- NT Libraries—Staff manuals
  - Sunday opening of libraries

Library school education
- USE Library education

Library school libraries
- USE Library science libraries

Library schools *(May Subd Geog)*
  ₍Z668-9₎
- BT Schools
- RT Library education
- NT Library science—Scholarships, fellowships, etc.
— **Accreditation**
— **Curricula**
— **Faculty**
  - BT College teachers

Library science *(May Subd Geog)*
  ₍Z665-718₎
- UF Librarianship
  - Libraries—Administration
  - Libraries—Organization
  - Library economy
- BT Documentation
  - Information science
- RT Bibliography
- SA *headings beginning with the word* Library
- NT Audio-visual library service
  - Cataloging
  - Charging systems (Libraries)
  - Classification—Books—Library science
  - Collectanea files
  - Collection development (Libraries)
  - Communication in library science
  - Comparative librarianship
  - Information storage and retrieval systems
  - International librarianship
  - Minorities in library science
  - Music librarianship
  - Open and closed shelves
  - Processing (Libraries)
  - Proposal writing in library science
  - Recataloging
  - Reclassification (Libraries)
  - Shelf-listing (Library science)
  - Women in library science
— **Anecdotes, facetiae, satire, etc.**
  ₍Z682.5₎
  - UF Library humor
— **Awards**
  - NT John Cotton Dana Library Public Relations Award
— **Bibliography**
  - RT Library science literature
— **Congresses**
  ₍Z672.5-673₎
  - UF Librarians—Congresses
    - Libraries—Congresses
    - Library conferences
— **Data processing**
  - NT Computer output microfilm devices—Library applications
    - Microcomputers—Library applications
    - Minicomputers—Library applications
— Fellowships
  - USE Library science—Scholarships, fellowships, etc.
— **Lexicography**
  - BT Lexicography
— **Research** *(May Subd Geog)*
  ₍Z669.7₎
  - UF Library research
— **Scholarships, fellowships, etc.**
  - UF Library science—Fellowships
  - BT Library schools
— **Societies, etc.**
  ₍Z673₎
  - UF Library associations
— Study and teaching
  - USE Library education

Library science libraries *(May Subd Geog)*
  ₍Z675.L5₎
- UF Libraries, Library science
  - Library school libraries
- BT Information science libraries

Library science literature
- UF Literature, Library science
- BT Communication in library science
- RT Information science literature
  - Library science—Bibliography
- NT Library publications

Library self-evaluation
- USE Libraries—Self-evaluation

Library service, Mail
- USE Direct delivery of books

Library service agencies *(May Subd Geog)*
  ₍Z679.8-679.83₎
- UF Agencies, Library service
  - Service agencies, Library
- BT Bibliographical services
  - Library fittings and supplies
  - Library planning
  - Processing (Libraries)
- NT Library consultants

Library service to intellectuals
- USE Libraries and intellectuals

Library service to metropolitan areas
- USE Libraries and metropolitan areas

Library service to Mexican Americans
- USE Mexican Americans and libraries

Library service to teachers
- USE Libraries and teachers

Library service to the unemployed
  USE Libraries and the unemployed
Library service to women
  USE Libraries and women
Library services to Afro-Americans
  USE Afro-Americans and libraries
Library services to Blacks
  USE Libraries and Blacks
Library services to foreign population
  USE Libraries and immigrants
Library services to handicapped children
  USE Libraries and handicapped children
Library services to Hispanic Americans
  USE Hispanic Americans and libraries
Library services to immigrants
  USE Libraries and immigrants
Library services to Indians
  USE Libraries and Indians
Library services to industry
  USE Libraries and industry
Library services to labor and laboring classes
  USE Libraries and labor
Library services to mentally handicapped
  children
    USE Libraries and mentally handicapped
      children
Library services to minorities
  USE Libraries and minorities
Library services to readers
  USE Libraries and readers
Library services to the blind
  USE Libraries and the blind
Library services to the deaf
  USE Libraries and the deaf
Library services to the handicapped
  USE Libraries and the handicapped
Library services to the hearing impaired
  USE Libraries and the hearing impaired
Library services to the mentally handicapped
  USE Libraries and the mentally
    handicapped
Library services to the physically handicapped
  USE Libraries and the physically
    handicapped
Library services to the socially handicapped
  USE Libraries and the socially handicapped
Library services to the visually handicapped
  USE Libraries and the visually handicapped
Library signs (May Subd Geog)
  [Z679.57]
  UF Libraries—Signs
    Signs in libraries
  BT Signs and signboards
Library sites
  UF Libraries—Location
    Library locations
  BT Building sites
Library skills
  USE Library orientation
Library space utilization
  USE Libraries—Space utilization
Library special collections
  USE Library resources
Library special collections, Administration of
  USE Libraries—Special collections
Library staff manuals
  USE Libraries—Staff manuals
Library stamps
  [Z689]
Library statistics
  [Z683]
  [Z711.3]
  Here are entered works on the compilation and
  study of statistics of libraries, or collections of general
  library statistics. Other collections of statistics are
  entered under Libraries—[place]; types of libraries,
  or names of individual libraries, with subdivision Sta-
  tistics, e.g. Libraries—Wisconsin—Statistics; Librar-
  ies, University and college—Statistics.
  UF Libraries—Statistical methods
    Libraries—Statistics
  BT Statistics

  RT Books—Statistics
  NT Bibliometrics
    Library use studies
Library students, Interchange of
  USE Librarians, Interchange of
Library supervisors, School
  USE School library supervisors
Library supplies
  USE Library fittings and supplies
Library surveys (May Subd Geog)
  Here are entered works on the methods and tech-
  niques employed in conducting library surveys, and
  reports of individual surveys. For the latter the head-
  ing may be subdivided by place; in such cases an
  additional subject entry is made under the heading
  Libraries—[local subdivision], e.g. 1. Libraries—
  United States. 2. Library surveys—United States. For
  library surveys on a special topic, the additional sub-
  ject entry is made under the special topic, e.g. 1.
  Inter-library loans—United States. 2. Library surveys
  —United States.
  UF Surveys, Library
  BT Surveys
Library technicians (May Subd Geog)
  UF Library assistants
    Library paraprofessionals
    Paraprofessionals in libraries
  BT Library employees
Library telephone reference services
  USE Telephone reference services
    (Libraries)
Library teletype systems
  USE Teletype in libraries
Library trustees
  USE Libraries—Trustees
Library use studies (May Subd Geog)
  [Z711.3]
  UF Libraries—Use studies
  BT Information services—Use studies
    Library statistics
  NT Agricultural libraries—Use studies
    Catalogs, Card—Use studies
    Catalogs, Subject—Use studies
    Government publications—Use studies
    Indexes—Use studies
    Libraries—Circulation analysis
    Libraries, Children's—Use studies
    Libraries, Technical college—Use
      studies
    Libraries, University and college—Use
      studies
    Libraries, Young people's—Use studies
    Library catalogs—Use studies
    Library catalogs on microfilm—Use
      studies
    Medical colleges—Information services
      —Use studies
    Medicine—Information services—Use
      studies
    Periodicals—Use studies
    Public libraries—Use studies
    Research libraries—Use studies
    Subject headings—Use studies
    Technology—Information services—
      Use studies
Library user orientation
  USE Library orientation
Library volunteers
  USE Volunteer workers in libraries
Library Week
  USE National Library Week
Libration of the moon
  USE Moon—Libration
Libration points
  USE Lagrangian points
Librettists (May Subd Geog)
  [ML2110]
  UF Opera—Librettists
  BT Dramatists
    Libretto
    Musicians

Libretto
  Here are entered works on the history and criti-
  cism of the libretto and on libretto-writing. Cf. note
  under Librettos.
  NT Librettists
Librettos
  [ML48-49]
  Here are entered collections of miscellaneous li-
  brettos. Collections of librettos limited to a specific
  form are entered under that form, e.g. Operas—Li-
  brettos; Oratorios—Librettos. Cf. note under Libret-
  to.
LIBRIS (Information retrieval system)
  UF Library Information System
  BT Information storage and retrieval
    systems
Libtako (Burkina Faso)
  USE Liptako (Burkina Faso)
Libtrot family
  USE Liptrap family
Liburnia
  [QL527.D44]
  BT Delphacidae
Liby (Saltvik, Finland) (Not Subd Geog)
  BT Farms—Finland
Libya
  — Antiquities
      NT Agora (Cyrene)
        Cyrene (Ancient city)
        Qaṣr aṣ-Ṣaḥābī (Libya)
        Sabratha (City)
        Sanctuary of Demeter and
          Persephone (Cyrene)
  — Antiquities, Roman
  — History (Not Subd Geog)
  — — To 642 (Not Subd Geog)
      [DT228]
  — — 642-1551 (Not Subd Geog)
      [DT229]
  — — 1551-1912 (Not Subd Geog)
      [DT231]
  — — 1912-1951 (Not Subd Geog)
  — — 1951-1969 (Not Subd Geog)
      [DT235.5]
  — — 1969- (Not Subd Geog)
      [DT236]
  — Languages
      NT Teda language
  — Politics and government
      (Not Subd Geog)
  — — 1969- (Not Subd Geog)
      [DT236]
Libyan Desert
  BT Deserts—Africa, North
    Sahara
  NT Western Desert (Egypt)
Libyan investments
  USE Investments, Libyan
Libyan languages
  USE Berber languages
Libyan literature
  USE Berber literature
    Folk literature, Arabic—Libya
    French literature—Libyan authors
Libyan newspapers (May Subd Geog)
Libyan students (May Subd Geog)
  BT Students
Libyans (May Subd Geog)
  BT Ethnology—Libya
  RT Berbers
Licancábur Volcano (Chile)
  UF Licancaur Volcano (Chile)
  BT Volcanoes—Chile
Licancaur Volcano (Chile)
  USE Licancábur Volcano (Chile)
Licania
  [QK495.C48 (Botany)]
  UF Moquilea
  BT Chrysobalanaceae
Licania macrophylla
  [QK495.C48 (Botany)]

Licchavi dynasty, Nepal, ca. 400-600
USE Nepal—History—Licchavi dynasty, ca. 400-600
Licchavis (Asian people)
UF Lichchhavis (Asian people)
BT Ethnology—India
Ethnology—Nepal
Lice *(May Subd Geog)*
[QL540 (Mallophaga)]
[QL570 (Anoplura)]
UF Louse
BT Insects
NT Anoplura
Cattle lice
Goat lice
Hog lice
Mallophaga
Pediculosis
Sheep lice
Lice, Book
USE Psocoptera
Lice as carriers of disease
[RA641.L6]
BT Insects as carriers of disease
Lice infestation
USE Pediculosis
License agreements *(May Subd Geog)*
UF Agreements, Licensing
Joint-venture agreements
Licensing agreements
BT Contracts
Industrial property
Intangible property
Licenses
NT Copyright licenses
Design protection
Exclusive licenses
Foreign licensing agreements
Merchandise licensing
Patent licenses
Trademark licenses
License system *(May Subd Geog)*
[HV5084-HV5087]
Here are entered works on control of the production, distribution, and sale of liquor. General works on permission granted in accordance with law by competent authority to engage in business or perform work are entered under Licenses.
UF High license
Liquor license system
BT Prohibition
Temperance
RT Liquor laws
Local option
Licensed beverage industry
USE Distilling industries
Licensed practical nurses
USE Practical nurses
Licensed vocational nurses
USE Practical nurses
Licenses *(May Subd Geog)*
[HD3629-HD3630 (Occupations and professions)]
[HJ5301-HJ5508 (Revenue)]
Here are entered general works on permission granted in accordance with law by competent authority to engage in business or perform work. Works on control of the production, distribution, and sale of liquor are entered under License system.
UF Permits
BT Administrative procedure
Commercial law
Intangible property
Internal revenue
Municipal finance
Taxation
Trade regulation
User charges
RT Concessions
Service industries—Taxation

SA *subdivision* Licenses *under types of industries and occupational groups, e.g.* Construction industry—Licenses; Medical personnel—Licenses
NT Banality (Law)
Environmental permits
Fish and game licenses
License agreements
— **Rates and tables**
Licenses, Export
USE Export controls
Licenses (Patents)
USE Patent licenses
Licensing, Merchandise
USE Merchandise licensing
Licensing agreements
USE License agreements
Licensing boards for health occupations
USE Health occupations licensing boards
Licensing of automobiles
USE Automobiles—Licenses
Licensing of dogs
USE Dogs—Taxation
Licentious persons in literature
USE Libertines in literature
Licentiousness
USE Lust
Lich-gates
[NA4950]
UF Lych-gates
BT Church architecture
Gates
Lichanura
[QL666.O63]
BT Boidae
Lichchhavis (Asian people)
USE Licchavis (Asian people)
Lichdi family
USE Leighty family
Lichee
USE Litchi
Litchi chinensis
Lichen planus
[RL291]
UF Lichen ruber planus
Lichen products *(May Subd Geog)*
[QK581 (Botany)]
Lichen ruber
[RL331]
Lichen ruber planus
USE Lichen planus
Lichens *(May Subd Geog)*
[QK581-597]
BT Cryptogams
Dye plants
NT Ascolichens
— **Anatomy**
[QK581]
Lichhavi dynasty, Nepal, ca. 400-600
USE Nepal—History—Licchavi dynasty, ca. 400-600
Lichi
USE Litchi
Litchi chinensis
Lichlyter family
USE Leckliter family
Lichtenberg figures
BT Electric spark
Lichtenstein, Roy, 1923-   Mural with blue brushstroke *(Not Subd Geog)*
[ND237.L627]
UF Mural with blue brushstroke (Mural painting)
BT Mural painting and decoration, American
Lichtenstein's hartebeest
[QL737.U53]
UF Alcelaphus lichtensteini
Hartebeest, Lichtenstein's
BT Hartebeests

Lichty family
USE Leighty family
Licinian laws
UF Lex Licinia
Licinidae
USE Carabidae
Licking River, South Fork (Ohio)
UF South Fork Licking River (Ohio)
BT Rivers—Ohio
Licklider family
USE Leckliter family
Lickliter family
USE Leckliter family
Licks, Earth
USE Salt licks
Licks, Mineral
USE Salt licks
Licks, Salt
USE Salt licks
Licorice
[RM666.L5 (Therapeutics)]
[SB295.L7 (Plant culture)]
UF Liquorice
Lictors
[DG83.5.L]
BT Rome—Officials and employees
Lida family
USE Lyda family
Lidar
USE Optical radar
Liday family
USE Lyda family
Liddel-Sherrington reflex
USE Stretch reflex
Liddell family
USE Little family
Liddeson family
USE Lett family
Liddle family
USE Little family
Lide family *(Not Subd Geog)*
RT Lyda family
Lidi family
USE Leedy family
Lido Key (Fla.)
BT Islands—Florida
Lidocaine
USE Xylocaine
Lidoflazine
UF Bisfluorophenylbutyl piperazineacetoxylidide
BT Piperazine
Vasodilators
Lids, Stein
USE Stein lids
Lidson family
USE Lett family
Lidzbark Castle (Lidzbark Warmiński, Poland)
USE Zamek biskupów warmińskich (Lidzbark Warmiński, Poland)
Lie (Obstetrics)
USE Fetal presentation
Lie-admissible algebras
[QC20.7.L54]
UF Algebras, Lie-admissible
BT Lie algebras
Lie algebras
[QA252.3]
UF Algebras, Lie
BT Algebra, Abstract
Algebras, Linear
RT Lie groups
NT Groups, Continuous
Lie-admissible algebras
Lie algebroids
Lie groups, Nilpotent
Universal enveloping algebras
Lie algebras, Exceptional
UF Exceptional Lie algebras

2152

Lie algebroids
  BT Algebroids
       Lie algebras
Lie detectors and detection
  (May Subd Geog)
  [HV8078]
  UF Polygraph
  BT Criminal investigation
       Evidence, Criminal
       Psychology, Forensic
       Truthfulness and falsehood
  NT Polygraph operators
Lie family (Not Subd Geog)
  UF Lier family
  RT Lee family
Lie groupoids
  BT Groupoids
       Lie groups
Lie groups
  [QA387]
  UF Groups, Lie
  BT Symmetric spaces
       Topological groups
  RT Lie algebras
  NT Homogeneous spaces
       Lie groupoids
       Lie groups, Nilpotent
       Pseudogroups
       Semisimple Lie groups
       Symmetric spaces, Hermitian
Lie groups, Nilpotent
  UF Nilpotent Lie groups
  BT Groups, Nilpotent
       Lie algebras
       Lie groups
Lie series
  USE Series, Lie
Liebenau Site (Germany) (Not Subd Geog)
  BT Germany (West)—Antiquities
Liebenguth family
  USE Levengood family
Liebfraumilch
  BT Wine and wine making
Liebieghaus Kopf (Statue)
  USE Liebieghaus kouros head (Statue)
Liebieghaus kouros head (Statue)
  UF Frankfurter Kopf (Statue)
       Frankfurter Kuroskopf (Statue)
       Liebieghaus Kopf (Statue)
  BT Sculpture, Greek
Liebig family (Not Subd Geog)
Liechtenstein, House of (Not Subd Geog)
  [DB891]
  UF House of Liechtenstein
  BT Liechtenstein—Kings and rulers
Liechtenstein
  — Description and travel
  — — 1981-
  — Kings and rulers
    NT Liechtenstein, House of
Liechtenstein Americans (May Subd Geog)
  BT Ethnology—United States
Liechtenstein art
  USE Art, Liechtenstein
Liechtenstein Castle (Austria)
  USE Burg Liechtenstein (Austria)
Liechtenstein cookery
  USE Cookery, Liechtenstein
Liechtenstein newspapers
Liechtenstein Palace (Austria)
  USE Schloss Liechtenstein (Austria)
Liechtenstein periodicals
Liechti family
  USE Leighty family
Liechty family
  USE Leighty family
Lied, Polyphonic
    Here are entered works on the polyphonic lied as
a musical form. Compositions in the form of the poly-
phonic lied are entered under the heading Lieder,
Polyphonic.

UF Polyphonic lied
Lied aus der Ferne (Painting)
  USE Hodler, Ferdinand, 1853-1918. Call
      from afar
Lieder, Polyphonic
    Here are entered compositions in the form of the
polyphonic lied. Works on the polyphonic lied as a
musical form are entered under the heading Lied,
Polyphonic.
  UF Polyphonic lieder
Liedke family
  USE Liedtke family
Liedtke family (Not Subd Geog)
  UF Liedke family
Liefdetuin (Painting)
  USE Rubens, Peter Paul, Sir, 1577-1640.
      Garden of love
Liège font
  USE Renier, de Huy, d. 1150. Liège font
Lieh-cho Peninsula (China)
  USE Luichow Peninsula (China)
Lieke family
  USE Leak family
Liemers (Netherlands)
  USE Lijmers (Netherlands)
Liens (May Subd Geog)
  UF Hypothecation
       Secret liens
  BT Bailments
       Chattel mortgages
       Commercial law
       Contracts, Maritime
       Encumbrances (Law)
       Personal property
       Real property
       Security (Law)
  RT Debtor and creditor
       Mortgages
       Pledges (Law)
       Priorities of claims and liens
       Sales, Conditional
  NT Maritime liens
       Mechanics' liens
       Railroad liens
       Stoppage in transitu
       Tax liens
       Trust receipts
Liens (Roman law)
Lier family
  USE Lie family
Lierle family
  USE Lyerly family
Liesegang rings
  [QD549]
  BT Precipitation (Chemistry)
Lietz family
  USE Litz family
Lieurance family
  USE Lawrence family
Lieutenant-governors
    Works on lieutenant-governors in the United
States are entered under the heading Lieutenant-gov-
ernors—United States. Works on lieutenant-gover-
nors in other countries are entered under the name of
the country with subdivision Lieutenant-governors,
e.g. Canada—Lieutenant-governors. Works on lieu-
tenant-governors of any state or province, including
collective biography, are entered under the name of
the state or province with subdivision Lieutenant-
governors, e.g. Texas—Lieutenant-governors.
  BT State governments
  — United States
  — — Powers and duties
Lievers family
  USE Livers family
Life
  [BD430-BD435 (Philosophy of life)]
  NT Birth (Philosophy)
       Death
       Jiva
       Philosophical anthropology
       Quality of life

  — Biblical teaching
    NT Christian life—Biblical teaching
  — Origin
    [QH325]
    UF Abiogenesis
         Biogenesis
         Germ theory
         Heterogenesis
         Life, Origin of
         Origin of life
         Plasmogeny
         Plasmogony
    BT Evolution
    RT Spontaneous generation
    NT Chemical evolution
Life, Book of
  USE Book of life
Life, Economic
  USE Economic life (of economic goods)
Life, Elixir of
  USE Elixir of life
Life, Future
  USE Future life
Life, Germfree
  USE Germfree life
Life, Jewish way of
  USE Jewish way of life
Life, Latent
  USE Cryptobiosis
Life, Long
  USE Longevity
Life, Origin of
  USE Life—Origin
Life, Quality of
  USE Quality of life
Life, Service (Engineering)
  USE Service life (Engineering)
Life, Spiritual
  USE Spiritual life
Life, Tree of
  USE Tree of life
Life (Biology)
  [QH325-QH349]
  [QP81 (Physiology)]
  RT Biology
  NT Biosphere
       Cryptobiosis
       Death (Biology)
       Dormancy (Biology)
       Genetics
       Longevity
       Mechanism (Philosophy)
       Protoplasm
       Reproduction
       Vital force
       Vitalism
Life after death
  USE Future life
       Immortality
Life and death, Power over
  [BJ1469]
  UF Death, Power over
       Power over life and death
  BT Ethics
       Free will and determinism
       Liberty
       Punishment
  NT Right to die
       Sallekhanā
  — Religious aspects
  — — Baptists, [Catholic Church, etc.]
  — — Buddhism, [Christianity, etc.]
Life-boats (May Subd Geog)
  [VK1473]
  UF Surf-boats
  BT Boats and boating
       Life-saving apparatus
       Merchant marine—Safety measures
  NT Lifeboat service
       United States. Navy—Boats
  — Motors

Life-boats
— **Motors** *(Continued)*
    BT Marine engines
Life care communities *(May Subd Geog)*
    Here are entered works on planned residential developments for the aged which also provide meal service, medical care, etc. Works on residential developments designed for the aged are entered under Retirement communities.
    UF Lifecare communities
    BT Aged—Dwellings
        Retirement communities
— **Law and legislation** *(May Subd Geog)*
Life change events *(May Subd Geog)*
    [BF637.L53 (Psychology)]
    [RC455.4.L53 (Psychiatry)]
    Here are entered works on those social, psychological and environmental occurrences which require an adjustment or effect a change in an individual's pattern of living.
    UF Events, Life change
        Experiences, Stressful life
        Life events, Stressful
        Life experiences, Stressful
        Stressful events
        Stressful life events
    BT Developmental psychology
        Experience
    RT Stress (Psychology)
Life cycle, Human
    UF Human life cycle
        Life stages, Human
        Lifecycle, Human
    BT Human growth
        Maturation (Psychology)
    RT Developmental psychology
    NT Adolescence
        Adulthood
        Children
        Infants
        Life span, Productive
        Life style
        Middle age
        Old age
— **Religious aspects**
— — **Buddhism, [Christianity, etc.]**
Life cycle, Product
    USE Product life cycle
Life events, Stressful
    USE Life change events
Life expectancy *(May Subd Geog)*
    BT Longevity
— **Sex differences**
Life experiences, Stressful
    USE Life change events
Life guards
    USE Lifeguards
Life histories
    USE *subdivision* Biography *under particular subjects, classes of persons and names of countries, cities, etc.*
        Biography
Life imprisonment *(May Subd Geog)*
    BT Prison sentences
        Prisoners
Life in art
Life insurance
    USE Insurance, Life
Life insurance stocks *(May Subd Geog)*
    BT Insurance stocks
Life insurance trusts *(May Subd Geog)*
    UF Insurance trusts
    BT Insurance, Life
        Trusts and trustees
— **Law and legislation** *(May Subd Geog)*
— **Self-insurance**
Life line (Physics)
    USE World line (Physics)
Life of Christ (Painting)
    USE Bailey, Jackson, 1927-   Life of Christ

Life of Louis XIV (Tapestries)
    USE History of the King (Tapestries)
Life of Marie de Médicis (Paintings)
    USE Rubens, Peter Paul, Sir, 1577-1640. Histories of Marie de Médicis
Life on other planets
    Here are entered works on the question of life in outer space. Works on the prospective use of the science of anthropology in dealing with intelligent beings in outer space, or establishing earth colonies on extraterrestrial bodies are entered under Extraterrestrial anthropology.
    UF Astrobiology
        Exobiology
        Extraterrestrial life
        Human beings on other planets
        Man on other planets
    BT Astronomy
        Cosmology
        Planets
        Space biology
        Stars
    RT Plurality of worlds
    NT Extraterrestrial anthropology
        Interstellar communication
        Religion and astronautics
Life-preservers
    [VK1477]
    BT Drowning—Prevention—Equipment and supplies
        Life-saving apparatus
Life-raft food packets
    USE Survival and emergency rations
Life rafts
    BT Life-saving apparatus
        Merchant marine—Safety measures
Life-rocket
    [VK1479]
    UF Rocket, Life
    BT Life-saving apparatus
Life-saving *(May Subd Geog)*
    [GV838.68-GV838.76 (Swimming)]
    [VK1300-VK1481 (Marine services)]
    BT Rescue work
    NT Aeronautics—Relief service
        Drowning—Prevention
        Drowning, Restoration from
        Life-saving stations
        Lifeboat crew members
        Lifeguards
        Lighthouses
        Rescues
        Search and rescue operations
        Survival (after airplane accidents, shipwrecks, etc.)
        Survival swimming
Life-saving apparatus
    [VK1460-1481]
    BT Shipwrecks
    NT Aircraft survival equipment
        Emergency vehicles
        Life-boats
        Life-preservers
        Life rafts
        Life-rocket
        Life-saving nets
        Line-throwing guns
        Submarine rescue vehicles
— **Law and legislation** *(May Subd Geog)*
Life-saving at fires *(May Subd Geog)*
    [TH9402-9418]
    BT Fire-escapes
        Fires
        Rescue work
Life-saving nets
    [TH9418]
    BT Fire-escapes
        Life-saving apparatus
Life-saving stations *(May Subd Geog)*
    [VK1460-1471]
    BT Life-saving

    NT Lifeboat service
Life science engineering
    USE Bioengineering
Life science publishing *(May Subd Geog)*
    BT Life sciences
        Publishers and publishing
        Science publishing
Life sciences *(May Subd Geog)*
    UF Biosciences
        Sciences, Life
    BT Science
    NT Agriculture
        Bioethics
        Biology
        Life science publishing
        Medical sciences
        Medicine
— **Bibliography**
    RT Life sciences literature
Life sciences ethics
    USE Bioethics
Life sciences libraries *(May Subd Geog)*
    UF Libraries, Life sciences
    BT Scientific libraries
    NT Agricultural libraries
        Biological libraries
        Medical libraries
Life sciences literature *(May Subd Geog)*
    [QH303.6]
    UF Literature, Life sciences
    BT Scientific literature
    RT Life sciences—Bibliography
    NT Agricultural literature
        Biological literature
        Medical literature
Life skills *(May Subd Geog)*
    Here are entered works that discuss a combination of the skills needed by an individual to exist in modern society, including skills related to education, employment, finance, health, housing, psychology, etc.
    UF Advice-for-living books
        Basic life skills
        Competencies, Functional
        Coping skills
        Everyday living skills
        Functional competencies
        Fundamental life skills
        Living skills
        Personal life skills
        Problems of everyday living, Skills for solving
        Skills, Life
    BT Interpersonal relations
        Social learning
        Success
    NT Conduct of life
        Self-help techniques
        Social skills
        Survival skills
— **Handbooks, manuals, etc.**
    UF Life skills guides
    SA *subdivision* Life skills guides *under classes of persons and ethnic groups*
— **United States**
    NT Hispanic Americans—Life skills guides
        Vietnamese Americans—Life skills guides
Life skills guides
    USE Life skills—Handbooks, manuals, etc.
Life span, Productive *(May Subd Geog)*
    UF Productive life span
        Working life
    BT Age and employment
        Aged
        Life cycle, Human
        Mortality
        Occupations

Life span prolongation
  USE Longevity
Life stages, Human
  USE Life cycle, Human
Life style
    Here are entered theoretical works on an in-
  dividual's distinctive, recognizable way of living, and
  the behavior that expresses it.
  UF Counter culture
      Lifestyle
      Social environment
      Style, Life
  BT Human behavior
      Life cycle, Human
      Manners and customs
      Quality of life
  NT Living alone
Life support systems (Critical care)
  (May Subd Geog)
  [RC86.7]
  BT Critical care medicine
Life support systems (Space environment)
  UF Man in space
  BT Bioengineering
      Environmental engineering
      Human engineering
      Space flight—Physiological effect
      Space medicine
  NT Closed ecological systems (Space
        environment)
      Extraterrestrial bases
      Project Apollo
      Project Mercury
      Space cabin atmospheres
      Space ships
      Space suits
      Space vehicles—Oxygen equipment
      Space vehicles—Water-supply
Life tables
  USE Mortality—Tables
Life time light (Portrait sculpture)
  USE Strong, Brett-Livingstone, 1953-
          Life time light
Life without death (Tale)
  USE Youth without age and life without
          death (Tale)
Life zones *(May Subd Geog)*
  [QH84]
  UF Biogeographic zones
      Zones, Life
  BT Biogeography
      Ecology
  RT Crop zones
Lifeboat crew members *(May Subd Geog)*
  BT Life-saving
      Lifeboat service
Lifeboat service *(May Subd Geog)*
  BT Life-boats
      Life-saving stations
  NT Lifeboat crew members
Lifecare communities
  USE Life care communities
Lifecycle, Human
  USE Life cycle, Human
Lifeguards *(May Subd Geog)*
  [GV838.72-838.74]
  UF Life guards
  BT Life-saving
      Swimmers
Lifelong education
  USE Continuing education
Lifestyle
  USE Life style
Lifou language
  USE Dehu language
Lift (Aerodynamics)
  UF Aerodynamic forces
  BT Aerodynamic load
      Aerodynamics
  RT Drag (Aerodynamics)
  NT Elevators (Airplanes)

Flaps (Airplanes)
      Ground-cushion phenomenon
      Stalling (Aerodynamics)
— **Computer programs**
Lift fans
  UF Fans, Lift
      Lifting fans
  BT Air jets
      Fans (Machinery)
  RT Ground-effect machines
  NT Fan-in-wing aircraft
Lift irrigation *(May Subd Geog)*
  BT Irrigation
Lift net fishing
  [SH344.6.L5]
  UF Dip net fishing
      Lift nets
  BT Fisheries
      Fishing nets
Lift nets
  USE Lift net fishing
Lift-off from the moon
  USE Artificial satellites—Lunar launching
Lift stations
  USE Pumping stations
Lifters, Vacuum
  USE Vacuum lifters
Lifthrop family
  USE Liptrap family
Lifting and carrying
  [T55.3.L5]
  UF Carrying weights
  BT Materials handling
  NT Slings and hitches
      Vacuum lifters
      Weight lifting
Lifting and carrying (Jewish law)
  BT Jewish law
      Prohibited work (Jewish law)
Lifting fans
  USE Lift fans
Lifting-jacks
  [TJ1425-1435]
  UF Jacks
  NT Fork lift trucks
      Hydraulic jacks
Lifting magnets
  UF Magnets, Lifting
  BT Electromagnets
Lifting theory
  BT Measure theory
Lifts
  USE Elevators
      Hoisting machinery
Lifts, Ski
  USE Ski lifts
Lifu language
  USE Dehu language
Ligament prostheses *(May Subd Geog)*
  UF Artificial ligaments
      Synthetic ligaments
  BT Ligaments
      Prosthesis
Ligaments
  [QL827 (Comparative anatomy)]
  [QM141 (Human anatomy)]
  [QM563 (Histology)]
  BT Bones
      Joints
      Muscles
  NT Cartilage
      Cruciate ligaments
      Ligament prostheses
      Periodontal ligament
— **Wounds and injuries**
Ligamentum cruciatum anterius
  USE Anterior cruciate ligament
Ligand binding assay (Biochemistry)
  USE Radioligand assay

Ligand field theory
  BT Complex compounds
      Coordination compounds
      Crystal field theory
      Transition metals
Ligands
  BT Complex compounds
      Metal ions
  NT Chelates
      Radioligand assay
Ligases
  [QP618]
  UF Synthetases
  BT Enzymes
  NT Aminoacyl-tRNA synthetases
      Glutamine synthetase
      Glutamyl-tRNA synthetase
      Lysyl-tRNA synthetase
      Pyruvate carboxylase
Ligation, Tubal
  USE Tubal sterilization
Ligation (Surgery)
  USE Ligature (Surgery)
Ligature (Music)
  USE Musical notation
      Neumes
Ligature (Surgery)
  [RD33]
  UF Ligation (Surgery)
  BT Surgery, Operative
  RT Sutures
  NT Arteries—Ligature
      Carotid artery—Ligature
      Catgut sutures
      Eustachian tube—Ligature
      Iliac artery—Ligature
      Staplers (Surgery)
      Umbilical cord—Ligature
      Veins—Ligature
Liggon family
  USE Ligon family
Light
  [QC350-495]
  BT Electromagnetic theory
      Electromagnetic waves
      Physics
      Vibration
      Waves
  RT Light sources
      Optics
      Photometry
      Radiation
      Spectrum analysis
  NT Absorption of light
      Artists' materials—Effect of light on
      Color
      Diffraction
      Doppler effect
      Electroluminescence
      Interference (Light)
      Lasers
      Light filters
      Luminescence
      N-rays
      Optical detectors
      Optical pumping
      Photobiology
      Photons
      Polarization (Light)
      Radioactivity
      Reflection (Optics)
      Refraction
      Transillumination
      Underwater light
      Will-o'-the-wisp
      X-rays
— **Chemical action**
      USE Photochemistry
— **Mythology**
— **Physiological effect**
      [GN197 (Anthropology)]

Light
— **Physiological effect** *(Continued)*
   [QH651 (Biology)]
   [QR84 (Bacteriology)]
   [RM838 (Phototherapy)]
   BT Photobiology
   SA *subdivision* Effect of light on *under*
        individual animals and groups of
        animals, e.g. Cattle—Effect of
        light on; Fishes—Effect of light
        on
   NT Color—Physiological effect
       Photodermatitis
       Photoperiodism
       Photosensitization, Biological
       Phototherapy
       Phototropism in animals
       Plants, Effect of light on
— **Religious aspects**
   NT Candles and lights
       Light and darkness in the Bible
— — **Buddhism, [Christianity, etc.]**
— — **Judaism**
     NT Candles and lights (Judaism)
        Hanukkah
— **Scattering**
   UF Light scattering
       Scattering of light
   BT Diffusion
       Particles
       Reflection (Optics)
       Refraction
   NT Brillouin scattering
       Critical opalescence
       Interstellar matter
       Photon correlation
       Quasielastic light scattering
       Rayleigh scattering
       Speckle
       Umkehr effect
— **Speed**
   [QC407]
   UF Speed of light
       Velocity of light
   NT Particles, Relativistic
— Therapeutic use
   USE Phototherapy
— **Transmission**
   [QC389]
— **Wave-length**
   [QC455]
Light, Black
  USE Ultraviolet radiation
Light, Blue
  USE Blue light
Light, Colored
   [RM835-RM844 (Therapeutics)]
  UF Colored light
  NT Blue light
— Therapeutic use
   USE Color—Therapeutic use
Light, Corpuscular theory of
   [QC402]
  UF Corpuscular theory of light
  BT Optics
      Wave-particle duality
Light, Electric
  USE Electric lighting
      Photometry
Light, Electromagnetic theory of
  USE Electromagnetic theory
Light, Gaussian
  USE Gaussian beams
Light, Inner
  USE Inner Light
Light, Ultraviolet
  USE Ultraviolet radiation
Light, Wave theory of
   [QC403]

   BT Optics
       Wave-motion, Theory of
       Wave-particle duality
   NT Electromagnetic theory
       Huygens' principle
       Optics, Physical
Light, Zodiacal
  USE Zodiacal light
Light (Easement)
  USE Light and air (Easement)
      Solar access rights
Light-activated pesticides *(May Subd Geog)*
   [SB951.145.L54]
  UF Photoactive pesticides
      Photodynamic pesticides
  BT Pesticides
Light alloys
  USE Light metal alloys
Light amplification by stimulated emission of
radiation
  USE Lasers
Light amplifiers
  UF Amplifiers, Light
  NT Lasers
Light and air (Easement) *(May Subd Geog)*
   [K]
   [TH7792]
  UF Air (Easement)
      Ancient lights
      Light (Easement)
  BT Adjoining landowners
      Lighting—Obstructions
      Real property
      Servitudes
  NT Solar access rights
Light and darkness in literature
  UF Darkness and light in literature
      Light in literature
Light and darkness in the Bible
   [BS680.L53]
  UF Darkness in the Bible
  BT Light—Religious aspects
      Polarity—Religious aspects
      Symbolism in the Bible
Light and shade
  USE Shades and shadows
Light-beam oscillograph
   [TK381]
  BT Oscillograph
Light beam splitters
  USE Beam splitters
Light beating spectroscopy
   [QC454.L63]
  UF Photon correlation spectroscopy
      Spectroscopy, Light beating
      Spectroscopy, Photon correlation
  BT Laser spectroscopy
      Quantum optics
      Spectrum analysis
Light Brigade, Charge of the
  USE Balaklava, Battle of, 1854
Light bulbs
  USE Electric lamps, Incandescent
Light coagulation
   [RE992.P]
  UF Photocoagulation
  BT Eye—Diseases and defects
      Phototherapy
  NT Laser coagulation
Light communication systems, Laser-based
  USE Laser communication systems
Light communications
  USE Optical communications
Light construction
  USE Lightweight construction
Light deflectors
  UF Beam deflectors, Light
      Deflectors, Light
  BT Optical instruments
      Optics

Light emitting diodes
  BT Diodes, Semiconductor
      Light sources
      Optical communications
      Optoelectronic devices
      Photoelectronic devices
Light-emitting organs
  USE Photophores
Light filters
   [QC373.L5]
  UF Filters, Light
  BT Light
      Optics
      Photographic optics
  NT Photography—Light filters
Light fishing
   [SH344.43.L5]
  UF Attracting fish by light
      Electric light fishing
      Fish attracting by light
  BT Fisheries
Light guides (Optical fibers)
  USE Optical fibers
Light in architecture
  BT Architecture
  RT Lighting, Architectural and decorative
Light in art
   [N8219.L5]
  RT Chiaroscuro
Light in literature
  USE Light and darkness in literature
Light intensity perception
  USE Brightness perception
Light lists
  USE Aids to navigation—Lists
Light metal alloys
   [TA484]
  UF Light alloys
  BT Alloys
— **Fatigue**
   [TA484]
Light metals
  BT Airplanes—Materials
      Metals
  NT Alkali metals
      Alkaline earth metals
      Aluminum
      Aluminum alloys
      Aluminum-magnesium alloys
      Magnesium
      Magnesium alloys
— **Founding**
— **Metallurgy**
   [TN773]
— **Welding**
Light metals industry *(May Subd Geog)*
  NT Aluminum industry and trade
Light meters
  BT Measuring instruments
Light modulators
   [TK8360.L5]
  UF Modulators, Light
      Photomodulators
  BT Electrooptics
      Photoelectronic devices
Light of the world (Painting)
  USE Hunt, William Holman, 1827-1910.
      Light of the world
Light pens
  UF Pens, Light
  BT Computer graphics
      Computers—Optical equipment
      Fiber optics
      Photoelectronic devices
Light production in animals and plants
  USE Bioluminescence
Light pulses, Picosecond
  USE Laser pulses, Ultrashort
Light pulses, Ultrashort
  USE Laser pulses, Ultrashort

Light quantum
  USE Photons
Light rail transit
  USE Street-railroads
Light railroads
  USE Railroads, Local and light
Light scattering
  USE Light—Scattering
Light scattering, Quasielastic
  USE Quasielastic light scattering
Light sensitive paper
  UF Paper, Light sensitive
    Sensitive paper, Light
Light-ships *(May Subd Geog)*
  ⌐VK1000-1246⌐
  BT Beacons
    Lighthouses
Light shows
  USE Lighting—Special effects
Light sources
  UF Sources of light
  RT Light
    Lighting
  NT Daylight
    Electric lamps
    Electric lighting
    Infrared sources
    Lamps
    Lasers
    Light emitting diodes
    Liquid crystals
    Luminescence
    Sun
Light sources for moving-picture projectors
  USE Moving-picture projectors—Light
    sources
Light therapy
  USE Phototherapy
Light transport planes
  USE Commuter aircraft
Light traps
  USE Insect traps
Light verse
  USE Humorous poetry
Light water graphite reactors
  ⌐TK9203.L45⌐
  UF Reactors, Light water graphite
  BT Light water reactors
    Nuclear reactors
Light water reactors *(May Subd Geog)*
  UF Reactors, Light water
  BT Nuclear reactors
    Water cooled reactors
  NT Light water graphite reactors
Light weight construction
  USE Lightweight construction
Light-year
  BT Astronomy, Spherical and practical
    Astrophysics
    Units
Lighter-aboard-ship vessels
  USE Barge-carrying ships
Lighter-than-air craft
  USE Airships
Lighterage *(May Subd Geog)*
  UF Lightering
  BT Cargo handling
    Freight and freightage
    Shipping
  NT Barge-carrying ships
Lightering
  USE Lighterage
Lightermen *(May Subd Geog)*
Lighters, Cigar
  USE Cigar lighters
Lightfishes
  USE Gonostomatidae
Lightfoot family *(Not Subd Geog)*
  UF Lightfoote family
Lightfoote family
  USE Lightfoot family

Lighthouse keepers *(May Subd Geog)*
Lighthouse tenders
  ⌐VK1000-VK1124 (Lighthouse service)⌐
  ⌐VM296 (Specifications)⌐
  BT Government vessels
    Lighthouses
    Ships
Lighthouse tubes
  USE Disk-seal tubes
Lighthouses *(May Subd Geog)*
  ⌐TC375-TC379 (Construction)⌐
  ⌐VK1000-VK1246⌐
  BT Aids to navigation
    Hydraulic structures
    Life-saving
    Marine service
    Navigation
  RT Beacons
  NT Bridge lights (Navigation)
    Light-ships
    Lighthouse tenders
  — **Law and legislation** *(May Subd Geog)*
    BT Maritime law
  — **Lighting**
    ⌐TC377⌐
    NT Holophote
  — **Delaware**
    NT Harbor of Refuge Lighthouse
      (Del.)
  — **Maine**
    NT Matinicus Rock Lighthouse
      (Matinicus Rock, Me.)
  — **Massachusetts**
    NT Boston Light (Mass.)
      Cape Ann Light Station (Thacher
        Island, Mass.)
  — **New Zealand**
    NT Tiritiri Lighthouse (N.Z.)
Lighting *(May Subd Geog)*
  ⌐GT440-GT445 (Manners and
    customs)⌐
  ⌐TH7700-TH7975 (Technology)⌐
  UF Illumination
  BT Buildings—Environmental engineering
    Sanitation, Household
  RT Gas-lighting
    Light sources
  SA subdivision Lighting under types of
    vehicles, structures, buildings,
    rooms, installations, etc., e.g.
    Factories—Lighting
  NT Acetylene
    Blackouts in war
    Candles
    Daylight
    Daylighting
    Electric lighting
    Emergency lighting
    Exterior lighting
    Flares
    Floodlighting
    Incandescent gas-lighting
    Interior lighting
    Lamps
    Lighting, Architectural and decorative
    Municipal lighting
    Reflectors, Lighting
    Sidewalk-lights
    Stage lighting
    Street-lighting
    Torches
  — **Law and legislation** *(May Subd Geog)*
    BT Building laws
  — **Obstructions**
    ⌐TH7792⌐
    NT Light and air (Easement)
  — **Special effects**
    UF Light shows
      Lighting—Visual effects
      Special effects (Lighting)
  — **Taxation** *(May Subd Geog)*

  UF Lighting tax
  — Visual effects
    USE Lighting—Special effects
Lighting, Architectural and decorative
  ⌐TH7703⌐
  UF Architectural lighting
    Decorative lighting
    Lighting, Decorative
  BT Architecture
    Electric lighting
    Exterior lighting
    Interior decoration
    Interior lighting
    Lighting
    Municipal lighting
  RT Light in architecture
  NT Garden lighting
Lighting, Decorative
  USE Lighting, Architectural and decorative
Lighting, Emergency
  USE Emergency lighting
Lighting, Exterior
  USE Exterior lighting
Lighting, Garden
  USE Garden lighting
Lighting reflectors
  USE Reflectors, Lighting
Lighting tax
  USE Lighting—Taxation
Lightning *(May Subd Geog)*
  ⌐GR630 (Folk-lore)⌐
  ⌐QC966 (General)⌐
  BT Accidents
    Electricity
    Meteorology
    Thunderstorms
  RT Atmospheric electricity
    Thunder
    Thunderstorm electricity
  NT Ball lightning
    Beaded lightning
    Electricity, Injuries from
    Transients (Electricity)
    Whistlers (Radio meteorology)
Lightning (BAC fighter plane)
  USE BAC Lightning (Fighter plane)
Lightning (Fighter planes)
  UF P-38 (Fighter planes)
  BT Fighter planes
Lightning-arresters
  ⌐TK3248⌐
  BT Electric apparatus and appliances—
    Protection
    Electric wiring
    Fire prevention
    Lightning protection
Lightning bugs
  USE Fireflies
Lightning-conductors
  ⌐TH9057-9092⌐
  UF Lightning-rods
  BT Fire prevention
    Lightning protection
Lightning in art
Lightning insurance
  USE Insurance, Lightning
Lightning interference
  USE Atmospherics
Lightning protection
  ⌐TH9057-9092⌐
  UF Protection from lightning
  BT Buildings—Protection
    Fire prevention
  NT Electric spark gaps
    Lightning-arresters
    Lightning-conductors
    Telephone lines—Lightning protection
Lightning-rods
  USE Lightning-conductors
Lightning war
  ⌐U167.5.L5⌐

Lightning war *(Continued)*
　UF　Blitzkrieg
　BT　Military art and science
　　　Tactics
Lightningbugs
　USE　Fireflies
Lights, Feast of
　USE　Hanukkah
Lights, Liturgical
　USE　Candles and lights
Lights, Signal
　USE　Signal lights
Lights and candles
　USE　Candles and lights
Lightweight concrete
　UF　Cellular concrete
　　　Concrete, Lightweight
　　　No-fines concrete
　　　Porous concrete
　BT　Concrete
　NT　Air-entrained concrete
Lightweight construction
　　⌈TA663⌉
　UF　Construction, Lightweight
　　　Light construction
　　　Light weight construction
　　　Minimum weight construction
　BT　Building
　　　Structures, Theory of
　SA　*particular structural forms and*
　　　　materials normally found in
　　　　lightweight construction, e.g. Shells
　　　(Engineering); Light metals
　NT　Air-supported structures
　　　Aluminum construction
　　　Monocoque construction
　　　Sandwich construction
　　　Sheet-metal work
　　　Tensile architecture
　　　Titanium construction
Ligia
　　⌈QL444.M34⌉
　UF　Lygia
　　　Rock slaters
　　　Sea slaters
　BT　Ligiidae
Ligia occidentalis
　　⌈QL444.M34⌉
Ligia oceanica
　　⌈QL444.M34⌉
Ligiidae
　　⌈QL444.M34⌉
　UF　Ligydidae
　BT　Isopoda
　NT　Ligia
Lignac's disease
　USE　Cystinosis
Lignans
　BT　Natural products
　　　Phenyl compounds
Ligne Maginot (France)
　USE　Maginot Line (France)
Ligni guaiaci, Oleum
　USE　Guaiac wood oil
Lignilites
　USE　Stylolites
Lignin
　　⌈QK647⌉
　RT　Wood—Chemistry
—**Biodegradation**
Lignite *(May Subd Geog)*
　　⌈HD9559.L4 (Economics)⌉
　　⌈TN831-TN834 (Mining)⌉
　　⌈TP329 (Fuel)⌉
　UF　Brown coal
　BT　Coal
　　　Fuel
　NT　Briquets (Fuel)
　　　Carbonization
—**Combustion**

Lignite industry *(May Subd Geog)*
　　⌈HD9559.L4-6⌉
Lignite leases *(May Subd Geog)*
　BT　Coal leases
Lignum, Paraguay
　USE　Bulnesia sarmienti
Lignum-vitæ
　　⌈SD397.L5 (Sylviculture)⌉
Ligon family *(Not Subd Geog)*
　UF　Leggon family
　　　Legon family
　　　Liggon family
　　　Ligons family
　　　Ligrand family
　　　Lygon family
Ligons family
　USE　Ligon family
Ligrand family
　USE　Ligon family
Liguria Alpina (Italy)
　USE　Ligurian Alps (Italy)
Ligurian Alps (Italy)
　UF　Alpi Liguri (Italy)
　　　Liguria Alpina (Italy)
　BT　Alps
　　　Mountains—Italy
Ligurian literature
　USE　Italian literature—Italy—Liguria
Ligurian race
　USE　Mediterranean race
Ligurians *(May Subd Geog)*
　　⌈DC82 (Gaul)⌉
　　⌈DG55.L5 (General and Italic)⌉
　BT　Basques
　　　Italic peoples
Liguus fasciatus
　　⌈QL430.5.B8⌉
Ligydidae
　USE　Ligiidae
Lihyanic inscriptions
　USE　Inscriptions, Lihyanic
Lijmers (Netherlands)
　UF　Liemers (Netherlands)
Lika Region (Croatia)
Likay
　USE　Likē
Likē *(May Subd Geog)*
　　Here are entered general works and those that
　deal solely with the presentation of Likē on the stage.
　The texts of Likē plays and works about them from
　a literary point of view are entered under Likē plays.
　UF　Likay
　　　Yīkē
　BT　Theater—Thailand
Likē plays *(May Subd Geog)*
　　Here are entered the texts of Likē plays and works
　about them from a literary point of view. General
　works and those that deal solely with the presentation
　of Likē plays on the stage are entered under Likē.
　BT　Thai drama
Likembe
　USE　Mbira
Lila, Operation, 1942
　USE　Operation Lila, 1942
Līla (Game)
　USE　Leela (Game)
Lilacs *(May Subd Geog)*
　　⌈QK495.O44 (Botany)⌉
　　⌈SB413.L65 (Ornamental plants)⌉
　UF　Syringa
　BT　Oleaceae
—**Varieties**
Lilaeopsis
　　⌈QK495.U48⌉
　BT　Umbelliferae
Lile
　　⌈QL638.C64⌉
　BT　Clupeidae
Lile family
　USE　Lyles family
Lile piquitinga
　　⌈QL638.C64⌉

Liles family
　USE　Lyles family
Liliaceae
　　⌈QK495.L72⌉
　BT　Liliales
　NT　Agapanthus
　　　Allium
　　　Aloe
　　　Aphyllanthes
　　　Asparagus
　　　Astroloba
　　　Bowiea
　　　Brodiaea
　　　Calochortus
　　　Convallaria
　　　Daylilies
　　　Dichelostemma
　　　Eremurus
　　　Haworthia
　　　Helonias
　　　Heloniopsis
　　　Hosta
　　　Lilies
　　　Luzuriaga
　　　Metanarthecium
　　　Narthecium
　　　Phormium
　　　Rohdea
　　　Sabadilla
　　　Sanseviera
　　　Smilax
　　　Tofieldia
　　　Triteleia
　　　Veratrum
Liliales
　　⌈QK495.A14⌉
　BT　Monocotyledons
　NT　Agavaceae
　　　Amaryllidaceae
　　　Burmanniaceae
　　　Corsiaceae
　　　Dioscoreaceae
　　　Iridaceae
　　　Liliaceae
　　　Pontederiaceae
　　　Taccaceae
Lilidahl family
　USE　Liljedahl family
Liliedahl family
　USE　Liljedahl family
Lilies *(May Subd Geog)*
　　⌈QK495.L72 (Botany)⌉
　　⌈SB413.L7 (Plant culture)⌉
　UF　Lilium
　　　Lily
　BT　Liliaceae
　NT　Calla
　　　Lilium superbum
—**Varieties**
Lilies, Day
　USE　Daylilies
Lilies, Fire
　USE　Cyrtanthus
Lilies, Flamingo
　USE　Anthuriums
Lilies, Sword
　USE　Gladiolus
Lilies-of-the-valley
　　⌈QK495.L72 (Botany)⌉
　　⌈SB413.L69 (Culture)⌉
　UF　Convallaria majalis
　　　Lily of the valley
Lilima language
　　⌈PL8454⌉
　BT　Bantu languages
　　　Shona language
Lilith (Semitic mythology)
　BT　Demonology, Semitic
　　　Mythology, Semitic
Lilium
　USE　Lilies

Lilium superbum
  [QK495.L72]
    UF Turks cap lily
        Turkscap lily
    BT Lilies
Liljedahl family (Not Subd Geog)
    UF Lilidahl family
        Liliedahl family
        Liljidahl family
        Lillidahl family
        Lilliedahl family
        Lilliedale family
        Lilliedoll family
Liljidahl family
    USE Liljedahl family
Lille Bælt (Denmark)
    UF Lille Belt (Denmark)
        Little Belt (Denmark)
    BT Straits—Denmark
    NT Als Island (Denmark)
Lille Belt (Denmark)
    USE Lille Bælt (Denmark)
Lille family
    USE Lilly family
Lille Street (Paris, France)
    USE Rue de Lille (Paris, France)
Lillegaard family (Not Subd Geog)
Lilley family
    USE Lilly family
Lillidahl family
    USE Liljedahl family
Lillie family
    USE Lilly family
Lilliedahl family
    USE Liljedahl family
Lilliedale family
    USE Liljedahl family
Lilliedoll family
    USE Liljedahl family
Lilliehöök family (Not Subd Geog)
Lillie's Cemetery (Bastard, Ont.)
    UF Chick's Cemetery (Bastard, Ont.)
        Old Lillie's Cemetery (Bastard, Ont.)
    BT Cemeteries—Ontario
Lilliputocoris
  [QL523.L9]
    BT Lygaeidae
Lillomarka (Oslo, Norway)
    (Not Subd Geog)
    UF Grefsenmarka (Oslo, Norway)
        Oslo (Norway). Grefsenmarka
        Oslo (Norway). Lillomarka
Lillön (Sweden)
    UF Helgö (Sweden)
    BT Islands—Sweden
Lillooet Indians
  [E99.L]
    UF Lilowat Indians
    BT Indians of North America
        Salishan Indians
Lillooet language
    UF Lilowat language
    BT Salishan languages
Lillooet River (B.C.)
    BT Rivers—British Columbia
Lilly family (Not Subd Geog)
    UF Lille family
        Lilley family
        Lillie family
Lilowat Indians
    USE Lillooet Indians
Lilowat language
    USE Lillooet language
Lilse language
    USE Kurumba language
Lily
    USE Lilies
Lily, Triplet
    USE Triteleia laxa
Lily of the valley
    USE Lilies-of-the-valley

Lim River (Montenegro-Bosnia and Hercegovina)
    BT Rivers—Yugoslavia
Lima bean
    UF Phaseolus limensis
        Phaseolus lunatus
    BT Beans
Lima-bean pod borer
    UF Etiella zinckenella
Lima Councils
    BT Councils and synods
Lima Verde family (Not Subd Geog)
Limacea, Fossil
    BT Pterioida, Fossil
Limacella
  [QK629.A53 (Botany)]
    BT Amanitaceae
Limacidae
    BT Stylommatophora
Limaciopsis
  [QK495.M537]
    BT Menispermaceae
Limaciopsis loangensis
  [QK495.M537 (Botany)]
Limacodidae
  [QL561.L54]
    UF Apodidae
        Cochlididae
        Cochlidiidae
        Cochliopodidae
        Eucleidae
        Slug caterpillars
    BT Lepidoptera
        Moths
    NT Monema
Limanda
  [QL638.P7]
    BT Pleuronectidae
    NT Limanda ferruginea
Limanda aspera
    USE Yellowfin sole
Limanda ferruginea
  [QL638.P7]
    UF Rusty dab
        Yellowtail flounder
    BT Limanda
Limanova, Battle of, 1914
  [D557.L5]
    BT World War, 1914-1918—Campaigns—Poland
Limantriidae
    USE Lymantriidae
Limay River (Argentina)
    UF Río Limay (Argentina)
    BT Rivers—Argentina
Limb, Phantom
    USE Phantom limb
Limb regeneration
    USE Extremities (Anatomy)—Regeneration
Limba (African people)
    BT Ethnology—Sierra Leone
Limba (Tree)
    USE Terminalia superba
Limba language
  [PL8455]
    BT Guinea—Languages
        Niger-Congo languages
        Sierra Leone—Languages
Limbakaraja language
    USE Iwaidji language
Limbic lobe
    USE Limbic system
Limbic system
    UF Limbic lobe
    BT Brain
    NT Amygdaloid body
        Hippocampus (Brain)
        Hypothalamus
Limbo
  [BT850-860]
    UF Limbus

    BT Eschatology
    RT Infant salvation
Limbo language
    USE Limbu language
Limbom language
    USE Limbum language
Limbs, Artificial
    USE Artificial limbs
Limbs, Phantom
    USE Phantom limb
Limbs (Anatomy)
    USE Extremities (Anatomy)
Limbu language
  [PL3801.L5]
    UF Limbo language
        Lumbu language
    BT Tibeto-Burman languages
Limbu women
    USE Women, Limbu
Limbum language (May Subd Geog)
    UF Limbom language
        Llimbumi language
        Ndzungle language
        Ndzungli language
        Njungene language
        Nsugni language
        Nsungali language
        Nsungli language
        Nsungni language
        Wimbum language
        Zungle language
    BT Cameroon—Languages
        Grasslands Bantu languages
Limbus
    USE Limbo
Limbus (Asian people)
    BT Ethnology—Nepal
    — Women
        USE Women, Limbu
Lime (May Subd Geog)
  [S643 (Fertilizers)]
  [TA434-TA435 (Properties, testing)]
  [TP886 (Technology)]
    UF Calcia
    BT Plaster of Paris
    NT Cement
        Lime industry
        Pisé
Lime, Chloride of
    USE Bleaching powder
Lime (Tree)
    USE Lime tree
Lime as a disinfectant
  [RA766.L7]
    BT Disinfection and disinfectants
Lime fruit (May Subd Geog)
  [SB370.L5 (Culture)]
    BT Citrus fruits
Lime fruit industry (May Subd Geog)
  [HD9259.L5-HD9259.L53]
Lime in agriculture
    USE Liming of soils
Lime industry (May Subd Geog)
    BT Lime
Lime-kilns
  [TP886]
    BT Kilns
Lime oil
    BT Citrus fruits—By-products
Lime Peak (Alaska) (Not Subd Geog)
    UF Rocky Mountain (Alaska)
    BT Mountains—Alaska
Lime-soda ash process (Water purification)
    USE Water—Purification—Lime-soda ash process
Lime tree (May Subd Geog)
  [QK495.R98 (Botany)]
  [SB370.L5 ((Culture))]

Lime tree *(Continued)*
  UF Citrus aurantifolia
      Citrus limetta
      Lime (Tree)
      Limonia aurantifolia
  BT Citrus
      Fruit trees
Lime tree, East Indian
  USE Elaeocarpus ganitrus
Lime tree, European
  USE Linden
Limenitis
  [QL561.N9]
  BT Nymphalidae
Limentra di Treppio River (Italy)
  USE Limentra River (Italy)
Limentra River (Italy)
  UF Limentra di Treppio River (Italy)
      Torrente Limentra di Treppio (Italy)
      Treppio River (Italy)
  BT Rivers—Italy
Limerick Atomic Power Station (Pa.)
  BT Nuclear power plants—Pennsylvania
Limerick Plantation (S.C.) *(Not Subd Geog)*
  BT Plantations—South Carolina
Limerick, Treaty of, 1691
  [DA946]
Limericks
  [PN6231.L5]
  BT Humorous poetry
      Poetry
      Wit and humor
  NT Nonsense-verses
  — Juvenile literature
      USE Limericks, Juvenile
Limericks, Juvenile
  [PN6231.L5]
  UF Children's limericks
      Juvenile limericks
      Limericks—Juvenile literature
  BT Children's poetry
      Wit and humor, Juvenile
Limes (Roman boundary) *(May Subd Geog)*
  BT Fortification
      Military architecture
Limestone *(May Subd Geog)*
  [TN967]
  BT Evaporites
      Rocks, Carbonate
  NT Gardens, Limestone
      Jasperoid
      Marble
      Travertine
Limestone Creek (N.C.)
  BT Rivers—North Carolina
Limestone gardens
  USE Gardens, Limestone
Limestone industry *(May Subd Geog)*
  [HD9621]
Limestone Plains (A.C.T.)
  BT Plains—Australia
Limestone quartzite
  USE Jasperoid
Limicolaria
  [QL430.5.A22]
  BT Achatinidae
Liming of soils *(May Subd Geog)*
  UF Lime in agriculture
      Soils—Liming
  BT Fertilizers
      Soil amendments
Limit analysis (Theory of structures)
  USE Plastic analysis (Theory of structures)
Limit dextrinase
  USE Dextranase
Limit theorems (Probability theory)
  BT Probabilities
  NT Central limit theorem
      Large deviations

Limitation of actions *(May Subd Geog)*
  Here are entered works on the so-called negative, or extinctive, prescription of Civil law. Works on prescription as a mode of acquiring title to incorporeal hereditaments by immemorial or long continued enjoyment and works on the so-called positive, or acquisitive, prescription of Civil law are entered under Prescription (Law).
  UF Limitations, Statute of
      Limitations (Law)
      Statute of limitations
  BT Actions and defenses
      Extinguishment of debts
  RT Prescription (Law)
      Time (Law)
  NT Adverse possession
      Natural obligations
Limitation of actions (Administrative law)
(May Subd Geog)
  BT Administrative law
Limitation of actions (Canon law)
Limitation of actions (Criminal law)
(May Subd Geog)
  BT Criminal law
Limitation of actions (Islamic law)
Limitation of actions (Jewish law)
Limitation of actions (Labor law)
(May Subd Geog)
  BT Labor courts
      Labor laws and legislation
Limitation of actions (Rif law)
Limitation of actions (Roman-Dutch law)
Limitation of actions (Roman law)
Limitation of actions (Taxation)
(May Subd Geog)
Limitation of armament
  USE Disarmament
Limitation of debate
  USE Cloture
      Legislative bodies—Freedom of debate
Limitations, Constitutional
  USE *subdivision* Constitutional law *under names of countries*
      Constitutional law
Limitations, Contractual
  USE Contracts
Limitations, Statute of
  USE Limitation of actions
Limitations, Tax and expenditure
  USE Tax and expenditure limitations
Limitations (Law)
  USE Entail
      Estates (Law)
      Limitation of actions
      Perpetuities
      Real property
      Remainders (Estates)
      Uses (Law)
Limited access highways
  USE Express highways
Limited auditing
  USE Auditing, Limited
Limited companies
  USE Corporations
Limited editions
  USE Bibliography—Limited editions
Limited editions (Art objects)
  USE Art objects—Limited editions
Limited editions (Prints)
  USE Prints—Limited editions
Limited editions (Small sculpture)
  USE Small sculpture—Limited editions
Limited entry in fisheries
  USE Fisheries—Licenses—Limited entry
Limited jurisdiction, Courts of
  USE Courts of special jurisdiction
Limited liability *(May Subd Geog)*
  UF Liability, Limited
  BT Commercial law
      Liability (Law)
  RT Carriers
  NT Abandonment (Maritime law)

      Limited partnership
      Private companies
Limited partnership *(May Subd Geog)*
  UF Partnership, Limited
  BT Corporation law
      Limited liability
      Partnership
      Stock companies
  RT Private companies
  NT Research and development partnership
Limited partnership (Islamic law)
(May Subd Geog)
  BT Islamic law
Limited partnership (Roman law)
Limited war
  [UA11.5]
  BT Military policy
      Strategy
      War
  RT Tactical nuclear weapons
  NT Low-intensity conflicts (Military science)
Limiter circuits
  UF Clipping circuits
      Limiters (Electronics)
  BT Electronic circuits
Limiters (Electronics)
  USE Limiter circuits
Limiting oxygen index of materials
  USE Oxygen index of materials
Limits, Confidence
  USE Confidence intervals
Limits (Mathematics)
  USE Calculus
Limnadidae
  USE Milkweed butterflies
Limnē Iōanninōn (Greece)
  USE Ioannina, Lake (Greece)
Limnebiidae
  USE Hydraenidae
Limnell family *(Not Subd Geog)*
Limnephilidae
  [QL518.L5]
  UF Limnophilidae
  BT Caddis-flies
  NT Halesus
      Stenophylax
Límni Trikhonís (Greece)
  USE Trichonis, Lake (Greece)
Limnia (Insect)
  [QL537.S365]
  BT Sciomyzidae
Limnichidae
  [QL596.L55]
  BT Beetles
Limniidae
  USE Elmidae
Limnocentropodidae
  [QL518.L]
  BT Caddis-flies
Limnochares
  [QL458.2.L54]
  BT Limnocharidae
Limnocharidae
  [QL458.2.L54]
  BT Mites
      Water mites
  NT Limnochares
Limnocyteridae
  USE Limnocytheridae
Limnocytheridae
  UF Limnocyteridae
  NT Bisulcocypris
      Theriosynoecum
      Timiriaseviinae
Limnodromus
  [QL696.C48]
  UF Dowitchers
      Lymnodromus
  BT Scolopacidae

Limnofregata
[QE872.P4]
BT Frigate-birds, Fossil
Limnofregata azygosternon
[QE872.P4]
Limnologists (May Subd Geog)
[QH96.3-96.35]
BT Limnology
Limnology (May Subd Geog)
[QH98 (Biology)]
BT Aquatic sciences
Lakes
RT Freshwater biology
Water chemistry
NT Eutrophication
Fisheries—Hydrologic factors
Lake ecology
Limnologists
Paleolimnology
Limnomys
[QL737.R666]
BT Muridae
Limnophilidae
USE Limnephilidae
Limnoria
[QL444.M34]
BT Limnoriidae
Limnoriidae
[QL444.M34]
BT Isopoda
NT Limnoria
Limnos Island (Greece)
USE Lemnos Island (Greece)
Limodorum autumnale
USE Spiranthes cernua
Limoges porcelain (May Subd Geog)
UF Porcelain, Limoges
Limon Bay (Panama)
UF Bahía de Limón (Panama)
Bahía Limón (Panama)
Bay of Limon (Panama)
Navy Bay (Panama)
BT Bays—Panama
Limonia aurantifolia
USE Lime tree
Limoniidae
USE Crane-flies
Limonite (May Subd Geog)
UF Brown hematite
BT Ferrous oxide
Limopsidae
BT Arcoida
Limosa
USE Godwits
Limosa aegocephala
USE Black-tailed godwit
Limosa limosa
USE Black-tailed godwit
Limosella
[QK495.S43]
BT Scrophulariaceae
Limosella aquatica
[QK495.S43]
Limosina
USE Leptocera
Limousin cattle (May Subd Geog)
[SF199.L]
BT Beef cattle
Limousine services (May Subd Geog)
BT Transportation, Automotive
Limousines (May Subd Geog)
[TL232.7]
BT Automobiles
NT Used limousines
LIMP (Computer program language)
Limpets
NT Acmaeidae
Limu
USE Algae
Marine algae as food
Mosses

Limulidae
[QL447.7]
BT Xiphosura
NT Limulus
Limulodidae
[QL596.L58]
BT Beetles
Limulus
[QL477.7]
UF Xiphosurus
BT Limulidae
Limulus amebocyte lysate test
USE Limulus test
Limulus polyphemus
UF Horseshoe crab, Atlantic
King crab, Atlantic
Xiphosurus sowerbyi
RT Limulus test
Limulus test
UF Limulus amebocyte lysate test
BT Biological assay
Diagnosis, Laboratory
Endotoxins—Analysis
RT Limulus polyphemus
Limuria
USE Chagos Islands
Mascarene Islands
Lin, Ch'un, 12th/13th cent. Bird on snowy plum blossoms and bamboo
UF Bird on snowy plum blossoms and bamboo (Fan painting)
Mei chu han ch'in t'u (Fan painting)
BT Fan painting, Chinese
Lin, Liang, ca. 1416-ca. 1480. Trees and birds (Not Subd Geog)
UF Kuan mu chi ch'in t'u (Scroll)
Trees and birds (Scroll)
BT Painting, Chinese
Scrolls, Chinese
Lin An-t'ai ku ts'o (Taipei, Taiwan)
UF Lin An-t'ai Old Homestead (Taipei, Taiwan)
Lin Old Homestead (Taipei, Taiwan)
BT Dwellings—Taiwan
Lin An-t'ai Old Homestead (Taipei, Taiwan)
USE Lin An-t'ai ku ts'o (Taipei, Taiwan)
Lin family (Not Subd Geog)
RT Lynn family
Lin Old Homestead (Taipei, Taiwan)
USE Lin An-t'ai ku ts'o (Taipei, Taiwan)
Linac, Heavy ion
USE Heavy ion accelerators
Linaceae
[QK495.L74]
BT Geraniales
Linacs
USE Linear accelerators
Linapi
USE Delaware Indians
Linaria
[QK495.S43]
BT Scrophulariaceae
Linaria minor
USE Chaenorrhinum minus
Linaria vulgaris
[QK495.S43]
UF Toadflax
Linberg family
USE Lindberg family
Linck family
USE Link family
Lincke family
USE Link family
Lincken family
USE Link family
Linckost family (Not Subd Geog)
RT Linkous family
Lincoln, Abraham, 1809-1865
[E457]
— Anecdotes
— Anniversaries, etc.

RT Lincoln Day
— Anniversaries, etc., [date]
— Assassination
— Autographs
— Birthplace
— Books and reading
— Burial
USE Lincoln, Abraham, 1809-1865—Death and burial
— Childhood and youth
[E457.32]
UF Lincoln, Abraham, 1809-1865—Youth
— Chronology
— Clothing
— Death and burial
UF Lincoln, Abraham, 1809-1865—Burial
Lincoln, Abraham, 1809-1865—Funeral
— Dictionaries, indexes, etc.
— Drama
RT Lincoln, Abraham, 1809-1865, in fiction, drama, poetry, etc.
— Family
— Fiction
RT Lincoln, Abraham, 1809-1865, in fiction, drama, poetry, etc.
— Funeral
USE Lincoln, Abraham, 1809-1865—Death and burial
— Funeral journey to Springfield
— Health
— Iconography
USE Lincoln, Abraham, 1809-1865—Pictorial works
— Inauguration
— Influence
— Journeys (May Subd Geog)
— Juvenile drama
— Language
— Literary art
— Medals
— Mental health
— Military leadership
— Museums, relics, etc. (May Subd Geog)
UF Lincoln, Abraham, 1809-1865—Relics
— Music
RT Lincoln, Abraham, 1809-1865—Songs and music
— Musical settings
— Oratory
Here are entered works on Lincoln as a public speaker.
UF Lincoln, Abraham, 1809-1865—Public speaking
— Philosophy
— Pictorial works
UF Lincoln, Abraham, 1809-1865—Iconography
— Poetry
RT Lincoln, Abraham, 1809-1865, in fiction, drama, poetry, etc.
— Political and social views
— Political career before 1861
NT Lincoln-Douglas debates, 1858
— Political career before [date]
— Public speaking
USE Lincoln, Abraham, 1809-1865—Oratory
— Quotations
[E457.99]
— Relations with Afro-Americans, [Relations with children, etc.]
— Relics
USE Lincoln, Abraham, 1809-1865—Museums, relics, etc.
— Religion
— Songs and music

Lincoln, Abraham, 1809-1865
— Songs and music (Continued)
    RT Lincoln, Abraham, 1809-1865—
        Music
— Study and teaching (May Subd Geog)
— — Outlines, syllabi, etc.
— Tomb
— Views on slavery, [Views on temperance,
    etc.]
— Youth
    USE Lincoln, Abraham, 1809-1865—
        Childhood and youth
Lincoln, Abraham, 1809-1865, in fiction,
  drama, poetry, etc.
    RT Lincoln, Abraham, 1809-1865—Drama
      Lincoln, Abraham, 1809-1865—Fiction
      Lincoln, Abraham, 1809-1865—Poetry
Lincoln, Battle of, 1217
   [DA227]
    BT Great Britain—History—Henry III,
        1216-1272
Lincoln (Bomber)
   [UG1242.B7]
    BT Bombers
Lincoln automobile
    NT Lincoln Continental automobile
Lincoln Boyhood National Memorial (Ind.)
    BT Monuments—Indiana
      National parks and reserves—Indiana
    NT Nancy Hanks Lincoln State Memorial
      (Ind.)
Lincoln Continental automobile
   [TL215.L]
    UF Continental automobile
    BT Lincoln automobile
Lincoln Day
   [E457.7]
    UF Lincoln's Birthday
    BT Holidays—United States
    RT Lincoln, Abraham, 1809-1865—
      Anniversaries, etc.
Lincoln Day addresses
    BT Speeches, addresses, etc., American
Lincoln-Douglas debates, 1858
   [E457.4]
    BT Lincoln, Abraham, 1809-1865—
      Political career before 1861
Lincoln Downs Brook (R.I.)
    BT Rivers—Rhode Island
Lincoln family (Not Subd Geog)
Lincoln Home National Historic Site
  (Springfield, Ill.)
    BT Historic sites—Illinois
      National parks and reserves—Illinois
Lincoln Memorial (Washington, D.C.)
   [F203.4.L73]
    BT Memorials—Washington (D.C.)
      National parks and reserves—
      Washington (D.C.)
Lincoln-Oseretsky motor development scale
    BT Motor ability—Testing
Lincoln Red cattle
   [SF199.L5]
    UF Lincoln Red Shorthorn cattle
Lincoln Red Shorthorn cattle
    USE Lincoln Red cattle
Lincoln State Park (Ind.)
    BT Parks—Indiana
Lincoln Township Cemetery (Lincoln, Cerro
  Gordo County, Iowa)
    BT Cemeteries—Iowa
Lincoln's Birthday
    USE Lincoln Day
Lincomycin
    BT Antibacterial agents
Lincos (Artificial language)
   [PM8508]
    UF Lingua cosmica
      Symbolic language
    BT Languages, Artificial
      Mathematical linguistics

Lincrusta-Walton
   [NK3505]
    BT Wall coverings
Lind family
    USE Lynn family
LINDA (Computer system)
    UF Line Drawing Analyzer (Computer
      system)
    BT Optical pattern recognition
Linda Creek (Calif.)
    BT Rivers—California
Linda dialect
    BT Banda language
      Central African Republic—Languages
Lindberg family (Not Subd Geog)
    UF Linberg family
      Lindbergh family
Lindbergh family
    USE Lindberg family
Lindbergh hop
    USE Lindy (Dance)
Lindblom family (Not Subd Geog)
Linde family
    USE Lynn family
Lindegaard family (Not Subd Geog)
    UF Lindegard family
Lindegard family
    USE Lindegaard family
Lindeman family (Not Subd Geog)
    UF Lenamon family
      Lenamond family
      Lendeman family
      Lenderman family
      Lindemann family
      Linderman family
Lindemann family
    USE Lindeman family
Linden (May Subd Geog)
   [QK495.T5 (Botany)]
   [SD397.L6 (Sylviculture)]
    UF Basswood
      European lime tree
      European linden
      Lime tree, European
      Tilia
      Tilia europaea
      Tilia vulgaris
Linden, Fossil
Linden family
    USE Lynn family
Linden oil
    UF Basswood oil
Lindenmayer developmental languages
    USE L systems
Lindenmayer systems
    USE L systems
Lindenmeier Site (Colo.) (Not Subd Geog)
    BT Colorado—Antiquities
Lindenschmit family (Not Subd Geog)
    UF Lindensmith family
      Lindesmith family
Lindensmith family
    USE Lindenschmit family
Linder family
    USE Lynn family
Linderman family
    USE Lindeman family
Lindesmith family
    USE Lindenschmit family
Lindgren family (Not Subd Geog)
Lindh family
    USE Lynn family
Lindley family (Not Subd Geog)
    RT Lindsay family
Lindley's Mill, Battle of, 1781
   [E241.L65]
    BT North Carolina—History—Revolution,
      1775-1783
      United States—History—Revolution,
      1775-1783—Campaigns

Lindmayer family (Not Subd Geog)
    UF Lindmayr family
      Lindmeir family
      Lindtmayer family
Lindmayr family
    USE Lindmayer family
Lindmeir family
    USE Lindmayer family
Lindow Man
   [GN780.22.G]
    BT Bog bodies—England
      England—Antiquities
Linds family
    USE Lynn family
Lindsay family (Not Subd Geog)
    UF Lindsey family
      Lindsy family
      Lindze family
      Lingsey family
      Linsay family
      Linsey family
      Linsy family
      Linzay family
      Linzee family
      Linzey family
      Lyndsay family
      Lyndsey family
    RT Lindley family
      Linse family
Lindscott family
    USE Linscott family
Lindsey family
    USE Lindsay family
Lindsy family
    USE Lindsay family
Lindtmayer family
    USE Lindmayer family
Lindy (Dance)
    UF Lindbergh hop
      Lindy hop
Lindy hop
    USE Lindy (Dance)
Lindze family
    USE Lindsay family
Line (Art)
    BT Art
Line and staff organization
  (May Subd Geog)
    UF Line-staff organization
      Staff and line organization
    BT Delegation of authority
      Management
      Organization
Line balancing (Assembly-lines)
    USE Assembly-line balancing
Line broadening, Spectral
    USE Spectral line broadening
Line Drawing Analyzer (Computer system)
    USE LINDA (Computer system)
Line drivers (Integrated circuits)
    UF Buffers, Tri-state (Integrated circuits)
      Drivers, Line (Integrated circuits)
      Tri-state buffers (Integrated circuits)
    BT Amplifiers (Electronics)
      Computer interfaces
      Integrated circuits
Line-engraving
    USE Engraving
Line formation, Spectral
    USE Spectral line formation
Line geometry
   [QA608]
    UF Geometry, Line
    RT Algebras, Linear
    NT Complexes
Line-item veto
    USE Item veto
Line of balance (Management)
    UF LOB technique

BT Graphic methods
    Production control
    Scheduling (Management)
Line of business reporting *(May Subd Geog)*
    [HG4028.B2]
    UF Lines of business reporting
        Segment reporting (Accounting)
    BT Corporation reports
        Financial statements
    — **Law and legislation** *(May Subd Geog)*
        BT Corporation law
Line of demarcation of Alexander VI
    USE Demarcation line of Alexander VI
Line-of-sight radio links *(May Subd Geog)*
    RT Microwave communication systems
Line play (Football)
    [GV951.2]
    BT Football
Line printers (Data processing systems)
    USE Printers (Data processing systems)
Line receivers (Integrated circuits)
    UF Receivers, Line (Integrated circuits)
    BT Computer interfaces
        Differential amplifiers
        Integrated circuits
Line source radiators
    USE Microwave pillboxes
Line-staff organization
    USE Line and staff organization
Line-throwing guns
    [VK1481.L55]
    UF Guns, Line-throwing
        Lyle guns
    BT Life-saving apparatus
Lineage of Buddhist priests
    USE Priests, Buddhist—Lineage
Lineage of lamas
    USE Lamas—Lineage
Lineage of Zen priests
    USE Priests, Zen—Lineage
Linear A inscriptions
    USE Inscriptions, Linear A
Linear accelerators
    [QC787.L5]
    UF Accelerators, Linear
        Linacs
    BT Particle accelerators
        Proton accelerators
    RT Recirculating electron accelerators
    NT Heavy ion accelerators
        Ion accelerators
        Meson factories
Linear accelerators in medicine
    (May Subd Geog)
    BT Medical instruments and apparatus
        Radiology, Medical—Instruments
Linear algebra
    USE Algebras, Linear
Linear algebraic groups
    UF Algebraic groups, Linear
    BT Geometry, Algebraic
        Groups, Theory of
    RT Algebraic varieties
    NT Adeles
        Arithmetic groups
        Chevalley groups
        Finite simple groups
        Symplectic groups
Linear B inscriptions
    USE Inscriptions, Linear B
Linear complementarity problem
    UF Complementarity problem, Linear
    BT Matrices
        Programming (Mathematics)
        Vector algebra
Linear complexes
    USE Complexes
Linear dichroism
    [QD473]
    BT Dichroism

Linear differential equations
    USE Differential equations, Linear
Linear digital filters (Mathematics)
    USE Digital filters (Mathematics)
Linear electric circuits
    USE Electric circuits, Linear
Linear electric motors
    USE Electric motors, Linear
Linear elliptic differential equations
    USE Differential equations, Elliptic
Linear energy transfer
    BT Nuclear physics
    RT Stopping power (Nuclear physics)
    NT Relative biological effectiveness
        (Radiobiology)
Linear filters (Mathematics)
    USE Digital filters (Mathematics)
Linear free energy relationship
    UF Correlation analysis (Chemistry)
        Correlation equation (Chemistry)
        Free energy relationship, Linear
    BT Chemical equilibrium
        Chemical reaction, Conditions and
            laws of
        Chemical reaction, Rate of
        Gibbs' free energy
    NT Hammett equation
Linear input logic
    USE Threshold logic
Linear integrated circuits
    [TK7874]
    UF Analog integrated circuits
    BT Integrated circuits
Linear maps
    USE Linear operators
Linear measurement
    USE Length measurement
Linear models (Statistics)
    UF Models, Linear (Statistics)
    BT Mathematical models
        Mathematical statistics
        Statistics
Linear momentum
    USE Momentum (Mechanics)
Linear normed spaces
    USE Normed linear spaces
Linear operators
    UF Linear maps
        Maps, Linear
        Operators, Linear
    BT Operator theory
    NT Closed graph theorems
        Closed operators
        Contraction operators
        Fredholm operators
        Hyponormal operators
        Markov operators
        Nonselfadjoint operators
        Normal operators
        Positive operators
        Selfadjoint operators
        Shift operators (Operator theory)
        Subnormal operators
        Symmetric operators
        Toeplitz operators
        Wiener-Hopf operators
    — **Generalized inverses**
        [QA329.2]
        UF Generalized inverses of linear
            operators
            Inverses of linear operators,
            Generalized
        RT Matrix inversion
Linear ordering (Grammar)
    USE Order (Grammar)
Linear orderings
    UF Orderings, Linear
    BT Combinatorial analysis
        Logic, Symbolic and mathematical
        Set theory

Linear oscillators
    USE Harmonic oscillators
Linear perspective
    USE Perspective
Linear Pottery culture
    USE Bandkeramik culture
Linear programming
    [T57.74]
    BT Matrices
        Programming (Mathematics)
        Scheduling (Management)
        Substitutions, Linear
        Transformations (Mathematics)
        Vector analysis
    SA *subdivision* Linear programming *under
        subjects, e.g.* Farm management—
            Linear programming
    NT Recursive programming
        Shadow prices
        Stochastic programming
    — **Data processing**
        NT PLATOFORM (Computer system)
Linear spaces
    USE Vector spaces
Linear substitutions
    USE Substitutions, Linear
Linear systems
    UF Systems, Linear
    BT System theory
    RT Differential equations, Linear
    NT Linear time invariant systems
Linear time invariant systems
    UF Systems, Linear time invariant
    BT Linear systems
    RT Discrete-time systems
Linear topological spaces
    UF Topological vector spaces
        Vector topology
    BT Topology
        Vector spaces
    NT Barrelled spaces
        Bases (Linear topological spaces)
        Bornological spaces
        Choquet theory
        Closed graph theorems
        Distributions, Theory of (Functional
            analysis)
        Fréchet spaces
        Locally convex spaces
        Pontriagin spaces
        Sequence spaces
        Topological algebras
        Webbed spaces
Linear topological spaces, Ordered
    [QA322]
    UF Ordered linear topological spaces
        Ordered topological vector spaces
        Topological vector spaces, Ordered
        Vector spaces, Ordered topological
    BT Functional analysis
        Ordered topological spaces
        Vector spaces
    NT Vector lattices, Archimedian
Linear vector spaces
    USE Vector spaces
Linearbandkeramik culture
    USE Bandkeramik culture
Linearly separable logic
    USE Threshold logic
Lineback family
    USE Leinbach family
Linebah family
    USE Leinbach family
Linebaugh family
    USE Leinbach family
Linel family
    USE Linnell family
Linell family
    USE Linnell family
Linen *(May Subd Geog)*
    [TS1710-1731]

Linen (Continued)
  BT Plant fibers
        Textile fabrics
  RT Flax
  NT Shaatnez
Linen closets
  UF Closets
Linen finishing
    [TS1725]
  BT Textile finishing
Linen industry (May Subd Geog)
    [HD9930]
Linen supply service (May Subd Geog)
  BT Laundry industry
  NT Hotel laundry service
  — **Law and legislation** (May Subd Geog)
Linens, Household
  USE Household linens
Liners
  USE Ocean liners
Lines, Boundary
  USE Boundaries
Lines, Instability (Meteorology)
  USE Squall lines
Lines, Meridian
  USE Meridian lines
Lines, Radio recombination
  USE Radio recombination lines
Lines, Squall
  USE Squall lines
Lines, Telecommunication
  USE Telecommunication lines
Lines, Wind-shift
  USE Squall lines
Lines of business reporting
  USE Line of business reporting
Linfield family
  USE Lynfield family
Ling (Artificial language)
    [PM8509]
  BT Languages, Artificial
Ling Canal (Hsing-an hsien, China)
  UF Hsiang-kuei Yün-ho (Hsing-an hsien,
        China)
        Hsing-an Yün-ho (Hsing-an hsien,
        China)
        Ling Ch'ü (Hsing-an hsien, China)
  BT Canals—China
Ling Ch'ü (Hsing-an hsien, China)
  USE Ling Canal (Hsing-an hsien, China)
Ling family
Ling-nan p'ai
  USE Ling-nan school of painting
Ling-nan school of painting
    [ND1043.53.L55]
  UF Ling-nan p'ai
  BT Painting, Chinese—Ming-Ch'ing
        dynasties, 1368-1912
Ling-Ting Yang
  USE Lingding Roads
Lingala language (May Subd Geog)
    [PL8456]
  UF Bangala language (Zaire)
        Mangala language (Zaire)
        Ngala language (Zaire)
  BT Bantu languages
        Congo (Brazzaville)—Languages
        Lingua francas
        Zaire—Languages
Lingala proverbs
  USE Proverbs, Lingala
Lingala songs
  USE Songs, Lingala
Lingayat cults (May Subd Geog)
    [BL1245.L5]
  BT Cults
Lingayat poetry, Kannada (May Subd Geog)
  UF Kannada Lingayat poetry
        Kannada Virasivaite poetry
        Virasivaite poetry, Kannada

  BT Kannada poetry
        Religious poetry, Kannada
Lingayatism
  USE Lingayats
Lingayats
    [BL1881.2-1881.292]
  UF Lingayatism
        Vīraśivaism
  BT Caste—India
        Hindu sects
        Sivaism
  NT Śaktiviśiṣṭādvaitavedānta
  — **Relations**
      [BL1245.L5]
Lingcod
    [QL638.H49]
  UF Cultus cod
        Green cod
        Ophiodon
        Ophiodon elongatus
        Ophiodontidae
  BT Hexagrammidae
Lingcod fisheries (May Subd Geog)
    [SH351.L5]
  BT Fisheries
Lingding Roads
  UF Ling-Ting Yang
        Lingding Yang
        Macao Roads
  BT Roadsteads—China
        Roadsteads—Hong Kong
        Roadsteads—Macao
Lingding Yang
  USE Lingding Roads
Linge River (Netherlands)
  BT Rivers—Netherlands
Lingel family
  USE Lengel family
Lingerie
    [TT670]
  UF Women's underwear
  BT Underwear
  NT Brassieres
Lingerie industry (May Subd Geog)
    [HD9948.3]
  BT Underwear industry
Linggardjati agreement
  USE Cheribon agreement, 1946
Lingk family
  USE Link family
Lingonberry
  USE Vaccinium vitis-idaea
Lingones
  UF Andematunnum
Lingsey family
  USE Lindsay family
Lingua cosmica
  USE Lincos (Artificial language)
Lingua Franca (Mediterranean region)
  BT Extinct languages
        Lingua francas
  NT Sabir
Lingua francas
    [PM7801-PM7895]
    Here are entered works discussing auxiliary,
  sometimes mixed, languages used among groups hav-
  ing no other language in common. Works discussing
  languages resulting from the intermingling of phono-
  logical, grammatical and/or lexical elements from
  different languages in areas of intensive language
  contact are entered under the heading Languages,
  Mixed. Works discussing lingua francas which are
  native to none of those using them and are character-
  ized by a simplified grammar and often mixed
  vocabulary are entered under the heading Pidgin languages. Works discussing pidgin languages that have
  become established as the native language of a speech
  community are entered under the heading Creole dialects.
  UF Contact vernaculars
        Trade languages
        Vehicular languages

  BT Languages in contact
  NT Fanakalo
        Kituba language
        Lingala language
        Lingua Franca (Mediterranean region)
        Mobilian trade language
        Ochweśnicki jargon
        Pidgin languages
        Sabir
        Sango language
Lingua infinitiva italiana
  USE Lingua italiana infinitiva
Lingua italiana infinitiva
    [PM8527]
  UF Lingua infinitiva italiana
  BT Language, Universal
Lingua philosophica (Artificial language)
    [PM8563]
  BT Languages, Artificial
Lingual bar major connectors (Dentistry)
  USE Partial dentures, Removable—Lingual
        bar major connectors
Lingual bone
  USE Hyoid bone
Lingual frenum
    [QM503]
  UF Frenulum linguae
        Frenum linguae
        Frenum of tongue
  BT Tongue
Lingual manifestations of general diseases
  USE Tongue manifestations of general
        diseases
Linguistic analogy
  USE Analogy (Linguistics)
Linguistic analysis (Linguistics)
  UF Analysis, Linguistic (Linguistics)
  BT Analysis (Philosophy)
        Grammar, Comparative and general
  NT Asymmetry (Linguistics)
        Binary principle (Linguistics)
        Componential analysis (Linguistics)
        Economy (Linguistics)
        Formalization (Linguistics)
        Glossematics
        Hierarchy (Linguistics)
        Metalanguage
        Minimal pair (Linguistics)
        Spectral analysis (Phonetics)
        Systemic grammar
        Tagmemics
Linguistic analysis (Philosophy)
  USE Analysis (Philosophy)
Linguistic anthropology
  USE Anthropological linguistics
Linguistic awareness
  USE Language awareness
Linguistic change
  UF Change, Linguistic
  BT Historical linguistics
        Language and languages
  NT Glottochronology
        Neogrammarians
Linguistic connotation
  USE Connotation (Linguistics)
Linguistic creativity
  USE Creativity (Linguistics)
Linguistic demography (May Subd Geog)
    [P40.5.D45]
  BT Demography
        Sociolinguistics
Linguistic economy
  USE Economy (Linguistics)
Linguistic geography
    [P375-P381]
  UF Dialect geography
        Geography, Linguistic
        Language geography
        Languages—Geography
  BT Areal linguistics
        Dialectology

SA *subdivisions* Dialects *and* Maps *under*
    names of languages; also subdivision
    Languages—Maps *under names of*
    countries, regions, etc.
NT Language surveys
Linguistic informants
  UF Informants, Linguistic
    Native speakers as linguistic
      informants
  BT Linguistics—Methodology
Linguistic interference
  USE Interference (Linguistics)
Linguistic minorities *(May Subd Geog)*
  UF Minority languages
  BT Languages—Political aspects
    Minorities
    Sociolinguistics
Linguistic models
  UF Models, Linguistic
  BT Linguistics
    Typology (Linguistics)
Linguistic paleontology *(May Subd Geog)*
  [P35]
  UF Paleontology (Linguistics)
  BT Anthropological linguistics
    Language and languages—Etymology
    Reconstruction (Linguistics)
Linguistic science
  USE Linguistics
Linguistic services
  USE Language services
Linguistic String Parser (Computer grammar)
  UF LSP (Computer grammar)
  BT English language—Data processing
    Grammar, Comparative and general
    Linguistics—Data processing
    Parsing (Computer grammar)
Linguistic surveys
  USE Language surveys
Linguistic taboo
  USE Taboo, Linguistic
Linguistic typology
  USE Typology (Linguistics)
Linguistics *(May Subd Geog)*
  [P121-141]
  Here are entered works dealing with the scientific
study of human speech, including phonetics, pho-
nemics, morphology, and syntax. Works dealing with
language in general, the origin and history of lan-
guage and surveys of languages, are entered under the
heading Language and languages.
  UF Linguistic science
    Science of language
  BT Language and languages
  NT Acceptability (Linguistics)
    Analogy (Linguistics)
    Anaphora (Linguistics)
    Anthropological linguistics
    Applied linguistics
    Archaisms (Linguistics)
    Areal linguistics
    Asymmetry (Linguistics)
    Autosegmental theory (Linguistics)
    Binary principle (Linguistics)
    Biolinguistics
    Cartesian linguistics
    Classification—Books—Linguistics
    Classifiers (Linguistics)
    Code switching (Linguistics)
    Communism and linguistics
    Componential analysis (Linguistics)
    Connotation (Linguistics)
    Context (Linguistics)
    Contrastive linguistics
    Creativity (Linguistics)
    Deep structure (Linguistics)
    Definiteness (Linguistics)
    Diglossia (Linguistics)
    Distinctive features (Linguistics)
    Economy (Linguistics)
    Emphasis (Linguistics)

Field theory (Linguistics)
Formalization (Linguistics)
Functionalism (Linguistics)
Government-binding theory
  (Linguistics)
Grammar, Comparative and general
Grammaticality (Linguistics)
Graphemics
Hesitation form (Linguistics)
Hierarchy (Linguistics)
Historical linguistics
Idioms
Juncture (Linguistics)
Language surveys
Linguistic models
Markedness (Linguistics)
Mathematical linguistics
Minimal pair (Linguistics)
Modality (Linguistics)
Naturalness (Linguistics)
Neurolinguistics
Neutralization (Linguistics)
Paralinguistics
Parallelism (Linguistics)
Phonetics
Prosodic analysis (Linguistics)
Psycholinguistics
Redundancy (Linguistics)
Reference (Linguistics)
Register (Linguistics)
Sociolinguistics
Speech acts (Linguistics)
Structural linguistics
Substratum (Linguistics)
Surface structure (Linguistics)
Transmutation (Linguistics)
Typology (Linguistics)
Universals (Linguistics)
Word (Linguistics)
— Computer programs
  NT BETA (Computer program)
    NEWCAT(Computer program)
    PARADIGM (Computer program)
— Data processing
  UF Computational linguistics
    Language and languages—Data
      processing
    Language data processing
  BT Applied linguistics
  RT Mathematical linguistics
  NT Automatic spelling-to-sound
      conversion
    Computer poetry
    Computer prose
    COMSKEE (Computer program
      language)
    Lexicography—Data processing
    Lexicology—Data processing
    Linguistic String Parser (Computer
      grammar)
    Machine translating
    MIND (Computer system)
    Network grammar
    Parsing (Computer grammar)
    Speech processing systems
    SUSY (Computer system)
— Graphic methods
  BT Mathematical linguistics
— History
— — 19th century
  NT Neogrammarians
— Intonation
  USE Intonation (Phonetics)
— Mathematical models
  USE Mathematical linguistics
— Methodology
  NT Linguistic informants
— Statistical methods
  [P138.5]

  UF Language and languages—
      Statistical methods
    Linguistics, Statistical
    Statistical linguistics
  BT Mathematical linguistics
  NT Language and languages—Word
      frequency
    Lexicostatistics
Linguistics, Experimental
  [P128.E94]
  UF Experimental linguistics
  NT Phonetics, Experimental
Linguistics, Mathematical
  USE Mathematical linguistics
Linguistics, Statistical
  USE Linguistics—Statistical methods
Linguistics, Structural
  USE Structural linguistics
Linguistics and anthropology
  USE Anthropological linguistics
Linguistics and history
  USE Language and history
Linguistics and logic
  USE Language and logic
Linguistics libraries *(May Subd Geog)*
  UF Libraries, Linguistics
  BT Humanities libraries
Linguists *(May Subd Geog)*
  [P83-85]
  RT Philologists
  NT Lexicographers
Linguists' literary writings
  BT Literature
Linguostylistics
  USE Language and languages—Style
Lingvo internacia (Artificial language)
  USE Esperanto
Linhas de Elvas, Battle of, 1659
  USE Elvas, Linhas de, Battle of, 1659
Linhof cameras
Liniel family
  USE Linnell family
Linings (Sewing)
  BT Dressmaking
    Sewing
  NT Interlinings (Sewing)
    Underlinings (Clothing)
Linings of blast-furnaces
  USE Blast-furnaces—Linings
Linings of chimneys
  USE Chimneys—Linings
Linings of electrolytic cells
  USE Electrolytic cells—Linings
Linings of foundry ladles
  USE Foundry ladles—Linings
Linings of irrigation canals
  USE Irrigation canals and flumes—Linings
Linings of pollution control equipment
  USE Pollution control equipment—Linings
Linings of pressure vessels
  USE Pressure vessels—Linings
Linings of reservoirs
  USE Reservoirs—Linings
Linings of sanitary landfills
  USE Sanitary landfills—Linings
Linings of tanks
  USE Tanks—Linings
LINK68 (Computer program)
  [QA76.8.M]
  BT Linking loaders (Computer programs)
Link-belting
  [TJ1119]
  UF Chain-belting
  BT Belts and belting

Link family *(Not Subd Geog)*
　UF　Linck family
　　　Lincke family
　　　Lincken family
　　　Lingk family
　　　Linke family
　　　Lynck family
　　　Lynk family
Link Mounds (Tenn.)
　USE　Link Site (Tenn.)
Link Site (Tenn.) *(Not Subd Geog)*
　UF　Link Mounds (Tenn.)
　BT　Tennessee—Antiquities
Link theory
　　[QA612.2]
　BT　Low-dimensional topology
　　　Piecewise linear topology
Link trainers
　　[TL697.T7]
　BT　Airplanes—Piloting
　　　Flight simulators
　　　Flight training
　　　Instrument flying
　　　Synthetic training devices
Linkage (Genetics)
　BT　Genetics
　　　Heredity
　RT　Chromosome mapping
　　　Chromosomes
　NT　Sex-linkage (Genetics)
Linke family
　USE　Link family
Linked verse
　USE　Renga
Linking loaders (Computer programs)
　UF　Loaders, Linking (Computer programs)
　NT　LINK68 (Computer program)
Linkous family *(Not Subd Geog)*
　RT　Linckost family
Links, Golf
　USE　Golf courses
Links and link-motion
　　[TJ182-3]
　BT　Mechanical movements
　NT　Steam-engines—Valve-gears
　　　Straight-line mechanisms
Linn Cove Viaduct (N.C.) *(Not Subd Geog)*
　BT　Viaducts—North Carolina
Linn family
　USE　Lynn family
Linnel family
　USE　Linnell family
Linnell family *(Not Subd Geog)*
　UF　Lanels family
　　　Lenel family
　　　Linel family
　　　Linell family
　　　Liniel family
　　　Linnel family
　　　Lynnell family
　RT　Lynn family
Linnets
　　[QL696.P2]
Linoleate oxygen oxidoreductases
　USE　Lipoxygenases
Linoleum
　　[TS1779.L5]
　BT　Floor coverings
　— Welding
Linoleum block-printing
　　[NE1330]
　UF　Block-printing, Linoleum
　BT　Block printing
　　　Color prints
　　　Engraving
　　　Wood-engraving
Linoleum block-printing, American,
　[Australian, etc.]
Linoleum block-printing, Cypriote
　(May Subd Geog)
　UF　Cypriote linoleum block-printing

Linoleum block-printing, English
　(May Subd Geog)
　UF　English linoleum block-printing
Linoleum block-printing, Polish
　(May Subd Geog)
　UF　Polish linoleum block-printing
Linoleum block-printing, Russian
　(May Subd Geog)
　UF　Russian linoleum block-printing
Linoleum block-printing, Spanish
　(May Subd Geog)
　UF　Spanish linoleum block-printing
Linoleum industry *(May Subd Geog)*
Linotype
　　[Z253]
　BT　Printing, Practical
　　　Printing machinery and supplies
　　　Type and type-founding
　　　Type-setting machines
　NT　Monotype
　— Societies, etc.
　　　USE　Printing—Societies, etc.
LINPACK (Computer system)
Lins family
　USE　Lynn family
Linsay family
　USE　Lindsay family
Linscot family
　USE　Linscott family
Linscott family *(Not Subd Geog)*
　UF　Lindscott family
　　　Linscot family
　　　Linscut family
　　　Linskit family
　　　Lynscott family
　　　Lynscotte family
Linscut family
　USE　Linscott family
Linse family *(Not Subd Geog)*
　RT　Lindsay family
Linseed
　USE　Flaxseed
Linseed-oil
　　[TP682]
　UF　Flaxseed oil
　BT　Drying oils
　　　Flaxseed
　　　Thinner (Paint mixing)
Linsey family
　USE　Lindsay family
Linshoten Islands (Japan)
　USE　Tokara Islands (Japan)
Linskit family
　USE　Linscott family
Linsy family
　USE　Lindsay family
Linters
　BT　Cotton
　　　Cottonseed
Linton family *(Not Subd Geog)*
Linum usitatissimum
　USE　Flax
Linvill family
　USE　Linville family
Linville family *(Not Subd Geog)*
　UF　Linvill family
　　　Linvilles family
　RT　Lynfield family
Linvilles family
　USE　Linville family
Linwood Park (Vermilion, Ohio)
　BT　Parks—Ohio
Linyphia
　　[QL458.42.L55]
　BT　Linyphiidae
Linyphiidae
　　[QL458.42.L55]
　UF　Dwarf spiders
　　　Erigonidae
　　　Micryphantidae
　　　Sheetweb spiders

　BT　Spiders
　NT　Centromerus
　　　Diplocentria
　　　Erigone
　　　Eulaira
　　　Linyphia
　　　Troglohyphantes
　　　Tunagyna
Linz Café (Linz, Austria)
　UF　Linz Coffeehouse (Linz, Austria)
　BT　Coffee-houses—Austria
Linz Castle (Linz, Austria)
　UF　Linzer Schloss (Linz, Austria)
　BT　Castles—Austria
Linz Coffeehouse (Linz, Austria)
　USE　Linz Café (Linz, Austria)
Linzay family
　USE　Lindsay family
Linzee family
　USE　Lindsay family
Linzer Schloss (Linz, Austria)
　USE　Linz Castle (Linz, Austria)
Linzey family
　USE　Lindsay family
Linzgau (Germany)
Liocephalus
　USE　Leiocephalus
Liodesidae
　USE　Leiodidae
Liodidae
　USE　Leiodidae
Lioi family
　USE　Lioy family
Liolaemus
　　[QL666.L25]
　BT　Iguanidae
Liolaemus duellmani
　　[QL666.L25]
Liomys
　　[QL737.R66]
　UF　Spiny pocket mice
　BT　Heteromyidae
　　　Pocket mice
Liomys spectabilis
　　[QL737.R66]
Lion attacks *(May Subd Geog)*
　　[QL737.C23]
　UF　Attacks by lions
　BT　Animal attacks
Lion family
　USE　Lyons family
Lion-headed eagles
　BT　Animals, Mythical
　　　Eagles—Mythology
Lion hunting *(May Subd Geog)*
　BT　Big game hunting
Lion Rosso (Florence, Italy)
　(Not Subd Geog)
　UF　Florence (Italy). Lion Rosso
Lion rugs *(May Subd Geog)*
　UF　Rugs, Lion
　BT　Rugs, Nomadic—Iran
　　　Rugs, Persian
Lion-tailed macaque
　　[QL737.P93]
　UF　Lion-tailed monkey
　　　Liontail macaque
　　　Macaca silenus
　BT　Macaques
Lion-tailed monkey
　USE　Lion-tailed macaque
Lion tamarin
　USE　Leontopithecus rosalia
Lionnet family *(Not Subd Geog)*
Lions *(May Subd Geog)*
　　[QL737.C23]
　UF　Leo leo
　　　Panthera leo
　BT　Panthera
　NT　Elsa (Lion)
　　　Joshua (Lion)

Leopons
Little Tyke (Lion)
— Pictorial works
— Religious aspects
NT Apedemak (Egyptian deity)
Lions (in numismatics) *(May Subd Geog)*
[CJ161.L56]
BT Numismatics
Lions family
USE Lyons family
Lions in art
BT Art
Lions in motion pictures
BT Moving-pictures
Liontail macaque
USE Lion-tailed macaque
Lionza, María (Legendary character)
[GR133.V]
UF Leonza, María (Legendary character)
María Leonza (Legendary character)
María Lionza (Legendary character)
BT Folklore—Venezuela
Liothyronine
USE Triiodothyronine
Liouville-Sturm equation
USE Sturm-Liouville equation
Lioy family *(Not Subd Geog)*
UF Lioi family
Lip-reading
USE Lipreading
Lip, s.a. Factory Occupation, 1973
[HD5375.W2]
Lipan, Battle of, 1434
[DB208]
BT Bohemia (Czechoslovakia)—History—
Hussite Wars, 1419-1436—
Campaigns
Lipan Indians
[E99.L]
BT Apache Indians
Athapascan Indians
Indians of North America
Lipara Island (Italy)
USE Lipari Island (Italy)
Lipari Acropolis (Lipari, Lipari Islands, Italy)
USE Acropolis of Lipari (Lipari, Lipari
Islands, Italy)
Lipari Island (Italy)
UF Isola di Lipari (Italy)
Isola Lipari (Italy)
Lipara Island (Italy)
BT Islands—Italy
Lipari Islands (Italy)
Lipari Islands (Italy)
UF Aeolian Islands (Italy)
Eolie Islands (Italy)
Isole Eolie (Italy)
Isole Lipari (Italy)
BT Islands—Italy
NT Lipari Island (Italy)
Liparidae (Insects)
USE Lymantriidae
Liparididae (Insects)
USE Lymantriidae
Liparis
USE Lymantria
Liparis (Fish)
[QL638.C9]
BT Cyclopteridae
Liparis monacha
USE Nun moth
Liparis salicis
USE Satin moth
Liparite
USE Rhyolite
Lipase
[QP601]
NT Lipoprotein lipase
Lipe family *(Not Subd Geog)*
UF Lipes family
RT Leib family

Lipectomy *(May Subd Geog)*
[RD119.5.L55]
UF Adipectomy
Dermolipectomy
BT Adipose tissues—Surgery
NT Suction lipectomy
Lipemia
[RB145]
BT Blood
Fat
Lipids
Lipes family
USE Lipe family
Lipica horse
USE Lipizzaner horse
Lipid bilayer membranes
USE Bilayer lipid membranes
Lipid bimolecular membranes
USE Bilayer lipid membranes
Lipid embolism
USE Fat embolism
Lipid emulsions, Intravenous
USE Fat emulsions, Intravenous
Lipid membranes
NT Bilayer lipid membranes
Lipid metabolism disorders
USE Lipids—Metabolism—Disorders
Lipid mobilizing factor, Pituitary
USE Lipotropin
Lipid research
USE Lipids—Research
Lipid synthesis
USE Lipids—Synthesis
Lipides
USE Lipids
Lipidosis
[RC627.L]
UF Lipoidosis
BT Lipids—Metabolism—Disorders
NT Sphingolipidoses
Lipids
[QP751]
UF Lipides
Lipins
Lipoids
BT Biological chemistry
Biomolecules
RT Steroids
NT Blood lipids
Fat
Lipemia
Lipoproteins
Membrane lipids
Microbial lipids
Phospholipids
Plant lipids
Sphingolipids
Sterols
Tumor lipids
— Metabolism
— — Disorders *(May Subd Geog)*
[RC632.L5]
UF Lipid metabolism disorders
NT Hyperlipidemia
Hypolipemia
Lipidosis
Xanthoma
— Research *(May Subd Geog)*
UF Lipid research
— Synthesis
UF Lipid synthesis
Lipids in human nutrition *(May Subd Geog)*
[QP751-QP752 (Biochemistry)]
[TX553.L5 (Food)]
BT Nutrition
Lipids in nutrition
[TX553.L5]
BT Nutrition
Lipingcott family
USE Lippincott family

Lipinia
[QL666.L28]
BT Skinks
Lipinia miota
USE Lipinia noctua
Lipinia noctua
[QL666.L28]
UF Lipinia miota
Lipinia rouxi
Lipinia rouxi
USE Lipinia noctua
Lipins
USE Lipids
Lipitsa horse
USE Lipizzaner horse
Lipizzaner horse
[SF293.L5]
UF Lipica horse
Lipitsa horse
Lippizana horse
Lippizaner horse
Lippizzaner horse
BT Horse breeds
Lipochromes
USE Carotenoids
Lipodystrophy, Intestinal
USE Whipple's disease
Lipofuscinosis, Neuronal ceroid
USE Neuronal ceroid-lipofuscinosis
Lipofuscins
[QP671.L]
UF Aging pigments
BT Animal pigments
Lipoidosis
USE Lipidosis
Lipoids
USE Lipids
Lipolysis
[QP601]
BT Enzymes
RT Lipotropin
Lipolytic hormones, Pituitary
USE Lipotropin
Lipomembranous polycystic osteodysplasia
(May Subd Geog)
[RC931.L5]
BT Bones—Diseases
Genetic disorders
Lipophagic intestinal granulomatosis
USE Whipple's disease
Lipopolysaccharides, Microbial
USE Endotoxins
Lipoprotein antibodies
UF Anti-lipoprotein antibodies
Antibodies against lipoproteins
BT Immunoglobulins
Lipoprotein deficiency syndromes
USE Hypolipoproteinemia
Lipoprotein lipase
UF Clearing factor
BT Lipase
Lipoproteins
BT Lipids
Proteins
NT Blood lipoproteins
Myelin sheath
Lipoproteins, HDL
USE High density lipoproteins
Lipoproteins, High density
USE High density lipoproteins
Lipoptera
USE Mallophaga
Liporrhopalum
[QL568.A23]
BT Agaonidae
Liposomes
UF Phospholipid vesicles
BT Cytoplasm
Membranes (Biology)
Membranes (Technology)
Phospholipids

Liposuctioning
  USE Suction lipectomy
Lipotes
    _QL737.C436_
  BT River dolphins
  NT Lipotes vexillifer
Lipotes vexillifer
    _QL737.C436_
  UF Chinese lake dolphin
    Chinese river dolphin
    White flag dolphin
  BT Lipotes
Lipotropic agents
  UF Lipotropic factors
  BT Chemotherapy
  NT Lipotropin
Lipotropic factors
  USE Lipotropic agents
Lipotropin
    _QP572.L56_
  UF Adipokinetic substances, Pituitary
    Appetite reversing factor, Pituitary
    Lipid mobilizing factor, Pituitary
    Lipolytic hormones, Pituitary
    Obesity reversing factor, Pituitary
    Pituitary lipotropin
  BT Lipotropic agents
    Peptide hormones
    Pituitary hormones
  RT Lipolysis
Lipovany
  USE Philippovtsi (Russian sect)
Lipoxidases
  USE Lipoxygenases
Lipoxygenases
  UF Carotene oxidases
    Linoleate oxygen oxidoreductases
    Lipoxidases
  BT Oxygenases
Lippard family
  USE Lippert family
Lippart family
  USE Lippert family
Lippert family _(Not Subd Geog)_
  UF Leaphart family
    Leibert family
    Leipert family
    Leiphardt family
    Leiphart family
    Leppard family
    Leppert family
    Libhart family
    Lippard family
    Lippart family
    Lipphard family
    Lipphardt family
Lipphard family
  USE Lippert family
Lipphardt family
  USE Lippert family
Lippincott family _(Not Subd Geog)_
  UF Lipingcott family
    Lippingcott family
Lippingcott family
  USE Lippincott family
Lippizana horse
  USE Lipizzaner horse
Lippizaner horse
  USE Lipizzaner horse
Lippizzaner horse
  USE Lipizzaner horse
Lippmann process
  USE Color photography—Lippmann process
Lipreading
    _HV2487_
  UF Lip-reading
    Speech-reading
    Speechreading
    Visual speech perception

  BT Deaf—Means of communication
    Speech perception
    Visual perception
Lips
    QL857 (Comparative anatomy)
    QM306 (Human anatomy)
  BT Mouth
  NT Labial frenulum
    Labiality (Phonetics)
— **Abnormalities** _(May Subd Geog)_
    NT Harelip
— **Cancer**
    _RC280.L46_
— **Surgery**
    UF Surgery, Oral
— **Tumors**
    _RC280.L_
    _RD662_
Lipscomb family _(Not Subd Geog)_
  UF Lascomb family
    Lascome family
    Lepscomb family
    Lescum family
    Lipscombe family
    Liscomb family
    Liscombe family
    Liscum family
    Lisecomb family
    Lisscomb family
    Luscomb family
    Luscombe family
    Lyscom family
Lipscombe family
  USE Lipscomb family
Lipstick tree
  USE Annatto tree
Liptako (Burkina Faso)
  UF Libtako (Burkina Faso)
    Liptako (Upper Volta)
Liptako (Upper Volta)
  USE Liptako (Burkina Faso)
Liptena
    _QL561.L8_
  BT Lycaenidae
Liptov Basin (Czechoslovakia)
  UF Liptov Valley (Czechoslovakia)
    Liptovská Kotlina (Czechoslovakia)
  BT Geology—Czechoslovakia
Liptov Valley (Czechoslovakia)
  USE Liptov Basin (Czechoslovakia)
Liptovská Kotlina (Czechoslovakia)
  USE Liptov Basin (Czechoslovakia)
Liptrap family _(Not Subd Geog)_
  UF Libtrot family
    Lifthrop family
    Liptrot family
Liptrot family
  USE Liptrap family
Lipuridae
  USE Onychiuridae
Lipusidae
  USE Psychidae
Liquation
  BT Fusion
    Phase rule and equilibrium
    Separation (Technology)
Liquefaction of coal
  USE Coal liquefaction
Liquefaction of gases
  USE Gases—Liquefaction
Liquefaction of soils
  USE Soil liquefaction
Liquefied gas carriers
    _VM456_
  UF Carriers, Liquefied gas
  BT Liquefied gases—Transportation
    Merchant ships
    Tankers
Liquefied gases
    _TP243_

  UF Gases, Liquefied
    Liquid gases
  BT Gases—Liquefaction
  NT Liquefied natural gas
    Liquefied petroleum gas
    Liquid air
    Liquid carbon dioxide
    Liquid chlorine
    Liquid hydrogen
    Liquid methane
    Liquid oxygen
— **Transportation**
    _TP243_
    NT Liquefied gas carriers
Liquefied natural gas _(May Subd Geog)_
  UF LNG
    Natural gas liquids
  BT Gas, Natural
    Gases—Liquefaction
    Liquefied gases
— **Law and legislation** _(May Subd Geog)_
— **Pipe lines**
— — **Law and legislation**
    (May Subd Geog)
— **Storage**
— **Transportation**
— — **Law and legislation**
    (May Subd Geog)
Liquefied natural gas industry
    (May Subd Geog)
    _HD9581.2.L57_
Liquefied petroleum gas
  UF Bottled gas
    Gas, Bottled
    LP gas
    LPG
    Petroleum gas, Liquefied
    Tank gas
  BT Gas, Natural
    Gas as fuel
    Gases—Liquefaction
    Gases, Compressed
    Liquefied gases
    Liquid fuels
  RT Butane
— **Law and legislation** _(May Subd Geog)_
    UF Liquefied petroleum gas industry—
      Law and legislation
— **Pipe lines**
— — **Law and legislation**
    (May Subd Geog)
Liquefied petroleum gas industry
    (May Subd Geog)
  BT Petroleum industry and trade
— Law and legislation
    USE Liquefied petroleum gas—Law
      and legislation
Liqueurs _(May Subd Geog)_
    _TP611_
  UF Cordials (Liquor)
  BT Liquors
  SA _names of liqueurs, e.g._ Absinthe
Liquid, Electron-hole
  USE Electron-hole droplets
Liquid air
    _QD535_
  UF Air, Liquid
  BT Chemistry
    Chemistry, Physical and theoretical
    Gases—Liquefaction
    Heat
    Liquefied gases
    Low temperature research
  NT Liquid oxygen
Liquid aluminum
  BT Liquid metals
Liquid ammonia
  BT Ammonia
  NT Metal ammonia solutions

Liquid argon
  BT Argon
     Gases—Liquefaction
Liquid assets
  USE Liquidity (Economics)
Liquid carbon dioxide
  [TP244.C1]
  BT Carbon dioxide
     Liquefied gases
Liquid chlorine
  [TP245.C5]
  BT Chlorine
     Liquefied gases
Liquid chromatography
  [QD79.C454 (Analytical chemistry)]
  [QD272.C447 (Organic chemistry)]
  [QH324.9.L5 (Biology)]
  BT Chromatographic analysis
  NT Capillary liquid chromatography
     Field-flow fractionation
     High performance liquid
        chromatography
Liquid copying processes
  USE Fluid copying processes
Liquid crystal devices
  [TS518]
  UF Crystal devices, Liquid
  BT Electrooptics
     Liquid crystals
  NT Kerr cell shutters
Liquid crystal polymers
  USE Polymer liquid crystals
Liquid crystalline polymers
  USE Polymer liquid crystals
Liquid crystalline solvents
  BT Liquid crystals
     Solvents
Liquid crystals
  [QD923]
  UF Crystals, Liquid
  BT Light sources
  NT Hexyloxyphenyl decyloxybenzoate
     Liquid crystal devices
     Liquid crystalline solvents
     Polymer liquid crystals
  — Spectra
     [QD923]
Liquid crystals, Polymer
  USE Polymer liquid crystals
Liquid dielectrics
  USE Dielectrics, Liquid
Liquid drop model, Nuclear
  USE Nuclear liquid drop model
Liquid droplet model, Nuclear
  USE Nuclear liquid drop model
Liquid farm manure
  USE Farm manure, Liquid
Liquid feeders
  [TP159.F4]
  UF Feeders, Liquid
     Liquid meters
     Meters, Liquid
  BT Process control
     Pumping machinery
Liquid fertilizer industry (May Subd Geog)
  BT Liquid fertilizers
Liquid fertilizers (May Subd Geog)
  UF Fluid fertilizers
  BT Fertilizers
  NT Farm manure, Liquid
     Liquid fertilizer industry
  — Additives
  — Application
     UF Application of liquid fertilizers
     NT Foliar feeding
Liquid films
  UF Films, Liquid
  BT Surfaces (Technology)
     Thin films

Liquid fluorine
  BT Fluorine
     Gases—Liquefaction
Liquid fuel rockets
  USE Liquid propellant rockets
Liquid fuels
  [TP343]
  UF Fuel, Liquid
  BT Fuel
     Motor fuels
  NT Alcohol as fuel
     Benzene as fuel
     Coal liquefaction
     Fuel, Colloidal
     Gasoline
     Hecter fuel
     Liquefied petroleum gas
     Liquid oxygen
     Petroleum, Synthetic
     Petroleum as fuel
     Petroleum products
  — Transportation
  — — Law and legislation
     (May Subd Geog)
Liquid gases
  USE Liquefied gases
Liquid helium
  BT Gases—Liquefaction
     Helium
     Helium at low temperatures
     Quantum liquids
  NT Second sound
     Superfluidity
  — Acoustic properties
Liquid honing
  UF Vapor blasting
  BT Grinding and polishing
     Honing
     Metals—Finishing
Liquid hydrogen
  BT Gases—Liquefaction
     Hydrogen
     Liquefied gases
Liquid inclusions
  USE Fluid inclusions
Liquid level gages
  USE Liquid level indicators
Liquid level indicators
  UF Electronic level gages
     Liquid level gages
     Tank-level gages
  BT Electronic apparatus and appliances
     Hydraulic engineering—Instruments
     Level indicators
     Liquids
     Radioisotopes—Industrial applications
     Stream-gaging stations
Liquid level indicators industry
  (May Subd Geog)
Liquid-liquid equilibrium
  UF Equilibrium, Liquid-liquid
  BT Phase rule and equilibrium
Liquid magnesium
  BT Liquid metals
     Magnesium
Liquid membranes
  BT Membranes (Technology)
Liquid metal cooled reactors
  [TK9203.L5]
  BT Nuclear reactors
  NT Liquid metal fast breeder reactors
     Sodium cooled reactors
     Sodium graphite reactors
Liquid metal fast breeder reactors
  [TK9203.B7]
  BT Breeder reactors
     Fast reactors
     Liquid metal cooled reactors
  — Containment
     BT Nuclear pressure vessels
  — — Linings

  — Cooling systems
     BT Cooling
  — — Leaks
Liquid metals
  UF Molten metals
  BT Liquids
     Metals
  NT Liquid aluminum
     Liquid magnesium
     Liquid sodium
     Mercury
     Metallic glasses
     Metals—Rapid solidification processing
  — Thermal properties
Liquid meters
  USE Liquid feeders
Liquid methane
  BT Liquefied gases
     Methane
Liquid nitrogen
  BT Gases—Liquefaction
     Nitrogen
Liquid oxygen
  [TP245.O9]
  UF LOX
     Oxygen, Liquid
  BT Explosives
     Gases—Liquefaction
     Liquefied gases
     Liquid air
     Liquid fuels
  RT Oxygen at low temperatures
Liquid potassium
  BT Potassium
Liquid propellant rockets
  UF Liquid fuel rockets
     Rocket motors, Liquid propellant
  BT Rockets (Aeronautics)
  NT Centaur rocket
     Hydrogen peroxide rockets
     Steam rockets
  — Control systems
     [TL784.C63]
  — Dynamics
  — Fuel systems
  — — Valves
     BT Valves
  — Vibration
Liquid propellants
  UF Liquid rocket propellants
  BT Propellants
     Rockets (Aeronautics)—Fuel
Liquid rocket propellants
  USE Liquid propellants
Liquid scintillation counters
  USE Liquid scintillation counting
Liquid scintillation counting
  [QC787.S34 (General)]
  [QH324.9.L53 (Biology)]
  UF Liquid scintillation counters
     Scintillation counting, Liquid
  BT Liquid scintillators
     Scintillation counters
Liquid scintillators
  [QC787.S34]
  UF Scintillators, Liquid
  BT Scintillators
  NT Liquid scintillation counting
Liquid semiconductors
  BT Semiconductors
Liquid sloshing
  USE Sloshing (Hydrodynamics)
Liquid sodium
  BT Liquid metals
     Sodium
Liquid sulphur
  BT Sulphur
Liquid-vapor equilibrium
  USE Vapor-liquid equilibrium
Liquidambar altingia
  USE Rasamala

2169

Liquidated damages (May Subd Geog)
  BT Damages
  RT Penalties, Contractual
Liquidation (May Subd Geog)
  ⌐HD2747⌐
  ⌐K⌐
    Here are entered works on the winding up of companies or of the affairs of an individual.
  UF Winding up of companies
  BT Accounting
    Bankruptcy
    Commercial law
    Corporation law
    Partnership
  RT Partition
  NT Inventories of decedents' estates
Liquidity (Economics)
  ⌐HG174⌐
  UF Assets, Frozen
    Assets, Liquid
    Frozen assets
    Liquid assets
  BT Banks and banking
    Capital
    Credit
    Finance
    Securities
  NT Cash flow
    International liquidity
    Monetary policy
Liquids
  ⌐QC141-159⌐
  BT Fluids
    Mechanics
    Physics
  RT Permeability
    Polywater
  NT Brownian movements
    Condensed matter
    Electric insulators and insulation—
      Liquids
    Hydraulics
    Hydrostatics
    Jets
    Liquid level indicators
    Liquid metals
    Meniscus (Liquids)
    Newtonian fluids
    Spheroidal state
    Splashes
    Supercooled liquids
    Surface tension
  — Acoustic properties
    ⌐QC145.4.A25⌐
  — Clarification
    ⌐TP156.C⌐
    UF Clarification of liquids
  — Compressibility
    USE Compressibility
  — Diffusion
    USE Diffusion
  — Effect of reduced gravity on
    UF Effect of reduced gravity on liquids
    BT Reduced gravity environments
  — Electric properties
  — Expansion
    USE Expansion of liquids
  — Optical properties
    ⌐QC145.4.O6⌐
    NT Sonoluminescence
  — Spectra
  — Thermal properties
  — Viscosity
    USE Viscosity
Liquids, Inflammable
  USE Inflammable liquids
Liquids, Kinetic theory of
  ⌐QC175.3⌐
  UF Kinetic theory of liquids

  BT Matter, Kinetic theory of
    Statistical mechanics
    Statistical physics
Liquids, Quantum
  USE Quantum liquids
Liquière Site (France)
  UF La Liquière Site (France)
  BT France—Antiquities
Liquimofono
  ⌐ML990.L54⌐
Liquor amnii
  USE Amniotic liquid
Liquor bottles (May Subd Geog)
  BT Beverage containers
    Bottles
    Liquors—Packaging
  NT Decanters
    Miniature bottles, Liquor
Liquor industry (May Subd Geog)
  ⌐HD9390-9395⌐
  UF Liquor traffic
  BT Liquors
Liquor laws (May Subd Geog)
  ⌐HV5074-5080⌐
  UF Alcoholic beverage control
    High license
    Law, Liquor
    Temperance—Law
  BT Alcohol—Law and legislation
    Beverages—Law and legislation
    Temperance
  RT License system
    Local option
    Prohibition
  NT Brewing industry—Law and legislation
    Distilleries—Law and legislation
    Drinking age—Law and legislation
    Gothenburg system
    Malt liquors—Law and legislation
    Wine and wine making—Law and
      legislation
  — Criminal provisions
Liquor laws (Islamic law) (May Subd Geog)
  BT Temperance and Islam
Liquor license system
  USE License system
Liquor miniature bottles
  USE Miniature bottles, Liquor
Liquor problem
  USE Alcoholism
    Drinking of alcoholic beverages
Liquor problem in the press
  USE Alcoholism in the press
Liquor traffic
  USE Alcoholic beverage industry
    Liquor industry
Liquorice
  USE Licorice
Liquors
  ⌐TP589-618⌐
  UF Distilled beverages
    Drinks
    Intoxicants
    Spirits, Alcoholic
    Spirituous liquors
  BT Alcohol
    Alcoholic beverages
    Stimulants
  RT Brewing
    Distillation
  SA names of liquors, e.g. Brandy, Rum,
    Whiskey
  NT Liqueurs
    Liquor industry
  — Flavor and odor
    BT Flavor
      Odors
  — Gaging and testing
    ⌐TP609⌐
    UF Alcoholometry

  RT Alcoholometer
    Gaging
  — Packaging
    NT Liquor bottles
  — Standards (May Subd Geog)
    UF Liquors—Tables, standards, etc.
  — Tables
    ⌐TP609⌐
    UF Liquors—Tables, standards, etc.
  — Tables, standards, etc.
    USE Liquors—Standards
      Liquors—Tables
  — Tariff
    USE Tariff on liquors
Liquors, Malt
  USE Malt liquors
Liquors, Refrigeration of
  ⌐TP658⌐
  BT Refrigeration and refrigerating
    machinery
Liri River (Italy)
  UF Liris River (Italy)
  BT Rivers—Italy
Liriodendron
  ⌐QK495.M24⌐
  BT Magnoliaceae
Liriodendron chinense
  ⌐QK495.M24⌐
  UF Chinese tulip tree
    Chinese tuliptree
    Tulip tree, Chinese
    Tuliptree, Chinese
Liriodendron tulipifera
  ⌐QK495.M24 (Botany)⌐
  ⌐SD397.L63 (Forestry)⌐
  UF Poplar, Tulip
    Poplar, Yellow
    Tulip poplar
    Tulip tree
    Tuliptree
    Tulipwood
    Whitewood
    Yellow poplar
Liriomyza
  ⌐QL537.A4⌐
  BT Agromyzidae
  NT Liriomyza mesnili
Liriomyza mesnili (May Subd Geog)
  ⌐QL537.A4⌐
  BT Liriomyza
Liriope (Coelenterata) (May Subd Geog)
  ⌐QL377.H9⌐
  BT Geryoniidae
Liriosma
  ⌐QK495.O35 (Botany)⌐
  BT Olacaceae
Liriosma egleri
  ⌐QK495.O35 (Botany)⌐
Liriosma papillosa
  ⌐QK495.O35 (Botany)⌐
Liris
  ⌐QL568.S7⌐
  BT Sphecidae
Liris River (Italy)
  USE Liri River (Italy)
Lirly family
  USE Lyerly family
Lis pendens (May Subd Geog)
  UF Res litigiosa
  BT Actions and defenses
    Exceptions (Law)
Lis pendens (Canon law)
  BT Civil procedure (Canon law)
Lis pendens (International law)
  BT International law
Lis pendens (Roman law)
Lisa computer
  ⌐QA76.8.L⌐
  UF Apple Lisa (Computer)
    Mac XL (Computer)
    Macintosh XL (Computer)

BT Apple computer
Lisango language
USE Shira language
Lisaw (Tibeto-Burman tribe)
USE Lisu (Tibeto-Burman tribe)
Lisaw language
USE Lisu language
Lisbon (Portugal)
— Description
— — 1951-1980
— — 1981-
Lisbon Expedition, 1589
⌐DA86.22.D7 (Drake)⌐
BT Great Britain—History, Naval—
Tudors, 1485-1603
Lischynsky family
USE Lishchyns′kyĭ family
Liscinsky family
USE Lishchyns′kyĭ family
Liscomb family
USE Lipscomb family
Liscombe family
USE Lipscomb family
Liscum family
USE Lipscomb family
Lisecomb family
USE Lipscomb family
Lishchyns′kyĭ family   *(Not Subd Geog)*
UF Lischynsky family
Liscinsky family
Lisira language
USE Shira language
Liskeard & Looe Union Canal, Eng.
BT Canals—England
Liskeard and Caradon Railway
BT Railroads—Great Britain
Liskeard and Looe Railway
BT Railroads—Great Britain
Liskey family   *(Not Subd Geog)*
Lisle family
USE Lyles family
L'Isle River (France)
USE Isle River (France)
Lisles family
USE Lyles family
Lisongo (African people)
USE Mbati (Central African Republic
people)
LISP (Computer program language)
UF List processing computer language
BT List processing (Electronic computers)
Lisping
UF Sigmatism
BT Articulation disorders
LISREL (Computer program)
BT Path analysis—Computer programs
Lissa, Battle of, 1866
⌐DG558⌐
BT Austro-Italian War, 1866
Lissajous' curves
⌐QC231⌐
BT Curves, Plane
Vibration
Lisscomb family
USE Lipscomb family
Lisser family   *(Not Subd Geog)*
Lissomidae
USE Elateridae
Lissone Prize
USE Premio Lissone
Lissongo (African people)
USE Mbati (Central African Republic
people)
List family   *(Not Subd Geog)*
List processing (Electronic computers)
UF Processing, List (Electronic computers)
BT Electronic data processing
Electronic digital computers—
Programming
File organization (Computer science)
Sorting (Electronic computers)

NT IPL (Computer program language)
LISP (Computer program language)
List processing computer language
USE LISP (Computer program language)
Listening
⌐BF323.L⌐
UF Auding
BT Attention
Comprehension
Educational psychology
RT Hearing
NT Eavesdropping
— **Religious aspects**
— — **Buddhism,** ⌐**Christianity, etc.**⌐
Listening comprehension tests
(May Subd Geog)
⌐LB3060.45⌐
UF Audio-lingual tests
BT Attention
Audio-lingual method (Language
teaching)
Comprehension
Listening devices, Unauthorized use of
USE Eavesdropping
Lister family   *(Not Subd Geog)*
UF Lyster family
Listera
USE Ophrys
Listerellosis
USE Listeriosis
Listerellosis in animals
USE Listeriosis in animals
Listeria infections
USE Listeriosis
Listeriosis
UF Listerellosis
Listeria infections
BT Bacterial diseases
NT Listeriosis in animals
Listeriosis in animals
⌐SF809.L5⌐
UF Listerellosis in animals
BT Communicable diseases in animals
Listeriosis
Veterinary bacteriology
Listerman family   *(Not Subd Geog)*
UF Listermann family
Listermann family
USE Listerman family
Listing of securities
USE Securities—Listing
Listings, Real estate
USE Real estate listings
Listland (Germany)
BT Sylt (Germany)
Listrochelus
USE Phyllophaga
Listroderes
⌐QL596.C9⌐
BT Curculionidae
Listroderes obliquus
USE Vegetable weevil
Listrophoridae
⌐QL458.2.L58⌐
BT Mites
Lists, Food exchange
USE Food exchange lists
Lists, Hospital waiting
USE Hospitals—Waiting lists
Lists, Mailing
USE Mailing lists
Lists, Tax
USE Taxation—Lists
Lists in rabbinical literature
UF Enumerations in rabbinical literature
Rabbinical literature—Lists
Lists in the Bible
UF Enumerations in the Bible
BT Bible—Criticism, Form
Lists of lights
USE Aids to navigation—Lists

Lists of objects
USE Catalogs
Lists of publications
USE Bibliography
Listwanite
⌐QE475.L57⌐
BT Rocks, Metamorphic
Lisu (Tibeto-Burman tribe)
(May Subd Geog)
UF Lisaw (Tibeto-Burman tribe)
Yawyin (Tibeto-Burman tribe)
NT Missions to Lisu (Tibeto-Burman tribe)
Lisu epic poetry
USE Epic poetry, Lisu
Lisu language
⌐PL4001.L6⌐
UF Lisaw language
Yawyin language
BT Loloish languages
Lisu literature   *(May Subd Geog)*
BT China—Literatures
NT Lisu poetry
Lisu poetry   *(May Subd Geog)*
BT Lisu literature
NT Epic poetry, Lisu
Lisuride
⌐RM666.L56⌐
UF Didehydromethylergolinyldiethylurea
Lysuride hydrogen maleate
Methylergol carbamide
BT Alkaloids
Dopamine
Dopamine—Agonists
Ergot
Heterocyclic compounds
Serotonin antagonists
Urea
Lit de justice
Here are entered works on the proceeding, in old
French law, whereby the king, accompanied by the
princes of the blood, the Chancellor, peers of France,
and high officials, seated on his throne, exercised his
powers as high justicier of France and made laws by
decree.
BT France—Constitutional law
France—Kings and rulers
Separation of powers—France
Litanies
BT Liturgies
— **Anglican Communion,** ⌐**Catholic Church,**
etc.⌐
Litanies (Music)
Litchi
⌐QK495.S19 (Botany)⌐
UF Leechee
Lichee
Lichi
Lychee
BT Sapindaceae
Litchi chinensis
⌐QK495.S19 (Botany)⌐
⌐SB379.L8 (Culture)⌐
UF Leechee
Lichee
Lichi
Lychee
Nephelium litchi
Liter
⌐QC104⌐
UF Litre
BT Metric system
Units
Volume (Cubic content)
Literacy   *(May Subd Geog)*
UF Illiteracy
BT Education
NT Computers and literacy
Elementary education of adults
Functional literacy
Intelligence tests for pre-literates
Libraries and new literates

Literacy *(Continued)*
  New literates, Writing for
  Public libraries—Services to the
    illiterate
  Right to Read program
  Visual literacy
Literacy, Computer
  USE Computer literacy
Literacy, Functional
  USE Functional literacy
Literacy, Visual
  USE Visual literacy
Literacy and computers
  USE Computers and literacy
Literacy testing
  USE Reading—Ability testing
Literacy tests (Election law)
  (May Subd Geog)
  UF Voting—Literacy tests
  BT Election law
    Suffrage
    Voting
Literary adaptations
  USE Literature—Adaptations
Literary agents *(May Subd Geog)*
  UF Agents, Literary
  BT Commercial agents
    Litterateurs
  RT Authors and publishers
    Theatrical agents
Literary anachronisms
  USE Errors and blunders, Literary
Literary anatomies
  UF Anatomies, Literary
  BT Literature
Literary awards
  USE Literary prizes
Literary blunders
  USE Errors and blunders, Literary
Literary book-plates
  USE Book-plates, Literary
Literary calendars
  UF Literature—Calendars
  BT Calendars
  SA *subdivision* Calendars *under names of
    individual literary authors, e.g.*
    Shakespeare, William, 1564-1616—
    Calendars
  NT Birthday books
Literary characters
  USE Characters and characteristics in
    literature
Literary classics
  USE Canon (Literature)
Literary collaboration
  USE Authorship—Collaboration
Literary competitions
  USE Literature—Competitions
Literary criticism
  USE Criticism
Literary criticism, Feminist
  USE Feminist literary criticism
Literary critics
  USE Critics
Literary curiosa
  UF Curiosa, Literary
  BT Curiosities and wonders
  NT Eccentric literature
    Literary forgeries and mystifications
Literary discourse analysis
  USE Discourse analysis, Literary
Literary errors and blunders
  USE Errors and blunders, Literary
Literary ethics
  [PN154]
  UF Ethics, Literary
  BT Literary forgeries and mystifications
  NT Plagiarism
Literary exchanges
  USE Exchanges, Literary and scientific

Literary feuds
  USE Literary quarrels
Literary forgeries and mystifications
  [PN171.F6-7]
  UF Frauds, Literary
    Literary frauds
    Literary mystifications
    Mystifications, Literary
  BT Authorship
    Bibliography
    Errors and blunders, Literary
    Forgery
    Literary curiosa
    Literature
  RT Anonyms and pseudonyms
    Imaginary books and libraries
    Imprints (in books), Fictitious
    Pasticcio
  NT Bookbinding—Forgeries
    History—Errors, inventions, etc.
    Literary ethics
Literary form
  [PN45.5]
  UF Form, Literary
    Genre (Literature)
    Literature—Forms
  SA *specific forms, e.g.* Drama
Literary frauds
  USE Literary forgeries and mystifications
Literary historians *(May Subd Geog)*
  BT Historians
    Literature—History and criticism—
      Theory, etc.
    Litterateurs
Literary influence
  USE Influence (Literary, artistic, etc.)
Literary journeys *(May Subd Geog)*
  UF Bibliographical journeys
Literary landmarks *(May Subd Geog)*
  [PN164]
  UF Authors—Homes and haunts
    Landmarks, Literary
  BT Historic buildings
    Literature—History and criticism
  SA *subdivision* Homes and haunts *under
    names of authors*
  NT Cities and towns in literature
    Poets' monuments
Literary language
  USE Standard language
Literary libraries *(May Subd Geog)*
  UF Libraries, Literary
  BT Libraries, Special
Literary life
  USE *subdivision* Intellectual life *under
    names of countries, cities, etc.*
    Litterateurs
Literary museums *(May Subd Geog)*
  UF Literature—Museums
  BT Museums
Literary mystifications
  USE Literary forgeries and mystifications
Literary piracy
  USE Copyright—Unauthorized reprints
Literary portraits
  USE Characters and characteristics in
    literature
Literary prizes *(May Subd Geog)*
  UF Book awards
    Book prizes
    Literary awards
    Literature—Awards
    Literature—Prizes
  BT Rewards (Prizes, etc.)
  SA *names of individual literary prizes*
  NT Cabotín prize
    Caldecott medal books
    Ciudad de Barcelona prizes
    Dimitrov prizes
    Kleist prize
    Leninskaia premiia v oblasti literatury

Library Association Carnegie Medal
    Literature—Competitions
    National Book Awards
    Newbery medal books
    Premio Ismael Pérez Pazmiño
    Premio letterario "Libera Stampa"
    Premio Nacional de Literatura
    Premio Viareggio
    Prix Essai-Poésie
    Prix Max Rose de poésie
    Pushkin prizes
    Regina medal books
    William Allen White children's book
      award
  — **Germany (West)**
    NT Ingeborg-Bachmann-Preis
  — **India**
    NT Bharatiya Jnanapitha
  — **Italy**
    NT Premio Antico Fattore
      Premio di narrativa fantastica
        "J.R.R. Tolkien"
      Premio Grinzane Cavour
  — **Japan**
    NT Naoki shō
  — **South Africa**
    NT Hertzogprys
  — **Spain**
    NT Lletra d'Or
      Premi Joan Crexells
  — **Switzerland**
    NT Schweizer Arbeiterliteraturpreis
  — **Venezuela**
    NT Premio Municipal de Literatura
Literary property
  USE Copyright
Literary quarrels *(May Subd Geog)*
  [PN165]
  UF Feuds, Literary
    Literary feuds
    Quarrels, Literary
Literary recreations
  [GV1493]
  UF Language games
    Recreations, Literary
  BT Amusements
    Literature—Miscellanea
  NT Charades
    Crossword puzzles
    Double-crostics
    Palindromes
    Plot-your-own stories
    Rebuses
    Riddles
    Utaawase
    Word games
Literary research
  USE Literature—Research
Literary reviews
  USE *subdivision* Book reviews *under
    individual literatures and genres of
    those literatures, e.g.* English
    literature—Book reviews
Literary sketch
  USE Essay
Literary societies
  USE *subdivision* Societies, etc. *under
    particular national literatures, e.g.*
    English literature—Societies, etc.
    Literature—Societies, etc.
Literary style
  USE Style, Literary
Literary terms
  USE Literature—Terminology
Literary terms, English
  USE English literature—Terminology
Literary tradition
  USE Ancients and moderns, Quarrel of
    Influence (Literary, artistic, etc.)
Literary transmission
  USE Transmission of texts

Literatura de cordel
  USE Chap-books, Brazilian
       Chap-books, Portuguese
       Chap-books, Spanish
Literature
  [PN45]
      Here are entered works dealing with literature in
  general, not limited to aesthetics, philosophy, history
  or any one aspect.
  UF Belles-lettres
       World literature
  BT Books
       Language and languages
  RT Authorship
       Books and reading
       Philology
  SA *headings of the type [topic] in*
       literature, e.g. Children in literature,
       Realism in literature; also headings
       of the type [language] literature,
       e.g. Swahili literature; *also headings*
       for national literatures, e.g.
       American literature, Mexican
       literature; and subdivision
       Literatures under names of
       countries, cities, etc.
  NT America—Literatures
       Anonymous writings
       Anthropologists' literary writings
       Apocalyptic literature
       Architecture and literature
       Art and literature
       Authors
       Autobiography
       Bible and literature
       Bilingualism and literature
       Bio-bibliography
       Buddhism and literature
       Campaign literature
       Catholic literature
       Children's literature
       Christian literature
       Classical literature
       Classicism
       Classification—Books—Literature
       College readers
       Conservatism and literature
       Copyright
       Cowboys' writings
       Creation (Literary, artistic, etc.)
       Criminals' writings
       Criticism
       Cubism and literature
       Cycles (Literature)
       Didactic literature
       Diseases and literature
       Divers' writings
       Drama
       Drugs and literature
       Epic literature
       Erotic literature
       Errors and blunders, Literary
       European literature
       Fables
       Fairy tales
       Fantastic fiction
       Fantastic literature
       Fascism and literature
       Feminism and literature
       Fiction
       First person narrative
       Folk literature
       Gothic literature
       Government employees' literary
         writings
       Ideology and literature
       Imitation (in literature)
       Industry and literature
       Influence (Literary, artistic, etc.)
       Journalism
       Judaism and literature

Kings' and rulers' writings
Laboring class writings
Legends
Legislative employees' literary writings
Legislators' literary writings
Letters
Lettrism
Linguists' literary writings
Literary anatomies
Literary forgeries and mystifications
Literature, Comparative—Occidental
  and Oriental
Literature, Comparative—Oriental and
  Occidental
Litterateurs
Liturgy and literature
Livres à clef
Lost literature
Macaronic literature
Mass media and literature
Mathematics and literature
Mock-heroic literature
Modernism (Literature)
Multilingualism and literature
Music and literature
National socialism and literature
Nationalism and literature
Nonsense literature
Nuclear warfare and literature
Originality (in literature)
Parodies
Pasticcio
Pastoral literature
Patriotic literature
Picaresque literature
Places of indeterminacy (Literature)
Plagiarism
Plots (Drama, novel, etc.)
Poetic justice
Poetry
Postage-stamps—Topics—Literature
Prose literature
Protestantism and literature
Psychological literature
Psychology and literature
Quotations
Radio and literature
Religious literature
Revolutionary literature
Romances
Romanticism
Sagas
Satire
Scientists' literary writings
Semiotics and literature
Sequels (Literature)
Setting (Literature)
Sincerity and literature
Sivaism and literature
Social psychology and literature
Socialism and literature
Style, Literary
Surrealism (Literature)
Tales
Triads (Literature)
Unanimism
Underground literature
Violence in literature
Visual literature
Wisdom literature
Wit and humor
Women and literature
Young adult literature
— Adaptations
  UF Adaptations, Literary
       Literary adaptations

  SA *subdivision* Adaptations *under*
       names of individual literary
       authors and individual works
       entered under title, and under
       individual literatures, e.g.
       Shakespeare, William, 1564-
       1616—Adaptations; Beowulf—
       Adaptations; English literature—
       Adaptations
  NT Film adaptations
       Radio adaptations
       Stage adaptations
       Television adaptations
— Aesthetics
  [PN45]
  BT Aesthetics
  RT Style, Literary
  NT Belief, Problem of (Literature)
       Rasas
— Anecdotes, facetiae, satire, etc.
  [PN165]
  [PN169]
  BT Authorship—Anecdotes, facetiae,
       satire, etc.
— Awards
  USE Literary prizes
— Bibliography
  [Z6511-6525]
— — Early
      Here are entered bibliographies issued
  before 1800.
— — First editions
  [Z6514.F5]
  BT Bibliography—First editions
— Black authors
  [PN6068 (Collections)]
  UF Black literature
  SA *subdivision* Black authors *under*
       headings for individual
       literatures and genres; and
       subdivision Afro-American
       authors *under headings in the*
       field of American literature, e.g.
       English poetry—Black authors;
       Drama—Black authors;
       American literature—Afro-
       American authors
— Calendars
  USE Literary calendars
— Cataloging
  USE Cataloging of literature
— Censorship
  USE Censorship
— Collections
  [PN6010-6078]
  UF Literature—Selections
  BT Anthologies
  SA *subdivision* Literary collections
       under special topics for
       collections including several
       literary forms, e.g. Cats—
       Literary collections; Political
       science—Literary collections
  NT Books, Condensed
— Competitions
  [PN171.P75]
  UF Literary competitions
  BT Literary prizes
  NT Floral games
— Evaluation
  USE Bibliography—Best books
       Books and reading
       Criticism
       Literature—History and criticism
— Examinations, questions, etc.
  UF Literature—Questions
— Exiled authors
  UF Exile literature
       Exiled authors' literature
       Expatriate literature
  BT Exiles

Literature
— **Exiled authors** *(Continued)*
   RT Authors, Exiled
   SA *individual literatures subdivided by place; and subdivision Foreign countries under individual literatures, e.g.* English literature —Foreign countries
— Film and video adaptations
   USE Film adaptations
          Television adaptations
— Forms
   USE Literary form
— **History and criticism**
   ⌜PN75-PN99 (Criticism)⌝
   ⌜PN441-PN595 (History)⌝
     Here are entered histories of literature and works evaluating the character and qualities of works of literature. Works on the principles of literary criticism are entered under the heading Criticism.
   UF Appraisal of books
          Books—Appraisal
          Evaluation of literature
          Literature—Evaluation
   BT Criticism
          Style, Literary
   NT Authors
          Canon (Literature)
          Literary landmarks
          Transmission of texts
— — **Periodicals**
   ⌜PN1-PN9⌝
   ⌜PN80⌝
   ⌜PN851 (Comparative literature)⌝
— — **Theory, etc.**
   ⌜PN441⌝
   NT Literary historians
— **Indian authors**
   SA *individual Indian literatures, e.g.* Aztec literature; *and subdivision* Indian authors *under individual non-Indian literatures, e.g.* Canadian literature—Indian authors
   NT Indian literature
— Influence
   USE Literature and morals
— Local color
   USE Local color in literature
— **Miscellanea**
   NT Literary recreations
— Moral and religious aspects
   USE Literature and morals
          Religion and literature
— Museums
   USE Literary museums
— **Periodicals**
   ⌜PN1-PN9⌝
   UF Literature—Yearbooks
— **Philosophy**
   ⌜PN45⌝
     Here are entered works on the theory of literature, including its aims, ideals, meaning, relations to philosophy, etc.
   UF Philosophy of literature
   NT Belief, Problem of (Literature)
          Phenomenology and literature
— Political aspects
   USE Politics and literature
— Prizes
   USE Literary prizes
— **Psychology**
   ⌜PN49⌝
   BT Psychology and literature
   RT Aesthetics
   NT Belief, Problem of (Literature)
          Comic books, strips, etc.— Psychological aspects
          Rhetoric and psychology
          Science fiction—Psychological aspects

— Publishing
   USE Literature publishing
— Questions
   USE Literature—Examinations, questions, etc.
— **Research** *(May Subd Geog)*
   UF Literary research
— Selections
   USE Literature—Collections
— Social aspects
   USE Literature and society
— **Societies, etc.**
   ⌜PN20-PN29⌝
   ⌜PN855 (Comparative literature)⌝
     Here are entered works about societies devoted to literature in general. Works about societies devoted to particular national literatures are entered under the national literature with the subdivision Societies, etc., e.g. English literature—Societies, etc.
   UF Literary societies
   NT Chambers of rhetoric
          Nonsense Club (Group of writers)
          Scriblerus Club (Group of writers)
— **Stories, plots, etc.**
   ⌜PN44⌝
— **Study and teaching** *(May Subd Geog)*
   ⌜PN59-72⌝
   UF Literature, Modern—Study and teaching
   BT Language arts
   NT Literature teachers
— Style
   USE Style, Literary
— **Terminology**
   UF Literary terms
          Terms, Literary
— Themes, motives
   USE Literature, Comparative— Themes, motives
— Therapeutic use
   USE Bibliotherapy
— Translating
   USE Translating and interpreting
— Translations
   USE Translations
— **Women authors**
   UF Literature, Modern—Women authors
   RT Feminism and literature
— Yearbooks
   USE Literature—Periodicals
Literature, Accounting
   USE Accounting literature
Literature, Ancient
   ⌜PN611-PN630 (History and criticism)⌝
   NT Classical literature
          Egyptian literature
Literature, Apocalyptic
   USE Apocalyptic literature
Literature, Archaeological
   USE Archaeological literature
Literature, Art
   USE Art literature
Literature, Baroque
   USE Baroque literature
Literature, Bibliographical
   USE Bibliographical literature
Literature, Bonpo
   USE Bonpo literature
Literature, Business
   USE Business literature
Literature, Classical
   USE Classical literature
Literature, Comic
   USE Burlesque (Literature)
          Comedy
          Commedia dell'arte
          Farce
          Parody
          Satire

Literature, Comparative
   ⌜PN851-PN883⌝
   ⌜PQ-PT (By country)⌝
     Subdivided by nationality of literatures compared, with duplicate entry, e.g. 1. Literature, Comparative —English and German. 2. Literature, Comparative— German and English.
   UF Comparative literature
   BT Philology
— Assyro-Babylonian and Hebrew
   USE Assyro-Babylonian literature— Relation to the Old Testament
— **Chinese and European**
   BT Chinese literature
          European literature
— **Classical and modern**
   BT Classical literature
          Literature, Modern
   NT Ancients and moderns, Quarrel of
— Egyptian and Hebrew
   USE Egyptian literature—Relation to the Old Testament
— **English and German**
— **European and Chinese**
   BT Chinese literature
          European literature
— **European and Kazakh**
— **German and American**
   BT German-American literature
— **German and English**
— Hebrew and Assyro-Babylonian
   USE Assyro-Babylonian literature— Relation to the Old Testament
— Hebrew and Egyptian
   USE Egyptian literature—Relation to the Old Testament
— **Modern and classical**
   BT Classical literature
          Literature, Modern
   NT Ancients and moderns, Quarrel of
— **Occidental and Oriental**
   BT Literature
          Oriental literature
— **Oriental and Occidental**
   BT Literature
          Oriental literature
— **Themes, motives**
   UF Literature—Themes, motives
   BT Plots (Drama, novel, etc.)
   RT Fairy tales—Classification
          Folk literature—Themes, motives
   SA *specific subjects, e.g.* Architecture in literature; Irish in literature; Social problems in literature; *and names of literary themes, e.g.* Prodigal son (Parable)
   NT Trickster in literature
Literature, Conservative
   USE Conservative literature
Literature, Cooperation
   USE Cooperation literature
Literature, Dental
   USE Dental literature
Literature, Didactic
   USE Didactic literature
Literature, Eccentric
   USE Eccentric literature
Literature, Ecological
   USE Environmental literature
Literature, Economics
   USE Economics literature
Literature, Electronics
   USE Electronics literature
Literature, Environmental
   USE Environmental literature
Literature, Epic
   USE Epic literature
Literature, Epilepsy
   USE Epilepsy literature
Literature, Erotic
   USE Erotic literature

Literature, European Economic Community
   USE European Economic Community
       literature
Literature, Experimental *(May Subd Geog)*
   UF Avant-garde literature
       Experimental literature
   BT Avant-garde (Aesthetics)
       Modernism (Literature)
       Style, Literary
   NT Experimental fiction
       Experimental poetry
Literature, Feminist
   USE Feminist literature
Literature, Film
   USE Moving-picture literature
Literature, Finance
   USE Finance literature
Literature, Gambling
   USE Gambling literature
Literature, Garden
   USE Horticultural literature
Literature, Gardening
   USE Horticultural literature
Literature, Genealogical
   USE Genealogical literature
Literature, Genetic
   USE Genetic literature
Literature, Gerontology
   USE Gerontology literature
Literature, Gothic
   USE Gothic literature
       Gothic revival (Literature)
Literature, Horticultural
   USE Horticultural literature
Literature, Housing
   USE Housing literature
Literature, Immoral
   [HQ471]
   [HV6727 (Social pathology)]
   [PN49 (Literature and ethics)]
   [Z659 (Copyright)]
   UF Immoral literature
       Obscene literature
   BT Erotica
       Pornography
       Vice
   RT Erotic literature
       Literature and morals
   NT Censorship
       Children and erotica
       Sex in literature
  — Law and legislation
     USE Obscenity (Law)
Literature, Industrial relations
   USE Industrial relations literature
Literature, Information science
   USE Information science literature
Literature, International relations
   USE International relations literature
Literature, Job satisfaction
   USE Job satisfaction literature
Literature, Job stress
   USE Job stress literature
Literature, Labor
   USE Labor literature
Literature, Legal
   USE Legal literature
Literature, Library science
   USE Library science literature
Literature, Life sciences
   USE Life sciences literature
Literature, Macaronic
   USE Macaronic literature
Literature, Management
   USE Management literature
Literature, Marketing
   USE Marketing literature
Literature, Mathematical
   USE Mathematical literature
Literature, Medical
   USE Medical literature

Literature, Medieval
   [PN665-694]
   UF European literature—Medieval, 500-
       1500
   BT Christian literature, Early
       Middle Ages
       Renaissance
   NT Chreiai
       Romances
  — **History and criticism**
     NT Questione della lingua
  — — **Theory, etc.**
  — **Stories, plots, etc.**
  — Translations
     USE Translations—Literature,
         Medieval
Literature, Mental health
   USE Mental health literature
Literature, Modern
   [PN695-779]
   UF Modern literature
   BT Arts, Modern
   NT European literature
       Futurism (Literary movement)
       Gothic revival (Literature)
       Literature, Comparative—Classical and
         modern
       Literature, Comparative—Modern and
         classical
       Neoclassicism (Literature)
       Symbolism (Literary movement)
  — **15th and 16th centuries**
     [PN661-739]
     BT Renaissance
     NT European literature—Renaissance,
         1450-1600
  — — **History and criticism**
     NT Questione della lingua
  — **17th century**
     [PN740-749]
  — **18th century**
     [PN750-759]
  — **19th century**
     [PN760-769]
     NT Negishi School
  — — **History and criticism**
     NT Aestheticism (Literature)
       Decadence (Literary movement)
  — **20th century**
     [PN771-9]
  — — **Explication**
  — — **History and criticism**
     NT Dadaism
  — **Appreciation** *(May Subd Geog)*
  — Cataloging
     USE Cataloging of modern literature
  — Study and teaching
     USE Literature—Study and teaching
  — Translations
     USE Translations—Literature, Modern
  — Women authors
     USE Literature—Women authors
Literature, Motion picture
   USE Moving-picture literature
Literature, Murder
   USE Murder literature
Literature, Nursing
   USE Nursing literature
Literature, Pastoral
   USE Pastoral literature
Literature, Pediatric
   USE Pediatric literature
Literature, Physics
   USE Physics literature
Literature, Picaresque
   USE Picaresque literature
Literature, Policy science
   USE Policy science literature
Literature, Political science
   USE Political science literature

Literature, Popular
   USE Popular literature
Literature, Poverty
   USE Poverty literature
Literature, Primitive
   USE Folk literature
Literature, Renaissance
   USE European literature—Renaissance,
       1450-1600
Literature, Rococo
   USE Rococo literature
Literature, Sex instruction
   USE Sex instruction literature
Literature, Social mobility
   USE Social mobility literature
Literature, Social science
   USE Social science literature
Literature, Social security
   USE Social security literature
Literature, Social service
   USE Social service literature
Literature, Socially handicapped
   USE Socially handicapped literature
Literature, Sociology
   USE Sociology literature
Literature, Sports
   USE Sports literature
Literature, Taxation
   USE Taxation literature
Literature, Technical
   USE Technical literature
Literature, Tennis
   USE Tennis literature
Literature, Trademark
   USE Trademark literature
Literature, Underground
   USE Underground literature
Literature, Unemployment
   USE Unemployment literature
Literature, Victorian
   USE English literature—19th century
Literature, Vocational rehabilitation
   USE Vocational rehabilitation literature
Literature, Work and family
   USE Work and family literature
Literature and anthropology
   (May Subd Geog)
   BT Anthropology
Literature and art
   USE Art and literature
Literature and capitalism
   USE Capitalism and literature
Literature and Christianity
   USE Christianity and literature
Literature and communism
   USE Communism and literature
Literature and conservatism
   USE Conservatism and literature
Literature and fascism
   USE Fascism and literature
Literature and folklore *(May Subd Geog)*
   BT Folklore
Literature and history
   [PN50]
   UF History and literature
       History and poetry
       Poetry and history
   NT Historical criticism (Literature)
       History in literature
Literature and homosexuality
   USE Homosexuality and literature
Literature and Islam
   USE Islam and literature
Literature and journalism
   USE Journalism and literature
Literature and Judaism
   USE Judaism and literature
Literature and law
   USE Law and literature
Literature and liturgy
   USE Liturgy and literature

Literature and medicine
    UF Medicine and literature
    BT Medicine and the humanities
    NT Medicine in literature
        Physicians as authors
Literature and mental illness
    UF Authors, Insane
        Mental illness and literature
        Poets, Insane
    NT Mentally ill, Writings of the
Literature and morals
    [PN49]
    UF Books and reading—Moral and
            religious aspects
        Literature—Influence
        Literature—Moral and religious
            aspects
        Morals and literature
    BT Arts and morals
        Ethics
        Religion in literature
    RT Literature, Immoral
    NT Belief, Problem of (Literature)
        Censorship
        Children's literature—Moral and
            religious aspects
        Didactic literature
Literature and moving-pictures
    USE Moving-pictures and literature
Literature and music
    USE Music and literature
Literature and mysticism
    USE Mysticism and literature
Literature and nationalism
    USE Nationalism and literature
Literature and painting
    USE Art and literature
Literature and photography
    (May Subd Geog)
    BT Photography
Literature and politics
    USE Politics and literature
Literature and psychoanalysis
    USE Psychoanalysis and literature
Literature and radio
    USE Radio and literature
Literature and religion
    USE Religion and literature
Literature and revolutions
    UF Revolutions and literature
    NT Revolutionary literature
Literature and science *(May Subd Geog)*
    [PN55 (General)]
    [PR149.S4 (English literature)]
    UF Poetry and science
        Science and literature
        Science and poetry
    BT Science and the humanities
    NT Science fiction
Literature and sculpture
    USE Art and literature
Literature and Shinto
    USE Shinto and literature
Literature and society *(May Subd Geog)*
    UF Literature—Social aspects
        Literature and sociology
        Society and literature
        Sociology and literature
    BT Sociolinguistics
    SA subdivision Social aspects *under*
            individual genres and national
            literatures, e.g. Poetry—Social
            aspects; English literature—Social
            aspects
Literature and sociology
    USE Literature and society
Literature and spiritualism
    [BF1275.L58]
    BT Spiritualism
Literature and state *(May Subd Geog)*
    [PN51]

    UF State and literature
    BT Cultural policy
    RT Authors and patrons
        Politics and literature
    NT Capitalism and literature
Literature and technology *(May Subd Geog)*
    UF Technology and literature
    BT Technology
Literature and totalitarianism
    USE Totalitarianism and literature
Literature and tuberculosis
    USE Tuberculosis and literature
Literature and war
    USE War and literature
Literature Manipulation System (Computer
    program)
    USE LITMAS (Computer program)
Literature of photography
    USE Photography literature
Literature on labor and laboring classes
    USE Labor literature
Literature publishing *(May Subd Geog)*
    UF Literature—Publishing
    BT Publishers and publishing
Literature teachers *(May Subd Geog)*
    BT Literature—Study and teaching
        Litterateurs
        Teachers
    NT Authors as teachers
Literatures of America
    USE America—Literatures
Literatures of the Soviet Union
    USE Soviet literature
Lithares Site (Greece)
    [DF221.L56]
    BT Greece—Antiquities
Lithic implements
    USE Stone implements
Lithic source areas
    USE Quarries and quarrying
Lithium
    [QD181.L5]
    [TP245.L5 (Chemical technology)]
    BT Tranquilizing drugs
    NT Soils—Lithium content
    — **Isotopes**
    — — **Spectra**
    — **Spectra**
Lithium alloys
    NT Aluminum-lithium alloys
        Lithium-lead alloys
        Magnesium-lithium alloys
Lithium-aluminum alloys
    USE Aluminum-lithium alloys
Lithium cells
    UF Batteries, Lithium
        Cells, Lithium
    BT Electric batteries
Lithium chloride
    BT Chlorides
Lithium hydride
    BT Hydrides
Lithium industry *(May Subd Geog)*
    [HD9539.L58-584]
Lithium iodate
    BT Iodates
Lithium-lead alloys
    UF Lead-lithium alloys
    BT Lead alloys
        Lithium alloys
Lithium-magnesium alloys
    USE Magnesium-lithium alloys
Lithium mines and mining *(May Subd Geog)*
Lithium niobate
    BT Niobates
Lithium ores *(May Subd Geog)*
Lithium organic compounds
    USE Organolithium compounds
Lithium silicates
    NT Petalite

Lithium tantalate
    BT Tantalates
Lithocenosis
    USE Lithotrity
Lithocolletidae
    USE Gracillariidae
Lithodidae
    [QL444.M33]
    BT Crabs
    NT Paralithodes
Lithodytes conspicillatus
    USE Eleutherodactylus conspicillatus
Lithofacies *(May Subd Geog)*
    BT Facies (Geology)
        Geology, Stratigraphic
        Petrology
        Rocks, Sedimentary
Lithognathus
    [QL638.S74]
    BT Sparidae
Lithognathus olivieri
    [QL638.S74]
Lithographers *(May Subd Geog)*
    [NE2301-NE2396 (Special countries)]
    [NE2410 (Collective)]
    BT Printmakers
    NT United States. Navy—Lithographers
Lithographic workshops *(May Subd Geog)*
    BT Lithography
        Workshops
Lithography *(May Subd Geog)*
    [NE2250-2529]
    BT Art
        Prints
    RT Chromolithography
    NT Algraphy
        Ion beam lithography
        Lithographic workshops
        Microlithography
        Nature-printing and nature-prints
        Offset printing
        Photolithography
        Tariff on lithography
        X-ray lithography
        Zincography
    — **19th century** *(May Subd Geog)*
    — **20th century** *(May Subd Geog)*
        NT Offset lithography
    — — **Norway**
            NT Munch, Edvard, 1863-1944.
                Alpha and Omega
    — **Metal plate processes**
        [NE2540-2560]
        UF Metal plate processes
                (Lithography)
        NT Offset lithography
            Offset printing
    — **Printing**
        [NE2860]
        BT Pictures—Printing
            Printing
    — — **Specimens**
            BT Printing—Specimens
    — **Private collections** *(May Subd Geog)*
    — **Tariff**
        USE Tariff on lithography
Lithography, American, [French, etc.]
Lithography, Direct
    [Z252.5.L5]
    UF Dilitho
        Direct lithography
    BT Printing
    RT Offset printing
Lithography, Electron beam
    UF Electron beam lithography
    BT Electron beams—Industrial
            applications
        Microelectronics
        Photolithography
Lithography, Estonian *(May Subd Geog)*
    UF Estonian lithography

Lithography, European
　UF European lithography
Lithography, Finnish (May Subd Geog)
　UF Finnish lithography
Lithography, French (May Subd Geog)
　UF French lithography
　NT Redon, Odilon, 1840-1916.
　　　Apocalypse of Saint John
Lithography, German (May Subd Geog)
　UF German lithography
Lithography, Japanese (May Subd Geog)
　UF Japanese lithography
Lithography, Lithuanian (May Subd Geog)
　UF Lithuanian lithography
Lithography, Mexican (May Subd Geog)
　UF Mexican lithography
Lithography, Offset
　USE Offset lithography
Litholapaxy
　USE Lithotrity
Lithology
　USE Petrology
Lithopedion
　[RG631]
　BT Fetal death
Lithophone (Paint)
　USE Lithopone
Lithophytes
　USE Corals
　　　Rock plants
Lithopone
　[HD9999.L6-HD9999.64 (Trade)]
　[TP936 (Technology)]
　UF Lithophone (Paint)
Lithoprinting
　USE Offset printing
Lithostrotionidae
　[QE778]
　BT Rugosa
Lithotomy
　[RD581]
　BT Bladder—Surgery
　　　Calculi, Urinary
　　　Surgery, Operative
　　　Urinary organs—Surgery
Lithotripsy
　USE Lithotrity
Lithotripsy, Shock-wave, Extracorporeal
　USE Ultrasonic lithotripsy
Lithotripsy, Ultrasonic
　USE Ultrasonic lithotripsy
Lithotrity
　[RD581]
　UF Lithocenosis
　　　Litholapaxy
　　　Lithotripsy
　BT Urinary organs—Surgery
　NT Ultrasonic lithotripsy
Lithozincography
　USE Zincography
Lithraea
　[QK495.A498 (Botany)]
　BT Anacardiaceae
Lithuania
— Anniversaries, etc.
　　NT Sixteenth of February
— Description and travel
— — 1981-
— Economic conditions
— — 1918-1945
— — 1945-
— History
　　NT Horodlo, Treaty of, 1413
　　　　Šiauliai (Lithuania), Battle of, 1236
　　　　Tannenberg, Battle of, 1410
— — Revolution, 1830-1832
— — Revolution, 1863
— — 20th century (Not Subd Geog)
— — Revolution of 1905
— — German occupation, 1915-1918
— — 1918-1945

— — Russian occupation, 1940-1941
— — German occupation, 1941-1944
— — 1945-
— Politics and government
— — 1918-1945
— — 1945-
— Social conditions
— — 1918-1945
— — 1945-
Lithuanian aesthetics
　USE Aesthetics, Lithuanian
Lithuanian American communists
　(May Subd Geog)
　UF Communists, Lithuanian American
Lithuanian-American literature
　(May Subd Geog)
　UF American literature (Lithuanian)
　BT Lithuanian literature
Lithuanian-American newspapers
　BT American newspapers
　　　Lithuanian newspapers
Lithuanian Americans (May Subd Geog)
　BT Ethnology—United States
　　　Lithuanians—United States
Lithuanian anonyms and pseudonyms
　USE Anonyms and pseudonyms, Lithuanian
Lithuanian art
　USE Art, Lithuanian
Lithuanian arts
　USE Arts, Lithuanian
Lithuanian authors
　USE Authors, Lithuanian
Lithuanian ballads
　USE Ballads, Lithuanian
Lithuanian book-plates
　USE Book-plates, Lithuanian
Lithuanian children's literature
　USE Children's literature, Lithuanian
Lithuanian children's plays
　USE Children's plays, Lithuanian
Lithuanian children's poetry
　USE Children's poetry, Lithuanian
Lithuanian cookery
　USE Cookery, Lithuanian
Lithuanian detective stories
　USE Detective and mystery stories,
　　　Lithuanian
Lithuanian didactic literature
　USE Didactic literature, Lithuanian
Lithuanian drama (May Subd Geog)
　[PG8709 (History)]
　[PG8713 (Collections)]
　NT Children's plays, Lithuanian
Lithuanian drama (Tragedy)
　[PG8709 (History)]
　[PG8713 (Collections)]
　BT Tragedy
Lithuanian encyclopedias and dictionaries
　USE Encyclopedias and dictionaries,
　　　Lithuanian
Lithuanian fiction
　NT Detective and mystery stories,
　　　Lithuanian
　　　Short stories, Lithuanian
Lithuanian folk dancing
　USE Folk dancing, Lithuanian
Lithuanian folk literature
　USE Folk literature, Lithuanian
Lithuanian folk-songs
　USE Folk-songs, Lithuanian
Lithuanian imprints (May Subd Geog)
Lithuanian Jews
　USE Jews, Lithuanian
Lithuanian language
　[PG8501-8693]
　BT Baltic languages
Lithuanian literature (May Subd Geog)
　[PG8701-8772]
　BT Baltic literature
　NT Children's literature, Lithuanian
　　　Didactic literature, Lithuanian

　　　Folk literature, Lithuanian
　　　Lithuanian-American literature
　　　Young adult literature, Lithuanian
— 20th century
　　[PG8701-PG8709 (History)]
　　[PG8713-PG8719 (Collections)]
— Illustrations
— Foreign countries
　　[PG8737]
　　UF Lithuanian literature in foreign
　　　　countries
Lithuanian literature in foreign countries
　USE Lithuanian literature—Foreign
　　　countries
Lithuanian lithography
　USE Lithography, Lithuanian
Lithuanian mystery stories
　USE Detective and mystery stories,
　　　Lithuanian
Lithuanian mythology
　USE Mythology, Baltic
Lithuanian narrative poetry
　USE Narrative poetry, Lithuanian
Lithuanian newspapers (May Subd Geog)
　NT Lithuanian-American newspapers
Lithuanian novelists
　USE Novelists, Lithuanian
Lithuanian patriotic poetry
　USE Patriotic poetry, Lithuanian
Lithuanian periodicals (May Subd Geog)
Lithuanian philology
　[PG8501-8693]
Lithuanian philosophy
　USE Philosophy, Lithuanian
Lithuanian poetry
　[PG8709 (History)]
　[PG8715 (Collections)]
　NT Children's poetry, Lithuanian
　　　Narrative poetry, Lithuanian
　　　Patriotic poetry, Lithuanian
　　　Religious poetry, Lithuanian
Lithuanian poets
　USE Poets, Lithuanian
Lithuanian prints
　USE Prints, Lithuanian
Lithuanian prose literature
　(May Subd Geog)
　NT School prose, Lithuanian
Lithuanian proverbs
　USE Proverbs, Lithuanian
Lithuanian religious poetry
　USE Religious poetry, Lithuanian
Lithuanian school prose
　USE School prose, Lithuanian
Lithuanian short stories
　USE Short stories, Lithuanian
Lithuanian watercolor painting
　USE Watercolor painting, Lithuanian
Lithuanian wit and humor (May Subd Geog)
Lithuanian wit and humor, Pictorial
Lithuanian women authors
　USE Women authors, Lithuanian
Lithuanian young adult literature
　USE Young adult literature, Lithuanian
Lithuanians (May Subd Geog)
　BT Balts (Indo-European people)
　　　Ethnology—Lithuania
— United States
　　NT Lithuanian Americans
Lithuanians in literature
Lithyphantes
　USE Steatoda
Litigants in person
　USE Pro se representation
Litigation
　USE subdivision Trials, litigation, etc. under
　　　names of individual persons,
　　　corporate bodies, or jurisdictions
　　　Actions and defenses
Litigation, Complex
　USE Complex litigation

Litigation, Government
  USE Government litigation
Litigation insurance
  USE Insurance, Litigation
Litigious paranoia
  UF Paranoia querulans
  BT Forensic psychiatry
     Insanity—Jurisprudence
     Paranoia
Litis contestatio
  USE Joinder of issue
Litiscontestation
  USE Joinder of issue
Litle family
  USE Little family
Litman family
  USE Littman family
LITMAS (Computer program)
  UF Literature Manipulation System
     (Computer program)
  BT Computer programs
     Data base management
     File organization (Computer science)
     Information storage and retrieval
     systems
Litolatria (Cult) *(May Subd Geog)*
  BT Cults—Brazil
Litopterna
  BT Ungulata, Fossil
Litopyllus
  ₍QL458.42.G5₎
  BT Gnaphosidae
Litoria citropa
  ₍QL668.E24₎
Litoria glandulosa
  ₍QL668.E24₎
Litotes
  USE Understatement
Litre
  USE Liter
Litsen family
  USE Lett family
Litson family
  USE Lett family
LITSYS (Information retrieval system)
  ₍Z699.4.L23₎
  BT Information storage and retrieval
     systems
Littel family
  USE Little family
Littell family
  USE Little family
Litter (Trash) *(May Subd Geog)*
  ₍TD813-870₎
  UF Littering
  BT Refuse and refuse disposal
Litter boxes, Cat
  USE Cat litter boxes
Littera family *(Not Subd Geog)*
  UF De Littera family
Litterateurs *(May Subd Geog)*
  ₍PN150-171₎
  UF Literary life
  BT Literature
  RT Authors
  SA *subdivision* Intellectual life *under*
     names of countries, cities, etc.; also
     headings for specific categories of
     authors, e.g. Dramatists, Poets, *etc.*
  NT Critics
     Dramatists
     Editors
     Literary agents
     Literary historians
     Literature teachers
     Poets
Litterateurs in literature
Littering
  USE Litter (Trash)

Litters
  UF Palanquins
     Stretchers
  BT Transport of sick and wounded
     Transportation, Primitive
     Vehicles
Little Armenia, Kingdom of, 1080-1375
  USE Cilicia—History—Armenian Kingdom,
     1080-1375
Little Baltic Union
  USE Baltic Entente, 1934-
Little Bear River (Utah)
  BT Rivers—Utah
  NT Hyrum Reservoir (Utah)
Little Belt (Denmark)
  USE Lille Bælt (Denmark)
Little Big Horn, Battle of the, 1876
  ₍E83.876₎
  BT Cheyenne Indians—Wars, 1876
     Dakota Indians—Wars, 1876
Little Big Horn, Battle of the, 1876, in art
Little Big Horn, Battle of the, 1876, in
literature
Little Bitterroot River (Mont.)
  (Not Subd Geog)
  BT Rivers—Montana
Little Black Sambo (Fictitious character)
  USE Sambo (Fictitious character)
Little blackfish
  USE Lagenorhynchus electra
Little Blitzen Gorge Wilderness (Or.)
  (Not Subd Geog)
  UF Little Blitzen Gorge Wilderness Study
     Area (Or.)
  BT National parks and reserves—Oregon
     Wilderness areas—Oregon
Little Blitzen Gorge Wilderness Study Area
  (Or.)
  USE Little Blitzen Gorge Wilderness (Or.)
Little blue penguin
  USE Eudyptula minor
Little Book Cliff Railway
  BT Railroads—United States
     Railroads, Narrow-gage—United States
Little Briar Rose (Tale)
  USE Sleeping Beauty (Tale)
Little brown bat
  USE Myotis lucifugus
Little brown myotis
  USE Myotis lucifugus
Little Bub (Horse)
  USE Justin Morgan (Horse)
Little Caney River (Okla. and Kan.)
  BT Rivers—Kansas
     Rivers—Oklahoma
Little collared fruit bats
  USE Myonycteris
Little Colorado River (N.M. and Ariz.)
  BT Rivers—Arizona
     Rivers—New Mexico
Little Conemaugh River (Pa.)
  BT Rivers—Pennsylvania
Little Contentnea Creek (N.C.)
  BT Rivers—North Carolina
Little Egg Harbor (N.J.)
  BT Harbors—New Jersey
     Inlets—New Jersey
Little Egg Harbor (N.J.), Battle of, 1778
  ₍E241.L7₎
  BT New Jersey—History—Revolution,
     1775-1783
     United States—History—Revolution,
     1775-1783—Campaigns
Little Egypt Site (Ga.)
  BT Georgia—Antiquities
Little Falls Branch (Md.)
  BT Rivers—Maryland

Little family *(Not Subd Geog)*
  UF Liddell family
     Liddle family
     Litle family
     Littel family
     Littell family
     Lyte family
     Lytell family
     Lytle family
     Lyttle family
Little grebe
  ₍QL696.P585₎
  UF Podiceps ruficollis
     Tachybaptus ruficollis
  BT Grebes
Little Humboldt River (Nev.)
  (Not Subd Geog)
  BT Rivers—Nevada
Little Humboldt River Wilderness (Nev.)
  USE North Fork of the Little Humboldt
     River Wilderness (Nev.)
Little Hunting Creek Plantation (Va.)
  USE Mount Vernon (Va. : Estate)
Little Italy (New York, N.Y.)
  (Not Subd Geog)
  UF New York (N.Y.).   Little Italy
Little Jacks Creek Wilderness (Idaho)
  (Not Subd Geog)
  UF Little Jacks Creek Wilderness Study
     Area (Idaho)
  BT National parks and reserves—Idaho
     Wilderness areas—Idaho
Little Jacks Creek Wilderness Study Area
  (Idaho)
  USE Little Jacks Creek Wilderness (Idaho)
Little Kanawha River (W. Va.)
  BT Rivers—West Virginia
Little King (Sculpture)
  USE Infant Jesus of Prague (Sculpture)
Little lady palm
  USE Rhapis excelsa
Little Lake Canyon Wilderness (Calif.)
  BT National parks and reserves—
     California
     Wilderness areas—California
Little leaf disease of pine
  NT Phytophthora cinnamomi
Little league baseball *(May Subd Geog)*
  ₍GV880.5₎
  BT Baseball for children
Little magazines *(May Subd Geog)*
  BT Periodicals
  NT Fanzines
Little mallow
  USE Malva parviflora
Little masters (Artists)
  ₍N6887₎
  UF Kleinmeister
  BT Art, Renaissance
     Artists
     Painters—Germany
Little Nemaha River (Neb.)
  BT Rivers—Nebraska
Little Orphan Annie (Fictitious character)
  UF Annie, Little Orphan (Fictitious
     character)
     Orphan Annie (Fictitious character)
Little Ottawa River (Ohio)
  BT Rivers—Ohio
Little Owyhee River Wilderness (Idaho)
  UF Little Owyhee River Wilderness Study
     Area (Idaho)
  BT National parks and reserves—Idaho
     Wilderness areas—Idaho
Little Owyhee River Wilderness Study Area
  (Idaho)
  USE Little Owyhee River Wilderness
     (Idaho)
Little painting
  USE Small painting

Little Para Dam (S. Aust.)
  BT Dams—Australia
Little Para River (S. Aust.)
  BT Rivers—Australia
Little penguin
  USE Eudyptula minor
Little piked whale
  USE Balaenoptera acutorostrata
Little press books
  [Z1033.L73 (Bibliography)]
  UF Books, Little press
      Small press books
  BT Little presses
Little presses (May Subd Geog)
  [Z231.5.L5]
  UF Presses, Little
      Printing—Little presses
      Small presses
  BT Publishers and publishing
  NT Little press books
Little Qualicum River Site (B.C.)
  (Not Subd Geog)
  BT British Columbia—Antiquities
**Little Raccoon Creek (Montgomery County
  and Parke County, Ind.)**
  UF Raccoon Creek, Little (Montgomery
      County and Parke County, Ind.)
  BT Rivers—Indiana
Little Red River (Ark.)
  BT Rivers—Arkansas
  NT Greers Ferry Lake (Ark.)
Little River (Ga.)
  BT Rivers—Georgia
Little River (Okla. and Ark.)
  BT Rivers—Arkansas
      Rivers—Oklahoma
  NT Millwood Lake (Ark.)
      Thunderbird, Lake (Okla.)
Little River Watershed Project
  BT Water resources development—Iowa
Little Rockies Wilderness (Utah)
  (Not Subd Geog)
  UF Little Rockies Wilderness Study Area
      (Utah)
  BT National parks and reserves—Utah
      Wilderness areas—Utah
Little Rockies Wilderness Study Area (Utah)
  USE Little Rockies Wilderness (Utah)
Little Saddleslut (Legendary character)
  USE Cinderella (Legendary character)
Little sail (Coelenterata)
  USE Velella velella
Little Schütt (Hungary)
  USE Szigetköz (Hungary)
Little skate
  [QL638.85.R3]
  UF Raja erinacea
  BT Skates (Fishes)
Little Smalltalk (Computer system)
  BT Electronic digital computers—
      Programming
Little Smokey (Bear)
  BT Bears
Little Snake River (Colo. and Wyo.)
  BT Rivers—Colorado
      Rivers—Wyoming
Little theater movement (May Subd Geog)
  [PN2267 (United States)]
  UF Community theater
      Nationwide theater
      Theater—Little theater movement
  BT Theater
  RT Amateur theater
      College theater
      Community plays, etc.
Little Thicket Nature Sanctuary (Tex.)
  BT Natural areas—Texas
      Sam Houston National Forest (Tex.)
Little Tibet (Pakistan)
  USE Baltistan (Pakistan)

Little Traverse Bay (Mich.)
  BT Bays—Michigan
Little Tybee Island (Ga.)
  USE Tybee Island (Ga. : Island)
Little Tyke (Lion)
  BT Lions
Little Union of the Baltic States
  USE Baltic Entente, 1934-
Little vehicle (Buddhism)
  USE Hinayana Buddhism
Little War, Cuba, 1879-1880
  USE Cuba—History—Revolution, 1879-
       1880
Little Whitestick Creek (W. Va.)
  BT Rivers—West Virginia
Little Wyaconda River (Mo.)
  BT Rivers—Missouri
Little's disease
  USE Cerebral palsy
Littleton Cemetery (Littleton, Colo.)
  BT Cemeteries—Colorado
Littman family (Not Subd Geog)
  UF Litman family
      Littmann family
Littmann family
  USE Littman family
Littoral drift (May Subd Geog)
  UF Drift, Littoral
      Shore drift
  BT Beaches
      Coasts
      Sedimentation and deposition
  NT Coast changes
Littoral flora
  USE Seashore flora
Littoral zonation, Intertidal
  USE Intertidal zonation
Littorina (May Subd Geog)
  [QL430.5.L58]
  BT Littorinidae
Littorinidae (May Subd Geog)
  [QL430.5.L58]
  BT Pectinibranchiata
  NT Littorina
Littrell family (Not Subd Geog)
Liturgical acclamations
  USE Acclamations (Liturgy)
Liturgical adaptation
  [BV178]
    Here are entered works on the modification or
  accommodation of liturgical forms to reflect particu-
  lar cultural and social conditions and to meet the
  need for a diversity of religious rites and forms.
  UF Adaptation, Liturgical
  BT Christianity and culture
      Liturgics
  — Baptists, [Catholic Church, etc.]
  — Catholic Church
      BT Catholic Church—Liturgy
Liturgical apostolate
  USE Liturgical movement—Catholic Church
Liturgical architecture
  USE Liturgy and architecture
Liturgical candles
  USE Candles and lights
Liturgical churches (May Subd Geog)
    Here are entered works on churches which use
  prescribed procedures in public worship in accord-
  ance with authorized or standard form.
  UF Churches, Liturgical
  BT Christian sects
  NT Evangelicalism and liturgical churches
Liturgical churches and evangelicalism
  USE Evangelicalism and liturgical churches
Liturgical colors
  USE Colors, Liturgical
Liturgical dance
  USE Religious dance, Modern
Liturgical drama
  UF Drama, Liturgical

  BT Bible plays
      Drama, Medieval
      Liturgy and drama
      Opera
  RT Mysteries and miracle-plays
Liturgical dramas
Liturgical dramas in art
Liturgical English
  USE Liturgical language—English
Liturgical gardens
  USE Church gardens
Liturgical language
  [BX1970 (Catholic)]
    Here are entered works on the language or lan-
  guages used in the liturgy of the church. Subdivided,
  if necessary, by the name of any particular language
  involved, e.g. Liturgical language—English.
  UF Language, Liturgical
      Language and languages—Religious
      aspects
  BT Languages—Religious aspects
      Liturgics
  NT Sexism in liturgical language
  — English
      [BX1970 (Catholic)]
      UF English language—Liturgical use
          Liturgical English
  — Latin
      [BX1970 (Catholic)]
      UF Latin language—Liturgical use
          Liturgical Latin
      RT Latin language—Church Latin
Liturgical Latin
  USE Latin language—Church Latin
       Liturgical language—Latin
Liturgical movement
    Here are entered works dealing with the revived
  interest in liturgical matters, which began about 1890
  in Catholic circles and spread over to Protestantism.
  The heading is to be subdivided by denomination
  whenever appropriate.
  BT Liturgics
  — Anglican Communion
      UF Anglican Communion—Liturgical
          movement
  — Catholic Church
      [BX1970]
      UF Apostolate, Liturgical
          Catholic Church—Liturgical
          movement
          Liturgical apostolate
  — Protestant churches
      [BV182]
Liturgical musicians
  USE Church musicians
Liturgical objects (May Subd Geog)
  UF Objects, Liturgical
  BT Ceremonial objects
      Religious articles
  RT Devotional objects
  SA subdivision Liturgical objects under
      names of religions and religious
      bodies, e.g. Buddhism—Liturgical
      objects; Orthodox Eastern Church—
      Liturgical objects
  NT Altar-cloths
      Bells
      Censers
      Chalices
      Church pennants
      Church plate
      Church vestments
      Crosses
      Religious supplies industry
      Staff, Pastoral
      Temple seas
Liturgical posture
  USE Posture in worship
Liturgical year
  USE Church year
Liturgics (May Subd Geog)
  [BV169-BV197]

Liturgics *(Continued)*
> Here are entered works on the historical and theological study of liturgies. Collections of procedures prescribed for public worship in accordance with authorized or standard forms are entered under Liturgies. Collections of services of any type for use in public worship are entered under Worship programs.
- UF Liturgiology
  - Liturgy
- BT Public worship
- RT Liturgies
- SA *subdivision* Liturgy *under* Judaism *and under names of individual Jewish and Christian sects and particular ceremonies, rituals, holidays, etc., e.g.* Catholic Church—Liturgy; *and subdivision* Rituals *under names of individual religions and sects other than* Judaism *and Jewish and Christian sects, e.g.* Buddhism—Rituals
- NT Ascensiontide (Liturgy)
  - Baptism (Liturgy)
  - Bible—Liturgical use
  - Chants (Plain, Gregorian, etc.)
  - Christian art and symbolism
  - Church in the liturgy
  - Church music
  - Communion of saints in the liturgy
  - Eastertide (Liturgy)
  - Fasts and feasts
  - Liturgical adaptation
  - Liturgical language
  - Liturgical movement
  - Lord's Supper (Liturgy)
  - Mary, Blessed Virgin, Saint, in the Koran
  - Ordination (Liturgy)
  - Responses (Liturgy)
  - Sacraments (Liturgy)
  - Vigils (Liturgy)
— Catholic Church
  - USE Catholic Church—Liturgy
Liturgics and Christian union
  ₍BX9.5.L55₎
- UF Public worship and Christian union
  - Worship and Christian union
- BT Christian union
Liturgies
  ₍BV170-BV199₎
  ₍BX (Particular denominations)₎
> Here are entered collections of procedures prescribed for public worship in accordance with authorized or standard forms. Collections of services of any type for use in public worship are entered under Worship programs. Works on the historical and theological study of liturgies are entered under Liturgics.
- UF Ecclesiastical rites and ceremonies
- RT Liturgics
- SA *subdivision* Liturgy—Texts *under* Judaism *and under names of individual Jewish and Christian sects and particular ceremonies, rituals, holidays, etc., e.g.* Catholic Church—Liturgy—Texts; *and subdivision* Rituals—Texts *under names of individual religions and sects other than* Judaism *and Jewish and Christian sects, e.g.* Buddhism—Rituals—Texts
- NT Acclamations (Liturgy)
  - Amen (Liturgy)
  - Breviaries
  - Canticles
  - Children's liturgies
  - Christmas service
  - Dedication services
  - Easter service
  - Exultets (Liturgy)
  - Fetal propitiatory rites
  - Funeral service
  - General intercessions

Graduals (Liturgical books)
Holy Week services
Hours, Books of
Hymns
Installation service (Church officers)
Kyrie eleison
Litanies
Marriage service
Mass
Memorial service
Missals
Occasional services
Ordinals (Liturgical books)
Prayer-books
Processionals (Liturgical books)
Propers (Liturgy)
Responsive worship
Ritual
Rituals (Liturgical books)
Trisagion (Liturgy)
— **Translations into English,** ₍etc.₎
Liturgies, Early Christian
  ₍BV185₎
- UF Early Christian liturgies
- NT Church orders, Ancient
Liturgies, Eastern churches
  USE Eastern churches—Liturgy
Liturgiology
  USE Liturgics
Liturgy
  USE Liturgics
Liturgy and architecture *(May Subd Geog)*
  ₍NA4605₎
- UF Architecture and liturgy
  - Liturgical architecture
- BT Architecture
Liturgy and drama
- UF Drama and liturgy
- BT Drama
- NT Liturgical drama
Liturgy and literature
  ₍PN49₎
- UF Literature and liturgy
- BT Literature
Liturgy and poetry
- UF Poetry and liturgy
- BT Poetry
Liturgy committees *(May Subd Geog)*
- UF Committees, Liturgy
- BT Church committees
— **Baptists,** ₍Catholic Church, etc.₎
Lituus (Staff)
- BT Emblems
  - Staffs (Sticks, canes, etc.)
Litz family *(Not Subd Geog)*
- UF Leitsch family
  - Leitz family
  - Lietz family
Liu family *(Not Subd Geog)*
Liu-p'an Mountains (China)
- UF Liu-p'an Shan (China)
- BT Mountains—China
Liu-p'an Shan (China)
  USE Liu-p'an Mountains (China)
Liu Sung dynasty, China, 420-479
  USE China—History—Liu Sung dynasty, 420-479
Liu-wan Site (China)
- BT China—Antiquities
Liuto attiorbato
  USE Archlute
Live animal collecting
  USE Wild animal collecting
Live-bearing reproduction
  USE Viviparity
Live birth
  USE Childbirth
Live loads (Bridges)
  USE Bridges—Live loads
Live loads (Pavements)
  USE Pavements—Live loads

Live loads in office buildings
  USE Office buildings—Live loads
Live loads on asphalt pavements
  USE Pavements, Asphalt—Live loads
Live loads on flexible pavements
  USE Pavements, Flexible—Live loads
Live oak
  ₍QK495.F14 (Botany)₎
  ₍SD397.L64 (Forestry)₎
- UF Live oak, Virginia
  - Quercus fusiformis
  - Quercus sempervirens
  - Quercus virginiana
  - Southern oak
  - Virginia live oak
- BT Oak
Live oak, California
  USE Coast live oak
Live oak, Coast
  USE Coast live oak
Live oak, Virginia
  USE Live oak
Live poliovirus vaccine
  USE Poliomyelitis vaccine
Live stock
  USE Livestock
Live television programs *(May Subd Geog)*
- UF Television programs, Live
- BT Television programs
Livebait fishing
  USE Bait fishing
Livebearers (Poeciliidae)
  USE Poeciliidae
Lively family *(Not Subd Geog)*
Livemore family
  USE Livermore family
Livenston family
  USE Livingston family
Liver
  ₍QL867 (Comparative anatomy)₎
  ₍QM351 (Human anatomy)₎
  ₍QP185 (Physiology)₎
- BT Abdomen
  - Biliary tract
- SA *headings beginning with the word* Hepatic
- NT Artificial liver
  - Cholagogues
  - Enterohepatic circulation
  - Foie gras
  - Liver cells
  - Somatomedin
— **Abscess**
  ₍RC848.A2₎
  - NT Liver abscess, Amebic
— **Atrophy**
  - USE Liver—Necrosis
— **Biopsy**
— **Blood-vessels**
— — **Radiography**
  - BT Angiography
— **Cancer**
  ₍RC280.L5₎
  - UF Hepatocellular carcinoma
— **Cirrhosis**
  ₍RC848.C5₎
  - UF Cirrhosis hepatis
    - Cirrhosis of the liver
    - Hepatic cirrhosis
  - BT Liver—Diseases
  - RT Portal hypertension
— **Diseases** *(May Subd Geog)*
  ₍RC845-RC848₎
  - NT Fatty liver
    - Fatty liver syndrome of chickens
    - Glycogenosis
    - Hepatic coma
    - Hepatitis
    - Hepatitis, Viral
    - Hepatitis B
    - Hepatolenticular degeneration

Hepatorenal syndrome
Liver—Cirrhosis
Liver—Failure
Liver—Necrosis
Liver—Radiography
— — **Diagnosis**
NT Liver—Puncture
Liver function tests
— — **Homeopathic treatment**
[RX333]
— **Displacement**
[RC846]
UF Hepatoptosis
Liver, Floating
— Extract
USE Liver extract
— **Failure** *(May Subd Geog)*
[RC848.F27]
UF Failure of the liver
Hepatic failure
Hepatic insufficiency
Liver failure
BT Liver—Diseases
RT Hepatic coma
— **Glycogenic function**
[QP185]
BT Glycogen
Sugar in the body
NT Glycogenosis
— **Hydatids**
[RC184.T6]
— Inflammation
USE Hepatitis
— **Necrosis**
[RC848.N4]
UF Liver—Atrophy
Yellow liver atrophy
BT Liver—Diseases
— **Puncture**
UF Hepatic puncture
BT Liver—Diseases—Diagnosis
— **Radiography**
BT Liver—Diseases
— **Regeneration**
UF Hepatic regeneration
Liver regeneration
BT Regeneration (Biology)
— **Surgery**
[RD546]
NT Hepatectomy
— **Syphilis**
[RC201.7.L5]
— **Transplantation**
UF Hepatic transplantation
— **Tumors**
[RC280.L5]
NT Hepatoma
— **Wounds and injuries**
[RC853]
Liver, Fat, of ducks and geese
USE Foie gras
Liver, Floating
USE Liver—Displacement
Liver abscess, Amebic
[RC848.A2]
UF Amebic liver abscess
Amoebic liver abscess
BT Amebiasis
Liver—Abscess
Liver cells
UF Hepatic cells
Hepatocytes
BT Cells
Liver
NT Fetal liver cells
Kupffer cells
— **Differentiation**
BT Cell differentiation
— **Inclusions**
UF Inclusion bodies in liver cells
BT Pathology, Cellular

NT Mallory bodies
Liver extract
UF Liver—Extract
BT Extracts
Liver failure
USE Liver—Failure
Liver flukes
UF Distoma
Distomum
Flukes, Liver
BT Trematoda
RT Distomatosis
NT Fasciola and fascioliasis
Liver function tests
[RC847]
UF Hepatic function tests
BT Function tests (Medicine)
Liver—Diseases—Diagnosis
Liver-oil shark
USE Galeorhinus galeus
Liver regeneration
USE Liver—Regeneration
Liver-rot
USE Distomatosis
Fasciola and fascioliasis
Livermar family
USE Livermore family
Livermoor family
USE Livermore family
Livermore family *(Not Subd Geog)*
UF Livemore family
Livermar family
Livermoor family
Liverpool (Merseyside). Toxteth
USE Toxteth (Liverpool, Merseyside)
Liverpool 8 (Liverpool, Merseyside)
USE Toxteth (Liverpool, Merseyside)
Liverpool and Manchester Railway
BT Railroads—Great Britain
Liverpool and National Steeplechase
USE Grand National Handicap Steeplechase
Liverpool Eight (Liverpool, Merseyside)
USE Toxteth (Liverpool, Merseyside)
Liverpool Plains (N.S.W.)
USE Liverpool Range (N.S.W.)
Liverpool porcelain
[NK4399.L]
UF Porcelain, Liverpool
Liverpool Range (N.S.W.)
UF Liverpool Plains (N.S.W.)
BT Mountains—Australia
Livers family *(Not Subd Geog)*
UF Lievers family
Lyvers family
Liverworts *(May Subd Geog)*
[QK551-563]
UF Hepaticae
BT Bryophytes
NT Anthocerotales
Jungermanniales
— **Spores**
BT Spores (Botany)
Livery
[TT626 (Tailoring)]
BT Clothing and dress
Costume
Domestics
Tailoring
Uniforms
NT Livery buttons
Livery buttons *(May Subd Geog)*
[NK3670]
BT Buttons
Heraldry
Livery
Livestock *(May Subd Geog)*
[SF1-SF121 (General)]
UF Animal husbandry
Farm animals
Live stock
Stock (Animals)

BT Agriculture
Animal culture
Animal industry
Domestic animals
RT Herders
Pounds
Range management
Rangelands
SA *headings beginning with the word*
Livestock
NT Cattle
Donkeys
Draft animals
Feral livestock
Goats
Horses
Male livestock
Mules
Pastures
Poultry
Sheep
Swine
— **Abnormalities** *(May Subd Geog)*
BT Animals—Abnormalities
— **Acclimatization**
[SF87]
BT Acclimatization
— Accounting
USE Animal industry—Accounting
— Anatomy
USE Veterinary anatomy
— Artificial insemination
USE Artificial insemination
— **Behavior**
[SF756.7]
UF Veterinary ethology
— Brands
USE Livestock brands
— **Breeding**
[SF105 (General)]
RT Livestock breeders
NT Animal mutation breeding
Artificial insemination
— **Carcasses**
[SF140.C37 (Animal culture)]
UF Carcases of livestock
Carcasses of livestock
SA *subdivision* Carcasses *under*
individual and groups of
domestic animals, e.g. Cattle—
Carcasses
— **Climatic factors**
[SF140.C57]
BT Meteorology, Agricultural
— **Cooperative marketing**
BT Agriculture, Cooperative
Animal industry
Cooperative marketing of farm
produce
Livestock—Marketing
— **Cytology**
[SF757.25]
BT Cytology
— **Development**
UF Development of livestock
BT Developmental biology
— **Diseases** *(May Subd Geog)*
[SF600-1100]
UF Veterinary diseases
RT Veterinary medicine
— — **Chemotherapy**
UF Chemotherapy, Veterinary
Veterinary chemotherapy
BT Chemotherapy
— **Ecology**
— **Embryos**
[SF767.5]
UF Embryos of livestock
BT Veterinary embryology
— — **Mortality**

Livestock
  — Embryos
    — — Mortality *(Continued)*
      ⌐SF767.5 *(Veterinary*
        embryology)⌐
      ⌐SF887 *(Veterinary obstetrics)*⌐
      UF Death of livestock embryos
          Embryo death in livestock
          Embryo loss in livestock
          Embryo mortality in livestock
          Embryonic death in livestock
          Embryonic loss in livestock
          Embryonic mortality in
            livestock
          Loss of livestock embryos
          Mortality of livestock embryos
      BT Mortality
    — — Transplantation
      ⌐SF887⌐
      BT Embryo transplantation
          Veterinary obstetrics
  — Exhibitions
    USE Livestock exhibitions
  — Feed utilization efficiency
    USE Feed utilization efficiency
  — Feeding and feeds
    USE Animal nutrition
          Feeds
  — Genetic engineering
    BT Animal genetic engineering
  — Genetics
    BT Animal genetics
  — Handling
  — Housing
    ⌐SF91⌐
    UF Livestock buildings
    BT Animal housing
    RT Farm buildings
    NT Livestock factories
          Stables
  — Infertility
  — Insurance
    USE Insurance, Agricultural—
          Livestock
  — Judging
    ⌐SF115⌐
    UF Stock-judging
    RT Livestock exhibitions
    SA *subdivision* Judging *under*
          particular livestock, e.g. Cattle—
          Judging; Sheep—Judging
  — Law and legislation
    USE Animal industry—Law and
          legislation
  — Losses *(May Subd Geog)*
    UF Losses, Livestock
    RT Agricultural estimating and
          reporting
          Insurance, Agricultural—Livestock
          Veterinary medicine
    NT Cattle—Losses
          Livestock—Mortality
  — Marketing
    UF Livestock marketing
          Marketing of livestock
    BT Animal industry
          Farm produce—Marketing
    NT Livestock—Cooperative marketing
          Stockyards
  — Mortality
    BT Livestock—Losses
  — Photography
    USE Photography of livestock
  — Physiology
    USE Veterinary physiology
  — Showing
    ⌐SF118⌐
    UF Showing of livestock
  — Societies, etc.
    ⌐SF1 *(General)*⌐
    ⌐SF17 *(State associations)*⌐

    UF Livestock associations
  — Stunning
    UF Stunning of livestock
    BT Animal immobilization
          Slaughtering and slaughter-houses
  — Subject headings
    USE Subject headings—Livestock
  — Transportation by rail
    USE Railroads—Livestock
          transportation
  — Trypanotolerance
    ⌐SF807⌐
    UF Trypanotolerance in livestock
          Trypanotolerant livestock
    BT Immunological tolerance
          Trypanosomiasis in animals—
            Immunological aspects
  — Wounds and injuries *(May Subd Geog)*
    ⌐SF914.3⌐
    BT Veterinary traumatology
Livestock, Feral
  USE Feral livestock
Livestock, Male
  USE Male livestock
Livestock, Photography of
  USE Photography of livestock
Livestock associations
  USE Livestock—Societies, etc.
Livestock brands *(May Subd Geog)*
  ⌐SF101⌐
  UF Branding of livestock
      Brands, Livestock
      Domestic animals—Brands
      Livestock—Brands
  NT Cattle brands
Livestock breeders *(May Subd Geog)*
  UF Breeders, Livestock
      Stock breeders
  BT Animal breeders
  RT Livestock—Breeding
  NT Cattle breeders
      Chicken breeders
      Donkey breeders
      Horse breeders
Livestock breeds *(May Subd Geog)*
  UF Stock breeds
  BT Animal breeds
  SA *names of particular kinds of livestock,*
      e.g. Cattle breeds, Horse breeds
Livestock buildings
  USE Livestock—Housing
Livestock exhibitions *(May Subd Geog)*
  ⌐SF114-121⌐
  UF Exhibitions, Livestock
      Livestock—Exhibitions
  BT Agricultural exhibitions
      Exhibitions
  RT Livestock—Judging
  NT Cattle—Grooming
      Cattle—Showing
      Horse-shows
      Sheep shows
  — Law and legislation *(May Subd Geog)*
Livestock factories *(May Subd Geog)*
  BT Animal industry
      Livestock—Housing
      Meat industry and trade
  NT Feedlots
      Poultry plants
Livestock industry
  USE Animal industry
Livestock marketing
  USE Livestock—Marketing
Livestock poisoning plants
  (May Subd Geog)
  ⌐QK100 *(Botany)*⌐
  ⌐SB617-SB618 *(Weeds)*⌐
  BT Poisonous plants
      Veterinary toxicology
      Weeds
  NT Astragalus earlei

      Cicuta
      Delphinium
      Halogeton glomeratus
      Helenium hoopesii
      Milkweed
      Oxytenia acerosa
      Prunus virginiana
      Quercus gambellie
      Quercus havardii
      Sarcobatus vermiculatus
      Tetradymia glabrata
      Triglochin maritima
      Zydadenus
Livestock productivity *(May Subd Geog)*
  UF Productivity, Livestock
  BT Agricultural productivity
Livestock waste
  USE Animal waste
Livestock workers *(May Subd Geog)*
  BT Agricultural laborers
  NT Wages—Livestock workers
Living, Cost of
  USE Cost and standard of living
Living, Standard of
  USE Cost and standard of living
Living alone *(May Subd Geog)*
  UF Alone, Living
      Living by oneself
      One-person households
      Single living
  BT Households
      Life style
Living by oneself
  USE Living alone
Living fossils
  ⌐QL88.5 *(Zoology)*⌐
  UF Fossils, Living
  BT Biology
      Evolution
      Paleontology
  SA *names of specific fossils, e.g.* Ginkgo,
      Platypus
Living historical farms
  USE Historic farms
Living in vans
  USE Van life
Living languages
  USE Languages, Modern
Living models
  USE Tableaux
Living newspaper
  BT Drama—20th century
Living pictures
  USE Tableaux
Living room furniture *(May Subd Geog)*
  ⌐NK2117.L5 *(Interior decoration)*⌐
  ⌐TT197.5.L5 *(Woodwork)*⌐
  UF Parlor furniture
      Sitting room furniture
  BT Furniture
Living rooms *(May Subd Geog)*
  UF Parlors
      Rooms, Living
      Sitting rooms
  BT Architecture, Domestic
Living skills
  USE Life skills
Living statues
  USE Tableaux
Living together
  USE Cohabitation
Living trusts *(May Subd Geog)*
  UF Inter vivos trusts
      Trusts inter vivos
  BT Trusts and trustees
  NT Revocable trusts
Living wills
  USE Right to die

Livingston family *(Not Subd Geog)*
  UF Lavingston family
      Libinston family
      Livenston family
      Livingstone family
      Livington family
      Livinston family
      Liviston family
Livingston Formation (Mont.)
(Not Subd Geog)
  BT Formations (Geology)—Montana
      Geology, Stratigraphic—Cretaceous
Livingston Manor (N.Y. : Estate)
  BT Manors—New York (State)
  RT Clermont State Park (N.Y.)
Livingstone family
  USE Livingston family
Livington family
  USE Livingston family
Livinston family
  USE Livingston family
Liviston family
  USE Livingston family
Livländische Aa River (Latvia and Estonia)
  USE Gauja River (Latvia and Estonia)
Livoneca
  ⌐QL444.M34⌐
  BT Cymothoidae
Livonian Aa River (Latvia and Estonia)
  USE Gauja River (Latvia and Estonia)
Livonian folk-songs
  USE Folk-songs, Livonian
Livonian language
  ⌐PH581-9⌐
  BT Baltic-Finnic languages
Livonian proverbs
  USE Proverbs, Livonian
Livonian War, 1557-1582
  BT Poland—History—Sigismund II
      Augustus, 1548-1572
      Poland—History—Elective monarchy,
      1572-1763
      Soviet Union—History—Ivan IV,
      1533-1584
Livonians
  ⌐DK511.L3-DK511.L4 (History)⌐
  ⌐GN585.R9 (Anthropology)⌐
  BT Ethnology—Latvia
      Finno-Ugrians
Livradois-Forez, Parc naturel régional (France)
  USE Parc naturel régional Livradois-Forez
      (France)
Livres à clef
  UF Drames à clef
      Romans à clef
  BT Bibliography
      Characters and characteristics in
      literature
      Literature
Livres d'artistes
  USE Artists' illustrated books
Livres de peintres
  USE Artists' illustrated books
Lixivium
  USE Leachate
Lixophaga
  ⌐QL537.T28⌐
  UF Erycioides
      Euzenillia
      Euzenilliopsis
      Prolixophaga
  BT Tachinidae
Lixophaga diatraeae
  ⌐QL537.T28⌐
Lixus (Ancient city)
  ⌐DT329.L59⌐
  BT Cities and towns, Ruined, extinct, etc.
      —Morocco
      Morocco—Antiquities
Lixus
  ⌐QL596.C9⌐

  BT Curculionidae
Liyang language
  ⌐PL4001.L75⌐
  UF Liang language
      Liangmai language
  BT Naga languages
      Tibeto-Burman languages
Liyongo (Legendary character)
  (May Subd Geog)
  BT Folklore—Africa, East
Liza (Fish)
  USE Mugil liza
Lizard fishes
  USE Synodontidae
Lizardfishes
  USE Synodontidae
Lizardite
  BT Serpentine
Lizards *(May Subd Geog)*
  ⌐QL666.L2⌐
  UF Lacertilia
      Sauria
  BT Squamata
  NT Agamidae
      Anguidae
      Anniellidae
      Chameleons
      Cordylidae
      Dibamidae
      Geckos
      Heloderma
      Helodermatidae
      Iguanidae
      Lacertidae
      Lanthanotidae
      Monitor lizards
      Pygopodidae
      Skinks
      Teiidae
      Xantusiidae
      Xenosauridae
  — **Anatomy**
  — **Mythology**
  — **Reproduction**
Lizards, Fossil
  ⌐QE862.L2⌐
  UF Sauria, Fossil
  BT Squamata, Fossil
  NT Helodermatidae, Fossil
      Hyporhinidae
      Mosasauridae
Lizards, Horned
  USE Horned toads
Lizards as pets
  BT Pets
Ljubljana (Slovenia).   Moste
  USE Moste (Ljubljana, Slovenia)
Llake family
  USE Lake family
Llamas
  ⌐QL737.U5⌐
  ⌐SF401.L6 (Animal culture)⌐
  UF Lama glama
  BT Lama (Genus)
Llamas as pets
  ⌐SF459.L52⌐
Llamas family *(Not Subd Geog)*
Llangollen Branch (England and Wales)
  USE Llangollen Canal (England and Wales)
Llangollen Canal (England and Wales)
  UF Llangollen Branch (England and
      Wales)
  BT Canals—England
      Canals—Wales
Llano de Bages (Spain)
  USE Bages (Spain)
Llano Estacado
  UF Estacado, Llano
      Staked Plain

  BT Plateaus—New Mexico
      Plateaus—Oklahoma
      Plateaus—Texas
Llanos *(May Subd Geog)*
  BT Grasslands
      Plains
  RT Prairies
      Steppes
  NT Tundras
  — **Colombia**
     NT Llanos Orientales (Colombia and
        Venezuela)
  — **Venezuela**
     NT Llanos Orientales (Colombia and
        Venezuela)
Llanos Orientales (Colombia and Venezuela)
  BT Llanos—Colombia
      Llanos—Venezuela
Llanos Region (Venezuela)
  UF Región de los Llanos (Venezuela)
Lletra d'Or
  BT Literary prizes—Spain
Llevant Coast (Spain)
  USE Maresme (Spain)
Llewellin family
  USE Llewellyn family
Llewellyn family *(Not Subd Geog)*
  UF Lewallen family
      Lewellen family
      Lewellin family
      Lewelling family
      Lewellyn family
      Llewellin family
  RT Wellons family
Llimbumi language
  USE Limbum language
Llinars del Vallès Castle Site (Llinás, Spain)
  USE Castell de Llinars del Vallès Site
      (Llinás, Spain)
Llinás Castle Site (Llinás, Spain)
  USE Castell de Llinars del Vallès Site
      (Llinás, Spain)
Llobregat River (Spain) *(Not Subd Geog)*
  UF Río Llobregat (Spain)
      Riu Llobregat (Spain)
  BT Rivers—Spain
Llogole language
  USE Logooli language
Llorona (Legendary character)
  ⌐GR114-133⌐
  BT Folklore—Latin America
Lloyd family *(Not Subd Geog)*
  UF Lloyde family
      Lloyds family
      Lloyed family
      Loyd family
      Loyde family
      Loyed family
Lloyd Manor House (Huntington, N.Y.)
  USE Henry Lloyd Manor House
      (Huntington, N.Y.)
Lloyde family
  USE Lloyd family
Lloyds associations
  ⌐HG8039⌐
    Here are entered works on combinations of in-
    dividual underwriters, operating mainly in the United
    States. Not to be confused with Lloyd's of London.
  BT Insurance companies
Lloyds family
  USE Lloyd family
Lloyed family
  USE Lloyd family
Llynfi River (Wales)
  BT Rivers—Wales
Llyr, King (Legendary character)
  USE Lear, King (Legendary character)
LNG
  USE Liquefied natural gas
Lo (African people)
  USE Guro (African people)

Lo-fu Mountains (China)
　　UF　Lofao Mountains (China)
　　BT　Mountains—China
Lo-pu-no-erh (China)
　　USE　Lop Nor (China)
Lo-tzu-sha Feng (China and Nepal)
　　USE　Lhotse (China and Nepal)
Loa diseases
　　USE　Loaiasis
Loa River (Chile)
　　UF　Río Loa (Chile)
　　BT　Rivers—Chile
Loaches
　　[QL638.C647]
　　UF　Acanthopsidae
　　　　Adiposiidae
　　　　Cobitidae
　　　　Cobitididae
　　BT　Catfishes
　　　　Cypriniformes
　　NT　Cobitis
　　　　Lepidocephalus
　　　　Nemachilus
Load (Electric power)
　　USE　Electric power-plants—Load
Load dispatching (Electric engineering)
　　USE　Electric power systems—Load
　　　　　dispatching
Load-line *(May Subd Geog)*
　　[VK237]
　　UF　Freeboard, Tables of
　　　　Plimsoll line
　　BT　Navigation
　　RT　Ships—Cargo
Loaders, Linking (Computer programs)
　　USE　Linking loaders (Computer programs)
Loaders (Machines)
　　UF　Loading machines
　　BT　Loading and unloading
　　NT　Straddle trucks
Loading, Dynamic (Materials)
　　USE　Materials—Dynamic testing
Loading, Static
　　USE　Dead loads (Mechanics)
Loading and unloading
　　[TS159]
　　UF　Stevedoring
　　　　Unloading
　　BT　Materials handling
　　NT　Bulk solids handling
　　　　Cargo handling
　　　　Fish handling—Loading and unloading
　　　　Lay days
　　　　Loaders (Machines)
　　　　Ore handling
　　　　Stevedores
　　　　Tankers—Loading and unloading
　　— Safety measures
Loading machines
　　USE　Loaders (Machines)
Loads, Axial
　　USE　Axial loads
Loads, Dead (Mechanics)
　　USE　Dead loads (Mechanics)
Loads, Dynamic (Materials)
　　USE　Materials—Dynamic testing
Loads, Eccentric
　　USE　Eccentric loads
Loads, Snow
　　USE　Snow loads
Loads, Static
　　USE　Dead loads (Mechanics)
Loaiasis *(May Subd Geog)*
　　UF　Loa diseases
　　　　Loiasis
　　BT　Filariasis
Loam soils
　　BT　Soils
　　NT　Sandy loam soils
　　　　Silt loam

Loamis family
　　USE　Loomis family
Loan associations
　　USE　Building and loan associations
Loan closing costs
　　USE　Settlement costs
Loan costs
　　USE　Loan servicing—Costs
Loan fees
　　USE　Loan servicing—Costs
Loan funds, Student
　　USE　Student loan funds
Loan insurance
　　USE　Insurance, Credit
Loan officers *(May Subd Geog)*
　　BT　Loans
Loan servicing *(May Subd Geog)*
　　UF　Servicing, Loan
　　BT　Loans
　　— Costs
　　　　UF　Loan costs
　　　　　　Loan fees
　　　　NT　Settlement costs
Loan sharking
　　USE　Usury
　　　　Usury laws
Loan-shifts
　　USE　Calques
Loan translations
　　USE　Calques
Loan words
　　USE　*subdivision* Foreign words and phrases
　　　　under individual languages, e.g.
　　　　English language—Foreign words
　　　　and phrases
Loangwa River (Zambia and Mozambique)
　　USE　Luangwa River (Zambia and
　　　　　Mozambique)
Loans *(May Subd Geog)*
　　[HG2053-HG2069]
　　UF　Lending
　　　　Loans for consumption
　　BT　Finance
　　RT　Credit
　　　　Investments
　　NT　Accounts receivable loans
　　　　Amortization
　　　　Bank loans
　　　　Capital market
　　　　Commercial loans
　　　　Debts, Public
　　　　Forced loans
　　　　Government lending
　　　　Interest
　　　　Inventory loans
　　　　Loan officers
　　　　Loan servicing
　　　　Loans, Foreign
　　　　Loans, Personal
　　　　Lombard loans
　　　　Mortgage loans
　　　　Repurchase agreements
　　　　Variable rate loans
　　— Conflict of laws
　　　　USE　Conflict of laws—Loans
　　— Government guaranty
　　　　UF　Federally guaranteed loans
　　　　　　Government guaranty of loans
　　　　　　Guaranteed loans, Federally
　　— — Law and legislation
　　　　　(May Subd Geog)
　　— Law and legislation *(May Subd Geog)*
　　　　BT　Commercial law
　　　　　　Real contracts (Civil law)
　　　　NT　Loans for use
　　　　　　Usury laws
Loans, American *(May Subd Geog)*
　　UF　American loans

Loans, American, [British, etc.]
　　(May Subd Geog)
　　　　Here are entered works on foreign loans originat-
　　ing in individual countries and made to the country,
　　if any, indicated by the subdivision. Works on loans
　　originating in several countries are entered under
　　Loans, Foreign.
Loans, Austrian *(May Subd Geog)*
　　UF　Austrian loans
Loans, British *(May Subd Geog)*
　　UF　British loans
Loans, Chinese *(May Subd Geog)*
　　UF　Chinese loans
Loans, Commercial
　　USE　Commercial loans
Loans, Compulsory
　　USE　Forced loans
Loans, Consumer
　　USE　Loans, Personal
Loans, Dutch *(May Subd Geog)*
　　UF　Dutch loans
Loans, Employee
　　USE　Employee loans
Loans, European *(May Subd Geog)*
　　UF　European loans
Loans, Forced
　　USE　Forced loans
Loans, Foreign *(May Subd Geog)*
　　　　Here are entered works on loans originating in
　　several countries. Works on foreign loans originating
　　in individual countries and made to the country, if
　　any, indicated by the subdivision are entered under
　　Loans, American, [British, etc.].
　　UF　Foreign loans
　　　　International loans
　　　　Loans, International
　　BT　Loans
　　RT　Insurance, Foreign loan
　　NT　Absorptive capacity (Economics)
　　　　Compensatory financing
　　— Law and legislation *(May Subd Geog)*
　　— Developing countries
　　　　NT　Cofinancing
Loans, French *(May Subd Geog)*
　　UF　French loans
Loans, German *(May Subd Geog)*
　　UF　German loans
Loans, Government
　　USE　Government lending
Loans, Gratuitous
　　USE　Loans for use
Loans, Inter-library
　　USE　Inter-library loans
Loans, International
　　USE　Loans, Foreign
Loans, Japanese *(May Subd Geog)*
　　UF　Japanese loans
Loans, Personal *(May Subd Geog)*
　　[HG3755-HG3756]
　　　　Here are entered works on loans to individuals for
　　personal rather than business uses, for consumption
　　rather than production purposes.
　　UF　Consumer loans
　　　　Loans, Consumer
　　　　Loans, Small
　　　　Personal loans
　　　　Small loans
　　BT　Consumer credit
　　　　Loans
　　NT　Banks and banking, Cooperative
　　　　Building and loan associations
　　　　Credit unions
　　　　Employee loans
　　　　Finance charges
　　　　Industrial loan associations
　　　　Pawnbroking
　　— Law and legislation *(May Subd Geog)*
Loans, Small
　　USE　Loans, Personal
Loans, Swiss *(May Subd Geog)*
　　UF　Swiss loans

Loans, Variable rate
  USE Variable rate loans
Loans (Greek law)
  BT Law, Greek
Loans (Islamic law) *(May Subd Geog)*
  BT Islamic law
Loans (Jewish law)
Loans (Roman-Dutch law)
Loans (Roman law)
Loans for consumption
  USE Loans
Loans for use *(May Subd Geog)*
  UF Commodates
    Loans, Gratuitous
    Loans for use—Law and legislation
  BT Bailments
    Loans—Law and legislation
  — Law and legislation
    USE Loans for use
Loans for use (Roman-Dutch law)
Loans for use (Roman law)
Loans to medical students
  USE Medical students—Loans
Loans to nursing students
  USE Nursing students—Loans
Loans to veterans
  USE Veterans—Loans
Loanwords
  USE *subdivision* Foreign words and phrases
    under individual languages, e.g.
    English language—Foreign words
    and phrases
    Language and languages—Foreign
    words and phrases
Loanwords, Translation
  USE Calques
Loar family
  USE Lohr family
Lob Nor (China)
  USE Lop Nor (China)
LOB technique
  USE Line of balance (Management)
Lobachevski geometry
  USE Geometry, Hyperbolic
Lobaje (African people)
  USE Bangandu (African people)
Lobar pneumonia
  USE Pneumonia, Pneumococcal
Lobaspis
  [QL596.C9]
  BT Curculionidae
Lobata *(May Subd Geog)*
  [QL380.5.T45]
  BT Tentaculata
  NT Bolinopsidae
Lobatschevski geometry
  USE Geometry, Hyperbolic
Lobb family *(Not Subd Geog)*
Lobbies, Hotel
  USE Hotel lobbies
Lobbying *(May Subd Geog)*
  [JK1118 (Congress)]
  [JK2498 (United States state
    legislatures)]
  BT Corruption (in politics)
    Politics, Practical
    Pressure groups
    Propaganda
    Social pressure
  NT Lobbyists
    Political action committees
    Political letter-writing
  — Law and legislation *(May Subd Geog)*
    UF Lobbyists—Legal status, laws, etc.
    BT Public relations and law
Lobbyists *(May Subd Geog)*
  UF Legislative advocates
  BT Lobbying
  NT Foreign agents
  — Legal status, laws, etc.
    USE Lobbying—Law and legislation

Lobedu
  UF Balobedu
    Lovedu
  BT Bantus
Lobelia plumieri
  USE Scaevola plumieri
Lobi (African people)
  [DT553.U7]
  BT Ethnology—Africa, West
  NT LoWiili (African people)
Lobi (African people) sculpture
  USE Sculpture, Lobi (African people)
Lobi dialects
  BT Gur languages
  NT Dyan dialect
Lobi folk-songs
  USE Folk-songs, Lobi
Lobianchia
  [QL638.M8]
  BT Lantern-fishes
Lobito Bay (Angola) *(Not Subd Geog)*
  UF Baía do Lobito (Angola)
  BT Bays—Angola
Lobivia
  [QK495.C11 (Botany)]
  BT Cactus
Loblolly-pine
  [QK495.C75]
  [SD397.P58 (Forestry)]
  UF Pinus taeda
  — Seed
Loblolly pine sawfly
  USE Neodiprion taedae
Lobolo
  USE Bride price
Lobopoda
  [QL596.A42]
  BT Alleculidae
Lobotidae
  [QL638.L6]
  BT Perciformes
Lobotomy, Frontal
  USE Frontal lobotomy
Lobotomy, Prefrontal
  USE Frontal lobotomy
Lobster-claw plants
  USE Heliconia
Lobster fisheries *(May Subd Geog)*
  [SH380]
  UF Crayfish fisheries, Marine
    Spiny lobster fisheries
  BT Fisheries
    Shellfish fisheries
  — Law and legislation *(May Subd Geog)*
    BT Fishery law and legislation
Lobster industry *(May Subd Geog)*
  [HD9472.L6-63]
  BT Lobsters
Lobster storage
  USE Lobsters—Storage
Lobsters *(May Subd Geog)*
  [QL444.M33]
  BT Crustacea
    Decapoda (Crustacea)
  NT American lobster
    Cookery (Lobsters)
    Homaridae
    Lobster industry
    Norway lobster
    Spiny lobsters
  — Storage *(May Subd Geog)*
    UF Lobster storage
Lobsters, Canned
  UF Canned lobsters
  BT Fishery products, Canned
Lobularia maritima
  USE Sweet alyssum
Local administration
  USE Local government
Local and light railroads
  USE Railroads, Local and light

Local anesthesia
  [RD84]
  UF Anesthesia, Local
    Anesthetics, Local
    Local anesthetics
  BT Conduction anesthesia
  NT Anesthesia, Intrapulpal
    Cocaine
    Holocain
    Impletol
    Novocaine
    Nupercaine
    Paravertebral anesthesia
    Xylocaine
Local anesthetics
  USE Local anesthesia
Local anti-infective agents
  USE Antiseptics
Local area networks (Computer networks)
  [TK5105.7]
  UF LAN's
  BT Computer networks
    Electronic data processing—
    Distributed processing
  NT Econet (Local area network system)
    Ethernet (Local area network system)
    ILLINET (Local area network system)
    Ring networks (Computer networks)
Local budgets *(May Subd Geog)*
  BT Budget
    Local finance
  NT County budgets
    Municipal budgets
  — Law and legislation *(May Subd Geog)*
Local-central government relations
  USE Central-local government relations
Local church councils
  [BV626]
  UF Church councils, Local
    Church federations, Local
    Federations, Local church
  BT Councils and synods
    Interdenominational cooperation
Local color in literature
  [PN56.L]
  UF Literature—Local color
  BT Manners and customs
    National characteristics
  NT Poetry of places
Local communication
  USE Local mass media
Local elections *(May Subd Geog)*
    Works on the electoral systems of individual cities
  or other local government units are entered under the
  headings Election law, or Elections, subdivided by
  the name of the respective city or other local govern-
  ment unit.
  UF County elections
    Elections, County
    Elections, Local
    Elections, Municipal
    Municipal elections
  BT Election law
    Elections
    Local government
    Municipal corporations
    Municipal government
  NT Elections, Nonpartisan
Local fields (Algebra)
  UF Fields, Local (Algebra)
  BT Fields, Algebraic
Local finance *(May Subd Geog)*
    Here are entered general works, including munici-
  pal finance, and works limited to the finance of coun-
  ties, townships, or other intermediate units of govern-
  ment. Works on the finance of an individual unit are
  entered under the heading Finance, Public, with local
  subdivision.
  UF County finance
    Finance, Local
    Township finance
  BT Finance, Public

Local finance *(Continued)*
  RT Grants-in-aid
      Municipal finance
  NT Local budgets
      Local taxation
      Metropolitan finance
      School districts—Finance
  — **Accounting**
    UF Local government—Accounting
  —— **Law and legislation**
      (May Subd Geog)
  — **Auditing**
  —— **Law and legislation**
      (May Subd Geog)
  — **Law and legislation** *(May Subd Geog)*
    NT Intergovernmental fiscal relations
Local geography
  [G75]
  UF Geography, Local
      Home geography
  BT Geography
Local government *(May Subd Geog)*
  [JS]
    Here are entered works which deal with local government of districts, counties, townships, etc. Works dealing with government of municipalities only are entered under Municipal government; those dealing with government of counties only are entered under County government.
  UF Local administration
      Subnational government
      Subnational politics
      Town-meeting
      Township government
  BT Community organization
      Political science
  RT Administrative and political divisions
      Decentralization in government
      Public administration
      Villages
  NT Annexation (County government)
      Annexation (Municipal government)
      Block wardens (Local government)
      Boroughs
      Cities and towns
      Community power
      County government
      Local elections
      Local officials and employees
      Mayors
      Metropolitan government
      Municipal government
      Municipal powers and services beyond
        corporate limits
      Neighborhood government
      Panchayat
      Parish councils (Local government)
      Parishes (Local government)
      Special districts
      State-local relations
      Supervisors (Local government)
      Veče
  — **Accounting**
    USE Local finance—Accounting
  — **Data processing**
    NT HAMPAS (Computer system)
  — **Labor productivity**
    BT Government productivity
  — **Law and legislation** *(May Subd Geog)*
    BT Administrative law
    RT Local laws
    NT Model ordinances
  — **State supervision**
    UF Municipal corporations—State
        supervision
      Municipal government—State
        supervision
      State control over local
        government
      State supervision over local
        government

  — **Communist countries**
    NT People's councils
  — **France**
    NT Conseillers généraux (French
        government)
  — **Rome**
    NT Forums, Roman
  — **Soviet Union**
Local government and the press
  (May Subd Geog)
  BT Government and the press
      Journalism
      Press
Local government bonds
  USE Municipal bonds
Local government documents
  (May Subd Geog)
  UF Documents, Local government
      Government documents, Local
  BT Government publications
      Public records
  SA *subdivision* Government publications
      under names of cities, counties, etc.
  NT Municipal documents
Local history
    Here are entered works on the writing and compiling of local histories. Collective histories of several local units are entered under names of countries, states, etc. with subdivision History, Local. Individual local histories are entered under [place]—History.
  UF History, Local
  BT Historiography
  NT Classification—Books—Local history
Local history (Cataloging)
  USE Cataloging of local history
Local independent unions
  USE Independent unions
Local junior colleges
  USE Community colleges
Local laws *(May Subd Geog)*
    Here are entered collections of texts of laws passed by state legislatures relating to several individual local jurisdictions and works about these laws. Collections of laws relating to an individual local jurisdiction are entered under Law—[place]. Nontopical collections of municipal ordinances of an individual municipality are entered under Ordinances, Municipal—[place].
  UF Law, Local
      Laws, Local
      Legislation, Local
      Local legislation
  BT Bills, Private
  RT Local government—Law and
      legislation
Local legislation
  USE Local laws
Local Library Cooperation Project
  BT Library cooperation—England
Local mass media *(May Subd Geog)*
  UF Community media
      Local communication
      Local media
  BT Communication
      Mass media
  NT Community newspapers
Local media
  USE Local mass media
Local officials and employees
  (May Subd Geog)
  BT Civil service
      Local government
      Public officers
  SA *subdivision* Officials and employees
      under names of provinces, districts,
      townships, etc.
  NT County officials and employees
      Intendants
      Municipal officials and employees
      Parish councils (Local government)

      Strikes and lockouts—Local officials
        and employees
  — **Collective bargaining**
    USE Collective bargaining—Local
        officials and employees
  — **Collective labor agreements**
    USE Collective labor agreements—
        Local officials and employees
  — **Health and hygiene**
    UF Local officials and employees—
        Medical care
    BT Hygiene
  — **Medical care**
    USE Local officials and employees—
        Health and hygiene
  — **Pensions** *(May Subd Geog)*
  —— **Law and legislation**
      (May Subd Geog)
  — **Salaries, allowances, etc.**
    USE Local officials and employees—
        Salaries, etc.
  — **Salaries, etc.** *(May Subd Geog)*
    UF Local officials and employees—
        Salaries, allowances, etc.
Local option *(May Subd Geog)*
  [HV5084-7]
  BT Prohibition
      Temperance
  RT License system
      Liquor laws
Local postage-stamps
  USE Postage-stamps, Local
Local redress rule (International law)
  USE Exhaustion of local remedies
      (International law)
Local remedy rule (International law)
  USE Exhaustion of local remedies
      (International law)
Local rings
  [QA251.38]
  UF Rings, Local
  BT Commutative rings
  NT Semilocal rings
Local service airlines *(May Subd Geog)*
  UF Air lines, Local service
      Airlines, Local service
      Feeder air lines
  BT Airlines
Local-state relations
  USE State-local relations
Local taxation *(May Subd Geog)*
    Here are entered general works on municipal taxation, and taxation by other units of local government. Works on taxation of individual cities, counties, etc. are entered under Taxation—[local subdivision]. Works on taxation of municipalities by federal or state governments are entered under Municipal corporations—Taxation.
  UF Municipal taxation
      Taxation, Local
      Taxation, Municipal
  BT Local finance
      Municipal finance
      Taxation
  NT Drainage tax
      Income tax, Municipal
      Octroi
      Real estate sales tax
      Visitors' taxes
  — **Law and legislation** *(May Subd Geog)*
Local transit *(May Subd Geog)*
    Here are entered works on the transit systems of urban areas, such as motor bus lines, subways, street-railroads, etc. Works on general transportation in urban areas, including local transit, private transportation, streets, roads, etc., are entered under Urban transportation. Works on the general transportation of individual cities, city regions, or metropolitan areas are entered under the heading Transportation with local subdivision.

UF City transit
     Mass transit
     Municipal transit
     Rapid transit
     Transit systems
     Urban transit
BT Transportation
     Urban transportation
RT Ridesharing
NT Bus lines
     Paratransit services
     Personal rapid transit
     Railroads, Elevated
     Street-railroads
     Strikes and lockouts—Local transit
     Subways
     Taxicabs
     Wages—Local transit
— Accounting
— — Law and legislation
     (May Subd Geog)
— Collective bargaining
    USE Collective bargaining—Local
         transit
— Collective labor agreements
    USE Collective labor agreements—
         Local transit
— Contracting out
    BT Contracting out
— Cost of operation
    UF Local transit—Operating costs
— Employees
    NT Strikes and lockouts—Local transit
— Fares
    BT Local transit—Rates
— Finance
— — Law and legislation
     (May Subd Geog)
— Law and legislation (May Subd Geog)
— Operating costs
    USE Local transit—Cost of operation
— Public opinion
— Rates
    NT Local transit—Fares
— Research (May Subd Geog)
    BT Transportation—Research
— Ridership
    UF Local transit ridership
        Ridership, Local transit
        Ridership, Transit
        Transit ridership
— Stations
— Illinois
    NT Chicago Central Area Transit
        Project
Local transit crime (May Subd Geog)
    UF Crimes aboard local transit
        Transit crime
    BT Offenses against public safety
    NT Crimes aboard buses
Local transit ridership
    USE Local transit—Ridership
Local unions
    USE Trade-unions—Local unions
Local value (Mathematics)
    USE Place value (Mathematics)
Localization of cerebral functions
    USE Brain—Localization of functions
Localization of sound
    USE Directional hearing
Localization theory
    BT Categories (Mathematics)
        Groups, Nilpotent
        Homotopy theory
Localized enzymes
    USE Immobilized enzymes
Localized proteins
    USE Immobilized proteins
Localizers, Runway
    USE Runway localizing beacons

Locally compact Abelian groups
    BT Compact Abelian groups
        Locally compact groups
        Topological groups
Locally compact groups
    BT Topological groups
    RT Compact groups
    NT Group algebras
        L1 algebras
        Locally compact Abelian groups
Locally compact spaces
    UF Compact spaces, Locally
        Spaces, Locally compact
    BT Compact spaces
        Spaces, Generalized
        Topology
    NT Harmonic spaces
Locally convex spaces
    UF Spaces, Locally convex
    BT Linear topological spaces
    NT Nuclear spaces (Functional analysis)
        Saks spaces
        Schwartz spaces
Locals (Philately)
    USE Postage-stamps, Local
Locals (Trade unions)
    USE Trade-unions—Local unions
Locard family
    USE Lockhart family
Locarno Lake (Italy and Switzerland)
    USE Maggiore, Lake (Italy and
        Switzerland)
Location in business
    USE Industry—Location
Location of airports
    USE Airports—Location
Location of crops and cultivated plants
    USE subdivision Location under individual
        and types of crops and cultivated
        plants, e.g. Corn—Location
Location of factories
    USE Factories—Location
Location of homes
    USE Homesites
Location of industries
    USE Industry—Location
Location of launch complexes
    USE Launch complexes (Astronautics)—
        Location
Location of nuclear facilities
    USE Nuclear facilities—Location
Location of offices
    USE Offices—Location
Location of roads
    USE Roads—Location
Location of stores
    USE Store location
Location of system faults
    USE Fault location (Engineering)
Location systems for motor vehicles,
  Automatic
    USE Motor vehicles—Automatic location
        systems
Locations (Motion pictures)
    USE Moving-picture locations
Loch a' Mhuilinn Nature Reserve (Scotland)
    UF Loch a'Mhuilinn Nature Reserve
        (Scotland)
    BT Natural areas—Scotland
Loch a'Mhuilinn Nature Reserve (Scotland)
    USE Loch a' Mhuilinn Nature Reserve
        (Scotland)
Loch family
    USE Locke family
Loch Lomond (Ark.)
    USE Lomond, Loch (Ark.)
Loch Lomond (Scotland)
    USE Lomond, Loch (Scotland)
Loch Menteith (Scotland)
    USE Menteith, Lake (Scotland)

Loch Ness (Scotland)
    USE Ness, Loch (Scotland)
Loch Ness monster
    UF Nessie
    BT Monsters
    RT Ness, Loch (Scotland)
Lochard family
    USE Lockhart family
Lochart family
    USE Lockhart family
Loche family
    USE Locke family
Lochner family (Not Subd Geog)
Loci (Mathematics)
    USE Locus (Mathematics)
Lock box banking (May Subd Geog)
    BT Banks and banking
Lock family
    USE Locke family
Lock-in amplifiers
    [TK7871.58.L57]
    UF Amplifiers, Lock-in
    BT Amplifiers (Electronics)
Lock picking
    UF Picking of locks
    BT Locks and keys
Lockard family
    USE Lockhart family
Lockart family
    USE Lockhart family
Locke family (Not Subd Geog)
    UF Loch family
        Loche family
        Lock family
        Locks family
        Loech family
        Lough family
Lockenhaus Castle (Austria)
    USE Burg Lockenhaus (Austria)
Locker hooking (May Subd Geog)
    [TT833]
    UF Australian locker hooking
        Hooking, Locker
    BT Textile crafts
Lockerbie family
    USE Lockerby family
Lockerby family (Not Subd Geog)
    UF Lockerbie family
Lockers, Coin operated
    USE Coin operated lockers
Lockhart family (Not Subd Geog)
    UF Locard family
        Lochard family
        Lochart family
        Lockard family
        Lockart family
        Lockheart family
Lockheart family
    USE Lockhart family
Lockheed airplanes
    NT Electra (Turboprop transports)
        Hudson (Bomber)
        Neptune (Reconnaissance aircraft)
        Shooting Star (Jet fighter plane)
        SR-71 (Jet reconnaissance plane)
        Starfire (Jet fighter plane)
        TriStar (Jet transport)
        U-2 (Reconnaissance aircraft)
        Ventura (Bomber)
Lockheed Constellation (Transport planes)
    USE Constellation (Transport planes)
Lockheed Electra
    USE Electra (Turboprop transports)
Lockheed Hercules
    USE Hercules (Turboprop transports)
Lockheed L-1011 (Jet transport)
    USE TriStar (Jet transport)
Lockheed Starfighter
    USE Starfighter (Fighter plane)
Lockheed StarLifter (Transport planes)
    USE StarLifter (Transport planes)

Lockheed SUE (Computer)
  [QA76.8.L]
  BT Electronic digital computers
    Minicomputers
— **Programming**
    [QA76.8.L]
    BT Minicomputers—Programming
Lockheed TriStar (Jet transport)
  USE TriStar (Jet transport)
Lockheed U-2 (Airplane)
  USE U-2 (Reconnaissance aircraft)
Locking devices
  USE Locks and keys
Locking up (Typography)
  USE Printing, Practical—Imposition, etc.
Lockjaw
  USE Trismus
Lockkeeper's House (Valley View, Cuyahoga
    County, Ohio)
  USE Locktender's House (Valley View,
      Cuyahoga County, Ohio)
Lockouts
  USE Strikes and lockouts
Locks, Electronic
  USE Electronic locking devices
Locks, Wooden
  BT Locks and keys
Locks (Canal)
  USE Locks (Hydraulic engineering)
Locks (Hydraulic engineering)
  (May Subd Geog)
  [TC761]
  UF Canals—Locks
    Locks (Canal)
    Sea-locks
  BT Hydraulic structures
— **Electric equipment**
— **Oklahoma**
    NT W.D. Mayo Lock (Okla.)
— **Panama**
    NT Miraflores Locks (Panama)
— **Pennsylvania**
    NT Davis Island Lock (Pa.)
Locks and keys (May Subd Geog)
  [TH2279 (Door fittings)]
  [TH9735 (Building protection)]
  [TS519-TS530 (Locksmithing)]
  UF Keys
    Locking devices
  BT Burglary protection
    Fasteners
    Hardware
  NT Cabinet hardware
    Electronic locking devices
    Lock picking
    Locks, Wooden
    Locksmiths
    Padlocks
    Watch keys
— **Tariff**
    USE Tariff on locks and keys
Locks family
  USE Locke family
Locksmithing (May Subd Geog)
  [TS519-TS530]
  BT Metal-work
Locksmiths (May Subd Geog)
  BT Locks and keys
  NT Trade-unions—Locksmiths
**Locktender's House (Valley View, Cuyahoga
    County, Ohio)**
  UF Hell's Half Acre (Valley View,
      Cuyahoga County, Ohio)
    Lockkeeper's House (Valley View,
      Cuyahoga County, Ohio)
  BT Dwellings—Ohio
Lockwood family (Not Subd Geog)
  UF Lackwood family
    Larkwood family
    Lorkwood family

Loco plants
  USE Astragalus (Plants)
Locomobile automobile
  [TL215.L65]
Locomotion
  [GT5220-GT5280 (Manners and
    customs)]
  [QP301-QP311 (Physiology)]
  [TL500-TL790 (Aeronautics)]
  NT Animal locomotion
    Automobiles
    Boats and boating
    Coaching
    Cycling
    Driving of horse-drawn vehicles
    Flight
    Horsemanship
    Human locomotion
    Navigation
    Transportation
— **Regulation**
    [QP303]
    UF Control, Locomotor
      Locomotor control
      Regulation of locomotion
    BT Biological control systems
Locomotion, Disordered
  [QP303 (Physiology)]
  [RD680 (Pathology)]
  UF Disorders of locomotion
    Gait disorders
    Locomotor disorders
  BT Human locomotion
    Movement disorders
    Neuromuscular diseases
    Orthopedia
Locomotion in cattle
  USE Cattle—Locomotion
Locomotion of leucocytes
  USE Leucocytes—Motility
Locomotive boiler explosions
  (May Subd Geog)
  UF Explosions, Locomotive boiler
  BT Steam-boiler explosions
  RT Locomotive boilers
Locomotive boilers
  [TJ642]
  BT Boilers
    Steam-boilers
  RT Locomotive boiler explosions
Locomotive diesels
  USE Diesel locomotives
Locomotive engineers (May Subd Geog)
    Here are entered works on persons engaged in
  driving locomotives. Works on engineers engaged in
  the location, construction and maintenance of rail-
  road structures are entered under Railroad engineers.
  BT Engineers
    Railroads—Employees
  NT Trade-unions—Locomotive engineers
Locomotive firemen (May Subd Geog)
  UF Firemen, Locomotive
  BT Railroads—Employees
Locomotive industry (May Subd Geog)
Locomotive rosters
  USE Locomotives—Registers
Locomotive sounds
  BT Locomotives
    Railroad sounds
    Sounds
Locomotive sparks
  [TJ656]
  BT Sparks
Locomotive works (May Subd Geog)
  [TJ680-683]
Locomotives (May Subd Geog)
  [TJ603-695]
  UF Rolling-stock

  BT Engines
    Machinery
    Railroads—Rolling-stock
    Steam engineering
    Steam-engines
  NT Baldwin locomotives
    Diesel locomotives
    Electric locomotives
    Gas-turbine locomotives
    Gasoline locomotives
    Hudson (Locomotive)
    Locomotive sounds
    Nuclear locomotives
    Railroad motor-cars
    Steam motor-cars
— **Ash-pans**
    [TJ647]
— **Bearings**
— **Boosters**
    [TJ669.B6]
    UF Boosters
— **Brakes**
    BT Railroads—Brakes
— **Compressors**
    [TJ669.C6]
    BT Air-compressors
— **Construction**
    [TJ635]
— **Cylinders**
    [TJ659]
— Drawing
    USE Locomotives—Drawings
— **Drawings**
    UF Locomotives—Drawing
    BT Mechanical drawing
— **Dynamics**
— **Early works to 1850**
    [TJ604]
— **Electric equipment**
— **Exhaust**
    [TJ650]
— **Fire-boxes**
    [TJ646]
    UF Fire-boxes
— **Fuel consumption**
    [TJ648]
    BT Railroads—Fuel
— **Headlights**
    [TJ668]
    UF Headlights
— **History**
— **Lubrication**
    [TJ675]
    BT Locomotives—Maintenance and
      repair
— **Lubrication systems**
    BT Lubrication systems
— **Maintenance and repair**
    UF Locomotives—Repairs
    BT Railroads—Maintenance and repair
      Railroads—Repair-shops
    NT Locomotives—Lubrication
— **Painting**
— **Performance**
    [TJ690]
— **Pictorial works**
— **Registers**
    UF Locomotive rosters
— Repairs
    USE Locomotives—Maintenance and
      repair
— **Scrapping**
    UF Scrapping of locomotives
    BT Salvage (Waste, etc.)
      Scrap metals
— **Transmission devices**
    BT Gearing
— **Valve-gears**
    [TJ665]
    UF Valve-gears
    NT Walschaert valve-gear

— Welding
— Germany
   NT Baureihe 61 (Locomotive)
— Great Britain
— Great Britain
   NT A4 (Locomotive)
      City of Truro (Locomotive)

Locomotives, Articulated *(May Subd Geog)*
⌐TJ608⌐
  UF Articulated locomotives
  NT Mallet locomotives

Locomotives, Compound
⌐TJ613⌐

Locomotives, Gas-turbine
  USE Gas-turbine locomotives

Locomotives, Nuclear
  USE Nuclear locomotives

Locomotives in art
  BT Railroads in art

Locomotor ataxia *(May Subd Geog)*
⌐RC203.T3⌐
  UF Tabes dorsalis
  BT Ataxia
    Neurosyphilis
    Spinal cord—Infections
  RT Paraplegia

Locomotor control
  USE Locomotion—Regulation

Locomotor disorders
  USE Locomotion, Disordered

Locosomidae
  USE Mimallonidae

Locoweed
  USE Astragalus (Plants)

Locoweed, Earl
  USE Astragalus earlei

Locri Epizefiri (Ancient city)
  USE Locri Epizephyrii (Ancient city)

Locri Epizephyrii (Ancient city)
(Not Subd Geog)
⌐DG70.L6⌐
  UF Locri Epizefiri (Ancient city)
    Lokroi Epizephyrioi (Ancient city)
  BT Cities and towns, Ruined, extinct, etc.
      —Italy
    Italy—Antiquities

Loculoascomycetes *(May Subd Geog)*
⌐QK623.A1 (Botany)⌐
  BT Ascomycetes
  NT Dothideales
    Hemisphaeriales
    Hysteriales
    Pleosporales

Locum tenens (Medicine)
  USE Substitute physicians

Locum tenens clergy
  USE Interim clergy

Locumba River (Peru)
  UF Río Locumba (Peru)
  BT Rivers—Peru

LOCUS (Computer operating system)
⌐QA76.76.O63⌐
  BT Operating systems (Computers)

Locus (Mathematics)
  UF Loci (Mathematics)
  BT Geometry
  SA *names of particular types, e.g.* Curves;
    Involutes (Mathematics)

Locus caeruleus
  USE Locus coeruleus

Locus ceruleus
  USE Locus coeruleus

Locus cinereus
  USE Locus coeruleus

Locus coeruleus
⌐QM455 (Anatomy)⌐
⌐QP377.5 (Physiology)⌐

  UF Blue place
    Locus caeruleus
    Locus ceruleus
    Locus cinereus
    Locus ferrugineus
    Nucleus pigmentosus pontis
  BT Neurons
    Pons Varolii

Locus ferrugineus
  USE Locus coeruleus

Locus method, Root
  USE Root-locus method

Locus regit actum
  UF Form of juristic acts
  BT Points of contact (Conflict of laws)

Locus standi *(May Subd Geog)*
  UF Standing in court
  BT Parties to actions
    Procedure (Law)

Locust, Black
  USE Black locust

Locust, Yellow
  USE Black locust

Locust-borer
⌐SB945.L72⌐
  UF Megacyllene robiniae

Locust leaf-miner
  BT Leaf-miners

Locust Site (Ohio)
  BT Ohio—Antiquities

Locust trees *(May Subd Geog)*
⌐QK495.L52 (Botany)⌐
  UF Locusts (Trees)
  BT Leguminosae
  NT Robinia

Locusta *(May Subd Geog)*
⌐QL508.A2⌐
  BT Acrididae
  NT Migratory locust

Locusta migratoria
  USE Migratory locust

Locustidae
  USE Acrididae
    Locusts

Locusts *(May Subd Geog)*
⌐QL508.A2⌐
⌐SB945.L7 (Economic entomology)⌐
  UF Grasshoppers
    Locustidae
  BT Orthoptera
  NT Acrididae
    Desert locust
    Red locust
    Rocky Mountain locust
— **Anatomy**
— **Control**
— — **Research**
— — — **Burkina Faso**
    NT Programme de recherches
      interdisciplinaire français
      sur les acridiens du Sahel
— — — **Niger**
    NT Programme de recherches
      interdisciplinaire français
      sur les acridiens du Sahel

Locusts, Shorthorned
  USE Acrididae

Locusts (Trees)
  USE Locust trees

Lodagaa (African people)
  USE Dagari (African people)

Lodberg family *(Not Subd Geog)*

Lode claims
  USE Mining claims

Loden family *(Not Subd Geog)*

Lodge family *(Not Subd Geog)*

Lodge-pole pine
⌐QK495.C75⌐
⌐SD397.P585 (Forestry)⌐
  UF Pinus contorta
— **Diseases and pests** *(May Subd Geog)*

    NT Lodgepole needle miner

Lodgepole needle miner
⌐QL561.G4⌐
  UF Recurvaria milleri
  BT Lodge-pole pine—Diseases and pests

Lodging-houses *(May Subd Geog)*
⌐HD7288 (Laboring classes)⌐
  UF Flophouses
    Rooming houses
  BT Hotels, taverns, etc.
    Housing
    Labor and laboring classes—Dwellings
  NT Tourist camps, hostels, etc.
— **Law and legislation** *(May Subd Geog)*

Lodging of grain
  BT Grain

Lodhas
⌐DS432.L6⌐
  BT Ethnology—India
    India—Denotified tribes
    Mundas

Lodi, Peace of, 1454
⌐DG537⌐
  BT Italy—History—15th century

Lodoicea *(May Subd Geog)*
⌐QK495.P17 (Botany)⌐
  BT Palms
  NT Sea coconut

Lodoicea callipyge
  USE Sea coconut

Lodoicea maldivica
  USE Sea coconut

Lodoicea sechellarum
  USE Sea coconut

Lodoicea seychellarum
  USE Sea coconut

Lodrigues family *(Not Subd Geog)*
  UF Lodriguss family
  RT Rodriguez family

Lodriguss family
  USE Lodrigues family

Łódź, Battle of, 1914
  BT World War, 1914-1918—Campaigns—
      Poland

Loe family
  USE Lowe family

Loech family
  USE Locke family

Loeffler family *(Not Subd Geog)*
  UF Loffler family
  RT Leffler family

Loehr family
  USE Lohr family

Loeloff family *(Not Subd Geog)*
  UF Loloff family
    Lueloff family
    Luloff family

Loening (Amphibian plane)
⌐TL684.1⌐
  BT Amphibian planes

Loesch family
  USE Lesh family

Loesche family
  USE Lesh family

Loess *(May Subd Geog)*
⌐QE697⌐
  BT Glacial epoch

Loew family
  USE Lowe family

Loewe family
  USE Lowe family

Loewen family *(Not Subd Geog)*
  UF Loewens family
    Lövens family
    Löwen family
    Löwens family
    Löwenz family

Loewengart family *(Not Subd Geog)*
  UF Lowengart family

Loewens family
  USE Loewen family

Lofao Mountains (China)
USE Lo-fu Mountains (China)
Loffler family
USE Loeffler family
Lofland family
USE Laughlin family
Loflin family
USE Laughlin family
Lofoten (Norway)
UF Lofoten Islands (Norway)
BT Islands—Norway
Lofoten Islands (Norway)
USE Lofoten (Norway)
LOFT (Nuclear reactor safety test facility)
UF Loss-of-Fluid-Test Facility
BT Nuclear reactors—Safety measures
Lofthouse family
USE Loftus family
Lofting (Shipbuilding)
USE Laying off (Shipbuilding)
Loftis family
USE Loftus family
Lofts *(May Subd Geog)*
[TH3000]
BT Buildings
Dwellings
RT Attics
— **Remodeling for other use**
UF Lofts—Renovation
— **Renovation**
USE Lofts—Remodeling for other use
Loftus family *(Not Subd Geog)*
UF Lofthouse family
Loftis family
Log-books
[VK211]
UF Logbooks
Logs (Books)
BT Nautical paraphernalia
Navigation
Ship's papers
Log brands *(May Subd Geog)*
[SD538.8-538.83]
UF Brands, Log
Brands, Timber
Log marks
Marks, Log
Marks, Timber
Timber—Brands
Timber—Trade-marks
Timber brands
Timber marks
BT Logging
Log buildings *(May Subd Geog)*
UF Buildings, Log
BT Building, Wooden
NT Log cabins
Log-end houses
Log cabins *(May Subd Geog)*
[NA8470]
UF Cabins
BT Dwellings
Log buildings
RT Log-end houses
— **Texas**
NT Walling Cabin Site (Tex.)
Log-chopping (Sports) *(May Subd Geog)*
UF Wood chopping (Sports)
BT Lumbermen—Recreation
Sports
Log driving *(May Subd Geog)*
[SD540]
UF Driving, Log
River driving
Stream driving
Timber driving
BT Log transportation
RT Booms (Log transportation)

Log-end houses *(May Subd Geog)*
UF Cordwood masonry houses
Houses, Log-end
Stovewood masonry
BT Building, Wooden
Dwellings
House construction
Log buildings
Masonry
RT Log cabins
Log hauling
USE Log transportation
Log-linear models
UF Models, Log-linear
BT Multivariate analysis
Regression analysis
— **Computer programs**
NT ANOHMI (Computer program)
Log marks
USE Log brands
Log normal distribution
USE Lognormal distribution
Log rolling (Aquatic sports)
USE Logrolling (Aquatic sports)
Log scaling
USE Forests and forestry—Mensuration
Log splitters (Machines)
UF Splitters, Log (Machines)
BT Hydraulic rams
Woodworking machinery
Log transportation *(May Subd Geog)*
[SD539]
UF Hauling, Log
Log hauling
Pulpwood—Transportation
Timber—Transportation
Transportation of logs
BT Logging
NT Booms (Log transportation)
Log driving
Logging, Aerial
Logging, Skyline
Logging railroads
Timber—Rafting
Logan (Fictitious character)
BT Characters and characteristics in
literature
RT Nolan, William F., 1928- —
Characters—Logan
Logan family *(Not Subd Geog)*
UF Logans family
Logen family
Loggan family
Loggans family
Loggin family
Loggins family
Login family
Logon family
Logan Plateau
BT Plateaus—Southern States
Loganberries
Loganiaceae
BT Gentianales
Loganiales
USE Gentianales
Logan's Cross Roads, Battle of, 1862
USE Mill Springs, Battle of, 1862
Logans family
USE Logan family
Logarithmic amplifiers
Logarithmic curves
USE Curves, Logarithmic
Logarithmic functions
[QA342]
UF Functions, Logarithmic
BT Logarithms
RT Functions, Exponential
Logarithmic integrals
USE Integrals, Logarithmic
Logarithmic normal distribution
USE Lognormal distribution

Logarithms
[QA55-QA59]
UF Logs (Logarithms)
Tables, Mathematical
BT Algebra
NT Dilogarithms
Functions, Exponential
Logarithmic functions
Logits
Slide-rule
Logbara (African tribe)
USE Lugbara (African people)
Logbara language
[PL8458]
UF Logbware language
Lugbara language
Luguaret language
Lugware language
BT Nilo-Saharan languages
Uganda—Languages
Logboats
USE Dugout canoes
Logbooks
USE Log-books
Logbware language
USE Logbara language
Logen family
USE Logan family
Loggan family
USE Logan family
Loggans family
USE Logan family
Logged-off lands
USE Cut-over lands
Loggerhead turtle
[QL666.C536]
UF Caretta
Caretta caretta
BT Cheloniidae
Loggers *(May Subd Geog)*
[HD8039.L9 (Labor)]
[SD537.5-SD537.540 (Logging)]
UF Buckers (Persons)
Fallers (Persons)
Lumberjacks
Timber buckers (Persons)
Timber fallers (Persons)
BT Logging
Lumbermen
NT Church work with loggers
Logging—Vocational guidance
Tie hacks
Women loggers
Loggin family
USE Logan family
Logging *(May Subd Geog)*
[SD538-SD538.3]
Here are entered works on the felling of trees
through the transporting of logs to sawmills or to a
place of sale. Works on the manufacturing of logs into
lumber are entered under Lumbering.
UF Pulpwood—Harvesting
Timber—Harvesting
BT Harvesting
Lumbering
RT Forestry engineering
Forests and forestry
NT Clear-cutting
Cull tree felling
Cut-over lands
Fishes—Effect of logging on
Log brands
Log transportation
Loggers
Slash (Logging)
Tree felling
— **Law and legislation** *(May Subd Geog)*
BT Forestry law and legislation
— **Machinery**
[SD388]

BT Forest machinery
    Harvesting machinery
— **Technological innovations**
    BT Forestry innovations
— **Vocational guidance** *(May Subd Geog)*
    [SD387.F6]
    BT Loggers
Logging, Aerial *(May Subd Geog)*
    [SD539.5]
  UF Aerial logging
  BT Log transportation
Logging, Geophysical well
  USE Geophysical well logging
Logging, Mud
  USE Mud logging
Logging, Oil well
  USE Oil well logging
Logging, Skyline *(May Subd Geog)*
    [SD539.57]
  UF Aerial skidding
    Cable logging, Skyline
    Cableway logging
    Carrier-cable logging
    High-line logging
    Skidding, Aerial
    Skyline cable logging
    Skyline logging
  BT Log transportation
    Wire-rope transportation
  NT Spartrees
Logging camps
  USE Lumber camps
Logging of wells, Radiation
  USE Radiation well logging
Logging railroads *(May Subd Geog)*
  UF Railroads, Logging
  BT Log transportation
    Railroads, Industrial
    Railroads, Narrow-gage
— **Wisconsin**
    NT Chippewa River and Menomonie
        Railway
Logging slash
  USE Slash (Logging)
Loggins family
  USE Logan family
Logia source (Synoptics criticism)
  USE Q hypothesis (Synoptics criticism)
Logic *(May Subd Geog)*
    [BC]
    Here are entered works on logic in general, deductive logic, and deductive and inductive logic combined. Works on inductive logic are entered under Induction (Logic).
  UF Argumentation
    Deduction (Logic)
    Deductive logic
    Dialectic (Logic)
    Logic, Deductive
  BT Intellect
    Philosophy
    Psychology
    Science—Methodology
  RT Reasoning
    Thought and thinking
  NT A priori
    Abduction (Logic)
    Abstraction
    Categories (Philosophy)
    Certainty
    Commands (Logic)
    Comprehension (Theory of knowledge)
    Conditionals (Logic)
    Counterfactuals (Logic)
    Definition (Logic)
    Dilemma
    Duality (Logic)
    Entailment (Logic)
    Enthymeme (Logic)
    Evidence
    Explanation (Philosophy)

Extension (Logic)
Fallacies (Logic)
Form (Logic)
Formalization (Philosophy)
Future contingents (Logic)
Hypothesis
Identity
Implication (Logic)
Inconsistency (Logic)
Induction (Logic)
Intention (Logic)
Judgment (Logic)
Knowledge, Theory of
Language and logic
Liar paradox
Logic diagrams
Logic machines
Logical atomism
Logical positivism
Modality (Logic)
Nominalism
Nyaya
Paralogism
Plausibility (Logic)
Possibility
Predicate (Logic)
Presupposition (Logic)
Proposition (Logic)
Question (Logic)
Refutation (Logic)
Relation (Philosophy)
Signification (Logic)
Sufficient reason
Syllogism
Tense (Logic)
Uniformity of nature
Universals (Philosophy)
Verification (Logic)
Vicious circle principle (Logic)
— Diagrams
  USE Logic diagrams
— Graphic methods
  USE Logic diagrams
Logic, Algebraic
  USE Algebraic logic
Logic, Ancient
    [BC25-BC32]
  UF Ancient logic
Logic, Bonpo
  USE Bonpo logic
Logic, Buddhist
  USE Buddhist logic
Logic, Combinatory
  USE Combinatory logic
Logic, Deductive
  USE Logic
Logic, Deontic
  USE Deontic logic
Logic, Hindu
  USE Hindu logic
Logic, Inductive
  USE Induction (Logic)
Logic, Jaina
  USE Jaina logic
Logic, Many-valued
  USE Many-valued logic
Logic, Medical
  USE Medical logic
Logic, Medieval
    [BC34-BC35]
  UF Medieval logic
  NT Insolubilia (Logic)
Logic, Modern
    [BC38-39]
  UF Modern logic
  NT First-order logic
— **16th century**
— **17th century**
— **18th century**
— **19th century**
— **20th century**

Logic, Multivalued
  USE Many-valued logic
Logic, Symbolic and mathematical
    [BC131-BC135 (Philosophy)]
    [QA9 (Mathematics)]
  UF Algebra of logic
    Logic, Universal
    Mathematical logic
    Symbolic and mathematical logic
  BT Mathematics
  RT Algebra, Abstract
    Metamathematics
    Set theory
    Syllogism
  NT Admissible sets
    Algebra, Boolean
    Algebraic logic
    Axiomatic set theory
    Categories (Mathematics)
    Combinatory logic
    Completeness theorem
    Computer programs—Correctness
    Constructive mathematics
    Cylindric algebras
    Decidability (Mathematical logic)
    Definability theory (Mathematical
      logic)
    First-order logic
    Gödel numbers
    Gödel's theorem
    Independence (Mathematics)
    Infinitary languages
    Lambda calculus
    Linear orderings
    Logic machines
    Machine theory
    Model theory
    Nonclassical mathematical logic
    Numbers, Cardinal
    Polyadic algebras
    Pragmatics
    Predicate calculus
    Proof theory
    Propositional calculus
    Reasoning
    Recursion theory
    Recursive functions
    Science—Methodology
    Semantics (Philosophy)
    Switching theory
    Threshold logic
    Truth-functions
    Type theory
    VL1 system
Logic, Tense
  USE Tense (Logic)
Logic, Threshold
  USE Threshold logic
Logic, Transcendental
  USE Transcendental logic
Logic, Universal
  USE Logic, Symbolic and mathematical
Logic, Variable-valued
  USE Many-valued logic
Logic and faith
  USE Faith and reason
Logic circuits
    [TK7868.L6 (General)]
    [TK7888.4 (Computer engineering)]
  UF Circuits, Logic
  BT Computers—Circuits
    Digital electronics
    Electronic circuits
    Switching circuits
    Switching theory
  RT Interface circuits
  NT Emitter-coupled logic circuits
    Integrated injection logic
    Logic design
    Metal oxide semiconductors,
      Complementary

Logic circuits   *(Continued)*
    Transistor-transistor logic circuits
Logic design
    UF Design, Logic
        Design of logic systems
    BT Digital electronics
        Electronic circuit design
        Logic circuits
        Machine theory
        Switching theory
    NT Fluid logic
  — Computer programs
    NT SIMPL (Computer program)
  — Data processing
    UF Computer assisted logic design
Logic devices
    [TK7872.L64]
    BT Electronic apparatus and appliances
    NT Programmable logic devices
Logic diagrams
    UF Diagrams, Logic
        Logic—Diagrams
        Logic—Graphic methods
    BT Logic
    NT Venn diagrams
Logic in language
    USE Language and logic
Logic in teaching
    [BC161.T4]
    BT Teaching
Logic machines
    [BC137-8]
    UF Intelligent machines
        Machines, Logic
    BT Logic
        Logic, Symbolic and mathematical
    NT Artificial intelligence
Logic of mathematics
    USE Mathematics—Philosophy
Logic-Oriented Language
    USE LOL (Computer program language)
Logic programming
    BT Programming (Electronic computers)
Logic structure tables
    USE Decision logic tables
Logical analysis
    USE Analysis (Philosophy)
Logical atomism
    [BC199.L6]
    UF Atomism (Logic)
    BT Logic
Logical Disk Operating System (Computer
    operating system)
    USE LDOS (Computer operating system)
Logical empiricism
    USE Logical positivism
Logical form
    USE Form (Logic)
Logical positivism
    [B824.6]
    UF Logical empiricism
        Neo-empiricism
        Neo-positivism
        Physicalism
        Positivism, Logical
        Unity of science movement
        Viennese circle
        Wiener Kreis
    BT Language and logic
        Logic
        Meaning (Psychology)
        Positivism
        Reductionism
        Relationism
        Science—Philosophy
    RT Analysis (Philosophy)
    NT Private language problem
        Semantics (Philosophy)
Logical semantics
    USE Formal languages—Semantics
        Semantics (Philosophy)

Logicians   *(May Subd Geog)*
    BT Philosophers
Logicians, Islamic
    USE Logicians, Muslim
Logicians, Muslim
    UF Islamic logicians
        Logicians, Islamic
        Muslim logicians
Logicians (Chinese philosophy)
    USE School of logicians (Chinese
        philosophy)
Login family
    USE Logan family
Logistae
    USE Curatores rei publicae
Logistic support, Integrated
    USE Integrated logistic support
Logistically orientated language
    USE LOGOL (Computer program language)
Logistics
    [U168]
    BT Military art and science
    SA *subdivision* Logistics *under individual*
        wars, e.g. World War, 1939-1945—
        Logistics; *and subdivision*
        Procurement *under names of*
        individual military services, e.g.
        United States.   Army—
        Procurement
    NT Air forces—Procurement
        Business logistics
        CAMCOS System
        Combat sustainability (Military
        science)
        Integrated logistic support
        Military supplies
        Quartermasters
        Transportation, Military
  — Computer programs
    NT AURA (Computer program)
        VIMCOS II (Computer program)
Logistics, Naval
    [V179]
    UF Naval logistics
    BT Naval art and science
        Naval tactics
    NT Naval auxiliary vessels
Logit transformation
    USE Logits
Logits
    UF Logit transformation
    BT Biomathematics
        Logarithms
        Transformations (Mathematics)
Loglan (Artificial language)
    [PM8590]
    BT Languages, Artificial
LOGLAN 82 (Computer program language)
    [QA76.73.L]
    BT Programming languages (Electronic
        computers)
Lognormal distribution
    UF Antilognormal distribution
        Log normal distribution
        Logarithmic normal distribution
    BT Distribution (Probability theory)
LOGO (Computer program language)
    [QA76.73.L]
    BT Programming languages (Electronic
        computers)
Logograms
    USE Logotype
Logography
    [Z253]
    BT Signs and symbols
Logokophosis
    USE Word deafness
LOGOL (Computer program language)
    UF Logistically orientated language
Logon family
    USE Logan family

Logooli language
    UF Llogole language
        Lougouli language
        Lugooli language
        Lulogooli language
        Luragoli language
    BT Bantu languages
Logos
    [BT210]
    UF Jesus Christ—Logos doctrine
    BT Jesus Christ
        Jesus Christ—Primacy
        Word of God (Theology)
    NT Alogi
        Jesus Christ—Pre-existence
        Memra (The word)
LOGOS (Information retrieval system)
    [Z699.5.P6]
    BT Information storage and retrieval
        systems—Political science
Logotherapy
    [RC489.L6]
    BT Existential psychology
        Phenomenological psychology
        Psychotherapy
    RT Meaning (Psychology)
Logotype
    UF Logograms
    BT Lettering
        Type and type-founding
    RT Nameplates of publications
        Trademarks
Logrolling (Aquatic sports)
    UF Log rolling (Aquatic sports)
    BT Aquatic sports
Logs (Books)
    USE Log-books
Logs (Logarithms)
    USE Logarithms
Logs (Nautical instruments)
    BT Speed-indicators
Logsden family
    USE Logsdon family
Logsdon family   *(Not Subd Geog)*
    UF Logsden family
Logue family   *(Not Subd Geog)*
Logwood
    [TP925.L7 (Dyes and dyeing)]
    BT Dye plants
Lohānās
    [DS432.L62]
    BT Caste—India
        Ethnology—India
        Merchants—India
Lohans
    USE Arhats
Lohars
    [DS432.L63]
    UF Belari
        Bhubalia
        Chittoriya Lohars
        Gadi Lohars
        Gaduliya Lohars
        Lohpitta
        Panchal Lohars
    BT Caste—India
        Ethnology—India
Lohei (Asian people)
    USE Lahu (Asian people)
Lohff-Johansen family   *(Not Subd Geog)*
    BT Johansson family
Lohmann's enzyme
    USE Creatine kinase
Lohne family
    USE Lone family
Lohpitta
    USE Lohars
Lohr family
    UF Loar family
        Loehr family
        Lower family

RT Lehr family
Lohrentz family
USE Lorenz family
Loi (Hainan people)
USE Li (Hainan people)
Loiasis
USE Loaiasis
Loigny-Poupry, Battle of, 1870
[DC309.L7]
BT Franco-German War, 1870-1871
Orléans, Battle of, 1870
Loir River (France)
BT Rivers—France
Loire River (France)
BT Rivers—France
Loire River Valley (France)
UF Loire Valley (France)
BT Valleys—France
Loire Valley (France)
USE Loire River Valley (France)
NT Paris Basin (France)
Løjtnant family *(Not Subd Geog)*
Lokāyata
[B132.L6]
BT Atheism
Hedonism
Humanism—20th century
Materialism
Philosophy, Hindu
Lokele (Bantu people)
BT Ethnology—Zaire
Loki (Norse deity)
[BL870.L6]
BT Gods, Norse
Lŏkk'i Group
BT Conglomerate corporations—Korea
(South)
Lokroi Epizephyrioi (Ancient city)
USE Locri Epizephyrii (Ancient city)
Lokskiĭ Massiv (Georgian S.S.R.)
USE Lokskiĭ Mountains (Georgian S.S.R.)
Lokskiĭ Mountains (Georgian S.S.R.)
UF Lokskiĭ Massiv (Georgian S.S.R.)
BT Mountains—Georgian S.S.R.
Lokundu language
USE Bakundu language
LOL (Computer program language)
UF Logic-Oriented Language
Lola cattle
USE Sahiwal cattle
loLeku dialect
USE Leko dialect
Loliginidae
[QL430.3.L8]
BT Cephalopoda
Squids
NT Loligo
Loligo
[QL430.3.L8]
BT Loliginidae
Loligo brasiliensis
[QL430.3.L8]
Loligo opalescens
[QL430.3.L8]
Loligo pealei
USE Loligo pealii
Loligo pealii
[QL430.3.L8]
UF Loligo pealei
Lolland (Denmark)
BT Islands—Denmark
Lollards
[BX4900-4906]
UF Poor priests
Wiclifites
Wyclifites
Lolly ice
USE Frazil ice
Lolo (Bantu language)
USE Mongo language

Lolo language
USE Yi language
Lolo languages
USE Loloish languages
Loloff family
USE Loeloff family
Loloish languages
[PL3916-3919]
UF Lolo languages
BT Tibeto-Burman languages
NT Lahu language
Lisu language
Moso language
Proto-Loloish language
Yi language
Lolos
USE Yi (Chinese people)
NT Moso (Tribe)
Loma language
UF Baru language
Buzi language
Toma language
BT Guinea—Languages
Liberia—Languages
Mande languages
Lomagne (France)
Lomariopsidaceae
[QK524.L64]
BT Filicales
NT Bolbitis
Elaphoglossum
Lomars family
USE Lambers family
Lomas family
USE Loomis family
Lomas Valentinas, Battle of, 1868
UF Valentinas Hills, Battle of, 1868
BT Paraguayan War, 1865-1870
Lomatium
[QK495.U48]
UF Cogswellia
BT Umbelliferae
Lomatium suksdorfii
[QK495.U48]
Lombard architecture
USE Architecture, Lombard
Lombard art
USE Art, Lombard
Lombard coins
USE Coins, Lombard
Lombard language
[PD1350]
Lombard law
USE Law, Lombard
Lombard League
[DG657.4]
UF League, Lombard
BT Lombardy (Italy)—History—To 1535
Lombard loans *(May Subd Geog)*
UF Collateral loans
BT Banks and banking
Banks and banking, Central
Loans
RT Pawnbroking
NT Warehouse loans
Warehouse receipts
Lombard manuscripts
USE Manuscripts, Lombard
Lombards *(May Subd Geog)*
[D145 (Europe)]
[DG511-DG514 (Italy)]
[DG657.2 (Lombardy)]
UF Langobards
Longobards
— **Kings and rulers**
— **Italy**
NT Italy—History—476-774
Lombardy (Italy)
— **History**
— — **To 1535**
[DG651-657]

NT Legnano, Battle of, 1176
Lombard League
— — **Spanish rule, 1535-1714**
[DG658.1]
— — **Austrian rule, 1714-1796**
[DG658.2]
— — **Napoleonic rule, 1796-1813**
[DG658.4]
— — **1813-1859**
[DG658.5]
Lombok (Indonesia)
UF Pulau Lombok (Indonesia)
BT Islands—Indonesia
Sunda Islands, Lesser (Indonesia)
Lomes family
USE Loomis family
Lomice family
USE Loomis family
Lomis family
USE Loomis family
Lomma River (Norway)
BT Rivers—Norway
Lommance family
USE Loomis family
Lommel functions
UF Functions, Lommel
BT Bessel functions
Lomond, Loch (Ark.) *(Not Subd Geog)*
UF Loch Lomond (Ark.)
BT Lakes—Arkansas
Reservoirs—Arkansas
Lomond, Loch (Scotland)
UF Loch Lomond (Scotland)
BT Lakes—Scotland
Lomongo (Bantu language)
USE Mongo language
Lomonosov prizes
[PG2020.L6]
Lomwe (African people)
UF Acilowe (African people)
Alomwe (African people)
Lomwe (Bantu people)
Nguru (African people)
Walomwe (African people)
BT Ethnology—Malawi
Ethnology—Mozambique
Lomwe (Bantu people)
USE Lomwe (African people)
Lonchistium
[QL638.O65]
BT Opisthognathidae
NT Lonchistium lemur
Lonchistium lemur
[QL638.O65]
BT Lonchistium
Lonchura
[QL696.P244]
UF Mannikins (Birds)
BT Estrildidae
London (England)
— **Description**
— — **To 1800**
[DA680-682]
— — **1801-1900**
[DA683]
— — **1901-1950**
[DA684]
— — **1951-1980**
[DA684.2]
— — **1981-**
— **History**
[DA675-689]
— — **To 1500**
— — **16th century**
— — **17th century**
— — **18th century**
— — **1800-1950**
NT Spa Fields Riot, 1816
— — **1951-**
— **Intellectual life**
— — **To 1500**

2193

London (England)
— Intellectual life (Continued)
— — 16th century
— — 17th century
— — 18th century
— — 19th century
— — 20th century
— Riot, 1816
USE Spa Fields Riot, 1816
— Riot, 1833
UF Clerkenwell Riot, 1833
Cold Bath Fields Riot, 1833
— Social life and customs
— — To 1500
— — 16th century
— — 17th century
— — 18th century
— — 19th century
— — 20th century
London (England). Adelphi
USE Adelphi, The (London, England)
London (England). Battersea
USE Battersea (London, England)
London (England). Covent Garden
USE Covent Garden (London, England)
London (England). East End
USE East End (London, England)
London (England). East London
USE East End (London, England)
London (England). Putney
USE Putney (London, England)
London (England). Puttney
USE Putney (London, England)
London (England). West End
USE West End (London, England)
London and Port Stanley Railway
BT Railroads—Canada
London Bridge (London, England)
  (Not Subd Geog)
BT Bridges—England
Thames River (England)—Bridges
London, Brighton and South Coast Railway
BT Railroads—Great Britain
London family (Not Subd Geog)
London Festival of Sail
BT Sailing ships
London-Mexico City World Cup Rally, 1970
USE Daily Mirror World Cup Rally, 1970
London Orbital Motorway (England)
UF M25 Motorway (England)
Orbital Motorway, London (England)
BT Beltways—England
London River (France and Switzerland)
UF Allondon River (France and
Switzerland)
BT Rivers—France
Rivers—Switzerland
London Silver Jubilee Walkway (London,
England)
UF Silver Jubilee Walkway (London,
England)
BT Trails—England
London-Sydney Marathon
BT Automobile racing
Automobile rallies
London, Tilbury and Southend Railway
BT Railroads—Great Britain
London, Tower of (London, England)
USE Tower of London (London, England)
Londonderry and Lough Swilly Railway
BT Railroads—Ireland
Railroads, Narrow-gage—Ireland
Lone family (Not Subd Geog)
UF Lohne family
Lono family
Lone Fir Cemetery (Portland, Or.)
BT Cemeteries—Oregon

Lone Ranger films
BT Characters and characteristics in
moving-pictures
Moving-pictures
Western films
Lone Star Trail (Tex.)
BT Trails—Texas
Loneliness
  [BF575.L7 (Psychology)]
  [BV4911 (Practical theology)]
BT Social isolation
Suffering
RT Solitude
NT Consolation
— Religious aspects
— — Baptists, [Catholic Church, etc.]
— — Buddhism, [Christianity, etc.]
Loneliness in children (May Subd Geog)
  [BF723.L64]
BT Child psychology
Loneliness in literature
Long, Robert Alexander, 1850-1934
— Homes and haunts
— — Missouri
NT Corinthian Hall (Kansas City,
Mo.)
Long-armed cross-stitch
USE Cross-stitch, Long-legged
Long Beach Island (N.J.)
BT Islands—New Jersey
Long-beaked dolphin
USE Stenella longirostris
Long-billed marsh wren
USE Telmatodytes palustris
Long Branch Lake (Mo.)
UF Long Branch Reservoir (Mo.)
BT Chariton River (Iowa and Mo.)
Lakes—Missouri
Reservoirs—Missouri
Long Branch Reservoir (Mo.)
USE Long Branch Lake (Mo.)
Long case clocks
USE Longcase clocks
Long clam
USE Mya arenaria
Long distance canoe racing
USE Canoe racing, Marathon
Long distance flying
USE Cross-country flying
Long-distance marriage
USE Commuter marriage
Long distance riding (Horsemanship)
USE Endurance riding (Horsemanship)
Trail riding—Competitions
Long distance swimming
USE Swimming, Long distance
Long distance telephone service
USE Telephone—Long distance
Long dogs
USE Deer-hounds
Greyhounds
Saluki
Long-Duration Exposure Facility (Artificial
satellite)
USE LDEF (Artificial satellite)
Long-eared bat, Common
USE Plecotus auritus
Long-eared bat, Grey
USE Plecotus austriacus
Long-eared bats
USE Plecotus
Long-eared owl
  [QL696.S83]
UF Asio otus
Asio wilsonianus
Northern long-eared owl
Long family (Not Subd Geog)
RT Lang family
Long-finned pilot whale
USE Globicephala melaena

Long hair cat
USE Persian cat
Long hair cats
USE Longhair cats
Long-haired cats
USE Longhair cats
Long hairs (Cats)
USE Longhair cats
Long-headed flour-beetle
  [SB608.G6]
BT Beetles
Long-horned beetles
USE Cerambycidae
Long-horned grasshoppers
USE Tettigoniidae
Long House (Kansas City, Mo.)
USE Corinthian Hall (Kansas City, Mo.)
Long Island (Bermuda Islands)
USE Bermuda Island (Bermuda Islands)
Long Island (N.Y.)
BT Islands—New York (State)
NT East End (Long Island, N.Y.)
— History
— — Revolution, 1775-1783
— Social life and customs
— — Colonial period, ca. 1600-1775
Long Island (Ont.)
USE Wolfe Island (Ont.)
Long Island, Battle of, 1776
  [E241.L8]
BT New York (State)—History—
Revolution, 1775-1783
United States—History—Revolution,
1775-1783—Campaigns
Long Island Sound (N.Y. and Conn.)
BT Sounds (Geomorphology)—
Connecticut
Sounds (Geomorphology)—New York
(State)
Long-jawed goby
USE Gillichthys mirabilis
Long jump
USE Broad jump
Long Jump, Operation
USE Operation Long Jump
Long Lake (Sask.)
USE Last Mountain Lake (Sask.)
Long-leaf pine
USE Longleaf pine
Long-legged cross-stitch
USE Cross-stitch, Long-legged
Long-legged flies
USE Dolichopodidae
Long life
USE Longevity
Long-line fishing
USE Longlining (Fisheries)
Long Man of Wilmington (East Sussex,
England)
UF Wilmington Giant (East Sussex,
England)
BT Hill figures—England
Long March, China, 1934-1935
USE China—History—Long March, 1934-
1935
Long moss
USE Spanish moss
Long-nosed armadillos
USE Dasypus
Long-nosed bats, Geoffroy's
USE Anoura (Mammals)
Long-nosed goblin
USE Tengu
Long Pond (N.J. and N.Y.)
USE Greenwood Lake (N.J. and N.Y.)
Long-range forecasting
USE Long-range weather forecasting
Long-range forecasts
USE Long-range weather forecasts
Long range navigation
USE Loran

Long range order (Solid state physics)
  BT Lattice dynamics
       Order-disorder models
       Solid state physics
Long-range weather forecasting
  (May Subd Geog)
  [QC997]
  UF Extended-range weather forecasting
       Long-range forecasting
       Medium-range weather forecasting
       Weather forecasting, Long-range
Long-range weather forecasts
  (May Subd Geog)
  [QC997]
  UF Extended range forecasts
       Forecasts, Long-range weather
       Long-range forecasts
       Weather forecasts, Long-range
  BT Meteorology
       Weather
Long rifle
  USE Kentucky rifle
Long River (China)
  USE Yangtze River (China)
Long-span bridges
  USE Bridges, Long-span
Long-suffering
  USE Meekness
Long-tailed duck
  USE Old-squaw
Long-tailed field mouse
  USE Apodemus sylvaticus
Long-tailed hermit hummingbird
  [QL696.A558]
  UF Phaethornis superciliosus
Long-tailed hutias
  USE Capromys
Long-tailed jaeger
  USE Stercorarius longicaudus
Long-tailed macaque
  USE Kra
Long-tailed nightjar
  [QL696.C23]
  UF Caprimulgus macrurus
       Large-tailed nightjar
Long-tailed shrew
  USE Sorex dispar
Long-tailed skua
  USE Stercorarius longicaudus
Long Tân (Vietnam : Village), Battle of, 1966
  [DS557.8.L66]
  UF Xã Long Tân (Vietnam), Battle of, 1966
  BT Vietnamese Conflict, 1961-1975—Campaigns—Vietnam
Long-term care facilities *(May Subd Geog)*
  [RA997-999]
  UF Extended care facilities
  BT Health facilities
       Hospitals—After care
       Long-term care of the sick
  NT Hospitals—Extended care units
       Hospitals, Convalescent
       Nursing homes
       Rest homes
       Sanatoriums
       Volunteer workers in long-term care facilities
  — Activity programs
     USE Long-term care facilities—Recreational activities
  — Admission
  — Bathing facilities
     BT Bathrooms
  — Complaints against
     UF Complaints against long-term care facilities
  — Law and legislation *(May Subd Geog)*
  — Medical records
     [RA999.M43]
     BT Medical records

  — Recreational activities
     [RA999.R42]
     UF Activity programs in long-term care facilities
         Long-term care facilities—Activity programs
         Recreational activities in long-term care facilities
     BT Recreational therapy
  — Toilet facilities
     BT Toilets
  — Utilization
     UF Utilization of long-term care facilities
Long term care of the aged
  USE Aged—Long term care
Long term care of the handicapped
  USE Handicapped—Long term care
Long-term care of the sick
  (May Subd Geog)
  BT Care of the sick
       Medical care
  NT Aged—Long term care
       Chronically ill—Care
       Continuum of care
       Handicapped—Long term care
       Long-term care facilities
       Nursing home care
Long-term skilled nursing facilities
  USE Nursing homes
Long-toed salamander
  USE Ambystoma macrodactylum
Long Valley (Mono County, Calif.)
  BT Valleys—California
Long Valley (Valley County, Idaho)
  BT Valleys—Idaho
Long waves (Economics) *(May Subd Geog)*
  [HB3729]
  UF Kondratieff cycles (Economics)
  BT Business cycles
       Economics
Long-winged grasshopper of the plains
  USE High plains grasshopper
Longacre family *(Not Subd Geog)*
  UF Longaker family
Longaker family
  USE Longacre family
Longan
  [SB379.L]
Longarim (African people)
  UF Boya (African people)
  BT Ethnology—Sudan
       Murle (African people)
Longbeak eucalyptus
  USE Eucalyptus camaldulensis
Longboat Key (Fla.). Spanish Main Yacht Club
  USE Spanish Main Yacht Club (Longboat Key, Fla.)
Longcase clocks *(May Subd Geog)*
  [NK7500.L65]
  UF Grandfather clocks
       Grandfather's clock
       Long case clocks
       Tall clocks
  BT Clocks and watches
Longdogs
  USE Deer-hounds
       Greyhounds
       Saluki
Longeing (Horsemanship)
  USE Lungeing (Horsemanship)
Longenbach family *(Not Subd Geog)*
Longeteig family *(Not Subd Geog)*
  UF Langeteig family
Longevialle family *(Not Subd Geog)*
  UF De Longvialle family
Longevity *(May Subd Geog)*
  [QP85 (Physiology)]

  UF Life, Long
       Life span prolongation
       Long life
       Prolongation of life span
  BT Age
       Health
       Life (Biology)
  RT Middle age
       Old age
  NT Aging
       Immortalism
       Life expectancy
       Plants—Longevity
       Vitality
  — Genetic aspects
  — Nutritional aspects
     BT Aging—Nutritional aspects
     NT Macrobiotic diet
Longevity of seeds
  USE Seeds—Viability
Longfin pilot whale
  USE Globicephala melaena
Longford Basin (Tas.)
  BT Geology—Australia
Longhair cat
  USE Persian cat
Longhair cat (Persian cat)
  USE Persian cat
Longhair cats *(May Subd Geog)*
  [SF449.L65]
  UF Long hair cats
       Long-haired cats
       Long hairs (Cats)
       Longhaired cats
       Longhairs (Cats)
  BT Cat breeds
       Cats
  NT Himalayan cat
       Maine coon cat
       Persian cat
       Turkish Angora cat
       Turkish cat
Longhair colorpoint cat
  USE Himalayan cat
Longhair Siamese cat
  USE Himalayan cat
Longhaired cats
  USE Longhair cats
Longhairs (Cats)
  USE Longhair cats
Longhi family *(Not Subd Geog)*
Longhorn beetles
  USE Cerambycidae
Longhorn cattle
  [SF199.L6]
  UF British longhorn cattle
       English longhorn cattle
  BT Cattle breeds
Longhorn cattle, Texas
  USE Texas longhorn cattle
Longibucca *(May Subd Geog)*
  [QL391.N4]
  BT Cylindrocorporidae
  NT Longibucca eptesica
Longibucca eptesica *(May Subd Geog)*
  [QL391.N4]
  BT Longibucca
Longicornia
  USE Cerambycidae
Longinus, Spear of
  USE Holy Lance
Longistigma
  [QL527.A64]
  BT Aphididae
Longitude
  [QB225-QB229 (Astronomy)]
  [VK565-VK567 (Navigation)]
  UF Degrees of latitude and longitude

Longitude *(Continued)*
 BT Astronomical geography
  Astronomy, Spherical and practical
  Earth
  Geodesy
  Geodetic astronomy
  Geography, Mathematical
  Nautical astronomy
  Navigation
  Occultations
 RT Geographical positions
 NT Moon—Tables
  Time
 — Prime meridian
   ⌜QB224⌝
  UF Meridian, Prime
   Prime meridian
  BT Time—Systems and standards
Longitudinal method
 UF Longitudinal research
  Longitudinal studies
 BT Methodology
  Psychometrics
  Research
  Social sciences—Research
  Sociometry
 SA *subdivision* Longitudinal studies *under
  topical headings and classes of
  persons*
Longitudinal research
 USE Longitudinal method
Longitudinal stability of airplanes
 USE Stability of airplanes, Longitudinal
Longitudinal studies
 USE Longitudinal method
Longjaw mudsucker
 USE Gillichthys mirabilis
Longjaw rockfish
 USE Pacific ocean perch
Longleaf pine
  ⌜QK495.C75⌝
  ⌜SB397.P59 (Forestry)⌝
 UF Georgia pine
  Long-leaf pine
  Pinus palustris
  Southern pine
Longley family
 USE Langley family
Longline fishing
 USE Longlining (Fisheries)
Longlining (Fisheries) *(May Subd Geog)*
  ⌜SH344.6.L⌝
 UF Long-line fishing
  Longline fishing
 BT Fisheries
  Fisheries—Equipment and supplies
 — Catch effort
Longly family
 USE Langley family
Longman's beaked whale
 USE Indopacetus pacificus
Longmire family *(Not Subd Geog)*
Longnose sucker
  ⌜QL638.C27⌝
 UF Catostomus catostomus
  Northern sucker
Longobards
 USE Lombards
Longone, Piazza di (Porto Azzurro, Italy)
 USE Piazza di Longone (Porto Azzurro,
  Italy)
Longs Peak (Colo.)
 BT Front Range (Colo. and Wyo.)
  Mountains—Colorado
  Rocky Mountain National Park (Colo.)
Longshore workers
 USE Stevedores
Longshoremen
 USE Stevedores

**Longshoremen's Strike, Antwerp, Belgium,
1907**
 BT Strikes and lockouts—Stevedores—
  Belgium
**Longshoremen's Strike, Montevideo, Uruguay,
1959**
 BT Strikes and lockouts—Stevedores—
  Uruguay
Longshoremen's Strike, 1971-1972
Longstaff family
 USE Langstaff family
Longstaffe family
 USE Langstaff family
Longstreet family *(Not Subd Geog)*
Longtin family *(Not Subd Geog)*
Longton Hall porcelain
  ⌜NK4399.L⌝
 UF Porcelain, Longton Hall
Longuda language
 UF Nunguda language
 BT Adamawa languages
  Nigeria—Languages
 NT Guyuk dialect
Longwall method of mining
 USE Longwall mining
Longwall mining *(May Subd Geog)*
 UF Longwall method of mining
  Mining, Longwall
 BT Coal mines and mining
Longways dance
 USE Country-dance
Longwing sculpins
 USE Cottocomephoridae
Longwood Gardens (Pa.)
 BT Gardens—Pennsylvania
Longwood Range (N.Z.)
 BT Mountains—New Zealand
Lonicera
 USE Honeysuckle
Lonicera japonica
 USE Japanese honeysuckle
Lonkengo language
 UF Nkengo language
 BT Bantu languages
Lonkundu language
 USE Nkundu language
Lono family
 USE Lone family
Lonomiidae
 USE Saturniidae
Lontar palm
 USE Borassus sundaica
  Palmyra palm
Lonwolwol dialect
 UF Fantig dialect
  Fanting dialect
 BT Ambrym language
Loo (Game)
  ⌜GV1295.L⌝
Loo Palace (Apeldoorn, Netherlands)
 USE Het Loo (Apeldoorn, Netherlands)
Lööf, Jan, 1940-   Felix (Comic strip)
 USE Felix (Comic strip)
Look-say method of reading
 USE Reading (Elementary)—Whole-word
  method
Looking-glasses
 USE Mirrors
Lookout Mountain, Battle of, 1863
  ⌜E475.97⌝
 BT Chattanooga, Battle of, 1863
Lookout stations, Fire
 USE Fire lookout stations
Lookout towers, Fire
 USE Fire lookout stations
Lookouts, Fire
 USE Fire lookouts
Loombo language
 USE Ombo language

Loomis family *(Not Subd Geog)*
 UF Laumiss family
  Loamis family
  Lomas family
  Lomes family
  Lomice family
  Lomis family
  Lommance family
  Loomise family
  Loomiss family
  Lumas family
  Lumis family
  Lummas family
  Lummis family
  Lummos family
  Lummus family
  Lummys family
  Lummyus family
Loomise family
 USE Loomis family
Loomiss family
 USE Loomis family
Looms
  ⌜TS1493⌝
 BT Cotton machinery
  Textile machinery
  Weaving
 NT Handlooms
  Jacquard weaving
  Pickers (Weaving)
  Ribbon loom
  Shuttles, Threading of
  Shuttles (Textile machinery)
Looney Site (Or.)
 BT Oregon—Antiquities
Loons *(May Subd Geog)*
 UF Colymbidae
  Gaviiformes
  Urinatoridae
 BT Divers (Birds)
  Procellariiformes
Loop Elevated Structure (Chicago, Ill.)
 USE Chicago Union Loop Elevated
  Structure (Chicago, Ill.)
Loop networks (Computer networks)
 USE Ring networks (Computer networks)
Loop spaces
 UF Spaces, Loop
 BT Homotopy theory
  Topological spaces
Loops, Button
 USE Button loops
Loops, Moufang
 USE Moufang loops
Loops, Phase-locked
 USE Phase-locked loops
Loops (Group theory)
  ⌜QA171⌝
 BT Groups, Theory of
 NT Moufang loops
Loos-en-Gohelle (France), Battle of, 1915
 BT World War, 1914-1918—Campaigns—
  France
Loos family
 USE Luce family
Loosahatchie River (Tenn.)
 BT Rivers—Tennessee
Loose family
 USE Luce family
Loose-leaf catalogs
 USE Catalogs, Sheaf
Loose-leaf Chinese cabbage
 USE Bok choy
Loose-leaf publications *(May Subd Geog)*
 UF Loose-leaf services
  Looseleafs
  Publications, Loose-leaf
 BT Books
  Serial publications
 NT Cataloging of loose-leaf publications

Loose-leaf publications, Legal
  (May Subd Geog)
    UF Loose-leaf services, Legal
        Looseleafs, Legal
    BT Legal literature
Loose-leaf services
  USE Loose-leaf publications
Loose-leaf services, Legal
  USE Loose-leaf publications, Legal
Loose teeth
  USE Teeth—Mobility
Looseleafs
  USE Loose-leaf publications
Looseleafs, Legal
  USE Loose-leaf publications, Legal
Looting
  USE Pillage
Loots family
  USE Lutz family
Lop Nor (China)
    UF Lo-pu-no-erh (China)
        Lob Nor (China)
    BT Lakes—China
Lop rabbits
    ⌐SF455.L64⌐
    BT Rabbit breeds
Lopadorhynchidae
    ⌐QL391.A6⌐
    UF Lopadorrhynchidae
    BT Phyllodocida
    NT Lopadorhynchus
Lopadorhynchus
    ⌐QL391.A6⌐
    UF Lopadorrhynchus
    BT Lopadorhynchidae
Lopadorrhynchidae
  USE Lopadorhynchidae
Lopadorrhynchus
  USE Lopadorhynchus
Lopaz family
  USE Lopez family
Lopeman family *(Not Subd Geog)*
Loperamide
    UF Chlorophenylhydroxyd
        imethyldiphenylpiper
        idinebutanamide
    BT Antidiarrheals
        Antiperistaltics
        Piperidine
Lopes family
  USE Lopez family
Lopez expeditions to Cuba
  USE Cuba—History—Insurrection, 1849-
        1851
Lopez family *(Not Subd Geog)*
    UF Lopaz family
        Lopes family
Lophiidae
    ⌐QL638.L75⌐
    UF Goosefishes
    BT Anglerfishes
    NT Lophius
Lophiiformes
  USE Anglerfishes
Lophiomys
    ⌐QL737.R638⌐
    BT Cricetidae
    NT Lophiomys ibeanus
Lophiomys ibeanus
    ⌐QL737.R638⌐
    BT Lophiomys
Lophiostomataceae
    BT Pleosporales
Lophius
    ⌐QL638.L75⌐
    BT Lophiidae
    NT Lophius budegassa
        Lophius piscatorius
Lophius americanus
    ⌐QL638.L75⌐

Lophius budegassa *(May Subd Geog)*
    ⌐QL638.L75⌐
    BT Lophius
Lophius piscatorius *(May Subd Geog)*
    ⌐QL638.L75⌐
    BT Lophius
Lophobranchii
  USE Gasterosteiformes
Lophocateridae
  USE Trogositidae
Lophocoleaceae
    ⌐QK555.L58⌐
    BT Jungermanniales
    NT Clasmatocolea
Lophortyx californicus
  USE California quail
Lophortyx gambelii
  USE Gambel's quail
Lophosaura
  USE Microsaura
Lophoziaceae
    NT Anastrophyllum
Lophyridae
  USE Diprionidae
Lopičić family *(Not Subd Geog)*
Lopoy Site (Kenya) *(Not Subd Geog)*
    BT Kenya—Antiquities
Loquat
    ⌐SB379.L85⌐
    UF Japanese medlar
        Medlar, Japanese
        Nispero
Loramore family
  USE Larrimore family
Loran
    ⌐VK560⌐
    UF Long range navigation
    BT Aeronautical radio stations
        Electronics in aeronautics
        Electronics in navigation
        Hyperbolic navigation
    — Maps
        USE Loran charts
    — Tables
        BT Navigation—Tables
            Navigation (Aeronautics)—Tables
Loran charts *(May Subd Geog)*
    UF Loran—Maps
    BT Aeronautical charts
        Electronics in navigation
        Hyperbolic navigation
        Nautical charts
Lorance family
  USE Lawrence family
Loranthaceae
    BT Santalales
Lorazepam
    UF Chlorochlorophenyldi
        hydrohydroxybenzodiazepinone
    BT Benzodiazepines
Lord, Day of the
  USE Day of Jehovah
Lord advocates
  USE Lawyers—Scotland
Lord Edgecombe Island (Solomon Islands)
  USE Utupua (Solomon Islands)
Lord family *(Not Subd Geog)*
    UF Laud family
        Lawd family
        Lawed family
        Lords family
Lord Howe Island (N.S.W.)
    BT Islands—Australia
Lord Peter Wimsey (Fictitious character)
  USE Wimsey, Peter, Lord (Fictitious
        character)
Lordalychus
  USE Hybalicus
Lordalycidae
    ⌐QL458.2.L67⌐
    NT Hybalicus

Lordotus
    ⌐QL537.B65⌐
    BT Bombyliidae
Lords' Canal (Amsterdam, Netherlands)
  USE Herengracht (Amsterdam,
        Netherlands)
Lord's Day
  USE Sabbath
        Sunday
Lords family
  USE Lord family
Lord's prayer (Music)
Lord's prayer
    ⌐BV230-BV233⌐
    UF Jesus Christ—Lord's prayer
    BT Bible—Prayers
    — **Illustrations**
        UF Lord's prayer—Pictures,
            illustrations, etc.
    — Pictures, illustrations, etc.
        USE Lord's prayer—Illustrations
Lord's prayer in art
Lord's Supper
    ⌐BV823-BV828⌐
    ⌐BX2215 (Catholic Church)⌐
    ⌐BX5149.C5 (Church of England)⌐
    UF Cena, Ultima
        Cenacolo
        Communion
        Eucharist
        Holy Communion
        Jesus Christ—Lord's Supper
        Sacrament of the Altar
    BT Blood—Religious aspects—Christianity
        Sacraments
        Sacred meals
    RT Last Supper
        Mass
    NT Aumbries
        Close and open communion
        Communion sermons
        Easter duties
        First communion
        Infant communion
        Monstrances
        Quartodecimans
        Sacrament houses
        Temperance—Biblical arguments
        Viaticum
    — **Admission age**
        NT First communion
    — **Admission of remarried persons**
        BT Remarriage—Religious aspects—
            Christianity
    — — **Catholic Church, ⌐Church of England,
        etc.⌐**
            BT Remarriage—Religious aspects—
                Baptists, ⌐Catholic Church,
                etc.⌐
    — **Adoration**
    — **Bread**
        UF Bread, Communion
            Bread, Consecrated
            Communion bread
            Consecrated bread
            Lord's Supper—Elements
        BT Bread—Religious aspects—
            Christianity
        NT Bread stamps (Liturgical objects)
    — **Bread and wine**
        UF Lord's Supper—Elements
    — **Catholic Church**
        NT Eucharistic congresses
    — — **Prayer-books and devotions**
        NT Forty hours' devotion
    — **Catholic Church, ⌐Presbyterian Church,
        etc.⌐**
    — **Celebration**
        NT Concelebration
            Mass—Celebration
            Private masses

Lord's Supper *(Continued)*
 — **Child participation**
   UF Child participation in communion
       Child participation in the Lord's
           Supper
       Children's communion
   BT Children—Religious life
   NT Infant communion
 — —**Catholic Church,** ⌈**Lutheran Church,**
       etc.⌉
 — **Communion in both elements**
   UF Communion in both elements
   BT Hussites
   NT Utraquists
 — Communion tokens
   USE Communion tokens
 — Consubstantiation
   USE Lord's Supper—Real presence
 — **Early works to 600**
   BT Christian literature, Early
 — Elements
   USE Lord's Supper—Bread
       Lord's Supper—Bread and wine
       Lord's Supper—Reservation
       Lord's Supper—Wine
 — **Exposition of elements**
 — **Fasting communion**
 — **Fasting communion (Canon law)**
 — First communion
   USE First communion
 — **Frequency of communion**
 — **History**
 — — **Early church, ca. 30-600**
 — — **Middle Ages, 600-1500**
 — Infant communion
   USE Infant communion
 — **Lay administration**
   UF Lay administration of the Lord's
           Supper
   BT Lay ministry
 — **Lay celebration**
   UF Lay celebration of the Lord's
           Supper
   BT Lay ministry
 — —**Church of England,** ⌈**Catholic Church,**
       etc.⌉
 — Liturgy
   USE Lord's Supper (Liturgy)
 — **Medieval works**
 — **Meditations**
 — **Miracles**
   BT Miracles
 — **Prayer-books and devotions**
   ⌈*BV823-BV828*⌉
   ⌈*BX2169 (Catholic Church)*⌉
   ⌈*BX5149.C5 (Church of England)*⌉
   Here are entered prayers and devotions for
   use by individuals receiving the sacrament of the
   Lord's Supper. Prayers in the liturgy of the
   Lord's Supper used by the celebrant to conse-
   crate the sacrament are entered under Eucharis-
   tic prayers.
 — —**English,** ⌈**French, German, etc.**⌉
 — **Real presence**
   ⌈*BV823-BV828*⌉
   ⌈*BX5149.C5 (Church of England)*⌉
   ⌈*BX8073 (Lutheran)*⌉
   Here are entered works on the doctrine that
   Christ is present in the sacrament of the Lord's
   Supper. Works on the Catholic doctrine that the
   substance of the elements of bread and wine is
   transformed into the substance of the body and
   blood of Christ after receiving priestly consecra-
   tion in the Mass are entered under Transubstan-
   tiation.
   UF Consubstantiation
       Lord's Supper—Consubstantiation
       Real presence
   BT Jesus Christ—Presence
   NT Transubstantiation
 — **Remains**
 — **Reservation**

Here are entered works on retention of a por-
tion of the consecrated eucharistic elements for
adoration by those worshiping at the church or
for administration of communion to the sick.
   UF Lord's Supper—Elements
       Reservation of the elements
           (Lord's Supper)
   NT Viaticum
 — **Sacrifice**
   UF Oblation (Lord's Supper)
   BT Sacrifice—Christianity
 — **Sermons**
   ⌈*BV827*⌉
   ⌈*BX2215 (Catholic Church)*⌉
   Here are entered sermons on the Lord's Sup-
   per itself. Sermons preached at, or in preparation
   for, a communion service are entered under the
   heading Communion sermons.
 — Table
   USE Communion table
 — **Wine**
   Here are entered works limited to the wine
   (and water where customary) used in the Lord's
   Supper.
   UF Communion wine
       Lord's Supper—Elements
   BT Wine—Religious aspects—
           Christianity
 — **Youth participation**
   UF Youth participation in communion
       Youth participation in the Lord's
           Supper
   BT Youth—Religious life
Lord's Supper (Canon law)
   ⌈*BX1939.L6*⌉
   RT Mass (Canon law)
Lord's Supper (Liturgy)
   UF Anaphora (Liturgy)
       Lord's Supper—Liturgy
   BT Liturgics
   NT Communion-service music
       Epiclesis
       Eucharistic prayers
       Mass (Music)
       Prefaces (Liturgy)
 — **Texts**
Lord's Supper and Christian union
   UF Christian union and the Lord's Supper
   BT Christian union
Lord's Supper in art
   NT Rubens, Peter Paul, Sir, 1577-1640.
       Triumph of the Eucharist
Lord's Supper in literature
   ⌈*PN49*⌉
   ⌈*PR145*⌉
   ⌈*PR275*⌉
   BT Christianity in literature
       Religion in literature
Loreing family
   USE Loring family
Loren Pope House (Falls Church, Va.)
   USE Pope-Leighey House (Va.)
Lorentz family
   USE Lorenz family
Lorentz groups
   UF Groups, Lorentz
   BT Groups, Continuous
       Groups, Theory of
   RT Lorentz transformations
Lorentz spaces
   UF Spaces, Lorentz
   BT Function spaces
       Interpolation spaces
   NT Lorentz-Zygmund spaces
Lorentz transformations
   ⌈*QC174.5*⌉
   BT Groups, Theory of
       Special relativity (Physics)
       Transformations (Mathematics)
   RT Lorentz groups
   NT World line (Physics)

Lorentz-Zygmund spaces
   UF Spaces, Lorentz-Zygmund
       Spaces, Zygmund-Lorentz
       Zygmund-Lorentz spaces
   BT Lorentz spaces
Lorentzen family *(Not Subd Geog)*
   UF Lorenzen family
   RT Lorenz family
Lorenz curve
   BT Income distribution—Mathematical
           models
Lorenz equations
   UF Equations, Lorenz
   BT Differential equations
Lorenz family *(Not Subd Geog)*
   UF Lerentz family
       Lohrentz family
       Lorentz family
   RT Lawrence family
       Lawrenz family
       Lorentzen family
Lorenzan Indians
   USE Amuesha Indians
Lorenzan language
   ⌈*PM6358*⌉
   UF Amueixa language
       Amuesa language
   BT Arawakan languages
       Indians of South America—Languages
Lorenzato family *(Not Subd Geog)*
   UF Lorenzatto family
Lorenzatto family
   USE Lorenzato family
Lorenzen family
   USE Lorentzen family
Lorenzini, Ampulla of
   USE Ampulla of Lorenzini
Lorey family
   USE Lowry family
Lorgeril family *(Not Subd Geog)*
   UF De Lorgeril family
Loricariidae
   ⌈*QL638.L785*⌉
   UF Armored catfishes
       Mailed catfishes
   BT Catfishes
   NT Hypostomus
       Scoloplax
Loricata (Reptiles)
   USE Crocodilia
Loricati
   USE Scorpaeniformes
Loricifera *(May Subd Geog)*
   ⌈*QL391.L67*⌉
   BT Animals
Lories
   ⌈*QL696.P688 (Zoology)*⌉
   ⌈*SF473.L57 (Cagebird)*⌉
   UF Brush-tongued parrots
       Loriidae
       Lorikeets
   BT Parrots
   NT Nymphicus
Loriidae
   USE Lories
Lorika (Hindu mythology)
   BT Mythology, Hindu
Lorikeets
   USE Lories
Lorimer family
   USE Larrimore family
Lorimor family
   USE Larrimore family
Lorin family
   USE Loring family
Loring family *(Not Subd Geog)*
   UF Loreing family
       Lorin family
       Lowring family
Lorises
   USE Lorisidae

Lorisidae
  [QL737.P955]
  UF Bushbabies
      Galagos
      Lorises
  BT Primates
  NT Galago
Lorkwood family
  USE Lockwood family
Lormin
  USE Chlormadinone
Lorne Forest Park (Vic.)
  BT Forest reserves—Australia
      Parks—Australia
Loroceridae
  USE Carabidae
Loroglossum hircinum
  USE Himantoglossum hircinum
Lorraine, House of *(Not Subd Geog)*
Lorraine (Belgium)
  UF Belgian Lorraine (Belgium)
      Lorraine belge (Belgium)
      Uplands of Lorraine (Belgium)
Lorraine, Parc naturel régional de (France)
  USE Parc naturel régional de Lorraine
       (France)
Lorraine, Cross of
  USE Cross of Lorraine
Lorraine belge (Belgium)
  USE Lorraine (Belgium)
Lorraine in art
Lorrainers *(May Subd Geog)*
  BT Ethnology—France
Lorrains, Notre-Dame des
  [BT660.L]
  UF Notre-Dame des Lorrains
  BT Mary, Blessed Virgin, Saint—Cult—
      France
Lorrentz family
  USE Lawrence family
Lorretto Indians
  USE Canelo Indians
Lorries (Motor vehicles)
  USE Trucks
Lorumor family
  USE Larrimore family
Los Angeles (Calif.)
  — History
  — — Civil War, 1861-1865
  — Riot, 1965
      UF Watts Riot, 1965
Los Angeles County Museum of Art Robert O.
  Anderson Building (Los Angeles, Calif.)
  USE Robert O. Anderson Building (Los
       Angeles, Calif.)
Los Angeles Pacific Railway
  BT Railroads—United States
Los Angeles Sleepy Lagoon Trial, 1942-1943
  USE Sleepy Lagoon Trial, Los Angeles,
       1942-1943
Los Angeles Transit
  BT Railroads—United States
**Los Baños (Los Baños, Laguna, Philippines :
  Concentration camp)**
  [D805.P6]
  BT World War, 1939-1945—
      Concentration camps—Philippines
Los Burros Mining District (Calif.)
  BT Gold mines and mining—California
      Mining districts—California
Los Cameros (Spain)
  USE Cameros (Spain)
Los Gavilanes Site (Peru)
  USE Gavilanes Site (Peru)
Los Glaciares National Park (Argentina)
  USE Parque Nacional Los Glaciares
       (Argentina)
Los Matachines (Dance)
  USE Matachines (Dance)
Los Monegros (Spain)
  USE Monegros (Spain)

Los Monjes Islands (Venezuela)
  USE Monjes Islands (Venezuela)
Los Negros (Philippines)
  USE Negros Island (Philippines)
Los Olmos Creek (Tex.)
  BT Rivers—Texas
Los Padres National Forest (Calif.)
  BT Forest reserves—California
      National parks and reserves—United
      States
Los Pedroches Region (Spain)
  USE Pedroches Region (Spain)
Lose family
  USE Luce family
Losengo language *(May Subd Geog)*
  UF Lusengo language
  BT Bantu languages
      Zaire—Languages
  NT Leko dialect
Losers *(May Subd Geog)*
  BT Failure (Psychology)
Loshad' (The Russian word)
  BT Russian language—Etymology
Losier family
  USE Lozier family
Losing (Psychology)
  USE Failure (Psychology)
Lošinj Island (Croatia) *(Not Subd Geog)*
  UF Lussino Island (Croatia)
  BT Islands—Yugoslavia
Loško pogorje (Slovenia)
  USE Škofja Loka Mountains (Slovenia)
Losna family *(Not Subd Geog)*
Lososina River (Poland) *(Not Subd Geog)*
  BT Rivers—Poland
Loss, Mass (Astrophysics)
  USE Mass loss (Astrophysics)
Loss (Psychology)
  [RC455.4.L67 (Psychiatry)]
  BT Psychology
  NT Bereavement
      Deprivation (Psychology)
      Grief
      Separation (Psychology)
Loss leader selling
  USE Loss leaders
Loss leaders *(May Subd Geog)*
  UF Below cost selling
      Loss leader selling
      Selling below cost
  BT Price cutting
      Price discrimination
Loss of appetite
  USE Anorexia
Loss of citizenship
  USE Citizenship, Loss of
Loss of consciousness
  UF Consciousness, Loss of
      Insensibility
      Unconsciousness
  BT Neurologic manifestations of general
      diseases
  NT Coma
      Inert gas narcosis
      Stupor
      Syncope (Pathology)
Loss of coolant in pressurized water reactors
  USE Pressurized water reactors—Loss of
       coolant
Loss-of-Fluid-Test Facility
  USE LOFT (Nuclear reactor safety test
       facility)
Loss of hope
  USE Despair
Loss of identity
  USE Depersonalization
Loss of livestock embryos
  USE Livestock—Embryos—Mortality
Loss of loved one by separation
  USE Separation (Psychology)

Loss of loved ones by death
  USE Bereavement
Loss of political rights
  USE Political rights, Loss of
Loss of tooth
  USE Tooth loss
Loss of weight
  USE Reducing
Losses, Business
  USE Business losses
Losses, Cattle
  USE Cattle—Losses
Losses, Crop
  USE Crop losses
Losses, Livestock
  USE Livestock—Losses
Losses as tax deductions
  USE Income tax—Deductions—Losses
Lost articles (Jewish law)
Lost articles (Law) *(May Subd Geog)*
  UF Finding lost property
  BT Bona vacantia
      Possession (Law)
  RT Res nullius
      Treasure-trove
Lost arts
  [T33]
  RT Industrial arts—History
Lost books
  [Z1024]
  BT Bibliography
Lost children
  USE Missing children
Lost circulation in oil well drilling
  USE Oil well drilling—Lost circulation
Lost coin (Parable)
  [BT378.L]
Lost continents
  [GN750-GN751]
  BT Continents
      Geographical myths
  NT Atlantis
      Lemuria
**Lost Creek (Gentry County and De Kalb
  County, Mo.)**
  BT Rivers—Missouri
Lost Creek (Okla.)
  BT Rivers—Oklahoma
Lost earnings damages *(May Subd Geog)*
  UF Damages for lost earnings
      Lost income damages
      Lost wages damages
  BT Damages
      Torts
      Wages
Lost income damages
  USE Lost earnings damages
Lost literature *(May Subd Geog)*
  UF Lost literature—History and criticism
  BT Literature
  — History and criticism
      USE Lost literature
Lost profits damages *(May Subd Geog)*
  UF Damages for lost profits
      Profit losses damages
  BT Business losses
      Contracts
      Damages
      Torts
Lost sheep (Parable)
Lost sheep (Parable) in art
Lost tribes of Israel
  [DS131]
  UF Israel, Ten lost tribes
      Jews—Lost tribes
      Jews—Ten lost tribes
      Ten lost tribes of Israel
  BT Tribes
  RT Anglo-Israelism
  NT Naphtali (Tribe of Israel)
      Twelve tribes of Israel

Lost wages damages
   USE Lost earnings damages
Lost-wax process
   USE Precision casting
Lost works of art   *(May Subd Geog)*
   UF Missing works of art
   BT Art
Lot, Choice by
   USE Choice by lot
Lot Exchange Dollar Credit Plan
   UF NAC Lot Exchange Dollar Credit
         Plan
   BT Cemeteries—Exchange credit plans
Lot family
   USE Lott family
Lot River (France)
   UF Oltis River (France)
   BT Rivers—France
Lot size determination
   USE Economic lot size
Lota
   BT Codfish
Lota lota
   USE Burbot
Lotha language
   USE Lhota language
Lothagam Site (Kenya)   *(Not Subd Geog)*
   BT Kenya—Antiquities
Lothorp family
   USE Lothrop family
Lothrop family   *(Not Subd Geog)*
   UF Lathrop family
         Lathrope family
         Lothorp family
         Lowthorp family
Lotru River (Romania)   *(Not Subd Geog)*
   UF Lotrul (Romania)
   BT Rivers—Romania
Lotrul (Romania)
   USE Lotru River (Romania)
Lots, Feast of
   USE Purim
Lötschen Thal (Switzerland)
   USE Lötschental (Switzerland)
Lötschen Valley (Switzerland)
   USE Lötschental (Switzerland)
Lötschental (Switzerland)
   UF Lötschen Thal (Switzerland)
         Lötschen Valley (Switzerland)
   BT Valleys—Switzerland
Lott family   *(Not Subd Geog)*
   UF Lot family
         Lotts family
         Lotz family
Lotteries   *(May Subd Geog)*
   ᵣHG6105-6270ᵧ
   BT Criminal law
         Gambling
   NT Lottery winners
   — Advertising
         USE Advertising—Lotteries
   — **Law and legislation**   *(May Subd Geog)*
Lottery winners   *(May Subd Geog)*
   ᵣHV6105-6270.9ᵧ
   UF Winners of lotteries
   BT Gamblers
         Lotteries
Lotto, Lorenzo, 1480?-1556?   Saint Jerome
   (Not Subd Geog)
   ᵣND623.L8ᵧ
   UF Saint Jerome (Painting)
         San Girolamo (Painting)
   BT Painting, Italian
Lotto
   ᵣGV1311.L6ᵧ
Lotts family
   USE Lott family
Lottsford Branch (Md.)
   BT Rivers—Maryland
Lotuho language
   USE Latuka language

Lotuka (African people)
   USE Latuka (African people)
Lotuko (African people)
   USE Latuka (African people)
Lotuko language
   USE Latuka language
Lotus
   ᵣQK495.L52 (Botany)ᵧ
   ᵣSB205.L7 (Forage plants)ᵧ
   UF Deervetch
         Lotus (Genus)
         Trefoils (Plants)
   BT Forage plants
         Leguminosae
Lotus, East Indian   *(May Subd Geog)*
   ᵣQK495.N97 (Botany)ᵧ
   UF East Indian lotus
         Indian lotus
         Nelumbo nucifera
         Nelumbo speciosa
Lotus (Genus)
   USE Lotus
Lotus automobile
   ᵣTL215.Lᵧ
   BT Automobiles
         Automobiles, Racing
         Sports cars
   NT Lotus Elan automobile
Lotus corniculatus
   ᵣQK495.L52 (Botany)ᵧ
   UF Bird's foot trefoil
         Birdsfoot trefoil
         Trefoil, Birdsfoot
Lotus Elan automobile
   ᵣTL215.Lᵧ
   BT Lotus automobile
Lotus major
   USE Big trefoil
Lotus sect
   USE Nichiren (Sect)
Lotus Symphony (Computer program)
   USE Symphony (Computer program)
Lotus tenuis
   USE Narrowleaf trefoil
Lotus uliginosus
   USE Big trefoil
Lotz family
   USE Lott family
Lou Gehrig's disease
   USE Amyotrophic lateral sclerosis
Loucheux Indians
   USE Kutchin Indians
Louck family
   USE Loucks family
Loucks family   *(Not Subd Geog)*
   UF Louck family
         Louk family
         Louks family
         Lowk family
         Lowks family
Loud family   *(Not Subd Geog)*
   UF Leod family
         Lowd family
         Lowde family
   RT Louden family
Loud-speaker cabinets
   USE Loudspeaker cabinets
Loud-speakers
   USE Loudspeakers
Loud-speakers, Direct radiator
   USE Direct radiator loudspeakers
Louden family   *(Not Subd Geog)*
   UF Loudin family
         Loudon family
         Lowdan family
         Lowden family
         Lowdon family
   RT Loud family
Loudermilch family
   USE Lowdermilk family

Loudermilk family
   USE Lowdermilk family
Loudin family
   USE Louden family
Loudon family
   USE Louden family
Loudoun Valley (Va.)
   BT Valleys—Virginia
Loudspeaker cabinets   *(May Subd Geog)*
   UF Enclosures, Loudspeaker
         Loud-speaker cabinets
         Speaker cabinets
   BT Cabinet-work
Loudspeakers   *(May Subd Geog)*
   ᵣTK5983ᵧ
   UF Loud-speakers
         Speakers (Loudspeakers)
   BT Electroacoustic transducers
         Sound—Equipment and supplies
   NT Direct radiator loudspeakers
Lough Corrib (Ireland)
   USE Corrib, Lough (Ireland)
Lough Erne (Northern Ireland)
   USE Erne, Lower Lough (Northern Ireland)
Lough family
   USE Locke family
**Loughborough War Memorial Tower and
   Carillon (Loughborough, Leicestershire)**
   UF War Memorial Carillon
         (Loughborough, Leicestershire)
   BT Bell towers—England
         Carillons—England
         War memorials—England
Lougheed Island (N.W.T.)
   BT Islands—Northwest Territories
Loughlin family
   USE Laughlin family
Loughrey family
   USE Lowry family
Lougouli language
   USE Logooli language
Louineau family
   USE Luneau family
Louineaux family
   USE Luneau family
Louis XIV, King of France, 1638-1715
   — Portraits
         UF Louis XIV, King of France, 1638-
               1715—Portraits, caricatures, etc.
   — Portraits, caricatures, etc.
         USE Louis XIV, King of France, 1638-
               1715—Portraits
Louis XVI, King of France, 1754-1793
   (Not Subd Geog)
   — Flight to Varennes, 1791
         ᵣDC137.O5ᵧ
         UF Flight of Louis XVI to Varennes,
               1791
               Varennes, Flight of Louis XVI to,
               1791
Louis (Name)
   BT Names, Personal
Louis-Bar syndrome
   USE Ataxia telangiectasia
Louis family
   USE Lewis family
Louis XV Plaza (Paris, France)
   USE Place de la Concorde (Paris, France)
Louisa (Game)
   ᵣGV1511.L8ᵧ
Louisbourg National Historic Park (Cape
   Breton Island, N.S.)
   USE Fortress of Louisbourg National
         Historic Park (Cape Breton Island,
         N.S.)
Louisburg National Historic Park (Cape Breton
   Island, N.S.)
   USE Fortress of Louisbourg National
         Historic Park (Cape Breton Island,
         N.S.)

Louise, Lake (Alta.)
  UF Lake Louise (Alta.)
  BT Lakes—Alberta
Louisets
  [BX4737]
  UF Incommunicants
      La Petite Église
      Stevenism
  BT Catholic Church—France
      Catholics—France
      Christian sects—France
  RT Nonjurors, French Catholic
Louisiana
  — Antiquities
      NT Eagle Hill II Site (La.)
          Elmwood Plantation Site (La.)
          Montrose Site (La.)
          Tchefuncte culture
          Trudeau Site (La.)
  — Description and travel
  — — To 1803
  — — 1803-1865
  — — 1865-1950
  — — 1951-1980
  — — 1981-
  — Governors
  — — Powers and duties
  — History
      [F366-380]
  — — To 1803
  — — 1803-1865
  — — War of 1812
      [E359.5.L8]
  — — Civil War, 1861-1865
      [E510]
      [E565]
  — — War of 1898
  — Languages
      NT Cajun French dialect
  — Politics and government
  — — To 1803
  — — 1803-1865
  — — Civil War, 1861-1865
  — — 1865-1950
  — — 1951-
Louisiana Acadian dialect
  USE Cajun French dialect
Louisiana French dialect
  USE Cajun French dialect
Louisiana Purchase
  [E333 (Diplomatic history)]
  [F351-F353 (Mississippi Valley)]
  [F366-F380 (Louisiana)]
Louisiana style of American cookery
  USE Cookery, American—Louisiana style
Louisville (Ky.)
  — History
  — — Civil War, 1861-1865
Louisville and Nashville Railroad
  BT Railroads—United States
Louk family
  USE Loucks family
Loukache family (Not Subd Geog)
Louks family
  USE Loucks family
Loungers
  USE Flaneurs
Lounsberry family
  USE Lounsbury family
Lounsbery family
  USE Lounsbury family
Lounsbury family (Not Subd Geog)
  UF Lounsberry family
      Lounsbery family
      Lownbury family
      Lownsberry family
      Lownsburry family
      Lownsbury family
Loupes
  USE Hand lenses

Louping-ill
  [SF968]
Loury family
  USE Lowry family
Lous family
  USE Luce family
Louse
  USE Lice
Louse family
  USE Luce family
Louse flies
  [QL537.H57]
  UF Hippoboscidae
  BT Diptera
Louseworts
  USE Pedicularis
Loutham family
  USE Louthan family
Louthan family (Not Subd Geog)
  UF Loutham family
      Louthian family
Louther family
  USE Luther family
Louthian family
  USE Louthan family
Louthrie family
  USE Lowther family
Louvell family
  USE Lovell family
Louviere family (Not Subd Geog)
Louvre (Paris, France)
      Here are entered works on the Louvre palace.
  Works on the museum housed within this building
  are entered under the name heading Musée du
  Louvre.
  UF Palais du Louvre (Paris, France)
  BT Palaces—France
Louw family (Not Subd Geog)
  RT Lowe family
Lovale (African people)
  USE Luvale (African people)
Lovan family
  USE Loving family
Lovari dialect
  [PK2899.Z9L]
  BT Romany language
Lovchorrite
  UF Lovtchorrite
  BT Silicates
Love
  [BD436 (Philosophy)]
  [BF575.L8 (Psychology)]
  [GR460 (Folklore)]
  [GT2600-GT2640 (Manners and
    customs)]
  [HQ61 (Love and religion)]
  UF Affection
  BT Emotions
  RT First loves
      Friendship
      Intimacy (Psychology)
  NT Attachment behavior
      Communism and love
      Courtly love
      Courtship
      Marriage
      Yoga, Bhakti
  — Religious aspects
      NT God—Love
          God—Worship and love
  — — Buddhism
          RT Compassion (Buddhism)
  — — Buddhism, [Christianity, etc.]
  — — Christianity
          NT Agape
              Love feasts
              Summary of the Law (Theology)
  — — Hinduism
          [BL1215.L]
          UF Love (Hinduism)
  — Terminology

NT Love names
Love, Courtly
  USE Courtly love
Love, Courts of
  USE Courts of love
Love, Maternal
  [HQ759]
  UF Maternal love
      Mother love
      Mother's love
  BT Mothers
  NT Maternal deprivation
      Maternal rejection
Love, Paternal
  [HQ756]
  UF Paternal love
  BT Father and child
      Fathers
  NT Paternal deprivation
Love, Platonic
  [B398.L9]
  UF Platonic love
Love (Hinduism)
  USE Love—Religious aspects—Hinduism
Love-birds
  USE Lovebirds
Love Canal Chemical Waste Landfill (Niagara
  Falls, N.Y.) (Not Subd Geog)
  BT Hazardous waste sites—New York
      (State)
      Sanitary landfills—New York (State)
Love family (Not Subd Geog)
  RT Loving family
Love feasts
      Here are entered works dealing with modern reli-
  gious services in imitation of the historic agape.
  BT Love—Religious aspects—Christianity
      Sacred meals
  RT Agape
Love grass
  [SB201.L]
  UF Eragrostis
      Lovegrass
  NT Weeping lovegrass
Love in art
  [N8220]
  NT Garden of love in art
Love in literature
  [PN56.L6]
  RT Erotic literature
      Sentimentalism in literature
      Sex in literature
Love in motion pictures
  BT Moving-pictures
Love-letters
  [HQ801.3-HQ801.5]
  [PN6140.L7 (General literature)]
  [PR1349.L8 (English literature)]
  [PS673.L6-PS673.L7 (American
    literature)]
  UF Correspondence
  BT Erotic literature
      Letter-writing
      Letters
  RT Courtship
  — Women authors
Love-lies-bleeding (Plant)
  USE Amaranthus caudatus
Love loss (Psychology)
  USE Separation (Psychology)
Love names (May Subd Geog)
  UF Endearment, Terms of
      Terms of endearment
  BT Epithets
      Love—Terminology
      Names
      Nicknames
Love of self (Theology)
  USE Self-love (Theology)
Love-philter
  USE Aphrodisiacs

Love-philtre
USE Aphrodisiacs
Love poetry
⌈*PN6110.L6 (General collections)*⌉
⌈*PR1184 (English literature)*⌉
⌈*PS595.L6 (American literature)*⌉
  BT Poetry
  NT Albas
      Epithalamia
      Erotic poetry
      Minnesingers
      Valentines
  — Women authors
Love poetry, Albanian *(May Subd Geog)*
  UF Albanian love poetry
  BT Albanian poetry
Love poetry, American *(May Subd Geog)*
  UF American love poetry
  BT American poetry
Love poetry, American, ⌈**English, French, etc.**⌉
Love poetry, Arabic *(May Subd Geog)*
  ⌈*PJ7542.L6 (History and criticism)*⌉
  ⌈*PJ7632.L6 (Collections)*⌉
  UF Arabic love poetry
  BT Arabic poetry
Love poetry, Argentine *(May Subd Geog)*
  UF Argentine love poetry
  BT Argentine poetry
Love poetry, Australian *(May Subd Geog)*
  UF Australian love poetry
  BT Australian poetry
Love poetry, Avaric *(May Subd Geog)*
  UF Avaric love poetry
  BT Avaric poetry
Love poetry, Basque *(May Subd Geog)*
  UF Basque love poetry
  BT Basque poetry
Love poetry, Bengali *(May Subd Geog)*
  UF Bengali love poetry
  BT Bengali poetry
Love poetry, Braj *(May Subd Geog)*
  UF Braj love poetry
  BT Braj poetry
Love poetry, Brazilian *(May Subd Geog)*
  UF Brazilian love poetry
  BT Brazilian poetry
Love poetry, Canadian *(May Subd Geog)*
  UF Canadian love poetry
  BT Canadian poetry
Love poetry, Canadian, ⌈**Danish, etc.**⌉
Love poetry, Chilean *(May Subd Geog)*
  UF Chilean love poetry
  BT Chilean poetry
Love poetry, Chinese *(May Subd Geog)*
  UF Chinese love poetry
  BT Chinese poetry
Love poetry, Classical *(May Subd Geog)*
  UF Classical love poetry
  BT Classical poetry
Love poetry, Colombian *(May Subd Geog)*
  UF Colombian love poetry
  BT Colombian poetry
Love poetry, Cuban *(May Subd Geog)*
  UF Cuban love poetry
  BT Cuban poetry
Love poetry, Dominican *(May Subd Geog)*
  UF Dominican love poetry
  BT Dominican poetry
Love poetry, Ecuadorian *(May Subd Geog)*
  UF Ecuadorian love poetry
  BT Ecuadorian poetry
Love poetry, Egyptian *(May Subd Geog)*
  UF Egyptian love poetry
  BT Egyptian poetry
Love poetry, English *(May Subd Geog)*
  UF English love poetry
  BT English poetry
Love poetry, Finnish *(May Subd Geog)*
  UF Finnish love poetry
  BT Finnish poetry

Love poetry, French *(May Subd Geog)*
  UF French love poetry
  BT French poetry
Love poetry, French-Canadian
  UF French-Canadian love poetry
Love poetry, German *(May Subd Geog)*
  UF German love poetry
  BT German poetry
Love poetry, Greek *(May Subd Geog)*
  UF Greek love poetry
  BT Greek poetry
Love poetry, Greek (Modern)
  (May Subd Geog)
  UF Greek love poetry, Modern
      Modern Greek love poetry
  BT Greek poetry, Modern
Love poetry, Gujarati *(May Subd Geog)*
  UF Gujarati love poetry
  BT Gujarati poetry
Love poetry, Hausa *(May Subd Geog)*
  UF Hausa love poetry
  BT Hausa poetry
Love poetry, Hebrew *(May Subd Geog)*
  UF Hebrew love poetry
  BT Hebrew poetry
Love poetry, Hindi *(May Subd Geog)*
  UF Hindi love poetry
  BT Hindi poetry
Love poetry, Hungarian *(May Subd Geog)*
  UF Hungarian love poetry
  BT Hungarian poetry
Love poetry, Indian *(May Subd Geog)*
  UF Indian love poetry
  BT Indian poetry
Love poetry, Indic *(May Subd Geog)*
  UF Indic love poetry
  BT Indic poetry
Love poetry, Irish *(May Subd Geog)*
  UF Irish love poetry
  BT Irish poetry
Love poetry, Italian *(May Subd Geog)*
  UF Italian love poetry
  BT Italian poetry
Love poetry, Japanese *(May Subd Geog)*
  UF Japanese love poetry
  BT Japanese poetry
Love poetry, Korean *(May Subd Geog)*
  UF Korean love poetry
  BT Korean poetry
Love poetry, Latin *(May Subd Geog)*
  UF Latin love poetry
  BT Latin poetry
Love poetry, Latin American
  (May Subd Geog)
  UF Latin American love poetry
  BT Latin American poetry
Love poetry, Latin (Medieval and modern)
  (May Subd Geog)
  UF Latin love poetry, Medieval and
      modern
  BT Latin poetry, Medieval and modern
Love poetry, Lushai *(May Subd Geog)*
  UF Lushai love poetry
  BT Lushai poetry
Love poetry, Nepali *(May Subd Geog)*
  UF Nepali love poetry
  BT Nepali poetry
Love poetry, Norwegian *(May Subd Geog)*
  ⌈*PT8695.L7*⌉
  UF Norwegian love poetry
  BT Norwegian poetry
Love poetry, Panamanian *(May Subd Geog)*
  UF Panamanian love poetry
  BT Panamanian poetry
Love poetry, Peruvian *(May Subd Geog)*
  UF Peruvian love poetry
  BT Peruvian poetry
Love poetry, Polish *(May Subd Geog)*
  UF Polish love poetry
  BT Polish poetry

Love poetry, Portuguese *(May Subd Geog)*
  UF Portuguese love poetry
  BT Portuguese poetry
Love poetry, Provençal *(May Subd Geog)*
  UF Provençal love poetry
  BT Provençal poetry
Love poetry, Puerto Rican
  (May Subd Geog)
  UF Puerto Rican love poetry
  BT Puerto Rican poetry
Love poetry, Romanian *(May Subd Geog)*
  UF Romanian love poetry
  BT Romanian poetry
Love poetry, Russian *(May Subd Geog)*
  UF Russian love poetry
  BT Russian poetry
Love poetry, Sanskrit *(May Subd Geog)*
  UF Sanskrit love poetry
  BT Sanskrit poetry
Love poetry, Serbian *(May Subd Geog)*
  UF Serbian love poetry
  BT Serbian poetry
Love poetry, Slovak *(May Subd Geog)*
  UF Slovak love poetry
  BT Slovak poetry
Love poetry, Spanish *(May Subd Geog)*
  UF Spanish love poetry
  BT Spanish poetry
Love poetry, Spanish American
  (May Subd Geog)
  UF Spanish American love poetry
  BT Spanish American poetry
Love poetry, Tamil *(May Subd Geog)*
  UF Tamil love poetry
  BT Tamil poetry
Love poetry, Thai *(May Subd Geog)*
  UF Thai love poetry
  BT Thai poetry
Love poetry, Tibetan *(May Subd Geog)*
  UF Tibetan love poetry
  BT Tibetan poetry
Love poetry, Turkish *(May Subd Geog)*
  UF Turkish love poetry
  BT Turkish poetry
Love poetry, Ukrainian *(May Subd Geog)*
  UF Ukrainian love poetry
  BT Ukrainian poetry
Love poetry, Vietnamese *(May Subd Geog)*
  UF Vietnamese love poetry
  BT Vietnamese poetry
Love-potion
USE Aphrodisiacs
Love songs *(May Subd Geog)*
  BT Songs
Love spoons *(May Subd Geog)*
  ⌈*GT2950 (Manners and customs)*⌉
  BT Spoons
Love stories *(May Subd Geog)*
  UF Romances (Love stories)
  BT Fiction
Love stories, American *(May Subd Geog)*
  UF American love stories
  BT American fiction
Love stories, Canadian *(May Subd Geog)*
  UF Canadian love stories
  BT Canadian fiction
Love stories, Chinese *(May Subd Geog)*
  ⌈*PL2419.L68 (History)*⌉
  ⌈*PL2629.L68 (Collections)*⌉
  UF Chinese love stories
  BT Chinese fiction
Love stories, Cuban *(May Subd Geog)*
  UF Cuban love stories
  BT Cuban fiction
Love stories, Czech *(May Subd Geog)*
  ⌈*PG5011 (History and criticism)*⌉
  ⌈*PG5029 (Collections)*⌉
  UF Czech love stories
  BT Czech fiction
Love stories, Danish
  UF Danish love stories

BT Danish fiction
Love stories, Dutch *(May Subd Geog)*
　UF Dutch love stories
　BT Dutch fiction
Love stories, English *(May Subd Geog)*
　UF English love stories
　BT English fiction
　— Philippine authors
　　USE Love stories, Philippine (English)
Love stories, French *(May Subd Geog)*
　UF French love stories
　BT French fiction
Love stories, French, ₁German, etc.₁
　(May Subd Geog)
Love stories, German *(May Subd Geog)*
　UF German love stories
　BT German fiction
Love stories, Greek *(May Subd Geog)*
　UF Greek love stories
　BT Greek fiction
Love stories, Hebrew *(May Subd Geog)*
　UF Hebrew love stories
　BT Hebrew fiction
Love stories, Indic (English)
　(May Subd Geog)
　UF Indic love stories (English)
　BT Indic fiction (English)
Love stories, Korean *(May Subd Geog)*
　UF Korean love stories
　BT Korean fiction
Love stories, Latvian *(May Subd Geog)*
　UF Latvian love stories
　BT Latvian fiction
Love stories, New Zealand
　(May Subd Geog)
　UF New Zealand love stories
　BT New Zealand fiction
Love stories, Philippine (English)
　(May Subd Geog)
　UF Love stories, English—Philippine
　　authors
　　Philippine love stories (English)
　BT Philippine fiction (English)
Love stories, Romanian *(May Subd Geog)*
　UF Romanian love stories
　BT Romanian fiction
Love stories, Spanish *(May Subd Geog)*
　UF Spanish love stories
　BT Spanish fiction
Love stories, Swedish *(May Subd Geog)*
　UF Swedish love stories
　BT Swedish fiction
Lovebirds
　₁QL696.P7₁
　UF Agapornis
　　Love-birds
　BT Parrots
　　Psittacidae
Loveday Brooke (Fictitious character)
　USE Brooke, Loveday (Fictitious character)
Lovedu
　USE Lobedu
Lovegrass
　USE Love grass
Lovein family
　USE Loving family
Loveing family
　USE Loving family
Lovejoy family *(Not Subd Geog)*
Lovel family
　USE Lovell family
Lovelace family *(Not Subd Geog)*
　UF Lovlace family
　　Luvlace family
Loveland family *(Not Subd Geog)*
Lovell family *(Not Subd Geog)*
　UF Louvell family
　　Lovel family
　　Lovewell family
　　Lovill family
　RT Lowell family

Lovemaking
　USE Sexual intercourse
Loven family
　USE Loving family
Lövens family
　USE Loewen family
Loveran family
　USE Lovering family
Loverein family
　USE Lovering family
Loverin family
　USE Lovering family
Lovering family *(Not Subd Geog)*
　UF Loveran family
　　Loverein family
　　Loverin family
　　Lovran family
　　Lovrin family
　　Lovring family
　RT Loving family
Lovern family
　USE Loving family
Lovers (Mistresses)
　USE Mistresses
Lovers of Teruel (Legend)
　₁PN687.L68₁
　UF Amantes de Teruel (Legend)
　　Martínez de Marcilla, Diego Juan,
　　　13th cent.—Legends
　　Segura, Isabel de, 13th cent.—Legends
　　Teruel, Lovers of (Legend)
　BT Legends—Spain
Loves, First
　USE First loves
Lovet family
　USE Lovett family
Lovett family *(Not Subd Geog)*
　UF Lovet family
　　Lovit family
　　Lovitt family
Lovewell family
　USE Lovell family
Lovewell's Fight, 1725
　USE Pigwacket Fight, 1725
Lovewell's Pond, Battle of
　USE Pigwacket Fight, 1725
Lovill family
　USE Lovell family
Lovin family
　USE Loving family
Loving family *(Not Subd Geog)*
　UF Lovan family
　　Lovein family
　　Loveing family
　　Loven family
　　Lovern family
　　Lovin family
　　Lovingern family
　　Lovorn family
　　Lovvorn family
　RT Love family
　　Lovering family
Loving kindness (Buddhism)
　USE Compassion (Buddhism)
Lovingern family
　USE Loving family
Lovinggood family
　USE Levengood family
Lovingood family
　USE Levengood family
Lovington Cemetery (Ill.)
　USE Kellar Cemetery (Ill.)
Lovis-Corinth-Preis
　BT Art—Competitions—Germany (West)
Loviştea (Romania)
　UF Detresiunea Lovistea (Romania)
　　Ţara Loviştei (Romania)
Lovit family
　USE Lovett family
Lovitt family
　USE Lovett family

Lovlace family
　USE Lovelace family
Lovö (Sweden)
　UF Lovön (Sweden)
　BT Islands—Sweden
Lovön (Sweden)
　USE Lovö (Sweden)
Lovorn family
　USE Loving family
Lovozero Mountain (R.S.F.S.R.)
　BT Mountains—Russian S.F.S.R.
Lovran family
　USE Lovering family
Lovrin family
　USE Lovering family
Lovring family
　USE Lovering family
Lovtchorrite
　USE Lovchorrite
Lovvorn family
　USE Loving family
Low birth weight
　USE Birth weight, Low
Low blood pressure
　USE Hypotension
Low blood sugar
　USE Hypoglycemia
Low blood sugar in children
　USE Hypoglycemia in children
Low body temperature
　USE Hypothermia
Low budget cookery
　UF Austerity cookery
　　Budget cookery, Low
　　Cheap cookery
　　Economy cookery
　　Low cost cookery
　BT Cookery
Low-calorie cookery
　USE Low-calorie diet—Recipes
Low-calorie diet
　₁RM222.2₁
　UF Diet, Low-calorie
　BT Reducing diets
　NT Low-carbohydrate diet
　　Low-fat diet
　　Sugar-free diet
　— Recipes
　　UF Low-calorie cookery
　　BT Cookery
Low-carbohydrate cookery
　USE Low-carbohydrate diet—Recipes
Low-carbohydrate diet
　UF Diet, Low-carbohydrate
　BT Carbohydrates
　　Low-calorie diet
　　Reducing diets
　NT Sugar-free diet
　— Recipes
　　UF Low-carbohydrate cookery
　　BT Cookery
Low-cholesterol cookery
　USE Low-cholesterol diet—Recipes
Low-cholesterol diet
　₁RM237.75₁
　UF Diet, Low-cholesterol
　BT Heart—Diseases—Diet therapy
　　Low-fat diet
　RT Cholesterol
　— Recipes
　　₁RM237.75₁
　　UF Low-cholesterol cookery
　　BT Cookery
Low cost cookery
　USE Low budget cookery
Low countries
　USE Benelux countries
Low-cut neckline
　USE Décolletage
Low-dimensional topology
　₁QA612.14₁

Low-dimensional topology *(Continued)*
  UF Topology, Low-dimensional
  BT Algebraic topology
    Manifolds (Mathematics)
  NT Braid theory
    Covering spaces (Topology)
    Four-manifolds (Topology)
    Knot theory
    Link theory
    Three-manifolds (Topology)
Low energy electron diffraction
  UF LEED (Solids)
  BT Electrons—Diffraction
Low family
  USE Lowe family
Low-fat cookery
  USE Low-fat diet—Recipes
Low-fat diet
  UF Diet, Low-fat
    Fat-free diet
  BT Cookery for the sick
    Diet in disease
    Fat
    Low-calorie diet
    Reducing diets
  NT Low-cholesterol diet
  — Recipes
    UF Low-fat cookery
    BT Cookery
Low German authors
  USE Authors, Low German
Low German children's literature
  USE Children's literature, Low German
Low German drama
  [PT4821 (History)]
  [PT4837-PT4838 (Collections)]
  — Stories, plots, etc.
Low German folk literature
  USE Folk literature, Low German
Low German folk-songs
  USE Folk-songs, Low German
Low German hymns
  USE Hymns, Low German
Low German language
  [PF5601-5844]
  UF Plattdeutsch
  BT German language
    Germanic languages
  NT Dutch language
    Friesian language
  — To 1500
    [PF5631-8]
    UF Low German language—Old Low
      German, 750-1050
      Low German language—Middle
      Low German, 1050-1500
    RT Old Saxon language
  — Old Low German, 750-1050
    USE Dutch language—To 1500
      Low German language—To 1500
      Old Saxon language
  — Middle Low German, 1050-1500
    USE Low German language—To 1500
Low German literature
  [PT4801-4899]
  BT German literature
  NT Children's literature, Low German
    Folk literature, Low German
    German literature—Germany,
      Northern
  — To 1500
    [PT4813]
  — Early to 1500
    [PT4813]
Low German philology
Low German poetry *(May Subd Geog)*
  [PT4817-PT4820 (History)]
  [PT4834-PT4836 (Collections)]
  — To 1500
    [PT4813]

Low German proverbs
  USE Proverbs, Low German
Low German songs
  USE Songs, Low German
Low German wit and humor
  (May Subd Geog)
  BT German wit and humor
Low gravity environments
  USE Reduced gravity environments
Low impact aerobic exercises
  (May Subd Geog)
  [RA781.15]
  UF Low impact aerobics
    Non impact aerobic exercises
    Non impact aerobics
    Soft aerobic exercises
    Soft aerobics
  BT Aerobic exercises
Low impact aerobics
  USE Low impact aerobic exercises
Low income housing
  USE Housing
    Public housing
Low income people
  USE Poor
Low-intensity conflicts (Military science)
  (May Subd Geog)
    Here are entered works on non-nuclear operations
  ranging from terrorism and small wars to revolutions
  and counterrevolutions, which require limited mili-
  tary, paramilitary, or mixed political-economic-mili-
  tary responses that are short of national mobilization
  and that often occur in conjunction with host regimes
  and third countries.
  UF Conflicts, Low-intensity (Military
      science)
    Low-intensity operations (Military
      science)
    Low-level conflicts (Military science)
    Operations, Low-intensity (Military
      science)
    Small wars
    Wars, Small
  BT Limited war
Low-intensity operations (Military science)
  USE Low-intensity conflicts (Military
      science)
Low intraocular pressure
  USE Ocular hypotony
Low-level conflicts (Military science)
  USE Low-intensity conflicts (Military
      science)
Low-level radiation *(May Subd Geog)*
  UF Radiation, Low-level
  BT Radiation
Low-light photography
  USE Photography, Available light
Low-luminosity stars
  USE Dwarf stars
Low-necked dress
  USE Décolletage
Low-observables military airplanes
  USE Stealth aircraft
Low-phenylalanine cookery
  USE Low-phenylalanine diet—Recipes
Low-phenylalanine diet *(May Subd Geog)*
  BT Low-protein diet
  RT Phenylalanine
  — Recipes
    UF Low-phenylalanine cookery
Low-phosphate diet
  BT Diet in disease
    Phosphates
Low-potassium cookery
  USE Low-potassium diet—Recipes
Low-potassium diet
  UF Diet, Low-potassium
    Potassium-free diet
  BT Diet therapy
    Potassium
  — Recipes
    UF Low-potassium cookery

  BT Cookery
Low power television *(May Subd Geog)*
  [HE8700.7-HE8700.72 (Broadcasting)]
  UF LPTV
    Television, Low power
  BT Television broadcasting
Low pressure systems (Meteorology)
  USE Lows (Meteorology)
Low-protein cookery
  USE Low-protein diet—Recipes
Low-protein diet
  UF Dietary proteins
  BT Diet in disease
    Proteins in human nutrition
  NT Low-phenylalanine diet
  — Recipes
    UF Low-protein cookery
    BT Cookery for the sick
Low radar signature military airplanes
  USE Stealth aircraft
Low signatures military airplanes
  USE Stealth aircraft
Low sodium cookery
  USE Salt-free diet—Recipes
Low sodium diet
  USE Salt-free diet
Low Sorbian language
  USE Lower Sorbian language
Low-sugar diet
  USE Sugar-free diet
Low temperature biochemistry
  USE Cryobiochemistry
Low temperature biology
  USE Cryobiology
Low temperature carbonization of coal
  USE Coal—Carbonization
Low temperature crystals
  USE Crystals at low temperatures
Low temperature engineering
  UF Cryogenic engineering
    Cryogenics
  BT Engineering
    Low temperatures
  NT Cryoelectronics
    Cryogenic gyroscopes
    Crystals at low temperatures
    Gases—Liquefaction
    Materials at low temperatures
    Plastics at low temperatures
    Refrigeration and refrigerating
      machinery
Low temperature materials
  USE Materials at low temperatures
Low temperature metals
  USE Metals at low temperatures
Low temperature physics
  USE Low temperatures
Low temperature plasmas
  [QC718]
  UF Cold plasmas
    Plasmas, Low temperature
  BT Plasma (Ionized gases)
Low temperature preservation of organs,
  tissues, etc.
  USE Cryopreservation of organs, tissues,
      etc.
Low temperature research *(May Subd Geog)*
  [QC278]
  UF Cryogenics
  BT Low temperatures
    Research
    Temperature
    Thermochemistry
  RT Cold
    Gases—Liquefaction
  NT Cryobiochemistry
    Liquid air
    Thermomagnetism
Low temperature sanitary engineering
  USE Sanitary engineering, Low temperature

Low temperatures
    [QC278 (Physics)]
    [QD515 (Chemistry)]
    UF Cryogenics
         Low temperature physics
         Temperatures, Low
    RT Cold
    NT Adiabatic demagnetization
         Cryobiology
         Cryochemistry
         Crystals at low temperatures
         Helium at low temperatures
         Low temperature engineering
         Low temperature research
         Materials at low temperatures
         Oxygen at low temperatures
         Quantum liquids
         Quantum solids
         Solid helium
         Spin waves
         Superfluidity
Low vision (May Subd Geog)
    [RE91]
        Here are entered works on impairment of vision
such that there is significant visual handicap but also
significant usable residual vision.
    UF Vision, Low
    BT Vision disorders
Low vocabulary-high interest books
    USE High interest-low vocabulary books
Low-volume highways
    USE Low-volume roads
Low-volume roads (May Subd Geog)
    [TE228.5]
    UF Low-volume highways
    BT Roads
Low water crossings
    USE Fords (Stream crossings)
Low-yeast diet
    USE Yeast-free diet
Lowd family
    USE Loud family
Lowdan family
    USE Louden family
Lowde family
    USE Loud family
Lowden family
    USE Louden family
Lowdermilch family
    USE Lowdermilk family
Lowdermilk family (Not Subd Geog)
    UF Laudermilch family
         Laudermilk family
         Lautermilch family
         Lautermilche family
         Lautermilk family
         Lauttermilch family
         Loudermilch family
         Loudermilk family
         Lowdermilch family
Lowdon family
    USE Louden family
Lowe family (Not Subd Geog)
    UF Loe family
         Loew family
         Loewe family
         Low family
    RT Louw family
Lowe syndrome
    USE Lowe's syndrome
Lowe-Terrey-MacLachlan syndrome
    USE Lowe's syndrome
Lowel family
    USE Lowell family
Lowell (Mass.)
  — **Industries**
        NT Lowell National Historical Park
            (Mass.)
Lowell family (Not Subd Geog)
    UF Lowel family
    RT Lovell family

Lowell Island (Alaska)
    USE Renard Island (Alaska)
Lowell National Historical Park (Mass.)
    BT Historic sites—Massachusetts
         Lowell (Mass.)—Industries
         National parks and reserves—United
            States
         Parks—Massachusetts
    NT Old City Hall (Lowell, Mass.)
Lowell Town House (Lowell, Mass.)
    USE Old City Hall (Lowell, Mass.)
Löwen family
    USE Loewen family
Lowenfeld mosaic test
    BT Personality tests
         Projective techniques
Lowengart family
    USE Loewengart family
Löwens family
    USE Loewen family
Löwenz family
    USE Loewen family
Lower Avon River (England)
    USE Avon, River (Gloucestershire-Avon)
Lower Bay (N.Y. and N.J.)
    BT Bays—New Jersey
         Bays—New York (State)
Lower California (Mexico)
    USE Baja California (Mexico)
Lower Carniola (Slovenia)
    USE Dolenjsko (Slovenia)
Lower Circassian language
    USE Adyghe language
Lower East Side (New York, N.Y.)
    (Not Subd Geog)
    UF East Side, Lower (New York, N.Y.)
         New York (N.Y.). Lower East Side
Lower family
    USE Lohr family
Lower Geyser Basin (Wyo.)
    UF Geyser Basin, Lower (Wyo.)
    BT Geysers—Wyoming
Lower Himalaya Mountains
    USE Lesser Himalaya Mountains
Lower ionosphere
    BT Ionosphere
    NT D region
         E region
Lower jaw
    USE Mandible
Lower larynx
    USE Syrinx (of birds)
Lower Lough Erne (Northern Ireland)
    USE Erne, Lower Lough (Northern Ireland)
Lower Manitou Lake (Ont.)
    UF Manitou Lake, Lower (Ont.)
    BT Lakes—Ontario
Lower Paleolithic period
    USE Paleolithic period, Lower
Lower Peninsula (Mich.)
    BT Peninsulas—Michigan
Lower Pima language
    USE Pima Bajo language
Lower Silesia (Poland and Germany)
    USE Silesia, Lower (Poland and Germany)
Lower Silurian period
    USE Geology, Stratigraphic—Ordovician
         Paleobotany—Ordovician
         Paleontology—Ordovician
Lower Sorbian language (May Subd Geog)
    UF Low Sorbian language
    BT Sorbian languages
Lower Styria (Slovenia)
    USE Styria, Lower (Slovenia)
Lower Town (Ottawa, Ont.)
    (Not Subd Geog)
    UF Ottawa (Ont.). Lower Town
Lower Umpqua language
    USE Kuitsh language
Lowery family
    USE Lowry family

Lowe's oculocerebrorenal syndrome
    USE Lowe's syndrome
Lowe's syndrome (May Subd Geog)
    [RJ399.L68 (Pediatrics)]
    UF Lowe syndrome
         Lowe-Terrey-MacLachlan syndrome
         Lowe's oculocerebrorenal syndrome
         Oculo-cerebro-renal syndrome
         Oculocerebrorenal syndrome
    BT Amino acids—Metabolism—Disorders
         Mental retardation
         Renal tubular transport, Disorders of
         Syndromes
         X chromosome—Abnormalities
Lowestoft, Oriental
    USE China trade porcelain
         Porcelain, Chinese
Lowestoft porcelain
    [NK4339.L7]
    UF Porcelain, Lowestoft
Lowestoft porcelain, Oriental
    USE Porcelain, Chinese
LoWiili (African people)
    UF Oulé (African people)
    BT Ethnology—Burkina Faso
         Lobi (African people)
LoWiili (African people) art
    USE Art, LoWiili (African people)
Lowk family
    USE Loucks family
Lowks family
    USE Loucks family
Lowland fir
    USE Abies grandis
Lowland paddy
    USE Rice
Lowland rice
    USE Rice
Lowland rice, Rainfed
    USE Rainfed lowland rice
Lowland Scots language
    USE Scots language
Lowland white fir
    USE Abies grandis
Lowlands (Scotland)
    UF Central Lowlands (Scotland)
         Scottish Lowlands (Scotland)
Lownbury family
    USE Lounsbury family
Lownsberry family
    USE Lounsbury family
Lownsburry family
    USE Lounsbury family
Lownsbury family
    USE Lounsbury family
Lowrance family
    USE Lawrence family
Lowrey family
    USE Lowry family
Lowrie family
    USE Lowry family
Lowring family
    USE Loring family
Lowry family (Not Subd Geog)
    UF Laure family
         Laury family
         Lawrey family
         Lawry family
         Lorey family
         Loughrey family
         Loury family
         Lowery family
         Lowrey family
         Lowrie family
Lows (Meteorology) (May Subd Geog)
    [QC880.4.L68]
    UF Depressions (Meteorology)
         Low pressure systems (Meteorology)
    BT Air masses
         Atmospheric pressure
         Cyclones

Lowth family *(Not Subd Geog)*
Lowther Castle (Lowther, Cumbria)
  UF Lowther Hall (Lowther, Cumbria)
  BT Castles—England
Lowther family *(Not Subd Geog)*
  UF Louthrie family
       Lowthre family
Lowther Hall (Lowther, Cumbria)
  USE Lowther Castle (Lowther, Cumbria)
Lowthorp family
  USE Lothrop family
Lowthre family
  USE Lowther family
LOX
  USE Liquid oxygen
Loxagrotis
  [QL561.N7]
  BT Noctuidae
Loxagrotis albicosta
  [QL561.N7]
  UF Bean cutworm
       Western bean cutworm
  BT Cutworms
Loxoceridae
  USE Psilidae
Loxodonta africana
  USE African elephant
Loxodrome
  UF Helix, Spherical
       Loxodromic spiral
       Rhumb-line
       Spherical helix
       Spiral, Loxodromic
  BT Curves
       Sphere
Loxodromic spiral
  USE Loxodrome
Loxops
  [QL696.P243]
  BT Drepanididae
Loxosceles
  [QL458.42.L6]
  UF Recluse spiders
  BT Loxoscelidae
Loxosceles reclusa
  [QL458.42.L6]
  UF Brown recluse spider
       Recluse spider, Brown
Loxosceles unicolor
  [QL458.42.L6]
Loxoscelidae
  [QL458.42.L6]
  UF Brown spiders
  BT Spiders
  NT Loxosceles
Loxosomatidae
  NT Loxosomella
Loxosomella
  [QL400.5.L6]
  BT Loxosomatidae
Loxosomella macginitieorum
  [QL400.5.L6]
Loxosomella prenanti
  [QL400.5.L6]
Loxostege
  [QL561.P9]
  BT Pyralidae
Loy family *(Not Subd Geog)*
Loyalists, Afrikaner
  USE Afrikaner loyalists
Loyalists, American
  USE American loyalists
Loyalists, United Empire
  USE United Empire loyalists
Loyalty
  [BJ1533.L8 (Ethics)]
  BT Conduct of life
  RT Constancy
  NT Allegiance
       Patriotism

Loyalty investigations
  USE Loyalty-security program, 1947-
Loyalty oaths *(May Subd Geog)*
  UF Loyalty tests
       Teachers' oaths
  BT Academic freedom
       Internal security
       Loyalty-security program, 1947-
       Oaths
Loyalty program
  USE Loyalty-security program, 1947-
Loyalty-security program, 1947-
  (May Subd Geog)
  UF Federal loyalty-security program,
       1947-
       Loyalty investigations
       Loyalty program
       Loyalty-security program, 1947- —
         United States
       Loyalty tests
       Security investigations
       Security program
       Security tests
  BT Internal security—United States
  SA *subdivision* Security measures *under*
       types of buildings, installations, and
       industries and names of individual
       corporate bodies
  NT Industrial security program (United
       States)
       Loyalty oaths
Loyalty-security program, 1947-
  — United States
      USE Loyalty-security program, 1947-
Loyalty tests
  USE Loyalty oaths
       Loyalty-security program, 1947-
Loyd family
  USE Lloyd family
Loyde family
  USE Lloyd family
Loyed family
  USE Lloyd family
Loygob language
  USE Kwafi language
Loykop language
  USE Kwafi language
Lozi (African people)
  [DT963.42]
  UF Barotse (African people)
       Barotsi (African people)
       Barozi (African people)
       Barutse (African people)
       Marotse (African people)
       Rotse (African people)
       Rozi (African people)
  BT Bantus
       Ethnology—Zambia
  NT Missions to Lozi (African people)
Lozi language
  [PL8460]
  UF Kololo language
       Sikololo language
       Silozi language
  BT Bantu languages
       Sotho-Tswana languages
Lozi law
  USE Law, Lozi
Lozier family *(Not Subd Geog)*
  UF Losier family
  RT Lasher family
       Le Sueur family
       Lesher family
LP gas
  USE Liquefied petroleum gas
Lp spaces
  UF Spaces, Lp
  BT Function spaces
       Functional analysis
LPAD (Psychological test)
  USE Learning Potential Assessment Device

LPG
  USE Liquefied petroleum gas
LPTV
  USE Low power television
LSD
  USE Lysergic acid diethylamide
LSI 11 (Computer)
  [QA76.8.L]
  BT Electronic digital computers
  — **Programming**
LSP (Computer grammar)
  USE Linguistic String Parser (Computer
         grammar)
LSR (Chemical reagents)
  USE Lanthanide shift reagents
LT Vz 35 (Tank)
  USE PzKpfw 35(t) (Tank)
Lu-ch'üan Shui (China)
  USE Hsiao River (China)
Lu family *(Not Subd Geog)*
  [CS1169.L]
Lu-ganda
  USE Ganda language
Lu Mountains (China)
  UF Li Shan (China)
       Lu Shan (China)
       Lu Shan Range (China)
  BT Mountains—China
Lu Shan (China)
  USE Lu Mountains (China)
Lu Shan Range (China)
  USE Lu Mountains (China)
Lü shih
  [PL2309.L83 (History)]
  [PL2519.L83 (Collections)]
  BT Chinese poetry
Lu-wumbu language
  USE Vili language
Lua' (Mon-Khmer tribe)
  USE Lawa (Mon-Khmer tribe)
Lua language
  USE Nielim language
Luaan language
  USE Bajau language
Luan He (China)
  USE Luan River (China)
Luan Ho (China)
  USE Luan River (China)
Luan River (China)
  UF Luan He (China)
       Luan Ho (China)
  BT Rivers—China
Luang River (Thailand)
  USE Huai Luang River (Thailand)
Luangiua language
  USE Leuangiua language
Luango language
  USE Yombe language
Luangwa River (Zambia and Mozambique)
  UF Aruângua River (Zambia and
         Mozambique)
       Loangwa River (Zambia and
         Mozambique)
       Rio Aruângua (Zambia and
         Mozambique)
  BT Rivers—Mozambique
       Rivers—Zambia
Luaniua language
  USE Leuangiua language
Luba (African people)
  [DT650.L8]
  UF Baluba (African people)
       Turruba (African people)
       Waluba (African people)
  BT Bantus
       Ethnology—Zaire
  NT Hemba (African people)
       Kaonde (African people)
       Songe (African people)
Luba folk literature
  USE Folk literature, Luba

Luba-Hemba (African people)
USE Hemba (African people)
Luba-Kaonde language
USE Kaonde language
Luba-Katanga language
UF Chiluba language (Luba-Katanga)
Katanga language
Kiluba language
Tshiluba language (Luba-Katanga)
BT Bantu languages
Luba language, Northeastern
USE Songe language
Luba language, Southern
USE Sanga language
Luba language, Western
USE Luba-Lulua language
Luba-Lulua language
UF Ciluba language
Kalebwe language (Luba-Lulua)
Luba language, Western
Lulua language
Luva language
Tshiluba language (Luba-Lulua)
Western Luba language
BT Bantu languages
Luba-Lulua proverbs
USE Proverbs, Luba-Lulua
Luba-Lulua riddles
USE Riddles, Luba-Lulua
Luba-Sanga language
USE Sanga language
Lubaantun (City) (Not Subd Geog)
[F1435.1.L83]
BT Belize—Antiquities
Cities and towns, Ruined, extinct, etc.
—Belize
NT Mitchell-Hedges skull
Lubavitch-Chabad
USE Habad
Lubbock Lake Site (Tex.)
BT Texas—Antiquities
Lubbockia
[QL444.C73]
BT Oncaeidae
Lübeck Bay (Germany)
UF Lübecker Bucht (Germany)
BT Bays—Germany (East)
Bays—Germany (West)
Lübeck-Büchener Eisenbahn
BT Railroads—Germany (West)
Lübeck-Elbe Canal (Germany)
USE Elbe-Lübeck Canal (Germany)
Lübeck law
UF Law, Lubish
Lubish law
BT Law—Germany
SA special legal headings with Lübeck law
added in parentheses, e.g.
Commercial law (Lübeck law)
Lübeck, Peace of, 1629
[D263]
BT Thirty Years' War, 1618-1648
Lübecker Bucht (Germany)
USE Lübeck Bay (Germany)
Lubéron Mountains (France)
UF Lébéron (France)
Montagne du Lubéron (France)
Montagnes du Lubéron (France)
BT Mountains—France
Lubish law
USE Lübeck law
Lublin Castle (Lublin, Poland)
USE Zamek Lubelski (Lublin, Poland)
Lubomirski Rebellion, 1665-1666
USE Poland—History—Rebellion of
Lubomirski, 1665-1666
Lubricants, Synthetic
USE Synthetic lubricants
Lubricating oil additives industry
(May Subd Geog)
[HD9660.L8-84]

BT Lubricating oils—Additives
Lubricating oils
UF Motor oils
Oils, Lubricating
BT Lubrication and lubricants
NT Oil filters
Synthetic lubricants
— **Additives**
NT Lubricating oil additives industry
— **Effect of temperature on**
— **Viscosity**
Lubricating systems
USE Lubrication systems
Lubrication and lubricants
[TJ1075-1081]
UF Grease
BT Friction
Machinery
Metals—Surfaces
Tribology
RT Bearings (Machinery)
Lubrication systems
Oils and fats
Petroleum products
SA names of lubricants, e.g. Olive oil;
Rosin oil; also subdivision
Lubrication under subjects, e.g.
Automobiles—Lubrication;
Locomotives—Lubrication
NT Fluid-film bearings
Lubricating oils
Metal-working lubricants
Oil-feeders
Solid lubricants
Synthetic lubricants industry
— **Additives**
— **Effect of temperature on**
— Tariff
USE Tariff on lubricants
Lubrication and lubricants industry
(May Subd Geog)
[HD9579.L8]
Lubrication systems
UF Lubricating systems
Lubricators
RT Lubrication and lubricants
NT Airplanes—Lubrication systems
Automobiles—Motors—Lubrication
systems
Compressors—Lubrication systems
Diesel motor—Lubrication systems
Excavating machinery—Lubrication
systems
Locomotives—Lubrication systems
Oil-feeders
Steam-turbines—Lubrication systems
Tractors—Lubrication systems
Turbogenerators—Lubrication systems
Lubricators
USE Lubrication systems
Lubukusu language
USE Bukusu language
Lubuska Region (Poland and Germany)
USE Lubusz Region (Poland and Germany)
Lubusz Land (Poland and Germany)
USE Lubusz Region (Poland and Germany)
Lubusz Region (Poland and Germany)
[DK4600.L86]
UF Lubuska Region (Poland and
Germany)
Lubusz Land (Poland and Germany)
Ziemia Lubuska (Poland and
Germany)
Lucani (Italic people)
BT Ethnology—Italy
Italic peoples
Lucania (Fish)
[QL638.C96]
BT Cyprinodontidae
Lucanidae
[QL596.L8]

BT Beetles
NT Lucanus
Lucanus
[QL596.L8]
BT Lucanidae
Lucarachne
USE Mysmenopsis
Lucas family (Not Subd Geog)
UF Lucass family
Luccus family
Lucus family
Lucust family
Lukas family
Lukess family
Lucass family
USE Lucas family
Lucayan Indians
[F1655]
UF Ceboynas
Lucayans
BT Indians of the West Indies
Lucayans
USE Lucayan Indians
Lucazi language
UF Luchazi language
Lujazi language
Ponda language
BT Bantu languages
Luccus family
USE Lucas family
Luce family (Not Subd Geog)
UF Loos family
Loose family
Lose family
Lous family
Louse family
Luice family
Luse family
RT Lucey family
Lucius family
Lucernariidae
USE Stauromedusae
Lucerne (Plant)
USE Alfalfa
Lucerne flea
[QL503.S6 (General)]
[SB945.L8 (Pest)]
UF Sminthurus viridis
Lucerne Lake (Switzerland)
UF Four Forest Cantons, Lake of
(Switzerland)
Lac des quatre cantons (Switzerland)
Lake Lucerne (Switzerland)
Vierwaldstätter-See (Switzerland)
BT Lakes—Switzerland
Lucey family (Not Subd Geog)
UF Lucie family
Lucy family
RT Luce family
Luchazi language
USE Lucazi language
Luchon Valley (France)
BT Valleys—France
Lucid (Computer program language)
[QA76.73.L]
BT Programming languages (Electronic
computers)
Lucie family
USE Lucey family
Lucifer
USE Devil
Lucilia
[QL537.C24]
BT Blowflies
Green-bottle flies
NT Lucilia cuprina
Lucilia cuprina (May Subd Geog)
[QL534.C24]
BT Lucilia
Lucinidae
NT Macrocallista

Luciobrama
  ₍QL638.C94₎
  BT Cyprinidae
Luciobrama macrocephalus
  ₍QL638.C94₎
  UF Luciobrama typus
      Synodus macrocephalus
Luciobrama typus
  USE Luciobrama macrocephalus
Lucioperca lucioperca
  USE Zander
Lucioperca sandra
  USE Zander
Lucite
  UF Methyl methacrylate resin
  BT Gums and resins, Synthetic
Lucius family (Not Subd Geog)
  RT Luce family
Luck, Seven gods of
  USE Seven gods of fortune
Luck family (Not Subd Geog)
  UF Lucke family
  RT Luckett family
Lucke family
  USE Luck family
Luckett family (Not Subd Geog)
  RT Luck family
Luckman, Stewart. Rokker V
  UF Rokker V (Sculpture)
  BT Steel sculpture—20th century—United
      States
      Steel sculpture, American
Lucky gods, Seven
  USE Seven gods of fortune
Luckynut thevetia
  USE Thevetia peruviana
Lucumí (Cultus)
  USE Santeria (Cultus)
Lucus family
  USE Lucas family
Lucus Feroniae (Italy : Ancient sanctuary)
  (Not Subd Geog)
  BT Italy—Antiquities
      Temples—Italy
Lucust family
  USE Lucas family
Lucy family
  USE Lucey family
Luddites
  ₍DA535₎
  BT Great Britain—History—1800-1837
      Labor and laboring classes—England
      Machinery in industry—Sabotage
Ludeman family (Not Subd Geog)
  UF Ludemann family
      Ludman family
      Ludmann family
Ludemann family
  USE Ludeman family
Ludendorff Bridge (Remagen, Germany)
  UF Remagen Bridge (Remagen, Germany)
  BT Bridges—Germany (West)
Luder family
  USE Luther family
Lüders bands
  ₍TA418.14₎
  UF Lüders lines
      Stretcher strains
  BT Strains and stresses
      Stress-strain curves
Lüders lines
  USE Lüders bands
Ludi saeculares
  USE Secular games
Ludi tarentini
  USE Secular games
Ludi terentini
  USE Secular games
Ludic dialect
  ₍PH531-539₎
  UF Lydi dialect

  BT Karelian language
Ludicrous, The
  USE Comic, The
      Wit and humor
Ludman family
  USE Ludeman family
Ludmann family
  USE Ludeman family
Ludruk
      Here are entered general works and those that
  deal solely with the presentation of Ludruk plays on
  the stage. The texts of the Ludruk plays and works
  treating of them from a literary point of view are
  entered under Ludruk plays.
Ludruk plays
      Here are entered the texts of the Ludruk plays and
  works treating of them from a literary point of view.
  General works and those that deal solely with the
  presentation of Ludruk plays on the stage are entered
  under Ludruk.
  BT Javanese drama
Ludwig-Donau-Main Canal (Germany)
  UF Ludwigs Kanal (Germany)
      Ludwigskanal (Germany)
  BT Canals—Germany (West)
Ludwigs Kanal (Germany)
  USE Ludwig-Donau-Main Canal (Germany)
Ludwigskanal (Germany)
  USE Ludwig-Donau-Main Canal (Germany)
Lueder family (Not Subd Geog)
  UF Lueders family
Lueders family
  USE Lueder family
Luehdorfia
  ₍QL561.P2₎
  BT Papilionidae
Luehdorfia japonica
  ₍QL561.P2₎
Luehdorfia puziloi
  ₍QL561.P2₎
Lueloff family
  USE Loeloff family
Luenas (African people)
  UF Luenas (Bantu tribe)
      Lwenas (African people)
  BT Bantus
      Ethnology—Angola
Luenas (Bantu tribe)
  USE Luenas (African people)
Luets family
  USE Lutz family
Luffkin family
  USE Lufkin family
Lufkin family (Not Subd Geog)
  UF Luffkin family
      Luftkin family
Luftkin family
  USE Lufkin family
Luganda language
  USE Ganda language
Lugar family (Not Subd Geog)
  UF Luger family
Lugbara (African people)
  UF Logbara (African tribe)
      Ma'di (African people)
  BT Ethnology—Uganda
      Ethnology—Zaire
  — Medicine
      BT Medicine, Primitive
Lugbara language
  USE Logbara language
Luger family
  USE Lugar family
Luger pistol
  ₍TS537₎
  BT Pistols
Luggage
  ₍TS2301.L₎
  UF Baggage
  BT Leather industry and trade
      Travel
  NT Airlines—Baggage

      Trunks (Luggage)
Luggage industry (May Subd Geog)
Lugier
  USE Lygii
Lugisu language
  USE Gisu language
Lugo family (Not Subd Geog)
Lugooli language
  USE Logooli language
Luguaret language
  USE Logbara language
Luguru (African people)
  UF Luguru (Bantu tribe)
      Ruguru (African people)
  BT Bantus
      Ethnology—Tanzania
Luguru (Bantu tribe)
  USE Luguru (African people)
Lugware language
  USE Logbara language
Luhanga dialect
  USE Hanga dialect (Kenya)
Luhya (African people)
  USE Luyia (African people)
Luhya language
  USE Luyia language
Luian language
  USE Luwian language
Luice family
  USE Luce family
Luichow Peninsula (China)
  UF Lei-chou Peninsula (China)
      Leizhou Peninsula (China)
      Lieh-cho Peninsula (China)
  BT Peninsulas—China
Luiseño Indians
  ₍E99.L9₎
  BT Indians of North America
  NT Agua Caliente Indians
  — Religion and mythology
      ₍E99.L9₎
  — Wars
Luiseño language
  BT Shoshonean languages
Lûish language
  USE Luwian language
Luisia
  ₍QK495.O64 (Botany)₎
  ₍SB409 (Culture)₎
  BT Orchids
Luisish languages
  USE Cupan languages
Luján, Nuestra Señora de
  USE Luján, Our Lady of
Luján, Our Lady of
  ₍BT660.L82₎
  UF Luján, Nuestra Señora de
      Nuestra Señora de Luján
      Our Lady of Luján
  BT Mary, Blessed Virgin, Saint—Cult—
      Argentina
Lujauvrite
  USE Lujavrite
Lujavrite (May Subd Geog)
  UF Lujauvrite
  BT Rocks, Igneous
Lujazi language
  USE Lucazi language
Lukanani
  USE Peacock bass
Lukas family
  USE Lucas family
Łukasiewicz algebras
  USE Algebras, Łukasiewicz
Luker family (Not Subd Geog)
Lukess family
  USE Lucas family
LuKete language
  USE Kete language
Lukhai language
  USE Lushai language

Lukiga language
  USE Kiga language
LuKisa dialect
  USE Kisa dialect
Lukö language
  USE Yakö language
Lukouchiao Incident, 1937
  USE Marco Polo Bridge Incident, 1937
Lukuba language
  USE Bushongo language
Lulab (Jewish cultus)
  USE Lulav
Lulav
  UF Lulab (Jewish cultus)
  BT Judaism—Liturgical objects
      Palms
Lule Indians
  [F2821]
  BT Indians of South America
  NT Tonocote Indians
      Vilela Indians
Lule language
  [PM6366]
  RT Tonocote language
  NT Cacán language
Lull family (Not Subd Geog)
Lullabies
  UF Cradle songs
      Slumber songs
  BT Children's poetry
      Children's songs
      Nursery rhymes
      Songs
Lullabies, American (May Subd Geog)
  UF American lullabies
Lullabies, Brazilian (May Subd Geog)
  UF Brazilian lullabies
Lullabies, Cuna (May Subd Geog)
  UF Cuna lullabies
Lullabies, English (May Subd Geog)
  UF English lullabies
Lullabies, French (May Subd Geog)
  UF French lullabies
Lullabies, German (May Subd Geog)
  UF German lullabies
Lullabies, Hindi (May Subd Geog)
  UF Hindi lullabies
Lullabies, Italian (May Subd Geog)
  UF Italian lullabies
Lullabies, Japanese (May Subd Geog)
  UF Japanese lullabies
Lullabies, Malay (May Subd Geog)
  UF Malay lullabies
Lullabies, Mongo (May Subd Geog)
  UF Mongo lullabies
Lullabies, Norwegian (May Subd Geog)
  UF Norwegian lullabies
Lullabies, Panjabi (May Subd Geog)
  UF Panjabi lullabies
Lullabies, Provençal (May Subd Geog)
  UF Provençal lullabies
Lullabies, Puerto Rican (May Subd Geog)
  UF Puerto Rican lullabies
Lullabies, Russian (May Subd Geog)
  UF Russian lullabies
Lullabies, Salvadorian (May Subd Geog)
  UF Salvadorian lullabies
Lullabies, Spanish (May Subd Geog)
  UF Spanish lullabies
Lullabies, Tamil (May Subd Geog)
  UF Tamil lullabies
Lullabies, Thai (May Subd Geog)
  UF Thai lullabies
Lullabies, Urdu (May Subd Geog)
  UF Urdu lullabies
Lullula arborea
  USE Wood lark
Luloff family
  USE Loeloff family
Lulogooli language
  USE Logooli language

Lulua language
  USE Luba-Lulua language
Luluhya language
  USE Luyia language
Lulumbamba Site (Ecuador)
  USE Pucará de Rumicucho Site (Ecuador)
Luluyia language
  USE Luyia language
Lumas family
  USE Loomis family
Lumasaaba language
  USE Gisu language
Lumbago
  USE Backache
Lumbar curve
  [QL821 (Comparative anatomy)]
  [QM111 (Human anatomy)]
  UF Curve, Lumbar
  BT Spine
Lumbar puncture
  USE Spine—Puncture
Lumbar vertebrae
  USE Vertebrae, Lumbar
Lumbee Indians
  [E99.C91]
  UF Croatan Indians
      Hatteras Indians
  BT Algonquian Indians
      Indians of North America
Lumber
  [TS800-TS837]
  BT Forests and forestry
      Wood products
  RT Timber
  SA kinds of lumber, e.g. Cypress; Walnut
  NT Hardwoods
      Pit-wood
      Planing-mills
      Sawmills
— Drying
    [TS837]
    UF Lumber—Seasoning
        Lumber drying
        Wood—Drying
    BT Wood—Preservation
— Law and legislation (May Subd Geog)
— Mensuration
— Rate-books
    [HE2116.L8]
— Seasoning
    USE Lumber—Drying
— Storage
— Transportation
    [HE199.5.L]
— — Law and legislation
      (May Subd Geog)
Lumber camps (May Subd Geog)
  UF Logging camps
  BT Camps
— Washington (State)
    NT Camp Grisdale (Wash.)
Lumber drying
  USE Lumber—Drying
Lumber industry and trade
  USE Lumber trade
Lumber sheds
  [TH4485]
Lumber trade (May Subd Geog)
  [HD9750-9769]
  UF Lumber industry and trade
  BT Forests and forestry
  RT Lumbering
  NT Pulpwood industry
      Staves and stave trade
      Strikes and lockouts—Lumber trade
      Timber
— Collective labor agreements
    USE Collective labor agreements—
         Lumber trade
— Credit guides
    [HF5585.L8]

— Tables
— United States
— — Credit guides
Lumber-yards (May Subd Geog)
  [TH4485]
Lumbering (May Subd Geog)
  [SD538-SD557 (Forestry)]
  [TS800-TS837 (Manufactures)]
    Here are entered works on the manufacturing of
  logs into lumber. Works on the felling of trees
  through the transporting of logs to sawmills or to a
  place of sale are entered under Logging.
  BT Forestry engineering
      Forests and forestry
      Trees
  RT Lumber trade
  NT Communication in lumbering
      Explosives in lumbering
      Logging
      Lumbermen
— Accidents
    NT Lumbering—Safety measures
— Cost control
— Fires and fire prevention
    USE Forest fires—Prevention and
         control
— Law and legislation (May Subd Geog)
— Machinery
    UF Lumbering machinery
    NT Woodworking machinery
— — Electric driving
      [TS850]
— — Parts
— Safety measures
    BT Lumbering—Accidents
— Vocational guidance
    [SD387.F6]
    BT Lumbermen
Lumbering in art
Lumbering machinery
  USE Lumbering—Machinery
Lumberjacks
  USE Loggers
Lumbermen (May Subd Geog)
  [HD8039.L9 (Labor)]
  [TS805-TS806]
  BT Lumbering
  NT Collective labor agreements—Lumber
        trade
      Loggers
      Lumbering—Vocational guidance
      Strikes and lockouts—Lumber trade
      Trade-unions—Lumbermen
      Wages—Lumbermen
— Recreation
    NT Log-chopping (Sports)
— Songs and music
    [M1977.L8]
    [M1978.L8]
    BT Labor and laboring classes—Songs
        and music
— Sweden
    NT Lumbermen's Strike, Sweden, 1975
Lumbermen's Strike, Sweden, 1975
  BT Lumbermen—Sweden
      Strikes and lockouts—Lumber trade—
        Sweden
      Strikes and lockouts—Sweden
Lumbosacral region
  BT Back
Lumbricidae
  NT Dendrobaena
Lumbricus terrestris
  USE Earthworms
Lumbu language
  USE Limbu language
Lumbu language (Gabon)
  UF Ilumbu language
  BT Bantu languages
Lumbus family
  USE Lambers family

Lumbwa (African people)
  USE Kipsigis (African people)
Luminescence
  BT Afterglow (Physics)
     Light
     Light sources
     Radiation
  NT Airglow
     Bioluminescence
     Chemiluminescence
     Electroluminescence
     Fluorescence
     Optical resonance
     Phosphorescence
     Phosphors
     Photoluminescence
     Scintillators
     Sonoluminescence
     Thermoluminescence
Luminescence, Animal
  USE Bioluminescence
Luminescence, Plant
  USE Plant luminescence
Luminescence analysis
  USE Fluorimetry
     Phosphorimetry
Luminescence spectroscopy
  $[QC476.6]$
  UF Spectroscopy, Luminescence
  BT Spectrum analysis
  NT Fluorescence spectroscopy
     Phosphorescence spectroscopy
Luminescent postage-stamps
  (May Subd Geog)
  UF Tagged postage-stamps
  BT Postage-stamps
Luminescent substances
  USE Phosphors
Luminism (Art) *(May Subd Geog)*
  $[ND1351.5]$
  BT Impressionism (Art)
     Landscape painting—19th century
     Landscape painting, American
Luminosity function of stars
  USE Stars—Luminosity function
Luminous bacteria
  USE Bacteria, Luminous
Luminous clouds
  USE Noctilucent clouds
Lumiprints
  $[NE2685]$
  UF Contact prints
  BT Cliché-verre
     Glass painting and staining
     Photography—Negatives
     Photography—Reproduction of plans,
        drawings, etc.
Lumis family
  USE Loomis family
Lumley family *(Not Subd Geog)*
Lummas family
  USE Loomis family
Lummi Indians
  $[E99.L95]$
  BT Coast Salish Indians
     Indians of North America
Lummi language
  $[PM1656]$
  BT Salishan languages
Lummis family
  USE Loomis family
Lummos family
  USE Loomis family
Lummus family
  USE Loomis family
Lummys family
  USE Loomis family
Lummyus family
  USE Loomis family
Lump-fish
  USE Lumpfish

Lump-fish fisheries
  USE Lumpfish fisheries
Lumpfish *(May Subd Geog)*
  $[QL638.C9]$
  UF Cyclopterus lumpus
     Lump-fish
  BT Cyclopterus
Lumpfish fisheries *(May Subd Geog)*
  $[SH351.L85]$
  UF Lump-fish fisheries
  BT Fisheries
Lumpsuckers
  USE Cyclopteridae
Lumpy jaw
  USE Actinomycosis
Lumpy skin disease *(May Subd Geog)*
  $[SF967.L8]$
  UF Pseudo-urticaria
  BT Cattle—Diseases
     Poxvirus diseases
     Veterinary virology
Lumpy skin disease virus
  BT Poxviruses
Luna flora
  USE Bread flowers
Luna moth
  BT Moths
Lunacy
  USE Insanity
Lunambe dialect
  UF Lunumbe dialect
  BT Asaro language
Lunar bases
  UF Lunar construction engineering
     Moon bases
     Moon settlements
  BT Extraterrestrial bases
  NT Lunar landing sites
     Moon—Exploration
     Tranquility Base (Moon)
Lunar basins
  UF Basins, Lunar
     Lunar multiring basins
     Lunar multiring crater structures
     Multiring basins, Lunar
     Multiring crater structures, Lunar
  BT Cratering
     Lunar craters
     Lunar geology
Lunar cars
  USE Moon cars
Lunar construction engineering
  USE Lunar bases
Lunar craters *(May Subd Geog)*
  $[QB591]$
  UF Craters, Lunar
  BT Cratering
     Moon—Surface
  NT Fra Mauro Crater (Moon)
     Lunar basins
Lunar eclipses
  USE Eclipses, Lunar
Lunar electric properties
  USE Moon—Electric properties
Lunar excursion module
  UF LEM
     Lunar module
  BT Project Apollo
     Space vehicles
  — Radar equipment
Lunar expeditions
  USE Space flight to the moon
Lunar exploration
  USE Moon—Exploration
Lunar figure
  USE Moon—Figure
Lunar flight
  USE Space flight to the moon
Lunar geodesy
  USE Selenodesy

Lunar geology *(May Subd Geog)*
  $[QB592]$
  UF Geology—Moon
     Geology, Lunar
  BT Moon
     Physical geology
  NT Lunar basins
     Lunar mineralogy
     Lunar petrology
     Lunar soil
     Lunar stratigraphy
Lunar globes
  USE Moon—Globes
Lunar gravitation
  USE Moon—Gravity
Lunar gravity
  USE Moon—Gravity
Lunar landing sites
  UF Moon landing sites
     Sites, Lunar landing
  BT Lunar bases
     Space vehicles—Landing
Lunar laser ranging
  UF Laser ranging, Lunar
     Ranging, Lunar laser
  BT Distances—Measurement
Lunar launching of artificial satellites
  USE Artificial satellites—Lunar launching
Lunar limb
  $[QB588]$
  UF Moon—Limb
Lunar magnetism
  USE Moon—Magnetic properties
Lunar mineralogy
  $[QB592]$
  BT Lunar geology
     Mineralogy
Lunar module
  USE Lunar excursion module
Lunar multiring basins
  USE Lunar basins
Lunar multiring crater structures
  USE Lunar basins
Lunar orbit
  USE Moon—Orbit
Lunar Orbiter (Artificial satellite)
  BT Artificial satellites—Moon
     Lunar probes
Lunar petrology *(May Subd Geog)*
  $[QB592]$
  UF Lunar rocks
     Moon rocks
  BT Lunar geology
     Petrology
Lunar photography
  UF Lunar spaceborne photography
     Moon photography
  BT Space photography
  NT Moon—Photographs
Lunar probes
  UF Moon probes
  BT Artificial satellites—Moon
     Outer space—Exploration
     Space probes
  NT Lunar Orbiter (Artificial satellite)
     Lunik (Lunar probes)
     Project Ranger
     Project Surveyor
Lunar Quarter Day (Buddhism)
  USE Uposatha Day
Lunar regolith
  USE Lunar soil
Lunar rocks
  USE Lunar petrology
Lunar satellite orbits
  USE Artificial satellites—Moon—Orbits
Lunar satellites
  USE Artificial satellites—Moon
Lunar soil
  $[QB592]$

UF Lunar regolith
    Soil, Lunar
BT Lunar geology
RT Moon—Surface
Lunar spaceborne photography
  USE Lunar photography
Lunar stratigraphic geology
  USE Lunar stratigraphy
Lunar stratigraphy
UF Lunar stratigraphic geology
    Moon—Stratigraphy
    Stratigraphy, Lunar
BT Geology, Stratigraphic
    Lunar geology
Lunar surface radio communication
    [TK6571.5.M6]
UF Radio—Installation on the moon
BT Moon
    Radio
Lunar surface vehicles
  USE Moon cars
Lunar tables
  USE Moon—Tables
Lunar tellurian
  USE Astronomical models
Lunar theory
  USE Moon, Theory of
Lunathyrium acrostichoides
  USE Deparia acrostichoides
Lunch bag cookery
  USE Lunchbox cookery
Lunch box cookery
  USE Lunchbox cookery
Lunch program (United States)
  USE National school lunch program
Lunch rooms
  USE Restaurants, lunch rooms, etc.
Lunchbag cookery
  USE Lunchbox cookery
Lunchbox cookery
    [TX735]
UF Brown bag lunch cookery
    Cookery, Lunchbox
    Lunch bag cookery
    Lunch box cookery
    Lunchbag cookery
    Packed lunch cookery
BT Cookery
    Luncheons
Luncheon of the boating party (Painting)
  USE Renoir, Auguste, 1841-1919.
      Luncheon of the boating party
Luncheons
    [TX735 (Home economics)]
BT Caterers and catering
    Cookery
    Entertaining
    Menus
    Table
RT Brunches
NT Lunchbox cookery
Lunchrooms
  USE Restaurants, lunch rooms, etc.
Lund, Battle of, 1676
    [DL728]
BT Scanian War, 1675-1679—Campaigns
    —Sweden
Lund family *(Not Subd Geog)*
UF Lunde family
Lund-Huntington chorea
  USE Huntington's chorea
Lunda, Northern (African people)
UF Alunda (African people)
    Arund (African people)
    Balunda (African people)
    Kalunda (African people)
    Valunda (African people)
BT Ethnology—Zaire
Lunda, Southern (African people)
UF Balunda (African people)

BT Ethnology—Angola
    Ethnology—Zambia
RT Ndembu (African people)
NT Missions to Southern Lunda (African
    people)
Lunda folk-songs
  USE Folk-songs, Lunda
Lunda language
    [PL8465]
BT Bantu languages
NT Luvale language
Lunda language, Northern
  USE Ruund language
Lundby I Site (Denmark)
  USE Lundby Site (Denmark)
Lundby II Site (Denmark)
  USE Lundby Site (Denmark)
Lundby III Site (Denmark)
  USE Lundby Site (Denmark)
Lundby Site (Denmark)
UF Lundby I Site (Denmark)
    Lundby II Site (Denmark)
    Lundby III Site (Denmark)
BT Denmark—Antiquities
Lunde family
  USE Lund family
Lundeen family
  USE Lundin family
Lundin family *(Not Subd Geog)*
UF Lundeen family
    Lundine family
    Lunding family
Lundine family
  USE Lundin family
Lunding family
  USE Lundin family
Lundquist family *(Not Subd Geog)*
UF Lundqvist family
    Lundqwist family
Lundqvist family
  USE Lundquist family
Lundqwist family
  USE Lundquist family
Lundsgård (Denmark)
BT Manors—Denmark
Lundu (Dance)
    [GV1796.L]
UF Aribú (Dance)
BT Folk dancing—Brazil
Lundy Island (England)
BT Islands—England
Lundy's Lane, Battle of, 1814
    [E356.L9]
UF Bridgewater, Battle of, 1814
    Cataract, Battle of the, 1814
    Niagara, Battle of, 1814
    Niagara Falls, Battle of, 1814
BT United States—History—War of 1812
    —Campaigns
Luneau family *(Not Subd Geog)*
UF Louineau family
    Louineaux family
Lüneburg Heath (Germany)
  USE Lüneburger Heide (Germany)
Lüneburger Heide (Germany)
UF Lüneburg Heath (Germany)
BT Moors and heaths—Germany (West)
NT Naturschutzpark Lüneburger Heide
    (Germany)
Lüneburger Heide, Naturschutzpark (Germany)
  USE Naturschutzpark Lüneburger Heide
    (Germany)
Lunéville, Treaty of, 1801
    [DC222.L8]
BT Austria—History—1789-1815
Lung
  USE Lungs
Lung cancer
  USE Lungs—Cancer
Lung-ch'tian celadon
  USE Lung-ch'tian ware

Lung-ch'tian ware *(May Subd Geog)*
    [NK4340.C44]
UF Lung-ch'tian celadon
BT Celadon ware
    Porcelain, Chinese
    Pottery, Chinese
Lung diseases, Obstructive
  USE Lungs—Diseases, Obstructive
Lung-fishes
    [QL638.3]
UF Lungfishes
Lung-fishes, Fossil
NT Lepidosirenidae
    Sagenodontidae
Lung function tests
  USE Pulmonary function tests
Lung-men Caves (China) *(Not Subd Geog)*
UF Lung-men shih k'u (China)
BT Cave temples, Buddhist—China
Lung-men shih k'u (China)
  USE Lung-men Caves (China)
Lung plague of cattle
  USE Pleuropneumonia of cattle
Lung-tu dialect
  USE Chinese language—Dialects—Lung-tu
Lung-worms
  USE Lungworms
Lungeing (Horsemanship)
    [SF287]
UF Longeing (Horsemanship)
BT Horsemanship
    Horses—Training
Lunger disease
  USE Pulmonary adenomatosis
Lunger family *(Not Subd Geog)*
Lungfishes
  USE Lung-fishes
Lungs
    [QL848 (Comparative anatomy)]
    [QM261 (Human anatomy)]
    [QP121 (Physiology)]
UF Lung
BT Chest
    Respiratory organs
RT Respiration
SA *headings beginning with* Pulmonary
NT Bronchi
    Docimasia pulmonum
    Pleura
    Pulmonary alveoli
    Pulmonary endothelium
— **Abscess**
    [RC776]
— **Aging**
— **Bacteriology**
    [QR171]
  NT Escherichia coli infections
— **Biopsy**
— **Blood-vessels**
  NT Pulmonary vein
— — **Diseases** *(May Subd Geog)*
    UF Pulmonary circulation disorders
— — **Radiography**
    UF Pneumoangiography
    BT Angiography
      Lungs—Radiography
— **Calcification**
— **Cancer** *(May Subd Geog)*
    UF Lung cancer
    NT Small cell lung cancer
— — **Complications and sequelae**
    NT Pancoast's syndrome
— — **Diagnosis**
— **Circulation**
    USE Pulmonary circulation
— **Collapse**
    USE Atelectasis
      Collapse therapy
      Pneumothorax
— **Congestion**
    [RC776]

Lungs
— **Congestion** (Continued)
  UF Congestion of the lungs
— **Diseases** (May Subd Geog)
    [RC756-776]
  UF Pulmonary diseases
  NT Atelectasis
    Chest—Diseases
    Cor pulmonale
    Cystic fibrosis
    Farmer's lung
    Hyaline membrane disease
    Injections, Bronchial
    Interstitial lung diseases
    Lungs—Diseases, Fungal
    Lungs—Diseases, Obstructive
    Lungs—Dust diseases
    Lungs—Hernia
    Lungs—Radiography
    Lungworms
    Pneumonia
    Pneumothorax
    Pulmonary adenomatosis
    Pulmonary aspergillosis
    Pulmonary edema
    Pulmonary fibrosis
    Pulmonary manifestations of
      general diseases
    Respiratory distress syndrome,
      Adult
    Respiratory insufficiency
    Tuberculosis
— — **Diagnosis**
    [RC733-4]
  NT Percussion
— — **Homeopathic treatment**
    [RX321]
— **Diseases, Fungal**
    [RC776.F8]
  UF Fungal lung diseases
    Fungous lung diseases
    Lungs—Fungal diseases
  BT Lungs—Diseases
    Mycoses
  NT Adiaspiromycosis
    Pulmonary aspergillosis
— **Diseases, Interstitial**
  USE Interstitial lung diseases
— **Diseases, Obstructive**
    (May Subd Geog)
    [RC776.O3]
  UF Chronic obstructive pulmonary
      disease
    COPD (Disease)
    Lung diseases, Obstructive
    Obstructive lung diseases
  BT Lungs—Diseases
    Respiratory organs—Obstructions
  NT Asthma
    Bronchitis
    Emphysema, Pulmonary
— **Dust diseases** (May Subd Geog)
    [HD7264 (Labor)]
    [RC773-RC775 (Internal medicine)]
  UF Anthracosis
    Black lung
    Chalicosis
    Dust diseases
    Pneumoconiosis
    Pneumokoniosis
  BT Lungs—Diseases
    Occupational diseases
  NT Asbestosis
    Byssinosis
    Miners' phthisis
    Silicosis
    Silicotuberculosis
— **Endothelium**
  USE Pulmonary endothelium
— **Foreign bodies**
— **Fungal diseases**

  USE Lungs—Diseases, Fungal
— **Gangrene**
    [RC776]
— **Hernia**
    [RD621]
  BT Lungs—Diseases
— **Hydatids**
    [RC184.T6]
— **Infections**
  NT Pneumonia, Pneumococcal
— **Inflammation**
  USE Pneumonia
— **Innervation**
— **Interstitial diseases**
  USE Interstitial lung diseases
— **Paracentesis**
— **Radiography**
  BT Lungs—Diseases
  NT Lungs—Blood-vessels—
      Radiography
— **Surgery**
  NT Pneumonectomy
— — **Complications and sequelae**
— **Transplantation**
— **Tuberculosis**
  USE Tuberculosis
— **Tumors**
    [RD667]
— **Wounds and injuries**
Lungs, Artificial
  USE Oxygenators
Lungs, Membrane
  USE Oxygenators, Membrane
Lungtu dialect
  USE Chinese language—Dialects—Lung-tu
Lungworms
    [SF810.L8 (Veterinary medicine)]
  UF Lung-worms
  BT Lungs—Diseases
    Worms, Intestinal and parasitic
  NT Dictyocaulidae
    Metastrongylidae
Lunigiana (Italy)
Lunik (Lunar probes)
  BT Lunar probes
Lunkundu language
  USE Nkundu language
Lunn family (Not Subd Geog)
Lunokhod lunar roving vehicles
    [TL480]
  BT Astronautics—Soviet Union
    Moon cars
Lunsford family (Not Subd Geog)
Lunumbe dialect
  USE Lunambe dialect
Lunyaneka language
  USE Nyaneka language
Lunyankole language
  USE Nyankole language
Lunyore language
  USE Nyore language
Lunyoro language
  USE Nyoro language
Luo (African people)
    [DT433.542 (Kenya)]
  UF Dho Luo (African people)
    Jaluo (African people)
    Jo Luo (African people)
    Kavirondo (Nilotic people)
    Nyifwa (African people)
  BT Ethnology—Africa, East
    Nilotic tribes
  NT Acoli (African people)
    Alur (African people)
    Anuaks
    Lango (African people)
    Maban (African people)
    Shilluks
Luo hymns
  USE Hymns, Luo

Luo language (Kenya and Tanzania)
  UF Dho Luo language
    Dholuo language
    Gaya language
    Jo Luo language
    Kavirondo language, Nilotic
    Nife language
    Nilotic Kavirondo language
    Nyife language
    Wagaya language
  BT Kenya—Languages
    Nilotic languages
    Tanzania—Languages
Luo language (Sudan)
  USE Lwo language (Sudan)
Luo law
  USE Law, Luo
Lupar River (Sarawak)
  UF Batang Lupar (Sarawak)
  BT Rivers—Malaysia
Lupastean family (Not Subd Geog)
  UF Lupastian family
    Lupastin family
    Lupostean family
    Lupostian family
  RT Lupton family
Lupastian family
  USE Lupastean family
Lupastin family
  USE Lupastean family
Lupercalia
    [BL815.L8]
  BT Cults—Rome
    Mythology, Roman
    Werewolves
Luperodes
    [QL596.C5]
  BT Chrysomelidae
Lupin
  USE Lupines
Lupine
  USE Lupines
  NT Lupinus luteus
Lupines (May Subd Geog)
    [QK495.L52 (Botany)]
    [SB177.L85 (Food crops)]
    [SB205.L9 (Forage plants)]
    [SB413.L86 (Ornamental plants)]
  UF Lupin
    Lupine
    Lupinus
  BT Leguminosae
  NT Bluebonnets (Lupines)
    Lupinus angustifolius
    Lupinus perennis
    Lupinus subcarnosus
    Lupinus texensis
Lupines as feed (May Subd Geog)
  BT Feeds
Lupines as food (May Subd Geog)
  BT Food
Lupinus
  USE Lupines
Lupinus angustifolius
    [QK495.L52]
  UF Blue lupine
    European blue lupine
  BT Lupines
Lupinus luteus
    [QK495.L52 (Botany)]
  UF European yellow lupine
    Yellow lupine
  BT Lupine
Lupinus perennis
    [QK495.L52 (Botany)]
    [SB284.4.L84 (Cover crop)]
  UF Blue lupine
    Perennial lupine
    Quaker bonnet (Plant)
    Sun-dial lupine
    Sundial lupine

BT Cover crops
 Lupines
Lupinus subcarnosus
 ₍QK495.L52 (Botany)₎
 UF Bluebonnet, Texas
 Texas bluebonnet
 BT Bluebonnets (Lupines)
 Lupines
Lupinus texensis
 ₍QK495.L52 (Botany)₎
 ₍SB413.L88 (Ornamental plant)₎
 UF Bluebonnet, Texas
 Texas bluebonnet
 BT Bluebonnets (Lupines)
 Lupines
Lupostean family
 USE Lupastean family
Lupostian family
 USE Lupastean family
Lupton family *(Not Subd Geog)*
 RT Lupastean family
Lupulinic acid
Lupus
 ₍RC312.5.S5₎
 BT Tuberculosis
 NT Phototherapy
Lupus erythematosus
 ₍RL201₎
 BT Collagen diseases
Lupus erythematosus, Systemic
 (May Subd Geog)
 ₍RC924.5.L85₎
 UF Libman-Sacks disease
 Lupus erythematosus disseminatus
 Systemic lupus erythematosus
 BT Blood-vessels—Diseases
 Collagen diseases
 Skin—Diseases
Lupus erythematosus disseminatus
 USE Lupus erythematosus, Systemic
Lur
 ₍ML990.L8₎
 BT Brass instruments
 Horn (Musical instrument)
 RT Alpenhorn
Lur language
 USE Alur language
Lur music
 ₍M175.L87₎
Luragoli language
 USE Logooli language
Lurcher
 ₍SF429.L87₎
 BT Gazehounds
Lures, Fishing
 USE Fishing lures
Luria-Nebraska Battery (Neuropsychology)
 USE Luria-Nebraska Neuropsychological
 Battery
Luria-Nebraska Neuropsychological Battery
 ₍RC386.6.L87₎
 UF Luria-Nebraska Battery
 (Neuropsychology)
 BT Neuropsychological tests
Lurín River (Peru)
 UF Río de Lurín (Peru)
 Río Lurín (Peru)
 BT Rivers—Peru
Luru (Indonesian people)
 USE Lara (Indonesian people)
Lurue family
 USE Larue family
Lusago language
 USE Lushai language
Lusaka (Zambia). Chainda
 USE Chainda (Lusaka, Zambia)
Lusaka (Zambia). Chawama
 USE Chawama (Lusaka, Zambia)
Lusaka (Zambia). George
 USE George (Lusaka, Zambia)

Lusalo
 BT Marriage customs and rites
Lusatia
 USE Lusatia (Germany)
Lusatia (Germany) *(Not Subd Geog)*
 As a geographic subdivision, this heading is used
 indirectly through Germany (East).
 UF Lausitz (Germany)
 Lusatia
 Łužice (Germany)
 Łużyca (Germany)
 — History *(Not Subd Geog)*
 — — Revolution, 1848-1849
 (Not Subd Geog)
 ₍DD209.L₎
Lusatia, Upper (Germany)
 UF Oberlausitz (Germany)
 Upper Lusatia (Germany)
Lusatian culture
 USE Lausitz culture
Lusatian Neisse River
 USE Neisse River
Lusatian Sorbian languages
 USE Sorbian languages
Lusatian Sorbs
 USE Sorbs
Lusby family *(Not Subd Geog)*
Lüscher test
 BT Color—Psychological aspects
 Personality tests
Luscinia *(May Subd Geog)*
 ₍QL696.P255₎
 BT Muscicapidae
Luscomb family
 USE Lipscomb family
Luscombe family
 USE Lipscomb family
Luse family
 USE Luce family
Lusengo language
 USE Losengo language
Lushai (Indic people)
 ₍DS432.L8₎
 UF Lushei (Indic people)
 Mizo (Indic people)
 BT Ethnology—India
 — Astronomy
 USE Astronomy, Lushai (Indic people)
 — Women
 USE Women, Lushai (Indic people)
Lushai (Indic people) astronomy
 USE Astronomy, Lushai (Indic people)
Lushai drama *(May Subd Geog)*
Lushai folk-songs
 USE Folk-songs, Lushai
Lushai hymns
 USE Hymns, Lushai
Lushai language
 ₍PL4001.L8₎
 UF Dulien language
 Lukhai language
 Lusago language
 Lushei language
 Mizo language
 Sailau language
 BT Bangladesh—Languages
 Burma—Languages
 China—Languages
 India—Languages
 Kuki-Chin languages
Lushai literature *(May Subd Geog)*
Lushai love poetry
 USE Love poetry, Lushai
Lushai poetry *(May Subd Geog)*
 NT Love poetry, Lushai
Lushai songs
 USE Songs, Lushai
Lushai women (Indic people)
 USE Women, Lushai (Indic people)
Lushei (Indic people)
 USE Lushai (Indic people)

Lushei language
 USE Lushai language
Lushisa dialect
 USE Kisa dialect
Lushootseed languages
 USE Puget Sound Salish languages
Lusi language
 ₍PL6253.L₎
 UF Kaliai language
 BT Melanesian languages
 Papua New Guinea—Languages
Lusiba language
 USE Ziba language
Lusignan family *(Not Subd Geog)*
Lusitanian gods
 USE Gods, Portuguese
Lusk family *(Not Subd Geog)*
Luso-Holandese cattle
 USE Turino cattle
Lusoga language
 USE Soga language
Lusonge language
 USE Songe language
Lusophone Africa
 USE Africa, Portuguese-speaking
Lussino Island (Croatia)
 USE Lošinj Island (Croatia)
Lust
 UF Carnal desire
 Concupiscence
 Lasciviousness
 Lechery
 Licentiousness
 Sexual lust
 BT Desire
 Sexual excitement
 — Religious aspects
 — — Buddhism, ₍Christianity, etc.₎
 — — Christianity
 BT Deadly sins
Luster
 ₍BF241 (Psychology)₎
 ₍QC425 (Optics)₎
Luster-ware *(May Subd Geog)*
 ₍NK4399.L9₎
 BT Glazes
 Pottery
 NT Wedgwood fairyland lustre
Luster-ware, Islamic *(May Subd Geog)*
 UF Islamic luster-ware
 — Spain
 UF Hispano-Moresque luster-ware
Lustrac Castle (Trentels, France)
 USE Château de Lustrac (Trentels, France)
Lustrations
 ₍BL619.L8₎
 BT Rites and ceremonies
 Water—Religious aspects
 NT Foot washing (Rite)
 Mikveh
Lusty family *(Not Subd Geog)*
Lusztig-Kazhdan polynomials
 USE Kazhdan-Lusztig polynomials
Lutao (Southeast Asian people)
 USE Bajau (Southeast Asian people)
Lute
 ₍ML1010-1013₎
 UF Colascione
 RT Vihuela
 NT Archlute
 Bağlama
 Bandura
 Bandurria
 Biwa
 Bouzouki
 Chitarrone
 Domra
 Harp-lute guitar
 Kobza
 Mandola
 Oud

2213

Lute *(Continued)*
    P'i p'a
    San hsien
    Sarod
    Tambura
    Tar (Musical instrument)
    Theorbo
Lute and cithern music
  USE Cithern and lute music
Lute and flute music
  USE Flute and lute music
Lute and glass-harmonica music
  USE Glass-harmonica and lute music
Lute and harp music
  USE Harp and lute music
Lute and harpsichord music
    ₍M282.L88₎
    ₍M283.L88₎
  UF Harpsichord and lute music
  BT Lute and piano music
  NT Sonatas (Lute and harpsichord)
Lute and organ music
    ₍M182-186₎
  UF Organ and lute music
Lute and piano music
    ₍M282.L88₎
    ₍M283.L88₎
  UF Piano and lute music
  NT Lute and harpsichord music
Lute and recorder music
  USE Recorder and lute music
Lute and viol music
  USE Viol and lute music
Lute and viola da gamba music
  USE Viola da gamba and lute music
Lute and viola d'amore music
  USE Viola d'amore and lute music
Lute and viola d'amore with string orchestra
    ₍M1140-1141₎
  RT Concertos (Lute and viola d'amore
      with string orchestra)
Lute and violin music
  USE Violin and lute music
Lute family
  USE Lutz family
Lute music
    ₍M140-141₎
  SA Concertos, Minuets, Sonatas, Suites,
    and similar headings with
    specification of instruments; Trios
    ₍Quartets, etc.₎ *followed by*
    specifications which include the
    lute; also Plectral ensembles *and*
    headings that begin with the words
    lute or lutes
  NT Canons, fugues, etc. (Lute)
    Domra music
    Mandola music
    Oud music
    Sarod music
    Sonatas (Lute)
    Suites (Lute)
    Tablature (Musical notation)
Lute music (Lutes (2))
    ₍M292-3₎
  NT Suites (Lutes (2))
Lute players
  USE Lutenists
Lute with string orchestra
    ₍M1105-6₎
  RT Concertos (Lute with string orchestra)
Luteal hormone
  USE Progesterone
Luteal inadequacy
  USE Luteal phase defects
Luteal insufficiency
  USE Luteal phase defects
Luteal phase
  UF Secretory phase (Menstrual cycle)
  BT Menstrual cycle
  RT Corpus luteum

Luteal phase defects *(May Subd Geog)*
    ₍RG205.L87₎
  UF Inadequate corpus luteum
    Inadequate luteal phase
    Luteal inadequacy
    Luteal insufficiency
    Luteal phase deficiency
    Luteal phase dysfunction
    Luteal phase inadequacy
    Luteal phase insufficiency
    Short luteal phase
  BT Endocrine gynecology
    Infertility, Female
Luteal phase deficiency
  USE Luteal phase defects
Luteal phase dysfunction
  USE Luteal phase defects
Luteal phase inadequacy
  USE Luteal phase defects
Luteal phase insufficiency
  USE Luteal phase defects
Lutecium
  USE Lutetium
Luteinizing hormone
    ₍QP572.L84₎
  UF Corpus luteum-stimulating hormone
    ICSH (Hormone)
    Interstitial cell-stimulating hormone
    LH (Hormone)
    Lutropin
    Metakentrin
    Pituitary B gonadotropin
  BT Gonadotropin
    Peptide hormones
    Pituitary hormones
  — **Receptors**
    BT Hormone receptors
Luteinizing hormone releasing hormone
    ₍QP572.L85₎
  UF LH-releasing factor
    LH-RH
  BT Peptide hormones
    Pituitary hormone releasing factors
  — **Agonists**
    UF Agonists, Luteinizing hormone
      releasing hormone
  — **Analogs**
    USE Luteinizing hormone releasing
      hormone—Derivatives
  — **Antagonists**
    UF Antagonists, Luteinizing hormone
      releasing hormone
    BT Hormone antagonists
  — **Derivatives**
    UF Luteinizing hormone releasing
      hormone—Analogs
Luteins
  USE Carotenoids
    Xanthophylls
Lutenists
    ₍ML399 (Biography: collective)₎
    ₍ML419 (individual)₎
  UF Lute players
Luteotropin
  USE Prolactin
Lutes (2) with string orchestra
    ₍M1137.4.L88₎
  RT Concertos (Lutes (2) with string
      orchestra)
Lutes family
  USE Lutz family
Lutetia
  BT Kelliellidae, Fossil
Lutetium
  UF Lutecium
  — **Isotopes**
    UF Isotopic lutetium
      Lutetium isotopes
  —— **Half-life**
  — **Spectra**

Lutetium isotopes
  USE Lutetium—Isotopes
Luth
  USE Leatherback turtle
Luther family *(Not Subd Geog)*
  UF Louther family
    Luder family
    Von Luder family
Lutheran Cemetery (Salisbury, N.C.)
  USE Old Lutheran Cemetery (Salisbury,
    N.C.)
Lutheran Church *(May Subd Geog)*
    ₍BX8001-BX8080₎
    Here are entered works on Lutheran denomina-
    tions treated collectively and works for which the
    individual Lutheran denomination cannot be identi-
    fied.
  BT Christian sects
  NT Women in the Lutheran Church
  — **Adult education**
  — **Bio-bibliography**
    ₍Z7845.L9₎
  — Biography
    USE Lutherans—Biography
  — **Charities**
    ₍BX8074.B4₎
  — **Clergy**
    ₍BX8071₎
    NT Superintendents (Lutheran Church)
  — **Discipline**
    NT Unionism (Lutheranism)
  — **Doctrines**
    NT Erlangen theology
      Syncretistic controversy
  — **Education**
    ₍LC573-LC574₎
    NT Lutheran universities and colleges
  — **Government**
    NT Superintendents (Lutheran Church)
  — **Hymns**
    ₍BV410₎
    ₍M2126 (Vocal music)₎
    NT Chorale
      Chorales
  — **Influence**
  — **Liturgy**
    ₍BX8067₎
  — **Membership**
  — **Missions**
    ₍BV2540₎
  — **Parties and movements**
  — **Prayer-books and devotions**
  — **Radio scripts**
  — Relation to the state
    USE Church and state—Lutheran
      Church
  — **Sermons**
    ₍BX8066₎
  — Work with youth
    USE Church work with youth—
      Lutheran Church
  — Youth, Work with
    USE Church work with youth—
      Lutheran Church
  — **Denmark**
    NT Grundtvigianism
Lutheran Church and art
    ₍N72.R4₎
  BT Art
    Art and religion
    Christian art and symbolism
Lutheran Church and state
  USE Church and state—Lutheran Church
Lutheran church buildings
  USE Churches, Lutheran
Lutheran Church orders
  USE Church orders, Lutheran
Lutheran churches
  USE Churches, Lutheran
Lutheran journalism
  USE Press, Lutheran

Lutheran literature (English)
  USE English literature—Lutheran authors
Lutheran monasticism and religious orders
  USE Monasticism and religious orders,
        Lutheran
      Monasticism and religious orders for
        women, Lutheran
Lutheran press
  USE Press, Lutheran
Lutheran universities and colleges
  (May Subd Geog)
  [LC573-LC574]
    BT Lutheran Church—Education
Lutheran women
  USE Women, Lutheran
Lutherans *(May Subd Geog)*
    BT Protestants
  — Biography
      UF Lutheran Church—Biography
  — Missouri
      NT Saxon emigration, 1838-1839
  — United States
      NT Afro-American Lutherans
Lutherans, Afro-American
  USE Afro-American Lutherans
Lutherans, Danish, [Polish, etc.]
  (May Subd Geog)
      Here are entered works on Lutherans living out-
    side their native country who use their native lan-
    guage in church services.
Lutherans, German *(May Subd Geog)*
  UF German Lutherans
Luthi family *(Not Subd Geog)*
  UF Luthin family
      Luthy family
  RT Leedy family
Luthin family
  USE Luthi family
Luthy family
  USE Luthi family
Lutianidae
  USE Lutjanidae
Lutianus
  USE Lutjanus
Lutici
  USE Veletians
Lutiger family *(Not Subd Geog)*
  UF Lutinger family
Lutinger family
  USE Lutiger family
Lutjanidae
  [QL638.L9]
  UF Lutianidae
      Snappers (Fish family)
  BT Perciformes
  NT Jordanichthys
      Lutjanus
Lutjanidae fisheries *(May Subd Geog)*
  BT Fisheries
Lutjanus
  [QL638.L9]
  UF Lutianus
  BT Lutjanidae
Lutjanus griseus
  USE Gray snapper
Lutjanus synagris
  USE Lane snapper
Lutoro language
  USE Tooro language
Lutra
  [QL737.C25]
  BT Mustelidae
      Otters
Lutra canadensis
  [QL737.C25]
  UF Canadian otter
      North American otter
      River otter
  BT Otters
Lutra lutra
  [QL737.C25]

UF Eurasian otter
    European otter
    Mustela lutra
Lutra maculicollis
  [QL737.C25]
  UF Hydrictis maculicollis
      Speckle-throated otter
      Spotted-necked otter
      Spotted-throated otter
Lutreola
  USE Mustela
Lutrinae
  USE Otters
Lutropin
  USE Luteinizing hormone
Luts family
  USE Lutz family
Lutse family
  USE Lutz family
Lutsk (Ukraine), Battle of, 1916
  [D552]
    BT World War, 1914-1918—Campaigns—
        Ukraine
Lutte family
  USE Lutz family
Lutter am Barenberge, Battle of, 1626
    BT Thirty Years' War, 1618-1648—
        Campaigns—Germany
Luttes family
  USE Lutz family
Lütticher Taufbecken
  USE Renier, de Huy, d. 1150.   Liège font
Lutton family *(Not Subd Geog)*
Lutts family
  USE Lutz family
Lutuamian Indians
  [E99.L]
    BT Indians of North America
    NT Klamath Indians
        Modoc Indians
Lutuamian languages
  [PM1661]
    RT Klamath language
Lutz family *(Not Subd Geog)*
  UF Loots family
      Luets family
      Lute family
      Lutes family
      Luts family
      Lutse family
      Lutte family
      Luttes family
      Lutts family
      Lutze family
      Lutzer family
Lutz-Splendore-Almeida disease
  USE Paracoccidioidomycosis
Lutze family
  USE Lutz family
Lützen, Battle of, 1632
    BT Thirty Years' War, 1618-1648
Lützen, Battle of, 1813
  [DC236.7.L8]
    BT Napoleonic Wars, 1800-1814—
        Campaigns—Germany (East)
        Saxony—History—1423-1815
Lutzer family
  USE Lutz family
Lutzomyia
  [QL537.P85]
    BT Psychodidae
        Sand flies
Lützow-Holm Bay (Antarctic regions)
  (Not Subd Geog)
    BT Bays—Antarctic regions
Luunda language
  USE Ruund language
LUV truck
  USE Chevrolet LUV truck
Luva language
  USE Luba-Lulua language

Luvale (African people)
  UF Balovale (African people)
      Lovale (African people)
      Luvale (Bantu tribe)
  BT Bantus
      Ethnology—Zambia
Luvale (Bantu tribe)
  USE Luvale (African people)
Luvale language
  [PL8473]
  BT Bantu languages
      Lunda language
Luvian language
  USE Luwian language
Luvlace family
  USE Lovelace family
Luwa language
  USE Lawa language (Thailand)
Luwi
  USE Luwians
Luwian inscriptions
  USE Inscriptions, Luwian
Luwian language
  [P961.L8]
  UF Luian language
      Lûish language
      Luvian language
  BT Anatolian languages
      Hittite language
Luwians
  UF Luwi
  BT Indo-Europeans
Luwumbu language
  USE Vili language
Luwunda language
  USE Ruund language
Luxations
  USE Dislocations
Luxembourg Americans *(May Subd Geog)*
  [E184.L88]
  UF Luxembourg Americans—United
      States
  BT Ethnology—United States
      Luxembourgers—United States
  — United States
      USE Luxembourg Americans
Luxembourg art
  USE Art, Luxembourg
Luxembourg coins
  USE Coins, Luxembourg
Luxembourg literature (English)
  USE English literature—Luxembourg
      authors
Luxembourg newspapers *(May Subd Geog)*
Luxembourg periodicals *(May Subd Geog)*
Luxembourgers *(May Subd Geog)*
  BT Ethnology—Luxembourg
  — United States
      NT Luxembourg Americans
Luxeuil script
  USE Writing, Luxeuil
Luxuries
  BT Commercial products
  — Taxation *(May Subd Geog)*
    [HJ5771-5797]
    UF Luxury duty
        Taxation of luxuries
    BT Taxation of articles of consumption
    NT Fur—Taxation
        Jewelry—Taxation
        Sales tax
        Toilet preparations—Taxation
  — — Law and legislation
      (May Subd Geog)
Luxury
  [HB841 (Economics)]
  BT Economics
      Wealth
  RT Cost and standard of living
      Leisure class
  NT Consumption (Economics)

Luxury *(Continued)*
    Sumptuary laws
    Wealth, Ethics of
Luxury duty
  USE Luxuries—Taxation
Luxury in literature
Luyana folk literature
  USE Folk literature, Luyana
Luyana language
  UF Luyi language
    SiLuyana language
  BT Bantu languages
  NT Mbukushu language
Luyi language
  USE Luyana language
Luyia (African people)
  [DT433.542]
  UF Abaluyia (African people)
    Baluyia (African people)
    Luhya (African people)
  BT Ethnology—Kenya
    Ethnology—Uganda
  — Rites and ceremonies
    NT Funeral rites and ceremonies,
      Luyia (African people)
Luyia (African people) funeral rites and
  ceremonies
  USE Funeral rites and ceremonies, Luyia
    (African people)
Luyia language
  UF Luhya language
    Luluhya language
    Luluyia language
    Oluluyia language
  BT Bantu languages
  NT Hanga dialect (Kenya)
    Kisa dialect
Luyia proverbs
  USE Proverbs, Luyia
Luz (Puebla, Mexico) *(Not Subd Geog)*
  UF La Luz (Puebla, Mexico)
    Puebla (Mexico). Luz
Luz Coast (Spain)
  USE Costa de la Luz (Spain)
Lužice (Germany)
  USE Lusatia (Germany)
Lužická Nisa River
  USE Neisse River
Luzius family *(Not Subd Geog)*
Luzon (Philippines)
  BT Islands—Philippines
Luzon wren-babbler
  USE Napothera rabori
Luzula
  [QK495.J87 (Botany)]
  UF Juncoides
    Wood rush
    Woodrush
  BT Juncaceae
Luzuriaga
  [QK495.L72]
  BT Liliaceae
Luzuriaga latifolia
  [QK495.L72]
Łuźyca (Germany)
  USE Lusatia (Germany)
Lvov, Battle of, 1914
  USE Lemberg, Battle of, 1914
Lvov-Volyn Basin (Ukraine)
  UF L'vovsko-Volynskiĭ ugol'nyĭ basseĭn
    (Ukraine)
  BT Geology—Ukraine
L'vovsko-Volynskiĭ ugol'nyĭ basseĭn (Ukraine)
  USE Lvov-Volyn Basin (Ukraine)
LVTs (Amphibian tractors)
  USE Tracked landing vehicles
L'wa language
  USE Lawa language (Thailand)
Lwenas (African people)
  USE Luenas (African people)

Lwo hymns (Sudan)
  USE Hymns, Lwo (Sudan)
Lwo language
  USE Acoli language
Lwo language (Sudan)
  UF Dhe Lwo language
    Dyur language
    Giur language
    Jo Lwo language
    Jur language
    Luo language (Sudan)
  BT Nilotic languages
    Sudan—Languages
Lyapunov functions
  USE Liapunov functions
Lyases
  [QP612-613]
  UF Desmolases
  BT Enzymes
  NT Adenylate cyclase
    Carbonic anhydrase
    Cystathionine gamma-lyase
    Decarboxylases
    Dopa decarboxylase
    Enolase
Lybarger family *(Not Subd Geog)*
  UF Leberger family
Lybeck family *(Not Subd Geog)*
Lycaconitin
  [QP921.L8 (Physiological effect)]
Lycaeides
  [QL561.L8]
  BT Lycaenidae
Lycaena
  [QL561.L8]
  BT Lycaenidae
Lycaena ferrisi
  [QL561.L8]
Lycaena phlaeas
  [QL561.L8]
Lycaena rubidus
  [QL561.L8]
  UF Ruddy copper butterfly
Lycaenidae
  [QL561.L8]
  UF Cupidinidae
    Plebejidae
    Ruralidae
  BT Butterflies
    Lepidoptera
  NT Aloeides
    Callophrys
    Celastrina
    Cycnus
    Drupadia
    Epidemia
    Glaucopsyche
    Liptena
    Lycaeides
    Lycaena
    Magnastigma
    Panthiades
    Philotes
    Plebejus
    Satyrium
    Spindasis
    Telipna
Lycalopex
  USE Dusicyon
Lycanthropy
  USE Werewolves
Lycaon
  [QL737.C22]
  BT Canidae
Lycaon pictus
  [QL737.C22]

  UF African hunting dog
    African wild dog
    Cape hunting dog
    Hunting dog, African
    Hyena, Painted
    Hyena dog
    Painted hyena
  BT Wild dogs
Lyce family
  USE Lyse family
Lycett family *(Not Subd Geog)*
  UF Lycette family
    Lysaght family
    Lysaught family
Lycette family
  USE Lycett family
Lyceums
  [LC6501-6560]
  BT Education
    University extension
  RT Lectures and lecturing
  NT Chautauquas
Lych-gates
  USE Lich-gates
Lychee
  USE Litchi
    Litchi chinensis
Lychniskida, Fossil
  [QE775]
  BT Hexactinellida, Fossil
Lycian language
  [P1008]
  BT Anatolian languages
Lycidae
  [QL596.L9]
  UF Net-winged beetles
  BT Beetles
Lycium chinense
  [QK495.S7 (Botany)]
  [RS165.L94 (Pharmacy)]
  [SB351.L (Culture)]
  UF Chinese matrimony vine
    Chinese wolfberry
    Matrimony vine, Chinese
    Wolfberry, Chinese
Lycodapodidae
  USE Zoarcidae
Lycodes
  [QL638.Z6]
  BT Zoarcidae
Lycodes sagittarius
  [QL638.Z6]
Lycodidae
  USE Zoarcidae
Lycogalopsis solmsii
  USE Morganella albina
Lyconidae
  USE Macrouridae
Lycopene
  UF Lycopin
  BT Carotenes
Lycoperdaceae
  [QK629.L9]
  BT Lycoperdales
  NT Acutocapillitium
    Calvatia
    Morganella
    Vascellum
Lycoperdales
  [QK629.L92]
  BT Gasteromycetes
  NT Geastraceae
    Lycoperdaceae
Lycoperdon
  USE Puffballs
Lycoperdon albinum
  USE Morganella albina
Lycoperdon perlatum
  [QK629.L9]
  BT Puffballs

Lycophidion

    [QL666.O636]

    BT Colubridae

    NT Lycophidion variegatum

Lycophidion variegatum

    [QL666.O636]

    BT Lycophidion

Lycopin

    USE Lycopene

Lycopodiaceae

    [QK524.L9]

    BT Lycopodiales

    NT Lycopodium

Lycopodiales

    [QK524.L]

    NT Lycopodiaceae

Lycopodiales, Fossil

Lycopodiatae

    USE Club-mosses

Lycopodineae

    USE Club-mosses

Lycopodiopsida

    USE Club-mosses

Lycopodium

    [QK524.L9]

    BT Lycopodiaceae

Lycopodium nudum

    USE Psilotum triquetrum

Lycopodium powder

    BT Club-mosses—Spores

           Powders

   — Electric ignition

        UF Electric ignition of lycopodium

             powder

Lycopsida

    USE Club-mosses

Lycoridae

    USE Nereidae

Lycoriidae

    USE Sciaridae

Lycosidae *(May Subd Geog)*

    [QL458.42.L9]

    UF Wolf spiders

    BT Spiders

    NT Pardosa

         Trochosa

Lyctidae

    [QL596.L92]

    UF Powder-post beetles

    BT Beetles

Lyda family *(Not Subd Geog)*

    UF Leidy family

         Lida family

         Liday family

         Lyday family

    RT Lide family

Lyday family

    USE Lyda family

Lydi dialect

    USE Ludic dialect

Lydia (Biblical character)

Lydian language

    [P1009]

    BT Anatolian languages

Lydidae

    USE Pamphiliidae

Lye

    [TP201]

    BT Alkalies

         Wood

Lyela (African people)

    USE Lele (African people)

Lyele dialect

    USE Lele dialect

Lyell's syndrome

    USE Toxic epidermal necrolysis

Lyerla family

    USE Lyerly family

Lyerly family *(Not Subd Geog)*

    UF Leyerla family

         Lierle family

         Lirly family

         Lyerla family

Lygaeidae

    [QL523.L9]

    UF Geocoridae

         Myodochidae

         Seed bugs

    BT Hemiptera

    NT Blissus

         Gastrodes (Insect)

         Geocoris

         Ischnodemus

         Isthmocoris

         Lilliputocoris

         Lygaeus

         Nysius

         Oncopeltus

Lygaeonematus

    USE Pristiphora

Lygaeonematus erichsonii

    USE Larch sawfly

Lygaeus

    [QL523.L9]

    BT Lygaeidae

Lygaeus equestris

    [QL523.L9]

Lygaeus kalmii

    [QL523.L9]

Lygia

    USE Ligia

Lygians

    USE Lygii

Lygii

    UF Lugier

         Lygians

    BT Germanic tribes

         Suevi

Lygodactylus

    [QL666.L245]

    BT Geckos

    NT Lygodactylus manni

Lygodactylus manni

    [QL666.L245]

    BT Lygodactylus

Lygodesmia

    [QK495.C74]

    BT Compositae

Lygon family

    USE Ligon family

Lygosoma

    [QL666.L28]

    BT Skinks

Lygosoma laterale

    [QL666.L28]

    UF Ground skink

Lygosoma palawanensis

    [QL666.L28]

    UF Sphenomorphus palawanensis

Lygromma

    [QL458.42.G5]

    BT Gnaphosidae

Lygus

    [QL523.M5]

    BT Miridae

Lygus lineolaris

    USE Tarnished plant bug

Lygus oblineatus

    USE Tarnished plant bug

Lygus pratensis

    USE Tarnished plant bug

Lying

    USE Mythomania

         Truthfulness and falsehood

Lying down position

    [GT2995 (Manners and customs)]

    UF Horizontal position (Posture)

    BT Posture

         Sleep positions

    NT Supine position

Lying-in hospitals

    USE Hospitals, Gynecologic and obstetric

Lying tales

    USE Tall tales

Lykken family *(Not Subd Geog)*

    UF Lykkja family

Lykkja family

    USE Lykken family

Lyle C. Roll Building (Battle Creek, Mich.)

    USE Roll Building (Battle Creek, Mich.)

Lyle family

    USE Lyles family

Lyle guns

    USE Line-throwing guns

Lyles family *(Not Subd Geog)*

    UF Lile family

         Liles family

         Lisle family

         Lisles family

         Lyle family

         Lysle family

Lyman family *(Not Subd Geog)*

    UF Leiman family

         Lymon family

         Lynan family

Lymantria

    [QL561.L9 (Zoology)]

    UF Liparis

    BT Lymantriidae

Lymantria dispar

    USE Gypsy moth

Lymantria monacha

    USE Nun moth

Lymantridae

    USE Lymantriidae

Lymantriidae

    [QL561.L9]

    UF Anaphidae

         Dasychiridae

         Gymnidae

         Hypogymnidae

         Leucomidae

         Limantriidae

         Liparidae (Insects)

         Liparididae (Insects)

         Lymantridae

         Ocneriidae

         Orgyidae

         Orgyiidae

         Tussock moths

    BT Lepidoptera

         Moths

    NT Bracharoa

         Hemerocampa

         Lymantria

         Nygmia

         Orgyia

         Porthetria

         Stilpnotia

Lymnadidae

    USE Milkweed butterflies

Lymnodromus

    USE Limnodromus

Lymon family

    USE Lyman family

Lymph

    BT Body fluids

         Lymphatics

    NT Perilymph

   — Circulation

        [QP115]

        UF Circulation of the lymph

            Lymph circulation

        BT Lymphatics

Lymph circulation

    USE Lymph—Circulation

Lymph node syndrome, Mucocutaneous

    USE Mucocutaneous lymph node syndrome

Lymph nodes
  UF Nodes, Lymph
      Nodus lymphaticus
  BT Lymphatics
  — **Diseases** *(May Subd Geog)*
      NT Mucocutaneous lymph node
           syndrome
Lymphadenitis
  UF Adenitis
  BT Lymphatics—Diseases
Lymphadenoma
  USE Hodgkin's disease
Lymphadenopathy-associated virus
  USE Human immunodeficiency viruses
Lymphadenopathy-associated virus antibodies
  USE Human immunodeficiency virus
      antibodies
Lymphangiography
  UF Lymphatics—Radiography
      Lymphography
  BT Angiography
      Radiography, Medical
Lymphatic duct, Right
    [QL841 (Comparative anatomy)]
    [QM197 (Human anatomy)]
    [QP115 (Physiology)]
  UF Ductus lymphaticus dexter
      Right lymphatic duct
  BT Thoracic duct
  — **Catheterization**
      BT Catheters
Lymphatic leukemia
  USE Lymphocytic leukemia
Lymphatic metastasis
  BT Metastasis
Lymphatic system
  USE Lymphatics
Lymphatics
    [QL841 (Comparative anatomy)]
    [QM197 (Human anatomy)]
    [QP115 (Physiology)]
  UF Lymphatic system
  BT Absorption (Physiology)
      Physiology
  NT Chyle
      Hemolymph
      Lymph
      Lymph—Circulation
      Lymph nodes
      Lymphoid tissue
      Thoracic duct
  — **Abnormalities**
      UF Angiodysplasia
  — **Cancer**
  — **Diseases** *(May Subd Geog)*
    [RC646]
      NT Elephantiasis
          Lymphadenitis
          Lymphatism
          Lymphedema
          Lymphoproliferative disorders
          Reticuloendotheliosis
          Scrofula
  — **Infections** *(May Subd Geog)*
      NT Lymphogranuloma venereum
  — **Puncture**
      BT Diagnosis
  — **Radiography**
      USE Lymphangiography
  — **Surgery**
  — **Syphilis**
  — **Tuberculosis**
    [RC312.5.L]
  — **Tumors**
Lymphatism
  UF Lymphoidotoxemia
      Lymphotoxemia
      Status lymphaticus
      Status thymicus
  BT Lymphatics—Diseases
      Thymus gland—Diseases

Lymphedema
  BT Edema
      Lymphatics—Diseases
  NT Elephantiasis
Lymphoblastic leukemia *(May Subd Geog)*
  UF Acute lymphocytic leukemia
      Leukemia, Lymphoblastic
  BT Lymphocytic leukemia
Lymphoblastic leukemia in children
  (May Subd Geog)
    [RJ416.L4]
  BT Leukemia in children
Lymphocyte activation products
  USE Lymphokines
Lymphocyte culture test, Mixed
  (May Subd Geog)
    [QR184.3]
  UF Leucocyte culture test, Mixed
      Mixed leucocyte culture test
      Mixed lymphocyte culture test
  BT Cell culture
      Histocompatibility testing
      Lymphocyte transformation
Lymphocyte factors
  USE Lymphokines
Lymphocyte mediators
  USE Lymphokines
Lymphocyte transformation
    [QR185.8.L9]
  BT Cell transformation
  NT Lymphocyte culture test, Mixed
Lymphocytes
  UF Leucocytes, Nongranular
      Nongranular leucocytes
  BT Leucocytes
  NT B cells
      Cell-mediated lympholysis
      Fc receptors
      Foà-Kurlov cells
      Hybridomas
      Interleukins
      Lymphokines
      T cells
Lymphocytic choriomeningitis
  UF Choriomeningitis, Lymphocytic
  BT Arenavirus diseases
      Meningitis
Lymphocytic choriomeningitis virus
    [QR201.L9]
  BT Arenaviruses
Lymphocytic leukemia *(May Subd Geog)*
    [RC643]
  UF Leukemia, Lymphocytic
      Lymphatic leukemia
      Lymphoid leukemia
  BT Leukemia
      Lymphoproliferative disorders
  NT Chronic lymphocytic leukemia
      Lymphoblastic leukemia
Lymphocytolysis, Cell-mediated
  USE Cell-mediated lympholysis
Lymphocytotoxicity, Cell-mediated
  USE Cell-mediated lympholysis
Lymphogranuloma
  USE Hodgkin's disease
Lymphogranuloma inguinale
  USE Lymphogranuloma venereum
Lymphogranuloma venereum
  (May Subd Geog)
    [RC203.L9]
  UF Lymphogranuloma inguinale
      Lymphopathia venereum
      Paradenolymphitis
  BT Chlamydia infections
      Lymphatics—Infections
      Sexually transmitted diseases
Lymphogranulomatosis
  USE Hodgkin's disease
Lymphogranulomatosis benigna
  USE Sarcoidosis

Lymphography
  USE Lymphangiography
Lymphoid leukemia
  USE Lymphocytic leukemia
Lymphoid tissue
  BT Immune system
      Lymphatics
      Tissues
  NT Adenoids
      Plasma cells
      Spleen
      Thymus gland
      Tonsils
Lymphoidotoxemia
  USE Lymphatism
Lymphokines
    [QR185.8.L93]
  UF Lymphocyte activation products
      Lymphocyte factors
      Lymphocyte mediators
      Soluble lymphocyte mediators
      Soluble lymphocyte products
      Soluble mediators of cellular immunity
      Soluble mediators of immunologic
        regulation
  BT Cellular immunity
      Immune response—Regulation
      Lymphocytes
  NT Interferon
      Transfer factor (Immunology)
Lympholysis, Cell-mediated
  USE Cell-mediated lympholysis
Lymphoma
  USE Lymphomas
Lymphomas *(May Subd Geog)*
    [RC280.L9]
  UF Germinoblastomas
      Immunoblastomas
      Lymphoma
      Reticulolymphosarcomas
      Sarcoma, Germinoblastic
      Sarcoma, Immunoblastic
  BT Reticulo-endothelial system—Tumors
  RT Lymphoproliferative disorders
  NT Adenolymphoma
      Burkitt's lymphoma
      Hodgkin's disease
      Plasmacytoma
      Reticuloendotheliosis
      Reticulum cell sarcoma
Lymphomatosis, Avian
  USE Marek's disease
Lymphopathia venereum
  USE Lymphogranuloma venereum
Lymphoproliferative disorders
  (May Subd Geog)
    [RC646.2]
  UF Immunoproliferative disorders
      Lymphoproliferative syndrome
  BT Cell proliferation
      Immunological deficiency syndromes
      Lymphatics—Diseases
  RT Lymphomas
  NT Agammaglobulinemia
      Amyloidosis
      Hodgkin's disease
      Leukemia, Hairy cell
      Lymphocytic leukemia
      Mycosis fungoides
      Sarcoidosis
Lymphoproliferative syndrome
  USE Lymphoproliferative disorders
Lymphosarcoma
  USE Hodgkin's disease
Lymphotoxemia
  USE Lymphatism
Lyn family
  USE Lynn family
Lynan family
  USE Lyman family

Lynceidae
USE Chydoridae
Lynch law
USE Lynching
Lynchburg, Battle of, 1864
  ₁E476.65₁
    BT United States—History—Civil War,
      1861-1865—Campaigns
Lynching *(May Subd Geog)*
  ₁HV6455-HV6471₁
    Here, without further subdivision, are entered
  general works on lynching, lynching in the United
  States as a whole, and in the Southern States.
    UF Lynch law
    BT Criminal justice, Administration of
    NT Vigilance committees
Lynck family
  USE Link family
Lynd family
  USE Lynn family
Lynde family
  USE Lynn family
Lyndes family
  USE Lynn family
Lyndon B. Johnson National Historic Site
  (Tex.)
    USE Lyndon B. Johnson National Historical
      Park (Tex.)
Lyndon B. Johnson National Historical Park
  (Tex.) *(Not Subd Geog)*
    UF Lyndon B. Johnson National Historic
      Site (Tex.)
    BT Historic sites—Texas
      National parks and reserves—Texas
    RT LBJ Ranch House (Tex.)
Lyndon B. Johnson Ranch House (Tex.)
  USE LBJ Ranch House (Tex.)
Lynds family
  USE Lynn family
Lyndsay family
  USE Lindsay family
Lyndsey family
  USE Lindsay family
Lyne family
  USE Lynn family
Lynes family
  USE Lynn family
Lynfield family *(Not Subd Geog)*
    UF Linfield family
    RT Linville family
Lyngby family *(Not Subd Geog)*
Lyngen Peninsula (Norway)
    (Not Subd Geog)
    UF Lyngsalpene (Norway)
    BT Peninsulas—Norway
Lyngsalpene (Norway)
  USE Lyngen Peninsula (Norway)
Lynk family
  USE Link family
Lynn family *(Not Subd Geog)*
    UF Lind family
      Linde family
      Linden family
      Linder family
      Lindh family
      Linds family
      Linn family
      Lins family
      Lyn family
      Lynd family
      Lynde family
      Lyndes family
      Lynds family
      Lyne family
      Lynes family
      Lynne family
    RT Lin family
      Linnell family
Lynne family
  USE Lynn family

Lynnell family
  USE Linnell family
Lynscott family
  USE Linscott family
Lynscotte family
  USE Linscott family
Lynton & Barnstaple Railway
    BT Railroads—Great Britain
Lynx (Tuvalu)
  USE Niutao (Tuvalu)
Lynx
  ₁QL737.C2₁
    NT Bobcat
Lynx, Fossil
Lynx automobile
  ₁TL215.L₁
    BT Mercury automobile
Lynx rufus
  USE Bobcat
Lynx spiders
  USE Oxyopidae
Lyø (Denmark)
    BT Islands—Denmark
Lyomeri
  USE Eels
Lyomeri, Fossil
  USE Eels, Fossil
Lyon (France)
  — History
  — — Insurrection, 1834
Lyon (France). Croix Rousse
  USE Croix Rousse (Lyon, France)
Lyon (France). La Croix Rousse
  USE Croix Rousse (Lyon, France)
Lyon family
  USE Lyons family
Lyon Inlet (N.W.T.)
    BT Inlets—Northwest Territories
Lyonetidae
  USE Lyonetiidae
Lyonetiidae
  ₁QL561.L95₁
    UF Bedellidae
      Bucculatrigidae
      Cemiostomatidae
      Cemiostomidae
      Hieroxestidae
      Leucopterygidae
      Lyonetidae
    BT Lepidoptera
      Moths
    NT Bucculatrix
      Leucoptera
Lyons Electronic Office computer
  USE Leo computer
Lyons family *(Not Subd Geog)*
    UF Lion family
      Lions family
      Lyon family
Lyophilization
  USE Freeze-drying
Lyopomi
  USE Notacanthiformes
Lyperosia irritans
  USE Horn fly
Lypusidae
  USE Yponomeutidae
Lyra viol
  ₁ML760₁
    UF Lyro-viol
      Viola bastarda
    BT Viola da gamba
Lyra-viol and continuo music
    UF Continuo and lyra-viol music
Lyra-viol music
  ₁M142.L₁
    NT Suites (Lute, violin, lyra viol)
      Suites (Theorbo, violin, lyra viol)
      Suites (Violin, lyra viol, continuo)
Lyra-viol music (Lyra-viols (2))
  ₁M990₁

Lyra-viol music (Lyra-viols (3))
  USE String trios (Lyra-viols (3))
Lyrceidae
  USE Geometridae
Lyre
  ₁ML162-9₁
    NT Lyre-guitar
Lyre-birds
  ₁QL696.P2₁
Lyre-guitar
  ₁ML1015-1018₁
    UF Apollo lyre
    BT Cithara
      Guitar
      Lyre
Lyre-guitar music
  ₁M135-7₁
    NT Trios (Flute, lyre-guitar, violin)
Lyre-guitar music (Lyre-guitars (2))
  ₁M292-3₁
Lyric drama
  USE Opera
Lyric poetry
  ₁PN691 (Medieval literature)₁
  ₁PN1351-PN1389 (History and
    criticism)₁
    Here are entered general works. The lyric poetry
  of individual countries is entered under English poe-
  try, French poetry, German poetry, etc.
    BT Poetry
    NT Albas
      Ballads
      Dithyramb
      Dramatic monologues
      Elegiac poetry
      Odes
      Songs
      Sonnets
Lyricists *(May Subd Geog)*
    UF Songwriters
    BT Poets
Lyro-viol
  USE Lyra viol
Lyrurus tetrix
  USE Black grouse
Lys, Battle of the, 1918
  ₁D542.L8₁
    BT World War, 1914-1918—Campaigns—
      France
Lysaght family
  USE Lycett family
Lysander (Army cooperation airplane)
  ₁UG1242.A27₁
    BT Airplanes, Military
Lysaught family
  USE Lycett family
Lyscom family
  USE Lipscomb family
Lyse family *(Not Subd Geog)*
    UF Lyce family
Lysergic acid diethylamide
    UF LSD
    BT Amides
      Diethylamine
      Hallucinogenic drugs
      Serotonin antagonists
  — Physiological effect
      BT Hallucinations and illusions
Lysimeter
  ₁S594₁
Lysine
  ₁QD305.A7₁
    BT Amino acids
    RT High-lysine diet
  — Synthesis
Lysine in animal nutrition
  ₁SF98.L9₁
    BT Amino acids in animal nutrition
      Feed additives
Lysiosquilla
  ₁QL444.M375₁

Lysiosquilla *(Continued)*
  BT Lysiosquillidae
Lysiosquillidae
  [QL444.M375]
  BT Stomatopoda
  NT Lysiosquilla
Lysle family
  USE Lyles family
Lysoform
  [RA766.L9 (Disinfectants)]
  BT Disinfection and disinfectants
Lysogenicity
  USE Lysogeny
Lysogeny
  UF Lysogenicity
  BT Bacterial genetics
  RT Bacteriophage
Lysokinase
  USE Plasminokinase
Lysolecithin
  BT Hemolysis and hemolysins
      Lecithin
Lysosomal disorders
  USE Lysosomal storage diseases
Lysosomal storage diseases
  (May Subd Geog)
  [RJ399.L95]
  UF Cell storage disorders
      Diseases, Lysosomal storage
      Lysosomal disorders
      Storage diseases, Lysosomal
  BT Metabolism, Inborn errors of
  RT Lysosomes
  NT Mucopolysaccharidosis
      Sphingolipidoses
Lysosomes
  BT Cell organelles
      Hydrolysis
  RT Lysosomal storage diseases
Lysozyme
  [QP609.L9]
  UF Mucopeptide glucohydrolase
      Muramidase
  BT Enzymes
      Proteins
Lyssa
  USE Rabies
Lyssomanes *(May Subd Geog)*
  [QL458.42.S24]
  BT Jumping spiders
Lyster family
  USE Lister family
Lysuride hydrogen maleate
  USE Lisuride
Lysyl ribonucleic acid synthetase
  USE Lysyl-tRNA synthetase
Lysyl T RNA synthetase
  USE Lysyl-tRNA synthetase
Lysyl-transfer ribonucleate synthetase
  USE Lysyl-tRNA synthetase
Lysyl-tRNA synthetase
  [QP619.L9]
  UF Lysyl ribonucleic acid synthetase
      Lysyl T RNA synthetase
      Lysyl-transfer ribonucleate synthetase
  BT Ligases
Lyte family
  USE Little family
Lytell family
  USE Little family
Lythraceae
  [QK495.L9 (Botany)]
  BT Myrtales
  NT Ammannia
      Diplusodon
      Lagerstroemia
      Lythrum
Lythrum
  [QK495.L9 (Botany)]
  BT Lythraceae

Lytle family
  USE Little family
Lytorhynchus
  [QL666.O636]
  BT Colubridae
Lytta
  [QL596.M38]
  BT Meloidae
Lyttidae
  USE Meloidae
Lyttle family
  USE Little family
Lyvers family
  USE Livers family
M1 (Tank)
  [UG446.5]
  UF Abrams (Tank)
      XM1 (Tank)
  BT Mechanization, Military—United
      States
      Tanks (Military science)
M1 carbine
  [UD395.M17]
  BT Rifles
M2 Bradley infantry fighting vehicle
  UF Bradley M2 infantry fighting vehicle
  BT Armored personnel carriers
      Mechanization, Military—United
      States
M4 Motorway (England and Wales)
  BT Express highways—England
      Express highways—Wales
M25 Motorway (England)
  USE London Orbital Motorway (England)
M26 (Tank)
  [UG446.5]
  UF Pershing (Tank)
  BT Mechanization, Military—United
      States
      Tanks (Military science)
M42 (Nebula)
  USE Orion Nebula
M46 (Tank)
  [UG446.5]
  UF Patton (Tank)
  BT Mechanization, Military—United
      States
      Tanks (Military science)
M48 (Tank)
  UF General Patton (Tank)
      Patton (Tank)
  BT Mechanization, Military—United
      States
      Tanks (Military science)
M60 (Tank)
  UF General Patton (Tank)
      Patton (Tank)
  BT Mechanization, Military—United
      States
      Tanks (Military science)
M60 machine-gun
  BT Machine-guns
M300 Workstation
  USE OCLC M300 Workstation
M6802 (Microprocessor)
  USE Motorola 6802 (Microprocessor)
M.A. degree
  USE Master of arts degree
M.B.A. degree
  USE Master of business administration
      degree
M-component hypergammaglobulinemia
  USE Gammopathies, Monoclonal
M.G. automobile
  [TL215.M]
  BT BLMC automobiles
  NT Magnette automobile
      Midget automobile
M. Gorkio Gatvė (Vilnius, Lithuania)
  USE Gorkio Gatvė (Vilnius, Lithuania)

"M.I. Hummel" figurines
  USE Hummel figurines
M.M.B.W. Farm (Werribee, Vic.)
  USE Melbourne and Metropolitan Board of
      Works Farm (Werribee, Vic.)
M stars
  BT Cool stars
  — Absolute magnitudes
      USE M stars—Magnitudes
  — Magnitudes
      UF M stars—Absolute magnitudes
  — Motion in line of sight
      UF M stars—Radial velocity
  — Radial velocity
      USE M stars—Motion in line of sight
  — Spectra
M-structure in Banach spaces
  USE Banach spaces—M-structure
M-X missile
  USE MX (Weapons system)
MA (Set theory)
  USE Martin's axiom
Ma' Betisék (Malaysian people)
  USE Mah-Meri (Malaysian people)
MA degree
  USE Master of arts degree
Ma family *(Not Subd Geog)*
Ma huang (Plant)
  USE Ephedra
Ma jong
  USE Mah jong
Ma language
  [PL8474.M3]
  UF Amadi language
      Madi language
      Madyo language
  BT Congo (Brazzaville)—Languages
      Niger-Congo languages
Ma-na-sa-lo-wu Ch'ih (China)
  USE Manasarowar Lake (China)
Ma t'ou ch'in
  USE Morin khuur
Ma-tri (Bonpo deity)
  BT Gods, Bonpo
Ma-tsu (Chinese goddess)
  BT Gods, Chinese
Ma-wang-tui Site (China)
  BT China—Antiquities
Mă-wi language
  USE Mano language
Maa language (Kenya and Tanzania)
  USE Masai language
Maagschap van Sint-Anna Altar (Sculpture)
  BT Altarpieces—Belgium
      Altarpieces, Gothic—Belgium
      Sculpture, Belgian
      Sculpture, Gothic—Belgium
Maale (African people)
  USE Male (African people)
Maanyan language
  BT Dyak language
  NT Dusun Deyah dialect
Maanyans (Bornean people)
  BT Dyaks
      Ethnology—Indonesia
Maar family *(Not Subd Geog)*
Maas family *(Not Subd Geog)*
  UF Maase family
      Maass family
Maas River
  USE Meuse River
Maasai language
  USE Masai language
Maasbanker
  USE Trachurus trachurus
Maase family
  USE Maas family
Ma'aseh merkavah
  USE Merkava
Maass family
  USE Maas family

MAAT (Electronic computer system)
  UF Maschinelle Analyse Altägyptischer
        Texte (Electronic computer system)

MAB
  USE Multidimensional Aptitude Battery

Maba language
  [PL8475]

  UF Dzema language
        Kursa language

  BT Chad—Languages
        Nilo-Saharan languages
        Sudan—Languages

Mabaan language
  USE Maban language

Maban (African people)
  UF Maban (Nilotic tribe)
        Meban (African people)

  BT Ethnology—Sudan
        Luo (African people)
        Nilotic tribes

Maban (Nilotic tribe)
  USE Maban (African people)

Maban language
  UF Mabaan language
        Meban language

  BT Nilotic languages
        Sudan—Languages

Mabaya language
  USE Mbaya language

Mabberry family
  USE Mabry family

Mabea (African people)
  USE Bisio (African people)

Mabea language
  USE Bisio language

Maberie family
  USE Mabry family

Maberies family
  USE Mabry family

Maberry family
  USE Mabry family

Mabery family
  USE Mabry family

Maberys family
  USE Mabry family

Mabi (African people)
  USE Bisio (African people)

Mabiha language
  USE Makonde language

Mabile Indians
  USE Mobile Indians

Mabillard family (Not Subd Geog)
Mabinza language
  USE Mbinsa language

Mabrey family
  USE Mabry family

Mabreys family
  USE Mabry family

Mabrie family
  USE Mabry family

Mabries family
  USE Mabry family

Mabrouk (Dog)
  BT Dogs

Mabry family (Not Subd Geog)
  UF Mabberry family
        Maberie family
        Maberies family
        Maberry family
        Mabery family
        Maberys family
        Mabrey family
        Mabreys family
        Mabrie family
        Mabries family
        Mabrys family
        Mabury family
        Mawbery family
        Mawbury family
        Maybary family
        Mayberry family
        Maybrey family
        Mayburry family
        Maybury family
        Mowbery family
        Mowbury family
Mabrys family
  USE Mabry family
MABU (Computer program language)
Mabuiag language
  BT Australia—Languages
        Australian languages
Mabury family
  USE Mabry family
Mabuso languages
  UF Madang languages
  BT Papua New Guinea—Languages
        Papuan languages
Mabuya
  [QL666.L28]
  BT Skinks
Mabuya capensis
  [QL666.L28]
Mabuya lacertiformis
  [QL666.L28]
Mabuya striata
  [QL666.L28]
  UF African striped skink
        Skink, African striped
Mac family
  USE Mack family
Mac-Robertson Land (Antarctic regions)
  UF Macrobertson Land (Antarctic regions)
Mac XL (Computer)
  USE Lisa computer
Macá Indians
  [F2679.2.M]
  UF Makka Indians
  BT Indians of South America
Maca language
  [PM6373]
  UF Maka language
  BT Indians of South America—Paraguay—
        Languages
        Paraguay—Languages
MaCabe family
  USE McCabe family
Macaca
  USE Macaques
Macaca fascicularis
  USE Kra
Macaca fuscata
  USE Japanese macaque
Macaca irus
  USE Kra
Macaca mulatta
  USE Rhesus monkey
Macaca nemestrina
  USE Pig-tailed macaque
Macaca silenus
  USE Lion-tailed macaque
Macaca sylvana
  USE Barbary ape
Macaca sylvanus
  USE Barbary ape

Macacus cynomolgus
  USE Kra
Macacus rhesus
  USE Rhesus monkey
MacAdam family
  USE McAdam family
Macadamia nut (May Subd Geog)
  [QK495.P957 (Botany)]
  [SB401.M32 (Culture)]
  UF Macadamia ternifolia
        Macadamia tree
        Queensland nut
  BT Nuts
  NT Cookery (Macadamia nuts)
Macadamia nut industry (May Subd Geog)
  [HD9259.M23]
Macadamia ternifolia
  USE Macadamia nut
Macadamia tree
  USE Macadamia nut
Macadamized roads
  USE Roads, Macadamized
MacAdams family
  USE McAdam family
Macafee family
  USE McAfee family
Macaffee family
  USE McAfee family
Maçahua language
  USE Mazahua language
Macallay family
  USE McCauley family
Macalpin family
  USE McAlpine family
Macalpine family
  USE McAlpine family
MacAlvay family
  USE McAlevy family
Macalvy family
  USE McAlevy family
Macan Markar family (Not Subd Geog)
Macanché Island Site (Guatemala)
  (Not Subd Geog)
  BT Guatemala—Antiquities
Macao
  — Civilization
  — — Portuguese influences
        BT Portugal—Civilization
Macao Roads
  USE Lingding Roads
Macaques
  [QL737.P93]
  UF Macaca
  BT Cercopithecidae
        Monkeys
  NT Barbary ape
        Japanese macaque
        Kra
        Lion-tailed macaque
        Pig-tailed macaque
        Rhesus monkey
        Stump-tailed macaque
Macara River (Peru) (Not Subd Geog)
  UF Río Macara (Peru)
  BT Rivers—Peru
Macareno Site (Spain)
  USE Cerro Macareno Site (Spain)
Macaroni craft
  UF Noodle craft
        Pasta craft
  BT Handicraft
Macaroni factories
  [TH4541]
  BT Factories
        Food processing plants
Macaroni industry (May Subd Geog)
  [HD9330.M32-324]
  BT Macaroni products
Macaroni penguin
  UF Eudyptes chrysocome
        Eudyptes chrysolophus

Macaroni penguin (Continued)
  BT Penguins
Macaroni products
  ⌐TS2157 (Manufacture)⌐
    Here are entered works on macaroni in a generic
  sense, including spaghetti, vermicelli, and related
  products. Specific products are entered under their
  individual names, e.g. Noodles.
  UF Alimentary pastes
    Italian paste
    Pasta
    Pastes, Alimentary
    Semolina products
  BT Cereal products
    Food
    Wheat products
  NT Cookery (Macaroni)
    Macaroni industry
    Noodles
Macaroni wheat
  USE Durum wheat
Macaronic literature
  ⌐PN1489 (Poetry)⌐
  UF Literature, Macaronic
  BT Literature
    Poetry
    Wit and humor
  NT Centos
MacArthur family (Not Subd Geog)
  UF Maccairter family
    Maccarter family
    McArtair family
    McArthur family
MacArthur harp
  USE Harp zither
Macassans (Indonesian people)
  USE Makasar (Indonesian people)
Macassar language
  USE Makasar language
Macaulay family
  USE McCauley family
Macauley family
  USE McCauley family
MacAuslane family
  USE McCausland family
Macaws
  ⌐QL696.P7 (Ornithology)⌐
  ⌐SF473.P3 (Cage-birds)⌐
  BT Parrots
  NT Ara
    Blue-and-yellow macaw
MacBean family
  USE Bean family
MacBride family
  USE McBride family
MACC-7-S (Computer)
  BT Electronic digital computers
Maccabe family
  USE McCabe family
Maccabee family
  USE McCabe family
Maccabees
  UF Asmoneans
    Hasmonaeans
  BT Jews—History—586 B.C.-70 A.D.
  NT Hanukkah
Maccabees, Feast of the
  USE Hanukkah
MacCain family
  USE McCain family
Maccairter family
  USE MacArthur family
Maccall family
  USE McCall family
MacCallum family
  USE McCollum family
MacCants family
  USE McCants family
Maccarter family
  USE MacArthur family

MacCarthy (Name)
MacCarthy family
  USE McCarthy family
Maccartley family
  USE McCarthy family
Maccarty family
  USE McCarthy family
Maccauly family
  USE McCauley family
MacCausland family
  USE McCausland family
Macceacharn family
  USE McEachern family
Macchi C.202 (Fighter plane)
  USE Folgore (Fighter plane)
Macchi C.205 (Fighter plane)
  USE Veltro (Fighter plane)
Macchi C.205N (Fighter plane)
  USE Orione (Fighter plane)
Macchiaioli
  BT Painters—Italy
    Painting, Modern—19th century—Italy
Macchruiter family
  USE McWhirt family
MacClamroch family (Not Subd Geog)
  UF McClamroch family
MacClanathan family
  USE McClanathan family
MacClaughry family
  USE McClaughry family
MacClave family
  USE McClave family
MacClenthen family
  USE McClanathan family
Macclintock family
  USE McClintock family
MacCloe family
  USE McClow family
MacCloud family
  USE McLeod family
MacClow family
  USE McClow family
Macclure family
  USE McClure family
MacCollum family
  USE McCollum family
Macconnell family
  USE McConnell family
MacCorcoran family
  USE Corcoran family
MacCorkill family
  USE McCorkle family
MacCorkle family
  USE McCorkle family
MacCormack family
  USE McCormick family
MacCormick family
  USE McCormick family
MacCormick's skua
  USE South polar skua
MacCosh family
  USE McCoach family
MacCown family
  USE McCown family
MacCurdie family
  USE McCurdy family
Maccurdy family
  USE McCurdy family
Macdaniel family
  USE McDaniel family
Macdaniels family
  USE McDaniel family
Macdermid family
  USE McDermott family
MacDermot family
  USE McDermott family
Macdermott family
  USE McDermott family
MacDiarmid family
  USE McDermott family

MacDonald, John D. (John Dann), 1916-
  — Characters
    —— Travis McGee (Not Subd Geog)
      BT McGee, Travis (Fictitious
        character)
MacDonald, John D. (John Dann), 1916-
1916-
  — Characters
MacDonald family
  USE McDonald family
Macdonald River (N.S.W.)
  (Not Subd Geog)
  BT Rivers—Australia
MacDougal family
  USE McDougall family
MacDougall family
  USE McDougall family
MacDowall family
  USE McDowell family
MacDowell family
  USE McDowell family
MacDraw (Computer program)
  BT Computer graphics—Computer
    programs
MacDuff family
  USE McDuff family
MacDuffee family
  USE McDuffie family
MacDuffie family
  USE McDuffie family
MacEachern family
  USE McEachern family
Macearchern family
  USE McEachern family
Macedo-Romanian dialect
  USE Aromanian dialect
Macedo-Romanians
  USE Aromanians
Macedo-Vlachs
  USE Aromanians
Macedon Forest Park (Vic.)
  BT Forest reserves—Australia
    Parks—Australia
Macedonia
    As a geographic subdivision, this heading is used
  directly.
  — Civilization
    NT Mosaics, Byzantine—Macedonian
      influences
      Mural painting and decoration,
        Byzantine—Macedonian
        influences
  — History
    ⌐DR701.M13-4⌐
    —— To 168 B.C.
      ⌐DF233-DF238⌐
      ⌐DF261.M2⌐
      NT Chaeronea, Battle of, 338 B.C.
        Gaugamela, Battle of, 331 B.C.
        Greece—History—Macedonian
          Expansion, 359-323 B.C.
        Greece—History—
          Chremonidean War, 267-262
          B.C.
        Macedonian War, 1st, 215-205
          B.C.
        Macedonian War, 2d, 200-196
          B.C.
        Macedonian War, 3d, 171-168
          B.C.
    —— Diadochi, 323-276 B.C.
      UF Diadochi
      RT Greece—History—Macedonian
        Hegemony, 323-281 B.C.
      NT Athens (Greece)—History—
        Revolution, 286 B.C.
    —— 168 B.C.-1389 A.D.
    —— 168 B.C.-1453 A.D.
    —— 1389-1912
      NT Haiduks
        Kresnensko Uprising, 1878

— — 1878-1912
— — Uprising of 1903
    UF Ilindensko vŭstanie, 1903
    RT Turkey—History—1878-1909
— — — Anniversaries, etc.
— — — Personal narratives
— — 1912-1945
— — 1945-
Macedonia (Greece)
  UF Aegean Macedonia
    Greek Macedonia
    Makedonia (Greece)
    Makedoniya (Greece)
Macedonian almanacs
  USE Almanacs, Macedonian
Macedonian Americans *(May Subd Geog)*
  [E184.M3]
  UF Macedonian Americans—United States
  BT Ethnology—United States
    Macedonians—United States
  — United States
    USE Macedonian Americans
Macedonian authors
  USE Authors, Macedonian
Macedonian Church Slavic language
  USE Church Slavic language—Macedonian
    recension
Macedonian Conquest, Iran, 334-325 B.C.
  USE Iran—History—Macedonian Conquest,
    334-325 B.C.
Macedonian drama *(May Subd Geog)*
  BT Yugoslav drama
Macedonian essays *(May Subd Geog)*
  BT Yugoslav essays
Macedonian Expansion, Greece, 359-323 B.C.
  USE Greece—History—Macedonian
    Expansion, 359-323 B.C.
Macedonian fantastic fiction
  USE Fantastic fiction, Macedonian
Macedonian fiction *(May Subd Geog)*
  NT Fantastic fiction, Macedonian
Macedonian folk literature
  USE Folk literature, Macedonian
Macedonian folk poetry
  USE Folk poetry, Macedonian
Macedonian folk-songs
  USE Folk-songs, Macedonian
Macedonian Hegemony, 323-281 B.C.
  USE Greece—History—Macedonian
    Hegemony, 323-281 B.C.
Macedonian imprints *(May Subd Geog)*
Macedonian language
  [PG1161-4]
  BT Slavic languages, Southern
Macedonian language (Ancient)
  [P1055]
  BT Indo-European languages
Macedonian literature *(May Subd Geog)*
  BT Yugoslav literature
  NT Damaskini
    Folk literature, Macedonian
  — To 1700
Macedonian painting
  USE Painting, Macedonian
Macedonian philology
Macedonian pine
  USE Balkan pine
Macedonian poetry *(May Subd Geog)*
  [PG1163.5 (History)]
  [PG1164.A2 (Collections)]
  NT Folk poetry, Macedonian
    Revolutionary poetry, Macedonian
    War poetry, Macedonian
Macedonian poets
  USE Poets, Macedonian
Macedonian prose literature
  (May Subd Geog)
  [PG1163.5 (History)]
  [PG1164.A2 (Collections)]
Macedonian question
  [D651.M3 (European War)]

[DR701.M4 (History)]
  RT Eastern question (Balkan)
Macedonian revolutionary poetry
  USE Revolutionary poetry, Macedonian
Macedonian War, 1st, 215-205 B.C.
  [DG251]
  BT Greece—History—281-146 B.C.
    Macedonia—History—To 168 B.C.
    Punic War, 2d, 218-201 B.C.
    Rome—History—Republic, 265-30
    B.C.
Macedonian War, 2d, 200-196 B.C.
  [DG251]
  BT Greece—History—281-146 B.C.
    Macedonia—History—To 168 B.C.
    Rome—History—Republic, 265-30
    B.C.
Macedonian War, 3d, 171-168 B.C.
  [DF238-DF238.9]
  [DG251.6]
  BT Greece—History—281-146 B.C.
    Macedonia—History—To 168 B.C.
    Rome—History—Republic, 265-30
    B.C.
  NT Pydna (Greece), Battle of, 168 B.C.
Macedonian war poetry
  USE War poetry, Macedonian
Macedonian wit and humor
  (May Subd Geog)
Macedonians *(May Subd Geog)*
  BT Ethnology—Macedonia
    Slavs, Southern
  — United States
    NT Macedonian Americans
Macedonians (Ancient) *(May Subd Geog)*
  [DF261.M2]
Macedonians (Christian sect)
  USE Pneumatomachi
MacEgan family
  USE Egan family
Macellicephala
  [QL391.A6]
  BT Polyniidae
MacElroy family
  USE McElroy family
MacEnery family
  USE McHenry family
MacEniry family
  USE McHenry family
Maceral *(May Subd Geog)*
  UF Coal—Organic constituents
  BT Coal
Maces, Ceremonial
  [NK7425]
  BT Emblems
    Insignia
    Municipal ceremonial
    Truncheons
MacEuen family
  USE McEwan family
Macevoy family
  USE McEvoy family
MacEwan family
  USE McEwan family
MacEwen family
  USE McEwan family
Macey family
  USE Macy family
MacFadden family
  USE McFadden family
MacFarlan family
  USE McFarland family
MacFarland family
  USE McFarland family
MacFarlane family
  USE McFarland family
Macfarlaniella
  [QL458.2.T36]
  BT False spider mites
  NT Macfarlaniella queenslandica

Macfarlaniella queenslandica
  [QL458.2.T36]
  UF Raoiella queenslandica
  BT Macfarlaniella
MacFarlen family
  USE McFarland family
MacFarlin family
  USE McFarland family
MacFarling family
  USE McFarland family
Macfee family
  USE McPhee family
Macfie family
  USE McPhee family
MacGartlan family
  USE Garland family
MacGartland family
  USE Garland family
MacGaughey family
  USE McGaughey family
MacGauley family
  USE McGauley family
MacGee family
  USE Magee family
MacGill family
  USE McGill family
MacGilvra family
  USE McGillivray family
MacGinnis family
  USE Guinness family
Macgorrie family
  USE McGory family
MacGory family
  USE McGory family
Macgowan family
  USE McGowan family
MacGrady family
  USE McGrady family
Macgrath family
  USE McGrath family
MacGregor family
  USE McGregor family
MacGuckin family
  USE McGuckin family
MacGuinness family
  USE Guinness family
Mach bands
  UF Mach rings
  BT Optics, Physiological
Mach family *(Not Subd Geog)*
Mach number
  BT Aerodynamics
    Compressibility
  NT Aerodynamics, Hypersonic
Mach rings
  USE Mach bands
Machaculi Indians
  USE Masacali Indians
Machado family *(Not Subd Geog)*
Machaerites
  [QL596.P8]
  BT Pselaphidae
Machaerotidae
  USE Cercopidae
Machan family
  USE McCann family
Machar Marshes (Sudan)
  UF Machar Swamp (Sudan)
  BT Marshes—Sudan
Machar Swamp (Sudan)
  USE Machar Marshes (Sudan)
MacHatton family *(Not Subd Geog)*
  UF McHatton family
Machchaj juyai language
  USE Callahuaya language
Machen (The German word)
  BT German language—Etymology
Machetes
  BT Knives
Machetes pugnax
  USE Ruff (Bird)

Macheyenga Indians
  USE Machiganga Indians
Machiavellianism (Psychology)
  BT Ethics
     Interpersonal relations
     Psychology
Machicui language
  USE Lengua-Mascoi language
Machida family *(Not Subd Geog)*
Machiganga Indians
  [F3430.1.M]
  UF Macheyenga Indians
     Machiguenga Indians
     Matshingenga Indians
     Matsigenga Indians
  BT Indians of South America
Machiganga language
  [PM6388]
  UF Matshingenga language
     Matsigenga language
  BT Indians of South America—Languages
Machiguenga Indians
  USE Machiganga Indians
Machilanus
  [QL503.8.M3]
  BT Machilidae
Machilidae
  [QL503.8.M3]
  BT Thysanura
  NT Machilanus
     Machilis
Machilis
  [QL503.8.M3]
  BT Machilidae
Machilis burgundiae
  [QL503.8.M3]
Machinability of metals
  USE Metals—Machinability
Machine appliqué *(May Subd Geog)*
  BT Appliqué
     Machine sewing
Machine assignments, Multiple
  USE Multimachine assignments
Machine breaking (Labor disputes)
  USE Machinery in industry—Sabotage
Machine ciphers
  BT Ciphers
Machine data storage and retrieval
  USE Information storage and retrieval
     systems
Machine design
  USE Machinery—Design
Machine embroidery
  USE Embroidery, Machine
Machine-gun drill and tactics
  [U167.5]
  [UF620]
  BT Machine-guns
     Tactics
  SA *subdivision* Machine-gun drill and
     tactics *under names of individual
     military services, e.g.* United States.
     Army—Machine-gun drill and
     tactics
Machine-guns
  [UF620]
  [VF410 (Naval)]
  UF Revolving cannon
  BT Firearms
     Ordnance
  NT Benet-Mercié machine-gun
     Beretta submachine gun
     Breda machine-gun
     Bren machine-gun
     Browning machine-gun
     Colt automatic machine-gun
     Degtîarev machine-gun
     Dreyse machine-gun
     Fiat machine-gun
     Gardner machine-gun
     Gatling guns

     Goriûnov machine-gun
     Hotchkiss machine-gun
     Hotchkiss revolving cannon
     Johnson light machine-gun
     Kalashnikov machine-gun
     Lewis machine-gun
     M60 machine-gun
     Machine-gun drill and tactics
     Maxim gun
     Mitrailleuses
     Nordenfelt machine-gun
     Sten machine carbine
     Submachine guns
     Thompson submachine gun
     Vickers machine-gun
Machine-Independent Organic Software Tools
  (Computer programs)
  USE MINT (Computer programs)
Machine industry
  USE Machinery industry
Machine intelligence
  USE Artificial intelligence
Machine knitting
  USE Knitting, Machine
Machine language
  USE Programming languages (Electronic
     computers)
Machine learning
  UF Learning, Machine
  BT Adaptive control systems
     Artificial intelligence
     Machine theory
     Self-organizing systems
Machine molding (Founding)
  BT Molding (Founding)
Machine parts *(May Subd Geog)*
     Here are entered general works on machine parts
  considered in themselves, not as directly related to
  complete machines. Works on parts of specific ma-
  chines are entered under the machine, e.g. Automo-
  biles—Parts. Special kinds of parts not peculiar and
  limited to specific types of machinery are entered
  under appropriate headings, e.g. Bolts and nuts,
  Cams.
  UF Machinery—Parts
     Parts, Machine
  BT Machinery
  RT Spare parts
  NT Airplanes—Parts
     Automobiles—Parts
     Automobiles—Transmission devices,
        Automatic—Parts
     Diesel motor—Parts
     Interchangeable mechanisms
     Marine engines—Carburetors—Parts
     Marine machinery—Parts
     Mining machinery—Parts
     Turbines—Parts
Machine parts industry *(May Subd Geog)*
  [HD9705.5.P37-374]
Machine quilting
  BT Machine sewing
     Quilting
  — Patterns
Machine-readable archival material
  USE Documents in machine-readable form
Machine-readable bibliographic data
  [Z699]
  UF Bibliographic data in machine-readable
        form
     Bibliographic records on magnetic tape
     Cataloging data in machine-readable
        form
     Computer-stored bibliographic data
     Machine-readable cataloging data
  BT Data bases
  SA *names of individual projects or
     systems, e.g.* MARC System
  NT BLAISE (Information retrieval system)
     CONSER Project
     ESTC Project
     On-line bibliographic searching

     PICA Project
     Retrospective conversion (Cataloging)
     UNIMARC System
  — Copyright
     USE Copyright—Machine-readable
        bibliographic data
Machine-readable Catalog System
  USE MARC System
Machine-readable cataloging data
  USE Machine-readable bibliographic data
Machine-readable data files
  USE Computer files
Machine-readable dictionaries
  UF Dictionaries, Machine-readable
  BT Encyclopedias and dictionaries
Machine-readable documents
  USE Documents in machine-readable form
Machine sewing
  [TT713]
  BT Sewing
  RT Sewing machines
  NT Embroidery, Machine
     Machine appliqué
     Machine quilting
Machine-shop mathematics
  USE Shop mathematics
Machine-shop practice
  [TJ1160-1167]
  UF Fitting (Engineering)
     Shop practice
  NT Indexing (Machine-shop practice)
     Laying-out (Machine-shop practice)
     Machining
  — **Data processing**
     NT MiCAPP (Computer system)
Machine shop practice
  — Mathematics
     USE Shop mathematics
Machine-shop practice
  — Vocational guidance
     USE Machine shops—Vocational
        guidance
Machine shops *(May Subd Geog)*
  [HD9700 (Economics)]
  [TJ1125-TJ1150 (General)]
  BT Workshops
Machine-shops
  NT Farm shops
Machine shops
  — **Automation**
     NT Machine-tools—Numerical control
  — **Electric equipment**
  — **Heating and ventilation**
     UF Machine shops—Ventilation
  — Job descriptions
     USE Machinists—Job descriptions
  — **Production standards**
  — Ventilation
     USE Machine shops—Heating and
        ventilation
  — **Vocational guidance**
     UF Machine-shop practice—Vocational
        guidance
     BT Machinists
Machine shorthand
  USE Stenotypy
Machine systems, Virtual
  USE Virtual computer systems
Machine theory
     Here are entered works on the abstract math-
  ematical models of devices which operate within a
  consistent logical system in accordance with a given
  algorithm; such mathematical theory can be used as
  a basis for design but is not concerned with hardware.
  UF Abstract automata
     Abstract machines
     Automata
     Mathematical machine theory

BT Algorithms
  Logic, Symbolic and mathematical
  Mathematical models
  Recursive functions
RT Robotics
NT Artificial intelligence
  Coding theory
  Computational complexity
  Computers
  Control theory
  Electronic data processing
  Formal languages
  L systems
  Logic design
  Machine learning
  Post machines
  Probabilistic automata
  Rewriting systems (Computer science)
  Sequential machine theory
  Switching theory
  Turing machines
Machine theory in literature
UF Automata in literature
Machine-tool industry *(May Subd Geog)*
  ⌐HD9703┐
BT Machine-tools
Machine-tool leasing
Machine-tools
  ⌐HD9703 (Economics)┐
  ⌐TJ1180-TJ1313┐
UF Automatic machine-tools
  Machine-tools, Automatic
  Transfer machines
BT Machinery
  Machinery, Automatic
  Metal-working machinery
  Tools
RT Machining
  Manufacturing processes
SA *specific machine-tools, e.g.* Planing-
    machines, Screw-cutting machines
NT Honing machines
  Indexing (Machine-shop practice)
  Jig borers
  Jigs and fixtures
  Machine-tool industry
  Metals—Machinability
  Spindles (Machine-tools)
  Tool-steel
— Advertising
  USE Advertising—Machine-tools
— Appraisal
  USE Machine-tools—Valuation
— **Bearings**
— **Design**
  ⌐TJ1185┐
— **Dynamics**
— **Electric driving**
  ⌐TK4058┐
— **Electric equipment**
— **Foundations**
  BT Foundations
— **Hydraulic drive**
  BT Oil hydraulic machinery
— **Lubrication**
— **Maintenance and repair**
— **Numerical control**
  ⌐TJ1189┐
  UF Tape-controlled machine-tools
  BT Automatic control
    Electronic control
    Electronic data processing
    Machine shops—Automation
— **Shock absorbers**
— **Transmission devices**
  BT Gearing
— **Valuation**
  ⌐TJ1185┐
  UF Machine-tools—Appraisal
— **Vibration**

Machine-tools, Automatic
USE Machine-tools
Machine-tractor stations *(May Subd Geog)*
UF Tractor stations
BT Farm mechanization, Cooperative
RT Agricultural machinery
— **Law and legislation** *(May Subd Geog)*
  BT Agricultural laws and legislation
Machine trade
USE Machinery industry
Machine translating
  ⌐P307-310┐
UF Automatic translating
  Computer translating
  Electronic translating
  Mechanical translating
BT Algorithms
  Applied linguistics
  Artificial intelligence
  Information theory
  Linguistics—Data processing
  Translating and interpreting
RT Translating machines
SA *subdivision* Machine translating *under
    names of languages, e.g.* Russian
    language—Machine translating
NT Garni computer
  United States. Air Force translator
  Ural computer
Machine vision
USE Computer vision
Machinery
  ⌐TJ┐
UF Machines
BT Engineering
  Industrial arts
  Manufactures
  Mills and mill-work
  Power (Mechanics)
  Technology
  Tools
RT Mechanical engineering
  Mechanics
  Motors
  Power transmission
SA *machinery used in particular industries
    or for special purposes, e.g.*
    Agricultural machinery; Folding-
    machines; Goffering-machines;
    Metal-working machinery; Milling
    machinery; Mining machinery;
    Mixing machinery; Screw-cutting
    machines; Tabulating machines;
    Woodworking machinery
NT Apartment houses—Mechanical
    equipment
  Balancing of machinery
  Bearings (Machinery)
  Belts and belting
  Beverage processing machinery
  Buildings—Mechanical equipment
  Clutches (Machinery)
  Construction equipment
  Couplings
  Electric engineering
  Electric machinery
  Engines
  Farm buildings—Mechanical
    equipment
  Feed mechanisms
  Food processing machinery
  Friction
  Gaskets
  Gearing
  Handles
  Hydraulic machinery
  Inclined planes
  Interchangeable mechanisms
  Inventions
  Locomotives
  Lubrication and lubricants

  Machine parts
  Machine-tools
  Mechanical drawing
  Packing (Mechanical engineering)
  Patents
  Replacement of industrial equipment
  Sealing (Technology)
  Shafting
  Simple machines
  Steam-engines
  Turning
  Used machinery
  Water-wheels
  Winding machines
  Windmills
— **Alignment**
  ⌐TJ177.5┐
  UF Alignment of machinery
  BT Machinery—Erecting work
    Shafting
  NT Optical tooling
— Appraisal
  USE Machinery—Valuation
— Balancing
  USE Balancing of machinery
— **Curious devices**
  ⌐TJ215┐
— **Design**
  ⌐TJ230-235┐
  UF Machine design
  NT Human engineering
    Machinery—Models
— Drawing
  USE Machinery—Drawings
— **Drawings**
  UF Machinery—Drawing
  BT Mechanical drawing
— **Effect of environment on**
— **Erecting work**
  ⌐TJ249┐
  NT Machinery—Alignment
    Machinery—Foundations
— **Foundations**
  ⌐TJ249┐
  BT Foundations
    Machinery—Erecting work
— — **Dynamics**
— — **Vibration**
— **Maintenance and repair**
  ⌐TJ153┐
  BT Plant maintenance
— Manufacture
  USE Machinery industry
— **Models**
  ⌐TJ248┐
  UF Mechanical models
    Models, Mechanical
  BT Machinery—Design
    Miniature objects
  RT Models (Patents)
— **Noise**
— **Painting**
  UF Machinery, Painting of
    Painting of machinery
— Parts
  USE Machine parts
— Products liability
  USE Products liability—Machinery
— **Quality control**
  UF Machinery industry—Quality
    control
— **Safety appliances**
  ⌐HD7273┐
  ⌐TJ1177 (Machine-shops)┐
— **Safety regulations** *(May Subd Geog)*
  NT Products liability—Machinery
— **Safety regulations, International**
— **Soundproofing**
— **Sounds**
  BT Sounds
— Tariff

Machinery
— Tariff *(Continued)*
    USE Duty-free importation of
        machinery
        Tariff on machinery
— **Terminology**
    UF Mechanical engineering—
        Terminology
— **Testing**
    [TJ148]
— Trade and manufacture
    USE Machinery industry
— **Valuation**
    [TJ153]
    UF Machinery—Appraisal
— **Vibration**
— **Work diagrams**
    [TJ173]
Machinery, Automatic
    [TJ212-TJ225]
    UF Automatic machinery
    BT Engineering instruments
    RT Automation
    NT Coin operated machines
        Machine-tools
        Robots, Industrial
        Screw machines, Automatic
        Vending machines
— **Buffer stocks**
    UF Buffer stocks (Transfer lines)
    BT Assembly-line methods
Machinery, Dynamics of
    [TJ170]
    BT Dynamics
    NT Machinery, Kinematics of
Machinery, Kinematics of
    [TJ175]
    UF Kinematics of machinery
    BT Machinery, Dynamics of
        Mechanical movements
    NT Rolling contact
Machinery, Marine
    USE Marine machinery
Machinery, Painting of
    USE Machinery—Painting
Machinery, Replacement of
    USE Replacement of industrial equipment
Machinery and civilization
    USE Technology and civilization
Machinery in art
    [N8222.M (Visual arts)]
    [NX650.M (Arts)]
    UF Bachelor machines
        Machines célibataires
    BT Art and technology
Machinery in industry
    [HD6331]
    BT Industry
        Technology and civilization
    RT Division of labor
        Labor productivity
        Technological innovations
        Technology—Philosophy
    NT Automation
        Capital productivity
        Factory system
        Farm mechanization
        Mechanization
        Technocracy
        Unemployment, Technological
— **Sabotage** *(May Subd Geog)*
    UF Machine breaking (Labor disputes)
        Sabotage of industrial machinery
    BT Sabotage
    NT Luddites
Machinery industry *(May Subd Geog)*
    [HD9705]
    UF Machine industry
        Machine trade
        Machinery—Manufacture
        Machinery—Trade and manufacture

— Collective bargaining
    USE Collective bargaining—Machinery
        industry
— Collective labor agreements
    USE Collective labor agreements—
        Machinery industry
— **Industrial capacity**
— **Information services** *(May Subd Geog)*
— **Law and legislation** *(May Subd Geog)*
— **Production standards** *(May Subd Geog)*
— Punched card systems
    USE Punched card systems—
        Machinery industry
— Quality control
    USE Machinery—Quality control
— Strikes and lockouts
    USE Strikes and lockouts—Machinery
        industry
— **Subcontracting**
— Wages
    USE Wages—Machinery industry
Machinery insurance
    USE Insurance, Machinery
Machines
    USE Machinery
Machines, Balancing of
    USE Balancing of machinery
Machines, Billing
    USE Billing machines
Machines, Blasting
    USE Blasting machines
Machines, Coin operated
    USE Coin operated machines
Machines, Logic
    USE Logic machines
Machines, Post
    USE Post machines
Machines, Simple
    USE Simple machines
Machines, Ticket printing
    USE Ticket printing machines
Machines, Water-wave
    USE Wave makers
Machines célibataires
    USE Machinery in art
Machining
    [TJ1185]
    Here are entered works on methods for changing
    the size or shape of a workpiece by means of ma-
    chine-operated cutting tools and including standard
    operations such as turning, shaping and planing, mill-
    ing, grinding, and drilling.
    UF Materials—Machining
    BT Machine-shop practice
        Manufacturing processes
    RT Cutting
        Machine-tools
    NT Ceramic materials—Machining
        Ceramics cutting
        Drilling and boring
        Electrochemical cutting
        Electron beam cutting
        Grinding and polishing
        Hard materials—Machining
        High-speed machining
        Laser beam cutting
        Metal-cutting
        Plastics cutting
        Stone-cutting
        Turning
        Ultrasonic cutting
        Woodwork
Machinists *(May Subd Geog)*
    [HD8039.M2-22]
    NT Machine shops—Vocational guidance
        Tool and die makers
— **Job descriptions**
    UF Machine shops—Job descriptions
— Trade-unions
    USE Trade-unions—Machinists

Machinist's mates (United States Navy)
    USE United States. Navy—Machinist's
        mates
Machinists' tools
    [TJ1195-1200]
    BT Tools
MacHone family
    USE McHone family
MacHose family
    USE McHose family
Machu Picchu (Peru) *(Not Subd Geog)*
    UF Machupijchu (Peru)
    BT Cities and towns, Ruined, extinct, etc.
        —Peru
        Peru—Antiquities
Machupijchu (Peru)
    USE Machu Picchu (Peru)
Machzorim
    USE Mahzorim
Machzors
    USE Mahzorim
Macias Nguema (Equatorial Guinea)
    USE Fernando Po (Equatorial Guinea)
Macinnes family
    USE McInnis family
Macinnis family
    USE McInnis family
Macintosh (Computer)
    [QA76.8.M]
    UF Apple Macintosh (Computer)
    BT Microcomputers
Macintosh family
    USE McIntosh family
Macintosh Toolbox (Computer programs)
    UF Toolbox, Macintosh (Computer
        programs)
    BT Computer programs
Macintosh XL (Computer)
    USE Lisa computer
MacIntyre family
    USE McIntyre family
Maciora family *(Not Subd Geog)*
MacIver family
    USE McIver family
MacIvor family
    USE McIver family
Mack family *(Not Subd Geog)*
    UF Mac family
        Macks family
    BT Mauck family
    RT McKey family
        Mock family
Mack trucks
    [TL230.5.M]
    BT Trucks
MacKale family
    USE McKale family
Mackan family
    USE McCann family
Mackaness family *(Not Subd Geog)*
    UF Mackarness family
        Mackerness family
        Makernes family
        Makernesse family
MacKanze family
    USE McCants family
Mackarness family
    USE Mackaness family
MacKay family
    USE McKay family
MacKays family
    USE McKay family
Macke family
    USE McKey family
MacKee family
    USE McKey family
MacKelvey family
    USE McKelvey family
Mackenzie clan
    USE Mackenzie family

Mackenzie family (Not Subd Geog)
UF Mackenzie clan
McKenzie family
Mackenzie Mountains (N.W.T. and Yukon)
UF Mackenzie Range (N.W.T. and Yukon)
BT Mountains—Northwest Territories
Mountains—Yukon Territory
Mackenzie Pipeline (N.W.T.)
USE Mackenzie Valley Pipeline (N.W.T.)
Mackenzie Range (N.W.T. and Yukon)
USE Mackenzie Mountains (N.W.T. and Yukon)
Mackenzie River (N.W.T.)
BT Rivers—Northwest Territories
NT Sans Sault Rapids (N.W.T.)
Mackenzie Valley pipeline
USE Mackenzie Valley Pipeline (N.W.T.)
Mackenzie Valley Pipeline (N.W.T.)
UF Mackenzie Pipeline (N.W.T.)
Mackenzie Valley pipeline
BT Gas, Natural—Northwest Territories—Pipe lines
Mackerel
[QL638.S35 (Zoology)]
[SH336.5.M (Fish processing)]
UF Atlantic mackerel
Scomber scombrus
NT Cookery (Mackerel)
Mackerel, Indian
USE Rastrelliger kanagurta
Mackerel fisheries (May Subd Geog)
[SH351.M2]
BT Fisheries
NT Bonito fisheries
Mackerel fishing
[SH691.M25]
BT Fishing
Mackerel sharks
USE Lamnidae
Mackerels, Snake
USE Gempylidae
Mackerness family
USE Mackaness family
Mackerras family (Not Subd Geog)
Mackey family
USE McKey family
Mackie family
USE McKey family
MacKim family
USE McKim family
Mackinac, Straits of (Mich.)
UF Straits of Mackinac (Mich.)
BT Straits—Michigan
— Bridges
NT Mackinac Bridge (Mich.)
Mackinac Bridge (Mich.)
BT Bridges—Michigan
Mackinac, Straits of (Mich.)—Bridges
Mackinac, Fort (Mackinac Island, Mich.)
USE Fort Mackinac (Mackinac Island, Mich.)
Mackinac Island (Mich. : Island)
BT Islands—Michigan
Mackinaw trout
USE Lake trout
MacKinlay family
USE McKinley family
MacKinley family
USE McKinley family
Mackinnon family
USE McKinnon family
Mackintosh family
USE McIntosh family
MacKirdy family
USE McCurdy family
Mackley family (Not Subd Geog)
Mackley River (N.Z.)
USE Orikaka River (N.Z.)

Macklin family (Not Subd Geog)
UF Mackling family
Mechlin family
Mechling family
Mackling family
USE Macklin family
MacKnight family
USE McKnight family
Mackoy family
USE McCoy family
Macks family
USE Mack family
Macky family
USE McKey family
Maclachlan family
USE McLaughlin family
MacLaine family
USE McLean family
Maclatzinca language
USE Ocuiltec language
Maclaughlin family
USE McLaughlin family
Maclaurin's series (Mathematics)
USE Series, Taylor's
MacLaury family
USE McClaughry family
MacLean family
USE McLean family
Macleay family (Not Subd Geog)
UF McLeay family
Maclennan family
USE McLennan family
MacLeod family
USE McLeod family
MacLevain family
USE McElwain family
MacManus family
USE McManus family
MacMillan family
USE McMillan family
MacMurray family
USE McMurray family
MacNachtan clan
USE McNaughton family
MacNaghten clan
USE McNaughton family
MacNair family
USE McNair family
MacNamara family
USE McNamara family
MacNauchtan clan
USE McNaughton family
MacNeal family
USE McNeil family
MacNeese family
USE McNeese family
MacNeil family
USE McNeil family
Macomber family
USE McCumber family
Macon, Fort (N.C.)
USE Fort Macon (N.C.)
Macon family
USE McCann family
Maconaghy family
USE McConaghy family
Maconde language
USE Makonde language
Mâconnais (France)
Macoushi Indians
USE Macusi Indians
Macoy family
USE McCoy family
MacPaint (Computer program)
BT Computer graphics—Computer programs
MacPeak family
USE McPeak family
MacPeake family
USE McPeak family

MacPeek family
USE McPeak family
MacPharlen family
USE McFarland family
Macphee family
USE McPhee family
Macpherson family
USE McPherson family
MacProject (Computer program)
[HD30.2]
BT Management—Computer programs
Macquarie, Lake (N.S.W.)
UF Lake Macquarie (N.S.W.)
BT Lakes—Australia
Macquarie Island (Tas.)
UF Macquarrie Island (Tas.)
BT Islands—Australia
Macquarrie Island (Tas.)
USE Macquarie Island (Tas.)
MacQuatty family
USE McQuitty family
Macqueen family
USE McQueen family
MacQuitty family
USE McQuitty family
Macracanthorhynchus (May Subd Geog)
[QL391.A2]
BT Oligacanthorhynchidae
NT Macracanthorhynchus hirudinaceus
Macracanthorhynchus hirudinaceus
(May Subd Geog)
[QL391.A2]
BT Macracanthorhynchus
MacRae family
USE McRae family
Macramé
[TT840]
UF Square knotting
BT Knots and splices
Lace and lace making
RT Ropework
— Patterns
MACRO-10 (Computer program language)
[QA76.73.M]
BT Assembler language (Computer program language)
DECsystem-10 (Computer)—Programming
MACRO-11 (Computer program language)
[QA76.73.M]
BT Assembler language (Computer program language)
PDP-11 (Computer)—Programming
Programming languages (Electronic computers)
Macro assembly programming
USE MAP (Computer program language)
Macro instructions (Electronic computers)
[QA76.6]
UF Macroinstructions (Electronic computers)
Macros (Electronic computers)
BT Electronic digital computers—Programming
Macroprogramming
NT MOPI (Computer system)
Macro Oriented Program Interpreter (Computer system)
USE MOPI (Computer system)
Macro-Penutian language phylum
USE Penutian languages
Macro processors
[QA76.6]
UF Processors, Macro
BT Electronic digital computers—Programming
Macroprogramming
RT Assembling (Electronic computers)
Compiling (Electronic computers)
Translators (Computer programs)

Macro-sociology
  USE Macrosociology
Macrobertson Land (Antarctic regions)
  USE Mac-Robertson Land (Antarctic
      regions)
Macrobiotic cookery
  USE Macrobiotic diet—Recipes
Macrobiotic diet
  ⌈RM235⌉
  UF Diet, Macrobiotic
      Macrobiotics
  BT Longevity—Nutritional aspects
      Vegetarianism
      Yin-yang
  — Recipes
      UF Cookery, Macrobiotic
          Macrobiotic cookery
      BT Vegetarian cookery
Macrobiotic restaurants (May Subd Geog)
  UF Restaurants, Macrobiotic
  BT Restaurants, lunch rooms, etc.
Macrobiotics
  USE Macrobiotic diet
Macrobrachium
  ⌈QL444.M33⌉
  BT Palaemonidae
Macrobrachium rosenbergii
  ⌈QL444.M33⌉
Macrocallista
  ⌈QL430.7.L8⌉
  BT Lucinidae
Macrocallista nimbosa
  ⌈QL430.7.L8⌉
  UF Sunray clam
      Sunray venus clam
      Venus clam, Sunray
Macrocentrus
  ⌈QL568.B8⌉
  BT Braconidae
Macrocephalidae
  USE Phymatidae
Macrochelys
  USE Alligator snapping turtle
Macrochires
  USE Apodiformes
Macrochirichthys
  ⌈QL638.C94⌉
  BT Cyprinidae
Macrochirichthys macrochirus
  ⌈QL638.C94⌉
Macroclemys
  USE Alligator snapping turtle
Macroclemys temminckii
  USE Alligator snapping turtle
Macrocosm and microcosm
  USE Microcosm and macrocosm
Macrocystis (May Subd Geog)
  ⌈QK569.L53 (Algology)⌉
  BT Lessoniaceae
  NT Giant kelp
      Macrocystis integrifolia
Macrocystis integrifolia (May Subd Geog)
  ⌈QK569.L53 (Algology)⌉
  BT Macrocystis
Macrocystis pyrifera
  USE Giant kelp
Macrodasyoidea
  ⌈QL391.G2⌉
  BT Gastrotricha
  NT Turbanella
Macrodiplactidae
  USE Libellulidae
Macroeconomics
  BT Economics
  NT IS-LM model (Macroeconomics)
  — Computer programs
      NT FAIRMODEL (Computer
          program)
Macrogenioglottus
  ⌈QL668.E257⌉
  BT Leptodactylidae

Macrogenioglottus alipioi
  ⌈QL668.E257⌉
Macrogeomys
  USE Orthogeomys
Macroglobulins
  BT Blood proteins
      Globulin
  NT Alpha macroglobulins
      Immunoglobulin M
Macroinstructions (Electronic computers)
  USE Macro instructions (Electronic
      computers)
Macrolepidoptera
  USE Lepidoptera
Macrolide antibiotics (May Subd Geog)
  ⌈RM666.M25 (Pharmacology)⌉
  UF Macrolides
  BT Antibiotics
      Lactones
  NT Erythromycin
      Nystatin
Macrolides
  USE Macrolide antibiotics
Macromolecules
  ⌈QD380-QD388 (Chemistry)⌉
  ⌈QP801.P64 (Biochemistry)⌉
  BT Molecules
      Polymers and polymerization
      Valence (Theoretical chemistry)
  NT Biopolymers
Macronyssidae
  ⌈QL458.2.M3⌉
  BT Mites
  NT Ophionyssus
Macrophage cell killing
  USE Antibody-dependent cell cytotoxicity
Macrophages
  ⌈QR185.8.M3⌉
  UF Mononuclear phagocytes
      Phagocytes, Mononuclear
  BT Cells
      Connective tissue cells
      Killer cells
      Phagocytes
      Reticulo-endothelial system
  RT Monocytes
  NT Fc receptors
      Kupffer cells
      Tumor necrosis factor
Macrophoma phaseoli
  USE Macrophomina phaseolina
Macrophoma phaseolina
  USE Macrophomina phaseolina
Macrophomina
  ⌈QK625.S5 (Botany)⌉
  BT Sphaeropsidaceae
Macrophomina phaseoli
  USE Macrophomina phaseolina
Macrophomina phaseolina
  ⌈QK625.S5 (Botany)⌉
  ⌈SB741.C (Phytopathogen)⌉
  UF Dothiorella phaseoli
      Macrophoma phaseoli
      Macrophoma phaseolina
      Macrophomina phaseoli
      Macrophomina philippinensis
  BT Fungi, Phytopathogenic
  RT Charcoal rot
Macrophomina philippinensis
  USE Macrophomina phaseolina
Macrophotography
  ⌈TR684⌉
  UF Photomacrography
  BT Photography
      Photography, Close-up
  NT Photomicrography
Macrophyllodromia
  ⌈QL505.7.E7⌉
  BT Epilampridae
Macropis
  ⌈QL568.M46⌉

  BT Melittidae
Macropis nuda
  ⌈QL568.M46⌉
Macropodidae
  USE Kangaroos
Macropodus
  ⌈QL638.B347⌉
  BT Belontiidae
Macropodus opercularis
  USE Paradise fish
Macropodus paradisi
  ⌈QL638.A5⌉
Macroprogramming
  BT Electronic digital computers—
      Programming
  NT Macro instructions (Electronic
      computers)
      Macro processors
Macropsidae
  USE Leafhoppers
Macropsis
  ⌈QL527.C49⌉
  BT Leafhoppers
Macropus
  ⌈QL737.M35⌉
  BT Kangaroos
Macropus canguru
  USE Grey kangaroo
Macropus eugenii
  ⌈QL737.M35⌉
  UF Dama wallaby
      Tammar
Macropus giganteus
  USE Grey kangaroo
Macropus major
  USE Grey kangaroo
Macropus rufus
  USE Red kangaroo
Macrorie family
  USE Macrory family
Macrorileya
  ⌈QL568.E85⌉
  BT Eurytomidae
  NT Macrorileya oecanthi
Macrorileya oecanthi
  ⌈QL596.E85⌉
  BT Macrorileya
Macrory family (Not Subd Geog)
  UF Macrorie family
Macros (Electronic computers)
  USE Macro instructions (Electronic
      computers)
Macroscelididae
  USE Elephant shrews
Macroscelididae, Fossil
  USE Elephant shrews, Fossil
Macrosiphum
  ⌈QL527.A64⌉
  BT Aphididae
Macrosiphum euphorbiae
  ⌈QL527.A64⌉
  BT Potatoes—Diseases and pests
Macrosiphum gei
  ⌈QL527.A64⌉
Macrosiphum pisi
  USE Pea aphid
Macrosiphum sanborni
  ⌈QL527.A64⌉
  UF Black chrysanthemum aphid
  BT Chrysanthemums—Diseases and pests
Macrosiphum solanifolii
  ⌈QL527.A64⌉
Macrosociology
  UF Macro-sociology
  BT Sociology
Macrosteles
  ⌈QL527.C49⌉
  BT Leafhoppers
Macrosteles divisus
  USE Six-spotted leaf-hopper

Macrosteles fascifrons
USE Six-spotted leaf-hopper
Macrostomida
  [QL391.P7]
  BT Turbellaria
Macrostomidae
  NT Acanthomacrostomum
    Psammomacrostomum
Macrotermes
  [QL529.3.T4]
  BT Termitidae
Macrothecidae
  USE Pyralidae
Macrothricidae *(May Subd Geog)*
  [QL444.B83]
  BT Cladocera
  NT Ilyocryptus
Macrouridae
  [QL638.M2]
  UF Coryphaenoididae
    Grenadiers (Fishes)
    Lyconidae
    Macrouroididae
    Macruridae
    Rat-tails (Fishes)
    Rattail fishes
  BT Gadiformes
  NT Coelorhynchus
    Hymenocephalus
    Mesobius
    Nezumia
    Squalogadus
    Trachyrhincus
Macrouroides inflaticeps
  [QL638.M2]
Macrouroididae
  USE Macrouridae
Macrura
  USE Shrimps
Macruridae
  USE Macrouridae
Macruriformes
  USE Gadiformes
MacSweeney family *(Not Subd Geog)*
  RT Sweeney family
MACSYMA (Computer system)
  [QA76.6]
Mactar (City)
  USE Mactaris (City)
Mactaris (City)
  [DT269.M28]
  UF Mactar (City)
  BT Cities and towns, Ruined, extinct, etc.
    —Tunisia
    Tunisia—Antiquities
Macú de cubeo language
  USE Cacua language
Macú de desano language
  USE Cacua language
Macú de guanano language
  USE Cacua language
Macú de tucano language
  USE Jupda language
Macú Indians (Papury River watershed)
  [F2520.1.M2]
  UF Mahacu Indians (Papury River
      watershed)
    Makú Indians (Papury River
      watershed)
    Maucu Indians (Papury River
      watershed)
  BT Indians of South America
    Indians of South America—Brazil
    Indians of South America—Colombia
Macú language
  [PM6393]
  BT Indians of South America—Languages
  NT Cacua language
    Jupda language
Macua (African people)
  USE Makua (African people)

Macua language
  USE Makua language
Macuchy Indians
  USE Macusi Indians
Macula lutea
  [QL949 (Comparative anatomy)]
  [QM551 (Human anatomy)]
  [QP479 (Physiology)]
  UF Macula retinae
  BT Retina
Macula retinae
  USE Macula lutea
Macular degeneration
  USE Retinal degeneration
Macumba (Cultus)
  USE Umbanda (Cultus)
Macumber family
  USE McCumber family
Macuna Indians
  UF Buhágana Indians
  BT Indians of South America
    Indians of South America—Brazil
    Indians of South America—Colombia
Macuna language
  [PM6394]
  UF Buhágana language
  BT Indians of South America—Languages
Macurda family
  USE McCurdy family
Macusi Indians
  [F2280.1.M (British Guiana)]
  UF Macoushi Indians
    Macuchy Indians
    Macuxi Indians
    Makuchi Indians
    Mokushi Indians
  BT Carib Indians
    Indians of South America
Macusi language
  [PM6397]
  UF Makuchi language
  BT Cariban languages
    Indians of South America—Languages
Macuxi Indians
  USE Macusi Indians
Mačva (Serbia)
MacVannel family
  USE McVannel family
MacWhorter family
  USE McWhorter family
Macwilliams family
  USE McWilliams family
Macwillian family
  USE McWilliams family
MacWrite (Computer program)
  BT Computer programs
    Word processing—Computer programs
Macy family *(Not Subd Geog)*
  UF Macey family
    Maisey family
    Masey family
MAD (Computer program language)
  [QA76.5]
  UF Algorithmic language
    Michigan algorithm decoder
    Symbolic language
Mad itch
  USE Pseudorabies
Mad Mullah Rebellion, British Somaliland,
    1900-1920
  USE Maxamad Cabdulle Xasan's Rebellion,
    British Somaliland, 1900-1920
Mad River (Calif.)
  BT Rivers—California
Mad River (Ohio)
  BT Rivers—Ohio
Mada (African people)
  USE Paduko (African people)
Madagascan . . .
  USE *subject headings beginning with the
    word* Malagasy

Madagascar
  UF Malagasy Republic
  — Description and travel
  — — 1981-
  — History
  — — To 1810
      [DT469.M31-313]
  — — Hova rule, 1810-1885
      [DT469.M32-.M335]
      UF Hova rule, 1810-1885
  — — 1885-1960
      [DT469.M34-342]
  — — French invasion, 1895
      UF French invasion of Madagascar,
        1895
  — — Menalamba Rebellion, 1895-1899
      [DT469.M34]
      UF Menalamba Rebellion,
        Madagascar, 1895-1899
        Red Shawls Rebellion,
        Madagascar, 1895-1899
  — — Revolution, 1947
      [DT469.M34]
  — Languages
      NT Tsimihety dialect
  — Politics and government
  — — 1947-1960
  — — 1960-
Madagascar groundnut
  USE Bambarra groundnut
Madagascar periwinkle
  UF Cape periwinkle
    Periwinkle, Madagascar
    Red periwinkle
Madaglashti dialect
  [PK6393.M]
Madama Palace (Turin, Italy)
  USE Palazzo Madama (Turin, Italy)
Madama Villa (Rome, Italy)
  USE Villa Madama (Rome, Italy)
Madame d'Haussonville (Portrait painting)
  USE Ingres, Jean-Auguste-Dominique,
    1780-1867. Comtesse
    d'Haussonville
Madame Moitessier (Portrait painting)
  USE Ingres, Jean-Auguste-Dominique,
    1780-1867. Madame Moitessier
Madang languages
  USE Mabuso languages
    Rai Coast languages
Madcalf family
  USE Metcalf family
Madden Lake (Panama)
  UF Alajuela Lake (Panama)
    Lago Alajuela (Panama)
    Lago Madden (Panama)
  BT Chagres River (Panama)
    Lakes—Panama
    Reservoirs—Panama
Madder
  [TP925.M2]
  BT Dyes and dyeing
  NT Alizarin
Maddina Volcanics (W.A.)
  BT Volcanoes—Australia
Maddock family
  USE Maddox family
Maddocks family
  USE Maddox family
Maddox family *(Not Subd Geog)*
  UF Maddock family
    Maddocks family
    Maddux family
    Madocks family
    Madox family
Maddux family
  USE Maddox family
Maddy family *(Not Subd Geog)*
Made in Occupied Japan collectibles
  USE Japan—History—Allied occupation,
    1945-1952—Collectibles

Madehsi Indians
  [E99.M115]
  UF Modesse Indians
      Pit River Indians
  BT Achomawi Indians
      Indians of North America
Madeira (Madeira Islands)
  UF Ilha da Madeira (Madeira Islands)
  BT Islands—Madeira Islands
  — History
  — — Revolution, 1931
        [DP702.M21]
Madeira and Mamoré Railway
  USE Madeira-Mamoré Railway
Madeira-Mamoré Railway
  UF Madeira and Mamoré Railway
  BT Railroads—Brazil
Madeira nut
  USE Walnut, English
Madeira River (Brazil)
  UF Rio Madeira (Brazil)
  BT Rivers—Brazil
Madeira wine
  [TP559.P8]
  BT Fortified wines
      Wine and wine making
Madeiran storm-petrel
  USE Oceanodroma castro
Maderaner Tal (Switzerland)
  USE Maderanertal (Switzerland)
Maderaner Valley (Switzerland)
  USE Maderanertal (Switzerland)
Maderanertal (Switzerland)
  UF Maderaner Tal (Switzerland)
      Maderaner Valley (Switzerland)
      Maderanerthal (Switzerland)
  BT Valleys—Switzerland
Maderanerthal (Switzerland)
  USE Maderanertal (Switzerland)
Madero Avenue (Mexico City, Mexico)
  USE Avenida Francisco I. Madero (Mexico
        City, Mexico)
Mādhvas (May Subd Geog)
  [BL1286.2-1286.292]
  BT Hindu sects
Madhyamā pratipad
  USE Middle Way (Buddhism)
Madhyamaka-Yogācāra Buddhism
  [BQ7479]
  UF Madhyamaka-Yogācāra School
      Mādhyamika-Yogācāra Buddhism
      Mādhyamika-Yogācāra School
      Yogācāra-Madhyamaka-Svātantrika
        Buddhism
  BT Mādhyamika (Buddhism)
      Mahayana Buddhism
      Yogācāra (Buddhism)
Madhyamaka-Yogācāra School
  USE Madhyamaka-Yogācāra Buddhism
Mādhyamika (Buddhism)
  UF Central philosophy (Buddhism)
      Chūgan shisō
      Mādhyamikaśāstra
      Middle doctrine school (Mahayana
        Buddhism)
      Middle school (Mahayana Buddhism)
      Sūnyavāda (Buddhism)
  BT Mahayana Buddhism
      Philosophy, Buddhist
  NT Madhyamaka-Yogācāra Buddhism
      Prāsaṅgika
      Sunyata
      Svātantrika
  — Relations
  — — Hinduism, [etc.]
Mādhyamika-Yogācāra Buddhism
  USE Madhyamaka-Yogācāra Buddhism
Mādhyamika-Yogācāra School
  USE Madhyamaka-Yogācāra Buddhism
Mādhyamikaśāstra
  USE Mādhyamika (Buddhism)

Ma'di (African people)
  USE Lugbara (African people)
Madí (Art movement) (May Subd Geog)
  BT Arts, Modern—20th century—Latin
        America—Societies, etc.
Madi language
  USE Ma language
Ma'di language (Uganda and Sudan)
  UF Madi-ti language (Uganda and Sudan)
  BT Nilo-Saharan languages
      Sudan—Languages
      Uganda—Languages
Madi-ti language (Uganda and Sudan)
  USE Ma'di language (Uganda and Sudan)
Madia (Indic people)
  USE Maria (Indic people)
Madigas
  [DS422.C3]
  UF Madigs
Madigs
  USE Madigas
Madiha Indians
  USE Culina Indians
Madik (Papuan people)
  BT Papuans
Madīnat al-Zahrā' (City)
  USE Medina Azahàra (City)
Madīnat Waṭifah, Kawm (Egypt)
  (Not Subd Geog)
  [DT73.M23]
  UF Kawm Madīnat Waṭifah (Egypt)
      Kom Madi (Egypt)
      Madînet Waṭfa (Egypt)
      Medinet Waṭfa (Egypt)
      Philo Teris (Egypt)
      Philoteris (Egypt)
  BT Egypt—Antiquities
Madînet Waṭfa (Egypt)
  USE Madīnat Waṭifah, Kawm (Egypt)
Madīq Hurmūz
  USE Hormuz, Strait of
Madīq Tīrān
  USE Tiran, Strait of
Madison Building, Library of Congress
    (Washington, D.C.)
  USE Library of Congress James Madison
        Memorial Building (Washington,
        D.C.)
Madison Island (Marquesas Islands)
  USE Nuka Hiva (Marquesas Islands)
Madison Range (Mont.)
  BT Mountains—Montana
Madison River (Mont. and Wyo.)
  BT Rivers—Montana
      Rivers—Wyoming
Madjinngay dialect
  USE Majingai dialect
Madkin family
  USE Matkins family
Madkins family
  USE Matkins family
Madloch family
  USE Matlock family
Madness
  USE Anger
      Insanity
      Mental illness
Madocks family
  USE Maddox family
Madoera Island (Indonesia)
  USE Madura Island (Indonesia)
MADOK (Information retrieval system)
  [Z699.4.M16]
  UF Magnetband-Austauschformat für
        Dokumentationszwecke
  BT Information storage and retrieval
        systems
Madokoro Mawatari Iseki (Ogi-machi, Ōita-
    ken, Japan)
  USE Madokoro Mawatari Site (Ogi-machi,
        Ōita-ken, Japan)

**Madokoro Mawatari Site (Ogi-machi, Ōita-
    ken, Japan)** (Not Subd Geog)
  UF Madokoro Mawatari Iseki (Ogi-machi,
        Ōita-ken, Japan)
  BT Japan—Antiquities
Madonna
  USE Mary, Blessed Virgin, Saint
Madonna dei fusi (Painting)
  USE Leonardo, da Vinci, 1452-1519.
        Virgin with the yarn winder
Madonna del parto (Mural painting)
  USE Francesca, Piero della, 1416?-1492.
        Madonna del parto
Madonna delle arpié (Panel painting)
  USE Sarto, Andrea del, 1486-1530.
        Madonna of the harpies
Madonna di Loretto (Painting)
  USE Raphael, 1483-1520. Madonna of
        Loretto
Madonna di Montevergine
  USE Montevergine, Madonna di
Madonna Incoronata di Foggia
  USE Foggia, Vergine Incoronata di
Madonna of Loretto (Painting)
  USE Raphael, 1483-1520. Madonna of
        Loretto
Madonna of the harpies (Panel painting)
  USE Sarto, Andrea del, 1486-1530.
        Madonna of the harpies
Madonna sistina (Painting)
  USE Raphael, 1483-1520. Sistine
        Madonna
Madonna von Werl
  USE Werl, Madonna von
Madoqua
  USE Dik-diks
Madoqua kirki
  [QL737.U53]
  UF Damara dik-dik
      Dik-dik, Kirk's
      Kirk's dik-dik
  BT Dik-diks
Madoryx
  [QL561.S7]
  BT Sphingidae
  NT Madoryx oiclus
Madoryx oiclus (May Subd Geog)
  [QL561.S7]
  UF Sphinx oiclus
  BT Madoryx
Madox family
  USE Maddox family
Madras (India : State)
  USE Tamil Nadu (India)
Madrazo family (Not Subd Geog)
Madre, Laguna (Tex.)
  USE Laguna Madre (Tex.)
Madre de Dios River (Peru and Bolivia)
  UF Río Madre de Dios (Peru and Bolivia)
  BT Rivers—Bolivia
      Rivers—Peru
Madreporaria
  USE Scleractinia
Madreporaria, Fossil
  USE Scleractinia, Fossil
Madresfield Court (Hereford and Worcester)
  BT Manors—England
Madri, Treaty of, 1750
  UF Treaty of Madri, 1750
  BT Brazil—Foreign relations—Treaties
Madrid (Spain)
  — Siege, 1936-1939
      USE Madrid (Spain)—History—Siege,
            1936-1939
  — Description
  — — 1951-
  — History (Not Subd Geog)
  — — Siege, 1936-1939

UF Madrid (Spain)—Siege, 1936-
         1939
      Madrid (Spain), Battle of, 1936-
         1939
   BT Spain—History—Civil War,
         1936-1939—Campaigns
Madrid (Spain). Pozo del Tío Raimundo
   USE Pozo del Tío Raimundo (Madrid,
         Spain)
Madrid (Spain), Battle of, 1936-1939
   USE Madrid (Spain)—History—Siege, 1936-
         1939
Madrid school of painting
   [ND808.5.M28]
   BT Painting—Spain
      Painting, Modern—20th century—
         Spain
      Painting, Spanish
Madrigal
   [PN1493]
   [PT581.M3 (German literature)]
      Here are entered works on the madrigal as a liter-
   ary or musical form. Collections of madrigals in liter-
   ature are entered under Madrigals. Musical works
   composed in the form of the madrigal are entered
   under Madrigals (Music).
   BT Choral music
      Part-songs
Madrigal comedies
      Here are entered musical works composed in the
   form of the madrigal comedy. A second heading for
   medium is assigned if a specific medium of performance is given in the work.
   UF Comedies, Madrigal
   BT Madrigals (Music), Italian
Madrigals
   [PR1195.M2 (English literature)]
      Here are entered collections of madrigals in litera-
   ture. Musical works composed in the form of the
   madrigal are entered under Madrigals (Music).
   Works on the madrigal as a literary or musical form
   are entered under Madrigal.
   BT Poetry
      Songs
      Vocal music
Madrigals (Music)
      Here are entered musical works composed in the
   form of the madrigal. The heading is qualified by
   language when the text is in one language only.
      A second heading for medium is assigned if a
   specific medium of performance is given in the work.
      Works on the madrigal as a literary or musical
   form are entered under Madrigal. Collections of ma-
   drigals in literature are entered under Madrigals.
   BT Part-songs
      Vocal duets
      Vocal ensembles
      Vocal nonets
      Vocal octets
      Vocal quartets
      Vocal quintets
      Vocal septets
      Vocal sextets
      Vocal trios
Madrigals (Music), English
   UF English madrigals (Music)
Madrigals (Music), English, [Spanish, etc.]
Madrigals (Music), Hungarian
   UF Hungarian madrigals (Music)
Madrigals (Music), Italian
   UF Italian madrigals (Music)
   NT Madrigal comedies
Madrigals (Music), Portuguese
   UF Portuguese madrigals (Music)
Madsen family (Not Subd Geog)
   UF Madson family
Madson family
   USE Madsen family
Madtom, Margined
   USE Margined madtom
Madtom, Pigmy
   USE Pigmy madtom

Madtoms
   USE Noturus
Madura foot
   USE Mycetoma
Madura Island (Indonesia)
   UF Madoera Island (Indonesia)
      Pulau Madura (Indonesia)
   BT Islands—Indonesia
Madurese language
   [PL5351-PL5354]
   BT Malayan languages
Maduromycosis
   USE Mycetoma
Madvig family (Not Subd Geog)
Madwort
   USE Alyssum
Madyo language
   USE Ma language
Mae-Enga
   USE Enga (New Guinea people)
Mae Klong River (Thailand)
   UF Khwae Yai River (Thailand)
      Klong River (Thailand)
      Meklong River (Thailand)
   BT Rivers—Thailand
Mae Nam Chao Buraya (Thailand)
   USE Chao Phraya River (Thailand)
Mae Nam Chao Praya (Thailand)
   USE Chao Phraya River (Thailand)
Mae Nam Khong
   USE Mekong River
Mae Nam Luang (Thailand)
   USE Huai Luang River (Thailand)
**Maea, José, 1759-1826. Portrait of Juan de
   Herrera**
   UF Juan de Herrera (Portrait drawing)
Maeander River (Turkey)
   USE Büyük Menderes River (Turkey)
Maecenatism
   USE Art patronage
      Authors and patrons
Maeda family (Not Subd Geog)
Maeder family
   USE Meador family
Maedi disease
   USE Visna-maedi
Maedi virus
   USE Visna-maedi
Maender River (Turkey)
   USE Büyük Menderes River (Turkey)
Maenge (Melanesian people)
   UF Mengen (Melanesian people)
   BT Ethnology—Papua New Guinea
Maenidae
   USE Centracanthidae
Maeotis Palus (Ukraine and R.S.F.S.R.)
   USE Azov, Sea of (Ukraine and R.S.F.S.R.)
Maes River
   USE Meuse River
Maesopsis
   [QK495.R45 (Botany)]
   BT Rhamnaceae
Maesopsis eminii
   [QK495.R45 (Botany)]
   [SD397.M16 (Forestry)]
Maestrazgo (Spain)
   UF El Maestrazgo (Spain)
Maestri comacini (Builders)
   USE Comacine Masters (Builders)
Mafa (African people)
   USE Matakam (African people)
Mafalda (Comic strip)
   USE Quino. Mafalda
Maffet family
   USE Moffett family
Mafia (May Subd Geog)
   [HV6441-6453]
   BT Crime and criminals
      Italian American criminals
      Organized crime

   RT Black Hand (United States)
      Camorra
Mafia in literature
Mafield family
   USE Mayfield family
Mafor language
   USE Nufor language
Mafulu language
   USE Fuyuge language
Mafulus
   [DU740 (History)]
   [GN671.N5 (Anthropology)]
   UF Fuyuge
      Mambule
Maga language
   USE Tumak language
Magahi language
   [PK1821-4]
   BT Bihari language
Magahi literature (May Subd Geog)
   [PK1823.5-1824]
   — 20th century
Magahi philology
Magan family (Not Subd Geog)
Magano Iseki (Matsubase-machi, Japan)
   USE Magano Site (Matsubase-machi, Japan)
Magano Site (Matsubase-machi, Japan)
   (Not Subd Geog)
   UF Magano Iseki (Matsubase-machi,
      Japan)
   BT Japan—Antiquities
Magar language
   [PL3801.M15]
   BT Tibeto-Burman languages
Magar women
   USE Women, Magar
Magarac, Joe (Legendary character)
   UF Joe Magarac (Legendary character)
   BT Folklore—United States
Magars
   BT Ethnology—Nepal
Magas Tátra (Czechoslovakia and Poland)
   USE Tatra Mountains (Czechoslovakia and
      Poland)
Magatama
   [GT2350]
   BT Beads
Magaw family
   USE McGaw family
Magawley family
   USE McGauley family
Magazine advertising
   USE Advertising, Magazine
Magazine covers (May Subd Geog)
   UF Covers (Magazine)
   BT Periodicals
   NT Comic book covers
Magazine design
   [Z253.5]
   UF Design, Magazine
      Periodical design
   BT Periodicals, Publishing of
   RT Printing, Practical—Layout
   NT Nameplates of publications
      Periodicals—Format
Magazine editing
   USE Journalism—Editing
Magazine illustration (May Subd Geog)
   [NC968 (General)]
   [NC975-NC995.8 (Special countries)]
   UF Illustration, Magazine
      Periodical illustration
   BT Illustrated periodicals
      Periodicals
   NT Journalism, Pictorial
   — 19th century (May Subd Geog)
   — 20th century (May Subd Geog)
Magazine publishing
   USE Periodicals, Publishing of
Magazine selection
   USE Periodical selection

Magazines
USE Periodicals
Magazines, Powder
USE Powder-magazines
Magdala Campaign, 1867-1868
USE Abyssinian Expedition, 1867-1868
Magdalena Mountains (N.M.)
(Not Subd Geog)
BT Mountains—New Mexico
NT South Baldy Peak (N.M.)
Magdalena Palace (Santander, Spain)
USE Palacio de la Magdalena (Santander, Spain)
Magdalena River (Colombia)
UF Río Magdalena (Colombia)
BT Rivers—Colombia
Magdalenian culture *(May Subd Geog)*
UF Reindeer period
BT Man, Prehistoric
Paleolithic period
Magdalensberg (Austria)
BT Mountains—Austria
Magdalis
[QL596.C9]
BT Curculionidae
Magdeburg dooms
USE Magdeburg law
Magdeburg experiments
[QC141]
BT Atmospheric pressure
Magdeburg law
UF Magdeburg dooms
BT Law—Germany
Law, Saxon
SA *special legal headings with* Magdeburg law *added in parentheses, e.g.*
Husband and wife (Magdeburg law); Inheritance and succession (Magdeburg law)
Mage family
USE Magee family
Magee family *(Not Subd Geog)*
UF MacGee family
Mage family
Magehee family
Maghee family
McGahee family
McGee family
McGehee family
McGhee family
McGhie family
Megee family
Megehee family
RT McKey family
Magee-Gutierrez Expedition, 1812-1813
USE Gutierrez-Magee Expedition, 1812-1813
Magehee family
USE Magee family
Magellan, Strait of (Chile and Argentina)
UF Estrecho de Magellanes (Chile and Argentina)
Strait of Magellan (Chile and Argentina)
BT Straits—Argentina
Straits—Chile
MAGELLAN (Computer programs)
BT Gravity—Measurement—Computer programs
Magellan Archipelago (Japan)
USE Volcano Islands (Japan)
Magellanic Clouds
[QB858.5.M33]
UF Clouds, Magellanic
Clouds of Magellan
Large Magellanic Cloud
Small Magellanic Cloud
BT Dwarf galaxies
Dwarf galaxies
Galaxies
Stars

Magen David
UF David's shield
Mogen David
Shield of David
Star of David
BT Jewish art and symbolism
Magen family
USE Maugans family
Magenis family
USE McInnis family
Magennis family
USE McInnis family
Magens family
USE Maugans family
Magenta, Battle of, 1859
[DG554.5.M2]
BT Italy—History—War of 1859—Campaigns
Magerøy family *(Not Subd Geog)*
Magerøy Island (Norway)
BT Islands—Norway
Magersfontein, South Africa, Battle of, 1899
[DT934.M22]
BT South African War, 1899-1902
Maggid (Cabala)
BT Cabala
Hallucinations and illusions
Psychology, Pathological
Psychology, Religious
Maggiore, Lake (Italy and Switzerland)
UF Lac de Locarno (Italy and Switzerland)
Lac Majeur (Italy and Switzerland)
Lago Maggiore (Italy and Switzerland)
Lake Maggiore (Italy and Switzerland)
Locarno Lake (Italy and Switzerland)
Majeur Lake (Italy and Switzerland)
Verbanus Lacus (Italy and Switzerland)
BT Lakes—Italy
Lakes—Switzerland
Maggots
BT Flies
Maggs Mountain (Tas.) *(Not Subd Geog)*
BT Mountains—Australia
Magh Rath, Battle of, 637
[DA932.4]
BT Ireland—History—To 1172
Maghee family
USE Magee family
Maghemite *(May Subd Geog)*
BT Iron ores
Maghreb
USE Africa, North
Maghrib
USE Africa, North
Maghs
[DS393.83.M3]
UF Arakanese in Bangladesh
Mags
Marma
Mogs
Mugs (Indic people)
BT Ethnology—Bangladesh
Magi
[BT315]
UF Three Kings (Magi)
Three Wise Men (Magi)
Wise Men (Magi)
BT Epiphany
NT Holy Innocents, Massacre of the
— Art
[N8110]
BT Jesus Christ—Art
Magi language (Central Province, Papua New Guinea)
USE Mailu language

Magi language (Southern Highlands Province, Papua New Guinea)
UF Angal Heneng language, South
Nembi language (Southern Highlands Province, Papua New Guinea)
South Angal Heneng language
BT Papua New Guinea—Languages
Papuan languages
Magic *(May Subd Geog)*
[BF1585-BF1623 (Occultism)]
[GN475.3 (Ethnology)]
Here are entered works on the use of charms, spells, etc., believed to have supernatural power to produce or prevent a particular result considered unobtainable by natural means. Works on a type of entertainment in which a performer does tricks of so-called magic are entered under Conjuring.
UF Necromancy
Sorcery
Spells
BT Occultism
NT Amulets
Cabala
Charms
Idols and images
Incantations
Magic drawings
Magical thinking
Mana
Medicine, Magic, mystic, and spagiric
Science and magic
Symbolism of numbers
Talismans
Tantrism
— Cataloging
USE Cataloging of magic literature
— **Religious aspects**
— — **Buddhism, [Christianity, etc.]**
— — **Christianity**
[BR115.M25]
UF Christianity and magic
Magic, Ancient
Magic, Anglo-Saxon
UF Anglo-Saxon magic
Magic, Assyro-Babylonian
[BF1591]
UF Assyro-Babylonian magic
Magic, Chaldean
NT Magic, Semitic
Magic, Buddhist
[BQ4570.M3]
UF Buddhist magic
NT Amulets (Buddhism)
Magic, Chaldean
USE Magic, Assyro-Babylonian
Magic, Coptic
UF Coptic magic
RT Magic, Egyptian
Magic, Egyptian
[BF1591]
UF Egyptian magic
RT Magic, Coptic
Magic, Ethiopian
NT Ethiopian magic scrolls
Magic, Germanic, [Gypsy, Hindu, etc.]
Magic, Gypsy
UF Gypsy magic
Magic, Hindu
NT Amulets (Hinduism)
Magic, Indian
USE Indians of Central America—Magic
Indians of North America—Magic
Magic, Islamic
UF Islamic magic
Magic, Muslim
Muslim magic
NT Amulets (Islam)
Zār
Magic, Jewish
UF Jewish magic
BT Magic, Semitic

NT Amulets (Judaism)
Magic, Muslim
  USE Magic, Islamic
Magic, Rubik's
  USE Rubik's Magic
Magic, Semitic
  [BF1591]
  UF Semitic magic
  BT Magic, Assyro-Babylonian
  NT Magic, Jewish
Magic and drugs
  [BF1623.D]
  BT Drugs
Magic and music
  USE Music and magic
Magic and poetry
  [PN1077]
  BT Poetry
      Religion and poetry
Magic Cube, Rubik's
  USE Rubik's Cube
Magic cubes
  [QA165]
      Here are entered works dealing with the three-
  dimensional array of integers which is counterpart to
  the two-dimensional magic square. Works on in-
  dividual three-dimensional geometric mathematical
  recreations are entered under Rubik's Cube; Rubik's
  Revenge; etc.
  UF Cubes, Magic
  BT Mathematical recreations
Magic drawings (May Subd Geog)
  UF Drawings, Magic
  BT Charms
      Magic
      Witchcraft
Magic drawings, Balinese (May Subd Geog)
  UF Balinese magic drawings
Magic flute (Ballet)
  UF Flûte enchantée (Ballet)
      Volshebnaĭa fleĭta (Ballet)
      Zauberflöte (Ballet)
  BT Ballets
Magic in art
  [N8222.M3]
Magic in literature
  RT Magic realism (Literature)
Magic lanterns
  USE Projectors
Magic medicine
  USE Medicine, Magic, mystic, and spagiric
Magic mirrors (May Subd Geog)
  [BF1325-BF1331]
  UF Catoptromancy
      Mirrors, Magic
  BT Fortune-telling
Magic mushroom, Starborn
  USE Psilocybe cubensis
Magic mushrooms
  USE Mushrooms, Hallucinogenic
Magic realism (Art) (May Subd Geog)
  [N6494.M3]
  UF Magischer Realismus (Art)
      Precise realism (Art)
      Realism, Magic (Art)
  BT Realism in art
      Surrealism
  RT New objectivity (Art)
  — **United States**
      BT Precisionism—Influence
Magic realism (Literature)
  BT Fantastic fiction
      Surrealism
  RT Magic in literature
      Marvelous, The, in literature
      Realism in literature
Magic scrolls, Ethiopian
  USE Ethiopian magic scrolls
Magic Snake, Rubik's
  USE Rubik's Snake

Magic squares
  [QA165]
  UF Latin squares and rectangles
      Squares, Magic
  BT Numbers, Theory of
  RT Mathematical recreations
  NT Rotas-Sator square
Magical thinking (May Subd Geog)
  UF Mystical-magic thinking
  BT Fantasy
      Magic
      Thought and thinking
  NT Charms
Magicians (May Subd Geog)
  [BF1597-BF1598 (Occult sciences)]
  [GV1545 (Conjuring)]
  UF Conjurers
      Enchanters
      Sorcerers
  BT Conjuring
      Entertainers
  RT Wizards
  NT Miracle workers
Magicicada
  USE Periodical cicada
Magill family
  USE McGill family
Magindanao Island (Philippines)
  USE Mindanao Island (Philippines)
Magindanao language
  [PL5911-5914]
  UF Magindanau language
      Maguindanao language
      Moro languages
  BT Philippine languages
Magindanaos (Philippine people)
  [DS666.M23]
  UF Magindanaus (Philippine people)
      Maguindanaos (Philippine people)
  BT Ethnology—Philippines
      Muslims—Philippines
Magindanau language
  USE Magindanao language
Magindanaus (Philippine people)
  USE Magindanaos (Philippine people)
Maginnis family
  USE McInnis family
Maginot Line (France)
  UF Ligne Maginot (France)
  BT Fortification—France
Magins family
  USE Maugans family
Magirus Deutz trucks
  USE Magirus trucks
Magirus trucks
  [TL230.5.M]
  UF Magirus Deutz trucks
  BT Trucks
Magischer Realismus (Art)
  USE Magic realism (Art)
Magister (Training planes)
  BT Training planes
Magisterium ecclesiae
  USE Catholic Church—Teaching office
Magisterium Summi Pontificis
  USE Popes—Teaching office
Magistracy, Roman
  USE Magistrates, Roman
Magistral
  BT Pyrites
      Silver—Metallurgy
Magistrates
  USE Judges
      Justices of the peace
      Police magistrates
Magistrates, Roman
  [DG83.5.M2]
  UF Magistracy, Roman
      Magistratus municipales
      Roman magistrates

  BT Rome—Officials and employees
      Rome—Politics and government
Magistrates, United States
  USE United States magistrates
Magistratus municipales
  USE Magistrates, Roman
Magistri officiorum (Roman officials)
  [DG83.5.M23]
  BT Rome—Officials and employees
      Rome—Politics and government
Maglemose (Denmark)
  BT Bogs—Denmark
      Natural areas—Denmark
Maglemosean culture (May Subd Geog)
  [GN774.2.M33]
  UF Big bog period
  BT Man, Prehistoric—Europe, Northern
      Mesolithic period—Europe, Northern
MAGLEV vehicles
  USE Magnetic levitation vehicles
Magmatism (May Subd Geog)
  [QE461]
  BT Rocks, Igneous
Magna Graecia (Italy)
  [DG55.M3]
  UF Magna Grecia (Italy)
  BT Greece—Colonies
Magna Grecia (Italy)
  USE Magna Graecia (Italy)
Magnacard data processing system
  UF Magnavox magnacard system
      Magnetic card systems
  BT Electronic data processing
      Information storage and retrieval
      systems
Magnan family
  USE Magnin family
Magnanimity
  [BJ1533.M3 (Ethics)]
  [BV4647.M2 (Christianity)]
  RT Generosity
Magnant family
  USE Maignien family
Magnastigma
  [QL561.L8]
  BT Lycaenidae
Magnavox magnacard system
  USE Magnacard data processing system
Magnesia
  [QD181.M4 (Chemistry)]
  [TP889 (Chemical technology)]
  — Dipole moments
Magnesia brick
  UF Brick, Magnesia
      Magnesia refractory brick
      Magnesite brick
  BT Fire-brick
Magnesia cement
  [TP884.M2]
  UF Cement, Magnesia
  BT Cement
      Stone, Artificial
Magnesia refractory brick
  USE Magnesia brick
Magnesians
  USE Magnetes
Magnesite (May Subd Geog)
  [TN948.M2]
  BT Spinel group
Magnesite brick
  USE Magnesia brick
Magnesium
  [QD181.M4 (Chemistry)]
  [TN799.M2 (Metallurgy)]
  [TP784.M2 (Lighting)]
  BT Light metals
  NT Liquid magnesium
      Plates, Magnesium
      Soils—Magnesium content
  — Electrometallurgy
  — Isotopes

2233

Magnesium
— **Isotopes** *(Continued)*
— — **Decay**
— — **Spectra**
— **Metabolism**
   NT Grass tetany
— **Metallurgy**
— **Physiological effect**
   NT Plants, Effect of magnesium on
— **Spectra**
Magnesium alloy plates
  USE Plates, Magnesium
Magnesium alloys
  [TN799.M2 (Metallurgy)]
  BT Light metals
  NT Aluminum-copper-magnesium alloys
     Aluminum-magnesium alloys
     Aluminum-magnesium-silicon alloys
     Aluminum-magnesium-zinc alloys
     Copper-magnesium alloys
     Copper-magnesium-silicon alloys
     Copper-tin-magnesium alloys
     Magnesium-cadmium alloys
     Magnesium-calcium-zinc alloys
     Magnesium-lithium alloys
     Magnesium-nickel alloys
     Magnesium-thorium-zinc-zirconium
      alloys
     Magnesium-yttrium alloys
— **Founding**
  [TS560]
— **Welding**
  [TS560]
Magnesium-aluminum alloys
  USE Aluminum-magnesium alloys
Magnesium-cadmium alloys
  UF Cadmium-magnesium alloys
  BT Cadmium alloys
    Magnesium alloys
Magnesium-calcium-zinc alloys
  BT Calcium alloys
    Magnesium alloys
    Zinc alloys
Magnesium carbonate
  [QD181.M4]
  NT Plants, Effect of magnesium carbonate
    on
— **Therapeutic use**
  [RM666.M314]
Magnesium castings
  BT Magnesium founding
    Metal castings
Magnesium-copper alloys
  USE Copper-magnesium alloys
Magnesium crystals
Magnesium deficiency diseases
  [RC627.M3]
  BT Deficiency diseases
Magnesium fertilizers *(May Subd Geog)*
  BT Fertilizers
Magnesium founding
  [TS630]
  BT Founding
  NT Magnesium castings
Magnesium group
  [QD172.M4]
Magnesium in soils
  USE Soils—Magnesium content
Magnesium in the body
Magnesium industry and trade
  (May Subd Geog)
  [HD9539.M26 (Economics)]
  [TN799.M3 (Technology)]
Magnesium-lithium alloys
  UF Lithium-magnesium alloys
  BT Lithium alloys
    Magnesium alloys
Magnesium-nickel alloys
  UF Nickel-magnesium alloys
  BT Magnesium alloys
    Nickel alloys

Magnesium organic compounds
  USE Organomagnesium compounds
Magnesium phosphate
  BT Phosphates
  NT Calcium magnesium phosphate
Magnesium plates
  USE Plates, Magnesium
Magnesium salts
  [QD181.M4 (Inorganic chemistry)]
  BT Salts
Magnesium sulphate
  [QD181.M4]
Magnesium-thorium-zinc-zirconium alloys
  BT Magnesium alloys
    Thorium alloys
    Zinc alloys
    Zirconium alloys
Magnesium-yttrium alloys
  [TA480.M3 (Materials)]
  [TN490.M2 (Ores and mining)]
  [TN693.M3 (Physical metallurgy)]
  [TN799.M2 (Extractive metallurgy)]
  [TS560 (Metal-work)]
  UF Yttrium-magnesium alloys
  BT Magnesium alloys
    Yttrium alloys
Magnesyn
  USE Synchros
Magnet centers
  USE Magnet schools
Magnet schools *(May Subd Geog)*
  [LB2818]
    Here are entered works on schools offering special
  courses not available in the regular school curriculum
  and designed, often as an aid to school desegregation,
  to attract students on a voluntary basis from all parts
  of a school district without reference to the usual
  attendance zone rules.
  UF Magnet centers
    Schools, Magnet
  BT Public schools
  RT School integration
Magnet winding
  USE Electromagnets
Magnetband-Austauschformat für
Dokumentationszwecke
  USE MADOK (Information retrieval
    system)
Magnetes
  UF Magnesians
    Magnetians
  BT Ethnology—Greece
Magnetians
  USE Magnetes
Magnetic alloys
  [TK454.4.M3]
  BT Alloys
    Magnetic materials
  NT Spin glasses
Magnetic amplifiers
  [TK2851]
  [TK7871.23 (Electronics)]
  UF Amplifiers, Magnetic
    Transductors
  BT Electric controllers
    Electric reactors
    Magnetic devices
Magnetic analyzers (Nuclear physics)
  [QC787.M3]
  UF Analyzers, Magnetic (Nuclear physics)
  BT Nuclear physics—Instruments
    Particles (Nuclear physics)
Magnetic anomalies *(May Subd Geog)*
  BT Magnetism, Terrestrial
Magnetic balance
  BT Balance
    Magnetic devices
Magnetic bearings
  USE Magnetic suspension
Magnetic brakes
  UF Electromagnetic brakes

  BT Brakes
    Magnetic devices
Magnetic bubble devices
  [TK7872.M25]
  UF Bubble devices, Magnetic
  BT Integrated circuits
    Magnetic bubbles
    Magnetic devices
Magnetic bubbles
  [QC754.2.M34]
  UF Bubbles, Magnetic
  BT Crystals—Magnetic properties
    Magnetization
  RT Domain structure
  NT Magnetic bubble devices
Magnetic card systems
  USE Magnacard data processing system
Magnetic circuits
  BT Electric circuits
    Magnetics
  NT Electric coils
    Magnetic cores
Magnetic circular dichroism
  UF MCD
  BT Circular dichroism
    Magneto-optics
    Spectrum analysis
Magnetic clutches
  UF Electromagnetic clutches
  BT Clutches (Machinery)
    Magnetic devices
Magnetic cooling
  USE Adiabatic demagnetization
Magnetic cores
  BT Magnetic circuits
    Magnetic memory (Calculating-
     machines)
  NT Ferrite cores
Magnetic crystals
  RT Crystals—Magnetic properties
Magnetic declination *(May Subd Geog)*
  [QC849]
  UF Declination, Magnetic
    Deviation, Magnetic
    Magnetic deviation
    Magnetic variation
    Variation, Magnetic
  BT Magnetic ranges
    Magnetism, Terrestrial
  RT Compass
Magnetic deflection systems (Television)
  USE Television—Magnetic deflection
    systems
Magnetic deviation
  USE Magnetic declination
Magnetic devices
  BT Electric engineering
    Magnetics
    Solid state electronics
  NT Ferrite devices
    Magnetic amplifiers
    Magnetic balance
    Magnetic brakes
    Magnetic bubble devices
    Magnetic clutches
    Magnetic drums
    Magnetic instruments
    Magnetic memory (Calculating-
     machines)
    Magnetic recorders and recording
    Magnetic variometer
    Television—Magnetic deflection
     systems
Magnetic dipoles
  [QC754.2.M3]
  UF Dipoles, Magnetic
    Doublets, Magnetic
    Magnetic doublets
  RT Dipole moments

Magnetic disk industry (May Subd Geog)
Magnetic disks
  UF Disks, Magnetic
  BT Magnetic memory (Calculating-
        machines)
  — **Library applications**
      [Z681.3.M34]
      UF Libraries and magnetic disks
            Library applications of magnetic
              disks
Magnetic domain
  USE Domain structure
Magnetic double refraction
  USE Voigt effect
Magnetic doublets
  USE Magnetic dipoles
Magnetic drums
  BT Computer storage devices
        Magnetic devices
        Magnetic memory (Calculating-
          machines)
        Magnetic recorders and recording
Magnetic energy storage
    [TK2985]
  BT Electric power
        Electromagnets
        Energy storage
        Superconducting magnets
Magnetic field annihilation
  USE Magnetic reconnection
Magnetic field line merging
  USE Magnetic reconnection
Magnetic fields
  UF Fields, Magnetic
  BT Field theory (Physics)
        Magnetics
        Magnetism, Terrestrial
        Magnetostatics
  SA subdivision Magnetic fields under
        individual parts of the body, e.g.
        Heart—Magnetic fields
  NT Body, Human—Magnetic fields
        Electromagnetic fields
        Galvanomagnetic effects
        Hyperfine interactions
        Magnetic flux
        Magnetic induction
        Magnetic lenses
        Magnetic levitation vehicles
        Magnetic mirrors
        Magnetic reconnection
        Magnetic resonance
        Magnetoresistance
        Pinch effect (Physics)
  — **Computer programs**
  — **Physiological effect**
      [QH656]
      UF Magnetism—Physiological effect
      BT Biomagnetism
Magnetic fields (Cosmic physics)
    [QC809.M25]
  BT Astrophysics
        Cosmic physics
        Space environment
  NT Dynamo theory (Cosmic physics)
        Electron precipitation
        Interplanetary magnetic fields
        Interstellar magnetic fields
        Magnetohydrodynamics
        Magnetopause
        Magnetosphere
        Solar magnetic field
        Stars—Corona—Magnetic fields
        Stars—Magnetic fields
Magnetic fields in the solar corona
  USE Sun—Corona—Magnetic fields
Magnetic films
  UF Films, Magnetic
  BT Magnetic materials
        Metallic films

Magnetic fluids
    [QC766.M36]
  UF Ferrofluids
  BT Fluids
        Magnetic materials
  — **Thermomechanical properties**
      UF Thermomechanics of magnetic
            fluids
      BT Mechanics
Magnetic flux
  UF Flux, Magnetic
  BT Magnetic fields
        Magnetic induction
Magnetic flux compression
  UF Compression, Magnetic flux
        Flux compression, Magnetic
Magnetic flux density
  USE Magnetic induction
Magnetic flux welding
  USE Gas metal arc welding
Magnetic forming
  BT High energy forming
        Metal-work
Magnetic glasses
  USE Spin glasses
Magnetic heads
  USE Magnetic recorders and recording—
          Heads
Magnetic healing
    [RZ422]
  UF Magnetotherapy
  BT Hypnotism
        Mental healing
        Spiritual healing
        Therapeutics, Physiological
        Therapeutics, Suggestive
  RT Animal magnetism
        Mesmerism
  NT Magnetism—Therapeutic use
        Tractors, Metallic
Magnetic induction
    [QC761]
  UF Induced magnetism
        Induction (Magnetism)
        Magnetic flux density
  BT Magnetic fields
  RT Electromagnets
        Induction, Electromagnetic
  NT Electromagnetism
        Hysteresis
        Hysteresis loop
        Magnetic flux
        Nuclear induction
Magnetic instruments
    [QC819 (Terrestrial magnetism)]
  UF Instruments, Magnetic
  BT Geophysical instruments
        Magnetic devices
        Physical instruments
        Scientific apparatus and instruments
  NT Dipping-needle
        Hysteresigraph
        Magnetometer
  — **Calibration**
Magnetic ions
    [QC754.2.M333]
  BT Ions
        Nuclear magnetism
Magnetic lenses
  BT Electron optics
        Lenses
        Magnetic fields
  RT Magnetic mirrors
  NT Electromagnetic lenses
        Electrostatic lenses
Magnetic levitation
  USE Magnetic suspension
Magnetic levitation vehicles
    [TF1600]
  UF MAGLEV vehicles
        Magnetic suspension vehicles

  BT Electric motors, Linear
        High speed ground transportation
        Magnetic fields
        Vehicles
Magnetic materials
    [QC761 (Physics)]
    [TK453 (Electric engineering)]
  UF Materials, Magnetic
  BT Electromagnetism
        Magnetics
  SA subdivision Magnetic properties under
        names of particular materials or
        substances, e.g. Steel—Magnetic
        properties
  NT Alnicos
        Copper ferrite
        Ferrites (Magnetic materials)
        Ferromagnetic materials
        Hysteresis loop
        Kondo effect
        Magnetic alloys
        Magnetic films
        Magnetic fluids
        Magnets
        Nonmagnetic steel
        Vanadium permendur
  — **Thermal properties**
Magnetic measurements
    [QC761]
    [QC818-QC849 (Terrestrial
      magnetism)]
  UF Measurements, Magnetic
  BT Magnetics
  NT Magnetic susceptibility—Measurement
        Magnetic units
        Magnetometer
        Permeameter
Magnetic memory (Calculating-machines)
    [TK7872.M4]
  UF Magnetic storage (Calculating-
          machines)
        Memory devices
        Storage elements (Calculating-
          machines)
  BT Computer storage devices
        Magnetic devices
  NT Data disk drives
        Magnetic cores
        Magnetic disks
        Magnetic drums
        Strela computer—Memory systems
  — **Testing**
  — — **Computer programs**
Magnetic mirrors
  BT Magnetic fields
        Mirrors
        Plasma confinement
  RT Magnetic lenses
Magnetic monopoles
    [QC760.4.M33]
  UF Monopoles, Magnetic
  BT Electromagnetism
        Magnetic pole
Magnetic needle
  USE Compass
Magnetic observations
  USE Magnetism, Terrestrial—Observations
Magnetic permeability
    [QC754.2.P4]
  UF Permeability, Magnetic
  BT Magnetism
Magnetic phonograph
  USE Telegraphone
Magnetic pole
  UF Pole, Magnetic
  BT Magnetism
        Magnets
  NT Magnetic monopoles

Magnetic properties of materials
USE *subdivision* Magnetic properties *under names of particular materials or substances, e.g.* Steel—Magnetic properties

Magnetic prospecting *(May Subd Geog)*
⌈TN269⌉
UF Prospecting, Magnetic
BT Magnetotelluric prospecting
Prospecting—Geophysical methods
NT Aeromagnetic prospecting
Magnetic variometer

Magnetic ranges
⌈QC849⌉
RT Compass
NT Magnetic declination
Magnetism of ships

Magnetic reconnection
UF Annihilation, Magnetic field
Magnetic field annihilation
Magnetic field line merging
Merging, Magnetic field line
Reconnection, Magnetic
BT Magnetic fields
Magnetosphere
Plasma (Ionized gases)

Magnetic recorders and recording
⌈TK5981⌉
UF Tape recorders
BT Electro-acoustics
Magnetic devices
Sound—Equipment and supplies
Sound—Recording and reproducing
NT Magnetic drums
Magnetic tapes
Nature sounds—Recording and reproducing
Video tape recorders and recording
— **Business applications**
BT Office equipment and supplies
— **Cassette recorders**
UF Cassette tape recorders
Tape recorders, Cassette
— **Fair use (Copyright)** *(May Subd Geog)*
BT Fair use (Copyright)
RT Copyright—Sound recordings
— **Heads**
⌈TK5984⌉
UF Magnetic heads
Magnetic recording heads
BT Electromagnets
— **Installation in automobiles**
UF Auto tape players
Tape players in automobiles
Magnetic recording heads
USE Magnetic recorders and recording—Heads
Magnetic recordings (Data storage)
USE Data tapes

Magnetic resonance
UF Resonance, Magnetic
BT Atoms
Magnetic fields
Nuclear spin
NT Electron paramagnetic resonance
Ferromagnetic resonance
Nuclear magnetic resonance
Magnetic resonance, Nuclear
USE Nuclear magnetic resonance
Magnetic resonance, Proton
USE Proton magnetic resonance
Magnetic resonance accelerator
USE Cyclotron
Magnetic resonance imaging
(May Subd Geog)
⌈RC78.7.N83⌉

UF Clinical magnetic resonance imaging
Diagnostic magnetic resonance imaging
Imaging, Magnetic resonance
Medical magnetic resonance imaging
NMR imaging
Nuclear magnetic resonance—Diagnostic use
Nuclear magnetic resonance imaging
BT Diagnostic imaging
Nuclear medicine

Magnetic semiconductors
⌈QC611.8.M25⌉
BT Semiconductors
NT Diluted magnetic semiconductors

Magnetic separation
⌈TP156.M26⌉
BT Separation (Technology)
NT Coal—Magnetic separation
Sewage—Purification—Magnetic separation

Magnetic separation of ores
⌈TN530⌉
UF Ores, Magnetic separation of
BT Metallurgy
Ore-dressing
Separation (Technology)
Magnetic separation of sewage
USE Sewage—Purification—Magnetic separation
Magnetic separators
USE Calutron

Magnetic shielding
⌈TK454.4.M33 (Magnetic shielding)⌉
UF Magnetostatic shielding
BT Shielding (Electricity)

Magnetic spectrometer
⌈QC787.S6⌉
BT Spectrometer

Magnetic stars
⌈QB843.M3⌉
BT Stars
Magnetic storage (Calculating-machines)
USE Magnetic memory (Calculating-machines)

Magnetic storms *(May Subd Geog)*
⌈QC835⌉
Subdivided by date, e.g. Magnetic storms—1909 (September)
UF Storms, Magnetic
BT Auroras
Magnetism, Terrestrial
Sun-spots
RT Auroral substorms
Magnetospheric substorms
Solar activity
NT Proton flares
— **1909 (September)**

Magnetic structure
⌈QC754.2.M336⌉
UF Structure, Magnetic
BT Crystallography
Nuclear spin
Magnetic survey maps
USE Magnetism, Terrestrial—Maps
Magnetic surveys
USE Magnetism, Terrestrial
Magnetic surveys (Archaeology)
USE Magnetometry in archaeology

Magnetic susceptibility
UF Susceptibility, Magnetic
— **Measurement**
BT Magnetic measurements

Magnetic suspension
UF Magnetic bearings
Magnetic levitation
Suspension, Magnetic
BT Bearings (Machinery)
Magnetics
Magnetic suspension vehicles
USE Magnetic levitation vehicles

Magnetic tape files
USE Data tapes
Magnetic tape industry *(May Subd Geog)*
⌈HD9697.M33-HD9697.M334⌉
Magnetic tape recordkeeping
USE Data tapes
Magnetic tapes
⌈TK5984⌉
UF Tapes, Magnetic
BT Magnetic recorders and recording
RT Data tapes
NT Phonotapes
Video tapes
— **Library applications**
⌈Z681.3.M34⌉
UF Libraries and magnetic tapes
Library applications of magnetic tapes

Magnetic testing
⌈QC761⌉
BT Magnetics
Non-destructive testing
Testing
Magnetic traps
UF Magnetic wells
Traps, Magnetic
Wells, Magnetic
BT Plasma confinement
Magnetic units
BT Magnetic measurements
Magnetic variation
USE Magnetic declination
Magnetic variations, Diurnal
USE Magnetism, Terrestrial—Diurnal variation
Magnetic variations, Secular
USE Magnetism, Terrestrial—Secular variation
Magnetic variometer
UF Variometer, Magnetic
BT Magnetic devices
Magnetic prospecting
Magnetometer
Prospecting—Geophysical methods
Magnetic wells
USE Magnetic traps
Magnetics
BT Electric engineering
RT Magnetism
NT Magnetic circuits
Magnetic devices
Magnetic fields
Magnetic materials
Magnetic measurements
Magnetic suspension
Magnetic testing
Magnets
Magnetism
⌈QC751-771⌉
BT Mathematical physics
Physics
RT Electricity
Magnetics
SA *headings beginning with the word* Magnetic
NT Animal magnetism
Compass
Cyclotron resonance
Diamagnetism
Electromagnetic theory
Electromagnetism
Electromagnets
Ferrimagnetism
Ferromagnetism
Hysteresis loop
Magnetic permeability
Magnetic pole
Magnetism, Band theory of
Magnetism of aircraft
Magnetization
Magnetochemistry

Magnets
Magnons
Nuclear magnetism
Paramagnetism
Thermomagnetism
— **Experiments**
⌐QC751-761¬
BT Physics—Experiments
— Physiological effect
USE Magnetic fields—Physiological
effect
— **Therapeutic use**
⌐RM893-6¬
UF Magnetotherapy
BT Magnetic healing
Therapeutics, Suggestive
Magnetism, Animal
USE Animal magnetism
Magnetism, Band theory of
⌐QC754.2.B35¬
UF Band model of magnetism
Band theory of magnetism
Itinerant-electron magnetism
BT Energy-band theory of solids
Free electron theory of metals
Magnetism
Magnetism, Biological
USE Biomagnetism
Magnetism, Human
USE Animal magnetism
Magnetism, Lunar
USE Moon—Magnetic properties
Magnetism, Solar
USE Solar magnetic field
Magnetism, Stellar
USE Stars—Magnetic fields
Magnetism, Terrestrial *(May Subd Geog)*
⌐QC811-QC849¬
UF Earth—Magnetism
Geomagnetic fields
Geomagnetism
Isogonic lines
Magnetic surveys
Surveys, Magnetic
Terrestrial magnetism
BT Geophysics
RT Auroras
Compass
Polar wandering
NT Earth resistance
Equatorial electrojet
Geomagnetic indexes
Geomagnetic micropulsations
Geomagnetic reversals
Ionospheric drift
Magnetic anomalies
Magnetic declination
Magnetic fields
Magnetic storms
Magnetometer
Magnetosphere
Magnetotelluric prospecting
Paleomagnetism
Rocks—Magnetic properties
Sun-spots
— **Diurnal variation**
⌐QC831¬
UF Diurnal variation of terrestrial
magnetism
Magnetic variations, Diurnal
— **Maps**
⌐QC822¬
UF Aeromagnetic maps
Geomagnetic maps
Magnetic survey maps
RT Geology—Maps
— **Observations**
⌐QC830-845¬
UF Magnetic observations
Observations, Magnetic
— **Observatories**

⌐QC818¬
BT Geophysical observatories
Observatories
— **Secular variation** *(May Subd Geog)*
⌐QC828¬
UF Magnetic variations, Secular
Secular variation (Terrestrial
magnetism)
Magnetism of aircraft
⌐QC849¬
UF Airplanes—Magnetic fields
BT Magnetism
Magnetism of ships
⌐QC849¬
UF Ships, Magnetism of
BT Magnetic ranges
NT Degaussing
Magnetite *(May Subd Geog)*
BT Iron ores
Magnetite crystals
— Spectra
Magnetization
BT Ferromagnetism
Magnetism
Paramagnetism
Thermomagnetism
NT Magnetic bubbles
Magnetization, Thermoremanent
USE Thermoremanent magnetization
Magneto
⌐TJ787 (Oil and gasoline engines)¬
⌐TL213 (Automobiles)¬
UF Ignition devices
BT Automobiles—Ignition
Internal combustion engines—Ignition
Magneto-electric machines
⌐TK9909 (Amateurs' manuals)¬
UF Electromagnetic machines
BT Electric apparatus and appliances
Electric generators
Electromagnetism
Electromagnets
Magneto-hydrodynamics
USE Magnetohydrodynamics
Magneto-ionic theory
BT Electromagnetism
Gases, Ionized
Polarization (Electricity)
RT Ionospheric radio wave propagation
Magneto-optics
⌐QC675¬
UF Optical phenomena, Influence of
magnetism on
BT Molecular rotation
Optics
RT Electromagnetic theory
Polarization (Light)
NT Electrons
Faraday effect
Magnetic circular dichroism
Voigt effect
Zeeman effect
Magneto-phonograph
USE Telegraphone
Magneto-resistance
USE Magnetoresistance
Magnetochemistry
⌐QD591¬
BT Electrochemistry
Magnetism
Magnetography (Photomechanical process)
USE Ferromagnetography
Magnetohydrodynamic generators
UF Generators, Magnetohydrodynamic
MHD generators
BT Direct energy conversion
Electric power production—
Magnetohydrodynamic generation
Magnetohydrodynamics
Plasma (Ionized gases)
Plasma devices

NT Electric rocket engines
Plasma generators
Plasma rockets
Project SNAP
— **Thermodynamics**
Magnetohydrodynamic instabilities
⌐QC718.5.M36¬
UF Hydromagnetic instabilities
Instabilities, Magnetohydrodynamic
MHD instabilities
BT Magnetohydrodynamics
Plasma instabilities
Magnetohydrodynamic power generation
USE Electric power production—
Magnetohydrodynamic generation
Magnetohydrodynamic waves
UF Alfvén waves
Alvén waves
Hydromagnetic waves
Waves, Magnetohydrodynamic
BT Magnetohydrodynamics
Plasma waves
Space plasmas
Magnetohydrodynamics
UF Magneto-hydrodynamics
BT Continuum mechanics
Cosmic physics
Electrodynamics
Electromagnetism
Fluid dynamics
Geophysics
Hydrodynamics
Magnetic fields (Cosmic physics)
Physics
RT Cosmic electrodynamics
Ion flow dynamics
Plasma dynamics
NT Dynamo theory (Cosmic physics)
Electric power production—
Magnetohydrodynamic generation
Field-coupled surface waves
Magnetohydrodynamic generators
Magnetohydrodynamic instabilities
Magnetohydrodynamic waves
Meteor trails
Pinch effect (Physics)
Plasma accelerators
Plasma electrodynamics
Plasma injection
Plasma instabilities
Plasma rockets
Plasma turbulence
Plasma waves
Stellarators
Synchrotron radiation
Van Allen radiation belts
Magnetometer
⌐QC819¬
BT Magnetic instruments
Magnetic measurements
Magnetism, Terrestrial
Metal detectors
NT Fluxgate magnetometer
Magnetic variometer
Magnetometry in archaeology
Nuclear magnetometer
Magnetometry in archaeology
(May Subd Geog)
UF Magnetic surveys (Archaeology)
BT Archaeology
Archaeology—Methodology
Magnetometer
Magnetopause
⌐QC809.M35¬
BT Atmosphere, Upper
Magnetic fields (Cosmic physics)
Magnetosphere
Magnetoplasma
USE Plasma (Ionized gases)
Magnetoresistance
UF Magneto-resistance

Magnetoresistance *(Continued)*
  BT Electric resistance
      Galvanomagnetic effects
      Magnetic fields
Magnetosphere
  [QC809.M35]
  BT Atmosphere, Upper
      Magnetic fields (Cosmic physics)
      Magnetism, Terrestrial
  NT Electron precipitation
      Magnetic reconnection
      Magnetopause
      Magnetospheric currents
      Magnetospheric substorms
      Magnetotails
      Polar cusp
      Proton precipitation
Magnetospheric current systems
  USE Magnetospheric currents
Magnetospheric currents
  [QC809.M35]
  UF Currents, Magnetospheric
      Magnetospheric current systems
  BT Electric fields
      Magnetosphere
  NT Magnetospheric substorms
Magnetospheric substorms
  [QC809.M35]
  UF Substorms, Magnetospheric
  BT Magnetosphere
      Magnetospheric currents
  RT Magnetic storms
  NT Auroral electrojet
      Auroral substorms
Magnetostatic shielding
  USE Magnetic shielding
Magnetostatics
  BT Electric charge and distribution
      Electromagnetism
  NT Magnetic fields
Magnetostriction
  [QC761]
Magnetotails
  BT Magnetosphere
Magnetotelluric prospecting
  (May Subd Geog)
  [TN269]
  UF Prospecting, Magnetotelluric
      Telluric current prospecting
  BT Earth currents
      Magnetism, Terrestrial
      Prospecting—Geophysical methods
  NT Electric prospecting
      Magnetic prospecting
Magnetotherapy
  USE Magnetic healing
      Magnetism—Therapeutic use
Magnetrons
  [TK7872.V3]
  BT Microwave tubes
      Oscillators, Electric
      Vacuum-tubes
Magnets
  [QC757]
  BT Magnetic materials
      Magnetics
      Magnetism
  RT Solenoids
  NT Ceramic magnets
      Electromagnets
      Magnetic pole
  — Thermal properties
Magnets, Lifting
  USE Lifting magnets
Magnets, Permanent
  [QC757.9]
  UF Permanent magnets
Magnets, Superconducting
  USE Superconducting magnets
Magnette automobile
  BT M.G. automobile

Magnien family
  USE Maignien family
Magnificat (Music)
  [M2079]
  BT Evening-service music
Magnification radiography
  USE Radiographic magnification
Magnifying glasses
  USE Hand lenses
Magnin family *(Not Subd Geog)*
  UF Magnan family
Magnitudes of stars
  USE Stars—Magnitudes
Magnolia
  [QK495.M24 (Botany)]
  [SB413.M34 (Culture)]
Magnolia Cemetery (Greenwood, S.C.)
  BT Cemeteries—South Carolina
Magnolia Cemetery (Mobile, Ala.)
  UF New City Cemetery (Mobile, Ala.)
  BT Cemeteries—Alabama
Magnolia Gardens (Charleston, S.C.)
  BT Gardens—South Carolina
Magnolia Mound Plantation (Baton Rouge, La.) *(Not Subd Geog)*
  BT Dwellings—Louisiana
      Plantations—Louisiana
Magnoliaceae
  [QK495.M24]
  BT Magnoliales
  NT Liriodendron
Magnoliales
  [QK495.A12 (Botany)]
  UF Annonales
      Canellales
      Illiciales
      Laurales
      Ranales
  BT Dicotyledons
  NT Annonaceae
      Hernandiaceae
      Magnoliaceae
      Myristicaceae
      Winteraceae
Magnoliophyta, Fossil
  USE Angiosperms, Fossil
Magnons
  [QC721]
  BT Magnetism
Magnus effect
  [TL574.M3]
  BT Aerodynamics
      Rotor ships
      Rotors
Magnusons Island (Minn.)
  UF Magnussen Island (Minn.)
  BT Islands—Minnesota
Magnussen Island (Minn.)
  USE Magnusons Island (Minn.)
Magomeni (Bagamoyo, Tanzania)
  (Not Subd Geog)
  UF Bagamoyo (Tanzania). Magomeni
Magong language
  USE !Xõ language
Magothy Aquifer *(Not Subd Geog)*
  BT Aquifers—Middle Atlantic States
Magoumaz, Cameroon
Magpie moth, European
  USE Abraxas grossulariata
Magpies
  [QL696.P2]
  NT Pica pica
      Yellow-billed magpie
Magra family
  USE Matra family
Mags
  USE Maghs
Magsaysay awards
  USE Ramon Magsaysay awards

Maguaga, Battle of, 1812
  USE Monguagon, Mich., Battle of, Aug. 9, 1812
Maguey
  USE Agave
Magui Iseki (Kanzaki-machi, Saga-ken, Japan)
  USE Magui Site (Kanzaki-machi, Saga-ken, Japan)
Magui Site (Kanzaki-machi, Saga-ken, Japan)
  (Not Subd Geog)
  UF Magui Iseki (Kanzaki-machi, Saga-ken, Japan)
  BT Japan—Antiquities
Maguindanao language
  USE Magindanao language
Maguindanaos (Philippine people)
  USE Magindanaos (Philippine people)
Maguire family
  USE McGuire family
Maguires, Molly
  USE Molly Maguires
Magura Cave (Romania)
  UF Peştera de la Magura (Romania)
  BT Caves—Romania
Maguzawa (African people)
  BT Ethnology—Nigeria
Magyar Államvasutak
  USE Railroads—Hungary
Magyar language
  USE Hungarian language
Magyar literature
  USE Hungarian literature
Magyar mythology
  USE Mythology, Finno-Ugrian
Magyar szent korona
  USE Holy Crown of Hungary
Magyar szentkorona
  USE Holy Crown of Hungary
Magyars
  [DB919]
  Here are entered works on the Magyars before their appearance in Europe.
  RT Hungarians
  NT Palocs
      Szeklers
Mah (African people)
  USE Mano (African people)
Mah jong
  [GV1299.M3]
  UF Ma jong
      Mahjong
      Pung chow
Mah-Meri (Malaysian people)
  [DS595.2.M]
  UF Besisi (Malaysian people)
      Betisék (Malaysian people)
      Cellate (Malaysian people)
      Hma Besisi (Malaysian people)
      Ma' Betisék (Malaysian people)
      Sisi (Malaysian people)
  BT Ethnology—Malaysia
      Senoi (Malaysian people)
  — Masks
Mahabharat Lekh (Nepal)
  USE Mahabharat Range (Nepal)
Mahabharat Range (Nepal)
  UF Mahabharat Lekh (Nepal)
  BT Himalaya Mountains
      Mountains—Nepal
Mahābhārata
  — Biography
      NT Aniruddha (Hindu mythology)
          Arjuna (Hindu mythology)
          Bhīma (Hindu mythology)
          Bhīṣma (Hindu mythology)
          Citraketu (Hindu mythology)
          Devayānī (Hindu mythology)
          Draupadī (Hindu mythology)
          Kakutstha (Hindu mythology)
          Kāma (Hindu deity)
          Kautsa (Hindu mythology)

Mārtaṇḍa (Hindu deity)
Nala (Hindu mythology)
Prabhāvatī (Hindu mythology)
Rukmāṅgada (Hindu mythology)
Śakuntalā (Hindu mythology)
Sītā (Hindu deity)
Tulādhāra
Mahābhārata. Bhagavadgītā and science
USE Bhagavadgītā and science
Mahacu Indians (Papury River watershed)
USE Macú Indians (Papury River watershed)
Mahafalay (Malagasy people)
USE Mahafaly (Malagasy people)
Mahafaly (Malagasy people)
 ⌈DT469.M277.M34⌉
 UF Mahafalay (Malagasy people)
 BT Ethnology—Madagascar
 — Rites and ceremonies
  NT Funeral rites and ceremonies, Mahafaly (Malagasy people)
Mahafaly (Malagasy people) funeral rites and ceremonies
 USE Funeral rites and ceremonies, Mahafaly (Malagasy people)
Mahaffay family
 USE Mahaffey family
Mahaffee family
 USE Mahaffey family
Mahaffey family (Not Subd Geog)
 UF Mahaffay family
  Mahaffee family
  Mahaffie family
  Mahaffy family
  Mehaffey family
  Mehaffie family
  Mehaffy family
Mahaffey Site (Okla.) (Not Subd Geog)
 BT Oklahoma—Antiquities
Mahaffie family
 USE Mahaffey family
Mahaffy family
 USE Mahaffey family
Mahaga language
 USE Bugotu language
Mahākāla (Buddhist deity)
 ⌈BQ4750.M35⌉
 BT Gods, Buddhist
Mahakam River (Kalimantan Timur, Indonesia)
 UF Koetai-rivier (Kalimantan Timur, Indonesia)
  Koetei River (Kalimantan Timur, Indonesia)
  Kutei River (Kalimantan Timur, Indonesia)
  Soengai Koetei (Kalimantan Timur, Indonesia)
  Sungai Kutai (Kalimantan Timur, Indonesia)
  Sungai Mahakam (Kalimantan Timur, Indonesia)
 BT Rivers—Indonesia
Mahali Mountains (Tanzania)
 UF Mahari Mountains (Tanzania)
 BT Mountains—Tanzania
Mahalis
 BT Ethnology—India
Mahāmudrā (Tantric rite)
 ⌈BQ8921.M35⌉
 BT Tantric Buddhism—Rituals
  Yoga (Tantric Buddhism)
Mahan family (Not Subd Geog)
 UF Mahen family
  Mahon family
  Mahone family
  Mayhon family
 RT Mohon family
Mahantango Creek (Pa.)
 USE Mahantongo Creek (Pa.)

Mahantongo Creek (Pa.) (Not Subd Geog)
 UF Mahantango Creek (Pa.)
 BT Rivers—Pennsylvania
Mahanubhava
 ⌈BL1245.M35⌉
 UF Mahatma pantha
  Manabhava
  Manbhaus
  Manbhav
 BT Hindu sects
  Vaishnavism
Mahāpradoṣa (Hindu rite)
 ⌈BL1226.82.M27⌉
 BT Hinduism—Rituals
Maharajahs
 USE India—Kings and rulers
Maharajas (Hindu sect)
 USE Vallabhachars
Maharashtra (India)
 — History
  NT Śilāhāras
Maharashtri language
 ⌈PK1231-1239⌉
 BT Prakrit languages
Mahari Mountains (Tanzania)
 USE Mahali Mountains (Tanzania)
Mahars
 ⌈DS422.C3⌉
 UF Mhâr
 BT Caste—India
Mahāsaṃghikas
 USE Mahāsāṅghikas
Mahāsāṅghika (Sect)
 USE Mahāsāṅghikas
Mahāsāṅghika School
 USE Mahāsāṅghikas
Mahāsāṅghikas
 ⌈BQ7255.M34⌉
 UF Mahāsaṃghikas
  Mahāsāṅghika (Sect)
  Mahāsāṅghika School
 BT Buddhist sects
  Hinayana Buddhism
Mahaseer
 USE Mahseer
Mahatma pantha
 USE Mahanubhava
Mahaveli River (Sri Lanka)
 USE Mahaweli River (Sri Lanka)
Mahawela River (Sri Lanka)
 USE Mahaweli River (Sri Lanka)
Mahaweli-ganga (Sri Lanka)
 USE Mahaweli River (Sri Lanka)
Mahaweli River (Sri Lanka)
 UF Mahaveli River (Sri Lanka)
  Mahawela River (Sri Lanka)
  Mahaweli-ganga (Sri Lanka)
  Mahawell River (Sri Lanka)
  Mahawelu River (Sri Lanka)
  Mahevilla River (Sri Lanka)
 BT Rivers—Sri Lanka
Mahawell River (Sri Lanka)
 USE Mahaweli River (Sri Lanka)
Mahawelu River (Sri Lanka)
 USE Mahaweli River (Sri Lanka)
Mahāyakṣa (Buddhist deity)
 (May Subd Geog)
 ⌈BQ4770-4775⌉
 BT Gods, Buddhist
  Yakṣas (Buddhist deities)
Mahayana Buddhism
 UF Greater vehicle
  Northern Buddhism
  Northern vehicle
 BT Buddhism
  Buddhist sects
 NT Hua-yen Buddhism
  Madhyamaka-Yogācāra Buddhism
  Mādhyamika (Buddhism)
  Pure Land Buddhism
  Religious life (Mahayana Buddhism)

San chieh (Sect)
Tantric Buddhism
T'ien-t'ai Buddhism
Yogācāra (Buddhism)
Zen Buddhism
 — Doctrines
  ⌈BQ7400-7420⌉
 — Essence, genius, nature
 — Relations
 — — Hinayana Buddhism, ⌈etc.⌉
  ⌈BQ7432⌉
 — Sacred books
  NT Aparamitāyurjñānahṛdaya
   Aparimitāyurjñāna nāmamahāyānasūtra
   Daśadigandhakāravidhvaṃsana
   Jen wang po je ching
   Kuan P'u-hsien p'u sa hsing fa ching
   Kuan wu liang shou ching
   Sandhinirmochana
   Saptatathāgatapūrvapraṇidhānaviśeṣ avistaraṇāmamahāyānasūtra
   Sarvapuṇyasamuccayasamādhisūtra
   Ssu shih erh chang ching
   Ta fang pien Fo pao en ching
   Tārābhaṭṭārikānāmāṣṭaśataka
Mahayana Buddhism in art
 ⌈N8193.3.M27⌉
Mahazorim
 USE Mahzorim
Mahdi
 ⌈BP166.93 (Islam)⌉
 ⌈DT108.3 (Sudan)⌉
 BT Panislamism
 RT Mahdism
Mahdism
 ⌈BP166.93⌉
 BT Eschatology, Islamic
  Islam
 RT Mahdi
Mahen family
 USE Mahan family
Maher family
 USE Myers family
Mahesri
 ⌈DS432.M16⌉
 UF Mahesvari
  Maheswari
 BT Businessmen—India
  Caste—India
  Ethnology—India
Mahesvari
 USE Mahesri
Maheswari
 USE Mahesri
Mahevilla River (Sri Lanka)
 USE Mahaweli River (Sri Lanka)
Mahew family
 USE Mayhew family
Mahican hymns
 USE Hymns, Mahican
Mahican Indians
 ⌈E99.M12⌉
 UF River Indians (New England)
 BT Algonquian Indians
  Indians of North America
 RT Mohegan Indians
 NT Brotherton Indians
  Moravian Indians
  Stockbridge Indians
Mahican language
 ⌈PM1671⌉
 BT Algonquian languages
  Indians of North America—Languages
  United States—Languages
Mahima Dharma
 ⌈BL1220.M3⌉
 UF Satya Mahima Dharma
 BT Hinduism

Mahisyas
  [DS432.M17]
  UF Hāliya Kaibarttas
      Hele Kaivartas
  BT Businessmen—India
      Caste—India
      Ethnology—India
      Vaisyas
Mahjong
  USE Mah jong
Mahlandt family (Not Subd Geog)
Maho family
  USE Mayo family
Mahogany
  [QK495.M52 (Botany)]
  [SD397.M2 (Culture)]
  NT Catechin
  — Labeling (May Subd Geog)
      BT Hardwoods—Labeling
Mahogany, Gaboon
  USE Aucoumea klaineana
Mahogany, White
  USE Khaya anthotheca
Mahon family
  USE Mahan family
Mahone Bay (N.S. : Bay)
  BT Bays—Nova Scotia
Mahone family
  USE Mahan family
Mahongwe (African people)
  USE Kota (African people)
Mahonia
  [QK495.B45]
  UF Odostemon
  BT Berberidaceae
Mahoning River (Ohio and Pa.)
  BT Rivers—Ohio
      Rivers—Pennsylvania
Mahorka
  USE Tobacco
Mahou dialect
  USE Mau dialect (Ivory Coast)
Mahra language
  USE Mahri language
Mahratta language
  USE Marathi language
Mahrattas
  USE Marathas
Mahratti language
  USE Marathi language
Mahre (Indic people)
  USE Buxas (Indic people)
Mahri language
  [PJ7111-7114]
  UF Mahra language
      Mehre language
  BT Arabic language
      South Arabic language
  NT Ḥarsūsī language
Mahseer
  [QL638.C94]
  UF Barbus mosal
      Mahaseer
      Mahsir
      Mahsur
  BT Barbel (Fish)
Mahseer fishing (May Subd Geog)
  [SH691.M3]
  BT Fishing
Mahser family
  USE Masear family
Mahsir
  USE Mahseer
Mahsud-Waziri Raids
Mahsuds (Pakistani people)
  BT Ethnology—Pakistan
      Pushtuns
Mahsur
  USE Mahseer
Mahu dialect
  USE Mau dialect (Ivory Coast)

Mahuang (Plant)
  USE Ephedra
Mahyeux family
  USE Mayeux family
Mahzorim
  UF Machzorim
      Machzors
      Mahazorim
      Mahzors
  BT Fasts and feasts—Judaism—Liturgy
      Judaism—Liturgy
Mahzors
  USE Mahzorim
Mai-chi Mountain Caves (China)
  USE Mai-chi-shan Caves (China)
Mai-chi-shan Caves (China)
  UF Mai-chi Mountain Caves (China)
      Mai-chi shan shih k'u (China)
  BT Caves—China
Mai-chi shan shih k'u (China)
  USE Mai-chi-shan Caves (China)
Mai family (Not Subd Geog)
Mai-Ndombe, Lake (Zaire)
  (Not Subd Geog)
  UF Lac Léopold II (Zaire)
      Lac Mai-Ndombe (Zaire)
      Lake Leopold II (Zaire)
      Lake Mai-Ndombe (Zaire)
      Leopold II, Lake (Zaire)
      Maindombe, Lake (Zaire)
  BT Lakes—Zaire
Maia
  USE Maja
Maibach family (Not Subd Geog)
Maiborg family
  USE Meiborg family
Maico motorcycle
  [TL448.M]
Maideh Indians
  USE Maidu Indians
Maiden aunts
  [HQ800.2]
  BT Aunts
      Single women
Maidenhair ferns (May Subd Geog)
  [QK524.A29 (Botany)]
  [SB413.M35 (Ornamental plants)]
  UF Adiantum
      Ferns, Maidenhair
  BT Adiantaceae
Maidenhair tree
  USE Ginkgo
Maidford River (R.I.)
  BT Rivers—Rhode Island
Maids, Hotel
  USE Hotel maids
Maids, House
  USE Women domestics
Maids of honor (Painting)
  USE Velázquez, Diego, 1599-1660. Maids
      of honor
Maidu Indians
  [E99.M18]
  UF Maideh Indians
      Meidoo Indians
      Pujunan Indians
  BT Indians of North America
  NT Nisenan Indians
  — Religion and mythology
      [E99.M18]
  — Reservations
Maidu language
  [PM1681]
  UF Pujunan languages
  NT Nisenan language
Maiella Mountains (Italy)
  UF Majella Mountains (Italy)
      Montagna della Maiella (Italy)
  BT Apennines (Italy)
      Mountains—Italy

Maigaard family
  USE Majgaard family
Maignard family
  USE Maynard family
Maignien family (Not Subd Geog)
  UF Magnant family
      Magnien family
Maigret, Jules (Fictitious character)
  BT Characters and characteristics in
      literature
Mail
  USE Postal service
Mail, Hate
  USE Hate mail
Mail art (May Subd Geog)
  [N6494.M35]
      Here are entered works on art created collabora-
  tively by using the postal service to transport a work
  in progress from one artist to another, and usually
  incorporating postal paraphernalia such as stamps,
  cancellations, etc. into the work.
  UF Art, Mail
      Correspondence art
      Postal art
  BT Art, Modern—20th century
      Artists' books
      Conceptual art
      Postal service in art
Mail-boats
  USE Packets
Mail carriers
  USE Postal service—Letter carriers
Mail-cars
  USE Railway mail service—Cars
Mail-cheeked fishes
  UF Cottoidei
      Scleroparei
      Scorpaenoidae
Mail-chutes
  [TJ1398]
Mail delivery of books
  USE Direct delivery of books
Mail drops
  USE Mail receiving and forwarding services
Mail handling, Letter
  USE Letter mail handling
Mail library service
  USE Direct delivery of books
Mail-messenger service
  USE Postal service—Mail-messenger service
Mail-order antique business
  (May Subd Geog)
  [NK1133.3]
  UF Antique mail-order business
  BT Antique dealers
      Mail-order business
Mail-order business (May Subd Geog)
  [HF5466]
  BT Business
      Direct selling
      Selling
  RT Advertising, Direct-mail
  NT Direct marketing
      Drop shipments
      Mail-order antique business
      Sales letters
  — Law and legislation (May Subd Geog)
  — Taxation (May Subd Geog)
  — — Law and legislation
      (May Subd Geog)
Mail planes
  USE Transport planes
Mail preparation
  RT Letter services
Mail procedures, Office
  USE Office mail procedures
Mail questionnaires
  USE Mail surveys
Mail receiving and forwarding services
  (May Subd Geog)
  [HE5999]

UF Forwarding services, Mail
      Mail drops
      Receiving services, Mail
BT Letter services

Mail recreations
USE Letter writing recreations

Mail service
USE Postal service

Mail sorting *(May Subd Geog)*
UF Sorting, Mail
BT Letter mail handling
      Postal service

Mail steamers *(May Subd Geog)*
   [HE6233]
   [HE6477 (United States)]
UF Steamship mail
BT Postal conventions
      Postal service
      Shipping
      Shipping bounties and subsidies
      Steamboats
NT Ocean mail stamps

Mail surveys *(May Subd Geog)*
UF Mail questionnaires
      Mailed surveys
      Surveys, Mail
BT Questionnaires
      Social sciences—Research
  — Response rate
      UF Response rate of mail surveys

Mail systems, Voice
USE Voice mail systems

Mailboxes *(May Subd Geog)*
UF Postal service—Mailboxes
  — Law and legislation *(May Subd Geog)*

Mailed catfishes
USE Loricariidae

Mailed surveys
USE Mail surveys

Mailing guides
USE Shippers' guides

Mailing lists *(May Subd Geog)*
UF Lists, Mailing
BT Advertising

Mailing services
USE Letter services

Maillard reaction
   [TP372.55.M35]
UF Browning reaction
BT Chemical reactions

Mailleux family
USE Mayeux family

Mailmen
USE Postal service—Letter carriers

MailMerge (Computer program)
BT Computer programs
      WordStar (Computer program)

Mailu
   [GN671.N5 (New Guinea)]

Mailu language
UF Magi language (Central Province,
      Papua New Guinea)
BT Papuan languages

Maïmecha River (R.S.F.S.R.)
UF Maymecha River (R.S.F.S.R.)
      Reka Maïmecha (R.S.F.S.R.)
BT Rivers—Russian S.F.S.R.

Maimuna
BT Jews, Moroccan
      Jews, Moroccan—Israel

**Main Building, Library of Congress
(Washington, D.C.)**
USE Library of Congress Thomas Jefferson
      Building (Washington, D.C.)

Main-Donau-Kanal (Germany)
USE Rhein-Main-Donau-Kanal (Germany)

Main-Donau-Wasserstrasse (Germany)
USE Rhein-Main-Donau-Kanal (Germany)

Main family *(Not Subd Geog)*
UF Maine family
      Maines family
      Mains family
      Mane family
      Manes family
      Mayne family
      Maynes family
      Mehn family

MAIN II (Computer program)

Main Island (Bermuda Islands)
USE Bermuda Island (Bermuda Islands)

Main Line (Pa.)

Main-Neckar-Eisenbahn
BT Railroads—Germany (West)

Main River (Germany)
BT Rivers—Germany (West)

Main Street (Bowling Green, Ky.)
BT Streets—Kentucky

Maina (Greece)
USE Mani (Greece)

Maina Indians
USE Mayna Indians

Mainard family
USE Maynard family

Maindombe, Lake (Zaire)
USE Mai-Ndombe, Lake (Zaire)

Maine
  — Antiquities
      NT Vail Site (Me.)
            Young Site (Alton, Me.)
  — Capital and capitol
      NT Maine State House (Augusta, Me.)
  — Description and travel
  — — 1951-1980
  — — 1981-
  — Governors
  — — Dwellings
      NT Blaine House (Augusta, Me.)
  — History
      [F16-30]
  — — Colonial period, ca. 1600-1775
      NT Eastern Indians, Wars with,
            1722-1726
  — — King William's War, 1689-1697
  — — King George's War, 1744-1748
  — — Revolution, 1775-1783
      [E263.M4]
  — — 1775-1865
  — — War of 1812
      [F24]
  — — Civil War, 1861-1865
      [E511]
  — — — Centennial celebrations, etc.
  — Politics and government
  — — Colonial period, ca. 1600-1775
  — — 1775-1865
  — — 1865-1950
  — — 1951-

Maine, Gulf of
BT Bays—North Atlantic Ocean

Maine cat
USE Maine coon cat

Maine coon cat
   [SF449.M34]
UF Coon cat
      Maine cat
BT Cat breeds
      Longhair cats

Maine family
USE Main family

Maine Forestry District
UF Forestry District, Me.
BT Fire protection districts—Maine
      Forest protection—Maine

Maine River (France)
UF Rivière de la Maine (France)
BT Rivers—France

Maine State Capitol (Augusta, Me.)
USE Maine State House (Augusta, Me.)

Maine State House (Augusta, Me.)
UF Maine State Capitol (Augusta, Me.)
      State Capitol (Augusta, Me.)
      State House (Augusta, Me.)
BT Maine—Capital and capitol

Maines family
USE Main family

Mainhard family
USE Maynard family

Mainōkyō
USE Kyōzuka

Mainor family
USE Maynard family

Mains family
USE Main family

Mainstreaming in education
  (May Subd Geog)
      Here are entered works on the placement of ex-
ceptional children in that part of the total public
school program not concerned with special education
services.
BT Education

Maintainability (Engineering)
UF Maintainability of equipment
BT Engineering
      Operations research
      Systems engineering
SA *subdivision* Maintainability *under types
      of equipment and machinery, e.g.*
      Electronic apparatus and appliances
      —Maintainability
NT Maintenance
      Nuclear power plants—Maintainability
      Reliability (Engineering)

Maintainability of equipment
USE Maintainability (Engineering)

**Maintaining, Preparing, and Producing
Executive Reports (Computer system)**
USE MAPPER (Computer system)

Maintenance
UF Preventive maintenance
      Upkeep
BT Maintainability (Engineering)
RT Repairing
      Service life (Engineering)
SA *subdivision* Maintenance and repair
      *under kinds of objects, including
      machinery, vehicles, structures, etc.,
      e.g.* Automobiles—Maintenance and
      repair; Dwellings—Maintenance and
      repair; Nuclear reactors—
      Maintenance and repair; *and
      subdivision* Maintenance *under
      special areas, e.g.* Parks—
      Maintenance; Recreation areas—
      Maintenance
NT Automatic checkout equipment
      Buildings—Repair and reconstruction
      Grounds maintenance
      Plant maintenance
  — Equipment and supplies
      NT Spare parts

Maintenance, Employee
USE Employee maintenance

Maintenance, Software
USE Software maintenance

Maintenance (Criminal law)
USE Maintenance and champerty

Maintenance (Domestic relations)
USE Support (Domestic relations)

Maintenance and champerty
UF Champerty
      Maintenance (Criminal law)
BT Criminal law
      Lawyers
      Legal ethics

Maintenance of prices
USE Price maintenance

Mainwaring family
USE Manwaring family

Mainyard family
USE Maynard family
Mainz Basin (Germany)
UF Mainzer Becken (Germany)
BT Geology—Germany (West)
Mainz Cathedral frescoes (Painting)
USE Veit, Philipp, 1793-1877. Mainz
Cathedral frescoes
Mainzer Becken (Germany)
USE Mainz Basin (Germany)
Mainzer Domfresken
USE Veit, Philipp, 1793-1877. Mainz
Cathedral frescoes
Maiolica
USE Majolica
Maiongking Indians
USE Yecuana Indians
Maipo, Battle of, 1818
[F3094]
UF Maipu, Battle of, 1818
BT Chile—History—War of Independence,
1810-1824—Campaigns
Maipu, Battle of, 1818
USE Maipo, Battle of, 1818
Maipua language
USE Purari language
Mair family
USE Myers family
Maire family
USE Myers family
Maires family
USE Myers family
Mairs family
USE Myers family
Mairy family
USE Merry family
Mais family
USE May family
Maise family
USE May family
Maisey family
USE Macy family
Maison du Roi (Brussels, Belgium)
UF Broodhuis (Brussels, Belgium)
BT Municipal buildings—Belgium
Maison Fornel (Québec, Québec)
UF Fornel House (Québec, Québec)
Maison Villeray (Québec, Québec)
Villeray House (Québec, Québec)
BT Dwellings—Québec (Province)
Villeray, Louis Rouer de, 1629-1700—
Homes and haunts—Québec
(Province)
**Maison Morand-Pasteur (Saillon,
Switzerland)**
UF Morand-Pasteur House (Saillon,
Switzerland)
BT Dwellings—Switzerland
Maison Saint-Gabriel (Montréal, Québec)
UF Marguerite Bourgeoys Farm
(Montréal, Québec)
Métairie de Marguerite Bourgeoys
(Montréal, Québec)
Saint-Gabriel House (Montréal,
Québec)
BT Dwellings—Québec (Province)
Farms—Québec (Province)
Maison Villeray (Québec, Québec)
USE Maison Fornel (Québec, Québec)
Maita family *(Not Subd Geog)*
Maithili authors
USE Authors, Maithili
Maithili drama *(May Subd Geog)*
Maithili epic poetry
USE Epic poetry, Maithili
Maithili fiction *(May Subd Geog)*
[PK1818.4 (History)]
[PK1818 (Collections)]
NT Short stories, Maithili
Maithili folk-songs
USE Folk-songs, Maithili

Maithili language
[PK1811-1819]
UF Tirhutia language
BT Bihari language
Maithili literature
[PK1818]
Maithili philology
Maithili poetry *(May Subd Geog)*
NT Epic poetry, Maithili
Religious poetry, Maithili
Vaishnava poetry, Maithili
— 20th century
Maithili poets
USE Poets, Maithili
Maithili prose literature *(May Subd Geog)*
Maithili religious poetry
USE Religious poetry, Maithili
Maithili short stories
USE Short stories, Maithili
Maithili songs
USE Songs, Maithili
Maithili Vaishnava poetry
USE Vaishnava poetry, Maithili
Maitonphi (Legendary character)
BT Folklore—India
Maitrakas
BT India—History—324 B.C.-1000 A.D.
Maître d's *(May Subd Geog)*
UF Headwaiters
Maîtres d'hôtel
Majordomos
BT Stewards
Waiters
Maîtres d'hôtel
USE Maître d's
Maitreya (Buddhist deity)
(May Subd Geog)
[BQ4690.M3]
UF Maitreya Bodhisattva
Maitreya Buddha
Metteyya (Buddhist deity)
BT Bodhisattvas
Buddhas
Gods, Buddhist
Maitreya Bodhisattva
USE Maitreya (Buddhist deity)
Maitreya Buddha
USE Maitreya (Buddhist deity)
Maitrī
USE Compassion (Buddhism)
Maîtrises
[ML3027]
BT Chapels (Music)
Choirs (Music)
Church music—Catholic Church
Church music—France
Conservatories of music
Music—Instruction and study—France
Maiya dialect
[PK7045.M3]
BT Pisacha languages
Maize
USE Corn
Maize bill-bug
[SB608.M2]
Maize family
USE May family
Maize paper
USE Paper, Maize
Maize root-rot
USE Root-rot of maize
Maize rough dwarf virus disease
[SB608.M2]
UF Rough dwarf virus disease of maize
BT Grasses—Diseases and pests
Maizuru Castle (Maizuru-shi, Japan)
USE Maizurujō (Maizuru-shi, Japan)
Maizurujō (Maizuru-shi, Japan)
UF Maizuru Castle (Maizuru-shi, Japan)
Tanabejō (Maizuru-shi, Japan)
Tango Tanabejō (Maizuru-shi, Japan)

BT Castles—Japan
Maja
[QL444.M33]
UF Maia
BT Majidae
Maja squinado
[QL444.M33]
Majangir (African people)
UF Masongo (African people)
Tama (African people)
Ujang (African people)
BT Ethnology—Ethiopia
Majardah River (Algeria and Tunisia)
USE Medjerda River (Algeria and Tunisia)
Majdanek (Poland : Concentration camp)
(Not Subd Geog)
BT Concentration camps—Poland
World War, 1939-1945—
Concentration camps—Poland
Majella Mountains (Italy)
USE Maiella Mountains (Italy)
Majenica Mountains (Bosnia and Hercegovina)
USE Majevica Mountains (Bosnia and
Hercegovina)
Majeur Lake (Italy and Switzerland)
USE Maggiore, Lake (Italy and
Switzerland)
**Majevica Mountains (Bosnia and
Hercegovina)**
UF Majenica Mountains (Bosnia and
Hercegovina)
Mayevitsa Mountains (Bosnia and
Hercegovina)
BT Mountains—Yugoslavia
Majgaard family *(Not Subd Geog)*
UF Maigaard family
Maji Maji Uprising, 1905-1907
BT Tanganyika—History
Majidae
[QL444.M33]
BT Oxyrhyncha
NT Chlorinoides
Maja
Tanner crabs
Majingai dialect
UF Madjinngay dialect
Midjinngay dialect
Modjinngay dialect
Moggingain dialect
Sar dialect
Sara-Majingai dialect
BT Central African Republic—Languages
Chad—Languages
Sara language
Majingai-Ngama language
USE Sara language
Majingai proverbs
USE Proverbs, Majingai
Majolica *(May Subd Geog)*
[NK4315-4320]
UF Maiolica
BT Pottery
— 16th century *(May Subd Geog)*
— 17th century *(May Subd Geog)*
— 18th century *(May Subd Geog)*
— 19th century *(May Subd Geog)*
— 20th century *(May Subd Geog)*
Majolica, American *(May Subd Geog)*
UF American majolica
Majolica, Baroque *(May Subd Geog)*
UF Baroque majolica
Majolica, Dutch, [Italian, etc.]
Majolica, Gothic *(May Subd Geog)*
[NK4315-4320]
UF Gothic majolica
Majolica, Islamic *(May Subd Geog)*
UF Islamic majolica
Majolica, Muslim
Muslim majolica
— Spain
UF Hispano-Moresque majolica

Majolica, Italian *(May Subd Geog)*
  UF Italian majolica
Majolica, Medieval *(May Subd Geog)*
  UF Medieval majolica
Majolica, Mexican *(May Subd Geog)*
  UF Mexican majolica
Majolica, Muslim
  USE Majolica, Islamic
Majolica, Renaissance *(May Subd Geog)*
  [NK4315-NK4320]
  UF Renaissance majolica
Majolica, Spanish *(May Subd Geog)*
  UF Spanish majolica
Majolica, Ukrainian *(May Subd Geog)*
  UF Ukrainian majolica
Majolier family *(Not Subd Geog)*
Major comes to woo (Painting)
  USE Fedotov, Pavel Andreevich, 1815-
    1852. Major comes to woo
Major histocompatibility complex
  [QR184.32]
  UF Histocompatibility complex
    Mhc (Immunogenetics)
  BT Immunogenetics
  RT HLA histocompatibility antigens
Major orders
  USE Bishops
    Clergy
Majorana
  USE Origanum
Majorca (Spain)
  UF Balearis Major (Spain)
    Isla de Mallorca (Spain)
    Majorica (Spain)
    Mallorca (Spain)
  BT Balearic Islands
    Islands—Spain
Majordomos
  USE Maître d's
Majorettes
  USE Drum majorettes
Majorica (Spain)
  USE Majorca (Spain)
Majorities
  [JF1051-JF1075 (Political rights)]
  BT Elections
    Representative government and
      representation
    Voting
  RT Minorities
Majorities (Canon law)
Majority leader, Senate
  USE United States. Congress. Senate—
    Majority leader
Majority logic
  USE Threshold logic
Majority whip, Senate
  USE United States. Congress. Senate—
    Majority whip
Majuba Hill (South Africa), Battle of, 1881
  BT Transvaal (South Africa)—History—
    War of 1880-1881
Majuro (Marshall Islands)
  BT Coral reefs and islands—Marshall
    Islands
Maka (African people)
  [DT571.M35]
  UF Makie (African people)
  BT Ethnology—Cameroon
Maka language
  USE Maca language
Makacari language
  USE Masacali language
Makah Indians
  [E99.M19]
  UF Cape Indians
    Classet Indians
    Clatset Indians
  BT Indians of North America
    Wakashan Indians

Makaira ampla
  USE Blue marlin
Makaira audax
  USE Striped marlin
Makaira mazara
  USE Blue marlin
Makaira mitsukurii
  USE Striped marlin
Makaira nigricans
  USE Blue marlin
Makama
  USE Maqamah
Makara
  [N7760 (Mythical monsters: art)]
  BT Mythology, Hindu
    Sea monsters
Makarub language
  USE Daribi language
Makasar (Indonesian people)
  UF Macassans (Indonesian people)
    Makassarese (Indonesian people)
  BT Ethnology—Indonesia
Makasar ethics
  USE Ethics, Makasar
Makasar language
  UF Macassar language
  BT Malayan languages
  RT Buginese language
  NT Kondjo dialect
Makasar literature *(May Subd Geog)*
  BT Indonesia—Literatures
  NT Makasar poetry
Makasar poetry *(May Subd Geog)*
  BT Makasar literature
Makassarese (Indonesian people)
  USE Makasar (Indonesian people)
Makaukau (African people)
  USE !Kung (African people)
Make (The English word)
  BT English language—Etymology
Make a picture story test
  USE Picture story tests
Make-buy decisions
  USE Make-or-buy decisions
Make-or-buy decisions
  UF Buy-make decisions
    Buy-or-make decisions
    Make-buy decisions
  BT Costs, Industrial
    Decision-making
    Industrial procurement
    Manufacturing processes
Make-up, Theatrical
  [PN2068]
  UF Acting—Make-up
    Makeup, Theatrical
    Stage make-up
    Theatrical make-up
  BT Actors
    Costume
  NT Film make-up
    Masks
    Prosthetic make-up, Theatrical
Make-up (Cosmetics)
  USE Cosmetics
Make-up (Typography)
  USE Printing, Practical—Make-up
Mak'edalā, Ethiopia, Battle of, 1868
  BT Abyssinian Expedition, 1867-1868
Makedonia (Greece)
  USE Macedonia (Greece)
Makedoniya (Greece)
  USE Macedonia (Greece)
Makee family
  USE McKey family
Makernes family
  USE Mackaness family
Makernesse family
  USE Mackaness family
Makers of crossword puzzles
  USE Crossword puzzle makers

Makeup, Theatrical
  USE Make-up, Theatrical
Makeup (Cosmetics)
  USE Cosmetics
Makeup (Typography)
  USE Printing, Practical—Make-up
Makey family
  USE McKey family
Makhanyas (African people)
  UF Makhanyas (Zulu tribe)
  BT Ethnology—South Africa
    Zulus
Makhanyas (Zulu tribe)
  USE Makhanyas (African people)
Makhorka
  USE Tobacco
Makhtesh Ramon (Israel)
  USE Ramon Crater (Israel)
Makian language, East
  USE East Makian language
Makian language, West
  USE West Makian language
Makie (African people)
  USE Maka (African people)
Makigaya kofun (Shizuoka-shi, Japan)
  USE Makigaya Site (Shizuoka-shi, Japan)
Makigaya Site (Shizuoka-shi, Japan)
  (Not Subd Geog)
  UF Makigaya kofun (Shizuoka-shi, Japan)
    Suruga Makigaya kofun (Shizuoka-shi,
      Japan)
  BT Japan—Antiquities
Makin, Battle of, 1943
  [D767.917]
  BT World War, 1939-1945—Campaigns—
    Kiribati
Making-choices stories
  USE Plot-your-own stories
Making decisions
  USE Decision-making
Making of beds
  USE Bedmaking
Making up trains
  USE Railroads—Making up trains
Makira (Solomon Islands)
  USE San Cristobal (Solomon Islands)
Makiritare Indians
  USE Yecuana Indians
Makiritare language
  USE Yecuana language
Makka Indians
  USE Macá Indians
Makkovik Bay (Nfld.)
  BT Bays—Newfoundland
Makoldi family *(Not Subd Geog)*
Makonde (African people)
  UF Konde (African people)
    Makonde (Bantu tribe)
  BT Bantus
    Ethnology—Africa, East
Makonde (African people) sculpture
  USE Sculpture, Makonde (African people)
Makonde (Bantu tribe)
  USE Makonde (African people)
Makonde language
  [PL8482.M8]
  UF Konde language
    Mabiha language
    Maconde language
    Mavia language
  BT Bantu languages
Makronēsos (Greece)
  UF Eléni (Greece)
    Makronísi (Greece)
    Makrónisos (Greece)
  BT Islands—Greece
Makronísi (Greece)
  USE Makronēsos (Greece)
Makrónisos (Greece)
  USE Makronēsos (Greece)

Maksim Gorky Street (Leningrad, R.S.F.S.R.)
  USE Prospekt Gor'kogo (Leningrad,
      R.S.F.S.R.)
Makú Indians (Papury River watershed)
  USE Macú Indians (Papury River
      watershed)
Makua (African people)
  [DT458.3.M35]
  UF Macua (African people)
      Makwa (African people)
      Wakua (African people)
      Wamakua (African people)
  BT Bantus
      Ethnology—Mozambique
Makua language
  [PL8483]
  UF Macua language
  BT Bantu languages
Makua proverbs
  USE Proverbs, Makua
Makuchi Cave (Japan)   (Not Subd Geog)
  UF Makuchi Dōkutsu (Japan)
      Makuchi Dōkutsu Iseki (Japan)
  BT Caves—Japan
Makuchi Dōkutsu (Japan)
  USE Makuchi Cave (Japan)
Makuchi Dōkutsu Iseki (Japan)
  USE Makuchi Cave (Japan)
Makuchi Indians
  USE Macusi Indians
Makuchi language
  USE Macusi language
Makurakotoba
  USE Japanese language—Epithets
Makwa (African people)
  USE Makua (African people)
Makwangwa (Bantu people)
  USE Kwangwa (Bantu people)
Mal de caderas
  BT Horses—Diseases
      Trypanosomiasis
Mal Paharias
  USE Malpaharias
Mala fides
  USE Bad faith (Law)
Mala language
  USE Mara language (Australia)
Mala Pandaram (Indic people)
  USE Malapandaram (Indic people)
Mala Plateau (India)
  USE Mālwa Plateau (India)
Mala River (Peru)
  UF Río de Mala (Peru)
      Río Mala (Peru)
  BT Rivers—Peru
Malabar Coast (India)
  BT Coasts—India
  — Rebellion, 1921
      UF Malabar Rebellion, Malabar Coast
          (India), 1921
Malabar language
  USE Malayalam language
      Tamil language
Malabar Rebellion, Malabar Coast (India),
1921
  USE Malabar Coast (India)—Rebellion,
      1921
Malabar rite (Catholic Church)
  USE Catholic Church—Malabar rite
Malabar rites
  [BX1995.M18]
      Here are entered works on indigenous rites and
  customs permitted by Jesuit missionaries in South
  India as an adaptation of Christianity to local culture
  until these practices were forbidden.
  UF Malabar rites controversy
      Rites, Malabar
  BT Catholic Church—Missions—India
Malabar rites controversy
  USE Malabar rites

Malabar simaltree
  USE Simal
Malabathrum
  [RS165.M35]
Malabsorption syndromes   (May Subd Geog)
  [RC862.M3]
  BT Intestines—Diseases
      Syndromes
  RT Intestinal absorption
  NT Blind loop syndrome
      Celiac disease
      Lactose intolerance
      Whipple's disease
Malacca, Strait of
  UF Malakka Strait
      Selat Malaka
      Straat Malaka
      Strait of Malacca
  BT Straits—Indonesia
      Straits—Malaysia
      Straits—Singapore
Malachiidae
  USE Melyridae
Malachite   (May Subd Geog)
Malachius
  [QL596.M43]
  BT Melyridae
Malaclemys
  USE Diamondback terrapin
Malaclemys terrapin
  USE Diamondback terrapin
Malacoctenus
  [QL638.C63]
  BT Clinidae
Malacoctenus aurolineatus
  [QL638.C.63]
  UF Blenny, Goldline
      Goldenlined blenny
      Goldline blenny
Malacoctenus erdmani
  [QL638.C63]
  UF Blenny, Graygreen
      Graygreen blenny
Malacoctenus triangulatus
  USE Saddled blenny
Malacodermidae
  USE Fireflies
Malacologists   (May Subd Geog)
  BT Zoologists
  NT Conchologists
Malacology
  USE Mollusks
Malacopterygii
  USE Osteichthyes
Malacosoma
  USE Tent-caterpillars
Malacosoma americana
  USE Eastern tent caterpillar
Malacosoma disstria
  USE Forest tent-caterpillar
Malacosoma fragile
  USE Great Basin tent caterpillar
Malacostraca
  [QL444.M]
  BT Crustacea
  NT Amphipoda
      Arthrostraca
      Cumacea
      Decapoda (Crustacea)
      Euphausiacea
      Isopoda
      Leptostraca
      Schizopoda
      Stomatopoda
      Tanaidacea
      Thoracostraca
Malacostraca, Fossil
  BT Crustacea, Fossil
  NT Shrimps, Fossil
Maladjusted children
  USE Problem children

Maladjustment (Psychology)
  USE Adjustment (Psychology)
Malag (Australian people)
  USE Murngin (Australian people)
Malagasy art
  USE Art, Malagasy
Malagasy astrology
  USE Astrology, Malagasy
Malagasy authors
  USE Authors, Malagasy
Malagasy fiction   (May Subd Geog)
Malagasy folk poetry
  USE Folk poetry, Malagasy
Malagasy folk-songs
  USE Folk-songs, Malagasy
Malagasy language
  [PL5371-PL5379]
  UF Hova dialect
      Malgache language
      Merina dialect
  BT Malayan languages
  NT Antaisaka dialect
      Antandroy dialect
      Bara dialect (Madagascar)
      Betsileo dialect
      Sakalava dialect
      Tsimihety dialect
  — Dialects
Malagasy literature   (May Subd Geog)
Malagasy literature (French)
  (May Subd Geog)
  UF French literature—Malagasy authors
Malagasy national characteristics
  USE National characteristics, Malagasy
Malagasy orations
  USE Speeches, addresses, etc., Malagasy
Malagasy periodicals   (May Subd Geog)
Malagasy philosophy
  USE Philosophy, Malagasy
Malagasy poetry
  NT Folk poetry, Malagasy
Malagasy poetry (French)
  UF French poetry—Malagasy authors
Malagasy pottery
  USE Pottery, Malagasy
Malagasy proverbs
  USE Proverbs, Malagasy
Malagasy Republic
  USE Madagascar
Malagasy songs
  USE Songs, Malagasy
Malagasy speeches
  USE Speeches, addresses, etc., Malagasy
Malagueta pepper
  USE Grains of paradise
Malaīā ėlektronnaīā schetnaīā mashina
  (Computer)
  USE MÉSM (Computer)
Malaīā Sos'va (R.S.F.S.R. : Preserve)
  (Not Subd Geog)
  UF Malaya Sos'va (R.S.F.S.R. : Preserve)
      Zapovednik Malaīā Sos'va (R.S.F.S.R.)
  BT National parks and reserves—Russian
      S.F.S.R.
      Natural areas—Russian S.F.S.R.
Malaiali
  USE Malaiyalis
Malaita (Solomon Islands)
  BT Islands—Solomon Islands
Malaiyalis
  [DS432.M24]
  UF Malaiali
  BT Caste—India
      Ethnology—India
Malaiyamān
  BT Tamil Nadu (India)—History
Mal'ak (The Hebrew word)
  USE Mal'akh (The Hebrew word)
Malakata Peshtera (Bulgaria)
  USE Bacho Kiro Cave (Bulgaria)

Mal'akh (The Hebrew word)
  UF Mal'ak (The Hebrew word)
  BT Hebrew language—Etymology
Malakka Strait
  USE Malacca, Strait of
Malakmalak language
  USE Mullukmulluk language
Malakula (Vanuatu)
  USE Malekula (Vanuatu)
Malalopidae
  USE Chrysomelidae
Malambo (Dance)
Malampuzha Project
  BT Dams—India
      Irrigation—India
      Reservoirs—India
      Water resources development—India
Malamute, Alaskan
  USE Alaskan Malamute
Malania anjouanae
  USE Coelacanth
Malankar rite (Catholic Church)
  USE Catholic Church—Malankar rite
Malans Castle (Malans, Haute-Saône, France)
  USE Château de Malans (Malans, Haute-Saône, France)
Malapandaram (Indic people)
  ₍DS432.M243₎
  UF Hill Pandaram (Indic people)
      Mala Pandaram (Indic people)
      Malapantaram (Indic people)
      Panturani (Indic people)
  BT Ethnology—India
Malapantaram (Indic people)
  USE Malapandaram (Indic people)
Malapropisms
  ₍PN6231.M19 (Wit and humor)₎
  BT Speech errors
Malapteruridae
  ₍QL638.M246₎
  BT Catfishes
Malar bone
  USE Cheek-bone
Mälar Lake (Sweden)
  UF Mälaren (Sweden)
  BT Lakes—Sweden
Mälaren (Sweden)
  USE Mälar Lake (Sweden)
Mälarhöjden (Stockholm, Sweden)
  (Not Subd Geog)
  UF Stockholm (Sweden). Mälarhöjden
Malaria (May Subd Geog)
  ₍RA644.M2 (Public health)₎
  ₍RC156-RC166 (General)₎
  UF Ague
      Chills and fever
      Intermittent fever
      Malarial fever
  BT Fever
      Medical protozoology
  NT Anopheles
      Antimalarials
      Blackwater fever
      Malariotherapy
      Plasmodium
      Plasmodium falciparum
  — Immunological aspects
  — Law and legislation
      BT Malaria—Prevention
  — Prevention
      NT Malaria—Law and legislation
Malaria, Avian
  USE Avian malaria
Malaria, Therapeutic
  USE Malariotherapy
Malaria therapy
  USE Malariotherapy
Malaria vaccine (May Subd Geog)
  BT Vaccines
Malarial fever
  USE Malaria

Malarial fever in birds
  USE Avian malaria
Malarial fever in poultry
  USE Avian malaria
Malariotherapy
  ₍RM868.5₎
  UF Malaria, Therapeutic
      Malaria therapy
  BT Fever therapy
      Malaria
Malartre family (Not Subd Geog)
Malary family
  USE Mallory family
Mālaśe family
  USE Malshe family
Malate dehydrogenase
  ₍QP603.D4₎
Malatesta Castle (Rimini, Italy)
  USE Castel Sismondo (Rimini, Italy)
Malatesta family (Not Subd Geog)
Malatesta Palace (Fano, Italy)
  USE Palazzo malatestiano (Fano, Italy)
Malatestiano Palace (Fano, Italy)
  USE Palazzo malatestiano (Fano, Italy)
Malau (Indonesian people)
  USE Maloh (Indonesian people)
Mālava (India)
  USE Malwa (India)
Mālavas
  ₍DS451₎
  UF Malli
      Malloi
  BT Ethnology—India
Malavi dialect
  USE Malvi dialect
Malawi
  UF Nyasaland
  — Foreign relations
  — — 1964-
  — History
  — — To 1891
  — — 1891-1953
  — — Chilembwe Rebellion, 1915
      ₍DT862₎
      UF Chilembwe Rebellion, 1915
  — — 1953-1964
  — — 1964-
      ₍DT862.2₎
  — Politics and government
  — — 1964-
Malawi, Lake
  USE Nyasa, Lake
Malawi cookery
  USE Cookery, Malawi
Malawi drama (English)
  ₍PR9385.3 (History)₎
  ₍PR9385.7 (Collections)₎
  UF English drama—Malawian authors
Malawi literature (May Subd Geog)
  ₍PL8014.M₎
Malawi literature (English)
  USE English literature—Malawi authors
Malawi Railways
Malay (Asian people) marriage customs and rites
  USE Marriage customs and rites, Malay (Asian people)
Malay alphabet
  USE Jawi alphabet
Malay anonyms and pseudonyms
  USE Anonyms and pseudonyms, Malay
Malay Archipelago
  Here are entered works dealing collectively with the island region consisting of Indonesia, Philippines, Borneo, and New Guinea.
  UF East Indian Archipelago
  BT Archipelagoes—Asia, Southeastern
      Asia, Southeastern
  NT Borneo
      New Guinea

Malay authors
  USE Authors, Malay
Malay bear
  USE Sun bear
Malay children's literature
  USE Children's literature, Malay
Malay children's plays
  USE Children's plays, Malay
Malay children's stories
  USE Children's stories, Malay
Malay children's writings
  USE Children's writings, Malay
Malay drama (May Subd Geog)
  NT Children's plays, Malay
      Radio plays, Malay
Malay essays (May Subd Geog)
Malay fiction (May Subd Geog)
  NT Children's stories, Malay
      Short stories, Malay
Malay folk literature
  USE Folk literature, Malay
Malay folk-songs
  USE Folk-songs, Malay
Malay hymns
  USE Hymns, Malay
Malay imprints (May Subd Geog)
Malay language (May Subd Geog)
  ₍PL5101-PL5129₎
  BT Malayan languages
  RT Indonesian language
  NT Besemah dialect
      Deli dialect
      Lembak Bilide dialect
      Manggarai language
      Musi dialect
      Ogan dialect
      Pasir dialect
      Pattani dialect (Thailand)
      Rawas dialect
      Semendo dialect
      Siladang dialect
      Urak Lawoi' language
  — Etymology
      NT Words, New—Malay
  — Asia, Southeastern
      UF Malay language in Southeastern Asia
Malay language in Southeastern Asia
  USE Malay language—Asia, Southeastern
Malay literature
  ₍PL5130-5149₎
  NT Children's literature, Malay
      Folk literature, Malay
  — To 1500
  — 1500-1800
  — 20th century
Malay lullabies
  USE Lullabies, Malay
Malay manuscripts
  USE Manuscripts, Malay
Malay newspapers (May Subd Geog)
Malay Peninsula
  BT Peninsulas—Asia, Southeastern
Malay periodicals (May Subd Geog)
Malay philology (May Subd Geog)
Malay poetry (May Subd Geog)
  NT Quatrains, Malay
  — 20th century
Malay-Polynesian languages
  USE Austronesian languages
Malay prose literature (May Subd Geog)
Malay proverbs
  USE Proverbs, Malay
Malay quatrains
  USE Quatrains, Malay
Malay radio plays
  USE Radio plays, Malay
Malay short stories
  USE Short stories, Malay
Malay subject headings
  USE Subject headings, Malay

Malaya

Here are entered works on the Federation of Malaya prior to its merger into Malaysia in 1963, as well as the present mainland states (i.e., those states located on the Malay Peninsula) of the country of Malaysia. Works on the country formed by the merger in 1963 of the Federation of Malaya, Sabah (formerly called North Borneo), and Sarawak are entered under Malaysia.

As a geographic subdivision, this heading is used indirectly through Malaysia.

  UF Federation of Malaya
      Malaysia, Peninsular
      Malaysia, West
      Malaysia Barat
      Peninsular Malaysia
      West Malaysia

  — **History**
    — — **Japanese occupation, 1942-1945**
        [DS596.6]
        UF Japanese occupation of Malaya, 1942-1945
    — — **Malayan Emergency, 1948-1960**
        [DS597]
        UF Communist Insurrection, Malayan, 1948-1960
             Malayan Communist Insurrection, 1948-1960
             Malayan Emergency, 1948-1960

Malaya Sos'va (R.S.F.S.R. : Preserve)
  USE Malaïa Sos'va (R.S.F.S.R. : Preserve)

Malayalam drama
  NT Folk-drama, Malayalam
      Kathakali plays

Malayalam dramatists
  USE Dramatists, Malayalam

Malayalam fiction *(May Subd Geog)*
  NT Short stories, Malayalam

Malayalam folk-drama
  USE Folk-drama, Malayalam

Malayalam folk-songs
  USE Folk-songs, Malayalam

Malayalam imprints *(May Subd Geog)*

Malayalam language
    [PL4711-PL4719]
  UF Malabar language
  BT Dravidian languages
  RT Manipravalam language (Malayalam)
  NT Ezhava dialect

Malayalam literature *(May Subd Geog)*
    [PL4718]

Malayalam manuscripts
  USE Manuscripts, Malayalam

Malayalam newspapers *(May Subd Geog)*
  BT Indic newspapers

Malayalam paleography
  USE Paleography, Malayalam

Malayalam periodicals *(May Subd Geog)*

Malayalam philology

Malayalam poetry *(May Subd Geog)*
  — **To 1500**
  — **1500-1800**
  — **Muslim authors**

Malayalam prose literature

Malayalam short stories
  USE Short stories, Malayalam

Malayalam wit and humor
  BT Indic wit and humor

Malayalees (Indic people)
  USE Malayalis (Indic people)

Malayalim (Indic people)
  USE Malayalis (Indic people)

Malayalis (Indic people)
    [DS432.M246]
  UF Malayalees (Indic people)
      Malayalim (Indic people)
  BT Ethnology—India

Malayan Communist Insurrection, 1948-1960
  USE Malaya—History—Malayan Emergency, 1948-1960

Malayan cookery
  USE Cookery, Malayan

Malayan drama *(May Subd Geog)*
    [PL5063 (History)]
    [PL5067 (Collections)]

Malayan Emergency, 1948-1960
  USE Malaya—History—Malayan Emergency, 1948-1960

Malayan languages *(May Subd Geog)*
    [PL5051-PL6135]

Here are entered works dealing with the Austronesian languages spoken in Madagascar, Sumatra, Java, Borneo, etc., the Philippine Islands, and parts of Taiwan and the Malay Peninsula.

  UF Hesperonesian languages
      Indonesian languages
      Western Austronesian languages
  BT Austronesian languages
  NT Achinese language
      Amboinese languages
      Atinggola language
      Bajau language
      Balaesang language
      Balinese language
      Banjarese language
      Barangas language
      Bareë dialect
      Batak language
      Biak language
      Bimanese language
      Bolaang Mongondo language
      Bolaang Mongondow language
      Buginese language
      Bukar Sadong language
      Buol language
      Chamic languages
      Chamorro language
      Dusun language
      Dyak language
      Enggano language
      Galelarese language
      Gayo language
      Gorontalo language
      Iban language
      Indonesian language
      Javanese language
      Katingan language
      Kawi language
      Kayan language
      Kemak language
      Kendayan language
      Kerinci language
      Kubu language
      Lampung language
      Madurese language
      Makasar language
      Malagasy language
      Malay language
      Mandar language
      Masenrempulu language
      Mentawai language
      Minangkabau language
      Mori language
      Muna language
      Murut language
      Napu language
      Ngada language
      Nias language
      Palauan language
      Philippine languages
      Proto-Malayan language
      Rejang language (Sumatra, Indonesia)
      Rottinese language
      Sangen language
      Sasak language
      Sawu language
      Serawai language
      Sigi language
      Simeulue language
      Sobojo language
      Sokop language
      Sumba language
      Sumbawa language
      Sundanese language
      Suwawa language
      Tae' language
      Taiwan languages
      Talaud language
      Tetum language
      Tidong dialects
      Timorese language
      Toba-Batak dialect
      Tolaki language
      Tondano language
      Toradja languages
      Toraja Sa'dan language
      Wandamen language
      Wolio language
      Yamdena language
  — **Alphabet**
    NT Jawi alphabet

Malayan literature
    [PL5060-5069]

Malayan manuscripts
  USE Manuscripts, Malayan

Malayan philology

Malayan poetry *(May Subd Geog)*
    [PL5062 (History)]
    [PL5066 (Collections)]

Malayan sun bear
  USE Sun bear

Malayo language
  UF Arosario language
      Maracasero language
      Marocasero language
      Sanja language
  BT Chibchan languages
      Colombia—Languages
      Indians of South America—Colombia—Languages

Malayo-Polynesian languages
  USE Austronesian languages

Malays (Asian people) *(May Subd Geog)*

Here are entered works on the people who inhabit the Malay Peninsula, eastern Sumatra, parts of Borneo, and some small adjacent islands, and who call themselves Orang Melayu.

  UF Melayu (Asian people)
      Orang Melayu (Asian people)
  BT Ethnology—Asia, Southeastern
  — **Medicine**
    BT Medicine, Primitive
  — **Rites and ceremonies**
    NT Marriage customs and rites, Malay (Asian people)

Malaysia

Here are entered works on the country formed by the merger in 1963 of the Federation of Malaya, Sabah (formerly called North Borneo), and Sarawak. Works on the Federation of Malaya prior to its merger into Malaysia in 1963, as well as the present mainland states (i.e., those states located on the Malay Peninsula) of the country of Malaysia are entered under Malaya.

  — **Anniversaries, etc.**
    NT Independence Day (Malaysia)
  — **Kings and rulers** *(Not Subd Geog)*
    NT Monarchy—Malaysia
  — **Languages**
    NT Bukar Sadong language
      Kayan language
      Urak Lawoi' language

Malaysia, East
  UF Eastern Malaysia
      Malaysia Timor

Malaysia, Peninsular
  USE Malaya

Malaysia, West
  USE Malaya

Malaysia Barat
  USE Malaya

Malaysia Timor
  USE Malaysia, East

Malaysian art
  USE Art, Malaysian

Malaysian arts
USE Arts, Malaysian
Malaysian atlases
USE Atlases, Malaysian
Malaysian civics
USE Civics, Malaysian
Malaysian coins
USE Coins, Malaysian
Malaysian cookery
USE Cookery, Malaysian
Malaysian fiction *(May Subd Geog)*
Malaysian fiction (English)
UF English fiction—Malaysian authors
NT Short stories, Malaysian (English)
Malaysian literature (English)
(May Subd Geog)
[PR9530.5 (Collections)]
[PR9530 (History)]
UF English literature—Malaysian authors
Malaysian monarchy
USE Monarchy—Malaysia
Malaysian newspapers *(May Subd Geog)*
Malaysian painting
USE Painting, Malaysian
Malaysian periodicals *(May Subd Geog)*
Malaysian poetry (English)
(May Subd Geog)
[PR9530.2 (History)]
[PR9530.6 (Collections)]
UF English poetry—Malaysian authors
NT Protest poetry, Malaysian (English)
Malaysian pottery
USE Pottery, Malaysian
Malaysian prose literature (English)
(May Subd Geog)
[PR9530.4 (History)]
[PR9530.8.P7 (Collections)]
UF English prose literature—Malaysian
authors
Malaysian protest poetry (English)
USE Protest poetry, Malaysian (English)
Malaysian short stories (English)
USE Short stories, Malaysian (English)
Malaysian students *(May Subd Geog)*
BT Students
Malaysian wit and humor, Pictorial
(May Subd Geog)
Malazgirt, Battle of, 1071
[DS27]
BT Byzantine Empire—History
Malbanc family
USE Malbon family
Malbank family
USE Malbon family
Malbedenc family
USE Malbon family
Malbedene family
USE Malbon family
Malbenge family
USE Malbon family
Malbon family *(Not Subd Geog)*
UF Malbanc family
Malbank family
Malbedenc family
Malbedene family
Malbenge family
Malcantone (Switzerland)
BT Alps
Mountains—Switzerland
Malchow family *(Not Subd Geog)*
Malcolm family *(Not Subd Geog)*
UF Malcom family
Malcomb family
Malcum family
Malcom family
USE Malcolm family
Malcomb family
USE Malcolm family
Malcontenta Villa (Mira, Italy)
USE Villa Foscari (Mira, Italy)

Malcum family
USE Malcolm family
Maldanidae
[QL391.A6]
BT Capitellida
NT Clymenella
Maldive Islands
USE Maldives
Maldives *(Not Subd Geog)*
UF Maldive Islands
BT Islands of the Indian Ocean
— **Languages** *(Not Subd Geog)*
NT Maldivian language
Maldivian language *(May Subd Geog)*
UF Divehi language
BT Indo-Aryan languages, Modern
Maldives—Languages
Male (African people)
[DT380.4.M32]
UF Maale (African people)
BT Ethnology—Ethiopia
Malê (Cult)
BT Cults—Brazil
Male actors
USE Men actors
Male birth control pills
USE Oral contraceptives, Male
Male change of life
USE Climacteric, Male
Male climacteric
USE Climacteric, Male
Male contraception *(May Subd Geog)*
UF Contraception, Male
BT Contraception
NT Vasectomy
Male contraceptive agents
USE Male contraceptives
Male contraceptive devices
USE Male contraceptives
Male contraceptives
UF Contraceptive agents, Male
Contraceptive devices, Male
Contraceptives, Male
Male contraceptive agents
Male contraceptive devices
BT Contraceptives
NT Condoms
Oral contraceptives, Male
Male figure in art
USE Men in art
Male generative organs
USE Generative organs, Male
Male grooming
USE Grooming for men
Male homosexual couples
USE Homosexual couples, Male
Male homosexuality
USE Homosexuality, Male
Male homosexuals
USE Homosexuals, Male
Male impersonators
USE Impersonators, Male
Male infertility
USE Infertility, Male
Male livestock *(May Subd Geog)*
UF Livestock, Male
BT Livestock
Males
NT Boars
Bulls
Rams
Roosters
Stallions
Male menopause
USE Climacteric, Male
Male nude *(May Subd Geog)*
UF Nude, Male
BT Men
Nudity
Male nurses
USE Men nurses

Male oral contraceptives
USE Oral contraceptives, Male
Male photography
USE Photography of men
Male pregnancy, Folklore of
USE Pregnant Man (Legendary character)
Male prostitution
USE Prostitution, Male
Male sex hormone
USE Hormones, Sex
Male sterility
USE Infertility, Male
Male sterility in plants *(May Subd Geog)*
[QK828]
BT Sterility in plants
NT Cytoplasmic male sterility
Male strip-tease
USE Strip-tease, Male
Male workers
USE Employment of men
Malecite Indians
[E99.M195]
UF Etchemin Indians
Maliseet Indians
Marashite Indians
Marechite Indians
Maricheet Indians
Melicete Indians
Milicete Indians
BT Abnaki Indians
Algonquian Indians
Indians of North America
Malecite language
USE Passamaquoddy language
Malediction
USE Blessing and cursing
Maleic acid
NT Maleic anhydride
Maleic anhydride
BT Anhydrides
Maleic acid
Malekula (Vanuatu)
UF Malakula (Vanuatu)
Mallicolo (Vanuatu)
BT Islands—Vanuatu
Malemute, Alaskan
USE Alaskan Malamute
Malengreau family *(Not Subd Geog)*
Maler (Hill tribe)
UF Sauria Paharias
BT Ethnology—India
Malery family
USE Mallory family
Males *(May Subd Geog)*
Here are entered works on male organisms in general. Works on the human male are entered under Men.
BT Sex
NT Male livestock
Men
Males, Human
USE Men
Malet family
USE Mallett family
Malette family
USE Mallett family
Malevich, Kazimir Severinovich, 1878-1935.
Black Square
[ND699.M224]
UF Black square (Painting)
Suprematist composition (Painting)
BT Black in art
Square in art
Suprematism in art
Malfatti's problem
[QA557]
Malfeasance in office
USE Misconduct in office
Malformations, Congenital
USE Abnormalities, Human

Malgache language
  USE Malagasy language
MALGOL (Computer program language)
  BT ALGOL (Computer program language)
Malheur National Forest (Or.)
  BT Forest reserves—Oregon
     National parks and reserves—United
      States
Mali
  UF French Sudan
     Sudan, French
     Sudanese Republic
  — History
     NT Mamadou Lamine, Rebellion of,
      1885-1887
  — — Coup d'état, 1968
     [DT551.8]
     UF Coup d'état, Mali, 1968
  — Languages
     NT Bobo Fing language
      Bozo language
Mali (Guinea)
  USE Niani (Guinea)
Mali empire
  UF Malinke empire
     Mandinga empire
  BT Mandingo (African people)
Mália Site (Crete) *(Not Subd Geog)*
  UF Mallia Site (Crete)
  BT Greece—Antiquities
Malibu automobile
  [TL215.M]
  BT Chevrolet automobile
Malibu million dollar rock (Portrait sculpture)
  USE Strong, Brett-Livingstone, 1953-
     Life time light
Malic acid
  [QD305.A2]
Malicious accusation *(May Subd Geog)*
  UF Accusation, Malicious
  BT Criminal law
     Torts
  RT Simulation of crimes
Malicious mischief *(May Subd Geog)*
  UF Destruction of property
     Mischief, Malicious
  BT Criminal law
     Offenses against property
  RT Vandalism
  NT Architecture—Mutilation, defacement,
     etc.
     Art—Mutilation, defacement, etc.
     Churches—Vandalism
     Painting—Mutilation, defacement, etc.
     Sabotage
     Sculpture—Mutilation, defacement,
     etc.
     Trials (Malicious mischief)
Malicious prosecution *(May Subd Geog)*
  UF Prosecution, Malicious
  BT Torts
  RT Simulation of crimes
  NT False imprisonment
Malicious prosecution (Canon law)
Malignant carcinoid syndrome
  BT Carcinoid
  NT Carcinoid heart disease
Malignant hemangioendothelioma
  USE Angiosarcoma
Malignant hyperpyrexia
  USE Malignant hyperthermia
Malignant hyperthermia
  [RD82.7.M3]
  UF Fulminant hyperthermia
     Hyperpyrexia, Malignant
     Hyperthermia, Malignant
     Malignant hyperpyrexia
  BT Anesthesia—Complications and
     sequelae
     Fever
     Physiology, Pathological

Malignant leucopenia
  USE Agranulocytosis
Malignant pustule
  USE Pustule, Malignant
Malignant tumors
  USE Cancer
Malignite
  [QE461]
Malikis
  BT Islamic law
     Islamic sects
     Sunnites
Malinda family
  USE Melendy family
Malingering
  [RA1146]
  UF Diseases, Feigned
     Feigned diseases
     Simulated diseases
     Simulation of diseases
  BT Medical jurisprudence
     Military offenses
  RT Self-mutilation
  NT Blindness, Feigned
Malinke empire
  USE Mali empire
Malinke language
  USE Mandingo language
Malinois sheepdog
  USE Belgian malinois
Maliseet Indians
  USE Malecite Indians
Maliseet language
  USE Passamaquoddy language
Malka
  USE Rubus chamaemorus
Malkata Site (Egypt)
  [DT73.M24]
  UF Malqata Site (Egypt)
  BT Egypt—Antiquities
Mall, The (Washington, D.C.)
  UF National Mall (Washington, D.C.)
     The Mall (Washington, D.C.)
  BT Parks—Washington (D.C.)
Malla dynasty *(Not Subd Geog)*
  BT Nepal—History—To 1768
Mallard
  [QL696.A52]
  UF Anas platyrhynchos
  BT Ducks
  NT Hawaiian duck
Mallary family
  USE Mallory family
Mallat family
  USE Mallett family
Malleability (Psychology)
  USE Adaptability (Psychology)
Mallee (Vic.)
Mallee
  USE Eucalyptus
Mallee, Blue-leaved
  USE Blue-leaved mallee
Mallee, Green
  USE Green mallee
Mallee fowl
  USE Leipoa ocellata
Malleoidosis
  USE Melioidosis
Mallery family
  USE Mallory family
Mallet family
  USE Mallett family
Mallet locomotives
  [TJ615]
  BT Locomotives, Articulated
Mallets Bay (Vt. : Bay)
  USE Malletts Bay (Vt. : Bay)

Mallett family *(Not Subd Geog)*
  UF Malet family
     Malette family
     Mallat family
     Mallet family
     Mallette family
     Mallit family
     Mellet family
     Mellett family
     Melot family
     Melott family
  RT Mullet family
Mallette family
  USE Mallett family
Malletts Bay (Vt. : Bay)
  UF Mallets Bay (Vt. : Bay)
  BT Bays—Vermont
Malleus (Ear)
  BT Ear ossicles
Malli
  USE Mālavas
Mallia Site (Crete)
  USE Mália Site (Crete)
Mallicolo (Vanuatu)
  USE Malekula (Vanuatu)
Mallit family
  USE Mallett family
Malloi
  USE Mālavas
Mallophaga *(May Subd Geog)*
  [QL540-540.42]
  UF Bird lice
     Biting lice
     Chewing lice
     Lipoptera
  BT Insects
     Lice
  NT Haematomyzidae
     Menoponidae
     Philopteridae
     Ricinidae
     Trichodectidae
Mallophora
  [QL537.A85]
  UF Megaphorus
  BT Robber flies
Mallorca (Spain)
  USE Majorca (Spain)
Mallory bodies *(May Subd Geog)*
  UF Alcohol hyaline
  BT Alcohol—Toxicology
     Liver cells—Inclusions
Mallory family *(Not Subd Geog)*
  UF Malary family
     Malery family
     Mallary family
     Mallery family
     Malory family
Mallotus *(May Subd Geog)*
  [QL638.O84]
  BT Smelts
Mallotus catervarius
  USE Capelin
Mallotus villosus
  USE Capelin
Mallow
  USE Malva
Mallow, Little
  USE Malva parviflora
Malloy family *(Not Subd Geog)*
  UF Molloy family
Malls, Pedestrian
  USE Shopping malls
Malls, Shopping
  USE Shopping malls
Malmaison (Rueil-Malmaison, France)
  UF Château de la Malmaison (Rueil-
     Malmaison, France)
     Malmaison Palace (Rueil-Malmaison,
     France)
  BT Palaces—France

Malmaison Palace (Rueil-Malmaison, France)
USE Malmaison (Rueil-Malmaison, France)
Malmani gold fields
BT Gold mines and mining—South Africa
Malmedy Massacre, 1944-1945
BT World War, 1939-1945—Atrocities
Malmesbury Railway
BT Railroads—Great Britain
Malmgren family *(Not Subd Geog)*
Malmignatte
USE Black widow spider
Malnutrition *(May Subd Geog)*
[RA645.N87 (Public health)]
[RC623 (Internal medicine)]
BT Nutrition disorders
RT Nutrition
Starvation
Malnutrition in children *(May Subd Geog)*
[RJ399.M26]
BT Children—Nutrition
Nutrition disorders in children
NT Fetal malnutrition
Kwashiorkor
Marasmus
Vitamin A deficiency in children
— **United States**
— — **Prevention**
Malnutrition in pregnancy
(May Subd Geog)
[RG580.M]
UF Prenatal malnutrition
BT Pregnancy—Nutritional aspects
Pregnancy, Complications of
NT Fetal malnutrition
— **United States**
— — **Prevention**
Malo (Indonesian people)
USE Maloh (Indonesian people)
Malocclusion *(May Subd Geog)*
BT Occlusion (Dentistry)
Orthodontics
Teeth—Abnormalities
RT Prognathism
NT Diastema (Teeth)
— Prevention
USE Orthodontics, Preventive
— **Treatment** *(May Subd Geog)*
NT Occlusal adjustment
Malocclusion in children *(May Subd Geog)*
[RK523]
BT Pedodontics
Maloh (Indonesian people)
[DS632.M275]
UF Ambalau (Indonesian people)
Ambaloh (Indonesian people)
Embaloh (Indonesian people)
Kalis (Indonesian people)
Malau (Indonesian people)
Malo (Indonesian people)
Maloo (Indonesian people)
Memaloh (Indonesian people)
Palin (Indonesian people)
BT Dyaks
Ethnology—Indonesia
Malone family *(Not Subd Geog)*
UF Melone family
Milone family
Maloo (Indonesian people)
USE Maloh (Indonesian people)
Małopolska (Poland)
UF Polonia Minor (Poland)
Malory family
USE Mallory family
Malou language (Solomon Islands)
USE Malu language (Solomon Islands)
Malpaharias
[DS432.M25]
UF Mal Paharias
BT Ethnology—India
Malpighiaceae
[QK495.M26]

BT Rutales
NT Banisteriopsis
Diplopterys
Malpighian glomerulus
USE Kidney glomerulus
Malpighian vessels
[QL494]
Malpighi's vesicles
USE Pulmonary alveoli
Malplaquet, Battle of, 1709
[D283.M]
BT Spanish Succession, War of, 1701-1714
Malpractice *(May Subd Geog)*
[RA1056.5]
UF Liability, Professional
Professional liability
Professions—Tort liability
Tort liability of professions
BT Liability (Law)
Negligence
Torts
SA subdivision Malpractice under names
of particular professionals, e.g.
Physicians—Malpractice; Nurses—
Malpractice
NT Anesthesiologists—Malpractice
Auditors—Malpractice
Cardiologists—Malpractice
Child welfare workers—Malpractice
Consultants—Malpractice
Correctional personnel—Malpractice
Criminal justice personnel—
Malpractice
Financial planners—Malpractice
Gynecologists—Malpractice
Immigration consultants—Malpractice
Insurance—Agents—Malpractice
Medical personnel—Malpractice
Neonatologists—Malpractice
Neurologists—Malpractice
Notaries—Malpractice
Obstetricians—Malpractice
Ophthalmologists—Malpractice
Orthopedists—Malpractice
Pharmacists—Malpractice
Public health personnel—Malpractice
Real estate appraisers—Malpractice
Social workers—Malpractice
Surveyors—Malpractice
Trials (Malpractice)
United States—Armed Forces—
Medical personnel—Malpractice
Malpractice by child welfare workers
USE Child welfare workers—Malpractice
Malpractice by correctional personnel
USE Correctional personnel—Malpractice
Malpractice by criminal justice personnel
USE Criminal justice personnel—
Malpractice
Malpractice by financial planners
USE Financial planners—Malpractice
Malpractice by neonatologists
USE Neonatologists—Malpractice
Malpractice by pharmacists
USE Pharmacists—Malpractice
Malpractice by public health personnel
USE Public health personnel—Malpractice
Malpractice by social workers
USE Social workers—Malpractice
Malpractice by United States Armed Forces
medical personnel
USE United States—Armed Forces—
Medical personnel—Malpractice
Malpractice insurance
USE Insurance, Malpractice
Malpractice insurance, Architects'
USE Insurance, Architects' liability
Malpractice insurance, Engineers'
USE Insurance, Engineers' liability
Malpractice insurance, Executive
USE Insurance, Executives' liability

Malpractice insurance, Medical
USE Insurance, Physicians' liability
Malpractice insurance, Police
USE Insurance, Police liability
Malpractice insurance, Psychiatrists'
USE Insurance, Psychiatrists' liability
Malqata Site (Egypt)
USE Malkata Site (Egypt)
Malshe family *(Not Subd Geog)*
UF Mālaśe family
Malt
[TP587 (Chemical technology)]
BT Ale
Beer
Brewing
Enzymes
NT Malt-extracts
Malt-extracts
[RM671.M2]
BT Beer
Malt
Malt industry *(May Subd Geog)*
Malt liquors
[TP569-587]
UF Liquors, Malt
NT Ale
Beer
Porter
— **Law and legislation** *(May Subd Geog)*
BT Liquor laws
Malta
[DG987-DG994 (Malta)]
[DR505-DR508 (Turkish history)]
As a geographic subdivision, this heading is used
directly.
— **Antiquities**
— **Description and travel**
— — **1981-**
[DG989.4]
— **History**
— — **To 870**
[DG992]
— — **870-1530**
[DG992.2]
— — **1530-1798**
[DG992.5]
— — **French occupation, 1798-1800**
[DG992.8]
BT France—History—1789-1815
— — **1798-1964**
[DG992.7]
NT Malta, Battle of, 1940-1943
— — **1964-**
[DG994]
— **Languages**
NT Maltese language
— **Politics and government**
— — **1798-1964**
— — **1964-**
Malta, Battle of, 1940-1943
[D756.5]
BT Malta—History—1798-1964
World War, 1939-1945—Aerial
operations
Malta fever
USE Brucellosis
Maltbie family
USE Maltby family
Maltby family *(Not Subd Geog)*
UF Maltbie family
Maltese *(May Subd Geog)*
BT Ethnology—Malta
— **United States**
NT Maltese Americans
Maltese Americans *(May Subd Geog)*
BT Ethnology—United States
Maltese—United States
Maltese children's literature
USE Children's literature, Maltese
Maltese cookery
USE Cookery, Maltese

2249

Maltese dialect
  USE Maltese language
Maltese dogs
  [SF429.M25]
  BT Toy dogs
Maltese language
  [PJ6891]
  UF Arabic language—Dialects—Malta
    Maltese dialect
  BT Malta—Languages
Maltese literature (May Subd Geog)
  [PJ8440-8458]
  UF Arabic literature—Malta
  NT Children's literature, Maltese
    Maltese poetry
  — **Italian influences**
    BT Italy—Civilization
Maltese missions
  USE Missions, Maltese
Maltese newspapers (May Subd Geog)
Maltese periodicals (May Subd Geog)
Maltese poetry (May Subd Geog)
  [PJ8450 (History and criticism)]
  [PJ8454 (Collections)]
  UF Arabic poetry—Malta
  BT Maltese literature
Maltese proverbs
  USE Proverbs, Maltese
Maltheidae
  USE Ogcocephalidae
Malthidae
  USE Ogcocephalidae
Malthusianism
  [HB861-3]
  BT Eugenics
  RT Population
Malto language
  [PL4731]
  BT Dravidian languages
Maltose
  [QD321]
  BT Sugar
Maltreated children
  USE Abused children
Maltreatment of children
  USE Child abuse
Maltzahn family (Not Subd Geog)
  UF Maltzan family
    Malzahn family
    Moltzahn family
    Moltzan family
    Molzahn family
Maltzan family
  USE Maltzahn family
Malu language (Solomon Islands)
  UF Malou language (Solomon Islands)
    Malu'u language (Solomon Islands)
    Toa ba'ita language
  BT Melanesian languages
Malugen family
  USE Melugin family
Malugin family
  USE Melugin family
Maluku (Indonesia)
  NT Ceram Island (Indonesia)
Malum epiphyseonecroticum vertebrale
  USE Scheuermann's disease
Malungeons
  USE Melungeons
Malus
  USE Apple
Malu'u language (Solomon Islands)
  USE Malu language (Solomon Islands)
Malva
  [QK495.M27 (Botany)]
  [SB261.M (Fiber plants)]
  UF Mallow
  BT Malvaceae
  NT Malva parviflora
Malva parviflora
  [QK495.M27 (Botany)]

  UF Little mallow
    Mallow, Little
  BT Malva
Malvaceae
  [QK495.M27 (Botany)]
  BT Malvales
  NT Hibiscus
    Lavatera
    Malva
    Urena
Malvales
  [QK495.A12 (Botany)]
  UF Columniferae
  BT Dicotyledons
  NT Bombacaceae
    Elaeocarpaceae
    Malvaceae
    Scytopetalaceae
    Sterculiaceae
    Tiliaceae
Malvani dialect
  USE Kudali dialect
Malven family
  USE Malvern family
Malvern family (Not Subd Geog)
  UF Malven family
    Malvin family
Malvern Hill, Battle of, 1862
  [E473.68]
  BT Peninsular Campaign, 1862
    Seven Days' Battles, 1862
    United States—History—Civil War,
      1861-1865—Campaigns
Malvern Hills (England)
  BT Mountains—England
Malversation
  USE Corruption (in politics)
Malvi dialect
  [PK2331-9]
  UF Malavi dialect
  BT Rajasthani language
Malvi folk literature
  USE Folk literature, Malvi
Malvi literature (May Subd Geog)
  NT Folk literature, Malvi
Malvi poetry (May Subd Geog)
  [PK2338.2 (History)]
  [PK2338.6 (Collections)]
Malvin family
  USE Malvern family
Malwa (India) (Not Subd Geog)
  UF Mālava (India)
Malwa painting (May Subd Geog)
  UF Painting, Malwa
  BT Miniature painting, Indic
    Rajput painting
Mālwa Plateau (India)
  UF Mala Plateau (India)
    Malwar Plateau (India)
  BT Plateaus—India
Malwar Plateau (India)
  USE Mālwa Plateau (India)
Malý Ostrov Žitný (Hungary)
  USE Szigetköz (Hungary)
Malzahn family
  USE Maltzahn family
Mam Indians
  BT Indians of Central America
    Indians of Mexico
    Mayas
Mam language
  [PM3936]
  UF Zaklohpakap language
Mamabolo (Bantu people)
  BT Bantus
    Ethnology—South Africa
Mamadou Lamine, Rebellion of, 1885-1887
  UF Insurrection of Mamadou Lamine,
      1885-1887
    Rebellion of Mamadou Lamine, 1885-
      1887

  BT Mali—History
    Senegambia—History
    Soninke (African people)
Mamaindê dialect (May Subd Geog)
  UF Tamainde dialect
  BT Brazil—Languages
    Indians of South America—Brazil—
      Languages
    Nambicuara language
Mamaindê Indians
  [F2520.1.M24]
  BT Indians of South America
    Indians of South America—Brazil
    Nambicuara Indians
Mamanua language
  USE Mamanwa language
Mamanuas (Philippine tribe)
  BT Ethnology—Philippines
    Negritos
Mamanwa language
  [PL5923]
  UF Mamanua language
    Manmanua language
  BT Philippine languages
Mambae (Indonesian people)
  USE Mambai (Indonesian people)
Mambai (Indonesian people)
  [DS632.M28]
  UF Mambae (Indonesian people)
    Manbae (Indonesian people)
  BT Ethnology—Indonesia
Mambas (May Subd Geog)
  [QL666.O64]
  UF Dendroaspis
  BT Elapidae
Mambere (African people)
  USE Mambila (African people)
Mambere language
  USE Mambila language
Mambila (African people)
  [DT515.42]
  UF Mambere (African people)
  BT Ethnology—Cameroon
    Ethnology—Nigeria
Mambila (African people) art
  USE Art, Mambila (African people)
Mambila language
  UF Lagubi language
    Mambere language
    Nor language
    Tagbo language
    Tongbo language
    Torbi language
  BT Benue-Congo languages
Mambo (Dance)
Mambukush language
  USE Mbukushu language
Mambule
  USE Mafulus
Mambuti
  USE Bambute
Mambwe (African people)
  UF Mambwe (Bantu tribe)
  BT Bantus
    Ethnology—Zambia
Mambwe (Bantu tribe)
  USE Mambwe (African people)
Mambwe language
  UF Cimambwe language
  BT Bantu languages
Mameluke architecture
  USE Architecture, Mameluke
Mameluke art
  USE Art, Mameluke
Mameluke illumination of books and
  manuscripts
  USE Illumination of books and manuscripts,
    Mameluke
Mamelukes
  [DT96]
  UF Mamluks

BT Egypt—History—1250-1517
  Islamic Empire
Mamenchisaurus
  ⌐QE862.S3⌐
  BT Titanosauridae
Mamertines
Mamey Hill Site (Belize)
  UF Mamie Hill Site (Belize)
  BT Belize—Antiquities
    Mounds—Belize
Mamezuka Iseki (Ichinomiya-ch-o, Yamanashi-
  ken, Japan)
  USE Mamezuka Site (Ichinomiya-ch-o,
    Yamanashi-ken, Japan)
**Mamezuka Site (Ichinomiya-ch-o, Yamanashi-
  ken, Japan)**
  UF Mamezuka Iseki (Ichinomiya-ch-o,
    Yamanashi-ken, Japan)
  BT Japan—Antiquities
Mamie Hill Site (Belize)
  USE Mamey Hill Site (Belize)
Mamillaria (Cactus)
  USE Mammillaria (Cactus)
Mamiya camera
  BT Twin-lens cameras
Mamluks
  USE Mamelukes
Mammagen
  USE Mammogen
Mammal pests *(May Subd Geog)*
  ⌐SB993.5-SB994 (Agricultural pests)⌐
  BT Mammals
    Vertebrate pests
Mammal populations *(May Subd Geog)*
  UF Populations, Mammal
  BT Animal populations
    Mammals—Geographical distribution
  NT Rodent populations
Mammalian oviduct
  USE Fallopian tubes
Mammalogical research
  USE Mammals—Research
Mammalogists *(May Subd Geog)*
  ⌐QL26.31⌐
  BT Zoologists
Mammals *(May Subd Geog)*
  ⌐QL701-739⌐
  BT Vertebrates
  SA *names of families, genera, species, etc.*
  NT Aquatic mammals
    Bats
    Bovidae
    Carnivora
    Cetacea
    Edentata
    Extinct mammals
    Feral mammals
    Flying lemurs
    Fur-bearing animals
    Hyracoidea
    Insectivora
    Lagomorpha
    Mammal pests
    Marine mammals
    Marsupialia
    Monotremata
    Pachydermata
    Primates
    Rare mammals
    Rodents
    Ruminants
    Sirenia
    Tubulidentata
    Ungulata
— **Age**
— **Anatomy**
  ⌐QL739⌐
  SA *subdivision* Mammals *under*
    Digestive organs, Nervous
    system
— **Behavior**

  SA *subdivision* Behavior *under names
    of particular mammals, e.g.*
    Foxes—Behavior
— **Catalogs and collections**
  ⌐QL708⌐
— — **Use studies**
— **Collection and preservation**
— **Cytology**
— **Evolution**
  BT Vertebrates—Evolution
— **Geographical distribution**
  NT Mammal populations
— **Nomenclature (Popular)**
  ⌐QL355⌐
— **Physiology**
— **Reproduction**
  RT Theriogenology
  NT Anestrus
    Estrus
— **Research** *(May Subd Geog)*
  UF Mammalogical research
Mammals, Fossil
  ⌐QE881-2⌐
  NT Amblypoda
    Desmostylia
    Docodonta
    Flying lemurs, Fossil
    Gallolestes
    Hyracoidea, Fossil
    Lagomorpha, Fossil
    Pantotheria
    Pholidota, Fossil
    Proteutheria
    Rodents, Fossil
    Sirenia, Fossil
    Theria
Mammaplasty *(May Subd Geog)*
  ⌐RD539.8⌐
  UF Mammoplasty
    Mastoplasty
  BT Breast—Surgery
    Surgery, Plastic
Mammary dysplasia
  USE Breast—Fibrocystic disease
Mammary glands
  ⌐QL944 (Comparative anatomy)⌐
  ⌐QM495 (Human anatomy)⌐
  ⌐QP188.M3 (Physiology)⌐
  UF Glands, Mammary
  BT Exocrine glands
  NT Breast
    Udder
— **Innervation**
Mammectomy
  USE Mastectomy
Mammies
  UF Mammies, Colored
Mammies, Colored
  USE Mammies
Mammilaria (Cactus)
  USE Mammillaria (Cactus)
Mammillaria (Cactus)
  ⌐QK495.C11 (Botany)⌐
  ⌐SB413.M (Ornamental plants)⌐
  UF Mamillaria (Cactus)
    Mammilaria (Cactus)
    Neomammillaria (Cactus)
    Pincushion cactus
    Strawberry cactus
  BT Cactus
Mammogen
  ⌐QP246⌐
  UF Mammagen
Mammography
  USE Breast—Radiography
Mammoplasty
  USE Mammaplasty
Mammoth
  ⌐QE882.U7⌐
  UF Elephas primigenius
  BT Proboscidea, Fossil

Mammoth Cave (Ky.)
  BT Caves—Kentucky
Mammoth Cave National Park (Ky.)
  BT National parks and reserves—United
    States
    Parks—Kentucky
Mammoth Mountain (Calif.)
  BT Mountains—California
Mammoth tree
  USE Giant sequoia
Mammotropin
  USE Prolactin
Mamoa 1 da Abogalheira Site (Portugal)
  (Not Subd Geog)
  UF Mamoa Number 1 da Abogalheira Site
    (Portugal)
  BT Portugal—Antiquities
Mamoa Number 1 da Abogalheira Site
  (Portugal)
  USE Mamoa 1 da Abogalheira Site
    (Portugal)
Mampituba River (Brazil)
  UF Rio Mampituba (Brazil)
  BT Rivers—Brazil
Mampruli language
  ⌐PL8485⌐
  UF Mamprusi language
  BT Gur languages
Mampruli proverbs
  USE Proverbs, Mampruli
Mamprusi (African people)
  UF Mamprusi (African tribe)
  BT Ethnology—Ghana
— **Kings and rulers**
Mamprusi (African tribe)
  USE Mamprusi (African people)
Mamprusi language
  USE Mampruli language
Mampukush language
  USE Mbukushu language
Mamry Lake (Poland)
  UF Jezioro Mamry (Poland)
    Mauer See (Poland)
  BT Lakes—Poland
Mamvu (African people)
  UF Mamvu (African tribe)
    Mangutu (African people)
    Momfu (African people)
    Momvou (African people)
    Monfou (African people)
    Mumvu (African people)
    Mvuba (African people)
  BT Ethnology—Africa, Central
  NT Balese (African people)
Mamvu (African tribe)
  USE Mamvu (African people)
Mamvu language
  UF Momvu language
    Monvu language
  BT Nilo-Saharan languages
    Uganda—Languages
    Zaire—Languages
Mamzer
  UF Illegitimacy (Jewish law)
  BT Jewish law
Man
  ⌐BD450 (Philosophy of life, BD430-
    435)⌐
  ⌐GN (Anthropology)⌐
  ⌐QH361-QH371 (Evolution)⌐
  UF Human beings
    Humans
    Mankind
  BT Primates
  RT Anthropology
    Creation
    Human-animal relationships
  SA *headings beginning with the word
    Human*
  NT Anthropometry
    Color of man

Man *(Continued)*
    Economic man
    Ethnology
    Heredity
    Human biology
    Men
    Men in literature
    Persons
    Philosophical anthropology
    Women
— **Age determination**
    ɾQP86 (Physiology)ɿ
    BT Age determination (Zoology)
    NT Gestational age—Testing
        Skeletal maturity
— **Animal nature**
    BT Body, Human
        Philosophical anthropology
    NT Sociobiology
— **Attitude and movement**
    ɾGN231ɿ
    UF Attitude and posture of man
        Man, Erect position of
    BT Equilibrium (Physiology)
        Human locomotion
    RT Posture
    NT Brachiation
        Movement education
— **Constitution**
    ɾBF698 (Personality)ɿ
    ɾBF795-BF811 (Temperament)ɿ
    ɾBF818 (Character)ɿ
    ɾGN60 (Anthropology)ɿ
    ɾRB150-RB151 (Theories of
        disease)ɿ
    UF Biological constitution of man
        Body constitution, Human
        Constitution, Human
        Physical constitution of man
    BT Constitutional diseases
        Heredity
    RT Temperament
    NT Body, Human
        Children—Constitution
        Heredity, Human
        Somatotypes
— Economic value
    USE Human capital
— Food habits
    USE Food habits
— **Influence of climate** *(May Subd Geog)*
    ɾGF71ɿ
    UF Climate, Influence of
    BT Anthropo-geography
        Bioclimatology
        Climatology
        Man—Influence of environment
    RT Acclimatization
        Climatology, Medical
    NT Industry and weather
        Weather—Psychological aspects
— **Influence of environment**
    (May Subd Geog)
    ɾBF353 (Psychology)ɿ
    ɾGF51-GF71 (Human ecology)ɿ
    ɾGN386-GN395 (Ethnography)ɿ
    ɾHM206-HM208 (Sociology)ɿ
    UF Environment
    BT Adaptation (Biology)
        Evolution
        Geography
        Human ecology
        Nature and nurture
        Physical anthropology
        Sociology
    RT Anthropo-geography
    NT Acclimatization
        Altitude, Influence of
        Architecture—Human factors
        Biopolitics
        Color of man

        Dwellings—Psychological aspects
        Environmental health
        Environmental psychology
        Euthenics
        Human comfort
        Man—Influence of climate
        Regionalism
        Survival skills
        Weightlessness
— **Influence on nature** *(May Subd Geog)*
    UF Earth, Effect of man on
        Environment
        Nature, Effect of man on
    BT Human ecology
        Nature
        Physical geography
    RT Environmental policy
    NT Desertification
        Habitat (Ecology)—Modification
        Pollution
        War—Environmental aspects
— **Migrations**
    ɾGF101 (Anthropo-geography)ɿ
    ɾGN370 (Ethnology)ɿ
    Here are entered works on the spread of population, largely in prehistoric times. Works on the mass migrations of peoples are entered under the heading Migrations of nations. Works dealing with migration from one country to another in modern times are entered under the heading Emigration and immigration. Works dealing with movement of population from one section to another section of the same country are entered under the heading Migration, Internal.
    UF Geographical distribution of man
        Migrations of man
    BT Anthropo-geography
        Emigration and immigration
        Ethnology
        History
        Population
    RT Migrations of nations
    NT Ethnic barriers
        Indians of North America—
            Transpacific influences
        Jews—Diaspora
        Migration, Internal
— **Origin**
    ɾQH361-371ɿ
    UF Antiquity of man
        Man, Antiquity of
        Origin of man
    BT Man, Prehistoric
        Physical anthropology
        Religion and science
    RT Anatomy, Comparative
        Evolution
    NT Brachiation
        Human evolution
        Monogenism and polygenism
— Parasites
    USE Medical parasitology
Man, Antiquity of
    USE Man—Origin
Man, Doctrine of
    USE Man (Theology)
Man, Erect position of
    USE Man—Attitude and movement
         Posture
Man, Fall of
    USE Fall of man
Man, Fossil
    USE Fossil man
Man, Prehistoric *(May Subd Geog)*
    ɾGN700-875ɿ

    UF Antiquities, Prehistoric
        Paleoanthropology
        Paleoethnography
        Prehistoric antiquities
        Prehistoric man
        Prehistory
        Skeletal remains
    BT Archaeology
        Craniology
        Ethnology
        Industries, Primitive
        Society, Primitive
        Stone age
    SA *subdivision* Antiquities *under names of*
        countries, cities, etc.
    NT Anthropology, Prehistoric
        Art, Prehistoric
        Aurignacian culture
        Bog bodies
        Bronze age
        Cave-dwellers
        Civilization, Subterranean
        Danilo culture
        Fossil man
        Ghassul culture
        Gravette points
        Hallstatt period
        La Téne period
        Lake-dwellers and lake-dwellings
        Land settlement patterns, Prehistoric
        Lausitz culture
        Magdalenian culture
        Man—Origin
        Megalithic monuments
        Tardenoisian culture
        Terremare
        Vinča culture
        Women, Prehistoric
— **Food**
    RT Agriculture, Prehistoric
— **Population**
    BT Demographic anthropology
— Textiles
    USE Textile fabrics, Prehistoric
— **Tools**
    UF Prehistoric tools
        Tools, Prehistoric
    BT Implements, utensils, etc.
        Industries, Primitive
        Tools
    NT Agricultural implements,
            Prehistoric
        Arms and armor, Prehistoric
        Harpoons, Prehistoric
        Knives, Prehistoric
        Pins and needles, Prehistoric
        Projectile points
        Razors, Prehistoric
        Spears, Prehistoric
        Stone implements
— **America**
    BT Indians—Antiquities
    NT Indians
        Paleo-Indians
— **Europe, Northern**
    NT Maglemosean culture
— **Philippines**
— **Spain**
Man, Prehistoric, in art
Man, Primitive
    ɾGN307-499ɿ
    RT Ethnology
        Society, Primitive
    NT Ethnopsychology
— **Diseases** *(May Subd Geog)*
    BT Medicine, Primitive
— **First contact with Occidental civilization**
    ɾGN368ɿ

UF Contact, First, of aboriginal
    peoples with Occidental
    civilization
    First contact of aboriginal peoples
    with Occidental civilization
BT Acculturation
    Civilization, Occidental
    Discoveries (in geography)
NT Indians of North America—First
    contact with Occidental
    civilization
— Food
Man, Wild
  USE Wild men
Man (Buddhism)
  UF Buddhist philosophical anthropology
    Kikon
  BT Buddhism—Doctrines
    Man (Theology)
    Philosophy, Buddhist
  NT Woman (Buddhism)
Man (Christian theology)
  [BT700-701.2]
    Here are entered works on the Christian theology
of humankind. Works on the theology of humankind
from the perspective of two or more of the world's
religions are entered under Man (Theology). Works
on the Christian theology of the male sex are entered
under Men (Christian theology). Works on the Christian
theology of the female sex are entered under
Woman (Christian theology)
  BT Man (Theology)
    Theology, Doctrinal
  NT Alienation (Theology)
    Children (Christian theology)
    Failure (Christian theology)
    Flesh (Theology)
    Innocence (Theology)
    Men (Christian theology)
    Sin
    Woman (Christian theology)
    Youth (Christian theology)
Man (Hinduism)
  [BL1215.M3]
  UF Hindu theological anthropology
  BT Hinduism
    Man (Theology)
  NT Soul (Hinduism)
Man (Islam)
  [BP166.7]
  UF Islamic theological anthropology
    Muslim theological anthropology
  BT Islam—Doctrines
    Man (Theology)
  NT Merit (Islam)
    Sin (Islam)
    Soul (Islam)
— Koranic teaching
    [BP134.M3]
    NT Koran—Ethnology
Man (Jewish theology)
  BT Man (Theology)
  NT Sin (Judaism)
    Soul (Judaism)
Man (Philosophy)
  USE Philosophical anthropology
Man (Shinto)
  BT Man (Theology)
    Shinto
Man (Sikhism)
  [BL2018.5.M35]
  BT Man (Theology)
    Sikhism—Doctrines
Man (Theology)
  [BL256 (Religion)]
  [BS661 (Bible)]
  [BT700-BT745 (Doctrinal theology)]

    Here are entered works on the theology of humankind
from the perspective of two or more of the
world's religions. Works on the theology of humankind
in a given religion are entered under Man
(Christian theology), Man (Jewish theology), Man
(Islam), Man (Hinduism), etc. Works on the Christian
theology of the male sex are entered under Men
(Christian theology). Works on the Christian theology
of the female sex are entered under Woman
(Christian theology).
  UF Anthropology, Biblical
    Anthropology, Doctrinal
    Anthropology, Theological
    Anthropology in the Bible
    Body and soul (Theology)
    Doctrinal anthropology
    Man, Doctrine of
    Theological anthropology
  BT Religious thought
  NT Decision (Christian theology)
    Fetus—Religious aspects
    Humanism, Religious
    Identification (Religion)
    Image of God
    Man (Buddhism)
    Man (Christian theology)
    Man (Hinduism)
    Man (Islam)
    Man (Jewish theology)
    Man (Shinto)
    Man (Sikhism)
    Man (Zoroastrianism)
    Soul
    Woman (Theology)
Man (Zoroastrianism)
  BT Man (Theology)
    Zoroastrianism
Man and animals
  USE Human-animal relationships
Man and the Biosphere Programme
  [GF26]
  UF Program on Man and the Biosphere
    Programme on Man and the Biosphere
  BT Conservation of natural resources—
    Research
    Environmental policy—Research
    Human ecology—Research
Man and wife
  USE Husband and wife
Man-animal communication
  USE Human-animal communication
Man-animal relationships
  USE Human-animal relationships
Man blind from his birth (Miracle)
  USE Healing of the man born blind
    (Miracle)
Man born blind (Miracle)
  USE Healing of the man born blind
    (Miracle)
Man-engines
  [TN339-TN340 (Mine transportation)]
  BT Mine hoisting
Man family
  USE Mann family
Man in art
  USE Humans in art
Man in space
  USE Life support systems (Space
    environment)
Man-in-space program
  USE Project Apollo
    Project Gemini
    Project Mercury
Man-machine control systems
  USE Man-machine systems
Man-machine systems
  [TA167]
  UF Human operators (Systems
    engineering)
    Human subsystems (Systems
    engineering)
    Man-machine control systems

  BT Automation
    Human engineering
    Systems engineering
  NT Control rooms
    Interactive computer systems
    Space vehicles—Piloting—
      Mathematical models
    Work design
— Manual control
    [TA167]
    UF Manual control systems
    BT Feedback control systems
Man-made chemicals industry
  USE Chemical industry
Man-made fibers industry *(May Subd Geog)*
  [TS1548.5]
  UF Synthetic fiber industry
  BT Fibers
    Textile fibers, Synthetic
    Textile industry
  RT Nonwoven fabrics industry
  NT Glass fiber industry
— Safety measures
Man-made lakes
  USE Reservoirs
Man-multimachine analysis
  USE Multimachine assignments
Man of the Year selections
  UF Time magazine's Man of the Year
    Time's Man of the Year selections
  BT Rewards (Prizes, etc.)—United States
Man-of-war birds
  USE Frigate-birds
Man-of-war names
  USE Warships—Names
Man on other planets
  USE Life on other planets
Man power
  USE Manpower
Man powered aircraft
  USE Human powered aircraft
Man sick of the palsy (Miracle)
  USE Healing of the man sick of the palsy
    (Miracle)
Man-to-man combat
  USE Hand-to-hand fighting
MAN trucks
  [TL230.5.M]
Mana
  [GN471]
  BT Magic
    Religion, Primitive
    Witchcraft
  NT Animism
    Barakah
Manabe family *(Not Subd Geog)*
Manabhava
  USE Mahanubhava
Manacica Indians
  [F3320.2.M26]
  UF Manasica Indians
  BT Chiquito Indians
    Indians of South America
Managalasi language
  [PL6621.M24]
  UF Managulasi language
    Mangulasi language
    Manugulasi language
  BT Papua New Guinea—Languages
    Papuan languages
MANAGD (Computer program)
  [SD381.5]
  BT Forest management—Computer
    programs
Managed care plans (Medical care)
  (May Subd Geog)
  [RA413-RA413.7]

Managed care plans (Medical care)
    (Continued)
      Here are entered works on alternative health care delivery and financing systems that integrate financing mechanisms, appropriate utilization management, and service delivery in contracting with employers and insurers to provide medical care.
    UF Managed care programs (Medical care)
        Managed care systems (Medical care)
        Plans, Managed care (Medical care)
        Programs, Managed care (Medical care)
        Systems, Managed care (Medical care)
    BT Medical care
    NT Health maintenance organizations
        Preferred provider organizations (Medical care)
Managed care programs (Medical care)
    USE Managed care plans (Medical care)
Managed care systems (Medical care)
    USE Managed care plans (Medical care)
Management *(May Subd Geog)*
    [HD31-HD37]
      Here are entered works on the principles of management as a discipline. Works on the application of systematic, logical, and mathematical methods and techniques to the solution of problems of management are entered under Management science.
    UF Administration
    RT Organization
    SA *subdivision* Management *under types of industries, industrial plants and processes, special activities, etc. and under names of corporate bodies, including individual government agencies, galleries, museums, parks, etc.; also subdivision* Administration *under types of institutions and names of individual institutions, especially libraries, health and social services, etc.; also subdivision* Politics and government *under names of countries, cities, etc.; and phrase headings for specific types of management or administration, e.g.* Industrial management; Police administration
    NT Accounting departments
        Advertising departments
        Bank management
        Baseball managing
        Business
        Campaign management
        Command and control systems
        Comparative management
        Computer programming management
        Conflict management
        Court administration
        Crisis management
        Decentralization in management
        Delegation of authority
        Drawing-room management
        Executives
        Facility management
        Farm management
        Finance departments
        Forest management
        Hospitals—Administration
        Housing management
        Industrial management
        Industrial project management
        Information resources management
        Institution management
        Kennel management
        Line and staff organization
        Management by objectives
        Management committees
        Management science
        Managerial economics
        Matrix organization
        Motel management
        Negotiation in business

        Office management
        Organizational behavior
        Organizational change
        Organizational effectiveness
        Personnel management
        Planning
        Police administration
        Prison administration
        Range management
        Resource allocation
        Risk management
        Scheduling (Management)
        School management and organization
        Secretariats
        Social sciences and management
        Social work administration
        Television in management
        Theater management
        Time management
        Water quality management
        Watershed management
        Work measurement
  — Bibliography
    RT Management literature
  — Communication systems
    [HD30.335]
    BT Communication in management
    RT Management information systems
  — Computer programs
    NT MacProject (Computer program)
  — Data processing
    NT DSS/A (Computer system)
  — Decision making
    USE Decision-making
  — Employee participation
    [HD5650-HD5660]
      Here are entered works on a variety of practices and institutional arrangements through which the employees of an enterprise or organization participate in or exercise control over the management of that enterprise or organization.
    UF Consultative management
        Economic democracy
        Employee participation in management
        Employees' representation in management
        Industrial democracy
        Labor participation in management
        Participative management
        Participatory management
        Self-management by employees
        Worker participation in management
        Workers' control
        Workers' participation in management
        Workers' self-management
    BT Guild socialism
        Personnel management
        Syndicalism
    RT Employee ownership
        Employees, Reporting to
        Producer cooperatives
    SA *subdivision* Employee participation *under individual headings for specific types of management, e.g.* Industrial management—Employee participation; *and subdivision* Management—Employee participation *under individual headings for specific industries, e.g.* Construction industry—Management—Employee participation
    NT Labor-management committees
        Libraries, University and college—Administration—Staff participation
        Library administration—Staff participation

        Works councils
  — — Law and legislation
    (May Subd Geog)
    BT Labor laws and legislation
  — Examinations
    NT Graduate Management Admission Test
  — Handbooks, manuals, etc.
    NT Administrative manuals
  — Religious aspects
  — — Baptists, [Catholic Church, etc.]
  — — Buddhism, [Christianity, etc.]
  — Research *(May Subd Geog)*
    UF Management research
  — Simulation methods
    BT Operations research
    NT Management games
  — Japan
    UF Japanese management
Management, Church
    USE Church management
Management, Game
    USE Wildlife management
Management, Industrial
    USE Industrial management
Management, Institution
    USE Institution management
Management, Issues
    USE Issues management
Management, Product
    USE Product management
Management, Sales
    USE Sales management
Management, Wildlife
    USE Wildlife management
Management accounting
    USE Managerial accounting
Management attitude surveys
    USE Employer attitude surveys
Management audit
    UF Audit, Management
        Management auditing
        Operational auditing
        Operations auditing
    BT Industrial management
Management auditing
    USE Management audit
Management buyouts *(May Subd Geog)*
    [HD2746.5]
      Here are entered works on the purchase of a company by its current management.
    UF Buy-outs, Management
        Buyouts, Management
    BT Leveraged buyouts
Management by exception
    BT Industrial management
Management by objectives
    BT Management
    NT Goal setting in personnel management
Management committees *(May Subd Geog)*
    UF Committees in management
    BT Committees
        Industrial management
        Management
    RT Labor-management committees
Management consultants
    USE Business consultants
Management contracts *(May Subd Geog)*
    UF Contracts, Management
    BT Contracts
        Corporation law
        Directors of corporations
    RT Delegation of authority
Management development programs
    USE Assessment centers (Personnel management procedure)
Management-employee relations in government
    USE Employee-management relations in government
Management engineering
    USE Industrial engineering

Management games
  [HD30.26]
  UF Business games
      Industrial gaming
      Industrial management games
  BT Decision-making
      Games of strategy (Mathematics)
      Industrial management
      Management—Simulation methods
  — Computer programs
      NT STRATPLAN (Computer program)
Management in literature
Management information systems
  [T58.6]
  UF Computer-based information systems
      MIS (Information systems)
  BT Information storage and retrieval
      systems
  RT Information resources management
      Management—Communication systems
  NT Decision support systems
      EMIS (Information retrieval system)
      SAMIS (Information retrieval system)
      SEMIS (Information retrieval system)
Management literature (May Subd Geog)
  UF Literature, Management
  RT Management—Bibliography
  NT Marketing literature
Management of conflict
  USE Conflict management
Management of factories
  USE Factory management
Management of flood plains
  USE Floodplain management
Management of floodplains
  USE Floodplain management
Management of Information through Natural
  Discourse (Computer system)
  USE MIND (Computer system)
Management prerogatives
  USE Management rights
Management research
  USE Management—Research
Management Review and Analysis Program
  BT Library administration—Research—
      United States
Management rights (May Subd Geog)
      Here are entered works dealing with the rights
  and powers essential to the operation of a business,
  such as hiring, production methods, and the like,
  which management may claim to be outside the scope
  of collective bargaining and over which management
  commonly maintains authority and responsibility.
  UF Management prerogatives
  BT Industrial management
      Industrial relations
  RT Restrictive practices in industrial
      relations
Management science
  [T55.4-T57.97]
      Here are entered works on the application of sys-
  tematic, logical, and mathematical methods and tech-
  niques to the solution of problems of management.
  Works on the principles of management as a disci-
  pline are entered under Management.
  UF Quantitative business analysis
  BT Management
      Problem solving
  RT Decision-making—Mathematical
      models
      Operations research
      Statistical decision
Management teams in schools
  USE School management teams
Managerial accounting (May Subd Geog)
  UF Management accounting
  BT Accounting
  RT Cost accounting
Managerial economics (May Subd Geog)
  [HD58.5]
  UF Business economics

  BT Economics
      Industrial management
      Management
      Microeconomics
Managerial finance
  USE Business enterprises—Finance
      Corporations—Finance
Managers
  USE Executives
Managers, Agricultural research
  USE Agricultural research managers
Managers, City
  USE City managers
Managers, Farm
  USE Farm managers
Managers, Grain elevator
  USE Grain elevator managers
Managers, Ranch
  USE Ranch managers
Managers, Soccer
  USE Soccer—Managers
Managers, Stage
  USE Stage managers
Managers, Theatrical
  USE Theatrical managers
Managing conflict
  USE Conflict management
Managing owners (Maritime law)
  USE Ship's husbands
Managing up
  USE Managing your boss
Managing your boss
  [HF5548.83]
  UF Boss management
      Managing up
      Managing your supervisor
  BT Industrial sociology
      Psychology, Industrial
  RT Supervisors
Managing Your Money (Computer program)
  BT Finance, Personal—Computer
      programs
Managing your supervisor
  USE Managing your boss
Managulasi language
  USE Managalasi language
Manahiki (Cook Islands)
  USE Manihiki Atoll (Cook Islands)
Manahoac Indians
  [E78.V7 (Virginia)]
  [E99.M]
  BT Algonquian Indians
      Indians of North America
Manakins (Birds)
  USE Pipridae
Manala (African people)
  BT Ethnology—South Africa
      Ndebele (African people)
Manali (Indic people)
  USE Kulu (Indic people)
Manam language
  [PL6254.M29]
  BT Melanesian languages
      Papua New Guinea—Languages
Manambu language
  BT Ndu languages
Manambu songs
  USE Songs, Manambu
Manard, Bayou (Okla.)
  UF Bayou Manard (Okla.)
  BT Bayous—Oklahoma
Manard family
  USE Maynard family
Manas Game Sanctuary (Bhutan)
  BT Game-preserves—Bhutan
      National parks and reserves—Bhutan
      Wildlife refuges—Bhutan
Manasā (Hindu deity)
  [BL1225.M3]
  BT Gods, Hindu

Manasarovar Lake (China)
  USE Manasarowar Lake (China)
Manasarowar Lake (China)
  UF Ma-na-sa-lo-wu Ch'ih (China)
      Manasarovar Lake (China)
  BT Lakes—China
Manasica Indians
  USE Manacica Indians
Manassas (Va.)
  — History
  — — Civil War, 1861-1865
Manassas, Battles of
  USE Bull Run, 1st Battle, 1861
      Bull Run, 2d Battle, 1862
Manassas National Battlefield Park (Va.)
  BT Battlefields—Virginia
      Bull Run, 1st Battle, 1861
      Bull Run, 2d Battle, 1862
      National parks and reserves—United
      States
      Parks—Virginia
      United States—History—Civil War,
      1861-1865—Battlefields
Manastirŭt v Tuzlalŭka (Preslav, Bulgaria)
  (Not Subd Geog)
  BT Bulgaria—Antiquities
      Monasteries—Bulgaria
Manatee, West Indian
  USE Trichechus manatus
Manatee River (Fla.)
  BT Rivers—Florida
Manatees
  [QL737.S63]
  UF Manatidae
      Trichechidae
      Trichechus
  BT Sirenia
  NT Trichechus manatus
Manatees, Fossil
  BT Sirenia, Fossil
Manatidae
  USE Manatees
Manavabhasha (Artificial language)
  BT Languages, Artificial
Manawatu River (N.Z.)
  BT Rivers—New Zealand
Manayunk (Philadelphia, Pa.)
  (Not Subd Geog)
  UF Philadelphia (Pa.). Manayunk
Manbae (Indonesian people)
  USE Mambai (Indonesian people)
Manbhaus
  USE Mahanubhava
Manbhav
  USE Mahanubhava
Mancagne language
  USE Mankanya language
Mancala (Game)
  NT Ayo (Game)
Mancanha language
  USE Mankanya language
Mancasellus
  [QL444.M34]
  BT Asellidae
Mancasellus danielsi
  [QL444.M34]
Mancha (Spain)
  UF La Mancha (Spain)
  BT Plains—Spain
Manche
  USE English Channel
Manche Indians
  USE Mopan Indians
Manche language
  USE Mopan language
Manchester (Greater Manchester)
  — Dock Strike, 1951
  — Peterloo Massacre, 1819
      [DA690.M4]

Manchester (Greater Manchester). Ancoats
USE Ancoats (Manchester, Greater Manchester)
Manchester scales of social adaptation
BT Maturation (Psychology)
Socialization
Manchester school of economics
BT Laissez-faire
Manchester terriers
[SF429.M]
BT Terriers
Manchineel
[QK495.E9 (Botany)]
UF Hippomane mancinella
BT Poisonous plants
Manchoukuo
USE Manchuria (China)
Manchu Buddhist literature
USE Buddhist literature, Manchu
Manchu imprints (May Subd Geog)
Manchu language
[PL471-9]
UF Manju language
BT Altaic languages
Tungus-Manchu languages
NT Ju-chen language
Manchu languages
USE Tungus-Manchu languages
Manchu literature
[PL480-489]
NT Buddhist literature, Manchu
Manchu manuscripts
USE Manuscripts, Manchu
Manchu-Tungus languages
USE Tungus-Manchu languages
Manchukuo
USE Manchuria (China)
Manchuria (China)
[DS781-784.2]
UF China, Northeast
Manchoukuo
Manchukuo
Northeast China
— **History**
— — Incident, 1931
USE Mukden Incident, 1931
— — 1931-1945
UF Manchurian question
— — 1945-
— **Languages**
NT Ju-chen language
Manchurian Incident, 1931
USE Mukden Incident, 1931
Manchurian pony
USE Mongolian pony
Manchurian question
USE Manchuria (China)—History—1931-1945
Manchus (Not Subd Geog)
[DS754-DS760 (Dynasty)]
[DS781-DS784 (Manchuria)]
BT Tatars
RT China—History—Ch'ing dynasty, 1644-1912
NT China—History—Tatar Conquest, 1643-1644
Mancipatio
USE Transfer (Roman law)
Manda Island (Kenya)
BT Islands—Kenya
Mandaean astrology
USE Astrology, Mandaean
Mandaean language
[PJ5321-9]
UF Mandaic language
BT Aramaic language
Mandaeans
[BT1405]

UF Christians of St. John
Disciples of St. John
Mendaeans
Nasoraeans
Sabians
St. John's Christians
BT Heresies, Christian—History—Early church, ca. 30-600
NT Missions to Mandaeans
Mandago language
USE Mandjak language
Mandaic language
USE Mandaean language
Mandailing dialect
[PL5401]
UF Angkola dialect
Ankola dialect
BT Batak language
Mandailing folk poetry
USE Folk poetry, Mandailing
Mandailing folk-songs
USE Folk-songs, Mandailing
Mandailing literature (May Subd Geog)
NT Mandailing poetry
Mandailing poetry (May Subd Geog)
BT Mandailing literature
NT Folk poetry, Mandailing
Mandailing proverbs
USE Proverbs, Mandailing
Mandak (Papua New Guinea people)
[DU740.42]
BT Ethnology—Papua New Guinea
Melanesians
Mandaka language
USE Mansaka language
Mandala
BT Circle—Religious aspects—Hinduism
Hindu sects
Mysticism—India
Symbolism
Mandala (Buddhism) (May Subd Geog)
BT Tantric Buddhism
— **Japan**
NT Ryōkai mandara zu (Den Shingon'in) (Painting)
Mandalas of the Two Worlds (Painting)
USE Ryōkai mandara zu (Den Shingon'in) (Painting)
Mandamus (May Subd Geog)
BT Administrative law
Extraordinary remedies
Writs
Mandan Indians
[E99.M2]
UF Wahtani Indians
BT Indians of North America
Siouan Indians
— **Antiquities**
— **Dances**
NT O-kee-pa (Religious ceremony)
— **Reservations**
NT Fort Berthold Indian Reservation (N.D.)
— **Rites and ceremonies**
NT O-kee-pa (Religious ceremony)
Mandan language
[PM1701]
Mandana (Art) (May Subd Geog)
BT Decoration and ornament—India
Folk art—India
Mandar language
[PL5402]
UF Andian language
BT Malayan languages
Mandar literature (May Subd Geog)
Mandara language
[PL8489]
UF Wandala language
BT Bari language
Chadic languages
NT Glavda language

Mandari (African people)
[DT132]
UF Wandala (African people)
BT Ethnology—Sudan
Mandarin (Fruit)
USE Tangerine
Mandarin dialects (May Subd Geog)
[PL1891-1900]
UF Northern Chinese dialects
BT Chinese language—Dialects
Mandarin duck
UF Aix galericulata
Anas galericulata
BT Ducks
Mandate (Contract) (May Subd Geog)
BT Bailments
Contracts
RT Agency (Law)
Hire
Negotiorum gestio
Mandate (Contract law, Roman)
BT Contracts (Roman law)
Mandates (May Subd Geog)
[D650.T4-D651 (European War questions)]
[JX1975.A49 (League of Nations documents)]
[JX4021-JX4023 (International law)]
UF League of Nations—Mandatory system
Mandates, Colonial
Mandates, International
BT International organization
Internationalized territories
RT International trusteeships
Protectorates
State succession
— **Syria**
BT Syria—History—20th century
Mandates, Colonial
USE Mandates
Mandates, International
USE Mandates
Mandatory retirement
USE Retirement, Mandatory
Mandaya (Philippine people)
BT Ethnology—Philippines
Mandaya language, Mansaka
USE Mansaka language
Mandé (African people)
USE Mandingo (African people)
Mande language
USE Mandingo language
Mande languages
[PL8490.M35]
BT Africa, West—Languages
Niger-Congo languages
NT Bobo Fing language
Bozo language
Busa language
Gbandi language
Kono language
Kpelle language
Loma language
Mandekan languages
Mende language
Sembla language
Soninke language
Southern Mande languages
Susu language
Vai language
Mande languages, Southern
USE Southern Mande languages
Mandeali dialect
[PK2610.M35]
BT Pahari languages
Mandeali folk literature
USE Folk literature, Mandeali
Mandegusu language
UF Eddystone language
BT Melanesian languages

Mandekan languages *(May Subd Geog)*
　[PL8490.M36]
　BT　Africa, West—Languages
　　　Mande languages
　NT　Bambara language
　　　Dyula language
　　　Mandingo language
Mandel family *(Not Subd Geog)*
　UF　Mandell family
　　　Mandl family
　　　Mandle family
　RT　Mendall family
Mandell family
　USE　Mandel family
Mandelonitrile glucuronoside
　USE　Laetrile
Mandenga language
　USE　Mandingo language
Mandeville family *(Not Subd Geog)*
　UF　Manvel family
　　　Manvell family
　　　Manville family
　　　Mundell family
Mandible
　UF　Jaw, Lower
　　　Lower jaw
　BT　Jaws
　NT　Alveolar process
　　　Dental arch
　　　Mandibular ramus
　　　Processus coronoideus mandibulae
　　　Submandibular triangle
— **Hinge axis determination**
　　[RK522]
　UF　Hinge axis determination of
　　　　mandible
　　　Mandibular hinge axis
　　　　determination
　BT　Jaw relation records
　　　Occlusion (Dentistry)
— **Surgery**
Mandibular condyle
　UF　Condyle of the mandible
　BT　Jaws
Mandibular coronoid process
　USE　Processus coronoideus mandibulae
Mandibular hinge axis determination
　USE　Mandible—Hinge axis determination
Mandibular joint
　USE　Temporomandibular joint
Mandibular prosthesis
　BT　Prosthodontics
Mandibular ramus
　UF　Ramus mandibulae
　BT　Mandible
Mandijildjara (Australian people)
　USE　Mandjildjara (Australian people)
Mandildjara (Australian people)
　USE　Mandjildjara (Australian people)
Mandinga empire
　USE　Mali empire
Mandinga Keys (Panama)
　BT　Islands—Panama
Mandingo (African people)
　UF　Mandé (African people)
　　　Mandinka (African people)
　NT　Bozo (African people)
　　　Kuranko (African people)
　　　Mali empire
　　　Niumi (Kingdom)
Mandingo (African people) sculpture
　USE　Sculpture, Mandingo (African people)
Mandingo (African people) terra-cotta
　sculpture
　USE　Terra-cotta sculpture, Mandingo
　　　　(African people)
Mandingo folk literature
　USE　Folk literature, Mandingo
Mandingo folk-songs
　USE　Folk-songs, Mandingo

Mandingo language
　[PL8491]
　UF　Malinke language
　　　Mande language
　　　Mandenga language
　　　Mandinka language
　　　Maninka language
　　　Meninka language
　BT　Africa, West—Languages
　　　Mandekan languages
　NT　Mau dialect (Ivory Coast)
Mandingo poetry
Mandinka (African people)
　USE　Mandingo (African people)
Mandinka language
　USE　Mandingo language
Mandioca
　USE　Cassava
Mandjack (African people)
　USE　Mandjak (African people)
Mandjack language
　USE　Mandjak language
Mandjak (African people)
　UF　Mandjack (African people)
　　　Mandjaks (African tribe)
　　　Mandyak (African people)
　　　Mandyako (African people)
　　　Manjaco (African people)
　　　Manjago (African people)
　　　Manjaku (African people)
　BT　Ethnology—Guinea-Bissau
　　　Ethnology—Senegal
Mandjak language
　[PL8493]
　UF　Kanop language
　　　Mandago language
　　　Mandjack language
　　　Manjacos language
　BT　Guinea—Languages
　　　Niger-Congo languages
　　　Senegal—Languages
Mandjaks (African tribe)
　USE　Mandjak (African people)
Mandjas
　[DT546 (History)]
　[GN652.M3 (Anthropology)]
　UF　Manjas
　　　Manza (African people)
Mandjildjara (Australian people)
　[DU125.M29]
　UF　Mandijildjara (Australian people)
　　　Mandildjara (Australian people)
　　　Mantjiltjara (Australian people)
　BT　Australian aborigines
　　　Ethnology—Australia
Mandl family
　USE　Mandel family
Mandle family
　USE　Mandel family
Mandobo
　BT　Ethnology—Indonesia
Mandola
　UF　Mandora
　　　Mandore
　BT　Lute
Mandola and Jew's harp with string orchestra
　[M1140-M1141]
　NT　Concertos (Mandola and Jew's harp
　　　with string orchestra)
Mandola music
　[M142.M25]
　BT　Lute music
　SA　Concertos, Minuets, Sonatas, Suites,
　　　and similar headings with
　　　specification of instruments; Trios
　　　[Quartets, etc.] *followed by*
　　　specifications which include the
　　　Mandola; also Plectral ensembles
　　　and headings that begin with the
　　　words Mandola *or* Mandolas

Mandolin
　[ML1015.M2 (History)]
　[MT600-MT608 (Instruction)]
　UF　Bandolim
　NT　Bağlama
— **Methods (Bluegrass)**
　　[MT602 (General)]
　　[MT608 (Self-instructors)]
Mandolin and continuo music
　UF　Continuo and mandolin music
　NT　Sonatas (Mandolin and continuo)
Mandolin and guitar music
　USE　Guitar and mandolin music
Mandolin and harpsichord music
　[M278-9]
　UF　Harpsichord and mandolin music
　BT　Mandolin and piano music
　NT　Sonatas (Mandolin and harpsichord)
Mandolin and piano music
　[M278-9]
　UF　Piano and mandolin music
　NT　Mandolin and harpsichord music
　　　Sonatas (Mandolin and piano)
　　　Suites (Mandolin and piano)
Mandolin and piano music, Arranged
　[M278-9]
　NT　Concertos (Mandolin)—Solo with
　　　　piano
　　　Concertos (Mandolin with string
　　　　orchestra)—Solo with piano
Mandolin and viola music
　USE　Viola and mandolin music
Mandolin bands
　USE　Mandolin orchestras
Mandolin music
　[M130-134]
　SA　Concertos, Minuets, Sonatas, Suites,
　　　and similar headings with
　　　specification of instruments; Trios
　　　[Quartets, etc.] *followed by*
　　　specifications which include the
　　　mandolin; also Plectral ensembles
　　　and headings that begin with the
　　　words mandolin or mandolins
Mandolin music (Jazz)
　[M130-134]
Mandolin music (Mandolins (2))
　[M292-3]
　NT　Concertos (Mandolins (2) with string
　　　　orchestra)
　　　Mandolins (2) with string orchestra
Mandolin orchestra music
　USE　Plectral ensembles
Mandolin orchestras *(May Subd Geog)*
　UF　Mandolin bands
　BT　Bands (Music)
　　　Orchestra
Mandolin players
　USE　Mandolinists
Mandolin with chamber orchestra
　[M1037.4.M3]
　NT　Suites (Mandolin with chamber
　　　　orchestra)
Mandolin with orchestra
　[M1037.4.M3]
　RT　Concertos (Mandolin)
Mandolin with string orchestra
　[M1105-6]
　RT　Concertos (Mandolin with string
　　　　orchestra)
Mandolinists
　[ML399 (Biography: collective)]
　[ML419 (individual)]
　UF　Mandolin players
Mandolins (2) with string orchestra
　[M1105-6]
　BT　Mandolin music (Mandolins (2))
　RT　Concertos (Mandolins (2) with string
　　　　orchestra)
Mandora
　USE　Mandola

Mandore
  USE Mandola
Mandrake
    ⌈GR790.M3 (Folk-lore)⌉
    BT Charms
       Hallucinogenic plants
Mandrels
  USE Arbors and mandrels
Mandua
  USE Ragi
Manduca
    ⌈QL561.S7⌉
    BT Sphingidae
Mandyak (African people)
  USE Mandjak (African people)
Mandyako (African people)
  USE Mandjak (African people)
Mane family
  USE Main family
Maneater shark
  USE White shark
Maned dog
  USE Maned wolf
Maned sheep
  USE Barbary sheep
Maned wolf
    ⌈QL737.C22⌉
    UF Chrysocyon brachyurus
       Chrysocyon jubatus
       Maned dog
Manegrs
    ⌈DK759.M3⌉
Maner family
  USE Maynard family
Manes family
  USE Main family
Manesfield family
  USE Mansfield family
Manet, Edouard, 1832-1883. Bar at the Folies-Bergère
    ⌈ND553.M3⌉
    UF Bar at the Folies-Bergère (Painting)
       Bar aux Folies-Bergère (Painting)
Manet, Edouard, 1832-1883. Gare Saint-Lazare (Not Subd Geog)
    ⌈ND553.M3⌉
    UF Gare Saint-Lazare (Painting)
       Railroad (Painting)
       Railway (Painting)
    BT Painting, French
Maneuver warfare
    Here are entered works on warfare concentrating on defeating the enemy by rapidly maneuvering so as to disrupt his cohesion and ability to react, rather than by physically destroying his forces.
    UF Warfare, Maneuver
    BT Military maneuvers
       Tactics
       Warfare, Conventional
Maneuverability of ships
  USE Ships—Maneuverability
Maneuvers, Military
  USE Military maneuvers
Maneuvers, Naval
  USE Naval maneuvers
Maneyard family
  USE Maynard family
Manfield family
  USE Mansfield family
Manfredinas
  USE Monferrinas
Manga (African people)
    UF Mangawa (African people)
    BT Ethnology—Niger
    — Women
        USE Women, Manga
Manga women
  USE Women, Manga
Mangabeys
    ⌈QL737.P93⌉

    UF Cercocebus
       Mangabys
       White-eyelid monkeys
    BT Cercopithecidae
Mangabys
  USE Mangabeys
Mangaia (Cook Islands)
    UF Mangara (Cook Islands)
       Mangea (Cook Islands)
    BT Islands—Cook Islands
Mangaian language
    ⌈PL6463⌉
    BT Polynesian languages
Mangala language (Zaire)
  USE Lingala language
Mangalarga horse
    ⌈SF293.M34⌉
    UF Junqueira horse
    BT Horse breeds
Mangan-amphibole
  USE Rhodonite
Mangan family
  USE Mangum family
     Maugans family
Manganates
    ⌈QD181.M6⌉
Manganese
    ⌈QD181.M6 (Chemistry)⌉
    ⌈TN490.M3 (Mining)⌉
    ⌈TN799.M3 (Metallurgy)⌉
    NT Manganese mines and mining
       Manganese mines and mining, Submarine
       Permanganates
       Plants, Effect of manganese on
       Soils—Manganese content
    — Electrometallurgy
    — Isotopes
        UF Isotopic manganese
           Manganese isotopes
    — — Decay
    — — Spectra
    — Metallurgy
        ⌈TN799.M3⌉
    — Spectra
Manganese, Deep-sea mining of
  USE Manganese mines and mining, Submarine
Manganese, Electrolytic
    UF Electrodeposited manganese
       Electrolytic manganese
Manganese alloys
    NT Aluminum-manganese alloys
       Chrome-manganese steel
       Copper-cobalt-manganese alloys
       Iron-manganese alloys
       Manganese-copper alloys
       Manganese-platinum alloys
       Manganese-silicon alloys
       Manganese-tellurium alloys
       Nickel-manganese alloys
Manganese-aluminum alloys
  USE Aluminum-manganese alloys
Manganese catalysts
    BT Catalysts
Manganese compounds
Manganese-copper alloys
    UF Copper-manganese alloys
    BT Copper alloys
       Manganese alloys
Manganese difluoride
  USE Manganous fluoride
Manganese dioxide electrodes
    UF Electrodes, Manganese dioxide
    BT Electrodes, Oxide
Manganese fluoride
  USE Manganous fluoride
Manganese geology
  USE Manganese ores—Geology
Manganese group
    BT Transition metals

Manganese in animal nutrition
    ⌈SF98.M⌉
Manganese in human nutrition
    BT Nutrition
Manganese in soils
  USE Soils—Manganese content
Manganese industry (May Subd Geog)
    ⌈HD9539.M3-34⌉
Manganese-iron alloys
  USE Iron-manganese alloys
Manganese isotopes
  USE Manganese—Isotopes
Manganese mines and mining (May Subd Geog)
    BT Manganese
    — Korea
        NT Janggun Mine (Korea)
Manganese mines and mining, Submarine (May Subd Geog)
    UF Manganese, Deep-sea mining of
    BT Manganese
       Ocean mining
    RT Dredging
       Hydraulic mining
       Manganese nodules
Manganese-nickel alloys
  USE Nickel-manganese alloys
Manganese nodules (May Subd Geog)
    UF Deep-sea manganese nodules
    BT Manganese ores
       Marine mineral resources
       Marine sediments
    RT Manganese mines and mining, Submarine
Manganese ore geology
  USE Manganese ores—Geology
Manganese ores (May Subd Geog)
    ⌈TN490.M3⌉
    NT Manganese nodules
    — Geology (May Subd Geog)
        ⌈TN490.M3⌉
        UF Manganese geology
           Manganese ore geology
        BT Geology
Manganese organic compounds
  USE Organomanganese compounds
Manganese oxides
    BT Oxides
    NT Manganic oxide
       Manganous oxide
Manganese-platinum alloys
    UF Platinum-manganese alloys
    BT Manganese alloys
       Platinum alloys
Manganese removal (Water purification)
  USE Water—Purification—Manganese removal
Manganese sesquioxide
  USE Manganic oxide
Manganese-silicon alloys
    UF Silicon-manganese alloys
    BT Manganese alloys
       Silicon alloys
Manganese spar
  USE Rhodonite
Manganese steel
    ⌈TN757.M3⌉
    BT Steel
    NT Chrome-manganese steel
Manganese sulphate
  USE Manganous sulphate
Manganese sulphide
    UF Manganous sulphide
    BT Sulphides
Manganese-tellurium alloys
    UF Tellurium-manganese alloys
    BT Manganese alloys
       Tellurium alloys
    — Electric properties
Manganese tetroxide
  USE Manganous oxide

Manganic manganous oxide
  USE Manganous oxide
Manganic oxide
  UF Manganese sesquioxide
  BT Manganese oxides
Mang'anja language
  USE Nyanja language
Mangankiesel
  USE Rhodonite
Manganolite
  USE Rhodonite
Manganomanganic oxide
  USE Manganous oxide
Manganous fluoride
  UF Manganese difluoride
      Manganese fluoride
  BT Fluorides
Manganous fluoride crystals
  BT Crystals
Manganous oxide
  UF Manganese tetroxide
      Manganic manganous oxide
      Manganomanganic oxide
  BT Manganese oxides
Manganous sulphate
  UF Manganese sulphate
  BT Sulphates
Manganous sulphide
  USE Manganese sulphide
Mangans family
  USE Maugans family
Mangapurua River (N.Z.) *(Not Subd Geog)*
  BT Rivers—New Zealand
Mangara (Cook Islands)
  USE Mangaia (Cook Islands)
Mangarai Island (Indonesia)
  USE Flores Island (Indonesia)
Mangareva language
  ₁PL6464₁
  BT Polynesian languages
Mangati (African people)
  UF Tatoga (African people)
  BT Ethnology—Tanzania
Mangatiti River (N.Z.) *(Not Subd Geog)*
  BT Rivers—New Zealand
Mangawa (African people)
  USE Manga (African people)
Mangbetu language
  UF Monbuttu language
  BT Nilo-Saharan languages
      Zaire—Languages
Mangbetus
  USE Monbuttus
Mangbuas
  USE Ababuas
Mange
  USE Scabies
Mangea (Cook Islands)
  USE Mangaia (Cook Islands)
Mangel-wurzel *(May Subd Geog)*
  ₁QK495.C46 (Botany)₁
  ₁SB207.M35 (Forage plant)₁
  UF Fodder beet
      Mangold-wurzel
  BT Beets
      Forage plants
Manger family
  USE Munger family
Manger in Christian art and tradition
  USE Crib in Christian art and tradition
Manger scenes (Crèches)
  USE Crèches (Nativity scenes)
Mangfall River (Germany)
  BT Rivers—Germany (West)
Manggarai language
  ₁PL5404₁
  BT Malay language
Manggarese people
  BT Ethnology—Indonesia
Mangham family
  USE Mangum family

Mangin family
  USE Mangum family
      Maugans family
Mangin mirror
  BT Optics, Geometrical
Mangins family
  USE Maugans family
Mangislak Peninsula (Kazakh S.S.R.)
  USE Mangyshlak Peninsula (Kazakh S.S.R.)
Mangium *(May Subd Geog)*
  ₁QK495.L52 (Botany)₁
  ₁SD397.M23 (Forestry)₁
  UF Acacia glaucescens
      Acacia mangium
      Black wattle
      Brown salwood
      Hickory wattle
      Mangium montanum
      Sabah salwood
      Salwood, Brown
      Salwood, Sabah
      Wattle, Black
      Wattle, Hickory
  BT Acacia
      Wattle (Tree)
Mangium montanum
  USE Mangium
Mangkunegara, House of *(Not Subd Geog)*
  UF Manku Negoro, House of
  BT Indonesia—Kings and rulers
Mango *(May Subd Geog)*
  ₁SB379.M2₁
  UF Mango tree
  NT Cookery (Mangos)
  — Varieties
Mango Gusor Range (Pakistan)
  BT Karakoram Range
      Mountains—Pakistan
Mango industry *(May Subd Geog)*
  ₁HD9259.M28-284₁
Mango pepper
  USE Bell pepper
Mango tree
  USE Mango
Mangold-wurzel
  USE Mangel-wurzel
Mangoni (African people)
  USE Ngoni (African people)
Mangoon
  USE Olcha
Mangora
  ₁QL458.42.A7₁
  BT Araneidae
Mangorongoro (Cook Islands)
  USE Penrhyn Atoll (Cook Islands)
Mangosteen
  ₁QK495.G87 (Botany)₁
  ₁SB379.M25 (Fruit-culture)₁
  UF Garcinia mangostana
      Mangostine
Mangostine
  USE Mangosteen
Mangram family
  USE Mangum family
Mangrove, Red
  USE Red mangrove
Mangrove forest flora
  USE Mangrove plants
Mangrove plants *(May Subd Geog)*
  ₁QK108-QK474.5 (Local)₁
  ₁QK938.M27 (General)₁
  ₁SD397.M25 (Forestry)₁
  UF Mangrove forest flora
      Mangrove swamp flora
      Mangroves

  BT Coastal flora
      Forest flora
      Halophytes
      Mangrove swamp ecology
      Mangrove swamps
      Plants
      Swamp flora
      Tropical plants
  NT Red mangrove
Mangrove swamp ecology *(May Subd Geog)*
  ₁QH541.5.M27₁
  BT Coastal ecology
      Swamp ecology
  NT Mangrove plants
Mangrove swamp flora
  USE Mangrove plants
Mangrove swamps *(May Subd Geog)*
  UF Mangroves
  BT Marshes, Tide
      Swamps
  NT Mangrove plants
Mangroves
  USE Mangrove plants
      Mangrove swamps
Mangrum family
  USE Mangum family
Mangrum Site (Ark.) *(Not Subd Geog)*
  BT Arkansas—Antiquities
Mangue Indians
  ₁F1434.3.M (Central America)₁
  UF Chorotega Indians
      Chorotegans
  BT Indians of Central America
Mangue language
  ₁PM3943₁
  UF Choluteca language
      Chorotega language
  BT Otomanguean languages
Manguian language
  USE Mangyan language
Mangulasi language
  USE Managalasi language
Mangum family *(Not Subd Geog)*
  UF Mangan family
      Mangham family
      Mangin family
      Mangram family
      Mangrum family
Mangun
  USE Olcha
Mangus family
  USE Menges family
Mangus-Tau (Kazakh S.S.R.)
  USE Mangyshlak Peninsula (Kazakh S.S.R.)
Mangutu (African people)
  USE Mamvu (African people)
Mangyan folk poetry
  USE Folk poetry, Mangyan
Mangyan language
  ₁PL5946₁
  UF Iraya language
      Manguian language
  BT Philippine languages
  NT Hanunóo language
Mangyan literature *(May Subd Geog)*
  NT Mangyan poetry
Mangyan poetry *(May Subd Geog)*
  BT Mangyan literature
Mangyans
  ₁DS666.M3₁
Mangyshlak Peninsula (Kazakh S.S.R.)
  UF Mangislak Peninsula (Kazakh S.S.R.)
      Mangus-Tau (Kazakh S.S.R.)
      Poluostrov Mangishlakskiy (Kazakh
      S.S.R.)
      Poluostrov Mangyshlak (Kazakh
      S.S.R.)
      Poluostrov Mangyshlakskiy (Kazakh
      S.S.R.)
  BT Peninsulas—Kazakh S.S.R.

Manhasset Neck (Long Island, N.Y.)
  UF Cow Neck Peninsula (Long Island, N.Y.)
  BT Peninsulas—New York (State)
Manhattan Indians
  [E99.M]
  BT Indians of North America
  NT Wappinger Indians
Manhole covers
  [TD696]
  UF Covers, Manhole
  BT Public utilities—Equipment and supplies
Manholes
  BT Holes
      Sewerage
      Water-supply engineering
Mani (Greece)
  UF Maina (Greece)
Mani (Guinea)
  USE Niani (Guinea)
Mania
  USE Manic-depressive psychoses
Maniba Indians
  USE Baniva Indians
Manic-depressive illness
  USE Manic-depressive psychoses
Manic-depressive psychoses
  (May Subd Geog)
  [RC516]
  UF Bipolar depression
      Depression, Bipolar
      Mania
      Manic-depressive illness
      Melancholia
  BT Affective disorders
      Psychology, Pathological
      Psychoses
  RT Depression, Mental
  NT Hypomania
Manichaean art
  USE Art, Manichaean
Manichaeism *(May Subd Geog)*
  [BT1410]
  BT Heresies, Christian—History—Early church, ca. 30-600
      Philosophy, Ancient
  — Hymns
Manicuring
  [RL94]
  BT Beauty, Personal
      Nails (Anatomy)—Care and hygiene
Manifee family
  USE Menefee family
Manifest destiny (United States)
  USE Messianism, Political—United States
      United States—Territorial expansion
Manifestation of conscience
  UF Conscience, Manifestation of
      Ratio conscientiae
  BT Canon law
      Monasticism and religious orders—Discipline
      Spiritual direction
MANIFILE (Information retrieval system)
  UF University of Manitoba computer-based file of world's nonferrous metallic deposits
  BT Information storage and retrieval systems—Mines and mineral resources
Manifold, River (England)
  UF River Manifold (England)
  BT Rivers—England
Manifold business forms industry
  (May Subd Geog)
  [HD9800.7]
  BT Business—Forms
Manifolding
  USE Copying processes

Manifolds, Almost complex
  USE Almost complex manifolds
Manifolds, Almost contact
  USE Almost contact manifolds
Manifolds, Banach
  USE Banach manifolds
Manifolds, Contact
  USE Contact manifolds
Manifolds, Einstein
  USE Einstein manifolds
Manifolds, Four dimensional
  USE Four-manifolds (Topology)
Manifolds, Grassmann
  USE Grassmann manifolds
Manifolds, Hyperbolic complex
  USE Hyperbolic spaces
Manifolds, Infinite-dimensional
  USE Infinite-dimensional manifolds
Manifolds, Nash
  USE Nash manifolds
Manifolds, Riemannian
  USE Riemannian manifolds
Manifolds, Sasakian
  USE Sasakian manifolds
Manifolds, Stiefel
  USE Stiefel manifolds
Manifolds, Symplectic
  USE Symplectic manifolds
Manifolds, Three dimensional (Topology)
  USE Three-manifolds (Topology)
Manifolds, Triangulating
  USE Triangulating manifolds
Manifolds (Mathematics)
  BT Geometry, Differential
      Topology
  NT Banach manifolds
      Catastrophes (Mathematics)
      Complex manifolds
      Differentiable manifolds
      Grassmann manifolds
      Homeomorphisms
      Immersions (Mathematics)
      Index theorems
      Jet bundles (Mathematics)
      Kählerian manifolds
      Low-dimensional topology
      Piecewise linear topology
      Riemannian manifolds
      Stiefel manifolds
      Submanifolds
      Submanifolds, Minimal
      Supermanifolds (Mathematics)
      Surgery (Topology)
      Symplectic manifolds
      Topological manifolds
      Topological transformation groups
      Torus (Geometry)
Manigault family *(Not Subd Geog)*
Manigotagan River (Ont. and Man.)
  BT Rivers—Manitoba
      Rivers—Ontario
Manihika (Cook Islands)
  USE Manihiki Atoll (Cook Islands)
Manihiki Atoll (Cook Islands)
  UF Humphrey (Cook Islands)
      Humphrey's Island (Cook Islands)
      Manahiki (Cook Islands)
      Manihika (Cook Islands)
      Manihiki Island (Cook Islands)
  BT Coral reefs and islands—Cook Islands
      Islands—Cook Islands
Manihiki Island (Cook Islands)
  USE Manihiki Atoll (Cook Islands)
Manihot *(May Subd Geog)*
  [QK495.E9 (Botany)]
  [SB211.M29 (Root-crops)]
  BT Euphorbiaceae
      Root-crops
Manihot esculenta
  USE Cassava

Manihot utilissima
  USE Cassava
Manika (Ancient city) *(Not Subd Geog)*
  [DF221.M35]
  BT Cities and towns, Ruined, extinct, etc.—Greece
      Greece—Antiquities
Manikins (Birds)
  USE Pipridae
Manikins (Figures)
  USE Mannequins (Figures)
Manila Bay, Battle of, 1898
  [E717.7]
  UF Cavite, Battle of, 1898
  BT United States—History—War of 1898—Campaigns—Philippines
Manila fibre
  USE Manila hemp
Manila hemp
  [QK495.M78 (Botany)]
  [SB261.M3 (Culture)]
  UF Abaca
      Hemp, Manila
      Manila fibre
  NT Manila hemp industry
Manila hemp industry *(May Subd Geog)*
  [HD9156.M35]
  BT Manila hemp
Manila rope
  USE Rope
Maning family
  USE Manning family
Maninka language
  USE Mandingo language
Manioc
  USE Cassava
Maniola
  [QL561.S3]
  BT Satyridae
  NT Maniola jurtina
Maniola jurtina
  [QL561.S3]
  BT Maniola
Manion family *(Not Subd Geog)*
  UF Mannion family
Manipravalam language (Malayalam)
  (May Subd Geog)
  BT India—Languages
      Languages, Mixed
  RT Malayalam language
      Sanskrit language
Manipravalam literature (Malayalam)
  (May Subd Geog)
  BT India—Literatures
Manipulation (Psychology)
  USE Manipulative behavior
Manipulation (Therapeutics)
  UF Orthopedic manipulation
  BT Orthopedia
      Physical therapy
  NT Cranial manipulation
      Craniosacral therapy
      Spinal adjustment
Manipulation of tables (Computer science)
  USE Table manipulation (Computer science)
Manipulative behavior *(May Subd Geog)*
  [BF632.5-BF633]
  UF Behavior, Manipulative
      Manipulation (Psychology)
  BT Human behavior
Manipulative books
  USE Toy and movable books
Manipulators (Mechanism)
  BT Robots, Industrial
  RT Robots
  — Optical equipment
      BT Optical instruments
Manipulators (Radioactive substances)
  UF Radioactive substances—Manipulators

BT Nuclear engineering—Instruments
  Nuclear engineering—Safety measures
  Radioisotopes—Safety measures
  Remote handling (Radioactive
   substances)
NT Glove boxes (Safety devices)
Manipuri (Indic people)
 USE Meitheis (Indic people)
Manipuri almanacs
 USE Almanacs, Manipuri
Manipuri authors
 USE Authors, Manipuri
Manipuri drama *(May Subd Geog)*
 NT Folk-drama, Manipuri
Manipuri fiction *(May Subd Geog)*
 NT Short stories, Manipuri
Manipuri folk-drama
 USE Folk-drama, Manipuri
Manipuri imprints *(May Subd Geog)*
Manipuri language
 [PL4001.M3]
 UF Meithei language
 BT Tibeto-Burman languages
 NT Bishnupuriya dialect
Manipuri literature *(May Subd Geog)*
Manipuri manuscripts
 USE Manuscripts, Manipuri
Manipuri paleography
 USE Paleography, Manipuri
Manipuri philology
Manipuri poetry *(May Subd Geog)*
Manipuri proverbs
 USE Proverbs, Manipuri
Manipuri short stories
 USE Short stories, Manipuri
Manipuri songs
 USE Songs, Manipuri
Manipuri wit and humor *(May Subd Geog)*
 BT Indic wit and humor
Maniti River (Peru)
 UF Río Maniti (Peru)
 BT Rivers—Peru
Manitoba
 — Antiquities
  NT Bjorklund Site (Man.)
   Childs Lake Site (Man.)
   Delorme House Site (Man.)
   Duck River Site (Man.)
   Garden Site (Man.)
   Kame Hills Site (Man.)
   Pine Fort Site (Man.)
   Sinnock Site (Man.)
   Stott Site (Man.)
   Swamp Site (Man.)
Manitou Experimental Forest (Colo.)
 BT Forest reserves—Colorado
  Forests and forestry—Colorado
Manitou Lake, Lower (Ont.)
 USE Lower Manitou Lake (Ont.)
Manitoulin Island (Ont.)
 UF Grand Manitou Island (Ont.)
  Grand Manitoulin Island (Ont.)
 BT Islands—Ontario
Maniva Indians
 USE Baniva Indians
Manix Lake (Calif.) *(Not Subd Geog)*
 BT Pluvial lakes—California
Manjaco (African people)
 USE Mandjak (African people)
Manjacos language
 USE Mandjak language
Manjago (African people)
 USE Mandjak (African people)
Manjaku (African people)
 USE Mandjak (African people)
Manjas
 USE Mandjas
Mañjirā River (India)
 USE Manjra River (India)
Manjra River (India)
 UF Mañjirā River (India)

BT Rivers—India
Manju language
 USE Manchu language
Mañjughoṣa (Buddhist deity)
 USE Mañjuśrī (Buddhist deity)
Mañjughsa (Buddhist deity)
 USE Mañjuśrī (Buddhist deity)
Mañjuśrī (Buddhist deity)
 [BQ4710.M4]
 UF Mañjughoṣa (Buddhist deity)
  Mañjughsa (Buddhist deity)
  Vāgīśvara (Buddhist deity)
  Vāsīśvara (Buddhist deity)
 BT Bodhisattvas
  Gods, Buddhist
 NT Yamāntaka (Buddhist deity)
 — Art
  NT Li, Kung-lin, 1049-1106. Wei
   Mo-ch'i (Vimalakirti) in
   conversation with Wen Shu
   (Manjusri)
Mankanya language
 UF Bola language (Portuguese Guinea)
  Brame language
  Bulama language
  Burama language
  Mancagne language
  Mancanha language
 BT Guinea—Languages
  Niger-Congo languages
Mankind
 USE Man
Mankind (Fictitious character)
 UF Mankynde (Fictitious character)
 BT Characters and characteristics in
  literature
Mankon language
 [PL8496.M35]
 BT Benue-Congo languages
Mankoya (African people)
 USE Nkoya (African people)
Manku Negoro, House of
 USE Mangkunegara, House of
Mankynde (Fictitious character)
 USE Mankind (Fictitious character)
Manley family *(Not Subd Geog)*
 UF Manly family
Manly family
 USE Manley family
Manmanua language
 USE Mamanwa language
Manmataṇ (Hindu deity)
 USE Kāma (Hindu deity)
Mann family *(Not Subd Geog)*
 UF Man family
  Manne family
  Manns family
 RT Manz family
Manna
 [BS1245 (Exodus)]
Manna gum
 USE Eucalyptus viminalis
Manna plants *(May Subd Geog)*
 [SB317.M33]
 UF Mannas (Plants)
 BT Botany, Economic
  Medicinal plants
  Plants, Edible
Mannan family
 USE Manning family
Mannas (Plants)
 USE Manna plants
Manne family
 USE Mann family
Manned exploration devices
 USE Oceanographic submersibles
Manned maneuvering units (Space flight)
 UF Extravehicular mobility units (Space
  flight)
 BT Extravehicular activity (Manned space
  flight)

Manned orbital laboratories
 USE Space stations
Manned space flight
 UF Space flight, Manned
 BT Astronautics
 RT Space medicine
 NT Apollo Soyuz Test Project
  Astronauts
  Extravehicular activity (Manned space
   flight)
  Outer space—Exploration
  Project Apollo
  Project Gemini
  Project Mercury
  Salyut-Soyuz Project
  Space flight training
  Space ships
  Space suits
  Space vehicles—Piloting
  Voskhod (Manned satellite)
  Vostok (Manned satellite)
  X-15 (Rocket aircraft)
 — Physiological effect
  USE Space flight—Physiological effect
 — Rescue work
  USE Space rescue operations
 — **Systems engineering**
Manned torpedoes
 USE Kaiten (Torpedoes)
  Midget submarines
Manned undersea research stations
 [GC66]
 UF Submarine research stations, Manned
  Under sea research stations, Manned
  Undersea research stations, Manned
 BT Diving, Submarine
  Ocean bottom
  Ocean engineering
  Oceanographic research stations
  Underwater exploration
 NT Project Sealab
  Project Tektite
 — **Rules for classification and construction**
Mannen family
 USE Manning family
Mannequins (Figures)
 UF Display figures
  Dummies (Figures)
  Manikins (Figures)
 BT Models and modelmaking
 NT Dress forms
  Museum manikins
Mannequins (Persons)
 USE Models, Fashion
Mannering family
 USE Manwaring family
Mannerism (Architecture) *(May Subd Geog)*
 BT Architecture
  Architecture, Renaissance
Mannerism (Art) *(May Subd Geog)*
 BT Art
Mannerism (Literature)
 BT Baroque literature
Mannerism (Music) *(May Subd Geog)*
 BT Music
Manners
 USE Courtesy
  Etiquette
Manners and customs
 [GT]
 Here are entered general works on folkways, cus-
 toms, ceremonies, festivals, popular traditions, etc.,
 treated collectively.
 UF Ceremonies
  Customs, Social
  Folkways
  Social customs
  Social life and customs
  Traditions
  Usages

Manners and customs *(Continued)*
  BT Civilization
     Ethnology
  RT Etiquette
     Rites and ceremonies
  SA *subdivision* Social life and customs
       under names of countries, cities,
       etc., and under names of ethnic
       groups, e.g. Afro-Americans—Social
       life and customs
  NT Aged, Killing of the
     Bees (Cooperative gatherings)
     Birth customs
     Body, Human—Social aspects
     Body-marking
     Bohemianism
     Caste
     Chivalry
     Clothing and dress
     Costume
     Country life
     Courts and courtiers
     Cries
     Dating (Social customs)
     Drinking customs
     Excuses
     Fads
     Fairs
     Farewells
     Festivals
     Folklore
     Foundation sacrifices
     Frontier and pioneer life
     Funeral rites and ceremonies
     Gifts
     Halloween
     Holidays
     Hugging
     Hunting customs
     Indians—Social life and customs
     Jews—Social life and customs
     Kissing
     Life style
     Local color in literature
     Marriage customs and rites
     May-pole
     Minstrels
     Mourning customs
     Necklaces
     Oaths
     Ordeal
     Outdoor life
     Political customs and rites
     Precedence
     Rings
     Salons
     Salutations
     Seafaring life
     Sex customs
     Sitting customs
     Sleeping customs
     Social norms
     Sounds
     Sports
     Table etiquette
     Taboo
     Tattooing
     Tipping
     Toasts
     Tournaments
     Travel
     Wayfaring life
     Women—History
Manners family *(Not Subd Geog)*
Mannheim slide-rule
  USE Slide-rule
Mannheimer biographical inventory
  [BF698.8.M]
  UF Biographical inventory, Mannheimer
  BT Psychological tests

Mannifield family
  USE Mansfield family
Mannikins (Birds)
  USE Lonchura
Mannila family *(Not Subd Geog)*
  UF Manninen family
Mannin family
  USE Manning family
Manninen family
  USE Mannila family
Manning family *(Not Subd Geog)*
  UF Maning family
     Mannan family
     Mannen family
     Mannin family
     Mannon family
     Mannun family
     Manon family
Manning of vessels
  USE Ships—Manning
Manning Park (B.C.)
  USE Manning Provincial Park (B.C.)
Manning Provincial Park (B.C.)
  UF Manning Park (B.C.)
  BT National parks and reserves—Canada
     Parks—British Columbia
Manningham Mills Strike, 1890-1891
  [HD5367.T42 1890B]
  BT Strikes and lockouts—Silk industry—
     Great Britain
     Strikes and lockouts—Great Britain
     Textile workers—Great Britain
Mannion family
  USE Manion family
Mannite
  [QD305.A4]
Mannlicher rifle
  [UD395.M28]
  BT Rifles
Mannon family
  USE Manning family
Mannose
  [QD321]
  BT Monosaccharides
  NT Sialic acids
Manns family
  USE Mann family
Mannun family
  USE Manning family
Mannus (Germanic deity)
  [BL870.M3]
  BT Gods, Germanic
Mano (African people)
  UF Mah (African people)
     Mano (African tribe)
  BT Ethnology—Guinea
     Ethnology—Liberia
Mano (African tribe)
  USE Mano (African people)
Mano language
  UF Mā-wi language
     Manon language
  BT Guinea—Languages
     Liberia—Languages
     Southern Mande languages
Mano Nera (United States)
  USE Black Hand (United States)
Manobo language
  [PL5955]
  BT Philippine languages
  RT Bukidnon language
     Dibabaon language
Manobo language, Bukidnon
  USE Bukidnon language
Manobo language, Dibabaon
  USE Dibabaon language
Manobos (Philippine people)
  UF Manuvùs (Philippine people)
  BT Ethnology—Philippines
Manoeuvers, Military
  USE Military maneuvers

Manoeuvers, Naval
  USE Naval maneuvers
Manohara family *(Not Subd Geog)*
Manometer
  [QC165]
  UF Micromanometer
  BT Pressure
     Pressure balance
  NT Sphygmomanometer
Manon family
  USE Manning family
Manon language
  USE Mano language
Manorial courts *(May Subd Geog)*
  UF Courts, Manorial
  RT Courts baron and courts leet
     Feudal courts
Manorial extents *(May Subd Geog)*
  UF Extents, Manorial
     Manorial registers
  BT Land titles—Registration and transfer
     Real property
     Real property—Valuation
     Real property tax
  RT Terriers (Law)
Manorial registers
  USE Manorial extents
Manors *(May Subd Geog)*
  BT Dwellings
     Real property
     Village communities
  NT Copyhold
— **Conservation and restoration**
    NT Manors—Remodeling for other use
— **Remodeling for other use**
    UF Manors—Renovation
    BT Manors—Conservation and
       restoration
— Renovation
    USE Manors—Remodeling for other
       use
— **Denmark**
    NT Brahetrolleborg (Denmark)
       Bratskov hovedgård (Brovst,
          Denmark)
       Dallund (Denmark)
       Erholm (Denmark)
       Flintholm (Denmark)
       Gyldensteen (Denmark)
       Herningsholm (Denmark)
       Hesselagergård (Denmark)
       Hjelmsø (Denmark)
       Juelsberg (Denmark)
       Krenkerup (Denmark)
       Lerchenborg (Denmark)
       Lundsgård (Denmark)
       Østrupgård (Denmark)
       Rødkilde (Denmark)
       Rugård (Denmark)
       Sæbygård, Denmark
       Serridslevgårde (Denmark)
       Skovsgård (Denmark)
       Søndergårde (Denmark)
       Tybjerggaard (Denmark)
— **England**
    NT Althorp (Northamptonshire)
       Beresford Hall (Staffordshire)
       East Lambrook Manor (Somerset)
       Farnborough Hill (Farnborough,
          Hampshire)
       Grafton House (Grafton Regis,
          Northamptonshire)
       Gravetye Manor (West Sussex)
       Halton House (Halton,
          Buckinghamshire)
       Ham House (Surrey)
       Hatfield House (Hertfordshire)
       High Ercall Manor (Shropshire)
       Houghton Hall (Norfolk)
       Kedleston Hall (Derbyshire)

Madresfield Court (Hereford and
Worcester)
Parham (Pulborough, West Sussex)
Stakes Hill Lodge (Hampshire)
Stansted (West Sussex)
Stourhead (Wiltshire)
Strawberry Hill (Twickenham,
Middlesex)
Waddesdon Manor (Waddesdon,
Buckinghamshire)
Wallington Hall (Northumberland)
Weston Hall (Hereford and
Worcester)
Whittington Estate (Lancashire)
— Estonia
NT Korps (Estonia)
— Germany (West)
NT Herrenhaus Steinhorst (Germany)
— Ireland
NT Umma-More (Westmeath)
— Japan
NT Tashibu no Shō (Japan)
— New York (State)
NT Livingston Manor (N.Y. : Estate)
— Norway
NT Skøien (Oslo, Norway)
— Poland
NT Torzeniec (Poland)
— Scotland
NT Glenfinnan Estate (Highland
Region, Scotland)
— Sweden
NT Huseby (Kronobergs län, Sweden)
— Virginia
NT Chatham Manor (Fredericksburg,
Va.)
Manors in art
Manostat
BT Gases
Manpower *(May Subd Geog)*
[UA17.5]
Here are entered general works on the strength of
a country in terms of available personnel, including
military and industrial requirements and reserves
from the non-working population. Works on person-
nel in specific fields are entered under specific head-
ings, e.g. Agricultural laborers; Chemists; etc.
UF Man power
RT Labor supply
SA *subdivision* Manpower *under names of
wars, e.g.* World War, 1939-1945—
Manpower
NT Armies
Pollution control personnel
MANPOWER (Computer program)
Manpower development and training
USE Occupational training
Manpower planning *(May Subd Geog)*
[HF5549.5.M3]
Here are entered works on management strategy
for the acquisition, utilization, and improvement of
the human resources of an enterprise. Works on gov-
ernment policy and effort to effect the development,
allocation, and utilization of human resources within
a labor market are entered under Manpower policy.
UF Manpower utilization planning
BT Personnel management
RT Organizational change
NT Employees, Relocation of
Recruiting of employees
Manpower policy *(May Subd Geog)*
Here are entered works on government policy and
effort to effect the development, allocation, and utili-
zation of human resources within a labor market.
Works on management strategy for the acquisition,
utilization, and improvement of the human resources
of an enterprise are entered under Manpower plan-
ning.
UF Human resource development
Manpower utilization
BT Economic policy
Employment (Economic theory)
Labor policy

RT Labor supply
Trade adjustment assistance
NT Enterprise zones
Full employment policies
Manpower policy, Rural
Occupational training
Public service employment
Unemployment
Vocational guidance
— United States
NT Work Incentive Program
Manpower policy, Rural *(May Subd Geog)*
UF Employment policy, Rural
Rural employment policy
Rural manpower policy
BT Manpower policy
NT Enterprise zones, Rural
Manpower training programs
USE Occupational training
Manpower utilization
USE Manpower policy
Personnel management
Manpower utilization planning
USE Manpower planning
Mans family
USE Manz family
Mansaka (Philippine people)
BT Ethnology—Philippines
Mansaka language *(May Subd Geog)*
UF Mandaka language
Mandaya language, Mansaka
Mansaka Mandaya language
BT Philippine languages
Philippines—Languages
Mansaka Mandaya language
USE Mansaka language
Mansei movement, 1919
USE Korea—History—Independence
movement, 1919
Mansen family
USE Munson family
Manservants
USE Butlers
Valets
Mansfeald family
USE Mansfield family
Mansfeil family
USE Mansfield family
Mansfeild family
USE Mansfield family
Mansfeld family
USE Mansfield family
Mansfield family *(Not Subd Geog)*
UF Manesfield family
Manfield family
Mannifield family
Mansfeald family
Mansfeil family
Mansfeild family
Mansfeld family
Mansfilld family
Mansfilld family
USE Mansfield family
Mansi
[DK759.M33]
UF Voguls
BT Ethnology—Russian S.F.S.R.
Finno-Ugrians
Mansi folk literature
USE Folk literature, Mansi
Mansi folk-songs
USE Folk-songs, Mansi
Mansi language
[PH1301-1309]
UF Vogul language
BT Ob-Ugric languages
Russian S.F.S.R.—Languages
Mansi literature *(May Subd Geog)*
[PH1308-1309]
NT Folk literature, Mansi

Mansi riddles
USE Riddles, Mansi
Mansions *(May Subd Geog)*
BT Dwellings
Manslaughter
USE Assassination
Homicide
Murder
Manson family
USE Munson family
Mansonia
[QL536]
BT Mosquitoes
Mansura, Battle of, 1250
BT Crusades—Seventh, 1248-1250
Mansura, Battle of, 1250, in literature
Mansurah (Pakistan)
UF al-Mansurah (Pakistan)
BT Arabs—Pakistan
Sind (Pakistan)—History
Manta Indians
[F3722.M3]
BT Indians of South America
Manta rays
USE Mobulidae
Mantarai (Legendary character)
USE Mantharā (Legendary character)
Mantaro River (Peru)
UF Río Mantaro (Peru)
BT Rivers—Peru
Mantels
[NA3050-NA3055 (Architecture)]
[TH2288 (Construction)]
UF Chimneypieces
BT Fireplaces
Manteo Bay (N.C.)
USE Shallowbag Bay (N.C.)
Mantey family
USE Manthey family
Mantharā (Legendary character)
UF Kūni (Legendary character)
Mantarai (Legendary character)
BT Folklore—India
Manthei family
USE Manthey family
Mantheiy family
USE Manthey family
Manthey family *(Not Subd Geog)*
UF Mantey family
Manthei family
Mantheiy family
Manthie family
Manthy family
Manthie family
USE Manthey family
Manthy family
USE Manthey family
**Manti La Sal National Forest (Utah and
Colo.)**
UF La Sals (Utah and Colo.)
BT Forest reserves—Colorado
Forest reserves—Utah
Manticoridae
USE Carabidae
Mantidae
[QL508.M2]
BT Orthoptera
NT Stagmomantis
Manting family *(Not Subd Geog)*
UF Mantingh family
Mantingh family
USE Manting family
Mantis religiosa
USE Praying mantis
Mantispa
[QL513.M3]
BT Mantispidae
Mantispa uhleri
[QL513.M3]
Mantispidae
[QL513.M3]

Mantispidae *(Continued)*
  BT Neuroptera
  NT Mantispa
Mantjiltjara (Australian people)
  USE Mandjildjara (Australian people)
Mantled howler monkey
    [QL737.P925]
  UF Alouatta palliata
      Alouatta villosa
      Central American howler monkey
      Guatemalan howler monkey
  BT Howler monkeys
Mantles, Ice
  USE Ice sheets
Mantoux test
  USE Tuberculin test
Mantrapping
  USE Human trapping
Mantras
    [BL1226.3]
  BT Incantations
  NT Bijas
      Buddhist mantras
      Om (Hinduism)
      Om (Sikhism)
      Sri Namaskara Mahaamantra
Mantras, Buddhist
  USE Buddhist mantras
Mantrayāna Buddhism
  USE Tantric Buddhism
Mantz family
  USE Manz family
Manu, Svārociṣa (Hindu mythology)
  USE Svārociṣa Manu (Hindu mythology)
Manuae (Cook Islands) *(Not Subd Geog)*
  UF Hervey Island (Cook Islands)
  BT Coral reefs and islands—Cook Islands
Manual alphabets
  USE Deaf—Means of communication
Manual control systems
  USE Man-machine systems—Manual
      control
Manual dexterity
  USE Motor ability
Manual labor *(May Subd Geog)*
  BT Labor and laboring classes
      Work
  RT Unskilled labor
Manual skill
  USE Motor ability
Manual training *(May Subd Geog)*
    [LB1595-LB1599 (Education)]
    [TT161-TT169 (Technology)]
  UF Education, Industrial
      Industrial education
      Industrial schools
      Training, Manual
  BT Industrial arts
      Schools
      Vocational education
  RT Arts and crafts movement
      Handicraft
      Sloyd
      Technical education
  NT Basket making
      Carpentry
      Design
      Drawing
      Models and modelmaking
      Needlework
      School shops
      Weaving (Manual training)
      Woodwork (Manual training)
  — **Methods and manuals**
      [TT168-9]
  — Woodwork
      USE Woodwork (Manual training)
Manualo
    [ML1055.M26]
  BT Musical instruments (Mechanical)
      Player-piano

Manuals, Administrative
  USE Administrative manuals
Manuals, Technical
  USE Technical manuals
Manuel Fort (S.D.)
  USE Fort Manuel (S.D.)
Manueline architecture
  USE Architecture, Manueline
Manufacture
  USE *subdivision* Manufacture *under specific*
      products
      Manufacturing processes
Manufacturers
  USE Businessmen
      Industrialists
Manufacturers' agents *(May Subd Geog)*
  UF Agents, Manufacturers'
      Factors
      Manufacturers' representatives
  BT Commission merchants
      Sales personnel
Manufacturers' liability
  USE Products liability
Manufacturers' liability insurance
  USE Insurance, Products liability
Manufacturers' representatives
  USE Manufacturers' agents
Manufacturers' retail outlets
    (May Subd Geog)
  UF Outlets, Manufacturers' retail
      Retail outlets, Manufacturers'
  BT Marketing
      Stores, Retail
Manufactures
    [HD9720-HD9739 (Economics)]
    [TS]
  UF Consumers' goods
      Manufacturing industries
      Manufacturing industry
      Products
      Products, Manufactured
  BT Commercial products
  RT Manufacturing processes
  SA *subdivision* Manufactures *under names*
      of countries, cities, etc. for works
      on products manufactured in those
      places; and headings for types of
      manufactured products
  NT Catalogs, Commercial
      Commerce
      Consular reports
      Factory system
      Generic products
      Home labor
      Industrial arts
      Industrial capacity
      Intermediate goods
      Machinery
      Mills and mill-work
      Patents
      Prices
      Product coding
      Production engineering
      Sweating system
      Value added
      Waste products
      Workshops
  — **Accounting**
      RT Factories—Accounting
      NT Product financing arrangements
          (Accounting)
  — **Costs**
      [HF5686.M3]
      UF Factory costs
      BT Costs, Industrial
      NT Markup
  — **Defects**
      UF Defective products
          Defects in manufactures
      NT Product recall
  — Life cycle

      USE Product life cycle
  — **Seasonal variations**
Manufacturing, Computer integrated
  USE Computer integrated manufacturing
      systems
Manufacturing capacity
  USE Industrial capacity
Manufacturing clause (Copyright law)
  USE Copyright—Manufacturing clause
Manufacturing engineering
  USE Production engineering
Manufacturing in space
  USE Space industrialization
Manufacturing industries
  USE Manufactures
Manufacturing industry
  USE Manufactures
Manufacturing management
  USE Production management
Manufacturing planning
  USE Production planning
Manufacturing processes *(May Subd Geog)*
      Here are entered works on the special manufac-
    turing methods by which raw materials are converted
    into usable product forms, including founding, turn-
    ing, forging, welding, etc.
  UF Industrial processing
      Manufacture
      Process engineering (Manufactures)
      Processes, Manufacturing
      Processing, Industrial
      Production processes
  BT Industrial arts
      Production engineering
  RT Machine-tools
      Manufactures
      Materials
  NT Assembly-line methods
      Chemical processes
      Extrusion process
      Fasteners
      Finishes and finishing
      Machining
      Make-or-buy decisions
      Mass production
      Metal-work
      Mills and mill-work
      Pelletizing
      Process control
      Turning
      Value added
      Welding
      Woodwork
Manufacturing systems, Flexible
  USE Flexible manufacturing systems
Manufacturing systems, Repetitive
  USE Repetitive manufacturing systems
Manugulasi language
  USE Managalasi language
Manukau Harbor (N.Z.) *(Not Subd Geog)*
  UF Manukau Harbour (N.Z.)
  BT Harbors—New Zealand
Manukau Harbour (N.Z.)
  USE Manukau Harbor (N.Z.)
Manumission of slaves
  USE Slavery—Emancipation
Manure crops, Green
  USE Green manure crops
Manure gases
  UF Gases in manure
  BT Farm manure
      Manures
  NT Methane
Manure handling
  BT Farm manure
      Materials handling
  SA *subdivision* Manure—Handling *under*
      names of particular animals, e.g.
      Cattle—Manure—Handling; Poultry
      —Manure—Handling

Manures (May Subd Geog)
  [S631-S667 (Fertilizers)]
  BT Animal waste
      Crop residues
      Fertilizers
      Organic fertilizers
  SA *subdivision* Manure *under individual*
      animals and groups of animals, e.g.
      Cattle—Manure; Poultry—Manure
  NT Farm manure
      Green manuring
      Guano
      Manure gases
      Night soil
  — **Disinfection**
      [S635]
      BT Disinfection and disinfectants
Manus (Papua New Guinea people)
  BT Ethnology—Papua New Guinea
Manuscript cancellations (Philately)
  USE Pen cancellations (Philately)
Manuscript dating
  UF Dating of manuscripts
  BT Manuscripts
Manuscript depositories
  USE Archives
Manuscript maps
  USE Maps, Manuscript
Manuscript preparation (Authorship)
  [PN160]
  UF Preparation of manuscripts
      (Authorship)
  BT Authorship—Handbooks, manuals, etc.
      Editing
  RT Printing, Practical—Style manuals
Manuscript repositories
  USE Archives
Manuscript transmission
  USE Transmission of texts
Manuscripts (May Subd Geog)
  [Z105-Z115]
  [Z6601-Z6625]
  UF Codices
  BT Archives
      Bibliography
      Books
      Library materials
  RT Archival materials
      Autographs
      Charters
      Diplomatics
      Illumination of books and manuscripts
      Marginalia
      Paleography
  SA *subdivision* Manuscripts *under subjects*
      and names of authors and individual
      works
  NT Cartularies
      Copyists
      Discarding of manuscripts, etc.
      Genizah
      Incipits
      Manuscript dating
      Manuscripts, Medieval
      Maps, Manuscript
      Music—Manuscripts
      Palm-leaf manuscripts
      Pecia
      Signatures (Writing)
      Transmission of texts
  — Cataloging
      USE Cataloging of manuscripts
  — **Certification**
      BT Forgery of manuscripts
          Transmission of texts
  — Classification
      USE Classification—Manuscripts
  — **Collections**
  — **Colophons**
      USE Colophons of manuscripts
  — **Conservation and restoration**

  [Z110.C7]
      UF Conservation of manuscripts
          Documents, Conservation of
          Manuscripts—Restoration
          Preservation of manuscripts
          Restoration of manuscripts
  — — **Tropical conditions**
  — Copyright
      USE Copyright—Manuscripts
  — Defacement
      USE Manuscripts—Mutilation,
          defacement, etc.
  — Depositories
      USE Archives
  — **Editing**
      BT Editing
  — **Exhibitions**
      RT Bibliographical exhibitions
      NT Music—Manuscripts—Exhibitions
  — **Facsimiles**
      [Z113-115]
      RT Diplomatics
      NT Paleography
  — Forgeries
      USE Forgery of manuscripts
  — **Mutilation, defacement, etc.**
      UF Defacement of manuscripts
          Manuscripts—Defacement
          Mutilation of manuscripts
      RT Books—Mutilation, defacement,
          etc.
  — **Prices**
      RT Books—Prices
  — Repositories
      USE Archives
  — **Reproduction**
      [Z110.R4]
      UF Photography of manuscripts
      BT Copying
      NT Manuscripts on microfilm
          Photocopying processes
          Scriptoria
  — Restoration
      USE Manuscripts—Conservation and
          restoration
  — **Rule marks**
      [Z110.R83]
      UF Rule marks (Manuscripts)
          Ruled lines (Manuscripts)
      BT Copying
          Paper ruling
Manuscripts, Abyssinian
  USE Manuscripts, Ethiopic
Manuscripts, American (May Subd Geog)
  UF American manuscripts
Manuscripts, Anglo-Saxon
  USE Manuscripts, English (Old)
Manuscripts, Arabic (May Subd Geog)
  UF Arabic manuscripts
Manuscripts, Arabic (Judeo-Arabic)
  USE Manuscripts, Judeo-Arabic
Manuscripts, Aramaic (May Subd Geog)
  UF Aramaic manuscripts
Manuscripts, Aramaic (Papyri)
  (May Subd Geog)
  UF Aramaic papyri
  BT Manuscripts (Papyri)
Manuscripts, Armenian (May Subd Geog)
  UF Armenian manuscripts
Manuscripts, Assamese (May Subd Geog)
  UF Assamese manuscripts
Manuscripts, Avesta
  UF Avesta manuscripts
      Zend manuscripts
Manuscripts, Azerbaijani (May Subd Geog)
  [Z6605.A96]
  UF Azerbaijani manuscripts
Manuscripts, Aztec
  [F1219]
  UF Aztec manuscripts
  BT Manuscripts, Mexican (Pre-Columbian)

Manuscripts, Baluchi (May Subd Geog)
  UF Baluchi manuscripts
Manuscripts, Bengali (May Subd Geog)
  [Z6605.B4]
  UF Bengali manuscripts
Manuscripts, Biblical
  USE Bible—Manuscripts
Manuscripts, Bohemian
  USE Manuscripts, Czech
Manuscripts, Bulgarian (May Subd Geog)
  UF Bulgarian manuscripts
Manuscripts, Burmese (May Subd Geog)
  [Z6605.B87]
  UF Burmese manuscripts
Manuscripts, Canadian (May Subd Geog)
  UF Canadian manuscripts
Manuscripts, Catalan (May Subd Geog)
  UF Catalan manuscripts
Manuscripts, Cham (May Subd Geog)
  UF Cham manuscripts
Manuscripts, Chinese (May Subd Geog)
  UF Chinese manuscripts
Manuscripts, Church Slavic
  (May Subd Geog)
  UF Manuscripts, Old Slovenian
      Manuscripts, Slovenian (Old)
Manuscripts, Classical (Papyri)
  UF Classical papyri
  BT Manuscripts (Papyri)
  NT Manuscripts, Greek (Papyri)
      Manuscripts, Latin (Papyri)
Manuscripts, Coptic (May Subd Geog)
  UF Coptic manuscripts
Manuscripts, Coptic (Papyri)
  BT Manuscripts (Papyri)
Manuscripts, Cyrillic (May Subd Geog)
  UF Cyrillic manuscripts
Manuscripts, Czech
  UF Czech manuscripts
      Manuscripts, Bohemian
Manuscripts, Demotic (Papyri)
  USE Egyptian language—Papyri, Demotic
Manuscripts, Dominican (May Subd Geog)
  UF Dominican manuscripts
Manuscripts, Dutch (May Subd Geog)
  UF Dutch manuscripts
Manuscripts, English (May Subd Geog)
  UF English manuscripts
Manuscripts, English, [Arabic, etc.]
  (May Subd Geog)
Manuscripts, English (Middle)
  (May Subd Geog)
  UF English manuscripts (Middle)
      Manuscripts, Middle English
      Middle English manuscripts
Manuscripts, English (Old)
  UF Anglo-Saxon manuscripts
      English manuscripts, Old
      Manuscripts, Anglo-Saxon
      Manuscripts, Old English
      Old English manuscripts
Manuscripts, Ethiopic
  UF Abyssinian manuscripts
      Ethiopic manuscripts
      Manuscripts, Abyssinian
Manuscripts, European (May Subd Geog)
  UF European manuscripts
Manuscripts, Finnish (May Subd Geog)
  UF Finnish manuscripts
Manuscripts, Forgery of
  USE Forgery of manuscripts
Manuscripts, French (May Subd Geog)
  UF French manuscripts
Manuscripts, French-Canadian
  (May Subd Geog)
  UF French-Canadian manuscripts
Manuscripts, German (May Subd Geog)
  UF German manuscripts
Manuscripts, Glagolitic (May Subd Geog)
  UF Glagolitic manuscripts

Manuscripts, Greek *(May Subd Geog)*
  UF Greek manuscripts
  BT Greek language
       Greek philology
Manuscripts, Greek (Medieval and modern)
(May Subd Geog)
  BT Manuscripts, Medieval
Manuscripts, Greek (Papyri)
  UF Greek papyri
       Papyri, Greek
  BT Manuscripts, Classical (Papyri)
       Manuscripts (Papyri)
Manuscripts, Gujarati *(May Subd Geog)*
  UF Gujarati manuscripts
  BT Manuscripts, Indic
Manuscripts, Hebrew *(May Subd Geog)*
  UF Hebrew manuscripts
  NT Cairo Genizah
Manuscripts, Hieratic (Papyri)
  USE Egyptian language—Papyri, Hieratic
Manuscripts, Hindi *(May Subd Geog)*
  UF Hindi manuscripts
Manuscripts, Hungarian *(May Subd Geog)*
  UF Hungarian manuscripts
Manuscripts, Illuminated
  USE Illumination of books and manuscripts
Manuscripts, Indic
  UF Indic manuscripts
       Indo-Aryan manuscripts
  NT Manuscripts, Gujarati
Manuscripts, Indonesian *(May Subd Geog)*
  UF Indonesian manuscripts
Manuscripts, Irish *(May Subd Geog)*
  UF Irish manuscripts
Manuscripts, Italian *(May Subd Geog)*
  UF Italian manuscripts
Manuscripts, Japanese *(May Subd Geog)*
  UF Japanese manuscripts
Manuscripts, Javanese *(May Subd Geog)*
  [Z6605.J37]
  UF Javanese manuscripts
Manuscripts, Judeo-Arabic
(May Subd Geog)
  UF Judeo-Arabic manuscripts
       Manuscripts, Arabic (Judeo-Arabic)
Manuscripts, Judeo-Persian
(May Subd Geog)
  UF Judeo-Persian manuscripts
       Manuscripts, Persian (Judeo-Persian)
Manuscripts, Kannada *(May Subd Geog)*
  UF Kannada manuscripts
Manuscripts, Karaite
  UF Caraite manuscripts
       Karaite manuscripts
Manuscripts, Khmer *(May Subd Geog)*
  UF Khmer manuscripts
Manuscripts, Latin
  UF Latin manuscripts
  BT Latin language
       Latin philology
Manuscripts, Latin (Medieval and modern)
(May Subd Geog)
  UF Medieval and modern Latin
       manuscripts
  BT Manuscripts, Medieval
Manuscripts, Latin (Papyri)
  UF Latin papyri
       Papyri, Latin
  BT Manuscripts, Classical (Papyri)
       Manuscripts (Papyri)
Manuscripts, Lombard *(May Subd Geog)*
  UF Lombard manuscripts
Manuscripts, Malay *(May Subd Geog)*
  UF Malay manuscripts
Manuscripts, Malayalam *(May Subd Geog)*
  UF Malayalam manuscripts
Manuscripts, Malayan *(May Subd Geog)*
  UF Malayan manuscripts
Manuscripts, Manchu *(May Subd Geog)*
  UF Manchu manuscripts

Manuscripts, Manipuri *(May Subd Geog)*
  UF Manipuri manuscripts
Manuscripts, Marathi *(May Subd Geog)*
  UF Manuscripts, Modi
       Marathi manuscripts
       Modi manuscripts
Manuscripts, Maya
  UF Maya manuscripts
  BT Manuscripts, Mexican (Pre-Columbian)
       Mayas—Writing
Manuscripts, Medieval *(May Subd Geog)*
  UF Medieval manuscripts
  BT Manuscripts
  NT Manuscripts, Greek (Medieval and
       modern)
       Manuscripts, Latin (Medieval and
       modern)
Manuscripts, Mexican *(May Subd Geog)*
  UF Mexican manuscripts
  NT Manuscripts, Tlaxcalan
Manuscripts, Mexican (Pre-Columbian)
  [F1219]
  UF Codices, Mexican (Pre-Columbian)
       Mexican manuscripts (Pre-Columbian)
  BT Picture-writing, Indian
  NT Manuscripts, Aztec
       Manuscripts, Maya
       Manuscripts, Mixtec
       Manuscripts, Zapotec
Manuscripts, Middle English
  USE Manuscripts, English (Middle)
Manuscripts, Mixtec
  [F1219]
  UF Mixtec manuscripts
  BT Manuscripts, Mexican (Pre-Columbian)
Manuscripts, Modi
  USE Manuscripts, Marathi
Manuscripts, Musical
  USE *subdivision* Manuscripts *under names*
      of composers, e.g. Wagner, Richard,
      1813-1883—Manuscripts
      Music—Manuscripts
Manuscripts, Newari *(May Subd Geog)*
  UF Newari manuscripts
Manuscripts, Old English
  USE Manuscripts, English (Old)
Manuscripts, Old Norse
  UF Old Norse manuscripts
  BT Old Norse literature
Manuscripts, Old Russian
  USE Manuscripts, Russian (Old)
Manuscripts, Old Slovenian
  USE Manuscripts, Church Slavic
Manuscripts, Oriental
  UF Oriental manuscripts
Manuscripts, Oriya *(May Subd Geog)*
  [Z6605.O77]
  UF Oriya manuscripts
Manuscripts, Pali *(May Subd Geog)*
  UF Pali manuscripts
Manuscripts, Palm-leaf
  USE Palm-leaf manuscripts
Manuscripts, Panjabi *(May Subd Geog)*
  UF Panjabi manuscripts
Manuscripts, Persian
  UF Persian manuscripts
  BT Persian literature
Manuscripts, Persian (Judeo-Persian)
  USE Manuscripts, Judeo-Persian
Manuscripts, Polish *(May Subd Geog)*
  UF Polish manuscripts
Manuscripts, Portuguese *(May Subd Geog)*
  UF Portuguese manuscripts
Manuscripts, Prakrit *(May Subd Geog)*
  UF Prakrit manuscripts
Manuscripts, Pushto *(May Subd Geog)*
  [Z6605.P97]
  UF Pushto manuscripts
Manuscripts, Rajasthani *(May Subd Geog)*
  UF Rajasthani manuscripts

Manuscripts, Renaissance *(May Subd Geog)*
  UF Renaissance manuscripts
Manuscripts, Romance *(May Subd Geog)*
  UF Romance manuscripts
Manuscripts, Russian (Old)
(May Subd Geog)
  UF Manuscripts, Old Russian
       Old Russian manuscripts
       Russian manuscripts (Old)
Manuscripts, Samaritan *(May Subd Geog)*
  UF Samaritan manuscripts
Manuscripts, Sanskrit *(May Subd Geog)*
  UF Sanskrit manuscripts
Manuscripts, Sasak *(May Subd Geog)*
  UF Sasak manuscripts
Manuscripts, Scottish *(May Subd Geog)*
  UF Scottish manuscripts
Manuscripts, Serbian *(May Subd Geog)*
  UF Serbian manuscripts
Manuscripts, Sindhi *(May Subd Geog)*
  UF Sindhi manuscripts
Manuscripts, Sinhalese *(May Subd Geog)*
  UF Sinhalese manuscripts
Manuscripts, Slavic *(May Subd Geog)*
  UF Slavic manuscripts
Manuscripts, Slovenian *(May Subd Geog)*
  UF Slovenian manuscripts
Manuscripts, Slovenian (Old)
  USE Manuscripts, Church Slavic
Manuscripts, Sogdian *(May Subd Geog)*
  UF Sogdian manuscripts
Manuscripts, Spanish *(May Subd Geog)*
  UF Spanish manuscripts
Manuscripts, Spanish American
(May Subd Geog)
  UF Spanish American manuscripts
Manuscripts, Swedish *(May Subd Geog)*
  UF Swedish manuscripts
Manuscripts, Syriac *(May Subd Geog)*
  UF Syriac manuscripts
  BT Syriac language
Manuscripts, Tamil *(May Subd Geog)*
  UF Tamil manuscripts
Manuscripts, Telugu *(May Subd Geog)*
  UF Telugu manuscripts
Manuscripts, Tlaxcalan *(May Subd Geog)*
  UF Tlaxcalan manuscripts
  BT Manuscripts, Mexican
       Tlaxcalan Indians—Writing
Manuscripts, Turkish *(May Subd Geog)*
  [Z6605.T8]
  UF Turkish manuscripts
Manuscripts, Ukrainian *(May Subd Geog)*
  UF Ukrainian manuscripts
Manuscripts, Urdu
  UF Urdu manuscripts
Manuscripts, Zapotec
  [F1219]
  UF Zapotec manuscripts
  BT Manuscripts, Mexican (Pre-Columbian)
Manuscripts (Palimpsests)
  Facsimiles of palimpsests have duplicate entry
under Manuscripts—Facsimiles, e.g. 1. Manuscripts
(Palimpsests) 2. Manuscripts—Facsimiles.
  UF Palimpsests
Manuscripts (Papyri)
  UF Papyri, Egyptian
       Papyrus manuscripts
  BT Paleography
       Writing—Materials and instruments
  SA *subdivision* Manuscripts (Papyri) *under*
      individual sacred works, e.g. Bible—
      Manuscripts (Papyri)
  NT Coptic language—Papyri
       Egyptian language—Papyri
       Manuscripts, Aramaic (Papyri)
       Manuscripts, Classical (Papyri)
       Manuscripts, Coptic (Papyri)
       Manuscripts, Greek (Papyri)
       Manuscripts, Latin (Papyri)

Manuscripts on microfilm *(May Subd Geog)*
  BT Manuscripts—Reproduction
       Microfilms
Manutius family
  USE Manuzio family
Manuvu language
  UF Bagobo language, Upper
      Obo language
      Upper Bagobo language
  BT Philippine languages
Manuvùs (Philippine people)
  USE Manobos (Philippine people)
Manuzio family *(Not Subd Geog)*
  UF Manutius family
Manvel family
  USE Mandeville family
Manvell family
  USE Mandeville family
Manville family
  USE Mandeville family
Manwaring family *(Not Subd Geog)*
  UF Mainwaring family
      Mannering family
      Manwarren family
      Manwarring family
  RT Warren family
Manwarren family
  USE Manwaring family
Manwarring family
  USE Manwaring family
Manx ballads
  USE Ballads, Manx
Manx Electric Railway
  BT Railroads—Great Britain
Manx folk-songs
  USE Folk-songs, Manx
Manx language
  [PB1801-1847]
  BT Celtic languages
      Gaelic language
      Goidelic languages
Manx literature *(May Subd Geog)*
  [PB1851 (History)]
  [PB1858 (Collections)]
Manx Northern Railway
  BT Railroads—Great Britain
      Railroads, Narrow-gage—Great Britain
Manx poetry *(May Subd Geog)*
  [PB1851 (History)]
  [PB1858 (Collections)]
Manx shearwater
  [QL696.P6]
Many (Philosophy)
  BT Philosophy
Many-body problem
  UF n-body problem
      Problem of many bodies
      Problem of n-bodies
  BT Mechanics, Analytic
      Mechanics, Celestial
      Perturbation (Astronomy)
      Quantum theory
  RT Few-body problem
  NT Feynman diagrams
      Hartree-Fock approximation
      Three-body problem
      Two-body problem
  — Numerical solutions
      BT Numerical analysis
Many-plume moths
  USE Alucitidae
Many-valley semiconductors
  [QC611.8.M27]
  BT Conduction band
      Semiconductors
Many-valued logic
  [BC126 (Philosophy)]
  [QA9.45 (Mathematics)]

  UF Logic, Many-valued
      Logic, Multivalued
      Logic, Variable-valued
      Multivalued logic
      Variable-valued logic
  BT Nonclassical mathematical logic
      Values
  NT AQVAL programs (Computer
       programs)
      Future contingents (Logic)
      INDUCE-1 (Computer program)
      SYM-1 (Computer program)
      SYM4 (Computer program)
      VL1 system
      VL21 system
  — Computer programs
      NT AQ7UNI (Computer program)
Manyukai (Indonesian people)
  USE Manyuke (Indonesian people)
Manyuke (Indonesian people)
  [DS632.M29]
  UF Manyukai (Indonesian people)
      Menjuke (Indonesian people)
      Menyukai (Indonesian people)
  BT Dyaks
      Ethnology—Indonesia
Manz family *(Not Subd Geog)*
  UF Mans family
      Mantz family
      Manze family
  RT Mann family
Manza (African people)
  USE Mandjas
Manzai (Comedy) *(May Subd Geog)*
  [PL746 (History)]
  [PL776 (Collections)]
  [PN2924.5.M36 (Performance)]
  BT Japanese drama (Comedy)
      Japanese wit and humor
      Theater—Japan
Manzai (Dance) *(May Subd Geog)*
  UF Mikawa manzai
      Owari manzai
Manzanares River (Spain)
  UF Río Manzanares (Spain)
  BT Rivers—Spain
Manzanillo Bay (Panama)
  UF Bahía de Manzanillo (Panama)
      Bahía Manzanillo (Panama)
  BT Bays—Panama
Manzanillo Island (Panama)
  UF Isla Manzanillo (Panama)
      Isleta (Panama)
      La Isleta (Panama)
  BT Islands—Panama
Manzanita
  USE Arctostaphylos
Manzano Mountains (N.M.)
  BT Mountains—New Mexico
Manze family
  USE Manz family
Manziano family *(Not Subd Geog)*
Manzoni family *(Not Subd Geog)*
Mao, Tse-tung, 1893-1976
  — Homes
      USE Mao, Tse-tung, 1893-1976—
        Homes and haunts
  — Homes and haunts *(May Subd Geog)*
      UF Mao, Tse-tung, 1893-1976—Homes
  — — China
MAO (Enzyme)
  USE Monoamine oxidase
Mao family *(Not Subd Geog)*
  UF Mau family
      Mow family
Mao language
  [PL4001.M32]
  UF Sopfomo language
      Sopvoma language
      Spowoma language
  BT Naga languages

Mao-nan (Chinese people)
  (May Subd Geog)
  [DS731.M36]
  UF Maonan (Chinese people)
  BT Ethnology—China
Mao-nan language
  USE Maonan language
Maoism
  USE Communism
Maonan (Chinese people)
  USE Mao-nan (Chinese people)
Maonan language
  [PL4251.M36]
  UF Mao-nan language
      Maunan language
  BT China—Languages
      Tai languages
Maori architecture
  USE Architecture, Maori
Maori art
  USE Art, Maori
Maori art objects
  USE Art objects, Maori
Maori astronomy
  USE Astronomy, Maori
Maori decorative arts
  USE Decorative arts, Maori
Maori folk-songs
  USE Folk-songs, Maori
Maori funeral rites and ceremonies
  USE Funeral rites and ceremonies, Maori
Maori imprints *(May Subd Geog)*
  [Z112.M35]
Maori language
  [PL6465]
  BT Polynesian languages
  RT Tahitian language
Maori language, Cook Islands
  USE Rarotongan language
Maori law
  USE Law, Maori
Maori literature
  [PL6465.Z7]
Maori marriage customs and rites
  USE Marriage customs and rites, Maori
Maori mythology
  USE Mythology, Maori
Maori physicians
  USE Physicians, Maori
Maori poetry
  [PL6465.Z77]
Maori psychologists
  USE Psychologists, Maori
Maori songs
  USE Songs, Maori
Maori textile fabrics
  USE Textile fabrics, Maori
Maori War, N.Z., 1845-1847
  USE New Zealand—History—Maori War,
      1845-1847
Maori Wars, 1843-1870
  USE New Zealand—History—1843-1870
Maori wood-carving
  USE Wood-carving, Maori
Maoris
  [DU423 (History)]
  [GN667.N9 (Anthropology)]
  BT Polynesians
  NT Missions to Maoris
      New Zealand—History—1843-1870
      Ngaa Rauru (Maori people)
      Ngaitahu (Maori tribe)
      Ngati Mamoe (Maori tribe)
      Ngāti Toa (Maori people)
      Patu
  — Agriculture
      [DU423.A35]
      BT Agriculture, Primitive—New
        Zealand
  — Amusements
      USE Maoris—Games

Maoris (Continued)
— Anthropometry
— Boats
    BT Boats, Primitive
       Canoes and canoeing
— Children
    BT Children
— Fishing
    [DU423.F5]
    BT Fishing, Primitive—New Zealand
— Games
    [DU423.G3]
    UF Maoris—Amusements
    BT Games, Primitive—New Zealand
— Government relations
— Hunting
    [DU423.H8]
    BT Hunting, Primitive—New Zealand
— Implements
    [DU423.I4]
— Land tenure
    [DU423.G6]
    BT Land tenure
— Medicine
    [DU423.M38]
    BT Medicine, Primitive
— Population
    [DU423.P66]
    BT Population
— Religion
    NT Maui (Polynesian deity)
— Rites and ceremonies
    UF Rites and ceremonies—Maori
    NT Funeral rites and ceremonies,
         Maori
       Marriage customs and rites, Maori
— Warfare
    [DU423.W35]
    UF Warfare, Maori
    NT New Zealand—History—Maori
         War, 1845-1847
— Youth
    BT Youth
Maou dialect
  USE Mau dialect (Ivory Coast)
MAP (Computer program language)
  UF Macro assembly programming
Map catalogers (May Subd Geog)
  BT Catalogers
Map collections (May Subd Geog)
  [GA193-GA197 (General)]
  [Z692.M3 (Map collections in
    libraries)]
  UF Libraries, Map
      Map libraries
  BT Libraries, Special
  SA subdivision Map collections under
      names of individual persons,
      families, and corporate bodies
Map-coloring problem
  [QA612.18]
  BT Color in cartography
      Graph theory
  NT Four-color problem
Map contours
  USE Contours (Cartography)
Map drawing
  [GA130]
    Here are entered works on the mapping of small
  areas and the drawing of maps in elementary schools.
  Works on the general science of map-making, includ-
  ing map-projection and the mapping of large areas are
  entered under the heading Cartography. Works about
  the maps themselves are entered under Maps.
  BT Drawing
  RT Surveys—Plotting
      Topographical drawing
  NT Protractors
Map grids
  USE Grids (Cartography)

Map industry and trade (May Subd Geog)
  UF Map trade
— Advertising
    USE Advertising—Map industry and
        trade
Map libraries
  USE Map collections
Map printing
  [GA150]
  UF Maps—Printing
      Maps, Printing of
  BT Cartography
      Maps—Reproduction
      Printing
— Equipment and supplies
    [GA150.5]
    BT Printing machinery and supplies
Map-projection
  [GA110-115]
  BT Geography, Mathematical
      Projection
  RT Cartography
      Surfaces, Representation of
  NT Aitoff's projection (Cartography)
      Azimuthal projection (Cartography)
      Conical projection (Cartography)
      Cylindrical projection (Cartography)
      Fuller projection (Cartography)
      Lambert conformal conic projection
        (Cartography)
      McBryde S3 equal-area projection
        (Cartography)
      Oblique Mercator projection
        (Cartography)
      Orthographic projection
      Peters projection (Cartography)
      Polymorphic projection (Cartography)
      Quincuncial projection (Cartography)
      Sinusoidal projection (Cartography)
      Space oblique Mercator projection
        (Cartography)
      Transverse Mercator projection
        (Cartography)
      Universal transverse Mercator
        projection (Cartography)
Map reading
  USE Maps
      Maps, Military
Map reproduction
  USE Maps—Reproduction
Map scales
  UF Scales (Cartography)
  BT Cartography
      Distances—Measurement
Map trade
  USE Map industry and trade
Mapel family
  USE Maples family
Mapels family
  USE Maples family
Mapepire
  USE Lachesis muta
Mapes family (Not Subd Geog)
Mapeshana Indians
  USE Wapisiana Indians
Mapimi Biosphere Reserve (Mexico)
  USE Reserva de la Biosfera de Mapimí
      (Mexico)
Maple (May Subd Geog)
  [QK495.A17 (Botany)]
  [SD397.M3 (Culture)]
  BT Aceraceae
  NT Fullmoon maple
      Japanese maple
      Red maple
      Sugar-maple
— Diseases and pests (May Subd Geog)
    NT Eutypella canker
       Maple worm
Maple, Fossil
  [QE983]

Maple family
  USE Maples family
Maple Grove Cemetery (Findlay, Ohio)
  BT Cemeteries—Ohio
Maple Grove Cemetery (Ovid, Mich.)
  BT Cemeteries—Michigan
Maple in art
Maple River Indian Reserve (Man.)
  USE Fort Alexander Indian Reserve (Man.)
Maple sugar
  [TP395]
  BT Sugar
      Sugar-maple
  NT Cookery (Maple sugar and syrup)
Maple sugar industry (May Subd Geog)
Maple syrup
  [TP395]
  BT Sugar-maple
  NT Cookery (Maple sugar and syrup)
Maple worm
  UF Anisota rubicunda
      Green-striped maple worm
      Mapleworm
  BT Maple—Diseases and pests
Maplelawn Cemetery (Elba, N.Y.)
  BT Cemeteries—New York (State)
Maples family (Not Subd Geog)
  UF Mapel family
      Mapels family
      Maple family
      Maypole family
Mapleworm
  USE Maple worm
Mapmakers
  USE Cartographers
Mapo
  USE Bathygobius soporator
Mapodi language
  USE Gude language
Maporese (Indonesian people)
  [DS632.M36]
  UF Mapurese (Indonesian people)
  BT Ethnology—Indonesia
Mapp family (Not Subd Geog)
  UF Mapps family
MAPPER (Computer system)
  UF Maintaining, Preparing, and Producing
      Executive Reports (Computer
      system)
  BT Electronic digital computers—
      Programming
Mappilas
  USE Moplahs
Mappin family (Not Subd Geog)
Mapping, Body surface
  USE Body surface mapping
Mapping, Conformal
  USE Conformal mapping
Mapping, Environmental
  USE Environmental mapping
Mapping (Cartography)
  USE Cartography
Mappings, Analytic
  USE Analytic mappings
Mappings, Biholomorphic
  USE Biholomorphic mappings
Mappings, Differentiable
  USE Differentiable mappings
Mappings, Holomorphic
  USE Holomorphic mappings
Mappings, Point (Mathematics)
  USE Point mappings (Mathematics)
Mappings, Quasiconformal
  USE Quasiconformal mappings
Mappings, Set-valued
  USE Set-valued maps
Mappings, Stratified
  USE Stratified sets
Mappings (Mathematics)
  UF Maps (Mathematics)

BT Functions
    Functions, Continuous
    Topology
    Transformations (Mathematics)
NT Analytic mappings
    Conformal mapping
    Differentiable mappings
    Gauss maps
    Harmonic maps
    Holomorphic mappings
    Immersions (Mathematics)
    Nonexpansive mappings
    Point mappings (Mathematics)
    Quasiconformal mappings
    Set-valued maps
    Shape theory (Topology)

Mapps family
USE Mapp family

Maprik language
USE Abulas language

Maps
UF Map reading
    Plans
BT Geography
    Government publications
    Library materials
SA *subdivision* Maps *under names of countries, cities, etc. and subjects for individual maps or collections of maps, e.g.* Africa—Climate—Maps; Africa, North—Economic conditions—Maps; Real property—Maps; *and headings beginning with the word* Map
NT Aeronautical charts
    Atlases
    Bathymetric maps
    Bottle-charts
    Cartography
    Cartometry
    Grids (Cartography)
    Index maps
    Maps, Comparative
    Maps, Statistical
    Maps, Tourist
    Mine maps
    Nautical charts
    Outline maps
    Road maps
    Topographic maps
    World maps
    Zoning maps
— **Bibliography**
    Here are entered works containing lists of maps.
    SA *subdivision* Maps—Bibliography *under names of countries, cities, etc., corporate bodies, and topical subjects*
— **Cataloging**
    USE Cataloging of maps
— **Classification**
    USE Classification—Maps
— **Conventional signs**
    USE Maps—Symbols
— **History**
    USE Cartography—History
— **Printing**
    USE Map printing
— **Reproduction**
    [GA150.7]
    UF Map reproduction
        Photography of maps
        Reproduction of maps
    BT Cartography
        Copying
        Photocopying processes
    NT Map printing
        Scribing (Cartography)
— **Symbols**

UF Cartography—Conventional signs
    Cartography—Symbols
    Maps—Conventional signs
RT Topographical drawing—
    Conventional signs
SA *subdivision* Maps—Symbols *under topical headings, e.g.* Soils—Maps—Symbols
— **Terminology**
    UF Cartography—Terminology
Maps, Acquisition of
USE Acquisition of maps
Maps, Agricultural
USE Agriculture—Maps
Maps, Cadastral
USE Real property—Maps
Maps, Comparative
UF Comparative area maps
BT Maps
SA *subdivision* Maps, Comparative *under countries, regions, cities, etc.*
Maps, Early
UF Early maps
BT Geography—History
SA *subdivision* Maps—To 1800 *under names of countries, cities, etc., e.g.* United States—Maps—To 1800
NT Geography, Ancient—Maps
Maps, Gauss
USE Gauss maps
Maps, Geological
USE Geology—Maps
Maps, Harmonic
USE Harmonic maps
Maps, Historical
USE *subdivision* Historical geography—Maps *under names of countries*
    Classical geography—Maps
    Geography, Ancient—Maps
    Geography, Historical—Maps
    Geography, Medieval—Maps
Maps, Linear
USE Linear operators
Maps, Manuscript
UF Manuscript maps
BT Manuscripts
SA *subdivision* Maps, Manuscript *under names of countries, regions, cities, etc.*
NT World maps, Manuscript
Maps, Memory (Computer science)
USE Memory maps (Computer science)
Maps, Mental
USE *subdivision* Maps, Mental *under names of countries, cities, etc.*
    Geographical perception
Maps, Meteorological
USE Meteorology—Charts, diagrams, etc.
Maps, Military
    [UA985-UA997 (Military geography)]
    [UG470 (Surveying, topography)]
UF Map reading
    Military maps
BT Cartography
    Military geography
RT Military topography
NT Military reconnaissance
— **Conventional signs**
    USE Maps, Military—Symbols
— **Symbols**
    [UG470-473]
    UF Maps, Military—Conventional signs
    BT Topographical drawing—Conventional signs
Maps, Mine
USE Mine maps
Maps, Oceanographic
USE Ocean—Maps
    Oceanography—Charts, diagrams, etc.

Maps, Outline and base
USE *subdivision* Maps, Outline and base *under names of countries, regions, etc.*
Maps, Physical
USE *subdivision* Maps, Physical *under names of countries, regions, etc.*
Maps, Pictorial
UF Pictorial maps
SA *subdivision* Maps, Pictorial *under names of countries, cities, etc.*
NT World maps, Pictorial
Maps, Printing of
USE Map printing
Maps, Set-valued
USE Set-valued maps
Maps, Statistical
    [GA109.8]
UF Maps of residuals
    Residuals, Maps of
    Statistical maps
BT Maps
    Statistics—Graphic methods
Maps, Topographic
USE Topographic maps
Maps, Tourist
    Here are entered maps designed for tourists. Maps illustrating the extent or state of tourism are entered under Tourist trade—Maps.
UF Tourist maps
    Travel—Maps
BT Maps
RT Road maps
SA *subdivision* Maps, Tourist *under names of countries, cities, etc.*
Maps, World
USE World maps
Maps, Zoning
USE Zoning maps
Maps (Mathematics)
USE Mappings (Mathematics)
MAPS design technology
UF Design technology, MAPS
    Multivariate Analysis, Participation and Structure
BT Social sciences—Research
    System analysis
Maps for the blind
UF Blind—Maps for
    Blind, Maps for the
BT Maps for the visually handicapped
SA *subdivision* Maps for the blind *under names of countries, cities, etc.*
Maps for the visually handicapped
    [GA135]
BT Visually handicapped
SA *subdivision* Maps for the visually handicapped *under names of countries, regions, cities, etc.*
NT Maps for the blind
Maps of residuals
USE Maps, Statistical
MAPS test
USE Picture story tests
MAPSIT (Computer program)
UF Modular Analysis Package for Systems of Income Transfers (Computer program)
BT Computer programs
    Income maintenance programs—Computer programs
Mapuche Indians
USE Araucanian Indians
Mapuche language
USE Araucanian language
Mapuda language
USE Gude language
Mapun language
USE Jama Mapun language
Mapungubwe Site (South Africa)
BT South Africa—Antiquities

Mapurese (Indonesian people)
USE Maporese (Indonesian people)
Maqamah
  ₍PJ7572.M3₎
  UF Makama
  BT Arabic prose literature
Maqamah, Hebrew
  UF Hebrew maqamah
    Mekamah
  BT Hebrew poetry
Maquettes
  USE Models (Clay, plaster, etc.)
Maquiladora industry
  USE Offshore assembly industry
Maquiladoras
  USE Offshore assembly industry
Maquiritare Indians
  USE Yecuana Indians
Maquiritare language
  USE Yecuana language
Maquis
  USE *subdivision* Underground movements
    under individual wars, e.g. World
    War, 1939-1945—Underground
    movements
    Guerrillas
Maquis ecology (May Subd Geog)
  BT Ecology
    Shrubland ecology
  RT Chaparral ecology
  NT Maquis flora
Maquis flora (May Subd Geog)
  UF Maquis flora—Mediterranean Region
  BT Botany
    Botany—Ecology
    Brush
    Maquis ecology
    Woody plants
  RT Chaparral
  — Mediterranean Region
    USE Maquis flora
Mar Cantabrico (France and Spain)
  USE Biscay, Bay of (France and Spain)
Mar Chiquita Lake (Córdoba, Argentina : Province)
  UF Laguna Mar Chiquita (Córdoba,
    Argentina : Province)
  BT Lakes—Argentina
Mar de Weddell (Antarctic regions)
  USE Weddell Sea (Antarctic regions)
Mar family
  USE Marrs family
Mar Menor (Spain) (Not Subd Geog)
  UF Marmenor (Spain)
    Menor Sea (Spain)
  BT Lagoons—Spain
Mar Morto (Israel and Jordan)
  USE Dead Sea (Israel and Jordan)
Mar Mountains (Brazil)
  UF Serra do Mar (Brazil)
  BT Mountains—Brazil
Mara Lake (N.W.T.)
  USE Nose Lake (N.W.T.)
Mara language (Australia)
  ₍PL7101.M26₎
  UF Leelalwarra language
    Leelawarra language
    Mala language
    Marra language
  BT Australia—Languages
    Australian languages
Mara language (India and Burma)
  USE Lakher language
Maraca
  BT Percussion instruments
Maraca music
  ₍M175.M₎
  NT Quintets (Electronic organs (4),
    maracas)
Maracaibo, Depresión de (Venezuela)
  USE Maracaibo Basin (Venezuela)

Maracaibo, Gulf of (Colombia and Venezuela)
  UF Venezuela, Gulf of (Colombia and
    Venezuela)
  BT Bays—Colombia
    Bays—Venezuela
Maracaibo Basin (Venezuela)
  UF Depresión de Maracaibo (Venezuela)
    Maracaibo, Depresión de (Venezuela)
    Maracaibo Lowlands (Venezuela)
    Zulia Basin (Venezuela)
  BT Geology—Venezuela
Maracaibo Lagoon (Venezuela)
  USE Maracaibo Lake (Venezuela)
Maracaibo Lake (Venezuela)
  UF Golfo de Maracaibo (Venezuela)
    Gran Lago de Maracaibo (Venezuela)
    Lago de Maracaibo (Venezuela)
    Lake Maracaibo (Venezuela)
    Maracaibo Lagoon (Venezuela)
  BT Lakes—Venezuela
Maracaibo Lake (Venezuela), Battle of, 1823
  UF Lake Maracaibo, Battle of, 1823
  BT Venezuela—History—War of
    Independence, 1810-1823—
    Campaigns
Maracaibo Lowlands (Venezuela)
  USE Maracaibo Basin (Venezuela)
Maracasero language
  USE Malayo language
Maradi River (Nigeria and Niger)
  UF Gada River (Nigeria and Niger)
    Goulbin Maradi (Nigeria and Niger)
    Gulbin Maradi (Nigeria and Niger)
  BT Rivers—Niger
    Rivers—Nigeria
Maragatos
  BT Astorga (Spain)—History
    Ethnology—Spain
Maraging steel
  UF Steel, Maraging
  BT Nickel steel
    Steel alloys
Maragua language
  USE Maue language
Maragwet (African people)
  USE Marakwet (African people)
Marais family (Not Subd Geog)
Marais Poitevin (France)
  USE Poitevin Marsh (France)
Marajó Island (Brazil)
  UF Ilha de Marajó (Brazil)
  BT Islands—Brazil
Maraka Indians
  USE Yuko Indians
Marakwet (African people)
  ₍DT433.542₎
  UF Maragwet (African people)
    Markweta (African people)
  BT Ethnology—Kenya
    Nilo-Hamitic tribes
Maram language
  ₍PL4001.M34₎
  BT Naga languages
Maramaldi family
  USE Maramaldo family
Maramaldo family (Not Subd Geog)
  UF Barramauro family
    de Marramauro family
    Maramaldi family
    Marmaldo family
    Marramaldo family
    Marramauro family
    Mauromaldo family
Maraña, Don Juan de (Legendary character)
  USE Don Juan (Legendary character)
Maranao (Philippine people)
  ₍DS666.M37₎
  UF Maranaw (Philippine people)
  BT Ethnology—Philippines
    Muslims—Philippines

Maranao (Philippine people) decoration and
  ornament
  USE Decoration and ornament, Maranao
    (Philippine people)
Maranao language
  ₍PL5957₎
  UF Maranaw language
    Moro languages
Maranaw (Philippine people)
  USE Maranao (Philippine people)
Maranaw language
  USE Maranao language
Marano Lagoon (Italy)
  UF Laguna di Marano (Italy)
  BT Lagoons—Italy
Marañón
  USE Cashew
Marañón River (Peru)
  UF Río Marañón (Peru)
  BT Rivers—Peru
Maranos
  USE Marranos
Marantaceae
  ₍QK495.M28 (Botany)₎
  BT Seitamineae
  NT Calathea
Maranungku language
  BT Australia—Languages
    Daly languages
Marari dialect (May Subd Geog)
  ₍PK1970.M37₎
  BT Bagheli dialect
    India—Languages
Mărăs
  USE Lakhers
Marasà, Sanctuary of (Locri Epizephyrii)
  USE Sanctuary of Marasà (Locri
    Epizephyrii)
Mărăşeşti (Romania), Battle of, 1917
  BT World War, 1914-1918—Campaigns—
    Romania
Mar'ashī family (Not Subd Geog)
Marashite Indians
  USE Malecite Indians
Marasmus (May Subd Geog)
  ₍RJ399.M35₎
  UF Athrepsia
    Atrophy, Infantile
    Infantile atrophy
    Protein-calorie malnutrition of infants
  BT Infants—Diseases
    Infants—Nutrition
    Malnutrition in children
    Protein deficiency
Maratha War, 1775-1782
  ₍DS473₎
  BT India—History—British occupation,
    1765-1947
Maratha War, 1803
  ₍DS475.3₎
  BT India—History—British occupation,
    1765-1947
Maratha War, 1816-1818
  ₍DS475.6₎
  BT India—History—British occupation,
    1765-1947
Maratha women
  USE Women, Maratha
Marathas
  ₍DS432.M2₎
  UF Mahrattas
  BT Ethnology—India
    India—History—1500-1765
  NT Panipat, Battle of, 1761
  — **History, Military**
  — **History, Naval**
  — Women
    USE Women, Maratha
Marathi arts
  USE Arts, Marathi

Marathi authors
  USE Authors, Marathi
Marathi drama
  NT Folk-drama, Marathi
      One-act plays, Marathi
      Radio plays, Marathi
Marathi dramatists
  USE Dramatists, Marathi
Marathi encyclopedias and dictionaries
  USE Encyclopedias and dictionaries,
      Marathi
Marathi essays *(May Subd Geog)*
Marathi fiction *(May Subd Geog)*
  NT Ghost stories, Marathi
      Historical fiction, Marathi
      Short stories, Marathi
Marathi folk-drama
  USE Folk-drama, Marathi
Marathi folk literature
  USE Folk literature, Marathi
Marathi folk-songs
  USE Folk-songs, Marathi
Marathi ghost stories
  USE Ghost stories, Marathi
Marathi Hindu hymns
  USE Hindu hymns, Marathi
Marathi Hindu literature
  USE Hindu literature, Marathi
Marathi historical fiction
  USE Historical fiction, Marathi
Marathi imprints *(May Subd Geog)*
Marathi language
  [PK2351-2378]
  UF Mahratta language
      Mahratti language
      Murathee language
  BT Indo-Aryan languages, Modern
  RT Halbi language
      Konkani language
  NT Koshti dialect (Marathi)
      Kunabi dialect
      Nagpuri dialect
  — Alphabet
      NT Modi alphabet
  — Dictionaries
      NT Picture dictionaries, Marathi
Marathi literature
  [PK2400-2458]
  NT Folk literature, Marathi
      Hindu literature, Marathi
      Protest literature, Marathi
  — To 1500
  — 1500-1800
  — 20th century
Marathi literature (English)
  USE English literature—Marathi authors
Marathi manuscripts
  USE Manuscripts, Marathi
Marathi mural painting and decoration
  USE Mural painting and decoration,
      Marathi
Marathi narrative poetry
  USE Narrative poetry, Marathi
Marathi newspapers *(May Subd Geog)*
Marathi one-act plays
  USE One-act plays, Marathi
Marathi paleography
  USE Paleography, Marathi
Marathi patriotic poetry
  USE Patriotic poetry, Marathi
Marathi periodicals *(May Subd Geog)*
Marathi philology
Marathi picture dictionaries
  USE Picture dictionaries, Marathi
Marathi poetry *(May Subd Geog)*
  NT Narrative poetry, Marathi
      Patriotic poetry, Marathi
      Religious poetry, Marathi
  — To 1500
  — 1500-1800

Marathi poets
  USE Poets, Marathi
Marathi prose literature *(May Subd Geog)*
Marathi protest literature
  USE Protest literature, Marathi
Marathi radio plays
  USE Radio plays, Marathi
Marathi religious poetry
  USE Religious poetry, Marathi
Marathi short stories
  USE Short stories, Marathi
Marathi songs
  USE Songs, Marathi
Marathi wit and humor
  BT Indic wit and humor
Marathi wit and humor, Pictorial
  (May Subd Geog)
Marathon, Battle of, 490 B.C.
  [DF225.4]
  BT Greece—History—Persian Wars, 500-
      449 B.C.—Campaigns
Marathon canoe racing
  USE Canoe racing, Marathon
Marathon running *(May Subd Geog)*
  [GV1065-GV1065.23]
  UF Distance running
      Marathoning (Running)
      Running, Marathon
  BT Running races
  NT Boston Marathon
  — Hawaii
      NT Honolulu Marathon
  — Japan
      NT Hakone Ekiden
  — New York (State)
      NT New York City Marathon, New
          York, N.Y.
  — New Zealand
      NT Comrades Marathon
Marathon swimming
  USE Swimming, Long distance
Marathoning (Running)
  USE Marathon running
Marauder (Bomber)
  [UG1242.B7]
  UF B-26 Marauder (Bomber)
  BT Bombers
      Martin airplanes
Maravans
  USE Maravars
Maravars
  [DS432.M26]
  UF Maravans
      Maravas
  BT Caste—India
      Ethnology—India
Maravas
  USE Maravars
Maravi (African people)
  USE Chewa (African people)
Marberry family *(Not Subd Geog)*
Marbits Torah
  [BM652]
  BT Judaism—Functionaries
      Rabbis
Marble *(May Subd Geog)*
  [TN967]
  BT Limestone
  NT Marezzo marble
      Onyx marble
  — Electric properties
  — Staining
      USE Stains and staining
Marble cutters
  USE Stone-cutters
Marble industry and trade
  (May Subd Geog)
  UF Marble quarrying
  BT Stone industry and trade
  — Law and legislation *(May Subd Geog)*
      BT Mining law

Marble papers
  USE Marbled papers
Marble quarrying
  USE Marble industry and trade
Marble sculpture *(May Subd Geog)*
  [NB1218]
  BT Sculpture
  — 20th century *(May Subd Geog)*
  — Greece
      NT Phigalian marbles
Marble sculpture, Belgian *(May Subd Geog)*
  UF Belgian marble sculpture
Marble sculpture, Classical
  (May Subd Geog)
  [NB144]
  UF Classical marble sculpture
  BT Sculpture, Classical
  NT Marble sculpture, Greek
      Townley marbles
  — Reproduction *(May Subd Geog)*
      UF Reproduction of classical marble
          sculpture
Marble sculpture, German *(May Subd Geog)*
  UF German marble sculpture
  NT Klinger, Max, 1857-1920. Salome
Marble sculpture, Greek
  BT Marble sculpture, Classical
  NT Kore statues
      Venus de Milo (Sculpture)
Marble sculpture, Greek, [etc.]
  (May Subd Geog)
Marble sculpture, Italian *(May Subd Geog)*
  UF Italian marble sculpture
  NT Michelangelo Buonarroti, 1475-1564.
      David
      Michelangelo Buonarroti, 1475-1564.
      Moses
      Michelangelo Buonarroti, 1475-1564.
      Pietà
      Michelangelo Buonarroti, 1475-1564.
      Saint John
Marble sculpture, Renaissance
  (May Subd Geog)
  UF Renaissance marble sculpture
  — Italy
      NT Michelangelo Buonarroti, 1475-
          1564. Moses
          Michelangelo Buonarroti, 1475-
          1564. Pietà
          Michelangelo Buonarroti, 1475-
          1564. Saint John
Marble sculpture, Roman *(May Subd Geog)*
  UF Roman marble sculpture
  — Expertising
Marbled cat
  [QL737.C2]
  UF Felis marmorata
      Pardofelis marmorata
Marbled papers *(May Subd Geog)*
  UF Marble papers
  BT Decorative paper
  RT Marbling (Bookbinding)
Marbled salamander
  USE Ambystoma opacum
Marbled seal
  USE Ringed seal
Marbled wood quail
  USE Odontophorus gujanensis
Marbles (Game)
  [GV1213]
Marbling
  [TT330 (Painting)]
  BT Painting, Industrial
Marbling (Bookbinding) *(May Subd Geog)*
  [Z271]
  UF Bookbinding—Marbling
  BT Bookbinding
      Endpapers
  RT Marbled papers
  NT Paste papers

Marburg, Lake (Pa.)   (Not Subd Geog)
  UF Lake Marburg (Pa.)
  BT Lakes—Pennsylvania
     Reservoirs—Pennsylvania
Marburg conference, 1529
  BT Disputations, Religious
Marburg Neo-Kantianism
  USE Marburg school of philosophy
Marburg school of philosophy
  UF Marburg Neo-Kantianism
  BT Philosophy, German—19th century
     Philosophy, German—20th century
  RT Neo-Kantianism
Marburg virus
  BT Rhabdoviruses
Marburg virus disease
  [RC167]
  BT Virus diseases
Marburger system (Computer system)
  [BF39.5]
Marc (Oenology)   (May Subd Geog)
  BT Wine and wine making
MARC-based automated serials system
  USE MASS (Serials control system)
MARC Project
  USE MARC System
MARC System   (May Subd Geog)
  [Z699.4.M2]
  UF Machine-readable Catalog System
     MARC Project
     Project MARC
  BT Libraries—Automation
  NT UNIMARC System
— Format
— Canada
  NT CATS System
— Finland
  UF FINMARC
— Great Britain
  UF BNB MARC
     U.K. MARC
— Korea (South)
  UF KOR MARC
— Poland
  NT APIN (Information retrieval
     system)
— South Africa
  UF SAMARC System
Marcahuasi Plateau (Peru)
  UF Meseta de Marcahuasi (Peru)
  BT Plateaus—Peru
Marcand family
  USE Marchand family
Marcasite   (May Subd Geog)
  [QE391.M3]
  BT Sulphide minerals
Marcelina Kué Site (Paraguay)
  BT Paraguay—Antiquities
Marcellus Village Cemetery (Marcellus, N.Y.)
  UF Village Cemetery (Marcellus, N.Y.)
  BT Cemeteries—New York (State)
Marcelo de Ridder Prize
  USE Premio Marcelo de Ridder
Marcey family
  USE Marcy family
March (Music)
  BT Military music—History and criticism
March Action, 1921 (Germany)
  USE Germany—History—March Uprising,
     1921
March family
  USE Marsh family
March flies
  USE Bibionidae
March Incident, 1931 (Japan)
  USE Japan—History—March and October
     Incidents, 1931

March of humanity on earth and toward the
  cosmos (Mural painting)
  USE Siqueiros, David Alfaro.   March of
     humanity on earth and toward the
     cosmos
March of the Ten Thousand, 401 B.C.
  USE Greece—History—Expedition of
     Cyrus, 401 B.C.
March on Rome, Italy, 1922
  USE Italy—History—March on Rome, 1922
**March on Washington for Jobs and Freedom,
1963**
  BT Afro-Americans—Civil rights
March out of the civil guard (Painting)
  USE Rembrandt Harmenszoon van Rijn,
     1606-1669.   Night watch
March Up-country, 401 B.C.
  USE Greece—History—Expedition of
     Cyrus, 401 B.C.
March Uprising, 1921 (Germany)
  USE Germany—History—March Uprising,
     1921
Marcha de la humanidad en la tiera y hacia el
  cosmos (Mural painting)
  USE Siqueiros, David Alfaro.   March of
     humanity on earth and toward the
     cosmos
Marchaliella
  USE Zopfia
Marchand family   (Not Subd Geog)
  UF Marcand family
     Marchant family
     Marchants family
     Marquand family
  RT Merchant family
     Mershon family
Marchand Island (Marquesas Islands)
  USE Nuka Hiva (Marquesas Islands)
Marchant family
  USE Marchand family
Marchantiales
  [QK555.M2]
Marchants family
  USE Marchand family
Marches
    Here are entered collections of march music for
various mediums. Individual marches and collections
of marches for a specific medium are entered under
the heading followed by specification of medium.
  UF Quick-steps
Marches (Accordion)
  [M175.A4]
  BT Accordion music
Marches (Band)
  [M1247]
  [M1260]
  BT Band music
Marches (Chamber orchestra)
  [M1046]
  [M1060]
  BT Chamber-orchestra music
Marches (Clarinet and piano)
  [M248-252]
  BT Clarinet and piano music
Marches (Flute)
  [M60-64]
  BT Flute music
Marches (Flute and continuo)
  BT Flute and continuo music
Marches (Flute and piano)
  [M240-244]
  BT Flute and piano music
Marches (Flutes (2))
  [M288-9]
  BT Flute music (Flutes (2))
Marches (Flutes (2), percussion)
  [M385]
Marches (Guitar and piano)
  [M276-7]
  BT Guitar and piano music

Marches (Harp)
  [M115-119]
  BT Harp music
Marches (Horn and piano)
  [M255-259]
  BT Horn and piano music
Marches (Instrumental ensemble)
  [M985]
Marches (Oboe and continuo)
  BT Oboe and continuo music
Marches (Orchestra)
  [M1046]
  [M1060]
  BT Orchestral music
Marches (Organ)
  [M6-M7]
  [M11-M13]
  BT Organ music
**Marches (Percussion, trombones (2), trumpets
(3), tuba)**
  [M785]
Marches (Piano)
  [M28]
  BT Piano music
Marches (Piano, 4 hands)
  [M200-M201]
  [M204]
  BT Piano music (4 hands)
Marches (Piano (4 hands) and reed-organ)
  [M191-5]
  BT Piano (4 hands) and reed-organ music
**Marches (Piano, bassoon, clarinet, flute, oboe,
trumpet, violin, viola, violoncello)**
  [M920-924]
  BT Nonets (Piano, bassoon, clarinet, flute,
     oboe, trumpet, violin, viola,
     violoncello)
Marches (Pianos (2))
  [M214-215]
  BT Piano music (Pianos (2))
Marches (Piccolo and piano)
  [M240-244]
  BT Piccolo and piano music
Marches (Salon orchestra)
  [M1350]
  BT Salon-orchestra music
Marches (Saxophone and piano)
  [M268-9]
  BT Saxophone and piano music
Marches (String orchestra)
  [M1145]
  [M1160]
  BT String-orchestra music
Marches (Trombone and piano)
  [M262-3]
  BT Trombone and piano music
Marches (Trumpet)
  [M85-89]
  BT Trumpet music
Marches (Trumpet and organ)
  [M182-186]
  BT Trumpet and organ music
Marches (Trumpet and piano)
  [M260-261]
  BT Trumpet and piano music
Marches (Tuba with instrumental ensemble)
  BT Tuba with instrumental ensemble
Marches (Tubas (2))
  [M288-M289]
  BT Tuba music (Tubas (2))
Marches (Ukulele and piano)
  [M282-3]
  BT Ukulele and piano music
Marches (Violin and continuo)
  BT Violin and continuo music
Marches (Violin and harpsichord)
  [M217-M218]
  [M221-M223]
  BT Violin and harpsichord music
Marches (Violin and piano)
  [M217-M218]

[M221-M223]
BT Violin and piano music
Marches (Violins (3))
[M349-353]
BT String trios (Violins (3))
Marches (Voice with piano)
BT Songs with piano
Marches (Wind ensemble)
[M955-7]
BT Wind ensembles
Marchfeld, Battle of, July 5-6, 1809
USE Wagram, Battle of, 1809
Marchfeld, Battle of, May 21-22, 1809
USE Aspern, Battle of, 1809
Marchi family *(Not Subd Geog)*
Marchia Nowa (Poland)
USE Nowa Marchia (Poland)
Marching
[UD310-315]
BT Military art and science
Marching bands
[MT733.4]
BT Bands (Music)
Drill (not military)
Drill and minor tactics
Marci family
USE Marcy family
Marcianites
USE Messalians
Marcipa
[QL561.N7]
BT Noctuidae
Marcipalina
[QL561.N7]
BT Noctuidae
Marck family *(Not Subd Geog)*
UF La Marck family
Lamarck family
Marck House (Paris, France)
USE Hôtel de La Marck (Paris, France)
Marckum family
USE Markham family
Marco Island (Fla. : Island)
UF Key Marco (Fla.)
BT Islands—Florida
Marco Polo Bridge Incident, 1937
UF Lukouchiao Incident, 1937
BT Sino-Japanese Conflict, 1937-1945
Marco Polo sheep
USE Argali
Marcom family
USE Markham family
Marcomanni
[DD78.M3 (Germany)]
BT Germanic tribes
Marcomannic War, 167-180
BT Germany—History—To 843
Marconi system of wireless telegraphy
USE Telegraph, Wireless—Marconi system
Marcot family
USE Marcotte family
Marcotte family *(Not Subd Geog)*
UF Marcot family
Marcq Saint Hilaire's method
USE Saint Hilaire method
Marcum family
USE Markham family
Marcy family *(Not Subd Geog)*
UF Marcey family
Marci family
Marsey family
Mardi Gras
USE Carnival
Mardikh, Tall (Syria)
USE Ebla (Ancient city)
Marduk (Babylonian deity)
[BL1625.M37]
BT Gods, Assyro-Babylonian
Mare (Papuan people)
USE Bunak (Papuan people)

Mare Adriatico
USE Adriatic Sea
Mare Crisium (Moon)
UF Crisium, Mare (Moon)
Sea of Crises (Moon)
BT Moon—Surface
Maré family *(Not Subd Geog)*
UF Maree family
Maré Island (New Caledonia)
UF Britannia Island (New Caledonia)
Mari Island (New Caledonia)
Mengöne Island (New Caledonia)
Nengone Island (New Caledonia)
BT Islands—New Caledonia
Mare language
USE Bunak language
Mare Tirreno
USE Tyrrhenian Sea
Mare Tyrrhenum
USE Tyrrhenian Sea
Marechite Indians
USE Malecite Indians
Maree family
USE Maré family
Mareganka River (Lithuania)
USE Merkys River (Lithuania)
Marek's disease *(May Subd Geog)*
[SF995.6.M33]
UF Acute leukosis of poultry
Avian lymphomatosis
Fowl paralysis
Lymphomatosis, Avian
Neurolymphomatosis gallinarum
BT Avian leukosis
Herpesvirus diseases in animals
Virus diseases in poultry
Marellia
[QL508.A2]
BT Acrididae
Marellia remipes
[QL508.A2]
Maremma (Italy)
Maremma, Parco nazionale della (Italy)
USE Parco nazionale della Maremma (Italy)
Mareng language
USE Maring language
Marengo, Battle of, 1800
[DC223.7]
BT Napoleonic Wars, 1800-1814—
Campaigns—Italy
Mareotis Lake (Egypt)
USE Maryūt, Lake (Egypt)
Marepotamo River (Italy)
BT Rivers—Italy
Mares
UF Dams (Horses)
BT Females
Horses
Mares family
USE Myers family
Maresma (Spain)
USE Maresme (Spain)
Maresme (Spain)
UF Costa de Levante (Spain)
Costa de Llevant (Spain)
Levante Coast (Spain)
Llevant Coast (Spain)
Maresma (Spain)
Marismas (Spain)
BT Coasts—Spain
Mareth Line
Marey family
USE Merry family
Marezzo marble
[TP871]
BT Marble
Marfan-Achard syndrome
USE Marfan syndrome
Marfan syndrome *(May Subd Geog)*
[RC580.M37]

UF Achrochondrohyperplasia
Arachnodactyly
Congenital mesodermal dystrophy
Dolichostenomelia
Dystrophia mesodermalis congenita
Hyperchondroplasia
Marfan-Achard syndrome
Marfan's syndrome
Spider fingers (Disease)
Strebdodactyly
BT Connective tissues—Diseases
Genetic disorders
Syndromes
Marfan's syndrome
USE Marfan syndrome
Marfleet family *(Not Subd Geog)*
Margamkali (Dance)
BT Dancing
Margaree River (N.S.)
BT Rivers—Nova Scotia
Margaric acid
[QD305.A2]
Margarin
USE Margarine
Margarine *(May Subd Geog)*
[TP684.M3 (Manufacture)]
UF Butter, Artificial
Margarin
Oleomargarine
BT Oils and fats, Edible
NT Vanaspati
— **Law and legislation** *(May Subd Geog)*
BT Food law and legislation
— Tariff
USE Tariff on margarine
Margarine industry *(May Subd Geog)*
[HD9330.M37-374]
Margarita Island (Venezuela)
UF Isla de Margarita (Venezuela)
BT Islands—Venezuela
Margarodes polonicus
USE Porphyrophora polonica
Margarodidae
[QL527.M37]
UF Monophlebidae
BT Homoptera
Scale-insects
NT Icerya
Matsucoccus
Porphyrophora
Sphaeraspis
Xylococcus
Margaronia
[QL561.P9]
BT Pyralidae
Margay cat
Margeride Mountains (France)
UF Montagnes de la Margeride (France)
BT Massif Central (France)
Mountains—France
Marget family
USE Merget family
Margett family
USE Merget family
Margetts family
USE Merget family
Margherita Palace (Rome, Italy)
USE Palazzo Margherita (Rome, Italy)
Marghi language
USE Margi language
Margi language
UF Marghi language
BT Chadic languages
Margin trading
USE Margins (Security trading)
Marginal costing
USE Direct costing
Marginal peoples
USE Marginality, Social
Marginal productivity
UF Productivity, Marginal

Marginal productivity *(Continued)*
  BT Economics
Marginal utility
    [HB201-5]
  UF Final utility
      Utility, Final
      Utility, Marginal
  BT Austrian school of economists
      Economics
      Utility theory
      Value
  NT Consumers' surplus
Marginalia
  UF Adversaria
  RT Autographs
      Books—Owners' marks
      Manuscripts
  NT Bibliography—Association books
Marginalist school of economics
  USE Austrian school of economists
Marginality, Social *(May Subd Geog)*
    [GN367 (Ethnology)]
    [HM136 (Sociology)]
    [HN50-HN942.5 (By country)]
  UF Marginal peoples
      Social marginality
  BT Assimilation (Sociology)
      Culture conflict
      Social isolation
      Sociology
  RT Socially handicapped
Margined madtom
    [QL638.I3]
  UF Madtom, Margined
      Noturus insignis
      Rabida insignis
Marginellidae
    [QL430.5.M3]
  BT Neogastropoda
Marginellidae, Fossil
  BT Neogastropoda, Fossil
Marginolamellidae, Fossil
  USE Globorotaliidae, Fossil
Margins, Continental
  USE Continental margins
Margins (Postage-stamps)
  USE Postage-stamps—Margins
Margins (Security trading)
  (May Subd Geog)
  UF Margin trading
      Stock margins
  BT Securities
      Speculation
      Stock-exchange
      Stocks
  — **Law and legislation** *(May Subd Geog)*
Margins in books
  UF Book margins
      Books—Margins
  BT Bibliography
      Printing, Practical—Imposition, etc.
Margoles family
  USE Margolis family
Margolies family
  USE Margolis family
Margolis family *(Not Subd Geog)*
  UF Margoles family
      Margolies family
Margosa
    [QK495.M52 (Botany)]
    [SB317.M34 (Culture)]
  UF Azadirachta indica
      Melia azadirachta
      Melia indica
      Melia parviflora
      Neem
      Nim
  BT Medicinal plants
      Oilseed plants
  NT Neem cake

Margosatubig Subanun dialect
  USE Southern Subanen dialect
Margret family
  USE Merget family
Marguerite Bourgeoys Farm (Montréal, Québec)
  USE Maison Saint-Gabriel (Montréal, Québec)
Marguot family
  USE Merget family
Mari (Ancient city) *(Not Subd Geog)*
    [DS99.M3]
  UF Hariri, Tall (Syria)
      Khirbat al-Marī (Syria)
      Tall Hariri (Syria)
      Tell Hariri (Syria)
  BT Cities and towns, Ruined, extinct, etc.
      —Syria
      Syria—Antiquities
Mari
    [DK34.M37]
  UF Cheremis
      Cheremisses
      Cheremissians
  BT Ethnology—Russian S.F.S.R.
      Finno-Ugrians
Mari art
  USE Art, Mari
Mari authors
  USE Authors, Mari
Mari children's stories
  USE Children's stories, Mari
Mari drama *(May Subd Geog)*
Mari fiction *(May Subd Geog)*
  NT Children's stories, Mari
      Short stories, Mari
Mari folk literature
  USE Folk literature, Mari
Mari folk-songs
  USE Folk-songs, Mari
Mari Island (New Caledonia)
  USE Maré Island (New Caledonia)
Mari language
    [PH801-807]
  UF Cheremis language
      Cheremissian language
  BT Finno-Ugric languages
      Russian S.F.S.R.—Languages
Mari literature *(May Subd Geog)*
    [PH811-836]
  NT Folk literature, Mari
Mari philology
Mari poetry *(May Subd Geog)*
Mari riddles
  USE Riddles, Mari
Mari short stories
  USE Short stories, Mari
Maria (Indic people) *(May Subd Geog)*
  UF Madia (Indic people)
      Mariya (Indic people)
  BT Ethnology—India
      Gonds
Maria da Fonte Uprising, 1846
  USE Portugal—History—Uprising, 1846
Maria Forest (Sumbawa, Indonesia)
  UF Hutan Maria (Sumbawa, Indonesia)
  BT Forests and forestry—Indonesia
María Leonza (Legendary character)
  USE Lionza, María (Legendary character)
María Lionza (Legendary character)
  USE Lionza, María (Legendary character)
Maria Theresa dollar
    [CJ2585]
Mariachi
    [ML3485]
  BT Bands (Music)
      Folk music—Mexico
Marian Year
    [BT646]
  UF Year, Marian

  BT Holy Year
      Indulgences
      Mary, Blessed Virgin, Saint—Cult
Mariaretabel van de O.-L.-V. Basiliek van Tongeren (Sculpture)
  USE Mariaretabel van Tongeren (Sculpture)
Mariaretabel van Tongeren (Sculpture)
  UF Mariaretabel van de O.-L.-V. Basiliek
      van Tongeren (Sculpture)
      O.-L.-V. Basiliek van Tongeren
      Mariaretabel (Sculpture)
      Our Lady of Tongeren retable
      (Sculpture)
      Tongeren Mariaretabel (Sculpture)
  BT Altarpieces, Flemish
      Sculpture, Flemish
Mariavites
    [BX4795.M2-28]
Maribyrnong River (Vic.)
  BT Rivers—Australia
Maricheet Indians
  USE Malecite Indians
Marīci
Maricopa Indians
    [E99.M]
  UF Cocomaricopa Indians
      Pipatsje Indians
  BT Indians of North America
      Yuman Indians
  — **Reservations**
      NT Salt River Indian Reservation
        (Ariz.)
Maricopa language
    [PM1711]
  BT Yuman languages
Maricopa Wells (Ariz.)
Maricopa Wells (Ariz.), Battle of, 1857
    [E83.8565]
  BT Indians of North America—Arizona—
      Wars
Mariculture *(May Subd Geog)*
    [SH138]
  UF Aquaculture, Marine
      Aquiculture, Marine
      Marine aquaculture
      Sea farming
  BT Aquaculture
      Biosaline resources
      Marine biology
  NT Fish-culture
      Marine algae culture
      Shellfish culture
Marie de Médicis, Queen, consort of Henry IV, King of France, 1573-1642
  — **Portraits**
      UF Marie de Médicis, Queen, consort
        of Henry IV, King of France,
        1573-1642—Portraits,
        caricatures, etc.
  — Portraits, caricatures, etc.
      USE Marie de Médicis, Queen,
        consort of Henry IV, King of
        France, 1573-1642—Portraits
Marie family
  USE Marye family
Marie-Struempell disease
  USE Ankylosing spondylitis
Mariée mise à nu par ses célibataires, même (Assemblage)
  USE Duchamp, Marcel, 1887-1968. Bride
      stripped bare by her bachelors, even
Mariel Boatlift, 1980
  UF Boatlift, Mariel, 1980
      Cuban Boatlift, 1980
      Cuban Sealift, 1980
      Flotilla, Freedom, 1980
      Freedom Flotilla, 1980
      Mariel-Key West Boatlift, 1980
      Mariel Sealift, 1980
      Sealift, Cuban, 1980
      Sealift, Mariel, 1980

BT Cuba—Emigration and immigration
    United States—Emigration and
      immigration
Mariel-Key West Boatlift, 1980
  USE Mariel Boatlift, 1980
Mariel Sealift, 1980
  USE Mariel Boatlift, 1980
Marienburg, Truce of, 1629
  USE Altmark, Truce of, 1629
Marigl dialect
  BT Dom dialects
  NT Golin dialect
Marigold
  USE Marigolds
Marigolds *(May Subd Geog)*
  ⌜*QK495.C74 (Botany)*⌝
  ⌜*SB413.M37 (Ornamental plant)*⌝
  UF Marigold
    Tagetes
  BT Compositae
  NT Tagetes lucida
Mariguana Island (Bahamas)
  USE Mayaguana Island (Bahamas)
Marihuana
  ⌜*HV5822.M3 (Social pathology)*⌝
  UF Ganja
    Marijuana
  BT Cannabis
    Drug abuse
  RT Marihuana industry
  NT Cookery (Marihuana)
  — Contamination
    UF Contamination of marihuana
  — Law and legislation *(May Subd Geog)*
  — Taxation *(May Subd Geog)*
  — — Law and legislation
    (May Subd Geog)
Marihuana industry *(May Subd Geog)*
  ⌜*HD9019.M38-382*⌝
  RT Marihuana
Mariinsk Waterway (R.S.F.S.R.)
  USE Volga-Baltic Waterway (R.S.F.S.R.)
Mariinskaia vodnaia sistema (R.S.F.S.R.)
  USE Volga-Baltic Waterway (R.S.F.S.R.)
Marijuana
  USE Marihuana
Marikina
  USE Saguinus
Marille (African people)
  USE Dasanetch (African people)
Marimba
  ⌜*ML1040*⌝
  UF Marimbaphone
  BT Percussion instruments
  RT Vibraphone
    Xylophone
Marimba and clarinet music
  USE Clarinet and marimba music
Marimba and euphonium music
  USE Euphonium and marimba music
Marimba and flute music
  USE Flute and marimba music
Marimba and organ music
  ⌜*M182-186*⌝
  UF Organ and marimba music
Marimba and piano music
  ⌜*M284-5*⌝
  UF Piano and marimba music
  NT Suites (Marimba and piano)
Marimba and piano music, Arranged
  ⌜*M284-5*⌝
  NT Concertos (Marimba)—Solo with piano
    Marimba with orchestra, Arranged—
      Solo with piano
    Suites (Marimba with orchestra)—Solo
      with piano
Marimba and piano with string orchestra
  ⌜*M1140-1141*⌝
  RT Concertos (Marimba and piano with
    string orchestra)

Marimba and saxophone music
  USE Saxophone and marimba music
Marimba and trumpet music
  USE Trumpet and marimba music
Marimba music
  ⌜*M175.X6*⌝
  SA Concertos, Minuets, Sonatas, Suites,
    and similar headings with
    specification of instruments; Trios
    ⌜*Quartets, etc.*⌝ *followed by*
    specifications which include the
    marimba; also Percussion ensembles,
    Percussion music, *and headings that*
    begin with the words marimba or
    marimbas
  NT Trios (Flute, guitar, marimba)
    Trios (Flute, marimba, vibraphone)
Marimba with band
  ⌜*M1205-M1206*⌝
  ⌜*M1257*⌝
  RT Concertos (Marimba with band)
Marimba with orchestra
  ⌜*M1038-9*⌝
  BT Orchestral music
  RT Concertos (Marimba)
  NT Suites (Marimba with orchestra)
Marimba with orchestra, Arranged
  ⌜*M1038-9*⌝
  — Solo with piano
    ⌜*M1039*⌝
    BT Marimba and piano music,
      Arranged
Marimba with string orchestra
  ⌜*M1138-1139*⌝
  RT Concertos (Marimba with string
    orchestra)
Marimbaphone
  USE Marimba
Marin Peninsula (Calif.)
  BT Peninsulas—California
Marina (Cagliari, Sardinia)
  USE Quartiere Marina (Cagliari, Sardinia)
Marina Island (Vanuatu)
  USE Espíritu Santo Island (Vanuatu)
Marinades
  ⌜*TX819.M26*⌝
  RT Sauces
Marinahua language
  USE Sharanahua language
Marinas *(May Subd Geog)*
  ⌜*TC353-TC373 (Hydraulic*
    engineering)⌝
  ⌜*VK369 (Navigation)*⌝
  UF Yacht basins
  BT Boats and boating
    Harbors
    Yachts and yachting
  RT Anchorage
  — Law and legislation *(May Subd Geog)*
  — Location
  — — Law and legislation
    (May Subd Geog)
Marinawa language
  USE Sharanahua language
Marinbata language
  USE Murinbata language
Marind tribes
  ⌜*DU744 (History)*⌝
  ⌜*GN671.N5 (New Guinea)*⌝
  BT Ethnology—Indonesia
Marindinese language
  ⌜*PL6621.M3*⌝
  UF Meraukese language
    Tugeri language
  BT Papuan languages
Marine accidents
  UF Accidents, Marine
    Ships—Accidents
  BT Accidents
    Maritime law

  NT Boats and boating—Accidents and
      injuries
    Collisions at sea
    Ships—Fires and fire prevention
    Shipwrecks
    Submarine disasters
  — Liability
    USE Liability for marine accidents
Marine aids
  USE Aids to navigation
Marine air conditioning
  USE Ships—Air conditioning
Marine algae *(May Subd Geog)*
  ⌜*QK570.2 (Botany)*⌝
  ⌜*SH390-SH390.5 (Fisheries)*⌝
  UF Algae, Marine
    Sea vegetables
    Seaweed
    Vegetables, Sea
  BT Algae
    Marine flora
    Marine phytoplankton
  NT Cookery (Marine algae)
  — Harvesting
Marine algae, Edible
  USE Marine algae as food
Marine algae as feed
  ⌜*SF99.M*⌝
  BT Algae as feed
Marine algae as fertilizer *(May Subd Geog)*
  ⌜*S661.2.M3*⌝
  BT Aquatic plants as fertilizer
Marine algae as food *(May Subd Geog)*
  UF Edible marine algae
    Edible seaweeds
    Limu
    Marine algae, Edible
    Seaweed as food
  BT Algae as food
  NT Agar as food
    Nori
Marine algae culture *(May Subd Geog)*
  ⌜*SH390-391.5*⌝
  UF Seaweed culture
  BT Algae culture
    Mariculture
    Salt-tolerant crops
Marine algae industry *(May Subd Geog)*
Marine animal oils
  UF Marine oils, Animal
  BT Oils and fats
  NT Fish oils
    Whale-oil
Marine anthropology
  USE Maritime anthropology
Marine aquaculture
  USE Mariculture
Marine aquarium fishes *(May Subd Geog)*
  ⌜*SF457.1*⌝
  UF Saltwater aquarium fishes
  BT Aquarium fishes
Marine aquariums
  UF Aquariums, Marine
    Aquariums, Saltwater
    Saltwater aquariums
  BT Aquariums
    Marine biology
    Marine fauna
    Marine flora
  NT Marine invertebrates as pets
Marine aquariums, Public *(May Subd Geog)*
  ⌜*QL78.5*⌝
  UF Oceanariums
    Public marine aquariums
Marine archaeologists *(May Subd Geog)*
  UF Archaeologists, Marine
    Underwater archaeologists
  BT Archaeologists
    Underwater archaeology
Marine archaeology
  USE Underwater archaeology

Marine architects
USE Naval architects
Marine architecture
USE Naval architecture
Marine art *(May Subd Geog)*
[N8230]
BT Art
NT Marine drawing
Marine painting
— **17th century** *(May Subd Geog)*
— **18th century** *(May Subd Geog)*
— **20th century** *(May Subd Geog)*
Marine art, American, [**British, etc.**]
(May Subd Geog)
Marine art, Dutch *(May Subd Geog)*
UF Dutch marine art
Marine art, English *(May Subd Geog)*
UF English marine art
— **Dutch influences**
BT Netherlands—Civilization
Marine art, German *(May Subd Geog)*
UF German marine art
Marine artists *(May Subd Geog)*
BT Artists
Marine bacteria *(May Subd Geog)*
[QR106]
UF Bacteria, Marine
BT Bacteria
Marine microbiology
Marine bacteriology
USE Marine microbiology
Marine biological laboratories
USE Marine laboratories
Marine biologists *(May Subd Geog)*
BT Aquatic biologists
Biologists
NT Marine biology—Vocational guidance
Marine biology *(May Subd Geog)*
[QH91-QH95 (Natural history)]
UF Biological oceanography
Deep-sea exploration
Hydrobiology
Ocean life
Sea life
BT Aquatic biology
Biology
Marine sciences
Natural history
Oceanography
Underwater exploration
RT Dredging (Biology)
NT Aquatic pests
Fishery oceanography
Mariculture
Marine aquariums
Marine ecology
Marine fauna
Marine flora
Marine laboratories
Marine microbiology
Marine pharmacology
Marine radioecology
Marine resources
Marine sediments
Nets
Ocean bottom
Photography, Submarine
Radioactive tracers in marine biology
Seashore biology
Ships—Fouling
— Information storage and retrieval systems
USE Information storage and retrieval
systems—Marine biology
— **Research** *(May Subd Geog)*
— **Vocational guidance** *(May Subd Geog)*
[QH91.45]
BT Marine biologists
Marine biology research vessels
(May Subd Geog)
BT Oceanographic research ships
Research vessels

NT Fishery research vessels
Marine boilers
USE Steam-boilers, Marine
Marine borers *(May Subd Geog)*
[TC201]
BT Aquatic pests
Marine fouling organisms
Wood—Deterioration
NT Ship-worms
Marine canvas work *(May Subd Geog)*
BT Boats and boating—Equipment and
supplies
Canvas
Textile crafts
Marine caves *(May Subd Geog)*
[GB601.8]
UF Sea caves
BT Caves
Marine chemistry
USE Chemical oceanography
Marine compressors
[VM821]
BT Compressors
Marine engines
Marine machinery
Marine refrigeration
Marine cookery
USE Cookery, Marine
Marine Corps wives *(May Subd Geog)*
UF Wives of Marine Corps personnel
BT Military wives
Marine corrosion
USE Sea-water corrosion
Ships—Corrosion
Marine deposits
USE Marine sediments
Marine diesel motors
[VM770]
BT Diesel motor
Marine engines
Motorboats—Motors
— **Bearings**
— **Cylinders**
— **Dynamics**
— **Fuel systems**
— **Lubrication**
— **Superchargers**
— **Vibration**
Marine disasters
USE Shipwrecks
Marine disposal of radioactive wastes
USE Radioactive waste disposal in the
ocean
Marine drawing *(May Subd Geog)*
[NC817]
UF Drawing, Marine
BT Drawing
Marine art
Marine drilling platforms
USE Drilling platforms
Marine ecology *(May Subd Geog)*
UF Biological oceanography
BT Aquatic ecology
Ecology
Marine biology
NT Coral reef ecology
Deep-sea ecology
Estuarine ecology
Hydrothermal vent ecology
Kelp bed ecology
Marine productivity
Marine radioecology
Red tide
Tide pool ecology
Marine electronics
USE Boats and boating—Electronic
equipment
Electronics in navigation
Ships—Electronic equipment
Marine engineering *(May Subd Geog)*
[VM595-VM989]

Here are entered general works on the application
of engineering to ships and their machinery. Works
on the engineering aspects of equipment and tech-
niques facilitating operations beneath the surface of
the ocean in order to exploit its resources are entered
under Ocean engineering.
UF Engineering, Marine
Marine technology
Naval engineering
BT Civil engineering
Engineering
Mechanical engineering
Naval architecture
Naval art and science
Steam-navigation
NT Electricity on ships
Marine machinery
Marine machinery industry
Marine pipe-fitting
Nautical instruments
Plastics in marine engineering
Ship propulsion
Ship resistance
Steering-gear
Underwater propulsion
Underwater welding and cutting
United States. Navy—Enginemen
Vibration (Marine engineering)
— **Vocational guidance** *(May Subd Geog)*
BT Marine engineers
Marine engineers *(May Subd Geog)*
UF Naval engineers
BT Engineers
Steam engineers
NT Marine engineering—Vocational
guidance
United States. Navy—Firemen
Marine engines
[VM731-775]
UF Steam-engines, Marine
BT Engines
Marine machinery
Steam-engines
NT Diesel motor
Junks—Motors
Life-boats—Motors
Marine compressors
Marine diesel motors
Marine gas-turbines
Marine nuclear reactor plants
Motorboats—Motors
Sailboats—Auxiliary engines
Steam-boilers, Marine
Steam-turbines, Marine
— **Carburetors**
— — **Parts**
BT Machine parts
— **Cooling**
UF Cooling of marine engines
BT Diesel motor—Cooling
Internal combustion engines—
Cooling
— **Dynamics**
— **Fluid dynamics**
— **Foundations**
BT Foundations
— **Fuel consumption**
— **Lubrication**
— **Maintenance and repair**
NT United States. Navy—Enginemen
United States. Navy—Machinist's
mates
— **Superchargers**
Marine environment pollution
USE Marine pollution
Marine ethnology
USE Maritime anthropology
Marine fauna *(May Subd Geog)*
[QL121-138]

UF Animals, Sea
　　Marine zoology
　　Sea animals
BT Aquatic animals
　　Corals
　　Marine biology
　　Zoology
NT Coral reef fauna
　　Dangerous marine animals
　　Echo scattering layers
　　Estuarine fauna
　　Insects, Marine
　　Interstitial fauna
　　Marine aquariums
　　Marine fishes
　　Marine fouling organisms
　　Marine invertebrates
　　Marine mammals
　　Sea monsters
— **Food**
— **Geographical distribution**
— **Physiology**
Marine fishes *(May Subd Geog)*
UF Sea fishes
BT Fishes
　　Marine fauna
NT Fishes, Deep-sea
— **Age**
— **Anatomy**
— **Development**
　　UF Marine fishes—Metamorphosis
— **Eggs**
— **Fecundity**
— **Food**
— **Geographical distribution**
— **Growth**
— **Metamorphosis**
　　USE Marine fishes—Development
— **Microbiology**
— **Migration**
— **Nomenclature (Popular)**
— **Physiology**
— **Reproduction**
Marine flora *(May Subd Geog)*
　　[QK103 (General)]
　　[QK931 (Ecology)]
BT Aquatic plants
　　Botany
　　Marine biology
RT Seashore flora
NT Coral reef flora
　　Marine algae
　　Marine aquariums
　　Phytoplankton
　　Primary productivity (Biology)
　　Seagrasses
Marine fouling organisms *(May Subd Geog)*
　　[QH91.8.M]
BT Fouling
　　Fouling organisms
　　Marine fauna
NT Marine borers
Marine fungi *(May Subd Geog)*
　　[QK604-QK615.7 (Local)]
　　[QK618.2 (Botany, General)]
UF Fungi, Marine
　　Thalassiomycetes
BT Aquatic fungi
Marine gas-turbines
BT Gas-turbines
　　Marine engines
— **Combustion**
Marine geodesy
BT Geodesy
Marine geology
USE Submarine geology
Marine geophysics
　　Subdivided by locality, e.g. Marine geophysics—
Atlantic Ocean.

BT Geophysics
　　Ocean bottom
　　Submarine geology
Marine geotechnique
UF Geotechnique, Marine
　　Marine soil mechanics
BT Marine sediments
　　Ocean engineering
　　Rock mechanics
　　Soil mechanics
　　Submarine geology
Marine hatchetfishes
USE Sternoptychidae
Marine hospitals
USE Hospitals, Naval and marine
Marine iguana
　　[QL666.L2]
UF Iguana, Marine
Marine insects
USE Insects, Marine
Marine instruments
USE Nautical instruments
　　Oceanographic instruments
Marine insurance
USE Insurance, Marine
Marine invertebrates *(May Subd Geog)*
BT Aquatic invertebrates
　　Invertebrates
　　Marine fauna
RT Seashore biology
NT Kinorhyncha
　　Pogonophora
　　Tube worms
— **Anatomy**
　　[QL363]
— **Cultures and culture media**
　　[QL362.8]
— **Metamorphosis**
　　[QL363.5]
　　BT Metamorphosis
— **Physiology**
Marine invertebrates as laboratory animals
　　[SF407.M37]
Marine invertebrates as pets
　　[SF457.1]
BT Invertebrates as pets
　　Marine aquariums
Marine jet engines
USE Jet boat engines
Marine jet propellers
USE Jet boat engines
Marine jet propulsion
USE Jet boat engines
Marine laboratories
　　[QH]
UF Marine biological laboratories
　　Marine stations
BT Biological laboratories
　　Marine biology
　　Oceanography
Marine law
USE Maritime law
Marine machinery
UF Machinery, Marine
　　Ship machinery
BT Marine engineering
　　Ships—Equipment and supplies
NT Deck machinery
　　Electricity on ships
　　Marine compressors
　　Marine engines
　　Marine pumps
　　Marine refrigeration
　　Ship propulsion
　　Ships—Air conditioning
　　Ships—Heating and ventilation
　　Ships—Transmission devices
— **Corrosion**
　　BT Corrosion and anti-corrosives
— **Hydraulic drive**
— **Maintenance and repair**

NT United States. Navy—Enginemen
— **Parts**
　　BT Machine parts
— **Unit construction**
— **Welding**
Marine machinery industry
　　(May Subd Geog)
BT Marine engineering
Marine mammals *(May Subd Geog)*
BT Aquatic mammals
　　Mammals
　　Marine fauna
SA *names of specific mammals, e.g.* Seals
　　(Animals); Whales
— **Anatomy**
— **Law and legislation** *(May Subd Geog)*
　　BT Fishery law and legislation
　　Game-laws
　　Wildlife conservation—Law and
　　legislation
Marine mammals, Fossil
Marine medicine
USE Medicine, Naval
Marine meteorological services
　　(May Subd Geog)
　　[QC875]
UF Marine weather services
BT Meteorological services
Marine meteorology
USE Meteorology, Maritime
Marine microbiology *(May Subd Geog)*
　　[QR106]
UF Marine bacteriology
　　Microbiology, Marine
　　Sea-water—Bacteriology
BT Aquatic microbiology
　　Marine biology
　　Microbiology
NT Marine bacteria
Marine mineral resources *(May Subd Geog)*
　　[GC1025]
UF Mineral resources, Marine
　　Ocean mineral resources
BT Marine resources
　　Mines and mineral resources
　　Ocean bottom
　　Ocean energy resources
RT Mineral resources in submerged lands
NT Manganese nodules
　　Ocean mining
— **Law and legislation** *(May Subd Geog)*
— **Taxation** *(May Subd Geog)*
— — **Law and legislation**
　　(May Subd Geog)
Marine mining
USE Ocean mining
Marine nuclear reactor plants
　　[VM774.3]
UF Atomic ship propulsion
　　Nuclear reactor plants, Marine
　　Ship propulsion, Atomic
BT Marine engines
　　Nuclear reactors
　　Nuclear ships
　　Pressurized water reactors
　　Ship propulsion
— **Employees**
　　NT United States. Navy—Nuclear
　　propulsion plant operators
— **Safety measures**
　　BT Radiation—Safety measures
— **Shielding (Radiation)**
Marine oil operations
USE Oil well drilling, Submarine
Marine oil pollution
USE Oil pollution of the sea
Marine oils, Animal
USE Marine animal oils
Marine outfalls
USE Ocean outfalls

Marine painters *(May Subd Geog)*
  UF Sea painters
Marine painting
    [ND1370]
    [ND2270 (Water-color)]
  BT Marine art
      Painting
      Sea in art
      Ships in art
  — 15th century *(May Subd Geog)*
  — 16th century *(May Subd Geog)*
  — 17th century *(May Subd Geog)*
  — 18th century *(May Subd Geog)*
  — 19th century *(May Subd Geog)*
  — 20th century *(May Subd Geog)*
  — Technique
Marine painting, American, [British, etc.]
  (May Subd Geog)
Marine painting, Brazilian
  (May Subd Geog)
  UF Brazilian marine painting
Marine painting, British *(May Subd Geog)*
  UF British marine painting
Marine painting, Danish *(May Subd Geog)*
  UF Danish marine painting
Marine painting, Dutch *(May Subd Geog)*
  UF Dutch marine painting
Marine painting, Flemish *(May Subd Geog)*
  UF Flemish marine painting
Marine painting, German *(May Subd Geog)*
  UF German marine painting
Marine painting, Minoan
  UF Minoan marine painting
Marine paraphernalia
  USE Nautical paraphernalia
Marine parks and reserves
  (May Subd Geog)
    [QH91.75]
  UF Marine sanctuaries
  BT Marine resources conservation
      National parks and reserves
      Wildlife conservation
  — California
    NT Point Reyes-Farallon Islands
        National Marine Sanctuary
        (Calif.)
  — Japan
    NT Ashizuri Uwakai Kokuritsu Kōen
        (Japan)
  — New Zealand
    NT Hauraki Gulf Maritime Park (N.Z.)
Marine pharmacognosy
  USE Marine pharmacology
Marine pharmacology *(May Subd Geog)*
    [RS160.7]
  UF Drugs from the sea
      Marine pharmacognosy
      Materia medica, Marine
  BT Marine biology
      Materia medica
      Pharmacognosy
  NT Marine toxins
Marine phytoplankton *(May Subd Geog)*
    [QK934]
  BT Marine plankton
      Phytoplankton
  NT Marine algae
Marine pipe-fitting
    [VM501]
  UF Pipe-fitting, Marine
      Ships—Pipe-fitting
      Ships—Pipe lines—Maintenance and
        repair
  BT Marine engineering
      Pipe-fitting
Marine pipe lines
  USE Underwater pipe lines
Marine plankton *(May Subd Geog)*
    [QH91.8.P5]
  BT Plankton
  NT Ebriida

      Marine phytoplankton
      Marine zooplankton
      Silicoflagellata
Marine pollution *(May Subd Geog)*
    [GC1080-1581]
  UF Marine environment pollution
      Marine water pollution
      Ocean pollution
      Offshore water pollution
      Sea pollution
      Sea-water—Pollution
  BT Coastal zone management
      Oceanography
      Pollution
      Water—Pollution
  RT Marine resources conservation
  NT Detergent pollution of the sea
      Estuarine pollution
      Oil pollution of the sea
      Radioactive pollution of the sea
      Sewage disposal in the ocean
      Waste disposal in the ocean
  — Law and legislation *(May Subd Geog)*
    BT Environmental law
Marine postal hand stamps
  USE Maritime postal hand stamps
Marine prints *(May Subd Geog)*
  UF Maritime prints
  BT Prints
  — 18th century *(May Subd Geog)*
  — 19th century *(May Subd Geog)*
Marine prints, American *(May Subd Geog)*
  UF American marine prints
Marine productivity *(May Subd Geog)*
    [QH91.8.M34]
  BT Biological productivity
      Marine ecology
      Primary productivity (Biology)
Marine protests *(May Subd Geog)*
  UF Protests (Maritime law)
      Ship's protests
  BT Maritime law
Marine pumps
    [VM821]
  BT Marine machinery
      Pumping machinery
Marine radar systems, Tariff on
  USE Tariff on marine radar systems
Marine radio
  USE Radio—Installation on ships
      Radio on boats
Marine radio stations *(May Subd Geog)*
    [VK397]
  UF Coast radio stations
      Navigation radio stations
      Ship radio stations
  BT Marine service
      Mobile communication systems
      Radio stations
  — Law and legislation *(May Subd Geog)*
Marine radioecology
    [QH543.6]
  BT Marine biology
      Marine ecology
      Radioecology
Marine railways
    [VM925]
  UF Railway docks
  BT Dry-docks
      Hoisting machinery
Marine refrigeration
    [VM485]
  UF Refrigeration, Marine
  BT Marine machinery
      Refrigeration and refrigerating
        machinery
  RT Cold storage on shipboard
      Refrigerator ships
  NT Fishing boats—Refrigeration
      Marine compressors

Marine resources *(May Subd Geog)*
  UF Ocean—Economic aspects
      Ocean resources
      Resources, Marine
      Sea resources
  BT Aquatic resources
      Commercial products
      Marine biology
      Natural resources
      Oceanography
  NT Amber
      Continental shelf—Economic aspects
      Fishery resources
      Marine mineral resources
      Ocean energy resources
      Ocean engineering
      Ocean thermal power plants
      Salt
      Sea-water—Fertilization
      Seafood
      Shell deposits
      Tidal power
  — Law and legislation
    USE Marine resources conservation—
        Law and legislation
  — United States
    NT National Sea Grant Program
Marine resources and state
  (May Subd Geog)
  UF State and marine resources
  NT Fishery policy
Marine resources conservation
  (May Subd Geog)
    [GC1018]
  UF Conservation of marine resources
  BT Conservation of natural resources
  RT Marine pollution
  NT Fishery conservation
      Marine parks and reserves
  — Law and legislation *(May Subd Geog)*
    UF Marine resources—Law and
        legislation
    BT Ocean bottom (Maritime law)
Marine safety
  USE Merchant marine—Safety measures
      Navigation—Safety measures
      Ships—Safety regulations
Marine sanctuaries
  USE Marine parks and reserves
Marine science libraries *(May Subd Geog)*
    [Z675.M35]
  UF Libraries, Marine science
  BT Scientific libraries
  NT Oceanographic libraries
Marine sciences *(May Subd Geog)*
  UF Ocean sciences
  BT Aquatic sciences
      Science
  NT Marine biology
      Oceanography
Marine sediments
    [GC380-399]
    Subdivided by locality, e.g. Marine sediments—
    Mexico, Gulf of; Marine sediments—Pacific Coast.
    Here are entered works on the accumulated min-
    erals and organic remains on the present ocean floor.
    Works on the unconsolidated mineral and organic
    sediments of the present land masses are entered
    under Sediments (Geology)
  UF Bottom deposits (Oceanography)
      Bottom sediments (Oceanography)
      Deep-sea deposits
      Deposits, Deep-sea
      Marine deposits
      Sediments, Marine
  BT Marine biology
      Ocean bottom
      Sedimentation and deposition
      Submarine geology
  RT Paleoceanography
      Sediments (Geology)
  NT Coccoliths

Dredging (Biology)
   Estuarine sediments
   Manganese nodules
   Marine geotechnique
— **Acoustic properties**
— **Bacteriology**
— **Gas content**
   [GC380.2.G3]
   UF Gases in marine sediments
— **Microbiology**
— **Sampling**
   [GC380.2.S28]
— **Mexico, Gulf of**
— **Pacific Coast**
Marine service *(May Subd Geog)*
   BT Naval art and science
   SA *names of individual navies, e.g.* United
        States. Navy
   NT Aids to navigation
        Beacons
        Buoys
        Lighthouses
        Marine radio stations
        Merchant marine
        Navigation
        Shipping
        Signals and signaling
— **United States**
   UF United States—Marine service
Marine shipping
   USE Shipping
Marine signals
   USE Aids to navigation
Marine soil mechanics
   USE Marine geotechnique
Marine stations
   USE Marine laboratories
Marine steam-boilers
   USE Steam-boilers, Marine
Marine stores
   USE Ship chandlers
Marine structures
   USE Offshore structures
Marine suppliers
   USE Ship chandlers
Marine surveying
   USE Boats and boating—Inspection
        Ships—Inspection
Marine surveyors
   USE Surveyors, Marine
Marine technology
   USE Marine engineering
Marine terminals *(May Subd Geog)*
   UF Port terminals
        Ship terminals
   BT Harbors
        Terminals (Transportation)
   NT Petroleum shipping terminals
— **Communication systems**
Marine terminals, Floating
   USE Floating harbors
Marine therapy
   USE Thalassotherapy
Marine toad
   USE Bufo marinus
Marine toxins
   [QP632.M37]
   BT Marine pharmacology
        Toxins
   RT Poisonous fishes
        Poisonous shellfish
   NT Saxitoxin
        Tetrodotoxin
Marine transportation
   USE Shipping
Marine trumpet
   USE Sea-trumpet
Marine turbines
   BT Turbines
   NT Steam-turbines, Marine
— **Blades**

— **Lubrication**
— **Transmission devices**
   BT Gearing
Marine turtles
   USE Sea turtles
Marine water pollution
   USE Marine pollution
Marine weather broadcasts
   (May Subd Geog)
   [QC877.5]
   UF Broadcasts, Marine weather
        Weather broadcasts, Marine
   BT Meteorology, Maritime
        Weather broadcasting
Marine weather services
   USE Marine meteorological services
Marine zoology
   USE Marine fauna
Marine zooplankton *(May Subd Geog)*
   [QL123]
   BT Marine plankton
        Zooplankton
   NT Chaetognatha
— **Geographical distribution**
**Marineland of the Pacific (Palos Verdes
Estates, Calif.)**
   BT Amusement parks—California
        Aquariums—California
Mariner bombers
   [UG1242.B6]
   UF PBM bombers
   BT Bombers
        Martin airplanes
Mariner project
   USE Project Mariner
Mariners
   USE Seamen
Mariner's compass
   USE Compass
Marines *(May Subd Geog)*
   [VE]
   BT Armed Forces
— **Insignia**
   [VC345]
— **Medals, badges, decorations, etc.**
   [VC345]
   BT Medals, Military and naval
**Marinette Knitting Mills Strike, Marinette,
Wis., 1951**
   BT Clothing workers—Wisconsin
        Strikes and lockouts—Clothing trade—
          Wisconsin
        Strikes and lockouts—Wisconsin
Maring, Tsembaga
   USE Tsembaga Maring
Maring (Indic people)
   [DS432.M27]
   BT Ethnology—India
Maring (New Guinea people)
   BT Ethnology—Papua New Guinea
Maring language
   UF Mareng language
        Yoadabe-Watoare language
   BT Papuan languages
Marinides
   USE Beni Marin dynasty
Marinism
   BT Baroque literature
        Italian literature—History and
          criticism
Marinker family *(Not Subd Geog)*
Marino Palace (Milan, Italy)
   USE Palazzo Marino (Milan, Italy)
Marinus family
   USE Mereness family
Mario Balzic (Fictitious character)
   USE Balzic, Mario (Fictitious character)
Mariology
   USE Mary, Blessed Virgin, Saint—Theology
Marion County Courthouse (Marion, Ohio)
   BT Court-houses—Ohio

Marion Island (Prince Edward Islands)
   BT Islands of the Indian Ocean
        Prince Edward Islands
Marionettes
   USE Puppets and puppet-plays
Mariotte's law
   USE Boyle's law
Mariposa lily
   USE Calochortus
Mariposa Site (Tex.)
   BT Texas—Antiquities
Mariposa tulip
   USE Calochortus
Mariposan Indians
   USE Yokuts Indians
Mariposan language
   USE Yokuts language
Mariquita (Dance)
   [GV1796.M34]
   UF Pala-pala (Dance)
Maris family *(Not Subd Geog)*
   RT Demaris family
MARISAT System
   UF Maritime Satellite System
   BT Artificial satellites in navigation
        Artificial satellites in
          telecommunication
Marismas (Spain)
   USE Maresme (Spain)
Marist Brothers *(May Subd Geog)*
   [BX3788]
   BT Monasticism and religious orders
Marital communication
   USE Communication in marriage
Marital condition
   USE Marital status
Marital counseling
   USE Marriage counseling
Marital counselors
   USE Marriage counselors
Marital deduction *(May Subd Geog)*
   UF Deduction for interspousal transfer of
          property
   BT Gifts—Taxation—Deductions
        Inheritance and transfer tax—
          Deductions
— **Law and legislation** *(May Subd Geog)*
Marital infidelity
   USE Adultery
Marital property *(May Subd Geog)*
   UF Matrimonial property
        Property, Marital
   BT Husband and wife
        Property
   NT Community property
        Equitable distribution of marital
          property
        Separate property
— Conflict of laws
   USE Conflict of laws—Marital
          property
Marital psychotherapy *(May Subd Geog)*
   [RC488.5]
   UF Couples psychotherapy
        Marriage psychotherapy
   BT Family psychotherapy
        Psychotherapy
   RT Marriage counseling
   NT Structural-strategic marital
          psychotherapy
Marital rape
   USE Rape in marriage
Marital separation
   USE Separation (Law)
Marital settlement agreements
   USE Divorce settlements
Marital status *(May Subd Geog)*
   UF Marital condition
        Status, Marital
   BT Marriage
        Social status

Marital status *(Continued)*
   NT Divorced people
        Married people
        Single people
        Widowers
        Widows
  — Statistics
      BT Vital statistics
Maritime Alps (France and Italy)
   UF Alpes Maritimes (France and Italy)
        Alpi Marittime (France and Italy)
   BT Alps, Western
        Mountains—France
        Mountains—Italy
Maritime anthropology
   [GN386]
   UF Marine anthropology
        Marine ethnology
        Maritime ethnology
   BT Anthropology
        Ethnology
   NT Fishing villages
Maritime capture
   USE Capture at sea
Maritime contracts
   USE Contracts, Maritime
Maritime discoveries
   USE Discoveries (in geography)
Maritime ethnology
   USE Maritime anthropology
Maritime history
   USE Navigation—History
Maritime journalism
   USE Journalism, Maritime
Maritime labor law
   USE Merchant seamen—Legal status, laws, etc.
Maritime law *(May Subd Geog)*
   [HE585-HE587 (Shipping laws)]
   [JX4408-JX4449 (International law)]
   [JX6311 (International law, Private)]
   UF Dominion of the sea
        High seas, Jurisdiction over
        Law, Maritime
        Law of the sea
        Marine law
        Merchant marine—Law
        Merchant ships—Law and legislation
        Navigation—Law and legislation
        Navigation laws
        Sea, Dominion of the
        Sea laws
        Shipping—Law
   BT Commerce
        International law
        Shipping
   RT Carriers
        Commercial law
        Naval law
        Territorial waters
        War, Maritime (International law)
   NT Abandonment (Maritime law)
        Access to the sea (International law)
        Admiralty
        Angary, Right of
        Archipelagoes—Law and legislation
        Armed merchant ships
        Arrest of ships
        Artificial satellites in navigation—Law and legislation
        Average (Maritime law)
        Barratry (Maritime law)
        Bays (International law)
        Bills of health
        C.I.F. clause
        Charter-parties
        Coastwise navigation—Law and legislation
        Coastwise shipping—Law and legislation
        Collisions at sea

        Contiguous zones (Maritime law)
        Contracts, Maritime
        Economic zones (Maritime law)
        Electricity on ships—Law and legislation
        F.O.B. clause
        Freedom of the seas
        Freight and freightage
        Government vessels
        Harbors—Law and legislation
        Harbors—Port charges
        Insurance, Marine
        Intercoastal shipping—Law and legislation
        Islands—Law and legislation
        Jurisdiction over ships at sea
        Lighthouses—Law and legislation
        Marine accidents
        Marine protests
        Maritime liens
        Merchant seamen—Legal status, laws, etc.
        Merchant ships—Passenger accommodation
        Nautical charts—Law and legislation
        Navicert system
        Nuclear ships—Law and legislation
        Ocean bottom (Maritime law)
        Ocean thermal power plants—Law and legislation
        Offshore structures—Law and legislation
        Offshore structures (International law)
        Offshore support vessels—Law and legislation
        Oil pollution of the sea—Law and legislation
        Petroleum shipping terminals—Law and legislation
        Pirates
        Prize law
        Radioactive pollution of the sea—Law and legislation
        Rule of the road at sea
        Salvage
        Search, Right of
        Seizure of vessels and cargoes
        Ship mortgages
        Ship transfers to foreign registry
        Shipmasters
        Shipping conferences—Law and legislation
        Ships—Health regulations
        Ships—Inspection
        Ships—Nationality
        Ships—Safety regulations
        Ship's husbands
        Ship's papers
        Slave-trade
        Steamboats—Law and legislation
        Steamboats—Passenger accommodation
        Tankers—Law and legislation
        Towing (International law)
        Underwater archaeology—Law and legislation
        Warships—Law and legislation
        Wreck
  — Cases
  —— Digests
      USE Maritime law—Digests
  — **Codification**
  — Conflict of laws
      USE Conflict of laws—Maritime law
  — **Criminal provisions**
  — **Digests**
      UF Maritime law—Cases—Digests
Maritime law (Adat law) *(May Subd Geog)*
Maritime law (Greek law)
   BT Law, Greek

Maritime law (Roman-Dutch law)
Maritime law (Roman law)
Maritime libraries
   USE Libraries, Naval
Maritime liens *(May Subd Geog)*
   BT Liens
        Maritime law
Maritime meteorology
   USE Meteorology, Maritime
Maritime museums
   USE Naval museums
Maritime operations (Naval forces)
   USE Sea control
Maritime paraphernalia
   USE Nautical paraphernalia
Maritime postal hand stamps
   (May Subd Geog)
   UF Marine postal hand stamps
   BT Hand stamps (Philately)
        Ship letters
Maritime prints
   USE Marine prints
Maritime Provinces
   Here are entered works dealing with the provinces of Nova Scotia, New Brunswick and Prince Edward Island.
   BT Atlantic Provinces
   NT New Brunswick
        Nova Scotia
Maritime saltwort
   USE Batis maritima
Maritime Satellite System
   USE MARISAT System
Maritime shipping
   USE Shipping
Maritime surveying
   USE Hydrographic surveying
Maritime war
   USE War, Maritime (International law)
Maritz's Rebellion, 1914-1915
   USE South Africa—History—Rebellion, 1914-1915
Mariut Lake (Egypt)
   USE Maryūt, Lake (Egypt)
Mariya (Indic people)
   USE Maria (Indic people)
Marjoulet family *(Not Subd Geog)*
Mark
   [JC20-JC45 (Primitive state)]
   BT Commons
        Land tenure
        Peasantry
        Village communities
Mark family
   USE Marks family
Mark I (Calculator)
   UF Automatic Sequence Controlled Calculator
        Harvard Mark I (Calculator)
        IBM Automatic Sequence Controlled Calculator
   BT Calculators
Mark Twain National Forest (Mo.)
   BT Forest reserves—Missouri
        National parks and reserves—United States
Markam family
   USE Markham family
Mārkaṇḍeya (Hindu mythology)
   UF Mārkkaṇṭaṇ (Hindu mythology)
   BT Mythology, Hindu
Markaz
   USE Muwashshah
Markdowns
   BT Retail trade
   RT Special sales
Marke family
   USE Marks family
Marked member (Linguistics)
   USE Markedness (Linguistics)

Markedness (Linguistics)
  [P299.M]
  UF Marked member (Linguistics)
  BT Distinctive features (Linguistics)
      Generative grammar
      Grammar, Comparative and general
      Linguistics
  SA subdivision Markedness under names
      of languages, e.g. English language
      —Markedness
Marker decoration, Felt
  USE Felt marker decoration
Marker drawing
  USE Dry marker drawing
Marker drawing, Felt
  USE Felt marker drawing
Markers, Biochemical
  USE Biochemical markers
Markers, Historical
  USE Historical markers
Markers, Tumor
  USE Tumor markers
Markerwaard (Netherlands)
  BT Polders—Netherlands
Markes family
  USE Marks family
Market, Capital
  USE Capital market
Market, Euro-dollar
  USE Euro-dollar market
Market gardening
  USE Truck farming
Market gunning
  USE Market hunting (Game hunting)
Market hunting (Game hunting)
  (May Subd Geog)
  UF Hunting game for sale
      Market gunning
  BT Hunting
  NT Punt gun
Market research
  USE Marketing research
Market segmentation
  BT Direct marketing
      Marketing
Market Square (Lake Forest, Ill.)
  BT Plazas—Illinois
Market Square (Washington, D.C.)
  BT Plazas—Washington (D.C.)
Market Street Railway
  BT Railroads—United States
Market structure
  USE Industrial organization (Economic
      theory)
Market surveys (May Subd Geog)
  [HC (Surveys)]
  [HF5415.3 (Technique)]
  UF Retail trading areas
  BT Advertising
      Consumption (Economics)—Surveys
      Economic surveys
      Marketing research
  RT Advertising campaigns
      Public opinion polls
  NT Consumer panels
      Consumers—Attitudes
      Consumers' preferences
      Store location
Market theory, Efficient
  USE Efficient market theory
Market towns (May Subd Geog)
      Here are entered works on small towns that have
  the privilege of holding a public market at stated
  times.
  UF Towns, Market
  BT Cities and towns
  RT Markets
Market women
  USE Women merchants
Marketeers, Black
  USE Black marketeers

Marketing (May Subd Geog)
  [HF5415-5416]
  BT Advertising
      Business
      Consumption (Economics)
      Industrial management
  RT Commodity exchanges
      Selling
  SA subdivision Marketing under names of
      commodities, e.g. Farm produce—
      Marketing; Fruit—Marketing
  NT Bank marketing
      Communication in marketing
      Comparative marketing
      Consumers
      Dealer aids
      Direct marketing
      Direct selling
      Distributive education
      Electronic marketing
      Export marketing
      Government marketing
      Industrial marketing
      Institutional market
      Manufacturers' retail outlets
      Market segmentation
      Merchandising
      New products
      Newspapers—Circulation
      Physical distribution of goods
      Pre-selling
      Pricing
      Product coding
      Product demonstrations
      Product life cycle
      Professions—Marketing
      Retail trade
      Sales management
      Sales promotion
      Samples (Commerce)
      Women in marketing
  — Bibliography
      RT Marketing literature
  — Costs
      BT Costs, Industrial
  — Decision making
      BT Decision-making
  — Key accounts
      UF Key accounts in marketing
          National accounts marketing
      BT Customer service
  — Law and legislation (May Subd Geog)
      BT Commercial law
  — Management
      [HF5415.13]
      UF Marketing management
      BT Business logistics
      NT Marketing audits
          Product management
  — — Data processing
          NT SalesCTRL (Computer system)
  — Mathematical models
      BT Business mathematics
  — Research
      USE Marketing research
  — Vocational guidance
Marketing, Comparative
  USE Comparative marketing
Marketing, Government
  USE Government marketing
Marketing, Multilevel
  USE Multilevel marketing
Marketing, Public sector
  USE Government marketing
Marketing, Vertical (May Subd Geog)
  UF Vertical marketing
Marketing (Home economics)
  (May Subd Geog)
  [TX356]

      Here are entered works limited to the purchase of
  provisions. Works on general household buying are
  entered under the headings Consumer education and
  Consumers.
  UF Buyers' guides
      Food—Purchasing
      Food buying
      Groceries—Purchasing
      Grocery shopping
  BT Home economics
      Purchasing
      Rationing, Consumer
  RT Consumer education
      Shopping
  NT Consumers
Marketing and Advertising Reference Service
  USE MARS (Information retrieval system)
Marketing auditing
  USE Marketing audits
Marketing audits
  UF Audits, Marketing
      Marketing auditing
  BT Marketing—Management
Marketing boards (May Subd Geog)
  [HD9000-9019]
  UF Boards, Marketing
      Commodity boards
  BT Produce trade
Marketing channels (May Subd Geog)
  UF Channels, Marketing
      Distribution channels
  RT Physical distribution of goods
Marketing literature (May Subd Geog)
  UF Literature, Marketing
  BT Management literature
  RT Marketing—Bibliography
Marketing management
  USE Marketing—Management
Marketing of consulting services
  USE Consultants—Marketing
Marketing of corn seeds
  USE Corn—Seeds—Marketing
Marketing of design services
  USE Design services—Marketing
Marketing of farm produce
  USE Farm produce—Marketing
Marketing of financial planning services
  USE Financial planners—Marketing
Marketing of fruit
  USE Fruit—Marketing
Marketing of legal services
  USE Lawyers—Marketing
Marketing of livestock
  USE Livestock—Marketing
Marketing of manuscripts (Authorship)
  USE Authorship—Marketing
Marketing of personal financial planning
  services
  USE Finance, Personal—Marketing
Marketing of photographic services
  USE Photographers—Marketing
Marketing of professional services
  USE Professions—Marketing
Marketing personnel (May Subd Geog)
  BT Businessmen
Marketing research (May Subd Geog)
  [HF5415.2]
  UF Market research
      Marketing—Research
      Markets—Research
  BT Research
      Research, Industrial
  NT Consumer panels
      Interviewing in marketing research
      Market surveys
      Motivation research (Marketing)
      Retail trade—Research
      Sales forecasting
Marketplaces (May Subd Geog)
  [NA9068 (City beautification)]

Marketplaces *(Continued)*
  Here are entered works dealing with the architectural aspects of the squares or places in town where markets or public sales are held.
    BT Markets
      Plazas
  — Decoration
    BT Decoration and ornament
  — Greece
    NT Agora (Athens, Greece)
  — Libya
    NT Agora (Cyrene)
Markets *(May Subd Geog)*
  ⌐HF5470-HF5475⌐
  Here are entered works on areas within which or arrangements by which many buyers and sellers are brought into contact with one another in order to exchange goods or services. Works on public gatherings at a stated time and place at which goods are exhibited and sold are entered under Fairs. Works on competitive exhibitions of farm products, livestock, baked goods, etc., with prizes for excellence, often combined with carnival-like entertainment, and held annually by states, counties, etc., are entered under Agricultural exhibitions.
    BT Commerce
    RT Fairs
      Market towns
    NT Bazaars, Oriental
      Commodity exchanges
      Flea markets
      Marketplaces
  — Conservation and restoration
  — Construction
    USE Markets—Design and construction
  — Design and construction
    UF Markets—Construction
  — Law and legislation *(May Subd Geog)*
    BT Trade regulation
    NT Wholesale trade—Law and legislation
  — Research
    USE Marketing research
  — Social aspects *(May Subd Geog)*
    UF Society and markets
  — Rome
    NT Forums, Roman
  — Washington (State)
    NT Pike Place Market (Seattle, Wash.)
Markham family *(Not Subd Geog)*
  UF Marckum family
    Marcom family
    Marcum family
    Markam family
    Markum family
Markham River (Papua New Guinea)
  BT Rivers—Papua New Guinea
Markidēs family *(Not Subd Geog)*
Marking (Students)
  USE Grading and marking (Students)
Marking devices
  ⌐TS2301.M3⌐
  BT Office equipment and supplies
  NT Labeling-machines
    Numbering-machines
    Rubber stamps
    Stencils and stencil cutting
Marking devices industry *(May Subd Geog)*
  ⌐HD9793⌐
Marking of animals
  USE Animal marking
Marking of bats
  USE Bat-banding
Marking of hydrants
  USE Hydrants—Marking
Marking of teeth
  USE Teeth—Marking
Marking-out
  USE Laying-out (Machine-shop practice)
Marking-out (Woodwork)
  USE Laying-out (Woodwork)

Markings, Transportation
  USE Transportation markings
Markings on firearms
  USE Firearms—Markings
Markings on freight-cars
  USE Railroads—Freight-cars—Markings
Markings on military vehicles
  USE Vehicles, Military—Markings
Märkische Schweiz (Germany)
Mārkkaṇṭaṇ (Hindu mythology)
  USE Mārkaṇḍeya (Hindu mythology)
Markle family
  USE Markley family
Markley family *(Not Subd Geog)*
  UF Markle family
    Markly family
  RT Merkel family
Markly family
  USE Markley family
Markoff processes
  USE Markov processes
Markon
  USE Markup
Markov chains
  USE Markov processes
Markov operators
  UF Operators, Markov
  BT Ergodic theory
    Linear operators
    Markov processes
Markov processes
  ⌐QA273⌐
  UF Markoff processes
    Markov chains
  BT Stochastic processes
  NT Birth and death processes (Stochastic processes)
    Brownian motion processes
    Diffusion processes
    Jump processes
    Markov operators
Marks, Armorers'
  USE Armorers' marks
Marks, Artists'
  USE Artists' marks
Marks, Banker
  USE Banker-marks
Marks, Bottle makers'
  USE Bottles—Marks
Marks, Cabinet-workers'
  USE Furniture—Marks
Marks, Calligraphers'
  USE Calligraphers' marks
Marks, Collectors'
  USE Collectors' marks
Marks, Engravers'
  USE Engravers' marks
Marks, Furniture
  USE Furniture—Marks
Marks, House
  USE House marks
Marks, Log
  USE Log brands
Marks, Masons'
  USE Banker-marks
Marks, Milk bottle makers'
  USE Milk bottles—Marks
Marks, Mortar makers'
  USE Mortars—Marks
Marks, Pewter
  USE Pewter—Marks
Marks, Potters'
  USE Pottery—Marks
Marks, Printers'
  USE Printers' marks
Marks, Standards
  USE Standardization—Marks
Marks, Swordsmiths'
  USE Swordsmiths' marks
Marks, Timber
  USE Log brands

Marks family *(Not Subd Geog)*
  UF Mark family
    Marke family
    Markes family
    Marx family
Marks in paper
  USE Water-marks
Marks of origin *(May Subd Geog)*
  ⌐HD3625-6⌐
  UF Origin, Marks of
  BT Competition, Unfair
    Industrial property
  RT Trademarks
  SA *subdivision* Marks of origin *under names of products, e.g.* Wine and wine making—Marks of origin
  NT Certificates of origin
    Cognac (Mark of origin)
    Furniture—Marks
Marks of the church
  USE Church—Marks
Marks on plate
  USE Hallmarks
Marks-Poling Cemetery (Millstone, Calhoun County, W. Va.)
  UF Poling-Marks Cemetery (Millstone, Calhoun County, W. Va.)
  BT Cemeteries—West Virginia
Marksmanship
  USE Shooting
Marksmen
  USE Shooters (of arms)
Markswomen
  USE Shooters (of arms)
Markum family
  USE Markham family
Markup *(May Subd Geog)*
  UF Markon
  BT Cost
    Manufactures—Costs
    Pricing
    Profit
    Retail trade
Markweta (African people)
  USE Marakwet (African people)
Markwith family *(Not Subd Geog)*
Marl *(May Subd Geog)*
  ⌐S643 (Fertilizers)⌐
  BT Clay
    Fertilizers
    Plaster of Paris
Marl Glaskasten Museum (Marl, Germany)
  USE Skulpturenmuseum Glaskasten (Marl, Germany)
Marlborough Sounds (N.Z.)
  BT Sounds (Geomorphology)—New Zealand
Marlett family *(Not Subd Geog)*
  UF Marlette family
Marlette family
  USE Marlett family
Marliani family *(Not Subd Geog)*
Marliani Palace (Milan, Italy)
  USE Casa Marliani (Milan, Italy)
Marlik Site (Iran) *(Not Subd Geog)*
  ⌐DS262.M37⌐
  UF Cheragh-Ali Tepe (Iran)
    Marlik Tepe (Iran)
  BT Iran—Antiquities
Marlik Tepe (Iran)
  USE Marlik Site (Iran)
Marlin
  ⌐QL638.I88⌐
  BT Istiophoridae
  NT Blue marlin
    Striped marlin
    White marlin
Marlin bombers
  ⌐UG1242.B6⌐
  UF P5M bombers

BT Bombers
    Martin airplanes
Marlin fisheries *(May Subd Geog)*
    [SH351.M]
    BT Fisheries
Marlin fishing
    BT Billfish fishing
       Fishing
    NT Blue marlin fishing
Marline spike seamanship
    [VM531-533]
    UF Marlinspike seamanship
    BT Seamanship
    RT Masts and rigging
    NT Knots and splices
       Rope
Marlinspike seamanship
    USE Marline spike seamanship
Marlowe, Philip (Fictitious character)
    UF Philip Marlowe (Fictitious character)
    BT Characters and characteristics in
       literature
    RT Chandler, Raymond, 1888-1959—
       Characters—Philip Marlowe
Marly Forest (France)
    UF Forêt de Marly (France)
    BT Forests and forestry—France
Marly-le-Roi Castle (Marly-le-Roi, France)
    USE Château de Marly-le-Roi (Marly-le-
       Roi, France)
Marma
    USE Maghs
Marmalade *(May Subd Geog)*
    [TX612.M37]
    BT Jam
       Jelly
Marmaldo family
    USE Maramaldo family
Marmara, Sea of (Turkey)
    UF Marmara Denizi (Turkey)
       Marmora, Sea of (Turkey)
       Propontis (Turkey)
       Sea of Marmara (Turkey)
       Sea of Marmora (Turkey)
Marmara Denizi (Turkey)
    USE Marmara, Sea of (Turkey)
Marmenor (Spain)
    USE Mar Menor (Spain)
Marmolada Mountains (Italy)
    UF Gruppo della Marmolada (Italy)
    BT Dolomite Alps (Italy)
       Mountains—Italy
Marmon automobile
    [TL215.M]
Marmor cucumeris
    USE Cucumber mosaic virus
Marmor dahliae
    USE Dahlia mosaic virus
Marmor laesifaciens
    USE Bean mosaic virus
Marmor persicae
    USE Peach mosaic virus
Marmor raphani
    USE Radish mosaic virus
Marmor rubi
    USE Red raspberry mosaic virus
Marmor tabaci
    USE Tobacco mosaic virus
Marmor trifolia
    USE Red clover vein mosaic virus
Marmora, Sea of (Turkey)
    USE Marmara, Sea of (Turkey)
Marmosets
    [QL737.P92]
    BT Callitrichidae
    NT Callithrix
Marmosets as laboratory animals
    [QL737.P92]
Marmots
    [QL737.R6]

    UF Bear-mice
       Ground-hogs
       Whistlers (Woodchucks)
       Woodchucks
    NT Woodchuck hunting
Marne, Battle of the, 1914
    [D545.M3]
    BT World War, 1914-1918—Campaigns—
       France
Marne, 2d Battle of the, 1918
    [D545.M35]
    BT World War, 1914-1918—Campaigns—
       France
Marne River (France)
    UF Matrona River (France)
    BT Rivers—France
Marnésia-Lézay family
    USE Lézay-Marnésia family
MARO (Computer program language)
    [QA76.73.M]
    UF Język maszynowe rozmowy
Maroba Indians
    USE Maruba Indians
Marocasero language
    USE Malayo language
Maroi (Malaysian people)
    USE Chewong (Malaysian people)
Maronite monasticism and religious orders
    USE Monasticism and religious orders,
       Maronite
Maronite rite (Catholic Church)
    USE Catholic Church—Maronite rite
Maronites *(May Subd Geog)*
    [BX180-BX189]
    BT Syriac Christians
    NT Catholic Church—Antiochene rite
       Dayr al Qamar, Lebanon, Massacre of,
         1860
       Monasticism and religious orders,
         Maronite
Maroon arts
    USE Arts, Maroon
Maroons *(May Subd Geog)*
    UF Cimarrones
    BT Blacks—West Indies
       Fugitive slaves—West Indies
    NT Jamaica—History—Maroon War,
         1795-1796
       Missions to Maroons
  — Jamaica
      BT Blacks—Jamaica
  — Surinam
      BT Blacks—Surinam
      NT Djuka people
        Saramacca (Surinam people)
Marotse (African people)
    USE Lozi (African people)
Marott family
    USE Marotta family
Marotta family *(Not Subd Geog)*
    UF Marott family
       Marotte family
Marotte (The German word)
    BT German language—Etymology
Marotte family
    USE Marotta family
Maroubra
    [QL638.S9]
    BT Pipefishes
       Syngnathidae
Maroubra perserrata
    [QL638.S9]
Marousek family *(Not Subd Geog)*
Marova Indians
    USE Maruba Indians
Marovoay Plain (Madagascar)
    UF Plaine de Marovoay (Madagascar)
    BT Plains—Madagascar

Marple, Jane (Fictitious character)
    UF Jane Marple (Fictitious character)
       Marple, Miss (Fictitious character)
       Miss Marple (Fictitious character)
    BT Characters and characteristics in
       literature
    RT Christie, Agatha, 1890-1976—
       Characters—Jane Marple
Marple, Miss (Fictitious character)
    USE Marple, Jane (Fictitious character)
Marple family *(Not Subd Geog)*
    UF Marples family
Marples family
    USE Marple family
Marprelate controversy
    [BR757]
    BT Church of England
       Puritans
Marquand family
    USE Marchand family
Marquard family
    USE Marquardt family
Marquardt family *(Not Subd Geog)*
    UF Marquard family
       Marquart family
Marquart family
    USE Marquardt family
Marque, Letters of
    USE Privateering
       Reprisals
Marques family
    USE Marquez family
Marquesan language
    [PL6471]
    BT Polynesian languages
    RT Nukahiva language
Marquesans *(May Subd Geog)*
    BT Ethnology—Marquesas Islands
       Polynesians
Marquesas de Mendoza
    USE Marquesas Islands
Marquesas Islands
    UF Archipel des Marquises
       Iles Marquises de Mendoça
       Islas Marquesas de Mendoza
       Marquesas de Mendoza
       Marquezas
       Mendaña
    BT Islands—French Polynesia
Marquetry *(May Subd Geog)*
    [NK2710 (Inlaid furniture)]
    [NK9920]
    UF Inlaying in wood
       Intarsia
    BT Cabinet-work
       Decoration and ornament
       Wood-carving
       Woodwork
Marquez family *(Not Subd Geog)*
    UF Marques family
Marquezas
    USE Marquesas Islands
Marquises of Villafranca
    USE Villafranca, Marquises of
Marr family
    USE Marrs family
Marra language
    USE Mara language (Australia)
Marramaldo family
    USE Maramaldo family
Marramauro family
    USE Maramaldo family
Marranos *(May Subd Geog)*
    UF Crypto-Jews
       Maranos
    BT Jewish Christians
    NT Sephardim
  — Puerto Rico
      USE Chuetas
  — Spain
  — — Majorca

Marranos
— Spain
— — Majorca *(Continued)*
USE Chuetas
Marrellida
ₜQE823.M3ₑ
BT Trilobites
Marriage *(May Subd Geog)*
ₜGN480 (Ethnology)ₑ
ₜGR465 (Folk-lore)ₑ
ₜHQ503-HQ1057ₑ
UF Matrimony
Nuptiality
Wedlock
BT Love
Sacraments
RT Betrothal
Courtship
Family
Home
SA *subdivision* Biography—Marriage
under names of individual literary
authors; and subdivision Marriage
under names of other individual
persons
NT Astrology and marriage
Beast marriage
Bigamy
Bisexuality in marriage
Bride price
Child marriage
Common law marriage
Communication in marriage
Commuter marriage
Concubinage
Deaf—Marriage
Divorce
Domestic relations
Endogamy and exogamy
Fortune hunters
Free love
Handicapped—Marriage
Honeymoon
Husbands
Intermarriage
Marital status
Married people
Mate selection
Matrimonial advertisements
Mentally handicapped—Marriage
Polyandry
Polygamy
Posthumous marriage
Remarriage
Sex in marriage
Teen-age marriage
Weddings
Wives
Wives—Effect of husband's
employment on
— **Annulment** *(May Subd Geog)*
ₜHQ822ₑ
ₜHQ1024 (Canon law)ₑ
UF Annulment of marriage
Nullity of marriage
BT Marriage law
Matrimonial actions
RT Divorce—Law and legislation
— **Annulment (Canon law)**
ₜHQ1024ₑ
BT Divorce (Canon law)
Marriage (Canon law)
Matrimonial actions (Canon law)
NT Defender of the marriage bond
— **Annulment (Church of England)**
— Compatibility tests
USE Marriage compatibility tests
— **Dispensations**
ₜBX1939.D6 (Canon law)ₑ
ₜHQ1021-HQ1024ₑ

BT Catholic Church—Discipline
Dispensations
Impediments to marriage
Marriage (Canon law)
NT Deathbed marriage (Canon law)
— **Druzes**
ₜHQ525.D78ₑ
UF Druzes—Marriage
— **Gift-books**
— Impediments
USE Impediments to marriage
— **Parental consent** *(May Subd Geog)*
BT Consent (Law)
Marriage law
— Prohibited degrees
USE Consanguinity
Marriage law
Marriage with deceased wife's
sister
— **Religious aspects**
— — **Baptists,** ₜCatholic Church, etc.ₑ
— — **Buddhism,** ₜChristianity, etc.ₑ
— **Sermons**
ₜBV837ₑ
UF Marriage sermons
RT Wedding sermons
— **United States**
NT Afro-Americans—Marriage
Marriage, Bisexual
USE Bisexuality in marriage
Marriage, Child
USE Child marriage
Marriage, Commuter
USE Commuter marriage
Marriage, Companionate
ₜHQ803ₑ
UF Companionate marriage
Marriage, Interfaith
USE Interfaith marriage
Marriage, Interracial
USE Interracial marriage
Marriage, Medical examination for
USE Premarital examinations
Marriage, Mixed
USE Interfaith marriage
Intermarriage
— **Law and legislation** *(May Subd Geog)*
BT Marriage law
Marriage, Mixed (Canon law)
USE Interfaith marriage (Canon law)
Marriage, Mixed, in literature
USE Interfaith marriage in literature
Marriage, Mixed (Islamic law)
USE Interfaith marriage (Islamic law)
Marriage, Mixed (Jewish law)
USE Interfaith marriage (Jewish law)
Marriage, Mixed (Roman law)
USE Interfaith marriage (Roman law)
Marriage, Morganatic
USE Marriages of royalty and nobility
Marriage, Promise of
USE Betrothal
Marriage, Sacred (Mythology)
USE Sacred marriage (Mythology)
Marriage (Adat law) *(May Subd Geog)*
BT Marriage law
Marriage (Ancient law)
Marriage (Aztec law)
BT Law, Aztec
Marriage law
Marriage (Canon law)
ₜHQ1021-4ₑ
BT Catholic Church—Discipline
Marriage law
NT Adultery (Canon law)
Bigamy (Canon law)
Clandestinity (Canon law)
Deathbed marriage (Canon law)
Defender of the marriage bond
Divorce (Canon law)
Impediments to marriage (Canon law)

Marriage—Annulment (Canon law)
Marriage—Dispensations
Matrimonial actions (Canon law)
Remarriage (Canon law)
Separation (Canon law)
Marriage (Canon law, Eastern)
BT Canon law, Eastern
Marriage (Canon law, Oriental)
BT Canon law, Oriental
Marriage (Canon law, Orthodox Eastern)
BT Canon law, Orthodox Eastern
Marriage law
NT Adultery (Canon law, Orthodox
Eastern)
Divorce (Canon law, Orthodox
Eastern)
Marriage (Canon law, Protestant Episcopal)
BT Canon law, Protestant Episcopal
Marriage (Frankish law)
BT Marriage law
Marriage (Germanic law)
BT Marriage law
Marriage (Greek law)
BT Marriage law
Marriage (Hindu law)
BT Marriage law
NT Levirate
Matrimonial actions (Hindu law)
Marriage (Igbo law)
BT Law, Igbo
Marriage (Islamic law) *(May Subd Geog)*
UF Marriage law (Islamic law)
NT Matrimonial actions (Islamic law)
Muta
Marriage (Jewish law)
BT Marriage law
NT Agunah
Ḥalitsah
Ketubah
Levirate
— **Cases**
Marriage (Karaite law)
BT Karaite law
Marriage (Luo law)
BT Law, Luo
Marriage law
Marriage (Maya law)
BT Law, Maya
Marriage law
Marriage (Primitive law)
BT Marriage law
Marriage (Roman-Dutch law)
BT Marriage law
Marriage (Roman law)
BT Marriage law
Marriage (Semitic law)
BT Marriage law
Marriage (Visigothic law)
BT Marriage law
Marriage (Yoruba law)
BT Marriage law
Marriage à la mode (Engravings)
USE Hogarth, William, 1697-1764.
Marriage à la mode
Marriage à la mode (Paintings)
USE Hogarth, William, 1697-1764.
Marriage à la mode
Marriage advertisements
USE Matrimonial advertisements
Marriage age *(May Subd Geog)*
BT Age
NT Child marriage
Teen-age marriage
— Law and legislation
USE Age of consent
Marriage and spiritualism
ₜBF1275.M3ₑ
UF Spiritualism and marriage
Marriage articles
USE Antenuptial contracts
Marriage at Cana
USE Marriage in Cana (Miracle)

Marriage bonds
USE Marriage licenses
Marriage brokerage *(May Subd Geog)*
UF Brokage, Marriage
Brokerage, Marriage
Brokers, Marriage
RT Mate selection
— **Law and legislation** *(May Subd Geog)*
Marriage by proxy *(May Subd Geog)*
BT Marriage law
Proxy
Marriage by proxy (Canon law)
Marriage compatibility tests
UF Compatibility tests, Marriage
Marriage—Compatibility tests
BT Character tests
Marriage counseling
Personality tests
Marriage contracts
USE Antenuptial contracts
Marriage counseling *(May Subd Geog)*
UF Marital counseling
Marriage guidance
Married people—Counseling of
Premarital counseling
BT Counseling
RT Marital psychotherapy
Sex counseling
NT Family psychotherapy
Marriage compatibility tests
Marriage counselors
Marriage counselors *(May Subd Geog)*
UF Counselors, Marriage
Marital counselors
BT Counselors
Marriage counseling
Marriage customs and rites
(May Subd Geog)
⌐GT2660-2800⌐
UF Bridal customs
BT Betrothal
Manners and customs
Rites and ceremonies
Weddings
NT Bridal crowns
Defloration
Indians of Central America—Marriage
customs and rites
Jus primae noctis
Lusalo
Shivaree
Wedding anniversaries
Wedding costume
Wedding etiquette
Wedding music
— Jews
USE Marriage customs and rites,
Jewish
— Malays (Asian people)
USE Marriage customs and rites,
Malay (Asian people)
— Maoris
USE Marriage customs and rites,
Maori
Marriage customs and rites, Anglo-Saxon
(May Subd Geog)
UF Anglo-Saxon marriage customs and
rites
BT Anglo-Saxons—Rites and ceremonies
Marriage customs and rites, Aromanian
(May Subd Geog)
⌐DR27.A8⌐
UF Aromanian marriage customs and rites
BT Aromanians—Rites and ceremonies
**Marriage customs and rites, Atoni (Indonesian
people)**
UF Atoni (Indonesian people) marriage
customs and rites

**Marriage customs and rites, Australian
aboriginal** *(May Subd Geog)*
UF Australian aboriginal marriage customs
and rites
BT Australian aborigines—Rites and
ceremonies
**Marriage customs and rites, Bagirmi (African
people)** *(May Subd Geog)*
⌐DT546.445.B34⌐
UF Bagirmi (African people) marriage
customs and rites
BT Bagirmi (African people)—Rites and
ceremonies
**Marriage customs and rites, Balinese
(Indonesian people)** *(May Subd Geog)*
UF Balinese (Indonesian people) marriage
customs and rites
BT Balinese (Indonesian people)—Rites
and ceremonies
Marriage customs and rites, Bambara
⌐DT551.42⌐
UF Bambara marriage customs and rites
Marriage customs and rites, Bantu
UF Bantu marriage customs and rites
Marriage customs and rites, Batak
(May Subd Geog)
UF Batak marriage customs and rites
BT Batak—Rites and ceremonies
Marriage customs and rites, Berber
⌐DT193⌐
UF Berber marriage customs and rites
BT Berbers—Rites and ceremonies
Marriage customs and rites, Buddhist
(May Subd Geog)
⌐BQ5015⌐
UF Buddhist marriage customs and rites
BT Buddhism—Rituals
**Marriage customs and rites, Bugis (Malay
people)**
⌐DS646.4⌐
UF Bugis (Malay people) marriage
customs and rites
BT Bugis (Malay people)—Rites and
ceremonies
**Marriage customs and rites, Dinka (African
people)** *(May Subd Geog)*
UF Dinka (African people) marriage
customs and rites
BT Dinka (African people)—Rites and
ceremonies
**Marriage customs and rites, Efik (African
people)**
UF Efik (African people) marriage
customs and rites
BT Efik (African people)—Rites and
ceremonies
**Marriage customs and rites, Ewe (African
people)** *(May Subd Geog)*
UF Ewe (African people) marriage
customs and rites
BT Ewe (African people)—Rites and
ceremonies
**Marriage customs and rites, Gayo (Indonesian
people)**
⌐DS632.G3⌐
UF Gayo (Indonesian people) marriage
customs and rites
BT Gayos (Indonesian people)—Rites and
ceremonies
Marriage customs and rites, Gujarati
(May Subd Geog)
UF Gujarati marriage customs and rites
BT Gujaratis (Indic people)—Rites and
ceremonies
Marriage customs and rites, Himba
(May Subd Geog)
⌐DT709⌐
UF Himba marriage customs and rites
BT Himba (Bantu people)—Rites and
ceremonies

Marriage customs and rites, Hindu
⌐BL1226.82.M3⌐
UF Hindu marriage customs and rites
BT Hinduism—Rituals
NT Marriage service (Hinduism)
**Marriage customs and rites, Iban (Bornean
people)**
UF Iban (Bornean people) marriage
customs and rites
BT Ibans (Bornean people)—Rites and
ceremonies
Marriage customs and rites, Ibibios
UF Ibibios marriage customs and rites
BT Ibibios—Rites and ceremonies
Marriage customs and rites, Indian
USE Indians—Marriage customs and rites
Indians of Mexico—Marriage customs
and rites
Indians of North America—Marriage
customs and rites
Indians of South America—Marriage
customs and rites
Marriage customs and rites, Islamic
(May Subd Geog)
⌐GT2695.M8⌐
UF Islamic marriage customs and rites
Marriage customs and rites, Muslim
Muslim marriage customs and rites
Marriage customs and rites, Javanese
(May Subd Geog)
UF Javanese marriage customs and rites
BT Javanese—Rites and ceremonies
Marriage customs and rites, Jewish
⌐BM713⌐
UF Jewish marriage customs and rites
Marriage customs and rites—Jews
BT Judaism—Customs and practices
NT Badḥanim
Marriage service (Judaism)
Marriage customs and rites, Khasi
UF Khasi marriage customs and rites
Marriage customs and rites, Kikuyu
⌐DT433.542⌐
UF Kikuyu marriage customs and rites
BT Kikuyu (African people)—Rites and
ceremonies
Marriage customs and rites, Kpelle
UF Kpelle marriage customs and rites
BT Kpelle—Rites and ceremonies
**Marriage customs and rites, Kwaya (African
people)** *(May Subd Geog)*
UF Kwaya (African people) marriage
customs and rites
BT Kwaya (African people)—Rites and
ceremonies
**Marriage customs and rites, Lamaholot
(Indonesian people)**
UF Lamaholot (Indonesian people)
marriage customs and rites
**Marriage customs and rites, Malay (Asian
people)** *(May Subd Geog)*
UF Malay (Asian people) marriage
customs and rites
Marriage customs and rites—Malays
(Asian people)
BT Malays (Asian people)—Rites and
ceremonies
Marriage customs and rites, Maori
UF Maori marriage customs and rites
Marriage customs and rites—Maoris
BT Maoris—Rites and ceremonies
Marriage customs and rites, Medieval
⌐GT2680⌐
UF Medieval marriage customs and rites
BT Civilization, Medieval
Marriage customs and rites, Minangkabau
(May Subd Geog)
⌐DS632.M4⌐
UF Minangkabau marriage customs and
rites

Marriage customs and rites, Minangkabau
(Continued)
    BT Minangkabau (Indonesian people)—
        Rites and ceremonies
Marriage customs and rites, Mossi (African
    people) *(May Subd Geog)*
    [DT555.45.M67]
    UF Mossi (African people) marriage
        customs and rites
    BT Mossi (African people)—Rites and
        ceremonies
Marriage customs and rites, Muslim
    USE Marriage customs and rites, Islamic
Marriage customs and rites, Nattukottai
    Chettiar *(May Subd Geog)*
    UF Nattukottai Chettiar marriage customs
        and rites
    BT Nattukottai Chettiars—Rites and
        cermonies
Marriage customs and rites, Ndonga (African
    people)
    [DT611.42 (Angola)]
    [DT709 (Namibia)]
    UF Ndonga (African people) marriage
        customs and rites
    BT Ndonga (African people)—Rites and
        ceremonies
Marriage customs and rites, Rifs (Berber
    people) *(May Subd Geog)*
    [DT313.3.R53 (Morocco)]
    UF Rifs (Berber people) marriage customs
        and rites
    BT Rifs (Berber people)—Rites and
        ceremonies
Marriage customs and rites, Rotuman
    [DU600]
    UF Rotuman marriage customs and rites
    BT Rotumans—Rites and ceremonies
Marriage customs and rites, Sikh
    UF Sikh marriage customs and rites
Marriage customs and rites, Slavic
    UF Slavic marriage customs and rites
Marriage customs and rites, Sumbanese
    (Indonesian people)
    UF Sumbanese (Indonesian people)
        marriage customs and rites
Marriage customs and rites, Sundanese
    (Indonesian people) *(May Subd Geog)*
    UF Sundanese (Indonesian people)
        marriage customs and rites
    BT Sundanese (Indonesian people)—Rites
        and ceremonies
Marriage customs and rites, Swazi (African
    people) *(May Subd Geog)*
    UF Swazi (African people) marriage
        customs and rites
    BT Swazi (African people)—Rites and
        ceremonies
Marriage customs and rites, Tamil
    (May Subd Geog)
    [DS432.T3]
    UF Tamil marriage customs and rites
    BT Tamils—Rites and ceremonies
Marriage customs and rites, Yoruba
    (May Subd Geog)
    UF Yoruba marriage customs and rites
    BT Yorubas—Rites and ceremonies
Marriage customs and rites, Zande (African
    people) *(May Subd Geog)*
    UF Zande (African people) marriage
        customs and rites
Marriage endowment insurance
    USE Insurance, Marriage endowment
Marriage guidance
    USE Marriage counseling
Marriage in art
Marriage in Cana (Miracle)
    UF Cana, Marriage in
        Marriage at Cana
        Wedding at Cana
        Wedding in Cana

    BT Jesus Christ—Miracles
Marriage in danger of death
    USE Deathbed marriage
Marriage in literature
    BT Social problems in literature
    NT Family in literature
Marriage in moving-pictures
    BT Moving-pictures
Marriage law *(May Subd Geog)*
    UF Law, Marriage
        Marriage—Prohibited degrees
    BT Domestic relations
        Sex and law
    RT Husband and wife
    NT Adultery
        Age (Law)
        Age of consent
        Alienation of affections
        Betrothal—Law and legislation
        Breach of promise
        Civil marriage
        Common law marriage
        Community property
        Concubinage
        Deathbed marriage
        Divorce—Law and legislation
        Dower
        Dowry
        Impediments to marriage
        Marriage—Annulment
        Marriage—Parental consent
        Marriage, Mixed—Law and legislation
        Marriage (Adat law)
        Marriage (Aztec law)
        Marriage (Canon law)
        Marriage (Canon law, Orthodox
         Eastern)
        Marriage (Frankish law)
        Marriage (Germanic law)
        Marriage (Greek law)
        Marriage (Hindu law)
        Marriage (Jewish law)
        Marriage (Luo law)
        Marriage (Maya law)
        Marriage (Primitive law)
        Marriage (Roman-Dutch law)
        Marriage (Roman law)
        Marriage (Semitic law)
        Marriage (Visigothic law)
        Marriage by proxy
        Marriage settlements
        Married women
        Matrimonial actions
        Miscegenation—Law and legislation
        Posthumous marriage
        Separation (Law)
  — Conflict of laws
      USE Conflict of laws—Marriage
  — Domicile
      USE Domicile in domestic relations
  — Germany
      UF Nuremberg laws
Marriage law (Islamic law)
    USE Marriage (Islamic law)
Marriage licenses *(May Subd Geog)*
    UF Marriage bonds
    BT Marriage records
Marriage of person to animal
    USE Beast marriage
Marriage of Saint Catherine (Painting)
    USE Correggio, 1489?-1534. Mystic
        marriage of Saint Catherine
Marriage of the deaf
    USE Deaf—Marriage
Marriage of the king's son (Parable)
    USE Great supper (Parable)
Marriage of the mentally handicapped
    USE Mentally handicapped—Marriage
Marriage proposals
    UF Proposals of marriage

Marriage psychotherapy
    USE Marital psychotherapy
Marriage records *(May Subd Geog)*
    BT Registers of births, etc.
    NT Marriage licenses
Marriage sermons
    USE Marriage—Sermons
Marriage service *(May Subd Geog)*
    [BX2250 (Catholic)]
    [BX5149.M2 (Church of England)]
    [BX5949.M3 (Protestant Episcopal)]
    [HQ745 (General)]
    UF Service, Marriage
        Wedding ceremony
        Wedding service
    BT Liturgies
        Weddings
        Worship programs
    NT Wedding sermons
Marriage service (Hinduism)
    [BL1226.82.M3]
    BT Hinduism—Rituals
        Marriage customs and rites, Hindu
Marriage service (Judaism)
    BT Marriage customs and rites, Jewish
    NT Synagogue music—Marriage services
Marriage settlements *(May Subd Geog)*
    UF Settlements (Law)
    BT Inheritance and succession
        Marriage law
    NT Antenuptial contracts
        Dower
Marriage statistics
    USE Vital statistics
Marriage subsidies *(May Subd Geog)*
    UF Subsidies, Marriage
Marriage theorem
    BT Combinatorial analysis
    RT Matching theory
Marriage with deceased wife's sister
    (May Subd Geog)
    [HQ1028]
    UF Deceased wife's sister, Marriage with
        Marriage—Prohibited degrees
    BT Affinity (Law)
        Impediments to marriage
        Remarriage
Marriages, International
    UF International marriages
    NT Marriages of royalty and nobility
Marriages of royalty and nobility
    (May Subd Geog)
    UF Marriage, Morganatic
        Morganatic marriage
    BT Kings and rulers—Succession
        Marriages, International
Married men
    USE Husbands
Married people *(May Subd Geog)*
    UF Couples, Married
        Married persons
        People, Married
        Persons, Married
    BT Marital status
        Marriage
    NT Church work with married people
        Married women
        Remarried people
  — Counseling of
      USE Marriage counseling
  — Employment *(May Subd Geog)*
      Here are entered works on the conditions of
      employment of married people. Works on fami-
      lies in which both husband and wife are pursuing
      careers and on how this affects their relationship
      and family life are entered under Dual-career
      families.
      NT Children of working parents
         Clergy couples
         Married people in missionary work
         Mothers—Employment

Wives—Employment
— **Religious life (Hinduism)**
  [BL1228.3.M3]
— **Religious life (Islam)**
  [BP188.3.M3]
Married people in church work
  (May Subd Geog)
  BT Church work
Married people in missionary work
  (May Subd Geog)
  BT Married people—Employment
    Missionaries
— **Baptists, [Catholic Church, etc.]**
Married persons
  USE Married people
Married students (May Subd Geog)
  [LB3616.M3]
  UF Student marriages
  BT Students
Married women (May Subd Geog)
     Here are entered works on the legal status of
  women during marriage, especially on the effect of
  marriage on their legal capacity. Works on legal rela-
  tions between husband and wife are entered under
  Husband and wife. For works on the legal conditions
  of women in general, see the heading Women—Legal
  status, laws, etc.
  UF Coverture
    Housewives—Legal status, laws, etc.
  BT Capacity and disability
    Marriage law
    Married people
    Wives
    Women
    Women—Legal status, laws, etc.
  RT Husband and wife
  NT Displaced homemakers—Legal status,
      laws, etc.
    Parent and child (Law)
    Widows
— Conflict of laws
    USE Conflict of laws—Married women
— Employment
    USE Wives—Employment
— **Nationality**
    BT Citizenship
      Conflict of laws—Citizenship
      Conflict of laws—Married women
— **India**
    NT Married women (Hindu law)
Married women (Hindu law)
  BT Married women—India
  RT Widows (Hindu law)
Married women (Ila law)
  BT Law, Ila (African people)
Married women (Islamic law)
Married women (Jewish law)
Married women (Roman law)
Marriotte's law
  USE Boyle's law
Marrow
  USE Bone marrow
Marrow cells
  USE Bone marrow cells
Marrs family (Not Subd Geog)
  UF Mar family
    Marr family
    Mars family
Marrubium
  [QK495.L25]
  BT Lamiaceae
Marry family
  USE Merry family
Mars (Planet) (Not Subd Geog)
  [QB376 (Theoretical astronomy)]
  [QB641 (Descriptive astronomy)]
  BT Planets
  NT Cydonia (Mars)
    Mars probes
    Space flight to Mars
— **Atmosphere**
    UF Martian atmosphere

— Charts, diagrams, etc.
— Diameters
    [QB641]
— Ephemerides
    [QB641]
    BT Ephemerides
— Exploration
    UF Mars exploration
    BT Space flight to Mars
    NT Viking Mars Program
— — **Equipment**
— — **Juvenile literature**
— Geology (May Subd Geog)
    UF Geology, Martian
      Martian geology
    BT Geology
— Globes
— Juvenile literature
— Maps
— Observations
— Opposition, 1849-1850, [1860, 1862, etc.]
    [QB516]
— Orbit
— Photographs
    BT Planets—Photographs
— **Photographs from space**
— — **Juvenile literature**
    [QB641]
— Spectra
    [QB775]
— Surface
    [QB641]
    UF Surface of Mars (Planet)
— Tables
    [QB376]
MARS (Information retrieval system)
  UF Marketing and Advertising Reference
      Service
  BT Information storage and retrieval
      systems—Advertising
    Information storage and retrieval
      systems—Marketing
Mars (Planet), Flight to
  USE Space flight to Mars
Mars (Roman deity)
  BT Gods, Roman
    Mythology, Roman
  RT Ares (Greek deity)
— **Art**
    NT Marte di Todi (Statue)
Mars exploration
  USE Mars (Planet)—Exploration
Mars family
  USE Marrs family
Mars-la-Tour, Battle of, 1870
  USE Vionville, Battle of, 1870
Mars probes
  UF Martian probes
  BT Mars (Planet)
    Outer space—Exploration
  NT Project Mariner
Marsala wine
  BT Fortified wines
    Wine and wine making
Marschall family
  USE Marshall family
Marsden family (Not Subd Geog)
  UF Marsdin family
    Marsdon family
    Marsten family
    Marstin family
    Marston family
    Marstone family
    Marstons family
    Masden family
    Masdon family
    Masten family
    Mastin family
    Maston family
    Morston family

Marsdin family
  USE Marsden family
Marsdon family
  USE Marsden family
Marseille (France). Quartier des Arcenaulx
  USE Quartier des Arcenaulx (Marseille,
      France)
Marseille, Battle of, 1944
  BT World War, 1939-1945—Campaigns—
      France
Marseille porcelain
  UF Porcelain, Marseille
  BT Porcelain, French
Marseille pottery
  UF Pottery, Marseille
  BT Pottery, French
Marsey family
  USE Marcy family
Marsh ecology (May Subd Geog)
  [QH541.5.M3]
  BT Ecology
    Freshwater ecology
    Marshes
  NT Tidemarsh ecology
Marsh family (Not Subd Geog)
  UF March family
    Marshe family
    Mersch family
    Mersh family
Marsh fauna (May Subd Geog)
  BT Freshwater fauna
    Marshes
    Zoology
  NT Tidemarsh fauna
Marsh flies
  USE Sciomyzidae
Marsh flora (May Subd Geog)
  [QK938.M3]
  BT Freshwater flora
    Wetland flora
  RT Bog flora
    Pond flora
  NT Tidemarsh flora
Marsh frog
  USE Rana ridibunda
Marsh-gas
  USE Fire-damp
Marsh hawk
  USE Circus cyaneas
Marsh horsetail
  [QK524.E6 (Botany)]
  [SB615.M3 (Weed)]
  UF Equisetum palustre
    Pewter grass
Marsh parsley
  USE Cryptotaenia canadensis
Marsh Saint John's-wort
  USE Triadenum virginicum
Marsh Saint Johnswort
  USE Triadenum virginicum
Marsh wren, Long-billed
  USE Telmatodytes palustris
Marshal family
  USE Marshall family
Marshall Day
  USE John Marshall Day
Marshall family (Not Subd Geog)
  UF Marschall family
    Marshal family
Marshall Ford Lake (Tex.)
  USE Travis, Lake (Tex.)
Marshall Islands
  NT Enewetak Atoll (Marshall Islands)
    Kwajalein Island (Marshall Islands)
Marshall language
  [PL6255]
  UF Ebon language
  BT Micronesian languages
Marshall Pass (Colo.)
  BT Mountain passes—Colorado
    Ouray, Mount (Colo.)—Passes

Marshallian economics
  USE Neoclassical school of economics
Marshalling yards
  USE Railroads—Yards
Marshals (May Subd Geog)
  UF Air marshals
     Field marshals
  BT Armies—Staffs
     Generals
Marshals, Court
  USE United States marshals
Marshals (Court officials)
  USE United States marshals
Marshburn family (Not Subd Geog)
  UF Masbourn family
     Mashburn family
Marshe family
  USE Marsh family
Marshes (May Subd Geog)
  [S621 (Agriculture)]
  [TC975 (Reclamation)]
  BT Drainage
     Reclamation of land
     Waste lands
     Wetlands
  RT Bogs
     Fens
     Moors and heaths
     Swamps
  NT Marsh ecology
     Marsh fauna
     Will-o'-the-wisp
  — Byelorussian S.S.R.
     NT Pripet Marshes (Byelorussian
        S.S.R. and Ukraine)
  — England
     NT Broads, The (England)
        Romney Marsh (England)
  — France
     NT Poitevin Marsh (France)
  — Hungary
     NT Ecsed Marsh (Hungary and
        Romania)
  — Italy
     NT Pontine Marshes (Italy)
  — Japan
     NT Oze Marsh (Japan)
        Teganuma Marsh (Japan)
  — New Jersey
     NT Meadowlands (N.J.)
  — Romania
     NT Ecsed Marsh (Hungary and
        Romania)
  — Sudan
     NT Machar Marshes (Sudan)
  — Ukraine
     NT Pripet Marshes (Byelorussian
        S.S.R. and Ukraine)
Marshes, Tide (May Subd Geog)
  [S621 (Agriculture)]
  [TC975 (Reclamation)]
  UF Salt-marshes
     Tidal marshes
     Tide-marshes
     Tidewater marshes
  BT Tidal flats
  NT Mangrove swamps
     Tidemarsh ecology
     Tidemarsh flora
Marshes in art
Marshfield Cemetery (Ohio)
  USE New Marshfield Cemetery (Ohio)
Marshpee Indians
  USE Mashpee Indians
Marsi
  [DG225.M3]
  BT Ethnology—Italy
     Italic peoples
Marsica (Italy)
Marsica Prize
  USE Premio Marsica

Marsiglia
  USE Marsilea
Marsilea
  [QK524.M4 (Botany)]
  UF Clover fern
     Marsiglia
     Marsilia
     Pepperwort
     Water clover
     Waterclover
  BT Marsileaceae
Marsilea drummondii
  [QK524.M4 (Botany)]
  UF Drummond pepperwort
Marsilea quadrifolia
  [QK524.M4 (Botany)]
  UF Marsilea quadrifoliata
Marsilea quadrifoliata
  USE Marsilea quadrifolia
Marsileaceae
  [QK524.M4 (Botany)]
  UF Marsiliaceae
  BT Marsileales
  NT Marsilea
     Regnellidium
Marsileales
  BT Ferns
     Water ferns
  NT Marsileaceae
Marsilia
  USE Marsilea
Marsiliaceae
  USE Marsileaceae
Marsteller family (Not Subd Geog)
Marsten family
  USE Marsden family
Marstin family
  USE Marsden family
Marston, William Moulton, 1893-1947.
  Wonder Woman
  UF Wonder Woman (Comic strip)
Marston family
  USE Marsden family
Marston Moor, Battle of, 1644
  [DA417]
  BT Great Britain—History—Civil War,
     1642-1649—Campaigns
Marstone family
  USE Marsden family
Marstonia
  [QL430.5.H9]
  BT Hydrobiidae
Marstons family
  USE Marsden family
Marsupialia (May Subd Geog)
  [QL737.M3]
  UF Pouched animals
  BT Mammals
  NT Brush-tailed phalangers
     Dasyuridae
     Flying phalangers
     Gliders (Mammals)
     Koalas
     Numbat
     Opossums
     Peramelidae
     Phalangeridae
     Wombats
Marsupialia, Fossil
  [QE882.M3]
  NT Borhyaenidae
     Ektopodontidae
     Microbiotheriidae
     Polydolopidae
Marsyas (Greek deity)
  [BL820.M26]
  BT Gods, Greek
     Mythology, Greek
Mart family (Not Subd Geog)
Martain family
  USE Martin family

Mārtaṇḍa (Hindu deity)
  BT Gods, Hindu
     Mahābhārata—Biography
Martanum (Ancient city)
  BT Cities and towns, Ruined, extinct, etc.
     —Italy
     Italy—Antiquities
Marte di Todi (Statue)
  BT Bronzes, Etruscan—Greek influences
     Etruria—Antiquities
     Mars (Roman deity)—Art
Marté shorthand
  USE Shorthand, Spanish—Marté
Martee family
  USE Marty family
Martello Collection (Italy)
  BT Art—Private collections—Italy
Martello towers (May Subd Geog)
  [UG407]
  BT Fortification
     Towers
Martelossi
  USE Martoloses
Marten family
  USE Martin family
Martenot (Musical instrument)
  USE Ondes Martenot
Martenot's ondes musicales
  USE Ondes Martenot
Martens
  [QL737.C2 (Zoology)]
  [SF405.M (Culture)]
  NT Fisher (Animal)
     Pine marten
     Stone marten
Martens family
  USE Martin family
Martensite
  [TN731]
  NT Martensitic stainless steel
     Martensitic transformations
Martensitic stainless steel
  BT Martensite
     Precipitation hardening
     Steel, Stainless
Martensitic transformations
  UF Transformations, Martensitic
  BT Martensite
     Phase rule and equilibrium
  NT Shape memory effect
Martes
  [QL737.C25]
  BT Mustelidae
Martes foina
  USE Stone marten
Martes martes
  USE Pine marten
Martes pennanti
  USE Fisher (Animal)
MARTHA (Computer program)
  BT Computer programs
     Electronic circuit design—Computer
        programs
Martha's Vineyard (Mass.)
  UF Martin Wyngaards Island (Mass.)
  BT Islands—Massachusetts
Marther family
  USE Mather family
Marthew family
  USE Matthews family
Marthews family
  USE Matthews family
Marti family
  USE Marty family
Martial artists (May Subd Geog)
  [GV1113]

UF Aikidoists
      Judo participants
      Judoists
      Judo
      Judoka
      Karateists
      Karateka
  BT Hand-to-hand fighting, Oriental

Martial arts *(May Subd Geog)*
  BT Combat
  RT Self-defense
  NT Archery
      Dueling
      Hand-to-hand fighting
      Shooting, Military
      Spear fighting
      Zen Buddhism and martial arts
  — Religious aspects
  — — Baptists, ⌜Catholic Church, etc.⌟
  — — Buddhism, ⌜Christianity, etc.⌟
  — Brazil
      NT Capoeira (Dance)

Martial arts fiction
  BT Fiction

Martial arts fiction, Chinese
  (May Subd Geog)
    ⌜PL2419.M37 (History)⌟
    ⌜PL2629.M37 (Collections)⌟
  UF Chinese martial arts fiction
  BT Chinese fiction

Martial arts schools *(May Subd Geog)*
    ⌜GV1102-1102.2⌟
  UF Schools, Martial arts
  BT Schools

Martial arts weapons *(May Subd Geog)*
    ⌜GV1101.5⌟
  UF Karate weapons
      Weapons in martial arts
  BT Arms and armor
  NT Nunchaku
  — Law and legislation *(May Subd Geog)*

Martial law *(May Subd Geog)*
    ⌜JK343-JK355 (United States)⌟
    ⌜JN261 (Constitutional history: Great
      Britain)⌟
    ⌜JX4595 (International law)⌟
  UF Law, Martial
  BT Constitutional law
      War
      War (International law)
  RT Military law
  NT Courts-martial and courts of inquiry
      Habeas corpus
      Military courts
      Military government of dependencies
      Requisitions, Military
      State of siege
  — United States
      UF United States—Martial law

Martian atmosphere
  USE Mars (Planet)—Atmosphere
Martian geology
  USE Mars (Planet)—Geology
Martian probes
  USE Mars probes
Martienssen's free-tailed bat
  USE Otomops martiensseni

Martin, Lake (Ala.)
  UF Lake Martin (Ala.)
  BT Lakes—Alabama
      Reservoirs—Alabama
      Tallapoosa River (Ga. and Ala.)

Martin airplanes
  NT Marauder (Bomber)
      Mariner bombers
      Marlin bombers

Martin family *(Not Subd Geog)*
  UF Martain family
      Marten family
      Martens family
      Martine family
      Marton family
      Martten family
      Martyn family
  RT Martínez family
      Martinson family
      Matusz family

Martín García, Battle of, 1814
  BT Argentina—History—War of
      Independence, 1810-1817—
      Campaigns

Martin-Gropius-Bau (Berlin, Germany)
  BT Exhibition buildings—Germany (West)

**Martin Luther King, Junior, National Historic
Site (Atlanta, Ga.)**
  UF King National Historic Site (Atlanta,
      Ga.)
  BT Historic sites—Georgia
      National parks and reserves—Georgia

Martin Viking (Rockets)
  USE Viking rocket
Martin Wyngaards Island (Mass.)
  USE Martha's Vineyard (Mass.)
Martine family
  USE Martin family

Martínez de Marcilla, Diego Juan, 13th cent.
  — Legends
      USE Lovers of Teruel (Legend)

Martínez del Río family *(Not Subd Geog)*

Martínez family *(Not Subd Geog)*
  RT Martin family

Martingales (Mathematics)
    ⌜QA274.5⌟
  BT Stochastic processes

Martini-Henry rifle
  BT Rifles

Martinique
    As a geographic subdivision, this heading is used
  directly.
  — Economic conditions
  — — 1918-
Martinique, Battle of, 1782
  USE Dominica, Battle of, 1782
Martinique art
  USE Art, Martinique
Martinique authors
  USE Authors, Martinique

Martinique fiction (French)
  (May Subd Geog)
    ⌜PQ3948.M3 (History)⌟
    ⌜PQ3948.M32 (Collections)⌟
  UF French fiction—Martinique authors

Martinique literature (French)
    ⌜PQ3948.5.M⌟
  UF French literature—Martinique authors

Martinique literature (French Creole)
  (May Subd Geog)
  UF Creole literature, Martinique French
      French Creole literature, Martinique

Martinique poetry (French)
  (May Subd Geog)
    ⌜PQ3948.5.M⌟
  UF French poetry—Martinique authors

Martinis
    ⌜TX951⌟
  BT Cocktails
Martinmas in winter
  USE Saint Martin's Day
Martins
  USE House-martin
      Purple martin

Martin's axiom
  UF MA (Set theory)
  BT Axiomatic set theory
      Continuity
      Numbers, Cardinal

Martin's Hundred Site (Va.)
  (Not Subd Geog)
  UF Merchant's Hundred Site (Va.)
  BT Virginia—Antiquities
Martinsen family
  USE Martinson family

Martinson family *(Not Subd Geog)*
  UF Martinsen family
  RT Martin family
Martirio di San Pietro (Painting)
  USE Michelangelo Buonarroti, 1475-1564.
      Crucifixion of Saint Peter

Martis culture *(May Subd Geog)*
  BT California—Antiquities
      Nevada—Antiquities
Martius babassu
  USE Babassu
Martlet (Fighter plane)
  USE Wildcat (Fighter plane)

Martoloses
  UF Armatoli
      Martelossi
      Mortoloses
Marton family
  USE Martin family
Martten family
  USE Martin family

Marty family *(Not Subd Geog)*
  UF Martee family
      Marti family
Martyn family
  USE Martin family

Martyniaceae
    ⌜QK495.M287 (Botany)⌟
  BT Tubiflorae

Martyr (The word)
  BT English language—Etymology

Martyrdom
  BT Death—Religious aspects
      Suffering—Religious aspects
  RT Martyrs
  NT Martyrdom (Christianity)

Martyrdom (Christianity)
  BT Martyrdom
  RT Christian martyrs

Martyrdom (Islam)
  RT Muslim martyrs

Martyrdom (Judaism)
    ⌜BM645.M34⌟
Martyrdom of Saint Erasmus (Painting)
  USE Poussin, Nicolas, 1594?-1665.
      Martydom of Saint Erasmus
Martyre de Saint Erasme (Painting)
  USE Poussin, Nicolas, 1594?-1665.
      Martydom of Saint Erasmus

Martyria *(May Subd Geog)*
  BT Architecture, Early Christian
      Christian martyrs—Cult
      Relics and reliquaries
      Shrines

Martyrologies
    ⌜BR1609⌟
    ⌜BX4660 (Catholic)⌟
  BT Necrologies

Martyrs *(May Subd Geog)*
  BT Heroes
      Persecution
      Saints
  RT Martyrdom
  NT Christian martyrs
      Hindu martyrs
      Muslim martyrs
      Refugees, Religious
      Sikh martyrs
  — Cult *(May Subd Geog)*
      UF Cult of martyrs
          Invocation of martyrs
          Veneration of martyrs
          Worship of martyrs
      BT Cults
  — Legends

Martyrs
— Legends *(Continued)*
[BR1600-BR1609]
[BX4654-BX4662 *(Catholic
Church)*]
— Prayer-books and devotions
— — English, [French, German, etc.]
[BX2166]
Martyrs, Buddhist
USE Buddhist martyrs
Martyrs, Christian
USE Christian martyrs
Martyrs, Islamic
USE Muslim martyrs
Martyrs, Jewish
USE Jewish martyrs
Martyrs, Muslim
USE Muslim martyrs
Martyrs in art
Martz family *(Not Subd Geog)*
UF Mertz family
Merz family
Maru-Kumbars
[DS432.M]
UF Kumbars, Maru
Kumbhars, Maru
BT Caste—India
Ethnology—India
Maruba Indians
[F2520.1.M26]
UF Maroba Indians
Marova Indians
Marubo Indians
BT Indians of South America
Indians of South America—Brazil
Marubo Indians
USE Maruba Indians
Maruina
[QL537.P85]
BT Moth-flies
Psychodidae
Maruki family *(Not Subd Geog)*
Marukoji (Japan)
USE Tsuta no Hosomichi (Japan)
Marum
USE Cat thyme
Marum syriacum
USE Cat thyme
Marum verum
USE Cat thyme
Marung language
USE Maung language
Maruyama-ha
USE Maruyama School
Maruyama School
[ND1053.6.M37]
UF Maruyama-ha
Maruyama school of painting
BT Painting, Japanese—Edo period, 1600-
1868
Maruyama school of painting
USE Maruyama School
Maruyamakyō
[BL2228.M37]
BT Cults—Japan
Mountain worship—Japan
Marvel family *(Not Subd Geog)*
UF Marvele family
Marvell family
Marvil family
Marvill family
Marvyle family
Mervaile family
Merveille family
Mervell family
Morvil family
Morvill family
Morville family
Marvele family
USE Marvel family

Marvell family
USE Marvel family
Marvelous, The
[BF775]
BT Supernatural
RT Miracles
Marvelous, The, in literature
RT Magic realism (Literature)
Marvil family
USE Marvel family
Marvill family
USE Marvel family
Marvin family *(Not Subd Geog)*
UF Marvine family
Marvins family
Marwine family
Marvine family
USE Marvin family
Marvins family
USE Marvin family
Marvyle family
USE Marvel family
Marwar sculpture
USE Mewar sculpture
Marwari folk-songs
USE Folk-songs, Marwari
Marwari language
[PK2461-2479]
BT Rajasthani language
NT Bikaneri dialect
Dingal language
Mewari dialect
Marwari poetry *(May Subd Geog)*
NT Vaishnava poetry, Marwari
Marwari songs
USE Songs, Marwari
Marwari Vaishnava poetry
USE Vaishnava poetry, Marwari
Marwaris
[DS432.M28]
BT Businessmen—India
Caste—India
Ethnology—India
Merchants—India
Marwine family
USE Marvin family
Marx family
USE Marks family
Marxian anthropology
USE Communism and anthropology
Marxian archaeology *(May Subd Geog)*
UF Archaeology, Marxian
Marxist archaeology
BT Archaeology—Methodology
Archaeology—Philosophy
Marxian criticism
USE Marxist criticism
Marxian economics
[HB97.5]
UF Radical economics
BT Communism
Economics
Socialism
NT Asiatic mode of production
Labor theory of value
Surplus value
Marxian historiography *(May Subd Geog)*
Here are entered works on the writing of history
from a historical materialist point of view. Works on
the Marxian theory of human history are entered
under Historical materialism.
UF Historiography, Marxian
Marxist historiography
BT Historiography
RT Historical materialism
Marxian philosophy
USE Philosophy, Marxist
Marxian school of sociology
(May Subd Geog)
UF Marxian sociology
Marxist sociology

BT Communism and society
Schools of sociology
RT Frankfurt school of sociology
Marxian sociology
USE Communism and society
Marxian school of sociology
Marxism
USE Communism
Socialism
Marxist aesthetics
USE Communist aesthetics
Marxist archaeology
USE Marxian archaeology
Marxist criticism *(May Subd Geog)*
UF Criticism, Marxist
Marxian criticism
Marxist literary criticism
BT Communism and literature
Communist aesthetics
Criticism
Marxist historiography
USE Marxian historiography
Marxist literary criticism
USE Marxist criticism
Marxist philosophy
USE Philosophy, Marxist
Marxist sociology
USE Marxian school of sociology
Mary, Blessed Virgin, Saint
[BT595-680]
UF Blessed Lady
Blessed Mother
Blessed Virgin Mary, Saint
Madonna
Mother of God
Our Lady
Theotokos
Virgin Mary
BT Christian saints
Ladybirds—Religious aspects—
Christianity
— Annunciation
[BT615]
UF Annunciation to the Blessed Virgin
Mary
— Apparitions and miracles
(May Subd Geog)
[BT650-660]
UF Mary, Blessed Virgin, Saint—
Miracles
BT Apparitions
Miracles
SA *names of particular apparitions and
miracles, e.g.* Fatima, Our Lady
of
NT Fatima, Our Lady of
— — Belgium
NT Beauraing, Notre-Dame de
— — Canary Islands
NT Pino, Virgen del
— — Mexico
NT Guadalupe, Our Lady of
Remedios, Nuestra Señora de
los
— Art
UF Mary, Blessed Virgin, Saint—
Iconography
NT Black Virgins
Bogomater' Donskaîa (Icon)
Chernigovskaîa Chudotvornaîa
Bogomater' (Icon)
Conquistadora (Statue)
Częstochowa, Our Lady of (Icon)
Goya, Francisco, 1746-1828.
Regina Martirum
Icons
Iverskaîa Svîataîa i Chudotvornaîa
Bogomater' (Icon)
Mary, Blessed Virgin, Saint—
Symbolism

2290

Michelangelo Buonarroti, 1475-
1564. Pietà
Pacher, Michael, 15th cent.   Gries
Altar
Pietà
Pochaïvs'ka Bohorodytsīā (Icon)
Raphael, 1483-1520.   Madonna of
Loretto
Sambirs'ka Bohorodytsīā (Icon)
Thaumatourgos Eikōn tēs
Prousiōtissēs (Icon)
Tikhvinskaīā Bogomater' (Icon)
Umilenīē TSaritsy Nebesnoĭ (Icon)
Uspenie (Icon)
Virga Jesse (Sculpture)
— Assumption
  ₍BT630₎
  UF Assumption of the Blessed Virgin
      Mary
      Mary, Blessed Virgin, Saint—
      Death
  RT Assumption of the Blessed Virgin
      Mary, Feast of the
— Biography
  ₍BT604-605.2₎
  NT Mysteries of the Rosary
— Coredemption
  ₍BT640₎
  UF Coredemption by the Blessed
      Virgin Mary
  NT Mary, Blessed Virgin, Saint—
      Mediation
      Mary, Blessed Virgin, Saint—
      Motherhood (Spiritual)
— Cult (May Subd Geog)
  ₍BT645-646₎
  UF Hyperdulia
      Mary, Blessed Virgin, Saint—
      Worship
  RT Mary, Blessed Virgin, Saint—
      Shrines
  NT Black Virgins
      Conquistadora (Statue)
      Marian Year
      Mary, Blessed Virgin, Saint—May
      devotions
      Mary, Blessed Virgin, Saint, in the
      liturgy
      Recouvrance, Notre Dame de
      Rosary, Our Lady of the
      Sacred Heart of Mary, Devotion to
      Sorrows of the Blessed Virgin
      Mary, Devotion to
— — Argentina
  NT Luján, Our Lady of
— — Chile
  NT Candelaria de Copiapó, Virgen
      de la
— — Costa Rica
  NT Angeles, Nuestra Señora de los
— — France
  NT Lorrains, Notre-Dame des
      Peinière, Notre-Dame de la
— — Germany (West)
  NT Werl, Madonna von
— — Italy
  NT Foggia, Vergine Incoronata di
      Montevergine, Madonna di
— — Mexico
  NT Guadalupe, Our Lady of
      Tepeyac, Virgen del
— — Poland
  NT Częstochowa, Our Lady of
      (Icon)
— — Portugal
  NT Fatima, Our Lady of
— — Spain
  NT Arboló, Nuestra Señora de
      Cabeza, Virgen de la
      Caridad, Virgen de la
      Montaña, Virgen de la

Nieves de Chinchilla, Virgen de
las
Peñarroya, Nuestra Señora de
Santa Maria de la Candela
Valpeñoso, Nuestra Señora de
Virtudes, Nuestra Señora de las
— — Venezuela
  NT Coromoto, Nuestra Señora de
— Death
  USE Mary, Blessed Virgin, Saint—
      Assumption
— Dolors
  USE Sorrows of the Blessed Virgin
      Mary, Devotion to
— Early works to 1800
— Feasts
  ₍BT645.5₎
  BT Church year
      Fasts and feasts
  SA names of individual feasts, e.g.
      Immaculate Conception, Feast
      of the
— History of doctrines
  ₍BT610-BT612₎
  UF Mary, Blessed Virgin, Saint—
      Theology—History of doctrines
— Iconography
  USE Mary, Blessed Virgin, Saint—Art
— Intercession
  USE Mary, Blessed Virgin, Saint—
      Mediation
— Interpretations, Islamic
  USE Mary, Blessed Virgin, Saint—
      Islamic interpretations
— Interpretations, Jewish
  USE Mary, Blessed Virgin, Saint—
      Jewish interpretations
— Islamic interpretations
  ₍BP172₎
  UF Mary, Blessed Virgin, Saint—
      Interpretations, Islamic
      Mary, Blessed Virgin, Saint, in
      Islam
  BT Christianity and other religions—
      Islam
      Islam—Relations—Christianity
  NT Mary, Blessed Virgin, Saint, in the
      Koran
— Jewish interpretations
  UF Mary, Blessed Virgin, Saint—
      Interpretations, Jewish
      Mary, Blessed Virgin, Saint, in
      Judaism
  BT Christianity and other religions—
      Judaism
      Judaism—Relations—Christianity
— Legends
— May devotions
  ₍BX2161₎
  UF May devotions to the Blessed
      Virgin Mary
  BT Mary, Blessed Virgin, Saint—Cult
      Mary, Blessed Virgin, Saint—
      Prayer-books and devotions
— Mediation
  ₍BT640₎
  UF Mary, Blessed Virgin, Saint—
      Intercession
  BT Mary, Blessed Virgin, Saint—
      Coredemption
      Mediation between God and man
      —Christianity
— Miracles
  USE Mary, Blessed Virgin, Saint—
      Apparitions and miracles
— Motherhood
— Motherhood (Spiritual)
  BT Mary, Blessed Virgin, Saint—
      Coredemption
— Name

USE Mary, Blessed Virgin, Saint—
    Titles
— Papal documents
— Prayer-books and devotions
  NT Mary, Blessed Virgin, Saint—May
      devotions
— — English
— Psychology
  ₍BT670.P75₎
  BT Psychology
— Purification
  ₍BT670.P8₎
  NT Candlemas
— Queenship
— Sacred Heart, Devotion to
  USE Sacred Heart of Mary, Devotion
      to
— Seven sorrows
  USE Sorrows of the Blessed Virgin
      Mary, Devotion to
— Shrines (May Subd Geog)
  ₍BT650-660₎
  BT Christian shrines
  RT Mary, Blessed Virgin, Saint—Cult
— Sinlessness
  ₍BT622₎
  UF Debitum peccati
      Sinlessness of the Blessed Virgin
      Mary
  RT Immaculate Conception
— Songs and music
  BT Church music
      Sacred vocal music
  NT Ave Maria (Music)
      Ave Maris Stella (Music)
      Ave Regina coelorum (Music)
      Regina Caeli laetare (Music)
      Salve Regina (Music)
      Stabat Mater dolorosa (Music)
— Sorrows
  USE Sorrows of the Blessed Virgin
      Mary, Devotion to
— Symbolism
  BT Christian art and symbolism
      Mary, Blessed Virgin, Saint—Art
      Symbolism
— Theology
  ₍BT613₎
  UF Mariology
— — History of doctrines
  USE Mary, Blessed Virgin, Saint—
      History of doctrines
— Titles
  ₍BT670.T5₎
  UF Mary, Blessed Virgin, Saint—Name
— Typology
  BT Typology (Theology)
— Virginity
  RT Jesus Christ—Brethren
      Virgin birth
— Visitation
  USE Visitation festival
— Worship
  USE Mary, Blessed Virgin, Saint—Cult
Mary, Blessed Virgin, Saint, and Christian
union
  BT Christian union
      Education
Mary, Blessed Virgin, Saint, and the church
  BT Church
Mary, Blessed Virgin, Saint, in Islam
  USE Mary, Blessed Virgin, Saint—Islamic
      interpretations
Mary, Blessed Virgin, Saint, in Judaism
  USE Mary, Blessed Virgin, Saint—Jewish
      interpretations
Mary, Blessed Virgin, Saint, in the Koran
  ₍BP133.7.M35₎
  UF Maryam (Koranic character)

Mary, Blessed Virgin, Saint, in the Koran
  (Continued)
  BT Koran—Biography
      Koran—Theology
      Liturgics
      Mary, Blessed Virgin, Saint—Islamic
        interpretations
Mary, Blessed Virgin, Saint, in the liturgy
  [BT645.3]
  BT Mary, Blessed Virgin, Saint—Cult
  — Catholic Church, [Orthodox Eastern
    Church, etc.]
Mary (Name)
**Mary Dunn Cemetery (Daufuskie Island,
  S.C.)**
  BT Cemeteries—South Carolina
Mary family
  USE Merry family
**Mary McLeod Bethune Council House
  (Washington, D.C.)**
  BT Dwellings—Washington (D.C.)
Maryam (Koranic character)
  USE Mary, Blessed Virgin, Saint, in the
    Koran
Marye family *(Not Subd Geog)*
  UF Marie family
Maryfield family
  USE Merrifield family
Maryland
  — Antiquities
      NT Hallowing Point Site (Md.)
          Moore Village Site (Md.)
          Oxon Hill Manor (Md.)
  — Boundaries
  — — Virginia
  — Claims vs. United States
  — Description and travel
  — — To 1775
  — — 1775-1865
  — — 1865-1950
  — — 1951-1980
  — — 1981-
  — History
      [F176-190]
  — — Colonial period, ca. 1600-1775
  — — — Juvenile literature
  — — French and Indian War, 1755-1763
  — — Revolution, 1775-1783
        [E263.M3]
  — — War of 1812
        [E395.5.M2]
  — — Civil War, 1861-1865
        [E512]
        [E566]
      NT Maryland Campaign, 1864
            (June-August)
          Monocacy, Battle of the, 1864
  — — War of 1898
  — Politics and government
  — — Colonial period, ca. 1600-1775
  — — Revolution, 1775-1783
  — — 1775-1865
  — — Civil War, 1861-1865
  — — 1865-1950
  — — 1951-
  — Social life and customs
  — — Colonial period, ca. 1600-1775
        [F184]
Maryland, Southern
      Here are entred works that discuss Anne Arundel,
    Calvert, St. Mary's, Charles, and Prince George's
    Counties collectively.
  UF Southern Maryland
Maryland, Western
      Here are entered works that discuss Washington,
    Allegany, and Garrett Counties collectively.
  UF Western Maryland
Maryland brook lamprey
  USE Least brook lamprey
Maryland Campaign, 1862
  [E474.61]

  UF Antietam Campaign
      Lee's 1st Northern Invasion
  BT United States—History—Civil War,
        1861-1865—Campaigns
      Virginia—History—Civil War, 1861-
        1865
Maryland Campaign, 1863
  USE Gettysburg Campaign, 1863
Maryland Campaign, 1864 (June-August)
  [E476.66]
  UF Early's Invasion of Maryland and
        Pennsylvania, 1864
      Pennsylvania Invasion, 1864
  BT Maryland—History—Civil War, 1861-
        1865
      United States—History—Civil War,
        1861-1865—Campaigns
Maryland, Delaware, and Virginia Railway
  BT Railroads—United States
Maryland Hunt Cup
  [SF359.7.M3]
  BT Rewards (Prizes, etc.)—Maryland
      Steeplechasing—Maryland
Maryland yellowthroat
  [QL696.P2]
  UF Geothlypis trichas
      Yellowthroat, Maryland
  BT Wood warblers
Marys family
  USE Merry family
Maryūt, Lake (Egypt) *(Not Subd Geog)*
  UF Buḥayrat Maryūt (Egypt)
      Lake Maryūt (Egypt)
      Mareotis Lake (Egypt)
      Mariut Lake (Egypt)
  BT Lakes—Egypt
Marzabotto Massacre, 1944
  UF Monte Sole Massacre, 1944
  BT World War, 1939-1945—Atrocities
Marzano Palace (Carinola, Italy)
  USE Palazzo Marzano (Carinola, Italy)
Marzio, Campo (Rome, Italy)
  USE Campo Marzio (Rome, Italy)
Marzipan *(May Subd Geog)*
  BT Confectionery
      Cookery (Almonds)
MAS (Computer system)
  UF Minerals availability system
  BT Electronic digital computers—
        Programming
      Mines and mineral resources—Data
        processing
Masa (African people)
  UF Massa (African people)
  BT Ethnology—Cameroon
      Ethnology—Chad
Masa language (Chadic) *(May Subd Geog)*
  [PL8499]
  UF Banaa language
      Banana language (Masa)
      Masana language
      Massa language
      Walai language
  BT Cameroon—Languages
      Chad—Languages
      Chadic languages
Masaba language
  USE Gisu language
Masacali Indians
  [F2520.1.M27]
  UF Machaculi Indians
      Mashacali Indians
      Maxakali Indians
  BT Indians of South America
Masacali language
  [PM6462]
  UF Makacari language
      Mashacali language
      Maxakali language
  BT Indians of South America—Languages

Masaccio, 1401-1428? Trinity
  UF Trinità (Mural painting)
      Trinity (Mural painting)
      Trinity with donors (Mural painting)
      Trinity with donors and skeleton
        (Mural painting)
  BT Mural painting and decoration, Italian
Masada Site (Israel) *(Not Subd Geog)*
  UF Ḥorvot Metsadah (Israel)
      Ḥorvot Meẓada (Israel)
      Massada Site (Israel)
      Mazada Site (Israel)
      Metsada Site (Israel)
      Metsadah Site (Israel)
      Meẓada Site (Israel)
      Sabba Site (Israel)
      Sebbe Site (Israel)
  BT Israel—Antiquities
  — Siege, 72-73
      BT Jews—History—Rebellion, 66-73
Masai
  [DT434.E2 (History, DT429)]
  [DT434.E2 (Kenya)]
  [GN659.M3 (Anthropology)]
  UF Elmoran
      Massai
  BT Ethnology—Tanganyika
      Hamites
  NT Arusha (African people)
      Missions to Masai
Masai folk literature
  USE Folk literature, Masai
Masai language
  [PL8501]
  UF Maa language (Kenya and Tanzania)
      Maasai language
  BT Kenya—Languages
      Nilo-Hamitic languages
      Tanzania—Languages
Masai literature *(May Subd Geog)*
  NT Folk literature, Masai
Masai Mara Game Reserve (Kenya)
  BT Game-preserves—Kenya
      National parks and reserves—Kenya
Masai women
  USE Women, Masai
Masakado's Revolt, 938-940
  USE Japan—History—Tengyō Revolt, 938-
        940
Masana language
  USE Masa language (Chadic)
Masango language
  USE Shira language
Masarete language
  USE Buru language
Masaridae
  [QL568.M3]
  UF Masarididae
  BT Hymenoptera
      Solitary wasps
  NT Pseudomasaris
Masarididae
  USE Masaridae
Masars family
  USE Masear family
Maşat Hüyük (Turkey)
  USE Maşat Mound (Turkey)
Maşat Mound (Turkey) *(Not Subd Geog)*
  [DS156.M]
  UF Maşat Hüyük (Turkey)
  BT Mounds—Turkey
      Turkey—Antiquities
Masbate language
  USE Masbateno language
Masbateno language *(May Subd Geog)*
  UF Masbate language
      Minasbate language
  BT Philippine languages
      Philippines—Languages
Masbourn family
  USE Marshburn family

Mascarene Islands
  UF Limuria
  BT Islands of the Indian Ocean
  NT Réunion
      Rodrigues Island (Mauritius)
Mascarene Islands literature
  USE Mascarene literature
Mascarene literature
  UF Mascarene Islands literature
  NT Mauritian literature (French)
      Réunion literature (French)
Mascarene white eye
  USE Zosterops borbonica
Masch Lake (Germany) *(Not Subd Geog)*
  UF Maschsee (Germany)
  BT Lakes—Germany (West)
Maschinelle Analyse Altägyptischer Texte
  (Electronic computer system)
  USE MAAT (Electronic computer system)
Maschsee (Germany)
  USE Masch Lake (Germany)
Masco Indians
  USE Mashco Indians
Masco language
  USE Mashco language
Mascoi language
  USE Lengua-Mascoi language
Mascots, Military
  USE *subdivision* Mascots *under specific*
         headings, e.g. Armed Forces—
         Mascots
Mascouten Indians
  ₍E99.M3₎
  BT Algonquian Indians
      Indians of North America
      Shawnee Indians
Masculinity (Psychology)
  BT Men—Psychology
      Sex (Psychology)
Masden family
  USE Marsden family
Masdon family
  USE Marsden family
Masear family *(Not Subd Geog)*
  UF Mahser family
      Masars family
      Maser family
Masen family
  USE Mason family
Masenrempulu language
  ₍PL5408₎
  BT Malayan languages
Maser family
  USE Masear family
Maserati automobile
  ₍TL215.M₎
Masers
  ₍TK7872.M45₎
  UF Microwave amplification by stimulated
         emission of radiation
      Quantum mechanical amplifiers
  BT Electromagnetism
      Electron tubes
      Infrared sources
      Microwave amplifiers
      Microwave devices
      Molecular dynamics
      Optical pumping
      Quantum electronics
  NT Negative temperature
Masers, Celestial
  UF Celestial masers
  BT Electromagnetism
      Interstellar matter
      Radiation
      Radio sources (Astronomy)
Masers, Optical
  USE Lasers
Masey family
  USE Macy family

MASH (Computer system)
Mashacali Indians
  USE Masacali Indians
Mashacali language
  USE Masacali language
Mashburn family
  USE Marshburn family
Mashco Indians
  UF Amarakaeri Indians
      Amarakaire Indians
      Harakmbet Indians
      Masco Indians
      Masko Indians
      Moeno Indians
  BT Arawakan Indians
      Indians of South America—Peru
Mashco language
  ₍PM6464.M3₎
  UF Harakmbet language
      Masco language
      Maško language
  BT Arawakan languages
      Indians of South America—Languages
Masherbrum Peak (Pakistan)
  BT Karakoram Range
      Mountains—Pakistan
Mashi language
  USE Shi language
Mashiko pottery *(May Subd Geog)*
  ₍NK4168.M₎
  UF Pottery, Mashiko
  BT Pottery, Japanese
Mashona
  ₍DT962.42₎
  UF Shona
  BT Bantus
      Ethnology—South Africa
      Ethnology—Zimbabwe
  NT Gova (Shona-speaking people)
      Karanga (African people)
      Missions to Mashona
      Tawara (African people)
      Zezuru (Bantu people)
  — Children
      BT Children—Zimbabwe
  — History
      NT Zimbabwe—History—Ndebele
          Insurrection, 1896-1897
  — Medicine
      ₍DT962.42₎
      BT Medicine, Primitive
Mashona law
  USE Law, Mashona
Mashona names
  USE Names, Mashona
Mashona sculpture
  USE Sculpture, Mashona
Mashpee Indians
  ₍E99.M4₎
  UF Marshpee Indians
  BT Algonquian Indians
      Indians of North America
Mashu-ko (Japan)
  USE Mashū Lake (Japan)
Mashū Lake (Japan)
  UF Mashu-ko (Japan)
      Mashun-ko (Japan)
  BT Lakes—Japan
Mashukolumbwe (African people)
  USE Ila (African people)
Mashun-ko (Japan)
  USE Mashū Lake (Japan)
Masiceridae
  USE Tachinidae
Masingale family
  USE Massengill family
Masingill family
  USE Massengill family
Masino Valley (Italy)
  UF Val Masino (Italy)
  BT Valleys—Italy

Masira Island (Oman)
  USE Masirah Island (Oman)
Masirah Island (Oman)
  UF Al Masira (Oman)
      Al Masīrah (Oman)
      Jazīrat al Masīrah (Oman)
      Jazīrat Masīrah (Oman)
      Masira Island (Oman)
      Mesirah Island (Oman)
  BT Islands—Oman
Masis (Turkey)
  USE Ararat, Mount (Turkey)
Masivul Ciucaş (Romania)
  USE Ciucaş Mountains (Romania)
Mask makers *(May Subd Geog)*
  UF Maskmakers
  BT Artisans
      Artists
Maskanah Site (Syria)
  USE Emar (Ancient city)
Masked bobwhite
  USE Bobwhite
Masked booby
  USE Sula dactylatra
Maskeeg
  USE Muskeg
Maskegon dialect
  USE Cree language
Masking (Chemistry)
  ₍QD63.M3₎
  BT Chemistry
  NT Complex compounds
      Sequestration (Chemistry)
Masking (Photography)
  USE Photography—Masking
Maskmakers
  USE Mask makers
Masko Indians
  USE Mashco Indians
Maško language
  USE Mashco language
Maskoki Indians
  USE Creek Indians
Maskoki language
  USE Creek language
Masks *(May Subd Geog)*
  ₍GN419.5 (Ethnology)₎
  ₍GT1747-GT1748 (Manners and
      customs)₎
  ₍PN2071.M37 (Theater)₎
  ₍TT898 (Handicraft)₎
  BT Make-up, Theatrical
  RT Carnival
  SA *subdivision* Masks *under ethnic groups*
  NT Mumming
  — Photographic measurements
  — Religious aspects
  — Japan
      NT Bugaku—Masks
          Kyōgen—Masks
  — Zaire
      NT Pende (African people)—Masks
Masks, Hockey
  USE Hockey masks
Masks, Pende
  USE Pende (African people)—Masks
Masks (Electronics)
  BT Electronics
  RT Photoresists
  NT Integrated circuits—Masks
Masks (Plays)
  USE Masques
Masks (Sculpture) *(May Subd Geog)*
  ₍NB1310₎
  UF Death-masks
  BT Busts
      Sculpture
  SA *subdivision* Death mask *under names*
      of individual persons

Masks in art
Maslov index
    UF Index, Maslov
    BT Forms, Quadratic
        Lagrangian functions
        Vector spaces
Masnavis
    UF Mathnawis
        Mesnevis
    BT Couplets
Masnavis, Urdu
    UF Urdu masnavis
    BT Urdu poetry
Masochism
    [RC553.M36 (Psychiatry)]
    UF Psychic masochism
        Sado-masochism
    BT Psychology, Pathological
    RT Self-destructive behavior
        Suffering
    NT Sexual masochism
Masochism in literature
Masochism in motion pictures
    [PN1995.9.M]
    BT Moving-pictures
Mason and Dixon's Line
    [F157.B7]
    BT Slavery—United States
Mason-bees
    [QL568.A6]
    UF Anthophora
    BT Bees
        Hymenoptera
    NT Anthophora bomboides
Mason City Oddfellows Home Cemetery
    (Mason City, Iowa)
    UF I.O.O.F. Cemetery (Mason City, Iowa)
        IOOF Cemetery (Mason City, Iowa)
        Oddfellows Home Cemetery (Mason
            City, Iowa)
    BT Cemeteries—Iowa
Mason family   (Not Subd Geog)
    UF Masen family
        Masons family
        Mayson family
Mason Farm (Chapel Hill, N.C.)
    BT Farms—North Carolina
        Wildlife refuges—North Carolina
Mason-Spinden Expedition, 1926
    [F1376]
Masongo (African people)
    USE Majangir (African people)
Masonic libraries
    UF Libraries, Masonic
    BT Libraries, Special
Masonic orders
    USE Freemasonry
Masonry   (May Subd Geog)
    [TA670-TA683.9 (Engineering)]
    [TH1199-TH1301 (Building)]
    [TH5311-TH5511 (Masonry work)]
    BT Bridge construction
        Building
        Civil engineering
        Engineering
        Stone
    RT Bricklaying
        Building stones
        Foundations
        Walls
    NT Arches
        Banker-marks
        Bricklaying
        Bridges—Foundations and piers
        Building, Brick
        Cement
        Concrete
        Concrete masonry
        Grouting
        Log-end houses
        Plastering

Reinforced masonry
Stone-cutting
Stonemasonry
— Joints
Masonry (Secret order)
    USE Freemasonry
Masonry bridges
    USE Bridges, Masonry
Masonry cutting tools
    UF Cutting tools, Masonry
    BT Building—Tools and implements
Masonry stoves
    USE Stoves, Masonry
Masons (Secret order)
    USE Freemasons
Masons (Trade)
    USE Bricklayers
        Stonemasons
Masons family
    USE Mason family
Masons' marks
    USE Banker-marks
Masora
    USE Masorah
Masorah
    [BS718]
    UF Masora
        Massora
        Massorah
    BT Bible. O.T.—Criticism, Textual
    NT Bible. O.T.—Accents and
        accentuation
Masoreidae
    USE Carabidae
Masovia (Poland)
    UF Masowien (Poland)
        Mazovia (Poland)
        Mazowsze (Poland)
Masowien (Poland)
    USE Masovia (Poland)
Masparro River (Venezuela)
    UF R'io Masparro (Venezuela)
    BT Rivers—Venezuela
Masquerades   (May Subd Geog)
    BT Amusements
    RT Mumming
Masques
    [PN1934]
    [PN6120.M3]
    UF Masks (Plays)
    BT Drama
        Pageants
        Theater
    NT Masques with music
        Mumming plays
Masques with music
    [M1520-M1526]
    BT Dramatic music
        Masques
— Excerpts, Arranged
— Vocal scores with piano
    [M1523]
Mass
    [BX2230-BX2233 (Catholic Church)]
    BT Liturgies
        Transubstantiation
    RT Lord's Supper
    NT Bination
        Children's mass
        Mass commentators
        Mass stipends
        Monstrances
        Red mass
— Celebration
        Here are entered works descriptive of the
    rites and ceremonies performed in the celebra-
    tion of Mass.
    BT Lord's Supper—Celebration
    NT Concelebration
        Private masses
— Celebration outside the church

    UF Mass in the home
— Frequency of celebration
— Prayer-books and devotions
        Subdivided by language.
Mass, Red
    USE Red mass
Mass, Standards of
    USE Standards of mass
Mass (Canon law)
    [BX1939.M23]
    RT Lord's Supper (Canon law)
    NT Bination (Canon law)
Mass (Chemistry)
    USE Atomic mass
Mass (Music)
    [ML3088]
    BT Church music
        Church music—Catholic Church
        Lord's Supper (Liturgy)
    NT Organ mass
Mass (Nuclear physics)
    USE Atomic mass
Mass (Physics)
    UF Gravitational mass
        Inertial mass
    BT Force and energy
        Gravitation
        Matter—Properties
        Mechanics
        Moments of inertia
    RT Inertia (Mechanics)
        Weight (Physics)
    NT Atomic mass
        Center of mass
        Earth—Mass
        Effective mass (Physics)
        Electromagnetic mass shift
        Gram (Unit)
        Mass spectrometry
        Mass transfer
        Renormalization (Physics)
        Venus (Planet)—Mass
— Measurement
    [QC106]
    UF Mass measurement
MASS (Serials control system)
    UF MARC-based automated serials system
    BT Serials control systems—Automation
Mass and charge renormalization
    USE Renormalization (Physics)
Mass attenuation coefficients
    [QC795.42]
    UF Absorption coefficients, Total
        Attenuation coefficients, Mass
        Total absorption coefficients
    BT Radiation
        Stopping power (Nuclear physics)
Mass BCG vaccination
    USE BCG vaccination
Mass behavior
    USE Collective behavior
Mass Book Deacidification Facility (Md.)
    USE Library of Congress Mass Book
        Deacidification Facility (Md.)
Mass budget (Geophysics)
    UF Budget, Mass (Geophysics)
    BT Geophysics
        Mass transfer
    NT Hydrologic cycle
        Ocean-atmosphere interaction
Mass casualties
    UF Casualties, Disaster
        Casualties, Mass
        Disaster casualties
    BT Civil defense
        Medical emergencies
        Medicine, Military
        Wounds and injuries
    NT Fires—Casualties
        Triage (Medicine)
— Medical records

[RA976]
  BT Medical records
— Treatment
    USE Disaster medicine
Mass commentators
    Here are entered works on the persons who direct worshippers during the celebration of Mass and provide comments explaining the various parts of the service.
  UF Commentators (Liturgy)
  BT Mass
Mass communication
  USE Communication
        Communication and traffic
        Mass media
        Telecommunication
Mass culture
  USE Popular culture
Mass energy relations
  USE Special relativity (Physics)
Mass feeding
  USE Emergency mass feeding
        Food service
Mass for children
  USE Children's mass
Mass hysteria
  USE Hysteria (Social psychology)
Mass in art
Mass in the home
  USE Mass—Celebration outside the church
Mass loss (Astrophysics)
  UF Loss, Mass (Astrophysics)
  BT Astrophysics
        Stars—Masses
Mass measurement
  USE Mass (Physics)—Measurement
Mass media *(May Subd Geog)*
    Here are entered works on the modern means of mass communication. Works on the communications industries treated collectively are entered under Communication and traffic. Works on human communication, including both the primary techniques of language, pictures, etc. and the secondary techniques, such as the press and radio, are entered under Communication.
  UF Mass communication
  BT Communication
  NT Africa in mass media
        Afro-Americans and mass media
        Aged in mass media
        Alcoholism in mass media
        Armed Forces and mass media
        Black English in mass media
        Bulgaria in mass media
        Children's mass media
        Collective bargaining—Effect of mass media on
        Communism and mass media
        Crime and criminals in mass media
        Criminal investigation in mass media
        Death in mass media
        Detectives in mass media
        Developing countries in mass media
        Deviant behavior in mass media
        Dinosaurs in mass media
        Documentary mass media
        Drugs and mass media
        Ethnic mass media
        Family in mass media
        Fantasy in mass media
        Geographical myths in mass media
        Germany (East) in mass media
        Gossip in mass media
        Healers in mass media
        Health in mass media
        Heroes in mass media
        Hispanic Americans and mass media
        Horror in mass media
        Housing law in mass media
        Indians of North America—Mass media
        Libraries and mass media

        Local mass media
        Mass media surveys
        Mickey Mouse (Cartoon character) in mass media
        Monsters in mass media
        Moving-pictures
        Newspapers
        Northern Ireland in mass media
        Nurses in mass media
        Oppression (Psychology) in mass media
        Police and mass media
        Radio broadcasting
        Sex in mass media
        Sex role in mass media
        Sexism in mass media
        Superman in mass media
        Tarzan in mass media
        Television broadcasting
        Terrorism in mass media
        Trade-unions—Mass media
        Trade-unions and mass media
        Villains in mass media
        Violence in mass media
        Voyages, Imaginary, in mass media
        West (U.S.) in mass media
        Women in mass media
        Women in the mass media industry
        Women's mass media
        Youth in mass media
— Audiences
    [P96.A83]
    UF Audiences, Mass media
    BT Audiences
        Mass media—Social aspects
— **Censorship** *(May Subd Geog)*
    NT Blacklisting of authors
— Evaluation
    USE Mass media criticism
— Government policy
    USE Mass media policy
— Influence
    [P94]
— International cooperation
    USE Communication—International cooperation
— **Law and legislation** *(May Subd Geog)*
    NT Right of reply
        Violence in mass media—Law and legislation
— Methodology
    NT Interviewing in mass media
— **Moral and religious aspects**
    NT Sex in mass media
— Objectivity
    BT Objectivity
— **Political aspects** *(May Subd Geog)*
    BT Communication in politics
— **Religious aspects**
    NT Mass media in religion
— — **Baptists, [Catholic Church, etc.]**
— — **Buddhism, [Christianity, etc.]**
— **Research** *(May Subd Geog)*
— **Social aspects**
    NT Mass media—Audiences
— Surveys
    USE Mass media surveys
— **United States**
    NT Afro-American mass media
Mass media, Afro-American
  USE Afro-American mass media
Mass media, Hispanic American
  USE Hispanic American mass media
Mass media and alien labor
  (May Subd Geog)
  [P94.5.A45]
  UF Alien labor and mass media
  BT Alien labor

Mass media and architecture
  (May Subd Geog)
  BT Architecture
    Communication in architectural design
Mass media and art *(May Subd Geog)*
  [N72.M28]
  BT Art
Mass media and business *(May Subd Geog)*
  BT Business
  RT Public relations
  NT Industrial publicity
Mass media and children *(May Subd Geog)*
  UF Children and mass media
  BT Children
  NT Moving-pictures and children
    Radio and children
    Television and children
Mass media and language *(May Subd Geog)*
  BT Language and languages
Mass media and literature
  (May Subd Geog)
  [P96.L5]
  BT Literature
Mass media and Mexican Americans
  USE Mexican Americans and mass media
Mass media and minorities
  (May Subd Geog)
  [P96.M5]
  BT Minorities
  NT Afro-Americans in the newspaper industry
    Ethnic press
    Mass media and race relations
    Minorities in the motion picture industry
    Minorities in the press
— **United States**
    NT Afro-Americans and mass media
    Hispanic Americans and mass media
Mass media and music
  [ML3849]
  UF Music and mass media
  BT Mass media and the arts
Mass media and race relations
  (May Subd Geog)
  BT Mass media and minorities
    Race relations
Mass media and social service
  (May Subd Geog)
  [HV42]
  BT Social service
  RT Public relations—Social service
Mass media and sports *(May Subd Geog)*
  [GV717.3]
  BT Popular culture
    Sports
  NT Radio broadcasting of sports
    Sports journalism
    Television and sports
    Television broadcasting of sports
Mass media and state
  USE Mass media policy
Mass media and the aged *(May Subd Geog)*
  [P94.5.A38]
  UF Aged and mass media
  BT Aged
Mass media and the arts *(May Subd Geog)*
  UF Arts and mass media
  NT Mass media and music
Mass media and the environment
  (May Subd Geog)
  UF Environment and mass media
Mass media and women *(May Subd Geog)*
  [P94.5.W65]
    Here are entered works discussing all aspects of women's involvement in the mass media. Works discussing women's employment in the mass media are entered under Women in the mass media industry. Works discussing the portrayal of women in the mass media are entered under Women in mass media.

Mass media and women *(Continued)*
  BT Women
  NT Women in mass media
        Women in the mass media industry
Mass media and youth *(May Subd Geog)*
  [HQ799.2.M35]
  UF Youth and mass media
Mass media and Zionism *(May Subd Geog)*
  UF Zionism and mass media
  BT Zionism
Mass media criticism *(May Subd Geog)*
  [P96.C76]
  UF Criticism of the mass media
        Mass media—Evaluation
  BT Criticism
Mass media for children
  USE Children's mass media
Mass media for women
  USE Women's mass media
Mass media in agricultural extension work
  (May Subd Geog)
  BT Agricultural extension work
Mass media in birth control
  (May Subd Geog)
  [HQ766.5]
  [HQ766]
  BT Birth control
        Communication in birth control
  NT Radio in birth control
        Television in birth control
Mass media in community development
  (May Subd Geog)
  BT Community development
Mass media in education *(May Subd Geog)*
  NT Newspapers in education
        Radio in education
        Television in education
Mass media in health education
  (May Subd Geog)
  BT Health education
  NT Radio in health education
        Television in health education
Mass media in mental health education
  (May Subd Geog)
  [RA790.87]
  BT Mental health education
Mass media in missionary work
  (May Subd Geog)
  [BV2082.M3]
  BT Missions
Mass media in religion *(May Subd Geog)*
  [BV652.95]
  BT Communication—Religious aspects
        Mass media—Religious aspects
  NT Advertising—Churches
        Journalism, Religious
        Moving-pictures in church work
        Religious broadcasting
        Religious newspapers and periodicals
Mass media in traffic safety
  (May Subd Geog)
  BT Traffic safety
Mass media policy *(May Subd Geog)*
  [P95.8]
  UF Mass media—Government policy
        Mass media and state
        State and mass media
  BT Communication policy
Mass media surveys *(May Subd Geog)*
    Here are entered works on the methods and techniques employed in conducting mass media surveys, and reports on individual surveys. For the latter the heading may be subdivided by place; in such cases an additional subject entry is made under the heading Mass media—[local subdivision], e.g. 1. Mass media—United States. 2. Mass media surveys—United States. For mass media surveys on a special topic, the additional entry is made under the special topic, e.g. 1. Mass media and minorities—United States. 2. Mass media surveys—United States.
  UF Mass media—Surveys

  BT Mass media
        Surveys
Mass medical screening
  USE Medical screening
Mass mortality of fishes
  USE Fish kills
Mass mortality of wildlife
  USE Die-off (Zoology)
Mass movement (Soil mechanics)
  USE Mass-wasting
Mass murder *(May Subd Geog)*
  UF Murder, Mass
  BT Murder
Mass nouns
  USE Grammar, Comparative and general—
        Mass nouns
Mass political behavior
  USE Political participation
        Political psychology
        Political sociology
        Politics, Practical
Mass production *(May Subd Geog)*
  BT Manufacturing processes
        Production engineering
  RT Standardization
  NT Assembly-line methods
Mass psychology
  USE Social psychology
Mass rearing of insects
  USE Insect rearing
Mass screening, Medical
  USE Medical screening
Mass shift, Electromagnetic
  USE Electromagnetic mass shift
Mass society
  BT Social history—Modern, 1500-
        Sociology
  NT Popular culture
Mass spectra
  USE Mass spectrometry
Mass spectrograph
  USE Mass spectrometry
Mass spectrometry
  UF Mass spectra
        Mass spectrograph
        Mass spectrum analysis
  BT Mass (Physics)
        Nuclear spectroscopy
        Spectrometer
        Spectrum analysis
  NT Calutron
        Chemical ionization mass spectrometry
        Field desorption mass spectrometry
        Field ionization mass spectrometry
        Ion cyclotron resonance spectrometry
        Molecular spectra
        Plasma desorption mass spectrometry
        Secondary ion mass spectrometry
        Time-of-flight mass spectrometry
  — Forensic applications
    UF Forensic applications of mass
        spectrometry
        Forensic mass spectrometry
        Mass spectrometry, Forensic
    BT Chemistry, Forensic
Mass spectrometry, Forensic
  USE Mass spectrometry—Forensic
        applications
Mass spectrum analysis
  USE Mass spectrometry
Mass stipends
  UF Stipends, Mass
  BT Canon law
        Catholic Church—Finance
        Fees, Ecclesiastical
        Mass
Mass suicide *(May Subd Geog)*
  [HV6547]
  UF Collective suicide
        Group suicide

  BT Collective behavior
        Suicide
Mass transfer
  UF Mass transport (Physics)
  BT Atomic mass
        Chemistry, Physical and theoretical
        Diffusion
        Fluid dynamics
        Mass (Physics)
        Transport theory
  NT Ablation (Aerothermodynamics)
        Charge transfer
        Mass budget (Geophysics)
        Nusselt number
Mass transit
  USE Local transit
Mass transport (Physics)
  USE Mass transfer
Mass-wasting *(May Subd Geog)*
  UF Mass movement (Soil mechanics)
  BT Slopes (Soil mechanics)
  NT Landslides
        Soils—Creep
        Solifluction
        Subsidences (Earth movements)
Massa (African people)
  USE Masa (African people)
Massa family
  USE Massey family
Massa language
  USE Masa language (Chadic)
Massa River (Morocco)
  UF Oued Massa (Morocco)
  BT Rivers—Morocco
Massachuset Indians
  [E99.M42]
  UF Massachusetts Indians
        Natick Indians
  BT Algonquian Indians
        Indians of North America
  — Missions
Massachuset language
  [PM1736-9]
  UF Natick language
        Niantic language
        Nonantum language
  RT Algonquian languages
Massachusetts
  — Antiquities
    NT Indian Neck Ossuary (Mass.)
        Shattuck Farm Site (Mass.)
        Wapanucket No. 6 Site
        (Middleborough, Mass.)
        Wheeler's Site (Mass.)
  — Description and travel
  — — 1951-1980
  — — 1981-
  — Governors
  — — Inability
      USE Massachusetts—Governors—
        Succession
  — — Succession
      UF Massachusetts—Governors—
        Inability
  — History
    [F61-75]
  — — Colonial period, ca. 1600-1775
    NT Eastern Indians, Wars with,
        1722-1726
        King Philip's War, 1675-1676
        Pigwacket Fight, 1725
  — — — Juvenile literature
  — — New Plymouth, 1620-1691
    UF New Plymouth Colony
        Plymouth Colony
    NT Pilgrims (New Plymouth
        Colony)
  — — — Juvenile literature
  — — Queen Anne's War, 1702-1713
    [E197]
  — — King George's War, 1744-1748

[E198]
— — **French and Indian War, 1755-1763**
[E199]
— — **Revolution, 1775-1783**
[E263.M4]
NT Boston Massacre, 1770
Boston Port Bill, 1774
Boston Tea Party, 1773
Bunker Hill, Battle of, 1775
Concord, Battle of, 1775
Lexington, Battle of, 1775
— — — **Juvenile literature**
— — **1775-1865**
NT Shays' Rebellion, 1786-1787
— — **War of 1812**
[E359.5.M3]
— — **Civil War, 1861-1865**
[E513]
— — — **Centennial celebrations, etc.**
— — **1865-**
— **Politics and government**
— — **Colonial period, ca. 1600-1775**
— — **New Plymouth, 1620-1691**
— — **French and Indian War, 1755-1763**
— — **Revolution, 1775-1783**
— — **1775-1865**
— — **War of 1812**
— — **Civil War, 1861-1865**
— — **1865-1950**
— — **1951-**
— **Social life and customs**
— — **Colonial period, ca. 1600-1775**
— — **19th century**
— **Surveys**
Massachusetts, Fort (Ship Island, Miss.)
USE Fort Massachusetts (Ship Island, Miss.)
Massachusetts General Hospital Utility Multiprogramming System (Computer program language)
USE MUMPS (Computer program language)
Massachusetts Indians
USE Massachuset Indians
Massachusetts trusts
UF Business trusts
BT Corporation law
Corporations
Partnership
Stock companies
Trusts and trustees
Massachusetts Turnpike (Mass.)
BT Express highways—Massachusetts
Toll roads—Massachusetts
Massacre of Saint Bartholomew's Day, France, 1572
USE Saint Bartholomew's Day, Massacre of, France, 1572
Massacre of the Innocents
USE Holy Innocents, Massacre of the
Massacre of the Innocents (Painting)
USE Stanzioni, Massimo, 1585-1656. Massacre of the Innocents
Massacres *(May Subd Geog)*
BT Atrocities
History
Persecution
SA *names of individual massacres, e.g.*
Saint Bartholomew's Day, Massacre of, France, 1572
— **France**
NT Saint Bartholomew's Day, Massacre of, France, 1572
— **India**
NT India—History—Amritsar Massacre, 1919
— **Ireland**
NT Gortroe Massacre, Ireland, 1834
— **Pennsylvania**
NT Conestoga Massacre, Pa., 1763
— **Utah**

NT Bear River Massacre, Utah, 1863
— **Zimbabwe**
NT Shangani River Massacre, 1893
Massacro degli Innocenti (Painting)
USE Stanzioni, Massimo, 1585-1656. Massacre of the Innocents
Massada Site (Israel)
USE Masada Site (Israel)
Massage *(May Subd Geog)*
[RA780.5 (Personal hygiene)]
[RM721-RM723 (Therapeutics)]
UF Chirotherapy
Pneumomassage
BT Physical therapy
Therapeutics, Physiological
RT Mechanotherapy
Osteopathy
Vibration (Therapeutics)
NT Acupressure
Cardiac massage
Electrotherapeutics
Massage parlors
Masseurs
Reflexotherapy
Spondylotherapy
Massage for children *(May Subd Geog)*
[RJ53.M35]
BT Physical therapy for children
Massage parlors *(May Subd Geog)*
BT Massage
Sex oriented businesses
Massagee family
USE Massegee family
Massagers
USE Masseurs
Massai
USE Masai
Massalians
USE Messalians
Massanutten Mountain (Va.)
BT Mountains—Virginia
Massapequa Indians
BT Algonquian Indians
Indians of North America
Massawomeke Indians
USE Iroquois Indians
Massay family
USE Massey family
Masse family
USE Massey family
Massegee family
UF Massagee family
Massengale family
USE Massengill family
Massengill family *(Not Subd Geog)*
UF Masingale family
Masingill family
Massengale family
Massengille family
Massingale family
Massingill family
Massengille family
USE Massengill family
Masses
[M2010-M2014.5]
Here are entered Masses for mixed voices and collections of Masses for various groups of voices (men's, mixed, women's, etc.).
BT Sacred vocal music
RT Communion-service music
NT Agnus Dei (Music)
Gloria in excelsis Deo (Music)
Kyrie eleison (Music)
Propers (Music)
Requiems
— **Juvenile**
[M2190]
UF Children's masses
— **Piano scores**
[M33]
BT Piano music, Arranged

Masses, Instrumental
USE Organ masses
Masses, Organ
USE Organ masses
Masses, Private
USE Private masses
Masses, Stellar
USE Stars—Masses
Masses, Unaccompanied
[M2011]
Masses, Water
USE Water masses
Masses (Children's voices)
Masses (Equal voices)
Masses (Men's voices)
Masses (Unison)
Masses (Women's voices)
Masses of stars
USE Stars—Masses
Masseter muscle
[QL831 (Comparative anatomy)]
[QM155 (Human anatomy)]
[QP321 (Physiology)]
Masseurs *(May Subd Geog)*
UF Massagers
BT Massage
Physical therapists
Massey family *(Not Subd Geog)*
UF Massa family
Massay family
Masse family
Massie family
Massy family
Massey Site (Ill.)
BT Illinois—Antiquities
Massie family
USE Massey family
Massif armoricain (France)
USE Armorican Massif (France)
Massif Central (France)
UF Central Massive (France)
BT Plateaus—France
NT Margeride Mountains (France)
Massif Ciucaş (Romania)
USE Ciucaş Mountains (Romania)
Massif de la Soufrière de Guadeloupe (Basse-Terre Island, Gaudeloupe)
USE Soufrière (Basse-Terre Island, Guadeloupe)
Massif de la Vanoise (France)
USE Vanoise Mountains (France)
Massif des Calanques (France)
USE Calanques (France)
Massif du Jorat (Switzerland)
USE Jorat Mountains (Switzerland)
Massif du Kaarta (Mali)
USE Kaarta (Mali)
Massif du Mercantour (France)
USE Mercantour Mountains (France)
Massim (Melanesian people)
BT Ethnology—Papua New Guinea
Melanesians
— **Commerce**
NT Kula exchange
— **Rites and ceremonies**
NT Kula exchange
Massim (Melanesian people) art
USE Art, Massim (Melanesian people)
Massingale family
USE Massengill family
Massingill family
USE Massengill family
Massive stars
USE Supergiant stars
Massora
USE Masorah
Massorah
USE Masorah
Massospondylus
[QE862.S3]
BT Anchisauridae

Massospondylus *(Continued)*
  NT Massospondylus carinatus
Massospondylus carinatus
  [QE862.S3]
  BT Massospondylus
Massy family
  USE Massey family
MAST (Pressure suit)
  USE Pressure suits
Mast cell disease
  UF Mastocytosis
  BT Connective tissues—Diseases
      Immunologic diseases
Mast cells
  BT Connective tissue cells
Mast churches
  USE Stave churches
Mast family *(Not Subd Geog)*
Mastabas
  USE Tombs—Egypt
Mastai family
  USE Masthay family
Mastaj family
  USE Masthay family
Mastay family
  USE Masthay family
Mastectomy *(May Subd Geog)*
  [RD667.5 (Cancer surgery)]
  UF Mammectomy
  BT Breast—Surgery
  — Complications and sequelae
Mastej family
  USE Masthay family
Masten family
  USE Marsden family
Master and servant *(May Subd Geog)*
  BT Contracts
      Family
  RT Agency (Law)
      Hire
      Independent contractors
  NT Apprentices
      Employers' liability
      Employment references
      Inventions, Employees'
      Negligence
      Respondeat superior
      Trade secrets
Master and servant (Jewish law)
Master and servant (Roman law)
Master and servant in literature
  BT Characters and characteristics in
      literature
Master antenna television
  USE Television, Master antenna
Master of arts degree
  [LB2385]
  UF Arts, Master of
      M.A. degree
      MA degree
      Master's degree
  BT Degrees, Academic
Master of business administration degree
  (May Subd Geog)
  UF Business administration, Master of
      M.B.A. degree
      MBA degree
  BT Business education
      Degrees, Academic
Master of novices
  UF Mistress of novices
      Novice masters
      Novice mistresses
  BT Superiors, Religious
  RT Novitiate
Master of novices (Canon law)
  BT Monasticism and religious orders
      (Canon law)
Master of the Housebook, 15th cent.
  Housebook
  [NE468.A5]

UF Hausbuch (Sketch-book)
    Mittelalterliche Hausbuch (Sketch-
    book)
BT Middle Ages in art
Masterpiece, Artistic
  [N72.5]
  Here are entered works which discuss the concept
of the artistic masterpiece.
  UF Artistic masterpiece
  BT Art
      Creation (Literary, artistic, etc.)
Masters, Flower
  USE Flower arrangers
Masters, Unnamed
  USE Anonymous painters
Masters, Whaling
  USE Whaling masters
Master's degree
  USE Master of arts degree
Masters in chancery *(May Subd Geog)*
  BT Courts—Officials and employees
      Equity pleading and procedure
Masters of ceremonies *(May Subd Geog)*
  BT Entertainers
Masters of ships
  USE Shipmasters
Mastery testing
  USE Criterion-referenced tests
Mastery tests
  USE Domain-referenced tests
Mastey family
  USE Masthay family
Masthay family *(Not Subd Geog)*
  UF Mastai family
      Mastaj family
      Mastay family
      Mastej family
      Mastey family
      Masti family
      Mastie family
Masti family
  USE Masthay family
Mastication
  UF Chewing
      Masticatory apparatus
  BT Digestion
      Jaws
      Oral habits
  NT Teeth—Abrasion
Mastication disorders *(May Subd Geog)*
  [RK480]
  BT Ingestion disorders
      Jaws—Diseases
      Teeth—Diseases
  NT Edentulous mouth
Masticatory apparatus
  USE Jaws
      Mastication
Masticophis
  [QL666.O636]
  BT Colubridae
Masticophis taeniatus
  [QL666.O636]
  UF Striped whipsnake
Mastie family
  USE Masthay family
Mastiff
  [SF429.M36]
  UF Old English mastiff
  NT Bullmastiff
      Fila Brasileiro
      Neapolitan mastiff
Mastiff bats, Typical
  USE Molossidae
Mastigograptus
  [QE840.5]
  BT Graptolites
Mastigophora
  USE Flagellata
Mastigosporella
  [QK625.Z9]

BT Zythiaceae
Mastin family
  USE Marsden family
Mastitis
  [SF967.M3]
  UF Bovine mastitis
      Colimastitis
  BT Cattle—Diseases
      Udder—Diseases
  RT Streptococcus agalactiae
  — Diagnosis
Mastitis, Cystic
  USE Breast—Fibrocystic disease
Mastocytosis
  USE Mast cell disease
Mastodon
  [QE882.U7]
  BT Proboscidea, Fossil
Mastodon angustidens
  USE Gomphotherium angustidens
Mastoid process
  BT Temporal bone
  — Diseases *(May Subd Geog)*
    [RF235]
    BT Ear—Diseases
       Temporal bone—Diseases
  — Radiography
Maston family
  USE Marsden family
Mastopathy, Fibrocystic
  USE Breast—Fibrocystic disease
Mastophora
  [QL458.42.A7]
  BT Araneidae
Mastoplasty
  USE Mammaplasty
Masts, Battle of, 655
  USE Dhāt al-Ṣawārī, Battle of, 655
Masts and rigging
  [VM531]
  UF Rigging
      Ships—Masts and rigging
      Tackling
  BT Naval architecture
      Navigation
  RT Marline spike seamanship
  NT Deadeyes
      Hoisting machinery—Rigging
  — Maintenance and repair
    NT Ditty bags
Mastuma, Tall (Syria)
  [DS99.M33]
  UF Tall Mastuma (Syria)
      Tell Mastuma (Syria)
  BT Syria—Antiquities
Masturbation
  [HQ447 (General works)]
  [RC560.M3 (Psychiatry)]
  UF Autoeroticism
      Autoerotism
      Onanism
  BT Sex
  NT Autoerotic death
  — Religious aspects
  — — Buddhism, [Christianity, etc.]
Masu (The Japanese word)
  [PL669.M]
  BT Japanese language—Etymology
Masuda family *(Not Subd Geog)*
Masuda Kaidō (Japan)
  USE Oyasu Kaidō (Japan)
Masuren (Poland)
  USE Mazury (Poland)
Masurenland (Poland)
  USE Mazury (Poland)
Masurenland, Battles of, 1914-1915
  BT World War, 1914-1918—Campaigns—
      Poland
  NT Tannenberg, Battle of, 1914
Masuria (Poland)
  USE Mazury (Poland)

Masurian Lakes Region (Poland)
  USE Mazury (Poland)
Masurium
  USE Technetium
Masyw Śnieżnika (Poland and Czechoslovakia)
  USE Śnieżnik Mountains (Poland and
        Czechoslovakia)
MAT
  USE Miller analogies test
Mat cutting (Pictures)
  BT Picture frames and framing
  NT Art—Matting
Mat industry *(May Subd Geog)*
Mat-making, Plants for
  USE Matwork plants
Matabele (African people)
  USE Ndebele (African people)
Matabele War, Zimbabwe, 1896-1897
  USE Zimbabwe—History—Ndebele
        Insurrection, 1896-1897
Matabele War, 1893
  ₁DT958₁
  BT Ndebele (African people)—History
  NT Shangani River Massacre, 1893
Matacapan Site (Mexico) *(Not Subd Geog)*
  BT Mexico—Antiquities
Matachines (Dance) *(May Subd Geog)*
  ₁GV1796.M35₁
  UF Los Matachines (Dance)
  BT Dancing
        Indians of Mexico—Dances
        Indians of North America—Southwest,
        New—Dances
Mataco Indians
  ₁F2821₁
  UF Mataguaya Indians
  BT Indians of South America
Mataco language
  ₁PM6466₁
  UF Mattacco language
  BT Indians of South America—Languages
Matador automobile
  ₁TL215.M₁
  BT American Motors automobiles
Matadors
  USE Bullfighters
Matagalpa language
  ₁PM3948₁
  UF Cacaopera language
  BT Central America—Languages
        Misumalpan languages
Matagorda Bay (Tex.)
  BT Bays—Texas
Mataguaya Indians
  USE Mataco Indians
Matahun family *(Not Subd Geog)*
Matakam (African people)
  ₁DT570₁
  UF Mafa (African people)
  BT Ethnology—East Cameroon
Matamoros Castle (Guatemala, Guatemala)
  USE Castillo de Matamoros (Guatemala,
        Guatemala)
Matanuska Glacier (Alaska)
  BT Glaciers—Alaska
Matanuska River (Alaska)
  BT Rivers—Alaska
Matapan, Battle of, 1941
  ₁D775.5.M₁
  UF Cape Matapan, Battle of, 1941
        Gavdo (Island), Battle of, 1941
        Tainaron, Cape, Battle of, 1941
  BT World War, 1939-1945—Naval
        operations
Matapi language
  USE Yucuna language
Mataplana family *(Not Subd Geog)*
Matauros (Ancient city) *(Not Subd Geog)*
  ₁DG70.M37₁
  UF Metauria (Ancient city)
        Metauros (Ancient city)

  BT Cities and towns, Ruined, extinct, etc.
    —Italy
    Italy—Antiquities
Mataveke-paya language
  USE Hualapai language
Matawara (African people)
  USE Tawara (African people)
Match box labels
  USE Matchbox labels
Match covers
  USE Matchcovers
Match fishing
  USE Tournament fishing
Match industry *(May Subd Geog)*
  BT Matches
  —Taxation *(May Subd Geog)*
    UF Matches—Taxation
Match industry workers *(May Subd Geog)*
Match makers (Boxing)
  USE Matchmakers (Boxing)
Match rifles
  USE Schuetzen rifles
Match safes
  USE Matchboxes
Match stamps *(May Subd Geog)*
  ₁HJ5315₁
  UF Stamps, Match
  BT Revenue-stamps
Matchbox labels *(May Subd Geog)*
  ₁NC1885₁
  UF Match box labels
  BT Labels
        Matches
        Smoking paraphernalia
  RT Matchcovers
Matchbox labels, Danish, ₁etc.₁
  (May Subd Geog)
Matchbox toys
  BT Toys
Matchboxes *(May Subd Geog)*
  UF Match safes
  BT Boxes
        Matches
Matchcovers
  ₁NC1885₁
  UF Book match covers
        Match covers
  BT Matches
        Smoking paraphernalia
  RT Matchbox labels
Matches
  ₁TP310₁
  NT Match industry
        Matchbox labels
        Matchboxes
        Matchcovers
  — Taxation
    USE Match industry—Taxation
Matches, Soccer
  USE Soccer—Matches
Matching theory
  BT Combinatorial analysis
  RT Marriage theorem
Matchless motorcycle
  ₁TL448.M₁
  BT Motorcycles
Matchmakers (Boxing) *(May Subd Geog)*
  UF Match makers (Boxing)
  BT Boxing
        Sports promoters
Matchstick games
  ₁GV1507.M2₁
  BT Games
Mate (Shrub) *(May Subd Geog)*
  ₁SB279.M4₁
  UF Yerba-mate
  BT Psychotropic plants
Mate (Tea)
  UF Ilex paraguensis
        Paraguay tea
  BT Tea

  — Law and legislation *(May Subd Geog)*
Mate (Tea) in art
  ₁N8222.M4₁
Mate (Tea) industry *(May Subd Geog)*
  ₁HD9198₁
Mate selection *(May Subd Geog)*
  BT Betrothal
        Courtship
        Husbands
        Marriage
        Remarriage
        Wives
  RT Marriage brokerage
  — Religious aspects
  — — Buddhism, ₁Christianity, etc.₁
Mate selection in animals
  USE Courtship of animals
Matema Group (Solomon Islands)
  USE Reef Islands (Solomon Islands)
Matema Islands (Solomon Islands)
  USE Reef Islands (Solomon Islands)
Mater Matuta (Roman deity)
  UF Matuta, Mater (Roman deity)
  BT Gods, Roman
        Mythology, Roman
Mater Matuta Temple (Satricum, Lazio, Italy)
  USE Temple of Mater Matuta (Satricum,
        Lazio, Italy)
Materia medica *(May Subd Geog)*
  ₁RM121-RM127 (Materia medica and
        therapeutics)₁
  ₁RS153-RS185₁
  ₁RV401-RV411 (Eclectic)₁
  BT Chemistry, Pharmaceutical
        Medicine
        Pharmacopoeias
        Therapeutics
  RT Drugs
        Pharmacy
  SA *names of drugs, e.g.* Belladonna,
        Strychnine
  NT Alteratives
        Antipyretics
        Aphrodisiacs
        Counter-irritants
        Drugs—Dosage
        Extracts
        Homeopathy—Materia medica and
        therapeutics
        Hypophosphites
        Marine pharmacology
        Materia medica, Animal
        Materia medica, Dental
        Materia medica, Ophthalmological
        Materia medica, Vegetable
        Medicine—Formulae, receipts,
        prescriptions
        Pharmacognosy
  — Juvenile literature
    USE Drugs—Juvenile literature
  — Museums
    USE Pharmaceutical museums
Materia medica, Animal *(May Subd Geog)*
  ₁RS162-163₁
  BT Materia medica
  RT Zoology, Medical
  NT Fishes—Therapeutic use
        Pantocrine
Materia medica, Arabic
  USE Medicine, Arabic
Materia medica, Dental
  ₁RK701₁
  UF Dental materia medica
  BT Materia medica
        Therapeutics, Dental
  RT Dental pharmacology
  NT Dentistry—Formulae, receipts,
        prescriptions
Materia medica, Marine
  USE Marine pharmacology

2299

Materia medica, Mineral
  USE Minerals in pharmacology
Materia medica, Ophthalmological
  [RE994]
  UF Ophthalmological materia medica
  BT Materia medica
     Ocular pharmacology
     Therapeutics, Ophthalmological
  NT Mydriatics
     Timolol maleate
Materia medica, Vegetable
  (May Subd Geog)
  [RS164-5]
  UF Botanical drugs
     Medicinal plants—Therapeutic use
     Phytotherapy
     Plant drugs
     Vegetable drugs
  BT Materia medica
  RT Botanical drug industry
     Botany, Medical
     Medicinal plants
  NT Arnica (Drug)
     Aromatic plants—Therapeutic use
     Essences and essential oils—
        Therapeutic use
     Herbalists
     Herbs—Therapeutic use
     Medicine, Medieval
     Phytohemagglutinins
Material accountability
  UF Accountability for materials
  BT Conservation of natural resources
     Environmental protection
     Inventory control
     Materials
  RT Materials management
Material balances (May Subd Geog)
  Here are entered works on the system of balances
  among materials, equipment, and consumer goods
  which is a component of central planning in the
  economies of communist countries.
  UF Balances, Material
  BT Central planning
Material culture (May Subd Geog)
  [GN406-GN442]
  Here are entered works on the objects made or
  used by people, especially the folk artifacts produced
  by traditional methods, as well as techniques of their
  production. Works limited to the techniques of production of pre-literate and folk cultures are entered
  under Industries, Primitive. Works on the material
  culture of particular ethnic groups are entered under
  the name of the group with the subdivision Material
  culture, e.g. Indians of North America—Material
  culture. Works on the industries of particular ethnic
  groups are entered under the name of the group with
  the subdivision Industries, e.g. Indians of North
  America—Industries.
    When this heading is divided by place an addition-
  al subject entry is made under the name of the place
  with an appropriate subdivision such as Industries,
  Social life and customs, Civilization, etc.
  BT Culture
  RT Folklore
     Technology
  NT Antiquities
     Indians of North America—Material
        culture
     Industries, Primitive
Material facts (Law) (May Subd Geog)
  UF Materiality (Law)
  BT Law and fact
Material handling
  USE Materials handling
Material science
  USE Materials
Materialism (May Subd Geog)
  BT Animism
     Philosophy
     Positivism

  RT Dualism
     Idealism
     Mechanism (Philosophy)
     Monism
     Realism
  NT Lokāyata
     Naturalism
Materialism, Dialectical
  USE Dialectical materialism
Materiality (Accounting)
  BT Accounting
Materiality (Law)
  USE Material facts (Law)
Materialization
  [BF1378]
  BT Apparitions
     Ghosts
     Spiritualism
Materials (May Subd Geog)
    Here are entered comprehensive works on the
  basic engineering and industrial materials used in the
  construction of devices, apparatus, structures, equip-
  ment, etc.
  UF Engineering—Materials
     Engineering materials
     Industrial materials
     Material science
  BT Engineering design
  RT Manufacturing processes
  SA subdivision Materials under scientific
        and technical disciplines and under
        types of equipment and
        construction, e.g. Electronics—
        Materials; and phrase headings for
        special types of materials, e.g.
        Building materials; Raw materials
  NT Acoustical materials
     Air classification of materials
     Binders (Materials)
     Biomedical materials
     Building materials
     Bulk solids
     Classification—Books—Materials
     Coatings
     Composite materials
     Finishes and finishing
     Foamed materials
     Friction materials
     Geosynthetics
     Granular materials
     Hard materials
     Hazardous substances
     Heat resistant materials
     Inhomogeneous materials
     Inorganic ion exchange materials
     Material accountability
     Materials at high temperatures
     Materials at low temperatures
     Materials management
     Materials science
     Microstructure
     Nonmetallic materials
     Optical materials
     Porous materials
     Road materials
     Slurry
     Strategic materials
     Superlattices as materials
— **Analysis**
     [QD130-131]
— **Appearance**
     [TA418.5]
     UF Appearance of materials
— **Biodeterioration**
     [TA418.74]
     UF Biodeterioration of materials
        Biological corrosion of materials
     BT Materials—Deterioration
     NT Materials—Microbiology
— **Brittleness**
     USE Brittleness

— **Compression testing**
     [TA417.7.C65]
     UF Compression testing of materials
     BT Materials—Testing
— **Creep**
     UF Creep of materials
     BT Deformations (Mechanics)
        Plasticity
        Rheology
        Strength of materials
        Stress relaxation
        Structural failures
     NT Concrete—Creep
        Copper—Creep
        Metals—Creep
        Rocks—Creep
        Soils—Creep
— **Cutting**
     USE Cutting
— **Deterioration**
     UF Deterioration of materials
        Materials—Disintegration
     BT Weathering
     SA subdivision Deterioration under
        kinds of substances, materials,
        products, etc., e.g. Paper—
        Deterioration
     NT Corrosion and anti-corrosives
        Materials—Biodeterioration
        Materials—Erosion
        Materials—Microbiology
— **Disintegration**
     USE Materials—Deterioration
— **Dynamic testing**
     [TA418.32-34]
     UF Dynamic loading (Materials)
        Dynamic testing (Materials)
        Loading, Dynamic (Materials)
        Loads, Dynamic (Materials)
     BT Dynamic testing
        Materials—Testing
        Testing
     RT Structural dynamics
     NT Concrete—Penetration resistance
        Impact
        Materials—Fatigue
        Mechanical wear
        Metals—Impact testing
        Notched bar testing
— **Effect of radiation on**
     UF Materials, Effect of radiation on
     BT Radiation
     NT Targets (Nuclear physics)
— **Effect of space environment on**
     [TA418.59]
     UF Effect of space environment on
        materials
     BT Space environment
— **Electric properties**
— **Erosion**
     UF Erosion of materials
     BT Materials—Deterioration
     NT Metals—Erosion
— **Fatigue**
     UF Fatigue of materials
        Fatigue testing
     BT Materials—Dynamic testing
        Materials—Testing
        Strains and stresses
        Strength of materials
        Structural failures
        Vibration
     RT Fracture mechanics
     SA subdivision Fatigue under specific
        materials, e.g. Concrete—
        Fatigue; Metals—Fatigue
     NT Airframes—Fatigue
        Composite construction—Fatigue
— **Fracture**
     USE Fracture mechanics
— **Handling and transportation**

USE Materials handling
— **Inventories**
— **Law and legislation** (May Subd Geog)
— Machining
USE Machining
— **Microbiology**
BT Materials—Biodeterioration
Materials—Deterioration
— **Microscopy**
— Oxygen index
USE Oxygen index of materials
— Radiography
USE Radiography, Industrial
— **Research** (May Subd Geog)
UF Materials research
— — **Law and legislation**
(May Subd Geog)
— Sensory evaluation
USE Sensory evaluation
— **Standards** (May Subd Geog)
BT Standards, Engineering
SA subdivision Standards under
specific kinds of materials of
engineering, e.g. Glass—
Standards; Pipe, Steel—
Standards
— Strengthening mechanisms
USE Strengthening mechanisms in
solids
— Surfaces
USE Surfaces (Technology)
— **Testing**
NT Acoustic emission
Brittleness
Materials—Compression testing
Materials—Dynamic testing
Materials—Fatigue
Moiré method
Non-destructive testing
Oxygen index of materials
— **Thermal properties**
UF Thermophysical properties
Materials, Archival
USE Archival materials
Materials, Condensed
USE Condensed matter
Materials, Core
USE Core materials
Materials, Effect of radiation on
USE Materials—Effect of radiation on
Materials, Fusible, in sewing
USE Fusible materials in sewing
Materials, Library
USE Library materials
Materials, Magnetic
USE Magnetic materials
Materials, Molding
USE Molding materials
Materials, Piezoelectric
USE Piezoelectric materials
Materials, Radioactive
USE Radioactive substances
Materials, Reflective
USE Reflective materials
Materials, Spatial property modulation
USE SPM materials
Materials, SPM
USE SPM materials
Materials, Strength of
USE Strength of materials
Materials at high pressures
BT High pressure (Technology)
Strength of materials
NT Plastics at high pressures
Materials at high temperatures
BT High temperatures
Materials
Strength of materials
NT Heat resistant materials
Metals at high temperatures
Plastic crystals

Materials at low temperatures
[TA407]
UF Low temperature materials
BT Low temperature engineering
Low temperatures
Materials
Strength of materials
Materials cutting
USE Cutting
Materials handling
UF Handling of materials
Material handling
Materials—Handling and
transportation
Mechanical handling
BT Plant engineering
Plant layout
Production engineering
Shipment of goods
NT Automated guided vehicle systems
Bins
Bulk solids handling
Cargo handling
Conveying machinery
Dairy products—Handling
Farm produce—Handling
Freight and freightage
Hydraulic conveying
Industrial electric trucks
Industrial power trucks
Lifting and carrying
Loading and unloading
Manure handling
Ore handling
Pallets (Shipping, storage, etc.)
Remote handling (Radioactive
substances)
Silage—Handling
Stacking machines
Storage racks
Trucks
Wages—Materials handling
Materials handling equipment industry
(May Subd Geog)
Materials literature searching
USE Information storage and retrieval
systems—Materials
Materials management (May Subd Geog)
[TS161]
UF Materiel management
BT Business logistics
Industrial management
Inventory control
Materials
RT Material accountability
NT Health facilities—Materials
management
Hospitals—Materials management
Purchasing
Surplus industrial property
Materials research
USE Materials—Research
Materials science
BT Materials
Materials testing reactors (May Subd Geog)
UF MTR
Reactors, Materials testing
BT Nuclear reactors
Nuclear reactors—Materials—Testing
NT BR-2 reactor
Fast Flux Test Facility Program
— In-pile loops
UF In-pile loops of materials testing
reactors
Materiel management
USE Materials management
Maternal age (May Subd Geog)
UF Mother's age at birth
BT Age
Childbirth
Mothers

NT Adolescent mothers
Childbirth in middle age
Maternal and child health services
USE Child health services
Maternal health services
Maternal and infant health services
USE Infant health services
Maternal health services
Maternal and infant welfare
(May Subd Geog)
[HV697-700]
UF Infant welfare
Infants—Charities, protection, etc.
Maternity welfare
BT Child welfare
Mothers
Women—Charities
RT Maternal health services
NT Child support
Infant health services
Insurance, Maternity
Mothers' pensions
Unmarried fathers
Unmarried mothers
— **Law and legislation** (May Subd Geog)
BT Labor laws and legislation
Women—Legal status, laws, etc.
Maternal behavior in animals
USE Parental behavior in animals
Maternal deprivation
UF Deprivation, Maternal
BT Love, Maternal
Mothers
Parent and child
Parental deprivation
Single-parent family
RT Maternal rejection
Maternal-fetal exchange
BT Fetus
Placenta
Pregnancy
NT Maternally acquired immunity
Maternal health care
USE Maternal health services
Maternal health services (May Subd Geog)
[RG940-RG991]
UF Maternal and child health services
Maternal and infant health services
Maternal health care
Maternity care
Mother and child health services
Mothers—Medical care
Perinatal care
BT Obstetrics
Women's health services
RT Maternal and infant welfare
NT Hospitals, Gynecologic and obstetric
Postnatal care
Prenatal care
— Federal aid
USE Federal aid to maternal health
services
— Finance
NT Federal aid to maternal health
services
— **Law and legislation** (May Subd Geog)
BT Medical laws and legislation
Maternal immunity
USE Maternally acquired immunity
Maternal love
USE Love, Maternal
Maternal mortality
USE Mothers—Mortality
Maternal nutrition
USE Mothers—Nutrition
Maternal rejection
UF Rejection, Maternal
BT Love, Maternal
Mother and child
Parental rejection
RT Maternal deprivation

Maternal weight gain
  USE Pregnant women—Weight gain
Maternally acquired immunity
  (May Subd Geog)
  [QR185.33]
  UF Fetal immunity, Maternally acquired
    Fetal passive immunity
    Immunity, Maternally acquired
    Maternal immunity
    Neonatal immunity, Maternally
      acquired
    Neonatal passive immunity
  BT Immunity
    Maternal-fetal exchange
Materne family *(Not Subd Geog)*
Maternity
  USE Motherhood
Maternity care
  USE Maternal health services
Maternity clothes
  [TT547]
  UF Clothes, Maternity
    Clothing, Maternity
    Pregnant women—Clothing
  BT Clothing and dress
Maternity homes *(May Subd Geog)*
  BT Hospitals, Gynecologic and obstetric
Maternity hospitals
  USE Hospitals, Gynecologic and obstetric
Maternity in art
Maternity insurance
  USE Insurance, Maternity
Maternity leave *(May Subd Geog)*
  BT Parental leave
  — Law and legislation *(May Subd Geog)*
    BT Labor laws and legislation
Maternity nursing
  USE Obstetrical nursing
Maternity welfare
  USE Maternal and infant welfare
Math
  USE Mathematics
Math anxiety
  USE Mathematics—Study and teaching—
    Psychological aspects
Mathelin family *(Not Subd Geog)*
Mathematical ability
  UF Arithmetical ability
    Number ability
  BT Ability
  NT Acalculia
    Mental calculators
    Numeracy
  — Testing
    UF Mathematics—Ability testing
    BT Ability—Testing
Mathematical analysis
  UF Analysis (Mathematics)
  RT Algebra
    Calculus
  NT Algebras, Linear
    Combinatorial analysis
    Duality theory (Mathematics)
    Engineering mathematics
    Fourier analysis
    Functions
    Functions, Special
    Harmonic analysis
    Mathematical optimization
    Nonlinear theories
    Numerical analysis
    Programming (Electronic computers)
    Random walks (Mathematics)
    Stochastic analysis
  — Foundations
    UF Foundations of mathematical
      analysis
    BT Axioms
      Mathematics—Philosophy
Mathematical analysis, Nonstandard
  [QA299.82]

  UF Analysis, Nonstandard mathematical
    Nonstandard mathematical analysis
  BT Model theory
Mathematical anthropology
  [GN34.3.M3]
  BT Anthropology
    Anthropology—Methodology
  NT Anthropology—Statistical methods
Mathematical constants
  UF Constants, Mathematical
  BT Functions
    Mathematics
  RT Variables (Mathematics)
Mathematical crystallography
  USE Crystallography, Mathematical
Mathematical drawing
  USE Geometrical drawing
    Mechanical drawing
Mathematical economics
  USE Economics, Mathematical
Mathematical equipollence
  USE Equipollence, Mathematical
Mathematical formulae
  USE Mathematics—Formulae
Mathematical geography
  USE Geography, Mathematical
Mathematical geology
  USE Geology—Mathematics
Mathematical induction
  USE Induction (Mathematics)
Mathematical instruments *(May Subd Geog)*
  [QA71-85]
  UF Instruments, Mathematical
  BT Scientific apparatus and instruments
  NT Abacus
    Analog computers
    Calculators
    Drawing instruments
    Planimeter
    Quipu
    Slide-rule
    Verniers
Mathematical learning models (Stochastic
  processes)
  USE Learning models (Stochastic processes)
Mathematical linguistics
  UF Algebraic linguistics
    Computational linguistics
    Language and languages—Statistical
      methods
    Linguistics—Mathematical models
    Linguistics, Mathematical
  BT Applied linguistics
    Information theory
    Linguistics
  RT Linguistics—Data processing
  NT Dependency grammar
    Glossematics
    Glottochronology
    Grammar, Comparative and general—
      Mathematical models
    IPL (Computer program language)
    Lincos (Artificial language)
    Linguistics—Graphic methods
    Linguistics—Statistical methods
    Semantics—Mathematical models
Mathematical literature
  [QA41.7]
  UF Literature, Mathematical
  RT Mathematics—Bibliography
Mathematical logic
  USE Logic, Symbolic and mathematical
Mathematical logic, Nonclassical
  USE Nonclassical mathematical logic
Mathematical machine theory
  USE Machine theory
Mathematical machines (Calculators)
  USE Calculators

Mathematical models
  Here are entered works on the representation of
  the operation of processes or systems in mathemati-
  cal terms.
  UF Models, Mathematical
  BT Simulation methods
  SA *subdivision* Mathematical models
    under subjects, e.g. Construction
    industry—Mathematical models
  NT Computer simulation
    Digital computer simulation
    Econometric models
    Fractals
    Game theory
    Hybrid computer simulation
    Linear models (Statistics)
    Machine theory
    Monte Carlo method
    Programming (Electronic computers)
    System analysis
  — Bibliography
    NT Information storage and retrieval
      systems—Mathematical models
Mathematical notation
  [QA41]
  UF Mathematical symbols
    Mathematics—Notation
    Mathematics—Symbols
    Notation, Mathematical
  NT AUTOMATH (Formal language)
    Quaternions
    Roman numerals
    Type and type-founding—
      Mathematical symbols
Mathematical Olympiad (U.S.)
  USE U.S.A. Mathematical Olympiad
Mathematical optimization
  UF Optimization (Mathematics)
    Optimization techniques
    Optimization theory
    Systems optimization
  BT Mathematical analysis
    Maxima and minima
    Operations research
    Simulation methods
  RT System analysis
  NT Combinatorial optimization
    Conjugate direction methods
    CONMIN (Computer program)
    Decision-making—Mathematical
      models
    Dynamic programming
    Experimental design
    Games of strategy (Mathematics)
    Lagrangian functions
    Programming (Mathematics)
  — Computer programs
Mathematical physics
  [QC20]
  UF Physical mathematics
    Physics—Mathematics
  BT Mechanics
    Physics
  NT Adiabatic invariants
    Boundary value problems
    Dimensional analysis
    Elasticity
    Electricity
    Electronics—Mathematics
    Engineering mathematics
    Ergodic theory
    Error functions
    Existence theorems
    Gases, Kinetic theory of
    Hypercircle method
    Invariant imbedding
    Magnetism
    Nonlinear theories
    Optics, Physical
    Perturbation (Mathematics)
    Phenomenological theory (Physics)

Potential, Theory of
Random walks (Mathematics)
Scalar field theory
Sound
Switching theory
System analysis
T-matrix
Thermodynamics
Transport theory
Mathematical readiness
  UF Arithmetical readiness
      Mathematics readiness
      Number readiness
      Readiness, Mathematical
  BT Arithmetic—Study and teaching
      Mathematics—Study and teaching
      Prediction of scholastic success
Mathematical recreations
    QA95
  UF Number games
      Recreations, Mathematical
  BT Amusements
      Puzzles
      Scientific recreations
  RT Games in mathematical education
      Magic squares
  NT Chess
      Magic cubes
      Pyraminx
      Rubik's Cube
      Rubik's Magic
      Rubik's Revenge
      Rubik's Snake
      Rubik's World
Mathematical research
  USE Mathematics—Research
Mathematical seismology
  USE Seismology—Mathematics
Mathematical sequences
  USE Sequences (Mathematics)
Mathematical sets
  USE Set theory
Mathematical sociology *(May Subd Geog)*
    HM24
  UF Sociology—Mathematics
  BT Sociology
      Sociology—Methodology
      Sociology—Statistical methods
  NT Sociometry
Mathematical statistics *(May Subd Geog)*
    QA276
  UF Mathematics—Statistical methods
      Statistical inference
      Statistics, Mathematical
  RT Biometry
      Probabilities
      Sampling (Statistics)
      Statistics
  NT Analysis of variance
      Asymptotic efficiencies (Statistics)
      Contingency tables
      Correlation (Statistics)
      Error analysis (Mathematics)
      Estimation theory
      Failure time data analysis
      Law of large numbers
      Least squares
      Linear models (Statistics)
      Moments method (Statistics)
      Multivariate analysis
      Nonparametric statistics
      Paired comparisons (Statistics)
      Ranking and selection (Statistics)
      Regression analysis
      Reliability (Engineering)—Statistical
        methods
      Robust statistics
      Sequential analysis
      Statistical astronomy
      Statistical functionals
      Statistical hypothesis testing

Statistical physics
Time-series analysis
— Asymptotic theory
  BT Asymptotic expansions
— Computer-assisted instruction
  BT Computer-assisted instruction
  NT SIMPLE (Computer program)
— Computer programs
  NT Interactive Statistical Programs
        (Computer programs)
      SITAFUES (Computer program)
      Statpal (Computer programs)
      UTILSTAT (Computer programs)
— Data processing
  NT Genstat (Computer system)
      IDA (Computer system)
      Minitab (Computer system)
      S (Computer system)
      SAS (Computer system)
Mathematical symbols
  USE Mathematical notation
Mathematical weather forecasting
  USE Numerical weather forecasting
Mathematicians *(May Subd Geog)*
    QA28-29
  BT Scientists
  NT Actuaries
      English language—Conversation and
        phrase books (for mathematicians)
      Mathematics—Vocational guidance
      Mathematics historians
      Mathematics teachers
      Women mathematicians
— Collective labor agreements
  USE Collective labor agreements—
        Mathematicians
Mathematicians, Afro-American
  USE Afro-American mathematicians
Mathematics *(May Subd Geog)*
    QA
  UF Math
  BT Science
  SA *subdivision Mathematics under topical*
      headings for the mathematics
      employed in those fields, e.g.
      Investments—Mathematics; also
      headings beginning with the word
      Mathematical and phrase headings
      for particular types of mathematics
  NT Algebra
      Arithmetic
      Associative law (Mathematics)
      Ausdehnungslehre
      Australian aborigines—Mathematics
      Axioms
      Binary system (Mathematics)
      Biomathematics
      Business mathematics
      Calculus
      Combinations
      Commutative law (Mathematics)
      Congruences (Geometry)
      Congruences and residues
      Conic sections
      Coordinates
      Curves
      Decomposition (Mathematics)
      Determinants
      Distributive law (Mathematics)
      Dynamics
      Economics, Mathematical
      Engineering mathematics
      Equations
      Factorization (Mathematics)
      Factors (Algebra)
      Fiberings (Mathematics)
      Filters (Mathematics)
      Forms (Mathematics)
      Fourth dimension
      Fractions
      Functions

Game theory
Geodesics (Mathematics)
Geography, Mathematical
Geometry
Graphic methods
Groups, Theory of
Harmonic analysis
Hyperspace
Index theory (Mathematics)
Indians of North America—
  Mathematics
Induction (Mathematics)
Information theory in mathematics
Interpolation
Interval analysis (Mathematics)
Intuitionistic mathematics
Kinematics
Least squares
Logic, Symbolic and mathematical
Mathematical constants
Maxima and minima
Mensuration
Metric system
Normal forms (Mathematics)
Numbers, Theory of
Numeracy
Numerals
Permutations
Potential, Theory of
Probabilities
Projection
Quaternions
Reciprocity theorems
Sequences (Mathematics)
Series
Set theory
Shop mathematics
Statics
Tiling (Mathematics)
Transformations (Mathematics)
Trigonometry
Variables (Mathematics)
Vector analysis
Women in mathematics
Word problems (Mathematics)
— 1961-
— Ability testing
  USE Mathematical ability—Testing
— Awards
  NT Fields prizes
— Bibliography
  RT Mathematical literature
— Charts, diagrams, etc.
  BT Graphic methods
      Nomography (Mathematics)
— Competitions
— — United States
  NT U.S.A. Mathematical Olympiad
— Data processing
    QA76.95
    Here are entered works on the use of elec-
  tronic data processing and computers in math-
  ematics. Works on those mathematical topics es-
  sential to the study of electronic data processing
  and computer science are entered under Elec-
  tronic data processing—Mathematics.
— Dictionaries
— — History and criticism
  USE Mathematics—Lexicography
— Formulae
    QA41
  UF Formulas (Mathematics)
      Mathematical formulae
— Historiography
  NT Mathematics historians
— Lexicography
  UF Mathematics—Dictionaries—
        History and criticism
  BT Lexicography
— Notation
  USE Mathematical notation

Mathematics *(Continued)*
— **Periodicals**
— — **Indexes**
— **Philosophy**
  ₍QA9₎
    UF Logic of mathematics
        Mathematics, Logic of
    NT Arithmetic—Foundations
        Continuity
        Geometry—Foundations
        Geometry, Projective—
          Foundations
        Mathematical analysis—
          Foundations
        Metamathematics
— **Problems, exercises, etc.**
  ₍QA43₎
— **Remedial teaching**
    UF Remedial mathematics
    BT Remedial teaching
— **Research** *(May Subd Geog)*
    UF Mathematical research
— **Statistical methods**
    USE Mathematical statistics
— **Study and teaching** *(May Subd Geog)*
    NT Games in mathematics education
        Mathematical readiness
        Mathematics laboratories
        Mathematics teachers
        Poetry in mathematics education
        Television in mathematics
          education
— — **Audio-visual aids**
    NT Cuisenaire rods
        Radio in mathematics education
— — **Law and legislation**
  (May Subd Geog)
    BT Educational law and legislation
— — **Psychological aspects**
    UF Math anxiety
— — **Africa, Sub-Saharan**
    NT African Mathematics Program
— — **United States**
    NT PRISM Project
— **Study and teaching (Elementary)**
  (May Subd Geog)
— **Study and teaching (Primary)**
  (May Subd Geog)
— — **Audio-visual aids**
    NT Radio Mathematics Project
— **Study and teaching (Secondary)**
  (May Subd Geog)
— — **Caribbean Area**
    NT Caribbean Mathematics Project
— **Symbols**
    USE Mathematical notation
— **Teacher training** *(May Subd Geog)*
— **Terminology**
  ₍QA5₎
    NT English language—Conversation
        and phrase books (for
        mathematicians)
— **Translating**
    UF Mathematics translating
— **Vocational guidance** *(May Subd Geog)*
  ₍QA10.5₎
    BT Mathematicians
Mathematics, Ancient
Mathematics, Arabic
  ₍QA27.A₎
    UF Arabic mathematics
Mathematics, Babylonian
  ₍QA22₎
Mathematics, Business
    USE Business mathematics
Mathematics, Chinese
  ₍QA27.C₎
Mathematics, Constructive
    USE Constructive mathematics
Mathematics, Egyptian
  ₍QA27.E3₎

Mathematics, Finger
    USE Finger calculation
Mathematics, German
    UF German mathematics
Mathematics, Greek
  ₍QA22₎
    UF Greek mathematics
    RT Geometry—Early works to 1800
Mathematics, Hindu
  ₍QA27.I4₎
Mathematics, Inca
    USE Incas—Mathematics
Mathematics, Indian
    USE Indians—Mathematics
Mathematics, Interval
    USE Interval analysis (Mathematics)
Mathematics, Japanese *(May Subd Geog)*
  ₍QA27.J3₎
Mathematics, Jewish
  ₍QA23₎
Mathematics, Logic of
    USE Mathematics—Philosophy
Mathematics, Maya
    USE Mayas—Mathematics
Mathematics, Primitive *(May Subd Geog)*
Mathematics and literature
    BT Literature
Mathematics historians
    BT Historians
        Mathematicians
        Mathematics—Historiography
Mathematics in the Koran
  ₍BP190.5.M34₎
    UF Koran—Mathematics
Mathematics laboratories *(May Subd Geog)*
      Here are entered works on the use of classroom
    activities and experiments in the study and teaching
    of mathematics. Works on facilities where numerical
    calculations are carried out, usually by computer, are
    entered under Computation laboratories.
    UF Laboratories, Mathematics
    BT Mathematics—Study and teaching
        Project method in teaching
Mathematics of finance
    USE Business mathematics
Mathematics of investment
    USE Investments—Mathematics
Mathematics printing
    BT Printing
    NT Type and type-founding—
        Mathematical symbols
Mathematics readiness
    USE Mathematical readiness
Mathematics teachers *(May Subd Geog)*
    UF Teachers, Mathematics
    BT Mathematicians
        Mathematics—Study and teaching
        Teachers
Mathematics translating
    USE Mathematics—Translating
Mathena family
    USE Matheny family
Mathenay family
    USE Matheny family
Matheney family
    USE Matheny family
Mathenia family
    USE Matheny family
Matheny family *(Not Subd Geog)*
    UF Mathena family
        Mathenay family
        Matheney family
        Mathenia family
        Methenay family
        Metheny family
        Metteneye family
Mather family *(Not Subd Geog)*
    UF Marther family
        Mathers family
        Matheys family

Mather Mine (Mich.)
    BT Iron mines and mining—Michigan
Mathers family
    USE Mather family
Mathes family
    USE Mathis family
Mathew family
    USE Matthews family
Mathewes family
    USE Matthews family
Mathews family
    USE Matthews family
Matheys family
    USE Mather family
Mathias family *(Not Subd Geog)*
    UF Mathies family
        Matthias family
        Matthies family
Mathies family
    USE Mathias family
Mathieu functions
  ₍QA405₎
    UF Functions, Mathieu
    BT Functions, Spheroidal
Mathieu groups
  ₍QA171₎
    UF Groups, Mathieu
    BT Finite groups
        Permutation groups
Mathis family *(Not Subd Geog)*
    UF Mathes family
    RT Matthews family
Mathnawis
    USE Masnavis
Mathurā sculpture
    USE Sculpture, Mathurā
Mathurā terra-cotta sculpture
    USE Terra-cotta sculpture, Mathurā
Matikainen family *(Not Subd Geog)*
Matilda Islands
    USE Mururoa Atoll
Mating behavior
    USE Courtship of animals
        Sexual behavior in animals
Mating cycle
    USE Sexual cycle
Matinicus Rock (Me.)
    BT Islands—Maine
Matinicus Rock Lighthouse (Matinicus Rock,
    Me.)
    BT Lighthouses—Maine
Matka Boska Częstochowska (Icon)
    USE Częstochowa, Our Lady of (Icon)
Matkin family
    USE Matkins family
Matkins family *(Not Subd Geog)*
    UF Madkin family
        Madkins family
        Matkin family
MATLAB (Computer program)
    UF Matrix Laboratory (Computer
        program)
    BT Matrices—Computer programs
Matlack family
    USE Matlock family
Matlak family
    USE Matlock family
Matlaltzinca language
    USE Matlatzinca language
Matlatzinca Indians
  ₍F1221.M₎
    BT Indians of Mexico
        Otomi Indians
Matlatzinca language
  ₍PM4193₎
    UF Matlaltzinca language
        Pirinda language
    BT Indians of Mexico—Languages
Matlazahua language
    USE Mazahua language

Matlick family
  USE Matlock family
Matloch family
  USE Matlock family
Matlock family *(Not Subd Geog)*
  UF Madloch family
    Matlack family
    Matlak family
    Matlick family
    Matloch family
    Matlocks family
    Meadlock family
    Medlock family
Matlocks family
  USE Matlock family
Mato Paha (S.D.)
  USE Bear Butte (S.D. : Mountain)
Matocks family
  USE Mattox family
Matoka (African people)
  USE Toka (African people)
Matopo Hills (Zimbabwe)
  UF Matopos (Zimbabwe)
    Matoppo Hills (Zimbabwe)
  BT Mountains—Zimbabwe
Matopos (Zimbabwe)
  USE Matopo Hills (Zimbabwe)
Matoppo Hills (Zimbabwe)
  USE Matopo Hills (Zimbabwe)
Matorral *(May Subd Geog)*
  BT Shrublands
Matorral ecology *(May Subd Geog)*
  BT Shrubland ecology
Matos family *(Not Subd Geog)*
Matous family
  USE Matusz family
Matozinhos, Santo Christo de (Crucifix)
  USE Bom Jesus de Bouças (Crucifix)
Matra family *(Not Subd Geog)*
  UF Magra family
Mátra Hegység (Hungary)
  USE Mátra Mountains (Hungary)
Mátra Mountains (Hungary)
  UF Mátra Hegység (Hungary)
  BT Mountains—Hungary
Matriarchs (Bible)
  [BS575]
  BT Bible. O.T.—Biography
    Women in the Bible
Matriarchy *(May Subd Geog)*
  [GN480.4]
  UF Gynecocracy
  BT Women
  RT Family
    Matrilineal kinship
  — **Mythology**
  — **Religious aspects**
Matrica Site (Hungary) *(Not Subd Geog)*
  BT Hungary—Antiquities, Roman
Matricaria
  [QK495.C74]
  BT Compositae
Matricaria capensis
  USE Feverfew
Matricaria chamomilla
  [QK495.C74]
  UF Chamomile, German
    Chamomilla matricaria
    German camomile
    German chamomile
    Hungarian chamomile
    Sweet false chamomile
    Wild chamomile
  BT Aromatic plants
Matricaria parthenium
  USE Feverfew
Matrices
  [QA263 (Mathematics)]

  UF Algebra, Matrix
    Cracovians (Mathematics)
    Matrix algebra
    Matrixes (Algebra)
  BT Algebra, Abstract
    Algebra, Universal
  NT Cayley-Hamilton theorem
    Eigenvalues
    Eigenvectors
    Feynman diagrams
    Games of strategy (Mathematics)
    Hadamard matrices
    Hadamard transform spectroscopy
    Jacobi method
    Jacobians
    Jordan matrix
    Kronecker products
    Linear complementarity problem
    Linear programming
    Matrices, Infinite
    Matrix derivatives
    Matrix groups
    Matrix inversion
    Matrix pencils
    Matrix rings
    Modular groups
    Multivariate analysis
    Non-negative matrices
    Permanents (Matrices)
    Racah algebra
    Random matrices
    Rayleigh quotient
    Resolvents (Mathematics)
    Sparse matrices
    Stochastic matrices
    Structures, Theory of—Matrix
      methods
    Symmetric matrices
    T-matrix
    Toeplitz matrices
    Zonal polynomials
  — **Computer programs**
    NT MATLAB (Computer program)
      Y12M (Computer program)
  — **Norms**
    UF Matrix norms
      Norms of matrices
Matrices, Density
  USE Density matrices
Matrices, Dental
  USE Dental matrices
Matrices, Infinite
  UF Infinite matrices
  BT Matrices
Matrices, Non-negative
  USE Non-negative matrices
Matrices, Nonnegative
  USE Non-negative matrices
Matrices, Random
  USE Random matrices
Matrices, Sparse
  USE Sparse matrices
Matrices, Stereotype
  USE Stereotype matrices
Matrices, Typefounding
  USE Typefounding matrices
Matricide
  USE Parricide
Matrilineal kinship *(May Subd Geog)*
  [GN480.4]
  UF Matriliny
  BT Kinship
  RT Matriarchy
Matrilineal kinship (Hindu law)
  (May Subd Geog)
  BT Hindu law
Matriliny
  USE Matrilineal kinship
Matrilocal residence *(May Subd Geog)*
  UF Matrilocality
    Uxorilocal residence

  BT Postnuptial residence (Ethnology)
Matrilocality
  USE Matrilocal residence
Matrimonial actions *(May Subd Geog)*
  UF Matrimonial causes
    Matrimonial suits
  BT Actions and defenses
    Civil procedure
    Marriage law
  NT Alimony
    Divorce suits
    Marriage—Annulment
    Separation (Law)
  — Conflict of laws
    USE Conflict of laws—Matrimonial
      actions
Matrimonial actions (Canon law)
  BT Civil procedure (Canon law)
    Marriage (Canon law)
  NT Defender of the marriage bond
    Divorce suits (Canon law)
    Marriage—Annulment (Canon law)
    Separation (Canon law)
Matrimonial actions (Hindu law)
  BT Marriage (Hindu law)
Matrimonial actions (Islamic law)
  (May Subd Geog)
  BT Civil procedure (Islamic law)
    Marriage (Islamic law)
Matrimonial advertisements
  (May Subd Geog)
  UF Advertising—Marriage
    Marriage advertisements
  BT Marriage
Matrimonial causes
  USE Matrimonial actions
Matrimonial cruelty
  USE Legal cruelty
Matrimonial domicile
  USE Domicile in domestic relations
Matrimonial property
  USE Marital property
Matrimonial regime
  USE Husband and wife
Matrimonial suits
  USE Matrimonial actions
Matrimony
  USE Marriage
Matrimony vine, Chinese
  USE Lycium chinense
Matrix, Dental
  USE Dental matrices
Matrix, Extracellular
  USE Extracellular matrix
Matrix, Interphotoreceptor
  USE Interphotoreceptor matrix
Matrix, Interstitial
  USE Interphotoreceptor matrix
Matrix, Jordan
  USE Jordan matrix
Matrix algebra
  USE Matrices
Matrix band (Dentistry)
  USE Dental matrices
Matrix derivatives
  UF Derivatives, Matrix
  BT Functions
    Matrices
Matrix groups
  BT Groups, Theory of
    Matrices
Matrix inversion
  UF Inverse matrices
    Inverse of a matrix
    Inversion, Matrix
  BT Matrices
  RT Linear operators—Generalized inverses
Matrix isolation spectroscopy
  BT Spectrum analysis
Matrix Laboratory (Computer program)
  USE MATLAB (Computer program)

Matrix management
  USE Matrix organization
Matrix mechanics
  ⌈QC174.3⌉
  RT Quantum statistics
     Wave mechanics
  NT Density matrices
     Quantum theory
     S-matrix theory
Matrix norms
  USE Matrices—Norms
Matrix organization
  ⌈HD58.5⌉
  UF Matrix management
  BT Industrial management
     Industrial organization
     Industrial project management
     Management
     Organization
Matrix pencils
  UF Pencils of matrices
  BT Matrices
Matrix rings
  UF Rings, Matrix
     Rings of matrices
  BT Associative rings
     Matrices
Matrixes (Algebra)
  USE Matrices
Matroids
  BT Combinatorial analysis
     Combinatorial designs and
       configurations
     Graph theory
Matrona River (France)
  USE Marne River (France)
Matrons of dormitories
  USE Housemothers
Matsang Tsangpo River
  USE Brahmaputra River
Matses language
  USE Mayoruna language
Matshaga (African people)
  UF Matshaga (African tribe)
  BT Ethnology—Zaire
Matshaga (African tribe)
  USE Matshaga (African people)
Matshingenga Indians
  USE Machiganga Indians
Matshingenga language
  USE Machiganga language
Matsigenga Indians
  USE Machiganga Indians
Matsigenga language
  USE Machiganga language
Matsu-take
  USE Tricholoma matsutake
Matsucoccus
  ⌈QL527.M37⌉
  BT Margarodidae
     Pine—Diseases and pests
  NT Matsucoccus josephi
     Matsucoccus resinosae
Matsucoccus josephi
  ⌈QL527.M37⌉
  BT Matsucoccus
Matsucoccus resinosae
  ⌈QL527.M37⌉
  UF Red pine scale
  BT Matsucoccus
Matsuda family (Not Subd Geog)
Matsudaira family (Not Subd Geog)
Matsudera Site (Kanazawa-shi, Japan)
  (Not Subd Geog)
  BT Japan—Antiquities
Matsue Castle (Matsue-shi, Japan)
  USE Matsuejō (Matsue-shi, Japan)
Matsuejō (Matsue-shi, Japan)
  UF Chidorijō (Matsue-shi, Japan)
     Matsue Castle (Matsue-shi, Japan)
  BT Castles—Japan

Matsugasako isekigun (Miyoshi-shi, Japan)
  USE Matsugasako Site (Miyoshi-shi, Japan)
Matsugasako Site (Miyoshi-shi, Japan)
  (Not Subd Geog)
  UF Matsugasako isekigun (Miyoshi-shi,
     Japan)
  BT Japan—Antiquities
Matsui family (Not Subd Geog)
Matsukata family (Not Subd Geog)
Matsukawa Railroad Accident, 1949
Matsumoto family (Not Subd Geog)
Matsumura family (Not Subd Geog)
Matsuno family (Not Subd Geog)
Matsuojō (Ueda-shi, Japan)
  USE Uedajō (Ueda-shi, Japan)
Matsura family
  USE Matsuura family
Matsushita Group
  BT Conglomerate corporations—Japan
Matsuura family (Not Subd Geog)
  UF Matsura family
Matsya
  ⌈QL638.C94⌉
  BT Cyprinidae
  NT Matsya sinensis
Matsya (Hindu deity) (May Subd Geog)
  BT Gods, Hindu
Matsya sinensis
  ⌈QL638.C94⌉
  UF Tsing-fish
     Tsing yu
  BT Matsya
Mattacco language
  USE Mataco language
Mattar family
  USE Matter family
Mattenley family
  USE Mattingly family
Mattenly family
  USE Mattingly family
Matter
  ⌈BD331 (Ontology)⌉
  ⌈BD493-BD708 (Cosmology)⌉
  ⌈QC171-QC197 (Physics)⌉
  BT Atoms
     Dynamics
     Gravitation
     Physics
  RT Substance (Philosophy)
  NT Condensed matter
     Form (Philosophy)
     Four elements (Philosophy)
     Hylomorphism
     Inhomogeneous materials
     Interstellar matter
     Occasionalism
     Order-disorder models
     Thomas-Fermi theory
— Classification
— Constitution
  ⌈QC173⌉
  UF Constitution of matter
     Corpuscular theory of matter
  NT Atoms
     Chemical structure
     Dipole moments
     Electrons
     Ether (of space)
     Matter, Nuclear
     Microstructure
     Molecular theory
     Neutrons
     Nuclear models
     Nuclear shell theory
     Protons
     Wave-particle duality
— Effect of reduced gravity on
  ⌈TA418.59 (Engineering)⌉
  UF Effect of reduced gravity on matter
     Matter, Effect of reduced gravity
       on

  BT Reduced gravity environments
— Properties
  ⌈QC171-197⌉
  UF Physical properties of matter
     Properties of matter
  BT Mechanics
  RT Diffusion
  NT Anisotropy
     Antimatter
     Atomic mass
     Brownian movements
     Capillarity
     Chemistry, Physical and theoretical
     Colloids
     Compressibility
     Critical point
     Dielectrophoresis
     Elasticity
     Equations of state
     Flocculation
     Gases
     Gravitation
     Ions
     Mass (Physics)
     Solution (Chemistry)
     Spheroidal state
     Stopping power (Nuclear physics)
     Surface energy
     Torsion
     Viscosity
Matter, Circumstellar
  USE Circumstellar matter
Matter, Effect of reduced gravity on
  USE Matter—Effect of reduced gravity on
Matter, Kinetic theory of
  ⌈QC175⌉
  UF Kinetic theory of matter
  BT Statistical mechanics
     Statistical physics
  NT Collisions (Physics)
     Gases, Kinetic theory of
     Liquids, Kinetic theory of
Matter, Nuclear
  UF Nuclear matter
  BT Matter—Constitution
  RT Nuclear structure
Matter (Buddhism)
  BT Abhidharma
     Cosmogony, Buddhist
     Philosophy, Buddhist
Matter and form
  USE Hylomorphism
Matter family (Not Subd Geog)
  UF Mattar family
     Metter family
Matter of state
  USE Act of state
Matterhorn (Switzerland and Italy)
  UF Cervin Mountain (Switzerland and
     Italy)
     Cervino Mountain (Switzerland and
     Italy)
     Mont Cervin (Switzerland and Italy)
     Monte Cervino (Switzerland and Italy)
  BT Alps
     Mountains—Italy
     Mountains—Switzerland
Matteria punctata
  USE Tuatara
Matterson family
  USE Mattison family
Mattes
  BT Smelting
     Sulphides
Mattes family
  USE Mattison family
Matteson family
  USE Mattison family
Matthäus-Passion (Ballet)
  USE Saint Matthew Passion (Ballet)

Matthäuspassion (Ballet)
USE Saint Matthew Passion (Ballet)
Matthew family
USE Matthews family
Matthews family *(Not Subd Geog)*
UF Marthew family
Marthews family
Mathew family
Mathewes family
Mathews family
Matthew family
RT Mathis family
Matthias family
USE Mathias family
Matthies family
USE Mathias family
Mattiello family *(Not Subd Geog)*
Matting
[TS1779.M2]
BT Industries, Primitive
Matting disease, Sugarcane
USE Sugarcane mosaic disease
Matting of works of art
USE Art—Matting
Mattingley family
USE Mattingly family
Mattingly family *(Not Subd Geog)*
UF Mattenley family
Mattenly family
Mattingley family
Mattinson (Tuvalu)
USE Niulakita (Tuvalu)
Mattiske family *(Not Subd Geog)*
Mattison family *(Not Subd Geog)*
UF Matterson family
Mattes family
Matteson family
Mattner family *(Not Subd Geog)*
Mattock family
USE Mattox family
Mattocks family
USE Mattox family
Mattokki (African people)
USE Kenuz (African people)
Mattoks family
USE Mattox family
Mattole language
[PM1745.M3]
Mattoon, Lake (Ill.)
UF Lake Mattoon (Ill.)
BT Lakes—Illinois
Mattox family *(Not Subd Geog)*
UF Matocks family
Mattock family
Mattocks family
Mattoks family
Mattress industry *(May Subd Geog)*
BT Mattresses
Mattresses
[TS1850]
BT Bedding
NT Mattress industry
Mattson family *(Not Subd Geog)*
UF Mattsson family
Mattsson family
USE Mattson family
Maturation (Psychology)
[BF710]
UF Growth (Psychology)
Personal development
Personal growth
BT Age (Psychology)
Developmental psychology
Genetic psychology
Psychology
NT Adulthood
Emotional maturity
Life cycle, Human
Manchester scales of social adaptation
Social maturity scales

Maturities
BT Contracts
Payment
Maturity, Emotional
USE Emotional maturity
Maturity, Skeletal
USE Skeletal maturity
Maturity onset diabetes
USE Non-insulin-dependent diabetes
Matus family
USE Matusz family
Matusz family *(Not Subd Geog)*
UF Matous family
Matus family
RT Martin family
Matuta
[QL444.M33]
BT Calappidae
Matuta, Mater (Roman deity)
USE Mater Matuta (Roman deity)
MATV
USE Television, Master antenna
Matwork plants *(May Subd Geog)*
[SB281-283]
UF Mat-making, Plants for
Plants, Matwork
BT Botany, Economic
Fiber plants
NT Juncus effusus
Matyó *(May Subd Geog)*
BT Ethnology—Hungary
Matzos
UF Matzoth
BT Bread—Religious aspects—Judaism
Passover
Matzoth
USE Matzos
Mau dialect (Ivory Coast)
UF Mahou dialect
Mahu dialect
Maou dialect
Mauka dialect
Maukakan dialect
BT Ivory Coast—Languages
Mandingo language
Mau family
USE Mao family
Maubile Indians
USE Mobile Indians
Mauchline, Scot., Battle of, 1648
Mauck family *(Not Subd Geog)*
UF Mauk family
Mauke family
RT Mack family
Mock family
NT Mack family
Mock family
Maucu Indians (Papury River watershed)
USE Macú Indians (Papury River watershed)
Maud Expedition, 1918-1925
[G690 1918]
Maudsley personality inventory
[BF698.8.M3]
UF Eysenck personality inventory
BT Extraversion
Introversion
Personality tests
Maue Indians
[F2520.1.M]
UF Maués
Mauhe Indians
BT Indians of South America
Maue language
UF Andira language
Arapium language
Maragua language
Mawe language
Satere language

BT Brazil—Languages
Indians of South America—Brazil—
Languages
Tupi languages
Mauer See (Poland)
USE Mamry Lake (Poland)
Maués
USE Maue Indians
Mauffray family *(Not Subd Geog)*
UF Mauffret family
Mauffrey family
Mauffret family
USE Mauffray family
Mauffrey family
USE Mauffray family
Maugan family
USE Maugans family
Maugans family *(Not Subd Geog)*
UF Magen family
Magens family
Magins family
Mangan family
Mangans family
Mangin family
Mangins family
Maugan family
Maugin family
Maugins family
RT Mogan family
Maugham family *(Not Subd Geog)*
Maughmer family *(Not Subd Geog)*
Maugin family
USE Maugans family
Maugins family
USE Maugans family
Mauhe Indians
USE Maue Indians
Maui (Hawaii)
BT Hawaii
Islands—Hawaii
Maui (Polynesian deity)
BT Maoris—Religion
Polynesians—Religion
Mauilla Indians
USE Mobile Indians
Mauk family
USE Mauck family
Mauka dialect
USE Mau dialect (Ivory Coast)
Maukakan dialect
USE Mau dialect (Ivory Coast)
Mauke family
USE Mauck family
Maukhari dynasty *(Not Subd Geog)*
UF Maukharis
BT India—History—324 B.C.-1000 A.D.
Maukharis
USE Maukhari dynasty
Maul family
USE Maule family
Maulden family
USE Mauldin family
Mauldin family *(Not Subd Geog)*
UF Maulden family
Maulding family
Maulding family
USE Mauldin family
Maule family *(Not Subd Geog)*
UF Maul family
Maumee River (Ind. and Ohio)
BT Rivers—Indiana
Rivers—Ohio
Mauna Kea (Hawaii) *(Not Subd Geog)*
BT Mountains—Hawaii
Volcanoes—Hawaii
Mauna Loa (Hawaii Island, Hawaii)
BT Mountains—Hawaii
Volcanoes—Hawaii
Mauna Ulu (Hawaii)
BT Mountains—Hawaii
Volcanoes—Hawaii

Maunan language
  USE Maonan language
Maundy coins
  BT Coins, English
Maundy Thursday
  [BV94]
  UF Holy Thursday
  BT Fasts and feasts
      Holy Week
  RT Last Supper
  NT In Coena Domini bulls
Maundy Thursday music
  [M2048.M35]
  [M2058.M35]
  BT Holy-Week music
Mauney family
  USE Mooney family
Maung (Australian people)
  [DU125.M33]
  BT Australian aborigines
      Ethnology—Australia
Maung language
  UF Marung language
  BT Australia—Languages
      Australian languages
Mauray family
  USE Morey family
Maurepas Fort (Ocean Springs, Miss.)
  USE Fort Maurepas (Ocean Springs, Miss.)
Maurer family (Not Subd Geog)
Maurey family
  USE Morey family
Mauri (African people)
  USE Mawri (African people)
Mauri family
  USE Morey family
Maurice family
  USE Morris family
Mauricie-Bois-Francs Region (Québec)
Maurison family
  USE Morrison family
Maurist architecture
  USE Architecture, Maurist
Mauritania
  — **Antiquities**
      NT Aoudaghost (City)
  — **Economic conditions**
  — — **1960-**
  — **Languages**
      NT Wolof language
  — **Politics and government**
  — — **1960-**
  — **Social conditions**
  — — **1960-**
Mauritia
  [QK495.P17 (Botany)]
  BT Palms
Mauritia flexuosa
  [QK495.P17 (Botany)]
  [SB317.M38 (Multiple use plant)]
  UF Aguaje palm
      Buriti
      Burity
      Mauritia setigera
      Mauritia vinifera
      Muriti palm
      Murity
      Wine Mauritia
Mauritia setigera
  USE Mauritia flexuosa
Mauritia vinifera
  USE Mauritia flexuosa
Mauritian authors
  USE Authors, Mauritian
Mauritian children's stories (French)
  USE Children's stories, Mauritian (French)
Mauritian children's stories (French Creole)
  USE Children's stories, Mauritian (French
      Creole)
Mauritian cookery
  USE Cookery, Mauritian

Mauritian fiction (English)
  (May Subd Geog)
  UF English fiction—Mauritian authors
  NT Horror tales, Mauritian (English)
Mauritian fiction (French)
  (May Subd Geog)
  UF French fiction—Mauritian authors
  NT Children's stories, Mauritian (French)
Mauritian fiction (French Creole)
  (May Subd Geog)
  UF Creole fiction, Mauritian French
      French Creole fiction, Mauritian
  NT Children's stories, Mauritian (French
      Creole)
Mauritian horror tales (English)
  USE Horror tales, Mauritian (English)
Mauritian literature (May Subd Geog)
  [PN849.M38]
Mauritian literature (English)
  (May Subd Geog)
  [PR9680.M3]
  UF English literature—Mauritian authors
Mauritian literature (French)
  [PQ3988.M3]
  UF French literature—Mauritian authors
  BT Mascarene literature
Mauritian newspapers (May Subd Geog)
Mauritian painting
  USE Painting, Mauritian
Mauritian poetry (English)
  (May Subd Geog)
  [PR9680.M3]
  UF English poetry—Mauritian authors
Mauritian poetry (French)
  [PQ3988.M3]
  UF French poetry—Mauritian authors
Mauritians (May Subd Geog)
  BT Ethnology—Mauritius
Mauritius (Not Subd Geog)
  As a geographic subdivision, this heading is used
  directly.
  BT Islands of the Indian Ocean
  — **Civilization**
  — — **Indic influences**
      BT India—Civilization
  — **Description and travel**
  — — **1981-**
  — **History**
  — — **To 1810**
  — **Politics and government**
  — — **To 1968**
  — — **1968-**
Maurolicidae
  USE Gonostomatidae
Mauromaldo family
  USE Maramaldo family
Maury Deep
  USE Aleutian Trench
Maury family
  USE Morey family
Maurya art
  USE Art, Maurya
Maus family
  USE Moss family
Mauser pistol
  BT Pistols
Mauser rifle
  BT Rifles
Mausolea
  USE Mausoleums
Mausoleion (Halicarnassus)
  USE Mausoleum (Halicarnassus)
Mausoleum (Halicarnassus)
  [DS156.H3]
  UF Mausoleion (Halicarnassus)
      Maussolleion (Halicarnassus)
  BT Architecture, Greek—Turkey
      Mausoleums—Turkey
      Seven Wonders of the World

**Mausoleum Crypt Exchange Dollar Credit
Plan**
  UF NAC Mausoleum Crypt Exchange
      Dollar Credit Plan
  BT Cemeteries—Exchange credit plans
Mausoleums (May Subd Geog)
  UF Mausolea
  BT Crypts
      Sepulchral monuments
      Tombs
  — **India**
      NT Taj Mahal (Agra, India)
  — **Turkey**
      NT Mausoleum (Halicarnassus)
Maussolleion (Halicarnassus)
  USE Mausoleum (Halicarnassus)
Mausy family
  USE Mauzy family
**Mauthausen (Mauthausen, Austria :
Concentration camp)** (Not Subd Geog)
  BT Concentration camps—Austria
      World War, 1939-1945—
      Concentration camps—Austria
      World War, 1939-1945—Prisoners and
      prisons, German
Mauvila Indians
  USE Mobile Indians
Mauzay family
  USE Mauzy family
Mauzee family
  USE Mauzy family
Mauzey faily
  USE Mauzy family
Mauzy family (Not Subd Geog)
  UF Mausy family
      Mauzay family
      Mauzee family
      Mauzey faily
      Mozea family
      Mozee family
      Mozzie family
      Mozzy family
MAVAR (Electronics)
  USE Parametric amplifiers
Mavars
  USE Parametric amplifiers
Maverick (Air-to-surface missile)
  BT Air-to-surface missiles
Maverick automobile
  BT Ford automobile
Maverick Basin (Tex. and Mexico)
  BT Geology—Mexico
      Geology—Texas
Mavia language
  USE Makonde language
Mavila Indians
  USE Mobile Indians
Mavone River (Italy)
  UF Fiume Mavone (Italy)
      Siciliano River (Italy)
  BT Rivers—Italy
Mawbery family
  USE Mabry family
Mawbury family
  USE Mabry family
Mawe language
  USE Maue language
Mawhiney family
  USE Mawhinney family
Mawhinney family (Not Subd Geog)
  UF Mawhiney family
Mawken
  [DS491.M4 (Mergui Archipelago)]
  BT Ethnology—Burma
Mawken (Southeast Asian people)
  USE Selung (Southeast Asian people)
Mawlawīyah
  USE Mevleviyeh
Mawlid al-Nabī
  [BP186.34]

UF Muḥammad, Prophet, d. 632—
      Birthday
BT Fasts and feasts—Islam
Mawlid al-Nabī in literature
Mawri (African people)
UF Mauri (African people)
BT Ethnology—Niger
      Hausa (African people)
 — Women
      USE Women, Mawri
Mawri women
   USE Women, Mawri
al-Mawṣilī family
Max Latin (Fictitious character)
   USE Latin, Max (Fictitious character)
Maxakali Indians
   USE Masacali Indians
Maxakali language
   USE Masacali language
**Maxamad Cabdulle Xasan's Rebellion, British
   Somaliland, 1900-1920**
   ₍DT404-404.3₎
   UF Dervish Rebellion, British Somaliland,
         1900-1920
      Mad Mullah Rebellion, British
         Somaliland, 1900-1920
   BT British Somaliland—History
Maxcy family
   USE Maxey family
Maxel family
   USE Mikesell family
Maxen family
   USE Maxson family
Maxey family *(Not Subd Geog)*
   UF Maxcy family
      Maxie family
      Maxxie family
      Maxy family
      Moxie family
      Moxy family
Maxfield family *(Not Subd Geog)*
Maxi automobile
   USE Morris Maxi automobile
Maxie family
   USE Maxey family
Maxilla
   UF Jaw, Upper
      Upper jaw
   BT Jaws
   NT Alveolar process
      Dental arch
      Maxillary expansion
      Palate
      Retromaxillary space
 — **Fractures**
 — **Surgery** *(May Subd Geog)*
Maxillary expansion
   ₍RK528.M37₎
   UF Expansion, Maxillary
      Expansion, Palatal
      Palatal expansion
      Rapid maxillary expansion
   BT Maxilla
      Orthodontics, Corrective
Maxillary sinus
   UF Antrum of Highmore
      Highmore's antrum
   BT Paranasal sinuses
 — **Abscess**
 — **Cancer**
 — **Diseases** *(May Subd Geog)*
      NT Fistula, Oroantral
 — **Examination**
      NT Antroscopy
 — **Tumors**
Maxillofacial prosthesis
   BT Prosthesis
      Prosthodontics
   NT Artificial palate
      Nasal prostheses

Maxillomandibular records
   USE Jaw relation records
Maxim family *(Not Subd Geog)*
   UF Maxime family
Maxim gun
   ₍UF620.M4₎
   BT Machine-guns
Maxim silencer
   ₍TS535₎
Maxima and minima
   ₍QA306 (Calculus)₎
   ₍QA563 (Geometry)₎
   UF Minima
   BT Mathematics
   RT Maximum principles (Mathematics)
   NT Calculus of variations
      Extremal problems (Mathematics)
      Mathematical optimization
      Maximal functions
      Surfaces, Minimal
 — **Computer programs**
Maxima automobile
   ₍TL215.M₎
   BT Nissan automobile
Maximal functions
   BT Fourier analysis
      Functions of several real variables
      Maxima and minima
Maximal subgroups
   UF Fitting subgroup
      Subgroup, Fitting
      Subgroups, Maximal
   BT Groups, Theory of
Maxime family
   USE Maxim family
Maxims
   ₍PN6299-6308₎
   UF Adages
      Ana
      Gnomes (Maxims)
      Sayings
   BT Epigrams
      Quotations
   RT Aphorisms and apothegms
      Proverbs
   SA *subdivision* Quotations, maxims, etc.
         under certain subjects, e.g. Music—
         Quotations, maxims, etc.
   NT Legal maxims
Maxims, American *(May Subd Geog)*
   UF American maxims
Maxims, Bengali *(May Subd Geog)*
   UF Bengali maxims
Maxims, Chinese *(May Subd Geog)*
   ₍PN6307.C₎
   UF Chinese maxims
Maxims, Colombian, ₍**French, etc.**₎
   (May Subd Geog)
Maxims, French *(May Subd Geog)*
   UF French maxims
 — Lebanese authors
      USE Maxims, Lebanese (French)
Maxims, German *(May Subd Geog)*
   UF German maxims
Maxims, Greek *(May Subd Geog)*
   UF Greek maxims
Maxims, Japanese *(May Subd Geog)*
   UF Japanese maxims
Maxims, Lebanese (French)
   (May Subd Geog)
   UF Lebanese maxims (French)
      Maxims, French—Lebanese authors
Maxims, Legal
   USE Legal maxims
Maxims, Oriental
   UF Oriental maxims
Maxims, Russian *(May Subd Geog)*
   UF Russian maxims
Maxims, Ryukyu *(May Subd Geog)*
   UF Ryukyu maxims

Maxims, Turkish *(May Subd Geog)*
   UF Turkish maxims
Maximum cards *(May Subd Geog)*
   ₍HE6184.M38₎
      Here are entered works on postcards bearing an
   adhesive stamp and an enlarged picture of the same
   stamp issued for sale to collectors with a cancellation
   of the stamp.
   UF Cards, Maximum
   BT Postcards
Maximum concentration values (Industrial
   toxicology)
   USE Threshold limit values (Industrial
      toxicology)
Maximum possible precipitation
   (Hydrometeorology)
   USE Probable maximum precipitation
      (Hydrometeorology)
Maximum precipitation, Probable
   (Hydrometeorology)
   USE Probable maximum precipitation
      (Hydrometeorology)
Maximum principles (Mathematics)
   BT Differential equations, Partial—
      Numerical solutions
      Harmonic functions
      Potential, Theory of
   RT Maxima and minima
Maximum usable frequency (Radio)
   UF Frequency, Maximum usable (Radio)
   BT Ionospheric radio wave propagation
      Radio, Short wave
      Radio frequency
Maxin family
   USE Maxson family
Maxixe (Dance)
Maxon family
   USE Maxson family
Maxson family *(Not Subd Geog)*
   UF Maxen family
      Maxin family
      Maxon family
Maxville (Jacksonville, Fla.)
   (Not Subd Geog)
   UF Jacksonville (Fla.). Maxville
Maxwel family
   USE Maxwell family
Maxwell-Boltzmann density function
   USE Maxwell-Boltzmann distribution law
Maxwell-Boltzmann distribution law
   ₍QC175.16.B6₎
   UF Boltzmann distribution law
      Maxwell-Boltzmann density function
      Maxwell distribution
   BT Distribution (Probability theory)
      Gases, Kinetic theory of
Maxwell distribution
   USE Maxwell-Boltzmann distribution law
Maxwell equations
   UF Equations, Maxwell
   BT Differential equations, Partial
      Electromagnetic theory
Maxwell family *(Not Subd Geog)*
   UF Maxwel family
      Maxwill family
      Meixwill family
Maxwell Land Grant (N.M. and Colo.)
   ₍F802.M38₎
   UF Beaubien-Miranda Grant (N.M. and
         Colo.)
      Miranda-Beaubien Grant (N.M. and
         Colo.)
   BT Land grants—Colorado
      Land grants—New Mexico
Maxwill family
   USE Maxwell family
Maxxie family
   USE Maxey family
Maxy family
   USE Maxey family

May, Isle of (Scotland)
  UF Isle of May (Scotland)
      May Island (Scotland)
  BT Islands—Scotland
May (Month) *(May Subd Geog)*
  — Folklore
      NT May Day
          May-pole
May 3 (Japanese holiday)
  USE Kempō Kinenbi (Japanese holiday)
May 15 Incident, 1932 (Japan)
  USE Japan—History—May Incident, 1932
       (May 15)
May Day *(May Subd Geog)*
  ₍GT4945₎
  BT Holidays
      May (Month)—Folklore
      Spring—Folklore
May Day (Labor holiday) *(May Subd Geog)*
  ₍HD7791₎
  UF First of May
      International Labor Day
  BT Holidays
  RT Labor Day
May devotions to the Blessed Virgin Mary
  USE Mary, Blessed Virgin, Saint—May
       devotions
May family *(Not Subd Geog)*
  UF Mais family
      Maise family
      Maize family
      Maye family
      Mayes family
      Mays family
      Mayse family
      Mayses family
      Mayze family
      Maze family
      Mey family
May Fourth Movement, 1919, China
  USE China—History—May Fourth
       Movement, 1919
May Island (Scotland)
  USE May, Isle of (Scotland)
May-may (African people)
  USE Rahanweyn (African people)
May-pole *(May Subd Geog)*
  ₍GT4945₎
  BT Manners and customs
      May (Month)—Folklore
May Revolution, Korea (South), 1961
  USE Korea (South)—History—May
       Revolution, 1961
May Thirtieth movement, China, 1925
  USE China—History—May Thirtieth
       movement, 1925
Maya (Hinduism)
  ₍B132.M₎
  BT Hinduism
      Philosophy, Hindu
      Vedanta
Maya art
  USE Mayas—Art
Maya cookery
  USE Cookery, Maya
Maya hieroglyphics
  USE Mayas—Writing
Maya hygiene
  USE Hygiene, Maya
Maya Indians
  USE Mayas
Maya inscriptions
  USE Mayas—Writing
Maya language
  ₍PM3961-9₎
  UF Yucatecan language

  BT Indians of Central America—
      Languages
      Indians of Central America—Belize—
      Languages
      Indians of Mexico—Languages
      Mayan languages
  NT Mopan language
Maya law
  USE Law, Maya
Maya literature
  ₍PM3968.1₎
Maya manuscripts
  USE Manuscripts, Maya
Maya mythology
  USE Mayas—Religion and mythology
Maya numeration
  USE Numeration, Maya
Maya poetry *(May Subd Geog)*
Maya terra-cotta sculpture
  USE Terra-cotta sculpture, Maya
Mayacaceae
  ₍QK495.M3₎
  BT Commelinales
Mayaguana Island (Bahamas)
  UF Mariguana Island (Bahamas)
  BT Islands—Bahamas
Mayaguez Crisis, May 1975
  ₍E865₎
  UF Mayaguez Incident
  BT United States—Foreign relations—
      1974-1977
Mayaguez Incident
  USE Mayaguez Crisis, May 1975
Mayailurus
  ₍QL737.C23₎
  BT Felidae
Mayailurus iriomotensis
  ₍QL737.C23₎
  UF Iriomote yamaneko
Mayaka (African people)
  USE Bayaka (African people)
Mayali (Australian people)
  USE Gunwinggu (Australian people)
Mayan cookery
  USE Cookery, Maya
Mayan languages
  ₍PM3961-9₎
  BT Indians of Central America—
      Languages
  NT Aguacatec language
      Choltí language
      Chorti language
      Chuj language
      Huastec language
      Ixil language
      Jacalteca language
      Kanjobal language
      Lacandon language
      Maya language
      Mochó language
      Pokomam language
      Pokonchi language
      Proto-Tzeltal-Tzotzil language
      Quichean languages
      Tzeltal language
      Tzotzil language
      Tzutuhil language
Mayan literature *(May Subd Geog)*
Mayan philology
  ₍PM3961-9₎
  BT Australia—Languages
Mayapic languages
  UF Bandjil languages
      Bundjil languages
      Mayi languages
  BT Australian languages
Mayas
  ₍F1435₎
  UF Maya Indians

  BT Indians of Central America
      Indians of Central America—Belize
      Indians of Mexico
  NT Cakchikel Indians
      Chañabal Indians
      Chol Indians
      Chorti Indians
      Huastec Indians
      Ixil Indians
      Jacalteca Indians
      Lacandon Indians
      Mam Indians
      Mopan Indians
      Pokomam Indians
      Pokonchi Indians
      Quichés
      Tzeltal Indians
      Tzotzil Indians
      Tzutuhil Indians
  — Antiquities
      ₍F1376 (Yucatan)₎
      ₍F1435 (Central America)₎
      NT Chultunes
          Copán Site (Honduras)
          Numeration, Maya
  — Art
      ₍F1435.3.A7₎
      UF Art, Maya
          Maya art
      BT Indians of Central America—Art
  — Astronomy
      UF Astronomy, Maya
  — Hygiene
      USE Hygiene, Maya
  — Law
      USE Law, Maya
  — Masks
  — Mathematics
      UF Mathematics, Maya
  — Numeration
      USE Numeration, Maya
  — Religion and mythology
      ₍F1435.3.R3₎
      UF Maya mythology
          Mythology, Maya
      BT Indians of Mexico—Religion and
          mythology
      NT Kukulcan
  — Wars
      ₍F1376₎
      NT Yucatán (Mexico : State)—History
          —Caste War, 1847-1855
  — Writing
      UF Hieroglyphics, Maya
          Inscriptions, Maya
          Maya hieroglyphics
          Maya inscriptions
          Picture-writing, Maya
      BT Indians of Central America—
          Writing
          Indians of Mexico—Writing
      NT Manuscripts, Maya
Maybach automobile
  ₍TL215.M₎
  BT Automobiles
Maybary family
  USE Mabry family
Mayberry family
  USE Mabry family
Maybrey family
  USE Mabry family
Mayburry family
  USE Mabry family
Maybury family
  USE Mabry family
Maycomber family
  USE McCumber family
Maye family
  USE May family

Mayell family (*Not Subd Geog*)
Mayer family
  USE Myers family
Mayers family
  USE Myers family
Mayes family
  USE May family
Mayetiola (*May Subd Geog*)
  [QL537.C33]
  BT Gall midges
Mayeus family
  USE Mayeux family
Mayeux family (*Not Subd Geog*)
  UF Mahyeux family
    Mailleux family
    Mayeus family
  RT Mayhew family
    Mayo family
Mayevitsa Mountains (Bosnia and
  Hercegovina)
  USE Majevica Mountains (Bosnia and
    Hercegovina)
Mayew family
  USE Mayhew family
Mayfeild family
  USE Mayfield family
Mayfield family (*Not Subd Geog*)
  UF Mafield family
    Mayfeild family
Mayflies (*May Subd Geog*)
  [QL505-505.42]
  UF Ephemerida
    Ephemeroptera
    Plectoptera (Order)
  BT Flies
    Insects
  NT Baetidae
    Baetiscidae
    Ephemerellidae
    Ephemeridae
    Heptageniidae
    Leptophlebiidae
    Palingeniidae
    Siphlonuridae
Mayhew, Elza. Column of the sea
  UF Column of the sea (Sculpture)
Mayhew family (*Not Subd Geog*)
  UF Mahew family
    Mayew family
    Mayhue family
    Mayhugh family
  RT Mayeux family
Mayho family
  USE Mayo family
Mayhon family
  USE Mahan family
Mayhr family
  USE Myers family
Mayhue family
  USE Mayhew family
Mayhugh family
  USE Mayhew family
Mayi languages
  USE Mayapic languages
Maymecha River (R.S.F.S.R.)
  USE Maĭmecha River (R.S.F.S.R.)
Maymont Park (Richmond, Va.)
  BT Parks—Virginia
  NT Italian Garden (Richmond, Va.)
Mayna Indians
  [F2230.2.M]
  UF Maina Indians
  BT Indians of South America
  — Missions

Maynard family (*Not Subd Geog*)
  UF Maignard family
    Mainard family
    Mainhard family
    Mainor family
    Mainyard family
    Manard family
    Maner family
    Maneyard family
    Maynord family
    Menard family
Mayne family
  USE Main family
Mayne Island (B.C.)
  BT Islands—British Columbia
Maynes family
  USE Main family
Maynord family
  USE Maynard family
Mayo Dam (Okla.)
  USE W.D. Mayo Dam (Okla.)
Mayo family (*Not Subd Geog*)
  UF Maho family
    Mayho family
    Mayos family
  RT Mayeux family
Mayo Indians
  [F1221.M]
  UF Mayos
  BT Indians of Mexico
    Piman Indians
  RT Cahita Indians
Mayo language (New Guinea)
  USE Yessan-Mayo language
Mayo language (Piman)
  [PM3972]
  BT Indians of Mexico—Languages
    Mexico—Languages
    Yaqui language
Mayo Lock (Okla.)
  USE W.D. Mayo Lock (Okla.)
Mayo River (Peru)
  UF Río Mayo (Peru)
  BT Rivers—Peru
Mayo-Yessan language
  USE Yessan-Mayo language
Mayombe
  [DT650 (History)]
  [GN654 (Anthropology)]
  BT Ethnology—Zaire
Mayonnaise
  RT Salad dressing
  NT Cookery (Mayonnaise)
Mayonnaise (Contract bridge)
  USE Goulasch (Contract bridge)
Mayor family
  USE Myers family
Mayor Island (N.Z.)
  UF Tuhua (N.Z.)
  BT Islands—New Zealand
Mayors (*May Subd Geog*)
  [JS143-JS163]
  [JS356-JS365 (United States)]
  [JS3155-JS3161 (Great Britain)]
  UF Alcaldes
  BT Local government
    Municipal corporations
    Municipal government
  RT Corregidors
  — Election
    BT Elections
  — United States
    NT Afro-American mayors
Mayors, Afro-American
  USE Afro-American mayors
Mayors' courts (*May Subd Geog*)
  BT Courts of first instance
    Justices of the peace
    Municipal courts
Mayors family
  USE Myers family

Mayoruna Indians
  [F3430.1.M45]
  BT Indians of South America
    Indians of South America—Brazil
    Indians of South America—Peru
    Panoan tribes
Mayoruna language (*May Subd Geog*)
  UF Matses language
  BT Brazil—Languages
    Indians of South America—Languages
    Panoan languages
    Peru—Languages
Mayos
  USE Mayo Indians
Mayos family
  USE Mayo family
Maypole family
  USE Maples family
Mayport (Jacksonville, Fla.)
  (*Not Subd Geog*)
  UF Jacksonville (Fla.). Mayport
Mayrinck family
  USE Mayrink family
Mayrink family (*Not Subd Geog*)
  UF Mayrinck family
    Meyerinck family
Mays family
  USE May family
Maysalūn, Battle of, 1920
  USE Khān Maysalūn, Battle of, 1920
Mayse family
  USE May family
Mayses family
  USE May family
Mayson family
  USE Mason family
Mayze family
  USE May family
Mazada Site (Israel)
  USE Masada Site (Israel)
Mazahua Indians
  BT Indians of Mexico
Mazahua language
  [PM3981]
  UF Maçahua language
    Matlazahua language
  BT Indians of Mexico—Languages
Mazama
  [QL737.U55]
  UF Brockets
    Coassus
  BT Cervidae
    Deer
Mazar, Tall al- (Jordan)
  [DS154.9.M]
  UF Mazar, Tell el- (Jordan)
    Tall al-Mazar (Jordan)
    Tell el-Mazar (Jordan)
  BT Jordan—Antiquities
Mazar, Tell el- (Jordan)
  USE Mazar, Tall al- (Jordan)
Mazarin family (*Not Subd Geog*)
Mazarinades
  BT Caricatures and cartoons
    Fronde
Mazarredo Sound (Vancouver Island, B.C.)
  USE Nootka Sound (Vancouver Island,
    B.C.)
Mazatec Indians
  BT Indians of Mexico
Mazateco language
  [PM3991]
  BT Indians of Mexico—Languages
    Popolocan languages
Mazateco poetry
  [PM3991]
Mazda 626 automobile
  [TL215.M]
  UF 626 automobile
  BT Mazda automobile

Mazda automobile
  [TL215.M]
  NT Mazda 626 automobile
      Mazda GLC automobile
      Mazda RX-7 automobile
      Mazda trucks
Mazda GLC automobile
  [TL215.M]
  UF GLC automobile
  BT Mazda automobile
Mazda RX-7 automobile
  [TL215.M]
  UF RX-7 automobile
  BT Mazda automobile
      Sports cars
Mazda trucks
  [TL230.5.M]
  BT Mazda automobile
      Trucks
Mazdaism
  USE Zoroastrianism
Mazdakism (May Subd Geog)
  [BL2280.M]
  BT Cults—Iran
      Iran—History—To 640
      Iran—Religion
      Sects—Iran
      Zoroastrianism
Mazdaznan
  [BP605.M37]
  BT Religions
Mazdeism
  USE Zoroastrianism
Mâze (The German word)
  BT German language—Etymology
Maze family
  USE May family
Maze gardens (May Subd Geog)
  [SB475]
  UF Labyrinth gardens
  BT Gardens
      Hedges
      Labyrinths
      Landscape gardening
Maze puzzles
  [GV1507.M3]
  UF Mazes
  BT Labyrinths
      Puzzles
Maze tests
  [BF433.M3]
  BT Animal intelligence—Testing
      Labyrinths
      Learning, Psychology of
      Memory
      Psychological tests
      Recognition (Psychology)
  NT Constant-choice perceptual maze test
      Porteus maze test
      Y maze
Mazelin family (Not Subd Geog)
Mazers (Drinking bowls)
  USE Drinking vessels
Mazes
  USE Maze puzzles
Mazon Creek (Ill.)
  USE Mazon River (Ill.)
Mazon River (Ill.)
  UF Mazon Creek (Ill.)
  BT Rivers—Illinois
Mazovia (Poland)
  USE Masovia (Poland)
Mazowsze (Poland)
  USE Masovia (Poland)
Mazuria (Poland)
  USE Mazury (Poland)
Mazurkas
  BT Dance music
  RT Redowas

Mazury (Poland)
  UF Masuren (Poland)
      Masurenland (Poland)
      Masuria (Poland)
      Masurian Lakes Region (Poland)
      Mazuria (Poland)
Mazut
  USE Petroleum as fuel
      Petroleum products
Mazyadids
  [DS76.4]
  BT Iraq—History—634-1534
Mazzard cherry
  USE Sweet cherry
MBA (Calculator)
  BT Programmable calculators
MBA (Computer program)
  USE Context MBA (Computer program)
MBA degree
  USE Master of business administration
      degree
Mba-tivi
  USE Tivi (African people)
Mbaï (African people)
  UF Bai (African people)
  BT Ethnology—Central African Republic
      Ethnology—Chad
Mbai language (Moissala)
  UF Mbay language (Moissala)
      Moissala Mbai language
      Sara Mbai language (Moissala)
  BT Central African Republic—Languages
      Chad—Languages
      Sara languages
Mbai proverbs (Moissala)
  USE Proverbs, Mbai (Moissala)
Mbala (Bantu people)
  UF Bambala (Bantu people)
      Gimbala (Bantu people)
      Rumbala (Bantu people)
  BT Bantus
      Ethnology—Zaire
Mbala language (Bandundu region, Zaire)
  UF Gimbala language
      Kimbala language
      Mumbala language
      Rumbala language
  BT Bantu languages
      Kongo language
      Zaire—Languages
  NT Hungana language
Mbam language
  USE Mbum language
Mbanderu (Bantu people)
  USE Mbandieru (Bantu people)
Mbandieru (Bantu people)
  [DT709]
  UF Mbanderu (Bantu people)
      Mbandyeru (Bantu people)
  BT Ethnology—Namibia
Mbandyeru (Bantu people)
  USE Mbandieru (Bantu people)
Mbata (African people)
  UF Ba-Mbata (African people)
  BT Bantus
      Ethnology—Zaire
  NT Missions to Mbata (African people)
Mbati (Central African Republic people)
  UF Isongo (African people)
      Lisongo (African people)
      Lissongo (African people)
      Songo (Central African Republic
      people)
  BT Bantus
      Ethnology—Central African Republic
Mbati language
  USE Ngbandi language
Mbay language (Moissala)
  USE Mbai language (Moissala)
Mbaya Indians
  [F2520.1.M]

  BT Guaycuru Indians
      Indians of South America
  NT Cadioéo Indians
Mbaya language
  [PM6485]
  UF Guaycururú language
      Mabaya language
  BT Indians of South America—Languages
  RT Guaycuruan languages
MBC-550 (Computer)
  USE Sanyo MBC-550 (Computer)
MBC-555 (Computer)
  USE Sanyo MBC-555 (Computer)
Mbede (African people)
  USE Mbete (African people)
Mbede language
  USE Mbete language
Mbeere (African people)
  USE Mbere (African people)
Mbem (African people)
  USE Mfumte (African people)
      Yamba (African people)
Mbem language
  USE Yamba language (Cameroon and
      Nigeria)
Mbembe (Cross River African people)
  UF Mbenbe (Cross River African people)
  BT Ethnology—Nigeria
Mbembe (Cross River African people) art
  USE Sculpture, Mbembe (Cross River
      African people)
Mbembe (Cross River African people) wood-
  carving
  USE Wood-carving, Mbembe (Cross River
      African people)
Mbembe language (Congo (Brazzaville))
  USE Bembe language (Congo (Brazzaville))
Mbenbe (Cross River African people)
  USE Mbembe (Cross River African people)
Mbere (African people)
  UF Emberre (African people)
      Mbeere (African people)
  BT Ethnology—Kenya
  — Land tenure
      [DT433.545.M]
      BT Land tenure
Mbete (African people)
  UF Ambete (African people)
      Bamba (African people)
      Bambete (African people)
      Mbede (African people)
      Obamba (African people)
      Umbete (African people)
  BT Ethnology—Congo (Brazzaville)
      Ethnology—Gabon
Mbete language
  UF Bamba language
      Mbede language
      Obamba language
  BT Bantu languages
Mbiem (African people)
  USE Yanzi (African people)
Mbinga (African people)
  USE Babinga (African people)
Mbinsa language
  [PL8504]
  UF Mabinza language
  BT Bantu languages
Mbira
  [ML1015-1018]
  UF Likembe
  BT Musical instruments—Africa
      Sanza
Mbira music
  [M142.M]
Mbita Point (Kenya)
  BT Peninsulas—Kenya
Mbo language (Cameroon)
  BT Bantu languages
  NT Bakossi dialect

2312

Mbochi (Bantu people)
　USE　Mbosi (Bantu people)
Mbocobi Indians
　USE　Mocobi Indians
Mboeti sect
　USE　Bwiti sect
Mbogedu language
　USE　Diriku language
Mbole (African people)
　₍DT650.M46₎
　UF　Bole (African people)
　　　Imona (African people)
　BT　Ethnology—Zaire
　　　Mongo (African people)
Mboshi language
　USE　Mbosi language
Mbosi (Bantu people)
　₍DT546.242₎
　UF　Mbochi (Bantu people)
　　　Ombosi (Bantu people)
　BT　Bantus
　　　Ethnology—Congo (Brazzaville)
Mbosi folk literature
　USE　Folk literature, Mbosi
Mbosi language
　UF　Mboshi language
　BT　Bantu languages
Mbosi literature　(May Subd Geog)
　NT　Folk literature, Mbosi
Mbouin (African people)
　USE　Gouin (African people)
Mbowamb
　₍DU742₎
　BT　Ethnology—New Guinea
MBTI (Personality test)
　USE　Myers-Briggs Type Indicator
Mbueti sect
　USE　Bwiti sect
Mbukuhu language
　USE　Mbukushu language
Mbukushu language
　₍PL8507₎
　UF　Goba language
　　　Gova language
　　　Mambukush language
　　　Mampukush language
　　　Mbukuhu language
　　　Mpukusu language
　BT　Botswana—Languages
　　　Luyana language
　　　Namibia—Languages
Mbulu (African people)
　USE　Iraqw (African people)
Mbum language
　UF　Bute language
　　　Mbam language
　　　Vouté language
　　　Vute language
　BT　Adamawa languages
　　　Cameroon—Languages
Mbunda language (Zambia)
　UF　Chimbunda language
　　　Gimbunda language
　　　Kimbunda language
　　　Mbuunda language
　BT　Bantu languages
Mbundu (African people)
　UF　Bimbundu (African people)
　　　Ovimbali (African people)
　　　Ovimbundu (African people)
　　　Umbundu (African people)
　　　Vakuanano (African people)
　BT　Ethnology—Angola
Mbundu language
　USE　Kimbundu language
Mbundu language (Benguela District, Angola)
　USE　Umbundu language
Mbuti
　USE　Bambute
Mbuunda language
　USE　Mbunda language (Zambia)

Mbwiha Indians
　USE　Mbya Indians
Mbya-Guarani language
　USE　Mbya language
Mbya Indians
　UF　Apytere Indians
　　　Ava-mbiha Indians
　　　Baticola Indians
　　　Caaygua Indians
　　　Mbwiha Indians
　BT　Caingua Indians
　　　Indians of South America
Mbya language
　UF　Mbya-Guarani language
　BT　Indians of South America—Languages
　　　Tupi languages
Mbya literature　(May Subd Geog)
　BT　Paraguay—Literatures
　NT　Mbya poetry
Mbya poetry　(May Subd Geog)
　BT　Mbya literature
MC-10 Micro Color Computer
　USE　TRS-80 MC-10 (Computer)
MC6800 (Computer)
　₍QA76.8.M₎
　BT　Electronic digital computers
　　　Microcomputers
　— Programming
MC68000 (Microprocessor)
　USE　Motorola 68000 (Microprocessor)
MC68010 (Microprocessor)
　USE　Motorola 68010 (Microprocessor)
MC68020 (Microprocessor)
　USE　Motorola 68020 (Microprocessor)
MC68851 (Microprocessor)
　USE　Motorola 68851 (Microprocessor)
McAdam family　(Not Subd Geog)
　UF　MacAdam family
　　　MacAdams family
　　　McAdams family
　　　McAddams family
　　　McCaddams family
McAdams family
　USE　McAdam family
McAddams family
　USE　McAdam family
McAdory art test
　BT　Art appreciation—Testing
McAfee family　(Not Subd Geog)
　UF　Macafee family
　　　Macaffee family
　　　McAffee family
　　　McEfee family
McAffee family
　USE　McAfee family
McAlaster family
　USE　McAllister family
McAlester family
　USE　McAllister family
McAlevy family
　UF　MacAlvay family
　　　Macalvy family
　　　McCalvy family
McAlister family
　USE　McAllister family
McAllaster family
　USE　McAllister family
McAllester family
　USE　McAllister family
McAlley family　(Not Subd Geog)
　UF　McAlyea family
　　　McCleyea family
　　　McElyea family
　　　McIlyhia family
　　　Muckleway family

McAllister family　(Not Subd Geog)
　UF　McAlaster family
　　　McAlester family
　　　McAlister family
　　　McAllaster family
　　　McAllester family
　　　McCalister family
　　　McCallister family
　　　McCollester family
　　　McCollister family
McAllum family
　USE　McCollum family
McAlpin family
　USE　McAlpine family
McAlpine family　(Not Subd Geog)
　UF　Macalpin family
　　　Macalpine family
　　　McAlpin family
McAlyea family
　USE　McAlley family
McAnall family
　USE　McAnally family
McAnally family　(Not Subd Geog)
　UF　McAnall family
　　　McAnelly family
　　　McAnnally family
McAnany family
　USE　McEnaney family
McAneaney family
　USE　McEnaney family
McAnelly family
　USE　McAnally family
McAneney family
　USE　McEnaney family
McAneny family
　USE　McEnaney family
McAnnally family
　USE　McAnally family
McArtair family
　USE　MacArthur family
McArthur family
　USE　MacArthur family
McArthy family
　USE　McCarthy family
McAuley family
　USE　McCauley family
McAully family
　USE　McCauley family
McAuly family
　USE　McCauley family
McAuslan family
　USE　McCausland family
McAuslane family
　USE　McCausland family
McAvoy family
　USE　McEvoy family
McBain family
　USE　Bean family
McBee family　(Not Subd Geog)
　NT　Bean family
McBride family　(Not Subd Geog)
　UF　MacBride family
McBroom family　(Not Subd Geog)
McBryde S3 equal-area projection (Cartography)　(May Subd Geog)
　BT　Map-projection
McCaa family　(Not Subd Geog)
McCabe family　(Not Subd Geog)
　UF　Cabe family
　　　MaCabe family
　　　Maccabe family
　　　Maccabee family
McCaddams family
　USE　McAdam family

McCain family *(Not Subd Geog)*
　UF　MacCain family
　　　McCane family
　　　McKain family
　　　McKane family
　　　McKean family
　　　McKeehan family
　　　McKeen family
McCalister family
　USE　McAllister family
McCall family *(Not Subd Geog)*
　UF　Maccall family
　　　McCaul family
　　　McCawl family
　　　McColl family
　RT　Call family
McCallam family
　USE　McCollum family
McCallay family
　USE　McCauley family
McCalley family
　USE　McCauley family
McCallister family
　USE　McAllister family
McCallum family
　USE　McCollum family
McCalvy family
　USE　McAlevy family
McCan family
　USE　McCann family
McCance family
　USE　McCants family
McCand family
　USE　McCann family
McCandeless family
　USE　McCandless family
McCandles family
　USE　McCandless family
McCandless family *(Not Subd Geog)*
　UF　McCandeless family
　　　McCandles family
　　　McCandlich family
　　　McCandlis family
　　　McCanless family
　　　McKanless family
　　　McKindles family
McCandlich family
　USE　McCandless family
McCandlis family
　USE　McCandless family
McCane family
　USE　McCain family
McCanless family
　USE　McCandless family
McCann family *(Not Subd Geog)*
　UF　Machan family
　　　Mackan family
　　　Macon family
　　　McCan family
　　　McCand family
　　　McConn family
　　　McKan family
　　　McKann family
McCanse family
　USE　McCants family
McCant family
　USE　McCants family
McCants family *(Not Subd Geog)*
　UF　MacCants family
　　　MacKanze family
　　　McCance family
　　　McCanse family
　　　McCant family
　　　McCantt family
　　　McCantz family
　　　McKanse family
　　　McKants family
McCantt family
　USE　McCants family
McCantz family
　USE　McCants family

McCarley family *(Not Subd Geog)*
McCarnick family
　USE　McCornack family
McCartee family
　USE　McCarthy family
McCartey family
　USE　McCarthy family
McCarthey family
　USE　McCarthy family
McCarthy-Army controversy, 1954
　ₜUB23ₕ
　UF　Army-McCarthy controversy, 1954
　BT　United States—National security
　　　United States—Politics and
　　　　government—1953-1961
McCarthy family *(Not Subd Geog)*
　UF　MacCarthy family
　　　Maccartley family
　　　Maccarty family
　　　McArthy family
　　　McCartee family
　　　McCartey family
　　　McCarthey family
　　　McCartie family
　　　McCarty family
　　　McCortey family
　RT　Carty family
McCartie family
　USE　McCarthy family
McCarty family
　USE　McCarthy family
McCashland family
　USE　McCausland family
McCasland family
　USE　McCausland family
McCaslen family
　USE　McCausland family
McCaslin family
　USE　McCausland family
McCasslin family
　USE　McCausland family
McCaul family
　USE　McCall family
McCauley family *(Not Subd Geog)*
　UF　Macallay family
　　　Macaulay family
　　　Macauley family
　　　Maccauly family
　　　McAuley family
　　　McAully family
　　　McAuly family
　　　McCallay family
　　　McCalley family
　　　McCaulley family
　　　McCaully family
　　　McCawley family
　RT　McGauley family
McCaulley family
　USE　McCauley family
McCaully family
　USE　McCauley family
McCausland family *(Not Subd Geog)*
　UF　MacAuslane family
　　　MacCausland family
　　　McAuslan family
　　　McAuslane family
　　　McCashland family
　　　McCasland family
　　　McCaslen family
　　　McCaslin family
　　　McCasslin family
　　　McCauslin family
　　　McCoslin family
McCauslin family
　USE　McCausland family
McCawl family
　USE　McCall family
McCawley family
　USE　McCauley family
McCee family
　USE　McKey family

McCelvie family
　USE　McKelvey family
McCelvy family
　USE　McKelvey family
McCinnan family
　USE　McKinnon family
McClaghry family
　USE　McClaughry family
McClaherry family
　USE　McClaughry family
McClaherty family
　USE　McClaughry family
McClahery family
　USE　McClaughry family
McClain family
　USE　McLean family
McClaland family
　USE　McClellan family
McClalen family
　USE　McClellan family
McClalin family
　USE　McClellan family
McClallan family
　USE　McClellan family
McClallen family
　USE　McClellan family
McClallin family
　USE　McClellan family
McClamroch family
　USE　MacClamroch family
McClanahan family *(Not Subd Geog)*
　UF　McClenaghan family
　　　McClenahan family
　　　McClenahen family
　　　McClenan family
　　　McCleneghan family
　　　McClennan family
　　　McClennen family
　RT　McLendon family
McClanathan family *(Not Subd Geog)*
　UF　MacClanathan family
　　　MacClenthen family
　　　McClenthen family
McClane family
　USE　McLean family
McClaskey family
　USE　McCloskey family
McClasky family
　USE　McCloskey family
McClauchrie family
　USE　McClaughry family
McClaughry family *(Not Subd Geog)*
　UF　MacClaughry family
　　　MacLaury family
　　　McClaghry family
　　　McClaherry family
　　　McClaherty family
　　　McClahery family
　　　McClauchrie family
　　　McLaury family
McClave family *(Not Subd Geog)*
　UF　MacClave family
McClayland family
　USE　McClellan family
McClean family
　USE　McLean family
McClelan family
　USE　McClellan family
McCleland family
　USE　McClellan family
McClelean family
　USE　McClellan family
McClelin family
　USE　McClellan family
McClellan Creek National Grassland (Tex.)
　(Not Subd Geog)
　BT　Grasslands—Texas
　　　National parks and reserves—Texas

McClellan family *(Not Subd Geog)*
   UF McClaland family
       McClalen family
       McClalin family
       McClallan family
       McClallen family
       McClallin family
       McClayland family
       McClelan family
       McCleland family
       McClelean family
       McClelin family
       McClelland family
       McClellen family
       McClelon family
       McLaland family
       McLallan family
       McLallen family
       McLeeland family
       McLeland family
       McLelen family
       McLellan family
       McLelland family
       McLellen family
       McLillan family
   RT McLennan family
McClelland family
   USE McClellan family
McClellen family
   USE McClellan family
McClelon family
   USE McClellan family
McClemore family
   USE McLemore family
McClenaghan family
   USE McClanahan family
McClenahan family
   USE McClanahan family
McClenahen family
   USE McClanahan family
McClenan family
   USE McClanahan family
McClendon family
   USE McLendon family
McCleneghan family
   USE McClanahan family
McClennan family
   USE McClanahan family
McClennen family
   USE McClanahan family
McClenthen family
   USE McClanathan family
McClentick family
   USE McClintock family
McClentock family
   USE McClintock family
McClentorick family
   USE McClintock family
McCleod family
   USE McCloud family
McCleskey family
   USE McCloskey family
McClesky family
   USE McCloskey family
McCleur family
   USE McClure family
McClewer family
   USE McClure family
McCleyea family
   USE McAlley family
McClurman family *(Not Subd Geog)*
McClintic family
   USE McClintock family
McClintick family
   USE McClintock family
McClintie family
   USE McClintock family
McClintoc family
   USE McClintock family
McClintoch family
   USE McClintock family

McClintock family *(Not Subd Geog)*
   UF Macclintock family
       McClentick family
       McClentock family
       McClentorick family
       McClintic family
       McClintick family
       McClintie family
       McClintoc family
       McClintoch family
       McClintuck family
       McLentock family
       McLintack family
       McLintock family
McClintuck family
   USE McClintock family
McClisky family
   USE McCloskey family
McCloe family
   USE McClow family
McCloskey family *(Not Subd Geog)*
   UF McClaskey family
       McClasky family
       McCleskey family
       McClesky family
       McClisky family
       McClosky family
       McCluskey family
       McClusky family
       McLoskey family
McClosky family
   USE McCloskey family
McCloud family *(Not Subd Geog)*
   UF McCleod family
McClour family
   USE McClure family
McCloure family
   USE McClure family
McClow family *(Not Subd Geog)*
   UF MacCloe family
       MacClow family
       McCloe family
       Mucklow family
McCluer family
   USE McClure family
McClung family *(Not Subd Geog)*
McClure family *(Not Subd Geog)*
   UF Macclure family
       McCleur family
       McClewer family
       McClour family
       McCloure family
       McCluer family
       McLlewer family
       McLure family
McCluskey family
   USE McCloskey family
McClusky family
   USE McCloskey family
McCoach family *(Not Subd Geog)*
   UF MacCosh family
McCoin family
   USE McKaughan family
McColgan family *(Not Subd Geog)*
   UF McColgin family
McColgin family
   USE McColgan family
McColl family
   USE McCall family
McCollah family
   USE McCullough family
McCollam family
   USE McCollum family
McCollester family
   USE McAllister family
McCollister family
   USE McAllister family
McColloch family
   USE McCullough family
McCollom family
   USE McCollum family

McCollum family *(Not Subd Geog)*
   UF MacCallum family
       MacCollum family
       McAllum family
       McCallam family
       McCallum family
       McCollam family
       McCollom family
       McCollums family
       McColm family
       McCullum family
McCollums family
   USE McCollum family
McColm family
   USE McCollum family
McCommons family *(Not Subd Geog)*
McConaghy family *(Not Subd Geog)*
   UF Maconaghy family
       McConnaha family
       McConnaughay family
       McConnaughey family
McConal family
   USE McConnell family
McConel family
   USE McConnell family
McConell family
   USE McConnell family
McConn family
   USE McCann family
McConnaha family
   USE McConaghy family
McConnal family
   USE McConnell family
McConnald family
   USE McConnell family
McConnaughay family
   USE McConaghy family
McConnaughey family
   USE McConaghy family
McConnell family *(Not Subd Geog)*
   UF Macconnell family
       McConal family
       McConel family
       McConell family
       McConnal family
       McConnald family
       McConyell family
       McKonnell family
McConyell family
   USE McConnell family
McCooey family
   USE McCoy family
McCorcoran family
   USE Corcoran family
McCord family *(Not Subd Geog)*
McCorkel family
   USE McCorkle family
McCorkell family
   USE McCorkle family
McCorkhill family
   USE McCorkle family
McCorkill family
   USE McCorkle family
McCorkle family *(Not Subd Geog)*
   UF MacCorkill family
       MacCorkle family
       McCorkel family
       McCorkell family
       McCorkhill family
       McCorkill family
       McCorquodales family
       McKorkell family
       McKorkle family
McCormack family
   USE McCormick family
McCormick family *(Not Subd Geog)*
   UF MacCormack family
       MacCormick family
       McCormack family
   RT McCornack family

McCormick's Creek State Park (Ind.)
BT Parks—Indiana
McCormilla family
USE McCormley family
McCormley family (Not Subd Geog)
UF McCormilla family
McCornack family (Not Subd Geog)
UF McCarnick family
McCornick family
McCornoch family
McCornock family
RT McCormick family
McCornick family
USE McCornack family
McCornoch family
USE McCornack family
McCornock family
USE McCornack family
McCorquodales family
USE McCorkle family
McCortey family
USE McCarthy family
Mccoskerichthys
[QL638.C4]
BT Chaenopsidae
Mccoskerichthys sandae
[QL638.C4]
McCoslin family
USE McCausland family
McCoun family
USE McCown family
McCowan family
USE McCown family
McCowen family
USE McCown family
McCowin family
USE McCown family
McCown family (Not Subd Geog)
UF MacCown family
McCoun family
McCowan family
McCowen family
McCowin family
McKowan family
McKowen family
McKown family
McOwen family
McOwn family
McCoy family (Not Subd Geog)
UF Mackoy family
Macoy family
McCooey family
McKoy family
RT McKay family
McKey family
NT Hatfield-McCoy Feud
McCoy-Hatfield Feud
USE Hatfield-McCoy Feud
McCracken (Name)
BT Names, Personal
McCracken family (Not Subd Geog)
UF McCrackin family
McCraken family
McCrackin family
USE McCracken family
McCrae family
USE McRae family
McCraken family
USE McCracken family
McCrary family
USE McCreery family
McCray family
USE McRae family
McCre family
USE McRae family
McCrea family
USE McRae family
McCreary family
USE McCreery family

McCreery family (Not Subd Geog)
UF McCrary family
McCreary family
McCrery family
RT Crary family
McCrery family
USE McCreery family
McCrimmon family (Not Subd Geog)
McCuan family
USE McEwan family
McCubbin, Frederick, 1855-1917. On the wallaby track
UF On the wallaby track (Painting)
McCulla family
USE McCullough family
McCullagh family
USE McCullough family
McCulloch family
USE McCullough family
McCullock family
USE McCullough family
McCulloh family
USE McCullough family
McCullough family (Not Subd Geog)
UF McCollah family
McColloch family
McCulla family
McCullagh family
McCulloch family
McCullock family
McCulloh family
McCullum family
USE McCollum family
McCully (Honolulu, Hawaii)
(Not Subd Geog)
UF Honolulu (Hawaii). McCully
McCumber family (Not Subd Geog)
UF Macomber family
Macumber family
Maycomber family
McOmber family
McCune family
USE McEwan family
McCurda family
USE McCurdy family
McCurday family
USE McCurdy family
McCurdey family
USE McCurdy family
McCurdie family
USE McCurdy family
McCurdy family (Not Subd Geog)
UF MacCurdie family
Maccurdy family
MacKirdy family
Macurda family
McCurda family
McCurday family
McCurdey family
McCurdie family
McKirdy family
McCurley family (Not Subd Geog)
RT Curley family
MCD
USE Magnetic circular dichroism
McDaniel (Name)
BT Names, Personal
McDaniel family (Not Subd Geog)
UF Macdaniel family
Macdaniels family
McDaniels family
McDaniels family
USE McDaniel family
McDermid family
USE McDermott family
McDermitt Caldera Complex (Nev. and Or.)
BT Calderas—Nevada
Calderas—Oregon

McDermott family (Not Subd Geog)
UF Macdermid family
MacDermot family
Macdermott family
MacDiarmid family
McDermid family
McDermut family
McDiarmid family
McDermut family
USE McDermott family
McDiarmid family
USE McDermott family
McDonagh family
USE McDonough family
Mcdonald, Gregory, 1937-
(Not Subd Geog)
1937-
— Characters
— — Fletch
RT Fletch (Fictitious character)
McDonald family (Not Subd Geog)
UF MacDonald family
McDonall family
McDonals family
McDonell family
McDonnel family
McDonnell family
McDonnold family
RT Donaldson family
McDonall family
USE McDonald family
McDonals family
USE McDonald family
McDonell family
USE McDonald family
McDonnel family
USE McDonald family
McDonnell airplanes
NT Banshee (Jet fighter plane)
Voodoo (Jet fighter plane)
McDonnell Douglas airplanes
BT Douglas airplanes
NT C-17 (Jet transport)
Eagle (Jet fighter plane)
Hornet (Jet fighter plane)
McDonnell Douglas DC-10 (Jet transport)
McDonnell Douglas Apache (Attack helicopter)
USE Apache (Attack helicopter)
McDonnell Douglas DC-9 Super 80 (Jet transport)
UF DC-9 Super 80 (Jet transport)
BT Jet transports
McDonnell Douglas DC-10 (Jet transport)
[TL686.M25]
UF DC-10 (Jet transport)
BT Jet transports
McDonnell Douglas airplanes
McDonnell family
USE McDonald family
McDonnold family
USE McDonald family
McDonoch family
USE McDonough family
McDonogh family
USE McDonough family
McDonough family (Not Subd Geog)
UF McDonagh family
McDonoch family
McDonogh family
McDougal family
USE McDougall family
McDougall clan
USE McDougall family

McDougall family *(Not Subd Geog)*
  UF MacDougal family
      MacDougall family
      McDougal family
      McDougall clan
      McDougle family
      McDugal family
      McDugald family
  RT Dougal family
McDougle family
  USE McDougall family
McDowal family
  USE McDowell family
McDowall family
  USE McDowell family
McDowel family
  USE McDowell family
McDowell family *(Not Subd Geog)*
  UF MacDowall family
      MacDowell family
      McDowal family
      McDowall family
      McDowel family
      McDowill family
      McDowl family
      McDowle family
      McDuel family
McDowill family
  USE McDowell family
McDowl family
  USE McDowell family
McDowle family
  USE McDowell family
McDuel family
  USE McDowell family
McDuff family *(Not Subd Geog)*
  UF MacDuff family
  RT McDuffie family
McDuffe family
  USE McDuffie family
McDuffee family
  USE McDuffie family
McDuffie family *(Not Subd Geog)*
  UF MacDuffee family
      MacDuffie family
      McDuffe family
      McDuffee family
      McDuffy family
  RT Duffy family
      McDuff family
McDuffy family
  USE McDuffie family
McDugal family
  USE McDougall family
McDugald family
  USE McDougall family
McEacheran family
  USE McEachern family
McEachern family *(Not Subd Geog)*
  UF Eachern family
      Macceacharn family
      MacEachern family
      Macearchern family
      McEacheran family
      McEachin family
      McEachran family
McEachin family
  USE McEachern family
McEachran family
  USE McEachern family
McEfee family
  USE McAfee family
McEgan family
  USE Egan family
McElroy family *(Not Subd Geog)*
  UF MacElroy family
      Muckelroy family
      Muckleroy family
      Muclaroy family
McElvain family
  USE McElwain family

McElvaney family
  USE McElwain family
McElvany family
  USE McElwain family
McElveen family
  USE McElwain family
McElven family
  USE McElwain family
McElvene family
  USE McElwain family
McElvin family
  USE McElwain family
McElvy family
  USE McKelvey family
McElwain family *(Not Subd Geog)*
  UF MacLevain family
      McElvain family
      McElvaney family
      McElvany family
      McElveen family
      McElven family
      McElvene family
      McElvin family
      McElwaine family
      McElwane family
      McElwaney family
      McElwean family
      McElwin family
      McIlvain family
      McIlvaine family
      McIlveen family
      McIlveene family
      McIlwain family
      McIlwaine family
      McLwain family
      Miklewane family
      Mucclewain family
      Mucclewane family
      Mucklewain family
McElwaine family
  USE McElwain family
McElwane family
  USE McElwain family
McElwaney family
  USE McElwain family
McElwean family
  USE McElwain family
McElwin family
  USE McElwain family
McElyea family
  USE McAlley family
McEnaney family *(Not Subd Geog)*
  UF McAnany family
      McAneaney family
      McAneney family
      McAneny family
      McEneaney family
      McEneany family
McEneaney family
  USE McEnaney family
McEneany family
  USE McEnaney family
McEntarfer family
  USE McInturff family
McEntee family *(Not Subd Geog)*
McEntire family
  USE McIntyre family
McEnturff family
  USE McInturff family
McEuen family
  USE McEwan family
McEune family
  USE McEwan family
McEver family
  USE McIver family
McEvers family
  USE McIver family
McEvoy family *(Not Subd Geog)*
  UF Macevoy family
      McAvoy family

McEwan family *(Not Subd Geog)*
  UF MacEuen family
      MacEwan family
      MacEwen family
      McCuan family
      McCune family
      McEuen family
      McEune family
      McEwen family
      McEwin family
      McEwing family
      McKewin family
      McKuen family
      McQuown family
McEwen family
  USE McEwan family
McEwin family
  USE McEwan family
McEwing family
  USE McEwan family
McFadan family
  USE McFadden family
McFadden family *(Not Subd Geog)*
  UF MacFadden family
      McFadan family
      McFaddin family
      McFadding family
      McFaddon family
      McFaden family
      McFadian family
      McFadien family
      McFadin family
      McFadion family
      McFadon family
      McFadyen family
      McFayden family
McFaddin family
  USE McFadden family
McFadding family
  USE McFadden family
McFaddon family
  USE McFadden family
McFaden family
  USE McFadden family
McFadian family
  USE McFadden family
McFadien family
  USE McFadden family
McFadin family
  USE McFadden family
McFadion family
  USE McFadden family
McFadon family
  USE McFadden family
McFadyen family
  USE McFadden family
McFarlan automobile
      ₜTL215.Mₗ
McFarlan family
  USE McFarland family
McFarland family *(Not Subd Geog)*
  UF MacFarlan family
      MacFarland family
      MacFarlane family
      MacFarlen family
      MacFarlin family
      MacFarling family
      MacPharlen family
      McFarlan family
      McFarlane family
      McFarlen family
      McFarlin family
      McFarling family
      McPharlen family
McFarland Site (Tenn.) *(Not Subd Geog)*
  BT Tennessee—Antiquities
McFarlane family
  USE McFarland family
McFarlen family
  USE McFarland family

2317

McFarlin family
  USE McFarland family
McFarling family
  USE McFarland family
McFayden family
  USE McFadden family
McFeaters family *(Not Subd Geog)*
  UF McFeatters family
    McFeeters family
    McFetridge family
McFeatters family
  USE McFeaters family
McFee family
  USE McPhee family
McFeeters family
  USE McFeaters family
McFercin family
  USE McPherson family
McFersin family
  USE McPherson family
McFerson family
  USE McPherson family
McFetridge family
  USE McFeaters family
McGahan family
  USE McKaughan family
McGahee family
  USE Magee family
McGara family
  USE McGarry family
McGarey family
  USE McGarry family
McGarry family *(Not Subd Geog)*
  UF McGara family
    McGarey family
    McGary family
    McGeary family
McGartlan family
  USE Garland family
McGartland family
  USE Garland family
McGary family
  USE McGarry family
McGaughan family
  USE McKaughan family
McGaughey family *(Not Subd Geog)*
  UF MacGaughey family
    McGaughy family
    McGauhy family
McGaughy family
  USE McGaughey family
McGauhy family
  USE McGaughey family
McGauley family *(Not Subd Geog)*
  UF MacGauley family
    Magawley family
    McGauly family
    McGawley family
  RT McCauley family
McGauly family
  USE McGauley family
McGavock family *(Not Subd Geog)*
McGaw family *(Not Subd Geog)*
  UF Magaw family
    Megaw family
McGawley family
  USE McGauley family
McGeary family
  USE McGarry family
McGee, Travis (Fictitious character)
  UF Travis McGee (Fictitious character)
  BT Characters and characteristics in
      literature
  RT MacDonald, John D. (John Dann),
      1916-   —Characters—Travis
      McGee
  NT MacDonald, John D. (John Dann),
      1916-   —Characters—Travis
      McGee
McGee family
  USE Magee family

McGehee family
  USE Magee family
McGennisken family *(Not Subd Geog)*
McGhee family
  USE Magee family
McGhie family
  USE Magee family
McGill family *(Not Subd Geog)*
  UF MacGill family
    Magill family
    Meagill family
    Megil family
    Megill family
McGill Pauper Cemetery (El Paso, Tex.)
  UF McGill Pauper's Cemetery (El Paso,
      Tex.)
    McGill's Pauper Cemetery (El Paso,
      Tex.)
  BT Cemeteries—Texas
    Poor—Texas
McGill Pauper's Cemetery (El Paso, Tex.)
  USE McGill Pauper Cemetery (El Paso,
      Tex.)
McGill University System for Interactive
  Computing (Computer system)
  USE MUSIC (Computer system)
McGillavry family
  USE McGillivray family
McGillivray family *(Not Subd Geog)*
  UF MacGilvra family
    McGillavry family
    McGillvray family
    McGilvary family
    McGilvery family
    McGilvray family
McGill's Pauper Cemetery (El Paso, Tex.)
  USE McGill Pauper Cemetery (El Paso,
      Tex.)
McGillvray family
  USE McGillivray family
McGilvary family
  USE McGillivray family
McGilvery family
  USE McGillivray family
McGilvray family
  USE McGillivray family
McGinnis family
  USE Guinness family
McGinty family *(Not Subd Geog)*
McGlinn family
  USE McGlynn family
McGlynn family *(Not Subd Geog)*
  UF McGlinn family
    McGlynne family
McGlynne family
  USE McGlynn family
McGoff family
  USE Goff family
McGonagle family
  USE McGonegle family
McGonegle family *(Not Subd Geog)*
  UF McGonagle family
    McGonigle family
McGonigle family
  USE McGonegle family
McGoogin family
  USE McGuckin family
McGookin family
  USE McGuckin family
McGorry family
  USE McGory family
McGory family *(Not Subd Geog)*
  UF Macgorrie family
    MacGory family
    McGorry family

McGowan family *(Not Subd Geog)*
  UF Macgowan family
    McGowen family
    McGowin family
    McGown family
    McGowns family
    Megowen family
McGowen family
  USE McGowan family
McGowin family
  USE McGowan family
McGown family
  USE McGowan family
McGowns family
  USE McGowan family
McGrady family *(Not Subd Geog)*
  UF MacGrady family
  RT Grady family
McGrath family *(Not Subd Geog)*
  UF Macgrath family
McGreal family
  USE McNeil family
McGreeger family
  USE McGregor family
McGreger family
  USE McGregor family
McGreggor family
  USE McGregor family
McGregor clan
  USE McGregor family
McGregor family *(Not Subd Geog)*
  UF MacGregor family
    McGreeger family
    McGreger family
    McGreggor family
    McGregor clan
    McGregory family
    McGriger family
    McGrigor family
    McGroeger family
  RT Gregory family
McGregory family
  USE McGregor family
McGriff family *(Not Subd Geog)*
McGriger family
  USE McGregor family
McGrigor family
  USE McGregor family
McGroeger family
  USE McGregor family
McGucken family
  USE McGuckin family
McGuckian family
  USE McGuckin family
McGuckin family *(Not Subd Geog)*
  UF MacGuckin family
    McGoogin family
    McGookin family
    McGucken family
    McGuckian family
    McGugan family
    McGuigan family
    McGurgan family
McGugan family
  USE McGuckin family
McGuigan family
  USE McGuckin family
McGuinness family
  USE Guinness family
McGuire family *(Not Subd Geog)*
  UF Maguire family
McGurgan family
  USE McGuckin family
McHarg family
  USE McHargue family
McHargue family *(Not Subd Geog)*
  UF McHarg family
McHatton family
  USE MacHatton family
McHenry, Fort (Baltimore, Md.)
  USE Fort McHenry (Baltimore, Md.)

McHenry family (Not Subd Geog)
 UF MacEnery family
  MacEniry family
McHenry-Langdon Home (Modesto, Calif.)
 USE McHenry Mansion (Modesto, Calif.)
McHenry Mansion (Modesto, Calif.)
 UF Langdon House (Modesto, Calif.)
  McHenry-Langdon Home (Modesto,
   Calif.)
 BT Dwellings—California
McHoes family
 USE McHose family
McHone family (Not Subd Geog)
 UF MacHone family
McHorter family
 USE McWhorter family
McHose family (Not Subd Geog)
 UF MacHose family
  McHoes family
McIlhany family
 USE McIlhenny family
McIlhenny family (Not Subd Geog)
 UF McIlhany family
  McIlnay family
McIlnay family
 USE McIlhenny family
McIlvain family
 USE McElwain family
McIlvaine family
 USE McElwain family
McIlveen family
 USE McElwain family
McIlveene family
 USE McElwain family
McIlwain family
 USE McElwain family
McIlwaine, Lake (Zimbabwe)
 UF Lake McIlwaine (Zimbabwe)
 BT Hunyani River (Zimbabwe and
   Mozambique)
  Lakes—Zimbabwe
  Reservoirs—Zimbabwe
McIlwaine family
 USE McElwain family
McIlyhia family
 USE McAlley family
McInnes family
 USE McInnis family
McInnis family (Not Subd Geog)
 UF Macinnes family
  Macinnis family
  Magenis family
  Magennis family
  Maginnis family
  McInnes family
McInteer family
 USE McIntyre family
McIntier family
 USE McIntyre family
McIntire family
 USE McIntyre family
McIntosh family (Not Subd Geog)
 UF Macintosh family
  Mackintosh family
McInturff family (Not Subd Geog)
 UF McEntarfer family
  McEnturff family
McIntyer family
 USE McIntyre family
McIntyre family (Not Subd Geog)
 UF MacIntyre family
  McEntire family
  McInteer family
  McIntier family
  McIntire family
  McIntyer family
McIntyre Site (Ont.)
 BT Ontario—Antiquities
McIvair family
 USE McIver family

McIver family (Not Subd Geog)
 UF MacIver family
  MacIvor family
  McEver family
  McEvers family
  McIvair family
  McIvers family
McIvers family
 USE McIver family
McJunkin family
 USE Jenkins family
McKain family
 USE McCain family
McKale family (Not Subd Geog)
 UF MacKale family
McKan family
 USE McCann family
McKane family
 USE McCain family
McKanless family
 USE McCandless family
McKann family
 USE McCann family
McKanse family
 USE McCants family
McKants family
 USE McCants family
McKaughan family (Not Subd Geog)
 UF McCoin family
  McGahan family
  McGaughan family
  McKoane family
  McKoin family
  McKone family
McKay family (Not Subd Geog)
 UF MacKay family
  MacKays family
  McKays family
 RT McCoy family
  McKey family
McKays family
 USE McKay family
McKean family
 USE McCain family
McKee family
 USE McKey family
McKeehan family
 USE McCain family
McKeen family
 USE McCain family
McKeithen Mounds (Fla.)
 USE McKeithen Site (Fla.)
McKeithen Site (Fla.) (Not Subd Geog)
 UF McKeithen Mounds (Fla.)
 BT Florida—Antiquities
McKelvey family (Not Subd Geog)
 UF MacKelvey family
  McCelvie family
  McCelvy family
  McElvy family
  McKelvie family
  McKelvy family
McKelvie family
 USE McKelvey family
McKelvy family
 USE McKelvey family
McKenna family (Not Subd Geog)
 UF McKenney family
  McKenny family
 RT McKinney family
McKenney family
 USE McKenna family
McKennon family
 USE McKinnon family
McKenny family
 USE McKenna family
McKenzie family
 USE Mackenzie family
McKettrick family
 USE McKittrick family

McKewin family
 USE McEwan family
McKey family (Not Subd Geog)
 UF Macke family
  MacKee family
  Mackey family
  Mackie family
  Macky family
  Makee family
  Makey family
  McCee family
  McKee family
  McKie family
 RT Mack family
  Magee family
  McCoy family
  McKay family
McKie family
 USE McKey family
McKim family (Not Subd Geog)
 UF MacKim family
McKindles family
 USE McCandless family
McKindley family
 USE McKinley family
McKinlay family
 USE McKinley family
McKinley, Mount (Alaska)
 UF Denali (Alaska)
  Mount McKinley (Alaska)
 BT Denali National Park and Preserve
   (Alaska)
  Mountains—Alaska
McKinley family (Not Subd Geog)
 UF MacKinlay family
  MacKinley family
  McKindley family
  McKinlay family
  McKinly family
McKinley National Park (Alaska)
 USE Denali National Park and Preserve
   (Alaska)
McKinley tariff
 [HF1755 (Discussion)]
 [HJ6085 1890 (Schedules)]
McKinly family
 USE McKinley family
McKinnen family
 USE McKinnon family
McKinney family (Not Subd Geog)
 RT McKenna family
McKinnin family
 USE McKinnon family
McKinnon family (Not Subd Geog)
 UF Mackinnon family
  McCinnan family
  McKennon family
  McKinnen family
  McKinnin family
  Miskimen family
  Miskimmin family
  Miskimmins family
  Miskimmon family
  Miskimmons family
McKirdy family
 USE McCurdy family
McKitrick family
 USE McKittrick family
McKitterick family
 USE McKittrick family
McKittrick family (Not Subd Geog)
 UF McKettrick family
  McKitrick family
  McKitterick family
 RT Ettrick family
McKneight family
 USE McKnight family

McKnight family *(Not Subd Geog)*
   UF MacKnight family
       McKneight family
       McKnite family
       McNight family
       McNite family
   RT McNaughton family
McKnite family
   USE McKnight family
McKoane family
   USE McKaughan family
McKoin family
   USE McKaughan family
McKone family
   USE McKaughan family
McKonnell family
   USE McConnell family
McKorkell family
   USE McCorkle family
McKorkle family
   USE McCorkle family
McKowan family
   USE McCown family
McKowen family
   USE McCown family
McKown family
   USE McCown family
McKoy family
   USE McCoy family
McKray family
   USE McRae family
McKuen family
   USE McEwan family
McLain family
   USE McLean family
McLaland family
   USE McClellan family
McLallan family
   USE McClellan family
McLallen family
   USE McClellan family
McLamar family
   USE McLemore family
McLamare family
   USE McLemore family
McLane family
   USE McLean family
McLane-Ocampo treaty
McLaren automobiles
   BT Automobiles, Racing
McLaughlan family
   USE McLaughlin family
McLaughlin family *(Not Subd Geog)*
   UF Maclachlan family
       Maclaughlin family
       McLaughlan family
       McLoughlin family
McLaury family
   USE McClaughry family
McLean family *(Not Subd Geog)*
   UF MacLaine family
       MacLean family
       McClain family
       McClane family
       McClean family
       McLain family
       McLane family
McLean Site (Ill.)
   BT Illinois—Antiquities
McLeay family
   USE Macleay family
McLeeland family
   USE McClellan family
McLeland family
   USE McClellan family
McLelen family
   USE McClellan family
McLellan family
   USE McClellan family
McLelland family
   USE McClellan family

McLellen family
   USE McClellan family
McLemoore family
   USE McLemore family
McLemore family *(Not Subd Geog)*
   UF McClemore family
       McLamar family
       McLamare family
       McLemoore family
McLenan family
   USE McLennan family
McLendon family *(Not Subd Geog)*
   UF McClendon family
   RT McClanahan family
       McLennan family
McLennan family *(Not Subd Geog)*
   UF Maclennan family
       McLenan family
       McLennen family
   RT McClellan family
       McLendon family
McLennen family
   USE McLennan family
McLentock family
   USE McClintock family
McLeod family *(Not Subd Geog)*
   UF MacCloud family
       MacLeod family
       McLoud family
   RT Cloud family
McLillan family
   USE McClellan family
McLintack family
   USE McClintock family
M'Clintock (N.W.T.)
   USE Prince Leopold Island (N.W.T.)
McLintock family
   USE McClintock family
McLlewer family
   USE McClure family
McLoskey family
   USE McCloskey family
McLoud family
   USE McLeod family
McLoughlin family
   USE McLaughlin family
MCLS (Disease)
   USE Mucocutaneous lymph node syndrome
McLure family
   USE McClure family
McLwain family
   USE McElwain family
McManus family *(Not Subd Geog)*
   UF MacManus family
McMellen family
   USE McMillan family
McMellens family
   USE McMillan family
McMillan family *(Not Subd Geog)*
   UF MacMillan family
       McMellen family
       McMellens family
       McMillen family
       McMillian family
       McMillin family
       McMillion family
       McMillon family
McMillen family
   USE McMillan family
McMillian family
   USE McMillan family
McMillin family
   USE McMillan family
McMillion family
   USE McMillan family
McMillon family
   USE McMillan family
McMin family
   USE McMinn family

McMinn family *(Not Subd Geog)*
   UF McMin family
       McMins family
McMins family
   USE McMinn family
McMonagle family *(Not Subd Geog)*
   UF McMoneagle family
       McMonigle family
McMoneagle family
   USE McMonagle family
McMonigle family
   USE McMonagle family
McMurdo Sound (Antarctic regions)
   (Not Subd Geog)
   BT Sounds (Geomorphology)—Antarctic
       regions
McMurey family
   USE McMurray family
McMurray family *(Not Subd Geog)*
   UF MacMurray family
       McMurey family
       McMurrey family
       McMurry family
McMurrey family
   USE McMurray family
McMurry family
   USE McMurray family
McMurtrey family
   USE McMurtry family
McMurtrie family
   USE McMurtry family
McMurtry family *(Not Subd Geog)*
   UF McMurtrey family
       McMurtrie family
McNacton family
   USE McNaughton family
McNair family *(Not Subd Geog)*
   UF MacNair family
       McNare family
       McNear family
       McNeer family
       McNeir family
McNamara family *(Not Subd Geog)*
   UF MacNamara family
McNare family
   USE McNair family
McNary Reservoir (Wash. and Or.)
   BT Reservoirs—Oregon
       Reservoirs—Washington (State)
McNattin family
   USE McNaughton family
McNatton family
   USE McNaughton family
McNaught family
   USE McNaughton family
McNaughtin family
   USE McNaughton family
McNaughton family *(Not Subd Geog)*
   UF MacNachtan clan
       MacNaghten clan
       MacNauchtan clan
       McNacton family
       McNattin family
       McNatton family
       McNaught family
       McNaughtin family
   RT McKnight family
McNeal family
   USE McNeil family
McNeall family
   USE McNeil family
McNear family
   USE McNair family
McNeel family
   USE McNeil family
McNeeley family *(Not Subd Geog)*
   RT McNeil family
McNeer family
   USE McNair family

McNeese family (Not Subd Geog)
  UF MacNeese family
      McNeise family
      McNess family
McNeil clan
  USE McNeil family
McNeil family (Not Subd Geog)
  UF MacNeal family
      MacNeil family
      McGreal family
      McNeal family
      McNeall family
      McNeel family
      McNeil clan
      McNeill family
      McNiel family
      McNiell family
  RT McNeeley family
McNeil River State Game Sanctuary (Alaska)
  BT Wildlife refuges—Alaska
McNeill family
  USE McNeil family
McNeir family
  USE McNair family
McNeise family
  USE McNeese family
McNess family
  USE McNeese family
McNichol family
  USE McNicholas family
McNicholas family (Not Subd Geog)
  UF McNichol family
      McNichols family
      McNickle family
      McNicoll family
McNichols family
  USE McNicholas family
McNickle family
  USE McNicholas family
McNicoll family
  USE McNicholas family
McNiel family
  USE McNeil family
McNiell family
  USE McNeil family
McNight family
  USE McKnight family
McNite family
  USE McKnight family
McNult family
  USE McNulty family
McNulty family (Not Subd Geog)
  UF McNult family
McNut family
  USE McNutt family
McNutt family (Not Subd Geog)
  UF McNut family
  RT Knott family
McOmber family
  USE McCumber family
McOwen family
  USE McCown family
McOwn family
  USE McCown family
MCPA (Herbicide)
    [SB952.M15 (Herbicide)]
  UF Chlorocresoxyacetic acid
      Chlorotolyloxyacetic acid
      Metaxon
      Methylchlorophenoxyacetic acid
  BT Chlorophenoxyacetic acid
      Herbicides
  NT Plants, Effect of MCPA on
McPeak family (Not Subd Geog)
  UF MacPeak family
      MacPeake family
      MacPeek family
      McPeake family
      McPeek family
McPeake family
  USE McPeak family

McPeek family
  USE McPeak family
McPharlen family
  USE McFarland family
McPhee family (Not Subd Geog)
  UF Macfee family
      Macfie family
      Macphee family
      McFee family
McPherson family (Not Subd Geog)
  UF Macpherson family
      McFercin family
      McFersin family
      McFerson family
McQuade family (Not Subd Geog)
  UF McQuaid family
      McQuaide family
McQuadie family
  USE McQuitty family
McQuady family
  USE McQuitty family
McQuaid family
  USE McQuade family
McQuaide family
  USE McQuade family
McQuattie family
  USE McQuitty family
McQuatty family
  USE McQuitty family
McQuaty family
  USE McQuitty family
McQueen family (Not Subd Geog)
  UF Macqueen family
      McQueyn family
      Mcquian family
McQueety family
  USE McQuitty family
McQueyn family
  USE McQueen family
Mcquian family
  USE McQueen family
McQuiddie family
  USE McQuitty family
McQuitty family (Not Subd Geog)
  UF MacQuatty family
      MacQuitty family
      McQuadie family
      McQuady family
      McQuattie family
      McQuatty family
      McQuaty family
      McQueety family
      McQuiddie family
      McWattie family
McQuown family
  USE McEwan family
McRa family
  USE McRae family
McRae family (Not Subd Geog)
  UF MacRae family
      McCrae family
      McCray family
      McCre family
      McCrea family
      McKray family
      McRa family
      McRay family
      McRea family
      McRee family
McRay family
  USE McRae family
McRea family
  USE McRae family
McRee family
  USE McRae family
McReynolds family (Not Subd Geog)
MCS (Computer program)
  USE Monitor Command System (Computer
       program)
McShannock family (Not Subd Geog)
  UF McShenoig family

McShenoig family
  USE McShannock family
McSpadden family (Not Subd Geog)
  UF McSpaden family
McSpaden family
  USE McSpadden family
MCTD (Disease)
  USE Mixed connective tissue disease
McTernan family (Not Subd Geog)
  UF McTiernan family
McTiernan family
  USE McTernan family
McVannel family (Not Subd Geog)
  UF MacVannel family
McWattie family
  USE McQuitty family
McWharton family
  USE McWhorter family
McWherter family
  USE McWhorter family
McWhinney family (Not Subd Geog)
  UF McWhinnie family
      Mewhinney family
McWhinnie family
  USE McWhinney family
McWhirt family (Not Subd Geog)
  UF Macchruiter family
      McWhirter family
McWhirter family
  USE McWhirt family
McWhorter family (Not Subd Geog)
  UF MacWhorter family
      McHorter family
      McWharton family
      McWherter family
      McWhurter family
      McWorter family
McWhurter family
  USE McWhorter family
McWilliam family
  USE McWilliams family
McWilliams family (Not Subd Geog)
  UF Macwilliams family
      Macwillian family
      McWilliam family
McWorter family
  USE McWhorter family
Mdaga Site (Chad) (Not Subd Geog)
  UF Midigui Site (Chad)
  BT Chad—Antiquities
Mdewakanton Indians
    [E99.M435]
  UF Medawakanton Indians
  BT Dakota Indians
      Indians of North America
      Santee Indians
  NT Kiyuksa Indians
  — Reservations
MDs
  USE Physicians
MDS (Computer system)
  UF Minerals data system of the U.S.
       Geological Survey
  BT Electronic digital computers—
       Programming
      Mines and mineral resources—Data
       processing
ME (Disease)
  USE Myalgic encephalomyelitis
Me-ri (Bonpo deity)
  BT Gods, Bonpo
Mea Shearim (Jerusalem) (Not Subd Geog)
    [DS109.8.M4]
  UF Jerusalem. Mea Shearim
      Jerusalem. Me'ah She'arim
      Me'ah She'arim (Jerusalem)

Meacham family *(Not Subd Geog)*
UF Meachem family
Meachum family
Mecham family
Mechem family
Mechum family
Meecham family
Meachem family
USE Meacham family
Meachum family
USE Meacham family
Mead, Lake (Ariz. and Nev.)
UF Lake Mead (Ariz. and Nev.)
Mead Reservoir (Ariz. and Nev.)
BT Lake Mead National Recreation Area
(Ariz. and Nev.)
Lakes—Arizona
Lakes—Nevada
Reservoirs—Arizona
Reservoirs—Nevada
Mead
UF Metheglin
BT Honey
RT Hydromel
Mead family *(Not Subd Geog)*
UF Meade family
Meades family
Meads family
Mede family
Medes family
Meed family
Meeds family
Meid family
Mead Reservoir (Ariz. and Nev.)
USE Mead, Lake (Ariz. and Nev.)
Meade family
USE Mead family
Meader family
USE Meador family
Meaders family
USE Meador family
Meades family
USE Mead family
Meadlock family
USE Matlock family
Meador family *(Not Subd Geog)*
UF Maeder family
Meader family
Meaders family
Meadors family
Meder family
Meeder family
RT Meadows family
Meadors family
USE Meador family
Meadow Creek (Fayette County, W. Va.)
BT Rivers—West Virginia
Meadow ecology *(May Subd Geog)*
[QH541.5.M4]
[QK938.M4]
BT Ecology
NT Meadow flora
Meadow family
USE Meadows family
Meadow fauna *(May Subd Geog)*
[QL115.5]
UF Field fauna
BT Meadows
Zoology
Meadow fescue *(May Subd Geog)*
[QK495.G74 (Botany)]
[SB201.M4 (Forage plant)]
UF Bluegrass, English
English bluegrass
Festuca elatior
Festuca pratensis
BT Fescue
Meadow flora *(May Subd Geog)*
[QK108-QK474.5 (Local)]
[QK938.M4 (General)]

BT Botany
Botany—Ecology
Meadow ecology
Meadow gardening *(May Subd Geog)*
UF Gardening, Meadow
BT Landscape gardening
Meadow-larks
[QL696.P2475]
Meadow mice
USE Microtus
Meadow spittlebug
USE Philaenus leucophthalmus
Meadow vole
USE Microtus pennsylvanicus
Meadow voles
USE Microtus
Meadowlands (N.J.)
UF Hackensack Meadowlands (N.J.)
Hackensack Meadows (N.J.)
BT Marshes—New Jersey
Meadows—New Jersey
Meadows *(May Subd Geog)*
[SB199]
UF Grassland farming
BT Agriculture
RT Grasses
Pastures
Rangelands
NT Meadow fauna
— **Fertilizers**
BT Fertilizers
— **Irrigation**
— **Mythology**
— **New Jersey**
NT Meadowlands (N.J.)
Meadows family *(Not Subd Geog)*
UF Meadow family
Medow family
Medows family
RT Meador family
Meads family
USE Mead family
Meagill family
USE McGill family
Me'ah She'arim (Jerusalem)
USE Mea Shearim (Jerusalem)
Meak family
USE Meeks family
Meake family
USE Meeks family
Meaker family
USE Meeker family
Meaks family
USE Meeks family
Meal
[TS2120-2159]
BT Cereal products
RT Grain—Milling
NT Canola meal
Corn meal
Corn oil meal
Cottonseed meal
Fish-meal
Oatmeal
Polenta
Soybean meal
Meal as feed
Meal beetles
USE Meal worms
Meal worms
UF Meal beetles
Mealworms
Mealer family
USE Meeler family
Meals, Sacred
USE Sacred meals
Meals for school children
USE School children—Food
Meals for the elderly
USE Meals on wheels programs

Meals on wheels programs
(May Subd Geog)
UF Home delivered meals
Meals for the elderly
BT Aged—Nutrition
Food relief
— **Law and legislation** *(May Subd Geog)*
Mealworms
USE Meal worms
Mealy bugs
[QL527.P83]
UF Mealybugs
BT Homoptera
Scale-insects
NT Eriococcidae
Pseudococcidae
Mealy plum aphis
[SB945.M45]
UF Hyalopterus arundinus
Hyalopterus pruni
Mealybugs
USE Mealy bugs
Mean, Golden
USE Moderation
Mean, Laws of the (Calculus)
USE Mean value theorems (Calculus)
Mean (Philosophy)
[B491.M36 (Aristotle)]
BT Average
Moderation
Philosophy
Mean family
USE Means family
Mean sea level
USE Sea level
Mean value theorems (Calculus)
UF Laws of the mean (Calculus)
Mean, Laws of the (Calculus)
BT Calculus
Meandering rivers *(May Subd Geog)*
[GB1205]
BT Rivers
Meanes family
USE Means family
Meaney family *(Not Subd Geog)*
UF Meany family
Meaning (Philosophy)
[B105.M4]
BT Philosophy
Semantics (Philosophy)
NT Relevance
Meaning (Psychology)
[BF455 (Thought and language)]
[BF778]
RT Logotherapy
Thought and thinking
NT Association tests
Connotation (Linguistics)
Definition (Logic)
Language and languages
Logical positivism
Relevance
Semantics
Semantics (Philosophy)
Meaninglessness (Philosophy)
[B825.2]
BT Nihilism (Philosophy)
Philosophy
Semantics (Philosophy)
Skepticism
Means (Buddhism)
USE Upāya (Buddhism)
Means and ends
USE Ends and means

Means family (Not Subd Geog)
  UF Mean family
      Meanes family
      Meeans family
      Meen family
      Meens family
      Mein family
      Menes family
Means of communication for the mentally
  handicapped
  USE Mentally handicapped—Means of
        communication
Means of communication for the visually
  handicapped
  USE Visually handicapped—Means of
        communication
Meany family
  USE Meaney family
Mear family
  USE Mears family
Meares family
  USE Mears family
Mears family (Not Subd Geog)
  UF Mear family
      Meares family
      Meers family
Measles (May Subd Geog)
  [RC168.M4]
  UF Rubeola
  BT Virus diseases
  NT Rubella
  — **Complications and sequelae**
    (May Subd Geog)
    NT Subacute sclerosing panencephalitis
  — **Preventive inoculation**
    [RA644.M5]
    NT Measles vaccine
Measles vaccine
  [QR180.5.M4]
  BT Measles—Preventive inoculation
      Viral vaccines
  NT Rubella vaccines
Measles virus (May Subd Geog)
  [QR201.M43]
  UF Morbilli virus
  BT Paramyxoviruses
Measurable sets
  USE Measure theory
Measure, Caratheodory
  USE Caratheodory measure
Measure algebras
  [QA403]
  UF Algebras, Measure
  BT Harmonic analysis
  RT Measure theory
Measure of a set
  USE Measure theory
Measure of damages
  USE Damages
Measure of information
  USE Information measurement
Measure of uncertainty (Information theory)
  USE Uncertainty (Information theory)
Measure-preserving transformations
  BT Ergodic theory
      Measure theory
      Transformations (Mathematics)
Measure theory
  UF Lebesgue measure
      Measurable sets
      Measure of a set
  BT Algebraic topology
      Integrals, Generalized
      Rings (Algebra)
  RT Measure algebras
  NT Bernoulli shifts
      Caratheodory measure
      Concentration functions
      Cylindrical probabilities
      Ergodic theory
      Gaussian measures

      Geometric measure theory
      Hausdorff measures
      Integrals, Haar
      Lebesgue-Radon-Nikodym theorems
      Lifting theory
      Measure-preserving transformations
      Operator-valued measures
      Pseudofunctions
      Radon measures
      Spaces of measures
      Spectral theory (Mathematics)
      Vector-valued measures
      Wiener integrals
Measure theory, Geometric
  USE Geometric measure theory
Measured drawing (May Subd Geog)
  [NA2712]
  UF Drawing, Measured
  BT Architectural drawing
Measured-mile trials (Ships)
  USE Ship trials
Measured music
  [ML174]
    The term is here restricted to medieval music in
  mensural notation.
  UF Music, Measured
  BT Music—500-1400
      Musical meter and rhythm
      Musical notation
Measurement
  USE subdivision Measurement under
      scientific and technical subjects for
      the technique of making
      measurements, e.g. Soil moisture—
      Measurement
      Mensuration
Measurement, Mental
  USE Psychometrics
Measurement, Psychological
  USE Psychometrics
Measurement of area
  USE Area measurement
Measurement of distances
  USE Distances—Measurement
Measurement of length
  USE Length measurement
Measurement of roundness
  USE Roundness measurement
Measurement of sound
  USE Sound—Measurement
Measurement of streams
  USE Stream measurements
Measurement of thickness
  USE Thickness measurement
Measurement of vibration
  USE Vibration—Measurement
Measurement of winds
  USE Winds—Measurement
Measurement of wool
  USE Wool—Measurement
Measurements, Aerodynamic
  USE Aerodynamic measurements
Measurements, Dielectric
  USE Dielectric measurements
Measurements, Electric
  USE Electric measurements
Measurements, Electromagnetic
  USE Electromagnetic measurements
Measurements, Electronic
  USE Electronic measurements
Measurements, Fluid dynamic
  USE Fluid dynamic measurements
Measurements, High pressure
  USE High pressure measurements
Measurements, Magnetic
  USE Magnetic measurements
Measurements, Optical
  USE Optical measurements
Measurements, Physical
  USE Physical measurements

Measurements, Type
  USE Type measurements
Measurements of women's clothing
  USE Clothing and dress measurements
Measures
  USE Weights and measures
Measures, Cylindrical (Probabilities)
  USE Cylindrical probabilities
Measures, Gaussian
  USE Gaussian measures
Measures, Operator-valued
  USE Operator-valued measures
Measures, Radon
  USE Radon measures
Measures, Spaces of
  USE Spaces of measures
Measures, Vector-valued
  USE Vector-valued measures
Measuring
  USE Mensuration
Measuring instruments (May Subd Geog)
  [QC100.5-QC100.8 (Physical
    instruments)]
  [TJ1313 (Machine-shop practice)]
  UF Instruments, Measuring
      Measuring tools
  BT Mensuration
      Weights and measures
  NT Calipers
      Chace air indicator
      Compasses (Mathematical instruments)
      Digital counters
      Distance measuring instruments,
        Electronic
      Gage blocks
      Gages
      Instrument manufacture
      Light meters
      Measuring microscopes
      Planimeter
      Rheometers
      Rotameters
      Rulers (Instruments)
      Slide-rule
      Tensiometers
      Torquemeters
      Verniers
  — Appraisal
    USE Measuring instruments—
        Valuation
  — **Maintenance and repair**
  — **Testing**
  — **Valuation**
    [TA165]
    UF Measuring instruments—Appraisal
Measuring instruments, Chinese
Measuring instruments industry
  (May Subd Geog)
  [HD9999.M34]
Measuring machines, Coordinate
  USE Coordinate measuring machines
Measuring microscopes
  UF Microscopes, Measuring
  BT Measuring instruments
      Microscope and microscopy
Measuring-pumps
  [QC104]
Measuring-tapes
  [TA579-TA581 (Surveying)]
  UF Steel measuring-tapes
  BT Surveyors' chains
Measuring tools
  USE Measuring instruments
Meat
  [TS1950-TS1975 (Animal products)]
  [TX371-TX389 (Food supply)]
  [TX555-TX556 (Food values)]
  [TX743-TX753 (Cookery)]
  BT Animal products
      Food
  NT Bacon

Meat *(Continued)*
    Beef
    Cookery (Meat)
    Horse meat
    Lamb (Meat)
    Meat, Precooked
    Mutton
    Pork
    Rabbit meat
    Veal
    Venison
    Wildlife as food
— **Bacteriology**
    [QR117]
    BT Meat—Microbiology
        Meat inspection
— **Boning**
    UF Boning of meat
        Deboning of meat
        Meat—Deboning
— **Color**
    USE Color of meat
— **Contamination**
    UF Contamination of meat
    BT Food contamination
— **Cutting**
    USE Meat cutting
— **Deboning**
    USE Meat—Boning
— **Inspection**
    USE Meat inspection
— **Labeling**
—— **Law and legislation**
    (May Subd Geog)
— **Microbiology**
    BT Meat inspection
    NT Meat—Bacteriology
— **Packaging**
—— **Law and legislation**
    (May Subd Geog)
— **Packing**
    Here are entered works on packing of meat
    for shipment. Works on meat packing, i.e., the
    wholesale meat industry, are entered under
    Packing-houses.
— **Preservation**
    [TX599-613]
    BT Food—Preservation
    NT Meat, Canned
        Meat, Smoked
— **Quality**
    UF Meat quality
— **Radiation preservation**
— **Religious aspects**
—— **Buddhism, [Christianity, etc.]**
— **Taxation** *(May Subd Geog)*
    UF Taxation of meat
    RT Slaughtering and slaughter-houses
        —Taxation
— **Thermal properties**
Meat, Canned
    UF Canned meat
    BT Food, Canned
        Meat—Preservation
    NT Beef, Canned
        Pork, Canned
Meat, Dried
    BT Food, Dried
    NT Pemmican
Meat, Frozen
    BT Food, Frozen
Meat, Precooked
    [TX556.M43 (Food values)]
    UF Precooked meat
    BT Food, Precooked
        Meat
— **Flavor and odor**
    BT Flavor
        Odors

Meat, Smoked
    UF Food, Smoked
        Smoked meat
    BT Cookery (Meat)
        Meat—Preservation
Meat consumption
    USE Meat industry and trade
Meat cuts
    BT Meat cutting
Meat cutting
    [TS1962]
    UF Meat—Cutting
        Meatcutting
    BT Butchers
    NT Carving (Meat, etc.)
        Meat cuts
Meat-eating animals
    USE Carnivora
Meat extract
    [TX389]
Meat grinders
    UF Grinders, Meat
    BT Grinding machines
Meat industry and trade *(May Subd Geog)*
    [HD9410-HD9441 (Economics)]
    [TS1950-TS1975 (Manufactures)]
    UF Meat consumption
        Packing industry
    BT Food supply
    RT Cold storage
    NT Animal gut industries
        Beef, Dried
        Beef packers
        Butchers
        Cattle trade
        Kosher food industry
        Livestock factories
        Packing-house products
        Packing-house workers
        Packing-houses
        Pork industry and trade
        Sausage casings
        Sausages
        Slaughtering and slaughter-houses
        Stockyards
        Strikes and lockouts—Meat industry
— Collective bargaining
    USE Collective bargaining—Meat
        industry
— Collective labor agreements
    USE Collective labor agreements—
        Meat industry
— **Government ownership**
    (May Subd Geog)
    UF Government ownership of the meat
        industry
— **Inventories**
    UF Meat inventories
— **Law and legislation** *(May Subd Geog)*
    UF Packing-houses—Law and
        legislation
    BT Food law and legislation
    NT Slaughtering and slaughter-houses
        —Law and legislation
— **Taxation**
    NT Slaughtering and slaughter-houses
        —Taxation
Meat inspection *(May Subd Geog)*
    [HD9410.9 (Economic aspects)]
    [TS1975 (Technical aspects)]
    UF Inspection of meat
        Meat—Inspection
    BT Food adulteration and inspection
    NT Meat—Bacteriology
        Meat—Microbiology
        Poultry—Inspection
— **Law and legislation** *(May Subd Geog)*
Meat inspection (Jewish law)
    BT Jews—Dietary laws
        Shehitah

Meat inspection stamps *(May Subd Geog)*
    [TS1975]
    UF Stamps, Meat inspection
    BT Rubber stamps
Meat inventories
    USE Meat industry and trade—Inventories
Meat packing industry
    USE Packing-houses
Meat production efficiency
    USE Feed utilization efficiency
Meat quality
    USE Meat—Quality
Meat substitutes
    [TX838]
    BT Food substitutes
        Vegetarianism
Meatballs
    BT Cookery (Meat)
Meatcutting
    USE Meat cutting
Meatless meals
    USE Lenten menus
        Vegetarianism
Meatus, Internal auditory
    USE Auditory meatus, Internal
Meban (African people)
    USE Maban (African people)
Meban language
    USE Maban language
Mebe language
    USE Dan language
Mebubarbital
    USE Pentobarbital
Mebumal
    USE Pentobarbital
Mecas
    [QL596.C4]
    BT Cerambycidae
Mecca, Pilgrimage to
    USE Muslim pilgrims and pilgrimages—
        Saudi Arabia—Mecca
Mech language
    USE Bara language
Mecham family
    USE Meacham family
Mechanic arts
    USE Industrial arts
Mechanical ability
    UF Ability, Mechanical
        Concrete intelligence
        Mechanical aptitude
        Mechanical intelligence
    BT Ability
        Mechanics
    RT Motor ability
— **Testing**
    [BF433.M4]
    UF Mechanical ability tests
    BT Ability—Testing
Mechanical ability tests
    USE Mechanical ability—Testing
Mechanical analogies in electricity
    USE Electromechanical analogies
Mechanical aptitude
    USE Mechanical ability
Mechanical brains
    USE Conscious automata
        Cybernetics
Mechanical chemistry
    UF Chemistry, Mechanical
        Mechanically induced chemical
        reactions
        Mechanochemistry
        Stress induced chemical reactions
    BT Chemistry, Physical and theoretical
Mechanical coin banks *(May Subd Geog)*
    BT Coin banks
Mechanical computers
    USE Calculators
Mechanical corn pickers
    USE Corn picking machinery

Mechanical dolls (May Subd Geog)
  [NK4894.3.M43]
  UF Dolls, Mechanical
  BT Dolls
      Toys, Mechanical
Mechanical draft
  [TJ335]
  UF Draft, Mechanical
      Draught, Mechanical
Mechanical drawing
  [T351-377]
  UF Drafting, Mechanical
      Engineering drawing
      Industrial drawing
      Mathematical drawing
      Plans
      Technical drawing
  BT Drawing
      Drawing instruments
      Engineering
      Machinery
      Pattern-making
  RT Design, Industrial
      Geometrical drawing
      Graphic statics
      Projection
      Technical illustration
  NT Aircraft drafting
      Architectural drawing
      Automotive drafting
      Bolts and nuts—Drawings
      Building—Tools and implements—
        Drawings
      Clocks and watches—Drawings
      Concrete plants—Equipment and
        supplies—Drawings
      Construction equipment—Drawings
      Conveying machinery—Drawings
      Dies (Metal-working)—Drawings
      Diesel motor—Drawings
      Drawing-room practice
      Drilling and boring machinery—
        Drawings
      Earthmoving machinery—Drawings
      Electric drafting
      Electronic drafting
      Engineering drawings
      Engineering graphics
      Excavating machinery—Drawings
      Forging machinery—Drawings
      Foundries—Equipment and supplies—
        Drawings
      Freehand technical sketching
      Furniture—Drawings
      Gas-turbines—Drawings
      Gearing—Drawings
      Graphic methods
      Grinding machines—Drawings
      Hoisting machinery—Drawings
      House painting—Equipment and
        supplies—Drawings
      Isometric projection
      Jigs and fixtures—Drawings
      Joints (Engineering)—Drawings
      Lathes—Drawings
      Lettering
      Locomotives—Drawings
      Machinery—Drawings
      Metal castings—Drawings
      Naval drafting
      Open-hearth furnaces—Drawings
      Optical instruments—Drawings
      Ordnance, Naval—Drawings
      Overlay drafting systems
      Paper-hanging—Equipment and
        supplies—Drawings
      Plastering—Equipment and supplies—
        Drawings
      Plumbing drafting
      Power presses—Drawings
      Railroads—Freight-cars—Drawings

      Railroads—Track—Drawings
      Rolling-mills—Drawings
      Screw-threads—Drawings
      Screws—Drawings
      Steam-turbines, Marine—Drawings
      Straight-line mechanisms
      Structural drawing
      Tanks—Drawings
      Tinting
      Tools—Drawings
      Tractors—Drawings
      United States. Navy—Draftsmen
      Woodwork (Manual training)—
        Drawings
      Woodworking machinery—Drawings
Mechanical drives
  USE Power transmission
Mechanical efficiency
  UF Efficiency, Mechanical
  BT Force and energy
      Power transmission
Mechanical engineering (May Subd Geog)
  [TJ]
    Here are entered works relating to the application
  of the principles of mechanics to the design, construc-
  tion, and operation of machinery. Works relating to
  the application of the principles of mechanics to engi-
  neering structures not of the nature of machines are
  entered under the heading Mechanics, Applied.
  UF Engineering, Mechanical
  BT Civil engineering
      Engineering
      Industrial arts
  RT Chemical engineering
      Machinery
      Steam engineering
  NT Agricultural mechanics
      Blades
      Communication in mechanical
        engineering
      Diaphragms (Mechanical devices)
      Diffusers
      Electric engineering
      Electromechanical devices
      Heat engineering
      Marine engineering
      Mechanical movements
      Power (Mechanics)
      Power transmission
      Production engineering
  — Laboratories
      USE Mechanical engineering
             laboratories
  — Terminology
      USE Machinery—Terminology
  — **Vocational guidance**
      [TJ157]
      BT Mechanical engineers
Mechanical engineering laboratories
  [TJ148]
  UF Mechanical engineering—Laboratories
  BT Engineering laboratories
Mechanical Engineering Laboratory's Turning
System
  USE MELTS (Computer system)
Mechanical engineers (May Subd Geog)
  BT Engineers
  NT Mechanical engineering—Vocational
        guidance
Mechanical equipment of apartment houses
  USE Apartment houses—Mechanical
         equipment
Mechanical equipment of buildings
  USE Buildings—Mechanical equipment
Mechanical equipment of farm buildings
  USE Farm buildings—Mechanical
         equipment
Mechanical equivalent of heat
  USE Heat, Mechanical equivalent of
Mechanical filters (Electrical engineering)
  [TK7872.F5]

  UF Electromechanical filters
  BT Electric filters
Mechanical handling
  USE Materials handling
Mechanical heart
  USE Heart, Mechanical
Mechanical impedance
  UF Impedance, Mechanical
  BT Oscillations
      Vibration
Mechanical intelligence
  USE Mechanical ability
Mechanical laboratories
  USE Engineering laboratories
Mechanical models
  USE Machinery—Models
Mechanical movements
  [TJ181-210]
  UF Mechanisms (Machinery)
  BT Kinematics
      Mechanical engineering
      Mechanics
      Motion
  RT Gearing
  NT Cams
      Geneva mechanisms
      Intermittent-motion mechanisms
      Links and link-motion
      Machinery, Kinematics of
      Orienting mechanisms
      Pedal-powered mechanisms
      Simple machines
      Splines
      Universal joints
Mechanical organs
  [ML1058 (History)]
  UF Automatic organs
  BT Musical instruments (Mechanical)
      Organ
  NT Band organ
      Barrel organ
      Calliope
      Musical clock
Mechanical painting
  USE Painting, Industrial
Mechanical perspective
  USE Perspective
Mechanical prestressing
  USE Residual stresses
Mechanical properties of biological membranes
  USE Membranes (Biology)—Mechanical
         properties
Mechanical properties of biological structures
  USE Biomechanics
Mechanical properties of bones
  USE Bones—Mechanical properties
Mechanical properties of farm produce
  USE Farm produce—Mechanical properties
Mechanical properties of metals
  USE Metals—Mechanical properties
Mechanical properties of polymers
  USE Polymers and polymerization—
         Mechanical properties
Mechanical properties of solid dosage forms
  USE Solid dosage forms—Mechanical
         properties
Mechanical properties testing
  USE Testing
Mechanical pulping process
  [TS1176.6.M4]
  UF Ground wood pulping process
      Groundwood pulping process
      Pulping process, Mechanical
  BT Wood-pulp
Mechanical quadrature
  USE Numerical integration
Mechanical shock
  USE Shock (Mechanics)
Mechanical snubbers
  USE Shock absorbers

Mechanical speech recognizer
  USE Automatic speech recognition
Mechanical stokers
  USE Stokers, Mechanical
Mechanical toys
  USE Toys, Mechanical
Mechanical translating
  USE Machine translating
Mechanical wear
  UF Scuffing
     Wear, Mechanical
     Wearing properties
  BT Friction
     Materials—Dynamic testing
     Strength of materials
     Tribology
  RT Hard materials
  NT Fretting corrosion
     Protective coverings
Mechanically boned poultry
  USE Poultry, Mechanically deboned
Mechanically deboned poultry
  USE Poultry, Mechanically deboned
Mechanically induced chemical reactions
  USE Mechanical chemistry
Mechanically-operated doors
  UF Automatic doors
  BT Doors
  NT Garage doors—Radio control
Mechanicoreceptors
  USE Mechanoreceptors
Mechanics
  ⌐QA801-QA935 (Theoretical)⌐
  ⌐QC122-QC168 (Experimental)⌐
  BT Physics
  RT Dynamics
     Engineering
     Force and energy
     Kinematics
     Machinery
     Motion
  NT Acceleration (Mechanics)
     Balance
     Biomechanics
     Center of mass
     Collisions (Physics)
     Deformations (Mechanics)
     Degree of freedom
     Elastic solids
     Elasticity
     Electromechanical analogies
     Equations of motion
     Fluids
     Forces and couples
     Friction
     Gases
     Hamilton-Jacobi equations
     Hydraulics
     Hydrostatics
     Ice mechanics
     Inertia (Mechanics)
     Least action
     Liquids
     Magnetic fluids—Thermomechanical
       properties
     Mass (Physics)
     Mathematical physics
     Matter—Properties
     Mechanical ability
     Mechanical movements
     Moments of inertia
     Pendulum
     Perpetual motion
     Photoelasticity
     Photoplasticity
     Potential, Theory of
     Power (Mechanics)
     Relativistic mechanics
     Rock mechanics
     Shock (Mechanics)
     Simple machines

Snow mechanics
Soil mechanics
Stability
Statics
Statistical mechanics
Steam-engines
Strains and stresses
Strength of materials
Superposition principle (Physics)
Thermodynamics
Torque
Torsion
Variational principles
Vibration
Viscosity
Wave mechanics
Wave-motion, Theory of
Work (Mechanics)
— Electric analogies
    USE Electromechanical analogies
Mechanics, Agricultural
  USE Agricultural mechanics
Mechanics, Analytic
  ⌐QA801-935⌐
  UF Analytical mechanics
     Kinetics
  NT Continuum mechanics
     Dynamics
     Elasticity
     Hydrostatics
     Kinematics
     Many-body problem
     Nonlinear mechanics
     Statics
     Statistical mechanics
Mechanics, Applied
  ⌐TA350⌐
  Here are entered works relating to the application
  of the principles of mechanics to engineering struc-
  tures not of the nature of machines. Works relating to
  the application of the principles of mechanics to the
  design, construction, and operation of machinery are
  entered under the heading Mechanical engineering.
  UF Applied mechanics
     Engineering, Mechanical
  BT Engineering mathematics
  NT Engineering models
     Motor vehicles—Dynamics
     Penetration mechanics
Mechanics, Celestial
  ⌐QB351-421⌐
  UF Celestial mechanics
  BT Astronomy
     Planets
     Stars
  RT Orbits
     Planets, Theory of
  NT Astrodynamics
     Comets—Orbits
     Lagrangian points
     Many-body problem
     Moon—Orbit
     Moon, Theory of
     Perturbation (Astronomy)
     Planets—Orbits
     Three-body problem
     Two-body problem
Mechanics, Farm
  USE Agricultural mechanics
Mechanics, Fracture
  USE Fracture mechanics
Mechanics, Nonlinear
  USE Nonlinear mechanics
Mechanics (Persons) *(May Subd Geog)*
  NT Automobile mechanics
     Aviation mechanics (Persons)
     Elevator mechanics
     Millwrights
     Trade-unions—Mechanics (Persons)
Mechanics consultants *(May Subd Geog)*
  BT Consultants

Mechanics' institutes
  ⌐HD6519 (United States: local)⌐
  ⌐HD8055⌐
  BT Technical education
Mechanics' lien foreclosure
  USE Foreclosure
Mechanics' liens *(May Subd Geog)*
  ⌐HD4934.M5-7⌐
  BT Improvements (Law)
     Liens
     Real property
  NT Foreclosure
Mechanics of continua
  USE Continuum mechanics
Mechanism (Philosophy)
  UF Mechanistic philosophy
     Philosophy, Mechanistic
  BT Biology—Philosophy
     Life (Biology)
     Philosophy
     Science—Philosophy
  RT Materialism
     Naturalism
     Vitalism
Mechanisms, Interchangeable
  USE Interchangeable mechanisms
Mechanisms, Orienting
  USE Orienting mechanisms
Mechanisms, Pedal-powered
  USE Pedal-powered mechanisms
Mechanisms, Straight-line
  USE Straight-line mechanisms
Mechanisms (Machinery)
  USE Mechanical movements
Mechanisms for intermittent motion
  USE Intermittent-motion mechanisms
Mechanisms of defense
  USE Defense mechanisms (Psychology)
Mechanistic philosophy
  USE Mechanism (Philosophy)
Mechanization *(May Subd Geog)*
  BT Efficiency, Industrial
     Machinery in industry
  NT Automation
     Robots, Industrial
Mechanization, Agricultural
  USE Farm mechanization
Mechanization, Military *(May Subd Geog)*
  Here are entered works on the equipping of a
  military force with armed and armored motor vehi-
  cles in which the force travels and engages in combat.
  Works on the equipping of a military force with
  motor vehicles for the purpose of transporting its per-
  sonnel, weapons and equipment are entered under
  Motorization, Military.
  UF Mechanized forces
     Mechanized warfare
     Warfare, Mechanized
  BT Military art and science
  RT Motorization, Military
  NT Armored troops
     Armored vehicles, Military
     Artillery, Self-propelled
     Tanks (Military science)
— Czechoslovakia
    NT PzKpfw 35(t) (Tank)
       PzKpfw 38(t) (Tank)
— Germany
    NT Panther (Tank)
       PzKpfw 35(t) (Tank)
       PzKpfw 38(t) (Tank)
       Tiger (Tank)
— Germany (West)
    NT Leopard (Tank)
— Great Britain
    NT Centurion (Tank)
       Chieftain (Tank)
       Cromwell (Tank)
— United States
    NT M1 (Tank)
       M2 Bradley infantry fighting
         vehicle

M26 (Tank)
    M46 (Tank)
    M48 (Tank)
    M60 (Tank)
    United States. Marine Corps—
      Motorcycle troops
Mechanization in agriculture
  USE Farm mechanization
Mechanization of library processes
  USE Libraries—Automation
Mechanized farming
  USE Farm mechanization
Mechanized forces
  USE Mechanization, Military
Mechanized hypothesis formation
  USE Automatic hypothesis formation
Mechanized information storage and retrieval
  systems
  USE Information storage and retrieval
      systems
Mechanized warfare
  USE Mechanization, Military
Mechanochemistry
  USE Mechanical chemistry
Mechanoreceptors
  [QL938.M3 (Comparative anatomy)]
  [QM471 (Human anatomy)]
  [QP369 (Physiology)]
  UF Mechanicoreceptors
  BT Neural receptors
Mechanotherapy
  [RM719-727]
  UF Kinesitherapy
    Movement cure
  BT Osteopathy
    Therapeutics, Physiological
  RT Exercise therapy
    Massage
  NT Vibration (Therapeutics)
Mechem family
  USE Meacham family
Meches
  [DS432.M]
  UF Mechhias
    Mes
  BT Bodos
    Ethnology—India
Mechhias
  USE Meches
Mechlin family
  USE Macklin family
Mechling family
  USE Macklin family
Mechum family
  USE Meacham family
Meckel family (Not Subd Geog)
Meckel's ganglion
  USE Pterygopalatine ganglion
Mecklenburg, House of (Not Subd Geog)
  UF House of Mecklenburg
  BT Germany—Kings and rulers
Mecklenburg (Germany : Region)
  — History
  —— Revolution, 1848-1849
Mecklenburg (Germany : Castle)
  UF Mecklenburg Castle (Germany)
  BT Castles—Germany (East)
Mecklenburg Castle (Germany)
  USE Mecklenburg (Germany : Castle)
Mecklenburg declaration of independence
  [E215.9]
Mecklenburg Lake Plateau (Germany)
  UF Mecklenburger Seenplatte (Germany)
    Mecklenburgische Seenplatte
      (Germany)
    Mecklenburgisher Landrücken
      (Germany)
  BT Plateaus—Germany (East)
Mecklenburger Seenplatte (Germany)
  USE Mecklenburg Lake Plateau (Germany)

Mecklenburgische Seenplatte (Germany)
  USE Mecklenburg Lake Plateau (Germany)
Mecklenburgisher Landrücken (Germany)
  USE Mecklenburg Lake Plateau (Germany)
Meckstroth family (Not Subd Geog)
Meclofenoxate
  USE Centrophenoxine
Meclophenoxate
  USE Centrophenoxine
Meco Indians
  USE Chichimeca-Jonaz Indians
Mecoceridae
  USE Geometridae
Meconium
  BT Feces
Mecoptera
  [QL601]
  BT Insects
  NT Bittacidae
    Boreidae
Mecrylate
  UF Cyanopropenoic acid methyl ester
    Methylcyanoacrylate
  BT Acids, Organic
    Adhesives in surgery
    Polymers in medicine
Mecsek Mountains (Hungary)
  UF Baranya Mountains (Hungary)
  BT Mountains—Hungary
Medaglia d'Oro
  [UB435.I]
  BT Italy. Esercito—Medals, badges,
    decorations, etc.
Medaille de Sainte-Hélène
  [UB435.F]
  BT Decorations of honor—France
    France—Armed Forces—Medals,
      badges, decorations, etc.
Médaille militaire (France)
  BT France. Armée—Medals, badges,
    decorations, etc.
Medaka
  USE Oryzias latipes
Medal, Miraculous
  USE Miraculous Medal
Medal of Honor
  [UB433]
  [VB333]
  UF Congressional Medal of Honor
  BT United States. Army—Medals,
    badges, decorations, etc.
    United States. Navy—Medals,
    badges, decorations, etc.
Medal of St. Benedict
  [BX2310.M5]
  BT Medals, Devotional
Medalists (May Subd Geog)
  [CJ5501-6651]
  BT Engravers
    Medals
  NT Medalists, Jewish
Medalists, Jewish (May Subd Geog)
  UF Jewish medalists
  BT Medalists
**Medalla de Honor Belisario Domínguez del
Senado de la Republica**
  UF Belisario Domínguez del Senado de la
    Republica Medalla de Honor
    Belisario Domínguez Medalla de
    Honor
  BT Decorations of honor—Mexico
Medalla Militar
  [UB435.S]
  BT Spain—Armed Forces—Medals,
    badges, decorations, etc.
Medallion portraits
  USE Portrait medallions
Medallions
  USE Medals

Medallions (Decorative arts)
  (May Subd Geog)
  BT Decoration and ornament
Medals (May Subd Geog)
  [CJ5501-6651]
  UF Badges of honor
    Medallions
    Medals—Collections
    Medals—Private collections
  BT Art metal-work
    Decorations of honor
    Glyptics
    History
    Numismatics
  SA subdivision Medals under subjects and
    names of individual persons and
    corporate bodies; and under names
    of individual wars, e.g. World War,
    1939-1945—Medals
  NT Chronograms
    Dufferin medals
    Medalists
    Medals, Religious
    Porcelain medals
    Portrait medallions
  — Collections
    USE Medals
  — **Law and legislation** (May Subd Geog)
  — Private collections
    USE Medals
  — **Soviet Union**
    NT Geroĭ Sovetskogo Soĭuza
Medals, Ancient
  [CJ5581-5690]
  BT Archaeology
  NT Medals, Greek
    Medals, Roman
Medals, Baroque
  UF Baroque medals
Medals, Bulgarian (May Subd Geog)
  UF Bulgarian medals
Medals, Czech, [French, etc.]
Medals, Devotional (May Subd Geog)
  Here are entered works dealing with "pieces of
  medal resembling coins, blessed by the church and
  used to increase devotion."
  UF Catholic Church—Medals
    Devotional medals
  RT Medals, Religious
  NT Medal of St. Benedict
    Medals, Papal
    Miraculous Medal
Medals, French (May Subd Geog)
  UF French medals
Medals, Greek (May Subd Geog)
  UF Greek medals
  BT Medals, Ancient
Medals, Jewish
  UF Jewish medals
Medals, Military and naval
  [UB430-UB435 (Military)]
  [VB330-VB335 (Naval)]
  UF Military decorations
    Military medals
    Naval medals
  BT Military paraphernalia
  SA subdivision Medals under names of
    individual wars, e.g. World War,
    1939-1945—Medals; and
    subdivision Medals, badges,
    decorations, etc. under names of
    individual military services, e.g.
    United States. Army—Medals,
    badges, decorations, etc.
  NT Air forces—Medals, badges,
    decorations, etc.
    Armies—Medals, badges, decorations,
      etc.
    Marines—Medals, badges, decorations,
      etc.

Medals, Papal
  [CR5577]
  UF Papal medals
  BT Medals, Devotional
Medals, Police (May Subd Geog)
  UF Police medals
  BT Police
Medals, Polish (May Subd Geog)
  UF Polish medals
Medals, Religious (May Subd Geog)
  [CJ5793.R34]
  UF Religious medals
  BT Medals
Medals, Renaissance
  UF Renaissance medals
Medals, Roman
  UF Roman medals
  BT Medals, Ancient
Medals, Slovenian (May Subd Geog)
  UF Slovenian medals
Medals, Turkish (May Subd Geog)
  UF Turkish medals
Medas Islands (Spain) (Not Subd Geog)
  UF Illes Medes (Spain)
      Islas Medas (Spain)
  BT Islands—Spain
Medawakanton Indians
  USE Mdewakanton Indians
Medcaff family
  USE Metcalf family
Medcalf family
  USE Metcalf family
Mede family
  USE Mead family
Medea (Ballet)
  [GV1790.M]
  BT Ballets
Medea (Greek mythology)
  [BL820.M37]
  BT Mythology, Greek
Medelpad (Sweden)
Meder family
  USE Meador family
Medes family
  USE Mead family
Medex
  USE Physicians' assistants
Medfly
  USE Mediterranean fruit-fly
Medi-Cal
  USE Medicaid—California
Medi-gap
  USE Medigap
Media, Condensed
  USE Condensed matter
Media, Culture (Biology)
  USE Culture media (Biology)
Media, Inhomogeneous
  USE Inhomogeneous materials
Media, Potting
  USE Potting soils
Media caña (Dance)
Media centers (Education)
  USE Instructional materials centers
Media planning in advertising
  USE Advertising media planning
Media programs (Education)
  (May Subd Geog)
  [LB1028.4]
  UF Educational media programs
      Instructional materials programs
      Multi media programs
      Programs, Media
      School media programs
  BT Educational technology
  RT Teaching—Aids and devices
Media selection
  USE Selection of non-book materials
Media service personnel in education
  USE Instructional materials personnel

Medial geniculate body
  [QL938.M43 (Comparative anatomy)]
  UF Corpus geniculatum mediale
  BT Prosencephalon
Median language
  UF Medic language
  BT Iranian languages
Median nerve
  BT Brachial plexus
  — Surgery
  — Wounds and injuries
      NT Carpal tunnel syndrome
Median strips
  UF Express highways—Medians
      Medians (Roads)
      Road medians
      Roads—Medians
  BT Roads—Safety measures
  NT Roads—Glare screens
Medians (Roads)
  USE Median strips
Mediastinoscopy
  BT Endoscope and endoscopy
      Mediastinum
Mediastinum
  [QM261 (Human anatomy)]
  BT Chest
  NT Mediastinoscopy
  — Blood-vessels
  — — Obstructions
      BT Mediastinum—Diseases
  — Diseases (May Subd Geog)
      [RC754]
      NT Mediastinum—Blood-vessels—
          Obstructions
          Mediastinum—Radiography
          Pneumomediastinum
  — Examination
  — Foreign bodies
  — Radiography
      BT Mediastinum—Diseases
  — Surgery
  — Tumors
      [RD667]
Mediation (May Subd Geog)
  Here are entered works on the voluntary process
  of conflict resolution between disputants by the inter-
  vention of an impartial third party, often involving
  joint problem solving.
  BT Conflict management
  RT Dispute resolution (Law)
  NT Environmental mediation
      Family mediation
      Indians of North America—Mediation
      Mediation, International
      Mediation and conciliation, Industrial
Mediation, Divorce
  USE Divorce mediation
Mediation, Environmental
  USE Environmental mediation
Mediation, Family
  USE Family mediation
Mediation, International
  [JX4475]
  UF Conciliation, International
      Good offices
      International conciliation
      International mediation
  BT International relations
      Mediation
      Pacific settlement of international
          disputes
      Peace
      Peaceful change (International
          relations)
      War (International law)
  RT Arbitration, International
  NT Aggression (International law)
Mediation, Natural resources
  USE Environmental mediation

Mediation and conciliation, Industrial
  (May Subd Geog)
  UF Conciliation, Industrial
      Industrial conciliation
      Industrial mediation
  BT Industrial relations
      Mediation
      Negotiation
Mediation between God and man
  UF Intercession between God and man
      Mediator between God and man
      Religious mediation
  BT Religion
  — Baptists, [Catholic Church, etc.]
  — Christianity
      BT Theology, Doctrinal
      NT Jesus Christ—Intercession
          Mary, Blessed Virgin, Saint—
              Mediation
  — Christianity, [Judaism, etc.]
Mediation in literature
Mediatized states
  BT Germany—Constitutional history
      Holy Roman Empire—Constitutional
          history
      Sovereignty
Mediator between God and man
  USE Mediation between God and man
Mediators of inflammation
  USE Inflammation—Mediators
Medic language
  USE Median language
Medicaid (May Subd Geog)
  UF Medicaid—United States
  BT Insurance, Health—United States
      Poor—Medical care—United States
  RT Medicare
  NT Early and Periodic Screening,
      Diagnosis, and Treatment Program
      System for Hospital Uniform
          Reporting
  — Law and legislation (May Subd Geog)
      UF Medicaid—Law and legislation—
          United States
      BT Medical laws and legislation
  — — Criminal provisions
      USE Medicaid fraud
  — — United States
      USE Medicaid—Law and legislation
  — California
      UF Medi-Cal
  — United States
      USE Medicaid
Medicaid fraud (May Subd Geog)
  UF Medicaid—Law and legislation—
      Criminal provisions
      Medicaid fraud—United States
  BT Fraud
      Swindlers and swindling
  — United States
      USE Medicaid fraud
Medical and health care industry
  USE Medical care
      Medical instruments and apparatus
          industry
Medical anthropology (May Subd Geog)
  BT Anthropology
  RT Medicine, Primitive
  NT Folk medicine
      Health and race
      Indians of Central America—Health
          and hygiene
      Indians of North America—Health
          and hygiene
      Indians of South America—Health and
          hygiene
      Paleopathology
Medical apparatus
  USE Medical instruments and apparatus

Medical appointments and schedules
(May Subd Geog)
  UF Appointments and schedules
        (Medicine)
      Schedules, Medical
  BT Hospitals—Administration
      Medical offices
      Medicine—Practice
  NT Hospitals—Waiting lists
  — Data processing
      NT ASCS (Computer system)
Medical archives
  USE Archives, Medical
Medical assistance (May Subd Geog)
  UF Medical technical assistance
  BT Technical assistance
  NT Medicine—International cooperation
      Missions, Medical
      Public health—International
        cooperation
Medical assistance, American
(May Subd Geog)
  UF American medical assistance
Medical assistance, American, [etc.]
(May Subd Geog)
Medical assistance, French
(May Subd Geog)
  UF French medical assistance
Medical assistance, Scandinavian
  — Tanzania
      NT Nordic Tanganyika Project
Medical assistants (May Subd Geog)
  [R728.8]
    Here are entered works on personnel who perform
  administrative and clerical duties in a physician's of-
  fice and may assist in routine clinical procedures.
  Works on personnel qualified to perform diagnostic
  and therapeutic procedures under the responsibility
  and supervision of a physician are entered under
  Physicians' assistants.
  UF Medical office assistants
  BT Allied health personnel
      Medical offices
  RT Medical secretaries
Medical astrology (May Subd Geog)
  [BF1718]
  UF Astrodiagnosis
      Astrology and medicine
  BT Astrology
      Medicine, Magic, mystic, and spagiric
Medical audit
  USE Medical care—Evaluation
Medical autoexperimentation
  USE Self-experimentation in medicine
Medical bacteriology
  USE Bacteriology, Medical
Medical biochemistry
  USE Clinical biochemistry
Medical book-plates
  USE Book-plates, Medical
Medical botanists (May Subd Geog)
  BT Botanists
      Botany, Medical
Medical care (May Subd Geog)
  UF Delivery of health care
      Delivery of medical care
      Health care
      Health care delivery
      Health services
      Medical and health care industry
      Medical services
      Personal health services
  BT Public health
  RT Insurance, Health

SA subdivision Medical care under names
      of individual military services and
      under individual wars, classes of
      persons, ethnic groups, and
      occupational groups, e.g. United
      States. Air Force—Medical care;
      World War, 1939-1945—Medical
      care; Aged—Medical care; Afro-
      Americans—Medical care;
      Construction industry—Employees
      —Medical care
NT Allied health personnel—Supply and
      demand
    Ambulatory medical care
    Charities, Medical
    Child health services
    Cleft palate services
    Dental care
    Diagnostic services
    Discrimination in medical care
    Emergency medical services
    Health facilities
    Health service areas
    Hospital care
    Long-term care of the sick
    Managed care plans (Medical care)
    Medical personnel
    Medical personnel—Supply and
      demand
    Medical social work
    Medically underserved areas
    Nurses—Supply and demand
    Nursing home care
    Nursing services
    Occupational health services
    Occupational therapy services
    Pharmaceutical services
    Physically handicapped services
    Physician services utilization
    Physicians—Supply and demand
    Preventive health services
    Regional medical programs
    Rural health services
    Self-care, Health
    Volunteer workers in medical care
    Women's health services
  — Administration
      USE Health services administration
           Public health administration
  — Contracting out
      BT Contracting out
  — Cost control
      BT Medical care, Cost of
  — — Law and legislation
          (May Subd Geog)
          BT Medical laws and legislation
  — Costs
      USE Medical care, Cost of
  — Cross-cultural studies
  — Economic aspects
      USE Medical economics
  — Evaluation
      UF Medical audit
      NT Medical care—Utilization review
          Patient satisfaction
          Professional standards review
            organizations (Medicine)
  — Finance
  — — Law and legislation
          (May Subd Geog)
  — Government policy
      USE Medical policy
  — Information storage and retrieval systems
      USE Information storage and retrieval
            systems—Medical care
  — Law and legislation (May Subd Geog)
      BT Medical laws and legislation
      NT Professional standards review
            organizations (Medicine)—Law
            and legislation
  — Management

USE Health services administration
  — Moral and ethical aspects
      USE Medical ethics
  — Needs assessment
      UF Assessment of medical care needs
          Needs assessment of medical care
      BT Health planning
          Needs assessment
  — Planning
      USE Health planning
  — Quality control
      NT Professional standards review
            organizations (Medicine)
  — — Citizen participation
  — Research
  — — Federal aid
          USE Federal aid to medical care
                research
  — — Finance
          NT Federal aid to medical care
                research
  — Social aspects
      USE Social medicine
  — Surveys
      USE Medical care surveys
  — Utilization
      [RA410.6.-410.9]
      UF Medical care use
          Utilization of medical care
      NT Drug utilization
          Mental health facilities—Utilization
  — — Reporting (May Subd Geog)
      UF Reporting of utilization of
            medical care
  — — Sex differences
  — Utilization review
      UF UR (Medical care)
          Utilization review (Medical care)
      BT Medical care—Evaluation
  — United States
      NT Afro-Americans—Medical care
Medical care, Cost of (May Subd Geog)
  UF Cost of medical care
      Health care costs
      Medical care—Costs
      Medical service, Cost of
      Medicine—Cost of medical care
  BT Medical economics
  NT Dental care, Cost of
      Hospitals—Rates
      Medical care—Cost control
      Medical fees
      Nursing homes—Rates
  — Law and legislation (May Subd Geog)
      BT Medical laws and legislation
Medical care, Military
  USE United States—Armed Forces—
            Medical care
Medical care, Prepaid
  USE Insurance, Health
Medical care, State
  USE Medicine, State
Medical care administrators
  USE Health services administrators
Medical care for the aged
  USE Aged—Medical care
Medical care of veterans
  USE Veterans—Medical care
Medical care planning
  USE Health planning
Medical care review organizations
  USE Professional standards review
            organizations (Medicine)

2329

Medical care surveys *(May Subd Geog)*
Here are entered works on the methods and techniques employed in conducting medical care surveys, and reports of individual surveys. For the latter the heading may be subdivided by place; in such cases an additional subject entry is made under the heading Medical care—[local subdivision], e.g. 1. Medical care—United States.   2. Medical care surveys—United States. For medical care surveys on a special topic, the additional subject entry is made under the special topic, e.g. 1. Ambulatory medical care—United States.   2. Medical care surveys—United States.
> UF   Health care surveys
>> Medical care—Surveys
> BT   Health surveys
> — Nonresponse
>> USE   Medical care surveys—Response rate
> **— Response rate**
>> UF   Medical care surveys—Nonresponse
>>> Response rate of medical care surveys

Medical care teams
> USE   Health care teams
Medical care use
> USE   Medical care—Utilization
Medical centers *(May Subd Geog)*
> BT   Health facilities
> RT   Hospitals
> NT   Clinics
>> Hospitals, Teaching
>> Hospitals, University
>> Medical colleges
> **— Administration**
>> [RA976]
>> BT   Health services administration
> **— Cost of construction**
> **— Cost of operation**
>> UF   Medical centers—Operating costs
> **— Operating costs**
>> USE   Medical centers—Cost of operation
> **— Planning**
>> NT   Medical centers—Space utilization
> **— Space utilization**
>> [R833]
>> UF   Space allocation in medical centers
>>> Space utilization in medical centers
>> BT   Medical centers—Planning
> **— United States**
>> NT   Area Health Education Centers Program

Medical charities
> USE   Charities, Medical
Medical chemistry
> USE   Chemistry, Clinical
>> Chemistry, Pharmaceutical
Medical Chinese
> USE   Chinese language—Medical Chinese
Medical cinematography
> USE   Cinematography, Medical
Medical climatology
> USE   Climatology, Medical
Medical clinics
> USE   Clinics
Medical college applicants
(May Subd Geog)
> [R838.4]
> UF   Applicants to medical college
> BT   Medical students
> RT   Medical colleges—Admission
Medical college libraries
> USE   Medical libraries
Medical colleges *(May Subd Geog)*
> [R735-832]
> UF   Medical schools

> BT   Health occupations schools
>> Medical centers
>> Medical education
>> Schools
>> Universities and colleges
>> Vocational education
> NT   Hospitals, University
>> Medicine—Scholarships, fellowships, etc.
>> Medicine—Study and teaching
>> Osteopathic schools
>> Pharmacy colleges
> **— Admission**
>> BT   Universities and colleges—Admission
>> RT   Medical college applicants
>>> Medical colleges—Entrance requirements
>> NT   Medical students—Transfer
> **— Construction**
> **— Entrance examinations**
>> BT   Medicine—Examinations
> **— Entrance requirements**
>> BT   Universities and colleges—Entrance requirements
>> RT   Medical colleges—Admission
>> NT   Premedical education
> **— Faculty**
>> BT   College teachers
> **— Information services** *(May Subd Geog)*
> **— — Use studies**
>> BT   Library use studies
> **— Planning**
>> NT   Medical colleges—Space utilization
> **— Space utilization**
>> [R833]
>> UF   Space allocation in medical colleges
>>> Space utilization in medical colleges
>> BT   Medical colleges—Planning
Medical communication
> USE   Communication in medicine
Medical competence testing
> USE   Medicine—Ability testing
Medical consultants *(May Subd Geog)*
> BT   Consultants
>> Medicine—Specialties and specialists
>> Physicians
> NT   Nursing consultants
Medical consultation *(May Subd Geog)*
> [R727.8]
> UF   Consultation, Medical
> BT   Medical cooperation
>> Medicine—Practice
> NT   Psychiatric consultation
> **— Law and legislation** *(May Subd Geog)*
>> BT   Medical laws and legislation
> **— New York (State)**
>> NT   Cornell-New York Hospital Second Opinion Program
Medical cooperation *(May Subd Geog)*
> UF   Cooperation, Medical
> BT   Social medicine
> NT   Consultation-liaison psychiatry
>> Group medical practice
>> Health care teams
>> Health facilities—Affiliations
>> Hospital-physician joint ventures
>> Hospitals—Shared services
>> Medical consultation
>> Medical referral
>> Patient compliance
>> Regional medical programs
Medical corporations *(May Subd Geog)*
> UF   Corporate practice of medicine
>> Corporations, Medical
> BT   Group medical practice
>> Professional corporations
> NT   Health facilities, Proprietary
>> Hospital management companies

Medical creativity
> USE   Creative ability in medicine
Medical delusions
> USE   Medical misconceptions
Medical devices
> USE   Medical instruments and apparatus
Medical diagnosis
> USE   Diagnosis
Medical diagnostic imaging
> USE   Diagnostic imaging
Medical digital radiography
> USE   Radiography, Medical—Digital techniques
Medical directories
> USE   Physicians—Directories
Medical disclosure
> USE   Informed consent (Medical law)
Medical disposables
> USE   Medical supplies, Disposable
Medical doctors
> USE   Physicians
Medical economics *(May Subd Geog)*
> [R728]
> [RA410-RA415]
> Here are entered comprehensive works on the economic aspects of medical service from the point of view of both the practitioner and the public. Works on special aspects of medical economics are entered under specific headings, e.g. Medical care, Cost of.
> UF   Economics, Medical
>> Health—Economic aspects
>> Health economics
>> Hygiene—Economic aspects
>> Medical care—Economic aspects
>> Medicine—Economic aspects
> NT   Dental economics
>> Group medical practice
>> Medical care, Cost of
>> Medically underserved areas
>> Prescription pricing
Medical editing
> USE   Medical literature—Editing
Medical education *(May Subd Geog)*
> Here are entered general works on education in the field of medicine. Works on methods of instruction and curricula are entered under Medicine—Study and teaching.
> UF   Medical personnel—Education
> NT   Discrimination in medical education
>> Health care teams—Training of
>> Health occupations schools
>> Hospitals—Staff—In-service training
>> Medical colleges
>> Medical students
>> Medical teaching personnel
>> Medicine—Scholarships, fellowships, etc.
>> Medicine—Study and teaching
>> Nursing—Study and teaching
>> Paramedical education
>> Premedical education
>> Public health personnel—Education
>> Regional medical programs
>> Sex discrimination in medical education
> **— Federal aid**
>> USE   Federal aid to medical education
> **— Finance**
>> NT   Federal aid to medical education
>>> Medical students—Loans
>>> State aid to medical education
> **— Government policy**
>> USE   Medical education policy
> **— International cooperation**
>> BT   Medicine—International cooperation
> **— Law and legislation** *(May Subd Geog)*
>> BT   Educational law and legislation
> **— Sex differences**
>> BT   Sex differences in education
> **— Social aspects** *(May Subd Geog)*
>> UF   Society and medical education

— State aid
USE State aid to medical education
Medical education and state
USE Medical education policy
Medical education policy *(May Subd Geog)*
UF Medical education—Government
policy
Medical education and state
State and medical education
BT Higher education and state
Medical policy
NT Federal aid to medical education
— **United States**
NT Area Health Education Centers
Program
Medical educators
USE Medical teaching personnel
Medical electricity
USE Electricity in medicine
Medical electronics
[R895]
UF Electronics in medicine
BT Biomedical engineering
Electronics
NT Electronics in cardiology
Electronics in psychiatry
Electronics in space medicine
Heart, Artificial—Power supply
Radiotherapy
Telemeter (Physiological apparatus)
— **Equipment and supplies**
NT Medical electronics equipment
industry
Medical electronics equipment industry
(May Subd Geog)
[HD9995.E4-44]
BT Medical electronics—Equipment and
supplies
Medical emergencies *(May Subd Geog)*
[RC86.7]
UF Emergencies, Medical
BT Diseases
Hospitals—Outpatient services
RT Accidents
Emergency medicine
First aid in illness and injury
NT Cardiovascular emergencies
Dental emergencies
Gastrointestinal emergencies
Gynecologic emergencies
Mass casualties
Obstetrical emergencies
Ophthalmologic emergencies
Orthopedic emergencies
Otolaryngologic emergencies
Pediatric emergencies
Psychiatric emergencies
Surgical emergencies
Toxicological emergencies
Veterinary emergencies
Medical emergency personnel
USE Emergency medical personnel
Medical engineering
USE Biomedical engineering
Medical English
USE English language—Medical English
Medical entomology
USE Insects as carriers of disease
Medical errors *(May Subd Geog)*
UF Errors, Medical
Medical mishaps
Mishaps, Medical
BT Errors
Errors, Scientific
Medicine—Practice
NT Diagnostic errors
Iatrogenic diseases
Medical misconceptions
Medical personnel—Malpractice
Medication errors
Psychiatric errors

Surgical errors
Medical ethics *(May Subd Geog)*
[R724-725]
UF Biomedical ethics
Ethics, Medical
Medical care—Moral and ethical
aspects
Medicine—Moral and ethical aspects
BT Bioethics
Ethics
Professional ethics
RT Nursing ethics
Social medicine
NT Advertising—Medicine
Children—Hospital care—Moral and
religious aspects
Confidential communications—
Physicians
Courts of honor
Dental ethics
Euthanasia
Human experimentation in medicine
Informed consent (Medical law)
Medical personnel—Malpractice
Medical records—Access control
Nurses—Malpractice
Orthopedists—Malpractice
Pharmaceutical ethics
Physicians—Discipline
Physicians—Malpractice
Psychiatric ethics
Psychiatrists—Malpractice
Psychotherapists—Malpractice
Sterilization (Birth control)—Moral
and religious aspects
Surgeons—Professional ethics
Veterinarians—Professional ethics
— **Cases**
— **Study and teaching** *(May Subd Geog)*
— — **Texas**
NT Value of Life Project
Medical examination of soldiers
USE subdivision Medical examinations
under armies, e.g. United States.
Army—Medical examinations
Medical examinations
USE subdivision Medical examinations
under classes of persons, e.g.
Airlines—Employees—Medical
examinations; Children—Medical
examinations; and individual
military services, e.g. United States.
Army—Medical examinations
Diagnosis
Medical screening
Pensions, Medical examinations for
Periodic health examinations
Self-examination, Medical
Medical examinations for marriage
USE Premarital examinations
Medical examinations in medical education
USE Medicine—Examinations
Medical examiners, Aviation
USE Aviation medical examiners
Medical examiners (Law) *(May Subd Geog)*
UF Post-mortem examiners
Postmortem examiners
BT Autopsy
Criminal justice, Administration of
Death—Causes
Death—Proof and certification
Forensic scientists
Medical jurisprudence
RT Coroners
Forensic pathology
NT Forensic pathologists
Medical experimentation on humans
USE Human experimentation in medicine
Medical experimentation on oneself
USE Self-experimentation in medicine

Medical facilities
USE Health facilities
Medical fees *(May Subd Geog)*
UF Fees, Medical
Medicine—Fees
Physicians—Fees
BT Fees, Professional
Medical care, Cost of
Physicians—Salaries, etc.
NT Medical laboratories—Fees
Optometrists—Fees
Surgeons—Fees
Medical fellowships
USE Medicine—Scholarships, fellowships,
etc.
Medical films
USE Moving-pictures in medicine
Medical folk-lore
USE Folk medicine
Medical food
USE Elemental diet
Medical formularies
USE Medicine—Formulae, receipts,
prescriptions
Medical French
USE French language—Medical French
Medical genetics *(May Subd Geog)*
[RB155]
UF Clinical genetics
Diseases—Genetic aspects
Genetics, Medical
Heredity of disease
BT Human genetics
Medical sciences
Pathology
RT Genetic disorders
SA subdivision Genetic aspects under
individual diseases, e.g. Cancer—
Genetic aspects; and subdivision
Diseases—Genetic aspects under
organs and regions of the body, e.g.
Heart—Diseases—Genetic aspects
NT Abnormalities, Human—Genetic
aspects
Children—Diseases—Genetic aspects
Genetic counseling
Genetic toxicology
Gynecology—Genetic aspects
Neurogenetics
Otolaryngology—Genetic aspects
Pharmacogenetics
Veterinary genetics
— **Law and legislation** *(May Subd Geog)*
BT Medical laws and legislation
— **Technique**
BT Diagnosis, Cytologic
Karyotypes
Medical geography *(May Subd Geog)*
[RA791-RA954]
Here are entered works on the geographical distri-
bution of diseases, and on pathology in relation to
conditions of geography and climate.
Works on the occurrence of a particular disease in
a locality are entered under the name of the disease
subdivided by the name of the place.
Works on the practice, history, or conditions of
medicine in any particular locality are entered under
Medicine—[local subdivision], e.g. Medicine—
Germany.
UF Diseases—Geographical distribution
Geographical distribution of diseases
Geographical pathology
Geography, Medical
Geomedicine
Medical topography
Pathology, Geographic
Topography, Medical
BT Geography
RT Climatology, Medical
World health
NT Endemic goiter
Environmentally induced diseases

Medical geography *(Continued)*
    Health service areas
    Soils and nutrition
    Veterinary medical geography
Medical Greek
  USE Greek language—Medical Greek
Medical group practice
  USE Group medical practice
Medical gymnastics
  USE Exercise therapy
Medical helminthology
  BT Helminthology
      Medical parasitology
  NT Helminthiasis
Medical historians *(May Subd Geog)*
  BT Historians
      Medicine—Historiography
Medical history taking
  [RC65]
  UF Medical interviewing
  BT Diagnosis
      Interviewing
      Medical records
  NT Interviewing in psychiatry
Medical holography
  USE Holography in medicine
Medical illustration
  [R836]
  UF Illustration, Medical
  BT Scientific illustration
  RT Medicine and art
  NT Moulage in medicine
Medical imaging
  USE Diagnostic imaging
Medical imaging equipment industry
(May Subd Geog)
  [HD9995.I56]
  BT Imaging systems in medicine—
      Equipment and supplies
Medical imaging systems
  USE Imaging systems in medicine
Medical indications
  USE Clinical indications
Medical innovations *(May Subd Geog)*
  UF Innovations, Medical
      Medicine—Innovations
      Medicine—Technological innovations
  BT Medical technology
      Technological innovations
  NT Health reformers
      Pharmaceutical industry—
        Technological innovations
  — **Social aspects** *(May Subd Geog)*
    [RA418.5.M4]
    UF Society and medical innovations
Medical inspection in schools
  USE Children—Medical examinations
Medical inspection of aliens
  USE Aliens—Medical examinations
Medical instruments and apparatus
(May Subd Geog)
  [R856-858]
  UF Apparatus, Medical
      Instruments, Medical
      Medical apparatus
      Medical devices
      Medical products
      Medicine—Apparatus
      Medicine—Equipment and supplies
      Medicine—Instruments
  BT Biomedical engineering
      Medical supplies
      Scientific apparatus and instruments
  RT Medical laboratories—Equipment and
      supplies
      Surgical instruments and apparatus

  SA *particular instruments and apparatus,*
    e.g. Hypodermic needles, Tilt table;
    also subdivision Apparatus and
    instruments *under special branches*
    of medicine, e.g. Dermatology—
    Apparatus and instruments
  NT Audiology—Instruments
      Biosensors
      Colloids in medicine
      Contraceptives
      Diagnosis, Ultrasonic—Instruments
      Electrocardiograph
      Endoscopes
      Holography in medicine
      Hypodermic jet injectors
      Imaging systems in medicine
      Lasers in medicine
      Linear accelerators in medicine
      Metals in medicine
      Plastics in medicine
      Polymers in medicine
      Radiology, Medical—Instruments
      Speech therapy—Instruments
      Stethoscopes
      Tourniquets
  — **Calibration**
  — **Microbiology**
  — Products liability
    USE Products liability—Medical
      instruments and apparatus
  — **Safety regulations** *(May Subd Geog)*
    NT Products liability—Medical
      instruments and apparatus
  — **Sterilization**
  — Tariff
    USE Tariff on medical instruments and
      apparatus
Medical instruments and apparatus industry
(May Subd Geog)
  UF Medical and health care industry
  NT Dental instruments and apparatus
      industry
      Hearing aid industry
      Orthopedic apparatus industry
Medical interns
  USE Interns (Medicine)
Medical interviewing
  USE Medical history taking
Medical journalism
  USE Journalism, Medical
Medical jurisprudence *(May Subd Geog)*
  [RA1001-1171]
  UF Forensic medicine
      Injuries (Law)
      Jurisprudence, Medical
      Legal medicine
      Medicine, Forensic
      Medicine, Legal
  BT Criminal investigation
      Evidence (Law)
      Medicine, State
      Personal injuries
      Surgery, Operative—Jurisprudence
  RT Chemistry, Forensic
      Identification
      Medical laws and legislation
  SA *subdivision* Jurisprudence *under*
    subjects to which medical
    jurisprudence is applicable, e.g.
    Insanity—Jurisprudence; Surgery,
    Operative—Jurisprudence
  NT Autopsy
      Dental jurisprudence
      Disability evaluation—Law and
      legislation
      Forensic anthropology
      Forensic audiology
      Forensic cardiology
      Forensic dermatology
      Forensic entomology
      Forensic genetics

      Forensic gynecology
      Forensic hematology
      Forensic neurology
      Forensic obstetrics
      Forensic oncology
      Forensic ophthalmology
      Forensic osteology
      Forensic pathology
      Forensic psychiatry
      Forensic radiography
      Forensic thermography
      Forensic toxicology
      Heart—Diseases—Law and legislation
      Malingering
      Medical examiners (Law)
      Paternity testing
      Psychology, Forensic
Medical jurisprudence (Canon law)
Medical laboratories *(May Subd Geog)*
  UF Laboratories, Medical
  BT Diagnosis, Laboratory
      Health facilities
  NT Dental laboratories
      Hospital laboratories
      Pathological laboratories
      Public health laboratories
      Toxicology laboratories
      Veterinary laboratories
  — **Equipment and supplies**
    RT Medical instruments and apparatus
    NT Medical laboratory equipment
      industry
  — **Fees**
    BT Medical fees
  — **Law and legislation** *(May Subd Geog)*
  — Technique
    USE Medical laboratory technology
  — **Utilization**
    UF Medical laboratory use
      Utilization of medical laboratories
Medical laboratory assistants
(May Subd Geog)
  BT Allied health personnel
      Medical technologists
Medical laboratory diagnosis
  USE Diagnosis, Laboratory
Medical laboratory equipment industry
(May Subd Geog)
  [HD9995.L3]
  BT Medical laboratories—Equipment and
      supplies
Medical laboratory technicians
  USE Medical technologists
Medical laboratory technology
(May Subd Geog)
  [RB37-RB56]
  UF Medical laboratories—Technique
      Medical technology (Medical
        laboratory technology)
      Technology, Medical laboratory
  BT Diagnosis, Laboratory
  RT Medical technologists
Medical laboratory use
  USE Medical laboratories—Utilization
Medical Latin
  USE Latin language—Medical Latin
Medical laws and legislation
(May Subd Geog)
  UF Law, Medical
      Medical personnel—Legal status, laws,
        etc.
      Medical registration and examination
      Medicine—Laws and legislation
      Physicians—Legal status, laws, etc.
      Surgeons—Legal status, laws, etc.
  BT Medical policy
  RT Medical jurisprudence
  NT Abortion services—Law and legislation
      Acupuncture—Law and legislation
      Advertising—Medicine—Law and
        legislation

Aged—Medical care—Law and
  legislation
Aliens—Medical care—Law and
  legislation
Allied health personnel—Legal status,
  laws, etc.
Ambulatory medical care—Law and
  legislation
Anesthesiology—Law and legislation
Burn care units—Law and legislation
Cancer—Law and legislation
Cardiologists—Malpractice
Child health services—Law and
  legislation
Children—Medical examinations—Law
  and legislation
Clitoridectomy—Law and legislation
Community health services—Law and
  legislation
Confidential communications—
  Physicians
Critical care medicine—Law and
  legislation
Cryonics—Law and legislation
Diagnosis related groups—Law and
  legislation
Donation of organs, tissues, etc.—Law
  and legislation
Emergency medical services—Law and
  legislation
Fertilization in vitro, Human—Law
  and legislation
Fetus—Research—Law and legislation
Genetic engineering—Law and
  legislation
Genetic recombination—Research—
  Law and legislation
Geriatrics—Law and legislation
Group medical practice—Law and
  legislation
Gynecology—Law and legislation
Health facilities—Certificate of need—
  Law and legislation
Health facilities—Licenses
Heart—Diseases—Law and legislation
Histocompatibility testing—Law and
  legislation
Home care services—Law and
  legislation
Homeopathy—Law and legislation
Hospice care—Law and legislation
Hospitals—Cost control—Law and
  legislation
Hospitals—Law and legislation
Hospitals—Licenses
Hospitals—Rates—Law and legislation
Human experimentation in medicine—
  Law and legislation
Intensive care units—Law and
  legislation
Maternal health services—Law and
  legislation
Medicaid—Law and legislation
Medical care—Cost control—Law and
  legislation
Medical care—Law and legislation
Medical care, Cost of—Law and
  legislation
Medical consultation—Law and
  legislation
Medical genetics—Law and legislation
Medical personnel—Malpractice
Medical records—Law and legislation
Medical screening—Law and
  legislation
Medical statistics—Law and legislation
Medicare—Law and legislation
Medicine—Research—Law and
  legislation
Medicine, Experimental—Law and
  legislation

Neonatal intensive care—Law and
  legislation
Neonatology—Law and legislation
Neurologists—Malpractice
Obstetrics—Law and legislation
Ophthalmologists—Malpractice
Ophthalmology—Law and legislation
Orthopedists—Legal status, laws, etc.
Osteopathy—Law and legislation
Paramedical education—Law and
  legislation
Pediatrics—Law and legislation
Phenylketonuria—Law and legislation
Physical therapy—Law and legislation
Physicians—Licenses
Physicians—Malpractice
Physicians, Foreign—Licenses
Plastic surgeons—Malpractice
Poor—Medical care—Law and
  legislation
Prisoners—Medical care—Law and
  legislation
Psychopharmacology—Law and
  legislation
Psychosurgery—Law and legislation
Psychotherapists—Malpractice
Public health laws
Right to die—Law and legislation
Rural health services—Law and
  legislation
Sex change—Law and legislation
Sickle cell anemia—Law and
  legislation
Terminal care—Law and legislation
United States—Armed Forces—
  Medical personnel—Malpractice
Vaccination—Law and legislation
Veterans—Medical care—Law and
  legislation
Vision—Testing—Law and legislation

Medical laws and legislation, International
  UF International medical laws and
        legislation
  BT International law
  NT Medicine—International cooperation
Medical laws and legislation (Canon law)
Medical laws and legislation (Jewish law)
  UF Medicine, Jewish—Law and legislation
  RT Medicine in the Talmud
Medical laws and legislation (Roman law)
Medical librarians (May Subd Geog)
    [Z675.M4]
  UF Librarians, Medical
  BT Special librarians
Medical libraries (May Subd Geog)
  UF Health sciences libraries
        Libraries, Health sciences
        Libraries, Medical
        Libraries, Medical college
        Medical college libraries
  BT Life sciences libraries
  RT Archives, Medical
  NT Dental libraries
        Hospital libraries
        Libraries, Public health
        Mental health libraries
        Nursing libraries
        Pharmaceutical libraries
        Veterinary libraries
— Federal aid
    USE Federal aid to medical libraries
Medical literature
    [R118.6]
  UF Literature, Medical
  BT Life sciences literature
        Medicine—History
  RT Medicine—Bibliography
  NT Dental literature
        Epilepsy literature
        Nursing literature
        Pediatric literature

— Acquisition
    USE Acquisition of medical literature
— **Editing**
    UF Medical editing
    BT Technical editing
— **Marketing**
    UF Medical manuscript marketing
    BT Medical writing
— Publishing
    USE Medical publishing
Medical Literature Analysis and Retrieval
  System
  USE MEDLARS
Medical literature searching
  USE Information storage and retrieval
        systems—Medicine
Medical logic
    [R723]
  UF Clinical reasoning
        Logic, Medical
        Medical reasoning
  BT Diagnosis
  RT Medicine—Philosophy
Medical magnetic resonance imaging
  USE Magnetic resonance imaging
Medical malpractice
  USE Medical personnel—Malpractice
Medical malpractice insurance
  USE Insurance, Physicians' liability
Medical manpower
  USE Medical personnel
        Public health personnel
Medical manuscript marketing
  USE Medical literature—Marketing
Medical materials
  USE Biomedical materials
Medical mathematics
  USE Medicine—Mathematics
Medical meteorology
  USE Climatology, Medical
Medical microbiology (May Subd Geog)
  UF Clinical microbiology
        Microbiology, Medical
  BT Body, Human—Microbiology
        Diagnosis, Laboratory
        Medical sciences
        Microbiology
  RT Micro-organisms, Pathogenic
  SA subdivision Microbiology under
        individual organs and regions of the
        body, e.g. Heart—Microbiology;
        Foot—Microbiology; and under
        individual diseases, e.g. Tuberculosis
        —Microbiology
  NT Bacteriology, Medical
        Communicable diseases
        Diagnostic microbiology
        Infection
        Medical mycology
        Medical protozoology
        Medical virology
        Mycoplasma diseases
        Rickettsial diseases
        Sanitary microbiology
Medical microscopy
  USE Microscopy, Medical
Medical microwave imaging
  USE Microwave imaging in medicine
Medical milk commissions
  USE Milk commissions, Medical
Medical misconceptions (May Subd Geog)
    [R729.9]
  UF Delusions, Medical
        Health misconceptions
        Medical delusions
        Medical superstitions
        Medicine—Superstitions
        Misconceptions, Medical
  BT Errors, Popular
        Medical errors

2333

Medical mishaps
  USE Medical errors
Medical missionaries
  USE Missionaries, Medical
Medical missions
  USE Missions, Medical
Medical museums *(May Subd Geog)*
  [R871-891]
  BT Museums
  NT Anatomical museums
     Pathological museums
     Pharmaceutical museums
Medical mycology *(May Subd Geog)*
  [RC117]
  BT Fungi—Economic aspects
     Medical microbiology
     Mycology
  RT Fungi, Pathogenic
     Mycoses
  SA *subdivision* Fungi *under names of*
     organs and regions of the body, e.g.
     Ear—Fungi
  NT Antifungal agents
Medical neurology
  USE Nervous system—Diseases
Medical occupations schools
  USE Health occupations schools
Medical office assistants
  USE Medical assistants
Medical office nursing *(May Subd Geog)*
  [RT120.09]
  UF Office nursing, Medical
  BT Nursing
  NT Nurse-physician joint practice
Medical offices *(May Subd Geog)*
  [R728]
  UF Doctors' offices
     Medical practice units
     Physicians' offices
  BT Health facilities
     Medicine—Practice
     Offices
  RT Clinics
  NT Chiropractic offices
     Dental offices
     Medical appointments and schedules
     Medical assistants
     Medical secretaries
     Psychotherapists' offices
  — **Planning**
     BT Office layout
Medical parasitology *(May Subd Geog)*
  UF Clinical parasitology
     Human parasitology
     Man—Parasites
  BT Medical sciences
     Parasites
     Parasitology
  SA *subdivision* Parasites *under names of*
     organs and regions of the body, e.g.
     Heart—Parasites
  NT Blood—Parasites
     Medical helminthology
     Medical protozoology
     Parasitic diseases
     Pediculosis
     Worms, Intestinal and parasitic
Medical partnership *(May Subd Geog)*
  [R729.5.P37]
  BT Medicine—Practice
     Partnership
Medical peer review organizations
  USE Professional standards review
     organizations (Medicine)

Medical personnel *(May Subd Geog)*
  UF Health care personnel
     Health manpower
     Health personnel
     Health professions
     Health sciences personnel
     Health services personnel
     Medical manpower
  BT Medical care
  SA Pharmacists; Physicians; Surgeons; *and*
     similar headings
  NT Allied health personnel
     Biomedical engineers
     Blacks in medicine
     Dental personnel
     Emergency medical personnel
     Eskimos in medicine
     Health care teams
     Health occupations students
     Health services administrators
     Hospitals—Staff
     Indians in medicine
     Medical research personnel
     Medical teaching personnel
     Medicine—Specialties and specialists
     Medicine—Vocational guidance
     Mental health personnel
     Midwives
     Nurses
     Operating room personnel
     Pharmacists
     Physicians
     Prosthetists
     Public health personnel
     Recovery room personnel
     Student volunteers in medical care
     United States—Armed Forces—
       Medical personnel
  — **Classification**
     BT Job analysis
  — Collective labor agreements
     USE Collective labor agreements—
       Medical personnel
  — **Discipline**
  — Education
     USE Medical education
  — **In-service training** *(May Subd Geog)*
     NT Nurses—In-service training
  — Information storage and retrieval systems
     USE Information storage and retrieval
       systems—Medical personnel
  — **Job stress**
  — Legal status, laws, etc.
     USE Medical laws and legislation
  — Licenses
     RT Health occupations licensing
       boards
  — — **California**
       NT Health Manpower Pilot Projects
         Program
  — **Malpractice** *(May Subd Geog)*
     UF Medical malpractice
        Medical personnel—Tort liability
        Tort liability of medical personnel
     BT Malpractice
        Medical errors
        Medical ethics
        Medical laws and legislation
     SA *subdivision* Malpractice *under*
        particular medical personnel,
        e.g. Physicians—Malpractice
     NT Informed consent (Medical law)
  — — **Cases**
  — — — Digests
         USE Medical personnel—
           Malpractice—Digests
  — — **Digests**
         UF Medical personnel—Malpractice
           —Cases—Digests
  — **Mental health** *(May Subd Geog)*
  — **Pensions** *(May Subd Geog)*

  [RA410.6-RA410.9]
     UF Medical personnel—Salaries,
        pensions, etc.
  — **Salaries, etc.** *(May Subd Geog)*
     [RA410.6-RA410.9]
     UF Medical personnel—Salaries,
        pensions, etc.
        Wages—Medical personnel
  — Salaries, pensions, etc.
     USE Medical personnel—Pensions
        Medical personnel—Salaries, etc.
  — **Supply and demand**
     [RA410.6-9]
     BT Medical care
        Medically underserved areas
  — **Taxation** *(May Subd Geog)*
  — — **Law and legislation**
        (May Subd Geog)
  — Tort liability
     USE Medical personnel—Malpractice
  — **United States**
     NT Afro-Americans in medicine
        Hispanic Americans in medicine
Medical personnel, Ayurvedic
  (May Subd Geog)
  UF Ayurvedic medical personnel
  BT Medicine, Ayurvedic
Medical personnel, Foreign
  (May Subd Geog)
  [R697.F6]
  UF Foreign medical personnel
     Foreign-trained medical personnel
  NT Nurses, Foreign
     Physicians, Foreign
Medical personnel and patient
  (May Subd Geog)
  UF Patient and medical personnel
  BT Interpersonal relations
     Sick
  NT Allied health personnel and patient
     Dental personnel and patient
     Health counseling
     Nurse and patient
     Patient education
     Patient representatives
     Patient satisfaction
     Pharmacist and patient
     Physician and patient
     Therapist and patient
Medical photogrammetry
  USE Photogrammetry in medicine
Medical photography
  USE Photography, Medical
Medical physics
  [R895]
  BT Biophysics
     Physics
  NT Radiology, Medical
Medical policy *(May Subd Geog)*
  UF Health policy
     Medical care—Government policy
     Medicine and state
     Policy, Medical
     Public health—Government policy
     State and medicine
  BT Science and state
     Social policy
  NT Dental policy
     Health planning
     Medical education policy
     Medical laws and legislation
     Medicine, State
     Mental health policy
     Pharmaceutical policy
  — **Business community participation**
     BT Business enterprises
        Industry—Social aspects
  — **Citizen participation**
Medical polymers
  USE Polymers in medicine

Medical polyurethanes
  USE Polyurethanes in medicine
Medical practice units
  USE Medical offices
Medical products
  USE Medical instruments and apparatus
      Medical supplies
Medical profession
  USE Medicine
      Physicians
Medical professional standards review
    organizations
  USE Professional standards review
      organizations (Medicine)
Medical professions schools
  USE Health occupations schools
Medical prognosis
  USE Prognosis
Medical programs, Regional
  USE Regional medical programs
Medical protocols
  [RC64]
  UF Clinical algorithms
      Clinical protocols
      Patient care plans
      Plans for patient care
      Protocols in medicine
  BT Communication in medicine
      Medical records
      Medicine, Clinical—Handbooks,
        manuals, etc.
  NT Nursing care plans
Medical protozoology
  UF Protozoan diseases
      Protozoan infections
  BT Medical microbiology
      Medical parasitology
      Parasitic diseases
      Protozoology
  RT Protozoa, Pathogenic
  NT Amebiasis
      Babesiosis
      Coccidiosis
      Giardiasis
      Leishmaniasis
      Malaria
      Toxoplasmosis
      Trichomoniasis
      Trypanosomiasis
Medical proverbs
  USE Medicine—Quotations, maxims, etc.
Medical publishing *(May Subd Geog)*
  UF Medical literature—Publishing
Medical radiography
  USE Radiography, Medical
Medical radiology
  USE Radiology, Medical
Medical reasoning
  USE Medical logic
Medical record librarians
  USE Medical record personnel
Medical record linkage *(May Subd Geog)*
  UF Record linkage, Medical
  BT Dual record systems
      Epidemiology
      Medical statistics
Medical record personnel *(May Subd Geog)*
  [RA976.5]
  UF Medical record librarians
  BT Allied health personnel
      Medical records—Management
Medical records *(May Subd Geog)*
  [R864 (General)]
  [RA976 (Hospital medical records)]
  UF Clinical records
      Health records
      Hospital medical records
      Patient care records
  BT Communication in medicine
      Hospital records
  NT Dental records

Long-term care facilities—Medical
      records
      Mass casualties—Medical records
      Medical history taking
      Medical protocols
      Mental health services—Medical
        records
      Nursing homes—Medical records
      Nursing records
      Psychiatry—Medical records
      Public health records
— **Abstracting and indexing**
— **Access control**
    BT Confidential communications—
          Physicians
        Medical ethics
— **Data processing**
— **Law and legislation** *(May Subd Geog)*
    BT Medical laws and legislation
— **Management** *(May Subd Geog)*
    [RA976]
    NT Medical record personnel
— **United States**
— — **Data processing**
        NT Professional Activity Study
Medical records equipment industry
  (May Subd Geog)
  [HD9995.M43-HD9995.M434]
Medical records on microfilm
  (May Subd Geog)
  BT Microfilms
Medical referral *(May Subd Geog)*
  [R727.8]
  UF Patient referral
      Referral, Medical
  BT Medical cooperation
      Medicine—Practice
Medical registration and examination
  USE Medical laws and legislation
Medical research
  USE Medicine—Research
Medical research personnel
  (May Subd Geog)
  UF Clinical investigators
      Medical researchers
  BT Medical personnel
      Medicine—Research
  NT Medical scientists
— **Supply and demand**
Medical researchers
  USE Medical research personnel
Medical residents
  USE Residents (Medicine)
Medical scholarships
  USE Medicine—Scholarships, fellowships,
      etc.
Medical schools
  USE Medical colleges
Medical sciences *(May Subd Geog)*
  Here are entered works discussing collectively the
scientific disciplines which are basic to the practice of
medicine and commonly covered in the preclinical
years of the medical curriculum.
  UF Basic medical sciences
      Basic sciences, Medical
      Biomedical sciences
      Preclinical sciences
      Sciences, Medical
  BT Life sciences
  RT Medicine
  NT Anatomy, Human
      Biological chemistry
      Biophysics
      Human physiology
      Medical genetics
      Medical microbiology
      Medical parasitology
      Pathology
      Pharmacology

Medical scientists *(May Subd Geog)*
  UF Biomedical scientists
      Health scientists
  BT Medical research personnel
      Scientists
  NT Anatomists
      Cardiologists
      Clinical chemists
      Endocrinologists
      Epidemiologists
      Hematologists
      Immunologists
      Oncologists
      Pharmacologists
      Physiologists
      Toxicologists
      Women medical scientists
Medical screening *(May Subd Geog)*
  [RA427.5]
  Here are entered works on mass examination of
the population to detect the existence of a particular
disease, as diabetes, tuberculosis, etc.
  UF Mass medical screening
      Mass screening, Medical
      Medical examinations
      Screening, Medical
  BT Diagnostic services
      Health risk assessment
  NT Drug testing
      Multiphasic health screening
      Nursing home applicants—
        Preadmission screening
      Triage (Medicine)
— **Law and legislation** *(May Subd Geog)*
    BT Medical laws and legislation
Medical secretaries *(May Subd Geog)*
  [R728]
  BT Allied health personnel
      Medical offices
      Secretaries
  RT Medical assistants
      Medical transcription
  NT Hospital secretaries
Medical self-care
  USE Self-care, Health
Medical self examination
  USE Self-examination, Medical
Medical self-experimentation
  USE Self-experimentation in medicine
Medical service, Cost of
  USE Medical care, Cost of
Medical service, Prepaid
  USE Insurance, Health
Medical services
  USE Medical care
Medical services, Rural
  USE Rural health services
Medical shorthand
  BT Medical transcription
      Shorthand
Medical slang
  USE Medicine—Slang
Medical social work *(May Subd Geog)*
  Here are entered works on social services that
supplement necessary medical and nursing care for
the needy sick. Works on the free provision of medi-
cal advice, drugs, and essential nursing are entered
under Charities, Medical.
  UF Hospital social work
      Social service, Medical
  BT Charities
      Medical care
      Public welfare
      Social medicine
      Social service
  RT Charities, Medical
      Psychiatric social work
  NT Hospitals—After care
      Hospitals—Case management services
      Social work with the terminally ill
      Visiting housekeepers
      Voluntary health agencies

Medical sociologists *(May Subd Geog)*
　　BT　Social medicine
　　　　Sociologists
Medical sociology
　　USE　Social medicine
Medical sounds
　　BT　Sounds
　　RT　Auscultation
　　SA　*subdivision* Sounds *under names of*
　　　　　organs or regions of the body, e.g.
　　　　　Heart—Sounds
Medical specialists
　　USE　Medicine—Specialties and specialists
Medical specialization
　　USE　Medicine—Specialties and specialists
Medical specialties
　　USE　Medicine—Specialties and specialists
Medical specimens
　　USE　Diagnostic specimens
Medical staff of hospitals
　　USE　Hospitals—Medical staff
Medical staff of public hospitals
　　USE　Hospitals, Public—Medical staff
Medical staff of veterans' hospitals
　　USE　Hospitals, Veterans'—Medical staff
Medical staff privileges
　　USE　Hospitals—Medical staff—Clinical
　　　　　privileges
Medical statistics *(Not Subd Geog)*
　　[RA407-RA409.5]
　　UF　Medicine—Statistical methods
　　BT　Statistics
　　SA　*subdivision* Statistics *under individual*
　　　　　diseases, e.g. Tuberculosis—
　　　　　Statistics; *and subdivision* Statistics,
　　　　　Medical *under names of countries,*
　　　　　cities, etc. for compilations of
　　　　　medical statistical data
　　NT　Diseases—Reporting
　　　　Health status indicators
　　　　Health surveys—Statistical methods
　　　　Medical record linkage
　　　　Public health records
　　— **Computer programs**
　　— Information storage and retrieval systems
　　　　USE　Information storage and retrieval
　　　　　　systems—Medical statistics
　　— **Law and legislation** *(May Subd Geog)*
　　　　BT　Medical laws and legislation
Medical stereophotogrammetry
　　USE　Photogrammetry in medicine
Medical students *(May Subd Geog)*
　　BT　Health occupations students
　　　　Medical education
　　　　Students
　　NT　Medical college applicants
　　　　Medical students, Foreign
　　　　Women medical students
　　— **Loans**
　　　　UF　Loans to medical students
　　　　BT　Medical education—Finance
　　　　　　Medicine—Scholarships,
　　　　　　　fellowships, etc.
　　　　　　Student loan funds
　　— **Transfer**
　　　　UF　Transfer of medical students
　　　　BT　Medical colleges—Admission
　　　　　　Students, Transfer of
Medical students, Foreign *(May Subd Geog)*
　　UF　Foreign medical students
　　BT　Medical students
　　　　Students, Foreign
Medical superstitions
　　USE　Medical misconceptions
Medical supplies *(May Subd Geog)*
　　[UH440-UH445 (Military)]
　　[VG290-VG295 (Naval)]
　　UF　Hospital supplies
　　　　Medical products
　　　　Medicine—Equipment and supplies
　　　　Supplies, Medical

　　RT　Health products
　　NT　Drugs
　　　　Medical instruments and apparatus
　　　　Plastics in medicine
　　　　Tampons
　　　　United States.　Army—Medical
　　　　　supplies
　　　　United States.　Navy—Medical
　　　　　supplies
　　— **Microbiology**
　　— **Sterilization**
Medical supplies, Disposable
　　(May Subd Geog)
　　[R857.D5]
　　UF　Disposable medical supplies
　　　　Medical disposables
　　　　Medical supplies, Single-use
　　　　Single-use medical supplies
　　RT　Health facilities—Waste disposal
　　NT　Disposable medical supplies industry
　　— **Sterilization**
Medical supplies, Single-use
　　USE　Medical supplies, Disposable
Medical supplies industry *(May Subd Geog)*
Medical symbolism
　　USE　Symbolism in medicine
Medical teaching personnel
　　(May Subd Geog)
　　UF　Medical educators
　　BT　Medical education
　　　　Medical personnel
　　　　Teachers
　　NT　Childbirth teachers
　　　　Dental auxiliary teachers
Medical technical assistance
　　USE　Medical assistance
Medical technicians
　　USE　Biomedical technicians
Medical technicians, Veterinary
　　USE　Animal health technicians
Medical technologists
　　UF　Clinical laboratory technicians
　　　　Medical laboratory technicians
　　　　Technologists, Medical
　　BT　Biomedical technicians
　　　　Laboratory technicians
　　RT　Medical laboratory technology
　　NT　Medical laboratory assistants
　　　　United States.　Navy—Medical
　　　　　technologists
Medical technology *(May Subd Geog)*
　　[R855-R855.5]
　　Here are entered works on the techniques, equip-
　　ment, drugs and procedures used to deliver medical
　　care and the systems within which such care is deliv-
　　ered.
　　UF　Health care technology
　　　　Health technology
　　　　Technology, Health
　　　　Technology, Medical
　　BT　Technology
　　NT　Medical innovations
　　— **Vocational guidance**
Medical technology (Medical laboratory
　　technology)
　　USE　Medical laboratory technology
Medical television
　　USE　Television in medicine
Medical thermography
　　[RC78.7.T5]
　　UF　Clinical thermography
　　　　Medicine—Thermographic methods
　　BT　Diagnostic imaging
　　　　Thermography
　　　　Thermometers and thermometry,
　　　　　Medical
　　NT　Body temperature
　　　　Forensic thermography
Medical thermometers
　　USE　Thermometers and thermometry,
　　　　　Medical

Medical topography
　　USE　Medical geography
Medical transcribing
　　USE　Medical transcription
Medical transcription *(May Subd Geog)*
　　[R728.8]
　　UF　Medical transcribing
　　　　Transcription, Medical
　　BT　Transcription
　　RT　Medical secretaries
　　NT　Medical shorthand
Medical transplantation
　　USE　Transplantation of organs, tissues, etc.
Medical Trial, Nuremberg, Germany, 1946-
　　1947
　　USE　Nuremberg Medical Trial, Nuremberg,
　　　　　Germany, 1946-1947
Medical ultrasonics
　　USE　Ultrasonics in medicine
Medical underservice areas
　　USE　Medically underserved areas
Medical virology *(May Subd Geog)*
　　UF　Virology, Medical
　　BT　Medical microbiology
　　　　Virology
　　RT　Virus diseases
　　NT　Diagnostic virology
Medical writing
　　[R119]
　　Here are entered guides to authorship in medical
　　writing. Similar guides in corresponding fields of en-
　　gineering, science, and technology are entered under
　　Technical writing.
　　UF　Hygiene—Authorship
　　　　Medicine—Authorship
　　　　Public health—Authorship
　　BT　Communication in medicine
　　　　Technical writing
　　RT　Medicine—Language
　　NT　Medical literature—Marketing
　　　　Nursing—Authorship
　　　　Prescription writing
　　　　Proposal writing in medicine
Medical zoology
　　USE　Zoology, Medical
Medically underserved areas
　　(May Subd Geog)
　　UF　Health service shortage areas
　　　　Medical underservice areas
　　　　Physician shortage areas
　　　　Underserved areas in medicine
　　BT　Health service areas
　　　　Medical care
　　　　Medical economics
　　　　Scarcity
　　NT　Health facilities—Location
　　　　Medical personnel—Supply and
　　　　　demand
Medicare *(May Subd Geog)*
　　UF　Medicare—United States
　　BT　Aged—Medical care—United States
　　　　Insurance, Health—United States
　　RT　Medicaid
　　　　Medigap
　　NT　System for Hospital Uniform
　　　　　Reporting
　　— **Claims administration**
　　　　UF　Administration of medicare claims
　　　　　　Claims administration in medicare
　　　　　　Claims processing in medicare
　　　　　　Processing of medicare claims
　　— **Law and legislation**
　　　　BT　Medical laws and legislation
　　— — Criminal provisions
　　　　　　USE　Medicare fraud
　　— United States
　　　　USE　Medicare
Medicare fraud *(May Subd Geog)*
　　UF　Medicare—Law and legislation—
　　　　　Criminal provisions
　　　　Medicare fraud—United States

BT Fraud
  Swindlers and swindling
— United States
  USE Medicare fraud
Medicare hospital prospective payment
  USE Hospitals—Prospective payment
Medicare nursing home prospective payment
  USE Nursing homes—Prospective payment
Medicare rural hospital prospective payment
  USE Hospitals, Rural—Prospective payment
Medicare supplemental health insurance
  USE Medigap
Medicated baths
  USE Baths, Medicated
Medicated feeds *(May Subd Geog)*
  ₍SF98.M4₎
  UF Drugs in animal feeds
  BT Feed additives
    Feeds
    Veterinary pharmacology
  NT Antibiotics in animal nutrition
    Tranquilizers in animal nutrition
— **Law and legislation** *(May Subd Geog)*
Medicated intrauterine contraceptives
  USE Intrauterine contraceptives, Medicated
Medicated plaster
  USE Plaster (Pharmacy)
Medication, Antiseptic
  USE Antiseptic medication
Medication, Intranasal
  USE Intranasal medication
Medication, Oral
  USE Oral medication
Medication, Preanesthetic
  USE Preanesthetic medication
Medication, Rectal
  USE Rectum, Medication by
Medication, Self
  USE Self medication
Medication, Vaginal
  USE Vagina, Medication by
Medication abuse *(May Subd Geog)*
  ₍RM146-RM146.7₎
    Here are entered works on the abuse or misuse of
  therapeutic drugs. Works on the abuse or misuse of
  drugs in a broad sense, such as aspirin, bromides,
  caffeine, sedatives, alcohol, LSD, marihuana, and
  narcotics, are entered under Drug abuse. Works lim-
  ited to addiction to narcotics such as opium, mor-
  phine, codeine and heroin, are entered under Narcot-
  ic habit.
  UF Abuse of medication
    Abuse of medicines
    Misuse of therapeutic drugs
    Pharmaceutical abuse
    Prescription drug abuse
  BT Drug abuse
    Drugs—Prescribing
    Medication errors
    Self medication
  RT Drugs—Overdosage
  NT Benzodiazepine abuse
    Methaqualone abuse
— **Complications and sequelae**
Medication errors *(May Subd Geog)*
  ₍RM146₎
  UF Drug errors
    Drug therapy errors
    Prescription errors
  BT Chemotherapy
    Drugs
    Medical errors
    Pharmacy
    Self medication
  RT Drugs—Overdosage
  NT Medication abuse
Medication use
  USE Drug utilization
Medici, House of *(Not Subd Geog)*
  ₍DG737.42₎
  UF House of Medici
  BT Italy—Kings and rulers

Medici cycle (Paintings)
  USE Rubens, Peter Paul, Sir, 1577-1640.
    Histories of Marie de Médicis
Medici Round House (Stabio, Switzerland)
  USE Casa rotonda (Stabio, Switzerland)
Medicinal herbs
  USE Herbs—Therapeutic use
Medicinal plant industry
  USE Botanical drug industry
Medicinal plants *(May Subd Geog)*
  ₍QK99 (Botany)₎
  ₍SB293-SB295 (Culture)₎
  UF Drug plants
    Plants, Drug
    Plants, Medicinal
  BT Botany, Medical
  RT Botanical drug industry
    Materia medica, Vegetable
    Psychotropic plants
  NT Aloe
    Atractylis ovata
    Ayahuasca
    Buxus madagascarica
    Camptotheca acuminata
    Cephaelis ipecacuanha
    Coptis japonica
    Ephedra
    Hay-fever plants
    Helenium mexicanum
    Herbals
    Jatropha gossypiifolia
    Manna plants
    Margosa
    Opium poppy
    Pyrethrum
    Rauvolfia serpentina
    Rosemary
    Viguiera buddleiaeformis
— Therapeutic use
  USE Materia medica, Vegetable
Medicinal powders
  USE Powders (Pharmacy)
Medicine *(May Subd Geog)*
  ₍R₎
  UF Medical profession
  BT Human biology
    Life sciences
  RT Medical sciences
    Pathology
    Physicians
    Therapeutic systems
  SA *headings beginning with the word*
    Medical
  NT Adolescent medicine
    Advertising—Medicine
    Automotive medicine
    Biomedical engineering
    Botany, Medical
    Broussaisism
    Circumpolar medicine
    Classification—Books—Medicine
    Climatology, Medical
    Creative ability in medicine
    Critical care medicine
    Dentistry
    Disaster medicine
    Diseases
    Diseases—Causes and theories of
      causation
    Diseases—Reporting
    Electricity in medicine
    Emergency medicine
    Family medicine
    Geriatrics
    Gynecology
    Healing
    Health
    Holistic medicine
    Homeopathy
    Internal medicine
    Materia medica

    Medicine, Physical
    Mind and body
    Minorities in medicine
    Missions, Medical
    Moving-pictures in medicine
    Nosology
    Nursing
    Optical fibers in medicine
    Pediatrics
    Pharmacy
    Podiatry
    Quacks and quackery
    Rademacherism
    Radio in medicine
    Sex discrimination in medicine
    Sexism in medicine
    Space medicine
    Sports medicine
    Surgery
    Toxicology
    Tropical medicine
    Urology
    Veterinary medicine
    Wit and humor in medicine
    Women in medicine
— **15th-18th centuries**
  ₍R128.6-R128.7 (General works)₎
  ₍R147-R148 (History)₎
  UF Medicine—Early works to 1800
  NT Brunonianism
    Iatrophysical school
— **Ability testing**
  UF Medical competence testing
  BT Medicine—Examinations
  RT Physicians—Rating of
— Advertising
  USE Advertising—Medicine
— **Anecdotes, facetiae, satire, etc.**
  ₍PN6231.M4₎
  ₍R705₎
  UF Anecdotes, Medical
    Operations, Surgical—Anecdotes,
      facetiae, satire, etc.
  NT Medicine—Quotations, maxims,
    etc.
— **Aphorisms**
  ₍R126₎
  ₍R128.7₎
    Here are entered only the older medical
  works made up of short precepts and instruc-
  tions, e.g. Aphorisms of Hippocrates.
  BT Aphorisms and apothegms
    Medicine—Quotations, maxims,
      etc.
— Apparatus
  USE Medical instruments and
    apparatus
— Authorship
  USE Medical writing
— **Awards**
  NT Albert Lasker Awards
    Paracelsus Ring
— **Bibliography**
  RT Medical literature
  NT Information storage and retrieval
    systems—Medicine
— — **Methodology**
— **Biography**
  ₍R134 (Collected)₎
  ₍R153-R684 (By country)₎
  NT Health-officers
— Cataloging
  USE Cataloging of medical literature
— **Communication systems**
  ₍R118₎
  UF Telemedicine
  BT Communication in medicine
    Telecommunication systems
  NT STARPAHC System
    Telephone in medicine
    Television in medicine

Medicine *(Continued)*
— Cost of medical care
    USE Medical care, Cost of
— **Data processing**
    UF Computers in medicine
    NT SUMEX-AIM (Computer system)
— **Documentation**
    NT Archives, Medical
— Early works to 1800
    USE Medicine—15th-18th centuries
          Medicine, Ancient
          Medicine, Medieval
— Economic aspects
    USE Medical economics
— Emblems and symbols
    USE Symbolism in medicine
— Equipment and supplies
    USE Medical instruments and
          apparatus
          Medical supplies
— **Examinations**
    [R837.E9]
    Here are entered works on the subject of ex-
    aminations and testing procedures in the study of
    medicine. Works on medical examinations of
    the body are entered under Diagnosis, Periodic
    health examinations, or the subdivision Medical
    examinations under topics or classes of people,
    e.g. Insurance, Accident—Medical examina-
    tions; Children—Medical examinations.
    UF Examinations, Medical, in medical
          education
          Medical examinations in medical
          education
    NT Medical colleges—Entrance
          examinations
          Medicine—Ability testing
— Fees
    USE Medical fees
— Fellowships
    USE Medicine—Scholarships,
          fellowships, etc.
— **Formulae, receipts, prescriptions**
    [RS125-7]
    UF Formularies, Medical
          Medical formularies
          Prescriptions
    BT Drugs
          Materia medica
          Therapeutics
    RT Dispensatories
          Pharmacopoeias
          Pharmacy
    SA *subdivision* Formulae, receipts,
          prescriptions *under specific*
          branches and systems of
          medicine, e.g. Dermatology—
          Formulae, receipts,
          prescriptions; Medicine, Chinese
          —Formulae, receipts,
          prescriptions
    NT Dentistry—Formulae, receipts,
          prescriptions
— — Prices
    USE Prescription pricing
— **Handbooks, manuals, etc.**
— **Historiography**
    NT Medical historians
— History
    [R131-684]
    SA Medicine, Ancient; Medicine,
          Arabic; Medicine, Medieval; *and*
          similar headings
    NT Medical literature
          Medicine, Ancient
          Medicine, Arabic
          Medicine, Medieval
— **Information services** *(May Subd Geog)*
    [R835]
    BT Communication in medicine
— — **Use studies**
    BT Library use studies

— Innovations
    USE Medical innovations
— Instruments
    USE Medical instruments and
          apparatus
          Surgical instruments and
          apparatus
— **International cooperation**
    BT International agencies
          Medical assistance
          Medical laws and legislation,
          International
    NT Medical education—International
          cooperation
— Jews
    USE Medicine, Jewish
— **Language**
    RT Medical writing
    NT English language—Conversation
          and phrase books (for medical
          personnel)
          French language—Medical French
          Greek language—Medical Greek
          Latin language—Medical Latin
          Medicine—Slang
— Laws and legislation
    USE Medical laws and legislation
— Materials
    USE Biomedical materials
— **Mathematical models**
    BT Biomathematics
— **Mathematics**
    UF Medical mathematics
— Moral and ethical aspects
    USE Medical ethics
— **Philosophy**
    [R723]
    UF Philosophy of medicine
    RT Medical logic
    NT Medicine, Empirical
— Popular works
    USE Medicine, Popular
— **Practice** *(May Subd Geog)*
    [R728-R729.5]
    UF Practice of medicine
    SA *subdivision* Practice *under*
          particular medical specialties,
          e.g. Surgery—Practice
    NT Clinics
          Group medical practice
          Internal medicine
          Medical appointments and
          schedules
          Medical consultation
          Medical errors
          Medical offices
          Medical partnership
          Medical referral
          Medicine, Clinical
          Medicine, Rural—Practice
          Nuclear medicine—Practice
          Nurse-physician joint practice
          Nursing—Practice
          Physicians—Malpractice
          Physicians (General practice)
          Substitute physicians
— — **Accounting**
    [HF5686.P9]
    UF Physicians—Accounting
— **Quotations, maxims, etc.**
    UF Medical proverbs
          Proverbs, Medical
    BT Medicine—Anecdotes, facetiae,
          satire, etc.
    NT Medicine—Aphorisms
— **Religious aspects**
    [BL65.M4]
    UF Medicine and religion
          Religion and medicine
    RT Pastoral medicine
    NT Medicine in the Bible

— — **Baptists, [Catholic Church, etc.]**
— — **Buddhism**
    NT Medicine, Buddhist
— — **Buddhism, [Christianity, etc.]**
— — **Islam**
    NT Medicine in the Koran
— — **Judaism**
    NT Medicine, Jewish
          Medicine in the Talmud
— **Research** *(May Subd Geog)*
    [R850-854]
    UF Medical research
    NT Human experimentation in
          medicine
          Medical research personnel
          Medicine, Experimental
— — Federal aid
    USE Federal aid to medical
          research
— — **Finance**
    NT Federal aid to medical research
— — **Law and legislation**
    (May Subd Geog)
    BT Medical laws and legislation
— **Scholarships, fellowships, etc.**
    (May Subd Geog)
    [R840]
    UF Medical fellowships
          Medical scholarships
          Medicine—Fellowships
    BT Medical colleges
          Medical education
    NT Medical students—Loans
— **Slang**
    UF Medical slang
    BT Medicine—Language
— Social aspects
    USE Social medicine
— **Societies, etc.**
— **Specialties and specialists**
    (May Subd Geog)
    [R729.5.S6]
    UF Medical specialists
          Medical specialization
          Medical specialties
          Specialists in medicine
          Specialties, Medical
    BT Medical personnel
    RT Physicians (General practice)
    NT Internists
          Medical consultants
          Nursing specialties
— Statistical methods
    USE Medical statistics
— **Study and teaching** *(May Subd Geog)*
    [R735-R832]
    Here are entered works on methods of in-
    struction and curricula in the teaching of medi-
    cine. General works on education in the field of
    medicine are entered under Medical education.
    BT Medical colleges
          Medical education
    NT Psychiatry—Study and teaching
          Television in medical education
— — **Audio-visual aids**
— — **Simulation methods**
    NT Simulated patients
— **Study and teaching (Preceptorship)**
    (May Subd Geog)
    UF Preceptorship medical education
— Superstitions
    USE Medical misconceptions
— Technological innovations
    USE Medical innovations
— **Terminology**
    [R123]
    NT French language—Medical French
          Greek language—Medical Greek
          Latin language—Medical Latin
— Thermographic methods
    USE Medical thermography

— Video tape catalogs
  [R835]
— Vocational guidance (May Subd Geog)
  BT Medical personnel
— — California
    NT Health Professions Career
        Opportunity Program
— Germany
— — Dutch influences
    BT Netherlands—Civilization
— Japan
— Netherlands
— — German influences
    BT Germany—Civilization
— Tropics
  USE Tropical medicine
— United States
— — German influences
    BT Germany—Civilization
Medicine, Adolescent
  USE Adolescent medicine
Medicine, Agasthya
  USE Medicine, Siddha
Medicine, Ancient
  [R135]
  UF Medicine—Early works to 1800
  BT Medicine—History
  NT Dentistry, Ancient
      Hospitals, Ancient
      Medicine, Assyro-Babylonian
      Medicine, Egyptian
      Medicine, Etruscan
      Medicine, Greek and Roman
      Medicine, Hittite
      Medicine, Persian
      Medicine, Scythian
      Paleopathology
Medicine, Anglo-Saxon
  UF Anglo-Saxon medicine
  BT Medicine, Medieval
Medicine, Arabic (May Subd Geog)
  UF Arabic medicine
      Materia medica, Arabic
      Medicine, Unani
      Unani medicine
  BT Medicine—History
      Medicine, Medieval
      Medicine, Oriental
— Formulae, receipts, prescriptions
Medicine, Arctic
  USE Arctic medicine
Medicine, Assyro-Babylonian
  UF Assyro-Babylonian medicine
  BT Medicine, Ancient
      Medicine, Oriental
Medicine, Ayurvedic (May Subd Geog)
  [R127.2 (Early works)]
  [R605-R608 (History)]
  UF Ayurvedic medicine
      Hindu medicine
      Medicine, Hindu
  BT Medicine, Oriental
  NT Medical personnel, Ayurvedic
— Formulae, receipts, prescriptions
  [RS131.68]
— Religious aspects
Medicine, Bhutan
  UF Bhutan medicine
      Bhutanese medicine
  BT Medicine, Oriental
Medicine, Biochemic
  [RZ422]
  UF Biochemic medicine
      Therapeutics, Biochemic
  BT Homeopathy
      Therapeutic systems
Medicine, Botanic
  [RV1-10]
  A system of medicine. Not to be confused with
medical botany.

UF Botanic medicine
    Thomsonianism
BT Therapeutic systems
RT Herbs—Therapeutic use
Medicine, Buddhist (May Subd Geog)
  [R135.6]
  UF Buddhist medicine
  BT Medicine—Religious aspects—
      Buddhism
Medicine, Chinese (May Subd Geog)
  UF Chinese medicine
  BT Medicine, Oriental
  NT Ch'i kung
— Biography
— Formulae, receipts, prescriptions
  [RS131.64]
Medicine, Chronothermal
  [RZ414]
  UF Chronothermal medicine
      Chronothermalism
  BT Therapeutic systems
Medicine, Circumpolar
  USE Circumpolar medicine
Medicine, Clerical
  USE Pastoral medicine
Medicine, Clincial
— Research
  NT Clinical trials
Medicine, Clinical (May Subd Geog)
  [RC61-69]
  UF Clinical medicine
  BT Medicine—Practice
  RT Diagnosis
  NT Charities, Medical
      Clinical indications
      Pathology
      Therapeutics
— Computer programs
  NT RX (Computer program)
— Handbooks, manuals, etc.
  NT Medical protocols
— Hospital reports
  [RC31]
  BT Hospitals
— Research
Medicine, Communication in
  USE Communication in medicine
Medicine, Comparative (May Subd Geog)
  UF Comparative medicine
  NT Anatomy, Comparative
      Diseases—Animal models
      Endocrinology, Comparative
      Pathology, Comparative
      Physiology, Comparative
      Psychiatry, Comparative
Medicine, Dental
  USE Teeth—Diseases
      Therapeutics, Dental
Medicine, Dosimetric
  [RZ416]
  UF Dosimetric medicine
  BT Therapeutic systems
      Therapeutics
  RT Alkaloids—Physiological effect
  SA subdivision Dosimetric treatment
      under individual diseases, e.g.
      Tuberculosis—Dosimetric treatment
  NT Constitutional diseases—Dosimetric
      treatment
Medicine, Eclectic
  [RV11-RV431]
  UF Eclectic medicine
  BT Therapeutic systems
  SA subdivision Eclectic treatment under
      individual diseases and groups of
      diseases. e.g. Cancer—Eclectic
      treatment
  NT Dispensatories, Eclectic
      Obstetrics, Eclectic
Medicine, Egyptian
  UF Egyptian medicine

  BT Medicine, Ancient
      Medicine, Oriental
Medicine, Electrolysis in
  USE Electrolysis in medicine
Medicine, Electromagnetism in
  USE Electromagnetism in medicine
Medicine, Emergency
  USE Emergency medicine
Medicine, Empirical (May Subd Geog)
  UF Empiric medicine
      Empirical medicine
  BT Empiricism
      Medicine—Philosophy
      Therapeutic systems
Medicine, Etruscan
  UF Etruscan medicine
  BT Medicine, Ancient
Medicine, Experimental
  [R850-854]
  UF Experimental medicine
  BT Medicine—Research
  NT Diseases—Animal models
      Hematology, Experimental
      Human experimentation in medicine
      Stomatology, Experimental
      Therapeutics, Experimental
      Vivisection
— Law and legislation (May Subd Geog)
  BT Medical laws and legislation
Medicine, Forensic
  USE Medical jurisprudence
Medicine, Greek and Roman
  UF Greek medicine
      Medicine, Roman
      Medicine, Unani
      Roman medicine
      Unani medicine
  BT Medicine, Ancient
Medicine, Gypsy
  UF Gypsy medicine
— Formulae, receipts, prescriptions
Medicine, Hindu
  USE Medicine, Ayurvedic
Medicine, Hittite
  [R135]
  UF Hittite medicine
  BT Medicine, Ancient
      Medicine, Oriental
Medicine, Industrial (May Subd Geog)
  [RC963-9]
  UF Industrial medicine
      Medicine, Occupational
      Occupational medicine
  RT Labor and laboring classes—Medical
      examinations
      Occupational diseases
  NT Disability evaluation
      Industrial dentistry
      Industrial hygiene
      Industrial nursing
      Industrial ophthalmology
      Industrial psychiatry
      Iron and steel workers—Medical
      examinations
      Occupational health services
— Law and legislation (May Subd Geog)
  BT Industrial hygiene—Law and
      legislation
Medicine, Intensive
  USE Critical care medicine
Medicine, Internal
  USE Internal medicine
Medicine, Jewish
  UF Hebrew medicine
      Jewish medicine
      Jews—Medicine
      Medicine—Jews
  BT Medicine—Religious aspects—Judaism
      Physicians, Jewish
  NT Medicine in the Talmud
— Law and legislation

Medicine, Jewish
  — Law and legislation *(Continued)*
     USE Medical laws and legislation
        (Jewish law)
Medicine, Korean
  UF Korean medicine
  BT Medicine, Oriental
Medicine, Laboratory
  USE Diagnosis, Laboratory
Medicine, Legal
  USE Medical jurisprudence
Medicine, Magic, mystic, and spagiric
  (May Subd Geog)
  UF Magic medicine
     Medicine, Mystic
     Medicine, Occult
     Medicine, Spagiric
     Mystic medicine
     Occult medicine
     Spagiric medicine
     Spagyric medicine
  BT Alchemy
     Amulets
     Magic
     Mental healing
     Spiritual healing
     Superstition
     Therapeutic systems
  NT Aphrodisiacs
     Coins—Therapeutic use
     Cramp-rings
     Folk dentistry
     Folk medicine
     Healing gods
     Incubation (Religion)
     Medical astrology
     Precious stones—Therapeutic use
     Royal touch
     Signatures (Medicine)
  — Formulae, receipts, prescriptions
Medicine, Marine
  USE Medicine, Naval
Medicine, Medieval *(May Subd Geog)*
  ⌈R128-R128.3 (General)⌉
  ⌈R141-R144 (History)⌉
  UF Medicine—Early works to 1800
     Medicine, Medieval—Early works to
     1800
  BT Botany, Medical
     Materia medica, Vegetable
     Medicine—History
  RT Botany—Pre-Linnean works
  NT Black death
     Elixir of life
     Hospitals, Medieval
     Medicine, Anglo-Saxon
     Medicine, Arabic
  — Early works to 1800
     USE Medicine, Medieval
Medicine, Military *(May Subd Geog)*
  ⌈RC970-RC971 (Medical practice)⌉
  ⌈UH (Military science)⌉
  UF Field hospitals
     Hospitals, Field
     Military medicine
  BT Armies—Medical and sanitary affairs
  RT Medicine, Naval
     Military hygiene
     War—Medical aspects
     War—Relief of sick and wounded
  SA *subdivision* Medical care *under names*
     of individual military services and
     individual wars, e.g. United States.
     Air Force—Medical care; World
     War, 1939-1945—Medical care
  NT Dentistry, Military
     Disability evaluation
     Hospitals, Military
     Mass casualties
     Military nursing
     Pharmacy, Military

     Surgery, Military
     Veterans, Disabled—Rehabilitation
  — **Study and teaching** *(May Subd Geog)*
  — — **Texas**
     NT Operation MENDEX
Medicine, Mongolian *(May Subd Geog)*
  UF Mongolian medicine
Medicine, Mystic
  USE Medicine, Magic, mystic, and spagiric
Medicine, Nautical
  USE Medicine, Naval
Medicine, Naval *(May Subd Geog)*
  ⌈RC981-RC986 (Medical practice)⌉
  ⌈VG (Naval science)⌉
  UF Marine medicine
     Medicine, Marine
     Medicine, Nautical
     Nautical medicine
     Naval medicine
     Navies—Medical service
     Shipboard medicine
  RT Boats and boating—Accidents and
     injuries
     Medicine, Military
     Naval hygiene
     War—Relief of sick and wounded
  SA *subdivision* Medical care *under names*
     of individual navies, e.g. United
     States. Navy—Medical care
  NT Hospitals, Naval and marine
     Ship physicians
     Surgery, Naval
     United States. Navy—Medical
     technologists
Medicine, Occult
  USE Medicine, Magic, mystic, and spagiric
Medicine, Occupational
  USE Medicine, Industrial
Medicine, Oriental *(May Subd Geog)*
  ⌈R581⌉
  UF Oriental medicine
  BT Therapeutic systems
  SA Medicine *subdivided by place, e.g.*
     Medicine—Japan
  NT Hygiene, Oriental
     Medicine, Arabic
     Medicine, Assyro-Babylonian
     Medicine, Ayurvedic
     Medicine, Bhutan
     Medicine, Chinese
     Medicine, Egyptian
     Medicine, Hittite
     Medicine, Korean
     Medicine, Persian
     Medicine, Siddha
     Medicine, Tibetan
Medicine, Osteopathic
  USE Osteopathy
Medicine, Pastoral
  USE Pastoral medicine
Medicine, Perinatal
  USE Perinatology
Medicine, Persian
  ⌈R135⌉
  UF Persian medicine
  BT Medicine, Ancient
     Medicine, Oriental
Medicine, Physical *(May Subd Geog)*
  ⌈RM695-951⌉
  UF Physiatrics
     Physical medicine
  BT Medicine
  RT Rehabilitation
  NT Physiatrists
     Physical therapy
Medicine, Physiomedical
  ⌈RM133⌉
  UF Physiomedicalism
Medicine, Polar
  USE Circumpolar medicine

Medicine, Popular
  ⌈RC81-82⌉
  UF Medicine—Popular works
  SA *subdivision* Popular works *under*
     medical disciplines and under
     individual diseases, e.g.
     Ophthalmology—Popular works;
     Cancer—Popular works; *and*
     subdivision Diseases—Popular
     works *under individual parts of the*
     body, e.g. Heart—Diseases—
     Popular works
  NT Self-care, Health
Medicine, Preventive *(May Subd Geog)*
  ⌈RA421-RA790⌉
  UF Diseases—Prevention
     Prevention of disease
     Preventive medicine
  RT Medicine, State
     Pathology
     Preventive health services
     Preventive medicine physicians
     Public health
  SA *subdivision* Prevention *under names of*
     diseases and groups of diseases, e.g.
     Diphtheria—Prevention;
     Communicable diseases—
     Prevention; *and subdivision*
     Diseases—Prevention *under*
     subjects, e.g. Heart—Diseases—
     Prevention
  NT Health risk assessment
     Hygiene
     Immunity
     Periodic health examinations
     Preventive dentistry
     Self-examination, Medical
     Serumtherapy
     Veterinary public health
  — **Authorship**
  — — **Competitions** *(May Subd Geog)*
     NT Prêmio Samuel Pessoa
  — **Law and legislation** *(May Subd Geog)*
Medicine, Primitive *(May Subd Geog)*
  ⌈GN477⌉
  UF Ethnomedicine
  RT Medical anthropology
  NT Ainu—Medicine
     Akans (African people)—Medicine
     Ando (African people)—Medicine
     Australian aborigines—Medicine
     Bakongo (African people)—Medicine
     Bambara (African people)—Medicine
     Bariba (African people)—Medicine
     Bedouins—Medicine
     Bisa (Burkinabe and Ghanaian people)
     —Medicine
     Evuzok (African people)—Medicine
     Fantis—Medicine
     Folk dentistry
     Folk medicine
     Gnau (Papua New Guinea people)—
     Medicine
     Hawaiians—Medicine
     Healers
     Indians—Medicine
     Indians of North America—Medicine
     Lugbara (African people)—Medicine
     Malays (Asian people)—Medicine
     Man, Primitive—Diseases
     Maoris—Medicine
     Mashona—Medicine
     Murngin (Australian people)—
     Medicine
     Paleopathology
     Samburu—Medicine
     Surgery, Primitive
     Swazi (African people)—Medicine
     Tamang (Nepalese people)—Medicine
     Yorubas—Medicine
     Zulus—Medicine

— Formulae, receipts, prescriptions
— **Botswana**
  NT Sotho (African people)—Medicine
— **Cameroon**
  NT Bamum (African people)—
      Medicine
— **Lesotho**
  NT Sotho (African people)—Medicine
— **Papua New Guinea**
  NT Fore (New Guinea people)—
      Medicine
— **Polynesia**
  NT Polynesians—Medicine
— **Samoan Islands**
  NT Samoans—Medicine
— **South Africa**
  NT Sotho (African people)—Medicine
Medicine, Psychosomatic
  [RC49-52]
  UF Psychosomatic medicine
      Somatopsychics
  BT Medicine and psychology
      Mind and body
      Neuroses
      Psychology, Pathological
  SA subdivision Diseases—Psychosomatic
      aspects under names of organs and
      regions of the body, e.g. Intestines
      —Diseases—Psychosomatic aspects;
      and subdivision Psychosomatic
      aspects under particular diseases,
      e.g. Tuberculosis—Psychosomatic
      aspects
  NT Consultation-liaison psychiatry
      Encopresis
      Enuresis
      Gynecology—Psychosomatic aspects
      Iatrogenic diseases
      Obstetrics—Psychosomatic aspects
      Pediatrics—Psychosomatic aspects
      Psychological manifestations of general
          diseases
      Puerperium—Psychological aspects
  — **Research** (May Subd Geog)
      [RC52]
      UF Psychosomatic research
Medicine, Roman
  USE Medicine, Greek and Roman
Medicine, Rural (May Subd Geog)
  UF Rural medicine
  RT Rural health
  NT Rural health services
  — **Practice**
      BT Medicine—Practice
Medicine, Scythian
  UF Scythian medicine
  BT Medicine, Ancient
Medicine, Shinto (May Subd Geog)
  [R135.8]
  UF Shinto medicine
Medicine, Siddha (May Subd Geog)
  UF Agasthya medicine
      Medicine, Agasthya
      Siddha medicine
  BT Medicine, Oriental
  — **Formulae, receipts, prescriptions**
Medicine, Social
  USE Social medicine
Medicine, Spagiric
  USE Medicine, Magic, mystic, and spagiric
Medicine, Sports
  USE Sports medicine
Medicine, State (May Subd Geog)
  [RA]
  UF Medical care, State
      Socialized medicine
      State medicine
  BT Medical policy
  RT Medicine, Preventive
      Public health
  NT Charities, Medical

Dentistry, State
Hospitals, Public
Medical jurisprudence
Quarantine
— **Great Britain**
  NT National Health Service (Great
      Britain)
Medicine, Submarine
  USE Submarine medicine
Medicine, Tibetan
  UF Tibetan medicine
  BT Medicine, Oriental
— **Formulae, receipts, prescriptions**
  [RS131.75.T]
Medicine, Transportation
  USE Transportation medicine
Medicine, Unani
  USE Medicine, Arabic
      Medicine, Greek and Roman
Medicine, Underwater
  USE Submarine medicine
Medicine, Veterinary
  USE Veterinary medicine
Medicine and art (May Subd Geog)
  [N8223]
  UF Art and medicine
      Doctors in art
      Medicine in art
      Physicians in art
  BT Art
      Art and science
      Medicine and the humanities
  RT Anatomy, Artistic
      Medical illustration
  NT Hospitals in art
      Physicians as artists
Medicine and communism
  USE Communism and medicine
Medicine and literature
  USE Literature and medicine
Medicine and psychology
  [R726.5]
  UF Behavioral medicine
      Psychology and medicine
  BT Psychology, Applied
  SA subdivision Psychological aspects
      under medical subjects, e.g. Cancer
      —Psychological aspects; Nursing—
      Psychological aspects
  NT Clinical health psychology
      Geriatrics—Psychological aspects
      Gynecology—Psychological aspects
      Health behavior
      Heart—Surgery—Psychological aspects
      Hospitals—Psychological aspects
      Isolation (Hospital care)—
          Psychological aspects
      Medicine, Psychosomatic
      Placebo (Medicine)
      Prescription writing—Psychological
          aspects
      Psychiatry
      Sick—Psychology
      Sick children—Psychology
      Youth—Diseases—Psychological
          aspects
Medicine and religion
  USE Medicine—Religious aspects
Medicine and sports
  USE Sports medicine
Medicine and state
  USE Medical policy
Medicine and the humanities
  BT Humanities
      Science and the humanities
  NT Literature and medicine
      Medicine and art
Medicine and war
  USE War—Medical aspects
Medicine-ball
  [GV1017.M5]

Medicine balls
  [GV496]
  BT Balls (Sporting goods)
Medicine bottles (May Subd Geog)
  BT Bottles
      Drugs—Packaging
Medicine bottles, Victorian
  (May Subd Geog)
  UF Victorian medicine bottles
Medicine Bow Mountains (Colo. and Wyo.)
  BT Front Range (Colo. and Wyo.)
      Mountains—Colorado
      Mountains—Wyoming
      Rocky Mountains
Medicine Bow National Forest (Wyo.)
  BT Forest reserves—Wyoming
      National parks and reserves—
          Wyoming
Medicine Creek Site (Or.) (Not Subd Geog)
  BT Oregon—Antiquities
Medicine in art
  USE Medicine and art
Medicine in literature
  [PN56.M]
  BT Literature and medicine
  RT Physicians in literature
  NT Pharmacy in literature
Medicine in television (May Subd Geog)
  UF Medicine on television
  BT Television
      Television programs
Medicine in the Bible
  [R135.5]
  UF Bible—Diseases
      Bible—Medicine
      Diseases in the Bible
  BT Medicine—Religious aspects
  NT Drugs in the Bible
      Healing in the Bible
Medicine in the Koran
  UF Koran—Medicine
  BT Medicine—Religious aspects—Islam
Medicine in the Talmud
  [R135.5]
  UF Diseases in the Talmud
      Talmud—Diseases
      Talmud—Medicine
  BT Medicine—Religious aspects—Judaism
      Medicine, Jewish
  RT Medical laws and legislation (Jewish
      law)
Medicine Lake National Wildlife Refuge
  (Mont.) (Not Subd Geog)
  BT National parks and reserves—Montana
      Wildlife refuges—Montana
Medicine Lake Wilderness (Mont.)
  (Not Subd Geog)
  BT National parks and reserves—Montana
      Wilderness areas—Montana
Medicine-man
  USE Shamans
Medicine men
  USE Shamans
Medicine on television
  USE Medicine in television
Medicine shows (May Subd Geog)
  [GV1801-1827]
  BT Peddlers and peddling
      Quacks and quackery
Medicine stamps (May Subd Geog)
  [HJ5315]
  UF Stamps, Medicine
  BT Revenue-stamps
Medicine women
  USE Shamans
Medicines, Patent, proprietary, etc.
  USE Patent medicines
Medicines, Specific
  [RS]
  UF Specific medicines

Medicolegal anthropology
  USE Forensic anthropology
Medicolegal audiology
  USE Forensic audiology
Medicolegal cardiology
  USE Forensic cardiology
Medicolegal dermatology
  USE Forensic dermatology
Medicolegal gynecology
  USE Forensic gynecology
Medicolegal hematology
  USE Forensic hematology
Medicolegal neurology
  USE Forensic neurology
Medicolegal neuropsychology
  USE Forensic neuropsychology
Medicolegal obstetrics
  USE Forensic obstetrics
Medicolegal oncology
  USE Forensic oncology
Medicolegal ophthalmology
  USE Forensic ophthalmology
Medicolegal osteology
  USE Forensic osteology
Medicolegal radiography
  USE Forensic radiography
Medicolegal serology
  USE Forensic serology
Medicolegal thermography
  USE Forensic thermography
Medicolegal toxicology
  USE Forensic toxicology
Medieval alabaster sculpture
  USE Alabaster sculpture—Medieval, 500-1500
Medieval altarpieces
  USE Altarpieces, Medieval
Medieval and modern Latin manuscripts
  USE Manuscripts, Latin (Medieval and modern)
Medieval art
  USE Art, Medieval
Medieval bookbinding
  USE Bookbinding, Medieval
Medieval bronze doors
  USE Bronze doors, Medieval
Medieval bronze fonts
  USE Bronze fonts, Medieval
Medieval busts
  USE Busts, Medieval
Medieval champlevé
  USE Champlevé, Medieval
Medieval Christian sects
  USE Christian sects, Medieval
Medieval church plate
  USE Church plate, Medieval
Medieval cities and towns
  USE Cities and towns, Medieval
Medieval cloisonné
  USE Cloisonné, Medieval
Medieval copperwork
  USE Copperwork, Medieval
Medieval cosmology
  USE Cosmology, Medieval
Medieval criticism
  USE Criticism, Medieval
Medieval decorative arts
  USE Decorative arts, Medieval
Medieval drawing
  USE Drawing, Medieval
Medieval ecclesiastical embroidery
  USE Ecclesiastical embroidery, Medieval
Medieval education of girls
  USE Women—Education, Medieval
Medieval education of nobility
  USE Nobility—Education, Medieval
Medieval education of women
  USE Women—Education, Medieval
Medieval enamel and enameling
  USE Enamel and enameling, Medieval

Medieval fiction
  USE Fiction, Medieval
Medieval furniture
  USE Furniture, Medieval
Medieval gardens
  USE Gardens, Medieval
Medieval glass underpainting
  USE Glass underpainting, Medieval
Medieval goldwork
  USE Goldwork, Medieval
Medieval Greece
  USE Greece—History—323-1453
Medieval history
  USE Middle Ages—History
Medieval ironwork
  USE Ironwork, Medieval
Medieval landscape painting
  USE Landscape painting, Medieval
Medieval learning and scholarship
  USE Learning and scholarship—History—Medieval, 500-1500
Medieval logic
  USE Logic, Medieval
Medieval majolica
  USE Majolica, Medieval
Medieval manuscripts
  USE Manuscripts, Medieval
Medieval marriage customs and rites
  USE Marriage customs and rites, Medieval
Medieval miniature painting
  USE Miniature painting, Medieval
Medieval music
  USE subdivisions 500-1400 and 15th century under music headings
      Music—500-1400
      Music—15th century
Medieval panel painting
  USE Panel painting, Medieval
Medieval period
  USE Middle Ages
Medieval philosophy
  USE Philosophy, Medieval
Medieval poetry
  USE Poetry, Medieval
Medieval portrait sculpture
  USE Portrait sculpture, Medieval
Medieval portraits
  USE Portraits, Medieval
Medieval prayers
  USE Prayers, Medieval
Medieval relief (Sculpture)
  USE Relief (Sculpture), Medieval
Medieval satire
  USE Satire, Medieval
Medieval ships
  USE Ships, Medieval
Medieval silver bowls
  USE Silver bowls, Medieval
Medieval silverwork
  USE Silverwork, Medieval
Medieval small sculpture
  USE Small sculpture, Medieval
Medieval textile fabrics
  USE Textile fabrics, Medieval
Medieval vaults (Architecture)
  USE Vaults (Architecture), Medieval
Medievalism (May Subd Geog)
  BT Civilization, Medieval
  RT Middle ages
Medievalists (May Subd Geog)
  BT Historians
      Middle Ages—Historiography
Medigap (May Subd Geog)
  [HD7101-HD7102]
      Here are entered works on insurance policies which pay all or part of the expenses for health care not covered by Medicare.

  UF Insurance, Medicare supplemental health
      Medi-gap
      Medicare supplemental health insurance
      Medigap—United States
      Supplemental health insurance to Medicare
  BT Insurance, Health—United States
  RT Medicare
  — **Law and legislation** (May Subd Geog)
      UF Medigap—Law and legislation—United States
      BT Insurance law—United States
  — — United States
        USE Medigap—Law and legislation
  — United States
      USE Medigap
Medimurje (Croatia)
  UF Medjimourie (Croatia)
      Medjimurje (Croatia)
      Medumurje (Croatia)
      Medzumurje (Croatia)
      Muraköz (Croatia)
      Murinsel (Croatia)
Medina, Battle of, Tex., 1813
  USE Medina River (Tex.), Battle of, 1813
Medina Az-Zahra (City)
  USE Medina Azahàra (City)
Medina Azahàra (City) (Not Subd Geog)
  [DP402.M15]
  UF Madīnat al-Zahrā' (City)
      Medina Az-Zahra (City)
      Medina Azzahara (City)
      Medina-Zahra (City)
  BT Cities and towns, Ruined, extinct, etc.—Spain
      Spain—Antiquities
Medina Azzahara (City)
  USE Medina Azahàra (City)
Medina Formation
  USE Medina Group
Medina Group (Not Subd Geog)
  UF Medina Formation
  BT Geology—Ontario
      Geology—United States
      Geology, Stratigraphic—Ordovician
      Geology, Stratigraphic—Silurian
Medina River (Tex.)
  BT Rivers—Texas
Medina River (Tex.), Battle of, 1813
  UF Encinal de Medina, Battle of, Tex., 1813
      First Texas Revolution, Tex., 1813
      Medina, Battle of, Tex., 1813
  BT Gutierrez-Magee Expedition, 1812-1813
Medina-Zahra (City)
  USE Medina Azahàra (City)
Medinet Madi Site (Egypt)
  [DT73.M35]
  UF Narmouthis (Ancient city)
  BT Cities and towns, Ruined, extinct, etc.—Egypt
      Egypt—Antiquities
Medinet Watfa (Egypt)
  USE Madīnat Wātifah, Kawm (Egypt)
Mediotarsal joint
  USE Chopart's joint
Medipest viruses
  BT Paramyxoviruses
  NT Canine distemper virus
      Rinderpest virus
Meditation
  [BL627 (Comparative religion)]
  [BV4813 (Christianity)]
      Here are entered works on mental prayer as a method of promoting the spiritual life. Collections of thoughts on spiritual truths for use in meditation are entered under Meditations.

UF Mental prayer
    Prayer, Mental
BT Prayer
    Spiritual life
RT Contemplation
NT Recollection (Theology)
    Transcendental Meditation
Meditation (Bonpo)
    [BQ7982.2]
BT Bonpo (Sect)
    Meditation (Buddhism)
NT Bonpo meditations
    Rdzogs-chen (Bonpo)
    Yoga (Bonpo)
Meditation (Buddhism)
UF Dhyāna (Meditation)
BT Buddhism
NT Ānāpānasmṛti
    Buddhist meditations
    Buddhist rosary
    Meditation (Bonpo)
    Meditation (Tantric Buddhism)
    Meditation (Zen Buddhism)
    Samadhi
    Śamatha (Buddhism)
    Satipaṭṭhāna (Buddhism)
    Vipaśyanā (Buddhism)
Meditation (Confucianism)
BT Confucianism
Meditation (Hinduism)
UF Dhyāna (Meditation)
BT Hinduism
    Yoga
NT Hindu meditations
    Om (Hinduism)
Meditation (Jainism)
BT Jainism
Meditation (Judaism)
NT Jewish meditations
Meditation (Tantric Buddhism)
BT Meditation (Buddhism)
Meditation (Taoism)
BT Taoism
NT Taoist meditations
Meditation (Zen Buddhism)
BT Meditation (Buddhism)
    Zen Buddhism
NT Koan
    Zen meditations
Meditation music
    USE Music for meditation
Meditations
    [BV4800-BV4870]
    [BX2177-BX2198 (Catholic Church)]
    Here are entered collections of thoughts on
    spiritual truths for use in meditation. Works on men-
    tal prayer as a method of promoting the spiritual life
    are entered under Meditation.
BT Devotional literature
SA subdivision Meditations under religious
    subjects, e.g. Bible—Meditations;
    Lord's Supper—Meditations
NT Bahai meditations
    Church year meditations
    Spiritual exercises
Meditations, Bahai
    USE Bahai meditations
Meditations, Bonpo
    USE Bonpo meditations
Meditations, Buddhist
    USE Buddhist meditations
Meditations, Hindu
    USE Hindu meditations
Meditations, Islamic
    USE Islamic meditations
Meditations, Jaina
    USE Jaina meditations
Meditations, Jewish
    USE Jewish meditations
Meditations, Muslim
    USE Islamic meditations

Meditations, Sufi
    USE Sufi meditations
Meditations, Taoist
    USE Taoist meditations
Meditations, Zen
    USE Zen meditations
Meditative music
    USE Minimal music
Mediterranean agreements, 1887
    [D397]
Mediterranean aloe
    USE Aloe barbadensis
Mediterranean anemia
    USE Thalassemia
Mediterranean climate
UF Mediterranean-type climate
BT Climatology
Mediterranean Coast (France)
BT Coasts—France
Mediterranean Coast (Spain)
BT Coasts—Spain
Mediterranean Coast (Turkey)
BT Coasts—Turkey
Mediterranean cookery
    USE Cookery, Mediterranean
Mediterranean disease
    USE Thalassemia
Mediterranean fever, Familial
    USE Periodic peritonitis
Mediterranean flour-moth
    [SB945.M5]
UF Mediterranean meal moth
BT Moths
Mediterranean fruit-fly
    [SB945.M54]
UF Medfly
BT Fruit-flies
Mediterranean meal moth
    USE Mediterranean flour-moth
Mediterranean monk seal
    [QL737.P64]
UF Monachus monachus
BT Monk seals
Mediterranean race
    [CB224 (Civilization)]
    [GN543]
UF Atlanto-Mediterranean race
    Ibero-Insular race
    Ligurian race
    Melanochroic race
BT Caucasian race
RT Latin peoples
NT Greeks
    Hamites
Mediterranean Region
UF Mediterranean Sea Region
— **Civilization**
    NT English literature—Mediterranean
        influences
        Great Britain—Civilization—
            Mediterranean influences
— **Description and travel**
— — **1981-**
— **Foreign relations**
— — **1945-**
— **Politics and government**
— — **1945-**
Mediterranean Region, Eastern
    USE Middle East
Mediterranean Region, Western
    USE Western Mediterranean
Mediterranean Sea
    NT Tyrrhenian Sea
Mediterranean Sea Region
    USE Mediterranean Region
Mediterranean-type climate
    USE Mediterranean climate
Mediterraneanpalm
    USE Chamaerops humilis
Medium format cameras
    [TR257]

Here are entered works on cameras which pro-
    duce images on film larger than 35mm but smaller
    than 2 1/4 x 3 1/4 sheet film.
UF Roll film cameras
BT Cameras
Medium-range weather forecasting
    USE Long-range weather forecasting
Medium scale integration of circuits
    USE Integrated circuits—Medium scale
        integration
Mediums *(May Subd Geog)*
    [BF1281]
BT Spiritualists
Medjerda River (Algeria and Tunisia)
UF Bagradas River (Algeria and Tunisia)
    Majardah River (Algeria and Tunisia)
    Medjerdah River (Algeria and Tunisia)
    Mejerda River (Algeria and Tunisia)
    Mejerdah River (Algeria and Tunisia)
BT Rivers—Algeria
    Rivers—Tunisia
Medjerdah River (Algeria and Tunisia)
    USE Medjerda River (Algeria and Tunisia)
Medjimourie (Croatia)
    USE Međimurje (Croatia)
Medjimurje (Croatia)
    USE Međimurje (Croatia)
Medkiff family
    USE Metcalf family
Medlar, Japanese
    USE Loquat
MEDLARS *(May Subd Geog)*
UF Medical Literature Analysis and
    Retrieval System
BT Information storage and retrieval
    systems—Medicine
NT MEDLINE
Medley relay (Swimming)
    USE Swimming, Medley
Medley swimming
    USE Swimming, Medley
Medleys, Musical
    USE Potpourris
MEDLINE
    [Z699.5.M39]
BT Library information networks
    MEDLARS
Medlock family
    USE Matlock family
Medlpa (Papua New Guinea people)
UF Hagen (Papua New Guinea people)
    Melpa (Papua New Guinea people)
    Moglei (Papua New Guinea people)
BT Ethnology—Papua New Guinea
NT Kawelka (New Guinea people)
Medlpa language
UF Hagen language
    Melpa language
    Moglei language
BT Papuan languages
Medma (Ancient city) *(Not Subd Geog)*
    [DG70.M43]
BT Cities and towns, Ruined, extinct, etc.
    —Italy
    Italy—Antiquities
Médoc (France)
Medow family
    USE Meadows family
Medows family
    USE Meadows family
Medraut
    USE Mordred
Medroxyprogesterone
UF Hydroxymethylpregnenedione
    Hydroxymethylprogesterone
    Methylhydroxyprogesterone
BT Hydroxyprogesterone
    Progestational hormones, Synthetic
Medulla oblongata
    [QL933 (Comparative anatomy)]
    [QM455 (Human anatomy)]

Medulla oblongata *(Continued)*
  ⌐QP377 (Physiology)¬
    BT Brain
        Nervous system
        Spinal cord
    NT Olivary nucleus
Medulla ossium
  USE Bone marrow
Medullary cone
  USE Conus medullaris
Medullary nailing
  USE Intramedullary fracture fixation
Medullary sheath (Nerve tissue)
  USE Myelin sheath
Medullated nerve fibers
  USE Myelinated neurofibrils
Medulloblastoma
  ⌐RC280.C¬
    BT Cerebellum—Tumors
        Gliomas
Medullosa noel
    BT Pteridospermae
Medumba language
    BT Bamileke languages
        Cameroon—Languages
Medumba proverbs
  USE Proverbs, Medumba
Međumurje (Croatia)
  USE Medimurje (Croatia)
Medusa (Computer system)
    BT Electronic data processing—
          Distributed processing
        Electronic digital computers—
          Programming
        Operating systems (Computers)
Medusa (Greek mythology)
    BT Mythology, Greek
Medusae
  ⌐QL375-9¬
    UF Jellyfish
    BT Coelenterata
    NT Hydromedusae
        Scyphozoa
Medusae, Fossil
  ⌐QE777-9¬
Medusahead (Weed)
  USE Medusahead wildrye
Medusahead wildrye *(May Subd Geog)*
  ⌐QK495.G74 (Botany)¬
  ⌐SB615.M38 (Weed)¬
    UF Elymus caput-medusae
        Medusahead (Weed)
        Medusa's head (Weed)
        Taeniatherum asperum
        Taeniatherum caput-medusae
        Wildrye, Medusahead
    BT Weeds
Medusa's head (Weed)
  USE Medusahead wildrye
**Medveditsa River (Kalininskaia oblast',
  R.S.F.S.R.)**
    UF Reka Medveditsa (Kalininskaia oblast',
          R.S.F.S.R.)
    BT Rivers—Russian S.F.S.R.
Medvednica Mountain (Croatia)
    BT Mountains—Yugoslavia
Medves Mountains (Hungary)
  (Not Subd Geog)
    BT Mountains—Hungary
Medway, River (England)
    UF River Medway (England)
    BT Rivers—England
Medworth family *(Not Subd Geog)*
Medzumurje (Croatia)
  USE Medimurje (Croatia)
MEE (Otolaryngology)
  USE Otitis media with effusion
Mee family *(Not Subd Geog)*
    UF Mey family
        Meye family

Meeans family
  USE Means family
Meech Lake (Québec)
    BT Lakes—Québec (Province)
Meecham family
  USE Meacham family
Meeck family
  USE Meeks family
Meecke family
  USE Meeks family
Meed family
  USE Mead family
Meeder family
  USE Meador family
Meeds family
  USE Mead family
Meegan family
  USE Meehan family
Meehan family *(Not Subd Geog)*
    UF Meegan family
        Mehan family
        Meigen family
        Meighan family
        Meighen family
        Meignan family
Meehanite metal
    BT Iron alloys
Meek family
  USE Meeks family
Meeke family
  USE Meeks family
Meeker family *(Not Subd Geog)*
    UF Meaker family
Meekness
  ⌐BV4647.M3 (Moral theology)¬
    UF Long-suffering
    RT Humility
Meeks family *(Not Subd Geog)*
    UF Meak family
        Meake family
        Meaks family
        Meeck family
        Meecke family
        Meek family
        Meeke family
Meeler family *(Not Subd Geog)*
    UF Mealer family
Meem family *(Not Subd Geog)*
Meen family
  USE Means family
Meenakshi (Hindu deity)
  USE Mīnākṣī (Hindu deity)
Meens family
  USE Means family
Meer, Van der family
  USE Vandermeer family
Meers family
  USE Mears family
Meerschaum *(May Subd Geog)*
  ⌐TN948.M5¬
    UF Sepiolite
    BT Silicates
Meerschaum tobacco-pipes
  USE Tobacco-pipes, Meerschaum
Mees family
  USE Meessen family
Meese family *(Not Subd Geog)*
Meess family
  USE Meessen family
Meessen family *(Not Subd Geog)*
    UF Mees family
        Meess family
Meessia
  ⌐QL561.T55¬
    BT Tineidae
Meeting-houses, Friends
  USE Churches, Quaker
Meeting-houses, Quaker
  USE Churches, Quaker
Meeting proceedings
  USE Conference proceedings

Meeting rooms
  USE Conference rooms
Meetings
    UF Business meetings
        Conferences
    BT Associations, institutions, etc.
        Congresses and conventions
        Social group work
    RT Discussion
        Leadership
    NT Committees
        Cooperative societies meetings
        Forums (Discussion and debate)
        Parliamentary practice
        Public meetings
        Religious gatherings
        Reunions
        Sales meetings
        Trade-union meetings
Meetings, Church
  USE Church meetings
Meetings, Corporate
  USE Corporate meetings
Meetings, Public
  USE Public meetings
Meetings, Religious
  USE Religious gatherings
Meetings, Stockholders'
  USE Stockholders' meetings
Meetings, Union
  USE Trade-union meetings
Meetings and the handicapped
  (May Subd Geog)
    BT Handicapped
Meetz family
  USE Metz family
Meetze family
  USE Metz family
Meewoc Indians
  USE Miwok Indians
Mefenamic acid
    UF Dimethylphenylaminobenzoic acid
        Xylylanthranilic acid
    BT Aminobenzoic acids
        Analgesics
        Nonsteroidal anti-inflammatory agents
Mefferd family
  USE Meffert family
Meffert family *(Not Subd Geog)*
    UF Mefferd family
        Mefford family
Mefford family
  USE Meffert family
Mefitis (Roman deity)
    BT Gods, Roman
Megacephala
  ⌐QL596.C56¬
    BT Cicindelidae
Megacephalidae
  USE Carabidae
Megaceroides
  USE Megaloceros
Megaceros
  USE Megaloceros
Megacerus *(May Subd Geog)*
  ⌐QL596.B7¬
    BT Bruchidae
Megaceryl alcyon
  USE Belted kingfisher
Megachile
  ⌐QL568.M4¬
    BT Megachilidae
Megachilidae
  ⌐QL568.M4¬
    UF Leafcutting bees
        Stelididae
    BT Bees
        Hymenoptera
    NT Coelioxys
        Dioxys
        Hoplitis

Megachile
Osmia
Parafidelia
Megacolon
[RC862.M35]
BT Colon (Anatomy)—Diseases
NT Hirschsprung's disease
Megacolon, Congenital
USE Hirschsprung's disease
Megacyllene robiniae
USE Locust-borer
Megakaryocytes
BT Bone marrow cells
NT Blood platelets
Megalaima
[QL696.P53]
BT Capitonidae
NT Megalaima virens
Megalaima virens
[QL696.P53]
UF Great barbet
BT Megalaima
Megalithic monuments *(May Subd Geog)*
[GN791-2]
UF Cyclopean remains
BT Man, Prehistoric
Monuments
Religion, Prehistoric
NT Cromlechs
Dolmens
Menhirs
— **Europe**
NT Passage Graves culture
— **Ireland**
— **Portugal**
Megalobatrachus
[QL668.C24]
BT Cryptobranchidae
Megalobatrachus japonicus
[QL668.C24]
UF Cryptobranchus maximus
Giant salamander
Megalobatrachus maximus
Megalobatrachus maximus
USE Megalobatrachus japonicus
Megaloblastic anemia
BT Anemia
Megaloceros
[QE882.U3]
UF Dolichodoryceros
Elk, Irish
Irish Elk
Megaceroides
Megaceros
Orthogonoceros
Sinomegaceroides
Sinomegacerus
BT Deer, Fossil
Megalodontacea
[QE812.M48]
BT Hippuritoida
Megalomania
[RC553.M43]
UF Delusions of grandeur
Grandeur, Delusions of
BT Hallucinations and illusions
Paranoia
Megalophrys
USE Megophrys
Megalopidae
[QL638.M33]
BT Elopiformes
NT Megalops
Megalopidae (Insects)
USE Anthribidae
Megalopolis (Ancient city) *(Not Subd Geog)*
[DF261.M4]
BT Cities and towns, Ruined, extinct, etc.
—Greece
Greece—Antiquities

Megalops
[QL638.M33]
BT Megalopidae
Megalops atlantica
USE Tarpon
Megalops cyprinoides
USE Oxeye tarpon
Megaloptera
USE Neuroptera
Megalosauridae
[QE862.S3]
BT Saurischia
NT Allosaurus
Dilophosaurus
Megalosporaceae
[QK585.M44]
BT Lecanorales
Megalothorax
[QL503.N4]
BT Neelidae
Meganomia
[QL568.M46]
BT Melittidae
Mégantic, Lake (Québec)
UF Lac Mégantic (Québec)
Lake Mégantic (Québec)
BT Lakes—Québec (Province)
Meganutrition
USE Orthomolecular therapy
Megaoryzomys
[QE882.R6]
BT Muridae, Fossil
Megaoryzomys curioi
[QE882.R6]
Megaphone
USE Speaking-trumpet
Megaphorus
USE Mallophora
Megapleuron
[QE852.D5]
BT Sagenodontidae
Megapleuron rochei
[QE852.D5]
Megapleuron zangerli
[QE852.D5]
Megapodes
USE Megapodiidae
Megapodiidae
[QL696.G25]
UF Brush turkeys
Megapodes
BT Galliformes
NT Leipoa
Talegalla
Megaptera nodosa
USE Humpback whale
Megaptera novaeangliae
USE Humpback whale
Megara Hyblaea (Ancient city)
[DG70.M44]
BT Cities and towns, Ruined, extinct, etc.
—Italy
Italy—Antiquities
Megarhinus
[QL536]
BT Mosquitoes
Megarhyssa
[QL568.I2]
BT Ichneumonidae
Megarian bowls *(May Subd Geog)*
UF Bowls, Megarian
BT Pottery, Hellenistic
Megarians (Greek philosophy)
[B285]
UF Eristics (Greek philosophy)
BT Philosophy, Ancient
Megarthroglossus
[QL599.7.H9]
BT Hystrichopsyllidae
Megascelidae
USE Chrysomelidae

Megascolecidae
[QL391.A6]
BT Opisthopora
NT Diplocardia
Diporochaeta
Megascolides
Metapheretima
Microscolex
Pheretima
Plutellus
Megascolides
[QL391.A6]
BT Megascolecidae
Megaselia
[QL537.P46]
UF Aphiochaeta
BT Phoridae
NT Megaselia ventralis
Megaselia ventralis *(May Subd Geog)*
[QL537.P46]
BT Megaselia
Megastructures *(May Subd Geog)*
[NA9053.M43]
Here are entered works on very large, adaptable,
multipurpose buildings containing most of the func-
tions of a city.
BT Architecture, Modern—20th century
City planning
Joint occupancy of buildings
Metabolism in architecture
(Movement)
Megathripidae
USE Phlaeothripidae
Megathymidae
[QL561.M42]
UF Skippers (Butterflies)
BT Butterflies
Lepidoptera
NT Megathymus
Megathymus
[QL561.M42]
BT Megathymidae
Megathymus coloradensis
[QL561.M]
Megathymus streckeri
[QL561.M42]
Megathymus texanus
[QL561.M42]
Megathymus ursus
[QL561.M42]
Megatomidae
USE Dermestidae
Megatrons
USE Disk-seal tubes
Megavitamin therapy
USE Orthomolecular therapy
Megavolt radiotherapy
USE Radiotherapy, High energy
Megaw family
USE McGaw family
Megeb dialect
BT Dagestanskaĭa A.S.S.R. (R.S.F.S.R.)—
Languages
Dargwa language
Megee family
USE Magee family
Megehee family
USE Magee family
Meghakumāra (Legendary character)
BT Legends, Jaina
Megi language
USE Sagara language
Megiddo (Ancient city) *(Not Subd Geog)*
[DS110.M4]
UF Megido (Ancient city)
Mutasallim, Tall al- (Israel)
Mutasallim, Tell el- (Israel)
Tall al-Mutasallim (Israel)
Tel Megiddo (Israel)
Tel Megido (Israel)
Tell el-Mutesellim (Israel)

Megiddo (Ancient city) *(Continued)*
    BT Cities and towns, Ruined, extinct, etc.
        —Israel
        Israel—Antiquities
Megiddo, Battle of, 1479 B.C.
    ⌐DT86¬
    BT Egypt—History—To 332 B.C.
Megido (Ancient city)
    USE Megiddo (Ancient city)
Megil family
    USE McGill family
Megili language
    USE Migili language
Megill family
    USE McGill family
Megimba (African people)
    USE Ngemba (African people)
Megimba language
    USE Ngemba language (Cameroon)
Megísti (Greece)
    USE Kastellorizo Island (Greece)
Megistopoda
    ⌐QL537.S86¬
    BT Streblidae
Megistopoda aranea
    ⌐QL537.S86¬
Megley family
    USE Megli family
Megli family *(Not Subd Geog)*
    UF Megley family
        Meglin family
        Moeglin family
        Moegling family
Meglin family
    USE Megli family
Megophrys
    ⌐QL668.E262¬
    UF Megalophrys
    BT Pelobatidae
Megophthalmidae
    USE Leafhoppers
Megowen family
    USE McGowan family
Megpunna
    ⌐DS422.M5¬
    BT Brigands and robbers
Megrelians
    USE Mingrelians
Megupsilon
    ⌐QL638.C96¬
    BT Cyprinodontidae
Megupsilon aporus
    ⌐QL638.C96¬
Mehaffey family
    USE Mahaffey family
Mehaffie family
    USE Mahaffey family
Mehaffy family
    USE Mahaffey family
Mehagen family *(Not Subd Geog)*
Mehan family
    USE Meehan family
Mehedenţi Mountains (Romania)
    UF Munţii Mehedenţi (Romania)
    BT Mountains—Romania
Meherrin River (Va. and N.C.)
    BT Rivers—North Carolina
        Rivers—Virginia
Mehinacu Indians
    ⌐F2520.1.M44¬
    UF Mehinkaku Indians
        Minaco Indians
    BT Indians of South America
        Indians of South America—Brazil
Mehinkaku Indians
    USE Mehinacu Indians

Mehlem family *(Not Subd Geog)*
Mehlem Haus (Beuel, Bonn, Germany)
    UF Mehlem House (Beuel, Bonn,
        Germany)
        Mehlem'sches Haus (Beuel, Bonn,
        Germany)
    BT Dwellings—Germany (West)
Mehlem House (Beuel, Bonn, Germany)
    USE Mehlem Haus (Beuel, Bonn, Germany)
Mehlem'sches Haus (Beuel, Bonn, Germany)
    USE Mehlem Haus (Beuel, Bonn, Germany)
Mehlhaff family *(Not Subd Geog)*
Mehn family
    USE Main family
Mehre (Indic people)
    USE Buxas (Indic people)
Mehre language
    USE Mahri language
Mei chu han ch'in t'u (Fan painting)
    USE Lin, Ch'un, 12th/13th cent. Bird on
        snowy plum blossoms and bamboo
Meibomia
    USE Desmodium
Meibomian glands
    UF Tarsal glands
    BT Eyelids
Meiborg family *(Not Subd Geog)*
    UF Maiborg family
Meichsel family
    USE Mikesell family
Meid family
    USE Mead family
Meidoo Indians
    USE Maidu Indians
Meier family
    USE Myers family
Meigen family
    USE Meehan family
Meighan family
    USE Meehan family
Meighen family
    USE Meehan family
Meignan family
    USE Meehan family
Meiji Restoration
    USE Japan—History—Restoration, 1853-
        1870
Meiji Seika Group
    BT Conglomerate corporations—Japan
Meikle family *(Not Subd Geog)*
Meilahn family *(Not Subd Geog)*
    UF Meilan family
        Meilen family
        Miglan family
Meilan family
    USE Meilahn family
Meilen family
    USE Meilahn family
Meili family
    USE Mylin family
Meilland family *(Not Subd Geog)*
Mein family
    USE Means family
Meincke family *(Not Subd Geog)*
Meiner family
    USE Meiners family
Meiners family *(Not Subd Geog)*
    UF Meiner family
        Meyner family
        Meyners family
    RT Meinhardt family
Meinert family
    USE Meinhardt family
Meinerte family
    USE Meinhardt family
Meinerts family
    USE Meinhardt family
Meinertz family
    USE Meinhardt family
Meinhard family
    USE Meinhardt family

Meinhardt family *(Not Subd Geog)*
    UF Meinert family
        Meinerte family
        Meinerts family
        Meinertz family
        Meinhard family
        Meinhart family
    RT Meiners family
Meinhart family
    USE Meinhardt family
Meinhold family
    USE Meinholz family
Meinholtz family
    USE Meinholz family
Meinholz family *(Not Subd Geog)*
    UF Meinhold family
        Meinholtz family
Meiocarpidium
    ⌐QK495.A6¬
    BT Annonaceae
Meiocarpidium lepidotum
    ⌐QK495.A6 (Botany)¬
Meiosis
    ⌐QH605¬
    UF Reduction division (Genetics)
    BT Cell division
    RT Karyokinesis
    NT Spindle (Cell division)
Meischer family
    USE Meisser family
Meiser family
    USE Meisser family
Meissen porcelain
    ⌐NK4380¬
    UF Porcelain, Meissen
    RT Dresden porcelain
Meissen stoneware
    USE Böttger ware
Meisser family *(Not Subd Geog)*
    UF Meischer family
        Meiser family
        Miser family
        Mizar family
        Mizer family
        Myser family
        Myzer family
Meissner Mountain (Germany)
    UF Hohenmeisner (Germany)
        Hoher Meissner (Germany)
    BT Mountains—Germany (West)
Meistersinger
    ⌐ML183 (Music)¬
    ⌐PT245 (Literature)¬
    BT Bards and bardism
        Minstrels
        Poets
    RT Minnesingers
Meiteis (Indic people)
    USE Meitheis (Indic people)
Meitetsu
    USE Nagoya Tetsudō
Meithei language
    USE Manipuri language
Meithei mythology
    USE Mythology, Meithei
Meitheis (Indic people)
    ⌐DS432.M33¬
    UF Manipuri (Indic people)
        Meiteis (Indic people)
    BT Ethnology—India
Meixel family
    USE Mikesell family
Meixell family
    USE Mikesell family
Meixsel family
    USE Mikesell family
Meixwill family
    USE Maxwell family
Méjannes-le-Clap Plateau (France)
    (Not Subd Geog)
    UF Plateau de Méjannes-le-Clap (France)

BT Plateaus—France
Mejbrat (Papuan people)
USE Mejprat (Papuan people)
Mejerda River (Algeria and Tunisia)
USE Medjerda River (Algeria and Tunisia)
Mejerdah River (Algeria and Tunisia)
USE Medjerda River (Algeria and Tunisia)
Mejillones, Bay of, Battle of, 1879
BT War of the Pacific, 1879-1884—
Campaigns—Chile
Mejora *(May Subd Geog)*
BT Inheritance and succession
Legacies
Legitime
Wills
Mejprat (Papuan people)
UF Mejbrat (Papuan people)
BT Ethnology—Indonesia
Papuans
Mekamah
USE Maqamah, Hebrew
Mekeo (Papua New Guinea people)
[DU740.42]
UF Bush Mekeo (Papua New Guinea
people)
BT Ethnology—Papua New Guinea
Mekhadma
[DT346.M4]
BT Ethnology—Sahara
Mekhiṭarists
[BX3795.M6]
Meklong River (Thailand)
USE Mae Klong River (Thailand)
Mekong River
UF Dza-chu
Lan-ts'ang Chiang
Lancang Jiang
Mae Nam Khong
Mékôngk
Mènam Khong
Song Tiên Giang
BT Rivers—Asia
Mékôngk
USE Mekong River
Mekranoti Indians
BT Cayapo Indians
Indians of South America
Mekusuky language
USE Mikasuki language
Mel Mountains (Rio Grande do Norte, Brazil)
(Not Subd Geog)
UF Serra do Mel (Rio Grande do Norte,
Brazil)
BT Mountains—Brazil
Melaena
[RC862]
BT Intestines—Diseases
Melaleuca
[QK495.M9 (Botany)]
UF Bottlebrush tea trees
Honey myrtles
Honeymyrtles
Paperbark trees
Swamp tea trees
Tea trees, Bottlebrush
Tea trees, Swamp
BT Myrtaceae
Melaleuca quinquenervia
[QK495.M9 (Botany)]
[SB615.M39 (Weed)]
UF Cajeput tree
Punk tree
Melalophidae
USE Notodontidae
Melamphaidae *(May Subd Geog)*
[QL638.M34]
UF Big-scale fishes
Bigscales (Fishes)
BT Beryciformes
Melampsora lini
USE Flax rust

Melampus (Greek mythology)
[BL820.M39]
BT Mythology, Greek
Melanalophidae
USE Geometridae
Melanargia
[QL561.S3]
BT Satyridae
Melanau (Malaysian people)
[DS597.367.M44]
BT Ethnology—Malaysia
Melancholia
USE Depression, Mental
Manic-depressive psychoses
Melancholy
UF Dejection
BT Emotions
RT Depression, Mental
Sadness
NT Homesickness
Melancholy in literature
Melanconiaceae
UF Melanconiales
NT Colletotrichum
Entomosporium
Gloeosporium
Melanconiales
USE Melanconiaceae
Melanconidaceae
[QK623.M38 (Botany)]
BT Diaporthales
NT Melanconis
Prosthecium
Melanconis
BT Melanconidaceae
Melanerpes
[QL696.P56]
UF Asyndesmus
BT Picidae
Woodpeckers
Melanerpes carolinus
USE Red-bellied woodpecker
Melanerpes herminieri
USE Guadelupe woodpecker
Melanerpes lewis
USE Lewis woodpecker
Melanerpes radiolatus
USE Jamaican woodpecker
Melanerpes striatus
USE Hispaniola woodpecker
Melanesia
BT Islands of the Pacific
Oceania
NT Bismarck Archipelago (Papua New
Guinea)
New Guinea
Melanesian art
USE Art, Melanesian
Melanesian imprints *(May Subd Geog)*
Melanesian languages *(May Subd Geog)*
[PL6201-PL6209]
Here are entered works on the Austronesian lan-
guages of Melanesia.
BT Austronesian languages
Oceania—Languages
Oceanic languages
Proto-Oceanic language
NT Ajie language
Ambrym language
Aneityum language
Anesu language
Aragure language
Areare language
Arosi language
Atchin language
Atsera language
Bambatana language
Big Nambas language
Buang language
Bugotu language
Bwaidoga language

Camuhi language
Dehu language
Dobu language
Dumbea language
Efate language
Eromanga language
Fijian language
Fiu language
Florida language
Gedaged language
Halia language
Hiri Motu language
Hula language
Iai language
Iamalele language
Jabim language
Kapone language
Kiriwinian language
Kuanua language
Kwaio language
Lusi language
Malu language (Solomon Islands)
Manam language
Mandegusu language
Misima language
Misima-Panayati language
Mono language
Mota language
Motu language
Mukawa language
Muyuw language
Nakanai language
Nemi language
Nenema language
Nengone language
Nguna language
Nogugu language
Nufor language
Paama language
Paici language
Pala language
Panayati language
Patep language
Petats language
Ponape language
Port Sandwich language
Roro language (New Guinea)
Rotuman language
Roviana language
Saa language
Sakau language
Sissano language
Suau language
Tanga language (Tanga Islands)
Tanna language
Teop language
Tigak language
Tubetube language
Ubir language
Ulawa language
Uripiv language
Vaturanga language
Wedau language
Melanesian mythology
USE Mythology, Melanesian
Melanesian pidgin English
USE Tok Pisin language
Melanesian poetry *(May Subd Geog)*
Melanesians *(May Subd Geog)*
BT Ethnology—Melanesia
Oceanians
NT Baegu (Melanesian people)
Gunantuna (Melanesian people)
Kalauna (Papua New Guinea people)
Kwaio (Melanesian people)
Lakalai (Melanesian people)
Mandak (Papua New Guinea people)
Massim (Melanesian people)
Me'udana (Melanesian people)
Pala (Melanesian people)
Rotumans

Melanesians *(Continued)*
    Solomon Islanders
    Tangas (Melanesian people)
    Wola (Papua New Guinea people)
Melanges (Petrology)
    [QE471.15.M44]
    BT Rocks, Sedimentary
Melanin
    BT Animal pigments
        Plant pigments
    RT Melanism
        Melanocytes
        Melanosis
  — Synthesis
      UF Melanogenesis
      BT Biosynthesis
Melanin-synthesizing cells
    USE Melanocytes
Melanism
    BT Color of animals
        Color of man
    RT Melanin
    NT Industrial melanism
Melanitta nigra
    USE Common scoter
Melanoblastoma
    BT Cancer
Melanochroic race
    USE Mediterranean race
Melanocyte stimulating hormone
    USE Intermedin
Melanocytes
    UF Melanin-synthesizing cells
    BT Epithelial cells
    RT Melanin
    NT Melanophores
Melanodidae
    USE Carabidae
Melanogenesis
    USE Melanin—Synthesis
Melanogrammus aeglefinus
    USE Haddock
Melanoma
    [RC262]
    BT Cancer
        Tumors
Melanophila
    [QL596.B8]
    BT Buprestidae
    NT Melanophila californica
        Melanophila fulvoguttata
Melanophila californica
    [QL596.B8]
    UF California flatheaded borer
    BT Melanophila
        Pine—Diseases and pests
Melanophila fulvoguttata
    [QL596.B8]
    UF Hemlock borer
    BT Eastern hemlock—Diseases and pests
        Melanophila
Melanophores
    BT Chromatophores
        Melanocytes
    NT Color of animals
Melanophryniscus
    [QL668.E227]
    BT Bufonidae
Melanophthalmidae
    USE Lathridiidae
Melanoplus
    [QL508.A2]
    BT Acrididae
    NT Melanoplus bilituratus
        Melanoplus differentialis
Melanoplus bilituratus
    [QL508.A2]
    BT Melanoplus
Melanoplus differentialis *(May Subd Geog)*
    [QL508.A2]
    UF Differential grasshopper

    BT Melanoplus
Melanoplus spretus
    USE Rocky Mountain locust
Melanosis
    [RL790]
    BT Color of animals
        Pigmentation disorders
    RT Melanin
Melanostomiatidae
    USE Melanostomiidae
Melanostomiidae
    [QL638.M3573]
    UF Black dragonfishes, Scaleless
        Dragonfishes, Scaleless
        Dragonfishes, Scaleless black
        Melanostomiatidae
        Scaleless black dragonfishes
        Scaleless dragonfishes
    BT Salmoniformes
    NT Eustomias
        Photonectes
Melanotekite *(May Subd Geog)*
    BT Silicates
Melanotropin
    USE Intermedin
Melaphyre
    [QE461]
Melasidae
    USE Eucnemidae
Melastomaceae
    USE Melastomataceae
Melastomataceae *(May Subd Geog)*
    [QK495.M514]
    UF Melastomaceae
    BT Myrtales
    NT Dactylocladus
        Monochaetum
        Osbeckia
        Votomita
Melatonin
    [QP572.M44 (Biochemistry)]
    UF Acetylmethoxytryptamine
        Methoxyindolylethylacetamide
    BT Pineal body
        Tryptamine
Melayu (Asian people)
    USE Malays (Asian people)
Melbourne and Metropolitan Board of Works Farm (Werribee, Vic.)
    UF M.M.B.W. Farm (Werribee, Vic.)
    BT Farms—Australia
Melbourne Cemetery, Old (Melbourne, Vic.)
    USE Old Melbourne Cemetery (Melbourne, Vic.)
Melbourne Cup (Horse race)
    [SF357.M]
Melbourne Hunt
    [SK287.M]
    BT Fox-hunting
Melcer family *(Not Subd Geog)*
Melchett family *(Not Subd Geog)*
    RT Mond family
Melchite Byzantine rite (Catholic Church)
    USE Catholic Church—Byzantine rite, Melchite
Melchizedek Priesthood (Mormon Church)
    [BX8659.6]
    BT Mormon Church
        Priesthood
    RT Aaronic Priesthood (Mormon Church)
    NT Patriarchs (Mormon theology)
Meldol family
    USE Mendall family
Meldon, Eng., Battle of, 991
    BT Great Britain—History—Ethelred II, 979-1016
Mele-Fila language
    [PL6475]
    UF Fila language
        Mele language
    BT Polynesian languages

Mele language
    USE Mele-Fila language
Meleager (Greek mythology)
  — Art
Meleager and Atalanta (Tapestry)
    BT Tapestry—Egypt
Melebuganon language *(May Subd Geog)*
    UF Milebuganon language
        Molbog language
    BT Philippine languages
        Philippines—Languages
Melegnano, Battle of, 1515
    BT Milan (Italy)—History—To 1535
Melegueta pepper
    USE Grains of paradise
Melendy family *(Not Subd Geog)*
    UF Malinda family
        Melinda family
        Melindy family
        Mellendy family
        Melody family
Meleoma
    [QL513.C5]
    BT Chrysopidae
Meles *(May Subd Geog)*
    [QL737.C25]
    BT Badgers
        Mustelidae
    NT Old World badger
Meles meles
    USE Old World badger
Meletin
    USE Quercetin
Meletski Tatars
    USE Chulyma Tatars
Melia
    [QK495.M52]
    BT Meliaceae
Melia azadirachta
    USE Margosa
Melia indica
    USE Margosa
Melia parviflora
    USE Margosa
Meliaceae
    [QK495.M52]
    BT Rutales
    NT Cedrela
        Chisocheton
        Entandrophragma
        Khaya
        Melia
        Trichilia
Meliandra
    USE Votomita
Melianthaceae
    [QK495.M524 (Botany)]
    BT Sapindales
    NT Melianthus
Melianthus
    [QK495.M524 (Botany)]
    BT Melianthaceae
Melicete Indians
    USE Malecite Indians
Meligethes
    [QL596.N58]
    BT Nitidulidae
Melilite
    BT Feldspathoid
        Silicates
    NT Akermanite
Melilot
    USE Sweet clover
Melilot, White
    USE White sweet clover
Melilotus
    USE Sweet clover
Melilotus alba
    USE White sweet clover
Melinae
    USE Badgers

Melinda family
  USE Melendy family
Melindy family
  USE Melendy family
Melinite
  [TP290.L8]
  BT Explosives
      Explosives, Military
Melioidosis
  [RC168.M45]
  UF Malleoidosis
  BT Glanders
Melioration of land
  USE Reclamation of land
Meliphagidae
  USE Honey eaters
Melipona
  [QL568.M456]
  BT Stingless bees
Melipona marginata
  [QL568.M456]
Meliponidae
  USE Stingless bees
Melitaea
  [QL561.N9]
  BT Nymphalidae
Melitoma
  [QL568.A53]
  BT Anthophoridae
Melitopol, Battle of, 1943
  BT World War, 1939-1945—Campaigns—
      Ukraine
Melittidae
  [QL568.M46]
  BT Hymenoptera
  NT Macropis
      Meganomia
Mellahs
  USE Jews—Morocco
Mellan Fryken Lake (Sweden)
  USE Frykensjöarna (Sweden)
Melle (France : Region)
  UF Mellois (France)
      Pays de Melle (France)
      Pays Mellois (France)
Mellein (The Greek word)
  BT Greek language—Etymology
Mellendy family
  USE Melendy family
Mellenthin family (Not Subd Geog)
Mellerio family (Not Subd Geog)
Mellet family
  USE Mallett family
Mellett family
  USE Mallett family
Mellin-Barnes functions, Generalized
  USE Fox's H-function
Mellin operators
  UF Operators, Mellin
  BT Operator theory
Mellin transform
  [QA432]
  UF Transform, Mellin
  BT Integral transforms
Mellingen family (Not Subd Geog)
Mellinidae
  USE Sphecidae
Mellois (France)
  USE Melle (France : Region)
Mellophone
  USE Alto horn
Mellorine
  BT Desserts, Frozen
Melo family, Guilherme de
  USE Guilherme de Melo family
Melocactus
  [QK495.C11]
  BT Cactus
Melocactus actinacanthus
  [QK495.C11]

Melochia
  [QK495.S8]
  BT Sterculiaceae
Melodeon (Button-key accordion)
  [MT681 (Instruction)]
  BT Button-key accordions
Melodeon (Reed organ)
  USE Reed-organ
Melodic analysis
  UF Analysis, Melodic
      Music—Melodic analysis
  BT Melody
      Musical analysis
Melodic dictation
  USE Musical dictation
Melodica
  [ML980]
  UF Scaletta
Melodrama
  [ML2050 (History)]
  [ML3861 (Music: aesthetics)]
  [PN1910-PN1919 (Literature)]
  BT Drama
      Music
      Opera
      Operetta
      Theater
Melody
  [ML440 (History)]
  [ML3834 (Psychology)]
  [ML3851 (Aesthetics)]
  [MT47 (Instruction)]
  BT Composition (Music)
      Harmony
      Music
      Music—Theory
  NT Melodic analysis
      Raga
Melody books
  USE Musical books
Melody family
  USE Melendy family
Melody flute
  BT Flageolet
      Penny whistle
Melody instrument music
  USE Unspecified instrument *used as part of
      the specification of medium in
      headings, e.g.* Sextets (Unspecified
      instruments (6)); Suites (Piano,
      unspecified instruments (2)); *also,*
      Duets, *with instrumental
      specification*
      Brass instrument music
      Solo instrument music
      String instrument music
      Wind instrument music
      Woodwind instrument music
Melody instruments
  USE *headings for melody instruments, e.g.*
      Flute; Recorder (Musical
      instrument); Violin
Meloe
  [QL596.M38]
  BT Meloidae
Melograph
  USE Music-recorders
Meloidae
  [QL596.M38]
  UF Blister beetles
      Cerocomatidae
      Horiinidae
      Lyttidae
      Tetraonycidae
  BT Beetles
  NT Cylindrothorax
      Epicauta
      Hornia
      Lytta
      Meloe
      Tricrania

Meloidogyne (May Subd Geog)
  [QL391.N4 (Nematology)]
  [SB998.M45 (Plant pests)]
  BT Nematoda
      Plant nematodes
      Root-knot
Meloidogyne incognita
  [QL391.N4 (Nematology)]
  [SB998.M45 (Plant pests)]
Melolontha
  USE Cockchafers
Melolonthidae
  USE Scarabaeidae
Melon, Snake
  USE Trichosanthes anguina
Melon, Tree
  USE Papaya
Melon fly
  [QL537.T42 (General)]
  [SB608.M4 (Pest)]
  UF Bactrocera cucurbitae
      Dacus cucurbitae
Melon-headed whale
  USE Lagenorhynchus electra
Melone family
  USE Malone family
Melons (May Subd Geog)
  [SB339]
  NT Cookery (Melons)
      Muskmelon
      Watermelons
Melos Island (Greece)
  UF Milo Island (Greece)
      Nísos Mílos (Greece)
  BT Cyclades (Greece)
      Islands—Greece
Melospiza melodia
  USE Song-sparrows
Melot family
  USE Mallett family
Melott family
  USE Mallett family
Melpa (Papua New Guinea people)
  USE Medlpa (Papua New Guinea people)
Melpa language
  USE Medlpa language
Melsom family (Not Subd Geog)
  RT Melson family
Melson family (Not Subd Geog)
  RT Melsom family
Melt extrusion
  USE Melt spinning
Melt spinning
  UF Melt extrusion
  BT Metals—Extrusion
      Spinning
  NT Metal fibers
Melting
  USE Fusion
Melting, Plasma arc
  USE Plasma arc melting
Melting points
  [QD518]
  BT Chemistry, Physical and theoretical
      Temperature
      Thermochemistry
  RT Solidification
  NT Ablation (Aerothermodynamics)
      Eutectics
Melton family
  USE Milton family
MELTS (Computer system)
  UF Mechanical Engineering Laboratory's
      Turning System
  BT Electronic digital computers—
      Programming
      Lathes—Numerical control
      Metal-work—Data processing
Melugin family (Not Subd Geog)
  UF Malugen family
      Malugin family

Melugin family *(Continued)*
  RT Mulligan family
Melungeons
  UF Malungeons
  BT Afro-Americans—Appalachian Region
      Ethnology—Appalachian Region
      Indians of North America—Mixed
        bloods
      Mulattoes
Melusine (Legendary character)
  BT Fairies
      Folklore—France
      Metamorphosis—Folklore
      Serpents—Folklore
Melusinidae
  USE Simuliidae
Melven family
  USE Melvin family
Melvill family
  USE Melville family
Melville, Lake (Nfld.)
  UF Lake Melville (Nfld.)
  BT Lakes—Newfoundland
Melville family *(Not Subd Geog)*
  UF Melvill family
Melville Island (N.W.T.)
  BT Arctic Archipelago (N.W.T.)
      Islands—Northwest Territories
      Queen Elizabeth Islands (N.W.T.)
Melville Sound (N.W.T.)
  USE Viscount Melville Sound (N.W.T.)
Melvin family *(Not Subd Geog)*
  UF Melven family
MELVYL (Information retrieval system)
  BT Information storage and retrieval
      systems
Melyridae
  ⌜QL596.M43⌝
  UF Dasytidae
      Malachiidae
      Prionoceridae
      Rhadalidae
  BT Beetles
  NT Malachius
MEM-SIM (Computer program)
  BT Computer programs
      Digital computer simulation
Mema Plain (Mali)
  BT Plains—Mali
Memaloh (Indonesian people)
  USE Maloh (Indonesian people)
Memba language
  ⌜PL4001.M37⌝
  BT Tibeto-Burman languages
Members, Angle
  USE Angles (Structural members)
Members of Congress (United States)
  USE Legislators—United States
Members of Congress (United States House of
  Representatives)
  USE Legislators—United States
      United States. Congress. House
Members of Congress (United States Senate)
  USE Legislators—United States
Membership
  USE *subdivision* Membership *under types of*
      corporate bodies and names of
      individual corporate bodies for
      works on the conditions of
      belonging to those organizations,
      e.g. Young Men's Christian
      associations—Membership; Catholic
      Church—Membership
Membership, Church
  USE Church membership
Membership campaigns
  UF Campaigns, Membership
      Drives, Membership
      Membership drives
  BT Associations, institutions, etc.
      Societies

Membership corporations
  USE Corporations, Nonprofit
Membership drives
  USE Membership campaigns
Membracidae
  ⌜QL527.M45⌝
  UF Treehoppers
  BT Homoptera
      Planthoppers
  NT Amastris
      Entylia
Membrana decidua
  USE Decidua
Membrana propria
  USE Membrane, Basement
Membrane, Basement
  ⌜QM561 (Histology)⌝
  ⌜QP88.4 (Physiology)⌝
  UF Basal lamina
      Basement lamina
      Basement membrane
      Basilemma
      Membrana propria
  BT Epithelium
      Membranes (Biology)
Membrane, Brush border
  USE Brush border membrane
Membrane, Germinal
  USE Blastoderm
Membrane disorders *(May Subd Geog)*
  UF Biological transport disorders
      Disorders of membranes
      Membrane pathology
      Membrane transport disorders
  BT Diseases
Membrane filters
  BT Filters and filtration
  NT Direct epifluorescent filter technique
Membrane filtration
  USE Membrane separation
Membrane fusion
  ⌜QH601⌝
  UF Fusion, Membrane
  BT Cell membranes
      Membranes (Biology)
  NT Cell adhesion
      Cell junctions
Membrane industry *(May Subd Geog)*
  ⌜HD9999.M42⌝
  BT Membranes (Technology)
Membrane lipids
  ⌜QP752.M45⌝
  BT Lipids
      Membranes (Biology)
  — **Peroxidation**
    UF Peroxidation of membrane lipids
    BT Active oxygen—Physiological
        effect
      Free radical reactions
Membrane lungs
  USE Oxygenators, Membrane
Membrane oxygenators
  USE Oxygenators, Membrane
Membrane pathology
  USE Membrane disorders
Membrane proteins
  ⌜QP552.M44⌝
  BT Membranes (Biology)
      Proteins
Membrane separation
  ⌜TP248.25.M46 (Biotechnology)⌝
  UF Filtration, Membrane
      Membrane filtration
      Separation, Membrane
  BT Separation (Technology)
Membrane transport
  USE Biological transport
Membrane transport disorders
  USE Membrane disorders
Membranes, Fetal
  USE Fetal membranes

Membranes, Synovial
  USE Synovial membranes
Membranes (Biology)
  UF Biological membranes
      Biomembranes
  BT Biological interfaces
      Protoplasm
  NT Basilar membrane
      Cell membranes
      Chloroplast membranes
      Egg cases (Zoology)
      Fetal membranes
      Liposomes
      Membrane, Basement
      Membrane fusion
      Membrane lipids
      Membrane proteins
      Mitochondrial membranes
      Mucous membrane
      Plant membranes
      Sarcolemma
      Synovial membranes
      Viral envelopes
  — **Electric properties**
  — **Mechanical properties**
    UF Mechanical properties of biological
        membranes
  — **Thermal properties**
Membranes (Technology)
  UF Artificial membranes
  BT Separation (Technology)
      Technology
  NT Diaphragms (Structural engineering)
      Ion-permeable membranes
      Liposomes
      Liquid membranes
      Membrane industry
      Saline water conversion—Reverse
        osmosis process
      Sewage—Purification—Reverse
        osmosis process
Membranous croup
  USE Croup
Memel Island (N.S.W.)
  USE Goat Island (N.S.W.)
Memel River
  USE Neman River
Memento Domine David (Music)
  USE Psalms (Music)—132d Psalm
Memnoniella
  ⌜QK625.D4⌝
  BT Dematiaceae
Memoirs
  USE *subdivision* History—Sources *under*
      names of countries, e.g. France—
      History—Sources
      Autobiography
      Biography
Memoranda
  USE Memorandums
Memorandums
  UF Memoranda
      Memos
  BT Commercial correspondence
      Government correspondence
      Public records
Memoria technica
  USE Mnemonics
Memorial Cemetery of the Pacific (Honolulu,
  Hawaii)
  USE National Memorial Cemetery of the
      Pacific (Honolulu, Hawaii)
Memorial certificates (Veterans)
  USE United States—Armed Forces—
      Memorial certificates
**Memorial Continental Hall (Washington,
D.C.)**
  UF National Headquarters of the
      Daughters of the American
      Revolution (Washington, D.C.)
  BT Halls—Washington (D.C.)

Memorial Day
  ₋E642₋
  UF Decoration Day
  BT Holidays
      Memorials
  NT Memorial Day sermons
Memorial Day, Confederate
  USE Confederate Memorial Day
Memorial Day (Israel)
  USE Yom ha-zikaron
Memorial Day addresses
  ₋E642₋
  BT Speeches, addresses, etc.
      Speeches, addresses, etc., American
Memorial Day addresses, Confederate
  USE Confederate Memorial Day addresses
Memorial Day sermons
  ₋BV4279₋
  UF Sermons, Memorial Day
  BT Memorial Day
      Occasional sermons
Memorial "Khatyn"' (Byelorussian S.S.R.)
  USE Khatyn' War Memorial (Byelorussian
       S.S.R.)
Memorial music
  BT Church music
      Music
      Sacred vocal music
  RT Funeral music
Memorial Park Cemetery (Mason City, Iowa)
  BT Cemeteries—Iowa
Memorial rites and ceremonies
  (May Subd Geog)
  UF Anniversary rites and ceremonies
  BT Rites and ceremonies
  NT Memorial service
Memorial rites and ceremonies, Buddhist
  (May Subd Geog)
  UF Buddhist memorial rites and
      ceremonies
  BT Buddhism—Rituals
  NT Memorial rites and ceremonies, Zen
      Ullambana
Memorial rites and ceremonies, Confucian
  (May Subd Geog)
  UF Confucian memorial rites and
      ceremonies
  BT Confucian rites and ceremonies
      Confucianism—Rituals
Memorial rites and ceremonies, Zen
  (May Subd Geog)
  ₋BQ9271.M4₋
  UF Zen Buddhism—Memorial rites and
      ceremonies
      Zen memorial rites and ceremonies
  BT Memorial rites and ceremonies,
      Buddhist
Memorial service
      Here are entered works on services in memory of
  persons without the presence of the body of the
  deceased. Works on services in the presence of the
  body of the deceased are entered under the heading
  Funeral service.
  UF Service, Memorial
  BT Liturgies
      Memorial rites and ceremonies
      Worship programs
Memorial tablets
  USE Sepulchral monuments
Memorial'nyï kompleks "Khatyn"'
  (Byelorussian S.S.R.)
  USE Khatyn' War Memorial (Byelorussian
       S.S.R.)
Memorials *(May Subd Geog)*
  UF Commemorations
  BT Historic sites
  RT Monuments
  NT Anniversaries
      Holidays
      Memorial Day
      War memorials

— Arkansas
  NT Arkansas Post National Memorial
      (Ark.)
— England
  NT Albert Memorial (London,
      England)
— Louisiana
  NT Archbishop Antoine Blanc
      Memorial (New Orleans, La.)
— Pennsylvania
  NT Johnstown Flood National
      Memorial (Pa.)
— Rhode Island
  NT Roger Williams National Memorial
      (Providence, R.I.)
— Russian S.F.S.R.
  NT Tysīācheletie Rossii (Novgorod,
      R.S.F.S.R.)
— South Dakota
  NT Mount Rushmore National
      Memorial (S.D.)
— Virginia
  NT Arlington House, the Robert E.
      Lee Memorial (Va.)
— Washington (D.C.)
  NT Lincoln Memorial (Washington,
      D.C.)
      Thomas Jefferson Memorial
      (Washington, D.C.)
      Washington Monument
      (Washington, D.C.)
Memories, Random access
  USE Random access storage
Memory
  ₋BF370-BF385 (Psychology)₋
  ₋LB1063 (Psychology, Educational)₋
  UF Forgetfulness
      Retention (Psychology)
  BT Brain
      Educational psychology
      Formal discipline
      Intellect
      Mental discipline
      Psychology
      Psychology, Physiological
      Thought and thinking
  RT Comprehension
      Mnemonics
      Perseveration (Psychology)
      Reproduction (Psychology)
  SA *subdivision* Memorizing *under*
      subjects, e.g. Music—Memorizing
  NT Amnesia
      Animal memory
      Association of ideas
      Association tests
      Attention
      Autobiographical memory
      Conservation (Psychology)
      Eidetic imagery
      Interruption (Psychology)
      Learning, Psychology of
      Maze tests
      Music—Memorizing
      Recognition (Psychology)
      Recollection (Psychology)
      Short-term memory
      Subconsciousness
— Age factors
  ₋BF378.A33 (Psychology)₋
  UF Age factors in memory
  BT Ability, Influence of age on
— Effect of drugs on
  BT Drugs—Physiological effect
      Psychopharmacology
Memory, Autobiographical
  USE Autobiographical memory
Memory, Disorders of
  ₋BF376₋
  UF Paramnesia
  BT Cognition disorders

  NT Amnesia
      Amusia
      Aphasia
      Fugue (Psychology)
Memory, Disorders of, in the aged
  USE Memory disorders in the aged
Memory, Immune
  USE Immunologic memory
Memory, Immunologic
  USE Immunologic memory
Memory, Virtual (Computer science)
  USE Virtual storage (Computer science)
Memory (Philosophy)
  ₋BD181.7₋
  BT Philosophy
Memory as a theme in literature
  USE Memory in literature
Memory cards
  USE Smart cards
Memory devices
  USE Ferroelectric storage cells
       Magnetic memory (Calculating-
       machines)
Memory disorders in the aged
  (May Subd Geog)
  UF Memory, Disorders of, in the aged
  BT Cognition disorders in the aged
Memory in children *(May Subd Geog)*
  ₋BF723.M4₋
  BT Child psychology
  — Cross-cultural studies
Memory in literature
  UF Memory as a theme in literature
Memory maps (Computer science)
  UF Maps, Memory (Computer science)
  BT Electronic digital computers—
      Programming
  RT Dynamic storage allocation (Computer
      science)
Memory training
  USE Mnemonics
Memory transfer
  UF Biochemical memory transfer
      Chemical memory transfer
      Interanimal memory transfer
      Transfer of memory
  BT Learning—Physiological aspects
      Learning, Psychology of
      Psychology, Physiological
Memory tubes
  USE Storage tubes
Memos
  USE Memorandums
Memotech MTX (Computer)
  ₋QA76.8.M₋
  BT Microcomputers
Memphis, Battle of, 1862
  BT Tennessee—History—Civil War, 1861-
      1865
      United States—History—Civil War,
      1861-1865—Campaigns
Memphis and Charleston Railroad
  BT Railroads—United States
Memphis, El Paso and Pacific Railroad
  BT Railroads—United States
Memra (The word)
  BT Aramaic language—Etymology
      God—Name
      Logos
Men *(May Subd Geog)*
      Here are entered works on the human male.
  Works on male organisms in general are entered
  under Males.
  UF Human males
      Males, Human
  BT Males
      Man
  RT Patriarchy
  NT Aged men
      Brotherhoods
      Brothers

Men *(Continued)*
    Church work with men
    English literature—Men authors
    Male nude
    Middle aged men
    Middle class men
    Sex instruction for men
    Short men
    Single men
    Strong men
    Young men
— **Diseases** *(May Subd Geog)*
    RT Andrology
— **Employment**
    USE Employment of men
— **Health and hygiene**
    BT Hygiene
    NT Exercise for men
       Grooming for men
       Men—Medical examinations
       Physical fitness for men
— **Medical examinations**
    BT Men—Health and hygiene
— **Mental health** *(May Subd Geog)*
    [RC451.4.M45]
— **Mortality**
    [RA408.M4 (Public health)]
— **Photography**
    USE Photography of men
— **Physical fitness**
    USE Physical fitness for men
— **Physiology**
    BT Human physiology
    RT Andrology
— **Prayer-books and devotions**
    [BV283.M4 (Prayers)]
    [BV4843 (Devotional works)]
— — **French,** [German, Italian, etc.]
— **Psychology**
    NT Anima (Psychoanalysis)
       Masculinity (Psychology)
— **Sexual behavior**
    NT Homosexuality, Male
       Prostitution, Male
— **Study and teaching** *(May Subd Geog)*
    NT Men's studies
Men, Afro-American
  USE Afro-American men
Men, Discrimination against
  USE Sex discrimination against men
Men, Short
  USE Short men
Men, White *(May Subd Geog)*
  UF White men
  BT Caucasian race
    Whites
  NT Wages—Men, White
Men (Christian theology)
    Here are entered works on the Christian theology of the male sex. Works on the theology of humankind from the perspective of two or more of the world's religions are entered under Man (Theology). Works on the Christian theology of humankind are entered under Man (Christian theology). Works on the Christian theology of the female sex are entered under Woman (Christian theology)
  BT Man (Christian theology)
Men actors *(May Subd Geog)*
    Here are entered works on men actors collectively. Works on women actors collectively are entered under Actresses. General works on both men and women actors collectively, works on both men and women stage actors collectively and works on individual men and women stage actors are entered under Actors. Works on actors, collectively or individually, specializing in particular media are entered under the appropriate specific heading, e.g. Television actors and actresses, with an additional heading for Men actors or Actresses, if necessary.
  UF Actors, Male
    Male actors
  BT Actors

Men and homemaking
  USE Househusbands
Men as antique collectors
  USE Men as collectors
Men as collectors
  UF Men as antique collectors
  BT Collectors and collecting
Men consumers *(May Subd Geog)*
  BT Consumers
Men dancers *(May Subd Geog)*
  BT Dancers
Men homemakers
  USE Househusbands
Men homosexuals
  USE Homosexuals, Male
Men in art
  [N7626-N7628]
  UF Male figure in art
  NT Pinup art
Men in church work
  BT Church work with men
    Laity
Men in literature
  BT Characters and characteristics in
      literature
    Man
Men in motion pictures
  [PN1995.9.M46]
  BT Moving-pictures
Men nurses
  UF Male nurses
  BT Nurses
Men weavers *(May Subd Geog)*
  BT Weavers
Menabe (Madagascan tribe)
  USE Menabe (Malagasy people)
Menabe (Malagasy people)
  UF Menabe (Madagascan tribe)
  BT Ethnology—Madagascar
    Sakalavas
Menacantite
  USE Ilmenite
Menaccanite
  USE Ilmenite
Menace, Operation
  USE Operation Menace
Menachanite
  USE Ilmenite
Menageries *(May Subd Geog)*
  [QL73]
  BT Zoos
  NT Animals, Training of
— **Japan**
    NT Mutsugoro's Animal Kingdom
      (Japan)
Menalamba Rebellion, Madagascar, 1895-1899
  USE Madagascar—History—Menalamba
    Rebellion, 1895-1899
Menam Chao Phya (Thailand)
  USE Chao Phraya River (Thailand)
Menam Chau Fya (Thailand)
  USE Chao Phraya River (Thailand)
Mènam Khong
  USE Mekong River
Menam River (Thailand)
  USE Chao Phraya River (Thailand)
Menangkabau (Indonesian people)
  USE Minangkabau (Indonesian people)
Menangkabau language
  USE Minangkabau language
Menapii
  [DH92.M]
Menarchal delay
  USE Amenorrhea, Primary
Menarche *(May Subd Geog)*
  [QP263 (Physiology)]
  [RJ145 (Pediatrics)]
  BT Adolescent girls—Physiology
    Menstruation
    Puberty
  NT Amenorrhea, Primary

Menard family
  USE Maynard family
Menaspis
  [QE852.C48]
  BT Chimaeriformes
Mendaeans
  USE Mandaeans
Mendal family
  USE Mendall family
Mendall family *(Not Subd Geog)*
  UF Meldol family
    Mendal family
    Mendel family
    Mendell family
    Mendle family
  RT Mandel family
Mendaña
  USE Marquesas Islands
Mende
  [DT516 (Sierra Leone)]
Mende (Papua New Guinea people)
  USE Mendi (Papua New Guinea people)
Mende art
  USE Art, Mende
Mende arts
  USE Arts, Mende
Mende language
  [PL8511]
  BT Mande languages
    Sierra Leone—Languages
Mendel family
  USE Mendall family
Mendell family
  USE Mendall family
Mendel's law
  [QH421-431]
  BT Breeding
    Variation (Biology)
  RT Heredity
    Hybridization
  NT Genetics
Mendenal family
  USE Mendenhall family
Mendenall family
  USE Mendenhall family
Mendenhall family *(Not Subd Geog)*
  UF Mendenal family
    Mendenall family
    Mendinall family
    Mendingall family
    Mendinghall family
    Mendinhall family
    Menhall family
    Meninall family
    Meningall family
    Mondenall family
Mendes (Ancient city) *(Not Subd Geog)*
  [DT73.M54]
  UF Per-banedjedet (Ancient city)
    Rub'a, Tall al- (Egypt)
    Tall al-Rub'a (Egypt)
    Tell el-Rub'a (Egypt)
  BT Cities and towns, Ruined, extinct, etc.
    —Egypt
    Egypt—Antiquities
MENDEX Operation
  USE Operation MENDEX
Mendi (Papua New Guinea people)
  UF Mende (Papua New Guinea people)
  BT Ethnology—Papua New Guinea
Mendicancy
  USE Begging
Mendicant orders
  USE Friars
Mendicants
  USE Beggars
Mendinall family
  USE Mendenhall family
Mending
  USE Repairing
    Reweaving

Mendingall family
    USE Mendenhall family
Mendinghall family
    USE Mendenhall family
Mendinhall family
    USE Mendenhall family
Mendip Hills (England)
    BT Mountains—England
Mendle family
    USE Mendall family
Mendon
    USE Nothosaurus
Mendota, Lake (Wis.)
    UF Fourth Lake (Wis.)
        Lake Mendota (Wis.)
    BT Lakes—Wisconsin
Mendoza family *(Not Subd Geog)*
Mendoza River (Argentina)
    UF Río Mendoza (Argentina)
    BT Rivers—Argentina
Mendzan
    USE Menzan
Menees family
    USE Menzies family
Menefee family *(Not Subd Geog)*
    UF Manifee family
        Menefie family
        Menifee family
        Mynyfie family
Menefie family
    USE Menefee family
Menein en (The Greek phrase)
    BT Greek language, Biblical—Terms and
        phrases
Menes family
    USE Means family
Meng-chiang-nü (Legendary character)
    BT Folklore—China
Meng-ku hui-hui (Chinese people)
    USE Tung-hsiang (Chinese people)
Mengen (Melanesian people)
    USE Maenge (Melanesian people)
Menges family *(Not Subd Geog)*
    UF Mangus family
        Mingos family
        Mingus family
Mengöne Island (New Caledonia)
    USE Maré Island (New Caledonia)
Mengücek, House of *(Not Subd Geog)*
    [DS27.53]
    UF House of Mengücek
        Mengücek Oğulları
    BT Turkey—Kings and rulers
Mengücek Oğulları
    USE Mengücek, House of
Mengwe Indians
    USE Iroquois Indians
Menhaden
    [QL638.C64]
    UF Brevoortia (Fishes)
    BT Clupeidae
    NT Atlantic menhaden
        Yellowfin menhaden
Menhaden fisheries *(May Subd Geog)*
    [SH351.M5]
    BT Fisheries
Menhall family
    USE Mendenhall family
Menhirs *(May Subd Geog)*
    [GN790-792]
    BT Megalithic monuments
    RT Cromlechs
        Dolmens
        Stele (Archaeology)
Menidia
    [QL638.A8]
    BT Silversides
Menidia audens
    [QL638.A8]
    UF Mississippi silverside

Menidia beryllina
    [QL638.A8]
    UF Tidewater silverside
Menidia menidia
    [QL638.A8]
    UF Common silverside
Ménière's disease
    [RF275]
    UF Aural vertigo
        Endolymphatic hydrops
        Labyrinthine hydrops
    BT Deafness
        Labyrinth (Ear)—Diseases
        Vertigo
Menifee family
    USE Menefee family
Meninall family
    USE Mendenhall family
Meninas (Painting)
    USE Velázquez, Diego, 1599-1660.   Maids
        of honor
Ménines (Painting)
    USE Picasso, Pablo, 1881-1973.   Ménines
Meningall family
    USE Mendenhall family
Meningeal artery
    [QL835]
    [QM191]
    BT Arteries
        Brain—Blood-vessels
Meninges
    [QL933-QL937 (Comparative
        anatomy)]
    [QM469 (Human anatomy)]
    BT Brain
        Nervous system
        Spinal cord
    NT Dura mater
        Subarachnoid space
— **Tuberculosis**
    UF Meningitis, Tuberculous
        Tuberculosis, Meningeal
Meningioma
    [RC280.M4]
    BT Brain—Tumors
Meningitis
    [RC124]
    [RC376]
    [SF799 (Veterinary medicine)]
    UF Leptomeningitis
    BT Central nervous system—Diseases
    RT Neisseria meningitidis
    NT Arachnoiditis
        Hemophilus meningitis
        Lymphocytic choriomeningitis
        Meningopneumonitis
        Pachymeningitis
— **Diagnosis**
Meningitis, Cerebrospinal *(May Subd Geog)*
    [RC124]
    UF Cerebrospinal fever
        Cerebrospinal meningitis
        Meningitis, Purulent
        Meningitis, Suppurative
        Meningococcic meningitis
        Purulent meningitis
        Suppurative meningitis
Meningitis, Purulent
    USE Meningitis, Cerebrospinal
Meningitis, Spinal
    UF Spinal meningitis
    BT Spinal cord—Diseases
Meningitis, Suppurative
    USE Meningitis, Cerebrospinal
Meningitis, Tuberculous
    USE Meninges—Tuberculosis
Meningitis in children *(May Subd Geog)*
    [RJ496.M45]
    BT Infection in children
        Pediatric neurology

Meningo-encephalocele
    BT Encephalocele
        Skull—Abnormalities
— **Surgery**
Meningo-encephalomyelitis
    USE Encephalomyelitis
Meningococcic meningitis
    USE Meningitis, Cerebrospinal
Meningococcus
    USE Neisseria meningitidis
Meningoencephalitis
    BT Central nervous system—Diseases
Meningomyelocele
    USE Myelomeningocele
Meningopneumonitis
    BT Meningitis
        Pneumonia
        Psittacosis
        Virus diseases
Meninka language
    USE Mandingo language
Menippe
    [QL444.M33]
    BT Xanthidae
Menippe mercenaria
    [QL444.M33]
    UF Stone crab
Meniscectomy *(May Subd Geog)*
    BT Meniscus (Anatomy)—Surgery
Meniscocytosis
    USE Sickle cell anemia
Meniscomys
    [QE882.R6]
    BT Aplodontidae, Fossil
Meniscus (Anatomy)
    UF Semilunar cartilage
    BT Cartilage
        Knee
— **Surgery**
    NT Meniscectomy
Meniscus (Liquids)
    [QC183]
    BT Capillarity
        Liquids
        Surface tension
        Surfaces
Menispermaceae
    [QK495.M537]
    BT Ranunculales
    NT Abuta
        Epinetrum
        Limaciopsis
Menja (African people)
    USE Kwegu (African people)
Menjuke (Indonesian people)
    USE Manyuke (Indonesian people)
Mennonite art
    USE Art, Mennonite
Mennonite authors *(May Subd Geog)*
    UF Authors, Mennonite
    SA *subdivision* Mennonite authors *under
        individual literatures, e.g.* English
        literature—Mennonite authors
Mennonite church buildings
    USE Churches, Mennonite
Mennonite churches
    USE Churches, Mennonite
Mennonite colonization
    USE Mennonites—Colonization
Mennonite converts
    USE Converts, Mennonite
Mennonite cookery
    USE Cookery, Mennonite
Mennonite furniture
    USE Furniture, Mennonite
Mennonite grass-burner
    [TH7458.G7]
    UF Grass-burner
    BT Fuel
        Stoves

Mennonite illumination of books and
   manuscripts
   USE Illumination of books and manuscripts,
       Mennonite
Mennonite quilts
   USE Quilts, Mennonite
Mennonite women
   USE Women, Mennonite
Mennonites *(May Subd Geog)*
   [BX8101-BX8143]
      Here are entered works on Mennonite denomina-
      tions treated collectively, works for which the in-
      dividual Mennonite denomination cannot be identi-
      fied, and works on Mennonites as a class of persons.
   UF Old Order Amish
   BT Anabaptists
       Baptists
       Christian sects
   NT Amish
       Old Colony Mennonites
       Old Order Mennonites
       Pentecostalism—Mennonites
   — **Colonization**
         [BX8128.C]
      UF Colonization, Mennonite
          Mennonite colonization
      BT Agricultural colonies
   — Converts
      USE Converts, Mennonite
   — **Parties and movements**
         [BX8129.A1]
   — **Relations**
   — **North America**
   — **United States**
         NT Afro-American Mennonites
             Hispanic American Mennonites
Mennonites, Afro-American
   USE Afro-American Mennonites
Mennonites, Hispanic American
   USE Hispanic American Mennonites
Menobranchus
   USE Necturus
Menominee Indians
   [E99.M44]
   BT Algonquian Indians
       Indians of North America
   — **Government relations**
Menominee language
   [PM1761]
   UF Menomoni language
   BT Algonquian languages
Menominee Range (Mich. and Wis.)
   BT Mountains—Michigan
       Mountains—Wisconsin
Menomoni language
   USE Menominee language
Menopause *(May Subd Geog)*
   [RG186]
   UF Change of life in women
       Climacteric, Female
       Female change of life
       Female climacteric
   BT Climacteric
       Menstruation
Menopause, Male
   USE Climacteric, Male
Menoponidae
   [QL540.3.M4]
   BT Mallophaga
   NT Dennyus
       Myrsidea
Menor Sea (Spain)
   USE Mar Menor (Spain)
Menorah
   [BM657.M]
   BT Art, Jewish
       Candles and lights
       Jewish art and symbolism
       Jews—Antiquities
       Judaism—Liturgical objects
       Worship in the Bible

   NT Hanukkah lamp
Menorca (Spain)
   USE Minorca (Spain)
Menorrhagia
   [RG176]
   BT Hemorrhage, Uterine
       Menstruation disorders
Menotti family *(Not Subd Geog)*
Men's apparel industry
   USE Men's clothing industry
Men's ballet dancing
   USE Ballet dancing for men
Men's clothing *(May Subd Geog)*
   UF Clothing, Men's
       Men's wear
       Menswear
   BT Clothing and dress
       Costume
       Fashion
       Grooming for men
       Tailoring
   SA *individual articles of apparel, e.g.*
          Coats, Hats, Trousers
   NT Men's furnishing goods
   — Pattern design
         USE Tailoring—Pattern design
Men's clothing industry *(May Subd Geog)*
   [HD9940 (Economics)]
   UF Men's apparel industry
       Men's wear industry
   BT Clothing trade
Men's etiquette
   USE Etiquette for men
Men's furnishing goods
   [TT572-630]
   UF Haberdashery
   BT Clothing trade
       Men's clothing
   NT Shirts, Men's
Men's gymnastics
   USE Gymnastics for men
Mens rea
   USE Criminal intent
Men's shirt industry *(May Subd Geog)*
   [HD9969.S5-7]
   RT Shirts, Men's
Men's studies *(May Subd Geog)*
   [HQ1088]
   UF Studies, Men's
   BT Men—Study and teaching
Men's wear
   USE Men's clothing
Men's wear industry
   USE Men's clothing industry
Men's writings
   USE *subdivision* Men authors *under*
          individual literatures and genres,
          e.g. English literature—Men
          authors; Fiction—Men authors
Mensa (African people)
   BT Ethnology—Ethiopia
Mensa Isiaca
   USE Isiac tablet
Menschenbild
   USE Humans in art
Menses
   USE Menstruation
Mensheviki
   USE Mensheviks
Mensheviks *(May Subd Geog)*
   UF Mensheviki
   BT Socialists—Soviet Union
   RT Soviet Union—Politics and
          government—20th century
Menshew family
   USE Mincey family
Menstrual cycle *(May Subd Geog)*
   [QP261-QP263 (Physiology)]
   [RG161-RG163 (Gynecology)]
   UF Sexual cycle of women

   BT Endocrine gynecology
       Sexual cycle
       Women—Physiology
   NT Luteal phase
       Menstruation
       Natural family planning
       Ovulation
       Premenstrual syndrome
   — **Psychological aspects**
      BT Psychology, Applied
          Sex (Psychology)
Menstrual disorders
   USE Menstruation disorders
Menstrual extraction
   USE Menstrual regulation
Menstrual induction
   USE Menstrual regulation
Menstrual regulation *(May Subd Geog)*
   [RG734]
   UF Atraumatic abortion
       Early abortion
       Extraction, Menstrual
       Induction, Menstrual
       Menstrual extraction
       Menstrual induction
       Preemptive abortion
   BT Abortion
Menstruation
   [RG161-186]
   UF Menses
   BT Menstrual cycle
       Ovaries
       Reproduction
   RT Emmenagogues
   NT Menarche
       Menopause
       Sanitary napkins
       Tampons
   — **Cross-cultural studies**
   — **Mythology**
Menstruation disorders
   UF Menstrual disorders
   BT Generative organs, Female—Diseases
   NT Amenorrhea
       Dysmenorrhea
       Menorrhagia
       Premenstrual syndrome
Menstruation inducing agents
   USE Emmenagogues
Mensuration
   [QA465 (Mathematics)]
   [T50-T51 (Technology)]
   UF Measurement
       Measuring
       Metrology
       Stereometry
   BT Engineering
       Mathematics
   RT Physical measurements
       Weights and measures
   SA *special measures, e.g.* Stadium
          (Standard of length); *and*
          subdivision Measurement *under*
          special subjects, e.g. Altitudes—
          Measurement; Ships—Measurement
   NT Area measurement
       Barometric hypsometry
       Classification—Books—Mensuration
       Colorimetry
       Flatness measurement
       Gaging
       Geodesy
       Length measurement
       Measuring instruments
       Planimeter
       Standards of length
       Standards of mass
       Surveying
       Thickness measurement
       Tolerance (Engineering)
       Volume (Cubic content)

— **Conversion tables**
   BT Ready-reckoners
— **Religious aspects**
Menswear
   USE Men's clothing
Mental ability and age
   USE Age and intelligence
Mental age (May Subd Geog)
   [LB1130.M5]
   BT Ability, Influence of age on
      Age and intelligence
      Developmental psychology
      Intelligence levels
   NT School age (Entrance age)
Mental arithmetic
   USE Arithmetic, Mental
Mental association
   USE Association of ideas
Mental calculators (May Subd Geog)
      Here are entered works on persons capable of ex-
   ecuting rapid mental mathematical calculations.
   UF Calculating prodigies
      Calculators, Mental
      Computers, Human
      Human computers
      Prodigies, Calculating
   BT Genius
      Mathematical ability
   RT Arithmetic, Mental
Mental chronometry
   USE Time perception
Mental content
   USE Content (Psychology)
Mental culture
   USE Mental discipline
Mental deficiency
   USE Mental retardation
Mental depression
   USE Depression, Mental
Mental disability evaluation
   USE Psychiatric disability evaluation
Mental discipline
   [BF632 (Psychology)]
   UF Discipline, Mental
      Mental culture
   BT Discipline
      Self-culture
   RT Education
   NT Memory
      Mnemonics
Mental diseases
   USE Mental illness
      Psychology, Pathological
      Psychoses
Mental disorders
   USE Mental illness
      Psychology, Pathological
      Psychoses
Mental epidemics
   USE Hysteria, Epidemic
Mental exhaustion
   USE Fatigue, Mental
Mental fatigue
   USE Fatigue, Mental
Mental healers
   USE Healers
Mental healing (May Subd Geog)
   [RZ400-RZ408]
      Here are entered works on the use of psychologi-
   cal or psychic means to treat illness. Works on the use
   of faith, prayer, or sacramental means to treat illness
   are entered under Spiritual healing.
   UF Absent treatment
      Health thoughts
      Mind-cure
      Psychic healing
   BT Healing
      Mesmerism
      Therapeutic systems

   RT Christian Science
      Mental suggestion
      Mind and body
      Psychic surgery
      Psychotherapy
      Spiritual healing
      Subconsciousness
      Therapeutics, Suggestive
   NT Emmanuel movement
      Healers
      Healing gods
      Jewish Science
      Magnetic healing
      Medicine, Magic, mystic, and spagiric
      New Thought
      Silva Mind Control
Mental health (May Subd Geog)
   [RA790-RA790.85]
   UF Emotional health
      Mental hygiene
   BT Happiness
      Health
      Public health
   RT Mental illness
      Psychiatry
      Psychology
      Psychology, Pathological
   SA subdivision Mental health under names
      of individual persons, and under
      classes of persons and ethnic
      groups, e.g. Women—Mental
      health; Afro-Americans—Mental
      health
   NT Child mental health
      Emotions
      Interviewing in mental health
      Mental health education
      Mental health personnel
      Mental health services
      Orthopsychiatry
      Personality
      Relaxation
      Self-actualization (Psychology)
      Social psychiatry
      Stress (Psychology)
      World Mental Health Year, 1960
— **Bibliography**
   RT Mental health literature
— **Research**
   USE Psychiatry—Research
— **Vocational guidance**
   USE Mental health services—
      Vocational guidance
— **United States**
Mental health and state
   USE Mental health policy
Mental health associates
   USE Allied mental health personnel
Mental health boards (May Subd Geog)
   UF Boards of mental health
   BT Health boards
Mental health care teams (May Subd Geog)
   [RC440.7]
   UF Team work in mental health
   BT Health care teams
      Mental health personnel
Mental health clinics
   USE Community mental health services
      Psychiatric clinics
Mental health consultation
   (May Subd Geog)
   [RA790.95]
   UF Consultation, Mental health
   BT Mental health services
   NT Psychiatric consultation
      Psychological consultation
Mental health counseling (May Subd Geog)
   [RC466]
   UF Counseling, Mental health
   BT Health counseling
      Mental health services

   RT Psychotherapy
Mental health education (May Subd Geog)
   BT Health education
      Mental health
   NT Mass media in mental health
      education
Mental health facilities (May Subd Geog)
   BT Health facilities
      Mental health services
   NT Pastoral counseling centers
      Psychiatric clinics
      Psychiatric hospitals
— **Admission and discharge**
   UF Admission to mental health
      facilities
      Discharge from mental health
      facilities
      Mental health facilities—Discharge
— **Discharge**
   USE Mental health facilities—
      Admission and discharge
— **Employees**
   UF Mental health services—Employees
— **Law and legislation** (May Subd Geog)
   BT Mental health laws
— **Utilization**
   BT Medical care—Utilization
   NT Psychiatric clinics—Utilization
Mental health insurance
   USE Insurance, Mental health
Mental health laws (May Subd Geog)
      Here are entered works on laws dealing with the
   care of the insane, the mentally ill, the mentally hand-
   icapped, alcoholics, epileptics, and narcotic addicts.
   Works dealing separately with alcoholics, epileptics,
   or narcotic addicts are entered under the specific
   headings. Works on the legal status of the insane are
   entered under the heading Insanity—Jurisprudence.
   UF Insane—Legal status, laws, etc.
      Law and mental illness
      Mental illness—Law and legislation
      Mental illness and law
      Mentally handicapped—Legal status,
      laws, etc.
      Mentally ill—Legal status, laws, etc.
   NT Behavior modification—Law and
      legislation
      Community mental health services—
      Law and legislation
      Insane—Commitment and detention
      Legal assistance to the mentally
      handicapped
      Mental health facilities—Law and
      legislation
      Mental health personnel—Malpractice
      Narcotic addicts—Legal status, laws,
      etc.
      Psychiatric hospitals—Law and
      legislation
      Psychosurgery—Law and legislation
      Therapeutic community—Law and
      legislation
Mental health libraries (May Subd Geog)
   [Z675.M43]
   UF Emotional health libraries
      Libraries, Mental health
      Mental hygiene libraries
   BT Medical libraries
Mental health literature
   UF Literature, Mental health
   RT Mental health—Bibliography
Mental health nursing
   USE Psychiatric nursing
Mental health personnel (May Subd Geog)
   UF Psychiatric personnel
   BT Medical personnel
      Mental health
   NT Aged in mental health
      Allied mental health personnel
      Clinical psychologists
      Community mental health personnel
      Mental health care teams

Mental health personnel *(Continued)*
  Mental health services—Vocational
   guidance
  Minority mental health personnel
  Psychiatric nursing
  Psychiatric social work
  Psychiatrists
  Psychotherapists
  Student volunteers in mental health
  Volunteer workers in mental health
 — **Legal status, laws, etc.**
  NT Mental health personnel—
   Malpractice
 — **Malpractice** *(May Subd Geog)*
  UF Mental health personnel—Tort
   liability
   Tort liability of mental health
   personnel
  BT Mental health laws
   Mental health personnel—Legal
   status, laws, etc.
 — **Pensions** *(May Subd Geog)*
  UF Mental health personnel—Salaries,
   pensions, etc.
 — **Salaries, etc.** *(May Subd Geog)*
  UF Mental health personnel—Salaries,
   pensions, etc.
   Wages—Mental health personnel
 — **Salaries, pensions, etc.**
  USE Mental health personnel—
   Pensions
   Mental health personnel—
   Salaries, etc.
 — **Tort liability**
  USE Mental health personnel—
   Malpractice
 — **United States**
  NT Asian American mental health
   personnel
   Hispanic American mental health
   personnel
Mental health personnel, Asian American
 USE Asian American mental health
  personnel
Mental health personnel, Community
 USE Community mental health personnel
Mental health personnel, Hispanic American
 USE Hispanic American mental health
  personnel
Mental health personnel, Minority
 USE Minority mental health personnel
Mental health planning *(May Subd Geog)*
 UF Mental health services—Planning
 BT Health planning
  Planning
 NT Community mental health services—
  Planning
Mental health policy *(May Subd Geog)*
 UF Mental health and state
  State and mental health
 BT Medical policy
 SA *subdivision* Government policy *under*
  special topics in mental health
 NT Citizens' advisory committees in
  mental health
Mental health services *(May Subd Geog)*
 [RA790]
 BT Mental health
  Public health
 SA *subdivision* Mental health services
  under classes of persons and ethnic
  groups, e.g. Indians of North
  America—Mental health services;
  and subdivision Students—Mental
  health services *under names of*
  individual educational institutions,
  e.g. Harvard University—Students—
  Mental health services
 NT Child mental health services
  Community mental health services
  Halfway houses

  Mental health consultation
  Mental health counseling
  Mental health facilities
  Psychiatric hospital care
  Rural mental health services
  Sexism in mental health services
 — **Citizen participation**
  NT Citizens' advisory committees in
   mental health
 — **Employees**
  USE Mental health facilities—
   Employees
 — **Finance**
 — **Medical records**
  BT Medical records
 — **Planning**
  USE Mental health planning
 — **Utilization**
  UF Utilization of mental health
   services
 — **Vocational guidance**
  [RA790.8]
  UF Mental health—Vocational
   guidance
  BT Mental health personnel
Mental health services, Rural
 USE Rural mental health services
Mental health services ethics
 USE Psychiatric ethics
Mental health services for children
 USE Child mental health services
Mental health surveys *(May Subd Geog)*
 Here are entered works on the techniques em-
ployed, and reports, etc. of individual surveys; the
latter are entered also under the heading Mental ill-
ness, subdivided by the name of a country or other
place concerned.
 BT Health surveys
Mental health volunteers
 USE Student volunteers in mental health
  Volunteer workers in mental health
Mental hospitals
 USE Psychiatric hospitals
Mental hygiene
 USE Mental health
Mental hygiene libraries
 USE Mental health libraries
Mental illness *(May Subd Geog)*
 Here are entered popular works and works on
regional or social aspects of mental disorders. Works
on the legal aspects of mental illness are entered
under Insanity. Systematic descriptions of mental
disorders are entered under Psychology, Pathologi-
cal. Works on clinical aspects of mental disorders,
including therapy, are entered under Psychiatry.
 UF Diseases, Mental
  Madness
  Mental diseases
  Mental disorders
 BT Diseases
  Psychiatry
  Psychology, Pathological
 RT Mental health
 NT Genius and mental illness
  Insanity
 — **Animal models**
  UF Animal mental illness models
   Animal models of mental illness in
   humans
  BT Animal psychopathology
   Diseases—Animal models
   Psychiatry, Comparative
 — **Bibliography**
 — **Classification**
  [RC455.2.C4]
  UF Psychology, Pathological—
   Classification
  BT Nosology
 — **Diagnosis**
  UF Psychiatric diagnosis
  BT Psychodiagnostics
   Psychological tests

  NT Psychiatric disability evaluation
   Szondi test
 — **Genetic aspects**
  UF Insanity—Genetic aspects
 — **Law and legislation**
  USE Insanity
   Mental health laws
 — **Nursing**
  USE Psychiatric nursing
 — **Nutritional aspects**
 — **Physiological aspects**
  UF Psychiatry, Physiological
  BT Psychological manifestations of
   general diseases
   Psychology, Physiological
 — **Public opinion**
  BT Social psychiatry
 — **Research**
  USE Psychiatry—Research
 — **Surgery**
  USE Psychosurgery
 — **Treatment**
 — — **Evaluation**
   NT Psychiatric rating scales
Mental illness and art
 USE Art and mental illness
Mental illness and law
 USE Insanity—Jurisprudence
  Mental health laws
Mental illness and literature
 USE Literature and mental illness
Mental illness in animals
 USE Animal psychopathology
Mental illness in art
 USE Psychiatry in art
Mental illness in children
 USE Child psychopathology
Mental illness in literature
 UF Insanity in literature
  Psychopathology in literature
 BT Mentally handicapped in literature
Mental illness in motion pictures
 [PN1995.9.M463]
 BT Moving-pictures
Mental illness in pregnancy
 (May Subd Geog)
 [RG588]
 BT Pregnancy, Complications of
  Women—Mental health
Mental illness insurance
 USE Insurance, Mental health
Mental imagery
 USE Imagery (Psychology)
  Imagination
Mental images
 USE Imagery (Psychology)
  Imagination
Mental institutions
 USE Mentally handicapped—Institutional
  care
  Psychiatric hospitals
Mental maps
 USE *subdivision* Maps, Mental *under names*
  of countries, cities, etc.
  Geographical perception
Mental mechanisms
 USE Defense mechanisms (Psychology)
Mental-motor relationship in education
 USE Perceptual-motor learning
Mental overwork
 USE Fatigue, Mental
Mental patients
 USE Mentally ill
  Psychotherapy patients
Mental patients, Former
 USE Ex-mental patients
Mental philosophy
 USE Philosophy
  Psychology
Mental prayer
 USE Contemplation

Meditation

Mental reservation
  ⌐BJ1429⌐
  UF Reservation, Mental
  BT Truthfulness and falsehood

Mental retardation *(May Subd Geog)*
  ⌐RC569.7-RC571 (General)⌐
  ⌐RJ506.M4 (Pediatrics)⌐
  UF Mental deficiency
      Retardation, Mental
  BT Developmental disabilities
      Psychology, Pathological
  RT Intellect
      Mentally handicapped
  NT Aspartylglycosaminuria
      Cretinism
      De Lange's syndrome
      Down's syndrome
      Fragile X syndrome
      Galactosemia
      Gangliosidoses
      Gaucher's disease
      Idiocy
      Idiot savants
      Kleeblattschädel syndrome
      Laurence-Moon-Biedl syndrome
      Lesch-Nyhan syndrome
      Leukodystrophy, Globoid cell
      Leukodystrophy, Metachromatic
      Lowe's syndrome
      Mucopolysaccharidosis
      Neurofibromatosis
      Neuronal ceroid-lipofuscinosis
      Phenylketonuria
      Prader-Willi syndrome
      Rett syndrome
      Spasms, Infantile
      Sphingolipidoses
      Tuberous sclerosis
  — Cross-cultural studies
  — Religious aspects

Mental retardation facilities
  (May Subd Geog)
  ⌐HV3004-8⌐
  UF Benevolent institutions
  BT Health facilities
      Mentally handicapped—Institutional
      care
  NT Architecture and mentally
      handicapped children
      Architecture and the mentally
      handicapped
  — Patients
      USE Mental retardation facilities
           patients
  — Utilization
      UF Utilization of mental retardation
          facilities

Mental retardation facilities patients
  (May Subd Geog)
  UF Mental retardation facilities—Patients
  BT Inmates of institutions
      Mentally handicapped
  — Suffrage *(May Subd Geog)*
    ⌐JK1872-JK1872.5⌐

Mental stereotype
  USE Stereotype (Psychology)
Mental stress
  USE Stress (Psychology)

Mental suggestion
  ⌐BF1111-1156⌐
  UF Autosuggestion
      Suggestion, Mental
  BT Mesmerism
      Mind and body
      Psychical research
      Subconsciousness
  RT Hypnotism
      Mental healing
      Therapeutics, Suggestive
  NT Animal magnetism

Autogenic training
Brainwashing
Silva Mind Control
Subliminal perception
Subliminal projection
Mental telepathy
  USE Telepathy
Mental tests
  USE Educational tests and measurements
       Intelligence tests
       Psychological tests
Mental types
  USE Typology (Psychology)

Mental work *(May Subd Geog)*
  UF Intellectual activity
  BT Thought and thinking
      Work
Mentally deficient
  USE Mentally handicapped

Mentally handicapped *(May Subd Geog)*
  UF Feeble-minded
      Imbecility
      Mentally deficient
      Mentally retarded
      Morons
  BT Developmentally disabled
      Handicapped
  RT Mental retardation
  NT Art museums and the mentally
      handicapped
      Artists, Mentally handicapped
      Christian education of the mentally
      handicapped
      Church work with the mentally
      handicapped
      Cookery for the mentally handicapped
      Day care centers for the mentally
      handicapped
      Handicraft for the mentally
      handicapped
      Idiocy
      Libraries and the mentally
      handicapped
      Mental retardation facilities patients
      Mentally ill
      Physical education for mentally
      handicapped persons
      Religious education of the mentally
      handicapped
      Sex instruction for the mentally
      handicapped
      Social work with the mentally
      handicapped
      Sports for the mentally handicapped
  — Abuse of
      UF Abuse of the mentally handicapped
  — Care *(May Subd Geog)*
      UF Mentally handicapped—Care and
          treatment
  — Care and treatment
      USE Mentally handicapped—Care
  — Education *(May Subd Geog)*
  — Home care *(May Subd Geog)*
  — Institutional care *(May Subd Geog)*
      UF Mental institutions
      NT Mental retardation facilities
  — Language
      BT Language and languages
          Psycholinguistics
  — Legal status, laws, etc.
      USE Mental health laws
  — Life skills guides
  — Marriage
      UF Marriage of the mentally
          handicapped
      BT Eugenics
          Heredity, Human
          Marriage
  — Means of communication
      ⌐HV3004.5⌐

      UF Means of communication for the
          mentally handicapped
      BT Communication
  — Mental health *(May Subd Geog)*
      ⌐RC451.4.M47⌐
  — Rehabilitation *(May Subd Geog)*
  — Sexual behavior
  — Surgery *(May Subd Geog)*
Mentally handicapped, Cookery for the
  USE Cookery for the mentally handicapped
Mentally handicapped, Legal assistance to the
  USE Legal assistance to the mentally
       handicapped
Mentally handicapped, Writings of the
  UF Writings of the mentally handicapped
**Mentally handicapped, Writings of the,
American**
  UF Writings of the mentally handicapped,
      American
Mentally handicapped and architecture
  USE Architecture and the mentally
       handicapped
Mentally handicapped and crime
  (May Subd Geog)
  UF Crime and the mentally handicapped
  BT Crime and criminals
Mentally handicapped and libraries
  USE Libraries and the mentally
       handicapped
Mentally handicapped and the Catholic Church
  USE Catholic Church and the mentally
       handicapped
Mentally handicapped artists
  USE Artists, Mentally handicapped
Mentally handicapped children
  (May Subd Geog)
  UF Backward children
      Children, Backward
      Children, Retarded
      Mentally retarded children
      Retarded children
  BT Child psychiatry
      Child psychopathology
      Developmentally disabled children
      Handicapped children
      Inefficiency, Intellectual
  NT Camps for mentally handicapped
      children
      Christian education of mentally
      handicapped children
      Church work with mentally
      handicapped children
      Cookery for mentally handicapped
      children
      Day care centers for mentally
      handicapped children
      Libraries and mentally handicapped
      children
      Mentally ill children
      Religious education of mentally
      handicapped children
      Sex instruction for mentally
      handicapped children
      Slow learning children
      Social work with mentally
      handicapped children
      Sports for mentally handicapped
      children
  — Economic conditions
      UF Mentally handicapped children—
          Socioeconomic status
  — Education *(May Subd Geog)*
      ⌐LC4601-4700⌐
      NT Teachers of mentally handicapped
          children
  — — Aims and objectives
  — — Dancing
      BT Dance therapy
          Dancing—Study and teaching
  — — English language, ⌐Reading, etc.⌐

Mentally handicapped children
(Continued)
— **Education (Elementary)**
  (May Subd Geog)
  [LC4603.3]
— **Education (Preschool)**
  (May Subd Geog)
  [LC4602.5]
  UF Preschool education of mentally
    handicapped children
  BT Education, Preschool
— **Education (Secondary)**
  (May Subd Geog)
  [LC4604]
— **Home care**
— **Life skills guides**
— **Psychological testing**
  UF Mentally handicapped children—
    Testing
  BT Psychological tests for children
— **Social conditions**
  UF Mentally handicapped children—
    Socioeconomic status
— Socioeconomic status
  USE Mentally handicapped children—
    Economic conditions
    Mentally handicapped children—
    Social conditions
— Testing
  USE Mentally handicapped children—
    Psychological testing
— **Vocational education** *(May Subd Geog)*
Mentally handicapped children, Cookery for
USE Cookery for mentally handicapped
  children
Mentally handicapped children, Teachers of
USE Teachers of mentally handicapped
  children
**Mentally handicapped children and
  architecture**
USE Architecture and mentally
  handicapped children
Mentally handicapped children and libraries
USE Libraries and mentally handicapped
  children
Mentally handicapped in literature
  NT Mental illness in literature
Mentally handicapped youth
  (May Subd Geog)
  BT Handicapped youth
— **Vocational education** *(May Subd Geog)*
  BT Vocational education
Mentally ill *(May Subd Geog)*
  UF Mental patients
  BT Mentally handicapped
    Sick
  RT Ex-mental patients
  NT Alcoholics
    Children of the mentally ill
    Church work with the mentally ill
    Police services for the mentally ill
    Psychiatric hospital patients
    Psychotherapy patients
    Schizophrenics
— **Abuse of**
  UF Abuse of the mentally ill
— **Care** *(May Subd Geog)*
  UF Insane—Care
    Mentally ill—Care and treatment
— Care and treatment
  USE Mentally ill—Care
— Commitment and detention
  USE Insane—Commitment and
    detention
— **Economic conditions**
  UF Mentally ill—Socioeconomic status
— **Employment**
  UF Employment of the mentally ill
  BT Mentally ill—Rehabilitation
— **Family relationships**
  [RC455.4.F3]

UF Families of the mentally ill
  BT Family
  RT Family psychotherapy
— Foster home care
  USE Mentally ill—Home care
— **Home care** *(May Subd Geog)*
  UF Mentally ill—Foster home care
  NT Schizophrenics—Home care
— Hospitals
  USE Psychiatric hospitals
— **Language**
  BT Speech, Disorders of
  NT Flight of ideas
— Legal status, laws, etc.
  USE Insanity—Jurisprudence
    Mental health laws
— **Life skills guides**
  [RC439.5]
— **Rehabilitation** *(May Subd Geog)*
  NT Halfway houses
    Mentally ill—Employment
— **Social conditions**
  UF Mentally ill—Socioeconomic status
— Socioeconomic status
  USE Mentally ill—Economic
    conditions
    Mentally ill—Social conditions
— **Surgery** *(May Subd Geog)*
    Here are entered works on any surgical opera-
    tions performed on the mentally ill. Works on
    brain surgery performed to treat psychiatric dis-
    orders are entered under Psychosurgery.
Mentally ill, Writings of the
  UF Writings of the mentally ill
  BT Literature and mental illness
Mentally ill, Writings of the, Canadian, [etc.]
Mentally ill, Writings of the, French-Canadian
  (May Subd Geog)
  UF French-Canadian writings of the
    mentally ill
  BT French-Canadian literature
Mentally ill, Writings of the, Italian
  (May Subd Geog)
  UF Italian writings of the mentally ill
  BT Italian literature
Mentally ill children *(May Subd Geog)*
    Here are entered works on mentally ill children
    themselves. Descriptive works on mental disorders of
    children are entered under Child psychopathology.
    Works on the clinical and therapeutic aspects of men-
    tal disorders in children are entered under Child psy-
    chiatry.
  UF Emotionally disturbed children
    Psychotic children
  BT Child psychiatry
    Child psychopathology
    Developmentally disabled children
    Mentally handicapped children
    Sick children
  NT Autistic children
    Emotional problems of children
    Mutism, Elective
— **Care** *(May Subd Geog)*
  UF Mentally ill children—Care and
    treatment
— Care and treatment
  USE Mentally ill children—Care
— **Education** *(May Subd Geog)*
  NT Flint Schools' Experimental
    Program for the Emotionally
    Handicapped
— **Recreation**
  NT Camps for mentally ill children
Mentally ill in literature
  NT Shakespeare, William, 1564-1616—
    Characters—Mentally ill
Mentally restored
  USE Ex-mental patients
Mentally retarded
  USE Mentally handicapped
Mentally retarded children
  USE Mentally handicapped children

Mentana, Battle of, 1867
  BT Papal States—History—1815-1870
Mentawai (Indonesian people)
  UF Mentaweians (Indonesian people)
    Mentawey (Indonesian people)
  BT Ethnology—Indonesia
Mentawai Islands (Indonesia)
  UF Kepulauan Mentawai (Indonesia)
    Mentawei Islands (Indonesia)
    Mentawi Islands (Indonesia)
  BT Islands—Indonesia
Mentawai language
  [PL5421]
  UF Mentawei language
    Mentawi language
  BT Indonesia—Languages
    Malayan languages
Mentawei Islands (Indonesia)
  USE Mentawai Islands (Indonesia)
Mentawei language
  USE Mentawai language
Mentaweians (Indonesian people)
  USE Mentawai (Indonesian people)
Mentawey (Indonesian people)
  USE Mentawai (Indonesian people)
Mentawi Islands (Indonesia)
  USE Mentawai Islands (Indonesia)
  NT Siberut (Indonesia)
Mentawi language
  USE Mentawai language
Menteith, Lake (Scotland)
  UF Lake Menteith (Scotland)
    Loch Menteith (Scotland)
  BT Lakes—Scotland
Menteith family
  USE Monteith family
Mentha
  [QK495.L25]
  BT Lamiaceae
  NT Mentha gentilis
Mentha gentilis
  [QK495.L25]
  BT Mentha
Menthaceae
  USE Lamiaceae
Menthenone
  UF Pulegone
  BT Ketones
Menthol
  [RM666.M (Therapeutics)]
  [RS165.M (Vegetable drugs)]
  UF Mint camphor
    Peppermint camphor
  RT Camphor
Menthon family *(Not Subd Geog)*
Menthone
  [QD341.K2]
Menticide
  USE Brainwashing
Menticirrhus
  [QL638.S34]
  UF King whitings
    Kingfishes
    Whiting (Fish)
  BT Sciaenidae
Menting family *(Not Subd Geog)*
Mentor Farm (Mentor, Ohio)
  USE James A. Garfield Home (Mentor,
    Ohio)
Mentors in business *(May Subd Geog)*
  BT Business
    Counseling
Mentors in education *(May Subd Geog)*
  BT Education
Mentors in science *(May Subd Geog)*
  BT Science
Mentors in the professions
  (May Subd Geog)
  BT Counseling
    Professions

Menus
  [TX727-8]
  UF Bills of fare
        Fare, Bills of
  BT Cookery
        Diet
        Gastronomy
        Table
  RT Caterers and catering
        Dinners and dining
  NT Breakfasts
        Buffets (Cookery)
        Lenten menus
        Luncheons
        Menus for space flight
        Reducing diets—Menus
        Suppers
        Wine lists
Menus for astronauts
  USE Menus for space flight
Menus for space flight
  UF Feeding programs (Space flight)
        In-flight feeding (Space flight)
        Menus for astronauts
  BT Menus
Menyukai (Indonesian people)
  USE Manyuke (Indonesian people)
Menzan
  [ML1040]
  UF Mendzan
  RT Xylophone
Menzies clan
  USE Menzies family
Menzies family *(Not Subd Geog)*
  UF Menees family
        Menzies clan
Meo (Asian people)
  USE Hmong (Asian people)
Meo language
  USE Hmong language
Meos (Indic people)
  BT Ethnology—India
Meos (Indic people) law
  USE Law, Meos (Indic people)
Mepacrine
  USE Quinacrine
Mepham family *(Not Subd Geog)*
Mephitinae
  USE Skunks
Mephitis
  USE Skunks
Mephitis macroura
  USE Hooded skunk
Mephitis mephitis
  USE Striped skunk
Mer, Double (Nfld.)
  USE Double Mer (Nfld.)
Mer Morte (Israel and Jordan)
  USE Dead Sea (Israel and Jordan)
Mer-wer (Egypt)
  USE Moeris, Lake (Egypt)
Meracantha
  [QL596.T2]
  BT Tenebrionidae
Merack family
  USE Merrick family
Meragh family
  USE Merrick family
Merak
  [QB805]
  BT Stars
Meralan Island (Vanuatu)
  USE Méré Lava (Vanuatu)
Meramec River (Mo.)
  BT Rivers—Missouri
Meraukese language
  USE Marindinese language
Mercantile agencies
  USE Credit bureaus
Mercantile buildings
  USE Commercial buildings

Mercantile law
  USE Commercial law
Mercantile marine
  USE Merchant marine
Mercantile system *(May Subd Geog)*
  [HB91]
  UF Cameralism
        Kameralism
  BT Economic policy
        Economics
        Industry and state
  RT Balance of trade
        Free trade and protection
Mercantile warrants
  USE Warehouse receipts
Mercantour Mountains (France)
  UF Massif du Mercantour (France)
  BT Mountains—France
Mercapto compounds
  NT Captopril
        Mercaptoethylguanidine
Mercaptoethylguanidine
  BT Guanidino compounds
        Mercapto compounds
Mercaptomethylpropanoylproline
  USE Captopril
Mercaptomethylpropionylproline
  USE Captopril
Mercaptovaline
  USE Penicillamine
Mercator projection, Space oblique
  (Cartography)
  USE Space oblique Mercator projection
          (Cartography)
Mercator projection, Transverse (Cartography)
  USE Transverse Mercator projection
          (Cartography)
Mercator projection, Universal transverse
  (Cartography)
  USE Universal transverse Mercator
          projection (Cartography)
Merced Peak (Calif.)
  BT Mountains—California
Merced River (Calif.)
  BT Rivers—California
Mercedes 300SL automobile
  [TL215.M4]
  UF 300SL automobile
        Gullwing automobile
  BT Mercedes automobile
Mercedes automobile
  UF Mercedes-Benz automobile
  NT Mercedes 300SL automobile
Mercedes-Benz automobile
  USE Mercedes automobile
Mercedes-Benz buses
  BT Buses
Mercenaries (Soldiers)
  USE Mercenary troops
Mercenary troops *(May Subd Geog)*
  UF Mercenaries (Soldiers)
        Troops, Mercenary
  BT Armies
        Soldiers
  RT Foreign enlistment
  NT Condottieri
        Galloglasses
        German mercenaries
        Greek mercenaries
        Gurkha soldiers
        Hanoverian mercenaries
        Hessian mercenaries
        Soldiers of fortune
        Swiss mercenaries
  — Haiti
      NT Cacos
Mercer family *(Not Subd Geog)*
  UF Mercier family
Mercerization
  [TS1515]

  BT Cotton finishing
        Cotton manufacture
Mercersburg theology *(May Subd Geog)*
  [BX9571]
  BT Calvinism
        Reformed Church—United States—
          Doctrines
        Theology, Doctrinal—United States
Mercês Palace (Salvador, Brazil)
  USE Palacete das Mercês (Salvador, Brazil)
Merchandise
  USE Commercial products
Merchandise, Branded
  USE Brand name products
Merchandise, Display of
  USE Display of merchandise
Merchandise in transit, Tariff on
  USE Duty-free transit
Merchandise licensing *(May Subd Geog)*
  UF Licensing, Merchandise
  BT License agreements
  RT Merchandising
Merchandising
  BT Marketing
  RT Merchandise licensing
  NT Fashion merchandising
Merchanka River (Lithuania)
  USE Merkys River (Lithuania)
Merchant banks *(May Subd Geog)*
  [HG1970-1971]
  BT Banks and banking
  RT Acceptances
        Investment banking
Merchant beetle
  USE Oryzaephilus mercator
Merchant companies
  USE Colonial companies
        Guilds
Merchant family *(Not Subd Geog)*
  RT Marchand family
Merchant grain beetle
  USE Oryzaephilus mercator
Merchant marine *(May Subd Geog)*
  [HE731-HE953 (Transportation)]
  [VK (Navigation)]
  UF Mercantile marine
  BT Commerce
        Marine service
        Seamen
        Ships
        Transportation
  RT Shipping
        Steamboat lines
  NT Armed merchant ships
        Cargo preference
        Coastwise navigation
        Coastwise shipping
        Insurance, Marine
        Merchant seamen
        Merchant ships
        Seatrains
        Ship transfers to foreign registry
        Shipping bounties and subsidies
        Ship's papers
        Tramp steamers
        Work boats
  — Accounting
      USE Shipping—Accounting
  — Administration
      USE Merchant marine—Management
  — Cargo
      USE Ships—Cargo
  — Collective bargaining
      USE Collective bargaining—Merchant
              marine
  — Collective labor agreements
      USE Collective labor agreements—
              Merchant marine
  — Law
      USE Maritime law
  — Lists of vessels

Merchant marine
— Lists of vessels *(Continued)*
  USE Ship registers
— **Management**
  UF Merchant marine—Administration
— Manning of vessels
  USE *subdivision* Manning of vessels
    under Merchant marine—
    ₍local subdivision₎, *e.g.*
    Merchant marine—Great
    Britain—Manning of vessels
    Ships—Manning
— **Medals, badges, decorations, etc.**
— **Officers**
  ₍VK221₎
  UF Ships—Officers
  NT Inland water transportation—
    Employees
    Shipmasters
— **Passenger traffic**
— Passes
  USE Shipping—Passes
— Personnel
  USE Merchant seamen
— Rates
  USE Shipping—Rates
— **Safety measures**
  ₍VK200₎
  UF Marine safety
    Merchant ships—Safety measures
    Ship safety
  RT Navigation—Safety measures
  NT Fishing boats—Safety measures
    Life-boats
    Life rafts
    Ships—Safety regulations
    Telegraph, Wireless
— Safety regulations
  USE Ships—Safety regulations
— Sanitary affairs
  USE Naval hygiene
— **Signaling**
  ₍VK381-397₎
  BT Signals and signaling
  NT Collisions at sea—Prevention
    Ships' lights
— Subsidies
  USE Shipping bounties and subsidies
— Taxation
  USE Shipping—Taxation
— **Vocational guidance** *(May Subd Geog)*
  ₍VK160₎
  BT Merchant seamen
— **Watch duty**
  ₍VK233₎
— **Great Britain**
— — **Manning of vessels**
— **United States**
  UF United States—Merchant marine
Merchant marks
USE Trademarks
Merchant seamen *(May Subd Geog)*
  Here are entered works on persons employed on
board of seagoing vessels as well as on vessels navi-
gating on inland waters.
  UF Merchant marine—Personnel
  BT Merchant marine
    Seamen
  RT Boatmen
  NT Collective bargaining—Merchant
    marine
    Collective labor agreements—Inland
    water transportation
    Collective labor agreements—
    Merchant marine
    Inland water transportation—
    Employees
    Merchant marine—Vocational
    guidance
    Shanghaiing
    Ships—Manning

    Strikes and lockouts—Merchant
    seamen
    Trade-unions—Merchant seamen
    Women merchant seamen
— **Accommodations on shipboard**
  ₍HE591₎
  UF Merchant ships—Crew
    accommodations
— **Biography**
— Charities
  USE Merchant seamen—Missions and
    charities
— **Effect of technological innovations on**
— **Legal status, laws, etc.**
  (May Subd Geog)
  UF Labor law, Maritime
    Maritime labor law
  BT Maritime law
— **Medical care** *(May Subd Geog)*
— **Missions and charities**
  (May Subd Geog)
  ₍BV2660-BV2678₎
  ₍HV3025-HV3163 (Charities)₎
  UF Merchant seamen—Charities
    Missions, Seamen's
    Seamen's missions
  BT Charities
— **Pensions** *(May Subd Geog)*
  UF Merchant seamen—Salaries,
    pensions, etc.
— — **Law and legislation**
  (May Subd Geog)
— **Salaries, etc.**
  UF Merchant seamen—Salaries,
    pensions, etc.
    Wages—Merchant seamen
— — **Law and legislation**
  (May Subd Geog)
— Salaries, pensions, etc.
  USE Merchant seamen—Pensions
    Merchant seamen—Salaries, etc.
— **Taxation** *(May Subd Geog)*
— — **Law and legislation**
  (May Subd Geog)
Merchant seamen, Afro-American
USE Afro-American merchant seamen
Merchant seamen, Women
USE Women merchant seamen
Merchant seamen's songs
USE Sea songs
Merchant seamen's writings
USE Sailors' writings
Merchant ship recognition
USE Merchant ships—Recognition
Merchant ships *(May Subd Geog)*
  UF Merchantmen
  BT Merchant marine
    Ships
  NT Armed merchant ships
    Barge-carrying ships
    Cargo ships
    Clipper-ships
    Coal-carrying vessels
    Coasters (Ships)
    Cogs (Sailing ships)
    Container ships
    Liquefied gas carriers
    Nuclear merchant ships
    Ocean liners
    Ore-bulk-oil ships
    Packets
    Passenger ships
    Steamboats
    Tankers
    Work boats
— Cargo
  USE Ships—Cargo
— Crew accommodations
  USE Merchant seamen—
    Accommodations on shipboard
— Law and legislation

    USE Maritime law
— Maintenance and repair
  USE Ships—Maintenance and repair
— **Passenger accommodation**
  UF Passenger accommodation
  BT Maritime law
— **Recognition**
  UF Merchant ship recognition
    Recognition of merchant ships
— Registers
  USE Ship registers
— Registration
  USE Ships—Registration and transfer
— Registry
  USE Ships—Nationality
— Safety measures
  USE Merchant marine—Safety
    measures
— **United States**
  NT Historic American Merchant
    Marine Survey
Merchant ships, Armed
USE Armed merchant ships
Merchant ships, Nuclear
USE Nuclear merchant ships
Merchant ship's papers
USE Ship's papers
Merchantmen
USE Merchant ships
Merchants *(May Subd Geog)*
  BT Business
    Businessmen
    Commerce
  NT Commission merchants
    English language—Conversation and
    phrase books (for merchants)
    Women merchants
— **Political activity**
  BT Politics, Practical
— **India**
  NT Lohānās
    Marwaris
    Poravālas
    Subarnabaniks
Merchants, Foreign *(May Subd Geog)*
  UF Foreign merchants
Merchants, Jewish *(May Subd Geog)*
  UF Jewish merchants
  NT Radanites
Merchants, Women
USE Women merchants
Merchant's Hundred Site (Va.)
USE Martin's Hundred Site (Va.)
Merchants in literature
USE Businessmen in literature
Merchel family
USE Merkel family
Mercier family
USE Mercer family
Mercle family
USE Merkel family
Mercuration
  BT Mercury
Mercurial diuretics
USE Diuretics, Mercurial
Mercuric oxide
  ₍QD181.H6₎
Mercurimetry
  BT Volumetric analysis
Mercurius (Roman deity)
USE Mercury (Roman deity)
Mercury (Planet) *(Not Subd Geog)*
  ₍QB371 (Theoretical astronomy)₎
  ₍QB611 (Descriptive astronomy)₎
  BT Planets
  NT Mercury probes
    Space flight to Mercury
— **Juvenile literature**
— **Surface**
Mercury *(May Subd Geog)*
  ₍QD181.H6 (Chemistry)₎

UF Quicksilver
BT Amalgamation
Liquid metals
NT Amalgams
Mercuration
— **Analysis**
— **Assaying**
— **Isotopes**
UF Isotopic mercury
Mercury isotopes
— — **Decay**
— **Metallurgy**
[TN790]
— **Spectra**
— **Toxicology**
[RA1231.M5]
UF Minamata disease
Mercury, Operation, 1941
USE Operation Mercury, 1941
Mercury, Sulphur compounds of
[QD181.H6]
Mercury (Planet), Transit of
[QB515]
Subdivided by date, e.g. Mercury (Planet), Transit
of—1861.
BT Transits
RT Parallax—Sun
Mercury (Roman deity)
UF Mercurius (Roman deity)
BT Gods, Roman
Mythology, Roman
RT Hermes (Greek deity)
Mercury arc
[QC705]
UF Arc, Mercury
BT Electric arc
Electric discharges through gases
Mercury-arc rectifiers
[TK2798]
BT Electric current rectifiers
NT Ignitrons
Mercury automobile
[TL215.M]
BT Ford automobile
NT Bobcat automobile
Comet automobile
Lynx automobile
Mercury Cougar automobile
Merkur automobile
Monarch automobile
Topaz automobile
Mercury cadmium tellurides
UF Cadmium mercury tellurides
BT Mercury telluride
Mercury compounds
[QD181.H6]
[QD412.H6 (Organic)]
Mercury Cougar automobile
[TL215.M]
UF Cougar automobile
BT Mercury automobile
Mercury dropping electrodes
USE Electrodes, Dropping mercury
Mercury electric light
USE Electric lighting, Mercury vapor
Mercury electrodes
USE Electrodes, Mercury
Mercury haloids
[QD181.H6]
Mercury-helium lasers
USE Helium-mercury lasers
Mercury in the body
Mercury industry and trade
(May Subd Geog)
Mercury isotopes
USE Mercury—Isotopes
Mercury miners (May Subd Geog)
[HD8039.M7]
BT Mercury mines and mining
Miners
NT Trade-unions—Mercury miners

Mercury mines and mining
(May Subd Geog)
[TN460-469]
NT Mercury miners
Mercury ores (May Subd Geog)
[TN460-469]
NT Cinnabar
Mercury organic compounds
USE Organomercury compounds
Mercury oxychlorides
[QD181.H6]
Mercury probes
BT Mercury (Planet)
Outer space—Exploration
Space flight to Mercury
NT Project Mariner
Mercury project
USE Project Mercury
Mercury sulphide
BT Sulphides
Mercury switches
[TK2831]
UF Switches, Mercury
BT Electric switchgear
Mercury telluride
[QC611.8.M38]
BT Tellurides
NT Mercury cadmium tellurides
Mercy
[BV4647.M4]
BT Ethics
Kindness
NT God—Mercy
God (Islam)—Mercy
Mercy, Corporal works of
USE Corporal works of mercy
Mercy death
USE Euthanasia
Mercy seat
USE Ark of the Covenant
Méré Lava (Vanuatu)
UF Ile Méralab (Vanuatu)
Ile Mwerlav (Vanuatu)
Ile Pic de l'Etoile (Vanuatu)
Meralan Island (Vanuatu)
Moraly (Vanuatu)
Star Peak (Vanuatu)
BT Islands—Vanuatu
Mere Mere (N.Z. : Mountain)
USE Meremere (N.Z. : Mountain)
Merechanka River (Lithuania)
USE Merkys River (Lithuania)
Mereczanka River (Lithuania)
USE Merkys River (Lithuania)
Meredeth family
USE Meredith family
Meredith family (Not Subd Geog)
UF Meredeth family
Merideth family
Meridith family
Merel family
USE Merrill family
Meremere (N.Z. : Mountain)
UF Mere Mere (N.Z. : Mountain)
BT Mountains—New Zealand
Meremon family
USE Merryman family
Mereness family (Not Subd Geog)
UF Marinus family
Morenus family
Merengue (Dance)
UF Meringue (Dance)
Merengues
BT Dance music
Meretsky family (Not Subd Geog)
Merett family
USE Merritt family
Merey family
USE Merry family
Merez River (Lithuania)
USE Merkys River (Lithuania)

Merfish
USE Mermen
Merganetta
USE Torrent ducks
Mergansers
[QL696.A5]
NT American merganser
— **Control**
Mergart family
USE Merget family
Merged transistor logic
USE Integrated injection logic
Merger (Criminal law)
USE Compound offenses
Merger of banks
USE Bank mergers
Merger of corporations
USE Consolidation and merger of
corporations
Merger of estates (May Subd Geog)
UF Confusion of titles
BT Estates (Law)
Merger of hospitals
USE Hospital mergers
Merger of rights
USE Confusion of rights
Merger of trade unions
USE Trade-unions—Consolidation
Mergers, Conglomerate
USE Conglomerate corporations
Mergers, Trade-union
USE Trade-unions—Consolidation
Mergert family
USE Merget family
Merget family (Not Subd Geog)
UF Marget family
Margett family
Margetts family
Margret family
Marguot family
Mergart family
Mergert family
Merging, Magnetic field line
USE Magnetic reconnection
Mergui Archipelago (Burma)
BT Archipelagoes—Burma
Mergus merganser
USE American merganser
Meri (Indic people)
USE Miri (Indic people)
Meriā
USE Merya (Finnish tribe)
Meriam family
USE Merriam family
Mericisca
[QL561.G6]
BT Geometridae
Merick family
USE Merrick family
Mérida, Cordillera de (Venezuela)
UF Andes de Mérida (Venezuela)
Cordillera de Mérida (Venezuela)
Cordillera Merideña (Venezuela)
Sierra de Mérida (Venezuela)
Sierra Nevada de Mérida (Venezuela)
BT Andes
Mountains—Venezuela
Merideth family
USE Meredith family
Meridian, Prime
USE Longitude—Prime meridian
Meridian acupuncture points
USE Acupuncture points
Meridian-circle
USE Transit-circle
Meridian lines
[QB207]
UF Lines, Meridian

Meridian lines *(Continued)*
    BT Astronomical geography
        Astronomy, Spherical and practical
        Azimuth
        Time—Systems and standards
    NT International date line
Meridian-marks
    ⌜QB101⌟
    BT Astronomical instruments
Meridith family
    USE Meredith family
Meriet family
    USE Merritt family
Meril family
    USE Merrill family
Merim Lagoon (Brazil and Uruguay)
    USE Mirim Lake (Brazil and Uruguay)
Meriman family
    USE Merryman family
Merimde-Benisalâme Site (Egypt)
    USE Merimde Site (Egypt)
Merimde Site (Egypt)
    UF Merimde-Benisalâme Site (Egypt)
    BT Egypt—Antiquities
Merina (African people)
    USE Hovas
Merina dialect
    USE Malagasy language
Meringue (Dance)
    USE Merengue (Dance)
Meringue cookery
    USE Cookery (Meringue)
Merinides
    USE Beni Marin dynasty
Merino sheep
    ⌜SF373.M5⌟
    NT Saxon merino sheep
Meris (Moth)
    ⌜QL561.G6⌟
    BT Geometridae
Meristem
    ⌜QK725⌟
    BT Plant cells and tissues
    RT Growth (Plants)
    NT Roots (Botany)—Anatomy
Meristem culture
    BT Plant tissue culture
Merit (Christianity)
    ⌜BT773⌟
    Here are entered works on the doctrine that the
    good works of those justified by God are worthy of
    further reward.
    UF Merit (Theology)
    BT Salvation
    RT Good works (Theology)
        Reward (Theology)
Merit (Ethics)
    ⌜BJ1500.M47⌟
    BT Ethics
Merit (Islam)
    ⌜BP166.33⌟
    BT Islam—Doctrines
        Man (Islam)
Merit (Jewish theology)
    ⌜BM645.M4⌟
    UF Merit of the fathers
    BT Ethics, Jewish
Merit (Theology)
    USE Merit (Christianity)
Merit family
    USE Merritt family
Merit of the fathers
    USE Merit (Jewish theology)
Merit scholarship qualifying test
    USE National merit scholarship qualifying
        test
Merit system
    USE Civil service reform
Merit-Tandy Farm (Switzerland County, Ind.)
    BT Farms—Indiana

Merit-Tandy House (Switzerland County, Ind.)
    BT Dwellings—Indiana
Mérite agricole
    UF Agricultural merit contest
    BT Agriculture—Awards
        Agriculture—Competitions
        Rewards (Prizes, etc.)—Québec
        (Province)
Mérite du défricheur
    UF Défricheur, Mérite du
    BT Agriculture—Québec (Province)—
        Awards
        Agriculture—Québec (Province)—
        Competitions
        Rewards (Prizes, etc.)—Québec
        (Province)
Meritt family
    USE Merritt family
Meriweather family
    USE Meriwether family
Meriwether family *(Not Subd Geog)*
    UF Meriweather family
        Merriweather family
        Merriwether family
        Merryweather family
Merkabah
    USE Merkava
Merkava
    UF Ma'aseh merkavah
        Merkabah
        Merkavah
    BT Mysticism—Judaism
    RT Throne of God
Merkava in rabbinical literature
    ⌜BM496.9.M⌟
    BT Rabbinical literature
Merkavah
    USE Merkava
Merkel family *(Not Subd Geog)*
    UF Merchel family
        Mercle family
        Merkele family
        Merkell family
        Merkil family
        Merkl family
        Merkle family
        Merkley family
        Murkle family
    RT Markley family
Merkele family
    USE Merkel family
Merkell family
    USE Merkel family
Merkem (Belgium), Battle of, 1918
    ⌜D542.M⌟
    BT World War, 1914-1918—Campaigns—
        Belgium
Merkil family
    USE Merkel family
Merkis River (Lithuania)
    USE Merkys River (Lithuania)
Merkl family
    USE Merkel family
Merkle family
    USE Merkel family
Merkley family
    USE Merkel family
Merkur automobile
    ⌜TL215.M⌟
    BT Mercury automobile
Merkus pine
    USE Pinus merkusii
Merkys River (Lithuania)
    UF Mareganka River (Lithuania)
        Merchanka River (Lithuania)
        Merechanka River (Lithuania)
        Mereczanka River (Lithuania)
        Merez River (Lithuania)
        Merkis River (Lithuania)
    BT Rivers—Lithuania

Merl
    USE European blackbird
Merlangius merlangus
    USE Gadus merlangus
Merlangus merlangus
    USE Gadus merlangus
Merlin
    USE Merlin (Legendary character)
Merlin (Legendary character)
    UF Merlin
    BT Arthurian romances
Merlucciidae
    USE Hake
Merluccius
    ⌜QL638.M4⌟
    BT Hake
Merluccius albidus
    ⌜QL638.G2⌟
Merluccius gayi
    ⌜QL638.M4⌟
    UF Merluccius gayii
Merluccius gayii
    USE Merluccius gayi
Merluccius hubbsi
    USE Merluccius merluccius
Merluccius merluccius
    ⌜QL638.M4⌟
    UF Merluccius hubbsi
Merluccius productus
    USE Pacific hake
MERMAC (Electronic computer system)
    BT IBM 360 (Computer)—Programming
Mermaids
    ⌜GR910⌟
    BT Animals, Mythical
        Ocean—Folklore
        Ocean—Mythology
        Pharaoh's army (in religion, folk-lore,
        etc.)
Mermen *(May Subd Geog)*
    ⌜GR910⌟
    UF Merfish
    BT Animals, Mythical
Merner family *(Not Subd Geog)*
    UF Murner family
Mero language
    USE Meru language
Merodon
    ⌜QL537.S9⌟
    BT Syrphidae
Meroe (Sudan) *(Not Subd Geog)*
    ⌜DT159.9.M47⌟
    BT Cities and towns, Ruined, extinct, etc.
        —Sudan
        Sudan—Antiquities
  — Civilization
  — — Indic influences
        BT India—Civilization
Meroitic inscriptions
    USE Inscriptions, Meroitic
Meroitic language
    ⌜PL8512.M45⌟
    BT African languages
        Nilo-Saharan languages
        Sudan—Languages
Merolepidae
    USE Centracanthidae
Merolu dialect
    USE Telugu language—Dialects—Merolu
Meromorphic functions
    USE Functions, Meromorphic
Meromyza *(May Subd Geog)*
    ⌜QL537.C46⌟
    BT Chloropidae
Merope, wife of Cresphontes
    BT Mythology, Greek
Merophysiidae
    USE Endomychidae
        Lathridiidae
Meropidae
    USE Bee eaters

Merosargus
⌐QL537.S84¬
BT Stratiomyidae
Merostomata
⌐QL447.7¬
BT Arachnida
Arachnida, Fossil
NT Xiphosura
Merovingian architecture
USE Architecture, Merovingian
Merovingian art
USE Art, Merovingian
Merovingian decoration and ornament
USE Decoration and ornament,
Merovingian
Merovingian goldwork
USE Goldwork, Merovingian
Merovingian numismatics
USE Numismatics, Merovingian
Merovingian pottery
USE Pottery, Merovingian
Merovingians *(May Subd Geog)*
⌐DC65-DC69 (France)¬
⌐DD128 (Germany)¬
RT France—History—To 987
NT Antrustions
— **Anthropometry**
Merphos
USE Tributylphosphorotrithioite
Merratt family
USE Merritt family
Merrefield family
USE Merrifield family
Merrell family
USE Merrill family
Merreman family
USE Merryman family
Merret family
USE Merritt family
Merrett family
USE Merritt family
Merrey family
USE Merry family
Merri River (Vic.)
BT Rivers—Australia
Merriam family *(Not Subd Geog)*
UF Meriam family
Miriam family
Merriam kangaroo rat
USE Merriam's kangaroo rat
Merriam's chipmunk
⌐QL737.R68¬
UF Tamias merriami
BT Chipmunks
Merriam's kangaroo rat
UF Dipodomys merriami
Merriam kangaroo rat
BT Kangaroo rats
Merriang Homestead (Vic.)
BT Dwellings—Australia
Merrick family *(Not Subd Geog)*
UF Merack family
Meragh family
Merick family
Merricks family
Merrik family
Mirach family
Mireck family
Mirich family
Mirick family
Miriek family
Mirrick family
Myrick family
Merricks family
USE Merrick family
Merrie family
USE Merry family
Merrifield family *(Not Subd Geog)*
UF Maryfield family
Merrefield family
Merryfield family

Merrik family
USE Merrick family
Merrill family *(Not Subd Geog)*
UF De Merle family
Merel family
Meril family
Merrell family
Merrimack River (N.H. and Mass.)
BT Rivers—Massachusetts
Rivers—New Hampshire
Merriman family
USE Merryman family
Merrit family
USE Merritt family
Merrits family
USE Merritt family
Merritt family *(Not Subd Geog)*
UF Merett family
Meriet family
Merit family
Meritt family
Merratt family
Merret family
Merrett family
Merrit family
Merrits family
Merrot family
Mirrit family
Mirritt family
Merriweather family
USE Meriwether family
Merriwether family
USE Meriwether family
Merrot family
USE Merritt family
Merry family *(Not Subd Geog)*
UF Mairy family
Marey family
Marry family
Mary family
Marys family
Merey family
Merrey family
Merrie family
Merry-go-round *(May Subd Geog)*
UF Carousel
Carrousel
BT Amusement rides
Merry-go-round art *(May Subd Geog)*
⌐NK5030-NK5035¬
UF Carousel art
Carrousel art
BT Fairground art
Merry-go-round music
USE Calliope music
Merryfield family
USE Merrifield family
Merryman family *(Not Subd Geog)*
UF Meremon family
Meriman family
Merreman family
Merriman family
Merrymon family
Merrymoon family
Merrymoone family
Miriman family
Mirriman family
Merrymon family
USE Merryman family
Merrymoon family
USE Merryman family
Merrymoone family
USE Merryman family
Merryweather family
USE Meriwether family
Mers-el-Kebir, Attack on, 1940
BT World War, 1939-1945—Campaigns—
Algeria
Mersch family
USE Marsh family

Mersey River (England)
BT Rivers—England
Mersh family
USE Marsh family
Mershon family *(Not Subd Geog)*
RT Marchand family
Merten family
USE Mertens family
Mertens family *(Not Subd Geog)*
UF Merten family
Merton family
MERTL (Computer program)
UF Multidrop Efficiency Regarding
Transmission Lines (Computer
program)
Merton family
USE Mertens family
Mertz family
USE Martz family
Mertzdorff family *(Not Subd Geog)*
Meru (African people)
⌐DT433.545.M47 (Kenya)¬
UF Mwere (African people)
Wameru (African people)
BT Ethnology—Kenya
Ethnology—Tanzania
Meru folk literature
USE Folk literature, Meru
Meru language
UF Kimeru language
Mero language
BT Bantu languages
Meru literature *(May Subd Geog)*
NT Folk literature, Meru
Mervaile family
USE Marvel family
Merveille family
USE Marvel family
Mervell family
USE Marvel family
Mervin family
USE Merwin family
Merwin family *(Not Subd Geog)*
UF Mervin family
Merya (Finnish tribe)
UF Meria
BT Ethnology—Soviet Union
Merycism
⌐RC840¬
UF Rumination in man
BT Stomach—Diseases
Merycoidodontidae
⌐QE882.U3¬
BT Ruminants, Fossil
Mery's glands
USE Cowper's glands
Merz family
USE Martz family
Mes
USE Meches
Mesa Verde National Park (Colo.)
BT Cliff-dwellings—Colorado
Colorado—Antiquities
National parks and reserves—United
States
Parks—Colorado
Mesaba Range (Minn.)
USE Mesabi Range (Minn.)
Mesabi Range (Minn.)
UF Mesaba Range (Minn.)
BT Mountains—Minnesota
Mesagroicus
⌐QL596.C9¬
BT Curculionidae
Mesas *(May Subd Geog)*
⌐GB571-578¬
BT Mountains
Plateaus
— **Arizona**
NT Black Mesa (Navajo County and
Apache County, Ariz.)

Mesas *(Continued)*
— **New Mexico**
  NT Gallegos Mesa (N.M.)
— **South Dakota**
  NT Cuny Table (S.D.)
— **Utah**
  NT White Mesa (Utah)
Mescal
  [TP607.M]
  Here are entered works dealing with the liquor
  distilled from the agave.
  UF Mezcal
  BT Agave
    Pulque
  NT Tequila
Mescal (Cactus)
  USE Peyote
Mescal bean plant
  USE Peyote
    Sophora secundiflora
Mescal beans
  USE Peyote
    Sophora secundiflora—Seed
Mescal buttons
  USE Peyote
Mescal plant (Lophophora)
  USE Peyote
Mescalbean plant
  USE Peyote
    Sophora secundiflora
Mescalbeans
  USE Peyote
    Sophora secundiflora—Seed
Mescalero Indians
  BT Apache Indians
    Indians of North America
Mescalero language
  BT Apache languages
    Indians of North America—New
      Mexico—Languages
    New Mexico—Languages
  RT Chiricahua language
Mescaline
  [BF209.M4 (Psychology)]
  UF Mezcalin
    Mezcaline
    Trimethoxybenzeneethanamine
    Trimethoxyphenethylamine
  BT Alkaloids
    Hallucinogenic drugs
    Peyote
    Phenethylamines
Mesembryanthemaceae
  USE Aizoaceae
Mesembryanthemum
  [QK495.A3 (Botany)]
Mesencephalon
  UF Midbrain
  BT Brain
  NT Cerebral peduncle
    Inferior colliculus
    Red nucleus
    Torus semicircularis
— **Surgery**
  UF Mesencephalotomy
Mesencephalotomy
  USE Mesencephalon—Surgery
Mesenchyme
  BT Connective tissues
    Tissues
  NT Reticulo-endothelial system
Mesenteric artery
  BT Arteries
Mesentery
  [QL864 (Comparative anatomy)]
  [QM367 (Human anatomy)]
  BT Intestines
— **Blood-vessels**
— — **Surgery**
    NT Mesocaval shunt
— **Surgery**

— **Tumors**
  [RD667]
Meser family
  USE Messer family
Meservey Cemetery (Wisner, Iowa)
  (Not Subd Geog)
  BT Cemeteries—Iowa
Meseta Central (Mexico)
  UF Anahuac (Mexico)
  BT Plateaus—Mexico
Meseta de Marcahuasi (Peru)
  USE Marcahuasi Plateau (Peru)
Meseta del Collao (Bolivia and Peru)
  USE Altiplano (Bolivia and Peru)
Meseta del Titicaca (Bolivia and Peru)
  USE Altiplano (Bolivia and Peru)
Méséta Marocaine (Morocco)
  BT Plateaus—Morocco
MESFET's
  USE Metal semiconductor field-effect
    transistors
Mesh generation, Numerical (Numerical
  analysis)
  USE Numerical grid generation (Numerical
    analysis)
Meshach (Biblical character)
Meshanticut Brook (R.I.)
  BT Rivers—Rhode Island
Meshchera (R.S.F.S.R.)
  USE Meshchera Lowland (R.S.F.S.R.)
Meshchera dialect
  USE Mishar dialect
Meshchera Lowland (R.S.F.S.R.)
  UF Meshchera (R.S.F.S.R.)
    Meshcherskaia nizina (R.S.F.S.R.)
    Meshcherskaia nizmennost'
      (R.S.F.S.R.)
    Meshcherskaya nizina (R.S.F.S.R.)
    Meshcherskaya nizmennost'
      (R.S.F.S.R.)
    Meshchora (R.S.F.S.R.)
Meshcherskaia nizina (R.S.F.S.R.)
  USE Meshchera Lowland (R.S.F.S.R.)
Meshcherskaia nizmennost' (R.S.F.S.R.)
  USE Meshchera Lowland (R.S.F.S.R.)
Meshcherskaya nizina (R.S.F.S.R.)
  USE Meshchera Lowland (R.S.F.S.R.)
Meshcherskaya nizmennost' (R.S.F.S.R.)
  USE Meshchera Lowland (R.S.F.S.R.)
Meshchora (R.S.F.S.R.)
  USE Meshchera Lowland (R.S.F.S.R.)
Meshwork
  USE Sprang
Mesier family
  USE Messer family
Mesirah Island (Oman)
  USE Masirah Island (Oman)
Mesitoderidae
  USE Centroderidae
Mesitylene
  [QD341.H9]
Meskéné Site (Syria)
  USE Emar (Ancient city)
Meskhetians *(May Subd Geog)*
  [DK34.M]
  BT Ethnology—Soviet Union
Meskwaki Indians
  USE Fox Indians
MÉSM (Computer)
  UF Malaia élektronnaia schetnaia mashina
    (Computer)
  BT Electronic digital computers
Mesmerism *(May Subd Geog)*
  [BF1111-BF1156 (Hypnotism)]
  [RM917-RM926 (Therapeutics)]
  BT Subconsciousness
    Therapeutic systems
  RT Animal magnetism
    Hypnotism
    Magnetic healing
    Therapeutics, Suggestive

  NT Mental healing
    Mental suggestion
    Mesmerists
Mesmerists *(May Subd Geog)*
  [BF1127]
  BT Mesmerism
Mesne profits
  USE Ejectment
Mesnevis
  USE Masnavis
Meso-America
  USE Indians of Central America
    Indians of Mexico
Meso-American Indians
  USE Indians of Central America
    Indians of Mexico
Mesoamerica
  USE Indians of Central America
    Indians of Mexico
Mesoamerican Indians
  USE Indians of Central America
    Indians of Mexico
Mesobius
  [QL638.M2]
  BT Macrouridae
Mesoblast
  USE Mesoderm
Mesoblastema
  USE Mesoderm
Mesocapromys
  USE Capromys
Mesocaval anastomosis
  USE Mesocaval shunt
Mesocaval shunt
  UF Anastomosis, Mesocaval
    Mesocaval anastomosis
    Shunt, Mesocaval
  BT Mesentery—Blood-vessels—Surgery
    Vena cava—Surgery
Mesocestoides
  [QL391.P7]
  BT Mesocestoididae
Mesocestoididae
  [QL391.P7]
  BT Cyclophyllidea
  NT Mesocestoides
Mesoclimate
  USE Mesoclimatology
Mesoclimatology
  [QC981.7.M4]
  UF Mesoclimate
  BT Climatology
  SA *subdivision* Climate *under names of*
    small valleys, towns, etc.
  NT Urban climatology
Mesocricetus *(May Subd Geog)*
  [QL737.R638]
  BT Cricetidae
    Hamsters
  NT Golden hamster
Mesocricetus auratus
  USE Golden hamster
Mesoderm
  UF Mesoblast
    Mesoblastema
  BT Embryology
Mesodon
  [QL430.5.P6]
  BT Polygyridae
Mesodon thyroidus
  [QL430.5.P6]
  UF Helix thyroidus
Mesogastropoda
  USE Pectinibranchiata
Mesogastropoda, Fossil
  USE Pectinibranchiata, Fossil
Mesoglia
  USE Microglia
    Oligodendroglia
Mesoinositol
  USE Inositol

Mesolcina Valley (Switzerland)
  UF Misox Valley (Switzerland)
      Misoxertal (Switzerland)
      Moësa Valley (Switzerland)
      Valle Mesolcina (Switzerland)
  BT Valleys—Switzerland
Mesolithic period *(May Subd Geog)*
  UF Middle Stone age
  BT Stone age
  NT Asturian culture
      Azilian culture
      Tardenoisian culture
      Wilton culture
  — Europe, Northern
      NT Maglemosean culture
  — Sweden
  — Yugoslavia
Mesomeric polarization
  USE Mesomerism
Mesomerism
  UF Mesomeric polarization
      Polarization, Mesomeric
      Resonance (Chemistry)
  BT Isomerism
      Polarization (Electricity)
  RT Tautomerism
  NT Hyperconjugation
Mesometeorology *(May Subd Geog)*
  [QC981]
  BT Meteorology
  RT Weather
  NT SESAME Project
Meson facilities
  USE Meson factories
Meson factories *(May Subd Geog)*
  UF Facilities, Meson
      Factories, Meson
      Meson facilities
  BT Linear accelerators
Meson-nucleon interactions
  UF Interactions, Meson-nucleon
      Meson-nucleon reactions
      Reactions, Meson-nucleon
  BT Nuclear reactions
Meson-nucleon reactions
  USE Meson-nucleon interactions
Meson resonance
  [QC721]
  UF Resonance mesons
  BT Mesons
      Nuclear magnetic resonance
Mesonephros
  USE Wolffian body
Mesones de Isuela Castle (Mesones de Isuela,
  Spain)
  USE Castillo de Mesones de Isuela
        (Mesones de Isuela, Spain)
Mesons
  UF Heavy electrons
      Mesotrons
  BT Cosmic rays
      Electrons
      Hadrons
  RT Muons
  NT Kaons
      Meson resonance
      Pions
  — Capture
  — Decay
  — Scattering
  — Spectra
Mesonychidae
  NT Mesonyx
Mesonyx
  [QE882.U8]
  BT Mesonychidae
  NT Mesonyx obtusidens
Mesonyx obtusidens
  [QE882.U8]
  BT Mesonyx

Mesoplodon
  [QL737.C438]
  BT Beaked whales
Mesoplodon carlhubbsi
  USE Hubb's beaked whale
Mesoplodon densirostris
  [QL737.C438]
  UF Blainville's beaked whale
      Dense-beaked whale
Mesoplodon europaeus
  [QL737.C438]
  UF Antillean beaked whale
      Gervais' beaked whale
      Gulf Stream beaked whale
      Mesoplodon gervaisi
Mesoplodon gervaisi
  USE Mesoplodon europaeus
Mesoplodon mirum
  USE True's beaked whale
Mesoplodon mirus
  USE True's beaked whale
Mesoplodon pacificus
  USE Indopacetus pacificus
Mesopotamia
  USE Iraq
Mesopotamia (Argentina)
  UF Mesopotamia Argentina (Argentina)
      Región de la Mesopotamia (Argentina)
Mesopotamia Argentina (Argentina)
  USE Mesopotamia (Argentina)
Mesosphaerocera
  [QL537.S7]
  BT Sphaeroceridae
Mesosphere
  BT Atmosphere
      Chemosphere
Mesostigmata
Mesosuchia
  BT Crocodiles, Fossil
Mesotaeniaceae *(May Subd Geog)*
  [QK569.M (Algology)]
  UF Desmids
      Gonatozygaceae
      Saccoderm desmids
  BT Zygnematales
Mesotermitidae
  USE Rhinotermitidae
Mesothelioma
  UF Mesothelium—Tumors
  BT Tumors
Mesothelium
  BT Epithelium
  — Tumors
      USE Mesothelioma
Mesothorium
  [QD181.T5]
  NT Radiothorium
      Radium paint
Mesotomy
  USE Resolution (Chemistry)
Mesotrons
  USE Mesons
Mesovelia
  [QL523.M4]
  BT Mesoveliidae
  NT Mesovelia mulsanti
Mesovelia mulsanti *(May Subd Geog)*
  [QL523.M4]
  BT Mesovelia
Mesoveliidae
  [QL523.M4]
  UF Water treaders (Insects)
  BT Hemiptera
  NT Mesovelia
Mesozoa
  [QL391.M]
  BT Invertebrates
Mesozoic period
  USE Geology, Stratigraphic—Mesozoic
      Paleobotany—Mesozoic
      Paleontology—Mesozoic

Mesquakie Indians
  USE Fox Indians
Mesquite *(May Subd Geog)*
  [QK495.L52 (Botany)]
  [SB317.M (Economic plants)]
  [SB615.M4 (Weeds)]
  UF Algaroba
      Prosopis
  BT Leguminosae
  NT Honey mesquite
      Tamarugo
Mess
  USE Armies—Commissariat
Mess management specialists (United States
  Navy)
  USE United States—Armed Forces—Food
        service specialists
Message handling (Telecommunication)
  USE Telecommunication—Message
        processing
Message processing (Telecommunication)
  USE Telecommunication—Message
        processing
Messages in bottles
  USE Ocean bottles
Messalians
  [BT1417]
  UF Adelphians
      Enthusiasts (Messalians)
      Euchites
      Lampetians
      Marcianites
      Massalians
  BT Heresies, Christian—History—Early
      church, ca. 30-600
Messapian inscriptions
  USE Inscriptions, Messapian
Messapian language
  [PA2394]
  UF Iapygian language
  BT Illyrian languages
Messapian Peninsula (Italy)
  USE Salentina Peninsula (Italy)
Messapians
  USE Messapii
Messapii
  [DG225.M4]
  UF Messapians
  BT Ethnology—Italy
Messar family
  USE Messer family
Messenger (Bronze sculpture)
  USE Wynne, David, 1926-   Messenger
Messenger ribonucleic acid
  UF Messenger RNA
      Ribonucleic acid, Messenger
      RNA, Messenger
  BT Genetic transcription
      Ribonucleic acid
  NT Genetic translation
Messenger RNA
  USE Messenger ribonucleic acid
Messengers
  BT Communication and traffic
  — Collective labor agreements
      USE Collective labor agreements—
         Messengers
Messengers-at-arms
Messengers in literature
  NT Divine messengers in literature
      Shakespeare, William, 1564-1616—
        Characters—Messengers
Messenian Wars
  USE Greece—History—Messenian Wars,
      735-460 B.C.
Messer family *(Not Subd Geog)*
  UF Meser family
      Mesier family
      Messar family
      Messers family

Messers family
    USE Messer family
Messerschmitt 108 (Airplane)
    [TL686.M]
    UF B.F.W. Me 108b "Taifun"
    BT Airplanes
       Messerschmitt airplanes
Messerschmitt 109 (Fighter planes)
    [TL686.M44]
    UF BF 109 (Fighter planes)
    BT Fighter planes
Messerschmitt 110 (Fighter planes)
    [TL686.M44]
    BT Fighter planes
Messerschmitt 163 (Fighter planes)
    [TL686.M44]
    UF Komet (Fighter planes)
    BT Fighter planes
       Rocket planes
Messerschmitt 262 (Fighter planes)
    [TL686.M44]
    BT Bombers
       Fighter planes
       Jet planes
Messerschmitt 321 (Glider)
    [TL686.M]
    BT Gliders (Aeronautics)
       Messerschmitt airplanes
Messerschmitt 323 (Transport planes)
    [TL686.M]
    UF Gigant (Transport planes)
    BT Messerschmitt airplanes
       Transport planes
Messerschmitt airplanes
    NT Messerschmitt 108 (Airplane)
       Messerschmitt 321 (Glider)
       Messerschmitt 323 (Transport planes)
Messiah
    [BL475 (Comparative religion)]
    [BM615-BM620 (Judaism)]
    [BT230-BT240]
    Here are entered general works on the conception of a messiah. Works dealing with prophecies in the Old Testament concerning a messiah are entered under Messiah—Prophecies. Works identifying Jesus Christ with the Messiah are entered under Jesus Christ—Messiahship.
    BT Jesus Christ
       Jesus Christ—Messiahship
       Judaism
    NT Messianic era (Judaism)
       Messianism
       Pseudo-Messiahs
       Superman
  — Legends
      BT Messianic era (Judaism)
  — Prophecies
      [BT235]
      UF Bible—Prophecies—Messiah
      NT Messianic Psalms
Messiah in literature
Messiahs, False
    USE Pseudo-Messiahs
Messianic cults
    USE Nativistic movements
Messianic era (Judaism)
    BT Eschatology, Jewish
       Jews—Restoration
       Messiah
    NT Messiah—Legends
Messianic Jews
    USE Jewish Christians
Messianic Psalms
    [BS1445.M4]
    UF Psalms, Messianic
    BT Messiah—Prophecies
Messianic secret (Bible)
    [BT245]
    UF Secret, Messianic (Bible)
    BT Jesus Christ—Messiahship

Messianism
    BT Messiah
       Nativistic movements
       Utopias
Messianism, Afro-American
    (May Subd Geog)
    [E185.625]
    UF Afro-American messianism
    BT Messianism, Political—United States
Messianism, Political (May Subd Geog)
    UF Political messianism
    BT Nationalism
    NT Sebastianism
  — United States
      UF Manifest destiny (United States)
      NT Messianism, Afro-American
Messina (Sicily)
  — History
  — — Rebellion, 1674-1678
Messina, Strait of (Italy)
    UF Fretum Siculum (Italy)
       Strait of Messina (Italy)
       Stretto di Messina (Italy)
    BT Straits—Italy
Messmer family
    USE Messner family
Messner family (Not Subd Geog)
    UF Messmer family
       Moessner family
Mesta
    USE Kenaf
Mestranol
    UF Ethinyl estradiol methyl ether
       Methoxynorpregnatrienynol
    BT Oral contraceptives
       Steroid hormones
       Sterols
MESY (Computer system)
    [TA345.5.M16]
Meta-abelian groups, Free
    USE Free metabelian groups
Meta-analysis
    BT Psychometrics
       Social sciences—Statistical methods
Meta knowledge
    USE Metacognition
Meta Language (Computer program language)
    USE ML (Computer program language)
Metabasite (May Subd Geog)
Metabelian groups, Free
    USE Free metabelian groups
Metabolic activation
    USE Biotransformation (Metabolism)
Metabolic antagonists
    USE Antimetabolites
Metabolic conjugation
    UF Conjugation, Metabolic
       Conjugation (Metabolism)
       Detoxication, Metabolic, by conjugation
       Detoxification, Metabolic, by conjugation
       Metabolic detoxication by conjugation
       Metabolic detoxification by conjugation
    BT Biotransformation (Metabolism)
       Metabolism
Metabolic control
    USE Metabolism—Regulation
Metabolic craniopathy
    USE Hyperostosis frontalis interna
Metabolic detoxication
    USE subdivision Metabolic detoxication under chemicals and other substances, e.g. Copper—Metabolic detoxication; Drugs—Metabolic detoxication
Metabolic detoxication by conjugation
    USE Metabolic conjugation

Metabolic detoxification
    USE subdivision Metabolic detoxication under chemicals and other substances, e.g. Copper—Metabolic detoxication; Drugs—Metabolic detoxication
Metabolic detoxification by conjugation
    USE Metabolic conjugation
Metabolic disorders
    USE Metabolism—Disorders
Metabolic disorders in children
    (May Subd Geog)
    [RJ390]
    BT Children—Diseases
       Metabolism—Disorders
    RT Children—Metabolism
    NT Acid-base imbalances in children
       Body fluid disorders in children
       Calcium metabolism disorders in children
       Carbohydrate metabolism disorders in children
       Diabetes in children
       Hyperlipidemia in children
       Hypoglycemia in children
       Lactose intolerance in children
       Obesity in children
       Phosphorus metabolism disorders in children
       Protein metabolism disorders in children
Metabolic inhibitors
    USE Enzyme inhibitors
Metabolic manifestations of general diseases
    [RB147]
    UF Metabolic symptoms of general diseases
    BT Metabolism—Disorders
       Symptomatology
Metabolic profile tests (May Subd Geog)
    [SF768 (Veterinary physiology)]
    UF Profile tests, Metabolic
    BT Metabolism—Testing
       Veterinary physiology
Metabolic regulation
    USE Metabolism—Regulation
Metabolic symptoms of general diseases
    USE Metabolic manifestations of general diseases
Metabolism
    [QH521 (Biology)]
    [QP171-QP177 (Physiology)]
    UF Anabolism
       Catabolism
       Metabolism, Primary
       Primary metabolism
    BT Biological chemistry
       Physiology
    SA subdivision Metabolism under individual chemicals and groups of chemicals, and individual organs and tissues, e.g. Copper—Metabolism; Heart—Metabolism
    NT Alloxuric substances
       Anaerobiosis
       Antimetabolites
       Basal metabolism
       Bioenergetics
       Biotransformation (Metabolism)
       Carbohydrates in the body
       Cell metabolism
       Children—Metabolism
       Crassulacean acid metabolism
       Dormancy (Biology)
       Drug-nutrient interactions
       Energy metabolism
       Enterohepatic circulation
       Fetus—Metabolism
       Gluconeogenesis
       Infants (Newborn)—Metabolism
       Ketogenic diet

Ketone body metabolism
Krebs cycle
Metabolic conjugation
Metabolism, Secondary
Microbial metabolism
Microbial metabolites
Mineral metabolism
Minerals in the body
Nitrogen in the body
Plants—Metabolism
Tissue metabolism
Urea
— Disorders (May Subd Geog)
    [RB147 (Pathology)]
    [RC627.5-RC632 (Internal
        medicine)]
    UF Disorders of metabolism
        Metabolic disorders
        Metabolism, Disorders of
    SA subdivision Metabolism—Disorders
        under individual chemicals and
        groups of chemicals, e.g. Copper
        —Metabolism—Disorders
    NT Achlorhydria
        Body fluid disorders
        Diabetes
        Growth disorders
        Metabolic disorders in children
        Metabolic manifestations of general
            diseases
        Metabolism, Inborn errors of
        Obesity
        Pigmentation disorders
— Drug effects
    USE Metabolism—Effect of drugs on
— Effect of drugs on
    UF Metabolism—Drug effects
    BT Drugs—Physiological effect
— Regulation
    [QP171]
    UF Control of metabolism
        Metabolic control
        Metabolic regulation
        Regulation of metabolism
    BT Biological control systems
        Enzymes
        Hormones
    SA subdivision Metabolism—
        Regulation under individual
        chemicals and groups of
        chemicals and individual organs
        and regions of the body, e.g.
        Copper—Metabolism—
        Regulation; Heart—Metabolism
        —Regulation
— Testing
    NT Metabolic profile tests
Metabolism, Bacterial
    USE Microbial metabolism
Metabolism, Disorders of
    USE Metabolism—Disorders
Metabolism, Inborn errors of
    (May Subd Geog)
    [RC627.8]
    UF Hereditary metabolic disorders
        Inborn errors of metabolism
    BT Genetic disorders
        Metabolism—Disorders
    NT Achondroplasia
        Adenosine deaminase deficiency
        Chronic granulomatous disease
        Gangliosidoses
        Glucosephosphate dehydrogenase
            deficiency
        Gout
        Hemochromatosis
        Hypophosphatemia, Familial
        Lesch-Nyhan syndrome
        Lysosomal storage diseases
        Neuronal ceroid-lipofuscinosis
        Prader-Willi syndrome

— Diagnosis
— Nutritional aspects
Metabolism, Primary
    USE Metabolism
Metabolism, Secondary
    [QH521 (Biology)]
    [QH634.5 (Cytology)]
    [QP171 (Physiology)]
    UF Secondary metabolism
    BT Metabolism
— Regulation
    UF Regulation of secondary
        metabolism
    BT Biological control systems
Metabolism (Group of architects)
    USE Metabolism in architecture
        (Movement)
Metabolism in architecture (Movement)
    UF Metabolism (Group of architects)
        Metabolist group (Architecture)
    BT Architecture, Modern—20th century—
        Japan
    NT Megastructures
Metabolist group (Architecture)
    USE Metabolism in architecture
        (Movement)
Metabolites, Plant
    USE Plant metabolites
Metabolites of micro-organisms
    USE Microbial metabolites
Metachandidae
    USE Oecophoridae
Metachirus
    [QL737.M34]
    BT Opossums
Metachroma
    [QL596.C5]
    BT Chrysomelidae
Metachromatic leukodystrophy
    USE Leukodystrophy, Metachromatic
Metacognition
    [BF311 (Psychology)]
    Here are entered works on awareness of one's own
    cognitive processes, such as knowledge or beliefs, and
    the monitoring of those processes.
    UF Meta knowledge
        Metamemory
    BT Cognition
        Self-control
        Self-perception
Metacyclopina
    [QL444.C73]
    BT Cyclopinidae
Metacyclopina brevisetosa
    [QL444.C73]
METADEX (Information retrieval system)
    BT Information storage and retrieval
        systems—Metals
Metafiction
    USE subdivision Criticism and
        interpretation under names of
        individual authors
        Fiction
        Fiction—Technique
METAFONT (Computer system)
    [Z250.8.M46]
    BT Type and type-founding—Data
        processing
Métairie de Marguerite Bourgeoys (Montréal,
    Québec)
    USE Maison Saint-Gabriel (Montréal,
        Québec)
Metakentrin
    USE Luteinizing hormone
Metal, Words for
    BT Language and languages
        Metals—Terminology
Metal-ammonia compounds
    [QD181.N15]
    SA specific metals, e.g. Chromium-
        ammonium compounds

NT Cisplatin
Metal ammonia solutions
    [QD544.5]
    UF Ammonia metal solutions
    BT Liquid ammonia
        Metals
        Solution (Chemistry)
Metal arc welding, Shielded
    USE Shielded metal arc welding
Metal arches
    USE Arches, Metal
Metal-base fuel
    UF Metal fuels
        Metal propellants
        Metallic fuels
    BT Fuel
        Solid propellants
Metal bonding
    [TS718]
    UF Metals—Bonding
    BT Adhesives
        Metallic composites
        Metals—Surfaces
        Sealing (Technology)
    SA subdivision Bonding under subjects,
        e.g. Aluminum wire—Bonding
    NT Aluminum alloys—Bonding
        Ceramic to metal bonding
        Diffusion bonding (Metals)
        Glass-metal sealing
        Rubber to metal bonding
Metal-bonding to glass
    USE Glass-metal sealing
Metal carboxylates
    USE Metallic soaps
Metal castings
    UF Castings, Metal
    BT Founding
    NT Aluminum castings
        Continuous casting
        Copper castings
        Die castings
        Magnesium castings
        Molybdenum castings
        Steel castings
        Titanium castings
— Drawing
    USE Metal castings—Drawings
— Drawings
    UF Metal castings—Drawing
    BT Mechanical drawing
— Shrinkage
— Thermal properties
— Welding
Metal castings industry (May Subd Geog)
Metal catalysts
    BT Catalysts
    NT Rare earth metal catalysts
        Transition metal catalysts
Metal-ceramic restorations (Dentistry)
    USE Dental ceramic metals
Metal ceramics
    USE Ceramic metals
Metal chasing
    USE Chasing (Metalwork)
Metal cladding
    UF Cladding
    BT Diffusion bonding (Metals)
        Metal coating
        Metals—Finishing
    NT Explosive cladding
        Nuclear fuel claddings
        Pressure vessels—Linings
Metal cleaning
    UF Metals—Cleaning
    BT Cleaning
        Metals—Finishing
    NT Descaling
        Metals—Pickling
        Shot blasting
        Steel, Stainless—Cleaning

Metal cleaning *(Continued)*
    Vapor degreasing
Metal cloth
  UF Lamé
      Metallic cloth
  BT Textile fabrics
  NT Cloth of gold
      Cloth of silver
Metal coating
  [TA491]
    Here are entered works on metals applied to the surfaces of objects for the sake of decoration, protection, etc.
  UF Coating, Metal
      Metallic coating
  BT Coatings
      Metallic composites
      Metallic films
      Metals
      Protective coatings
      Refractory coating
      Surfaces (Technology)
  RT Plating
  NT Aluminum coating
      Electroless plating
      Iron, Galvanized
      Metal cladding
      Metal spraying
      Metallizing
      Plasma spraying
      Pressure vessels—Linings
      Steel, Galvanized
      Zinc coating
Metal coloring
  USE Metals—Coloring
Metal composites
  USE Metallic composites
Metal corrosion
  USE Corrosion and anti-corrosives
Metal crystals
  BT Metallography
  NT Body-centered cubic metals
      Dendritic crystals
      Metallic whiskers
  — **Growth**
    UF Grain growth in metals
    NT Recrystallization (Metallurgy)
Metal curtain walls *(May Subd Geog)*
  BT Curtain walls
Metal-cutting
  [TJ1215-TJ1240 (Machine-tools)]
  UF Cutting of metals
      Metals—Machining
  BT Cutting
      Machining
  RT Metals—Machinability
  NT Broaching
      Broaching machines
      Cutting machines
      Electric metal-cutting
      Electrochemical cutting
      Electron beam cutting
      Hacksaws
      Knurling
      Laser beam cutting
      Metal-cutting tools
      Milling (Metal-work)
      Oxyacetylene welding and cutting
      Reaming
      Slitting (Metal-work)
      Spot facing
      Thread cutting
      Ultrasonic metal-cutting
      Underwater welding and cutting
  — **Chip disposal**
    UF Chip disposal (Metal-cutting)
        Swarf (Metal-cutting)
    BT Scrap metals

Metal-cutting tools
    Here are entered works on attachments to machine-tools, such as drills, milling-cutters, reamers, etc. Works on cutting tools used independently are entered under the specific tool or machine, e.g. Cutting machines, Knives, Machine-tools, Milling-machines.
  BT Cutting machines
      Metal-cutting
  NT Milling cutters
  — **Welding**
Metal-cutting tools industry
  (May Subd Geog)
Metal detection
  USE Metal detectors
Metal detectors
  [TK7882.M4]
  UF Metal detection
      Metal locators
      Metals—Detection
  BT Detectors
      Electronic apparatus and appliances
      Proximity detectors
  NT Magnetometer
  — **Law and legislation** *(May Subd Geog)*
Metal doors
  UF Doors, Metal
  BT Doors
  NT Bronze doors
Metal-drawing machinery
  UF Drawbenches
  BT Drawing (Metal-work)
      Metal-working machinery
  NT Wiredrawing machines
Metal engravers
  USE Engravers
Metal fibers
  UF Filaments, Metal
      Metal filaments
  BT Fibers
      Melt spinning
Metal filaments
  USE Metal fibers
Metal-filled plastics
  [TA445.P55]
  UF Composites, Metal-polymer
      Metal-filled polymers
      Metal-polymer composites
      Metallized plastics
      Metalloplastics
      Plastics, Metal-filled
      Polymers, Metal-filled
  BT Reinforced plastics
Metal-filled polymers
  USE Metal-filled plastics
Metal finishing
  USE Metals—Finishing
Metal foils
  [TS360]
  UF Foils, Metal
      Metal leaf
  BT Sheet-metal
  NT Aluminum foil
      Copper foil
      Gold foil
Metal fuels
  USE Metal-base fuel
Metal furniture
  BT Furniture
  NT Steel furniture
      Wrought-iron furniture
Metal-glass sealing
  USE Glass-metal sealing
Metal halides
  BT Halides
  NT Indium halides
Metal implants
  USE Metals in surgery
Metal industries
  USE Metal trade
      Metal-work

      Mineral industries
Metal inert gas welding
  USE Gas metal arc welding
Metal insulator semiconductors
  [TK7871.99.M4]
  BT Metal oxide semiconductors
      Semiconductors
Metal-insulator transitions
  UF Transitions, Metal-insulator
  BT Anderson model
      Electric insulators and insulation
      Free electron theory of metals
      Phase transformations (Statistical physics)
      Transition metals
Metal inventories
  USE Metal trade—Inventories
Metal ions
  BT Ions
  NT Ligands
  — **Spectra**
Metal leaf
  USE Metal foils
Metal locators
  USE Metal detectors
Metal matrix composites
  USE Metallic composites
Metal-metal bonds
  [QD461]
  UF Metal-to-metal bonds
  BT Chemical bonds
Metal molds (Cookery) *(May Subd Geog)*
  [NK8490 (Decorative arts)]
  BT Molds (Cookware)
Metal oxide semiconductor field-effect transistors
  UF MOSFET
  BT Field-effect transistors
      Metal oxide semiconductors
Metal oxide semiconductors
  [TK7871.85]
  UF Unipolar transistors
  BT Semiconductors
      Transistors
  RT Charge coupled devices
  NT Metal insulator semiconductors
      Metal oxide semiconductor field-effect transistors
Metal oxide semiconductors, Complementary
  [TK871.99.M44]
  UF Complementary metal oxide semiconductors
      Semiconductors, Complementary metal oxide
  BT Digital electronics
      Logic circuits
  RT Transistor-transistor logic circuits
Metal oxide semiconductors, Vertical
  [TK7871.99.M44]
  UF Semiconductors, Vertical metal oxide
      Vertical metal oxide semiconductors
Metal oxides
  USE Metallic oxides
Metal painting
  USE Metals—Painting
Metal plate processes (Lithography)
  USE Lithography—Metal plate processes
Metal plating
  USE Plating
Metal-polymer composites
  USE Metal-filled plastics
Metal powder products
  BT Metal powders
      Powder metallurgy
Metal powder rolling
  [TS245]
  UF Powder rolling
      Rolling of metal powders
  BT Powder metallurgy—Pressing
      Rolling (Metal-work)
  RT Roll compacting

Metal powders
  UF Metals, Powdered
     Powdered metals
  BT Powder metallurgy
     Powders
  NT Aluminum powder
     Copper powder
     Iron powder
     Metal powder products
     Zinc powder
  — **Analysis**
  — **Combustion**
  — **Optical properties**
Metal products
  UF Products, Metal
  — **Marking**
Metal products tariff
  USE Tariff on metal products
Metal propellants
  USE Metal-base fuel
Metal recycling
  USE Metals—Recycling
     Scrap metals—Recycling
Metal-rolling
  USE Rolling (Metal-work)
Metal scaffolding
  USE Scaffolding, Metal
Metal sculpture *(May Subd Geog)*
  ₍NB1220₎
  BT Metal-work
     Sculpture
  NT Iron sculpture
     Steel sculpture
     Welded sculpture
Metal sculpture, American
  (May Subd Geog)
  UF American metal sculpture
Metal sculpture, French *(May Subd Geog)*
  UF French metal sculpture
Metal sculpture, German *(May Subd Geog)*
  UF German metal sculpture
Metal sculpture, Italian *(May Subd Geog)*
  UF Italian metal sculpture
Metal sculpture, Italian, ₍etc.₎
  (May Subd Geog)
Metal sculpture, Japanese *(May Subd Geog)*
  UF Japanese metal sculpture
Metal-semiconductor boundaries
  USE Semiconductor-metal boundaries
Metal semiconductor field-effect transistors
  UF MESFET's
     Schottky gate field-effect transistors
  BT Field-effect transistors
Metal-spinning
  ₍TT206₎
  UF Flow turning (Metalwork)
     Spinning, Metal
  BT Roll forming (Metalwork)
     Sheet-metal work
Metal spraying
  ₍TS655₎
  UF Spraying, Metal
  BT Metal coating
     Surface hardening
  NT Aluminum coating
     Metals—Finishing
     Zinc coating
Metal stamping
  ₍TS253₎
  UF Press forming of metals
     Press working of metals
     Pressworking of metals
     Stamping (Metal-work)
  BT Metal-work
     Plate-metal work
     Sheet-metal work
  RT Forging
  NT Dies (Metal-working)
     Drawing (Metal-work)
     Power presses
     Punching machinery

Metal straightening
  ₍TJ1300₎
  UF Straightening, Metal
  BT Metal-work
Metal sulfides
  USE Metal sulphides
Metal sulphides
  UF Metal sulfides
     Metallic sulfides
     Metallic sulphides
  BT Sulphides
Metal surfaces
  USE Metals—Surfaces
Metal to ceramic bonding
  USE Ceramic to metal bonding
Metal-to-glass sealing
  USE Glass-metal sealing
Metal-to-metal bonds
  USE Metal-metal bonds
Metal toys *(May Subd Geog)*
  ₍NK8454 (Decorative arts)₎
  BT Toys
  NT Tin toys
Metal trade *(May Subd Geog)*
  ₍HD9506-9539₎
  UF Metal industries
  SA Iron industry and trade; Steel industry
     and trade; *and similar headings*
  NT Forging industry
     Hardware
     Iron industry and trade
     Steel industry and trade
  — Collective labor agreements
     USE Collective labor agreements—
        Metal industry
  — **Inventories**
     UF Metal inventories
  — **Law and legislation** *(May Subd Geog)*
Metal vapors
  BT Vapors
Metal whiskers
  USE Metallic whiskers
Metal windows
  BT Windows
  NT Aluminum windows
Metal-work *(May Subd Geog)*
  ₍HD9743-HD9747 (Economics)₎
  ₍NK6400-NK8450 (Fine arts)₎
  ₍TS200-TS770 (Manufactures)₎
  ₍TT205-TT273 (Mechanic trades)₎
  UF Metal industries
     Metalwork
  BT Arts and crafts movement
     Decoration and ornament
     Manufacturing processes
  RT Metals—Coloring
  NT Aluminum forming
     Aluminum work
     Architectural metal-work
     Art metal-work
     Bending
     Brasswork
     Brazing
     Chasing (Metalwork)
     Classification—Books—Metal-work
     Copperwork
     Deburring
     Electroplating
     Embossing (Metal-work)
     Engraving (Metal-work)
     Eyelets (Metal-work)
     Forging
     Founding
     Goldwork
     Hammers
     Horse brasses
     Indians—Metal-work
     Indians of Central America—Metal-
        work
     Indians of Mexico—Metal-work

     Indians of North America—Metal-
        work
     Indians of South America—Metal-
        work
     Ironwork
     Lead-work
     Locksmithing
     Magnetic forming
     Metal sculpture
     Metal stamping
     Metal straightening
     Metal-working lubricants
     Metals—Cold working
     Metals—Finishing
     Metals—Formability
     Metals—Heating
     Metals—Hot working
     Milling (Metal-work)
     Nail craft
     Plate-metal work
     Roll forming (Metalwork)
     Sheet-metal work
     Shipfitting
     Shot peening
     Silverwork
     Slitting (Metal-work)
     Solder and soldering
     Steelwork
     Superplastic forming (Metal-work)
     Swaging
     Welding
     Wire craft
  — **Data processing**
     NT MELTS (Computer system)
Metal-work, Architectural
  USE Architectural metal-work
Metal-work, Art
  USE Art metal-work
Metal-work, Etruscan *(May Subd Geog)*
  UF Etruscan metal-work
Metal-work, Islamic *(May Subd Geog)*
  UF Islamic metal-work
     Metal-work, Muslim
     Muslim metal-work
Metal-work, Muslim
  USE Metal-work, Islamic
Metal-work, Oriental
Metal-work, Prehistoric *(May Subd Geog)*
  UF Prehistoric metal-work
Metal-workers *(May Subd Geog)*
  ₍HD8039.M5₎
  NT Art metal-workers
     Collective labor agreements—Metal
        industry
     Foundrymen
     Iron and steel workers
     Pewterers
     Strikes and lockouts—Metal-workers
     Trade-unions—Metal-workers
     Turning—Vocational guidance
     Wages—Metal-workers
     Women metal-workers
  — Collective bargaining
     USE Collective bargaining—Metal-
        workers
  — **France**
     NT Metal-Workers' Strike, France,
        1905
  — **Germany (West)**
     NT Metal-workers' Strike, Hesse,
        Germany, 1951
  — **Italy**
     NT Metal-Workers' Strike, Italy, 1920
**Metal-Workers' Strike, Baden-Württemberg,
Germany, 1971**
  ₍HD5379.M5₎
  BT Strikes and lockouts—Metal-workers—
     Germany (West)

Metal-Workers' Strike, France, 1905
    BT Iron and steel workers—France
        Metal-workers—France
        Strikes and lockouts—Iron industry—
          France
        Strikes and lockouts—Metal-workers—
          France
        Strikes and lockouts—France
Metal-workers' Strike, Hesse, Germany, 1951
    [HD5379.M5]
    BT Metal-workers—Germany (West)
        Strikes and lockouts—Metal-workers—
          Germany (West)
        Strikes and lockouts—Germany (West)
Metal-Workers' Strike, Italy, 1920
    BT Metal-workers—Italy
        Strikes and lockouts—Metal-workers—
          Italy
        Strikes and lockouts—Italy
Metal-workers' Strike, Rio de Janeiro, Brazil, 1979
    [HD5354.M5]
    BT Strikes and lockouts—Metal-workers—
        Brazil
Metal-workers' Strike, São Paulo, Brazil, 1980
    [HD5354.M5]
    UF ABC Strike, São Paulo, Brazil, 1980
    BT Strikes and lockouts—Metal-workers—
        Brazil
Metal-workers' Strike, U.S., 1935
    BT Strikes and lockouts—Metal-workers—
        United States
Metal-working lubricants
    UF Cutting fluids
        Cutting lubricants
        Metalworking lubricants
    BT Lubrication and lubricants
        Metal-work
Metal-working machinery
    [HD9705 (Trade)]
    [TJ1180-TJ1338 (Machine-tools)]
    BT Power presses
    NT Drill presses
        Electric cutting machinery
        Forging machinery
        Machine-tools
        Metal-drawing machinery
        Rolling-mill machinery
        Sheet metal working machinery
        Straightening machines
    — Appraisal
        USE Metal-working machinery—
          Valuation
    — Electric driving
    — Electric equipment
    — Erecting work
    — Tariff
        USE Tariff on metal-working
          machinery
    — Valuation
        [TS215]
        UF Metal-working machinery—
          Appraisal
Metal-working machinery industry
(May Subd Geog)
    [HD9705]
Metalanguage
    [P128.M48]
    UF Second-order language
    BT Linguistic analysis (Linguistics)
Metalinguistic knowledge
    USE Language awareness
Metallic alloys
    USE Alloys
Metallic ceramics
    USE Ceramic metals
Metallic cloth
    USE Metal cloth
Metallic coating
    USE Metal coating

Metallic composites
    [TA481]
    UF Metal composites
        Metal matrix composites
    BT Composite materials
        Metals
    NT Alloys
        Metal bonding
        Metal coating
    — Fracture
Metallic films
    [TN690 (Metallography)]
    UF Films, Metallic
    BT Metals
        Surfaces (Technology)
        Thin films
    NT Aluminum films
        Cathode sputtering (Plating process)
        Chromium films
        Gold films
        Magnetic films
        Metal coating
        Nickel films
        Selenium films
        Tantalum films
    — Electric properties
    — Magnetic properties
    — Optical properties
    — Size effects
        UF Size effects in metallic films
        BT Surfaces (Physics)
          Surfaces (Technology)
Metallic fuels
    USE Metal-base fuel
Metallic glasses
    [TN693.M4]
    UF Glasses, Metallic
        Glassy alloys
        Glassy metals
    BT Alloys
        Amorphous substances
        Liquid metals
Metallic meteorites
    USE Meteorites, Iron
Metallic oxides
    UF Metal oxides
    BT Metals
        Oxides
    NT Electric insulators and insulation—
          Metallic oxides
        Metals—Anodic oxidation
        Orthoferrites
    — Magnetic properties
        [QC766.M4]
    — Spectra
Metallic silhouette shooting
    USE Silhouette shooting
Metallic soaps
    [TP992]
    UF Metal carboxylates
        Soaps, Metallic
    BT Colloids
        Soap
    NT Napalm
    — Spectra
Metallic sulfides
    USE Metal sulphides
Metallic sulphides
    USE Metal sulphides
Metallic surfaces
    USE Metals—Surfaces
Metallic tractors
    USE Tractors, Metallic
Metallic whiskers
    UF Metal whiskers
        Whiskers, Metallic
    BT Crystal whiskers
        Metal crystals
Metallic wood borers (Insects)
    USE Buprestidae

Metallized dyes
    [TP918.M37]
    BT Dyes and dyeing
Metallized plastics
    USE Metal-filled plastics
Metallizing
    [TS655]
    BT Metal coating
    NT Electrochemical metallizing
Metallo-organic chemistry
    USE Organometallic chemistry
Metallo-organic compounds
    USE Organometallic compounds
Metallocenes
    [QD410-QD412.5 (Chemistry)]
    [TP248.M45 (Chemical technology)]
    BT Organometallic compounds
    NT Ferrocene
Metallochromy
    USE Metals—Coloring
Metalloenzymes
    [QP601.7-601.75]
    BT Enzymes
        Metalloproteins
    NT Catalase
        Collagenases
        Copper enzymes
        Cytochrome oxidase
        Cytochrome P-450
        Molybdenum enzymes
        Monoamine oxidase
        Oxygenases
        Peroxidase
        Zinc enzymes
Metallographic specimens
    [TN690.7]
    UF Metallography—Specimens
        Specimens, Metallographic
    BT Grinding and polishing
        Metallography
Metallography
    [TN690-693]
    UF Analysis, Microscopic
        Metals—Microscopic structure
        Micrographic analysis
        Microscopic analysis
    BT Industrial microscopy
        Metals
        Microstructure
        Physical metallurgy
    SA subdivision Metallography *under*
        particular metals or groups of
        metals, e.g. Iron—Metallography;
        Nonferrous metals—Metallography
    NT Electron metallography
        Fractography
        Metal crystals
        Metallographic specimens
        Metals—Surfaces
        X-rays—Industrial applications
    — Specimens
        USE Metallographic specimens
Metalloids
    USE Semimetals
Metalloids, Organic
    USE Organometallic compounds
Metalloplastics
    USE Metal-filled plastics
Metalloproteins
    [QP552.M46]
    BT Organometallic compounds
        Proteins
    NT Copper proteins
        Hemoproteins
        Iron proteins
        Metalloenzymes
        Metallothionein
Metallothein
    USE Metallothionein
Metallothionein
    [QP552.M47]

UF Metallothein
BT Metalloproteins
Organometallic compounds
Organosulphur compounds
Metallurgic chemistry
USE Chemistry, Metallurgic
Metallurgical analysis
[QD133 (Chemistry)]
[TN565 (Assaying)]
Here are entered works dealing collectively with the analysis of metals, ores, slags, etc. Works limited to the analysis of metals are entered under Metals—Analysis.
UF Analysis, Metallurgical
BT Chemistry, Technical
Metals—Analysis
RT Chemistry, Analytic
SA *subdivision* Analysis *under substances, e.g.* Copper—Analysis; Alloys—Analysis; Iron ores—Analysis
NT Alloys
Assaying
Blowpipe
Mineralogy, Determinative
Metallurgical furnaces
BT Furnaces
NT Bessemer process
Blast-furnaces
Continuous furnaces
Cupola-furnaces
Cyclone furnaces
Electron beam furnaces
Open-hearth furnaces
Pernot steel furnaces
Puddling-furnaces
Refractory materials
Roller hearth furnaces
Rotary hearth furnaces
Salt bath furnaces
Smelting furnaces
Soaking pits
— **Combustion**
— **Maintenance and repair**
— **Models**
BT Hydraulic models
— **Protective atmospheres**
UF Furnace atmospheres
BT Protective atmospheres
Metallurgical laboratories *(May Subd Geog)*
[TN570-571]
UF Laboratories, Metallurgical
Metallurgical libraries *(May Subd Geog)*
[Z675.M44]
UF Metals libraries
Metallurgical literature
[TN610.5]
UF Metals literature
Metallurgical literature searching
USE Information storage and retrieval systems—Metallurgy
Metallurgical plants *(May Subd Geog)*
[TN677]
BT Factories
NT Aluminum plants
— **Automation**
UF Metallurgy—Automation
— **Electric equipment**
— **Equipment and supplies**
NT Foundry ladles
— — **Appraisal**
USE Metallurgical plants—Equipment and supplies—Valuation
— — **Lubrication**
— — **Valuation**
[TN675.5]
UF Metallurgical plants—Equipment and supplies—Appraisal
— **Fuel**
— **Fuel consumption**
— **Heating and ventilation**

BT Factories—Heating and ventilation
— **Maintenance and repair**
— **Pilot plants**
— **Waste disposal**
NT Slimes (Metallurgy)
Metallurgical research *(May Subd Geog)*
[TN207]
UF Metallurgy—Research
BT Research, Industrial
Metallurgists *(May Subd Geog)*
[TN139-140]
Metallurgy *(May Subd Geog)*
[TN600-799]
Cf. note under Mineral industries.
BT Ores
Oxygen—Industrial applications
RT Alloys
Chemical engineering
Smelting
SA *subdivision* Metallurgy *under names of metals and groups of metals, e.g.* Copper—Metallurgy; Gold—Metallurgy; Nonferrous metals—Metallurgy; Precious metals—Metallurgy
NT Aluminothermy
Cementation (Metallurgy)
Chemistry, Technical
Classification—Books—Metallurgy
Cyanide process
Dental metallurgy
Electrometallurgy
Hydrometallurgy
Magnetic separation of ores
Metals
Metals—Heat treatment
Metals—Pickling
Metals at high temperatures
Metals at low temperatures
Physical metallurgy
Powder metallurgy
Pyrometallurgy
Radioactive tracers in metallurgy
Radioisotopes in metallurgy
Refractory materials
Sinter (Metallurgy)
Ultrasonics in metallurgy
Vacuum metallurgy
Zone melting
— Automation
USE Metallurgical plants—Automation
— Costs
USE Metallurgy—Estimates and costs
— **Estimates and costs** *(May Subd Geog)*
UF Metallurgy—Costs
— — **Computer programs**
— **Graphic methods**
— **Ion exchange process**
[TN688.3.165]
BT Hydrometallurgy
Ion exchange
— **Laser use in**
BT Lasers
— Research
USE Metallurgical research
— **Study and teaching** *(May Subd Geog)*
— Subject headings
USE Subject headings—Metallurgy
— **Tables**
[TN671]
UF Metallurgy—Tables, calculations, etc.
— Tables, calculations, etc.
USE Metallurgy—Tables
Metallurgy, Dental
USE Dental metallurgy
Metallurgy, Physical
USE Physical metallurgy
Metallurgy, Powder
USE Powder metallurgy

Metallurgy, Vacuum
USE Vacuum metallurgy
Metallurgy in the Bible
UF Bible—Metallurgy
Metalorganic compounds
USE Organometallic compounds
Metals
[QD171-QD172 (Chemistry)]
[TN400-TN490 (Mining)]
BT Chemistry, Inorganic
Metallurgy
Ores
SA *particular metals and metal groups, e.g.* Gold, Iron group, Platinum group
NT Alloys
Amalgamation
Amalgams
Assaying
Astrology and metals
Bauschinger effect
Binary systems (Metallurgy)
Blowpipe
Body-centered cubic metals
Earths, Rare
Filler metal
Free electron theory of metals
Getters
Glass-metal sealing
Heavy metals
Intermetallic compounds
Laminated metals
Light metals
Liquid metals
Metal ammonia solutions
Metal coating
Metallic composites
Metallic films
Metallic oxides
Metallography
Metals, Effect of temperature on
Nonferrous metals
Passivity (Chemistry)
Precious metals
Segregation (Metallurgy)
Semimetals
Solder and soldering
Transition metals
— **Acoustic properties**
— **Analysis**
[QD133-7]
NT Gases in metals
Metallurgical analysis
— — **Automation**
— **Anodic oxidation**
UF Anodic oxidation of metals
Anodizing
Metals—Oxidation, Anodic
BT Metallic oxides
Oxidation, Electrolytic
Oxide coating
Protective coatings
SA *subdivision* Anodic oxidation *under names of particular metals, e.g.* Aluminum—Anodic oxidation
— Bonding
USE Metal bonding
— **Brittleness**
BT Metals—Fracture
Metals—Testing
— **Carbon content**
UF Carbon in metals
BT Carbon
— Cleaning
USE Metal cleaning
— **Cobalt content**
UF Cobalt in metals
BT Cobalt
— **Cold working**
[TS462]
UF Cold working of metals
Metals, Cold working of

Metals
   — Cold working *(Continued)*
      BT Metal-work
      SA *subdivision* Cold working *under*
          names of metals, e.g. Brass—
          Cold working
      NT Bulging (Metalwork)
          Cold welding
          Deep drawing (Metal-work)
          Stored energy of cold work
          Strain hardening
   — — Safety measures
   — Coloring
      [TS710]
      UF Coloring of metals
          Metal coloring
          Metallochromy
      BT Metals—Finishing
          Plating
      RT Bronzing
          Gilding
          Metal-work
      NT Copper—Coloring
   — Combustion
      [TA459]
   — Conservation *(May Subd Geog)*
      UF Conservation of metals
          Metals conservation
      BT Conservation of natural resources
          Mineral resources conservation
      RT Scrap metals
      NT Substitute products
   — Corrosion
      USE Corrosion and anti-corrosives
   — Corrosion fatigue
      [TA462]
      UF Fatigue of metals
      BT Corrosion and anti-corrosives
          Metals—Fatigue
   — Creep
      BT Dislocations in metals
          Materials—Creep
          Metals—Plastic properties
   — Deep drawing
      USE Deep drawing (Metal-work)
   — Defects
      NT Scarfing (Metals)
          Steel—Defects
   — — Reporting *(May Subd Geog)*
   — Degassing
      USE Degassing of metals
   — Deoxidizing
      UF Deoxidization of metals
          Deoxidizing of metals
      BT Degassing of metals
          Metals—Oxygen content
   — Desulphurization
      BT Desulphuration
   — Detection
      USE Metal detectors
   — Diffusion coatings
      USE Diffusion coatings
   — Ductility
      UF Ductility of metals
      BT Metals—Testing
      NT Superplasticity
   — Effect of radiation on
      BT Radiation
   — Electric properties
   — Embrittlement
      UF Embrittlement of metals
      NT Metals—Hydrogen embrittlement
   — Environmental aspects
      (May Subd Geog)
      UF Trace metal protection
   — Erosion
      UF Erosion of metals
      BT Materials—Erosion
      NT Airplanes—Rain erosion
   — Etching
      [NE2700]

   — Explosive forming
      USE Explosive forming
   — Extrusion
      UF Extrusion (Metals)
      BT High energy forming
      NT Hydrostatic extrusion
          Melt spinning
   — Failure
      USE Metals—Fracture
   — Fatigue
      [TA460]
      UF Fatigue of metals
      BT Metals—Fracture
          Metals—Testing
      SA *subdivision* Fatigue *under*
          particular metals, e.g. Steel—
          Fatigue
      NT Fatigue testing machines
          Metals—Corrosion fatigue
          Residual stresses
          Stress corrosion
          Welded joints—Fatigue
   — Finishing
      [TS213]
      UF Metal finishing
      BT Electroplating
          Etching
          Finishes and finishing
          Grinding and polishing
          Japanning
          Lacquer and lacquering
          Metal spraying
          Metal-work
          Metals—Surfaces
          Plating
      SA *subdivision* Finishing *under*
          particular metals, e.g. Aluminum
          —Finishing
      NT Burnishing
          Diamond burnishing
          Electrolytic polishing
          Embossing (Metal-work)
          Enamel and enameling
          Hard-facing
          Ion plating
          Liquid honing
          Metal cladding
          Metal cleaning
          Metals—Coloring
          Patina of metals
          Phosphate coating
          Scarfing (Metals)
          Shot peening
          Spot facing
          Surface hardening
          Tumbling (Metal finishing)
          Vibratory finishing (Metal work)
   — — Equipment and supplies
   — — Safety measures
   — — Standards *(May Subd Geog)*
   — — Vocational guidance
      (May Subd Geog)
   — — Waste disposal
   — Flammability
      BT Combustion
   — Formability
      UF Bendability of metals
          Deformability of metals
          Formability of metals
          Workability of metals
      BT Metal-work
   — Fracture
      UF Failure of metals
          Fracture of metals
          Metals—Failure
      BT Fracture mechanics
          Metals—Testing
      SA *subdivision* Fracture *under*
          particular metals, e.g. Steel—
          Fracture
      NT Fractography

          Metals—Brittleness
          Metals—Fatigue
          R-curves
   — Hard-facing
      USE Hard-facing
   — Hardenability
      UF Hardenability of metals
      BT Hardness
          Metals—Quenching
          Strengthening mechanisms in solids
      NT Dispersion strengthening
          Precipitation hardening
          Strain hardening
          Surface hardening
   — Heat treatment
      Here are entered works dealing with the heating of metals to obtain certain desired properties. Works on the heating of metals for the purpose of hot working are entered under Metals—Heating. Works on the heat treatment of specific metals are entered under the name of the metal with subdivision Heat treatment, e.g. Steel—Heat treatment.
      UF Heat treatment of metals
      BT Metallurgy
      NT Annealing of metals
          Carbonitriding
          Case hardening
          Flame hardening
          Germanium—Quenching
          Induction hardening
          Metals—Quenching
          Metals—Thermomechanical
          treatment
          Precipitation hardening
          Recrystallization (Metallurgy)
          Residual stresses
          Siliconizing (Metallurgy)
          Sulphonitriding
          Surface hardening
          Tempering
   — — Production standards
      (May Subd Geog)
   — Heating
      [TS209]
      Here are entered works on the heating of metals for the purpose of hot working. Works on the heating of metals to obtain certain desired properties are entered under Metals—Heat treatment. Works on the heating of specific metals are entered under the name of the metal with subdivision Heating, e.g. Steel—Heating.
      UF Reheating of metals
      BT Metal-work
      RT Metals—Hot working
      NT Steel—Heating
   — High energy forming
      USE High energy forming
   — Hot reduction
      USE Metals—Hot working
   — Hot working
      [TS209.5]
      UF Hot reduction of metals
          Hot working of metals
          Metals—Hot reduction
      BT Metal-work
      RT Metals—Heating
   — Hydrogen content
      UF Hydrogen in metals
      BT Gases in metals
          Hydrogen
      NT Metals—Hydrogen embrittlement
   — Hydrogen embrittlement
      UF Embrittlement of metals, Hydrogen
          Hydrogen embrittlement of metals
      BT Metals—Embrittlement
          Metals—Hydrogen content
   — Impact testing
      UF Drop testing (Metals)
          Drop weight testing (Metals)

BT Impact
    Materials—Dynamic testing
    Metals—Testing
— Impurities
    USE Metals—Inclusions
— **Inclusions**
    UF Impurities in metals
        Inclusions in metals
        Metals—Impurities
    NT Copper—Lead content
— **Information services** *(May Subd Geog)*
— **Machinability**
    UF Machinability of metals
    BT Machine-tools
    RT Metal-cutting
— Machining
    USE Metal-cutting
— **Magnetic properties**
— **Mechanical properties**
    UF Mechanical properties of metals
— **Microbiology**
— Microscopic structure
    USE Metallography
— **Nitrogen content**
    UF Nitrogen in metals
    BT Gases in metals
        Nitrogen
— **Notation**
— **Optical properties**
— Oxidation, Anodic
    USE Metals—Anodic oxidation
— **Oxygen content**
    BT Gases in metals
        Oxygen
    NT Metals—Deoxidizing
— **Painting**
    UF Metal painting
        Metals painting
        Painting, Metal
        Painting of metals
    BT Painting, Industrial
        Protective coatings
    RT Painting, Structural
— Peening
    USE Shot peening
— **Physiological effect**
    ⌜QP903-913⌝
    RT Metals as antiseptics
    NT Plants, Effect of metals on
— **Pickling**
    ⌜TA467⌝
    UF Chemical polishing of metals
        Electrolytic pickling of metals
        Pickling (Metals)
    BT Corrosion and anti-corrosives
        Electroplating
        Galvanizing
        Metal cleaning
        Metallurgy
        Tin plate
    NT Steel—Pickling
— — **By-products**
— — **Safety measures**
— — **Waste disposal**
— **Plastic properties**
    ⌜TA460⌝
    NT Cylinders—Plastic properties
        Dislocations in metals
        Metals—Creep
        Photoplasticity
        Strain hardening
— **Prices** *(May Subd Geog)*
    NT Metals as an investment
— Printing
    USE Printing on metals
— **Quenching**
    UF Quenching of metals
    BT Cooling
        Metals—Heat treatment

    SA *subdivision* Quenching *under*
        specific metals, e.g. Steel—
        Quenching
    NT Metals—Hardenability
        Metals—Rapid solidification
        processing
— **Radiography**
— **Rapid solidification processing**
    ⌜TS247⌝
    Here are entered works on cooling of metals
from the liquid to the solid at rates fast enough
to achieve compositions, phases or microstruc-
tures not normally obtained at solidification rates
of conventional ingots or castings.
    UF Rapid quenching processing of
        metals
        Rapid solidification processing of
        metals
    BT Founding
        Liquid metals
        Metals—Quenching
        Solidification
— **Recycling**
    UF Metal recycling
    BT Recycling (Waste, etc.)
— **Refining**
    UF Purification of metals
        Refining of metals
    NT Plasma arc melting
— **Religious aspects**
— Residual stresses
    USE Residual stresses
— **Societies, etc.**
— **Solubility**
— **Spectra**
— **Standards** *(May Subd Geog)*
— **Stress corrosion**
    BT Stress corrosion
— Surface properties
    USE Metals—Surfaces
— **Surfaces**
    UF Metal surfaces
        Metallic surfaces
        Metals—Surface properties
    BT Metallography
        Surface chemistry
    NT Corrosion and anti-corrosives
        Diffusion coatings
        Lubrication and lubricants
        Metal bonding
        Metals—Finishing
— — **Defects**
— — **Optical properties**
— **Terminology**
    NT Metal, Words for
— **Testing**
    ⌜TA459-492⌝
    NT Brinell test
        Metals—Brittleness
        Metals—Ductility
        Metals—Fatigue
        Metals—Fracture
        Metals—Impact testing
        Rockwell hardness
        Spark tests
— — **Automation**
— — **Patents**
— — **Statistical methods**
— **Texture**
    BT Texture (Crystallography)
— **Therapeutic use**
    BT Metals in medicine
    NT Metals as antiseptics
        Tractors, Metallic
— **Thermal fatigue**
    UF Thermal fatigue of metals
    BT Thermal stresses
— **Thermal properties**
    ⌜TA460⌝
    BT Metals, Effect of temperature on
— **Thermomechanical properties**

    UF Thermomechanical properties of
        metals
— **Thermomechanical treatment**
    ⌜TN752.T54⌝
    UF Thermomechanical processing of
        metals
        Thermomechanical strengthening
        of metals
        Thermomechanical treatment of
        metals
    BT Metals—Heat treatment
        Strain hardening
— **Toxicology** *(May Subd Geog)*
— **War use**
— **Weldability**
    BT Welding
Metals, Cold working of
    USE Metals—Cold working
Metals, Dental
    USE Dental metallurgy
Metals, Effect of temperature on
    UF Metals and temperature
    BT Metals
    NT Electron work function
        Metals—Thermal properties
        Metals at high temperatures
        Metals at low temperatures
        Thermionic emission
Metals, Free electron theory of
    USE Free electron theory of metals
Metals, Gases in
    USE Gases in metals
Metals, Heat resistant
    USE Heat resistant alloys
Metals, Nonferrous
    USE Nonferrous metals
Metals, Powdered
    USE Metal powders
Metals, Printing on
    USE Printing on metals
Metals, Scrap
    USE Scrap metals
Metals, Transmutation of
    USE Alchemy
        Transmutation (Chemistry)
Metals and astrology
    USE Astrology and metals
Metals and temperature
    USE Metals, Effect of temperature on
Metals as an investment *(May Subd Geog)*
    ⌜HD9506⌝
    BT Investments
        Metals—Prices
Metals as antiseptics
    ⌜RD91.5.M⌝
    BT Antiseptics
        Metals—Therapeutic use
    RT Metals—Physiological effect
Metals at high temperatures
    UF High temperature metallurgy
    BT Heat
        High temperatures
        Materials at high temperatures
        Metallurgy
        Metals, Effect of temperature on
    RT Gas-turbines—Materials
    NT Heat resistant alloys
        Nimonic alloys
Metals at low temperatures
    UF Low temperature metals
    BT Cold
        Metallurgy
        Metals, Effect of temperature on
— **Optical properties**
Metals conservation
    USE Metals—Conservation
Metals in dentistry
    USE Dental metallurgy
Metals in medicine *(May Subd Geog)*
    BT Biomedical materials
        Medical instruments and apparatus

Metals in medicine *(Continued)*
NT Metals—Therapeutic use
Metals in surgery
Metals in stage setting
[PN2091.M48]
BT Theaters—Stage-setting and scenery
Metals in surgery
UF Metal implants
BT Metals in medicine
Prosthesis
Surgical instruments and apparatus
Metals in the body
[QP531]
BT Biological chemistry
NT Chelation therapy
Metals libraries
USE Metallurgical libraries
Metals literature
USE Metallurgical literature
Metals painting
USE Metals—Painting
Metalsmiths, Naval
USE United States. Navy—Metalsmiths
Metalwork
USE Metal-work
Metalworking lubricants
USE Metal-working lubricants
Metamasius
[QL596.C9]
BT Curculionidae
Metamathematics
[QA9]
BT Mathematics—Philosophy
RT Logic, Symbolic and mathematical
Metamemory
USE Metacognition
Metamere
USE Somite
Metamorphic rocks
USE Rocks, Metamorphic
Metamorphism (Geology) *(May Subd Geog)*
BT Geodynamics
RT Rocks, Metamorphic
Metamorphosis
[QL981]
BT Embryology
NT Amphibians—Metamorphosis
Butterflies—Metamorphosis
Cyclomorphosis
Insects—Metamorphosis
Marine invertebrates—Metamorphosis
— **Folklore**
NT Leopard men
Melusine (Legendary character)
Swan-maidens
Werewolves
— **Religious aspects**
Metamorphosis in literature
Metanarthecium
[QK495.L72]
BT Liliaceae
Metanarthecium luteoviride
[QK495.L72]
UF Nogi-ran
Metandrocarpa *(May Subd Geog)*
[QL613]
BT Styelidae
NT Metandrocarpa taylori
Metandrocarpa taylori *(May Subd Geog)*
[QL613]
BT Metandrocarpa
Metapenaeopsis
[QL444.M33]
BT Penaeidae
Metapenaeus
[QL444.M33]
BT Penaeidae
Metapenaeus bennettae
[QL444.M33]
UF Greentail prawn
Prawn, Greentail

Metapenaeus macleayi
[QL444.M33]
UF Prawn, School
School prawn
Metapheretima
[QL391.A6]
BT Megascolecidae
Metapheretima elongata
[QL391.A6]
Metaphor
[PN228.M4]
Here are entered general works and works on
metaphor in particular literatures.
UF Parabole
RT Simile
— **Religious aspects**
Metaphor in the Bible
BT Bible—Language, style
Metaphysical painting
USE Metaphysical school (Art movement)
Metaphysical school (Art movement)
(May Subd Geog)
UF Metaphysical painting
BT Art, Modern—20th century
NT Surrealism
Metaphysics
[BD]
BT Philosophy
RT God
Ontology
SA *subdivision* Metaphysics *under names
of philosophers*
NT Absolute, The
Causation
Cosmology
First philosophy
Form (Philosophy)
Hylomorphism
Immanence (Philosophy)
Knowledge, Theory of
Space and time
Substance (Philosophy)
Sufficient reason
Values
Metaplasia
[RB140]
BT Diseases—Causes and theories of
causation
Pathology
Tissues
NT Metaplastic ossification
Myeloid metaplasia
Metaplastic ossification *(May Subd Geog)*
[RC931.M47]
UF Soft tissue ossification
BT Metaplasia
Ossification
Metapolycope
[QL444.O85]
BT Polycopidae
Metapolycope hartmanni
[QL444.O85]
Metapolycope microthrix
[QL444.O85]
Metapontum (Ancient city)
BT Cities and towns, Ruined, extinct, etc.
—Italy
Italy—Antiquities
Metapsychology
USE Psychical research
Spiritualism
Metarbelidae
USE Cossidae
Metargon
[QD181.A6]
BT Argon
Metasequoia
[QK494.5.T3]
BT Taxodiaceae
Metasequoia disticha
USE Dawn redwood

Metasequoia glyptostroboides
USE Dawn redwood
Metasomatism (Mineralogy)
UF Metasomatosis
BT Mineralogy
Petrology
Metasomatosis
USE Metasomatism (Mineralogy)
Metastasis
Here are entered works on the transfer of cancer
to an organ or part of the body remote from the
primary site. Works on the ability of cancer to infil-
trate and actively destroy surrounding tissue are en-
tered under Cancer invasiveness.
UF Cancer metastasis
Dissemination of cancer
Neoplasm metastasis
Spread of cancer
Tumor dissemination
Tumor metastasis
Tumor spread
BT Pathology
RT Cancer invasiveness
NT Lymphatic metastasis
Metastigmata
USE Ticks
Metastoma
[QL430.5.U68]
BT Urocoptidae
Metastrongylidae *(May Subd Geog)*
[QL391.N4]
BT Lungworms
Strongylida
Metate industry *(May Subd Geog)*
BT Metates
Metatermitidae
USE Termitidae
Metates
BT Indians of Mexico—Implements
Millstones
NT Metate industry
Metatetranychus citri
USE Citrus red mite
Metatetranychus ulmi
USE European red mite
Metatheory
BT Theory (Philosophy)
Metathesis
BT Phonemics
Metauria (Ancient city)
USE Matauros (Ancient city)
Metauros (Ancient city)
USE Matauros (Ancient city)
Metavampyressa
USE Vampyressa
Metaxaglaea
[QL561.N7]
BT Noctuidae
Metaxon
USE MCPA (Herbicide)
Métayer system *(May Subd Geog)*
[HD1478]
UF Farming on shares
BT Agriculture
Contracts, Agricultural
Farm tenancy
Land tenure
Metazoa
[QL45-50]
— **Anatomy**
Metazygia
[QL458.42.A7]
BT Araneidae

Metcalf family *(Not Subd Geog)*
  UF Madcalf family
     Medcaff family
     Medcalf family
     Medkiff family
     Metcalfe family
     Metcoff family
     Midcalf family
     Mitcalf family
Metcalf Management Area (Mont.)
  USE Lee Metcalf Management Area
     (Mont.)
Metcalf Wilderness (Mont.)
  USE Lee Metcalf Wilderness (Mont.)
Metcalfe family
  USE Metcalf family
Metcoff family
  USE Metcalf family
Metelino Island (Greece)
  USE Lesbos Island (Greece)
Metelli family *(Not Subd Geog)*
Metempsychosis
  USE Transmigration
Meteor (Fighter planes)
  UF Gloster Meteor
  BT Fighter planes
     Gloster aircraft
     Jet planes
Meteor Crater (Ariz.)
  UF Coon Butte (Ariz.)
     Crater Mound (Ariz.)
     Diablo Crater (Ariz.)
  BT Meteorite craters—Arizona
Meteor streams
  ₍QB748.2₎
  BT Meteors
  RT Meteor trails
Meteor trails *(May Subd Geog)*
  UF Ion columns
  BT Ionization of gases
     Magnetohydrodynamics
     Meteors
     Plasma (Ionized gases)
     Radio meteorology
  RT Meteor streams
Meteoric glass
  USE Tektite
Meteoric iron
  USE Meteorites, Iron
Meteorite craters *(May Subd Geog)*
  ₍QB755-6₎
  UF Craters, Meteorite
  BT Cratering
     Meteorites
  — Arizona
     NT Meteor Crater (Ariz.)
Meteorite Orgueil
  USE Orgueil meteorite
Meteorites *(May Subd Geog)*
  ₍QB755 (Astronomy)₎
  ₍QE395 (Mineralogy)₎
  BT Astronomy
     Meteors
     Mineralogy
  NT Achondrites
     Chondrites (Meteorites)
     Cryptoexplosion structures
     Meteorite craters
     Sikhote-Alin meteorite
     Tunguska meteorite
  — Age
     UF Age of meteorites
        Dating of meteorites
  — Mexico
     NT Allende meteorite
Meteorites, Iron
  UF Iron meteorites
     Irons (Meteorites)
     Metallic meteorites
     Meteoric iron

  BT Iron
     Siderite
  NT Schreibersite
Meteoritic hypothesis
  ₍QB981₎
  BT Astronomy
     Cosmogony
Meteorograph
  ₍QC876₎
  UF Aerograph
  BT Meteorological instruments
Meteorological imaging systems
  USE Imaging systems in meteorology
Meteorological instruments
  ₍QC876₎
  UF Instruments, Meteorological
  BT Physical instruments
     Scientific apparatus and instruments
  RT Geophysical instruments
     Meteorological satellites
  NT Actinometer
     Air sampling apparatus
     Altimeter
     Anemoclinometer
     Anemometer
     Aneroid barometer
     Barometer
     Bolometer
     Cascade impactors (Meteorological
        instruments)
     Ceilometer
     Cyclonometer
     Densitometer (Meteorological
        instrument)
     Density altitude computers
     Frigorimeter
     Hygrometers
     Ice crystal replicators
     Imaging systems in meteorology
     Kites (Meteorology)
     Meteorograph
     Meteorology—Observers' manuals
     Ozonesondes
     Precipitation gauges
     Pressure probe (Meteorological
        instrument)
     Radioactive snow gages
     Radiometersondes
     Radiosondes
     Rain gauges
     Riometer
     Sunshine-recorder
     Thermometers and thermometry
     Weather vanes
  — Appraisal
     USE Meteorological instruments—
        Valuation
  — **Calibration**
  — **Valuation**
     UF Meteorological instruments—
        Appraisal
Meteorological libraries
  ₍Z675.M₎
  UF Libraries, Meteorological
  BT Scientific libraries
Meteorological literature searching
  USE Information storage and retrieval
     systems—Meteorology
Meteorological maps
  USE Meteorology—Charts, diagrams, etc.
Meteorological observations
  USE Meteorology—Observations
Meteorological observatories
  USE Meteorological stations
Meteorological optics *(May Subd Geog)*
  ₍QC975-6₎
  UF Atmospheric optics
     Optics, Meteorological
  BT Interferometry
  RT Air—Optical properties
  NT Airglow

     Airports—Visibility
     Atmospheric transparency
     Atmospheric turbidity
     Auroras
     Counterglow
     Dewbow
     Electrooptical devices—Atmospheric
        effects
     Fogbow
     Green flash
     Halos (Meteorology)
     Infrared radiation—Atmospheric
        effects
     Laser beams—Atmospheric effects
     Millimeter waves—Atmospheric effects
     Noctilucent clouds
     Rainbow
     Refraction
     Twilight
     Visibility
     Zodiacal light
Meteorological photography
  UF Photography, Meteorological
  BT Photography—Scientific applications
  NT Photography of clouds
Meteorological reports, Radio
  USE Weather reporting, Radio
Meteorological research
  USE Meteorology—Research
Meteorological Rocket Network
  ₍QC879.562.U₎
  UF MRN
  BT Atmosphere, Upper—Rocket
        observations
     Information networks
     Meteorological stations
     Rockets, Sounding
Meteorological satellites
  ₍TL798.M4₎
  UF Weather satellites
  BT Artificial satellites
     Astronautics in meteorology
  RT Meteorological instruments
     Meteorological stations
     Satellite meteorology
  NT Clouds—Photographs from space
     Himawari (Meteorological satellite)
     ISIS-II (Artificial satellite)
     ISS-b (Artificial satellite)
     Nimbus (Meteorological satellite)
     Project Nimbus
     Project POSSUM
     Tiros (Meteorological satellite)
Meteorological services *(May Subd Geog)*
  ₍QC875₎
  UF Weather bureaus
     Weather services
  NT Hydrometeorological services
     Marine meteorological services
     Tornado warning systems
  — **Employees**
  — —Collective labor agreements
        USE Collective labor agreements—
           Meteorological employees
Meteorological stations *(May Subd Geog)*
  ₍QC875₎
  UF Meteorological observatories
     Meteorology—Observatories
     Observatories, Meteorological
     Stations, Meteorological
     Weather stations
  BT Geophysical observatories
  RT Meteorological satellites
  NT Automatic meteorological stations
     Meteorological Rocket Network
Meteorological stations, Radar
  (May Subd Geog)
  ₍QC973.62₎

2375

Meteorological stations, Radar
(Continued)
  UF Meterological radar stations
      Radar meteorological stations
      Radar stations, Meteorological
      Radar stations, Weather
      Radar weather stations
      Weather radar stations
      Weather stations, Radar
  BT Radar meteorology
Meteorologists *(May Subd Geog)*
  BT Earth scientists
      Geophysicists
  NT English language—Conversation and
        phrase books (for meteorologists)
      Meteorology—Vocational guidance
 — Collective labor agreements
      USE Collective labor agreements—
           Meteorological employees
Meteorology *(May Subd Geog)*
  [QC851-999]
  UF Aerology
  BT Earth
      Earth sciences
      Geophysics
      Physical geography
      Physics
      Science
  RT Atmosphere
      Atmospheric physics
      Climatology
      Rain and rainfall
      Storms
      Weather
  SA *headings beginning with the word*
      Meteorological
  NT Aeronautics in meteorology
      Air
      Air—Pollution—Meteorological
        aspects
      Art and meteorology
      Astrology and meteorology
      Astronautics in meteorology
      Atmosphere, Upper—Rocket
        observations
      Atmospheric circulation
      Atmospheric electricity
      Atmospheric nucleation
      Atmospheric pressure
      Atmospheric temperature
      Baroclinicity
      Barometric hypsometry
      Boundary layer (Meteorology)
      Classification—Books—Meteorology
      Clouds
      Cooling power (Meteorology)
      Cyclones
      Dew
      Droughts
      Dust-fall
      Dynamic meteorology
      Engineering meteorology
      Evaporation
      Evaporation (Meteorology)
      Floods
      Fog
      Forest meteorology
      Fronts (Meteorology)
      Frost
      Hail
      Humidity
      Hurricanes
      Hydrometeorology
      Hygrometry
      Ice on rivers, lakes, etc.
      Icing (Meteorology)
      Jet stream
      Lakes—Temperature
      Lightning
      Long-range weather forecasts
      Mesometeorology

Meteorology, Military
METROMEX
Micrometeorology
Noise pollution—Meteorological
  aspects
Nuclear energy and meteorology
Planetary meteorology
Radar meteorology
Radio meteorology
Rainbow
Rivers—Temperature
Sea breeze
Seasons
Snow
Solar radiation
Statistical weather forecasting
Sun-spots
Sunshine
Synoptic meteorology
Thunderstorms
Tornadoes
Trade-winds
Typhoons
Van Allen radiation belts
Waterspouts
Weather control
Weather forecasting
Weather telegraphy
Winds
— **Bibliography**
  NT Information storage and retrieval
      systems—Meteorology
— **Charts, diagrams, etc.**
  [QC878]
  UF Maps, Meteorological
      Meteorological maps
  NT Thickness charts (Meteorology)
— Cipher and telegraph codes
  USE Cipher and telegraph codes—
        Meteorology
— **Communication systems**
— **Diurnal variation**
  UF Diurnal meteorological variation
      Diurnal variation in meteorology
— **International cooperation**
  NT Global Observing System
      (Meteorology)
      World Climate Programme
— **Mathematical models**
  NT Hydrodynamic weather forecasting
— **Methodology**
  NT Atmosphere—Laser observations
      Atmosphere, Upper—Radiosonde
        observations
      Atmosphere, Upper—Rocket
        observations
— **Observation blanks**
  [QC871]
— **Observations**
  [QC871-QC874 (Methods)]
  [QC983-QC994 (Reports)]
  UF Meteorological observations
      Observations, Meteorological
  NT Global Observing System
      (Meteorology)
      Weather reporting, Radio
      Weather telegraphy
— Observatories
  USE Meteorological stations
— **Observers' manuals**
  [QC871]
  BT Meteorological instruments
  NT Weather telegraphy
— **Periodicity**
  [QC883]
  UF Periodicity in meteorology
  RT Dendrochronology
  NT Clouds—Diurnal variation
— **Research** *(May Subd Geog)*

  UF Meteorological research
      Weather—Research
      Weather research
  NT First GARP Global Experiment
      Geophysical Monitoring for
        Climatic Change
      Global Observing System
        (Meteorology)
      Global Weather Experiment
        Project
      Monsoon Experiment
      SESAME Project
      Typhoon Operational Experiment
      West African Monsoon Experiment
      World Climate Programme
      World Climate Programme, 1980-
        1983
— — **South Africa**
      NT Bethlehem Weather
           Modification Experiment
— — **Tropics**
      NT Atlantic Tropical Experiment
           Program, 1974
— **Rocket observations**
  BT Aeronautics in meteorology
      Astronautics in meteorology
      Rockets, Sounding
— **Statistical methods**
  NT Precipitation variability
— **Study and teaching** *(May Subd Geog)*
  NT Interns (Meteorology)
— **Terminology**
  NT English language—Conversation
      and phrase books (for
      meteorologists)
— **Vocational guidance** *(May Subd Geog)*
  [QC869.5]
  BT Meteorologists
— **Indonesia**
  NT Aeronautical Meteorology and
      Related Field of Activity Project
— **Tropics**
Meteorology, Agricultural *(May Subd Geog)*
  [S600 (Crops and climate)]
  UF Agricultural meteorology
      Agrometeorology
      Plant biometeorology
  BT Bioclimatology
  RT Crops and climate
  SA *subdivision* Climatic factors *under*
      individual and groups of domestic
      animals and plants, e.g. Cattle—
      Climatic factors; Cattle—Feeding
      and feeds—Climatic factors; Corn—
      Climatic factors
  NT Irrigation farming—Climatic factors
      Livestock—Climatic factors
Meteorology, Forest
  USE Forest meteorology
Meteorology, Maritime *(May Subd Geog)*
  [QC994]
  UF Marine meteorology
      Maritime meteorology
  BT Oceanography
  NT Armada, 1588—Weather conditions
      Hurricanes
      Marine weather broadcasts
      Ocean-atmosphere interaction
      Optimum ship routing
      Trade-winds
      Typhoons
      Waterspouts
Meteorology, Medical
  USE Climatology, Medical
Meteorology, Military *(May Subd Geog)*
  [UG467]
  UF Military meteorology
  BT Meteorology
      Military art and science
  NT Weather control—War use

Meteorology, Planetary
  USE Planetary meteorology
Meteorology, Satellite
  USE Satellite meteorology
Meteorology in aeronautics
  (May Subd Geog)
  [*TL556-TL558*]
      Here are entered works on the study of weather
  conditions for aeronautical purposes.
    BT Aeronautics
        Engineering meteorology
        Weather control
        Weather forecasting
    RT Aeronautics in meteorology
        Aids to air navigation
    NT Airplanes—Climatic factors
        Airports—Visibility
        Condensation trails
        Density altitude computers
        Mountain wave
        Pressure pattern flying
        Standard atmosphere
Meteorology in engineering
  USE Engineering meteorology
Meteorology in literature
Meteorology in rocketry
    BT Ballistics
        Rocketry
Meteoroscope
  [*QB85*]
    BT Astronomical instruments
Meteors
  [*QB741-755*]
    UF Astronomical meteors
        Falling-stars
        Fire balls
        Meteors, Astronomical
        Shooting-stars
        Stars, Falling
    BT Astronomy
        Solar system
        Stars
    NT Meteor streams
        Meteor trails
        Meteorites
        Space vehicles—Meteoroid protection
  — August
      [*QB746*]
  — November
      [*QB745*]
  — Orbits
      [*QB748-751*]
      BT Orbits
  — Photographic measurements
      BT Photography—Scientific
          applications
  — Photographs
Meteors, Astronomical
  USE Meteors
Metepeira
  [*QL458.42.A7*]
    BT Araneidae
Meter
  USE *subdivision* Metrics and rhythmics
        under names of ancient languages,
        e.g. Greek language—Metrics and
        rhythmics; Sanskrit language—
        Metrics and rhythmics
        Musical meter and rhythm
        Versification
Meter (Unit)
  [*QC102*]
    UF Metre (Unit)
    BT Length measurement
        Metric system
        Units
Metered mail
  USE Postal service—Metered mail
Metering pumps
  [*TJ916*]

    UF Controlled-volume pumps
        Proportional pumps
        Proportioning pumps
        Pumps, Metering
    BT Flow meters
        Pumping machinery
        Reciprocating pumps
    NT Spinning pumps (Textile machinery)
Meterological radar stations
  USE Meteorological stations, Radar
Meters, Capacitance
  USE Capacitance meters
Meters, Electric
  USE Electric meters
Meters, Flow
  USE Flow meters
Meters, Frequency
  USE Frequency meters
Meters, Frequency-deviation
  USE Frequency-deviation meters
Meters, Gas
  USE Gas-meters
Meters, Liquid
  USE Liquid feeders
Meters, Parking
  USE Parking meters
Meters, Quality factor
  USE Quality factor meters
Meters, Road
  USE Road meters
Meters, Smoke
  USE Smokemeters
Meters, Taxi
  USE Taximeters
Meters, Water
  USE Water-meters
Meth (Drug)
  USE Methamphetamine
Methadone hydrochloride
    RT Methadone maintenance
  — Therapeutic use
      USE Methadone maintenance
Methadone maintenance *(May Subd Geog)*
  [*RC568.M4*]
    UF Methadone hydrochloride—
        Therapeutic use
        Methadone treatment programs
    BT Drug abuse—Treatment
    RT Methadone hydrochloride
    NT Methadyl acetate
  — Complications and sequelae
      USE Methadone maintenance—Side
          effects
  — Side effects
      UF Methadone maintenance—
          Complications and sequelae
Methadone treatment programs
  USE Methadone maintenance
Methadyl acetate *(May Subd Geog)*
    UF Acemethadone
        Acetylmethadol
        Alphacetylmethadol
        Amidolacetate
        Dimethylaminodiphenylheptanol
        acetate
        Dimethylaminopropyle
        thylphenylbenzeneethanol acetate
    BT Acetates
        Analgesics
        Methadone maintenance
        Narcotics
        Phenyl compounds
Methamphetamine *(May Subd Geog)*
    UF Deoxyephedrine
        Dimethylphenethylamine
        Meth (Drug)
        Methylamphetamine
        Phenylmethylaminopropane
        Speed (Drug)
    BT Amphetamines

Methanation
  [*TP156.M45 (Chemical engineering)*]
    BT Fischer-Tropsch process
        Hydrogenation
    RT Methane
Methane *(May Subd Geog)*
  [*QD305.H6*]
    BT Manure gases
    RT Methanation
    NT Biogas
        Bromotrifluoromethane
        Chlorofluoromethane
        Chloroform
        Coalbed methane
        Dibenzoylmethane
        Dichloromethane
        Dimethyl sulphoxide
        Fluorene
        Fluoroform
        Liquid methane
  — Spectra
  — Thermal properties
Methane drainage, Coalbed
  USE Coalbed methane drainage
Methane industry *(May Subd Geog)*
Methanobacteriaceae *(May Subd Geog)*
    UF Methanogenic bacteria
    BT Archaebacteria
    NT Methanobacterium
Methanobacterium *(May Subd Geog)*
    BT Methanobacteriaceae
    NT Methanobacterium
        thermoautotrophicum
Methanobacterium thermoautotrophicum
  (May Subd Geog)
    UF Methanobacterium
        thermoautotrophicus
    BT Methanobacterium
Methanobacterium thermoautotrophicus
  USE Methanobacterium
        thermoautotrophicum
Methanogenic bacteria
  USE Methanobacteriaceae
Methanol
    UF Carbinol
        Colonial spirit (Alcohol)
        Columbian spirit (Alcohol)
        Hydroxymethyl
        Methyl alcohol
        Methyl hydroxide
        Pyroxylic spirit
        Wood alcohol
        Wood naphtha
        Wood spirit (Alcohol)
    BT Alcohols
Methanol as fuel *(May Subd Geog)*
    BT Alcohol as fuel
        Fuel
    NT Methanol fuel industry
Methanol fuel industry *(May Subd Geog)*
  [*HD9502.5.M47-474*]
    BT Methanol as fuel
Methanol industry *(May Subd Geog)*
  [*HD9660.M57-574*]
Methanomonadaceae
  USE Methylomonadaceae
Methaqualone
    UF Methylmethylphenylquinazolinone
        Metolquizolone
        Ortonal
    BT Quinazoline
        Sedatives
Methaqualone abuse *(May Subd Geog)*
  [*RC568.M45 (Psychiatry)*]
    UF Abuse of methaqualone
    BT Medication abuse
Metheglin
  USE Mead
Methemoglobinemia
  [*RC647.M*]
    BT Blood—Diseases

Methenay family
USE Matheny family
Methene compounds
USE Carbenes (Methylene compounds)
Metheny family
USE Matheny family
Methenyl compounds
USE Carbynes
Methenyl trichloride
USE Chloroform
Metheral family (Not Subd Geog)
UF Metherell family
Metherell family
USE Metheral family
Methindione
USE Metindione
Methine compounds
USE Carbynes
Methionine
BT Sulphur amino acids
NT Adenosylmethionine
Methionine, Active
USE Adenosylmethionine
Methocidae
USE Tiphiidae
Method, Decomposition
USE Decomposition method
Method, Pullman
USE Pullman method
Method (Acting)
[PN2062]
UF Stanislavsky method
BT Acting
Method of averaging (Differential equations)
USE Averaging method (Differential equations)
Method of least squares
USE Least squares
Method of moments (Statistics)
USE Moments method (Statistics)
Method of study
USE Study, Method of
Method of the hypercircle
USE Hypercircle method
Method of work
USE Methods engineering
Work
Methodism
[BX8201-8495]
BT Arminianism
Church polity
Dissenters, Religious
Episcopacy
Evangelical Revival
NT Camp-meetings
Itinerancy (Church polity)—Methodist Church
Methodist Cemetery (Greenwood, S.C.)
USE Greenwood Cemetery (Greenwood, S.C.)
Methodist Church (May Subd Geog)
[BX8201-BX8495]
Here are entered works on Methodist denominations treated collectively and works for which the individual Methodist denomination cannot be identified.
BT Christian sects
— **Anniversaries, etc.**
— Biography
USE Methodists—Biography
— **Clergy**
NT District superintendents (Methodist)
Theological seminaries, Methodist
— **Education**
NT Theological seminaries, Methodist
Wesley foundations
— **Government**
NT Class meetings, Methodist
District superintendents (Methodist)

— **Hymns**
— **Influence**
— **Membership**
— **Missions**
— **Publishing**
— **Relations**
— — **Puritans, [etc.]**
— **Sermons**
RT Preaching, Methodist
Methodist church buildings
USE Churches, Methodist
Methodist churches
USE Churches, Methodist
Methodist class meetings
USE Class meetings, Methodist
Methodist Episcopal Church
(May Subd Geog)
[BX8380-8389]
— **History**
— — **Civil War, 1861-1865**
Methodist homiletics
USE Preaching, Methodist
Methodist preaching
USE Preaching, Methodist
Methodist theological seminaries
USE Theological seminaries, Methodist
Methodist women
USE Women, Methodist
Methodists (May Subd Geog)
[BX8201-8495]
RT Calvinistic Methodists
— **Biography**
UF Methodist Church—Biography
— **United States**
NT Afro-American Methodists
Methodists, Afro-American
USE Afro-American Methodists
Methodists, Calvinistic
USE Calvinistic Methodists
Methodists, German (May Subd Geog)
[BX8247.G]
UF German Methodists
Methodists, Swedish (May Subd Geog)
UF Swedish Methodists
Methodology
[BD240-BD241]
UF Philosophy—Methodology
RT Research
SA subdivision Methodology under names of disciplines for works on both the theory and practice of procedures to be followed, e.g. Science—Methodology; Theology—Methodology
NT Analysis (Philosophy)
Classification of sciences
Formalization (Philosophy)
Heuristic
Interdisciplinary approach to knowledge
Longitudinal method
Performative (Philosophy)
Problem solving
Social sciences—Comparative method
Sociology—Comparative method
Methods (Computer system)
BT Microcomputers—Programming
Methods (Industrial engineering)
USE Methods engineering
Methods engineering
UF Method of work
Methods (Industrial engineering)
Simplification of work
Work, Method of
Work methods
Work simplification
BT Industrial engineering
RT Work measurement
NT Motion study
Multimachine assignments
Work design

Methods of defect correction (Numerical analysis)
USE Defect correction methods (Numerical analysis)
Methods-time measurement
UF MTM (Work measurement)
BT Predetermined motion time systems
Methomyl
[SB952.M]
UF Lannate (Insecticide)
Methylmethylaminocar bonyloxyethanimidothioate
Methylmethylcarbamoy loxythioacetimidate
Methylthioacetaldehy demethylcarbamoyloxime
Methylthioethylidene aminomethylcarbamate
BT Carbamates
Methotrexate
[RC271.M44]
UF Amethopterin
Aminomethylfolic acid
Aminomethylpteroylglutamic acid
Diaminopteridinylmet hylmethylaminobenzoylglutamic acid
BT Aminobenzoic acids
Antineoplastic agents
Folic acid—Antagonists
Heterocyclic compounds
Immunosuppressive agents
Pteridines
Methoxyflurane
USE Penthrane
Methoxyhydroxyphenethyleneglycol
USE Methoxyhydroxyphenylglycol
Methoxyhydroxyphenylethyleleneglycol
USE Methoxyhydroxyphenylglycol
Methoxyhydroxyphenylglycol
[QP801.M42]
UF Hydroxymethoxyphenylglycol
Methoxyhydroxyphenethyleneglycol
Methoxyhydroxyphenyl ethyleleneglycol
MHPG
MOPEG
BT Glycols
Phenyl compounds
Methoxyindolylethylacetamide
USE Melatonin
Methoxymethane
USE Methyl ether
Methoxymethylnaphthaleneacetic acid
USE Naproxen
Methoxynaphthyl carbamate
USE Carbaryl
Methoxynorpregnatrienynol
USE Mestranol
Methoxytrimethylphenylnonatetraenoic acid ethyl ester
USE Etretinate
Methyl alcohol
USE Methanol
Methyl chloroform
USE Trichloroethane
Methyl ether
UF Dimethyl ether
Methoxymethane
Methyl oxide
Oxybismethane
Wood ether
BT Ether
NT Dichloromethyl ether
Isoflurane
Methyl ethylene oxide
USE Propylene oxide
Methyl groups
BT Hydrocarbons
NT Adenosylmethionine
Methylation

Methylxanthines
    Transmethylation
— **Spectra**
Methyl hydroxide
    USE Methanol
Methyl isocyanate
    UF Isocyanatomethane
        MIC (Chemical)
    BT Isocyanates
Methyl mercury
    USE Methylmercury
Methyl methacrylate resin
    USE Lucite
Methyl oxide
    USE Methyl ether
Methyl oxirane
    USE Propylene oxide
Methyl sulfate
    USE Dimethyl sulphate
Methyl sulfoxide
    USE Dimethyl sulphoxide
Methyl sulphoxide
    USE Dimethyl sulphoxide
Methyl yellow
    USE Dimethylaminoazobenzene
Methylamines
    ₍QD305.A8₎
Methylamphetamine
    USE Methamphetamine
Methylases
    USE Methyltransferases
Methylated spirit
    USE Alcohol, Denatured
Methylation
    BT Alkylation
        Methyl groups
    NT Transmethylation
Methylbutylaminocarbonylbenzidazolylcarb
    amate
    USE Benomyl
Methylbutylcarbamoylbenzidazolylcarbamate
    USE Benomyl
Methylchloroform
    USE Trichloroethane
Methylchlorophenoxyacetic acid
    USE MCPA (Herbicide)
Methylcyanoacrylate
    USE Mecrylate
Methylene blue
    BT Indicators and test-papers
        Thiazine dyes
        Wright's stain
Methylene chloride
    USE Dichloromethane
Methylene compounds
    USE Carbenes (Methylene compounds)
Methylene diphenylene oxide
    USE Xanthene
Methylenebishydroxybenzopyranone
    USE Dicumarol
Methylenebishydroxycoumarin
    USE Dicumarol
Methylergol carbamide
    USE Lisuride
Methylethylidenebisthiobisbisdimethyleth
    ylphenol
    USE Probucol
Methylferases
    USE Methyltransferases
Methylglycinevalinealanineangiotensin II
    USE Saralasin
Methylgylcylarginylvalyltyrosylvalylhist
    idylprolylalanine
    USE Saralasin
Methylhydroxyhydroxydimethyloctenyloxocy
    clopentylheptenoate
    USE Gemeprost
Methylhydroxyprogesterone
    USE Medroxyprogesterone
Methylidyne compounds
    USE Carbynes

Methylkinases
    USE Methyltransferases
Methylmercury
    UF Methyl mercury
    BT Organomercury compounds
Methylmethylaminocarbonyloxyethanimidoth
    ioate
    USE Methomyl
Methylmethylcarbamoyloxythioacetimidate
    USE Methomyl
Methylmethylphenylquinazolinone
    USE Methaqualone
Methylnitroethanol imidazole
    USE Metronidazole
Methylomonadaceae *(May Subd Geog)*
    ₍QR82.M4₎
    UF Methanomonadaceae
    BT Bacteria, Aerobic
        Gram negative bacteria
Methylotrophic bacteria
    USE Bacteria, Methylotrophic
Methylphenyltetrahydropyridine
    UF MPTP (Neurotoxin)
    BT Neurotoxic agents
        Pyridine—Derivatives
Methylpiperidylethylmethylthiophenothiazine
    USE Thioridazine
Methylpyrimidinedione
    USE Thymine
Methyltaurine
    BT Taurine
Methyltheobromine
    USE Caffeine
Methylthioacetaldehydemethylcarbamoyloxime
    USE Methomyl
Methylthioethylideneaminomethylcarbamate
    USE Methomyl
Methylthiomethylnitrofurfurylideneaminoo
    xazolidinone
    USE Nifuratel
Methyltoluoylpyrroleacetic acid
    USE Tolmetin
Methyltransferases
    ₍QP606.M48₎
    UF Methylases
        Methylferases
        Methylkinases
        Transmethylases
    BT Transferases
    RT Transmethylation
Methylxanthines
    ₍QP801.M425 (Biochemistry)₎
    BT Methyl groups
        Xanthine
    NT Caffeine
        Theophylline
Methylxylyloxyethylamine
    USE Mexiletine
Methypranol
    USE Metipranolol
Metics
    ₍DF277₎
Metindione
    ₍RC374.M48 (Medicine)₎
    UF Ethylmethylaminoindandione
        Methindione
    BT Amino compounds
        Anticonvulsants
        Indan
        Psychotropic drugs
Metipranolol
    UF Hydroxymethylethylam
            inopropoxytrimethylphenol acetate
        Hydroxytrimethylphen
            oxyisopropylaminopropanol acetate
        Methypranol
        Trimepranol
    BT Hypotensive agents
Métis (Canadian people)
    USE Indians of North America—Canada—
        Mixed bloods

Métis Rebellion, 1869-1870
    USE Red River Rebellion, 1869-1870
Métis Rebellion, 1885
    USE Riel Rebellion, 1885
Metochia (Serbia)
    USE Metohija (Serbia)
Metohija (Serbia)
    UF Metochia (Serbia)
        Metokhiya (Serbia)
Metokhiya (Serbia)
    USE Metohija (Serbia)
Metolquizolone
    USE Methaqualone
Metonyms
    UF Metonymy
    BT Figures of speech
    SA *subdivision* Metonyms *under*
            individual languages and groups of
            languages, e.g. English language—
            Metonyms
Metonymy
    USE Metonyms
Metopes
    BT Decoration and ornament,
            Architectural
        Friezes
Metopiidae
    USE Sarcophagidae
Metopium
    ₍QK495.A498 (Botany)₎
    UF Poisontree
    BT Anacardiaceae
        Poisonous plants
Metopium toxifera
    ₍QK495.A498 (Botany)₎
    UF Florida poisontree
        Poisonwood
        Rhus metopium
Metoposcopy
    USE Physiognomy
Metoprolol
    UF Isopropylaminomethox
            yethylphenoxypropanol
    BT Adrenergic beta blockers
        Amino alcohols
        Cardiovascular agents
        Propanols
Metrarabdotos
    BT Adeonidae
Metre (Unit)
    USE Meter (Unit)
Metribuzin
    UF Aminobutyldihydromet
            hylthiotriazinone
        Aminobutylmethylthiotriazinone
        Aminodihydromethylth
            iobutyltriazinone
        Aminodimethylethylme
            thylthiotriazinone
    BT Herbicides
        Triazines
Metric rings
    USE Banach algebras
Metric spaces
    UF Spaces, Metric
    BT Set theory
        Spaces, Generalized
        Topology
    NT Distance geometry
        G-spaces
Metric system *(May Subd Geog)*
    ₍QC91-QC94 (Weights and measures)₎
    UF International metric system
        International system of units
        SI
        SI-metric
    BT Arithmetic
        Mathematics
        Units
    RT Weights and measures
    NT Carat (Unit of weight)

Metric system *(Continued)*
    Celsius thermometer
    Gram (Unit)
    Liter
    Meter (Unit)
  — **Conversion tables**
      [QC94]
      BT Weights and measures—Tables
  — **Law and legislation** *(May Subd Geog)*
Metric topology
  USE Distance geometry
Metrics
  USE Versification
Metridiidae
    [QL444.C72]
  BT Calanoida
  NT Pleuromamma
Metriidae
  USE Carabidae
Metrizamide
  UF Acetamidomethylaceta
      midotriiodobenzamidodeoxyglucose
    Acetamidotriiodometh
      ylacetamidobenzamidodeoxyglucose
  BT Benzamide
    Contrast media
    Glucose
    Iodobenzene
Metro automobile
    [TL215.M]
  BT BLMC automobiles
Metroliners
  USE High speed trains
Metrology
  USE Mensuration
    Weights and measures
Metrology, Speckle
  USE Speckle metrology
Metrometer
  USE Metronome
METROMEX
  UF Metropolitan meteorological
      experiment
  BT Meteorology
    Precipitation (Meteorology)
    Urban climatology
Metronidazole
    [RM666.M547]
  UF Methylnitroethanol imidazole
    Trichopal
  BT Antiparasitic agents
    Nitroimidazoles
Metronome
    [ML1080]
  UF Chronometer (Music)
    Metrometer
  BT Tempo (Music)
Metropolis (Ancient city) *(Not Subd Geog)*
    [DS156.M]
  BT Cities and towns, Ruined, extinct, etc.
      —Turkey
    Turkey—Antiquities
Metropolitan areas *(May Subd Geog)*
  UF Conurbations
    Urban areas
  BT Cities and towns—Growth
  SA *names of individual metropolitan areas*
  NT Annexation (Municipal government)
    Metropolitan finance
    Metropolitan government
    Municipal powers and services beyond
      corporate limits
    Open spaces
    Suburbs
    Urban renewal
  — **Law and legislation** *(May Subd Geog)*
  — **United States**
    NT New York Metropolitan Area
      Washington Metropolitan Area
Metropolitan areas and libraries
  USE Libraries and metropolitan areas

Metropolitan automobile
  USE Nash Metropolitan automobile
Metropolitan finance *(May Subd Geog)*
    Here are entered general works on public finance
of metropolitan areas. Works on the finance of an
individual metropolitan area are entered under Fi-
nance, Public, with local subdivision e.g. Finance,
Public—Washington Metropolitan Area.
  BT Finance, Public
    Local finance
    Metropolitan areas
    Metropolitan government
    Municipal finance
  — **Law and legislation** *(May Subd Geog)*
Metropolitan government *(May Subd Geog)*
  UF Consolidation of local governments
    Urban politics
  BT Local government
    Metropolitan areas
  RT Municipal corporations
    Municipal government
  SA *subdivision* Politics and government
      under names of metropolitan areas
  NT Annexation (Municipal government)
    Metropolitan finance
    Municipal powers and services beyond
      corporate limits
    Special districts
    State-local relations
Metropolitan helicopter services
  (May Subd Geog)
  BT Aeronautics, Commercial
    Helicopters
Metropolitan lighting
  USE Municipal lighting
Metropolitan meteorological experiment
  USE METROMEX
Metropolitan transportation
  USE Urban transportation
Metropolitans *(May Subd Geog)*
    Here are entered works on metropolitan jurisdic-
tion in the Catholic Church. Works on local history
and biography are entered under the heading Bish-
ops.
  UF Archbishops
  BT Bishops
    Catholic Church—Government
Metrosalpingography
  USE Hysterosalpingography
Metrosideros
    [QK495.M9]
  UF Bottle brushes (Plants)
    Bottlebrushes (Plants)
    Iron trees
  BT Myrtaceae
Metrosideros collina
  USE Ohia-lehua
Metrosideros polymorpha
  USE Ohia-lehua
Metrotubography
  USE Hysterosalpingography
Metroxylon
    [QK495.P17]
  UF Ivory nut palms
    Ivory palms
    Ivorynutpalms
  BT Palms
    Sago palms
Metroxylon laeve
  USE Swamp sago
Metroxylon sagu
  USE Swamp sago
Mets family
  USE Metz family
Metsada Site (Israel)
  USE Masada Site (Israel)
Metsadah Site (Israel)
  USE Masada Site (Israel)
Metsgar family
  USE Metzger family
Metsger family
  USE Metzger family

Metsker family
  USE Metzger family
Mett family
  USE Metz family
Mettā
  USE Compassion (Buddhism)
Mettawee River (Vt. and N.Y.)
  BT Rivers—New York (State)
    Rivers—Vermont
Metteneye family
  USE Matheny family
Metter family
  USE Matter family
Metteyya (Buddhist deity)
  USE Maitreya (Buddhist deity)
Mettre (The French word)
  BT French language—Etymology
Metts family
  USE Metz family
Metz, Battle of, 1944
    [D756.5.M]
  BT World War, 1939-1945—Campaigns—
      France
Metz family *(Not Subd Geog)*
  UF Meetz family
    Meetze family
    Mets family
    Mett family
    Metts family
    Metze family
    Metzer family
    Muetze family
    Mutz family
    Mutze family
Metz-Strasbourg Expressway (France)
  USE Autoroute Metz-Strasbourg (France)
Metze family
  USE Metz family
Metzear family
  USE Metzger family
Metzer family
  USE Metz family
    Metzger family
Metzgar family
  USE Metzger family
Metzger family *(Not Subd Geog)*
  UF Metsgar family
    Metsger family
    Metsker family
    Metzear family
    Metzer family
    Metzgar family
    Metzker family
    Metzler family
Metzker family
  USE Metzger family
Metzler family
  USE Metzger family
Metzograph
  USE Mezzograph
Me'udana (Melanesian people)
  BT Ethnology—Papua New Guinea
    Melanesians
Meulen family
  USE Van der Meulen family
Meuse, Battle of the, 1940
    [D756.5.M4]
  BT World War, 1939-1945—Campaigns—
      France
  — **Monthermé**
      [D756.5.M4]
Meuse River
  UF Maas River
    Maes River
    Mosa River
  BT Rivers—Belgium
    Rivers—France
    Rivers—Netherlands
Mevadi dialect
  USE Mewari dialect

Mevalonic acid
  UF Dihydroxymethylpentanoic acid
  BT Carboxylic acids
Mevlevi order
  USE Mevleviyeh
Mevleviyeh *(May Subd Geog)*
  [BP189.7.M4-42]
  UF Mawlawīyah
      Mevlevi order
      Whirling Dervishes
  BT Dervishes
      Sufism
Mevleviyeh members *(May Subd Geog)*
  [BP189.7.M4-42]
Mew gull
  USE Larus canus
Mewa dialect
  USE Mewari dialect
Mewadi dialect
  USE Mewari dialect
Mewan Indians
  USE Miwok Indians
Mewan languages
  USE Miwok languages
Mewar painting *(May Subd Geog)*
  UF Painting, Mewar
  BT Miniature painting, Indic
      Rajput painting
Mewar sculpture *(May Subd Geog)*
  UF Marwar sculpture
      Sculpture, Marwar
      Sculpture, Mewar
  BT Sculpture, Indic
Mewari dialect
  [PK2469.M4]
  UF Mevadi dialect
      Mewa dialect
      Mewadi dialect
  BT India—Languages
      Marwari language
Mewati dialect
  BT India—Languages
      Rajasthani language
Mewes family
  USE Muse family
Mewhinney family
  USE McWhinney family
Mewite tribe
  BT Australian aborigines
Mews family
  USE Muse family
Mexēs family *(Not Subd Geog)*
Mexican alien labor
  USE Alien labor, Mexican
Mexican almanacs
  USE Almanacs, Mexican
Mexican American aged *(May Subd Geog)*
  UF Aged, Mexican American
  BT Aged—United States
Mexican American agricultural laborers
  (May Subd Geog)
  UF Agricultural laborers, Mexican
      American
  BT Agricultural laborers—United States
Mexican American architecture
  (May Subd Geog)
  UF Architecture, Mexican American
  BT Ethnic architecture—United States
Mexican American art *(May Subd Geog)*
  UF Art, Mexican American
  BT Ethnic art—United States
Mexican American artists *(May Subd Geog)*
  UF Artists, Mexican American
Mexican American arts *(May Subd Geog)*
  UF Arts, Mexican American
Mexican American authors
  (May Subd Geog)
  UF Authors, Chicano
      Authors, Mexican American
      Chicano authors
  BT Authors, American

Mexican-American Border Region
  UF American-Mexican Border Region
      Borderlands, American-Mexican
      Borderlands, Mexican-American
      Borderlands, United States-Mexico
      Mexico-United States Border Region
      United States-Mexico Border Region
  BT Mexico—Boundaries—United States
      United States—Boundaries—Mexico
**Mexican-American Border Region in motion
pictures**
  BT Moving-pictures
Mexican American Catholics
  (May Subd Geog)
  UF Catholics, Mexican American
      Chicano Catholics
  BT Hispanic American Catholics
      Mexican Americans—Religion
Mexican American children
  (May Subd Geog)
  UF Children, Mexican American
  BT Children—United States
      Hispanic American children
  NT Mexican American youth
  — Games
      USE Mexican American children's
          games
Mexican American children's games
  [GR104 (Folklore)]
  [GV1204.12 (Recreation)]
  UF Children's games, Mexican American
      Mexican American children—Games
  BT Games—United States
Mexican American cookery
  USE Cookery, Mexican American
Mexican American drama (English)
  USE American drama—Mexican American
      authors
Mexican American families
  (May Subd Geog)
  [E184.M5]
  UF Families, Mexican American
  BT Family—United States
Mexican American fiction (Spanish)
  (May Subd Geog)
  NT Short stories, Mexican American
      (Spanish)
Mexican American folk art
  (May Subd Geog)
  UF Folk art, Mexican American
  BT Folk art—United States
Mexican American leadership
  (May Subd Geog)
  [E184.M5]
  UF Leadership, Mexican American
  BT Leadership
Mexican-American libraries
  USE Mexican Americans and libraries
Mexican American literature (English)
  USE American literature—Mexican
      American authors
Mexican American literature (Spanish)
  (May Subd Geog)
  UF Chicano literature (Spanish)
      Spanish literature—Mexican American
      authors
Mexican American names
  USE Names, Mexican American
Mexican American periodicals
  (May Subd Geog)
  BT American periodicals
      Mexican periodicals
Mexican American poetry (English)
  USE American poetry—Mexican American
      authors
Mexican American poets *(May Subd Geog)*
  UF Chicano poets
      Poets, Chicano
      Poets, Mexican American
  BT Poets, American

Mexican American prisoners
  (May Subd Geog)
  UF Prisoners, Mexican American
  BT Prisoners
Mexican American proverbs
  (May Subd Geog)
  UF Proverbs, Mexican American
  BT Proverbs, American
Mexican American short stories (English)
  USE Short stories, American—Mexican
      American authors
Mexican American short stories (Spanish)
  USE Short stories, Mexican American
      (Spanish)
Mexican American studies
  USE Mexican Americans—Study and
      teaching
Mexican American theater
  (May Subd Geog)
  [PN2270.M48]
  UF Chicano theater
      Theater, Chicano
      Theater, Mexican American
  BT Theater
  NT American drama—Mexican American
      authors
Mexican American women
  (May Subd Geog)
  [E184.M5]
  UF Mexican Americans—Women
      Women, Mexican American
  BT Hispanic American women
Mexican American youth *(May Subd Geog)*
  UF Youth, Mexican American
  BT Mexican American children
Mexican Americans *(May Subd Geog)*
  UF Chicanos
      Hispanos
      Mexican Americans—United States
  BT Ethnology—United States
      Hispanic Americans
      Mexicans—United States
  NT Missions to Mexican Americans
  — **Books and reading**
      [Z1039.M5]
  — **Civil rights** *(May Subd Geog)*
  — **Education** *(May Subd Geog)*
      NT Teachers of Mexican Americans
  — — **Language arts,** [etc.]
  — **Education (Higher)** *(May Subd Geog)*
      [LC2683.6]
  — **Ethnic identity**
      [E184.M5]
  — **Health and hygiene** *(May Subd Geog)*
      NT Mexican Americans—Mental
          health
  — **Mental health** *(May Subd Geog)*
      [RC451.5.M48]
      BT Mexican Americans—Health and
          hygiene
  — **Mental health services**
      (May Subd Geog)
  — **Religion**
      NT Mexican American Catholics
  — **Study and teaching** *(May Subd Geog)*
      UF Mexican American studies
  — Subject headings
      USE Subject headings—Mexican
          Americans
  — Women
      USE Mexican American women
  — United States
      USE Mexican Americans
Mexican Americans and libraries
  (May Subd Geog)
  [Z711.92.M47]
  UF Libraries, Mexican-American
      Libraries and Mexican Americans
      Library service to Mexican Americans
      Mexican-American libraries
  BT Libraries and minorities

Mexican Americans and mass media
    UF Mass media and Mexican Americans
    BT Hispanic Americans and mass media
Mexican Americans and television
    (May Subd Geog)
    BT Television
        Television audiences
        Television broadcasting
        Television programs
Mexican Americans in motion pictures
    ₁PN1995.9.M49₁
    BT Moving-pictures
Mexican anonyms and pseudonyms
    USE Anonyms and pseudonyms, Mexican
Mexican art
    USE Art, Mexican
Mexican atlases
    USE Atlases, Mexican
Mexican authors
    USE Authors, Mexican
Mexican bean beetle
    ₁SB945.M59₁
    UF Bean beetle
        Bean ladybird
        Epilachna corrupta
        Epilachna varivestis
    BT Ladybirds
Mexican bedbug
    USE Triatoma lecticularius
Mexican boll weevil
    USE Boll weevil
Mexican chronology
    USE Chronology, Mexican
Mexican coins
    USE Coins, Mexican
Mexican cookery
    USE Cookery, Mexican
Mexican cotton boll weevil
    USE Boll weevil
Mexican cypress
    USE Cupressus lusitanica
Mexican detective stories
    USE Detective and mystery stories,
        Mexican
Mexican drama *(May Subd Geog)*
    ₁PQ7183-PQ7195 (History)₁
    ₁PQ7264-PQ7270 (Collections)₁
    NT American drama—Mexican American
        authors
        Pastoral drama, Mexican
    — **20th century**
Mexican drawing
    USE Drawing, Mexican
Mexican duck
    USE Anas diazi
Mexican erotic poetry
    USE Erotic poetry, Mexican
Mexican fantastic fiction
    USE Fantastic fiction, Mexican
Mexican fiction
    ₁PQ7197-PQ7207 (History)₁
    ₁PQ7275-PQ7276 (Collections)₁
    NT Detective and mystery stories,
        Mexican
        Fantastic fiction, Mexican
        Historical fiction, Mexican
        Picaresque literature, Mexican
        Political fiction, Mexican
        Short stories, Mexican
    — **19th century**
    — **20th century**
Mexican free-tailed bat
    USE Tadarida brasiliensis
Mexican fruit-fly
    UF Mexican fruitworm
        Mexican orange maggot
    BT Fruit-flies
Mexican fruitworm
    USE Mexican fruit-fly
Mexican hieroglyphics
    USE Indians of Mexico—Writing

Mexican historical fiction
    USE Historical fiction, Mexican
Mexican language
    USE Aztec language
Mexican literature *(May Subd Geog)*
    ₁PQ7100-PQ7221 (History)₁
    ₁PQ7231-PQ7293 (Collections)₁
        For the Spanish literature of Mexico. The litera-
    ture of the Aztecs is entered under Aztec literature.
    BT Spanish American literature
    — **To 1800**
Mexican lithography
    USE Lithography, Mexican
Mexican majolica
    USE Majolica, Mexican
Mexican manuscripts
    USE Manuscripts, Mexican
Mexican manuscripts (Pre-Columbian)
    USE Manuscripts, Mexican (Pre-Columbian)
Mexican marigold, Sweet-scented
    USE Tagetes lucida
Mexican mural painting and decoration
    USE Mural painting and decoration,
        Mexican
Mexican mystery stories
    USE Detective and mystery stories,
        Mexican
Mexican national characteristics
    USE National characteristics, Mexican
Mexican newspapers *(May Subd Geog)*
    ₁PN4961-PN4979 (History)₁
Mexican nut pine
    USE Pinus cembroides
Mexican orange maggot
    USE Mexican fruit-fly
Mexican orations
    USE Speeches, addresses, etc., Mexican
Mexican paleography
    USE Paleography, Mexican
Mexican pastoral drama
    USE Pastoral drama, Mexican
Mexican pastoral poetry
    USE Pastoral poetry, Mexican
Mexican patriotic poetry
    USE Patriotic poetry, Mexican
Mexican periodicals *(May Subd Geog)*
    NT Mexican American periodicals
        Women's periodicals, Mexican
    — **Circulation**
Mexican philosophy
    USE Philosophy, Mexican
Mexican picaresque literature
    USE Picaresque literature, Mexican
Mexican pinyon pine
    USE Pinus cembroides
Mexican poetry *(May Subd Geog)*
    ₁PQ7161-PQ7181 (History)₁
    ₁PQ7249-PQ7263 (Collections)₁
    NT Erotic poetry, Mexican
        Pastoral poetry, Mexican
        Patriotic poetry, Mexican
        Revolutionary poetry, Mexican
        Sonnets, Mexican
    — **19th century**
    — **20th century**
    — **Indian authors**
Mexican poets
    USE Poets, Mexican
Mexican political fiction
    USE Political fiction, Mexican
Mexican portrait painting
    USE Portrait painting, Mexican
Mexican pottery
    USE Pottery, Mexican
Mexican prose literature
    ₁PQ7197-PQ7221 (History)₁
    ₁PQ7272-PQ7287 (Collections)₁
Mexican proverbs
    USE Proverbs, Mexican
Mexican quail
    USE Callipepla squamata

Mexican red-bellied squirrel
    USE Sciurus aureogaster
Mexican revolutionary poetry
    USE Revolutionary poetry, Mexican
Mexican riddles
    USE Riddles, Mexican
Mexican sculpture
    USE Sculpture, Mexican
Mexican sea bass
    USE Totoaba
Mexican short stories
    USE Short stories, Mexican
Mexican sisal
    USE Henequen
Mexican sonnets
    USE Sonnets, Mexican
Mexican speeches
    USE Speeches, addresses, etc., Mexican
Mexican stone pine
    USE Pinus cembroides
Mexican students *(May Subd Geog)*
    BT Students
Mexican tetra
    USE Astyanax mexicanus
Mexican War, 1845-1848
    USE United States—History—War with
        Mexico, 1845-1848
Mexican watercolor painting
    USE Watercolor painting, Mexican
Mexican weeping pine
    USE Pinus patula
Mexican wit and humor
    ₁PN6222.M4 (Collections)₁
    ₁PQ7215 (History)₁
    ₁PQ7286₁
        Here are entered collections from several authors
    and individual authors who have not written in other
    literary forms.
Mexican wit and humor, Pictorial
    (May Subd Geog)
Mexican women's periodicals
    USE Women's periodicals, Mexican
Mexican wood rat
    UF Neotoma mexicana
    BT Wood rats
Mexicans *(May Subd Geog)*
    BT Ethnology—Mexico
    — **United States**
        NT Mexican Americans
Mexicans in literature
Mexico
    — **Anniversaries, etc.**
        NT Independence Day (Mexico)
    — **Antiquities**
        NT Acanceh Site (Mexico)
            Alta Vista Site (Mexico)
            Andasolos Cave (Mexico)
            Becan Site (Mexico)
            Bonampak Site (Mexico)
            Casas Grandes Site (Mexico)
            Chalcatzingo Site (Mexico)
            Chiapa de Corso Site (Mexico)
            Chichén Itzá Site (Mexico)
            Chingú Site (Mexico)
            Chinkultic Site (Mexico)
            Cobá Site (Mexico)
            Cuarenta Casas Site (Mexico)
            Dzibilchaltún Site (Mexico)
            Dzibilnocac Site (Mexico)
            Edzná Site (Mexico)
            Guilá Naquitz Cave (Mexico)
            Izapa Site (Mexico)
            Jmetic Lubton Site (Mexico)
            Kabah Site (Mexico)
            Kohunlich Site (Mexico)
            Labná Site (Mexico)
            Laguna Francesa Site (Mexico)
            Matacapan Site (Mexico)
            Mirador Site (Mexico)
            Monte Albán (Mexico)
            Pajón Site (Mexico)

Palenque Site (Mexico)
Pilas Site (Jonacatepec, Mexico)
Sayil Site (Mexico)
Tancah Site (Mexico)
Templo Mayor (Mexico City, Mexico)
Teotihuacán Site (San Juan Teotihuacán, Mexico)
Texcal Cave (Mexico)
Tinganio Site (Mexico)
Tlatilco Site (Naucalpan de Juarez, Mexico)
Tomaltepec Site (Mexico)
Tonina (Mexico)
Tulum Site (Mexico)
Uxmal Site (Mexico)
Xlapak Site (Mexico)
Xoc Site (Mexico)
— Boundaries
— — Belize
    NT Belize question
— — United States
    NT Mexican-American Border Region
— Church history
— — 16th century
— — 18th century
— — 19th century
— — 20th century
— Civilization
— — Classical influences
    [F1210]
    BT Civilization, Classical
— — Spanish influences
    BT Spain—Civilization
— Description and travel
— — 1951-1980
— — 1981-
— Economic conditions
— — 1540-1810
— — 19th century
— — 1918-
— — 1970-
— Economic policy
— — 1970-
— Foreign relations
— — 1821-1861
— — 1861-1867
— — 1867-1910
— — 1910-
— — 1910-1946
— — 1946-
— — 1946-1970
— — 1970-
— Frontier troubles
— — To 1910
    [F391 (Texas)]
    [F786 (New Southwest)]
    [F1234]
— — 1910-
    [F391 (Texas)]
    [F786 (New Southwest)]
    [F1234]
    BT Mexico—History—1910-1946
    United States—History—20th century
    NT United States. Army—History—Punitive Expedition into Mexico, 1916
— History
    [F1203-1409]
— — To 1519
    NT Champotón, Battle of, 1517
— — To 1810
— — Conquest, 1519-1540
    NT Tenochtitlán, Battle of, 1521
— — — Juvenile literature
— — — Naval operations
— — — — Juvenile literature
— — Spanish colony, 1540-1810
    NT Pueblo Revolt, 1680

Yaqui Indians—Wars, 1740
— — 1810-
— — Wars of Independence, 1810-1821
    UF Spain—History—Revolution of American colonies, 1806-1830
    NT Arroyo Hondo, Battle of, 1821
— — — Campaigns *(Not Subd Geog)*
    NT Monte de las Cruces, Battle of, 1810
— — 1821-1861
— — — Anecdotes, facetiae, satire, etc.
— — War with the United States, 1845-1848
    USE United States—History—War with Mexico, 1845-1848
— — European intervention, 1861-1867
    NT Juchitán, Battle of, 1866
    Pachuca, Battle of, 1861
    Shelby's Expedition to Mexico, 1865
— — — Foreign public opinion
— — — Juvenile literature
— — — Pictorial works
— — 1867-1910
— — 20th century
— — Revolution, 1910-1920
    [F1234]
— — — Campaigns *(Not Subd Geog)*
    NT Celaya, Battle of, 1915
    El Ebano, Battle of, 1915
    Torréon, Battle of, 1914
    Veracruz Llave (Mexico)—History—American occupation, 1914
    Zacatecas, Battle of, 1914
— — 1910-1946
    NT Cristero Rebellion, 1926-1929
    Mexico—Frontier troubles—1910-
— — — Anecdotes, facetiae, satire, etc.
— — — Juvenile literature
— — Revolution, 1923-1924
— — 1946-
— — 1946-1970
— — 1970-
— Intellectual life
— — 20th century
— Languages
    NT Chiricahua language
    Cocopa language
    Kiliwa language
    Mayo language (Piman)
    Mochó language
    Ocuiltec language
    Pima Bajo language
    Popoloca language
    Tepehuan language
    Tlapanec language
    Totonac language
— Literatures
    NT Zapotec literature
— Politics and government
— — To 1519
— — 1540-1810
— — 19th century
— — 1810-
— — 1810-1821
— — 1821-1861
— — 1861-1867
— — 1867-1910
— — 20th century
— — 1910-1946
— — 1946-1970
— — 1970-
— Presidents
— — Dwellings
    NT Castillo de San Juan de Ulúa (San Juan de Ulúa Island, Mexico)
— Social conditions
— — To 1810

— — 1970-
Mexico, Gulf of
    UF Gulf of Mexico
    BT Bays—Mexico
    Bays—United States
    NT Campeche, Bay of (Mexico)
Mexico, Valley of (Mexico)
    UF Valley of Mexico (Mexico)
    BT Valleys—Mexico
Mexico City (Mexico)
— History
— — To 1519
— — American occupation, 1847-1848
    BT United States—History—War with Mexico, 1845-1848
Mexico City (Mexico). Buenos Aires
    USE Buenos Aires (Mexico City, Mexico)
Mexico-United States Border Region
    USE Mexican-American Border Region
Mexilana
    [QL444.M34]
    BT Cirolanidae
Mexilana saluposi
    [QL444.M34]
Mexiletine
    [RM666.M]
    UF Methylxylyloxyethylamine
    BT Ethylamines
    Myocardial depressants
Mey family
    USE May family
    Mee family
Meye family
    USE Mee family
Meyer family
    USE Myers family
Meyerinck family
    USE Mayrink family
Meyers family
    USE Myers family
Meygal Mountain (France)
    UF Montagne du Mégal (France)
    Montagne du Meygal (France)
    BT Mountains—France
Meyner family
    USE Meiners family
Meyners family
    USE Meiners family
Meyor family
    USE Myers family
Meyors family
    USE Myers family
Meyssel family
    USE Mikesell family
Meyuhas family *(Not Subd Geog)*
Meyvali (Sect) *(May Subd Geog)*
    [BL1295.M47]
    BT Hindu sects
Mezada Site (Israel)
    USE Masada Site (Israel)
Mezcal
    USE Mescal
Mezcalapa River (Mexico)
    USE Grijalva River (Mexico)
Mezcalin
    USE Mescaline
Mezcaline
    USE Mescaline
Mézenc Mount (France)
    UF Mont Mézenc (France)
    Mont Mézène (France)
    BT Mountains—France
Meziad Cave (Romania)
    UF Peştera Meziad (Romania)
    Peştera Meziadului (Romania)
    BT Caves—Romania
Mezinárodní systém vědeckých a technických informací classification
    USE Classification, MSVTI

Mezőföld (Hungary)
Mezquital River (Mexico)
    UF Río Mezquital (Mexico)
    BT Rivers—Mexico
Mezuzah
    [BM657.M4]
    BT Judaism—Liturgical objects
    NT Scribes, Jewish—Handbooks, manuals,
          etc.
Mezzograph
    [TR976]
    UF Metzograph
    BT Photoengraving—Halftone process
          Photomechanical processes
Mezzotint engraving
    [NE1815]
    UF Mezzotints
    BT Engraving
  — 17th century *(May Subd Geog)*
  — 18th century *(May Subd Geog)*
  — 20th century *(May Subd Geog)*
Mezzotint engraving, British, [**English, etc.**]
Mezzotint engraving, English
    (May Subd Geog)
    UF English mezzotint engraving
Mezzotinters
    [NE1815]
    BT Engravers
Mezzotints
    USE Mezzotint engraving
Mfecane
    USE Bantus—Migrations
Mfengos
    USE Fingos
Mfumte (African people)
    UF Kaka (African people)
          Mbem (African people)
    BT Ethnology—Cameroon
          Ethnology—Nigeria
          Tikar (African people)
Mgeni River (South Africa)
    UF Umgeni River (South Africa)
    BT Rivers—South Africa
Mgon-po Bse-khrab-can (Buddhist deity)
    [BQ4890.M]
    UF Bse-khrab-can (Buddhist deity)
    BT Gods, Buddhist
Mhâr
    USE Mahars
Mhar (Hill tribe)
    USE Hmar (Hill tribe)
Mhar language
    USE Hmar language
Mhaskara family
Mhc (Immunogenetics)
    USE Major histocompatibility complex
MHD generators
    USE Magnetohydrodynamic generators
MHD instabilities
    USE Magnetohydrodynamic instabilities
Mhire family
    USE Myers family
MHPG
    USE Methoxyhydroxyphenylglycol
Mi, Wan-chung, chin shih 1595. Shao yüan
**   hsiu hsi t'u**
    UF Mi Garden (Painting)
          Shao yüan hsiu hsi t'u (Painting)
          Shao yüan t'u (Painting)
    BT Architecture, Domestic, in art
          Gardens in art
          Painting, Chinese—Ming-Ch'ing
            dynasties, 1368-1912
Mi-1 (Helicopters)
    UF Hare (Helicopters)
    BT Helicopters
Mi-6A (Helicopter)
    BT Helicopters
Mi-8 (Helicopters)
    [TL716.9.M]
    BT Helicopters

Mi Garden (Painting)
    USE Mi, Wan-chung, chin shih 1595.
          Shao yüan hsiu hsi t'u
Mi-koshi
    USE Mikoshi
MIA families
    USE Missing in action—Family
          relationships
Mial family
    USE Miles family
Mials family
    USE Miles family
Miami (Fla.). Coconut Grove
    USE Coconut Grove (Miami, Fla.)
Miami (Fla.). Fort Dallas Park
    USE Fort Dallas Park (Miami, Fla.)
Miami Indians
    [E99.M48]
    UF Twightwees
    BT Algonquian Indians
          Indians of North America
    NT Piankashaw Indians
  — Missions
Miami language
    [PM1781]
    BT Algonquian languages
Miami Purchase
    [F483]
    BT Northwest, Old—History—1775-1865
Miami River (Fla.)
    BT Rivers—Florida
Miami River (Ohio)
    UF Great Miami River (Ohio)
    BT Rivers—Ohio
Mianmin (Papua New Guinea people)
    UF Miyanmin (Papua New Guinea people)
    BT Ethnology—Papua New Guinea
Mianmin language
    BT Papuan languages
Miao (Asian people)
    USE Hmong (Asian people)
Miao language
    USE Hmong language
Miao-shan (Legendary character)
    BT Legends, Buddhist
Miao ying ssu (Peking, China)
  — Pai t'a
      UF Pai t'a, Miao ying ssu (Peking,
          China)
          Śvetacaitya, Miao ying ssu (Peking,
          China)
          White Dagoba, Miao ying ssu
          (Peking, China)
      BT Stūpas—China
Miar family
    USE Myers family
Miargyrite *(May Subd Geog)*
    BT Sulphide minerals
Miars family
    USE Myers family
MIA's
    USE Missing in action
Miastor
    [QL537.C33]
    BT Gall-gnats
Miastor metraloas
    [QL537.C33]
Mibu family *(Not Subd Geog)*
MIC (Chemical)
    USE Methyl isocyanate
Mica *(May Subd Geog)*
    [TN933]
    UF Biotite-granite
    BT Rock-forming minerals
    NT Biotite
          Celadonite
          Electric insulators and insulation—
            Mica
          Fluorine mica
          Illite
          Lepidolite

          Muscovite
          Phlogopite
          Phyllite
          Vermiculite
Mica crystals
  — Cleavage
Mica industry *(May Subd Geog)*
    [HD9585.M5-53]
Mica miners *(May Subd Geog)*
    BT Miners
Mica mines and mining *(May Subd Geog)*
    [TN933]
MiCAPP (Computer system)
    UF MiCAPP Manufacturing Cost
          Estimating Software System
          (Computer system)
    BT Machine-shop practice—Data
          processing
MiCAPP Manufacturing Cost Estimating
    Software System (Computer system)
    USE MiCAPP (Computer system)
Miccosukee Indians
    USE Mikasuki Indians
Miccosukee language
    USE Mikasuki language
Mice
    [QL737.R6]
    UF Mouse
          Mus musculus
    BT Rodents
    NT Brush mouse
          Cricetidae
          Dancing mice
          Dormice
          Nude mouse
          Oldfield mouse
          Piñon mouse
          Plateau mouse
          Pocket mice
          Sitka mouse
          Woodland jumping mouse
  — Anatomy
  — Control *(May Subd Geog)*
      [SB994.M5]
      UF Mice—Extermination
  — Diseases *(May Subd Geog)*
      NT Mouse leukemia complex
  — Extermination
      USE Mice—Control
Mice as carriers of disease
    (May Subd Geog)
    BT Rodents as carriers of disease
Mice as laboratory animals
Mice as pets
    [SF459.M5]
Mice family
    USE Mize family
Micelles
    RT Colloids
    NT Critical micelle concentration
Mich family
    USE Michel family
Michael (Archangel)
    [BT968.M5]
    BT Angels
Michael (Name)
    UF Michel (Name)
    BT Names, Personal
Michael family *(Not Subd Geog)*
    UF Michaels family
          Mickel family
          Mickell family
          Mickels family
          Mickles family
          Mikell family
    RT Michaelis family
          Michel family
          Michelson family
          Mickle family
Michaels family
    USE Michael family

Michaelsen family
USE Michelson family
Michaelson family
USE Michelson family
Michaud family *(Not Subd Geog)*
UF Michaux family
Micheau family
Micheaux family
Michaux family
USE Michaud family
Micheau family
USE Michaud family
Micheaux family
USE Michaud family
Michel (Name)
USE Michael (Name)
Michel family *(Not Subd Geog)*
UF Mich family
Michell family
Michels family
Michill family
Michl family
Michle family
RT Michael family
Michelson family
Mitchell family
**Michelangelo Buonarroti, 1475-1564.
Conversion of Saint Paul**
[ND623.B9]
UF Conversion of Saint Paul (Painting)
Conversione di San Paolo (Painting)
BT Painting, Italian
**Michelangelo Buonarroti, 1475-1564.
Crucifixion of Saint Peter**
[ND623.B9]
UF Crucifixion of Saint Peter (Painting)
Martirio di San Pietro (Painting)
BT Peter, the Apostle, Saint—Art
Michelangelo Buonarroti, 1475-1564. David
(Not Subd Geog)
UF David (Sculpture)
BT Marble sculpture, Italian
**Michelangelo Buonarroti, 1475-1564. Last
judgment**
[ND623.B9]
UF Giudizio universale (Painting)
Last judgment (Painting)
BT Judgment Day in art
Michelangelo Buonarroti, 1475-1564. Moses
[NB623.B9]
UF Mosè (Sculpture)
Moses (Sculpture)
BT Marble sculpture, Italian
Marble sculpture, Renaissance—Italy
Moses (Biblical leader)—Art
Michelangelo Buonarroti, 1475-1564. Pietà
[NB623.B9]
UF Pietà (Sculpture)
BT Jesus Christ—Art
Marble sculpture, Italian
Marble sculpture, Renaissance—Italy
Mary, Blessed Virgin, Saint—Art
**Michelangelo Buonarroti, 1475-1564. Saint
John**
[NB623.B9]
UF Saint John (Sculpture)
San Giovannino (Sculpture)
St. John (Sculpture)
BT John, the Baptist, Saint—Art
Marble sculpture, Italian
Marble sculpture, Renaissance—Italy
Michelena Salon, Valencia, Venezuela
USE Salón Arturo Michelena, Valencia,
Venezuela
Michelet family
USE Mickley family
Michell family
USE Michel family
Michels family
USE Michel family

Michelsberg culture *(May Subd Geog)*
[GN776.2.M5]
BT Europe—Antiquities
Neolithic period—Europe
Michelsen family
USE Michelson family
Michelsohn family
USE Michelson family
Michelson family *(Not Subd Geog)*
UF Michaelsen family
Michaelson family
Michelsen family
Michelsohn family
Mickelsen family
Mickelson family
Mikkelsen family
RT Michael family
Michel family
Michi
USE Tivi (African people)
Michif language
[PM7895.M53]
UF Cree language, French
French Cree language
Mitchif language
BT Canada—Languages
Creole dialects, French
Indians of North America—Languages
North Dakota—Languages
Michigan
— Antiquities
NT Copper Falls (Mich.)
Fletcher Site (Mich.)
French Farm Lake Site (Mich.)
Schultz Site (Mich.)
— **Description and travel**
— — **1951-1980**
— — **1981-**
— **History**
[F561-575]
— — **To 1837**
— — **War of 1812**
[E359.5.M]
NT Raisin River, Battle of, 1813
— — **1837-**
— — **Civil War, 1861-1865**
— **Politics and government**
— — **To 1837**
— — **1837-1950**
— — **1951-**
Michigan, Lake
UF Lake Michigan
BT Great Lakes
Lakes—United States
— **Temperature**
— **Water diversion**
Michigan algorithm decoder
USE MAD (Computer program language)
Michigan Basin (Mich. and Ont.)
BT Geology—Michigan
Geology—Ontario
Michigan digital automatic computer
USE Seac computer
Michigan grayling
USE Arctic grayling
Michigan picture test
[BF698.8.M44]
BT Personality tests
Psychological tests for children
Michigan Southern Railroad
BT Railroads—United States
Michihli
USE Chinese cabbage
Michilimackinac, Fort (Mich.)
USE Fort Michilimackinac (Mich.)
Michill family
USE Michel family
Michl family
USE Michel family
Michle family
USE Michel family

Michoacana language
USE Tarascan language
Michot family *(Not Subd Geog)*
Michuacana language
USE Tarascan language
Mickel family
USE Michael family
Mickell family
USE Michael family
Mickeln Castle (Düsseldorf, Germany)
USE Schloss Mickeln (Düsseldorf,
Germany)
Mickels family
USE Michael family
Mickelsen family
USE Michelson family
Mickelson family
USE Michelson family
Mickey Mouse (Cartoon character)
BT Moving-picture cartoons
— **Collectibles** *(May Subd Geog)*
**Mickey Mouse (Cartoon character) in mass
media** *(May Subd Geog)*
[P96.M53]
BT Mass media
Mickle family *(Not Subd Geog)*
RT Michael family
Mickley family
Mickles family
USE Michael family
Mickley family *(Not Subd Geog)*
UF Michelet family
Mickly family
RT Mickle family
Mickly family
USE Mickley family
Mickmak Indians
USE Micmac Indians
Micmac Indians
[E99.M6]
UF Mickmak Indians
BT Algonquian Indians
Indians of North America
Micmac language
[PM1791-4]
RT Algonquian languages
Mico
USE Callithrix
Micom (Word processor)
USE Philips/Micom (Word processor)
Miconazole
UF Dichlorodichlorobenz
yloxyphenethylimidazole
Dichlorophenyldichlo
rophenylmethoxyethylimidazole
BT Antifungal agents
Imidazole
Micrampelis
USE Echinocystis
Micranthes
USE Saxifraga
Micrasterias
[QK569.D46]
BT Desmidiaceae
Micrasterias torreyi
[QK569.D46]
Micrathena
[QL458.42.A7]
UF Acrosoma
BT Araneidae
Micrathene
[QL696.S83]
BT Strigidae
Micrathene whitneyi
USE Elf owl
Micro Business Computer 550
USE Sanyo MBC-550 (Computer)
Micro Business Computer 555
USE Sanyo MBC-555 (Computer)
Micro computers
USE Microcomputers

Micro-DSS/ANALYSIS (Computer system)
　USE　DSS/A (Computer system)
Micro-DSS/FINANCE (Computer system)
　USE　DSS/F (Computer system)
Micro-DYNAMO (Computer program language)
　BT　Digital computer simulation
　　　DYNAMO (Computer program language)
　　　Programming languages (Electronic computers)
　　　System analysis—Data processing
Micro-nutrient fertilizers
　USE　Micronutrient fertilizers
Micro-organisms　*(May Subd Geog)*
　[QH201-QH277 (Microscopy)]
　[QR (Bacteriology)]
　UF　Germs
　　　Microbes
　　　Microscopic organisms
　RT　Microbiology
　NT　Animalcules
　　　Bacteria
　　　Chlamydiales
　　　Fungi
　　　Micro-organisms, Alkalophilic
　　　Micro-organisms, Nitrogen-fixing
　　　Microbial cell cycle
　　　Microbial ecology
　　　Microbial mutation
　　　Microbial populations
　　　Microbiological chemistry
　　　Microscope and microscopy
　　　Mycoplasmatales
　　　Prokaryotes
　　　Protozoa
　　　Rickettsia
　　　Unicellular organisms
　　　Viruses
　— Aggregation
　　　USE　Microbial aggregation
　— Anatomy
　　　USE　Micro-organisms—Morphology
　— Catalogs and collections
　　　UF　Microbial culture collections
　　　　　Microbiology—Cultures and culture media—Catalogs and collections
　— Classification
　　　USE　Microbiology—Classification
　— Counting
　　　UF　Counting of micro-organisms
　　　NT　Direct epifluorescent filter technique
　— Development
　　　[QR73.4]
　　　UF　Microbial development
　　　BT　Developmental biology
　— Dispersal
　　　[QR102]
　　　UF　Dispersal of micro-organisms
　　　BT　Air—Microbiology
　　　　　Water—Microbiology
　— Drying
　　　[QR69]
　　　UF　Micro-organisms—Freezing and drying
　— Effect of antibiotics on
　　　UF　Micro-organisms, Effect of antibiotics on
　　　BT　Antibiotics—Physiological effect
　　　RT　Microbial sensitivity tests
　— Effect of drugs on
　　　UF　Micro-organisms, Effect of drugs on
　　　BT　Drugs—Physiological effect
　　　RT　Microbial sensitivity tests
　— Effect of xenobiotics on
　　　[QR97.X46]
　　　BT　Xenobiotics
　— Electric properties

　[QR69.E43]
　— Evolution
　　　UF　Microbial evolution
　　　BT　Evolution
　— Freezing and drying
　　　USE　Micro-organisms—Drying
　— Genetics
　　　USE　Microbial genetics
　— Host plants
　　　USE　Micro-organisms, Phytopathogenic—Host plants
　— Identification
　　　Here are entered works on the identification of micro-organisms. Works on differentiation in function and/or morphology of micro-organisms are entered under Microbial differentiation.
　— Morphology
　　　UF　Micro-organisms—Anatomy
　— Motility
　　　UF　Microbial motility
　　　　　Motility of micro-organisms
　　　NT　Bacteria—Motility
　　　　　Cells—Motility
　　　　　Cilia and ciliary motion
　　　　　Flagella (Microbiology)
　　　　　Protozoa—Motility
　— Physiology
　　　NT　Microbial metabolism
　— Respiration
　　　USE　Microbial respiration
Micro-organisms, Alkalophilic
　UF　Alkalophilic micro-organisms
　BT　Micro-organisms
Micro-organisms, Effect of antibiotics on
　USE　Micro-organisms—Effect of antibiotics on
Micro-organisms, Effect of drugs on
　USE　Micro-organisms—Effect of drugs on
Micro-organisms, Effect of temperature on
　BT　Temperature—Physiological effect
Micro-organisms, Halophilic
　UF　Halophilic micro-organisms
　　　Halophils
　BT　Salt
　NT　Halobacterium
Micro-organisms, Immobilized
　UF　Immobilized micro-organisms
　BT　Industrial microbiology
Micro-organisms, Mutation of
　USE　Microbial mutation
Micro-organisms, Nitrogen-fixing
　(May Subd Geog)
　[QR89.7]
　UF　Nitrogen-fixing micro-organisms
　BT　Micro-organisms
　RT　Nitrogen—Fixation
　NT　Azotobacteraceae
　　　Nitrogen-fixing algae
Micro-organisms, Pathogenic
　[QR175-351]
　UF　Pathogenic micro-organisms
　　　Pathogens
　RT　Medical microbiology
　　　Veterinary microbiology
　　　Virulence (Microbiology)
　NT　Bacteria, Pathogenic
　　　Fungi, Pathogenic
　　　Protozoa, Pathogenic
　— Identification
　　　RT　Diagnostic microbiology
　— Type specimens
　　　BT　Type specimens (Natural history)
Micro-organisms, Phytopathogenic
　(May Subd Geog)
　UF　Phytopathogenic micro-organisms
　　　Plant pathogens
　BT　Agricultural microbiology
　　　Plant parasites
　RT　Plant diseases
　NT　Bacteria, Phytopathogenic
　　　Fungi, Phytopathogenic

　　　Mycoplasma-like organisms, Phytopathogenic
　　　Plant viruses
　— Host plants
　　　UF　Micro-organisms—Host plants
Micro-organisms, Thermophilic
　UF　Thermophilic micro-organisms
　NT　Bacteria, Thermophilic
　　　Fungi, Thermophilic
Micro-organisms in food
　USE　Food—Microbiology
Micro-PROLOG (Computer program language)
　BT　Programming languages (Electronic computers)
　RT　Prolog (Computer program language)
Micro-sociology
　USE　Microsociology
micro TSP (Computer program)
　USE　microTSP (Computer program)
MicroAce (Computer)
　[QA76.8.M]
　BT　Electronic digital computers
Microanalysis (Chemistry)
　USE　Microchemistry
Microbalance
　[QC107]
　BT　Balance
　NT　Quartz crystal microbalances
　　　Vacuum microbalance
Microbes
　USE　Bacteria
　　　Bacteriology
　　　Germ theory of disease
　　　Micro-organisms
　　　Viruses
Microbial aggregation
　[QR73.6]
　UF　Aggregation, Microbial
　　　Micro-organisms—Aggregation
　RT　Cell aggregation
Microbial antitoxins
　BT　Antitoxins
　NT　Bacterial antitoxins
Microbial assay
　USE　Microbiological assay
Microbial biology
　USE　Microbiology
Microbial biomass proteins
　USE　Single cell proteins
Microbial cell cycle
　[QR73.7]
　BT　Cell cycle
　　　Micro-organisms
Microbial chemistry
　USE　Microbiological chemistry
Microbial culture collections
　USE　Micro-organisms—Catalogs and collections
Microbial cultures
　USE　Microbiology—Cultures and culture media
Microbial development
　USE　Micro-organisms—Development
Microbial differentiation
　[QR73.5]
　　　Here are entered works on differentiation in function and/or morphology of micro-organisms. Works on the identification of micro-organisms are entered under Micro-organisms—Identification.
　BT　Cell differentiation
　NT　Fungi—Differentiation
Microbial diseases in animals
　USE　Communicable diseases in animals
Microbial diseases in man
　USE　Communicable diseases
Microbial diseases in plants
　USE　Plant diseases
Microbial drug resistance
　USE　Drug resistance in micro-organisms

Microbial ecology

[QR100]

BT Ecology

Micro-organisms

NT Bacteria—Ecology

Microbial energy conversion

USE Biomass energy

Microbial enzymes

[QR90]

BT Enzymes

Microbiological chemistry

NT Beta lactamases

Subtilisins

Microbial evolution

USE Micro-organisms—Evolution

Microbial fouling

USE Fouling

Microbial genetic engineering

(May Subd Geog)

UF Genetic engineering, Microbial

BT Genetic engineering

Microbial genetics

UF Micro-organisms—Genetics

BT Genetics

Microbiology

NT Bacterial genetics

Bacterial transformation

Drug resistance in micro-organisms

Genetic transformation

Microbial mutation

Microbial mutation breeding

Transduction

Viral genetics

Microbial growth

BT Growth

Growth (Plants)

RT Microbiology—Cultures and culture
media

NT Bacterial growth

Microbial insecticides (May Subd Geog)

UF Insecticides, Microbial

BT Insect pests—Biological control

Insecticides

NT Viral insecticides

Microbial insecticides industry

(May Subd Geog)

Microbial lipids

[QR92.L5]

BT Lipids

NT Endotoxins

Microbial lipopolysaccharides

USE Endotoxins

Microbial metabolism

[QR88]

UF Bacterial metabolism

Metabolism, Bacterial

BT Metabolism

Micro-organisms—Physiology

NT Microbial metabolites

Microbial respiration

— **Regulation**

UF Regulation of microbial metabolism

BT Biological control systems

Microbial metabolites

UF Metabolites of micro-organisms

BT Biological chemistry

Metabolism

Microbial metabolism

Microbiological synthesis

Microbiology

RT Fungal metabolites

NT Antibiotics

Bestatin

Biosynthesis

Microbial surfactants

Microbial motility

USE Micro-organisms—Motility

Microbial mutation

[QH434]

UF Micro-organisms, Mutation of

Mutation of micro-organisms

BT Micro-organisms

Microbial genetics

Mutation (Biology)

NT Gene fusion

Tn elements

Microbial mutation breeding

BT Industrial microbiology

Microbial genetics

Mutation breeding

Microbial peptides

[QR92.P]

UF Peptides, Microbial

BT Microbiological chemistry

Peptides

Microbial pigments

BT Pigments (Biology)

NT Bacterial pigments

Microbial polysaccharides

[QR92.P6]

UF Polysaccharides, Microbial

BT Microbiological chemistry

NT Endotoxins

Peptidoglycans

Microbial populations

UF Populations, Microbial

BT Micro-organisms

Population

Microbial proteins

BT Microbiological chemistry

Proteins

NT Bacterial proteins

Single cell proteins

Microbial respiration

[QR89]

UF Bacteria—Respiration

Bacterial respiration

Micro-organisms—Respiration

Respiration, Microbial

BT Microbial metabolism

Respiration

RT Energy metabolism

Microbial sensitivity tests

[QR69.A57]

UF Antibiotic sensitivity tests

Antimicrobial sensitivity tests

Bacterial sensitivity tests

Microbial susceptibility tests

Sensitivity tests, Microbial

Sensitivity tests (Microbiology)

BT Microbiology—Technique

RT Micro-organisms—Effect of antibiotics
on

Micro-organisms—Effect of drugs on

Microbial serine proteinases

USE Subtilisins

Microbial surface active agents

USE Microbial surfactants

Microbial surfactants (May Subd Geog)

UF Microbial surface active agents

BT Biosurfactants

Microbial metabolites

Microbial susceptibility tests

USE Microbial sensitivity tests

Microbial synthesis

USE Microbiological synthesis

Microbial technology

USE Biotechnology

Microbial toxins

BT Toxins

NT Bacterial toxins

Mycotoxins

Microbial transformation of chemical
compounds

USE Microbiological synthesis

Microbiological assay

[QR69.P6]

UF Assay, Microbiological

Microbial assay

BT Biological assay

NT Plaque assay technique

Microbiological chemistry

UF Microbial chemistry

BT Biological chemistry

Micro-organisms

NT Microbial enzymes

Microbial peptides

Microbial polysaccharides

Microbial proteins

Siderophores

Microbiological geology

USE Geomicrobiology

Microbiological laboratories

(May Subd Geog)

UF Laboratories, Microbiological

BT Pharmaceutical microbiology

NT Bacteriological laboratories

— **Safety measures**

NT Biological safety cabinets

Microbiological research

USE Microbiology—Research

Microbiological synthesis

UF Bacterial synthesis

Microbial synthesis

Microbial transformation of chemical
compounds

BT Biochemical engineering

Biosynthesis

Industrial microbiology

Pharmaceutical microbiology

NT Fermentation

Microbial metabolites

Microbiologists (May Subd Geog)

[QR31]

BT Biologists

Scientists

NT Bacteriologists

Geneticists

Parasitologists

Virologists

— **Supply and demand**

Microbiology (May Subd Geog)

[QR]

UF Microbial biology

BT Biology

RT Micro-organisms

Microscope and microscopy

SA subdivision Microbiology under
subjects, e.g. Fishery products—
Microbiology; Foot—Microbiology;
Metals—Microbiology

NT Agricultural microbiology

Algology

Aquatic microbiology

Bacteriology

Biodegradation

Biotechnology

Dairy microbiology

Freshwater microbiology

Geomicrobiology

Germfree life

Industrial microbiology

Marine microbiology

Medical microbiology

Microbial genetics

Microbial metabolites

Mycology

Protozoology

Radioisotopes in microbiology

Sanitary microbiology

Seafood—Microbiology

Soil microbiology

Veterinary microbiology

Virology

— **Classification**

UF Micro-organisms—Classification

— **Cultures and culture media**

UF Microbial cultures

RT Microbial growth

NT Blood agar

— — Catalogs and collections

Microbiology
— **Cultures and culture media**
— — Catalogs and collections
(Continued)
USE Micro-organisms—Catalogs
and collections
— **Experiments**
— Industrial applications
USE Industrial microbiology
— **Research**
UF Microbiological research
— **Technique**
NT Microbial sensitivity tests
Micrurgy
Plaque assay technique
— **Variation**
BT Variation (Biology)
Microbiology, Agricultural
USE Agricultural microbiology
Microbiology, Clinical
USE Diagnostic microbiology
Microbiology, Diagnostic
USE Diagnostic microbiology
Microbiology, Geological
USE Geomicrobiology
Microbiology, Industrial
USE Industrial microbiology
Microbiology, Marine
USE Marine microbiology
Microbiology, Medical
USE Medical microbiology
Microbiology, Pharmaceutical
USE Pharmaceutical microbiology
Microbiology, Sanitary
USE Sanitary microbiology
Microbiotheriidae
[QE882.M3]
BT Marsupialia, Fossil
Microbodies
[QH603.M35]
UF Cytoplasmic bodies, type I
Peroxisomes
BT Cell organelles
NT Catalase
Plant cell microbodies
MICROBOOK (Computer system)
BT Apple II (Computer)—Programming
Data base management
Electronic digital computers—
Programming
PASCAL (Computer program
language)
Microbore liquid chromatography
USE Capillary liquid chromatography
Microbracon
[QL568.B8]
BT Braconidae
Microbuses (Computers)
USE Microcomputers—Buses
Microcalorimetry
USE Calorimeters and calorimetry
Microcards
BT Microforms
Micrographics
— **Catalogs**
SA *subdivision* Microform catalogs
under subjects
— Reader-printers
USE Reader-printers
(Microphotography)
Microcebus
[QL737.P933]
UF Mouse lemurs
BT Cheirogaleidae
NT Microcebus murinus
Microcebus murinus
[QL737.P933]
UF Lesser mouse lemur
Mouse lemur, Lesser
BT Microcebus

Microcellular striatal syndrome
USE Huntington's chorea
Microcephalia
USE Microcephaly
Microcephalism
USE Microcephaly
Microcephaly
[QM691]
UF Microcephalia
Microcephalism
BT Craniology
Head—Abnormalities
Microcheilinella
BT Pachydomellidae
Microchemistry
UF Microanalysis (Chemistry)
BT Chemistry
NT Microprobe analysis
Spot tests (Chemistry)
Microchips
USE Integrated circuits
Microcinematography
UF Cinematomicrography
Cinemicrography
Cinephotomicrography
Moving photomicrography
BT Cinematography
Microscope and microscopy
Photomicrography
Microcirculation
BT Blood—Circulation
NT Arteriovenous anastomosis
Capillaries
Microclimatology *(May Subd Geog)*
[QC982.7 (Meteorology)]
[QH543 (Ecology)]
BT Climatology
Ecology
NT Animal housing—Climate
Cave climates
Forest microclimatology
Greenhouses—Climate
Micrococcus gonorrhoea
USE Neisseria gonorrhoeae
Micrococcus melitensis
USE Brucella melitensis
Micrococcus pneumoniae
USE Streptococcus pneumoniae
Microcolumn chromatography
USE Capillary liquid chromatography
Microcomputer buses
USE Microcomputers—Buses
Microcomputer interfaces, Programmable
peripheral
USE Microcomputers—Programmable
peripheral interfaces
Microcomputer software, Cataloging of
USE Cataloging of microcomputer software
Microcomputer workstations
(May Subd Geog)
UF Microprocessor-based workstations
Personal computer workstations
Work stations, Microcomputer
Work stations (Electronic office
machines)
Workstations, Microcomputer
Workstations, Microprocessor-based
BT Microcomputers
NT OCLC workstations
Microcomputers *(May Subd Geog)*
UF Home computers
Micro computers
Personal computers
Small computers
BT Minicomputers
NT Adam (Computer)
Alice (Computer)
Alice-90 (Computer)
Amiga (Computer)
Amstrad Microcomputer
Apple computer

Apple IIc (Computer)
AT&T PC 6300 (Computer)
Atari computer
BBC Microcomputer
Burroughs B 20 (Computer)
Casio FX-702P (Computer)
Cataloging of microcomputer software
Commodore Plus/4 (Computer)
COMPAQ Portable Computer
Cromemco C-10 (Computer)
Cromemco Z-2D (Computer)
DEC microcomputers
DEC Professional 350 (Computer)
Dragon 32 (Computer)
Eagle computers
Electron Microcomputer
Epson computers
Exidy Sorcerer (Computer)
Expansion boards (Microcomputers)
Franklin Ace 1000 (Computer)
Heathkit H-8 (Computer)
HHC (Computer)
HP 150 (Computer)
Hyperion (Computer)
IBM microcomputers
Intel 8048 (Computer)
Kaypro 10 (Computer)
Kaypro II (Computer)
Macintosh (Computer)
MC6800 (Computer)
Memotech MTX (Computer)
Microcomputer workstations
MO5 (Computer)
Morrow computers
Motorola 6801 (Computer)
Motorola 6803 (Computer)
Motorola 6809 (Computer)
Motorola 68701 (Computer)
Motorola computers
Motorola M6800 series (Computers)
NEC PC-8200 (Computer)
NEC PC-8201 (Computer)
NEC PC-8201A (Computer)
Olivetti M-10 (Computer)
Olivetti M-24 (Computer)
Oric 1 (Computer)
Oric Atmos (Computer)
Osborne 1 (Computer)
Panasonic Jr-200 (Computer)
PC-1211 (Computer)
PC-1500 (Computer)
Portable computers
S6800 (Computer)
Sanyo MBC-550 (Computer)
Sanyo MBC-555 (Computer)
Selling—Microcomputers
Sharp pocket computers
Sinclair QL (Computer)
Smart cards
Spectravideo SV-318 (Computer)
Spectravideo SV-328 (Computer)
Synertek SYM-1 (Computer)
TI 99/2 (Computer)
TI Professional Computer
Timex 1000 (Computer)
Timex Sinclair 2068 (Computer)
TRS-80 Color Computer
TRS-80 Color Computer 2
TRS-80 computers
TRS-80 MC-10 (Computer)
TRS-80 Model 4 (Computer)
TRS-80 Model 4P (Computer)
TRS-80 Model 16 (Computer)
TRS-80 Model 100 (Computer)
TRS-80 Model I (Computer)
TRS-80 Model II (Computer)
TRS-80 Model III (Computer)
TRS-80 PC-1 (Computer)
TRS&80 PC-2 (Computer)
Used microcomputers
Victor 9000 (Computer)

Wang Professional Computer
Workslate (Computer)
Zenith Z-100 (Computer)
— Access control
    BT Data protection
— — Computer programs
      NT Double Agent (Computer
         program)
— Buses
    [TK7895.B87]
    UF Buses (Microcomputers)
        Microbuses (Computers)
        Microcomputer buses
    BT Bus conductors (Electricity)
        Data transmission systems
— Equipment and supplies
    NT Computer furniture
— Library applications
    UF Libraries and microcomputers
        Library applications of
         microcomputers
    BT Information storage and retrieval
        systems
        Library science—Data processing
— Programmable peripheral interfaces
    UF Interfaces, Programmable
        peripheral microcomputer
        Microcomputer interfaces,
        Programmable peripheral
    BT Computer input-output equipment
        Computer interfaces
— Programming
    NT Methods (Computer system)
        MicroTex (Computer system)
— Purchasing
— Study and teaching (May Subd Geog)
    NT Computer camps
Microcomputers and the arts
(May Subd Geog)
    BT Arts
Microcosm and macrocosm
[BD493-523]
    UF Macrocosm and microcosm
    BT Cosmology
        Monadology
Microcrystal polymers
    USE Microcrystalline polymers
Microcrystalline polymers
[TP1183.M5]
    UF Microcrystal polymers
        Polymer microcrystals
    BT Colloids
        Polymers and polymerization
Microctonus
[QL568.B8]
    BT Braconidae
    NT Microctonus vittatae
Microctonus vittatae (May Subd Geog)
[QL568.B8]
    BT Microctonus
Microcyprini
    USE Atheriniformes
Microcytic hypochromic anemia
    USE Hypochromic anemia
Microdensitometry
    BT Photography—Negatives
Microdesmidae
[QL638.M5]
    UF Wormfishes
    BT Perciformes
Microdosimetry
[QC795.32.R3]
    BT Radiation dosimetry
Microeconomics
    UF Price theory
    BT Economics
    NT Demand (Economic theory)
        Industrial organization (Economic
        theory)
        Managerial economics
        Production (Economic theory)

Microelectrodes
    UF Electrodes, Miniature
        Miniature electrodes
    BT Electrodes
Microelectronic packaging
    [TK7874]
    UF Packaging (Microelectronics)
    BT Electronic packaging
        Microelectronics
Microelectronics
    UF Microminiature electronic equipment
        Microminiaturization (Electronics)
    BT Electronics
        Semiconductors
    RT Miniature electronic equipment
    NT Integrated circuits
        Lithography, Electron beam
        Microelectronic packaging
        Molecular electronics
        Photoresists
        Printed circuits
        Semiconductor wafers
        Thick-film circuits
        Thick films
        Thin-film circuits
— Charts, diagrams, etc.
    UF Microelectronics—Diagrams
— Diagrams
    USE Microelectronics—Charts,
        diagrams, etc.
— Research (May Subd Geog)
    UF Microelectronics research
Microelectronics industry (May Subd Geog)
[HD9696]
Microelectronics research
    USE Microelectronics—Research
Microelements
    USE Trace elements
Microencapsulation
    UF Encapsulation, Particle
        Particle encapsulation
    BT Packaging
Microfarad meters
    USE Capacitance meters
Microfibrils
[QK725 (Botany)]
    BT Cells
        Plant cell walls
Microfiche services
    BT Micrographics
        Microphotography
    RT Microfilm services
Microfiches
    BT Microforms
        Micrographics
    RT Microfilms
    NT Herbaria on microfiche
        Library catalogs on microfiche
        Pamphlets on microfiche
        Periodicals on microfiche
        Technical reports on microfiche
— Format
    UF Format of microfiches
— Image quality
    UF Image quality of microfiches
        Quality of images on microfiches
    BT Images, Photographic
Microfilaments
    USE Cytoplasmic filaments
Microfilm aperture card systems
    UF Aperture card systems
        IBM aperture card systems
    BT Computer storage devices
        Electronic data processing
        Information storage and retrieval
        systems
        Micrographics
        Punched card systems
— Engineering drawings
    BT Drawing-room practice
        Engineering drawings

Microfilm atlases
    USE Atlases on microfilm
Microfilm books
    USE Books on microfilm
Microfilm devices, Computer output
    USE Computer output microfilm devices
Microfilm industry (May Subd Geog)
    BT Micrographics
        Microphotography
Microfilm projectors
    BT Microphotography—Equipment and
        supplies
        Projectors
    NT Reader-printers (Microphotography)
Microfilm readers
    [TR835]
    UF Microfilm viewers
        Readers, Microfilm
    BT Microphotography—Equipment and
        supplies
Microfilm services (May Subd Geog)
    BT Micrographics
        Microphotography
    RT Microfiche services
    NT Photocopying services
Microfilm viewers
    USE Microfilm readers
Microfilming
    USE Microphotography
Microfilms
    UF Films
    BT Microforms
        Micrographics
        Photography—Films
    RT Microfiches
    NT Atlases on microfilm
        Bank records on microfilm
        Books on microfilm
        Church records on microfilm
        Computer output microfilm
        Court records on microfilm
        Diazo microfilm
        Documents on microfilm
        Gazettes on microfilm
        Hospital records on microfilm
        Library catalogs on microfilm
        Manuscripts on microfilm
        Medical records on microfilm
        Newspapers on microfilm
        Out-of-print books on microfilm
        Pamphlets on microfilm
        Periodicals on microfilm
        Projected books
        Rare books on microfilm
        VSMF microfilm system
— Deterioration
    UF Deterioration of microfilms
— Library applications
    [Z681.3.M53]
    UF Libraries and microfilms
        Library applications of microfilms
— Reader-printers
    USE Reader-printers
        (Microphotography)
Microform reader-printers
    USE Reader-printers (Microphotography)
Microforms
    UF Micropublications
    RT Micrographics
        Microphotography
    NT Acquisition of microforms
        Cataloging of microforms
        Documents in microform
        Gazettes in microform
        Libraries—Special collections—
         Microforms
        Microcards
        Microfiches
        Microfilms
        Micropublishing
        Newspapers in microform

Microforms *(Continued)*
    Pamphlets in microform
    Periodicals in microform
  — **Catalogs**
    SA *subdivision* Microform catalogs
        under subjects
  — **Preservation and storage**
    UF Preservation of microforms
      Storage of microforms
Microforms in education *(May Subd Geog)*
  [LB1043.9]
  BT Education
    Teaching—Aids and devices
    Visual education
Microfractography
  USE Fractography
Microgaster
  [QL568.B8]
  BT Braconidae
Microglia
  UF Mesoglia
  BT Neuroglia
    Phagocytes
Micrognathia
  [QM691]
  [RD526 (Surgery)]
  BT Jaws
Micrognathus
  [QL638.S9]
  NT Micrognathus dawsoni
Micrognathus dawsoni
  [QL638.S9]
  BT Micrognathus
Microgobius
  [QL638.G7]
  BT Gobiidae
Microgobius signatus
  [QL638.G7]
Microgramma
  USE Polypodium
Micrographic analysis
  USE Metallography
    Microscope and microscopy
Micrographics *(May Subd Geog)*
  [TR835 (Photography)]
  [Z265 (General)]
  Here are entered works on the production and use
of microforms, including microphotography, mi-
cropublishing, computer output microfilm, document
retrieval systems, library applications, etc.
  BT Graphic arts
  RT Microforms
    Microphotography
  NT Computer output microfilm devices
    Microcards
    Microfiche services
    Microfiches
    Microfilm aperture card systems
    Microfilm industry
    Microfilm services
    Microfilms
    Micropublishing
  — **Library applications**
    UF Libraries and micrographics
      Library applications of
        micrographics
Micrographics industry *(May Subd Geog)*
  [HD9999.M47]
Microhabitat
  USE Niche (Ecology)
Microhardness
  BT Hardness
Microhylidae
  [QL668.E26]
  BT Anura
    Frogs
  NT Chiasmocleis
    Cophixalus
    Hypopachus

Microincineration
  BT Microscope and microscopy—
    Technique
Microinjections
  BT Injections
Microlepidoptera
  USE Lepidoptera
Microlithography *(May Subd Geog)*
  BT Lithography
Micromalthidae
  [QL596.M47]
  BT Beetles
  NT Micromalthus
Micromalthus
  [QL596.M47]
  BT Micromalthidae
Micromanipulation
  USE Micrurgy
Micromanometer
  USE Manometer
Micromechanics
  [QC176.8.M5]
  BT Composite materials
    Solid state physics
  RT Microstructure
Micromeles
  USE Sorbus
Micromesistius poutassou
  USE Gadus poutassou
Micrometeorology *(May Subd Geog)*
  BT Meteorology
Micrometer
  [QB113 (Astronomy)]
  [QC102]
  BT Thickness measurement
Microminiature electronic equipment
  USE Microelectronics
Microminiaturization (Electronics)
  USE Microelectronics
    Miniature electronic equipment
Micromonospora
  BT Streptomycetaceae
Micromus
  [QL513.H5]
  BT Hemerobiidae
Micromygale
  [QL458.42.M5]
  BT Microstigmatidae
Micromygale diblemma
  [QL458.42.M5]
Micromys
  [QL737.R666]
  BT Muridae
Micromys minutus
  [QL737.R666]
  UF Harvest mouse, European
    Red mouse
    Red ranny
Micronecta
  [QL523.C75]
  BT Corixidae
Micronesia
  Here are entered works on the division of Oceania
which consists of Guam, the Trust Territory of the
Pacific Islands, Nauru, and the Gilbert Islands.
Works on the Trust Territory of the Pacific Islands,
which consists of the island groups of the Marianas
(except Guam), the Carolines, and the Marshalls, are
entered under Pacific Islands (Trust Territory).
Works on the Federated States of Micronesia, which
consists of the four administrative districts of Truk,
Yap, Ponape, and Kosrae, are entered under Micronesia (Federated States).
  BT Oceania

Micronesia (Federated States)
  Here are entered works on the Federated States of
Micronesia, which consists of the four administrative
districts of Truk, Yap, Ponape, and Kosrae. Works on
the division of Oceania which consists of Guam, the
Trust Territory of the Pacific Islands, Nauru, and the
Gilbert Islands, are entered under Micronesia. Works
on the Trust Territory of the Pacific Islands, which
consists of the island groups of the Marianas (except
Guam), the Carolines, and the Marshalls, are entered
under Pacific Islands (Trust Territory).
  NT Kosrae (Micronesia)
    Truk Islands (Micronesia)
Micronesian art
  USE Art, Micronesian
Micronesian arts
  USE Arts, Micronesian
Micronesian cookery
  USE Cookery, Micronesian
Micronesian languages
  [PL6191-5]
  Here are entered works dealing with the lan-
guages spoken in the Caroline, Marshall, Gilbert, La-
drone, and other islands of Micronesia. Linguistically
they appear to be partly Malayan and partly Melane-
sian.
  BT Oceania—Languages
    Oceanic languages
    Proto-Oceanic language
  NT Chamorro language
    Gilbertese language
    Kapingamarangi language
    Kusaie language
    Marshall language
    Mokilese language
    Mortlock language
    Nauru language
    Ponape language
    Puluwat language
    Sonsorol-Tobi language
    Truk language
    Ulithi language
    Woleai language
    Yap language
Micronesians
  [DU500 (History)]
  [GN669 (Anthropology)]
  BT Ethnology—Micronesia
    Oceanians
  NT Chamorros
Micronidae
  USE Geometridae
Micronutrient fertilizer industry
  (May Subd Geog)
  [HD9484.M53-534]
  BT Micronutrient fertilizers
Micronutrient fertilizers *(May Subd Geog)*
  [S653.4 (Agriculture)]
  UF Micro-nutrient fertilizers
  BT Fertilizers
    Trace elements
  NT Micronutrient fertilizer industry
    Zinc fertilizers
Micronutrients
  USE Trace elements in nutrition
Micronycteris
  [QL737.C57]
  BT Phyllostomatidae
Micronycteris brachyotis
  [QL737.C57]
Micronycteris nicefori
  [QL737.C57]
Micropaleontology *(May Subd Geog)*
  [QE719]
  BT Microscope and microscopy
    Paleontology
  RT Palynology
  NT Discoasters
    Pollen, Fossil
    Protozoa, Fossil
    Spores (Botany), Fossil

Microparamys
  ₜQE882.R6ₜ
  BT Ischyromyidae
Micropedology
  USE Soil micromorphology
Micropezidae *(May Subd Geog)*
  ₜQL537.M43ₜ
  UF Calobatidae
    Stilt-legged flies
    Trepidariidae
    Tylidae
  BT Diptera
Microphanurus semistriatus
  USE Asolcus semistriatus
Microphone
  ₜTK6478ₜ
  BT Sound—Equipment and supplies
    Transducers
  NT Electrostatic microphone
— **Calibration**
Microphone, Electrostatic
  USE Electrostatic microphone
Microphotography
  ₜTR835ₜ
  ₜZ265 (Library science)ₜ
  Here are entered works on the photographing of
  objects of any size upon a microscopic or very small
  scale. To be distinguished from Photomicrography,
  the photographing of minute objects enlarged by
  means of the microscope.
  UF Microfilming
  BT Photography
  RT Microforms
    Micrographics
  NT Filmstrips
    Microfiche services
    Microfilm industry
    Microfilm services
— **Apparatus and supplies**
    USE Microphotography—Equipment
      and supplies
— **Equipment and supplies**
    UF Microphotography—Apparatus and
      supplies
      Microreproduction equipment
    NT Microfilm projectors
      Microfilm readers
      Reader-printers
      (Microphotography)
Microphotometer
  ₜQC391ₜ
  BT Microphotometry
    Photometry
  NT Microspectrophotometry
Microphotometry
  ₜQC391ₜ
  UF Microscope photometry
  BT Microscope and microscopy
    Photometry
  NT Microphotometer
Microphthalmus
  ₜQL391.A6ₜ
  BT Hesionidae
Microphthalmus arenarius
  ₜQL391.A6ₜ
Microphthalmus bermudensis
  ₜQL391.A6ₜ
Microphysidae
  ₜQL523.M47ₜ
  BT Hemiptera
Micropipets
  USE Micropipettes
Micropipettes
  ₜQH585.5.M52 (Cytology)ₜ
  UF Micropipets
  BT Pipettes
Microplitis
  ₜQL568.B8ₜ
  BT Braconidae
Micropodidae
  USE Swifts

Micropodiformes
  USE Apodiformes
Micropogon
  ₜQL638.S34ₜ
  BT Sciaenidae
Micropogon (Fish)
  USE Micropogonias
Micropogon undulatus
  USE Atlantic croaker
Micropogonias
  ₜQL638.S34ₜ
  UF Micropogon (Fish)
  BT Sciaenidae
Micropogonias undulatus
  USE Atlantic croaker
Micropolar elasticity
  ₜQA932ₜ
  BT Elasticity
Micropollutants *(May Subd Geog)*
  BT Pollutants
Microprobe analysis
  ₜQH324.9.M5ₜ
  UF Analysis, Microprobe
  BT Microchemistry
    Probes (Electronic instruments)
  NT Electron probe microanalysis
    X-ray microanalysis
Microprocessor-based workstations
  USE Microcomputer workstations
Microprocessors *(May Subd Geog)*
  BT Minicomputers
  NT 65x series microprocessors
    Bit slice microprocessors
    CLIPPER (Microprocessor)
    Intel 8080 (Microprocessor)
    Intel 8085 (Microprocessor)
    Intel 8085A (Microprocessor)
    Intel 8086 (Microprocessor)
    Intel 8087 (Microprocessor)
    Intel 8088 (Microprocessor)
    Intel 8089 (Microprocessor)
    Intel 8096 (Microprocessor)
    Intel 80286 (Microprocessor)
    Intel 80287 (Microprocessor)
    Intel 80386 (Microprocessor)
    Intel 80387 (Microprocessor)
    Intel SDK-85 (Microprocessor)
    Intel SDK-86 (Microprocessor)
    Motorola 6800 (Microprocessor)
    Motorola 6802 (Microprocessor)
    MUMS (Computer)
    NS32000 series (Microprocessors)
    NSC800 (Computer)
    Programmable array logic
    TI 99000 (Microprocessor)
    TMS9900 family (Computer)
    Zilog Z-80 (Microprocessor)
    Zilog Z8000 (Microprocessor)
— **Programming**
  ₜQA76.6ₜ
Microprogramming
  ₜQA76.6ₜ
  BT Electronic digital computers—
    Programming
  NT Emulators (Computer programs)
Microprojection
  UF Microprojector
  BT Lantern projection
    Microscope and microscopy
    Projectors
Microprojector
  USE Microprojection
Microprolactinoma
  USE Prolactinoma
Micropropagation, Plant
  USE Plant propagation—In vitro
Micropteridae
  USE Centrarchidae
Micropterus
  ₜQL638.C3ₜ

  UF Bass, Centrarchid
    Centrarchid basses
  BT Bass
    Centrarchidae
    Sunfishes
  NT Spotted bass
Micropterus dolomieu
  USE Smallmouth bass
Micropterus pseudoplites
  USE Spotted bass
Micropterus punctulatus
  USE Spotted bass
Micropterus salmoides
  USE Largemouth bass
Micropublications
  USE Microforms
Micropublishing *(May Subd Geog)*
  ₜZ286.M5ₜ
  BT Microforms
    Micrographics
    Publishers and publishing
— **Advertising**
    USE Advertising—Micropublishing
Micropulsations, Geomagnetic
  USE Geomagnetic micropulsations
Micropyrometer
  ₜQC277ₜ
  BT Pyrometers and pyrometry
Microradiography
  BT Photomicrography
    Radiography
Microreader-printers
  USE Reader-printers (Microphotography)
Microreproduction equipment
  USE Microphotography—Equipment and
    supplies
Microrespirometer
  USE Respirometer
Microsaura
  ₜQL666.L23ₜ
  UF Lophosaura
  BT Chameleons
Microsaura pumila
  ₜQL666.L23ₜ
  UF Cape dwarf chameleon
    Chamaeleo pumilus
    Dwarf chameleon
Microsauria
  ₜQE868.M53ₜ
  BT Amphibians, Fossil
  NT Gymnarthridae
Microscolex
  ₜQL391.A6ₜ
  BT Megascolecidae
Microscolex elegans
  ₜQL391.A6ₜ
Microscope and microscopy
  ₜQH201-277ₜ
  UF Analysis, Microscopic
    Micrographic analysis
    Microscopic analysis
  BT Animalcules
    Biology
    Botany
    Micro-organisms
    Optical instruments
  RT Histology
    Microbiology
    Photomicrography
  NT Acoustic microscopes
    Apertometer
    Biological apparatus and supplies
    Botanical microscopy
    Chemical microscopy
    Classification—Books—Microscope
      and microscopy
    Colpomicroscopes
    Compound microscope
    Dissecting microscope
    Electron microscope
    Electron microscope, Transmission

Microscope and microscopy *(Continued)*
    Electron microscopy
    Field ion microscope
    Fluorescence microscopy
    Hot stage microscope
    Industrial microscopy
    Interference microscope
    Measuring microscopes
    Microcinematography
    Micropaleontology
    Microphotometry
    Microprojection
    Microscopy, Medical
    Micrurgy
    Phase microscope
    Polarizing microscope
    Proton microscope
    Resinography
    Stains and staining (Microscopy)
    Video microscopy
    X-ray microscope
  — Technique
    [QH207]
    UF Microscopical technique
        Microtechnique
    BT Natural history—Technique
    NT Freeze-etching
        Microincineration
        Microtome
        Microtomy
        Mounting of microscope specimens
Microscope photometry
  USE Microphotometry
Microscope specimens, Mounting of
  USE Mounting of microscope specimens
Microscopes, Acoustic
  USE Acoustic microscopes
Microscopes, Measuring
  USE Measuring microscopes
Microscopic analysis
  USE Metallography
       Microscope and microscopy
Microscopic anatomy
  USE Histology
Microscopic books
  USE Miniature books
Microscopic editions
  USE Miniature books
Microscopic organisms
  USE Micro-organisms
Microscopical technique
  USE Microscope and microscopy—
       Technique
Microscopy, Botanical
  USE Botanical microscopy
Microscopy, Chemical
  USE Chemical microscopy
Microscopy, Industrial
  USE Industrial microscopy
Microscopy, Medical
  [RB43]
  UF Medical microscopy
  BT Diagnosis, Laboratory
       Microscope and microscopy
  NT Colpomicroscopy
       Diagnosis, Electron microscopic
       Microsurgery
       Ocular biomicroscopy
       Urine—Examination
Microscopy, Quantitative
  USE Stereology
Microscopy, Video
  USE Video microscopy
Microseisms *(May Subd Geog)*
  [QE539.2.M5]
  UF Seismic noise
  BT Seismology
Microseris
  [QK495.C74]
  BT Compositae

Microsociology
  UF Micro-sociology
  BT Sociology
Microsoft Business BASIC Compiler (Computer program)
  BT Computer programs
Microsoft Chart (Computer program)
  UF Chart (Computer program)
  BT Computer graphics—Computer
       programs
Microsoft Disk Operating System (Computer operating system)
  USE MS-DOS (Computer operating system)
Microsoft File (Computer program)
  BT Electronic filing systems—Computer
       programs
Microsoft MS-DOS (Computer operating system)
  USE MS-DOS (Computer operating system)
Microsoft QuickBASIC (Computer program)
  UF QuickBASIC (Computer program)
  BT Compilers (Computer programs)
Microsoft Windows (Computer programs)
  UF MS Windows (Computer programs)
  BT Computer programs
Microsoft Word (Computer program)
  UF Word (Computer program)
  BT Computer programs
       Word processing—Computer programs
Microsoft Works (Computer program)
  UF Works (Computer program)
  BT Computer programs
Microsomes
  [QH603.M4]
  BT Cells
       Protoplasm
  RT Ribosomes
Microsomia, Hemifacial
  USE Hemifacial microsomia
Microsorium
  USE Polypodium
Microspectrophotometry
  BT Microphotometer
       Spectrophotometer
Microspheres
  BT Foraminifera
Microspheres (Pharmacy)
  [RS201.M53]
  BT Drugs—Vehicles
Microsporidia
  NT Nosematidae
Microstigmatidae
  [QL458.42.M5]
  BT Spiders
  NT Micromygale
Microstomatidae
  USE Bathylagidae
Microstomidae
  USE Bathylagidae
Microstomus
  [QL638.P7]
  BT Pleuronectidae
  NT Microstomus kitt
Microstomus kitt
  [QL638.P7]
  UF Lemon dab
       Lemon sole
       Pleuronectes microcephalus
  BT Microstomus
Microstomus pacificus
  [QL638.P7]
  UF Dover sole, Pacific
       Slime sole
Microstrabismus *(May Subd Geog)*
  [RE771]
  UF Microtropia
  BT Strabismus
Microstraining of sewage
  USE Sewage—Purification—Microstraining
Microstrip
  USE Microwave wiring

       Strip transmission lines
Microstructure
  BT Materials
       Matter—Constitution
       Morphology
  RT Micromechanics
       Stereology
  NT Metallography
       Ultrastructure (Biology)
Microsurgery
  [RD33.6]
  BT Microscopy, Medical
       Surgery
  NT Cerebral revascularization
       Endoscopic surgery
       Experimental microsurgery
Microsurgical revascularization, Cerebral
  USE Cerebral revascularization
microSURVEY (Computer programs)
  BT Surveying—Computer-assisted
       instruction—Computer programs
Microteaching
  BT Education—Simulation methods
       Interaction analysis in education
       Teachers—Training of
       Teaching
Microtechnique
  USE Microscope and microscopy—
       Technique
MicroTex (Computer system)
  [Z253.4.M53]
  BT Microcomputers—Programming
       Printing, Practical—Data processing
Microthyriaceae
  BT Hemisphaeriales
Microthyriales
  USE Hemisphaeriales
Microtinae
  USE Lemmings
       Voles
Microtini
  USE Voles
Microtome
  [QH233]
  BT Microscope and microscopy—
       Technique
Microtomy
  [QH233]
  UF Section-cutting
       Sectioning (Microscopy)
  BT Histology—Technique
       Microscope and microscopy—
       Technique
  NT Cryotomy
       Frozen tissue sections
Microtones
  Here is entered material on musical intervals smaller than the semitone.
  UF Quarter-tones
       Third-tones
  BT Microtonic music
       Music—Acoustics and physics
       Tonality
  RT Musical intervals and scales
  NT Bichromatic harmonium
Microtonic music
  This heading is used (1) for discussion of music employing microtones, and (2) as additional heading for compositions employing microtones. Thus a sonata composed for a quarter-tone piano is entered under two headings: 1. Sonatas (Piano) 2. Microtonic music.
  UF Music, Microtonic
       Music, Quarter-tone
       Quarter-tone music
  BT Music
  NT Microtones
Microtropia
  USE Microstrabismus
microTSP (Computer program)
  UF micro TSP (Computer program)

BT Computer programs
    Econometrics—Computer programs
    Economic forecasting—Computer
      programs
    Regression analysis—Computer
      programs

Microtubules
    [QH603.M44]
  UF Cytotubules
  BT Cell organelles

Microtus
    [QL737.R638]
  UF Field mice
    Grass voles
    Meadow mice
    Meadow voles
  BT Cricetidae
    Voles
  NT Microtus agrestis
    Microtus arvalis
    Microtus guentheri
    Microtus montanus
    Microtus pennsylvanicus
    Microtus socialis

Microtus agrestis
    [QL737.R638]
  UF European field vole
    Field vole, European
  BT Microtus

Microtus arvalis
    [QL737.R638]
  UF Common vole
    Vole, Common
  BT Microtus

Microtus breweri
  USE Beach vole
    Microtus pennsylvanicus

Microtus californicus
  USE California vole

Microtus guentheri
    [QL737.R638]
  UF Gunther's vole
    Levant vole
    Yesreel vole
  BT Microtus

Microtus montanus
    [QL737.R638]
  UF Montane vole
    Mountain vole
  BT Microtus

Microtus ochrogaster
  USE Prairie vole

Microtus pennsylvanicus
    [QL737.R638]
  UF Meadow vole
    Microtus breweri
    Pennsylvania meadow mouse
  BT Microtus

Microtus pinetorum
  USE Pitymys pinetorum

Microtus socialis
    [QL737.R638]
  UF Social vole
  BT Microtus

Microvelia
    [QL523.V45]
  BT Veliidae

Microvelia chanita
    [QL523.V45]

Microvelia inquilina
    [QL523.V45]

Microwave amplification by stimulated
  emission of radiation
  USE Masers

Microwave amplification by variable reactance
  USE Parametric amplifiers

Microwave amplifiers
  BT Microwave devices
  NT Amplifiers, Crossed-field
    Masers
    Parametric amplifiers

Microwave antennas
    [TK7871.6]
  BT Antennas (Electronics)
    Microwave devices
  NT Microwave pillboxes

Microwave attenuation
  USE Microwaves—Attenuation

Microwave circuits
  UF Circuits, Microwave
  BT Electronics
    Microwave devices
  NT Gyrators
    Microwave integrated circuits

Microwave communication systems
  (May Subd Geog)
  BT Intercommunication systems
    Microwave devices
    Telecommunication systems
  RT Line-of-sight radio links
  SA *subdivision* Communication systems
    under subjects, e.g. Railroads—
    Communication systems
  NT Closed-circuit television
    Industrial television
    Millimeter wave communication
      systems
    Mobile radio stations
    Police communication systems
    Radiotelephone
  — Receivers and reception
    USE Microwave receivers

Microwave cookery
    [TX832]
  UF Cookery, Microwave
  BT Electric cookery
    Microwave heating

Microwave detectors
    [TK7876]
  UF Detectors, Microwave
  BT Detectors
  NT Bolometer

Microwave devices
    [TK7876]
  BT Electronic apparatus and appliances
    Microwaves
  NT Cavity resonators
    Circulators, Wave-guide
    Dielectric resonators
    Masers
    Microwave amplifiers
    Microwave antennas
    Microwave circuits
    Microwave communication systems
    Microwave equipment industry
    Microwave filters
    Microwave lenses
    Microwave mixers
    Microwave ovens
    Microwave pillboxes
    Microwave receivers
    Microwave tubes
    Millimeter wave devices
    Moisture meters, Microwave
    Oscillators, Microwave
    Parametric amplifiers
    Transistors, Microwave

Microwave equipment industry
  (May Subd Geog)
    [HD9696.M53-534]
  BT Microwave devices

Microwave filters
    [TK7872.F5]
  BT Electric filters
    Microwave devices
    Wave guides
  NT Electric filters, Wave-guide

Microwave heating
    [TK4601]
  UF Heating, Microwave

BT Dielectrics
    Direct energy conversion
    Electric heating
    Microwaves
  NT Microwave cookery

Microwave holography
    [TA1552]
  BT Holography

Microwave imaging *(May Subd Geog)*
  UF Imaging, Microwave
  BT Imaging systems

Microwave imaging in medicine
    [RC78.7.M53]
  UF Medical microwave imaging
  BT Diagnostic imaging

Microwave integrated circuits
    [TK7876]
  BT Integrated circuits
    Microwave circuits

Microwave landing systems
  UF Landing systems, Microwave
  BT Airplanes—Landing
    Electronics in aeronautics
    Instrument flying
    Landing aids (Aeronautics)

Microwave lenses
    [QC447 (Physics)]
    [TK6590.M5 (Radar)]
  UF Lenses, Microwave
  BT Antennas (Electronics)
    Electron optics
    Lens antennas
    Microwave devices

Microwave measurements
  BT Electronic measurements

Microwave meteorology
  USE Radio meteorology

Microwave mixers
    [TK7872.M5]
  UF Mixers, Microwave
  BT Microwave devices
    Mixing circuits

Microwave moisture meters
  USE Moisture meters, Microwave

Microwave optics
    [QC675.8]
  UF Optics, Microwave
  BT Optics, Physical

Microwave oscillators
  USE Oscillators, Microwave

Microwave ovens
  UF Ovens, Microwave
  BT Microwave devices
    Stoves

Microwave pillboxes
  UF Cheese antennas
    Line source radiators
    Pillbox antennas
  BT Antennas (Electronics)
    Microwave antennas
    Microwave devices
    Radar

Microwave receivers
  UF Microwave communication systems—
    Receivers and reception
    Receivers, Microwave
  BT Microwave devices

Microwave relay systems
  USE Radio relay systems

Microwave spectroscopy
  BT Molecular spectroscopy
    Radiofrequency spectroscopy

Microwave transistors
  USE Transistors, Microwave

Microwave transmission lines
    [TK7876]
  UF Transmission lines, Microwave
  BT Electric lines
    Telecommunication lines
  NT Coaxial cables
    Wave guides

Microwave tubes
  BT Electron tubes
     Microwave devices
  NT Backward-wave tubes
     Disk-seal tubes
     Gyrotrons
     Klystrons
     Magnetrons
     Traveling-wave tubes
Microwave wiring
     [TK7870]
  UF Microstrip
     Plumbing for microwaves
     Strip conductors
  BT Electric conductors
     Electronic apparatus and appliances
     Microwaves
Microwaves
  UF Hertzian waves
  BT Electric waves
     Electromagnetic waves
     Geomagnetic micropulsations
     Radio, Short wave
     Radio waves
  SA *headings beginning with the word*
     Microwave
  NT Centimeter waves
     Coherent radar
     Decimeter waves
     Microwave devices
     Microwave heating
     Microwave wiring
     Millimeter waves
     Quantum electronics
     Strip transmission lines
  — **Attenuation**
     UF Attenuation of microwaves
        Microwave attenuation
  — **Military applications**
        [UG485]
Micrurgy
     Here are entered works dealing with basic tech-
     nique adapted to the manipulation and observation of
     micro-objects, animate or inanimate.
  UF Micromanipulation
  BT Bacteriology—Technique
     Cytology—Technique
     Microbiology—Technique
     Microscope and microscopy
Micrurus *(May Subd Geog)*
     [QL666.O64]
  UF Coral snakes
  BT Elapidae
Micrurus annellatus
     [QL666.O64]
  UF Elaps annellatus
Micrurus averyi
     [QL666.O64]
Micrurus hemprichi
     [QL666.O64]
  UF Hemprich's coral snake
Micrurus nigrocinctus
     [QL666.O64]
Micrurus spixi
     [QL666.O64]
  UF Amazonian coral snake
Micrurus surinamus
     [QL666.O64]
Micryphantidae
  USE Linyphiidae
Micthel family
  USE Mitchell family
Micturation disorders
  USE Urination disorders
Micturition
  USE Urination
Mid-Atlantic Bight
  BT Coasts—United States
     Continental margins—United States
Mid-Atlantic Cordillera
  USE Mid-Atlantic Ridge

Mid-Atlantic Ridge
  UF Atlantic Ridge
     Atlantis Cordillera
     Challenger Rise
     Dolphin Rise
     Mid-Atlantic Cordillera
     Mid-Atlantic Swell
     Mid-Ocean Ridge
     Mid-Oceanic Ridge
  BT Submarine topography—Atlantic
     Ocean
Mid-Atlantic Ridge Rift Valley
  BT Submarine valleys
Mid-Atlantic States
  USE Middle Atlantic States
Mid-Atlantic Swell
  USE Mid-Atlantic Ridge
Mid-career changes
  USE Career changes
Mid-life career changes
  USE Career changes
Mid-Ocean Ridge
  USE Mid-Atlantic Ridge
Mid-Oceanic Ridge
  USE Mid-Atlantic Ridge
Mid-Waria language
  USE Guhu-Samane language
MIDAC computer
  USE Seac computer
Midas
     [BL820.M55]
  BT Mythology, Classical
MIDAS (Computer system)
  UF Mine inspection data analysis system
  BT Electronic digital computers—
     Programming
     Mine inspection—Data processing
Midasidae
  USE Mydidae
Midbar Yehuda
  USE Judaea, Wilderness of
Midbar Yehudah
  USE Judaea, Wilderness of
Midbrain
  USE Mesencephalon
Midcalf family
  USE Metcalf family
Middag family
  USE Middaugh family
Middagh family
  USE Middaugh family
Middaugh family *(Not Subd Geog)*
  UF Middag family
     Middagh family
Midday
  USE Noon
Middendorf family *(Not Subd Geog)*
  UF Middendorff family
Middendorff family
  USE Middendorf family
Middens, Kitchen
  USE Kitchen-middens
Middle age *(May Subd Geog)*
     [HQ1059.4-HQ1059.5 (Social groups)]
     [RA777.5 (Hygiene)]
  UF Middle aged persons
     Midlife
  BT Adulthood
     Age
     Life cycle, Human
  RT Longevity
     Old age
  NT Aging
     Climacteric
  — **Nutrition**
     [TX361.M47]
  — **Psychological aspects**
     [BF724.6]
     BT Aged—Psychology
        Aging—Psychological aspects
  — **Sexual behavior**

Middle age and employment
  USE Age and employment
Middle age in motion pictures
  BT Moving-pictures
Middle aged children
  USE Adult children
Middle aged men *(May Subd Geog)*
  UF Older men
  BT Men
Middle aged persons
  USE Middle age
Middle aged women *(May Subd Geog)*
  UF Older women
  BT Women
  NT Childbirth in middle age
     Pregnancy in middle age
  — **Life skills guides**
  — **Sexual behavior**
Middle aged workers
  USE Age and employment
Middle Ages
     [CB351-CB355 (Civilization)]
  UF Dark Ages
     Medieval period
  BT Civilization, Medieval
  RT Medievalism
     Renaissance
  SA Archaeology, Medieval; Church
     history—Middle Ages, 600-1500;
     Civilization, Medieval; Education,
     Medieval; Geography, Medieval;
     Literature, Medieval; Science,
     Medieval; *and similar headings*
  NT Archaeology, Medieval
     Architecture, Medieval
     Art, Medieval
     Church history—Middle Ages, 600-
     1500
     Education, Medieval
     Geography, Medieval
     Literature, Medieval
     Science, Medieval
  — Biblical influences
     USE Bible—Influence—Civilization,
        Medieval
  — **Biography**
     USE Biography—Middle Ages, 500-
        1500
  — **Historiography**
     NT Feudalism—Historiography
        Medievalists
  — **History**
     [D111-D203]
     UF History, Medieval
        Medieval history
        World history, Medieval
     BT World history
     RT Europe—History—476-1492
     NT Chivalry
        Crusades
        Eleventh century
        Europe—History—392-814
        Feudalism
        Fifteenth century
        Fourteenth century
        Holy Roman Empire
        Knights and knighthood
        Migrations of nations
        Seventh century
        Tenth century
        Thirteenth century
        Twelfth century
  — — **Juvenile literature**
        UF Middle Ages—History, Juvenile
  — — Maps
        USE Geography, Medieval—Maps
  — History, Juvenile
     USE Middle Ages—History—Juvenile
        literature

Middle Ages in art
  NT Master of the Housebook, 15th cent.
        Housebook
Middle Ages in literature
Middle Asian golden eagle
  USE Himalayan golden eagle
Middle Atlantic Region
  USE Middle Atlantic States
Middle Atlantic States
    Here are entered works dealing collectively with
  New York, New Jersey, Pennsylvania, Delaware,
  Maryland, and Washington, D.C.
  UF Mid-Atlantic States
        Middle Atlantic Region
        Middle Colonies
        Middle States
  BT Atlantic States
  — History
  —— Colonial period, ca. 1600-1775
  —— Revolution, 1775-1783
Middle atmosphere *(May Subd Geog)*
  ₍QC881.2.M53₎
  UF Atmosphere, Middle
  BT Atmosphere
  NT Chemosphere
        Tropopause
  — Rocket observations
        BT Rockets, Sounding
Middle Chinese language, 1200-1919
  USE Chinese language—Middle Chinese,
        1200-1919
Middle class men *(May Subd Geog)*
  BT Men
        Middle classes
Middle class women *(May Subd Geog)*
  BT Middle classes
        Women
Middle classes *(May Subd Geog)*
  ₍HT680-HT690₎
  UF Bourgeoisie
        Commons (Social order)
  BT Social classes
  NT Middle class men
        Middle class women
        Proletariat
  — Political activity
        BT Political participation
            Politics, Practical
Middle classes in literature
  NT Domestic drama
Middle Colonies
  USE Middle Atlantic States
Middle Columbia Salish Indians
  USE Sinkiuse-Columbia Indians
Middle Congo
  USE Congo (Brazzaville)
Middle Creek Cemetery (Winnebago, Ill.)
  BT Cemeteries—Illinois
Middle doctrine school (Mahayana Buddhism)
  USE Mādhyamika (Buddhism)
Middle ear
  ₍QL948 (Comparative anatomy)₎
  ₍QM507 (Human anatomy)₎
  ₍QP461 (Physiology)₎
  UF Tympanic cavity
        Tympanum
  BT Ear
  NT Ear ossicles
        Eustachian tube
        Tympanic membrane
  — Anatomy
  — Diseases *(May Subd Geog)*
        ₍RF220-228₎
        NT Middle ear—Radiography
            Otitis media
  — Radiography
        BT Middle ear—Diseases
  — Surgery
        NT Tympanoplasty
Middle ear effusion
  USE Otitis media with effusion

Middle Earth (Imaginary place)
  BT Geographical myths
Middle East *(Not Subd Geog)*
    Here are entered works on the region consisting
  of Asia west of Pakistan, northeastern Africa, and
  occasionally Greece and Pakistan. Works treating
  collectively the Arabic-speaking countries of Asia
  and Africa, or of Asia only, are entered under Arab
  countries.
  UF Asia, Western
        East (Middle East)
        Eastern Mediterranean
        Fertile crescent
        Levant
        Mediterranean Region, Eastern
        Mideast
        Near East
        Northern Tier (Middle East)
  BT Orient
  NT Arab countries
        Latin Orient
  — Civilization
        NT Art, Medieval—Middle Eastern
              influences
            Ireland—Civilization—Middle
              Eastern influences
  —— To 622
        ₍DS57₎
  — Economic conditions *(Not Subd Geog)*
  —— 19th century *(Not Subd Geog)*
  — Foreign relations
  —— Europe
        NT Eastern question
  — History
  —— To 622
        UF Arab countries—History—To
              622
        NT Sea Peoples
  —— 622-1517
        USE Islamic Empire
  —— 1517-
        NT Eastern question
  —— 20th century
  — Languages
        UF Middle Eastern languages
  — Literatures
        USE Middle Eastern literature
  — Politics and government
  —— 1914-1945
        ₍DS63₎
  —— 1945-
        ₍DS63-DS63.1₎
  — Study and teaching *(May Subd Geog)*
        ₍DS61.8-DS61.9₎
        UF Middle East studies
            Middle Eastern studies
            Oriental studies
        RT Arabic studies
            Orientalists
Middle East studies
  USE Middle East—Study and teaching
Middle Eastern bread
  USE Pita bread
Middle Eastern cookery
  USE Cookery, Middle Eastern
Middle Eastern languages
  USE Middle East—Languages
Middle Eastern literature
  UF Middle East—Literatures
        Near Eastern literature
  NT Semitic literature
Middle Eastern periodicals
  UF Near Eastern periodicals
Middle Eastern philology
  ₍PJ₎
    Here are entered works on the ancient and/or
  modern languages and literatures of the Middle East,
  which may include material on South Asia and North
  Africa. Works on the ancient and/or modern Orien-
  tal languages and literatures of Asia as a whole, or of
  the Far East only are entered under Oriental philolo-
  gy.

  UF Near Eastern philology
  BT Oriental philology
  NT Semitic philology
Middle Eastern proverbs
  USE Proverbs, Middle Eastern
Middle Eastern students *(May Subd Geog)*
  UF Near East students
        Near Eastern students
  BT Students
Middle Eastern studies
  USE Middle East—Study and teaching
Middle English
  USE English language—Middle English,
        1100-1500
Middle English Bibles
  USE Bible. English (Middle English)
Middle English Christian literature
  USE Christian literature, English (Middle)
Middle English Christian poetry
  USE Christian poetry, English (Middle)
Middle English literature
  USE English literature—Middle English,
        1100-1500
Middle English manuscripts
  USE Manuscripts, English (Middle)
Middle English part-songs
  USE Part-songs, Middle English
Middle English religious poetry
  USE Religious poetry, English (Middle)
Middle English sermons
  USE Sermons, English (Middle)
Middle English songs
  USE Songs, Middle English
Middle Fabius River (Mo.)
  UF Fabius River, Middle (Mo.)
  BT Rivers—Missouri
Middle Fork, Eel River (Calif.)
  USE Eel River, Middle Fork (Calif.)
Middle Fork, Salmon River (Idaho)
  USE Salmon River, Middle Fork (Idaho)
Middle games
  USE Chess—Middle games
        Chinese chess—Middle games
Middle High German language
  USE German language—Middle High
        German, 1050-1500
Middle High German literature
  USE German literature—Middle High
        German, 1050-1500
Middle High German songs
  USE Songs, German (Middle High German)
Middle Himalaya Mountains
  USE Lesser Himalaya Mountains
Middle Indo-Aryan languages
  USE Indo-Aryan languages, Middle
Middle Iranian languages
  USE Iranian languages, Middle
Middle Khotanese language
  USE Khotanese language
Middle Korean literature
  USE Korean literature—Middle Korean,
        935-1500
Middle-level managers
  USE Middle managers
Middle manager unions
  USE Trade-unions—Middle managers
Middle managers *(May Subd Geog)*
  UF Middle-level managers
  BT Executives
  NT Trade-unions—Middle managers
        Women middle managers
Middle managers, Retired *(May Subd Geog)*
  ₍HD6279₎
  UF Retired middle managers
  BT Retirement
Middle Path (Buddhism)
  USE Middle Way (Buddhism)

Middle powers
    Here are entered works on states which are weak-
er than the great powers in the world but significantly
stronger than the minor powers and small states with
which they normally interact.
    UF Middle-ranking powers
        Middle-sized powers
        Powers, Middle
    BT International relations
        States, Size of
        World politics
    RT Great powers
        States, Small
Middle-ranking powers
    USE Middle powers
Middle school (Mahayana Buddhism)
    USE Mādhyamika (Buddhism)
Middle schools *(May Subd Geog)*
    UF Intermediate schools
    BT Education, Secondary
        Elementary schools
        Junior high schools
Middle-sized powers
    USE Middle powers
Middle States
    USE Middle Atlantic States
Middle Stone age
    USE Mesolithic period
Middle Tennessee
    USE Tennessee, Middle
Middle things
    USE Adiaphora
Middle Way (Buddhism)
    ₁BQ4280₁
    UF Madhyamā pratipad
        Middle Path (Buddhism)
    BT Buddhism—Doctrines
Middle West
    UF Midwest
        Midwestern States
        North Central States
    BT Mississippi River Valley
        Northwest, Old
    NT Lake States
Middleburg Island (Tonga)
    USE Eua Island (Tonga)
Middlegate Gap (Nev.)
    BT Mountain passes—Nevada
Middleton family *(Not Subd Geog)*
    UF Middletown family
        Midelton family
        Midleton family
        Myddelton family
        Myddleton family
Middletown, Va., Battle of, 1864
    USE Cedar Creek, Battle of, 1864
Middletown family
    USE Middleton family
Mideast
    USE Middle East
Midelton family
    USE Middleton family
Midge, Pine gall
    USE Pine gall midge
Midges
    USE Diptera
Midges, Biting
    USE Ceratopogonidae
Midges, Bloodsucking
    USE Ceratopogonidae
Midges, Gall
    USE Gall midges
Midges, Net-winged
    USE Net-winged midges
Midges, Non-biting
    USE Chironomidae
Midges, Phantom
    USE Chaoboridae
Midges, True
    USE Chironomidae

Midget automobile
    BT M.G. automobile
Midget cars
    USE Karts (Midget cars)
Midget submarines
    UF Human torpedoes
        Manned torpedoes
        Submarines, Midget
    BT Mines, Submarine
        Submarine boats
        Torpedoes
        World War, 1939-1945—Naval
            operations—Submarine
    NT Bathyscaphe
        Kaiten (Torpedoes)
Midget vegetables
    UF Dwarf vegetables
        Miniature vegetables
    BT Dwarfism in plants
        Miniature plants
        Vegetables
Midgets
    USE Dwarfs
Midgley family *(Not Subd Geog)*
Midhi (Indic people)
    USE Idu (Indic people)
MIDI (Standard)
    UF Musical Instrument Digital Interface
    BT Analog-to-digital converters—
        Standards
Midi Canal (France)
    USE Canal du Midi (France)
Midigui Site (Chad)
    USE Mdaga Site (Chad)
Midilli Island (Greece)
    USE Lesbos Island (Greece)
Midillü Island (Greece)
    USE Lesbos Island (Greece)
MIDIM (Computer system)
    BT Electronic digital computers—
        Programming
        Music—Data processing
    NT DESC7 (Computer program)
        MIDIM7 (Computer program)
MIDIM7 (Computer program)
    BT Computer programs
        MIDIM (Computer system)
        Music—Computer programs
    RT DESC7 (Computer program)
Midjinngay dialect
    USE Majingai dialect
Midland and South Western Junction Railway
    BT Railroads—Great Britain
Midland Basin (Tex. and N.M.)
    BT Geology—New Mexico
        Geology—Texas
Midland Great Western Railway
    BT Railroads—Ireland
Midlands (England)
Midlands (Ireland)
    UF Central Plain (Ireland)
Midleton family
    USE Middleton family
Midlife
    USE Middle age
Midlothian Lake (Ont.)
    BT Lakes—Ontario
Midorihon
    USE Tanrokubon
Midrash
    ₁BM511-BM518₁
    Here are entered general works on the Midrash.
Works on the treatment of specific topics in the Mi-
drash are entered under headings of the type ₁top-
ic₁ in rabbinical literature, e.g. Brazen serpent in
rabbinical literature.
    BT Bible. O.T.—Criticism, interpretation,
            etc., Jewish
        Jewish literature
        Jewish sermons
        Rabbinical literature

    NT Bible. O.T.—Quotations in rabbinical
            literature
        Burning bush in rabbinical literature
        Tannaim
    — **Folklore**
        NT Folklore in rabbinical literature
    — **Indexes, Topical**
    — **Language, style**
    — **Legends**
        BT Legends, Jewish
Midrash Halakah
    USE Halakhic Midrashim
Midrashim, Halakhic
    USE Halakhic Midrashim
Midrashim, Tannaitic
    USE Halakhic Midrashim
Midrashim, Yelammedenu
    USE Yelammedenu Midrashim
Midshipmen
    ₁V415₁
    ₁VB315.G7 (Great Britain)₁
    BT Seamen
Midsummer night's dream (Ballet)
    BT Ballets
Midtrimester of pregnancy
    USE Pregnancy—Trimester, Second
Midu (Indic people)
    USE Idu (Indic people)
Midway, Battle of, 1942
    ₁D774.M5₁
    BT World War, 1939-1945—Naval
        operations
Midway Islands
    BT Coral reefs and islands
        Islands of the Pacific
Midweek services
    USE Church-night services
Midwest
    USE Middle West
Midwestern States
    USE Middle West
Midwife toad
    USE Alytes obstetricans
Midwifery
    USE Obstetrics
Midwives *(May Subd Geog)*
    ₁RG950₁
    UF Birth attendants
        Nurse midwives
        Traditional birth attendants
    BT Medical personnel
        Obstetrics
    — **Supply and demand**
Mie scattering
    ₁QC425₁
    UF Mie theory
        Scattering, Mie
    BT Brillouin scattering
        Electromagnetic waves—Scattering
    NT Rayleigh scattering
Mie theory
    USE Mie scattering
Mier Expedition, 1842
    ₁F390₁
    UF Texan Mier Expedition, 1842
Mier family
    USE Myers family
Miers family
    USE Myers family
Miexell family
    USE Mikesell family
Mifepristone
    ₁RG137.6.M53 (Gynecology)₁
    BT Abortifacients
        Contraceptive drugs
        Progesterone—Antagonists
Mifflin, Fort (Philadelphia, Pa.)
    USE Fort Mifflin (Philadelphia, Pa.)
MIG (Fighter planes)
    BT Fighter planes
    NT Fishbed (Jet fighter planes)

MIG-25 (Jet fighter plane)
MIG-21 (Jet fighter planes)
  USE Fishbed (Jet fighter planes)
MIG-25 (Jet fighter plane)
  BT Fighter planes
      Jet planes, Military
      MIG (Fighter planes)
MIG welding
  USE Gas metal arc welding
Migadopidae
  USE Carabidae
Migaru Page Daribi
  USE Daribi
Migili language
  UF Koro Lafia language
      Megili language
  BT Plateau languages (Nigeria)
Miglan family
  USE Meilahn family
Migmatite *(May Subd Geog)*
  UF Injection-gneiss
Migraine
  BT Headache
  RT Cluster headache
Migrainous neuralgia
  USE Cluster headache
Migrant agricultural laborers
  (May Subd Geog)
  UF Agricultural laborers, Migrant
      Agricultural migrants
      Migrant agricultural workers
      Migrant farm workers
  BT Agricultural laborers
      Migrant labor
  — Nutrition
Migrant agricultural workers
  USE Migrant agricultural laborers
Migrant farm workers
  USE Migrant agricultural laborers
Migrant labor *(May Subd Geog)*
  ₁HD5855-6₁
      Here are entered works on laborers who migrate
  from one section to another section of the same coun-
  try. Works on laborers who migrate from one country
  to another are entered under Alien labor.
  UF Labor, Migrant
      Migrant workers
      Migratory workers
      Transient labor
  BT Homelessness
      Labor and laboring classes
      Seasonal industries
      Unemployment, Seasonal
  RT Casual labor
  NT Children of migrant laborers
      Church work with migrant labor
      Labor mobility
      Migrant agricultural laborers
      Migration, Internal
  — Medical care *(May Subd Geog)*
Migrant remittances *(May Subd Geog)*
      Here are entered works on the transfer of funds by
  migrants to their place of origin within the same
  country. Works on the transfer of funds by emigrants
  to their country of origin are entered under Emigrant
  remittances.
  UF Remittances, Migrant
      Remittances, Urban-rural
      Transfers, Urban-rural
      Urban-rural income transfers
  BT Income
Migrant workers
  USE Migrant labor
Migration, Internal *(May Subd Geog)*
  ₁HB1952₁
      Here are entered works on the movement of popu-
  lation from one section to another section of the same
  country. Works dealing with migration from one
  country to another, or from one section of a country
  to another country or to a section of another country
  are entered under Emigration and immigration.

  UF Internal migration
      Mobility
  BT Colonization
      Emigration and immigration
      Man—Migrations
      Migrant labor
      Population
      Population geography
  NT Cities and towns—Growth
      Labor mobility
      Population density
      Residential mobility
      Rural-urban migration
      Student mobility
      Urban-rural migration
  — Sex differences
Migration, Internal, in literature
Migration, International
  USE Emigration and immigration
Migration, Polar
  USE Polar wandering
Migration, Return
  USE Return migration
Migration, Rural-urban
  USE Rural-urban migration
Migration, Urban-rural
  USE Urban-rural migration
Migration art (Frankish)
  USE Decorative arts, Frankish
Migration of animals
  USE Animal migration
Migration of bats
  USE Bats—Migration
Migration of birds
  USE Birds—Migration
Migration of cells
  USE Cell migration
Migration of college students
  USE College student mobility
Migration of fishes
  USE Fishes—Migration
Migration of fluids
  USE Fluids—Migration
Migration of graduate students
  USE Graduate student mobility
Migration of insects
  USE Insects—Migration
Migration of ions
  USE Ions—Migration and velocity
Migration of natural gas
  USE Gas, Natural—Migration
Migration of petroleum
  USE Petroleum—Migration
Migration of plants
  USE Plants—Migration
Migration of radioisotopes
  USE Radioisotopes—Migration
Migration of thorium
  USE Thorium—Migration
Migration of uranium
  USE Uranium—Migration
Migrations, Jewish
  USE Jews—Migrations
Migrations of man
  USE Man—Migrations
Migrations of nations
  ₁D135-149₁
      Here are entered works on mass migrations of
  peoples. Works on the spread of population largely in
  prehistoric times are entered under the heading Man
  —Migrations; in modern times, under Emigration
  and immigration.
  UF Nations, Migrations of
  BT Civilization
      Europe—History—392-814
      History
      Middle Ages—History
  RT Man—Migrations
  NT Bantus—Migrations
      Europeans—Migrations
      Germanic tribes

      Jews—Migrations
      Ngoni (African people)—Migrations
      Rome—History—Germanic Invasions,
        3d-6th centuries
Migratory bird hunting stamps
  USE Duck stamps
Migratory birds, Protection of
  USE Birds, Protection of
Migratory locust *(May Subd Geog)*
  ₁QL508.A2 (Zoology)₁
  UF Locusta migratoria
  BT Locusta
Migratory workers
  USE Migrant labor
Mihalchan family *(Not Subd Geog)*
Mihara family *(Not Subd Geog)*
  UF Mizuhara family
Miharada Iseki (Akagi-mura, Japan)
  USE Miharada Site (Akagi-mura, Japan)
Miharada Site (Akagi-mura, Japan)
  (Not Subd Geog)
  UF Miharada Iseki (Akagi-mura, Japan)
  BT Japan—Antiquities
Mihlhauser family *(Not Subd Geog)*
Miḥna
  ₁BP175.M6₁
  UF Inquisition, Islamic
      Inquisition, Motazilite
      Motazilite Inquisition
  BT Islam
Miiaks
  USE Mijaks
Mijaks
  UF Miiaks
  BT Ethnology—Yugoslavia
Mije Indians
  USE Mixe Indians
Mije language
  USE Mixe language
Miji language *(May Subd Geog)*
  ₁PL4001.M49₁
  BT India—Languages
      Tibeto-Burman languages
Mijikenda (African people)
  USE Nika (African people)
Mijolla family *(Not Subd Geog)*
Miju dialect *(May Subd Geog)*
  ₁PL4001.M5595M₁
  BT India—Languages
      Mishmi language
Mik family *(Not Subd Geog)*
Mikado (Name)
  BT Names, Japanese
Mikami Mountain (Shiga-ken, Japan)
  UF Mikami-yama (Shiga-ken, Japan)
      Ōmi-Fuji (Shiga-ken, Japan)
  BT Mountains—Japan
Mikami-yama (Shiga-ken, Japan)
  USE Mikami Mountain (Shiga-ken, Japan)
Mikania
  ₁QK495.C74₁
  BT Compositae
Mikania scandens
  USE Climbing hempweed
Mikaru
  USE Daribi
Mikaru language
  USE Daribi language
Mikasuki Indians
  UF Miccosukee Indians
  BT Indians of North America
      Muskhogean Indians
      Seminole Indians
Mikasuki language *(May Subd Geog)*
  UF Mekusuky language
      Miccosukee language
  BT Florida—Languages
      Muskhogean languages
      Oklahoma—Languages

Mikatagahara, Battle of, 1572
  BT Japan—History—Azuchi-Momoyama
       period, 1568-1603
Mikawa Bay (Japan)
  UF Mikawa-wan (Japan)
  BT Bays—Japan
Mikawa manzai
  USE Manzai (Dance)
Mikawa no Kuni (Japan)
  USE Mikawa Region (Japan)
Mikawa Region (Japan) *(Not Subd Geog)*
  UF Mikawa no Kuni (Japan)
Mikawa-wan (Japan)
  USE Mikawa Bay (Japan)
Mikawachi porcelain
  USE Hirado porcelain
Mike Hammer (Fictitious character)
  USE Hammer, Mike (Fictitious character)
Mikell family
  USE Michael family
Mikesel family
  USE Mikesell family
Mikesell family *(Not Subd Geog)*
  UF Maxel family
      Meichsel family
      Meixel family
      Meixell family
      Meixsel family
      Meyssel family
      Miexell family
      Mikesel family
      Miksel family
      Mixel family
      Mixsell family
Mikgware Hills (Botswana)
  USE Mokgware Hills (Botswana)
Miki Castle (Miki-shi, Japan)
  USE Mikijō (Miki-shi, Japan)
Miki family *(Not Subd Geog)*
Mikijō (Miki-shi, Japan)
  UF Besshojō (Miki-shi, Japan)
      Kamiyamajō (Miki-shi, Japan)
      Miki Castle (Miki-shi, Japan)
  BT Castles—Japan
Mikínai (Ancient city)
  USE Mycenae (Ancient city)
Mikir language
  [PL4001.M5]
  UF Karbi language
  BT Naga languages
      Tibeto-Burman languages
Mikirs
  BT Ethnology—India
Mikkelsen family
  USE Michelson family
Mikkyō
  USE Tantric Buddhism
Miklewane family
  USE McElwain family
Míkonos Island (Greece)
  USE Mykonos Island (Greece)
Mikoshi *(May Subd Geog)*
  [BL2227.8.M54]
  UF Mi-koshi
  BT Festivals—Japan
      Processions, Religious—Shinto
      Shinto—Liturgical objects
Mikrá Dhílos (Greece)
  USE Delos Island (Greece)
Miksel family
  USE Mikesell family
Mikumo Iseki (Maebaru-machi, Japan)
  USE Mikumo Site (Maebaru-machi, Japan)
Mikumo Site (Maebaru-machi, Japan)
  (Not Subd Geog)
  UF Mikumo Iseki (Maebaru-machi, Japan)
  BT Japan—Antiquities
Mikveh *(May Subd Geog)*
  UF Mikwa
      Mikweh
      Miqvah

  BT Baths
      Lustrations
      Purity, Ritual (Judaism)
Mikwa
  USE Mikveh
Mikweh
  USE Mikveh
Milagin family
  USE Milligan family
Milagro 1 Site (Ecuador)
  BT Ecuador—Antiquities
Milagros, Señor de los
  [BT580.L55]
  UF Señor de los Milagros
  BT Jesus Christ—Cult—Peru
Milam family *(Not Subd Geog)*
  UF Mileham family
      Millam family
      Milum family
Milan (Italy)
— **History**
— — **To 1535**
      NT Melegnano, Battle of, 1515
          Patarines
— — **1535-1859**
— — **Revolution of 1848**
— — **1859-1945**
    [DG661]
— — **1945-**
    [DG662]
— **Politics and government**
— — **1859-1945**
— — **1945-**
Milan (Italy).   Quartiere Gallaratese
  USE Quartiere Gallaratese (Milan, Italy)
Milanese rite (Catholic Church)
  USE Catholic Church—Ambrosian rite
Milang language
  [PL4001.M53]
  BT Abor language
      India—Languages
Milar Site (Ill.) *(Not Subd Geog)*
  BT Illinois—Antiquities
Milaw family
  USE Miller family
Milby family *(Not Subd Geog)*
Milch cattle
  USE Dairy cattle
Milch glass
  USE Milk glass
Milch Trial, Nuremberg, Germany, 1946-1947
  UF Subsequent proceedings, Nuremberg
      War Crime Trials, case no. 2
  BT Nuremberg War Crime Trials, 1946-
      1949
Mild hypertension *(May Subd Geog)*
  [RC685.H8]
  UF Borderline hypertension
      Labile hypertension
  BT Hypertension
Mildew
  [SB741.M65]
  BT Fungi
  NT Powdery mildew diseases
Mile, Nautical
  [VK572]
  UF Nautical mile
  BT Navigation
Mile, Roman
  [G86]
  UF Roman mile
Mileage tickets
  USE Railroads—Fares
      Railroads—Tickets
Milebuganon language
  USE Melebuganon language
Milegan family
  USE Milligan family
Mileham family
  USE Milam family

Milekin family
  USE Milligan family
Mileposts
  USE Milestones
Miler family
  USE Miller family
Miles airplanes
  [TL686.M]
  BT Airplanes
Miles family *(Not Subd Geog)*
  UF Mial family
      Mials family
      Myles family
Milešovka Mountain (Czechoslovakia)
  UF Donners Berg (Czechoslovakia)
  BT Mountains—Czechoslovakia
Milestones *(May Subd Geog)*
  UF Mileposts
  BT Boundary stones
      Street signs
Milford family *(Not Subd Geog)*
  UF Millford family
Milford Track (N.Z.)
  BT Trails—New Zealand
Milham family *(Not Subd Geog)*
  UF Millham family
Milholan family
  USE Milhollan family
Milholen family
  USE Milhollan family
Milhollan family *(Not Subd Geog)*
  UF Milholan family
      Milholen family
      Millholland family
      Millhollon family
Milhous family *(Not Subd Geog)*
  UF Milhouse family
      Millhouse family
      Mulhausen family
      Mulhouse family
Milhouse family
  USE Milhous family
Milicete Indians
  USE Malecite Indians
Milieu therapy
  [RC489.M5]
  BT Psychotherapy
  NT Therapeutic community
Miligan family
  USE Milligan family
Milikan family
  USE Milligan family
Miliken family
  USE Milligan family
Milikin family
  USE Milligan family
Miliolidae, Fossil
  [QE772]
  BT Foraminifera, Fossil
Militaire Willems-Orde (Medal)
  [UB435.N]
  BT Netherlands—Armed Forces—Medals,
      badges, decorations, etc.
Militant organizations, Black
  USE Black militant organizations
Militarism *(May Subd Geog)*
  [JX1937-JX1964]
  [U21]
  [UA10]
  UF Antimilitarism
  BT Armies
      Military policy
      Sociology, Military
      War
  RT Chauvinism and jingoism
      Disarmament
      Imperialism
  NT War, Cost of
— **History**
— **Religious aspects**
— — **Buddhism, [Christianity, etc.]**

Militarism in literature

Military administration
[UB]
RT Military law
SA *subdivision* Armed Forces—
Management *under names of*
countries, e.g. United States—
Armed Forces—Management; *and*
subdivision Management *under*
names of individual military
services, e.g. United States. Army
—Management
NT Military planning

Military aeronautics
USE Aeronautics, Military

Military aeronautics equipment industry
(May Subd Geog)
[HD9711-9711.5]
BT Aeronautics, Military—Equipment and
supplies

Military aid
USE Military assistance

Military air bases
USE Air bases

Military air pilots
USE Air pilots, Military

Military air stations
USE Air bases

Military airlift
USE Airlift, Military

Military airplanes
USE Airplanes, Military

Military airplanes, Undetectable
USE Stealth aircraft

Military and civilian power
USE Civil-military relations

Military anti-shock trousers
USE Pressure suits

Military antiquities in Rome
USE Rome—Military antiquities

Military appointments
USE *subdivision* Appointments and
retirements *under names of*
individual military services, e.g.
United States. Army—
Appointments and retirements

Military architecture *(May Subd Geog)*
[NA490-NA497 *(Architecture)*]
[UG460 *(Military science)*]
UF Architecture, Military
BT Architecture
RT Fortification
Military engineering
NT Armories
Arsenals
Barracks
Limes (Roman boundary)

Military art and science *(May Subd Geog)*
[U]
UF Fighting
Military power
Military science
RT Armies
Drill and minor tactics
Naval art and science
Soldiers
Strategy
War
SA *subdivision* Military aspects *under*
types of industries; and headings
beginning with the word Military
NT Aeronautics, Military
Air warfare
Airtankers (Military science)
Armaments
Armed Forces
Armies
Armored trains
Arms and armor
Artillery drill and tactics
Attack and defense (Military science)

Battles
Biological warfare
Briefing, Military
Camouflage (Military science)
Camps (Military)
Cavalry drill and tactics
Chemical warfare
Classification—Books—Military art
and science
Combat patrols
Combat sustainability (Military
science)
Combined operations (Military
science)
Command of troops
Demolition, Military
Desert warfare
Disarmament
Engines of war
Envelopment (Military science)
Escalation (Military science)
Field service (Military science)
Fortification
Gases, Asphyxiating and poisonous—
War use
Guard duty
Guerrilla warfare
Gunnery
Hospitals, Military
Imaginary wars and battles
Industrial mobilization
Infantry drill and tactics
Infiltration (Military science)
Intrenchments
Jungle warfare
Lightning war
Logistics
Marching
Mechanization, Military
Meteorology, Military
Military hydrology
Mines, Military
Morale
Motorization, Military
Mountain warfare
Night fighting (Military science)
Ninjutsu
Nuclear warfare
Obstacles (Military science)
Operational readiness (Military
science)
Orders, Preparation of (Military
science)
Ordnance
Paramilitary forces
Preemptive attack (Military science)
Psychical research—Military aspects
Psychological warfare
Raids (Military science)
Range-finding
Rearguard action (Military science)
Requisitions, Military
Scouts and scouting
Sharpshooting (Military science)
Shooting, Military
Sieges
Signals and signaling
Special forces (Military science)
Special operations (Military science)
Spies
Street fighting (Military science)
Swordplay
Tactics
Tank destroyers
Tank warfare
Terrain study (Military science)
Transportation, Military
Unified operations (Military science)
United States. Air Force—Combat
sustainability
Veterans

War, Cost of
War games
Warfare, Primitive
Winter warfare
— Abbreviations
[U26]
NT Naval art and science—
Abbreviations
— Automation
UF Computers—Military applications
RT Electronics in military engineering
— Computer programs
NT TAGS (Computer program)
TAGS-V (Computer program)
TALLY (Computer program)
TOTEM (Computer program)
— Data processing
UF Computers—Military applications
NT AGATE (Computer war game)
BETA Project
Red Agent (Computer war game)
Scenario Agent (Computer war
game)
— Dictionaries
[U24-26]
UF Military terms
— Exhibitions
— History
[U27-43]
BT Military history
Naval history
— — Exhibitions
— Officers' handbooks
[U130-135]
SA *subdivision* Officers' handbooks
under armies, e.g. United States.
Army—Officers' handbooks
— Soldiers' handbooks
[U110-U115]
Here are entered general soldiers' handbooks
not limited to one country.
UF Soldiers' handbooks
SA *subdivision* Handbooks, manuals,
etc. *under armies, e.g.* United
States. Army—Handbooks,
manuals, etc.
— Statistical methods
USE Military statistics
— Study and teaching
USE Military education
— Terminology
[U26]
UF Military terms
— Vocational guidance
USE Armed Forces—Vocational
guidance

Military art and science in the Koran
[BP134.W29]
UF Koran—Military art and science

Military assets
USE Military capital

Military assistance
UF Arms aid
Arms sales
Foreign aid program
Foreign assistance
Foreign military sales
Military aid
Military sales
Mutual defense assistance program
Sale of military equipment
BT Asia—Defenses
Europe—Defenses
United States—Defenses
NT Exchanges of patents and technical
information

Military assistance, American
(May Subd Geog)
BT Mutual security program, 1951-
NT Offshore procurement program, 1951-
Security Assistance Program

Military assistance, American
(Continued)
— **Iran**
NT Iran-Contra Affair, 1985-
— **Nicaragua**
NT Iran-Contra Affair, 1985-
Military assistance, Australian
(May Subd Geog)
UF Australian military assistance
Military assistance, British, ⌐Portuguese, etc.⌐
(May Subd Geog)
Military assistance, Chinese
(May Subd Geog)
UF Chinese military assistance
Military assistance, Communist
(May Subd Geog)
UF Communist military assistance
Military assistance, French
(May Subd Geog)
UF French military assistance
Military assistance, Israeli
(May Subd Geog)
UF Israeli military assistance
Military assistance, Russian
(May Subd Geog)
UF Russian military assistance
Military assistance, South Korean
(May Subd Geog)
UF South Korean military assistance
Military astronautics
USE Astronautics, Military
Military atrocities
USE *subdivision* Atrocities *under names of*
wars, e.g. World War, 1939-1945—
Atrocities
Military attachés (May Subd Geog)
UF Air attachés
Armed forces attachés
Attachés
Naval attachés
BT Diplomatic and consular service
Diplomats
Military automatic checkout equipment
BT Automatic checkout equipment
**Military automatic checkout equipment
industry** (May Subd Geog)
⌐HD9706.7⌐
Military automobiles
USE Automobiles, Military
Military aviation
USE Aeronautics, Military
Military balloons
USE Balloons
Military banks and banking
USE Banks and banking, Military
Military bases (May Subd Geog)
UF Bases, Military
Military facilities
Military installations
NT Air bases
Guided missile bases
Military posts
Navy-yards and naval stations
— **Law and legislation** (May Subd Geog)
BT Military law
— **Water-supply**
⌐UC780⌐
UF Water-supply, Military
Military bases, American (May Subd Geog)
UF American military bases
— **Law and legislation** (May Subd Geog)
**Military bases, American, ⌐British, Russian,
etc.⌐** (May Subd Geog)
Military bases, Dutch (May Subd Geog)
UF Dutch military bases
Military bases, Japanese (May Subd Geog)
UF Japanese military bases
Military bases, Russian (May Subd Geog)
UF Russian military bases
Military basic training
USE Military education—Basic training

Military bicycles
USE Military cycling
Military biography
⌐U51-55⌐
BT Biography
Military history
Soldiers
RT Generals
SA *subdivision* Biography *under armies,*
e.g. United States. Army—
Biography
Military book-plates
USE Book-plates, Military
Military bounties
USE Bounties, Military
Military bridges
⌐UG335⌐
UF Bridges, Military
BT Bridges
Military engineering
Military railroads
Stream crossing, Military
Transportation, Military
RT Bridges, Prefabricated
NT Pontoon-bridges
Military briefing
USE Briefing, Military
Military calls
⌐M1270⌐
⌐UH40-UH45⌐
UF Calls, Military
Drum and bugle-calls
Military signaling
BT Military music
Signals and signaling
RT Bugle-calls
Fanfares
Trumpet-calls
Military camps
USE Camps (Military)
Military capital (May Subd Geog)
⌐UA17⌐
Here are entered works on the aggregate value of
the durable physical assets of the defense establish-
ment, including the military equipment, facilities,
spare parts, and ordnance that provide military capa-
bility over an extended period of time.
UF Armed Forces—Military assets
Armed Forces—Military capital
Military assets
BT Armed Forces—Procurement
Armies, Cost of
Capital
SA *subdivision* Military capital *under*
names of armies, navies, etc., e.g.
United States. Army—Military
capital
Military capitulations
USE Capitulations, Military
Military cemeteries and funerals
USE Military funerals
National cemeteries
Military ceremonies, honors, and salutes
(May Subd Geog)
⌐U350-365⌐
UF Military courtesy
Military honors
Military salutes
Salutes, Military
BT Etiquette
NT Military funerals
Naval ceremonies, honors, and salutes
Weddings, Military
Military chaplains
USE Chaplains, Military
Military chaplains' wives
USE Chaplains, Military—Wives
Military chess
⌐GV1469.M6⌐
BT Chess—Variants

Military children
USE Children of military personnel
Military civic action
USE Armed Forces—Civic action
Military-civil relations
USE Civil-military relations
Military combat
USE Combat
Military commissions
USE Military courts
Military communication equipment industry
(May Subd Geog)
BT Communications, Military—Equipment
and supplies
Military communications
USE Communications, Military
Military compensation
USE *subdivision* Pay, allowances, etc. *under*
armies, navies, etc., e.g. United
States. Army—Pay, allowances,
etc.
Pensions, Military
Military conscription
USE Draft
Military construction
USE *subdivision* Military construction
operations *under armies, navies,*
etc., e.g. United States. Army—
Military construction operations
Military contracts
USE Defense contracts
Military contributions
USE Requisitions, Military
Military cookery
USE Cookery, Military
Military correspondence
USE *subdivision* Records and
correspondence *under armies, e.g.*
United States. Army—Records
and correspondence
Military costume
USE *subdivision* Uniforms *under armies and*
navies, e.g. United States. Army—
Uniforms; United States. Navy—
Uniforms
Uniforms, Military
Military courtesy
USE Military ceremonies, honors, and
salutes
Military courts (May Subd Geog)
Here are entered works on courts established to
administer martial law, mainly in occupied territory,
and to try prisoners of war. Works on courts estab-
lished to try members of a country's Armed Forces
for military offenses are entered under the heading
Courts-martial and courts of inquiry.
UF Military commissions
Military government courts
Military tribunals
BT Martial law
RT Courts-martial and courts of inquiry
Military crimes
USE Military offenses
Military currency (May Subd Geog)
⌐HG353.5⌐
UF Currency, Military
Military money
Military payment certificates
Scrip
BT Money
RT Emergency currency
Occupation currency
SA *subdivision* Military currency *under*
individual wars, e.g. World War,
1939-1945—Military currency
Military cycling
⌐UH30-35⌐
UF Bicycles, Military
Military bicycles
BT Cycling

Military decorations
USE *subdivision* Medals, badges,
decorations, etc. *under armies,
navies, etc.*
Medals, Military and naval
Military demolition
USE Demolition, Military
Military dental care
USE Dentistry, Military
Military dentistry
USE Dentistry, Military
Military departments and divisions
(May Subd Geog)
⌈UA⌉
— United States
UF United States—Military
departments and divisions
United States. Army—Military
departments and divisions
Military dependents *(May Subd Geog)*
⌈UB400-405⌉
UF Dependents, Military
Dependents of military personnel
Families of military personnel
Military families
BT Soldiers
NT Children of military personnel
Military wives
Missing in action—Family
relationships
Non-commissioned officers' wives
Officers' wives
Prisoners of war—Family relationships
Military deserters
USE Deserters, Military
Military desertion
USE Desertion, Military
Military diplomas (Rome) *(May Subd Geog)*
⌈DG89⌉
UF Diplomas, Military (Rome)
Diplomata militaria
Roman military diplomas
BT Citizenship—Rome
Military discharge—Rome
Rome—Army—Medals, badges,
decorations, etc.
Military discharge *(May Subd Geog)*
UF Armed Forces—Discharge
Discharge, Military
Mustering out
BT Recruiting and enlistment
— Rome
NT Military diplomas (Rome)
Military discipline *(May Subd Geog)*
⌈UB790-UB795⌉
Here are entered works on the maintenance of
discipline, military disciplinary power, and offenses
subject to disciplinary action. Works on criminal of-
fenses subject to adjudication by courts-martial are
entered under Military offenses.
UF Armies—Discipline
Discipline, Military
BT Disciplinary power
Discipline
NT Naval discipline
Military draft
USE Draft
Military draft registration
USE Draft registration
Military drill
USE Drill and minor tactics
Military education *(May Subd Geog)*
⌈U400-714⌉
UF Army schools
Education, Military
Military art and science—Study and
teaching
Military schools
Military training
Schools, Military
BT Education

NT Aeronautics, Military—Study and
teaching
Military missions
Military training camps
Moving-pictures in military education
Occupational training, Military
Physical education and training,
Military
Sand tables (Military science)
Soldiers—Education, Non-military
Staff rides
Synthetic training devices
Television in military education
— Aids and devices
— Basic training
UF Basic training (Military education)
Military basic training
— Law and legislation *(May Subd Geog)*
BT Educational law and legislation
— United States
NT Experimental Volunteer Army
Training Program
Military engineering *(May Subd Geog)*
⌈UG⌉
UF Engineering, Military
BT Civil engineering
Engineering
RT Fortification
Military architecture
SA *subdivision* Engineering and
construction *under individual wars,
e.g.* World War, 1939-1945—
Engineering and construction
NT Artificial intelligence—Military
applications
Attack and defense (Military science)
Coast defenses
Combat engineer vehicles
Earthwork
Electricity in military engineering
Electronics in military engineering
Fortification, Field
Infrared radiation—Military
applications
Intrenchments
Lasers—Military applications
Military bridges
Military field engineering
Military railroads
Mines, Military
Roadblocks (Military science)
Robotics—Military applications
Sapping
Spain—History—Civil War, 1936-1939
—Engineering and construction
Topographical surveying
Ultrasonic waves—Military
applications
Military engineers *(May Subd Geog)*
⌈UG⌉
BT Engineers
NT Tank engineers
Military engines
USE Engines of war
Military equipment, supplies, etc.
USE *subdivisions* Commissariat, Equipment,
Supplies and stores, Uniforms *under
armies*
Armies—Commissariat
Armies—Equipment
Military supplies
Uniforms, Military
Military ethics *(May Subd Geog)*
UF Ethics, Military
BT Ethics
Morale
NT Soldiers—Conduct of life
Military explosives
USE Explosives, Military
Military facilities
USE Military bases

Military families
USE Military dependents
Soldiers—Family relationships
Military fever
USE Sweating-sickness
Military field engineering
⌈UG360-390⌉
BT Military engineering
RT Topographical surveying
NT Camps (Military)
Demolition, Military
Intrenchments
Obstacles (Military science)
Military fireworks
⌈UF860⌉
BT Fireworks
Signals and signaling
NT Incendiary weapons
Military flight navigators
USE Flight navigators, Military
Military funerals *(May Subd Geog)*
UF Military cemeteries and funerals
Naval funerals
BT Funeral rites and ceremonies
Military ceremonies, honors, and
salutes
Naval ceremonies, honors, and salutes
Military geography *(May Subd Geog)*
⌈UA985-997⌉
UF Geography, Military
BT Geography
RT Military topography
SA *subdivision* Strategic aspects *under
names of regions, countries, cities,
etc.*
NT Africa—Strategic aspects
Africa, Northeast—Strategic aspects
Africa, Sub-Saharan—Strategic aspects
Arctic Ocean—Strategic aspects
Arctic regions—Strategic aspects
East Asia—Strategic aspects
Greenland—Strategic aspects
Indian Ocean—Strategic aspects
Maps, Military
North Atlantic Region—Strategic
aspects
Persian Gulf Region—Strategic aspects
Scandinavia—Strategic aspects
Military geology
⌈UG465⌉
UF Geology, Military
War geology
BT Geology
Military government *(May Subd Geog)*
BT Public administration
RT Civil-military relations
Military occupation
NT Military government of dependencies
Military government courts
USE Military courts
Military government of dependencies
⌈JV423⌉
BT Colonies—Administration
Martial law
Military government
Political science
NT Military occupation
Military graves
USE Soldiers' bodies, Disposition of
Military grid system
USE Grids (Cartography)
Military half-tracks
USE Half-track vehicles, Military
Military headquarters
USE *subdivision* Headquarters *under armies,
navies, etc., e.g.* United States—
Armed Forces—Headquarters
Military helicopters
⌈TL716⌉

2401

Military helicopters *(Continued)*
  BT Aeronautics, Military
      Airplanes, Military
      Helicopters
  NT Apache (Attack helicopter)
Military history
  [D25]
  [U27-U43 (Military science)]
  UF History, Military
      Wars
  BT History
  RT Naval history
  SA *subdivision* History, Military *under*
      names of countries, cities, etc.;
      names of particular wars, battles,
      sieges, etc.; and subdivision History
      under names of individual armies,
      e.g. United States. Army—History
  NT Battles
      Military art and science—History
      Military biography
      Military policy
      Naval art and science—History
      Sieges
      United States. Air Force—
        Historiography
Military history, Ancient
  [U29-35]
  NT Military history in the Bible
Military history, Medieval
  [U37]
  — **Exhibitions**
Military history, Modern
  [U39-42]
  — **16th century**
  — **17th century**
  — **18th century**
  — **19th century**
  — **20th century**
Military history in the Bible
  UF Battles in the Bible
      Bible—Military history
      Wars in the Bible
  BT Military history, Ancient
Military honors
  USE Military ceremonies, honors, and
      salutes
Military hospitals
  USE Hospitals, Military
Military housing
  USE *subdivision* Barracks and quarters
      under armies, navies, etc.
      Barracks
      Soldiers—Billeting
Military hydrology
  [UG468]
  BT Hydrology
      Military art and science
Military hygiene *(May Subd Geog)*
  [UH600-UH625]
  UF Health, Military
      Hygiene, Military
      Soldiers—Hygiene
  BT Hygiene
      Sanitation
  RT Medicine, Military
  SA *subdivision* Sanitary affairs *under*
      names of individual military
      services, e.g. United States. Army
      —Sanitary affairs; *and subdivision*
      Health aspects *under individual*
      wars, e.g. World War, 1939-1945—
      Health aspects
  NT Physical education and training,
      Military
  — **Law and legislation** *(May Subd Geog)*
Military inspectors general
  (May Subd Geog)
  [UB240-UB245]
  UF Inspectors general, Military
  BT Generals

Military installations
  USE Military bases
Military intelligence *(May Subd Geog)*
  [UB250-270]
  BT Intelligence service
  SA *subdivision* Military intelligence *under*
      individual wars, e.g. World War,
      1939-1945—Military intelligence
  NT Electronic intelligence
      Jennifer Project
      Military surveillance
      Photographic interpretation (Military
      science)
      Propaganda analysis
      U-2 Incident, 1960
      United States. Navy—Intelligence
      specialists
  — **Equipment and supplies**
    NT Military intelligence equipment
      industry
  — **Finance**
  — — **Law and legislation**
      (May Subd Geog)
Military intelligence equipment industry
  (May Subd Geog)
  BT Military intelligence—Equipment and
      supplies
Military intervention
  USE Intervention (International law)
Military jets
  USE Jet planes, Military
Military journalism
  USE Journalism, Military
Military justice
  USE Courts-martial and courts of inquiry
Military laundries
  USE Laundries, Military
Military law *(May Subd Geog)*
  [UB461-736]
    Not to be confused with subdivision Regulations
  under armies. Duplicate entry to be made if neces-
  sary, e.g. l. Military law—United States. 2. United
  States. Army—Regulations
  UF Articles of war
      Law, Military
      War, Articles of
  BT International law
      Public law
      War
      War (International law)
  RT Martial law
      Military administration
      National security—Law and legislation
      Naval law
  SA *subdivision* Defenses—Law and
      legislation *under names of*
      countries, etc.
  NT Air Force law
      Armies—Organization
      Astronautics, Military—Law and
      legislation
      Capitulations, Military
      Combatants and noncombatants
      (International law)
      Complaints (Military law)
      Courts-martial and courts of inquiry
      Draft—Law and legislation
      Hospitals, Military—Law and
      legislation
      Military bases—Law and legislation
      Military offenses
      Military privileges and immunities
      Military service, Voluntary—Law and
      legislation
      Military training camps—Law and
      legislation
      Military unions—Law and legislation
      Pharmacy, Military—Law and
      legislation
      Post exchanges—Law and legislation

      United States—Armed Forces—
        Recruiting, enlistment, etc.—Law
        and legislation
  — **Codification**
  — **United States**
    NT United States—Armed Forces—
      Pay, allowances, etc.—Law and
      legislation
Military law (Greek law) *(May Subd Geog)*
  BT Law, Greek
Military law (Jewish law)
Military law (Roman law)
Military leadership
  USE Command of troops
Military leaves and furloughs
  USE *subdivision* Leaves and furloughs
      under names of individual military
      services
Military legal assistance
  USE Legal assistance to servicemen
Military libraries *(May Subd Geog)*
  [Z675.M5]
    Here are entered works on libraries whose collec-
  tions focus on military art and science. Works on
  library collections for personal use by soldiers or
  naval personnel, especially during wars, are entered
  under Soldiers' libraries. Works on libraries located
  within military institutions or branches of the mili-
  tary service are entered under Military libraries and-
  /or Soldiers' libraries, depending on their purpose
  and subject focus.
  UF Libraries, Military
  BT Libraries, Special
  NT Libraries, Naval
      Military post libraries
      Soldiers' libraries
Military life
  USE *subdivision* Military life *under names*
      of individual military services, e.g.
      United States. Army—Military life
      Soldiers
Military maneuvers *(May Subd Geog)*
  [U250-U255 (General)]
  [UD460-UD465 (Infantry)]
  UF Armies—Maneuvers
      Maneuvers, Military
      Manoeuvers, Military
  BT Tactics
  SA *subdivision* Maneuvers *under armies,*
      e.g. United States. Army—
      Maneuvers
  NT Maneuver warfare
      War games
Military maps
  USE Maps, Military
Military mascots
  USE *subdivision* Mascots *under specific*
      headings, e.g. Armed Forces—
      Mascots
Military medals
  USE Medals, Military and naval
Military medicine
  USE Medicine, Military
Military meteorology
  USE Meteorology, Military
Military mines
  USE Mines, Military
Military miniatures *(May Subd Geog)*
  UF Military models
      Miniatures, Military
      Model soldiers
      Models, Military
      Toy soldiers
  BT Miniature objects
  NT Fortification—Models
      Miniature arms
      Paper soldiers
Military missions
  [UA16]
  UF Missions, Military
      Missions, Naval
      Naval missions

BT Government missions
International relations
Military education
SA *names of individual military missions*
Military mobilization
USE Armed Forces—Mobilization
Military models
USE Military miniatures
Military money
USE Military currency
Military motorcycles
USE Motorcycles, Military
Military motorization
USE Motorization, Military
Military museums *(May Subd Geog)*
[U13]
Here are entered works on collections and exhibitions, including modern army equipment, arms, uniforms, supplies, records, etc.
UF Artillery—Museums
War museums
BT Museums
RT Armories
Arms and armor—Exhibitions
Arsenals
Military music *(May Subd Geog)*
[M1270]
UF Armies—Music
Music, Military
BT Instrumental music
Music
RT Band music
SA *subdivision* Songs and music *under individual wars and names of individual military services, e.g.* World War, 1939-1945—Songs and music; United States. Army—Songs and music
NT Bugle-calls
Fanfares
Military calls
Pipe band music
Trumpet-calls
War-songs
— **Handbooks, manuals, etc.**
UF Military music—Manuals, textbooks, etc.
— **History and criticism**
[ML1300-1354]
RT Music and war
Music in the army
NT Bands (Music)
Instrumentation and orchestration (Band)
March (Music)
— **Manuals, text-books, etc.**
[MT735]
USE Military music—Handbooks, manuals, etc.
Military necessity
[JX5135.M5]
UF Necessity, Military
BT Necessity (International law)
War (International law)
Military nursing *(May Subd Geog)*
BT Medicine, Military
Nursing
Military occupation
[JX4093]
[JX5003]
UF Belligerent occupation
De facto doctrine (International law)
Occupation, Military
Occupied territory
BT Armed Forces in foreign countries
Military government of dependencies
War (International law)
RT Conquest, Right of
Military government
Territory, National

SA *subdivisions* History *and* Politics and government *under names of territories occupied, e.g.* France—History—German occupation, 1914-1918; *and subdivision* Occupied territories *under individual wars, e.g.* World War, 1939-1945—Occupied territories
NT Booty (International law)
De facto doctrine
Israel-Arab War, 1967—Occupied territories
Military occupation damages
Occupation currency
Russo-Japanese War, 1904-1905—Occupied territories
Military occupation damages *(May Subd Geog)*
UF Occupation damages, Military
BT Claims
Enemy property
Military occupation
Requisitions, Military
War damage compensation
Military occupational specialties (United States Armed Forces)
USE United States—Armed Forces—Occupational specialties
Military occupational specialties (United States Army)
USE United States. Army—Job descriptions
Military occupational training
USE Occupational training, Military
Military oceanography *(May Subd Geog)*
[V396-396.5]
UF Oceanography, Military
BT Naval art and science
Military offenses *(May Subd Geog)*
Here are entered works on criminal offenses subject to adjudication by courts-martial. Works on the maintenance of discipline, military disciplinary power, and offenses subject to disciplinary action are entered under Military discipline.
UF Crimes, Military
Military crimes
Offenses, Military
BT Criminal law
Military law
NT Absence without leave
Desertion, Military
Foreign enlistment
Guerrillas—Law and legislation
Insubordination
Malingering
Mutiny
Naval offenses
Pillage
Trials (Military offenses)
— **Statistics**
BT Criminal statistics
— **United States**
UF United States. Army—Crimes and misdemeanors
Military offenses (Roman law)
Military offensive (Military strategy)
USE Offensive (Military strategy)
Military officers, Retired
USE Retired military personnel
Military operations, Special
USE Special operations (Military science)
Military paraphernalia *(May Subd Geog)*
UF Paraphernalia, Military
Soldiers—Paraphernalia
NT Arms and armor
Decorations of honor
Medals, Military and naval
Uniforms, Military
Military parks *(May Subd Geog)*
UF National military parks

BT Historic sites
Parks
RT Battlefields
National cemeteries
Soldiers' monuments
War memorials
— **Mississippi**
NT Vicksburg National Military Park (Miss.)
— **North Carolina**
NT Moores Creek National Military Park (N.C.)
— **Pennsylvania**
NT Gettysburg National Military Park (Pa.)
— **Virginia**
Military passes
[UB280-285]
UF Passes, Military
RT Safe-conducts
Military pay
USE *subdivision* Pay, allowances, etc. *under names of armies, navies, etc., e.g.* United States—Armed Forces—Pay, allowances, etc.
Military payment certificates
USE Military currency
Military pensions
USE Pensions, Military
Military personnel
USE Soldiers
Military personnel, Retired
USE Retired military personnel
Military personnel, Unknown
USE Unknown military personnel
Military pharmacy
USE Pharmacy, Military
Military photography
USE Photography, Military
Military physical education and training
USE Physical education and training, Military
Military planning *(May Subd Geog)*
UF Planning, Military
BT Military administration
Military policy
— **Computer programs**
NT TATR (Computer program)
TSAR (Computer program)
Military police
USE *subdivision* Armed Forces—Military police *under names of countries, and subdivisions* Military police *under names of armies,* Shore patrol *under names of navies,* Air police *under names of air forces*
Military policy
[UA11]
UF Defense policy
BT Military history
Sociology, Military
War
RT National security
SA *subdivision* Military policy *under names of countries*
NT Aircraft industry—Military aspects
Defense information, Classified
Deterrence (Strategy)
Hospitals—Military aspects
Limited war
Militarism
Military planning
Offensive (Military strategy)
Ship transfers to foreign registry
Strategic materials
Warfare, Conventional
Military post exchanges
USE Post exchanges
Military post libraries *(May Subd Geog)*
[Z675.M6]
BT Military libraries

Military post schools
  UF Army schools
      Overseas dependents schools
  BT Schools
Military post schools, American
  (May Subd Geog)
  UF American military post schools
Military post schools, British
  (May Subd Geog)
    [LC5082.G]
  UF British military post schools
Military postal service
  USE *subdivision* Postal service *under names*
      of individual military services, e.g.
      United States. Army—Postal
      service
Military posts *(May Subd Geog)*
  [UA26 (United States)]
  UF Army posts
      Military stations
      Posts, Military
      Stations, Military
  BT Military bases
  — **United States**
      UF United States. Army—Military
          posts
Military power
  USE Air forces
      Air power
      Armies
      Disarmament
      Military art and science
      Navies
      Sea-power
Military prisons
  USE *subdivision* Prisons *under armies, e.g.*
      United States. Army—Prisons
      Prisons, Military
Military privileges and immunities
  (May Subd Geog)
  UF Privileges and immunities, Military
  BT Military law
      Privileges and immunities
      Soldiers—Civil status
Military procurement
  USE *subdivision* Procurement *under armies,*
      navies, etc., e.g. United States—
      Armed Forces—Procurement;
      United States. Navy—
      Procurement
      Air forces—Procurement
      Armed Forces—Procurement
Military promotions
  USE *subdivision* Promotions *under names*
      of individual military services, e.g.
      United States. Army—Promotions
Military psychiatry
  USE Psychiatry, Military
Military psychology
  USE Psychology, Military
Military public works
  USE *subdivision* Military construction
      operations *under names of*
      individual military services, e.g.
      United States. Army—Military
      construction operations
Military radio
  USE Radio, Military
Military railroads *(May Subd Geog)*
  [UG345]
  UF Railroads, Military
  BT Military engineering
      Railroads
      Transportation, Military
  NT Military bridges
Military rearguard action
  USE Rearguard action (Military science)
Military reconnaissance
  [U220]
  UF Reconnaissance, Military
      Reconnaissance, War

  BT Maps, Military
      Military surveillance
  RT Military topography
      Scouts and scouting
  SA *subdivision* Reconnaissance operations
      under individual wars, e.g. World
      War, 1939-1945—Reconnaissance
      operations
  NT Aerial reconnaissance
      Combat patrols
      Naval reconnaissance
      Photographic reconnaissance systems
      Terrain study (Military science)
      U-2 Incident, 1960
Military relations
  USE *subdivision* Military relations *under*
      names of countries, cities, etc.
Military religious orders *(May Subd Geog)*
  [CR4701-4785]
  UF Knighthood, Orders of
      Religious orders
  BT Monasticism and religious orders
      Orders of knighthood and chivalry
  NT Hospitalers
      Templars
      Teutonic Knights
  — **Insignia**
      [CR4653]
      [CR4705]
      BT Insignia
Military requisitions
  USE Requisitions, Military
Military research *(May Subd Geog)*
  [U390-395]
  UF Defense research
      Research, Military
  BT Research
  RT Research and development contracts,
      Government
  NT Aeronautics, Military—Research
      Transportation, Military—Research
  — **United States**
      NT ARPA computer network
Military reservations *(May Subd Geog)*
  [UB390-395]
  UF Reservations, Military
  RT National parks and reserves
Military reserves
  USE Armed Forces—Reserves
Military retirements
  USE *subdivision* Appointments and
      retirements *under names of*
      individual military services, e.g.
      United States. Army—
      Appointments and retirements
Military roads *(May Subd Geog)*
  [UG330]
  UF Roads, Military
  BT Roads
  — **Vermont**
      NT Bayley-Hazen Military Road (Vt.)
Military sales
  USE Military assistance
      Munitions
Military salutes
  USE Military ceremonies, honors, and
      salutes
Military schools
  USE Military education
Military science
  USE Military art and science
Military scientists *(May Subd Geog)*
Military secrets
  USE Defense information, Classified
Military service, Compulsory
  USE Draft
Military service, Voluntary
  (May Subd Geog)
  [UB320-325]

  UF All-volunteer forces
      Voluntary military service
      Volunteer army
  BT Armed Forces
      National service
      Recruiting and enlistment
  SA *subdivision* Recruiting, enlistment, etc.
      under armies, navies, etc., e.g.
      United States—Armed Forces—
      Recruiting, enlistment, etc.; United
      States. Army—Recruiting,
      enlistment, etc.; United States.
      Navy—Recruiting, enlistment, etc.
  — **Law and legislation** *(May Subd Geog)*
      BT Military law
  — **United States**
      NT Experimental Volunteer Army
          Training Program
          VOLAR Project
Military service as a profession
  USE Armed Forces—Vocational guidance
Military shooting
  USE Shooting, Military
Military signaling
  USE *subdivision* Signaling *under armies, e.g.*
      United States. Army—Signaling
      Military calls
      Signals and signaling
Military sketching
  UF Sketching, Military
  BT Drawing
      Military topography
      Topographical drawing
Military slang
  USE Soldiers—Language (New words,
      slang, etc.)
Military social work *(May Subd Geog)*
  [UH750-769]
  UF Social service, Military
      Social service and military
      mobilization
      United States—Armed Forces—Social
      services
  BT Public welfare
      Social service
  SA *subdivision* Social services *under*
      armies, navies, etc., e.g. United
      States. Army—Social services;
      United States. Navy—Social
      services
  NT Missing in action—Family
      relationships
      Prisoners of war—Family relationships
Military sociology
  USE Sociology, Military
Military space surveillance
  USE Space surveillance
Military spending
  USE *subdivision* Appropriations and
      expenditures *under names of*
      individual defense agencies, e.g.
      United States. Dept. of Defense—
      Appropriations and expenditures;
      and subdivision *Armed Forces—*
      Appropriations and expenditures
      under names of countries, e.g.
      United States—Armed Forces—
      Appropriations and expenditures
Military sports
  BT Sports
  SA *subdivision* Sports *under names of*
      individual military services, e.g.
      United States. Army—Sports
  NT Zarnitsa
Military staffs
  USE *names of individual general staffs*
      Armies—Staffs
Military standards
  USE Standards, Military
Military stations
  USE Military posts

Military statistics
    [UA19 (Theory)]
    UF Military art and science—Statistical
         methods
    BT Statistics
    SA *subdivision* Statistics *under armies, e.g.*
         United States. Army—Statistics
    NT Armies
Military strategy
    USE Strategy
Military stream crossing
    USE Stream crossing, Military
Military supplies
    [UC260-267]
    UF Armies—Supplies
         Army supplies
         Military equipment, supplies, etc.
         Subsistence stores
         Supplies, Military
    BT Industrial mobilization
         Logistics
    SA *subdivisions* Equipment *and* Supplies
         and stores *under names of*
         individual military services, e.g.
         United States. Army—Equipment;
         United States. Army—Supplies
         and stores; *and subdivision*
         Equipment and supplies *under*
         individual wars, e.g. World War,
         1939-1945—Equipment and
         supplies
    NT Armies—Commissariat
         Quartermasters
         Requisitions, Military
         Surplus military property
    — Mothballing
         USE Military supplies—Preservation
    — **Packing**
         [UC277]
         BT Packing for shipment
    — **Preservation**
         UF Military supplies—Mothballing
              Mothballing of military supplies
              Preservation of military supplies
Military surgery
    USE Surgery, Military
Military surplus stores
    USE Army-Navy stores
Military surpluses
    USE Surplus military property
Military surveillance *(May Subd Geog)*
    [UG475]
    UF Surveillance, Military
    BT Detectors
         Military intelligence
    NT Military reconnaissance
         Space surveillance
Military surveying
    USE Military topography
Military symbols
    [U26]
    BT Signs and symbols
    NT Armed Forces—Insignia
         Vehicles, Military—Markings
Military tactics
    USE Tactics
Military telegraph *(May Subd Geog)*
    [UG590-610]
    UF Field telegraph
         Telegraph, Military
    BT Communications, Military
         Signals and signaling
         Telegraph
Military telephone *(May Subd Geog)*
    [UG620]
    UF Telephone, Military
    BT Communications, Military
         Signals and signaling
         Telephone
Military television
    [UG623]

    UF Combat television
         Television, Military
    BT Communications, Military
         Television
    NT Television in military education
         Television in naval education
Military terms
    USE Military art and science—Dictionaries
         Military art and science—Terminology
Military testaments
    USE Wills, Military
Military topography *(May Subd Geog)*
    [UG470]
         Here are entered works on the detailed mapping
    or surveying of the features of an area for military
    purposes.
    UF Military surveying
         Surveying, Military
         Topography, Military
    BT Cartography
         Topographical surveying
    RT Maps, Military
         Military geography
         Military reconnaissance
    NT Military sketching
         Terrain study (Military science)
    — **Instruments**
         UF Instruments, Military topography
Military towns *(May Subd Geog)*
         Here are entered works on cities and towns on
    which the military has had a pervasive influence.
    UF Garrison towns
         Towns, Garrison
         Towns, Military
    BT Cities and towns
Military training
    USE Military education
Military training, Universal
    USE Draft
Military training camps *(May Subd Geog)*
    [U290-295]
    UF Camps of instruction
         Instruction, Camps of
         Students' military training camps
         Training camps, Military
    BT Military education
    — **Law and legislation** *(May Subd Geog)*
         BT Military law
    — **Sounds**
         BT Sounds
Military transportation
    USE Transportation, Military
Military tribunals
    USE Courts-martial and courts of inquiry
         Military courts
Military trophies
    USE Trophies, Military
Military trucks
    USE Trucks, Military
Military uniforms
    USE Uniforms, Military
Military unions *(May Subd Geog)*
    UF Army unions
         Soldiers' unions
         Unions, Military
    BT Soldiers
         Trade-unions
    — **Law and legislation** *(May Subd Geog)*
         BT Labor laws and legislation
              Military law
Military vehicle industry *(May Subd Geog)*
    [HD9744.V43-HD9744.V434]
    RT Vehicles, Military
Military vehicles
    USE Vehicles, Military
Military veterinary service
    USE Veterinary service, Military
Military wagons
    USE Vehicles, Military
Military weddings
    USE Weddings, Military

Military wills
    USE Wills, Military
Military wives *(May Subd Geog)*
    UF Wives, Military
         Wives of military personnel
    BT Military dependents
         Wives
    NT Air Force wives
         Army wives
         Marine Corps wives
         Navy wives
         War widows
Militia
    USE *subdivision* Militia *under names of*
         regions, countries, states, etc.
Militia (Minutemen)
    USE Minutemen (Militia)
Milk
    [SF251-262]
    BT Dairying
         Exocrine glands—Secretions
    RT Cream
    NT Butter
         Camel milk
         Cheese
         Cookery (Milk)
         Cookery (Sour cream and milk)
         Cream-separators
         Creameries
         Goat's milk
         Kephir
         Kumiss
         Milk, Human
         Milkshakes
         School milk programs
         Sheep milk
         Soybean milk
         Whey
    — **Bacteriology**
         [QR121]
         BT Bacteriology, Agricultural
              Cheese—Bacteriology
              Milk hygiene
         RT Dairy bacteriology
         NT Milk—Sterilization
              Streptococcus thermophilus
              Udder—Bacteriology
    — Care and handling
         USE Milk hygiene
    — **Composition**
         [SF251]
         NT Butterfat
              Milk proteins
    — **Containers**
         UF Milk containers
         BT Milk trade
         NT Milk bottles
              Milk tanks
    — Contamination
         USE Milk contamination
    — **Cooling**
         [SF247]
         UF Milk—Refrigeration
         BT Refrigeration and refrigerating
              machinery
    — — **Equipment and supplies**
         [SF247]
         UF Milk coolers
    — **Cooperative marketing**
         BT Cooperative marketing of farm
              produce
              Milk trade
    — **Flavor and odor**
         UF Milk—Odor
         BT Flavor
              Odors
    — **Fluoridation** *(May Subd Geog)*
         [RK331]
         UF Fluoridation of milk

Milk
— **Fluoridation** *(Continued)*
   BT Fluorides
      Fluorine—Physiological effect
      Preventive dentistry
— **Grading and standardization**
— Homogenization
   USE Milk, Homogenized
— Law and legislation
   USE Dairy laws
— Marketing
   USE Milk trade
— Odor
   USE Milk—Flavor and odor
— **Pasteurization**
   ⌜SF259⌝
   UF Milk, Pasteurized
      Pasteurization of milk
   BT Milk hygiene
— Processing
   USE Dairy processing
— Production
   USE Milk production
— **Quality**
   UF Milk quality
— Radioactive contamination
   USE Radioactive contamination of
       milk
— Refrigeration
   USE Milk—Cooling
— Sanitation
   USE Milk hygiene
— Secretion
   USE Lactation
— **Sterilization**
   ⌜SF259⌝
   BT Dairy bacteriology
      Milk—Bacteriology
      Milk hygiene
— Tanks
   USE Milk tanks
— **Transportation**
   NT Milk tanks
— **Weight and measurement**
— **Weights and measures**
   BT Weights and measures
Milk, Concentrated
   UF Concentrated milk
      Milk concentrates
   NT Milk, Condensed
      Milk, Dried
      Milk, Evaporated
— **Law and legislation** *(May Subd Geog)*
   BT Dairy laws
Milk, Condensed *(May Subd Geog)*
   ⌜SF259⌝
   UF Condensed milk
   BT Milk, Concentrated
Milk, Dehydrated
   USE Milk, Dried
Milk, Desiccated
   USE Milk, Dried
Milk, Dried
   ⌜SF259⌝
   UF Dehydrated milk
      Dried milk
      Milk, Dehydrated
      Milk, Desiccated
      Milk, Powdered
      Powdered milk
   BT Milk, Concentrated
   NT Dried milk industry
Milk, Evaporated
   UF Evaporated milk
   BT Milk, Concentrated
Milk, Fermented
   ⌜RM234⌝
   RT Lactic acid
   NT Kephir
      Kumiss

Milk, Frozen
   UF Frozen milk
   BT Food, Frozen
Milk, Homogenized
   ⌜SF259⌝
   UF Homogenized milk
      Milk—Homogenization
Milk, Human
   ⌜QP246⌝
   BT Milk
   RT Breast feeding
      Lactation
   NT Colostrum
      Infants—Nutrition
— **Contamination**
   BT Milk contamination
Milk, Pasteurized
   USE Milk—Pasteurization
Milk, Powdered
   USE Milk, Dried
Milk, Recombined
   USE Milk, Remade
Milk, Reconstituted
   USE Milk, Remade
Milk, Remade
   UF Milk, Recombined
      Milk, Reconstituted
      Recombined milk
      Reconstituted milk
      Remade milk
— **Flavor and odor**
   UF Milk, Remade—Odor
   BT Flavor
      Odors
— Odor
   USE Milk, Remade—Flavor and odor
Milk, Skimmed
   USE Skim milk
Milk as feed
   BT Calves—Feeding and feeds
Milk as food *(May Subd Geog)*
   BT Food
Milk bottle makers' marks
   USE Milk bottles—Marks
Milk bottles *(May Subd Geog)*
   UF Milkbottles
   BT Beverage containers
      Bottles
      Milk—Containers
— **Marks**
   UF Marks, Milk bottle makers'
      Milk bottle makers' marks
Milk commissions, Medical
   ⌜SF255⌝
   UF Medical milk commissions
   BT Food adulteration and inspection
Milk concentrates
   USE Milk, Concentrated
Milk consumption *(May Subd Geog)*
   BT Milk supply
Milk containers
   USE Milk—Containers
Milk contamination *(May Subd Geog)*
   UF Contamination, Milk
      Milk—Contamination
   BT Dairy products—Contamination
      Food contamination
   NT Milk, Human—Contamination
      Radioactive contamination of milk
Milk coolers
   USE Milk—Cooling—Equipment and
       supplies
Milk dating
   UF Dating of milk
   BT Milk trade
Milk depots
   ⌜HD4501.M5 (Economics)⌝
   BT Child welfare
      Infants—Nutrition
      Social settlements

Milk fat
   USE Butterfat
Milk fat globules
   USE Butterfat—Fat globules
Milk fever
   ⌜RG871.M5⌝
   BT Lactation
Milk fever in animals *(May Subd Geog)*
   ⌜SF967.M5⌝
   UF Parturient hypocalcemia
      Parturient paresis
   BT Calcium—Metabolism—Disorders
      Cattle—Diseases
      Deficiency diseases in domestic
       animals
Milk-free cookery
   USE Milk-free diet—Recipes
Milk-free diet
   ⌜RM234.5⌝
   UF Diet, Milk-free
      Milkless diet
   BT Diet in disease
      Lactose intolerance
— **Recipes**
   UF Milk-free cookery
      Milkless cookery
   BT Cookery for the sick
Milk glass *(May Subd Geog)*
   ⌜NK5439.M54⌝
   UF Glass, Milk
      Glass, Opaque
      Lattimo
      Milch glass
      Opaque glass
   BT Glassware
Milk goats
   USE Goats
Milk hygiene *(May Subd Geog)*
   UF Milk—Care and handling
      Milk—Sanitation
      Milk sanitation
   BT Dairy inspection
      Food adulteration and inspection
      Milk supply
      Veterinary hygiene
   NT Milk—Bacteriology
      Milk—Pasteurization
      Milk—Sterilization
— Law and legislation
   USE Dairy laws
Milk inspection
   USE Dairy inspection
Milk plants *(May Subd Geog)*
   UF Dairies
      Dairy
   BT Beverage processing plants
      Dairy plants
   RT Dairy processing
   NT Dairy workers
— Construction
   USE Milk plants—Design and
       construction
— **Design and construction**
   UF Milk plants—Construction
Milk production *(May Subd Geog)*
   Here are entered works on the quantity of milk
   produced by a cow or herd. Works on milk produc-
   tion as an industry are entered under Dairying.
   UF Cattle—Milk production
      Cows—Milk production
      Dairy cattle—Milk production
      Milk—Production
      Milk yield
   BT Cows
      Dairy cattle
      Dairying
   SA *subdivision* Milk production *under*
      particular animals other than cattle,
      e.g. Sheep—Milk production
   NT Lactation

Milk products
    USE Dairy products
Milk proteins
    BT Milk—Composition
    NT Casein
Milk quality
    USE Milk—Quality
Milk sanitation
    USE Milk hygiene
Milk secretion
    USE Lactation
Milk-sickness
Milk snake, Common
    USE Lampropeltis triangulum
Milk snakes
    USE Lampropeltis
Milk substitutes
    USE Food substitutes
Milk sugar
    USE Lactose
Milk supply *(May Subd Geog)*
    ₍SF257-8₎
    NT Milk consumption
        Milk hygiene
Milk tanks
    UF Bulk milk tanks
        Milk—Tanks
    BT Milk—Containers
        Milk—Transportation
Milk teeth
    USE Teeth, Deciduous
Milk trade *(May Subd Geog)*
    ₍HD9282 (Economics)₎
    UF Milk—Marketing
    NT Dairy workers
        Milk—Containers
        Milk—Cooperative marketing
        Milk dating
        Wages—Dairy workers
    — Law and legislation
        USE Dairy laws
Milk vetch
    USE Astragalus (Plants)
Milk yield
    USE Milk production
Milkbottles
    USE Milk bottles
Milkfish
    ₍QL638.C484₎
    UF Awa
        Bangos
        Bangus
        Banyos
        Chanos chanos
    BT Chanos
Milkfish industry *(May Subd Geog)*
    ₍HD9469.M56-HD9469.M564₎
Milking
    ₍SF250₎
    UF Cattle—Milking
        Cows—Milking
        Dairy cattle—Milking
    SA *subdivision* Milking *under particular*
        animals other than cattle, e.g.
        Sheep—Milking
    NT Sheep—Milking
Milking machines
    ₍SF247₎
    UF Cattle—Milking—Machinery
    BT Agricultural machinery
        Dairying—Equipment and supplies
    SA *subdivision* Milking—Machinery *under*
        particular animals other than cattle,
        e.g. Sheep—Milking—Machinery
    NT Sheep—Milking—Machinery
Milking parlors *(May Subd Geog)*
    ₍SF247₎
    UF Parlors, Milking
    BT Dairy barns
Milkless cookery
    USE Milk-free diet—Recipes

Milkless diet
    USE Milk-free diet
Milkovic family
    USE Milkovich family
Milkovich family *(Not Subd Geog)*
    UF Milkovic family
Milkshakes
    ₍TX817.M₎
    BT Ice cream, ices, etc.
        Milk
Milkvetch
    USE Astragalus (Plants)
Milkweed
    ₍QK495.A815 (Botany)₎
    ₍SB618.M5 (Poisonous plants)₎
    UF Silkweed
    BT Livestock poisoning plants
        Rubber plants
    NT Asclepias curassavica
Milkweed beetles
    USE Tetraopes
Milkweed bug
    USE Oncopeltus fasciatus
Milkweed butterflies
    ₍QL561.D3₎
    UF Danaidae
        Danaididae
        Euploeidae
        Limnadidae
        Lymnadidae
    BT Butterflies
        Lepidoptera
    NT Danaus
Milky Way
    ₍QB857.7₎
    UF Galaxy (Milky Way)
    BT Galaxies
    NT Galactic center
        Galactic windows
        Solar system
        Stars—Distribution
    — Atlases
Mill Creek (Crook County, Or.)
    BT Rivers—Oregon
Mill Creek culture
    BT Great Plains—Antiquities
        Indians of North America—Great
            Plains—Antiquities
        Indians of North America—Iowa—
            Antiquities
        Iowa—Antiquities
Mill Creek Indians
    ₍E83.858 (Wars)₎
    ₍E99.M₎
    BT Indians of North America
    — Wars, 1857-1865
        BT Indians of North America—Wars—
            1815-1875
            Pacific Coast Indians, Wars with,
            1847-1865
Mill family
    USE Mills family
Mill River Disaster, 1874
    ₍F72.H3₎
Mill Springs, Battle of, 1862
    UF Fishing Creek, Battle of, 1862
        Logan's Cross Roads, Battle of, 1862
    BT United States—History—Civil War,
        1861-1865—Campaigns
Mill tailings, Uranium
    USE Uranium mill tailings
Mill work (Woodwork)
    USE Millwork (Woodwork)
Milla family
    USE Miller family
Millagan family
    USE Milligan family
Millage family
    USE Millidge family
Millam family
    USE Milam family

Millan family
    USE Milne family
Millar family
    USE Miller family
Millare family
    USE Miller family
Millar's asthma
    USE Laryngismus stridulus
Millcayac language
    ₍PM6511₎
Mille Lacs Indian Reservation (Minn.)
    UF Thousand Lakes Indian Reservation
        (Minn.)
    BT Chippewa Indians—Reservations
        Indians of North America—Minnesota
        —Reservations
Mille Miglia
    ₍GV1034.51.M₎
    UF Mille Miglia Race
        Mille Miglia Rally
    BT Automobile racing—Italy
        Automobile rallies—Italy
Mille Miglia Race
    USE Mille Miglia
Mille Miglia Rally
    USE Mille Miglia
Milled lead
    USE Sheet-lead
Milledge family
    USE Millidge family
Millefiori canes (Paperweights)
    (May Subd Geog)
    ₍NK5440.P3₎
    BT Paperweights
Millefiori glass
    USE Glass, Millefiori
Millegan family
    USE Milligan family
Millegen family
    USE Milligan family
Millen family
    USE Milne family
Millenarianism
    USE Millennialism
Millennialism *(May Subd Geog)*
    UF Amillennialism
        Millenarianism
        Millennianism
        Postmillennialism
        Premillennialism
    BT Dispensationalism
    RT Millennium
    — Indonesia
        NT Sawito Affair, Indonesia, 1976
Millennianism
    USE Millennialism
Millennium
    ₍BT890-891₎
    UF Chiliasm
    BT Eschatology
    RT Millennialism
        Second Advent
    NT Dispensationalism
        One thousand, A.D.
        Rapture (Christian eschatology)
Millepedes
    USE Millepeds
Millepeds *(May Subd Geog)*
    ₍QL449.6₎
    UF Diplopoda
        Millepedes
        Millipedes
    BT Myriapoda
    NT Chordeumida
        Platydesmida
        Spirostreptida
    — Geographical distribution
Miller analogies test
    ₍LB2367₎
    UF Analogies test, Miller
        MAT

Miller analogies test *(Continued)*
  BT Scholastic aptitude test
     Universities and colleges—United
        States—Examinations
Miller family *(Not Subd Geog)*
  UF De la Miller family
     Milaw family
     Miler family
     Milla family
     Millar family
     Millare family
     Millers family
     Millir family
     Millor family
     Millr family
  RT Milner family
     Moeller family
     Mounier family
     Mueller family
Miller Site (Wash.)
  USE Strawberry Island Village Site (Wash.)
Miller-Yoder Language Comprehension Test
  ₍LB3060.33.M54₎
  UF MY
  BT Comprehension—Testing
     Educational tests and measurements
     Language acquisition—Testing
Millericrinida, Fossil
  ₍QE782₎
  BT Crinoidea, Fossil
Millerism
  USE Millerite movement
Millerite movement *(May Subd Geog)*
     Here are entered works on the pre-1845 followers
  of William Miller. Works on the post-1845 Adventist
  groups are entered under Adventists.
  UF Millerism
     Millerites
  RT Adventists
Millerites
  USE Millerite movement
Millers *(May Subd Geog)*
Millers family
  USE Miller family
Millers River (Mass.)
  BT Rivers—Massachusetts
Miller's-thumb (Fish)
  USE Cottus
Millersville State College Old Library
     (Millersville, Pa.)
  USE Biemesderfer Executive Center
        (Millersville, Pa.)
Milles family
  USE Mills family
Millet, Jean François, 1814-1875. Angelus
  ₍ND553.M6₎
  UF Angelus (Painting)
  BT Peasants in art
Millet *(May Subd Geog)*
  ₍SB191.M5₎
  BT Forage plants
  RT Millet industry
  NT Pearl millet
     Ragi
  — Diseases and pests *(May Subd Geog)*
  ₍SB608.M₎
Millet, Indian
  USE Durra
Millet as feed
Millet industry *(May Subd Geog)*
  ₍HD9049.M5-6₎
  RT Millet
Millford family
  USE Milford family
Millham family
  USE Milham family
Millholland family
  USE Milhollan family
Millhollon family
  USE Milhollan family

Millhouse family
  USE Milhous family
Millican family
  USE Milligan family
Millicon family
  USE Milligan family
Millidge family *(Not Subd Geog)*
  UF Millage family
     Milledge family
Milligan family *(Not Subd Geog)*
  UF Milagin family
     Milegan family
     Milekin family
     Miligan family
     Milikan family
     Miliken family
     Milikin family
     Millagan family
     Millegan family
     Millegen family
     Millican family
     Millicon family
     Milligen family
     Millikan family
     Milliken family
     Millikin family
Milligen family
  USE Milligan family
Millikan family
  USE Milligan family
Millikan rays
  USE Cosmic rays
Milliken family
  USE Milligan family
Milliken's Bend, Battle of, 1863
  ₍E475.2₎
  BT United States—History—Civil War,
        1861-1865—Campaigns
Millikin family
  USE Milligan family
Millimeter wave communication systems
  (May Subd Geog)
  UF Communication systems, Millimeter
        wave
     Telecommunication systems,
        Millimeter wave
  BT Microwave communication systems
     Radio, Short wave
     Telecommunication systems
Millimeter wave devices
  BT Electronic apparatus and appliances
     Microwave devices
     Millimeter waves
Millimeter waves
  ₍TK7876₎
  BT Microwaves
  NT Millimeter wave devices
  — Atmospheric effects
     UF Atmospheric effects on millimeter
           waves
     BT Meteorological optics
Millin family
  USE Milne family
Millinery *(May Subd Geog)*
  ₍HD9999.M5 (Trade)₎
  ₍TT650-TT665 (Technical works)₎
  BT Costume
  RT Hats
     Head-gear
  NT Artificial flowers
     Dress accessories
     Millinery workers
Millinery workers *(May Subd Geog)*
  BT Millinery
  NT Wages—Millinery workers
Milling, Barley
  USE Barley—Milling
Milling, Rice
  USE Rice—Milling

Milling (Metal-work)
  BT Metal-cutting
     Metal-work
  NT Chemical milling
     Milling-machines
     Spiral milling
Milling (Metallurgy)
  USE Ore-dressing
Milling cutters
  ₍TJ1227₎
  UF Cutters, Milling
  BT Metal-cutting tools
     Milling-machines
Milling machinery
  ₍TJ1345₎
     Here are entered works on machinery used in the
  process of grinding, etc.
  UF Pulverizers
  BT Grain—Milling
  RT Crushing machinery
     Mills and mill-work
  NT Autogenous grinding
     Ball mills
     Feed mills
     Flour-mills
     Jet mills
     Oil mills
  — Appraisal
     USE Milling machinery—Valuation
  — Valuation
     ₍TJ1345₎
     UF Milling machinery—Appraisal
Milling-machines
  ₍TJ1225₎
     Here are entered works on machine-tools used in
  shaping metal by means of rotary cutters.
  BT Milling (Metal-work)
  NT Milling cutters
     Spiral milling
  — Numerical control
     ₍TJ1225₎
     UF Milling-machines—Punched tape
           control
        Milling-machines, Tape-controlled
        Numerically controlled milling-
           machines
        Robot milling-machines
        Tape-controlled milling-machines
     BT Automatic control
        Electronic control
        Punched card systems
  — Punched tape control
     USE Milling-machines—Numerical
           control
  — Vibration
Milling-machines, Tape-controlled
  USE Milling-machines—Numerical control
Milling of grain
  USE Grain—Milling
Milling trade
  USE Flour and feed trade
Million (The number)
  BT Symbolism of numbers
Millionaires *(May Subd Geog)*
  RT Capitalists and financiers
     Wealth
  NT Millionairesses
Millionairesses *(May Subd Geog)*
  BT Capitalists and financiers
     Millionaires
     Wealth
     Women
Millipedes
  USE Millepeds
Millir family
  USE Miller family
Millivoltmeter
  ₍TK321₎
  BT Voltmeter
Millor family
  USE Miller family

Millr family
  USE Miller family
Mills, Mini
  USE Steel minimills
Mills, Small
  USE Steel minimills
Mills (Buildings)
  USE Factories
Mills and mill-work (May Subd Geog)
    ₎TJ1040-1119₎
    BT Industrial arts
        Manufactures
        Manufacturing processes
        Technology
    RT Factories
        Milling machinery
    SA types of mills, e.g. Flour-mills, Planing-
        mills
    NT Horse mills
        Machinery
        Millstones
        Millwork (Woodwork)
        Millwrights
        Size reduction of materials
        Steel minimills
        Windmills
Mills and mill-work in art
Mills bill
    ₎HF1755 (Discussion)₎
    ₎HJ6085-HJ6086 (Schedules)₎
Mills family (Not Subd Geog)
    UF De Myll family
        DeMyll family
        Mill family
        Milles family
        Mils family
        Myill family
        Myll family
        Mylles family
Mills-Nixon effect
    BT Benzene
        Chemical bonds
Millspaugh family (Not Subd Geog)
    UF Millspough family
        Milspaw family
Millspough family
    USE Millspaugh family
Millstones (May Subd Geog)
    BT Mills and mill-work
        Stone
    NT Metates
Millwood Lake (Ark.)
    UF Millwood Reservoir (Ark.)
    BT Lakes—Arkansas
        Little River (Okla. and Ark.)
        Reservoirs—Arkansas
Millwood Reservoir (Ark.)
    USE Millwood Lake (Ark.)
Millwork (Woodwork)
    ₎TS878₎
    UF Mill work (Woodwork)
    BT Mills and mill-work
        Planing-machines
        Woodwork
    SA names of special products, e.g. Doors;
        Sashes
Millwrights (May Subd Geog)
    ₎HD8039.M59₎
    UF Industrial mechanics
    BT Mechanics (Persons)
        Mills and mill-work
Milly family
    USE De Milly family
Miln family
    USE Milne family
**Milne, David Brown, 1882-1953. Painting
  place**
    ₎ND249.M5₎
    UF Coin pour peindre (Painting)

Milne family (Not Subd Geog)
    UF Millan family
        Millen family
        Millin family
        Miln family
        Milnes family
        Mylne family
Milne Land (Greenland)
    BT Islands—Greenland
Milner Dam (Idaho) (Not Subd Geog)
    BT Dams—Idaho
Milner family (Not Subd Geog)
    UF Milnor family
    RT Miller family
Milnes family
    USE Milne family
Milnor family
    USE Milner family
Milo
    ₎QK495.G74 (Botany)₎
    ₎SB191.S7 (Culture)₎
    BT Sorghum
Milo industry (May Subd Geog)
Milo Island (Greece)
    USE Melos Island (Greece)
Milon d'Angers
    UF Milone d'Anglante
    BT Legends—Europe
Milone d'Anglante
    USE Milon d'Angers
Milone family
    USE Malone family
Milrinone
    ₎RC684.M55₎
    UF Dihydromethyloxobipy
        ridinonecarbonitrile
    BT Bipyridine
        Cardiotonic agents
        Nitriles
        Vasodilators
MILS (Information retrieval system)
    ₎Z699.5.M5₎
    UF Mineral Industry Location System of
        the Federal Bureau of Mines
        United States Bureau of Mines
        Mineral Industry Location System
        (MILS)
    BT Information storage and retrieval
        systems—Mines and mineral
        resources
Mils family
    USE Mills family
Milspaw family
    USE Millspaugh family
Milt of fishes
    USE Fishes—Spermatozoa
Milten family
    USE Milton family
Milti (The word)
    BT German language—Old High German,
        750-1050—Etymology
Milton family (Not Subd Geog)
    UF Melton family
        Milten family
Miltzow family (Not Subd Geog)
Miluk Indians
    USE Coquille Indians
Milum family
    USE Milam family
Milvion Bridge, Battle of, 312
    USE Saxa Rubra, Battle of, 312
Milwaukee (Wis.). Bay View
    USE Bay View (Milwaukee, Wis.)
Milwaukee (Wis.). East Side
    USE East Side (Milwaukee, Wis.)
Milwaukee (Wis.). North Point
    USE North Point (Milwaukee, Wis.)
Milwaukee (Wis.). West Milwaukee
    USE West Milwaukee (Milwaukee, Wis.)
Milwaukee (Wis.). Sherman Park
    USE Sherman Park (Milwaukee, Wis.)

Milyeringidae
    USE Gobiidae
Mimallo
    ₎QL561.M5₎
    BT Mimallonidae
Mimallonidae
    ₎QL561.M5₎
    UF Cicinnidae
        Lacosomidae
        Lascosomatidae
        Locosomidae
        Perophoridae
        Protopsychidae
        Ptochopsychidae
        Sack-bearers
    BT Lepidoptera
        Moths
    NT Mimallo
Mimamsa
    ₎B132.M5₎
    BT Hinduism
        Philosophy, Hindu
Mimbreño Indians
    ₎E99.M63₎
    UF Coppermine Apache Indians
    BT Apache Indians
        Indians of North America
Mimbres culture
    USE Mogollon culture
Mimbres Mountains (N.M.)
    BT Mountains—New Mexico
Mimbres River (N.M.)
    BT Rivers—New Mexico
Mime
    ₎PA3029 (Classical)₎
    ₎PA6071.M5 (Latin)₎
    ₎PN2071.G4₎
    BT Acting
        Puppets and puppet-plays
    RT Pantomime
Mimeograph
    ₎Z48₎
    BT Copying processes
        Stencil work
Mimes (May Subd Geog)
    ₎PN1986₎
    BT Actors
        Entertainers
Mimesis in literature
    UF Representation (Literature)
    RT Imitation (in literature)
        Realism in literature
Mimetics, GABA
    USE GABA—Agonists
Mimetidae
    ₎QL458.42.M54₎
    BT Spiders
Mimetite
    ₎QE391.M₎
Mimetomyia
    USE Tripteroides
Mimic theater
    USE Toy theaters
Mimic thrushes
    USE Mimidae
Mimicry
    USE Imitation
Mimicry (Biology)
    ₎QH546₎
    UF Resemblance, Protective
    BT Animal defenses
        Biology
        Color-variation (Biology)
        Evolution
    RT Camouflage (Biology)
        Color of animals
Mimidae
    ₎QL696.P25₎
    UF Mimic thrushes
    BT Passeriformes
    NT Dumetella

Mimidae (Continued)
   Toxostoma
Mimika (Indonesian people)
   BT Ethnology—Indonesia
Mimika (Indonesian people) art
   USE Art, Mimika (Indonesian people)
Mimosa
   [QK495.L52 (Botany)]
   BT Leguminosae
Mimosa glauca
   USE Lead tree
Mimosa pigra
   [QK495.L52 (Botany)]
   [SB615.M46 (Weed)]
   UF Giant sensitive plant
      Sensitive plant, Giant
      Sensitive plant, Thorny
      Thorny sensitive plant
   BT Weeds
Mimosa tree (Albizzia julibrissin)
   USE Silk tree
Mimosine
   UF Aminohydroxyoxopyridinepropionic
         acid
      Leucenine
      Leucenol
   BT Alanine
      Lead tree
      Pyridone
Mimpei pottery
   USE Awaji pottery
Min (Egyptian deity)
   [BL2450.M55]
   UF Amsu (Egyptian deity)
   BT Gods, Egyptian
Min-chia
   USE Pai (Chinese people)
Min-chia language
   USE Pai language
Min-chia literature
   USE Pai literature
Min-kia-tze
   USE Pai (Chinese people)
Min-nan dialects
   USE Southern Min dialects
Min-pei dialects
   USE Northern Min dialects
Min tsu i shu hsin ch'uan chiang
   BT Folk art—Taiwan—Awards
Mina, Portuguese
   USE Ghana—History—Portuguese rule,
         1469-1637
Mina (African people)
   UF Gaingbe (African people)
      Ge (African people)
      Guingbe (African people)
      Popo (African people)
   BT Ethnology—Benin
      Ethnology—Ghana
      Ethnology—Togo
      Ewe (African people)
Mina dialect
   [PL8164.Z9]
   UF Gẽ dialect
      Gen dialect
      Gengbe dialect
      Guen dialect
   BT Ewe language
Mina language
   USE Muna language
Mina proverbs
   USE Proverbs, Mina
Minaco Indians
   USE Mehinacu Indians
Minahasa (Indonesian people)
   BT Ethnology—Indonesia
Minahoshi
   USE Sanka (Social class)
Mīnākṣī (Hindu deity)
   [BL1225.M48]
   UF Meenakshi (Hindu deity)

   BT Gods, Hindu
Minakuchijō (Minakuchi-chō, Japan)
   USE Okayamajō (Minakuchi-chō, Japan)
Minamata disease
   USE Mercury—Toxicology
Minami Manshū Tetsudō
   BT Railroads—China
Minamihanada Iseki (Sakai-shi, Japan)
   USE Minamihanada Site (Sakai-shi, Japan)
Minamihanada Site (Sakai-shi, Japan)
   (Not Subd Geog)
   UF Minamihanada Iseki (Sakai-shi, Japan)
   BT Japan—Antiquities
Minamishinbo Sanmaida Iseki (Kanazawa-shi,
   Japan)
   USE Minamishinbo Sanmaida Site
        (Kanazawa-shi, Japan)
**Minamishinbo Sanmaida Site (Kanazawa-shi,
Japan)** (Not Subd Geog)
   UF Minamishinbo Sanmaida Iseki
        (Kanazawa-shi, Japan)
   BT Japan—Antiquities
Minamishinpo Iseki (Kanazawa-shi, Japan)
   USE Minamishinpo Site (Kanazawa-shi,
        Japan)
Minamishinpo Site (Kanazawa-shi, Japan)
   UF Minamishinpo Iseki (Kanazawa-shi,
        Japan)
   BT Japan—Antiquities
Minamoto family (Not Subd Geog)
Minangkabau (Indonesian people)
   UF Menangkabau (Indonesian people)
   BT Ethnology—Indonesia
   NT English literature—Minangkabau
      influences
   — Rites and ceremonies
      NT Marriage customs and rites,
         Minangkabau
Minangkabau (Indonesian people) architecture
   USE Architecture, Minangkabau
      (Indonesian people)
Minangkabau (Indonesian people) philosophy
   USE Philosophy, Minangkabau (Indonesian
      people)
Minangkabau (Indonesian people) textile
   fabrics
   USE Textile fabrics, Minangkabau
      (Indonesian people)
Minangkabau drama (May Subd Geog)
Minangkabau fiction (May Subd Geog)
Minangkabau folk literature
   USE Folk literature, Minangkabau
Minangkabau folk poetry
   USE Folk poetry, Minangkabau
Minangkabau language
   [PL5415]
   UF Menangkabau language
   BT Malayan languages
   NT Kubuang Tigo Baleh dialect
Minangkabau literature (May Subd Geog)
   BT Indonesia—Literatures
   NT Minangkabau poetry
Minangkabau marriage customs and rites
   USE Marriage customs and rites,
      Minangkabau
Minangkabau orations (May Subd Geog)
Minangkabau poetry (May Subd Geog)
   BT Minangkabau literature
   NT Folk poetry, Minangkabau
Minangkabau proverbs
   USE Proverbs, Minangkabau
Minarets (May Subd Geog)
   [NA2930]
   BT Architecture, Islamic
      Mosques
      Towers
Minaro (Indic people)
   UF Anderkaro (Indic people)
   BT Ethnology—India

Minas (N.S.) Expedition, 1747
   BT United States—History—King
      George's War, 1744-1748
Minas
   BT Caste—India
      Ethnology—India
Minas Basin (N.S.) (Not Subd Geog)
   BT Fundy, Bay of
Minas Canaria S.A. Strike, 1980
   BT Miners—Peru
      Strikes and lockouts—Miners—Peru
      Strikes and lockouts—Peru
Minas Gerais (Brazil)
   — History
   — — Revolution, 1789
      UF Brazil—History—Revolution,
         1789
         Conjuração mineira, Minas
           Gerais (Brazil), 1789
         Inconfidencia mineira, Minas
           Gerais (Brazil), 1789
         Revolta do Tiradentes, Minas
           Gerais (Brazil), 1789
      BT Brazil—History—1763-1821
Minasbate language
   USE Masbateno language
Mince family
   USE Mincey family
Mince meat
   USE Mincemeat
Mincemeat
   [TX389]
   UF Mince meat
Mincemeat, Operation
   USE Operation Mincemeat
Mincey family (Not Subd Geog)
   UF Menshew family
      Mince family
      Mincy family
      Minsey family
Minch Moor (Scotland)
   BT Moors and heaths—Scotland
      Mountains—Scotland
Minck family
   USE Minkler family
Minckler family
   USE Minkler family
Minckley family
   USE Minkler family
Mincopi (Indic people)
   USE Andamanese (Indic people)
Mincy family
   USE Mincey family
Mind
   USE Brain
      Intellect
      Knowledge, Theory of
      Mind and body
      Psychology
      Reason
      Thought and thinking
Mind, Peace of
   USE Peace of mind
MIND (Computer system)
   UF Management of Information through
        Natural Discourse (Computer
        system)
   BT Data base management
      Electronic digital computers—
        Programming
      Information storage and retrieval
        systems
      Linguistics—Data processing
Mind and body
   [BF150-BF171 (Psychology)]
   UF Body, Human—Psychological aspects
      Body and mind
      Body and soul (Philosophy)
      Mind
      Mind-cure
      Somatopsychics

BT Brain
    Dualism
    Medicine
    Philosophical anthropology
    Psychical research
RT Body, Human
    Holistic medicine
    Mental healing
    Parousia (Philosophy)
    Phrenology
    Psychology, Physiological
    Self
SA *subdivision* Psychophysiology *under individual parts of the body, e.g.*
    Heart—Psychophysiology
NT Ability, Influence of age on
    Alexander technique
    Bioenergetic psychotherapy
    Biofeedback training
    Body, Human (Philosophy)
    Body and soul in literature
    Body image
    Consciousness
    Emmanuel movement
    Fatigue, Mental
    Intentionality (Philosophy)
    Medicine, Psychosomatic
    Mental suggestion
    Mind-brain identity theory
    Nervous system
    No-mind (Buddhism)
    Occasionalism
    Other minds (Theory of knowledge)
    Rolfing
    Sleep
    Somatotypes—Psychological aspects
    Temperament
— Early works to 1850
Mind and body therapies *(May Subd Geog)*
  [RC489.M53]
BT Psychotherapy
    Therapeutics
NT Bioenergetic psychotherapy
    Movement therapy
Mind-brain identity theory
  [B105.M55]
UF Brain-mind identity theory
BT Brain
    Identity
    Mind and body
Mind control
  USE Brainwashing
Mind-cure
  USE Animal magnetism
      Christian Science
      Mental healing
      Mind and body
Mind-distorting drugs
  USE Hallucinogenic drugs
Mind Jogger (Game)
BT Psychological games
Mind-only (Buddhism)
  USE Vijñaptimātratā
Mind-reading
  USE Telepathy
Mindanao Island (Philippines)
UF Magindanao Island (Philippines)
    Mindinao Island (Philippines)
BT Islands—Philippines
Mindfulness of breathing
  USE Ānāpānasmṛti
Mindinao Island (Philippines)
  USE Mindanao Island (Philippines)
Mindler family
  USE Mündler family
Mindoro (Philippines)
BT Islands—Philippines
Minds of others (Theory of knowledge)
  USE Other minds (Theory of knowledge)
Minduumo language
  USE Ndumu language

Mine accidents *(May Subd Geog)*
  [TN311-TN319]
UF Mining accidents
BT Disasters
    Industrial accidents
RT Mine rescue work
SA *names of specific mine accidents, e.g.*
    Monongah Mines Disaster,
    Monongah, W.Va., 1907
NT Coal mines and mining—Accidents
    Gas bursts
    Mine explosions
    Mine fires
    Rock bursts
    Safety-lamp
— Liability
  USE Liability for mine accidents
— Prevention
  USE Mine safety
— Kentucky
  NT Scotia Mine Disaster, Oven Fork,
      Ky., 1976
Mine acid drainage
  USE Acid mine drainage
Mine buildings
  [TH4561]
NT Mine shafts
    Tipples
— **Maintenance and repair**
Mine cars
  USE Mine railroads—Cars
Mine communication systems
UF Mine signaling systems
    Telecommunication in mining
BT Signals and signaling
    Telecommunication systems
NT Radio in mining
    Telephone in mining
Mine drainage *(May Subd Geog)*
  [TN321-325]
UF Drainage of mines
BT Drainage
NT Acid mine drainage
    Slimes (Mining)
— **Law and legislation** *(May Subd Geog)*
  BT Drainage laws
    Mining law
Mine dusts
BT Mineral dusts
NT Coal mines and mining—Dust control
    Dust explosion
    Strip mining—Dust control
Mine examination
  [TN272]
UF Examination of mines
RT Mine surveying
    Mine valuation
    Prospecting
Mine explosions *(May Subd Geog)*
  [TN313]
BT Explosions
    Mine accidents
NT Hillcrest Mine Disaster, Hillcrest,
    Alta., 1914
    Safety-lamp
Mine filling *(May Subd Geog)*
  [TN292]
UF Back-filling
    Goafing (Mining)
    Gobbing (Mining)
    Mine stowage
    Packing (Mining)
    Stowage, Mine
BT Mining engineering
Mine fire control
  USE Mine fires—Prevention and control
Mine fire fighting
  USE Mine fires—Prevention and control
Mine fire prevention
  USE Mine fires—Prevention and control

Mine fires *(May Subd Geog)*
  [TN315]
BT Fires
    Mine accidents
NT Combustion, Spontaneous
— Control
  USE Mine fires—Prevention and
      control
— Extinction
  USE Mine fires—Prevention and
      control
— **Prevention and control**
  UF Mine fire control
    Mine fire fighting
    Mine fire prevention
    Mine fires—Control
    Mine fires—Extinction
  BT Fire extinction
    Fire prevention
  NT Stench fire-warning system in
      mines
Mine gases *(May Subd Geog)*
  [TN305-TN306]
UF Gases in mines
BT Gases, Asphyxiating and poisonous
NT Coalbed methane
    Fire-damp
    Gas bursts
    Hydrogen sulphide
    Safety-lamp
Mine haulage
  [TN331-342]
BT Mining machinery
NT Gasoline locomotives
    Mine railroads
    Shuttle cars (Mine haulage)
    Tipples
    Winches
— **Safety appliances**
  BT Mine safety
Mine hoisting
  [TN339-340]
BT Hoisting machinery
NT Man-engines
— **Electric driving**
— **Safety appliances**
  [TN339-340]
  BT Mine safety
Mine inspection *(May Subd Geog)*
  [TN]
UF Inspection of mines
    Mines and mineral resources—
      Inspection
— **Data processing**
  NT MIDAS (Computer system)
Mine inspection data analysis system
  USE MIDAS (Computer system)
Mine Iseki (Yasu-machi, Fukuoka-ken, Japan)
  USE Mine Site (Yasu-machi, Fukuoka-ken,
      Japan)
Mine lighting
  [TN307-9]
BT Electricity in mining
NT Electric lamps, Portable
Mine management
  [TN274]
BT Mineral industries
RT Mining engineering
Mine maps
  [TN273]
UF Maps, Mine
BT Maps
Mine planting
  USE Mines, Military
Mine pumps
  [TN325]
BT Mining machinery
    Pumping machinery
Mine railroads *(May Subd Geog)*
  [TN336]
UF Railroads, Mine

Mine railroads *(Continued)*
  BT Mine haulage
     Railroads
     Railroads, Industrial
     Railroads, Local and light
  — Cars
     [TN342]
     UF Mine cars
        Ore cars
     NT Dump cars
  — **Electronic equipment**
     [TN336]
  — **Power supply**
     BT Electric power
  — **Track**
     [TN336]
  — **Trains**
     [TN336]
  — — **Dynamics**
     [TN336]
Mine rescue work *(May Subd Geog)*
  [TN297]
  BT Rescue work
  RT Mine accidents
  — **Equipment and supplies**
     NT Self-contained self-rescuer (Mine
        rescue equipment)
Mine roof bolting
  UF Bolting, Mine roof
     Skyhooks
  BT Ground control (Mining)
     Mine roof control
     Rock bolts
  RT Mine timbering
  NT Gypsum-bonded mine roof bolts
     Mine roof bolts, Resin
Mine roof bolts, Resin
  UF Bolts, Resin mine roof
     Resin bolts, Mine roof
     Resined mine roof bolts
     Roof bolts, Resin mine
  BT Mine roof bolting
     Rock bolts
Mine roof control
  UF Roof control, Mine
     Strata control in mines
  BT Ground control (Mining)
     Rock mechanics
  NT Kettlebottoms (Mining)
     Mine roof bolting
Mine safety *(May Subd Geog)*
  UF Mine accidents—Prevention
     Mining engineering—Safety measures
     Mining safety
  BT Industrial safety
     Mineral industries—Safety measures
  SA *subdivision* Safety measures *under
     specific types of mining operations,
     e.g.* Coal mines and mining—Safety
     measures
  NT Coalbed methane drainage
     Mine haulage—Safety appliances
     Mine hoisting—Safety appliances
     Petroleum industry and trade—Safety
        measures
     Quarries and quarrying—Safety
        measures
  — **Equipment and supplies**
     UF Mine safety appliances
     NT Geophone
        Mining machinery—Blind-area
           viewers
        Safety-lamp
  — **Law and legislation** *(May Subd Geog)*
     UF Mineral industries—Safety
        regulations
        Mining engineering—Safety
           regulations

     BT Industrial safety—Law and
        legislation
        Mining law
        Safety regulations
     SA *subdivision* Safety regulations
        *under specific types of mining
        operations, e.g.* Coal miners and
        mining—Safety regulations
     NT Explosives—Law and legislation
Mine safety appliances
  USE Mine safety—Equipment and supplies
Mine sanitation *(May Subd Geog)*
  [TN295-309]
  BT Industrial hygiene
     Sanitation
  — **Law and legislation** *(May Subd Geog)*
     BT Mining law
Mine shafts
  BT Mine buildings
     Shafts (Excavations)
  NT Raise drilling
     Shaft sinking
Mine signaling systems
  USE Mine communication systems
Mine Site (Yasu-machi, Fukuoka-ken, Japan)
  UF Mine Iseki (Yasu-machi, Fukuoka-ken,
     Japan)
  BT Japan—Antiquities
Mine soils *(May Subd Geog)*
  UF Mine-spoil soils
     Soils, Mine
  BT Soils
Mine-spoil soils
  USE Mine soils
Mine stench fire-warning system
  USE Stench fire-warning system in mines
Mine stowage
  USE Mine filling
Mine subsidences *(May Subd Geog)*
  [TN319]
  UF Mining subsidences
  BT Subsidences (Earth movements)
  NT Ground control (Mining)
Mine supports, Concrete
  USE Concrete mine supports
Mine supports, Reinforced concrete
  USE Concrete mine supports
Mine surveying
  [TN273]
  UF Mineral land surveying
  BT Mining engineering
     Prospecting
     Surveying
  RT Mine examination
Mine sweepers *(May Subd Geog)*
  UF Mine sweeping
     Minesweepers
  BT Mines, Submarine
Mine sweeping
  USE Mine sweepers
Mine throwers
  USE Trench mortars
Mine timbering
  [TN289]
  UF Timbering of mines
  BT Ground control (Mining)
     Mining engineering
     Wood poles
  RT Mine roof bolting
  NT Pit-wood
Mine tools
  [TN345-7]
  BT Tools
Mine valuation *(May Subd Geog)*
  [TN272]
  RT Mine examination
     Prospecting
Mine ventilation
  [TN301-TN303]
  BT Ventilation
  NT Concrete stoppings (Mining)

  — **Equipment and supplies**
     NT Brattices (Mining)
Mine water
  [TN318]
  UF Water in mines
  BT Water, Underground
Mine wives
  USE Miners' wives
Mineck family
  USE Minnick family
Miner family
  USE Minor family
Mineral aggregates
  USE Aggregates (Building materials)
Mineral collecting
  USE Mineralogy—Collectors and collecting
Mineral content of food
  USE Food—Mineral content
Mineral cycle (Biogeochemistry)
  (May Subd Geog)
  BT Biogeochemical cycles
Mineral dressing
  USE Ore-dressing
Mineral dusts *(May Subd Geog)*
  UF Rock dusts
  BT Dust
  NT Asbestos dust
     Mine dusts
     Mineral industries—Dust control
     Quartz dust
Mineral impurities in coal
  USE Coal—Mineral inclusions
Mineral inclusions in coal
  USE Coal—Mineral inclusions
Mineral industries *(May Subd Geog)*
  [HD9506-HD9585 (Economics)]
  [TN (Mining engineering)]
    This is a general heading, covering technical and
  economic works on mining, metallurgy, and minerals
  of economic value. Works dealing only with mining
  are entered under Mining engineering and those deal-
  ing only with metallurgy are entered under Metallur-
  gy. Works on mining and metallurgy of specific met-
  als are entered under names of metals, e.g. Lead
  mines and mining, Lead—Metallurgy.
    Descriptive and statistical works are entered
  under Mines and mineral resources.
  UF Metal industries
     Mines and mining
     Mining
     Mining industry
  BT Technology
  NT Ceramic industries
     Ceramics
     Cobalt industry
     Mine management
     Refractories industry
  — **Automation**
  — **Bibliography**
     NT Mining literature
  — **Capital productivity**
  — Collective bargaining
     USE Collective bargaining—Mining
        industry
  — Collective labor agreements
     USE Collective labor agreements—
        Mining industry
  — **Defense measures**
     BT Factories—Protection
        War damage, Industrial
  — **Dictionaries**
     [TN9-10]
  — **Directories**
     [TN12]
     UF Mines and mineral resources—
        Directories
        Mining directories
        Mining engineering—Directories
  — **Dust control**
     BT Mineral dusts
  — **Environmental aspects**
     (May Subd Geog)

2412

Mineralogy, Optical
   USE Optical mineralogy
Mineralogy in archaeology
   (May Subd Geog)
     UF Archaeological mineralogy
     BT Archaeology—Methodology
Minerals
   USE Mineralogy
         Mines and mineral resources
Minerals, Artificial
   USE Artificial minerals
Minerals, Carbonate
   USE Carbonate minerals
Minerals, Clay
   USE Clay minerals
Minerals, Dietary
   USE Minerals in nutrition
Minerals, Energy
   USE Energy minerals
Minerals, Heavy
   USE Heavy minerals
Minerals, Industrial
   USE Industrial minerals
Minerals, Nonfuel
   USE Nonfuel minerals
Minerals, Nonmetallic
   USE Nonmetallic minerals
Minerals, Radioactive
   USE Radioactive substances
Minerals, Refractive index of
   USE Refractive index of minerals
Minerals, Rock-forming
   USE Rock-forming minerals
Minerals, Silicate
   USE Silicate minerals
Minerals, Sulphide
   USE Sulphide minerals
Minerals, Synthetic
   USE Artificial minerals
Minerals availability system
   USE MAS (Computer system)
Minerals data system of the U.S. Geological
   Survey
   USE MDS (Computer system)
Minerals in animal nutrition
   (May Subd Geog)
   [SF98.M5]
     UF Feeds—Mineral content
     NT Salt in animal nutrition
         Salt licks
Minerals in food
   USE Minerals in nutrition
Minerals in human nutrition
     BT Nutrition
Minerals in nutrition
     UF Minerals, Dietary
         Minerals in food
     BT Nutrition
     NT Food—Mineral content
         Mineral metabolism
Minerals in pharmacology *(May Subd Geog)*
     UF Materia medica, Mineral
     BT Mineralogy
         Pharmacology
Minerals in plants
   USE Plants—Assimilation
Minerals in rabbinical literature
     BT Rabbinical literature
Minerals in soil
   USE Soil mineralogy
Minerals in the Bible
   [BS667]
     UF Bible—Minerals
         Gems in the Bible
         Precious stones in the Bible
     BT Gems—Religious aspects
         Mineralogy—Religious aspects
         Mines and mineral resources—
            Religious aspects
         Nature in the Bible

Minerals in the body
     BT Biological chemistry
         Metabolism
     RT Mineral metabolism
     SA *names of specific minerals in the body,*
         e.g. Calcium in the body; Iron in
         the body
     NT Biomineralization
         Trace elements in the body
Minerisporites
   [QE996]
     BT Spores (Botany), Fossil
Miners *(May Subd Geog)*
   [HD8039.M6-HD8039.M7 (Labor)]
     NT Coal miners
         Collective bargaining—Mining industry
         Collective labor agreements—Mining
            industry
         Copper miners
         Diamond miners
         Gold miners
         Graphite miners
         Iron miners
         Lead miners
         Mercury miners
         Mica miners
         Minority miners
         Phosphate miners
         Potash miners
         Silver miners
         Strikes and lockouts—Miners
         Strikes and lockouts—Zinc mining
         Sulphur miners
         Tin miners
         Trade-unions—Miners
         Wages—Miners
         Women miners
   — **Songs and music**
     [M1977.M5 (Music)]
     [ML3780 (Musical history)]
     [PS595.M5 (American literature)]
     BT Labor and laboring classes—Songs
         and music
   — **Greenland**
     NT Greenex (Firm) Strike, 1977
   — **Peru**
     NT Minas Canaria S.A. Strike, 1980
Miners' consumption
   USE Miners' phthisis
Miners family
   USE Minor family
Miners in motion pictures
   [PN1995.9.M54]
     BT Moving-pictures
Miners' nystagmus
   USE Nystagmus
Miners' phthisis *(May Subd Geog)*
   [HD7269.M6-61]
     UF Miners' consumption
         Phthisis, Miners'
     BT Lungs—Dust diseases
         Occupational diseases
         Tuberculosis
**Miners' Strike, Mineral del Monte, Mexico,
1766**
     BT Strikes and lockouts—Miners—Mexico
Miners' wives *(May Subd Geog)*
     UF Mine wives
     BT Wives
Minerva (Roman deity)
   [BL820.M6]
     BT Gods, Roman
         Mythology, Roman
     RT Athena (Greek deity)
Minervois (France)
     UF Monts du Minervois (France)
Mines, Military
   [UG490]
     UF Booby traps (Military science)
         Military mines
         Mine planting

     BT Attack and defense (Military science)
         Coast defenses
         Explosives
         Explosives, Military
         Fortification
         Intrenchments
         Military art and science
         Military engineering
         Obstacles (Military science)
         Torpedoes
         Tunnels
     RT Blasting
     NT Mines, Submarine
         Sapping
Mines, Submarine *(May Subd Geog)*
   [UG490-497]
     UF Submarine mines
     BT Anti-submarine warfare
         Mines, Military
     RT Submarine warfare
     NT Degaussing
         Midget submarines
         Mine sweepers
Mines and mineral resources
   (May Subd Geog)
     [TN]
     Here are entered descriptive and statistical works.
   Cf. note under Mineral industries.
     UF Mineral resources
         Minerals
         Mines and mining
         Mining
     BT Concessions
         Geology, Economic
         Natural resources
         Ores
     SA *specific types of mines and mining,*
         e.g. Coal mines and mining, Gold
         mines and mining; *and headings*
         beginning with the word Mine
     NT Asbestos mines and mining
         Ceramic materials
         Chalk mines and mining
         Coal mines and mining
         Energy minerals
         Gas fields
         Gypsum mines and mining
         Industrial minerals
         Marine mineral resources
         Mineral lands
         Mineral resources conservation
         Mineral resources in submerged lands
         Mining engineering
         Mining law
         Nonfuel minerals
         Nonmetallic minerals
         Ore-deposits
         Ores—Sampling and estimation
         Precious metals
         Prospecting
         Raw materials
         Rutile mines and mining
         Sapphire mines and mining
         Trona mines and mining
         Zircon mines and mining
   — **Computer programs**
     NT NCHARAN (Computer program)
   — **Data processing**
     NT MAS (Computer system)
         MDS (Computer system)
         MuPROSPECTOR (Computer
            system)
   — Directories
     USE Mineral industries—Directories
   — Education
     USE Mining schools and education
   — **Electric equipment**
   — Exhibitions
     USE Mineral industries—Exhibitions
   — **Government ownership**
     (May Subd Geog)

[HD9506-9559]
  UF Government ownership of mines
— — **Law and legislation**
      (May Subd Geog)
      BT Mining law
— **History**
— Inspection
      USE Mine inspection
— Law
      USE Mining law
— **Religious aspects**
      NT Minerals in the Bible
— **Research** (May Subd Geog)
— — **Law and legislation**
      (May Subd Geog)
— Societies, etc.
      USE Mineral industries—Societies, etc.
— Study and teaching
      USE Mining schools and education
— Tariff
      USE Tariff on minerals
— **Taxation** (May Subd Geog)
      [HJ4169]
      BT Real property tax
          Severance tax
— — **Law and legislation**
      (May Subd Geog)
— **Arkansas**
      NT Sparta Mine (Ark.)
— **Nevada**
      NT Comstock Lode (Nev.)
— **North Carolina**
      NT Lee Creek Mine (N.C.)
— **Washington (State)**
      NT Holden Mine (Wash.)
Mines and mineral resources (in numismatics)
      (May Subd Geog)
      [CJ161.M]
      BT Numismatics
Mines and mineral resources in art
Mines and mining
      USE Mineral industries
          Mines and mineral resources
          Mining engineering
Minesweepers
      USE Mine sweepers
Ming ch'i
      [GT3238 (Chinese burial customs)]
      [NK4165 (Chinese art objects)]
      UF Chinese tomb figures
          Statuettes
      BT Figurines
          Idols and images
      RT Ushabti
— **Private collections** (May Subd Geog)
Ming porcelain (May Subd Geog)
      [NK4565.5]
      UF Porcelain, Ming
      BT Porcelain, Chinese
          Porcelain, Chinese—Ming-Manchu
          (Ch'ing) dynasties, 1368-1912
— **Expertising**
Ming Tombs (China)
      [DS793.S]
      UF 13 Tombs (China)
          Shih-san-ling (China)
          Shisan Ling (China)
          Shisanling (China)
          Thirteen Tombs (China)
          Valley of the Ming Tombs (China)
      BT Tombs—China
Mingan Islands (Québec)
      UF Isles de Mingan (Québec)
      BT Islands—Québec (Province)
Mingin
      UF Urinary trypsin inhibitor
      BT Enzyme inhibitors
          Trypsin
Mingo Indians
      [E99.M64]
      BT Indians of North America

NT Iroquois Indians
Mingos family
      USE Menges family
Mingrelian language
      [PK9141]
      BT Kartvelian languages
Mingrelians
      UF Megrelians
      BT Ethnology—Caucasus
Mingus family
      USE Menges family
Minhag Ari
      USE Judaism—Ari rite
Minhag Frankfurt
      USE Judaism—Frankfurt rite
Minhag ha-Romanyoṭim
      USE Judaism—Romaniot rite
Minhag Ḥasidim
      USE Judaism—Hasidic rite
Minhag Sefarad
      USE Judaism—Sephardic rite
Minhagim
      USE Judaism—Customs and practices
Minhasa language
      USE Bolaang Mongondow language
Minhassa language
      USE Bolaang Mongondow language
Mini automobiles
      [TL215.M]
      UF Austin Mini automobiles
          Morris Mini Minor automobile
      BT BLMC automobiles
      NT Mini-Cooper automobiles
Mini computers
      USE Minicomputers
Mini-Cooper automobiles
      [TL215.M]
      UF Austin Mini-Cooper automobiles
          Morris Mini-Cooper automobiles
      BT Mini automobiles
Mini-mills, Steel
      USE Steel minimills
Mini-Numerical Taxonomy System (Computer
      program)
      USE MINTS (Computer program)
MINI-REGRESSION (Computer program)
      [QA278.2]
Mini-storage facilities
      USE Self-service storage facilities
Mini-warehouses
      USE Self-service storage facilities
Minianka (African people)
      BT Ethnology—Ivory Coast
          Ethnology—Mali
          Senufo (African people)
Minianka dialect
      [PL8658.95.M]
      UF Bamana dialect (Senufo)
          Bambara dialect (Senufo)
      BT Senufo language
Minianka proverbs
      USE Proverbs, Minianka
Miniature arms
      [NK8475.A7]
      BT Arms and armor
          Military miniatures
          Miniature objects
Miniature beer bottles
      USE Miniature bottles, Beer
Miniature beer cans
      USE Miniature cans, Beer
Miniature book-plates
      USE Book-plates, Miniature
Miniature books (May Subd Geog)
      [Z1033.M6]
          Here are entered works on books 10 centimeters
      or less in both height and width. Actual specimens of
      such books are entered under Miniature books—
      Specimens, a form heading assigned without geo-
      graphic subdivision.

UF Bibliography—Microscopic and
          miniature editions
          Books—Microscopic editions
          Books—Miniature editions
          Books, Microscopic
          Books, Miniature
          Diamond editions
          Editions, Diamond
          Microscopic books
          Microscopic editions
          Miniature editions
      BT Books—Format
          Miniature objects
      RT Books—Sizes
          Pocket editions
      NT Bible—Thumb Bibles
— **Specimens**
          Here are entered actual specimens of books
      10 centimeters or less in both height and width.
      This form heading is assigned without geograph-
      ic subdivision. Works on such books are entered
      under Miniature books.
Miniature bottles
      BT Bottles
          Miniature objects
Miniature bottles, Beer (May Subd Geog)
      [NK8475.B6]
      UF Beer miniature bottles
          Miniature beer bottles
      BT Beer bottles
Miniature bottles, Liquor (May Subd Geog)
      [NK8475.B6]
      UF Liquor miniature bottles
          Miniature liquor bottles
      BT Liquor bottles
Miniature cameras (May Subd Geog)
      UF Subminiature cameras
          Ultra-miniature cameras
      BT Cameras
      SA individual makes of miniature cameras,
          e.g. Bolsey camera, Retina camera
      NT 35mm cameras
Miniature cans (May Subd Geog)
      UF Cans, Miniature
Miniature cans, Beer (May Subd Geog)
      UF Beer miniature cans
          Miniature beer cans
      BT Beer cans
Miniature car racing
      USE Model car racing
Miniature cases (May Subd Geog)
      UF Cases, Miniature
      BT Miniature objects
          Picture frames and framing
Miniature cases, American, [etc.]
      (May Subd Geog)
Miniature computers
      USE Minicomputers
Miniature craft
      [TT178]
      UF Miniatures
      BT Handicraft
          Models and modelmaking
      RT Miniature objects
      NT Miniature flower arrangement
Miniature dachshund
      [SF429.D255]
      BT Dachshund
Miniature decorative design
      [NK1520]
      UF Decorative design, Miniature
      BT Decoration and ornament
Miniature dolls (May Subd Geog)
      UF Doll house dolls
      BT Dolls
          Miniature objects
Miniature editions
      USE Miniature books
Miniature electric railroads
      USE Electric railroads, Miniature

Miniature electrodes
USE Microelectrodes
Miniature electronic equipment
[TK7870]
UF Electronic equipment, Miniature
Microminiaturization (Electronics)
Miniaturization (Electronics)
Subminiature electronic equipment
Subminiaturization (Electronics)
BT Electronic apparatus and appliances
Electronics
RT Microelectronics
SA *names of instruments, e.g.* Telemeter
(Physiological apparatus)
NT Minicomputers
Printed circuits
Transistor radios
— **Bonding**
— **Welding**
Miniature fan palm
USE Rhapis excelsa
Miniature flower arrangement
(May Subd Geog)
[SB449.5.M56]
BT Flower arrangement
Miniature craft
Miniature objects
Miniature furniture *(May Subd Geog)*
UF Furniture—Models
BT Furniture
Miniature objects
NT Doll furniture
Miniature gardens
USE Gardens, Miniature
Miniature glassware
[NK8475.G55]
BT Glassware
Miniature objects
Miniature golf
USE Golf, Miniature
Miniature heraldic porcelain
(May Subd Geog)
UF Heraldic models
Heraldic porcelain, Miniature
BT Miniature objects
Porcelain
World War, 1914-1918—Collectibles
Miniature horses
[SF293.M56]
BT Horse breeds
Horses
Miniature houses
USE Doll-houses
Miniature lamps
[NK8475.L3]
BT Lamps
Miniature objects
Miniature liquor bottles
USE Miniature bottles, Liquor
Miniature mosaics *(May Subd Geog)*
[NK8475.M66]
BT Mosaics
Miniature objects *(May Subd Geog)*
[NK492 (Art)]
UF Miniatures
Objects, Miniature
Tiny objects
BT Art objects
RT Miniature craft
Toys
SA *subdivision* Models *under names of
objects, mainly mechanical, e.g.*
Aeroplanes—Models
NT Architectural models
Doll-houses
Electric railroads, Miniature
Gardens, Miniature
Machinery—Models
Military miniatures
Miniature arms
Miniature books

Miniature bottles
Miniature cases
Miniature dolls
Miniature flower arrangement
Miniature furniture
Miniature glassware
Miniature heraldic porcelain
Miniature lamps
Miniature plants
Miniature porcelain
Miniature pottery
Miniature quilts
Miniature rooms
Miniature silverwork
Miniature tableware
Miniature wood-carving
Models (Patents)
Models and modelmaking
Sebastian miniatures
Ship models
Souvenir buildings
Miniature orchids *(May Subd Geog)*
[QK495.O64 (Botany)]
[SB409 (Culture)]
BT Miniature plants
Orchids
Miniature painters *(May Subd Geog)*
UF Miniaturists
Painters, Miniature
Miniature painting *(May Subd Geog)*
[N7616 (Portraits)]
[ND1330-ND1337 (Painting)]
UF Miniature paintings
BT Art
Illumination of books and manuscripts
Painting
Portraits
RT Portrait painting
NT Icon painting
Portrait miniatures
— **Reproductions, facsimiles, etc.**
[N7616]
Miniature painting, Celtic, [**Indic, etc.**]
(May Subd Geog)
Miniature painting, French
(May Subd Geog)
UF French miniature painting
Miniature painting, Indic *(May Subd Geog)*
UF Indic miniature painting
NT Guler painting
Malwa painting
Mewar painting
Miniature painting, Islamic
(May Subd Geog)
UF Islamic miniature painting
Miniature painting, Muslim
Muslim miniature painting
Miniature painting, Jaina *(May Subd Geog)*
UF Jaina miniature painting
Miniature painting, Medieval
(May Subd Geog)
UF Medieval miniature painting
Miniature painting, Mogul
(May Subd Geog)
UF Mogul miniature painting
Miniature painting, Muslim
USE Miniature painting, Islamic
Miniature painting, Rococo
(May Subd Geog)
UF Rococo miniature painting
Miniature painting, Russian
(May Subd Geog)
UF Russian miniature painting
Miniature painting, Thai *(May Subd Geog)*
UF Thai miniature painting
Miniature painting, Turkish
(May Subd Geog)
UF Turkish miniature painting
Miniature paintings
USE Miniature painting

Miniature pinschers
[SF429.M56]
UF Pinschers, Miniature
BT Dog breeds
Toy dogs
Miniature plants
UF Miniature trees
Plants, Miniature
BT Glass gardens
Miniature objects
Plants, Ornamental
RT Gardens, Miniature
NT Bonsai
Midget vegetables
Miniature orchids
Miniature porcelain *(May Subd Geog)*
[NK8475.P65]
BT Miniature objects
Porcelain
Miniature portraits
USE Portrait miniatures
Miniature pottery *(May Subd Geog)*
[NK8475.P65]
BT Miniature objects
Pottery
Miniature printing *(May Subd Geog)*
BT Printing
Prints
Miniature quilts *(May Subd Geog)*
BT Miniature objects
Quilts
Miniature railroads
USE Railroads, Miniature
Miniature rooms *(May Subd Geog)*
UF Rooms in miniature
BT Architectural models
Miniature objects
Miniature roses
[SB411]
BT Roses
Miniature schnauzers
BT Schnauzers
Miniature sheets (Philately)
USE Postage-stamps—Miniature sheets
Miniature silverwork *(May Subd Geog)*
BT Miniature objects
Silverwork
Miniature stūpas
USE Stūpas, Miniature
Miniature tableware
[NK8475.T33]
BT Miniature objects
Tableware
Miniature theaters
USE Theaters, Miniature
Miniature trees
USE Bonsai
Miniature plants
Miniature vegetables
USE Midget vegetables
Miniature wood-carving *(May Subd Geog)*
[NK8475.W66]
BT Miniature objects
Wood-carving
Miniatures
USE Miniature craft
Miniature objects
Miniatures, Military
USE Military miniatures
Miniatures (Illumination of books and
manuscripts)
USE Illumination of books and manuscripts
Miniaturists
USE Miniature painters
Miniaturization (Electronics)
USE Miniature electronic equipment
Minibike racing *(May Subd Geog)*
[GV1060.125]
BT Minibikes
Motorcycle racing

Minibikes
  [TL443]
  BT Bicycles
    Motorcycles
  NT Minibike racing
Minica automobile
Minich family
  USE Minnick family
Minick family
  USE Minnick family
Minicks family
  USE Minnick family
Minicomputers *(May Subd Geog)*
  UF Mini computers
    Miniature computers
    Small computers
  BT Electronic digital computers
    Miniature electronic equipment
  NT HP/1000 (Computer)
    Lockheed SUE (Computer)
    Microcomputers
    Microprocessors
    Network Access Machine (Computer)
    PDP computers
    Visible record computers
— **Circuits**
    BT Electronic circuits
— **Library applications**
    UF Libraries and minicomputers
      Library applications of
        minicomputers
    BT Library science—Data processing
— **Programming**
    BT Programming (Electronic
      computers)
    NT Csmini (Computer system)
      ICGS (Electronic computer
        system)
      Lockheed SUE (Computer)—
        Programming
      PDP-11 (Computer)—
        Programming
— **Purchasing**
Miniconjou Indians
  [E99.M642]
  UF Minneconjon Indians
  BT Dakota Indians
    Indians of North America
    Teton Indians
MINICS project *(May Subd Geog)*
  [Z699.4.M23]
  UF Minimal-Input Cataloguing System
  BT Libraries—Automation
Minicycles
  [TL443]
  BT Bicycles
    Motorcycles
Minidoka Relocation Center (Idaho :
  Concentration camp) *(Not Subd Geog)*
  BT Concentration camps—Idaho
    Japanese Americans—Evacuation and
      relocation, 1942-1945
    World War, 1939-1945—Japanese
      Americans
Minima
  USE Maxima and minima
Minimal art *(May Subd Geog)*
  [N6494.M5]
  UF Art, Minimal
    Systematic painting
  BT Art, Abstract
    Art, Modern—20th century
  NT Serial art
Minimal brain dysfunction
  (May Subd Geog)
  [RC394.M55]
  UF Brain dysfunction, Minimal
  BT Brain damage
Minimal brain dysfunction in children
  (May Subd Geog)
  [RJ496.B7]

  UF Brain dysfunction in children, Minimal
  BT Brain-damaged children
    Children—Diseases
  RT Learning disabilities
  NT Attention deficit disorders
    Hyperactive child syndrome
Minimal competency tests
  USE Competency based educational tests
Minimal-Input Cataloguing System
  USE MINICS project
Minimal music *(May Subd Geog)*
  UF Meditative music
    Music, Minimal
    Repetitive music
    Systematic music
  BT Music
Minimal pair (Linguistics)
  UF Contrastive pair (Linguistics)
  BT Linguistic analysis (Linguistics)
    Linguistics
    Phonemics
Minimal principles
  USE Variational principles
Minimal sculpture *(May Subd Geog)*
  UF Primary structures
    Sculpture, Minimal
  BT Constructivism (Art)
    Sculpture, Modern—20th century
Minimal submanifolds
  USE Submanifolds, Minimal
Minimal surfaces
  USE Surfaces, Minimal
Minimax approximation
  USE Chebyshev approximation
Minimills, Steel
  USE Steel minimills
Minimum drinking age
  USE Drinking age
Minimum income
  USE Income maintenance programs
Minimum temperature forecasting
  USE Temperature forecasting, Minimum
Minimum wage
  USE Wages—Minimum wage
Minimum weight construction
  USE Lightweight construction
Mining
  USE Mineral industries
    Mines and mineral resources
    Mining engineering
Mining, Electric
  USE Electricity in mining
Mining, Longwall
  USE Longwall mining
Mining, Ocean
  USE Ocean mining
Mining, Photography in
  USE Photography in mining
Mining accidents
  USE Mine accidents
Mining claims *(May Subd Geog)*
  UF Annual assessment work on mining
    claims
    Assessment work on mining claims
    Lode claims
    Placer claims
  BT Mining law
Mining companies
  USE Mining corporations
Mining corporations *(May Subd Geog)*
  UF Mining companies
  BT Corporation law
    Corporations
    Mining law
Mining courts *(May Subd Geog)*
  BT Courts of special jurisdiction
    Mining law
Mining directories
  USE Mineral industries—Directories
Mining districts *(May Subd Geog)*
  BT Special districts

— **California**
    NT Los Burros Mining District (Calif.)
Mining education
  USE Mining schools and education
Mining engineering *(May Subd Geog)*
  [TN]
  Here are entered works dealing only with mining.
  Cf. note under Mineral industries.
  UF Engineering, Mining
    Mines and mining
    Mining
  BT Civil engineering
    Engineering
    Mines and mineral resources
    Underground areas
  RT Electricity in mining
    Mine management
  NT Blasting
    Borehole mining
    Boring
    Ground control (Mining)
    Hydraulic mining
    In situ processing (Mining)
    Lasers in mining
    Mine filling
    Mine surveying
    Mine timbering
    Mining machinery
    Moving-pictures in mining
    Ocean mining
    Petroleum engineering
    Photography in mining
    Pillaring (Mining)
    Plastics in mining
    Radio in mining
    Rock bursts
    Rock-drills
    Rock pressure
    Shaft sinking
    Solution mining
    Strip mining
    Tunneling
— **Cold weather conditions**
— **Directories**
    USE Mineral industries—Directories
— **Environmental aspects**
    USE Mineral industries—
      Environmental aspects
— **Patents**
    NT Coal mines and mining—Patents
— **Safety measures**
    USE Mine safety
— **Safety regulations**
    USE Mine safety—Law and legislation
— **Societies, etc.**
    USE Mineral industries—Societies, etc.
— **Study and teaching**
    USE Mining schools and education
Mining engineers *(May Subd Geog)*
  [TN139-140]
  BT Engineers
Mining geology
  [TN260]
  UF Geology, Mining
  BT Geology, Economic
Mining industry
  USE Mineral industries
Mining journalism
  USE Journalism, Mining
Mining law *(May Subd Geog)*
  [TN215-255]
  UF Law, Mining
    Mines and mineral resources—Law
    Subsoil rights
  BT Concessions
    Labor laws and legislation
    Mines and mineral resources
    Power resources—Law and legislation
    Real property
  NT Coal mines and mining—Law and
    legislation

2417

Mining law *(Continued)*
        Indians of North America—Mines and
           mining—Law and legislation
        Iron mines and mining—Law and
           legislation
        Liability for mine accidents
        Marble industry and trade—Law and
           legislation
        Mine drainage—Law and legislation
        Mine safety—Law and legislation
        Mine sanitation—Law and legislation
        Mines and mineral resources—
           Government ownership—Law and
           legislation
        Mining claims
        Mining corporations
        Mining courts
        Mining leases
        Mining partnership
        Ocean mining—Law and legislation
        Petroleum law and legislation
        Phosphate mines and mining—Law
           and legislation
        Quarries and quarrying—Law and
           legislation
        Radioactive substances—Law and
           legislation
        Salt mines and mining—Law and
           legislation
        Strip mining—Law and legislation
        Subsidences (Earth movements)
        Uranium mines and mining—Law and
           legislation
  — Colonies
     USE Mining law, Colonial
  — Conflict of laws
     USE Conflict of laws—Mining law
Mining law, Colonial
    Here are entered general and comparative works
only. Works on mining law of the colonies of an
individual country are entered under the heading
Mining law with subdivision ⌐country¬—Colonies.
Works dealing with a specific colony are entered
under the same heading, subdivided by the name of
the colony.
  UF Colonial mining law
     Colonies—Mining law
     Mining law—Colonies
Mining law (Roman law)
Mining leases *(May Subd Geog)*
  BT Leases
     Mining law
  NT Coal leases
     Oil and gas leases
     Phosphate leases
Mining libraries *(May Subd Geog)*
  UF Libraries, Mining
  BT Technical libraries
Mining literature
  BT Mineral industries—Bibliography
     Mineral industries—History
Mining machinery
  ⌐TN345-7¬
  BT Conveying machinery
     Mining engineering
  RT Hoisting machinery
  NT Electricity in mining
     Mine haulage
     Mine pumps
     Peat machinery
     Petroleum industry and trade—
       Equipment and supplies
     Rock-drills
     Rock splitters (Machines)
  — Appraisal
     USE Mining machinery—Valuation
  — Blind-area viewers
     ⌐TN345¬
     UF Blind-area viewers for mining
       machinery
       Viewers, Blind-area, for mining
       machinery

     BT Mine safety—Equipment and
       supplies
       Optical instruments
  — Cutter bars
     UF Bar cutters of mining machinery
       Cutter bars of mining machinery
     BT Cutting machines
       Mining machinery—Parts
  — Dynamics
  — Electric driving
  — Electric equipment
     BT Electricity in mining
  — Hydraulic drive
  — Parts
     BT Machine parts
     NT Mining machinery—Cutter bars
  — Testing
  — Transmission devices
     ⌐TN345¬
     BT Gearing
  — Valuation
     ⌐TN345¬
     UF Mining machinery—Appraisal
Mining machinery industry
  (May Subd Geog)
Mining of marine mineral resources
  USE Ocean mining
Mining partnership *(May Subd Geog)*
  BT Mining law
     Partnership
Mining safety
  USE Mine safety
Mining schools and education
  (May Subd Geog)
  ⌐TN165-213¬
  UF Education, Mining
     Mines and mineral resources—
       Education
     Mines and mineral resources—Study
       and teaching
     Mining education
     Mining engineering—Study and
       teaching
  BT Education
     Schools
     Technical education
     Vocational education
  — Law and legislation *(May Subd Geog)*
Mining subsidences
  USE Mine subsidences
Minisink (N.Y.), Battle of, 1779
  ⌐E241.M6¬
  BT United States—History—Revolution,
     1775-1783—Campaigns
Minisink Indians
  ⌐E99.M¬
  UF Minusing Indians
  BT Algonquian Indians
     Indians of North America
MINISIS (Information retrieval system)
  ⌐Z699.4.I19¬
  BT Automatic indexing
     Information storage and retrieval
       systems—Archival material
Ministerial responsibility *(May Subd Geog)*
  ⌐JF341¬
  UF Countersignature (Constitutional law)
     Responsibility, Ministerial
  BT Cabinet officers
     Cabinet system
     Legislative bodies
     Monarchy
     Political science
     Representative government and
       representation
  NT Interpellation
     Official secrets
Ministerials
  ⌐JC116.M4¬

     BT Estates (Social orders)
       Feudalism
       Knights and knighthood
Ministers (Diplomatic agents)
  USE Ambassadors
     Diplomatic and consular service
Ministers as authors
  USE Clergymen as authors
Ministers as writers
  USE Clergymen as authors
Ministers of Christian education
  USE Christian education directors
Ministers of religious education
  USE Directors of religious education
Ministers of State
  USE Cabinet officers
Ministers of the gospel
  USE Clergy
Ministorage facilities
  USE Self-service storage facilities
Ministries Trial, Nuremberg, Germany, 1948-1949
  UF Subsequent proceedings, Nuremberg
     War Crime Trials, case no. 11
     Wilhelmstrasse Trial, Nuremberg,
       Germany, 1948-1949
  BT Nuremberg War Crime Trials, 1946-
     1949
Ministry
  USE Church work
     Clergy—Office
     Pastoral theology
Ministry, Coffee house
  USE Coffee house ministry
Ministry, Cooperative
  USE Cooperative ministry
Ministry, Country
  USE Rural clergy
Ministry, Doctor of
  USE Doctor of ministry degree
Ministry, Group
  USE Group ministry
Ministry, Lay
  USE Lay ministry
Ministry, Urban
  USE City clergy
Minitab (Computer system)
  BT Mathematical statistics—Data
     processing
     Statistics—Data processing
Minitaree Indians
  USE Hidatsa Indians
Miniwarehouses
  USE Self-service storage facilities
Minjur Aquifer (Saudi Arabia)
  BT Aquifers—Saudi Arabia
Mink Aleutian disease *(May Subd Geog)*
  UF Aleutian disease of minks
     Plasmacytosis, Viral
     Viral plasmacytosis
  BT Minks—Diseases
     Veterinary virology
     Virus diseases, Slow
Mink family
  USE Minkler family
Mink farming *(May Subd Geog)*
  ⌐SF405.M6¬
  BT Fur farming
     Mink fur industry
     Minks
  NT Tariff on mink fur
Mink fur, Tariff on
  USE Tariff on mink fur
Mink fur industry *(May Subd Geog)*
  ⌐HD9944¬
  UF Mink industry
  BT Fur trade
     Minks
  NT Mink farming
  — Advertising
     USE Advertising—Mink fur industry

Mink industry
  USE Mink fur industry
Minke whale
  USE Balaenoptera acutorostrata
Minkel family
  USE Minkler family
Minkia language
  USE Pai language
Minkler family *(Not Subd Geog)*
  UF Minck family
     Minckler family
     Minckley family
     Mink family
     Minkel family
     Minkley family
Minkley family
  USE Minkler family
Minkowski space
  USE Spaces, Generalized
Minks *(May Subd Geog)*
     ₍QL737.C25₎
     ₍SF405.M6 (Breeding)₎
  UF Mustela vison
  BT Mustela
  NT Mink farming
     Mink fur industry
  — **Diseases**
     NT Mink Aleutian disease
  — **Feeding and feeds**
Minneapolis Metropolitan Area (Minn.)
  UF Twin Cities Metropolitan Area (Minn.)
Minneconjon Indians
  USE Miniconjou Indians
Minnelia family *(Not Subd Geog)*
Minner family
  USE Minor family
Minnesingers
     ₍GT3650 (Manners and customs)₎
     ₍PT217 (History)₎
     ₍PT1419-PT1426 (German literature:
       collections)₎
  BT Bards and bardism
     Love poetry
     Minstrels
     Poets
     Scalds and scaldic poetry
  RT Courtly love
     Meistersinger
     Troubadours
     Trouvères
Minnesingers in art
Minnesota
  — **Antiquities**
     NT Fort Saint Charles Archaeological
        Site (Magnusons Island, Minn.)
        Kensington Rune Stone
  — **Description and travel**
  — — **To 1858**
  — — **1858-1950**
  — — **1951-1980**
  — — **1981-**
  — **History**
     ₍F601-615₎
  — — **To 1858**
  — — **1858-**
  — — **Civil War, 1861-1865**
       ₍E515₎
  — — — **Centennial celebrations, etc.**
  — **Politics and government**
  — — **To 1858**
  — — **1858-1950**
  — — **Civil War, 1861-1865**
  — — **1951-**
Minnesota Fortran (Computer program)
  USE MNF (Computer program)
Minnesota Multiphasic Personality Inventory
     ₍BF698.8.M5 (Psychology)₎
     ₍RC473.M5 (Psychiatry)₎
  UF Minnesota Personality Scale
     MMPI (Personality test)
  BT Personality tests

Minnesota Personality Scale
  USE Minnesota Multiphasic Personality
     Inventory
Minnesota River (S.D. and Minn.)
  BT Rivers—Minnesota
     Rivers—South Dakota
Minnesota Union List of Serials System
  USE MULS System
**Minnesota Valley National Wildlife Refuge
  (Minn.)**
  BT National parks and reserves—
     Minnesota
     Wildlife refuges—Minnesota
Minnesota vocational interest inventory
     ₍LB1027.5₎
  BT Vocational guidance
Minnetaree Indians
  USE Hidatsa Indians
Minnetonka, Lake (Minn.)
     (Not Subd Geog)
  UF Lake Minnetonka (Minn.)
  BT Lakes—Minnesota
Minney family *(Not Subd Geog)*
Minnich family
  USE Minnick family
Minnick family *(Not Subd Geog)*
  UF Mineck family
     Minich family
     Minick family
     Minicks family
     Minnich family
Minnor family
  USE Minor family
Minnow, Bluntnose
  USE Bluntnose minnow
Minnow, Fathead
  USE Fathead minnow
Minnow, Pugnose
  USE Pugnose minnow
Minnows
     ₍QL638.C94₎
  BT Cyprinidae
  NT Bluntnose minnow
Mino-Owari Plain (Japan)
  USE Nōbi Plain (Japan)
Mino pottery
  UF Pottery, Mino
  BT Pottery, Japanese
Minoan architecture
  USE Architecture, Minoan
Minoan art
  USE Art, Minoan
Minoan bronze figurines
  USE Bronze figurines, Minoan
Minoan funeral rites and ceremonies
  USE Funeral rites and ceremonies, Minoan
Minoan gods
  USE Gods, Minoan
Minoan goldwork
  USE Goldwork, Minoan
Minoan marine painting
  USE Marine painting, Minoan
Minoan medicine
  USE Minoans—Medicine
Minoan mural painting and decoration
  USE Mural painting and decoration,
     Minoan
Minoan painting
  USE Painting, Minoan
Minoan Palace (Knossos)
  USE Palace of Knossos (Knossos)
Minoan pottery
  USE Pottery, Minoan
Minoan sculpture
  USE Sculpture, Minoan
Minoan silverwork
  USE Silverwork, Minoan
Minoan vases
  USE Vases, Minoan
Minoan writing
  USE Inscriptions—Greece—Crete

     Inscriptions, Linear A
     Inscriptions, Linear B
Minoans *(May Subd Geog)*
     ₍DF221.C8₎
  UF Civilization, Minoan
  BT Civilization, Aegean
     Cretans
  — **Medicine**
     ₍R137.3₎
     UF Minoan medicine
  — **Rites and ceremonies**
     NT Funeral rites and ceremonies,
        Minoan
Minolta camera
Minoo Mountain (Japan) *(Not Subd Geog)*
  UF Minoo-yama (Japan)
     Minoosan (Japan)
  BT Mountains—Japan
Minoo-yama (Japan)
  USE Minoo Mountain (Japan)
Minoosan (Japan)
  USE Minoo Mountain (Japan)
Minor arts
  USE Decorative arts
Minor automobile
  USE Morris Minor automobile
Minor canons, Cathedral, collegiate, etc.
  UF Canons, Minor
     Choral vicars
     Priest vicars
     Vicars, Priest
     Vicars choral
  BT Canons, Cathedral, collegiate, etc.
     Chapters, Cathedral, collegiate, etc.
     Clergy
Minor family *(Not Subd Geog)*
  UF Miner family
     Miners family
     Minner family
     Minnor family
     Myner family
Minor planets
  USE Planets, Minor
Minor prophets
  USE Prophets
Minor surgery
  USE Surgery, Minor
Minor tactics
  USE Drill and minor tactics
Minorca (Spain)
  UF Balearis Minor (Spain)
     Isla de Menorca (Spain)
     Menorca (Spain)
  BT Balearic Islands
     Islands—Spain
  — **History**
  — — **Invasions**
       ₍DP302.B281₎
     UF Invasions of Minorca (Spain)
Minorcan Americans *(May Subd Geog)*
  BT Ethnology—United States
     Minorcans—United States
Minorcans *(May Subd Geog)*
  BT Ethnology—Spain
  — **United States**
     NT Minorcan Americans
Minorcas (Poultry)
     ₍SF489.M6₎
Minorites
  USE Franciscans
Minorities *(May Subd Geog)*
     ₍D655 (European War and
       reconstruction)₎
     ₍JC311 (Nationalism)₎
     Here are entered works dealing with the condi-
     tion, protection, rights, etc. of racial, religious and
     other minorities. Material on the representation of
     minorities is entered under Proportional representa-
     tion.
  UF Foreign population
     Minority groups

Minorities *(Continued)*
    BT Ethnic groups
    RT Assimilation (Sociology)
        Discrimination
        Ethnic relations
        Majorities
        Nationalism
        Plebiscite
        Proportional representation
        Race relations
        Segregation
        Self-determination, National
    SA *names of individual races, ethnic*
        groups, or other minority groups,
        e.g. German Americans;
        Handicapped; *etc.; and subdivisions*
        Ethnic relations *and* Race relations
        under names of countries, cities,
        etc.
    NT Catholics—Non-Catholic countries
        Children of minorities
        Church and minorities
        Church work with minorities
        English literature—Minority authors
        Ethnic art
        Ethnic attitudes
        Ethnic mass media
        Ethnic press
        Ethnic theater
        Instructional materials centers—
            Services to minorities
        Jews—Diaspora
        Libraries and minorities
        Linguistic minorities
        Mass media and minorities
        Minorities as artists
        Minorities in engineering
        Minorities in medicine
        Minority aged
        Minority authors
        Minority business enterprises
        Minority college graduates
        Minority farmers
        Minority lawyers
        Minority students
        Minority television audiences
        Minority women
        Muslims—Non-Muslim countries
        Nationalities, Principle of
        Population transfers
        Race discrimination
        Social work with minorities
    — Anecdotes, facetiae, satire, etc.
        USE Ethnic wit and humor
    — **Crimes against**
        UF Crimes against minorities
            Minorities, Crimes against
            Minority victims of crime
    — **Economic conditions**
        UF Minorities—Socioeconomic status
    — **Education** *(May Subd Geog)*
        NT Education, Bilingual
            Minorities—Scholarships,
                fellowships, etc.
    — — **Language arts,** ₍etc.₎
    — — **Law and legislation**
        (May Subd Geog)
        BT Educational law and legislation
    — **Education (Elementary)**
        (May Subd Geog)
    — **Education (Graduate)**
    — — **California**
        NT Health Professions Career
            Opportunity Program
    — **Education (Higher)** *(May Subd Geog)*
    — **Education (Preschool)**
    — **Education (Primary)**
    — **Education (Secondary)**
    — **Employment** *(May Subd Geog)*
        ₍HD6305.M5₎
        UF Minority employment

    RT Affirmative action programs
    NT Airlines—Minority employment
        Civil service—Minority
            employment
        Minorities in the motion picture
            industry
        Minorities in the television
            industry
        Trade-unions—Minority
            membership
        Vocational guidance for minorities
    — Fellowships
        USE Minorities—Scholarships,
            fellowships, etc.
    — **Health and hygiene** *(May Subd Geog)*
        RT Minorities—Medical care
    — **Housing** *(May Subd Geog)*
        BT Discrimination in housing
            Housing
    — **Legal status, laws, etc.**
        (May Subd Geog)
        UF Minority rights
    — **Medical care** *(May Subd Geog)*
        RT Minorities—Health and hygiene
    — **Political activity**
        UF Ethnic politics
        BT Political participation
    — **Population**
    — **Psychology**
        BT Social psychology
        NT Psychological tests for minorities
    — **Scholarships, fellowships, etc.**
        (May Subd Geog)
        UF Minorities—Fellowships
            Minority fellowships
            Minority scholarships
        BT Minorities—Education
    — **Services for**
        NT Public libraries—Services to
            minorities
    — **Social conditions**
        UF Minorities—Socioeconomic status
    — Socioeconomic status
        USE Minorities—Economic conditions
            Minorities—Social conditions
    — **Study and teaching** *(May Subd Geog)*
        UF Ethnic studies
        SA *subdivision* Study and teaching
            under ethnic groups
    — **Substance use**
    — **Suffrage** *(May Subd Geog)*
    — Testing
        USE Psychological tests for minorities
    — **Islamic Empire**
        NT Dhimmis
    — **United States**
        NT United States. Navy—Minorities
Minorities, Crimes against
    USE Minorities—Crimes against
Minorities, Public library services to
    USE Public libraries—Services to minorities
Minorities, School library services to
    USE School libraries—Services to minorities
Minorities and libraries
    USE Libraries and minorities
Minorities as a theme in literature
    USE Minorities in literature
Minorities as artists *(May Subd Geog)*
    BT Artists
        Minorities
    NT Minorities in the arts
Minorities as consumers *(May Subd Geog)*
    UF Minority consumers
    BT Consumers
    — **United States**
        SA *particular minority groups as*
            consumers, e.g. Afro-Americans
            as consumers
Minorities in architecture *(May Subd Geog)*
    UF Minority groups in architecture
    BT Architecture

    NT Minority-owned architectural firms
Minorities in broadcasting
    (May Subd Geog)
    BT Broadcasting
Minorities in dentistry *(May Subd Geog)*
    BT Dentistry
        Minorities in medicine
    — **United States**
        NT Afro-Americans in dentistry
Minorities in engineering *(May Subd Geog)*
    UF Minority groups in engineering
    BT Engineering
        Minorities
    NT Minority-owned engineering firms
        Women in engineering
Minorities in films
    USE Minorities in motion pictures
Minorities in government advertising
    (May Subd Geog)
        Here are entered works discussing the portrayal of
    minorities in government advertising.
    BT Government advertising
Minorities in librarianship
    USE Minorities in library science
Minorities in library science
    (May Subd Geog)
    UF Minorities in librarianship
        Minority groups in library science
    BT Library science
    NT Afro-American librarians
Minorities in literature
    UF Minorities as a theme in literature
Minorities in medicine *(May Subd Geog)*
    ₍R693-695₎
    UF Minority groups in medicine
    BT Medicine
        Minorities
    NT Minorities in dentistry
        Minorities in nursing
    — **California**
        NT Health Professions Career
            Opportunity Program
    — **United States**
        NT Afro-Americans in medicine
Minorities in motion pictures
    (May Subd Geog)
    ₍PN1995.9.M₎
        Here are entered works discussing the portrayal of
    minorities in motion pictures. Works discussing all
    aspects of minority involvement in motion pictures
    are entered under Minorities in the motion picture
    industry.
    UF Minorities in films
    BT Minorities in the motion picture
            industry
        Moving-picture industry
        Moving-pictures
    SA *specific minority groups in motion*
            pictures
    NT Racism in motion pictures
Minorities in nursing *(May Subd Geog)*
    ₍RT83.3₎
    BT Minorities in medicine
        Nursing
Minorities in science *(May Subd Geog)*
    UF Minority groups in science
    BT Science
    NT Women in science
Minorities in social work education
    (May Subd Geog)
    BT Social work education
    NT Women in social work education
Minorities in technology *(May Subd Geog)*
    UF Minority groups in technology
    BT Technology
Minorities in television *(May Subd Geog)*
        Here are entered works discussing the portrayal of
    minorities on television. Works discussing all aspects
    of minority involvement in television are entered
    under Minorities in the television industry.
    UF Minorities on television
    BT Television

Minorities in the arts *(May Subd Geog)*
  BT Arts
     Minorities as artists
Minorities in the civil service
  USE Civil service—Minority employment
Minorities in the motion picture industry
  (May Subd Geog)
     Here are entered works discussing all aspects of minority involvement in motion pictures. Works discussing the portrayal of minorities in motion pictures are entered under Minorities in motion pictures.
  BT Mass media and minorities
     Minorities—Employment
     Moving-picture industry
  NT Minorities in motion pictures
Minorities in the press *(May Subd Geog)*
     Here are entered works discussing the portrayal of minorities by the press.
  BT Journalism
     Mass media and minorities
     Press
Minorities in the professions
  (May Subd Geog)
  BT Professions
  NT Minority women in the professions
Minorities in the television industry
  (May Subd Geog)
     Here are entered works discussing all aspects of minority involvement in television. Works discussing the portrayal of minorities on television are entered under Minorities in television.
  BT Minorities—Employment
     Television industry
Minorities in the United States Navy
  USE United States. Navy—Minorities
Minorities in trade-unions
  USE Trade-unions—Minority membership
Minorities on television
  USE Minorities in television
Minority aged *(May Subd Geog)*
  UF Ethnic aged
  BT Aged
     Minorities
  NT Jewish aged
  — United States
     NT Afro-American aged
        Chinese American aged
        Hispanic American aged
Minority arts facilities *(May Subd Geog)*
  BT Arts facilities
Minority authors *(May Subd Geog)*
  BT Authors
     Minorities
  SA *subdivision* Minority authors *under individual literatures, e.g.* English literature—Minority authors
Minority business enterprises
  (May Subd Geog)
  UF Business enterprises, Minority
  BT Business
     Minorities
  NT Black business enterprises
     East Indian American business enterprises
     East Indian business enterprises
     Indians of North America—Business enterprises
     Minority-owned architectural firms
     Minority-owned engineering firms
  — Federal aid
     USE Federal aid to minority business enterprises
  — **Finance**
     NT Federal aid to minority business enterprises
  — **Law and legislation** *(May Subd Geog)*
     BT Commercial law
  — **United States**
     NT Afro-American business enterprises
        Afro-Americans in business
        Asian Americans in business
        Chinese Americans in business

        Filipino Americans in business
        Hispanic American business enterprises
        Hispanic Americans in business
        Indochinese American business enterprises
        Korean American business enterprises
        Ukrainian American business enterprises
        Vietnamese American business enterprises
Minority children
  USE Children of minorities
Minority college administrators
  (May Subd Geog)
  BT College administrators
     Minority executives
Minority college graduates
  (May Subd Geog)
  BT College graduates
     Minorities
  NT Minority women college graduates
Minority college students *(May Subd Geog)*
  UF College students, Minority
  BT College students
     Minority students
Minority consultants *(May Subd Geog)*
  BT Consultants
Minority consumers
  USE Minorities as consumers
Minority employment
  USE Minorities—Employment
Minority executives *(May Subd Geog)*
  UF Executives, Minority
  BT Executives
  NT Afro-American executives
     Minority college administrators
     Minority women executives
Minority farmers *(May Subd Geog)*
  BT Farmers
     Minorities
Minority fellowships
  USE Minorities—Scholarships, fellowships, etc.
Minority groups
  USE Minorities
Minority groups in architecture
  USE Minorities in architecture
Minority groups in engineering
  USE Minorities in engineering
Minority groups in library science
  USE Minorities in library science
Minority groups in medicine
  USE Minorities in medicine
Minority groups in science
  USE Minorities in science
Minority groups in technology
  USE Minorities in technology
Minority journalists *(May Subd Geog)*
  UF Journalists, Minority
  BT Journalists
Minority languages
  USE Linguistic minorities
Minority lawyers *(May Subd Geog)*
  BT Lawyers
     Minorities
  NT Afro-American lawyers
     Lawyers, Blind
     Women lawyers
Minority leader, Senate
  USE United States. Congress. Senate— Minority leader
Minority literature (American)
  USE American literature—Minority authors
     American poetry—Minority authors
Minority mass media
  USE Ethnic mass media
Minority mental health personnel
  (May Subd Geog)
  UF Mental health personnel, Minority

     BT Mental health personnel
Minority miners *(May Subd Geog)*
  BT Miners
Minority-owned architectural firms
  (May Subd Geog)
  BT Architectural firms
     Minorities in architecture
     Minority business enterprises
Minority-owned engineering firms
  (May Subd Geog)
  BT Engineering firms
     Minorities in engineering
     Minority business enterprises
Minority performing arts
  USE Ethnic performing arts
Minority press
  USE Ethnic press
Minority radio broadcasting
  USE Ethnic radio broadcasting
Minority rights
  USE Minorities—Legal status, laws, etc.
Minority scholarships
  USE Minorities—Scholarships, fellowships, etc.
Minority shareholders
  USE Minority stockholders
Minority stockholders *(May Subd Geog)*
  UF Minority shareholders
  BT Corporation law
     Stockholders
Minority students *(May Subd Geog)*
  UF Students, Minority
  BT Minorities
     Students
  NT Minority college students
Minority television audiences
  (May Subd Geog)
  BT Minorities
     Television audiences
Minority television broadcasting
  USE Ethnic television broadcasting
Minority theater
  USE Ethnic theater
Minority victims of crime
  USE Minorities—Crimes against
Minority whip, Senate
  USE United States. Congress. Senate— Minority whip
Minority women *(May Subd Geog)*
  UF Women, Minority
     Women minorities
  BT Minorities
     Women
Minority women college graduates
  (May Subd Geog)
  BT Minority college graduates
     Women college graduates
Minority women executives
  (May Subd Geog)
  BT Minority executives
     Women executives
Minority women in motion pictures
     Here are entered works discussing the portrayal of minority women in motion pictures.
  BT Moving-pictures
Minority women in the professions
  (May Subd Geog)
  BT Minorities in the professions
     Women in the professions
Minority youth *(May Subd Geog)*
  BT Youth
Minors
  USE Children
Minotaur (Greek mythology)
  [BL820.M63]
  UF Minotauros (Greek mythology)
  BT Monsters
     Mythology, Greek
Minotauros (Greek mythology)
  USE Minotaur (Greek mythology)

Minowa Castle (Misato-machi, Japan)
  USE Minowajō (Misato-machi, Japan)
Minowajō (Misato-machi, Japan)
  UF Minowa Castle (Misato-machi, Japan)
  BT Castles—Japan
Minox camera
Minquiers and Ecrehos case
  UF Ecrehos and Minquiers case
  BT Acquisition of territory—Cases
     Sovereignty—Cases
Minsey family
  USE Mincey family
Minshall-Estey organ
  [ML597]
  BT Electronic organ
  — Methods
     [MT192]
Minsi language
  USE Munsee language
MINSK-ARDIS (Information retrieval system)
  BT Documentation
     Information storage and retrieval
        systems
Minsk computer
  [QA76.8.M5]
  BT Electronic digital computers
  — Programming
Minstrel shows
  UF Afro-American minstrel shows
     Blackfaced minstrel shows
     Negro minstrel shows
  BT Afro-Americans in the performing arts
     Musical revues, comedies, etc.
     Vaudeville—United States
  RT Blackface entertainers
Minstrels *(May Subd Geog)*
  [GT3650 (Manners and customs)]
  [ML2870 (Modern) (Musical history,
     ML182-183 (Medieval))]
  UF Jongleurs
  BT Manners and customs
     Poets
  RT Bards and bardism
  NT Charans
     Meistersinger
     Minnesingers
     Troubadours
     Trouvères
  — Japan
     NT Goze
MINT (Computer programs)
  UF Machine-Independent Organic
     Software Tools (Computer
     programs)
     SNIBBOL (Computer programs)
  BT Computer programs
Mint camphor
  USE Menthol
Mint julep
Mint weed
  USE Salvia reflexa
Mintern family
  USE Minturn family
Minters *(May Subd Geog)*
  BT Mints
Minters, Jewish *(May Subd Geog)*
  UF Jewish minters
Minton (Game)
  [GV1017.M6]
Mints *(May Subd Geog)*
  [HG321]
  [HG451-HG461 (United States)]
  BT Money
  RT Coinage
  NT Minters
MINTS (Computer program)
  UF Mini-Numerical Taxonomy System
     (Computer program)
  BT Cluster analysis—Computer programs
     Computer programs

Minturn family *(Not Subd Geog)*
  UF Mintern family
Minué Federal (Dance)
  USE Montonero (Dance)
Minuet
  [GV1796.M5 (Dancing)]
  [ML3465 (Musical form: history)]
  [MT64 (instruction)]
  RT Scherzo
Minuets
     Here are entered collections of minuet music for
  various mediums. Individual minuets and collections
  of minuets for a specific medium are entered under
  the heading followed by specification of medium.
  BT Dance music
Minuets (Accordion ensemble)
  [M1362]
  BT Accordion ensembles
Minuets (Band)
  [M1249]
  [M1266]
  BT Band music
Minuets (Bassoon, flute, guitar)
  [M375-9]
  BT Trios (Bassoon, flute, guitar)
Minuets (Bassoons (2), clarinets (2), horns (2), oboes (2))
  [M855-9]
Minuets (Clarinet and piano)
  [M248-252]
  BT Clarinet and piano music
Minuets (Double bass and piano)
  [M237-238]
  BT Double-bass and piano music
Minuets (Flute and continuo)
  BT Flute and continuo music
Minuets (Flute and harpsichord)
  [M240-244]
  BT Flute and harpsichord music
Minuets (Flute and violoncello)
  [M290-291]
  BT Flute and violoncello music
Minuets (Flutes (2))
  [M288-289]
  BT Flute music (Flutes (2))
Minuets (Guitar)
  [M125-9]
  BT Guitar music
Minuets (Harpsichord)
  [M32]
  BT Harpsichord music
     Minuets (Piano)
Minuets (Oboe and continuo)
  BT Oboe and continuo music
Minuets (Orchestra)
  [M1049]
  [M1060]
  BT Orchestral music
Minuets (Organ)
  [M6-M7]
  [M11-M13]
  BT Organ music
Minuets (Piano)
  [M32]
  BT Piano music
  NT Minuets (Harpsichord)
Minuets (Piano, 4 hands)
  [M204]
  [M211]
  BT Piano music (4 hands)
Minuets (Piano trio)
  [M310-314]
  BT Piano trios
Minuets (Pianos (2))
  [M214-215]
  BT Piano music (Pianos (2))
Minuets (Recorder)
  [M60-64]
  BT Recorder music
Minuets (Recorder and piano)
  [M240-244]

  BT Recorder and piano music
Minuets (Recorders (2))
  [M288-289]
  BT Recorder music (Recorders (2))
Minuets (Recorders (2) with plectral ensemble)
  [M1360]
  BT Recorders (2) with plectral ensemble
Minuets (String orchestra)
  [M1145]
  [M1160]
  BT String-orchestra music
Minuets (String quartet)
  [M450-454]
  BT String quartets
Minuets (String trio)
  [M349-353]
  BT String trios
Minuets (Violin and continuo)
  BT Violin and continuo music
Minuets (Violin and piano)
  [M217-M218]
  [M221-M223]
  BT Violin and piano music
Minuets (Violins (2), viola)
  [M349-353]
  BT String trios (Violins (2), viola)
Minuets (Violins (2), violoncello)
  [M349-353]
  BT String trios (Violins (2), violoncello)
Minuets (Violins (3))
  [M349-353]
  BT String trios (Violins (3))
Minuets (Violoncello and piano)
  [M229-M230]
  [M233-M236]
  BT Violoncello and piano music
Minuscule writing
  USE Writing, Minuscule
Minusing Indians
  USE Minisink Indians
Minusinsk Basin (R.S.F.S.R.)
  UF Minusinskaĭa kotlovina (R.S.F.S.R.)
     Minusinskaya kotlovina (R.S.F.S.R.)
  BT Valleys—Russian S.F.S.R.
Minusinskaĭa kotlovina (R.S.F.S.R.)
  USE Minusinsk Basin (R.S.F.S.R.)
Minusinskaya kotlovina (R.S.F.S.R.)
  USE Minusinsk Basin (R.S.F.S.R.)
Minute Man National Historical Park (Mass.)
  BT Historic sites—Massachusetts
     National parks and reserves—United
        States
     Parks—Massachusetts
Minute men
  USE Minutemen (Militia)
Minute pirate bugs
  USE Anthocoridae
Minuteman (Missile)
Minutemen (Militia) *(May Subd Geog)*
     Here are entered works on American Revolution-
  ary War militiamen who were ready to turn out for
  service with little advance warning.
  UF Militia (Minutemen)
     Minute men
  BT United States—History—Revolution,
        1775-1783
     United States—Militia
Minutes, Corporate
  USE Corporate minutes
Minx automobile
  [TL215.M5]
  BT Hillman automobile
Miny language
  USE Dehu language
Minya Gonkar (China)
  USE Minya Konka (China)

Minya Konka (China)
  UF Bokonka (China)
     Bokunka (China)
     Gongga Mountains (China)
     Kung-ka Mountains (China)
     Minya Gonkar (China)
  BT Mountains—China
Minyung language
  USE Bandjalang language
Miocene period
  USE Geology, Stratigraphic—Miocene
     Paleobotany—Miocene
     Paleontology—Miocene
Miomote-gawa (Japan)
  USE Miomote River (Japan)
Miomote River (Japan) *(Not Subd Geog)*
  UF Miomote-gawa (Japan)
     Miomotegawa (Japan)
  BT Rivers—Japan
Miomotegawa (Japan)
  USE Miomote River (Japan)
Miqvah
  USE Mikveh
Mir
     [*HD1289.R9 (Russian, HD715)*]
  BT Commons
     Communism
     Land tenure
     Peasantry
     Village communities
Mir computer
  BT Electronic digital computers
Mirach family
  USE Merrick family
Miracle-plays
  USE Mysteries and miracle-plays
Miracle workers *(May Subd Geog)*
  UF Thaumaturges
     Wonder workers
     Workers of miracles
  BT Magicians
     Prophets
  RT Miracles
Miracles
     [*BS1199.M5 (Old Testament)*]
     [*BS2545.M5 (New Testament)*]
     [*BT97 (Theology, Doctrinal)*]
  UF Bible—Miracles
  BT God
  RT Marvelous, The
     Miracle workers
     Supernatural
  NT Holy wells
     Jesus Christ—Miracles
     Lord's Supper—Miracles
     Mary, Blessed Virgin, Saint—
        Apparitions and miracles
     Saints—Legends
     Shrines
     Spiritual healing
     Stigmatization
Miracles (Buddhism)
  BT Buddhism
Miracles (Greek mythology)
  BT Mythology, Greek
Miracles (Hinduism)
  BT Hinduism
Miracles (Islam)
     [*BP166.65*]
  BT Islam—Doctrines
  NT Muḥammad, Prophet, d. 632—
        Miracles
Miracles in art
Miraculous draught of fishes (Miracle)
  UF Draught of fishes (Miracle)
     Fishes, Draught of (Miracle)
  BT Jesus Christ—Miracles
Miraculous draught of fishes (Miracle) in art
Miraculous Medal
  UF Medal, Miraculous
  BT Medals, Devotional

Mirador Site (Mexico)
  BT Mexico—Antiquities
Mirafiori (Turin, Italy) *(Not Subd Geog)*
  UF Turin (Italy). Mirafiori
Miraflores, Peru (Lima), Battle of, 1881
     [*F3097*]
  BT War of the Pacific, 1879-1884—
        Campaigns—Peru
Miraflores Lake (Panama)
  UF Lago de Miraflores (Panama)
  BT Lakes—Panama
  NT Miraflores Locks (Panama)
Miraflores Locks (Panama)
  BT Locks (Hydraulic engineering)—
        Panama
     Miraflores Lake (Panama)
     Panama Canal (Panama)
Mirage (Fighter planes)
     [*TL685.3*]
  UF Dassault Mirage (Fighter planes)
     Mirage III (Fighter planes)
  BT Dassault Breguet airplanes
     Fighter planes
Mirage III (Fighter planes)
  USE Mirage (Fighter planes)
Mirages
  BT Air, Rarefied
     Hallucinations and illusions
     Reflection (Optics)
Mi'rāj
  USE Muḥammad, Prophet, d. 632—Isrā'
     and Mi'rāj
Mi'rāj, Laylat
  USE Laylat al-Mi'rāj
Miramichi River (N.B.)
  BT Rivers—New Brunswick
Miranda-Beaubien Grant (N.M. and Colo.)
  USE Maxwell Land Grant (N.M. and Colo.)
Miranda camera
  BT Single-lens reflex cameras
**Miranda de Ebro (Spain : Concentration
  camp)**
  BT Concentration camps—Spain
     World War, 1939-1945—
        Concentration camps—Spain
     World War, 1939-1945—Prisoners and
        prisons, Spanish
Mirandese dialect
     [*PC5401-4*]
  BT Portuguese language
Mire family
  USE Myers family
Mireck family
  USE Merrick family
Miremont Cave (France)
  USE Rouffignac Cave (France)
Mires family
  USE Myers family
Mirex
     [*SB952.M*]
  UF Dechlorane
     Dodecachlorooctahydr
        omethenocyclobutapentalene
     Hexachlorocyclopentadiene dimer
  BT Organochlorine compounds
Miri (Indic people)
     [*DS432.M44*]
  UF Meri (Indic people)
     Mishing (Indic people)
     Mishings (Indic people)
  BT Ethnology—India
Miri language
  USE Abor language
Miriam family
  USE Merriam family
Mirich family
  USE Merrick family
Mirick family
  USE Merrick family

Miridae
  UF Capsidae
     Isometopidae
     Phytocoridae
     Termatophylidae
  BT Hemiptera
  NT Beamerella
     Chlamydatus
     Cimex
     Cyrtorhinus
     Globiceps
     Hambletoniola
     Helopeltis
     Lygus
     Myrmecophyes
     Neaphaenops
     Psallus
     Pseudanophthalmus
     Trigonotylus
Miriek family
  USE Merrick family
Mirim Lake (Brazil and Uruguay)
  UF Lagoa Mirim (Brazil and Uruguay)
     Laguna Merín (Brazil and Uruguay)
     Laguna Mirim (Brazil and Uruguay)
     Lake Mirim (Brazil and Uruguay)
     Merim Lagoon (Brazil and Uruguay)
  BT Lakes—Brazil
     Lakes—Uruguay
Miriman family
  USE Merryman family
Mirliton
  BT Wind instruments
  NT Kazoo
Miró, Joan, 1893-   Woman
  UF Femme (Tapestry)
     Woman (Tapestry)
  BT Tapestry—Spain
Miró Quesada family *(Not Subd Geog)*
Miroglio, Valerio. Last judgment
     [*ND623.M*]
  UF Giudizio universale (Painting)
     Last judgment (Painting)
  BT Judgment Day in art
Mirones Cave (Spain)
  USE Rascaño Cave (Spain)
Mirounga angustirostris
  USE Northern elephant seal
Mirrick family
  USE Merrick family
Mirriman family
  USE Merryman family
Mirrit family
  USE Merritt family
Mirritt family
  USE Merritt family
Mirror-cases
     [*NK9955.M5*]
  BT Mirrors—Frames
Mirror embroidery, Indian
  USE Shisha mirror embroidery
Mirror embroidery, Shisha
  USE Shisha mirror embroidery
Mirror-image isomers
  USE Enantiomers
Mirror images
  UF Images, Mirror
  BT Images, Optical
     Mirrors
Mirror Lake (Grafton County, N.H.)
  BT Lakes—New Hampshire
Mirror lenses
  USE Catadioptric systems
Mirror nuclei
     [*QC173*]
  UF Nuclei, Mirror
  BT Neutrons
     Nuclear forces (Physics)
     Nuclear shell theory
     Protons
     Symmetry (Physics)

Mirror-tracing test
  BT Projective techniques
Mirror-writing
  [BF456.W8]
  BT Left- and right-handedness
      Writing
Mirrors (May Subd Geog)
  [NK8440 (Art)]
  [QC385 (Optics)]
  [TP867 (Technology)]
  UF Aberration, Chromatic and spherical
      Looking-glasses
  BT Furniture
      Optical instruments
  NT Automobiles—Rearview mirrors
      Bronze mirrors
      Lasers—Mirrors
      Magnetic mirrors
      Mirror images
      Rotating mirrors
      Telescope, Reflecting
  — **Frames**
      [TP867]
      NT Mirror-cases
  — **Religious aspects**
Mirrors, Burning
  USE Burning-mirrors
Mirrors, Colonial (May Subd Geog)
  UF Colonial mirrors
Mirrors, Etruscan (May Subd Geog)
  UF Etruscan mirrors
Mirrors, Magic
  USE Magic mirrors
Mirrors in architecture (May Subd Geog)
  [NA2796]
  UF Architectural mirrors
  BT Architecture
Mirrors in art
  [N8224.M6]
Mirrors in literature
MIRV
  USE Multiple independently targetable
      reentry vehicles
MIS (Information systems)
  USE Management information systems
Misanthropy
  BT Cynicism
      Hate
  NT Misogyny
Misanthropy in literature
Misarticulations
  USE Articulation disorders
Misayama 2 Iseki (Minowa-machi, Nagano-ken, Japan)
  USE Misayama Daini Site (Minowa-machi, Nagano-ken, Japan)
Misayama Daini Iseki (Minowa-machi, Nagano-ken, Japan)
  USE Misayama Daini Site (Minowa-machi, Nagano-ken, Japan)
Misayama Daini Site (Minowa-machi, Nagano-ken, Japan) (Not Subd Geog)
  UF Misayama 2 Iseki (Minowa-machi, Nagano-ken, Japan)
      Misayama Daini Iseki (Minowa-machi, Nagano-ken, Japan)
  BT Japan—Antiquities
Miscarriage (May Subd Geog)
  [RG648]
  UF Abortion, Spontaneous
      Spontaneous abortion
  BT Pregnancy, Complications of
Miscarriage of justice
  USE Judicial error
Miscegenation (May Subd Geog)
  [E185.62 (Afro-Americans)]
  [GN254 (Ethnology)]
      Here are entered works on marriage or sexual re-
  lations between persons of different races and on the
  resulting mixture or hybridity of races.

  UF Hybridity of races
      Racial amalgamation
      Racial crossing
  BT Race relations
  NT Anglo-Indians
      Australian aborigines—Mixed bloods
      Colored people (South Africa)
      Creoles
      Eurasians
      Griquas
      Indians—Mixed bloods
      Mulattoes
  — **Law and legislation** (May Subd Geog)
      BT Marriage law
Miscellanea
  USE subdivision Miscellanea under subjects
Miscellaneous facts
  USE Almanacs
      Curiosities and wonders
      Handbooks, vade-mecums, etc.
      Questions and answers
Misch metal
  USE Mischmetal
Mischel family
  USE Mitchell family
Mischief, Malicious
  USE Malicious mischief
Mischmetal
  [TN693.R3 (Physical metallurgy)]
  UF Misch metal
  BT Cerium alloys
      Rare earth metal alloys
Mischocyttarus
  [QL568.V5]
  BT Vespidae
Mischocyttarus drewseni
  [QL568.V5]
Mischocyttarus labiatus
  [QL568.V5]
Miscible displacement (Petroleum engineering)
  UF Displacement, Miscible (Petroleum engineering)
      Miscible flooding
  BT Oil field flooding
Miscible flooding
  USE Miscible displacement (Petroleum engineering)
Miscogastridae
  USE Pteromalidae
Misconceptions, Medical
  USE Medical misconceptions
Misconceptions, Popular
  USE Errors, Popular
Misconduct in office (May Subd Geog)
      Here are entered works on criminal offenses com-
  mitted by government officials in the performance of
  their duties. Works on offenses against professional
  ethics or against discipline are entered under names
  of countries, cities, government departments, etc.
  with subdivision Officials and employees—Discipline. Works on specific offenses are entered under
  the name of the offense, e.g. Bribery. Works on the
  personal liability of government officials to the state
  or to individuals for wrongful acts committed in office are entered under Administrative responsibility.
  Works on the liability of the state for wrongful acts
  of officials are entered under Government liability.
  UF Malfeasance in office
      Misfeasance in office
      Official misconduct
  BT Administrative responsibility
      Criminal law
  RT Corruption (in politics)
  NT Denial of justice
      False certification
      Government liability
      Judicial corruption
      Police corruption
      Prevarication (Law)
      Trials (Misconduct in office)

Misconduct in office (Frankish law)
Misconduct in office (Roman law)
Miscue analysis
  BT Reading
      Reading—Code emphasis approaches
Misdemeanors (Law)
  USE Criminal law
Misdiagnosis
  USE Diagnostic errors
Mise family
  USE Mize family
Misener family
  USE Misner family
Miser family
  USE Meisser family
Miserere mei, Deus, miserere mei (Music)
  USE Psalms (Music)—57th Psalm
Miserere mei, Deus, secundum magnum misericordiam (Music)
  USE Psalms (Music)—51st Psalm
Misereres (Seats)
  USE Choir-stalls
Misericordias Domine (Music)
  USE Psalms (Music)—89th Psalm
Misericords (May Subd Geog)
  BT Choir-stalls
Misers
  [HB838]
  BT Avarice
      Hoarding of money
      Wealth
Misfeasance in office
  USE Misconduct in office
Misfueling of automobiles
  USE Automobiles—Misfueling
Mishaps, Medical
  USE Medical errors
Mishar dialect
  UF Meshchera dialect
      Mishcheriāk dialect
      Misher dialect
      Western Tatar dialect
  BT Russian S.F.S.R.—Languages
      Tatar language
Mishar Tatars
  BT Tatars
Mishcheriāk dialect
  USE Mishar dialect
Misher dialect
  USE Mishar dialect
Mishikhwutmetunne Indians
  USE Coquille Indians
Mishimi
  USE Mishmis
Mishing (Indic people)
  USE Miri (Indic people)
Mishing language
  USE Abor language
Mishings (Indic people)
  USE Miri (Indic people)
Mishirosugō Iseki (Shingū-machi, Fukuoka-ken, Japan)
  USE Mishirosugō Site (Shingū-machi, Fukuoka-ken, Japan)
Mishirosugō Site (Shingū-machi, Fukuoka-ken, Japan)
  UF Mishirosugō Iseki (Shingū-machi, Fukuoka-ken, Japan)
  BT Japan—Antiquities
Mishkin family (Not Subd Geog)
  UF Mishkind family
Mishkind family
  USE Mishkin family
Mishmar Wadi (Israel)
  UF Naḥal Mishmar (Israel)
  BT Wadis—Israel
Mishmi language
  [PL4001.M55]
  BT India—Languages
      Tibeto-Burman languages
  NT Miju dialect

2424

Mishmis
  [DS485.A86]
    UF Mishimi
    BT Ethnology—India
Mishnah
  — Animals
      USE Animals in the Mishnah
  — Plants
      USE Plants in the Mishnah
Mishōryū ikebana
    USE Flower arrangement, Japanese—
          Mishōryū school
Misima language
    BT Melanesian languages
    RT Misima-Panayati language
Misima-Panayati language
    BT Melanesian languages
    RT Misima language
        Panayati language
Misinformation
    USE Errors, Popular
Mising language
    USE Abor language
Miskigula Indians
    USE Pascagoula Indians
Miskimen family
    USE McKinnon family
Miskimmin family
    USE McKinnon family
Miskimmins family
    USE McKinnon family
Miskimmon family
    USE McKinnon family
Miskimmons family
    USE McKinnon family
Miskito Coast (Nicaragua and Honduras)
    USE Mosquitia (Nicaragua and Honduras)
Miskito Indians
    USE Mosquito Indians
Miskito language
    USE Mosquito language
Misleading advertising
    USE Advertising, Fraudulent
Misleading financial statements
    USE Financial statements, Misleading
Misner family (Not Subd Geog)
    UF Misener family
        Mizner family
Miso (May Subd Geog)
  [TP438.S6]
    BT Soybean as food
    NT Cookery (Miso)
Miso industry (May Subd Geog)
    BT Soybean products
Misogi (Shinto)
  [BL2224.25.M57]
    BT Shinto—Rituals
Misogyny (May Subd Geog)
    UF Women-hating
    BT Misanthropy
    RT Women
Misokuri
    USE Sanka (Social class)
Misonne family (Not Subd Geog)
Misox Valley (Switzerland)
    USE Mesolcina Valley (Switzerland)
Misoxertal (Switzerland)
    USE Mesolcina Valley (Switzerland)
Mispagel family (Not Subd Geog)
Misprints
    USE Errata (in books)
Misprision (May Subd Geog)
    BT Criminal law
        Omission, Criminal
Misrepresentation (Law)
    USE Fraud
Misrepresentations in financial statements
    USE Financial statements, Misleading

Misrian (City)
    BT Cities and towns, Ruined, extinct, etc.
        —Turkmen S.S.R.
        Turkmen S.S.R.—Antiquities
Miss America Pageant, Atlantic City, N.J.
    BT Beauty contests—United States
Miss Joaquim Vanda
    USE Vanda Miss Joaquim
Miss Marple (Fictitious character)
    USE Marple, Jane (Fictitious character)
Miss Nancy (Legendary character)
    USE Anansi (Legendary character)
Miss One Dot (Dog)
    UF Dot (Dog)
    BT Dogs
Missals
  [BX2015]
    [ND3375 (Illuminated manuscripts)]
    BT Liturgies
        Prayer-books
    RT Illumination of books and manuscripts
Missals for children
    USE Children's missals
Missed labor
    USE Pregnancy, Protracted
Missen family (Not Subd Geog)
Missile attack warning systems
    (May Subd Geog)
    UF Warning systems, Missile attack
    BT Air defenses, Military
        Radar defense networks
    RT Ballistic missile defenses
    NT Ballistic missile early warning system
Missile bases
    USE Guided missile bases
Missile control systems
    USE Guided missiles—Control systems
Missile fire control technicians (United States
    Navy)
    USE United States. Navy—Fire control
          technicians (Missile)
Missile guidance systems
    USE Guided missiles—Guidance systems
Missile industry
    USE Guided missile industries
Missile ranges
    USE Guided missile ranges
Missile silos
    USE Guided missile silos
Missile tracking
    USE Guided missiles—Tracking
Missile warheads
    USE Multiple independently targetable
          reentry vehicles
Missiles, Air-to-surface
    USE Air-to-surface missiles
Missiles, Antiaircraft
    USE Antiaircraft missiles
Missiles, Antitank
    USE Antitank missiles
Missiles, Ballistic
    USE Ballistic missiles
Missiles, Cruise
    USE Cruise missiles
Missiles, Guided
    USE Guided missiles
Missiles, Surface-to-surface
    USE Surface-to-surface missiles
Missing blood syndrome
    USE Anemia, Hypovolemic
Missing children (May Subd Geog)
    UF Children, Missing
        Lost children
    BT Children
        Missing persons
Missing data (Statistics)
    USE Missing observations (Statistics)
Missing in action
    UF MIA's
        Servicemen missing in action

    BT Battle casualties
        Prisoners of war
        Soldiers
    SA subdivision Missing in action under
        individual wars, e.g. World War,
        1939-1945—Missing in action
  — Family relationships
      UF Families of military personnel
          Families of servicemen missing in
            action
          MIA families
      BT Military dependents
          Military social work
          Soldiers—Family relationships
Missing link
  [QH368]
    BT Evolution
    NT Neanderthal race
Missing observations (Statistics)
    UF Data, Missing (Statistics)
        Missing data (Statistics)
        Observations, Missing (Statistics)
    BT Estimation theory
        Multivariate analysis
    RT Multiple imputation (Statistics)
Missing persons (May Subd Geog)
    UF Desaparecidos
        Disappeared persons
        Persons, Missing
        Skip tracers
    BT Persons
    NT Absence and presumption of death
        Missing children
  — Investigation
      BT Investigations
  — Registers, lists, etc.
Missing persons (International law)
    BT International law
Missing works of art
    USE Lost works of art
Missinnipi River (Sask. and Man.)
    USE Churchill River (Sask. and Man.)
Missiology
    USE Missions—Theory
Mission buildings, Spanish
    USE Spanish mission buildings
Mission furniture
    USE Furniture, Mission
Mission Indians of California
    USE Indians of North America—California
Mission Mountains Wilderness (Mont.)
    (Not Subd Geog)
    BT National parks and reserves—Montana
        Wilderness areas—Montana
Mission oak furniture
    USE Furniture, Mission
Mission of the church
  [BV601.8]
    Here are entered works on the chief objective and
    responsibility of the church as viewed in its entirety.
    Works on missionary work are entered under Mis-
    sions.
    UF Church—Mission
        Church—Purpose
    BT Church
    NT Apostolate (Christian theology)
        Church and the world
Mission of the twelve apostles
    USE Jesus Christ—Sending of the twelve
Mission sermons
    USE Missions—Sermons
Mission style (Domestic architecture)
    USE Architecture, Domestic—Mission style
Mission Viejo Ranch (Calif.)
    USE Rancho Mission Viejo (Calif.)
Missionaries (May Subd Geog)
  [BV3700-BV3705 (General biography)]
    BT Christian biography
        Clergy
        Missions
    NT Children of missionaries

Missionaries *(Continued)*
        Married people in missionary work
        Missionaries, Lay
        Women missionaries
  — Appointment, call, and election
      [BV2063]
      [BV2180 (Catholic Church)]
      UF Missionaries—Vocation
      BT Clergy—Appointment, call, and
          election
          Vocation, Ecclesiastical
  — Furloughs
      USE Missionaries—Leaves and
          furloughs
  — Leaves and furloughs
      UF Furloughs
          Missionaries—Furloughs
          Missionaries on furlough
  — Pensions *(May Subd Geog)*
      [BV2081]
      UF Missionaries—Salaries, pensions,
          etc.
  — Salaries, etc. *(May Subd Geog)*
      [BV2081]
      UF Missionaries—Salaries, pensions,
          etc.
  — Salaries, pensions, etc.
      USE Missionaries—Pensions
          Missionaries—Salaries, etc.
  — Training of *(May Subd Geog)*
      UF Missionaries, Training of
  — Vocation
      USE Missionaries—Appointment, call,
          and election
  — Wives
      USE Missionaries' wives
  — United States
      NT Afro-American missionaries
Missionaries, Afro-American
  USE Afro-American missionaries
Missionaries, Buddhist
  USE Buddhist missionaries
Missionaries, Lay
  UF Lay missionaries
      Missions—Lay workers
  BT Missionaries
  NT Missionaries, Part-time
Missionaries, Medical *(May Subd Geog)*
  [R722]
  UF Medical missionaries
  BT Missions, Medical
Missionaries, Part-time *(May Subd Geog)*
  UF Part-time missionaries
      Self-supporting missionaries
      Tentmakers (Missionaries)
  BT Missionaries, Lay
Missionaries, Resignation of
  UF Missionaries, Withdrawal of
      Resignation of missionaries
      Withdrawal of missionaries
  BT Missions
Missionaries, Tenrikyō
  USE Tenrikyō missionaries
Missionaries, Training of
  USE Missionaries—Training of
Missionaries, Withdrawal of
  USE Missionaries, Resignation of
Missionaries' children
  USE Children of missionaries
Missionaries on furlough
  USE Missionaries—Leaves and furloughs
Missionaries' wives *(May Subd Geog)*
  [BV2611]
  UF Missionaries—Wives
  BT Wives
      Women in church work
Missionary education
  USE Missions—Study and teaching
Missionary medicine
  USE Missions, Medical

Missionary plays
  [BV2086]
  BT Religious drama
Missionary Ridge, Battle of, 1863
  [E475.97]
  RT Chattanooga, Battle of, 1863
Missionary Sisters of the Sacred Heart
  (May Subd Geog)
  [BX4408]
  BT Monasticism and religious orders for
      women
Missionary stories
  [BV2087]
  BT Children's stories
Missionary work of youth
  USE Youth in missionary work
Missions *(May Subd Geog)*
  [BV2000-BV3705]
  UF Missions, Foreign
  BT Religion
      Theology, Practical
  SA *subdivision* Missions *under names of*
      religions, religious denominations,
      etc., e.g. Buddhism—Missions;
      Catholic Church—Missions; Baptists
      —Missions; Jesuits—Missions
  NT Aeronautics in missionary work
      Boats and boating in missionary work
      Church growth
      College students in missionary work
      Indians of North America—Missions
      Language in missionary work
      Mass media in missionary work
      Missionaries
      Missionaries, Resignation of
      Moving-pictures in missionary work
      Radio in missionary work
      Sound recordings in missionary work
      Spanish mission buildings
      Women in missionary work
      Young adults in missionary work
      Youth in missionary work
      Zenana missions
  — Agricultural work
      [S532]
      UF Agricultural work of missions
      BT Agricultural education
  — Anthropological aspects
      BT Anthropology
  — Biblical teaching
      [BV2073]
      NT Great Commission (Bible)
          Kerygma
  — Chronology
      USE Missions—History—Chronology
  — Cooperative movement
      USE Missions—Interdenominational
          cooperation
  — Devolution
      USE Indigenous church administration
  — Early works to 1800
      UF Catholic Church—Missions—Early
          works to 1800
  — Educational work
      [BV2630]
      UF Educational missions
      BT Church and education
  — Exercises, recitations, etc.
  — Finance
  — Geography
      BT Religion and geography
  — — Maps
      UF Missions—Maps
  — Germanic tribes
      BT Germanic tribes
  — History
  — — Early church, ca. 30-600
      [BR165]
  — — Chronology
      UF Missions—Chronology
  — Hymns

      [BV465.M5]
  — Industrial work
      UF Industrial missions
      BT Technical education
  — Interdenominational cooperation
      [BV2082.I6]
      UF Missions—Cooperative movement
      BT Interdenominational cooperation
  — Lay workers
      USE Missionaries, Lay
  — Maps
      USE Missions—Geography—Maps
  — Music
  — Public relations
      USE Public relations—Missions
  — Rural work
      UF Missions—Village work
          Missions, Rural
          Rural missions
  — Sermons
      [BV2075]
      UF Mission sermons
  — Societies, etc.
  — Study and teaching *(May Subd Geog)*
      UF Missionary education
  — Theory
      [BV2063]
      UF Missiology
  — Village work
      USE Missions—Rural work
  — Asia
      Here are entered works on missions in Asia.
      Works on missions to Asians residing outside of
      Asia are entered under Missions to Asians.
  — South Africa
      NT Ethiopian movement (South
          Africa)
  — United States
  — — To Mexican Americans
      USE Missions to Mexican
          Americans
Missions, American *(May Subd Geog)*
  UF American missions
Missions, American, [Belgian, Spanish, etc.]
  (May Subd Geog)
Missions, Asian *(May Subd Geog)*
  UF Asian missions
Missions, Australian *(May Subd Geog)*
  UF Australian missions
Missions, Austrian *(May Subd Geog)*
  UF Austrian missions
Missions, Belgian *(May Subd Geog)*
  UF Belgian missions
Missions, Breton *(May Subd Geog)*
  UF Breton missions
Missions, British *(May Subd Geog)*
  [BV2200 (Catholic)]
  [BV2420 (Protestant)]
  UF British missions
  NT Missions, Scottish
Missions, Bulgarian *(May Subd Geog)*
  UF Bulgarian missions
Missions, Canadian *(May Subd Geog)*
  UF Canadian missions
Missions, City
  USE City missions
Missions, Czech *(May Subd Geog)*
  [BV2470.C]
  UF Czech missions
Missions, Danish *(May Subd Geog)*
  UF Danish missions
Missions, Domestic
  USE Missions, Home
Missions, Dutch *(May Subd Geog)*
  [BV2240.N]
  UF Dutch missions
Missions, English *(May Subd Geog)*
  UF English missions
Missions, European *(May Subd Geog)*
  UF European missions

Missions, Finnish (May Subd Geog)
  UF Finnish missions
Missions, Foreign
  USE Missions
Missions, French (May Subd Geog)
  UF French missions
Missions, German (May Subd Geog)
  [BV2440]
  UF German missions
Missions, Government
  USE Government missions
Missions, Home
  [BV2495-BV2595 (By denomination)]
  [BV2650]
  [BV2750-BV3697 (By country)]
  UF Church extension
      Domestic missions
      Home missions
      Missions, Domestic
  NT City missions
      Inner missions
      Institutional missions
Missions, Indian
  USE subdivision Missions under names of
       tribes, e.g. Dakota Indians—
       Missions
       Indians—Missions
Missions, Indic (May Subd Geog)
  UF Indic missions
Missions, Inner
  USE Inner missions
Missions, Institutional
  USE Institutional missions
Missions, Irish (May Subd Geog)
  UF Irish missions
Missions, Islamic
  USE Islam—Missions
Missions, Italian (May Subd Geog)
  UF Italian missions
Missions, Japanese (May Subd Geog)
  UF Japanese missions
Missions, Latin American (May Subd Geog)
  UF Latin American missions
Missions, Maltese (May Subd Geog)
  UF Maltese missions
Missions, Medical (May Subd Geog)
  [RA390-392]
  UF Medical missions
      Missionary medicine
  BT Medical assistance
      Medicine
  NT Missionaries, Medical
      Zenana missions
Missions, Military
  USE Military missions
Missions, Muslim
  USE Islam—Missions
Missions, Naval
  USE Military missions
Missions, New Zealand (May Subd Geog)
  UF New Zealand missions
Missions, Norwegian (May Subd Geog)
  UF Norwegian missions
Missions, Parish
  USE Parish missions
Missions, Parochial
  USE Parish missions
Missions, Polish (May Subd Geog)
  UF Polish missions
Missions, Popular
  USE Parish missions
Missions, Portuguese (May Subd Geog)
  UF Portuguese missions
Missions, Rural
  USE Missions—Rural work
Missions, Russian (May Subd Geog)
  UF Russian missions
Missions, Scandinavian (May Subd Geog)
  UF Scandinavian missions
Missions, Scottish (May Subd Geog)
  [BV2200 (Catholic)]

  [BV2420 (Protestant)]
  UF Scottish missions
  BT Missions, British
Missions, Seamen's
  USE Merchant seamen—Missions and
       charities
Missions, Slovak (May Subd Geog)
  UF Slovak missions
Missions, South Korean (May Subd Geog)
  UF South Korean missions
Missions, Spanish (May Subd Geog)
  UF Spanish missions
Missions, Swedish (May Subd Geog)
  UF Swedish missions
Missions, Swiss (May Subd Geog)
  [BV2460]
  UF Swiss missions
Missions, Tamil (May Subd Geog)
  UF Tamil missions
Missions (Canon law)
  BT Catholic Church—Missions
Missions and Christian union
  [BX9.5.M5]
  UF Christian union and missions
  BT Christian union
Missions in literature
  BT Religion in literature
Missions of Piritu
  [F2319.3.M5]
  UF Piritu missions
  BT Franciscans—Missions
      Indians of South America—Missions
Missions to Afro-Americans
  (May Subd Geog)
  [BV2783]
  BT Afro-Americans
      Afro-Americans—Religion
Missions to Ahoms (Indic people)
  BT Ahoms (Indic people)
Missions to Akans (African people)
  [BV3630.A4]
  BT Akans (African people)
Missions to Angoni
  USE Missions to Ngoni (African people)
Missions to Armenians (May Subd Geog)
  [BV2628.A7]
  BT Armenians
Missions to Asians (May Subd Geog)
      Here are entered works on missions to Asians
  residing outside of Asia. Works on missions in Asia
  are entered under Missions—Asia.
  BT Asians
Missions to Australian aborigines
  (May Subd Geog)
  [BV3650-3660]
  BT Australian aborigines
Missions to Bachama (African people)
  [BV3630.B23]
  BT Bachama (African people)
Missions to Bakongo (African people)
  [BV3630.B24]
  BT Bakongo (African people)
Missions to Bamangwato
  BT Bamangwato
Missions to Bantus (May Subd Geog)
  [BV3630.B3]
  BT Bantus
Missions to Batak
  BT Batak
Missions to Bayaka (African people)
  [BV3630.B69]
  BT Bayaka (African people)
Missions to Bemba (African people)
  [BV3630.B46]
  BT Bemba (African people)
Missions to Blacks (May Subd Geog)
  BT Blacks
      Blacks—Religion
Missions to Bororo (African people)
  [BV3630.B]
  BT Bororo (African people)

Missions to Buddhists (May Subd Geog)
  [BV2618]
      Here are entered works on Christian missionary
  activity among Buddhists. Works on the spread of
  Buddhism are entered under Buddhism—Missions.
  BT Buddhists
      Christianity and other religions—
      Buddhism
  NT Converts from Buddhism
Missions to Buriats
  BT Buriats
Missions to Chinese (May Subd Geog)
  BT Chinese
Missions to Confucians
  BT Christianity and other religions—
      Confucianism
  NT Converts from Confucianism
Missions to Dani (New Guinea people)
  BT Dani (New Guinea people)
Missions to Dyaks
  BT Dyaks
Missions to Filipino Americans
  (May Subd Geog)
  [BV2788.F5]
  BT Filipino Americans
Missions to Fingos
  [BV3630.F]
  BT Fingos
Missions to French-Canadians
  (May Subd Geog)
  BT French-Canadians
Missions to Garo (Indic people)
  BT Garo (Indic people)
Missions to Germans (May Subd Geog)
  BT Germans
Missions to Gypsies
  [BV3697]
  BT Gypsies
Missions to Hakkas (May Subd Geog)
  BT Hakkas
Missions to Hindus (May Subd Geog)
      Here are entered works on Christian missions
  among Hindus. Works on Hindu missionary activity
  are entered under Hinduism—Missions.
  BT Christianity and other religions—
      Hinduism
      Hinduism—Relations—Christianity
      Hindus
  NT Converts from Hinduism
Missions to Hispanic Americans
  (May Subd Geog)
  BT Hispanic Americans
Missions to Hottentots
  USE Missions to Khoikhoi
Missions to Igbo (African people)
  [BV3630.I2]
  BT Igbo (African people)
Missions to immigrants
  USE Church work with immigrants
Missions to Indians of North America
  USE Indians of North America—Missions
Missions to Iranian Americans
  (May Subd Geog)
  [BV2788.I73]
  BT Iranian Americans
Missions to Iranians (May Subd Geog)
  BT Iranians
Missions to Iraqw (African people)
  UF Missions to Wambulu (African tribe)
  BT Iraqw (African people)
Missions to Italians (May Subd Geog)
  BT Italians
Missions to Jalé (Papuan people)
  [BV3373.J35]
  BT Jalé (Papuan people)
Missions to Japanese (May Subd Geog)
  BT Japanese
Missions to Japanese Americans
  (May Subd Geog)
  BT Japanese Americans

Missions to Jews *(May Subd Geog)*
  [BV2619-BV2623]
  BT Christianity and other religions—
        Judaism
      Jews
  NT Converts from Judaism
Missions to Kachin (Asian people)
  (May Subd Geog)
  UF Missions to Kachin tribes
  BT Kachin (Asian people)
Missions to Kachin tribes
  USE Missions to Kachin (Asian people)
Missions to Kagoro (African people)
  UF Missions to Kagoro (African tribe)
  BT Kagoro (African people)
Missions to Kagoro (African tribe)
  USE Missions to Kagoro (African people)
Missions to Kaguru (African people)
  [BV3630.K32]
  BT Kaguru (African people)
Missions to Kamwe (African people)
  [BV3630.K35]
  BT Kamwe (African people)
Missions to Kandhs
  BT Kandhs
Missions to Karens
  BT Karens
Missions to Karo-Batak *(May Subd Geog)*
  [BV3365]
  BT Karo-Batak
Missions to Kgatla (African people)
  BT Kgatla (African people)
Missions to Khasis
  [BV3280.K]
  BT Khasis
Missions to Khoikhoi
  [BV3630.K47]
  UF Missions to Hottentots
  BT Khoikhoi (African people)
Missions to Kikuyu (African people)
  BT Kikuyu (African people)
Missions to Kpelle (African people)
  (May Subd Geog)
  BT Kpelle (African people)
Missions to Lalungs (Indic people)
  BT Lalungs (Indic people)
Missions to Lambas
  [BV3630.L]
  BT Lambas
Missions to lepers *(May Subd Geog)*
  [BV2637]
  BT Leprosy
Missions to Lisu (Tibeto-Burman tribe)
  BT Lisu (Tibeto-Burman tribe)
Missions to Lolos
  USE Missions to Yi (Chinese people)
Missions to Lozi (African people)
  (May Subd Geog)
  [BV3630.L]
  BT Lozi (African people)
Missions to Mandaeans
  BT Mandaeans
Missions to Maoris
  BT Maoris
Missions to Maroons *(May Subd Geog)*
  BT Maroons
Missions to Masai *(May Subd Geog)*
  [BV3630.M3]
  BT Masai
Missions to Mashona
  BT Mashona
Missions to Mbata (African people)
  [BV3630.M35]
  BT Mbata (African people)
Missions to Mexican Americans
  (May Subd Geog)
  [BV2788.M4]
  UF Missions—United States—To Mexican
        Americans
  BT Mexican Americans

Missions to Mongo (African people)
  [BV3630.M64]
  BT Mongo (African people)
Missions to Mormons
  [BV2627]
  BT Mormons
Missions to Murngin (Australian people)
  BT Murngin (Australian people)
Missions to Muslims *(May Subd Geog)*
  [BV2625]
  Here are entered works on Christian missions
among Muslims. Works on Islamic missionary activi-
ty are entered under Islam—Missions.
  BT Christianity and other religions—Islam
      Islam—Relations—Christianity
      Muslims
  NT Converts from Islam
Missions to Nestorians *(May Subd Geog)*
  [BV2628.N4-5]
  BT Nestorians
Missions to Ngoni (African people)
  UF Missions to Angoni
  BT Ngoni (African people)
Missions to Oraons *(May Subd Geog)*
  [BV3280.O]
  BT Oraons
Missions to Oromo (African people)
  [BV3630.G3]
  BT Oromo (African people)
Missions to Pygmies *(May Subd Geog)*
  BT Pygmies
Missions to Santals (Indic people)
  (May Subd Geog)
  [BV3280.S3]
  BT Santals (Indic people)
Missions to Sawi (Indonesian people)
  [BV3373.S]
  BT Sawi (Indonesian people)
Missions to Sikhs *(May Subd Geog)*
  [BV2628.S]
  BT Sikhs
Missions to Southern Lunda (African people)
  BT Lunda, Southern (African people)
Missions to Tboli (Philippine people)
  BT Tboli (Philippine people)
Missions to the blind *(May Subd Geog)*
  BT Blind
Missions to Uhunduni (Indonesian people)
  [BV3373.U35]
  BT Uhunduni (Indonesian people)
Missions to Wambulu (African tribe)
  USE Missions to Iraqw (African people)
Missions to Wape (Papua New Guinea people)
  BT Wape (Papua New Guinea people)
Missions to Worora tribe
  BT Worora tribe
Missions to Xhosa (African people)
  [BV3630.X65]
  BT Xhosa (African people)
Missions to Yi (Chinese people)
  UF Missions to Lolos
  BT Yi (Chinese people)
Missions to Yorubas
  [BV3630.Y6]
  BT Yorubas
Missions to Zulus *(May Subd Geog)*
  [BV3630.Z8]
  BT Zulus
Missisauga Indians
  [E99.M68]
  BT Algonquian Indians
      Chippewa Indians
      Indians of North America
Missisauga language
  [PM1831]
  RT Algonquian languages
Mississauga City Hall (Mississauga, Ont.)
  BT City halls—Ontario
Mississauga Fort (Niagara-on-the-Lake, Ont.)
  USE Fort Mississauga (Niagara-on-the-
        Lake, Ont.)

Mississinewa, Battle of, 1812
  BT Indiana—History—War of 1812
      United States—History—War of 1812
        —Campaigns
Mississippi
  — Antiquities
      NT F. L. Brinkley Midden (Miss.)
          Fatherland Site (Miss.)
          Lake George Site (Miss.)
  — Description and travel
  — — 1951-1980
  — — 1981-
  — Governors
  — — Dwellings
        NT Mississippi Governor's Mansion
            (Jackson, Miss.)
  — History
      [F336-350]
  — — To 1803
  — — War of 1812
  — — Civil War, 1861-1865
        [E516]
        [E568]
        NT Grierson's Cavalry Raid, 1863
  — Politics and government
  — — To 1865
  — — Civil War, 1861-1865
  — — 1865-1950
  — — 1951-
  — Public buildings
      USE Public buildings—Mississippi
Mississippi and Iowa Central Railroad
  BT Railroads—United States
Mississippi Embayment
  BT Geosynclines—United States
      Mississippi River
Mississippi Governor's Mansion (Jackson,
  Miss.)
  BT Dwellings—Mississippi
      Mississippi—Governors—Dwellings
Mississippi kite
  UF Ictinia mississippiensis
Mississippi paddlefish
  USE Paddlefish
Mississippi River *(Not Subd Geog)*
  BT Rivers—United States
  NT Mississippi Embayment
  — Alluvial plain
  — Delta
      NT Mud lumps
  — Jetties
Mississippi River Parkway
  USE Great River Road
Mississippi River Valley
  UF Mississippi Valley
  BT Valleys—United States
  NT American Bottom (Ill.)
      Middle West
  — History
  — — To 1803
        [F352]
        UF New France—History
  — — Revolution, 1775-1783
        [E230.5]
  — — 1803-1865
        [F353]
  — — Civil War, 1861-1865
        [E470.8]
  — — 1865-
Mississippi silverside
  USE Menidia audens
Mississippi Sound
  BT Sounds (Geomorphology)—Alabama
      Sounds (Geomorphology)—Louisiana
      Sounds (Geomorphology)—Mississippi
Mississippi Valley
  USE Mississippi River Valley
Mississippian culture
  UF Temple Mound culture
  BT Indians of North America—Antiquities
      Mound-builders

NT Cemochechobee Archaeological
District (Ga.)
Oneota Indians (Great Plains)
Mississippian epoch
USE Geology, Stratigraphic—Mississippian
Paleontology—Mississippian
Misskito language
USE Mosquito language
Missoula, Lake (Not Subd Geog)
UF Glacial Lake Missoula
Lake Missoula
BT Glacial lakes—Idaho
Glacial lakes—Montana
Glacial lakes—Washington (State)
Missouri
— Antiquities
NT Callahan-Thompson Site (Mo.)
Hess Site (Mo.)
Nebo Hill Site (Mo.)
Turner Site (Mo.)
— Description and travel
— — 1951-1980
— — 1981-
— History
[F461-475]
— — Civil War, 1861-1865
[E517]
[E569]
NT Big Blue, Battle of the, 1864
Palmyra (Mo.)—Execution of
citizens, 1862
Pilot Knob, Battle of, 1864
Price's Missouri Expedition,
1864
— Politics and government
— — To 1865
— — Civil War, 1861-1865
— — 1865-1950
— — 1951-
— Public buildings
USE Public buildings—Missouri
Missouri compromise
[E373]
BT Slavery—United States
NT Kansas-Nebraska bill
Missouri Indians
[E99.M]
UF Missouria Indians
BT Indians of North America
Missouri Pacific Number 2 Site (Ill.)
(Not Subd Geog)
BT Illinois—Antiquities
Missouri River
BT Rivers—United States
Missouri River Basin project. Garrison
Diversion Unit
UF Garrison Diversion Unit (Missouri
River Watershed)
BT Water resources development—North
Dakota
Missouria Indians
USE Missouri Indians
Misspellings
USE Spelling errors
Mist-poeffers
USE Acoustic phenomena in nature
Mist propagation
[SB123.75]
UF Propagation, Mist
BT Plant propagation
Mistake (Canon law)
[BX1939.M]
Mistake (Criminal law) (May Subd Geog)
UF Error (Criminal law)
BT Criminal intent
Criminal law
Criminal liability
Mistake (Law)

Mistake (Islamic law)
Mistake (Jewish law)
Mistake (Law) (May Subd Geog)
UF Error (Law)
BT Consent (Law)
Declaration of intention
RT Fraud
Good faith (Law)
Ignorance (Law)
Motive (Law)
NT False demonstration (Law)
Mistake (Criminal law)
Reformation of instruments
Rescission (Law)
Mistake (Roman law)
Mistakes
USE Errors
Errors, Popular
Errors, Scientific
Errors and blunders, Literary
Mistassin Indians
[E99.M683]
BT Algonquian Indians
Cree Indians
Indians of North America
Montagnais Indians
Mistassini Lake (Québec)
UF Lac Mistassini (Québec)
Lake Mistassini (Québec)
Lake Mistassinie (Québec)
BT Lakes—Québec (Province)
Mistbow
USE Fogbow
MISTIC (Computer)
USE Illiac computer
Mistichthys
[QL638.G7]
BT Gobiidae
Mistik Creek (Man.)
BT Rivers—Manitoba
Mistletoe (May Subd Geog)
[QK495.L87 (Botany)]
[SB615.M5 (Pests)]
NT Dwarf mistletoe
European mistletoe
Mistletoe fungus
[SB615.M51]
Mistpouffers
USE Acoustic phenomena in nature
Mistral (Turbojet fighter planes)
USE Vampire (Turbojet fighter planes)
Mistral family (Not Subd Geog)
Mistreatment of animals
USE Animals, Treatment of
Mistreatment of the aged
USE Aged—Abuse of
Mistress of novices
USE Master of novices
Mistresses (May Subd Geog)
UF Lovers (Mistresses)
Paramours (Mistresses)
BT Concubinage
Unmarried couples
RT Adultery
NT Kings and rulers—Mistresses
Presidents—Mistresses
Presidents—United States—Mistresses
Misty Fjords National Monument (Alaska)
BT National monuments—Alaska
Misu Haiji Iseki (Tanabe-shi, Japan)
USE Misu Haiji Site (Tanabe-shi, Japan)
Misu Haiji Site (Tanabe-shi, Japan)
(Not Subd Geog)
UF Misu Haiji Iseki (Tanabe-shi, Japan)
BT Japan—Antiquities
Misumalpan languages
BT Central America—Languages
NT Matagalpa language
Mosquito language
Sumo language

Misuse of therapeutic drugs
USE Medication abuse
MIT time-sharing system (Electronic
computers)
USE Compatible time-sharing system
(Electronic computers)
Mitake Mountain (Japan)
UF Mitake-san (Japan)
Mitakesan (Japan)
BT Mountains—Japan
Mitake-san (Japan)
USE Mitake Mountain (Japan)
Mitakesan (Japan)
USE Mitake Mountain (Japan)
Mitama Ōtsuka Kofun (Kisa-chō, Japan)
USE Mitama Ōtsuka Site (Kisa-chō, Japan)
Mitama Ōtsuka Site (Kisa-chō, Japan)
(Not Subd Geog)
UF Mitama Ōtsuka Kofun (Kisa-chō,
Japan)
BT Japan—Antiquities
Mitama Region (Japan)
USE Tama Region (Japan)
Mitani language
USE Hurrian language
Mitannian language
USE Hurrian language
Mitannians
NT Hurrians
Subarians
Mitarai family (Not Subd Geog)
Mitcalf family
USE Metcalf family
Mitchael family
USE Mitchell family
Mitchal family
USE Mitchell family
Mitchall family
USE Mitchell family
Mitchel family
USE Mitchell family
Mitchell bomber
UF B-25 bomber
BT Bombers
North American airplanes (Military
aircraft)
Mitchell City Cemetery (Mitchell, Neb.)
BT Cemeteries—Nebraska
Mitchell family (Not Subd Geog)
UF Micthel family
Mischel family
Mitchael family
Mitchal family
Mitchall family
Mitchel family
Mitchels family
Mitchiell family
Mitchil family
Mittchel family
RT Michel family
Mitchell grass
[QK495.G74 (Botany)]
[SB201.M5 (Forage crop)]
Mitchell-Hedges skull
BT Lubaantun (City)
Mitchell Island (Tuvalu)
USE Nukulaelae Atoll (Tuvalu)
Mitchell Plateau (W.A.)
BT Plateaus—Australia
Mitchell Valley Cemetery (Neb.)
BT Cemeteries—Nebraska
Mitchels family
USE Mitchell family
Mitchiell family
USE Mitchell family
Mitchif language
USE Michif language
Mitchil family
USE Mitchell family
Mite control
USE Mites—Control

Miter-gages
  ⌐TH5618⌐
  BT Gages
      Mitering
Mitering
  ⌐TH5691 (Carpentry)⌐
  UF Mitring
  BT Carpentry
  NT Miter-gages
Miters
  UF Mitra (Head-gear)
      Mitres
  BT Head-gear
Mites (May Subd Geog)
  ⌐QL458⌐
  UF Acari
      Acarida
      Acaridea
      Acariformes
      Acarina
      Opilioacariformes
      Oribatei
      Parasitiformes
      Tetranychoidea
  BT Arachnida
  RT Acarology
  SA names of specific mites, e.g. Broad
      mite; Citrus rust mite
  NT Acaridae
      Ameronothridae
      Analgesidae
      Anystidae
      Argasidae
      Arrenuridae
      Brachychthoniidae
      Caeculidae
      Cercomegistidae
      Cheyletidae
      Dermanyssidae
      Epidermoptidae
      Eremaeidae
      Eriophyidae
      Eupodidae
      Eustathiidae
      False spider mites
      Galumnidae
      Glycyphagidae
      Halacaridae
      Hermanniidae
      Heterocheylidae
      Hydrachnidae
      Hygrobatidae
      Ixodidae
      Labidocarpidae
      Laelapidae
      Lebertiidae
      Leeuwenhoekiidae
      Limnocharidae
      Listrophoridae
      Macronyssidae
      Myocoptidae
      Oribatidae
      Parasitidae
      Penthaleidae
      Phytoseiidae
      Pionidae
      Plant mites
      Proctophyllodidae
      Pterygosomatidae
      Pyemotidae
      Pyroglyphidae
      Rhagidiidae
      Rosensteiniidae
      Sarcoptidae
      Spinturnicidae
      Stigmaeidae
      Syringophilidae
      Tarsonemidae
      Tetranychidae
      Ticks
      Trombiculidae

      Trombidiidae
      Varroidae
      Water mites
      Zerconidae
  — Acaricide resistance
      USE Acaricide resistance
  — **Biological control** (May Subd Geog)
      BT Mites—Control
      NT Plant mites—Biological control
  — **Control** (May Subd Geog)
      ⌐RA641.M5 (Public health)⌐
      ⌐SB940 (Plant culture)⌐
      ⌐SF810.T5 (Veterinary medicine)⌐
      UF Mite control
          Mites as carriers of disease—
              Control
      RT Acaricides
      NT Chiggers (Mites)—Control
          Mites—Biological control
  — **Physiology**
  — **Resistance to acaricides**
      USE Acaricide resistance
Mites as carriers of disease
  ⌐RA641.M5⌐
  BT Arachnida as carriers of disease
  NT Plant mites as carriers of disease
      Ticks as carriers of disease
  — **Control**
      USE Mites—Control
Mites as carriers of plant disease
  USE Plant mites as carriers of disease
Mitford-Barberton family (Not Subd Geog)
  RT Mitford family
Mitford family (Not Subd Geog)
  RT Mitford-Barberton family
Mithan
  USE Gayal
Mithen family
  USE Mitten family
Mithraea (May Subd Geog)
  UF Mithraeums
  BT Cave temples
  — **Italy**
      NT Mithraeum of the Castra
          Peregrinorum (Rome, Italy)
Mithraeum of the Castra Peregrinorum
  (Rome, Italy)
  UF Mitreo dei Castra Peregrinorum
      (Rome, Italy)
  BT Mithraea—Italy
Mithraeums
  USE Mithraea
Mithraism (May Subd Geog)
  ⌐BL1585⌐
  RT Zoroastrianism
  NT Rider-gods
Mithridatic Wars, 88-63 B.C.
  USE Rome—History—Mithridatic Wars,
      88-63 B.C.
Mitiaro (Cook Islands)
  BT Coral reefs and islands—Cook Islands
      Islands—Cook Islands
Miticides
  USE Acaricides
Mitigation (Law)
  USE Extenuating circumstances
Mitilini Island (Greece)
  USE Lesbos Island (Greece)
Mito Castle (Mito-shi, Japan)
  USE Mitojō (Mito-shi, Japan)
Mito-dōri (Japan)
  USE Mito Kaidō (Japan)
Mito Kaidō (Japan) (Not Subd Geog)
  UF Aizu Kaidō (Japan)
      Hitachiōta Kaidō (Japan)
      Ibaraki Kaidō (Japan)
      Mito-dōri (Japan)
      Tanakura Kaidō (Japan)
  BT Roads—Japan
Mitochondria
  UF Chondriosomes

  BT Cell organelles
      Protoplasm
  RT Extrachromosomal DNA
  NT Plant mitochondria
Mitochondrial membranes
  ⌐QH603.M5⌐
  BT Cell membranes
      Membranes (Biology)
  — **Abnormalities** (May Subd Geog)
      BT Pathology, Cellular
Mitogaku
  BT Philosophy, Japanese
Mitogens
  BT Lectins
      Mitosis
  NT Pokeweed mitogens
Mitojō (Mito-shi, Japan)
  UF Babajō (Mito-shi, Japan)
      Mito Castle (Mito-shi, Japan)
  BT Castles—Japan
Mitoko Matsubara Iseki (Shima-machi, Japan)
  USE Mitoko Matsubara Site (Shima-machi,
      Japan)
Mitoko Matsubara Site (Shima-machi, Japan)
  (Not Subd Geog)
  UF Mitoko Matsubara Iseki (Shima-machi,
      Japan)
  BT Japan—Antiquities
Mitomycin C
  ⌐RC271.M53 (Cancer chemotherapy)⌐
  UF Aminohexahydrohydrox
      ymethylmethoxymethyl
      azirinopyrroloindoledione carbamate
      (ester)
  BT Amino compounds
      Antibiotics
      Antineoplastic agents
      Carbamates
      Immunosuppressive agents
      Indole
      Streptomyces
Mitopus
  ⌐QL458.52.P45⌐
  BT Phalangiidae
Mitopus morio
  ⌐QL458.52.P45⌐
Mitosis
  ⌐QH605⌐
  BT Cell cycle
      Cell division
      Karyokinesis
  NT Antimitotic agents
      Mitogens
      Premature chromosome condensation
      Spindle (Cell division)
Mitotic cycle
  USE Cell cycle
Mitoura
  USE Callophrys
Mitoxantrone hydrochloride
  ⌐RC271.M57⌐
  UF Dihydroxybishydroxye
      thylaminoethylaminoa
      nthracenedione dihydrochloride
      Dihydroxybishydroxye
      thylaminoethylaminoanthraquinone
      dihydrochloride
  BT Anthracene
      Antineoplastic agents
      Cyclic compounds
      Quinone
Mitra (Head-gear)
  USE Miters
Mitra (Hindu deity)
  BT Gods, Hindu
Mitrailleuses
  ⌐UF620.M7⌐
  BT Machine-guns
  NT Gatling guns
Mitral incompetence
  USE Mitral valve insufficiency

2430

Mitral regurgitation
  USE Mitral valve insufficiency
Mitral stenosis
  BT Mitral valve—Diseases
Mitral valve
  UF Bicuspid valve
  BT Heart—Valves
  — **Diseases** *(May Subd Geog)*
    NT Mitral stenosis
        Mitral valve insufficiency
  — **Displacement**
    UF Barlow's syndrome
        Click murmur syndrome
        Displacement of the mitral valve
        Floppy mitral valve syndrome
        Mitral valve—Prolapse
        Mitral valve prolapse
        MVP (Heart disease)
        Prolapse of the mitral valve
  — **Prolapse**
        USE Mitral valve—Displacement
  — **Surgery**
    UF Mitral valvotomy
        Mitral valvulotomy
Mitral valve insufficiency *(May Subd Geog)*
    [RC685.V2]
  UF Incompetence, Mitral
      Mitral incompetence
      Mitral regurgitation
      Regurgitation, Mitral
  BT Mitral valve—Diseases
Mitral valve prolapse
  USE Mitral valve—Displacement
Mitral valvotomy
  USE Mitral valve—Surgery
Mitral valvulotomy
  USE Mitral valve—Surgery
Mitreo dei Castra Peregrinorum (Rome, Italy)
  USE Mithraeum of the Castra Peregrinorum
        (Rome, Italy)
Mitres
  USE Miters
Mitridae
    [QL430.5.M57]
  BT Prosobranchiata
Mitring
  USE Mitering
Mitsogho (African people)
  UF Apindji (African people)
      Ashogo (African people)
      Isogo (African people)
      Shogo (African people)
      Tsogho (African people)
  BT Ethnology—Gabon
Mitsogho (African people) art
  USE Art, Mitsogho (African people)
Mitsogo language
  USE Tsogo language
Mitsu family *(Not Subd Geog)*
Mitsubishi airplanes
  BT Airplanes
  NT Raiden (Fighter plane)
Mitsubishi automobiles
    [TL215.M]
  BT Automobiles
Mitsubishi Group
  BT Conglomerate corporations—Japan
Mitsubishi J2M (Fighter plane)
  USE Raiden (Fighter plane)
Mitsubishi Zaibatsu
  BT Trusts, Industrial—Japan
Mitsuhashi family *(Not Subd Geog)*
Mitsui Zaibatsu
Mitsukurina
  USE Goblin shark
Mitsukurinidae
    [QL638.95.M58]
  BT Lamniformes
  NT Goblin shark
Mitsumata
    [SB261.M6]

Mitsuwa Iseki (Hatogaya-shi, Japan)
  USE Mitsuwa Site (Hatogaya-shi, Japan)
Mitsuwa Site (Hatogaya-shi, Japan)
  UF Mitsuwa Iseki (Hatogaya-shi, Japan)
  BT Japan—Antiquities
Mitsvah
  USE Commandments (Judaism)
Mitsvot
  USE Commandments (Judaism)
Mittan family
  USE Mitten family
Mittchel family
  USE Mitchell family
Mittelalterliche Hausbuch (Sketch-book)
  USE Master of the Housebook, 15th cent.
        Housebook
Mittelgebirge (Czechoslovakia)
  USE České středohoří (Czechoslovakia)
Mitten family *(Not Subd Geog)*
  UF Mithen family
      Mittan family
      Mittin family
      Mitton family
      Mydon family
      Mythen family
      Myton family
Mittendorf family *(Not Subd Geog)*
Mittens *(May Subd Geog)*
  BT Gloves
Mittenwaldbahn
  BT Railroads—Austria
      Railroads—Germany (West)
Mittin family
  USE Mitten family
Mitton family
  USE Mitten family
Mituku language
  BT Bantu languages
Mitzvah
  USE Commandments (Judaism)
Mitzvot
  USE Commandments (Judaism)
Miura family *(Not Subd Geog)*
Miura-hantō (Japan)
  USE Miura Peninsula (Japan)
Miura Peninsula (Japan)
  UF Miura-hantō (Japan)
  BT Peninsulas—Japan
Miwa family *(Not Subd Geog)*
Miwok Indians
    [E99.M69]
  UF Awani Indians
      Meewoc Indians
      Mewan Indians
      Yosemite Indians
  BT Indians of North America
      Moquelumnan Indians
  NT Saclan Indians
Miwok languages
    [PM1845]
  UF Mewan languages
      Moquelumnan languages
  BT California—Languages
  NT Bodega Miwok language
      Northern Sierra Miwok language
      Plains Miwok language
Mix family *(Not Subd Geog)*
  UF Mixon family
      Mixson family
Mixe Indians
    [F1221.M67]
  UF Mije Indians
  BT Indians of Mexico
Mixe language
    [PM4011]
  UF Ayook language
      Mije language
  BT Indians of Mexico—Languages
Mixed Abelian groups
  BT Abelian groups

Mixed bloods (American Indians)
  USE Indians—Mixed bloods
Mixed bloods (Australian aborigines)
  USE Australian aborigines—Mixed bloods
Mixed communion
  USE Close and open communion
Mixed connective tissue disease
    (May Subd Geog)
    [RC924.5.M58]
  UF MCTD (Disease)
  BT Connective tissues—Diseases
Mixed cycloids (Chemistry)
  USE Heterocyclic compounds
Mixed distributions (Probability theory)
  USE Mixture distributions (Probability
        theory)
Mixed economy *(May Subd Geog)*
    Here are entered works on economic systems in
  which characteristics of both capitalism and social-
  ism are found. When this heading is subdivided by
  place, a second heading is assigned for the name of
  the place subdivided by Economic conditions.
  UF Economy, Mixed
  BT Capitalism
      Socialism
Mixed languages
  USE Languages, Mixed
Mixed leucocyte culture test
  USE Lymphocyte culture test, Mixed
Mixed lymphocyte culture test
  USE Lymphocyte culture test, Mixed
Mixed marriage
  USE Interfaith marriage
      Intermarriage
Mixed media painting
  BT Painting
Mixed race adoption
  USE Interracial adoption
Mixed race children
  USE Children of interracial marriage
Mixed schizophrenic and affective psychosis
  USE Schizoaffective disorders
Mixed spaces
  USE Saks spaces
Mixed use of buildings
  USE Joint occupancy of buildings
Mixel family
  USE Mikesell family
Mixers, Microwave
  USE Microwave mixers
Mixers (Cookery)
    [TX840.M5]
  BT Kitchen utensils
      Mixing machinery
  NT Food mixes
Mixers (Electronics)
  USE Mixing circuits
Mixers (Machinery)
  USE Mixing machinery
Mixes (Cookery)
  USE Food mixes
Mixing
  UF Blending
  BT Chemical engineering
      Fluid dynamics
      Hydrodynamics
  NT Concrete—Mixing
      Density currents
      Fireproofing agents—Mixing
      Heat of mixing
      Plastics—Mixing
Mixing, Oceanic
  USE Oceanic mixing
Mixing circuits
  UF Mixers (Electronics)
  BT Electronic circuits
  NT Microwave mixers
Mixing distributions (Probability theory)
  USE Mixture distributions (Probability
        theory)

Mixing machinery
[TP156.M5]
UF Agitators (Machinery)
Kneading machinery
Mixers (Machinery)
Stirrers (Machinery)
NT Blenders (Cookery)
Concrete mixers
Farinographs
Mixers (Cookery)
Mixomatosis
USE Myxomatosis
Mixon family
USE Mix family
Mixsell family
USE Mikesell family
Mixson family
USE Mix family
Mixtec Indians
[F1221.M]
BT Indians of Mexico
— Antiquities
— Land tenure
— Writing
[F1219]
BT Indians of Mexico—Writing
Mixtec language
[PM4016]
BT Indians of Mexico—Languages
Otomanguean languages
RT Proto-Popotecan language
NT Amishgo language
Cuicatec language
Ixcateco language
Trique language
Mixtec manuscripts
USE Manuscripts, Mixtec
Mixton War, 1541-1542
[F1231]
BT Indians of Mexico—Wars
Mixture distributions (Probability theory)
UF Compound distributions (Probability theory)
Distributions, Mixture (Probability theory)
Mixed distributions (Probability theory)
Mixing distributions (Probability theory)
Mixtures of distributions (Probability theory)
BT Distribution (Probability theory)
Mixture stops
UF Compound stops
Mixtures (Organ stops)
Stops, Mixture
BT Organ stops
Mixtures
NT Asphalt emulsion mixtures
Azeotropes
Emulsions
Eutectics
Fertilizer-pesticide mixtures
Solution (Chemistry)
Mixtures (Organ stops)
USE Mixture stops
Mixtures of distributions (Probability theory)
USE Mixture distributions (Probability theory)
Miyagawa family *(Not Subd Geog)*
Miyagi Plain (Japan) *(Not Subd Geog)*
UF Kokubugahara (Japan)
Miyagino (Japan)
Miyaginohara (Japan)
BT Plains—Japan
Miyagino (Japan)
USE Miyagi Plain (Japan)
Miyaginohara (Japan)
USE Miyagi Plain (Japan)

Miyake Island (Japan)
UF Miyake-jima (Japan)
Miyake Sima (Japan)
Miyakejima (Japan)
Miyakezima (Japan)
BT Islands—Japan
Miyake Island Earthquake, 1962
UF Oyama, Eruption of, 1962
Miyake-jima (Japan)
USE Miyake Island (Japan)
Miyake Sima (Japan)
USE Miyake Island (Japan)
Miyakejima (Japan)
USE Miyake Island (Japan)
Miyakezima (Japan)
USE Miyake Island (Japan)
Miyakō
USE Miyaza
Miyako Island (Japan)
UF Miyako-jima (Japan)
Miyako-shima (Japan)
BT Islands—Japan
Ryukyu Islands
Miyako-jima (Japan)
USE Miyako Island (Japan)
Miyako-machi Kita Iseki (Kudamatsu-shi, Japan)
USE Miyako-machi Kita Site (Kudamatsu-shi, Japan)
Miyako-machi Kita Site (Kudamatsu-shi, Japan) *(Not Subd Geog)*
UF Miyako-machi Kita Iseki (Kudamatsu-shi, Japan)
BT Japan—Antiquities
Miyako-shima (Japan)
USE Miyako Island (Japan)
Miyanakama
USE Miyaza
Miyanmin (Papua New Guinea people)
USE Mianmin (Papua New Guinea people)
Miyanohara Iseki (Ajimu-machi, Japan)
USE Miyanohara Site (Ajimu-machi, Japan)
Miyanohara Site (Ajimu-machi, Japan)
UF Miyanohara Iseki (Ajimu-machi, Japan)
BT Japan—Antiquities
Miyanosako Iseki (Japan)
USE Miyanosako Site (Japan)
Miyanosako Site (Japan) *(Not Subd Geog)*
UF Miyanosako Iseki (Japan)
BT Japan—Antiquities
Miyauchi family *(Not Subd Geog)*
Miyauchi Kita Iseki (Oyama-shi, Japan)
USE Miyauchi Kita Site (Oyama-shi, Japan)
Miyauchi Kita Site (Oyama-shi, Japan) *(Not Subd Geog)*
UF Miyauchi Kita Iseki (Oyama-shi, Japan)
BT Japan—Antiquities
Miyaza
[BL2211.M5]
UF Miyakō
Miyanakama
BT Shinto
Shinto shrines—Organization and administration
Miyazaki family *(Not Subd Geog)*
Miyazu-han Peasant Uprising, 1822
UF Tango no Kuni Bunsei gonen Miyazuryō ikki, 1822
Miyoshi family *(Not Subd Geog)*
Mizar family
USE Meisser family
Mize family *(Not Subd Geog)*
UF Mice family
Mise family
Myse family
Myze family
Mizel family
USE Mizell family

Mizell family *(Not Subd Geog)*
UF Mizel family
Mizelle family
Mizelle family
USE Mizell family
Mizer family
USE Meisser family
Mizner family
USE Misner family
Mizo (Indic people)
USE Lushai (Indic people)
Mizo language
USE Lushai language
Mizote family *(Not Subd Geog)*
Mizugo kuyō
USE Fetal propitiatory rites—Buddhism
Mizuhara family
USE Mihara family
Mizuho Iseki (Fukuoka-shi, Japan)
USE Mizuho Site (Fukuoka-shi, Japan)
Mizuho Plateau (Antarctic regions)
BT Plateaus—Antarctic regions
Mizuho Site (Fukuoka-shi, Japan) *(Not Subd Geog)*
UF Hie Daichi Site (Fukuoka-shi, Japan)
Hiedaichi Site (Fukuoka-shi, Japan)
Mizuho Iseki (Fukuoka-shi, Japan)
BT Japan—Antiquities
Mizuiri Iseki (Tagajō-shi, Japan)
USE Takasaki Mizuiri Site (Tagajō-shi, Japan)
Mizuko kuyō
USE Fetal propitiatory rites—Buddhism
Mizukuki Okayamajō (Japan)
UF Okayamajō (Japan)
Ōmi Mizukukijō (Japan)
Ōmi Okayamajō (Japan)
BT Castles—Japan
Mizuno family *(Not Subd Geog)*
Mizutori
USE Omizutori
Mizwahs, Six hundred and thirteen
USE Commandments, Six hundred and thirteen
Mjillem language
USE Nielim language
Mjøsa Lake (Norway)
UF Mjøsen Lake (Norway)
BT Lakes—Norway
Mjøsen Lake (Norway)
USE Mjøsa Lake (Norway)
Mkata Plain, North (Tanzania)
USE North Mkata Plain (Tanzania)
ML (Computer program language)
[QA76.73.M]
UF Meta Language (Computer program language)
BT Programming languages (Electronic computers)
Mlada Bosna movement
Mladeck family
USE Mladek family
Mladek family *(Not Subd Geog)*
UF Mladeck family
MLNS (Disease)
USE Mucocutaneous lymph node syndrome
Młoda Polska
BT Polish literature—History and criticism
Mmfo language
USE Mo language (Ghana and Ivory Coast)
MMPI (Personality test)
USE Minnesota Multiphasic Personality Inventory
MN blood group system
USE Blood groups—MNSs system
Mnemiopsis *(May Subd Geog)*
[QL380.5.T45]
BT Bolinopsidae
NT Mnemiopsis leidyi
Mnemiopsis leidyi *(May Subd Geog)*
[QL380.5.T45]

BT Mnemiopsis
Mnemonics
[BF380-BF385 (Psychology)]
UF Memoria technica
Memory training
Training of the memory
BT Mental discipline
Self-culture
RT Memory
Reproduction (Psychology)
NT Bible—Mnemonic devices
Music—Memorizing
Talmud—Mnemonic devices
— **Early works to 1850**
[BF383]
MNF (Computer program)
UF Minnesota Fortran (Computer
program)
BT Compilers (Computer programs)
Mniotiltidae
USE Wood warblers
Mnong (Indochinese tribe)
BT Ethnology—Vietnam
Mnong language, Eastern
[PL4351.M62]
UF Eastern Mnong language
BT Mon-Khmer languages
MNSs blood group system
USE Blood groups—MNSs system
MO5 (Computer)
[QA76.8.M]
BT Microcomputers
Mo family
USE Moe family
Mo language (Ghana and Ivory Coast)
UF Buru language (Ghana and Ivory
Coast)
Deg language
Degha language
Mmfo language
BT Ghana—Languages
Gurunsi dialects
Ivory Coast—Languages
Mo-peds
USE Mopeds
Moa
UF Dinornis
Dinornithiformes
BT Birds, Extinct
Moa language
USE Moba language
Moaaga (African people)
USE Mossi (African people)
Moaaga languages
USE Mossi languages
Moabite stone
[PJ4149]
UF Inscriptions, Moabitic
Moache Indians
[E99.M]
UF Muache Indians
BT Indians of North America
Ute Indians
Moats (May Subd Geog)
[NA490-NA497 (Military
architecture)]
[NA660 (English castles)]
BT Castles
— **Denmark**
NT Vestvolden (Copenhagen,
Denmark)
Moba (African people)
UF Mwaba (African people)
BT Ethnology—Nigeria
Moba language
[PL8516]
UF Bimoba language
Moa language
BT Gur languages
Gurma language

Moba proverbs
USE Proverbs, Moba
Mobenge language
USE Benge language
Moberget family (Not Subd Geog)
Moberly family
USE Mobley family
Mobile (Ala.)
— **History**
— — **Civil War, 1861-1865**
Mobile banks
USE Banks and banking, Mobile
Mobile Bay, Battle of, 1864
[E476.85]
BT United States—History—Civil War,
1861-1865—Campaigns
United States—History—Civil War,
1861-1865—Naval operations
Mobile breakwaters
USE Breakwaters, Mobile
Mobile Catholic Cemetery (Mobile, Ala.)
USE Catholic Cemetery (Mobile, Ala.)
Mobile communication systems
(May Subd Geog)
[TK7882.M6]
UF Vehicles—Communication systems
Vehicular communication systems
BT Communications, Military
Radio
Telecommunication systems
NT Aeronautical radio stations
Airplanes—Radio equipment
Automobiles—Radio equipment
Cellular radio
Marine radio stations
Mobile radio stations
Police communication systems
Public safety radio service
Radio—Installation in tanks
Radio—Installation on ships
Radio, Military
Railroads—Communication systems
Walkie-talkies
Mobile community centers
USE Community centers, Mobile
Mobile coronary care units
USE Coronary care units, Mobile
Mobile home industry (May Subd Geog)
[HD9715.7]
Mobile home living (May Subd Geog)
[TX1100-1105]
BT Home economics
Mobile homes
RT Van life
NT Church work with mobile home
dwellers
Trailer camps
Mobile home parks (May Subd Geog)
BT Mobile homes
Trailer camps
— **Law and legislation** (May Subd Geog)
Mobile homes (May Subd Geog)
UF Homes, Mobile
House trailers
BT Automobiles—Trailers
Dwellings
Housing
Trailers
NT Mobile home living
Mobile home parks
Used mobile homes
— **Foundations**
BT Foundations
— **Inspection**
BT Building inspection
— **Insulation**
BT Insulation (Heat)
— **Law and legislation** (May Subd Geog)
— **Registration and transfer**
(May Subd Geog)
BT Recording and registration

— **Taxation** (May Subd Geog)
— — **Law and legislation**
(May Subd Geog)
Mobile hospitals
USE Hospitals, Mobile
Mobile Indians
[E99.M698]
UF Mabile Indians
Maubile Indians
Mauilla Indians
Mauvila Indians
Mavila Indians
Mouile Indians
BT Indians of North America
Indians of North America—Alabama
Mobile intensive care units
USE Intensive care units, Mobile
Mobile occupational training centers
USE Occupational training centers, Mobile
Mobile post offices (May Subd Geog)
UF Traveling post offices
BT Postal service
NT Highway post offices
Railway mail service
Mobile radio stations (May Subd Geog)
UF Mobile stations (Radio)
Radio stations, Mobile
BT Microwave communication systems
Mobile communication systems
Radio stations
Radiotelephone
RT Citizens band radio
SA subjects for particular types and
applications, e.g. Aeronautical radio
stations; Police communication
systems; Radio, Military
— **Law and legislation** (May Subd Geog)
Mobile schools
USE Schools, Traveling
Mobile sea launching base (Satellites)
USE Satellite launching ships
Mobile stations (Radio)
USE Mobile radio stations
Mobiles (Sculpture) (May Subd Geog)
[NB1315]
UF Sculpture, Mobile
Sculpture, Moving
BT Art
Sculpture
RT Kinetic sculpture
Mobilian jargon
USE Mobilian trade language
Mobilian trade language
[PM1855]
UF Chickasaw trade language
Choctaw jargon
Mobilian jargon
BT Alabama language
Choctaw language
Indians of North America—Languages
Lingua francas
Mobility
USE College teacher mobility
Graduate student mobility
Labor mobility
Migration, Internal
Occupational mobility
Residential mobility
Social mobility
Student mobility
Mobility, Drift
USE Drift mobility
Mobility of electrons
USE Electron mobility
Mobility of ions
USE Ionic mobility
Mobility of teeth
USE Teeth—Mobility
Mobilization, Industrial
USE Industrial mobilization

2433

Mobilization, Military
　USE Armed Forces—Mobilization
Mobima language
　USE Movima language
Möbius function
　UF Function, Möbius
　BT Numerical functions
Möbius transformations
　BT Transformations (Mathematics)
Mobley family *(Not Subd Geog)*
　UF Moberly family
　　Mobly family
Mobly family
　USE Mobley family
Mobray family
　USE Mowbray family
Mobs *(May Subd Geog)*
　[HM281-HM283 (Psychology)]
　[HV6474-HV6485]
　BT Crowds
　RT Riots
Mobulidae
　[QL638.85.M6]
　UF Devilfish (Manta rays)
　　Manta rays
　BT Rajiformes
　　Rays (Fishes)
Mocă language
　USE Mocha language
Moçambique (Dance) *(May Subd Geog)*
　[GV1796.M]
　BT Folk dancing—Brazil
Moçambique Channel
　USE Mozambique Channel
Moçâmedes Desert (Angola)
　UF Deserto de Moçâmedes (Angola)
　　Deserto de Mossâmedes (Angola)
　　Mossâmedes Desert (Angola)
　BT Deserts—Angola
Moccasins
　[E98.C8]
　UF Indians of North America—Footwear
　BT Indians of North America—Costume
　　and adornment
　　Shoes
Moce Island (Fiji)
　USE Mothe Island (Fiji)
Mocenigo family *(Not Subd Geog)*
Mocha language
　UF Mocă language
　BT Omotic languages
Möchda language (Tucanan)
　USE Carapana language (Tucanan)
Moche Indians
　USE Mochica Indians
Moche River (Peru)
　UF Río Moche (Peru)
　BT Rivers—Peru
Mochica Indians
　[F3430.1.M6]
　UF Moche Indians
　BT Indians of South America
　　Yunca Indians
Mochica language
　USE Yunca language
Mochida family
Mochó language
　[PM4040.M6]
　UF Motochintlec language
　　Mototzintlec language
　　Motozintlec language
　　Tuzantec language
　BT Mayan languages
　　Mexico—Languages
Mocho Mountains (Jamaica)
　(Not Subd Geog)
　BT Mountains—Jamaica
Mochochidae
　USE Mochokidae
Mochocidae
　USE Mochokidae

Mochockidae
　USE Mochokidae
Mochokidae
　[QL638.M6]
　UF Mochochidae
　　Mochocidae
　　Mochockidae
　　Synodidae
　　Upside-down catfishes
　BT Catfishes
　NT Synodontis
Mock cucumber
　USE Echinocystis lobata
Mock epic literature
　USE Mock-heroic literature
Mock family *(Not Subd Geog)*
　BT Mauck family
　RT Mack family
Mock-heroic literature
　[PN6149.M55 (History)]
　UF Comic epic literature
　　Heroi-comical literature
　　Mock epic literature
　BT Epic literature
　　Literature
　　Wit and humor
Mock trials
　　Here are entered works on and collections of
　mock trials.
　BT Trial practice
　　Trials
　RT Moot courts
Mock trumpet
　USE Chalumeau (Single-reed musical
　　instrument)
Mocking-birds
　[QL696.P2]
Mocking of Christ (Painting)
　USE Grünewald, Matthias, 16th cent.
　　Mocking of Christ
Mocobi Indians
　[F2823.M]
　UF Mbocobi Indians
　　Mocovi Indians
　BT Guaycuru Indians
　　Indians of South America
Mocovi Indians
　USE Mocobi Indians
Modal choice in transportation
　USE Choice of transportation
Modal split (Transportation)
　USE Choice of transportation
Modality (Linguistics)
　BT Linguistics
　SA *subdivision* Modality *under names of*
　　languages and groups of languages,
　　e.g. English language—Modality
Modality (Logic)
　BT Logic
　　Nonclassical mathematical logic
　NT Deontic logic
Modality (Theory of knowledge)
　BT Knowledge, Theory of
Modang (Indonesian people)
　[DS646.32.M64]
　BT Ethnology—Indonesia
Modderdam (Cape Town, South Africa)
　(Not Subd Geog)
　UF Cape Town (South Africa).
　　Modderdam
Mode (Grammar)
　USE Grammar, Comparative and general—
　　Mood
Mode-locked lasers
　[TA1688]
　UF Phase-locked lasers
　BT Lasers
Model
　USE Example
Model, Anderson
　USE Anderson model

Model, Nilsson
　USE Nilsson model
MODEL (Computer program language)
　[QA76.73.M]
Model A Ford automobile
　USE Ford Model A automobile
Model agencies
　USE Modeling agencies
Model airplane motors
　USE Airplanes—Models—Motors
　　Airplanes—Models—Rubber motors
Model airplane racing
　[GV761.5]
　BT Airplane racing
　　Airplanes—Models
Model airplanes
　USE Airplanes—Models
Model apartments *(May Subd Geog)*
　BT Apartments
　　Architectural models
Model artists
　USE Tableaux
Model auto racing
　USE Model car racing
Model basins
　USE Towing basins
Model car racing
　[GV1570]
　UF Miniature car racing
　　Model auto racing
　BT Automobile racing
　　Automobiles—Models
　NT Automobiles, Racing—Models
Model cars
　USE Automobiles—Models
Model cities
　USE City planning
　　Urban renewal
Model homes
　USE Model houses
Model houses *(May Subd Geog)*
　UF Houses, Model
　　Model homes
　BT Architectural models
　　Architecture, Domestic
　　Dwellings
　— **Law and legislation** *(May Subd Geog)*
Model-making
　USE Models and modelmaking
Model networks
　USE Electric lines—Models
　　Electric network analyzers
Model ordinances *(May Subd Geog)*
　UF Ordinances, Model
　BT Local government—Law and
　　legislation
　　Municipal corporations
　　Ordinances, Municipal
Model railroads
　USE Railroads—Models
Model sampling
　USE Monte Carlo method
Model schools
　USE Laboratory schools
Model ship-building
　USE Ship models
Model ships
　USE Ship models
Model soldiers
　USE Military miniatures
Model space vehicles
　USE Space vehicles—Models
Model T automobile
　USE Ford Model T automobile
Model theory
　BT Logic, Symbolic and mathematical
　NT Admissible sets
　　Completeness theorem
　　Definability theory (Mathematical
　　logic)
　　Forcing (Model theory)

Mathematical analysis, Nonstandard

Modeling
[*NB1180-NB1185 (Sculpture)*]
  UF Clay modeling
       Modelling
       Molding (Clay, plaster, etc.)
  BT Arts and crafts movement
       Clay
       Sculpture
  RT Sculpture—Technique
  NT Earth casting
       Prosthetic make-up, Theatrical
       Soap sculpture
  — **Therapeutic use**
     UF Plastotherapy
     BT Art therapy
         Occupational therapy
         Psychotherapy
Modeling, Geological
  USE Geological modeling
Modeling, Topographical
  USE Relief models
Modeling agencies *(May Subd Geog)*
[*HD9999.M64*]
  UF Agencies, Modeling
       Model agencies
  BT Employment agencies
  RT Models, Fashion
Modeling in wax
  USE Wax-modeling
Modelling
  USE Modeling
Modelmakers *(May Subd Geog)*
  BT Models and modelmaking
Modelmaking
  USE Models and modelmaking
Modelmaking industry *(May Subd Geog)*
  RT Models and modelmaking
Models, Acoustic
  USE Acoustic models
Models, Architectural
  USE Architectural models
Models, Artists' *(May Subd Geog)*
[*N7434*]
  UF Artists' models
  BT Women in art
  NT Models, Fashion
Models, Astronomical
  USE Astronomical models
Models, Biological
  USE Biological models
Models, Chemical
  USE Chemical models
Models, Clothing
  USE Models, Fashion
Models, Communication
  USE Communication models
Models, Dressmaker's
  USE Dress forms
Models, Fashion *(May Subd Geog)*
[*HD6073.M7*]
  UF Fashion models
       Mannequins (Persons)
       Models, Clothing
  BT Clothing and dress
       Models, Artists'
  RT Modeling agencies
  — **Vocational guidance**
Models, Historical
  USE Historical models
Models, Hydraulic
  USE Hydraulic models
Models, Learning (Stochastic processes)
  USE Learning models (Stochastic processes)
Models, Linear (Statistics)
  USE Linear models (Statistics)
Models, Linguistic
  USE Linguistic models
Models, Log-linear
  USE Log-linear models

Models, Mathematical
  USE Mathematical models
Models, Mechanical
  USE Machinery—Models
Models, Military
  USE Military miniatures
Models, Nuclear
  USE Nuclear models
Models, Order-disorder
  USE Order-disorder models
Models, Quark
  USE Quark models
Models, Ship
  USE Ship models
Models, String
  USE String models
Models, Unified nuclear
  USE Unified nuclear models
Models, Zoological
  USE Zoological models
Models (Clay, plaster, etc.)
  UF Maquettes
  BT Artists' preparatory studies
       Sculpture
  NT Moulage in medicine
       Plaster casts
Models (Patents) *(May Subd Geog)*
[*T324*]
  UF Patent models
  BT Engineering models
       Industrial property
       Miniature objects
       Models and modelmaking
       Patents
  RT Machinery—Models
Models and artists in art
  USE Artists and models in art
Models and modelmaking *(May Subd Geog)*
[*TT154*]
  UF Model-making
       Modelmaking
  BT Handicraft
       Manual training
       Miniature objects
  RT Modelmaking industry
  SA *subdivision* Models *under types of
       objects, e.g.* Automobiles—Models;
       Machinery—Models; *and phrase
       headings for types of models, e.g.*
       Wind tunnel models
  NT Architectural models
       Engineering models
       Geological modeling
       Geometrical models
       Historical models
       Hydraulic models
       Hydrologic models
       Mannequins (Figures)
       Miniature craft
       Modelmakers
       Models (Patents)
       Paradigms (Social sciences)
       Pattern-making
       Relief models
       Ship models
       Simulation methods
       Surfaces, Models of
       Wind tunnel models
       Zoological models
  — **Motors**
  — **Radio control systems**
     [*TT154*]
     BT Citizens band radio
         Radio control
Models in art
  USE Artists and models in art
Models of surfaces
  USE Surfaces, Models of
Modems
  UF Modulate/demodulate units

  BT Computer input-output equipment
       Data transmission systems
       Modulators (Electronics)
Moderated reactors, Organic
  USE Organic moderated reactors
Moderation
  UF Golden mean
       Mean, Golden
  NT Mean (Philosophy)
       Temperance (Virtue)
  — **Religious aspects**
  — — **Buddhism,** [**Christianity, etc.**]
Moderation (Buddhism)
[*BQ4420.M6*]
  BT Buddhism—Doctrines
       Virtues (Buddhism)
Moderators, Nuclear reactor
  USE Reactor moderators
Modern aesthetics
  USE Aesthetics, Modern
Modern architecture
  USE Architecture, Modern
Modern art
  USE Art, Modern
       Modernism (Art)
Modern arts
  USE Arts, Modern
Modern Chinese language, 1919-
  USE Chinese language—Modern Chinese,
       1919-
Modern civilization
  USE Civilization, Modern
Modern dance *(May Subd Geog)*
[*GV1783*]
  UF Classical dancing
       Interpretive dancing
  BT Dancing
  NT Religious dance, Modern
Modern ethics
  USE Ethics, Modern
Modern geometry
  USE Geometry, Modern
Modern Greek anonyms and pseudonyms
  USE Anonyms and pseudonyms, Greek
       (Modern)
Modern Greek authors
  USE Authors, Greek (Modern)
Modern Greek chap-books
  USE Chap-books, Greek (Modern)
Modern Greek children's literature
  USE Children's literature, Greek (Modern)
Modern Greek children's plays
  USE Children's plays, Greek (Modern)
Modern Greek children's poetry
  USE Children's poetry, Greek (Modern)
Modern Greek children's stories
  USE Children's stories, Greek (Modern)
Modern Greek children's writings
  USE Children's writings, Greek (Modern)
Modern Greek Christian poetry
  USE Christian poetry, Greek (Modern)
Modern Greek detective and mystery stories
  USE Detective and mystery stories, Greek
       (Modern)
Modern Greek dramatists
  USE Dramatists, Greek (Modern)
Modern Greek elegiac poetry
  USE Elegiac poetry, Greek (Modern)
Modern Greek erotic poetry
  USE Erotic poetry, Greek (Modern)
Modern Greek erotic stories
  USE Erotic stories, Greek (Modern)
Modern Greek fables
  USE Fables, Greek (Modern)
Modern Greek folk-drama
  USE Folk-drama, Greek (Modern)
Modern Greek folk poetry
  USE Folk poetry, Greek (Modern)
Modern Greek folk-songs
  USE Folk-songs, Greek (Modern)

Modern Greek landscape painting
  USE Landscape painting, Greek (Modern)
Modern Greek love poetry
  USE Love poetry, Greek (Modern)
Modern Greek mystery stories
  USE Detective and mystery stories, Greek
    (Modern)
Modern Greek narrative poetry
  USE Narrative poetry, Greek (Modern)
Modern Greek one-act plays
  USE One-act plays, Greek (Modern)
Modern Greek pastoral poetry
  USE Pastoral poetry, Greek (Modern)
Modern Greek poets
  USE Poets, Greek (Modern)
Modern Greek proverbs
  USE Proverbs, Greek (Modern)
Modern Greek quotations
  USE Quotations, Greek (Modern)
Modern Greek revolutionary literature
  USE Revolutionary literature, Greek
    (Modern)
Modern Greek satire
  USE Satire, Greek (Modern)
Modern Greek sea stories
  USE Sea stories, Greek (Modern)
Modern Greek short stories
  USE Short stories, Greek (Modern)
Modern Greek songs
  USE Songs, Greek (Modern)
Modern Greek sonnets
  USE Sonnets, Greek (Modern)
Modern Greek verse satire
  USE Verse satire, Greek (Modern)
Modern Greek war stories
  USE War stories, Greek (Modern)
Modern history
  USE History, Modern
Modern language fellowships
  USE Languages, Modern—Scholarships,
    fellowships, etc.
Modern language scholarships
  USE Languages, Modern—Scholarships,
    fellowships, etc.
Modern languages
  USE Languages, Modern
Modern literature
  USE Literature, Modern
Modern logic
  USE Logic, Modern
Modern painting
  USE Painting, Modern
Modern philosophers
  USE Philosophers, Modern
Modern philosophy
  USE Philosophy, Modern
Modern poetry
  USE Poetry, Modern
Modern religious dance
  USE Religious dance, Modern
Modern sculpture
  USE Sculpture, Modern
Modern style (France)
  USE Art nouveau
Modernism
  [BT82]
  Here are entered works on a movement that arose
in the late 19th century which seeks to establish the
meaning of the Christian faith in relation to present
human experience and to reconcile traditional theo-
logical concepts with the requirements of modern
knowledge.
  BT Theology, Doctrinal—History—19th
    century
    Theology, Doctrinal—History—20th
    century
  RT Modernist-fundamentalist controversy
  — **Catholic Church** (May Subd Geog)
    [BX1396]
    UF Catholic Church—Modernism

    RT Americanism (Catholic
     controversy)
  — **Church of England**
    [BX5126]
    UF Church of England—Modernism
    BT Church of England—Parties and
     movements
Modernism (Aesthetics) (May Subd Geog)
  [BH301.M54]
  BT Aesthetics
Modernism (Art) (May Subd Geog)
  [N6490]
  UF Art, Modernist
    Modern art
    Modernism in art
    Modernist art
  BT Aesthetic movement (British art)
  RT Art, Modern—20th century
  NT Art, Abstract
    Avant-garde (Aesthetics)
    Cubism
    Dadaism
    Expressionism (Art)
    Fauvism
    Futurism (Art)
    Impressionism (Art)
    Post-impressionism (Art)
    Postmodernism
    Surrealism
Modernism (Literature) (May Subd Geog)
  UF Crepuscolarismo
  BT Literature
  NT Literature, Experimental
    Postmodernism
Modernism in art
  USE Modernism (Art)
Modernist art
  USE Modernism (Art)
Modernist-fundamentalist controversy
  [BT82.3]
  Here are entered works on the conflict between
modernists and fundamentalists in the interpretation
of Christian doctrine.
  BT Theology, Doctrinal—History—20th
    century
  RT Fundamentalism
    Modernism
  NT Creationism
Moderns and ancients, Quarrel of
  USE Ancients and moderns, Quarrel of
Modes, Musical
  USE Musical intervals and scales
Modesse Indians
  USE Madehsi Indians
Modesty (May Subd Geog)
  [BJ1533.M73]
  BT Conduct of life
  — **Religious aspects**
  — — **Buddhism, [Christianity, etc.]**
  — — **Islam**
    [BP188.16.M6]
    UF Modesty (Islam)
     Naẓar (Islam)
  — — **Judaism**
    UF Modesty (Judaism)
Modesty (Islam)
  USE Modesty—Religious aspects—Islam
Modesty (Judaism)
  USE Modesty—Religious aspects—Judaism
Modesty Blaise (Fictitious character)
  USE Blaise, Modesty (Fictitious character)
Modi alphabet
  [PK2361]
  BT Alphabet
    Marathi language—Alphabet
Modi manuscripts
  USE Manuscripts, Marathi
Modi paleography
  USE Paleography, Marathi

Modification, Precipitation (Meteorology)
  USE Precipitation (Meteorology)—
    Modification
Modification of automobile motors
  USE Automobiles—Motors—Modification
Modification of commercial products for export
  USE Commercial products—Modification
    for export
Modification of firearms
  USE Firearms—Modification
Modification of habitat (Ecology)
  USE Habitat (Ecology)—Modification
Modified water
  USE Polywater
Modifiers, Biological response
  USE Biological response modifiers
Modistic grammar
  USE Speculative grammar
Modjinngay dialect
  USE Majingai dialect
Modoc Indians
  [E99.M7]
  BT Indians of North America
    Lutuamian Indians
  — **Religion and mythology**
    [E99.M7]
  — **Wars, 1873**
    [E83.87]
    BT Indians of North America—Wars—
     1866-1895
Modoc National Forest (Calif.)
  BT Forest reserves—California
    National parks and reserves—
     California
Modred
  USE Mordred
Modula-2 (Computer program language)
  [QA76.73.M]
  BT Programming languages (Electronic
    computers)
Modular Analysis Package for Systems of
  Income Transfers (Computer program)
  USE MAPSIT (Computer program)
Modular approach in education
  USE Independent study
Modular arithmetic
  [QA247.35]
  UF Finite arithmetic
    Residue arithmetic
  BT Modules (Algebra)
Modular building
  USE Modular construction
Modular construction
  [TH1098]
  UF Construction, Modular
    Modular building
    Modular structures
    Structures, Modular
  BT Buildings, Prefabricated
    Industrialized building
    Modular coordination (Architecture)
    Unit construction
Modular construction industry
  (May Subd Geog)
  BT Construction industry
Modular coordination (Architecture)
  [NA2700 (Drafting)]
  [NA2760 (Design)]
  [TH860 (Building)]
  UF Architecture—Modular design
    Building—Modular coordination
    Dimensional coordination in building
    Modular design
  BT Architecture
    Building
    Simplification in industry
    Standardization
  NT Building materials—Standards
    Modular construction
Modular curves
  USE Curves, Modular

Modular design
USE Modular coordination (Architecture)
Modular fields (Algebra)
USE Finite fields (Algebra)
Modular forms
USE Forms, Modular
Modular functions
USE Functions, Modular
Modular groups
BT Groups, Theory of
Matrices
Numbers, Theory of
NT Arithmetic groups
Modular integrated utility systems
UF Integrated utility systems, Modular
Utility systems, Modular integrated
BT Environmental protection
Public utilities
Sanitary engineering
Modular Integrated Utility Systems Program
BT Environmental protection—United
States
Public utilities—United States
Sanitary engineering—United States
Modular lattices
UF Symmetric lattices
BT Lattice theory
NT Continuous geometries
Orthomodular lattices
Modular programming
⌜QA76.6⌝
BT Electronic digital computers—
Programming
Modular representations of groups
BT Representations of groups
Modular structures
USE Modular construction
Modular surfaces, Hilbert
USE Hilbert modular surfaces
Modular systems (Algebra)
USE Modules (Algebra)
Modulate/demodulate units
USE Modems
Modulation, Pulse amplitude
USE Pulse amplitude modulation
Modulation, Velocity
USE Velocity modulation
Modulation (Electronics)
UF Radio modulation
BT Electronics
Modulation theory
Radio
Signal theory (Telecommunication)
NT Amplitude modulation
Angle modulation
Carrier control systems
Carrier waves
Demodulation (Electronics)
Digital modulation
Modulators (Electronics)
Pulse modulation (Electronics)
Radio frequency modulation
Radio pulse time modulation
Velocity modulation
Modulation (Music)
⌜MT52 (Music)⌝
BT Harmony
Music—Instruction and study
Music—Theory
Musical accompaniment
Modulation detectors, Amplitude
USE Amplitude modulation detectors
Modulation spectroscopy
UF Spectroscopy, Modulation
BT Spectrum analysis
Modulation theory
BT Information theory
NT Modulation (Electronics)
Speech processing systems
Modulators, Biological response
USE Biological response modifiers

Modulators, Light
USE Light modulators
Modulators (Electronics)
BT Modulation (Electronics)
Pulse circuits
Radio—Transmitters and transmission
NT Modems
Module structure in Banach spaces
USE Banach spaces—M-structure
Modules, Projective (Algebra)
USE Projective modules (Algebra)
Modules (Algebra)
UF Finite number systems
Modular systems (Algebra)
BT Algebra
Rings (Algebra)
RT Finite groups
NT Artin algebras
Banach modules (Algebra)
Banach spaces—M-structure
Divisor theory
Filtered modules
Finite fields (Algebra)
Graded modules
Injective modules (Algebra)
Modular arithmetic
Projective modules (Algebra)
Theory of descent (Mathematics)
Torsion theory (Algebra)
Verma modules
Modules to simulate in PL/I (Computer
programs)
USE MOSIM (Computer programs)
Moduli theory
UF Theory of moduli
BT Analytic spaces
Functions of several complex variables
Geometry, Algebraic
Modus (Civil law) *(May Subd Geog)*
BT Gifts
Wills
RT Conditions (Law)
Mody family
USE Moody family
Moe family *(Not Subd Geog)*
UF Mo family
Moeglin family
USE Megli family
Moegling family
USE Megli family
Moehai Peninsula (N.Z.)
USE Coromandel Peninsula (N.Z.)
Moehau Peninsula (N.Z.)
USE Coromandel Peninsula (N.Z.)
Moehlenberg family
USE Moellenberg family
Moejoe (New Guinea tribe)
USE Muiu (New Guinea tribe)
Moelck family
USE Moelk family
Moele family
USE Mullis family
Moelis family
USE Mullis family
Moelk family *(Not Subd Geog)*
UF Moelck family
Mölck family
Mölk family
Moellenberg family *(Not Subd Geog)*
UF Moehlenberg family
Mollenberg family
Moeller family *(Not Subd Geog)*
UF Möller family
RT Miller family
Mueller family
Moen (Denmark)
UF Møn (Denmark)
BT Islands—Denmark
Moen Island (Micronesia)
UF Haru Island (Micronesia)
Wééné Island (Micronesia)

BT Islands—Micronesia (Federated States)
Moen jo Daro Site (Pakistan)
USE Mohenjo-Daro Site (Pakistan)
Moenkopi Plateau (Ariz.) *(Not Subd Geog)*
BT Plateaus—Arizona
Moeno Indians
USE Mashco Indians
Moeresoen family
USE Moyersoen family
Moeris, Lake (Egypt) *(Not Subd Geog)*
UF Lake Moeris (Egypt)
Mer-wer (Egypt)
BT Lakes—Egypt
Moerman d'Harlebeke family
(Not Subd Geog)
UF Moerman family
Moerman family
USE Moerman d'Harlebeke family
Moers family
USE Moore family
Moersoon family
USE Moyersoen family
Moësa River (Switzerland)
BT Rivers—Switzerland
Moësa Valley (Switzerland)
USE Mesolcina Valley (Switzerland)
Moess family
USE Moss family
Moesselman family
USE Musselman family
Moessner family
USE Messner family
Moeyrson family
USE Moyersoen family
Moffat family
USE Moffett family
Moffatt family
USE Moffett family
Moffet family
USE Moffett family
Moffett family *(Not Subd Geog)*
UF Maffet family
Moffat family
Moffatt family
Moffet family
Moffit family
Moffitt family
Mofit family
Morfett family
Morfetts family
Morfitt family
Morfitts family
Moffit family
USE Moffett family
Moffitt family
USE Moffett family
Mofit family
USE Moffett family
Mofu-Gudur language *(May Subd Geog)*
UF Mofu language
BT Cameroon—Languages
Chadic languages
Mofu language
USE Mofu-Gudur language
Mogami Region (Japan)
Mogamijō (Yamagata-shi, Japan)
USE Yamagatajō (Yamagata-shi, Japan)
Mogan family *(Not Subd Geog)*
RT Maugans family
Mogen David
USE Magen David
Mogensen family *(Not Subd Geog)*
UF Mogenson family
Morgensen family
Morgenson family
Mogenson family
USE Mogensen family
Moggingain dialect
USE Majingai dialect

Mögingen Castle (Radolfzell am Bodensee, Germany)
  USE Schloss Mögingen (Radolfzell am Bodensee, Germany)
Moghal Empire
  USE Mogul Empire
Moghas
  USE Rabaris
Moghol language
  [PL431.M57]
  UF Mogol language
  BT Mongolian languages
Mogi-Guaçu River (Brazil)
  UF Mogí-Guassú River (Brazil)
      Mogy Guassú River (Brazil)
      Moji Guaçu River (Brazil)
  BT Rivers—Brazil
Mogí-Guassú River (Brazil)
  USE Mogi-Guaçu River (Brazil)
Mogimba (African people)
  USE Ngemba (African people)
Mogimba language
  USE Ngemba language (Cameroon)
Moglei (Papua New Guinea people)
  USE Medlpa (Papua New Guinea people)
Moglei language
  USE Medlpa language
Mogol language
  USE Moghol language
Mogollon culture
  UF Mimbres culture
  BT Indians of North America—Southwest, New—Antiquities
      Southwest, New—Antiquities
Mogollon Indians
  [E99.M76]
  BT Apache Indians
      Indians of North America
Mogoreb language
  USE Baria language
Mogs
  USE Maghs
Moguex Indians
  UF Gambía Indians
      Gambiano Indians
      Guambia Indians
      Guambiano Indians
      Silvia Indians
  BT Indians of South America
Moguex language (May Subd Geog)
  UF Cuambia language
      Guambia language
      Guambiano language
      Moguez language
  BT Chibchan languages
      Colombia—Languages
      Indians of South America—Colombia
          —Languages
Moguez language
  USE Moguex language
Mogul architecture
  USE Architecture, Mogul
Mogul art
  USE Art, Mogul
Mogul calligraphy
  USE Calligraphy, Mogul
Mogul Empire
  [DS461]
  UF Moghal Empire
      Mughal Empire
  BT India—History—1500-1765
Mogul gardens
  USE Gardens, Mogul
Mogul illumination of books and manuscripts
  USE Illumination of books and manuscripts, Mogul
Mogul miniature painting
  USE Miniature painting, Mogul
Mogul painting
  USE Painting, Mogul

Mogul portraits
  USE Portraits, Mogul
Mogy Guassú River (Brazil)
  USE Mogi-Guaçu River (Brazil)
Moha Indians
  USE Moxo Indians
Mohács, Battle of, 1526
  [DR507]
  BT Turkey—History—1453-1683
Mohair
  BT Angora goat
  RT Mohair industry
Mohair industry (May Subd Geog)
  RT Mohair
Mohammedan . . .
  USE subject headings beginning with the word Muslim or Islamic
Mohammedanism
  USE Islam
Mohammedans
  USE Muslims
Mohanārānī (Legendary character)
  BT Folklore—India
Mohave, Lake (Nev.) (Not Subd Geog)
  UF Lake Mohave (Nev.)
  BT Lakes—Nevada
Mohave Apache Indians
  USE Yavapai Indians
Mohave Desert (Calif.)
  UF Mojave Desert (Calif.)
  BT Deserts—California
Mohave Indians
  [E99.M77]
  BT Indians of North America
      Yuman Indians
  — Law
      USE Law, Mohave
  — **Reservations**
      NT Colorado River Indian Reservation (Ariz. and Calif.)
Mohave language
  [PM1871]
  BT Yuman languages
Mohave law
  USE Law, Mohave
Mohave River (Calif.)
  USE Mojave River (Calif.)
Mohave Road (Calif. and Nev.)
  USE Mojave Road (Calif. and Nev.)
Mohawk Canyon (Ariz.)
  BT Canyons—Arizona
Mohawk Indians
  [E99.M8]
  UF Canienga Indians
  BT Indians of North America
      Iroquoian Indians
      Iroquois Indians
  NT Caughnawaga Indians
      St. Regis Indians
  — **Land tenure**
Mohawk language
  [PM1881-4]
  RT Iroquoian languages
Mohawk River (N.Y.)
  BT Rivers—New York (State)
Mohawk River (Or.)
  BT Rivers—Oregon
Mohawk Valley Railroad
  BT Railroads—United States
Mohegan Indians
  [E99.M83]
  UF Mohican Indians
      River Indians (New England)
  BT Algonquian Indians
      Indians of North America
  RT Mahican Indians
  NT Brotherton Indians
      Moravian Indians
      Scaticook Indians
      Stockbridge Indians
  — **Missions**

Mohegan language
  [PM1885]
  UF Pequot language
  RT Algonquian languages
Mohenjo-Daro Site (Pakistan)
  (Not Subd Geog)
  [DS392.M6]
  UF Moen jo Daro Site (Pakistan)
  BT Pakistan—Antiquities
Mohican Indians
  USE Mohegan Indians
Mohism
  USE Moism
Mohmands
  [DS432.M]
  BT Pushtuns
Moho
  USE Mohorovicic discontinuity
Mohole project
  UF Project Mohole
  BT Earth—Crust
      Earth—Mantle
      Oceanography—Research
      Submarine geology
Mohon family (Not Subd Geog)
  RT Mahan family
Mohongia language
  USE Nocte language
Mohorovicic discontinuity
  UF Moho
  BT Earth—Internal structure
Moi (Southeast-Asiatic people)
  [DS539.M6]
  UF Kha (Southeast-Asiatic people)
      Pnong (Southeast-Asiatic people)
  BT Ethnology—Indochina, French
Moier family
  USE Moyer family
Moiliili (Honolulu, Hawaii)
  (Not Subd Geog)
  UF Honolulu (Hawaii). Moiliili
Moïltyn am Site (Mongolia)
  (Not Subd Geog)
  UF Moil'tyn um Site (Mongolia)
  BT Mongolia—Antiquities
Moil'tyn um Site (Mongolia)
  USE Moïltyn am Site (Mongolia)
Moir family
  USE Moyer family
Moira (The Greek word)
  BT Greek language—Etymology
Moiré method
  UF Fringe method, Moiré
  BT Diffraction gratings
      Materials—Testing
      Strains and stresses
Moisi languages
  USE Mossi languages
Moism (May Subd Geog)
  [B127.M65]
  UF Mohism
  BT Philosophy, Chinese
Moissala Mbai language
  USE Mbai language (Moissala)
Moissanite (May Subd Geog)
  [QE391.M67]
  BT Silicon carbide
Moisture (May Subd Geog)
  [QC915-QC929 (Meteorology)]
  BT Condensation
      Rain and rainfall
      Water
  RT Condensation (Meteorology)
      Humidity
  SA subdivision Moisture under types of farm produce, inanimate objects, technical equipment, etc. for works on their moisture content, e.g. Concrete—Moisture; Corn—Moisture
  NT Evaporation

Humectants
Water vapor, Atmospheric
— **Measurement**
NT Moisture meters
Moisture control in buildings
USE Dampness in buildings
Moisture controlling agents
USE Humectants
Moisture in textiles
UF Textile fabrics—Moisture
Textiles, Moisture in
Moisture index
[QC915]
[S594]
UF Precipitation effectiveness index
BT Climatic classification
Hydrometeorology
Plants, Effect of soil moisture on
Moisture meters
[TA418.64]
UF Humidity meters
BT Moisture—Measurement
RT Hygrometers
— **Calibration**
Moisture meters, Microwave
(May Subd Geog)
[SD388.5 (Forestry)]
UF Microwave moisture meters
BT Microwave devices
Moisture of soils
USE Soil moisture
Moisture Utilization in Semi-Arid Tropics: Summer Rainfall Agriculture Project
UF Summer Rainfall Agriculture Project
BT Information storage and retrieval systems—Agriculture
Moja Indians
USE Moxo Indians
Moja language
USE Moxo language
Mojave Desert (Calif.)
USE Mohave Desert (Calif.)
Mojave River (Calif.) *(Not Subd Geog)*
UF Mohave River (Calif.)
BT Rivers—California
Mojave Road (Calif. and Nev.)
UF Mohave Road (Calif. and Nev.)
Old Government Road (Calif. and Nev.)
BT Roads—California
Roads—Nevada
Moji family *(Not Subd Geog)*
Moji Guaçu River (Brazil)
USE Mogi-Guaçu River (Brazil)
Mojkovac (Montenegro), Battle of, 1916
BT World War, 1914-1918—Campaigns—Yugoslavia
Mojo Indians
USE Moxo Indians
Mojo language
USE Moxo language
Mojung language
USE Chang language
Mokar (African people)
USE Gaanda (African people)
Mokele-mbembe *(May Subd Geog)*
[QL89.2.M58]
BT Dinosaurs
Monsters
Moken (Southeast Asian people)
USE Selung (Southeast Asian people)
Mokgware Hills (Botswana)
UF Mikgware Hills (Botswana)
BT Mountains—Botswana
Mokhe (Asian people)
BT Ethnology—Russian S.F.S.R.
Tunguses
Mokhev people
USE Mokhevtsy
Mokhevtsy
[DK34.M58]

UF Mokhev people
BT Ethnology—Georgian S.S.R.
Moki Indians
USE Hopi Indians
Moki language
USE Hopi language
Mokihinui River (N.Z.)
BT Rivers—New Zealand
Mokilese language
[PL6256.M83]
BT Micronesian languages
Moklum dialect
[PL4001.M64]
BT India—Languages
Tangsa language
Mōko shūrai ekotoba (Scrolls)
[ND1053.4]
UF Takezaki Suenaga ekotoba (Scrolls)
BT Japan—History—Attempted Mongol invasions, 1274-1281—Pictorial works
Painting, Japanese—Kamakura-Momoyama periods, 1185-1600
Scrolls, Japanese
Mokpe
USE Bakwiri (African people)
Mokpe language
USE Bakwiri language
Mokṣa
UF Mukti
BT Philosophy, Indic
Reincarnation
Self (Philosophy)
Soul
Moksha dialect
[PH778.M6]
BT Mordvin language
Mokushi Indians
USE Macusi Indians
Molala Indians
[E99.M84]
UF Molel Indians
BT Indians of North America
— **Antiquities**
Molannidae
[QL5188.M6]
BT Caddis-flies
Molar teeth
USE Molars
Molars
UF Molar teeth
BT Teeth
NT Third molars
Molas *(May Subd Geog)*
BT Cuna Indians—Art
Indians of Central America—Panama—Art
Wall hangings—Panama
Molas (Fishes)
USE Molidae
Molasse *(May Subd Geog)*
BT Geology, Stratigraphic—Cenozoic
Sandstone
Molasses
[HD9119.M6 (Trade)]
[TP413 (Manufacture)]
BT Sugar
Sugarcane products
NT Cookery (Molasses)
Molasses as feed
BT Feeds
Molasses as fertilizer
BT Fertilizers
Molasses industry *(May Subd Geog)*
Molbog language
USE Melebuganon language
Mølby family *(Not Subd Geog)*
Mölck family
USE Moelk family
Mold, Vegetable
USE Humus

Soils
Mold (Botany)
USE Molds (Botany)
Mold coatings (Founding)
USE Foundry coatings
Mold control
USE Molds (Botany)—Control
Mold dressings (Founding)
USE Foundry coatings
Mold facings (Founding)
USE Foundry coatings
Mold washes (Founding)
USE Foundry coatings
Moldau River (Czechoslovakia)
USE Vltava River (Czechoslovakia)
Moldavia
Here are entered works on the historical principality and on the region of eastern Romania. Works on the area of the constituent republic of the U.S.S.R. are entered under Moldavian S.S.R.
As a geographic subdivision, this heading is used indirectly through Romania.
— **History**
NT Muşatin dynasty, 1363-1704
Moldavian art
USE Art, Moldavian
Moldavian arts
USE Arts, Moldavian
Moldavian authors
USE Authors, Moldavian
Moldavian dialect
[PC794.M6]
BT Romanian language
Moldavian fiction *(May Subd Geog)*
Moldavian folk dancing
USE Folk dancing, Moldavian
Moldavian folk poetry
USE Folk poetry, Moldavian
Moldavian folk-songs
USE Folk-songs, Moldavian
Moldavian literature *(May Subd Geog)*
[PC794.M65 (History)]
[PC794.M66-PC794.M69 (Collections)]
Moldavian mural painting and decoration
USE Mural painting and decoration, Moldavian
Moldavian painting
USE Painting, Moldavian
Moldavian philology
[PC794.M6]
Moldavian poetry *(May Subd Geog)*
[PC794.M65 (History)]
[PC794.M67 (Collections)]
Moldavian portrait painting
USE Portrait painting, Moldavian
Moldavian portrait sculpture
USE Portrait sculpture, Moldavian
Moldavian prints
USE Prints, Moldavian
Moldavian prose literature
(May Subd Geog)
Moldavian proverbs
USE Proverbs, Moldavian
Moldavian S.S.R.
Here are entered works on the area of the constituent republic of the U.S.S.R. Works on the historical principality and on the region of eastern Romania are entered under Moldavia.
— **Antiquities**
NT Trinka Site (Moldavian S.S.R.)
— **Civilization**
NT Arts, Russian—Moldavian influences
— — **Russian influences**
BT Russian S.F.S.R.—Civilization
— — **Ukrainian influences**
BT Ukraine—Civilization
— **History** *(Not Subd Geog)*
— — **Revolution, 1917-1921**
(Not Subd Geog)
Moldavian S.S.R. in motion pictures
BT Moving-pictures

Moldavian wit and humor *(May Subd Geog)*
Moldavian wit and humor, Pictorial
    (May Subd Geog)
Moldavite *(May Subd Geog)*
    ⌐QE461⌐
    BT Tektite
Molded dishes (Cookery)
    USE Cookery (Molded dishes)
Molding (Chemical technology)
    UF Casting (Chemical technology)
    BT Chemical engineering
    SA *subdivision* Molding *under particular*
        chemical products, e.g. Plastics—
        Molding
    NT Pelletizing
Molding (Clay, plaster, etc.)
    USE Modeling
        Moulage in medicine
        Sculpture—Technique
Molding (Founding)
    UF Molding (Metal)
        Moulding (Metal)
    BT Founding
        Pattern-making
    NT Coremaking
        Foundry coatings
        Machine molding (Founding)
        Molding materials
        Shell molding (Founding)
Molding (Metal)
    USE Molding (Founding)
Molding (Plastics)
    USE Plastics—Molding
Molding materials
    ⌐TS243.5⌐
    UF Materials, Molding
    BT Molding (Founding)
    NT Core materials
        Glass manufacture—Molds
        Plastics—Molds
        Sand, Foundry
Molding sand
    USE Sand, Foundry
Moldings *(May Subd Geog)*
    ⌐NA2960 (Architecture)⌐
    ⌐TH2482-TH2483 (Building: exterior)⌐
    ⌐TH2553 (Interior)⌐
    UF Mouldings
    BT Architecture—Details
        Building
        Carpentry
        Decoration and ornament
Moldo-Wallachians
    USE Romanians
Molds, Glassmaking
    USE Glass manufacture—Molds
Molds (Botany)
    ⌐QK621⌐
    UF Mold (Botany)
        Mould (Botany)
    BT Fermentation
    RT Fungi
    NT Myxomycetes
        Penicillium
    — **Control** *(May Subd Geog)*
        UF Mold control
Molds (Cookware) *(May Subd Geog)*
    ⌐NK8490 (Decorative arts)⌐
    UF Moulds (Cookware)
    BT Cookware
    NT Bread molds (Baking)
        Butter molds
        Cookie molds
        Metal molds (Cookery)
Molds (for plastics)
    USE Plastics—Molds
Mole, Adrian (Fictitious character)
    UF Adrian Mole (Fictitious character)
    BT Characters and characteristics in
        literature

RT Townsend, Sue—Characters—Adrian
        Mole
Mole, Uterine
    USE Pregnancy, Molar
Mole (Animal)
    USE Moles (Animals)
Mole (Chemistry)
    ⌐QD461⌐
    UF Gram-atom
        Gram-atomic weight
        Gram-formula weight
        Gram-molecular weight
        Gram-molecule
    BT Molecular theory
Mole (Dermatology)
    ⌐BF861.M65 (Physiognomy)⌐
    ⌐RL793⌐
    UF Moles (Dermatology)
        Naevus
        Nevus
    BT Skin
    NT Birthmarks
        Fortune-telling by moles
Mole-crickets
    ⌐QL508.G87 (Zoology)⌐
    ⌐SB945.M7 (Control)⌐
    UF Crickets, Mole
        Gryllotalpidae
        Gryllotalpinae
    BT Orthoptera
    NT Gryllotalpa
        Scapteriscus
Mole crickets, Pigmy
    USE Tridactylidae
Mole language
    USE Moré language
Mole languages
    USE Mossi languages
Mole rats, African
    USE Bathyergidae
Mole rats, Palearctic
    USE Spalacidae
Molectronics
    USE Molecular electronics
Molecular acoustics
    UF Acoustics
    BT Fluid dynamics
        Molecules
        Sound-waves
Molecular association
    BT Chemistry, Physical and theoretical
        Polymers and polymerization
        Solvation
    NT Hydrogen bonding
Molecular astrophysics
    ⌐QB462.6⌐
    BT Astrophysics
    NT Interstellar molecules
Molecular asymmetry
    USE Stereochemistry
Molecular beam epitaxy
    BT Crystals—Growth
        Epitaxy
        Molecular beams
Molecular beams
    UF Molecular rays
        Positive rays
    BT Molecular dynamics
    NT Molecular beam epitaxy
    — **Scattering**
Molecular biochemistry
    USE Molecular biology
Molecular biologists *(May Subd Geog)*
    BT Biologists
        Molecular biology
    NT Women molecular biologists
Molecular biology *(May Subd Geog)*
    ⌐QH506⌐
    UF Biology, Molecular
        Molecular biochemistry
        Molecular biophysics

    BT Biological chemistry
        Histochemistry
    NT Biomolecules
        Fungal molecular biology
        Genetic code
        Molecular biologists
        Molecular electronics
        Molecular endocrinology
        Molecular genetics
        Molecular neurobiology
        Molecular pharmacology
        Pathology, Molecular
        Plant molecular biology
    — **Research** *(May Subd Geog)*
        ⌐QH506⌐
    — **Technique**
        NT Spin labels
Molecular biology, Fungal
    USE Fungal molecular biology
Molecular biology, Plant
    USE Plant molecular biology
Molecular biophysics
    USE Molecular biology
Molecular cloning
    ⌐QH442⌐
    UF Cloning, Molecular
        DNA cloning
        Gene cloning
    BT Cloning
        Genetic engineering
        Molecular genetics
    RT Clone cells
    NT Antibodies, Monoclonal
        Genetic vectors
Molecular crystals
    BT Molecules
    — **Optical properties**
Molecular distillation
    USE Distillation, Molecular
Molecular dynamics
    ⌐QC173⌐
    ⌐QC183 (Capillarity)⌐
    UF Dynamics, Molecular
    BT Physics
    RT Quantum theory
    NT Gases, Kinetic theory of
        Irreversible processes
        Masers
        Molecular beams
        Molecular rotation
        Monomolecular films
        Wave mechanics
Molecular electronics
    UF Molectronics
    BT Electronics
        Microelectronics
        Molecular biology
        Switching circuits
Molecular endocrinology *(May Subd Geog)*
    ⌐QP187.3.M64⌐
    BT Endocrinology
        Molecular biology
Molecular evolution
    USE Chemical evolution
Molecular films
    USE Monomolecular films
Molecular gas lasers
    UF Molecular lasers
    BT Gas lasers
        Lasers
Molecular genetics
    BT Genetics
        Molecular biology
    NT Biochemical genetics
        Episomes
        Genetic code
        Genetic regulation
        Insertion elements, DNA
        Molecular cloning
        Plant molecular genetics
        Repressors, Genetic

Molecular genetics, Plant
  USE Plant molecular genetics
Molecular lasers
  USE Molecular gas lasers
Molecular metals
  USE Organic conductors
Molecular models
  USE Molecules—Models
Molecular neurobiology (May Subd Geog)
  ₍QP365.2₎
  UF Molecular neurology
  BT Molecular biology
     Neurobiology
Molecular neurology
  USE Molecular neurobiology
Molecular orbitals
  UF Orbitals, Molecular
  BT Chemical bonds
     Electrons
     Molecules
     Quantum chemistry
     Valence (Theoretical chemistry)
     Wave mechanics
  RT Overlap integral
  NT Basis sets (Quantum mechanics)
     Conservation of orbital symmetry
     Hückel molecular orbitals
     Molecular structure
     Photoelectron spectroscopy
     Self-consistent field theory
Molecular pathology
  USE Pathology, Molecular
Molecular pharmacology (May Subd Geog)
  ₍RM301.65₎
  BT Molecular biology
     Pharmacology
Molecular phytobiology
  USE Plant molecular biology
Molecular rays
  USE Molecular beams
Molecular rearrangements
  USE Rearrangements (Chemistry)
Molecular relaxation
  BT Relaxation phenomena
Molecular rotation
  ₍QD481₎
  UF Hindered rotation theory
     Internal rotation (Molecular)
     Molecules—Internal rotation
     Rotation spectra
  BT Molecular dynamics
     Stereochemistry
  SA subdivision Molecular rotation under
     substances, e.g. Proteins—Molecular
     rotation
  NT Conformational analysis
     Isomerism
     Magneto-optics
     Optical rotation
     Spin labels
Molecular sieves
  BT Chemical engineering
     Drying agents
     Sieves
     Sorbents
  NT Clathrate compounds
     Zeolites
Molecular spectra
  UF Molecules—Spectra
     Spectrum, Molecular
  BT Absorption spectra
     Mass spectrometry
     Nuclear spectroscopy
     Raman spectroscopy
     Spectrum analysis
  RT Molecular spectroscopy
  NT Photoelectron spectroscopy
     Vibrational spectra
Molecular spectroscopy
  ₍QC454.M6 (Physics)₎
  ₍QD96.M65 (Qualitative analysis)₎

  UF Spectroscopy, Molecular
  BT Spectrum analysis
  RT Molecular spectra
  NT Absorption spectra
     Emission spectroscopy
     Infrared spectroscopy
     Microwave spectroscopy
     Molecular structure
     Photoelectron spectroscopy
     Ultraviolet spectroscopy
     Vibrational spectra
     X-ray spectroscopy
Molecular stills
  UF Stills, Molecular
  BT Distillation, Molecular
Molecular structure
  ₍QD461₎
  UF Structure, Molecular
  BT Chemical structure
     Molecular orbitals
     Molecular spectroscopy
     Molecules
  RT Atomic structure
  SA subdivision Structure under individual
     chemicals and groups of chemicals,
     e.g. Insulin—Structure
Molecular theory
  ₍QD461 (Chemistry)₎
  BT Chemistry, Physical and theoretical
     Matter—Constitution
  NT Gases, Kinetic theory of
     Mole (Chemistry)
Molecular weights
  ₍QD545₎
  UF Freezing points of solutions
  BT Chemistry, Physical and theoretical
  RT Atomic weights
     Cryoscopy
  NT Boiling-points
     Vapor density
Molecule-electron collisions
  USE Electron-molecule collisions
Molecule-electron interactions
  USE Electron-molecule collisions
Molecule-electron scattering
  USE Electron-molecule scattering
Molecules
  ₍QC173₎
  ₍QC179₎
  SA headings beginning with the word
     Molecular
  NT Avogadro's hypothesis
     Biomolecules
     Dipole moments
     Electron-molecule collisions
     Electron-molecule scattering
     Energy-band theory of solids
     Intermolecular forces
     Interstellar molecules
     Macromolecules
     Molecular acoustics
     Molecular crystals
     Molecular orbitals
     Molecular structure
     Quasimolecules
     Van der Waals forces
  — Internal rotation
     USE Molecular rotation
  — Models
     UF Molecular models
     BT Chemical models
  — Spectra
     USE Molecular spectra
Molecules, Biological
  USE Biomolecules
Molecules, Interstellar
  USE Interstellar molecules
Molel Indians
  USE Molala Indians
Moles (Animals)
  ₍QL737.I5₎

  UF Mole (Animal)
     Talpidae
  BT Insectivora
  NT Desmana
     Galemys
     Scalopus
     Scapanus
     Talpa
Moles (Animals), Fossil
  ₍QE882.I5₎
Moles (Dermatology)
  USE Mole (Dermatology)
Moleson family
  USE Mullison family
Molesting of children
  USE Child molesting
Moleton family
  USE Moulton family
Molge
  USE Triturus
Molgulidae (May Subd Geog)
  ₍QL613₎
  UF Caesiridae
  BT Stolidobranchia
Molidae
  ₍QL638.M64₎
  UF Molas (Fishes)
  BT Tetraodontiformes
  NT Orthagoriscus
     Ranzania
Molineaux family
  USE Mullineaux family
Molines family
  USE Mullineaux family
Molineu family
  USE Mullineaux family
Molineux family
  USE Mullineaux family
Molinism
  ₍BT762₎
  BT Catholic Church—Doctrines
     Free will and determinism
     Grace (Theology)
Molis family
  USE Mullis family
Molison family
  USE Mullison family
Mölk family
  USE Moelk family
Molla Nasreddin (Legendary character)
  USE Nasreddin Hoca (Legendary character)
Mollenberg family
  USE Moellenberg family
Möller family
  USE Moeller family
Molleson family
  USE Mullison family
Molleston family
  USE Mullison family
Mollet family (Not Subd Geog)
  UF Mollett family
Molletson family
  USE Mullison family
Mollett family
  USE Mollet family
Mollienesia
  USE Poecilia
Mollier charts
  USE Mollier diagrams
Mollier diagrams
  UF Diagrams, Enthalpy-entropy
     Diagrams, Mollier
     Enthalpy-entropy diagrams
     Mollier charts
     Mollier steam diagrams
  BT Enthalpy—Charts, diagrams, etc.
     Entropy—Charts, diagrams, etc.
Mollier steam diagrams
  USE Mollier diagrams
Mollin
  ₍RS201.O3₎

Mollin (Continued)
  BT Ointments
Mollineux family
  USE Mullineaux family
Mollison family
  USE Mullison family
Mollisone family
  USE Mullison family
Mollissen family
  USE Mullison family
Molliston family
  USE Mullison family
Mollo culture (May Subd Geog)
  ₍F3320.2.M57₎
  BT Bolivia—Antiquities
       Peru—Antiquities
Molloy family
  USE Malloy family
Mölltal cattle
  USE Pinzgauer cattle
Molluginaceae
  ₍QK495.M6₎
  BT Centrospermae
  NT Glinus
       Mollugo
Mollugo
  ₍QK495.M6₎
  BT Molluginaceae
Mollugo hirta
  USE Glinus lotoides
Mollugo oppositifolia
  USE Glinus oppositifolius
Mollugo pentaphylla
  ₍QK495.M6₎
  UF Mollugo stricta
Mollugo spergula
  USE Glinus oppositifolius
Mollugo stricta
  USE Mollugo pentaphylla
Molluscacides
  USE Molluscicides
Molluscicides
  UF Molluscacides
  BT Pesticides
  NT Plant molluscicides
Mollusk fisheries
  USE Shellfish fisheries
Mollusks (May Subd Geog)
  ₍QL401-432₎
  UF Conchology
       Malacology
  BT Invertebrates
       Shellfish
  NT Amphineura
       Bivalvia
       Cephalopoda
       Dibranchiata
       Gasteropoda
       Monoplacophora
       Pulmonata
       Scaphopoda
       Shells
       Snails
       Solenogastres
       Squids
       Tetrabranchiata
  — Anatomy
       ₍QL431₎
     SA subdivision Mollusks under
          Digestive organs, Nervous
          system, Sense-organs
     NT Radula
  — Evolution
  — Geographical distribution
  — Physiology
       ₍QL431₎
Mollusks, Fossil (May Subd Geog)
  ₍QE801-813₎
  NT Ammonoidea
       Amphineura, Fossil
       Bivalvia, Fossil

Cephalopoda, Fossil
       Gasteropoda, Fossil
       Inoceramidae
       Rostroconchia
       Scaphopoda, Fossil
       Tetrabranchiata, Fossil
  — Type specimens
       ₍QE801₎
     BT Paleontology—Catalogs and
          collections
          Type specimens (Natural history)
Mollusks as carriers of disease
  (May Subd Geog)
  ₍RA641.M6₎
  BT Invertebrates as carriers of disease
       Shellfish as carriers of disease
  NT Gasteropoda as carriers of disease
Molly Maguires
  ₍HV6441-6453₎
  UF Maguires, Molly
  BT Crime and criminals
Mollyneaux family
  USE Mullineaux family
Mollyneux family
  USE Mullineaux family
Molodova Site (Ukraine) (Not Subd Geog)
  BT Ukraine—Antiquities
Molokai (Hawaii)
  BT Hawaii
       Islands—Hawaii
Molossians
  BT Greece—History—To 146 B.C.
Molossidae
  ₍QL737.C54₎
  UF Free-tailed bats
       Mastiff bats, Typical
  BT Bats
  NT Eumops
       Molossus
       Otomops
       Tadarida
Molossus
  ₍QL737.C54₎
  BT Molossidae
  NT Molossus molossus
Molossus molossus
  ₍QL737.C54₎
  UF Molossus tropidorhynchus
       Pallas' mastiff-bat
  BT Molossus
Molossus tropidorhynchus
  USE Molossus molossus
Molothrus aeneus
  USE Bronzed cowbird
Molpadia
  ₍QL384.H7₎
  BT Molpadiidae
Molpadiida
  ₍QL384.H7₎
  UF Molpadonia
  BT Holothurians
  NT Molpadiidae
Molpadiidae
  ₍QL384.H7₎
  BT Molpadiida
  NT Molpadia
Molpadonia
  USE Molpadiida
Molson family (Not Subd Geog)
  UF Moulson family
Mølsted family (Not Subd Geog)
Molten family
  USE Moulton family
Molten metals
  USE Liquid metals
Molten salt electrolysis
  USE Fused salt electrolysis
Molten salt reactors
  UF Reactors, Molten salt
  BT Nuclear reactors

Molten salts
  USE Fused salts
Molthen family
  USE Moulton family
Molting
  UF Moulting
       Shedding (Zoology)
  BT Feathers
       Fur
       Hair
       Horns, Cutaneous
       Insects—Development
       Shells
       Skin
  NT Ecdysis
Molting hormone
  USE Ecdysone
Molting in arthropods and reptiles
  USE Ecdysis
Moltke family (Not Subd Geog)
Molton family
  USE Moulton family
Moltumyr family (Not Subd Geog)
Moltzahn family
  USE Maltzahn family
Moltzan family
  USE Maltzahn family
Moltzen family
  USE Molzen family
Moluccans (May Subd Geog)
  UF Moluccans, South
       South Moluccans
  BT Ethnology—Indonesia
Moluccans, South
  USE Moluccans
Moluche language
  ₍PM6541₎
  BT Araucanian language
Molybdates
  BT Molybdenum compounds
Molybdenite (May Subd Geog)
  ₍QE391.M7₎
  BT Molybdenum ores
       Sulphide minerals
Molybdenum
  ₍QD181.M7 (Chemistry)₎
  ₍TN490.M7 (Mining)₎
  ₍TN799.M7 (Metallurgy)₎
  BT Chromium group
  RT Molybdenum industry
  NT Plants, Effect of molybdenum on
       Soils—Molybdenum content
  — Isotopes
  — — Decay
  — Metallurgy
Molybdenum alloys
  NT Chromium-cobalt-nickel-molybdenum
          alloys
       Chromium-molybdenum-iron alloys
       Chromium-molybdenum steel
       Iron-molybdenum alloys
       Iron-molybdenum-aluminum alloys
       Tungsten-molybdenum alloys
Molybdenum castings
  UF Castings, Molybdenum
  BT Metal castings
Molybdenum compounds
  NT Molybdates
Molybdenum enzymes
  ₍QP601.75.M64₎
  UF Enzymes, Molybdenum
  BT Metalloenzymes
Molybdenum halides
  BT Halides
Molybdenum in soils
  USE Soils—Molybdenum content
Molybdenum industry (May Subd Geog)
  ₍HD9539.M6-64₎
  RT Molybdenum
Molybdenum ions
  BT Ions

Molybdenum-iron alloys
  USE Iron-molybdenum alloys
Molybdenum mines and mining
  (May Subd Geog)
Molybdenum ores *(May Subd Geog)*
  ⌜TN490.M7⌝
  NT Molybdenite
Molybdenum organic compounds
  USE Organomolybdenum compounds
Molybdenum-steel alloys
  USE Iron-molybdenum alloys
Molybdenum-tungsten alloys
  USE Tungsten-molybdenum alloys
Molybdite
  ⌜TN799.M⌝
Molyneaux family
  USE Mullineaux family
Molyneux family
  USE Mullineaux family
Molzahn family
  USE Maltzahn family
Molzen family *(Not Subd Geog)*
  UF Moltzen family
MOM (Otolaryngology)
  USE Otitis media with effusion
Mom and pop business enterprises
  USE Couple-owned business enterprises
Mombasa (Kenya)
  — History
  — — Uprising, 1631
Mombasa (Kenya). Old Town
  USE Old Town (Mombasa, Kenya)
Mombuttus
  USE Monbuttus
Moment of force
  USE Torque
Moment of momentum
  USE Angular momentum
Moment problems (Mathematics)
  BT Calculus, Operational
Moment spaces
  BT Conformal mapping
    Polynomials
    Spaces, Generalized
    Topology
Moments, Quadrupole
  USE Quadrupole moments
Moments method (Statistics)
  UF Method of moments (Statistics)
  BT Mathematical statistics
    Spectral energy distribution
Moments of inertia
  ⌜QA839 (Analytic mechanics)⌝
  ⌜TG265-TG267 (Engineering)⌝
  UF Inertia, Moments of
    Inertia, Products of
    Products of inertia
  BT Dynamics, Rigid
    Mechanics
  RT Angular momentum
  NT Mass (Physics)
Momentum, Angular
  USE Angular momentum
Momentum (Mechanics)
  UF Linear momentum
  BT Inertia (Mechanics)
  NT Angular momentum
Momentum pumps
  USE Jet pumps
Momentum transfer
  UF Transfer, Momentum
  BT Transport theory
Momentum wave function
  ⌜QC174.26.W3⌝
  BT Angular momentum
    Wave function
Momfu (African people)
  USE Mamvu (African people)
Momotidae
  ⌜QL696.C756⌝

  UF Motmotidae
    Motmots
  BT Coraciiformes
Mompa (Indic people)
  USE Monpa (Indic people)
Mompesson family *(Not Subd Geog)*
Momvou (African people)
  USE Mamvu (African people)
Momvu language
  USE Mamvu language
Møn (Denmark)
  USE Moen (Denmark)
Mon (Game)
  ⌜GV1511⌝
Mon (Southeast-Asiatic people)
  ⌜DS570.M⌝
  UF Mons (Southeast-Asiatic people)
  BT Ethnology—Asia, Southeastern
Mon-Anam languages
  USE Mon-Khmer languages
Mon-Khmer languages
  ⌜PL4301-9⌝
  UF Mon-Anam languages
  BT Austroasiatic languages
    Indic languages
  RT Sino-Tibetan languages
  NT Bahnar language
    Chrau language
    Cua language
    Jarai language
    Jeh language
    Katu language
    Khmer language
    Khmu' language
    Kui language (Mon-Khmer)
Mon Khmer languages
  NT Lawa language (Thailand)
Mon-Khmer languages
  NT Mnong language, Eastern
    Mon language
    Nyah Kur language
    Pacoh language
    Pear language
    Proto-Mon-Khmer language
    Proto-North-Bahnaric language
    Rengao language
    Sedang language
    Srê language
    Stieng language
Mon language
  ⌜PL4331-9⌝
  UF Peguan language
    Talaing language
  BT Mon-Khmer languages
Mon River (W. Va. and Pa.)
  USE Monongahela River (W. Va. and Pa.)
Mona Island (P.R.)
  BT Islands—Puerto Rico
Mona Lisa (Game)
  USE Joconde (Game)
Mona Reclamation Experimental Project
  BT Agriculture and state—Pakistan
    Reclamation of land—Pakistan
Monacan Indians
  ⌜E99.M85⌝
  BT Indians of North America
Monacanthidae
  ⌜QL638.M645⌝
  BT Tetraodontiformes
  NT Acreichthys
Monachism
  USE Monasticism and religious orders
Monachus
  USE Monk seals
Monachus monachus
  USE Mediterranean monk seal
Monachus schauinslandi
  USE Hawaiian monk seal
Monachus tropicalis
  ⌜QL737.P64⌝

  UF Caribbean monk seal
    West India seal
  BT Monk seals
Monacle family
  USE Monical family
Monaco Grand Prix Race
  BT Automobile racing
    Grand Prix racing
Monad (Symbol)
  USE Yin Yang symbol
Monadenium
  ⌜QK495.E9⌝
  BT Euphorbiaceae
    Succulent plants
Monadology
  ⌜B2599.M8 (Leibnitz)⌝
  UF Monads (Philosophy)
  BT Cosmology
    Philosophy
  RT Pluralism
  NT Microcosm and macrocosm
Monads (Mathematics)
  USE Triples, Theory of
Monads (Philosophy)
  USE Monadology
Monagham family
  USE Monahan family
Monaghan family
  USE Monahan family
Monaham family
  USE Mooneyham family
Monahan family *(Not Subd Geog)*
  UF Monagham family
    Monaghan family
Monahans Sandhills State Park (Tex.)
  (Not Subd Geog)
  BT Parks—Texas
Monamine oxidase
  USE Monoamine oxidase
Monarch automobile
  ⌜TL215.M⌝
  BT Mercury automobile
Monarch butterfly
  ⌜QL561.D3⌝
  UF Anosia plexippus
    Danaus archippus
    Danaus plexippus
  BT Butterflies
Monarchianism
  ⌜BT1420⌝
  BT Heresies, Christian—History—Early
    church, ca. 30-600
Monarchists
  USE Royalists
Monarchs
  USE Kings and rulers
Monarchy *(May Subd Geog)*
  ⌜JC374-JC408⌝
  UF Sovereigns
  BT Executive power
  RT Democracy
    Despotism
    Royalists
  NT Divine right of kings
    Emperors
    Kings and rulers—Succession
    Ministerial responsibility
    Prerogative, Royal
    Queens
    Sovereignty
  — Denmark
    UF Danish monarchy
      Monarchy, Danish
    BT Denmark—Kings and rulers
  — France
    UF French monarchy
      Monarchy, French
    BT France—Kings and rulers
  — Great Britain
    UF British monarchy
      Monarchy, British

Monarchy
— **Great Britain** *(Continued)*
    BT Great Britain—Kings and rulers
— **Malaysia**
    UF Malaysian monarchy
        Monarchy, Malaysian
    BT Malaysia—Kings and rulers
— **Poland**
    UF Monarchy, Polish
        Polish monarchy
    BT Poland—Kings and rulers
— **Soviet Union**
    ⌐JN6540⌐
    UF Monarchy, Russian
        Russian monarchy
    BT Soviet Union—Kings and rulers
— **Spain**
    UF Monarchy, Spanish
        Spanish monarchy
    BT Spain—Kings and rulers
— **Thailand**
    UF Monarchy, Thai
        Thai monarchy
    BT Thailand—Kings and rulers
Monarchy, British
  USE Monarchy—Great Britain
Monarchy, Danish
  USE Monarchy—Denmark
Monarchy, French
  USE Monarchy—France
Monarchy, Malaysian
  USE Monarchy—Malaysia
Monarchy, Polish
  USE Monarchy—Poland
Monarchy, Russian
  USE Monarchy—Soviet Union
Monarchy, Spanish
  USE Monarchy—Spain
Monarchy, Thai
  USE Monarchy—Thailand
Monasa
  USE Nun-birds
Monascaceae
    ⌐QK623.M⌐
  BT Eurotiales
  NT Monascus
Monascidae
  USE Fellodistomidae
Monascus
  BT Monascaceae
Monasteries *(May Subd Geog)*
    ⌐BX2460-2749 (Catholic Church)⌐
    ⌐NA5201-6113 (Architecture,
    NA4850)⌐
  UF Cloisters
  BT Charities
      Church property
  RT Abbeys
      Convents and nunneries
      Monasticism and religious orders
  NT Cave monasteries
      Enclosure (Monasticism)
      Hermitages
      Houses of prayer
      Music in monasteries
      Priories
      Secularization
— **Seals**
    UF Monastic seals
    BT Religious and ecclesiastical
        institutions—Seals
— **Bulgaria**
    NT Manastirŭt v Tuzlalŭka (Preslav,
        Bulgaria)
— **Spain**
    NT Monasterio de Rueda, Spain
— **Sri Lanka**
    NT Alahana Parivena Site
        (Polonnaruwa, Sri Lanka)
Monasteries, Armenian *(May Subd Geog)*
  UF Armenian Church monasteries

Monasteries, Buddhist *(May Subd Geog)*
  UF Buddhist monasteries
  BT Buddhism
      Monasticism and religious orders,
        Buddhist
  NT Convents and nunneries, Buddhist
— **Japan**
    NT Kōyasan Monasteries (Japan)
Monasteries, Cave
  USE Cave monasteries
Monasteries, Coptic *(May Subd Geog)*
  UF Coptic monasteries
  BT Monasticism and religious orders,
      Coptic
Monasteries, Franciscan *(May Subd Geog)*
  UF Franciscan monasteries
Monasteries, Hindu *(May Subd Geog)*
    ⌐BL1226.9⌐
  UF Hindu monasteries
  BT Hinduism
Monasteries, Jaina *(May Subd Geog)*
    ⌐BL1378⌐
  UF Jaina monasteries
  BT Jainism
Monasteries, Orthodox Eastern
  (May Subd Geog)
  UF Orthodox Eastern monasteries
  BT Monasticism and religious orders,
      Orthodox Eastern
      Orthodox Eastern Church
Monasteries and state *(May Subd Geog)*
  UF State and monasteries
  BT Church and state
Monasterio de Rueda, Spain
  UF Abadía de Nuestra Señora de Rueda,
      Spain
  BT Monasteries—Spain
Monastic and religious life
    ⌐BX2435⌐
  UF Monastic life
      Religious life
      Spirituality (in religious orders,
        congregations, etc.)
  BT Monasticism and religious orders
      Spiritual life
  RT Vows
  SA *subdivision* Spiritual life *under names*
      of individual religious orders,
      congregations, etc., e.g. Jesuits—
      Spiritual life
  NT Celibacy—Christianity
      Eremitic life
      Evangelical counsels
      Hermits
      Retreats for members of religious
        orders
      Spiritual direction
      Superiors, Religious
— **History**
— — **Early church, ca. 30-600**
    ⌐BX2465⌐
— — **Middle Ages, 600-1500**
Monastic and religious life (Buddhism)
  (May Subd Geog)
  BT Monasticism and religious orders,
      Buddhist
      Religious life (Buddhism)
  NT Spiritual life (Buddhism)
      Trisaṃvara (Buddhism)
Monastic and religious life (Canon law)
  BT Canon law
Monastic and religious life (Hinduism)
  (May Subd Geog)
    ⌐BL1226.85⌐
  UF Hindu monastic and religious life
  BT Hinduism
Monastic and religious life (Jainism)
  BT Jainism
Monastic and religious life (Zen Buddhism)
  (May Subd Geog)
  BT Zen Buddhism

  NT Monasticism and religious orders, Zen
      Spiritual life (Zen Buddhism)
Monastic and religious life in art
Monastic and religious life of women
    ⌐BX4210⌐
  UF Monastic life
      Religious life
  BT Monasticism and religious orders for
        women
      Spiritual life
  NT Celibacy—Christianity
      Nuns in campus ministry
— **History**
— — **Middle Ages, 600-1500**
— **Psychology**
    ⌐BV4205⌐
  UF Monasticism and religious orders
        for women—Psychology
Monastic libraries *(May Subd Geog)*
    ⌐Z675.M⌐
  UF Libraries, Monastic
  BT Religious libraries
  RT Scriptoria
Monastic life
  USE Monastic and religious life
      Monastic and religious life of women
Monastic orders
  USE Monasticism and religious orders
Monastic poverty
  USE Monasticism and religious orders—
      Common life
Monastic profession
  USE Profession (in religious orders,
      congregations, etc.)
Monastic seals
  USE Monasteries—Seals
Monastic vocation
  USE Vocation (in religious orders,
      congregations, etc.)
Monasticism and religious orders
  (May Subd Geog)
    ⌐BX385 (Greek Church)⌐
    ⌐BX580-BX583 (Russian Church)⌐
    ⌐BX2410-BX4560 (Catholic Church)⌐
    Here are entered works on groups of Christians
  who live together under religious vows. Works on
  groups of Christians who live together without vows
  are entered under Societies living in common without
  vows. Works on groups of Christians who live and/or
  work together to achieve common spiritual and social
  objectives are entered under Christian communities.
  UF Monachism
      Monastic orders
      Monasticism and religious orders for
        men
      Monasticism and religious orders of
        men
      Orders, Monastic
      Religious orders
  BT Brotherhoods
      Christian communities
  RT Brothers (in religious orders,
      congregations, etc.)
      Friars
      Monasteries
      Monks
  SA *names of individual orders, e.g.* Jesuits
  NT Augustinians
      Beghards
      Benedictines
      Birgittines
      Brothers Hospitallers of St. John of
        God
      Brothers of Charity
      Brothers of the Common Life
      Carmelites
      Clerks Regular of Somaschi
      Confraternities
      Contemplative orders
      Culdees
      Doctrinarians
      Dominicans

Ex-monks
Franciscans
Gilbertines
Hospitalers
Jesuits
Marist Brothers
Military religious orders
Monastic and religious life
Novitiate
Postulancy
Profession (in religious orders,
   congregations, etc.)
Superiors, Religious
Third orders
Vallombrosans
Vocation (in religious orders,
   congregations, etc.)
— Brothers
   USE Brothers (in religious orders,
      congregations, etc.)
— **Common life**
   UF Common life
      Monastic poverty
      Poverty, Monastic
   BT Poverty, Vow of
— **Dietary rules**
   BT Asceticism
      Diet
      Food—Religious aspects
   RT Vegetarianism—Religious aspects
— **Discipline**
   [BX2435]
   BT Church discipline
   NT Manifestation of conscience
— **Education**
   BT Catholic Church—Education
   NT Juniorate
      Monasticism and religious orders
       for women—Education
— **Government**
   [BX2410-2440]
   NT General chapters
— **Habit**
   [BX2790]
   [BX4223 (Sisterhoods)]
   UF Ecclesiastical costume
      Habit, Monastic
   BT Church vestments
      Clergy—Costume
      Costume
   NT Scapulars
— **History**
— — **Early church, ca. 30-600**
      [BX2465]
      BT Church history—Primitive and
         early church, ca. 30-600
— — **Middle Ages, 600-1500**
      [BX2470]
      BT Church history—Middle Ages,
         600-1500
— Lay brothers
   USE Lay brothers
— **Liturgy and ritual**
   [BX2049.A1]
— **Missions**
   BT Catholic Church—Missions
   SA *subdivision* Missions *under names*
      of individual monastic and
      religious orders, e.g. Jesuits—
      Missions
— **Occupations**
   Here are entered works on lay occupations
   performed by members of orders, e.g. building,
   farming, etc.
   BT Occupations
   SA *subdivision* Occupation *under*
      names of individual orders, with
      or without local subdivisions,
      e.g. Jesuits—Occupations
— Provision for old age

   USE Monasticism and religious orders
      —Retirement
— **Retirement**
   [BX2437.5]
   UF Monasticism and religious orders—
      Provision for old age
— **Rules**
   [BX2436-7]
   SA *subdivision* Rules *under names of*
      individual orders, e.g. Jesuits—
      Rules
   NT Monasticism and religious orders
      for women—Rules
— Third orders
   USE Third orders
— Vows
   USE Vows
Monasticism and religious orders, Anglican
   UF Anglican monasticism and religious
      orders
   NT Franciscan movement (Anglican
      Communion)
      Monasticism and religious orders for
      women, Anglican
Monasticism and religious orders, Buddhist
   (May Subd Geog)
   UF Buddhist monasticism and religious
      orders
   BT Buddhism
   NT Amarapura (Sect)
      Buddhist monks
      Buddhist novices
      Koan
      Monasteries, Buddhist
      Monastic and religious life (Buddhism)
      Monasticism and religious orders, Zen
      Monasticism and religious orders for
      women, Buddhist
      Profession (Buddhist monastic orders)
— **Dietary rules**
   BT Asceticism
      Diet
      Food—Religious aspects—
      Buddhism
— **Education** *(May Subd Geog)*
   BT Buddhism—Education
— **Habit**
   UF Habit, Monastic
   BT Costume
— **Ordination**
   USE Ordination (Buddhism)
— **Rules**
— **Vows**
   USE Vows (Buddhism)
Monasticism and religious orders, Coptic
   UF Coptic monasticism and religious
      orders
   NT Monasteries, Coptic
Monasticism and religious orders, Hindu
   (May Subd Geog)
   UF Hindu monasticism and religious
      orders
— **Rules**
   [BL1238.76]
Monasticism and religious orders, Islamic
   (May Subd Geog)
   [BP189.2-7]
   UF Islamic monasticism and religious
      orders
      Monasticism and religious orders,
      Muslim
      Muslim monasticism and religious
      orders
   NT Senussites
Monasticism and religious orders, Jaina
   [BL1378]
   UF Jaina monasticism and religious orders
   BT Jainism
— **Rules**

Monasticism and religious orders, Lutheran
   UF Lutheran monasticism and religious
      orders
   NT Monasticism and religious orders for
      women, Lutheran
Monasticism and religious orders, Maronite
   UF Maronite monasticism and religious
      orders
   BT Maronites
Monasticism and religious orders, Muslim
   USE Monasticism and religious orders,
      Islamic
Monasticism and religious orders, Nestorian
   UF Nestorian monasticism and religious
      orders
**Monasticism and religious orders, Orthodox
Eastern** *(May Subd Geog)*
   UF Orthodox Eastern monasticism and
      religious orders
   NT Monasteries, Orthodox Eastern
— **Rules**
Monasticism and religious orders, Protestant
   [BV4405-6]
   UF Protestant monasticism and religious
      orders
— **Rules**
Monasticism and religious orders, Taoist
   UF Taoist monasticism and religious
      orders
Monasticism and religious orders, Zen
   UF Zen monasticism and religious orders
   BT Monastic and religious life (Zen
      Buddhism)
      Monasticism and religious orders,
      Buddhist
      Zen Buddhism
— **Rules**
Monasticism and religious orders (Canon law)
   [BX2427]
   NT Abbots (Canon law)
      Dowry (Canon law)
      Exclaustration
      Master of novices (Canon law)
      Novitiate (Canon law)
**Monasticism and religious orders (Canon law,
Oriental)**
   BT Canon law, Oriental
**Monasticism and religious orders (Canon law,
Orthodox Eastern)**
Monasticism and religious orders for men
   USE Monasticism and religious orders
Monasticism and religious orders for women
   (May Subd Geog)
   [BX4200-4560]
   BT Women in Christianity
   RT Convents and nunneries
      Ex-nuns
      Nuns
      Sisterhoods
   NT Beguinages
      Beguines
      Benedictine nuns
      Carmelite Nuns
      Cistercian nuns
      Consecration of virgins
      Daughters of Mary, Help of Christians
      Dominican Sisters
      Missionary Sisters of the Sacred Heart
      Monastic and religious life of women
      Mothers general
— **Education**
   [BX4210.5]
   BT Monasticism and religious orders—
      Education
— **History**
— — **Middle Ages, 600-1500**
— **Psychology**
   USE Monastic and religious life of
      women—Psychology
— **Rules**

Monasticism and religious orders for women
— Rules *(Continued)*
    BT Monasticism and religious orders—
        Rules
    SA *subdivision* Rules *under names of*
        individual orders
— Belgium
    NT Zwarte Zusters van Sint-
        Augustinus
Monasticism and religious orders for women,
Anglican *(May Subd Geog)*
    UF Anglican monasticism and religious
        orders
    BT Monasticism and religious orders,
        Anglican
Monasticism and religious orders for women,
Buddhist *(May Subd Geog)*
    UF Buddhist monasticism and religious
        orders
    BT Monasticism and religious orders,
        Buddhist
— Rules
Monasticism and religious orders for women,
Lutheran
    UF Lutheran monasticism and religious
        orders
    BT Monasticism and religious orders,
        Lutheran
Monasticism and religious orders for women,
Orthodox Eastern *(May Subd Geog)*
    UF Orthodox Eastern monasticism and
        religious orders for women
Monasticism and religious orders for women
(Canon law)
Monasticism and religious orders of men
    USE Monasticism and religious orders
Monay family
    USE Monet family
Monazite *(May Subd Geog)*
    [TN948.M7]
Monba (Indic people)
    USE Monpa (Indic people)
Monba language
    USE Monpa language
Monbuttu language
    USE Mangbetu language
Monbuttu
    [GN654]
    UF Mangbetus
        Mombuttus
    BT Ethnology—Zaire
Moncada Barracks Attack, Cuba, 1953
    USE Cuba—History—Moncada Barracks
        Attack, 1953
Moncada family
    USE Montcada family
Moncada Palace (Mexico City, Mexico)
    USE Palacio de Iturbide (Mexico City,
        Mexico)
Monceau, Parc (Paris, France)
    USE Parc Monceau (Paris, France)
Mönckeberg family *(Not Subd Geog)*
Monckton's Expedition to St. John River, Me.
and N.B., 1758
    [E199]
Moncreiff family
    USE Moncrief family
Moncreiffe family
    USE Moncrief family
Moncrief family *(Not Subd Geog)*
    UF Moncreiff family
        Moncreiffe family
        Moncrieff family
        Muncrief family
        Muncriep family
        Muncriffe family
Moncrieff family
    USE Moncrief family
Moncure family *(Not Subd Geog)*
Mond family *(Not Subd Geog)*
    RT Melchett family

Mondale family *(Not Subd Geog)*
    UF Mundal family
        Mundale family
Monday family
    USE Mundy family
MONDEB (Computer program)
    BT Debugging in computer science
Mondego River (Portugal)
    UF Rio Mondego (Portugal)
    BT Rivers—Portugal
Mondenall family
    USE Mendenhall family
Mondi linguo (Artificial language)
    [PM8629]
    UF Mondilingwo (Artificial language)
    BT Languages, Artificial
Mondial (Artificial language)
    [PM8630]
    BT Languages, Artificial
Mondilingwo (Artificial language)
    USE Mondi linguo (Artificial language)
Mondorocu Indians
    USE Mundurucu Indians
Mone family
    USE Monet family
Monee family
    USE Monet family
Monegres (Spain)
    USE Monegros (Spain)
Monegros (Spain)
    UF Los Monegros (Spain)
        Monegres (Spain)
Monel metal
    [TA490 (Testing)]
    [TS650 (Manufacture)]
    BT Nickel alloys
Monell family *(Not Subd Geog)*
Monella
    USE Cyrtanthus
Monema
    [QL561.E9]
    BT Limacodidae
    NT Monema flavescens
Monema flavescens *(May Subd Geog)*
    [QL561.E9]
    BT Monema
Moneron Island (R.S.F.S.R.)
    (Not Subd Geog)
    UF Kaiba-to (R.S.F.S.R.)
        Ostrov Moneron (R.S.F.S.R.)
    BT Islands—Russian S.F.S.R.
Monet family *(Not Subd Geog)*
    UF DeMoneia family
        DeMoney family
        DeMonia family
        LeMoine family
        Monay family
        Mone family
        Monee family
        Money family
        Monnet family
        Mony family
Monetarism
    USE Chicago school of economics
Monetary correction
    USE Indexation (Economics)
Monetary gold confiscations
    BT Booty (International law)
        Confiscations
        Gold
        World War, 1939-1945—Confiscations
        and contributions
        World War, 1939-1945—Reparations
Monetary management
    USE Monetary policy
Monetary policy *(May Subd Geog)*
    UF Monetary management
    BT Banks and banking, Central
        Currency question
        Economic policy
        Liquidity (Economics)

    RT Fiscal policy
        Money supply
    NT Credit control
        Devaluation of currency
Monetary question
    USE Currency question
        Money
Monetary reformers *(May Subd Geog)*
    UF Reformers, Monetary
    BT Money
Monetary unions
    UF Common currencies
        Currency areas
        Optimum currency areas
    BT Currency question
        Money
    SA *names of individual monetary unions*
    NT Coinage, International
        French franc area
        Sterling area
MONEX
    USE Monsoon Experiment
Money *(May Subd Geog)*
    [GN436.2 (Primitive)]
    [HG201-HG1490]
    UF Currency
        Monetary question
        Specie
        Standard of value
    BT Commerce
        Economics
        Exchange
        Value
    RT Banks and banking
        Coinage
        Currency question
        Finance
        Finance, Public
        Gold
        Legal tender
        Silver
        Silver question
        Wealth
    SA *subdivision* Military currency *under*
        individual wars, e.g. World War,
        1939-1945—Military currency
    NT Bank deposits
        Bank-notes
        Banks and banking, Central
        Barter
        Bills of exchange
        Bimetallism
        Black market—Foreign exchange
        Capital
        Children's allowances
        Circular velocity of money
        Coinage, International
        Coins
        Counterfeits and counterfeiting
        Credit
        Currency convertibility
        Deflation (Finance)
        Demand for money
        Emergency currency
        Foreign exchange
        Gold standard
        Gresham's law
        Hoarding of money
        Indians of North America—Money
        Inflation (Finance)
        Military currency
        Mints
        Monetary reformers
        Monetary unions
        Money, Primitive
        Money market
        Money supply
        Occupation currency
        Paper money
        Precious metals
        Prices

Purchasing power
Quantity theory of money
Reproduction of money, documents, etc.
Social credit
Tokens
— Congresses
[HG203-5]
— Devaluation
USE Devaluation of currency
— Law and legislation *(May Subd Geog)*
NT Banking law
— — Criminal provisions
NT Money laundering
— Tables
[HG219]
UF Cambistry tables
Foreign exchange—Tables
— Confederate States of America
UF Confederate States of America—Money
— European Economic Community countries
NT European currency unit
— United States
NT Dollar, American
— — History
— — — Colonial period, ca. 1600-1775
UF Continental money
Money, Circular velocity of
USE Circular velocity of money
Money, Hoarding of
USE Hoarding of money
Money, International
USE Coinage, International
Money, Primitive
BT Money
NT Coal money
Fur money
Shell money
Stone money
Tin money
Wampum
Wooden money
Money, Quantity theory of
USE Quantity theory of money
Money changing machines (Coins)
USE Coin changing machines
Money family
USE Monet family
Money in art
Money in literature
BT Economics in literature
Money laundering *(May Subd Geog)*
Here are entered works on the practice of channeling illegally-obtained money through a third party in order to conceal the true source and cause it to appear legitimate.
UF Laundering of money
Money washing
Washing of money
BT Money—Law and legislation—Criminal provisions
Money laundering investigation
(May Subd Geog)
[HV8079.M64]
BT Criminal investigation
Money-making projects for children
(May Subd Geog)
UF Children's business enterprises
Children's money-making projects
BT Business enterprises
Children—Employment
RT Children's allowances
Money market *(May Subd Geog)*
BT Finance
Financial institutions
Money
NT Capital market
Interest rate futures
Money market certificates
USE Certificates of deposit

Money market funds *(May Subd Geog)*
UF Funds, Money market
BT Mutual funds
— Law and legislation *(May Subd Geog)*
— Reserves
UF Reserves, Money market fund
— — Law and legislation
(May Subd Geog)
Money orders *(May Subd Geog)*
BT Drafts
Letters of credit
Negotiable instruments
NT Postal service—Money-orders
Money raising
USE Fund raising
Money stock
USE Money supply
Money supply *(May Subd Geog)*
UF Money stock
Quantity of money
Supply of money
BT Money
RT Demand for money
Monetary policy
— Seasonal variations
Money washing
USE Money laundering
Moneyham family
USE Mooneyham family
Monferrato (Italy)
UF Montferrat (Italy)
Monferrato War, 1613-1618
BT Savoy (France and Italy)—History
Spain—History—Philip III, 1598-1621
Monferrinas
UF Manfredinas
Monfredas
Monfrinas
Montferrine
BT Country-dances
Dance music—Italy
Monfou (African people)
USE Mamvu (African people)
Monfredas
USE Monferrinas
Monfrinas
USE Monferrinas
Mong language
USE Hmong language
Monge-Ampère equations
UF Equations, Monge-Ampère
BT Differential equations, Partial
Monger family
USE Munger family
Monges Islands (Venezuela)
USE Monjes Islands (Venezuela)
Mongibello (Sicily)
USE Etna, Mount (Sicily)
Mongo (African people)
[DT650.M65]
UF Balolo (African people)
BT Bantus
Ethnology—Zaire
NT Mbole (African people)
Missions to Mongo (African people)
Mongo language
[PL8518]
UF Bamongo
Lolo (Bantu language)
Lomongo (Bantu language)
BT Bantu languages
Mongo lullabies
USE Lullabies, Mongo
Mongo poetry *(May Subd Geog)*
Mongol Invasion, Poland, 1241
USE Poland—History—Mongol Invasion, 1241
Mongolia
— Antiquities
NT Moïltyn am Site (Mongolia)
— Languages

NT Oirat language
Mongolian art
USE Art, Mongolian
Mongolian astrology
USE Astrology, Mongolian
Mongolian ballads
USE Ballads, Mongolian
Mongolian birthmark
UF Birthmark, Mongolian
Mongolian Buddhist literature
USE Buddhist literature, Mongolian
Mongolian cookery
USE Cookery, Mongolian
Mongolian ephedra
USE Ephedra equisetina
Mongolian epic literature
USE Epic literature, Mongolian
Mongolian epic poetry
USE Epic poetry, Mongolian
Mongolian fiction *(May Subd Geog)*
NT Short stories, Mongolian
Mongolian folk art
USE Folk art, Mongolian
Mongolian folk literature
USE Folk literature, Mongolian
Mongolian folk poetry
USE Folk poetry, Mongolian
Mongolian folk-songs
USE Folk-songs, Mongolian
Mongolian imprints *(May Subd Geog)*
Mongolian inscriptions
USE Inscriptions, Mongolian
Mongolian language
[PL401-9]
BT Mongolian languages
NT Chahar dialect
Khalkha dialect
Ordos dialect
— Middle Mongolian, 13th century-16th century
— Alphabet
NT hPhags-pa alphabet
Mongolian languages *(May Subd Geog)*
BT Altaic languages
Mongolian philology
RT Buriat language
NT Dagur language
Eastern Yuku language
Jarut language
Kalmyk language
Khitan language
Moghol language
Mongolian language
Monguor language
Oirat language
Pao-an language
Proto-Mongolian language
Tung-hsiang language
Mongolian law
USE Law, Mongolian
Mongolian literature
[PL410-419]
NT Buddhist literature, Mongolian
Epic literature, Mongolian
Folk literature, Mongolian
Mongolian literature (English)
USE English literature—Mongolian authors
Mongolian medicine
USE Medicine, Mongolian
Mongolian mythology
USE Mythology, Mongolian
Mongolian newspapers *(May Subd Geog)*
Mongolian philology
SA *individual Mongolian languages and literatures, e.g.* Buriat language, Mongolian language, Mongolian literature
NT Mongolian languages
Mongolian poetry *(May Subd Geog)*
[PL412 (History)]
[PL416 (Collections)]

Mongolian poetry *(Continued)*
  NT Epic poetry, Mongolian
       Folk poetry, Mongolian
Mongolian pony
  [SF315.2.M]
  UF Manchurian pony
  BT Ponies
Mongolian proverbs
  USE Proverbs, Mongolian
Mongolian short stories
  USE Short stories, Mongolian
Mongolian songs
  USE Songs, Mongolian
Mongolian watercolor painting
  USE Watercolor painting, Mongolian
Mongolians
  USE Mongols
Mongolism (Disease)
  USE Down's syndrome
Mongoloid race *(May Subd Geog)*
  [GN548]
  UF Yellow race
  BT Race
Mongols *(May Subd Geog)*
  [DS19-DS23 (History)]
  [GN548 (Ethnography)]
  UF Mongolians
  BT Ethnology—Asia
  NT Buriats
       Hazāras
       Kalmyks
       Khitan Mongols
       Monguors
       Oirats
       Ordos (Mongolian tribe)
       Tanawalis (Pakistani people)
       Tatars
 — History
    NT 'Ayn Jālūt, Battle of, 1260
        Golden Horde
        Legnica, Battle of, 1241
        Turkey—History—Invasion of
          Timur, 1402
        Wahlstatt, Battle of, 1241
Mongols, Western
  USE Oirats
Mongols in art
Mongomery family
  USE Montgomery family
Mongondou language
  USE Bolaang Mongondow language
Mongondow language
  USE Bolaang Mongondow language
Mongoose lemur
  [QL737.P95]
  UF Lemur mongoz
  BT Lemur
Mongooses
  [QL737.C28]
  UF Herpestinae
  BT Viverridae
  NT Banded mongoose
       Mungos
Mongooses, Dwarf
  USE Helogale
Mongooses, Pigmy
  USE Helogale
Mongos Islands (Venezuela)
  USE Monjes Islands (Venezuela)
Mongsen dialect
  USE Ao language
Monguagon, Mich., Battle of, Aug. 9, 1812
  [E356.M]
  UF Brownstown, Mich., Battle of, Aug. 9,
      1812
      Maguaga, Battle of, 1812
Monguor language
  [PL431.M6]
  BT Mongolian languages
Monguors
  [DS731.M65]

UF T'u-jen
BT Ethnology—China
     Mongols
Mongwandi language
  USE Ngbandi language
Monhysterida
  [QL391.N4]
  UF Monhysteroidea
  BT Adenophorea
      Nematoda
  NT Monhysteridae
Monhysteridae
  [QL391.N4]
  BT Monhysterida
  NT Rhynchonema
Monhysteroidea
  USE Monhysterida
Monical family *(Not Subd Geog)*
  UF Monacle family
      Monicale family
      Monicul family
      Monnicle family
      Monnicul family
Monicale family
  USE Monical family
Monicul family
  USE Monical family
Moniezia
  [QL391.P7]
  BT Anoplocephalidae
Monilia
  USE Candida
Moniliaceae
  [QK625.M7]
  UF Mucedinaceae
  BT Moniliales
  NT Aspergillus
      Penicillium
      Trichoderma
Moniliales
  [QK625.M74]
  UF Hyphomycetales
  BT Hyphomycetes
  NT Dematiaceae
      Moniliaceae
Moniliasis
  USE Candidiasis
Moniliasis, Oral
  USE Thrush (Mouth disease)
Monilinia
  [QK623.S3 (Botany)]
  BT Sclerotiniaceae
  NT Brown rot fungi of fruit
Monilinia fructicola
  [QK623.S3 (Botany)]
  [SB608.F8 (Phytopathogen)]
  UF American brown rot fungus
      Sclerotinia americana
      Sclerotinia cinerea
      Sclerotinia fructicola
  BT Brown rot fungi of fruit
Monilinia fructigena
  [QK623.S3 (Botany)]
  [SB608.F8 (Phytopathogen)]
  UF Sclerotinia fructigena
  BT Brown rot fungi of fruit
Monilinia laxa
  [QK623.S3 (Botany)]
  [SB608.F8 (Phytopathogen)]
  UF Sclerotinia cinerea
      Sclerotinia laxa
  BT Brown rot fungi of fruit
Monin family *(Not Subd Geog)*
Monishia
  [QL638.G7]
  BT Gobiidae
Monishia william
  [QL638.G7]
Monism
  [B827]
  [B851-B4695 (By country)]

BT Philosophy
     Reality
RT Dualism
     Materialism
     Pluralism
NT Idealism
Monitor Command System (Computer program)
  UF MCS (Computer program)
  BT Intel 8080 (Microprocessor)—
      Programming
      Utilities (Computer programs)
Monitor lizards
  [QL666.L29]
  UF Dragon lizards
      Goannas
      Varanidae
  BT Lizards
  NT Varanus
Monitor Valley (Nev.)
  BT Valleys—Nevada
Monitorial system of education
  [LB1029.M7]
  UF Lancasterian system
  BT Education
      School discipline
      School management and organization
      Teaching
Monitoring, Biological
  USE Biological monitoring
Monitoring, Drug use
  USE Drug utilization
Monitoring, Environmental
  USE Environmental monitoring
Monitoring, Patient
  USE Patient monitoring
Monitoring, Physiological
  USE Patient monitoring
Monitoring (Hospital care)
  USE Patient monitoring
Monitoring (Psychology)
  USE Vigilance (Psychology)
Monitoring in flight of turbojet engines
  USE Airplanes—Turbojet engines—In-flight
      monitoring
Monitoring of electric machinery
  USE Electric machinery—Monitoring
Monitoring of plant performance
  USE Plant performance—Monitoring
Monitoring radio receivers
  USE Radio—Monitoring receivers
Monitors (Warships)
  USE Turret ships
Monjes Islands (Venezuela)
  UF Archipiélago de Los Monjes
      (Venezuela)
      Los Monjes Islands (Venezuela)
      Monges Islands (Venezuela)
      Mongos Islands (Venezuela)
  BT Islands—Venezuela
Monjombo (African people)
  UF Monzombo (African people)
  BT Ethnology—Central African Republic
      Ethnology—Congo (Brazzaville)
      Ethnology—Zaire
Monk seals
  [QL737.P64]
  UF Monachus
  BT Seals (Animals)
  NT Hawaiian monk seal
      Mediterranean monk seal
      Monachus tropicalis
Monkey eating eagle
  [QL696.F32]
  UF Pithecophaga jefferyi
Monkey grasshoppers, American
  USE Eumastacidae
Monkey peach
  USE Kiwi fruit
Monkeys *(May Subd Geog)*
  [QE882.P7 (Fossil)]

[QL737.P9 (Zoology)]
UF Haplorhini
BT Primates
NT Capuchin monkeys
Cebidae
Cercopithecidae
Macaques
Squirrel monkeys
— Anatomy
— Folklore
NT Three monkeys (Motif)
— Physiology
— Religious aspects
NT Kōshin
Monkeys, Fossil
Monkeys, Three (Motif)
USE Three monkeys (Motif)
Monkeys as aids for the handicapped
(May Subd Geog)
BT Handicapped
Monkeys as laboratory animals
Monkeys as pets
[SF459.M6]
Monkeys in art
Monkland & Kirkintilloch Railway
BT Railroads—Great Britain
Monks *(May Subd Geog)*
BT Christian biography
RT Ex-monks
Monasticism and religious orders
Monks basil
USE Ocimum sanctum
Monks in art
Monksfield (Race horse)
BT Race horses
Monmouth, Battle of, 1778
[E241.M7]
BT New Jersey—History—Revolution,
1775-1783
United States—History—Revolution,
1775-1783—Campaigns
Monmouth Battlefield State Historic Park
(N.J.)
USE Monmouth Battlefield State Park
(N.J.)
Monmouth Battlefield State Park (N.J.)
UF Monmouth Battlefield State Historic
Park (N.J.)
BT Battlefields—New Jersey
Parks—New Jersey
United States—History—Revolution,
1775-1783—Battlefields
Monmouth's Rebellion, 1685
[DA448.9]
BT Great Britain—History—Charles II,
1660-1685
NT Bloody Assizes, 1685
Sedgemoor (England), Battle of, 1685
Monmouthshire and Brecon Canal (Wales)
BT Canals—Wales
Monnaie Street (Lille, France)
USE Rue de la Monnaie (Lille, France)
Monnerat family *(Not Subd Geog)*
Monnet family
USE Monet family
Monnicle family
USE Monical family
Monnicul family
USE Monical family
Mono (Disease)
USE Mononucleosis
Mono-acting
USE Multiple role acting
Mono Indians
[E99.M]
BT Indians of North America
Numic Indians
Mono Lake (Calif.)
BT Lakes—California
Saline waters—California

Mono language
BT Melanesian languages
Monoamine oxidase
[QP603.M6]
UF Adrenalin oxidase
Benzylamine oxidase
MAO (Enzyme)
Monamine oxidase
Tyraminase
Tyramine oxidase
BT Amine oxidase
Metalloenzymes
— Inhibitors
UF Inhibitors, Monoamine oxidase
Monoamine oxidase inhibitors
BT Enzyme inhibitors
Monoamine oxidase inhibitors
USE Monoamine oxidase—Inhibitors
Monobathrida
BT Crinoidea, Fossil
NT Platycrinitidae
Monobia
[QL568.E84]
BT Eumenidae
Monoblepharella
BT Gonapodyaceae
Monoblepharidales
[QK621]
UF Monoblepharidineae
BT Chytridiomycetes
NT Gonapodyaceae
Monoblepharidineae
USE Monoblepharidales
Monocacy, Battle of the, 1864
[E476.66]
BT Maryland—History—Civil War, 1861-
1865
United States—History—Civil War,
1861-1865—Campaigns
Monocentridae
[QL638.M65]
BT Beryciformes
NT Monocentris
Monocentris
[QL638.M65]
BT Monocentridae
NT Monocentris reedi
Monocentris reedi
[QL638.M65]
BT Monocentris
Monochaetum *(May Subd Geog)*
[QK495.M514 (Botany)]
BT Melastomataceae
Monochlorobenzene
USE Chlorobenzene
Monochord
[ML3809]
BT Music—Acoustics and physics
Musical temperament
Monochromator
[QC467]
BT Spectrophotometer
Spectrum analysis—Instruments
MONOCLE project *(May Subd Geog)*
[Z699.4.M25]
BT Libraries—Automation
Monoclonal antibodies
USE Antibodies, Monoclonal
Monoclonal gammopathies
USE Gammopathies, Monoclonal
Monoclonal immunoglobulinopathies
USE Gammopathies, Monoclonal
Monoclonal immunoglobulins
USE Antibodies, Monoclonal
Monocoque construction
UF Reinforced monocoque construction
Semi-monocoque construction
BT Lightweight construction
Monocotyledons
[QK495.A14]
BT Angiosperms

NT Bromeliales
Commelinales
Cyperales
Helobiae
Juncales
Liliales
Pandanales
Scitamineae
Seagrasses
Spathiflorae
Monocotyledons, Fossil
BT Paleobotany
Monocrotaline alkaloids
USE Pyrrolizidines
Monoctenidae
USE Geometridae
Monocteniidae
USE Geometridae
Monocular blindness
USE Vision, Monocular
Monocular vision
USE Vision, Monocular
Monoculicoides variipennis
USE Culicoides variipennis
Monocyclia, Fossil
USE Anthozoa, Fossil
Monocytes
UF Leucocytes, Nongranular
Mononuclear phagocytes
Nongranular leucocytes
Phagocytes, Mononuclear
BT Leucocytes
Phagocytes
RT Macrophages
Reticulo-endothelial system
NT Monocytopoiesis
Monocytosis
Monokines
Monocytic leukemia
BT Nonlymphoid leukemia
Monocytopoiesis
[QP95]
BT Hematopoiesis
Monocytes
Monocytosis *(May Subd Geog)*
BT Leucocytosis
Monocytes
Monodon
USE Narwhal
Monodon monoceros
USE Narwhal
Monodontidae
[QL737.C433]
BT Cetacea
Whales
NT Narwhal
White whale
Monodontomerus
[QL568.T6]
BT Torymidae
NT Monodontomerus obscurus
Monodontomerus obscurus
(May Subd Geog)
[QL568.T6]
BT Monodontomerus
Monodramas *(May Subd Geog)*
[PN1936 (History)]
BT Drama
Monologues
Monodromy preserving deformation
USE Isomonodromic deformation method
Monogenic functions
[QA331]
UF Functions, Monogenic
BT Analytic functions
Functions of complex variables
Monogenism and polygenism
[GN353-6]
UF Polygenism
BT Man—Origin

Monoglycerides
  BT Glycerides
Monognathiformes
  USE Eels
Monognathiformes, Fossil
  USE Eels, Fossil
Monograms
  [NE2710 (Engraving)]
  [NK3640]
  UF Ciphers (Lettering)
  BT Decoration and ornament
      Inscriptions
      Lettering
  RT Alphabets
      Initials
  NT Anagrams
      Artists' marks
      Chi Rho symbol
Monographic series
  UF Bibliography—Books issued in series
      Books issued in series
      Series, Monographic
  BT Series (Publications)
  RT Serial publications
  SA subdivision Collected works under
        subjects
  — Cataloging
      USE Cataloging of monographic series
Monohelea
  [QL537.C37]
  BT Ceratopogonidae
Monoids
  BT Semigroups
Monokines
  BT Cellular immunity
      Immune response—Regulation
      Monocytes
Monokutuba language
  USE Kituba language
Monolayers
  USE Monomolecular films
Monolithic churches
  USE Cave churches
Monologue
  [PN1530]
  UF Monopolylogue
  BT Dialogue
      Drama
  NT Dramatic monologues
      Jōruri
      Sekkyō jōruri
      Soliloquy
Monologues
  [PN4305.M6]
    Here are entered collections of monologues.
Works on the monologue as a literary form are en-
tered under the heading Monologue. Monologues re-
corded with incidental musical background are en-
tered under Monologues—Readings with music.
Musical works in which spoken language is an inte-
gral part are entered under Monologues with music.
  BT Recitations
  NT Dramatic monologues
      Monodramas
  — **Readings with music**
Monologues, French (May Subd Geog)
  UF French monologues
Monologues, Humorous
  USE Humorous recitations
Monologues, Spanish (May Subd Geog)
  UF Spanish monologues
Monologues in literature
Monologues with music
  [M1625-6]
    Here, followed by specification of accompanying
medium, are entered secular musical works in which
spoken language is an integral part. The specification
(Instrumental ensemble) stands for two or more dif-
ferent solo instruments; (Voice) for a solo voice of
high, low, or medium range; and (Chorus) for men's,
mixed, women's, or children's voices in two or more
parts. Sacred works are entered under Sacred monologues with music.

Headings are printed below only if specific cross
references are needed.
  UF Declamation, Musical
      Musical declamation
      Narration with music
      Recitations with music
      Speaking with music
  BT Music
  NT Katarimono
      Rapping (Music)
      Sacred monologues with music
      Sekkyō jōruri
Monologues with music, Sacred
  USE Sacred monologues with music
Monologues with music (Chorus with band)
  BT Choruses with band
**Monologues with music (Chorus with chamber
orchestra)**
  BT Choruses with chamber orchestra
  — **Vocal scores with piano**
**Monologues with music (Chorus with
electronic music)**
  [M1625]
  BT Choruses with electronic music
**Monologues with music (Chorus with
instrumental ensemble)**
  BT Choruses with instrumental ensemble
**Monologues with music (Chorus with
orchestra)**
  BT Choruses with orchestra
  — **Scores**
Monologues with music (Chorus with piano)
  [M1626]
  BT Choruses with piano
**Monologues with music (Chorus with piano, 4
hands)**
  BT Choruses with piano, 4 hands
Monologues with music (Concrete music)
  [M1625]
  BT Concrete music
**Monologues with music (Double bass with
orchestra)**
  [M1625]
  BT Double bass with orchestra
Monologues with music (Electronic music)
  [M1625]
  BT Electronic music
**Monologues with music (Jazz ensemble with
chamber orchestra)**
  [M1625-6]
  BT Jazz ensemble with chamber orchestra
  — **Scores**
    [M1625]
Monologues with music (Jazz quintet)
  [M1625]
  BT Jazz quintets
Monologues with music (Orchestra)
  [M1625]
  BT Orchestral music
Monologues with music (Piano)
  [M1626]
  BT Piano music
Monologues with music (Piano, 4 hands)
  [M1626]
  BT Piano music (4 hands)
**Monologues with music (Pianos (2) with
chamber orchestra)**
  [M1625]
  BT Piano music (Pianos (2))
      Pianos (2) with chamber orchestra
Monologues with music (Plectral ensemble)
  [M1625]
  BT Plectral ensembles
Monologues with music (Shamisen)
  BT Shamisen music
  NT Jōruri
      Katōbushi
      Naniwabushi
      Shinnai

**Monologues with music (Violin with
orchestra)**
  [M1625]
  BT Violin with orchestra
**Monologues with music (Vocal duet with
instrumental ensemble)**
  [M1625-1626]
  BT Vocal duets with instrumental
      ensemble
**Monologues with music (Vocal octet with
chamber orchestra)**
  [M1625-6]
**Monologues with music (Vocal quartet with
instrumental ensemble)**
  [M1625-1626]
  BT Vocal quartets with instrumental
      ensemble
**Monologues with music (Vocal trio with
orchestra)**
  [M1625-6]
  BT Vocal trios with orchestra
**Monologues with music (Voice with
instrumental ensemble)**
  [M1625]
Monomania
  UF Fixed ideas
  BT Psychology, Pathological
Monomers
  BT Polymers and polymerization
Monomizuka Iseki (Kushigata-machi, Japan)
  USE Monomizuka Site (Kushigata-machi,
        Japan)
Monomizuka Site (Kushigata-machi, Japan)
  UF Monomizuka Iseki (Kushigata-machi,
        Japan)
  BT Japan—Antiquities
Monomolecular films
  [QD506 (Chemistry)]
  [TD397 (Water supply)]
  UF Films, Monomolecular
      Molecular films
      Monolayers
      Unilayers
  BT Molecular dynamics
      Surface chemistry
      Thin films
      Thin films, Multilayered
Monomorium
  [QL568.F7]
  BT Ants
**Monongah Mines Disaster, Monongah, W.Va.,
1907**
  [TN313]
Monongahela, Battle of the, 1755
  [E199]
  BT Braddock's Campaign, 1755
Monongahela (Fish)
  [QE852.D5]
  BT Lepidosirenidae
Monongahela dunkardensis
  [QE852.D5]
Monongahela River (W. Va. and Pa.)
  UF Mon River (W. Va. and Pa.)
  BT Rivers—Pennsylvania
      Rivers—West Virginia
Mononuclear leucocytosis
  USE Mononucleosis
Mononuclear phagocytes
  USE Macrophages
      Monocytes
Mononucleosis (May Subd Geog)
  [RC147.G6]
  UF Glandular fever
      Infectious mononucleosis
      Mono (Disease)
      Mononuclear leucocytosis
      Pfeiffer's disease
  BT Blood—Diseases
      Epstein-Barr virus diseases
      Leucocytosis

Mononychidae
USE Gelastocoridae
Monooxygenase, Cholesterol
USE Cholesterol hydroxylase
Monopeltis
⌐QL666.L224⌐
BT Amphisbaenidae
Monopeltis luandae
⌐QL666.L224⌐
Monopeltis perplexus
⌐QL666.L224⌐
Monophlebidae
USE Margarodidae
Monophthalmus
USE Cyclopia
Monophthongization
BT Phonetics
Monophysites *(May Subd Geog)*
⌐BT1425⌐
Here are entered works on the followers of
Eutyches. Works on the Syrian Jacobite, Armenian,
Coptic, Ethiopian, and Indian Orthodox churches
treated collectively are entered under Oriental Or-
thodox churches.
BT Heresies, Christian—History—Early
church, ca. 30-600
RT Oriental Orthodox churches
NT Jacobites (Syrian Christians)
Monothelitism
Schism, Acacian, 484-519
Monoplacophora
BT Mollusks
Monoplacophora, Fossil
Monopoles, Magnetic
USE Magnetic monopoles
Monopolies *(May Subd Geog)*
⌐HD2709-2930⌐
UF Combinations in restraint of trade
Commercial corners
Corners, Commercial
Engrossing
Forestalling
BT Capital
Commerce
Commercial crimes
Economics
Trade regulation
RT Competition
Monopolistic competition
Monopsonies
Restraint of trade
Trusts, Industrial
NT Banality (Law)
Cartels
Competition, Imperfect
Corporation law
Duopolies
Exclusive contracts
Exclusive licenses
Government monopolies
Oligopolies
Press monopolies
Railroads—Consolidation
Shipping conferences
— Computer programs
NT SMS (Computer program)
Monopolies, Government
USE Government monopolies
Monopolies, Partial
USE Duopolies
Oligopolies
Monopolies (Jewish law)
Monopolistic competition *(May Subd Geog)*
⌐HB238⌐
Here are entered works on the competition among
sellers whose products are similar, emphasizing prod-
uct differentiation and advertising rather than price.
UF Competition, Monopolistic
BT Competition
RT Monopolies
Monopoly (Game)
⌐GV1469.M65⌐

BT Board games
Monopolylogue
USE Monologue
Monoprint
USE Monotype (Engraving)
Monopsonies *(May Subd Geog)*
UF Buyers' monopolies
BT Competition
Industrial concentration
RT Monopolies
Monopsyllus
⌐QL599.7.C47⌐
BT Ceratophyllidae
Fleas
Monopulse radar
⌐TK6592.M6⌐
UF Direction finding by simultaneous
lobing
Simultaneous-lobing techniques
BT Pulse techniques (Electronics)
Radar
Monorail conveyors
UF Conveyors, Monorail
BT Conveying machinery
Monorail railroads *(May Subd Geog)*
⌐TF694⌐
UF Railroads, Monorail
Railroads, Single-rail
Single-rail railroads
BT Railroads
Monoraphidium griffithii
USE Ankistrodesmus falcatus
Monorchis
USE Cryptorchism
Monosaccharides
BT Saccharides
NT Fructose
Galactose
Glucose
Mannose
Oligosaccharides
Pentoses
Uronic acids
Monosodium glutamate *(May Subd Geog)*
⌐QP562.G5 (Physiology)⌐
UF MSG (Food additive)
Sodium glutamate
BT Food additives
Glutamic acid
Sodium salts
Monostiche
USE Calathea
Monosyllables
SA *subdivision* Monosyllables *under*
names of languages and groups of
languages, e.g. English language—
Monosyllables
Monotaxidae
USE Lethrinidae
Monoterpenes
BT Terpenes
Monotheism
⌐BL221⌐
BT Pantheism
Religion
Theism
Theology
Trinity
RT God
Polytheism
NT God—Incomparability
Monotheism (Islam)
USE God (Islam)
Monothelitism
BT Heresies, Christian—History—Early
church, ca. 30-600
Jesus Christ—History of doctrines—
Early church, ca. 30-600
Monophysites
Monotone operators
BT Operator theory

Monotonic functions
UF Functions, Monotonic
BT Functions of real variables
Monotremata *(May Subd Geog)*
⌐QL737.M7⌐
BT Mammals
NT Platypus
Tachyglossidae
Monotype
⌐Z253⌐
BT Linotype
Printing, Practical
Printing machinery and supplies
Type and type-founding
Type-setting machines
Monotype (Engraving) *(May Subd Geog)*
UF Monoprint
BT Engraving
Painting
— 20th century *(May Subd Geog)*
Monotype (Engraving), American
(May Subd Geog)
⌐NE2245⌐
UF American monotype (Engraving)
Monotype (Engraving), American, ⌐etc.⌐
(May Subd Geog)
Monoxia
⌐QL596.C5⌐
BT Chrysomelidae
Monpa (Indic people)
⌐DS432.M63⌐
UF Mompa (Indic people)
Monba (Indic people)
BT Ethnology—India
Monpa language
UF Monba language
BT Tibeto-Burman languages
Monrad family *(Not Subd Geog)*
Monro family
USE Monroe family
Monroe doctrine
⌐JX1425⌐
BT International relations
Intervention (International law)
Latin America—Foreign relations—
United States
Pan-Americanism
United States—Foreign relations—
Latin America
NT Drago doctrine
Monroe family *(Not Subd Geog)*
UF Monro family
Munro clan
Munro family
Munroe family
Monrosier family
USE Monrozier family
Monrozier family *(Not Subd Geog)*
UF Monrosier family
Mons, Battle of, 1914
⌐D542.M7⌐
BT World War, 1914-1918—Campaigns—
Belgium
Mons (Southeast-Asiatic people)
USE Mon (Southeast-Asiatic people)
Mons Albus (France and Italy)
USE Blanc, Mont (France and Italy)
Monselice Castle (Monselice, Italy)
USE Castello di Monselice (Monselice,
Italy)
Monsen family
USE Munson family
Monseny Mountains (Spain)
USE Montseny Mountains (Spain)
Monserrat (Spain)
USE Montserrat (Spain)
Monsey language
USE Munsee language
Monson family
USE Munson family

Monsoon Experiment
UF MONEX
BT Meteorology—Research
Monsoons
Monsoons *(May Subd Geog)*
 ₍QC939.M7₎
BT Winds
NT Monsoon Experiment
West African Monsoon Experiment
Monsters *(May Subd Geog)*
 ₍GR825-GR830 (Folklore)₎
 ₍QL991 (Animals)₎
 ₍QM691-QM699 (Human anatomy)₎
UF Freaks
Monstrosities
Teratology
BT Animals—Folklore
Curiosities and wonders
Folklore
RT Abnormalities, Human
Animals—Abnormalities
NT Bunyips
Cerberus (Greek mythology)
Cucafera
Dicephalism
Dragons
Dwarfs
Geryon (Classical mythology)
Ghouls and ogres
Giants
Gorgons
Loch Ness monster
Minotaur (Greek mythology)
Mokele-mbembe
Sea monsters
Yeti
— **Symbolic aspects**
BT Symbolism
Monsters in art
Monsters in literature
Monsters in mass media
 ₍P96.M6₎
BT Mass media
Monsters in motion pictures
BT Moving-pictures
Monsters in the Bible
UF Bible—Monsters
Monstrances
 ₍NK7215₎
BT Church plate
Lord's Supper
Mass
Monstrilloida
 ₍QL444.C756₎
BT Copepoda
Monstrosities
USE Monsters
Monsú Site (Colombia) *(Not Subd Geog)*
BT Colombia—Antiquities
Mounds—Colombia
Mont Bego (France)
USE Bego Mountain (France)
Mont Blanc (France and Italy)
USE Blanc, Mont (France and Italy)
Mont Castleguard (Alta.)
USE Castleguard, Mount (Alta.)
Mont Cervin (Switzerland and Italy)
USE Matterhorn (Switzerland and Italy)
Mont Chemin (Switzerland)
USE Chemin Mountain (Switzerland)
Mont family
USE Mount family
Mont Mézenc (France)
USE Mézenc Mount (France)
Mont Mézène (France)
USE Mézenc Mount (France)
Mont-Orford Park (Québec)
USE Parc du Mont-Orford (Québec)
Mont Pelée (Martinique)
USE Pelée, Mount (Martinique)

Mont Pilat (France)
USE Pilat Mountain (France)
Mont Revelstoke, Parc national du (B.C.)
USE Mount Revelstoke National Park
(B.C.)
Mont Ventoux (France)
USE Ventoux Mountain (France)
Montafon (Austria)
USE Montafon Valley (Austria)
Montafon Valley (Austria)
UF Montafon (Austria)
Montafontal (Austria)
Montavon (Austria)
Montavon Thal (Austria)
BT Valleys—Austria
Montafontal (Austria)
USE Montafon Valley (Austria)
Montagna della Maiella (Italy)
USE Maiella Mountains (Italy)
Montagna family *(Not Subd Geog)*
UF Montegna family
RT Montague family
Montagnaea
USE Montanoa
Montagnais (Athapascan) language
USE Chipewyan language
Montagnais Indians
 ₍E99.M87₎
UF Mountaineer Indians
BT Algonquian Indians
Indians of North America
NT Mistassin Indians
— **Missions**
— **Religion and mythology**
Montagnais language
 ₍PM1921-4₎
UF Mountainee language
RT Algonquian languages
Montagnard (Vietnamese people) arts
USE Arts, Montagnard (Vietnamese people)
Montagnards
 ₍DC180₎
BT France—History—Revolution, 1789-
1799—Clubs
Montagnards (Vietnamese people)
UF Nguoi Thuong (Vietnamese people)
BT Ethnology—Vietnam
Montagne de Reims (France)
USE Reims Mountain (France)
Montagne du Lubéron (France)
USE Lubéron Mountains (France)
Montagne du Mégal (France)
USE Meygal Mountain (France)
Montagne du Meygal (France)
USE Meygal Mountain (France)
Montagne Noire (France)
USE Noires Mountains (France)
Montagne Pelée (Martinique)
USE Pelée, Mount (Martinique)
Montagnes de la Chartreuse (France)
USE Chartreuse Mountains (France)
Montagnes de la Grande Chartreuse (France)
USE Chartreuse Mountains (France)
Montagnes de la Margeride (France)
USE Margeride Mountains (France)
Montagnes du Lubéron (France)
USE Lubéron Mountains (France)
Montagnes Noires (France)
USE Noires Mountains (France)
Montagu family
USE Montague family
Montagua River (Guatemala)
USE Motagua River (Guatemala)
Montague family *(Not Subd Geog)*
UF Montagu family
Montaigue family
Montauge family
Montgue family
Montigue family
Mountague family
RT Montagna family

Montague grammar
 ₍P158.5₎
BT Generative grammar
Language and logic
Semantics (Philosophy)
Montaigne-Preis
BT Rewards (Prizes, etc.)—Germany
(West)
Montaigue family
USE Montague family
Montaiguillon-en-Brie Castle (France)
USE Château de Montaiguillon-en-Brie
(France)
Montal Castle (Saint-Céré, France)
USE Château de Montal (Saint-Céré,
France)
Montalto family *(Not Subd Geog)*
Montana
— **Antiquities**
NT Bootlegger Trail Site (Mont.)
— **Description and travel**
— — **1951-1980**
— — **1981-**
Montaña, Nuestra Señora de la
USE Montaña, Virgen de la
Montaña, Virgen de la
UF Montaña, Nuestra Señora de la
Nuestra Señora de la Montaña
Virgen de la Montaña
BT Mary, Blessed Virgin, Saint—Cult—
Spain
Montana family *(Not Subd Geog)*
RT Montaney family
Montana formation
USE Geology, Stratigraphic—Cretaceous
Paleobotany—Cretaceous
Paleontology—Cretaceous
Montana grayling
USE Arctic grayling
Montane vole
USE Microtus montanus
Montaney family *(Not Subd Geog)*
UF Montanye family
RT Montana family
Montanism
 ₍BT1435₎
BT Heresies, Christian—History—Early
church, ca. 30-600
Montanoa
 ₍QK495.C74₎
UF Eriocarpha
Eriocoma
Montagnaea
Uhdea
BT Compositae
Montanye family
USE Montaney family
Montaperto, Battle of, 1260
 ₍DG737.2-DG737.22 (Florence)₎
 ₍DG975.S5 (Siena)₎
Montasio cheese
 ₍SF272.M6₎
BT Cheese—Varieties
Montauge family
USE Montague family
Montauk Indians
 ₍E99.M₎
BT Algonquian Indians
Indians of North America
NT Brotherton Indians
Montavon (Austria)
USE Montafon Valley (Austria)
Montavon Thal (Austria)
USE Montafon Valley (Austria)
Montcada family *(Not Subd Geog)*
UF Moncada family
Montcornet family *(Not Subd Geog)*
Montdidier (Somme, France), Battle of, 1918
 ₍D545.M75₎
BT World War, 1914-1918—Campaigns—
France

Monte Albán (Mexico) *(Not Subd Geog)*
  UF Albán, Monte (Mexico)
  BT Cities and towns, Ruined, extinct, etc.
      —Mexico
      Mexico—Antiquities
Monte Altuzzo, Battle of, 1944
  USE Altuzzo, Battle of, 1944
Monte Amiata (Italy)
  USE Amiata, Monte (Italy)
Monte Baldo (Italy)
  USE Baldo Mountains (Italy)
Monte Bianco (France and Italy)
  USE Blanc, Mont (France and Italy)
Monte Carlo automobile
  BT Chevrolet automobile
Monte Carlo method
  UF Artificial sampling
      Model sampling
      Stochastic sampling
  BT Games of chance (Mathematics)
      Mathematical models
      Numerical analysis
      Numerical calculations
      Stochastic processes
  — Computer programs
      NT RAVAGE (Computer programs)
          TESTRAND (Computer programs)
Monte Cassino (Italy), Battle of, 1944
  USE Cassino (Italy), Battle of, 1944
Monte Castellier degli Elleri (Italy)
  USE Castellier degli Elleri Mountain (Italy)
Monte, Castello del (Italy)
  USE Castello del Monte (Italy)
Monte Cervino (Switzerland and Italy)
  USE Matterhorn (Switzerland and Italy)
Monte Cimone, Battle of, 1916
  BT World War, 1914-1918—Campaigns—
      Italy
Monte das Tabocas, Battle of, 1645
  USE Tabocas, Battle of, 1645
Monte de las Cruces, Battle of, 1810
  ₍F1232₎
  BT Mexico—History—Wars of
      Independence, 1810-1821—
      Campaigns
Monte Etna (Sicily)
  USE Etna, Mount (Sicily)
Monte Gargano (Italy)
  USE Gargano Promontory (Italy)
Monte Iato (Sicily)
  USE Iato Mountain (Sicily)
Monte Irazú (Costa Rica)
  USE Irazú Volcano (Costa Rica)
Monte Jato (Sicily)
  USE Iato Mountain (Sicily)
Monte Lazzu (Corsica)
  USE Lazzu Mountain (Corsica)
Monte Novegno, Battle of, 1916
  BT World War, 1914-1918—Campaigns—
      Italy
Monte Pascoal National Park (Brazil)
  USE Parque Nacional de Monte Pascoal
      (Brazil)
Monte Pelée (Martinique)
  USE Pelée, Mount (Martinique)
Monte Piano, Battles of, 1915-1917
  BT World War, 1914-1918—Campaigns—
      Italy
Monte Pollino (Italy)
  USE Pollino, Mount (Italy)
Monte Roraima
  USE Roraima, Mount
Monte San Giorgio (Switzerland)
  USE San Giorgio Mountain (Switzerland)
Monte Sannace (Italy)
  USE Sannace Mountain (Italy)
Monte Sole Massacre, 1944
  USE Marzabotto Massacre, 1944

Monte Vista National Wildlife Refuge (Colo.)
  (Not Subd Geog)
  BT National parks and reserves—Colorado
      Wildlife refuges—Colorado
Monteath family
  USE Monteith family
Montebello Chateau (Québec)
  USE Château Montebello (Québec)
Montee family
  USE Monty family
Montegna family
  USE Montagna family
Monteith bowls
  USE Monteiths (Silverwork)
Monteith family *(Not Subd Geog)*
  UF Menteith family
      Monteath family
      Monteiths family
Monteiths (Silverwork) *(May Subd Geog)*
  ₍NK7236.M65₎
  UF Bowls, Monteith
      Monteith bowls
  BT Silverwork
Monteiths family
  USE Monteith family
Montello (Italy)
  UF Il Montello (Italy)
  BT Mountains—Italy
      Plateaus—Italy
Montello, Battle of, 1918
  BT World War, 1914-1918—Campaigns—
      Italy
Montelupich (Kraków, Poland : Concentration camp)
  BT World War, 1939-1945—
      Concentration camps—Poland
Montenegrin art
  USE Art, Montenegrin
Montenegrin newspapers *(May Subd Geog)*
  BT Yugoslav newspapers
Montenegrin periodicals *(May Subd Geog)*
  BT Yugoslav periodicals
Montenegrin-Turkish War, 1858
  USE Turco-Montenegrin War, 1858
Montenegrin-Turkish War, 1876-1878
  USE Turco-Montenegrin War, 1876-1878
Montenegrin-Turkish Wars, 1711-1714
  USE Turco-Montenegrin Wars, 1711-1714
Montenegrin wit and humor
  (May Subd Geog)
  ₍PN6222.Y (Collections)₎
  BT Yugoslav wit and humor
Montenegrins
  BT Yugoslavs
Montenegro
  —Description and travel
  — —To 1918
  — —1918-1980
  — —1981-
  —History
  — —To 1516
  — —1516-1782 *(Not Subd Geog)*
  — —Petar I, 1782-1830
  — —1782-1918
  — —Petar II, 1830-1851
  — —Nicholas I, 1860-1918
  — —1918-1945
  — Kings and rulers
      NT Petrović-Njegoš, House of
Monteny family
  USE Mounteney family
Monterey, Battle of, 1846
  ₍E406.M7₎
  BT United States—History—War with
      Mexico, 1845-1848—Campaigns
Monterey Bay (Calif.)
  BT Bays—California
Monterey Peninsula (Calif.)
  BT Peninsulas—California
Monterey pine
  USE Pinus radiata

Monterey pine engraver
  USE Ips radiatae
Montes Claros, Battle of, 1665
  ₍DP635₎
  BT Portugal—History—Alfonso VI, 1656-
      1683
Montes de Oca Avenue (Buenos Aires,
    Argentina)
  USE Avenida Montes de Oca (Buenos
      Aires, Argentina)
Montes de Toledo (Spain)
  USE Toledo Mountains (Spain)
Montesa motorcycle
  ₍TL448.M₎
Montessori method of education
  ₍LB775.M8₎
  BT Education of children
      Kindergarten
      Teaching
Montevergine, Madonna di
  UF Madonna di Montevergine
  BT Mary, Blessed Virgin, Saint—Cult—
      Italy
Montezuma Castle (Ariz.)
  BT Cliff-dwellings—Arizona
  RT Montezuma Castle National
      Monument (Ariz.)
**Montezuma Castle National Monument
    (Ariz.)** *(Not Subd Geog)*
  BT National monuments—Arizona
  RT Montezuma Castle (Ariz.)
Montezuma Well (Ariz.)
  BT Wells—Arizona
  RT Montezuma Well National Monument
      (Ariz.)
Montezuma Well National Monument (Ariz.)
  (Not Subd Geog)
  BT National monuments—Arizona
  RT Montezuma Well (Ariz.)
Montferland (Netherlands)
Montferrat (Italy)
  USE Monferrato (Italy)
Montferrine
  USE Monferrinas
Montford (Asheville, N.C.)
  (Not Subd Geog)
  UF Asheville (N.C.).   Montford
      Montford Hills (Asheville, N.C.)
Montford Hills (Asheville, N.C.)
  USE Montford (Asheville, N.C.)
Montgomary family
  USE Montgomery family
Montgomerie family
  USE Montgomery family
Montgomery cattle
  USE Sahiwal cattle
Montgomery family *(Not Subd Geog)*
  UF Mongomery family
      Montgomary family
      Montgomerie family
      Montgomry family
      Mountgomery family
Montgomery Rights March, 1965
  USE Selma-Montgomery Rights March,
      1965
Montgomry family
  USE Montgomery family
Montgue family
  USE Montague family
Months
  BT Calendar
      Chronology
      Year
  SA *names of individual months, e.g. July*
Months in art
Monti Appennini (Italy)
  USE Apennines (Italy)
Monti Caronie (Sicily)
  USE Nebrodi Mountains (Sicily)
Monti Chianti (Italy)
  USE Chianti Mountains (Italy)

Monti del Chianti (Italy)
  USE Chianti Mountains (Italy)
Monti del Cilento (Italy)
  USE Cilento Mountains (Italy)
Monti Lepini (Italy)
  USE Lepini Mountains (Italy)
Monti Lessini (Italy)
  USE Lessini Mountains (Italy)
Monti Nebrodi (Sicily)
  USE Nebrodi Mountains (Sicily)
Monti Volsini (Italy)
  USE Volsini Mountains (Italy)
Monticchiello (Italy), Battle of, 1943
      BT Italy—History—German occupation,
          1943-1945
          World War, 1939-1945—Campaigns—
          Italy
Monticello (Va.)
      BT Dwellings—Virginia
Monticello Cemetery (Monticello, Ill.)
      BT Cemeteries—Illinois
**Monticello Nuclear Power Generating Plant
(Minn.)**
      BT Nuclear power plants—Minnesota
Monticola
      [QL696.P288]
      UF Rock thrushes
      BT Turdidae
Monticola saxatilis
  USE Rufous-tailed rock thrush
Montigue family
  USE Montague family
Montlhéry, Battle of, 1465
      [DC106.3]
      BT France—History—Louis XI, 1461-
          1483
Montmartre (Paris, France)
      (Not Subd Geog)
      [DC752.M7]
      UF Paris (France).   Montmartre
Montmorency cherry
  USE Sour cherry
Montmorillonite   (May Subd Geog)
      BT Clay
          Mineralogy
Montmorillonite catalysts
      BT Catalysts
Montmusard Castle (Dijon, France)
  USE Château de Montmusard (Dijon,
        France)
Montonero (Dance)
      UF Minué Federal (Dance)
Montréal Island (Québec)
      UF Ile de Montréal (Québec)
      BT Islands—Québec (Province)
Montreal River (Ont.)
      BT Rivers—Ontario
**Montreuil-Bellay (Montreuil-Bellay, France :
Concentration camp)**
      BT Concentration camps—France
          World War, 1939-1945—
              Concentration camps—France
          World War, 1939-1945—Prisoners and
              prisons, German
Montreuil-Bellay (France), Battle of, 1793
      BT Vendean War, 1793-1800—Campaigns
          —France
Montreux-Berner Oberland-Bahn
  USE Chemin de fer Montreux-Oberland
        Bernois
Montreux, Switzerland, Treaty of, 1936
      [D462 1936]
      BT Turkey—Foreign relations—1918-1960
          —Treaties
Montrose Site (La.)   (Not Subd Geog)
      BT Louisiana—Antiquities
Monts Alantika (Nigeria and Cameroon)
  USE Alantika Mountains (Nigeria and
        Cameroon)
Monts Belgica (Antarctic regions)
  USE Belgica Mountains (Antarctic regions)

Monts Ciucaş (Romania)
  USE Ciucaş Mountains (Romania)
Monts-de-piété
  USE Pawnbroking
Monts de Rodna (Romania)
  USE Rodna Mountains (Romania)
Monts Dômes (France)
  USE Dômes Mountains (France)
Monts du Jura (France and Switzerland)
  USE Jura Mountains (France and
        Switzerland)
Monts du Minervois (France)
  USE Minervois (France)
Monts Jura (France and Switzerland)
  USE Jura Mountains (France and
        Switzerland)
Montseny, Sierra de (Spain)
  USE Montseny Mountains (Spain)
Montseny Mountains (Spain)
      UF Monseny Mountains (Spain)
          Montseny, Sierra de (Spain)
          Sierra de Monseny (Spain)
          Sierra de Montseny (Spain)
      BT Mountains—Spain
Montserrat (Spain)
      UF Monserrat (Spain)
      BT Mountains—Spain
Montsià Region (Spain)   (Not Subd Geog)
      UF Comarca de Montsià (Spain)
          El Montsià (Spain)
Monty family   (Not Subd Geog)
      UF Montee family
Montz family
  USE Mount family
Monumbo language
      [PL6621.M6]
      BT Papuan languages
Monument Commemorating the 1,000th
Anniversary of Russia (Novgorod,
R.S.F.S.R.)
  USE Tysiacheletie Rossii (Novgorod,
        R.S.F.S.R.)
Monument of Philopappos (Athens, Greece)
  USE Monument of Philopappus (Athens,
        Greece)
Monument of Philopappus (Athens, Greece)
      [DF287.M65]
      UF Monument of Philopappos (Athens,
          Greece)
          Philopappos, Monument of (Athens,
          Greece)
          Philopappus, Monument of (Athens,
          Greece)
      BT Sepulchral monuments—Greece
Monument of the Ampheion (Th-evai, Greece)
  USE Tomb of Amphion and Zethos
        (Th-evai, Greece)
Monument to the People's Heroes (Peking,
China)
  USE Jen min ying hsiung chi nien pei
        (Peking, China)
Monument to the Third International
(Sculpture)
  USE Tatlin, Vladimir Evgrafovich, 1885-
        1953.   Monument to the Third
        International
Monument Valley (Ariz. and Utah)
      BT Valleys—Arizona
          Valleys—Utah
Monumental brasses
  USE Brasses
Monumental theology
  USE Bible—Antiquities
        Christian antiquities
**Monumento a Túpac Amaru II (Yanaoca,
Peru)**
      UF Túpac Amaru II Monument (Yanaoca,
          Peru)
      BT Monuments—Peru
          Statues—Peru

**Monumento ao Christo Redemptor (Rio de
Janeiro, Brazil)**
      [NA9355.R]
      UF Christ the Redeemer Monument (Rio
          de Janeiro, Brazil)
          Corcovado's Christ (Rio de Janeiro,
          Brazil)
          Cristo do Corcovado (Rio de Janeiro,
          Brazil)
          Statue of Christ the Redeemer (Rio de
          Janeiro, Brazil)
      BT Statues—Brazil
Monumento de Mafra (Mafra, Portugal)
      UF National Monument (Mafra, Portugal)
          Palácio Nacional (Mafra, Portugal)
          Royal Palace (Mafra, Portugal)
      BT Monuments—Portugal
**Monumento Nacional de Santa Cruz del Valle
de los Caídos (Spain)**
      UF Valle de los Caídos Monument (Spain)
          Valley of the Fallen Monument
          (Spain)
      BT Spain—History—Civil War, 1936-1939
          War memorials—Spain
Monumentos Historicos Nacionales de San
Juan (San Juan, P.R.)
  USE San Juan National Historic Site (San
        Juan, P.R.)
Monuments   (May Subd Geog)
      [NA9335-NA9355 (Municipal art)]
      [NB1330-NB1885 (Sculpture)]
      UF Historical monuments
      BT Architecture
          Sculpture
      RT Historic sites
          Memorials
          Public sculpture
          Statues
      SA subdivision Monuments under classes
          of persons, ethnic groups, and under
          names of individual persons and
          families; and names of individual
          monuments
      NT Arches, Triumphal
          Artists' monuments
          Historic buildings
          Historical markers
          Megalithic monuments
          National monuments
          Natural monuments
          Obelisks
          Poets' monuments
          Pyramids
          Sepulchral monuments
          Soldiers' monuments
          Stūpas
          War memorials
          Workers' monuments
    — **Conservation and restoration**
          [N8850-N9084 (Art)]
          UF Conservation of monuments
              Monuments—Preservation
              Preservation of monuments
    — — **Law and legislation**
          (May Subd Geog)
    — Preservation
          USE Monuments—Conservation and
              restoration
    — **Recording**
          UF Recording of monuments
          BT Archaeology—Methodology
              Cultural property, Protection of
    — **California**
          NT Pioneer Monument (Calif.)
    — **China**
          NT Jen min ying hsiung chi nien pei
              (Peking, China)
    — **Colorado**
          NT Hovenweep National Monument
              (Utah and Colo.)
    — **Germany (West)**

2454

NT Herkules-Bauwerk (Kassel, Germany)
— **Indiana**
  NT Lincoln Boyhood National Memorial (Ind.)
      Nancy Hanks Lincoln State Memorial (Ind.)
— **Italy**
  NT Trajan's Column (Rome, Italy)
— **Japan**
  NT Onna no Hi (Kyoto, Japan)
— **Peru**
  NT Monumento a Túpac Amaru II (Yanaoca, Peru)
— **Portugal**
  NT Monumento de Mafra (Mafra, Portugal)
— **Romania**
  NT Tropaeum Traiani (Adamclisi, Romania)
— **Ukraine**
  NT Pamiatnik Velikomu Oktiabriu (Kiev, Ukraine)
— **Utah**
  NT Hovenweep National Monument (Utah and Colo.)
— **Washington (D.C.)**
  NT Thomas Jefferson Memorial (Washington, D.C.)
Monuments, National
  USE National monuments
Monuments, Natural
  USE Natural monuments
Monuments, Sepulchral
  USE Sepulchral monuments
Monumentul triumfal (Adamclisi, Romania)
  USE Tropaeum Traiani (Adamclisi, Romania)
Monvu language
  USE Mamvu language
Mony family
  USE Monet family
Monza automobile
  [TL215.M]
  BT Chevrolet automobile
Monzombo (African people)
  USE Monjombo (African people)
Monzonite *(May Subd Geog)*
  [QE462.M6]
  BT Rocks, Igneous
Mooar family
  USE Moore family
Mood (Grammar)
  USE Grammar, Comparative and general—Mood
Mood (Psychology)
  BT Emotions
      Personality
  NT Rasas
Mood disorders
  USE Affective disorders
Moodey family
  USE Moody family
Moodie family
  USE Moody family
Moody family *(Not Subd Geog)*
  UF Mody family
      Moodey family
      Moodie family
      Moodye family
      Mooty family
      Moudy family
Moodye family
  USE Moody family
Moomaw Lake (Va.)
  UF Gathright Lake (Va.)
  BT Lakes—Virginia
      Reservoirs—Virginia
Moon
  [QB581-595]
  UF Selenology

BT Astronomy
  Satellites
  Solar system
NT Fra Mauro Crater (Moon)
  Lunar geology
  Lunar surface radio communication
  Moon—Gravity
  Occultations
  Plants, Effect of the moon on
  Selenodesy
  Sinus Medii (Moon)
  Space flight to the moon
  Tides
  Tranquility Base (Moon)
— **Anecdotes, facetiae, satire, etc.**
— **Brightness**
  [QB588]
  BT Photometry, Astronomical
— **Caricatures and cartoons**
— **Charts, diagrams, etc.**
— **Early works to 1800**
— Eclipses
  USE Eclipses, Lunar
— **Electric properties**
  UF Electric properties, Lunar
      Lunar electric properties
— **Ephemerides**
  [QB583]
  BT Ephemerides
— **Exploration**
  UF Lunar exploration
  BT Lunar bases
      Space flight to the moon
  NT Apollo Lunar Surface Experiments Package
— — **Juvenile literature**
— **Exploration (Jewish theology)**
  [BM538.A75]
  BT Judaism and astronautics
— **Figure**
  UF Lunar figure
  BT Geodesy
— **Globes**
  UF Globes, Lunar
      Lunar globes
  BT Moon—Maps
— **Gravity**
  UF Gravitational field of the moon
      Lunar gravitation
      Lunar gravity
  BT Moon
— **Influence on man**
  [BF1723]
  BT Astrology
  NT Solunar theory
— Influence on weather
  USE Weather, Influence of the moon on
— **Internal structure**
  [QB592]
— **Juvenile literature**
— **Libration**
  [QB585]
  UF Libration of the moon
— Limb
  USE Lunar limb
— **Literary collections**
— **Magnetic properties**
  UF Lunar magnetism
      Magnetism, Lunar
— **Maps**
  NT Moon—Globes
— — **Early works to 1800**
  [QB595]
— **Mass**
  [QB591]
— **Mythology**
— **Observations**
  [QB397-QB399 (Lunar theory)]
  [QB581-QB595]
  BT Astronomy—Observations

— **Orbit**
  UF Lunar orbit
  BT Mechanics, Celestial
      Orbits
— — **Tables**
  UF Moon—Orbit—Tables, etc.
— — **Tables, etc.**
  USE Moon—Orbit—Tables
— **Origin**
— Parallax
  USE Parallax—Moon
— **Phases**
  UF Phases of the moon
— — **Tables**
— **Photographs**
  BT Astronomy—Charts, diagrams, etc.
      Lunar photography
— **Photographs from space**
— **Religious aspects**
  NT Moon worship
— — **Hinduism**
  NT Gangaur
— — **Judaism**
  NT New moon (Judaism)
— **Rotation**
  [QB585]
— Stratigraphy
  USE Lunar stratigraphy
— **Surface**
  [QB591]
  RT Lunar soil
  NT Apollo Lunar Surface Experiments Package
      Lunar craters
      Mare Crisium (Moon)
— — **Tables**
  [QB591]
— **Tables**
  [QB399 (Lunar theory)]
  [VK563-VK567 (Navigation)]
  UF Lunar tables
      Tables, Lunar
  BT Longitude
      Nautical astronomy
— **Temperature and radiation**
  [QB588]
  BT Temperature
Moon, Flight to the
  USE Space flight to the moon
Moon, Theory of
  [QB391-9]
  UF Lunar theory
  BT Mechanics, Celestial
Moon, Voyages to
  USE Interplanetary voyages
Moon bases
  USE Lunar bases
Moon bear
  USE Selenarctos thibetanus
Moon cars
  [TL480]
  Here are entered works on vehicles for travel on the surface of the moon.
  UF Lunar cars
      Lunar surface vehicles
  BT Motor vehicles
      Roving vehicles (Astronautics)
      Vehicles, Remotely piloted
  NT Lunokhod lunar roving vehicles
Moon family *(Not Subd Geog)*
  UF Moone family
Moon in art
Moon jelly (Coelenterata)
  [QL377.S4]
  UF Aurelia aurita
Moon landing sites
  USE Lunar landing sites
Moon photography
  USE Lunar photography
Moon Pies
  BT Cookies

Moon probes
USE Lunar probes
Moon rocks
USE Lunar petrology
Moon settlements
USE Lunar bases
Moon shells, Fossil
USE Naticidae, Fossil
Moon Sound (Estonia)
USE Muhu Sound (Estonia)
Moon system
USE Blind—Printing and writing systems
Moon worship
⌈BL438⌉
BT Moon—Religious aspects
Worship
Moondyne Nature Reserve (W.A.)
(Not Subd Geog)
BT Natural areas—Australia
Moone family
USE Moon family
Mooney airplanes
⌈TL686.M⌉
BT Airplanes
Mooney family (Not Subd Geog)
UF Mauney family
Moonie family
Moony family
Mooneyham family (Not Subd Geog)
UF Monaham family
Moneyham family
Mooningham family
Moonie family
USE Mooney family
Moonies
USE Unificationists
Mooningham family
USE Mooneyham family
Moonlighting
USE Supplementary employment
Moonrat
USE Echinosorex gymnurus
Moon's type for the blind
USE Blind—Printing and writing systems
Moonsee language
USE Munsee language
Moonshining
USE Distilling, Illicit
Moonstones
BT Adularia
Moonstones (Architecture)
BT Architecture—Details
Moony family
USE Mooney family
Moor ecology (May Subd Geog)
⌈QH541.5.M6⌉
UF Heath ecology
BT Ecology
Moors and heaths
Shrubland ecology
NT Moor flora
Moor family
USE Moore family
Moor fauna (May Subd Geog)
UF Heath fauna
Moorland fauna
BT Moors and heaths
Zoology
Moor flora (May Subd Geog)
⌈QK108-QK474.5 (Local)⌉
⌈QK938.M6 (Botany, General)⌉
UF Heath flora
BT Botany
Botany—Ecology
Moor ecology
Moors and heaths
Moor Park (Surrey)
BT Country homes—England
Moore, Henry, 1898-   Hill arches
⌈NB497.M⌉
UF Hill arches (Sculpture)

Moore, Henry, 1898-   Large two forms
⌈NB497.M6⌉
UF Large two forms (Sculpture)
Moore, Camp (La.)
USE Camp Moore (La.)
Moore family (Not Subd Geog)
UF Moers family
Mooar family
Moor family
Moores family
Moors family
More family
Mores family
Moure family
Moore Park (Easton, Pa.)
USE Hugh Moore Park (Easton, Pa.)
Moore River (W.A.)
BT Rivers—Australia
Moore-Smith convergence
USE Nets (Mathematics)
Moore Village Site (Md.) (Not Subd Geog)
BT Maryland—Antiquities
Moored oceanographic buoys
USE Oceanographic buoys
Moorehead family
USE Morehead family
Moores Creek (Chambers County, Ala.)
BT Rivers—Alabama
Moores Creek National Military Park (N.C.)
UF Moores Creek National Park (N.C.)
BT Military parks—North Carolina
National parks and reserves—United States
Parks—North Carolina
Moores Creek National Park (N.C.)
USE Moores Creek National Military Park (N.C.)
Moores family
USE Moore family
Moorey family
USE Morey family
Moorhead family
USE Morehead family
Moorhen, Gray
USE Gallinula chloropus
Mooring of drilling platforms
USE Drilling platforms—Anchorage
Mooring of ships (May Subd Geog)
⌈VK361-365⌉
UF Berthing of ships
Ship mooring
Ships—Mooring
BT Docks
Harbors
NT Anchorage
Deep-sea moorings
Single-point moorings
Moorings, Deep-sea
USE Deep-sea moorings
Moorings, Single-point
USE Single-point moorings
Moorings, Swinging
USE Single-point moorings
Moorish architecture
USE Architecture, Islamic
Architecture, Islamic—Spain
Moorish art
USE Art, Islamic—Africa, North
Art, Islamic—Spain
Moorish language (India)
USE Urdu language
Moorish occupation, Spain, 711-1492
USE Spain—History—711-1516
Moorland fauna
USE Moor fauna
Moors
USE Muslims
Moors and Christians, Dance of
USE Moros y Cristianos (Dance)
Moors and heaths (May Subd Geog)
⌈GB621-8⌉

⌈S621 (Agriculture, HD1665-1683)⌉
UF Heaths
BT Drainage
Shrublands
Waste lands
Wetlands
RT Bogs
Fens
Marshes
NT Moor ecology
Moor fauna
Moor flora
Peat bogs
— **Fires and fire prevention**
BT Ground cover fires
— **Belgium**
NT Hautes Fagnes (Belgium and Germany)
— **England**
NT Bodmin Moor (England)
Dartmoor (England)
Exmoor National Park (England)
North York Moors (England)
North York Moors National Park (England)
Sedgemoor (England)
Soyland Moor (England)
— **Germany (East)**
NT Dübener Heide (Germany)
— **Germany (West)**
NT Hautes Fagnes (Belgium and Germany)
Lüneburger Heide (Germany)
Naturpark Südheide (Germany)
Naturschutzpark Lüneburger Heide (Germany)
Teufelsmoor (Germany)
— **Netherlands**
NT Dwingelderveld (Netherlands)
— **Scotland**
NT Minch Moor (Scotland)
Moors family
USE Moore family
Moorse family
USE Morse family
Moorundee language
USE Murundi language
Moose (May Subd Geog)
⌈QL737.U5⌉
UF Elk, European
European elk
Moose hunting (May Subd Geog)
⌈SK301⌉
Moose Lake Provincial Recreation Park (Man.)
BT Parks—Manitoba
Recreation areas—Manitoba
Moose River (Me.)
BT Rivers—Maine
Moose River (Ont.)
BT Rivers—Ontario
Moosehead Lake (Me.)
BT Lakes—Maine
Moot
⌈DA140⌉
Moot courts
BT Law—Study and teaching
RT Mock trials
SA individual moot courts, e.g. Columbia University. School of Law. Blackstone Moot Court
Mooty family
USE Moody family
Mopan Indians
UF Manche Indians
BT Indians of Central America
Mayas
Mopan language
⌈PM3941⌉
UF Manche language

2456

BT Indians of Central America—
    Languages
    Maya language
Moped industry *(May Subd Geog)*
   [HD9710.6]
Mopeds *(May Subd Geog)*
  UF Mo-peds
    Motorized bicycles
  BT Bicycles
    Motorcycles
  NT Batavus moped
    Garelli moped
    Peugeot moped
    Puch moped
    Solex moped
    Used mopeds
MOPEG
  USE Methoxyhydroxyphenylglycol
MOPI (Computer system)
  UF Macro Oriented Program Interpreter
    (Computer system)
  BT Electronic digital computers—
    Programming
    Interpreters (Computer programs)
    Macro instructions (Electronic
    computers)
Mopin
  [DS432.A19]
  BT Abors—Rites and ceremonies
    Festivals—India
Moplah arts
  USE Arts, Moplah
Moplahs
  UF Mappilas
    Moplas
  BT Caste—India
    Ethnology—India
    Muslims—India
Moplas
  USE Moplahs
Mopping
  USE Mops and mopsticks
Mops and mopsticks
  UF Dustmops
    Mopping
    Mopsticks
    Wet mops
  BT Cleaning
Mopsticks
  USE Mops and mopsticks
Moquegua River (Peru)
  UF Río Moquegua (Peru)
  BT Rivers—Peru
Moquelumnan Indians
  [E99.M]
  UF Olon-ko Indians
  BT Indians of North America
  NT Miwok Indians
Moquelumnan languages
  USE Miwok languages
Moquette
  [HD9909.M (Economics)]
  [TS1772-TS1776 (Textile
    manufacturers)]
  BT Carpets
Moqui Indians
  USE Hopi Indians
Moquilea
  USE Licania
Mora (Civil law)
  USE Performance (Law)
Mora (The Latin word)
  BT Latin language—Etymology
Moraceae
  [QK495.M73]
  NT Dorstenia
    Ficus (Plants)
    Humulus
    Mulberry
Moradas *(May Subd Geog)*
  BT Church architecture

Moraine family
  USE Moran family
Moraine State Park (Pa.)
  BT Moraines—Pennsylvania
    Parks—Pennsylvania
Moraines *(May Subd Geog)*
  [QE578]
  BT Glacial landforms
  — **Pennsylvania**
    NT Moraine State Park (Pa.)
  — **Poland**
    NT Oksywie Hill (Poland)
Moral conditions *(Not Subd Geog)*
  UF Morals
  BT Social history
    Social norms
  SA *subdivision* Moral conditions *under
    names of countries, cities, etc., e.g.*
    United States—Moral conditions
  NT Crimes without victims
    Sex customs
Moral development *(May Subd Geog)*
  [BF723.M54]
  UF Ethical development
  BT Child psychology
    Moral education
Moral education *(May Subd Geog)*
  [LC251-LC318]
  [LC2751 (Negro)]
  UF Character education
    Education, Character
    Education, Ethical
    Education, Moral
    Ethical education
  BT Child rearing
    Education
    Ethics
  RT Religious education
  NT Euthenics
    Humane education
    Islamic religious education
    Jewish religious education
    Kentucky movement
    Moral development
    Student ethics
  — **Law and legislation** *(May Subd Geog)*
    BT Educational law and legislation
Moral education (Elementary)
  (May Subd Geog)
Moral education (Secondary)
  (May Subd Geog)
Moral insanity
  USE Insanity, Moral
Moral judgment
  USE Judgment (Ethics)
Moral philosophy
  USE Ethics
Moral proof of God
  USE God—Proof, Moral
Moral rearmament
  [BJ10.M6]
  BT Ethics
    Oxford Group
    World War, 1939-1945—Moral and
    ethical aspects
Moral rights (Copyright law)
  USE Copyright—Moral rights
Moral theology
  USE Christian ethics
Moral virtues
  USE Cardinal virtues
Morale
  [U22]
  BT Courage
    Military art and science
    Social psychology
    Sociology, Military
  RT Psychology, Military
  NT Employee morale
    Fortitude
    Military ethics

    Psychological warfare
    Psychology, Naval
    Soldiers—Recreation
    Teacher morale
    War—Psychological aspects
Morale, Employee
  USE Employee morale
Morales family *(Not Subd Geog)*
  UF Moralez family
Moralez family
  USE Morales family
Moralists
  USE Ethicists
Moralities
  [PN1771]
  UF Morality plays
  BT Drama
    Religious drama
    Theater
  RT Drama, Medieval
    Mysteries and miracle-plays
Moralities, English
  BT English drama
Moralities, French
  BT French drama
Moralities, Hebrew
  UF Hebrew moralities
  BT Hebrew drama
Moralities, Hungarian *(May Subd Geog)*
  UF Hungarian moralities
  BT Hungarian drama
Morality
  USE Ethics
Morality plays
  USE Moralities
Morals
  USE Conduct of life
    Ethics
    Moral conditions
Morals and art
  USE Art and morals
Morals and law
  USE Law and ethics
Morals and literature
  USE Literature and morals
Morals and music
  USE Music and morals
Morals and the arts
  USE Arts and morals
Morals offenses
  USE Crimes without victims
Moraly (Vanuatu)
  USE Méré Lava (Vanuatu)
Morama
  USE Bauhinia esculenta
Moran family *(Not Subd Geog)*
  UF Moraine family
    Morane family
    Morang family
    Morans family
Morand-Pasteur House (Saillon, Switzerland)
  USE Maison Morand-Pasteur (Saillon,
    Switzerland)
Morandière family *(Not Subd Geog)*
  UF La Morandière family
Morane family
  USE Moran family
Morang family
  USE Moran family
Morans family
  USE Moran family
Morason family
  USE Morrison family
Morat, Lake of (Switzerland)
  UF Lac de Morat (Switzerland)
    Lake of Morat (Switzerland)
    Murtensee (Switzerland)
  BT Lakes—Switzerland
Morat, Battle of, 1476
  [DQ104]
  UF Murten, Battle of, 1476

Morata (Papua New Guinea)
  USE Goodenough Island (Papua New
        Guinea)
Morato language
  USE Candoshi language
Moratorium *(May Subd Geog)*
    ⌈*JX5271.M6*⌉
  UF Moratory law
  BT Commercial law
       Credit
       Debt
       Debtor and creditor
Moratorium (Roman law)
Moratory law
  USE Moratorium
Moravia (Czechoslovakia)
  UF Great Moravia (Czechoslovakia)
  — History
  — — To 906
Moravia in art
Moravian architecture
  USE Architecture, Moravian
Moravian ballads and songs
    (May Subd Geog)
Moravian Church *(May Subd Geog)*
    ⌈*BX8551-8593*⌉
  — Education
  — Government
Moravian cookery
  USE Cookery, Moravian
Moravian decorative arts
  USE Decorative arts, Moravian
Moravian Indians
    ⌈*E99.M9*⌉
  UF Christian Indians (Moravian)
  BT Algonquian Indians
       Delaware Indians
       Indians of North America
       Mahican Indians
       Mohegan Indians
       Munsee Indians
  — Missions
Moravian pottery
  USE Pottery, Moravian
Moravians *(May Subd Geog)*
    ⌈*BX8551-8593*⌉
      Here are entered works dealing with the Moravi-
    ans as an element in the population. Works on the
    Moravian Church are entered under the heading
    Moravian Church.
  UF Brethren, United
       Hernhutters
       Herrnhuter
       Unitas Fratrum
       United Brethren
  BT Hussites
  RT Bohemian Brethren
Moray eels
  USE Morays
Moray family
  USE Morey family
Moray Firth (Scotland)
  BT Estuaries—Scotland
Morays
  UF Moray eels
       Muraenidae
  BT Eels
  NT Gymnothorax
Morbid anatomy
  USE Anatomy, Pathological
Morbidity
  USE Diseases
Morbidity reporting
  USE Diseases—Reporting
Morbihan Gulf (France)
  UF Golfe du Morbihan (France)
       Gulf of Morbihan (France)
  BT Bays—France
Morbilli virus
  USE Measles virus

Morbus Blount
  USE Blount's disease
Morbus haemolyticus neonatorum
  USE Hemorrhagic disease of newborn
Morchella
  USE Morels
Morchellaceae *(May Subd Geog)*
    ⌈*QK623.M65*⌉
  BT Pezizales
  NT Morels
Morda language
  USE Baria language
Mordacq family *(Not Subd Geog)*
Mordants
    ⌈*TP927*⌉
Mordellidae
    ⌈*QL596.M6*⌉
  UF Anaspidae
  BT Beetles
Mordenite *(May Subd Geog)*
    ⌈*QE391.M*⌉
Mordovians
  USE Mordvins
Mordred
  UF Medraut
       Modred
       Mordret
  BT Arthurian romances
Mordret
  USE Mordred
Mordva
  USE Mordvins
Mordva language
  USE Mordvin language
Mordvin art
  USE Art, Mordvin
Mordvin language
    ⌈*PH751-779*⌉
  UF Mordva language
       Mordvinian language
  BT Finno-Ugric languages
       Russian S.F.S.R.—Languages
  NT Erzya dialect
       Moksha dialect
Mordvin literature *(May Subd Geog)*
    ⌈*PH781-785*⌉
Mordvin poetry *(May Subd Geog)*
Mordvin poets
  USE Poets, Mordvin
Mordvinian language
  USE Mordvin language
Mordvinians
  USE Mordvins
Mordvins
    ⌈*DK34.M6*⌉
  UF Mordovians
       Mordva
       Mordvinians
  BT Ethnology—Russian S.F.S.R.
       Finno-Ugrians
Mordwilkoja
    ⌈*QL527.A64*⌉
  BT Aphididae
  NT Mordwilkoja vagabunda
Mordwilkoja vagabunda
    ⌈*QL527.A64*⌉
  UF Vagabond gall-aphid
  BT Mordwilkoja
Möre (Sweden)
More family
  USE Moore family
Moré Indians
  USE Itenez Indians
Moré language
    ⌈*PL8521*⌉
  UF Mole language
       Moshi language
       Mossi language
  BT Mossi languages
More languages
  USE Mossi languages

Moré proverbs
  USE Proverbs, Moré
Morea (Greece)
  USE Peloponnesus (Greece)
Moreau family *(Not Subd Geog)*
Morehead family *(Not Subd Geog)*
  UF Moorehead family
       Moorhead family
       Morehed family
       Morhead family
       Muirhead family
Morehed family
  USE Morehead family
Morehouse family *(Not Subd Geog)*
Morehouse's comet
    ⌈*QB723.M*⌉
Morel family
  USE Morrill family
Moreland family *(Not Subd Geog)*
  UF Morland family
Morell family
  USE Morrill family
Morella
  USE Myrica
Morels *(May Subd Geog)*
    ⌈*QK623.M65 (Mycology)*⌉
  UF Morchella
  BT Morchellaceae
  RT Cookery (Morels)
Morel's syndrome
  USE Hyperostosis frontalis interna
Morenus family
  USE Mereness family
Morery family
  USE Morey family
Mores family
  USE Moore family
Moresby Island (B.C.)
  BT Islands—British Columbia
       Queen Charlotte Islands (B.C.)
Moreton Bay District (Qld.)
  UF Moreton District (Qld.)
       Moreton Region (Qld.)
Moreton Bay pine
  USE Araucaria cunninghamii
Moreton District (Qld.)
  USE Moreton Bay District (Qld.)
Moreton Island (Qld.)
  BT Islands—Australia
Moreton Region (Qld.)
  USE Moreton Bay District (Qld.)
Moretus family *(Not Subd Geog)*
Morey family *(Not Subd Geog)*
  UF Mauray family
       Maurey family
       Mauri family
       Maury family
       Moorey family
       Moray family
       Morery family
       Morrey family
       Morrie family
       Morry family
       Mory family
       Mourey family
       Mowery family
       Mowra family
       Mowre family
       Mowrey family
       Mowry family
Morey Peak Wilderness (Nev.)
  UF Morey Peak Wilderness Study Area
        (Nev.)
  BT National parks and reserves—Nevada
       Wilderness areas—Nevada
Morey Peak Wilderness Study Area (Nev.)
  USE Morey Peak Wilderness (Nev.)
Morf family
  USE Murff family
Morfett family
  USE Moffett family

Morfetts family
  USE Moffett family
Morfey family
  USE Murphy family
Morff family
  USE Murff family
Morfitt family
  USE Moffett family
Morfitts family
  USE Moffett family
Morgagni-Adams-Stokes syndrome
  USE Adams-Stokes syndrome
Morgagni's syndrome
  USE Hyperostosis frontalis interna
Morgain family
  USE Morgan family
Morgain le Fay (Legendary character)
  USE Morgan le Fay (Legendary character)
Morgaine family
  USE Morgan family
Morgan, Justin (Horse)
  USE Justin Morgan (Horse)
Morgan automobile
  ⌐TL215.M¬
Morgan family *(Not Subd Geog)*
  UF Morgain family
     Morgaine family
     Morgen family
     Morghen family
     Morgon family
Morgan horse
  ⌐SF293.M8¬
  BT Horse breeds
Morgan la Fée (Legendary character)
  USE Morgan le Fay (Legendary character)
Morgan le Fay (Legendary character)
  UF Morgain le Fay (Legendary character)
     Morgan la Fée (Legendary character)
     Morgane le Fay (Legendary character)
     Morgue la Fée (Legendary character)
  BT Characters and characteristics in
     literature
     Fairies
Morgan Line
Morganatic marriage
  USE Marriages of royalty and nobility
Morgane le Fay (Legendary character)
  USE Morgan le Fay (Legendary character)
Morganella
  ⌐QK629.L9¬
  BT Lycoperdaceae
Morganella albina
  ⌐QK629.L9¬
  UF Lycogalopsis solmsii
     Lycoperdon albinum
Morgan's Paint Prize
  USE Premio Morgan's Paint
Morgan's Raid, 1863
  ⌐E475.18¬
  BT United States—History—Civil War,
     1861-1865—Campaigns
Morganstern family
  USE Morgenstern family
Morgarten, Battle of, 1315
  ⌐DQ94¬
  BT Switzerland—History—1032-1499
Morgen family
  USE Morgan family
Morgen-Kleine Fassung (Painting)
  USE Runge, Philipp Otto, 1777-1810.
     Small morning
Morgensen family
  USE Mogensen family
Morgenson family
  USE Mogensen family
Morgenstern family *(Not Subd Geog)*
  UF Morganstern family
Morges, Front
  USE Front Morges
Morghen family
  USE Morgan family

Morgon family
  USE Morgan family
Morgue la Fée (Legendary character)
  USE Morgan le Fay (Legendary character)
Morgues *(May Subd Geog)*
  ⌐RA620-621¬
Morgues (Newspaper libraries)
  USE Newspaper office libraries
Morhead family
  USE Morehead family
Mori family *(Not Subd Geog)*
Mori language *(May Subd Geog)*
  UF Aikoa language
  BT Indonesia—Languages
     Malayan languages
Moriah, Mount (Jerusalem)
  USE Temple Mount (Jerusalem)
Moriarty submarine boat
  ⌐VM365¬
  BT Submarine boats
Morice family
  USE Morris family
Moridae
  ⌐QL638.M67¬
  BT Gadiformes
  NT Antimora
     Lepidion
Morikawa family *(Not Subd Geog)*
Morill family
  USE Morrill family
Morimoto family *(Not Subd Geog)*
Morin family *(Not Subd Geog)*
Morin khuur
  ⌐ML927.M67¬
  UF Khil-khuur
     Ma t'ou ch'in
  BT Musical instruments—Asia, Central
     Stringed instruments, Bowed
Morina
  USE Chesiadodes
Moringua
  ⌐QL638.M675¬
  BT Moringuidae
Moringuidae
  ⌐QL638.M675¬
  UF Anguillichthyidae
     Ratabouridae
     Spaghetti eels
     Stilbiscidae
     Whip eels
  BT Eels
  NT Moringua
Morini (Celtic people) *(May Subd Geog)*
  ⌐DC62.2.M67¬
  BT Celts—France
     Ethnology—France
Morioka Castle (Morioka-shi, Japan)
  USE Moriokajō (Morioka-shi, Japan)
Moriokajō (Morioka-shi, Japan)
  UF Kozukatajō (Morioka-shi, Japan)
     Morioka Castle (Morioka-shi, Japan)
  BT Castles—Japan
Morioris
  BT Polynesians
 — Antiquities
Moris family
  USE Morris family
Morisca (Dance)
  USE Moros y Cristianos (Dance)
Moriscos *(May Subd Geog)*
  ⌐DP104¬
     Here are entered works on Muslims in Spain after
     about 1492 who were converted to Christianity by
     decree. Works on Muslims living in Spain under
     Christian protection before 1492 who did not convert
     to Christianity are entered under the heading Mudé-
     jares. Works including both Mudéjares and Moriscos
     are entered under Moriscos.
  BT Muslims—Spain
  RT Mudéjares
Moriset family
  USE Morrissett family

Morisette family
  USE Morrissett family
Morison family
  USE Morrison family
Moriss family
  USE Morris family
Morisset family
  USE Morrissett family
Morita family *(Not Subd Geog)*
Morita psychotherapy *(May Subd Geog)*
  ⌐RC489.M65¬
  UF Morita therapy
  BT Psychotherapy
Morita therapy
  USE Morita psychotherapy
Morizet family
  USE Morrissett family
Mørkris Valley (Norway)
  USE Mørkrisdalen (Norway)
Mørkrisdalen (Norway)
  UF Mørkris Valley (Norway)
  BT Valleys—Norway
Morlaks
  ⌐DB34.S5 (Slavs of Austria-Hungary)¬
  BT Ethnology—Yugoslavia
Morland family
  USE Moreland family
Morlock family *(Not Subd Geog)*
Mormon arts
  USE Arts, Mormon
Mormon authors
  UF Authors, Mormon
  SA *subdivision* Mormon authors *under*
     individual literatures, e.g. English
     literature—Mormon authors
Mormon Church *(May Subd Geog)*
  ⌐BX8601-BX8695¬
     Here are entered works on Mormon denomina-
     tions treated collectively and works for which the
     individual Mormon denomination cannot be identi-
     fied.
  UF Mormonism
  BT Christian sects
  RT Mormons
  NT Aaronic Priesthood (Mormon Church)
     Cataloging of Mormon literature
     Church of the First Born (Morrisites)
     Converts, Mormon
     Danites (Mormon theology)
     Family home evenings (Mormon
       Church)
     Hygiene, Mormon
     Jesus Christ—Mormon interpretations
     Kingdom of God (Mormon theology)
     Melchizedek Priesthood (Mormon
       Church)
     Mormon Fundamentalism
     Nephites
     Prophets (Mormon theology)
     Revelation (Mormon theology)
     Sociology, Christian (Mormon)
     Temples, Mormon
     Tithes—Mormon Church
     Woman (Mormon theology)
     Women in the Mormon Church
 — Apostles
     UF Apostles (Mormon Church)
        Council of the Twelve (Mormon
          Church)
        Quorum of the Twelve Apostles
          (Mormon Church)
     BT Apostles
 — Doctrines
     NT Jaredites (Mormon Church)
        Lamanites (Mormon Church)
 — History
     NT Mountain Meadows Massacre,
          1857
        Nauvoo (Ill.)—Expulsion of the
          Mormons
        Utah Expedition, 1857-1858

Mormon Church *(Continued)*
— **Presidents**
    UF Presidents (Mormon Church)
— Relation to the state
    USE Church and state—Mormon
        Church
— **Sacred books**
    NT Book of Mormon
        Doctrine and covenants
— — **Inspiration**
    [BX8622]
Mormon church buildings
    USE Churches, Mormon
Mormon churches
    USE Churches, Mormon
Mormon converts
    USE Converts, Mormon
Mormon cookery
    USE Cookery, Mormon
Mormon cricket
    USE Anabrus simplex
Mormon decorative arts
    USE Decorative arts, Mormon
Mormon Fundamentalism *(May Subd Geog)*
    [BX8680.M5-BX8680.M58]
    BT Fundamentalism
        Mormon Church
Mormon furniture
    USE Furniture, Mormon
Mormon hygiene
    USE Hygiene, Mormon
Mormon literature, Cataloging of
    USE Cataloging of Mormon literature
Mormon painting
    USE Painting, Mormon
Mormon pilgrims and pilgrimages
  (May Subd Geog)
    UF Pilgrims and pilgrimages, Mormon
    BT Pilgrims and pilgrimages
    NT Mormon shrines
Mormon shrines *(May Subd Geog)*
    UF Shrines, Mormon
    BT Mormon pilgrims and pilgrimages
Mormon tabernacles
    USE Tabernacles, Mormon
Mormon temples
    USE Temples, Mormon
Mormon Trail
    BT Mormons—West (U.S.)—History
        Trails—United States
Mormon women
    USE Women, Mormon
Mormonism
    USE Mormon Church
Mormons *(May Subd Geog)*
    UF Latter-Day Saints
    RT Mormon Church
    NT Converts, Mormon
        Missions to Mormons
— **Women**
    USE Women, Mormon
— **United States**
    NT Afro-American Mormons
— **Utah**
— — **History**
    NT Morrisite War, 1862
— **West (U.S.)**
— — **History**
    NT Mormon Trail
Mormons, Afro-American
    USE Afro-American Mormons
Mormoopidae
    [QL737.C543]
    BT Bats
    NT Mormoops
        Pteronotus
Mormoops
    [QL737.C543]
    UF Ghost-faced bats
    BT Mormoopidae

Mormyridae
    [QL638.M676]
    BT Mormyriformes
    NT Gnathonemus
        Mormyrops
        Mormyrus
Mormyriformes
    [QL637.9.M6]
    UF Scyphophori
    BT Osteichthyes
    NT Gymnarchidae
        Mormyridae
Mormyrops
    [QL638.M676]
    BT Mormyridae
Mormyrops deliciosus
    [QL638.M676]
    UF Cornish jack (Fish)
Mormyrus
    [QL638.M676]
    BT Mormyridae
Mormyrus longirostris
    [QL638.M676]
    UF Bottlenose (Fish)
Morne Trois Pitons National Park (Dominica)
    BT National parks and reserves—
        Dominica
        Parks—Dominica
Morning after pills
    USE Contraceptives, Postcoital
Morning glories *(May Subd Geog)*
    [QK495.C78 (Botany)]
    [SB413.M67 (Ornamental plants)]
    BT Ipomoea
    NT Japanese morning glory
Morning prayer (Anglican)
    BT Public worship
Morning-service music
    BT Sacred vocal music
    NT Lauds (Music)
Mornington Peninsula (Vic.)
  (Not Subd Geog)
    BT Peninsulas—Australia
Morno River (Greece)
    USE Mornos River (Greece)
Mornos Potamos (Greece)
    USE Mornos River (Greece)
Mornos River (Greece) *(Not Subd Geog)*
    UF Dhafnous Potamos (Greece)
        Morno River (Greece)
        Mornos Potamos (Greece)
    BT Rivers—Greece
Moro family *(Not Subd Geog)*
Moro Indians
    [F2679.2.M6]
    UF Ayoweo Indians
    BT Indians of South America
— **Missions**
Moro language (South America)
    UF Ayoweo language
        Morotoco language
    BT Indians of South America—Bolivia—
        Languages
Moro language (Sudan)
Moro languages
    USE Lanao Moro dialect
        Magindanao language
        Maranao language
        Sulu language
Moro-moro
    USE Philippine drama (Comedy)
Moroccan alien labor
    USE Alien labor, Moroccan
Moroccan art
    USE Art, Moroccan
Moroccan cookery
    USE Cookery, Moroccan
Moroccan Crisis, 1904-1906
    BT Europe—History—20th century
Moroccan Crisis, 1911
    USE Agadir Incident, 1911

Moroccan fiction (Spanish)
  (May Subd Geog)
    UF Spanish fiction—Moroccan authors
    NT Short stories, Moroccan (Spanish)
Moroccan Jews
    USE Jews, Moroccan
Moroccan literature (French)
  (May Subd Geog)
    [PQ3988.M]
    UF French literature—Moroccan authors
Moroccan painting
    USE Painting, Moroccan
Moroccan poetry (French)
    UF French poetry—Moroccan authors
Moroccan short stories (Spanish)
    USE Short stories, Moroccan (Spanish)
Moroccan-Spanish War, 1859-1860
    USE Spanish-Moroccan War, 1859-1860
Moroccans *(May Subd Geog)*
    BT Ethnology—Morocco
Morocco
— **Antiquities**
    NT Lixus (Ancient city)
        Volubilis (City)
— **Description and travel**
— — **1981-**
— **History**
— — **To 647**
— — **647-1516**
    NT Beni Marin dynasty
        Wattasids
— — **1516-1830**
    NT Kassr-el-Kebir, Battle of, 1578
— — **19th century**
    NT Spanish-Moroccan War, 1859-
        1860
— — **20th century**
    NT Agadir Incident, 1911
        Casablanca Massacre, 1907
        Rif Revolt, 1909
        Rif Revolt, 1921-1926
— **Languages**
    NT Ḥakétia language
Morocco leather
    BT Leather
        Tanning
Morochocos
    USE Morochucan Indians
Morochucan Indians
    UF Morochocos
        Morochucans
        Morochucos
    BT Indians of South America
Morochucans
    USE Morochucan Indians
Morochucos
    USE Morochucan Indians
Morocosi language
    USE Moxo language
Moroe family
    USE Morrow family
Morone
    [QL638.P358]
    UF Roccus
    BT Percichthyidae
    NT Yellow bass
Morone americana
    [QL638.P358]
    UF White perch, Anadromous
    RT White perch fishing
Morone chrysops
    USE White bass
Morone interrupta
    USE Yellow bass
Morone saxatilis
    USE Striped bass
Morongo Wilderness (Calif.)
  (Not Subd Geog)
    UF Morongo Wilderness Study Area
        (Calif.)

BT National parks and reserves—
    California
    Wilderness areas—California
Morongo Wilderness Study Area (Calif.)
  USE Morongo Wilderness (Calif.)
Morons
  USE Mentally handicapped
Moros
  USE Muslims—Philippines
Moros y Cristianos, Fiesta de
  USE Moros y Cristianos (Dance)
Moros y Cristianos (Dance)
  (May Subd Geog)
  UF Christians and Moors, Dance of
    Conquista (Dance)
    Cristianos y Moros (Dance)
    Moors and Christians, Dance of
    Morisca (Dance)
    Moros y Cristianos, Fiesta de
    Santiagos (Dance)
  BT Indians of Central America—Dances
    Indians of Mexico—Dances
    Spain—History—711-1516
Morotoco language
  USE Moro language (South America)
Morow family
  USE Morrow family
Morozov Strike of 1885
  BT Textile workers—Soviet Union
Morphemes
  USE Morphemics
Morphemics
  UF Morphemes
  BT Grammar, Comparative and general—
    Morphology
  SA *subdivision* Morphemics *under*
    individual languages and groups of
    languages, e.g. English language—
    Morphemics
  NT Morphophonemics
Morphia
  USE Morphine
Morphine
  [QP921.M8 (Physiological effects)]
  [RA1238.M8 (Toxicology)]
  [RM666.M8 (Therapeutics)]
  UF Morphia
  BT Narcotics
  RT Opium
  NT Apomorphine
    Buprenorphine
    Heroin
    Naloxone
Morphine habit
  [HV5813]
  [RC568.O6 (Medicine)]
  BT Narcotic habit
  — **Jurisprudence** *(May Subd Geog)*
Morphine receptors
  USE Endorphins—Receptors
Morphisms (Mathematics)
  BT Categories (Mathematics)
    Set theory
  NT Isomorphisms (Mathematics)
Morphogenesis
  [QH491]
  UF Morphogeny
    Organogenesis
  BT Biology
    Embryology
  RT Morphology
  NT Cell differentiation
    Plant morphogenesis
Morphogeny
  USE Morphogenesis
Morphology
  [QH351 (General biology)]

UF Biological form
  Biological structure
  Comparative morphology
  Form in biology
  Structure in biology
BT Anatomy, Comparative
RT Morphogenesis
NT Abnormalities, Human
  Bacteria—Morphology
  Botany—Morphology
  Cells—Morphology
  Homology (Biology)
  Microstructure
  Morphology (Animals)
  Vestigial organs
  Viruses—Morphology
Morphology (Animals)
  [QL799]
  Here are entered works devoted to general discussion of the principles of structure in the animal kingdom. General works on animal anatomy and morphology are entered under Anatomy, Comparative.
  UF Animal morphology
    Body form in animals
    Zoology—Morphology
  BT Morphology
    Zoology
  SA *subdivision* Morphology *under names*
    of animals and groups of animals,
    e.g. Fishes—Morphology; Insects—
    Morphology
  NT Animals—Abnormalities
    Body size
    Dimorphism (Animals)
    Embryology
    Growth
Morphology (Linguistics)
  USE *subdivisions* Inflection *and* Word
    formation *under names of languages*
    Grammar, Comparative and general—
    Morphology
Morphology (Plants)
  USE Botany—Morphology
Morphophonemics
  UF Allomorphs (Linguistics)
    Morphophonology
  BT Morphemics
    Phonemics
  SA *subdivision* Morphophonemics *under*
    individual languages and groups of
    languages, e.g. English language—
    Morphophonemics
Morphophonology
  USE Morphophonemics
Morphy family
  USE Murphy family
Morral family
  USE Morrill family
Morrall family
  USE Morrill family
Morraw family
  USE Morrow family
Morrel family
  USE Morrill family
Morrell family
  USE Morrill family
Morres family
  USE Morris family
Morreson family
  USE Morrison family
Morrey family
  USE Morey family
Morrice family
  USE Morris family
Morrie family
  USE Morey family
Morril family
  USE Morrill family

Morrill family *(Not Subd Geog)*
  UF Morel family
    Morell family
    Morill family
    Morral family
    Morrall family
    Morrel family
    Morrell family
    Morril family
Morris, Robert, 1931-   Grand Rapids
Project
  UF Grand Rapids Project (Environment
    (Art))
Morris (Cat)
  BT Cats
Morris (Name)
  BT Names, Personal
Morris automobile
  BT BLMC automobiles
  NT Morris Maxi automobile
    Morris Minor automobile
Morris Canal (N.J.)
  BT Canals—New Jersey
Morris Creek (W. Va.)
  USE Turtle Creek (W. Va.)
Morris-dance
  [GV1796.M7]
Morris-dances
  BT Dance music
Morris family *(Not Subd Geog)*
  UF Maurice family
    Morice family
    Moris family
    Moriss family
    Morres family
    Morrice family
    Morriss family
  RT Morrison family
Morris Maxi automobile
  [TL215.M]
  UF Maxi automobile
  BT Morris automobile
Morris Mini-Cooper automobiles
  USE Mini-Cooper automobiles
Morris Mini Minor automobile
  USE Mini automobiles
Morris Minor automobile
  UF Minor automobile
  BT Morris automobile
Morriset family
  USE Morrissett family
Morrisite War, 1862
  BT Church of the First Born (Morrisites)
    —History
    Mormons—Utah—History
    Utah—History
Morrisites
  USE Church of the First Born (Morrisites)
Morrison family *(Not Subd Geog)*
  UF Maurison family
    Morason family
    Morison family
    Morreson family
    Morrisson family
    Morriston family
    Morrosen family
    Morroson family
    Morrowson family
  RT Morris family
Morrison Formation
  BT Formations (Geology)—West (U.S.)
    Geology, Stratigraphic—Jurassic
Morriss family
  USE Morris family
Morrissett family *(Not Subd Geog)*
  UF Moriset family
    Morisette family
    Morisset family
    Morizet family
    Morriset family

Morrisson family
USE Morrison family
Morriston family
USE Morrison family
Morristown National Historical Park (N.J.)
BT Historic sites—New Jersey
National parks and reserves—United
States
Parks—New Jersey
NT Ford Powder Mill Site (Morristown,
N.J.)
Morrosen family
USE Morrison family
Morroson family
USE Morrison family
Morrow computers
[QA76.8.M]
BT Microcomputers
Morrow family *(Not Subd Geog)*
UF Moroe family
Morow family
Morraw family
Morrows family
Murrow family
Morrow Point Dam (Colo.)
(Not Subd Geog)
BT Dams—Colorado
Morrows family
USE Morrow family
Morrowson family
USE Morrison family
Morry family
USE Morey family
Mors family
USE Morse family
Morse
USE Walruses
Morse alphabet
USE Morse code
Morse code
UF Morse alphabet
Morse radiotelegraph code
Morse telegraph code
BT Cipher and telegraph codes
Radio
Signals and signaling
Telegraph—Alphabets
Morse family *(Not Subd Geog)*
UF Moorse family
Mors family
Morss family
RT Moss family
Morse radiotelegraph code
USE Morse code
Morse telegraph code
USE Morse code
Morskie Oko (Poland)
UF Rybie Jezioro (Poland)
BT Lakes—Poland
Morss family
USE Morse family
Morston family
USE Marsden family
Mort de Jane Grey (Portrait painting)
USE Delaroche, Paul, 1797-1856.
Execution of Lady Jane Grey
Mort family *(Not Subd Geog)*
UF Morte family
Morts family
Mortt family
Morty family
Mortz family
Mortain family
USE Morton family
Mortal sin
USE Sin, Mortal
Mortalism
USE Annihilationism
Mortality *(May Subd Geog)*
[HB1321-HB1530 (Demography)]
[HG8783-HG8787 (Insurance)]

When subdivided by place, assign a second subject
heading for place with subdivision Statistics, Vital,
e.g. 1. Mortality—United States. 2. United States—
Statistics, Vital.
UF Burial statistics
Death rate
Mortuary statistics
BT Death
Death—Causes
Demographic transition
Demography
Population
Vital statistics
RT Death (Biology)
SA *subdivision* Mortality *under individual*
animals, diseases, classes of persons,
and ethnic groups for works that list
or discuss the number of deaths
during a given time due to a
particular cause or occurring in a
particular group, e.g. Fishes—
Mortality; Cancer—Mortality;
Indians of North America—
Mortality
NT Die-off (Zoology)
Fetal death
Insurance, Life—Mathematics
Life span, Productive
Livestock—Embryos—Mortality
Occupational mortality
Perinatal mortality
Sudden death
Violent deaths
War—Casualties (Statistics, etc.)
— **Sex differences**
— **Tables**
UF Life tables
— **United States**
Mortality, Business
USE Business failures
Mortality, Law of
[HB1321]
UF Law of mortality
BT Insurance, Life
Vital statistics
Mortality and race *(May Subd Geog)*
BT Race
Mortality of livestock embryos
USE Livestock—Embryos—Mortality
Mortar
[TA436-TA437 (Properties, testing)]
[TP887 (Manufacture)]
BT Adhesives
Binders (Materials)
Plaster
NT Grout (Mortar)
Grouting
Gunite
Polymer-impregnated mortar
— **Additives**
UF Mortar admixtures
Mortar admixtures
USE Mortar—Additives
Mortar makers' marks
USE Mortars—Marks
Mortars *(May Subd Geog)*
— **Marks**
UF Marks, Mortar makers'
Mortar makers' marks
Mortars (Ordnance)
[UF560-565]
BT Ordnance
NT Trench mortars
Morte family
USE Mort family
Morten family
USE Morton family
Mortensen family *(Not Subd Geog)*
UF Mortenson family
Mortenson family
USE Mortensen family

Mortgage-backed securities
USE Mortgage bonds
Mortgage banks *(May Subd Geog)*
[HD1439-HD1440 (Theory)]
[HG2041-HG2051]
UF Agricultural banks
Mortgage companies
BT Banks and banking
RT Agricultural credit
Mortgage loans
NT Mortgage bonds
— **Accounting**
— — **Law and legislation**
(May Subd Geog)
Mortgage bonds *(May Subd Geog)*
UF First-mortgage bonds
Mortgage-backed securities
Mortgage certificates
Mortgage-participation certificates
Pass-through certificates
BT Bonds
Mortgage banks
— **Law and legislation** *(May Subd Geog)*
Mortgage bonds, Tax-exempt
(May Subd Geog)
UF Tax-exempt mortgage bonds
BT Securities, Tax-exempt
Taxation, Exemption from
— **Law and legislation** *(May Subd Geog)*
Mortgage certificates
USE Mortgage bonds
Mortgage closing costs
USE Settlement costs
Mortgage companies
USE Mortgage banks
Mortgage foreclosure
USE Foreclosure
Mortgage guaranty insurance
USE Insurance, Mortgage guaranty
Mortgage lending
USE Mortgage loans
Mortgage loans *(May Subd Geog)*
UF Mortgage lending
Real estate loans
BT Loans
RT Mortgage banks
Mortgages
Secondary mortgage market
NT Discrimination in mortgage loans
Home improvement loans
Veterans—Loans
— **Refinancing**
UF Mortgage refinancing
Refinancing of mortgage loans
Mortgage loans, Equity sharing
(May Subd Geog)
UF Equity sharing mortgage loans
Shared appreciation mortgages
Mortgage loans, Reverse *(May Subd Geog)*
[HG2040-2040.5]
UF Reverse annuity mortgages
Reverse mortgage loans
NT Home equity conversion
Mortgage loans, Variable rate
(May Subd Geog)
UF Graduated payment mortgage loans
Renegotiable rate mortgage loans
Variable rate mortgage loans
BT Floating rate notes
Variable rate loans
— **Law and legislation** *(May Subd Geog)*
BT Mortgages
Mortgage market, Secondary
USE Secondary mortgage market
Mortgage-participation certificates
USE Mortgage bonds
Mortgage refinancing
USE Mortgage loans—Refinancing
Mortgages *(May Subd Geog)*
[HD1443 (Farm economics)]
[HG5095 (Investments, HG4655)]

UF Hypothecation
BT Accessory obligations
Commercial law
Contracts
Deeds
Encumbrances (Law)
Investments
Land titles
Real obligations
Real property
Securities
Security (Law)
RT Conveyancing
Housing—Finance—Law and
legislation
Liens
Mortgage loans
Priorities of claims and liens
NT Antichresis
Bottomry and respondentia
Buildings—Repair and reconstruction
—Finance
Chattel mortgages
Deeds of trust
Foreclosure
Housing—Finance
Housing, Rural—Finance
Insurance, Mortgage guaranty
Insurance, Mortgage life
Mortgage loans, Variable rate—Law
and legislation
Secondary mortgage market—Law and
legislation
Veterans—Loans—Law and legislation
— Taxation (May Subd Geog)
[HJ5901-5919]
NT Taxation of bonds, securities, etc.
Mortgages, Aircraft
USE Aircraft mortgages
Mortgages (Adat law) (May Subd Geog)
Mortgages (Byzantine law)
Mortgages (Canon law)
[BX1939.M68]
BT Church property (Canon law)
Mortgages (Greek law)
Mortgages (Islamic law) (May Subd Geog)
Mortgages (Jewish law)
Mortgages (Roman-Dutch law)
Mortgages (Roman law)
NT Fiducia
Morthimer family
USE Mortimer family
Morticians
USE Undertakers and undertaking
Mortification (Pathology)
USE Gangrene
Mortimer family (Not Subd Geog)
UF Morthimer family
Mortimore family
Mortimore family
USE Mortimer family
Mortin family
USE Morton family
Mortlock language
[PL6256.M85]
BT Micronesian languages
Mortmain (May Subd Geog)
[BX1939.M7 (Canon law)]
[HJ5521-HJ5529]
BT Charitable uses, trusts, and foundations
Land tenure—Law and legislation
NT Church lands
Religious trusts
Mortoloses
USE Martoloses
Morton family (Not Subd Geog)
UF Mortain family
Morten family
Mortin family
Mortorn family

Morton Ranch (Wyo.)
BT Ranches—Wyoming
Mortonagrion
[QL520.3.C64]
BT Coenagrionidae
Mortorn family
USE Morton family
Morts family
USE Mort family
Mortt family
USE Mort family
Mortuary chapels
USE Sepulchral chapels
Mortuary cosmetology (May Subd Geog)
[RA623.5]
UF Cosmetology, Mortuary
Post-mortem cosmetology
Postmortem cosmetology
BT Beauty culture
Embalming
Mortuary customs
USE Indians—Mortuary customs; Indians of
North America—Mortuary customs;
and similar headings
Burial
Cremation
Dead
Embalming
Funeral rites and ceremonies
Indians—Mortuary customs
Indians of North America—Mortuary
customs
Mourning customs
Undertakers and undertaking
Urn burial
Mortuary law
USE Burial laws
Mortuary practice
USE Undertakers and undertaking
Mortuary statistics
USE Mortality
Vital statistics
Morty family
USE Mort family
Mortz family
USE Mort family
Moru language
BT Nilo-Saharan languages
Sudan—Languages
Morus (Plants)
USE Mulberry
Morus bassanus
USE Northern gannet
Morus cathayana
[QK495.M73 (Botany)]
[SF557 (Culture)]
UF Chinese mulberry
BT Mulberry
Morvan, Parc naturel régional du (France)
USE Parc naturel régional du Morvan
(France)
Morvan in art
Morvil family
USE Marvel family
Morvill family
USE Marvel family
Morville family
USE Marvel family
Mory family
USE Morey family
Mosa River
USE Meuse River
Mosaic (Genetics)
USE Mosaicism
Mosaic bindings
USE Bookbinding—Mosaic bindings
Mosaic diseases
BT Plant diseases
Plant viruses

SA mosaic diseases affecting specific
plants or groups of plants, e.g.
Potato mosaic virus
NT Cymbidium mosaic diseases
Sugarcane mosaic disease
Mosaic floors
USE Floors, Mosaic
Mosaic law
USE Jewish law
Mosaic pavements
USE Pavements, Mosaic
Mosaicism
UF Chimaera (Genetics)
Chimera (Genetics)
Mosaic (Genetics)
BT Genetics
Mosaicists (May Subd Geog)
UF Mosaists
Mosaics (May Subd Geog)
[NA3750-NA3850 (Architectural
decoration)]
[NK5430 (Glass)]
[NK8500 (Ornaments and jewelry)]
BT Art
Arts and crafts movement
Christian art and symbolism
Church decoration and ornament
Decoration and ornament
Decorative arts
RT Mural painting and decoration
NT Floors, Mosaic
Miniature mosaics
Pavements, Mosaic
— 20th century (May Subd Geog)
— Copying
BT Art—Reproduction
Copying
NT Nile mosaic (Palestrina)—Copying
— Expertising
— Italy
NT Fish mosaic (Palestrina)
Nile mosaic (Palestrina)
Otranto mosaic
— Syria
NT Amazon mosaic (Apamea, Syria)
Mosaics, Ancient (May Subd Geog)
Mosaics, Byzantine (May Subd Geog)
UF Byzantine mosaics
— Expertising
— Macedonian influences
BT Macedonia—Civilization
Mosaics, Carlovingian (May Subd Geog)
UF Carlovingian mosaics
Mosaics, Early Christian (May Subd Geog)
UF Early Christian mosaics
Mosaics, German, [Greco-Roman, Italian, etc.]
(May Subd Geog)
Mosaics, Greek (May Subd Geog)
UF Greek mosaics
Mosaics, Hellenistic (May Subd Geog)
UF Hellenistic mosaics
Mosaics, Islamic (May Subd Geog)
UF Islamic mosaics
Mosaics, Muslim
Muslim mosaics
Mosaics, Italian (May Subd Geog)
[NA3790 (Medieval)]
[NA3820 (Modern)]
UF Italian mosaics
Mosaics, Medieval (May Subd Geog)
— Byzantine [etc.] influences
Mosaics, Muslim
USE Mosaics, Islamic
Mosaics, Roman (May Subd Geog)
— Expertising
— Italy
NT Fish mosaic (Palestrina)
Nile mosaic (Palestrina)
Mosaik von Otranto
USE Otranto mosaic

Mosaïque aux amazones chasseresses (Apamea,
    Syria)
    USE Amazon mosaic (Apamea, Syria)
Mosaists
    USE Mosaicists
Mosasauridae
    UF Pythonomorpha
    BT Lizards, Fossil
    NT Globidens
Moscas
    USE Chibcha Indians
Mosce family
    USE Moss family
Moscoso family *(Not Subd Geog)*
Moscow (R.S.F.S.R.)
    — History
    — — Uprising, 1662
        USE Moscow Uprising, 1662
    — — Revolution of 1905
    — — 1917-1921
    — Siege, 1941-1942
        USE Moscow, Battle of, 1941-1942
Moscow, Battle of, 1941-1942
    ₍D764₎
    UF Moscow (R.S.F.S.R.)—Siege, 1941-
        1942
    BT World War, 1939-1945—Campaigns—
        Russian S.F.S.R.
Moscow Canal (R.S.F.S.R.)
    UF Kanal imeni Moskvy (R.S.F.S.R.)
        Kanal Moskva-Volga (R.S.F.S.R.)
        Moscow-Volga Canal (R.S.F.S.R.)
        Volga Canal (R.S.F.S.R.)
        Volga-Moscow Canal (R.S.F.S.R.)
    BT Canals—Russian S.F.S.R
Moscow River (R.S.F.S.R.)
    USE Moskva River (R.S.F.S.R.)
Moscow school of icon painting
    BT Icon painting—Russian S.F.S.R.
        Icons, Russian
Moscow Sea (R.S.F.S.R.)
    USE Ivan'kovo Reservoir (R.S.F.S.R.)
Moscow Trial, 1945
    ₍D802.P6₎
    BT Poland—History—Occupation, 1939-
        1945
**Moscow Trials, Moscow, R.S.F.S.R., 1936-
1937**
    UF Moscow Trials, 1936-1937
    BT Trials (Political crimes and offenses)—
        Russian S.F.S.R.
Moscow Trials, 1936-1937
    USE Moscow Trials, Moscow, R.S.F.S.R.,
        1936-1937
Moscow Uprising, 1662
    UF Moscow (R.S.F.S.R.)—History—
        Uprising, 1662
Moscow-Volga Canal (R.S.F.S.R.)
    USE Moscow Canal (R.S.F.S.R.)
Mosè (Sculpture)
    USE Michelangelo Buonarroti, 1475-1564.
        Moses
Mose family
    USE Moses family
Mosel River
    USE Moselle River
Moseley family
    USE Mosley family
Mosella River
    USE Moselle River
Moselle River
    UF La Moselle Rivière
        Mosel River
        Mosella River
    BT Rivers—France
        Rivers—Germany (West)
        Rivers—Luxembourg
Moselle River, Battle of the, 1944
    USE Arnaville, Battle of, 1944
Mosely family
    USE Mosley family

Mosenthal family *(Not Subd Geog)*
Moser family *(Not Subd Geog)*
    UF Mossir family
        Mozer family
    RT Mosher family
Moseria
    USE Iponemus
Moses (Biblical leader)
    — Art
        NT Michelangelo Buonarroti, 1475-
            1564. Moses
Moses (Sculpture)
    USE Michelangelo Buonarroti, 1475-1564.
        Moses
Moses family *(Not Subd Geog)*
    UF Mose family
        Moseson family
Moseson family
    USE Moses family
Moseteno language
    ₍PM6561₎
    RT Chimane language
Mosetenos
    ₍F3320.2.M (Bolivian Indians)₎
MOSFET
    USE Metal oxide semiconductor field-effect
        transistors
Mosgrove family
    USE Musgrave family
Moshav shitufi
    UF Collective settlements—Israel
    BT Agriculture, Cooperative—Israel
    RT Kibbutzim
Moshavim
    ₍HD1491.I7₎
    BT Agriculture, Cooperative—Israel
Mosher family *(Not Subd Geog)*
    UF Moshier family
        Moshure family
        Mosier family
        Mosser family
        Mosure family
        Mosyer family
        Mozier family
    RT Moser family
Moshi language
    USE Moré language
Moshi languages
    USE Mossi languages
Moshier family
    USE Mosher family
Moshure family
    USE Mosher family
Mosier family
    USE Mosher family
MOSIM (Computer programs)
    ₍QA76.9.C65₎
    UF Modules to simulate in PL/I
        (Computer programs)
    BT Digital computer simulation
        PL/I (Computer program language)
Moskito (Fighter plane)
    ₍UG1242.F5₎
    UF Focke-Wulf Moskito (Fighter plane)
        Focke-Wulf Ta 154 (Fighter plane)
        Ta 154 (Fighter plane)
    BT Fighter planes
        Focke-Wulf airplanes
Moskovskoe more (R.S.F.S.R.)
    USE Ivan'kovo Reservoir (R.S.F.S.R.)
Moskovskoye more (R.S.F.S.R.)
    USE Ivan'kovo Reservoir (R.S.F.S.R.)
Moskva River (R.S.F.S.R.)
    UF Moscow River (R.S.F.S.R.)
    BT Rivers—Russian S.F.S.R.
Moskvich automobile
    ₍TL215.M63₎
Moslem . . .
    USE *subject headings beginning with the
        word* Muslim *or* Islamic

Moslems
    USE Muslims
Mosley, Zack. Smilin' Jack
    UF Smilin' Jack (Comic strip)
    BT Comic books, strips, etc.
Mosley family *(Not Subd Geog)*
    UF Moseley family
        Mosely family
        Mossley family
        Mossly family
Moso (Tribe)
    UF Djiong
        Giong
        Lashis
        Mossos
        Mousseux
        Mussu
        Musu (Asiatic tribe)
        Na-khi
        Nashis
    BT Ethnology—China
        Lolos
Moso epic poetry
    USE Epic poetry, Moso
Moso language
    ₍PL3311.M7₎
    BT Loloish languages
Moso literature
    NT Moso poetry
Moso poetry *(May Subd Geog)*
    BT Moso literature
    NT Epic poetry, Moso
Mosque etiquette
    ₍BJ2019.5.I8₎
    UF Etiquette, Mosque
    BT Islamic etiquette
Mosque libraries *(May Subd Geog)*
    ₍Z675.I84₎
    UF Libraries, Mosque
    BT Islamic libraries
Mosques *(May Subd Geog)*
    ₍NA4670 (Architecture)₎
    UF Religious art
    BT Architecture
        Architecture, Islamic
        Architecture, Oriental
        Church architecture
        Religious and ecclesiastical institutions
        Temples
    NT Adobe mosques
        Minarets
    — Organization and administration
        BT Islam—Government
        NT Pastoral theology (Islam)
Mosques, Adobe
    USE Adobe mosques
Mosques as community centers
    ₍BP190₎
    BT Community centers
Mosquitia (Nicaragua and Honduras)
    UF Costa de Mosquitos (Nicaragua and
            Honduras)
        Miskito Coast (Nicaragua and
            Honduras)
        Mosquito Coast (Nicaragua and
            Honduras)
Mosquito (Bombers)
    BT Bombers
        De Havilland aircraft
Mosquito Coast (Nicaragua and Honduras)
    USE Mosquitia (Nicaragua and Honduras)
Mosquito control
    USE Mosquitoes—Control
Mosquito ferns
    USE Azolla
Mosquito Indians
    ₍F1529.M9₎
    UF Miskito Indians
    BT Indians of Central America
Mosquito language
    ₍PM4036-PM4039₎

UF Miskito language
    Misskito language
BT Central America—Languages
    Misumalpan languages
Mosquito larvae
  USE Mosquitoes—Larvae
Mosquito vectors
  USE Mosquitoes as carriers of disease
Mosquitoes *(May Subd Geog)*
  [QL536]
  UF Culicidae
  BT Diptera
  NT Acartomyia
    Aedes
    Conchyliastes
    Culex
    Culiseta
    Deinocerites
    Mansonia
    Megarhinus
    Psorophora
    Stegomyia
    Topomyia
    Tripteroides
    Zeugnomyia
  — **Anatomy**
  — **Control** *(May Subd Geog)*
    [RA640]
    UF Mosquito control
    NT Aeronautics in mosquito control
  — — **Finance**
  — — — **Law and legislation**
      (May Subd Geog)
  — **Integrated control** *(May Subd Geog)*
  — **Larvae**
    UF Mosquito larvae
Mosquitoes as carriers of disease
  (May Subd Geog)
  [RA640]
  UF Mosquito vectors
  BT Insects as carriers of disease
Mosquitofish
  USE Gambusia affinis
Moss animals
  USE Bryozoa
Moss family *(Not Subd Geog)*
  UF Maus family
    Moess family
    Mosce family
    Mosse family
  RT Morse family
Moss Neck Swamp (N.C.)
  BT Rivers—North Carolina
    Swamps—North Carolina
Moss, Norway, Convention of, 1814
  [DL500-501]
Moss Site (Ill.) *(Not Subd Geog)*
  BT Illinois—Antiquities
Mossa Indians
  USE Moxo Indians
Mossâmedes Desert (Angola)
  USE Moçâmedes Desert (Angola)
Mössbauer effect
  BT Fluorescence
    Nuclear physics
    Photons
    Quantum theory
    Radiation
  RT Mössbauer spectroscopy
Mössbauer spectroscopy
  UF Spectroscopy, Mössbauer
  BT Spectrum analysis
  RT Mössbauer effect
Mosse family
  USE Moss family
Mosser family
  USE Mosher family
Mosses *(May Subd Geog)*
  [QK534-549]

UF Acrogens
    Brypsida
    Limu
    Musci
BT Bryology
    Bryophytes
    Cryptogams
NT Dicranales
    Grimmiales
    Hookeriales
    Hypnobryales
    Isobryales
    Peat mosses
    Peristome (Botany)
— **Anatomy**
Mosses, Fossil
  [QE959]
Mossi (African people)
  [DT553.U7]
  UF Moaaga (African people)
  — **History**
    NT Yatenga (Kingdom)
  — **Rites and ceremonies**
    NT Marriage customs and rites, Mossi
      (African people)
Mossi (African people) marriage customs and
  rites
  USE Marriage customs and rites, Mossi
    (African people)
Mossi language
  USE Moré language
Mossi languages
  UF Moaaga languages
    Moisi languages
    Mole languages
    More languages
    Moshi languages
  BT Gur languages
  NT Dagari language
    Dagomba language
    Kussassi language
    Moré language
Mossi law
  USE Law, Mossi
Mossi proverbs
  USE Proverbs, Mossi
Mossie (Bird)
  USE Passer melanurus
Mossir family
  USE Moser family
Mossley family
  USE Mosley family
Mossly family
  USE Mosley family
Mossoró (Race horse)
  BT Race horses
Mossos
  USE Moso (Tribe)
**Mossy Creek, Battle of, Jefferson City, Tenn.,
1863**
  BT Tennessee—History—Civil War, 1861-
    1865
    United States—History—Civil War,
    1861-1865—Campaigns
Most favored nation clause
  USE Favored nation clause
MOST I (Computer program language)
Mostaganem Plateau (Algeria)
  UF Haḍbat Mustaghānim (Algeria)
    Mustaghānim Plateau (Algeria)
    Plateau de Mostaganem (Algeria)
  BT Plateaus—Algeria
Moste (Ljubljana, Slovenia)
  (Not Subd Geog)
  UF Ljubljana (Slovenia). Moste
Mosto Palace (Reggio Emilia, Italy)
  USE Palazzo da Mosto (Reggio Emilia,
    Italy)
Mosure family
  USE Mosher family

Mosyer family
  USE Mosher family
Mot (Semitic god)
  BT Gods, Semitic
Mot family
  USE Mott family
Mota language
  [PL6256.M87]
  BT Melanesian languages
Motacilla
  [QL696.P252]
  BT Wagtails
  NT Motacilla alba
    Motacilla flava
Motacilla alba
  [QL696.P252]
  UF Pied wagtail
    White wagtail
  BT Motacilla
Motacilla flava
  [QL696.P252]
  UF Blue-headed wagtail
    Yellow wagtail
  BT Motacilla
Motacillidae
  [QL696.P252]
  BT Passeriformes
  NT Wagtails
Motagua River (Guatemala)
  UF Grande River (Guatemala)
    Montagua River (Guatemala)
    Río Grande (Guatemala)
    Río Montagua (Guatemala)
    Río Motagua (Guatemala)
    Río Selapec (Guatemala)
    Selapec River (Guatemala)
  BT Rivers—Guatemala
Motazilite Inquisition
  USE Miḥna
Motazilites
  UF Mutazilites
  BT Islamic sects
Mote and the beam (Parable)
  [BT378.M]
Mote family
  USE Mott family
Motel administration
  USE Motel management
Motel bellmen
  USE Hotel bellmen
Motel doormen
  USE Hotel doormen
Motel maids
  USE Hotel maids
Motel management *(May Subd Geog)*
  UF Motel administration
    Motels—Management
  BT Hotel management
    Management
  — **Vocational guidance**
    UF Motel management as a profession
Motel management as a profession
  USE Motel management—Vocational
    guidance
Motels *(May Subd Geog)*
  UF Auto courts
    Motor courts
    Motor hotels
    Motor inns
    Motor lodges
    Tourist courts
  BT Hotels, taverns, etc.
    Tourist camps, hostels, etc.
  — **Employees**
    USE Hotels, taverns, etc.—Employees
  — **Law and legislation** *(May Subd Geog)*
  — **Management**
    USE Motel management
  — **Mathematics**
    USE Business mathematics—Motels
  — **Parking facilities**

Motels
— **Parking facilities**   *(Continued)*
  BT Automobile parking
Motels, Pet
  USE Pet boarding facilities
Motes family
  USE Mott family
Motet
  Here are entered works on the motet as a musical form. Musical works composed in the form are entered under Motets.
  BT Choral music
    Church music
    Church music—Catholic Church
    Part-songs
    Part-songs, Sacred
Motets
  Here are entered musical works composed in the form of the motet. Works on the motet as a musical form are entered under Motet.
  A second heading for medium is assigned if a specific medium of performance is given in the work.
  BT Part-songs
    Part-songs, Sacred
    Sacred duets
    Sacred nonets
    Sacred octets
    Sacred quartets
    Sacred quintets
    Sacred septets
    Sacred sextets
    Sacred trios
  NT Anthems
Moth-flies
  ₍QL537.P85₎
  UF Moth gnats
    Moth midges
    Psychodinae
  BT Psychodidae
  NT Maruina
Moth gnats
  USE Moth-flies
Moth midges
  USE Moth-flies
Mothballing of military supplies
  USE Military supplies—Preservation
Mothballing of ships
  USE Ships—Preservation
Mothe Island (Fiji)   *(Not Subd Geog)*
  UF Moce Island (Fiji)
  BT Islands—Fiji
Mother and child   *(May Subd Geog)*
  UF Child and mother
    Mother-child relationship
  BT Parent and child
  NT Maternal rejection
    Mother and infant
    Mothers and daughters
    Mothers and sons
    Play groups
— **Cross-cultural studies**
— Hospital care
    USE Hospitals, Gynecologic and obstetric
Mother and child health services
  USE Child health services
    Maternal health services
Mother and child in art
  USE Mothers in art
Mother and infant   *(May Subd Geog)*
  ₍BF720.M68₎
  UF Infant and mother
    Mother-infant relationship
  BT Mother and child
Mother-child relationship
  USE Mother and child
Mother-goddesses   *(May Subd Geog)*
  ₍BL325.M6₎
  UF Goddesses, Mother
    Mothers (in religion, folklore, etc.)

  BT Goddesses
    Mysteries, Religious
    Mythology
    Sex—Religious aspects
  NT Pacamama (Goddess)
    Sekhmet (Egyptian deity)
Mother goddesses, Greek
  ₍BL820.M65₎
  UF Greek mother goddesses
  BT Gods, Greek
Mother-in-law
  USE Mothers-in-law
Mother-in-law apartments
  USE Accessory apartments
Mother-infant relationship
  USE Mother and infant
Mother love
  USE Love, Maternal
Mother of God
  USE Mary, Blessed Virgin, Saint
Mother-of-pearl
  ₍QL432 (Zoology)₎
  ₍SH377.5 (Fisheries)₎
  NT Pearl button industry
    Trochus shell fisheries
Mother tongue
  USE Native language
Motherhood   *(May Subd Geog)*
  ₍HQ759₎
  UF Maternity
  BT Parenthood
  RT Mothers
— **Religious aspects**
— — **Baptists, ₍Catholic Church, etc.₎**
— — **Buddhism, ₍Christianity, etc.₎**
Motherhood insurance
  USE Insurance, Maternity
Motherhood of God
  USE God—Motherhood
Mothers   *(May Subd Geog)*
  ₍HQ759 (Social sciences)₎
  ₍PN6071.M7 (Literary extracts)₎
  BT Family
    Parents
    Women
  RT Housewives
    Motherhood
    Pregnant women
  NT Absentee mothers
    Adolescent mothers
    Authors, English—Mothers
    Divorced mothers
    Grandparents
    Kings and rulers—Mothers
    Lesbian mothers
    Love, Maternal
    Maternal age
    Maternal and infant welfare
    Maternal deprivation
    Presidents—Mothers
    Single parents
    Stepmothers
    Surrogate mothers
    Working mothers
— **Anthropometry**
— Biblical teaching
    USE Women in the Bible
— **Employment**   *(May Subd Geog)*
    Here are entered works on the conditions of employment of mothers. Works on the social conditions of mothers apart form their workplace and how work affects the quality of life of mothers are entered under Working mothers.
    BT Married people—Employment
    NT Children of working mothers
— — **Law and legislation**
    (May Subd Geog)
    BT Labor laws and legislation
— Medical care
    USE Maternal health services
— **Mortality**

  ₍HB1322.5 (Vital statistics)₎
  ₍RG530-RG530.3 (Obstetrics)₎
  UF Maternal mortality
  BT Pregnancy, Complications of
— **Nutrition**
  UF Maternal nutrition
  RT Pregnancy—Nutritional aspects
  NT Puerperium—Nutritional aspects
— **Poetry**
  ₍PN6110.H6₎
— **Portraits**
  BT Mothers in art
    Women—Portraits
— **Religious life**
  NT Churching of women
— **Time management**
— **United States**
— — **Nutrition**
Mothers, Employed
  USE Working mothers
Mothers, Unmarried
  USE Unmarried mothers
Mothers, Working
  USE Working mothers
Mothers (in religion, folklore, etc.)
  USE Mother-goddesses
Mother's age at birth
  USE Maternal age
Mothers and daughters   *(May Subd Geog)*
  UF Daughters and mothers
  BT Daughters
    Girls
    Mother and child
Mothers and sons   *(May Subd Geog)*
  UF Sons and mothers
  BT Boys
    Mother and child
  NT Oedipus complex
Mother's Day   *(May Subd Geog)*
  ₍HQ759.2₎
  BT Holidays
  NT Mother's Day sermons
— **Exercises, recitations, etc.**
— Sermons
    USE Mother's Day sermons
— **Songs and music**
Mother's Day sermons
  UF Mother's Day—Sermons
    Sermons, Mother's Day
  BT Mother's Day
    Occasional sermons
Mothers general
  BT Convents and nunneries
    Monasticism and religious orders for women
Mothers in art
  ₍N7630₎
  UF Mother and child in art
  NT Mothers—Portraits
Mothers-in-law   *(May Subd Geog)*
  UF Mother-in-law
  BT Family
    Parents-in-law
Mothers in literature
Mother's love
  USE Love, Maternal
Mothers' pensions   *(May Subd Geog)*
  ₍HV697-HV700₎
  UF Widows—Pensions
    Widows' pensions
  BT Child welfare
    Maternal and infant welfare
    Pensions
    Survivors' benefits
  NT Family allowances
— **Law and legislation**   *(May Subd Geog)*
Motherwell, Robert. Reconciliation elegy
  UF Reconciliation elegy (Painting)

Motherwell Farmstead National Historic Park
(Sask.)
USE W. R. Motherwell Farmstead National
Historic Park (Sask.)
Motherwell House (Sask.)
USE W. R. Motherwell Stone House (Sask.)
Motherwell Stone House (Sask.)
USE W. R. Motherwell Stone House (Sask.)
Motherwort
USE Leonurus cardiaca
Mothproofing
[TS1523]
BT Insecticides
Moths
Moths *(May Subd Geog)*
[QL541-562]
UF Heterocera
Lepidoptera nocturna
BT Insects
Lepidoptera
NT Acrolepiidae
Agaristidae
Ailanthus moth
Alucitidae
Anomologidae
Argyresthiidae
Bombycidae
Brown-tail moth
Bud-moth
Carposinidae
Caterpillars
Cecropia moth
Clearwing moths
Clothes moths
Clover-worm
Cochylidae
Codling-moth
Coleophoridae
Cossidae
Cutworms
Diamond-back moth
Dioptidae
Douglas fir pitch moth
Douglas-fir tussock moth
Drepanidae
Eastern tent caterpillar
Elachistidae
Epipyropidae
Ethmiidae
Gelechiidae
Gracillariidae
Holcopogonidae
Incurvariidae
Lasiocampidae
Lecithoceridae
Limacodidae
Luna moth
Lymantriidae
Lyonetiidae
Mediterranean flour-moth
Mimallonidae
Mothproofing
Nantucket pine moth
Neopseustidae
Nepticulidae
Notodontidae
Nun moth
Ochsenheimeriidae
Oecophoridae
Palaephatidae
Peppered moth
Pine brown-tail moth
Pine-moth
Promethea moth
Psychidae
Pterophoridae
Pyralidae
Satin moth
Saturniidae
Scythridae
Sphingidae

Stenomidae
Symmocidae
Tent-caterpillars
Thyrididae
Tineidae
Tortricidae
Uraniidae
Western grape-leaf skeletonizer
White-marked tussock moth
Winter moth
Xylorictidae
Yponomeutidae
Yucca moths
Zygaenidae
— **Cultures and culture media**
[SF562.M6 (Culture)]
BT Insect rearing
Moți (Romanian people)
UF Motzi (Romanian people)
BT Ethnology—Romania
Romanians
Motia (Ancient city)
USE Motya (Ancient city)
Motility, Colon (Anatomy)
USE Colon (Anatomy)—Motility
Motility, Esophageal
USE Esophagus—Motility
Motility, Foot
USE Foot—Movements
Motility, Gastric
USE Stomach—Motility
Motility, Gastrointestinal
USE Gastrointestinal system—Motility
Motility disorders, Esophageal
USE Esophagus—Motility—Disorders
Motility disorders, Gastrointestinal
USE Gastrointestinal system—Motility—
Disorders
Motility of bacteria
USE Bacteria—Motility
Motility of cancer cells
USE Cancer cells—Motility
Motility of cells
USE Cells—Motility
Motility of leucocytes
USE Leucocytes—Motility
Motility of micro-organisms
USE Micro-organisms—Motility
Motility of muscles
USE Muscles—Motility
Motility of protozoa
USE Protozoa—Motility
Motility of spermatozoa
USE Spermatozoa—Motility
Motility of the Fallopian tube
USE Fallopian tubes—Motility
Motilon Indians
UF Bari Indians
Chake Indians
Motilone Indians
Motilones
Mutilones
BT Indians of South America
NT Yupa Indians
Motilon language
[PM6571]
UF Bari language (Venezuela)
BT Indians of South America—Languages
Motilone Indians
USE Motilon Indians
Motilones
USE Motilon Indians
Motion
[QA801-QA935 (Analytic mechanics)]
[QC122-QC168 (Physics)]
UF Kinetics
BT Dynamics
Physics
RT Force and energy
Kinematics
Mechanics

NT Acceleration (Mechanics)
Centripetal force
Harmonic motion
Impetus theory
Liapunov functions
Mechanical movements
Movement, Psychology of
Perpetual motion
Robots—Motion
Rotational motion
Speed
Stability
Motion, Chandler
USE Polar wandering
Motion, Compensatory
USE Irritability
Motion, Perpetual
USE Perpetual motion
Motion control, Incremental
USE Incremental motion control
Motion equations
USE Equations of motion
Motion in line of sight of stars
USE Stars—Motion in line of sight
Motion of stars in line of sight
USE Stars—Motion in line of sight
Motion of the solar system in space
USE Solar system—Motion in space
Motion perception (Vision)
UF Speed perception
BT Movement, Psychology of
Vision
Visual perception
Motion-picture . . .
USE *subject headings beginning with the
words* Moving-picture
Motion pictures
USE Moving-pictures
Motion sickness
[RC103.M6]
UF Airsickness
Car sickness
Seasickness
Motion study
[T60.M65]
BT Methods engineering
Personnel management
Production standards
RT Movement, Psychology of
Time study
NT Therbligs
Motions (Law) *(May Subd Geog)*
BT Civil procedure
Criminal procedure
Trial practice
NT Arrest of judgment
Motivation, Intrinsic
USE Intrinsic motivation
Motivation (Psychology)
[BF199 (Physiological psychology)]
[BF683 (Comparative psychology)]
UF Drive (Psychology)
BT Psychology
NT Achievement motivation
Burn out (Psychology)
Cognitive dissonance
Competition (Psychology)
Conflict (Psychology)
Employee motivation
Expectation (Psychology)
Goal (Psychology)
Incentive (Psychology)
Interruption (Psychology)
Intimidation
Intrinsic motivation
Job enrichment
Motivation in adult education
Motivation in education
Motivation research (Marketing)
Need (Psychology)
Punishment (Psychology)

Motivation (Psychology) *(Continued)*
    Remotivation therapy
    Reward (Psychology)
    Risk-taking (Psychology)
    Self-actualization (Psychology)
    Social desirability
    Social facilitation
    Threat (Psychology)
    Wishes
  — **Testing**
    BT Psychological tests
  — **Therapeutic use**
    USE Remotivation therapy
Motivation in adult education
  (May Subd Geog)
  UF Adult education—Motivation
  BT Motivation (Psychology)
Motivation in Christian education
  BT Christian education
Motivation in education
  UF Academic motivation
  BT Academic achievement
    Learning, Psychology of
    Motivation (Psychology)
Motivation in industry
  USE Employee motivation
Motivation in religious education
  UF Religious education—Motivation
  BT Religious education
    Religious education—Psychology
Motivation in sports
  USE Sports—Psychological aspects
Motivation research (Marketing)
  BT Advertising—Psychological aspects
    Marketing research
    Motivation (Psychology)
    Research
Motive (Islamic law)
Motive (Law) *(May Subd Geog)*
  BT Declaration of intention
  RT Consideration (Law)
    Mistake (Law)
Motives, themes
  USE *subdivisions* Themes, motives *under
    literary or art forms or under names
    of persons other than literary
    authors and* Themes, motives,
    Literary *under music compositions
    for general discussions of the
    themes, etc., occurring or possible
    in the form or in the person's
    creative work*
Motley
  BT Fools and jesters
Motmotidae
  USE Momotidae
Motmots
  USE Momotidae
Moto-cross
  USE Motocross
Moto Guzzi motorcycle
  [TL448.M]
  UF Guzzi motorcycle
  BT Motorcycles
Motochintlec language
  USE Mochó language
Motocross *(May Subd Geog)*
  [GV1060.12]
  UF Cross-country motorcycle racing
    Enduro motorcycle racing
    Moto-cross
  BT All terrain vehicle racing
    Motorcycle racing
  NT Bicycle motocross
Motojuku Iseki (Japan)
  USE Motojuku Site (Japan)
Motojuku Site (Japan) *(Not Subd Geog)*
  UF Motojuku Iseki (Japan)
  BT Japan—Antiquities
Motoneuron transmission
  USE Neuromuscular transmission

Motoneurons
  USE Motor neurons
Motor ability
  UF Agility
    Dexterity
    Manual dexterity
    Manual skill
    Motor dexterity
    Motor skill
    Muscular coordination
  BT Ability
    Movement, Psychology of
  RT Kinesiology
    Mechanical ability
  NT Clumsiness
  — **Testing**
    UF Psychomotor tests
    BT Ability—Testing
    NT Lincoln-Oseretsky motor
      development scale
Motor ability and intelligence
  (May Subd Geog)
  [BF433.M68 (Psychology)]
  UF Intelligence and motor ability
  BT Intellect
Motor ability in children
  [BF723.M6 (Child psychology)]
  UF Motor development in children
  BT Child development
    Perceptual-motor learning
  RT Physical education for children
  NT Movement disorders in children
Motor-boat engines
  USE Motorboats—Motors
Motor-boat racing
  USE Motorboat racing
Motor-boats
  USE Motorboats
Motor buses
  USE Buses
Motor carriages, Gun
  USE Tank destroyers
Motor carrier rates
  USE Transportation, Automotive—Rates
Motor carriers
  USE Transportation, Automotive
Motor-cars
  USE Automobiles
    Railroad motor-cars
    Steam motor-cars
Motor cortex
  BT Frontal lobes
Motor courts
  USE Motels
Motor development in children
  USE Motor ability in children
Motor dexterity
  USE Motor ability
Motor disorders, Esophageal
  USE Esophagus—Motility—Disorders
Motor end plate
  USE Myoneural junction
Motor engines
  USE Motors
Motor fleets
  USE Motor vehicle fleets
Motor fuel additives industry
  (May Subd Geog)
  [HD9660.M77-774]
  BT Motor fuels—Additives
Motor fuels
  [TP343]
  UF Automotive fuels
  BT Fuel
  RT Automobiles—Misfueling
  NT Acetylene as fuel
    Airplanes—Fuel
    Alcohol as fuel
    Automobiles—Fuel consumption
    Benzene as fuel
    Diesel fuels

    Internal combustion engines, Spark
      ignition—Alternate fuels
    Jet planes—Fuel
    Liquid fuels
    Motorboats—Fuel
    Petroleum as fuel
    Petroleum products
  — **Additives**
    [TP343]
    NT Motor fuel additives industry
  — **Anti-knock and anti-knock mixtures**
    UF Anti-knock compounds
      Octane number
    RT Automobiles—Motors—Knock
    NT Gasoline—Anti-knock and anti-
      knock mixtures
  — **Taxation** *(May Subd Geog)*
    [HD9579.G4 (Gasoline)]
    Here are entered works on the taxation of
    gasoline as a motor fuel. General works on the
    taxation of gasoline are entered under Gasoline
    —Taxation.
    UF Highway taxes
  — — **Law and legislation**
    (May Subd Geog)
Motor graders
  USE Graders (Earthmoving machinery)
Motor homes
  USE Campers and coaches, Truck
Motor hotels
  USE Motels
Motor industry *(May Subd Geog)*
  [HD9705.5.M67-HD9705.5.M674]
Motor inns
  USE Motels
Motor learning
  UF Motor skill learning
  BT Learning, Psychology of
    Movement, Psychology of
    Physical education and training
  RT Movement education
  NT Perceptual-motor learning
Motor lodges
  USE Motels
Motor nervous system
  USE Efferent pathways
Motor neuron transmission
  USE Neuromuscular transmission
Motor neurons
  UF Anterior horn cells
    Brain motor cells
    Motoneurons
  BT Brain
    Cells
    Neurons
    Spinal cord
Motor oils
  USE Lubricating oils
Motor pathways
  USE Efferent pathways
Motor psychology
  USE Movement, Psychology of
Motor sailers
  UF Motorsailers
  BT Boats and boating
    Motorboats
    Sailboats
Motor scooters
  [TL450]
  UF Scooters, Motor
  BT Motorcycles
  SA *names of motor scooters, e.g.*
    Lambretta motor scooter
  NT Honda motor scooters
    Tul'skiĭ motor scooter
Motor-ships *(May Subd Geog)*
  [VM315]
Motor skill
  USE Motor ability
Motor skill learning
  USE Motor learning

Motor sledges
  UF Aerosleighs
  BT Sleighs and sledges
Motor sports
  USE Motorsports
Motor torpedo boats
  USE Torpedo-boats
Motor tracts
  USE Efferent pathways
Motor transportation
  USE Transportation, Automotive
Motor-truck drivers
  USE Truck drivers
Motor-truck driving
  USE Truck driving
Motor-truck parking
  USE Truck parking
Motor-truck terminals
  USE Truck terminals
Motor-trucks
  USE Trucks
Motor-trucks, Military
  USE Trucks, Military
Motor vehicle bearings
  USE Motor vehicles—Bearings
Motor vehicle bodies
  USE Motor vehicles—Bodies
Motor vehicle drivers *(May Subd Geog)*
  UF Drivers, Motor vehicle
      Motor vehicle operators
      Operators, Motor vehicle
  RT Motor vehicle driving
  NT Ambulance drivers
      Automobile drivers
      Bus drivers
      Motorcyclists
      Postal service—Motor vehicle
        operators
      Truck drivers
Motor vehicle driving
  UF Driving, Motor vehicle
      Motor vehicle operation
  BT Motor vehicles
  RT Motor vehicle drivers
  NT Ambulance driving
      Automobile driving
      Fire engine driving
      Tractor driving
      Truck driving
  — Vocational guidance
Motor vehicle fleets
  [TL165]
  UF Automotive fleets
      Fleets, Motor vehicle
      Motor fleets
  BT Motor vehicles
  — Safety measures
    BT Traffic safety
Motor vehicle fuel systems
  USE Motor vehicles—Fuel systems
Motor vehicle operation
  USE Motor vehicle driving
Motor vehicle operators
  USE Motor vehicle drivers
Motor vehicle scales *(May Subd Geog)*
  UF Automobile scales
      Roads—Weigh stations
      Truck scales
      Weigh stations (Motor vehicles)
  BT Scales (Weighing instruments)
Motor vehicle sports
  USE Motorsports
Motor vehicle sun visors, Tariff on
  USE Tariff on motor vehicle sun visors
Motor vehicle transmissions
  USE Motor vehicles—Transmission devices
Motor vehicles *(May Subd Geog)*
  [TL]
  UF Automotive vehicles
  BT Transportation, Automotive
      Vehicles

  NT All terrain vehicles
      Automobiles
      Commercial vehicles
      Disabled vehicles on express highways
      Dune buggies
      Electric vehicles
      Emergency vehicles
      Graders (Earthmoving machinery)
      Ground-effect machines
      Hearses (Vehicles)
      Moon cars
      Motor vehicle driving
      Motor vehicle fleets
      Motor vehicles, Amphibious
      Motorcycles
      Police vehicles
      Road-rail vehicles
      Roving vehicles (Astronautics)
      Trafficability
      Trucks
  — Appraisal
    USE Motor vehicles—Valuation
  — **Automatic location systems**
    UF Automatic location systems for
        motor vehicles
        Location systems for motor
          vehicles, Automatic
        Vehicle locator systems
  — **Batteries**
    [TL272]
  — **Bearings**
    UF Motor vehicle bearings
  — **Bodies**
    UF Motor vehicle bodies
    BT Motor vehicles—Design and
        construction
  — **Brakes**
  — **Cold weather operation**
    NT Automobiles—Cold weather
        operation
  — **Design and construction**
    NT Motor vehicles—Bodies
  — Diesel motors
    USE Motor vehicles—Motors (Diesel)
  — **Dynamics**
    BT Mechanics, Applied
    NT Motor vehicles—Skidding
  — **Electric equipment**
  — **Electronic equipment**
    [TL272.5]
    UF Automotive electronics
  — Emission control devices
    USE Motor vehicles—Pollution control
        devices
  — Exhaust control devices
    USE Motor vehicles—Pollution control
        devices
  — **Fuel consumption**
  — **Fuel systems**
    UF Motor vehicle fuel systems
    BT Fuel pumps
  — Gearing
    USE Motor vehicles—Transmission
        devices
  — **Inspection** *(May Subd Geog)*
    BT Traffic safety
  — **Lubrication**
    NT Automobiles—Lubrication
  — **Maintenance and repair**
    UF Motor vehicles—Repairing
        Motor vehicles—Servicing
  — **Models**
    [TL237]
    NT Corgi toys
  — — **Radio control**
  — **Motors**
  — — **Air filters**
      BT Air filters
  — — **Carburetors**
  — — **Superchargers**
      UF Motor vehicles—Superchargers

  — **Motors (Diesel)**
    UF Motor vehicles—Diesel motors
      Motor vehicles, Diesel
  — **Painting**
  — **Pneumatic equipment**
  — **Pollution control devices**
    [TL214.P6]
    UF Emission control devices (Motor
        vehicles)
      Exhaust control devices (Motor
        vehicles)
      Motor vehicles—Emission control
        devices
      Motor vehicles—Exhaust control
        devices
      Motor vehicles—Smog control
        devices
      Pollution control devices (Motor
        vehicles)
      Smog control devices (Motor
        vehicles)
    BT Air—Pollution
      Pollution control equipment
  — Products liability
    USE Products liability—Motor
        vehicles
  — **Recreational use**
    Here are entered works on the use of various
    vehicles for recreational purposes, such as snow-
    mobiles, dune buggies, etc. Works on vehicles for
    recreational travel living, such as motor homes,
    campers, etc., are entered under Recreational
    vehicles.
    UF Recreational motor vehicles
    RT Recreational vehicles
    NT Motorsports
  — Repairing
    USE Motor vehicles—Maintenance
        and repair
  — Servicing
    USE Motor vehicles—Maintenance
        and repair
  — **Shock absorbers**
    UF Shock absorbers, Motor vehicle
  — **Skidding**
    UF Skidding of automobiles
    BT Motor vehicles—Dynamics
      Motor vehicles—Tires
      Roads
      Slush on pavements, runways, etc.
      Traffic accidents
    RT Tires, Rubber—Traction
    NT Pavements—Skid resistance
  — Smog control devices
    USE Motor vehicles—Pollution control
        devices
  — **Springs and suspension**
    UF Motor vehicles—Suspension
  — **Standards** *(May Subd Geog)*
  — — **Law and legislation**
      (May Subd Geog)
  — **Steering-gear**
    BT Steering-gear
  — Superchargers
    USE Motor vehicles—Motors—
        Superchargers
  — Suspension
    USE Motor vehicles—Springs and
        suspension
  — **Testing**
    [TL285]
  — **Tires**
    NT Automobiles—Tires
      Motor vehicles—Skidding
  — — **Law and legislation**
      (May Subd Geog)
  — **Transmission devices**
    UF Motor vehicle transmissions
      Motor vehicles—Gearing
    BT Gearing
  — **Transmission devices, Automatic**

Motor vehicles *(Continued)*
— **Valuation**
    UF Motor vehicles—Appraisal
— **Vibration**
— **Welding**
Motor vehicles, American, ⌜**British, Russian, etc.**⌝
Motor vehicles, Amphibious
    ⌜*TL229.A*⌝
    ⌜*V880 (Naval science)*⌝
    UF Amphibious motor vehicles
    BT Motor vehicles
        Vehicles, Military
    NT Landing craft
        Tracked landing vehicles
Motor vehicles, Diesel
    USE Motor vehicles—Motors (Diesel)
Motor vehicles in motion pictures
    BT Moving-pictures
Motor vehicles in war
    USE Automobiles, Military
        Motorization, Military
        Tanks (Military science)
        Transportation, Military
Motorboat engines
    USE Motorboats—Motors
Motorboat racing *(May Subd Geog)*
    ⌜*GV835.9*⌝
    UF Boat-racing
        Motor-boat racing
    BT Racing
Motorboats *(May Subd Geog)*
    ⌜*GV833.5-GV835.9 (Sports)*⌝
    ⌜*VM340-VM349 (Naval architecture)*⌝
    UF Cabin cruisers
        Motor-boats
        Powerboats
        Speedboats
    BT Boats and boating
    NT Hydroplanes
        Jet boats
        Launches
        Motor sailers
        Outboard motorboats
— **Accidents**
— **Fuel**
    BT Motor fuels
— — **Taxation** *(May Subd Geog)*
— — — **Law and legislation**
        (May Subd Geog)
— **Gasoline engines**
    ⌜*VM771*⌝
    BT Motorboats—Motors
    NT Outboard motors
— **Models**
    ⌜*VM342*⌝
    BT Ship models
— — **Radio control**
— **Motors**
    UF Motor-boat engines
        Motorboat engines
    BT Internal combustion engines
        Marine engines
    NT Inboard-outboard engines
        Jet boat engines
        Marine diesel motors
        Motorboats—Gasoline engines
        Outboard motors
— **Registration and transfer**
    (May Subd Geog)
    UF Registration of motorboats
    BT Recording and registration
— **Speed**
    UF Speed of motorboats
    NT Motorboats—Speed records
— **Speed records**
    UF Speed records of motorboats
    BT Motorboats—Speed
Motorcycle accessories industry
    USE Motorcycle supplies industry

Motorcycle gangs *(May Subd Geog)*
    ⌜*HV6486-6491*⌝
    UF Gangs, Motorcycle
    BT Motorcycles—Societies, etc.
Motorcycle industry *(May Subd Geog)*
    NT Motorcycle industry workers
Motorcycle industry workers
    (May Subd Geog)
    ⌜*HD8039.M84*⌝
    BT Motorcycle industry
    NT Trade-unions—Motorcycle industry
        workers
Motorcycle parking *(May Subd Geog)*
    UF Motorcycles—Parking
        Parking, Motorcycle
Motorcycle parts industry
    USE Motorcycle supplies industry
Motorcycle prices
    USE Motorcycles—Prices
Motorcycle racing *(May Subd Geog)*
    ⌜*GV1060*⌝
    BT Motorsports
        Racing
    NT International Six Days Trial
        Minibike racing
        Motocross
        Sidecar motorcycle racing
        Speedway motorcycle racing
        Tourist Trophy Road Race
— **Florida**
    NT Daytona 200 Motorcycle Race
Motorcycle racing on ice
    BT Winter sports
Motorcycle soccer
    ⌜*GV1060.15*⌝
    BT Soccer
Motorcycle stealing
    USE Motorcycle theft
Motorcycle supplies industry
    (May Subd Geog)
    UF Motorcycle accessories industry
        Motorcycle parts industry
    BT Motorcycles—Equipment and supplies
        Motorcycles—Parts
Motorcycle theft *(May Subd Geog)*
    UF Motorcycle stealing
    BT Crime and criminals
        Larceny
        Motorcycles
    NT Motorcycle theft investigation
Motorcycle theft investigation
    (May Subd Geog)
    BT Criminal investigation
        Motorcycle theft
Motorcycle troops of United States Marine Corps
    USE United States. Marine Corps—
        Motorcycle troops
Motorcycles *(May Subd Geog)*
    ⌜*TL439-448*⌝
    UF Bikes
        Cycles, Motor
    BT Automobiles
        Motor vehicles
        Vehicles
    RT Bicycles
    SA *names of motorcycles, e.g.* Vespa
        motorcycle
    NT Ariel motorcycle
        Brough Superior motorcycle
        Cycle-cars
        CZ motorcycle
        Husqvarna motorcycle
        Matchless motorcycle
        Minibikes
        Minicycles
        Mopeds
        Moto Guzzi motorcycle
        Motor scooters
        Motorcycle theft
        Motorcycles, Military

        Motorcycles, Racing
        Motorcycling
        MV Agusta motorcycle
        Royal Enfield motorcycle
        Sunbeam motorcycle
        Used motorcycles
— **Electric equipment**
    ⌜*TL445*⌝
— **Equipment and supplies**
    NT Motorcycle supplies industry
— **Law and legislation** *(May Subd Geog)*
— **Maintenance and repair**
    UF Motorcycles—Repairing
— **Motors**
— — **Carburetors**
— **Motors (Two-stroke cycle)**
    UF Motorcycles—Two-stroke cycle
        motors
        Two-stroke cycle motorcycle
        motors
— **Parking**
    USE Motorcycle parking
— **Parts**
    NT Motorcycle supplies industry
— **Prices** *(May Subd Geog)*
    ⌜*HD9710.5*⌝
    UF Motorcycle prices
— **Repairing**
    USE Motorcycles—Maintenance and
        repair
— **Societies, etc.**
    NT Motorcycle gangs
— **Two-stroke cycle motors**
    USE Motorcycles—Motors (Two-
        stroke cycle)
Motorcycles, American, ⌜**British, Russian, etc.**⌝
Motorcycles, British
    NT Vincent H.R.D. motorcycle
Motorcycles, Military *(May Subd Geog)*
    ⌜*UG615-UG620*⌝
    UF Military motorcycles
    BT Motorcycles
        Vehicles, Military
Motorcycles, Racing *(May Subd Geog)*
    UF Racing motorcycles
    BT Motorcycles
    NT MV Agusta motorcycle
Motorcycling *(May Subd Geog)*
    ⌜*GV1059.5*⌝
    BT Cycling
        Motorcycles
    NT Stunt cycling
Motorcyclists *(May Subd Geog)*
    ⌜*TL440.2*⌝
    BT Motor vehicle drivers
    NT Women motorcyclists
— **Personality**
    USE Motorcyclists—Psychology
— **Psychology**
    UF Motorcyclists—Personality
Motorists
    USE Automobile drivers
Motorization, Military *(May Subd Geog)*
    ⌜*UC340-UC345*⌝
    Here are entered works on the equipping of a military force with motor vehicles for the purpose of transporting its personnel, weapons and equipment. Works on the equipping of a military force with armed and armored motor vehicles in which the force travels and engages in combat are entered under Mechanization, Military.
    UF Armies—Motorization
        Army motorization
        Military motorization
        Motor vehicles in war
        Motorized troops
    BT Military art and science
        Tanks (Military science)
        Transportation, Automotive
        Transportation, Military
    RT Mechanization, Military

NT Automobiles, Military
   Trucks, Military
Motorized bicycles
  USE Mopeds
Motorized troops
  USE Motorization, Military
Motorless flight
  USE Gliding and soaring
Motorola 6800 (Microprocessor)
  QA76.8.M
  BT Microprocessors
Motorola 6801 (Computer)
  QA76.8.M
  BT Microcomputers
     Motorola computers
— **Programming**
Motorola 6802 (Microprocessor)
  QA76.8.M
  UF M6802 (Microprocessor)
  BT Microprocessors
Motorola 6803 (Computer)
  QA76.8.M
  BT Microcomputers
     Motorola computers
— **Programming**
Motorola 6809 (Computer)
  QA76.8.M
  BT Microcomputers
     Motorola computers
Motorola 68000 (Microprocessor)
  UF 68000 (Microprocessor)
     MC68000 (Microprocessor)
  BT Motorola 68000 series microprocessors
Motorola 68000 series microprocessors
  NT Motorola 68000 (Microprocessor)
     Motorola 68010 (Microprocessor)
     Motorola 68020 (Microprocessor)
     Motorola 68851 (Microprocessor)
Motorola 68010 (Microprocessor)
  UF 68010 (Microprocessor)
     MC68010 (Microprocessor)
  BT Motorola 68000 series microprocessors
Motorola 68020 (Microprocessor)
  QA76.8.M
  UF 68020 (Microprocessor)
     MC68020 (Microprocessor)
  BT Motorola 68000 series microprocessors
Motorola 68701 (Computer)
  QA76.8.M
  BT Microcomputers
     Motorola computers
— **Programming**
Motorola 68851 (Microprocessor)
  QA76.8.M
  UF 68851 (Microprocessor)
     MC68851 (Microprocessor)
  BT Motorola 68000 series microprocessors
Motorola computers
  QA76.8.M
  BT Microcomputers
  NT Motorola 6801 (Computer)
     Motorola 6803 (Computer)
     Motorola 6809 (Computer)
     Motorola 68701 (Computer)
     Motorola M6800 series (Computers)
— **Programming**
Motorola M6800 series (Computers)
  BT Microcomputers
     Motorola computers
Motors
  HD9685-HD9712 (Economics)
  TJ (Technology)
  UF Motor engines
  BT Engines
     Power (Mechanics)
     Power transmission
  RT Machinery
  SA *subdivision* Motors *under subjects, e.g.*
     Automobiles—Motors; Models and
     modelmaking—Motors
  NT Airplanes, Home-built—Motors

Alcohol motors
Diesel motor
Electric motors
Electric railway motors
Hydraulic motors
Internal combustion engines
Internal combustion engines, Spark
  ignition
Outboard motors
Motorsailers
  USE Motor sailers
Motorsports *(May Subd Geog)*
  GV1019.2
  UF Motor sports
     Motor vehicle sports
  BT Motor vehicles—Recreational use
     Sports
  NT All terrain vehicle racing
     Automobile racing
     Automobile rallies
     Motorcycle racing
Motorways
  USE Express highways
Mototzintlec language
  USE Mochó language
Motozintlec language
  USE Mochó language
Mott family *(Not Subd Geog)*
  UF Mot family
     Mote family
     Motes family
     Motte family
     Motts family
     Motz family
Motte family
  USE Mott family
Mottle-leaf
  SB608.C5 (Citrus diseases)
Mottled enamel
  RK341
  UF Dental fluorosis
     Endemic dental fluorosis
  BT Fluorine—Physiological effect
     Fluorosis
     Teeth—Discoloration
     Teeth—Diseases
Mottled sculpin
  USE Cottus bairdii
Mottled swift
  UF Apus aequatorialis
Mottoes
  CR73-CR75 (Heraldry)
  PN6309-PN6318
  BT Emblems
     Heraldry
     Proverbs
  RT Devices
  NT Slogans
Motts family
  USE Mott family
Motu (Papua New Guinea people)
  BT Ethnology—Papua New Guinea
Motu language
  PL6257
  BT Melanesian languages
  NT Hiri Motu language
Motu-Motu (Papua New Guinea people)
  USE Toaripi (Papua New Guinea people)
Motugaugau (Cook Islands)
  USE Nassau Island (Cook Islands)
Motuna language
  USE Siwai language
Motya (Ancient city) *(Not Subd Geog)*
  DG70.M67
  UF Motia (Ancient city)
     Motye (Ancient city)
     Mozia (Ancient city)
  BT Cities and towns, Ruined, extinct, etc.
     —Italy
     Italy—Antiquities

Motye (Ancient city)
  USE Motya (Ancient city)
Motz family
  USE Mott family
Motzi (Romanian people)
  USE Moţi (Romanian people)
Mou (Southeast Asian people)
  USE Khmu' (Southeast Asian people)
Moubray family
  USE Mowbray family
Moubrey family
  USE Mowbray family
Mouchy Castle (Mouchy-le-Châtel, France)
  USE Château de Mouchy (Mouchy-le-
     Châtel, France)
Moudy family
  USE Moody family
Moufang loops
  UF Loops, Moufang
  BT Loops (Group theory)
Moufflon
  USE Mouflon
Mouflon
  UF Moufflon
     Muflon
     Ovis musimon
  BT Mountain sheep
Mouile Indians
  USE Mobile Indians
Moulage in medicine
  QM33 (Human anatomy)
  RB35 (Pathology)
  UF Molding (Clay, plaster, etc.)
  BT Biological models
     Medical illustration
     Models (Clay, plaster, etc.)
  NT Anatomy, Human—Models
     Dental impressions
     Plaster casts, Surgical
     Prosthesis
Mould, Vegetable
  USE Humus
     Soils
Mould (Botany)
  USE Molds (Botany)
Mould family *(Not Subd Geog)*
  UF Moulder family
Moulder family
  USE Mould family
Moulding (Metal)
  USE Molding (Founding)
Moulding sand
  USE Sand, Foundry
Mouldings
  USE Moldings
Moulds (Cookware)
  USE Molds (Cookware)
Moulison family
  USE Mullison family
Moulsham Street (Chelmsford, Essex)
  BT Streets—England
Moulson family
  USE Molson family
     Mullison family
Moulten family
  USE Moulton family
Moulting
  USE Molting
Moulting hormone
  USE Ecdysone
Moulting in arthropods and reptiles
  USE Ecdysis
Moulton family *(Not Subd Geog)*
  UF Moleton family
     Molten family
     Molthen family
     Molton family
     Moulten family
     Multon family
Moulton planes
  UF Planes, Moulton

Moulton planes *(Continued)*
  BT Geometry, Affine
Moultrie, Fort, Battle of, 1776
  [E241.M9]
  UF Sullivan's Island, Battle of
  BT Charleston (S.C.)—History—
      Revolution, 1775-1783
      South Carolina—History—Revolution,
      1775-1783
      United States—History—Revolution,
      1775-1783—Campaigns
Mounce family
  USE Mount family
Mound-builders *(May Subd Geog)*
  [E73-74]
  BT Indians of North America
      Indians of North America—Antiquities
  NT Adena culture
      Bocootawwonauke Indians
      Hopewell culture
      Mississippian culture
  — Art
    [E73]
    BT Indians of North America—Art
  — Implements
    [E73]
  — Iowa
  — Louisiana
    NT Tchefuncte culture
  — Southern States
    NT Poverty Point culture
Mound Cemetery (Marietta, Ohio)
  BT Cemeteries—Ohio
      Mounds—Ohio
Mound Grove Memorial Park (Evansville, Minn.)
  BT Parks—Minnesota
Mound State Monument (Ala.)
  (Not Subd Geog)
  UF Moundville site (Ala.)
  BT Alabama—Antiquities
      Mounds—Alabama
      Parks—Alabama
Moundan (African people)
  USE Mundang (African people)
Moundang (African people)
  USE Mundang (African people)
Mounds *(May Subd Geog)*
  [GN795-6]
  UF Barrows
      Graves
      Tumuli
  BT Archaeology
      Burial
      Cairns
      Dead
      Fortification, Primitive
      Indians of North America—Antiquities
      Tombs
  RT Earthworks (Archaeology)
      Kitchen-middens
  NT Ship burial
  — Alabama
    NT Mound State Monument (Ala.)
      Murphy Hill Site (Ala.)
  — Arkansas
  — Belize
    NT Mamey Hill Site (Belize)
  — Colombia
    NT Monsú Site (Colombia)
  — Ecuador
  — England
  — Europe
    NT Tumulus culture
  — Florida
  — Guatemala
    NT Culebra, Gran Monticulo de la
      (Guatemala, Guatemala)
  — Illinois
  — Iowa
  — Mississippi

    NT Lake George Site (Miss.)
  — Ohio
    NT Edwin Harness Mound (Ohio)
      Mound Cemetery (Marietta, Ohio)
  — Oklahoma
  — Rhine River Valley
    BT Hallstatt period
      La Téne period
  — Tennessee
    NT Pinson Mounds Site (Tenn.)
  — Turkey
    NT Maşat Mound (Turkey)
  — Utah
Mounds State Park (Ind.)
  BT Parks—Indiana
Moundville site (Ala.)
  USE Mound State Monument (Ala.)
Mounier family *(Not Subd Geog)*
  UF Mousnier family
  RT Miller family
Mount Aconcagua (Argentina)
  USE Aconcagua, Mount (Argentina)
Mount Ainslie (A.C.T.)
  UF Mt. Ainslie (A.C.T.)
  BT Mountains—Australia
Mount Alexander (Vic.)
  USE Alexander, Mount (Vic.)
Mount Anchesmos (Greece)
  USE Tourkovouni (Greece)
Mount Ararat (Turkey)
  USE Ararat, Mount (Turkey)
Mount Aspiring National Park (N.Z.)
  BT National parks and reserves—New
      Zealand
      Parks—New Zealand
Mount Assiniboine Provincial Park (B.C.)
  UF Mt. Assiniboine Provincial Park (B.C.)
  BT Parks—British Columbia
Mount Auburn Catholic Cemetery (Watertown, Mass.)
  UF Mt. Auburn Catholic Cemetery
      (Watertown, Mass.)
      Sand Banks Cemetery (Watertown,
      Mass.)
  BT Cemeteries—Massachusetts
Mount Auckland (Korea)
  USE Halla Mountain (Korea)
Mount Baker (Wash.)
  USE Baker, Mount (Wash.)
Mount Buffalo National Park (Vic.)
  BT National parks and reserves—Australia
Mount Calvary Cemetery (Baltimore, Md.)
  BT Cemeteries—Maryland
Mount Carmel (Israel)
  USE Carmel, Mount (Israel)
Mount Carmel Cemetery (El Paso, Tex.)
  UF Mt. Carmel Cemetery (El Paso, Tex.)
  BT Cemeteries—Texas
Mount Castleguard (Alta.)
  USE Castleguard, Mount (Alta.)
Mount Clare (Baltimore, Md. : Building)
  BT Dwellings—Maryland
Mount Comfort Plantation (Va.)
  UF Mt. Comfort Plantation (Va.)
  BT Plantations—Virginia
Mount Cook National Park (N.Z.)
  BT National parks and reserves—New
      Zealand
      Parks—New Zealand
Mount Cotopaxi (Ecuador)
  USE Cotopaxi Mountain (Ecuador)
Mount Cuchama (Calif.)
  USE Tecate Peak (Calif.)
Mount Desert Island (Me.)
  BT Islands—Maine
  NT Acadia National Park (Me.)
Mount Egmont National Park (N.Z.)
  USE Egmont National Park (N.Z.)
Mount Etna (Sicily)
  USE Etna, Mount (Sicily)

Mount Everest (China and Nepal)
  USE Everest, Mount (China and Nepal)
Mount Everest Expedition, 1921
  [DS486.E8]
Mount Everest Expedition, 1922
  [DS486.E8]
Mount Everest Expedition, 1924
  [DS486.E8]
Mount Everest Expedition, 1938
  [DS486.E8]
Mount Everest National Park (Nepal)
  USE Sagarmāthā National Park (Nepal)
Mount family *(Not Subd Geog)*
  UF Mont family
      Montz family
      Mounce family
      Mounts family
      Mountz family
Mount Field National Park (Tas.)
  BT National parks and reserves—Australia
Mount Fuji (Japan)
  USE Fuji, Mount (Japan)
Mount Godwin Austen (Pakistan)
  USE K2 (Pakistan : Mountain)
Mount Goverla (Ukraine)
  USE Goverla, Mount (Ukraine)
Mount Grafton Wilderness (Nev.)
  (Not Subd Geog)
  UF Mount Grafton Wilderness Study Area
      (Nev.)
  BT National parks and reserves—Nevada
      Wilderness areas—Nevada
Mount Grafton Wilderness Study Area (Nev.)
  USE Mount Grafton Wilderness (Nev.)
Mount Greylock State Reservation (Mass.)
  UF Greylock Reservation (Mass.)
  BT Parks—Massachusetts
Mount Hakone (Japan)
  USE Hakone, Mount (Japan)
Mount Halla (Korea)
  USE Halla Mountain (Korea)
Mount Hamilton Range (Calif.)
  USE Hamilton Range, Mount (Calif.)
Mount Hármashatár (Budapest, Hungary)
  USE Hármashatár, Mount (Budapest,
      Hungary)
Mount Hood (Or.)
  USE Hood, Mount (Or.)
Mount Hope Cemetery (Kitchener, Ont.)
  USE Kitchener Mount Hope Cemetery
      (Kitchener, Ont.)
Mount Isa Mines, ltd. Strike, 1964-1965
Mount Ishizuchi (Japan)
  USE Ishizuchi, Mount (Japan)
Mount Island Lake (N.C.)
  USE Mountain Island Lake (N.C.)
Mount Jefferson Wilderness (Or.)
  BT National parks and reserves—United
      States
      Wilderness areas—Oregon
Mount Katahdin (Me.)
  USE Katahdin, Mount (Me.)
Mount Kenya (Kenya)
  USE Kenya, Mount (Kenya)
Mount Kilimanjaro (Tanzania)
  USE Kilimanjaro, Mount (Tanzania)
Mount Kongur (China)
  USE Konger Mount (China)
Mount Ktaadn (Me.)
  USE Katahdin, Mount (Me.)
Mount Kuju (Japan)
  USE Kuju, Mount (Japan)
Mount Kulal (Kenya)
  USE Kulal, Mount (Kenya)
Mount Lassen (Calif.)
  USE Lassen Peak (Calif.)
Mount Le Conte (Tenn.)
  USE LeConte, Mount (Tenn.)
Mount LeConte (Tenn.)
  USE LeConte, Mount (Tenn.)

Mount Lemmon (Ariz.)
  USE Lemmon, Mount (Ariz.)
Mount Lemon (Ariz.)
  USE Lemmon, Mount (Ariz.)
Mount Limbo Wilderness (Nev.)
  UF Mount Limbo Wilderness Study Area
      (Nev.)
  BT National parks and reserves—Nevada
      Wilderness areas—Nevada
Mount Limbo Wilderness Study Area (Nev.)
  USE Mount Limbo Wilderness (Nev.)
Mount McKinley (Alaska)
  USE McKinley, Mount (Alaska)
Mount McKinley National Park (Alaska)
  USE Denali National Park and Preserve
      (Alaska)
Mount Mitchell (N.C.) *(Not Subd Geog)*
  UF Mt. Mitchell (N.C.)
  BT Black Mountains (N.C.)
      Mountains—North Carolina
Mount Moriah (Deadwood, S.D.)
  BT Cemeteries—South Dakota
Mount Moriah (Jerusalem)
  USE Temple Mount (Jerusalem)
Mount Odae (Korea)
  USE Odae Mountain (Korea)
Mount of Olives (Jerusalem)
  UF Har ha-Zetim (Jerusalem)
      Mount of Olivet (Jerusalem)
      Olives, Mount of (Jerusalem)
      Olivet, Mount of (Jerusalem)
      Ṭūr, Jabal al- (Jerusalem)
      Zaytūn, Jabal al- (Jerusalem)
      Zetim, Har ha- (Jerusalem)
  BT Mountains—Jerusalem
Mount of Olivet (Jerusalem)
  USE Mount of Olives (Jerusalem)
Mount Olivet Cemetery (Fowlerville, Mich.)
  UF Mt. Olivet Cemetery (Fowlerville,
      Mich.)
  BT Cemeteries—Michigan
Mount Olympus (Greece)
  USE Olympus, Mount (Greece)
Mount Olympus National Monument (Wash.)
  USE Olympic National Park (Wash.)
Mount Olympus National Park (Wash.)
  USE Olympic National Park (Wash.)
Mount Orford Park (Québec)
  USE Parc du Mont-Orford (Québec)
Mount Otoko (Japan)
  USE Otoko Mountain (Japan)
Mount Ouray (Colo.)
  USE Ouray, Mount (Colo.)
Mount Parnassus (Greece)
  USE Parnassus, Mount (Greece)
Mount Pelée (Martinique)
  USE Pelée, Mount (Martinique)
Mount Pilot Festival
  ₍ML37₎
  BT Music festivals—North Carolina
Mount Pollino (Italy)
  USE Pollino, Mount (Italy)
Mount Popa (Burma)
  USE Popa, Mount (Burma)
Mount Prospect Graveyard and Cemetery
  (Mount Pleasant, Washington County, Pa.)
  (Not Subd Geog)
  BT Cemeteries—Pennsylvania
Mount Rae (Alta.)
  USE Rae, Mount (Alta.)
Mount Rainier (Wash.)
  USE Rainier, Mount (Wash.)
Mount Rainier National Park (Wash.)
  UF Rainier National Park (Wash.)
  BT National parks and reserves—United
      States
      Parks—Washington (State)
  RT Rainier, Mount (Wash.)
Mount Rest Cemetery (Newport, Ill.)
  USE Newport Mount Rest Cemetery
      (Newport, Ill.)

Mount Revelstoke National Park (B.C.)
  UF Mont Revelstoke, Parc national du
      (B.C.)
      Parc national du mont Revelstoke
      (B.C.)
  BT National parks and reserves—British
      Columbia
Mount Richmond State Forest Park (N.Z.)
  (Not Subd Geog)
  UF Mt. Richmond State Forest Park
      (N.Z.)
  BT Forest reserves—New Zealand
      Parks—New Zealand
Mount Rip (Czechoslovakia)
  USE Rip, Mount (Czechoslovakia)
Mount Robson Park (B.C.)
  USE Mount Robson Provincial Park (B.C.)
Mount Robson Provincial Park (B.C.)
  UF Mount Robson Park (B.C.)
      Mt. Robson Provincial Park (B.C.)
  BT Parks—British Columbia
Mount Rogers National Recreation Area (Va.)
  BT National parks and reserves—United
      States
      Recreation areas—Virginia
Mount Roraima
  USE Roraima, Mount
Mount Rushmore National Memorial (S.D.)
  BT Memorials—South Dakota
      National parks and reserves—United
      States
      Parks—South Dakota
      Portrait sculpture—South Dakota
      Presidents—United States—Portraits
Mount Saint Helena (Calif.)
  USE Saint Helena, Mount (Calif.)
Mount Saint Helens (Wash.)
  USE Saint Helens, Mount (Wash.)
Mount Saint Helens National Volcanic Area
  (Wash.)
  USE Mount Saint Helens National Volcanic
      Monument (Wash.)
Mount Saint Helens National Volcanic
  Monument (Wash.)
  UF Mount Saint Helens National Volcanic
      Area (Wash.)
  BT National monuments—Washington
      (State)
  RT Saint Helens, Mount (Wash.)
Mount Shasta (Calif. : Mountain)
  USE Shasta, Mount (Calif.)
Mount Shasta Wilderness (Calif.)
  BT National parks and reserves—United
      States
      Wilderness areas—California
Mount Sinai (Egypt)
  USE Sinai, Mount (Egypt)
Mount Sorenson (Alaska)
  USE Sorenson, Mount (Alaska)
Mount St. Helens (Wash.)
  USE Saint Helens, Mount (Wash.)
Mount Stirling Wilderness (Nev.)
  (Not Subd Geog)
  UF Mount Stirling Wilderness Study Area
      (Nev.)
      Mt. Stirling Wilderness (Nev.)
  BT National parks and reserves—Nevada
      Wilderness areas—Nevada
Mount Stirling Wilderness Study Area (Nev.)
  USE Mount Stirling Wilderness (Nev.)
Mount Suckling (Papua New Guinea)
  USE Suckling, Mount (Papua New Guinea)
Mount Szrenica (Poland)
  USE Szrenica, Mount (Poland)
Mount Taal (Volcano Island, Philippines)
  USE Taal, Mount (Volcano Island,
      Philippines)
Mount Tacoma (Wash.)
  USE Rainier, Mount (Wash.)
Mount Tamalpais (Calif.)
  USE Tamalpais, Mount (Calif.)

Mount Tamalpais and Muir Woods Railroad
  USE Mt. Tamalpais and Muir Woods
      Railroad
Mount Tambora (Sumbawa, Indonesia)
  USE Tambora, Mount (Sumbawa,
      Indonesia)
Mount Taylor (N.M.)
  USE Taylor, Mount (N.M.)
Mount Tecate (Calif.)
  USE Tecate Peak (Calif.)
Mount Toby (Mass.)
  USE Toby, Mount (Mass.)
Mount Tokaj (Hungary)
  USE Tokaj, Mount (Hungary)
Mount Tom (Mass.)
  USE Tom, Mount (Mass.)
Mount Tom State Park (Mass.)
  USE Mount Tom State Reservation (Mass.)
Mount Tom State Reservation (Mass.)
  UF Mount Tom State Park (Mass.)
      Mt. Tom State Park (Mass.)
      Mt. Tom State Reservation (Mass.)
  BT Natural areas—Massachusetts
      Parks—Massachusetts
  RT Tom, Mount (Mass.)
Mount Troodos (Cyprus)
  USE Troodos Mountains (Cyprus)
Mount Tuomuer (China)
  USE Tuomuer Peak (China)
Mount Vernon (Va. : Estate)
  (Not Subd Geog)
  UF Epsewasson (Va.)
      Little Hunting Creek Plantation (Va.)
      Mt. Vernon (Va. : Estate)
  BT Dwellings—Virginia
      Plantations—Virginia
Mount Vernon Memorial Highway (Va.)
  (Not Subd Geog)
  BT George Washington Memorial
      Parkway
      National parks and reserves—Virginia
      Parkways—Virginia
Mount Vernon Place (Baltimore, Md.)
  BT Plazas—Maryland
Mount Vernon Trail (Va.)
  BT George Washington Memorial
      Parkway
      Trails—Virginia
Mount Washington (Baltimore, Md.)
  (Not Subd Geog)
  UF Baltimore (Md.). Mount Washington
Mount Washington (N.H.)
  USE Washington, Mount (N.H.)
Mount Washington Railway
  BT Rack-railroads—United States
      Railroads—United States
Mount Washusett (Mass.)
  USE Wachusett Mountain (Mass.)
Mount Wellington (Tas.)
  USE Wellington, Mount (Tas.)
Mount Whitney (Calif.)
  USE Whitney, Mount (Calif.)
Mount Xixia Bangma (China)
  USE Hsi-hsia-pang-ma Peak (China)
Mount Zion Cemetery (Washington, D.C.)
  UF Female Union Band Society Burying
      Ground (Washington, D.C.)
      Old Methodist Burial Ground
      (Washington, D.C.)
  BT Cemeteries—Washington (D.C.)
Mountague family
  USE Montague family
Mountain agriculture
  USE Hill farming
Mountain alyssum *(May Subd Geog)*
  ₍QK495.C9 (Botany)₎
  UF Alyssum montanum
      Alyssum pedemontanum
  BT Alyssum
Mountain architecture
  USE Hillside architecture

Mountain arnica
    USE Arnica montana
Mountain artillery
    USE Artillery, Field and mountain
Mountain aspen
    USE Populus tremuloides
Mountain beaver
    USE Aplodontia
Mountain bluebird
    ⌈QL696.P288⌉
    UF Sialia currucoides
Mountain churches *(May Subd Geog)*
    BT Churches
Mountain climate
    ⌈QC993.6⌉
    UF Climate, Highland
       Climate, Mountain
       Highland climate
    BT Climatology
       Weather, Influence of mountains on
    SA *subdivision* Climate *under names of*
       individual mountains and mountain
       ranges
    NT Orographic clouds
Mountain climbers
    USE Mountaineers
Mountain climbing
    USE Mountaineering
Mountain collie
    USE Bearded collie
Mountain cranberry
    USE Vaccinium vitis-idaea
Mountain dogs, Swiss
    USE Sennenhunde
Mountain driving
    USE Automobile driving on mountain roads
Mountain dulcimer
    USE Appalachian dulcimer
Mountain ecology *(May Subd Geog)*
    UF Alpine ecology
    BT Ecology
    NT Alpine flora
       Timberline
Mountain farming
    USE Hill farming
Mountain fauna
    USE Alpine fauna
Mountain flora
    USE Alpine flora
Mountain flying
    ⌈TL711.M68⌉
    UF Flying, Mountain
    BT Airplanes—Piloting
Mountain fog
    USE Fog, Mountain
Mountain gem, Green-throated
    USE Lampornis viridipallens
Mountain goat
    USE Rocky Mountain goat
Mountain-gods *(May Subd Geog)*
    ⌈BL325⌉
    BT Gods
       Mountains—Religious aspects
       Mythology
Mountain grouse
    USE Spruce grouse
Mountain guides (Persons)
    USE Mountaineering guides (Persons)
Mountain guns
    ⌈UF440-445⌉
    UF Gun, Mountain
       Guns, Mountain
    BT Artillery, Field and mountain
       Firearms
Mountain Hanra (Korea)
    USE Halla Mountain (Korea)
Mountain hemlock *(May Subd Geog)*
    UF Black hemlock
       Hemlock, Black
       Hemlock, Mountain
       Tsuga mertensiana

Mountain Island Lake (N.C.)
    UF Mount Island Lake (N.C.)
    BT Catawba River (N.C. and S.C.)
       Lakes—North Carolina
       Reservoirs—North Carolina
Mountain Koiali language
    USE Mountain Koiari language
Mountain Koiari language *(May Subd Geog)*
    UF Koiali language, Mountain
       Koiari language, Mountain
       Mountain Koiali language
    BT Papua New Guinea—Languages
       Papuan languages
Mountain laurel
    ⌈QK495.E68 (Botany)⌉
    ⌈SB413.K3 (Culture)⌉
    UF Kalmia latifolia
Mountain life *(May Subd Geog)*
    ⌈GT3490⌉
    BT Country life
Mountain life in art
Mountain lions
    USE Pumas
Mountain Meadows Massacre, 1857
    ⌈F826⌉
    BT Mormon Church—History
Mountain muhly *(May Subd Geog)*
    ⌈QK495.G74⌉
    UF Muhlenbergia montana
Mountain mullet
    USE Agonostomus monticola
Mountain parrot
    USE Kea
Mountain passes *(May Subd Geog)*
    UF Notches
       Passes
    SA *subdivision* Passes *under names of*
       mountains, e.g. Alps—Passes; *also*
       names of specific passes, e.g.
       Brenner Pass
— **Alberta**
       NT Crowsnest Pass (Alta. and B.C.)
— **Austria**
       NT Untersulzbachtörl (Austria)
— **British Columbia**
       NT Crowsnest Pass (Alta. and B.C.)
— **California**
       NT Cajon Pass (Calif.)
          Tehachapi Pass (Calif.)
— **Colorado**
       NT Arapaho Pass (Boulder County and
          Grand County, Colo.)
          Marshall Pass (Colo.)
          Raton Pass (Colo. and N.M.)
— **Czechoslovakia**
       NT Dukla Pass (Czechoslovakia and
          Poland)
— **Greece**
       NT Thermopylae (Greece)
— **Nevada**
       NT Middlegate Gap (Nev.)
— **New Hampshire**
       NT Crawford Notch (N.H.)
— **New Mexico**
       NT Raton Pass (Colo. and N.M.)
— **New Zealand**
       NT Arthur's Pass (N.Z.)
— **Poland**
       NT Dukla Pass (Czechoslovakia and
          Poland)
— **Switzerland**
       NT Rawil Pass (Switzerland)
          Saint Gotthard Pass (Switzerland)
— **Washington (State)**
       NT Snoqualmie Pass (Wash.)
Mountain pediments
    USE Pediments (Geology)
Mountain people *(May Subd Geog)*
    ⌈GN392⌉
    BT Ethnology
    RT Mountaineers

— **Southern States**
       NT Mountain whites (Southern States)
Mountain people (Ramapo Mountains)
    USE Ramapo Mountain people
Mountain photography
    USE Photography of mountains
Mountain pine beetle *(May Subd Geog)*
    ⌈QL596.S35 (Entomology)⌉
    ⌈SB945.M78 (Pest)⌉
    UF Black Hills beetle
       Dendroctonus ponderosae
Mountain railroads *(May Subd Geog)*
    ⌈HE4051-HE4071 (Transportation)⌉
    ⌈TF680-TF688 (Engineering)⌉
    UF Railroads, Mountain
    BT Railroads
    RT Railroads, Cable
    NT Rack-railroads
— **Japan**
       NT Rokkō Maya Tetsudō
— **United States**
       NT Mt. Tamalpais and Muir Woods
          Railroad
Mountain ranges
    USE Mountains
Mountain ridges
    USE Mountains
Mountain River
    USE Liard River
Mountain roads *(May Subd Geog)*
    ⌈TE153⌉
    UF Roads, Mountain
    BT Roads
Mountain Seolag (Korea)
    USE Sorak Mountain (Korea)
Mountain sheep
    ⌈QL737.U5 (Zoology)⌉
    ⌈SK305.M (Hunting)⌉
    BT Sheep
    NT Argali
       Barbary sheep
       Bighorn sheep
       Dall sheep
       Mouflon
Mountain sheep hunting *(May Subd Geog)*
    ⌈SK305.M6⌉
    NT Argali hunting
Mountain shelters *(May Subd Geog)*
    UF Shelters, Mountain
    BT Mountaineering
Mountain sickness *(May Subd Geog)*
    ⌈RC103.A4⌉
    BT Altitude, Influence of
Mountain soils *(May Subd Geog)*
    ⌈S592.17.M (General)⌉
    ⌈S599-S599.9 (Local)⌉
    UF Alpine soils
    BT Soils
Mountain spinach
    USE Orach
Mountain vole
    USE Microtus montanus
Mountain warfare
    ⌈U240⌉
    BT Military art and science
       Strategy
       Tactics
       War
    NT Ski troops
Mountain wave *(May Subd Geog)*
    ⌈QC939.M8⌉
    ⌈TL557.A5 (Aeronautics)⌉
    UF Lee waves
    BT Atmospheric turbulence
       Meteorology in aeronautics
       Weather, Influence of mountains on
       Winds
Mountain whitefish
    UF Prosopium williamsoni

Mountain whites (Southern States)
(May Subd Geog)
[F210]
UF Appalachian people (Southern States)
BT Ethnology—Appalachian Region
Mountain people—Southern States
Mountain whites (Southern States) in literature
Mountain worship *(May Subd Geog)*
[BL447]
BT Mountains—Religious aspects
Nature worship
Religion, Primitive
— Japan
NT Maruyamakyō
Mountain yellow-legged frog
USE Rana muscosa
Mountainee language
USE Montagnais language
Mountaineer Indians
USE Montagnais Indians
Mountaineering *(May Subd Geog)*
[GV199.8-200.3]
UF Mountain climbing
BT Hiking
Mountains
Outdoor life
Voyages and travels
RT Rock climbing
NT Mountain shelters
Mountaineers
Mountains—Difficulty of ascent
Photography of mountains
Prusiking
Rappelling
Snow and ice climbing
Trails
— Accidents and injuries
UF Mountaineering—Injuries
Mountaineering accidents
— Biography
USE Mountaineers
— Injuries
USE Mountaineering—Accidents and injuries
— Physiological aspects
[RC1220.M6]
BT Sports—Physiological aspects
— Search and rescue operations
[GV200.183]
BT Search and rescue operations
— Societies, etc.
UF Alpine clubs
Mountaineering societies
Mountaineering accidents
USE Mountaineering—Accidents and injuries
Mountaineering guides (Persons)
(May Subd Geog)
UF Guides for mountaineering (Persons)
Mountain guides (Persons)
BT Mountaineers
Mountaineering societies
USE Mountaineering—Societies, etc.
Mountaineers *(May Subd Geog)*
[GA512.A2]
UF Mountain climbers
Mountaineering—Biography
Rock climbers
BT Mountaineering
RT Mountain people
NT Mountaineering guides (Persons)
Women mountaineers
Mountains *(May Subd Geog)*
[GB501-GB553 (Physical geography)]
[GR660 (Folklore)]

UF Hills
Mountain ranges
Mountain ridges
Orography
Orology
Peaks
Ranges, Mountain
Ridges, Mountain
BT Geology
Physical geography
RT Geology, Structural
SA *headings beginning with the words* Hill *or* Mountain
NT Alpine regions
Buried hills
Fog, Mountain
Inselbergs
Mesas
Mountaineering
Orogeny
Pediments (Geology)
Photography of mountains
Pingos
Plateaus
Seamounts
Watersheds
— Difficulty of ascent
[G510]
UF Difficulty of ascent
BT Mountaineering
— Influence on weather
USE Weather, Influence of mountains on
— Mythology
— Recreational use
BT Outdoor recreation
— Religious aspects
[BL447]
UF Holy mountains
Sacred mountains
NT Mountain-gods
Mountain worship
Mountains in the Bible
— Afghanistan
NT Hindu Kush Mountains (Afghanistan and Pakistan)
Pamir-Alai Mountains
— Africa, North
NT Atlas Mountains
— Alaska
NT Alaska Range (Alaska)
Augustine Volcano (Augustine Island, Alaska)
Brooks Range (Alaska)
Clearwater Mountains (Alaska)
Darby Mountains (Alaska)
Kantishna Hills (Alaska)
Ketchem Dome (Alaska)
Lime Peak (Alaska)
McKinley, Mount (Alaska)
Philip Smith Mountains (Alaska)
Quartz Hill (Alaska)
Ray Mountains (Alaska)
Sorenson, Mount (Alaska)
Table Mountain (Yukon-Koyukuk Borough, Alaska)
Wrangell Mountains (Alaska)
Yantarni Volcano (Alaska)
— Albania
NT Dinaric Alps
— Alberta
NT Canadian Rockies (B.C. and Alta.)
Castleguard, Mount (Alta.)
Rae, Mount (Alta.)
— Algeria
NT Ahaggar Mountains (Algeria)
Blida Atlas Mountains (Algeria)
— Antarctic regions
NT Belgica Mountains (Antarctic regions)
Bunger Hills (Antarctic regions)

Coalsack Bluff (Antarctic regions)
Queen Alexandra Range (Antarctic regions)
Queen Fabiola Mountains (Antarctic regions)
Queen Maud Mountains (Antarctic regions)
Transantarctic Mountains (Antarctic regions)
Vestfold Hills (Antarctic regions)
— Argentina
NT Aconcagua, Mount (Argentina)
Pie de Palo Mountains (Argentina)
Sierra de Córdoba (Argentina)
— Arizona
NT Brady Butte (Ariz.)
Dos Cabezas Mountains (Ariz.)
Lemmon, Mount (Ariz.)
Peloncillo Mountains (Ariz. and N.M.)
San Francisco Peaks (Ariz.)
Santa Catalina Mountains (Ariz.)
Santa Rita Mountains (Ariz.)
South Mountains (Ariz.)
Superstition Mountains (Ariz.)
— Arkansas
NT Crowley's Ridge (Ark. and Mo.)
Ouachita Mountains (Ark. and Okla.)
Ozark Mountains
— Armenian S.S.R.
NT Gegam Range (Armenian S.S.R.)
— Asia
NT Altai Mountains
Himalaya Mountains
Karakoram Range
Kumaun Himalaya
Lesser Himalaya Mountains
Pamir
— Australia
NT Alexander, Mount (Vic.)
Australian Alps (N.S.W. and Vic.)
Barrington Tops (N.S.W.)
Bindoon Hill (W.A.)
Blue Mountains (N.S.W.)
Budawang Range (N.S.W.)
Cradle Mountain (Tas.)
Darling Range (W.A.)
Denison Range (S. Aust.)
Flinders Range (S. Aust.)
Flinders Ranges (S. Aust.)
Frenchmans Cap (Tas.)
Great Dividing Range
Liverpool Range (N.S.W.)
Maggs Mountain (Tas.)
Mount Ainslie (A.C.T.)
Otway Ranges (Vic.)
Peake Range (S. Aust.)
Porongurup Range (W.A.)
Reynolds Range (N.T.)
Snowy Mountains (N.S.W.)
Stirling Range (W.A.)
Wellington, Mount (Tas.)
— Austria
NT Allgäu Alps (Germany and Austria)
Alps, Austrian (Austria)
Bohemian Forest
Carnic Alps (Italy and Austria)
Dachstein Mountains (Austria)
Ennstal Alps (Austria)
Hagengebirge (Austria)
Hochschwab Alps (Austria)
Hohe Tauern (Austria)
Hoher Göll (Austria and Germany)
Karawanken (Austria and Slovenia)
Magdalensberg (Austria)
Radstädter Tauern (Austria)
Rossfeld (Austria)
Salzburg Alps (Austria and Germany)

Mountains
— **Austria** *(Continued)*
    Stubay Alps (Austria)
    Totes Gebirge (Austria)
    Zillertal Alps (Austria and Italy)
— **Azerbaijan S.S.R.**
  NT Talish Mountains (Azerbaijan
     S.S.R. and Iran)
— **Balkan Peninsula**
  NT Rhodope Mountains
— **Belgium**
  NT Hautes Fagnes (Belgium and
     Germany)
— **Bhutan**
  NT Chomo Lhari (Bhutan and China)
— **Botswana**
  NT Mokgware Hills (Botswana)
— **Brazil**
  NT Carajás Mountains (Brazil)
    João do Vale Hills (Brazil)
    Mar Mountains (Brazil)
    Mel Mountains (Rio Grande do
     Norte, Brazil)
    Roraima, Mount
    Teixeira Mountains (Brazil)
— **British Columbia**
  NT Canadian Rockies (B.C. and Alta.)
    Cariboo Mountains (B.C.)
    Cassiar Mountains (B.C.)
    Hozameen Range (B.C.)
    Selkirk Range
    Tahtsa Range (B.C.)
— **Bulgaria**
  NT Balkan Mountains (Bulgaria)
    Batashka Mountains (Bulgaria)
    Belemeto Mountains (Bulgaria)
    Chernatitsa Mountains (Bulgaria)
    Eledzhik Mountains (Bulgaria)
    Golema Mountains (Bulgaria)
    Istranca Mountains (Turkey and
     Bulgaria)
    Lakavishki Hills (Bulgaria)
    Pirin Mountains (Bulgaria)
    Plana Mountains (Bulgaria)
    Ravnogor Mountains (Bulgaria)
    Rila Mountains (Bulgaria)
    Sakar Mountains (Bulgaria)
    Sredna Gora Mountains (Bulgaria)
    Verila Mountains (Bulgaria)
    Vitosha Mountains (Bulgaria)
    Zlatishko-Teteven Mountains
     (Bulgaria)
— **Burma**
  NT Popa, Mount (Burma)
— **California**
  NT Argus Range (Calif.)
    Baldwin Hills (Calif.)
    Berkeley Hills (Calif.)
    Chocolate Mountains (Calif.)
    Coso Range (Calif.)
    Cowtrack Mountain (Calif.)
    Diablo Range (Calif.)
    Glass Mountain (Mono County,
     Calif.)
    Hamilton Range, Mount (Calif.)
    Inyo Mountains (Calif.)
    Kingston Range (Calif.)
    Klamath Mountains (Calif. and
     Or.)
    Lassen Peak (Calif.)
    Mammoth Mountain (Calif.)
    Merced Peak (Calif.)
    Saint Helena, Mount (Calif.)
    San Bernardino Mountains (Calif.)
    San Emigdio Mountains (Calif.)
    San Gabriel Mountains (Calif.)
    Santa Ana Mountains (Calif.)
    Santa Cruz Mountains (Calif.)
    Santa Lucia Range (Calif.)
    Santa Monica Mountains (Calif.)
    Santa Rosa Mountains (Calif.)

    Shasta, Mount (Calif.)
    Sierra Nevada Mountains (Calif.
     and Nev.)
    Simi Hills (Calif.)
    Sweeney Ridge (Calif.)
    Tamalpais, Mount (Calif.)
    Tecate Peak (Calif.)
    Tehachapi Mountains (Calif.)
    Transverse Ranges (Calif.)
    Trinity Alps (Calif.)
    White Mountains (Calif. and Nev.)
    Whitney, Mount (Calif.)
— **Cameroon**
  NT Alantika Mountains (Nigeria and
     Cameroon)
— **Canada**
  NT Appalachian Mountains
    Coast Ranges
    Rocky Mountains
— **Canary Islands**
  NT Teide, Pico de (Tenerife, Canary
     Islands)
— **Central Europe**
  NT Alps
— **Chad**
  NT Tibesti Mountains
— **China**
  NT Ch'ang-pai Mountains (China and
     Korea)
    Ch'i-lien Mountains (China)
    Ch'i-lin Mountains (China)
    Ch'ien Mountains (China)
    Ch'in-ling Mountains (China)
    Ch'ing-ch'eng Mountain (China)
    Ching Mountain (China)
    Ch'ing-yen Mountains (China)
    Chiu-hua Mountains (China)
    Chiu-jih Mountains (China)
    Chomo Lhari (Bhutan and China)
    Everest, Mount (China and Nepal)
    Fu-ch'un Mountains (China)
    Greater Khingan Range (China)
    Heng Mountains (China)
    Hsi-ch'iao Mountains (China)
    Hsi-hsia-pang-ma Peak (China)
    Hsi Mountain (China)
    Hsi Mountains (China)
    Hua Mountains (China)
    Huang Mountains (China)
    Hui Mountains (China)
    I-meng Mountains (China)
    Kailas Mountain (China)
    Konger Mount (China)
    Ku Mountain (China)
    Lao Mountain (China)
    Lhotse (China and Nepal)
    Liang Mountains (China)
    Liu-p'an Mountains (China)
    Lo-fu Mountains (China)
    Lu Mountains (China)
    Minya Konka (China)
    O-mei Mountain (China)
    Pamir-Alai Mountains
    P'an Mountain (China)
    Pao-hua Mountain (China)
    Po-ko-to Mountains (China)
    She Mountain (China)
    Sung Mountains (China)
    Ta-ch'ing Mountains (China)
    Ta-pieh Mountains (China)
    T'ai Mountains (China)
    Tarbagataĭ Range (Kazakh S.S.R.
     and China)
    T'ien-chu Mountains (China)
    T'ien-mu Mountains (China)
    Tien Shan
    T'ien-t'ai Mountains (China)
    Tuomuer Peak (China)
    Wu-chih Mountains (China)
    Wu-i Mountains (China)
    Wu-ling Mountain (China)

    Wu-t'ai Mountains (China)
    Wu-tang Mountains (China)
    Yang Mountain (China)
    Yen-tang Mountains (China)
    Yin-ch'üeh Mountain (China)
    Yü-t'ai Mountain (China)
    Yüeh-lu Mountains (China)
    Zaskar Range (India and China)
— **Colombia**
  NT Aspavé Highlands (Panama and
     Colombia)
    Ejón Hill (Colombia)
    Nevado del Ruiz (Colombia)
    Perija Mountains (Colombia and
     Venezuela)
    Santa Marta Range (Colombia)
— **Colorado**
  NT Eagle Mountain Wilderness (Colo.)
    Front Range (Colo. and Wyo.)
    Laramie Mountains (Wyo. and
     Colo.)
    Longs Peak (Colo.)
    Medicine Bow Mountains (Colo.
     and Wyo.)
    Old Man Mountain (Colo.)
    Ouray, Mount (Colo.)
    Park Range (Colo. and Wyo.)
    Pikes Peak (Colo.)
    Puma Hills (Colo.)
    San Juan Mountains (Colo. and
     N.M.)
    Sangre de Cristo Mountains (Colo.
     and N.M.)
    Tarryall Mountains (Colo.)
    Wet Mountains (Colo.)
— **Costa Rica**
  NT Barra Honda Mountain (Costa
     Rica)
    Irazú Volcano (Costa Rica)
    Talamanca Mountains (Costa Rica)
— **Cyprus**
  NT Troodos Mountains (Cyprus)
— **Czechoslovakia**
  NT Beskid Śląski (Poland and
     Czechoslovakia)
    Beskid Żywiecki (Poland and
     Czechoslovakia)
    Beskids (Poland and
     Czechoslovakia)
    Bialskie Mountains (Poland and
     Czechoslovakia)
    Bohemian Forest
    Bohemian-Moravian Highlands
     (Czechoslovakia)
    Brdy Mountains (Czechoslovakia)
    České středohoří (Czechoslovakia)
    East Beskids (Poland and
     Czechoslovakia)
    Elbe Sandstone Rocks
     (Czechoslovakia and Germany)
    Erzgebirge (Czechoslovakia and
     Germany)
    Fichtelgebirge (Germany and
     Czechoslovakia)
    Izerskie Mountains (Poland and
     Czechoslovakia)
    Jeseníky Mountains
     (Czechoslovakia)
    Klínovec Mountain
     (Czechoslovakia)
    Krkonoše (Czechoslovakia and
     Poland)
    Krupina Plateau (Czechoslovakia)
    Milešovka Mountain
     (Czechoslovakia)
    Oblík (Czechoslovakia)
    Orlické Mountains
     (Czechoslovakia)
    Pavlovské Hills (Czechoslovakia)
    Pieniny Range (Poland and
     Czechoslovakia)

Pohronský Inovec Mountains
(Czechoslovakia)
Rip, Mount (Czechoslovakia)
Slovak Ore Mountains
(Czechoslovakia)
Śnieżnik Mountains (Poland and
Czechoslovakia)
Strážov Mountains
(Czechoslovakia)
Sudeten
Šumava (Czechoslovakia)
Tatra Mountains (Czechoslovakia
and Poland)
Tokaj-Eperjes Mountains
(Czechoslovakia and Hungary)
Tríbeč Mountains (Czechoslovakia)
Veľká Fatra (Czechoslovakia)
Złote Mountains (Poland and
Czechoslovakia)
— Ecuador
NT Condor Range (Ecuador and Peru)
Cotopaxi Mountain (Ecuador)
Cutucú Mountains (Ecuador)
— Egypt
NT Ataqa Mountains (Egypt)
Sinai, Mount (Egypt)
— England
NT Baugh Fell (England)
Bredon Hill (England)
Chiltern Hills (England)
Cotswold Hills (England)
Dartmoor (England)
Howgill Fells (England)
Kinder Scout (England)
Langdale Fell (England)
Malvern Hills (England)
Mendip Hills (England)
North York Moors (England)
Pennine Chain (England)
Scafell Pike (England)
Wild Boar Fell (England)
Yorkshire Dales (England)
— Ethiopia
NT Simen Mountains (Ethiopia)
— Europe
NT Alps
— Europe, Eastern
NT Carpathian Mountains
— Finland
NT Rautuvaara Mountains (Finland)
— France
NT Alps, French (France)
Armorican Massif (France)
Auvergne Mountains (France)
Bego Mountain (France)
Blanc, Mont (France and Italy)
Calanques (France)
Causses (France)
Cévennes Mountains (France)
Chartreuse Mountains (France)
Corbières Mountains (France)
Dauphiné Alps (France)
Dômes Mountains (France)
Graian Alps (France and Italy)
Jura Mountains (France and
Switzerland)
Lazzu Mountain (Corsica)
Lévezou (France)
Lubéron Mountains (France)
Margeride Mountains (France)
Maritime Alps (France and Italy)
Mercantour Mountains (France)
Meygal Mountain (France)
Mézenc Mount (France)
Noires Mountains (France)
Pilat Mountain (France)
Pyrenees (France and Spain)
Reims Mountain (France)
Revermont (France)
Vanoise Mountains (France)
Ventoux Mountain (France)

Vercors (France)
Voirons (France)
Vosges Mountains (France)
— French Guiana
NT Fumée Mountain (French Guiana)
— Georgia
NT Soapstone Ridge (Ga.)
— Georgian S.S.R.
NT Dalar Mountain (Georgian S.S.R.
and R.S.F.S.R.)
Keli Range (Georgian S.S.R.)
Lokskiĭ Mountains (Georgian
S.S.R.)
Svanetian Mountains (Georgian
S.S.R.)
Trialet Range (Georgian S.S.R.)
— Germany (East)
NT Adlersberg (Germany : Hill)
Aschberg (Karl-Marx-Stadt,
Germany : Mountain)
Elbe Sandstone Rocks
(Czechoslovakia and Germany)
Erzgebirge (Czechoslovakia and
Germany)
Fichtelberg (Karl-Marx-Stadt,
Germany : Bezirk)
Harz Mountains (Germany)
Oberharz Mountains (Germany)
Rhön (Germany)
Steinsburg (Germany)
Sudeten
Thuringian Forest (Germany)
Zittauer Gebirge (Germany)
— Germany (West)
NT Allgäu Alps (Germany and
Austria)
Alps, Bavarian (Germany)
Bavarian Forest (Germany)
Black Forest (Germany)
Bohemian Forest
Deister (Germany)
Eggegebirge (Germany)
Eifel (Germany)
Fichtelgebirge (Germany and
Czechoslovakia)
Frankenwald (Germany)
Fränkische Alb (Germany)
Frauenberg (Germany)
Grosser Feldberg (Germany)
Harz Mountains (Germany)
Hautes Fagnes (Belgium and
Germany)
Hils Ridge (Germany)
Hoher Göll (Austria and Germany)
Hunsrück (Germany)
Ith Ridge (Germany)
Meissner Mountain (Germany)
Naturpark Siebengebirge
(Germany)
Niederwald (Germany)
Oberharz Mountains (Germany)
Odenwald (Germany)
Rammelsberg (Germany)
Reinhardswald (Germany)
Rheinisches Schiefergebirge
(Germany)
Rhön (Germany)
Salzburg Alps (Austria and
Germany)
Samerberg (Germany)
Siebengebirge (Germany)
Spessart (Germany)
Steigerwald (Germany)
Swabian Alps (Germany)
Taunus (Germany)
Teutoburg Forest (Germany)
Vogelsberg (Germany)
Wesergebirge (Germany)
— Greece
NT Olympus, Mount (Greece)
Parnassus, Mount (Greece)

Pelion Mountains (Greece)
Peratí Mountain (Greece)
Pieria Mountains (Greece)
Pindus Mountains (Greece)
Taygetus Mountains (Greece)
Tourkovouni (Greece)
— Greenland
NT Ilimaussaq Mountain (Greenland)
Werner Mountain (Greenland)
— Guadeloupe
NT Soufrière (Basse-Terre Island,
Guadeloupe)
— Guyana
NT Roraima, Mount
— Hawaii
NT Mauna Kea (Hawaii)
Mauna Loa (Hawaii Island,
Hawaii)
Mauna Ulu (Hawaii)
— Hungary
NT Bakony Mountains (Hungary)
Buda Mountains (Hungary)
Bükk Mountains (Hungary)
Cserhát Mountains (Hungary)
Gerecse Mountains (Hungary)
Göcsej Hills (Hungary)
Hármashatár, Mount (Budapest,
Hungary)
Keszthely Mountains (Hungary)
Mátra Mountains (Hungary)
Mecsek Mountains (Hungary)
Medves Mountains (Hungary)
Pilis Mountains (Hungary)
Tokaj, Mount (Hungary)
Tokaj-Eperjes Mountains
(Czechoslovakia and Hungary)
Velence Mountains (Hungary)
Vértes Mountains (Hungary)
— Iceland
NT Hekla (Iceland)
— Idaho
NT Bitterroot Range (Idaho and
Mont.)
Black Pine Mountains (Idaho)
Coeur d'Alene Mountains (Idaho
and Mont.)
Hoodoo Mountains (Idaho)
Selkirk Range
Teton Range (Wyo. and Idaho)
Wasatch Range (Utah and Idaho)
— India
NT Changabang Mountain (India)
Jaintia Hills (India)
Kānchenjunga (Nepal and India)
Kinner Kailash (India)
Nanda Devi (India)
Nanga Parbat (India)
Nilgiri Hills (India)
Palni Hills (India)
Saser Kangri (India)
Trango Tower
Vindhya Range (India)
Western Ghats (India)
Zaskar Range (India and China)
— Indonesia
NT Barisan Mountains (Sumatra,
Indonesia)
Patiayam Mountain (Java,
Indonesia)
Tambora, Mount (Sumbawa,
Indonesia)
Tengger Mountains (Java,
Indonesia)
— Iran
NT Baḥtiyārī Mountains (Iran)
Bozqūsh Mountains (Iran)
Elburz Mountains (Iran)
Kopet Dag (Turkmen S.S.R. and
Iran)
Talish Mountains (Azerbaijan
S.S.R. and Iran)

Mountains

— Iran *(Continued)*
    Zagros Mountains (Iran)
— Ireland
  NT Blue Stack Mountains (Ireland)
      Derryveagh Mountains (Ireland)
— Israel
  NT Carmel, Mount (Israel)
      Karkom Mountain (Israel)
— Italy
  NT Adamello Mountains (Italy)
      Alps, Italian (Italy)
      Amiata, Monte (Italy)
      Apennines (Italy)
      Asolo Hills (Italy)
      Aspromonte (Italy)
      Baldo Mountains (Italy)
      Blanc, Mont (France and Italy)
      Carnic Alps (Italy and Austria)
      Castellier degli Elleri Mountain (Italy)
      Chianti Mountains (Italy)
      Cilento Mountains (Italy)
      Dinaric Alps
      Dolomite Alps (Italy)
      Euganean Hills (Italy)
      Gargano Promontory (Italy)
      Graian Alps (France and Italy)
      Iato Mountain (Sicily)
      Julian Alps (Slovenia and Italy)
      Lepini Mountains (Italy)
      Lessini Mountains (Italy)
      Ligurian Alps (Italy)
      Maiella Mountains (Italy)
      Maritime Alps (France and Italy)
      Marmolada Mountains (Italy)
      Matterhorn (Switzerland and Italy)
      Montello (Italy)
      Nebrodi Mountains (Sicily)
      Ortler (Italy)
      Palermo Mountains (Sicily)
      Pennine Alps (Italy and Switzerland)
      Pollino, Mount (Italy)
      Sannace Mountain (Italy)
      Vesuvius (Italy)
      Volsini Mountains (Italy)
      Zillertal Alps (Austria and Italy)
— Jamaica
  NT Hellshire Hills (Jamaica)
      Mocho Mountains (Jamaica)
— Japan
  NT Akagi Mountain (Japan)
      Asahi Mountain Range (Japan)
      Asama Mountain (Japan)
      Ashitaka Mountain (Japan)
      Aso Mountains (Japan)
      Chōkai Mountain (Japan)
      Daisen (Japan)
      Daisetsu Mountains (Japan)
      Fuji, Mount (Japan)
      Gagyū Hill (Japan)
      Haguro Mountain (Japan)
      Hakkōda Mountain (Japan)
      Hakone, Mount (Japan)
      Haku Mountain (Japan)
      Hayachine Mountain (Japan)
      Hidaka Mountain Range (Japan)
      Hiko Mountain (Japan)
      Hira Mountains (Japan)
      Hiru Mountain (Japan)
      Hotaka Mountain (Japan)
      Iide Mountain (Japan)
      Iide Mountain Range (Japan)
      Ishizuchi, Mount (Japan)
      Iwaki Mountain (Japan)
      Japanese Alps (Japan)
      Kinshō Mountain (Japan)
      Kiyomizu Mountain (Japan)
      Kuju, Mount (Japan)

Mikami Mountain (Shiga-ken, Japan)
Minoo Mountain (Japan)
Mitake Mountain (Japan)
Myōgi Mountain (Japan)
Nijō Mountain (Japan)
Ōmine Mountains (Japan)
Ontake Mountain (Japan)
Osore Mountains (Japan)
Otoko Mountain (Japan)
Rokkō Mountain (Japan)
Sayama Hills (Japan)
Shirakami Mountains (Japan)
Shirane Mountain (Gunma-ken, Japan)
Suzuka Mountain Range (Japan)
Takago Mountain (Japan)
Takezawa Mountain (Japan)
Tanzawa Mountains (Japan)
Tate Mountain (Japan)
Togakushi Mountain (Japan)
Usu Mountain (Japan)
Yahiko Mountain (Japan)
Yake Mountain (Niigata-ken, Japan)
Yari Mountain (Japan)
Yatsuga Mountain (Japan)
Yoshino Mountain (Japan)
Zaō Mountains (Japan)
— Jerusalem
  NT Mount of Olives (Jerusalem)
— Kazakh S.S.R.
  NT Chatkal Range
      Chingiztau (Kazakh S.S.R.)
      Kara-Tau (Kazakh S.S.R.)
      Kirgizskiĭ Range (Kirghiz S.S.R. and Kazakh S.S.R.)
      Tarbagataĭ Range (Kazakh S.S.R. and China)
— Kenya
  NT Kenya, Mount (Kenya)
      Kenya Highlands (Kenya)
      Kulal, Mount (Kenya)
      Taita Hills (Kenya)
— Kirghiz S.S.R.
  NT Fergana Range (Kirghiz S.S.R.)
      Kirgizskiĭ Range (Kirghiz S.S.R. and Kazakh S.S.R.)
— Korea
  NT Ch'ang-pai Mountains (China and Korea)
      Halla Mountain (Korea)
— Korea (North)
  NT Diamond Mountains (Korea)
      Myohyang Mountain (Korea)
      Paektu Mountain (Korea)
— Korea (South)
  NT Chiri Mountain (Korea)
      Chuwang Mountain (Korea)
      Naejang Mountain (Korea)
      Odae Mountain (Korea)
      Songni Mountain (Korea)
      Sorak Mountain (Korea)
— Lebanon
  NT 'Āmil Mountains (Lebanon)
— Lesotho
  NT Drakensberg Mountains
— Libya
  NT Akhḍar Mountains (Libya)
      Tibesti Mountains
— Maine
  NT Katahdin, Mount (Me.)
      Oxford Hills (Me.)
      Saddleback Mountain (Franklin County, Me.)
      White Mountains (N.H. and Me.)
— Mali
  NT Sarnyéré (Mali)
— Manitoba
  NT Pembina Hills (Man. and N.D.)
— Martinique

  NT Pelée, Mount (Martinique)
— Massachusetts
  NT Berkshire Hills (Mass.)
      Holyoke Range (Mass.)
      Toby, Mount (Mass.)
      Tom, Mount (Mass.)
      Wachusett Mountain (Mass.)
— Mexico
  NT Chichon (Mexico)
      Iztaccihuatl (Mexico)
      Laguna Mountains (Mexico)
      Pinacate Mountain (Mexico)
      Sierra Madre del Sur (Mexico)
      Sierra Madre Occidental (Mexico)
      Teotepec Mountain (Mexico)
— Michigan
  NT Menominee Range (Mich. and Wis.)
— Minnesota
  NT Cuyuna Range (Minn.)
      Mesabi Range (Minn.)
      Vermilion Range (Minn.)
— Missouri
  NT Crowley's Ridge (Ark. and Mo.)
      Ozark Mountains
— Mongolia
  NT Khangai Mountains (Mongolia)
— Montana
  NT Absaroka Range (Mont. and Wyo.)
      Bearpaw Mountains (Mont.)
      Beartooth Mountains (Mont. and Wyo.)
      Bitterroot Range (Idaho and Mont.)
      Coeur d'Alene Mountains (Idaho and Mont.)
      Madison Range (Mont.)
      Pioneer Mountains (Mont.)
      Selkirk Range
      Tendoy Mountains (Mont.)
      Tobacco Root Mountains (Mont.)
— Morocco
  NT Anti-Atlas Mountains (Morocco)
      Rif Mountains (Morocco)
— Nepal
  NT Annapurna (Nepal)
      Dhaulāgiri (Nepal)
      Everest, Mount (China and Nepal)
      Kānchenjunga (Nepal and India)
      Lhotse (China and Nepal)
      Mahabharat Range (Nepal)
      Pumori (Nepal)
— Nevada
  NT Antelope Range (Nev.)
      Desert Peak (Nev.)
      Sierra Nevada Mountains (Calif. and Nev.)
      Toquima Range (Nev.)
      Tuscarora Mountains (Nev.)
      White Mountains (Calif. and Nev.)
      Yucca Mountain (Nev.)
— New Hampshire
  NT Cannon Mountain (N.H.)
      Presidential Range (N.H.)
      Washington, Mount (N.H.)
      White Mountains (N.H. and Me.)
— New Jersey
  NT Somerset Hills (N.J.)
— New Mexico
  NT Big Hatchet Peak (N.M.)
      Black Range (N.M.)
      Hueco Mountains (Tex. and N.M.)
      Magdalena Mountains (N.M.)
      Manzano Mountains (N.M.)
      Mimbres Mountains (N.M.)
      Organ Mountains (N.M.)
      Peloncillo Mountains (Ariz. and N.M.)
      Sacramento Mountains (N.M.)
      San Andres Mountains (N.M.)

San Juan Mountains (Colo. and
N.M.)
San Mateo Mountains (Valencia
County, N.M.)
Sandia Mountains (N.M.)
Sangre de Cristo Mountains (Colo.
and N.M.)
Ship Rock (N.M.)
Sierra Blanca Range (N.M.)
South Baldy Peak (N.M.)
Taylor, Mount (N.M.)
Tusas Ridge (N.M.)
— **New York (State)**
NT Adirondack Mountains (N.Y.)
Catskill Mountains (N.Y.)
Shawangunk Mountains (N.Y.)
Tug Hill (N.Y.)
— **New Zealand**
NT Hauhungaroa Range (N.Z.)
Hector Mountains (New Zealand)
Longwood Range (N.Z.)
Meremere (N.Z. : Mountain)
Port Hills (N.Z.)
Rangitoto Range (N.Z.)
Remarkables, The (New Zealand)
Ruahine Range (N.Z.)
Ruapehu Mountain (N.Z.)
Southern Alps (N.Z.)
Tauhara (N.Z.)
Te Maru (N.Z.)
Waitakere Ranges (N.Z.)
— **Niger**
NT Tibesti Mountains
— **Nigeria**
NT Alantika Mountains (Nigeria and
Cameroon)
— **North Carolina**
NT Black Mountains (N.C.)
Brushy Mountains (N.C.)
Great Smoky Mountains (N.C. and
Tenn.)
Mount Mitchell (N.C.)
— **North Dakota**
NT Pembina Hills (Man. and N.D.)
— **Northern Ireland**
NT Mourne Mountains (Northern
Ireland)
Slieve Gullion (Northern Ireland)
— **Northwest, Pacific**
NT Cascade Range
— **Northwest Territories**
NT Cathedral Mountain (N.W.T.)
Mackenzie Mountains (N.W.T. and
Yukon)
Prince Albert Hills (N.W.T.)
Richardson Mountains (N.W.T.)
Selwyn Mountains (Yukon and
N.W.T.)
— **Norway**
NT Kölen Mountains (Sweden and
Norway)
Rondane Mountains (Norway)
— **Nova Scotia**
NT Cobequid Mountains (N.S.)
— **Oklahoma**
NT Arbuckle Mountains (Okla.)
Ouachita Mountains (Ark. and
Okla.)
Ozark Mountains
Wichita Mountains (Okla.)
— **Oregon**
NT Blue Mountains (Or. and Wash.)
Hood, Mount (Or.)
Klamath Mountains (Calif. and
Or.)
Spencer Butte (Or.)
— **Pakistan**
NT Gasherbrum I (Pakistan)
Haramosh (Pakistan)
Hindu Kush Mountains
(Afghanistan and Pakistan)

K2 (Pakistan : Mountain)
Mango Gusor Range (Pakistan)
Masherbrum Peak (Pakistan)
Salt Range (Pakistan)
Tirich Mīr Mountain (Pakistan)
Trango Tower
— **Panama**
NT Aspavé Highlands (Panama and
Colombia)
San Blas, Cordillera de (Panama)
— **Papua New Guinea**
NT Suckling, Mount (Papua New
Guinea)
— **Pennsylvania**
NT Pocono Mountains (Pa.)
— **Peru**
NT Blanca, Cordillera (Peru)
Condor Range (Ecuador and Peru)
Cordillera Central (Peru)
Cordillera Occidental (Peru)
Cordillera Oriental (Peru)
Huayhuash, Cordillera (Peru)
Sarapo Mountain (Peru)
Vilcabamba Mountains (Peru)
— **Philippines**
NT Taal, Mount (Volcano Island,
Philippines)
— **Poland**
NT Bardo Mountains (Poland)
Beshchady Mountains (Poland and
Ukraine)
Beskid Makowski (Poland)
Beskid Mały (Poland)
Beskid Sądecki (Poland)
Beskid Śląski (Poland and
Czechoslovakia)
Beskid Żywiecki (Poland and
Czechoslovakia)
Beskids (Poland and
Czechoslovakia)
Bialskie Mountains (Poland and
Czechoslovakia)
Bystrzyca Mountains (Poland)
East Beskids (Poland and
Czechoslovakia)
Izerskie Mountains (Poland and
Czechoslovakia)
Kaczawa Mountains (Poland)
Kamienne Mountains (Poland)
Kraków-Częstochowa Highland
(Poland)
Krkonoše (Czechoslovakia and
Poland)
Pieniny Range (Poland and
Czechoslovakia)
Roztocze Range (Poland and
Ukraine)
Śnieżnik Mountains (Poland and
Czechoslovakia)
Sowie Mountains (Poland)
Stołowe Mountains (Poland)
Sudeten
Świętokrzyskie Mountains (Poland)
Szrenica, Mount (Poland)
Tatra Mountains (Czechoslovakia
and Poland)
Wałbrzych Mountains (Poland)
Złote Mountains (Poland and
Czechoslovakia)
— **Portugal**
NT Sintra Mountains (Portugal)
— **Québec (Province)**
NT Laurentian Mountains (Québec)
— **Romania**
NT Apuseni Mountains (Romania)
Baiului Mountains (Romania)
Bucegi Mountains (Romania)
Buzău Mountains (Romania)
Ciucaș Mountains (Romania)
Făgăraș Mountains (Romania)
Godeanu Mountains (Romania)

Gutîi Mountains (Romania)
Iezer Mountains (Romania)
Mehedenți Mountains (Romania)
Oaș Mountains (Romania)
Parîng Mountains (Romania)
Piatra Craiului (Romania)
Poiana Rusca Mountains
(Romania)
Retezat Mountains (Romania)
Rodna Mountains (Romania)
Semenic Mountains (Romania)
Transylvanian Alps (Romania)
Zarandului Mountains (Romania)
— **Russian S.F.S.R.**
NT Aldan Plateau (R.S.F.S.R.)
Alkhanai Mountain (R.S.F.S.R.)
Cherskiĭ Range (R.S.F.S.R.)
Dalar Mountain (Georgian S.S.R.
and R.S.F.S.R.)
Gornaīa Shoriīa (R.S.F.S.R.)
Khibiny Mountains (R.S.F.S.R.)
Koryak Range (R.S.F.S.R.)
Kuznetsk Alatau (R.S.F.S.R.)
Lovozero Mountain (R.S.F.S.R.)
Paĭ-Khoĭ Range (R.S.F.S.R.)
Pripolīarnyĭ Ural Mountains
(R.S.F.S.R.)
Putorana Plateau (R.S.F.S.R.)
Salair Ridge (R.S.F.S.R.)
Sayan Mountains (R.S.F.S.R.)
Sette-Daban Range (R.S.F.S.R.)
Sikhote-Alin' Range (R.S.F.S.R.)
Stanovoi Range (R.S.F.S.R.)
Timan Ridge (R.S.F.S.R.)
Tolbachik Volcano (R.S.F.S.R.)
Udokan Range (R.S.F.S.R.)
Ural Mountains (R.S.F.S.R.)
Valdai Hills (R.S.F.S.R.)
Verkhoīansk Range (R.S.F.S.R.)
Zhiguli Mountains (R.S.F.S.R.)
— **Saudi Arabia**
NT Șa'id Mountain (Saudi Arabia)
— **Scotland**
NT Ben Nevis (Scotland)
Cairngorms (Scotland)
Grampians (Scotland)
Minch Moor (Scotland)
Pentland Hills (Scotland)
— **South Africa**
NT Cathedral Peak (South Africa)
Drakensberg Mountains
Hottentots Holland Mountains
(South Africa)
Stormberg Range (South Africa)
Table Mountain (Cape of Good
Hope, South Africa)
— **South America**
NT Andes
— **South Dakota**
NT Bear Butte (S.D. : Mountain)
Black Hills (S.D. and Wyo.)
Slim Buttes (S.D.)
— **Soviet Central Asia**
NT Turkestan Range
— **Soviet Union**
NT Caucasus
Pamir-Alai Mountains
Tien Shan
— **Spain**
NT Aitana Mountain (Spain)
Alhamilla Mountains (Spain)
Aneto, Pico de (Spain)
Aralar Mountain Range (Spain)
Aubenç Mountain Range (Spain)
Benéticos Range (Spain)
Cabrera Mountains (Spain)
Cantabrian Mountains (Spain)
Cazorla Mountains (Spain)
Cebollera Mountains (Spain)
Demanda Mountains (Spain)
Duranguesado, Peñas del (Spain)

Mountains
— **Spain** *(Continued)*
    Els Moletons (Spain)
    Espadán Mountains (Spain)
    Gredos Mountains (Spain)
    Guadarrama Mountains (Spain)
    Javalambre Mountains (Spain)
    Montseny Mountains (Spain)
    Montserrat (Spain)
    Picos de Europa (Spain)
    Pyrenees (France and Spain)
    Ronda Mountains (Spain)
    Segura Mountains (Spain)
    Sierra Nevada (Spain)
    Toledo Mountains (Spain)
— **Sri Lanka**
— **Sudan**
  NT Nuba Mountains (Sudan)
— **Swaziland**
  NT Drakensberg Mountains
— **Sweden**
  NT Kölen Mountains (Sweden and Norway)
— **Switzerland**
  NT Aarmassiv (Switzerland)
    Alps, Swiss (Switzerland)
    Bernese Alps (Switzerland)
    Chemin Mountain (Switzerland)
    Eiger (Switzerland)
    Gantrisch (Switzerland)
    Glarner Alps (Switzerland)
    Jorat Mountains (Switzerland)
    Jungfrau (Switzerland)
    Jura Mountains (France and Switzerland)
    Malcantone (Switzerland)
    Matterhorn (Switzerland and Italy)
    Pennine Alps (Italy and Switzerland)
    Pilatus (Switzerland)
    Rigi Mountain (Switzerland)
    San Giorgio Mountain (Switzerland)
    Toggenburg Mountains (Switzerland)
    Valais Alps (Switzerland)
    Weissenstein Mountain (Switzerland)
    Zurich Oberland (Switzerland)
— **Tajik S.S.R.**
  NT Chatkal Range
    Gissar Range (Tajik S.S.R. and Uzbek S.S.R.)
    Kurama Range (Uzbek S.S.R. and Tajik S.S.R.)
    Zeravshan Range (Tajik S.S.R. and Uzbek S.S.R.)
— **Tanzania**
  NT Kilimanjaro, Mount (Tanzania)
    Mahali Mountains (Tanzania)
    Nguru Mountains (Tanzania)
    Southern Highlands (Tanzania)
— **Tennessee**
  NT Great Smoky Mountains (N.C. and Tenn.)
    LeConte, Mount (Tenn.)
— **Texas**
  NT Chinati Mountains (Tex.)
    Finlay Mountains (Tex.)
    Gyp Hill (Tex.)
    Hueco Mountains (Tex. and N.M.)
    Sierra Diablo (Tex.)
— **Thailand**
  NT Phetchabun Mountain Range (Thailand)
— **Turkey**
  NT Ararat, Mount (Turkey)
    Istranca Mountains (Turkey and Bulgaria)
    Kop Mountains (Turkey)
    Kure Mountains (Turkey)

    Taurus Mountains (Turkey)
— **Turkmen S.S.R.**
  NT Kopet Dag (Turkmen S.S.R. and Iran)
— **Ukraine**
  NT Beshchady Mountains (Poland and Ukraine)
    Goverla, Mount (Ukraine)
    Hutsul Alps (Ukraine)
    Pop Ivan (Ukraine)
    Roztocze Range (Poland and Ukraine)
    Volyn-Podolian Upland (Ukraine)
— **United States**
  NT Appalachian Mountains
    Blue Ridge Mountains
    Coast Ranges
    Cumberland Mountains
— **Uruguay**
  NT Cerro (Montevideo, Uruguay)
— **Utah**
  NT San Rafael Swell (Utah)
    Tushar Mountains (Utah)
    Uinta Mountains (Utah and Wyo.)
    Wah Wah Mountains (Utah)
    Wasatch Range (Utah and Idaho)
— **Uzbek S.S.R.**
  NT Chatkal Range
    Gissar Range (Tajik S.S.R. and Uzbek S.S.R.)
    Kurama Range (Uzbek S.S.R. and Tajik S.S.R.)
    Zeravshan Range (Tajik S.S.R. and Uzbek S.S.R.)
— **Venezuela**
  NT Mérida, Cordillera de (Venezuela)
    Perija Mountains (Colombia and Venezuela)
    Roraima, Mount
— **Virginia**
  NT Dean Mountain (Va.)
    Jones Mountain (Va.)
    Massanutten Mountain (Va.)
— **Wales**
  NT Rhinog Fach (Wales)
    Rhinog Fawr (Wales)
— **Washington (State)**
  NT Baker, Mount (Wash.)
    Blue Mountains (Or. and Wash.)
    Horse Heaven Hills (Wash.)
    Olympic Mountains (Wash.)
    Rainier, Mount (Wash.)
    Saint Helens, Mount (Wash.)
    Stensgar Mountain (Wash.)
    Willapa Hills (Wash.)
— **West (U.S.)**
  NT Rocky Mountains
— **West Virginia**
  NT Canaan Mountain (W. Va.)
    Cheat Mountain (W. Va.)
— **Wisconsin**
  NT Menominee Range (Mich. and Wis.)
— **Wyoming**
  NT Absaroka Range (Mont. and Wyo.)
    Bear Lodge Mountains (Wyo.)
    Beartooth Mountains (Mont. and Wyo.)
    Black Hills (S.D. and Wyo.)
    Casper Mountain (Wyo.)
    Como Bluff (Wyo.)
    Front Range (Colo. and Wyo.)
    Grand Teton National Park (Wyo.)
    Laramie Mountains (Wyo. and Colo.)
    Medicine Bow Mountains (Colo. and Wyo.)
    Owl Creek Mountains (Wyo.)
    Park Range (Colo. and Wyo.)
    Rendezvous Mountain (Wyo.)
    Sherman Hill (Wyo.)

    Teton Range (Wyo. and Idaho)
    Uinta Mountains (Utah and Wyo.)
— **Yugoslavia**
  NT Bilo Mountains (Croatia)
    Dinaric Alps
    Fruška Mountains (Serbia)
    Julian Alps (Slovenia and Italy)
    Kalnik Mountain (Croatia)
    Karawanken (Austria and Slovenia)
    Kopaonik Mountains (Serbia)
    Kozara Mountains (Bosnia and Hercegovina)
    Majevica Mountains (Bosnia and Hercegovina)
    Medvednica Mountain (Croatia)
    Petrova Mountains (Croatia)
    Škofja Loka Mountains (Slovenia)
    Velebit Mountains (Croatia)
— **Yukon Territory**
  NT Mackenzie Mountains (N.W.T. and Yukon)
    Pelly Mountains (Yukon)
    Selwyn Mountains (Yukon and N.W.T.)
— **Zaire**
  NT Katekelayi Hill (Zaire)
— **Zambia**
  NT Bungua Hill (Zambia)
    Chafukuma Hill (Zambia)
— **Zimbabwe**
  NT Matopo Hills (Zimbabwe)
Mountains in art
  [N8213]
Mountains in literature
  [PN56.M7]
  BT Landscape
    Nature in literature
  NT Mountains in the Bible
Mountains in the Bible
  [BS630]
  BT Bible—Geography
    Mountains—Religious aspects
    Mountains in literature
Mountainy family
  USE Mounteney family
Mountaney family
  USE Mounteney family
Mountany family
  USE Mounteney family
Mounted police *(May Subd Geog)*
  UF Police, Mounted
  RT Police horses
Mounted sports
  USE Horse sports
Mountenay family
  USE Mounteney family
Mounteney family *(Not Subd Geog)*
  UF Monteny family
    Mountainy family
    Mountaney family
    Mountany family
    Mountenay family
    Mounteny family
    Mountnay family
    Mountney family
    Mountny family
Mounteny family
  USE Mounteney family
Mountgomery family
  USE Montgomery family
Mounting of microscope specimens
  [QH239]
  UF Microscope specimens, Mounting of
  BT Microscope and microscopy— Technique
Mountings, Jewelry
  USE Jewelry settings
Mountings, Sword
  USE Sword mountings
Mountnay family
  USE Mounteney family

Mountney family
  USE Mounteney family
Mountny family
  USE Mounteney family
Mounts, Lens
  USE Lens mounts
Mounts (Decorative arts) (May Subd Geog)
  BT Art metal-work
     Decoration and ornament
  NT Jewelry settings
Mounts Bay (England)
  UF Mount's Bay (England)
  BT Bays—England
Mount's Bay (England)
  USE Mounts Bay (England)
Mounts family
  USE Mount family
Mountz family
  USE Mount family
Moura Cave (Portugal)
  UF Cova da Moura (Portugal)
  BT Caves—Portugal
     Portugal—Antiquities
Moure family
  USE Moore family
Mourey family
  USE Morey family
Mourides
  USE Murīdīyah
Mouritsen family (Not Subd Geog)
Mourne Mountains (Northern Ireland)
  BT Mountains—Northern Ireland
Mourners, Professional
  USE Weepers (Mourners)
Mourners Sarcophagus (Sidon, Lebanon)
  ₍NB1810₎
  UF Klagefrauensarkophag (Sidon,
       Lebanon)
     Weeping Women Sarcophagus (Sidon,
       Lebanon)
  BT Lebanon—Antiquities, Phoenician
     Phoenicians—Lebanon
     Sarcophagi—Lebanon
     Sarcophagi, Greek—Lebanon
     Sarcophagi, Phoenician—Lebanon
Mourning
  USE Bereavement—Psychological aspects
     Grief
Mourning customs (May Subd Geog)
  ₍GT3390₎
  UF Mortuary customs
  BT Manners and customs
     Rites and ceremonies
  RT Funeral rites and ceremonies
  NT Laments
     Mourning etiquette
     Weepers (Mourners)
Mourning customs, Jewish
  ₍BM712₎
  UF Jewish mourning customs
  BT Funeral rites and ceremonies, Jewish
     Jewish law
Mourning dove
  ₍QL696.C63₎
  UF Dove, Mourning
     Turtledove, American
     Zenaida macroura
     Zenaidura caroliensis
     Zenaidura macroura caroliensis
  BT Zenaida
Mourning dove shooting
  ₍SK325.M65₎
  UF Dove shooting
  BT Upland game bird shooting
Mourning etiquette (May Subd Geog)
  ₍BJ2070-75₎
  UF Funeral etiquette
  BT Etiquette
     Mourning customs

Mourouzēs family (Not Subd Geog)
Mouse
  USE Mice
Mouse, Hazel
  USE Hazel mouse
Mouse (Computer program language)
  ₍QA76.73.M₎
  BT Programming languages (Electronic
     computers)
Mouse-deer
  ₍QL737.U5₎
  BT Deer
Mouse lemur, Lesser
  USE Microcebus murinus
Mouse lemurs
  USE Microcebus
Mouse leukemia complex
  UF Leukosis, Mouse
     Mouse leukosis
     Murine leukemia
  BT Leukemia in animals
     Mice—Diseases
Mouse leukemia viruses
  UF Murine leukemia viruses
  BT Retroviruses
  NT Friend virus
Mouse leukosis
  USE Mouse leukemia complex
Mouse sarcoma viruses
  USE Murine sarcoma viruses
Mousebirds
  USE Colius
Mouser family (Not Subd Geog)
  RT Musser family
Mousnier family
  USE Mounier family
Mousses
  ₍TX773₎
  BT Cookery (Cold dishes)
     Desserts
Mousseux
  USE Moso (Tribe)
Moussoulens, Saint-Jean family
  USE Saint-Jean Moussoulens family
Moustache
  USE Mustache
Moustached bats
  USE Pteronotus
Mousterian culture (May Subd Geog)
  ₍GN772.2.M6₎
  BT Neanderthal race
     Paleolithic period
Moutan peony
  USE Tree peony
Mouth
  ₍QL857 (Anatomy)₎
  ₍QM306 (Human anatomy)₎
  BT Dentistry
     Face
     Head
  NT Edentulous mouth
     Jaws
     Lips
     Mouth floor
     Oral habits
     Oral mucosa
     Periodontium
     Saliva
     Salivary glands
     Teeth
     Tongue
  — Abnormalities
     NT Velopharyngeal insufficiency
  — Bacteriology
     USE Mouth—Microbiology
  — Cancer
     ₍RC261₎
  — — Diagnosis
  — Care and hygiene (May Subd Geog)
     UF Oral hygiene
     BT Hygiene

  RT Oral hygiene products
  — Diseases (May Subd Geog)
     ₍RC815₎
     NT Fistula, Oroantral
        Gums—Diseases
        Ingestion disorders
        Mouth—Sepsis
        Oral manifestations of general
          diseases
        Orofacial pain
        Stomatitis
        Stomatology
        Thrush (Mouth disease)
  — — Diagnosis
        UF Oral diagnosis
        NT Mouth—Radiography
  — — Genetic aspects
  — — Immunological aspects
  — Examination
     UF Oral examination (Medicine)
  — Hemorrhage
     USE Oral hemorrhage
  — Innervation
  — Microbiology
     ₍QR47₎
     UF Dental microbiology
        Mouth—Bacteriology
        Oral microbiology
     NT Dental plaque
  — Radiography
     BT Mouth—Diseases—Diagnosis
  — Sepsis
     ₍RK305₎
     UF Mouth, Infections from
        Oral sepsis
     BT Mouth—Diseases
        Teeth—Diseases
  — Surgery
     ₍RK529-533₎
     UF Dental surgery
        Oral surgery
        Surgery, Dental
        Surgery, Oral
     NT Gag (Surgical instrument)
        Implant dentures
        Oral surgeons
        Teeth—Extraction
        Teeth—Transplantation
        Vestibuloplasty
  — Tuberculosis
  — Tumors
     ₍RD662₎
     NT Odontogenic cysts
        Odontogenic tumors
  — Ulcers
     UF Oral ulcerations
Mouth, Infections from
  USE Mouth—Sepsis
Mouth, Medication by
  USE Oral medication
Mouth breathing
  BT Oral habits
     Respiration
     Respiratory organs—Diseases
  NT Snoring
Mouth floor
  ₍QL857 (Comparative anatomy)₎
  ₍QM306 (Human anatomy)₎
  ₍QP146 (Physiology)₎
  UF Floor of mouth
     Sublingual region
  BT Mouth
Mouth gag
  USE Gag (Surgical instrument)
Mouth habits
  USE Oral habits
Mouth harmonica
  USE Harmonica
Mouth organ
  USE Harmonica

2481

Mouth organs
  [ML1088]
  BT Musical instruments
  NT Harmonica
    Kaen
    Sheng (Musical instrument)
    Shō
Mouth protectors
  [GV749.M6]
  BT Athletics—Equipment and supplies
Mouthpieces (Music)
  USE Brass instruments—Mouthpieces
Mouthwashes *(May Subd Geog)*
  UF Collutorium
    Oral antiseptics
  BT Antiseptics in dentistry
    Oral hygiene products
Mouton family *(Not Subd Geog)*
Mouvement Wallon
  USE Walloon Movement
Mouyeng (African people)
  [DT570]
  BT Ethnology—Cameroon
Mouyer family
  USE Moyer family
Movable books
  USE Toy and movable books
Move games
  USE Board games
Moveable books
  USE Toy and movable books
Movement, Aesthetic
  USE Aesthetic movement (British art)
Movement, Aesthetics of
  BT Aesthetics
    Movement, Psychology of
  RT Rhythm
  NT Eurythmy
Movement, Cursillo
  USE Cursillo movement
Movement, Disorders of
  USE Movement disorders
Movement, Ecumenical
  USE Ecumenical movement
Movement, Freedom of
  USE Freedom of movement
Movement, Notation of
  USE Movement notation
Movement, Psychology of
  [BF295]
  UF Motor psychology
  BT Motion
    Psychology, Physiological
    Will
  RT Motion study
    Movement education
    Muscular sense
  NT Drinking behavior
    Motion perception (Vision)
    Motor ability
    Motor learning
    Movement, Aesthetics of
    Movement therapy
    Perceptual-motor processes
    Rhythm
    Rhythm—Psychological aspects
    Sleep movements
Movement, Sanctuary
  USE Sanctuary movement
Movement, The (English poetry)
  [PR605.M68]
  UF The Movement (English poetry)
  BT English poetry—20th century
Movement (Acting)
  UF Movement on the stage
  BT Acting
  NT Gesture
    Nonverbal communication in motion
      pictures
    Stage fighting

Movement (Philosophy)
  [B105.M65]
  BT Philosophy
Movement cure
  USE Mechanotherapy
Movement disorders
  UF Dyskinesia
    Movement, Disorders of
  BT Nervous system—Diseases
  NT Ataxia
    Athetosis
    Chorea
    Dystonia musculorum deformans
    Eye—Movement disorders
    Hypokinesia
    Joints—Hypermobility
    Locomotion, Disordered
    Muscle hypotonia
    Muscle rigidity
    Mutism, Akinetic
    Paralysis
    Parkinsonism
    Psychomotor disorders
    Spasticity
    Tremor
Movement disorders, Drug-induced
  USE Tardive dyskinesia
Movement disorders in children
  (May Subd Geog)
  [RJ496.M]
  BT Children—Diseases
    Motor ability in children
    Pediatric neurology
  NT Cerebral palsied children
    Muscle hypotonia in children
    Psychomotor disorders in children
Movement education *(May Subd Geog)*
  [GV452]
  UF Education, Movement
  BT Kinesiology
    Man—Attitude and movement
    Physical education and training
    Physical education for children
  RT Motor learning
    Movement, Psychology of
Movement notation
  [GV1587]
  UF Kinetography
    Movement, Notation of
  NT Dance notation
Movement of fertilizers in soils
  USE Soils—Fertilizer movement
Movement of herbicides in soils
  USE Soils—Herbicide movement
Movement of robots
  USE Robots—Motion
Movement on the stage
  USE Movement (Acting)
Movement therapy *(May Subd Geog)*
  BT Mind and body therapies
    Movement, Psychology of
    Psychotherapy
  RT Dance therapy
    Exercise therapy
Movements, Foot
  USE Foot—Movements
Movements, Human
  USE Human mechanics
Movements against apartheid
  USE Anti-apartheid movements
Movements in sleep
  USE Sleep movements
Movements of animals
  USE Animal locomotion
    Animal mechanics
    Irritability
Movements of plants
  USE Plants—Irritability and movements
Movie . . .
  USE *subject headings beginning with the
    words* Moving-picture

Movie cameras
  USE Moving-picture cameras
Movie loops
  USE Moving-pictures, Loop
Moviegoers
  USE Moving-picture audiences
Movies
  USE Moving-pictures
Movietone
  USE Moving-pictures, Talking
Movima language
  [PM6573]
  UF Mobima language
    Moyma language
  BT Indians of South America—Languages
Moving, Household *(May Subd Geog)*
  UF Household moving
    Relocation (Household moving)
Moving industry
  USE Storage and moving trade
Moving loads (Bridges)
  USE Bridges—Live loads
Moving loads (Pavements)
  USE Pavements—Live loads
Moving of buildings, bridges, etc.
  [TH153 (Building)]
  UF Buildings, Moving of
    House moving
Moving photomicrography
  USE Microcinematography
Moving-picture academy awards
  USE Academy awards (Moving-pictures)
Moving-picture acting
  UF Acting for moving-pictures
    Film acting
  BT Acting
    Moving-pictures
  NT Moving-picture actors and actresses
    Nonverbal communication in motion
      pictures
Moving-picture actors and actresses
  (May Subd Geog)
  UF Film actors
    Film stars
    Moving-picture stars
    Women as moving-picture actresses
  BT Actors
    Actresses
    Moving-picture acting
    Moving-pictures—Biography
    Women in the motion picture industry
  — Auditions
    USE Screen tests
  — **Credits**
    UF Credits of motion picture actors
        and actresses
      Film credits of motion picture
        actors and actresses
      Moving-picture credits of actors
        and actresses
Moving-picture actors and actresses, Afro-
  American
  USE Afro-American motion picture actors
    and actresses
Moving-picture adaptations
  USE Film adaptations
Moving-picture archives
  USE Archives, Motion picture
Moving-picture art directors
  (May Subd Geog)
  UF Art directors, Motion picture
  BT Moving-picture producers and
    directors
Moving-picture audiences *(May Subd Geog)*
  UF Film audiences
    Filmgoers
    Moviegoers
    Moving-pictures—Audiences

2482

BT Moving-picture industry
    Moving-pictures—Social aspects
    Performing arts—Audiences
    Theater audiences
Moving-picture authorship
  [PN1996]
  UF Film authorship
    Moving-picture plays—Authorship
    Moving-picture writing
    Moving-pictures—Play-writing
    Screenwriting
    Scriptwriting, Motion picture
  BT Authorship
  RT Screenwriters
  NT Moving-picture plays—Technique
Moving-picture awards
  USE Moving-pictures—Awards
    Moving-pictures, Documentary—
      Awards
Moving-picture cameramen
  USE Cinematographers
Moving-picture cameras
  [TR880]
  UF Movie cameras
  BT Cameras
    Cinematography
  SA *individual makes of moving-picture*
    cameras, e.g. Revere moving-picture
    camera
  NT Arriflex 16SR moving-picture camera
    Electronic cameras
    Kinetograph
Moving-picture cartoons *(May Subd Geog)*
  [NC1765 (Drawing)]
  [PN1997.5 (Scenarios)]
  Here are entered animated cartoons, including
those featuring animals. Individual fiction films in
which animals are the principal characters are en-
tered under Animal films.
  UF Animated cartoons
  BT Caricatures and cartoons
    Short films
  RT Animation (Cinematography)
  NT Comedy films
    Computer animation
    Donald Duck (Cartoon character)
    Mickey Mouse (Cartoon character)
    Television broadcasting of motion
      picture cartoons
Moving-picture cartoons, American, [German,
etc.] *(May Subd Geog)*
Moving-picture cartoons, Bulgarian
(May Subd Geog)
  UF Bulgarian moving-picture cartoons
Moving-picture cartoons, French
(May Subd Geog)
  UF French moving-picture cartoons
Moving-picture cartoons, Hungarian
(May Subd Geog)
  UF Hungarian moving-picture cartoons
Moving-picture cartoons, Kazakh
(May Subd Geog)
  UF Kazakh motion picture cartoons
Moving-picture cartoons, Russian
(May Subd Geog)
  UF Russian motion-picture cartoons
Moving-picture cartoons, Swiss
(May Subd Geog)
  UF Swiss moving-picture cartoons
Moving-picture cartoons, Ukrainian
(May Subd Geog)
  UF Ukrainian moving-picture cartoons
Moving-picture cartoons, Vietnamese
(May Subd Geog)
  UF Vietnamese moving-picture cartoons
Moving-picture characters
  USE Characters and characteristics in
      moving-pictures
Moving-picture circulation
  USE Moving-pictures—Distribution

Moving-picture collections
  USE Moving-picture film collections
Moving-picture comedies
  USE Comedy films
Moving-picture credits of actors and actresses
  USE Moving-picture actors and actresses—
      Credits
Moving-picture credits of producers and
directors
  USE Moving-picture producers and
      directors—Credits
Moving-picture criticism *(May Subd Geog)*
  [PN1995]
  Here are entered works dealing with the tech-
nique of moving-picture reviewing. Works dealing
with criticism of screenplays are entered under Mov-
ing-picture plays—History and criticism. Collections
of reviews are entered under Moving-pictures—Re-
views.
  UF Moving-pictures—Criticism
  BT Criticism
    Dramatic criticism
  RT Moving-pictures—Evaluation
  NT Moving-picture critics
    Newspapers—Sections, columns, etc.—
      Reviews
Moving-picture critics *(May Subd Geog)*
  UF Film critics
  BT Critics
    Moving-picture criticism
  NT Women motion picture critics
Moving-picture direction
  USE Moving-pictures—Production and
      direction
Moving-picture directors and producers
  USE Moving-picture producers and
      directors
Moving-picture distribution
  USE Moving-pictures—Distribution
Moving-picture editing
  USE Moving-pictures—Editing
Moving-picture editors *(May Subd Geog)*
  UF Editors, Moving-picture
  BT Moving-pictures—Editing
Moving-picture festivals *(May Subd Geog)*
  UF Film festivals
    Moving-pictures—Festivals
  BT Art festivals
    Festivals
    Performing arts festivals
Moving-picture film
  UF Cinematograph film
    Cinematographic film
    Films, Cinematographic
    Moving-pictures—Film
  BT Cinematography
    Photography—Films
  — Preservation and storage
    [TR886.3]
    UF Preservation of moving-picture film
  — Splicing
    [TR886.5]
    UF Splicing (Moving-picture film)
Moving-picture film collections
(May Subd Geog)
  UF Film collections
    Film libraries
    Libraries, Film
    Libraries, Motion picture
    Moving-picture collections
    Moving-picture libraries
  BT Libraries, Special
  RT Archives, Motion picture
    Libraries and moving-pictures
  NT Danmarks Radio Film Collection
    George Kleine Film Collection
Moving-picture film coupons
  USE UNESCO film coupons
Moving-picture film editing
  USE Moving-pictures—Editing

Moving-picture genres
  USE Film genres
Moving-picture industry *(May Subd Geog)*
  UF Film industry (Motion pictures)
  NT Blacks in the motion picture industry
    Minorities in motion pictures
    Minorities in the motion picture
      industry
    Moving-picture audiences
    Moving-pictures—Distribution
    Moving-pictures—Production and
      direction
    Moving-pictures, American, [French,
      etc.]
    Strikes and lockouts—Moving-picture
      industry
    Trade-unions—Moving-picture
      industry
    UNESCO film coupons
    Women in the motion picture industry
  — Biography
    USE Moving-pictures—Biography
  — **Collectibles** *(May Subd Geog)*
  — Collective bargaining
    USE Collective bargaining—Moving-
      picture industry
  — Collective labor agreements
    USE Collective labor agreements—
      Moving-picture industry
  — **Employees**
    NT Collective labor agreements—
      Moving-picture industry
      Wages—Moving-picture industry
  — Federal aid
    USE Federal aid to the motion picture
      industry
  — **Finance**
    UF Moving-pictures—Finance
    NT Federal aid to the motion picture
      industry
  — Public relations
    USE Public relations—Moving-picture
      industry
  — **Taxation** *(May Subd Geog)*
    RT Amusements—Taxation
  — **United States**
    NT Afro-Americans in the motion
      picture industry
Moving-picture industry in motion-pictures
  BT Moving-pictures
Moving-picture insurance
  USE Insurance, Moving-picture
Moving-picture journalism
(May Subd Geog)
  UF Moving-pictures—Journalism
    Newsreel
  BT Journalism
    Journalism and moving-pictures
    Moving-pictures
  RT Newsreels
  NT News photographers
Moving-picture libraries
  USE Moving-picture film collections
Moving-picture literature *(May Subd Geog)*
  UF Film literature
    Literature, Film
    Literature, Motion picture
  RT Moving-pictures—Bibliography
  — Cataloging
    USE Cataloging of motion picture
      literature
Moving-picture locations *(May Subd Geog)*
  UF Filming on location
    Locations (Motion pictures)
  BT Moving-pictures
    Moving-pictures—Production and
      direction
    Moving-pictures—Setting and scenery
Moving-picture loops
  USE Moving-pictures, Loop

Moving-picture make-up
  USE Film make-up
Moving-picture music *(May Subd Geog)*
  ₍ML2075₎
  UF Film music
      Moving-pictures—Musical
        accompaniment
  BT Moving-pictures, Musical
      Music
      Musical accompaniment
  RT Silent film music
  — Copyright
      USE Copyright—Moving-picture music
  — Excerpts
  — — Vocal scores with accordion
      ₍M1507-8₎
  — — Vocal scores with piano
      ₍M1507-8₎
      UF Moving-picture music—Vocal
          scores with piano—Excerpts
  — Piano scores
      ₍M1527₎
      BT Piano music, Arranged
  — Scores
      ₍M1527₎
      UF Moving-pictures—Musical scores
          Moving-pictures, Musical—Scores
  — Vocal scores with piano
      ₍M1507-8₎
  — — Excerpts
      USE Moving-picture music—
          Excerpts—Vocal scores
          with piano
Moving-picture music, Arranged
Moving-picture paraphernalia
  USE Moving-pictures—Collectibles
Moving-picture plays
  ₍PN1996-PN1997₎
  UF Filmscripts
      Photoplays
      Scenarios
      Screenplays
  BT Drama
  NT Comedy films
      Film adaptations
      Shakespeare, William, 1564-1616—
        Moving-picture plays
  — Authorship
      USE Moving-picture authorship
  — History and criticism
  — Production and direction
      USE Moving-pictures—Production and
          direction
  — Reviews
      USE Moving-pictures—Reviews
  — Stories, plots, etc.
      USE Moving-pictures—Plots, themes,
          etc.
  — Technique
      BT Moving-picture authorship
Moving-picture plots
  USE Moving-pictures—Plots, themes, etc.
Moving-picture posters
  USE Film posters
Moving-picture producers and directors
  (May Subd Geog)
  ₍PN1998.A2₎
  UF Directors, Moving-picture
      Film directors
      Film producers and directors
      Moving-picture directors and
        producers
      Producers, Moving-picture
  BT Moving-pictures—Biography
      Moving-pictures—Production and
        direction
  NT Afro-American motion picture
        producers and directors
      Casting directors
      Moving-picture art directors

      Women motion picture producers and
        directors
  — Credits
      UF Credits of motion picture
          producers and directors
          Film credits of motion picture
          producers and directors
          Moving-picture credits of
          producers and directors
Moving-picture production
  USE Moving-pictures—Production and
      direction
Moving-picture programs *(May Subd Geog)*
  ₍PN1995.9.P5₎
  UF Film programs
  BT Playbills
Moving-picture projection
  ₍TR890₎
  UF Bioscope
      Projection, Moving-picture
  BT Lantern projection
      Moving-picture theaters
      Moving-pictures
  NT Moving-picture projectors
  — Safety regulations *(May Subd Geog)*
      BT Moving-picture theaters—Law and
          legislation
      NT Safety film—Law and legislation
Moving-picture projectors
  BT Moving-picture projection
      Projectors
  — Light sources
      UF Light sources for moving-picture
          projectors
      BT Electric lamps
  — — Power supply
      BT Electric power
Moving-picture remakes
  ₍PN1995.9.R45₎
  UF Moving-pictures—Remakes
      Remakes, Moving-picture
  BT Moving-pictures
Moving-picture reviews
  USE Moving-pictures—Reviews
Moving-picture sequels
  ₍PN1995.9.S29₎
  UF Moving-pictures—Sequels
      Sequels, Moving-picture
      Sequels (Moving-pictures)
  BT Moving-pictures
Moving-picture serials
  UF Moving-pictures—Serials
      Serials, Moving-picture
Moving-picture stars
  USE Moving-picture actors and actresses
Moving-picture story editors
  USE Story editors (Motion pictures)
Moving-picture studios *(May Subd Geog)*
  NT Moving-pictures—Setting and scenery
Moving-picture theater managers
  (May Subd Geog)
  BT Moving-picture theaters—Management
Moving-picture theaters *(May Subd Geog)*
  ₍NA6845 (Architecture)₎
  ₍PN1993-PN1999₎
  UF Cinemas
      Theaters, Moving-picture
  BT Architecture
      Theaters
  NT Drive-in theaters
      Moving-picture projection
      Wages—Moving-picture theaters
  — Conservation and restoration
      NT Moving-picture theaters—
          Remodeling for other use
  — Law and legislation *(May Subd Geog)*
      NT Moving-picture projection—Safety
          regulations
  — Management
      NT Moving-picture theater managers
  — Remodeling for other use

      UF Moving-picture theaters—
          Renovation
          Remodeling of moving-picture
          theaters for other use
          Renovation of moving-picture
          theaters
      BT Moving-picture theaters—
          Conservation and restoration
  — Renovation
      USE Moving-picture theaters—
          Remodeling for other use
  — California
      NT Paramount Theatre (Oakland,
          Calif.)
  — Japan
      NT Jinseiza (Tokyo, Japan)
Moving-picture titling
  USE Moving-pictures—Titling
Moving-picture writing
  USE Moving-picture authorship
Moving-pictures *(May Subd Geog)*
  ₍PN1992-PN1999₎
      Here are entered general works on moving-pic-
  tures themselves, including moving-pictures as an art
  form, copyrighting, distribution, editing, plots, pro-
  duction, etc. Works on the technical aspects of mak-
  ing moving-pictures and their projection on to a
  screen are entered under Cinematography.
  UF Cinema
      Films
      Motion pictures
      Movies
      Moving-pictures—History and
        criticism
      Photography—Animated pictures
      Photography—Moving-pictures
  BT Audio-visual materials
      Mass media
      Photographs
  NT Adventure films
      Africa, North, in motion pictures
      Africa in moving-pictures
      Afro-Americans in motion pictures
      Alien labor in motion pictures
      Alienation (Social psychology) in
        moving-pictures
      Animals in moving-pictures
      Anti-Nazi movement in motion
        pictures
      Antiheroes in motion pictures
      Antisemitism in motion pictures
      Apes in motion pictures
      Architecture in motion pictures
      Art in moving-pictures
      Asians in motion pictures
      Atomic bomb victims in motion
        pictures
      Automobiles in moving-pictures
      Ballet in moving-pictures, television,
        etc.
      Baths in moving-pictures
      Bible films
      Biko, Stephen, 1946-1977, in motion
        pictures
      Biographical films
      Blacks in motion pictures
      Boats and boating in motion pictures
      Bondage (Sexual behavior) in motion
        pictures
      Bowery Boys films
      Brooklyn (New York, N.Y.) in motion
        pictures
      Bullfights in motion pictures
      Canada in motion pictures
      Catholic Church in motion pictures
      Catholics in motion pictures
      Characters and characteristics in
        moving-pictures
      Charlie Chan films
      Children in motion pictures
      Children's films

China in motion pictures
Cities and towns in motion pictures
City and town life in motion pictures
Civilization, Ancient, in motion
  pictures
Clay animation films
Clergy in moving-pictures
College life films
Color moving-pictures
Comedy films
Comic strip characters in motion
  pictures
Country life in motion pictures
Cruelty in motion pictures
Dadaism in motion pictures
Dancing in moving-pictures, television,
  etc.
Death in motion pictures
Detective and mystery films
Developing countries in motion
  pictures
Disasters in motion pictures
Dogs in motion pictures
Doubles in motion pictures
Drifters in motion pictures
Drugs in motion pictures
English language—Study and teaching
  —Audio-visual aids
Entertainers in motion pictures
Erotic films
Existentialism in motion pictures
Experimental films
Family in motion pictures
Farm life in moving-pictures
Fascism and motion pictures
Feature films
Feminism and motion pictures
Feminist motion pictures
Film genres
Films by children
Films noirs
Flight in motion pictures
Frankenstein films
Gangster films
German reunification question (1949-
) in motion pictures
Grand Prix racing in motion pictures
Hand-to-hand fighting, Oriental, in
  motion pictures
Heroes in motion pictures
Historical films
Hồ Chí Minh, 1890-1969, in motion
  pictures
Holocaust, Jewish (1939-1945), in
  motion pictures
Homosexuality in motion pictures
Horror films
Horses in moving-pictures
Identity (Psychology) in motion
  pictures
Impersonators, Female, in motion
  pictures
Impersonators, Male, in motion
  pictures
Impressionism in motion pictures
India in motion pictures
Indians in motion pictures
Ireland in motion pictures
Israel-Arab War, 1973, in motion
  pictures
Italian Americans in motion pictures
James Bond films
Japan in motion pictures
Jesus Christ in moving-pictures
Jewish-Arab relations in motion
  pictures
Jews in motion pictures
Journalists in motion-pictures
Justice, Administration of, in motion
  pictures
Juvenile delinquency films

Karate in motion-pictures
Labor and laboring classes in motion
  pictures
Latin America in motion pictures
Lenin, Vladimir Ilích, 1870-1924, in
  motion pictures
Libraries and moving-pictures
Lions in motion pictures
Lone Ranger films
Love in motion pictures
Marriage in moving-pictures
Masochism in motion pictures
Men in motion pictures
Mental illness in motion pictures
Mexican-American Border Region in
  motion pictures
Mexican Americans in motion pictures
Middle age in motion pictures
Miners in motion pictures
Minorities in motion pictures
Minority women in motion pictures
Moldavian S.S.R. in motion pictures
Monsters in motion pictures
Motor vehicles in motion pictures
Moving-picture acting
Moving-picture industry in motion-
  pictures
Moving-picture journalism
Moving-picture locations
Moving-picture projection
Moving-picture remakes
Moving-picture sequels
Moving-pictures, Musical
Moving-pictures and television
Mukhtār, 'Umar, 1860?-1931, in
  motion pictures
Myth in motion pictures
Mythology in motion pictures
National characteristics, American, in
  motion pictures
National socialism and motion pictures
National socialism in motion pictures
New Deal, 1933-1939, in motion
  pictures
Newsreels
Nonverbal communication in motion
  pictures
Nuclear warfare in motion pictures
Our Gang films
Outlaws in motion pictures
Painting and motion pictures
Paris (France) in motion pictures
Peasants in motion pictures
Phenakistoscope
Poland in motion pictures
Politics in motion pictures
Prehistoric animals in motion pictures
Prussia (Germany) in motion pictures
Psychiatry in motion pictures
Racism in motion pictures
Railroads in moving-pictures
Realism in moving-pictures
Regeneration in motion pictures
Religion and motion pictures
Religion in motion pictures
Religious films
Repetition in motion pictures
Revolutions in motion pictures
Sadism in moving-pictures
Samurai films
Science fiction films
Science films
Scotland in motion pictures
Screen tests
Script clerks
Sea in motion pictures
Sensationalism in motion pictures
Sex in moving-pictures
Sherlock Holmes films
Short films
Silent films

Social problems in motion pictures
Socialism and motion pictures
Socialist realism in motion pictures
Southern States in motion pictures
Sports films
Sports in motion pictures
Spy films
Star Trek films
Star Wars films
Superman films
Supernatural in moving-pictures
Surrealism in motion pictures
Swordsmen in motion pictures
Tarzan films
Teachers in moving-pictures
Texas in motion pictures
Three Stooges films
Time in motion pictures
Trial in motion pictures
Ukrainians in motion pictures
Underground movements in motion
  pictures
United States in motion pictures
Vampire films
Villains in motion pictures
Violence in motion pictures
War films
Werewolf films
Western films
Women in motion pictures
Woods, Donald, 1933-   , in motion
  pictures
Young adult films
Youth in moving-pictures
— Academy awards
   USE Academy awards (Moving-
          pictures)
— Advertising
   USE Advertising—Motion pictures
— **Aesthetics**
   BT Aesthetics
— **Appreciation**
   UF Appreciation of moving-pictures
— **Archival resources** *(May Subd Geog)*
   BT Moving-pictures—Bibliography
— Audiences
   USE Moving-picture audiences
— **Awards**
   UF Moving-picture awards
   BT Rewards (Prizes, etc.)
   NT Academy awards (Moving-pictures)
        Bayerischer Filmpreis
— **Bibliography**
   RT Moving-picture literature
   NT Moving-pictures—Archival
         resources
— **Biography**
   ₍PN1998.A2-3₎
   UF Moving-picture industry—
         Biography
   NT Moving-picture actors and
         actresses
        Moving-picture producers and
         directors
— **Casting**
   ₍PN1995.9.C34₎
   UF Casting of motion pictures
   BT Moving-pictures—Production and
         direction
— Cataloging
   USE Cataloging of moving-pictures
— **Catalogs**
   UF Catalogs, Film
        Film catalogs
        Filmography
   SA *subdivision* Film catalogs *under
         specific subjects, e.g.* Geology—
         Film catalogs; Hygiene—Film
         catalogs
— **Censorship** *(May Subd Geog)*
   ₍PN1994.A1-5₎

Moving-pictures
— **Censorship** *(Continued)*
    BT Freedom of information
— Circulation
    USE Moving-pictures—Distribution
— **Collectibles** *(May Subd Geog)*
    [PN1995.P.C53]
    UF Moving-picture paraphernalia
— **Competitions**
    NT Cinematography—Competitions
— Copyright
    USE Copyright—Moving-pictures
— Costume
    USE Costume
— Criticism
    USE Moving-picture criticism
— Direction
    USE Moving-pictures—Production and
        direction
— **Distribution**
    UF Moving-picture circulation
        Moving-picture distribution
        Moving-pictures—Circulation
    BT Moving-picture industry
    NT Block booking
        Moving-pictures, Documentary—
        Distribution
— — **Law and legislation**
    (May Subd Geog)
    BT Contracts
— Dubbing
    USE Dubbing of moving-pictures
— **Editing**
    UF Film editing (Cinematography)
        Moving-picture editing
        Moving-picture film editing
        Moving-pictures—Film editing
        Moving-pictures—Montage
    BT Editing
    NT Moving-picture editors
— **Evaluation**
    [PN1995.9.E9]
    UF Moving-pictures, Documentary—
        Evaluation
    BT Moving-pictures, Documentary
        Moving-pictures in education
    RT Moving-picture criticism
— Fantastic films
    USE Fantastic films
— Festivals
    USE Moving-picture festivals
— Film
    USE Moving-picture film
— Film editing
    USE Moving-pictures—Editing
— Finance
    USE Moving-picture industry—
        Finance
— **History**
    UF Moving-pictures—History and
        criticism
— History and criticism
    USE Moving-pictures
        Moving-pictures—History
— Industrial applications
    USE Moving-pictures in industry
— Insurance
    USE Insurance, Moving-picture
— Journalism
    USE Moving-picture journalism
— **Law and legislation** *(May Subd Geog)*
    NT Copyright—Moving-pictures
        Moving-pictures—Registration
— Lighting
    USE Cinematography—Lighting
— Montage
    USE Moving-pictures—Editing
— **Moral and ethical aspects**
    [PN1995.5]
    UF Moving-pictures—Moral and
        religious aspects

— Moral and religious aspects
    USE Moving-pictures—Moral and
        ethical aspects
— Musical accompaniment
    USE Moving-picture music
— Musical scores
    USE Moving-picture music—Scores
— **Periodicals**
    UF Fan magazines
— Play-writing
    USE Moving-picture authorship
— **Plots, themes, etc.**
    Films on specific topics are entered under
    specific headings, e.g. Horror films; War films;
    Children in motion pictures; Death in motion
    pictures.
    UF Moving-picture plays—Stories,
        plots, etc.
        Moving-picture plots
        Moving-pictures—Stories, plots,
        etc.
        Moving-pictures—Themes, motives
    BT Plots (Drama, novel, etc.)
    RT Film genres
— Posters
    USE Film posters
— **Production and direction**
    UF Moving-picture direction
        Moving-picture plays—Production
        and direction
        Moving-picture production
        Moving-pictures—Direction
    BT Moving-picture industry
    NT Moving-picture locations
        Moving-picture producers and
        directors
        Moving-pictures—Casting
        Script clerks
— — **Biography**
    Here are entered collective biographies of
    the occupations involved in the production of
    motion pictures.
— **Registration** *(May Subd Geog)*
    UF Moving-pictures, Registration of
    BT Moving-pictures—Law and
        legislation
— **Religious aspects**
— — **Baptists, [Catholic Church, etc.]**
— — **Buddhism, [Christianity, etc.]**
— — **Catholic Church**
    UF Catholic Church and moving-
        pictures
        Moving-pictures and Catholic
        Church
— Remakes
    USE Moving-picture remakes
— **Reviews**
    [PN1995]
    UF Moving-picture plays—Reviews
        Moving-picture reviews
        Reviews of moving-pictures
— Scientific applications
    USE Cinematography—Scientific
        applications
— **Semiotics**
    [PN1995]
    UF Semiotics of motion pictures
    BT Semiotics
— Sequels
    USE Moving-picture sequels
— Serials
    USE Moving-picture serials
— **Setting and scenery**
    [PN1995]
    UF Scenery (Stage)
        Setting (Stage)
        Stage scenery
        Stage-setting
        Staging
    BT Moving-picture studios

    RT Scene painting
        Television—Stage-setting and
        scenery
        Theaters—Stage-setting and
        scenery
    NT Moving-picture locations
        Stage props
— **Social aspects** *(May Subd Geog)*
    [PN1995.9.S6]
    NT Moving-picture audiences
— Sound
    USE Moving-pictures, Talking
— **Sound effects**
    BT Moving-pictures, Talking
        Sounds
— Special effects
    USE Cinematography—Special effects
— Stories, plots, etc.
    USE Moving-pictures—Plots, themes,
        etc.
— Themes, motives
    USE Moving-pictures—Plots, themes,
        etc.
— Therapeutic use
    USE Moving-pictures in psychotherapy
— Titles
    USE Moving-pictures—Titling
— **Titling**
    [TR899]
    UF Moving-picture titling
        Moving-pictures—Titles
        Titles (Moving-pictures)
— **Vocational guidance**
    UF Moving-pictures as a profession
— **United States**
Moving-pictures, Amateur
    USE Amateur moving-pictures
Moving-pictures, American
    (May Subd Geog)
    UF American motion pictures
Moving-pictures, American, [French, etc.]
    (May Subd Geog)
    Here are entered works dealing with moving-pic-
    tures produced by the moving-picture industry of an
    individual country and shown outside the country.
    Works on moving-pictures produced by the moving-
    picture industry of an individual country or on the
    moving pictures shown in an individual country are
    entered under Moving-pictures—[local subdivi-
    sion], e.g. Moving pictures—United States.
    BT Moving-picture industry
Moving-pictures, Australian
    (May Subd Geog)
    UF Australian motion pictures
Moving-pictures, Canadian
    (May Subd Geog)
    UF Canadian motion pictures
Moving-pictures, Continuous
    USE Moving-pictures, Loop
Moving-pictures, Documentary
    (May Subd Geog)
    UF Documentary films
        Documentary moving-pictures
    BT Documentary mass media
    NT Moving-pictures—Evaluation
— **Awards**
    UF Moving-picture awards
    BT Rewards (Prizes, etc.)
— **Distribution**
    BT Moving-pictures—Distribution
    RT Libraries and moving-pictures
    NT Museums and moving-pictures
— Evaluation
    USE Moving-pictures—Evaluation
— **International cooperation**
    UF International cooperation in
        documentary moving-pictures
— **Production and direction**
Moving-pictures, Educational
    USE Moving-pictures in education
Moving-pictures, Erotic
    USE Erotic films

Moving-pictures, Experimental
  USE Experimental films
Moving-pictures, Loop
  UF Film loops
      Movie loops
      Moving-picture loops
      Moving-pictures, Continuous
  BT Moving-pictures in education
Moving-pictures, Musical *(May Subd Geog)*
  [PN1995.9.M86]
  UF Musical moving-pictures
      Musicals (Motion pictures)
      Operatic moving-pictures
  BT Moving-pictures
  NT Moving-picture music
      Operas—Film and video adaptations
      Rock films
  — **History and criticism**
  — Scores
        USE Moving-picture music—Scores
Moving-pictures, Portuguese
  (May Subd Geog)
  UF Portuguese moving-pictures
Moving-pictures, Registration of
  USE Moving-pictures—Registration
Moving-pictures, Religious
  USE Religious films
Moving-pictures, Silent
  USE Silent films
Moving-pictures, Stereoscopic
  USE Moving-pictures, Three-dimensional
Moving-pictures, Swiss *(May Subd Geog)*
  UF Swiss motion pictures
Moving-pictures, Talking
  [PN1995.7]
  UF Kinetophone
      Movietone
      Moving-pictures—Sound
      Photophone
      Radiomovies
      Sound motion pictures
      Sound pictures
      Talkies
      Talking movies
      Talking pictures
      Vitaphone
  NT Dubbing of moving-pictures
      Moving-pictures—Sound effects
      Sound—Recording and reproducing
      Video tapes
Moving-pictures, Three-dimensional
  UF Cinematography, Stereoscopic
      Moving-pictures, Stereoscopic
      Stereoscopic moving-pictures
      Three-dimensional moving-pictures
  BT Three-dimensional display systems
  NT Wide-screen processes
        (Cinematography)
Moving-pictures, Ukrainian
  (May Subd Geog)
  UF Ukrainian motion pictures
Moving-pictures, Wide-screen
  USE Wide-screen processes
        (Cinematography)
Moving-pictures, Yiddish *(May Subd Geog)*
  [PN1995.9.Y54]
  UF Yiddish motion pictures
Moving-pictures about art
  USE Art in moving-pictures
Moving-pictures and art
  USE Art and moving-pictures
Moving-pictures and Catholic Church
  USE Moving-pictures—Religious aspects—
        Catholic Church
Moving-pictures and children
  (May Subd Geog)
  UF Children and moving-pictures
  BT Arts and children
      Children
      Mass media and children
  RT Moving-pictures for children

  NT Children in motion pictures
      Films by children
      Moving-pictures and youth
Moving-pictures and communism
  USE Communism and moving-pictures
Moving-pictures and dancing
  USE Dancing in moving-pictures, television,
        etc.
Moving-pictures and history
  [PN1995.2]
  UF History and moving-pictures
  BT History
  RT Historical films
Moving-pictures and journalism
  USE Journalism and moving-pictures
Moving-pictures and libraries
  USE Libraries and moving-pictures
Moving-pictures and literature
  (May Subd Geog)
  [PN1995.3]
  UF Literature and moving-pictures
      Moving-pictures and poetry
      Poetry and moving-pictures
  BT Moving-pictures and the arts
  NT Moving-pictures in literature
Moving-pictures and museums
  USE Museums and moving-pictures
Moving-pictures and music
  UF Music and moving-pictures
  BT Moving-pictures and the arts
Moving-pictures and painting
  USE Painting and motion pictures
Moving-pictures and poetry
  USE Moving-pictures and literature
Moving-pictures and socialism
  USE Socialism and motion pictures
Moving-pictures and television
  UF Television and moving-pictures
  BT Moving-pictures
      Television
      Television broadcasting
  NT Television broadcasting of films
      Television film
Moving-pictures and the arts
  (May Subd Geog)
  [PN1995.25]
  BT Arts
  NT Art and moving-pictures
      Dancing in moving-pictures, television,
        etc.
      Moving-pictures and literature
      Moving-pictures and music
      Moving-pictures and theater
Moving-pictures and theater
  (May Subd Geog)
  UF Theater and moving-pictures
  BT Moving-pictures and the arts
Moving-pictures and war
  USE *subdivisions* Motion pictures and the
        war, Motion pictures and the
        revolution, *etc. under individual
        wars, e.g.* World War, 1939-1945—
        Motion pictures and the war
Moving-pictures and youth
  (May Subd Geog)
  UF Youth and moving-pictures
  BT Moving-pictures and children
Moving-pictures as a profession
  USE Moving-pictures—Vocational guidance
Moving-pictures for children
  (May Subd Geog)
    Here are entered works which discuss collectively
  fiction and non-fiction films for children. Individual
  fiction films for children are entered under Children's
  films. Works discussing fiction films for children are
  entered under Children's films—History and criti-
  cism.
  UF Children's moving-pictures
  BT Children's mass media
  RT Moving-pictures and children

  SA *subdivision* Juvenile films *under
        subjects*
  NT Children's films
Moving-pictures for the deaf
  USE Films for the hearing impaired
Moving-pictures for the hearing impaired
  USE Films for the hearing impaired
Moving-pictures for women
  (May Subd Geog)
  [PN1995.9.W6]
  BT Women
Moving-pictures for young adults
  USE Young adult films
Moving-pictures in ability testing
  BT Ability—Testing
Moving-pictures in advertising
  UF Advertising, Moving-pictures in
Moving-pictures in aeronautics
  BT Aeronautics
      Aeronautics—Study and teaching
Moving-pictures in agriculture
  (May Subd Geog)
  BT Agriculture—Study and teaching—
        Audio-visual aids
Moving-pictures in business
  USE Moving-pictures in industry
Moving-pictures in chemical engineering
  BT Chemical engineering
      Moving-pictures in industry
Moving-pictures in child study
  BT Child development
Moving-pictures in church work
  (May Subd Geog)
  [BV652.82]
  BT Mass media in religion
  NT Moving-pictures in religious education
Moving-pictures in dentistry
  [RK76]
  BT Dentistry—Study and teaching
Moving-pictures in education
  (May Subd Geog)
  [LB1044]
  UF Educational films
      Moving-pictures, Educational
  BT Education
      Teaching—Aids and devices
      Visual education
  NT Libraries and moving-pictures
      Moving-pictures—Evaluation
      Moving-pictures, Loop
      Moving-pictures in higher education
      Moving-pictures in nursing education
      Moving-pictures in technical education
      Museums and moving-pictures
Moving-pictures in ethnology
  BT Ethnology
Moving-pictures in evangelistic work
  (May Subd Geog)
  BT Evangelistic work
Moving-pictures in forestry
  BT Forests and forestry
Moving-pictures in higher education
  (May Subd Geog)
  BT Education, Higher
      Moving-pictures in education
Moving-pictures in historiography
  BT Historiography
Moving-pictures in industry
  (May Subd Geog)
  UF Industrial films
      Moving-pictures—Industrial
        applications
      Moving-pictures in business
  BT Business
      Employees, Training of
      Industry
      Technical education
  NT Moving-pictures in chemical
        engineering
      Moving-pictures in mining

Moving-pictures in libraries
USE Libraries and moving-pictures
Moving-pictures in literature
BT Moving-pictures and literature
Moving-pictures in medicine
(May Subd Geog)
[R835]
UF Medical films
BT Medicine
Visual education
Moving-pictures in military education
(May Subd Geog)
[U408.3]
BT Military education
Moving-pictures in mining
BT Mining engineering
Moving-pictures in industry
Moving-pictures in missionary work
(May Subd Geog)
BT Missions
Moving-pictures in museums
USE Museums and moving-pictures
Moving-pictures in nursing education
BT Moving-pictures in education
Nursing—Study and teaching—Audio-
visual aids
Moving-pictures in physics
Moving-pictures in propaganda
(May Subd Geog)
UF Propaganda in moving-pictures
BT Propaganda
Moving-pictures in psychology
(May Subd Geog)
[BF80.3 (Psychology)]
BT Psychology
Moving-pictures in psychotherapy
UF Moving-pictures—Therapeutic use
BT Group psychotherapy
Psychotherapy
RT Psychodrama
Moving-pictures in religious education
[BV1535.4]
BT Moving-pictures in church work
Religious education—Audio-visual aids
Moving-pictures in science
Moving-pictures in sports
BT Coaching (Athletics)
Moving-pictures in teacher training
BT Teachers—Training of
Moving-pictures in technical education
(May Subd Geog)
[T65.5.M6]
BT Moving-pictures in education
Technology—Study and teaching—
Audio-visual aids
Moving-pictures in television
USE Television broadcasting of films
Moving-pictures in the social sciences
BT Social sciences—Study and teaching
Moving-pictures on television
USE Television broadcasting of films
Moving sidewalks
USE Passenger conveyors
Moving target indicator radar
[TK6592.M67]
BT Radar
Moving trade
USE Storage and moving trade
Moviya (African people)
USE Eviya (African people)
Mow family
USE Mao family
Mowbery family
USE Mabry family
Mowbray family (Not Subd Geog)
UF Mobray family
Moubray family
Moubrey family
Mowbury family
USE Mabry family

Mowers, Power lawn
USE Power lawn mowers
Mowery family
USE Morey family
Mowing machines (May Subd Geog)
[S695-S697]
BT Agricultural machinery
NT Power lawn mowers
Mowra family
USE Morey family
Mowre family
USE Morey family
Mowrey family
USE Morey family
Mowry family
USE Morey family
Moxa (May Subd Geog)
[RM306 (Therapeutics)]
BT Counter-irritants
RT Acupuncture points
— **Law and legislation** (May Subd Geog)
Moxa Indians
USE Moxo Indians
Moxa language
USE Moxo language
Moxeño language
USE Moxo language
Moxie family
USE Maxey family
Moxitae
USE Moxo Indians
Moxley family (Not Subd Geog)
UF Muxley family
Moxness family (Not Subd Geog)
Moxo Indians
[F3319]
UF Moha Indians
Moja Indians
Mojo Indians
Mossa Indians
Moxa Indians
Moxitae
Musu Indians
BT Arawak Indians
Indians of South America
Moxo language
[PM6576]
UF Moja language
Mojo language
Morocosi language
Moxa language
Moxeño language
BT Arawakan languages
Bolivia—Languages
Brazil—Languages
Paraguay—Languages
Moxy family
USE Maxey family
Moya family (Not Subd Geog)
UF De Moya family
DeMoya family
Moyamoya disease (May Subd Geog)
[RC388.5]
BT Arterial occlusions
Carotid artery—Diseases
Cerebrovascular disease
Moyar family
USE Moyer family
Moye (African people)
USE Nunu (African people)
Moyensoen family
USE Moyersoen family
Moyensone family
USE Moyersoen family

Moyer family (Not Subd Geog)
UF Moier family
Moir family
Mouyer family
Moyar family
Moyers family
Moyr family
Moyre family
RT Moyersoen family
Myers family
Moyers family
USE Moyer family
Moyersoen family (Not Subd Geog)
UF Moeresoen family
Moersoon family
Moeyrson family
Moyensoen family
Moyensone family
Moyson family
RT Moyer family
Moyma language
USE Movima language
Moyr family
USE Moyer family
Moyre family
USE Moyer family
Moyson family
USE Moyersoen family
Mozabite language
USE Mzab language
Mozaffarids
USE Muzaffarids
Mozambican alien labor
USE Alien labor, Mozambican
Mozambican cookery
USE Cookery, Mozambican
Mozambican fables
USE Fables, Mozambican
Mozambican periodicals (May Subd Geog)
Mozambican poetry (Portuguese)
(May Subd Geog)
UF Portuguese poetry—Mozambican
authors
Mozambicans (May Subd Geog)
BT Ethnology—Mozambique
Mozambique
— **Description and travel**
(Not Subd Geog)
— — **1981-** (Not Subd Geog)
— **Economic conditions**
— — **To 1975**
— — **1975-**
— **History**
— — **To 1505**
[DT461-461.3]
— — **1505-1698**
[DT461.5-461.8]
— — **1698-1891**
[DT462-462.7]
— — **1891-1975**
[DT463-463.3]
— — **War of 1894-1895**
[DT463]
— — **Revolution, 1964-1975**
[DT463-DT463.3]
— — **1975-**
[DT463.5-463.8]
— **Languages**
NT Tswa language
— **Politics and government**
— — **To 1975**
— — **1975-**
— **Social conditions**
— — **To 1975**
— — **1975-**
Mozambique Channel
UF Canal de Moçambique
Canal de Mozambique
Moçambique Channel
BT Straits—Madagascar
Straits—Mozambique

Mozambique tilapia
  USE Sarotherodon mossambicus
Mozarabic architecture
  USE Architecture, Mozarabic
Mozarabic art
  USE Art, Mozarabic
Mozarabic arts
  USE Arts, Mozarabic
Mozarabic illumination of books and
    manuscripts
  USE Illumination of books and manuscripts,
      Mozarabic
Mozarabic literature *(May Subd Geog)*
  UF Arabic-Spanish literature
      Spanish-Arabic literature
Mozarabic painting
  USE Painting, Mozarabic
Mozarabic poetry
  [PQ6056]
  UF Arabic-Spanish poetry
      Spanish-Arabic poetry
  NT Muwashshah
Mozarabic rite (Catholic Church)
  USE Catholic Church—Mozarabic rite
Mozarabs
  [BR1024]
  BT Christians—Spain
Mozart Preis
  USE Wolfgang Amadeus Mozart Preis
Mozartiana (Ballet)
  BT Ballets
Mozea family
  USE Mauzy family
Mozee family
  USE Mauzy family
Mozer family
  USE Moser family
Mozia (Ancient city)
  USE Motya (Ancient city)
Mozier family
  USE Mosher family
Mozingo Creek (Mo.)
  BT Rivers—Missouri
Mozzie family
  USE Mauzy family
Mozzy family
  USE Mauzy family
MP/M (Computer operating system)
  UF MultiProgramming Monitor (Computer
      operating system)
  BT Operating systems (Computers)
Mpangwe (West African people)
  USE Fang (West African people)
Mpika Dairy Settlement Scheme (Zambia)
  BT Dairy farms—Zambia
      Ranches—Zambia
Mpondos
  USE Pondos
Mpongwe (African people)
  [DT546.145.M66]
  UF Bayugu (African people)
      Empoongwe (African people)
      Mpungwe (African people)
      Npongwe (African people)
      Pongo (African people)
  BT Ethnology—Gabon
      Myene (African people)
  NT Nkomi (African people)
Mpongwe language
  [PL8531]
  UF Pongwe language
  BT Bantu languages
MPTP (Neurotoxin)
  USE Methylphenyltetrahydropyridine
Mpukusu language
  USE Mbukushu language
Mpungwe (African people)
  USE Mpongwe (African people)
Mpur dialect
  UF Mputu dialect

BT Yanzi language
    Zaire—Languages
Mputu (African people) *(May Subd Geog)*
  BT Ethnology—Zaire
Mputu dialect
  USE Mpur dialect
MR2 automobile
  USE Toyota MR2 automobile
Mr. Collins (Fictitious character)
  USE Collins, Mr. (Fictitious character)
Mrdangam
  USE Mridanga
MRDS (Information retrieval system)
  UF Mineral Resource Data System
  BT Information storage and retrieval
      systems—Mines and mineral
      resources
Mridanga
  [ML1035]
  UF Mrdangam
  BT Drum
Mridanga and vina music
  USE Vina and mridanga music
Mridanga and violin music
  USE Violin and mridanga music
Mridanga music
  [M146]
  BT Percussion music
MRN
  USE Meteorological Rocket Network
Mrtyuñjaya homa
  [BL1126.82.M7]
  BT Death—Religious aspects—Hinduism
      Hinduism—Rituals
Mrung language
  USE Tipura language
MS (Disease)
  USE Multiple sclerosis
MS-DOS (Computer operating system)
  UF Microsoft Disk Operating System
      (Computer operating system)
      Microsoft MS-DOS (Computer
      operating system)
  BT Operating systems (Computers)
  RT PC DOS (Computer operating system)
MS-LIB (Computer program)
  UF MS-LIB Library Manager (Computer
      program)
  BT Utilities (Computer programs)
MS-LIB Library Manager (Computer program)
  USE MS-LIB (Computer program)
MS Windows (Computer programs)
  USE Microsoft Windows (Computer
      programs)
MSG (Food additive)
  USE Monosodium glutamate
MSIS (Information retrieval system)
  USE Multi-State Information System
Msta River (R.S.F.S.R.)
  UF Reka Msta (R.S.F.S.R.)
  BT Rivers—Russian S.F.S.R.
Mstěnice (City)
  BT Cities and towns, Ruined, extinct, etc.
      —Czechoslovakia
      Czechoslovakia—Antiquities
MSVTI classification
  USE Classification, MSVTI
MSX-BASIC (Computer program language)
  [QA76.73.M]
  BT Programming languages (Electronic
      computers)
MSX computers
  [QA76.8.M]
  BT Electronic digital computers
Mt. Ainslie (A.C.T.)
  USE Mount Ainslie (A.C.T.)
Mt. Assiniboine Provincial Park (B.C.)
  USE Mount Assiniboine Provincial Park
      (B.C.)

Mt. Auburn Catholic Cemetery (Watertown,
    Mass.)
  USE Mount Auburn Catholic Cemetery
      (Watertown, Mass.)
Mt. Carmel Cemetery (El Paso, Tex.)
  USE Mount Carmel Cemetery (El Paso,
      Tex.)
Mt. Castleguard (Alta.)
  USE Castleguard, Mount (Alta.)
Mt. Comfort Plantation (Va.)
  USE Mount Comfort Plantation (Va.)
Mt. Everest National Park (Nepal)
  USE Sagarmāthā National Park (Nepal)
Mt. Le Conte (Tenn.)
  USE LeConte, Mount (Tenn.)
Mt. LeConte (Tenn.)
  USE LeConte, Mount (Tenn.)
Mt. Mitchell (N.C.)
  USE Mount Mitchell (N.C.)
Mt. Olivet Cemetery (Fowlerville, Mich.)
  USE Mount Olivet Cemetery (Fowlerville,
      Mich.)
Mt. Otoko (Japan)
  USE Otoko Mountain (Japan)
Mt. Rae (Alta.)
  USE Rae, Mount (Alta.)
Mt. Rest Cemetery (Newport, Ill.)
  USE Newport Mount Rest Cemetery
      (Newport, Ill.)
Mt. Richmond State Forest Park (N.Z.)
  USE Mount Richmond State Forest Park
      (N.Z.)
Mt. Robson Provincial Park (B.C.)
  USE Mount Robson Provincial Park (B.C.)
Mt. St. Helens (Wash.)
  USE Saint Helens, Mount (Wash.)
Mt. Stirling Wilderness (Nev.)
  USE Mount Stirling Wilderness (Nev.)
Mt. Tamalpais and Muir Woods Railroad
  UF Mount Tamalpais and Muir Woods
      Railroad
  BT Mountain railroads—United States
      Railroads—United States
Mt. Taylor (N.M.)
  USE Taylor, Mount (N.M.)
Mt. Toby (Mass.)
  USE Toby, Mount (Mass.)
Mt. Tom (Mass.)
  USE Tom, Mount (Mass.)
Mt. Tom State Park (Mass.)
  USE Mount Tom State Reservation (Mass.)
Mt. Tom State Reservation (Mass.)
  USE Mount Tom State Reservation (Mass.)
Mt. Tuomuer (China)
  USE Tuomuer Peak (China)
Mt. Vernon (Va. : Estate)
  USE Mount Vernon (Va. : Estate)
Mt. Washington (N.H.)
  USE Washington, Mount (N.H.)
Mtir (Berber people)
  USE Ndhir (Berber people)
Mtiuli
  BT Ethnology—Georgian S.S.R.
MTM (Work measurement)
  USE Methods-time measurement
Mtongwe Site (Kenya)
  BT Kenya—Antiquities
MTR
  USE Materials testing reactors
MU5 (Computer)
  [QA76.8.M]
  BT Electronic digital computers
Mu bacteriophage
  USE Bacteriophage mu
Mu family *(Not Subd Geog)*
Mu-kao Caves (China)
  USE Tun-huang Caves (China)
Mu mesons
  USE Muons
Mu phage
  USE Bacteriophage mu

2489

Muache Indians
USE Moache Indians
Muana language
BT Ivory Coast—Languages
Muatiamvua language
USE Ruund language
Muʻaṭṭilah
[BP195.M]
BT Islamic sects
Mucclewain family
USE McElwain family
Mucclewane family
USE McElwain family
Mucedinaceae
USE Moniliaceae
Muchopi (African people)
USE Chopi (African people)
Mucilage
[TP970]
RT Adhesives
Mucins
[QP551]
NT Mucopolysaccharides
— **Analysis**
Muck
USE Humus
Muckaluck Indians
USE Klamath Indians
Muckelroy family
USE McElroy family
Muckleroy family
USE McElroy family
Muckleshoot Indians
[E99.M917]
BT Indians of North America
Indians of North America—
Washington (State)
Salishan Indians
Mucklewain family
USE McElwain family
Muckleway family
USE McAlley family
Muckley family
USE Muggli family
Muckli family
USE Muggli family
Mucklow family
USE McClow family
Muclaroy family
USE McElroy family
Mucocutaneous leishmaniasis
USE Leishmaniasis, Mucocutaneous
Mucocutaneous lymph node syndrome
(May Subd Geog)
[RJ406.M83]
UF Acute febrile mucocutaneous lymph
node syndrome
Kawasaki disease
Kawasaki's disease
Lymph node syndrome,
Mucocutaneous
MCLS (Disease)
MLNS (Disease)
BT Arteritis
Communicable diseases in children
Connective tissue diseases in children
Lymph nodes—Diseases
Mucous membrane—Diseases
Syndromes in children
Mucoid, Interstitial
USE Interphotoreceptor matrix
Mucoids
[QP551]
Mucopeptide glucohydrolase
USE Lysozyme
Mucopeptides
USE Peptidoglycans
Mucopolysaccharides
BT Mucins
Polysaccharides
NT Glycosaminoglycans

Hyaluronic acid
Mucopolysaccharidosis
BT Carbohydrates—Metabolism—
Disorders
Lysosomal storage diseases
Mental retardation
Mucor miehei
[QK621.M94 (Botany)]
Mucoraceae (May Subd Geog)
[QK621.M94 (Mycology)]
BT Mucorales
NT Phycomyces
Mucorales (May Subd Geog)
[QK621.M96 (Mycology)]
BT Zygomycetes
NT Choanephoraceae
Mucoraceae
Mucormycosis (May Subd Geog)
UF Phycomycosis
BT Mycoses
Mucosa
USE Mucous membrane
Mucosa, Gastric
USE Gastric mucosa
Mucosa, Nasal
USE Nasal mucosa
Mucosa, Oral
USE Oral mucosa
Mucosal diseases of cattle (May Subd Geog)
[SF967.M78]
BT Cattle—Diseases
Veterinary virology
NT Infectious bovine rhinotracheitis
Mucosal relief radiography
USE Radiography, Double-contrast
Mucous colitis
USE Irritable colon
Mucous membrane
[QM561 (Histology)]
UF Mucosa
BT Epithelium
Membranes (Biology)
NT Endometrium
Gastric mucosa
Nasal mucosa
Oral mucosa
— **Diseases** (May Subd Geog)
NT Leukoplakia
Mucocutaneous lymph node
syndrome
Mucous otitis media
USE Otitis media with effusion
Mucoviscidosis
USE Cystic fibrosis
Mucronothrus
[QL458.2.C74]
BT Oribatidae
Mucronothrus nasalis
[QL458.2.O74]
Mucuna (May Subd Geog)
[QK495.L52]
BT Leguminosae
Mucuna pruriens
USE Cowhage
Mucus
[QP215]
BT Body fluids
Exocrine glands—Secretions
NT Cervix mucus
Mud (May Subd Geog)
BT Sediments (Geology)
Soil science
Mud baths
USE Baths, Moor and mud
Mud eels
USE Amphiumidae
Mud family
USE Mudd family
Mud flat ecology
[QH541.5.M]
BT Ecology

Mud flows
USE Mudflows
Mud fuel
[TP360]
BT Fuel
RT Briquets (Fuel)
NT Sewage-sludge fuel
Mud Glyph Cave (Tenn.)
BT Caves—Tennessee
Tennessee—Antiquities
Mud-laden fluids
USE Drilling muds
Mud logging (May Subd Geog)
[TN871.35]
UF Logging, Mud
BT Drilling muds
Oil well logging
Mud lumps
UF Mudlumps
BT Mississippi River—Delta
Mud pumps
UF Drilling muds—Pumping
Pumps, Drilling mud
Pumps, Mud
Pumps, Slush
Slush pumps
BT Oil wells—Equipment and supplies
Pumping machinery
Mud puppies
USE Necturus
Mud rock
USE Mudstone
Mud roofs
USE Roofs, Mud
Mud Run Disaster, Oct. 10, 1888
[HE1781.M8]
Mud-scows
USE Scows
Mud turtles
USE Kinosternidae
Mud volcanoes (May Subd Geog)
BT Petroleum—Geology
Volcanoes
Muda River (Kedah)
UF Sungai Muda (Kedah)
BT Rivers—Malaysia
Mudd family (Not Subd Geog)
UF Mud family
Muddās (Buddhism)
USE Mudrās (Buddhism)
Muddy Creek (Daviess County, Mo.)
BT Rivers—Missouri
Muddy Creek (Duplin County, N.C.)
BT Rivers—North Carolina
Muddy Run Park (Pa.)
USE Muddy Run Recreation Park (Pa.)
Muddy Run Recreation Park (Pa.)
UF Muddy Run Park (Pa.)
BT Parks—Pennsylvania
Recreation areas—Pennsylvania
Mudéjar architecture
USE Architecture, Mudéjar
Mudéjar art
USE Art, Mudéjar
Mudéjar decoration and ornament
USE Decoration and ornament, Mudéjar
Mudéjar wood-carving
USE Wood-carving, Mudéjar
Mudéjares
[DP104]
Here are entered works on Muslims living in
Spain under Christian protection before 1492 who
did not convert to Christianity. Works on Muslims in
Spain after about 1492 who were converted to Chris-
tianity by decree are entered under the heading
Moriscos. Works including both Mudéjares and
Moriscos are entered under Moriscos.
RT Moriscos
NT Architecture—Portugal—Mudéjar
influences
Architecture, Romanesque—Mudéjar
influences

Church architecture—Spain—
Salamanca (Province)—Mudéjar
influences
Mudflows *(May Subd Geog)*
 ⌐QE598-598.2⌐
 UF   Mud flows
 BT   Earth movements
 RT   Earthflows
 NT   Lahars
Mudflows, Volcanic
 USE   Lahars
Mudiraj
 USE   Muthurajas
Mudjatik River (Sask.)
 BT   Rivers—Saskatchewan
Mudlumps
 USE   Mud lumps
Mudpuppies
 USE   Necturus
Mudra
 USE   Gesture
Mudrās (Buddhism)
 ⌐BQ5125.M8⌐
 UF   Gestures (Buddhism)
    Muddās (Buddhism)
 BT   Buddhism—Doctrines
    Buddhist art and symbolism
Mudrās (Hinduism)
 ⌐BL1226.82.M93⌐
 BT   Hinduism—Rituals
Muds, Drilling
 USE   Drilling muds
Mudstone *(May Subd Geog)*
 ⌐QE471.15.M83⌐
 UF   Mud rock
 BT   Rocks, Sedimentary
Muduva dialect
 BT   India—Languages
    Tamil language
Muelis family
 USE   Mullis family
Mueller family *(Not Subd Geog)*
 UF   Muller family
 RT   Miller family
    Moeller family
Muenane language
 USE   Muinane language
Muetze family
 USE   Metz family
Muffins
 BT   Baking
Mufflers (Airplane motors)
 USE   Airplanes—Motors—Mufflers
Mufflers (Automobile motors)
 USE   Automobiles—Motors—Mufflers
Mufflers (Internal combustion engines)
 USE   Internal combustion engines—Mufflers
Mufflers (Jet engines)
 USE   Airplanes—Turbojet engines—Mufflers
Muffs
 ⌐GT2190 (Costume)⌐
Muflon
 USE   Mouflon
Mufti of Istanbul
 USE   Shaykh al-Islām—Turkey
Muftilik
 USE   Shaykh al-Islām—Turkey
Muga moth *(May Subd Geog)*
 ⌐QL561.S2 (Entomology)⌐
 ⌐SF560.M84 (Sericulture)⌐
 UF   Antheraea assamensis
 BT   Silkworms, Non-mulberry
Mugello Valley (Italy)
 BT   Valleys—Italy
Mugging *(May Subd Geog)*
 ⌐HV6646-6665⌐
 BT   Brigands and robbers
    Criminal law
    Offenses against the person
 RT   Robbery

Muggins (Game)
 ⌐GV1299.M (Card games)⌐
 ⌐GV1467 (Dominoes)⌐
Muggletonians
 ⌐BX8698⌐
 BT   Christian sects—England
Muggli family *(Not Subd Geog)*
 UF   Muckley family
    Muckli family
Mughal architecture
 USE   Architecture, Mogul
Mughal Empire
 USE   Mogul Empire
Mugil
 ⌐QL638.M8⌐
 BT   Gray mullets
Mugil capito
 ⌐QL638.M8⌐
Mugil cephalus
 ⌐QL638.M8⌐
 UF   Black mullet
    Striped mullet
Mugil curema
 ⌐QL638.M8⌐
 UF   Silver mullet
    White mullet
Mugil dobula
 ⌐QL638.M8⌐
Mugil liza
 ⌐QL638.M8⌐
 UF   Liza (Fish)
Mugilidae
 USE   Gray mullets
Mugiloididae
 ⌐QL638.M84⌐
 UF   Parapercichthyidae
    Parapercidae
    Pinguipedidae
    Sandperches
 BT   Perciformes
 NT   Parapercis
Mugo pine
 ⌐QK495.P66 (Botany)⌐
 UF   Pinus montana
    Pinus mugo
    Swiss mountain pine
Mugs *(May Subd Geog)*
 BT   Drinking vessels
Mugs (Indic people)
 USE   Maghs
Mugu Lagoon (Calif.) *(Not Subd Geog)*
 BT   Lagoons—California
Mugwort
 USE   Artemisia vulgaris
Muḥammad, d. 632
 USE   Muḥammad, Prophet, d. 632
 — Military leadership
    ⌐BP77.7⌐
Muḥammad, Prophet, d. 632
 ⌐BP75-BP77.5⌐
 UF   Muḥammad, d. 632
 — Ascension
    USE   Muḥammad, Prophet, d. 632—
       Isrā' and Mi'rāj
 — Birthday
    USE   Mawlid al-Nabī
 — Companions
    ⌐BP75.5 (Biography)⌐
    UF   Companions of Muḥammad,
       Prophet, d. 632
       Muḥammad, Prophet, d. 632—
          Ṣaḥābah
       Ṣaḥābah
    BT   Hadith—Authorities
       Muḥammad, Prophet, d. 632—
          Friends and associates
    NT   Ansar
 — Flight from Mecca
    USE   Muḥammad, Prophet, d. 632—
       Hijrah
 — Friends and associates

 ⌐BP76.9⌐
    NT   Muḥammad, Prophet, d. 632—
       Companions
 — Hijrah
    ⌐BP77.5⌐
    UF   Hegirah
       Hejira
       Higrah
       Hijrah
       Muḥammad, Prophet, d. 632—
          Flight from Mecca
 — Isrā' and Mi'rāj
    ⌐BP166.57⌐
    UF   Isrā'
       Mi'rāj
       Muḥammad, Prophet, d. 632—
          Ascension
       Muḥammad, Prophet, d. 632—
          Mi'rāj and Isrā'
       Muḥammad, Prophet, d. 632—
          Night journey to Jerusalem
 — Khatm āl-nabīyīn
    USE   Muḥammad, Prophet, d. 632—
       Prophetic office
 — Miracles
    ⌐BP75.8⌐
    BT   Miracles (Islam)
 — Mi'rāj and Isrā'
    USE   Muḥammad, Prophet, d. 632—
       Isrā' and Mi'rāj
 — Night journey to Jerusalem
    USE   Muḥammad, Prophet, d. 632—
       Isrā' and Mi'rāj
 — Prophethood
    USE   Muḥammad, Prophet, d. 632—
       Prophetic office
 — Prophetic office
    ⌐BP166.5-BP166.55⌐
    UF   Muḥammad, Prophet, d. 632—
          Khatm āl-nabīyīn
       Muḥammad, Prophet, d. 632—
          Prophethood
       Muḥammad, Prophet, d. 632—Seal
          of the prophets
 — Ṣaḥābah
    USE   Muḥammad, Prophet, d. 632—
       Companions
 — Seal of the prophets
    USE   Muḥammad, Prophet, d. 632—
       Prophetic office
Muhammadanism
 USE   Islam
Muhammadans
 USE   Muslims
Muhanha (African people)
 USE   Hanya (African people)
Muḥarram, Tenth of
 USE   Tenth of Muḥarram
Mühlbacher family *(Not Subd Geog)*
Mühldorf, Battle of, 1322
 UF   Ampfing, Battle of, 1322
 BT   Austria—History—1273-1519
    Germany—History—1273-1517
Muhlenbergia montana
 USE   Mountain muhly
Mühlviertel (Austria)
Muhs family
 USE   Muse family
Muhso language
 USE   Lahu language
Muḥtasib *(May Subd Geog)*
 UF   Ḥisbah
 BT   Municipal officials and employees—
    Islamic countries
Muhu Sound (Estonia)
 UF   Moon Sound (Estonia)
    Muhu väin (Estonia)
    Mukhu Sound (Estonia)
 BT   Sounds (Geomorphology)—Estonia
Muhu väin (Estonia)
 USE   Muhu Sound (Estonia)

Mui tsai
  USE Slavery
Muila (Bantu people)
  USE Mwila (Bantu people)
Muinane language
  UF Muenane language
  BT Indians of South America—Languages
  RT Witoto language
Muir Woods National Monument (Calif.)
  BT National monuments—California
Muirhead family
  USE Morehead family
Muiscas
  USE Chibcha Indians
Muiu (New Guinea tribe)
  UF Moejoe (New Guinea tribe)
    Muyu (New Guinea tribe)
  BT Ethnology—New Guinea
Muiza (Zambian people)
  USE Bisa (Zambian people)
Mujinaoka iseki (Kushigata-machi, Japan)
  USE Mujinaoka Site (Kushigata-machi,
    Japan)
Mujinaoka Site (Kushigata-machi, Japan)
  (Not Subd Geog)
  UF Mujinaoka iseki (Kushigata-machi,
    Japan)
  BT Japan—Antiquities
Mukaffirat (Islam)
  USE Kufr (Islam)
Mukaihara Iseki (Hiratsuka-shi, Japan)
  USE Mukaihara Site (Hiratsuka-shi, Japan)
Mukaihara Site (Hiratsuka-shi, Japan)
  (Not Subd Geog)
  UF Mukaihara Iseki (Hiratsuka-shi, Japan)
  BT Japan—Antiquities
Mukaiyama Iseki (Hamamatsu-shi, Japan)
  USE Mukaiyama Site (Hamamatsu-shi,
    Japan)
Mukaiyama Site (Hamamatsu-shi, Japan)
  (Not Subd Geog)
  UF Mukaiyama Iseki (Hamamatsu-shi,
    Japan)
  BT Japan—Antiquities
Mukawa language
  UF Kapikapi language
  BT Melanesian languages
Mukden, Battle of, 1905
  [DS517.4]
  BT Russo-Japanese War, 1904-1905
Mukden Incident, 1931
  [DS783.8]
  UF Manchuria (China)—History—
    Incident, 1931
    Manchurian Incident, 1931
  — Battles, sieges, etc.
    USE Mukden Incident, 1931—
      Campaigns
  — **Campaigns** *(May Subd Geog)*
    [DS783.8]
    UF Mukden Incident, 1931—Battles,
      sieges, etc.
      Mukden Incident, 1931—Military
      operations
  — Military operations
    USE Mukden Incident, 1931—
      Campaigns
Mukenai (Ancient city)
  USE Mycenae (Ancient city)
Mukhayyam Tall az Za'tar, Battle of, 1976
  BT Lebanon—History—Civil War, 1975-
    1976
**Mukhtār, 'Umar, 1860?-1931, in motion
  pictures**
  BT Moving-pictures
Mukhu Sound (Estonia)
  USE Muhu Sound (Estonia)
Mukkulattor dialect
  USE Kallan dialect
Mukōjima Hyakkaen (Tokyo, Japan)
  BT Parks—Japan

Mukri dialect
  BT Kurdish language
Mukti
  USE Mokṣa
Muḳtseh
  USE Mukẓeh
Muktza
  USE Mukẓeh
Muku (Melanesian people)
  USE Lakalai (Melanesian people)
Mukulehe (African people)
  UF Mukulehe (African tribe)
  BT Ethnology—Cameroon
Mukulehe (African tribe)
  USE Mukulehe (African people)
Mukẓeh
  [BM685]
  UF Muḳtseh
    Muktza
  BT Sabbath (Jewish law)
Mulam (Chinese people)
  USE Mulao (Chinese people)
Mulam language
  USE Mulao language
Mulao (Chinese people) *(May Subd Geog)*
  [DS731.M84]
  UF Mulam (Chinese people)
  BT Ethnology—China
Mulao language
  [PL4251.M85]
  UF Mulam language
  BT China—Languages
    Tai languages
Mūlasarvāstivāda (Sect)
  USE Sarvāstivādins
Mūlasarvāstivāda School
  USE Sarvāstivādins
Mūlasarvāstivādins
  USE Sarvāstivādins
Mulattoes *(May Subd Geog)*
  [E185.62 (United States)]
  [GN645 (Anthropology)]
  UF Octoroons
    Quadroons
  BT Afro-Americans
    Blacks
    Miscegenation
  NT Melungeons
    Ramapo Mountain people
    Wesorts
  — United States
    NT Black Seminoles
Mulberry *(May Subd Geog)*
  [QK495.M73 (Botany)]
  [SF557 (Culture)]
  UF Morus (Plants)
    Mulberry tree
  BT Moraceae
  NT Morus cathayana
    Paper mulberry
  — **Diseases and pests** *(May Subd Geog)*
    [SB608.M8]
    NT Mulberry blight
Mulberry, Dwarf
  USE Rubus chamaemorus
Mulberry bacterial blight
  USE Mulberry blight
Mulberry blight
  [SB741.M]
  UF Mulberry bacterial blight
  BT Mulberry—Diseases and pests
Mulberry harbors
  BT World War, 1939-1945—Campaigns—
    France—Normandy
    World War, 1939-1945—Naval
    operations
Mulberry Island (Va.)
  BT Peninsulas—Virginia
Mulberry tree
  USE Mulberry

Mulching *(May Subd Geog)*
  [S661.5]
  UF Mulsh
    Soil mulching
  BT Gardening
    Horticulture
    Soil management
    Soils
  NT Stubble mulching
    Wood waste as mulch, soil conditioner,
    etc.
Mulde River (Germany)
  BT Rivers—Germany (East)
Mule deer
  UF Black-tailed deer
    Blacktail deer
    Cariacus macrotis
    Dama hemionus
    Odocoileus columbianus
    Odocoileus hemionus
    Odocoileus hemionus sitkensis
    Sitka black-tailed deer
  BT Deer
Mule deer hunting *(May Subd Geog)*
  [SK301]
  BT Deer hunting
Mule drivers
  USE Muleteers
Mule skinners
  USE Muleteers
Mulert family *(Not Subd Geog)*
Mules *(May Subd Geog)*
  [SF362 (Culture)]
  [UC600-UC695 (Military use)]
  BT Donkeys
    Horses
    Livestock
  NT Muleteers
Mules (Spinning machinery)
  USE Spinning machinery
Muleteers *(May Subd Geog)*
  UF Mule drivers
    Mule skinners
  BT Mules
Mülhausen, War of, 1468
  USE Waldshut, War of, 1468
Mulhausen family
  USE Milhous family
Mulherakara Deśmukha family
  (Not Subd Geog)
Mulholland family *(Not Subd Geog)*
Mulhouse family
  USE Milhous family
MULI (Electronic computer system)
  [QA76.6]
  UF Multi level dialog system
Muligen family
  USE Mulligan family
Mulisas
  USE Mulizas
Mulison family
  USE Mullison family
Mulizas
  UF Mulisas
  BT Folk-songs, Spanish—Peru
Mulkey family *(Not Subd Geog)*
Mull, Island of (Scotland)
  UF Isle of Mull (Scotland)
  BT Inner Hebrides (Scotland)
    Islands—Scotland
Mulla Nasreddin (Legendary character)
  USE Nasreddin Hoca (Legendary character)
Mullan family
  USE Mullen family
Mullein thrips
  [QL503.T5]
  UF Haplothrips verbasci
  BT Thrips

Mullen family *(Not Subd Geog)*
 UF Mullan family
  Mullenax family
  Mullin family
  Mulling family
  Mullings family
  Mullins family
  Mullon family
Mullenax family
 USE Mullen family
Mulleneox family
 USE Mullineaux family
Mullenix family
 USE Mullineaux family
Mullenneix family
 USE Mullineaux family
Mullenneux family
 USE Mullineaux family
Mullennex family
 USE Mullineaux family
Muller family
 USE Mueller family
Mullet family *(Not Subd Geog)*
 RT Mallett family
Mullet fisheries
 BT Fisheries
  Gray mullets
Mullet fishing
 ⌜SH691.M78⌝
 BT Fishing
Mullets, Gray
 USE Gray mullets
Mullets, Red
 USE Mullidae
Mullica River (N.J.)
 UF Atsion River (N.J.)
  Mullicas River (N.J.)
  Mullicus River (N.J.)
 BT Rivers—New Jersey
Mullican family
 USE Mulligan family
Mullicas River (N.J.)
 USE Mullica River (N.J.)
Mullicus River (N.J.)
 USE Mullica River (N.J.)
Mullidae
 ⌜QL638.M85⌝
 UF Goatfishes
  Mullets, Red
  Red mullets
  Surmullets
 BT Perciformes
 NT Mullus
  Upeneus
Mullies family
 USE Mullis family
Mulligan family *(Not Subd Geog)*
 UF Muligen family
  Mullican family
  Mulliken family
  Mullikin family
  Mullokin family
 RT Melugin family
Mulliken family
 USE Mulligan family
Mullikin family
 USE Mulligan family
Mullin family
 USE Mullen family
Mullinax family
 USE Mullineaux family

Mullineaux family *(Not Subd Geog)*
 UF Molineaux family
  Molines family
  Molineu family
  Molineux family
  Mollineux family
  Mollyneaux family
  Mollyneux family
  Molyneaux family
  Molyneux family
  Mulleneox family
  Mullenix family
  Mullenneix family
  Mullenneux family
  Mullennex family
  Mullinax family
  Mullineux family
  Mullinex family
  Mullinix family
  Mulniks family
  Mulnix family
Mullineux family
 USE Mullineaux family
Mullinex family
 USE Mullineaux family
Mulling family
 USE Mullen family
Mullings family
 USE Mullen family
Mullinix family
 USE Mullineaux family
Mullins family
 USE Mullen family
Mullins Lectures on Preaching
 USE E. Y. Mullins Lectures on Preaching
Mullinson family
 USE Mullison family
Mullis family *(Not Subd Geog)*
 UF Moele family
  Moelis family
  Molis family
  Muelis family
  Mullies family
Mullison family *(Not Subd Geog)*
 UF Moleson family
  Molison family
  Molleson family
  Molleston family
  Molletson family
  Mollison family
  Mollisone family
  Mollissen family
  Molliston family
  Moulison family
  Moulson family
  Mulison family
  Mullinson family
Mullite
 ⌜QD181.A4⌝
 BT Aluminum silicates
Mullokin family
 USE Mulligan family
Mullon family
 USE Mullen family
Mulluk Indians
 USE Coquille Indians
Mullukmulluk language
 ⌜PL7101.M77⌝
 UF Malakmalak language
 BT Australia—Languages
  Daly languages
Mullus
 ⌜QL638.M85⌝
 BT Mullidae
 NT Mullus barbatus
Mullus barbatus
 ⌜QL638.M85⌝
 BT Mullus
Mulniks family
 USE Mullineaux family

Mulnix family
 USE Mullineaux family
Mulreadies (Philately)
 BT Covers (Philately)
  Postal stationery
MULS System
 UF Minnesota Union List of Serials
  System
 BT Catalogs, Union—Minnesota—
  Automation
  Serials control systems—Automation
Mulsh
 USE Mulching
Multi-acting
 USE Multiple role acting
Multi-age grouping
 USE Nongraded schools
Multi-Batch (Electronic computer system)
 ⌜QA76.8.P2⌝
 BT Multiprocessors
  Multiprogramming (Electronic
  computers)
  PDP-11 (Computer)—Programming
Multi-family housing
 USE Apartment houses
Multi-hospital systems
 USE Multihospital systems
Multi-institutional hospital systems
 USE Multihospital systems
Multi-institutional systems, Hospital
 USE Multihospital systems
Multi level dialog system
 USE MULI (Electronic computer system)
Multi media programs
 USE Media programs (Education)
Multi-State Information System
 UF MSIS (Information retrieval system)
 BT Information storage and retrieval
  systems
Multichannel communication
 UF Communication, Multichannel
 BT Telecommunication
 NT Teleconferencing
Multicollinearity
 ⌜QA278.2⌝
 BT Correlation (Statistics)
  Estimation theory
  Regression analysis
 RT Ridge regression (Statistics)
Multicolored approach to reading
 USE Words in color
Multicomponent flow
 USE Multiphase flow
Multicultural mass media
 USE Ethnic mass media
Multiculturalism
 USE Pluralism (Social sciences)
Multidimensional Aptitude Battery
 ⌜BF432.5.M85⌝
 UF MAB
 BT Intelligence tests
Multidimensional phonology
 USE Prosodic analysis (Linguistics)
Multidimensional scaling
 BT Psychometrics
  Scaling (Social sciences)
Multidimensional symbol test
 ⌜BF698.8.M8⌝
 BT Projective techniques
Multidrop Efficiency Regarding Transmission
 Lines (Computer program)
 USE MERTL (Computer program)
Multiflora bean
 USE Scarlet runner bean
Multigraph
 ⌜Z48⌝
 UF Multilith
 BT Copying processes
Multigrid methods (Numerical analysis)
 BT Numerical analysis

Multigroup diffusion (Neutron transport)
  USE Neutron transport theory
Multihadron production
  USE Hadrons—Multiplicity
Multihospital systems *(May Subd Geog)*
  UF Hospital systems, Multi-institutional
      Multi-hospital systems
      Multi-institutional hospital systems
      Multi-institutional systems, Hospital
      Multiple hospital systems
      Systems, Multihospital
  BT Health facilities—Affiliations
      Hospitals
      Hospitals—Administration
      Interorganizational relations
  NT Hospital mergers
      Hospitals—Shared services
Multihull sailboats *(May Subd Geog)*
  ⌜GV811.55⌝
  BT Boats and boating
      Sailboats
      Yachts and yachting
  NT Catamarans
      Trimarans
Multihull Transpacific Yacht Race
  ⌜GV832⌝
  UF Transpacific Catamaran Race
  BT Catamarans
      Yacht racing
Multilayered thin films
  USE Thin films, Multilayered
Multilevel distributorship
  USE Multilevel marketing
Multilevel marketing *(May Subd Geog)*
  ⌜HF5415.126⌝
  UF Distributorship, Multilevel
      Marketing, Multilevel
      Multilevel distributorship
      Multilevel sales companies
      Pyramid sales clubs
  BT Direct marketing
      Direct selling
Multilevel sales companies
  USE Multilevel marketing
Multilinear algebra
  ⌜QA199.5⌝
  BT Algebra
Multilingual dictionaries
  USE Dictionaries, Polyglot
Multilingualism *(May Subd Geog)*
  UF Plurilingualism
      Polyglottism
  BT Language and languages
  NT Bilingualism
Multilingualism and literature
  BT Literature
Multilith
  USE Multigraph
Multilocular adipose tissue
  USE Brown adipose tissue
Multilocular fat
  USE Brown adipose tissue
Multimachine assignments
  UF Machine assignments, Multiple
      Man-multimachine analysis
      Multiple machine assignments
  BT Methods engineering
      Work measurement
MultiMate (Computer program)
  BT Computer programs
      Word processing—Computer programs
MultiMate Advantage (Computer program)
  ⌜Z52.5.M85⌝
  BT Word processing—Computer programs
Multinational corporations
  USE International business enterprises
Multiparticle hadrodynamics
  USE Hadrons—Multiplicity

Multiphase flow
  UF Flow, Multiphase
      Flow, Polyphase
      Multicomponent flow
      Polyphase flow
  BT Fluid dynamics
  NT Two-phase flow
Multiphase materials
  USE Composite materials
Multiphasic health screening
  (May Subd Geog)
  ⌜RA427.6⌝
  UF Automated multiphasic health testing
      Health testing, Multiphasic
      Multiphasic health testing
  BT Medical screening
Multiphasic health testing
  USE Multiphasic health screening
Multiphoton processes
  UF Multiple photon processes
      Processes, Multiphoton
  BT Excited state chemistry
      Lasers in chemistry
      Photochemistry
      Quantum electrodynamics
      Quantum optics
Multiplan (Computer program)
  BT Computer programs
Multiplan-86 (Computer program)
  BT Computer programs
Multiple algebra
  USE Algebra, Universal
Multiple art *(May Subd Geog)*
  UF Art, Multiple
      Multiples (Art)
  BT Art, Modern—20th century
Multiple birth
  USE Birth, Multiple
Multiple-choice examinations
  BT Examinations
Multiple comparisons (Statistics)
  ⌜QA278.4⌝
  UF Comparisons, Multiple (Statistics)
  BT Correlation (Statistics)
      Regression analysis
Multiple cropping *(May Subd Geog)*
  ⌜S603.7⌝
  BT Cropping systems
  RT Agroforestry
  NT Double cropping
Multiple effect boiling distillation (Saline water
  conversion)
  USE Saline water conversion—Multiple
          effect distillation
Multiple employment
  USE Supplementary employment
Multiple endocrine adenomatosis
  USE Adenomatosis, Familial endocrine
Multiple generation of hadrons
  USE Hadrons—Multiplicity
Multiple hemorrhagic sarcoma
  USE Kaposi's sarcoma
Multiple hospital systems
  USE Multihospital systems
Multiple imputation (Statistics)
  UF Imputation, Multiple (Statistics)
  BT Social sciences—Statistical methods
      Social surveys—Response rate
  RT Missing observations (Statistics)
**Multiple independently targetable reentry
  vehicles**
  UF MIRV
      Missile warheads
Multiple integrals
  USE Integrals, Multiple
Multiple-line insurance
  USE Insurance, Multiple-line
Multiple listing *(May Subd Geog)*
  BT Real estate agents
      Real estate business
      Real estate listings

Multiple machine assignments
  USE Multimachine assignments
Multiple marriage
  USE Bigamy
      Polygamy
Multiple molecular forms of hormones
  USE Isohormones
Multiple myeloma *(May Subd Geog)*
  UF Kahler's disease
      Plasma cell myeloma
  BT Gammopathies, Monoclonal
      Plasmacytoma
Multiple particle production
  USE Particles (Nuclear physics)—
          Multiplicity
Multiple personality *(May Subd Geog)*
  ⌜RC569.5.M8⌝
  UF Consciousness, Multiple
      Double consciousness
      Personality, Multiple
  BT Personality, Disorders of
      Psychology, Pathological
  NT Multiple personality in children
Multiple personality in children
  (May Subd Geog)
  ⌜RJ506.M84⌝
  BT Multiple personality
      Personality disorders in children
Multiple photon processes
  USE Multiphoton processes
Multiple plot stories
  USE Plot-your-own stories
Multiple pregnancy
  USE Pregnancy, Multiple
Multiple printing
  ⌜Z252.5.M8⌝
  Here are entered works describing the printing of
  two or more texts on the same page.
  UF Twin printing
  BT Printing
Multiple production of hadrons
  USE Hadrons—Multiplicity
Multiple psychotherapy *(May Subd Geog)*
  ⌜RC489.M85⌝
  UF Co-therapy
      Multiple therapy
      Psychotherapy, Multiple
  BT Psychotherapy
Multiple role acting
  UF Mono-acting
      Multi-acting
  BT Acting
Multiple scattering (Physics)
  ⌜QC173.4.M85⌝
  UF Scattering, Multiple (Physics)
  BT Particles
      Scattering (Mathematics)
      Scattering (Physics)
Multiple sclerosis *(May Subd Geog)*
  ⌜RC377⌝
  UF MS (Disease)
      Sclerosis, Multiple
  BT Demyelination
      Myelin sheath—Diseases
      Virus diseases
  — **Psychological aspects**
      BT Sick—Psychology
  — **Research** *(May Subd Geog)*
Multiple sclerosis in children
  (May Subd Geog)
  ⌜RJ496.M84⌝
  BT Pediatric neurology
Multiple staff ministry
  USE Group ministry
Multiple star systems
  USE Multiple stars
Multiple stars
  ⌜QB821-QB829⌝
  UF Multiple star systems
      Multiple stars, Visual
      Visual multiple stars

BT Stars
NT Stars, Double
    Stars, Triple
Multiple stars, Visual
  USE Multiple stars
Multiple therapy
  USE Multiple psychotherapy
Multiple tumors
  BT Tumors
  NT Adenomatosis, Familial endocrine
      Basal cell nevus syndrome
      Phakomatoses
Multiple use of buildings
  USE Joint occupancy of buildings
Multiple use of cemeteries
  USE Cemeteries—Multiple use
Multiple use of forest lands
  USE Forests and forestry—Multiple use
Multiple use of forest reserves
  USE Forest reserves—Multiple use
Multiple use of geothermal resources
  USE Geothermal resources—Multiple use
Multiple use of national parks and reserves
  USE National parks and reserves—Multiple
      use
Multiple use of rangelands
  USE Rangelands—Multiple use
Multiple use of rights of way
  USE Public utilities—Right of way—
      Multiple use
      Railroads—Right of way—Multiple use
      Roads—Right of way—Multiple use
Multiple use of watersheds
  USE Watersheds—Multiple use
Multiple Virtual Storages (Computer system)
  USE MVS (Computer system)
Multiples (Art)
  USE Multiple art
Multiplex broadcasting
  USE Stereophonic broadcasting
Multiplex spectrometry
  USE Fourier transform spectroscopy
      Hadamard transform spectroscopy
Multiplexing
  BT Telecommunication
  NT Stereophonic broadcasting
      Telephone—Multiplex systems
Multiplication
  [QA115 (Mathematics)]
  BT Arithmetic
      Ready-reckoners
  — Tables
      [QA49]
      UF Tables, Mathematical
Multiplication, Complex
  UF Complex multiplication
  BT Geometry, Algebraic
Multiplicity (Nuclear physics)
  USE Particles (Nuclear physics)—
      Multiplicity
Multiplicity of hadrons
  USE Hadrons—Multiplicity
Multiplier, Schur
  USE Schur multiplier
Multiplier (Economics)
  UF Economic multiplier
  BT Business cycles
      Economics
      Income
      National income
  RT Circular velocity of money
Multiplier phototubes
  USE Photoelectric multipliers
Multipliers (Electronic calculating-machines)
  USE Analog multipliers
Multipliers (Mathematical analysis)
  BT Functional analysis
      Harmonic analysis
Multiply transitive groups
  USE Groups, Multiply transitive

Multipole resonance, Giant
  USE Giant multipole resonance
Multiprocessors
  [QA76.5]
  BT Electronic digital computers
  RT Multiprogramming (Electronic
      computers)
      Parallel processing (Electronic
      computers)
  NT Array processors
      Cm* (Computer system)
      Multi-Batch (Electronic computer
      system)
Multiprogramming (Electronic computers)
  BT Electronic data processing
      Electronic digital computers—
      Programming
      Time-sharing computer systems
  RT Multiprocessors
  NT Multi-Batch (Electronic computer
      system)
MultiProgramming Monitor (Computer
  operating system)
  USE MP/M (Computer operating system)
Multipurpose buildings
  USE Joint occupancy of buildings
Multipurpose plant species
  USE Multipurpose plants
Multipurpose plants *(May Subd Geog)*
  UF Multipurpose plant species
      Plants, Multipurpose
  BT Plants, Useful
  NT Multipurpose trees
Multipurpose tree species
  USE Multipurpose trees
Multipurpose trees *(May Subd Geog)*
  [SB172]
      Here are entered works dealing with trees which
  are deliberately grown or kept and managed for more
  than one intended use to provide economical or eco-
  logical products or services in a multipurpose land
  use system.
  UF Multipurpose tree species
      Tree species, Multipurpose
      Trees, Multipurpose
  BT Multipurpose plants
      Tree crops
Multiring basins, Lunar
  USE Lunar basins
Multiring crater structures, Lunar
  USE Lunar basins
Multispectral photography
  UF Photography, Multispectral
  BT Photography
      Remote sensing
      Space optics
Multistate alliances, Hospital
  USE Hospitals—Regional alliances
Multistate hospital alliances
  USE Hospitals—Regional alliances
Multistory buildings
  USE Tall buildings
Multistory housing
  USE High-rise apartment buildings
Multistory school buildings
  USE School buildings, High rise
Multivalued logic
  USE Many-valued logic
MULTIVARIANCE (Computer program)
  BT Computer programs
      Multivariate analysis—Computer
      programs
Multivariate analysis
  UF Multivariate distributions
      Multivariate statistical analysis
      Statistical analysis, Multivariate
  BT Analysis of variance
      Mathematical statistics
      Matrices
  NT Cluster analysis
      Discriminant analysis

      Latent structure analysis
      Latent variables
      Log-linear models
      Missing observations (Statistics)
  — Computer programs
      NT MULTIVARIANCE (Computer
        program)
Multivariate Analysis, Participation and
  Structure
  USE MAPS design technology
Multivariate distributions
  USE Multivariate analysis
Multivariate statistical analysis
  USE Multivariate analysis
Multivibrators
  [TK7872.O7]
  BT Relaxation oscillators
Multnomah Indians
  [E99.M92]
  BT Chinookan Indians
      Indians of North America
Multon family
  USE Moulton family
Mulu National Park, Gunung (Sarawak)
  USE Gunung Mulu National Park
      (Sarawak)
Mulvad family *(Not Subd Geog)*
Mulvaney family *(Not Subd Geog)*
  UF Mulvania family
      Mulvanny family
      Mulvany family
      Mulvenny family
Mulvania family
  USE Mulvaney family
Mulvanny family
  USE Mulvaney family
Mulvany family
  USE Mulvaney family
Mulvenny family
  USE Mulvaney family
Mulwi dialect
  USE Vulum dialect
Muma
  USE Myositis tropica
Mumbala language
  USE Mbala language (Bandundu region,
      Zaire)
Mumbo (Cult) *(May Subd Geog)*
  BT Cults—Kenya
      Religion, Primitive—Kenya
Mumma family *(Not Subd Geog)*
Mummies *(May Subd Geog)*
  [DT62.M7 (Egyptology)]
  BT Archaeology
      Burial
      Egypt—Antiquities
  RT Embalming
  — Radiography
      BT Radiography in archaeology
Mumming *(May Subd Geog)*
  [GT4895 (Christmas customs)]
  [PR635.F6 (English folk-drama)]
  BT Carnival
      Masks
      Theater
  RT Masquerades
Mumming plays
  BT Carnival plays
      Christmas plays
      Folk-drama, English
      Masques
Mummy cases *(May Subd Geog)*
  [DT62.M7]
  UF Cases, Mummy
  BT Coffins
Mummy portraits *(May Subd Geog)*
  UF Fayum portraits
  BT Portraits, Ancient
Mumps *(May Subd Geog)*
  [RC168.M8]

Mumps (Continued)
  BT Parotid glands—Diseases
       Parotitis
  — Preventive inoculation
       [RA644.M8]
MUMPS (Computer program language)
  [QA76.73.M]
  UF Massachusetts General Hospital Utility
       Multiprogramming System
       (Computer program language)
MUMS (Computer)
  [QA76.8.M]
  BT Microprocessors
Mumuye language
  BT Adamawa languages
       Cameroon—Languages
       Nigeria—Languages
Mumuyes
  BT Ethnology—Nigeria
Mumvu (African people)
  USE Mamvu (African people)
Mun River (Thailand)
  UF Nam Mun (Thailand)
  BT Rivers—Thailand
Muna language (May Subd Geog)
  UF Mina language
  BT Indonesia—Languages
       Malayan languages
MUNAP (Computer)
  [QA76.8.M]
  BT Electronic digital computers
Muncey language
  USE Munsee language
Munch, Edvard, 1863-1944. Alpha and
       Omega
  UF Alpha and Omega (Lithography)
  BT Lithography—20th century—Norway
Muncrief family
  USE Moncrief family
Muncriep family
  USE Moncrief family
Muncriffe family
  USE Moncrief family
Mund Site (Ill.) (Not Subd Geog)
  BT American Bottom (Ill.)—Antiquities
       Illinois—Antiquities
Munda folk poetry
  USE Folk poetry, Munda
Munda languages
  [PL4501-9]
  UF Kolarian languages
  BT Austroasiatic languages
       Indic languages
  RT Kherwari language
       Kurku language
       Santali language
  NT Bonda language
       Ho language
       Kharia language
       Mundari language
       Nahali language
       Parengi language
       Savara language
Munda poetry (May Subd Geog)
  NT Folk poetry, Munda
Mundal (Artificial language)
  [PM8637]
  BT Languages, Artificial
Mundal family
  USE Mondale family
Mundale family
  USE Mondale family
Mundang (African people)
  [DT546.445.M85 (Chad)]
  UF Moundan (African people)
       Moundang (African people)
  BT Ethnology—Cameroon
       Ethnology—Chad
Mundari folk poetry
  USE Folk poetry, Mundari

Mundari folk-songs
  USE Folk-songs, Mundari
Mundari language
  [PL4559]
  UF Kohl language
       Kol language
  BT Munda languages
Mundari literature (May Subd Geog)
Mundari poetry (May Subd Geog)
  NT Folk poetry, Mundari
Mundas
  [DS432.M8]
  UF Kols
  BT Civilization, Dravidian
       Ethnology—India
  NT Asurs
       Baigas
       Bhils
       Bhuiyas
       Didayi (Indic people)
       Hos
       Juang (Indic people)
       Kharias
       Lodhas
       Santals (Indic people)
Munday family
  USE Mundy family
Mundbjerg family (Not Subd Geog)
Munde family
  USE Mundy family
Mundell family
  USE Mandeville family
Mundie family
  USE Mundy family
Mundju language
  USE Bamougoun-Bamenjou language
Mündler family (Not Subd Geog)
  UF Mindler family
Mundo (African people)
  USE Bongo (African people)
Mundrucu Indians
  USE Mundurucu Indians
Mundu language
  BT Niger-Congo languages
       Sudan—Languages
       Zaire—Languages
Mundu language (Philippines)
  USE Sulod language
Mundugamor (Papua New Guinea people)
  [DU740.42]
  BT Ethnology—Papua New Guinea
Mundurucu Indians
  [F2520.1.M]
  UF Mondorocu Indians
       Mundrucu Indians
       Pari Indians
  BT Indians of South America
Mundurucu language
  [PM6596]
  UF Pari language
  BT Indians of South America—Languages
       Tupi languages
Mundy family (Not Subd Geog)
  UF Monday family
       Munday family
       Munde family
       Mundie family
Mundzhan language
  USE Munji language
Mung bean
  [QK495.L52 (Botany)]
  [SB317.M85 (Culture)]
  UF Azukia radiata
       Green gram
       Mungbean
       Mungo bean
       Phaseolus aureus
       Phaseolus radiatus
       Vigna radiata
  BT Beans

Mungar family
  USE Munger family
Mungarai (Australian tribe)
  [DU397.5]
  UF Mungari (Australian tribe)
  BT Australian aborigines
Mungari (Australian tribe)
  USE Mungarai (Australian tribe)
Mungbean
  USE Mung bean
Munger family (Not Subd Geog)
  UF Manger family
       Monger family
       Mungar family
Munggan language
  USE Wik-Munkan language
Munggava language
  USE Rennellese language
Mungkan language
  USE Wik-Munkan language
Mungo bean
  USE Mung bean
Mungos
  [QL737.C28]
  BT Mongooses
       Viverridae
Mungsen dialect
  USE Ao language
Munich (Germany)
  — History
  — — Beer Hall Putsch, 1923
       USE Germany—History—Beer Hall
            Putsch, 1923
Munich school of painting
  [ND567.5.M85]
  BT Painting, German
       Painting, Modern—19th century—
            Germany
  NT Leibl-Kreis
Municipal accounting
  USE Municipal finance—Accounting
Municipal administration
  USE Municipal government
Municipal and international law
  USE International and municipal law
Municipal annexation
  USE Annexation (Municipal government)
Municipal art
  USE Art, Municipal
Municipal bankruptcy (May Subd Geog)
  UF Bankruptcy, Municipal
  BT Bankruptcy
Municipal bonds (May Subd Geog)
  [HG4726]
  [HG4951-HG4953 (United States)]
  [HG5151-HG5890 (10) or (7) under
       country (Other countries)]
  Works on the bonds of an individual city, town,
  village, etc. are entered under the heading Bonds,
  with local subdivision.
  UF Bonds, Municipal
       Local government bonds
  BT Bonds
       Government securities
       Municipal finance
       Securities
  NT Industrial development bonds
       Library bonds
       School bonds
  — Law and legislation (May Subd Geog)
  — Ratings (May Subd Geog)
       UF Municipal bonds, Rating of
            Rating of municipal bonds
  — — Law and legislation
       (May Subd Geog)
  — Taxation (May Subd Geog)
       BT Taxation of bonds, securities, etc.
  — — Law and legislation
       (May Subd Geog)
Municipal bonds, Rating of
  USE Municipal bonds—Ratings

Municipal budgets *(May Subd Geog)*
  UF Budgets, Municipal
  BT Local budgets
       Municipal finance
  — Law and legislation *(May Subd Geog)*
Municipal buildings *(May Subd Geog)*
  ⌈JS201-JS208⌉
  ⌈NA4430-NA4437 (Architecture)⌉
  UF Buildings, Municipal
  BT Architecture
       Art, Municipal
       Public buildings
       Public works
  RT Civic centers
  NT City halls
  — Austria
     NT Künstlerhaus (Graz, Austria)
  — Belgium
     NT Maison du Roi (Brussels, Belgium)
  — France
     NT Kursaal-Cirque (Besançon, France)
  — Germany (East)
     NT Sport- und Ausstellungszentrum
         (Frankfurt an der Oder,
         Germany)
  — Germany (West)
     NT Altes Rathaus (Göttingen,
         Germany)
        Haus am Checkpoint Charlie
         (Berlin, Germany)
        Haus Bitz (Frechen, Germany)
        Kubus Hannover (Hannover,
         Germany)
        Rathaus (Mainz, Rhineland-
         Palatinate, Germany)
        Schwörhaus (Ulm, Germany)
        Skulpturenmuseum Glaskasten
         (Marl, Germany)
  — Italy
     NT Palazzo Madama (Turin, Italy)
  — Switzerland
     NT Haus zum Rechberg (Zurich,
         Switzerland)
        Rathaus des Äusseren Standes
         (Bern, Switzerland)
        Stadthaus Olten (Olten,
         Switzerland)
  — Wales
     NT Guildhall (Swansea, West
         Glamorgan)
Municipal centers
  USE Civic centers
Municipal ceremonial *(May Subd Geog)*
  UF Ceremonial, Municipal
       Civic ceremonial
  BT Municipal corporations
       Municipal government
       Rites and ceremonies
  RT Precedence
  NT Maces, Ceremonial
Municipal charters *(May Subd Geog)*
  UF Charters, Municipal
  BT Charters
       Municipal corporations
  SA *subdivision* Charters *under names of*
       cities of the United States; and
       subdivision Charters, grants,
       privileges *under names of foreign*
       cities
Municipal civil service
  USE Municipal officials and employees
Municipal contracts
  USE Public contracts
Municipal corporations *(May Subd Geog)*
  ⌈JS⌉

Here are entered legal treatises and collections of statutes regarding municipal corporations. Works on the formation of a municipal corporation are entered under the heading Municipal incorporation. For general works prefer Municipal government. Works on public service corporations in cities are entered under Municipal franchises, Public utilities, etc. Cf. note under Cities and towns.
  UF Cities and towns—Law and legislation
       Corporations, Public
       Municipal government—Law and
         legislation
       Municipal law (Municipal
         corporations)
       Public corporations
  BT Corporations
  RT Metropolitan government
       Municipal government
  NT Annexation (Municipal government)
       Boroughs—Law and legislation
       City attorneys
       Community organization—Law and
         legislation
       De facto doctrine
       Local elections
       Mayors
       Model ordinances
       Municipal ceremonial
       Municipal charters
       Municipal finance
       Municipal incorporation
       Municipal powers and services beyond
         corporate limits
       Municipal services—Law and
         legislation
       Parishes (Local government)
       Police power
       Special assessments
       Special assessments—Law and
         legislation
       Ultra vires
  — State supervision
     USE Local government—State
         supervision
  — Taxation *(May Subd Geog)*

Here are entered works on taxation of municipalities by federal or state governments. Works on municipal taxation and taxation by other units of local government are entered under Local taxation.
  — Tort liability
     USE Tort liability of municipal
         corporations
Municipal corporations (Germanic law)
Municipal corporations (Roman law)
Municipal courts *(May Subd Geog)*

Here are entered general works. Works on an individual court are entered under the name of the court.
  UF Corporation courts
       Courts, Municipal
  BT Courts
       Courts of first instance
  NT Mayors' courts
Municipal default *(May Subd Geog)*

Here are entered general works on city, town, borough, or village financial default. Works on the financial default of an individual city or town are entered under the heading Default (Finance) with local subdivision.
  BT Default (Finance)
       Municipal finance
Municipal documents *(May Subd Geog)*
  UF Documents
  BT Government publications
       Local government documents
       Municipal government
Municipal elections
  USE Local elections
Municipal employees
  USE Municipal officials and employees
Municipal engineering *(May Subd Geog)*
  ⌈TD⌉

  UF Engineering, Municipal
  BT Engineering
       Public works
  NT Aerial photography in municipal
         engineering
       Bridges
       Municipal engineers
       Municipal lighting
       Municipal water supply
       Parks
       Refuse and refuse disposal
       Sewerage
       Street cleaning
       Streets
       Underground utility lines
       Water-supply
  — Equipment and supplies
     NT Public works equipment
Municipal engineers *(May Subd Geog)*
  BT Municipal engineering
Municipal finance *(May Subd Geog)*
  ⌈HJ9000-9697⌉

Here are entered general works on city, town, borough, or village finance. Works on the finance of an individual city or town are entered under the heading Finance, Public, with local subdivision.
  UF Finance, Municipal
  BT Municipal corporations
       Municipal government
  RT Local finance
  NT Licenses
       Local taxation
       Metropolitan finance
       Municipal bonds
       Municipal budgets
       Municipal default
       Municipal revenue
       Octroi
  — Accounting
     ⌈HJ9771-9⌉
     UF Municipal accounting
        Public accounting
     BT Accounting
  — — Law and legislation
       (May Subd Geog)
  — Auditing
  — — Law and legislation
       (May Subd Geog)
  — Law and legislation *(May Subd Geog)*
Municipal franchises *(May Subd Geog)*
  ⌈HD2763-8⌉
  UF Franchises, Municipal
  BT Corporations
  RT Concessions
  NT Public service commissions
       Public utilities
       Public utilities—Law and legislation
Municipal government *(May Subd Geog)*
  ⌈JS⌉

Here are entered theoretical and practical works on city government and administration. Collections of statutes are entered under Municipal corporations. Works on local government not municipal are entered under Local government. Cf. note under Cities and towns.
  UF City government
       Municipal administration
       Municipalities
       Urban politics
  BT Local government
       Urban policy
  RT Metropolitan government
       Municipal corporations
  SA *subdivision* Politics and government
       under names of cities
  NT Annexation (Municipal government)
       Boroughs
       Boroughs (Municipal subdivision)
       City councils
       City-states
       Classification—Books—Municipal
         government

Municipal government *(Continued)*
    Corregidors
    Federal-city relations
    Freemen
    Local elections
    Mayors
    Municipal ceremonial
    Municipal documents
    Municipal finance
    Municipal home rule
    Municipal incorporation
    Municipal officials and employees
    Municipal powers and services beyond
        corporate limits
    Municipal reports
    Municipal services
    State-local relations
    Strikes and lockouts—Municipal
        government
— Law and legislation
    USE Municipal corporations
— Public relations
    USE Public relations—Municipal
        government
— **Records and correspondence**
    UF Municipal records
    BT Public records
— — **Indexing**
    BT Indexing
— State supervision
    USE Local government—State
        supervision
— **Vocational guidance** *(May Subd Geog)*
    BT Municipal officials and employees
— **Brazil**
    NT Coronelismo
— **Iowa**
    UF Des Moines plan of city
        government
— **Rome**
    NT Decurions (Roman municipal
        government)
Municipal government by city manager
(May Subd Geog)
    [JS344.C5 (United States)]
    UF Commission government with city
        manager
    RT City managers
Municipal government by commission
    [JS342-JS343 (United States)]
    UF Commission government
        Des Moines plan of city government
        Government by commission
    SA *subdivision* Politics and government
        under names of cities
Municipal home rule *(May Subd Geog)*
    [JS113 (General)]
    UF City and state, Relation of
        Home rule for cities
        Self-government for cities
    BT Municipal government
    NT Home rule (District of Columbia)
Municipal improvement
    USE Civic improvement
Municipal improvements
    USE Art, Municipal
Municipal income tax
    USE Income tax, Municipal
Municipal incorporation *(May Subd Geog)*
    Cf. note under Municipal corporations.
    UF Incorporation, Municipal
    BT Incorporation
        Municipal corporations
        Municipal government
    NT Annexation (Municipal government)
Municipal insignia
    UF Insignia, Municipal
    SA *subdivision* Insignia *under names of*
        cities and towns
Municipal junior colleges
    USE Community colleges

Municipal laundries
    USE Laundries, Public
Municipal law (Municipal corporations)
    USE Municipal corporations
Municipal law officers
    USE City attorneys
Municipal lighting *(May Subd Geog)*
    Here are entered works on city, town, borough, or
    village lighting. Works on the lighting of an individu-
    al city or town are entered under the heading Light-
    ing with local subdivision.
    UF Cities and towns—Lighting
        City lighting
        Metropolitan lighting
        Public lighting
    BT Lighting
        Municipal engineering
    NT Bridges—Lighting
        Lighting, Architectural and decorative
        Sidewalk-lights
        Street-lighting
        Tunnels—Lighting
Municipal officers
    USE Municipal officials and employees
Municipal officials and employees
(May Subd Geog)
    UF Civil service, Municipal
        Municipal civil service
        Municipal employees
        Municipal officers
        Town officers
    BT Civil service
        Local officials and employees
        Municipal government
        Public officers
    SA *subdivision* Officials and employees
        under names of cities
    NT City council members
        Collective labor agreements—
            Municipal employees
        Corregidors
        Municipal government—Vocational
            guidance
        Selectmen
        Strikes and lockouts—Municipal
            government
        Town clerks
— Collective bargaining
    USE Collective bargaining—Municipal
        employees
— **Discipline** *(May Subd Geog)*
    BT Disciplinary power
— **Residence requirements**
    UF Residence requirements for
        municipal officials and
        employees
    SA *subdivision* Officials and employees
        —Residence requirements *under*
        names of cities
— Salaries, allowances, etc.
    USE Municipal officials and employees
        —Salaries, etc.
— **Salaries, etc.** *(May Subd Geog)*
    UF Municipal officials and employees
        —Salaries, allowances, etc.
— Trade-unions
    USE Trade-unions—Municipal
        employees
— **Islamic countries**
    NT Muḥtasib
Municipal officials and employees, Honorary
(May Subd Geog)
    UF Honorary municipal officials and
        employees
Municipal ordinances
    USE Ordinances, Municipal
Municipal ownership *(May Subd Geog)*
    [HD4421-4730]
    UF Public ownership

    BT Economic policy
        Government business enterprises
        Government ownership
    NT Service at cost (Public utilities)
**Municipal powers and services beyond
corporate limits** *(May Subd Geog)*
    UF Extraterritorial powers of
        municipalities
        Municipal services beyond corporate
        limits
    BT Local government
        Metropolitan areas
        Metropolitan government
        Municipal corporations
        Municipal government
        Suburbs
    RT Public utilities—Law and legislation
Municipal records
    USE Municipal government—Records and
        correspondence
Municipal reference libraries
(May Subd Geog)
    [Z675.M9]
    UF Libraries, Municipal reference
    BT Libraries, Governmental,
        administrative, etc.
Municipal reports
    [JS163]
    BT Municipal government
        Report writing
Municipal research
    USE Cities and towns—Research
Municipal revenue *(May Subd Geog)*
    [HJ9115-HJ9123]
    BT Municipal finance
        Revenue
Municipal services *(May Subd Geog)*
    [HD4421-4730.7]
    UF Municipal services within corporate
        limits
        Public services
    BT City planning
        Municipal government
        Public utilities
    SA *specific services, e.g.* Fire-departments;
        Police
    NT Discrimination in municipal services
        Homeowners' associations
        User charges
— **Contracting out**
    BT Contracting out
— **Finance**
— **Law and legislation** *(May Subd Geog)*
    BT Municipal corporations
Municipal services beyond corporate limits
    USE Municipal powers and services beyond
        corporate limits
Municipal services within corporate limits
    USE Municipal services
Municipal Stadium (Cleveland, Ohio)
    USE Cleveland Municipal Stadium
        (Cleveland, Ohio)
Municipal taxation
    USE Local taxation
Municipal theater
    USE Theater, Municipal
Municipal transit
    USE Local transit
Municipal transportation
    USE Urban transportation
Municipal universities and colleges
(May Subd Geog)
    [LB2329]
    UF County colleges (English)
        Urban universities
    BT Universities and colleges
— **Law and legislation** *(May Subd Geog)*
    BT Educational law and legislation
Municipal university and college libraries
    [Z675.M]

UF Libraries, Municipal university and
college
BT Libraries, University and college
Municipal utilities
USE Public utilities
Municipal water supply *(May Subd Geog)*
[TD201-TD500]
Here are entered general works on city, town,
borough, or village water supply. Works on the water
supply of an individual city or town are entered under
the heading Water-supply with local subdivision.
UF Cities and towns—Water-supply
Urban water
Water, Municipal
Water, Urban
BT Municipal engineering
Water-supply
Municipalities
USE Cities and towns
Municipal government
Munition workers
[HD7269.M8]
NT Strikes and lockouts—Munitions
industry
Trade-unions—Munition workers
Wages—Munition workers
Munitions *(May Subd Geog)*
[HD9743 (Economics)]
[JX5390 (International law)]
[UF530-UF537 (Manufacture)]
Here are entered general works on the imple-
ments of war and the industries producing them.
Works on military strength including military person-
nel, munitions, natural resources and industrial war
potential are entered under the heading Armaments.
UF Arms sales
Foreign military sales
Instruments of war
Military sales
Munitions trade
Sale of military equipment
BT Armaments
Industrial mobilization
War—Economic aspects
RT Arms race
SA *subdivision* Equipment and supplies
under individual wars, e.g. World
War, 1939-1945—Equipment and
supplies
NT Firearms industry and trade
Hot shot
Offshore procurement program, 1951-
Precision guided munitions
Space weapons
Weapons systems
— Advertising
USE Advertising—Munitions
— **Law and legislation** *(May Subd Geog)*
BT Neutrality
War, Maritime (International law)
War (International law)
— **Religious aspects**
— — **Buddhism,** [**Christianity, etc.**]
Munitions, Tear gas
USE Tear gas munitions
Munitions trade
USE Munitions
Munjani language
USE Munji language
Munji language
[PK6996.M8]
UF Mundzhan language
Munjani language
BT Afghanistan—Languages
Pakistan—Languages
Pamir languages
Munju language
USE Bamougoun-Bamenjou language
Munkan tribe
UF Wik-Munkan tribe
BT Australian aborigines

Munker family *(Not Subd Geog)*
Münkü Indians
USE Iranxe Indians
Munro clan
USE Monroe family
Munro family
USE Monroe family
Munroe charges
USE Shaped charges
Munroe family
USE Monroe family
Munsee Indians
[E99.M93]
BT Algonquian Indians
Indians of North America
NT Esopus Indians
Moravian Indians
Munsee language
[PM1961]
UF Esopus language
Minsi language
Monsey language
Moonsee language
Muncey language
RT Algonquian languages
Delaware language
Munsen family
USE Munson family
Munshi
USE Tivi (African people)
Munsi
USE Tivi (African people)
Munson family *(Not Subd Geog)*
UF Mansen family
Manson family
Monsen family
Monson family
Munsen family
RT Edmondson family
Munson shorthand
USE Shorthand—Munson
Münster family *(Not Subd Geog)*
Münster Rathaus (Münster in Westfalen,
Germany)
USE Rathaus zu Münster (Münster in
Westfalen, Germany)
Munster Union Cemetery (Goulbourn, Ont.)
BT Cemeteries—Ontario
Muntele Paringul (Romania)
USE Parîng Mountains (Romania)
Muntiacus
[QL737.U55]
BT Cervidae
Deer
Muntiacus reevesi
UF Chinese muntjac
Reeves' muntjac
Munţii Apuseni (Romania)
USE Apuseni Mountains (Romania)
Munţii Baiului (Romania)
USE Baiului Mountains (Romania)
Munţii Buzăului (Romania)
USE Buzău Mountains (Romania)
Munţii Ciucaş (Romania)
USE Ciucaş Mountains (Romania)
Munţii Făgăraşului (Romania)
USE Făgăraş Mountains (Romania)
Munţii Godeanu (Romania)
USE Godeanu Mountains (Romania)
Munţii Gutăiului (Romania)
USE Gutîi Mountains (Romania)
Munţii Gutîi (Romania)
USE Gutîi Mountains (Romania)
Munţii Gutîiului (Romania)
USE Gutîi Mountains (Romania)
Munţii Gutinului (Romania)
USE Gutîi Mountains (Romania)
Munţii Iezer (Romania)
USE Iezer Mountains (Romania)
Munţii Mehedenţi (Romania)
USE Mehedenţi Mountains (Romania)

Munţii Oaşului (Romania)
USE Oaş Mountains (Romania)
Munţii Ouaş (Romania)
USE Oaş Mountains (Romania)
Munţii Ouaşului (Romania)
USE Oaş Mountains (Romania)
Munţii Parângu (Romania)
USE Parîng Mountains (Romania)
Munţii Parângului (Romania)
USE Parîng Mountains (Romania)
Munţii Paring (Romania)
USE Parîng Mountains (Romania)
Munţii Parîngului (Romania)
USE Parîng Mountains (Romania)
Munţii Poiana Ruscă (Romania)
USE Poiana Rusca Mountains (Romania)
Munţii Retezat (Romania)
USE Retezat Mountains (Romania)
Munţii Rodnei (Romania)
USE Rodna Mountains (Romania)
Munţii Semenic (Romania)
USE Semenic Mountains (Romania)
Munţii Semenicului (Romania)
USE Semenic Mountains (Romania)
Munţii Zarandului (Romania)
USE Zarandului Mountains (Romania)
Munukutuba language
USE Kituba language
Münzenberg family *(Not Subd Geog)*
UF Münzenberger family
Münzenburg family
Münzenberger family
USE Münzenberg family
Münzenburg family
USE Münzenberg family
Muon spin relaxation
USE Muon spin rotation
Muon spin resonance
USE Muon spin rotation
Muon spin rotation
UF Muon spin relaxation
Muon spin resonance
Relaxation, Muon spin
Resonance, Muon spin
Rotation, Muon spin
BT Muons—Decay
Muons—Depolarization
Spin-lattice relaxation
Muong (Vietnamese people)
BT Ethnology—Vietnam
Muong fiction *(May Subd Geog)*
NT Short stories, Muong
Muong folk poetry
USE Folk poetry, Muong
Muong language
[PL4392]
BT Austroasiatic languages
Muong poetry *(May Subd Geog)*
NT Folk poetry, Muong
Muong short stories
USE Short stories, Muong
Muonium
BT Electrons
Muons
Nuclear reactions
Muons
UF Mu mesons
BT Leptons (Nuclear physics)
RT Kaons
Mesons
Pions
NT Cosmic ray muons
Exotic atoms
Muonium
— **Capture**
[QC721]
— **Decay**
NT Muon spin rotation
— **Depolarization**
UF Depolarization of muons
BT Polarization (Nuclear physics)

Muons
— **Depolarization** *(Continued)*
   NT Muon spin rotation
— **Scattering**
— **Spectra**
Mupirocin
  UF Pseudomonic acid A
     Trans-pseudomonic acid
  BT Antibiotics
     Carboxylic acids
     Dermatologic agents
  RT Pseudomonas fluorescens
MuPROSPECTOR (Computer system)
  BT Expert systems (Computer science)
     Mines and mineral resources—Data
       processing
     Prospecting—Data processing
Muqayyar, Tall al- (Iraq)
  USE Ur (Ancient city)
Mur de l'Atlantique (France and Belgium)
  USE Atlantic Wall (France and Belgium)
Mur River *(Not Subd Geog)*
  UF Mura River
  BT Rivers—Austria
     Rivers—Hungary
     Rivers—Yugoslavia
Mura River
  USE Mur River
Muraenesocidae
  [QL638.M87]
  UF Pike congers
     Sauromuraenesocidae
  BT Eels
  NT Muraenesox
     Paraxenomystax
Muraenesox
  [QL638.M87]
  BT Muraenesocidae
Muraenichthyidae
  USE Xenocongridae
Muraenidae
  USE Morays
Muraenosaurus
  USE Nettastoma
Muraenosaurus guntheri
  USE Nettastoma melanurum
Murakami family *(Not Subd Geog)*
Muraköz (Croatia)
  USE Medimurje (Croatia)
Mural painting and decoration
  (May Subd Geog)
  [ND2550-2876]
  UF Ceilings, Painted
     Fresco painting
     Murals
     Painted ceilings
     Painting, Decorative
     Wall decoration
     Wall-painting
  BT Art
     Arts and crafts movement
     Ceilings
     Church decoration and ornament
     Decoration and ornament
     Interior decoration
     Painting
     Walls
  RT Mosaics
  NT Cave-drawings
     Encaustic painting
     Graffito decoration
— **16th century** *(May Subd Geog)*
— **17th century** *(May Subd Geog)*
— **18th century** *(May Subd Geog)*
— **19th century** *(May Subd Geog)*
— **20th century** *(May Subd Geog)*
   NT Street art
— — **Austria**
— **Attribution**

  UF Attribution of mural painting and
     decoration
     Mural painting and decoration—
      Reattribution
  BT Mural painting and decoration—
     Expertising
— **Conservation and restoration**
  (May Subd Geog)
  UF Conservation of mural painting and
     decoration
     Preservation of mural painting and
      decoration
     Restoration of mural painting and
      decoration
— **Deterioration**
  [ND2551]
  UF Deterioration of mural painting
     and decoration
— **Expertising**
  NT Mural painting and decoration—
     Attribution
— **Reattribution**
  USE Mural painting and decoration—
     Attribution
— **India**
  NT Pahari mural painting and
     decoration
— **Italy**
  NT Bramante, Donato, 1444?-1514.
     Casa Panigarola frescoes
     Perino, del Vaga, 1500 or 1501-
      1547. Sala Paolina frescoes
     Raphael, 1483-1520. School of
      Athens
     Salimbeni, Ventura, 1568-1613.
      Apocalypse frescoes
— **Washington (D.C.)**
  NT Peacock Room
Mural painting and decoration, American
  NT Benton, Thomas Hart, 1889-1975.
     America today
     Lichtenstein, Roy, 1923-   Mural
     with blue brushstroke
— **Washington (D.C.)**
  NT Peacock Room
Mural painting and decoration, American,
[Greco-Roman, Italian, etc.]
(May Subd Geog)
Mural painting and decoration, Ancient
Mural painting and decoration, Argentine
  (May Subd Geog)
  UF Argentine mural painting and
     decoration
Mural painting and decoration, Armenian
  (May Subd Geog)
  UF Armenian mural painting and
     decoration
Mural painting and decoration, Austrian
  (May Subd Geog)
  UF Austrian mural painting and
     decoration
Mural painting and decoration, Baroque
  (May Subd Geog)
  UF Baroque mural painting and decoration
— **Italy**
  NT Salimbeni, Ventura, 1568-1613.
     Apocalypse frescoes
Mural painting and decoration, Belgian
  (May Subd Geog)
  UF Belgian mural painting and decoration
Mural painting and decoration, Brazilian
  (May Subd Geog)
  UF Brazilian mural painting and
     decoration
Mural painting and decoration, British
  (May Subd Geog)
  UF British mural painting and decoration
Mural painting and decoration, Buddhist
  (May Subd Geog)
  UF Buddhist mural painting and
     decoration

Mural painting and decoration, Bulgarian
  (May Subd Geog)
  UF Bulgarian mural painting and
     decoration
Mural painting and decoration, Byelorussian
  (May Subd Geog)
  UF Byelorussian mural painting and
     decoration
Mural painting and decoration, Byzantine
  (May Subd Geog)
  UF Byzantine mural painting and
     decoration
— **Expertising**
— **Macedonian influences**
  BT Macedonia—Civilization
Mural painting and decoration, Carlovingian
  (May Subd Geog)
  UF Carlovingian mural painting and
     decoration
Mural painting and decoration, Chinese
  (May Subd Geog)
  UF Chinese mural painting and decoration
— **Three kingdoms-Sui dynasty, 220-618**
  UF Mural painting and decoration,
     Chinese—Three kingdoms, six
     dynasties-Sui dynasty, 220-618
— Three kingdoms, six dynasties-Sui
  dynasty, 220-618
  USE Mural painting and decoration,
     Chinese—Three kingdoms-Sui
     dynasty, 220-618
— **Ch'in-Han dynasties, 221 B.C.-220 A.D.**
  [ND2868]
— **T'ang-Five dynasties, 618-960**
  [ND2868]
— **Sung-Yüan dynasties, 960-1368**
  NT T'ai shan shen ch'i pi hui luan t'u
     (Mural)
— **Ming-Ch'ing dynasties, 1368-1912**
— **20th century**
— **Reproduction**
  BT Art—Reproduction
Mural painting and decoration, Colonial
  (May Subd Geog)
  UF Colonial mural painting and decoration
Mural painting and decoration, Coptic
  (May Subd Geog)
  UF Coptic mural painting and decoration
Mural painting and decoration, Danish
  (May Subd Geog)
  UF Danish mural painting and decoration
Mural painting and decoration, Early
Christian *(May Subd Geog)*
  UF Early Christian mural painting and
     decoration
Mural painting and decoration, Egyptian
  (May Subd Geog)
  UF Egyptian mural painting and
     decoration
Mural painting and decoration, Etruscan
  (May Subd Geog)
  UF Etruscan mural painting and
     decoration
Mural painting and decoration, European
  UF European mural painting and
     decoration
Mural painting and decoration, Finnish
  (May Subd Geog)
  UF Finnish mural painting and decoration
Mural painting and decoration, Gallo-Roman
  (May Subd Geog)
  UF Gallo-Roman mural painting and
     decoration
Mural painting and decoration, Georgian
  (May Subd Geog)
  UF Georgian mural painting and
     decoration

Mural painting and decoration, Georgian (Georgian S.S.R.) *(May Subd Geog)*
  UF Georgian (Georgian S.S.R.) mural painting and decoration
     Mural painting and decoration, Georgian (Transcaucasia)
  — **Byzantine influences**
     BT Byzantine Empire—Civilization
Mural painting and decoration, Georgian (Transcaucasia)
  USE Mural painting and decoration, Georgian (Georgian S.S.R.)
Mural painting and decoration, German *(May Subd Geog)*
  UF German mural painting and decoration
Mural painting and decoration, Gothic *(May Subd Geog)*
  UF Gothic mural painting and decoration
  — **Attribution**
     UF Attribution of Gothic mural painting and decoration
        Mural painting and decoration, Gothic—Reattribution
     BT Mural painting and decoration, Gothic—Expertising
  — **Expertising**
     NT Mural painting and decoration, Gothic—Attribution
  — **Italian influences**
     BT Italy—Civilization
  — **Reattribution**
     USE Mural painting and decoration, Gothic—Attribution
Mural painting and decoration, Greek *(May Subd Geog)*
  UF Greek mural painting and decoration
  — **Expertising**
Mural painting and decoration, Hellenistic *(May Subd Geog)*
  UF Hellenistic mural painting and decoration
Mural painting and decoration, Hungarian *(May Subd Geog)*
  UF Hungarian mural painting and decoration
Mural painting and decoration, Indic *(May Subd Geog)*
  UF Indic mural painting and decoration
  NT Pahari mural painting and decoration
Mural painting and decoration, Islamic
  UF Islamic mural painting and decoration
     Mural painting and decoration, Muslim
     Muslim mural painting and decoration
Mural painting and decoration, Italian *(May Subd Geog)*
  UF Italian mural painting and decoration
  NT Francesca, Piero della, 1416?-1492. Madonna del parto
     Francesca, Piero della, 1416?-1492. Sigismund Malatesta kneeling before Saint Sigismund
     Masaccio, 1401-1428? Trinity
     Nelli, Ottaviano, ca. 1370-ca. 1446. Incoronazione della Vergine
     Perino, del Vaga, 1500 or 1501-1547. Sala Paolina frescoes
     Pontormo, Jacopo Carucci, 1494-ca. 1556. Passion frescoes
     Raphael, 1483-1520. School of Athens
     Salimbeni, Ventura, 1568-1613. Apocalypse frescoes
  — **Attribution**
     UF Attribution of Italian mural painting and decoration
        Mural painting and decoration, Italian—Reattribution
     BT Mural painting and decoration, Italian—Expertising
  — **Expertising**

     NT Mural painting and decoration, Italian—Attribution
  — **Inscriptions**
     UF Inscriptions on Italian mural painting
     BT Inscriptions
  — **Reattribution**
     USE Mural painting and decoration, Italian—Attribution
Mural painting and decoration, Jaina *(May Subd Geog)*
  UF Jaina mural painting and decoration
Mural painting and decoration, Japanese *(May Subd Geog)*
  — **To 794**
  — **To 1868**
  — **Kamakura-Momoyama periods, 1185-1600**
  — **Edo period, 1600-1868**
     [ND2851]
Mural painting and decoration, Khmer *(May Subd Geog)*
  UF Khmer mural painting and decoration
Mural painting and decoration, Korean *(May Subd Geog)*
  UF Korean mural painting and decoration
Mural painting and decoration, Marathi *(May Subd Geog)*
  UF Marathi mural painting and decoration
Mural painting and decoration, Medieval *(May Subd Geog)*
  — **Byzantine [etc.] influences**
Mural painting and decoration, Mexican *(May Subd Geog)*
  UF Mexican mural painting and decoration
  NT Siqueiros, David Alfaro. March of humanity on earth and toward the cosmos
Mural painting and decoration, Minoan *(May Subd Geog)*
  UF Minoan mural painting and decoration
Mural painting and decoration, Mogul
  NT Pahari mural painting and decoration
Mural painting and decoration, Moldavian *(May Subd Geog)*
  UF Moldavian mural painting and decoration
Mural painting and decoration, Muslim
  USE Mural painting and decoration, Islamic
Mural painting and decoration, Mycenaean *(May Subd Geog)*
  UF Mycenaean mural painting and decoration
Mural painting and decoration, Pahari
  USE Pahari mural painting and decoration
Mural painting and decoration, Portuguese *(May Subd Geog)*
  UF Portuguese mural painting and decoration
Mural painting and decoration, Renaissance *(May Subd Geog)*
  UF Renaissance mural painting and decoration
  — **Inscriptions**
     UF Inscriptions on Renaissance mural painting
     BT Inscriptions
  — **Italy**
     NT Bramante, Donato, 1444?-1514. Casa Panigarola frescoes
     Neroni, Bartolomeo, ca. 1505-1571. Fondi Monument fresco
     Perino, del Vaga, 1500 or 1501-1547. Sala Paolina frescoes
     Raphael, 1483-1520. School of Athens
Mural painting and decoration, Rococo *(May Subd Geog)*
  UF Rococo mural painting and decoration

Mural painting and decoration, Roman *(May Subd Geog)*
  UF Roman mural painting and decoration
  — **Expertising**
Mural painting and decoration, Romanesque *(May Subd Geog)*
  UF Romanesque mural painting and decoration
  — **Byzantine [etc.] influences**
  — **Expertising**
Mural painting and decoration, Romanian *(May Subd Geog)*
  UF Romanian mural painting and decoration
Mural painting and decoration, Russian *(May Subd Geog)*
  UF Russian mural painting and decoration
  NT Glazunov, Il'ia Sergeevich. Gift of the USSR to UNESCO
Mural painting and decoration, Serbian *(May Subd Geog)*
  UF Serbian mural painting and decoration
  — **Copying**
     BT Copying
  — **Expertising**
Mural painting and decoration, Slovak *(May Subd Geog)*
  UF Slovak mural painting and decoration
Mural painting and decoration, Sogdian *(May Subd Geog)*
  UF Sogdian mural painting and decoration
Mural painting and decoration, Spanish *(May Subd Geog)*
  UF Spanish mural painting and decoration
  — **Expertising**
Mural painting and decoration, Sri Lankan *(May Subd Geog)*
  UF Sri Lankan mural painting and decoration
Mural painting and decoration, Swedish *(May Subd Geog)*
  UF Swedish mural painting and decoration
Mural painting and decoration, Swiss *(May Subd Geog)*
  UF Swiss mural painting and decoration
Mural painting and decoration, Tantric-Buddhist *(May Subd Geog)*
  UF Tantric-Buddhist mural painting and decoration
Mural painting and decoration, Taoist *(May Subd Geog)*
  UF Taoist mural painting and decoration
Mural painting and decoration, Thai *(May Subd Geog)*
  UF Thai mural painting and decoration
  — **Expertising**
Mural painting and decoration, Vijayanagara *(May Subd Geog)*
  UF Vijayanagara mural painting and decoration
Mural with blue brushstroke (Mural painting)
  USE Lichtenstein, Roy, 1923- Mural with blue brushstroke
Murals
  USE Mural painting and decoration
Muramidase
  USE Lysozyme
Murasaki Shikibu, b. 978? Genji monogatari
  — **Illustrations**
     NT Genji monogatari emaki (Scrolls)
Murathee language
  USE Marathi language
Murato language
  USE Candoshi language
Muray family
  USE Murray family
Murayama family *(Not Subd Geog)*
Murchison family *(Not Subd Geog)*
Murchisoniata
  BT Gasteropoda, Fossil

Murder *(May Subd Geog)*
⌐HV6499-6542⌐
UF Manslaughter
BT Crimes against humanity
Criminal law
Offenses against the person
Violent deaths
RT Assassination
Homicide
NT Aged, Killing of the
Filicide
Fratricide
Infanticide
Mass murder
Parricide
Poisoning
Police murders
Prison homicide
Strangling
Trials (Murder)
Uxoricide
— **Biblical teaching**
NT Ten commandments—Murder
— **Bibliography**
RT Murder literature
— **Investigation**
BT Homicide investigation
Murder, Mass
USE Mass murder
Murder, Ritual
USE Blood accusation
Murder (Islamic law)
Murder (Jewish law)
Murder (Roman law)
NT Senatus consultum Silanianum
Murder literature *(May Subd Geog)*
UF Literature, Murder
BT Sociology literature
RT Murder—Bibliography
Murder trials
USE Trials (Murder)
Murderkill River (Del.)
BT Rivers—Delaware
Murein
USE Peptidoglycans
Murein sacculus
USE Peptidoglycans
Muren family *(Not Subd Geog)*
Muret, Battle of, 1213
⌐DC611.L3⌐
BT Albigenses
Murex *(May Subd Geog)*
⌐QL430.5.M9⌐
BT Muricidae
Murex trunculus
⌐QL430.5.M9⌐
Murey family
USE Murray family
Murfee family
USE Murphy family
Murfey family
USE Murphy family
Murff family *(Not Subd Geog)*
UF Morf family
Morff family
Murph family
Murfree family
USE Murphy family
Murfreesboro, Battle of, 1862-1863
⌐E474.77⌐
UF Stone River, Battle of, 1862-1863
Stones River, Battle of, 1862-1863
BT United States—History—Civil War,
1861-1865—Campaigns
Murfrey family
USE Murphy family
Murfy family
USE Murphy family
Muria
⌐DS432.M⌐
BT Gonds

Muriatic acid
USE Hydrochloric acid
Muricidae
⌐QL430.5.M9⌐
BT Neogastropoda
NT Murex
Pterynotus
Rapana
Thais (Mollusk)
Urosalpinx
Muricidae, Fossil
⌐QE809.M85⌐
BT Neogastropoda, Fossil
Muridae
⌐QL737.R666⌐
BT Rodents
NT Abditomys
Andalgalomys
Apodemus
Apomys
Chiropodomys
Crunomys
Limnomys
Micromys
Mus
Papagomys
Paraleptomys
Rattus
Shrew rats
Muridae, Fossil
NT Megaoryzomys
Nonomys simplicidens
Murīdīyah
⌐BP195.M⌐
UF Mourides
Murids
BT Islamic sects
Murids
USE Murīdīyah
Murillo family *(Not Subd Geog)*
Murinbata language *(May Subd Geog)*
UF Marinbata language
Murrinh-patha language
BT Australia—Languages
Australian languages
Murine leukemia
USE Mouse leukemia complex
Murine leukemia viruses
USE Mouse leukemia viruses
Murine sarcoma viruses
UF Mouse sarcoma viruses
BT Retroviruses
Murine typhus
USE Typhus, Endemic flea-borne
Murinsel (Croatia)
USE Medimurje (Croatia)
Muriti palm
USE Mauritia flexuosa
Murity
USE Mauritia flexuosa
Murkle family
USE Merkel family
Murle (African people)
UF Agibba (African people)
Ajibba (African people)
Beir (African people)
Irenge (African people)
Murule (African people)
BT Ethnology—Sudan
NT Longarim (African people)
Murle language
UF Beir language
BT Ethiopia—Languages
Nilo-Saharan languages
Sudan—Languages
Murlo Site (Italy)
USE Poggio Civitate Site (Italy)
Murmansk Peninsula (R.S.F.S.R.)
USE Kola Peninsula (R.S.F.S.R.)
Murmi language
USE Tamang language

Murmurs, Heart
USE Heart murmurs
Murner family
USE Merner family
Murngin (Australian people)
⌐DU125.M8⌐
UF Malag (Australian people)
Ulamba (Australian people)
Walamba (Australian people)
Wulamba (Australian people)
Yolngu (Australian people)
BT Australian aborigines
Ethnology—Australia
NT Missions to Murngin (Australian
people)
— **Land tenure**
BT Land tenure
— **Medicine**
BT Medicine, Primitive
— **Rites and ceremonies**
NT Funeral rites and ceremonies,
Murngin (Australian people)
Murngin (Australian people) funeral rites and
ceremonies
USE Funeral rites and ceremonies, Murngin
(Australian people)
Murngin (Australian people) law
USE Law, Murngin (Australian people)
Muromachi Bakufu
USE Japan—Politics and government—
1336-1573
Muromeẗs (Bomber)
USE Il'ia Muromeẗs (Bomber)
Muroto Cape (Japan)
UF Muroto Point (Japan)
Muroto-saki (Japan)
Muroto-zaki (Japan)
Murotosaki (Japan)
Murotozaki (Japan)
BT Capes (Coasts)—Japan
Muroto Point (Japan)
USE Muroto Cape (Japan)
Muroto-saki (Japan)
USE Muroto Cape (Japan)
Muroto-zaki (Japan)
USE Muroto Cape (Japan)
Murotosaki (Japan)
USE Muroto Cape (Japan)
Murotozaki (Japan)
USE Muroto Cape (Japan)
Murph family
USE Murff family
Murphey family
USE Murphy family
Murphree family
USE Murphy family
Murphrey family
USE Murphy family
Murphry family
USE Murphy family
Murphy (Name)
Murphy family *(Not Subd Geog)*
UF Morfey family
Morphy family
Murfee family
Murfey family
Murfree family
Murfrey family
Murfy family
Murphey family
Murphree family
Murphrey family
Murphry family
Murprey family
Murpry family
Murpy family
Murphy Hill Site (Ala.)
BT Alabama—Antiquities
Mounds—Alabama

Murphy's law
  BT Chance
      Disasters
      Fate and fatalism
      Pessimism
Murprey family
  USE Murphy family
Murpry family
  USE Murphy family
Murpy family
  USE Murphy family
Murrah family
  USE Murray family
Murray family *(Not Subd Geog)*
  UF Muray family
      Murey family
      Murrah family
      Murree family
      Murrey family
      Murrie family
      Murry family
Murray red gum tree
  USE Eucalyptus camaldulensis
Murray River (N.S.W.-S. Aust.)
  UF River Murray (N.S.W.-S. Aust.)
  BT Rivers—Australia
Murray River language
  USE Murundi language
Murre, Common
  USE Common murre
Murree family
  USE Murray family
Murres
    ₍QL696.C42₎
  UF Uria
  BT Alcidae
  NT Common murre
      Thick-billed murre
Murrey family
  USE Murray family
Murrie family
  USE Murray family
Murrina
  BT Horses—Diseases
      Trypanosomiasis
Murrinh-patha language
  USE Murinbata language
Murrow family
  USE Morrow family
Murrumbidgee River (N.S.W.)
  BT Rivers—Australia
Murrumbidgee tribes
  BT Australian aborigines
Murry family
  USE Murray family
Murtafaʿāt al Jawlān
  USE Golan Heights
Murtalbahn
  BT Railroads—Austria
Murten, Battle of, 1476
  USE Morat, Battle of, 1476
Murtensee (Switzerland)
  USE Morat, Lake of (Switzerland)
Murua Island (Papua New Guinea)
  USE Woodlark Island (Papua New Guinea)
Murua language
  USE Muyuw language
Murugan (Hindu deity)
  UF Subrahmaṇya (Hindu deity)
  BT Gods, Hindu
  — Cult
      NT Thaipusam
Murui language
  BT Indians of South America—Languages
  RT Witoto language
Murule (African people)
  USE Murle (African people)
Murundi language
    ₍PL7101.M8₎
  UF Moorundee language
      Murray River language

  BT Australia—Languages
      Australian languages
Mururea Atoll
  USE Mururoa Atoll
Mururoa Atoll
  UF Atoll Mururoa
      Braburgh
      Ile Mururoa
      Matilda Islands
      Mururea Atoll
      Osnaburg
  BT Coral reefs and islands—French
      Polynesia
Murut language
  BT Malayan languages
Muruts
    ₍DS646.33 (Borneo)₎
  NT Kelabit (Malaysian people)
      Timoguns (Bornean people)
Muruwari (Australian people)
    ₍DU125.M83₎
  BT Australian aborigines
      Ethnology—Australia
Murvale Cemetery (Portland, Ont.)
  BT Cemeteries—Ontario
Muryōji B Iseki (Kanazawa-shi, Japan)
  USE Muryōji B Site (Kanazawa-shi, Japan)
Muryōji B Site (Kanazawa-shi, Japan)
  (Not Subd Geog)
  UF Kanazawa-shi Muryōji B Iseki
      (Kanazawa-shi, Japan)
      Muryōji B Iseki (Kanazawa-shi, Japan)
  BT Japan—Antiquities
Muryōji Iseki (Kanazawa-shi, Japan)
  USE Muryōji Site (Kanazawa-shi, Japan)
Muryōji Site (Kanazawa-shi, Japan)
  UF Muryōji Iseki (Kanazawa-shi, Japan)
  BT Japan—Antiquities
Mus
    ₍QL737.R666₎
  BT Muridae
Mus coypus
  USE Coypu
Mus musculus
  USE Mice
Musa
  USE Banana
Musa paradisiaca
  USE Plantain banana
Musa sapientum
  USE Banana
Musaceae
    ₍QK495.M78₎
  BT Scitamineae
  NT Banana
      Heliconia
Musales
  USE Scitamineae
Musalmans
  USE Muslims
Musar movement
    ₍BJ1285.5.M8₎
  UF Musarnikes
  BT Ethics, Jewish
Musarnikes
  USE Musar movement
Musashi family *(Not Subd Geog)*
Musashi Plain (Japan)
  USE Musashi Region (Japan)
Musashi Region (Japan)
  UF Musashi Plain (Japan)
Musashigaoka Iseki (Machida-shi, Japan)
  USE Musashigaoka Site (Machida-shi,
      Japan)
Musashigaoka Site (Machida-shi, Japan)
  (Not Subd Geog)
  UF Musashigaoka Iseki (Machida-shi,
      Japan)
  BT Japan—Antiquities
Muṣat dynasty, 1363-1704
  USE Muṣatin dynasty, 1363-1704

Muṣătesci, Dynasty of, 1363-1704
  USE Muṣatin dynasty, 1363-1704
Muṣatin dynasty, 1363-1704
  (Not Subd Geog)
    ₍DR240₎
  UF Muṣat dynasty, 1363-1704
      Muṣătesci, Dynasty of, 1363-1704
      Muṣatini, Dynasty of, 1363-1704
  BT Moldavia—History
      Romania—History—To 1711
Muṣatini, Dynasty of, 1363-1704
  USE Muṣatin dynasty, 1363-1704
Musca
    ₍QL537.M8₎
  BT Muscidae
Musca autumnalis
  USE Face fly
Musca domestica
  USE Housefly
Muscadine grape *(May Subd Geog)*
    ₍QK495.V84₎
    ₍SB389₎
  UF Scuppernong
      Vitis rotundifolia
  BT Grapes
Muscardinidae
  USE Dormice
Muscardinus
  USE Hazel mouse
Muscardinus avellanarius
  USE Hazel mouse
Muscaria
  USE Saxifraga
Muscarine
Muscarinic receptors
    ₍QP364.7₎
  UF Receptors, Muscarinic
  BT Cholinergic receptors
Muschelkalk (Germany)
Musci
  USE Mosses
Muscicapa
    ₍QL696.P255₎
  BT Muscicapidae
  NT Muscicapa gabela
Muscicapa gabela *(May Subd Geog)*
    ₍QL696.P255₎
  BT Muscicapa
Muscicapidae
    ₍QL696.P255₎
  BT Passeriformes
  NT Batis (Bird)
      Catharus
      Hylocichla
      Luscinia
      Muscicapa
      Polioptila
      Rhipidura
Muscidae
    ₍QL537.M8₎
  BT Diptera
  NT Chaetophlepsis
      Fannia
      Haematobia
      Leptohylemia
      Musca
      Opsodexia
      Passeromyia
      Stomoxys
Muscineae
    ₍QK534-563₎
Muscle
  USE Muscles
Muscle, Vascular
  USE Vascular smooth muscle
Muscle cars *(May Subd Geog)*
  BT Automobiles
Muscle cells
  UF Myocytes
  BT Cells
  NT Sarcoplasmic reticulum

Muscle compartment syndrome
  USE Compartment syndrome
Muscle contraction
  UF Muscles—Contraction
  BT Contractility (Biology)
     Muscles—Motility
  NT Actomyosin
     Heart—Contraction
     Muscle tone
     Peristalsis
  — **Regulation**
     UF Regulation of muscle contraction
     BT Biological control systems
Muscle flaccidity
  USE Muscle hypotonia
Muscle hypotonia *(May Subd Geog)*
  UF Flaccidity, Muscle
     Hypotonia, Muscle
     Muscle flaccidity
  BT Movement disorders
     Muscle tone
     Muscles—Diseases
Muscle hypotonia in children
  (May Subd Geog)
  BT Movement disorders in children
Muscle pain
  USE Myalgia
Muscle proteins
  BT Proteins
  NT Actomyosin
     Myoglobin
     Myosin
Muscle receptors
  ⌐QL931 (Comparative anatomy)¬
  ⌐QM471 (Human anatomy)¬
  ⌐QP369 (Physiology)¬
  BT Neural receptors
  NT Cardiac receptors
Muscle relaxants
  UF Drugs, Muscle relaxant
     Relaxants (Drugs)
  BT Shock therapy
  NT Anticonvulsants
     Antispasmodics
     Carisoprodol
     Dantrolene
     Neuromuscular blocking agents
     Prazosin
Muscle rigidity
  ⌐QP320 (Physiology)¬
  ⌐RC925 (Medicine)¬
  UF Rigidity, Muscle
  BT Movement disorders
     Muscles—Diseases
Muscle spasticity
  USE Spasticity
Muscle strength
  UF Strength of muscles
  BT Exercise
     Muscles
     Physical fitness
Muscle stretch reflex
  USE Stretch reflex
Muscle tone
  UF Tone, Muscle
     Tonus, Muscle
  BT Muscle contraction
     Stretch reflex
  NT Muscle hypotonia
Muscles
  ⌐QL831 (Anatomy)¬
  ⌐QM151-QM165 (Human anatomy)¬
  ⌐QM571 (Histology)¬
  ⌐QP321 (Physiology)¬
  UF Muscle
     Musculature
     Myodynamics
     Myology
  BT Musculoskeletal system

  SA *names of muscles, e.g.* Tensor tympani
     muscle; and subdivision Muscles
     under names of organs and regions
     of the body, e.g. Foot—Muscles;
     also headings beginning with the
     word Muscle
  NT Abdominal compression reaction
     Eye—Muscles
     Facial muscles
     Heart—Muscle
     Intercostal muscles
     Larynx—Muscles
     Ligaments
     Muscle strength
     Myometrium
     Myoneural junction
     Neuromuscular transmission
     Respiratory muscles
     Rigor mortis
     Sarcolemma
     Sarcoplasm
     Smooth muscle
     Striated muscle
     Tendons
  — Contraction
     USE Muscle contraction
  — **Diseases** *(May Subd Geog)*
     ⌐RC925-RC927¬
     ⌐RC935¬
     ⌐RD688¬
     UF Myopathy
     NT Compartment syndrome
       Contracture (Pathology)
       Dystonia
       Dystonia musculorum deformans
       Muscle hypotonia
       Muscle rigidity
       Myalgia
       Myoglobinuria
       Myositis
       Myositis tropica
       Myotonia
       Neuromuscular diseases
       Scalenus anticus syndrome
       Spasticity
  — Inflammation
     USE Myositis
  — **Motility**
     UF Motility of muscles
     NT Muscle contraction
  — **Regeneration**
     BT Regeneration (Biology)
  — **Tumors**
     UF Myoma
     NT Rhabdomyosarcoma
Muscogee Indians
  USE Creek Indians
Muscogee language
  USE Creek language
Muscology
  USE Bryology
Muscovite
  ⌐QE391.M (Mineralogy)¬
  BT Mica
Muscular atrophy
  USE Atrophy, Muscular
Muscular atrophy, Peroneal
  USE Charcot-Marie-Tooth disease
Muscular coordination
  USE Motor ability
Muscular dystrophies
  USE Muscular dystrophy
Muscular dystrophy
  UF Muscular dystrophies
  BT Dystrophy
     Neuromuscular diseases
  — **Genetic aspects**
Muscular dystrophy in children
  (May Subd Geog)
  ⌐RJ482.D9¬
  BT Neuromuscular diseases in children

  NT Duchenne muscular dystrophy
Muscular pain
  USE Myalgia
Muscular sense
  ⌐BF285¬
  UF Kinesthesia
     Myesthesia
  BT Proprioception
     Psychology, Physiological
     Senses and sensation
  RT Movement, Psychology of
Muscular triangle
  USE Carotid triangle, Inferior
Musculature
  USE Muscles
Musculocutaneous nerve
  — **Surgery**
Musculoskeletal system
  NT Bones
     Connective tissues
     Muscles
  — **Diseases** *(May Subd Geog)*
     NT Rheumatism
       Torticollis
  — **Wounds and injuries**
Muse family *(Not Subd Geog)*
  UF Mewes family
     Mews family
     Muhs family
Muse River (France) *(Not Subd Geog)*
  BT Rivers—France
Musei language
  UF Musey language
  BT Chadic languages
Museku language
  USE Musgu language
Musele dialect
  USE Mussele dialect
Muselman family
  USE Musselman family
Museology
  USE Museum techniques
Muser family
  USE Musser family
Muses (Greek deities)
  BT Goddesses, Greek
  NT Urania (Greek deity)
Musette
  USE Bagpipe
Museum acquisitions
  USE Museums—Acquisitions
Museum architecture *(May Subd Geog)*
  UF Architecture, Museum
  BT Architecture
  NT Art museum architecture
  — **Washington (D.C.)**
Museum archives *(May Subd Geog)*
  ⌐AM158¬
  BT Archives
  RT Museum libraries
Museum attendance *(May Subd Geog)*
  UF Attendance, Museum
     Museum audiences
     Museums—Attendance
  NT Art museums—Visitors
Museum audiences
  USE Museum attendance
Museum buildings *(May Subd Geog)*
  UF Buildings, Museum
  BT Buildings
  — **California**
     NT Robert O. Anderson Building (Los
       Angeles, Calif.)
  — **Washington (D.C.)**
     NT Halls of the Ancients (Washington,
       D.C.)
       Smithsonian Institution Building
       (Washington, D.C.)
Museum conservation methods
  (May Subd Geog)
  ⌐AM141-148¬

UF Conservation methods, Museum
BT Museum techniques
NT Museums—Climatic factors
Museum curators *(May Subd Geog)*
  UF Curators, Museum
  BT Museums—Employees
  NT Art museum curators
      Museums—Vocational guidance
      Women museum curators
Museum directors *(May Subd Geog)*
  UF Directors, Museum
      Directors of museums
  BT Museums—Employees
  NT Art museum directors
Museum finance *(May Subd Geog)*
  [AM122]
  UF Museums—Finance
  BT Finance
  NT Federal aid to museums
Museum labels *(May Subd Geog)*
  [AM157]
  UF Exhibit labels
      Exhibition labels
  BT Labels
Museum libraries *(May Subd Geog)*
  [Z675.M]
  UF Libraries, Museum
  BT Libraries, Special
  RT Libraries and museums
      Museum archives
Museum manikins
  BT Mannequins (Figures)
Museum publications *(May Subd Geog)*
  UF Publications, Museum
  BT Publishers and publishing
Museum publicity
  USE Public relations—Museums
Museum registrars *(May Subd Geog)*
  UF Registrars, Museum
  BT Museums—Employees
Museum registration methods
  [AM139]
  UF Museums—Accessioning
      Museums—Registration
  BT Museum techniques
  NT Classification—Museums
Museum shops
  USE Museum stores
Museum stores *(May Subd Geog)*
  UF Museum shops
      Shops, Museum
      Stores, Museum
  BT Museums
      Specialty stores
Museum techniques
  [AM151-3]
  UF Display techniques
      Museology
  BT Exhibitions
      Museums
  NT Art—Exhibition techniques
      Costume—Conservation and
        restoration
      Museum conservation methods
      Museum registration methods
Museum trustees
  USE Museums—Trustees
Museum volunteers
  USE Volunteer workers in museums
Museums *(May Subd Geog)*
  [AM]
  BT Documentation
      Public institutions
      Records

SA *subdivision* Museums *under subjects,*
     names of wars and corporate bodies,
     e.g. Indians of North America—
     Museums; World War, 1939-1945—
     Museums; Harvard University—
     Museums; *also subdivision*
     Museums, relics, etc. *under names*
     of individual persons and families;
     and names of individual museums
NT Aeronautical museums
     Agricultural museums
     Anatomical museums
     Anthropological museums and
       collections
     Archaeological museums and
       collections
     Architectural museums
     Art museums
     Astronautical museums
     Astronomical museums
     Botanical museums
     Children's museums
     Commercial museums
     Dance museums
     Ethnological museums and collections
     Geographical museums
     Geological museums
     Halls of fame
     Historical museums
     Hunting—Museums and collections
     Hunting museums
     Industrial museums
     International museums
     Jewish museums
     Libraries and museums
     Literary museums
     Medical museums
     Military museums
     Mineralogical museums
     Museum stores
     Museum techniques
     Music museums
     Natural history museums
     Naval museums
     Numismatic museums
     Open-air museums
     Performing arts in museums
     Postal museums
     Railroad museums
     Safety museums
     Science museums
     Sports museums
     Textile museums
     Theater—Museums and collections
     Transportation museums
     Waxworks
     Zoological museums
— **Access for the physically handicapped**
    [NA2545.P5]
  BT Architecture and the physically
      handicapped
— Accessioning
  USE Museum registration methods
— **Accreditation**
— **Acquisitions**
    [AM135]
  UF Acquisitions, Museum
      Museum acquisitions
— Attendance
  USE Museum attendance
— Classification
  USE Classification—Museums
— **Climatic factors**
  BT Buildings—Environmental
      engineering
      Engineering meteorology
      Museum conservation methods
— **Educational aspects**
    [AM7]
  BT Education
      Visual education

— **Employees**
  NT Museum curators
      Museum directors
      Museum registrars
— Federal aid
  USE Federal aid to museums
— Finance
  USE Museum finance
— **Furniture, equipment, etc.**
    [AM127-9]
— **Law and legislation** *(May Subd Geog)*
  NT Federal aid to museums
— Public relations
  USE Public relations—Museums
— Registration
  USE Museum registration methods
— **Trustees**
    [AM121]
  UF Museum trustees
      Trustees, Museum
— **Vocational guidance** *(May Subd Geog)*
  BT Museum curators
— **Germany (East)**
— **Italy**
  NT Palazzo Madama (Turin, Italy)
— **Massachusetts**
  NT Harvard University—Museums
Museums, Children's
  USE Children's museums
Museums, Dance
  USE Dance museums
Museums, Music
  USE Music museums
Museums and moving-pictures
  UF Moving-pictures and museums
      Moving-pictures in museums
  BT Moving-pictures, Documentary—
      Distribution
      Moving-pictures in education
Museums and schools *(May Subd Geog)*
  UF Schools and museums
  BT Schools
      Visual education
  RT Children's museums
Museums and the handicapped
  (May Subd Geog)
  [AM160]
  BT Handicapped
Museums and the visually handicapped
  (May Subd Geog)
  [AM160]
  BT Visually handicapped
Museums for children
  USE Children's museums
Musey language
  USE Musei language
Musgoy language
  USE Daba language
Musgrave family *(Not Subd Geog)*
  UF Mosgrove family
      Musgrove family
Musgrove family
  USE Musgrave family
Musgu language
  [PL8535]
  UF Museku language
      Musuk language
      Muzuk language
  BT Chadic languages
  NT Vulum dialect
Mush
  USE Porridge
Musha Rebellion, 1930
  UF Wu-shê Rebellion, 1930
  BT Taiwan—History—1895-1945
Mūshaka dynasty *(Not Subd Geog)*
  UF Mūshika dynasty
      Mūṣika dynasty
  BT Kerala (India)—History
Mushakōji family *(Not Subd Geog)*
  UF Mushanokōji family

Mushakōji Senke school of Japanese tea
　　ceremony
　　USE　Japanese tea ceremony—Mushanokōji
　　　　　Senke school
Mushanokōji family
　　USE　Mushakōji family
Mushanokōji Senke school of Japanese tea
　　ceremony
　　USE　Japanese tea ceremony—Mushanokōji
　　　　　Senke school
Musha'sha'ids
　　BT　Iraq—History—1534-1921
Mushers　*(May Subd Geog)*
　　UF　Dog mushers
　　RT　Dogsledding
　　　　Sled dog racing
　　NT　Women mushers
Mushiake pottery
　　UF　Pottery, Mushiake
　　BT　Pottery, Japanese
Mūshika dynasty
　　USE　Mūshaka dynasty
Mushroom ceremony
　　BT　Hallucinogenic drugs and religious
　　　　　experience
　　　　Mushrooms—Religious aspects
　　　　Mushrooms, Hallucinogenic
Mushroom corals
　　USE　Fungiidae
Mushroom culture　*(May Subd Geog)*
　　[SB353]
　　UF　Mushrooms—Culture
　　BT　Horticulture
　　　　Mushrooms, Edible
　　RT　Mushroom industry
　　NT　Casing soils
Mushroom industry　*(May Subd Geog)*
　　[HD9235.M95-952]
　　BT　Mushrooms, Edible
　　RT　Mushroom culture
Mushrooms　*(May Subd Geog)*
　　[QK617]
　　UF　Champignons
　　　　Toadstools
　　BT　Basidiomycetes
　　RT　Fungi
　　NT　Cookery (Mushrooms)
　　— Culture
　　　　USE　Mushroom culture
　　— Mythology
　　— Pictorial works
　　　　BT　Fungi—Pictorial works
　　— Preservation
　　— Religious aspects
　　　　NT　Mushroom ceremony
　　　　　　Mushrooms, Hallucinogenic
　　— Soils
　　　　BT　Fungi—Cultures and culture media
　　　　NT　Casing soils
　　— Tariff
　　　　USE　Tariff on mushrooms
Mushrooms, Canned　*(May Subd Geog)*
　　[HD9330.M87]
　　UF　Canned mushrooms
　　BT　Vegetables, Canned
Mushrooms, Edible　*(May Subd Geog)*
　　[QK617]
　　UF　Edible mushrooms
　　BT　Fungi—Economic aspects
　　　　Fungi, Edible
　　　　Plants, Edible
　　NT　Cookery (Mushrooms)
　　　　Lentinus edodes
　　　　Mushroom culture
　　　　Mushroom industry
　　　　Pleurotus
　　　　Tricholoma matsutake
　　　　Volvariella
　　— Tariff
　　　　USE　Tariff on mushrooms

Mushrooms, Hallucinogenic
(May Subd Geog)
　　[QK600-QK635 (Botany)]
　　[SB293-SB295 (Culture)]
　　UF　Hallucinogenic mushrooms
　　　　Magic mushrooms
　　　　Psychedelic mushrooms
　　　　Sacred mushrooms
　　BT　Hallucinogenic plants
　　　　Mushrooms—Religious aspects
　　RT　Hallucinogenic drugs
　　NT　Mushroom ceremony
　　　　Panaeolus
　　　　Psilocybe
Mushrooms, Poisonous　*(May Subd Geog)*
　　[QK617]
　　UF　Poisonous mushrooms
　　BT　Toxigenic fungi
　　— Toxicology
　　　　BT　Mycotoxicoses
Musi dialect　*(May Subd Geog)*
　　[PL5128.M87]
　　BT　Indonesia—Languages
　　　　Malay language
Music　*(May Subd Geog)*
　　For works consisting of music of an individual
　　ethnic group, additional subject entry is made under
　　the heading [ethnic group]—[place]—Music.
　　UF　Classical music
　　　　Music, Classical
　　SA　*subdivision* Songs and music *under*
　　　　　individual subjects, classes of
　　　　　persons, names of individuals,
　　　　　institutions, societies, etc., e.g.
　　　　　Aeronautics—Songs and music;
　　　　　subdivision Music *under individual*
　　　　　ethnic groups, e.g. Afro-Americans
　　　　　—Music; Navajo Indians—Music;
　　　　　and headings beginning with the
　　　　　words Music *or* Musical
　　NT　Advent music
　　　　Arrangement (Music)
　　　　Ascension Day music
　　　　Bands (Music)
　　　　Big band music
　　　　Big bands
　　　　Blind, Music for the
　　　　Carillons
　　　　Chamber music
　　　　Chance compositions
　　　　Chimes
　　　　Choral music
　　　　Christmas music
　　　　Church music
　　　　Composition (Music)
　　　　Computer music
　　　　Concerts
　　　　Concrete music
　　　　Conservatories of music
　　　　Coronation music
　　　　Counterpoint
　　　　Dance music
　　　　Dance orchestras
　　　　Death in music
　　　　Dramatic music
　　　　Easter music
　　　　Electronic music
　　　　Epiphany music
　　　　Feminism and music
　　　　Folk dance music
　　　　Folk music
　　　　Folk-songs
　　　　Funeral music
　　　　Harmony
　　　　Harmony (Aesthetics)
　　　　Hunting music
　　　　Impressionism (Music)
　　　　Improvisation (Music)
　　　　Information theory in music
　　　　Instrumental music
　　　　Instrumentation and orchestration

　　　　Jazz music
　　　　Kindergarten—Music
　　　　Leitmotiv
　　　　Mannerism (Music)
　　　　Melodrama
　　　　Melody
　　　　Memorial music
　　　　Microtonic music
　　　　Military music
　　　　Minimal music
　　　　Monologues with music
　　　　Moving-picture music
　　　　National music
　　　　National socialism and music
　　　　National songs
　　　　New Age music
　　　　Paleography, Musical
　　　　Pantomimes with music
　　　　Passion-music
　　　　Pastoral music (Secular)
　　　　Patriotic music
　　　　Peru in music
　　　　Popular music
　　　　Program music
　　　　Radio music
　　　　Realism in music
　　　　Romanticism in music
　　　　Sacred monologues with music
　　　　School music
　　　　Singing
　　　　Solmization
　　　　Songs
　　　　Sound
　　　　Street music and musicians
　　　　Symbolism in music
　　　　Symphony orchestras
　　　　Television music
　　　　Titles of musical compositions
　　　　Tragedy in music
　　　　Transposition (Music)
　　　　Vibrato
　　　　Virtuosity in music
　　　　Vocal music
　　　　Voice
　　　　Wedding music
— To 500
　　UF　Ancient music
　　　　Music, Ancient
　　SA　*subdivision* To 500 *under music*
　　　　　headings
　　NT　Music, Greek and Roman
　　　　Music in the Bible
—— Theory
　　　　USE　Music—Theory—To 500
— 500-1400
　　UF　Medieval music
　　　　Music, Medieval
　　SA　*subdivision* 500-1400 *under music*
　　　　　headings
　　NT　Chants (Plain, Gregorian, etc.)
　　　　Measured music
　　　　Organum
　　　　Tonus peregrinus
—— Theory
　　　　USE　Music—Theory—500-1400
— 15th century
　　UF　Medieval music
　　　　Music, Medieval
　　　　Music, Renaissance
　　　　Renaissance music
　　SA　*subdivision* 15th century *under*
　　　　　music headings
—— Theory
　　　　USE　Music—Theory—15th century
— 16th century
　　UF　Music, Renaissance
　　　　Renaissance music
　　SA　*subdivision* 16th century *under*
　　　　　music headings
—— Theory
　　　　USE　Music—Theory—16th century

— 17th century
  UF Baroque music
      Music, Baroque
      Music, Renaissance
      Renaissance music
  SA *subdivision* 17th century *under*
      music headings
— — Theory
  USE Music—Theory—17th century
— 18th century
  UF Baroque music
      Classical period music
      Music, Baroque
      Music, Classical period
  SA *subdivision* 18th century *under*
      music headings
— — Theory
  USE Music—Theory—18th century
— 19th century
  UF Classical period music
      Music, Classical period
      Music, Romantic period
      Romantic period music
  SA *subdivision* 19th century *under*
      music headings
— — Theory
  USE Music—Theory—19th century
— 20th century
  SA *subdivision* 20th century *under*
      music headings
— — Theory
  USE Music—Theory—20th century
— Acoustics and physics
  [ML3805-3817]
  UF Acoustics
      Physiological acoustics
  BT Acoustical engineering
      Music—Theory
      Physics
  RT Sound
  NT Electro-acoustics
      Harmonics (Music)
      Microtones
      Monochord
      Musical intervals and scales
      Musical temperament
      Tone color (Music)
— Aesthetics
  USE Music—Philosophy and aesthetics
— Almanacs, yearbooks, etc.
  [ML13-21]
  UF Music—Yearbooks
  BT Almanacs
      Yearbooks
  RT Music—Chronology
  NT Music calendars
— Analysis, appreciation
  USE Music appreciation
      Musical analysis
— Analytical guides
  USE Music appreciation
      Musical analysis
— Anecdotes, facetiae, satire, etc.
  [ML65]
  UF Anecdotes, Musical
      Musicians—Anecdotes, facetiae,
      satire, etc.
— Appreciation
  USE Music appreciation
— Bibliography
  [ML111-158]
  NT International inventory of musical
      sources
      Music—First performances
— — Catalogs, Microfilm
— — Catalogs, Publishers'
  (May Subd Geog)
  [ML145]
  NT Music printing—Plate numbers
— — Graded lists
  UF Music—Graded lists

— Bio-bibliography
  [ML105-ML107 (Dictionaries)]
  [ML385-ML429 (History and
      criticism)]
  UF Composers—Dictionaries
      Music—Biography
      Musicians—Dictionaries
  BT Musicians
— Biography
  USE Flute-players, Organists, Pianists,
      and similar headings
      Composers
      Conductors (Music)
      Flute-players
      Music—Bio-bibliography
      Music teachers
      Musicians
      Organists
      Pianists
      Singers
— Cataloging
  USE Cataloging of music
— Chinese influences
  BT China—Civilization
— Chronology
  [ML161]
  BT Music—History and criticism
  RT Music—Almanacs, yearbooks, etc.
  NT Music printing—Plate numbers
— Classification
  USE Classification—Music
— Competitions
  [ML76]
  BT Music—Examinations, questions,
      etc.
      Music festivals
— Composition
  USE Composition (Music)
— Computer programs
  NT DESC7 (Computer program)
      MIDIM7 (Computer program)
      Music Major (Computer program)
      PR1XM (Computer program)
— Conservatories
  USE Conservatories of music
— Copyright
  USE Copyright—Music
— Data processing
  NT MIDIM (Computer system)
— Dictionaries
  [ML100-110]
  SA *subdivision* Dictionaries *under*
      various headings, e.g. Chamber
      music—Dictionaries; Opera—
      Dictionaries
  NT Music—Terminology
— Dictionaries, Juvenile
— Discography
  [ML156]
— Dynamics, phrasing
  USE Music—Interpretation (Phrasing,
      dynamics, etc.)
— Economic aspects *(May Subd Geog)*
— Editing
  [ML63]
  BT Editing
      Musicology
— Elementary theory
  USE Music—Theory, Elementary
— Endowments
  BT Endowments
— Examinations, questions, etc.
  [MT9]
  NT Music—Competitions
      Musical ability—Testing
— Exhibitions
  [ML141 (Catalogs)]
  [ML462 (Instruments)]
  BT Music museums
  NT Music—Manuscripts—Exhibitions

      Musical instruments—Catalogs and
      collections
      Musical instruments—Exhibitions
— First performances *(May Subd Geog)*
  UF First performances of musical
      works
      Music—Premiere performances
      Premiere performances of musical
      works
  BT Music—Bibliography
  SA *subdivision* First performances
      under headings for music
      compositions, e.g. Operas—First
      performances
— Graded lists
  USE Music—Bibliography—Graded
      lists
— Handbooks, manuals, etc.
  UF Music—Manuals, text-books, etc.
— Harmonic analysis
  USE Harmonic analysis (Music)
— Historiography
  [ML]
  UF Music—History and criticism—
      Methods
      Music—History and criticism—
      Theory, etc.
  RT Musicology
  NT Musical criticism
— History and criticism
  [ML159-3795]
  BT Criticism
  SA *headings of the type* Music—
      [period subdivision]—History
      and criticism; Songs—[period
      subdivision]—History and
      criticism
  NT Music—Chronology
      Music—Performance—History
      Music, Origin of
— — Methods
  USE Music—Historiography
      Musical criticism
— — Outlines, syllabi, etc.
  UF Music—Outlines, syllabi, etc.
— — Theory, etc.
  USE Music—Historiography
      Musical criticism
— Iconography
  USE Music in art
— Incunabula
  USE Incunabula—Music
— Indians
  USE Indians—Music
— Instruction and study
  (May Subd Geog)
  [MT]
  UF Education, Musical
      Music—Study and teaching
      Music education
      Musical education
      Musical instruction
  SA *subdivision* Instruction and study
      under names of musical
      instruments, e.g. Piano—
      Instruction and study
  NT Chromatic alteration (Music)
      Composition (Music)
      Conducting
      Conservatories of music
      Counterpoint
      Ear training
      Embellishment (Music)
      Embellishment (Vocal music)
      Galin-Paris-Chevé method (Music)
      Harmony
      Instrumental music—Instruction
      and study
      Instrumentation and orchestration
      Kindergarten—Music
      Modulation (Music)

Music
— **Instruction and study**
    (Continued)
        Music—Interpretation (Phrasing,
          dynamics, etc.)
        Music—Manuals, text-books, etc.
        Music—Memorizing
        Music—Teacher training
        Music appreciation
        Music in universities and colleges
        Music teachers
        Musical accompaniment
        Musical form
        Sight-reading (Music)
        Singing—Instruction and study
        Tempo (Music)
        Thorough bass
        Transposition (Music)
        Virtuosity in music
— — **Juvenile**
    BT Music—Juvenile literature
    NT Handicapped children—
        Education—Music
— — **France**
    NT Maîtrises
— **Interpretation (Phrasing, dynamics, etc.)**
    UF Dynamics (Music)
       Interpretation, Musical
       Music—Dynamics, phrasing
       Music—Phrasing, dynamics
       Musical interpretation
       Phrasing (Music)
    BT Music—Instruction and study
       Music—Performance
— **Inventions and patents**
    USE Musical inventions and patents
— **Juvenile**
    UF Children's music
       Juvenile music
       Music, Children's
       Music, Juvenile
    SA *subdivision* Juvenile *under*
       headings for music compositions
       for works to be performed by
       children, e.g. Operas—Juvenile
    NT Children's songs
— **Juvenile literature**
    [ML3930]
    NT Music—Instruction and study—
       Juvenile
       Musical instruments—Juvenile
       literature
— **Kindergarten**
    USE Kindergarten—Music
— **Manuals, text-books, etc.**
    [MT6-10]
    BT Music—Instruction and study
    USE Music—Handbooks, manuals, etc.
— **Manuscripts** *(May Subd Geog)*
    [ML93-98]
    UF Manuscripts, Musical
    BT Manuscripts
    RT Paleography, Musical
    SA *subdivision* Manuscripts *under*
       names of composers, e.g.
       Wagner, Richard, 1813-1883—
       Manuscripts
— — **Exhibitions**
    BT Manuscripts—Exhibitions
       Music—Exhibitions
— **Melodic analysis**
    USE Melodic analysis
— **Memorizing**
    [MT82]
    BT Memory
       Mnemonics
       Music—Instruction and study
— **Modes**
    USE Musical intervals and scales
— **Museums**
    USE Music museums

— **Notation**
    USE Musical notation
— **Nursery schools**
    USE Nursery schools—Music
— **Outlines, syllabi, etc.**
    USE Music—History and criticism—
       Outlines, syllabi, etc.
— **Performance**
    [ML457]
    UF Musical performance
    BT Embellishment (Music)
       Embellishment (Vocal music)
    RT Concerts
       Conducting
    NT Improvisation (Music)
       Music—Interpretation (Phrasing,
         dynamics, etc.)
       Notes inégales
       Piano—Performance
       Rehearsals (Music)
       Singing
       Tonguing (Wind instrument
         playing)
       Violin—Performance
       Virtuosity in music
— — **History**
    BT Music—History and criticism
— **Philosophy and aesthetics**
    [ML3800-3920]
    UF Music—Aesthetics
    BT Aesthetics
       Music—Theory
    NT Classicism in music
       Harmony (Aesthetics)
       Impressionism (Music)
       Music and architecture
       Realism in music
       Romanticism in music
       Style, Musical
       Symbolism in music
— **Phrasing, dynamics**
    USE Music—Interpretation (Phrasing,
       dynamics, etc.)
— **Physiological aspects**
    [ML3820-3822]
    UF Physiological aspects of music
    BT Senses and sensation
    NT Amusia
       Hearing
       Music—Physiological effect
       Music, Influence of
       Music therapy
       Vocal registers
       Voice
— **Physiological effect**
    [ML3920]
    UF Music, Effect of
       Music, Physical effect of
       Music, Physiological effect of
    BT Music—Physiological aspects
       Music, Influence of
    NT Music therapy
       Plants, Effect of music on
— **Plagiarism**
    USE Plagiarism in music
— **Poetry**
    UF Musicians—Poetry
    BT Music and literature
    NT Music—Quotations, maxims, etc.
— **Premiere performances**
    USE Music—First performances
— **Proofreading**
    USE Proofreading—Music
— **Psychology**
    [ML3830-3838]
    NT Amusia
       Music and color
       Music therapy
       Musical ability—Testing
       Symbolism in music
— **Publishing** *(May Subd Geog)*

    [ML112-ML112.5]
    UF Music publishing
    BT Publishers and publishing
    NT Popular music—Writing and
       publishing
— **Quotations, maxims, etc.**
    [ML66]
    BT Music—Poetry
       Music and literature
— **Reading**
    USE Score reading and playing
       Sight-reading (Music)
— **Religious aspects**
    UF Religion and music
— — **Baptists, [Catholic Church, etc.]**
— — **Buddhism**
    UF Buddhism and music
    NT Music, Buddhist
— — **Buddhism, [Christianity, etc.]**
— — **Christianity**
    NT Church music
       Music in churches
— — **Islam**
    UF Islam and music
    NT Music, Islamic
— — **Judaism**
    NT Music in synagogues
       Synagogue music
— **Rudiments**
    USE Music—Theory, Elementary
— **Sketches**
    USE Musical sketches
— **Societies, etc.**
    [ML25-28]
    UF Clubs, Musical
       Music clubs
       Music societies
       Musical clubs
       Musical societies
    NT Choral societies
       Church music—Societies, etc.
— **Study and teaching**
    USE Music—Instruction and study
— **Sunday-schools**
    USE Sunday-schools—Hymns
— **Teacher training** *(May Subd Geog)*
    UF Music teachers, Training of
    BT Music—Instruction and study
— **Terminology**
    [ML108]
    BT Music—Dictionaries
    NT English language—Conversation
       and phrase books (for musicians,
       musicologists, etc.)
— **Thematic catalogs**
    UF Thematic catalogs (Music)
    SA *subdivision* Thematic catalogs
       under names of individual
       composers and under special
       musical forms, e.g. Symphonies
       —Thematic catalogs
— **Theory**
    UF Music theory
       Theory of music
    NT Chants (Plain, Gregorian, etc.)—
       Instruction and study
       Chromatic alteration (Music)
       Composition (Music)
       Counterpoint
       Harmonic analysis (Music)
       Harmony
       Instrumentation and orchestration
       Melody
       Modulation (Music)
       Music—Acoustics and physics
       Music—Philosophy and aesthetics
       Musical analysis
       Musical form
       Musical intervals and scales
       Musical meter and rhythm
       Musical temperament

Schenkerian analysis
Thorough bass
Transposition (Music)
Twelve-tone system
— — **To 500**
    UF Music—To 500—Theory
— — **500-1400**
    UF Music—500-1400—Theory
— — **15th century**
    UF Music—15th century—Theory
— — **16th century**
    UF Music—16th century—Theory
— — **17th century**
    UF Music—17th century—Theory
— — **18th century**
    UF Music—18th century—Theory
— — **19th century**
    UF Music—19th century—Theory
— — **20th century**
    UF Music—20th century—Theory
— — **Computer-assisted instruction**
    NT Music Major (Computer program)
— **Theory, Elementary**
    [MT7]
    UF Music—Elementary theory
       Music—Rudiments
— Therapeutic use
    USE Music therapy
— Yearbooks
    USE Music—Almanacs, yearbooks, etc.
— **Egypt**
    NT Sistrum
— **Flanders**
    BT Music—France
— **France**
    NT Music—Flanders
— **India**
    NT Music, Hindustani
       Music, Karnatic
       Raga
       Vedas—Recitation
— **Japan**
    NT Gagaku
       Kabuki music
       Katarimono
       Nō music
       Shigin
— **Latin America**
— **Scotland**
    NT Bagpipe
       Pibroch
       Pibrochs
— **United States**
    NT Music Week
— **Wales**
    NT Pennillion singing
Music, Aleatory
    USE Chance composition
        Chance compositions
Music, Ancient
    USE *subdivision* To 500 *under music headings*
        Music—To 500
Music, Baroque
    USE *subdivisions* 17th century *and* 18th century *under music headings*
        Music—17th century
        Music—18th century
Music, Buddhist *(May Subd Geog)*
    UF Buddhist music
       Buddhists—Music
    BT Music—Religious aspects—Buddhism
    NT Chants (Buddhist)
Music, Byzantine
    UF Byzantine music
    BT Music, Greek and Roman
Music, Chance
    USE Chance composition
        Chance compositions

Music, Children's
    USE Music—Juvenile
Music, Chiming clock
    USE Chiming clock music
Music, Choral
    USE Choral music
Music, Classical
    USE Music
Music, Classical period
    USE *subdivisions* 18th century *and* 19th century *under music headings*
        Music—18th century
        Music—19th century
Music, Community
    USE Community music
Music, Computer
    USE Computer music
Music, Concrete
    USE Concrete music
Music, Disco
    USE Disco music
Music, Dixieland
    USE Dixieland music
Music, Dramatic
    USE Dramatic music
Music, Effect of
    USE Music—Physiological effect
        Music, Influence of
        Music and morals
        Music therapy
Music, Electronic
    USE Electronic music
Music, Gospel
    USE Gospel music
Music, Greek (Ancient)
    USE Music, Greek and Roman
Music, Greek and Roman
    UF Greek music
       Music, Greek (Ancient)
       Music, Roman
       Roman music
    BT Music—To 500
    NT Greek drama—Incidental music
       Hymns to Apollo
       Music, Byzantine
Music, Hebrew
    USE Jews—Music
Music, Hindustani
    [M1808-9]
    Here is entered vocal or instrumental music of the Hindustani system, native to northern India, as differentiated from the Karnatic system, native to southern India.
    UF Hindustani music
    BT Music—India
    NT Khyāl (Musical form)
Music, Imitation in
    USE Imitation (in music)
Music, Impressionism in
    USE Impressionism (Music)
Music, Inca
    USE Incas—Music
Music, Incidental
    [ML2000 (History)]
    [ML3860 (Aesthetics)]
    UF Incidental music
    BT Dramatic music
       Music in theaters
    NT Entr'acte music
       Greek drama—Incidental music
       Overture
       Pageants
       Radio plays with music
— **Excerpts**
— — **Vocal scores with piano**
    [M1518]
    UF Music, Incidental—Vocal scores with piano—Excerpts
— **Excerpts, Arranged**
— **Piano scores**
    [M1513]

— **Vocal scores with piano**
    [M1513]
— — **Excerpts**
    USE Music, Incidental—Excerpts—Vocal scores with piano
Music, Influence of
    [ML3920]
    UF Music, Effect of
    BT Music—Physiological aspects
    NT Music—Physiological effect
       Music and morals
       Music in the army
       Music therapy
Music, Instrumental
    USE Instrumental music
Music, Islamic *(May Subd Geog)*
    UF Music, Muslim
       Muslim music
       Muslims—Music
    BT Music—Religious aspects—Islam
    NT Koran—Recitation
Music, Jewish
    USE Jews—Music
Music, Juvenile
    USE Music—Juvenile
Music, Karnatic *(May Subd Geog)*
    [M1808-1809]
    Here is entered vocal or instrumental music of the Karnatic system, native to southern India, as differentiated from the Hindustani system, native to northern India.
    UF Carnatic music
       Karnatic music
    BT Music—India
— **Theory**
Music, Magical use of
    USE Music and magic
Music, Measured
    USE Measured music
Music, Medieval
    USE *subdivisions* 500-1400 *and* 15th century *under music headings*
        Music—500-1400
        Music—15th century
Music, Microtonic
    USE Microtonic music
Music, Military
    USE Military music
Music, Minimal
    USE Minimal music
Music, Muslim
    USE Music, Islamic
Music, National
    USE National music
Music, Origin of
    [ML3800]
    BT Music—History and criticism
Music, Passover
    USE Passover music
Music, Pastoral
    USE Pastoral music (Secular)
Music, Patriotic
    USE Patriotic music
Music, Physical effect of
    USE Music—Physiological effect
        Music therapy
Music, Physiological effect of
    USE Music—Physiological effect
Music, Plagiarism in
    USE Plagiarism in music
Music, Popular
    USE Popular music
Music, Popular (Songs, etc.)
    USE Popular music
— **Japan**
    NT Enka
Music, Printing of
    USE Music printing
Music, Quarter-tone
    USE Microtonic music

Music, Religious
  USE Church music
      Synagogue music
Music, Renaissance
  USE *subdivisions* 15th century, 16th
      century, *and* 17th century *under*
      music headings
      Music—15th century
      Music—16th century
      Music—17th century
Music, Rhythm and blues
  USE Rhythm and blues music
Music, Roman
  USE Music, Greek and Roman
Music, Romantic period
  USE *subdivision* 19th century *under music*
      headings
      Music—19th century
Music, Sacred
  USE Church music
      Synagogue music
Music, Soul
  USE Soul music
Music, Sufi *(May Subd Geog)*
  UF Sufi music
Music, Theatrical
  USE Dramatic music
Music, Turkmen *(May Subd Geog)*
  UF Turkmen music
Music, Vocal
  USE Vocal music
MUSIC (Computer system)
  [QA76.9.I58]
  UF McGill University System for
      Interactive Computing (Computer
      system)
  BT Electronic digital computers—
      Programming
      Interactive computer systems
Music analysis
  USE Musical analysis
Music and architecture
  [ML3849]
  UF Architecture and music
  BT Aesthetics
      Music—Philosophy and aesthetics
      Musical form
Music and art
  USE Art and music
Music and color
  [ML3840]
  UF Color and music
      Color-music
      Music of colors
  BT Color
      Color-hearing
      Music—Psychology
      Wave-motion, Theory of
Music and communism
  USE Communism and music
Music and erotica
  BT Erotica
  NT Erotic songs
Music and industry
  USE Music in industry
Music and language
  [ML3849]
  UF Language and music
  BT Language and languages
  RT Music and literature
      Musical accentuation
Music and literature
  [ML80]
  [ML3849]
  UF Literature and music
      Music and poetry
      Poetry and music
  BT Literature
  RT Music and language
      Musicians in literature
  NT Music—Poetry

Music—Quotations, maxims, etc.
  Musical fiction
  Musicians as authors
Music and magic
  UF Magic and music
      Music, Magical use of
Music and mass media
  USE Mass media and music
Music and morals
  [ML3920]
  UF Morals and music
      Music, Effect of
  BT Art and morals
      Arts and morals
      Ethics
      Music, Influence of
      Music and society
Music and moving-pictures
  USE Moving-pictures and music
Music and mythology
  [ML80]
  [ML3849]
  UF Mythology and music
Music and poetry
  USE Music and literature
Music and race
  UF Race and music
  BT Ethnopsychology
      Nationalism in music
Music and radio
  USE Radio and music
Music and romanticism
  USE Romanticism in music
Music and society
  UF Society and music
      Sociology and music
  NT Music and morals
      Music and state
Music and state *(May Subd Geog)*
  [ML3795]
  UF State and music
  BT Cultural policy
      Music and society
  NT Musicians—Legal status, laws, etc.
Music and television
  USE Television and music
Music and war
  UF War and music
  RT Military music—History and criticism
      Music in the army
  SA *subdivisions* Music and the war, Music
      and the revolution, *etc. and* Songs
      and music *under individual wars,*
      e.g. World War, 1939-1945—Music
      and the war; World War, 1939-1945
      —Songs and music
Music and youth *(May Subd Geog)*
  UF Youth and music
  BT Youth
Music appreciation
  UF Analytical guides (Music)
      Appreciation of music
      Music—Analysis, appreciation
      Music—Analytical guides
      Music—Appreciation
      Musical appreciation
  BT Music—Instruction and study
  RT Musical analysis
  SA *subdivision* Analysis, appreciation
      under headings for music
      compositions
— **Music collections**
  [MT6.5]
Music archaeology *(May Subd Geog)*
  UF Archaeology, Music
      Archaeomusicology
      Archeo-musicology
  BT Archaeology
      Musicology

Music as recreation
  BT Community music
      Hobbies
      Music in the home
  NT Musical recreations
Music audiences *(May Subd Geog)*
  BT Performing arts—Audiences
  NT Jazz audiences
Music box
  [ML1066]
  UF Musical box
  BT Musical instruments (Mechanical)
Music box books
  USE Musical books
Music box music
  [M174.M85]
Music calendars
  [ML13-21]
  BT Calendars
      Music—Almanacs, yearbooks, etc.
Music chapels
  USE Chapels (Music)
Music clubs
  USE Music—Societies, etc.
Music conductors
  USE Conductors (Music)
Music conservatories
  USE Conservatories of music
Music critics *(May Subd Geog)*
  BT Critics
      Musical criticism
      Musicians
Music education
  USE Music—Instruction and study
Music festivals *(May Subd Geog)*
  [ML35-38]
  UF Musical festivals
  BT Art festivals
      Festivals
      Performing arts festivals
  RT Concerts
  NT Festivals of Male Voice Praise
      Hymn festivals
      Jazz festivals
      Music—Competitions
      Music Week
      Saint Cecilia's Day
— **Canada**
  NT Latvian Song Festival
— **Germany (West)**
  NT Ostdeutsche Musiktage
— **Indiana**
  NT Battle Ground Fiddlers' Gathering,
      Battle Ground, Ind.
— **New York (State)**
  NT Eastman School Festival of
      American Music
— **North Carolina**
  NT Mount Pilot Festival
— **United States**
  NT Latvian Song Festival
Music for meditation
  UF Meditation music
Music for playgrounds
  USE Playground music
Music for silent films
  USE Silent film music
Music for the blind
  USE Blind, Music for the
Music for the visually handicapped
  BT Visually handicapped
  NT Blind, Music for the
Music-halls *(May Subd Geog)*
  [NA6820-NA6840 (Architecture)]
  UF Concert halls
  BT Arts facilities
      Auditoriums
      Centers for the performing arts
      Halls
  RT Theaters
— **Scotland**

NT Saint Cecilia's Hall (Edinburgh, Lothian)
— Switzerland
  NT Casino (Bern, Switzerland)
Music-halls (Variety-theaters, cabarets, etc.)
  (May Subd Geog)
  [PN1960-1969]
  UF Cabarets
    Café theater
    Night clubs
    Nightclubs
    Variety shows (Theater)
    Variety-theaters
  BT Hotels, taverns, etc.
  RT Vaudeville
  NT Burlesque (Theater)
    Discotheques
    Strip-tease
— Law and legislation *(May Subd Geog)*
Music-halls (Variety theaters, cabarets, etc.)
— England
  NT Penny theaters
Music-halls (Variety-theaters, cabarets, etc.)
— Japan
  NT Yose
Music in advertising
  BT Advertising
  NT Singing commercials
Music in armies
  USE Music in the army
Music in art
  [ML85]
  [N8226]
  Here are entered works dealing with the representation of musical subjects in art.
  UF Music—Iconography
    Musical iconography
  BT Art
  RT Art and music
  NT Musical instruments in art
    Rāgamālā painting
Music in book-plates *(May Subd Geog)*
  [Z994.5.M87]
  BT Book-plates
Music in Christian education
  BT Christian education
    Church music
    Music in religious education
Music in churches
  [ML3001]
  Here are entered discussions as to the desirability, etc. of having music in the church.
  BT Music—Religious aspects—Christianity
  RT Church music
    Psalmody
  NT Music in synagogues
Music in education
  BT Education
Music in industry
  UF Industry and music
    Music and industry
Music in monasteries *(May Subd Geog)*
  BT Church music
    Monasteries
Music in physical education
  [ML3923]
  UF Physical education and music
  BT Dancing
    Physical education and training
Music in prisons
  [ML3920]
  UF Prisons, Music in
  BT Prisons
Music in religious education
  BT Religious education
  NT Music in Christian education
Music in synagogues
  [M3195]
  BT Jews—Music
    Music—Religious aspects—Judaism
    Music in churches

Music in the army
  [UH40-UH45 (Military science)]
  UF Armies—Music
    Music in armies
  BT Community music
    Music, Influence of
  RT Military music—History and criticism
    Music and war
    War-songs
Music in the Bible
  [ML166]
  Here are entered works on music and musical instruments in the Bible.
  UF Bible—Music
    Bible—Musical instruments
    Bible. O.T. Psalms—Music
    Musical instruments in the Bible
  BT Jews—Music
    Music—To 500
Music in the home
  [ML67]
  BT Chamber music—History and criticism
  NT Music as recreation
Music in theaters
  Here are entered works on music as an adjunct to theatrical productions.
  BT Dramatic music
    Theater
  NT Music, Incidental
Music in universities and colleges
  (May Subd Geog)
  [ML63]
  [MT18 (Instruction)]
  BT Music—Instruction and study
    Universities and colleges
  RT Students' songs
  SA *subdivision* Songs and music *under names of universities and colleges, e.g.* Harvard University—Songs and music
Music librarianship
  [ML111]
  BT Library science
  NT Cataloging of music
    Cataloging of sound recordings
    Classification—Music
    Classification—Sound recordings
    Subject headings—Music
— Awards
  NT Ida Rosen Prize
Music libraries *(May Subd Geog)*
  [ML111 (Forming of libraries)]
  [ML136-ML139 (Catalogs)]
  UF Libraries, Music
  BT Libraries, Special
  NT Sound recording libraries
— Shelving
  USE Shelving (for music)
Music Major (Computer program)
  BT Computer programs
    Music—Computer programs
    Music—Theory—Computer-assisted instruction
Music museums *(May Subd Geog)*
  [ML136-ML141 (Libraries, exhibitions)]
  [ML462 (Instruments)]
  UF Museums, Music
    Music—Museums
  BT Museums
  NT Music—Exhibitions
    Musical instruments—Catalogs and collections
    Theater—Museums and collections
Music of colors
  USE Music and color
Music of the spheres
  USE Harmony of the spheres
Music plate numbers
  USE Music printing—Plate numbers

Music printing *(May Subd Geog)*
  [ML112-ML112.5]
  UF Music, Printing of
    Type and type-founding—Music-type
  BT Printing
  NT Music title-pages
— Law and legislation *(May Subd Geog)*
— Plate numbers
  UF Music plate numbers
    Plate numbers, Music
  BT Music—Bibliography—Catalogs, Publishers'
    Music—Chronology
Music publishers *(May Subd Geog)*
  BT Publishers and publishing
Music publishing
  USE Music—Publishing
Music reading
  USE Score reading and playing
    Sight-reading (Music)
Music-recorders
  [ML1090]
  UF Melograph
    Pianograph
  BT Musical instruments (Mechanical)
    Piano
Music Room from Norfolk House (Interior decoration)
  USE Brettingham, Matthew, 1699-1769. Norfolk House Music Room
Music rooms and equipment
  UF Rooms, Music
Music schools
  USE Conservatories of music
Music societies
  USE Music—Societies, etc.
Music supervision in schools
  USE School music supervision
Music teachers *(May Subd Geog)*
  [ML3795]
  UF Music—Biography
  BT Music—Instruction and study
    Musicians
    Teachers
Music teachers, Training of
  USE Music—Teacher training
Music theory
  USE Music—Theory
Music therapy *(May Subd Geog)*
  [ML3919-ML3920]
  UF Music—Therapeutic use
    Music, Effect of
    Music, Physical effect of
    Musical therapy
  BT Music—Physiological aspects
    Music—Physiological effect
    Music—Psychology
    Music, Influence of
    Occupational therapy
    Recreational therapy
    Therapeutics, Physiological
  NT Musical instruments for the handicapped
    Tarantella
Music title-pages *(May Subd Geog)*
  UF Sheet-music covers
  BT Music printing
    Title-page
Music trade *(May Subd Geog)*
  [ML3790]
  NT Musical instruments—Catalogs, Manufacturers'
— Credit guides
Music video direction
  USE Music videos—Production and direction
Music video production
  USE Music videos—Production and direction
Music videos *(May Subd Geog)*
  [PN1992.8.M87]

Music videos *(Continued)*
  UF Videos, Music
  BT Television programs
      Video recordings
  RT Television music
  NT Rock videos
  — Direction
      USE Music videos—Production and
           direction
  — **Production and direction**
      UF Music video direction
          Music video production
          Music videos—Direction
Music Week
    [ML200.5]
  UF National Music Week
  BT Music—United States
      Music festivals
  RT Community music
Musica ficta
  USE Chromatic alteration (Music)
Música norteña
  USE Popular music—Mexico
       Popular music—Texas
Musical ability
  UF Ability, Musical
      Musical talent
  BT Ability
  — Testing
      BT Ability—Testing
          Music—Examinations, questions,
           etc.
          Music—Psychology
Musical accentuation
  UF Accentuation (Music)
      Declamation, Musical
      Musical declamation
  RT Music and language
      Singing—Diction
Musical accompaniment
    [MT68 (Instruction)]
    [MT190 (Organ)]
    [MT239 (Piano)]
  UF Accompaniment, Musical
  BT Composition (Music)
      Music—Instruction and study
      Piano—Instruction and study
  NT Chants (Plain, Gregorian, etc.)—
       Accompaniment
      Folk-songs—Accompaniment
      Hymns—Accompaniment
      Modulation (Music)
      Moving-picture music
      Songs—Accompaniment
      Thorough bass
      Transposition (Music)
Musical analysis
  UF Analysis, Musical
      Analytical guides (Music)
      Music—Analysis, appreciation
      Music—Analytical guides
      Music analysis
  BT Music—Theory
  RT Music appreciation
  SA subdivision Analysis, appreciation
       under headings for music
       compositions
  NT Harmonic analysis (Music)
      Melodic analysis
      Schenkerian analysis
  — **Music collections**
      [MT6.5]
Musical appreciation
  USE Music appreciation
Musical books *(May Subd Geog)*
  UF Melody books
      Music box books
  BT Books
Musical box
  USE Music box

Musical card games
    [M1985]
  UF Card games
  BT Games with music
      Musical recreations
Musical clock
    [ML1067 (History)]
      Here are entered works about clocks equipped
    with mechanical organs. Works about clocks
    equipped with carillons or other chiming mechanisms
    are entered under the heading Chiming clocks.
  UF Clock, Musical
      Flötenuhr
      Flötenwerk
      Flute clock
      Flute-playing clock
      Laufwerk
      Spieluhr
  BT Mechanical organs
Musical clock music
    [M174.M]
Musical clubs
  USE Music—Societies, etc.
Musical comedies
  USE Musical revues, comedies, etc.
Musical comedy
  USE Musical revue, comedy, etc.
Musical composition
  USE Composition (Music)
Musical compositions, Titles of
  USE Titles of musical compositions
Musical criticism *(May Subd Geog)*
    [ML3880-3916]
  UF Music—History and criticism—
       Methods
      Music—History and criticism—
       Theory, etc.
  BT Criticism
      Journalism
      Music—Historiography
      Musicology
  NT Music critics
      Newspapers—Sections, columns, etc.—
       Reviews
Musical declamation
  USE Monologues with music
       Musical accentuation
       Singing—Diction
Musical dictation
    [MT35]
  UF Dictation, Musical
      Harmonic dictation
      Melodic dictation
  RT Ear training
Musical education
  USE Music—Instruction and study
Musical ensembles
  USE Musical groups
Musical extravaganza
  USE Musical revue, comedy, etc.
Musical farce
  USE Musical revue, comedy, etc.
       Operetta
Musical festivals
  USE Music festivals
Musical fiction
  UF Musical novels
  BT Fiction
      Music and literature
  NT Musicians in literature
      Wagner, Richard, 1813-1883, in
       fiction, drama, poetry, etc
Musical form
    [ML448 (History)]
    [MT58-MT64 (Instruction)]
  UF Form, Musical
  BT Composition (Music)
      Music—Instruction and study
      Music—Theory
  SA names of particular musical forms, e.g.
       Fugue; Motet; Opera; Sonata

  NT Cadence (Music)
      Coda (Music)
      Music and architecture
      Parody (Music)
      Scherzo
Musical glasses
  USE Glass harmonica
Musical groups *(May Subd Geog)*
  UF Ensembles, Musical
      Groups, Musical
      Musical ensembles
  NT Bands (Music)
      Brass bands
      Chamber music groups
      Chamber orchestra
      Choirs (Music)
      Choral societies
      Country music groups
      Dance orchestras
      Folk music groups
      Rock groups
      Symphony orchestras
Musical iconography
  USE Music in art
Musical instruction
  USE Music—Instruction and study
Musical instrument collections
  USE Musical instruments—Catalogs and
       collections
Musical Instrument Digital Interface
  USE MIDI (Standard)
Musical instrument makers
    (May Subd Geog)
  UF Musical instruments—Makers
  BT Musicians
  NT Clavichord makers
      Harpsichord makers
      Organ-builders
      Piano makers
      Stringed instrument makers
      Wind instrument makers
Musical instruments *(May Subd Geog)*
    [HD9999.M8 (Industry)]
    [ML460-ML1055 (History)]
    [ML462 (Collections, descriptive
     catalogs, exhibitions)]
    [MT170-MT805 (Instruction)]
      For works about musical instruments of an in-
    dividual ethnic group, additional subject entry is
    made under the heading [ethnic group]—[place]
    —Music.
  UF Instruments, Musical
      Organology (Music)
  BT Classical antiquities
  RT Instrumental music—History and
       criticism
      Instrumentation and orchestration
  SA groups of instruments, e.g. Percussion
       instruments; Stringed instruments;
       Stringed instruments, Bowed; Wind
       instruments; also names of
       individual musical instruments, e.g.
       Accordion, Harpsichord, Organ,
       Piano
  NT Hurdy-gurdy
      Jew's harp
      Mouth organs
      Musical instruments, Electronic
      Orchestra
      Tuning
  — **Catalogs and collections**
      (May Subd Geog)
      [ML461-462]
      UF Musical instrument collections
          Musical instruments—Collections
      BT Music—Exhibitions
          Music museums
      SA subdivision Musical instrument
           collections under names of
           persons, families, and corporate
           bodies

— Catalogs, Manufacturers'
  [ML155]
  BT Music trade
— Collections
  USE Musical instruments—Catalogs
       and collections
— Construction
— Dictionaries
  [ML102]
  SA *subdivision* Dictionaries *under*
      names of instruments, e.g. Piano
      —Dictionaries
— Exhibitions
  [ML462]
  BT Music—Exhibitions
— Indians
  USE Indians—Music
— Juvenile literature
  [ML3930]
  BT Music—Juvenile literature
  NT Rhythm bands and orchestras
— Makers
  USE Musical instrument makers
— Studies and exercises
— Studies and exercises (Jazz)
— Tariff
  USE Tariff on stringed instruments
       Tariff on wind instruments
— Africa
  NT Goura (Musical instrument)
      Kora (Musical instrument)
      Mbira
      Sanza
— Africa, French-speaking West
  NT Balo
— Andes Region
  NT Charango
— Asia, Central
  NT Morin khuur
— Brazil
  NT Berimbau
— China
  NT Cheng (Musical instrument)
      Ch'in (Musical instrument)
      Erh hu
      Hsüan (Musical instrument)
      Hu ch'in
      Huang chung (Musical instrument)
      Nan hu
      Pan hu
      Sheng (Musical instrument)
      So na
      Yang ch'in
      Yüeh ch'in
— Cuba
  NT Conga (Drum)
— Greece
  NT Bouzouki
— India
  NT Bānsurī
      Daph
      Sarod
      Shehnai
      Sitar
      Tabla
— Indonesia
  NT Angklung
      Gender (Musical instrument)
      Kolintang
— Iran
  NT Santūr
      Tunbūk
— Ireland
  NT Bodhran
— Japan
  NT Biwa
      Hichiriki
      Ichigenkin
      Kei
      Koto
      Kotsuzumi

Ryūteki
Shakuhachi
Shamisen
Shinobue
Shō
— Kenya
  NT Zumari
— Korea
  NT Changgo
      Haegŭm
      Hyŏn'gŭm
      Kayakeum
      Komunko
      P'illyul
      Taegŭm
      Tanso
— Laos
  NT Kaen
— Latvia
  NT Kokle
— Lithuania
  NT Kanklės
— Nepal
  NT Gumlā
— Pakistan
  NT Bānsurī
— Puerto Rico
  NT Cuatro puertorriqueño
— Russian S.F.S.R.
  NT Russian horn
— Soviet Union
  NT Bayan
— Spain
  NT Alboka
      Dulzaina
— Sweden
  NT Keyed fiddle
      Tambi
— Thailand
  NT Kaen
— Turkey
  NT Saz
— Ukraine
  NT Kobza
— Yugoslavia
  NT Tambura
Musical instruments, Ancient
  (May Subd Geog)
  [ML162-169]
  UF Ancient musical instruments
  NT Psaltery
— Greece
  NT Aulos
      Cithara
— Rome
  NT Tibia (Musical instrument)
Musical instruments, Electronic
  [ML1092]
  UF Electric musical instruments
      Electronic musical instruments
      Electrophonic musical instruments
  BT Household electronics
      Musical instruments
      Musical instruments (Mechanical)
  RT Electro-acoustics
  NT Clavioline
      Electric guitar
      Electronic harpsichord
      Electronic organ
      Electronic piano
      Ondes Martenot
      Synthesizer (Musical instrument)
      Trautonium
Musical instruments (Mechanical)
  [ML1050-ML1055 (History)]
  [MT700 (Instruction)]
  NT Aeolian-vocalion
      Jukeboxes
      Manualo
      Mechanical organs
      Music box

Music-recorders
Musical instruments, Electronic
Organina
Pianola
Player-organ
Player-piano
Pyrophone
Violano-virtuoso
Musical instruments for the handicapped
  BT Handicapped
      Music therapy
Musical instruments in art
  BT Music in art
Musical instruments in the Bible
  USE Music in the Bible
Musical instruments industry
  (May Subd Geog)
  [HD9999.M8]
Musical interpretation
  USE Music—Interpretation (Phrasing,
       dynamics, etc.)
Musical intervals and scales
  [ML3809]
  UF Intervals (Music)
      Modes, Musical
      Music—Modes
      Musical modes
      Scales (Music)
  BT Harmony
      Music—Acoustics and physics
      Music—Theory
  RT Microtones
  NT Raga
      Tonality
      Tonus peregrinus
      Twelve-tone system
Musical inventions and patents
  UF Music—Inventions and patents
  BT Inventions
      Patents
Musical jaw bone
  USE Jaw bone, Musical
Musical landmarks (May Subd Geog)
  [ML198-370]
  BT Historic buildings
Musical medleys
  USE Potpourris
Musical meter and rhythm
  [ML437 (History of composition)]
  [ML3813 (Physics: acoustics)]
  [ML3832 (Psychology)]
  [ML3850 (Aesthetics)]
  [MT42 (Instruction in composition)]
  [MT233 (Piano)]
  UF Meter
  BT Music—Theory
      Rhythm
  NT Chants (Plain, Gregorian, etc.)—
      Instruction and study
      Measured music
      Musical notation
      Neumes
      Syncopation
      Tempo (Music)
— Studies and exercises
  [MT42]
Musical modes
  USE Musical intervals and scales
Musical moving-pictures
  USE Moving-pictures, Musical
Musical notation
  [ML431 (History)]
  [ML432 (Reform)]
  [MT35 (Instruction)]
  UF Ligature (Music)
      Music—Notation
      Notation, Musical
  BT Musical meter and rhythm
  NT Braille music-notation
      Embellishment (Music)
      Galin-Paris-Chevé method (Music)

Musical notation *(Continued)*
     Measured music
     Musical shorthand
     Neumes
     Notes inégales
     Paleography, Musical
     Solmization
     Tablature (Musical notation)
     Tone-word system
     Tonic sol-fa
Musical novels
  USE Musical fiction
Musical paleography
  USE Paleography, Musical
Musical parodies
  USE Wit and humor, Musical
Musical parody
  USE Parody (Music)
Musical performance
  USE Music—Performance
Musical pitch
  [ML3807-ML3809 (Acoustics)]
  [ML3830 (Psychology)]
  UF Pitch, Musical
  BT Tuning
  NT Organ-pipes
Musical play
  USE Musical revue, comedy, etc.
Musical radio programs
  USE Radio programs, Musical
Musical realism
  USE Realism in music
Musical recreations
  UF Recreations, Musical
  BT Amusements
     Music as recreation
  NT Musical card games
Musical research
  USE Musicology
Musical revue, comedy, etc.
  (May Subd Geog)
     Here are entered works on musical revue, comedy, etc. Musical works composed for Musical revues, comedies, etc. are entered under Musical revues, comedies, etc.
  UF Musical comedy
     Musical extravaganza
     Musical farce
     Musical play
  BT Dramatic music
     Zarzuela
  NT Pantomime (Christmas entertainment)
  — Authorship
     USE Musical revue, comedy, etc.—
         Writing and publishing
  — Direction
     USE Musical revue, comedy, etc.—
         Production and direction
  — **Production and direction**
     [MT955]
     UF Musical revue, comedy, etc.—
         Direction
  — **Writing and publishing**
     UF Musical revue, comedy, etc.—
         Authorship
     BT Composition (Music)
Musical revues, comedies, etc.
  [M1500-M1508]
     Here are entered musical works composed for musical revues, comedies, etc. Works on musical revue, comedy, etc., are entered under Musical revue, comedy, etc.
  UF Musical comedies
     Operettas
  BT Dramatic music
     Feature films
  NT College operas, revues, etc.
     Minstrel shows
     Tonadillas
  — **Stage guides**
     [MT955]
  — **Stories, plots, etc.**

  BT Plots (Drama, novel, etc.)
Musical saw
  [ML1055]
  UF Saw, Musical
Musical saw music
  [M175.M9]
  NT Septets (Piano, guitar, clavioline, musical saw, percussion, vibraphone, xylophone)
Musical settings
  USE *subdivision* Musical settings *under headings for authors, e.g.* Shakespeare, William, 1564-1616—Musical settings; *also under headings for literature, poetry, drama, etc., e.g.* English literature—Musical settings *for musical scores or sound recordings in which the writings or words of an author or authors have been set to music*
Musical shorthand
  [MT35]
  BT Musical notation
     Shorthand
Musical sketches
     Here are entered tentative drafts or preliminary studies, in manuscript, facsimile or transcription, for musical works.
  UF Composers' sketches
     Music—Sketches
     Sketches, Musical
Musical societies
  USE Music—Societies, etc.
Musical style
  USE Style, Musical
Musical talent
  USE Musical ability
Musical temperament
  [ML3809]
  UF Temperament, Musical
  BT Music—Acoustics and physics
     Music—Theory
     Tuning
  NT Monochord
Musical therapy
  USE Music therapy
Musical time
  USE Tempo (Music)
Musical variation
  USE Variation (Music)
Musical wit and humor
  USE Wit and humor, Musical
Musicals (Motion pictures)
  USE Moving-pictures, Musical
Musicians *(May Subd Geog)*
  [ML385-403]
  UF Music—Biography
  BT Artists
     Entertainers
  SA Flute-players, Pianists, Singers, *and similar headings*
  NT Aged musicians
     Bagpipers
     Bandsmen
     Biwa players
     Blues musicians
     Calypso musicians
     Children as musicians
     Church musicians
     Composers
     Conductors (Music)
     Country musicians
     Disco musicians
     Double-bassists
     Drummers (Musicians)
     Flute-players
     Gospel musicians
     Harmonica players
     Harpsichordists
     Jazz musicians
     Kobzari

     Librettists
     Music—Bio-bibliography
     Music critics
     Music teachers
     Musical instrument makers
     Musicologists
     Oboe players
     Physically handicapped musicians
     Physicians as musicians
     Pianists
     Reggae musicians
     Rock musicians
     Singers
     Sitar players
     Soul musicians
     Stadtpfeifer
     Street music and musicians
     Trade-unions—Musicians
     Trumpet players
     Viol players
     Violinists
     Violists
     Violoncellists
     Women musicians
  — Anecdotes, facetiae, satire, etc.
     USE Music—Anecdotes, facetiae, satire, etc.
  — **Autographs**
     [ML93-98]
  — Dictionaries
     USE Music—Bio-bibliography
  — **Legal status, laws, etc.**
     (May Subd Geog)
     [ML63]
     BT Copyright—Music
         Music and state
  — **Pensions** *(May Subd Geog)*
     UF Musicians—Salaries, pensions, etc.
  — Poetry
     USE Music—Poetry
  — **Salaries, etc.** *(May Subd Geog)*
     [ML3795]
     UF Musicians—Salaries, pensions, etc.
  — Salaries, pensions, etc.
     USE Musicians—Pensions
         Musicians—Salaries, etc.
  — **France**
  — — **Portraits**
     NT Titon du Tillet, Évrard, 1677-1762. Parnasse françois
  — **Great Britain**
     NT Waits
  — **Japan**
     NT Shakuhachi players
  — **Korea**
     NT Kayakeum players
Musicians, Afro-American
  USE Afro-American musicians
Musicians, Basque
  UF Basque musicians
Musicians, Black *(May Subd Geog)*
  UF Black musicians
  BT Blacks in the performing arts
Musicians, Blind
  USE Blind musicians
Musicians, Celtic
  UF Celtic musicians
Musicians, Gipsy
  USE Musicians, Gypsy
Musicians, Gypsy
  UF Gipsy musicians
     Gypsy musicians
     Musicians, Gipsy
Musicians, Jewish
  UF Jewish musicians
  NT Cantors, Jewish
Musicians, Physically handicapped
  USE Physically handicapped musicians
Musicians, Street
  USE Street music and musicians

Musicians, Town
　USE Stadtpfeifer
　　　Waits
Musicians, Women
　USE Women musicians
Musicians as authors
　BT Authors
　　　Music and literature
Musicians in literature
　BT Musical fiction
　RT Music and literature
Musicians' wives *(May Subd Geog)*
　BT Wives
　NT Rock musicians' wives
Musico-callisthenics
　[GV464 (Callisthenics, GV463)]
　[M1993 (Music)]
　BT Callisthenics
　　　Dancing
Musicologists *(May Subd Geog)*
　BT Musicians
　　　Scholars
　RT Musicology
　NT Ethnomusicologists
Musicology *(May Subd Geog)*
　[ML]
　UF Musical research
　　　Research, Musical
　RT Music—Historiography
　　　Musicologists
　NT Ethnomusicology
　　　Music—Editing
　　　Music archaeology
　　　Musical criticism
　　　Paleography, Musical
　— **Almanacs, yearbooks, etc.**
　　　UF Musicology—Yearbooks
　— **Yearbooks**
　　　USE Musicology—Almanacs,
　　　　　　yearbooks, etc.
Mūṣika dynasty
　USE Mūshaka dynasty
Musique concrète
　USE Concrete music
Musk
　[RM666.M85 (Therapeutics)]
　[TP983 (Perfumery)]
Musk-deer
　[QL737.U5]
　BT Deer
Musk Hog Canyon (Tex.)
　BT Canyons—Texas
Musk ox
　[QL737.U5]
　UF Ovibos
Musk ox, Fossil
Musk turtle, Southern
　USE Southern musk turtle
Musk turtles
　USE Kinosternidae
Muskeg *(May Subd Geog)*
　[GB621-628]
　UF Grassy bog
　　　Maskeeg
　BT Bogs
　　　Wetlands
Muskeg flora *(May Subd Geog)*
　[QK108-QK474.5 (Local)]
　[QK938.M (General)]
　BT Wetland flora
Muskellunge *(May Subd Geog)*
　[QL638.E7 (Zoology)]
　UF Muskies (Fish)
　　　Musky (Fish)
Muskellunge fishing
　[SH691.M8]
　BT Fishing
　　　Pike fishing
Musketry
　USE Shooting, Military

Muskhogean Indians
　[E99.M]
　BT Indians of North America
　NT Alibamu Indians
　　　Apalachee Indians
　　　Chickasaw Indians
　　　Choctaw Indians
　　　Creek Indians
　　　Koasati Indians
　　　Mikasuki Indians
　　　Seminole Indians
　　　Yuchi Indians
Muskhogean languages
　[PM1971-4]
　UF Muskoki languages
　RT Choctaw language
　　　Creek language
　NT Alabama language
　　　Apalachee language
　　　Chickasaw language
　　　Mikasuki language
　　　Seminole language
Muskies (Fish)
　USE Muskellunge
Muskingum River (Ohio)
　BT Rivers—Ohio
Muskmelon *(May Subd Geog)*
　UF Cantaloupe
　　　Cantelope
　　　Cucumis melo
　　　Netted melon
　　　Nutmeg melon
　　　Persian melon
　BT Melons
Muskmelon industry *(May Subd Geog)*
　[HD9259.M86-864]
Muskogee Indians
　USE Creek Indians
Muskoki Indians
　USE Creek Indians
Muskoki language
　USE Creek language
Muskoki languages
　USE Muskhogean languages
Muskrats *(May Subd Geog)*
　[QL737.R6]
　UF Ondatra zibethica
　BT Cricetidae
　　　Voles
Muskwaki Indians
　USE Fox Indians
Musky (Fish)
　USE Muskellunge
Muslim angelology
　USE Angels (Islam)
Muslim antiquities
　USE Islamic antiquities
Muslim apologetics
　USE Islam—Apologetic works
Muslim architects
　USE Architects, Muslim
Muslim architecture
　USE Architecture, Islamic
Muslim arms and armor
　USE Arms and armor, Islamic
Muslim art
　USE Art, Islamic
Muslim art metal-work
　USE Art metal-work, Islamic
Muslim art objects
　USE Art objects, Islamic
Muslim artists
　USE Artists, Muslim
Muslim arts
　USE Arts, Islamic
Muslim authors
　UF Authors, Islamic
　　　Authors, Muslim
　　　Islamic authors
　BT Islamic literature

Muslim bookbinding
　USE Bookbinding, Islamic
Muslim calendar
　USE Calendar, Islamic
Muslim calligraphers
　USE Calligraphers, Muslim
Muslim children *(May Subd Geog)*
　UF Children, Islamic
　　　Children, Muslim
　　　Islamic children
　BT Children
　— **Religious life**
　　　[BP188.3.C5]
　　　UF Children—Religious life (Islam)
　　　BT Religious life (Islam)
Muslim chronology
　USE Chronology, Islamic
Muslim cities and towns
　USE Cities and towns, Islamic
Muslim civilization
　USE Civilization, Islamic
Muslim coins
　USE Coins, Islamic
Muslim converts *(May Subd Geog)*
　[BP170.5]
　UF Converts, Islamic
　　　Converts, Muslim
　　　Converts to Islam
　　　Islamic converts
Muslim converts from Christianity
　[BP170.5]
　UF Converts from Christianity to Islam
Muslim converts from Judaism
　(May Subd Geog)
　UF Jewish converts to Islam
Muslim converts to Christianity
　USE Converts from Islam
Muslim cosmology
　USE Cosmology, Islamic
Muslim costume
　USE Costume, Islamic
Muslim countries
　USE Islamic countries
Muslim courts
　USE Courts, Islamic
Muslim Croatian literature
　USE Croatian literature—Muslim authors
Muslim Croatian poetry
　USE Croatian poetry—Muslim authors
Muslim decoration and ornament
　USE Decoration and ornament, Islamic
Muslim decorative arts
　USE Decorative arts, Islamic
Muslim demonology
　USE Demonology, Islamic
Muslim devotional calendars
　USE Islamic devotional calendars
Muslim education
　USE Islam—Education
Muslim educators
　USE Educators, Muslim
Muslim Empire
　USE Islamic Empire
Muslim enamel and enameling
　USE Enamel and enameling, Islamic
Muslim eschatology
　USE Eschatology, Islamic
Muslim ethics
　USE Islamic ethics
Muslim etiquette
　USE Islamic etiquette
Muslim exempla
　USE Exempla, Islamic
Muslim fasts and feasts
　USE Fasts and feasts—Islam
Muslim funeral rites and ceremonies
　USE Funeral rites and ceremonies, Islamic
Muslim glassware
　USE Glassware, Islamic
Muslim heresies
　USE Heresies, Islamic

Muslim heretics
  USE Heretics, Muslim
Muslim holy war
  USE Jihad
Muslim homiletical illustrations
  USE Homiletical illustrations, Islamic
Muslim homiletics
  USE Preaching, Islamic
Muslim hygiene
  USE Hygiene, Islamic
Muslim hymns
  USE Islamic hymns
Muslim illumination of books and manuscripts
  USE Illumination of books and manuscripts,
      Islamic
Muslim inscriptions
  USE Inscriptions, Islamic
Muslim ivories
  USE Ivories, Islamic
Muslim learning and scholarship
  USE Islamic learning and scholarship
Muslim legends
  USE Legends, Islamic
Muslim libraries
  USE Islamic libraries
Muslim literature
  USE Islamic literature
Muslim logicians
  USE Logicians, Muslim
Muslim magic
  USE Magic, Islamic
Muslim majolica
  USE Majolica, Islamic
Muslim marriage customs and rites
  USE Marriage customs and rites, Islamic
Muslim martyrs (May Subd Geog)
  [BP72]
  UF Islamic martyrs
     Martyrs, Islamic
     Martyrs, Muslim
  BT Martyrs
  RT Martyrdom (Islam)
  NT Shiites—Persecutions
Muslim meditations
  USE Islamic meditations
Muslim metal-work
  USE Metal-work, Islamic
Muslim miniature painting
  USE Miniature painting, Islamic
Muslim missions
  USE Islam—Missions
Muslim monasticism and religious orders
  USE Monasticism and religious orders,
     Islamic
Muslim mosaics
  USE Mosaics, Islamic
Muslim mural painting and decoration
  USE Mural painting and decoration, Islamic
Muslim music
  USE Music, Islamic
Muslim mysticism
  USE Mysticism—Islam
Muslim names
  USE Names, Personal—Islamic
Muslim New Year
  USE Islamic New Year
Muslim numismatics
  USE Numismatics, Islamic
Muslim orders of knighthood and chivalry
  USE Orders of knighthood and chivalry,
     Islamic
Muslim painting
  USE Painting, Islamic
Muslim pastoral theology
  USE Pastoral theology (Islam)
Muslim philosophers
  USE Philosophers, Muslim
Muslim philosophy
  USE Philosophy, Islamic
Muslim physicians
  USE Physicians, Muslim

Muslim pilgrims and pilgrimages
  (May Subd Geog)
  [BP187]
  UF Islamic pilgrims and pilgrimages
     Pilgrims and pilgrimages, Muslim
  BT Pilgrims and pilgrimages
  NT Islamic shrines
     Muslim saints
  — **Law and legislation** (May Subd Geog)
    BT Religious law and legislation
  — **Saudi Arabia**
  — — **Mecca**
      [BP187.3]
      UF Hajj
        Mecca, Pilgrimage to
      BT Pillars of Islam
Muslim pottery
  USE Pottery, Islamic
Muslim preaching
  USE Preaching, Islamic
Muslim press
  USE Press, Islamic
Muslim psychology
  USE Islam—Psychology
Muslim public finance
  USE Finance, Public—Islamic countries
Muslim religious education
  USE Islamic religious education
Muslim religious functionaries
  USE Islam—Functionaries
Muslim religious practice
  USE Islamic religious practice
Muslim research
  USE Islam—Research
Muslim rugs
  USE Rugs, Islamic
Muslim saints (May Subd Geog)
  [BP189.33]
  UF Islamic saints
     Saints, Islamic
     Saints, Muslim
     Saints, Sufi
     Sufi saints
  BT Islam
     Muslim pilgrims and pilgrimages
     Sufism
  — **Cult**
Muslim saints, Women (May Subd Geog)
  UF Islamic women saints
     Muslim women saints
     Women saints, Muslim
  BT Saints, Women
     Women, Muslim
     Women in Islam
Muslim scholars
  USE Scholars, Muslim
Muslim scientists
  USE Scientists, Muslim
Muslim sculpture
  USE Sculpture, Islamic
Muslim sects
  USE Islamic sects
Muslim Serbian literature
  USE Serbian literature—Muslim authors
Muslim Serbian poetry
  USE Serbian poetry—Muslim authors
Muslim sermons
  USE Islamic sermons
Muslim shrines
  USE Islamic shrines
Muslim sociology
  USE Sociology, Islamic
Muslim students
  USE Students, Muslim
Muslim taxation
  USE Taxation—Islamic countries
Muslim teachers
  [LC905.T42]
  UF Teachers, Muslim
  BT Islam—Education

Muslim textile fabrics
  USE Textile fabrics, Islamic
Muslim theologians
  USE Theologians, Muslim
Muslim theological anthropology
  USE Man (Islam)
Muslim theology
  USE Islam—Doctrines
Muslim wedding sermons
  USE Wedding sermons, Islamic
Muslim women
  USE Women, Muslim
Muslim women saints
  USE Muslim saints, Women
Muslim wood-carving
  USE Wood-carving, Islamic
Muslim youth
  USE Youth, Muslim
Muslimism
  USE Islam
Muslims (May Subd Geog)
  [DS38]
  UF Mohammedans
     Moors
     Moslems
     Muhammadans
     Musalmans
     Mussulmen
  BT Islam
  NT Hamdanids
     Missions to Muslims
  — **Art patronage**
    BT Art patronage
  — **Dietary laws**
    UF Dietary laws, Islamic
      Dietary laws, Muslim
    BT Diet
      Food—Religious aspects—Islam
      Nutrition—Religious aspects—
        Islam
  — Education
    USE Islam—Education
  — **Intellectual life**
    RT Islamic learning and scholarship
    NT Scholars, Muslim
  — Learning and scholarship
    USE Islamic learning and scholarship
  — **Life skills guides**
  — Music
    USE Music, Islamic
  — Women
    USE Women, Muslim
  — **France**
    NT Poitiers, Battle of, 732
  — **India**
    NT Aligarh movement
      Khaksar Movement
      Khilafat Movement
      Moplahs
      Navayats
      Siddiquis (South Asian people)
      Sumarā (Indic people)
  — — **Politics and government**
     NT Pakistan movement
      Razakars
  — **Non-Muslim countries**
    Here are entered works on Muslims living in
    predominantly non-Muslim countries treated
    collectively. Works on Muslims living in in-
    dividual non-Muslim countries are entered under
    Muslims—[place].
    UF Muslims in non-Muslim countries
    BT Minorities
  — **Philippines**
    UF Moros
    NT Dajo, Mount, Battle of, 1906
      Magindanaos (Philippine people)
      Maranao (Philippine people)
      Tausugs
  — **Spain**
    NT Moriscos

Spain—Civilization, Islamic
— United States
    NT Black Muslims
Muslims, Black
    ⌈BP62.N4⌉
        Here are entered works on persons of the Black
    race who are Muslims. Works on the movement
    known as the Nation of Islam or Black Muslims are
    entered under Black Muslims.
    BT Blacks—Religion
Muslims (in heraldry)
Muslims as scientists
    USE Scientists, Muslim
Muslims in non-Muslim countries
    USE Muslims—Non-Muslim countries
Musotimidae
    USE Pyralidae
Musquakie Indians
    USE Fox Indians
Mussara Site (Spain)
    UF La Mussara Site (Spain)
    BT Spain—Antiquities
Mussel culture *(May Subd Geog)*
    ⌈SH372.5⌉
    BT Shellfish culture
Mussel fisheries *(May Subd Geog)*
    BT Shellfish fisheries
Mussel scale
    USE Oyster-shell scale
Mussel Slough Tragedy, 1880
    BT Kings County (Calif.)—History
        Railroads—California—History—19th
            century
Mussele dialect
    ⌈PL8755.95.M⌉
    UF Musele dialect
    BT Umbundu language
Musselman family *(Not Subd Geog)*
    UF Moesselman family
        Muselman family
        Mussselmann family
        Mussilman family
        Musslman family
        Mussulman family
Musselmann family
    USE Musselman family
Mussels *(May Subd Geog)*
    ⌈SH373⌉
    NT Cookery (Mussels)
Mussels, Fresh-water *(May Subd Geog)*
    ⌈SH378⌉
        Here are entered works of economic interest. Sys-
    tematic studies are entered under the heading Un-
    ionidae.
    UF Fresh-water mussels
    BT Shellfish fisheries
Musser family *(Not Subd Geog)*
    UF Muser family
    RT Mouser family
Musserongo dialect
    USE Solongo dialect
Mussetter family *(Not Subd Geog)*
Mussey family
    USE Muzzy family
Mussilman family
    USE Musselman family
Musslman family
    USE Musselman family
Musso, War of, 1531-1532
    ⌈DQ114⌉
    ⌈DQ398 (Basel)⌉
    ⌈DQ498 (Grisons)⌉
    BT Switzerland—History—1499-1648
Musso (Asian people)
    USE Lahu (Asian people)
Mussolini family *(Not Subd Geog)*
Mussolini's March on Rome, Italy, 1922
    USE Italy—History—March on Rome, 1922
Mussu
    USE Moso (Tribe)
Mussulman family
    USE Musselman family

Mussulmanism
    USE Islam
Mussulmen
    USE Muslims
Must
    BT Fruit juices
        Wine and wine making
Mustache
    ⌈GT2318⌉
    UF Moustache
    BT Hair
    NT Mustache cups
Mustache cups *(May Subd Geog)*
    ⌈NK4695.M8⌉
    UF Cups, Mustache
    BT Drinking cups
        Mustache
Mustache lifters
    BT Beard
Mustaghānim Plateau (Algeria)
    USE Mostaganem Plateau (Algeria)
Mustang
    BT Horses
        Wild horses
    NT Indian ponies
Mustang (Fighter planes)
    ⌈TL685.3⌉
    UF A-36 (Fighter-bomber planes)
        F-51 (Fighter planes)
        P-51 (Fighter planes)
    BT Fighter planes
        North American airplanes (Military
            aircraft)
Mustang automobile
    ⌈TL215.M8⌉
    BT Ford automobile
Mustangs in art
Mustard *(May Subd Geog)*
    ⌈QK495.C9 (Botany)⌉
    ⌈SB307.M87 (Condiment plant)⌉
    UF Black mustard
        Brassica nigra
    BT Brassica
— Advertising
    USE Advertising—Mustard
— Seeds
    UF Mustard seed
Mustard (Condiment)
    ⌈TP420 (Manufacture)⌉
    ⌈TX407.M (Food)⌉
    ⌈TX819.M (Cookery)⌉
    RT Cookery (Mustard)
Mustard cabbage, Chinese white
    USE Bok choy
Mustard cabbage, White Chinese
    USE Bok choy
Mustard family *(Not Subd Geog)*
Mustard gas
    ⌈RA1247.M8 (Toxicology)⌉
    ⌈UG447.5.M8 (Military science)⌉
    UF Yperite (Poison gas)
    BT Gases, Asphyxiating and poisonous
Mustard oils
    UF Oleum sinapis volatile
    BT Thiocyanates
Mustard pots *(May Subd Geog)*
    BT Pots
Mustard seed
    USE Mustard—Seeds
Mustard seed (Parable)
    ⌈BT378.M8⌉
    BT Jesus Christ—Parables
Mustela
    ⌈QL737.C25⌉
    UF Grammogale
        Lutreola
        Putorius
    BT Mustelidae
    NT Black-footed ferret
        European polecat
        Minks

Mustela erminea
        Mustela nivalis
Mustela erminea
    ⌈QL737.C25⌉
    UF Ermine
        Stoat
    BT Mustela
Mustela lutra
    USE Lutra lutra
Mustela nigripes
    USE Black-footed ferret
Mustela nivalis
    ⌈QL737.C25⌉
    UF Least weasel
        Mustela rixosa
        Weasel, Common
    BT Mustela
        Weasels
Mustela putorius
    USE European polecat
Mustela rixosa
    USE Mustela nivalis
Mustela vison
    USE Minks
Mustelidae
    ⌈QL737.C25⌉
    BT Carnivora
    NT Amblonyx
        Badgers
        Enhydra
        Gulo
        Lutra
        Martes
        Meles
        Mustela
        Otters
        Skunks
        Taxidea
        Weasels
Mustelus
    ⌈QL638.95.T75⌉
    UF Smoothhound dogfish
        Smoothhound sharks
    BT Carcharhinidae
        Dogfish
        Triakidae
    NT Mustelus canis
Mustelus canis
    ⌈QL638.95.C3⌉
    UF Dogfish, Smooth
        Smooth dogfish
    BT Mustelus
Muster family *(Not Subd Geog)*
Mustering out
    USE Military discharge
Mustering-out pay
    USE Bounties, Military—United States
Musu (Asiatic tribe)
    USE Moso (Tribe)
Musu Indians
    USE Moxo Indians
Musuk language
    USE Musgu language
Mût (The Hebrew root)
    USE Myt (The Hebrew root)
Muta
    BT Marriage (Islamic law)
Mutagen testing
    USE Mutagenicity testing
Mutagenesis
    BT Mutation (Biology)
    RT Radiogenetics
        Teratogenesis
    NT Antimitotic agents
        Antimutagens
        Chemical mutagenesis
        Mutagens
        X-ray mutagenesis
— Testing
    USE Mutagenicity testing

Mutagenic agents
  USE Mutagens
Mutagenicity testing
    ⌐QH465 (Genetics)¬
    ⌐RA1224.4.M86 (Toxicology)¬
  UF Mutagen testing
      Mutagenesis—Testing
      Mutagens—Testing
  BT Toxicity testing
Mutagens *(May Subd Geog)*
    ⌐QH465¬
  UF Mutagenic agents
  BT Mutagenesis
      Mutation (Biology)
  RT Teratogenic agents
  — Testing
      USE Mutagenicity testing
Mutasallim, Tall al- (Israel)
  USE Megiddo (Ancient city)
Mutasellim, Tell el- (Israel)
  USE Megiddo (Ancient city)
Mutation (Biology)
  RT Genetics
      Variation (Biology)
  NT Animal mutation
      Chromosome abnormalities
      Evolution
      Genetic load
      Lethal mutation
      Microbial mutation
      Mutagenesis
      Mutagens
      Nonsense mutation
      Nonsense suppression (Genetics)
      Plant mutation
Mutation (Phonetics)
  UF Grammar, Comparative and general—
        Mutation
      Lenition (Phonetics)
  BT Grammar, Comparative and general—
        Phonology
      Phonetics
  SA *subdivision* Mutation *under individual*
      languages and groups of languages,
      e.g. English language—Mutation
Mutation breeding
  UF Induced mutations in breeding
  BT Breeding
  NT Animal mutation breeding
      Microbial mutation breeding
      Plant mutation breeding
Mutation of animals
  USE Animal mutation
Mutation of micro-organisms
  USE Microbial mutation
Mutation of plants
  USE Plant mutation
Mutazilites
  USE Motazilites
Mute swan
  UF Cygnus olor
  BT Swans
Muthurajas
  UF Ambalakaran
      Mudiraj
      Muttarachas
  BT Ethnology—India
  — Anthropometry
Mutilation
    ⌐GN419.2 (Ethnology)¬
  RT Self-mutilation
  NT Architecture—Mutilation, defacement,
        etc.
      Art—Mutilation, defacement, etc.
      Christian art and symbolism—
        Mutilation, defacement, etc.
      Churches—Vandalism
      Deformities, Artificial
      Painting—Mutilation, defacement, etc.
      Sculpture—Mutilation, defacement,
        etc.

      Tattooing
Mutilation in literature
Mutilation of art
  USE Art—Mutilation, defacement, etc.
Mutilation of books
  USE Books—Mutilation, defacement, etc.
Mutilation of Christian art
  USE Christian art and symbolism—
        Mutilation, defacement, etc.
Mutilation of manuscripts
  USE Manuscripts—Mutilation, defacement,
        etc.
Mutillidae *(May Subd Geog)*
    ⌐QL568.M8¬
  UF Velvet ants
  BT Hymenoptera
      Wasps
  NT Sphaeropthalma
Mutilones
  USE Motilon Indians
Mutiny *(May Subd Geog)*
    ⌐UB787 (Military)¬
    ⌐VB860-VB867 (Naval)¬
  BT Insubordination
      Military offenses
      Naval offenses
  SA *particular mutinies, e.g.* Globe Mutiny,
      1824
  NT Trials (Mutiny)
  — **England**
      NT Newhaven Mutiny, 1795
  — **Great Britain**
      NT Étaples (France), Mutiny, 1917
  — **United States**
      NT Somers Mutiny, 1842
Mutisia
    ⌐QK495.C74¬
  BT Compositae
Mutism *(May Subd Geog)*
      Here are entered works on the inability to speak
    whether from any functional or physical cause other
    than deafness. Works on the lack of sense of hearing,
    including the lack combined with the inability to
    speak, i.e. deaf-mutism, are entered under Deafness.
  UF Dumbness
      Speechlessness
  BT Speech, Disorders of
  NT Mutism, Elective
Mutism, Akinetic *(May Subd Geog)*
    ⌐RC394.A43¬
  UF Akinetic mutism
      Apallic syndrome
  BT Brain stem—Diseases
      Movement disorders
      Neuropsychiatry
Mutism, Elective
    ⌐RJ506.M87¬
  UF Elective mutism
  BT Mentally ill children
      Mutism
      Psychology, Pathological
      Speech, Disorders of
Mutō family *(Not Subd Geog)*
Mutsugorō no dōbutsu ōkoku (Japan)
  USE Mutsugoro's Animal Kingdom (Japan)
Mutsugoro's Animal Kingdom (Japan)
    (Not Subd Geog)
  UF Animal Kingdom, Mutsugoro's (Japan)
      Mutsugorō no dōbutsu ōkoku (Japan)
  BT Menageries—Japan
Mutsun language
    ⌐PM1976-9¬
Muttarachas
  USE Muthurajas
Muttaraiyar
  BT Tamil Nadu (India)—History
Mutton
  BT Meat
      Sheep
  RT Lamb (Meat)
  NT Cookery (Lamb and mutton)

Mutton industry *(May Subd Geog)*
    ⌐HD9436¬
Mutual aid societies
  USE Friendly societies
Mutual arrangements
  USE Deals
Mutual benefit associations
  USE Friendly societies
Mutual defense assistance program
  USE Military assistance
      Mutual security program, 1951-
Mutual funds *(May Subd Geog)*
    ⌐HG4530-HG4930 (United States)¬
  UF Closed-end mutual funds
      Investment companies
      Investment trusts
      Open-end mutual funds
      Profit-sharing trusts
      Unit trusts
  BT Investments
  RT Investment clubs
  NT Face-amount certificate companies
      Money market funds
      Real estate investment trusts
Mutual housing
  USE Housing, Cooperative
Mutual inductance
    ⌐QC638¬
  BT Electric measurements
      Electrodynamics
      Electromagnetism
      Inductance
      Induction coils
Mutual insurance
  USE Insurance
Mutual intelligibility of related languages
  USE Languages, Modern—Mutual
        intelligibility
Mutual security program, 1951-
    ⌐UA12¬
  UF Mutual defense assistance program
  BT Security, International
  NT Economic assistance, American
      Military assistance, American
      Offshore procurement program, 1951-
      Technical assistance, American
  — **Appropriations and expenditures**
Mutualism
    ⌐HD2951-HD3570 (Economics)¬
    ⌐HM131 (Sociology)¬
  BT Cooperation
      Economics
      Socialism
Mutualism (Biology) *(May Subd Geog)*
    ⌐QH548.3¬
  BT Symbiosis
Mutz family
  USE Metz family
Mutze family
  USE Metz family
Muwāḥ ḥadis
  USE Almohades
Muwashshah
    ⌐PJ7542.M8 (Arabic poetry)¬
    ⌐PQ6056 (Spanish literature)¬
  UF Jarchas
      Jaryas
      Kharjas
      Markaz
      Tawshīh
  BT Mozarabic poetry
Muwisa (Wŏrha-ri, Sŏngjŏn-myŏn, Korea)
  — **Kungnakchŏn**
      UF Kungnakchŏn, Muwisa (Wŏrha-ri,
          Sŏngjŏn-myŏn, Korea)
      BT Temples, Buddhist—Korea (South)
Muxley family
  USE Moxley family
Muysca Indians
  USE Chibcha Indians

Muyu (New Guinea tribe)
  USE Muiu (New Guinea tribe)
Muyuw language
  UF Murua language
  BT Melanesian languages
Muzaffarids
  UF Mozaffarids
  BT Iran—History—640-1500
Muzo Indians
  BT Chibcha Indians
      Indians of South America
Muztagh-Karakoram
  USE Karakoram Range
Muztāgh River (Pakistan)
  UF Kelechin River (Pakistan)
      K'olo-ch'ung Ho (Pakistan)
      Shaksgam River (Pakistan)
  BT Rivers—Pakistan
Muzuk language
  USE Musgu language
Muzy family
  USE Muzzy family
Muzze family
  USE Muzzy family
Muzzey family
  USE Muzzy family
Muzzi family
  USE Muzzy family
Muzzle-loaders
  USE Muzzle-loading firearms
Muzzle-loading firearms
  UF Muzzle-loaders
  BT Firearms
  NT Kentucky rifle
Muzzles (Firearms)
  BT Firearms
  NT Silencers (Firearms)
Muzzy family *(Not Subd Geog)*
  UF Mussey family
      Muzy family
      Muzze family
      Muzzey family
      Muzzi family
MV Agusta motorcycle
  ₍TL448.M₎
  BT Motorcycles
      Motorcycles, Racing
MVP (Heart disease)
  USE Mitral valve—Displacement
MVS (Computer system)
  UF Multiple Virtual Storages (Computer
      system)
  BT IBM 360 (Computer)—Programming
      IBM 370 (Computer)—Programming
      Operating systems (Computers)
  NT WINDOWS (Computer program)
Mγt (The Hebrew root)
  UF Mût (The Hebrew root)
  BT Hebrew language—Roots
Mvuba (African people)
  USE Mamvu (African people)
Mwaba (African people)
  USE Moba (African people)
Mwamba language
  ₍PL8538₎
  UF Iki-kukwe language
      Swciri language
      Wanda language
  BT Bantu languages
      Ngonde language
Mwanabantu (African people)
  USE Safwa (African people)
Mwera language
  ₍PL8539₎
  BT Bantu languages
Mwere (African people)
  USE Meru (African people)
Mwila (Bantu people)
  UF Muila (Bantu people)
  BT Bantus
      Ethnology—Angola

MX (Weapons system)
  UF M-X missile
      MX missile
      Peacekeeper (Missile)
  BT Guided missiles
      Intercontinental ballistic missiles
      United States.   Air Force—Weapons
      systems
MX missile
  USE MX (Weapons system)
MY
  USE Miller-Yoder Language
      Comprehension Test
My Castle (Belgium)
  USE Château de My (Belgium)
Mya
  ₍QL430.7.M9₎
  BT Myidae
Mya arenaria
  ₍QL430.7.M9₎
  UF Long clam
      Soft-shell clam
Myacidae
  USE Myidae
Myalgia
  UF Muscle pain
      Muscular pain
      Myodynia
      Myosalgia
  BT Muscles—Diseases
      Pain
  NT Myalgic encephalomyelitis
Myalgic encephalomyelitis
  (May Subd Geog)
  ₍RC370₎
  UF Akureyri disease
      Benign myalgic encephalomyelitis
      Epidemic myalgic encephalomyelitis
      Epidemic neuromyasthenia
      Iceland disease
      Icelandic disease
      ME (Disease)
      Neuromyasthenia, Epidemic
      Post-viral fatique syndrome
  BT Encephalomyelitis
      Myalgia
      Neuromuscular diseases
      Virus diseases
Myall Lakes National Park (N.S.W.)
  BT National parks and reserves—Australia
Myang language
  USE Northern Thai language
Myars family
  USE Myers family
Myà's disease
  USE Hirschsprung's disease
Myas family
  USE Myers family
Myasthenia angiosclerotica
  USE Intermittent claudication
Myasthenia gravis
  BT Neuromuscular diseases
Mycelium
  ₍QK601₎
  NT Fungi—Hyphae
      Sclerotium (Mycelium)
Mycena (Ancient city)
  USE Mycenae (Ancient city)
Mycenae (Ancient city) *(Not Subd Geog)*
  ₍DF221.M9₎
  UF Mikínai (Ancient city)
      Mukenai (Ancient city)
      Mycena (Ancient city)
      Mycenes (Ancient city)
  BT Cities and towns, Ruined, extinct, etc.
      —Greece
      Greece—Antiquities
Mycenaean architecture
  USE Architecture, Mycenaean
Mycenaean arms and armor
  USE Arms and armor, Mycenaean

Mycenaean art
  USE Art, Mycenaean
Mycenaean civilization
  USE Civilization, Mycenaean
Mycenaean gods
  USE Gods, Mycenaean
Mycenaean goldwork
  USE Goldwork, Mycenaean
Mycenaean mural painting and decoration
  USE Mural painting and decoration,
      Mycenaean
Mycenaean Palace (Knossos)
  USE Palace of Knossos (Knossos)
Mycenaean pottery
  USE Pottery, Mycenaean
Mycenaean silverwork
  USE Silverwork, Mycenaean
Mycenaean vase-painting
  USE Vase-painting, Mycenaean
Mycenaean vases
  USE Vases, Mycenaean
Mycenes (Ancient city)
  USE Mycenae (Ancient city)
Mycetaeidae
  USE Endomychidae
Mycetoma *(May Subd Geog)*
  ₍RC168.M9₎
  UF Madura foot
      Maduromycosis
  BT Dermatomycoses
      Foot—Infections
Mycetophilidae
  ₍QL537.M92₎
  UF Bolitophilidae
      Diadocidiidae
      Ditomyiidae
      Fungivoridae
      Fungus gnats
      Keroplatidae
  BT Diptera
  NT Australosymmerus
      Symmerus
Mycetozoa
  USE Myxomycetes
MYCIN (Computer system)
  ₍QR46₎
Mycobacteria
  ₍QR82.M8₎
  UF Mycobacteriaceae
  RT Mycobacterial diseases
  NT Mycobacteria, Atypical
      Mycobacterium
— **Identification**
  RT Ziehl-Neelsen stain
Mycobacteria, Anonymous
  USE Mycobacteria, Atypical
Mycobacteria, Atypical
  ₍QR82.M8₎
  UF Anonymous mycobacteria
      Atypical mycobacteria
      Mycobacteria, Anonymous
      Mycobacteria, Unclassified
      Unclassified mycobacteria
  BT Mycobacteria
  NT Mycobacterial diseases
      Mycobacterium marinum
      Mycobacterium phlei
Mycobacteria, Unclassified
  USE Mycobacteria, Atypical
Mycobacteriaceae
  USE Mycobacteria
Mycobacterial diseases *(May Subd Geog)*
  ₍RC116.M8₎
  UF Mycobacterial infections
      Mycobacterioses
  BT Bacterial diseases
      Mycobacteria, Atypical
  RT Mycobacteria
  NT Leprosy
      Tuberculosis

Mycobacterial infections
  USE Mycobacterial diseases
Mycobacterioses
  USE Mycobacterial diseases
Mycobacterium
  BT Mycobacteria
Mycobacterium agreste
  USE Nocardia corallina
Mycobacterium balnei
  USE Mycobacterium marinum
Mycobacterium marinum
  ⌈QR82.M8⌉
  UF Mycobacterium balnei
      Mycobacterium platypoecilus
  BT Mycobacteria, Atypical
Mycobacterium phlei
  BT Mycobacteria, Atypical
Mycobacterium platypoecilus
  USE Mycobacterium marinum
Mycobacterium tuberculosis
  RT Tuberculin
Mycogenetics
  USE Fungi—Genetics
Mycologists *(May Subd Geog)*
  BT Mycology
Mycology
  BT Botany
      Microbiology
  RT Fungi
  NT Medical mycology
      Mycologists
      Veterinary mycology
  — Catalogs and collections
      UF Fungi—Catalogs and collections
  — Cultures and culture media
      USE Fungi—Cultures and culture
          media
Mycoplasma diseases
  BT Medical microbiology
  NT Mycoplasma diseases in plants
Mycoplasma diseases in animals
  (May Subd Geog)
  ⌈SF809.M9⌉
  BT Veterinary microbiology
Mycoplasma diseases in plants
  (May Subd Geog)
  ⌈SB737⌉
  BT Mycoplasma diseases
      Mycoplasmatales
      Plant diseases
  NT Cotton phyllody
Mycoplasma-like diseases of plants
  (May Subd Geog)
  ⌈SB738⌉
  BT Plant diseases
  RT Mycoplasma-like organisms,
      Phytopathogenic
Mycoplasma-like organisms
  (May Subd Geog)
  RT Mycoplasmatales
Mycoplasma-like organisms, Phytopathogenic
  (May Subd Geog)
  ⌈SB738 (Plant diseases)⌉
  UF Phytopathogenic mycoplasma-like
      organisms
  BT Micro-organisms, Phytopathogenic
      Plant parasites
  RT Mycoplasma-like diseases of plants
Mycoplasmas
  USE Mycoplasmatales
Mycoplasmatales
  ⌈QR352⌉
  UF Mycoplasmas
      Pleuropneumonia-like organisms
  BT Micro-organisms
      Pleuropneumonia
  RT Mycoplasma-like organisms
  NT Mycoplasma diseases in plants
Mycorhiza
  USE Mycorrhiza

Mycorrhiza *(May Subd Geog)*
  ⌈QK604 (Mycology)⌉
  ⌈QK918 (Botany)⌉
  UF Mycorhiza
  BT Symbiosis
  RT Roots (Botany)
      Soil fungi
  NT Ectomycorrhiza
      Endomycorrhiza
Mycorrhizal plants *(May Subd Geog)*
  ⌈QK918⌉
  BT Plants
Mycoses *(May Subd Geog)*
  ⌈RC117⌉
  UF Fungal diseases
      Fungous diseases
      Mycotic diseases
  RT Antifungal agents
      Fungi, Pathogenic
      Medical mycology
  NT Blastomycosis
      Candidiasis
      Coccidioidomycosis
      Dermatomycoses
      Histoplasmosis
      Hyphomycosis
      Lungs—Diseases, Fungal
      Mucormycosis
      Mycotoxicoses
      Paracoccidioidomycosis
      Rhinosporidiosis
      Sporotrichosis
      Torulosis
Mycosis fungoides *(May Subd Geog)*
  UF Fungoid mycosis
      Granuloma fungoides
  BT Lymphoproliferative disorders
Mycosphaerella *(May Subd Geog)*
  ⌈QK623.D72⌉
  BT Dothideaceae
Mycostatin
  USE Nystatin
Mycotic diseases
  USE Mycoses
Mycotic skin diseases
  USE Dermatomycoses
Mycotoxic fungi
  USE Toxigenic fungi
Mycotoxicoses *(May Subd Geog)*
  ⌈RA1250⌉
  UF Fungi—Toxicology
      Mycotoxins—Toxicology
      Toxigenic fungi—Toxicology
  BT Mycoses
      Poisoning
  RT Mycotoxins
  NT Ergotism
      Mushrooms, Poisonous—Toxicology
Mycotoxicoses in animals *(May Subd Geog)*
  BT Veterinary mycology
      Veterinary toxicology
Mycotoxigenic fungi
  USE Toxigenic fungi
Mycotoxin-producing fungi
  USE Toxigenic fungi
Mycotoxins
  UF Fungal toxins
  BT Fungal metabolites
      Microbial toxins
  RT Mycotoxicoses
      Toxigenic fungi
  NT Aflatoxins
      Amanitins
      Cytochalasins
      Phalloidine
      Trichothecenes
  — Physiological effect
      NT Plants, Effect of mycotoxins on
  — Synthesis
  — Toxicology
      USE Mycotoxicoses

Mycotrophy
  BT Fungi
      Plants—Nutrition
Mycotrupes
  ⌈QL596.S3⌉
  BT Scarabaeidae
Mycoviruses
  USE Fungal viruses
Mycteria americana
  USE Wood stork
Mycteroperca microlepis
  USE Gag (Fish)
Mycterosaurus
  ⌈QE862.P3⌉
  BT Varanopsidae
Mycterosaurus longiceps
  ⌈QE862.P3⌉
Myctophidae
  USE Lantern-fishes
Myctophiformes
  ⌈QL637.9.M93⌉
  UF Iniomi
  BT Osteichthyes
  NT Anotopteridae
      Evermannellidae
      Harpadontidae
      Lantern-fishes
      Notosudidae
      Scopelarchidae
      Synodontidae
Mydaidae
  USE Mydidae
Mydas
  ⌈QL537.M93⌉
  BT Mydidae
Mydasidae
  USE Mydidae
Myddelton family
  USE Middleton family
Myddleton family
  USE Middleton family
Mydidae
  ⌈QL537.M93⌉
  UF Midasidae
      Mydaidae
      Mydasidae
  BT Diptera
  NT Mydas
Mydon family
  USE Mitten family
Mydopholeus
  ⌈QL458.2.R66⌉
  BT Rosensteiniidae
  NT Mydopholeus capillus
Mydopholeus capillus
  ⌈QL458.2.R66⌉
  BT Mydopholeus
Mydriatics
  ⌈RE994-7⌉
  BT Materia medica, Ophthalmological
  NT Atropine
      Belladonna
      Homatropin
Myelin sheath
  ⌈QP752.M9 (Biochemistry)⌉
  ⌈RC366 (Neuropathology)⌉
  UF Medullary sheath (Nerve tissue)
      Schwann's white substance
      White substance of Schwann
  BT Cell membranes
      Lipoproteins
      Nerve tissue
  RT Myelination
  NT Myelinated neurofibrils
  — Diseases *(May Subd Geog)*
      NT Demyelination
          Multiple sclerosis
Myelin sheath formation
  USE Myelination
Myelinated neurofibrils
  ⌈QM575⌉

UF Medullated nerve fibers
      Nerve fibers, Myelinated
BT Myelin sheath
      Neurofibrils

Myelination
  UF Myelin sheath formation
      Myelinization
      Myelinogenesis
  RT Demyelination
      Myelin sheath

Myelinization
  USE Myelination

Myelinoclasia
  USE Encephalomyelitis

Myelinogenesis
  USE Myelination

Myelitis
  USE Spinal cord—Inflammation

Myelocytic leukemia *(May Subd Geog)*
  BT Bone marrow—Diseases
      Nonlymphoid leukemia

Myelofibrosis *(May Subd Geog)*
    [*RC645.76*]
  UF Myelosclerosis
  BT Myeloproliferative disorders

Myelogram
  USE Myelography

Myelographic cisternography
  USE Myelography

Myelography
    [*RC402.2.M94*]
  UF Cisternography, Myelographic
      Myelogram
      Myelographic cisternography
  BT Contrast media
      Spinal cord—Radiography
  NT Pneumomyelography

Myeloid metaplasia *(May Subd Geog)*
  UF Agnogenic myeloid metaplasia
      Aleukemic myelosis
      Leukoerythroblastic anemia
      Nonleukemic myelosis
      Symptomatic myeloid metaplasia
  BT Anemia
      Metaplasia
      Myeloproliferative disorders

Myelois venipars
  USE Navel orangeworm

Myeloma proteins
  BT Tumor proteins
  NT Immunoglobulin idiotypes

Myeloma-spleen cell hybrids
  USE Hybridomas

Myelomeningocele
  UF Meningomyelocele
      Spina bifida cystica
  BT Spina bifida

Myelooticoneuropathy, Subacute
  USE Subacute myelooptic neuropathy

Myeloproliferative disorders
  (May Subd Geog)
    [*RC645.75-RC645.76*]
  UF Myeloproliferative syndrome
  BT Bone marrow—Diseases
  NT Myelofibrosis
      Myeloid metaplasia
      Polycythemia

Myeloproliferative syndrome
  USE Myeloproliferative disorders

Myelosclerosis
  USE Myelofibrosis

Myene (African people)
    [*DT546.145.M93*]
  UF Ngwemyene (African people)
      Omyene (African people)
  BT Ethnology—Gabon
  NT Galwa (African people)
      Mpongwe (African people)
      Orungu (African people)

Myenteric plexus
  UF Auerbach's plexus

BT Ganglia, Autonomic
      Intestines

Myer family
  USE Myers family

Myers-Briggs Type Indicator
    [*BF698.8.M94 (Psychology)*]
  UF MBTI (Personality test)
  BT Personality tests
      Typology (Psychology)

Myers family *(Not Subd Geog)*
  UF Maher family
      Mair family
      Maire family
      Maires family
      Mairs family
      Mares family
      Mayer family
      Mayers family
      Mayhr family
      Mayor family
      Mayors family
      Meier family
      Meyer family
      Meyers family
      Meyor family
      Meyors family
      Mhire family
      Miar family
      Miars family
      Mier family
      Miers family
      Mire family
      Mires family
      Myars family
      Myas family
      Myer family
      Myor family
      Myre family
      Myres family
      Myrs family
  RT Moyer family

Myesthesia
  USE Muscular sense

Myhra family
  USE Myhre family

Myhre family *(Not Subd Geog)*
  UF Myhra family

Myiarchus
    [*QL696.P289*]
  BT Tyrannidae

Myiasis
  BT Ectoparasitic infestations

Myidae
    [*QL430.7.M9*]
  UF Myacidae
  BT Clams
      Myoida
  NT Mya

Myill family
  USE Mills family

Myiochanes virens
  USE Wood pewee

Myiozetetes
    [*QL696.P289*]
  BT Tyrannidae

Myiozetetes luteiventris
    [*QL696.P289*]

Myitis
  USE Myositis

Myitkyinā (Burma), Battle of, 1944
  BT World War, 1939-1945—Campaigns—
      Burma

Mykonos Island (Greece)
  UF Míkonos Island (Greece)
      Nísos Míkonos (Greece)
  BT Cyclades (Greece)
      Islands—Greece

Mylabridae
  USE Bruchidae

Mylabris
  USE Bruchus

Myles family
  USE Miles family

Mylin family *(Not Subd Geog)*
  UF Meili family

Myliobatidae
    [*QL638.85.M9*]
  UF Aetobatidae
      Bat rays
      Eagle rays
  BT Rajiformes
      Rays (Fishes)
      Stingrays
  NT Aetobatus

Myll family
  USE Mills family

Mylles family
  USE Mills family

Mylne family
  USE Milne family

Mylne's Court (Edinburgh, Lothian)
  BT Dormitories—Scotland
      Dwellings—Scotland

Mylonite *(May Subd Geog)*
    [*QE475.M95*]

Mymaridae
    [*QL568.M94*]
  UF Fairyflies
  BT Chalcid wasps
      Hymenoptera

Mynahs
    [*QL795.B57*]
  UF Mynas
  BT Blackbirds
      Starlings
      Sturnidae
  NT Leucopsar

Mynas
  USE Mynahs

Myner family
  USE Minor family

Mynyfie family
  USE Menefee family

Myobatrachidae
    [*QL668.E2615*]
  BT Anura
      Frogs

Myocardial contraction
  USE Heart—Contraction

Myocardial depressants
    [*RM347*]
  UF Antiarrhythmia agents
      Antifibrillatory agents
      Cardiac inotropic agents, Negative
      Defibrillatory agents
      Inotropic agents, Negative cardiac
      Negative cardiac inotropic agents
  BT Cardiovascular agents
  NT Aconite
      Amiodarone
      Bretylium tosylate
      Disopyramide
      Fendiline
      Gallopamil
      Mexiletine
      Nadolol
      Perhexiline
      Phenytoin
      Propafenone
      Quinidine
      Sparteine
      Timolol maleate

Myocardial diseases
  USE Heart—Muscle—Diseases

Myocardial infarction
  USE Heart—Infarction

Myocardial metabolism
  USE Heart—Metabolism

Myocardial revascularization
    [*RD598*]
  UF Revascularization, Myocardial

Myocardial revascularization *(Continued)*
  BT Coronary heart disease—Surgery
        Heart—Surgery
  NT Aortocoronary bypass
Myocardial stimulants
  USE Cardiotonic agents
Myocardioplasty
  USE Cardiomyoplasty
Myocarditis *(May Subd Geog)*
  [RC685.M9]
  UF Heart—Muscle—Inflammation
  BT Heart—Muscle—Diseases
        Myositis
Myocardium
  USE Heart—Muscle
Myocastor
  [QL737.R668]
  BT Myocastoridae
Myocastor coypus
  USE Coypu
Myocastoridae
  [QL737.R668]
  BT Rodents
  NT Myocastor
Myochrous
  [QL596.C5]
  BT Chrysomelidae
Myoclonic epilepsy, Infantile
  USE Spasms, Infantile
Myoclonic seizures
  USE Myoclonus
Myoclonus
  UF Myoclonic seizures
  BT Epilepsy
        Spasms
  — **Genetic aspects**
Myocoptidae
  [QL458.2.M93]
  BT Mites
Myocytes
  USE Muscle cells
Myodites
  USE Rhipiphorus
Myodocarpa
  USE Myodocopida
Myodochidae
  USE Lygaeidae
Myodocopa
  USE Myodocopida
Myodocopida
  [QL444.O85]
  UF Myodocarpa
        Myodocopa
        Myodocopina
  BT Ostracoda
  NT Cylindroleberididae
        Cypridinidae
        Halocyprididae
        Philomedidae
        Polycopidae
        Rutidermatidae
        Sarsiellidae
        Thaumatocyprididae
Myodocopida, Fossil
  [QE817.O8]
  BT Ostracoda, Fossil
  NT Thaumatocyprididae, Fossil
Myodocopina
  USE Myodocopida
Myodynamics
  USE Muscles
Myodynia
  USE Myalgia
Myodystrophia fetalis deformans
  USE Arthrogryposis
Myoelectric prosthesis
  UF Myoelectrically controlled prosthesis
  BT Biomedical engineering
        Prosthesis
Myoelectrically controlled prosthesis
  USE Myoelectric prosthesis

Myofilaments
  USE Cytoplasmic filaments
Myogenesis
  BT Embryology
Myōgi Mountain (Japan)
  UF Myogi-san (Japan)
  BT Mountains—Japan
Myogi-san (Japan)
  USE Myōgi Mountain (Japan)
Myoglobin
  UF Myohemoglobin
  BT Blood proteins
        Hemoproteins
        Muscle proteins
Myoglobinuria
  BT Muscles—Diseases
        Physiology, Pathological
Myohemoglobin
  USE Myoglobin
Myohyang Mountain (Korea)
  UF Myohyang-san (Korea)
        Myohyangsan (Korea)
  BT Mountains—Korea (North)
Myohyang-san (Korea)
  USE Myohyang Mountain (Korea)
Myohyangsan (Korea)
  USE Myohyang Mountain (Korea)
Myoida *(May Subd Geog)*
  [QL430.6]
  BT Bivalvia
  NT Myidae
Myoida, Fossil
  [QE812.P]
  BT Bivalvia, Fossil
Myoinositol
  USE Inositol
Myōkōnin
  BT Shin (Sect)
Myology
  USE Muscles
Myoma
  USE Muscles—Tumors
Myoma previum
  USE Leiomyoma uteri
Myōmae Site (Japan) *(Not Subd Geog)*
  BT Japan—Antiquities
Myometrium
  UF Uterine muscle
  BT Muscles
        Uterus
  — **Tumors** *(May Subd Geog)*
    NT Leiomyoma uteri
Myoneural blocking agents
  USE Neuromuscular blocking agents
Myoneural junction
  UF Motor end plate
        Neuromuscular end plate
        Neuromuscular junction
  BT Muscles
        Nerve endings
        Nerves
Myŏng-dong (Seoul, Korea)
  BT Streets—Korea (South)
Myŏngsŏng Group
  BT Conglomerate corporations—Korea
        (South)
Myonycteris *(May Subd Geog)*
  [QL737.C575]
  UF Collared fruit bats, Little
        Fruit bats, Little collared
        Little collared fruit bats
  BT Pteropidae
Myonycteris relicta *(May Subd Geog)*
  [QL737.C575]
  UF Collared fruit bat, Relict
        Fruit bat, Relict collared
        Relict collared fruit bat
Myopathy
  USE Muscles—Diseases
Myophoria
  BT Myophoriidae

Myophoriidae *(Not Subd Geog)*
  BT Trigonioida, Fossil
  NT Myophoria
Myopia
  [RE938]
  UF Nearsightedness
        Short-sightedness
        Shortsightedness
  BT Eye—Refractive errors
Myoporaceae
  [QK495.M8 (Botany)]
  BT Tubiflorae
  NT Eremophila
        Myoporum
Myoporum
  [QK495.M8]
  BT Myoporaceae
Myopotamus coypus
  USE Coypu
Myopus
  [QL737.R638]
  BT Cricetidae
Myopus schisticolor
  USE Wood lemming
Myor family
  USE Myers family
Myosalgia
  USE Myalgia
Myosin
  BT Globulin
        Muscle proteins
Myositis
  UF Muscles—Inflammation
        Myitis
  BT Inflammation
        Muscles—Diseases
        Nonarticular rheumatism
  NT Dermatomyositis
        Myocarditis
        Polymyositis
Myositis purulenta tropica
  USE Myositis tropica
Myositis tropica
  UF Muma
        Myositis purulenta tropica
  BT Muscles—Diseases
Myotatic reflex
  USE Stretch reflex
Myotis
  [QL737.C595]
  BT Vespertilionidae
  NT Myotis californicus
        Myotis grisescens
        Myotis lucifugus
        Myotis sodalis
        Myotis velifer
        Myotis vivesi
Myotis californicus
  [QL737.C595]
  UF California myotis
  BT Myotis
Myotis grisescens
  [QL737.C595]
  UF Gray bat
  BT Myotis
Myotis leucifugus
  USE Myotis lucifugus
Myotis lucifugus
  [QL737.C595]
  UF Little brown bat
        Little brown myotis
        Myotis leucifugus
  BT Myotis
Myotis sodalis
  [QL737.C595]
  UF Indiana bat
        Indiana myotis
  BT Myotis
Myotis velifer
  [QL737.C595]
  UF Cave myotis

BT Myotis
Myotis vivesi
[QL737.C595]
UF American fish-eating bat
Fish-eating bat
Fishing bat
Pizonyx vivesi
BT Myotis
Myotonia
[RC935.M95 (Internal medicine)]
[RD688 (Surgery)]
BT Muscles—Diseases
Myotonia atrophica
UF Deleage's disease
Dystrophia myotonica
Myotonic dystrophy
Steinert's disease
BT Neuromuscular diseases
Myotonia congenita
UF Amyotonia congenita
Eulenburg's disease
Myotonia hereditaria
Paramyotonia congenita
Thomsen's disease
BT Neuromuscular diseases
Myotonia hereditaria
USE Myotonia congenita
Myotonic dystrophy
USE Myotonia atrophica
Myoxus glis
USE Edible dormouse
Myra (Ancient city) *(Not Subd Geog)*
BT Cities and towns, Ruined, extinct, etc.
—Turkey
Turkey—Antiquities
Myrceugenia
[QK495.M9]
BT Myrtaceae
Myrcia oil
USE Bay oil
Mýrdalsjökull (Iceland)
BT Glaciers—Iceland
Myre family
USE Myers family
Myrelaion (Istanbul, Turkey)
BT Architecture, Byzantine—Turkey
Churches—Turkey
Myres family
USE Myers family
Myriapoda *(May Subd Geog)*
[QL449]
UF Myriopoda
BT Arthropoda
NT Centipedes
Colobognatha
Millepeds
Pauropoda
— Development
NT Ecdysis
Myrica
[QK495.M83]
UF Bayberries
Cerothamnus
Morella
Waxmyrtles
BT Myricaceae
Myrica faya
[QK495.M83 (Botany)]
[SB615.M94 (Weed)]
UF Canary Islands waxmyrtle
Candleberry myrtle
Firetree
Myrtle, Candleberry
Waxmyrtle, Canary Islands
BT Weeds
Myricaceae
[QK495.M83]
BT Juglandales
NT Myrica
Myrick family
USE Merrick family

Myridae
USE Snake eels
Xenocongridae
Myridium
USE Laetinaevia
Myringoplasty *(May Subd Geog)*
[RF126]
BT Surgery, Plastic
Tympanic membrane—Surgery
Tympanoplasty
Myriophyllum spicatum
USE Eurasian watermilfoil
Myriopoda
USE Myriapoda
Myripristidae
USE Squirrelfishes
Myripristis
[QL638.H64]
BT Squirrelfishes
Myristica
[QK495.M85]
BT Myristicaceae
Myristica fragrans
USE Nutmeg
Myristica officinalis
USE Nutmeg
Myristicaceae
[QK495.M85]
BT Magnoliales
NT Myristica
Myrmarachne
[QL458.42.S24]
BT Jumping spiders
Myrmecia *(May Subd Geog)*
[QL568.F7]
UF Bulldog ants
BT Ants
Myrmecobiidae
USE Numbat
Myrmecobius fasciatus
USE Numbat
Myrmecobius rufus
USE Numbat
Myrmecocystus
USE Honey-ants
Myrmecocystus melliger
[QL568.F7]
Myrmecodema
[QL596.T2]
UF Myrmecosoma
BT Tenebrionidae
Myrmecophaga
[QL737.E24]
UF Ant bear
Anteater, Giant
Anteater, Great
Giant anteater
Great anteater
Tamanoir
BT Myrmecophagidae
Myrmecophagidae
[QL737.E24]
UF American anteaters
Anteaters, American
BT Edentata
NT Myrmecophaga
Tamandua
Myrmecophila
[QL508.M9]
BT Crickets
Myrmecophilous plants
UF Plants, Myrmecophilous
BT Ants
Botany
Plants
Symbiosis
Myrmecophyes
[QL523.M5]
BT Miridae
Myrmecophyes oregonensis
[QL523.M5]

Myrmecosoma
USE Myrmecodema
Myrmeleon
[QL513.M9]
BT Ant lions
Myrmeleonidae
USE Ant lions
Myrmeleontidae
USE Ant lions
Myrmosidae
[QL568.M97]
BT Hymenoptera
Myrobalan, Belleric
USE Belleric myrobalan
Myrobalan, Black
USE Terminalia chebula
Myrobalan, Chebulic
USE Terminalia chebula
Myrobalan, Indian almond
USE Terminalia catappa
Myrobalan plum
USE Cherry plum
Myron
USE Chrism
Myrophidae
USE Snake eels
Myrothamnaceae
USE Myrothamnus
Myrothamnus
[QK495.M86 (Botany)]
UF Myrothamnaceae
BT Rosales
Myrrh
Myrrhidendron
[QK495.U48]
BT Umbelliferae
Myrs family
USE Myers family
Myrsidea
[QL540.3.M4]
BT Menoponidae
Myrsinaceae *(May Subd Geog)*
[QK495.M87 (Botany)]
BT Primulales
NT Cybianthus
Myrtaceae
[QK495.M9 (Botany)]
BT Myrtales
NT Callistemon
Eucalyptus
Melaleuca
Metrosideros
Myrceugenia
Psidium
Myrtales
[QK495.A12 (Botany)]
UF Myrtiflorae
BT Dicotyledons
NT Combretaceae
Lecythidaceae
Lythraceae
Melastomataceae
Myrtaceae
Onagraceae
Myrtales, Fossil
[QE983]
BT Dicotyledons, Fossil
NT Onagraceae, Fossil
Myrtiflorae
USE Myrtales
Myrtle, Candleberry
USE Myrica faya
Myrtle (Jewish cultus)
USE Myrtle (Sukkot)
Myrtle (Sukkot)
UF Myrtle (Jewish cultus)
BT Judaism—Liturgical objects
Myrtle whortleberry
USE Vaccinium myrtillus
Mys Pitsunda (Georgian S.S.R.)
USE Pitsunda Cape (Georgian S.S.R.)

Mysaleles
USE Capromys
Myse family
USE Mize family
Myser family
USE Meisser family
Mysian language
[P1054.5]
UF Daco-Mysian language
BT Anatolian languages
RT Dacian language
Mysidacea *(May Subd Geog)*
[QL444.M35]
UF Opossum shrimps
BT Crustacea
NT Mysidae
Mysidae
[QL444.M35]
BT Mysidacea
NT Mysis
Mysis
[QL444.M35]
BT Mysidae
Mysis relicta
[QL444.M35]
Mysmenidae
[QL458.42.M97]
BT Spiders
NT Mysmenopsis
Mysmenopsis
[QL458.42.M97]
UF Lucarachne
BT Mysmenidae
Mysore War, 1790-1792
USE India—History—Mysore War, 1790-
1792
Mysore War, 1799
USE India—History—Mysore War, 1799
Mystacocarida
[QL444.M]
BT Entomostraca
Mysteries, Religious
[BL610 (Comparative religion)]
[HS491 (Freemasonry and ancient
mysteries)]
UF Religious mysteries
BT Religion
Secret societies
RT Rites and ceremonies
NT Cabiri
Eleusinian mysteries
Mother-goddesses
Oracles
Mysteries, Religious, in art
Mysteries (Dramatic)
USE Mysteries and miracle-plays
Mysteries and miracle-plays
[PN1761 (History and criticism)]
UF Bible—Drama
Bible—History of Biblical events—
Drama
Miracle-plays
Mysteries (Dramatic)
Saint plays
Saint's plays
BT Drama
Easter—Drama
Pageants
Passion-plays
Religious drama
Theater
RT Drama, Medieval
Liturgical drama
Moralities
NT Bible plays
Mysteries and miracle-plays, Cornish
(May Subd Geog)
UF Cornish miracle-plays
Cornish mysteries and miracle-plays
BT Cornish drama

Mysteries and miracle-plays, English
(May Subd Geog)
UF English miracle-plays
English mysteries and miracle-plays
BT English drama
**Mysteries and miracle-plays, English, [French,
German, etc.]**
Duplicate entry is made under English [French,
German, etc.] drama—To 1500
Mysteries and miracle-plays, French
(May Subd Geog)
UF French miracle-plays
French mysteries and miracle-plays
BT French drama
Mysteries and miracle-plays, Hungarian
(May Subd Geog)
UF Hungarian miracle-plays
Hungarian mysteries and miracle-plays
BT Hungarian drama
Mysteries and miracle-plays, Italian
(May Subd Geog)
UF Italian miracle-plays
Italian mysteries and miracle-plays
BT Italian drama
Mysteries and miracle-plays, Provençal
(May Subd Geog)
UF Provençal miracle-plays
Provençal mysteries and miracle-plays
BT Provençal drama
Mysteries of the Rosary
[BT303]
BT Jesus Christ—Biography
Mary, Blessed Virgin, Saint—
Biography
Rosary
Mysterion (The Greek word)
BT Greek language—Etymology
Mysterium (The Latin word)
BT Latin language—Etymology
Mystery
[BT127.5]
BT Revelation
Mystery and detective television programs
USE Detective and mystery television
programs
Mystery plays (Modern)
USE Detective and mystery plays
Mystery stories
USE Adventure and adventurers
Detective and mystery stories
Mystic marriage of Saint Catherine (Painting)
USE Correggio, 1489?-1534. Mystic
marriage of Saint Catherine
Mystic medicine
USE Medicine, Magic, mystic, and spagiric
Mystic River (Mass.)
UF Mytic River (Mass.)
BT Rivers—Massachusetts
Mystic union
USE Mystical union
Mystical body of Christ
USE Jesus Christ—Mystical body
Mystical-magic thinking
USE Magical thinking
Mystical theology
USE Mysticism—Catholic Church,
[Orthodox Eastern Church, etc.]
Mysticism
Mystical union
[BT769]
Here are entered works on the relationship be-
tween God and the individual Christian at the highest
level of mystical experience. Works on the Christian
doctrine that the church is the mystical body of
Christ are entered under Jesus Christ—Mystical
body.
UF God and man, Mystical union of
Indwelling of God
Mystic union
Unio mystica
Union, Mystical
Union with Christ

BT Immanence of God
Mysticism
NT Adoption (Theology)
Children of God
Temple of God
Mysticism *(May Subd Geog)*
[B728 (Medieval philosophy)]
[B828 (Modern philosophy)]
[BL625 (Comparative religion)]
[BV5070-BV5095 (Christianity)]
UF Dark night of the soul
Mystical theology
Theology, Mystical
BT Spiritual life
RT Mystics
NT Alumbrados
Christian art and symbolism
Contemplation
Depersonalization—Religious aspects
Illuminati
Mystical union
Perfection
Private revelations
Quietism
Rosicrucians
Symbolism of numbers
Tantrism
— **Brahmanism, [Judaism, Nestorian
Church, etc.]**
— **Buddhism**
BT Buddhism—Doctrines
— **Catholic Church, [Orthodox Eastern
Church, etc.]**
UF Theology, Mystical
— **Hinduism**
[BL1215.M9]
UF Hindu mysticism
BT Hinduism
Mysticism—India
NT Ecstasy (Hinduism)
Om (Hinduism)
Samadhi
— **History**
UF Mysticism—History of doctrines
— — **Early church, ca. 30-600**
[BV5075]
BT Church history—Primitive and
early church, ca. 30-600
— — **Middle Ages, 600-1500**
[BV5075]
BT Church history—Middle Ages,
600-1500
NT Devotio moderna
— History of doctrines
USE Mysticism—History
— **Islam** *(May Subd Geog)*
[BP189]
UF Islamic mysticism
Muslim mysticism
BT Islam—Doctrines
Islamic religious practice
NT Barakah
Sufism
— **Jainism**
[BL1378.8]
UF Jaina mysticism
BT Jainism
NT Samadhi (Jainism)
— **Judaism**
BT Judaism
NT Dybbuk
Ecstasy (Judaism)
Golem
Hasidism
Merkava
— **Orthodox Eastern Church**
NT Hesychasm
— **Sikhism** *(May Subd Geog)*
[BL2018.43]
UF Sikh mysticism
NT Om (Sikhism)

— Zoroastrianism
  [BL1590.M9]
  UF Zoroastrian mysticism
  BT Zoroastrianism
— India
  NT Mandala
     Mysticism—Hinduism
— Indonesia
  NT Sawito Affair, Indonesia, 1976
Mysticism and art (May Subd Geog)
  [N72.M85]
  UF Art and mysticism
  BT Art
Mysticism and literature
  UF Literature and mysticism
  BT Religion and literature
Mysticism and poetry
  UF Poetry and mysticism
Mysticism in literature
  [PN49]
  [PR145 (English literature)]
  NT Chayavada
Mystics (May Subd Geog)
  [BV5095]
  BT Religious biography
  RT Mysticism
  NT Women mystics
Mystics, Women
  USE Women mystics
Mystifications, Literary
  USE Literary forgeries and mystifications
Mystique of sin
  Here are entered works on the idea that sin and
  evil are a necessary stage in the development of a
  mature human life.
  UF Sin mysticism
  BT Sin
Myszyniecka Puszcza (Poland)
  USE Kurpiowska Forest (Poland)
Myth
  BT Demythologization
     God
     Gods
     Religion
  RT Mythology
Myth in literature
  [PN56.M94]
  Here are entered works dealing with the use in
  literature of stories invented as a veiled explanation
  of a truth. Works concerning the use in literature of
  traditional or legendary themes are entered under
  Mythology in literature.
  NT Demythologization (Literature)
Myth in motion pictures
  BT Moving-pictures
Myth in the Bible
  [BS520.5]
  UF Bible—Mythology
  RT Demythologization
  NT Myth in the Old Testament
Myth in the Old Testament
  [BS1183]
  UF Bible. O.T.—Mythology
  BT Demythologization
     Myth in the Bible
     Mythology
Myth of the cave (Allegory)
  USE Plato's cave (Allegory)
Mythe family
Mythen family
  USE Mitten family
Mythical animals
  USE Animals, Mythical
Mythical places
  USE Geographical myths
Mythology
  [BL300-BL325 (Comparative)]
  UF Myths

BT Archaeology
   God
   Legends
   Religion
   Religions
RT Folklore
   Gods
   Heroes
   Myth
SA *subdivision* Mythology *under subjects;*
   and subdivision Religion and
   mythology *under the headings*
   Indians, Indians of North America,
   and similar headings; and under
   individual Indian tribes
NT Animals, Mythical
   Art and mythology
   Curetes
   Dryads
   Furies
   Geographical myths
   Gorgons
   Healing gods
   Mother-goddesses
   Mountain-gods
   Myth in the Old Testament
   Rainbow serpent
   Religion, Primitive
   Sacred marriage (Mythology)
   Sirens (Mythology)
   Sky-gods
   Sphinxes (Mythology)
   Symbolism
   Titans (Mythology)
   Totemism
   Tutelaries (Shinto)
   Water spirits
   Wind gods
— Dictionaries
  [BL303]
  UF Gods—Dictionaries
Mythology, African
  NT Mythology, East African
     Mythology, West African
Mythology, Arctic (May Subd Geog)
  UF Arctic mythology
  BT Arctic races
Mythology, Armenian, [Dravidian, Egyptian,
etc.]
Mythology, Asian (May Subd Geog)
  UF Asian mythology
Mythology, Assyro-Babylonian
  UF Assyro-Babylonian mythology
     Babylonian mythology
     Mythology, Babylonian
  BT Mythology, Semitic
Mythology, Australian aboriginal
  UF Australian aborigines—Mythology
     Australian mythology
Mythology, Aztec
  USE Aztecs—Religion and mythology
Mythology, Babylonian
  USE Mythology, Assyro-Babylonian
Mythology, Balinese (May Subd Geog)
  UF Balinese mythology
Mythology, Baltic
  [BL945]
  UF Latvian mythology
     Lithuanian mythology
     Mythology, Latvian
     Mythology, Lithuanian
     Mythology, Prussian (Baltic tribe)
     Mythology, Yatvyag
     Prussian mythology (Baltic tribe)
     Yatvyag mythology
Mythology, Basa (Cameroon people)
  [BL2480.B337]
  UF Basa (Cameroon people) mythology
Mythology, Basque
  UF Basque mythology

Mythology, Bolivian (May Subd Geog)
  UF Bolivian mythology
Mythology, Boma (May Subd Geog)
  UF Boma mythology
Mythology, Brahman
  USE Mythology, Hindu
     Vedas
Mythology, British
  UF British mythology
  NT Mythology, Welsh
Mythology, Buddhist (May Subd Geog)
  [BQ5741-5755]
  UF Buddhist mythology
Mythology, Bulgarian
  USE Mythology, Slavic
Mythology, Canaanite
  UF Canaanite mythology
Mythology, Celtic
  BT Druids and Druidism
Mythology, Chinese
  NT Hayagrīva
     Mythology, Taoist
Mythology, Classical
  [BL700-820]
  UF Classical mythology
  BT Classical antiquities
  SA *names of mythological persons and*
     objects
  NT Centaurs
     Curetes
     Furies
     Geryon (Classical mythology)
     Gods
     Golden age (Mythology)
     Gorgons
     Heroes
     Midas
     Mythology, Greek
     Mythology, Roman
     Sirens (Mythology)
     Sphinxes (Mythology)
     Titans (Mythology)
Mythology, Classical, in art
  NT Titon du Tillet, Évrard, 1677-1762.
     Parnasse françois
Mythology, Czech
  USE Mythology, Slavic
Mythology, Dagari (May Subd Geog)
  [BL2430.D3]
  UF Dagari mythology
Mythology, East African
  [BL2464]
  BT Mythology, African
Mythology, Egyptian
  NT Egypt—Queens—Mythology
     Osiris (Egyptian deity)
Mythology, Estonian
  USE Mythology, Finno-Ugrian
Mythology, Finnish
  USE Mythology, Finno-Ugrian
Mythology, Finno-Ugrian
  UF Estonian mythology
     Finnish mythology
     Hungarian mythology
     Lappish mythology
     Magyar mythology
     Mythology, Estonian
     Mythology, Finnish
     Mythology, Hungarian
     Mythology, Lappish
     Mythology, Magyar
     Mythology, Vogul
     Vogul mythology
Mythology, Germanic
  UF Germanic mythology
     Teutonic mythology
  BT Germanic tribes—Religion
  NT Mythology, Norse
Mythology, Greek
  BT Mythology, Classical
  NT Achilles (Greek mythology)

Mythology, Greek *(Continued)*
    Adonis (Greek deity)
    Adrastus (Greek mythology)
    Aeneas (Legendary character)
    Aesculapius (Greek deity)
    Agamemnon (Greek mythology)
    Alcestis (Greek mythology)
    Amphitryon (Greek mythology)
    Anchises (Greek mythology)
    Andromeda (Greek mythology)
    Aphrodite (Greek deity)
    Apollo (Greek deity)
    Ares (Greek deity)
    Argonauts (Greek mythology)
    Ariadne (Greek mythology)
    Atalanta (Greek mythology)
    Athena (Greek deity)
    Baucis and Philemon (Greek
      mythology)
    Bellerophon (Greek mythology)
    Cadmus (Greek mythology)
    Cassandra (Greek mythology)
    Cerberus (Greek mythology)
    Charon (Greek mythology)
    Chimera (Greek mythology)
    Clytemnestra (Greek mythology)
    Cronus (Greek deity)
    Cyclopes (Greek mythology)
    Daedalus (Greek mythology)
    Daphnis (Greek mythology)
    Demeter (Greek deity)
    Dionysus (Greek deity)
    Eileithyia (Greek deity)
    Electra (Greek mythology)
    Erinyes (Greek mythology)
    Eros (Greek deity)
    Europa (Greek mythology)
    Eurydice (Greek mythology)
    Ganymede (Greek mythology)
    Helen of Troy (Greek mythology)
    Hephaestus (Greek deity)
    Hera (Greek deity)
    Heracles (Greek mythology)
    Hermes (Greek deity)
    Hero
    Hippolytus (Greek mythology)
    Icarus (Greek mythology)
    Inachus (Greek deity)
    Io (Greek mythology)
    Ion (Greek mythology)
    Iphigeneia (Greek mythology)
    Ixion (Greek mythology)
    Jason (Greek mythology)
    Leander
    Leda (Greek mythology)
    Marsyas (Greek deity)
    Medea (Greek mythology)
    Medusa (Greek mythology)
    Melampus (Greek mythology)
    Merope, wife of Cresphontes
    Minotaur (Greek mythology)
    Miracles (Greek mythology)
    Narcissus (Greek mythology)
    Nike (Greek deity)
    Odysseus (Greek mythology)
    Oedipus (Greek mythology)
    Orestes (Greek mythology)
    Orion (Greek mythology)
    Orpheus (Greek mythology)
    Pandora (Greek mythology)
    Paris (Greek mythology)
    Patroclus (Greek mythology)
    Pegasus (Greek mythology)
    Penelope (Greek mythology)
    Penthesilea (Greek mythology)
    Persephone (Greek deity)
    Perseus (Greek mythology)
    Phaedra (Greek mythology)
    Phaethon (Greek mythology)
    Pluto (Greek deity)
    Poseidon (Greek deity)

    Procrustes (Greek mythology)
    Prometheus (Greek mythology)
    Psyche (Greek deity)
    Pygmalion (Greek mythology)
    Satyrs (Greek mythology)
    Seven against Thebes (Greek
      mythology)
    Sisyphus (Greek mythology)
    Telegonus (Greek mythology)
    Telemachus (Greek mythology)
    Theseus (Greek mythology)
    Tithonus (Greek mythology)
    Troilus (Greek mythology)
    Trojan War
    Zephyrus (Greek deity)
    Zeus (Greek deity)
Mythology, Greek, in art
Mythology, Hebrew
  USE Mythology, Jewish
Mythology, Hindu
  UF Brahman mythology
     Mythology, Brahman
     Mythology, Vedic
     Vedic mythology
  BT Mythology, Indic
  NT Ambā (Hindu mythology)
     Aniruddha (Hindu mythology)
     Arjuna (Hindu mythology)
     Bali (Hindu mythology)
     Bhīma (Hindu mythology)
     Bhīṣma (Hindu mythology)
     Citraketu (Hindu mythology)
     Cosmogony, Hindu
     Damayantī (Hindu mythology)
     Devayānī (Hindu mythology)
     Draupadī (Hindu mythology)
     Droṇa (Hindu mythology)
     Ekāvalī (Hindu mythology)
     Hariścandra (Hindu mythology)
     Jalandhara (Hindu mythology)
     Jarāsandha (Hindu mythology)
     Kaikeyī (Hindu mythology)
     Kakutstha (Hindu mythology)
     Karṇa (Hindu mythology)
     Kautsa (Hindu mythology)
     Kīcaka (Hindu mythology)
     Kuśa (Hindu mythology)
     Lava (Hindu mythology)
     Lorika (Hindu mythology)
     Makara
     Mārkaṇḍeya (Hindu mythology)
     Mythology, Meithei
     Mythology, Tamil
     Nala (Hindu mythology)
     Prabhāvatī (Hindu mythology)
     Prahlāda (Hindu mythology)
     Rāvaṇa (Hindu mythology)
     Ṛsyaśṛṅga (Hindu mythology)
     Rukmāṅgada (Hindu mythology)
     Rukmiṇī (Hindu mythology)
     Śakuntalā (Hindu mythology)
     Śatrughna (Hindu mythology)
     Sudāmā (Hindu mythology)
     Sugrīva (Hindu mythology)
     Sulakṣaṇā (Hindu mythology)
     Svārociṣa Manu (Hindu mythology)
     Symbolism of numbers
     Ūṣā (Hindu mythology)
     Vidhṛtā (Hindu mythology)
     Viśvāmitra (Hindu mythology)
Mythology, Hittite
  UF Hittite mythology
Mythology, Hungarian
  USE Mythology, Finno-Ugrian
Mythology, Igbo (African people)
  (May Subd Geog)
    UF Igbo (African people) mythology
Mythology, Indian (American Indian)
  USE Indians—Religion and mythology
Mythology, Indic
  [BL2000-2015]

  NT Guha (Mythological character)
     Mythology, Hindu
     Mythology, Meithei
     Mythology, Tamil
Mythology, Indo-European
  [BL660]
  UF Indo-European mythology
  NT Soma
Mythology, Indonesian
  UF Indonesian mythology
Mythology, Iranian
  UF Iranian mythology
     Mythology, Persian
     Persian mythology
Mythology, Japanese
  NT Cosmogony, Shinto
     Ōkuninushi no kami
     Seven gods of fortune
     Susanoo no Mikoto (Shinto deity)
     Takamagahara
Mythology, Jewish
  UF Mythology, Hebrew
  BT Judaism
     Mythology, Semitic
Mythology, Korean
  UF Korean mythology
Mythology, Lappish
  USE Mythology, Finno-Ugrian
Mythology, Latvian
  USE Mythology, Baltic
Mythology, Lithuanian
  USE Mythology, Baltic
Mythology, Magyar
  USE Mythology, Finno-Ugrian
Mythology, Manipuri
  USE Mythology, Meithei
Mythology, Maori *(May Subd Geog)*
  [BL2615]
  UF Maori mythology
Mythology, Maya
  USE Mayas—Religion and mythology
Mythology, Meithei
  UF Meithei mythology
     Mythology, Manipuri
  BT Mythology, Hindu
     Mythology, Indic
Mythology, Meitheis
  NT Yāithiṃ Konu (Meitheis mythology)
Mythology, Melanesian *(May Subd Geog)*
  UF Melanesian mythology
Mythology, Mongolian *(May Subd Geog)*
  UF Mongolian mythology
Mythology, Nahuatl
  USE Nahuas—Religion and mythology
Mythology, Near Eastern
  USE Mythology, Oriental
Mythology, Nepali *(May Subd Geog)*
  UF Nepali mythology
Mythology, Norse
  BT Germanic tribes—Religion
     Mythology, Germanic
  NT Valkyries (Norse mythology)
Mythology, Oriental
  [BL1000-2370]
  UF Mythology, Near Eastern
     Oriental mythology
  NT Mythology, Semitic
Mythology, Oriental, in art
Mythology, Oriya *(May Subd Geog)*
  UF Oriya mythology
  NT Śvetabasanta (Oriya mythology)
Mythology, Panamanian *(May Subd Geog)*
  UF Panamanian mythology
Mythology, Papuan
  UF Papuan mythology
Mythology, Persian
  USE Mythology, Iranian
Mythology, Philippine *(May Subd Geog)*
  [BL2130]
  UF Philippine mythology

Mythology, Phoenician
  UF Phoenician mythology
Mythology, Phrygian
  UF Phrygian mythology
  NT Sabazius (Thraco-Phrygian deity)
Mythology, Polish
  USE Mythology, Slavic
Mythology, Polynesian
  ₂BL2620.P6₃
  UF Polynesian mythology
Mythology, Portuguese
  ₂BL980.P₃
  UF Portuguese mythology
Mythology, Prussian (Baltic tribe)
  USE Mythology, Baltic
Mythology, Roman
  BT Mythology, Classical
  NT Aeneas (Legendary character)
      Cacus (Roman deity)
      Camilla (Roman mythology)
      Ceres (Roman deity)
      Cupid (Roman deity)
      Fortuna (Roman deity)
      Genius (Companion spirit)
      Hercules (Roman mythology)
      Juno (Roman deity)
      Jupiter (Roman deity)
      Liber Pater (Roman deity)
      Lupercalia
      Mars (Roman deity)
      Mater Matuta (Roman deity)
      Mercury (Roman deity)
      Minerva (Roman deity)
      Neptune (Roman deity)
      Ops (Roman deity)
      Proserpina (Roman deity)
      Regifugium
      Roman she-wolf (Legendary character)
      Saturn (Roman deity)
      Venus (Roman deity)
      Victoria (Roman deity)
      Vulcan (Roman deity)
Mythology, Romanian
  ₂BL980.R₃
  UF Romanian mythology
Mythology, Russian
  USE Mythology, Slavic
Mythology, Samoyedic
  UF Mythology, Yurak
      Yurak mythology
Mythology, Semitic
  BT Mythology, Oriental
  NT Lilith (Semitic mythology)
      Mythology, Assyro-Babylonian
      Mythology, Jewish
      Mythology, Ugaritic
Mythology, Slavic
  UF Bulgarian mythology
      Czech mythology
      Mythology, Bulgarian
      Mythology, Czech
      Mythology, Polish
      Mythology, Russian
      Mythology, Slovak
      Mythology, Wendic
      Polish mythology
      Russian mythology
      Slovak mythology
      Sorbian mythology
Mythology, Slovak
  USE Mythology, Slavic
Mythology, Spanish *(May Subd Geog)*
  UF Spanish mythology
Mythology, Sri Lankan *(May Subd Geog)*
  ₂BL2030.C5₃
  UF Sri Lankan mythology
Mythology, Sub-Saharan African
  (May Subd Geog)
  ₂BL2462.5₃
  UF Sub-Saharan African mythology

Mythology, Sumerian
  ₂BL1615₃
  UF Sumerian mythology
  NT Inanna (Sumerian deity)
Mythology, Tamil
  ₂BL2370.T25₃
  UF Tamil mythology
  BT Mythology, Hindu
      Mythology, Indic
Mythology, Taoist
  BT Mythology, Chinese
Mythology, Thracian
  UF Thracian mythology
  NT Bendida (Thracian deity)
      Sabazius (Thraco-Phrygian deity)
Mythology, Turkish *(May Subd Geog)*
  UF Turkish mythology
Mythology, Ugaritic *(May Subd Geog)*
  UF Ugaritic mythology
  BT Mythology, Semitic
Mythology, Vedic
  USE Mythology, Hindu
      Vedas
Mythology, Vogul
  USE Mythology, Finno-Ugrian
Mythology, Welsh
  UF Welsh mythology
  BT Mythology, British
Mythology, Wendic
  USE Mythology, Slavic
Mythology, West African
  ₂BL2465₃
  UF West African mythology
  BT Mythology, African
Mythology, Yatvyag
  USE Mythology, Baltic
Mythology, Yurak
  USE Mythology, Samoyedic
Mythology and music
  USE Music and mythology
Mythology in art
  USE Art and mythology
Mythology in literature
  ₂PN56.M₃
  ₂PQ145.1.M9 (French literature)₃
  ₂PR508.M9 (English literature,
      PR149.M)₃
  ₂PT135 (German literature)₃
  NT Demythologization (Literature)
Mythology in motion pictures
  ₂PN1995.9.M₃
  BT Moving-pictures
Mythomania
  UF Lying
      Pseudologia phantastica
  BT Psychology, Forensic
      Psychology, Pathological
      Truthfulness and falsehood
Mythopoeic displacement
  USE Demythologization (Literature)
Myths
  USE Mythology
Mytic River (Mass.)
  USE Mystic River (Mass.)
Mytilaspis
  USE Lepidosaphes
Mytilēnē Island (Greece)
  USE Lesbos Island (Greece)
Mytilidae
  NT Aulacomya
      Mytilus
Mytilidae, Fossil
  ₂QE812.M94₃
  NT Mytilus, Fossil
Mytilini Island (Greece)
  USE Lesbos Island (Greece)
Mytilus
  ₂QL430.7.M95₃
  BT Mytilidae
Mytilus, Fossil
  ₂QE812.M94₃

  BT Mytilidae, Fossil
Mytilus edulis
  ₂QL430.7.M95₃
  UF Blue mussel
      Common mussel
Myton family
  USE Mitten family
Myxedema *(May Subd Geog)*
  ₂RC657₃
  BT Hypothyroidism
Myxine
  ₂QL638.15.M9₃
  BT Myxinidae
Myxine glutinosa
  USE Atlantic hagfish
Myxinidae
  ₂QL638.15.M9₃
  UF Eptatetridae
  BT Hagfishes
  NT Eptatretus
      Myxine
Myxiniformes
  USE Hagfishes
Myxinoidei
  USE Hagfishes
Myxobacterales
  ₂QR81₃
  UF Gliding bacteria
      Myxobacteria
  BT Bacteria
  NT Myxococcaceae
Myxobacteria
  USE Myxobacterales
Myxococcaceae
  ₂QR82.M95₃
  BT Myxobacterales
  NT Myxococcus
Myxococcus
  ₂QR82.M95₃
  BT Myxococcaceae
Myxococcus xanthus
  ₂QR82.M95₃
Myxogastres
  USE Myxomycetes
Myxoma
  BT Tumors
Myxomatosis *(May Subd Geog)*
  UF Bighead (Disease)
      Mixomatosis
  BT Poxvirus diseases
      Rabbits—Diseases
Myxomembranous colitis
  USE Irritable colon
Myxomycetes *(May Subd Geog)*
  ₂QK635₃
  UF Aerogastres
      Mycetozoa
      Myxogastres
      Slime fungi
      Slime molds
  BT Fungi
      Molds (Botany)
      Protozoa
  NT Coenobic plants
      Physarales
      Plasmodiophorales
      Plasmodium (Myxomycetes)
Myxophyceae
  USE Cyanobacteria
Myxophyta
  USE Cyanobacteria
Myxosporidia
  NT Chloromyxidae
Myxoviruses
  UF Orthomyxoviruses
  BT Viruses, RNA
  RT Paramyxoviruses
  NT Fowl plague virus
      Influenza viruses
Myze family
  USE Mize family

Myzer family
  USE Meisser family
Myzine
  USE Myzinum
Myzinidae
  USE Tiphiidae
Myzinum
    ₍QL568.T5₎
  UF Elis
      Myzine
  BT Tiphiidae
Myzocallis
    ₍QL527.A64₎
  BT Aphididae
Myzomyia
  USE Anopheles
Myzornis
    ₍QL696.P285₎
  BT Timaliidae
Myzostomaria
  USE Myzostomida
Myzostomida *(May Subd Geog)*
    ₍QL391.A6₎
  UF Myzostomaria
  BT Polychaeta
Myzus
    ₍QL527.A64₎
  BT Aphididae
Myzus lythri
    ₍QL527.A64₎
  UF Aphis mahaleb
      Myzus mahaleb
      Plum plant-louse
Myzus mahaleb
  USE Myzus lythri
Myzus persicae
  USE Green peach aphid
Myzus pseudosolani
  USE Foxglove aphid
Myzus solani
  USE Foxglove aphid
Mzab (Algeria)
  BT Oases—Algeria
Mzab language *(May Subd Geog)*
  UF Mozabite language
      Mzabi language
  BT Algeria—Languages
      Berber languages
Mzabi language
  USE Mzab language
N-3 fatty acids
  USE Omega-3 fatty acids
n-body problem
  USE Many-body problem
N-carboxy-aminoacid-anhydrides
  USE Amino acid anhydrides
N.F.T.
  USE Nutrient film culture
N-rays
    ₍QC485₎
    ₍RM862.N2 (Therapeutics)₎
  BT Light
      Radiation
      X-rays
N stars
    ₍QB843.N12₎
  UF Carbon stars
  BT Cool stars
  — Spectra
N-way algebra
  USE Algebra, Universal
N.Y.C. Marathon, New York, N.Y.
  USE New York City Marathon, New York,
       N.Y.
Na (Kingdom)
  USE Na no Kuni
Na Ayutthaya family *(Not Subd Geog)*
Na-Dene languages
    ₍PM1980₎
  BT Indians of North America—Languages
  NT Athapascan languages

Eyak language
Haida language
Tlingit language
Na-khi
  USE Moso (Tribe)
Na-len-dra-pa (Sect) *(May Subd Geog)*
    ₍BQ7675₎
  UF Na-lendra-pa (Sect)
      Nalendrapa (Sect)
  BT Buddhist sects
      Sa-skya-pa (Sect)
Na-lendra-pa (Sect)
  USE Na-len-dra-pa (Sect)
Na no Kuni
  UF Na (Kingdom)
      Wa no Na no Kuni
  BT Japan—History—To 645
Naab River (Germany)
  UF Nab River (Germany)
  BT Rivers—Germany (West)
Na'ar (The Hebrew word)
  BT Hebrew language—Etymology
Naas family
  USE Nassau family
Naassenes
    ₍BT1437₎
  BT Gnosticism
Nāatas
  USE Navayats
Nab River (Germany)
  USE Naab River (Germany)
Naba language
  USE Nabak language
Nabagraha (Hindu deity)
  BT Gods, Hindu
Nabak language *(May Subd Geog)*
  UF Naba language
      Wain language
  BT Finisterre-Huon languages
      Papua New Guinea—Languages
Nabaloi dialect
    ₍PL5981₎
  UF Benguet Igorot dialect
      Ibadoy dialect
      Ibaloi dialect
      Inibaloi dialect
  BT Iloko language
      Philippine languages
Nabataean inscriptions
  USE Inscriptions, Nabataean
Nabataean pottery
  USE Pottery, Nabataean
Nabataeans
  UF Nabathites
Nabathites
  USE Nabataeans
Nabdam (African people)
  USE Namnam (African people)
Nabe language
  USE Kulango language
Naber family
  USE Neighbors family
Nabers family
  USE Neighbors family
Nabeshima family *(Not Subd Geog)*
Nabeshima porcelain *(May Subd Geog)*
    ₍NK4399.N25₎
  UF Porcelain, Nabeshima
  BT Porcelain, Japanese
Nabesna language
  USE Upper Tanana language
Nabesnatana Indians
  USE Tanana Indians
Nabokoff family
  USE Nabokov family
Nabokov family *(Not Subd Geog)*
  UF Nabokoff family
Nabor (Horse)
  USE *Naborr (Horse)
Nabor family
  USE Neighbors family

*Naborr (Horse)
  UF Nabor (Horse)
  BT Arabian horse
      Horses
Nabors family
  USE Neighbors family
Nabour family
  USE Neighbors family
Nabours family
  USE Neighbors family
NAC Lot Exchange Dollar Credit Plan
  USE Lot Exchange Dollar Credit Plan
NAC Mausoleum Crypt Exchange Dollar
    Credit Plan
  USE Mausoleum Crypt Exchange Dollar
       Credit Plan
Nac-nanuc Indians
  USE Tapuya Indians
Nacelles (Airplane)
  USE Airplanes—Nacelles
Nach-Expressionismus (Art)
  USE New objectivity (Art)
Nachbin-Hewitt spaces
  USE Hewitt-Nachbin spaces
Nachiketas
  USE Nāciketa (Character)
Nachtwacht (Painting)
  USE Rembrandt Harmenszoon van Rijn,
       1606-1669. Night watch
Nāciketa (Character)
  UF Nachiketas
Nadaf family
  USE Nadav family
Nadars
  UF Shanars
  BT Caste—India
Nadav family *(Not Subd Geog)*
  UF Alnadaf family
      Nadaf family
Nadeau family *(Not Subd Geog)*
NADH2 oxidase deficiency
  USE Chronic granulomatous disease
Nadj (Saudi Arabia)
  USE Najd (Saudi Arabia)
Nadolol *(May Subd Geog)*
    ₍RM666.N32₎
  UF Dimethylethylaminohy
      droxypropoxytetrahyd
      ronaphthalenediol
  BT Adrenergic beta blockers
      Cardiovascular agents
      Myocardial depressants
Nadowessioux Indians
  USE Dakota Indians
Naeff family
  USE Neff family
Naegel family
  USE Nagel family
Naegele family
  USE Nagel family
Naejang Mountain (Korea)
  UF Naejang San (Korea)
      Naejangsan (Korea)
  BT Mountains—Korea (South)
Naejang San (Korea)
  USE Naejang Mountain (Korea)
Naejangsan (Korea)
  USE Naejang Mountain (Korea)
Naematoloma caerulescens
  USE Psilocybe cubensis
Naemorhedus
  USE Gorals
Naeogaeidae
  USE Hebridae
Naert family *(Not Subd Geog)*
Næss family
  USE Ness family
Naevus
  USE Mole (Dermatology)
Nafalan
    ₍QP915.N2 (Physiological effects)₎

[RM666.N (Therapeutics)]
BT Naphtha
Näfels, Switzerland, Battle of, 1388
[DQ97]
BT Switzerland—History—1032-1499
Naff family
USE Neff family
Naffziger's syndrome
USE Scalenus anticus syndrome
Thoracic outlet syndrome
Nafzger family
USE Nafziger family
Nafziger family (Not Subd Geog)
UF Nafzger family
NAG Library (Computer programs)
UF Numerical Algorithms Group Library
(Computer programs)
BT Numerical analysis—Computer
programs
Naga-Assamese language
USE Naga Pidgin
Naga languages
[PL3881-4]
BT Tibeto-Burman languages
NT Angami language
Ao language
Chakhesang language
Chang language
Kabui language
Khezha language
Konyak language
Lhota language
Liyang language
Mao language
Maram language
Mikir language
Naga Pidgin
Nocte language
Phom language
Pochury language
Rengma language
Sangtam language
Sema language
Simte language
Tangkhul language
Tangsa language
Wancho language
Yimchungru language
Zeliang language
Naga Pidgin
[PM7895.N3]
UF Naga-Assamese language
Nagamese language
BT Assamese language
Naga languages
Pidgin languages
Naga-Tangkhuls
USE Tangkhuls
Nagahama Castle (Nagahama-shi, Japan)
USE Nagahamajō (Nagahama-shi, Japan)
Nagahamajō (Nagahama-shi, Japan)
UF Nagahama Castle (Nagahama-shi,
Japan)
BT Castles—Japan
Nagaki family (Not Subd Geog)
Nāgakumāra (Jaina deity)
BT Gods, Jaina
Nagamese language
USE Naga Pidgin
Nagami language
USE Angami language
Nagana
USE Trypanosomiasis in cattle
Nagano Dentetsu
BT Electric railroads—Japan
Railroads—Japan
Nagano Iseki (Ikarigaseki-mura, Japan)
USE Nagano Site (Ikarigaseki-mura, Japan)
Nagano-ken (Japan)
— History
— — Iiyama Peasant Uprising, 1837

UF Iiyama Peasant Uprising,
Nagano-ken (Japan), 1837
Nagano Site (Ikarigaseki-mura, Japan)
UF Nagano Iseki (Ikarigaseki-mura, Japan)
BT Japan—Antiquities
Nagao family (Not Subd Geog)
Nagaoka-kyō Site (Kyoto, Japan)
UF Nagaoka-kyōseki (Kyoto, Japan)
BT Japan—Antiquities
Nagaoka-kyōseki (Kyoto, Japan)
USE Nagaoka-kyō Site (Kyoto, Japan)
Nagar Brahmans
[DS432.N28]
BT Brahmans
Caste—India
Ethnology—India
Nagarathars
USE Nattukottai Chettiars
Nagarnooks
[DU122.N3]
[GN665 (Anthropology)]
BT Australian aborigines
Nagarse proteinase
USE Subtilisins
Nagas
[DS432.N3]
BT Ethnology—India
NT Anal (Indic people)
Angami (Indic people)
Ao (Indic people)
Rengma (Indic people)
Tangkhuls
Nagasaki byōbu
USE Namban screen painting
Nagasako Iseki (Fukuyama-shi, Japan)
USE Nagasako Site (Fukuyama-shi, Japan)
Nagasako Site (Fukuyama-shi, Japan)
(Not Subd Geog)
UF Nagasako Iseki (Fukuyama-shi, Japan)
BT Japan—Antiquities
Nagase B Iseki (Ninohe-shi, Japan)
USE Nagase B Site (Ninohe-shi, Japan)
Nagase B Site (Ninohe-shi, Japan)
(Not Subd Geog)
UF Nagase B Iseki (Ninohe-shi, Japan)
BT Japan—Antiquities
Nagase C Iseki (Japan)
USE Nagase C Site (Japan)
Nagase C Site (Japan) (Not Subd Geog)
UF Nagase C Iseki (Japan)
BT Japan—Antiquities
Nagase D Iseki (Japan)
USE Nagase D Site (Japan)
Nagase D Site (Japan) (Not Subd Geog)
UF Nagase D Iseki (Japan)
BT Japan—Antiquities
Nagashino, Battle of, 1575
BT Japan—History—Azuchi-Momoyama
period, 1568-1603
Nagashino, Battle of, 1575, in art
NT Nagashino kassen zu (Screen painting)
Nagashino kassen zu (Screen painting)
[ND1059.6]
BT Nagashino, Battle of, 1575, in art
Painting, Japanese—Edo period, 1600-
1868
Screen painting, Japanese
Nagashinojō (Hōrai-chō, Japan)
UF Ōgijō (Hōrai-chō, Japan)
Suehirojō (Hōrai-chō, Japan)
BT Castles—Japan
Nagauta
BT Ballads, Japanese
Songs, Japanese
Nagel camera
BT Cameras

Nagel family (Not Subd Geog)
UF Naegel family
Naegele family
Nagele family
Nagell family
Nagl family
Nagle family
Naglee family
Nagler family
Naigly family
Negley family
Negly family
Nagele family
USE Nagel family
Nagell family
USE Nagel family
Nagesar (Indic people)
USE Nagesia (Indic people)
Nagesh sect
[BL1245.N3]
BT Advaita
Hindu sects
Pushtuns
Nagesia (Indic people)
[DS432.N]
UF Kisan (Indic people)
Nagesar (Indic people)
BT Ethnology—India
Nagid
BT Jews—Islamic countries
Nagino Kofungun (Setaka-machi, Japan)
USE Nagino Site (Setaka-machi, Japan)
Nagino Site (Setaka-machi, Japan)
(Not Subd Geog)
UF Nagino Kofungun (Setaka-machi,
Japan)
BT Japan—Antiquities
Nagl family
USE Nagel family
Nagle family
USE Nagel family
Naglee family
USE Nagel family
Nagler family
USE Nagel family
Nago language
USE Yoruba language
Nagorcka family (Not Subd Geog)
Nagovisi (Papuan people)
[DU85]
UF Sibbe (Papuan people)
BT Ethnology—Solomon Islands
Nagoya Castle (Nagoya-shi, Japan)
USE Nagoyajō (Nagoya-shi, Japan)
Nagoya Daigaku
Nagoya Plain (Japan)
USE Nōbi Plain (Japan)
Nagoya Tetsudō
UF Meitetsu
BT Railroads—Japan
Street-railroads—Japan
Nagoyajō (Nagoya-shi, Japan)
UF Nagoya Castle (Nagoya-shi, Japan)
BT Castles—Japan
Nagpuri dialect
[PK2378.N]
BT Marathi language
Nagpuriā dialect
BT Bhojpuri language
Nagpuria literature (May Subd Geog)
Nagpuria philology
Nagualism
[GN470]
BT Indians of Mexico—Religion and
mythology
Religion, Primitive
Religions
Superstition
Nagy Alföld
USE Great Alföld

Nagy Magyar Alföld
USE Great Alföld
Nagykunság (Hungary) *(Not Subd Geog)*
Naḥal Mishmar (Israel)
USE Mishmar Wadi (Israel)
Nahali language
[PL4585]
UF Nihali language
Nimaree language
BT Munda languages
Nahane Indians
UF Nahani Indians
Nahauni Indians
BT Athapascan Indians
Indians of North America
NT Kaska Indians
Nahani Indians
USE Nahane Indians
Nahauni Indians
USE Nahane Indians
Nahāvand, Iran, Battle of, 642
[DS38.1]
BT Iran—History—640-1500
Islamic Empire—History—622-661
Nahe River (Germany)
BT Rivers—Germany (West)
Nahe Valley in art
Nahoas
USE Nahuas
Nahr al-Urdunn
USE Jordan River
Nahr an Nīl
USE Nile River
Nahr Dijlah
USE Tigris River
Nahr Diyālá (Iran and Iraq)
USE Diyala River (Iran and Iraq)
Nahua Indians
USE Nahuas
Nahua law
USE Law, Nahua
Nahuas
[F1219]
UF Nahoas
Nahua Indians
Nahuatl Indians
Nahuatlecas
BT Aztecs
Indians of Mexico
Toltecs
Uto-Aztecan Indians
NT Nicarao Indians
Tepanecas
— **Religion and mythology**
UF Mythology, Nahuatl
Nahuatl mythology
BT Indians of Mexico—Religion and
mythology
Nahuat language
USE Pipil language
Nahuatl Indians
USE Nahuas
Nahuatl language
USE Aztec language
Nahuatl-Spanish dialect
Nahuatl literature
USE Aztec literature
Nahuatl mythology
USE Nahuas—Religion and mythology
Nahuatl philology
USE Aztec philology
Nahuatl-Spanish dialect
[PM4070]
UF Nahuatl language
BT Aztec language
Nahuatlecas
USE Nahuas
Nahuel Huapí National Park (Argentina)
USE Parque Nacional Nahuel Huapí
(Argentina)

Nahuṣa
UF Nahusha
Nahusha
USE Nahuṣa
Nai
USE Panpipes
Naiadales
USE Helobiae
Naigly family
USE Nagel family
Naikan psychotherapy *(May Subd Geog)*
UF Naikan therapy
BT Psychotherapy
Naikan therapy
USE Naikan psychotherapy
Naikas
UF Naikdas
Nayaks
BT Ethnology—India
Naikdas
USE Naikas
Nail-biting *(May Subd Geog)*
[HQ784.N3 (Child development)]
UF Biting of nails
Fingernail biting
BT Neuroses
Oral habits
Nail craft
[TT213.6]
BT Handicraft
Metal-work
Nails and spikes
Nail industry *(May Subd Geog)*
[HD9529.N32-324]
BT Nails and spikes
Nail makers *(May Subd Geog)*
BT Nails and spikes
Nail manifestations of general diseases
(May Subd Geog)
[RL169]
UF Nail symptoms of general diseases
Ungual manifestations of general
diseases
BT Cutaneous manifestations of general
diseases
Nail symptoms of general diseases
USE Nail manifestations of general diseases
Nailer family
USE Naylor family
Nailers *(May Subd Geog)*
BT Nails and spikes
Nailing
USE Nails and spikes
Nailing, Intramedullary
USE Intramedullary fracture fixation
Nailing, Medullary
USE Intramedullary fracture fixation
Nailor family
USE Naylor family
Nails, Ingrowing
[RD563]
UF Ingrowing nails
BT Foot—Diseases
Toes—Abnormalities
Nails (Anatomy)
[QL942 (Comparative anatomy)]
[QM488 (Human anatomy)]
UF Claws
BT Skin
Toes
NT Fingernails
— **Care and hygiene**
NT Manicuring
Nails and spikes
[HD9529.N32-HD9529.N324
(Economics)]
[TA492.N2 (Testing)]
[TS440 (Manufacture)]
UF Nailing
Spikes
BT Hardware

NT Bone nails (Orthopedics)
Nail craft
Nail industry
Nail makers
Nailers
Naipali language
USE Nepali language
Nairi computer
BT Electronic digital computers
— **Programming**
Nairobi National Park (Kenya)
BT National parks and reserves—Kenya
Parks—Kenya
Nairs
[DS432.N324]
UF Nayars
BT Caste—India
Ethnology—India
Naissaar Island (Estonia) *(Not Subd Geog)*
UF Naissar Island (Estonia)
Nayssar Island (Estonia)
BT Islands—Estonia
Naissar Island (Estonia)
USE Naissaar Island (Estonia)
Naiteas
USE Navayats
Naītias
USE Navayats
Naitō Iseki (Shari-chō, Japan)
USE Naitō Site (Shari-chō, Japan)
Naitō Site (Shari-chō, Japan)
(Not Subd Geog)
UF Naitō Iseki (Shari-chō, Japan)
BT Japan—Antiquities
Naitonal parks and reserves
— **Utah**
NT Cache National Forest (Utah and
Idaho)
Naive art
USE Primitivism in art
Naïveté
USE Innocence (Psychology)
Naja
USE Cobras
Naja hannah
USE King cobra
Naja nigricollis
[QL666.O64]
BT Cobras
Najd (Saudi Arabia)
UF Nadj (Saudi Arabia)
Nejd (Saudi Arabia)
Nájera family *(Not Subd Geog)*
Nakabayashi family *(Not Subd Geog)*
Nakabyō Kōshinzuka Iseki (Abiko-shi, Japan)
USE Nakabyō Kōshinzuka Site (Abiko-shi,
Japan)
Nakabyō Kōshinzuka Site (Abiko-shi, Japan)
(Not Subd Geog)
UF Nakabyō Kōshinzuka Iseki (Abiko-shi,
Japan)
Nakabyō Stone Marker Site (Abiko-
shi, Japan)
BT Japan—Antiquities
Nakabyō Stone Marker Site (Abiko-shi, Japan)
USE Nakabyō Kōshinzuka Site (Abiko-shi,
Japan)
Nakahira Iseki (Hamamatsu-shi, Japan)
USE Nakahira Site (Hamamatsu-shi, Japan)
Nakahira Site (Hamamatsu-shi, Japan)
(Not Subd Geog)
UF Nakahira Iseki (Hamamatsu-shi,
Japan)
Nishikamoe Nakahara Iseki
(Hamamatsu-shi, Japan)
Nakai family
Nakajima Hayate (Fighter planes)
USE Hayate (Fighter planes)
Nakajima J1N1-S (Night fighter plane)
USE Irving (Night fighter plane)

Nakajima Ki. 27 (Fighter planes)
  USE 97 Sen (Fighter planes)
Nakajima Ki 43 (Fighter planes)
  USE Hayabusa (Fighter planes)
Nakajima Ki 84 (Fighter planes)
  USE Hayate (Fighter planes)
Nakajima kikka
  USE Kikka (Jet fighter plane)
Nakambala Sugar Estates (Zambia)
  BT Plantations—Zambia
Nakamura (Name)
Nakamura family *(Not Subd Geog)*
Nakanai language
  ⌐PL6262¬
  UF Lakalai language
  BT Melanesian languages
      Papua New Guinea—Languages
Nakanais (Melanesian people)
  USE Lakalai (Melanesian people)
Nakane family *(Not Subd Geog)*
Nakanishi family *(Not Subd Geog)*
Nakano Iseki (Neba-mura, Japan)
  USE Nakano Site (Neba-mura, Japan)
Nakano Iseki (Tondabayashi, Japan)
  USE Nakano Site (Tondabayashi-shi, Japan)
Nakano Site (Neba-mura, Japan)
  (Not Subd Geog)
  UF Nakano Iseki (Neba-mura, Japan)
  BT Japan—Antiquities
Nakano Site (Tondabayashi-shi, Japan)
  (Not Subd Geog)
  UF Nakano Iseki (Tondabayashi, Japan)
  BT Japan—Antiquities
Nakasai Iseki (Mishima-machi, Fukushima-ken,
  Japan)
  USE Nakasai Site (Mishima-machi,
       Fukushima-ken, Japan)
**Nakasai Site (Mishima-machi, Fukushima-ken,
  Japan)** *(Not Subd Geog)*
  UF Nakasai Iseki (Mishima-machi,
       Fukushima-ken, Japan)
  BT Japan—Antiquities
Nakasendō (Japan)
  ⌐DS894.59N36¬
  UF Hida-Kaidō (Japan)
      Kiso-kaidō (Japan)
      Kisoji (Japan)
      Nomugi Kaidō (Japan)
  BT Roads—Japan
Nakasuji Iseki (Nose-chō, Japan)
  USE Nakasuji Site (Nose-chō, Japan)
Nakasuji Site (Nose-chō, Japan)
  (Not Subd Geog)
  UF Nakasuji Iseki (Nose-chō, Japan)
  BT Japan—Antiquities
Nakatomi Iseki (Kyoto, Japan)
  USE Nakatomi Site (Kyoto, Japan)
Nakatomi Site (Kyoto, Japan)
  (Not Subd Geog)
  UF Nakatomi Iseki (Kyoto, Japan)
  BT Japan—Antiquities
Nakaya Iseki (Kanazawa-shi, Japan)
  USE Nakaya Site (Kanazawa-shi, Japan)
Nakaya Site (Kanazawa-shi, Japan)
  (Not Subd Geog)
  UF Nakaya Iseki (Kanazawa-shi, Japan)
  BT Japan—Antiquities
Nakazato Maehara Iseki (Japan)
  USE Nakazato Maehara Site (Japan)
Nakazato Maehara Site (Japan)
  (Not Subd Geog)
  UF Nakazato Maehara Iseki (Japan)
  BT Japan—Antiquities
Nakazawa family *(Not Subd Geog)*
Naked-backed bats
  USE Pteronotus
Naked clothes moth
  USE Tineola bisselliella
Naked singularities (Cosmology)
  ⌐QB991.N34¬
  UF Singularities, Naked (Cosmology)

  BT Astrophysics
      Cosmology
      Space and time
Nakedness
  USE Nudity
Nakh languages
  ⌐PK9050¬
  UF Central Caucasian languages
      Kist languages
      Northeast Caucasian languages
      Samurian languages
      Veinakh languages
      Vejnax languages
  BT Caucasian languages
  NT Bats language
      Chechen language
      Ingush language
Nakiri Iseki (Gōnoura-chō, Japan)
  USE Nakiri Site (Gōnoura-chō, Japan)
Nakiri Site (Gōnoura-chō, Japan)
  UF Nakiri Iseki (Gōnoura-chō, Japan)
  BT Japan—Antiquities
Naktong Bulge (Korea), Battle of, 1950
  USE Naktong River (Korea), Battle of,
       1950
Naktong-gang (Korea)
  USE Naktong River (Korea)
Naktong River (Korea)
  UF Naktong-gang (Korea)
      Naktonggang (Korea)
  BT Rivers—Korea (South)
Naktong River (Korea), Battle of, 1950
  ⌐DS918.2¬
  UF Naktong Bulge (Korea), Battle of,
       1950
  BT Korean War, 1950-1953—Campaigns
Naktonggang (Korea)
  USE Naktong River (Korea)
Nala (Hindu mythology)
  BT Mahābhārata—Biography
      Mythology, Hindu
Nālandā Site (India) *(Not Subd Geog)*
  ⌐DS486.N266¬
  BT India—Antiquities
Naldi family *(Not Subd Geog)*
Nale family
  USE Nall family
Nałęcz family *(Not Subd Geog)*
Naled (Insecticide)
  UF Dibromodichloroethyl dimethyl
       phosphate
  BT Acaricides
      Organophosphorus compounds
Naled (Meteorology)
  USE Aufeis
Nalendrapa (Sect)
  USE Na-len-dra-pa (Sect)
Naler family
  USE Naylor family
Nalganga River Valley Project
  BT Water resources development—India
Naligh family
  USE Nalley family
Nall family *(Not Subd Geog)*
  UF Nale family
      Nalle family
      Nalls family
      Naul family
      Nayle family
Nalle family
  USE Nall family
Nalley family *(Not Subd Geog)*
  UF Naligh family
      Nally family
Nalls family
  USE Nall family
Nally family
  USE Nalley family
Nalou (African people)
  USE Nalu (African people)

Naloxone
  UF Allylepoxydihydroxymorphinan
      Naltrexone
  BT Morphine
      Narcotic antagonists
Naltrexone
  USE Naloxone
Nalu (African people)
  ⌐DT543.42 (Guinea)¬
  ⌐DT613.42 (Guinea-Bissau)¬
  UF Nalou (African people)
  BT Ethnology—Guinea
      Ethnology—Guinea-Bissau
Nalum (New Guinea people)
  BT Ethnology—Indonesia
Nam Chi (Thailand)
  USE Chi River (Thailand)
Nam-gang (Kyŏngsang-namdo, Korea)
  USE Nam River (Kyŏngsang-namdo, Korea)
Nam language
  ⌐PL3801.N4¬
  BT Tibeto-Burman languages
Nam Louang (Thailand)
  USE Huai Luang River (Thailand)
Nam Luang (Thailand)
  USE Huai Luang River (Thailand)
Nam Mun (Thailand)
  USE Mun River (Thailand)
Nam Ngum Reservoir (Laos)
  BT Reservoirs—Laos
Nam Pong River (Thailand)
  BT Rivers—Thailand
Nam River (Kyŏngsang-namdo, Korea)
  UF Nam-gang (Kyŏngsang-namdo, Korea)
      Namgang (Kyŏngsang-namdo, Korea)
      South River (Kyŏngsang-namdo,
       Korea)
  BT Rivers—Korea (South)
Nama (African people) *(May Subd Geog)*
  UF Namaqua (African people)
  BT Ethnology—Namibia
      Ethnology—South Africa
      Khoikhoi (African people)
Nama language
  ⌐PL8541¬
  BT Khoikhoi language
      Namibia—Languages
      South Africa—Languages
  — Tone
    BT Tone (Phonetics)
Namaqua (African people)
  USE Nama (African people)
Namartham
  USE Benami transactions
Namasudras
  ⌐DS432.N35¬
  BT Caste—India
      Ethnology—Bangladesh
      Ethnology—India
Namau language
  USE Purari language
Namazlik
  USE Rugs, Prayer
Nambai language
  USE Kulango language
Namban art *(May Subd Geog)*
  UF Art, Namban
      Art, Nanban
      Nanban art
  BT Art, Japanese
  NT Namban screen painting
Namban byōbu
  USE Namban screen painting

Namban screen painting *(May Subd Geog)*
  UF Kokusen byōbu
      Nagasaki byōbu
      Namban byōbu
      Namban screens
      Nanban byōbu
      Nanban screens
      Screen painting, Namban
      Screen painting, Nanban
  BT Namban art
Namban screens
  USE Namban screen painting
Nambas language, Big
  USE Big Nambas language
Nambicuara Indians
  UF Nanbikuara Indians
  BT Indians of South America
  NT Mamaindê Indians
Nambicuara language
    [PM6643]
  UF Nambikuara language
      Nambiquara language
      Nanbikuara language
      Nhambicuara language
  BT Brazil—Languages
      Indians of South America—Brazil—
        Languages
  NT Mamaindê dialect
Nambikuara language
  USE Nambicuara language
Nambiquara language
  USE Nambicuara language
Nambu family *(Not Subd Geog)*
  UF Nanbu family
Nambudiri
  UF Nambudri
      Namburi
      Nambutiri
      Nampudiri
  BT Brahmans
      Caste—India
      Ethnology—India
Nambudri
  USE Nambudiri
Namburi
  USE Nambudiri
Nambutiri
  USE Nambudiri
Namchi (African people)
  USE Dowayo (African people)
Namdharis
  UF Kukas
  BT Sikhism
Name plates of publications
  USE Nameplates of publications
Nameless Ones (Christian sect)
  USE Two-by-Two's (Christian sect)
Nameplates of publications
  (May Subd Geog)
  UF Name plates of publications
  BT Graphic arts
      Magazine design
      Newspaper layout and typography
  RT Logotype
      Title-page
Names *(May Subd Geog)*
  UF Nomenclature
      Proper names
      Terminology
  BT Language and languages—Etymology
  RT Epithets
  SA *subdivisions* Name *or* Names *under*
      subjects, e.g. America—Name;
      Catholic Church—Name; United
      States—History—Civil War, 1861-
      1865—Name; Jews—Name; Sects—
      Names; Stars—Names
  NT Boat names
      Business names
      Code names
      House names

      Love names
      Names, Geographical
      Names, Personal
      Onomastics
      Ship names
      Terms and phrases
  — Pronunciation
  — Transliteration
Names, African
  UF African languages—Names
      African names
  BT African languages—Etymology—
      Names
Names, Ainu
  UF Ainu language—Names
      Ainu names
  BT Ainu language—Etymology—Names
Names, Amharic
  UF Amharic language—Names
      Amharic names
Names, Anglo-Saxon
  USE Names, English (Old)
Names, Celtiberian
  UF Celtiberian names
Names, Christian
  USE Names, Personal
Names, Circassian *(May Subd Geog)*
  UF Circassian languages—Names
      Circassian names
  BT Circassian languages—Etymology—
      Names
Names, Code
  USE Code names
Names, Cornish *(May Subd Geog)*
  UF Cornish language—Names
      Cornish names
Names, Corporate (Cataloging)
  USE Corporate headings (Cataloging)
Names, Dagari (African people)
    [DT510.42 (Ghana)]
  UF Dagari names
Names, Dutch *(May Subd Geog)*
  UF Dutch language—Names
      Dutch names
  BT Dutch language—Etymology—Names
Names, English
  UF English language—Names
      English names
  NT English language—Etymology—Names
Names, English, [Arabic, Celtic, etc.]
Names, English (Old)
  UF Anglo-Saxon names
      English language—Old English, ca.
        450-1100—Names
      English names, Old
      Names, Anglo-Saxon
      Names, Old English
      Old English names
Names, Ethnic
  USE Names, Ethnological
Names, Ethnological *(May Subd Geog)*
  UF Ethnic group names
      Ethnological names
      Ethnology—Names
      Names, Ethnic
      Names of peoples
      Tribal names
  BT Onomastics
Names, Family
  USE Names, Personal
Names, Fictitious
  USE Anonyms and pseudonyms
Names, French
Names, Geographical *(May Subd Geog)*
    [G104-8]
  UF Geographical names
      Place-names
  BT Names
      Onomastics
  RT Geography—Terminology
      Toponymy

  SA *subdivision* Name *under names of*
      countries, cities, etc.
  NT Andover (Name)
      Field names
      Hanover (Name)
      Hydronymy
      Street names
      Tatsuta (Name)
  — Cataloging
    USE Names, Geographical
      (Cataloging)
  — Dictionaries
    USE Gazetteers
  — English, [Celtic, Latin, etc.]
  — Indians
    USE Indians—Names
  — Indians of North America
    USE Indians of North America—
      Names
  — Information storage and retrieval systems
    USE Information storage and retrieval
      systems—Names,
      Geographical
  — Law and legislation *(May Subd Geog)*
  — Pronunciation
  — Punched card systems
    USE Punched card systems—Names,
      Geographical
  — Transliteration
    BT Transliteration
Names, Geographical (Cataloging)
    [Z695.1.G4]
  UF Cataloging of geographical names
      Names, Geographical—Cataloging
Names, German *(May Subd Geog)*
  UF German language—Names
      German names
Names, Germanic *(May Subd Geog)*
  UF Germanic languages—Names
      Germanic names
Names, Hungarian *(May Subd Geog)*
  UF Hungarian language—Names
      Hungarian names
  BT Hungarian language—Etymology—
      Names
Names, Indian
  USE Indians—Names
Names, Indo-European *(May Subd Geog)*
  UF Indo-European names
Names, Irish *(May Subd Geog)*
  UF Irish language—Names
      Irish names
Names, Islamic
  USE Names, Personal—Islamic
Names, Italian
  UF Italian language—Names
      Italian names
  BT Italian language—Etymology—Names
Names, Japanese *(May Subd Geog)*
  UF Japanese language—Names
      Japanese names
  NT Mikado (Name)
Names, Jewish
  USE Names, Personal—Jewish
Names, Kazakh *(May Subd Geog)*
  UF Kazakh language—Names
      Kazakh names
  BT Kazakh language—Etymology—Names
Names, Khoikhoi *(May Subd Geog)*
  UF Khoikhoi language—Names
      Khoikhoi names
Names, Korean *(May Subd Geog)*
  UF Korean language—Names
      Korean names
  BT Korean language—Etymology—Names
Names, Langue d'oc *(May Subd Geog)*
  UF Langue d'oc—Names
      Langue d'oc names
Names, Latin *(May Subd Geog)*
  UF Latin language—Names
      Latin names

Names, Mashona *(May Subd Geog)*
  UF Mashona names
       Shona language—Names
Names, Mexican American
  UF Mexican American names
  BT Names, Personal
Names, Muslim
  USE Names, Personal—Islamic
Names, North American Indian
  USE Indians of North America—Names
Names, Old English
  USE Names, English (Old)
Names, Personal *(May Subd Geog)*
    ⌜CS2300-2389⌝
  UF Anthroponomy
       Baby names
       Christian names
       Family names
       Forenames
       Names, Christian
       Names, Family
       Names of families
       Names of persons
       Personal names
       Surnames
  BT Names
       Onomastics
  SA *subdivision* Name *under names of*
       individual persons; and individual
       personal and family names, e.g.
       Mary (Name)
  NT Anne (Name)
       Anonyms and pseudonyms
       Anthony (Name)
       DeLage (Name)
       Drake (Name)
       Fick (Name)
       Fortune-telling by names
       Ingemar (Name)
       John (Name)
       Louis (Name)
       McCracken (Name)
       McDaniel (Name)
       Michael (Name)
       Morris (Name)
       Names, Mexican American
       Nicknames
       Oliver (Name)
       Peter (Name)
       Tatsuta (Name)
       Vincent (Name)
       William (Name)
  — Cataloging
      USE Names, Personal (Cataloging)
  — Conflict of laws
      USE Conflict of laws—Names,
            Personal
  — Islamic *(May Subd Geog)*
      ⌜CS2970⌝
      UF Islamic names
           Islamic personal names
           Muslim names
           Names, Islamic
           Names, Muslim
  — Jewish *(May Subd Geog)*
      ⌜CS3010⌝
      UF Jewish names
           Jewish personal names
           Names, Jewish
  — Law and legislation *(May Subd Geog)*
      BT Personality (Law)
  — Pronunciation
  — Religious aspects
  — — Buddhism
        NT Buddhist posthumous names
  — — Buddhism, ⌜Christianity, etc.⌝
  — Scottish, ⌜Spanish, Welsh, etc.⌝
Names, Personal (Cataloging)
    (May Subd Geog)
    ⌜Z695.1.P4⌝

  UF Cataloging of personal names
       Names, Personal—Cataloging
Names, Personal, in art
  NT Names carved on trees
Names, Personal (Jewish law)
Names, Personal (Roman law)
Names, Portuguese *(May Subd Geog)*
  UF Portuguese language—Names
       Portuguese names
  BT Portuguese language—Etymology—
       Names
Names, Posthumous, Buddhist
  USE Buddhist posthumous names
Names, Romance *(May Subd Geog)*
  UF Romance languages—Names
       Romance names
Names, School of (Chinese philosophy)
  USE School of logicians (Chinese
        philosophy)
Names, Sorbian *(May Subd Geog)*
  UF Sorbian names
  BT Sorbian languages—Names
Names, Spanish *(May Subd Geog)*
  UF Spanish language—Names
       Spanish names
  BT Spanish language—Etymology—Names
Names, Welsh *(May Subd Geog)*
  UF Welsh language—Names
       Welsh names
Names carved on trees
  UF Initials on trees
       Names on trees
  BT Art—Themes, motives
       Names, Personal, in art
       Trees in art
       Wood-carving
Names derived from animals
  BT Onomastics
       Zoology—Nomenclature (Popular)
Names in poetry
  BT Poetry
Names in the Bible
    ⌜BS435⌝
  UF Bible—Names
  NT God—Name
       Israel—Name
       Jesus Christ—Name
       Jews—Name
  — Pronunciation
Names in the Book of Mormon
  UF Book of Mormon—Names
Names in the Talmud
    ⌜BM509.N3⌝
  UF Talmud—Names
Names of animals, Common
  USE Zoology—Nomenclature (Popular)
Names of animals, Scientific
  USE Zoology—Nomenclature
Names of corporate bodies
  USE *subdivision* Name *under names of*
        individual corporate bodies; and
        subdivision Names *under types of*
        corporate bodies, e.g. Universities
        and colleges—Names
Names of families
  USE Names, Personal
Names of peoples
  USE Names, Ethnological
Names of persons
  USE Names, Personal
Names of plants, Common
  USE Plant names, Popular
Names of plants, Scientific
  USE Botany—Nomenclature
Names of poems
  USE Titles of poems
Names on trees
  USE Names carved on trees
Namgang (Kyŏngsang-namdo, Korea)
  USE Nam River (Kyŏngsang-namdo, Korea)

Namib Desert (Namibia)
  BT Deserts—Namibia
Namibia
    ⌜DT701-DT720 (History)⌝
  UF Africa, German Southwest
       Africa, Southwest
       German Southwest Africa
       South-West Africa
       Southwest Africa
  — Description and travel
  — — 1981-
  — History
  — — To 1884
  — — 1884-1915
  — — Herero Revolt, 1904-1907
        UF Herero Revolt, Namibia, 1904-
             1907
        BT Hereros—History
  — — 1915-1946
        NT Bondelswarts Rebellion, 1922
             Rehoboth Basters Rebellion,
             1925
  — — 1946-
  — Languages
      NT Mbukushu language
           Nama language
           !Xõ language
           !Xũ language
  — Politics and government
  — — 1884-1915
  — — 1946-
Namibian arts
  USE Arts, Namibian
Namibian students *(May Subd Geog)*
  UF South-West African students
  BT Students
  — Foreign countries
      UF South-West African students in
           foreign countries
      BT Students, Foreign
Naming (Semantics)
  USE Onomasiology
Namnam (African people)
  UF Nabdam (African people)
  BT Ethnology—Ghana
Nampudiri
  USE Nambudiri
Namshi (African people)
  USE Dowayo (African people)
Namu (Whale)
    ⌜QL795.W5⌝
  BT Killer whale
Nan family *(Not Subd Geog)*
Nan Hai
  USE South China Sea
Nan Han, China, 917-971
  USE China—History—Southern Han
        kingdom, 917-971
Nan hsün t'u (Scroll)
  USE Wang, Hui, 1632-1717. Imperial
        inspection tour of the South
Nan hu
    ⌜ML927.N⌝
  BT Hu ch'in
       Musical instruments—China
       Stringed instruments, Bowed
  RT Erh hu
Nan hu music
    ⌜M59.N⌝
Nan Kai
  USE South China Sea
Nan Shan (China)
  USE Ch'i-lien Mountains (China)
Nan-shan Shan-mo (China)
  USE Ch'i-lien Mountains (China)
Nan T'ang, China, 937-975
  USE China—History—Southern T'ang
        kingdom, 937-975
Nan-t'ung dialect
  USE Chinese language—Dialects—China—
        Nan-t'ung-shih

Nanai language
  [PL481.N34]
  UF Goldi language
     Goldian language
  BT China—Languages
     Tungus-Manchu languages
Nanaita Iseki (Yasu-machi, Fukuoka-ken,
  Japan)
  USE Nanaita Site (Yasu-machi, Fukuoka-
       ken, Japan)
**Nanaita Site (Yasu-machi, Fukuoka-ken,
  Japan)**
  UF Nanaita Iseki (Yasu-machi, Fukuoka-
     ken, Japan)
  BT Japan—Antiquities
Nanawa, Battle of, 1933 (Jan. 20-24)
  BT Chaco War, 1932-1935
Nanawa, Battle of, 1933 (July 4-6)
  BT Chaco War, 1932-1935
Nanban art
  USE Namban art
Nanban byōbu
  USE Namban screen painting
Nanban screens
  USE Namban screen painting
Nanbikuara Indians
  USE Nambicuara Indians
Nanbikuara language
  USE Nambicuara language
Nanbu family
  USE Nambu family
Nanbumichi (Japan)
  USE Heiwa Kaidō (Japan)
Nance family (Not Subd Geog)
  UF Nans family
     Nantz family
Nancere language (May Subd Geog)
  UF Nanchere language
     Nantcere language
     Nantjere language
  BT Central African Republic—Languages
     Chad—Languages
     Chadic languages
Nanchere language
  USE Nancere language
Nancy, Battle of, 1477
  [DC106.3]
  BT France—History—Louis XI, 1461-
     1483
Nancy Drew (Fictitious character)
  USE Drew, Nancy (Fictitious character)
Nancy Hanks Lincoln State Memorial (Ind.)
  BT Lincoln Boyhood National Memorial
     (Ind.)
     Monuments—Indiana
Nanda Devi (India) (Not Subd Geog)
  BT Himalaya Mountains
     Mountains—India
Nande (Zairian people)
  [DT650.N34]
  UF Banande (Zairian people)
     Konjo (Zairian people)
     Nandi (Zairian people)
     Ndande (Zairian people)
     Ndgandi (Zairian people)
     Wahondjo (Zairian people)
     Wanande (Zairian people)
  BT Ethnology—Zaire
Nande language
  [PL8544]
  BT Bantu languages
Nandi (African people)
  [DT433.545.N34]
  UF Cemual (African people)
  BT Ethnology—Kenya
     Ethnology—Tanzania
     Ethnology—Uganda
     Nilo-Hamitic tribes
Nandi (Zairian people)
  USE Nande (Zairian people)

Nandi language
  BT Kalenjin language
     Kenya—Languages
     Nandi languages
  NT Kipsikis dialect
Nandi languages (May Subd Geog)
  UF Nandi-Suk languages
     Southern Nilotic languages
  BT Kenya—Languages
     Nilo-Hamitic languages
     Tanzania—Languages
     Uganda—Languages
  NT Kalenjin language
     Nandi language
     Suk language
Nandi law
  USE Law, Nandi
Nandi-Suk languages
  USE Nandi languages
Nandidae
  [QL638.N25]
  BT Perciformes
Nanga
  UF Nanshūga
  BT Watercolor painting, Japanese
Nanga Parbat (India)
  UF Diamir (India)
  BT Himalaya Mountains
     Mountains—India
Nanga Poroja
  USE Bondos
Ñangatú language
  USE Tupi language
Nangudi Vellalas
  [DS432.N36]
  UF Savalai Pillais
     Sevalai Pillaimars
  BT Caste—India
     Ethnology—India
     Vellalas
Nani (Guinea)
  USE Niani (Guinea)
Naniwa Kyū (Osaka, Japan)
  (Not Subd Geog)
  UF Naniwa no Miya (Osaka, Japan)
     Naniwa Palace (Osaka, Japan)
     Naniwa Palaces (Osaka, Japan)
  BT Japan—Antiquities
     Palaces—Japan
Naniwa no Miya (Osaka, Japan)
  USE Naniwa Kyū (Osaka, Japan)
Naniwa Palace (Osaka, Japan)
  USE Naniwa Kyū (Osaka, Japan)
Naniwa Palaces (Osaka, Japan)
  USE Naniwa Kyū (Osaka, Japan)
Naniwabushi
  BT Monologues with music (Shamisen)
     Sekkyō jōruri
Naniwabushi reciters
Nanjō family (Not Subd Geog)
Nankai Denki Tetsudō
  BT Railroads—Japan
     Street-railroads—Japan
Nankai Trough
  UF Kyusyu Zhelob
  BT Submarine topography—Pacific Ocean
Nankanse language
  [PL8546]
  UF Frafra language
     Gurenne language
     Gurune language
  BT Gur languages
Nankeen night heron
  USE Rufous night heron
Nannippus phlegon
  BT Horses, Fossil
Nannopterum harrisi
  USE Flightless cormorant
Nannorhamdia
  [QL638.P6]
  BT Pimelodidae

  NT Nannorhamdia lineata
Nannorhamdia lineata
  [QL638.P6]
  BT Nannorhamdia
Nannosquilla
  [QL444.M375]
  BT Nannosquillidae
Nannosquillidae
  [QL444.M375]
  BT Stomatopoda
  NT Nannosquilla
Nanobius
  [QL596.S75]
  BT Staphylinidae
Nanomana (Tuvalu)
  USE Nanumanga (Tuvalu)
Nanoo (Solomon Islands)
  USE Utupua (Solomon Islands)
Nanoparticles (May Subd Geog)
  [RS201.N35 (Pharmacy)]
  BT Particles
Nans family
  USE Nance family
Nanse (Legendary character)
  USE Anansi (Legendary character)
Nansen passports
  USE Passports, Refugee
Nansha Islands
  USE Spratly Islands
Nanshūga
  USE Nanga
Nansi (Legendary character)
  USE Anansi (Legendary character)
Nantahala National Forest (N.C.)
  BT Forest reserves—North Carolina
     National parks and reserves—United
     States
Nantahala River (N.C.)
  BT Rivers—North Carolina
Nantcere language
  USE Nancere language
Nantes à Brest Canal (France)
  UF Brest-Nantes Canal (France)
     Canal de Nantes à Brest (France)
     Nantes-Brest Canal (France)
  BT Canals—France
Nantes-Brest Canal (France)
  USE Nantes à Brest Canal (France)
Nantes, Edict of
  USE Edict of Nantes
Nantgarw porcelain
  [NK4399.N]
Nantgarw pottery
  [NK4399.N3]
  BT Pottery—Wales
Nantican Island (Mass.)
  USE Nantucket Island (Mass.)
Nanticoke Indians
  [E99.N14]
  BT Indians of North America
  — Land transfers
Nanticoke language
  [PM2001]
Nanticoke River (Del. and Md.)
  BT Rivers—Delaware
     Rivers—Maryland
Nantjere language
  USE Nancere language
Nantocket Island (Mass.)
  USE Nantucket Island (Mass.)
Nantoe Island (Mass.)
  USE Nantucket Island (Mass.)

Nantucket Island (Mass.)
  UF Nantican Island (Mass.)
      Nantocket Island (Mass.)
      Nantoe Island (Mass.)
      Nantuket Island (Mass.)
      Nantukket Island (Mass.)
      Natace Island (Mass.)
      Natocke Island (Mass.)
      Natocko Island (Mass.)
      Nauticon Island (Mass.)
      Neutocket Island (Mass.)
      Siasconset Island (Mass.)
  BT Islands—Massachusetts
Nantucket pine moth
  UF Rhyacionia frustrana
  BT Moths
Nantuket Island (Mass.)
  USE Nantucket Island (Mass.)
Nantukket Island (Mass.)
  USE Nantucket Island (Mass.)
Nantz family
  USE Nance family
Nanumaga (Tuvalu)
  USE Nanumanga (Tuvalu)
Nanumanaga (Tuvalu)
  USE Nanumanga (Tuvalu)
Nanumanga (Tuvalu)
  UF Hudson Island (Tuvalu)
      Nanomana (Tuvalu)
      Nanumaga (Tuvalu)
      Nanumanaga (Tuvalu)
  BT Coral reefs and islands—Tuvalu
Nanumea Atoll (Tuvalu)
  BT Coral reefs and islands—Tuvalu
Nanzi (Legendary character)
  USE Anansi (Legendary character)
Naoki Sanjūgo shō
  USE Naoki shō
Naoki shō
  UF Naoki Sanjūgo shō
  BT Japanese fiction—Competitions—Japan
      Literary prizes—Japan
Naouru language
  USE Nauru language
Nap family
  USE Knapp family
Napa cabbage
  USE Chinese cabbage
Napa River (Calif.)
  BT Rivers—California
Napaeozapus insignis
  USE Woodland jumping mouse
Napalm
  BT Incendiary weapons
      Metallic soaps
Napata (Ancient city)
  BT Cities and towns, Ruined, extinct, etc.
      —Sudan
      Sudan—Antiquities
Napeague Dunes (Long Island, N.Y.)
  BT Sand-dunes—New York (State)
Naphtali (Tribe of Israel)
  BT Jews
      Lost tribes of Israel
      Twelve tribes of Israel
Naphtha
  [QP915.N2 (Physiological effects)]
  [TP692.4.N3 (Technology)]
  UF Naptha
  NT Nafalan
  — Tariff
    USE Tariff on naphtha
Naphtha industry (May Subd Geog)
  [HD9579.N3-5]
Naphtha-launches
  [GV835 (Boating)]
  [VM341 (Construction)]
  BT Launches
Naphthacridinone
  UF Ceramidone
      Ceramidonine

  BT Acridine
      Heterocyclic compounds
Naphthalene
  [QD391]
  BT Polycyclic aromatic hydrocarbons
  NT Copper naphthenate
      Decahydronaphthalene
      Naphthoquinone
      Propoxyphene napsylate
Naphthaleneacetic acid
  NT Naproxen
Naphthanthracene
  USE Benzanthracenes
Naphthaquinone
  USE Naphthoquinone
Naphthazarin
  [TP918.N2 (Dyes)]
  UF Alizarin black
  BT Coal-tar colors
Naphthenic acids
  BT Acids, Organic
      Cycloparaffins
Naphthoquinone
  [QC463.N35 (Spectra)]
  UF Naphthaquinone
  BT Naphthalene
Naphthylamines
  BT Amines
Napier Expedition, 1867-1868
  USE Abyssinian Expedition, 1867-1868
Napipi Expedition, 1875
  [TC773]
Napipí River (Colombia)
  UF Río Napipí (Colombia)
  BT Rivers—Colombia
Napkin folding
  UF Folding of napkins
  BT Table setting and decoration
Napkin rings (May Subd Geog)
  BT Rings
Napkin rings, Victorian (May Subd Geog)
  UF Victorian napkin rings
Napkins, Sanitary
  USE Sanitary napkins
Naples (Italy)
  — History
  — — To 1503
  — — 1503-1734
  — — 1734-1860
  — — 1860-1945
  — — 1945-
  — Politics and government
  — — 1860-1945
  — — 1945-
Naples (Kingdom)
  NT Italy, Southern
  — Economic conditions
  — — 18th century
      [HC307.N3]
  — History
  — — To 1016
      [DG847.1-847.11]
  — — 1016-1268
      NT Italy—History—Germanic rule,
          962-1268
  — — Anjou dynasty, 1268-1442
  — — Jane I, 1343-1382
  — — Spanish rule, 1442-1707
      [DG848.1-DG848.15]
      BT Aragon (Spain)—History—John
          II, 1458-1479
      NT Palermo (Sicily)—History—
          Rebellion, 1647
  — — Rebellion, 1485-1487
      [DG848.115]
  — — 1735-1861
      [DG848.3]
      NT Expedition of the Thousand,
          1860
          Naples (Kingdom)—History—
          Jacobin Conspiracy, 1794

          Naples (Kingdom)—History—
          Sapri expedition, 1857
  — — Jacobin Conspiracy, 1794
      UF Jacobin Conspiracy, Naples,
          1794
      BT Jacobins
          Naples (Kingdom)—History—
          1735-1861
  — — Joseph Bonaparte, 1806-1808
      [DG848.44]
  — — Joachim Murat, 1808-1815
      [DG848.45]
  — — War of 1815
      [DG848.45]
      BT Austria—History—1789-1815
          Italy—History—1789-1815
  — — Revolution, 1820-1821
      [DG848.51]
  — — Revolution, 1848
  — — 1848-1861
      [DG848.55-848.57]
  — — Sapri expedition, 1857
      [DG848.55]
      UF Sapri expedition, 1857
          Sapri Rebellion, 1857
      BT Naples (Kingdom)—History—
          1735-1861
Naples, Bay of (Italy) (Not Subd Geog)
  UF Bay of Naples (Italy)
      Golfo di Napoli (Italy)
  BT Bays—Italy
Napo Indians
  USE Canelo Indians
      Quijo Indians
Napo River (Ecuador and Peru)
  (Not Subd Geog)
  UF Río Napo (Ecuador and Peru)
  BT Rivers—Ecuador
      Rivers—Peru
**Napoleon I, Emperor of the French, 1769-
1821**
  — Abdication, 1814
      [DC238]
  — Art patronage
      BT Art patronage
          Art patrons
  — Assassination attempt, 1800 (December
    24)
  — Captivity, 1815-1821
      [DC211]
  — Consulate, 1799-1804
      USE France—History—Consulate and
          Empire, 1799-1815
  — Coronation
      [DC206]
  — Death mask
  — Drama
      RT Napoleon I, Emperor of the
          French, 1769-1821, in fiction,
          drama, poetry, etc.
  — Elba and the Hundred Days, 1814-1815
      UF Hundred Days, 1815
  — Empire, 1804-1814
      USE France—History—Consulate and
          Empire, 1799-1815
  — Fiction
      RT Napoleon I, Emperor of the
          French, 1769-1821, in fiction,
          drama, poetry, etc.
  — Friends and associates
  — Headquarters (May Subd Geog)
  — Palaces (May Subd Geog)
      BT Palaces—France
      NT Palais du Roi de Rome (Paris,
          France)
  — Poetry
      RT Napoleon I, Emperor of the
          French, 1769-1821, in fiction,
          drama, poetry, etc.
  — Relations with women
      [DC204]

2535

Napoleon I, Emperor of the French, 1769-1821
— **Relations with women** *(Continued)*
UF Napoleon I, Emperor of the French, 1769-1821—Women
— **Will**
[DC214.3]
— **Women**
USE Napoleon I, Emperor of the French, 1769-1821—Relations with women
Napoleon I, Emperor of the French, 1769-1821, in fiction, drama, poetry, etc.
RT Napoleon I, Emperor of the French, 1769-1821—Drama
Napoleon I, Emperor of the French, 1769-1821—Fiction
Napoleon I, Emperor of the French, 1769-1821—Poetry
Napoleon, Continental system of
USE Continental system of Napoleon
Napoleon Hollow Site (Ill.)
BT Illinois—Antiquities
Napoleonic Wars, 1800-1814
BT Europe—History—1789-1815
France—History—Consulate and Empire, 1799-1815
NT First Coalition, War of the, 1792-1797
Peninsular War, 1807-1814
Second Coalition, War of the, 1798-1801
Walcheren Expedition, 1809
Wars of Liberation, 1813-1814
— **Campaigns** *(May Subd Geog)*
— — **Austria**
NT Aspern, Battle of, 1809
Dürnstein, Battle of, 1805
Hollabrunn (Hollabrunn, Austria), Battle of, 1805
Tyrol (Austria)—History—Uprising of 1809
Wagram, Battle of, 1809
— — **Czechoslovakia**
NT Austerlitz, Battle of, 1805
Znojmo (Czechoslovakia), Battle of, 1809
— — **France**
NT Paris (France)—History—Capitulation, 1814
— — **Germany (East)**
NT Bautzen, Battle of, 1813
Dennewitz, Battle of, 1813
Dresden, Battle of, 1813
Grossbeeren, Battle of, 1813
Jena, Battle of, 1806
Leipzig, Battle of, 1813
Lützen, Battle of, 1813
— — **Germany (West)**
NT Ebelsberg, Battle of, 1809
Elchingen, Battle of, 1805
Ulm (Germany)—History—Capitulation, 1805
— — **Italy**
NT Gaeta (Italy), Battle of, 1806
Marengo, Battle of, 1800
Rivoli, Battle of, 1797
— — **Russian S.F.S.R.**
NT Preussisch-Eylau, Battle of, 1807
— — **Soviet Union**
UF Soviet Union—History—Invasion, 1812
— **Proposed invasion of England, 1793-1805**
BT Great Britain—History—1789-1820
Napolitana
USE Strambotto
Napothera
[QL696.P285]
BT Timaliidae
NT Napothera rabori
Napothera rabori
[QL696.P285]

UF Luzon wren-babbler
Rabor's wren-babbler
BT Napothera
Napp family
USE Knapp family
Nappe family
USE Knapp family
Napper family *(Not Subd Geog)*
UF Knapper family
RT Knapp family
Nappes (Geology) *(May Subd Geog)*
[QE606]
UF Decke (Geology)
BT Faults (Geology)
Folds (Geology)
Napping (Textiles)
[TS1510]
UF Gigging (Textiles)
Raising (Textiles)
BT Textile finishing
Napping machines
BT Textile machinery
Naprapathy
BT Therapeutics, Physiological
Naproxen
[RM666.N]
UF Methoxymethylnaphthaleneacetic acid
BT Antiarthritic agents
Antipyretics
Bicyclic compounds
Naphthaleneacetic acid
Nonsteroidal anti-inflammatory agents
Naptha
USE Naphtha
Napu language *(May Subd Geog)*
UF Bara language (Indonesia)
BT Indonesia—Languages
Malayan languages
Naqshabandīyah *(May Subd Geog)*
[BP189.7.N35-352]
UF Naqshbandīyah
BT Dervishes
Sufism
Naqshabandīyah members *(May Subd Geog)*
Naqshbandīyah
USE Naqshabandīyah
Nar (African people)
[DT546.445.N35]
UF Sara Nar (African people)
BT Ethnology—Chad
Sara (African people)
Nara Imperial Palace (Nara-shi, Japan)
USE Heijōkyū (Nara-shi, Japan)
Nara language
USE Baria language
Nara no Miya (Nara-shi, Japan)
USE Heijōkyū (Nara-shi, Japan)
Narak language
[PL6621.N35]
UF Gandja language
Ganja language (Papua New Guinea)
Kandawo language
Kol language (Papua New Guinea)
BT Papuan languages
Narangga (Australian people)
[DU125.N36]
UF Adjadura (Australian people)
Narrangga (Australian people)
Narunga (Australian people)
Turra (Australian people)
Wallarod (Australian people)
BT Australian aborigines
Naranjilla
[SB379.N3]
UF Solanum quitoense
Naranjo agrio
USE Citrus aurantium
Naranjo amargo
USE Citrus aurantium
Naranjo Site (Guatemala) *(Not Subd Geog)*
[F1435.1.N37]

BT Guatemala—Antiquities
Narasiṃha (Hindu deity) *(May Subd Geog)*
UF Nṛsiṃha (Hindu deity)
BT Gods, Hindu
Nārāyaṇa (Hindu deity) *(May Subd Geog)*
BT Gods, Hindu
Vishnu (Hindu deity)
Narbada River (India)
USE Narmada River (India)
Narbona family *(Not Subd Geog)*
Narbonne House (Salem, Mass.)
BT Dwellings—Massachusetts
NARC (Electronic computer system)
UF Numerical Analysis of Rectangularly Configured Plane Strain
Narcissism
[BF575.N35 (Psychology)]
[RC553.N36 (Psychiatry)]
UF Self-love (Psychology)
BT Egoism
Psychology, Pathological
Narcissism in children *(May Subd Geog)*
BT Child psychopathology
Narcissus
USE Daffodils
Narcissus (Greek mythology)
BT Mythology, Greek
Narcissus bulb fly
UF Bulb fly
Daffodil fly
Narcissus fly
BT Bulbs—Diseases and pests
Daffodils—Diseases and pests
Narcissus fly
USE Narcissus bulb fly
Narcoanalysis
UF Truth serums
BT Narcotics
Psychoanalysis
Narcolepsy
BT Sleep
Sleep disorders
Narcopsychotherapy
USE Narcotherapy
Narcosis, Inert gas
USE Inert gas narcosis
Narcotherapy
[RC489.N3]
UF Narcopsychotherapy
BT Narcotics
Psychotherapy
Therapeutics, Suggestive
Narcotic addiction
USE Narcotic habit
Narcotic addicts *(May Subd Geog)*
For works on particular ethnic groups or classes of persons as narcotic addicts, assign as an additional heading [group or class]—Drug use, e.g. 1. Narcotic addicts. 2. Youth—Drug use.
UF Addicts, Narcotic
Drug addicts
BT Narcotic habit
Narcotics, Control of
NT Children of narcotic addicts
Church work with narcotic addicts
Narcotics and crime
— Hospitals and asylums
USE Narcotic habit—Hospitals
— **Legal status, laws, etc.**
(May Subd Geog)
BT Mental health laws
— **Rehabilitation** *(May Subd Geog)*
BT Drug abuse counseling
Narcotic addicts' adult children
USE Adult children of narcotic addicts
Narcotic agents (Persons)
USE Narcotic enforcement agents
Narcotic antagonists
BT Drug antagonism
Narcotics
NT Buprenorphine

Endorphin antagonists
Naloxone
Narcotic clinics *(May Subd Geog)*
⌐RA974.5⌐
  BT Clinics
Narcotic dealers
  USE Narcotics dealers
Narcotic enforcement agents
(May Subd Geog)
  UF Agents, Narcotic enforcement
    Narcotic agents (Persons)
    Narcs
  BT Law enforcement
Narcotic enforcement agents' wives
(May Subd Geog)
  BT Wives
Narcotic habit *(May Subd Geog)*
⌐HV5800-HV5840 (Economics)⌐
⌐RC566⌐
    Here are entered works limited to addiction to
  narcotics such as opium, morphine, codeine and he-
  roin. Works on the abuse or misuse of drugs in a
  broad sense, such as aspirin, bromides, caffeine, seda-
  tives, alcohol, LSD, marihuana, and narcotics, are
  entered under Drug abuse. Works on the abuse or
  misuse of therapeutic drugs are entered under Medi-
  cation abuse.
  UF Addiction to narcotics
    Drug addiction
    Drug habit
    Intoxication
    Narcotic addiction
  BT Drug abuse
    Habit
    Narcotics, Control of
    Temperance
  NT Chloral habit
    Cocaine habit
    Drug withdrawal symptoms
    Heroin habit
    Morphine habit
    Narcotic addicts
    Narcotics dealers
    Opium habit
— **Complications and sequelae**
— **Hospitals** *(May Subd Geog)*
  UF Narcotic addicts—Hospitals and
    asylums
— **Treatment** *(May Subd Geog)*
⌐RA1242.M3 (Toxicology)⌐
⌐RC566-RC568 (Psychiatry)⌐
Narcotic laws *(May Subd Geog)*
⌐RA402 (Public health)⌐
  BT Drugs—Law and legislation
  RT Narcotics, Control of
    Pharmacy—Law and legislation
  NT Designer drugs—Law and legislation
    Opium trade—Law and legislation
    Trials (Narcotic laws)
Narcotic laws (Islamic law)
(May Subd Geog)
  BT Islamic law
Narcotic receptors
  USE Endorphins—Receptors
Narcotic trade
  USE Narcotics, Control of
Narcotic traffic
  USE Narcotics, Control of
Narcotics *(May Subd Geog)*
⌐GT3010 (Manners and customs)⌐
⌐RM328 (Therapeutics)⌐
  UF Opiates
  BT Central nervous system depressants
  NT Bhang (Drug)
    Chloral
    Cocaine
    Endorphins
    Fentanyl
    Hashish
    Heroin
    Isonipecaine
    Lactucarium

Methadyl acetate
Morphine
Narcoanalysis
Narcotherapy
Narcotic antagonists
Narcotics, Control of
Opium
Qat
— **Overdosage**
  UF Overdosage of narcotics
— **Physiological effect**
— — **Genetic aspects**
  BT Drugs—Toxicology
— **Psychological aspects**
  BT Psychology, Applied
Narcotics, Control of *(May Subd Geog)*
  UF Drug traffic control
    Narcotic trade
    Narcotic traffic
  BT Narcotics
  RT Narcotic laws
  NT Narcotic addicts
    Narcotic habit
Narcotics and crime *(May Subd Geog)*
  UF Crime and narcotics
  BT Crime and criminals
    Narcotic addicts
Narcotics and youth *(May Subd Geog)*
  UF Youth and narcotics
  BT Youth
Narcotics dealers *(May Subd Geog)*
  UF Dealers, Narcotics
    Drug dealers
    Drug pushers
    Narcotic dealers
  BT Drug abuse
    Narcotic habit
Narcotics in literature
Narcs
  USE Narcotic enforcement agents
Narenta River (Bosnia and Hercegovina and
  Croatia)
  USE Neretva River (Bosnia and
    Hercegovina and Croatia)
Narev River (Byelorussian S.S.R. and Poland)
  USE Narew River (Byelorussian S.S.R. and
    Poland)
**Narew River (Byelorussian S.S.R. and
  Poland)**
  UF Narev River (Byelorussian S.S.R. and
    Poland)
  BT Rivers—Byelorussian S.S.R.
    Rivers—Poland
Narikawa Iseki (Japan)
  USE Narikawa Site (Japan)
Narikawa Site (Japan) *(Not Subd Geog)*
  UF Narikawa Iseki (Japan)
  BT Japan—Antiquities
Narinjari language
  USE Narrinyeri language
Narita family *(Not Subd Geog)*
Narmada River (India)
  UF Narbada River (India)
    Nerbudda River (India)
  BT Rivers—India
Narmouthis (Ancient city)
  USE Medinet Madi Site (Egypt)
Naro (African people)
  USE Naron (African people)
Naro River (Bosnia and Hercegovina and
  Croatia)
  USE Neretva River (Bosnia and
    Hercegovina and Croatia)
Naron (African people)
⌐DT709 (Namibia)⌐
⌐DT797 (Botswana)⌐
  UF Naro (African people)
    Naron tribe
    Nharo (African people)
    Nhauru (African people)
    Nhaurun (African people)

  BT Ethnology—Africa, Southern
    San (African people)
Naron tribe
  USE Naron (African people)
Narraganset Indians
⌐E99.N16⌐
  UF Narragansett Indians
  BT Algonquian Indians
    Indians of North America
  NT Brotherton Indians
Narraganset language
⌐PM2003⌐
  RT Algonquian languages
Narragansett Bay (R.I.)
  BT Bays—Rhode Island
Narragansett Indians
  USE Narraganset Indians
Narrangga (Australian people)
  USE Narangga (Australian people)
Narration (Rhetoric)
⌐PE1425 (English rhetoric)⌐
  UF Narrative writing
  BT Rhetoric
  RT Discourse analysis, Narrative
  NT First person narrative
    Free indirect speech
    Grammar, Comparative and general—
      Indirect discourse
    Narration in the Bible
    Point of view (Literature)
Narration in the Bible
  UF Bible—Narration
  BT Bible—Language, style
    Narration (Rhetoric)
Narration with music
  USE subdivision Readings with music *under*
      subjects, e.g. American poetry—
      20th century—Readings with music;
      Monologues—Readings with music
    Monologues with music
    Sacred monologues with music
Narrative, First person
  USE First person narrative
Narrative art *(May Subd Geog)*
⌐N7433.93⌐
  UF Art, Narrative
    Narrative art (Visual arts)
  BT Genre (Art)
  NT Stories without words
— **18th century** *(May Subd Geog)*
— **19th century** *(May Subd Geog)*
Narrative art, British *(May Subd Geog)*
  UF British narrative art
Narrative art, French *(May Subd Geog)*
  UF French narrative art
Narrative art, Italian *(May Subd Geog)*
  UF Italian narrative art
Narrative art, Renaissance
(May Subd Geog)
  UF Renaissance narrative art
Narrative art, Spanish *(May Subd Geog)*
  UF Spanish narrative art
Narrative art (Art movement)
(May Subd Geog)
⌐N6494.N3⌐
  UF Narrative art (Visual arts)
    Narrative figuration (Art movement)
  BT Art, Modern—20th century
Narrative art (Visual arts)
  USE Narrative art
    Narrative art (Art movement)
Narrative discourse analysis
  USE Discourse analysis, Narrative
Narrative figuration (Art movement)
  USE Narrative art (Art movement)
Narrative painting *(May Subd Geog)*
  UF Painting, Narrative
  BT Genre painting
    Painting
— **18th century** *(May Subd Geog)*
— **19th century** *(May Subd Geog)*

Narrative painting
— **19th century** *(Continued)*
    NT Narrative painting, Victorian
— **Japan**
    NT Saigyō monogatari emaki (Scrolls)
       Sōshun, fl. 1299-1303. Ippen
        Shōnin engi
       Tachibana, Moribe, 1781-1849.
        Taketori monogatari emaki
       Taketori monogatari emaki
        (Scrolls)
Narrative painting, British
(May Subd Geog)
    UF British narrative painting
Narrative painting, Dutch *(May Subd Geog)*
    UF Dutch narrative painting
Narrative painting, Flemish
(May Subd Geog)
    UF Flemish narrative painting
Narrative painting, French
(May Subd Geog)
    UF French narrative painting
Narrative painting, Gothic
(May Subd Geog)
    UF Gothic narrative painting
Narrative painting, Italian
(May Subd Geog)
    UF Italian narrative painting
Narrative painting, Japanese
(May Subd Geog)
    UF Japanese narrative painting
    NT Shigisan engi emaki (Scrolls)
— **To 1868**
— **Kamakura-Momoyama periods, 1185-1600**
— **Heian period, 794-1185**
— **20th century**
— **Taishō period, 1912-1926**
Narrative painting, Renaissance
(May Subd Geog)
    UF Renaissance narrative painting
Narrative painting, Spanish
(May Subd Geog)
    UF Spanish narrative painting
Narrative painting, Victorian
(May Subd Geog)
    UF Victorian narrative painting
    BT Narrative painting—19th century
Narrative poetry
    [PN6110.N17 (Collections)]
    BT Poetry
    RT Epic poetry
    NT Novelle
Narrative poetry, American
(May Subd Geog)
    UF American narrative poetry
Narrative poetry, American, [English, etc.]
(May Subd Geog)
Narrative poetry, Arabic *(May Subd Geog)*
    [PJ7542.N27]
    UF Arabic narrative poetry
    BT Arabic poetry
Narrative poetry, Australian
(May Subd Geog)
    [PR9615.85.N2 (Collections)]
    UF Australian narrative poetry
    BT Australian poetry
Narrative poetry, Bengali *(May Subd Geog)*
    UF Bengali narrative poetry
    BT Bengali poetry
Narrative poetry, Catalan *(May Subd Geog)*
    UF Catalan narrative poetry
    BT Catalan poetry
Narrative poetry, Chinese *(May Subd Geog)*
    [PL2309.N47 (History)]
    [PL2519.N47 (Collections)]
    UF Chinese narrative poetry
    BT Chinese poetry
Narrative poetry, English *(May Subd Geog)*
    UF English narrative poetry
    BT English poetry

Narrative poetry, French *(May Subd Geog)*
    UF French narrative poetry
    BT French poetry
Narrative poetry, German *(May Subd Geog)*
    UF German narrative poetry
    BT German poetry
Narrative poetry, Greek (Modern)
(May Subd Geog)
    UF Greek narrative poetry (Modern)
       Modern Greek narrative poetry
    BT Greek poetry, Modern
Narrative poetry, Gujarati
(May Subd Geog)
    UF Gujarati narrative poetry
    BT Gujarati poetry
Narrative poetry, Hindi *(May Subd Geog)*
    UF Hindi narrative poetry
    BT Hindi poetry
Narrative poetry, Latvian *(May Subd Geog)*
    UF Latvian narrative poetry
    BT Latvian poetry
Narrative poetry, Lithuanian
(May Subd Geog)
    UF Lithuanian narrative poetry
    BT Lithuanian poetry
Narrative poetry, Marathi
(May Subd Geog)
    UF Marathi narrative poetry
    BT Marathi poetry
Narrative poetry, Pai *(May Subd Geog)*
    UF Pai narrative poetry
    BT Pai poetry
Narrative poetry, Panjabi *(May Subd Geog)*
    UF Panjabi narrative poetry
    BT Panjabi poetry
Narrative poetry, Polish *(May Subd Geog)*
    UF Polish narrative poetry
    BT Polish poetry
Narrative poetry, Russian *(May Subd Geog)*
    UF Russian narrative poetry
    BT Russian poetry
Narrative poetry, Scottish *(May Subd Geog)*
    UF Scottish narrative poetry
    BT Scottish poetry
Narrative poetry, Swedish *(May Subd Geog)*
    UF Swedish narrative poetry
    BT Swedish poetry
Narrative poetry, Ukrainian
(May Subd Geog)
    UF Ukrainian narrative poetry
    BT Ukrainian poetry
Narrative writing
    USE Narration (Rhetoric)
Narratives, Passion (Gospels)
    USE Passion narratives (Gospels)
Narrinyeri (Australian people)
    [DU125.N37]
    UF Ngarrindjeri (Australian people)
    BT Australian aborigines
Narrinyeri language
    UF Narinjari language
    BT Australia—Languages
       Australian languages
Narris family
    USE Norris family
Narrow-band DME
    USE Distance measuring equipment
       (Aircraft to ground station)
Narrow-band radio frequency modulation
    USE Radio frequency modulation, Narrow-band
Narrow-gage railroads
    USE Railroads, Narrow-gage
Narrow gap semiconductors
    [QC611.8.N35]
    BT Conduction band
       Energy gap (Physics)
       Semiconductors
       Valence (Theoretical chemistry)
Narrow-leaved black peppermint (Tree)
    USE Eucalyptus nicholii

Narrow-leaved dock
    USE Rumex crispus
Narrow-leaved peppermint (Tree)
    USE Eucalyptus radiata
Narrow Mountain Brook (N.B.)
    BT Rivers—New Brunswick
Narrow-snouted dolphin
    USE Stenella attenuata
Narrow-winged damselflies
    USE Coenagrionidae
Narrowleaf ironbark eucalyptus
    USE Eucalyptus creba
Narrowleaf trefoil *(May Subd Geog)*
    [QK495.L52 (Botany)]
    UF Lotus tenuis
       Trefoil, Narrowleaf
    BT Forage plants
Narrows, The (Qld.)
    UF The Narrows (Qld.)
    BT River channels—Australia
Narthecium
    [QK495.L72]
    UF Asphodel, Bog
       Bog asphodel
    BT Liliaceae
Narthex
    BT Church architecture
Narunga (Australian people)
    USE Narangga (Australian people)
Narva, Battle of, 1700
    [DL743.N]
    BT Northern War, 1700-1721
Narvik, Battle of, 1940
    [D763.N6]
    BT World War, 1939-1945—Campaigns—Norway
Narwal
    USE Narwhal
Narwhal
    [QL737.C433]
    UF Monodon
       Monodon monoceros
       Narwal
       Narwhale
       Narwhals
    BT Monodontidae
Narwhale
    USE Narwhal
Narwhals
    USE Narwhal
NASA Structural Analysis Computer System
    USE NASTRAN (Computer program)
Nasal bone
    [QL947 (Comparative anatomy)]
    [QM505 (Human anatomy)]
    BT Facial bones
       Nose
Nasal capsule
    BT Cartilage
       Nose
Nasal cavity
    USE Nasal fossa
Nasal fossa
    [QL947 (Comparative anatomy)]
    [QM505 (Human anatomy)]
    UF Nasal cavity
    BT Nose
    NT Turbinate bones
Nasal gland for salt regulation
    USE Salt gland
Nasal medication
    USE Intranasal medication
Nasal mucosa
    UF Mucosa, Nasal
    BT Mucous membrane
       Nose
    NT Olfactory mucosa
— Inflammation
    USE Rhinitis
Nasal ornaments
    USE Nose ornaments

Nasal polyps
  BT Nose—Tumors
      Polyps (Pathology)
Nasal prostheses *(May Subd Geog)*
  BT Maxillofacial prosthesis
      Nose
      Prosthesis
  — Color
    UF Color of nasal prostheses
    BT Color of man
Nasal sinuses
  USE Paranasal sinuses
Nasal sounds (Phonetics)
  USE Nasality (Phonetics)
Nasalis
  [QL737.P93]
  UF Simias
  BT Cercopithecidae
  NT Proboscis monkey
Nasalis larvatus
  USE Proboscis monkey
Nasality (Phonetics)
  UF Nasal sounds (Phonetics)
      Nasalization (Phonetics)
  BT Grammar, Comparative and general—
      Phonology
      Sonorants (Phonetics)
      Voice
  SA *subdivision* Nasality *under names of*
      languages and groups of languages,
      e.g. English language—Nasality
Nasalization (Phonetics)
  USE Nasality (Phonetics)
Nasami Indians
  USE Coquille Indians
Nasca Site (Peru)
  USE Nazca Site (Peru)
Nascapee Indians
  [E99.N18]
  UF Nasquapee Indians
  BT Algonquian Indians
      Indians of North America
Nascapee language
  [PM2004.N3]
  BT Algonquian languages
Nasciturus
  USE Unborn children (Law)
NASDAQ Market System
  UF NASDAQ System
      National Association of Securities
        Dealers Automated Quotations
        Systems
  BT Stock-exchange—Data processing
      Stocks—Prices—Data bases
NASDAQ System
  USE NASDAQ Market System
Nase family
  USE Nassau family
Nasella trichotoma
  USE Serrated tussock
Nash family *(Not Subd Geog)*
Nash manifolds
  UF Manifolds, Nash
  BT Differentiable manifolds
Nash Metropolitan automobile
  [TL215.N]
  UF Metropolitan automobile
  BT American Motors automobiles
Nashis
  USE Moso (Tribe)
Nashua and Lowell Railroad
  BT Railroads—United States
Nashua River (Mass. and N.H.)
  BT Rivers—Massachusetts
      Rivers—New Hampshire
Nashville, Battle of, 1864
  [E477.52]
  BT United States—History—Civil War,
      1861-1865—Campaigns
Nasi
  UF Patriarchs and patriarchate (Jewish)

  BT Sanhedrin
Nasidae
  USE Surgeonfishes
Nasioi (Melanesian people)
  BT Ethnology—Papua New Guinea
Nasioi language
  [PL6621.N36]
  BT Papuan languages
Nasionale Kruger Wildtuin (South Africa)
  USE Kruger National Park (South Africa)
Nasoendoscopy
  USE Nasoscopy
Nasoni family *(Not Subd Geog)*
Nasopharyngitis *(May Subd Geog)*
  [RF361]
  UF Nasopharynx—Inflammation
  BT Nasopharynx—Diseases
      Pharyngitis
Nasopharyngoscopy *(May Subd Geog)*
  [RF345]
  BT Nasopharynx—Examination
      Rhinolaryngoscopy
Nasopharynx
  [QM505 (Human anatomy)]
  UF Rhinopharynx
  BT Nose
      Pharynx
      Throat
  NT Adenoids
  — Bacteriology
  — Cancer *(May Subd Geog)*
    [RC280.P4]
  — Diseases *(May Subd Geog)*
    NT Nasopharyngitis
  — Examination
    NT Nasopharyngoscopy
  — Inflammation
    USE Nasopharyngitis
  — Tumors
    [RC280.N6]
Nasoraeans
  USE Mandaeans
Nasoscopy *(May Subd Geog)*
  [RF345]
  UF Nasoendoscopy
  BT Nose—Examination
      Rhinolaryngoscopy
Nasqua language
  USE Niska language
Nasquapee Indians
  USE Nascapee Indians
Naṣr al-Dīn, Khwājah (Legendary character)
  USE Nasreddin Hoca (Legendary character)
Naṣr al-Dīn, Mullā (Legendary character)
  USE Nasreddin Hoca (Legendary character)
Nasreddin Hoca (Legendary character)
  [PN6231.N27 (Humor)]
  UF Molla Nasreddin (Legendary
      character)
      Mulla Nasreddin (Legendary
      character)
      Naṣr al-Dīn, Khwājah (Legendary
      character)
      Naṣr al-Dīn, Mullā (Legendary
      character)
      Nasrudin, Mulla (Legendary character)
  BT Folklore—Middle East
      Folklore—Turkey
Nasrides
  UF Alahmares
      Alhamarides
Nasrudin, Mulla (Legendary character)
  USE Nasreddin Hoca (Legendary character)
Nass family
  USE Nassau family
Nass River Indians
  USE Niska Indians
Nassau (Duchy)
  — History
  —— Revolution, 1848-1849
    [DD209.N]

  BT Germany—History—Revolution,
      1848-1849
Nassau family *(Not Subd Geog)*
  UF Naas family
      Nase family
      Nass family
      Nauss family
Nassau Island (Cook Islands)
  UF Motugaugau (Cook Islands)
  BT Islands—Cook Islands
Nassauische Kleinbahn
  BT Railroads—Germany (West)
Nasser, Lake (Egypt and Sudan)
  UF Lake Nasser (Egypt and Sudan)
  BT Lakes—Egypt
      Lakes—Sudan
      Reservoirs—Egypt
      Reservoirs—Sudan
NASTRAN (Computer program)
  UF NASA Structural Analysis Computer
      System
  BT Structures, Theory of—Computer
      programs
Nasturtium (Garden flower)
  USE Nasturtiums
Nasturtium (Genus)
  [QK495.C9]
  BT Cruciferae
  NT Watercress
Nasturtium mosaic
  USE Turnip mosaic virus
Nasturtium officinale
  USE Watercress
Nasturtiums
  [SB413.N (Culture)]
  UF Garden nasturtiums
      Nasturtium (Garden flower)
      Tall nasturtiums
      Tropaeolum majus
Nasu Chihō (Japan)
  USE Nasu Region (Japan)
Nasu Region (Japan)
  UF Nasu Chihō (Japan)
Nasua
  USE Coatis
Na't
  USE Elegiac poetry, Arabic
Nat Turner's Insurrection
  USE Southampton Insurrection, 1831
Natace Island (Mass.)
  USE Nantucket Island (Mass.)
Natal (South Africa)
  — History
  —— To 1843
  —— 1843-1893
      NT Langalibalele Rebellion, 1873
  —— 1893-1910
  —— 1910-
  — Politics and government
  —— 1910-
NATAL (Computer program language)
  [QA76.73.N]
  BT Programming languages (Electronic
      computers)
Natal Lake (Ont.)
  BT Lakes—Ontario
Natal stones
  USE Birthstones
Natality
  USE Fertility, Human
Natan family
  USE Nathan family
Natantia (Decapoda)
  USE Shrimps
Natchesan Indians
  [E99.N]
  BT Indians of North America
  NT Natchez Indians
      Taensa Indians
Natchez (Miss.)
  — History

Natchez (Miss.)
— History   (Continued)
— — Civil War, 1861-1865
Natchez City Cemetery (Natchez, Miss.)
    BT Cemeteries—Mississippi
Natchez Indians
    [E99.N2]
    BT Indians of North America
        Natchesan Indians
    NT Taensa Indians
— Antiquities
— Wars, 1716
        [E83.716]
        BT Indians of North America—Wars—
            1600-1750
Natchez language
    [PM2004.N4]
Natchez Trace
    BT Roads—Alabama
        Roads—Mississippi
        Roads—Tennessee
Nate family
    USE Neat family
Nath language
    USE Nuer language
Natha sect
    [BL1278.5-1278.592]
    BT Hindu sects
Nathan family   (Not Subd Geog)
    UF Natan family
        Nathans family
        Nathanson family
Nathan Hale, Fort (New Haven, Conn.)
    USE Fort Nathan Hale (New Haven,
         Conn.)
Nathan Söderblom vicarage (Sweden)
    USE Stabby prästgård (Sweden)
Nathans family
    USE Nathan family
Nathanson family
    USE Nathan family
Nather family
    USE Nethers family
Nathers family
    USE Nethers family
Naticidae, Fossil
    [QE809.N32]
    UF Moon shells, Fossil
    BT Pectinibranchiata, Fossil
Natick Indians
    USE Massachuset Indians
Natick language
    USE Massachuset language
Nation family   (Not Subd Geog)
    UF Nations family
Nation of Islam
    USE Black Muslims
Nation-state
    USE National state
National accounting
    USE National income—Accounting
National accounts marketing
    USE Marketing—Key accounts
National achievement award
    BT Rewards (Prizes, etc.)—United States
National Antarctic Expedition, 1901-1904
    [G850 1901]
    [Q115]
National anthems
    USE National songs
National Assessment of Educational Progress
    (Project)
    BT Academic achievement
        Educational tests and measurements—
        United States
National Association of Securities Dealers
    Automated Quotations Systems
    USE NASDAQ Market System
National bank notes
    [HG607-HG609 (United States)]

[HG651-HG1490 (15) or (7) under
    country (Other countries)]
    RT Bank-notes
National bankruptcy
    USE State bankruptcy
National banks (United States)
    [HG2545-2557]
    BT Banks and banking—United States
        Banks of issue—United States
National bibliography
    USE Bibliography, National
National Book Awards
    BT Literary prizes
National book week   (May Subd Geog)
    UF Book week, National
    BT Books and reading
        National Library Week
National Botanic Garden (Luzon, Philippines)
    USE National Botanic Garden of the
         Philippines (Luzon, Philippines)
National Botanic Garden of the Philippines
    (Luzon, Philippines)
    UF National Botanic Garden (Luzon,
        Philippines)
    BT Botanical gardens—Philippines
National Bureau of Standards Load
    Determination (Computer program)
    USE NBSLD (Computer program)
National Capitol (Washington, D.C.)
    USE United States Capitol (Washington,
         D.C.)
National cemeteries   (May Subd Geog)
    UF Military cemeteries and funerals
    RT Military parks
— Contracting out
        BT Contracting out
— Law and legislation   (May Subd Geog)
— Maryland
        NT Antietam National Cemetery (Md.)
— United States
        [E160]
        [E494]
        [UB393-UB394]
        UF United States—National cemeteries
        BT Cemeteries
        RT Soldiers' bodies, Disposition of
        NT National Memorial Cemetery of
            the Pacific (Honolulu, Hawaii)
— Virginia
        NT Arlington National Cemetery (Va.)
National cemeteries, American, [British, etc.]
    (May Subd Geog)
National Cemetery of the Pacific (Honolulu,
    Hawaii)
    USE National Memorial Cemetery of the
         Pacific (Honolulu, Hawaii)
National Championship Air Races, Reno, Nev.
    [GV759.2.N37]
    UF Reno Air Races, Reno, Nev.
        Reno National Championship Air
        Races, Reno, Nev.
    BT Airplane racing—Nevada
National characteristics
    [CB195-CB197]
    [CB203 (Europe)]
    UF Characteristics
        National images
        National psychology
        Psychology, National
    BT Anthropology
        Nationalism
        Social psychology
    RT Ethnopsychology
    NT Local color in literature
— Anecdotes, facetiae, satire, etc.
        USE Ethnic wit and humor
National characteristics, African
    UF African national characteristics
National characteristics, American
    UF American national characteristics
    NT Uncle Sam (Nickname)

National characteristics, American, in motion
    pictures   (May Subd Geog)
    UF American national characteristics in
        motion pictures
    BT Moving-pictures
National characteristics, Antillean
    UF Antillean national characteristics
National characteristics, Arab
    UF Arab national characteristics
National characteristics, Argentine
    (May Subd Geog)
    UF Argentine national characteristics
National characteristics, Australian
    UF Australian national characteristics
National characteristics, Basque
    UF Basque national characteristics
National characteristics, Belgian
    UF Belgian national characteristics
National characteristics, Brazilian
    UF Brazilian national characteristics
National characteristics, Breton
    UF Breton national characteristics
National characteristics, British
    UF British national characteristics
    NT National characteristics, English
National characteristics, Bulgarian
    UF Bulgarian national characteristics
National characteristics, Canadian
    UF Canadian national characteristics
National characteristics, Catalan
    UF Catalan national characteristics
National characteristics, Chilean
    UF Chilean national characteristics
National characteristics, Chinese
    UF Chinese national characteristics
National characteristics, Chinese, [French,
    Russian, etc.]
National characteristics, Costa Rican
    UF Costa Rican national characteristics
National characteristics, Cuban
    UF Cuban national characteristics
National characteristics, East German
    UF East German national characteristics
National characteristics, East Indian
    UF East Indian national characteristics
        Indic national characteristics
        National characteristics, Indic
National characteristics, Egyptian
    [DT70]
    UF Egyptian national characteristics
National characteristics, English
    UF English national characteristics
    BT National characteristics, British
National characteristics, Eritrean
    UF Eritrean national characteristics
National characteristics, European
    UF European national characteristics
National characteristics, Finnish
    UF Finnish national characteristics
National characteristics, French
    UF French national characteristics
National characteristics, Gallegan
    UF Gallegan national characteristics
National characteristics, German
    UF German national characteristics
National characteristics, Greek
    UF Greek national characteristics
National characteristics, Hungarian
    UF Hungarian national characteristics
National characteristics, Indic
    USE National characteristics, East Indian
National characteristics, Indonesian
    UF Indonesian national characteristics
National characteristics, Irish
    UF Irish national characteristics
National characteristics, Israeli
    UF Israeli national characteristics
National characteristics, Italian
    UF Italian national characteristics
National characteristics, Japanese
    NT Bushido

National characteristics, Korean
  NT Hwarangdo
National characteristics, Latin American
  UF Latin American national characteristics
National characteristics, Malagasy
  UF Malagasy national characteristics
National characteristics, Mexican
  [F1210]
  UF Mexican national characteristics
National characteristics, New Zealand
  UF New Zealand national characteristics
National characteristics, Nigerian
  UF Nigerian national characteristics
National characteristics, Panamanian
  UF Panamanian national characteristics
National characteristics, Paraguayan
  UF Paraguayan national characteristics
National characteristics, Philippine
  UF Philippine national characteristics
National characteristics, Prussian
  [DD350]
  UF Prussian national characteristics
National characteristics, Puerto Rican
  [F1960]
  UF Puerto Rican national characteristics
National characteristics, Romanian
  UF Romanian national characteristics
National characteristics, Russian
  UF Russian national characteristics
National characteristics, Scandinavian
  UF Scandinavian national characteristics
National characteristics, Scottish
  UF Scottish national characteristics
National characteristics, Serbian
  UF Serbian national characteristics
National characteristics, Singapore
  UF Singapore national characteristics
National characteristics, Spanish
  [DP52]
  UF Spanish national characteristics
National characteristics, Sudanese
  UF Sudanese national characteristics
National characteristics, Swedish
  UF Swedish national characteristics
National characteristics, Swiss
  UF Swiss national characteristics
National characteristics, Thai
  UF Thai national characteristics
National characteristics, Ukrainian
  UF Ukrainian national characteristics
National characteristics, Venezuelan
  [F2310]
  UF Venezuelan national characteristics
National characteristics, Vietnamese
  UF Vietnamese national characteristics
National characteristics, Welsh
  UF Welsh national characteristics
National characteristics, West German
  UF West German national characteristics
National characteristics in literature
National churches
  USE Established churches
National Climate Program
  BT Climatology—Research—United States
      United States—Climate
National Coal Resources Data System
  [Z699.5.C57]
  UF NCRDS (Information retrieval system)
National consciousness
  USE Nationalism
National dances
  USE Folk dance music
      Folk dancing
National debts
  USE Debts, Public
National defenses
  USE subdivision Defenses under names of
      countries, etc.
National domain
  USE Public domain

National Elk Refuge (Wyo.)
  (Not Subd Geog)
  BT National parks and reserves—
      Wyoming
      Wildlife refuges—Wyoming
National emblems
  USE Emblems, National
National emergency legislation
  USE War and emergency legislation
National Environmental Specimen Bank
  UF Environmental Specimen Bank,
      National
      Specimen Bank, National
      Environmental
  BT Environmental specimen banking—
      United States
National environmental study areas
  (May Subd Geog)
  UF Environmental study areas, National
  BT Ecology—Study and teaching
      National parks and reserves
      Natural areas
National flowers   (May Subd Geog)
  [QK84.8-QK85.3]
  BT Emblems, National
      Flowers
National forests
  USE Forest reserves
National Foundation Day
  USE Kenkoku Kinen no hi
National Greenback Party
  [HG604-5]
  UF Greenback Party
      "Greenbackers"
      Independent Party
  RT Greenbacks
National Guard (United States)
  USE United States—National Guard
National Guard air units
  USE United States—Air National Guard
National Headquarters of the Daughters of the
  American Revolution (Washington, D.C.)
  USE Memorial Continental Hall
      (Washington, D.C.)
National Health Service (Great Britain)
  UF British National Health Service (Great
      Britain)
      Great Britain—National Health
      Service
  BT Medicine, State—Great Britain
      Public health—Great Britain
National holidays
  USE particular national holidays, e.g.
      Memorial Day
      Holidays
National hospitals
  USE Hospitals, Public
National hysteria
  USE Hysteria (Social psychology)
National images
  USE National characteristics
National income   (May Subd Geog)
  UF Net national product
  BT Flow of funds
      Income
  RT Gross national product
  NT Multiplier (Economics)
  — Accounting
      UF National accounting
          National income accounting
      BT Income accounting
      RT Social accounting
      NT Input-output analysis
          Transfer payments
  — — Effect of inflation on
      BT Inflation (Finance)
National income accounting
  USE National income—Accounting

National League for Nursing Pre-Nursing and
  Guidance Examination
  USE Pre-Nursing and Guidance
      Examination
National Learning Movement
  USE Kokugaku
National liberation movements
  (May Subd Geog)
    Here are entered works dealing with minority or
  other groups in armed rebellion against a colonial
  government, or against a national government
  charged with corruption or foreign domination. In
  general this heading is applicable only to the post
  World War II period.
  UF Liberation movements, National
  BT Nationalism
      Native races
      Revolutions
  RT Anti-imperialist movements
      Self-determination, National
  NT Guerrillas
National libraries
  USE Libraries, National
National Library Week
  UF Library Week
  RT Library Day
  NT National book week
National Mall (Washington, D.C.)
  USE Mall, The (Washington, D.C.)
National Measurement System for Time and
  Frequency
  BT Frequency standards
      Time—Systems and standards
      Weights and measures—United States
National Memorial Cemetery of the Pacific
  (Honolulu, Hawaii)
  UF Memorial Cemetery of the Pacific
      (Honolulu, Hawaii)
      National Cemetery of the Pacific
      (Honolulu, Hawaii)
      Punchbowl Cemetery (Honolulu,
      Hawaii)
  BT Cemeteries—Hawaii
      National cemeteries—United States
National merit scholarship qualifying test
  UF Merit scholarship qualifying test
      Scholarship qualifying test
  BT Scholarships—United States
      Universities and colleges—Entrance
      examinations
      Universities and colleges—United
      States—Examinations
National military parks
  USE Military parks
      National parks and reserves
National Monument (Mafra, Portugal)
  USE Monumento de Mafra (Mafra,
      Portugal)
National monuments   (May Subd Geog)
  UF Monuments, National
  BT Monuments
      National parks and reserves
  SA names of individual national
      monuments
  — Alaska
      NT Cape Krusenstern National
          Monument (Alaska)
          Misty Fjords National Monument
          (Alaska)
  — Arizona
      NT Canyon de Chelly National
          Monument (Ariz.)
          Chiricahua National Monument
          (Ariz.)
          Montezuma Castle National
          Monument (Ariz.)
          Montezuma Well National
          Monument (Ariz.)
          Organ Pipe Cactus National
          Monument (Ariz.)

2541

National monuments
— **Arizona** *(Continued)*
    Saguaro National Monument
        (Ariz.)
    Sunset Crater National Monument
        (Ariz.)
    Tuzigoot National Monument
        (Ariz.)
— **California**
    NT Death Valley National Monument
        (Calif. and Nev.)
        Devils Postpile National
            Monument (Calif.)
        Joshua Tree National Monument
            (Calif.)
        Lava Beds National Monument
            (Calif.)
        Muir Woods National Monument
            (Calif.)
        Pinnacles National Monument
            (Calif.)
— **Colorado**
    NT Black Canyon of the Gunnison
            National Monument (Colo.)
        Colorado National Monument
            (Colo.)
        Dinosaur National Monument
            (Colo. and Utah)
        Great Sand Dunes National
            Monument (Colo.)
— **Florida**
    NT Castillo de San Marcos National
            Monument (Saint Augustine,
            Fla.)
— **Georgia**
    NT Fort Pulaski National Monument
            (Ga.)
— **Idaho**
    NT Craters of the Moon National
            Monument (Idaho)
— **Iowa**
    NT Effigy Mounds National
            Monument (Iowa)
— **Maryland**
    NT Fort McHenry National
            Monument and Historic Shrine
            (Baltimore, Md.)
— **Nevada**
    NT Death Valley National Monument
            (Calif. and Nev.)
— **New Mexico**
    NT Aztec Ruins National Monument
            (N.M.)
        Bandelier National Monument
            (N.M.)
        Capulin Mountain National
            Monument (N.M.)
        El Morro National Monument
            (N.M.)
        Pecos National Monument (N.M.)
— **New York (State)**
    NT Statue of Liberty National
            Monument (New York, N.Y.)
— **Oregon**
    NT Oregon Caves National Monument
            (Or.)
— **South Carolina**
    NT Fort Sumter National Monument
            (Charleston, S.C.)
— **Texas**
    NT Alibates Flint Quarries and Texas
            Panhandle Pueblo Culture
            National Monument (Tex.)
— **Utah**
    NT Cedar Breaks National Monument
            (Utah)
        Dinosaur National Monument
            (Colo. and Utah)
        Natural Bridges National
            Monument (Utah)
— **Washington (D.C.)**

    NT Washington Monument
            (Washington, D.C.)
— **Washington (State)**
    NT Mount Saint Helens National
            Volcanic Monument (Wash.)
— **Wyoming**
    NT Devils Tower National Monument
            (Wyo.)
National music *(May Subd Geog)*
    ₍M1627-1844₎
    UF Music, National
    BT Music
    RT Patriotic music
    SA *subdivision* Songs and music *under*
            armies and navies, e.g. United
            States. Army—Songs and music;
            United States. Navy—Songs and
            music
    NT Folk dancing
        Folk music
        Folk-songs
        National songs
— **History and criticism**
    ₍ML3545₎
    RT Nationalism in music
National Music Week
    USE Music Week
National Old Trail Road
    USE Cumberland Road
National Palace (Madrid, Spain)
    USE Palacio Real (Madrid, Spain)
National Palace (Mexico City, Mexico)
    USE Palacio Nacional (Mexico City,
            Mexico)
National Park Aso (Japan)
    USE Aso Kokuritsu Kōen (Japan)
National Park Washington-Slagbaai (Bonaire)
    UF Slagbaai, National Park Washington-
            (Bonaire)
        Washington-Slagbaai National Park
            (Bonaire)
    BT National parks and reserves—
            Netherlands
        Parks—Bonaire
National parks and reserves
    (May Subd Geog)
    ₍SB481-SB484₎
    UF National military parks
        National reserves
        Parks, National
        Reserves, National
    BT Conservation of natural resources
        Parks
        Public lands
    RT Forest reserves
        Military reservations
        Natural areas
        Natural monuments
    SA *names of parks*
    NT Inholdings
        Marine parks and reserves
        National environmental study areas
        National monuments
        Park rangers
        Wild and scenic rivers
        Wilderness areas
— Administration
    USE National parks and reserves—
            Management
— **Fees**
    BT User charges
— **Interpretive programs**
    ₍SB481-SB485 (Local)₎
    ₍SB486.I57 (General)₎
    UF Interpretation, Park
        Interpretive programs of national
            parks and reserves
        Park interpretation
— **Law and legislation** *(May Subd Geog)*
— **Management**

    UF National parks and reserves—
            Administration
— **Multiple use**
    UF Multiple use of national parks and
            reserves
— **Planning**
    UF Park planning, National
— **Transportation**
    BT Transportation
    SA *subdivision* Transportation *under*
            individual national parks
— **Visitors**
    UF Visitors to national parks
— **Alabama**
    NT Talladega National Forest (Ala.)
— **Alaska**
    NT Alaska Maritime National Wildlife
            Refuge (Alaska)
        Chugach National Forest (Alaska)
        Iditarod National Historic Trail
            (Alaska)
        Katmai National Park and Preserve
            (Alaska)
        Kenai Fjords National Park
            (Alaska)
        Noatak National Preserve (Alaska)
— **Alberta**
    NT Banff National Park (Alta.)
        Elk Island National Park (Alta.)
        Jasper National Park (Alta.)
        Wood Buffalo National Park (Alta.
            and N.W.T.)
— **Argentina**
    NT Parque Nacional Los Glaciares
            (Argentina)
        Parque Nacional Nahuel Huapí
            (Argentina)
— **Arizona**
    NT Apache National Forest (Ariz.)
        Big Horn Mountains Wilderness
            (Ariz.)
        Black Rock Wilderness (Ariz.)
        Coconino National Forest (Ariz.)
        Coronado National Forest (Ariz.
            and N.M.)
        Dos Cabezas Mountains
            Wilderness (Ariz.)
        Fishhooks Wilderness (Ariz.)
        Hubbell Trading Post National
            Historic Site (Ganado, Ariz.)
        Needles Eye Wilderness (Ariz.)
        Paria Canyon Primitive Area (Ariz.
            and Utah)
        Pusch Ridge Wilderness (Ariz.)
        San Pedro Riparian National
            Conservation Area (Ariz.)
        Sitgreaves National Forest (Ariz.)
        Superstition Wilderness (Ariz.)
— **Arkansas**
    NT Caney Creek Wilderness (Ark.)
        Felsenthal National Wildlife
            Refuge (Ark.)
        Ouachita National Forest (Ark.
            and Okla.)
— **Australia**
    NT Carnarvon National Park (Qld.)
        Cradle Mountain-Lake Saint Clair
            National Park (Tas.)
        Freycinet National Park (Tas.)
        Geikie Gorge National Park
            (W.A.)
        Hattah Lakes National Park (Vic.)
        Heathcote National Park (N.S.W.)
        Kakadu National Park (N.T.)
        Keep River National Park (N.T.)
        Kosciusko National Park (N.S.W.)
        Ku-ring-gai Chase National Park
            (N.S.W.)
        Mount Buffalo National Park (Vic.)
        Mount Field National Park (Tas.)

Myall Lakes National Park
(N.S.W.)
Royal National Park (N.S.W.)
Shannon Forest and
D'Entrecasteaux National Park
(W.A.)
Walls of Jerusalem National Park
(Tas.)
Warrumbungle National Park
(N.S.W.)
Wilsons Promontory National Park
(Vic.)
Wollemi National Park (N.S.W.)
— **Austria**
NT Nationalpark Hohe Tauern
(Austria)
— **Azerbaijan S.S.R.**
NT Zakatal'skiĭ zapovednik (Azerbaijan
S.S.R.)
— **Bhutan**
NT Manas Game Sanctuary (Bhutan)
— **Brazil**
NT Floresta Nacional de São Francisco
de Paula (Brazil)
Itatiaia National Park (Brazil)
Parque Nacional da Serra da
Canastra (Brazil)
Parque Nacional da Tijuca (Brazil)
Parque Nacional das Emas (Brazil)
Parque Nacional de Aparados da
Serra (Brazil)
Parque Nacional de Brasília
(Brazil)
Parque Nacional de Monte Pascoal
(Brazil)
Parque Nacional de Sete Cidades
(Brazil)
Parque Nacional de Ubajara
(Brazil)
Parque Nacional do Amazonas
(Brazil)
Parque Nacional do Caparaó
(Brazil)
Parque Nacional do Iguaçu (Brazil)
— **British Columbia**
NT Glacier National Park (B.C.)
Kootenay National Park (B.C.)
Mount Revelstoke National Park
(B.C.)
Pacific Rim National Park
(Vancouver Island, B.C.)
Yoho National Park (B.C.)
— **Byelorussian S.S.R.**
NT Berezinskiĭ zapovednik
(Byelorussian S.S.R.)
— **California**
NT Bristol/Granite Mountains
Wilderness (Calif.)
Carrizo Gorge/Eastern McCain
Valley Wilderness (Calif.)
Castle Peaks Wilderness (Calif.)
Cinder Cones Wilderness (Calif.)
Cleveland National Forest (Calif.)
Desolation Wilderness (Calif.)
Emigrant Wilderness (Calif.)
Fish Creek Mountains Wilderness
(Calif.)
Fort Piute Wilderness (Calif.)
Funeral Mountains Wilderness
(Calif.)
Golden Trout Wilderness (Calif.)
Greenwater Valley Wilderness
(Calif.)
Indian Pass Wilderness (Calif.)
Jacumba/In-ko-pah Wilderness
(Calif.)
Kingston Range Wilderness (Calif.)
Little Lake Canyon Wilderness
(Calif.)
Modoc National Forest (Calif.)
Morongo Wilderness (Calif.)

Newberry Mountains Wilderness
(Calif.)
Nopah Range Wilderness (Calif.)
Owens Peak Wilderness (Calif.)
Phillip Burton Wilderness (Calif.)
Picacho Peak Wilderness (Calif.)
Pinnacles Wilderness Contiguous
Wilderness (Calif.)
Point Reyes-Farallon Islands
National Marine Sanctuary
(Calif.)
Providence Mountains Wilderness
(Calif.)
Rogue River National Forest (Or.
and Calif.)
Sawtooth Mountains Wilderness
(Calif.)
South Sierra Wilderness (Calif.)
South Warner Wilderness (Calif.)
Southern Inyo Wilderness (Calif.)
Stanislaus National Forest (Calif.)
Trinity Alps Wilderness (Calif.)
— **Canada**
NT Fortress of Louisbourg National
Historic Park (Cape Breton
Island, N.S.)
Gatineau Park (Québec)
Grasslands National Park (Sask.)
Kluane National Park (Yukon)
Manning Provincial Park (B.C.)
Waterton Lakes National Park
(Alta.)
— **Chile**
NT Parque Nacional Puyehue (Chile)
— **Colorado**
NT Alamosa National Wildlife Refuge
(Colo.)
American Flats Wilderness (Colo.)
Arapaho National Forest (Colo.)
Arapaho National Wildlife Refuge
(Colo.)
Browns Canyon Wilderness (Colo.)
Browns Park National Wildlife
Refuge (Colo.)
Bull Canyon Wilderness (Colo. and
Utah)
Bull Gulch Wilderness (Colo.)
Comanche National Grassland
(Colo.)
Curecanti National Recreation
Area (Colo.)
Eagle Mountain Wilderness (Colo.)
Grand Mesa National Forest
(Colo.)
Hovenweep National Monument
(Utah and Colo.)
Monte Vista National Wildlife
Refuge (Colo.)
Papa Keal Wilderness (Colo.)
Pawnee National Grassland (Colo.)
Pike National Forest (Colo.)
Roosevelt National Forest (Colo.)
Routt National Forest (Colo.)
San Isabel National Forest (Colo.)
Zapata Creek Wilderness (Colo.)
Zapata Creek Wilderness (Colo.)
— **Costa Rica**
NT Parque Nacional Santa Rosa (Costa
Rica)
— **Czechoslovakia**
NT Štátna prírodná rezervácia
Dobročský prales
(Czechoslovakia)
— **Dominica**
NT Morne Trois Pitons National Park
(Dominica)
— **England**
NT Dartmoor National Park (England)
Exmoor National Park (England)
— **Finland**

NT Urho Kekkosen kansallispuisto
(Finland)
— **Florida**
NT Florida Panther National Wildlife
Refuge (Fla.)
— **France**
NT Parc national de Port-Cros
(France)
Parc national des Cévennes
(France)
Parc national des Ecrins (France)
Parc national des Pyrénées
occidentales (France)
— **Georgia**
NT Martin Luther King, Junior,
National Historic Site (Atlanta,
Ga.)
— **Germany (West)**
NT Deutsch-Luxemburgischer
Naturpark (Germany and
Luxembourg)
Nationalpark Bayerischer Wald
(Germany)
Nationalpark Berchtesgaden
(Germany)
— **Great Britain**
NT Brecon Beacons National Park
(Wales)
Lake District National Park
(England)
North York Moors National Park
(England)
Peak District National Park
(England)
Yorkshire Dales National Park
(England)
— **Hawaii**
NT Haleakala National Park (Hawaii)
Pu'uhōnua o Honaunau National
Historical Park (Hawaii)
— **Hungary**
NT Bükki Nemzeti Park (Hungary)
Hortobágyi Nemzeti Park
(Hungary)
— **Idaho**
NT Battle Creek Wilderness (Idaho)
Big Jacks Creek Wilderness
(Idaho)
Boise National Forest (Idaho)
Cache National Forest (Utah and
Idaho)
Caribou National Forest
Coeur d'Alene National Forest
(Idaho)
Curlew National Grassland (Idaho)
Deep Creek-Owyhee River
Wilderness (Idaho)
Duncan Creek Wilderness (Idaho)
Gooding City of Rocks East
Wilderness (Idaho)
Gooding City of Rocks West
Wilderness (Idaho)
Hells Canyon National Recreation
Area (Or. and Idaho)
Hell's Half Acre Wilderness
(Idaho)
Juniper Creek Wilderness (Idaho)
Kaniksu National Forest
King Hill Creek Wilderness (Idaho)
Little Jacks Creek Wilderness
(Idaho)
Little Owyhee River Wilderness
(Idaho)
Nezperce National Forest (Idaho)
North Fork Owyhee River
Wilderness (Idaho)
Owyhee River Canyon Wilderness
(Idaho)
Payette National Forest (Idaho)
Raven's Eye Wilderness (Idaho)
Saint Joe National Forest (Idaho)

National parks and reserves
  — Idaho *(Continued)*
        Salmon National Forest (Idaho)
        Sand Butte Wilderness (Idaho)
        Snake River Birds of Prey Natural
            Area (Idaho)
        South Fork Owyhee River
            Wilderness (Idaho and Nev.)
        Targhee National Forest (Idaho
            and Wyo.)
        Upper Deep Creek Wilderness
            (Idaho)
        Yatahoney Creek Wilderness
            (Idaho)
  — Illinois
  NT Lincoln Home National Historic
            Site (Springfield, Ill.)
        Shawnee National Forest (Ill.)
  — India
  NT Bori Forest Range (India)
        Corbett National Park (India)
        Pachmarhi Forest Range (India)
        Tiger Haven Reserve (India)
  — Indiana
  NT Hoosier National Forest (Ind.)
        Lincoln Boyhood National
            Memorial (Ind.)
  — Italy
  NT Parco nazionale d'Abruzzo (Italy)
        Parco nazionale del Circeo (Italy)
        Parco nazionale del Gran Paradiso
            (Italy)
        Parco nazionale della Maremma
            (Italy)
  — Ivory Coast
  NT Parc National du Banco (Ivory
            Coast)
  — Japan
  NT Ashizuri Uwakai Kokuritsu Kōen
            (Japan)
        Aso Kokuritsu Kōen (Japan)
        Daisetsuzan Kokuritsu Kōen
            (Japan)
        Fuji-Hakone-Izu-Kokuritsu Kōen
            (Japan)
        Jōshin'etsu Kōgen Kokuritsu Kōen
            (Japan)
        Nikkō Kokuritsu Kōen (Japan)
        Shinjuku Gyoen (Tokyo, Japan)
        Tanzawa Ōyama Kokuritsu Kōen
            (Japan)
        Towada-Hachimantai National
            Park (Japan)
  — Kentucky
  NT Big South Fork National River and
            Recreation Area (Tenn. and
            Ky.)
        Cumberland Gap National
            Historical Park
        Daniel Boone National Forest
            (Ky.)
        Land Between the Lakes (Ky. and
            Tenn.)
  — Kenya
  NT Kakamega Forest Reserve (Kenya)
        Masai Mara Game Reserve
            (Kenya)
        Nairobi National Park (Kenya)
        Tsavo National Park (Kenya)
  — Korea (South)
  NT Chirisan Kungnip Kongwŏn
            (Korea)
        Chuwang Mountain (Korea)
        Odaesan Kungnip Kongwŏn
            (Korea)
        Sŏraksan Kungnip Kongwŏn
            (Korea)
  — Louisiana
  NT Bayou Sauvage Urban National
            Wildlife Refuge (La.)

Jean Lafitte National Historical
    Park and Preserve (La.)
  — Luxembourg
  NT Deutsch-Luxemburgischer
            Naturpark (Germany and
            Luxembourg)
  — Malaysia
  NT Gunung Mulu National Park
            (Sarawak)
  — Maryland
  NT Antietam National Battlefield
            (Md.)
        Assateague Island National
            Seashore (Md. and Va.)
        Chesapeake and Ohio Canal
            National Historical Park
        George Washington Memorial
            Parkway
  — Massachusetts
  NT Frederick Law Olmsted National
            Historic Site (Brookline, Mass.)
        Saugus Iron Works National
            Historic Site (Saugus, Mass.)
  — Michigan
  NT Huron National Forest (Mich.)
        Ottawa National Forest (Mich.)
  — Minnesota
  NT Chippewa National Forest (Minn.)
        Minnesota Valley National Wildlife
            Refuge (Minn.)
  — Mississippi
  NT De Soto National Forest (Miss.)
        Delta National Forest (Miss.)
        Tombigbee National Forest (Miss.)
  — Missouri
  NT Ozark National Scenic Riverways
            (Mo.)
  — Mongolia
  NT Ih Gobiin barhan zaazpai gazar
            (Mongolia)
  — Montana
  NT Absaroka-Beartooth Wilderness
            (Mont. and Wyo.)
        Anaconda-Pintler Wilderness
            (Mont.)
        Bighorn Canyon National
            Recreation Area (Mont. and
            Wyo.)
        Black Coulee National Wildlife
            Refuge (Mont.)
         Blacktail Mountains Wilderness
            (Mont.)
        Bowdoin National Wildlife Refuge
            (Mont.)
        Burnt Lodge Wilderness (Mont.)
        Charles M. Russell National
            Wildlife Refuge (Mont.)
        Creedman Coulee National
            Wildlife Refuge (Mont.)
        Deerlodge National Forest (Mont.)
        Farlin Creek Wilderness (Mont.)
        Flathead National Forest (Mont.)
        Hailstone National Wildlife Refuge
            (Mont.)
        Halfbreed Lake National Wildlife
            Refuge (Mont.)
        Helena National Forest (Mont.)
        Hewitt Lake National Wildlife
            Refuge (Mont.)
        Kaniksu National Forest
        Lake Mason National Wildlife
            Refuge (Mont.)
        Lake Thibadeau National Wildlife
            Refuge (Mont.)
        Lamesteer National Wildlife
            Refuge (Mont.)
        Lee Metcalf National Wildlife
            Refuge (Mont.)
        Medicine Lake National Wildlife
            Refuge (Mont.)
        Medicine Lake Wilderness (Mont.)

Mission Mountains Wilderness
    (Mont.)
Ninepipe National Wildlife Refuge
    (Mont.)
Pablo National Wildlife Refuge
    (Mont.)
Red Rock Lakes National Wildlife
    Refuge (Mont.)
Red Rock Lakes Wilderness
    (Mont.)
Ruby Mountains Wilderness
    (Mont.)
Swan River National Wildlife
    Refuge (Mont.)
U L Bend National Wildlife Refuge
    (Mont.)
War Horse National Wildlife
    Refuge (Mont.)
  — Namibia
  NT Etosha National Park (Namibia)
  — Nepal
  NT Royal Chitwan National Park
            (Nepal)
        Sagarmāthā National Park (Nepal)
  — Netherlands
  NT National Park Washington-Slagbaai
            (Bonaire)
  — Nevada
  NT Antelope Wilderness (Nev.)
        Bad Lands Wilderness (Nev.)
        Blue Eagle Wilderness (Nev.)
        Blue Lakes Wilderness (Nev.)
        Bluebell Wilderness (Nev.)
        Desatoya Mountains Wilderness
            (Nev.)
        Fandango Wilderness (Nev.)
        Far South Egans Wilderness (Nev.)
        Goshute Peak Wilderness (Nev.)
        High Rock Lake Wilderness (Nev.)
        La Madre Mountains Wilderness
            (Nev.)
        Morey Peak Wilderness (Nev.)
        Mount Grafton Wilderness (Nev.)
        Mount Limbo Wilderness (Nev.)
        Mount Stirling Wilderness (Nev.)
        North Fork of the Little Humboldt
            River Wilderness (Nev.)
        Owyhee Canyon Wilderness (Nev.)
        Pahute Peak Wilderness (Nev.)
        Palisade Mesa Wilderness (Nev.)
        Park Range Wilderness (Nev.)
        Parsnip Peak Wilderness (Nev.)
        Pueblo Mountain Wilderness (Or.
            and Nev.)
        Roberts Mountains Wilderness
            (Nev.)
        South Fork Owyhee River
            Wilderness (Idaho and Nev.)
        South Jackson Mountains
            Wilderness (Nev.)
        South Pequop Wilderness (Nev.)
        South Reveille Wilderness (Nev.)
        Wall Wilderness (Nev.)
        Weepah Spring Wilderness (Nev.)
        White Rock Range Wilderness
            (Nev. and Utah)
        Worthington Mountains Wilderness
            (Nev.)
  — New Brunswick
  NT Fundy National Park (N.B.)
        Kouchibouguac National Park
            (N.B.)
  — New Jersey
  NT Delaware Water Gap National
            Recreation Area (N.J. and Pa.)
        Pinelands National Reserve (N.J.)
  — New Mexico
  NT Antelope Wilderness (N.M.)
        Cabezon Wilderness (N.M.)
        Coronado National Forest (Ariz.
            and N.M.)

Jornada del Muerto Wilderness
(N.M.)
Kiowa National Grassland (N.M.)
Ojito Wilderness (N.M.)
Sabinoso Wilderness (N.M.)
— **New York (State)**
NT Fire Island National Seashore
(N.Y.)
Sagamore Hill National Historic
Site (Oyster Bay, N.Y.)
Vanderbilt Mansion National
Historic Site (Hyde Park,
Dutchess County, N.Y.)
— **New Zealand**
NT Abel Tasman National Park (N.Z.)
Arthur's Pass National Park (N.Z.)
Egmont National Park (N.Z.)
Fiordland National Park (N.Z.)
Hauraki Gulf Maritime Park (N.Z.)
Mount Aspiring National Park
(N.Z.)
Mount Cook National Park (N.Z.)
Nelson Lakes National Park (N.Z.)
Tongariro National Park (N.Z.)
Westland National Park (N.Z.)
— **North Carolina**
NT Croatan National Forest (N.C.)
Fort Raleigh National Historic Site
(Roanoke Island, N.C.)
— **Northwest Territories**
NT Wood Buffalo National Park (Alta.
and N.W.T.)
— **Ohio**
NT Cuyahoga Valley National
Recreation Area (Ohio)
James A. Garfield National
Historic Site (Mentor, Ohio)
Wayne National Forest (Ohio)
William Howard Taft National
Historic Site (Cincinnati, Ohio)
— **Oklahoma**
NT Black Kettle National Grassland
(Okla. and Tex.)
Ouachita National Forest (Ark.
and Okla.)
Rita Blanca National Grassland
(Okla. and Tex.)
— **Oregon**
NT Columbia Gorge National Scenic
Area (Or. and Wash.)
Crater Lake National Park (Or.)
Hells Canyon National Recreation
Area (Or. and Idaho)
High Steens Wilderness (Or.)
Honeycombs Wilderness (Or.)
Little Blitzen Gorge Wilderness
(Or.)
Owyhee Canyon Wilderness (Or.)
Pueblo Mountain Wilderness (Or.
and Nev.)
Rogue River National Forest (Or.
and Calif.)
Wallowa National Forest (Or.)
Whitman National Forest (Or.)
— **Paraguay**
NT Parque Nacional Cerro Corá
(Paraguay)
Parque Nacional Ybycuí
(Paraguay)
— **Pennsylvania**
NT Delaware Water Gap National
Recreation Area (N.J. and Pa.)
Hopewell Furnace National
Historic Site (Pa.)
Independence National Historical
Park (Philadelphia, Pa.)
Johnstown Flood National
Memorial (Pa.)
— **Poland**
NT Kampinoski Park Narodowy
(Poland)

Karkonoski Park Narodowy
(Poland)
Ojcowski Park Narodowy (Poland)
Pieniński Park Narodowy (Poland)
Tatrzański Park Narodowy
(Poland)
Wielkopolski Park Narodowy
(Poland)
— **Rhode Island**
NT Roger Williams National Memorial
(Providence, R.I.)
— **Russian S.F.S.R.**
NT Kandalakshskiĭ zapovednik
(R.S.F.S.R.)
Kavkazskiĭ zapovednik (R.S.F.S.R.)
Kedrovaĭa pad' (R.S.F.S.R.)
Laplandskiĭ zapovednik
(R.S.F.S.R.)
Malaĭa Sos'va (R.S.F.S.R. :
Preserve)
— **Saskatchewan**
NT W. R. Motherwell Farmstead
National Historic Park (Sask.)
— **Saudi Arabia**
NT Asir National Park (Saudi Arabia)
— **South Africa**
NT Cape Flats Nature Reserve (South
Africa)
Kruger National Park (South
Africa)
— **Soviet Union**
NT Gaujas nacionālais parks (Latvia)
Lahemaa Rahvuspark (Estonia)
— **Spain**
NT Parque Nacional de Doñana
(Spain)
— **Sri Lanka**
NT Wilpattu National Park (Sri Lanka)
Yala National Park (Sri Lanka)
— **Taiwan**
NT K'en-ting kuo chia kung yüan
(Taiwan)
T'ai-lu-ko kuo chia kung yüan
(Taiwan)
Yang-ming-shan kuo chia kung
yüan (Taiwan)
Yü-shan kuo chia kung yüan
(Taiwan)
— **Tanzania**
NT Gombe Stream National Park
(Tanzania)
Ngorongoro Game Control Area
Reserve (Tanzania)
Selous Game Reserve (Tanzania)
Serengeti National Park (Tanzania)
— **Tennessee**
NT Big South Fork National River and
Recreation Area (Tenn. and
Ky.)
Cumberland Gap National
Historical Park
Land Between the Lakes (Ky. and
Tenn.)
— **Texas**
NT Angelina National Forest (Tex.)
Big Bend National Park (Tex.)
Big Thicket National Preserve
(Tex.)
Black Kettle National Grassland
(Okla. and Tex.)
Fort Davis National Historic Site
(Tex.)
Lyndon B. Johnson National
Historical Park (Tex.)
McClellan Creek National
Grassland (Tex.)
Rita Blanca National Grassland
(Okla. and Tex.)
Sabine National Forest (Tex.)
— **Turkmen S.S.R.**

NT Repetekskiĭ zapovednik (Turkmen
S.S.R.)
— **Uganda**
NT Kibale Forest Reserve (Uganda)
— **United States**
NT Acadia National Park (Me.)
Adams National Historic Site
(Quincy, Mass.)
Allegheny National Forest (Pa.)
Alpine Lakes Wilderness (Wash.)
Andersonville National Historic
Site (Ga.)
Apalachicola National Forest (Fla.)
Apostle Islands National Lakeshore
(Wis.)
Arches National Park (Utah)
Arctic National Wildlife Refuge
(Alaska)
Arkansas Post National Memorial
(Ark.)
Back Bay National Wildlife Refuge
(Va.)
Badlands National Park (S.D.)
Beaver Creek Wilderness (Colo.)
Bent's Old Fort National Historic
Site (Colo.)
Bering Land Bridge National
Preserve (Alaska)
Bienville National Forest (Miss.)
Big Cypress National Preserve
(Fla.)
Big Sur Coast National Scenic
Area (Calif.)
Biscayne National Park (Fla.)
Black Hills National Forest (S.D.
and Wyo.)
Boston African American National
Historic Site (Boston, Mass.)
Boston National Historical Park
(Boston, Mass.)
Bridger National Forest (Wyo.)
Buffalo National River (Ark.)
California Desert National
Conservation Area (Calif.)
Canyonlands National Park (Utah)
Cape Cod National Seashore
(Mass.)
Cape Hatteras National Seashore
(N.C.)
Capitol Reef National Park (Utah)
Carl Sandburg Home National
Historic Site (Flat Rock, N.C.)
Carlsbad Caverns National Park
(N.M.)
Chama-Southern San Juan
Mountains Wilderness (Colo.)
Channel Islands National Park
(Calif.)
Charles C. Deam Wilderness (Ind.)
Charles Sheldon Wilderness (Nev.
and Or.)
Chattahoochee National Forest
(Ga.)
Chattahoochee River National
Recreation Area (Ga.)
Cheaha Wilderness (Ala.)
Cherokee National Forest (Tenn.)
Cibola National Forest (N.M.)
Citico Creek Wilderness (Tenn.)
Clearwater National Forest (Idaho)
Cloud Peak Primitive Area (Wyo.)
Colonial National Historical Park
(Va.)
Connecticut River National
Parkway and Recreation Area
Cumberland Island National
Seashore (Ga.)
Davy Crockett National Forest
(Tex.)
Denali National Park and Preserve
(Alaska)

North Cascades National Park
(Wash.)
Ross Lake National Recreation
Area (Wash.)
San Juan Island National Historical
Park (San Juan Island, Wash.)
— **West Virginia**
  NT Chesapeake and Ohio Canal
  National Historical Park
— **Wisconsin**
  NT Chequamegon National Forest
  (Wis.)
— **Wyoming**
  NT Absaroka-Beartooth Wilderness
  (Mont. and Wyo.)
  Bamforth National Wildlife Refuge
  (Wyo.)
  Bighorn Canyon National
  Recreation Area (Mont. and
  Wyo.)
  Caribou National Forest
  Honeycomb Buttes Wilderness
  (Wyo.)
  Hutton Lake National Wildlife
  Refuge (Wyo.)
  Medicine Bow National Forest
  (Wyo.)
  National Elk Refuge (Wyo.)
  Pathfinder National Wildlife
  Refuge (Wyo.)
  Sand Dunes Wilderness (Wyo.)
  Seedskadee National Wildlife
  Refuge (Wyo.)
  Targhee National Forest (Idaho
  and Wyo.)
  Teton Wilderness (Wyo.)
  Wasatch National Forest (Utah
  and Wyo.)
— **Yugoslavia**
  NT Triglavski narodni park (Slovenia)
— **Zaire**
  NT Parc National des Virunga (Zaire)
National Petroleum Reserve (Alaska)
  UF Naval Petroleum Reserve-No. 4
  (Alaska)
  Pet-4 (Alaska)
  BT National parks and reserves—United
  States
  Petroleum—Alaska—Reserves
  Petroleum—United States—Reserves
National planning
  USE subdivisions Economic policy and
  Social policy under names of
  countries
  Central planning
  Economic policy
  Social policy
National Postpartum Program, Bangladesh
  USE Bangladesh Postpartum Family
  Planning Program
National poultry improvement plan
  (May Subd Geog)
  BT Game bird culture—United States
  Poultry—United States—Breeding
National Preventive Dentistry Demonstration
Program
  ⌜*RK60.7*⌝
  BT Preventive dentistry—United States
  School children—Dental care—United
  States
National product, Gross
  USE Gross national product
National Program for Acquisitions and
Cataloging
  ⌜*Z688.5*⌝
  UF NPAC
  Shared cataloging program
  BT Acquisitions, Cooperative (Libraries)
  Acquisitions (Libraries)
  Cataloging, Cooperative
  Library cooperation

National psychology
  USE Ethnopsychology
  National characteristics
National Railways of Zimbabwe
  USE Railroads—Zimbabwe
National reserves
  USE National parks and reserves
National resources
  USE subdivision Economic conditions under
  names of countries, regions, etc.,
  e.g. France—Economic conditions
  Natural resources
National Road (Cumberland Road)
  USE Cumberland Road
National school lunch program
  UF Lunch program (United States)
  School lunch program (United States)
  BT School children—Food
— **Law and legislation** *(May Subd Geog)*
  UF National school lunch program—
  Law and legislation—United
  States
  BT Educational law and legislation—
  United States
— — United States
  USE National school lunch program
  —Law and legislation
National Sea Grant Program
  UF Sea Grant Program
  BT Marine resources—United States
  Oceanography—Research—United
  States
National security
  RT Economic policy
  International relations
  Military policy
  SA subdivision National security under
  names of countries, e.g. United
  States—National security
— **Finance**
— — **Law and legislation**
  SA subdivision National security—
  Finance—Law and legislation
  under names of countries
— **Law and legislation**
  RT Military law
  SA subdivision National security—Law
  and legislation under names of
  countries
— **Religious aspects**
— — **Baptists,** ⌜**Catholic Church, etc.**⌝
— — **Buddhism,** ⌜**Christianity, etc.**⌝
National self-determination
  USE Self-determination, National
National Semiconductor 32000 series
  (Microprocessors)
  USE NS32000 series (Microprocessors)
National Semiconductor Corporation 800
  (Computer)
  USE NSC800 (Computer)
National service *(May Subd Geog)*
  UF Alternative military service
  Service, Alternative military
  Service, National
  BT Armed Forces
  Conscientious objectors
  Public welfare
  Recruiting and enlistment
  Social service
  NT Draft
  Economic assistance, Domestic
  Military service, Voluntary
  Service, Compulsory non-military
  Technical assistance
  Voluntarism
  Volunteer workers in community
  development
  Volunteer workers in education
  Volunteer workers in hospitals
  Volunteer workers in law enforcement
  Volunteer workers in social service

Youth volunteers in social service
— **Law and legislation** *(May Subd Geog)*
National socialism
  ⌜*DD253 (Germany)*⌝
  UF Nazism
  BT Authoritarianism
  RT Fascism
  Socialism
  Totalitarianism
  World War, 1939-1945—Causes
  NT Anti-Nazi movement
  Fascism—Germany
  German-Christian movement
  Libraries and national socialism
  National socialists
— **Religious aspects**
National socialism and architecture
  ⌜*NA1068.5.N37*⌝
  UF Nazi architecture
  BT Architecture
National socialism and art
  ⌜*N6868.5.N37*⌝
  UF Nazi art
  BT Art
  NT Fascism in art
National socialism and education
  UF Education and national socialism
  Nazi education
  BT Education—Germany
  Education and state—Germany
National socialism and literature
  BT Literature
National socialism and motion pictures
  ⌜*PN1995.9.N36*⌝
  BT Moving-pictures
National socialism and music
  UF Nazi music
  BT Music
National socialism and occult sciences
  USE National socialism and occultism
National socialism and occultism
  ⌜*DD256.5*⌝
  UF National socialism and occult sciences
  Occultism and national socialism
  BT Occultism
National socialism in literature
  BT Politics in literature
National socialism in motion pictures
  BT Moving-pictures
  NT Anti-Nazi movement in motion
  pictures
National socialists *(May Subd Geog)*
  UF Nazis
  BT Fascists—Germany
  National socialism
  Socialists—Germany
National songs *(May Subd Geog)*
  UF Anthems, National
  National anthems
  Patriotic songs
  Songs, National
  Songs, Patriotic
  BT Emblems, National
  Music
  National music
  Patriotic music
  Songs
  RT Folk-songs
  NT Patriotic poetry
  Political ballads and songs
  War-songs
— **United States**
  NT State songs
National Standard Reference Data System
  UF NSRDS
  Standard Reference Data Program
  BT Chemistry—Information services
  Physics—Information services

National Standard Theatre (Shoreditch, London, England)
USE Standard Theatre (Shoreditch, London, England)
National state
UF Nation-state
BT Nationalism
State, The
NT Nationalities, Principle of
National Steeplechase, Grand
USE Grand National Handicap Steeplechase
National Stream Quality Accounting Network
BT Water quality—United States
National System of Interstate and Defense Highways
USE Interstate Highway System
National teacher examinations
UF Teacher examinations, National
BT Examinations
National teacher of the year award
National territory
USE Territory, National
National Theatre (Washington, D.C.)
BT Theaters—Washington (D.C.)
National trees *(May Subd Geog)*
[QK84.8-QK85.3]
BT Emblems, National
Trees
National Voluntary Laboratory Accreditation Program
BT Testing laboratories—United States—Accreditation
Nationalism *(May Subd Geog)*
[JC311-JC323 (Political science)]
UF National consciousness
BT International relations
Patriotism
Political science
RT Internationalism
Minorities
NT Cargo movement
Chauvinism and jingoism
Ethnocentrism
Folklore and nationalism
Languages—Political aspects
Messianism, Political
National characteristics
National liberation movements
National state
Nationalists
Nationalities, Principle of
Nativistic movements
Regionalism
Self-determination, National
— Blacks
USE Black nationalism
— Jews
USE Jewish nationalism
— **Religious aspects**
UF Nationalism and religion
NT Civil religion
— — **Baptists, [Catholic Church, etc.]**
— — **Buddhism, [Christianity, etc.]**
— **France**
NT Occitan movement
— **Iran**
NT Shu'-ub-iyah
Nationalism, Black
USE Black nationalism
Nationalism, Jewish
USE Jewish nationalism
Nationalism and architecture
(May Subd Geog)
UF Architecture and nationalism
Nationalism in architecture
BT Architecture
Nationalism and art *(May Subd Geog)*
UF Art and nationalism
BT Art

Nationalism and education
(May Subd Geog)
[LC71]
UF Education and nationalism
Nationalism in education
BT Education
Nationalism and literature
(May Subd Geog)
[PN51]
UF Literature and nationalism
BT Literature
NT Nationalism in literature
Nationalism and music
USE Nationalism in music
Nationalism and religion
USE Nationalism—Religious aspects
Nationalism and socialism *(May Subd Geog)*
UF Socialism and nationalism
BT Socialism
Nationalism in architecture
USE Nationalism and architecture
Nationalism in education
USE Nationalism and education
Nationalism in literature
BT Nationalism and literature
Nationalism in music
UF Nationalism and music
RT National music—History and criticism
NT Music and race
Nationalists *(May Subd Geog)*
BT Nationalism
RT Revolutionists
Nationalities, Principle of
UF Nationality, Principle of
Principle of nationalities
BT Minorities
National state
Nationalism
RT Self-determination, National
Nationality, Dual
USE Dual nationality
Nationality, Option of
USE Option of nationality
Nationality, Plural
USE Dual nationality
Nationality, Principle of
USE Nationalities, Principle of
Nationality (Citizenship)
USE Citizenship
Nationality of airplanes
USE Airplanes—Nationality
Nationality of ships
USE Ships—Nationality
Nationalization
USE Government ownership
Nationalization of alien property
USE Eminent domain (International law)
Nationalization of land
USE Land, Nationalization of
Nationalization of railroads
USE Railroads and state
Nationalpark Bayerischer Wald (Germany)
UF Bayerischer Wald National Park (Germany)
BT Forests and forestry—Germany (West)
National parks and reserves—Germany (West)
Parks—Germany (West)
Nationalpark Berchtesgaden (Germany)
UF Berchtesgaden, Nationalpark (Germany)
BT National parks and reserves—Germany (West)
Nationalpark Hohe Tauern (Austria)
UF Hohe Tauern, Nationalpark (Austria)
BT National parks and reserves—Austria
RT Hohe Tauern (Austria)
Nationalsozialistische Deutsche Arbeiter-Partei
NT Church and state—Germany—History—1933-1945

Denazification
— **Party work**
BT Propaganda, German
Nations, Comity of
USE Comity of nations
Nations, Law of
USE International law
Nations, Migrations of
USE Migrations of nations
Nations, Small
USE States, Small
Nations' Cup
USE Prix des Nations
Nations family
USE Nation family
Nationwide theater
USE Little theater movement
Native Americans
USE Indians of North America
Native church administration
USE Indigenous church administration
Native clergy
USE Clergy
Native immunity
USE Natural immunity
Native labor
Works dealing with native labor in particular colonial areas are entered under the heading Labor and laboring classes, with appropriate regional subdivision.
UF Indigenous labor
BT Labor and laboring classes
Native races
RT Labor laws and legislation, Colonial
NT Contract labor
Forced labor
Native land (Theology)
USE Homeland (Theology)
Native language
UF Mother tongue
Vernacular language
BT Language and languages
— **Study and teaching** *(May Subd Geog)*
BT Language and education
— Use in schools
USE Native language and education
Native language and education
(May Subd Geog)
UF Native language—Use in schools
BT Education
Language and education
Native Market, Santa Fe, N.M.
[HF5472]
BT Handicraft—New Mexico—Marketing
Native plant gardening *(May Subd Geog)*
[SB439-SB439.26]
BT Gardening
NT Wild flower gardening
Native plant industry *(May Subd Geog)*
[SB439.3-SB439.35]
Native plants
USE Botany
Native plants for cultivation
(May Subd Geog)
[SB439-SB439.26 (Gardening)]
BT Plants, Cultivated
Native races
[HV3176-HV3177 (Protection)]
[JV305-JV317 (Colonization)]
Here are entered works on the relations between the governing authorities and the aboriginal inhabitants of colonial or other areas.
UF Aborigines
RT Ethnology
SA *subdivision* Government relations *under* Indians of North America *and under names of tribes, e.g.* Dakota Indians—Government relations; *and subdivision* Native races *under names of continents, countries, etc., e.g.* Africa—Native races; Angola—Native races

NT National liberation movements
    Native labor
— Education
    USE Education, Colonial
— — Law and legislation
      USE Educational law and
          legislation, Colonial
Native speakers as linguistic informants
   USE Linguistic informants
Nativism
    Here are entered works on the policy of favoring
  the native inhabitants of a country over immigrants
  and, particularly in American history, of favoring na-
  tive Protestants over Catholic immigrants.
   BT Anti-Catholicism—United States
      Catholics—United States
   NT Ku Klux Klan (1915-   )
Nativistic movements *(May Subd Geog)*
   UF Cults, Messianic
      Cults, Prophetistic
      Ethnic revivals
      Messianic cults
      Prophetistic movements
      Revivals, Ethnic
      Sects, Nativistic
   BT Cults
      Ethnology
      Nationalism
      Religion, Primitive
   NT Cargo movement
      Ghost dance
      Messianism
— South Africa
    NT Ethiopian movement (South
       Africa)
Natività (Painting)
   USE Giorgione, 1477-1511. Nativity
Natività mistica (Painting)
   USE Botticelli, Sandro, 1444 or 5-1510.
       Nativity
Nativity (Painting)
   USE Botticelli, Sandro, 1444 or 5-1510.
       Nativity
      Giorgione, 1477-1511. Nativity
Nativity of Christ
   USE Jesus Christ—Nativity
Nativity scenes (Crèches)
   USE Crèches (Nativity scenes)
Natkutai Chetti
   USE Nattukottai Chettiars
Natocke Island (Mass.)
   USE Nantucket Island (Mass.)
Natocko Island (Mass.)
   USE Nantucket Island (Mass.)
Natricidae
   USE Colubridae
Natriciteres
   [QL666.O636]
   BT Colubridae
Natriuresis
   [QP211]
   UF Natruresis
   BT Diuresis
      Sodium—Metabolism
— Regulation
    UF Regulation of natriuresis
    BT Biological control systems
Natriuretic factors, Atrial
   USE Atrial natriuretic peptides
Natriuretic peptides, Atrial
   USE Atrial natriuretic peptides
Natrix
   [QL666.O636]
   UF Tropidonotus
   BT Colubridae
   NT Natrix natrix
      Natrix pryeri
      Natrix vibakari
Natrix fasciata
   [QL666.O636]

Natrix natrix
   [QL666.O636]
   UF Grass snake, European
      Ring snake
      Ringed snake
      Ringelnatter
   BT Natrix
Natrix pryeri
   [QL666.O636]
   BT Natrix
Natrix sipedon
   [QL666.O636]
Natrix vibakari
   [QL666.O636]
   BT Natrix
Natrolite *(May Subd Geog)*
   [QE391.N27]
   BT Zeolites
Natron Valley (Egypt)
   USE Natrun Valley (Egypt)
Natrun Valley (Egypt)
   UF Natron Valley (Egypt)
      Wādī al-Naṭrūn (Egypt)
   BT Wadis—Egypt
Natruresis
   USE Natriuresis
Natsionalʹnyĭ park Gauia (Latvia)
   USE Gaujas nacionālais parks (Latvia)
Natsitkutchin Indians
   [E99.N22]
   UF Chandalar Kutchin Indians
      Netsikutchin Indians
   BT Indians of North America
      Kutchin Indians
Natsushima Iseki (Yokosuka-shi, Japan)
   USE Natsushima Shell Mounds (Yokosuka-
       shi, Japan)
Natsushima Kaizuka (Yokosuka-shi, Japan)
   USE Natsushima Shell Mounds (Yokosuka-
       shi, Japan)
**Natsushima Shell Mounds (Yokosuka-shi,
Japan)** *(Not Subd Geog)*
   UF Natsushima Iseki (Yokosuka-shi,
      Japan)
      Natsushima Kaizuka (Yokosuka-shi,
      Japan)
   BT Japan—Antiquities
      Kitchen-middens—Japan
Natta-Ziegler catalysts
   USE Ziegler-Natta catalysts
Natterjack toad
   [QL668.E227]
   UF Bufo calamita
Nattō *(May Subd Geog)*
   [TP438.S36 (Manufacture)]
   [TX558.S6 (Nutrition)]
   BT Fermentation
      Soybean as food
      Soybean products
Nattō industry *(May Subd Geog)*
Nattukottai Chettiar marriage customs and
rites
   USE Marriage customs and rites,
       Nattukottai Chettiar
Nattukottai Chettiars
   [DS432.N38 (India)]
   [DS489.25.N (Sri Lanka)]
   UF Chetti, Natkutai
      Chettiars, Nattukottai
      Nagarathars
      Natkutai Chetti
   BT Caste—India
      Caste—Sri Lanka
      Ethnology—India
      Ethnology—Sri Lanka
      Vaisyas
— Rites and ceremonies
— Rites and cermonies
    NT Marriage customs and rites,
       Nattukottai Chettiar

Nātu family *(Not Subd Geog)*
Natural arches
   USE Natural bridges
Natural areas *(May Subd Geog)*
   [QH75-77]
   UF Nature reserves
   BT Nature conservation
   RT National parks and reserves
   NT National environmental study areas
      Natural monuments
      Nature centers
      Research natural areas
      Wilderness areas
      Wildlife management areas
      Wildlife refuges
— Law and legislation *(May Subd Geog)*
   BT Environmental law
— Arizona
   NT San Pedro Riparian National
       Conservation Area (Ariz.)
— Australia
   NT Moondyne Nature Reserve (W.A.)
       Thomsons Lake Nature Reserve
       (W.A.)
— Azerbaijan S.S.R.
   NT Zakatalʹskiĭ zapovednik (Azerbaijan
       S.S.R.)
— California
   NT Big Sur Coast National Scenic
       Area (Calif.)
      California Desert National
       Conservation Area (Calif.)
      Coachella Valley Preserve (Calif.)
— Czechoslovakia
   NT Štátna prírodná rezervácia
       Dobročský prales
       (Czechoslovakia)
— Denmark
   NT Maglemose (Denmark)
— England
   NT Box Hill Country Park (England)
— France
   NT Parc naturel régional de Camargue
       (France)
      Parc naturel régional de Lorraine
       (France)
      Parc naturel régional du Morvan
       (France)
      Parc naturel régional Livradois-
       Forez (France)
— Germany (West)
   NT Deutsch-Luxemburgischer
       Naturpark (Germany and
       Luxembourg)
      Naturpark Arnsberger Wald
       (Germany)
      Naturpark Bergstrasse-Odenwald
       (Germany)
      Naturpark Diemelsee (Germany)
      Naturpark Eggegebirge-Südlicher
       Teutoburger Wald (Germany)
      Naturpark Harburger Berge
       (Germany)
      Naturpark Harz (Germany)
      Naturpark Homert (Germany)
      Naturpark Kottenforst-Ville
       (Germany)
      Naturpark Lauenburgische Seen
       (Germany)
      Naturpark Pfälzerwald (Germany)
      Naturpark Rothaargebirge
       (Germany)
      Naturpark Schwalm-Nette
       (Germany)
      Naturpark Siebengebirge
       (Germany)
      Naturpark Südheide (Germany)
      Naturschutzgebiet Hiddeser Bent-
       Donoper Teich (Germany)
      Naturschutzpark Lüneburger Heide
       (Germany)

Natural areas *(Continued)*
— **Idaho**
  NT Snake River Birds of Prey Natural
       Area (Idaho)
— **Italy**
  NT Parco naturale Alta Valsesia (Italy)
       Parco naturale de Rimigliano
       (Italy)
       Riserva naturale orientata Valle
       dell'Orfento (Italy)
— **Luxembourg**
  NT Deutsch-Luxemburgischer
       Naturpark (Germany and
       Luxembourg)
       Parc naturel de la Haute-Sûre
       (Luxembourg)
— **Massachusetts**
  NT Mount Tom State Reservation
       (Mass.)
— **Mexico**
  NT Reserva de la Biosfera de Mapimí
       (Mexico)
— **Mongolia**
  NT Ih Gobiin barhan zaazpai gazar
       (Mongolia)
— **Oregon**
  NT Columbia Gorge National Scenic
       Area (Or. and Wash.)
— **Pennsylvania**
  NT Bowman's Hill State Wildflower
       Preserve (Pa.)
— **Russian S.F.S.R.**
  NT Kandalakshskiĭ zapovednik
       (R.S.F.S.R.)
       Kedrovaiā pad' (R.S.F.S.R.)
       Laplandskiĭ zapovednik
       (R.S.F.S.R.)
       Malaiā Sos'va (R.S.F.S.R. :
       Preserve)
— **Scotland**
  NT Loch a' Mhuilinn Nature Reserve
       (Scotland)
— **Switzerland**
  NT Freiberg am Kärpf (Switzerland)
— **Texas**
  NT Big Thicket National Preserve
       (Tex.)
       Little Thicket Nature Sanctuary
       (Tex.)
— **Turkmen S.S.R.**
  NT Repetekskiĭ zapovednik (Turkmen
       S.S.R.)
— **Washington (State)**
  NT Columbia Gorge National Scenic
       Area (Or. and Wash.)
— **Wisconsin**
  NT Apostle Islands National Lakeshore
       (Wis.)
       Ice Age National Scientific
       Reserve (Wis.)
Natural beauty conservation
  USE Landscape protection
Natural boundaries
  USE Boundaries
Natural bridges *(May Subd Geog)*
  [GB561-568]
  UF Bridges, Natural
     Karst bridge
     Natural arches
  BT Landforms
     Natural monuments
— **Utah**
  NT Arches National Park (Utah)
Natural Bridges National Monument (Utah)
  BT National monuments—Utah
Natural calamities
  USE Natural disasters
Natural childbirth *(May Subd Geog)*
  [RG661]

  UF Childbirth, Natural
     Labor, Painless (Obstetrics)
     Lamaze method of childbirth
     Painless labor (Obstetrics)
     Psychoprophylactic childbirth
  BT Childbirth
     Labor (Obstetrics)
  NT Childbirth at home
Natural class (Linguistics)
  USE Naturalness (Linguistics)
Natural communities
  USE Biotic communities
Natural convection
  USE Heat—Convection, Natural
Natural death (Right to die)
  USE Right to die
Natural disaster warning systems
(May Subd Geog)
  UF Disaster warning systems, Natural
     Warning systems, Natural disaster
  BT Civil defense—Warning systems
     Emergency communication systems
     Natural disasters
  NT Tornado warning systems
— **Pacific Ocean**
  NT Tsunami Warning System
Natural disasters *(May Subd Geog)*
  UF Natural calamities
  BT Disasters
  NT Archaeology and natural disasters
     Avalanches
     Bores (Tidal phenomena)
     Buildings—Natural disaster effects
     Earth movements
     Earthquakes
     Electric power systems—Natural
       disaster effects
     Floods
     Forest fires
     Geophysical prediction
     Natural disaster warning systems
     Nuclear power plants—Natural
       disaster effects
     Railroads—Natural disaster effects
     Storm surges
     Storms
     Tsunamis
     Volcanism
— Information storage and retrieval systems
  USE Information storage and retrieval
     systems—Natural disasters
— **Law and legislation** *(May Subd Geog)*
Natural disasters and archaeology
  USE Archaeology and natural disasters
Natural electronic business language
  USE NEBULA (Computer program
     language)
Natural family planning *(May Subd Geog)*
  [RG136.5]
    Here are entered works on techniques for plan-
  ning or preventing pregnancies by observation of the
  naturally occurring signs and symptoms of the fertile
  and infertile phases of the menstrual cycle.
  UF Behavioral methods of birth control
     Family planning, Natural
     Sympto-thermal method of birth
       control
  BT Birth control
     Contraception
     Menstrual cycle
  NT Sexual abstinence
— Basal body temperature method
  USE Natural family planning—
     Temperature method
— Billings ovulation method
  USE Natural family planning—
     Ovulation method
— **Calendar method**

  UF Calendar method of birth control
     Natural family planning—Rhythm
       method
     Rhythm method of birth control
— Cervical mucus method
  USE Natural family planning—
     Ovulation method
— **Ovulation method**
  UF Billings ovulation method of birth
       control
     Cervical mucus method of birth
       control
     Natural family planning—Billings
       ovulation method
     Natural family planning—Cervical
       mucus method
     Ovulation method of birth control
  BT Cervix mucus
     Ovulation—Detection
— Rhythm method
  USE Natural family planning—
     Calendar method
— **Temperature method**
  UF Basal body temperature method of
       birth control
     Natural family planning—Basal
       body temperature method
     Temperature method of birth
       control
  BT Body temperature—Measurement
Natural food
  USE Food, Natural
Natural food cookery
  USE Cookery (Natural foods)
Natural food restaurants *(May Subd Geog)*
  UF Restaurants, Natural food
  BT Restaurants, lunch rooms, etc.
  RT Food, Natural
Natural foods industry *(May Subd Geog)*
  [HD9000-9019]
  UF Health foods industry
  BT Food, Natural
Natural gardening
  USE Organic gardening
Natural gardens, American
(May Subd Geog)
  [SB457.53]
  UF American natural gardens
     Naturalistic gardens, American
Natural gardens, English
  USE Gardens, English
Natural gas
  USE Gas, Natural
Natural gas, Compressed
  USE Compressed natural gas
Natural gas conservation
  USE Gas, Natural—Conservation
Natural gas fields
  USE Gas fields
Natural gas liquids
  USE Liquefied natural gas
Natural gas reserves
  USE Gas, Natural—Reserves
Natural gas wells
  USE Gas wells
Natural history *(May Subd Geog)*
  [QH]
  UF History, Natural
     Natural science
     Physiophilosophy
  BT Science
  RT Biology
  NT Biogeography
     Botany
     Desert biology
     Geology
     Marine biology
     Soil biology
     Zoology
— **Bibliography**
  NT Natural history literature

— Catalogs and collections
  (May Subd Geog)
  UF Natural history collections
  SA *subdivision* Natural history
      collections *under names of*
      individuals, families, and
      corporate bodies
— Classification
  [QH83]
  UF Classification—Natural history
  BT Botany—Classification
      Zoology—Classification
  NT Classification—Books—Natural
      history
      Type specimens (Natural history)
— Dictionaries, Juvenile
— Early works to 1735
  USE Natural history—Pre-Linnean
      works
— Museums
  USE Natural history museums
— Nomenclature
  [QH83]
  BT Biology—Nomenclature
  NT Botany—Nomenclature
      Zoology—Nomenclature
— Organography
  [QH41-48]
  UF Organography
— Outdoor books
  [QH81]
  BT Forests and forestry
      Nature study
      Outdoor education
      Outdoor life
      Science—Study and teaching
  NT Phenology
— Pictorial works
  [QH46]
  NT Botany—Pictorial works
      Nature photography
      Zoology—Pictorial works
— Pre-Linnean works
  [QH41]
  UF Natural history—Early works to
      1735
  RT Zoology—Pre-Linnean works
  NT Botany—Pre-Linnean works
— Record blanks
  [QH61]
— Societies, etc.
  UF Natural history societies
— Stories
  USE Nature stories
— Study and teaching *(May Subd Geog)*
  [QH51-53]
  RT Nature study
  NT Research natural areas
— Technique
  [QH60]
  UF Preservation (Natural history)
      Specimens, Preservation of
  SA *subdivision* Collection and
      preservation *under* Zoological
      specimens, *and* Birds, Insects,
      Plants, *and similar headings*
  NT Aquariums
      Dredging (Biology)
      Microscope and microscopy—
      Technique
      Nature photography
      Taxidermy
— Terminology
  [QH83]
  BT Biology—Terminology
— Vocational guidance *(May Subd Geog)*
  BT Naturalists
Natural history, Koranic
USE Koran—Natural history
Natural history (in numismatics)
  BT Numismatics

Natural history collections
USE Natural history—Catalogs and
      collections
Natural history illustration
  (May Subd Geog)
  [QH46.5]
  UF Nature illustration
  BT Scientific illustration
  NT Biological illustration
      Botanical illustration
      Zoological illustration
Natural history illustrators
  (May Subd Geog)
  BT Scientific illustrators
Natural history libraries *(May Subd Geog)*
  UF Libraries, Natural history
  BT Scientific libraries
Natural history literature *(May Subd Geog)*
  BT Natural history—Bibliography
Natural history museums *(May Subd Geog)*
  [QH70-71]
  UF Natural history—Museums
  BT Museums
  NT Botanical museums
      Type specimens (Natural history)
      Zoological museums
Natural history societies
USE Natural history—Societies, etc.
Natural immunity *(May Subd Geog)*
  [QR185.2]
  UF Disease resistance
      Host resistance
      Innate immunity
      Innate resistance
      Native immunity
      Natural resistance
      Nonspecific immunity
      Resistance to disease
  BT Immunity
Natural killer cells
USE Killer cells
Natural law
  [JC571-JC609]
  UF Law, Natural
      Law of nature
      Natural rights
      Nature, Law of
      Rights, Natural
  BT Ethics
      Law
  RT International law
  NT Free-law movement
      International law—Philosophy
      Jurisprudence
      Law—Philosophy
      Liberty
      Political ethics
Natural monuments *(May Subd Geog)*
  [QH75-77]
  UF Conservation of natural monuments
      Landmarks, Preservation of
      Monuments, Natural
      Preservation of landmarks
      Preservation of natural monuments
      Protection of natural monuments
  BT Landscape
      Landscape protection
      Monuments
      Natural areas
      Nature conservation
      Wildlife conservation
  RT National parks and reserves
  NT Forest reserves
      Natural bridges
      Wilderness areas
— Law and legislation *(May Subd Geog)*
  BT Wildlife conservation—Law and
      legislation
— Alaska
  NT Glacier Bay National Park and
      Preserve (Alaska)

— New Hampshire
  NT Old Man of the Mountain (N.H.)
Natural numbers
USE Numbers, Natural
Natural obligations *(May Subd Geog)*
  UF Obligations, Natural
  BT Contracts
      Limitation of actions
      Obligations (Law)
Natural obligations (Roman law)
Natural parents
USE Birthparents
Natural pest control agents
USE Natural pesticides
Natural pesticides *(May Subd Geog)*
  [SB951.145.N37]
  UF Natural pest control agents
      Naturally occurring pesticides
  BT Natural products
      Pesticides
  RT Insect hormones
      Plant hormones
      Plants, Insecticidal
Natural philosophy
USE Physics
Natural products
  UF Products, Natural
  BT Raw materials
  NT Biological products
      Lignans
      Natural pesticides
      Plant products
— Spectra
Natural purification of streams
USE Stream self-purification
Natural radiation
USE Radiation, Background
Natural religion
USE Natural theology
Natural resistance
USE Natural immunity
Natural resources *(May Subd Geog)*
  [HC]
  UF National resources
      Natural resources—Economic aspects
      Resources, Natural
  RT Resource-based communities
  NT Afforestation
      Agricultural resources
      Aquatic resources
      Biosaline resources
      Commercial products
      Conservation of natural resources
      Desert resources development
      Factor proportions
      Fisheries
      Forests and forestry
      Geothermal resources
      Germplasm resources
      Icebergs—Utilization
      Landsat satellites
      Marine resources
      Mines and mineral resources
      Nonrenewable natural resources
      Power resources
      Renewable natural resources
      Water-power
      Water resources development
      Water-supply
      Wind power
— Economic aspects
  USE Natural resources
— International cooperation
  NT United States-Japan Cooperative
      Program in Natural Resources
— Law and legislation *(May Subd Geog)*
  BT Environmental law
  NT Forestry law and legislation
      Petroleum law and legislation
      Shore protection—Law and
      legislation

Natural resources
— **Law and legislation** *(Continued)*
   Wildlife conservation—Law and
   legislation
— **Study and teaching** *(May Subd Geog)*
   UF Conservation education
— **Taxation** *(May Subd Geog)*
   RT Severance tax
— — **Law and legislation**
   (May Subd Geog)
— **Japan**
   NT United States-Japan Cooperative
   Program in Natural Resources
— **United States**
   NT United States-Japan Cooperative
   Program in Natural Resources
Natural resources, Communal
(May Subd Geog)
   UF Communal natural resources
   Community-owned natural resources
   BT Collective settlements
   Village communities
   RT Commons
   Public lands
   NT Community forests
   Pasture, Right of
   Water-rights
Natural resources, Nonrenewable
   USE Nonrenewable natural resources
Natural resources, Renewable
   USE Renewable natural resources
Natural resources mediation
   USE Environmental mediation
Natural rights
   USE Natural law
Natural scenery
   USE *subdivision* Description and travel
   under names of countries, states,
   regions, etc., e.g. Ohio—Description
   and travel
   Landscape
   Views
Natural science
   USE Natural history
   Physics
   Science
Natural selection
   [QH365-7]
   UF Selection, Natural
   BT Genetics
   Variation (Biology)
   RT Evolution
   Heredity
   NT Kin selection (Evolution)
   Sexual selection in animals
Natural shorthand
   USE Shorthand—Thomas
Natural spawning of fishes
   USE Fishes—Spawning
Natural sweeteners
   UF Nutritive sweeteners
   BT Sweeteners
   NT Honey
   Sugar
   Sugars
Natural theology
   [BL175-190]
   UF Natural religion
   Theology, Natural
   BT Apologetics
   God
   Religion
   Religion and science
   Theology
   RT Philosophy of nature
   NT Creation
   Teleology
— **Early works to 1900**
— **History of doctrines**
Natural therapy
   USE Naturopathy

Natural toxicants
   USE Toxins
Natural trumpet
   USE Trumpet
Natural water chemistry
   USE Water chemistry
Naturalism
   [B828.2]
   BT Materialism
   Philosophy
   Positivism
   Science—Philosophy
   RT Mechanism (Philosophy)
   NT Banality (Philosophy)
Naturalism in art *(May Subd Geog)*
   BT Aesthetics
   Art
   Painting
   RT Idealism in art
   Realism in art
   Romanticism in art
Naturalism in literature
   [PN56.R3 (Theory)]
   [PN601 (General history)]
   BT Aesthetics
   RT Idealism in literature
   Realism in literature
   Romanticism
   NT Verism (Italian literature)
Naturalistic ethics
   USE Ethics, Evolutionary
Naturalistic fallacy
   UF Fallacy, Naturalistic
   BT Ethics
Naturalistic gardens, American
   USE Natural gardens, American
Naturalists *(May Subd Geog)*
   [QH26-QH35 (Biography)]
   BT Scientists
   NT Animal specialists
   Biologists
   Bird watchers
   Botanists
   Ecologists
   Entomologists
   Geologists
   Natural history—Vocational guidance
   Ornithologists
   Women naturalists
   Zoologists
— Directories
   USE Scientists—Directories
Naturalization *(May Subd Geog)*
   [JF811 (Theory)]
   [JK1800-JK1836 (United States)]
   [JX4216 (International law)]
   UF Foreigners
   BT Allegiance
   Emigration and immigration
   International law
   Suffrage
   RT Aliens
   Citizenship
   Expatriation
   NT Dual nationality
— Records
   USE Naturalization records
— **United States**
   UF United States—Naturalization
Naturalization records *(May Subd Geog)*
   UF Naturalization—Records
   BT Recording and registration
Naturally occurring pesticides
   USE Natural pesticides
Naturalness (Linguistics)
   UF Natural class (Linguistics)
   BT Linguistics
Nature
   NT Landscape
   Man—Influence on nature
— Nurture

   USE Nature and nurture
— Philosophy
   USE Philosophy of nature
— **Religious aspects**
   BT Philosophy of nature
   Religion and science
   NT Nature in the Bible
   Nature worship
— — **Buddhism, [Christianity, etc.]**
— Stories
   USE Nature stories
Nature, Acoustic phenomena in
   USE Acoustic phenomena in nature
Nature, Effect of man on
   USE Man—Influence on nature
Nature, Healing power of
   [R723]
   BT Healing
   Therapeutics, Physiological
   RT Naturopathy
Nature, Law of
   USE Natural law
Nature, Philosophy of
   USE Philosophy of nature
Nature, Uniformity of
   USE Uniformity of nature
Nature (Aesthetics)
   [BH301.N3]
   Here are entered works on aesthetic aspects of
   nature, nature in art, etc.
   UF Art and nature
   Nature in art
   BT Aesthetics
   Philosophy of nature
   RT Landscape
Nature and nurture
   UF Environment
   Genetics and environment
   Heredity and environment
   Nature—Nurture
   Nature versus nurture
   Nurture and nature
   BT Genetics
   Heredity
   NT Man—Influence of environment
Nature centers *(May Subd Geog)*
   [QH75-77]
   BT Natural areas
   Nature conservation
   Nature study
   RT Nature trails
Nature conservation *(May Subd Geog)*
   [QH75]
   UF Conservation of nature
   Nature protection
   Protection of nature
   BT Conservation of natural resources
   NT Endangered species
   Germplasm resources
   Landscape protection
   Natural areas
   Natural monuments
   Nature centers
   Plant conservation
   Stream conservation
   Wetland conservation
   Wildlife conservation
Nature craft
   BT Handicraft
   SA *specific crafts using natural materials,*
   e.g. Cornhusk craft; Eggshell craft
   NT Grasswork
   Potpourris (Scented floral mixtures)
   Preserved flower pictures
Nature illustration
   USE Natural history illustration
Nature in art
   USE Nature (Aesthetics)
Nature in literature
   [PN48 (General)]
   [PQ145.3 (French literature)]

[PR143 (English literature)]
[PS163 (American literature)]
[PT139 (German literature)]
UF Nature in poetry
BT Landscape
NT Birds in literature
Forests in literature
Mountains in literature
Sea in literature
Seasons in literature
Weather in literature
Nature in music
USE Program music
Nature in ornament
USE Decoration and ornament
Nature in poetry
USE Nature in literature
Nature in the Bible
[BS660-667]
UF Bible—Gardens
Bible—Natural history
Bible—Nature
BT Nature—Religious aspects
NT Animals in the Bible
Minerals in the Bible
Plants in the Bible
Nature in the Koran
BT Koran
Nature in the Tripiṭaka
[BQ1136.N38]
UF Tripiṭaka—Gardens
Tripiṭaka—Natural history
Tripiṭaka—Nature
NT Plants in the Tripiṭaka
Nature photography
[TR721]
UF Photography of nature
BT Natural history—Pictorial works
Natural history—Technique
Nature study
Photography
Photography—Scientific applications
Photography, Biological
RT Outdoor photography
NT Photography of animals
Photography of birds
Photography of clouds
Photography of fungi
Photography of insects
Photography of leaves
Photography of mountains
Photography of plants
Photography of rocks
Nature-printing and nature-prints
[Z259]
UF Nature-prints
Physiotypy
Phytoglyphy
BT Engraving
Lithography
Printing, Practical
Nature-prints
USE Nature-printing and nature-prints
Nature protection
USE Nature conservation
Nature reserves
USE Natural areas
Nature sounds *(May Subd Geog)*
BT Bioacoustics
Sounds
NT Animal sounds
Insect sounds
Sound production by animals
— **Recording and reproducing**
BT Magnetic recorders and recording
Nature stories
UF Natural history—Stories
Nature—Stories
BT Fiction
Nature study
[LB1185 (Kindergarten)]

[LB1532 (Primary schools)]
[LB1585 (Elementary schools)]
[QH51-QH53]
BT Education
Human ecology—Study and teaching
Science—Juvenile literature
Science—Study and teaching
RT Biology—Field work
Natural history—Study and teaching
NT Natural history—Outdoor books
Nature centers
Nature photography
Nature trails
School gardens
Wildlife watching
Zoology
Nature trails *(May Subd Geog)*
[QH58]
BT Biology—Field work
Nature study
Trails
RT Nature centers
Nature trails for the visually handicapped
USE Visually handicapped, Nature trails for the
Nature versus nurture
USE Nature and nurture
Nature worship *(May Subd Geog)*
[BL435-457]
BT Nature—Religious aspects
Worship
NT Animal worship
Mountain worship
Phallicism
Stone worship
Sun worship
Tree worship
Naturopathic practitioners
USE Naturopaths
Naturopathic schools *(May Subd Geog)*
BT Health occupations schools
Naturopathy
Schools
Naturopaths *(May Subd Geog)*
[RZ440]
UF Naturopathic practitioners
BT Healers
Naturopathy
Naturopathy *(May Subd Geog)*
[RZ440-445]
UF Natural therapy
BT Chiropractic
Therapeutic systems
Therapeutics, Physiological
RT Nature, Healing power of
NT Naturopathic schools
Naturopaths
Naturpark Arnsberger Wald (Germany)
UF Arnsberger Wald, Naturpark (Germany)
BT Forest reserves—Germany (West)
Natural areas—Germany (West)
Parks—Germany (West)
Naturpark Bergstrasse-Odenwald (Germany)
UF Bergstrasse-Odenwald, Naturpark (Germany)
Odenwald, Naturpark Bergstrasse (Germany)
BT Natural areas—Germany (West)
Parks—Germany (West)
RT Odenwald (Germany)
Naturpark Diemelsee (Germany)
UF Diemelsee, Naturpark (Germany)
BT Natural areas—Germany (West)
Parks—Germany (West)
Naturpark Eggegebirge-Südlicher Teutoburger Wald (Germany)
UF Eggegebirge-Südlicher Teutoburger Wald, Naturpark (Germany)
Südlicher Teutoburger Wald, Naturpark Eggegebirge (Germany)

BT Forest reserves—Germany (West)
Natural areas—Germany (West)
Parks—Germany (West)
RT Eggegebirge (Germany)
Teutoburg Forest (Germany)
Naturpark Harburger Berge (Germany)
(Not Subd Geog)
UF Harburger Berge, Naturpark (Germany)
BT Natural areas—Germany (West)
Parks—Germany (West)
Naturpark Harz (Germany)
UF Harz, Naturpark (Germany)
BT Natural areas—Germany (West)
Parks—Germany (West)
Naturpark Homert (Germany)
UF Homert, Naturpark (Germany)
BT Natural areas—Germany (West)
Parks—Germany (West)
Naturpark Kottenforst (Germany)
USE Naturpark Kottenforst-Ville (Germany)
Naturpark Kottenforst-Ville (Germany)
UF Kottenforst-Ville, Naturpark (Germany)
Naturpark Kottenforst (Germany)
BT Forest reserves—Germany (West)
Natural areas—Germany (West)
Parks—Germany (West)
Naturpark Lauenburgische Seen (Germany)
UF Lauenburgische Seen, Naturpark (Germany)
BT Lakes—Germany (West)
Natural areas—Germany (West)
Parks—Germany (West)
Naturpark Pfälzerwald (Germany)
UF Pfälzerwald, Naturpark (Germany)
BT Forest reserves—Germany (West)
Natural areas—Germany (West)
Parks—Germany (West)
Naturpark Rothaargebirge (Germany)
UF Rothaargebirge, Naturpark (Germany)
BT Forest reserves—Germany (West)
Natural areas—Germany (West)
Parks—Germany (West)
Naturpark Schwalm-Nette (Germany)
UF Nette, Naturpark Schwalm- (Germany)
Schwalm-Nette, Naturpark (Germany)
BT Natural areas—Germany (West)
Parks—Germany (West)
Naturpark Siebengebirge (Germany)
UF Siebengebirge, Naturpark (Germany)
BT Mountains—Germany (West)
Natural areas—Germany (West)
Parks—Germany (West)
Siebengebirge (Germany)
Naturpark Südeifel (Germany and Luxembourg)
USE Deutsch-Luxemburgischer Naturpark (Germany and Luxembourg)
Naturpark Südheide (Germany)
UF Südheide (Germany)
Südheide, Naturpark (Germany)
BT Moors and heaths—Germany (West)
Natural areas—Germany (West)
Parks—Germany (West)
Naturschutzgebiet Hiddeser Bent-Donoper Teich (Germany)
UF Donoper Teich-Hiddeser Bent, Naturschutzgebiet (Germany)
Hiddeser Bent-Donoper Teich, Naturschutzgebiet (Germany)
BT Natural areas—Germany (West)
Teutoburg Forest (Germany)
Naturschutzpark Lüneburger Heide (Germany)
UF Lüneburger Heide, Naturschutzpark (Germany)

Naturschutzpark Lüneburger Heide
(Germany) (Continued)
  BT Lüneburger Heide (Germany)
      Moors and heaths—Germany (West)
      Natural areas—Germany (West)
      Parks—Germany (West)
Natzke family *(Not Subd Geog)*
Naucoridae
  [QL523.N4]
  UF Aphelocheiridae
      Creeping waterbugs
      Water bugs, Creeping
  BT Hemiptera
  NT Ambrysus
      Aphelocheirus
Naudowessie Indians
  USE Dakota Indians
Naugatuck River (Conn.)
  BT Rivers—Connecticut
Nauheim bath
  [RM822.N3]
  BT Baths
Naujakasite
Naukam family
Naul family
  USE Nall family
Nault family *(Not Subd Geog)*
Nauman family
  USE Newman family
Naumann family
  USE Newman family
Nauphoeta
  [QL505.7.B4]
  BT Blaberidae
  NT Nauphoeta cinerea
Nauphoeta cinerea
  [QL505.7.B4]
  BT Nauphoeta
Nauru language
  UF Naouru language
  BT Micronesian languages
Nausea *(May Subd Geog)*
  BT Gastrointestinal system—Diseases
      Symptomatology
  RT Vomiting
Nauset Indians
  [E99.N25]
  BT Algonquian Indians
      Indians of North America
Naushon Island (Mass.)
  BT Elizabeth Islands (Mass.)
      Islands—Massachusetts
Nauss family
  USE Nassau family
Nautarachna
  [QL458.2.H9]
  UF Nautarachnidae
  BT Hydrachnidae
Nautarachnidae
  USE Nautarachna
Nauthars (Nepalese people)
  [DS493.9.N35]
  BT Ethnology—Nepal
Nautical almanacs
  [QB8]
  UF Astronomy—Ephemerides
  BT Almanacs
      Astronomy
      Nautical paraphernalia
      Navigation
  RT Ephemerides
Nautical astronomy
  [VK549-587]
  UF Astronomy, Nautical
      Celestial navigation
  BT Astronomy
      Astronomy, Spherical and practical
      Geography, Mathematical
  RT Navigation
  NT Latitude
      Longitude

      Moon—Tables
      Time
Nautical charts *(May Subd Geog)*
  UF Charts, Nautical
      Hydrographic charts
      Inland navigation—Maps
      Navigation—Maps
      Navigation charts
      Navigation maps
      Pilot charts
  BT Aids to navigation
      Cartography
      Maps
      Nautical paraphernalia
      Navigation
  NT Loran charts
      Plotting charts
  — Conventional signs
      USE Nautical charts—Symbols
  — **Law and legislation** *(May Subd Geog)*
      BT Maritime law
  — **Symbols**
      UF Nautical charts—Conventional
         signs
      BT Topographical drawing—
         Conventional signs
Nautical influences on United States
architecture
  USE Architecture—United States—Nautical
      influences
Nautical instruments
  [VK573-585]
  UF Instruments, Marine
      Instruments, Nautical
      Marine instruments
  BT Aids to navigation
      Marine engineering
      Nautical paraphernalia
      Navigation
  SA *names of nautical instruments, e.g.*
      Sextant, Station-pointer
  NT Gyroscopic instruments
      Horizons, Artificial
      Inertial navigation
      Inertial navigation systems
Nautical medicine
  USE Medicine, Naval
Nautical mile
  USE Mile, Nautical
Nautical museums
  USE Naval museums
Nautical paraphernalia *(May Subd Geog)*
  UF Marine paraphernalia
      Maritime paraphernalia
      Naval paraphernalia
      Paraphernalia, Nautical
      Seamen's paraphernalia
  BT Naval art and science
      Navigation
      Ships
  NT Log-books
      Nautical almanacs
      Nautical charts
      Nautical instruments
      Ships—Equipment and supplies
Nautical surveying
  USE Hydrographic surveying
Nautical terms
  USE Naval art and science—Dictionaries
      Naval art and science—Terminology
Nautical training-schools *(May Subd Geog)*
  [VK525-529]
  UF Naval art and science—Study and
      teaching
      Naval training-schools
  BT Naval education
  RT Training-ships
Nautichthys
  [QL638.C8]
  BT Cottidae

Nautichthys robustus
  [QL638.C8]
Nauticon Island (Mass.)
  USE Nantucket Island (Mass.)
Nautilida *(May Subd Geog)*
  [QL430.2]
  UF Ectochoclia
      Nautiloida
  BT Cephalopoda
  NT Nautilidae
Nautilidae *(May Subd Geog)*
  [QL430.3.N4]
  BT Nautilida
  NT Nautilus
Nautiloida
  USE Nautilida
Nautiloidea, Fossil
  NT Discosorida
Nautilus *(May Subd Geog)*
  [QL430.3.N4]
  UF Chambered nautilus
  BT Nautilidae
Nautilus fitness training
  USE Nautilus training
Nautilus training *(May Subd Geog)*
  UF Fitness training, Nautilus
      Nautilus fitness training
      Training, Nautilus
  BT Weight lifting
Nauvoo (Ill.)
  — **Expulsion of the Mormons**
      BT Mormon Church—History
Navaho Indian Reservation
  USE Navajo Indian Reservation
Navaho Indians
  USE Navajo Indians
Navaho language
  USE Navajo language
Navāits
  USE Navayats
Navajo artists
  USE Artists, Navajo
Navajo Dam (N.M.) *(Not Subd Geog)*
  BT Dams—New Mexico
Navajo Formation
  USE Navajo Sandstone
Navajo Indian Irrigation Project
Navajo Indian Reservation
  UF Navaho Indian Reservation
  BT Indians of North America—
      Reservations
      Navajo Indians—Reservations
Navajo Indians
  [E99.N3]
  UF Navaho Indians
  BT Athapascan Indians
      Indians of North America
  — **Art**
      NT Artists, Navajo
         Sandpaintings
  — **Law**
      USE Law, Navajo
  — **Music**
  — **Reservations**
      NT Navajo Indian Reservation
  — **Rites and ceremonies**
      NT Ajilee (Navajo rite)
  — **Rugs**
      USE Navajo Indians—Textile industry
         and fabrics
  — **Textile industry and fabrics**
      UF Navajo Indians—Rugs
         Navajo rugs
Navajo language
  [PM2006-2009]
  UF Navaho language
  BT Apache languages
      Athapascan languages
      Indians of North America—Languages
      Southwest, New—Languages

Navajo law
    USE Law, Navajo
Navajo poetry
    [PM2008.5-2009]
Navajo rugs
    USE Navajo Indians—Textile industry and
        fabrics
Navajo sandpaintings
    USE Sandpaintings
Navajo Sandstone *(Not Subd Geog)*
    UF Navajo Formation
    BT Formations (Geology)—West (U.S.)
        Geology, Stratigraphic—Jurassic
        Geology, Stratigraphic—Triassic
        Sandstone—West (U.S.)
Naval administration
    USE France. Marine; United States.
        Navy; *and similar headings*
        Naval art and science
        United States. Navy
Naval aeronautical materials
    USE United States. Navy—Aviation
        supplies and stores
Naval aeronautics
    USE Naval aviation
Naval air bases
    USE Air bases
Naval air stations
    USE Air bases
Naval appropriation bills
    USE *subdivision* Appropriations and
        expenditures *under navies, e.g.*
        United States. Navy—
        Appropriations and expenditures
Naval architects *(May Subd Geog)*
    [VM139-VM140 (Biography)]
    UF Architects, Naval
        Marine architects
    BT Architects
        Naval architecture
    NT Yacht designers
Naval architecture
    [VM]
    UF Architecture, Naval
        Marine architecture
        Ships—Design
    BT Architecture
    RT Shipbuilding
    SA *types of vessels, e.g.* Launches, Steam-
        boats, Torpedo-boats
    NT Architecture—United States—Nautical
        influences
        Armored vessels
        Boatbuilding
        Bulk carrier cargo ships—Rules for
        classification and construction
        Bulkheads (Naval architecture)
        Displacement (Ships)
        Electricity on ships
        Hulls (Naval architecture)
        Keels
        Marine engineering
        Masts and rigging
        Naval architects
        Ship propulsion
        Ship resistance
        Ships—Hydrodynamics
        Ships—Ratproof construction
        Ships—Rules for classification and
        construction
        Ships—Seakeeping
        Ships, Aluminum
        Ships, Concrete
        Ships, Iron and steel
        Ships, Wooden
        Stability of ships
        Stacks (Naval architecture)
        Trim (of ships)
        Warships
        Yacht building
    — Designs and plans

    RT Naval drafting
Naval art and science
    [V]
    UF Fighting
        Naval administration
        Naval science
        Naval warfare
        Navy
        War, Maritime
    BT War
    RT Military art and science
        Navies
        Navigation
    SA *headings beginning with the word*
        Naval
    NT Armor-plate
        Armored vessels
        Camouflage (Military science)
        Classification—Books—Naval art and
        science
        Floating batteries
        Hospitals, Naval and marine
        Imaginary wars and battles
        Logistics, Naval
        Marine engineering
        Marine service
        Military oceanography
        Nautical paraphernalia
        Naval battle groups
        Naval strategy
        Navy-yards and naval stations
        Nuclear warfare
        Ordnance, Naval
        Privateering
        Range-finding
        Riverine operations
        Sea control
        Sea-power
        Seamanship
        Seamen
        Signals and signaling
        Submarine boats
        Submarine warfare
        Torpedo-boats
        Torpedoes
        War games, Naval
        Warships
        Warships, Scuttling of
    — Abbreviations
        BT Military art and science—
            Abbreviations
    — Biography
        USE Naval biography
    — Data processing
        NT United States. Navy—Data
            systems technicians
    — Dictionaries
        [V23-24]
        UF Nautical terms
            Navigation—Dictionaries
    — History
        [V25-55]
        BT Military history
            Naval history
    — Study and teaching
        USE Nautical training-schools
            Naval education
            Navigation—Study and teaching
            Training-ships
    — Terminology
        [V23-24]
        UF Nautical terms
Naval art and science in the Bible
    UF Bible—Naval art and science
Naval artificers
    [VG600-605]
Naval artillery
    USE Artillery
Naval astronautics
    USE Astronautics, Military

Naval attachés
    USE Military attachés
Naval auxiliary vessels *(May Subd Geog)*
    [V865]
    UF Fleet train
        Ships of the train
    BT Logistics, Naval
        Navies
    NT Range instrumentation ships
        Repair ships
Naval aviation
    [VG90-95]
    UF Aeronautics, Naval
        Aviation, Naval
        Naval aeronautics
    BT Aeronautics, Military
    SA *subdivision* Aviation *under navies, e.g.*
        United States. Navy—Aviation; *and*
        subdivision Aerial operations *under*
        wars, e.g. World War, 1939-1945—
        Aerial operations
    NT Aircraft carriers
        Electronics in naval aviation
        United States. Marine Corps—
        Aviation
Naval bases
    USE Navy-yards and naval stations
Naval battle groups *(May Subd Geog)*
    UF Battle groups, Naval
    BT Naval art and science
Naval battles *(May Subd Geog)*
    [D27]
    UF Battles, Naval
        Naval warfare
        War, Maritime
    BT Sea control
        Sea-power
    RT Battles
        Naval history
    SA *subdivision* History, Naval *under*
        names of countries, etc.; subdivision
        Naval operations *under individual*
        wars, e.g. World War, 1939-1945—
        Naval operations; *names of*
        individual naval battles; and names
        of individual ships
Naval battles in art
Naval biography *(May Subd Geog)*
    [D-F (By country)]
    [V61-V65 (General)]
    Here are entered works on persons engaged in any
    area of naval and maritime activity, including civilian
    members of the naval establishment, political leaders,
    members of merchant marines, navies, etc. For bio-
    graphical works on individual classes of persons en-
    gaged in such activities, see the subdivision Biogra-
    phy under classes of persons, e.g. Admirals—Biogra-
    phy; Merchant seamen—Biography. For biographies
    of members of navies, see subdivision Biography
    under names of individual navies.
    UF Naval art and science—Biography
    BT Biography
        Naval history
    RT Seamen
    NT Admirals
Naval boilers
    USE Steam-boilers, Marine
Naval career
    USE *subdivision* Vocational guidance *under*
        navies, e.g. United States. Navy—
        Vocational guidance
Naval ceremonies, honors, and salutes
    (May Subd Geog)
    [V310]
    UF Naval courtesy
        Naval honors
        Naval salutes
        Salutes, Naval
    BT Military ceremonies, honors, and
        salutes
    NT Military funerals
        Warships—Visits to foreign ports

Naval chaplains
  USE Chaplains, Military
Naval communications
  USE *subdivision* Communication systems
      under armies and navies, e.g.
      United States. Navy—
      Communication systems
      Communications, Military
Naval construction
  USE Shipbuilding
Naval convoys *(May Subd Geog)*
  [V182]
  UF Convoy
     Convoys, Naval
  BT Naval tactics
     Shipping
Naval convoys (International law)
  [JX5268]
  UF Convoy
     Convoys, Naval (International law)
  BT War, Maritime (International law)
Naval cookery
  USE Cookery, Marine
Naval correspondence
  USE *subdivision* Records and
      correspondence *under navies, e.g.*
      United States. Navy—Records and
      correspondence
Naval courtesy
  USE Naval ceremonies, honors, and salutes
Naval crimes
  USE Naval offenses
Naval dentistry
  USE Dentistry, Naval
Naval desertion
  USE Desertion, Naval
Naval discipline *(May Subd Geog)*
  UF Discipline, Naval
  BT Discipline
     Military discipline
Naval districts *(May Subd Geog)*
  [VA]
  — **United States**
     [VA62.5-7]
     UF Naval river commands
        United States—Naval districts and
        river commands
        United States. Navy—Naval
        districts and river commands
     SA *names of specific districts and*
        commands, e.g. United States.
        Navy. 5th Naval District;
        United States. Navy. Severn
        River Naval Command
Naval drafting
  [VM297]
  UF Drafting, Naval
     Drafting, Ship
     Drawing, Naval
     Naval drawing
     Ship drafting
  BT Mechanical drawing
  RT Naval architecture—Designs and plans
  NT Ships—Drawings
Naval drawing
  USE Naval drafting
Naval education *(May Subd Geog)*
  [V400-695]
  UF Education, Naval
     Naval art and science—Study and
     teaching
     Naval schools
  BT Education
  NT International Sail Training Races
     Nautical training-schools
     Navigation—Study and teaching
     Synthetic training devices
     Television in naval education
     Training-ships
     United States. Navy—Tradevmen
  — **Confederate States of America**

     UF Confederate States of America—
        Naval education
Naval engineering
  USE Marine engineering
Naval engineers
  USE Marine engineers
Naval funerals
  USE Military funerals
Naval gunners
  USE *subdivision* Gunners *under names of*
      individual navies, e.g. United States.
      Navy—Gunners
Naval gunnery
  [VF]
  BT Gunnery
     Ordnance, Naval
  NT Ballistics
     Fire control (Naval gunnery)
     Range-finding
Naval history
  [D27]
  [D-F (Naval history, wars, and battles of
     particular countries)]
  UF History, Naval
     Wars
  BT History
  RT Military history
     Naval battles
     Sea-power
  SA *subdivision* History, Naval *under*
      names of countries; subdivision
      History *under names of individual*
      navies, e.g. United States. Navy—
      History; *names of naval battles, e.g.*
      Jutland, Battle of, 1916; *and names*
      of ships
  NT Buccaneers
     Impressment
     Military art and science—History
     Naval art and science—History
     Naval biography
     Pirates
     Privateering
     Warships, Scuttling of
Naval history, Ancient
  [D95]
Naval history, Modern
  — **20th century**
     [D436]
Naval honors
  USE Naval ceremonies, honors, and salutes
Naval hospitals
  USE Hospitals, Naval and marine
Naval housing
  USE United States. Navy—Barracks and
      quarters
Naval hygiene *(May Subd Geog)*
  [VG470-VG475]
  UF Hygiene, Naval
     Merchant marine—Sanitary affairs
  BT Hygiene
     Sanitation
  RT Medicine, Naval
  SA *subdivision* Sanitary affairs *under*
      names of individual navies, e.g.
      United States. Navy—Sanitary
      affairs
  NT Quarantine
     Ships—Sanitation
  — **Law and legislation** *(May Subd Geog)*
Naval laundries
  USE Laundries, Military
Naval law *(May Subd Geog)*
  [VB350-785]
  Not to be confused with subdivision Regulations
  under navies. Duplicate entry is made if necessary,
  e.g. 1. Naval law—United States. 2. United States.
  Navy—Regulations
  UF Law, Naval

  BT International law
     Navigation
     Public law
  RT Maritime law
     Military law
     War, Maritime (International law)
  NT Courts-martial and courts of inquiry
     Naval offenses
     Prize money
     Warships—Law and legislation
  — **United States**
Naval libraries
  USE Libraries, Naval
Naval literature searching
  USE Information storage and retrieval
      systems—Naval art and science
Naval logistics
  USE Logistics, Naval
Naval maneuvers
  [V245]
  UF Maneuvers, Naval
     Manoeuvers, Naval
  BT Tactics
  SA *subdivision* Maneuvers *under navies,*
      e.g. United States. Navy—
      Maneuvers
  NT War games, Naval
Naval medals
  USE Medals, Military and naval
Naval medicine
  USE Medicine, Naval
Naval militia
  USE *subdivision* Naval militia *under names*
      of regions, countries, states, etc.
Naval missions
  USE Military missions
Naval museums *(May Subd Geog)*
  [V13]
  UF Maritime museums
     Nautical museums
  BT Museums
Naval offenses *(May Subd Geog)*
  [K]
  [VB850-VB880]
  UF Crimes, Naval
     Naval crimes
     Offenses, Naval
  BT Criminal law
     Military offenses
     Naval law
  NT Desertion, Naval
     Insubordination
     Mutiny
     Trials (Naval offenses)
  — **United States**
     UF United States. Navy—Crimes and
        misdemeanors
Naval officers
  USE Navies—Officers
Naval operations
  USE Sea control
Naval ordnance
  USE Ordnance, Naval
Naval paraphernalia
  USE Nautical paraphernalia
Naval pensions
  USE Pensions, Military
Naval Petroleum Reserve-No. 4 (Alaska)
  USE National Petroleum Reserve (Alaska)
Naval policy
  USE *subdivision* Defenses *under names of*
      countries, e.g. United States—
      Defenses; *and* France. Marine;
      United States. Navy; *and similar*
      headings
     Sea-power
     United States. Navy
Naval porcelain *(May Subd Geog)*
  UF Porcelain, Naval
Naval pottery *(May Subd Geog)*
  UF Pottery, Naval

Naval prints
  [NE957]
  BT Engraving
    Ships in art
Naval prints, English *(May Subd Geog)*
  UF English naval prints
Naval prints, European *(May Subd Geog)*
  UF European naval prints
Naval prisons
  USE Prisons, Military
Naval psychology
  USE Psychology, Naval
Naval radio
  USE Radio, Military
Naval ratings
  USE *subdivision* Petty officers *under navies,*
    e.g. United States. Navy—Petty
    officers
Naval reconnaissance
  [V190]
  UF Reconnaissance, Naval
  BT Military reconnaissance
    Scouts and scouting
  NT Kites (Military and naval
    reconnaissance)
    United States. Navy—Photographers
Naval research *(May Subd Geog)*
  UF Research, Naval
  BT Research
    Research, Industrial
  — United States
    NT Philadelphia Experiment, 1943
Naval reserves
  [VA]
  UF Reserves, Naval
  SA *subdivision* Naval militia *under* United
    States *and under names of states*
Naval river commands
  USE Naval districts—United States
Naval salutes
  USE Naval ceremonies, honors, and salutes
Naval schools
  USE Naval education
Naval science
  USE Naval art and science
Naval shiphandling
  USE Warships—Handling
Naval ships
  USE Warships
Naval shipyards
  USE Navy-yards and naval stations
Naval signaling
  USE Signals and signaling
Naval signalling
  USE *subdivision* Signaling *under navies, e.g.*
    United States. Navy—Signaling
Naval stations
  USE Navy-yards and naval stations
Naval stores
  [TP977-TP978]
  Here are entered works on turpentine, resin, tar,
  etc., collectively.
  BT Gums and resins
    Turpentine
    Wood-tar
Naval strategy
  [V160-165]
  BT Naval art and science
    Strategy
  RT Sea-power
  NT Sea control
Naval surgery
  USE Surgery, Naval
Naval tactics
  [V167-178]
  UF Naval warfare
    War, Maritime
  BT Tactics
  NT Logistics, Naval
    Naval convoys
    Sea control

War games, Naval
Naval training-schools
  USE Nautical training-schools
Naval training-ships
  USE Training-ships
Naval visits to foreign ports
  USE Warships—Visits to foreign ports
Naval war games
  USE War games, Naval
Naval warfare
  USE Naval art and science
    Naval battles
    Naval tactics
    War, Maritime (International law)
Naval weapons systems
  USE United States. Navy—Weapons
    systems
Navarin Basin
  BT Submarine topography—Bering Sea
Navarino, Battle of, 1827
  [DF810.N3]
  BT Turkey—History—1683-1829
Navas de Tolosa, Battle of, 1212
  [DP114.3]
  UF Tolosa, Battle of, 1212
  BT Spain—History—711-1516
Navayats
  [DS432.N42]
  UF Nāatas
    Naiteas
    Nāītias
    Navāits
    Nevayets
    Nevoyats
    Newayetahs
    Novyts
  BT Ethnology—India
    Muslims—India
Navel
  [QM543]
  UF Belly button
    Omphalos
    Umbilicus
  BT Abdomen
  RT Umbilical cord
  — Hemorrhage
    UF Omphalorrhagia
  — Hernia
    UF Omphalocele
      Umbilical hernia
  — Religious aspects
  — — Baptists, [Catholic Church, etc.]
  — — Orthodox Eastern Church
Navel orangeworm *(May Subd Geog)*
  [QL561.P45 (Zoology)]
  [SB945.N (Pest)]
  UF Myelois venipars
    Orange worm, Navel
    Orangeworm, Navel
    Paramyelois transitella
  BT Walnut—Diseases and pests
Navesink River (N.J.)
  UF North Shrewsbury River (N.J.)
  BT Rivers—New Jersey
Navicert system
  UF Navigation certificates
  BT Blockade
    Contraband of war
    Maritime law
    Neutral trade with belligerents
    Prize law—Great Britain
    Search, Right of
    War, Maritime (International law)
Navicula
  BT Naviculaceae
Naviculaceae
  [QK569.N37 (Botany)]
  BT Naviculales
  NT Gomphonema
    Navicula
    Pinnularia

Pleurosigma
Naviculales
  [QK569.N (Botany)]
  BT Diatoms
  NT Naviculaceae
Navidad River (Tex.)
  BT Rivers—Texas
  NT Palmetto Bend Reservoir (Tex.)
Navier-Stokes equations
  UF Equations, Navier-Stokes
  BT Differential equations, Partial
    Fluid dynamics
    Viscous flow
  NT Burgers equation
  — Numerical solutions
    BT Numerical analysis
Navies *(May Subd Geog)*
  [VA37-42]
  UF Military power
    Navy
  BT Armaments
    Armed Forces
    Ships
    War
  RT Armies
    Naval art and science
    Sea-power
    Warships
  SA France. Marine; United States.
    Navy; *and similar headings*
  NT Armored vessels
    Coaling-stations
    Disarmament
    Naval auxiliary vessels
    Seamen
    Submarine forces
    United States. Navy
  — Medical service
    USE Medicine, Naval
  — Officers
    [VB310]
    UF Naval officers
    SA *subdivision* Officers *under navies,*
      e.g. United States. Navy—
      Officers
Navies, Cost of
  [VA20-VA25]
  [VA60-VA750 (Particular countries)]
  UF Cost of navies
  BT Disarmament
    Peace
  RT War, Cost of
Navigation *(May Subd Geog)*
  [VK]
  BT Astronomy, Spherical and practical
    Hydrography
    Locomotion
    Marine service
    Oceanography
    Orientation
    Ships
  RT Hydrographic surveying
    Nautical astronomy
    Naval art and science
    Pilots and pilotage
    Sailing
    Seamanship
    Steam-navigation
  SA *names of nautical instruments, e.g.*
    Compass, Sextant; *and subdivision*
    Navigation *under names of bodies*
    of water, e.g. Ohio River—
    Navigation
  NT Aids to navigation
    Animal navigation
    Astronautics in navigation
    Azimuth
    Ballast (Ships)
    Beacons
    Buoys
    Coastwise navigation

Navigation *(Continued)*
　　　　Collisions at sea
　　　　Dead reckoning (Navigation)
　　　　Derelicts
　　　　Electronics in navigation
　　　　Fisheries navigation
　　　　Fog-bells
　　　　Fog-signals
　　　　Great-circle sailing
　　　　Hyperbolic navigation
　　　　Ice navigation
　　　　Inertial navigation
　　　　Inland navigation
　　　　Knots and splices
　　　　Latitude
　　　　Lighthouses
　　　　Load-line
　　　　Log-books
　　　　Longitude
　　　　Masts and rigging
　　　　Mile, Nautical
　　　　Nautical almanacs
　　　　Nautical charts
　　　　Nautical instruments
　　　　Nautical paraphernalia
　　　　Naval law
　　　　Navigation (Astronautics)
　　　　Notices to mariners
　　　　Ocean currents
　　　　Optimum ship routing
　　　　Pilot guides
　　　　Proportional navigation
　　　　Rule of the road at sea
　　　　Saint Hilaire method
　　　　Ship handling
　　　　Shipwrecks
　　　　Signals and signaling
　　　　Sounding and soundings
　　　　Stowage
　　　　Stranding of ships
　　　　Stream channelization
　　　　Submarine boats
　　　　Submarine topography
　　　　Sumner's method
　　　　Tides
　　　　Underwater navigation
　　　　Waves, Calming of
　　　　Winds
　　　　Yachts and yachting
— Dictionaries
　　　USE Naval art and science—
　　　　　Dictionaries
— Equipment and supplies
　　　NT Navigation equipment industry
— History
　　　UF Maritime history
— Law and legislation
　　　USE Inland navigation—Law and
　　　　　legislation
　　　　　Maritime law
— Maps
　　　USE Nautical charts
— Research
　　　UF Navigation research
　　　BT Research, Industrial
— Safety measures
　　　⌐VK200⌐
　　　UF Marine safety
　　　RT Merchant marine—Safety measures
　　　NT Navigational warnings, Special
　　　　　Radio in navigation
— Study and teaching *(May Subd Geog)*
　　　⌐VK401-529⌐
　　　UF Naval art and science—Study and
　　　　　teaching
　　　BT Naval education
— Tables
　　　⌐VK563⌐
　　　NT Loran—Tables
　　　　　Traverse tables

Navigation, Aerial
　　USE Navigation (Aeronautics)
Navigation, Electronics in
　　USE Electronics in navigation
Navigation, Inertial
　　USE Inertial navigation
Navigation, Inertial (Aeronautics)
　　USE Inertial navigation (Aeronautics)
Navigation, Inertial (Astronautics)
　　USE Inertial navigation (Astronautics)
Navigation, Inland
　　USE Inland navigation
Navigation, Primitive *(May Subd Geog)*
　　⌐GN440⌐
　　BT Archaeology
　　　　Ethnology
　　NT Boats, Prehistoric
　　　　Boats, Primitive
　　　　Indians—Boats
　　　　Indians of Central America—Boats
　　　　Indians of North America—Boats
　　　　Indians of South America—Boats
Navigation, Radar in
　　USE Radar in navigation
Navigation, Steam
　　USE Steam-navigation
Navigation, Underwater
　　USE Underwater navigation
Navigation (Aeronautics)
　　⌐TL586-9⌐
　　UF Aerial navigation
　　　　Aeronautical navigation
　　　　Aeronautics—Navigation
　　　　Air navigation
　　　　Avigation
　　　　Navigation, Aerial
　　BT Aeronautics
　　NT Aeronautical charts
　　　　Aids to air navigation
　　　　Course-line computers
　　　　Doppler navigation
　　　　Electronics in aeronautics
　　　　Guidance systems (Flight)
　　　　Inertial navigation (Aeronautics)
　　　　Landing aids (Aeronautics)
　　　　Omnirange system
　　　　Pressure pattern flying
　　　　Radar in aeronautics
　　　　Radio direction finders
　　　　Tacan
— Equipment and supplies
　　NT Navigation equipment industry
— Tables
　　NT Loran—Tables
Navigation (Astronautics)
　　⌐TL1065⌐
　　UF Astrogation
　　　　Astronavigation
　　　　Space navigation
　　BT Astrodynamics
　　　　Astronautics
　　　　Navigation
　　RT Space flight
　　NT Astronautical instruments
　　　　Inertial navigation (Astronautics)
　　　　Space flight training
　　　　Space vehicles
　　　　Space vehicles—Piloting
— Charts, diagrams, etc.
　　USE Astronautical charts
Navigation (Underwater)
　　USE Underwater navigation
Navigation acts, 1649-1696
　　UF Acts of trade and navigation, 1649-
　　　　1696
Navigation by birds
　　USE Bird navigation
Navigation certificates
　　USE Navicert system
Navigation charts
　　USE Nautical charts

Navigation clearances (Bridges)
　　USE Bridges—Navigation clearances
Navigation computer (Aeronautical instrument)
　　BT Aeronautical instruments
　　　　Slide-rule
Navigation equipment industry
　　(May Subd Geog)
　　BT Navigation—Equipment and supplies
　　　　Navigation (Aeronautics)—Equipment
　　　　and supplies
Navigation laws
　　USE Inland navigation—Law and legislation
　　　　Maritime law
Navigation lights, Aircraft
　　USE Airplanes—Lighting
Navigation maps
　　USE Nautical charts
Navigation radio stations
　　USE Marine radio stations
Navigation research
　　USE Navigation—Research
Navigation Satellite Timing and Ranging
　　Global Positioning System
　　USE Global Positioning System
Navigational aids (Aeronautics)
　　USE Aids to air navigation
Navigational clearances (Bridges)
　　USE Bridges—Navigation clearances
Navigational warnings, Special
　　(May Subd Geog)
　　UF Special navigational warnings
　　BT Aids to navigation
　　　　Navigation—Safety measures
　　　　Notices to mariners
　　　　Warnings, Special navigational
Navigators
　　USE Explorers
　　　　Seamen
Navigators Islands
　　USE Samoan Islands
Naviti (Fiji)
　　USE Viti Levu (Fiji)
Naviti Levu (Fiji)
　　USE Viti Levu (Fiji)
NAVSTAR GPS
　　USE Global Positioning System
Navua River (Viti Levu, Fiji)
　　BT Rivers—Fiji
Navvies
　　USE Labor and laboring classes
Navy
　　USE France. Marine; *and similar headings*
　　　　Naval art and science
　　　　Navies
　　　　Sea-power
Navy appropriation bills
　　USE *subdivision* Appropriations and
　　　　　expenditures *under navies, e.g.*
　　　　　United States. Navy—
　　　　　Appropriations and expenditures
Navy Bay (Panama)
　　USE Limon Bay (Panama)
Navy bean
　　USE Kidney bean
Navy clearance diving teams
　　USE Underwater demolition teams
Navy Cross (Medal)
　　BT United States. Navy—Medals,
　　　　badges, decorations, etc.
Navy Day
　　USE Armed Forces Day
Navy exchanges (United States Navy)
　　USE Ship's stores and Navy exchanges
　　　　(United States Navy)
Navy Hall (Niagara-on-the-Lake, Ont.)
　　BT Navy-yards and naval stations—
　　　　Ontario
Navy Island Campaign, 1837-1838
　　⌐F1032⌐

Navy organization
   USE *subdivision* Organization *under navies,*
      e.g. United States. Navy—
      Organization
Navy wives
   UF Wives of Navy personnel
   BT Military wives
Navy-yards and naval stations
   (May Subd Geog)
      ₍V220-V240₎
      ₍VA67-VA70 (By country)₎
   UF Dockyards
      Naval bases
      Naval shipyards
      Naval stations
      Stations, Navy-yards and naval
   BT Military bases
      Naval art and science
   RT Coaling-stations
   — Inventory control
   — Ontario
      NT Navy Hall (Niagara-on-the-Lake,
         Ont.)
   — United States
      UF United States—Navy-yards and
         naval stations
         United States. Navy—Navy-yards
         and naval stations
      RT Navy-yards and naval stations,
         American
      NT United States. Navy—Barracks
         and quarters
Navy-yards and naval stations, American
   (May Subd Geog)
   RT Navy-yards and naval stations—United
      States
Nawar
      ₍DX289₎
   UF Nowâr
      Zoot
      Zutt
   BT Gypsies
   — Language
      USE Nuri dialect
Nawariyi language
   USE Wandarang language
Nawazi-Moñtji Indians
   USE Chimane Indians
Nawazi-Moñtji language
   USE Chimane language
Nawdowissnee Indians
   USE Dakota Indians
Nawp language
   USE Daga language
Nawrūz
   USE New Year
Naxalite Movement
   BT Communism—India
Naxos Island (Greece)
   BT Cyclades (Greece)
      Islands—Greece
Nāy
      ₍ML990.N₎
   UF Ney
      Quṣaba
   BT Flute
Nāy and zarb music
   UF Zarb and nāy music
Nayak dynasty of Madurai, 1529-1739
   (Not Subd Geog)
      ₍DS485.M29₎
   UF Nayaks of Madurai
Nayaks
   USE Naikas
Nayaks of Madurai
   USE Nayak dynasty of Madurai, 1529-1739
Nayanars
   UF Nayanmars
   BT Sivaism
Nayanmars
   USE Nayanars

Nayarit Indians
   USE Cora Indians
Nayarita language
   USE Cora language
Nayars
   USE Nairs
Nayerits
   USE Cora Indians
Nayle family
   USE Nall family
Nayler family
   USE Naylor family
Naylor family *(Not Subd Geog)*
   UF Nailer family
      Nailor family
      Naler family
      Nayler family
Nayssar Island (Estonia)
   USE Naissaar Island (Estonia)
Naẓar (Islam)
   USE Modesty—Religious aspects—Islam
Nazarene frescoes (Painting)
   USE Veit, Philipp, 1793-1877. Mainz
      Cathedral frescoes
Nazarenes (German painters)
   BT Painters—Germany
      Painting, Modern—19th century—
      Germany
Nazarenes (Wirz) *(May Subd Geog)*
      ₍BX8699.N4₎
Nazarite (Judaism)
   UF Nazirite (Judaism)
Nazca Site (Peru) *(Not Subd Geog)*
   UF Nasca Site (Peru)
   BT Peru—Antiquities
Nazi architecture
   USE National socialism and architecture
Nazi art
   USE National socialism and art
Nazi education
   USE National socialism and education
Nazi music
   USE National socialism and music
Nazi Putsch, Vienna, July 1934
   USE Austria—History—Nazi Putsch, July
      1934
Nazirite (Judaism)
   USE Nazarite (Judaism)
Nazis
   USE National socialists
Nazism
   USE National socialism
NBSLD (Computer program)
   UF National Bureau of Standards Load
      Determination (Computer program)
NCHARAN (Computer program)
      ₍QE48.8₎
   UF New Characteristic Analysis
      (Computer program)
   BT Computer programs
      Geology—Computer programs
      Mines and mineral resources—
      Computer programs
Nchimburu language
   USE Nchumburu language
NCHS' general well-being schedule
   USE General well-being schedule
Nchumburu language
   UF Nchimburu language
   BT Gonja language
NCR VRX OLPD (Computer program)
   BT Computer programs
      Utilities (Computer programs)
NCRDS (Information retrieval system)
   USE National Coal Resources Data System

Nd-YAG lasers *(May Subd Geog)*
   UF Neodymium-aluminum yttrium garnet
      lasers
      Neodymium-doped YAG lasers
      Neodymium-YAG lasers
      Neodymium-yttrium aluminum garnet
      lasers
   BT Rare earth lasers
      Solid-state lasers
N'Dama cattle
      ₍SF199.N19₎
   UF Fouta cattle
      Futa cattle
Ndande (Zairian people)
   USE Nande (Zairian people)
Ndani (New Guinea people)
   USE Dani (New Guinea people)
Ndau language
   USE Chindau language
Ndebele (African people)
   UF Amandebele (African people)
      Matabele (African people)
   BT Ethnology—South Africa
      Ethnology—Zimbabwe
      Nguni (African people)
      Zulus
   NT Manala (African people)
   — History
      NT Matabele War, 1893
         Zimbabwe—History—Ndebele
         Insurrection, 1896-1897
Ndebele (African people) art
   USE Art, Ndebele (African people)
Ndebele children's stories (Zimbabwe)
   USE Children's stories, Ndebele
      (Zimbabwe)
Ndebele fiction (Zimbabwe)
   (May Subd Geog)
   NT Children's stories, Ndebele
      (Zimbabwe)
Ndebele folk literature (Zimbabwe)
   USE Folk literature, Ndebele (Zimbabwe)
Ndebele Insurrection, Zimbabwe, 1896-1897
   USE Zimbabwe—History—Ndebele
      Insurrection, 1896-1897
Ndebele language (South Africa)
   UF Ndebele-Sotho language
      Ndzundza language
      Nrebele language (South Africa)
      Transvaal Ndebele language
   BT Bantu languages
      Northern Sotho language
      South Africa—Languages
      Zulu language
Ndebele language (Zimbabwe)
   UF IsiNdebele language
      Nrebele language (Zimbabwe)
      Sindebele language
      Tabele language
      Tebele language
   BT Nguni languages
      Zimbabwe—Languages
      Zulu language
Ndebele literature (Zimbabwe)
   (May Subd Geog)
   BT Zimbabwean literature
   NT Folk literature, Ndebele (Zimbabwe)
Ndebele nursery rhymes (Zimbabwe)
   USE Nursery rhymes, Ndebele (Zimbabwe)
Ndebele poetry (Zimbabwe)
   (May Subd Geog)
   BT Zimbabwean poetry
   NT Nursery rhymes, Ndebele (Zimbabwe)
Ndebele prose literature (Zimbabwe)
   (May Subd Geog)
   NT School prose, Ndebele (Zimbabwe)
Ndebele proverbs (Zimbabwe)
   USE Proverbs, Ndebele (Zimbabwe)
Ndebele school prose (Zimbabwe)
   USE School prose, Ndebele (Zimbabwe)

Ndebele songs (Zimbabwe)
  USE Songs, Ndebele (Zimbabwe)
Ndebele-Sotho language
  USE Ndebele language (South Africa)
Ndembu (African people)
  UF Andembu (African people)
      Bandempo (African people)
      Dembo (African people)
      Ndembu (African tribe)
  BT Ethnology—Angola
      Ethnology—Zaire
      Ethnology—Zambia
  RT Lunda, Southern (African people)
  — **Rites and ceremonies**
        NT Chihamba
Ndembu (African tribe)
  USE Ndembu (African people)
Ndendeuli (African people)
    ₍DT443₎
  BT Ethnology—Tanzania
Ndeni (Solomon Islands)
  USE Nendö (Solomon Islands)
Ndeni Island (Solomon Islands)
  USE Nendö (Solomon Islands)
Ndeu (African people)
  USE Bana (African people)
Ndgandi (Zairian people)
  USE Nande (Zairian people)
Ndhir (Berber people)
    ₍DT313.3.N4₎
  UF Ait Ndhir (Berber people)
      Beni Mtir (Berber people)
      Mtir (Berber people)
  BT Berbers
      Ethnology—Morocco
Ndiki (African people)
  UF Ndiki (African tribe)
  BT Banen (African people)
      Ethnology—Cameroon
Ndiki (African tribe)
  USE Ndiki (African people)
Ndja (African people)
  USE Bandja (African people)
Ndjĕ (African people)
  USE Bandja (African people)
Ndjuka language
  USE Djuka language
Ndo River (Kenya)
  USE Kerio River (Kenya)
Ndogo-Sere languages
  BT Niger-Congo languages
Ndondakusuka, Battle of, South Africa, 1856
  BT Zululand (South Africa)—History—To
        1879
Ndonga (African people)
    ₍DT611.42 (Angola)₎
    ₍DT709 (Namibia)₎
  UF Ondonga (African people)
  BT Ethnology—Angola
      Ethnology—Namibia
      Ovambo (African people)
  — **Rites and ceremonies**
        NT Marriage customs and rites,
              Ndonga (African people)
Ndonga (African people) marriage customs and
    rites
  USE Marriage customs and rites, Ndonga
        (African people)
Ndonga language
    ₍PL8547.N4₎
  UF Oshindonga language
      Oshiwambo language
      Ovambo language
  BT Bantu languages
Ndu languages
  BT Papuan languages
  NT Abulas language
      Boiken language
      Iatmul language
      Manambu language

Ndumbo language
  USE Ndumu language
Ndumu language
  UF Doumbou language
      Minduumo language
      Ndumbo language
      Ondoumbo language
  BT Bantu languages
Ndzundza language
  USE Ndebele language (South Africa)
Ndzungle language
  USE Limbum language
Ndzungli language
  USE Limbum language
Né (African people)
  USE Bana (African people)
Ne (The Russian word)
  BT Russian language—Etymology
Ne bis in idem
  USE Double jeopardy
Ne exeat *(May Subd Geog)*
  BT Writs
Nea Paphos (Ancient city)
  USE New Paphos (Ancient city)
NEAC 2200 (Computer)
    ₍QA76.8.N₎
  BT Electronic digital computers
Nead family
  USE Need family
Neagle family *(Not Subd Geog)*
  UF Neagles family
Neagles family
  USE Neagle family
Neai chōrai (Greece)
  USE New Lands (Greece)
Neal family *(Not Subd Geog)*
  UF Neale family
      Neall family
      Neals family
      Neel family
      Neil family
      Neill family
      Niel family
      Niele family
      Niell family
      Nielle family
      Niels family
  RT O'Neill family
Neale family
  USE Neal family
Nealella
    ₍QL444.O85₎
  BT Sarsiellidae
Nealella muelleri
    ₍QL444.O85₎
Nealey family
  USE Neely family
Neall family
  USE Neal family
Neals family
  USE Neal family
Nealy family
  USE Neely family
Neanderthal race
    ₍GN285₎
  BT Fossil man
      Missing link
  NT Mousterian culture
      Petralona man
      Rhodesian man
Neaphaenops
    ₍QL523.M5₎
  BT Miridae
Neaphaenops tellkampfi
    ₍QL523.M5₎
Neapolitan mastiff
    ₍SF429.N33₎
  UF Italian mastiff
  BT Mastiff
Near algebras
  UF Algebras, Near

  BT Associative algebras
Near death
  USE Death, Apparent
Near-death experiences *(May Subd Geog)*
      Here are entered works on the paranormal experi-
    ences of those who have survived near death or ap-
    parent death.
  UF Experiences, Near-death
  BT Death, Apparent
  — **Religious aspects**
        RT Future life
  — — **Buddhism, ₍Christianity, etc.₎**
Near East
  USE Middle East
Near East students
  USE Middle Eastern students
Near Eastern cookery
  USE Cookery, Middle Eastern
Near Eastern literature
  USE Middle Eastern literature
Near Eastern periodicals
  USE Middle Eastern periodicals
Near Eastern philology
  USE Middle Eastern philology
Near Eastern students
  USE Middle Eastern students
Near edge structure, X-ray absorption
  USE X-ray absorption near edge structure
Near-fields
  BT Fields, Algebraic
Near-rings
  UF Rings, Near
  BT Associative rings
Nearby stars
  UF Common stars, Nearby
  BT Stars
Nearsightedness
  USE Myopia
Neasbit family
  USE Nesbitt family
Neaspilota
    ₍QL537.T42₎
  BT Tephritidae
Neat family *(Not Subd Geog)*
  UF Nate family
      Neate family
Neatby family *(Not Subd Geog)*
Neate family
  USE Neat family
Neatness
  USE Orderliness
Neave family *(Not Subd Geog)*
  NT Neave-Hill family
Neave-Hill family *(Not Subd Geog)*
  BT Hill family
      Neave family
Neavel family
  USE Neville family
Neavill family
  USE Neville family
Neb-wenenef
  BT Priests, Egyptian
Nebbio (Corsica)
Nebel family *(Not Subd Geog)*
  UF Neibel family
      Niebel family
Nebo Hill Site (Mo.)
  BT Missouri—Antiquities
Nebome language
  USE Pima Bajo language
Nebramycin factor 6
  USE Tobramycin
Nebraska
  — **Description and travel**
  — — **1951-1980**
  — — **1981-**
  — **History**
  — — **War of 1812**
Nebriidae
  USE Carabidae

2560

Nebrodi Mountains (Sicily)
  UF Caronie Mountains (Sicily)
      Monti Caronie (Sicily)
      Monti Nebrodi (Sicily)
  BT Mountains—Italy
NEBULA (Computer program language)
  [HF5548.5.N2]
  UF Natural electronic business language
Nebulae
  [QB855-QB855.9 (General)]
  [QB891 (Spectra)]
  UF Galactic nebulae
      Gaseous nebulae
      Nebulas
  BT Galaxies
  NT Andromeda (Nebula)
      Crab Nebula
      H II regions (Astrophysics)
      Orion Nebula
Nebulae, Extragalactic
  USE Galaxies
Nebulae, Planetary
  USE Planetary nebulae
Nebular hypothesis
  [QB981]
  BT Solar system
Nebulas
  USE Nebulae
Nebulizers
  USE Aerosols
NEC 8200 (Computer)
  USE NEC PC-8200 (Computer)
NEC PC-8200 (Computer)
  [QA76.8.N]
  UF NEC 8200 (Computer)
      Nippon Electric Company PC-8200
        (Computer)
  BT Microcomputers
      Portable computers
NEC PC-8201 (Computer)
  [QA76.8.N]
  UF Nippon Electric Company PC-8201
        (Computer)
      PC-8201 (Computer)
      Small Wonder (Computer)
  BT Microcomputers
NEC PC-8201A (Computer)
  [QA76.8.N]
  UF Nippon Electric Company PC-8201A
        (Computer)
      PC-8201A (Computer)
  BT Microcomputers
      Portable computers
Necator
  [QL391.N4]
  BT Hookworms
Necator americanus
  [QL391.N4]
Nece Site (Iowa)
  USE Chan-ya-ta Site (Iowa)
Necessities of life
  USE Basic needs
Necessity, Fort, Battle of, 1754
  [E199]
  UF Great Meadows, Battle of, 1754
  RT Washington's Expedition to the Ohio,
      2d, 1754
Necessity, Military
  USE Military necessity
Necessity (International law)
  [JX4079.N4]
  BT International law
  NT Military necessity
Necessity (Islamic law)
Necessity (Jewish law)
Necessity (Law) *(May Subd Geog)*
  UF State of necessity

  BT Assistance in emergencies
      Criminal liability
      Justification (Law)
      Liability (Law)
      Self-help (Law)
  RT Duress (Law)
      Self-defense (Law)
  NT Justifiable homicide
Necessity (Philosophy)
  [B187.N4 (Greek philosophy)]
  [BD417 (Ontology)]
  [BF620-BF628 (Psychology)]
  RT Causation
      Chance
      Fate and fatalism
      Free will and determinism
      Ontology
      Predestination
      Teleology
      Truth
Necessity (Roman law)
  BT Roman law
Necessity money
  USE Emergency currency
Nechanicky family *(Not Subd Geog)*
Nechernozem'e (R.S.F.S.R.)
  USE Non-Chernozem Region (R.S.F.S.R.)
Nechernozemnaîa zona (R.S.F.S.R.)
  USE Non-Chernozem Region (R.S.F.S.R.)
Nechernozemnaya zona (R.S.F.S.R.)
  USE Non-Chernozem Region (R.S.F.S.R.)
Nechernozemnyĭ raĭon (R.S.F.S.R.)
  USE Non-Chernozem Region (R.S.F.S.R.)
Nechernozemnyy rayon (R.S.F.S.R.)
  USE Non-Chernozem Region (R.S.F.S.R.)
Neches River (Tex.)
  BT Rivers—Texas
Neck
  [QL950.4 (Comparative anatomy)]
  [QM535 (Human anatomy, QM155)]
  NT Carotid triangle
      Carotid triangle, Inferior
      Submandibular triangle
      Submental triangle
      Throat
  — Abscess
      [RD641-2]
    UF Angina Ludovici
    BT Neck—Diseases
  — Cancer
  — Diseases *(May Subd Geog)*
      [RC936]
    NT Neck—Abscess
      Neck pain
      Torticollis
  — Radiography
  — Surgery
      [RD531]
  — Tumors
      [RD661]
  — Wounds and injuries
    NT Whiplash injuries
  —— Complications and sequelae
Neck breathers (Persons)
  USE Tracheotomy—Patients
Neck family *(Not Subd Geog)*
Neck of the uterus
  USE Cervix uteri
Neck pain *(May Subd Geog)*
  UF Cervical pain
      Cervicodynia
      Neckache
  BT Neck—Diseases
      Pain
  NT Cervico-brachial neuralgia
Neckache
  USE Neck pain
Neckar River (Germany)
  BT Rivers—Germany (West)

Neckarhausen (Nürtingen, Germany)
  (Not Subd Geog)
  UF Nürtingen (Germany). Neckarhausen
Necklaces *(May Subd Geog)*
  [GT2260]
  BT Jewelry
      Manners and customs
      Neckwear
Necks (Geology) *(May Subd Geog)*
  [QE611]
  BT Intrusions (Geology)
      Volcanism
  NT Volcanic plugs
  — New Mexico
    NT Ship Rock (N.M.)
Neckties
  [GT2120 (Manners and customs)]
  [TT616 (Clothing manufacture)]
  UF Cravats
      Ties (Neckwear)
  BT Neckwear
  NT Bola ties
Neckwear *(May Subd Geog)*
  BT Clothing and dress
  NT Bola ties
      Collars
      Necklaces
      Neckties
      Scarves
Necro
  USE Necrotic enteritis
Necrologies
    Here are entered registers of deaths in ecclesiasti-
  cal or other organizations or registers of anniversary
  days when services are performed for the dead.
  Works on announcements of death either published
  in the press or mailed individually are entered under
  Death notices. Works on short biographical sketches,
  especially in newspapers, published upon a person's
  death are entered under Obituaries.
  UF Deaths, Registers of
      Registers of deaths
  BT Church records and registers
  SA subdivision Necrology *under names of*
      individual orders, e.g. Jesuits—
      Necrology
  NT Martyrologies
Necromancy
  USE Magic
Necrophilia
  UF Necrophilism
  BT Psychology, Pathological
Necrophilism
  USE Necrophilia
Necrophoridae
  USE Silphidae
Necrópolis C. Colón (Havana, Cuba)
  USE Necrópolis Cristóbal Colón (Havana,
      Cuba)
Necrópolis Cristóbal Colón (Havana, Cuba)
  UF Cementerio Cristóbal Colón (Havana,
      Cuba)
      Cementerio de Colón (Havana, Cuba)
      Colón Cemetery (Havana, Cuba)
      Cristóbal Colón Cemetery (Havana,
      Cuba)
      Necrópolis C. Colón (Havana, Cuba)
  BT Cemeteries—Cuba
Necropsy
  USE Autopsy
Necroscopy
  USE Autopsy
Necrosing arteritis
  USE Periarteritis nodosa
Necrosis
  [RB133]
  RT Gangrene
  SA subdivision Necrosis *under names of*
      organs and regions of the body, e.g.
      Heart—Necrosis; Foot—Necrosis
  NT Fat necrosis
  — Bacteriology

Necrosis
— **Bacteriology** *(Continued)*
  $[QR201.N4]$
    BT Bacteria, Pathogenic
Necrosis, Fat
  USE Fat necrosis
Necrotic enteritis
  UF Infectious enteritis in pigs
      Necro
      Swine typhoid
Necrotizing enterocolitis, Neonatal
  USE Enterocolitis, Neonatal necrotizing
Necrotizing ulcerative gingivitis
  USE Gingivitis, Necrotizing ulcerative
Nectar
  BT Nectaries
  RT Honey
Nectar-eating animals
  USE Nectarivores
Nectar plants
  USE Honey plants
Nectarberry
  USE Arctic raspberry
Nectaries
  $[QK657]$
  BT Flowers
  NT Nectar
Nectarine *(May Subd Geog)*
  UF Nectarine tree
  BT Peach
Nectarine industry *(May Subd Geog)*
  $[HD9259.N43-434]$
Nectarine tree
  USE Nectarine
Nectarivores *(May Subd Geog)*
  UF Honey-eating animals
      Nectar-eating animals
      Nectarivorous animals
  BT Animals
  NT Bees
      Honey eaters
Nectarivorous animals
  USE Nectarivores
Nectarophora
  $[QL527.A64]$
  BT Aphididae
Nectocarcinus
  $[QL444.M33]$
  BT Portunidae
Nectocarcinus bennetti
  $[QL444.M33]$
Nectomys
  $[QL737.R638]$
  BT Cricetidae
Necton
  USE Nekton
Nectria galligena
  USE European canker
Nectrioidaceae
  USE Zythiaceae
Necturus
  $[QL668.C277]$
  UF Menobranchus
      Mud puppies
      Mudpuppies
  BT Proteidae
  NT Necturus maculosus
Necturus louisianensis
  USE Necturus maculosus
Necturus maculosus
  $[QL668.C277]$
  UF Necturus louisianensis
      Necturus stictus
  BT Necturus
Necturus stictus
  USE Necturus maculosus

Nederlandsche Grofsmederij Strike, 1978
  BT Forging industry—Netherlands—
      Employees
      Strikes and lockouts—Forging industry
      —Netherlands
      Strikes and lockouts—Netherlands
Nederlandse Pool-Expeditie, 1882-1883
Nederlandse Hervormde Kerk
— **Parties and movements**
    NT Doleantie
        Ethical movement (Dutch
        Reformed Church)
Nederlandse Waddeneilanden (Netherlands)
  USE West Frisian Islands (Netherlands)
NEDIS (Computer program language)
  $[QA76.73.N]$
Nedre Fryken Lake (Sweden)
  USE Frykensjöarna (Sweden)
Nee (African people)
  USE Bana (African people)
Neece family
  USE Neese family
Need (Philosophy)
  $[B105.N]$
  BT Philosophy
Need (Psychology)
  UF Psychogenic needs
  BT Motivation (Psychology)
Need certification for health facilities
  USE Health facilities—Certificate of need
Need family
  UF Nead family
Needle biopsy
  USE Biopsy, Needle
Needle Eye Wilderness (Ariz.)
  USE Needles Eye Wilderness (Ariz.)
Needle grasses
  USE Stipa
Needle-holders
  $[RD73.N5 (Surgery)]$
Needle ice
  USE Frazil ice
Needle lace
  USE Needlepoint lace
Needle penetration test of soils
  USE Soil penetration test
Needlefish fishing
  $[SH691.N]$
  BT Fishing
Needlefishes
  $[QL638.B34]$
  UF Belonidae
      Esocesidae
      Petalichthyidae
      Tylosuridae
  BT Atheriniformes
  NT Belone
      Tylosurus
Needlegrasses
  USE Stipa
Needlepoint canvas work
  USE Canvas embroidery
Needlepoint embroidery
  USE Canvas embroidery
Needlepoint lace *(May Subd Geog)*
  UF Needle lace
  BT Lace and lace making
Needles
  USE Pins and needles
Needles, Phonograph
  USE Phonograph needles
Needles Eye Wilderness (Ariz.)
  UF Needle Eye Wilderness (Ariz.)
      Needles Eye Wilderness Study Area
      (Ariz.)
  BT National parks and reserves—Arizona
      Wilderness areas—Arizona
Needles Eye Wilderness Study Area (Ariz.)
  USE Needles Eye Wilderness (Ariz.)

Needles Range Group (Utah and Nev.)
  (Not Subd Geog)
  BT Geology—Nevada
      Geology—Utah
      Geology, Stratigraphic—Oligocene
Needless surgery
  USE Surgery, Unnecessary
Needlework *(May Subd Geog)*
  $[NK8800-NK9499 (Art needlework)]$
  $[TT700-TT845]$
  BT Arts and crafts movement
      Decoration and ornament
      Decorative arts
      Home economics
      Manual training
      Textile crafts
  RT Dressmaking
      Embroidery
      Fancy work
      Sewing
  NT Appliqué
      Assisi embroidery
      Counted thread embroidery
      Cross-stitch
      Cross-stitch, Long-legged
      Drawn-work
      Fabric pictures
      Hardanger needlework
      Lace and lace making
      Needlework industry and trade
      Netting
      Patchwork
      Punched work
      Quilting
      Reweaving
      Samplers
      Stump work
      Tapestry
      White work embroidery
— **Implements and appliances**
    $[TT715]$
— **Patterns**
    $[TT753]$
Needlework, Edwardian
  UF Edwardian needlework
Needlework, Hmong (Asian people)
  (May Subd Geog)
  UF Hmong (Asian people) needlework
Needlework, Jewish *(May Subd Geog)*
  UF Jewish needlework
Needlework, Turkmen *(May Subd Geog)*
  UF Turkmen needlework
Needlework, Victorian
  UF Victorian needlework
Needlework boxes *(May Subd Geog)*
  BT Boxes
Needlework industry and trade
  (May Subd Geog)
  BT Needlework
Needs, Basic
  USE Basic needs
Needs, Nutritional
  USE Nutrition—Requirements
Needs, Training
  USE Training needs
Needs assessment *(May Subd Geog)*
    Here are entered works on the methods and tech-
  niques employed in assessing the need for programs,
  projects, or products.
  UF Assessment of needs
      Needs assessment—Methodology
  BT Planning
  NT Medical care—Needs assessment
— Methodology
    USE Needs assessment
Needs assessment of medical care
  USE Medical care—Needs assessment
Neel family
  USE Neal family
Neeley family
  USE Neely family

2562

Neelidae
  [QL503.N4]
  BT Collembola
  NT Megalothorax
Neely family (Not Subd Geog)
  UF Kneely family
     Nealey family
     Nealy family
     Neeley family
     Neily family
Neem
  USE Margosa
Neem cake (May Subd Geog)
  UF Neem oil-cake
  BT Margosa
     Oil cake
Neem oil-cake
  USE Neem cake
Neenchelidae
  USE Neenchelyidae
Neenchelyidae
  [QL638.N3]
  UF Neenchelidae
  BT Eels
Ñeengatú language
  USE Tupi language
Neerwinden, Belgium, Battle of, 1693
  BT Belgium—History—1648-1794
Neerwinden, Belgium, Battle of, 1793
  BT Belgium—History—1648-1794
Nees family
  USE Neese family
Neesbit family
  USE Nesbitt family
Neese family (Not Subd Geog)
  UF Neece family
     Nees family
     Niece family
  RT Niess family
Neethling family (Not Subd Geog)
Nefas (The Latin word)
  BT Latin language—Etymology
Nefesh (The Hebrew word)
  BT Hebrew language—Etymology
Neff family (Not Subd Geog)
  UF Naeff family
     Naff family
Nefs
  BT Silverwork
Negation (Logic)
  UF Negative propositions
  BT Judgment (Logic)
Negation (Logic) in literature
Negation of negation (Dialectical materialism)
  UF Law of negation of negation
     (Dialectical materialism)
  BT Dialectical materialism, Laws of
     Philosophy
Negative absolute temperature
  USE Negative temperature
Negative assurance (Accounting)
  (May Subd Geog)
  UF Assurance, Negative (Accounting)
  BT Accounting
     Auditing
Negative binomial distribution
  UF Pascal distribution
  BT Binomial distribution
  NT Binomial theorem
Negative cardiac inotropic agents
  USE Myocardial depressants
Negative engraving (Cartography)
  USE Scribing (Cartography)
Negative income tax (May Subd Geog)
  BT Economic assistance, Domestic
     Economic security
     Guaranteed annual income
     Income
     Income maintenance programs
  RT Wages—Annual wage

Negative ion vacancy
  USE Holes (Electron deficiencies)
Negative ions
  USE Anions
Negative numbers
  USE Numbers, Negative
Negative propositions
  USE Negation (Logic)
Negative resistance devices
  [TK7872.N4]
  UF Negatrons
  BT Electric resistance
     Electronic apparatus and appliances
  NT Tetrodes
     Thyristors
     Tunnel diodes
     Unijunction transistors
Negative scribing (Cartography)
  USE Scribing (Cartography)
Negative temperature
  UF Negative absolute temperature
  BT Lasers
     Masers
     Nuclear spin
     Temperature
     Thermodynamics
Negatives
  USE Photography—Negatives
Negatives (Grammar)
  USE subdivision Negatives under names of
     languages and groups of languages
     Grammar, Comparative and general—
     Negatives
Negativism
  BT Personality
     Psychology, Pathological
Negativity (Philosophy)
  BT Philosophy
Negatrons
  USE Negative resistance devices
Negda
  USE Nigidals
Negeb (Israel)
  USE Negev (Israel)
Negev (Israel)
  UF Negeb (Israel)
Negidal language (May Subd Geog)
  [PL481.N45]
  BT Russian S.F.S.R.—Languages
     Tungus-Manchu languages
Negidals
  USE Nigidals
Negishi family (Not Subd Geog)
Negishi School
  BT Art criticism—Japan
     Japanese literature—Meiji period,
     1868-1912
     Literature, Modern—19th century
Neglect of animals
  USE Animals, Treatment of
Neglect of the aged
  USE Aged—Abuse of
Negley family
  USE Nagel family
Negligence (May Subd Geog)
  BT Guilt (Law)
     Liability (Law)
     Master and servant
     Railroad law
     Railroads—Accidents
  RT Accident law
     Damages
     Dolus (Civil law)
     Negligence, Contributory
     Torts
  NT Attractive nuisance
     Employers' liability
     Liability for building accidents
     Liability for condition and use of land
     Liability for fire damages
     Liability for landslide damages

     Liability for slip and fall accidents
     Malpractice
     Negligence, Comparative
     Negligence, Criminal
     Occupations, Dangerous
     Omission, Criminal
     Products liability
     Proximate cause (Law)
     Res ipsa loquitur doctrine
     Tort liability of charitable
     organizations
     Tort liability of corporations
     Tort liability of highway departments
     Tort liability of hospitals
     Tort liability of insurance companies
     Tort liability of municipal corporations
     Tort liability of parks
     Tort liability of partnerships
     Tort liability of recreation agencies
     Tort liability of social service agencies
     Tort liability of trade-unions
     Tort liability of unincorporated
     societies
     Tort liability of universities and
     colleges
     Tort liability of works councils
Negligence, Comparative (May Subd Geog)
  UF Comparative negligence
  BT Negligence
  RT Negligence, Contributory
Negligence, Contributory (May Subd Geog)
  UF Contributory negligence
  BT Accident law
     Damages
  RT Negligence
     Negligence, Comparative
  SA Negligence, and references under that
     heading
  NT Last clear chance
Negligence, Criminal (May Subd Geog)
  UF Criminal negligence
  BT Negligence
  NT Danger (Law)
Negligence (Byzantine law)
Negligence (Canon law)
Negligence (Ethics)
Negligence (Islamic law)
Negligence (Jewish law)
Negligence (Roman law)
Negligence in financial statements
  USE Financial statements, Misleading
Negly family
  USE Nagel family
Negotiable instruments (May Subd Geog)
  [HF1259 (United States)]
  [JX6288-JX6289 (International law)]
  UF Bills and notes
     Bills of credit
     Commercial paper
     Instruments, Negotiable
  BT Banking law
     Banks and banking
     Choses in action
     Commercial documents
     Commercial law
     Contracts
     Delegation (Civil law)
     Legal instruments
  RT Drafts
  NT Acceptances
     Bills of exchange
     Bonds
     Certificates of deposit
     Checks
     Currency exchanges (Domestic)
     Documentary credit
     Holder in due course
     Indorsements
     Letters of credit
     Money orders
     Postal service—Money-orders

Negotiable instruments *(Continued)*
        Promissory notes
        Protests (Negotiable instruments)
        Warehouse receipts
  — **Cancellation** *(May Subd Geog)*
    UF Cancellation of negotiable
           instruments
  — Taxation
    USE Bills of exchange—Taxation
           Taxation of bonds, securities, etc.
  — **United States**
  — — **States**
Negotiable order of withdrawal accounts
  USE NOW accounts
Negotiation
  [BF637.N4]
  UF Bargaining
  BT Discussion
      Psychology, Applied
  NT Arbitration, International
      Conflict management
      Deals
      Hostage negotiations
      Mediation and conciliation, Industrial
      Treaties
Negotiation in business *(May Subd Geog)*
  [HD58.6]
  BT Business
      Management
  NT Collective bargaining
Negotiations in international disputes
  USE Diplomatic negotiations in
        international disputes
Negotiorum gestio *(May Subd Geog)*
  BT Contracts
      Quasi contracts
  RT Mandate (Contract)
  NT Betterments
      Improvements (Law)
Negotiorum gestio (Jewish law)
Negotiorum gestio (Roman law)
  BT Roman law
Negrillos
  [DT16.P8]
  UF Nigrillos
  BT Pygmies
  RT Bagelli tribe
      Bambute
      Negritos
Negrinho do pastoreio (Brazilian brownie)
  BT Fairies
Negrito languages (Philippine)
  [PL5501-5525]
  BT Philippine languages
  NT Agta language
Negritos
  [DS666.N4 (Philippine Islands)]
  [GN664.N3 (Anthropology)]
  BT Pygmies
  RT Negrillos
  NT Aeta (Philippine people)
      Andamanese (Indic people)
      Mamanuas (Philippine tribe)
      Semang (Malayan people)
Negritos (Dance)
  [GV1796.N4]
Negritude
  USE Afro-Americans—Race identity
        Blacks—Race identity
Negro-Dutch dialects
  USE Creole dialects, Dutch
Negro-English dialects
  USE Creole dialects, English
Negro minstrel shows
  USE Minstrel shows
Negro race
  USE Black race
Negro River (Brazil and Uruguay)
  USE Rio Negro (Brazil and Uruguay)
Negro spirituals
  USE Spirituals (Songs)

Negro yam
  USE Dioscorea cayenensis
Negroes
  USE Blacks
Negroes (United States)
  USE Afro-Americans
Negropont Island (Greece)
  USE Euboea Island (Greece)
Negroponte Island (Greece)
  USE Euboea Island (Greece)
Negros Island (Philippines)
  UF Buglas Island (Philippines)
      Los Negros (Philippines)
  BT Islands—Philippines
      Visayan Islands (Philippines)
Nehalem Indians
  [E99.N45]
  BT Indians of North America
      Salishan Indians
Nehan (Sect)
  USE Nieh p'an (Sect)
Nehanshū
  USE Nieh p'an (Sect)
Nehru family *(Not Subd Geog)*
Neibel family
  USE Nebel family
Neididae
  USE Berytidae
Neighbor family
  USE Neighbors family
Neighborhood *(May Subd Geog)*
  BT Community life
      Social groups
  NT Neighborhood government
Neighborhood art projects
  USE Community art projects
Neighborhood centers
  USE Social settlements
Neighborhood councils
  USE Neighborhood government
Neighborhood gardens
  USE Community gardens
Neighborhood government *(May Subd Geog)*
  UF Government, Neighborhood
      Neighborhood councils
  BT Local government
      Neighborhood
  RT Citizens' associations
  NT Homeowners' associations
Neighborhood health centers
  USE Community health services
Neighborhood improvement programs
  USE Community development, Urban
Neighborhood Information Center Project
  BT Information services—United States
Neighborhood justice centers
  (May Subd Geog)
  UF Community justice centers
  BT Arbitration and award
      Compromise (Law)
      Courts
      Justice, Administration of
      Small claims courts
      Third parties (Law)
  RT Dispute resolution (Law)
Neighborhood newspapers
  USE Community newspapers
Neighborhood schools
  USE Community schools
Neighboring rights (Copyright)
  USE Copyright—Neighboring rights
Neighborliness
  BT Friendship
  — **Religious aspects**
  — — **Buddhism, [Christianity, etc.]**

Neighbors family *(Not Subd Geog)*
  UF Naber family
      Nabers family
      Nabor family
      Nabors family
      Nabour family
      Nabours family
      Neighbor family
      Neighbour family
      Neighbours family
Neighbor's rights
  USE Adjoining landowners
Neighbour family
  USE Neighbors family
Neighbours family
  USE Neighbors family
Neil family
  USE Neal family
Neill family
  USE Neal family
Neilsen family
  USE Nelson family
Neilson family
  USE Nelson family
Neily family
  USE Neely family
Nein family
  USE Neun family
Neis family
  UF Nise family
  RT Neus family
      Nice family
Neisbet family
  USE Nesbitt family
Neisbit family
  USE Nesbitt family
Neisbitt family
  USE Nesbitt family
Neisse River
  UF Lausitzer Neisse River
      Lusatian Neisse River
      Lužická Nisa River
      Nysa Łużycka River
  BT Rivers—Czechoslovakia
      Rivers—Germany (East)
      Rivers—Poland
  NT Oder-Neisse Line (Germany and
      Poland)
Neisseria
  [QR82.N4]
  BT Neisseriaceae
  NT Neisseria flavescens
      Neisseria gonorrhoeae
      Neisseria meningitidis
      Neisseria sicca
Neisseria flavescens
  [QR82.N4]
  BT Neisseria
Neisseria gonorrhoeae
  [QR82.N4]
  UF Diplococcus gonorrhoeae
      Gonococcus
      Micrococcus gonorrhoea
      Neisser's coccus
  BT Neisseria
  RT Gonorrhea
Neisseria meningitidis
  [QR82.N4]
  UF Meningococcus
  BT Neisseria
  RT Meningitis
Neisseria sicca
  [QR82.N4]
  UF Diplococcus siccus
  BT Neisseria
Neisseriaceae
  [QR82.N4]
  BT Bacteria
      Bacteria, Pathogenic
  NT Neisseria

Neisser's coccus
  USE Neisseria gonorrhoeae
Neit (Egyptian deity)
  USE Neith (Egyptian deity)
Neith (Egyptian deity)
  ₎BL2450.N45₎
  UF Neit (Egyptian deity)
      Net (Egyptian deity)
  BT Gods, Egyptian
Nejd (Saudi Arabia)
  USE Najd (Saudi Arabia)
Nekete language
  USE Anesu language
Nekli͡udov family (Not Subd Geog)
Nekton (May Subd Geog)
  ₎QH90.8.N44₎
  UF Necton
  BT Aquatic animals
NELIAC (Computer program language)
  BT ALGOL (Computer program language)
Nelli, Ottaviano, ca. 1370-ca. 1446.
  Incoronazione della Vergine
  (Not Subd Geog)
  UF Incoronazione della Vergine (Mural
      painting)
  BT Mural painting and decoration, Italian
Nellson family
  USE Nelson family
Nelly Sachs Preis
Nelmes family
  USE Nelms family
Nelms family (Not Subd Geog)
  UF Nelmes family
Nelsen family
  USE Nelson family
Nelson Brook (Mass.)
  BT Rivers—Massachusetts
Nelson family (Not Subd Geog)
  UF Neilsen family
      Neilson family
      Nellson family
      Nelsen family
  RT Nielsen family
      Nilsen family
Nelson House (Yorktown, Va.)
  BT Colonial National Historical Park (Va.)
      Dwellings—Virginia
Nelson Island (Alaska)
  BT Islands—Alaska
Nelson Lake (Sask.)
  BT Lakes—Saskatchewan
Nelson Lakes National Park (N.Z.)
  BT National parks and reserves—New
      Zealand
      Parks—New Zealand
Nelson River (Banks Island, N.W.T.)
  BT Rivers—Northwest Territories
Nelson River (Man.)
  BT Rivers—Manitoba
Nelson's Mountains
  USE Selkirk Range
Nelumbicum
  USE Nelumbo
Nelumbium
  USE Nelumbo
Nelumbo
  ₎QK495.N97 (Botany)₎
  UF Nelumbicum
      Nelumbium
  BT Nymphaeaceae
Nelumbo nucifera
  USE Lotus, East Indian
Nelumbo speciosa
  USE Lotus, East Indian
Nemacheilus
  USE Nemachilus
Nemachilus
  ₎QL638.C647₎
  UF Nemacheilus
  BT Loaches
  NT Nemachilus barbatulus

Nemachilus fasciatus
Nemachilus barbatulus
  ₎QL638.C647₎
  BT Nemachilus
Nemachilus fasciatus
  ₎QL638.C647₎
  BT Nemachilus
Nemacides
  USE Nematocides
Nemadi dialect
  USE Nimadi dialect
Nemaliales (May Subd Geog)
  ₎QK569.N₎
  UF Nemalionales
  BT Red algae
  NT Acrochaetiaceae
Nemalionales
  USE Nemaliales
Neman River
  UF Memel River
      Nemunas River
      Niemen River
      Nyeman River
      Russ River
  BT Rivers—Byelorussian S.S.R.
      Rivers—Lithuania
      Rivers—Russian S.F.S.R.
Nemanja dynasty (Not Subd Geog)
  UF Nemanjić dynasty
      Nemanjid dynasty
      Nemanya dynasty
  BT Serbia—History—To 1456
Nemanjić dynasty
  USE Nemanja dynasty
Nemanjid dynasty
  USE Nemanja dynasty
Nemanya dynasty
  USE Nemanja dynasty
Nemastomatidae
  ₎QL458.52.N4₎
  BT Opiliones
Nemathelminthes
  ₎QL391.N2₎
  BT Helminths
      Worms
  NT Acanthocephala
      Gordiacea
      Nematoda
Nematicides
  USE Nematocides
Nematidae
  USE Tenthredinidae
Nematistiidae
  ₎QL638.N33₎
  BT Perciformes
  NT Nematistius
Nematistius
  ₎QL638.N33₎
  BT Nematistiidae
Nematistius pectoralis
  USE Roosterfish
Nematocera
  USE Diptera
Nematocides
  UF Nemacides
      Nematicides
  BT Anthelmintics
      Pesticides
Nematocysts
  UF Cnidae
      Cnidocysts
  BT Coelenterata—Anatomy
Nematoda (May Subd Geog)
  ₎QL391.N4₎
  UF Eelworms
  BT Nemathelminthes
  NT Adenophorea
      Ascaridida
      Chromadorida
      Desmodorida
      Dorylaimida

      Dracunculida
      Enoplida
      Filarioida
      Hemicycliophoridae
      Hookworms
      Meloidogyne
      Monhysterida
      Nematoidea
      Oxyurida
      Plant nematodes
      Roundworm
      Soil nematodes
      Spirurida
      Trichinellida
      Tylenchida
  — Anatomy
  — Biological control
  — Food
  — Host plants
  — Research (May Subd Geog)
      UF Nematological research
Nematode-destroying fungi
  USE Fungi, Nematode-destroying
Nematode diseases of plants
  (May Subd Geog)
  ₎SB998.N4₎
  BT Agricultural pests
      Plant diseases
  RT Plant nematodes
  NT Root-knot
Nematode-trapping fungi
  USE Fungi, Nematode-destroying
Nematode vectors
  USE Plant nematodes as carriers of disease
Nematodes, Phytopathogenic
  USE Plant nematodes
Nematodes as carriers of plant disease
  USE Plant nematodes as carriers of disease
Nematognathi
  USE Catfishes
Nematoidea
  ₎QL391.N4₎
  UF Phasmidea
      Secernentea
  BT Nematoda
  NT Rhabditoidea
      Strongylida
Nematological research
  USE Nematoda—Research
Nematologists (May Subd Geog)
  ₎QL26-31₎
  BT Zoologists
Nematomorpha (May Subd Geog)
  ₎QL391.N5₎
  UF Gordioidea
  BT Gordiacea
  NT Gordioida
Nematophagous fungi
  USE Fungi, Nematode-destroying
Nematophycus
  USE Nematophyton
Nematophyton
  ₎QE989₎
  UF Nematophycus
Nematoscelis
  ₎QL444.M338₎
  BT Euphausiidae
Nematoscelis difficilis
  ₎QL444.M338₎
Nematospora
  USE Yeast
Nematus
  USE Pristiphora
Nematus erichsonii
  USE Larch sawfly
Nembe language
  ₎PL8548₎
  UF Nimbi language
  BT Ijo language

Nembi language (Southern Highlands Province,
      Papua New Guinea)
   USE Magi language (Southern Highlands
            Province, Papua New Guinea)
Nembutsu
   BT Pure Land Buddhism
         Shin (Sect)
Nemeobiidae
   USE Riodinidae
Nemeris
      ₍QL561.G6₎
   BT Geometridae
Nemertea
   USE Nemertinea
Nemertinea *(May Subd Geog)*
      ₍QL391.N6₎
   UF Nemertea
         Nemertini
         Proboscis worms
         Rhynchocoela
   BT Worms
   NT Enopla
Nemertini
   USE Nemertinea
Nemi folk literature
   USE Folk literature, Nemi
Nemi language
   BT Melanesian languages
         New Caledonia—Languages
Nemi literature *(May Subd Geog)*
   NT Folk literature, Nemi
Nemipteridae
      ₍QL638.N347₎
   UF Denticidae
   BT Perciformes
   NT Argyrozona
Nemkey family *(Not Subd Geog)*
Nemopalpus *(May Subd Geog)*
      ₍QL537.P85₎
   BT Psychodidae
Nemophididae
   USE Blenniidae
Nemophoridae
   USE Incurvariidae
Nemorhaedus
   USE Gorals
Nemoura
      ₍QL530.3.N4₎
   BT Nemouridae
Nemouridae
      ₍QL530.3.N4₎
   BT Stoneflies
   NT Amphinemura
         Nemoura
Nemunas River
   USE Neman River
Nemuro-hantō (Japan)
   USE Nemuro Peninsula (Japan)
Nemuro Peninsula (Japan)
   UF Nemuro-hantō (Japan)
   BT Peninsulas—Japan
Nen River (England)
   USE Nene River (England)
Nenadović family *(Not Subd Geog)*
Nendiume Site (Mexico)
   USE Chiapa de Corso Site (Mexico)
Nendö (Solomon Islands)
   UF Egmont Island (Solomon Islands)
         Ndeni (Solomon Islands)
         Ndeni Island (Solomon Islands)
         New Guernsey (Solomon Islands)
         Nitendi (Solomon Islands)
         Santa Cruz Island (Solomon Islands)
   BT Islands—Solomon Islands
         Santa Cruz Islands (Solomon Islands)
Nene
      ₍QL696.A52₎
   UF Anser sandvicensis
         Branta sandvicensis
         Hawaiian goose
         Nesochen sandvicensis

   BT Branta
Nene River (England)
   UF Nen River (England)
   BT Rivers—England
Nene Valley Railway
   BT Railroads—Great Britain
Nenema language
   BT Melanesian languages
Nenets language
      ₍PL16.Y8₎
   UF Jurak language
         Yurak language
   BT Samoyedic languages
Nenets people
   USE Nentsy
Nengone folk literature
   USE Folk literature, Nengone
Nengone Island (New Caledonia)
   USE Maré Island (New Caledonia)
Nengone language
      ₍PL6268₎
   BT Melanesian languages
Neni-nesu (Ancient city)
   USE Heracleopolis Magna (Ancient city)
Nenjū gyōji emaki (Scrolls)
      ₍ND1059.6.N₎
   BT Japan—Court and courtiers—Pictorial
            works
         Japan—Social life and customs—To
            1600—Pictorial works
         Painting, Japanese—Heian period, 794-
            1185
         Painting, Japanese—Edo period, 1600-
            1868
         Scrolls, Japanese
Nentsy
      ₍DK34.N4₎
   UF Nenets people
         Yuraks
   BT Ethnology—Soviet Union
         Samoyeds
Neo (Artificial language)
      ₍PM8670₎
   BT Languages, Artificial
Neo-Caroline script
   USE Writing, Humanistic
Neo-Confucianism *(May Subd Geog)*
      ₍B127.N4₎
   BT Confucianism
         Philosophy, Chinese
Neo-Dadaism
   USE Pop art
Neo-empiricism
   USE Logical positivism
Neo-fascism
   USE Fascism
Neo-Firthian linguistics
   USE Systemic grammar
Neo-Greek literature
   USE Greek literature, Modern
Neo-impressionism (Art) *(May Subd Geog)*
      ₍N6465.N44 (General)₎
   UF Divisionism
         Pointillism
   BT Art, Modern—19th century
         Dots (Art)
         Impressionism (Art)
         Painting, Modern—19th century
   NT Post-impressionism (Art)
Neo-Kantianism
      ₍B3192 (Germany)₎
   BT Idealism
         Transcendentalism
   RT Marburg school of philosophy
Neo-Latin languages
   USE Romance languages
Néo-latine, Langue internationale
   USE Langue internationale néo-latine
            (Artificial language)
Neo-literates, Writing for
   USE New literates, Writing for

Neo-Melanesian language
   USE Tok Pisin language
Neo-Melanesian poetry
   USE Tok Pisin poetry
Neo-Nazism
   USE Fascism—Germany
Neo-orthodoxy
      Here are entered works on a mid-twentieth cen-
   tury trend in Christian theology that emphasizes the
   transcendence of God, human sinfulness, and justifi-
   cation by faith.
   BT Dialectical theology
Neo-positivism
   USE Logical positivism
Neo-romanticism (Art movement)
   USE Neoromanticism (Art movement)
Neo-Scholasticism
      ₍B839₎
   UF Neo-Thomism
         Thomism (Modern philosophy)
   BT Philosophy, Modern
         Scholasticism
Neo-Slavism
   USE Panslavism
Neo-Thomism
   USE Neo-Scholasticism
Neobalidae
   USE Leafhoppers
Neobarrettia
      ₍QL508.T4₎
   BT Tettigoniidae
Neobidessus
      ₍QL596.D9₎
   BT Dytiscidae
Neobomolochus
      ₍QL444.C73₎
   BT Bomolochidae
Neobythites grandis
   USE Parabassogigas grandis
Neocapritermes
      ₍QL529.3.T4₎
   BT Termitidae
Neocene epoch
   USE Geology, Stratigraphic—Neocene
         Paleobotany—Neocene
         Paleontology—Neocene
Neochloromyxum
   USE Kudoa
Neoclassical school of economics
      ₍HB98.2₎
   UF Cambridge school of economics
         Marshallian economics
   BT Classical school of economics
         Economics
   NT Chicago school of economics
Neoclassicism (Architecture)
(May Subd Geog)
      Here are entered works on the revival of classical
   principles in architecture during the late 18th and
   early 19th centuries.
   BT Architecture, Classical
         Architecture, Modern
         Classicism in architecture
         Revival movements (Art)
   NT Egyptian revival (Architecture)
         Greek revival (Architecture)
Neoclassicism (Art) *(May Subd Geog)*
      Here are entered works on the revival of classical
   principles in art during the late 18th and early 19th
   centuries.
   BT Art, Modern
         Classicism in art
         Revival movements (Art)
   NT Decoration and ornament—
            Neoclassicism
         Egyptian Revival (Art)
Neoclassicism (Literature)
   BT Classicism
         Literature, Modern
         Revival movements (Art)
Neocoelidiidae
   USE Leafhoppers

Neocolonialism
  USE *subdivision* Colonial influence *under*
      regions and countries
      Colonies
      Imperialism
Neocortex
  USE Neopallium
Neocteniza
  [QL458.42.A28]
  BT Actinopodidae
Neodecanoic acid
  BT Carboxylic acids
Neodiprion
  [QL568.D5]
  BT Diprionidae
  NT Neodiprion excitans
      Neodiprion nanulus
      Neodiprion pratti
      Neodiprion sertifer
      Neodiprion taedae
Neodiprion excitans *(May Subd Geog)*
  [QL568.D5]
  UF Blackheaded pine sawfly
  BT Neodiprion
Neodiprion nanulus *(May Subd Geog)*
  [QL568.D5]
  UF Red pine sawfly
  BT Neodiprion
Neodiprion pratti *(May Subd Geog)*
  [QL568.D5]
  BT Neodiprion
Neodiprion sertifer *(May Subd Geog)*
  [QL568.D5]
  UF European pine sawfly
  BT Neodiprion
Neodiprion taedae *(May Subd Geog)*
  [QL568.D5]
  UF Loblolly pine sawfly
  BT Neodiprion
Neodymium
  [QD181.N4]
  — **Spectra**
Neodymium-aluminum yttrium garnet lasers
  USE Nd-YAG lasers
Neodymium-doped YAG lasers
  USE Nd-YAG lasers
Neodymium glass lasers
  BT Lasers
      Solid-state lasers
Neodymium-YAG lasers
  USE Nd-YAG lasers
Neodymium-yttrium aluminum garnet lasers
  USE Nd-YAG lasers
Neofascism in Italy
  USE Fascism—Italy—1945-
Neofelis nebulosa
  USE Clouded leopard
Neofiber
  [QL737.R638]
  BT Cricetidae
  NT Neofiber alleni
Neofiber alleni
  [QL737.R638]
  UF Florida water rat
      Roundtailed muskrat
  BT Neofiber
Neofidelia
  [QL568.F47]
  BT Fideliidae
Neofidelia profuga
  [QL568.F47]
Neogastropoda *(May Subd Geog)*
  [QL430.4]
  UF Stenoglossa
  BT Prosobranchiata
  NT Cancellariidae
      Conidae
      Marginellidae
      Muricidae
Neogastropoda, Fossil
  BT Prosobranchiata, Fossil

  NT Cancellariidae, Fossil
      Marginellidae, Fossil
      Muricidae, Fossil
      Turridae, Fossil
Neoglify (Picture language)
  BT Language, Universal
      Languages, Artificial
      Pasigraphy
Neogrammarians
  [P75]
  UF Junggrammatiker
      Leipzig School (Linguistics)
      Young grammarians
  BT Linguistic change
      Linguistics—History—19th century
Neohellenists *(May Subd Geog)*
  [DF505.7 (Byzantine specialists)]
  [DF755.7-Modern Greek specialists]
  BT Scholars
Neoispano (Artificial language)
  BT Languages, Artificial
Neolatinus (Artificial language)
  BT Languages, Artificial
Neolepidozia grossiseta
  USE Telaranea grossiseta
Neolethrinidae
  USE Lethrinidae
Neolithic period *(May Subd Geog)*
  UF New Stone age
  BT Stone age
  NT Beaker cultures
      Danilo culture
      Funnel-beaker culture
      Ghassul culture
      Horgen culture
      Jōmon culture
      Okhotsk culture
      Vinča culture
      Yayoi culture
  — **Cyprus**
  — **England**
  — **Europe**
    NT Bandkeramik culture
       Corded Ware culture
       Michelsberg culture
       Passage Graves culture
  — **Europe, Eastern**
    NT Cotofeni culture
  — **Greece**
  — **India**
  — **Iran**
  — **Iraq**
  — **Ireland**
  — **Italy**
  — **Japan**
  — **Kenya**
  — **Romania**
    NT Cucuteni-Tripolye culture
  — **Scotland**
  — **Spain**
  — **Sweden**
  — **Switzerland**
    NT Pfyn culture
  — **Ukraine**
    NT Cucuteni-Tripolye culture
  — **Yugoslavia**
Neologisms
  USE Words, New
Neomammillaria (Cactus)
  USE Mammillaria (Cactus)
Neomeris phocaenoides
  USE Finless porpoise
Neomochtherus
  [QL537.A85]
  BT Robber flies
Neomycin
  [RM666.N35]
  BT Aminoglycosides
      Antibacterial agents
      Antibiotics

Neon
  [QD181.N5]
  BT Gases, Rare
  RT Argon
  — **Isotopes**
  — — **Decay**
  — — **Spectra**
  — **Spectra**
Neon-helium lasers
  USE Helium-neon lasers
Neon lamps
  [TK4383]
  BT Electric discharge lighting
  RT Electric lamps, Incandescent
      Electric lighting
Neon sculpture *(May Subd Geog)*
  [NB1270.N45]
  UF Sculpture, Neon
  BT Glass sculpture
Neon tetra
  [QL638.C5 (Zoology)]
  [SF458.T4 (Culture)]
  BT Aquarium fishes
Neon tubes
  [TK4383]
Neonatal anatomy
  USE Infants (Newborn)—Anatomy
Neonatal Behavioral Assessment Scale,
  Brazelton
  USE Brazelton Neonatal Behavioral
      Assessment Scale
Neonatal death
  USE Infants (Newborn)—Death
Neonatal hepatitis
  USE Hepatitis, Neonatal
Neonatal immunity, Maternally acquired
  USE Maternally acquired immunity
Neonatal intensive care *(May Subd Geog)*
  [RJ253.5]
  UF Intensive care, Neonatal
      Intensive care of the newborn
      Newborn intensive care
  BT Infant health services
      Infants (Newborn)—Hospital care
      Pediatric intensive care
  NT Incubators (Pediatrics)
  — **Law and legislation** *(May Subd Geog)*
    BT Medical laws and legislation
Neonatal jaundice
  USE Jaundice, Neonatal
Neonatal mortality
  USE Infants (Newborn)—Mortality
Neonatal necrotizing enterocolitis
  USE Enterocolitis, Neonatal necrotizing
Neonatal passive immunity
  USE Maternally acquired immunity
Neonatal pediatrics
  USE Neonatology
Neonatal pharmacology
  USE Infants (Newborn)—Effect of drugs on
Neonatal respiratory therapy
  USE Respiratory therapy for newborn
      infants
Neonatal surgery
  USE Infants (Newborn)—Surgery
Neonates
  USE Infants (Newborn)
Neonatologists *(May Subd Geog)*
  BT Pediatricians
  — **Malpractice** *(May Subd Geog)*
    UF Malpractice by neonatologists
       Tort liability of neonatologists
    BT Malpractice
       Neonatology—Law and legislation
Neonatology *(May Subd Geog)*
  [RJ251-RJ325]
  UF Neonatal pediatrics
  BT Perinatology
  RT Infants (Newborn)
  NT Infants (Newborn)—Diseases
  — **Law and legislation** *(May Subd Geog)*

Neonatology
— **Law and legislation** *(Continued)*
    BT Medical laws and legislation
    NT Neonatologists—Malpractice
Neonomianism
  BT Antinomianism
      Arminianism
      Calvinism
      Law (Theology)
      Law and gospel
Neopallium
  [QL938.N45 *(Comparative anatomy)*]
  [QM455 *(Human anatomy)*]
  UF Homogenetic cortex
      Isocortex
      Laminated cortex
      Neocortex
  BT Cerebral cortex
Neopanorpa
  [QL598.7.P3]
  BT Panorpidae
Neophasia
  [QL561.P5]
  BT Pieridae
Neophocaena phocaenoides
  USE Finless porpoise
Neoplasm growth
  USE Tumors—Growth
Neoplasm invasiveness
  USE Cancer invasiveness
Neoplasm metastasis
  USE Metastasis
Neoplasm regression, Spontaneous
  USE Cancer regression, Spontaneous
Neoplasms
  USE Tumors
Neoplastic endocrine-like syndromes
  [RC254.5]
  UF Hormone producing tumors
  BT Endocrine glands—Diseases
      Tumors
Neoplasticism *(May Subd Geog)*
  BT Art, Abstract
      Art, Modern—20th century
      Arts, Modern—20th century
      Painting, Abstract
Neoplatonism
  [B517]
  [B645]
  BT Church history—Primitive and early
        church, ca. 30-600
      Hellenism
      Philosophy
      Philosophy, Ancient
      Platonists
      Theosophy
  RT Alexandrian school
Neopositivism in law
  USE Legal positivism
Neoprene
  USE Rubber, Artificial
Neopseustidae *(May Subd Geog)*
  [QL561.N38]
  BT Lepidoptera
      Moths
Neorealism (Literature)
  USE Realism in literature
Neorhabdocoela
  [QL391.P7]
  BT Turbellaria
  NT Karkinorhynchidae
Neoromanticism (Art movement)
  (May Subd Geog)
  [N6494.N46]
  UF Neo-romanticism (Art movement)
  BT Art, Modern—20th century
Neoscona
  [QL458.42.A7]
  BT Araneidae
Neoseps
  [QL666.L28]

  BT Skinks
Neosho River (Kan. and Okla.)
  UF Grand River (Kan. and Okla.)
  BT Rivers—Kansas
      Rivers—Oklahoma
Neosphaerocera
  [QL537.S7]
  BT Sphaeroceridae
Neostethidae
  [QL638.N387]
  BT Atheriniformes
  NT Ceratostethus
Neostriatum
  BT Corpus striatum
  NT Caudate nucleus
Neotamias
  USE Chipmunks
Neotenin
  USE Juvenile hormones
Neoteny
  BT Embryology
  RT Axolotls
Neotestudina
  USE Zopfia
Neothallis
  [QL596.E7]
  BT Erotylidae
Neothunnus argentivittatus
  USE Yellowfin tuna
Neothunnus macropterus
  USE Yellowfin tuna
Neotoma
  [QL737.R638]
  BT Cricetidae
Neotoma albigula
  USE White-throated wood rat
Neotoma cinerea
  USE Bushy-tailed wood rat
Neotoma floridana
  USE Eastern wood rat
Neotoma fuscipes
  USE Dusky-footed wood rat
Neotoma goldmani
  USE Goldman's wood rat
Neotoma lepida
  USE Desert wood rat
Neotoma mexicana
  USE Mexican wood rat
Neotoma micropus
  USE Southern plains wood rat
Neotomys
  [QL737.R638]
  BT Cricetidae
Neotropic cormorant
  [QL696.P4745]
  UF Phalacrocorax olivaceus
  BT Cormorants
Neottia cernua
  USE Spiranthes cernua
Neovascularization
  UF Angiogenesis
  BT Blood-vessels—Growth
Neozimiris
  [QL458.42.G5]
  BT Ganaphosidae
Nepal
— **Antiquities** *(Not Subd Geog)*
    NT Kapilavastu (Ancient city)
— **History**
— — **To 1768**
    [DS495]
    NT Karnata dynasty of Mithila and
        Nepal, ca. 1097-1325
      Malla dynasty
— — **Licchavi dynasty, ca. 400-600**
    UF Licchavi dynasty, Nepal, ca.
        400-600
      Lichhavi dynasty, Nepal, ca.
        400-600
— — **1768-1951**
    [DS495.3]

    NT Nepalese War, 1814-1816
      Shah dynasty, 1768-
— — **1951-**
    NT Shah dynasty, 1768-
— **Languages**
    NT Danuwar Rai language
      Lhomi language
      Pahri dialect
      Rajbangsi dialect
      Sherpa language
Nepal barley
  USE Barley
Nepal Valley (Nepal)
  USE Kathmandu Valley (Nepal)
Nepalese cookery
  USE Cookery, Nepali
Nepalese in Assam, [etc.]
Nepalese language
  USE Nepali language
Nepalese War, 1814-1816
  [DS485.N4]
  BT India—History—British occupation,
      1765-1947
      Nepal—History—1768-1951
Nepali art
  USE Art, Nepali
Nepali authors
  USE Authors, Nepali
Nepali bronzes
  USE Bronzes, Nepali
Nepali cookery
  USE Cookery, Nepali
Nepali drama *(May Subd Geog)*
  [PK2597.5 *(History)*]
  [PK2598.A2 *(Collections)*]
  NT One-act plays, Nepali
Nepali erotic poetry
  USE Erotic poetry, Nepali
Nepali essays *(May Subd Geog)*
Nepali fiction *(May Subd Geog)*
  NT Short stories, Nepali
Nepali folk dancing
  USE Folk dancing, Nepali
Nepali folk literature
  USE Folk literature, Nepali
Nepali ghazals
  USE Ghazals, Nepali
Nepali imprints *(May Subd Geog)*
Nepali inscriptions
  USE Inscriptions, Nepali
Nepali language
  [PK2595-9]
  UF Gorkhali language
      Gurkhali language
      Khas language
      Naipali language
      Nepalese language
      Parbate language
      Parbatiya language
      Purbutti language
  BT Indo-Aryan languages, Modern
      Pahari languages
Nepali literature *(May Subd Geog)*
  [PK2597.5 *(History)*]
  [PK2598 *(Collections)*]
  NT Folk literature, Nepali
Nepali love poetry
  USE Love poetry, Nepali
Nepali mythology
  USE Mythology, Nepali
Nepali newspapers *(May Subd Geog)*
Nepali one-act plays
  USE One-act plays, Nepali
Nepali painting
  USE Painting, Nepali
Nepali periodicals *(May Subd Geog)*
Nepali philology *(May Subd Geog)*
Nepali poetry *(May Subd Geog)*
  NT Erotic poetry, Nepali
      Ghazals, Nepali
      Love poetry, Nepali

— To 1500
— 1500-1800
Nepali poetry (English)
 UF English poetry—Nepali authors
Nepali poets
 USE Poets, Nepali
Nepali prose literature
Nepali proverbs
 USE Proverbs, Nepali
Nepali riddles
 USE Riddles, Nepali
Nepali sculpture
 USE Sculpture, Nepali
Nepali short stories
 USE Short stories, Nepali
Nepali songs
 USE Songs, Nepali
Nepali wit and humor *(May Subd Geog)*
Nepean River (N.S.W.)
 BT Rivers—Australia
Nepeña River (Peru)
 UF Río Nepeña (Peru)
 BT Rivers—Peru
Nepenthaceae
 USE Nepenthes
Nepenthales
 USE Sarraceniales
Nepenthes
 [QK495.N35 (Botany)]
 UF Nepenthaceae
 BT Pitcher plants
 Sarraceniales
Nepenthes khasiana
 [QK495.N35]
Nepeta
 [QK495.L25]
 BT Lamiaceae
 NT Catnip
Nepeta cataria
 USE Catnip
Nepeta hederacea
 USE Ground ivy
Nepetaceae
 USE Lamiaceae
Nephanalysis (Meteorology)
 [QC874]
 BT Clouds
 Precipitation (Meteorology)—
 Measurement
 Synoptic meteorology
Nephantis *(May Subd Geog)*
 [QL561.X9]
 BT Xylorictidae
 NT Nephantis serinopa
Nephantis serinopa *(May Subd Geog)*
 [QL561.X9]
 BT Nephantis
Nepheline
 USE Nephelite
Nephelinite
 [QE461]
 BT Basalt
Nephelite *(May Subd Geog)*
 UF Nepheline
 BT Feldspathoid
 Silicates
 NT Teschenite
 Urtite
Nephelium litchi
 USE Litchi chinensis
Nephi City Cemetery (Nephi, Utah)
 UF Old City Cemetery (Nephi, Utah)
 BT Cemeteries—Utah
Nephila
 [QL458.42.A7]
 BT Araneidae
Nephila maculata
 [QL458.42.A7]
 UF Golden orb-weaving spider
NEPHIS (Indexing system)
 [Z695.92]

 UF Nested Phrase Indexing System
 BT Automatic indexing
 Permutation indexes
Nephites
 BT Book of Mormon
 Indians—Origin
 Mormon Church
Nephrite
 USE Jade
Nephritic calculi
 USE Kidneys—Calculi
Nephritis
 USE Kidneys—Diseases
Nephritis, Interstitial *(May Subd Geog)*
 [RC918.I56]
 UF Interstitial nephritis
 Nephropathies, Interstitial
 BT Kidneys—Diseases
Nephroblastoma
 UF Wilms' tumor
 BT Kidneys—Cancer
 Tumors, Embryonal
 Tumors in children
Nephrolithiasis
 USE Kidneys—Calculi
Nephrological services in hospitals
 USE Hospitals—Nephrological services
Nephrologists *(May Subd Geog)*
 BT Internists
 Kidneys—Diseases
 Physicians
 Urologists
Nephrology *(May Subd Geog)*
 [RC902]
 BT Internal medicine
 RT Kidneys
 NT Geriatric nephrology
 Pediatric nephrology
 Radioisotopes in nephrology
 Veterinary nephrology
Nephron
 USE Kidney tubules
Nephropathies, Interstitial
 USE Nephritis, Interstitial
Nephropathy
 USE Kidneys—Diseases
Nephropathy, IgA
 USE IgA glomerulonephritis
Nephropidae
 USE Homaridae
Nephrops norvegicus
 USE Norway lobster
Nephropsidae
 USE Homaridae
Nephroptosis
 USE Kidneys—Displacement
Nephrosclerosis
 [RC918.N4]
 BT Hypertension
 Kidneys—Diseases
Nephrostomy *(May Subd Geog)*
 [RD575]
 UF Ostomy, Renal
 Renal ostomy
 Renal stoma
 Stoma, Renal
 BT Kidneys—Surgery
Nephrotic syndrome
 BT Kidneys—Diseases
 Renal manifestations of general
 diseases
 Syndromes
Nephrotic syndrome in children
 (May Subd Geog)
 [RJ476.N]
 BT Pediatric nephrology
 Syndromes in children
Nephrotomy
 USE Kidneys—Surgery
Nephus
 [QL596.C65]

 BT Ladybirds
Népi írók mozgalom
 BT Hungarian literature—20th century
Neponset River (Mass.)
 BT Rivers—Massachusetts
Nepotism *(May Subd Geog)*
 BT Business ethics
 Political ethics
— **Law and legislation** *(May Subd Geog)*
Neppia
 [QL391.P7]
 BT Dugesiidae
Nepterotaea
 [QL561.G6]
 BT Geometridae
Nepticula
 [QL561.N4]
 BT Nepticulidae
 NT Nepticula braunella
Nepticula braunella *(May Subd Geog)*
 [QL561.N4]
 BT Nepticula
Nepticulidae
 [QL561.N4]
 UF Stigmellidae
 BT Lepidoptera
 Moths
 NT Nepticula
Neptune (Planet)
 [QB388 (Planetary theory)]
 [QB407 (Satellites)]
 [QB691 (Descriptive astronomy)]
 BT Outer planets
 Planets
Neptune (Antisubmarine aircraft)
 UF P2V (Antisubmarine aircraft)
 BT Antisubmarine aircraft
Neptune (Reconnaissance aircraft)
 [UG1242.R4]
 UF P-2 (Reconnaissance aircraft)
 P2V (Reconnaissance aircraft)
 BT Airplanes, Military
 Lockheed airplanes
 Reconnaissance aircraft
Neptune (Roman deity)
 UF Neptunus (Roman deity)
 BT Gods, Roman
 Mythology, Roman
 RT Poseidon (Greek deity)
Neptune project
 USE Project Neptune
Neptunea
 [QL430.5.B75]
 UF Chrysodomus
 BT Buccinidae
Neptunium
 BT Radioactive substances
— **Isotopes**
Neptunus (Roman deity)
 USE Neptune (Roman deity)
Nerbudda River (India)
 USE Narmada River (India)
Nerchinsk, Treaty of, 1689
Nere language
 USE Baria language
Nereidae
 [QL391.A6]
 UF Lycoridae
 Nereididae
 BT Phyllodocida
 NT Laeonereis
 Leptonereis
 Nereis
 Nicon
 Platynereis
Nereididae
 USE Nereidae
Nereis
 [QL391.A6]
 BT Nereidae

Nereis succinea
  ⌈QL391.A6⌉
Nereocystis *(May Subd Geog)*
  ⌈QK569.L53 (Algology)⌉
  BT Lessoniaceae
  NT Nereocystis luetkeana
Nereocystis luetkeana *(May Subd Geog)*
  ⌈QK569.L53 (Algology)⌉
  ⌈SH391.N47 (Fisheries)⌉
  UF Bladder kelp
      Cabbage, Sea-otter's
      Sea-otter's-cabbage
  BT Nereocystis
Neretva River (Bosnia and Hercegovina and Croatia)
  UF Narenta River (Bosnia and
      Hercegovina and Croatia)
      Naro River (Bosnia and Hercegovina
      and Croatia)
  BT Rivers—Yugoslavia
Neretva River, Battle of the, 1943
  BT World War, 1939-1945—Campaigns—
      Yugoslavia
Nerim family *(Not Subd Geog)*
Neritidae, Fossil
  BT Gasteropoda, Fossil
Nernst lamp
  ⌈TK4371⌉
  BT Electric lamps, Incandescent
Nero, Arch of (Rome, Italy)
  USE Arch of Nero (Rome, Italy)
Nero Wolfe (Fictitious character)
  USE Wolfe, Nero (Fictitious character)
Neroni, Bartolomeo, ca. 1505-1571. Fondi Monument fresco
  UF Fondi-Grabmal Fresko (Mural painting
      and decoration)
      Fondi Monument fresco (Mural
      painting and decoration)
  BT Mural painting and decoration,
      Renaissance—Italy
      Sepulchral monuments, Renaissance—
      Italy
Nero's Arch (Rome, Italy)
  USE Arch of Nero (Rome, Italy)
NERS (Computer program)
  UF Nursing Examination Review Software
  BT Nursing—Examinations—Computer
      programs
Nerthridae
  USE Gelastocoridae
Nerve, Accessory
  USE Accessory nerve
Nerve, Spinal accessory
  USE Accessory nerve
Nerve axons
  USE Axons
Nerve block
  UF Neural blockade
  BT Conduction anesthesia
Nerve-cells
  USE Nerves
      Neurons
Nerve compression injury
  USE Entrapment neuropathies
Nerve conduction
  USE Neural conduction
Nerve degeneration
  USE Nervous system—Degeneration
Nerve endings
  BT Nervous system
  NT Myoneural junction
      Neural receptors
      Neuromuscular transmission
      Synapses
Nerve fibers
  USE Neurofibrils
Nerve fibers, Myelinated
  USE Myelinated neurofibrils

Nerve grafting
  UF Grafting of nerves
      Nerves—Grafting
      Nerves—Transplantation
  BT Nervous system—Surgery
  NT Nervous system—Regeneration
Nerve growth factor
  BT Growth promoting substances
  RT Nervous system—Regeneration
Nerve net
  USE Neural circuitry
Nerve network
  USE Neural circuitry
Nerve proteins
  UF Nerve tissue proteins
      Neural proteins
      Neuroproteins
  BT Neurochemistry
      Proteins
  NT Cerebrospinal fluid proteins
      Neuropeptides
Nerve regeneration
  USE Nervous system—Regeneration
Nerve stimulation
  USE Neural stimulation
Nerve stimulation, Transcutaneous electrical
  USE Transcutaneous electrical nerve
      stimulation
Nerve tissue
  UF Nervous tissue
      Neural tissue
  BT Nervous system
      Tissues
  NT Fetal nerve tissue
      Myelin sheath
      Neuroglia
      Neurons
  — Cultures and culture media
Nerve tissue proteins
  USE Nerve proteins
Nerve transmission
  USE Neural transmission
Nerve transmitter substances
  USE Neurotransmitters
Nerves
  ⌈QM575 (Histology)⌉
  ⌈QP331 (Physiology)⌉
  UF Nerve-cells
  BT Electrophysiology
  RT Nervous system
  NT Myoneural junction
      Neuroglia
      Nissl bodies
      Nodes of Ranvier
      Purkinje cells
      Synapses
  — Anatomy
      USE Neuroanatomy
  — Diseases
      USE Nervous system—Diseases
  — Grafting
      USE Nerve grafting
  — Growth
      BT Developmental neurology
  — Radiography
      BT Nervous system—Diseases—
          Diagnosis
  — Secretions
      USE Neurosecretion
  — Surgery
      USE Nervous system—Surgery
  — Transplantation
      USE Nerve grafting
  — Wounds and injuries
      USE Nervous system—Wounds and
          injuries
Nerves, Brachial
  USE Arm—Innervation
Nerves, Cranial
  UF Cranial nerves
  BT Nerves, Peripheral

  NT Accessory nerve
      Acoustic nerve
      Facial nerve
      Glossopharyngeal nerve
      Hypoglossal nerve
      Olfactory nerve
      Optic nerve
      Trigeminal nerve
      Vagus nerve
Nerves, Peripheral
  UF Nervous system, Peripheral
      Peripheral nerves
      Peripheral nervous system
  BT Nervous system
  SA *subdivision* Innervation *under names*
      of organs and regions of the body,
      e.g. Heart—Innervation; Foot—
      Innervation
  NT Nerves, Cranial
      Nerves, Spinal
  — Diseases *(May Subd Geog)*
      NT Diabetic neuropathies
          Entrapment neuropathies
          Neuralgia
          Neuritis
          Polyneuropathies
  — — Diagnosis
  — Surgery
  — Tumors
      NT Neurofibroma
  — Wounds and injuries
Nerves, Sacral
  UF Sacral nerves
Nerves, Spinal
  UF Spinal nerves
  BT Nerves, Peripheral
  NT Brachial plexus
      Cauda equina
      Sciatic nerve
      Spinal shock
  — Diseases *(May Subd Geog)*
      NT Cervical syndrome
  — Roots
      ⌈QM471 (Anatomy)⌉
      ⌈QP367 (Physiology)⌉
      ⌈RC411 (Diseases)⌉
      UF Radices spinales nervi
          Roots, Spinal nerve
          Spinal nerve radicles
          Spinal nerve roots
  — — Diseases *(May Subd Geog)*
      NT Radiculitis
  — — Radiography
      UF Radiculography
          Radiculosaccography
Nerves, Splanchnic
  ⌈QL939⌉
  ⌈QM471⌉
  UF Splanchnic nerves
  BT Nervous system, Sympathetic
  — Surgery
Nervous activity, Higher
  USE Higher nervous activity
Nervous breakdown
  USE Neurasthenia
Nervous exhaustion
  USE Neurasthenia
Nervous prostration
  USE Neurasthenia
Nervous system
  ⌈QL921-QL939 (Comparative
    anatomy)⌉
  ⌈QM451-QM471 (Human anatomy)⌉
  ⌈QP351-QP425 (Physiology)⌉
  BT Anatomy
      Mind and body
      Neurology
      Physiology
  RT Nerves
      Spinal cord

SA *subdivision* Innervation *under names*
of organs and regions of the body,
e.g. Heart—Innervation; Foot—
Innervation
NT Biological control systems
Central nervous system
Excitation (Physiology)
Medulla oblongata
Meninges
Nerve endings
Nerve tissue
Nerves, Peripheral
Neural circuitry
Neural crest
Neural tube
Neuroanatomy
Neurogenetics
Neurohemal organs
Neurologic examination
Neurophysiology
Neurosecretion
Oligodendroglia
Pudendal nerve
Pyramidal tract
Shock
Spinal ganglia
— **Abnormalities** *(May Subd Geog)*
NT Dysraphia
— **Aging**
— **Amphibians,** ₍**Birds, Fishes, etc.**₎
Works on the nervous system of a particular
class, order, family, genus, or species are entered
under Nervous system, subdivided by the larger
zoological groups only. When the monograph
treats of one of the smaller divisions, additional
entry is made under the particular group, e.g. 1.
Nervous system—Amphibians. 2. Frogs.
— **Blood-vessels**
— — Diseases
USE Neurovascular diseases
— — **Surgery**
UF Neurovascular surgery
Surgery, Neurovascular
— Congresses
USE Neurology—Congresses
— **Degeneration**
UF Degeneration, Nerve
Nerve degeneration
Nervous system degeneration
Neuron degeneration
Nissl degeneration
Retrograde degeneration
Wallerian degeneration
BT Degeneration (Pathology)
RT Nervous system—Regeneration
— **Diseases** *(May Subd Geog)*
₍RC321-429₎
UF Medical neurology
Nerves—Diseases
Neuropathology
BT Brain—Diseases
SA *specific diseases, e.g.* Insanity,
Neurasthenia
NT Communicative disorders
Demyelination
Gangliosidoses
Movement disorders
Nervous system—Radiography
Neural transmission—Disorders
Neurocutaneous disorders
Neurologic manifestations of
general diseases
Neurological nursing
Neuromuscular diseases
Neurovascular diseases
Pediatric neurology
Perception, Disorders of
Psychomotor disorders
Sleep disorders
Sphingolipidoses
Spondylotherapy
Veterinary neurology

— — **Diagnosis**
₍RC348₎
NT Nerves—Radiography
Psychodiagnostics
Reflexes, Abnormal
— — **Dispensaries**
₍RC328₎
BT Dispensaries
— — **Homeopathic treatment**
₍RX281-301₎
— — **Hospitals**
₍RC328₎
BT Hospitals
— — **Immunological aspects**
BT Neuroimmunology
— — Nursing
USE Neurological nursing
— — **Psychosomatic aspects**
UF Psychosomatic neuropathology
— Drug effects
USE Neuropharmacology
— **Evolution**
UF Evolutionary neurology
BT Evolution
RT Developmental neurology
— Genetic aspects
USE Neurogenetics
— **Growth**
Here are entered works limited to the growth
of the nervous system. Works on the growth and
differentiation of the nervous system are entered
under Developmental neurology.
BT Developmental neurology
— Nomenclature
USE Neurology—Terminology
— **Radiography**
BT Nervous system—Diseases
— **Regeneration**
UF Nerve regeneration
Nervous system regeneration
Neuron regeneration
Regeneration, Nerve
BT Nerve grafting
Regeneration (Biology)
RT Nerve growth factor
Nervous system—Degeneration
— Secretions
USE Neurosecretion
— **Surgery**
₍RD593₎
UF Nerves—Surgery
Neurosurgery
NT Anesthesia in neurology
Brain—Surgery
Denervation
Nerve grafting
Neurosurgeons
Spinal cord—Surgery
— — **Complications and sequelae**
— Syphilis
USE Neurosyphilis
— Terminology
USE Neurology—Terminology
— **Tumors**
₍RD663₎
NT Gliomas
Neuroblastoma
Nonchromaffin paraganglioma
— **Wounds and injuries**
₍RD593-5₎
UF Nerves—Wounds and injuries
Nervous system, Autonomic
₍QL939 (Comparative anatomy)₎
₍QM471 (Human anatomy)₎
₍QP368 (Physiology)₎
UF Autonomic nervous system
Nervous system, Vegetative
Vegetative nervous system
NT Nervous system, Parasympathetic
Nervous system, Sympathetic
Nonchromaffin paraganglia

— **Diseases** *(May Subd Geog)*
NT Dysautonomia
Reflex sympathetic dystrophy
— — **Diagnosis**
— **Surgery**
Nervous system, Central
USE Central nervous system
Nervous system, Effect of drugs on
USE Neuropharmacology
Nervous system, Parasympathetic
UF Parasympathetic nervous system
BT Nervous system, Autonomic
NT Cholinergic mechanisms
Ganglia, Autonomic
Pterygopalatine ganglion
Vagus nerve
Nervous system, Peripheral
USE Nerves, Peripheral
Nervous system, Sympathetic
₍QL939 (Comparative anatomy)₎
₍QM471 (Human anatomy)₎
₍QP368 (Physiology)₎
UF Sympathetic nervous system
BT Nervous system, Autonomic
NT Adrenergic receptors
Chromaffin cells
Ganglia, Autonomic
Nerves, Splanchnic
Nervous system, Vasomotor
— **Surgery**
₍RD593₎
NT Sympathectomy
Nervous system, Vasomotor
₍QP109 (Physiology)₎
UF Vasomotor nervous system
BT Cardiovascular system
Nervous system, Sympathetic
Nervous system, Vegetative
USE Nervous system, Autonomic
Nervous system degeneration
USE Nervous system—Degeneration
Nervous system plasticity
USE Neuroplasticity
Nervous system regeneration
USE Nervous system—Regeneration
Nervous tissue
USE Nerve tissue
Nervous transmission
USE Neural transmission
Nervus hypoglossus
USE Hypoglossal nerve
Nesbet family
USE Nesbitt family
Nesbett family
USE Nesbitt family
Nesbit family
USE Nesbitt family
Nesbitt family *(Not Subd Geog)*
UF Neasbit family
Neesbit family
Neisbet family
Neisbit family
Neisbitt family
Nesbet family
Nesbett family
Nesbit family
Nisbet family
Nisbett family
Nisbit family
Nisbitt family
Neshaminy Creek (Pa.)
BT Rivers—Pennsylvania
Neshaminy State Park (Pa.)
BT Parks—Pennsylvania
Neshter family
USE Nestor family
Neshtor family
USE Nestor family
Nesiotes, fl. 480-460 B.C. Tyrant-slayers
USE Critius, fl. 480-460 B.C. Tyrant-
slayers

Nesochen sandvicensis
USE Nene
Nesoctites
[QL696.P56]
BT Picidae
NT Antillean piculet
Nesoctites micromegas
USE Antillean piculet
Nesoryzomys
[QL737.R638]
BT Cricetidae
NT Nesoryzomys swarthi
Nesoryzomys swarthi
[QL737.R638]
BT Nesoryzomys
Nēsos Paxoi (Greece)
USE Paxos Island (Greece)
Nesothrips
[QL598.3.P45]
BT Phlaeothripidae
Nespelim Indians
[E99.N]
BT Indians of North America
Salishan Indians
Nesque River (France)
BT Rivers—France
Ness, Loch (Scotland)
UF Loch Ness (Scotland)
BT Lakes—Scotland
RT Loch Ness monster
Ness family *(Not Subd Geog)*
UF Næss family
Nesse family
Noss family
Nesse family
USE Ness family
Nessie
USE Loch Ness monster
Nest building
UF Nidification
BT Animal behavior
Animals—Habitations
NT Fishes—Nests
Nested Phrase Indexing System
USE NEPHIS (Indexing system)
Nester family
USE Nestor family
Nesticidae
[QL458.42.N4]
BT Spiders
Nestlings (Birds)
USE Birds—Nestlings
Nestor family *(Not Subd Geog)*
UF Neshter family
Neshtor family
Nester family
Nestor notabilis
USE Kea
Nestorian Church *(May Subd Geog)*
[BX150-159]
UF Chaldean Church
East Syrian Church
BT Eastern churches
Nestorians
Syrian Church
Nestorian monasticism and religious orders
USE Monasticism and religious orders,
Nestorian
Nestorians *(May Subd Geog)*
[BT1440]
BT Heresies, Christian—History—Early
church, ca. 30-600
Syriac Christians
NT Assyrians
Chaldean Catholics
Missions to Nestorians
Nestorian Church
Nests of fishes
USE Fishes—Nests
Net (Egyptian deity)
USE Neith (Egyptian deity)

Net blotch disease of barley
USE Barley net-spot blotch disease
Net equations
USE Nets (Mathematics)
Net methods (Mathematics)
USE Nets (Mathematics)
Net national product
USE National income
Net-spinning caddisflies
USE Hydropsychidae
Net-spot blotch disease of barley
USE Barley net-spot blotch disease
Net structures, Cable
USE Cable structures
Net-throwing spiders
USE Dinopis
Net-winged beetles
USE Lycidae
Net-winged midges
[QL537.B56]
UF Blephariceridae
Blepharoceridae
Midges, Net-winged
NT Blepharicera
Dioptopsis
Net worth tax
USE Wealth tax
Netball
[GV887]
BT Basketball
Neth family
USE Nethers family
Nether family
USE Nethers family
Netherland family *(Not Subd Geog)*
Netherland Island (Tuvalu)
USE Nui (Tuvalu)
Netherlandic language
USE Dutch language
Netherlands
UF Holland
NT Dutch
— Antiquities
NT Bovenkarspel Het Valkje Site
(Netherlands)
— Armed Forces
— — **Medals, badges, decorations, etc.**
NT Militaire Willems-Orde (Medal)
— Capital and capitol
NT Binnenhof (Hague, Netherlands)
— Church history
— — **Middle Ages, 843-1555**
— — **16th century**
— — **17th century**
— — **18th century**
— — **19th century**
— — **20th century**
— Civilization
NT Architecture—England—Dutch
influences
Arts, Belgian—Dutch influences
Arts, German—Dutch influences
Brazil—Civilization—Dutch
influences
Civilization, Occidental—Dutch
influences
Japan—Civilization—Dutch
influences
Marine art, English—Dutch
influences
Medicine—Germany—Dutch
influences
Painting, Austrian—Dutch
influences
Painting, French—Dutch influences
Painting, Modern—17th-18th
centuries—Dutch influences
— — **Venetian influences**
BT Venice (Italy)—Civilization
— Description and travel
— — **1945-1977**

[DJ40]
— — **1978-**
— **Economic conditions**
— — **1918-1945**
— — **1945-**
— **Flood, 1570**
UF Allerheiligenvloed, 1570
— **Foreign relations**
— — **1556-1648**
— — **1648-1714**
— — **1648-1795**
— — **1714-1795**
— — **1778-1783**
— — **1815-**
[DJ147]
— — **1830-1898**
[DJ241-263]
— — **1898-1948**
[DJ281-286]
— — **1948-**
[DJ288]
— **History**
[DH1-DH207]
[DH401-DH811 (Belgium)]
[DJ (Holland)]
— — **To 1384**
— — **House of Burgundy, 1384-1477**
— — **House of Habsburg, 1477-1556**
— — **Charles V, 1506-1555**
— — **Wars of Independence, 1556-1648**
NT Netherlands—History—Twelve
Years' Truce, 1609-1621
Southampton, Treaty of, 1625
Vervins, Peace of, 1598
— — — **Campaigns** *(Not Subd Geog)*
NT Downs, Battle of the, 1639
Heiligerlee, Battle of, 1568
Nieuport, Battle of, 1600
— — — **Poetry**
NT Gueux—Songs and music
— — **Twelve Years' Truce, 1609-1621**
[DH201]
BT Netherlands—History—Wars of
Independence, 1556-1648
— — **1648-1714**
NT Beachy Head, Battle of, 1690
Dutch War, 1672-1678
— — **1648-1795**
— — **1714-1795**
— — **1789-1900**
— — **Batavian Republic, 1795-1806**
— — **1795-1815**
NT Walcheren Expedition, 1809
— — **1815-1830**
— — **1830-**
— — **1830-1849**
— — **William II, 1840-1849**
— — **1849-**
— — **William III, 1849-1890**
[DJ261]
— — **Wilhelmina, 1898-1948**
— — **German occupation, 1940-1945**
UF German occupation of
Netherlands, 1940-1945
— — — **Juvenile literature**
— — — **Pictorial works**
— — **1945-**
— **Kings and rulers**
NT Orange-Nassau, House of
Stadholders
— **Politics and government**
NT Stadholders
— — **1477-1556**
— — **1556-1648**
— — **1648-1714**
— — **1648-1795**
— — **1714-1795**
— — **1795-1815**
— — **1830-**
— — **1830-1898**
— — **1898-1948**

—— 1940-1945
—— 1945-
— Public buildings
  USE Public buildings—Netherlands
— **Social conditions**
—— **1945-**
  ⌈HN517⌉
Netherlands Antilleans *(May Subd Geog)*
  BT Ethnology—Netherlands Antilles
Nethers family *(Not Subd Geog)*
  UF Nather family
    Nathers family
    Neth family
    Nether family
Netherton family
NETL (Computer system)
  BT Parallel processing (Electronic
    computers)
Netlakapamuk Indians
  USE Ntlakyapamuk Indians
Netlakapamuk language
  USE Ntlakyapamuk language
Nets
  BT Industries, Primitive
    Marine biology
    Zoological specimens—Collection and
      preservation
  NT Fishing nets
Nets, Petri
  USE Petri nets
Nets (Geodesy) *(May Subd Geog)*
  UF Level nets
    Triangulation nets
  BT Leveling
    Triangulation
Nets (Mathematics)
  UF Moore-Smith convergence
    Net equations
    Net methods (Mathematics)
  BT Convergence
    Set theory
    Topology
  NT Numerical grid generation (Numerical
      analysis)
    Petri nets
Netsikutchin Indians
  USE Natsitkutchin Indians
Netsuke carvers *(May Subd Geog)*
  UF Carvers, Netsuke
  BT Netsukes
Netsuke carving *(May Subd Geog)*
  ⌈NK6050-6052⌉
  BT Carving (Decorative arts)
Netsukes *(May Subd Geog)*
  ⌈NK6050⌉
  BT Figurines
    Glyptics
    Inro
    Ivories
  NT Netsuke carvers
    Ojime
Nettastoma
  ⌈QL638.N46⌉
  UF Muraenosaurus
  BT Nettastomatidae
  NT Nettastoma melanurum
Nettastoma melanurum
  ⌈QL638.N46⌉
  UF Muraenosaurus guntheri
  BT Nettastoma
Nettastomatidae
  ⌈QL638.N46⌉
  UF Duckbill eels
    Nettastomidae
  BT Eels
  NT Facciolella
    Nettastoma
Nettastomidae
  USE Nettastomatidae
Nette, Naturpark Schwalm- (Germany)
  USE Naturpark Schwalm-Nette (Germany)

Netted melon
  USE Muskmelon
Nettels family
  USE Nettles family
Netterville family *(Not Subd Geog)*
Nettesheim family *(Not Subd Geog)*
Netting
  ⌈TT840 (Fancy work)⌉
  BT Fancy work
    Needlework
  RT Netting industry
Netting, Knotless
  USE Sprang
Netting industry *(May Subd Geog)*
  ⌈HD9869.N47-474⌉
  RT Netting
Nettl family
  USE Nettles family
Nettle, Roman
  USE Roman nettle
Nettle family
  USE Nettles family
Nettle-rash
  USE Urticaria
Nettles
  ⌈QK495.47 (Botany)⌉
  UF Urtica
  BT Urticaceae
  NT Roman nettle
    Stinging nettle
    Urtica urens
Nettles, Hedge
  USE Stachys
Nettles family *(Not Subd Geog)*
  UF Nettels family
    Nettl family
    Nettle family
Nettlespurge, Bellyache
  USE Jatropha gossypiifolia
Nettleton Scrubb Site (Nettleton, Wiltshire)
  UF Apollo Shrine Site (Nettleton,
      Wiltshire)
    Nettleton Shrub Site (Nettleton,
      Wiltshire)
    Shrine of Apollo Site (Nettleton,
      Wiltshire)
  BT England—Antiquities
Nettleton Shrub Site (Nettleton, Wiltshire)
  USE Nettleton Scrubb Site (Nettleton,
      Wiltshire)
NETTRA (Computer programs)
  BT Electronic circuit design—Data
      processing
NETTRA-E1 (Computer program)
  BT Computer programs
    Electronic circuit design—Data
      processing
NETTRA-E2 (Computer program)
  BT Computer programs
    Electronic circuit design—Data
      processing
NETTRA-E3 (Computer program)
  BT Computer programs
    Electronic circuit design—Data
      processing
NETTRA-G1 (Computer program)
NETTRA-G1-FIFO (Computer program)
NETTRA-G2 (Computer program)
NETTRA-G2-FIFO (Computer program)
NETTRA-G3 (Computer program)
NETTRA-G3-FIFO (Computer program)
NETTRA-G4 (Computer program)
NETTRA-P1 (Computer program)
NETTRA-P2 (Computer program)
NETTRA-PG1 (Computer program)
NETTRA-PG1-FIFO (Computer program)
NetWare (Computer operating system)
  BT Operating systems (Computers)
Network Access Machine (Computer)
  ⌈QA76.8.N⌉

  BT Computer networks
    Electronic digital computers
    Minicomputers
    On-line data processing
Network analysis (Anthropo-geography)
  USE Anthropo-geography—Network
      analysis
Network analysis (Communication)
  USE Communication—Network analysis
Network analysis (Geography)
  USE Geography—Network analysis
Network analysis (Planning)
  ⌈T57.85 (Operations research)⌉
  UF Project networks
  BT Graph theory
    Industrial project management
    Operations research
    Production planning
    Scheduling (Management)
  NT Branch and bound algorithms
    Critical path analysis
    GERT (Network analysis)
    INTEGRAL (Network analysis)
    PERT (Network analysis)
— Computer programs
Network analysis (Semantics)
  USE Semantics—Network analysis
Network analysis (Social sciences)
  USE Social sciences—Network analysis
Network analysis (Sociolinguistics)
  USE Sociolinguistics—Network analysis
Network analyzers
  USE Electric network analyzers
Network architectures, Computer
  USE Computer network architectures
Network grammar
  ⌈P98⌉
  UF Augmented transition network
      grammar
    Procedural grammar
    Transition network grammar
  BT Grammar, Comparative and general
    Linguistics—Data processing
Network theory
  USE Electric networks
    System analysis
Network topology (Electrical engineering)
  USE Electric network topology
Networks, Active
  USE Electric networks, Active
Networks, Computer
  USE Computer networks
Networks, Electric
  USE Electric networks
Networks, Information
  USE Information networks
Networks, New-girl
  USE Women—Social networks
Networks, Parent's
  USE Parents—Social networks
Networks, Passive
  USE Electric networks, Passive
Networks, Self-help
  USE Self-help groups
Networks, Social
  USE Social networks
Networks, Women's
  USE Women—Social networks
Networks (Associations, institutions, etc.)
  USE Associations, institutions, etc.
Networks of libraries
  USE Library information networks
Neu family
  USE New family
Neu Pommern language
  USE Kuanua language
Neubauer family *(Not Subd Geog)*
  UF Neuber family
Neuber family
  USE Neubauer family

2573

Neuces River (Tex.)
USE Nueces River (Tex.)
Neuchâtel, Lake of (Switzerland)
UF Lac de Neuchâtel (Switzerland)
Lago di Neuchâtel (Switzerland)
Lake of Neuchâtel (Switzerland)
Neuenburg (Switzerland)
Neuenburger See (Switzerland)
BT Lakes—Switzerland
Neue Bremm (Saarbrücken, Germany :
Concentration camp)
[D805.G3]
BT World War, 1939-1945—
Concentration camps—Germany
(West)
Neue Reichskanzlei (Berlin, Germany :
Building)
USE Reichskanzlei (Berlin, Germany :
Building)
Neue Sachlichkeit (Art)
USE New objectivity (Art)
Neue Salome (Sculpture)
USE Klinger, Max, 1857-1920. Salome
Neue Unglücke des Krieges (Aquatint)
USE Baumgartner, Fritz. New disasters of
war
Neuenburg (Switzerland)
USE Neuchâtel, Lake of (Switzerland)
Neuenburger See (Switzerland)
USE Neuchâtel, Lake of (Switzerland)
Neuengamme (Hamburg, Germany :
Concentration camp)
[D805.G3]
BT Concentration camps—Germany
(West)
World War, 1939-1945—
Concentration camps—Germany
(West)
World War, 1939-1945—Prisoners and
prisons, German
Neuenschwander family (Not Subd Geog)
Neufchâteau, Battle of, 1914
[D545.N4]
BT World War, 1914-1918—Campaigns—
France
Neufchâtel cheese
[SF272.N]
Neuhaus family
USE Neuhauser family
Neuhauser family (Not Subd Geog)
UF Neuhaus family
Neuin family
USE Neun family
Neuins family
USE Neun family
Neukirk family
USE Newkirk family
Neuman family
USE Newman family
Neumann algebras
USE Von Neumann algebras
Neumann family
USE Newman family
Neumann problem
BT Boundary value problems
Differential equations, Partial
Neumark (Poland)
USE Nowa Marchia (Poland)
Neumes
[ML174]
UF Ligature (Music)
BT Chants (Plain, Gregorian, etc.)—
Instruction and study
Musical meter and rhythm
Musical notation
RT Paleography, Musical
Neun family (Not Subd Geog)
UF Nein family
Neuin family
Neuins family
Nuyn family

RT Nine family
Neural adaptation
USE Neuroplasticity
Neural analyzers
UF Analysor, Neural
Analyzers, Neural
BT Central nervous system
Senses and sensation
Neural blockade
USE Nerve block
Neural circuitry (May Subd Geog)
[QP363.3]
UF Circuitry, Neural
Nerve net
Nerve network
Neural networks
Neurocircuitry
Neuronal circuitry
BT Cybernetics
Electrophysiology
Nervous system
RT Reflexes
NT Neural transmission
Synapses
— **Adaptation**
UF Adaptation of neural circuitry
BT Adaptation (Physiology)
Developmental neurology
Neuroplasticity
Neural conduction
UF Nerve conduction
BT Neurophysiology
Neural crest
[QL938.N48]
UF Crest, Neural
Ganglionic crest
Ganglionic ridge
BT Embryology
Nervous system
Neural networks
USE Neural circuitry
Neural plasticity
USE Neuroplasticity
Neural proteins
USE Nerve proteins
Neural receptors
UF Neuroreceptors
Receptors, Neural
BT Nerve endings
NT Chemoreceptors
Cholinergic receptors
Corti's organ
Electroreceptors
Mechanoreceptors
Muscle receptors
Neuromuscular spindles
Neurotransmitter receptors
Nociceptors
Proprioceptors
Thermoreceptors
Neural stimulation (May Subd Geog)
[RC350.N48 (Therapeutics)]
UF Nerve stimulation
Stimulation, Neural
BT Electric stimulation
Electrophysiology
RT Electrodiagnosis
Electrotherapeutics
NT Brain stimulation
Transcutaneous electrical nerve
stimulation
Neural tissue
USE Nerve tissue
Neural transmission
UF Nerve transmission
Nervous transmission
Neurotransmission
Synaptic transmission
Transmission of nerve impulses

BT Neural circuitry
Neurochemistry
Neurophysiology
NT Neuromuscular transmission
Neurotransmitters
Synapses
— **Disorders** (May Subd Geog)
UF Neural transmission disorders
Neurohumoral transmission
disorders
Neurotransmitter disorders
BT Nervous system—Diseases
— **Regulation**
UF Regulation of neural transmission
BT Biological control systems
Neural transmission disorders
USE Neural transmission—Disorders
Neural transmitters
USE Neurotransmitters
Neural tube
BT Embryology
Nervous system
Neuralgia
[RC412]
BT Nerves, Peripheral—Diseases
Pain
NT Causalgia
Cervico-brachial neuralgia
Erythromelalgia
— **Homeopathic treatment**
[RX301.N5]
Neuralgia, Cranial
UF Cranial neuralgia
Neuralgia, Facial
[RC412]
UF Facial neuralgia
Tic-douloureux
BT Facial pain
Tic
— **Homeopathic treatment**
[RX301.N5]
Neuralgia, Sciatic
USE Sciatica
Neuralgia, Traumatic
[RC412]
BT Traumatism
Neuralgia, Trigeminal
UF Trigeminal neuralgia
Neurasthenia
[RC552.N5]
UF Nervous breakdown
Nervous exhaustion
Nervous prostration
RT Fatigue, Mental
NT Astasia and astasia-abasia
Brain—Anemia
Depression, Mental
— **Somatization** (May Subd Geog)
UF Somatization of neurasthenia
BT Somatoform disorders
Neureclipsis
[QL518.P6]
BT Polycentropodidae
NT Neureclipsis bimaculata
Neureclipsis bimaculata
[QL518.P6]
BT Neureclipsis
Neuritis
[RC416]
BT Nerves, Peripheral—Diseases
Nonarticular rheumatism
NT Radiculitis
Neuritis, Multiple
[RC416]
UF Polyneuritis
NT Diphtheric polyneuritis
Polyradiculitis
Polyradiculoneuritis
Neuro-arthropathy
USE Charcot joints

Neuro-linguistic programming
   USE Neurolinguistic programming
Neuro-linguistics
   USE Neurolinguistics
Neuro-ophthalmological diagnosis
   USE Neuro-ophthalmology—Diagnosis
Neuro-ophthalmology *(May Subd Geog)*
     [RE725-RE780]
   UF Neuroophthalmology
   BT Ophthalmology
   NT Eye—Movement disorders
       Oculomotor paralysis
       Optic nerve—Diseases
  — Diagnosis
     UF Diagnosis, Neuro-ophthalmological
        Neuro-ophthalmological diagnosis
     BT Diagnosis
Neuro-psychopharmacology
   USE Neuropsychopharmacology
Neuroanatomy
     [QM451]
   UF Nerves—Anatomy
   BT Nervous system
Neurobehavioral toxicology
   USE Behavioral toxicology
Neurobiology
   BT Neurology
   NT Molecular neurobiology
Neurobiology, Developmental
   USE Developmental neurology
Neuroblastoma *(May Subd Geog)*
     [RC280.N4]
   UF Hutchinson's syndrome
       Pepper's syndrome
       Sympathicoblastoma
   BT Nervous system—Tumors
       Sarcoma
       Tumors in children
   NT Retinoblastoma
Neuroblastoma, Retinal
   USE Retinoblastoma
Neurochemistry
     [QP356]
   BT Neurology
   NT Brain chemistry
       Nerve proteins
       Neural transmission
       Neurotransmitters
Neurocircuitry
   USE Neural circuitry
Neurocutaneous disorders
   UF Dermatoneurosis
       Neurodermatitis
   BT Nervous system—Diseases
       Skin—Diseases
   NT Phakomatoses
Neurocyte
   USE Neurons
Neurodermatitis
   USE Neurocutaneous disorders
Neuroendocrine cells
   USE Paraneurons
Neuroendocrinology
   BT Endocrinology
       Neurology
   NT Hypothalamo-hypophyseal system
       Neurohemal organs
       Psychoneuroendocrinology
Neurofibrils
   UF Nerve fibers
   BT Neurons
   NT Myelinated neurofibrils
Neurofibroma
   BT Fibromas
       Nerves, Peripheral—Tumors
   NT Neurofibromatosis
Neurofibromatosis
   UF Recklinghausen's disease
   BT Mental retardation
       Neurofibroma
       Phakomatoses

Neurofilaments
   USE Cytoplasmic filaments
Neurogenesis
   USE Developmental neurology
Neurogenetics
   UF Nervous system—Genetic aspects
   BT Genetics
       Medical genetics
       Nervous system
Neurogenic arthropathy
   USE Charcot joints
Neurogenic bladder
     [RC921.N4]
   BT Bladder—Diseases
       Neurologic manifestations of general
         diseases
Neuroglia
   UF Glial cells
   BT Nerve tissue
       Nerves
   NT Astrocytes
       Microglia
Neurohemal organs
   BT Nervous system
       Neuroendocrinology
       Neurosecretion
       Neurotransmitters
Neurohumoral transmission disorders
   USE Neural transmission—Disorders
Neurohumors
   USE Neurotransmitters
Neurohypophysis
   UF Posterior pituitary gland
   BT Circumventricular organs
       Pituitary gland
Neuroimmunology *(May Subd Geog)*
     [QP356.47]
   BT Immunology
       Neurology
   NT Nervous system—Diseases—
         Immunological aspects
Neurokeratin
   USE Keratin
Neurokopion (Greece) *(Not Subd Geog)*
Neurokopion (Greece), Battle of, 1941
   BT World War, 1939-1945—Campaigns—
        Greece
Neuroleptanalgesia
   USE Neuroleptanesthesia
Neuroleptanesthesia
     [RD85.N4]
   UF Anesthesia, Neurolept
       Neuroleptanalgesia
   BT Autonomic drugs
Neuroleptic drugs
   USE Neuropsychopharmacology
Neurolinguistic programming
    (May Subd Geog)
     [BF637.N46 (Psychology)]
     [RC489.N47 (Psychiatry)]
    Here are entered works about a set of procedures
    developed by Richard Bandler, John Grinder, and
    others, by which to organize subjective experience in
    order to define and achieve a desired behavioral out-
    come.
   UF Neuro-linguistic programming
       NLP (Psychology)
       Programming, Neuro-linguistic
       Programming, Neurolinguistic
   BT Change (Psychology)
       Psychotherapy
Neurolinguistics *(May Subd Geog)*
     [QP399]
   UF Neuro-linguistics
   BT Biolinguistics
       Higher nervous activity
       Language and languages—
         Physiological aspects
       Linguistics
       Neuropsychology
   RT Psycholinguistics

Neurologic examination
     [RC348-349]
   BT Nervous system
       Physical diagnosis
   NT Neuropsychological tests
       Reflexes
       Reflexes—Testing
Neurologic manifestations of general diseases
   UF Neurologic symptoms of general
        diseases
   BT Nervous system—Diseases
       Symptomatology
   RT Neuromuscular manifestations of
        general diseases
   NT Loss of consciousness
       Neurogenic bladder
       Reflexes, Abnormal
       Tremor
       Vertigo
Neurologic symptoms of general diseases
   USE Neurologic manifestations of general
        diseases
Neurological anesthesia
   USE Anesthesia in neurology
Neurological equipment industry
    (May Subd Geog)
     [HD9995.N48]
   BT Neurology—Equipment and supplies
Neurological nursing
     [RC350.5 (Neurology)]
     [RD596 (Neurosurgery)]
   UF Nervous system—Diseases—Nursing
       Neurosurgical nursing
   BT Nervous system—Diseases
       Nursing
Neurologists *(May Subd Geog)*
     [RC339.5-RC339.52 (Biography)]
   BT Physicians
   RT Psychiatrists
   NT Neurosurgeons
  — Legal status, laws, etc.
     NT Neurologists—Malpractice
  — Malpractice *(May Subd Geog)*
     UF Tort liability of neurologists
     BT Malpractice
        Medical laws and legislation
        Neurologists—Legal status, laws,
         etc.
  — Supply and demand
Neurology *(May Subd Geog)*
   UF Neurosciences
   RT Neuropsychiatry
   NT Anesthesia in neurology
       Developmental neurology
       Electrophysiology
       Geriatric neurology
       Inhibition
       Nervous system
       Neurobiology
       Neurochemistry
       Neuroendocrinology
       Neuroimmunology
       Neuropsychopharmacology
       Pediatric neurology
       Psychology, Pathological
       Psychology, Physiological
       Radioisotopes in neurology
       Veterinary neurology
  — Congresses
     UF Nervous system—Congresses
  — Equipment and supplies
     NT Neurological equipment industry
  — Jurisprudence
     USE Forensic neurology
  — Research *(May Subd Geog)*
     NT Neuropsychology—Research
  — Terminology
     UF Nervous system—Nomenclature
        Nervous system—Terminology
Neurology, Behavioral
   USE Clinical neuropsychology

Neurology, Developmental
  USE Developmental neurology
Neurology, Forensic
  USE Forensic neurology
Neurolymphomatosis gallinarum
  USE Marek's disease
Neuromotor disorders
  USE Neuromuscular diseases
Neuromuscular blocking agents
    [RD83.5 (Anesthesiology)]
    [RM312 (Pharmacology)]
  UF Blocking agents, Neuromuscular
      Myoneural blocking agents
  BT Anesthesia
      Autonomic drugs
      Muscle relaxants
  NT Bungarotoxin
      Curare-like agents
      Neuromuscular depolarizing agents
      Vecuronium bromide
Neuromuscular depolarizing agents
  UF Depolarizing agents, Neuromuscular
      Depolarizing muscle relaxants
      Leptocucares
  BT Neuromuscular blocking agents
Neuromuscular diseases
  UF Neuromotor disorders
  BT Muscles—Diseases
      Nervous system—Diseases
  NT Amyotrophic lateral sclerosis
      Atrophy, Muscular
      Ingestion disorders
      Locomotion, Disordered
      Muscular dystrophy
      Myalgic encephalomyelitis
      Myasthenia gravis
      Myotonia atrophica
      Myotonia congenita
      Neuromuscular manifestations of
        general diseases
      Paralysis, Spastic
  — **Diagnosis**
Neuromuscular diseases in children
    [RJ496.N49]
  BT Pediatric neurology
  NT Atrophy, Muscular, in children
      Muscular dystrophy in children
      Paralysis, Spastic, in children
Neuromuscular end plate
  USE Myoneural junction
Neuromuscular junction
  USE Myoneural junction
Neuromuscular manifestations of general
  diseases (May Subd Geog)
    [RC925.55]
  UF Neuromuscular symptoms of general
        diseases
  BT Neuromuscular diseases
      Symptomatology
  RT Neurologic manifestations of general
        diseases
Neuromuscular nondepolarizing agents
  USE Curare-like agents
Neuromuscular spindles
  BT Neural receptors
      Neuromuscular transmission
Neuromuscular symptoms of general diseases
  USE Neuromuscular manifestations of
        general diseases
Neuromuscular transmission
  UF Motoneuron transmission
      Motor neuron transmission
  BT Muscles
      Nerve endings
      Neural transmission
  NT Neuromuscular spindles
Neuromyasthenia, Epidemic
  USE Myalgic encephalomyelitis
Neuron degeneration
  USE Nervous system—Degeneration

Neuron regeneration
  USE Nervous system—Regeneration
Neuronal adaptation
  USE Neuroplasticity
Neuronal ceroid-lipofuscinosis
    (May Subd Geog)
    [RC632.N47]
  UF Amaurotic familial idiocy
      Batten-Spielmeyer-Vogt disease
      Batten's disease
      Ceroid-lipofuscinosis, Neuronal
      Jansky-Bielschowsky disease
      Kufs disease
      Lipofuscinosis, Neuronal ceroid
  BT Demyelination
      Mental retardation
      Metabolism, Inborn errors of
Neuronal circuitry
  USE Neural circuitry
Neuronal plasticity
  USE Neuroplasticity
Neurons
  UF Nerve-cells
      Neurocyte
  BT Nerve tissue
  NT Axons
      Dendrites
      Ganglia, Sensory
      Locus coeruleus
      Motor neurons
      Neurofibrils
      Nissl bodies
      Olivary nucleus
      Paraneurons
      Purkinje cells
      Satellite cells
  — **Growth**
      BT Developmental neurology
          Neurotrophic functions
Neuroophthalmology
  USE Neuro-ophthalmology
Neuropathic joint
  USE Charcot joints
Neuropathic muscular atrophy
  USE Charcot-Marie-Tooth disease
Neuropathies, Entrapment
  USE Entrapment neuropathies
Neuropathology
  USE Nervous system—Diseases
Neuropathy
    [RZ399.N5 (Therapeutic system)]
  BT Osteopathy
Neuropeptides
    [QP552.N39]
  UF Brain peptides
  BT Nerve proteins
      Peptides
  RT Neurotransmitters
  NT Endorphins
      Hypothalamic hormones
      Pituitary hormones
      Tachykinins
Neuropharmacology
  UF Nervous system—Drug effects
      Nervous system, Effect of drugs on
      Neurotropic drugs
  BT Pharmacology
  NT Autonomic drugs
      Neuropsychopharmacology
      Neurotoxic agents
Neurophysins
    [QP552.N4]
  BT Pituitary hormones
      Proteins
Neurophysiology
    [QP355.2]
  BT Nervous system
      Physiology
  NT Higher nervous activity
      Language and languages—
        Physiological aspects

      Neural conduction
      Neural transmission
      Neuroplasticity
      Neurotrophic functions
      Reflexes
      Senses and sensation
      Spreading cortical depression
Neuroplasmic flow
  USE Axonal transport
Neuroplasticity
      Here are entered works on the functional and
    morphologic adjustment and adaptation of the nerv-
    ous system to various stimulating factors and lesions.
  UF Nervous system plasticity
      Neural adaptation
      Neural plasticity
      Neuronal adaptation
      Neuronal plasticity
      Plasticity, Nervous system
      Soft-wired nervous system
      Synaptic plasticity
  BT Adaptation (Physiology)
      Neurophysiology
  RT Developmental neurology
  NT Neural circuitry—Adaptation
Neuropoisons
  USE Neurotoxic agents
Neuroproteins
  USE Nerve proteins
Neuropsychiatry (May Subd Geog)
  UF Behavioral neurology
  BT Biological psychiatry
  RT Neurology
  NT Mutism, Akinetic
Neuropsychoendocrinology
  USE Psychoneuroendocrinology
Neuropsychoimmunoendocrinology
  USE Psychoneuroimmunoendocrinology
Neuropsychological assessment
  USE Neuropsychological tests
Neuropsychological evaluation
  USE Neuropsychological tests
Neuropsychological tests (May Subd Geog)
  UF Neuropsychological assessment
      Neuropsychological evaluation
      Tests, Neuropsychological
  BT Clinical neuropsychology
      Neurologic examination
      Psychological tests
  NT Halstead-Reitan Neuropsychological
        Test Battery
      Luria-Nebraska Neuropsychological
        Battery
Neuropsychological toxicology
  USE Behavioral toxicology
Neuropsychology (May Subd Geog)
    [QP360]
  BT Brain
      Psychology, Physiological
  NT Clinical neuropsychology
      Forensic neuropsychology
      Learning—Physiological aspects
      Neurolinguistics
      Psychoneuroendocrinology
  — **Research** (May Subd Geog)
      BT Neurology—Research
Neuropsychopharmacology
    (May Subd Geog)
    [RM315]
  UF Neuro-psychopharmacology
      Neuroleptic drugs
  BT Neurology
      Neuropharmacology
      Psychopharmacology
  NT Benzodiazepines
      Central nervous system depressants
      Chlorophenylalanine
      Neurotransmitters
      Phenothiazine
Neuroptera (May Subd Geog)
    [QL511-514]

2576

UF Megaloptera
BT Insects
NT Alderflies
Ant lions
Chrysopidae
Coniopterygidae
Corydalidae
Hemerobiidae
Lacewing flies
Mantispidae
Osmylidae
Pseudoneuroptera
Raphidiidae
Neuroptera, Fossil
Neuroreceptors
USE Neural receptors
Neurosciences
USE Neurology
Neurosecretion
UF Nerves—Secretions
Nervous system—Secretions
BT Nervous system
Secretion
NT Neurohemal organs
Neurotransmitters
Pituitary hormone releasing factors
Neuroses
  ⌈RC530-552⌉
UF Psychoneuroses
BT Psychology, Pathological
RT Personality, Disorders of
Psychoses
SA *particular neuroses, e.g.* Anxiety,
Hysteria
NT Depression, Mental
Fear of success
Inferiority complex
Medicine, Psychosomatic
Nail-biting
Neurotics
Obsessive-compulsive neurosis
Occupational neuroses
Phobias
Psychological manifestations of general
diseases
Traumatic neuroses
— **Diagnosis**
BT Psychological tests
NT Personality tests
Neuroses in literature
Neurospora
  ⌈QK623.S6⌉
BT Sordariaceae
Neurospora crassa
  ⌈QK623.S6⌉
UF Bread mold, Pink
Pink bread mold
Neurospora sitophila
  ⌈QK623.S6⌉
Neurospora tetrasperma
  ⌈QK623.S6⌉
Neurosurgeons *(May Subd Geog)*
BT Nervous system—Surgery
Neurologists
Surgeons
Neurosurgery
USE Nervous system—Surgery
Neurosurgical nursing
USE Neurological nursing
Neurosyphilis
UF Nervous system—Syphilis
BT Central nervous system—Diseases
Syphilis
NT Locomotor ataxia
Neurotensin
  ⌈QP572.N47⌉
BT Gastrointestinal hormones
Hypothalamic hormones
Peptide hormones
Neurotics
  ⌈RC530-RC552⌉

This heading is used only with subdivisions.
BT Neuroses
Neurotics in literature
BT Characters and characteristics in
literature
Neurotoechus
USE Paullinia
Neurotoxic agents *(May Subd Geog)*
UF Neuropoisons
Neurotoxicants
Neurotoxins
BT Neuropharmacology
Poisons
NT Behavioral toxicology
Kainic acid
Methylphenyltetrahydropyridine
Ototoxic agents
Saxitoxin
Tetrodotoxin
Neurotoxicants
USE Neurotoxic agents
Neurotoxins
USE Neurotoxic agents
Neurotransmission
USE Neural transmission
Neurotransmitter disorders
USE Neural transmission—Disorders
Neurotransmitter receptors
  ⌈QP364.7⌉
UF Receptors, Neurotransmitter
BT Cell receptors
Hormone receptors
Neural receptors
NT Acetylcholine—Receptors
Dopamine—Receptors
GABA—Receptors
Neurotransmitters
  ⌈QP364.7⌉
UF Chemical nerve transmitters
Nerve transmitter substances
Neural transmitters
Neurohumors
Synaptic transmitters
Transmitters, Chemical nerve
Transmitters, Synaptic
BT Neural transmission
Neurochemistry
Neuropsychopharmacology
Neurosecretion
Synapses
RT Neuropeptides
NT Acetylcholine
Adrenalin
Dopamine
Endorphins
GABA
Glutamic acid
Glycine
Neurohemal organs
Noradrenalin
Serotonin
Substance P
Vasoactive intestinal peptides
Neurotrophic functions
  ⌈QP363⌉
BT Neurophysiology
NT Neurons—Growth
Neurotropic drugs
USE Neuropharmacology
Neurovascular diseases *(May Subd Geog)*
UF Nervous system—Blood-vessels—
Diseases
BT Blood-vessels—Diseases
Nervous system—Diseases
Neurovascular surgery
USE Nervous system—Blood-vessels—
Surgery
Neus family *(Not Subd Geog)*
UF Neuss family
RT Neis family
Nice family

Neuschwanstein Castle (Germany)
USE Schloss Neuschwanstein (Germany)
Neuse River (N.C.)
BT Rivers—North Carolina
Neusiedler Lake (Austria and Hungary)
UF Fertő tó (Austria and Hungary)
Neusiedler See (Austria and Hungary)
Neusiedlersee (Austria and Hungary)
BT Lakes—Austria
Lakes—Hungary
Neusiedler See (Austria and Hungary)
USE Neusiedler Lake (Austria and
Hungary)
Neusiedlersee (Austria and Hungary)
USE Neusiedler Lake (Austria and
Hungary)
Neuss family
USE Neus family
Neusticurus
  ⌈QL666.L285⌉
BT Teiidae
Neuston
  ⌈QH91.8.N4⌉
BT Aquatic biology
Neutocket Island (Mass.)
USE Nantucket Island (Mass.)
Neuton family
USE Newton family
Neutral beams
UF Beams, Neutral
Neutral particle beams
BT Particle beams
NT Neutron beams
Neutral Buffer Zone, Korean (Korea)
USE Korean Demilitarized Zone (Korea)
Neutral money
USE Commodity dollar
Neutral Nation Indians
  ⌈E99.N⌉
UF Attiwendaronk Indians
BT Indians of North America
Iroquoian Indians
— **Antiquities**
Neutral particle beams
USE Neutral beams
Neutral trade with belligerents
BT Commerce
Neutrality
War, Maritime (International law)
War (International law)
RT Blockade
Contraband of war
NT Continuous voyages (International law)
Navicert system
Neutralism
USE Neutrality
Nonalignment
Neutrality
  ⌈JX5355-JX5397⌉
Here are entered works on the status of states
resulting from their adoption of impartiality towards
belligerent states, and on the consequent rights and
duties created between the neutral states and the bel-
ligerents under international law. Works on the for-
eign policy of states who do not identify themselves
with the major power blocs but retain the option of
becoming aligned when necessary are entered under
Nonalignment.
UF Isolationism
Neutralism
BT Commerce
International law
Privateering
Security, International
States, Small
RT Buffer states
Intervention (International law)
Nonalignment
Prize law
Region of war
War, Maritime (International law)
War (International law)

2577

Neutrality *(Continued)*
- SA *subdivision* Neutrality *under names of countries and of neutralized areas, e.g.* Belgium—Neutrality, Great Lakes—Neutrality; *and particular cases involving the principle of neutrality, e.g.* Alabama claims
- NT Asylum, Right of
  - Contraband of war
  - Guaranty, Treaties of
  - Munitions—Law and legislation
  - Neutral trade with belligerents
  - Passage of troops
  - Recruiting and enlistment
  - Search, Right of
  - Transit by land (International law)
  - Unneutral service
  - Warships, Internment of

Neutrality, Armed
- ⌐D295 (Armed neutrality of 1780)⌐
- ⌐JX5383 (International law)⌐
- UF Armed Neutrality, 1780 and 1800
  - Leagues of armed neutrality
- BT International relations
  - War (International law)

Neutralization (Chemistry)
- BT Acids
  - Bases (Chemistry)
  - Hydrogen-ion concentration
- NT Antacids
  - Sewage—Purification—Neutralization

Neutralization (Linguistics)
- BT Grammar, Comparative and general— Phonology
  - Linguistics

Neutret
- USE Neutrinos

Neutrino astronomy
- USE Neutrino astrophysics

Neutrino astrophysics
- ⌐QB464.2⌐
- UF Astrophysics, Neutrino
  - Neutrino astronomy
- BT Neutrinos
  - Nuclear astrophysics

Neutrinos
- UF Neutret
- BT Leptons (Nuclear physics)
  - Neutrons
- NT Antineutrinos
  - Neutrino astrophysics
  - Solar neutrinos
- — Scattering

Neutrinos, Solar
- USE Solar neutrinos

Neutron activation analysis
- USE Radioactivation analysis

Neutron albedo
- ⌐QC793.5.N4626⌐
- UF Albedo, Neutron
- BT Albedo

Neutron beams
- ⌐QC793.5.N4622⌐
- UF Beams, Neutron
- BT Neutral beams
- — Polarization

Neutron bomb
- ⌐UG1282.N48⌐
- BT Bombs
  - Neutron weapons

Neutron bombardment
- USE Neutron irradiation

Neutron capture
- USE Neutrons—Capture

Neutron capture gamma ray spectroscopy
- ⌐QC793.5.N4627⌐
- UF Capture gamma ray spectroscopy, Neutron
  - Neutron capture spectroscopy
  - Spectroscopy, Neutron capture

- BT Gamma ray spectrometry
  - Interferometry, Neutron
- RT Neutrons—Capture
- NT Fast neutrons—Capture
  - Thermal neutrons—Capture

Neutron capture spectroscopy
- USE Neutron capture gamma ray spectroscopy

Neutron capture therapy
- USE Boron-neutron capture therapy

Neutron counters
- ⌐QC787.C6⌐
- UF Neutron detectors
- BT Nuclear counters
- — Calibration

Neutron cross section standards
- ⌐QC793.5.N4628⌐
- UF Standard neutron cross sections

Neutron cross sections
- ⌐QC793.5.N4628⌐
- UF Cross sections, Neutron
- BT Collisions (Nuclear physics)
  - Fission cross sections

Neutron detectors
- USE Neutron counters

Neutron diffraction
- USE Neutrons—Diffraction

Neutron diffusion theory
- USE Neutron transport theory

Neutron flux
- ⌐QC793.5.N4626⌐
- UF Flux, Neutron

Neutron flux standards
- ⌐QC793.5.N4626⌐
- UF Standard neutron flux

Neutron generators
- USE Neutron sources

Neutron interferometry
- USE Interferometry, Neutron

Neutron irradiation
- UF Bombardment, Neutron
  - Neutron bombardment
- BT Irradiation
  - Nuclear reactions
- NT Semiconductor doping, Neutron transmutation

Neutron-proton interactions
- UF Interactions, Neutron-proton
  - Interactions, Proton-neutron
  - Proton-neutron interactions
- BT Neutrons
  - Nuclear reactions
  - Protons

Neutron radiography
- ⌐QC793.5.N4628 (Physics)⌐
- ⌐TA417.25 (Industrial radiography)⌐
- BT Radiography, Industrial
  - Thermal neutrons

Neutron resonance
- ⌐QC793.5.N4624⌐
- BT Nuclear magnetic resonance
  - Resonance
- NT Neutron spin echoes

Neutron resonance integral
- USE Resonance integral

Neutron sources
- UF Neutron generators
  - Neutrons—Sources
- BT Nuclear reactors
  - Radiation sources
  - Radioisotopes
- NT Pulsed neutron techniques
- — Spectra

Neutron spin echoes
- UF Echoes, Neutron spin
  - Spin echoes, Neutron
- BT Neutron resonance

Neutron stars
- ⌐QB843.N4⌐
- BT Stars
- RT Pulsars

— Atmospheres

Neutron transmutation doping of semiconductors
- USE Semiconductor doping, Neutron transmutation

Neutron transport theory
- UF Multigroup diffusion (Neutron transport)
  - Neutron diffusion theory
- BT Nuclear fission
  - Nuclear fusion
  - Transport theory
- RT Nuclear reactors

Neutron weapons
- UF Enhanced radiation weapons
  - Weapons, Enhanced radiation
  - Weapons, Neutron
- BT Nuclear weapons
- NT Neutron bomb

Neutrons
- ⌐QC173⌐
- BT Baryons
  - Matter—Constitution
  - Quantum theory
- RT Atoms
  - Electrons
  - Positrons
  - Protons
- SA *headings beginning with the word* Neutron
- NT Alpha rays
  - Cold neutrons
  - Cosmic ray neutrons
  - Delayed neutrons
  - Fast neutrons
  - Heavy water reactors—Exponential measurements
  - Mirror nuclei
  - Neutrinos
  - Neutron-proton interactions
  - Prompt neutrons
  - Stripping reaction (Nuclear physics)
  - Thermal neutrons
- — Capture
  - UF Neutron capture
  - BT Nuclear physics
  - RT Neutron capture gamma ray spectroscopy
- — Diffraction
  - ⌐QC721⌐
  - UF Neutron diffraction
- — Energy spectra
  - USE Neutrons—Spectra
- — Measurement
  - BT Radioactivity—Measurement
  - NT Resonance integral
    - Time-of-flight mass spectrometry
- — Physiological effect
  - ⌐QH652⌐
  - BT Radiation—Physiological effect
- — Polarization
- — Scattering
  - ⌐QH324.9.N48 (Biology)⌐
  - BT Nucleon-nucleon scattering
    - Potential scattering
- — Sources
  - USE Neutron sources
- — Spectra
  - UF Neutrons—Energy spectra
  - BT Nuclear spectroscopy
  - NT Interferometry, Neutron

Neutrophilic leucocytes
- USE Neutrophils

Neutrophils
- UF Neutrophilic leucocytes
  - Polymorphonuclear leucocytes
  - Polynuclear leucocytes
- BT Granulocytes
  - Leucocytes
  - Phagocytes

Neuwerk movement (Christianity)
  [BV4487.N48]
  BT Christianity—Germany
     Church and social problems—Germany
Neva Bay (R.S.F.S.R.)
  UF Nevskaĭa guba (R.S.F.S.R.)
     Nevskaya guba (R.S.F.S.R.)
  BT Bays—Russian S.F.S.R.
Neva River (R.S.F.S.R.)
  BT Rivers—Russian S.F.S.R.
Nevada
  — Antiquities
     NT Fort Sage Drift Fence Site (Nev.)
        Martis culture
  — Capital and capitol
     NT Nevada State Capitol (Carson City,
        Nev.)
  — Description and travel
  — — 1951-1980
  — — 1981-
  — Governors
  — — Dwellings
        NT Nevada Governor's Mansion
           (Carson City, Nev.)
  — Public buildings
     USE Public buildings—Nevada
Nevada Governor's Mansion (Carson City,
     Nev.)
  UF Governor's Mansion (Carson City,
     Nev.)
  BT Dwellings—Nevada
     Nevada—Governors—Dwellings
Nevada State Capitol (Carson City, Nev.)
  BT Nevada—Capital and capitol
Nevado del Ruiz (Colombia)
  (Not Subd Geog)
  [QE523.N]
  UF Nevado el Ruiz (Colombia)
  BT Mountains—Colombia
     Volcanoes—Colombia
Nevado el Ruiz (Colombia)
  USE Nevado del Ruiz (Colombia)
Nevado Sarapo (Peru)
  USE Sarapo Mountain (Peru)
Nevanlinna theory
  BT Functions, Meromorphic
     Value distribution theory
Nevayets
  USE Navayats
Neveil family
  USE Neville family
Nevell family
  USE Neville family
Nevels family
  USE Neville family
Nevet family
  USE Neveu family
Neveu family   (Not Subd Geog)
  UF Nevet family
     Neveux family
     Nevoit family
     Nevouet family
Neveux family
  USE Neveu family
Nevil family
  USE Neville family
Nevill family
  USE Neville family
Neville family   (Not Subd Geog)
  UF Neavel family
     Neavill family
     Neveil family
     Nevell family
     Nevels family
     Nevil family
     Nevill family
Nevoid basal cell carcinoma syndrome
  USE Basal cell nevus syndrome
Nevoid basalioma syndrome
  USE Basal cell nevus syndrome

Nevoit family
  USE Neveu family
Nevoma language
  USE Pima Bajo language
Nevome language
  USE Pima Bajo language
Nevouet family
  USE Neveu family
Nevoyats
  USE Navayats
Nevskaĭa guba (R.S.F.S.R.)
  USE Neva Bay (R.S.F.S.R.)
Nevskaya guba (R.S.F.S.R.)
  USE Neva Bay (R.S.F.S.R.)
Nevskiĭ prospekt (Leningrad, R.S.F.S.R.)
  UF Nevsky Boulevard (Leningrad,
     R.S.F.S.R.)
     Nevsky prospekt (Leningrad,
     R.S.F.S.R.)
  BT Streets—Russian S.F.S.R.
Nevsky Boulevard (Leningrad, R.S.F.S.R.)
  USE Nevskiĭ prospekt (Leningrad,
     R.S.F.S.R.)
Nevsky prospekt (Leningrad, R.S.F.S.R.)
  USE Nevskiĭ prospekt (Leningrad,
     R.S.F.S.R.)
Nevus
  USE Birthmarks
     Mole (Dermatology)
Nevus syndrome, Basal cell
  USE Basal cell nevus syndrome
New, The
  [B105.N4]
  BT Philosophy
New Age movement   (May Subd Geog)
  [BP605.N48]
     Here are entered works on a group of post-1970
  cults and organizations influenced by Eastern and
  Native American religions, occult beliefs and prac-
  tices, mysticism, etc. and employing techniques, such
  as meditation, to enhance consciousness and develop
  human potential.
  UF Aquarian Age movement
  BT Cults
     Social movements
New Age music
  [ML3529]
  BT Music
New Alderney (Solomon Islands)
  USE Vanikolo (Solomon Islands)
New Armenia, Kingdom of, 1080-1375
  USE Cilicia—History—Armenian Kingdom,
     1080-1375
New Bell (Douala, Cameroon)
  (Not Subd Geog)
  UF Douala (Cameroon). New Bell
New birth (Theology)
  USE Regeneration (Theology)
New Bond Street (London, England)
  USE Bond Street (London, England)
New Britain Island (Papua New Guinea)
  BT Bismarck Archipelago (Papua New
     Guinea)
     Islands—Papua New Guinea
New Britain language
  USE Kuanua language
New Brunswick
  BT Acadia
     Maritime Provinces
New brutalism (Architecture)
  USE Brutalism (Architecture)
New business enterprises   (May Subd Geog)
  UF Business enterprises, New
     How to start a business
     Starting a business
  BT Business enterprises
     Industry
     Small business
  — Finance
  — — Law and legislation
        (May Subd Geog)

New Caledonia
     As a geographic subdivision, this heading is used
  directly.
  — Languages
     NT Camuhi language
        Nemi language
        Paici language
New categorial approach (Computer program)
  USE NEWCAT(Computer program)
New Cemetery (Hampden, Mass.)
  USE Prospect Hill Cemetery (Hampden,
     Mass.)
New Chancellery (Berlin, Germany : Building)
  USE Reichskanzlei (Berlin, Germany :
     Building)
New Characteristic Analysis (Computer
     program)
  USE NCHARAN (Computer program)
New Church
  USE New Jerusalem Church
New churches
  USE Church development, New
New City Cemetery (Mobile, Ala.)
  USE Magnolia Cemetery (Mobile, Ala.)
New color canaries
  USE Color canaries
New communities
  USE New towns
New Criticism   (May Subd Geog)
  [PN98.N4]
  BT Criticism
New Deal, 1933-1939   (May Subd Geog)
     Here are entered works on the domestic programs
  of the administration of President Franklin D. Roose-
  velt during the Great Depression of the 1930's. When
  this heading is assigned, additional subject entries are
  made under one or more of the following headings as
  appropriate: United States—Economic conditions—
  1918-1945; United States—Economic policy—1933-
  1945; United States—Politics and government—
  1933-1945; United States—Social conditions—1933-
  1945.
  UF New Deal, 1933-1939—United States
  BT United States—Economic conditions—
     1918-1945
     United States—Economic policy—
     1933-1945
     United States—History—1933-1945
     United States—Politics and
     government—1933-1945
     United States—Social conditions—
     1933-1945
  — United States
     USE New Deal, 1933-1939
New Deal, 1933-1939, in motion pictures
  BT Moving-pictures
New devotions
  USE Devotio moderna
New disasters of war (Aquatint)
  USE Baumgartner, Fritz. New disasters of
     war
New England
  BT Northeastern States
  — Description and travel
  — — To 1775
  — — 1775-1865
  — — 1865-1950
  — — 1951-1980
  — — 1981-
  — History
     [F1-15]
  — — Colonial period, ca. 1600-1775
        NT King Philip's War, 1675-1676
  — — French and Indian War, 1755-1763
        [E199]
  — — Revolution, 1775-1783
  — — 1775-1865
  — — War of 1812
        [E357-9]
  — Intellectual life
     NT Transcendentalism (New England)
  — Politics and government

New England
— Politics and government (Continued)
—— Colonial period, ca. 1600-1775
    NT Freemen (American colonies)
—— 1775-1865
—— War of 1812
— Social life and customs
—— Colonial period, ca. 1600-1775
New England District (N.S.W.)
New England eucalypt dieback
USE Eucalypt dieback
New England Offshore Mining Environmental
    Study
    UF NOMES Project
        Project NOMES
    BT Ocean mining—Environmental aspects
New England style of American cookery
    USE Cookery, American—New England
        style
New England theology
    ₍BX7250₎
        Here are entered works on the Calvinistic theo-
    logical movement prominent in American Congrega-
    tional churches in the late eighteenth and early nine-
    teenth centuries.
    UF Theology, New England
    BT Calvinism
        Congregational churches—Doctrines
New England transcendentalism
    USE Transcendentalism (New England)
New England transcendentalists
    USE Transcendentalists (New England)
New England witchcraft
    USE Witchcraft—New England
New Englanders (May Subd Geog)
    UF Yankees
    BT Ethnology—New England
New Era Cemetery (New Era, Mich.)
    UF New Era City Cemetery (New Era,
        Mich.)
    BT Cemeteries—Michigan
New Era City Cemetery (New Era, Mich.)
    USE New Era Cemetery (New Era, Mich.)
New family
    UF Knew family
        Neu family
        Newce family
        Newe family
        News family
        Nuse family
    RT Nye family
New Forest (England)
    BT Forests and forestry—England
New Forest pony
    ₍SF315.2.N49₎
    UF Foresters (Ponies)
    BT Ponies
New Found, Lake (N.H.)
    USE Newfound Lake (N.H.)
New Fourth Army Incident, China, 1941
    USE China—History—Southern Anhui
        Incident, 1941
New France
    NT Canada
    — History
        USE Canada—History—To 1763 (New
            France)
            Mississippi River Valley—History
            —To 1803
New Germany State Park (Md.)
    BT Parks—Maryland
New-girl networks
    USE Women—Social networks
New Grange Mound (Ireland)
    USE Newgrange Site (Ireland)
New Grange Site (Ireland)
    USE Newgrange Site (Ireland)
New Guernsey (Solomon Islands)
    USE Nendö (Solomon Islands)

New Guinea
    BT Malay Archipelago
        Melanesia
New Guinea pidgin English
    USE Tok Pisin language
New Hall porcelain
    ₍NK4399.N4₎
    UF Porcelain, New Hall
New Hampshire
    — Antiquities
    — Description and travel
    —— 1951-1980
    —— 1981-
    — History
        ₍F31-45₎
    —— Colonial period, ca. 1600-1775
    ——— Juvenile literature
    —— King George's War, 1744-1748
        ₍E198₎
    —— Revolution, 1775-1783
        ₍E263.N4₎
    —— 1775-1865
    —— Civil War, 1861-1865
        ₍E520₎
    — Juvenile literature
    — Politics and government
    —— Colonial period, ca. 1600-1775
    —— Revolution, 1775-1783
    —— 1775-1865
    —— War of 1812
    —— Civil War, 1861-1865
    —— 1865-1950
    —— 1951-
New Hampshires (Chickens)
    ₍SF489.N₎
New Haven (Conn.)
    — History
    —— Colonial period, ca. 1600-1775
    —— Revolution, 1775-1783
    — Invasion, 1779
New Haven River (Vt.)
    BT Rivers—Vermont
New Haven theology (May Subd Geog)
    ₍BX7252.N5₎
    UF Taylorism (New Haven theology)
        Theology, New Haven
    BT Congregational churches—Doctrines
New Hebrides
    USE Vanuatu
New Hebrides poetry (English)
    (May Subd Geog)
    UF English poetry—New Hebrides authors
New Helvetius (Sacramento, Calif.)
    USE Sutter's Fort (Sacramento, Calif.)
New Hope & Ivyland Railroad
    BT Railroads—United States
New Hope Lake (N.C.)
    USE B. Everett Jordan Lake (N.C.)
New Hope Reservoir (N.C.)
    USE B. Everett Jordan Lake (N.C.)
New Hope River (N.C.)
    BT Rivers—North Carolina
    NT B. Everett Jordan Lake (N.C.)
New international communication order
    USE Communication—International
        cooperation
New international economic order
    USE International economic relations
New international information order
    USE Communication—International
        cooperation
New Jersey
    — Antiquities
        NT Ford Powder Mill Site
            (Morristown, N.J.)
    — Description and travel
    —— 1951-1980
    —— 1981-
    — History
        ₍F131-145₎
    —— Colonial period, ca. 1600-1775

——— Juvenile literature
—— Revolution, 1775-1783
    ₍E263.N5₎
    NT Bound Brook, Battle of, 1777
        Little Egg Harbor (N.J.), Battle
            of, 1778
        Monmouth, Battle of, 1778
        Princeton, Battle of, 1777
        Trenton, Battle of, 1776
—— 1775-1865
—— Expedition against the Indians, 1791
    USE St. Clair's Campaign, 1791
—— Civil War, 1861-1865
    ₍E521₎
——— Centennial celebrations, etc.
—— 1865-
—— War of 1898
— Politics and government
—— Colonial period, ca. 1600-1775
—— Revolution, 1775-1783
—— 1775-1865
—— War of 1812
—— Civil War, 1861-1865
—— 1865-1950
—— 1951-
— Social life and customs
—— Colonial period, ca. 1600-1775
    ₍F137₎
New Jersey tea
New Jerusalem Church
    ₍BX8701-BX8749₎
        Here are entered works on Swedenborgian
    denominations treated collectively and works for
    which the individual Swedenborgian denomination
    cannot be identified.
    UF Church of the New Jerusalem
        New Church
        Swedenborgianism
    BT Christian sects
    NT Bible-Christian Church
        Swedenborgians
New jobs tax credit (May Subd Geog)
    UF Jobs tax credit
        Targeted jobs tax credit
    BT Employment tax credit
    — Law and legislation (May Subd Geog)
New journalism
    USE Journalism—United States
        Nonfiction novel
New Kirghiz horse
    USE Novokirghiz horse
New Lanark Establishment
    ₍HX696₎
New Lands (Greece)
    UF Neai chōrai (Greece)
        New Territories (Greece)
New Lauenburg (Tokelau Islands)
    USE Atafu Atoll (Tokelau Islands)
New Left
    USE College students—Political activity
        Communism—1945-
        Radicalism
        Right and left (Political science)
New literates, Writing for
    UF Neo-literates, Writing for
        Writing for new literates
    BT Authorship
        Children's literature—Technique
        Literacy
    NT Readers for new literates
New literates and libraries
    USE Libraries and new literates
New London (Conn.)
    — Burning by the British, 1781
        BT United States—History—
            Revolution, 1775-1783—
            Campaigns
    — History
    —— Revolution, 1775-1783
New Mark (Poland)
    USE Nowa Marchia (Poland)

New Market (Philadelphia, Pa.)
  USE Newmarket (Philadelphia, Pa.)
New Market, Battle of, 1864
  ₍E476.64₎
  BT United States—History—Civil War,
    1861-1865—Campaigns
New Marshfield Cemetery (Ohio)
  UF Marshfield Cemetery (Ohio)
  BT Cemeteries—Ohio
New matter (Civil procedure)
  (May Subd Geog)
  BT Appellate procedure
    Civil procedure
    Pleading
New Mexican duck
  USE Anas diazi
New Mexico
  — Antiquities
      NT Arroyo Hondo Site (N.M.)
        Aztec Ruins National Monument
          (N.M.)
        Baca Site (N.M.)
        Bis sa'ani Pueblo (N.M.)
        Galaz Site (N.M.)
        Garnsey Site (N.M.)
        Garnsey Spring Site (N.M.)
        Guadalupe Ruin (N.M.)
        Henderson Site (N.M.)
        Las Huertas Site (N.M.)
        Salmon Site (N.M.)
        Sandia Cave (N.M.)
  — Description and travel
  — — 1951-1980
  — — 1981-
  — History
      ₍F791-805₎
  — — To 1848
      NT Pueblo Revolt, 1680
  — — — Juvenile literature
  — — War with Mexico, 1845-1848
      ₍E405.2₎
  — — 1848-
  — — Civil War, 1861-1865
      ₍E522₎
      ₍E571₎
  — Juvenile literature
  — Languages
      NT Chiricahua language
        Mescalero language
  — Politics and government
  — — 1848-1950
  — — 1951-
New Mexico range caterpillar
New moon (Judaism)
  UF Rosh Hodesh
  BT Calendar, Jewish
    Moon—Religious aspects—Judaism
New Negro Movement
  USE Harlem Renaissance
New New York naturalism
  USE Photo-realism
New objectivity (Art) *(May Subd Geog)*
  UF Nach-Expressionismus (Art)
    Neue Sachlichkeit (Art)
    Post-expressionism (Art)
  BT Art, Modern—20th century
  RT Magic realism (Art)
New optics
  USE Photonics
New Orleans (La.)
  — Description
  — — 1981-
  — History
  — — Civil War, 1861-1865
New Orleans, Battle of, 1815
  ₍E356.N5₎
  BT United States—History—War of 1812
    —Campaigns
New Orleans, Battle of, 1862
  ₍E472.88₎

  BT United States—History—Civil War,
    1861-1865—Campaigns
    United States—History—Civil War,
    1861-1865—Naval operations
New painting of the mountains around Fu-
  ch'un (Watercolor painting)
  USE Yeh, Ch'ien-yü, 1907-   New
    painting of the mountains around
    Fu-ch'un
New Paphos (Ancient city)
  UF Nea Paphos (Ancient city)
    Paphos (Ancient city)
  BT Cities and towns, Ruined, extinct, etc.
    —Cyprus
    Cyprus—Antiquities
New Plymouth Colony
  USE Massachusetts—History—New
    Plymouth, 1620-1691
New Plymouth Purchase, Maine
  USE Kennebec Patent
New Product Announcements (Data base)
  ₍HF5415.153₎
  UF NPA (Data base)
  BT New products—Data bases
    Predicasts Terminal System
      (Information retrieval system)
New products
  UF Products, New
  BT Commercial products
    Marketing
    Product management
    Research, Industrial
    Technological forecasting
    Technology transfer
  NT Design, Industrial
  — Data bases
      NT New Product Announcements
        (Data base)
New Providence Island (Bahamas)
  BT Islands—Bahamas
  — History
  — — British Conquest, 1783
      BT United States—History—
        Revolution, 1775-1783—
        Campaigns
New realism
  USE Photo-realism
New River (Ariz.)
  BT Rivers—Arizona
New River (Mexico and Calif.)
  BT Rivers—California
    Rivers—Mexico
New River (N.C.-W. Va.)
  BT Rivers—North Carolina
    Rivers—Virginia
    Rivers—West Virginia
New River language
  ₍PM2017.N8₎
  RT Shastan languages
New San'yo Line
  USE San'yo Shinkansen
New Sark (Solomon Islands)
  USE Utupua (Solomon Islands)
New schools
  UF Schools, New
  BT School buildings
    School management and organization
New sculpture (Art movement)
  (May Subd Geog)
  ₍NB467.5.N48₎
  BT Sculpture, British
    Sculpture, Modern—19th century—
      Great Britain
    Sculpture, Modern—20th century—
      Great Britain
    Sculpture, Victorian—Great Britain
New South Wales
  — Church history
  — — 20th century
      ₍BR1483.N5₎

New Standard Theatre (Shoreditch, London,
  England)
  USE Standard Theatre (Shoreditch, London,
    England)
New stars
  USE Stars, New
New states
  USE States, New
New Stone age
  USE Neolithic period
New Street (Genoa, Italy)
  USE Via Garibaldi (Genoa, Italy)
**New Street Station (Birmingham, West
  Midlands, England)**
  BT Railroads—England—Stations
New super-realism
  USE Pop art
New Sweden Tercentenary Celebration, 1938
New Territories (Greece)
  USE New Lands (Greece)
New Testament apocryphal books
  USE Apocryphal books (New Testament)
New Testament Greek
  USE Greek language, Biblical
New Testament scholars *(May Subd Geog)*
  ₍BS2351₎
  UF Bible scholars (New Testament)
    Biblical scholars (New Testament)
    Scholars, New Testament
  BT Biblical scholars
New Thought
  ₍BF638-645₎
  UF Thought, New
  BT Mental healing
    Psychology
    Therapeutics, Suggestive
  NT Jesus Christ—New Thought
      interpretations
    Psychology, Applied
New Tokaido Line
  USE Tōkaidō Shinkansen
New towns *(May Subd Geog)*
  ₍HT169.55-HT169.57 (City planning)₎
  ₍NA9053.N (Architecture)₎
  UF New communities
    Satellite cities
  BT Cities and towns
New trials *(May Subd Geog)*
  BT Appellate procedure
    Civil procedure
    Criminal procedure
    Trials
New Vriesland Cemetery (Zeeland, Mich.)
  BT Cemeteries—Michigan
New Waterway (Netherlands)
  UF Nieuwe Waterweg (Netherlands)
  BT Canals—Netherlands
    Channels (Hydraulic engineering)—
      Netherlands
New wave music *(May Subd Geog)*
  BT Rock music
  RT Punk rock music
New words
  USE Words, New
New world communication order
  USE Communication—International
    cooperation
New world information order
  USE Communication—International
    cooperation
New World Island (Nfld.)
  BT Islands—Newfoundland
New-World monkeys
  USE Cebidae
New World orioles
  USE Icterus (Birds)
New world porcupines
  USE Erethizontidae
New Year *(May Subd Geog)*
  ₍GT4905₎
  UF Nawrūz

New Year *(Continued)*
  BT Holidays
  NT Baisakhi (Festival)
      New Year sermons
      Watch night
  — Songs and music
      USE New Year music
New Year, Islamic
  USE Islamic New Year
New Year, Jewish
  USE Rosh ha-Shanah
New Year, Muslim
  USE Islamic New Year
New Year cards *(May Subd Geog)*
  UF Cards, New Year
      New Year's cards
  BT Greeting cards
New Year decorations, etc.
  (May Subd Geog)
  BT Holiday decorations
New Year for Trees
  USE Tu bi-Shevat
New Year in literature
New Year music
  UF New Year—Songs and music
  NT Synagogue music—Rosh ha-Shanah
      services
New Year sermons
  [BV4282]
  UF Sermons, New Year
  BT New Year
      Occasional sermons
New Year's cards
  USE New Year cards
New York (N.Y.)
  As a geographic subdivision, this heading is used directly.
  — Description
  — — 1951-1980
  — — 1981-
  — Draft Riot, 1863
      USE Draft Riot, 1863
  — History
      [F128]
  — — Colonial period, ca. 1600-1775
      NT New York (N.Y.)—Negro plot, 1741
  — — Revolution, 1775-1783
      [E230.5-E289]
      [E263.N6]
      NT Harlem Heights, Battle of, 1776
      Hickey Plot, 1776
  — — 1775-1865
  — — War of 1812
      [E359.5.N6]
  — — Civil War, 1861-1865
      NT Draft Riot, 1863
  — — 1865-1898
  — — 1898-1951
  — — 1951-
  — Mayors
  — — Dwellings
      NT Gracie Mansion (New York, N.Y.)
  — Negro plot, 1741
      BT New York (N.Y.)—History—Colonial period, ca. 1600-1775
  — Politics and government
  — — To 1898
      NT Tweed Ring
  — — 1898-1951
  — — 1951-
  — Social life and customs
  — — Colonial period, ca. 1600-1775
New York (N.Y.). Chinatown
  USE Chinatown (New York, N.Y.)
New York (N.Y.). East Harlem
  USE East Harlem (New York, N.Y.)
New York (N.Y.). East Village
  USE East Village (New York, N.Y.)

New York (N.Y.). Flushing
  USE Flushing (New York, N.Y.)
New York (N.Y.). Forest Hills
  USE Forest Hills (New York, N.Y.)
New York (N.Y.). Greenwich Village
  USE Greenwich Village (New York, N.Y.)
New York (N.Y.). Little Italy
  USE Little Italy (New York, N.Y.)
New York (N.Y.). Lower East Side
  USE Lower East Side (New York, N.Y.)
New York (N.Y.). Rochdale Village
  USE Rochdale Village (New York, N.Y.)
New York (N.Y.). SoHo
  USE SoHo (New York, N.Y.)
New York (N.Y.). Times Square
  USE Times Square (New York, N.Y.)
New York (N.Y.). Washington Heights
  USE Washington Heights (New York, N.Y.)
New York (N.Y.). West Side
  USE West Side (New York, N.Y.)
New York (State)
  — Altitudes
  — Antiquities *(Not Subd Geog)*
      NT Ganondagan State Historic Site (N.Y.)
  — Capital and capitol
      NT New York State Capitol (Albany, N.Y.)
  — Constitutional history
  — Description and travel
  — — 1951-1980
  — — 1981-
  — Governors
  — — Children
  — — Election
  — — Wives
  — History
      [F116-130]
  — — Colonial period, ca. 1600-1775
      NT Champlain-Iroquois Battle, 1615
      Esopus Indians—Wars, 1663-1664
  — — King William's War, 1689-1697
      [E196]
  — — Queen Anne's War, 1702-1713
      [E197]
  — — French and Indian War, 1755-1763
      NT Abercrombie's Ticonderoga Campaign, 1758
  — — Revolution, 1775-1783
      [E263.N6]
      NT Bedford, N.Y. (Westchester Co.), Battle of, 1779
      Burgoyne's Invasion, 1777
      Clinton's Hudson River Expedition, 1777
      Evacuation Day, Nov. 25, 1783
      Harlem Heights, Battle of, 1776
      Long Island, Battle of, 1776
      Oriskany, Battle of, 1777
      Pell's Point, Battle of, 1776
      Saratoga Campaign, 1777
      St. Leger's Expedition, 1777
      Sullivan's Indian Campaign, 1779
      Valcour Island, Battle of, 1776
      White Plains, Battle of, 1776
  — — — Juvenile literature
  — — 1775-1865
  — — War of 1812
      [E359.5.N6]
      NT Plattsburgh (N.Y.), Battle of, 1814
  — — Civil War, 1861-1865
      [E523]
  — — — Centennial celebrations, etc.
  — — 1865-
  — — War of 1898
      [E726.N5]
  — Juvenile literature
  — Officials and employees

  — — Accidents
  — Politics and government
  — — Colonial period, ca. 1600-1775
  — — Revolution, 1775-1783
  — — 1775-1865
  — — War of 1812
  — — Civil War, 1861-1865
  — — 1865-1950
  — — 1951-
  — Public buildings
      USE Public buildings—New York (State)
  — Social life and customs
  — — Colonial period, ca. 1600-1775
New York 21 Trial, New York, N.Y., 1970-1971
  USE Black Panthers Trial, New York, N.Y., 1970-1971
New York air-brake
  [TF430]
  BT Air-brakes
New York Bight (N.J. and N.Y.)
  BT Bays—New Jersey
      Bays—New York (State)
New York Central Railroad
  NT 20th Century Limited (Express train)
New York, Chicago, and St. Louis Railroad
  UF Nickel Plate Road
  BT Railroads—United States
New York City Bomb Conspiracy Trial, New York, N.Y.,1970-1971
  USE Black Panthers Trial, New York, N.Y., 1970-1971
New York City Marathon, New York, N.Y.
  UF N.Y.C. Marathon, New York, N.Y.
      New York Marathon, New York, N.Y.
  BT Marathon running—New York (State)
New York-London Air Race, 1969
  USE Daily Mail Transatlantic Air Race, 1969
New York Marathon, New York, N.Y.
  USE New York City Marathon, New York, N.Y.
New York Metropolitan Area
  As a geographic subdivision, this heading is used directly.
  BT Metropolitan areas—United States
  RT New York Region
      New York Suburban Area
New York, Ontario and Western Railway
  BT Railroads—United States
New York point system
  USE Blind—Printing and writing systems
New York Region
  As a geographic subdivision, this heading is used directly.
  RT New York Metropolitan Area
      New York Suburban Area
New York School
  USE New York school of art
New York school of art
  UF New York School
  BT Art, American
      Art, Modern—20th century—United States
New York State Barge Canal System (N.Y.)
  (Not Subd Geog)
  UF Barge Canal (N.Y.)
  BT Canals—New York (State)
New York State Capitol (Albany, N.Y.)
  UF State Capitol (Albany, N.Y.)
  BT New York (State)—Capital and capitol
New York State Forest Preserve (N.Y.)
  UF Forest Preserve of New York State (N.Y.)
  BT Forest reserves—New York (State)
  NT Adirondack Forest Preserve (N.Y.)
      Adirondack Park (N.Y.)
New York State North Country
  USE North Country (N.Y.)

New York State Thruway (N.Y.)
  UF Dewey Thruway (N.Y.)
      Governor Thomas E. Dewey Thruway
        (N.Y.)
      Thomas E. Dewey Thruway (N.Y.)
      Thruway (N.Y.)
  BT Express highways—New York (State)
      Toll roads—New York (State)
New York Stock Exchange
  NT Wall Street
New York Suburban Area
    As a geographic subdivision, this heading is used
  directly.
  BT Suburbs—United States
  RT New York Metropolitan Area
      New York Region
New York times
  — Indexes
New Zealand
  — Antiquities
      NT Ruahihi Pa Site (N.Z.)
  — Description and travel
  — — To 1840
  — — 1840-1950
  — — 1951-1980
  — — 1981-
  — Economic conditions
  — — 1918-
  — — 1945-
  — Foreign relations
  — — 1945-
  — History
  — — To 1843
  — — 1843-1870
      UF Maori Wars, 1843-1870
      BT Maoris
      NT Hone Heke's Rebellion, 1844-
          1846
        Te Porere, Battle of, 1869
  — — — Juvenile literature
  — — — Pictorial works
  — — Maori War, 1845-1847
      UF Maori War, N.Z., 1845-1847
      BT Maoris—Warfare
  — — 1870-
  — Juvenile literature
  — Politics and government
  — — 1972-
  — Public buildings
      USE Public buildings—New Zealand
New Zealand agricultural assistance
  USE Agricultural assistance, New Zealand
New Zealand alien labor
  USE Alien labor, New Zealand
New Zealand art
  USE Art, New Zealand
New Zealand artificial satellites
  USE Artificial satellites, New Zealand
New Zealand atlases
  USE Atlases, New Zealand
New Zealand authors
  USE Authors, New Zealand
New Zealand beech
  USE Nothofagus
New Zealand children's stories
  USE Children's stories, New Zealand
New Zealand college prose
  USE College prose, New Zealand
New Zealand cookery
  USE Cookery, New Zealand
New Zealand Cup (Horse race)
  USE New Zealand Trotting Cup
New Zealand drama
New Zealand economic assistance
  USE Economic assistance, New Zealand
New Zealand fiberlily
  USE Phormium tenax
New Zealand fiction *(May Subd Geog)*
  UF English fiction—New Zealand
  NT Children's stories, New Zealand
      Love stories, New Zealand

    War stories, New Zealand
New Zealand flax
  USE Phormium tenax
New Zealand fur seal
  ⌐QL737.P63⌐
  UF Arctocephalus forsteri
New Zealand historical prints
  USE Historical prints, New Zealand
New Zealand investments
  USE Investments, New Zealand
New Zealand kauri
  USE Kauri
New Zealand landscape painting
  USE Landscape painting, New Zealand
New Zealand literature *(May Subd Geog)*
  UF English literature—New Zealand
  — 20th century
New Zealand love stories
  USE Love stories, New Zealand
New Zealand missions
  USE Missions, New Zealand
New Zealand national characteristics
  USE National characteristics, New Zealand
New Zealand newspapers
  ⌐PN5591-PN5600 (History)⌐
  UF English newspapers—New Zealand
New Zealand painting
  USE Painting, New Zealand
New Zealand poetry *(May Subd Geog)*
  UF English poetry—New Zealand
  — 20th century
New Zealand poets
  USE Poets, New Zealand
New Zealand prose literature
  (May Subd Geog)
  ⌐PR9635-PR9639 (History)⌐
  ⌐PR9678-PR9679 (Collections)⌐
  NT College prose, New Zealand
New Zealand technical assistance
  USE Technical assistance, New Zealand
New Zealand Trotting Cup
  ⌐SF345.N48⌐
  UF New Zealand Cup (Horse race)
  BT Harness racing—New Zealand
New Zealand war stories
  USE War stories, New Zealand
New Zealand watercolor painting
  USE Watercolor painting, New Zealand
New Zealand whitebait fisheries
  USE Galaxias fisheries
New Zealand wit and humor
  (May Subd Geog)
  ⌐PN6178.N4 (Minor collections)⌐
    Here are entered collections from several authors
  and individual authors who have not written in other
  literary forms.
New Zealand wit and humor, Pictorial
New Zealanders *(May Subd Geog)*
  BT Ethnology—New Zealand
Newal family
  USE Newell family
Newall family
  USE Newell family
Newar women
  USE Women, Newar
Newari architecture
  USE Architecture, Newari
Newari art
  USE Art, Newari
Newari Buddhist literature
  USE Buddhist literature, Newari
Newari drama *(May Subd Geog)*
  — To 1500
  — 1500-1800
Newari essays *(May Subd Geog)*
Newari fiction *(May Subd Geog)*
  NT Short stories, Newari
Newari language
  ⌐PL3801.N5⌐
  BT Tibeto-Burman languages
  NT Pahri dialect

Newari literature *(May Subd Geog)*
  NT Buddhist literature, Newari
Newari manuscripts
  USE Manuscripts, Newari
Newari periodicals *(May Subd Geog)*
Newari philology
Newari poetry *(May Subd Geog)*
  — 20th century
Newari prose literature *(May Subd Geog)*
Newari proverbs
  USE Proverbs, Newari
Newari satire
  USE Satire, Newari
Newari short stories
  USE Short stories, Newari
Newari songs
  USE Songs, Newari
Newars
  BT Ethnology—Nepal
Newayetahs
  USE Navayats
Newberry family
  USE Newbury family
Newberry Mountains Wilderness (Calif.)
  (Not Subd Geog)
  UF Newberry Mountains Wilderness
      Study Area (Calif.)
  BT National parks and reserves—
      California
      Wilderness areas—California
Newberry Mountains Wilderness Study Area
  (Calif.)
  USE Newberry Mountains Wilderness
      (Calif.)
Newbery family
  USE Newbury family
Newbery medal books
  UF John Newbery medal books
      Newbery prize books
  BT Children's literature
      Literary prizes
Newbery prize books
  USE Newbery medal books
Newbold family *(Not Subd Geog)*
  UF Newbolt family
Newbolt family
  USE Newbold family
Newborn infants
  USE Infants (Newborn)
Newborn intensive care
  USE Neonatal intensive care
Newborn respiratory therapy
  USE Respiratory therapy for newborn
      infants
Newbry family
  USE Newbury family
Newbury family *(Not Subd Geog)*
  UF Newberry family
      Newbery family
      Newbry family
Newburyport (Mass.). Plum Island
  USE Plum Island (Newburyport, Mass.)
Newby family *(Not Subd Geog)*
Newcastle and Carlisle Railway
  BT Railroads—Great Britain
Newcastle disease *(May Subd Geog)*
  ⌐SF995.6.N4⌐
  UF Avian pneumoencephalitis
      Fowl pest
  BT Virus diseases in poultry
Newcastle disease vaccine
  ⌐SF995.6.N4⌐
  BT Viral vaccines
Newcastle disease virus
  ⌐QR201.N5⌐
  BT Paramyxoviruses
NEWCAT(Computer program)
  UF New categorial approach (Computer
      program)
  BT Linguistics—Computer programs

Newce family
    USE New family
Newcom family
    USE Newcomer family
Newcomb family
    USE Newcomer family
Newcomb pottery
    ₍NK340.N47₎
    BT Pottery—Louisiana
Newcombe family
    USE Newcomer family
Newcome family
    USE Newcomer family
Newcomer family *(Not Subd Geog)*
    UF Newcom family
        Newcomb family
        Newcombe family
        Newcome family
        Newcumber family
        Newcumer family
        Newkomer family
        Nicomer family
        Niewcomer family
Newcumber family
    USE Newcomer family
Newcumer family
    USE Newcomer family
Newdigate family
    USE Newgate family
Newe family
    USE New family
Newel family
    USE Newell family
Newell family *(Not Subd Geog)*
    UF Newal family
        Newall family
        Newel family
        Newhall family
        Newil family
        Newill family
        Nuel family
Newfound Lake (N.H.)
    UF Lake New Found (N.H.)
        Lake Newfound (N.H.)
        New Found, Lake (N.H.)
    BT Lakes—New Hampshire
Newfoundland
    — **Antiquities**
Newfoundland dogs
    ₍SF429.N4₎
Newgate family *(Not Subd Geog)*
    UF Newdigate family
Newgrange Mound (Ireland)
    USE Newgrange Site (Ireland)
Newgrange Site (Ireland) *(Not Subd Geog)*
    UF New Grange Mound (Ireland)
        New Grange Site (Ireland)
        Newgrange Mound (Ireland)
    BT Ireland—Antiquities
Newhall family
    USE Newell family
Newhaven Mutiny, 1795
    BT Mutiny—England
Newil family
    USE Newell family
Newill family
    USE Newell family
Newkerk family
    USE Newkirk family
Newkirk family
    UF Neukirk family
        Newkerk family
Newkomer family
    USE Newcomer family
Newlan family
    USE Newland family

Newland family *(Not Subd Geog)*
    UF Newlan family
        Newlander family
        Newlands family
        Newlin family
        Newling family
        Nuland family
Newlander family
    USE Newland family
Newlands family
    USE Newland family
Newlin family
    USE Newland family
Newling family
    USE Newland family
Newly industrializing countries
    USE Developing countries
Newlyn school of painting
    ₍ND467.5.N48₎
    BT Artist colonies—England
        Painting, English
        Painting, Modern—19th century—
            England
Newman family *(Not Subd Geog)*
    UF Nauman family
        Naumann family
        Neuman family
        Neumann family
        Newmann family
        Newmen family
        Newmon family
        Nieuman family
        Nouman family
        Numan family
        Numans family
        Numon family
Newmann family
    USE Newman family
Newmarket (Philadelphia, Pa.)
    (Not Subd Geog)
    UF New Market (Philadelphia, Pa.)
        Philadelphia (Pa.). Newmarket
Newmarket and Thurlow Hunt
    USE Puckeridge and Thurlow Hunt
Newmarket cough
    USE Equine influenza
Newmen family
    USE Newman family
Newmon family
    USE Newman family
Newport (N.C.)
    — **History**
    — — **Civil War, 1861-1865**
        ₍F264.N₎
Newport Burying Ground (Newport, Ill.)
    USE Newport Mount Rest Cemetery
        (Newport, Ill.)
Newport Common Burial Ground (Newport,
    R.I.)
    USE Common Burial Ground (Newport,
        R.I.)
**Newport Mount Rest Cemetery (Newport,
Ill.)**
    UF Mount Rest Cemetery (Newport, Ill.)
        Mt. Rest Cemetery (Newport, Ill.)
        Newport Burying Ground (Newport,
            Ill.)
        Newport Mt. Rest Cemetery
            (Newport, Ill.)
    BT Cemeteries—Illinois
Newport Mt. Rest Cemetery (Newport, Ill.)
    USE Newport Mount Rest Cemetery
        (Newport, Ill.)
Newport to Ensenada, International Yacht
Race
    USE Ensenada Race
Newport Uprising, Wales, 1839
    UF Chartist Riots, Wales, 1839
    BT Labor disputes—Wales
        Riots—Wales
        Wales—History

News, Attribution of
    USE Attribution of news
News, Foreign
    USE Foreign news
News, Science
    USE Science news
News agencies *(May Subd Geog)*
    UF News-gathering organizations
        News services
        Wire services
    BT Newspapers
        Press
    NT Foreign news
News agencies (Wholesale trade)
    USE Newspaper and periodical wholesalers
News broadcasting
    USE Broadcast journalism
News dealers
    USE Newspaper vendors
News editing
    USE Journalism—Editing
News family
    USE New family
News films
    USE Newsreels
News flow, International
    USE Communication—International
            cooperation
        Foreign news
News-gathering organizations
    USE News agencies
News-letters
    USE Newsletters
News photographers *(May Subd Geog)*
    UF Newsreel photographers
        Press photographers
    BT Journalists
        Moving-picture journalism
        Newsreels
        Photographers
        Photography, Journalistic
        Reporters and reporting
News photography
    USE Photography, Journalistic
News radio stations *(May Subd Geog)*
    UF All-news radio stations
    BT Radio journalism
        Radio stations
News recordings
        Subdivided by date, e.g. News recordings—1958.
    BT History—Yearbooks
    — **1958**
News services
    USE News agencies
News source identification
    USE Attribution of news
News vendors
    USE Newspaper vendors
Newsboys
    USE Newspaper carriers
        Newspaper vendors
Newsletters *(May Subd Geog)*
    ₍PN4784.N5₎
    UF News-letters
    BT Journalism
        Newspapers
    NT Church newsletters
Newsman's privilege
    USE Confidential communications—Press
Newsom family
    USE Newsome family
Newsome family *(Not Subd Geog)*
    UF Newsom family
        Newsum family
Newspaper advertising
    USE Advertising, Newspaper
Newspaper agents *(May Subd Geog)*
    ₍PN4784.C6₎
    BT Book industries and trade

2584

Newspaper and periodical libraries
  (*May Subd Geog*)
  ₍Z675.N37₎
  UF Libraries, Newspaper
      Libraries, Periodical
      Newspaper libraries
      Periodical libraries
  BT Libraries, Special
  RT Serials control systems
Newspaper and periodical wholesalers
  (*May Subd Geog*)
  UF News agencies (Wholesale trade)
      Newspaper distributors
      Newspaper wholesalers
      Periodical distributors
      Periodical wholesalers
  BT Newspapers
      Periodicals
      Periodicals—Marketing
Newspaper buildings (*May Subd Geog*)
  UF Buildings, Newspaper
      Newspaper printing plants
      Plants, Newspaper printing
  BT Printing plants
Newspaper carriers
  ₍HD6247.N5₎
  UF Newsboys
      Paper carriers
  BT Boys
      Children—Employment
      Newspaper vendors
Newspaper circulation
  USE Newspapers—Circulation
Newspaper clipping bureaus
  USE Clipping bureaus
Newspaper clippings
  USE Clippings (Books, newspapers, etc.)
Newspaper court reporting
  (*May Subd Geog*)
  UF Court reporting (by newspapers)
      Gag rule
      Trial reporting
      Trials in the press
  BT Free press and fair trial
      Journalism
      Journalism, Legal
      Reporters and reporting
  RT Crime and the press
  NT Contempt of court
      Courtroom art
Newspaper dealers
  USE Newspaper vendors
Newspaper distributors
  USE Newspaper and periodical wholesalers
Newspaper layout and typography
  UF Layout and typography, Newspaper
  BT Journalism
      Journalism—Editing
      Newspapers
      Printing
      Printing, Practical—Layout
      Type and type-founding
      Type-setting
  NT Advertising layout and typography
      Nameplates of publications
Newspaper libraries
  USE Newspaper and periodical libraries
      Newspaper office libraries
Newspaper office libraries (*May Subd Geog*)
  ₍Z675.N4₎
  UF Journalistic libraries
      Libraries, Journalistic
      Libraries, Newspaper office
      Morgues (Newspaper libraries)
      Newspaper libraries
  BT Libraries, Special
Newspaper ownership
  USE Newspapers—Ownership
Newspaper presses
  ₍Z249₎
  UF Newspaper printing presses

BT Printing-press
Newspaper printing, Offset
  USE Offset printing of newspapers
Newspaper printing plants
  USE Newspaper buildings
Newspaper printing presses
  USE Newspaper presses
Newspaper publishing (*May Subd Geog*)
  UF Newspapers, Publishing of
      Publishing of newspapers
  BT Journalism
      Newspapers
      Publishers and publishing
  RT Periodicals, Publishing of
  NT Newspapers—Ownership
      Wages—Newspaper publishing
Newspaper reading
  UF Newspapers, Reading of
      Reading of newspapers
  BT Journalism
      Newspapers
      Newspapers in education
      Reading interests
Newspaper reporting
  USE Reporters and reporting
Newspaper Strike, Bremen, Germany, 1977
  BT Strikes and lockouts—Newspapers—
      Germany (West)
Newspaper style
  USE *subdivision* Language *under types of*
      newspapers
      Journalism—Style manuals
Newspaper syndicates
  USE Syndicates (Journalism)
Newspaper vendors (*May Subd Geog*)
  UF News dealers
      News vendors
      Newsboys
      Newspaper dealers
      Newsstands
  NT Newspaper carriers
Newspaper wholesalers
  USE Newspaper and periodical wholesalers
Newspapers
  ₍AN₎
  ₍PN4700-PN4899 (History)₎
  Here are entered works on the newspapers of the
  world and, with appropriate subdivisions, works on
  special aspects or sections of newspapers. Works on
  newspapers in a specific language, or in a specific
  country or larger area, are entered under the adjecti-
  val form of the language or area, e.g. Afrikaans
  ₍American, German-American, Hebrew, Israeli,
  Southeast Asian, Ukrainian, etc.₎ newspapers.
  BT Journalism
      Library materials
      Mass media
      Serial publications
      Street literature
  RT Periodicals
      Press
  NT Advertising, Newspaper
      Afro-Americans in the newspaper
        industry
      American newspapers
      Black newspapers
      Clippings (Books, newspapers, etc.)
      Feuilletons
      Free circulation newspapers and
        periodicals
      French newspapers
      News agencies
      Newsletters
      Newspaper and periodical wholesalers
      Newspaper layout and typography
      Newspaper publishing
      Newspaper reading
      Offset printing of newspapers
      Phototypesetting of newspapers
      Postal service—Second-class matter
      Press law
      Reporters and reporting

Stamp-duties—Newspapers
      Stereotype matrices
      Strikes and lockouts—Newspapers
      Student newspapers and periodicals
      Tabloid newspapers
      Virgin Islands newspapers
      Wall newspapers
  —**Abstracting and indexing**
    BT Abstracting
        Indexing
    NT Subject headings—Newspapers
  —**Abstracts**
  —**Accounting**
  —Advertising
    USE Advertising—Newspapers
  —**Anniversary editions**
    ₍PN4784.A5₎
    UF Anniversary editions of newspapers
  —**Bibliography**
    ₍Z6941₎
  ——**Catalogs**
  ——**Methodology**
    UF Newspapers—Bibliography—
        Theory, methods, etc.
  ——Theory, methods, etc.
    USE Newspapers—Bibliography—
        Methodology
  ——**Union lists**
  —Cataloging
    USE Cataloging of newspapers
  —**Circulation**
    ₍PN4784.C6₎
    UF Circulation of newspapers
        Newspaper circulation
    BT Marketing
        Periodicals—Circulation
    SA *subdivision* Circulation *under*
        special language or area
        newspapers, e.g. English
        newspapers—Circulation;
        American newspapers—
        Circulation
  —Collective bargaining
    USE Collective bargaining—Journalists
        Collective bargaining—
        Newspapers
  —Collective labor agreements
    USE Collective labor agreements—
        Newspapers
  —**Collectors and collecting**
    (*May Subd Geog*)
  —**Conservation and restoration**
  —**Directories**
  —Editing
    USE Journalism—Editing
  —**Employees**
    NT Collective bargaining—Newspapers
        Trade-unions—Newspaper
        employees
  ——Collective bargaining
    USE Collective bargaining—
        Newspapers
  ——Collective labor agreements
    USE Collective labor agreements—
        Newspapers
  —**Exhibitions**
  —**Extra editions**
    UF Extras (Newspapers)
        Newspapers—Special editions
  —**Facsimiles**
  —**Headlines**
    ₍PN4784.H4₎
    UF Headline writing
  —**Illustrations**
    ₍NC970₎
    BT Journalism, Pictorial
    RT Illustrated periodicals
  —**Indexes**
    ₍AI21₎

Newspapers
— Indexes (Continued)
    Indexes of individual newspapers are entered under the name of the newspaper followed by the subdivision Indexes, e.g. New York times—Indexes.
— Information storage and retrieval systems
    USE Information storage and retrieval systems—Newspapers
— **Language**
— **Library resources** (May Subd Geog)
— **Local editions**
    [PN4784.L6]
    Here are entered works on special editions, or sections of newspapers published to meet local needs of smaller areas within the territory covered by the newspaper.
    UF Newspapers—Sections, columns, etc.—Local
— **Marketing**
    [PN4784.C6]
— **Microform catalogs**
    UF Newspapers in microform—Catalogs
       Newspapers on microfilm—Catalogs
— **Objectivity**
    BT Journalistic ethics
       Objectivity
— **Ownership**
    UF Newspaper ownership
       Ownership of newspapers
    BT Newspaper publishing
    RT Press monopolies
— Public relations
    USE Public relations—Newspapers
— **Sections, columns, etc.**
    Here are entered works dealing with specific newspaper sections, their writing and editing as well as their understanding and interpretation by the reading public. Works on papers devoted to one particular field are entered under the heading Journalism qualified by the field, e.g. Journalism, Agricultural; Sports journalism.
    Subdivided by subject, e.g. Newspapers—Sections, columns, etc.—Fashion; Newspapers—Sections, columns, etc.—Food.
    UF Periodicals—Sections, columns, etc.
    SA subdivision Sections, columns, etc. under American [English, French, etc.] newspapers
    NT American newspapers—Sections, columns, etc.
       English newspapers—Sections, columns, etc.
       French newspapers—Sections, columns, etc.
       Syndicates (Journalism)
— — **Advice**
    UF Advice columns
       Problem pages
    BT Counseling
— — **Arts**
    BT Arts
— — Book section
    USE Book reviewing
       Newspapers—Sections, columns, etc.—Reviews
— — **Comics**
    BT Comic books, strips, etc.
— — **Corrections**
    UF Correction of errors in newspapers
       Errata (in newspapers)
       Retraction of errors in newspapers
    BT Errors
— — Death notices
    USE Death notices
— — **Editorials**
    BT Editorials
— — **Fashion**

    BT Clothing and dress
       Dressmaking
       Fashion writing
— — **Fiction**
    BT Feuilletons
— — **Finance**
    [PN4784.F5]
    UF Financial news
— — **Food**
    UF Food pages of newspapers
       Food sections of newspapers
— — **Front pages** (Not Subd Geog)
    UF Front pages of newspapers
— — **Genealogy**
    BT Genealogy
— — **Letters to the editor**
    UF Letters to the editor
— — Local
    USE Newspapers—Local editions
— — Obituaries
    USE Obituaries
— — **Op-ed pages**
    UF Op-ed pages of newspapers
— — **Reviews**
    [PN4784.R4]
    UF Newspapers—Sections, columns, etc.—Book section
       Reviews
    BT Art criticism
       Book reviewing
       Criticism
       Dramatic criticism
       Journalism and literature
       Moving-picture criticism
       Musical criticism
— — **Sports**
    UF Sports pages (Newspapers)
    BT Sports journalism
— — **Women**
— Societies, etc.
    USE Journalism—Societies, etc.
— Special editions
    USE Newspapers—Extra editions
— Subject headings
    USE Subject headings—Newspapers
— **Taxation**
    NT American newspapers—Taxation
       German newspapers—Taxation
— **Transportation**
Newspapers, Black
    USE Black newspapers
Newspapers, Community
    USE Community newspapers
Newspapers, Phototypesetting of
    USE Phototypesetting of newspapers
Newspapers, Publishing of
    USE Newspaper publishing
Newspapers, Reading of
    USE Newspaper reading
Newspapers, Suburban
    USE Community newspapers
Newspapers, Talking
    USE Talking newspapers
Newspapers and children
    [HQ784.N4]
    UF Children and newspapers
       Newspapers and youth
       Youth and newspapers
    BT Children
Newspapers and youth
    USE Newspapers and children
Newspapers for the visually handicapped
    (May Subd Geog)
    BT Visually handicapped
    NT Talking newspapers
Newspapers in education (May Subd Geog)
    [LB1044.9.N4]
    BT Journalism and education
       Mass media in education
       Teaching—Aids and devices
       Visual education

    NT Newspaper reading
Newspapers in genealogy (May Subd Geog)
    BT Genealogy
Newspapers in literature
Newspapers in microform
    BT Microforms
    NT Newspapers on filmstrips
       Newspapers on microfilm
— Catalogs
    USE Newspapers—Microform catalogs
Newspapers on filmstrips
    BT Filmstrips
       Newspapers in microform
Newspapers on microfilm
    [Z265]
    BT Microfilms
       Newspapers in microform
— Catalogs
    USE Newspapers—Microform catalogs
Newspapers on phonorecords
    USE Talking newspapers
Newspapers on phonotapes
    USE Talking newspapers
Newsprint (May Subd Geog)
    BT Bagasse
       Wood-pulp
— Tariff
    USE Tariff on paper
Newsprint industry (May Subd Geog)
    [HD9839.N4-44]
Newsreel
    USE Moving-picture journalism
       Newsreels
Newsreel photographers
    USE News photographers
Newsreels
    UF Filmstrips, Newsreel
       News films
       Newsreel
    BT Moving-pictures
    RT Moving-picture journalism
       Photography, Journalistic
    NT News photographers
Newsstands
    USE Newspaper vendors
Newsum family
    USE Newsome family
Newth family (Not Subd Geog)
    UF Nuth family
Newton Creek (N.Y.)
    USE Newtown Creek (Chemung County, N.Y.)
Newton family
    UF Neuton family
       Newtown family
       Nuton family
Newtonian fluids
    UF Newtonian liquids
    BT Fluid dynamics
       Fluids
       Liquids
    RT Non-Newtonian fluids
Newtonian liquids
    USE Newtonian fluids
Newtonian reflector
    USE Newtonian telescope
Newtonian telescope
    UF Newtonian reflector
       Reflector, Newtonian
       Telescope, Newtonian
    BT Telescope, Reflecting
Newton's rings
    USE Interference (Light)
Newtown Creek (Chemung County, N.Y.)
    UF Newton Creek (N.Y.)
    BT Rivers—New York (State)
Newtown family
    USE Newton family
Newts
    [QL668.C2]
    BT Salamandridae

NT Notophthalmus
Taricha
Triturus
Newts as pets
[SF459.N]
Ney
USE Nāy
Ney family
USE Nye family
Nez Percé Indians
[E99.N5]
UF Chopunnish Indians
Nimapu
Nimipu
Numipu
Sahaptin Indians
BT Indians of North America
Shahaptian Indians
NT Nez Perce National Historical Park
(Idaho)
— Antiquities
— Wars, 1877
[E83.877]
BT Indians of North America—Wars—
1866-1895
NT Big Hole, Battle of the, 1877
Nez Percé language
[PM2019]
UF Numipu language
Sahaptin languages
RT Shahaptian languages
Nez Perce National Forest (Idaho)
USE Nezperce National Forest (Idaho)
Nez Perce National Historical Park (Idaho)
BT Historic sites—Idaho
National parks and reserves—United
States
Nez Percé Indians
Parks—Idaho
Nezame monogatari emaki (Scrolls)
[ND1059.6.N]
BT Painting, Japanese—Kamakura-
Momoyama periods, 1185-1600
Painting, Japanese—Heian period, 794-
1185
Scrolls, Japanese
Nezara
[QL523.P5]
BT Pentatomidae
NT Nezara viridula
Nezara viridula *(May Subd Geog)*
[QL523.P5]
UF Southern green stink bug
Stink bug, Southern green
BT Nezara
Nezperce National Forest (Idaho)
(Not Subd Geog)
UF Nez Perce National Forest (Idaho)
BT Forest reserves—Idaho
National parks and reserves—Idaho
Nezumia
[QL638.M2]
UF Kuronezumia
BT Macrouridae
Nezumia bubonis
[QL638.M2]
Ngaa Rauru (Maori people)
[DU424.N37]
UF Ngaa Rauru Kiitahi (Maori people)
BT Ethnology—New Zealand
Maoris
Ngaa Rauru Kiitahi (Maori people)
USE Ngaa Rauru (Maori people)
Ngaaka (African people)
USE Bali (African people)
Ngaanyatjara language
[PL7101.N43]
UF Nyanganyatjara language
BT Australia—Languages
Pitjandjara language
Western desert language

Ngada language
[PL5432]
UF Ngadha language
BT Malayan languages
Ngada people
UF Ngadha people
BT Ethnology—Indonesia
Ngadha language
USE Ngada language
Ngadha people
USE Ngada people
Ngadju (Indonesian people)
USE Ngaju (Indonesian people)
Ngadju dialect
USE Ngaju language
Ngadju language (Australia)
[PL7101.N44]
UF Ngadjumaja language
BT Australia—Languages
Australian languages
Languages, Mixed
Ngadju language (Indonesia)
USE Ngaju language
Ngadjumaja language
USE Ngadju language (Australia)
Ngaitahu (Maori tribe)
BT Ethnology—New Zealand
Maoris
Ngaju (Indonesian people)
UF Biadju (Indonesian people)
Ngadju (Indonesian people)
Olo Ngadjoe (Indonesian people)
BT Dyaks
Ethnology—Indonesia
— Rites and ceremonies
NT Funeral rites and ceremonies,
Ngaju (Indonesian people)
Ngaju (Indonesian people) funeral rites and
ceremonies
USE Funeral rites and ceremonies, Ngaju
(Indonesian people)
Ngaju Dayak language
USE Ngaju language
Ngaju language
UF Biadju language
Ngadju dialect
Ngadju language (Indonesia)
Ngaju Dayak language
BT Dyak language
Indonesia—Languages
NT Bakumpai dialect
Ngala language (Zaire)
USE Lingala language
Ngalagan language
USE Ngalakan language
Ngalakan language *(May Subd Geog)*
[PL7101.N447]
UF Hongalla language
Ngalagan language
Ngalbon language
Nullakun language
Nullikin language
BT Australia—Languages
Australian languages
Ngalbon language
USE Ngalakan language
Ngalia Basin (N.T.)
BT Geology—Australia
Ngaloi (African people)
USE Galwa (African people)
Ngam dialect
USE Ngama dialect
Ngama dialect *(May Subd Geog)*
UF Ngam dialect
Sara Ngama dialect
BT Central African Republic—Languages
Chad—Languages
Sara language
Ngambai dialect
USE Gambai dialect

Ngambaye (African people)
USE Gambaye (African people)
Nganasan language
[PH3818]
UF Tavgi language
BT Samoyedic languages
Nganasani
[DK759.N4]
BT Ethnology—Soviet Union
Samoyeds
Ngandi language
[PL7101.N45]
BT Australia—Languages
Australian languages
Ngando-Kota (African people)
USE Bangandu (African people)
Ngandu (African people)
USE Bangandu (African people)
Ng'anga language
USE Nyanja language
Ngangela (Bantu people)
[DT611.42 (Angola)]
[DT963.42 (Zambia)]
UF Banguella (Bantu people)
Benguella (Bantu people)
Ganguella (Bantu people)
Va Ngangela (Bantu people)
BT Ethnology—Angola
Ethnology—Zambia
Ngangela language
USE Ganguela language
Ngarinjin language
UF Ungarinjin language
Wungarinjin language
BT Australia—Languages
Wororan languages
Ngarluma language
BT Australia—Languages
Australian languages
Ngarrindjeri (Australian people)
USE Narrinyeri (Australian people)
Ngas (African people)
USE Angas (African people)
Ngati Mamoe (Maori tribe)
BT Maoris
Ngāti Toa (Maori people)
[DU424.N44]
UF Ngatitoa (Maori people)
BT Ethnology—New Zealand
Maoris
Ngatitoa (Maori people)
USE Ngāti Toa (Maori people)
Ngazam language
USE Ngizim language
Ngbaka (African people)
[DT650.N45]
UF Bwaka (African people)
Gbaka (African people)
Gmbwaga (African people)
Gwaka (African people)
BT Ethnology—Central African Republic
Ethnology—Zaire
NT Bangandu (African people)
Ngbaka-Ma'bo (African people)
Ngbaka Gbaya language
USE Gbaya language
Ngbaka limba language
USE Ngbaka ma'bo language
Ngbaka Lobaye (African people)
USE Bangandu (African people)
Ngbaka-Ma'bo (African people)
BT Ethnology—Central African Republic
Ngbaka (African people)
Ngbaka ma'bo folk-songs
USE Folk-songs, Ngbaka ma'bo
Ngbaka ma'bo language
[PL8548.5]
UF Ngbaka limba language
BT Central African Republic—Languages
Niger-Congo languages
Zaire—Languages

Ngbaka ma'bo literature *(May Subd Geog)*
  [PL8548.5]
Ngbandi language
  UF Gbandi language (Zaire)
      Mbati language
      Mongwandi language
  BT Congo (Brazzaville)—Languages
      Niger-Congo languages
  RT Yakoma language
  NT Sango language
Ngbanya (African people)
  USE Gonja (African people)
Ngbanyito (African people)
  USE Gonja (African people)
NGC 1976 (Nebula)
  USE Orion Nebula
Ngemba (African people)
  [DT515.42 (Nigeria)]
  [DT570 (Cameroon)]
  UF Megimba (African people)
      Mogimba (African people)
      Ngomba (African people)
      Widerkum (African people)
  BT Ethnology—Cameroon
      Ethnology—Nigeria
Ngemba language (Australia)
  USE Wongaibon language
Ngemba language (Cameroon)
  UF Megimba language
      Mogimba language
      Ngomba language
      Nguemba language
      Ngyemboon language
  BT Benue-Congo languages
      Cameroon—Languages
Ngere (African people)
  USE Gere (African people)
Ngere (Kru-speaking African people)
  USE Wobe (African people)
Ngeumba language
  USE Wongaibon language
Ngezzim language
  USE Ngizim language
Nggela language
  USE Florida language
Nggerikudi language
  [PL7101.N5]
  BT Australia—Languages
      Australian languages
Ngiyambaa language
  USE Wongaibon language
Ngizim language
  [PL8548.67]
  UF Gwazum language
      Kirdiwat language
      Ngazam language
      Ngezzim language
      Ngodjin language
      Nugzum language
      Walu language
  BT Chadic languages
      Nigeria—Languages
Ngjamba language
  USE Wongaibon language
Ngo language
  [PL8548.68]
  UF Babungo language
  BT Benue-Congo languages
      Cameroon—Languages
Ngodjin language
  USE Ngizim language
Ngok (Malayan people)
  USE Semang (Malayan people)
Ngomba (African people)
  USE Ngemba (African people)
Ngomba language
  USE Ngemba language (Cameroon)
Ngombe (African people)
  [DT650.N48]
  UF Ngombe (Bantu tribe)

BT Bantus
    Ethnology—Zaire
Ngombe (Bantu tribe)
  USE Ngombe (African people)
Ngombe language
  BT Bantu languages
Ngonde (African people)
  UF Konde (African people)
      Nkhonde (African people)
      Nkonde (African people)
      Wangonde (African people)
  BT Bantus
      Ethnology—Malawi
      Ethnology—Tanzania
  RT Nyakyusa (African people)
Ngonde folk literature
  USE Folk literature, Ngonde
Ngonde language
  [PL8549]
  UF Ikinyi-Kiusa language
      Kiusa language
      Konde language
      Nkonde language
      Nyakyusa language
  BT Bantu languages
  NT Mwamba language
Ngongo (African people)
  UF Bangongo (African people)
  BT Ethnology—Zaire
Ngoni (African people)
  UF Angoni
      Mangoni (African people)
      Wangoni (African people)
  BT Ethnology—Africa, Eastern
      Nguni (African people)
  NT Bhaca (African people)
      Missions to Ngoni (African people)
  — Migrations
      BT Migrations of nations
Ngoni (African people) law
  USE Law, Ngoni (African people)
Ngorongoro Conservation Area (Tanzania)
  USE Ngorongoro Game Control Area
       Reserve (Tanzania)
Ngorongoro Game Control Area Reserve
(Tanzania)
  UF Ngorongoro Conservation Area
      (Tanzania)
  BT Game-preserves—Tanzania
      National parks and reserves—Tanzania
NGOs (International agencies)
  USE Non-governmental organizations
Ngueba language
  USE Bamougoun-Bamenjou language
Nguemba language
  USE Ngemba language (Cameroon)
Nguere (Kru-speaking African people)
  USE Wobe (African people)
Ngũgĩ wa Thiong'o, 1938-
  (Not Subd Geog)
  1938-
  — Characters
  — — Wanja
      RT Wanja (Fictitious character)
Ngulu (Tanzanian people)
  [DT443]
  UF Nguru (Tanzanian people)
  BT Ethnology—Tanzania
Nguna language
  UF Nguna-Tongoa language
      Ngunese language
  BT Melanesian languages
Nguna-Tongoa language
  USE Nguna language
Ngundjan dialects
  USE Gundjun dialects
Ngunese language
  USE Nguna language
Nguni (African people)
  BT Bantus
      Ethnology—Africa, Southern

NT Ndebele (African people)
    Ngoni (African people)
    Swazi (African people)
    Tembu (African people)
    Xhosa (African people)
    Zulus
— Food
  BT Food
Nguni languages
  [PL8550.N44]
  BT Africa, Southern—Languages
      Bantu languages
  NT Ndebele language (Zimbabwe)
      Swazi language
      Xhosa language
      Zulu language
— Tone
  BT Tone (Phonetics)
Nguoi Thuong (Vietnamese people)
  USE Montagnards (Vietnamese people)
Nguru (African people)
  USE Lomwe (African people)
Nguru (Tanzanian people)
  USE Ngulu (Tanzanian people)
Nguru Mountains (Tanzania)
  (Not Subd Geog)
  BT Mountains—Tanzania
Nguruman Forest (Kenya) *(Not Subd Geog)*
  BT Forests and forestry—Kenya
Ngwa dialect *(May Subd Geog)*
  BT Igbo language
      Nigeria—Languages
Ngwala language
  USE Kulango language
Ngwato (African people)
  USE Bamangwato
Ngwemyene (African people)
  USE Myene (African people)
Ngyemboon language
  USE Ngemba language (Cameroon)
Nhambicuara language
  USE Nambicuara language
Nhamundá River (Brazil)
  UF Jamundá River (Brazil)
      Yamundá River (Brazil)
  BT Rivers—Brazil
Nharo (African people)
  USE Naron (African people)
Nhauru (African people)
  USE Naron (African people)
Nhaurun (African people)
  USE Naron (African people)
NHP (Health profile)
  USE Nottingham Health Profile
Ni (The Russian word)
  BT Russian language—Etymology
Ni (The Swedish word)
  BT Swedish language—Etymology
Nī-nīroku jiken, Japan, 1936
  USE Japan—History—February Incident,
       1936 (February 26)
Nia-kuoll language
  USE Nyah Kur language
Niabua language
  USE Nyabwa language
Niacin
  [QP772.N48]
  UF Antipellagra vitamin
      Carboxypyridine
      Nicotinic acid
      P.P. factor
      Pellagra preventive factor
      Pyridinecarboxylic acid
  BT Carboxylic acids
      Nicotine
      Pyridine
      Vitamin B complex
  RT Isonicotinic acid
  NT Vitamin PP
Niacin amide
  USE Vitamin PP

Niagara, Fort (N.Y.)
 USE Old Fort Niagara (N.Y.)
Niagara, Battle of, 1814
 USE Lundy's Lane, Battle of, 1814
Niagara Falls (N.Y.)
 — Public works
Niagara Falls (N.Y. and Ont.)
 BT Niagara River (N.Y. and Ont.)
  Waterfalls—New York (State)
  Waterfalls—Ontario
Niagara Falls, Battle of, 1814
 USE Lundy's Lane, Battle of, 1814
Niagara Frontier (N.Y.)
Niagara Peninsula (Ont.)
 BT Peninsulas—Ontario
Niagara River (N.Y. and Ont.)
 BT Rivers—New York (State)
  Rivers—Ontario
 NT Niagara Falls (N.Y. and Ont.)
Niakuol language
 USE Nyah Kur language
Nialuok language
 USE Nyah Kur language
Niam-Niam (African people)
 USE Zande (African people)
Niangua darter
 [QL638.P4]
 UF Etheostoma nianguae
 BT Darters (Fishes)
Niangua River (Mo.)
 BT Rivers—Missouri
Niani (Guinea) *(Not Subd Geog)*
 UF Mali (Guinea)
  Mani (Guinea)
  Nani (Guinea)
  Nianimadougou (Guinea)
  Yani (Guinea)
 BT Cities and towns, Ruined, extinct, etc.
   —Guinea
  Guinea—Antiquities
Nianimadougou (Guinea)
 USE Niani (Guinea)
Niantic language
 USE Massachuset language
Nias Island (Indonesia)
 UF Pulau Nias (Indonesia)
 BT Islands—Indonesia
Nias language
 [PL5433]
 BT Malayan languages
Nias proverbs
 USE Proverbs, Nias
Niasese (Indonesian people)
 [DS632.N52]
 UF Niassans (Indonesian people)
 BT Ethnology—Indonesia
Niassa, Lake
 USE Nyasa, Lake
Niassans (Indonesian people)
 USE Niasese (Indonesian people)
Niblo family *(Not Subd Geog)*
Nibulu dialect
 USE Nunuma dialect
Nicaragua
 — Antiquities
  NT Acahualinca Site (Nicaragua)
 — Description and travel
 — — 1951-1980
 — — 1981-
 — Economic conditions
 — — 1918-
 — — 1918-1979
 — — 1979-
 — Foreign relations
 — — 1979-
 — History
  [F1521-7]
 — — To 1838
 — — English invasion, 1780-1781
 — — 1838-1909
 — — Filibuster War, 1855-1860

 UF Filibuster War, Nicaraguan
 BT Filibusters
 NT Rivas, Battle of, 1856
  Santa Rosa, Battle of, 1856
 — — Revolution, 1909-1910
  [F1526.3]
 — — 1909-1937
 — — Revolution of 1912
 — — Revolution, 1926-1929
 — — 1937-1979
 — — Uprising, 1978
 — — 1979-
 — — Revolution, 1979
 — Languages
  NT Sumo language
 — Politics and government
 — — To 1838
 — — 1838-1909
 — — 1909-1937
 — — 1937-1979
 — — 1979-
 — Social conditions
 — — 1979-
Nicaragua Canal (Nicaragua)
 BT Canals—Nicaragua
Nicaragua chocolatetree
 USE Patashte
Nicaraguan art
 USE Art, Nicaraguan
Nicaraguan authors
 USE Authors, Nicaraguan
Nicaraguan drama *(May Subd Geog)*
 [PQ7513 (History)]
 [PQ7517 (Collections)]
Nicaraguan fiction *(May Subd Geog)*
 NT Short stories, Nicaraguan
Nicaraguan literature
 [PQ7510-7519]
Nicaraguan painting
 USE Painting, Nicaraguan
Nicaraguan periodicals *(May Subd Geog)*
Nicaraguan poetry *(May Subd Geog)*
 [PQ7512 (History)]
 [PQ7516 (Collections)]
 NT Political poetry, Nicaraguan
  Revolutionary poetry, Nicaraguan
  War poetry, Nicaraguan
Nicaraguan poets
 USE Poets, Nicaraguan
Nicaraguan political poetry
 USE Political poetry, Nicaraguan
Nicaraguan revolutionary poetry
 USE Revolutionary poetry, Nicaraguan
Nicaraguan short stories
 USE Short stories, Nicaraguan
Nicaraguan war poetry
 USE War poetry, Nicaraguan
Nicaraguan wit and humor, Pictorial
 (May Subd Geog)
Nicaraguans *(May Subd Geog)*
 BT Ethnology—Nicaragua
Nicarao Indians
 UF Niquiranos
  Niquiras
 BT Indians of Central America
  Nahuas
 — Religion and mythology
Nicarbing
 USE Carbonitriding
Nicaria Island (Greece)
 USE Ikaria Island (Greece)
Nice (France)
 — Antiquities
  NT Terra Amata Site (France)
Nice (France). Cimiez
 USE Cimiez (Nice, France)
Nice family *(Not Subd Geog)*
 UF De Nice family
  Nyce family
 RT Neis family
  Neus family

Niceforonia
 [QL668.E257]
 BT Leptodactylidae
Nicene Creed (Music)
 USE Credo (Music)
Nicergoline
 UF Nicotergoline
  Nimergoline
 BT Alkaloids
  Carboxylic acids
  Esters
  Pyridine
  Vasodilators
Nichals family
 USE Nichols family
Nichalson family
 USE Nicholson family
Niche (Ecology)
 UF Microhabitat
 BT Biotic communities
  Competition (Biology)
  Ecology
  Habitat (Ecology)
 NT Food chains (Ecology)
  Resource partitioning (Ecology)
Nichelson family
 USE Nicholson family
Niches (Architecture) *(May Subd Geog)*
 [NA2942]
 BT Architecture
  Walls
Nichiren (Sect) *(May Subd Geog)*
 UF Lotus sect
  Nichiren-shū
 BT Buddhist sects
 NT Fuju-fuse (Sect)
  Hommon Butsuryū (Sect)
  Honzon (Nichiren)
  Kenpon Hokkeshū
  Nichiren Buddhists
  Nichiren Shōshū
  Priests, Nichiren
  Reiyūkai
  Sōka Gakkai
 — Ceremonies and practices
 — Doctrines
 — — Introductions
  [BQ8318.5]
 — Missions *(May Subd Geog)*
 — Relation to the state
  USE Buddhism and state—Nichiren
   (Sect)
 — Relations
 — — Christianity, [etc.]
Nichiren (Sect) and state
 USE Buddhism and state—Nichiren (Sect)
Nichiren Buddhists *(May Subd Geog)*
 [BQ8348]
 BT Buddhists
  Nichiren (Sect)
 NT Priests, Nichiren
  Reiyūkai Buddhists
Nichiren priests
 USE Priests, Nichiren
Nichiren Shō (Sect)
 USE Nichiren Shōshū
Nichiren-shō-shū
 USE Nichiren Shōshū
Nichiren Shōshū *(May Subd Geog)*
 [BQ8400-8449]
 UF Fuji (Sect)
  Nichiren Shō (Sect)
  Nichiren-shō-shū
  Nichiren Shōshū (Sect)
 BT Buddhist sects
  Nichiren (Sect)
 RT Sōka Gakkai
Nichiren Shōshū (Sect)
 USE Nichiren Shōshū
Nichiren-shū
 USE Nichiren (Sect)

Nicholason family
USE Nicholson family
Nicholdson family
USE Nicholson family
Nicholls family
USE Nichols family
Nichols family *(Not Subd Geog)*
UF Nichals family
Nicholls family
Nickals family
Nickell family
Nickels family
Nickles family
Nickols family
Nicol family
Nicoll family
Nicols family
RT Nicholson family
Nicholsen family
USE Nicholson family
Nicholsin family
USE Nicholson family
Nicholson family *(Not Subd Geog)*
UF Nichalson family
Nichelson family
Nicholason family
Nicholdson family
Nicholsen family
Nicholsin family
Nickelsen family
Nickelson family
Nickleson family
Nickolson family
Nicolson family
RT Nicolaisen family
Nicolajsen family
Nick (Japanese fighter plane)
USE Toryū (Fighter plane)
Nick Adams (Fictitious character)
USE Adams, Nick (Fictitious character)
Nickals family
USE Nichols family
Nickel
 ₋HD9539.N (Economics)₋
 ₋QD181.N6 (Chemistry)₋
 ₋TN799.N6 (Metallurgy)₋
NT Nickel compounds
Nickel steel
Soils—Nickel content
— **Electrometallurgy**
— **Isotopes**
— **Metallurgy**
— **Spectra**
— **Welding**
Nickel (Coin)
UF Nickle (Coin)
Nickel-alloy steel
USE Nickel steel
Nickel alloys
 ₋TA480.N6 (Properties)₋
 ₋TS650 (Manufacture)₋
BT Alloys
NT Chrome-nickel steel
Chromium-cobalt-nickel-molybdenum
alloys
Chromium-copper-nickel alloys
Chromium-iron-nickel alloys
Cobalt-nickel alloys
Cobalt-nickel-silicon alloys
Copper-nickel alloys
Copper-nickel-tin alloys
Copper-nickel-zinc alloys
Iron-nickel alloys
Iron-nickel-cobalt alloys
Iron-nickel-phosphorus alloys
Magnesium-nickel alloys
Monel metal
Nickel-aluminum alloys
Nickel-chromium alloys
Nickel-chromium-aluminum alloys
Nickel-manganese alloys

Nickel silver
Nickel-tin alloys
Nickel-titanium alloys
Nickel-titanium-carbon alloys
— **Welding**
Nickel-aluminum alloys
UF Aluminum-nickel alloys
BT Aluminum alloys
Nickel alloys
Nickel bronze
USE Nickel silver
Nickel-cadmium batteries
UF Batteries, Nickel-cadmium
Cadmium-nickel batteries
Nickel-cadmium cells
BT Storage batteries
Nickel-cadmium cells
USE Nickel-cadmium batteries
Nickel catalysts
BT Catalysts
Nickel chromite
 ₋QD181.N6₋
UF Chromium nickel oxide
BT Chromium compounds
Nickel-chromium alloys
UF Chromium-nickel alloys
BT Chromium alloys
Nickel alloys
NT Nimonic alloys
— **Electric properties**
Nickel-chromium-aluminum alloys
BT Aluminum alloys
Chromium alloys
Nickel alloys
Nickel-chromium-iron alloys
USE Chromium-iron-nickel alloys
Nickel-cobalt alloys
USE Cobalt-nickel alloys
Nickel compounds
BT Nickel
Nickel-copper alloys
USE Copper-nickel alloys
Nickel electrodes
USE Electrodes, Nickel
Nickel films
BT Metallic films
Nickel industry *(May Subd Geog)*
NT Strikes and lockouts—Nickel industry
— **Ontario**
— — **Employees**
NT Inco Metals Company Strike,
Sudbury, Ont., 1978-1979
Nickel-magnesium alloys
USE Magnesium-nickel alloys
Nickel-manganese alloys
UF Manganese-nickel alloys
BT Manganese alloys
Nickel alloys
Nickel mines and mining *(May Subd Geog)*
 ₋TN490.N6₋
Nickel nitrate
 ₋QD181.N6₋
Nickel ores *(May Subd Geog)*
NT Skutterudite
Nickel organic compounds
USE Organonickel compounds
Nickel Plate Road
USE New York, Chicago, and St. Louis
Railroad
Nickel-plating
 ₋TS690₋
Nickel silver
UF German silver
Nickel bronze
White bronze
BT Copper alloys
Copper-nickel-zinc alloys
Nickel alloys
Zinc alloys
Nickel steel
 ₋TN757.N5 (Metallurgy)₋

UF Nickel-alloy steel
BT Nickel
Steel
NT Chrome-nickel steel
Maraging steel
Nickel sulphide
BT Sulphides
Nickel-tin alloys
UF Tin-nickel alloys
BT Nickel alloys
Tin alloys
Nickel-titanium alloys
UF Titanium-nickel alloys
BT Nickel alloys
Titanium alloys
Nickel-titanium-carbon alloys
BT Nickel alloys
Titanium alloys
Titanium carbide
Nickell family
USE Nichols family
Nickels family
USE Nichols family
Nickelsen family
USE Nicholson family
Nickelson family
USE Nicholson family
Nickle (Coin)
USE Nickel (Coin)
Nickles family
USE Nichols family
Nickleson family
USE Nicholson family
Nicknames *(May Subd Geog)*
 ₋CT108 (English)₋
UF Sobriquets
Soubriquets
BT Names, Personal
RT Epithets
SA *subdivision* Nicknames *under subjects,*
e.g. Kings and rulers—Nicknames;
also special nicknames, e.g. Hoosier
(Nickname), Uncle Sam
(Nickname)
NT Brother Jonathan (Nickname)
Butternut (Nickname)
Copperhead (Nickname)
Love names
Nickols family
USE Nichols family
Nickolson family
USE Nicholson family
Niclausse boiler
USE Steam-boilers, Marine—Niclausse
Nicobarese language
 ₋PL4471₋
UF Nikobar language
BT Austroasiatic languages
Nicodemites
BT Converts, Protestant
Dissenters, Religious
Protestantism—History
NICOL (Computer program language)
BT Nonprocedural languages
(Programming languages)
Nicol family
USE Nichols family
Nicolai family *(Not Subd Geog)*
Nicolaisen family *(Not Subd Geog)*
RT Nicholson family
Nicolajsen family
Nicolajsen family *(Not Subd Geog)*
UF Nicolaysen family
RT Nicholson family
Nicolaisen family
Nicolaysen family
USE Nicolajsen family
Nicoleño Indians
BT Indians of North America

Nicolet family *(Not Subd Geog)*
Nicolet National Forest (Wis.)
   BT Forest reserves—Wisconsin
        National parks and reserves—United
         States
Nicoletia
   ₜQL503.8.N5ⱼ
   BT Nicoletiidae
Nicoletia texensis
   USE Texoreddellia texensis
Nicoletiidae
   ₜQL503.8.N5ⱼ
   BT Thysanura
   NT Coletinia
        Lepidospora
        Nicoletia
        Texoreddellia
Nicoll family
   USE Nichols family
Nicols family
   USE Nichols family
Nicolson family
   USE Nicholson family
Nicolson pavements
   USE Pavements, Wooden
Nicomer family
   USE Newcomer family
Nicon
   ₜQL391.A6ⱼ
   BT Nereidae
Nicopolis, Battle of, 1396
   USE Nikopoli, Battle of, 1396
Nicotergoline
   USE Nicergoline
Nicotiana
   ₜQK495.S7 (Botany)ⱼ
   BT Solanaceae
Nicotiana tabacum
   USE Tobacco
Nicotinamide
   USE Vitamin PP
Nicotine
   RT Tobacco
   NT Niacin
Nicotinic acid
   USE Niacin
Nicotinic acid amide
   USE Vitamin PP
Nicoya Peninsula (Costa Rica)
   BT Peninsulas—Costa Rica
Níd (The Old Norse word)
   BT Old Norse language—Etymology
Nidation
   USE Ovum implantation
NIDDM
   USE Non-insulin-dependent diabetes
Nidification
   USE Nest building
Nidula Island (Papua New Guinea)
   USE Goodenough Island (Papua New
        Guinea)
Nidulariales
   ₜQK629.Nⱼ
   BT Gasteromycetes
Nie family
   USE Nye family
Nieb family *(Not Subd Geog)*
Niebel family
   USE Nebel family
Nieblas family *(Not Subd Geog)*
Niebling family
   USE Nübling family
Niebuhr family *(Not Subd Geog)*
   UF Niebur family
Niebur family
   USE Niebuhr family
Niece family
   USE Neese family
Nieces *(May Subd Geog)*
   BT Family
        Women

Niederkrain (Slovenia)
   USE Dolenjsko (Slovenia)
Niederschlesien (Poland and Germany)
   USE Silesia, Lower (Poland and Germany)
Niederwald (Germany)
   BT Mountains—Germany (West)
        Taunus (Germany)
Nieh p'an (Sect)
   ₜBQ8450-8459ⱼ
   UF Nehan (Sect)
        Nehanshū
        Nieh p'an tsung
   BT Buddhist sects
Nieh p'an tsung
   USE Nieh p'an (Sect)
Niejalke family *(Not Subd Geog)*
   UF Niesalke family
Niel family
   USE Neal family
Niele family
   USE Neal family
Nielim language
   ₜPL8550.N53ⱼ
   UF Lua language
        Mjillem language
        Niellim language
        Nyilem language
   BT Bua languages
        Chad—Languages
Niell family
   USE Neal family
Nielle family
   USE Neal family
Niellim language
   USE Nielim language
Niello *(May Subd Geog)*
   ₜNK6525ⱼ
   BT Art metal-work
        Engraving
Niels family
   USE Neal family
Nielsen family *(Not Subd Geog)*
   UF Nielson family
   RT Nelson family
        Nilsen family
Nielson family
   USE Nielsen family
Nieman family
   USE Niemann family
Niemand family
   USE Niemann family
Niemann family *(Not Subd Geog)*
   UF Nieman family
        Niemand family
Niemen River
   USE Neman River
Niementowski reaction
   BT Chemical reactions
Nien Rebellion, China, 1853-1868
   USE China—History—Nien Rebellion,
        1853-1868
Niende (African people)
   USE Nyende (African people)
Niepolomice Forest (Poland)
   UF Puszcza Niepołomicka (Poland)
   BT Forests and forestry—Poland
Niernberger family *(Not Subd Geog)*
   UF Nurnberg family
        Nurnberger family
Niesalke family
   USE Niejalke family
Niess family *(Not Subd Geog)*
   RT Neese family
Nietzsche family *(Not Subd Geog)*
Nieuman family
   USE Newman family
Nieuport, Battle of, 1600
   ₜDH199.N4ⱼ
   BT Netherlands—History—Wars of
        Independence, 1556-1648—
        Campaigns

Nieuport-Macchi 11 (Fighter plane)
   ₜUG1242.F5ⱼ
   BT Fighter planes
Nieuport-Macchi 17 (Fighter plane)
   ₜUG1242.F5ⱼ
   BT Fighter planes
Nieuw-Waldeck (Hague, Netherlands)
   (Not Subd Geog)
   UF Hague (Netherlands). Nieuw-
        Waldeck
Nieuwe Waterweg (Netherlands)
   USE New Waterway (Netherlands)
Nieves de Chinchilla, Virgen de las
   ₜBT660.N47ⱼ
   UF Chinchilla, Virgen de las Nieves de
        Virgen de las Nieves de Chinchilla
   BT Mary, Blessed Virgin, Saint—Cult—
        Spain
Nievole River (Italy)
   UF Fiume Nievole (Italy)
   BT Rivers—Italy
Niewcomer family
   USE Newcomer family
Nife language
   USE Luo language (Kenya and Tanzania)
Nifedipine
   ₜRM666.N53ⱼ
   UF Dihydrodimethylnitro
        phenylpyridinedicarboxylic acid
        dimethyl ester
        Dimethyldihydrodimet
        hylnitrophenylpyridinedicarboxylate
        Nitrophenyldimethyld
        icarbomethoxydihydropyridine
   BT Calcium—Antagonists
        Carboxylic acids
        Esters
        Pyridine
        Vasodilators
Niffer (Ancient city)
   USE Nippur (Ancient city)
Nifuratel
   UF Methylthiomethylnitr
        ofurfurylideneaminooxazolidinone
   BT Nitrofurans
Nigatsudō shunie
   USE Omizutori
Niger
  — **Description and travel**
    (Not Subd Geog)
  —— **1981-** *(Not Subd Geog)*
  — **History**
    NT Senussite Rebellion, 1916-1918
  —— **To 1960**
  — **Languages**
    NT Daza language
        Dendi dialect
        Zarma dialect
  —— **Terms and phrases**
Niger-Congo languages
   BT Africa—Languages
        African languages
   NT Adamawa languages
        Badyaranke language
        Baka language (Cameroon)
        Balante language
        Banda languages
        Bedik language
        Benue-Congo languages
        Bullom language
        Cangin languages
        Diola language
        Feroge languages
        Fulah language
        Gbaya language
        Gola language
        Gur languages
        Kissi language
        Kwa languages
        Limba language
        Ma language

Niger-Congo languages *(Continued)*
    Mande languages
    Mandjak language
    Mankanya language
    Mundu language
    Ndogo-Sere languages
    Ngbaka ma'bo language
    Ngbandi language
    Sango language
    Serer language
    Timne language
    Wolof language
    Yakoma language
    Zande languages

Niger Expedition, 1841-1842
  [DT360]

Niger fiction (French) *(May Subd Geog)*
  [PQ3988.N5]
  UF French fiction—Niger authors
      French fiction—Nigerien authors
      Nigerien fiction (French)
  NT Short stories, Niger (French)

Niger lapis (Rome, Italy)
  USE Lapis niger (Rome, Italy)

Niger poetry (French) *(May Subd Geog)*
  [PQ3988.N5 (Collections)]
  [PQ3988.N5 (History)]
  UF French poetry—Niger authors
      French poetry—Nigerien authors
      Nigerien poetry (French)

Niger River
  UF River Niger
  BT Rivers—Africa, West
  NT Kainji Reservoir (Nigeria)

Niger short stories (French)
  USE Short stories, Niger (French)

Nigeria
  — Civilization
  — — Occidental influences
      BT Civilization, Occidental
  — Description and travel
  — — 1981-
  — Economic conditions
  — — To 1960
  — — 1960-
  — — 1970-
  — Foreign relations
  — — 1960-
  — History
      NT Senussite Rebellion, 1916-1918
  — — To 1851
      [DT515.65-515.66]
  — — 1851-1899
      [DT515.7-515.72]
  — — 1900-1960
      [DT515.7-515.76]
  — — 1960-
  — — Coup d'état, 1966 (January 15)
      BT Coups d'état—Nigeria
  — — Coup d'état, 1966 (July 29)
      (Not Subd Geog)
      BT Coups d'état—Nigeria
  — — Civil War, 1967-1970
      UF Biafran Conflict, 1967-1970
  — — — Causes
  — — — Charities
      USE Nigeria—History—Civil
          War, 1967-1970—War
          work
  — — — Civilian relief
      NT Nigeria—History—Civil War,
          1967-1970—War work
  — — — — Destruction and pillage
  — — — — Foreign public opinion
  — — — — Personal narratives
  — — — — Pictorial works
  — — — — Social work
      USE Nigeria—History—Civil
          War, 1967-1970—War
          work
  — — — War work

      UF Nigeria—History—Civil War,
          1967-1970—Charities
          Nigeria—History—Civil War,
          1967-1970—Social work
      BT Nigeria—History—Civil War,
          1967-1970—Civilian relief
  — — — — — Red Cross
      BT Red Cross
          War—Relief of sick and
          wounded
  — — Coup d'état, 1983
      BT Coups d'état—Nigeria
  — Languages
      NT Adamawa languages
          Bolewa languages
          Busa language
          Dendi dialect
          Efik language
          Etsako language
          Gbagyi language
          Guyuk dialect
          Ibibio language
          Igbo language
          Jukunoid languages
          Kamwe language
          Kanuri language
          Laamang language
          Longuda language
          Mumuye language
          Ngizim language
          Ngwa dialect
          Okpe language
          Pero language
          Plateau languages (Nigeria)
          Southern Bauchi languages
          Teda language
          Yamba language (Cameroon and
          Nigeria)
          Zarma dialect
  — Politics and government
  — — To 1960
  — — 1960-
  — — 1960-1975
  — — 1975-1979
  — — 1979-1983 *(Not Subd Geog)*
  — — 1984- *(May Subd Geog)*
  — Religion
      NT Godianism (Cult)
  — Social conditions
  — — 1960-

Nigeria, Eastern *(Not Subd Geog)*
  UF Eastern Nigera

Nigeria, Northern
  UF Northern Nigeria (Region)

Nigerian art
  USE Art, Nigerian

Nigerian atlases
  USE Atlases, Nigerian

Nigerian authors
  USE Authors, Nigerian

Nigerian chap-books
  USE Chap-books, Nigerian

Nigerian college verse (English)
  USE College verse, Nigerian (English)

Nigerian cookery
  USE Cookery, Nigerian

Nigerian drama *(May Subd Geog)*

Nigerian fiction (English)
  UF English fiction—Nigerian authors
  NT Short stories, Nigerian (English)

Nigerian folk poetry
  USE Folk poetry, Nigerian

Nigerian literature

Nigerian literature (English)
  [PR9387.5 (Collections)]
  [PR9387 (History)]
  UF English literature—Nigerian authors

Nigerian national characteristics
  USE National characteristics, Nigerian

Nigerian newspapers

Nigerian periodicals

Nigerian poetry *(May Subd Geog)*
  NT Folk poetry, Nigerian

Nigerian poetry (English) *(May Subd Geog)*
  UF English poetry—Nigerian authors
  NT College verse, Nigerian (English)

Nigerian poets
  USE Poets, Nigerian

Nigerian satire (English)
  USE Satire, Nigerian (English)

Nigerian sculpture
  USE Sculpture, Nigerian

Nigerian short stories (English)
  USE Short stories, Nigerian (English)

Nigerian soldiers' writings (English)
  USE Soldiers' writings, Nigerian (English)

Nigerian terra-cotta sculpture
  USE Terra-cotta sculpture, Nigerian

Nigerian toad
  USE Bufo regularis

Nigerians *(May Subd Geog)*
  BT Ethnology—Nigeria
  — Zaire
      NT Zaire—History—Civil War, 1960-
          1965—Participation, Nigerian

Nigerien fiction (French)
  USE Niger fiction (French)

Nigerien poetry (French)
  USE Niger poetry (French)

Nigerien short stories (French)
  USE Short stories, Niger (French)

Nigh family
  USE Nye family

Night
  BT Chronology
      Day
      Time

Night airglow
  USE Airglow

Night care in hospitals
  USE Hospitals—Night care

Night clubs
  USE Music-halls (Variety-theaters, cabarets,
      etc.)

Night depositories (Banking)
  USE Banks and banking—Night and curb
      depositories

Night driving
  USE Automobile driving at night

Night Ferry (Express train)
  UF Ferry Boat du Nuit (Express train)
  BT Railroads—Belgium—Express-trains
      Railroads—France—Express-trains
      Railroads—Great Britain—Express-
      trains

Night fighter planes
  [UG1242.F5]
  UF Night fighters (Airplanes)
  BT Fighter planes
  NT Irving (Night fighter plane)

Night fighters (Airplanes)
  USE Night fighter planes

Night fighting (Military science)
  [U167.5.N5]
  UF Fighting
  BT Drill and minor tactics
      Infantry drill and tactics
      Military art and science
      Tactics
  NT Night vision devices

Night fighting equipment industry
  (May Subd Geog)
  [HD9744.N53-HD9744.N534]

Night flying
  [TL711.N5]
  UF Flying, Night
  BT Instrument flying

Night in art
Night in literature
Night lamps *(May Subd Geog)*
  BT Lamps
Night lizards
  USE Xantusiidae
Night monkey
  USE Aotes trivirgatus
Night of mid-Shaʻbān
  USE Laylat al-Barāʼah
Night of the barāʼah
  USE Laylat al-Barāʼah
Night of the Long Knives, 1934
  USE Germany—History—Great Blood
      Purge, 1934
Night owls (Persons)
  USE Night people
Night people *(May Subd Geog)*
  UF Night owls (Persons)
      Nighttime people
      Nocturnal people
  BT Persons
Night photography
  USE Photography, Night
Night school students
  USE Evening and continuation school
      students
Night-schools
  USE Evening and continuation schools
Night soil
  [S657]
  BT Manures
      Organic fertilizers
      Organic wastes as fertilizer
Night sticks
  USE Truncheons
Night vision
  UF Dark adaptation (Vision)
  BT Eye—Adaptation
      Vision
  NT Automobile driving at night
Night vision devices
  BT Night fighting (Military science)
      Optical instruments
      Police—Equipment and supplies
  NT Starlight scopes
Night watch (Painting)
  USE Rembrandt Harmenszoon van Rijn,
      1606-1669. Night watch
Night watchmen
  USE Watchmen
Night work *(May Subd Geog)*
  [HD5113]
  BT Hours of labor
  NT Hospitals—Night care
      Shift systems
  — **Law and legislation** *(May Subd Geog)*
Nightclothes
  USE Sleepwear
Nightclubs
  USE Music-halls (Variety-theaters, cabarets,
      etc.)
Nightengale family
  USE Nightingale family
Nightfire Island Site (Calif.)
  (Not Subd Geog)
  BT California—Antiquities
Nightgowns
  USE Sleepwear
Nightingale award
  BT Nursing—Awards
Nightingale family *(Not Subd Geog)*
  UF Nightengale family
Nightingales
  [QL696.P2]
Nightmares *(May Subd Geog)*
  [BF1099.N53]
  UF Bad dreams
  BT Dreams

Nightmares in art
Nightshade, Black
  USE Solanum nigrum
Nightshade, Common
  USE Solanum nigrum
Nightshade family (Botany)
  USE Solanaceae
Nightshirts
  USE Sleepwear
Nighttime people
  USE Night people
Nightwear
  USE Sleepwear
Nightwear, Children's
  USE Children's sleepwear
Nigidal
  USE Nigidals
Nigidals
  UF Negda
      Negidals
      Nigidal
  BT Ethnology—Russian S.F.S.R.
      Tunguses
Nigorikawa Kaidō (Japan)
  BT Roads—Japan
Nigrillos
  USE Negrillos
Nigrosine
  BT Dyes and dyeing
Nigrospora
  [QK625.D4]
  BT Dematiaceae
Nigrospora musae
  [QK625.D4]
  RT Banana squirter disease
Nihali language
  USE Nahali language
Nihilianism
  UF Nihilism (Theology)
  BT Heresies, Christian—History—Middle
      Ages, 600-1500
Nihilism
  [HX914-HX917 (Russia)]
  UF Nihilists
  BT Political crimes and offenses
  RT Anarchism
  NT Soviet Union—History—19th century
Nihilism (Philosophy)
  BT Philosophy
  NT Meaninglessness (Philosophy)
      Nothing (Philosophy)
Nihilism (Theology)
  USE Nihilianism
Nihilism in literature
Nihilists
  USE Nihilism
Nihon Arupusu (Japan)
  USE Japanese Alps (Japan)
Nihon Gakushiin shō
Nihon Geijutsuin shō
  BT Arts—Competitions
Nihon-kai
  USE Japan, Sea of
Nihon Rōdō Kumiai Sōhyōgikai shō
  USE Sōhyō bungakushō
Nihon Rōru Strike, 1964
Nihongi Iseki (Ōno-machi, Ōita-ken, Japan)
  USE Nihongi Site (Ōno-machi, Ōita-ken,
      Japan)
Nihongi Site (Ōno-machi, Ōita-ken, Japan)
  (Not Subd Geog)
  UF Nihongi Iseki (Ōno-machi, Ōita-ken,
      Japan)
  BT Japan—Antiquities
Nihongi Wachino Iseki (Hakusan-chō, Mie-
  ken, Japan)
  USE Wachino Site (Hakusan-chō, Mie-ken,
      Japan)

Nihongi Wachino Site (Hakusan-chō, Mie-ken,
  Japan)
  USE Wachino Site (Hakusan-chō, Mie-ken,
      Japan)
Nii Island (Japan)
  UF Niishima (Japan)
  BT Islands—Japan
      Izu Islands (Japan)
Nii language
  UF Ek Nii language
  BT Papuan languages
Niigata Lowlands (Japan)
  USE Echigo Plain (Japan)
Niihama Iseki (Shiogama-shi, Japan)
  USE Niihama Site (Shiogama-shi, Japan)
Niihama Site (Shiogama-shi, Japan)
  (Not Subd Geog)
  UF Niihama Iseki (Shiogama-shi, Japan)
  BT Japan—Antiquities
Niihau (Hawaii)
  BT Hawaii
      Islands—Hawaii
Niinamesai
  BT Shinto—Rituals
Niishima (Japan)
  USE Nii Island (Japan)
Nijinsky (Race horse)
  BT Horses
Nijmegen, Peace of, 1678-1679
  [D278.5]
  BT Dutch War, 1672-1678
Nijō Castle (Kyoto, Japan)
  USE Nijōjō (Kyoto, Japan)
Nijō Mountain (Japan)
  UF Nijō-san (Japan)
  BT Mountains—Japan
Nijō-san (Japan)
  USE Nijō Mountain (Japan)
Nijōjō (Kyoto, Japan)
  UF Nijō Castle (Kyoto, Japan)
  BT Castles—Japan
Nika (African people)
  UF Mijikenda (African people)
      Nyika (African people)
      Wanika (African people)
  BT Ethnology—Kenya
      Ethnology—Tanzania
  NT Giryama (African people)
      Ribe (African people)
Nika language
  BT Bantu languages
  NT Digo language
      Giryama language
Nikaria Island (Greece)
  USE Ikaria Island (Greece)
Nikbolu, Battle of, 1396
  USE Nikopoli, Battle of, 1396
Nike (Greek deity)
  BT Gods, Greek
      Mythology, Greek
  RT Victoria (Roman deity)
Nike-Ajax rocket
  USE Nike rocket
Nike-Hercules rocket
  USE Nike rocket
Nike rocket
  UF Nike-Ajax rocket
      Nike-Hercules rocket
  BT Antiaircraft missiles
      Rockets (Ordnance)
      Surface-to-air missiles
Niken'ya Iseki (Japan)
  USE Niken'ya Site (Japan)
Niken'ya Site (Japan)
  UF Niken'ya Iseki (Japan)
  BT Excavations (Archaeology)—Japan
      Japan—Antiquities
Nikhak Site (Alaska)
  USE Kijik Site (Alaska)
Nikhkak Site (Alaska)
  USE Kijik Site (Alaska)

Nikkō Dōchū (Japan)
  USE Nikkō Kaidō (Japan)
Nikkō Higashi Dōchū (Japan)
  USE Nikkō Kaidō (Japan)
Nikkō Kaidō (Japan)
  UF Higashi Nikkō Kaidō (Japan)
      Nikkō Dōchū (Japan)
      Nikkō Higashi Dōchū (Japan)
  BT Roads—Japan
Nikkō Kokuritsu Kōen (Japan)
  UF Nikko National Park (Japan)
  BT National parks and reserves—Japan
Nikko National Park (Japan)
  USE Nikkō Kokuritsu Kōen (Japan)
Nikkorex camera
  USE Nikkormat camera
Nikkormat camera
  [TR263.N]
  UF Nikkorex camera
  BT Cameras
      Nikon camera
Nikobar language
  USE Nicobarese language
Nikolayevsk-na-Amure Incident, 1920
  [DK265.8.N5]
  BT Soviet Union—History—Allied
      intervention, 1918-1920
Nikon camera
  NT Nikkormat camera
      Nikonos camera
Nikonos camera
  [TR263.N]
  BT Nikon camera
Nikopoli, Battle of, 1396
  [DR496]
  UF Nicopolis, Battle of, 1396
      Nikbolu, Battle of, 1396
  BT Turkey—History—1288-1453
Nīl River
  USE Nile River
Nilamba language
  UF Ilamba language
      Iramba language
      Kiniramba language
      Nilyamba language
      Niramba language
  BT Bantu languages
Nile, Battle of the, 1798
  [DC226.N5]
  UF Aboukir, Battle of, 1798
  BT Second Coalition, War of the, 1798-
      1801—Campaigns—Egypt
Nile family
  USE Niles family
Nile mosaic (Palestrina)
  [NA3770]
  UF Barberini mosaic
      Nilotic mosaic
      Palestrina mosaic
  BT Mosaics—Italy
      Mosaics, Roman—Italy
      Pavements, Mosaic—Italy
  — Adaptation
      USE Nile mosaic (Palestrina)—
          Copying
  — Copying
      UF Nile mosaic (Palestrina)—
          Adaptation
      BT Mosaics—Copying
Nile perch
  [QL638.C34]
  UF Capitaine
      Lates niloticus
Nile River
  UF Bahr en Nīl
      Nahr an Nīl
      Nīl River
      Nilus River
  BT Rivers—Africa
  — **Barrages**
  — **Regulation**

— **Religious aspects**
Nile River, Blue (Ethiopia and Sudan)
  USE Blue Nile River (Ethiopia and Sudan)
Niles family *(Not Subd Geog)*
  UF Nile family
      Nilles family
      Niols family
      Nyles family
Nilgiri Hills (India)
  UF Nilgiris (India)
  BT Mountains—India
Nilgiris (India)
  USE Nilgiri Hills (India)
Nilles family
  USE Niles family
Nilo-Hamitic languages
  BT Africa, Eastern—Languages
      Hamitic languages
      Nilo-Saharan languages
      Nilotic languages
  NT Bari language
      Baria language
      Karamojong language
      Latuka language
      Masai language
      Nandi languages
      Teso language
      Toposa language
      Turkana language
Nilo-Hamitic tribes
  [GN659.N5]
  BT Ethnology—Africa, East
  NT Alur (African people)
      Barabaig (African people)
      Dodoth (African people)
      Dorobo (African people)
      Hamites
      Jie (African people)
      Kipsigis (African people)
      Marakwet (African people)
      Nandi (African people)
      Samburu
      Sandawe
      Sapiny (African people)
      Suk (African people)
      Teso tribe
      Turkana (African people)
Nilo-Saharan languages
  BT Africa—Languages
      African languages
  NT Balese language
      Birri language
      Bongo-Bagirmi languages
      Daza language
      Fur language
      Ingassana language
      Kanuri language
      Kunama language
      Logbara language
      Maba language
      Ma'di language (Uganda and Sudan)
      Mamvu language
      Mangbetu language
      Meroitic language
      Moru language
      Murle language
      Nilo-Hamitic languages
      Nilotic languages
      Nubian language
      Songhai language
      Teda language
      Teuso languages
      Uduk language
Nilotaspis
  [QL527.D44]
  BT Delphacidae
  NT Nilotaspis halli
Nilotaspis halli
  [QL527.D44]
  UF Hall scale
  BT Nilotaspis

Nilotes
  USE Nilotic tribes
Nilotic Kavirondo language
  USE Luo language (Kenya and Tanzania)
Nilotic languages
  [PL8026]
  BT Africa, Eastern—Languages
      Nilo-Saharan languages
  NT Acoli language
      Alur language
      Anuak language
      Dinka language
      Lango language
      Luo language (Kenya and Tanzania)
      Lwo language (Sudan)
      Maban language
      Nilo-Hamitic languages
      Nuer language
      Päri language (Sudan)
      Shilluk language
Nilotic mosaic
  USE Nile mosaic (Palestrina)
Nilotic position
  USE One-leg resting position
Nilotic tribes
  [DT132]
  UF Nilotes
  BT Ethnology—Sudan
      Ethnology—Uganda
  NT Atuot (African people)
      Dinka (African people)
      Luo (African people)
      Maban (African people)
      Nuer (African people)
Nilpotent groups
  USE Groups, Nilpotent
Nilpotent Lie groups
  USE Lie groups, Nilpotent
Nilsen family *(Not Subd Geog)*
  UF Nilson family
      Nilsson family
  RT Nelson family
      Nielsen family
Nilson family
  USE Nilsen family
Nilsson family
  USE Nilsen family
Nilsson model
  UF Deformed shell model
      Model, Nilsson
      Shell model, Deformed
  BT Nuclear models
      Nuclear shell theory
      Nuclear spectroscopy
      Nuclear structure
Nilus River
  USE Nile River
Nilyamba language
  USE Nilamba language
Nim
  USE Margosa
Nim (Chimpanzee)
  USE Nim Chimpsky (Chimpanzee)
Nim Chimpsky (Chimpanzee)
  [QL737.P96]
  UF Nim (Chimpanzee)
  BT Chimpanzees
Nimadi dialect
  [PK2521]
  UF Nemadi dialect
      Nimari dialect
  BT India—Languages
      Rajasthani language
Nimadi folk-songs
  USE Folk-songs, Nimadi
Nimadi poetry *(May Subd Geog)*
Nimadi proverbs
  USE Proverbs, Nimadi
Nimapu
  USE Nez Percé Indians

Nimaree language
  USE Nahali language
Nimari dialect
  USE Nimadi dialect
Nīmāvats
  USE Nimbarka (Sect)
Nimbarka (Sect)
  _[BL1286.5-1286.592]_
  UF Nīmāvats
      Sanaka (Sect)
  BT Hindu sects
      Vaishnavism
Nimbi language
  USE Nembe language
Nimboran language
  BT Papuan languages
Nimbus
Nimbus (Art)
  [N8160 (Christian art)]
  [N8193.3.N54 (Buddhist art)]
  UF Aureola (Art)
      Halo (Art)
  BT Art
      Buddhist art and symbolism
      Christian art and symbolism
      Symbolism in art
Nimbus (Meteorological satellite)
  _[TL798.M4]_
  BT Meteorological satellites
      Project Nimbus
Nimbus Dam (Calif.) _(Not Subd Geog)_
  BT Dams—California
Nimbus project
  USE Project Nimbus
Nimergoline
  USE Nicergoline
Nimipu
  USE Nez Percé Indians
Nimmo family _(Not Subd Geog)_
Nimonic alloys
  BT Heat resistant alloys
      Metals at high temperatures
      Nickel-chromium alloys
Nimrod Lake (Ark.)
  UF Nimrod Reservoir (Ark.)
  BT Fourche La Fave River (Ark.)
      Lakes—Arkansas
      Reservoirs—Arkansas
Nimrod Reservoir (Ark.)
  USE Nimrod Lake (Ark.)
Nimrud (Iraq)
  USE Calah (Ancient city)
Nimrud ivories
  USE Ivories, Assyro-Babylonian
Nims family _(Not Subd Geog)_
Nine, Rule of the, Siena (Italy), 1287-1355
  USE Siena (Italy)—History—Rule of the
      Nine, 1287-1355
Nine (The number)
  _[QA142]_
  BT Symbolism of numbers
Nine-banded armadillo
  _[QL737.E23]_
  UF Dasypus novemcinctus
      Peba
  BT Dasypus
Nine family _(Not Subd Geog)_
  RT Neun family
Nine Mile Point Nuclear Power Plant (N.Y.)
  USE James A. FitzPatrick/Nine Mile Point
      Nuclear Power Plant (N.Y.)
Nine-pipe National Wildlife Refuge (Mont.)
  USE Ninepipe National Wildlife Refuge
      (Mont.)
Nine Years' War, 1689-1697
  USE Grand Alliance, War of the, 1689-
      1697
Ninepins
  _[GV910.5.N5]_
  BT Bowling games

Ninepipe National Wildlife Refuge (Mont.)
  (Not Subd Geog)
  UF Nine-pipe National Wildlife Refuge
      (Mont.)
  BT National parks and reserves—Montana
      Wildlife refuges—Montana
Nineteen hundred thirty-nine, A.D.
  USE Nineteen thirty-nine, A.D.
Nineteen thirty-nine, A.D.
  UF 1939 A.D.
      Nineteen hundred thirty-nine, A.D.
  BT Twentieth century
Nineteenth century
  [CB415-CB417 (Civilization)]
  _[D351-D363]_
  NT Civilization, Modern—19th century
      Eighteen forty-four, A.D.
  — Biography
      USE Biography—19th century
Ninety-nine (Game)
  _[GV1469.N5]_
Ninety-Six Ranch (Nev.) _(Not Subd Geog)_
  BT Ranches—Nevada
Nineveh (Ancient city)
  _[DS70.N47]_
  UF Ninos (Ancient city)
      Ninus (Ancient city)
  BT Cities and towns, Ruined, extinct, etc.
      —Iraq
      Iraq—Antiquities
Ningmapa
  USE Rñiṅ-ma-pa (Sect)
Ningpo River (Chekiang Province, China)
  USE Yung River (Chekiang Province,
      China)
Ninia
  _[QL666.O636]_
  BT Colubridae
Ninia sebae
  _[QL666.O636]_
  UF Coffee snake, Seba's
      Seba's coffee snake
Ninjitsu
  USE Ninjutsu
Ninjutsu
  _[UB271.J3]_
  UF Ninjitsu
  BT Espionage
      Military art and science
Niño Current
  USE El Niño Current
Ninos (Ancient city)
  USE Nineveh (Ancient city)
Ninstints Site (B.C.) _(Not Subd Geog)_
  UF Quee-ah Site (B.C.)
      Red Cod Island Town (B.C.)
      Sqa'ngwa-i Inaga'i (B.C.)
  BT British Columbia—Antiquities
Ninth grade (Education)
  UF Freshman class (High school)
  BT Education, Secondary
Ninth of Av
  USE Tish'ah be-Av
Nintooa
  USE Honeysuckle
Ninus (Ancient city)
  USE Nineveh (Ancient city)
Niō (Buddhist deity)
  USE Vajradhara (Buddhist deity)
Nio Island (Greece)
  USE Ios Island (Greece)
Niobates
  UF Columbates
  NT Lithium niobate
Niobium _(May Subd Geog)_
  UF Columbium
  — Isotopes
  — — Decay
  — Magnetic properties
  — Metallography
  — Metallurgy

  — Spectra
      _[QC462.M3]_
Niobium alloys
  NT Niobium-tantalum alloys
      Niobium-zirconium alloys
      Tungsten-niobium alloys
  — Metallography
Niobium industry _(May Subd Geog)_
  _[HD9539.N54-HD9539.N544]_
Niobium ores _(May Subd Geog)_
  UF Columbium ores
Niobium-tantalum alloys
  UF Tantalum-niobium alloys
  BT Niobium alloys
      Tantalum alloys
Niobium-tungsten alloys
  USE Tungsten-niobium alloys
Niobium-zirconium alloys
  UF Zirconium-niobium alloys
  BT Niobium alloys
      Zirconium alloys
Niobrara Formation _(Not Subd Geog)_
  UF Niobrara Limestone
  BT Formations (Geology)—West (U.S.)
      Geology, Stratigraphic—Cretaceous
Niobrara Limestone
  USE Niobrara Formation
Niols family
  USE Niles family
Nios Island (Greece)
  USE Ios Island (Greece)
Nipa (Plant)
  USE Nypa
Niphogeton
  _[QK495.U48]_
  BT Umbelliferae
Nipissing, Lake (Ont.)
  UF Lake Nipissing (Ont.)
  BT Lakes—Ontario
Nipissing Indians
  _[E99.N]_
  BT Algonquian Indians
      Indians of North America
  NT Oka Indians
Nipissing language
  _[PM2025]_
  RT Algonquian languages
Nipmuc Indians
  _[E99.N7]_
  BT Algonquian Indians
      Indians of North America
Nipper (Dog)
  BT Dogs
Nippers
Nippon Electric Company PC-8200
  (Computer)
  USE NEC PC-8200 (Computer)
Nippon Electric Company PC-8201
  (Computer)
  USE NEC PC-8201 (Computer)
Nippon Electric Company PC-8201A
  (Computer)
  USE NEC PC-8201A (Computer)
Nippon-kai
  USE Japan, Sea of
Nipponia
  _[QL696.C585]_
  BT Threskiornithidae
Nipponia nippon
  _[QL696.C585]_
  UF Crested ibis
      Japanese crested ibis
Nippostrongylus _(May Subd Geog)_
  _[QL391.N4]_
  BT Trichostrongylidae
  NT Nippostrongylus brasiliensis
      Nippostrongylus muris
Nippostrongylus brasiliensis
  (May Subd Geog)
  _[QL391.N4]_
  BT Nippostrongylus

Nippostrongylus muris *(May Subd Geog)*
  ₍QL391.N4₎
  BT Nippostrongylus
Nippur (Ancient city) *(Not Subd Geog)*
  UF Niffer (Ancient city)
      Nuffar (Ancient city)
  BT Cities and towns, Ruined, extinct, etc.
      —Iraq
      Iraq—Antiquities
Niquiranos
  USE Nicarao Indians
Niquiras
  USE Nicarao Indians
Niquitao, Battle of, 1813
  ₍E2324₎
  BT Venezuela—History—War of
      Independence, 1810-1823—
      Campaigns
Niramalas
  USE Nirmalas
Niramba language
  USE Nilamba language
Niranjanis
  ₍BL1245.N55₎
  BT Hindu sects
Nirankari gurus *(May Subd Geog)*
  UF Gurus, Nirankari
Nirankaris
  ₍BL2018.7.N₎
  BT Sikh sects
Nirātman
  USE Anātman
Nirere dialect
  UF Abri dialect (Sudan)
Nirmalas *(May Subd Geog)*
  ₍BL2018.7.N59₎
  UF Niramalas
      Nirmālins
  BT Sikh sects
Nirmālins
  USE Nirmalas
Nirmāṇakāya (Buddhism)
  USE Buddha (The concept)
Nirodha-samāpatti
  USE Nirodhasamāpatti
Nirodhasamāpatti
  ₍BQ4327₎
  UF Attainment of cessation (Buddhism)
      Attainment of extinction (Buddhism)
      Cessation, Attainment of (Buddhism)
      Extinction, Attainment of (Buddhism)
      Nirodha-samāpatti
  BT Buddhism—Doctrines
      Consciousness—Religious aspects—
      Buddhism
Nirvana
  BT Eightfold Path
      Eschatology
  NT Enlightenment (Buddhism)
Nirvanidae
  USE Leafhoppers
Nisbet family
  USE Nesbitt family
Nisbett family
  USE Nesbitt family
Nisbit family
  USE Nesbitt family
Nisbitt family
  USE Nesbitt family
Nise family
  USE Neis family
Nisei
  USE Japanese Americans
Nisenan Indians
  UF Nishinam Indians
  BT Indians of North America—California
      Maidu Indians
Nisenan language
  UF Nishinam language
  BT Maidu language

Nishga Indians
  USE Niska Indians
Nishi Miyayama Kofun (Tatsuno-shi, Japan)
  USE Nishi Miyayama Tomb (Tatsuno-shi,
      Japan)
Nishi Miyayama Tomb (Tatsuno-shi, Japan)
  (Not Subd Geog)
  UF Nishi Miyayama Kofun (Tatsuno-shi,
      Japan)
  BT Japan—Antiquities
      Tombs—Japan
Nishi Nihon Tetsudo
  BT Bus lines—Japan
      Electric railroads—Japan
      Railroads—Japan
Nishi-omote-shima (Japan)
  USE Iriomote Island (Japan)
Nishi-ura (Japan)
  USE Kasumigaura (Japan)
Nishigōchi Kami Iseki (Ochiai-chō, Japan)
  USE Nishigōchi Kami Site (Ochiai-chō,
      Japan)
Nishigōchi Kami Site (Ochiai-chō, Japan)
  (Not Subd Geog)
  UF Nishigōchi Kami Iseki (Ochiai-chō,
      Japan)
  BT Japan—Antiquities
Nishikamoe Nakahara Iseki (Hamamatsu-shi,
  Japan)
  USE Nakahira Site (Hamamatsu-shi, Japan)
Nishikiori Iseki (Tondabayashi-shi, Japan)
  USE Nishikiori Site (Tondabayashi-shi,
      Japan)
Nishikiori Site (Tondabayashi-shi, Japan)
  (Not Subd Geog)
  UF Nishikiori Iseki (Tondabayashi-shi,
      Japan)
  BT Japan—Antiquities
Nishina family *(Not Subd Geog)*
Nishinahua language
  USE Jaminaua language
Nishinam Indians
  USE Nisenan Indians
Nishinam language
  USE Nisenan language
Nishing (Indic people)
  USE Dafla (Indic people)
Nishioku Iseki (Mitsu-chō, Okayama-ken,
  Japan)
  USE Nishioku Site (Mitsu-chō, Okayama-
      ken, Japan)
Nishioku Site (Mitsu-chō, Okayama-ken,
  Japan) *(Not Subd Geog)*
  UF Nishioku Iseki (Mitsu-chō, Okayama-
      ken, Japan)
  BT Japan—Antiquities
Nishisaigyō Iseki (Azuchi-chō, Japan)
  USE Nishisaigyō Site (Azuchi-chō, Japan)
Nishisaigyō Site (Azuchi-chō, Japan)
  UF Nishisaigyō Iseki (Azuchi-chō, Japan)
  BT Japan—Antiquities
Nishiyama Iseki (Suwa-shi, Japan)
  USE Nishiyama Site (Suwa-shi, Japan)
Nishiyama Site (Suwa-shi, Japan)
  (Not Subd Geog)
  UF Nishiyama Iseki (Suwa-shi, Japan)
  BT Japan—Antiquities
Nisi Dominus (Music)
  USE Psalms (Music)—127th Psalm
Nisi prius
  BT Actions and defenses
      Civil procedure
      Jury
Nisin
  BT Antibiotics
Nisiro Island (Greece)
  USE Nisyros Island (Greece)
Nisiros Island (Greece)
  USE Nisyros Island (Greece)

Niska Indians
  UF Nass River Indians
      Nishga Indians
  BT Chimmesyan Indians
      Indians of North America
Niska language
  ₍PM2026.N3₎
  UF Nasqua language
  RT Chimmesyan languages
Nísos Aíyina (Greece)
  USE Aegina Island (Greece)
Nísos Alónnisos (Greece)
  USE Alónnisos Island (Greece)
Nísos Amorgós (Greece)
  USE Amorgos Island (Greece)
Nísos Andíparos (Greece)
  USE Antiparos Island (Greece)
Nísos Andros (Greece)
  USE Andros Island (Greece)
Nísos Chálkē (Greece)
  USE Khalki Island (Greece)
Nísos Dhflos (Greece)
  USE Delos Island (Greece)
Nísos Évvoia (Greece)
  USE Euboea Island (Greece)
Nísos Ikaría (Greece)
  USE Ikaria Island (Greece)
Nísos Íos (Greece)
  USE Ios Island (Greece)
Nísos Itháki (Greece)
  USE Ithaca Island (Greece)
Nísos Kárpathos (Greece)
  USE Karpathos Island (Greece)
Nísos Kásos (Greece)
  USE Kasos Island (Greece)
Nísos Kefallinía (Greece)
  USE Cephalonia Island (Greece)
Nísos Kérkira (Greece)
  USE Corfu Island (Greece)
Nísos Khíos (Greece)
  USE Chios Island (Greece)
Nisos Kithira (Greece)
  USE Kythēra Island (Greece)
Nísos Kos (Greece)
  USE Kos Island (Greece)
Nísos Lésvos (Greece)
  USE Lesbos Island (Greece)
Nísos Levkás (Greece)
  USE Levkás Island (Greece)
Nísos Megisti (Greece)
  USE Kastellorizo Island (Greece)
Nísos Míkonos (Greece)
  USE Mykonos Island (Greece)
Nísos Mílos (Greece)
  USE Melos Island (Greece)
Nísos Nísiros (Greece)
  USE Nisyros Island (Greece)
Nísos Páros (Greece)
  USE Paros Island (Greece)
Nísos Pátmos (Greece)
  USE Patmos Island (Greece)
Nísos Paxoí (Greece)
  USE Paxos Island (Greece)
Nisos Peristera (Greece)
  USE Peristera Island (Greece)
Nísos Ródhos (Greece)
  USE Rhodes (Greece : Island)
Nísos Sámos (Greece)
  USE Samos Island (Greece)
Nísos Samothráki (Greece)
  USE Samothrace Island (Greece)
Nísos Sariá (Greece)
  USE Saria Island (Greece)
Nísos Sími (Greece)
  USE Sími Island (Greece)
Nisos Siros (Greece)
  USE Syros Island (Greece)
Nisos Skiathos (Greece)
  USE Skiathos Island (Greece)
Nísos Skíros (Greece)
  USE Skyros Island (Greece)

Nísos Skópelos (Greece)
USE Skopelos Island (Greece)
Nísos Thásos (Greece)
USE Thasos Island (Greece)
Nísos Thíra (Greece)
USE Thera Island (Greece)
Nísos Tílos (Greece)
USE Telos Island (Greece)
Nísos Tínos (Greece)
USE Tinos Island (Greece)
Nísos tōn Iōanninōn (Greece)
USE Iōannina Island (Greece)
Nísos Yíaros (Greece)
USE Gyaros Island (Greece)
Nísos Yioúra (Greece)
USE Gyaros Island (Greece)
Nisos Zakinthos (Greece)
USE Zakynthos Island (Greece)
Nispero
USE Loquat
Nisqualli Indians
⌈E99.N74⌉
BT Coast Salish Indians
Indians of North America
Nisqualli language
⌈PM2026.N5⌉
BT Salishan languages
Nissan automobile
BT Automobiles
NT Bluebird automobile
Datsun automobile
Maxima automobile
Sentra automobile
Nissan Group
BT Conglomerate corporations—Japan
Nissan Sentra automobile
USE Sentra automobile
Nissan trucks
⌈TL230.5.N⌉
BT Trucks
NT Datsun truck
Nissen family
UF Nisson family
Nissi (Indic people)
USE Dafla (Indic people)
Nissl bodies
UF Tigroid bodies
BT Nerves
Neurons
Nissl degeneration
USE Nervous system—Degeneration
Nisson family
USE Nissen family
Nistru River (Ukraine and Moldavian S.S.R.)
USE Dniester River (Ukraine and
Moldavian S.S.R.)
Nistrul River (Ukraine and Moldavian S.S.R.)
USE Dniester River (Ukraine and
Moldavian S.S.R.)
Nisyros Island (Greece)
UF Nisiro Island (Greece)
Nisiros Island (Greece)
Nísos Nísiros (Greece)
BT Dodecanese
Islands—Greece
Nitendi (Solomon Islands)
USE Nendö (Solomon Islands)
Niter
USE Saltpeter
Nitidulidae
⌈QL596.N58⌉
UF Cateretidae
Sap beetles
Smicripidae
BT Beetles
NT Meligethes
Stelidota
Niton
USE Radon
Nitramines
USE Nitroamines

Nitrate industry (May Subd Geog)
⌈HD9660.N3-5⌉
BT Nitrates
Nitrate of iron
USE Ferric nitrate
Nitrate of potash
USE Saltpeter
Nitrate of silver
USE Silver nitrate
Nitrate of soda
USE Saltpeter, Chile
Nitrate-reducing bacteria
USE Bacteria, Denitrifying
Nitrates
⌈QD181.N1 (Chemistry)⌉
⌈QP535.N1 (Physiological chemistry)⌉
⌈S651 (Fertilizers)⌉
⌈TN911 (Mineral industries)⌉
⌈TP237-TP238 (Chemical technology)⌉
NT Aluminum nitrate
Ammonium nitrate
Nitrate industry
Nitroglycerin
Rare earth nitrates
— Physiological effect
⌈QP913.N1⌉
NT Plants, Effect of nitrates on
— Spectra
Nitration
⌈QD63.N (Chemistry)⌉
⌈QD281.N5 (Organic chemistry)⌉
Nitre
USE Saltpeter
Nitrendipine
UF Ethyl methyl dihydrodimethylnitro
phenylpyridinedicarboxylate
BT Calcium—Antagonists
Carboxylic acids
Hypotensive agents
Pyridine
Nitrenes
UF Imidogen derivatives
BT Nitrogen compounds
Nitric acid
⌈QD181.N1⌉
⌈TP217.N5 (Chemical technology)⌉
Nitric acid ammonium salt
USE Ammonium nitrate
Nitrides
BT Heat resistant alloys
Surface hardening
NT Boron nitride
Silicon nitride
Transition metal nitrides
Nitriding
BT Case hardening
Surface hardening
RT Carbonitriding
Nitrification
⌈S651-S652 (Agriculture)⌉
⌈TD433 (Water-supply)⌉
Here are entered works dealing with the forma-
tion of nitrites and nitrates in soil, sewage sludge, etc.
from other nitrogenous compounds by micro-organ-
isms. Works dealing with the uptake of free nitrogen,
either by micro-organisms or by some technical or
natural processes, are entered under the heading Ni-
trogen—Fixation.
BT Oxidation
RT Bacteria, Nitrifying
Denitrification
Nitrification inhibitors (May Subd Geog)
⌈SB951.45 (Agriculture)⌉
UF Inhibitors, Nitrification
Nitrification suppressants
BT Nitrogen—Fixation
Nitrification suppressants
USE Nitrification inhibitors
Nitrifying bacteria
USE Bacteria, Nitrifying
Nitrile rubber
BT Rubber, Artificial

Nitriles
⌈QD305.N7⌉
⌈QD341.N7⌉
NT Acrylonitrile
Gallopamil
Milrinone
Phenylbutyronitrile
Succinonitrile
Nitriloside
USE Laetrile
Nitrilotriacetic acid
BT Acetic acid
Nitrites
⌈QD181.N1⌉
Nitro compounds
⌈QD305.N8⌉
⌈QD341.A8⌉
NT Nitroimidazoles
Nitroquinoline oxide
Nitroamines
⌈QD305.A8⌉
⌈QD341.A8⌉
UF Nitramines
Nitrobacteria
USE Bacteria, Nitrifying
Nitrobenzoic acid
⌈QD341.A2⌉
Nitrocellulose
⌈TP276⌉
UF Cellulose nitrates
BT Cellulose
RT Guncotton
NT Explosives
Nitrofurans
BT Furans
NT Nifuratel
Nitrogen
⌈QD181.N1 (Chemistry)⌉
⌈TP261.N7 (Electrochemistry)⌉
BT Nonmetals
NT Active nitrogen
Liquid nitrogen
Metals—Nitrogen content
Protein nitrogen
Soils—Nitrogen content
Steel—Nitrogen content
Water—Nitrogen content
— Assimilation and excretion
USE Nitrogen excretion
— Excretion
USE Nitrogen excretion
— Fixation
⌈QR89.7 (Microbiology)⌉
⌈TP245.N8 (Chemical technology)⌉
Here are entered works dealing with the proc-
ess of taking up free nitrogen, either by micro-
organisms or by some technical or natural pro-
cesses. Works dealing with the formation of ni-
trites and nitrates in soil, sewage sludge, etc.
from other nitrogenous compounds by micro-or-
ganisms are entered under the heading Nitrifica-
tion.
UF Dinitrogen fixation
Fixation of nitrogen
Nitrogen fixation
BT Biogeochemical cycles
RT Micro-organisms, Nitrogen-fixing
NT Green manuring
Nitrification inhibitors
— Isotopes
UF Nitrogen isotopes
— Optical properties
— Physiological effect
NT Plants, Effect of nitrogen on
— Spectra
— Thermal properties
Nitrogen compounds
⌈QD181.N1⌉
⌈TP245.N8 (Chemical technology)⌉
NT Alkaloids
Amic acids
Carbenicillin

Nitrogen compounds *(Continued)*
 Nitrenes
 Nitrogen mustards
 Organonitrogen compounds
— **Spectra**
Nitrogen cycle *(May Subd Geog)*
 BT Biogeochemical cycles
Nitrogen dioxide
 BT Nitrogen oxides
 Oxides
Nitrogen excretion
 [QP211]
 UF Nitrogen—Assimilation and excretion
 Nitrogen—Excretion
 BT Excretion
 NT Alloxuric substances
 Urea
 Xanthine
Nitrogen fertilizers *(May Subd Geog)*
 [S651 (Agriculture)]
 BT Fertilizers
 NT Urea as fertilizer
— **Control**
 UF Control of nitrogen fertilizer use
 Restricted use of nitrogen
 fertilizers
Nitrogen fixation
 USE Nitrogen—Fixation
Nitrogen-fixing algae *(May Subd Geog)*
 BT Algae
 Micro-organisms, Nitrogen-fixing
Nitrogen-fixing algae as fertilizer
 (May Subd Geog)
 BT Fertilizers
Nitrogen-fixing micro-organisms
 USE Micro-organisms, Nitrogen-fixing
Nitrogen in animal nutrition
 [SF98.N5]
 BT Animal nutrition
Nitrogen in metals
 USE Metals—Nitrogen content
Nitrogen in soils
 USE Soils—Nitrogen content
Nitrogen in steel
 USE Steel—Nitrogen content
Nitrogen in the body
 [QP535.N1]
 BT Metabolism
 NT Azotemia
Nitrogen in water
 USE Water—Nitrogen content
Nitrogen industries *(May Subd Geog)*
 NT Fertilizer industry
 Saltpeter
Nitrogen isotopes
 USE Nitrogen—Isotopes
Nitrogen mustards
 BT Antineoplastic agents
 Nitrogen compounds
Nitrogen organic compounds
 USE Organonitrogen compounds
Nitrogen oxides
 BT Oxides
 NT Nitrogen dioxide
 Nitrous oxide
Nitrogen oxychlorides
 BT Oxychlorides
 NT Chlorine nitrate
 Nitrosyl chloride
Nitrogen removal (Sewage purification)
 USE Sewage—Purification—Nitrogen
 removal
Nitrogen removal (Water purification)
 USE Water—Purification—Nitrogen
 removal
Nitrogen supersaturation *(May Subd Geog)*
 UF Dissolved nitrogen supersaturation
 Supersaturated nitrogen
 BT Dams—Environmental aspects
 Spillways—Design and construction
 Water—Nitrogen content

 NT Gas bubble disease in fish
Nitroglycerin
 [TP285]
 UF Blasting oil
 Glonoin
 Glyceryl trinitrate
 Trinitrin
 BT Explosives
 Glycerin
 Nitrates
— **Therapeutic use**
 [RM666.N725]
 BT Vasodilators
Nitroimidazoles
 [QD401 (Organic chemistry)]
 [RM666.N727 (Pharmacology)]
 BT Imidazole
 Nitro compounds
 Radiation-sensitizing agents
 NT Metronidazole
Nitroparaffins
Nitrophenyldimethyldicarbomethoxydihydro
 pyridine
 USE Nifedipine
Nitrophenylfuranylmethyleneaminoimidazol
 idinedione
 USE Dantrolene
Nitroprusside
 USE Sodium nitroferricyanide
Nitroprusside, Sodium
 USE Sodium nitroferricyanide
Nitroquinoline oxide
 [RC268.7.N57 (Carcinogen)]
 BT Nitro compounds
 Organonitrogen compounds
 Oxides
 Quinoline
Nitrosamides
 BT Amides
 Nitroso-compounds
— **Decontamination**
Nitrosamines
 USE Nitrosoamines
Nitrosation
 BT Chemical reactions
 RT Nitroso-compounds
Nitroso-compounds
 [QD305.N8]
 [QD341.N8]
 RT Nitrosation
 NT Nitrosamides
 Nitrosoamines
 Nitrosoureas
— **Spectra**
Nitrosoamines
 UF Nitrosamines
 BT Amines
 Nitroso-compounds
Nitrosoureas
 [RC271.N56]
 BT Antineoplastic agents
 Nitroso-compounds
 Urea
 NT Streptozotocin
Nitrosyl chloride
 BT Nitrogen oxychlorides
Nitrous acid
 [QD181.N1]
Nitrous oxide
 [QD181.N1]
 [RD86.N7 (Anesthetics)]
 UF Laughing-gas
 BT Anesthetics
 Nitrogen oxides
Nitrous oxide, Atmospheric
 UF Atmospheric nitrous oxide
 BT Atmosphere
Nitta family *(Not Subd Geog)*
Niuaks
 USE Anuaks

Niué language
 USE Niuean language
Niuean language
 UF Niué language
 BT Polynesian languages
Niulakita (Tuvalu)
 UF Independence (Tuvalu)
 Mattinson (Tuvalu)
 Nukulakita (Tuvalu)
 Nurakito (Tuvalu)
 Rocky Island (Tuvalu)
 Sophia Island (Tuvalu)
 BT Coral reefs and islands—Tuvalu
Niumi (Kingdom)
 [DT532.23]
 BT Gambia—History
 Mandingo (African people)
 Senegal—History
Niutao (Tuvalu)
 UF Lynx (Tuvalu)
 Sepper Island (Tuvalu)
 Speiden Island (Tuvalu)
 BT Coral reefs and islands—Tuvalu
Niva automobile
 [TL215.N]
 BT Automobiles—Soviet Union
Nivacle language
 USE Chulupí language
Nivation *(May Subd Geog)*
 BT Weathering
Nivkh
 USE Gilyaks
Nivkh language
 USE Gilyak language
Nivkhi
 USE Gilyaks
Nizhegorodsko-Syzranskaĭa zheleznaĭa doroga
 BT Railroads—Soviet Union
Nizinne czerwono-biała bydło
 USE Polish red and white lowland cattle
Nizip, Battle of, 1839
 [DT104]
 BT Egypt—History—19th century
 Turkey—History—1829-1878
Nizke Beskydy (Poland and Czechoslovakia)
 USE East Beskids (Poland and
 Czechoslovakia)
Nizo camera
Njangamada language
 USE Nyangumata language
Njangomada language
 USE Nyangumata language
Njangumada language
 USE Nyangumata language
Njangumarda language
 USE Nyangumata language
Njangumata language
 USE Nyangumata language
Njarasa, Lake (Tanzania)
 USE Eyasi, Lake (Tanzania)
Njassa See
 USE Nyasa, Lake
Njavi (African people)
 USE Nzabi (African people)
Njawi (African people)
 USE Nzabi (African people)
Njemps (African people)
 UF Njempsian (African people)
 Tiamus (African people)
 BT Ethnology—Kenya
Njempsian (African people)
 USE Njemps (African people)
Njuṇar dialects
 USE Nyungar dialects
Njungene language
 USE Limbum language
NK cells
 USE Killer cells
Nkâmi (African people)
 USE Nkomi (African people)

Nkengo language
  USE Lonkengo language
Nkhonde (African people)
  USE Ngonde (African people)
Nkole language
  USE Nyankole language
Nkom (African people)
  USE Kom (African people)
Nkomi (African people)
  ₍DT546.145.N56₎
  UF Camma (African people)
    Commi (African people)
    Nkâmi (African people)
  BT Ethnology—Gabon
    Mpongwe (African people)
Nkonde (African people)
  USE Ngonde (African people)
Nkonde language
  USE Ngonde language
Nkonya language
  USE Nkunya language
Nkore-Kiga language
  USE Nyankore-Kiga language
Nkore language
  USE Nyankole language
Nkosi (Bantu people)
  USE Bakossi (Bantu people)
Nkosi dialect
  USE Bakossi dialect
Nkoya (African people)
  UF Mankoya (African people)
    Shinkoya (African people)
  BT Ethnology—Zambia
Nkundo (African people)
  USE Nkundu (African people)
Nkundo language
  USE Nkundu language
Nkundu (African people)
  UF Gundo (African people)
    Inkundo (African people)
    Kundu (African people)
    Nkundo (African people)
  BT Ethnology—Zaire
Nkundu language
  UF Lonkundu language
    Lunkundu language
    Nkundo language
  BT Bantu languages
Nkunya language
  UF Nkonya language
  BT Gonja language
Nkurange language
  USE Kulango language
Nkwaleni River (South Africa)
  USE Nkwalini River (South Africa)
Nkwalini River (South Africa)
  UF Nkwaleni River (South Africa)
  BT Rivers—South Africa
NL Industries Strike, Sayreville, N.J., 1975
  BT Pigments industry—United States—
    Employees
    Strikes and lockouts—Pigments
    industry—United States
    Strikes and lockouts—United States
NLN Pre-Nursing and Guidance Examination
  USE Pre-Nursing and Guidance
    Examination
NLP (Psychology)
  USE Neurolinguistic programming
NMR imaging
  USE Magnetic resonance imaging
NMR shift reagents, Lanthanide
  USE Lanthanide shift reagents
NMR spectroscopy
  USE Nuclear magnetic resonance
    spectroscopy
NN-278-gō Koyō Iseki (Japan)
  USE NN-278 Koyō Site (Japan)
NN-278 Koyō Site (Japan)
  (Not Subd Geog)
  UF NN-278-gō Koyō Iseki (Japan)

BT Japan—Antiquities
NN-314-gō Koyō Iseki (Japan)
  USE NN-314 Koyō Site (Japan)
NN-314 Koyō Site (Japan)
  (Not Subd Geog)
  UF NN-314-gō Koyō Iseki (Japan)
  BT Japan—Antiquities
Nō (May Subd Geog)
    Here are entered general works and those that
  deal with the presentation of Nō plays on the stage.
  The text of the Nō plays and works treating of them
  from a literary point of view are entered under Nō
  plays.
  UF Noh
    Shimai
  BT Theater—Japan
  NT Hōshō school
    Kanze school
    Kyōgen
    Sarugaku
    Umewaka school
    Utai
  — Costume
    BT Costume—Japan
  — Masks
  — Stage-setting and scenery
No (The English word)
  BT English language—Etymology
No. 10 Downing Street (London, England)
  USE Number 10 Downing Street (London,
    England)
No-bond resonance
  USE Hyperconjugation
No confidence motions (May Subd Geog)
  UF Censure motions (Parliamentary
    practice)
    Government dissolution (Parliamentary
    practice)
    Votes of no confidence
  BT Confidence voting
No-eye pea
  USE Pigeon-pea
No family (Not Subd Geog)
No-fault automobile insurance
  USE Insurance, No-fault automobile
No-fines concrete
  USE Lightweight concrete
No first use (Nuclear strategy)
  ₍U264₎
    Here are entered works on the principle that a
  military power, in the event of war, would not be the
  first to resort to the tactical or strategic use of nuclear
  weapons. Works on preemptive strategic nuclear at-
  tacks designed to destroy the enemy's strategic forces
  before they can be used against one's own strategic
  forces are entered under First strike (Nuclear strate-
  gy).
  BT Deterrence (Strategy)
  RT First strike (Nuclear strategy)
    Nuclear warfare
    Nuclear weapons
No-hitter (Baseball)
  UF Baseball no-hitter
  BT Baseball
    Pitching (Baseball)
Nō kyōgen
  USE Kyōgen
Nō kyōgen plays
  USE Kyōgen plays
No-mind (Buddhism)
  BT Anātman
    Mind and body
    Philosophy, Buddhist
Nō music
  BT Music—Japan
  NT Utai
No-par stocks
  USE No-par-value stocks

No-par-value stocks (May Subd Geog)
  UF No-par stocks
    Non-par stocks
    Non-par-value stocks
    Stocks without par value
  BT Stocks
  — Law and legislation (May Subd Geog)
Nō plays
  ₍PL735₎
  ₍PL765 (Collections)₎
    Here are entered the texts of the Nō plays and
  works treating of them from a literary point of view.
  General works and those that deal solely with the
  presentation of Nō plays on the stage are entered
  under Nō.
  BT Japanese drama
  NT Utai
No-Popery Riots, 1780
  USE Gordon Riots, 1780
No pork diet
  USE Pork-free diet
No-see-ums (Insects)
  USE Ceratopogonidae
No smoking areas
  USE Nonsmoking areas
No smoking hotel rooms
  USE Hotels, taverns, etc.—Nonsmoking
    areas
No-strike clause (May Subd Geog)
  UF Peace clause
  BT Clauses (Law)
    Collective labor agreements
    Strikes and lockouts
No. Ten Downing Street (London, England)
  USE Number 10 Downing Street (London,
    England)
No-tillage (May Subd Geog)
  ₍S604₎
  UF Zero tillage
  BT Conservation tillage
  RT Tillage
Noachian Laws
  USE Noahide Laws
Noachide Laws
  USE Noahide Laws
Noahide Laws
  ₍BM520.73₎
  UF Noachian Laws
    Noachide Laws
  BT Jewish law
Noah's ark
  ₍BL325.D4₎
  ₍BS658₎
  UF Ark, Noah's
  BT Deluge
Noah's ark in art
Noamlaki Indians
  USE Nomlaki Indians
Noanama Indians
  USE Choco Indians
Noanama language
  USE Waunana language
Noardske balke
  USE Noordsche balk
Noatak National Preserve (Alaska)
  (Not Subd Geog)
  BT National parks and reserves—Alaska
    Wilderness areas—Alaska
Noatia (Indic people)
  ₍DS432.N62₎
  UF Katal (Indic people)
  BT Ethnology—India
    India—Scheduled tribes
Nobel family
  USE Noble family
Nobel prizes
  ₍AS911₎
Nōbi-heiya (Japan)
  USE Nōbi Plain (Japan)

Nōbi Plain (Japan)
    UF Mino-Owari Plain (Japan)
         Nagoya Plain (Japan)
         Nōbi-heiya (Japan)
    BT Plains—Japan
Nobidome Canal (Japan) *(Not Subd Geog)*
    BT Canals—Japan
Nobility
    ⌈HT647-HT650 (Social classes)⌉
    ⌈JC411-JC417 (Political theory)⌉
    RT Aristocracy
         Peerage
         Titles of honor and nobility
    SA *subdivision* Nobility *under names of*
           regions, countries, etc.
    NT Duchies
         Knights and knighthood
         Sicily—Nobility
  — **Education, Medieval** *(May Subd Geog)*
       ⌈LC4929-4949⌉
    UF Medieval education of nobility
    BT Education, Medieval
  — **Genealogy**
       ⌈CS28⌉
       ⌈CS42-CS2209 (By country)⌉
    BT Genealogy
  — **Heraldry**
    BT Heraldry
    SA *subdivision* Nobility—Heraldry
           under names of countries, etc.
Nobility, Frankish
    USE Franks—Nobility
Nobility, Papal *(May Subd Geog)*
    ⌈CR5547-CR5577 (Orders,
       decorations)⌉
    UF Catholic Church—Nobility
         Papal nobility
Nobility in literature
    BT Characters and characteristics in
         literature
Nobility of character
    ⌈BJ1533⌉
    BT Character
Noble (Coin)
Noble family *(Not Subd Geog)*
    UF Nobel family
    BT Nobles family
Noble fir
    ⌈QK494.5.P66 (Botany)⌉
    UF Abies nobilis
         Abies procera
    BT Fir
Noble gas solids
    USE Solid rare gases
Noble gases
    USE Gases, Rare
Noble metals
    USE Precious metals
Noble savage
    UF Savage, Noble
    BT Ethnology—Philosophy
         Primitivism in literature
Noble Truths, Four
    USE Four Noble Truths
Nobleman's son (Miracle)
    USE Healing of the nobleman's son
         (Miracle)
Nobles family *(Not Subd Geog)*
    NT Noble family
Noblit family
    USE Noblitt family
Noblitt family *(Not Subd Geog)*
    UF Noblit family
Noc family
    USE Knox family
Nocardia
    ⌈QR82.N6⌉
    BT Actinomycetaceae
Nocardia corallina
    ⌈QR82.N6⌉

    UF Bacillus mycoides corallinus
         Mycobacterium agreste
         Proactinomyces agrestis
         Proactinomyces corallinus
         Serratia corallina

Nocardia opaca
    ⌈QR82.N6⌉

Noch family
    USE Knox family

Nociceptors
    ⌈QP451.4⌉

    UF Pain receptors

    BT Neural receptors
         Pain—Physiological aspects

Nock family
    USE Knox family

Nockamixon, Lake (Pa.)
    UF Lake Nockamixon (Pa.)

    BT Lakes—Pennsylvania
         Reservoirs—Pennsylvania
         Tohickon Creek (Pa.)

Nockamixon State Park (Pa.)
    BT Parks—Pennsylvania

Nocks family
    USE Knox family

Nocomis
    ⌈QL638.C94⌉

    BT Cyprinidae

Nocomis biguttatus
    ⌈QL638.C94⌉

Nocomis leptocephalus
    USE Bluehead chub

Nocte language
    ⌈PL4001.N63⌉

    UF Borduaria language
         Mohongia language
         Paniduaria language

    BT Naga languages

Noctilucent clouds *(May Subd Geog)*
    ⌈QC976.N6⌉

    UF Luminous clouds

    BT Atmosphere, Upper
         Clouds
         Meteorological optics

Noctuidae
    ⌈QL561.N7⌉

    UF Acontidae
         Agrotidae
         Alypiidae
         Amphigonidae
         Amphipyridae
         Anthrophilidae
         Apamidae
         Bendidae
         Boletobidae
         Bolinidae
         Bombycoidae
         Bryophilidae
         Calpidae
         Caradrinidae
         Catephidae
         Catocalidae
         Chloeophoridae
         Cosmidae
         Dyopsidae
         Erebidae
         Eriopidae
         Eucocytiidae
         Eurhipidae
         Euschemidae
         Focillidae
         Gonopteridae
         Gortynidae
         Graptolithidae
         Hadenidae
         Haemerosidae
         Heliothidae
         Hemerosidae
         Herminidae
         Homopteridae
         Hulodidae
         Hypenidae
         Hypocalidae
         Hypogrammidae
         Hypopyridae
         Leucanidae
         Nycteolidae
         Ommatophoridae
         Ophideridae
         Ophiusidae
         Orthosidae
         Palindidae
         Phalaenidae
         Phalaenoididae
         Phyllodidae
         Placodidae
         Platydidae
         Plusidae
         Plusiidae
         Poaphilidae
         Polydesmidae
         Pseudodeltoidae
         Quadrifidae
         Remigidae
         Stilbidae
         Strepsimanidae
         Thermesidae
         Toxocampidae
         Trifidae
         Xylinidae
         Xylophasidae
    BT Lepidoptera
         Moths
    NT Agrotis
         Diparopsis
         Gonodonta
         Heliothis
         Loxagrotis
         Marcipa
         Marcipalina
         Metaxaglaea
         Othreis
         Panolis
         Polia
         Prodenia
         Pseudaletia
         Sacadodes

Schinia
Sesamia
Spodoptera
Spodoptera
Tanocryx
Trichoplusia
Noctule bats
USE Nyctalus
Noctules
USE Nyctalus
Nocturnal animals *(May Subd Geog)*
UF Animals, Nocturnal
BT Animal behavior
Zoology
Nocturnal E (Ionosphere)
USE Sporadic E (Ionosphere)
Nocturnal people
USE Night people
Noda Shōyu Kabushiki Kaisha Strike, 1927-1928
Nodai Iseki (Nagaizumi-chō, Japan)
USE Nodai Site (Nagaizumi-chō, Japan)
Nodai Site (Nagaizumi-chō, Japan)
(Not Subd Geog)
UF Nodai Iseki (Nagaizumi-chō, Japan)
BT Japan—Antiquities
Node, Sinoatrial
USE Sinoatrial node
Node of Keith and Flack
USE Sinoatrial node
Nodes, Lymph
USE Lymph nodes
Nodes of Ranvier
UF Ranvier's nodes
BT Nerves
Nodocion
[QL458.42.G5]
BT Gnaphosidae
Nodonota
[QL596.C5]
BT Chrysomelidae
Nodular disease
[SF968]
UF Nodular worm disease
Nodule disease
Nodular fasciitis *(May Subd Geog)*
UF Fasciitis, Nodular
Fasciitis, Proliferative
Fasciitis, Pseudosarcomatous
Proliferative fasciitis
Pseudosarcomatous fasciitis
BT Cell proliferation
Fasciae (Anatomy)—Inflammation
Nodular iron
USE Iron, Nodular
Nodular worm disease
USE Nodular disease
Nodule disease
USE Nodular disease
Nodulus caroticus
USE Carotid body
Nodus lymphaticus
USE Lymph nodes
Nodus sinuatrialis
USE Sinoatrial node
Noel-Baker family *(Not Subd Geog)*
UF Baker-Noel family
RT Baker family
Noel family
Noel family *(Not Subd Geog)*
UF Noell family
Noelle family
RT Noel-Baker family
Noell family
USE Noel family
Noelle family
USE Noel family
Noels
USE Carols, French
Noenama language
USE Waunana language

Noergaard family
USE Nørgaard family
Noetherian rings
UF Rings, Noetherian
BT Associative rings
Commutative rings
Noftsger family *(Not Subd Geog)*
Nogai
[DK34.N64]
UF Nogaĭtsy
BT Ethnology—Soviet Union
Nogai language
[PL65.N]
BT Turkic languages
Turkic languages, Northwest
Nogai literature *(May Subd Geog)*
Nogaĭtsy
USE Nogai
Nogaret family *(Not Subd Geog)*
Nogi-ran
USE Metanarthecium luteoviride
Nogn (Malaysian people)
USE Batek (Malaysian people)
Noguchi family *(Not Subd Geog)*
Noguera (Spain)
UF La Noguera (Spain)
Noguera Ribagorçana River (Spain)
USE Noguera Ribagorzana River (Spain)
Noguera Ribagorzana River (Spain)
UF Noguera Ribagorçana River (Spain)
Noguera Rivagoranzo River (Spain)
Río Noguera Ribagorzana (Spain)
BT Rivers—Spain
Noguera Rivagoranzo River (Spain)
USE Noguera Ribagorzana River (Spain)
Nogugu language
BT Melanesian languages
Noh
USE Nō
Nohawus (S.D.)
USE Bear Butte (S.D. : Mountain)
Nohmul Site (Belize)
BT Belize—Antiquities
Noho (African people)
USE Tanga (African people)
Noice family
USE Noyes family
Noir Lake (Switzerland)
USE Schwarzsee (Switzerland : Lake)
Noire Mountain (France)
USE Noires Mountains (France)
Noire River (France and Belgium)
USE Eau Noire River (France and Belgium)
Noires Mountains (France)
UF Montagne Noire (France)
Montagnes Noires (France)
Noire Mountain (France)
BT Mountains—France
Noirmoutier Island (France)
(Not Subd Geog)
UF Ile de Noirmoutier (France)
BT Islands—France
Nois family
USE Noyes family
Noise *(May Subd Geog)*
[BF205.N6 (Psychology)]
[QC243 (Sound waves)]
[RA772.N7 (Hygiene)]
[TJ153 (Machinery)]
BT Sound
RT Silence
SA *subdivision* Noise *under subjects, e.g.*
Automobiles—Noise; Construction
industry—Noise; *and phrase
headings for specific types of noise,
including its control, e.g.* Traffic
noise
NT Aerodynamic noise
Airport noise
Anechoic chambers
Boundary layer noise

Cavitation noise
City noise
Electromagnetic noise
Industrial noise
Noise control
Rock noise
Soundproofing
Transportation noise
— Measurement
NT Sound analyzers
— Physiological effect
NT Acoustic trauma
Deafness, Noise induced
Noise, Current
USE Current noise (Electricity)
Noise, Electric
USE Electric noise
Noise, Electronic
USE Electronic noise
Noise, Radio
USE Radio noise
Noise, Random
USE Random noise theory
Noise barriers
[TD892]
UF Barriers, Noise
BT Noise control
NT Plants as noise barriers
Noise control *(May Subd Geog)*
Here are entered general works on the reduction
or elimination of noise. Works on noise in types of
institutions and industries and generated by types of
vehicles, machinery, equipment, etc., and efforts to
reduce or eliminate it, are entered under the appro-
priate heading with the subdivision Noise.
UF Noise prevention
BT Acoustical engineering
Environmental engineering
Noise
SA *subdivision* Noise *under subjects, e.g.*
Automobiles—Noise; Construction
industry—Noise
NT Noise barriers
Soundproofing
— Equipment and supplies
NT Noise control products industry
— Law and legislation *(May Subd Geog)*
BT Environmental law
Nuisances
Noise control products industry
(May Subd Geog)
[HD9718.5.N64]
BT Noise control—Equipment and
supplies
Noise generators (Electronics)
[TK7872.N6]
UF Noise source (Electronics)
BT Oscillators, Electric
Noise induced deafness
USE Deafness, Noise induced
Noise induced hearing loss
USE Deafness, Noise induced
Noise pollution *(May Subd Geog)*
[TD891-893.5]
BT Pollution
— Meteorological aspects
BT Meteorology
Noise pollution damages, Liability for
USE Liability for noise pollution damages
Noise prevention
USE Noise control
Noise source (Electronics)
USE Noise generators (Electronics)
Noise storms, Solar
USE Solar noise storms
Noise word lists in automatic indexing
USE Exclusion lists in automatic indexing
Noisseville, Battle of, 1870
[DC303.8]
BT Franco-German War, 1870-1871

Noisy circuits
    USE Electronic circuits—Noise
Noji Onoyama Iseki (Kusatsu-shi, Japan)
    USE Noji Onoyama Site (Kusatsu-shi,
            Japan)
Noji Onoyama Site (Kusatsu-shi, Japan)
    (Not Subd Geog)
    UF Noji Onoyama Iseki (Kusatsu-shi,
            Japan)
    BT Japan—Antiquities
Nojiri Lake (Japan) *(Not Subd Geog)*
    UF Nojiriko (Japan)
    BT Lakes—Japan
Nojiriko (Japan)
    USE Nojiri Lake (Japan)
Nok terra-cotta sculpture
    USE Terra-cotta sculpture, Nok
Nokuhiva (Marquesas Islands)
    USE Nuka Hiva (Marquesas Islands)
Nolambas
Nolan, William F., 1928-
    (Not Subd Geog)
1928-
    — Characters
    — — Logan
        RT Logan (Ficitious character)
Nolan family *(Not Subd Geog)*
    UF Knowland family
        Knowlon family
        Noland family
        Nolen family
        Nolland family
        Nowlan family
        Nowland family
        Nowlen family
        Nowlin family
    RT Nollen family
Nolana
    BT Nolanaceae
Nolanaceae
    [QK495.N6 (Botany)]
    BT Tubiflorae
    NT Nolana
Noland family
    USE Nolan family
Nolde family *(Not Subd Geog)*
    UF Von Nolde family
Nolden House (Mayen, Germany)
    USE Haus Dr. Nolden (Mayen, Germany)
Nolen family
    USE Nolan family
Noli aemulari (Music)
    USE Psalms (Music)—37th Psalm
Nolin Lake (Ky.)
    BT Lakes—Kentucky
        Nolin River (Ky.)
        Reservoirs—Kentucky
Nolin River (Ky.)
    BT Rivers—Kentucky
    NT Nolin Lake (Ky.)
Noll family *(Not Subd Geog)*
    UF Nolle family
    RT Knoll family
Nolland family
    USE Nolan family
Nolle family
    USE Noll family
Nolleman family
    USE Nollen family
Nollen family *(Not Subd Geog)*
    UF Nolleman family
    RT Nolan family
Nolten family
    USE Knowlton family
Nolton family
    USE Knowlton family
NOMAD (Computer program)
    BT Data base management—Computer
            programs
Nomad automobile
    [TL215.N]

BT Chevrolet automobile
Nomadacris septemfasciata
    USE Red locust
Nomadic rugs
    USE Rugs, Nomadic
Nomadopsis *(May Subd Geog)*
    [QL568.A4]
    BT Andrenidae
Nomads *(May Subd Geog)*
    [GN387]
    UF Horde
        Pastoral peoples
        Vagabonds
    BT Anthropology
        Society, Primitive
    RT Herders
    SA *names of nomadic tribes, e.g.*
            Bedouins, Kirghiz
    NT Gypsies
        Transhumance
    — Sedentarisation
        UF Sedentarisation of nomads
            Settlement of nomads
Nomads in art
Nomatsiguenga Indians
    USE Campa Indians
Nomatsiguenga language
    UF Pangoa language
    BT Campa languages
        Indians of South America—Languages
Nomenclature
    USE *subdivisions* Nomenclature *and*
            Nomenclature (Popular) *under*
            names of scientific or technical
            disciplines and types of substances,
            plants, and animals for systemically
            derived lists of names or
            designations that have been
            formally adopted or sanctioned or
            for discussions of the principles
            involved in the creation and
            application of such names, e.g. Corn
            —Nomenclature; Fishes—
            Nomenclature (Popular)
        Names
NOMES Project
    USE New England Offshore Mining
            Environmental Study
Nomifensine
    [RC483.5.N66 (Psychiatry)]
    UF Aminotetrahydromethy
            lphenylisoquinoline
    BT Anticonvulsants
        Antidepressants
        Antiparkinsonian agents
        Heterocyclic compounds
        Isoquinoline
        Stimulants
Nominalism
    [B731]
    BT Logic
        Philosophy
        Scholasticism
        Universals (Philosophy)
    RT Conceptualism
        Realism
        Reality
Nominals (Grammar)
    USE Grammar, Comparative and general—
            Nominals
Nomination (Semantics)
    USE Onomasiology
Nomination of governors
    USE Governors—United States—
            Nomination
Nomination of presidents
    USE Presidents—United States—
            Nomination
Nominations for office *(May Subd Geog)*
    [JF2081 (Constitutional history)]
    [JK2053-JK2096 (United States)]

UF Office, Nominations for
        Office, Qualifications for
        Qualifications for office
    BT Election law
        Elections
        Politics, Practical
        Representative government and
            representation
    RT Political conventions
        Primaries
    NT Caucus
        Governors—United States—
            Nomination
        Presidents—United States—
            Nomination
Nominees for president
    USE Presidential candidates
Nominees for Vice-President
    USE Vice-Presidential candidates
Nomlaki Indians
    UF Noamlaki Indians
    BT Indians of North America
        Wintun Indians
Nomocanon
    [BX343]
    BT Canon law, Orthodox Eastern
Nomograms
    USE Nomography (Mathematics)
Nomographs
    USE Nomography (Mathematics)
Nomography (Mathematics)
    [QA90]
    UF Alignment charts
        Nomograms
        Nomographs
    BT Graphic methods
        Graphic statics
        Numerical analysis
    NT Mathematics—Charts, diagrams, etc.
Nomonhan Incident, 1939
    USE Halhaiin Gol, Battle of, 1939
Noms de plume
    USE Anonyms and pseudonyms
Nomugi Kaidō (Japan)
    USE Nakasendō (Japan)
Nomura Zaibatsu
    [HD2907]
    BT Trusts, Industrial—Japan
Non-A, non-B hepatitis
    USE Hepatitis, Non-A, non-B
Non-Abelian groups
    UF Groups, Non-Abelian
        Groups, Nonabelian
        Nonabelian groups
    BT Abelian groups
        Groups, Theory of
Non-aligned nations
    USE Nonalignment
Non-alignment
    USE Nonalignment
Non-Aristotelian philosophy
    USE General semantics
Non-belief
    USE Irreligion
Non bis in idem
    USE Double jeopardy
Non-Black Earth Region (R.S.F.S.R.)
    USE Non-Chernozem Region (R.S.F.S.R.)
Non-book materials, Acquisition of
    USE Acquisition of non-book materials
Non-book materials, Cataloging of
    USE Cataloging of non-book materials
Non-book materials, Classification of
    USE Classification—Non-book materials
Non-book materials, Library collections of
    USE Libraries—Special collections—Non-
            book materials
Non-book materials, Shelving for
    USE Shelving (for non-book materials)
Non-book materials selection
    USE Selection of non-book materials

Non-Chernozem Region (R.S.F.S.R.)
- UF Nechernozem'e (R.S.F.S.R.)
  - Nechernozemnaiā zona (R.S.F.S.R.)
  - Nechernozemnaya zona (R.S.F.S.R.)
  - Nechernozemnyĭ raĭon (R.S.F.S.R.)
  - Nechernozemnyy rayon (R.S.F.S.R.)
  - Non-Black Earth Region (R.S.F.S.R.)
  - Nonchernozem Region (R.S.F.S.R.)

Non church-affiliated people
- *(May Subd Geog)*
- UF Unchurched, The
- BT Irreligion
- NT Ex-church members

Non-classical mathematical logic
- USE Nonclassical mathematical logic

Non-commercial broadcasting
- USE Public broadcasting

Non-commercial radio
- USE Public radio

Non-commercial television
- USE Public television

Non-commissioned officers' wives
- BT Military dependents
  - Wives

Non-Conformist Cemetery (Canterbury, Kent)
- USE Canterbury Cemetery (Canterbury, Kent)

Non-contentious jurisdiction
- *(May Subd Geog)*
- UF Jurisdiction, Non-contentious
  - Jurisdiction, Voluntary
  - Voluntary jurisdiction
- BT Civil procedure
  - Procedure (Law)
- RT Notaries
  - Recording and registration
- NT Agricultural courts and procedure
  - Airplanes—Registration and transfer
  - Authentication
  - Business enterprises—Registration and transfer
  - Land titles—Registration and transfer
  - Legalization
  - Ordinaries
  - Ships—Registration and transfer

Non-contentious jurisdiction (Roman law)

Non-dairy frozen desserts
- UF Frozen desserts, Non-dairy
- BT Desserts, Frozen
- NT Soy ice cream

Non-destructive testing
- BT Engineering inspection
  - Materials—Testing
  - Testing
- NT Acoustic emission testing
  - Automatic checkout equipment
  - Holographic testing
  - Magnetic testing
  - Penetrant inspection
  - Plant performance—Monitoring
  - Radiography, Industrial
  - Speckle metrology
  - Ultrasonic testing

Non-differentiable functions
- USE Nondifferentiable functions

Non-equilibrium thermodynamics
- USE Nonequilibrium thermodynamics

Non-Euclidean geometry
- USE Geometry, Non-Euclidean

Non-flam film
- USE Safety film

Non-formal education *(May Subd Geog)*
- [LC45-45.8]
- UF Alternative education
  - Education, Non-formal
  - Education, Non-traditional
  - Non-traditional education
  - Nonformal education
  - Nontraditional education

- BT Adult education
  - Educational innovations
  - Occupational training
- NT Women—Non-formal education

Non-formal education of women
- USE Women—Non-formal education

Non-frontal scenography
- USE Theater, Environmental

Non-governmental organizations
- *(May Subd Geog)*
- Here are entered works dealing with international organizations created and financed independent of governments and having a non-profit function in the developing countries.
- UF NGOs (International agencies)
  - Nongovernmental organizations
  - Organizations, Non-governmental (International agencies)
  - Private and voluntary organizations (International agencies)
  - PVOs (International agencies)
- BT Corporations, Nonprofit
  - International agencies

Non-harming (Ethics)
- USE Ahiṃsā

Non-histone chromosomal proteins
- USE Nonhistone chromosomal proteins

Non-Hopfian groups
- UF Groups, Non-Hopfian
- BT Groups, Theory of

Non impact aerobic exercises
- USE Low impact aerobic exercises

Non impact aerobics
- USE Low impact aerobic exercises

Non-impact printing
- USE Nonimpact printing

Non-importation agreements, 1768-1769
- [E215.3]
- BT United States—History—Colonial period, ca. 1600-1775

Non-injury (Ethics)
- USE Ahiṃsā

Non-institutional churches
- *(May Subd Geog)*
- [BV601.9]
- UF Avant-garde churches
  - Church—Non-institutional forms
  - Churches, Avant-garde
  - Churches, Non-institutional
- BT Independent churches
- NT House churches

Non-insulin-dependent diabetes
- *(May Subd Geog)*
- [RC660-RC662]
- UF Adult onset diabetes
  - Ketosis resistant diabetes
  - Maturity onset diabetes
  - NIDDM
  - Noninsulin-dependent diabetes
  - Stable diabetes
  - Type 2 diabetes
- BT Diabetes

Non-interest banks, Islamic
- USE Banks and banking—Islamic countries

Non-ionizing radiation
- USE Nonionizing radiation

Non-language adaptability test
- USE Purdue non-language adaptability test

Non-linear . . .
- USE *subject headings beginning with the word* Nonlinear

Non-lymphoid leukemia
- USE Nonlymphoid leukemia

Non-mulberry silkworms
- USE Silkworms, Non-mulberry

Non-negative matrices
- [QA188]
- UF Matrices, Non-negative
  - Matrices, Nonnegative
  - Nonnegative matrices
- BT Matrices

Non-Newtonian fluids
- BT Rheology
  - Viscous flow
- RT Newtonian fluids

Non nobis, Domine (Music)
- USE Psalms (Music)—115th Psalm

Non-nutritive sweeteners
- USE Nonnutritive sweeteners

Non-objective art
- USE Art, Abstract

Non-objective drawing
- USE Drawing, Abstract

Non-objective painting
- USE Painting, Abstract

Non-par stocks
- USE No-par-value stocks

Non-par-value stocks
- USE No-par-value stocks

Non-pension benefits
- USE Postemployment benefits

Non-performance (Law)
- USE Breach of contract

Non-postal labels
- USE Seals and labels (Philately)

Non-postal stamps
- USE Cinderella materials (Philately)
  - Duck stamps
  - Revenue-stamps
  - Seals and labels (Philately)
  - Telegraph stamps

Non procedural languages (Programming languages)
- USE Nonprocedural languages (Programming languages)

Non-profit corporations
- USE Corporations, Nonprofit

Non-profit private hospitals
- USE Hospitals, Voluntary

Non-promotion (School)
- USE Grade repetition
  - Promotion (School)

Non-resistance to evil
- USE Evil, Non-resistance to

Non-resistance to government
- USE Government, Resistance to

Non-self
- USE Anātman

Non-shatterable glass
- USE Glass, Safety

Non-significant words in automatic indexing
- USE Exclusion lists in automatic indexing

Non-smoking areas
- USE Nonsmoking areas

Non-social-realist art
- — Soviet Union
  - USE Dissident art—Soviet Union

Non-steroid anti-inflammatory agents
- USE Nonsteroidal anti-inflammatory agents

Non-support
- USE Desertion and non-support

Non-traditional education
- USE Non-formal education

Non-urgent surgery
- USE Surgery, Elective

Non-verbal communication
- USE Nonverbal communication

Non-verbal intelligence tests
- *(May Subd Geog)*
- UF Performance tests
- BT Intelligence tests
- NT Kohs block design test
  - Leiter International Performance Scale
  - Purdue non-language adaptability test
  - Stanford-Ohwaki-Kohs tactile block design intelligence test for the blind

Non-victim crimes
- USE Crimes without victims

Non-violence
- USE Nonviolence

Non-wage payments
- USE Employee fringe benefits

Nonabelian groups
USE Non-Abelian groups
Nonacho Lake (N.W.T.)
BT Lakes—Northwest Territories
Nonaka family *(Not Subd Geog)*
Nonaligned nations
USE Nonalignment
Nonalignment
[*JX1393.N54 (International relations)*]
Here are entered works on the foreign policy of states who do not identify themselves with the major power blocs but retain the option of becoming aligned when necessary. Works on the status of states resulting from their adoption of impartiality towards belligerent states, and on the consequent rights and duties created between the neutral states and the belligerents under international law are entered under Neutrality.
UF Neutralism
Non-aligned nations
Non-alignment
Nonaligned nations
BT International relations
RT Neutrality
SA *subdivision* Nonalignment *under names of regions, countries, etc.*
Nonama language
USE Waunana language
Nonamaker family
USE Nonnenmacher family
Nonantum language
USE Massachuset language
Nonaqueous solvents
[*QD544.5*]
[*TP247.5*]
BT Solvents
NT Organic solvents
Nonarticular rheumatic disease
USE Nonarticular rheumatism
Nonarticular rheumatism *(May Subd Geog)*
[*RC927.5.N65*]
UF Nonarticular rheumatic disease
Rheumatism, Nonarticular
Soft tissue rheumatism
BT Rheumatism
NT Bursitis
Myositis
Neuritis
Tendinitis
Tenosynovitis
Nonassociative algebras
UF Algebras, Nonassociative
BT Algebra, Abstract
Algebras, Linear
NT Cayley algebras
Nonassociative rings
[*QA252*]
BT Rings (Algebra)
Nonbook . . .
USE *subject headings beginning with the word* Non-book
Nonbroadcast television
USE Video recordings
Nonchernozem Region (R.S.F.S.R.)
USE Non-Chernozem Region (R.S.F.S.R.)
Nonchromaffin paraganglia
UF Paraganglia, Nonchromaffin
BT Nervous system, Autonomic
NT Carotid body
Glomus jugulare
— Tumors
USE Nonchromaffin paraganglioma
Nonchromaffin paraganglioma
UF Chemodectoma
Nonchromaffin paraganglia—Tumors
Paraganglioma, Nonchromaffin
BT Nervous system—Tumors
NT Glomus jugulare—Tumors
Nonclassical mathematical logic
[*QA9.4*]
UF Mathematical logic, Nonclassical
Non-classical mathematical logic

BT Logic, Symbolic and mathematical
NT Combinatory logic
Many-valued logic
Modality (Logic)
Noncombatants (International law)
USE Combatants and noncombatants (International law)
Noncommercial broadcasting
USE Public broadcasting
Noncommercial radio
USE Public radio
Noncommercial television
USE Public television
Noncommutative algebras
[*QA251.4*]
UF Algebras, Noncommutative
Noncommutative rings
[*QA251.5*]
BT Associative rings
— **Chain conditions**
UF Chain conditions in noncommutative rings
Nonconformist art
USE Dissident art
Nonconformist arts
USE Dissident arts
Nonconformists
USE Dissenters
Nonconformists, Religious
USE Dissenters, Religious
Nonconformity
USE Conformity
Nonconformity (Religion)
USE Dissenters, Religious
Free churches
Nonconsensual sexual intercourse
USE Rape
Nonconservation of parity
USE Parity nonconservation
Noncontiguous possessions of the United States
USE United States—Insular possessions
United States—Territories and possessions
Noncrystalline semiconductors
USE Amorphous semiconductors
Noncustodial mothers
USE Absentee mothers
Nondenominational churches
USE Independent churches
Nondepolarizing agents, Neuromuscular
USE Curare-like agents
Nondepolarizing muscle relaxants
USE Curare-like agents
Nondifferentiable functions
UF Functions, Nondifferentiable
Non-differentiable functions
BT Functions of real variables
Nondimensional numbers
USE Dimensionless numbers
Nondirective counseling
USE Client-centered psychotherapy
Nondirective psychotherapy
USE Client-centered psychotherapy
Nondirective therapy
USE Client-centered psychotherapy
Nonelectrolytic plating
USE Electroless plating
Nonemacher family
USE Nonnenmacher family
Nonemacker family
USE Nonnenmacher family
Nonemaker family
USE Nonnenmacher family
Nonenmacher family
USE Nonnenmacher family
Nonequilibrium thermodynamics
[*QC318.I7*]
UF Irreversible thermodynamics
Non-equilibrium thermodynamics
Thermodynamics of the steady state

BT Thermodynamics
RT Irreversible processes
Nonerasable storage
USE Read-only storage
Nonets
[*M900-986*]
Here are entered collections of compositions for nine instruments belonging to various families and in various combinations; and compositions for nine specific instruments belonging to various families, followed by specification of instruments (including the specification Unspecified instrument(s))
Compositions for nine bowed stringed instruments are entered under String nonets; for nine wind instruments under Wind nonets; for nine brass instruments under Brass nonets; and for nine woodwind instruments under Woodwind nonets, with or without specification of instruments in each case.
Compositions for nine plectral instruments are entered under Plectral ensembles, except those for guitars and/or harps, which are entered under Nonets followed by specification of instruments.
Compositions for nine percussionists are entered under Percussion ensembles.
Compositions for nine solo voices are entered under Sacred nonets or Vocal nonets.
Headings with specification of instruments are printed below only if specific cross references are needed.
SA Suites, Variations, Waltzes, *and similar headings with specification of instruments*
Nonets, Brass
USE Brass nonets
Nonets, Sacred
USE Sacred nonets
Nonets, Secular
USE Vocal nonets
Nonets, String
USE String nonets
Nonets, Vocal
USE Vocal nonets
Nonets, Wind
USE Wind nonets
Nonets, Woodwind
USE Woodwind nonets
Nonets (Bassoon, clarinet, flute, horn, oboe, violin, viola, violoncello, double bass)
[*M960-962*]
NT Suites (Bassoon, clarinet, flute, horn, oboe, violin, viola, violoncello, double bass)
Nonets (Bassoon, clarinet, flute, horn, oboe, violins (2), viola, violoncello)
[*M960-962*]
Nonets (Bassoon, clarinet, flute, horn, violins (2), viola, violoncello, double bass)
[*M960-962*]
NT Variations (Bassoon, clarinet, flute, horn, violins (2), viola, violoncello, double bass)
Nonets (Bassoon, clarinet, flute, oboe, trumpet, violin, viola, violoncello, double bass)
[*M960-962*]
NT Suites (Bassoon, clarinet, flute, oboe, trumpet, violin, viola, violoncello, double bass)
Nonets (Bassoon, clarinet, flute, oboe, violins (2), viola, violoncello, double bass)
[*M960-962*]
NT Suites (Bassoon, clarinet, flute, oboe, violins (2), viola, violoncello, double bass)
Nonets (Bassoon, clarinet, oboe, percussion, violins (2), viola, violoncello, double bass)
[*M985*]
NT Suites (Bassoon, clarinet, oboe, percussion, violins (2), viola, violoncello, double bass)
Nonets (Bassoon, clarinets (3), flute, trombone, trumpets (2), percussion)
[*M985*]

Nonets (Bassoon, flute, horn, piccolo,
trombone, trumpet, viola, violoncello,
double bass)
[M960-962]
Nonets (Clarinet, flute, guitar, percussion,
violin, viola, violoncello)
[M985]
Nonets (Clarinet, flute, trumpet, mandolin,
xylophone, violins (2), viola, violoncello)
[M985]
Nonets (Clarinets (2), horns (2), hurdy-gurdies
(2), violas (2), violoncello)
[M985]
Nonets (Clarinets (2), horns (2), violins (2),
violas (2), violoncello)
[M960-962]
  NT Suites (Clarinets (2), horns (2), violins
       (2), violas (2), violoncello)
Nonets (Clarinets (3), cornet, trombone,
trumpet, violin, viola, violoncello)
[M960-962]
  NT Suites (Clarinets (3), cornet, trombone,
       trumpet, violin, viola, violoncello)
Nonets (Flute, horns (2), oboe, violins (2),
violas (2), violoncello)
[M960-962]
Nonets (Flute, horns (2), oboe, violins (2),
violas (2), violoncello), Arranged
[M963-4]
Nonets (Harpsichord, bassoon, clarinets (2),
horns (2), oboes (2), percussion)
[M935]
  NT Suites (Harpsichord, bassoon, clarinets
       (2), horns (2), oboes (2), percussion)
Nonets (Harpsichord, violins (4), violas (3),
violoncello)
[M910-912]
  BT Nonets (Piano, violins (4), violas (3),
       violoncello)
Nonets (Harpsichord, violins (4), violas (3),
violoncello), Arranged
[M913-914]
Nonets (Horns (2), oboes (2), violins (2),
violas (2), violoncello)
[M960-962]
  NT Suites (Horns (2), oboes (2), violins
       (2), violas (2), violoncello)
Nonets (Percussion, violins (2), viola,
violoncello)
[M985]
  NT Suites (Percussion, violins (2), viola,
       violoncello)
Nonets (Piano, bassoon, clarinet, flute, horn,
oboe, trombone, trumpet, tuba)
[M915-917]
Nonets (Piano, bassoon, clarinet, flute, horn,
trombone, trumpet, violin, violoncello)
[M920-922]
Nonets (Piano, bassoon, clarinet, flute, oboe,
trumpet, violin, viola, violoncello)
[M920-922]
  NT Marches (Piano, bassoon, clarinet,
       flute, oboe, trumpet, violin, viola,
       violoncello)
Nonets (Piano, bassoon, clarinet, flute, oboe,
violins (2), viola, violoncello)
[M920-922]
Nonets (Piano, bassoon, clarinet, flutes (2),
horn, oboe, trombone, trumpet)
[M915-917]
Nonets (Piano, bassoon, clarinets (2), English
horn, flute, horn, oboe, trumpet)
[M915-917]
  NT Suites (Piano, bassoon, clarinets (2),
       English horn, flute, horn, oboe,
       trumpet)
Nonets (Piano, bassoon, clarinets (2), English
horn, oboe, piccolo, violin, violoncello)
[M920-922]

Nonets (Piano, bassoon, clarinets (2), trumpet,
violins (2), violoncello, double bass)
[M920-922]
Nonets (Piano, bassoons (2), flute, horn, oboe,
violin, violoncello, double bass)
[M920-922]
  NT Variations (Piano, bassoons (2), flute,
       horn, oboe, violin, violoncello,
       double bass)
Nonets (Piano, clarinet, English horn, flute,
trombones (2), percussion, violin)
[M947]
Nonets (Piano, clarinet, flute, horn, oboe,
trombone, trumpet, violin, viola)
[M920-922]
Nonets (Piano, clarinets (2), flute, percussion,
violins (2), viola, violoncello)
[M985]
Nonets (Piano, flute, percussion, violin, viola,
violoncello)
[M985]
Nonets (Piano, horn, trombone, tuba,
percussion, viola, violoncello, double bass)
[M945-7]
Nonets (Piano, horn, trombone, tuba,
percussion, violin, violoncello, double bass)
[M945-7]
Nonets (Piano, violins (4), violas (3),
violoncello)
[M910-912]
  NT Nonets (Harpsichord, violins (4),
       violas (3), violoncello)
Nonets (Pianos (2), bassoon, flutes (4),
trombone, percussion)
[M985]
Nonets (Pianos (2), flutes (3), trumpet,
violoncellos (3))
[M920-922]
Nonets (Saxophone, guitar, percussion, violins
(2), viola, violoncello, double basses (2))
[M985]
Nonexistent objects (Philosophy)
  UF Objects, Nonexistent (Philosophy)
  BT Object (Philosophy)
       Philosophy
Nonexpansive mappings
  BT Mappings (Mathematics)
       Nonlinear operators
Nonfeasance
  USE Omission, Criminal
Nonferrous alloys
  UF Alloys, Nonferrous
  BT Alloys
— Brittleness
— Heat treatment
     [TN758]
— Metallography
— Spectra
— Welding
Nonferrous ingots
  UF Ingots, Nonferrous
  BT Nonferrous metals
Nonferrous metal industries
  (May Subd Geog)
  BT Nonferrous metals
  NT Strikes and lockouts—Nonferrous
       metal industries
       Wages—Nonferrous metal industries
— Collective bargaining
     USE Collective bargaining—
            Nonferrous metal industries
— Electric equipment
— Safety measures
     UF Nonferrous metals—Metallurgy—
            Safety measures
Nonferrous metals (May Subd Geog)
  [TN758]
  UF Metals, Nonferrous
       Rare metals
  BT Metals
  NT Nonferrous ingots

Nonferrous metal industries
Rare earth metals
— Brittleness
— Electrometallurgy
— Etching
     [TN690.7 (Metallography)]
     [TS371 (Metal finishing)]
— Founding
— Heat treatment
— Hydrogen content
     BT Gases in metals
          Hydrogen
— Metallography
— Metallurgy
— — Oxygen processes
     BT Oxygen—Industrial applications
— — Safety measures
     USE Nonferrous metal industries—
            Safety measures
— Pickling
     [TS371]
— Welding
Nonfiction novel
  [PS374.N6 (American fiction)]
  UF Documentary story
       Journalistic novel
       New journalism
       Novel, Nonfiction
  BT Fiction
       Prose literature
Nonfiction novel, Japanese
  (May Subd Geog)
  UF Japanese nonfiction novel
  BT Japanese fiction
       Japanese prose literature
Nonformal education
  USE Non-formal education
Nonfossil fuels
  USE Synthetic fuels
Nonfuel minerals (May Subd Geog)
  UF Minerals, Nonfuel
  BT Mines and mineral resources
  NT Industrial minerals
Nonfuel minerals industry (May Subd Geog)
Nongazer family
  USE Nungezer family
Nongonococcal urethritis
  USE Urethritis, Nongonococcal
Nongovernmental organizations
  USE Non-governmental organizations
Nongraded schools
  [LB1029.N6]
  UF Multi-age grouping
       Schools, Nongraded
       Schools, Ungraded
       Ungraded schools
  BT Ability grouping in education
       Education—Experimental methods
Nongranular leucocytes
  USE Lymphocytes
       Monocytes
Nonhistone chromosomal proteins
  [QP552.N62]
  UF Acidic chromosomal proteins
       Chromosomal nonhistone proteins
       Chromosomal proteins, Nonhistone
       Non-histone chromosomal proteins
       Nonhistone nucleoproteins
       Nonhistone proteins, Chromosomal
  BT Chromatin
       Chromosomal proteins
Nonhistone nucleoproteins
  USE Nonhistone chromosomal proteins
Nonhistone proteins, Chromosomal
  USE Nonhistone chromosomal proteins
Nonimmigrants, Admission of
  USE Admission of nonimmigrants
Nonimpact printer industry
  (May Subd Geog)
  [HD9696.C6-64]
  BT Nonimpact printers

Nonimpact printers
UF Printers, Nonimpact
BT Printers (Data processing systems)
NT Nonimpact printer industry
Nonimpact printing *(May Subd Geog)*
⌜Z252.5.N46⌝
UF Impactless printing
Non-impact printing
Printing, Impactless
Printing, Non-impact
Printing, Nonimpact
BT Printing, Practical
NT Electrostatic printing
Printing, Ink jet
Printing, Practical—Laser use in
Noninsulin-dependent diabetes
USE Non-insulin-dependent diabetes
Noninvasive diagnosis
USE Diagnosis, Noninvasive
Noninvasive diagnostic tests
USE Diagnosis, Noninvasive
Noninvasive lithotripsy
USE Ultrasonic lithotripsy
Noninvasive medical imaging
USE Diagnostic imaging
Nonionizing radiation *(May Subd Geog)*
⌜QP82.2.N64 (Physiology)⌝
UF Non-ionizing radiation
Radiation, Nonionizing
BT Radiation
Nonius horse
⌜SF293.N66⌝
UF Nóniusz horse
BT Horse breeds
Nóniusz horse
USE Nonius horse
Nonjurors
⌜BX5087⌝
BT Church of England
Jacobites
Nonjurors, English Catholic
⌜DA499 (18th century)⌝
UF Catholic nonjurors, English
English Catholic nonjurors
BT Catholics—England
Nonjurors, French Catholic
UF Catholic nonjurors, French
French Catholic nonjurors
BT Catholic Church—France
Catholics—France
France—History—Revolution, 1789-
1799—Religious history
RT Louisets
Nonleukemic myelosis
USE Myeloid metaplasia
Nonlinear acoustics
UF Acoustics, Nonlinear
BT Nonlinear theories
Sound-waves
Nonlinear differential equations
USE Differential equations, Nonlinear
Nonlinear diffusion equation
USE Burgers equation
Nonlinear electric circuits
USE Electric circuits, Nonlinear
Nonlinear electric networks
USE Electric networks, Nonlinear
Nonlinear equations of evolution
USE Evolution equations, Nonlinear
Nonlinear evolution equations
USE Evolution equations, Nonlinear
Nonlinear functional analysis
⌜QA321.5⌝
UF Functional analysis, Nonlinear
BT Functional analysis
Nonlinear theories
Nonlinear heat flow equation
USE Burgers equation
Nonlinear integral equations
USE Integral equations, Nonlinear

Nonlinear mechanics
UF Mechanics, Nonlinear
BT Mechanics, Analytic
Nonlinear operator equations
USE Operator equations, Nonlinear
Nonlinear operators
UF Operators, Nonlinear
BT Operator theory
NT Fixed point theory
Nonexpansive mappings
Nonlinear optics
UF Optics, Nonlinear
RT Lasers
NT Optical phase conjugation
Nonlinear oscillations
BT Nonlinear theories
Oscillations
Nonlinear oscillators
UF Oscillators, Nonlinear
BT Oscillators, Electric
Nonlinear problems
USE Nonlinear theories
Nonlinear programming
⌜T57.8⌝
BT Programming (Mathematics)
NT Quadratic programming
Nonlinear theories
UF Nonlinear problems
Nonlinearity (Mathematics)
BT Calculus
Mathematical analysis
Mathematical physics
RT System analysis
NT Chaotic behavior in systems
Differential equations, Nonlinear
Electric networks, Nonlinear
Integral equations, Nonlinear
Nonlinear acoustics
Nonlinear functional analysis
Nonlinear oscillations
Nonlinear waves
Solitons
Nonlinear waves
BT Nonlinear theories
Wave-motion, Theory of
Waves
Nonlinearity (Mathematics)
USE Nonlinear theories
Nonlipid histiocytosis
USE Letterer-Siwe disease
Nonlymphoid leukemia *(May Subd Geog)*
UF Leukemia, Nonlymphoid
Non-lymphoid leukemia
BT Leukemia
NT Monocytic leukemia
Myelocytic leukemia
Nonlymphoid leukemia in children
Nonlymphoid leukemia in children
(May Subd Geog)
⌜RJ416.L4⌝
BT Leukemia in children
Nonlymphoid leukemia
Nonmacher family
USE Nonnenmacher family
Nonmagnetic steel
⌜TA478⌝
BT Magnetic materials
Steel
Nonmaker family
USE Nonnenmacher family
Nonmetallic bearings
⌜TJ1072⌝
BT Bearings (Machinery)
NT Jewel bearings
Nonmetallic elements
USE Nonmetals
Nonmetallic materials
BT Materials
NT Pipe, Nonmetallic
— **Brittleness**
— **Thermal properties**

Nonmetallic minerals *(May Subd Geog)*
UF Minerals, Nonmetallic
BT Mineralogy
Mines and mineral resources
NT Diaspore
Industrial minerals
Witherite
Nonmetallic minerals industry
(May Subd Geog)
Nonmetallic pipe
USE Pipe, Nonmetallic
Nonmetals
⌜QD161⌝
UF Elements, Nonmetallic
Nonmetallic elements
BT Chemical elements
NT Boron
Carbon
Gases, Rare
Halogens
Hydrogen
Nitrogen
Oxygen
Phosphorus
Selenium
Silicon
Sulphur
Nonnamaker family
USE Nonnenmacher family
Nonnegative matrices
USE Non-negative matrices
Nonnemacher family
USE Nonnenmacher family
Nonnenmacher family *(Not Subd Geog)*
UF Nonamaker family
Nonemacher family
Nonemacker family
Nonemaker family
Nonenmacher family
Nonmacher family
Nonmaker family
Nonnamaker family
Nonnemacher family
RT Nunnemacher family
Nonneutral plasma
⌜QC718.5.N4⌝
UF Plasma, Nonneutral
BT Plasma (Ionized gases)
Nonnuclear warfare
USE Warfare, Conventional
Nonnutritive sweeteners
UF Artificial sweeteners
Non-nutritive sweeteners
Synthetic sweeteners
BT Sweeteners
NT Aspartame
Cyclamates
Saccharin
Nonobjective photography
USE Photography, Abstract
Nonomys simplicidens
BT Muridae, Fossil
Nonpar banking *(May Subd Geog)*
UF Banks and banking—Nonpar banking
BT Banks and banking—Service charges
Nonparametric detection of signals
USE Nonparametric signal detection
Nonparametric signal detection
UF Detection, Nonparametric signal
Nonparametric detection of signals
BT Signal detection
Nonparametric statistics
UF Statistics, Nonparametric
BT Mathematical statistics
NT Order statistics
— **Asymptotic theory**
⌜QA278.8⌝
UF Asymptotic theory of
nonparametric statistics
BT Asymptotic expansions
— **Data processing**

2606

NT GMDH algorithms
Nonpartisan elections
  USE Elections, Nonpartisan
Nonpenetrating wounds
  USE Wounds, Nonpenetrating
Nonprescription drug industry
  (May Subd Geog)
  ₁HD9665-9675₁
  BT Drugs, Nonprescription
Nonprescription drugs
  USE Drugs, Nonprescription
Nonprint materials, Cataloging of
  USE Cataloging of non-book materials
NonProcedural Language (Computer program
  language)
  USE NPL (Computer program language)
**Nonprocedural languages (Programming
  languages)**
  UF Languages, Non procedural
      (Programming languages)
    Languages, Nonprocedural
      (Programming languages)
    Non procedural languages
      (Programming languages)
  BT Programming languages (Electronic
      computers)
  NT APT (Computer program language)
    NICOL (Computer program language)
    NPL (Computer program language)
    RPG (Computer program language)
Nonprofessional theater
  USE Amateur theater
Nonprofessionalism
  USE Amateurism
Nonprofessionals in social service
  USE Paraprofessionals in social service
Nonprofit corporations
  USE Corporations, Nonprofit
Nonprofit organizations
  USE Corporations, Nonprofit
Nonprofit private hospitals
  USE Hospitals, Voluntary
Nonprofitable drugs
  USE Orphan drugs
Nonproliferation, Nuclear
  USE Nuclear nonproliferation
Nonrachitic bowleg
  USE Blount's disease
Nonradiative transitions
  USE Radiationless transitions
Nonrealistic photography
  USE Photography, Abstract
Nonrecognition of governments
  USE Recognition (International law)
Nonrenewable natural resources
  (May Subd Geog)
  UF Exhaustible resources
    Natural resources, Nonrenewable
    Nonrenewable natural resources—
      Economic aspects
  BT Natural resources
  — Economic aspects
      USE Nonrenewable natural resources
Nonselective college admission
  USE Universities and colleges—Open
      admission
Nonselfadjoint operators
  UF Operators, Nonselfadjoint
  BT Linear operators
    Selfadjoint operators
Nonselfgoverning territories
  USE Colonies
    International trusteeships
Nonsense Club (Group of writers)
  ₁PR448.N66₁
  BT Literature—Societies, etc.
Nonsense literature *(May Subd Geog)*
  BT Literature
    Wit and humor
  NT Nonsense-verses

Nonsense literature, Bengali
  (May Subd Geog)
  UF Bengali nonsense literature
  BT Bengali literature
Nonsense literature, English, ₁etc.₁
  (May Subd Geog)
Nonsense mutation
  ₁QH462.5₁
  BT Mutation (Biology)
Nonsense songs
  BT Humorous songs
Nonsense suppression (Genetics)
  UF Suppression, Nonsense
  BT Genetic translation
    Mutation (Biology)
Nonsense-verses
  ₁PN1525 (History)₁
  ₁PN6110.N6 (Collections)₁
  BT Humorous poetry
    Limericks
    Nonsense literature
    Wit and humor
  NT Schnaderhüpfel
    Tongue twisters
Nonsense-verses, American
  (May Subd Geog)
  UF American nonsense-verses
  BT American poetry
    American wit and humor
Nonsense-verses, American, ₁English, etc.₁
  (May Subd Geog)
Nonsense-verses, English *(May Subd Geog)*
  UF English nonsense-verses
  BT English poetry
    English wit and humor
Nonsexist communication
  USE Sexism in communication
Nonsexist language
  USE Sexism in language
Nonsmoking areas *(May Subd Geog)*
  UF No smoking areas
    Non-smoking areas
    Smoke-free areas
  NT Hotels, taverns, etc.—Nonsmoking
      areas
    Restaurants, lunch rooms, etc.—
      Nonsmoking areas
Nonsmoking hotel rooms
  USE Hotels, taverns, etc.—Nonsmoking
      areas
Nonspecific immunity
  USE Natural immunity
Nonspecific urethritis
  USE Urethritis, Nongonococcal
Nonstandard mathematical analysis
  USE Mathematical analysis, Nonstandard
Nonsteroidal anti-inflammatory agents
  (May Subd Geog)
  UF Anti-inflammatory agents,
      Nonsteroidal
    Non-steroid anti-inflammatory agents
    NSAID's (Pharmacology)
  BT Anti-inflammatory agents
  NT Aspirin
    Diflunisal
    Indomethacin
    Mefenamic acid
    Naproxen
    Phenylbutazone
    Piroxicam
    Sulindac
    Tolmetin
Nonstipendiary clergy
  USE Clergy, Part-time
Nonsuch Island (Bermuda Islands)
  (Not Subd Geog)
  BT Islands—Bermuda Islands
Nonsuit
  USE Dismissal and nonsuit
Nonsuppressible insulinlike activity
  USE Somatomedin

Nontariff distortions of trade
  USE Nontariff trade barriers
Nontariff trade barriers *(May Subd Geog)*
  ₁HF1430₁
  UF Nontariff distortions of trade
    Trade barriers, Nontariff
  BT Commercial policy
  RT Tariff
  NT Antidumping duties
    Buy national policy
    Government purchasing
    Import quotas
    Standardization
    Subsidies
Nonterm
  USE Terms of court
Nontraditional education
  USE Non-formal education
Nontronite
  ₁QE391.N₁
  ₁TN948.N₁
  BT Silicates
Nonvascular plants
  USE Cryptogams
Nonverbal communication *(May Subd Geog)*
  UF Non-verbal communication
  BT Communication
  RT Expression
  NT Drum language
    Gesture
    Paralinguistics
    PONS test
Nonverbal communication (Psychology)
  (May Subd Geog)
  ₁BF637.N66₁
  UF Body language
    Kinesics
  BT Interpersonal communication
  NT Eye contact
    Gaze—Psychological aspects
    Hugging
    Personal space
Nonverbal communication in children
  (May Subd Geog)
  ₁BF723.C57₁
  BT Interpersonal communication in
      children
Nonverbal communication in education
  (May Subd Geog)
  ₁LB1027₁
  BT Communication in education
Nonverbal communication in motion pictures
  UF Film kinesics
  BT Movement (Acting)
    Moving-picture acting
    Moving-pictures
Nonviolence
  UF Non-violence
  RT Pacifism
    Passive resistance
  NT Ahiṃsā
    Hunger strikes
  — **Religious aspects**
  — — **Baptists, ₁Catholic Church, etc.₁**
  — — — **Buddhism, ₁Christianity, etc.₁**
Nonviolence and communism
  USE Communism and nonviolence
Nonviolent noncooperation
  USE Passive resistance
Nonwoven fabrics
  ₁TS1828₁
  UF Fabrics, Nonwoven
  BT Synthetic fabrics
    Textile fabrics
  NT Flocking, Electrostatic
Nonwoven fabrics in medicine
  (May Subd Geog)
  ₁R857.N65₁
  BT Biomedical materials

Nonwoven fabrics industry
(May Subd Geog)
[HD9869.N64]
BT Textile industry
RT Man-made fibers industry
Noodle craft
USE Macaroni craft
Noodles
[TS2157]
BT Macaroni products
RT Dumplings
Noodles industry (May Subd Geog)
Nooga (Australian people)
USE Nyunga (Australian people)
Nooksack Indians
BT Coast Salish Indians
Indians of North America
Noon
UF Midday
Noontime
BT Day
Time
Noonga (Australian people)
USE Nyunga (Australian people)
Noontime
USE Noon
Noord-Zuid-Hollandse Vervoer
BT Railroads—Netherlands
Noordsche balk
[ML760]
UF Hommel
Hummel
Langleik
Noardske balke
Scheitholt
BT Zither
Noordzeekanaal (Netherlands)
USE North Sea Canal (Netherlands)
Noos (The Greek word)
UF Nous (The Greek word)
BT Greek language—Etymology
Nootka falsecypress
USE Chamaecyparis nootkatensis
Nootka Indians
[E99.N85]
UF Aht Indians
Noutka Indians
Nutka Indians
Nuu-chah-nulth Indians
BT Indians of North America
Wakashan Indians
NT Clayoquot Indians
Nootka language
[PM2031]
UF Aht language
Noutka language
Nutka language
RT Wakashan languages
Nootka Sound (Vancouver Island, B.C.)
UF Mazarredo Sound (Vancouver Island, B.C.)
Nutka Sound (Vancouver Island, B.C.)
BT Sounds (Geomorphology)—British Columbia
Nopah Range Wilderness (Calif.)
UF Nopah Range Wilderness Study Area (Calif.)
BT National parks and reserves—California
Wilderness areas—California
Nopah Range Wilderness Study Area (Calif.)
USE Nopah Range Wilderness (Calif.)
Nopalea
BT Cactus
Dactylopius—Host plants
Nope language
USE Nupe language
Nopiming Provincial Park (Man.)
(Not Subd Geog)
BT Parks—Manitoba

Nor language
USE Mambila language
Nora (Ancient city) (Not Subd Geog)
[DG70.N64]
BT Cities and towns, Ruined, extinct, etc.
—Italy
Italy—Antiquities
Nōrā (Dance)
[GV1796.N67]
BT Dancing—Thailand
Folk dancing—Thailand
Noradrenalin
UF Noradrenaline
Norepinephrine
BT Catecholamines
Neurotransmitters
Noradrenaline
USE Noradrenalin
Norba (Puglia, Italy : Ancient city)
(Not Subd Geog)
[DG70.N643]
UF Norve (Puglia, Italy : Ancient city)
BT Cities and towns, Ruined, extinct, etc.
—Italy
Italy—Antiquities
Norbeck family (Not Subd Geog)
Norby family
USE Nordby family
Norcross family (Not Subd Geog)
Nord-Norgebanen
BT Railroads—Norway
Nord-Ostsee Kanal (Germany)
USE Kiel Canal (Germany)
Nordan family (Not Subd Geog)
UF Nordeen family
Norden family
Nordin family
Nordås Waters (Norway)
USE Nordåsvannet (Norway)
Nordåsvannet (Norway) (Not Subd Geog)
UF Nordås Waters (Norway)
BT Lakes—Norway
Nordbeck's and Rystedt's mapping system (Electronic computer system)
USE NORMAP (Electronic computer system)
Nordby family (Not Subd Geog)
UF Norby family
Nordbye family
Nordbye family
USE Nordby family
Nordeen family
USE Nordan family
Norden
USE Scandinavia
Norden family
USE Nordan family
Nordenbrock family (Not Subd Geog)
Nordenfelt machine-gun
[UF620.N8]
BT Machine-guns
Nordenflycht family (Not Subd Geog)
UF De Nordenflycht family
Nordenskiöld (Spitsbergen Island, Norway)
USE Nordenskiöld Land (Spitsbergen Island, Norway)
Nordenskiöld Land (Spitsbergen Island, Norway) (Not Subd Geog)
UF Nordenskiöld (Spitsbergen Island, Norway)
Nordenskiölds Land (Spitsbergen Island, Norway)
BT Peninsulas—Norway
Nordenskiölds Land (Spitsbergen Island, Norway)
USE Nordenskiöld Land (Spitsbergen Island, Norway)
Nordfriesische Inseln (Denmark and Germany)
USE North Frisian Islands (Denmark and Germany)

Nordfriesland (Germany)
USE North Friesland (Germany)
Nordfriislon (Germany)
USE North Friesland (Germany)
Nordfrisiske Øer (Denmark and Germany)
USE North Frisian Islands (Denmark and Germany)
Nordic race
USE Teutonic race
Nordic skiing
USE Cross-country skiing
Ski jumping
Nordic Tanganyika Project
BT Medical assistance, Scandinavian—Tanzania
Technical assistance, Scandinavian—Tanzania
Nordiidae
[QL391.N4]
BT Dorylaimida
NT Enchodelus
Nordin family
USE Nordan family
Nordkapp (Magerøy Island, Norway)
USE North Cape (Magerøy Island, Norway)
Nordkirchen Palace (Germany)
USE Schloss Nordkirchen (Germany)
Nördlingen, Battle of, 1634
[D267.N7]
BT Thirty Years' War, 1618-1648
Nördlinger Ries (Germany)
USE Ries (Germany)
Nordnes family (Not Subd Geog)
Nordpol-Spiel
USE Englandspiel
Nordquist family (Not Subd Geog)
Nore Mutiny, 1797
[DA87.7]
Norem family (Not Subd Geog)
Norephedrine
USE Phenylpropanolamine
Norepinephrine
USE Noradrenalin
Norethindrone
[RG137.6.N67]
UF Ethinylnortestosterone
Hydroxynorpregnenyone
Norethisterone
Norpregneninolone
BT Oral contraceptives
Progestational hormones, Synthetic
Steroid hormones
Norethisterone
USE Norethindrone
Norfloxacin
UF Ethylfluorodihydroox opiperazinylquinolinecarboxylic acid
BT Antibacterial agents
Carboxylic acids
Quinoline
Norfolk, Dukes of (Not Subd Geog)
BT England—Nobility
Norfolk Broads (England)
USE Broads, The (England)
Norfolk House Music Room (Interior decoration)
USE Brettingham, Matthew, 1699-1769.
Norfolk House Music Room
Norfolk Island pine
UF Araucaria excelsa
Norfolk-Virginia Beach Toll Road (Va.)
USE Virginia Beach-Norfolk Expressway (Va.)
Norfolk wherries
USE Wherries
Nørgaard family (Not Subd Geog)
UF Noergaard family
Norgard family
Norgard family
USE Nørgaard family

2608

Norgestrel
    BT Progestational hormones
Nori *(May Subd Geog)*
    [QK569.B2 (Botany)]
    [SH391.N65 (Culture)]
    UF Amanori
          Haet'ae
          Kim
    BT Marine algae as food
          Porphyra
Noric cattle
    USE Pinzgauer cattle
Noris family
    USE Norris family
Norm (Linguistics)
    USE Standard language
Norm (Philosophy)
    [B105.N65]
    BT Philosophy
Norm based tests
    USE Norm-referenced tests
Norm-referenced tests *(May Subd Geog)*
    [LB3060.32.N67]
    UF Norm based tests
    BT Achievement tests
          Educational tests and measurements
          Examinations
Normal distribution
    USE Gaussian distribution
Normal forms (Mathematics)
    UF Forms, Normal (Mathematics)
    BT Mathematics
Normal institutes
    USE Teachers' institutes
Normal numbers
    BT Numbers, Theory of
          Series, Geometric
Normal operators
    UF Operators, Normal
    BT Linear operators
Normal schools
    USE Teachers colleges
Normal varieties (Algebraic geometry)
    UF Varieties, Normal (Algebraic
          geometry)
    BT Algebraic varieties
    NT Picard number
Norman, Lake (N.C.)
    UF Lake Norman (N.C.)
    BT Catawba River (N.C. and S.C.)
          Lakes—North Carolina
          Reservoirs—North Carolina
Norman architecture
    USE Architecture, Norman
Norman art
    USE Art, Norman
Norman family *(Not Subd Geog)*
    UF Normand family
          Normann family
          Normant family
          Norment family
Norman horse
    USE Percheron horse
Norman illumination of books and manuscripts
    USE Illumination of books and manuscripts,
          Norman
Norman style of French cookery
    USE Cookery, French—Normandy style
Normand Bocage (France)
    USE Bocage normand (France)
Normand family
    USE Norman family
Normandie Expressway (France)
    USE Autoroute de Normandie (France)
Normandy, Dukes of *(Not Subd Geog)*
    UF Dukes of Normandy
    BT France—Nobility
          Great Britain—Nobility
Normandy (France)
— History
— — To 1515

Normandy Archaeological Project
    [E78.T3]
    BT Indians of North America—Tennessee
          —Antiquities
          Tennessee—Antiquities
Normandy cattle
    [SF193.N8 (Herd-books)]
    [SF199.N]
Normandy Expressway (France)
    USE Autoroute de Normandie (France)
Normandy Invasion, 1944 (Military operation)
    USE World War, 1939-1945—Campaigns—
          France—Normandy
Normandy Invasion, 1944 (Planning)
    USE Operation Overlord
Normandy Lake (Tenn.)
    USE Normandy Reservoir (Tenn.)
Normandy Reservoir (Tenn.)
    UF Normandy Lake (Tenn.)
    BT Duck River (Tenn.)
          Lakes—Tennessee
          Reservoirs—Tennessee
Normandy Reservoir Region (Tenn.)
— Antiquities
        NT Duke I Site (Tenn.)
            Eoff I Site (Tenn.)
            Ewell III Site (Tenn.)
            Jernigan II Site (Tenn.)
            Parks Site (Tenn.)
Normandy style of French cookery
    USE Cookery, French—Normandy style
Normann family
    USE Norman family
Normans *(May Subd Geog)*
    UF Northmen—France
    BT Northmen
Normant family
    USE Norman family
NORMAP (Electronic computer system)
    [GA106.3]
    UF Nordbeck's and Rystedt's mapping
          system (Electronic computer
          system)
Normative grammar
    USE Standard language
Normed linear spaces
    UF Linear normed spaces
          Normed vector spaces
    BT Banach spaces
          Functional analysis
          Vector analysis
Normed rings
    USE Banach algebras
Normed vector spaces
    USE Normed linear spaces
Norment family
    USE Norman family
Normichthys
    [QL638.S47]
    BT Searsidae
    NT Normichthys yahganorum
Normichthys yahganorum
    [QL638.S47]
    BT Normichthys
Norms, Social
    USE Social norms
Norms of matrices
    USE Matrices—Norms
Norn dialect
    [PD2485]
    BT Old Norse language
Noro family *(Not Subd Geog)*
Norops
    [QL666.L25]
    BT Iguanidae
Nororiental (Venezuela)
    USE Venezuela, Northeast
Norpregnatrienynediol
    USE Ethinyl estradiol
Norpregneninolone
    USE Norethindrone

Norrbotten (Sweden)
Norre Port (Halmstad, Sweden)
    UF North Gate (Halmstad, Sweden)
    BT Gates—Sweden
Nørrebro (Copenhagen, Denmark)
    (Not Subd Geog)
    UF Copenhagen (Denmark).   Nørrebro
Norress family
    USE Norris family
Norrice family
    USE Norris family
Norridgewock Indians
    [E78.M4]
    [E99.N]
    UF Kennebec Indians
          Norridgwalk Indians
          Norridgwog Indians
    BT Algonquian Indians
          Indians of North America
Norridgwalk Indians
    USE Norridgewock Indians
Norridgwog Indians
    USE Norridgewock Indians
Norrie's disease *(May Subd Geog)*
    UF Heredo-retinopathia congenitalis
    BT Eye—Diseases and defects
          Genetic disorders
Norrington family *(Not Subd Geog)*
Norris Basin (Wyo.)
    USE Norris Geyser Basin (Wyo.)
Norris family *(Not Subd Geog)*
    UF Narris family
          Noris family
          Norress family
          Norrice family
          Norrise family
          Norrish family
          Norriss family
Norris Geyser Basin (Wyo.)
    (Not Subd Geog)
    UF Norris Basin (Wyo.)
    BT Geysers—Wyoming
Norris Lake (Tenn.)
    UF Norris Reservoir (Tenn.)
    BT Clinch River (Va. and Tenn.)
          Lakes—Tennessee
          Powell River (Va. and Tenn.)
          Reservoirs—Tennessee
Norris Reservoir (Tenn.)
    USE Norris Lake (Tenn.)
Norrise family
    USE Norris family
Norrish family
    USE Norris family
Norriss family
    USE Norris family
Norrland (Sweden)
Norrmalm (Stockholm, Sweden)
    (Not Subd Geog)
    UF Stockholm (Sweden).   Norrmalm
Norse architecture
    USE Architecture, Norse
Norse cults *(May Subd Geog)*
    BT Cults
Norse decoration and ornament
    USE Decoration and ornament, Norse
Norse gods
    USE Gods, Norse
Norse illumination of books and manuscripts
    USE Illumination of books and manuscripts,
          Norse
Norse inscriptions
    USE Inscriptions, Norse
Norse languages
    USE Old Norse language
          Scandinavian languages
Norsemen
    USE Northmen
Norskehavet
    USE Norwegian Sea

Norte Chico Region (Chile)
Norteno music
  USE Popular music—Mexico
        Popular music—Texas
North (The word)
  ⌈G108.N8⌉
  BT Cardinal points
North Adams (Mass.). Blackinton
  USE Blackinton (North Adams, Mass.)
North Africa
  USE Africa, North
North Africa specialists
  USE North Africanists
North African alien labor
  USE Alien labor, North African
North African authors
  USE Authors, North African
North African cookery
  USE Cookery, North African
North African fiction (French)
  ⌈PQ3988.N⌉
  UF French fiction—North African authors
North African Jews
  USE Jews, North African
North African literature (French)
  UF French literature—North African
       authors
North African poetry (French)
  ⌈PQ3988.N6⌉
  UF French poetry—North African authors
North Africanists *(May Subd Geog)*
  UF North Africa specialists
  BT Africa, North—Study and teaching
North Africans *(May Subd Geog)*
  RT Arabs
  NT Arabs—Africa, North
      Bedouins
      Berbers
North America
  — Antiquities
    NT Blackduck culture
  — Description and travel
  — — 1951-1980
  — — 1981-
  — History
  — — Colonial period, ca. 1600-1775
  — Population
    NT Indians of North America—
        Population
North American airplanes (Military aircraft)
  ⌈TL686.N6⌉
  UF North American-Rockwell airplanes
  NT B-1 bomber
      Mitchell bomber
      Mustang (Fighter planes)
      Sabre (Jet fighter planes)
      T-6 (Training planes)
      Vigilante bomber
      X-15 (Rocket aircraft)
North American badger
  USE American badger
North American black snake
  USE Coluber constrictor
North American blastomycosis
  USE Blastomycosis
North American cattle tick
  USE Cattle tick
North American Indians
  USE Indians of North America
North American language
  ⌈PM8679⌉
  BT Languages, Artificial
North American manatee
  USE Trichechus manatus
North American otter
  USE Lutra canadensis
North American porcupine
  ⌈QL737.R652⌉
  UF Canada porcupine
      Erethizon dorsatum
  BT Porcupines

North American raccoon
  USE Raccoons
North American-Rockwell airplanes
  USE North American airplanes (Military
      aircraft)
      Rockwell airplanes (Civil aircraft)
North American X-15 (Rocket aircraft)
  USE X-15 (Rocket aircraft)
North and south
  ⌈CB261⌉
  Here are entered works on both acculturation and
  culture conflict between civilizations of colder and
  warmer areas.
  UF South and north
  BT Acculturation
      Culture conflict
North Anna River (Va.)
  BT Rivers—Virginia
  NT Anna, Lake (Va.)
North Anna River (Va.), Battle of, 1864
  UF Hanover Junction (Va.), Battle of,
      1864
      Jericho Bridge (Va.), Battle of, 1864
      Jericho Ford (Va.), Battle of, 1864
      Jericho Mills (Va.), Battle of, 1864
      Taylor's Bridge (Va.), Battle of, 1864
  BT United States—History—Civil War,
      1861-1865—Campaigns
North Aryan language
  USE Khotanese language
North Atlantic Ocean
  BT Atlantic Ocean
  NT Baffin Bay (North Atlantic Ocean)
      Bermuda Triangle
      Caribbean Sea
      Irish Sea
      Labrador Sea
      Norwegian Sea
      Sargasso Sea
North Atlantic pact, 1949
  USE North Atlantic treaty, 1949
North Atlantic Region
  — Strategic aspects
    BT Military geography
      Strategy
North Atlantic treaty, 1949
  UF Atlantic pact, 1949
      North Atlantic pact, 1949
North Atlantic Treaty Organization
  (May Subd Geog)
  — Armed Forces *(May Subd Geog)*
  — — Uniforms
North-Bahnaric language, Proto-
  USE Proto-North-Bahnaric language
North Branch Canal (Pa.)
  BT Canals—Pennsylvania
North Brazil
  USE Brazil, North
North Canadian River (Okla.)
  UF Canadian River, North (Okla.)
  BT Rivers—Oklahoma
North Cape (Magerøy Island, Norway)
  UF Nordkapp (Magerøy Island, Norway)
  BT Capes (Coasts)—Norway
North Cape Coral Industrial Park (Cape Coral, Fla.)
  BT Industrial districts—Florida
North Carolina
  — Description and travel
  — — 1951-1980
  — — 1981-
  — Governors
  — — Dwellings
    NT Tryon Palace (New Bern, N.C.)
  — History
    ⌈F251-265⌉
  — — Colonial period, ca. 1600-1775
    NT Culpeper's Rebellion, 1677-1679
      Raleigh's Roanoke colonies,
      1584-1590
      St. Augustine Expedition, 1740

      Tuscarora Indians—Wars, 1711-
      1713
  — — — Juvenile literature
  — — French and Indian War, 1755-1763
  — — Regulator Insurrection, 1766-1771
    UF Regulator Insurrection, North
      Carolina, 1766-1771
  — — — Campaigns *(Not Subd Geog)*
    NT Alamance, Battle of, 1771
  — — Revolution, 1775-1783
    ⌈E263.N8⌉
    NT Cowan's Ford, Battle of, 1781
      Guilford Court House, Battle of,
      1781
      Lindley's Mill, Battle of, 1781
      Ramsour's Mill, Battle of, 1780
  — — 1775-1865
  — — War of 1812
  — — Civil War, 1861-1865
    ⌈E524⌉
    ⌈E573⌉
    NT Roanoke Island (N.C.)—
      Capture, 1862
      Sherman's March through the
      Carolinas
  — — 1865-
  — Politics and government
  — — Colonial period, ca. 1600-1775
  — — Revolution, 1775-1783
  — — 1775-1865
  — — Civil War, 1861-1865
  — — 1865-1950
  — — 1951-
  — Social life and customs
  — — Colonial period, ca. 1600-1775
North Carolina Day
  ⌈LB3541⌉
North Cascades National Park (Wash.)
  BT National parks and reserves—
      Washington (State)
North Central States
  USE Middle West
North Channel (Huron, Lake, Mich. and Ont.)
  BT Huron, Lake (Mich. and Ont.)
      Sounds (Geomorphology)—Michigan
      Sounds (Geomorphology)—Ontario
North Cornwall Island (N.W.T.)
  USE Cornwall Island (N.W.T.)
North Country (N.Y.)
  UF New York State North Country
North Dakota
  — Antiquities
    NT Beaver Creek Site (N.D.)
  — Description and travel
  — — 1951-
  — Languages
    NT Michif language
North Dakota pottery
  USE University of North Dakota pottery
North Delaney Lake (Colo.)
  (Not Subd Geog)
  BT Lakes—Colorado
North Downs Way (England)
  BT Trails—England
North End (Boston, Mass.)
  (Not Subd Geog)
  UF Boston (Mass.). North End
North England
  USE England, Northern
North family *(Not Subd Geog)*
  UF Northan family
      Northen family
      Northern family
      Noth family
North Fork, Coeur d'Alene River (Idaho)
  USE Coeur d'Alene River, North Fork
      (Idaho)
North Fork, Solomon River (Kan.)
  USE Solomon River, North Fork (Kan.)

North Fork of the Little Humboldt River Wilderness (Nev.) *(Not Subd Geog)*
  UF Little Humboldt River Wilderness (Nev.)
     North Fork of the Little Humboldt River Wilderness Study Area (Nev.)
  BT National parks and reserves—Nevada
     Wilderness areas—Nevada
North Fork of the Little Humboldt River Wilderness Study Area (Nev.)
  USE North Fork of the Little Humboldt River Wilderness (Nev.)
North Fork Owyhee River Wilderness (Idaho) *(Not Subd Geog)*
  UF North Fork Owyhee River Wilderness Study Area (Idaho)
     Owyhee River Wilderness, North Fork (Idaho)
  BT National parks and reserves—Idaho
     Wilderness areas—Idaho
North Fork Owyhee River Wilderness Study Area (Idaho)
  USE North Fork Owyhee River Wilderness (Idaho)
North Fork Skokomish River (Wash.)
  USE Skokomish River, North Fork (Wash.)
North Fork Swan Creek (Neb.)
  USE Swan Creek, North Fork (Neb.)
North Friesian Islands (Denmark and Germany)
  USE North Frisian Islands (Denmark and Germany)
North Friesland (Germany)
  UF Friesland, North (Germany)
     Nordfriesland (Germany)
     Nordfriislon (Germany)
  NT North Frisian Islands (Denmark and Germany)
North Frisian Islands (Denmark and Germany)
  UF Frisian Islands, North (Denmark and Germany)
     Nordfriesische Inseln (Denmark and Germany)
     Nordfrisiske Øer (Denmark and Germany)
     North Friesian Islands (Denmark and Germany)
  BT Frisian Islands
     Islands—Denmark
     Islands—Germany (West)
     North Friesland (Germany)
  NT Föhr (Germany)
     Rømø (Denmark)
     Sylt (Germany)
North Gate (Halmstad, Sweden)
  USE Norre Port (Halmstad, Sweden)
North Halmaheran languages
  USE Halmaheran languages
North Island (N.Z.)
  BT Islands—New Zealand
North Korea
  USE Korea (North)
North Korean espionage
  USE Espionage, North Korean
North Land (R.S.F.S.R.)
  USE Severnaĭa Zemlĭa (R.S.F.S.R.)
North Lawndale (Chicago, Ill.) *(Not Subd Geog)*
  UF Chicago (Ill.).   North Lawndale
North London Railway
  BT Railroads—Great Britain
North Mkata Plain (Tanzania)
  UF Mkata Plain, North (Tanzania)
  BT Plains—Tanzania
North Pacific Ocean
  BT Pacific Ocean
North Pender Island (B.C.)
  UF Pender Island, North (B.C.)
  BT Islands—British Columbia

North Platte River
  BT Rivers—Colorado
     Rivers—Nebraska
     Rivers—Wyoming
North Point (Milwaukee, Wis.) *(Not Subd Geog)*
  UF Milwaukee (Wis.).   North Point
North Point, Battle of, 1814
  [E356.B2]
  UF Patapsco Neck, Battle of, 1814
  BT Baltimore, Battle of, 1814
     United States—History—War of 1812—Campaigns
North Pole
  [G600-700]
  BT Polar regions
  RT Arctic regions
North pole star
  USE Polestar
North Puget Sound Salish language
  USE Puget Sound Salish languages
North River (Plymouth County, Mass.)
  BT Rivers—Massachusetts
North Ronaldsay (Scotland)
  [DA880.O5-DA880.O6]
  UF Ronaldsay, North (Scotland)
  BT Islands—Scotland
     Orkney
North Saskatchewan River (Alta. and Sask.)
  UF Saskatchewan River, North (Alta. and Sask.)
  BT Rivers—Alberta
     Rivers—Saskatchewan
North Sea
North Sea-Baltic Canal (Germany)
  USE Kiel Canal (Germany)
North Sea Canal (Netherlands)
  UF Noordzeekanaal (Netherlands)
  BT Canals—Netherlands
North Shore Railroad
  BT Railroads—United States
North Shrewsbury River (N.J.)
  USE Navesink River (N.J.)
North Slope (Alaska)
North star
  USE Polestar
North Star (Transport plane)
  USE Canadair DC-4M (Transport plane)
North Thailand
  USE Thailand, Northern
North Toe River (N.C.)
  UF Estatoe River (N.C.)
     Toe River (N.C.)
  BT Rivers—North Carolina
North Vietnamese literature (French)
  USE French literature—North Vietnamese authors
North Wales
  USE Wales, North
North Wales Coast Road (Wales)
  BT Roads—Wales
North York Moors (England)
  BT Moors and heaths—England
     Mountains—England
     North York Moors National Park (England)
North York Moors National Park (England)
  BT Moors and heaths—England
     National parks and reserves—Great Britain
     Parks—England
  NT North York Moors (England)
North Yorkshire Moors Railway
  BT Railroads—Great Britain
Northan family
  USE North family
Northeast Africa
  USE Africa, Northeast
Northeast boundary of the United States *(Not Subd Geog)*
  [E398]

  NT Aroostook War, 1839
Northeast Brazil
  USE Brazil, Northeast
Northeast Bulgarian fine-wooled sheep
  [SF373.N67]
  UF Bulgarian fine-wooled sheep, Northeast
Northeast Caucasian languages
  USE Daghestan languages
     Nakh languages
Northeast China
  USE Manchuria (China)
Northeast India
  USE India, Northeastern
Northeast Passage
  [G680-690]
  BT Arctic regions
     Discoveries (in geography)
     Voyages and travels
Northeast Thailand
  USE Thailand, Northeastern
Northeast Venezuela
  USE Venezuela, Northeast
Northeastern India
  USE India, Northeastern
Northeastern Luba language
  USE Songe language
Northeastern Region (Thailand)
  USE Thailand, Northeastern
Northeastern Siberia (R.S.F.S.R.)
  USE Siberia, Northeastern (R.S.F.S.R.)
Northeastern States
  Here are entered works on that part of the United States lying north of the Ohio and the Potomac Rivers, and east of the Mississippi River.
  NT Atlantic States
     New England
     Northwest, Old
Northeastern Thailand
  USE Thailand, Northeastern
Northen family
  USE North family
Northern Altai language
  BT Altai language
     Russian S.F.S.R.—Languages
     Turkic languages, Northeast
Northern anchovy
  [QL638.E55]
  UF Engraulis mordax
  BT Anchovies
Northern and Southern dynasties, China, 386-589
  USE China—History—Northern and Southern dynasties, 386-589
Northern birch mouse
  USE Sicista betulina
Northern Border Pipeline
  BT Gas, Natural—United States—Pipe lines
Northern Border War, 1st, South Africa, 1868-1870
  USE Korana War, 1st, 1868-1870
Northern Border War, 2nd, South Africa, 1878-1879
  USE Korana War, 2nd, 1878-1879
Northern boundary of the United States *(Not Subd Geog)*
  [F551]
  [F597]
  BT United States—Boundaries
Northern Buddhism
  USE Mahayana Buddhism
Northern Cagayan Negrito language
  USE Atta language
Northern California
  USE California, Northern
Northern Canada
  USE Canada, Northern
Northern Carrier language
  USE Babine language
Northern Caucasus (R.S.F.S.R.)
  USE Caucasus, Northern (R.S.F.S.R.)

Northern Central Semitic languages
  USE Semitic languages, Northwest
Northern Ch'i dynasty, 550-577
  USE China—History—Northern Ch'i
     dynasty, 550-577
Northern Chinese dialects
  USE Mandarin dialects
Northern Chou dynasty, 557-581
  USE China—History—Northern Chou
     dynasty, 557-581
Northern Circars (India)
  UF Circars, Northern (India)
     Northern Sarkārs (India)
     Sarkārs, Northern (India)
Northern corn rootworm
  UF Corn rootworm, Northern
Northern dogs
  USE Spitz dogs
Northern Donets River (R.S.F.S.R. and
  Ukraine)
  USE Donets River (R.S.F.S.R. and Ukraine)
Northern eagle owl
  USE Bubo bubo
Northern Electric Street Railway
  BT Railroads—United States
     Street-railroads—United States
Northern elephant seal
  UF Elephant seal, Northern
     Mirounga angustirostris
  BT Elephant seals
Northern England
  USE England, Northern
Northern Epera language
  USE Catio language
Northern Europe
  USE Europe, Northern
Northern Expedition, 1926-1928
  USE China—History—Northern Expedition,
     1926-1928
Northern family
  USE North family
Northern flicker
  USE Colaptes auratus
Northern fulmar
  USE Fulmarus glacialis
Northern fur seal
  UF Callorhinus ursinus
     Fur seal, Northern
  BT Eared seals
  — Law and legislation *(May Subd Geog)*
Northern gannet
  [QL696.P48]
  UF Morus bassanus
     Sula bassanus
  BT Gannets
Northern Germany
  USE Germany, Northern
Northern harrier
  USE Circus cyaneas
Northern Hemisphere
  UF Hemisphere, Northern
  BT Earth
Northern Illinois Railroad
  BT Railroads—United States
Northern Ireland
  — Description and travel
  — — 1981-
  — History
  — — 1969-
  — — 1969-
  — — — Anecdotes, facetiae, satire, etc.
     (Not Subd Geog)
  — Politics and government
  — — 1969-
  — Social conditions
  — — 1969-
Northern Ireland in mass media
  (May Subd Geog)
  BT Mass media
Northern Italian style of cookery
  USE Cookery, Italian—Northern style

Northern Italy
  USE Italy, Northern
Northern Karoo (South Africa)
  USE Northern Karroo (South Africa)
Northern Karroo (South Africa)
  UF High Veld (South Africa)
     Highveld (South Africa)
     Karoo, Northern (South Africa)
     Karoo, Upper (South Africa)
     Karroo, Northern (South Africa)
     Northern Karoo (South Africa)
     Upper Karoo (South Africa)
  BT Plateaus—South Africa
Northern Kimberley languages
  USE Wororan languages
Northern leopard frog
  USE Rana pipiens
Northern lights
  USE Auroras
Northern long-eared owl
  USE Long-eared owl
Northern Lunda language
  USE Ruund language
Northern marsh harrier
  USE Circus cyaneas
Northern midshipman
  UF Porichthys notatus
  BT Toadfishes
Northern Min dialects *(May Subd Geog)*
  [PL1681-1690]
  UF Min-pei dialects
  BT Chinese language—Dialects
Northern Miwok language
  USE Northern Sierra Miwok language
Northern mountain cranberry
  USE Vaccinium vitis-idaea
Northern Neck (Va.)
  BT Peninsulas—Virginia
Northern Nigeria (Region)
  USE Nigeria, Northern
Northern oriole
  [QL696.P2475]
  UF Abeille's oriole
     Baltimore bird
     Baltimore oriole (Bird)
     Bullock's oriole
     Coracius galbula
     Golden robin
     Hangnest
     Icterus abeillei
     Icterus bullockii
     Icterus galbula
     Oriole, Baltimore (Bird)
     Oriole, Northern
  BT Icterus (Birds)
Northern Pacific Railway
  BT Railroads—United States
Northern Peninsula (Mich.)
  USE Upper Peninsula (Mich.)
Northern pike
  USE Pike
Northern pocket gopher
  USE Thomomys talpoides
Northern Puget Sound Salish language
  USE Puget Sound Salish languages
Northern red-backed vole
  USE Clethrionomys rutilus
Northern red oak
  USE Red oak
Northern Rhodesia
  USE Zambia
Northern Russia
  USE Soviet Union, Northern
Northern Sarkārs (India)
  USE Northern Circars (India)
Northern sea cow
  USE Steller's sea cow
Northern sea lion
  USE Eumetopias jubata
Northern Seven Years' War, 1563-1570
  [DL188.5 (Denmark)]

  UF Denmark—History—Northern Seven
     Years' War, 1563-1570
     Norway—History—Northern Seven
     Years' War, 1563-1570
     Sweden—History—Northern Seven
     Years' War, 1563-1570
     Three Crowns' War, 1563-1570
Northern shoveler
  USE Anas clypeata
Northern shrimp
  USE Pandalus borealis
Northern shrimp, Deepsea
  USE Pandalus borealis
Northern Sierra Miwok language
  (May Subd Geog)
  [PM1845]
  UF Northern Miwok language
  BT California—Languages
     Miwok languages
Northern Sinama dialect
  USE Balangingì dialect
Northern song-tales (Chinese drama)
  USE Ku tz'u
Northern Sotho language
  [PL8690]
  UF Pedi language
     Sepedi language
     Sotho language, Northern
     Transvaal Sotho language
  BT Sotho-Tswana languages
  NT Ndebele language (South Africa)
Northern Sotho philology
  [PL8690]
Northern Soviet Union
  USE Soviet Union, Northern
Northern Spain
  USE Spain, Northern
Northern squawfish
  USE Ptychocheilus oregonensis
Northern style of Indic cookery
  USE Cookery, Indic—Northern style
Northern style of Italian cookery
  USE Cookery, Italian—Northern style
Northern sucker
  USE Longnose sucker
Northern tehuelche language
  USE Pampa language
Northern Thai language
  [PL4251.N63]
  UF Kammyang language
     Lanna Thai language
     Myang language
     Phayap language
     Thai language, Northern
     Thai Yuan language
     Yuan language
  BT Laos—Languages
     Tai languages
     Thailand—Languages
Northern Thai literature *(May Subd Geog)*
Northern Thai proverbs
  USE Proverbs, Northern Thai
Northern Thailand
  USE Thailand, Northern
Northern three-toed woodpecker
  [QL696.P56]
  UF Picoides tridactylus
  BT Woodpeckers
Northern Tier
  USE Iran
     Turkey
Northern Tier (Middle East)
  USE Middle East
Northern Tier Pipeline
  UF Northern Tier pipeline, Wash.-Minn.
  BT Petroleum—United States—Pipe lines
  — Earthquake effects
     BT Earthquakes
Northern Tier pipeline, Wash.-Minn.
  USE Northern Tier Pipeline

Northern Turkic languages
USE Turkic languages, Northeast
Northern tzoneca language
USE Pampa language
Northern vehicle
USE Mahayana Buddhism
Northern War, 1700-1721
[DL733-DL743 (Sweden)]
UF Great Northern War, 1700-1721
Sweden—History—Northern War,
1700-1721
NT Hangö, Battle of, 1714
Narva, Battle of, 1700
Poltava, Battle of, 1709
Vyborg, Battle of, 1710
— **Campaigns**
— — **Sweden**
NT Helsingborg, Battle of, 1710
— **Prisoners and prisons**
Northern Wei dynasty
USE China—History—Northern Wei
dynasty, 386-534
Northern wheatear
[QL696.P288]
UF Oenanthe oenanthe
Wheatear, Northern
BT Wheatears
Northern white cedar
USE Thuja occidentalis
Northern white-tailed prairie dog
USE Cynomys leucurus
Northern winter moth
USE Operophthera fagata
Northland (N.Z.)
Northmen (May Subd Geog)
Here are entered works on the inhabitants of
Scandinavia prior to the 10th century. Works on the
Scandinavian sea-warriors who plundered the north-
ern and western coasts of Europe from the 8th to the
10th centuries are entered under Vikings. Works on
the inhabitants of Scandinavia since the 10th century
are entered under Scandinavians.
UF Norsemen
BT Ethnology—Scandinavia
NT Normans
Vikings
— **America**
USE America—Discovery and
exploration—Norse
— **France**
USE Normans
— **Soviet Union**
USE Varangians
Northoop family
USE Northrup family
Northorp family
USE Northrup family
Northrip family
USE Northrup family
Northrop aircraft
[TL686.N]
NT Black widow (Fighter planes)
Northrop black widow (Fighter planes)
USE Black widow (Fighter planes)
Northrop family
USE Northrup family
Northrope family
USE Northrup family
Northroup family
USE Northrup family
Northrup family (Not Subd Geog)
UF Northoop family
Northorp family
Northrip family
Northrop family
Northrope family
Northroup family
Northup family
Nortrip family
Nortrup family
Nothrop family

Northumberland Strait (Not Subd Geog)
BT Straits—New Brunswick
Straits—Nova Scotia
Straits—Prince Edward Island
Northup family
USE Northrup family
Northview Cemetery (Dearborn, Mich.)
BT Cemeteries—Michigan
Northville-Lake Placid Trail (N.Y.)
(Not Subd Geog)
BT Trails—New York (State)
Northwest, Canadian
[F1060]
Here are entered works on the area of Canada
west of Ontario and Hudson Bay.
UF Canadian Northwest
West (Canada)
RT Canada, Western
NT Great Plains
— **Description and travel**
— — **To 1821**
— — **1821-1867**
— — **1867-1950**
— — **1951-1980**
— — **1981-**
Northwest, New
USE Northwestern States
Northwest, Old
[F476-485]
Used for the region between the Ohio and Missis-
sippi rivers and the Great Lakes.
BT Northeastern States
NT Middle West
— **History**
[F476-485]
— — **To 1775**
— — **Revolution, 1775-1783**
[E263.N84]
NT Clark's Expedition against
Detroit, 1781
Clark's Expedition to the
Illinois, 1778-1779
— — **1775-1865**
NT Lewis Cass Expedition, 1820
Miami Purchase
Wayne's Campaign, 1794
— — **War of 1812**
[E355.2]
[E355.4]
— — **Civil War, 1861-1865**
— — **1865-**
Northwest, Pacific
[F851-F852]
Here are entered works on the old Oregon coun-
try, comprising the present states of Oregon, Wash-
ington and Idaho, parts of Montana and Wyoming
and the province of British Columbia.
UF Oregon Country
Pacific Northwest
— **Description and travel**
— — **1951-1980**
— — **1981-**
— **Storm, 1962**
Northwest Africa
USE Africa, Northwest
Northwest boundary of the United States
(Not Subd Geog)
[F854 (1846-)]
[F880 (To 1846)]
RT Oregon question
Northwest Branch Anacostia River (Md.)
USE Anacostia River, Northwest Branch
(Md.)
Northwest Caucasian languages
USE Abkhazo-Adyghian languages
Northwest China
USE China, Northwest
Northwest Coast of North America
Here are entered works limited to the coastal re-
gion extending from Northern California to Southern
Alaska.
UF West Coast (U.S. and B.C.)

BT Coasts—North America
Pacific Coast (North America)
RT Pacific Coast (U.S.)
NT Pacific Coast (B.C.)
Northwest Palace (Calah)
BT Iraq—Antiquities
Palaces—Iraq
Northwest Passage
[G640-665]
BT Arctic regions
Discoveries (in geography)
Voyages and travels
Northwest Rebellion, 1885
USE Riel Rebellion, 1885
Northwest River (Va. and N.C.)
BT Rivers—North Carolina
Rivers—Virginia
Northwest school of artists
BT Art, American—Northwestern States
Art, Modern—20th century—
Northwestern States
Artist colonies—Northwestern States
Northwest Semitic languages
USE Semitic languages, Northwest
Northwest Territories
— **Antiquities**
NT Brooman Point Site (N.W.T.)
DeBlicquy Site (N.W.T.)
Lagoon Site (Banks Island,
N.W.T.)
Tunirmiut Site (N.W.T.)
Northwest Trek Park (Wash.)
BT Parks—Washington (State)
Wildlife refuges—Washington (State)
Northwest Turkic languages
USE Turkic languages, Northwest
Northwestern Conspiracy, 1864
[E458.8]
BT United States—History—Civil War,
1861-1865
Northwestern Pennsylvania Railway
BT Railroads—United States
Northwestern Russia
USE Soviet Union, Northwestern
Northwestern Semitic languages
USE Semitic languages, Northwest
Northwestern Soviet Union
USE Soviet Union, Northwestern
Northwestern States
[F597]
UF Northwest, New
— **History**
— — **Civil War, 1861-1865**
Northwood family (Not Subd Geog)
Nortin family
USE Norton family
Nortine family
USE Norton family
Norton Basin (Not Subd Geog)
BT Submarine topography—Bering Sea
Norton family (Not Subd Geog)
UF Nortin family
Nortine family
Noten family
Noton family
Norton motorcycle
Norton Reservoir (Mass.)
BT Reservoirs—Massachusetts
Rumford River (Mass.)
Norton Sound (Alaska)
BT Sounds (Geomorphology)—Alaska
Nortrip family
USE Northrup family
Nortrup family
USE Northrup family
Norve (Puglia, Italy : Ancient city)
USE Norba (Puglia, Italy : Ancient city)
Norwalk (Conn.)
— **Burning by the British, 1779**

Norwalk (Conn.)
— Burning by the British, 1779
  (Continued)
    BT United States—History—
        Revolution, 1775-1783—
        Campaigns
Norway
  NT Classification—Books—Norway
— Anniversaries, etc.
    NT Independence Day (Norway)
— Antiquities
    NT Kaupang Site (Norway)
        Soløy Farm Mound Site (Soløy,
        Norway)
— Civilization
— — Greek influences
    BT Greece—Civilization
— — Roman influences
    BT Rome—Civilization
— Description and travel
— — 1945-
— — 1945-1980
— — 1981-
— Economic conditions
— — 1918-
— — 1945-
— Foreign relations
— — 1808-1814
— — 1814-1905
— — 1905-
— — 1905-1945
      ₍DL530₎
— — 1945-
      ₍DL533-534₎
— History
    ₍DL401-596₎
— — To 1030
    NT Havsfjord, Battle of, 872
        Stiklestad, Battle of, 1030
— — 1030-1397
— — Magnus I, 1035-1047
— — Sigurd Jorsalafari, 1103-1130
— — Sverre, 1177-1202
— — Haakon Gamli, 1204-1263
— — Magnus VII Eriksson, 1319-1343
— — 1397-1814
    NT Kalmar, Union of, 1397
— — Eric III, 1400-1442
— — Christian I, 1448-1481
— — Frederick I, 1523-1533
— — Christian III, 1537-1559
— — Northern Seven Years' War, 1563-1570
      USE Northern Seven Years' War,
          1563-1570
— — Christian IV, 1588-1648
— — Scottish Expedition, 1612
— — Hannibal's War, 1644-1645
— — Frederick III, 1648-1670
— — 1660-1814
— — Christian V, 1670-1699
      ₍DL195-DL195.8₎
— — Frederick IV, 1699-1730
— — Christian VI, 1730-1746
— — Frederick V, 1746-1766
— — Christian VII, 1766-1808
— — War of 1807-1814
— — Frederick VI, 1808-1814
— — Christian Frederick, 1814
— — 1814-1905
— — Oscar I, 1844-1859
— — Charles IV, 1859-1872
— — Oscar II, 1872-1905
— — Separation from Sweden, 1905
      ₍DL525₎
      BT Sweden—History—1905-
— — 1905-1940
— — German occupation, 1940-1945
      ₍DL532₎
      UF German occupation of Norway,
          1940-1945
— — 1945-

  ₍DL533₎
— Politics and government
— — 1397-1660
— — 1397-1814
— — 1766-1808
— — 1814-1905
— — 1905-
— — 1940-1945
— — 1945-
— Social conditions
— — 16th century
— — 17th century
— — 18th century
— — 19th century
— — 20th century
— — 1945-
— Social life and customs
— — 19th century
— — 20th century
Norway, West (Norway)
  USE Vestlandet (Norway)
Norway Bay Anglican Cemetery (Bristol,
    Québec)
  BT Cemeteries—Québec (Province)
Norway Bay United Cemetery (Bristol,
    Québec)
  BT Cemeteries—Québec (Province)
Norway Cup (Soccer)
  BT Soccer for children—Tournaments—
      Norway
Norway lemming
  UF Lemmus lemmus
      Norwegian lemming
  BT Lemmings
Norway lobster
  UF Nephrops norvegicus
  BT Lobsters
Norway pine
  USE Red pine
Norway pout
  UF Gadus esmarkii
      Pout, Norway
      Trisopterus esmarkii
Norway rat
  USE Rattus norvegicus
Norway saltpeter
  USE Ammonium nitrate
Norway spruce (May Subd Geog)
  ₍SD397.N6₎
  UF Abies picea
      Picea abies
      Picea excelsa
      Pinus excelsa
  BT Spruce
— Seed
Norwegian agricultural assistance
  USE Agricultural assistance, Norwegian
Norwegian-American fiction
  BT Norwegian-American literature
      Norwegian fiction
Norwegian-American literature
  ₍PT9131-9150₎
  BT Norwegian literature
  NT Norwegian-American fiction
Norwegian-American newspapers
  ₍PN4885.N6₎
  BT American newspapers
      Norwegian newspapers
Norwegian-American periodicals
  ₍PN4885.N6₎
  BT American periodicals
      Norwegian periodicals
Norwegian American wood-carving
    (May Subd Geog)
  UF Wood-carving, Norwegian American
  BT Wood-carving—United States
Norwegian Americans (May Subd Geog)
  BT Ethnology—United States
      Norwegians—United States
      Scandinavian Americans
— Ethnic identity

Norwegian anonyms and pseudonyms
  USE Anonyms and pseudonyms, Norwegian
Norwegian architecture
  USE Architecture, Norwegian
Norwegian art
  USE Art, Norwegian
Norwegian arts
  USE Arts, Norwegian
Norwegian atlases
  USE Atlases, Norwegian
Norwegian authors
  USE Authors, Norwegian
Norwegian ballads
  USE Ballads, Norwegian
Norwegian Basin
  UF Norwegian Deep
  BT Geology—Arctic Ocean
      Submarine topography—Arctic Ocean
Norwegian book-plates
  USE Book-plates, Norwegian
Norwegian bronze sculpture
  USE Bronze sculpture, Norwegian
Norwegian children's literature
  USE Children's literature, Norwegian
Norwegian children's poetry
  USE Children's poetry, Norwegian
Norwegian coins
  USE Coins, Norwegian
Norwegian corporations
  USE Corporations, Norwegian
Norwegian Deep
  USE Norwegian Basin
Norwegian diaries (May Subd Geog)
  BT Diaries
Norwegian drama
  ₍PT8500-PT8534 (History)₎
  ₍PT8699-PT8718 (Collections)₎
Norwegian drama (Nynorsk)
Norwegian dramatists
  USE Dramatists, Norwegian
Norwegian drawn work
  USE Hardanger needlework
Norwegian economic assistance
  USE Economic assistance, Norwegian
Norwegian elkhounds
  ₍SF429.N6₎
  UF Elkhounds
  BT Dog breeds
      Spitz dogs
Norwegian encyclopedias and dictionaries
  USE Encyclopedias and dictionaries,
      Norwegian
Norwegian essays (May Subd Geog)
Norwegian fantastic fiction
  USE Fantastic fiction, Norwegian
Norwegian fiction
  ₍PT8555-PT8567 (History)₎
  ₍PT8720-PT8722 (Collections)₎
  NT Fantastic fiction, Norwegian
      Ghost stories, Norwegian
      Norwegian-American fiction
      Science fiction, Norwegian
      Short stories, Norwegian
— 20th century
Norwegian folk literature
  USE Folk literature, Norwegian
Norwegian folk-songs
  USE Folk-songs, Norwegian
Norwegian ghost stories
  USE Ghost stories, Norwegian
Norwegian haddock
  USE Rosefish
Norwegian humorous poetry
  USE Humorous poetry, Norwegian
Norwegian hymns
  USE Hymns, Norwegian
Norwegian investments
  USE Investments, Norwegian
Norwegian laboring class writings
  USE Laboring class writings, Norwegian

Norwegian landscape painting
  USE Landscape painting, Norwegian
Norwegian language
  ⌐PD2571-2699⌐
  UF Bokmål language
      Dano-Norwegian language
      Norwegian language—Bokmål
      Norwegian language (Bokmål)
  BT Germanic languages
      Scandinavian languages
  NT Danish language
  — To 1350
      USE Old Norse language
  — Bokmål
      USE Norwegian language
  — Landsmaal
      USE Norwegian language (Nynorsk)
  — Nynorsk
      USE Norwegian language (Nynorsk)
Norwegian language (Bokmål)
  USE Norwegian language
Norwegian language (Landsmaal)
  USE Norwegian language (Nynorsk)
Norwegian language (Nynorsk)
  ⌐PD2900-2999⌐
  UF Landsmaal
      Norwegian language—Landsmaal
      Norwegian language—Nynorsk
      Norwegian language (Landsmaal)
      Nynorsk
  BT Scandinavian languages
Norwegian lemming
  USE Norway lemming
Norwegian letters (May Subd Geog)
Norwegian literature
  ⌐PT8301-PT8610 (History)⌐
  ⌐PT8615-PT8733 (Collections)⌐
  UF Bokmål literature
      Norwegian literature—Bokmål
      Norwegian literature (Bokmål)
  BT Scandinavian literature
  NT Children's literature, Norwegian
      Folk literature, Norwegian
      Laboring class writings, Norwegian
      Norwegian-American literature
      Old Norse literature
      Youths' writings, Norwegian
  — **19th century**
  — **Bokmål**
      USE Norwegian literature
  — Landsmaal
      USE Norwegian literature (Nynorsk)
  — Nynorsk
      USE Norwegian literature (Nynorsk)
  — **Women authors**
Norwegian literature (Bokmål)
  USE Norwegian literature
Norwegian literature (Landsmaal)
  USE Norwegian literature (Nynorsk)
Norwegian literature (Nynorsk)
  (May Subd Geog)
  ⌐PT9000-9094⌐
  UF Landsmaal literature
      Norwegian literature—Landsmaal
      Norwegian literature—Nynorsk
      Norwegian literature (Landsmaal)
      Nynorsk literature
  BT Scandinavian literature
Norwegian love poetry
  USE Love poetry, Norwegian
Norwegian lullabies
  USE Lullabies, Norwegian
Norwegian missions
  USE Missions, Norwegian
Norwegian newspapers (May Subd Geog)
  ⌐PN5291-PN5299 (History)⌐
  NT Norwegian-American newspapers
Norwegian novelists
  USE Novelists, Norwegian
Norwegian nursery rhymes
  USE Nursery rhymes, Norwegian

Norwegian painting
  USE Painting, Norwegian
Norwegian paleography
  USE Paleography, Norwegian
Norwegian periodicals (May Subd Geog)
  ⌐PN5291-PN5300 (History)⌐
  NT Norwegian-American periodicals
Norwegian philology
  ⌐PD2501-PD2999 (Language)⌐
  ⌐PT8301-PT9155 (Literature)⌐
  BT Scandinavian philology
Norwegian poetry (May Subd Geog)
  ⌐PT8460-PT8490 (History)⌐
  ⌐PT8675-PT8695 (Collections)⌐
  BT Scandinavian poetry
  NT Children's poetry, Norwegian
      Humorous poetry, Norwegian
      Love poetry, Norwegian
      Nursery rhymes, Norwegian
      Political poetry, Norwegian
      Protest poetry, Norwegian
      Revolutionary poetry, Norwegian
  — **19th century**
  — **20th century**
  — Landsmaal
      USE Norwegian poetry (Nynorsk)
  — Nynorsk
      USE Norwegian poetry (Nynorsk)
Norwegian poetry (Landsmaal)
  USE Norwegian poetry (Nynorsk)
Norwegian poetry (Nynorsk)
  (May Subd Geog)
  UF Landsmaal poetry
      Norwegian poetry—Landsmaal
      Norwegian poetry—Nynorsk
      Norwegian poetry (Landsmaal)
      Nynorsk poetry
  BT Scandinavian poetry
  — **20th century**
Norwegian political poetry
  USE Political poetry, Norwegian
Norwegian political posters
  USE Political posters, Norwegian
Norwegian portrait sculpture
  USE Portrait sculpture, Norwegian
Norwegian prose literature
  (May Subd Geog)
  — **20th century**
Norwegian protest poetry
  USE Protest poetry, Norwegian
Norwegian revolutionary poetry
  USE Revolutionary poetry, Norwegian
Norwegian science fiction
  USE Science fiction, Norwegian
Norwegian sculpture
  USE Sculpture, Norwegian
Norwegian Sea
  UF Norskehavet
  BT Arctic Ocean
      North Atlantic Ocean
Norwegian short stories
  USE Short stories, Norwegian
Norwegian students (May Subd Geog)
  BT Students
  — **Foreign countries**
      UF Norwegian students in foreign
          countries
      BT Students, Foreign
Norwegian students in foreign countries
  USE Norwegian students—Foreign
      countries
Norwegian technical assistance
  USE Technical assistance, Norwegian
Norwegian wit and humor (May Subd Geog)
Norwegian wit and humor, Pictorial
  (May Subd Geog)
Norwegian women authors
  USE Women authors, Norwegian
Norwegian women novelists
  USE Women novelists, Norwegian

Norwegian youths' writings
  USE Youths' writings, Norwegian
Norwegians (May Subd Geog)
  BT Ethnology—Norway
      Scandinavians
  — **United States**
      NT Norwegian Americans
Norwich school of painting
  BT Landscape painting—19th century—
          England
      Landscape painting, English
Norwich terriers
  ⌐SF429.N65⌐
  BT Terriers
Norwood family (Not Subd Geog)
Nosairians
  ⌐BP195.N7⌐
  UF Alawites
      'Alawīyīn
      Ansarii
      Nossarii
      Nusayris
  BT Assassins (Ismailites)
      Ethnology—Syria
      Islamic sects
      Ismailites
      Shī'ah
Nōsayama pottery (May Subd Geog)
  ⌐NK4168.K⌐
  UF Pottery, Nōsayama
  BT Pottery, Japanese
  RT Odo pottery
Nose
  ⌐QP458 (Physiology)⌐
  UF Rhinology
  BT Face
      Head
  RT Smell
  NT Cribriform plate
      Frontal sinus
      Jacobson's organ
      Nasal bone
      Nasal capsule
      Nasal fossa
      Nasal mucosa
      Nasal prostheses
      Nasopharynx
      Olfactory nerve
      Paranasal sinuses
      Shanghai gesture
  — **Anatomy**
      ⌐QL947 (Comparative anatomy)⌐
      ⌐QM505 (Human anatomy)⌐
      NT Bowman's glands
  — **Diseases** (May Subd Geog)
      ⌐RF341-437⌐
      BT Otolaryngology
      NT Catarrh
          Hay-fever
          Nose—Radiography
          Rhinitis
          Rhinosporidiosis
          Smell disorders
  — — **Homeopathic treatment**
      ⌐RX451⌐
  — — **Hospitals**
      ⌐RF6⌐
      BT Hospitals
  — **Examination**
      BT Otolaryngologic examination
      NT Nasoscopy
  — **Larvae and insects**
      ⌐RF435⌐
  — **Radiography**
      BT Nose—Diseases
  — **Secretions**
  — **Surgery**
      ⌐RF51⌐
      ⌐RF451 (Restoration)⌐
      BT Otolaryngology, Operative
      NT Dacryocystorhinostomy

Nose
— Surgery   *(Continued)*
          Paraffin injections
          Rhinoplasty
— Tuberculosis
     [RC312.5.N6]
— Tumors
     [RC280.N6]
     NT Nasal polyps
Nose, Accessory sinuses of
  USE Paranasal sinuses
Nose cones (Aircraft)
  USE Noses (Aircraft)
Nose cones (Space vehicles)
  USE Noses (Space vehicles)
Nose Lake (N.W.T.)
  UF Mara Lake (N.W.T.)
  BT Lakes—Northwest Territories
Nose ornaments
  UF Nasal ornaments
  BT Decoration and ornament
      Jewelry
Nose paintings on military airplanes
  USE Airplanes, Military—Decoration
Nose thumbing
  USE Shanghai gesture
Nosebleed
  UF Epistaxis
  BT Hemorrhage
Nosema
     [QL368.M5 (Zoology)]
  BT Nosematidae
Nosēma (The Greek word)
  BT Greek language—Etymology
Nosema bombycis
     [QL368.M5 (Zoology)]
  NT Pebrine
Nosematidae
     [QL368.M5 (Zoology)]
  BT Microsporidia
  NT Nosema
Noses (Aircraft)
  UF Nose cones (Aircraft)
  BT Airplanes—Fuselage
      Airplanes—Nacelles
      Shells (Engineering)
Noses (Space vehicles)
  UF Nose cones (Space vehicles)
      Space vehicles—Nose cones
Nōso Site (Japan)   *(Not Subd Geog)*
  BT Japan—Antiquities
Nosocomial infections   *(May Subd Geog)*
  UF Hospital-acquired infections
      Hospital infections
  BT Cross infection
      Hospitals
      Infection
  NT Surgical wound infections
Nosology
     [RB115]
  UF Classification—Diseases
      Diseases—Classification
  BT Medicine
  NT Child psychiatry—Classification
      Children—Diseases—Classification
      Mental illness—Classification
      Operations, Surgical—Classification
Nosophobia
  UF Disease phobia
      Diseases—Fear
      Diseases, Fear of
      Fear of diseases
      Pathophobia
  BT Phobias
      Sick—Psychology
Noss family
  USE Ness family
Nossa Senhora da Fátima
  USE Fatima, Our Lady of
Nossarii
  USE Nosairians

Nostalgia
     [BF575.N6]
  NT Homesickness
Nostoc
     [QK569.N75]
  BT Nostocaceae
  NT Nostoc verrucosum
Nostoc verrucosum
     [QK569.N75 (Botany)]
  BT Nostoc
Nostocaceae   *(May Subd Geog)*
     [QR99.7.N67]
  BT Oscillatoriales
  NT Nostoc
Nostocales
  USE Oscillatoriales
Nostratic community of languages theory
  USE Nostratic hypothesis
Nostratic hypothesis
     [P143]
  UF Nostratic community of languages
      theory
  BT Comparative linguistics
      Language and languages—
      Classification
Not family
  USE Knott family
Notacanthidae
     [QL638.N58]
  BT Albuliformes
  NT Notacanthus
Notacanthiformes
     [QL637.9.N6]
  UF Halosauriformes
      Heteromi
      Lyopomi
  BT Osteichthyes
Notacanthus
     [QL638.N58]
  BT Notacanthidae
Notacanthus bonapartei
     [QL638.N58]
Notaries   *(May Subd Geog)*
  RT Acknowledgments
      Justices of the peace
      Non-contentious jurisdiction
— Confidential communications
      USE Confidential communications—
           Notaries
— Fees
      BT Costs (Law)
— Malpractice   *(May Subd Geog)*
      UF Notaries—Tort liability
          Tort liability of notaries
      BT Malpractice
— Tort liability
      USE Notaries—Malpractice
Notaries (Canon law)
  NT Chancellors, Diocesan
Notaries (Islamic law)
Notaries (Roman law)
Notaries in art
Notaries in literature
  BT Lawyers in literature
Notarii (Roman officials)
     [DG83.5.N68]
  BT Rome—Officials and employees
Notation, Mathematical
  USE Mathematical notation
Notation, Musical
  USE Musical notation
Notation (for books in libraries)
  USE Shelf-listing (Library science)
Notch bar testing
  USE Notched bar testing
Notch effect
     [TA418.17]
  BT Brittleness
      Strains and stresses
      Strength of materials
  NT Notched bar testing

Notched bar testing
     [TA418.17]
  UF Notch bar testing
  BT Materials—Dynamic testing
      Notch effect
      Testing
Notched rattle
     [GN477.R]
  UF Bone rattle
      Rattle, Notched
  BT Percussion instruments
Notched sticks
  USE Tallies
Notches
  USE Mountain passes
Note-taking
     [LB2395 (Students)]
  UF Keeping notes
      Notekeeping
      Notetaking
      Taking notes
  BT Report writing
      Reporters and reporting
      Study, Method of
Notebooks   *(May Subd Geog)*
  BT Books
  SA *subdivision* Notebooks, sketchbooks,
      etc. *under names of individual*
      persons
  NT Laboratory notebooks
      School notebooks
Notebooks, Laboratory
  USE Laboratory notebooks
Notebooks, School
  USE School notebooks
Notekeeping
  USE Note-taking
Noten family
  USE Norton family
Notes, Floating rate
  USE Floating rate notes
Notes, Nurses'
  USE Nursing records
Notes, Promissory
  USE Promissory notes
Notes, Thank-you
  USE Thank-you notes
Notes (Cataloging)
      Here are entered works on concise statements
      after the physical description and series areas on catalog-
      ing records containing useful descriptive and con-
      tents information that cannot be fitted into other
      areas of the description.
  UF Cataloging notes
      Descriptive notes (Cataloging)
      Drop notes (Cataloging)
  BT Descriptive cataloging
Notes inégales
  BT Music—Performance
      Musical notation
Notes of the church
  USE Church—Marks
Notetaking
  USE Note-taking
Notgrass family   *(Not Subd Geog)*
  RT Snodgrass family
Noth family
  USE North family
Notharctidae
  USE Adapidae
Nothing (Philosophy)
  UF Nothingness (Philosophy)
  BT Nihilism (Philosophy)
      Ontology
Nothingness (Philosophy)
  USE Nothing (Philosophy)
Nothingness (Sunyata)
  USE Sunyata
Nothingness in literature
  UF Void in literature

Nothofagus
  [QK495.F14 (Botany)]
  [SD397.N64 (Culture)]
  UF Evergreen beech
      False beech
      New Zealand beech
  BT Beech
      Fagaceae
Nothofagus dombeyi
  [QK495.F14 (Botany)]
  UF Coigüe
      Southern falsebeech
Nothofagus obliqua
  [QK495.F14 (Botany)]
  [SD397.N (Culture)]
Nothofagus procera
  [QK495.F14 (Botany)]
  [SD397.N65 (Culture)]
  UF Chilean beech
Nothosauridae
  [QE862.S33]
  BT Sauropterygia
  NT Nothosaurus
Nothosaurus
  [QE862.S33]
  UF Chonchiosaurus
      Chondriosaurus
      Dracontosaurus
      Dracosaururus
      Dracosaurus
      Kolposaurus
      Mendon
      Oligolychus
  BT Nothosauridae
Nothrop family
  USE Northrup family
Nothura
  [QL696.T4]
  BT Tinamidae
Notice, Judicial
  USE Judicial notice
Notice (Law) *(May Subd Geog)*
  BT Civil procedure
  NT Legal advertising
      Time (Law)
Notice of dismissal
  USE Employees, Dismissal of
Notices, Death
  USE Death notices
Notices to mariners *(May Subd Geog)*
  [VK798]
  BT Navigation
  RT Aids to navigation
      Pilot guides
  NT Navigational warnings, Special
Notification (International relations)
  BT Diplomacy
      International law
      International relations
Notikewin River (Alta.)
  UF Battle River (Alta.)
  BT Rivers—Alberta
Notiomys
  [QL737.R638]
  BT Cricetidae
Notions (Merchandise)
  NT Novelties
Notions (Philosophy)
  BT Philosophy
Notiphila
  [QL537.E7]
  BT Ephydridae
Noto-hantō (Japan)
  USE Noto Peninsula (Japan)
Noto Peninsula (Japan)
  UF Noto-hantō (Japan)
  BT Peninsulas—Japan
Notochord
  UF Chorda dorsalis
      Chorda vertebralis
      Head process

  BT Chordata
      Embryology
  NT Chordoma
Notodelphyoida
  [QL444.C76]
  BT Copepoda
Notodontidae
  [QL561.N8]
  UF Ceruridae
      Dicranuridae
      Hemiceridae
      Melalophidae
      Ptilodontidae
      Pygaeridae
  BT Lepidoptera
      Moths
  NT Automolis
      Cerura
      Heterocampa
      Induba
      Streblota
      Thaumetopoea
      Umncumbata
Notolophus
  USE Orgyia
Notolophus antiqua
  USE Orgyia antiqua
Noton family
  USE Norton family
Notoncus *(May Subd Geog)*
  [QL568.F7]
  BT Ants
Notophthalmus
  [QL668.C28]
  UF Diemictylus
  BT Newts
      Salamandridae
Notophthalmus viridescens
  [QL668.C28]
  UF Diemictylus viridescens
      Red-spotted newt
      Triturus viridescens
Notoriety (Law)
  USE Judicial notice
Notostraca
  UF Tadpole shrimps
  BT Branchiopoda
Notosudidae
  [QL638.N5873]
  UF Scopelosauridae
  BT Myctophiformes
Nototheniidae
  [QL638.N6]
  UF Cod icefishes
      Gelididae
  BT Perciformes
  NT Trematomus
Notoungulata
  [QE882.N6]
  BT Ungulata, Fossil
  NT Hegetotheriidae
      Pyrotheria
Notoxidae
  USE Anthicidae
Notre-Dame de Beauraing
  USE Beauraing, Notre-Dame de
Notre-Dame de la Peinière
  USE Peinière, Notre-Dame de la
Notre Dame de Recouvrance
  USE Recouvrance, Notre Dame de
Notre-Dame des Lorrains
  USE Lorrains, Notre-Dame des
Notropis
  [QL638.C94]
  BT Cyprinidae
Notropis aguirrepequenoi
  [QL638.C94]
Notropis candidus
  USE Silverside shiner
Notropis emiliae
  USE Pugnose minnow

Notropis hubbsi
  USE Bluehead shiner
Notropis lutrensis
  USE Red shiner
Notropis phenacobius
  USE Sand shiner
Notropis reticulatus
  USE Sand shiner
Notropis rubellus
  USE Rosyface shiner
Notropis shumardi
  USE Silverband shiner
Notropis stramineus
  USE Sand shiner
Notropis welaka
  USE Bluenose shiner
Nottingham family *(Not Subd Geog)*
Nottingham Health Profile
  UF NHP (Health profile)
  BT Health status indicators
Notu language
  UF Ewage language
  BT Papua New Guinea—Languages
      Papuan languages
Notukeu Creek (Sask.)
  BT Rivers—Saskatchewan
Noturus
  [QL638.I3]
  UF Madtoms
  BT Ictaluridae
Noturus flavus
  USE Stonecat
Noturus insignis
  USE Margined madtom
Noturus stanauli
  USE Pigmy madtom
Nougats *(May Subd Geog)*
  [HD9999.C72 (Trade)]
  [TX784-TX791 (Cookery)]
  BT Candy
Noughts and crosses
  USE Tic-tac-toe
Noulton family
  USE Knowlton family
Nouman family
  USE Newman family
Noun
  USE *subdivision* Noun *under names of*
        languages and groups of languages
        Grammar, Comparative and general—
        Noun
Noun-equivalents (Grammar)
  USE Grammar, Comparative and general—
        Nominals
Noun phrase
  USE Grammar, Comparative and general—
        Noun phrase
Nouni dialect
  USE Nunuma dialect
Nouns, Mass
  USE Grammar, Comparative and general—
        Mass nouns
Nourse family *(Not Subd Geog)*
  UF Nurse family
      Nurss family
Nous (The Greek word)
  USE Noos (The Greek word)
Nousos (The Greek word)
  BT Greek language—Etymology
Noutka Indians
  USE Nootka Indians
Noutka language
  USE Nootka language
Nouvelles
  USE Novelle
Nova automobile
  BT Chevrolet automobile
Nova Cygni 1975
  UF Star V1500 Cygni
  BT Stars, New
      Stars, Variable

Nova Cygni 1975 *(Continued)*
— Spectra
Nova Scotia
　　BT Acadia
　　　　Maritime Provinces
　— Antiquities
　　　　NT Debert Site (N.S.)
　— Church history
　— — 18th century
　　　　[BR575]
　— Economic conditions
　— — 1918-
　— History
　　　　[F1036-1039.5]
　— — To 1763
　— — 1603-1713
　— — 1713-1763
　— — 1763-
　— — 1763-1867
　— — 1775-1783
　　　　[E263.N9]
　— — 1867-
　— Politics and government
　— — 1713-1763
　— — 1763-1867
　— — 1867-
Novac family
　USE Novak family
Novacek family
　USE Novak family
Novack family
　USE Novak family
Novaculite
　　[QE391.N]
　BT Rocks, Sedimentary
　RT Chert
Novae (Ancient city) *(Not Subd Geog)*
　UF Novensis Moesia Civitas (Ancient
　　　　city)
　　　Staklen (Ancient city)
　BT Bulgaria—Antiquities, Roman
　　　Cities and towns, Ruined, extinct, etc.
　　　　—Bulgaria
Novae
　USE Stars, New
Novae, Dwarf
　USE Dwarf novae
Novaiā Zemliā (R.S.F.S.R.)
　UF Novaya Zemlya (R.S.F.S.R.)
　BT Islands of the Arctic
Novak family *(Not Subd Geog)*
　UF Novac family
　　　Novacek family
　　　Novack family
　RT Nowak family
Novara, Battle of, 1513
　　[DQ109]
　BT Italy—History—1492-1559
　　　Switzerland—History—1499-1648
Novara, Battle of, 1849
　　[DG553.5.N7]
　BT Austro-Sardinian War, 1848-1849
Novara Expedition, 1857-1859
　　[Q115.N]
Novation *(May Subd Geog)*
　BT Accord and satisfaction
　　　Civil law
　　　Contracts
　　　Debtor and creditor
　　　Discharge of contracts
　　　Extinguishment of debts
　NT Delegation (Civil law)
　　　Expromission
Novation (Roman-Dutch law)
Novation (Roman law)
Novaya Zemlya (R.S.F.S.R.)
　USE Novaiā Zemliā (R.S.F.S.R.)
Novel, Nonfiction
　USE Nonfiction novel
Novelists
　BT Fiction

NT Women novelists
Novelists, Afro-American
　USE Afro-American novelists
Novelists, American *(May Subd Geog)*
　UF American novelists
　NT Afro-American novelists
Novelists, American, [French, Russian, etc.]
　(May Subd Geog)
　— 18th century
　— 19th century
　— 20th century
Novelists, Australian *(May Subd Geog)*
　UF Australian novelists
Novelists, Barbadian *(May Subd Geog)*
　UF Barbadian novelists
Novelists, Belgian *(May Subd Geog)*
　UF Belgian novelists
Novelists, Bengali *(May Subd Geog)*
　UF Bengali novelists
Novelists, Brazilian *(May Subd Geog)*
　UF Brazilian novelists
Novelists, Byelorussian *(May Subd Geog)*
　UF Byelorussian novelists
　　　Novelists, White Russian
Novelists, Catalan *(May Subd Geog)*
　UF Catalan novelists
Novelists, Chilean *(May Subd Geog)*
　UF Chilean novelists
Novelists, Colombian *(May Subd Geog)*
　UF Colombian novelists
Novelists, English
　UF English fiction—Biography
　— 19th century
Novelists, French *(May Subd Geog)*
　UF French novelists
Novelists, French-Canadian
　(May Subd Geog)
　UF French-Canadian novelists
Novelists, German *(May Subd Geog)*
　UF German novelists
Novelists, Indic *(May Subd Geog)*
　UF Indic novelists
Novelists, Indonesian *(May Subd Geog)*
　UF Indonesian novelists
Novelists, Italian *(May Subd Geog)*
　UF Italian novelists
Novelists, Japanese *(May Subd Geog)*
　UF Japanese novelists
Novelists, Kannada *(May Subd Geog)*
　UF Kannada novelists
Novelists, Lithuanian *(May Subd Geog)*
　UF Lithuanian novelists
Novelists, Norwegian *(May Subd Geog)*
　UF Norwegian novelists
Novelists, Pakistani *(May Subd Geog)*
　UF Pakistani novelists
Novelists, Polish *(May Subd Geog)*
　UF Polish novelists
Novelists, Portuguese *(May Subd Geog)*
　UF Portuguese novelists
Novelists, Romanian *(May Subd Geog)*
　UF Romanian novelists
Novelists, Russian *(May Subd Geog)*
　UF Russian novelists
Novelists, Scottish *(May Subd Geog)*
　UF Scottish novelists
Novelists, Serbian *(May Subd Geog)*
　UF Serbian novelists
Novelists, Spanish *(May Subd Geog)*
　UF Spanish novelists
Novelists, Swedish *(May Subd Geog)*
　UF Swedish novelists
Novelists, Swiss *(May Subd Geog)*
　UF Swiss novelists
Novelists, Ukrainian *(May Subd Geog)*
　UF Ukrainian novelists
Novelists, Urdu *(May Subd Geog)*
　UF Urdu novelists
Novelists, Venezuelan *(May Subd Geog)*
　UF Venezuelan novelists

Novelists, White Russian
　USE Novelists, Byelorussian
Novelists in literature
　NT Shakespeare, William, 1564-1616—
　　　　Characters—Novelists
Novellas (Early literary form)
　USE Novelle
Novellas (Short novels)
　USE Fiction
Novelle
　　Here are entered works on the brief fictional yet
　realistic narrative form, moral or satiric, in prose or
　poetry, popular in medieval and Renaissance times.
　UF Nouvelles
　　　Novellas (Early literary form)
　BT Fiction
　　　Narrative poetry
Novels
　USE Fiction
　　　Plots (Drama, novel, etc.)
Novels, Three-decker
　USE Three-decker novels
Novels in letters
　USE Epistolary fiction
Novelties
　　[TS2301.N55]
　BT Notions (Merchandise)
Novelty books
　USE Toy and movable books
Novelty tooth saws
　USE Planer saws
November devotions
　USE Prayers for the dead—November
　　　　devotions
November treaty, 1855
　USE Stockholm, Treaty of, 1855
Novenas
　　[BX2170.N7]
　BT Catholic Church—Prayer-books and
　　　　devotions
Novensis Moesia Civitas (Ancient city)
　USE Novae (Ancient city)
Noveschi, Rule of the, Siena (Italy), 1287-1355
　USE Siena (Italy)—History—Rule of the
　　　　Nine, 1287-1355
Novgorod birch bark inscriptions
　USE Bark inscriptions
Novgorodskaiā oblast' (R.S.F.S.R.)
　— History
　— — Revolution of 1905
　　　　[DK264.2.N]
Novi automobile
Novi Pazar (Serbia and Montenegro)
　USE Sandžak (Serbia and Montenegro)
Novial (Artificial language)
　　[PM8685]
　BT Languages, Artificial
Novice masters
　USE Master of novices
Novice mistresses
　USE Master of novices
Novices, Buddhist
　USE Buddhist novices
Noviciate
　USE Novitiate
Novikov gearing
　USE Gearing, Novikov
Novitiate
　UF Noviciate
　BT Monasticism and religious orders
　RT Master of novices
　NT Buddhist novices
Novitiate (Canon law)
　BT Monasticism and religious orders
　　　　(Canon law)
Novocaine
　　[RD86.N8]
　　[RK510 (Dentistry)]
　UF Procaine
　BT Local anesthesia
　NT Impletol

Novokirghiz horse
[SF293.N68]
UF Kirghiz horse, New
New Kirghiz horse
BT Horse breeds

Novolingua
[PM8688]
BT Languages, Artificial

Novorossiĭsk (R.S.F.S.R.), Battle of, 1943
BT World War, 1939-1945—Campaigns—
Russian S.F.S.R.

Novosibirsk (R.S.F.S.R.). Akademgorodok
USE Akademgorodok (Novosibirsk,
R.S.F.S.R.)

Novosibirskiĭ nauchnyĭ tsentr (Novosibirsk,
R.S.F.S.R.)
USE Akademgorodok (Novosibirsk,
R.S.F.S.R.)

Novosibirskiy nauchnyy tsentr (Novosibirsk,
R.S.F.S.R.)
USE Akademgorodok (Novosibirsk,
R.S.F.S.R.)

Novumbra
[QL638.U5]
BT Umbridae, Fossil

Novumbridae
USE Umbridae

Novyts
USE Navayats

NOW accounts (May Subd Geog)
[HG1660]
UF Negotiable order of withdrawal
accounts
BT Bank accounts
Bank deposits
Interest

— **Law and legislation** (May Subd Geog)
BT Banking law

Nowa Marchia (Poland)
UF Marchia Nowa (Poland)
Neumark (Poland)
New Mark (Poland)

Nowak family (Not Subd Geog)
RT Novak family

Nowâr
USE Nawar

Nowcasting (Meteorology)
(May Subd Geog)
[QC997.75]
Here are entered works on the technique of de-
scribing in detail the current weather and forecasting
the weather by extrapolation for the next few hours.
BT Weather forecasting

Nowgong (Indic people)
USE Ao (Indic people)

Nowlan family
USE Nolan family

Nowland family
USE Nolan family

Nowlen family
USE Nolan family

Nowlin family
USE Nolan family

Nox family
USE Knox family

Noya River (Spain)
UF Anoia River (Spain)
Anoya River (Spain)
La Noya River (Spain)
Río Noya (Spain)
BT Rivers—Spain

Noyce family
USE Noyes family

Noye family
USE Noyes family

Noyes family (Not Subd Geog)
UF Noice family
Nois family
Noyce family
Noye family
Noys family
Noyse family

Noyon (France), Battle of, 1917-1918
[D545.N7]
BT World War, 1914-1918—Campaigns—
France

Noys family
USE Noyes family

Noyse family
USE Noyes family

Nozzles
[TC173 (Hydraulics)]
[TH9380 (Fire hose)]
BT Atomizers
Hydraulics
NT Airplanes—Ramjet engines—Nozzles
Fire streams
Jet nozzles
Pitot tubes
Rockets (Aeronautics)—Nozzles
Spray nozzles
Sprinklers
Supersonic nozzles
Venturi tubes

— **Fluid dynamics**

NPA (Data base)
USE New Product Announcements (Data
base)

NPAC
USE National Program for Acquisitions and
Cataloging

NPL (Computer program language)
UF NonProcedural Language (Computer
program language)
BT Nonprocedural languages
(Programming languages)
Programming languages (Electronic
computers)

Npongwe (African people)
USE Mpongwe (African people)

Nrebele language (South Africa)
USE Ndebele language (South Africa)

Nrebele language (Zimbabwe)
USE Ndebele language (Zimbabwe)

nroff (Computer program)
BT Text editors (Computer programs)

Nṛsiṃha (Hindu deity)
USE Narasiṃha (Hindu deity)

NS32000 series (Microprocessors)
UF National Semiconductor 32000 series
(Microprocessors)
BT Microprocessors

NSAID's (Pharmacology)
USE Nonsteroidal anti-inflammatory agents

Nsaw (African people)
USE Nso (African people)

NSC800 (Computer)
[QA76.8.N]
UF National Semiconductor Corporation
800 (Computer)
BT Electronic digital computers
Microprocessors

— **Programming**

Nsenga language
USE Senga language

Nsima language
USE Nzima language

Nso (African people)
UF Bansaw (African people)
Banso (African people)
Lamnso (African people)
Lamso (African people)
Nsaw (African people)
BT Ethnology—Cameroon

NSRDS
USE National Standard Reference Data
System

NSU automobile
[TL215.N76]

Nsugni language
USE Limbum language

Nsungali language
USE Limbum language

Nsungli language
USE Limbum language

Nsungni language
USE Limbum language

Ntaandu dialect
UF Kintaandu dialect
Kintandu dialect
Kisantu dialect
Ntandu dialect
Santu dialect
BT Kongo language
Zaire—Languages

Ntandu dialect
USE Ntaandu dialect

Ntlakyapamuk Indians
[E99.N96]
UF Netlakapamuk Indians
Thompson Indians
Thompson River Indians
BT Indians of North America
Salishan Indians

— **Religion and mythology**

Ntlakyapamuk language
[PM2045]
UF Netlakapamuk language
Thompson language
RT Salishan languages

Ntn (The Hebrew root)
BT Hebrew language—Roots

Ntomba language
[PL8568]
UF Ntumba language
Tomba language
BT Bantu languages
RT Bolia language

Ntumba language
USE Ntomba language

Nü-chen language
USE Ju-chen language

Nu nu mouse
USE Nude mouse

Nuaulu (Indonesian people)
[DS632.N83]
UF Patakai (Indonesian people)
BT Ethnology—Indonesia

Nuba (African people)
BT Ethnology—Sudan

Nuba (African people) art
USE Art, Nuba (African people)

Nuba Mountains (Sudan)
UF Jibāl an Nūbah (Sudan)
Nūbah, Jibāl an (Sudan)
BT Mountains—Sudan

Nūbah, Jibāl an (Sudan)
USE Nuba Mountains (Sudan)

Nubi language (May Subd Geog)
[PM7895.N83]
UF KiNubi language
BT Creole dialects, Arabic—Kenya
Creole dialects, Arabic—Uganda
Kenya—Languages
Uganda—Languages

Nubia
— **Antiquities**

Nubian goats
[SF386.N83]
UF Anglo-Nubian goats
BT Goat breeds

Nubian language
[PL8571-5]

Nubian language *(Continued)*
  BT Egypt—Languages
     Nilo-Saharan languages
     Sudan—Languages
  NT Kenuz dialect
Nubian pottery
  USE Pottery, Nubian
Nubians *(May Subd Geog)*
    [DT159.6.N83]
  BT Ethnology—Egypt
     Ethnology—Sudan
  NT Danagla (African people)
— **Ethnic identity**
Nübling family *(Not Subd Geog)*
  UF Niebling family
Nubson family *(Not Subd Geog)*
Nuckles family
  USE Nuckols family
Nuckolls family
  USE Nuckols family
Nuckols family *(Not Subd Geog)*
  UF Nuckles family
     Nuckolls family
Nuclear aircraft *(May Subd Geog)*
  UF Aircraft, Nuclear
     Atomic aircraft
     Nuclear airplanes
     Nuclear planes
     Nuclear propelled aircraft
  BT Airplanes
     Nuclear propulsion
  RT Airplanes—Nuclear power plants
Nuclear aircraft carriers *(May Subd Geog)*
  UF Aircraft carriers, Nuclear
     Atomic aircraft carriers
     Nuclear-powered aircraft carriers
  BT Aircraft carriers
     Nuclear warships
Nuclear aircraft engines
  USE Airplanes—Nuclear power plants
Nuclear airplanes
  USE Nuclear aircraft
Nuclear arms control *(May Subd Geog)*
    [JX1947.7-1974.76]
  UF Nuclear weapons control
  BT Arms control
  RT Nuclear nonproliferation
     Nuclear weapons
— **Verification**
    [UA12.5]
  UF Verification of nuclear arms control
Nuclear assaying of boreholes
  USE Radiation well logging
Nuclear astrophysics
    [QB464]
  BT Astrophysics
     Nuclear physics
  NT Neutrino astrophysics
Nuclear barrier
  USE Potential barrier
Nuclear batteries
    [TK2965]
  UF Atomic batteries
     Batteries, Nuclear
     Radioisotope batteries
     Radioisotopic generators
  BT Electric batteries
     Isotopic power generators
     Nuclear energy
Nuclear binding energy
  USE Binding energy
Nuclear bomb (International law)
  USE Nuclear weapons (International law)
Nuclear bomb shelters *(May Subd Geog)*
  UF Atomic bomb shelters
     Atomic shelters
     Bomb shelters
     Shelters, Nuclear bomb

  BT Air raid shelters
     Building, Bombproof
     Nuclear weapons—Safety measures
     Public shelters
  NT Fallout shelters
— **Law and legislation** *(May Subd Geog)*
  BT Building laws
Nuclear cargo ships *(May Subd Geog)*
  UF Atomic cargo ships
     Atomic freighters
     Nuclear freighters
     Nuclear-powered cargo ships
  BT Cargo ships
     Nuclear merchant ships
Nuclear charge
    [QC173]
  UF Charge, Nuclear
  BT Nuclear physics
Nuclear chemistry *(May Subd Geog)*
    [QD601-QD608]
    Here are entered works on the application of
  chemical techniques to the study of the structure and
  properties of atomic nuclei, their transformations and
  reactions. Works on the chemical effects of high ener-
  gy radiation on matter are entered under Radiation
  chemistry. Works on the chemical properties of radi-
  oactive substances and their use in chemical studies
  are entered under Radiochemistry.
  UF Chemistry, Nuclear
  BT Chemistry, Physical and theoretical
  RT Nuclear physics
     Radiation chemistry
     Radiochemistry
  NT Hot-atom chemistry
Nuclear collective models
  UF Collective models, Nuclear
     Nuclear collective motion
  BT Nuclear physics
  RT Nuclear models
     Nuclear shell theory
Nuclear collective motion
  USE Nuclear collective models
Nuclear collisions
  USE Collisions (Nuclear physics)
Nuclear counters
    [QC787.C6]
  UF Radiation counters
  BT Detectors
     Nuclear physics
     Radioactivity—Instruments
  RT Dosimeters
     Ionization chambers
     Particle tracks (Nuclear physics)
     Period meter (Nuclear engineering)
  NT Cherenkov counters
     Coincidence circuits
     Cold cathode tubes
     Geiger-Müller counters
     Neutron counters
     Nuclear emulsions
     Nuclear track detectors
     Photon detectors
     Position sensitive particle detectors
     Proportional counters
     Pulse height analyzers
     Radiation dosimetry
     Radioactive prospecting
     Scintillation counters
     Semiconductor nuclear counters
— **Computer programs**
Nuclear cranking model
  UF Cranking model, Nuclear
  BT Nuclear models
Nuclear cratering
  USE Nuclear excavation
Nuclear crisis control *(May Subd Geog)*
    [JX1974.8]
  UF Control of nuclear crises
     Crisis control, Nuclear
  BT Crisis management
     International relations

  RT Nuclear energy
     Nuclear warfare
Nuclear crisis stability
    [U263]
  UF Crisis stability (Nuclear warfare)
     Stability, Nuclear crisis
  BT Nuclear warfare
  RT Deterrence (Strategy)
Nuclear cross sections
  USE Cross sections (Nuclear physics)
Nuclear cycle (Cytology)
  USE Cell cycle
Nuclear damages, Liability for
  USE Liability for nuclear damages
Nuclear direct reactions
  USE Direct reactions (Nuclear physics)
Nuclear disarmament *(May Subd Geog)*
    [JX1974.7-1974.76]
  UF Atomic bomb and disarmament
     Atomic weapons and disarmament
     Disarmament, Nuclear
     Nuclear weapons disarmament
  BT Disarmament
  RT Antinuclear movement
     Nuclear nonproliferation
     Nuclear weapons
  NT Nuclear-weapon-free zones
Nuclear division (Cytology)
  USE Karyokinesis
Nuclear electromagnetic pulse
  USE Electromagnetic pulse
Nuclear emulsions
    [QC787.N78]
  UF Emulsions, Nuclear
  BT Nuclear counters
     Particles (Nuclear physics)
     Photographic emulsions
     Photography in nuclear physics
  NT Nuclear track detectors
Nuclear energy *(May Subd Geog)*
    [QC791.9-792.8]
  UF Atomic energy
     Atomic power
     Energy, Atomic
     Energy, Nuclear
     Nuclear power
     Power, Atomic
     Power, Nuclear
  BT Force and energy
     Nuclear physics
     Power resources
  RT Nuclear crisis control
     Nuclear engineering
     Nuclear facilities
     Nuclear power plants
  NT Binding energy
     Nuclear batteries
     Nuclear excavation
     Nuclear industry
     Nuclear propulsion
     Nuclear reactions
     Nuclear reactors
— **Government policy** *(May Subd Geog)*
  UF Atomic energy policy
— **Law and legislation** *(May Subd Geog)*
  NT Liability for nuclear damages
     Radioactive substances—Safety
       regulations
— **Religious aspects**
— — **Baptists,** [Catholic Church, etc.]
— — **Buddhism,** [Christianity, etc.]
— **Research** *(May Subd Geog)*
— — **International cooperation**
  NT Dragon Project
— — **Laboratories**
  UF Atomic research laboratories
     Laboratories, Nuclear energy
       research
  BT Chemical laboratories
     Nuclear facilities
     Physical laboratories

NT Hot laboratories (Radioactive
   substances)
Nuclear energy and meteorology
  (May Subd Geog)
  UF Atomic energy and meteorology
  BT Engineering meteorology
    Meteorology
  RT Atmospheric radioactivity
    Radioactive pollution of the
     atmosphere
  NT Radioactive fallout
Nuclear energy industry
  USE Nuclear industry
Nuclear engineering *(May Subd Geog)*
  [TK9001-9401]
  UF Atomic power engineering
  BT Engineering
    Nuclear physics
  RT Nuclear energy
  NT Criticality (Nuclear engineering)
    Heavy water reactors—Exponential
     measurements
    Nuclear facilities
    Nuclear fuel elements
    Nuclear fuels
    Nuclear reactors
    Radioactive wastes
    Radioisotopes
    Shielding (Radiation)
    Ultrasonics in nuclear engineering
  — Computer programs
    NT THERM (Computer program)
  — Instruments
    NT Manipulators (Radioactive
     substances)
    Period meter (Nuclear engineering)
  — Microcard catalogs
    [Z7144.N8]
  — Safety measures
    [TK9152]
    NT Manipulators (Radioactive
     substances)
    Radiation—Dosage
    Radioactive decontamination
    Radioactive waste disposal
    Shielding (Radiation)
  — Belgium
    NT BR-2 reactor
Nuclear envelope
  USE Nuclear membranes
Nuclear excavation
  UF Atomic blasting
    Cratering, Nuclear
    Nuclear cratering
  BT Blasting
    Excavation
    Nuclear energy
    Underground nuclear explosions
  NT Project Plowshare
Nuclear excitation
  [QC794]
  UF Excitation, Nuclear
  BT Nuclear physics
  RT Energy levels (Quantum mechanics)
    Exciton theory
  NT Coulomb excitation
    Cross section fluctuations (Nuclear
     physics)
    Spin excitations
Nuclear explosions
  UF Atomic explosions
  BT Explosions
  NT Climatic changes—Effect of nuclear
     explosions on
    Electromagnetic pulse
    Project Argus
    Underground nuclear explosions
Nuclear exports
  USE Nuclear nonproliferation

Nuclear facilities *(May Subd Geog)*
  UF Atomic facilities
    Facilities, Nuclear
    Nuclear installations
  BT Nuclear engineering
  RT Nuclear energy
  NT Antinuclear movement
    Gaseous diffusion plants
    Hot laboratories (Radioactive
     substances)
    Nuclear energy—Research—
     Laboratories
    Nuclear power plants
    Nuclear reactors
    Nuclear saline water conversion plants
    Radioactive waste disposal
    Radiochemical laboratories
    Radium processing plants
  — Decommissioning
    UF Decommissioning of nuclear
     facilities
  — Law and legislation *(May Subd Geog)*
  — Location
    UF Location of nuclear facilities
  — — Law and legislation
    (May Subd Geog)
  — Washington (State)
    NT Fast Flux Test Facility Program
Nuclear fission
  UF Fission, Nuclear
  BT Nuclear reactions
  RT Spontaneous fission
  NT Delayed neutrons
    Delayed protons
    Fission cross sections
    Fission products
    Neutron transport theory
    Photofission
    Prompt neutrons
Nuclear forces (Physics)
  [QC173]
  UF Specifically nuclear forces
  BT Nuclear physics
    Particles (Nuclear physics)
  RT Binding energy
  NT Coulomb functions
    Mirror nuclei
Nuclear-free zones
  USE Nuclear-weapon-free zones
Nuclear freeze movement
  USE Antinuclear movement
Nuclear freighters
  USE Nuclear cargo ships
Nuclear fuel claddings
  [TK9207.5]
  UF Claddings, Nuclear fuel
    Fuel claddings, Nuclear
  BT Metal cladding
    Nuclear fuel elements
    Nuclear fuels
  — Effect of radiation on
    UF Nuclear fuel claddings, Effect of
     radiation on
    BT Radiation
Nuclear fuel claddings, Effect of radiation on
  USE Nuclear fuel claddings—Effect of
    radiation on
Nuclear fuel elements
  UF Fuel elements
    Nuclear reactors—Fuel elements
    Reactor fuel elements
  BT Nuclear engineering
    Nuclear fuels
  NT Nuclear fuel claddings
    Nuclear fuel rods
  — Computer programs
  — Thermal properties
Nuclear fuel rods
  [TK9207]

  UF Fuel rods, Nuclear
    Reactor fuel rods
    Rods, Nuclear fuel
  BT Nuclear fuel elements
  — Thermal properties
Nuclear fuels *(May Subd Geog)*
  [TK9360]
  UF Atomic fuel
    Nuclear reactors—Fuel
    Reactor fuels
  BT Isotope separation
    Nuclear engineering
    Nuclear reactors—Materials
    Radioactive substances
  RT Plutonium
    Thorium
    Uranium
  NT Criticality (Nuclear engineering)
    Fuel burnup (Nuclear engineering)
    Heavy water reactors—Exponential
     measurements
    Nuclear fuel claddings
    Nuclear fuel elements
    Nuclear nonproliferation
    Nuclear reactors—Reactivity
    Reactor fuel reprocessing
    Spent reactor fuels
    Thermonuclear fuels
  — Breeding
    UF Breeding of nuclear fuels
    NT Breeder reactors
  — Law and legislation *(May Subd Geog)*
Nuclear fusion
  [QC791]
    Here are entered works on the nuclear reaction
  between two light nuclei to form a heavier nucleus
  with release of binding energy. Works on the transi-
  tion from a frozen to an unfrozen state by warming
  are entered under Thawing. Works on the change of
  the state of a substance from the solid phase to the
  liquid phase are entered under Fusion.
  UF Fusion, Nuclear
    Fusion reactions
  BT Fusion
    Nuclear reactions
  NT Controlled fusion
    Heavy ion fusion reactions
    Hydrogen bomb
    Neutron transport theory
Nuclear fusion, Controlled
  USE Controlled fusion
Nuclear gages
  USE Radioactive gages
Nuclear geochemistry
  USE Isotope geology
Nuclear geology
  USE Isotope geology
Nuclear geophysics
  USE Isotope geology
Nuclear hazards insurance
  USE Insurance, Nuclear hazards
Nuclear icebreakers *(May Subd Geog)*
  UF Atomic icebreakers
    Ice-breaking vessels, Nuclear
    Icebreakers, Nuclear
    Nuclear-powered icebreaking vessels
  BT Ice-breaking vessels
    Nuclear ships
Nuclear induction
  BT Electromagnetic theory
    Magnetic induction
    Nuclear magnetic resonance
    Nuclear moments
Nuclear industry *(May Subd Geog)*
  [HD9698-HD9698.5 (Economics)]
  [TK9001-TK9401 (Technology)]
  UF Atomic energy industries
    Atomic industry
    Atomic power industry
    Nuclear energy industry
    Nuclear power industry

Nuclear industry *(Continued)*
  BT Energy industries
      Nuclear energy
  NT Strikes and lockouts—Nuclear industry
      Wages—Nuclear industry
  — Employees
    UF Atomic workers
    NT Trade-unions—Nuclear industry
        employees
  — Public relations
    USE Public relations—Nuclear
        industry
Nuclear industry in the press
  (May Subd Geog)
  UF Atomic power industry in the press
  BT Journalism
      Press
Nuclear installations
  USE Nuclear facilities
Nuclear insurance
  USE Insurance, Nuclear hazards
Nuclear isobars
  [QC173]
  UF Isobars, Nuclear
  BT Isotopes
      Nuclides
Nuclear isomers
  UF Isomerism (Nuclear physics)
      Isomers, Nuclear
      Isomers (Nuclear physics)
  BT Nuclear physics
      Nuclides
Nuclear jaundice
  USE Kernicterus
Nuclear liquid drop model
  UF Drop model, Nuclear
      Droplet model, Nuclear
      Liquid drop model, Nuclear
      Liquid droplet model, Nuclear
  BT Nuclear models
Nuclear locomotives *(May Subd Geog)*
  UF Atomic locomotives
      Locomotives, Nuclear
  BT Locomotives
      Nuclear propulsion
Nuclear magnetic resonance
  UF Magnetic resonance, Nuclear
  BT Magnetic resonance
      Nuclear moments
      Relaxation (Nuclear physics)
      Resonance
      Spectrum analysis
      Spin temperature
  RT Nuclear magnetism
      Nuclear quadrupole resonance
  NT Baryon resonance
      Cyclotron
      Electron nuclear double resonance
      Giant multipole resonance
      Knight shift
      Meson resonance
      Neutron resonance
      Nuclear induction
      Nuclear magnetic resonance, Giant
      Overhauser effect (Nuclear physics)
      Paramagnetism
      Photon-echo nuclear double resonance
      Proton magnetic resonance
      Raman effect, Resonance
  — Diagnostic use
    USE Magnetic resonance imaging
Nuclear magnetic resonance, Giant
  UF Giant nuclear magnetic resonance
      Giant resonance (Nuclear physics)
  BT Nuclear magnetic resonance
Nuclear magnetic resonance, Pulsed
  UF Pulse nuclear magnetic resonance
      Pulsed nuclear magnetic resonance
      Pulsed nuclear resonance
Nuclear magnetic resonance imaging
  USE Magnetic resonance imaging

Nuclear magnetic resonance spectroscopy
  [QC490 (Physics)]
  [QD96.N8 (Chemistry)]
  UF NMR spectroscopy
      Spectroscopy, NMR
      Spectroscopy, Nuclear magnetic
        resonance
  BT Nuclear spectroscopy
  RT Knight shift
  NT Deuteron magnetic resonance
        spectroscopy
      Proton magnetic resonance
        spectroscopy
Nuclear magnetism
  [QC762]
  BT Magnetism
      Nuclear moments
      Nuclear physics
  RT Nuclear magnetic resonance
  NT Hyperfine interactions
      Magnetic ions
      Spin temperature
Nuclear magnetometer
  UF Proton precession magnetometer
  BT Magnetometer
Nuclear masses
  USE Atomic mass
Nuclear matter
  USE Matter, Nuclear
Nuclear medicine *(May Subd Geog)*
  [R895]
  UF Atomic medicine
      Radioisotopes in medicine
  BT Radioactive tracers
      Radiology, Medical
  RT Radioactivity—Physiological effect
  NT Magnetic resonance imaging
      Radioisotopes—Therapeutic use
      Radioisotopes in cardiology
      Radioisotopes in dermatology
      Radioisotopes in endocrinology
      Radioisotopes in gastroenterology
      Radioisotopes in hematology
      Radioisotopes in medical diagnosis
      Radioisotopes in nephrology
      Radioisotopes in neurology
      Radioisotopes in obstetrics
      Radioisotopes in ophthalmology
      Radioisotopes in pediatrics
      Radioisotopes in pharmacology
      Radioisotopes in urology
  — Equipment and supplies
    NT Nuclear medicine equipment
        industry
  — Practice
    BT Medicine—Practice
Nuclear medicine equipment industry
  (May Subd Geog)
  [HD9995.N83-834]
  BT Nuclear medicine—Equipment and
      supplies
Nuclear medicine physicians
  (May Subd Geog)
  UF Nuclear medicine specialists
  BT Physicians
Nuclear medicine specialists
  USE Nuclear medicine physicians
Nuclear membranes
  [QH601.2]
  UF Nuclear envelope
  BT Cell membranes
      Cell nuclei
Nuclear merchant ships *(May Subd Geog)*
  UF Atomic merchant ships
      Merchant ships, Nuclear
      Nuclear-powered merchant ships
  BT Merchant ships
      Nuclear ships
  NT Nuclear cargo ships
Nuclear models
  UF Models, Nuclear

  BT Atoms
      Matter—Constitution
      Nuclear physics
  RT Cluster theory (Nuclear physics)
      Nuclear collective models
      Nuclear structure
  NT Nilsson model
      Nuclear cranking model
      Nuclear liquid drop model
      Nuclear optical models
      Nuclear shell theory
      Quark models
      Quark-parton model
      Unified nuclear models
Nuclear moments
  [QC794]
  BT Nuclear physics
  NT Angular momentum (Nuclear physics)
      Hyperfine structure
      Nuclear induction
      Nuclear magnetic resonance
      Nuclear magnetism
      Nuclear spin
      Paramagnetism
Nuclear nonproliferation
  Here are entered works on international control
over the transfer and use of nuclear equipment,
material, and technology, aimed at preventing the
spread of nuclear explosive capability.
  UF Export of nuclear materials
      Export of nuclear technology
      Nonproliferation, Nuclear
      Nuclear exports
      Nuclear proliferation
      Proliferation, Nuclear
  BT Nuclear fuels
      Nuclear reactors
      Technology transfer
  RT Arms control
      Nuclear arms control
      Nuclear disarmament
      Nuclear-weapon-free zones
Nuclear optical models
  UF Optical models, Nuclear
  BT Nuclear models
      Nuclear reactions
      Nuclear structure
      Potential, Theory of
  RT Nuclear optical potentials
Nuclear optical potentials
  UF Optical potentials, Nuclear
  RT Nuclear optical models
      Potential scattering
Nuclear orientation
  [QC173]
  BT Angular momentum (Nuclear physics)
      Nuclear physics
      Nuclear spin
Nuclear particles
  USE Particles (Nuclear physics)
Nuclear physics
  [QC173]
  UF Atomic nuclei
      Atoms, Nuclei of
      Nucleus of the atom
      Physics, Nuclear
  BT Atoms
  RT Chemistry, Physical and theoretical
      Compound nucleus
      Nuclear chemistry
      Radioactivity
  NT Analog resonance
      Angular momentum (Nuclear physics)
      Atomic mass
      Atomic transition probabilities
      Atomic units
      Auger effect
      Binding energy
      Bound states (Quantum mechanics)
      Cascade shower
      Causality (Physics)

Cluster theory (Nuclear physics)
Collisions (Nuclear physics)
Cosmic rays
Criticality (Nuclear engineering)
Cyclotron
Deuterons
Dispersion relations
Electric discharges
Electrons—Capture
Energy levels (Quantum mechanics)
Few-body problem
Finite nuclei
Internal conversion (Nuclear physics)
Isobaric spin
Linear energy transfer
Mössbauer effect
Neutrons—Capture
Nuclear astrophysics
Nuclear charge
Nuclear collective models
Nuclear counters
Nuclear energy
Nuclear engineering
Nuclear excitation
Nuclear forces (Physics)
Nuclear isomers
Nuclear magnetism
Nuclear models
Nuclear moments
Nuclear orientation
Nuclear reactions
Nuclear reactors
Nuclear shell theory
Nuclear size (Physics)
Nuclear spin
Nuclear structure
Parity nonconservation
Particle beams
Particles (Nuclear physics)
Polarized targets (Nuclear physics)
Potential barrier
Protons—Capture
Quantum electrodynamics
Radiobiology
Scattering (Physics)
Synchrocyclotron
Targets (Nuclear physics)
Time reversal
Transmutation (Chemistry)
Triplet state
Tritons (Nuclear physics)
Unified nuclear models
Unitary operators
— **Computer programs**
— **Instruments**
    NT Ion sources
        Magnetic analyzers (Nuclear
          physics)
        Particle accelerators
— **Research** *(May Subd Geog)*
    UF Nuclear research
— **Tables**
    UF Nuclear physics—Tables, etc.
— Tables, etc.
    USE Nuclear physics—Tables
Nuclear physics, Photography in
   USE Photography in nuclear physics
Nuclear planes
   USE Nuclear aircraft
Nuclear polarization
   USE Polarization (Nuclear physics)
Nuclear pollution
   USE Radioactive pollution
Nuclear power
   USE Nuclear energy
Nuclear power industry
   USE Nuclear industry
Nuclear power plant operators
   UF Operators, Nuclear power plant
   BT Nuclear power plants—Employees

Nuclear power plants *(May Subd Geog)*
   [TK1078]
   UF Atomic power plants
      Nuclear power stations
      Power plants, Nuclear
   BT Electric power-plants
      Nuclear facilities
   RT Antinuclear movement
      Nuclear energy
   NT Offshore nuclear power plants
      Underground nuclear power plants
— **Control rooms**
    [TK9220]
    UF Control rooms in nuclear power
       plants
    BT Control rooms
— **Control rooms**
— — **Human factors**
      BT Human engineering
— **Decommissioning**
    UF Decommissioning of nuclear power
       plants
— **Design and construction**
— — **Finance**
— — — **Law and legislation**
      (May Subd Geog)
— — **Law and legislation**
      (May Subd Geog)
— **Earthquake effects**
    UF Earthquakes and atomic power
       plants
    BT Earthquakes
— **Electronic equipment**
— **Employees**
    NT Nuclear power plant operators
— **Environmental aspects**
    (May Subd Geog)
— **Equipment and supplies**
— — **Vibration**
      BT Vibration
— — **Welding**
      BT Welding
— **Human factors**
    BT Human engineering
— **Instruments**
    [TK9178-9183]
    UF Instruments, Nuclear power plant
    BT Engineering instruments
— **Law and legislation** *(May Subd Geog)*
— **Location**
— — **Law and legislation**
      (May Subd Geog)
— **Maintainability**
    BT Maintainability (Engineering)
— **Natural disaster effects**
    BT Natural disasters
— **Painting**
    BT Painting, Industrial
— **Pipe lines**
— — **Valves**
      BT Valves
— **Risk assessment**
    BT Risk assessment
— **Shielding (Radiation)**
    BT Shielding (Radiation)
— **Shock absorbers**
    BT Shock absorbers
— **Thermodynamics**
    BT Thermodynamics
— **California**
    NT Diablo Canyon Nuclear
       Powerplant (Calif.)
— **Germany (West)**
    NT Obrigheim Nuclear Power Plant
       (Germany)
— **Ireland**
    NT Carnsore Nuclear Power Station
       (Wexford)
— **Massachusetts**
    NT Pilgrim Nuclear Power Station
       (Mass.)

— **Minnesota**
    NT Monticello Nuclear Power
       Generating Plant (Minn.)
— **Mississippi**
    NT Grand Gulf Nuclear Powerplant
       (Miss.)
       Yellow Creek Nuclear Power Plant
       (Miss.)
— **New York (State)**
    NT Indian Point Nuclear Power Plant
       (N.Y.)
       James A. FitzPatrick/Nine Mile
       Point Nuclear Power Plant
       (N.Y.)
       Shoreham Nuclear Powerplant
       (N.Y.)
— **Ohio**
    NT Davis-Besse Nuclear Power Plant
       (Ohio)
— **Pennsylvania**
    NT Limerick Atomic Power Station
       (Pa.)
       Three Mile Island Nuclear Power
       Plant (Pa.)
— **Sweden**
    NT Barsebäck kärnkraftverk (Sweden)
— **Tennessee**
    NT Clinch River Breeder Reactor
       Demonstration Power Plant
       (Tenn.)
— **Texas**
    NT Allens Creek Nuclear Generating
       Station (Tex.)
— **Ukraine**
— — **Accidents**
      NT Chernobyl Nuclear Accident,
        Chernobyl', Ukraine, 1986
Nuclear power stations
   USE Nuclear power plants
Nuclear-powered aircraft carriers
   USE Nuclear aircraft carriers
Nuclear-powered cargo ships
   USE Nuclear cargo ships
Nuclear-powered icebreaking vessels
   USE Nuclear icebreakers
Nuclear-powered merchant ships
   USE Nuclear merchant ships
Nuclear-powered saline water conversion plants
   USE Nuclear saline water conversion plants
Nuclear-powered ships
   USE Nuclear ships
Nuclear-powered submarines
   USE Nuclear submarines
Nuclear-powered vehicles
   USE Nuclear propulsion
Nuclear-powered warships
   USE Nuclear warships
Nuclear pressure vessels
   BT Nuclear reactors
      Pressure vessels
   RT Nuclear reactors—Containment
   NT Liquid metal fast breeder reactors—
      Containment
— **Inspection**
    BT Engineering inspection
— **Welding**
Nuclear proliferation
   USE Nuclear nonproliferation
Nuclear propelled aircraft
   USE Nuclear aircraft
Nuclear propulsion
   [TK9230]
   UF Atomic-powered vehicles
      Nuclear-powered vehicles
   BT Nuclear energy
   RT Nuclear reactors
   NT Airplanes—Nuclear power plants
      Nuclear aircraft
      Nuclear locomotives
      Nuclear rockets
      Nuclear ships

Nuclear propulsion plant operators (United States Navy)
    USE United States. Navy—Nuclear propulsion plant operators
Nuclear propulsion systems (Airplane)
    USE Airplanes—Nuclear power plants
Nuclear-pumped lasers
    BT Lasers
    NT X-ray lasers
Nuclear quadrupole resonance
    UF Resonance, Nuclear quadrupole
    BT Quadrupole moments
    RT Nuclear magnetic resonance
Nuclear quadrupole resonance spectroscopy
    [QD95 (Inorganic analysis)]
    [QD276.S6 (Organic analysis)]
    BT Radiofrequency spectroscopy
    Spectrum analysis
Nuclear radius (Physics)
    USE Nuclear size (Physics)
Nuclear reactions
    UF Nuclear transformations
    Nuclear transmutation
    BT Collisions (Nuclear physics)
    Nuclear energy
    Nuclear physics
    RT Compound nucleus
    SA *subdivision* Capture *under names of particles, e.g.* Neutrons—Capture; *and subdivision* Decay *under radioactive substances, e.g.* Radium—Decay
    NT Angular correlations (Nuclear physics)
    Angular distribution (Nuclear physics)
    Annihilation reactions
    Branching ratios (Nuclear physics)
    Bremsstrahlung
    Cross section fluctuations (Nuclear physics)
    Deep inelastic collisions
    Deuteron reactions
    Direct reactions (Nuclear physics)
    Duality (Nuclear physics)
    Effective interactions (Nuclear physics)
    Electromagnetic interactions
    Grand unified theories (Nuclear physics)
    Hadron interactions
    Hadrons—Multiplicity
    Inclusive processes (Nuclear physics)
    Inclusive reactions (Nuclear physics)
    Induced radioactivity
    Jets (Nuclear physics)
    Lepton interactions
    Meson-nucleon interactions
    Muonium
    Neutron irradiation
    Neutron-proton interactions
    Nuclear fission
    Nuclear fusion
    Nuclear optical models
    Nuclear spectroscopy
    Nucleon-antinucleon interactions
    Nucleon-nucleon interactions
    Pair production
    Particle beams, Colliding
    Particles (Nuclear physics)—Multiplicity
    Photonuclear reactions
    Pion-pion interactions
    Positronium
    Proton-antiproton interactions
    Quark-gluon interactions
    Radiative capture
    Radioactive decay
    Radioactivity
    Resonance integral
    Scaling laws (Nuclear physics)
    Spallation (Nuclear physics)
    Stopping power (Nuclear physics)

    String models
    Stripping reaction (Nuclear physics)
    Weak interactions (Nuclear physics)
Nuclear reactor calculations
    USE Nuclear reactors—Computer programs
Nuclear reactor containment buildings
    USE Nuclear reactors—Containment
Nuclear reactor fuel reprocessing
    USE Reactor fuel reprocessing
Nuclear reactor kinetics
    UF Kinetic theory, Nuclear reactor
    Nuclear reactors—Kinetics
    NT Nuclear reactors—Reactivity
Nuclear reactor plants, Marine
    USE Marine nuclear reactor plants
Nuclear reactor programs (Electronic computers)
    USE Nuclear reactors—Computer programs
Nuclear reactor reactivity
    USE Nuclear reactors—Reactivity
Nuclear reactor shielding
    USE Nuclear reactors—Shielding (Radiation)
Nuclear reactor stability
    USE Nuclear reactors—Stability
Nuclear reactors *(May Subd Geog)*
    [QC786 (Physics)]
    [TK9202 (Technology)]
    UF Atomic piles
    Chain reaction piles
    Reactors (Nuclear physics)
    BT Nuclear energy
    Nuclear engineering
    Nuclear facilities
    Nuclear physics
    RT Neutron transport theory
    Nuclear propulsion
    NT Airplanes—Nuclear power plants
    Armour Research Reactor
    Army package power reactors
    Boiling water reactors
    Breeder reactors
    Dragon Project
    Engineering test reactors
    Fast reactors
    Fluid fuel reactors
    Fluidized reactors
    Fusion reactors
    Gas cooled reactors
    Heavy water reactors
    Light water graphite reactors
    Light water reactors
    Liquid metal cooled reactors
    Marine nuclear reactor plants
    Materials testing reactors
    Molten salt reactors
    Neutron sources
    Nuclear nonproliferation
    Nuclear pressure vessels
    Organic cooled reactors
    Organic moderated reactors
    Pebble bed reactors
    Pressurized water reactors
    Project SNAP
    Pulsed reactors
    Resonance integral
    Sodium cooled reactors
    Sodium graphite reactors
    Solid fuel reactors
    Superheating reactors
    Swimming pool reactors
    Thermal neutrons
    Water boiler reactors
    Water cooled reactors
— Accidents
    Subdivided by date, e.g. Nuclear reactors—Accidents—1961.
— — **1961**
    UF Accidental nuclear excursions
— **Brazing**
— **Buckling**

    UF Buckling (Nuclear reactors)
— Computer codes
    USE Nuclear reactors—Computer programs
— **Computer programs**
    [QC783.4]
    UF Nuclear reactor calculations
    Nuclear reactor programs (Electronic computers)
    Nuclear reactors—Computer codes
— Construction
    USE Nuclear reactors—Design and construction
— **Containment**
    [TK9211]
    UF Nuclear reactor containment buildings
    Reactor containment buildings
    BT Industrial buildings
    RT Nuclear pressure vessels
— — **Painting**
— **Control**
— **Cooling**
    [TK9212]
— **Decommissioning**
    UF Decommissioning of nuclear reactors
— **Design and construction**
    UF Nuclear reactors—Construction
— **Fluid dynamics**
— Fuel
    USE Nuclear fuels
— Fuel elements
    USE Nuclear fuel elements
— **Incrustations**
— Kinetics
    USE Nuclear reactor kinetics
— **Maintenance and repair**
— **Materials**
    [TK9202]
    NT Nuclear fuels
— — **Testing**
    NT Engineering test reactors
    Materials testing reactors
— — **Thermal properties**
— **Models**
— Moderators
    USE Reactor moderators
— **Noise**
    BT Random noise theory
— **Power distribution**
    UF Power distribution in nuclear reactors
— **Reactivity**
    UF Nuclear reactor reactivity
    Reactivity of nuclear reactors
    BT Criticality (Nuclear engineering)
    Nuclear fuels
    Nuclear reactor kinetics
— **Refueling**
    UF Refueling of nuclear reactors
— **Safety measures**
    NT LOFT (Nuclear reactor safety test facility)
— **Shielding (Radiation)**
    UF Nuclear reactor shielding
— — **Computer programs**
— **Stability**
    UF Nuclear reactor stability
    Stability of nuclear reactors
    BT Stability
— **Tables**
    UF Nuclear reactors—Tables, calculations, etc.
— Tables, calculations, etc.
    USE Nuclear reactors—Tables
— **Vibration**
— **Welding**
— **United States**
    NT Vallecitos Superheat Reactor

Nuclear research
  USE Nuclear physics—Research
Nuclear rockets
  [TL783.5]
  UF Rockets, Atomic powered
  BT Direct energy conversion
     Nuclear propulsion
     Rockets (Aeronautics)
     Space ships
     Space vehicles—Propulsion systems
  NT Photon rockets
     Project Rover
Nuclear saline water conversion plants
  (May Subd Geog)
  [TD479.6]
  UF Atomic power-plants (Saline water
     conversion)
     Atomic saline water conversion plants
     Nuclear-powered saline water
     conversion plants
  BT Nuclear facilities
     Saline water conversion plants
Nuclear scattering
  USE Scattering (Physics)
Nuclear shape (Physics)
  USE Nuclear size (Physics)
Nuclear shell models
  USE Nuclear shell theory
Nuclear shell structure
  USE Nuclear shell theory
Nuclear shell theory
  [QC173]
  UF Nuclear shell models
     Nuclear shell structure
     Shell models (Nuclear physics)
  BT Atoms
     Cluster theory (Nuclear physics)
     Matter—Constitution
     Nuclear models
     Nuclear physics
  RT Nuclear collective models
     Nuclear structure
  NT Inner-shell ionization
     Mirror nuclei
     Nilsson model
Nuclear shielding
  USE Shielding (Radiation)
Nuclear ships *(May Subd Geog)*
  [VM317]
  UF Atomic ships
     Nuclear-powered ships
  BT Nuclear propulsion
     Ships
  NT Marine nuclear reactor plants
     Nuclear icebreakers
     Nuclear merchant ships
     Nuclear warships
  — **Law and legislation** *(May Subd Geog)*
     BT Maritime law
Nuclear ships (International law)
  UF Atomic ships (International law)
  BT International law
Nuclear size (Physics)
  UF Nuclear radius (Physics)
     Nuclear shape (Physics)
     Nucleus size (Physics)
     Radius, Nuclear (Physics)
     Shape, Nuclear (Physics)
     Size, Nuclear (Physics)
  BT Nuclear physics
     Nuclear structure
Nuclear size measurements
  USE Karyometry
Nuclear spaces (Functional analysis)
  UF Spaces, Nuclear (Functional analysis)
  BT Locally convex spaces
  NT Conuclear spaces
Nuclear spectroscopy
  [QC454.N8]
  UF Spectroscopy, Nuclear

  BT Nuclear reactions
     Radiation
     Spectrum analysis
  NT Atomic spectra
     Gamma ray spectrometry
     Hadron spectroscopy
     Hyperfine interactions
     Inner-shell ionization
     Isotone shift
     Mass spectrometry
     Molecular spectra
     Neutrons—Spectra
     Nilsson model
     Nuclear magnetic resonance
      spectroscopy
     Quantum flavor dynamics
     Radiofrequency spectroscopy
     Scintillation spectrometry
     Supermultiplets
Nuclear spin
  BT Angular momentum (Nuclear physics)
     Eightfold way (Nuclear physics)
     Nuclear moments
     Nuclear physics
  NT Magnetic resonance
     Magnetic structure
     Negative temperature
     Nuclear orientation
     Pauli exclusion principle
     Polarization (Nuclear physics)
     Spin exchange
     Spin excitations
     Spin glasses
     Spin-lattice relaxation
     Spin temperature
     Spin waves
Nuclear strategy
  USE Nuclear warfare
Nuclear structure
  [QC793.3.S8]
  UF Structure, Nuclear
  BT Atomic theory
     Nuclear physics
  RT Atomic structure
     Matter, Nuclear
     Nuclear models
     Nuclear shell theory
  NT Hyperfragments
     Nilsson model
     Nuclear optical models
     Nuclear size (Physics)
Nuclear submarines *(May Subd Geog)*
  [V857.5]
  UF Atomic submarines
     Nuclear-powered submarines
  BT Nuclear warships
     Submarine boats
  RT Fleet ballistic missile weapons systems
  NT Trident (Weapons systems)
Nuclear targeting
  USE Targeting (Nuclear strategy)
Nuclear terrorism *(May Subd Geog)*
    Here are entered works on terrorism targeted at
  nuclear sites or involving threats to use nuclear weap-
  ons.
  UF Terrorism, Nuclear
  BT Terrorism
Nuclear track detectors
  [QC787.N83]
  UF Detectors, Nuclear track
     Particle track detectors
     Track detectors, Nuclear
  BT Nuclear counters
     Nuclear emulsions
     Particle tracks (Nuclear physics)
  NT Time projection chambers (Nuclear
     physics)
Nuclear transfer
  USE Cell nuclei—Transplantation
Nuclear transformations
  USE Nuclear reactions

Nuclear transmutation
  USE Nuclear reactions
Nuclear transplantation
  USE Cell nuclei—Transplantation
Nuclear underground explosions
  USE Underground nuclear explosions
Nuclear warfare
  [U263]
  UF Atomic warfare
     CBR warfare
     Nuclear strategy
  BT Military art and science
     Naval art and science
     War
  RT No first use (Nuclear strategy)
     Nuclear crisis control
     Nuclear weapons
  NT Art and nuclear warfare
     Communism and nuclear warfare
     Dropshot Plan
     Nuclear crisis stability
     Targeting (Nuclear strategy)
  — **Environmental aspects**
     (May Subd Geog)
     NT Nuclear winter
  — **Religious aspects**
  — — **Baptists,** [**Catholic Church, etc.**]
  — — **Buddhism,** [**Christianity, etc.**]
  — **Social aspects** *(May Subd Geog)*
     UF Atomic warfare and society
  — **Targeting**
     USE Targeting (Nuclear strategy)
  — **Termination**
     [U263]
     UF Termination of nuclear warfare
Nuclear warfare (International law)
  USE Nuclear weapons (International law)
Nuclear warfare and literature
  (May Subd Geog)
  UF Atomic warfare and literature
  BT Literature
     War and literature
Nuclear warfare in motion pictures
  UF Atomic warfare in motion pictures
  BT Moving-pictures
  RT War films
Nuclear warships *(May Subd Geog)*
  UF Atomic warships
     Nuclear-powered warships
     Warships, Nuclear
  BT Nuclear ships
     Warships
  NT Nuclear aircraft carriers
     Nuclear submarines
Nuclear waste disposal
  USE Radioactive waste disposal
Nuclear wastes
  USE Radioactive wastes
Nuclear-weapon-free zones
  (May Subd Geog)
  [JX1974.735-1974.74]
  UF Atom-free zones
     Atomic-weapon-free zones
     Denuclearized zones
     Nuclear-free zones
     Zones, Denuclearized
     Zones, Nuclear-weapon-free
  BT Nuclear disarmament
  RT Nuclear nonproliferation
  — **Europe**
     NT Rapacki plan
Nuclear weapons *(May Subd Geog)*
  [U264]
  UF Atomic weapons
     Weapons, Nuclear
  BT Ordnance
  RT No first use (Nuclear strategy)
     Nuclear arms control
     Nuclear disarmament
     Nuclear warfare
     Nuclear weapons industry

Nuclear weapons (Continued)
  NT Atomic bomb
      Hydrogen bomb
      Neutron weapons
      Tactical nuclear weapons
      United States. Navy—Gunner's mate
        technicians
  — **Inventory control**
  — **Safety measures**
    NT Nuclear bomb shelters
  — **Testing**
    NT Cannikin Project
        Operation Crossroads, 1946
        Operation Hardtack, 1958
        Operation Sandstone, 1948
        Project Argus
        Underground nuclear explosions
  — — **Detection**
      UF Detection of nuclear weapons
        tests
  — **Nevada**
  — — **Testing**
      NT Baneberry Nuclear Test, Nev.,
        1970
Nuclear weapons, Tactical
  USE Tactical nuclear weapons
Nuclear weapons (International law)
  UF Atomic bomb (International law)
      Atomic weapons (International law)
      Nuclear bomb (International law)
      Nuclear warfare (International law)
  BT War (International law)
Nuclear weapons control
  USE Nuclear arms control
Nuclear weapons disarmament
  USE Nuclear disarmament
Nuclear weapons industry (May Subd Geog)
  [HD9744.N83-834]
  RT Nuclear weapons
Nuclear weapons information
  (May Subd Geog)
  UF Atomic weapons information
      Exchange of nuclear weapons
        information
  BT Defense information, Classified
  — **Law and legislation** (May Subd Geog)
Nuclear weapons information, American
  (May Subd Geog)
  UF American nuclear weapons information
Nuclear weapons information, French
  (May Subd Geog)
  UF French nuclear weapons information
Nuclear weapons testing victims
  (May Subd Geog)
    Here are entered works on the victims of nuclear
  weapons tests. Works on the victims of atomic bomb
  warfare are entered under Atomic bomb victims.
  UF Atomic weapons testing victims
      Victims of nuclear weapons testing
  BT Victims
Nuclear weaponsmen (United States Navy)
  USE United States. Navy—Gunner's mate
      technicians
Nuclear well logging
  USE Radiation well logging
Nuclear winter (May Subd Geog)
  UF Winter, Nuclear
  BT Nuclear warfare—Environmental
      aspects
Nucleases
  BT Hydrolases
  NT Deoxyribonucleases
Nucleate boiling
  UF Boiling, Nucleate
  BT Ebullition
Nucleation
  BT Chemistry, Physical and theoretical
Nucleation, Atmospheric
  USE Atmospheric nucleation
Nuclei, Finite
  USE Finite nuclei

Nuclei, Galactic
  USE Galactic nuclei
Nuclei, Ice
  USE Ice nuclei
Nuclei, Mirror
  USE Mirror nuclei
Nuclei, Rare earth
  USE Rare earth nuclei
Nuclei, Vestibular
  USE Vestibular nuclei
Nucleic acid fractionation
  USE Nucleic acids—Separation
Nucleic acid hybridization
  BT Cytogenetics
      Cytology—Technique
      Hybridization
Nucleic acid separation
  USE Nucleic acids—Separation
Nucleic acid sequence analysis
  USE Nucleotide sequence
Nucleic acid synthesis
  USE Nucleic acids—Synthesis
Nucleic acids
  [QD341.A2]
  UF Polynucleotides
  BT Biomolecules
  NT Deoxyribonucleic acid
      Genetic transformation
      Nucleoproteins
      Nucleotides
      Ribonucleic acid
      Transfection
  — **Analysis**
    NT Nucleotide sequence
  — **Fractionation**
    USE Nucleic acids—Separation
  — **Separation**
    UF Fractionation of nucleic acids
       Nucleic acid fractionation
       Nucleic acid separation
       Nucleic acids—Fractionation
  — **Spectra**
  — **Synthesis**
    UF Nucleic acid synthesis
Nuclein
  [QP551]
Nucleogenesis
  USE Nucleosynthesis
Nucleoids
  BT Cell nuclei
      Deoxyribonucleic acid
Nucleolus
  UF Cell nucleolus
      Plasmosome
  BT Cell nuclei
      Cell organelles
Nucleon-antinucleon interactions
  UF Antinucleon-nucleon interactions
      Interactions, Nucleon-antinucleon
  BT Nuclear reactions
Nucleon-lepton scattering
  USE Lepton-nucleon scattering
Nucleon-nucleon interactions
  UF Interactions, Nucleon-nucleon
  BT Nuclear reactions
      Particles (Nuclear physics)
  NT Nucleon-nucleon scattering
Nucleon-nucleon scattering
  [QC793.5.N828]
  UF Nucleon scattering
  BT Nucleon-nucleon interactions
      Scattering (Physics)
  NT Neutrons—Scattering
      Protons—Scattering
Nucleon scattering
  USE Nucleon-nucleon scattering
Nucleons
  USE Particles (Nuclear physics)
Nucleophilic reactions
  UF Nucleophilicity
      Reactions, Nucleophilic

  BT Chemical reactions
Nucleophilicity
  USE Nucleophilic reactions
Nucleoproteins
  UF Ribonucleoproteins
  BT Nucleic acids
      Proteins
  NT Chromatin
      Chromosomal proteins
      Histones
      Ribosomes
      Volutin
Nucleosidases
Nucleosides
  BT Nucleotides
  NT Bromodeoxyuridine
      Ribavirin
      Tunicamycin
Nucleosynthesis
  [QB450]
  UF Nucleogenesis
  BT Chemical elements
      Cosmochemistry
Nucleotide fractionation
  USE Nucleotides—Separation
Nucleotide separation
  USE Nucleotides—Separation
Nucleotide sequence
  [QP625.N89]
  UF Analysis, Nucleic acid sequence
      Analysis, Nucleotide sequence
      Base sequence (Nucleic acids)
      Nucleic acid sequence analysis
      Nucleotide sequence analysis
      Sequence, Nucleotide
  BT Nucleic acids—Analysis
      Nucleotides—Analysis
  — Information storage and retrieval systems
    USE Information storage and retrieval
      systems—Nucleotide sequence
Nucleotide sequence analysis
  USE Nucleotide sequence
Nucleotides
  BT Nucleic acids
  NT Deoxyribonucleotides
      Interferon inducers
      Nucleosides
      Promoters (Genetics)
      Purine nucleotides
      Pyridine nucleotides
      Pyrimidine nucleotides
  — **Analysis**
    NT Nucleotide sequence
  — **Fractionation**
    USE Nucleotides—Separation
  — **Separation**
    UF Fractionation of nucleotides
       Nucleotide fractionation
       Nucleotide separation
       Nucleotides—Fractionation
Nucleotides, Pyridine
  USE Pyridine nucleotides
Nucleotidyltransferases, Deoxyribonucleate
  USE DNA polymerases
Nucleus, Caudate
  USE Caudate nucleus
Nucleus, Compound
  USE Compound nucleus
Nucleus, Olivary
  USE Olivary nucleus
Nucleus (Cells)
  USE Cell nuclei
Nucleus dentatus cerebelli
  USE Dentate nucleus
Nucleus magnocellularis
  USE Lateral vestibular nucleus
Nucleus of the atom
  USE Nuclear physics
Nucleus pigmentosus pontis
  USE Locus coeruleus

Nucleus size (Physics)
  USE Nuclear size (Physics)
Nuclide generators
  USE Radionuclide generators
Nuclides
  BT Atoms
  NT Isotopes
      Nuclear isobars
      Nuclear isomers
Nucras
  [QL666.L255]
  BT Lacertidae
Nucras tessellata
  [QL666.L255]
Nuctenea
  [QL458.42.A7]
  BT Araneidae
Nuculoida
  [QL430.6]
  BT Bivalvia
Nuculoida, Fossil
  [QE812.N]
  BT Bivalvia, Fossil
  NT Ctenodontidae, Fossil
Nuda (May Subd Geog)
  [QL380.5.N8]
  UF Atentaculata
  BT Ctenophora
  NT Beroida
Nudaurelia
  USE Imbrasia
Nude
  USE Nudity
Nude, Male
  USE Male nude
Nude culture
  USE Nudism
Nude in art
  [N7572]
  BT Human figure in art
  RT Art and morals
  NT Anatomy, Artistic
      Figure drawing
      Figure painting
      Photography of the nude
Nude in book-plates
  UF Erotic book-plates
  BT Book-plates
  RT Book-plates, Erotic
Nude mouse
  UF Athymic mouse
      Nu nu mouse
      Thymusless mouse
  BT Laboratory animals
      Mice
Nude photography
  USE Photography of the nude
Nudibranchiata
  [QL430.4]
  UF Gymnobranchiata
  NT Phyllirhoidae
Nudism (May Subd Geog)
  [GV450]
    Here are entered works on the physical culture
  aspects of nudity. Works on the moral, psychological
  and theological aspects of nakedness are entered
  under Nudity.
  UF Nude culture
      Nudity culture
      Sunbathing
  BT Physical education and training
  NT Nudist camps
      Nudity
Nudist camps (May Subd Geog)
  [GV451]
  BT Camps
      Nudism
Nudity
  [BJ1500.N8 (Ethics)]

    Here are entered works on the moral, psychologi-
  cal and theological aspects of nakedness. Works on
  the physical culture aspects of nudity are entered
  under Nudism.
  UF Nakedness
      Nude
  BT Nudism
  NT Male nude
  — **Religious aspects**
  — — **Baptists, [Catholic Church, etc.]**
Nudity culture
  USE Nudism
Nudity in dance (May Subd Geog)
  BT Dancing
Nudity in the performing arts
  BT Performing arts
Nueces Bay (Tex.) (Not Subd Geog)
  BT Bays—Texas
Nueces River (Tex.)
  UF East Nueces River (Tex.)
      Neuces River (Tex.)
  BT Rivers—Texas
  NT Corpus Christi, Lake (Tex.)
Nueces River, Battle of, 1862
  BT United States—History—Civil War,
      1861-1865—Campaigns
Nuel family
  USE Newell family
Nuer (African people)
  [DT155.2.N85]
  BT Ethnology—Sudan
      Nilotic tribes
Nuer (African people) law
  USE Law, Nuer (African people)
Nuer (African people) women
  USE Women, Nuer (African people)
Nuer folk-songs
  USE Folk-songs, Nuer
Nuer language
  [PL8576.N4]
  UF Abigar language
      Nath language
  BT Ethiopia—Languages
      Nilotic languages
      Sudan—Languages
Nuer law
  USE Law, Nuer (African people)
Nuestra Señora d'Arboló
  USE Arboló, Nuestra Señora de
Nuestra Señora de Coromoto
  USE Coromoto, Nuestra Señora de
Nuestra Señora de Guadalupe
  USE Guadalupe, Our Lady of
Nuestra Señora de la Montaña
  USE Montaña, Virgen de la
Nuestra Señora de las Virtudes
  USE Virtudes, Nuestra Señora de las
Nuestra Señora de los Angeles
  USE Angeles, Nuestra Señora de los
Nuestra Señora de los Remedios
  USE Remedios, Nuestra Señora de los
Nuestra Señora de Luján
  USE Luján, Our Lady of
Nuestra Señora de Nuria
  USE Nuria, Nuestra Señora de
Nuestra Señora de Peñarroya
  USE Peñarroya, Nuestra Señora de
Nuestra Señora de Sales Site (Viladecáns,
    Spain)
  USE Ermita de Nuestra Señora de Sales
      Site (Viladecáns, Spain)
Nuestra Señora de Valpeñoso
  USE Valpeñoso, Nuestra Señora de
Nuestra Señora del Buen Viaje
  USE Buen Viaje, Nuestra Señora del
Nuestra Señora del Rosario
  USE Rosary, Our Lady of the
Nueva Caledonia, 1698-1700
  USE Darien Scots' Colony, 1698-1700
Nuffar (Ancient city)
  USE Nippur (Ancient city)

Nuffield Mathematics Project
  UF Project Nuffield (Mathematics)
Nufi language
  USE Fe'fe' language
Nufor language
  [PL6279]
  UF Mafor language
      Nuforian language
  BT Melanesian languages
Nuforian language
  USE Nufor language
Nugunu language
  USE Gunu language
Nugzum language
  USE Ngizim language
Nuhalk Indians
  USE Bella Coola Indians
Nui (Tuvalu)
  UF Netherland Island (Tuvalu)
      Tnaguinui (Tuvalu)
  BT Coral reefs and islands—Tuvalu
Nuisance, Attractive
  USE Attractive nuisance
Nuisances (May Subd Geog)
  BT Adjoining landowners
      Self-help (Law)
      Torts
  NT Gases, Asphyxiating and poisonous—
      Law and legislation
      Noise control—Law and legislation
      Odors
      Smoke prevention
Nuisances (International law)
  [JX4147]
  BT International law
Nuisances (Jewish law)
Nuka Hiva (Marquesas Islands)
  UF Adams (Marquesas Islands)
      Baux (Marquesas Islands)
      Ile Nouka-Hiva (Marquesas Islands)
      Ile Nuku-Hiva (Marquesas Islands)
      Madison Island (Marquesas Islands)
      Marchand Island (Marquesas Islands)
      Nokuhiva (Marquesas Islands)
      Nukahiva (Marquesas Islands)
      Nuku Hiva (Marquesas Islands)
      Nukuhiva (Marquesas Islands)
      Sir Henry Martin's (Marquesas
      Islands)
      Tah Nuuhiva (Marquesas Islands)
  BT Islands—Marquesas Islands
Nukahiva (Marquesas Islands)
  USE Nuka Hiva (Marquesas Islands)
Nukahiva language
  [PL6471]
  UF Nukuhiva language
  BT Polynesian languages
  RT Marquesan language
Nukazuka Iseki (Takayama-shi, Japan)
  USE Nukazuka Site (Takayama-shi, Japan)
Nukazuka Site (Takayama-shi, Japan)
  UF Nukazuka Iseki (Takayama-shi, Japan)
  BT Japan—Antiquities
Nuko Nono Atoll (Tokelau Islands)
  USE Nukunonu Atoll (Tokelau Islands)
Nuku Hiva (Marquesas Islands)
  USE Nuka Hiva (Marquesas Islands)
Nukufetau Atoll (Tuvalu)
  UF De Peyster Group (Tuvalu)
      De Peyster Island (Tuvalu)
      De Peysters Island (Tuvalu)
      Depeyster Island (Tuvalu)
      Peyster's Group (Tuvalu)
  BT Coral reefs and islands—Tuvalu
Nukuhiva (Marquesas Islands)
  USE Nuka Hiva (Marquesas Islands)
Nukuhiva language
  USE Nukahiva language
Nukulaelae Atoll (Tuvalu)
  UF Mitchell Island (Tuvalu)
      Nukulailai Atoll (Tuvalu)

Nukulaelae Atoll (Tuvalu) *(Continued)*
  BT Coral reefs and islands—Tuvalu
Nukulailai Atoll (Tuvalu)
  USE Nukulaelae Atoll (Tuvalu)
Nukulakita (Tuvalu)
  USE Niulakita (Tuvalu)
Nukuno (Tokelau Islands)
  USE Nukunonu Atoll (Tokelau Islands)
Nukunono Atoll (Tokelau Islands)
  USE Nukunonu Atoll (Tokelau Islands)
Nukunonu Atoll (Tokelau Islands)
  UF Duke of Clarence Island (Tokelau
       Islands)
     Nuko Nono Atoll (Tokelau Islands)
     Nukuno (Tokelau Islands)
     Nukunono Atoll (Tokelau Islands)
  BT Coral reefs and islands—Tokelau
       Islands
Nukuoro (Polynesian people)
  BT Ethnology—Caroline Islands
     Polynesians
Nukuoro language
  BT Polynesian languages
Nula (Artificial language)
  [PM8693]
  BT Languages, Artificial
Nuland family
  USE Newland family
Null cell killing
  USE Antibody-dependent cell cytotoxicity
Nulla poena sine lege doctrine
  USE Ex post facto laws
Nullakun language
  USE Ngalakan language
Nullibrotheas
  [QL458.72.V4]
  BT Vejovidae
Nullification
  [E384.3]
  [JK310-JK325 (Constitutional history)]
  RT Kentucky and Virginia resolutions of
       1798
     Secession
     State rights
Nullikin language
  USE Ngalakan language
Nullipores
  USE Coralline algae
Nullity *(May Subd Geog)*
  BT Civil law
  RT Revocation
     Sanctions (Law)
  NT Condicio juris
     Illegal contracts
     Illegal juristic acts
     Rescission (Law)
Nullity (Canon law)
  [BX1939.N]
Nullity (Canon law, Orthodox Eastern)
  BT Canon law, Orthodox Eastern
Nullity (Islamic law)
Nullity (Roman law)
Nullity of marriage
  USE Marriage—Annulment
Nullum crimen sine lege doctrine
  USE Ex post facto laws
NULOAD (Computer program)
  BT Computer programs
     Roads—Maintenance and repair—
       Computer programs
Numa Indians
  USE Numic Indians
Numan family
  USE Newman family
Numancia (Ancient city)
  USE Numantia (Ancient city)
Numans family
  USE Newman family
Numantia (Ancient city) *(Not Subd Geog)*
  [DP95]
  UF Numancia (Ancient city)

  BT Cities and towns, Ruined, extinct, etc.
     —Spain
     Spain—Antiquities
Numantine War, 143-133 B.C.
  [DG252.8]
  BT Rome—History—Republic, 265-30
       B.C.
Numata Kaidō (Japan) *(Not Subd Geog)*
  BT Roads—Japan
NUMAUDO (Computer program language)
  UF Audible numbers
     Numerus and audire
  BT Languages, Artificial
     Speech processing systems
Numbat
  [QL737.M33]
  UF Banded anteater
     Myrmecobiidae
     Myrmecobius fasciatus
     Myrmecobius rufus
  BT Dasyuridae
     Marsupialia
Number, Nusselt
  USE Nusselt number
Number, Picard
  USE Picard number
Number, Platonic
  USE Platonic number
Number, Rayleigh
  USE Rayleigh number
Number (Grammar)
  USE *subdivision* Number *under names of
       languages*
     Grammar, Comparative and general—
       Number
**Number 10 Downing Street (London,
England)**
  UF 10 Downing Street (London, England)
     No. 10 Downing Street (London,
       England)
     No. Ten Downing Street (London,
       England)
     Number Ten Downing Street (London,
       England)
     Ten Downing Street (London,
       England)
  BT Dwellings—England
     Prime ministers—Great Britain—
       Dwellings
Number ability
  USE Mathematical ability
Number concept
  [QA141.15]
  Here are entered works on the psychology of nu-
  meration. Works on counting, including counting
  books, are entered under Counting. Works on the
  theory and systems of numbering are entered under
  Numeration.
  BT Apperception
     Psychology
  NT Number concept in children
     Signed numbers
Number concept in children
  (May Subd Geog)
  [BF723.N8]
  BT Cognition in children
     Number concept
Number games
  USE Arithmetic—Study and teaching
       (Primary)
     Mathematical recreations
Number line
  BT Arithmetic
     Numbers, Real
Number readiness
  USE Mathematical readiness
Number rhymes
  USE Counting-out rhymes
Number sieves
  USE Sieves (Mathematics)

Number study
  USE Arithmetic—Study and teaching
       (Primary)
     Numbers, Theory of
Number symbolism
  USE Symbolism of numbers
Number Ten Downing Street (London,
England)
  USE Number 10 Downing Street (London,
       England)
Number theory
  USE Numbers, Theory of
Number theory, Combinatorial
  USE Combinatorial number theory
Numbering-machines
  [Z249]
  BT Marking devices
     Printing machinery and supplies
Numbers, Bernoullian
  USE Bernoullian numbers
Numbers, Cardinal
  [QA248]
  UF Cardinal numbers
  BT Logic, Symbolic and mathematical
     Numbers, Theory of
     Numbers, Transfinite
     Set theory
  NT Martin's axiom
Numbers, Complex
  [QA255]
  UF Complex numbers
     Imaginary quantities
     Quantities, Imaginary
  RT Algebra, Universal
     Quaternions
     Vector analysis
  NT Ausdehnungslehre
     Functions
     Numbers, Real
Numbers, Dimensionless
  USE Dimensionless numbers
Numbers, Divisibility of
  [QA242]
  NT Perfect numbers
Numbers, Euler's
  USE Euler's numbers
Numbers, Figurate
  USE Numbers, Polygonal
Numbers, Fortune-telling by
  USE Fortune-telling by numbers
Numbers, Fuzzy
  USE Fuzzy numbers
Numbers, Geometry of
  USE Geometry of numbers
Numbers, Gödel
  USE Gödel numbers
Numbers, House
  USE Street addresses
Numbers, Index
  USE Index numbers (Economics)
Numbers, Irrational
  [QA247.5]
  UF Irrational numbers
  NT Numbers, Transcendental
Numbers, Large
  USE Law of large numbers
Numbers, Natural
  UF Natural numbers
     Numbers, Whole
     Whole numbers
  BT Numbers, Rational
  NT Greatest integer function
     Numbers, Prime
     Numbers, Theory of
     Sequences, Aliquot
Numbers, Negative
  UF Negative numbers
Numbers, Nondimensional
  USE Dimensionless numbers
Numbers, Ordinal
  UF Ordinal numbers

Numerical analysis *(Continued)*
    Functional equations—Numerical
      solutions
    Galerkin methods
    Hamilton-Jacobi equations—Numerical
      solutions
    Heat equation—Numerical solutions
    Helmholtz equation—Numerical
      solutions
    Initial value problems—Numerical
      solutions
    Integral equations, Nonlinear—
      Numerical solutions
    Integro-differential equations—
      Numerical solutions
    Interpolation
    Interval analysis (Mathematics)
    Inverse problems (Differential
      equations)—Numerical solutions
    Iterative methods (Mathematics)
    Lagrange equations—Numerical
      solutions
    Many-body problem—Numerical
      solutions
    Monte Carlo method
    Multigrid methods (Numerical
      analysis)
    Navier-Stokes equations—Numerical
      solutions
    Nomography (Mathematics)
    Numerical calculations
    Numerical differentiation
    Numerical grid generation (Numerical
      analysis)
    Numerical integration
    Operator equations—Numerical
      solutions
    Operator equations, Nonlinear—
      Numerical solutions
    Painlevé equations—Numerical
      solutions
    Poisson's equation—Numerical
      solutions
    Pseudoinverses
    Random walks (Mathematics)
    Relaxation methods (Mathematics)
    Roundoff errors
    Runge-Kutta formulas
    Smoothing (Numerical analysis)
    Volterra equations—Numerical
      solutions
    Wave equation—Numerical solutions
— **Acceleration of convergence**
  UF Acceleration of convergence in
      numerical analysis
      Numerical analysis—Convergence
      acceleration
  BT Convergence
— **Computer programs**
  NT FEED (Computer program)
      NAG Library (Computer
      programs)
      TEAPACK (Computer programs)
— Convergence acceleration
  USE Numerical analysis—Acceleration
      of convergence
— **Improperly posed problems**
  UF Improperly posed problems in
      numerical analysis
Numerical analysis laboratories
  USE Computation laboratories
Numerical Analysis of Rectangularly
  Configurated Plane Strain
  USE NARC (Electronic computer system)
Numerical analysis programs
  USE Numerical calculations—Computer
      programs
Numerical calculations
  ⌈QA297⌉
  BT Numerical analysis
  NT Computation laboratories

    Differential equations—Numerical
      solutions
    Differential equations, Linear—
      Numerical solutions
    Differential equations, Partial—
      Numerical solutions
    Digital filters (Mathematics)
    Integral equations—Numerical
      solutions
    Monte Carlo method
— **Computer programs**
  ⌈QA297⌉
  UF Numerical analysis programs
Numerical coordinate generation (Numerical
  analysis)
  USE Numerical grid generation (Numerical
      analysis)
Numerical differentiation
  ⌈QA355⌉
  UF Graphic differentiation
  BT Functions
      Numerical analysis
Numerical filters
  USE Digital filters (Mathematics)
Numerical functions
  ⌈QA246⌉
  UF Functions, Numerical
  NT Bernoullian numbers
      Gaussian sums
      Möbius function
Numerical grid generation (Numerical
analysis)
  UF Coordinate generation, Numerical
      (Numerical analysis)
      Generation of numerical grids
      (Numerical analysis)
      Grid generation, Numerical
      (Numerical analysis)
      Mesh generation, Numerical
      (Numerical analysis)
      Numerical coordinate generation
      (Numerical analysis)
      Numerical mesh generation
      (Numerical analysis)
  BT Boundary value problems—Numerical
      solutions
      Differential equations, Partial—
      Numerical solutions
      Nets (Mathematics)
      Numerical analysis
Numerical integration
  ⌈QA299.3⌉
  UF Integration, Numerical
      Mechanical quadrature
      Quadrature, Mechanical
  BT Integrals, Definite
      Interpolation
      Numerical analysis
  NT Cubature formulas
      Gaussian quadrature formulas
— **Computer programs**
  NT QUADPACK (Computer
      programs)
Numerical languages
  USE Cesges de damis (Artificial language)
      Pasigraphy
      Translingua script
Numerical mesh generation (Numerical
  analysis)
  USE Numerical grid generation (Numerical
      analysis)
Numerical roots
  USE Roots, Numerical
Numerical sequences
  USE Sequences (Mathematics)
Numerical taxonomy *(May Subd Geog)*
  ⌈QH83⌉

  UF Phenetic taxonomy
      Phenograms
      Quantitative taxonomy
      Taximetrics
      Taxonomy, Numerical
      Taxonomy, Quantitative
  BT Biology—Classification
  NT Plant numerical taxonomy
Numerical weather forecasting
  ⌈QC996⌉
  UF Mathematical weather forecasting
      Physical weather forecasting
      Weather forecasting, Numerical
  BT Baroclinic models
      Hydrodynamic weather forecasting
Numerically controlled milling-machines
  USE Milling-machines—Numerical control
Numerology
  USE Symbolism of numbers
Numerus and audire
  USE NUMAUDO (Computer program
      language)
Numerus clausus *(May Subd Geog)*
  BT Universities and colleges—Admission
Numic Indians
  ⌈E99.N97⌉
  UF Numa Indians
      Plateau Shoshonean Indians
  BT Indians of North America
      Shoshonean Indians
  NT Bannock Indians
      Comanche Indians
      Gosiute Indians
      Kawaiisu Indians
      Mono Indians
      Paiute Indians
      Shoshoni Indians
      Ute Indians
Numic languages
  UF Plateau Shoshonean languages
  BT Shoshonean languages
  NT Chemehuevi language
      Comanche language
      Kawaiisu language
      Shoshoni language
      Ute language
Numinous, The
  USE Holy, The
Numipu
  USE Nez Percé Indians
Numipu language
  USE Nez Percé language
Numismatic collections
  USE Numismatic museums
      Numismatics—Private collections
Numismatic errors
  USE Numismatics—Errors
Numismatic libraries *(May Subd Geog)*
  UF Libraries, Numismatic
  BT Libraries, Special
Numismatic museums *(May Subd Geog)*
  ⌈CJ43-45⌉
  UF Numismatic collections
  BT Museums
Numismatic portraits
  USE Portrait sculpture (in numismatics)
Numismatics *(May Subd Geog)*
  ⌈CJ⌉
      Here are entered works on the study of coins,
  medals, tokens, etc. collectively. Works on the study
  of coins only are entered under Coins.
  BT Archaeology
      Auxiliary sciences of history
      History
      History, Ancient
  SA *subdivision* Numismatics *under names*
      of individual persons
  NT Animals (in numismatics)
      Architecture (in numismatics)
      Arms and armor (in numismatics)
      Bible (in numismatics)

Birds (in numismatics)
Castles (in numismatics)
Cistophorus (Coin)
Coins
Counterstamp (Numismatics)
Dollar sign
Donkeys (in numismatics)
Elephant (in numismatics)
Gods (in numismatics)
Heroes (in numismatics)
Horsemen and horsewomen (in
  numismatics)
Horses (in numismatics)
Hunting (in numismatics)
Jettons
Kings and rulers (in numismatics)
Lions (in numismatics)
Medals
Mines and mineral resources (in
  numismatics)
Natural history (in numismatics)
Olympics (in numismatics)
Painting (in numismatics)
Portrait sculpture (in numismatics)
Seals (Numismatics)
Ships (in numismatics)
Sports (in numismatics)
Transportation (in numismatics)
Washington, George, 1732-1799—
  Numismatics
Wine and wine making (in
  numismatics)
Women (in numismatics)
— **Collectors and collecting**
    NT Coins as an investment
       Numismatics—Private collections
       Numismatists
— — **Law and legislation**
    (May Subd Geog)
— Dealers
    USE Coin dealers
— Designers
    USE Coin designers
— **Errors**
    UF Errors, Numismatic
       Numismatic errors
    SA *subdivision* Errors *under names of*
       coins, e.g. Cent—Errors
— **Private collections**
    UF Numismatic collections
    BT Numismatics—Collectors and
       collecting
    SA *subdivision* Numismatic collections
       under names of individual
       persons, families. and corporate
       bodies
Numismatics, Ancient *(May Subd Geog)*
  ₍CJ201-1397₎
Numismatics, Arabic, ₍**Phoenician, Punic, etc.**₎
Numismatics, Etruscan *(May Subd Geog)*
    UF Etruscan numismatics
Numismatics, Greek *(May Subd Geog)*
    BT Classical antiquities
Numismatics, Islamic
    UF Islamic numismatics
       Muslim numismatics
       Numismatics, Muslim
Numismatics, Italic *(May Subd Geog)*
    UF Italic numismatics
Numismatics, Jewish *(May Subd Geog)*
  ₍CJ1375₎
    UF Jewish numismatics
    BT Coins, Jewish
       Jews—Antiquities
Numismatics, Medieval
  ₍CJ1601-1715₎
    NT Tremissis
Numismatics, Merovingian
    UF Merovingian numismatics
Numismatics, Muslim
    USE Numismatics, Islamic

Numismatics, Roman *(May Subd Geog)*
    BT Classical antiquities
Numismatics in literature
Numismatists *(May Subd Geog)*
    BT Coins—Collectors and collecting
       Numismatics—Collectors and
         collecting
Nummulites
  ₍QL368.F6₎
Nummulites, Fossil
  ₍QE772₎
    BT Nummulitidae, Fossil
Nummulitidae, Fossil
  ₍QE772₎
    BT Foraminifera, Fossil
    NT Nummulites, Fossil
Numon family
    USE Newman family
Numsimatics
    NT Bridges (in numismatics)
Nūn, Wādī (Morocco)
    UF Oued Noun (Morocco)
       Wādī Nūn (Morocco)
       Wedi Noon (Morocco)
       Wedinoon (Morocco)
    BT Wadis—Morocco
Nun-birds
  ₍QL696.P5₎
    UF Monasa
Nun moth
  ₍SB945.N₎
    UF Liparis monacha
       Lymantria monacha
       Psilura monacha
    BT Moths
Nuna dialect (Burkina Faso)
    USE Nunuma dialect
Nunally family
    USE Nunley family
Nunamaker family
    USE Nunnemacher family
Nunamiut (Eskimo people)
  ₍E99.E7₎
    UF Nunatogmiut (Eskimo people)
    BT Eskimos—Alaska
Nunan family
    USE Nunn family
Nunane family
    USE Nunn family
Nunatogmiut (Eskimo people)
    USE Nunamiut (Eskimo people)
Nunc dimittis (Music)
    BT Canticles
Nunchaku
  ₍GV1142.6₎
    BT Martial arts weapons
       Stick fighting
Nunciature controversy
    USE Nuncios, Papal
Nuncios, Papal *(May Subd Geog)*
  ₍BX1908₎
    UF Nunciature controversy
       Nuntios, Papal
       Papal nuncios
    BT Ambassadors
       Catholic Church—Diplomatic service
       Catholic Church—Relations
         (diplomatic)
       Diplomatic and consular service
       Diplomats
    RT Legates, Papal
Nune family
    USE Nunn family
Nunemacher family
    USE Nunnemacher family
Nunemaker family
    USE Nunnemacher family
Nunenmaker family
    USE Nunnemacher family
Nuner family
    USE Nunn family

Nung arts
    USE Arts, Nung
Nung language
  ₍PL4001.N8₎
    UF Khunung language
    BT Kachin dialects
Nungazer family
    USE Nungezer family
Nungesser family
    USE Nungezer family
Nungezer family *(Not Subd Geog)*
    UF Nongazer family
       Nungazer family
       Nungesser family
       Nunngesser family
Nunggubuju language
    USE Nunggubuyu language
Nunggubuyu (Australian people)
  ₍DU125.N94₎
    UF Nungubuju (Australian people)
    BT Australian aborigines
       Ethnology—Australia
Nunggubuyu language
  ₍PL7101.N8₎
    UF Nunggubuju language
       Wubuy language
    BT Australia—Languages
       Australian languages
Nungs
  ₍DS556.45.N85 (Vietnam)₎
    BT Ethnology—China
       Ethnology—Vietnam
Nungubuju (Australian people)
    USE Nunggubuyu (Australian people)
Nunguda language
    USE Longuda language
Nunley family *(Not Subd Geog)*
    UF Nunally family
       Nunnally family
       Nunnelly family
Nunmaker family
    USE Nunnemacher family
Nunn family *(Not Subd Geog)*
    UF Nunan family
       Nunane family
       Nune family
       Nuner family
       Nunne family
Nunnally family
    USE Nunley family
Nunne family
    USE Nunn family
Nunnelly family
    USE Nunley family
Nunnemacher family *(Not Subd Geog)*
    UF Nunamaker family
       Nunemacher family
       Nunemaker family
       Nunenmaker family
       Nunmaker family
       Nunnenmacker family
    RT Nonnenmacher family
Nunnenmacker family
    USE Nunnemacher family
Nunneries
    USE Convents and nunneries
Nunngesser family
    USE Nungezer family
Nuns *(May Subd Geog)*
    UF Sisters (in religious orders,
         congregations, etc.)
    BT Christian biography
    RT Ex-nuns
       Monasticism and religious orders for
         women
    NT Buddhist nuns
       Consecration of nuns
       Lesbian nuns
Nuns, Benedictine
    USE Benedictine nuns

Nuns, Cistercian
    USE Cistercian nuns
Nuns, Lesbian
    USE Lesbian nuns
Nuns as authors
    BT Authors
        Women authors
    NT Nuns' writings
Nuns as public school teachers
    BT Teachers
Nun's fiddle
    USE Sea-trumpet
Nuns in campus ministry
    BT Chaplains, University and college
        Monastic and religious life of women
        Women in campus ministry
Nuns in literature
    BT Women in literature
Nuns' writings *(May Subd Geog)*
    UF Writings of nuns
    BT Nuns as authors
Nuns' writings, American *(May Subd Geog)*
    UF American nuns' writings
Nuns' writings, English *(May Subd Geog)*
    UF English nuns' writings
Nuntios, Papal
    USE Nuncios, Papal
Nunu (African people)
    [DT546.245.N86]
    UF Banunu (African people)
        Moye (African people)
    BT Ethnology—Congo (Brazzaville)
Nunuma dialect
    UF Nibulu dialect
        Nouni dialect
        Nuna dialect (Burkina Faso)
        Nuruma dialect
    BT Burkina Faso—Languages
        Gurunsi dialects
        Kasena dialect
Nupe (African people)
    BT Ethnology—Nigeria
Nupe language
    [PL8577]
    UF Nope language
    BT Kwa languages
Nupercaine
    UF Percaine
    BT Anesthetics
        Local anesthesia
Nuphar
    [QK495.N97]
    BT Nymphaeaceae
Nuphar lutum
    [QK495.N97 (Botany)]
    UF European cowlily
        Yellow water lily
Nuprl (Computer system)
    BT Automatic theorem proving
Nuptiality
    USE Marriage
Nuraghi
    [DG55.S2]
    BT Fortification—Italy
        Italy—Antiquities
        Towers—Italy
    NT Nuraghic language
Nuraghi culture *(May Subd Geog)*
    BT Bronze age—Italy
        Sardinia—Antiquities
  — **Sumerian influences**
        BT Sumerians
Nuraghic language *(May Subd Geog)*
    [P1079]
    UF Paleosardic language
    BT Nuraghi
        Sardinia—Languages
Nurakito (Tuvalu)
    USE Niulakita (Tuvalu)
Nurculuk
    [BP251-253]

    UF Enlightenment (Turkish religious
        movement)
Nuremberg laws
    USE Citizenship—Germany
        Jews—Legal status, laws, etc.—
        Germany
        Marriage law—Germany
**Nuremberg Medical Trial, Nuremberg,
Germany, 1946-1947**
    UF Medical Trial, Nuremberg, Germany,
        1946-1947
        Nuremberg Medical Trial, 1946-1947
        Subsequent proceedings, Nuremberg
        War Crime Trials, case no. 1
    BT Nuremberg War Crime Trials,
        Nuremberg, Germany, 1946-1949
Nuremberg Medical Trial, 1946-1947
    USE Nuremberg Medical Trial, Nuremberg,
        Germany, 1946-1947
**Nuremberg Trial of Major German War
Criminals, Nuremberg, Germany, 1945-1946**
    UF Nuremberg Trial of Major German
        War Criminals, 1945-1946
        Nuremberg War Crime Trials,
        Nuremberg, Germany, 1945-1946
    BT War crime trials—Germany (West)
Nuremberg Trial of Major German War
Criminals, 1945-1946
    USE Nuremberg Trial of Major German
        War Criminals, Nuremberg,
        Germany, 1945-1946
    NT Operation Edelweiss
Nuremberg War Crime Trials, Nuremberg,
Germany, 1945-1946
    USE Nuremberg Trial of Major German
        War Criminals, Nuremberg,
        Germany, 1945-1946
**Nuremberg War Crime Trials, Nuremberg,
Germany, 1946-1949**
    UF Nuremberg War Crime Trials, 1946-
        1949
        Subsequent proceedings, Nuremberg
        War Crime Trials
    BT War crime trials—Germany (West)
    NT Krupp Trial, Nuremberg, Germany,
        1947-1948
        Nuremberg Medical Trial, Nuremberg,
        Germany, 1946-1947
Nuremberg War Crime Trials, 1946-1949
    USE Nuremberg War Crime Trials,
        Nuremberg, Germany, 1946-1949
    NT Einsatzgruppen Trial, Nuremberg,
        Germany, 1947-1948
        Flick Trial, Nuremberg, Germany,
        1947-1949
        High Command Trial, Nuremberg,
        Germany, 1948-1949
        Hostage Trial, Nuremberg, Germany,
        1947-1949
        I.G. Farben Trial, Nuremberg, 1947-
        1948
        Justice Trial, Nuremberg, Germany,
        1947
        Milch Trial, Nuremberg, Germany,
        1946-1947
        Ministries Trial, Nuremberg, Germany,
        1948-1949
Nuri dialect
    [PK2899.Z9N]
    UF Nawar—Language
    BT Romany language
Nuria, Nuestra Señora de
    [BT660.N84]
    UF Nuestra Señora de Nuria
    RT Mary, Blessed Virgin, Saint—Cult—
        Spain
Nurnberg family
    USE Niernberger family
Nurnberger family
    USE Niernberger family

Nürnberger Rathaus (Nuremberg, Germany)
    BT City halls—Germany (West)
Nurse administrators *(May Subd Geog)*
    [RT89]
    UF Administrators, Nurse
        Head nurses
        Nurse managers
        Nursing administrators
        Nursing managers
    BT Health services administrators
        Nurses
    NT Nursing school administrators
Nurse and patient *(May Subd Geog)*
    UF Nurse-patient relationship
        Patient and nurse
    BT Medical personnel and patient
        Nurses
        Nursing
Nurse and physician *(May Subd Geog)*
    [RT86.4]
    UF Nurse-physician relationship
        Physician and nurse
        Physician-nurse relationship
    BT Interpersonal relations
        Nurses
        Physicians
    NT Nurse-physician joint practice
Nurse anesthetists *(May Subd Geog)*
    UF Anesthetists, Nurse
    BT Nurses
        Operating room nursing
        Operating room personnel
Nurse clinicians
    USE Nurse practitioners
Nurse consultants
    USE Nursing consultants
Nurse family
    USE Nourse family
Nurse frog
    USE Alytes obstetricans
Nurse managers
    USE Nurse administrators
Nurse midwives
    USE Midwives
Nurse-patient relationship
    USE Nurse and patient
Nurse-physician collaboration
    USE Nurse-physician joint practice
Nurse-physician joint practice
    (May Subd Geog)
    [R729.5.N87]
    UF Joint practice of nurses and physicians
        Nurse-physician collaboration
        Physician-nurse collaboration
        Physician-nurse joint practice
    BT Health care teams
        Medical office nursing
        Medicine—Practice
        Nurse and physician
        Nursing—Practice
Nurse-physician relationship
    USE Nurse and physician
Nurse practitioners *(May Subd Geog)*
    UF Clinical nurse specialists
        Nurse clinicians
    BT Nurses
        Nursing—Practice
        Physicians' assistants
  — **Supply and demand**
Nurse supply and demand
    USE Nurses—Supply and demand
Nurseries *(May Subd Geog)*
    BT Children's rooms
    NT Hospitals—Nurseries
  — **Equipment and supplies**
        RT Infants' supplies
Nurseries, Forest
    USE Forest nurseries
Nurseries (Forestry)
    USE Forest nurseries

Nurseries (Horticulture)   *(May Subd Geog)*
  ₍SB₎
  BT Fruit-culture
     Horticulture
     Ornamental horticulture
     Trees
  RT Arboriculture
     Garden centers (Retail trade)
     Nursery dealers
     Nursery growers
     Nursery stock
     Ornamental plant industry
  NT Landscape nurseries
     Plant propagation
  — **Law and legislation**   *(May Subd Geog)*
     BT Agricultural laws and legislation
  — **Machinery**
     ₍S678.7₎
     BT Horticultural machinery
  — **Vocational guidance**
Nursery care of primates
  USE Primates—Nursery care
Nursery dealers   *(May Subd Geog)*
  ₍SB88.5-89₎
  BT Nursery stock—Marketing
  RT Florists
     Garden centers (Retail trade)
     House plant industry
     Nurseries (Horticulture)
     Nursery growers
Nursery farmers
  USE Nursery growers
Nursery growers   *(May Subd Geog)*
  UF Nursery farmers
     Nursery managers
     Nurserymen
  BT Horticulturists
  RT Nurseries (Horticulture)
     Nursery dealers
Nursery-infant teachers
  USE Preschool teachers
Nursery managers
  USE Nursery growers
Nursery rearing of primates
  USE Primates—Nursery care
Nursery rhymes
  ₍PN6110.C4₎
  ₍PZ8.3₎
  UF Poetry for children
  BT Children's poetry
     Children's songs
     Folk literature
     Folk poetry
     Picture-books for children
     Poetry
  NT Alphabet rhymes
     Counting-out rhymes
     Jump rope rhymes
     Lullabies
Nursery rhymes, Burmese   *(May Subd Geog)*
  UF Burmese nursery rhymes
  BT Burmese poetry
Nursery rhymes, Chinese   *(May Subd Geog)*
  UF Chinese nursery rhymes
  BT Chinese poetry
Nursery rhymes, Chinese, ₍**French, German,**
  etc.₎
Nursery rhymes, English
  UF English nursery rhymes
Nursery rhymes, German   *(May Subd Geog)*
  UF German nursery rhymes
Nursery rhymes, Hungarian
  (May Subd Geog)
  UF Hungarian nursery rhymes
  BT Hungarian poetry
Nursery rhymes, Japanese
  (May Subd Geog)
  UF Japanese nursery rhymes
  BT Japanese poetry
Nursery rhymes, Kannada   *(May Subd Geog)*
  UF Kannada nursery rhymes

  BT Kannada poetry
Nursery rhymes, Khasi   *(May Subd Geog)*
  UF Khasi nursery rhymes
  BT Khasi poetry
Nursery rhymes, Ndebele (Zimbabwe)
  (May Subd Geog)
  UF Ndebele nursery rhymes (Zimbabwe)
  BT Ndebele poetry (Zimbabwe)
Nursery rhymes, Norwegian
  (May Subd Geog)
  UF Norwegian nursery rhymes
  BT Norwegian poetry
Nursery rhymes, Polish   *(May Subd Geog)*
  UF Polish nursery rhymes
  BT Polish poetry
Nursery rhymes, Spanish   *(May Subd Geog)*
  UF Spanish nursery rhymes
Nursery rhymes, Spanish American
  (May Subd Geog)
  UF Spanish American nursery rhymes
Nursery rhymes, Yiddish   *(May Subd Geog)*
  UF Yiddish nursery rhymes
  BT Yiddish poetry
Nursery school facilities
  ₍LB3325.N8₎
  BT School facilities
Nursery school teachers
  USE Preschool teachers
Nursery school teachers, Training of
  USE Preschool teachers—Training of
Nursery schools   *(May Subd Geog)*
  ₍LB1140₎
  BT Schools
  RT Day care centers
     Education, Preschool
     Kindergarten
  NT Cooperative nursery schools
     Play schools
  — **Law and legislation**   *(May Subd Geog)*
     BT Educational law and legislation
  — **Music**
     UF Music—Nursery schools
     BT Children's songs
        Kindergarten—Music
Nursery stock   *(May Subd Geog)*
  RT Nurseries (Horticulture)
     Ornamental plant industry
     Plants, Ornamental
  NT Shrubs
     Trees
  — **Marketing**
     BT Garden centers (Retail trade)
     NT Nursery dealers
Nursery-web spiders
  USE Pisauridae
Nurserymen
  USE Nursery growers
Nurses   *(May Subd Geog)*
  UF RNs
  BT Medical personnel
  NT Associate degree nurses
     Deaconesses
     Men nurses
     Nurse administrators
     Nurse and patient
     Nurse and physician
     Nurse anesthetists
     Nurse practitioners
     Nurses' aides
     Nursing—Vocational guidance
     Nursing consultants
     Nursing students
     Practical nurses
     Prison nurses
     Public health nurses
     Strikes and lockouts—Nursing
     Trade-unions—Nurses
     Visiting nurses
  — **Attitudes**
     BT Attitude (Psychology)
  — **Collective labor agreements**

     USE Collective labor agreements—
        Nurses
  — **In-service training**   *(May Subd Geog)*
     BT Medical personnel—In-service
        training
        Nursing—Study and teaching
        Nursing—Study and teaching
        (Continuing education)
  — **Job satisfaction**
     BT Job satisfaction
  — **Job stress**
  — Legal status, laws, etc.
     USE Nursing—Law and legislation
  — **Malpractice**   *(May Subd Geog)*
     UF Nurses—Tort liability
        Tort liability of nurses
     BT Medical ethics
        Nursing—Law and legislation
        Nursing—Practice
  — **Pensions**   *(May Subd Geog)*
     UF Nurses—Salaries, pensions, etc.
  — — **Law and legislation**
        (May Subd Geog)
  — **Rating of**
     ₍RT85.5₎
     UF Nurses, Rating of
        Rating of nurses
  — **Salaries, etc.**   *(May Subd Geog)*
     UF Nurses—Salaries, pensions, etc.
  — — **Law and legislation**
        (May Subd Geog)
  — Salaries, pensions, etc.
     USE Nurses—Pensions
        Nurses—Salaries, etc.
  — **Supply and demand**
     UF Nurse supply and demand
     BT Medical care
  — Tort liability
     USE Nurses—Malpractice
Nurses, Afro-American
  USE Afro-American nurses
Nurses, Foreign   *(May Subd Geog)*
  UF Foreign nurses
  BT Medical personnel, Foreign
  — **Licenses**   *(May Subd Geog)*
     BT Nursing—Law and legislation
Nurses, Rating of
  USE Nurses—Rating of
Nurses' aides   *(May Subd Geog)*
  ₍RT84₎
  UF Nursing assistants
  BT Allied health personnel
     Nurses
Nurses in mass media   *(May Subd Geog)*
  BT Mass media
Nurses in television
  ₍PN1992.8.N87₎
  UF Nurses on television
  BT Television
Nurses' notes
  USE Nursing records
Nurses on television
  USE Nurses in television
Nursing   *(May Subd Geog)*
  ₍RT₎
  BT Care of the sick
     Medicine
  SA *subdivision* Nursing *under names of*
     diseases or procedures, e.g. Cancer
     —Nursing; Enterostomy—Nursing;
     Heart—Surgery—Nursing
  NT Aviation nursing
     Camp nursing
     Cardiovascular disease nursing
     Communication in nursing
     Community health nursing
     Dermatologic nursing
     Disaster nursing
     Emergency nursing
     Geriatric nursing
     Gynecologic nursing

Nursing *(Continued)*
    Home nursing
    Industrial nursing
    Intensive care nursing
    Medical office nursing
    Military nursing
    Minorities in nursing
    Neurological nursing
    Nurse and patient
    Obstetrical nursing
    Ophthalmic nursing
    Orthopedic nursing
    Otolaryngological nursing
    Pediatric nursing
    Poliomyelitis nursing
    Practical nursing
    Private duty nursing
    Psychiatric nursing
    Public health nursing
    Rehabilitation nursing
    Respiratory disease nursing
    School nursing
    Strikes and lockouts—Nursing
    Surgical nursing
    Team nursing
    Urological nursing
    Veterinary nursing
— **Ability testing**
    NT Pre-Nursing and Guidance
        Examination
— Administration
    USE Nursing services—Administration
— **Authorship**
    [RT24]
    BT Medical writing
— **Awards**
    BT Rewards (Prizes, etc.)
    NT Nightingale award
— **Bibliography**
    RT Nursing literature
— Collective bargaining
    USE Collective bargaining—Nursing
— **Cross-cultural studies**
— **Endowments**
    BT Charities, Medical
— Evaluation
    USE Nursing audit
— **Examinations**
— — **Computer programs**
    NT NERS (Computer program)
— **Examinations, questions, etc.**
    NT Nursing schools—Entrance
        examinations
— **Law and legislation** *(May Subd Geog)*
    UF Nurses—Legal status, laws, etc.
        Nursing law
    NT Nurses—Malpractice
        Nurses, Foreign—Licenses
— **Practice**
    [RT86.7]
    BT Medicine—Practice
    NT Nurse-physician joint practice
        Nurse practitioners
        Nurses—Malpractice
        Private duty nursing
— **Psychological aspects**
    [RT86]
    UF Nursing psychology
    NT Nursing students—Psychology
— **Research**
— — **Moral and religious aspects**
    BT Nursing ethics
— **Scholarships, fellowships, etc.**
    NT Nursing students—Loans
— **Social aspects** *(May Subd Geog)*
    UF Society and nursing
— Specialties
    USE Nursing specialties
— **Standards**
    NT Nursing audit
— **Study and teaching** *(May Subd Geog)*

[RT71-81]
    BT Medical education
    NT Nurses—In-service training
        Nursing schools
        Nursing students
— — **Audio-visual aids**
    NT Moving-pictures in nursing
        education
        Television in nursing education
— — Federal aid
    USE Federal aid to nursing
        education
— — **Finance**
    NT Federal aid to nursing education
— **Study and teaching (Associate degree)**
    (May Subd Geog)
    [RT74.5]
    UF Associate degree nursing education
    BT Junior colleges
    RT Associate degree nurses
— **Study and teaching (Continuing**
    education) *(May Subd Geog)*
    [RT76]
    NT Nurses—In-service training
— **Vocational guidance** *(May Subd Geog)*
    BT Nurses
Nursing, Aviation
    USE Aviation nursing
Nursing (Infant feeding)
    USE Bottle feeding
        Breast feeding
Nursing administration
    USE Nursing services—Administration
Nursing administrators
    USE Nurse administrators
Nursing agencies
    USE Nursing services
Nursing assistants
    USE Nurses' aides
Nursing audit
    [RT85.5]
    UF Audit, Nursing
        Nursing—Evaluation
    BT Nursing—Standards
Nursing care plans *(May Subd Geog)*
    [RT49]
    UF Plans, Nursing care
    BT Medical protocols
Nursing consultants *(May Subd Geog)*
    UF Nurse consultants
    BT Consultants
        Medical consultants
        Nurses
Nursing ethics *(May Subd Geog)*
    [RT85]
    BT Ethics
        Professional ethics
    RT Medical ethics
    NT Nursing—Research—Moral and
        religious aspects
Nursing Examination Review Software
    USE NERS (Computer program)
Nursing facilities, Skilled
    USE Nursing homes
Nursing home administrators
    (May Subd Geog)
    BT Allied health personnel
        Health services administrators
        Hospital administrators
        Nursing homes—Administration
        Nursing homes—Employees
Nursing home applicants *(May Subd Geog)*
    UF Applicants to nursing homes
    BT Nursing home patients
— **Preadmission screening**

    UF PAS for nursing homes
        Pre-admission screening for nursing
        homes
        Preadmission screening for nursing
        homes
        Screening, Pre-admission, for
        nursing homes
        Screening, Preadmission, for
        nursing homes
    BT Medical screening
Nursing home benefactors *(May Subd Geog)*
    UF Nursing home philanthropists
    BT Benefactors
        Hospital benefactors
        Nursing homes—Endowments
Nursing home care *(May Subd Geog)*
    BT Institutional care
        Long-term care of the sick
        Medical care
    NT Nursing home patients—Abuse of
        Nursing homes—Complaints against
Nursing home care, Cost of
    USE Nursing homes—Rates
Nursing home charges
    USE Nursing homes—Rates
Nursing home patients *(May Subd Geog)*
    UF Nursing home residents
        Patients, Nursing home
    BT Chronically ill
        Hospital patients
        Nursing homes
    NT Nursing home applicants
        Nursing homes—Complaints against
— **Abuse of**
    UF Abuse of nursing home patients
    BT Nursing home care
— Relocation
    USE Nursing home patients—Transfer
— **Transfer**
    UF Nursing home patients—Relocation
        Relocation of nursing home
        patients
        Transfer of nursing home patients
    BT Nursing homes—Admission
Nursing home pharmacies
    USE Nursing homes—Pharmaceutical
        services
Nursing home philanthropists
    USE Nursing home benefactors
Nursing home prospective payment
    USE Nursing homes—Prospective payment
Nursing home rates
    USE Nursing homes—Rates
Nursing home residents
    USE Nursing home patients
Nursing home use
    USE Nursing homes—Utilization
Nursing homes *(May Subd Geog)*
    [RA997-RA999]
    UF Long-term skilled nursing facilities
        Nursing facilities, Skilled
        Skilled nursing facilities
    BT Long-term care facilities
    NT Nursing home patients
        Teaching nursing homes
        Violence in nursing homes
— Activity programs
    USE Nursing homes—Recreational
        activities
— **Administration**
    UF Nursing homes—Management and
        regulation
    BT Health services administration
    NT Nursing home administrators
        Nursing homes—Complaints
        against
— — **Citizen participation**
— **Admission**
    NT Nursing home patients—Transfer
— **Bed capacity**

UF Bed capacity of nursing homes
    Nursing homes—Size
    Size of nursing homes
— Charges
    USE Nursing homes—Rates
— **Complaints against**
    UF Complaints against nursing homes
    BT Nursing home care
       Nursing home patients
       Nursing homes—Administration
— Cost control
— — **Law and legislation**
    (May Subd Geog)
— Employees
    NT Nursing home administrators
— Endowments
    NT Nursing home benefactors
— **Evacuation**
    UF Evacuation of nursing homes
    BT Transport of sick and wounded
— Federal aid
    USE Federal aid to nursing homes
— **Finance**
    NT Federal aid to nursing homes
— Hygiene
    USE Nursing homes—Sanitation
— **Law and legislation** *(May Subd Geog)*
— — **Criminal provisions**
— Management and regulation
    USE Nursing homes—Administration
— **Medical records**
    [RA999.M43]
    BT Medical records
— **Pharmaceutical services**
    UF Nursing home pharmacies
       Nursing homes—Pharmacy
         departments
    BT Pharmaceutical services
       Pharmacy
— Pharmacy departments
    USE Nursing homes—Pharmaceutical
        services
— **Prospective payment**
    UF Medicare nursing home prospective
        payment
       Nursing home prospective payment
       Payment, Prospective, Nursing
        home
       PPS (Medical care)
       Prospective payment, Nursing
        home
       Prospective reimbursement,
        Nursing home
       Reimbursement, Prospective,
        Nursing home
    BT Insurance, Hospitalization
       Nursing homes—Rates
— **Rates**
    UF Nursing home care, Cost of
       Nursing home charges
       Nursing home rates
       Nursing homes—Charges
    BT Medical care, Cost of
    NT Nursing homes—Prospective
        payment
— **Recreational activities**
    [RA999.R42]
    UF Activity programs in nursing
        homes
       Nursing homes—Activity programs
       Recreational activities in nursing
        homes
    BT Recreational therapy
— **Sanitation**
    [RA999.S36]
    UF Nursing homes—Hygiene
— Size
    USE Nursing homes—Bed capacity
— **Utilization**
    UF Nursing home use
       Utilization of nursing homes

Nursing homes, Investor-owned
    USE Nursing homes, Proprietary
Nursing homes, Private for profit
    USE Nursing homes, Proprietary
Nursing homes, Proprietary
    (May Subd Geog)
    UF For profit nursing homes
       Investor-owned nursing homes
       Nursing homes, Investor-owned
       Nursing homes, Private for profit
       Private for profit nursing homes
       Proprietary nursing homes
    BT Health facilities, Proprietary
Nursing homes, Teaching
    USE Teaching nursing homes
Nursing law
    USE Nursing—Law and legislation
Nursing libraries
    [Z675.N8]
    UF Libraries, Nursing
    BT Medical libraries
    NT Nursing school libraries
Nursing literature
    UF Literature, Nursing
    BT Medical literature
    RT Nursing—Bibliography
Nursing literature searching
    USE Information storage and retrieval
        systems—Nursing
Nursing managers
    USE Nurse administrators
Nursing psychology
    USE Nursing—Psychological aspects
Nursing records *(May Subd Geog)*
    [RT50]
    UF Notes, Nurses'
       Nurses' notes
    BT Communication in nursing
       Medical records
Nursing school administrators
    (May Subd Geog)
    UF Administrators, Nursing school
    BT College administrators
       Nurse administrators
       Nursing schools—Administration
Nursing school benefactors
    (May Subd Geog)
    UF Nursing school philanthropists
    BT Benefactors
       Nursing schools—Endowments
Nursing school dropouts *(May Subd Geog)*
    BT Dropouts
       Nursing schools
       Nursing students
Nursing school libraries
    [Z675.N8]
    UF Libraries, Nursing school
    BT Libraries, University and college
       Nursing libraries
Nursing school philanthropists
    USE Nursing school benefactors
Nursing schools *(May Subd Geog)*
    [RT71-81]
    UF Hospital training-schools
       Schools of nursing
       Training schools for nurses
    BT Health occupations schools
       Nursing—Study and teaching
    NT Nursing school dropouts
— **Accreditation**
— **Administration**
    NT Nursing school administrators
— **Admission**
    RT Nursing schools—Entrance
        requirements
— **Endowments**
    NT Nursing school benefactors
— **Entrance examinations**
    BT Nursing—Examinations, questions,
        etc.
— **Entrance requirements**

    RT Nursing schools—Admission
— **Faculty**
— — **Work load**
    USE Nursing schools—Faculty—
        Workload
— — **Workload**
    UF Nursing schools—Faculty—
        Work load
       Workload of nursing school
        faculty
— **United States**
— — **Entrance examinations**
    NT Pre-Nursing and Guidance
        Examination
Nursing service administration
    USE Nursing services—Administration
Nursing services *(May Subd Geog)*
    UF Nursing agencies
       Services, Nursing
    BT Medical care
— **Administration**
    [RT89]
    UF Administration, Nursing service
       Nursing—Administration
       Nursing administration
       Nursing service administration
       Supervisory nursing
    BT Health services administration
    NT GRASP System
       Nursing services—Business
        management
— **Business management**
    [RT86.7-RT86.75]
    UF Business management in nursing
        services
    BT Nursing services—Administration
Nursing specialties *(May Subd Geog)*
    [RT86.7-RT86.75]
    UF Nursing—Specialties
       Specialties, Nursing
    BT Medicine—Specialties and specialists
Nursing students *(May Subd Geog)*
    [RT71-81]
    UF Student nurses
    BT Health occupations students
       Nurses
       Nursing—Study and teaching
       Students
    NT Nursing school dropouts
— **Loans**
    UF Loans to nursing students
    BT Nursing—Scholarships, fellowships,
        etc.
       Student loan funds
— **Psychology**
    BT Nursing—Psychological aspects
Nursing students, Foreign *(May Subd Geog)*
    UF Foreign nursing students
    BT Students, Foreign
Nursing team
    USE Team nursing
Nurss family
    USE Nourse family
Nürtingen (Germany). Neckarhausen
    USE Neckarhausen (Nürtingen, Germany)
Nurturance
    USE Nurturing behavior
Nurture and nature
    USE Nature and nurture
Nurturing behavior *(May Subd Geog)*
    UF Behavior, Nurturing
       Nurturance
    BT Human behavior
    NT Nurturing behavior in children
Nurturing behavior in children
    (May Subd Geog)
    [BF723.N84 (Psychology)]
    BT Child psychology
       Nurturing behavior
Nuruma dialect
    USE Nunuma dialect

Nusa Tenggara (Indonesia)
USE Sunda Islands, Lesser (Indonesia)
Nusaḥ Ari
USE Judaism—Ari rite
Nusaḥ Franḳfurṭ
USE Judaism—Frankfurt rite
Nusaḥ ha-Romanyoṭim
USE Judaism—Romaniot rite
Nusaḥ Ḥasidim
USE Judaism—Hasidic rite
Nusaḥ Sefarad
USE Judaism—Sephardic rite
Nusayris
USE Nosairians
Nusbaum family *(Not Subd Geog)*
UF Nusbaumer family
Nussbaum family
Nussbaumer family
Nusbaumer family
USE Nusbaum family
Nuse family
USE New family
Nussbaum family
USE Nusbaum family
Nussbaumer family
USE Nusbaum family
Nusselt number
UF Heat transfer coefficient
Number, Nusselt
BT Mass transfer
Thermodynamics
Nussknacker (Ballet)
USE Nutcracker (Ballet)
Nut, Bambara
USE Bambarra groundnut
Nut, Bambarra
USE Bambarra groundnut
Nut, Earth
USE Bambarra groundnut
Nut, Peach
USE Peach palm
Nut culture
USE Nuts
Nut family
USE Knott family
Nut grass
USE Nutgrass
Nut industry *(May Subd Geog)*
[HD9259.N68-HD9259.N7]
Nut pine
USE Pinus edulis
Nut pine, Mexican
USE Pinus cembroides
Nut pines
USE Pinyon pines
Nut products *(May Subd Geog)*
[TP439]
BT Nuts
Seed products
Nut runners and setters
UF Setters and nut runners
BT Power tools
Wrenches
Nut trees *(May Subd Geog)*
Here are entered works on the description of nut-bearing trees or their nursery production. Works on nut growing or nuts as food are entered under Nuts.
BT Nuts
Trees
SA *individual nut trees, e.g.* Pecan; Walnut
NT Cashew
Tree crops
— Diseases and pests
USE Nuts—Diseases and pests
Nutakkamuushupe-yama (Japan)
USE Daisetsu Mountains (Japan)
Nutation
[QB165 (Astronomy)]
BT Astronomy
Astronomy, Spherical and practical

Nutcracker (Ballet)
UF Casse-Noisette (Ballet)
Nussknacker (Ballet)
Shchelkunchik (Ballet)
Stschelkunschick (Ballet)
The nutcracker (Ballet)
BT Ballets
Nute family
USE Knott family
Nutgrass
[QK495.C997]
UF Cyperus rotundus
Nut grass
Nutsedge
Nuth family
USE Newth family
Nuthatches
[QL696.P2]
UF Certhiomorphae
NT Giant nuthatch
Tichodroma
White-breasted nuthatch
Nutka Indians
USE Nootka Indians
Nutka language
USE Nootka language
Nutka Sound (Vancouver Island, B.C.)
USE Nootka Sound (Vancouver Island, B.C.)
Nutmeg
[QK495.M85 (Botany)]
[SB307.N8 (Culture)]
UF Myristica fragrans
Myristica officinalis
Nutmeg tree
Nutmeg graters
UF Graters, Nutmeg
BT Kitchen utensils
Nutmeg industry *(May Subd Geog)*
[HD9211.N88]
BT Spice trade
Nutmeg melon
USE Muskmelon
Nutmeg tree
USE Nutmeg
Nuton family
USE Newton family
Nutria
USE Coypu
Nutriculture gardening
USE Hydroponics
Nutrient-drug interactions
USE Drug-nutrient interactions
Nutrient film culture *(May Subd Geog)*
[SB126.5-126.57]
UF N.F.T.
Nutrient film technique
Nutrient film technology
BT Hydroponics
Nutrient film technique
USE Nutrient film culture
Nutrient film technology
USE Nutrient film culture
Nutrient intake
USE Ingestion
Nutrient media (Biology)
USE Culture media (Biology)
Nutrient requirements
USE Nutrition—Requirements
Nutrient supplements
USE Dietary supplements
Nutrition *(May Subd Geog)*
[QP141-QP185.3 (Physiology)]
[RA784 (Personal health)]
[TX341-TX641 (Home economics)]

Here are entered works on the sum of the physiological processes involved in the assimilation and utilization of nutrients for proper body functioning and health. This heading may be subdivided by place to indicate the nutritional status of a group of people in the place. Works on the food and drink regularly consumed by an individual or group of people are entered under Diet.
UF Alimentation
BT Health
Physiology
RT Diet
Dietetics
Digestion
Food
Food habits
Malnutrition
SA *subdivision* Nutrition *under classes of persons and ethnic groups; and subdivision* Nutritional aspects *under topics, e.g.* Cancer—Nutritional aspects
NT Absorption (Physiology)
Amino acids in human nutrition
Amino acids in nutrition
Animal nutrition
Antibiotics in nutrition
Artificial feeding
Chromium in human nutrition
Dietary supplements
Drug-nutrient interactions
Elemental diet
Fiber in human nutrition
Fish oils in human nutrition
Folic acid in human nutrition
Food preferences
Fructose in human nutrition
Heart—Surgery—Nutritional aspects
Human behavior—Nutritional aspects
Lipids in human nutrition
Lipids in nutrition
Manganese in human nutrition
Minerals in human nutrition
Minerals in nutrition
Nutritionists
Parenteral feeding
Proteins in human nutrition
Puerperium—Nutritional aspects
Selenium in human nutrition
Sex (Biology)—Nutritional aspects
Soils and nutrition
Stress (Physiology)—Nutritional aspects
Sugars in human nutrition
Sulphur in nutrition
Surgery—Nutritional aspects
Survival and emergency rations
Trace elements in nutrition
Unsaturated fatty acids in human nutrition
Vitamin A in human nutrition
Vitamin B in human nutrition
Vitamin D in human nutrition
Vitamin tolerance
Vitamins
Vitamins in human nutrition
Women in nutrition
— Aging effect
USE Aging—Nutritional aspects
— **Evaluation**
UF Nutritional status measurement
— **Exhibitions**
[TX535]
UF Nutrition exhibits
— **Genetic aspects**
— **Psychological aspects**
RT Appetite
Food habits
Food preferences
NT Children—Nutrition—Psychological aspects
— **Religious aspects**

— —**Baptists,** ⌈Catholic Church, etc.⌉
— —**Buddhism,** ⌈Christianity, etc.⌉
— —**Islam**
      NT Black Muslims—Dietary laws
           Muslims—Dietary laws
— —**Jainism**
      NT Jains—Dietary laws
— —**Judaism**
      NT Jews—Dietary laws
— —**Sikhism**
      NT Sikhs—Dietary laws
— **Requirements**
    UF Dietary requirements
        Food requirements, Dietary
        Needs, Nutritional
        Nutrient requirements
        Nutrition requirements
        Nutritional needs
        Nutritional requirements
        Requirements, Nutritional
    SA *subdivision* Nutrition—
        Requirements *under classes of*
        persons, e.g. Infants—Nutrition
        —Requirements
— **Research** *(May Subd Geog)*
    ⌈TX537⌉
    UF Nutrition research
— —**Law and legislation**
    (May Subd Geog)
— **Study and teaching** *(May Subd Geog)*
    ⌈TX364-365⌉
    NT Nutrition extension work
— —**United States**
      NT Expanded Food and Nutrition
           Education Program
Nutrition, Clinical
    USE Diet therapy
Nutrition and dental health
    (May Subd Geog)
    ⌈RK281⌉
    UF Dental health and nutrition
        Dentistry and nutrition
        Teeth—Diseases—Nutritional aspects
    BT Diet in disease
        Teeth
    NT Periodontal disease—Nutritional
        aspects
Nutrition and sex
    USE Sex (Biology)—Nutritional aspects
Nutrition and state
    USE Nutrition policy
Nutrition disorders *(May Subd Geog)*
    ⌈RA645.N87 (Public health)⌉
    ⌈RC620-RC627 (Internal medicine)⌉
    UF Disorders of nutrition
    BT Diseases
    NT Appetite disorders
        Deficiency diseases
        Ingestion disorders
        Malnutrition
        Nutritionally induced diseases
        Obesity
        Pica (Pathology)
Nutrition disorders in children
    (May Subd Geog)
    ⌈RJ399.N8⌉
    BT Children—Diseases
    NT Anorexia in children
        Malnutrition in children
        Nutrition disorders in infants
        Nutritionally induced diseases in
        children
        Obesity in children
        Trace element deficiency diseases in
        children
Nutrition disorders in infants
    (May Subd Geog)
    UF Infant nutrition disorders
    BT Infants—Diseases
        Nutrition disorders in children

Nutrition exhibits
    USE Nutrition—Exhibitions
Nutrition extension work *(May Subd Geog)*
    UF Extension work, Nutrition
    BT Home economics extension work
        Nutrition—Study and teaching
Nutrition in pre- and post-surgery
    USE Surgery—Nutritional aspects
Nutrition in pregnancy
    USE Pregnancy—Nutritional aspects
Nutrition in space flight
    USE Astronauts—Nutrition
Nutrition of astronauts
    USE Astronauts—Nutrition
Nutrition of athletes
    USE Athletes—Nutrition
Nutrition of children
    USE Children—Nutrition
        Infants—Nutrition
Nutrition of plants
    USE Plants—Nutrition
Nutrition policy *(May Subd Geog)*
    ⌈TX359-360⌉
    UF Food policy
        Nutrition and state
        State and nutrition
    BT Social policy
Nutrition requirements
    USE Nutrition—Requirements
Nutrition research
    USE Nutrition—Research
Nutrition surveys *(May Subd Geog)*
    UF Food consumption surveys
    BT Surveys
— **Law and legislation** *(May Subd Geog)*
— **United States**
      NT Health and Nutrition Examination
           Survey
Nutritional causes of aging
    USE Aging—Nutritional aspects
Nutritional disorders in plants
    USE Nutritionally induced diseases in
        plants
Nutritional exchange lists
    USE Food exchange lists
Nutritional needs
    USE Nutrition—Requirements
Nutritional requirements
    USE Nutrition—Requirements
Nutritional status measurement
    USE Nutrition—Evaluation
Nutritionally induced diseases
    (May Subd Geog)
    ⌈RA645.N87 (Public health)⌉
    ⌈RC622 (Internal medicine)⌉
    UF Diet—Adverse effects
        Diet and disease
        Dietary causes of disease
        Diseases—Dietary aspects
    BT Diseases—Causes and theories of
        causation
        Nutrition disorders
    NT Carbohydrates, Refined
        Nutritionally induced diseases in
        children
Nutritionally induced diseases in animals
    (May Subd Geog)
    BT Animal nutrition
        Diet in veterinary medicine
        Veterinary medicine
    RT Deficiency diseases in domestic
        animals
Nutritionally induced diseases in children
    (May Subd Geog)
    BT Nutrition disorders in children
        Nutritionally induced diseases
Nutritionally induced diseases in plants
    (May Subd Geog)
    UF Nutritional disorders in plants
    BT Plant diseases—Nutritional apsects
    NT Deficiency diseases in plants

Nutritionists *(May Subd Geog)*
    BT Nutrition
        Physiologists
    RT Dietitians
Nutritive sweeteners
    USE Natural sweeteners
Nuts *(May Subd Geog)*
    ⌈SB401⌉
    Here are entered works on nut growing or nuts as
    food. Works on the description of nut-bearing trees or
    their nursery production are entered under Nut trees.
    UF Nut culture
    BT Food
        Food crops
        Horticultural crops
        Seed crops
    SA *names of nuts, e.g.* Chestnut, Pecan
    NT American chestnut
        Chinese chestnut
        Cookery (Nuts)
        Macadamia nut
        Nut products
        Nut trees
— **Diseases and pests** *(May Subd Geog)*
    ⌈SB608.N⌉
    UF Nut trees—Diseases and pests
    BT Trees—Diseases and pests
    SA *names of pests, e.g.* Chestnut-
        weevil, Walnut span-worm
— **Varieties**
Nuts (Machinery)
    USE Bolts and nuts
Nutsedge
    USE Nutgrass
Nutshell (Computer program)
    USE Leading Edge Nutshell (Computer
        program)
Nutt family
    USE Knott family
Nutter family
    USE Knott family
Nutts family
    USE Knott family
Nuu-chah-nulth Indians
    USE Nootka Indians
Nux vomica
    BT Strychnine
Nuxalk Indians
    USE Bella Coola Indians
Nuy River (South Africa)
    BT Rivers—South Africa
Nuyn family
    USE Neun family
Nuzi (Ancient city)
    ⌈DS70.5.N9⌉
    UF Gasur (Ancient city)
        Nuzi (Iraq)
        Nuzu (Ancient city)
        Yorghan Tepe (Iraq)
    BT Cities and towns, Ruined, extinct, etc.
        —Iraq
        Iraq—Antiquities
Nuzi (Iraq)
    USE Nuzi (Ancient city)
Nuzu (Ancient city)
    USE Nuzi (Ancient city)
Nyabingi (African deity) *(May Subd Geog)*
    BT Gods, African
Nyabungu language
    USE Shi language
Nyabwa language
    UF Niabua language
    BT Bete language
        Ivory Coast—Languages
        Kru languages
Nyah Kur language *(May Subd Geog)*
    ⌈PL4351.N93⌉

Nyah Kur language *(Continued)*
  UF Chao Bon language
       Chao Bun language
       Chaobon language
       Chaobun language
       Chhao-bon language
       Nia-kuoll language
       Niakuol language
       Nialuok language
  BT Mon-Khmer languages
       Thailand—Languages
Nyai language
  USE Tete language
Nyakyusa (African people)
       [DT443]
  UF Sokile (African people)
  BT Bantus
       Ethnology—Tanzania
  RT Ngonde (African people)
Nyakyusa language
  USE Ngonde language
Nyala
  USE Tragelaphus
Nyam-Nyam (African people)
  USE Zande (African people)
Nyam-Nyam language
  USE Zande language
Nyamwezi
  USE Nyamwezi (African people)
Nyamwezi (African people)
       [DT443.3.N93]
  UF Banyamwezi (African people)
       Nyamwezi
       Wanyamwezi (African people)
  BT Bantus
       Ethnology—Tanzania
Nyamwezi language
       [PL8591]
  BT Bantu languages
Nyandja language
  USE Nyanja language
Nyaneka language
  UF Lunyaneka language
       Olunyaneka language
  BT Bantu languages
Nyanga (African people)
  BT Ethnology—Africa, West
Nyanga language *(May Subd Geog)*
  UF KiNyanga language
  BT Bantu languages
       Zaire—Languages
Nyangamada language
  USE Nyangumata language
Nyanganyatjara language
  USE Ngaanyatjara language
Nyangatom (African people)
       [DT380.4.N83]
  UF Dongiro (African people)
       Donyiro (African people)
       Idongiro (African people)
       Toposa (African people)
  BT Ethnology—Ethiopia
       Ethnology—Sudan
Nyangumata language
       [PL7101.N9]
  UF Njangamada language
       Njangomada language
       Njangumada language
       Njangumarda language
       Njangumata language
       Nyangamada language
  BT Australia—Languages
       Australian languages
Nyanja (African people)
  UF Nyanja (African tribe)
  BT Ethnology—Malawi
Nyanja (African tribe)
  USE Nyanja (African people)
Nyanja imprints *(May Subd Geog)*
Nyanja language
       [PL8593]

  UF Chinyanja language
       Kiniassa language
       Mang'anja language
       Ng'anga language
       Nyandja language
       Nyassa language
  BT Bantu languages
  RT Chewa dialect
       Sena language
       Tete language
       Tumbuka language
Nyanja literature *(May Subd Geog)*
Nyankole
  USE Banyankole
Nyankole language
  UF Lunyankole language
       Nkole language
       Nkore language
       Nyankore language
       Runyankore language
  BT Bantu languages
  RT Nyankore-Kiga language
Nyankole poetry
Nyankore-Kiga language
  UF Nkore-Kiga language
       Runyankore-Rukiga language
  BT Bantu languages
  RT Kiga language
       Nyankole language
Nyankore language
  USE Nyankole language
Nyasa, Lake
  UF Lake Malawi
       Lake Nyasa
       Lake Nyassa
       Malawi, Lake
       Niassa, Lake
       Njassa See
       Nyassa, Lake
  BT Lakes—Malawi
       Lakes—Mozambique
       Lakes—Tanzania
Nyasaland
  USE Malawi
Nyassa, Lake
  USE Nyasa, Lake
Nyassa language
  USE Nyanja language
Nyaya
       [B132.N8]
  BT Hinduism
       Logic
       Philosophy, Hindu
  NT Jaina logic
Nyce family
  USE Nice family
Nyckelgiga
  USE Keyed fiddle
Nyckelharpa
  USE Keyed fiddle
Nycora collaris
  USE Ring-necked duck
Nyctaginaceae
       [QK495.N9]
  BT Centrospermae
  NT Boerhavia
Nyctalemonidae
  USE Uraniidae
Nyctalus
       [QL737.C595]
  UF Noctule bats
       Noctules
  BT Vespertilionidae
Nyctalus noctula
       [QL737.C595]
Nyctanassa violacea
  USE Yellow-crowned night heron
Nyctea
       [QL696.S83]
  BT Strigidae

Nyctea nyctea
  USE Snowy owl
Nyctea scandiaca
  USE Snowy owl
Nycteribiidae
       [QL537.N9]
  UF Bat flies
  BT Diptera
  NT Basilia (Insect)
Nycteribosca *(May Subd Geog)*
       [QL537.S86]
  BT Streblidae
  NT Nycteribosca amboinensis
Nycteribosca amboinensis *(May Subd Geog)*
       [QL537.S86]
  BT Nycteribosca
Nycteridopsylla
       [QL599.7.I3]
  BT Ischnopsyllidae
Nycticorax
       [QL696.C52]
  BT Ardeidae
       Herons
Nycticorax caledonicus
  USE Rufous night heron
Nycticorax nycticorax
  USE Black-crowned night heron
Nycticorax violaceus
  USE Yellow-crowned night heron
Nyctimantis
       [QL668.E24]
  BT Hylidae
Nyctimantis rugiceps
       [QL668.E24]
Nyctinomops femorosaccus
  USE Tadarida femorosacca
Nyctitheriidae, Fossil
       [QE882.I5]
  BT Insectivora, Fossil
Nyctomys
       [QL737.R638]
  BT Cricetidae
  NT Nyctomys sumichrasti
Nyctomys sumichrasti
       [QL737.R638]
  UF Sumichrast vesper rat
       Vesper rat, Sumichrast
  BT Nyctomys
Nye family *(Not Subd Geog)*
  UF Ney family
       Nie family
       Nigh family
  RT New family
Nyeman River
  USE Neman River
Nyenchen Tanglha (China)
  USE Kailas Mountain (China)
Nyende (African people)
       [DT541.42]
  UF Niende (African people)
  BT Ethnology—Benin
Nygaard family
  USE Nygard family
Nygard family *(Not Subd Geog)*
  UF Nygaard family
       Nygårds family
Nygårds family
  USE Nygard family
Nygmia
       [QL561.L9]
  UF Euproctis
  BT Lymantriidae
Nygmia phaeorrhoea
  USE Brown-tail moth
Nyholm family *(Not Subd Geog)*
Nyidi (African people)
  USE Kwegu (African people)
Nyife language
  USE Luo language (Kenya and Tanzania)
Nyifwa (African people)
  USE Luo (African people)

Nyika (African people)
  USE Nika (African people)
Nyilem language
  USE Nielim language
Nying-ma (Sect)
  USE Rñiṅ-ma-pa (Sect)
Nying-ma-pa
  USE Rñiṅ-ma-pa (Sect)
Nyírség (Hungary)
Nyising (Indic people)
  USE Dafla (Indic people)
Nylander family *(Not Subd Geog)*
Nyles family
  USE Niles family
Nylon
  ₁TS1688₁
  UF Capron
      Kapron
  BT Polyamide fibers
      Polyamides
      Synthetic fabrics
      Textile fibers, Synthetic
  RT Rayon
  NT Electric insulators and insulation—
      Nylon
  — Thermal properties
Nylon dyeing
  USE Dyes and dyeing—Nylon
Nylon hosiery
  USE Hosiery, Nylon
Nylon yarns
  UF Yarns, Nylon
  BT Yarn
Nymoen family *(Not Subd Geog)*
Nymphaea
  ₁QK495.N97₁
  BT Nymphaeaceae
Nymphaea advena
  ₁QK495.N97₁
Nymphaea in art
Nymphaeaceae
  ₁QK495.N97₁
  BT Ranunculales
  NT Brasenia
      Nelumbo
      Nuphar
      Nymphaea
      Victoria (Plants)
Nymphalidae
  ₁QL561.N9₁
  UF Aegyreidae
      Brushfooted butterflies
  BT Butterflies
      Lepidoptera
  NT Adelpha
      Agrias
      Anaea
      Anartia
      Antanartia
      Apatura
      Archimestra
      Bassaris
      Boloria
      Brenthis
      Charaxes
      Cynthia (Insects)
      Dynamine
      Euphydryas
      Hypolimnas
      Junonia (Insect)
      Limenitis
      Melitaea
      Polygonia
      Polyura
      Prepona
      Sais
      Sasakia
      Speyeria
      Vanessa (Insects)

Nymphenburg Castle (Munich, Germany)
  USE Schloss Nymphenburg (Munich,
      Germany)
Nymphenburger Park (Munich, Germany)
  USE Schloss Nymphenburg (Munich,
      Germany)
Nymphicus
  BT Lories
  NT Cockatiel
Nymphicus hollandicus
  USE Cockatiel
Nymphomania *(May Subd Geog)*
  ₁RC560.N9₁
  BT Psychosexual disorders
      Sex
Nymphs (Insects)
  BT Insects—Larvae
Nymphulidae
  USE Pyralidae
Nynorsk
  USE Norwegian language (Nynorsk)
Nynorsk literature
  USE Norwegian literature (Nynorsk)
Nynorsk poetry
  USE Norwegian poetry (Nynorsk)
Nyolcak (Group of artists)
  ₁N6820.5.N93₁
  UF Eight (Group of artists)
  BT Art, Hungarian
Nyole language
  USE Nyore language
Nyon porcelain
  ₁NK4399.N9₁
  UF Porcelain, Nyon
Nyonga (African people)
  USE Bali (African people)
Nyoraikyō (Sect) *(May Subd Geog)*
  ₁BQ9800.N96₁
  UF Isson Kyōdai (Sect)
      Nyoraishū (Sect)
  BT Buddhist sects
Nyoraishū (Sect)
  USE Nyoraikyō (Sect)
Nyore language
  UF Lunyore language
      Nyole language
      Olunyore language
  BT Bantu languages
Nyoro (Bantu people)
  USE Banyoro
Nyoro language
  ₁PL8595₁
  UF Lunyoro language
      Urunyoro language
  BT Bantu languages
  RT Nyoro-Tooro language
Nyoro-Tooro language
  UF Runyoro-Rutooro language
  BT Bantu languages
  RT Nyoro language
      Tooro language
Nypa
  ₁QK495.P17₁
  UF Nipa (Plant)
  BT Palms
Nypa, Fossil
  BT Palms, Fossil
Nyroca valisineria
  USE Canvasback
Nysa Łużycka River
  USE Neisse River
Nysius
  ₁QL523.L9₁
  BT Lygaeidae
Nysius ericae
  USE False chinch bug
Nysius groenlandicus
  ₁QL523.L9₁
Nysson
  ₁QL568.S7₁
  BT Sphecidae

Nyssonidae
  ₁QL568.N9₁
  BT Hymenoptera
Nystad, Finland, Treaty of, 1721
  ₁DL743.N8₁
Nystagmus
  ₁RE748₁
  UF Miners' nystagmus
  BT Eye—Movement disorders
      Occupational diseases
  NT Electronystagmography
Nystatin
  UF Mycostatin
  BT Antifungal agents
      Macrolide antibiotics
Nyū family *(Not Subd Geog)*
Nyunga (Australian people)
  ₁DU125.N97₁
  UF Nooga (Australian people)
      Noonga (Australian people)
      Nyungar (Australian people)
  BT Australian aborigines
      Ethnology—Australia
Nyungar (Australian people)
  USE Nyunga (Australian people)
Nyungar dialects
  UF Njuṇar dialects
  BT Australia—Languages
      Australian languages
Nyungwe language
  USE Tete language
Nzabi (African people)
  ₁DT546.145.N93 (Gabon)₁
  UF Bandzabi (African people)
      Banjabi (African people)
      Njavi (African people)
      Njawi (African people)
      Nzebi (African people)
  BT Bantus
      Ethnology—Congo (Brazzaville)
      Ethnology—Gabon
Nzakara (African people)
  BT Ethnology—Central African Republic
Nzakara dialect
  ₁PL8828.95N₁
  UF Sakara dialect
  BT Zande language
Nzakara poetry *(May Subd Geog)*
Nzebi (African people)
  USE Nzabi (African people)
Nzema language
  USE Nzima language
Nzima (African people)
  UF Zema (African people)
  BT Ethnology—Ghana
Nzima language
  ₁PL8597₁
  UF Amanaya language
      Nsima language
      Nzema language
      Zema language
      Zimba language
  BT Kwa languages
Nzombo dialect
  USE Zoombo dialect
Nzoombo dialect
  USE Zoombo dialect
O Doine family
  USE O Doyne family
O Doyne family *(Not Subd Geog)*
  UF Doine family
      Doyne family
      Duinn family
      O Doine family
      O Duinn family
  RT Dunn family
O Duinn family
  USE O Doyne family
O-er-do-su Basin (China)
  USE Ordos Desert (China)

O-er-do-su Desert (China)
USE Ordos Desert (China)
O-erh-to-ssu Basin (China)
USE Ordos Desert (China)
O-erh-to-ssu Desert (China)
USE Ordos Desert (China)
O family (Not Subd Geog)
O-kee-pa (Religious ceremony)
⌐E99.M2 (Mandan Indians)¬
BT Indians of North America—Dances
Mandan Indians—Dances
Mandan Indians—Rites and
ceremonies
O.-L.-V. Basiliek van Tongeren Mariaretabel
(Sculpture)
USE Mariaretabel van Tongeren (Sculpture)
O-luan-pi Park (Taiwan)
BT Parks—Taiwan
O-mei Mountain (China)
UF O-mei Shan (China)
Omei Shan (China)
Omi Shan (China)
BT Mountains—China
O-mei Shan (China)
USE O-mei Mountain (China)
O stars
⌐QB843.O12¬
BT Early stars
— Spectra
O-wen-k'o (Tribe)
UF Owenke (Tribe)
Owenk'o (Tribe)
BT Ethnology—China
Oa language
USE Pamoa language
Oadell family
USE O'Dell family
Oahu (Hawaii)
BT Hawaii
Islands—Hawaii
Oaica Indians
USE Waica Indians
Oajana Indians
USE Oyana Indians
Oak (May Subd Geog)
⌐QK495.F14 (Botany)¬
⌐SB413.O34 (Ornamental plants)¬
⌐SD397.O12 (Forestry)¬
UF Quercus
NT Acorns
Aleppo oak
Bartram oak
Black oak
Bur oak
California black oak
Coast live oak
Cork-tree
Durmast oak
English oak
European Turkey oak
Furniture, Oak
Holm oak
Live oak
Pin oak
Pyrenean oak
Quercus prinus
Red oak
Valonia oak
White oak
— Diseases and pests (May Subd Geog)
⌐SB608.O115¬
SA names of specific diseases and
pests, e.g. Oak wilt
Oak family
USE Oakes family
Oak Grove Cemetery (Bowling Green, Ohio)
BT Cemeteries—Ohio
Oak Grove Cemetery (Howell, Mich.)
USE Lakeview Cemetery (Howell, Mich.)

Oak Grove Cemetery (Oakley, Mich.)
(Not Subd Geog)
BT Cemeteries—Michigan
Oak Hill Cemetery (Clear Lake, Ill.)
BT Cemeteries—Illinois
Oak Hill Cemetery (Mich.)
BT Cemeteries—Michigan
Oak Hill Cemetery (Palmyra, Ill.)
BT Cemeteries—Illinois
Oak leaf caterpillar, Variable
USE Variable oak leaf caterpillar
Oak Park (Calif.)
BT Parks—California
Oak Ridge Cemetery (Somonauk, Ill.)
UF Union Cemetery (Somonauk, Ill.)
BT Cemeteries—Illinois
Oak silkworm, Chinese
USE Chinese oak silkworm
Oak silkworm moth, Japanese
USE Yamamai
Oak wilt (May Subd Geog)
⌐SB608.O115¬
BT Wilt diseases
RT Ceratocystis fagacearum
Oak wilt fungus
USE Ceratocystis fagacearum
Oakes family (Not Subd Geog)
UF Oak family
Oaks family
Okes family
Oakham Canal (England)
BT Canals—England
Oakland (Pittsburgh, Pa.) (Not Subd Geog)
UF Pittsburgh (Pa.). Oakland
Oakland automobile
⌐TL215¬
BT Automobiles
Oakland Bay Bridge (Oakland and San
Francisco, Calif.)
USE San Francisco-Oakland Bay Bridge
(Oakland and San Francisco, Calif.)
Oakland Cemetery (De Kalb, Ill.)
USE Oakwood Cemetery (De Kalb, Ill.)
Oakland Paramount Theatre (Oakland, Calif.)
USE Paramount Theatre (Oakland, Calif.)
Oakleaf poison ivy
USE Poison oak
Oakley family (Not Subd Geog)
UF Oakly family
Okeley family
Okely family
Oakly family
USE Oakley family
Oaks family
USE Oakes family
Oakum
⌐TS1747.O3 (Manufacture)¬
Oakville Aquifer (Tex.)
BT Aquifers—Texas
Oakville Creek (Ont.)
BT Rivers—Ontario
Oakwood Cemetery (De Kalb, Ill.)
UF Oakland Cemetery (De Kalb, Ill.)
BT Cemeteries—Illinois
Oakwood Cemetery (Plymouth, Iowa)
BT Cemeteries—Iowa
Oakwood Cemetery (Tacoma, Wash.)
UF Prairie Cemetery (Tacoma, Wash.)
BT Cemeteries—Washington (State)
Oaldham family
USE Oldham family
Oaldhum family
USE Oldham family
Oalds family
USE Olds family
OAO
USE Orbiting astronomical observatories
Oar family
USE Orr family
Oarsmen
USE Rowers

Oaş Mountains (Romania)
UF Munţii Oaşului (Romania)
Munţii Ouaş (Romania)
Munţii Ouaşului (Romania)
Ouaşul (Romania)
BT Mountains—Romania
Oases (May Subd Geog)
⌐GB611-618¬
BT Deserts
— Algeria
NT Mzab (Algeria)
— Egypt
NT Bir Kiseiba (Egypt)
Dakhla Oasis (Egypt)
— Niger
NT Kaouar (Niger)
— Saudi Arabia
NT Hasa Oasis (Saudi Arabia)
OASIS (Computer operating system)
USE THEOS (Computer operating system)
Oat, Common
USE Oats
Oat aphis
⌐SB608.O2¬
Oat blue dwarf disease (May Subd Geog)
⌐SB608.02¬
BT Oats—Diseases and pests
Oat mosaic
BT Oats—Diseases and pests
Oatafu (Tokelau Islands)
USE Atafu Atoll (Tokelau Islands)
Oath of allegiance, 1601
UF Disabilities, Political (Great Britain)
Oath of allegiance, 1606
UF Allegiance, Oath of, 1606
Oath of obedience, 1606
Obedience, Oath of, 1606
Political disabilities (Great Britain)
BT Catholic Church—Great Britain
Catholics—Great Britain
Church and state—England
Oath of obedience, 1606
USE Oath of allegiance, 1606
Oath of the tennis court (Painting)
USE David, Jacques Louis, 1748-1825.
Oath of the tennis court
Oaths (May Subd Geog)
⌐GN493 (Anthropology)¬
⌐GT3080 (Manners and customs)¬
Here are entered works on judicial or official
oaths. Works on profane language are entered under
Swearing. Works on blasphemy in the legal and theo-
logical sense of maliciously reviling God or religion,
are entered under Blasphemy.
BT Manners and customs
RT Vows
NT Affidavits
Ephebic oath
Loyalty oaths
Perjury
Poor debtor's oath
— Biblical teaching
NT Ten commandments—False witness
— Jews
Here are entered works on the special oath
which Jews were required to take in courts of law
before their emancipation. Works on oaths in
Jewish religious courts are entered under Oaths
(Jewish law)
BT Jews—Legal status, laws, etc.
— Koranic teaching
USE Oaths in the Koran
Oaths (Canon law)
⌐BX1939.O2¬
Oaths (Greek law)
Oaths (Islamic law) (May Subd Geog)
Oaths (Jewish law)
Here are entered works on oaths in Jewish reli-
gious courts. Works on the special oath which Jews
were required to take in courts of law before their
emancipation are entered under Oaths—Jews.

Oaths (Roman law)
Oaths in rabbinical literature
  BT Rabbinical literature
Oaths in the Bible
  UF Bible—Oaths
Oaths in the Koran
  UF Koran—Oaths
    Oaths—Koranic teaching
Oatman family (Not Subd Geog)
  UF Othman family
    Otman family
    Outman family
Oatmeal
  ⌐TS2159.O (Milling)⌐
  ⌐TX393 (Food-supply)⌐
  BT Meal
    Oats
Oats (May Subd Geog)
  ⌐QK495.G74 (Botany)⌐
  ⌐SB191.O2 (Culture)⌐
  UF Avena
    Avena sativa
    Common oat
    Oat, Common
  BT Flour
    Grain
    Grasses
  NT Cookery (Granola)
    Oatmeal
    Wild oat
  — Disease and pest resistance
    (May Subd Geog)
  — Diseases and pests (May Subd Geog)
    NT Oat blue dwarf disease
      Oat mosaic
  — Genetics
  — Varieties
Oats as feed
Oats as food
  ⌐TX558.O3⌐
  BT Food
Oaxaca Valley (Mexico)
  UF Valle de Oaxaca (Mexico)
  BT Valleys—Mexico
Oaza Bungera (Antarctic regions)
  USE Bunger Hills (Antarctic regions)
Ob' River (R.S.F.S.R.)
  BT Rivers—Russian S.F.S.R.
Ob-Ugrian languages
  USE Ob-Ugric languages
Ob-Ugrian poetry (May Subd Geog)
Ob-Ugrian textile fabrics
  USE Textile fabrics, Ob-Ugrian
Ob-Ugric languages
  ⌐PH1251-1254⌐
  UF Ob-Ugrian languages
  BT Finno-Ugric languages
  NT Khanty language
    Mansi language
Ōba family (Not Subd Geog)
Ōba Kita Iseki (Moriguchi-shi, Japan)
  USE Ōba Kita Site (Moriguchi-shi, Japan)
Ōba Kita Site (Moriguchi-shi, Japan)
  (Not Subd Geog)
  UF Ōba Kita Iseki (Moriguchi-shi, Japan)
  BT Japan—Antiquities
Ōbaku (Sect) (May Subd Geog)
  ⌐BQ9310-9319⌐
  BT Buddhist sects
    Zen Buddhism
Ōbaku ink painting
  USE Ink painting, Ōbaku
Obamayama Iseki (Nagato-shi, Japan)
  USE Obamayama Site (Nagato-shi, Japan)
Obamayama Site (Nagato-shi, Japan)
  (Not Subd Geog)
  UF Obamayama Iseki (Nagato-shi, Japan)
  BT Japan—Antiquities
Obamba (African people)
  USE Mbete (African people)

Obamba language
  USE Mbete language
Oban Line Railroad
  BT Railroads—Great Britain
O'Bar family
  USE O'Barr family
O'Barr family (Not Subd Geog)
  UF O'Bar family
Obata family (Not Subd Geog)
Obdeijn family
  USE Op 't Eijnde family
Obduracy
  USE Hardness of heart
Obeah (Cult) (May Subd Geog)
  ⌐BL2532.O23⌐
  UF Roots (Cult)
  BT Cults
    Voodooism
    Witchcraft
Obeche
  UF Arere
    Ayous
Obed River (Tenn.)
  BT Rivers—Tennessee
  NT Obed Wild and Scenic River (Tenn.)
Obed Wild and Scenic River (Tenn.)
  BT National parks and reserves—United
    States
    Obed River (Tenn.)
    Wild and scenic rivers—Tennessee
Obedience
  BT Conduct of life
  — Religious aspects
  — — Biblical teaching
    NT Ten commandments—Parents
  — — Buddhism, ⌐Christianity, etc.⌐
  — — Christianity
    BT Evangelical counsels
Obedience, Oath of, 1606
  USE Oath of allegiance, 1606
Obedience, Vow of
  UF Vow of obedience
  BT Vows
Obedience (Canon law)
  BT Catholic Church—Discipline
Obedience trials for dogs
  USE Dogs—Obedience trials
Obee family (Not Subd Geog)
Obel family (Not Subd Geog)
Obelia (May Subd Geog)
  ⌐QL377.H9⌐
  BT Campanulariidae
  NT Obelia dichotoma
Obelia dichotoma (May Subd Geog)
  ⌐QL377.H9⌐
  BT Obelia
Obelisks (May Subd Geog)
  ⌐DT62.O2⌐
  BT Archaeology
    Architecture
    Monuments
    Pyramids
Oberg family (Not Subd Geog)
Oberharz Mountains (Germany)
  (Not Subd Geog)
  UF Upper Harz Mountains (Germany)
  BT Harz Mountains (Germany)
    Mountains—Germany (East)
    Mountains—Germany (West)
Oberholtz family
  USE Oberholtzer family

Oberholtzer family (Not Subd Geog)
  UF Oberholtz family
    Oberholz family
    Oberholzer family
    Overholser family
    Overholt family
    Overholts family
    Overholtz family
    Overholtzer family
    Overholzer family
    Overhults family
Oberholz family
  USE Oberholtzer family
Oberholzer family
  USE Oberholtzer family
Oberinntal cattle
  USE Grey Tirolean cattle
Oberkrain (Slovenia)
  USE Gorenjsko (Slovenia)
Oberland bernois (Switzerland)
  USE Bernese Alps (Switzerland)
Oberländische Kanal (Poland)
  USE Elbląg Canal (Poland)
Oberlausitz (Germany)
  USE Lusatia, Upper (Germany)
Oberlin (Ohio) (Not Subd Geog)
  — History (Not Subd Geog)
    NT Oberlin-Wellington Rescue, 1858
Oberlin-Wellington Rescue, 1858
  ⌐E450⌐
  BT Fugitive slaves—Ohio—History
    Oberlin (Ohio)—History
    Wellington (Ohio)—History
Obermaier family
  USE Obermayer family
Obermair family
  USE Obermayer family
Oberman family (Not Subd Geog)
  UF Obermann family
Obermann family
  USE Oberman family
Obermayer family (Not Subd Geog)
  UF Obermaier family
    Obermair family
    Obermeier family
    Obermeyer family
    Obermier family
    Overmayer family
    Overmeyer family
    Overmire family
    Overmyer family
Obermeier family
  USE Obermayer family
Obermeyer family
  USE Obermayer family
Obermier family
  USE Obermayer family
Oberonia
  ⌐QK495.O64⌐
  BT Orchids
Oberrheinische Eisenbahn
  BT Railroads—Germany (West)
Oberschlesien (Poland and Czechoslovakia)
  USE Silesia, Upper (Poland and
    Czechoslovakia)
Oberschwaben (Germany)
Obersee (Switzerland)
  USE Zurich, Lake of (Switzerland)
Obertin, Battle of, 1531
  BT Poland—History—Sigismund I, 1506-
    1548
Obese-hyperglycemic syndrome
  UF Hyperglycemic-obese syndrome
  BT Endocrine glands—Diseases
    Hyperglycemia
    Obesity
Obesity (May Subd Geog)
  ⌐RC628-RC628.5⌐

Obesity *(Continued)*
　UF　Adiposity
　　　Corpulence
　　　Fatness
　　　Overweight
　BT　Body weight
　　　Metabolism—Disorders
　　　Nutrition disorders
　NT　Obese-hyperglycemic syndrome
　　　Obesity in children
　　　Pickwickian syndrome
　　　Prader-Willi syndrome
　— Control
　　USE　Reducing
　— Diet therapy
　　USE　Reducing diets
　— **Psychological aspects**
　　　BT　Gluttony
　— **Surgery**
　　　UF　Bariatric surgery
　　　　　Surgery, Bariatric
Obesity in children *(May Subd Geog)*
　　[RJ399.C6]
　BT　Metabolic disorders in children
　　　Nutrition disorders in children
　　　Obesity
Obesity reversing factor, Pituitary
　USE　Lipotropin
Obi
　　[GT1560]
　BT　Kimonos
　　　Sashes (Costume)
Obion River (Tenn.)
　BT　Rivers—Tennessee
Obituaries *(May Subd Geog)*
　　Here are entered short biographical sketches, especially in newspapers, published upon a person's death. Works on announcements of death either published in the press or mailed individually are entered under Death notices. Works on registers of deaths in ecclesiastical or other organizations or registers of anniversary days when services are performed for the dead are entered under Necrologies.
　UF　Newspapers—Sections, columns, etc.—
　　　　Obituaries
　BT　Biography
　　　Dead
　RT　Death notices
　— **Indexes**
　　　UF　Deaths, Registers of
　　　　　Registers of deaths
　　　BT　Registers of births, etc.
Object (Aesthetics)
　　[BH301.O24]
　UF　Aesthetic object
　BT　Aesthetics
　NT　Art objects
Object (Philosophy)
　BT　Philosophy
　NT　Nonexistent objects (Philosophy)
Object constancy (Psychoanalysis)
　　[RC489.O24 (Psychiatry)]
　UF　Constancy, Object (Psychoanalysis)
　BT　Psychoanalysis
Object relations (Psychoanalysis)
　　(May Subd Geog)
　　[BF175.5.O24]
　　Here are entered works on the psychoanalytic description of emotional attachments formed between one person and another, as opposed to interest in and love for oneself.
　UF　Object relations theory
　　　　(Psychoanalysis)
　BT　Psychoanalysis
　RT　Interpersonal relations
Object relations theory (Psychoanalysis)
　USE　Object relations (Psychoanalysis)
Object-teaching
　　[LB1519-LB1520 (Primary education)]
　BT　Education of children
　　　Kindergarten
　　　Teaching

　NT　Project method in teaching
　　　Visual education
Objections (Evidence) *(May Subd Geog)*
　BT　Evidence (Law)
　　　Examination of witnesses
　NT　Confidential communications
　　　Evidence, Hearsay
Objective-analytic test
　　[BF698.8.O24]
　BT　Personality tests
Objective tests *(May Subd Geog)*
　　[LB3060.32.O35]
　BT　Achievement tests
　　　Examinations
　NT　Domain-referenced tests
Objectivity
　BT　Knowledge, Theory of
　　　Reality
　NT　Journalism—Objectivity
　　　Mass media—Objectivity
　　　Newspapers—Objectivity
Objectors, Conscientious
　USE　Conscientious objectors
Objects, Art
　USE　Art objects
Objects, Ceremonial
　USE　Ceremonial objects
Objects, Found (Art)
　USE　Found objects (Art)
Objects, Liturgical
　USE　Liturgical objects
Objects, Miniature
　USE　Miniature objects
Objects, Nonexistent (Philosophy)
　USE　Nonexistent objects (Philosophy)
Objects, Religious
　USE　Religious articles
Objects, Transitional (Psychology)
　USE　Transitional objects (Psychology)
Objets d'art
　USE　Art objects
Oblation (Lord's Supper)
　USE　Lord's Supper—Sacrifice
Obligado, Battle of, 1845
　　[F2846]
　BT　Argentina—History—1817-1860
Obligation
　USE　Duty
　　　Responsibility
Obligation, Political
　USE　Political obligation
Obligations, Natural
　USE　Natural obligations
Obligations (Greek law)
Obligations (Islamic law)
Obligations (Jewish law)
Obligations (Law) *(May Subd Geog)*
　UF　Personal obligations
　BT　Civil law
　RT　Promise (Law)
　NT　Accessory obligations
　　　Contracts
　　　Correality and solidarity
　　　Damages
　　　Debtor and creditor
　　　Jus ad rem
　　　Liability (Law)
　　　Natural obligations
　　　Quasi contracts
　　　Real obligations
　　　Torts
　— **Cases**
　— — Digests
　　　　USE　Obligations (Law)—Digests
　— Conflict of laws
　　　USE　Conflict of laws—Obligations
　— **Digests**
　　　　UF　Obligations (Law)—Cases—Digests
Obligations (Roman-Dutch law)
Obligations (Roman law)
　NT　Retentio (Roman law)

Oblík (Czechoslovakia)
　UF　Hoblik (Czechoslovakia)
　BT　České středohoří (Czechoslovakia)
　　　Mountains—Czechoslovakia
Oblique arches
　USE　Arches, Oblique
Oblique coordinates
　USE　Coordinates, Oblique
**Oblique cylindrical orthomorphic projection
　(Cartography)**
　USE　Oblique Mercator projection
　　　　(Cartography)
Oblique Mercator projection (Cartography)
　UF　Oblique cylindrical orthomorphic
　　　　projection (Cartography)
　BT　Map-projection
Oblique projection
　　[T365]
　UF　Projection, Oblique
　BT　Projection
Oblitacythereis
　　[QE817.O8]
　BT　Trachyleberididae, Fossil
Obliterative arteriosclerosis
　USE　Arteriosclerosis obliterans
Obo language
　USE　Manuvu language
OBO ships
　USE　Ore-bulk-oil ships
Oboe
　　[ML940-ML943 (History and
　　　construction)]
　BT　Woodwind instruments
　RT　English horn
　NT　Crumhorn
　　　Heckelphone
　　　Hichiriki
　　　Pommer
　　　Shawm
　　　Shehnai
　　　So na
　— **Orchestra studies**
　　　[MT366]
　　　BT　Oboe—Studies and exercises
　— **Reeds**
　— **Studies and exercises**
　　　[MT365]
　　　NT　Oboe—Orchestra studies
Oboe, Pastoral
　USE　Pipe (Musical instrument)
Oboe and bassoon music
　USE　Bassoon and oboe music
Oboe and clarinet music
　USE　Clarinet and oboe music
Oboe and claves music *(May Subd Geog)*
　　[M298]
　UF　Claves and oboe music
Oboe and continuo music
　UF　Continuo and oboe music
　NT　Marches (Oboe and continuo)
　　　Minuets (Oboe and continuo)
　　　Sonatas (Oboe and continuo)
　　　Suites (Oboe and continuo)
　　　Variations (Oboe and continuo)
Oboe and double-bass music
　　[M290-291]
　UF　Double-bass and oboe music
Oboe and English horn music
　USE　English horn and oboe music
Oboe and flute music
　USE　Flute and oboe music
Oboe and guitar music
　　[M296-7]
　UF　Guitar and oboe music
　NT　Sonatas (Oboe and guitar)
　　　Variations (Oboe and guitar)
Oboe and harp music
　　[M296-7]
　UF　Harp and oboe music
　NT　Concertos (Oboe and harp)

Concertos (Oboe and harp with string
orchestra)
Oboe and harp with orchestra
Oboe and harp with string orchestra
Sonatas (Oboe and harp)
Oboe and harp with chamber orchestra
[*M1040-1041*]
RT Concertos (Oboe and harp with
chamber orchestra)
Oboe and harp with orchestra
[*M1040-1041*]
BT Oboe and harp music
RT Concertos (Oboe and harp)
Oboe and harp with string orchestra
[*M1105-6*]
BT Oboe and harp music
RT Concertos (Oboe and harp with string
orchestra)
— **Scores and parts**
[*M1105*]
Oboe and harpsichord music
[*M245-6*]
UF Harpsichord and oboe music
NT Concertos (Oboe and harpsichord with
string orchestra)
Oboe and harpsichord with string
orchestra
Sonatas (Oboe and harpsichord)
Suites (Oboe and harpsichord)
Variations (Oboe and harpsichord)
Oboe and harpsichord with string orchestra
[*M1105-6*]
BT Oboe and harpsichord music
RT Concertos (Oboe and harpsichord with
string orchestra)
Oboe and horn music
USE Horn and oboe music
Oboe and keyboard instrument music
[*M245-M246*]
UF Keyboard instrument and oboe music
Oboe and organ music
[*M182-4*]
UF Organ and oboe music
NT Chorale preludes (Oboe and organ)
Sonatas (Oboe and organ)
Suites (Oboe and organ)
Variations (Oboe and organ)
Oboe and percussion music
[*M298*]
UF Percussion and oboe music
Oboe and percussion with string orchestra
[*M1140-1141*]
RT Concertos (Oboe and percussion with
string orchestra)
Oboe and piano music
[*M245-6*]
UF Piano and oboe music
NT Rondos (Oboe and piano)
Sonatas (Oboe and piano)
Suites (Oboe and piano)
Variations (Oboe and piano)
Oboe and piano music, Arranged
[*M247*]
NT Concertos (Oboe)—Solo with piano
Concertos (Oboe), Arranged—Solo
with piano
Concertos (Oboe with chamber
orchestra)—Solo with piano
Concertos (Oboe with string orchestra)
—Solo with piano
Oboe with band—Solo with piano
Oboe with chamber orchestra—Solo
with piano
Oboe with orchestra—Solo with piano
Oboe with string orchestra—Solo with
piano
Suites (Oboe with chamber orchestra)
—Solo with piano
Suites (Oboe with string orchestra)—
Solo with piano

Variations (Oboe with band)—Solo
with piano
Oboe and piano with string ensemble
NT Concertos (Oboe and piano with string
ensemble)
Oboe and piccolo music
[*M288-289*]
UF Piccolo and oboe music
Oboe and recorder music
[*M288-9*]
UF Recorder and oboe music
NT Concertos (Oboe and recorder with
string orchestra)
Oboe and recorder with string
orchestra
Oboe and recorder with string orchestra
[*M1105-6*]
BT Oboe and recorder music
RT Concertos (Oboe and recorder with
string orchestra)
Oboe and theorbo music
[*M296-297*]
UF Theorbo and oboe music
NT Suites (Oboe and theorbo)
Oboe and trombone music
[*M288-289*]
UF Trombone and oboe music
Oboe and trumpet music
[*M288-9*]
UF Trumpet and oboe music
NT Concertos (Oboe and trumpet with
string orchestra)
Oboe and trumpet with string
orchestra
Oboe and trumpet with string orchestra
[*M1105-6*]
BT Oboe and trumpet music
RT Concertos (Oboe and trumpet with
string orchestra)
Oboe and viola music
[*M290-291*]
UF Viola and oboe music
NT Concertos (Oboe and viola with string
orchestra)
Oboe and viola with string orchestra
Oboe and viola with string orchestra
[*M1105-6*]
BT Oboe and viola music
RT Concertos (Oboe and viola with string
orchestra)
Oboe and violin music
[*M290-291*]
UF Violin and oboe music
NT Concertos (Oboe and violin)
Concertos (Oboe and violin with
chamber orchestra)
Concertos (Oboe and violin with string
orchestra)
Oboe and violin with chamber
orchestra
Oboe and violin with orchestra
Oboe and violin with string orchestra
Oboe and violin with chamber orchestra
[*M1040-1041*]
BT Chamber-orchestra music
Oboe and violin music
RT Concertos (Oboe and violin with
chamber orchestra)
Oboe and violin with orchestra
[*M1040-1041*]
BT Oboe and violin music
Orchestral music
RT Concertos (Oboe and violin)
Oboe and violin with string orchestra
[*M1105-6*]
BT Oboe and violin music
RT Concertos (Oboe and violin with string
orchestra)
Oboe and violoncello music
[*M290-291*]

NT Oboe and violoncello with string
orchestra
Suites (Oboe and violoncello)
Variations (Oboe and violoncello)
Oboe and violoncello with orchestra
[*M1040-1041*]
RT Concertos (Oboe and violoncello)
Oboe and violoncello with string orchestra
[*M1140-1141*]
BT Oboe and violoncello music
NT Suites (Oboe and violoncello with
string orchestra)
Oboe d'amore and continuo music
UF Continuo and oboe d'amore music
NT Suites (Oboe d'amore and continuo)
Oboe d'amore and guitar music
[*M296-297*]
UF Guitar and oboe d'amore music
Oboe d'amore and harpsichord music
[*M270.O26*]
[*M271.O26*]
UF Harpsichord and oboe d'amore music
Oboe d'amore and piano music
[*M270.O26*]
[*M271.O26*]
UF Piano and oboe d'amore music
Oboe d'amore and piano music, Arranged
[*M270.O26*]
[*M271.O26*]
NT Concertos (Oboe d'amore)—Solo with
piano
Oboe d'amore music
[*M65-69*]
SA Concertos, Minuets, Sonatas, Suites,
*and similar headings with
specification of instruments;* Trios
[*Quartets, etc.*], Wind trios
[*quartets, etc.*], *and* Woodwind
trios [*quartets, etc.*] *followed by
specifications which include the
oboe d'amore; also* Wind ensembles,
Woodwind ensembles, *and headings
that begin with the words* Oboe
d'amore *or* Oboi d'amore
NT Trios (Flute, oboe d'amore, percussion)
Trios (Harpsichord, flute, oboe
d'amore)
Oboe d'amore with orchestra
[*M1034.O26*]
[*M1035.O26*]
RT Concertos (Oboe d'amore)
Oboe d'amore with string orchestra
[*M1105-6*]
RT Concertos (Oboe d'amore with string
orchestra)
— **Scores**
[*M1105*]
Oboe music
[*M65-69*]
SA Concertos, Minuets, Sonatas, Suites,
*and similar headings with
specification of instruments;* Trios
[*Quartets, etc.*], Wind trios
[*quartets, etc.*], *and* Woodwind
trios [*quartets, etc.*] *followed by
specifications which include the
oboe; also* Wind ensembles,
Woodwind ensembles, *and headings
that begin with the words* oboe *or*
oboes
NT Recorded accompaniments (Oboe)
Sonatas (Oboe)
Suites (Oboe)
Oboe music (Oboes (2))
[*M288-9*]
NT Concertos (Oboes (2) with string
orchestra)
Oboes (2) with string orchestra
Sonatas (Oboes (2))
Suites (Oboes (2))

Oboe music (Oboes (3))
  USE Woodwind trios (Oboes (3))
Oboe music (Oboes (4))
  USE Woodwind quartets (Oboes (4))
Oboe players *(May Subd Geog)*
  UF Oboists
  BT Musicians
Oboe, violin, violoncello with orchestra
  [M1040-1041]
  BT Trios (Oboe, violin, violoncello)
  RT Concertos (Oboe, violin, violoncello)
Oboe, violin, violoncello with string orchestra
  [M1105-6]
  BT Trios (Oboe, violin, violoncello)
  RT Concertos (Oboe, violin, violoncello
      with string orchestra)
Oboe with band
  [M1205-6]
  BT Band music
  RT Concertos (Oboe with band)
  NT Variations (Oboe with band)
  — Solo with piano
      [M1206]
      BT Oboe and piano music, Arranged
Oboe with chamber orchestra
  [M1022-3]
  BT Chamber-orchestra music
  RT Concertos (Oboe with chamber
      orchestra)
  NT Suites (Oboe with chamber orchestra)
      Variations (Oboe with chamber
      orchestra)
  — Solo with piano
      [M1023]
      BT Oboe and piano music, Arranged
Oboe with instrumental ensemble
  RT Concertos (Oboe with instrumental
      ensemble)
Oboe with orchestra
  [M1022-3]
  RT Concertos (Oboe)
  NT Variations (Oboe with orchestra)
  — Solo with piano
      [M1023]
      BT Oboe and piano music, Arranged
Oboe with orchestra, Arranged
  [M1022-3]
Oboe with string ensemble
  [M960-962]
  RT Concertos (Oboe with string ensemble)
Oboe with string orchestra
  [M1105-6]
  RT Concertos (Oboe with string orchestra)
  NT Canons, fugues, etc. (Oboe with string
      orchestra)
      Passacaglias (Oboe with string
      orchestra)
      Suites (Oboe with string orchestra)
      Variations (Oboe with string orchestra)
  — Solo with piano
      [M1106]
      BT Oboe and piano music, Arranged
Oboe with string orchestra, Arranged
  [M1105-6]
  — Scores and parts
      [M1105-6]
Oboes (2), trumpet with string orchestra
  [M1140-1141]
  BT Wind trios (Oboes (2), trumpet)
  RT Concertos (Oboes (2), trumpet with
      string orchestra)
Oboes (2) with orchestra
  [M1022-1023]
  RT Concertos (Oboes (2))
Oboes (2) with string orchestra
  [M1105-6]
  BT Oboe music (Oboes (2))
  RT Concertos (Oboes (2) with string
      orchestra)
Oboes (3) with string orchestra
  [M1122-1123]

BT Woodwind trios (Oboes (3))
RT Concertos (Oboes (3) with string
    orchestra)
NT Suites (Oboes (3) with string
    orchestra)
Oboes (4) with string orchestra
  [M1122-3]
  BT Woodwind quartets (Oboes (4))
  RT Concertos (Oboes (4) with string
      orchestra)
Oboi d'amore (2) with string orchestra
  [M1134.O26]
  [M1135.O26]
  RT Concertos (Oboi d'amore (2) with
      string orchestra)
Oboists
  USE Oboe players
O'Brian family
  USE O'Brien family
O'Brien family *(Not Subd Geog)*
  UF O'Brian family
      O'Brion family
      O'Bryan family
      O'Bryant family
      O'Bryen family
      O'Bryon family
Obrigheim Nuclear Power Plant (Germany)
  BT Nuclear power plants—Germany
      (West)
O'Brion family
  USE O'Brien family
O'Bryan family
  USE O'Brien family
O'Bryant family
  USE O'Brien family
O'Bryen family
  USE O'Brien family
O'Bryon family
  USE O'Brien family
Obscene literature
  USE Literature, Immoral
Obscene words
  USE Words, Obscene
Obscenity (Law) *(May Subd Geog)*
  UF Erotic art—Law and legislation
      Literature, Immoral—Law and
      legislation
  BT Crimes without victims
      Criminal law
      Erotic literature
      Erotica
      Law and literature
      Pornography
      Press law
      Publicity (Law)
  NT Postal service—Law and legislation
      Trials (Obscenity)
Obsci
  USE Oscans
OBSCIS (Information retrieval system)
  [Z699.5.C6]
  UF Offender-Based State Corrections
      Information System
  BT Information storage and retrieval
      systems—Corrections
Obsequies
  USE Funeral rites and ceremonies
Observability (Control theory)
  USE Observers (Control theory)
Observation (Educational method)
  UF Classroom observation
  BT Teachers—Training of
  NT Interaction analysis in education
Observation (Psychology)
  BT Knowledge, Theory of
      Psychology
  NT Critical incident technique
      Introspection
      Participant observation

Observation (Scientific method)
  USE *subdivision* Observations *under*
      scientific headings for works
      consisting of numerical data
      obtained by the observation of
      natural phenomena or for
      discussions on the processing and
      use of these data, e.g. Astronomy—
      Observations
Observations, Astronomical
  USE Astronomy—Observations
Observations, Geodetic
  USE Geodesy—Observations
Observations, Geophysical
  USE Geophysics—Observations
Observations, Magnetic
  USE Magnetism, Terrestrial—Observations
Observations, Meteorological
  USE Meteorology—Observations
Observations, Missing (Statistics)
  USE Missing observations (Statistics)
Observations, Oceanographic
  USE Oceanography—Observations
Observatories
  [QB81-QB84 (Astronomical)]
  [QC818 (Magnetic)]
  [QC875 (Meteorological)]
  [QE540 (Seismological)]
  NT Geophysical observatories
      Magnetism, Terrestrial—Observatories
      Scientific satellites
      Seismology—Observatories
Observatories, Astronomical
  USE Astronomical observatories
Observatories, Geophysical
  USE Geophysical observatories
Observatories, Hydrometeorological
  USE Hydrometeorological stations
Observatories, Meteorological
  USE Meteorological stations
Observatory domes
  [QB84]
  UF Domes, Observatory
Observer Singlehanded Transatlantic Sailing
Race
  USE Observer Transatlantic Singlehanded
      Sailing Race
**Observer Transatlantic Singlehanded Sailing
Race**
  UF Observer Singlehanded Transatlantic
      Sailing Race
      Plymouth-Newport Singlehanded
      Sailing Race
      Singlehanded Transatlantic Sailing
      Race
      Transatlantic Singlehanded Sailing
      Race
  BT Yacht racing
Observers (Control theory)
  [QA402.3]
  UF Observability (Control theory)
      State estimator (Control theory)
      State observer (Control theory)
  BT Control theory
Observers' manuals
  USE *subdivision* Observers' manuals *under*
      scientific headings for instruction
      books on making observations of
      natural phenomena
Obsession (Psychology)
  USE Obsessive-compulsive neurosis
Obsessive-compulsive neurosis
  [RC533]
  UF Compulsive neurosis
      Fixed ideas
      Obsession (Psychology)
  BT Neuroses
  RT Compulsive behavior
Obsidian *(May Subd Geog)*
  BT Volcanic ash, tuff, etc.

Obsidian dating
 USE Hydration rind dating
Obsidian hydration dating
 USE Hydration rind dating
Obsidional coins *(May Subd Geog)*
 ₍CJ1539₎
 UF Siege coins
 BT Coins
Obsolescence, Product
 USE Product obsolescence
Obsolescence (Accounting)
 USE Depreciation
Obsolescence of books, periodicals, etc.
 (May Subd Geog)
 UF Obsolete books, periodicals, etc.
  Obsolete information in books,
   periodicals, etc.
  Out-of-date books, periodicals, etc.
 BT Books
  Collection development (Libraries)
  Periodicals
Obsolete books, periodicals, etc.
 USE Obsolescence of books, periodicals,
  etc.
Obsolete information in books, periodicals, etc.
 USE Obsolescence of books, periodicals,
  etc.
Obsolete securities
 USE Securities, Obsolete
Obstacle courses (Horse sports)
 USE Courses (Horse sports)
Obstacle racing
 BT Running races
 NT Hurdle-racing
Obstacles (Military science)
 ₍UG375₎
 UF Barriers (Military science)
  Obstruction (Military science)
 BT Military art and science
  Military field engineering
 NT Demolition, Military
  Intrenchments
  Mines, Military
  Roadblocks (Military science)
  Wire obstacles
Obstetric anesthesia
 USE Anesthesia in obstetrics
Obstetric emergencies
 USE Obstetrical emergencies
Obstetric endocrinology
 USE Obstetrical endocrinology
Obstetric nursing
 USE Obstetrical nursing
Obstetric palsy
 USE Obstetrical paralysis
Obstetric paralysis
 USE Obstetrical paralysis
Obstetrical diagnosis
 USE Obstetrics—Diagnosis
Obstetrical emergencies *(May Subd Geog)*
 ₍RG571-591₎
 UF Emergencies, Obstetrical
  Emergency obstetrics
  Obstetric emergencies
 BT Medical emergencies
  Obstetrics
 NT Labor, Complicated
  Pregnancy, Complications of
Obstetrical endocrinology
 ₍RG558.5₎
 UF Endocrine obstetrics
  Obstetric endocrinology
 BT Endocrine gynecology
  Endocrinology
  Human reproduction—Endocrine
   aspects
  Obstetrics
 NT Placental hormones
Obstetrical extraction
 ₍RG741₎

UF Extraction, Obstetrical
 Vacuum extraction, Obstetrical
BT Delivery (Obstetrics)
 Labor, Complicated
Obstetrical nursing
 ₍RG951₎
 UF Maternity nursing
  Obstetric nursing
 BT Nursing
  Obstetrics
 NT Cesarean section—Nursing
— **Administration**
Obstetrical paralysis
 UF Obstetric palsy
  Obstetric paralysis
  Paralysis, Obstetrical
 BT Paralysis
Obstetrical pharmacology
 ₍RG528₎
 BT Obstetrics
  Pharmacology
 NT Abortifacients
  Alcoholism in pregnancy
  Anesthesia in obstetrics
  Drug abuse in pregnancy
  Fetus—Effect of drugs on
  Human embryo—Effect of drugs on
  Infants (Newborn)—Effect of drugs on
Obstetrical practice
 USE Obstetrics—Practice
Obstetrical roentgenology
 USE Radiography in obstetrics
Obstetrical toad
 USE Alytes obstetricans
Obstetricians *(May Subd Geog)*
 UF Birth attendants
— **Attitudes**
  BT Attitude (Psychology)
— **Legal status, laws, etc.**
  NT Obstetricians—Malpractice
— **Malpractice** *(May Subd Geog)*
  UF Tort liability of obstetricians
  BT Malpractice
   Obstetricians—Legal status, laws,
    etc.
   Obstetrics—Law and legislation
Obstetrics *(May Subd Geog)*
 ₍RG₎
 UF Midwifery
 BT Fetus
  Generative organs, Female
 RT Pregnancy
 NT Anesthesia in obstetrics
  Birth, Multiple
  Childbirth
  Delivery (Obstetrics)
  Hypnotism in obstetrics
  Labor (Obstetrics)
  Maternal health services
  Midwives
  Obstetrical emergencies
  Obstetrical endocrinology
  Obstetrical nursing
  Obstetrical pharmacology
  Perinatology
  Puerperal disorders
  Puerperium
  Radiography in obstetrics
  Radioisotopes in obstetrics
  Ultrasonics in obstetrics
  Veterinary obstetrics
— **Apparatus and instruments**
  ₍RG545₎
  NT Forceps, Obstetric
— **Atlases**
— **Case studies**
  ₍RG529₎
  UF Obstetrics—Cases, clinical reports,
   statistics
— Cases, clinical reports, statistics
  USE Obstetrics—Case studies

  Obstetrics—Statistics
— **Diagnosis**
  UF Diagnosis, Obstetrical
   Obstetrical diagnosis
  BT Diagnosis
  NT Pregnancy—Signs and diagnosis
   Prenatal diagnosis
   Radiography in obstetrics
— **Formulae, receipts, prescriptions**
  ₍RG528₎
— Hospitals
  USE Hospitals, Gynecologic and
   obstetric
— **Immunological aspects**
— Jurisprudence
  USE Forensic obstetrics
— **Law and legislation** *(May Subd Geog)*
  BT Medical laws and legislation
  NT Obstetricians—Malpractice
— **Practice**
  UF Obstetrical practice
— **Psychosomatic aspects**
  BT Medicine, Psychosomatic
— **Research**
— — **United States**
— **Social aspects** *(May Subd Geog)*
  UF Society and obstetrics
— **Statistics**
  ₍RG530-RG530.3₎
  UF Obstetrics—Cases, clinical reports,
   statistics
— **Study and teaching** *(May Subd Geog)*
  ₍RG141-RG149₎
  Here are entered works on professional edu-
  cation in obstetrics. Works on public education
  in childbirth, including classes for expectant par-
  ents, are entered under Childbirth—Study and
  teaching.
— **Surgery**
  ₍RG725-RG791₎
  Here are entered works on obstetrical opera-
  tions. Works on non-obstetrical operations per-
  formed on pregnant women are entered under
  Pregnant women—Surgery.
  UF Obstetrics, Operative
   Operative obstetrics
  BT Gynecology, Operative
   Surgery
   Surgery, Operative
  NT Abortion
   Abortion, Therapeutic
   Amniocentesis
   Cesarean section
   Craniotomy
   Episiotomy
   Labor, Induced (Obstetrics)
   Symphyseotomy
— — **Complications and sequelae**
   (May Subd Geog)
Obstetrics, Anesthetics in
 USE Anesthesia in obstetrics
Obstetrics, Antiseptics in
 USE Antiseptics in obstetrics
Obstetrics, Eclectic
 ₍RV365₎
 UF Eclectic obstetrics
 BT Medicine, Eclectic
Obstetrics, Forensic
 USE Forensic obstetrics
Obstetrics, Homeopathic
 ₍RX476₎
 BT Homeopathy
Obstetrics, Operative
 USE Obstetrics—Surgery
Obstetrics, Veterinary
 USE Veterinary obstetrics
Obstinacy
 UF Stubbornness
 RT Toughness (Personality trait)
 NT Hardness of heart
Obstruction (Military science)
 USE Obstacles (Military science)

Obstruction theory
 [QA612.79]
 BT Algebraic topology
Obstructions, Intestinal
 USE Intestines—Obstructions
Obstructions, Ureteral
 USE Ureters—Obstructions
Obstructive jaundice
 USE Jaundice, Obstructive
Obstructive lung diseases
 USE Lungs—Diseases, Obstructive
Obturators, Palatal
 USE Artificial palate
Obugezi (The Ganda word)
 BT Ganda language—Etymology
Ocaina language
 [PM6682]
 UF Okaina language
 BT Indians of South America—Languages
Ocala National Forest (Fla.)
 BT Forest reserves—Florida
 National parks and reserves—United
 States
O'Callanane family
 USE Callahan family
O'Callinan family
 USE Callahan family
O'Cannan family
 USE Cannon family
Ocarina
 [ML990.O3]
 BT Woodwind instruments
 — **Methods**
 [MT526]
 — — **Self-instruction**
 [MT526]
 UF Ocarina—Self-instruction
 — Self-instruction
 USE Ocarina—Methods—Self-
 instruction
Ocarina and piano music
 [M270-271]
 UF Piano and ocarina music
Ocarina music
 [M110.O3]
occam (Computer program language)
 [QA76.73.O]
 BT Programmming languages (Electronic
 computers)
occam2 (Computer program language)
 [QA76.73.O]
 BT Programming languages (Electronic
 computers)
Occanichi Indians
 USE Occoneechee Indians
Occanuchee Indians
 USE Occoneechee Indians
Occasional criminals
 BT Crime and criminals
 Criminal psychology
Occasional poetry
 USE Occasional verse
Occasional sermons
 [BV4254.2]
 Here are entered works containing sermons
 preached on special days or for special occasions, e.g.
 Christmas, Easter, dedications, anniversaries, etc.
 Single sermons, or works containing sermons of one
 kind only, are entered under the specific subject, e.g.
 Confirmation sermons.
 UF Sermons, Occasional
 BT Occasional services
 Sermons
 NT Baptismal sermons
 Canonization sermons
 Church dedication sermons
 Communion sermons
 Confirmation sermons
 Coronation sermons
 Evangelistic sermons
 Execution sermons

 Farewell sermons
 Fast-day sermons
 First communion sermons
 Funeral sermons
 Memorial Day sermons
 Mother's Day sermons
 New Year sermons
 Ordination sermons
 Red mass
 Wedding sermons
Occasional sermons, Jewish
 [BM744]
Occasional services
 [BV199]
 UF Services, Occasional
 BT Liturgies
 Worship programs
 NT Occasional sermons
 — **Anglican Communion,** [**Catholic Church,**
 etc.]
Occasional verse
 UF Epideictic poetry
 Occasional poetry
 BT Poetry
Occasional verse, Classical
 (May Subd Geog)
 UF Classical occasional verse
 BT Classical poetry
Occasional verse, Dutch (May Subd Geog)
 UF Dutch occasional verse
 BT Dutch poetry
Occasional verse, English (May Subd Geog)
 UF English occasional verse
 BT English poetry
Occasional verse, Estonian
 (May Subd Geog)
 UF Estonian occasional verse
 BT Estonian poetry
Occasional verse, Estonian [**etc.**]
 (May Subd Geog)
Occasional verse, Latin (Medieval and
 modern) (May Subd Geog)
 UF Latin occasional verse, Medieval and
 modern
 BT Latin poetry, Medieval and modern
Occasional verse, Swedish (May Subd Geog)
 UF Swedish occasional verse
 BT Swedish poetry
Occasionalism
 BT Causation
 Fate and fatalism
 God
 Matter
 Mind and body
 RT Dualism
Occidental (Artificial language)
 [PM8702]
 BT Languages, Artificial
Occidental art
 USE Art
Occidental civilization
 USE Civilization, Occidental
Occidental imprints (May Subd Geog)
Occidentals in Oriental art
 BT Art, Oriental
 East and West
Occipital bone
 [QL821]
 [QM105]
 BT Craniology
 Skull
 NT Atlanto-occipital joint
 Basioccipital bone
Occipital lobes
 [QP382.O22 (Physiology)]
 BT Cerebral cortex
 NT Visual cortex
Occipitoatlantal joint
 USE Atlanto-occipital joint
Occitan language
 USE Langue d'oc

 Provençal language
Occitan movement
 [DC607.9]
 UF Occitanian movement
 BT France, Southern—History—
 Autonomy and independence
 movements
 France, Southern—Politics and
 government
 Nationalism—France
 Regionalism—France
Occitanian movement
 USE Occitan movement
Occluded fronts (Meteorology)
 (May Subd Geog)
 [QC880.4.F7]
 UF Frontal occlusion (Meteorology)
 Occlusion (Meteorology)
 BT Fronts (Meteorology)
Occlusal adjustment (May Subd Geog)
 UF Adjustment, Occlusal
 Equilibration, Occlusal
 Grinding of occlusal tooth surfaces,
 Selective
 Occlusal equilibration
 Selective grinding of occlusal tooth
 surfaces
 Teeth—Grinding of occlusal surfaces,
 Selective
 BT Malocclusion—Treatment
Occlusal bite plane splints
 USE Splints, Bite plane
Occlusal equilibration
 USE Occlusal adjustment
Occlusal sealants
 USE Pit and fissure sealants (Dentistry)
Occlusion (Dentistry)
 UF Dental occlusion
 Teeth—Occlusion
 BT Dentistry
 NT Dental articulators
 Jaw relation records
 Malocclusion
 Mandible—Hinge axis determination
Occlusion (Meteorology)
 USE Occluded fronts (Meteorology)
Occlusion of gases
 USE Gases—Occlusion
Occlusion of the vas deferens
 USE Vas occlusion
Occlusive bandages
 USE Occlusive surgical dressings
Occlusive dressings (Surgery)
 USE Occlusive surgical dressings
Occlusive surgical dressings
 (May Subd Geog)
 [RD113.4.O22]
 UF Bandages, Occlusive
 Occlusive bandages
 Occlusive dressings (Surgery)
 Surgical dressings, Occlusive
 BT Surgical dressings
 NT Hydrocolloid surgical dressings
Occoneechee Indians
 UF Occanichi Indians
 Occanuchee Indians
 Ocheneechees
 BT Indians of North America
Occoquan Creek (Va.)
 USE Occoquan River (Va.)
Occoquan Reservoir (Va.)
 BT Occoquan River (Va.)
 Reservoirs—Virginia
Occoquan River (Va.)
 UF Occoquan Creek (Va.)
 Occoquon Creek (Va.)
 BT Rivers—Virginia
 NT Occoquan Reservoir (Va.)
Occoquon Creek (Va.)
 USE Occoquan River (Va.)

Occult, The
  USE Occultism
OCCULT (Computer program)
  UF Ordered Computer Collation of
    Unprepared Literary Text
Occult medicine
  USE Medicine, Magic, mystic, and spagiric
Occult sciences
  USE Occultism
  — Biography
    USE Occultists
Occult sciences, Muslim
  USE Occultism, Islamic
Occult sciences and criminal investigation
  USE Occultism and criminal investigation
Occultations
    ₜQB175 (Calculation)₁
  BT Astronomy
    Astronomy, Spherical and practical
    Moon
    Planets
  RT Eclipses
    Transits
  NT Longitude
Occultism *(May Subd Geog)*
    ₜBF1405-BF1999₁
  UF Occult, The
    Occult sciences
  BT Religions
    Supernatural
  RT Psychical research
  NT Alchemy
    Astrology
    Divination
    Fortune-telling
    Hermetism
    Kuṇḍalinī
    Magic
    National socialism and occultism
    Oracles
    Prophecies (Occultism)
    Psychometry (Occultism)
    Satanism
    Spiritualism
    Stock-exchange and occultism
    Witchcraft
  — **Early works to 1900**
  — **Religious aspects**
  — — **Baptists, ₜCatholic Church, etc.₁**
  — — **Buddhism, ₜChristianity, etc.₁**
  — — **Catholic Church**
  — — **Christianity**
Occultism, Islamic *(May Subd Geog)*
  UF Islamic occultism
    Occult sciences, Muslim
Occultism and criminal investigation
  UF Criminal investigation and occultism
    Occult sciences and criminal
      investigation
  BT Criminal investigation
Occultism and national socialism
  USE National socialism and occultism
Occultism and stock-exchange
  USE Stock-exchange and occultism
Occultism in art
Occultism in literature
Occultists *(May Subd Geog)*
  UF Occult sciences—Biography
  BT Religious biography
  NT Spiritualists
Occupancy (International law)
  BT Acquisition of territory
    International law
Occupancy (Law) *(May Subd Geog)*
  BT Acquisition of property
  NT Squatters
Occupancy (Roman law)
Occupancy of buildings, Joint
  USE Joint occupancy of buildings
Occupation, Choice of
  USE Vocational guidance

Occupation, Free choice of
  USE Free choice of employment
Occupation, Military
  USE Military occupation
Occupation and personality
  USE Personality and occupation
Occupation currency *(May Subd Geog)*
  UF Currency, Occupation
  BT Emergency currency
    Military occupation
    Money
  RT Military currency
**Occupation currency, American, ₜBritish,
  Japanese, etc.₁** *(May Subd Geog)*
Occupation damages, Military
  USE Military occupation damages
Occupation diseases
  USE Occupational diseases
Occupation of factories
  USE Sit-down strikes
Occupation tax
  USE Business tax
Occupation therapy
  USE Occupational therapy
Occupational accidents
  USE Industrial accidents
Occupational aptitude tests
    ₜHF5381.7₁
  BT Ability—Testing
  RT Employment tests
    Vocational qualifications
  NT Theological school inventory
Occupational aspirations
  USE Vocational interests
Occupational crimes
  USE White collar crimes
Occupational dermatitis *(May Subd Geog)*
    ₜRL241₁
  UF Industrial dermatitis
  BT Occupational diseases
    Skin—Inflammation
**Occupational disease diagnostic equipment
  industry** *(May Subd Geog)*
    ₜHD9995.O34-344₁
  BT Occupational diseases—Diagnosis—
    Equipment and supplies
Occupational diseases *(May Subd Geog)*
  UF Diseases of occupations
    Industrial diseases
    Occupation diseases
    Occupations—Diseases
  BT Diseases
  RT Medicine, Industrial
    Occupations, Dangerous
  SA *subdivision* Diseases *under
    occupational groups, e.g.* Printers—
    Diseases; *and subdivision*
    Employees—Diseases *under types
    of industries, e.g.* Construction
    industry—Employees—Diseases
  NT Anthrax
    Arsenic poisoning
    Decompression sickness
    Industrial toxicology
    Inert gas narcosis
    Laboratory infections
    Lead-poisoning
    Lungs—Dust diseases
    Miners' phthisis
    Nystagmus
    Occupational dermatitis
    Occupational mortality
    Occupational neuroses
    Phosphorus—Toxicology
    Vibration syndrome
    Weil's disease
    Workers' compensation
  — **Diagnosis**
  — — **Equipment and supplies**
      NT Occupational disease diagnostic
        equipment industry

  — **Psychosomatic aspects**
  — **Reporting** *(May Subd Geog)*
Occupational health and safety
  USE Industrial hygiene
    Industrial safety
Occupational health libraries
  (May Subd Geog)
    ₜZ675.O22₁
  UF Industrial hygiene libraries
    Industrial safety libraries
    Libraries, Industrial hygiene
    Libraries, Industrial safety
    Libraries, Occupational health
    Libraries, Occupational safety
    Occupational safety libraries
  BT Libraries, Public health
Occupational health nursing
  USE Industrial nursing
Occupational health services
  (May Subd Geog)
    ₜRC968-RC969 (Industrial medicine)₁
    Here are entered works on health services for em-
  ployees, usually provided at the place of work.
  UF Employee health services
  BT Medical care
    Medicine, Industrial
  SA *subdivision* Employees—Medical care
    under types of industries, e.g.
    Construction industry—Employees
    —Medical care; *and subdivision*
    Medical care *under occupational
    groups, e.g.* Merchant seamen—
    Medical care
Occupational hierarchy
  USE Occupational prestige
Occupational interests inventories
  USE Occupational values inventory
Occupational literacy
  USE Functional literacy
Occupational medicine
  USE Medicine, Industrial
Occupational mobility *(May Subd Geog)*
  UF Job mobility
    Mobility
  BT Occupations
    Social mobility
    Vocational interests
  NT Career changes
    Teacher mobility
Occupational mortality *(May Subd Geog)*
  BT Death—Causes
    Mortality
    Occupational diseases
    Occupations
    Vital statistics
  SA *subdivision* Mortality *under
    occupational groups, e.g.* Iron and
    steel workers—Mortality
Occupational neuroses
    ₜRC552.O3₁
  BT Neuroses
    Occupational diseases
  NT Telegraphers' cramp
    Writers' cramp
Occupational physicians *(May Subd Geog)*
  UF Company doctors
    Company physicians
    Factory doctors
    Factory physicians
    Industrial doctors
    Industrial physicians
    Physicians, Occupational
  BT Physicians
Occupational poisoning
  USE Industrial toxicology
Occupational prestige *(May Subd Geog)*
  UF Occupational hierarchy
  BT Prestige
Occupational representation
  USE Functional representation

Occupational retraining (May Subd Geog)

Here are entered works on retraining persons with obsolete vocational skills. Works on on-the-job training of employees are entered under Employees, Training of. Works on vocational instruction within the standard educational system, usually at the secondary level, are entered under Vocational education. Works on the efforts of educational institutions and the community to teach individuals the values of a work-oriented society in preparation for meaningful employment are entered under Career education. Works on the process of training individuals in a particular skill after termination of their formal education are entered under Occupational training.

  UF Retraining, Occupational

  BT Employees, Training of

       Occupational training

 — **Law and legislation** (May Subd Geog)

Occupational safety and health

  USE Industrial hygiene

       Industrial safety

Occupational safety libraries

  USE Occupational health libraries

Occupational specialties (United States Armed Forces)

  USE United States—Armed Forces—

       Occupational specialties

Occupational stress

  USE Job stress

Occupational surveys

Here are entered works on the methods and techniques employed. Individual surveys are entered under names of cities, etc. with subdivision Occupations.

  BT Occupations

       Social surveys

Occupational therapists (May Subd Geog)

  NT Occupational therapy—Vocational

       guidance

Occupational therapy (May Subd Geog)

  [RC487 (Psychotherapy)]

  [RM735-RM735.7 (Rehabilitation)]

  UF Activity programs, Therapeutic effect of

       Occupation therapy

       Work, Therapeutic effect of

  BT Physical therapy

       Psychotherapy

       Rehabilitation

       Therapeutics, Physiological

  RT Invalids—Occupations

  NT Art therapy

       Gardening—Therapeutic use

       Handicraft

       Handicraft—Therapeutic use

       Knitting—Therapeutic use

       Modeling—Therapeutic use

       Music therapy

       Occupational therapy services

       Puppets and puppet-plays—

         Therapeutic use

       Recreational therapy

 — **Vocational guidance** (May Subd Geog)

    UF Occupational therapy as a profession

    BT Occupational therapists

Occupational therapy as a profession

  USE Occupational therapy—Vocational

       guidance

Occupational therapy assistants (May Subd Geog)

  BT Allied health personnel

Occupational therapy for children (May Subd Geog)

  [RJ53.O25]

  BT Children—Diseases—Treatment

Occupational therapy for the aged (May Subd Geog)

  [RC953.8.O22]

  UF Geriatric occupational therapy

  BT Aged—Diseases—Treatment

Occupational therapy services (May Subd Geog)

  BT Medical care

       Occupational therapy

Occupational toxicology

  USE Industrial toxicology

Occupational training (May Subd Geog)

  [HD5715-5715.5]

Here are entered works on the vocationally oriented process of endowing people with a skill after either completion or termination of their formal education. Works on vocational instruction within the standard educational system are entered under Vocational education. Works on retraining persons with obsolete vocational skills are entered under Occupational retraining. Works on training of employees on the job are entered under Employees, Training of.

  UF Job training

       Manpower development and training

       Manpower training programs

       Training, Occupational

       Training, Vocational

       Vocational training

  BT Manpower policy

       Technical education

       Vocational education

  NT Employees, Training of

       Non-formal education

       Occupational retraining

       Training needs

 — **Law and legislation** (May Subd Geog)

Occupational training, Military (May Subd Geog)

  UF Military occupational training

  BT Military education

       Soldiers—Education, Non-military

  SA individual military occupational specialties under names of armies, navies, etc., e.g. United States. Army—Photographers; United States. Navy—Draftsmen

Occupational training centers, Mobile (May Subd Geog)

  [HD5715-5715.5]

  UF Mobile occupational training centers

Occupational training for Jews (May Subd Geog)

  BT Jews—Economic conditions

Occupational training for women (May Subd Geog)

  BT Women—Employment

Occupational values inventory

  UF Occupational interests inventories

  BT Values—Testing

       Vocational interests—Testing

Occupations

  [GR890-GR920 (Folklore)]

  [GT5750-GT6390 (Manners and customs)]

  [HB2581-HB2790 (Statistics)]

  [HF5381 (Choice of)]

  [HJ5645-HJ5651 (Taxation)]

  [HT675-HT690 (Social classes)]

  UF Career patterns

       Careers

       Jobs

       Trades

  BT Business

       Labor and laboring classes

  RT Handicraft

       Vocational guidance

  SA subdivision Vocational guidance under subjects, e.g. Agriculture—Vocational guidance; also subdivision Occupations under names of countries, cities, etc.; also subdivision Biography—Careers under names of individual literary authors; and subdivision Career in [field] under names of other individual persons

  NT Civil service positions

       Invalids—Occupations

       Job descriptions

       Job evaluation

       Life span, Productive

       Monasticism and religious orders—Occupations

       Occupational mobility

       Occupational mortality

       Occupational surveys

       Occupations and race

       Personality and occupation

       Professions

       Vocation

       Vocational interests

       Vocational qualifications

 — **Classification**

    NT United States—Armed Forces—Occupational specialties

 — Diseases

    USE Occupational diseases

 — **Early works to 1900**

 — Health aspects

    USE Industrial hygiene

 — **Licenses**

    SA subdivision Occupations—Licenses under names of countries, cities, etc.

Occupations, Dangerous

  [HD3623-HD3624 (Legislation)]

  [HD7262]

  [T54 (Technology)]

  UF Dangerous occupations

       Injurious occupations

  BT Accidents

       Industrial arts

       Industrial laws and legislation

       Labor and laboring classes

       Negligence

  RT Employers' liability

       Industrial accidents

       Occupational diseases

  SA individual occupations and industries, e.g., Bronzing; Chemical industry; Tinning

  NT Accident law

 — **Safety appliances**

    [HD7273]

    SA subdivisions Safety appliances and Safety measures under particular subjects, e.g. Machinery—Safety appliances; Coal mines and mining—Safety measures

    NT Accidents—Prevention

       Clothing, Protective

Occupations and busy work

  USE Creative activities and seat work

Occupations and race

  UF Race and occupations

  BT Occupations

       Race

       Vocational guidance

Occupations as a theme in art

  USE Occupations in art

Occupations in art

  UF Occupations as a theme in art

       Professions in art

Occupations in literature

  UF Professions in literature

  SA similar headings

  NT Actors in literature

       Lawyers in literature

Occupations in television

  [PN1992.8.O27]

Here are entered works on the portrayal of occupations on television. Works on the occupational opportunities in the field of television are entered under Television—Vocational guidance.

  UF Occupations on television

  BT Television

Occupations on television

  USE Occupations in television

Occupied Japan collectibles
USE Japan—History—Allied occupation,
1945-1952—Collectibles
Occupied territory
USE Military occupation
Ocean
Here are entered geographical descriptions of the world's oceans, including popular accounts of their various features and "mysteries." Works on the scientific study of the ocean and its phenomena are entered under Oceanography.
UF Sea
BT Earth
Physical geography
Water
RT Oceanography
SA *names of oceans, e.g.* Arctic Ocean,
Atlantic Ocean
NT Diving, Submarine
Radioactive waste disposal in the
ocean
Underwater exploration
Women and the sea
— Economic aspects
USE Marine resources
Shipping
— Fiction
USE Sea stories
— **Folklore**
NT Flying Dutchman
Mermaids
Sea monsters
Shellbacks
— **Maps**
UF Maps, Oceanographic
Oceanographic maps
RT Oceanography—Charts, diagrams,
etc.
SA *subdivision* Maps *under individual
oceans and seas, e.g.* Pacific
Ocean—Maps
— **Mythology**
NT Mermaids
Sea monsters
— Poetry
USE Sea poetry
— **Quotations, maxims, etc.**
NT Sea proverbs
— **Religious aspects**
— Research
USE Oceanography—Research
Ocean and civilization
[CB465]
UF Civilization and ocean
BT Civilization
Ocean-atmosphere interaction
UF Air-sea interaction
Atmosphere-ocean interaction
Interaction of atmosphere and ocean
Ocean-meteorological relations
Sea-air interaction
BT Energy budget (Geophysics)
Mass budget (Geophysics)
Meteorology, Maritime
Oceanography
Solar radiation
NT Land breeze
Ocean waves
Sea breeze
Southern oscillation
Thermoclines (Oceanography)
Ocean birds
USE Sea birds
Ocean bonito
USE Skipjack tuna
Ocean bottles
UF Bottles, Messages in
Messages in bottles
Seagoing bottles
RT Drift bottles

Ocean bottom *(May Subd Geog)*
[GC83]
UF Ocean floor
Sea bed
Sea floor
Seabed
BT Marine biology
Oceanography
RT Abyssal zone
Submarine geology
Submarine topography
NT Benthos
Manned undersea research stations
Marine geophysics
Marine mineral resources
Marine sediments
Sea-floor spreading
Submarine valleys
Ocean bottom (Maritime law)
[JX4426]
UF Suboceanic lands (Maritime law)
Subsoil (Maritime law)
BT International law
Maritime law
RT Economic zones (Maritime law)
NT Continental shelf
Marine resources conservation—Law
and legislation
Ocean mining—Law and legislation
Oil well drilling, Submarine
Ocean cables
USE Cables, Submarine
Ocean circulation *(May Subd Geog)*
[GC228.5-GC228.6]
UF Circulation, Ocean
BT Oceanography
RT Oceanic mixing
NT Ocean currents
Water masses
— Indian Ocean
Ocean currents *(May Subd Geog)*
[GC231-296]
Subdivided by body of water, e.g. Ocean currents
—Atlantic Ocean.
UF Currents, Oceanic
BT Hydrography
Navigation
Ocean circulation
Oceanography
Physical geography
NT Bottle-charts
Guinea Current
Gulf Stream
Kuroshio
Paleocurrents
Sea ice drift
Tidal currents
Turbidity currents
Upwelling (Oceanography)
— Atlantic Ocean
— Pacific Ocean
NT El Niño Current
Peru Current
Ocean drilling platforms
USE Drilling platforms
Ocean drilling ships
USE Deep-sea drilling ships
Ocean dumping
USE Waste disposal in the ocean
Ocean energy resources
UF Energy from the ocean
BT Marine resources
Ocean engineering
Power resources
NT Gas, Natural, in submerged lands
Marine mineral resources
Ocean thermal power plants
Ocean wave power
Petroleum in submerged lands
Tidal power

Ocean engineering *(May Subd Geog)*
Here are entered works on the engineering aspects of equipment and techniques facilitating operations beneath the surface of the ocean in order to exploit its resources. General works on the application of engineering to ships and their machinery are entered under Marine engineering.
UF Deep-sea engineering
Oceaneering
Submarine engineering
Underwater engineering
BT Engineering
Marine resources
Oceanography
Oceanography—Equipment and
supplies
NT Diving, Submarine—Equipment and
supplies
Manned undersea research stations
Marine geotechnique
Ocean energy resources
Ocean mining
Ocean wave power
Oceanographic instruments
Offshore structures
Ocean fertilization
USE Sea-water—Fertilization
Ocean fishing
USE Saltwater fishing
Ocean floor
USE Ocean bottom
Ocean floor mining
USE Ocean mining
Ocean floor spreading
USE Sea-floor spreading
Ocean freight forwarders *(May Subd Geog)*
UF Foreign freight forwarders
Independent ocean freight forwarders
International forwarding agents
BT Contracts, Maritime
Freight forwarders
RT Customhouse brokers
Ocean freight rates
USE Shipping—Rates
Ocean freighters
USE Cargo ships
Ocean Highway
USE Ocean Hiway
Ocean Hiway
Here are entered works on the named highway running along the Atlantic Coast from Maine to Florida.
UF Ocean Highway
BT Roads—Atlantic States
Ocean in art
USE Sea in art
Ocean in literature
USE Sea in literature
Ocean in motion pictures
USE Sea in motion pictures
Ocean life
USE Marine biology
Ocean liners *(May Subd Geog)*
UF Liners
BT Merchant ships
Passenger ships
Ships
Steamboat lines
RT Cruise ships
— **Decoration**
[VM382]
BT Ship decoration
— **Registers**
Ocean mail stamps *(May Subd Geog)*
BT Mail steamers
Postage-stamps
Ocean-meteorological relations
USE Ocean-atmosphere interaction
Ocean mineral resources
USE Marine mineral resources

Ocean mining *(May Subd Geog)*
UF Deep-sea mining
　　Marine mining
　　Mining, Ocean
　　Mining of marine mineral resources
　　Ocean floor mining
　　Seabed mining
BT Marine mineral resources
　　Mining engineering
　　Ocean engineering
NT Manganese mines and mining,
　　　Submarine
　　Oil well drilling, Submarine
　　Shell deposits
— **Environmental aspects**
　(May Subd Geog)
　NT New England Offshore Mining
　　　　Environmental Study
— **Law and legislation** *(May Subd Geog)*
　BT Mining law
　　　Ocean bottom (Maritime law)
Ocean outfalls *(May Subd Geog)*
UF Marine outfalls
　　Outfalls, Ocean
BT Hydraulic structures
　　Waste disposal in the ocean
Ocean perch, Pacific
USE Pacific ocean perch
Ocean pollution
USE Marine pollution
Ocean Ranger (Drilling rig)
BT Oil well drilling rigs
Ocean resources
USE Marine resources
Ocean routes
USE Trade routes
Ocean sciences
USE Marine sciences
Ocean sounds
UF Sea sounds
BT Oceanography
　　Sounds
NT Waterfront sounds
Ocean temperature *(May Subd Geog)*
　[GC161-177]
　　Subdivided by locality, e.g. Ocean temperature—
　Atlantic Ocean.
UF Sea-water—Temperature
BT Oceanography
　　Sea-water—Thermodynamics
　　Temperature
RT Deep-sea temperature
　　Heat budget (Geophysics)
NT Bathythermograph
　　Thermoclines (Oceanography)
— **Atlantic Ocean**
Ocean thermal power plants
　(May Subd Geog)
UF Ocean thermal power systems
　　Sea thermal power plants
　　Solar sea power plants
BT Electric power-plants
　　Marine resources
　　Ocean energy resources
　　Power resources
　　Renewable energy sources
　　Solar energy
　　Solar power plants
　　Thermoclines (Oceanography)
— **Law and legislation** *(May Subd Geog)*
　BT Maritime law
Ocean thermal power systems
USE Ocean thermal power plants
Ocean transportation
USE Shipping
Ocean travel
　[G153]
　[G550]
　[RA793 (Hygiene)]

UF Cruises
　　Routes of travel
　　Sea travel
BT Communication and traffic
　　Transportation
　　Travel
　　Voyages and travels
RT Steamboats—Passenger
　　　accommodation
NT Shipping conferences
　　Steamboat lines
　　Yachts and yachting
Ocean travel in literature
Ocean trenches
USE Submarine trenches
Ocean View Avenue (Monterey, Calif.)
USE Cannery Row (Monterey, Calif.)
Ocean water masses
USE Water masses
Ocean wave power *(May Subd Geog)*
UF Power, Ocean wave
　　Wave power, Ocean
BT Hydroelectric power plants
　　Ocean energy resources
　　Ocean engineering
　　Ocean waves
　　Power resources
　　Water-power
Ocean waves *(May Subd Geog)*
　[GC211]
　　This heading may be subdivided by bodies of wa-
　ter, e.g. Ocean waves—Atlantic Ocean.
UF Breakers
　　Sea waves
　　Surf
　　Swell
BT Coasts
　　Ocean-atmosphere interaction
　　Oceanography
　　Water waves
　　Wind waves
NT Internal waves
　　Ocean wave power
　　Storm surges
　　Tsunamis
　　Wave resistance (Hydrodynamics)
— **Atlantic Ocean**
Oceanariums
USE Marine aquariums, Public
Oceaneering
USE Ocean engineering
Oceanfront gardening
USE Seaside gardening
Oceania
　　Here are entered comprehensive works on the is-
　lands of the Pacific Ocean belonging to the island
　groups of Melanesia, Micronesia, and Polynesia.
　Comprehensive works on all of the islands of the
　Pacific Ocean are entered under Islands of the Pacif-
　ic.
UF Oceanica
　　South Pacific
　　South Pacific Region
　　South Sea Islands
　　South Seas
　　Southwest Pacific Region
BT Islands of the Pacific
NT Melanesia
　　Micronesia
　　Polynesia
— **Description and travel**
— — **1951-1980**
— — **1981-**
— **Languages**
　NT Australian languages
　　　Melanesian languages
　　　Micronesian languages
　　　Oceanic languages
　　　Papuan languages
　　　Polynesian languages
　　　Tasmanian languages
— **Literatures**

USE Oceanian literature
Oceanian American librarians
　(May Subd Geog)
UF Librarians, Oceanian American
BT Librarians—United States
Oceanian Americans *(May Subd Geog)*
BT Ethnology—United States
　　Oceanians—United States
— **Mental health** *(May Subd Geog)*
Oceanian literature
　[PN849.O26]
UF Oceania—Literatures
Oceanian literature (English)
UF English literature—Oceanian authors
　　English literature—South Pacific
　　　authors
　　South Pacific literature (English)
Oceanian newspapers
Oceanian periodicals *(May Subd Geog)*
Oceanians *(May Subd Geog)*
UF Pacific Islanders (Oceania)
BT Ethnology—Oceania
NT Melanesians
　　Micronesians
　　Polynesians
— **United States**
　NT Oceanian Americans
Oceanic bonito
USE Skipjack tuna
Oceanic disposal of radioactive wastes
USE Radioactive waste disposal in the
　　　ocean
Oceanic drilling ships
USE Deep-sea drilling ships
Oceanic hot springs
USE Hydrothermal vents
Oceanic languages
　[PL6171-PL6175]
　　Here are entered works dealing collectively with
　the Polynesian, Melanesian and Micronesian lan-
　guages.
UF Eastern Austronesian languages
BT Austronesian languages
　　Oceania—Languages
RT Proto-Oceanic language
NT Melanesian languages
　　Micronesian languages
　　Polynesian languages
Oceanic mixing
　[GC299]
UF Mixing, Oceanic
BT Oceanography
RT Diffusion in hydrology
　　Ocean circulation
Oceanic pipelines
USE Underwater pipe lines
Oceanica
USE Oceania
Oceanodroma
　[QL696.P64]
BT Hydrobatidae
Oceanodroma castro
　[QL696.P64]
UF Band-rumped storm-petrel
　　Harcourt's storm-petrel
　　Madeiran storm-petrel
Oceanodroma leucorhoa
　[QL696.P64]
UF Leach petrel
　　Leach's storm-petrel
Oceanodroma tethys
　[QL696.P64]
UF Galapagos storm-petrel
　　Wedge-rumped storm-petrel
Oceanographers *(May Subd Geog)*
　[GC30]
BT Earth scientists
　　Geophysicists
　　Oceanography
NT Oceanography—Vocational guidance

Oceanographic buoys
  ₍GC41₎
  UF Floating instrument platforms
      Instrument platforms, Floating
      Moored oceanographic buoys
      Unmanned floating instrument
        platforms
  BT Buoys
      Oceanographic instruments
      Oceanographic research stations
  NT Deep-sea moorings
Oceanographic information, Exchange of
  USE Exchange of oceanographic
        information
Oceanographic instruments
  ₍GC41₎
  UF Instruments, Oceanographic
      Marine instruments
      Oceanography—Instruments
  BT Ocean engineering
      Oceanography—Equipment and
        supplies
      Physical instruments
      Scientific apparatus and instruments
  NT Drift bottles
      Oceanographic buoys
Oceanographic laboratories
  USE Oceanographic research stations
Oceanographic libraries *(May Subd Geog)*
  ₍Z675.O23₎
  UF Libraries, Oceanographic
  BT Marine science libraries
Oceanographic maps
  USE Ocean—Maps
      Oceanography—Charts, diagrams, etc.
Oceanographic observations
  USE Oceanography—Observations
Oceanographic research
  USE Oceanography—Research
Oceanographic research ships
  (May Subd Geog)
  UF Oceanographic ships
  BT Hydrographic surveying
      Oceanography—Research
      Research vessels
      Ships
  SA *names of individual oceanographic
        research ships*
  NT Deep-sea drilling ships
      Marine biology research vessels
      Oceanographic submersibles
Oceanographic research stations
  (May Subd Geog)
  UF Anchor stations (Oceanography)
      Deep-sea instrument stations
      Oceanographic laboratories
      Stations, Oceanographic research
      Unmanned instrument stations
        (Oceanography)
  BT Oceanography—Research
  NT Drifting ice stations
      Manned undersea research stations
      Oceanographic buoys
      Tide stations
  — Anchorage
      USE Deep-sea moorings
Oceanographic ships
  USE Oceanographic research ships
Oceanographic submersibles
  (May Subd Geog)
  ₍GC67₎
  UF Deep diving vehicles
      Deep-sea research vessels
      Deep submergence vehicles
      Manned exploration devices
      Submersibles, Oceanographic
  BT Oceanographic research ships
      Submarine boats
  NT Bathyscaphe
      Diving-bells
      Submarine rescue vehicles

— Electric equipment
— **Rules for classification and construction**
    ₍VM453₎
Oceanography *(May Subd Geog)*
  ₍GC₎
    Here are entered works on the scientific study of
  the ocean and its phenomena. Geographical descrip-
  tions of the world's oceans, including popular ac-
  counts of their various features and "mysteries" are
  entered under Ocean.
  UF Oceanography, Physical
      Oceanology
      Physical oceanography
      Thalassography
  BT Earth sciences
      Geology
      Geophysics
      Hydrology
      Marine sciences
      Physical geography
      Water
  RT Ocean
  NT Abyssal zone
      Aeronautics in oceanography
      Astronautics in oceanography
      Chemical oceanography
      Coasts
      Diving, Submarine
      Estuarine oceanography
      Fisheries—Hydrologic factors
      Fishery oceanography
      Hydrography
      Marine biology
      Marine laboratories
      Marine pollution
      Marine resources
      Meteorology, Maritime
      Navigation
      Ocean-atmosphere interaction
      Ocean bottom
      Ocean circulation
      Ocean currents
      Ocean engineering
      Ocean sounds
      Ocean temperature
      Ocean waves
      Oceanic mixing
      Oceanographers
      Optical oceanography
      Paleoceanography
      Photography in oceanography
      Radio in oceanography
      Radioactive tracers in oceanography
      Radioisotopes in oceanography
      Rossby waves
      Sea ice
      Sea level
      Sea-water
      Sounding and soundings
      Submarine geology
      Television in oceanography
      Tides
      Underwater exploration
      Water masses
— **Charts, diagrams, etc.**
    UF Maps, Oceanographic
        Oceanographic maps
        Oceanography—Maps
    RT Ocean—Maps
— **Computer programs**
— **Equipment and supplies**
    NT Ocean engineering
        Oceanographic instruments
— **Experiments**
— Instruments
    USE Oceanographic instruments
— **International cooperation**
    NT Exchange of oceanographic
          information
— Maps

      USE Oceanography—Charts, diagrams,
            etc.
— **Observations**
    UF Observations, Oceanographic
        Oceanographic observations
    NT Exchange of oceanographic
          information
— **Research** *(May Subd Geog)*
    ₍GC57-59₎
      This heading may be subdivided by the geo-
    graphical area investigated, e.g. Oceanography—
    Research—Pacific Ocean. Where applicable,
    also make a second subject entry for the country
    conducting the research, .e.g. Oceanography—
    Research—Denmark.
    UF Ocean—Research
        Oceanographic research
    RT Exploratory fishing
        Underwater exploration
    NT International Decade of Ocean
          Exploration, 1970-1980
        Mohole project
        Oceanographic research ships
        Oceanographic research stations
— — **Law and legislation**
      (May Subd Geog)
— — **Denmark**
— — **Pacific Ocean**
— — **United States**
      NT National Sea Grant Program
— **Vocational guidance** *(May Subd Geog)*
    ₍QC30.5₎
    BT Oceanographers
— **Atlantic Ocean**
— **Caribbean Sea**
— **Chesapeake Bay**
Oceanography, Military
  USE Military oceanography
Oceanography, Physical
  USE Oceanography
Oceanography and state *(May Subd Geog)*
  UF State and oceanography
Oceanology
  USE Oceanography
Ocellated antbird
  ₍QL696.P2455₎
  UF Ocellated antthrush
      Phaenostictus mcleannani
  BT Phaenostictus
Ocellated antthrush
  USE Ocellated antbird
Ocelots
  UF Felis pardalis
Ocelots as pets
  ₍SF459.O2₎
  BT Pets
Ochakov, Battle of, 1737
  ₍DR548₎
  BT Russo-Turkish War, 1736-1739
Ochanomizu (Tokyo, Japan)
  (Not Subd Geog)
  UF Tokyo (Japan). Ochanomizu
Ochekwu (African people)
  USE Idoma (African people)
Ocheneechees
  USE Occoneechee Indians
Ochenrider family
  USE Oxenreider family
Ocher *(May Subd Geog)*
  ₍TN948.O2₎
Ochi Day (Greek holiday)
  USE Hēmera tou Ochi (Greek holiday)
Ochi family *(Not Subd Geog)*
Ochipawa Indians
  USE Chippewa Indians
Ochlockonee River (Ga. and Fla.)
  BT Rivers—Florida
      Rivers—Georgia
  NT Talquin, Lake (Fla.)
Ocho reales
  USE Piece of eight

Ochodaeidae
  USE Scarabaeidae
Ochotona
  USE Pikas
Ochotonidae
  [QL737.L33]
  BT Lagomorpha
  NT Pikas
Ochrolechia
  [QK585.L37 (Botany)]
  BT Lecanoraceae
Ochroma lagopus
  USE Balsa wood
Ochrotrichia
  [QL518.H95]
  BT Hydroptilidae
Ochsenheimeria *(May Subd Geog)*
  [QL561.O26]
  BT Ochsenheimeriidae
  NT Ochsenheimeria vacculella
Ochsenheimeria vacculella
  (May Subd Geog)
  [QL561.O26]
  BT Ochsenheimeria
Ochsenheimeriidae *(May Subd Geog)*
  [QL561.O26]
  BT Lepidoptera
    Moths
  NT Ochsenheimeria
Ochsenreider family
  USE Oxenreider family
Ochsenreiter family
  USE Oxenreider family
Ochsenreither family
  USE Oxenreider family
Ochsenreuter family
  USE Oxenreider family
Ochteridae
  [QL523.O3]
  UF Pelogonidae
  BT Hemiptera
  NT Ochterus
Ochterus
  [QL523.O3]
  UF Pelogonus
  BT Ochteridae
Ochterus minor
  [QL523.O3]
Ochterus piliferus
  [QL523.O3]
Ochthiphilidae
  USE Chamaemyiidae
Ochweśnicki jargon
  [PM7895.O3]
  UF Argot des marchands d'images
  BT Lingua francas
Ocimum
  USE Basil
Ocimum sanctum
  [QK495.L15 (Botany)]
  UF Monks basil
    Purple-stalked basil
    Sacred basil
    Toolsi
    Toolsy
    Tulasī
    Tulsi
Ocklawaha River (Fla.)
  USE Oklawaha River (Fla.)
Ocksrider family
  USE Oxenreider family
Oclawaha River (Fla.)
  USE Oklawaha River (Fla.)
OCLC Acquisitions Subsystem
  BT Acquisitions (Libraries)—Automation
OCLC Cataloging Subsystem
  [Z699.4.O29]
  BT Cataloging, Cooperative—Data
    processing
    On-line data processing

OCLC Interlibrary Loan Subsystem
  [Z674.82.O15]
  BT Inter-library loans—United States
OCLC M300 Workstation
  UF M300 Workstation
  BT IBM Personal Computer
    OCLC workstations
OCLC Serials Control Subsystem
  BT Serials control systems—Automation
OCLC workstations
  UF Workstations, OCLC
  BT Microcomputer workstations
  NT OCLC M300 Workstation
Ocmulgee Wildlife Management Area (Ga.)
  BT Shooting preserves—Georgia
    Wildlife management areas—Georgia
Ocneria
  USE Porthetria
Ocneriidae
  USE Lymantriidae
Ocoee River (Tenn.)
  BT Rivers—Tennessee
O'Coffey family
  USE Coffey family
Ocoña River (Peru)
  UF Río de Ocoña (Peru)
    Río Ocoña (Peru)
  BT Rivers—Peru
Oconee National Forest (Ga.)
  BT Forest reserves—Georgia
    National parks and reserves—United
      States
O'Conner family
  USE O'Connor family
O'Connor family
  UF Coner family
    Conner family
    Conners family
    Connor family
    Connors family
    Conors family
    O'Conner family
    O'Conor family
O'Conor family
  USE O'Connor family
O'Corcoran family
  USE Corcoran family
OCR devices
  USE Optical character recognition devices
OCRYSP (Computer program)
  UF Optimisation of Crystal Positions
    (Computer program)
Octadecanoic acid
  USE Oleic acid
Octadecenoic acid
  USE Oleic acid
Octagon House (Watertown, Wis.)
  BT Dwellings—Wisconsin
Octagonal buildings
  USE Buildings, Octagonal
Octagonal houses *(May Subd Geog)*
  UF Houses, Octagonal
  BT Buildings, Octagonal
    Dwellings
Octahedrite
  USE Titanium dioxide
Octal system
  [QA141]
  UF Base eight numeration
    Numeration, Base eight
    Octimal system
  BT Arithmetic
    Numeration
Octane number
  USE Gasoline—Anti-knock and anti-knock
    mixtures
    Motor fuels—Anti-knock and anti-
      knock mixtures
Octdon family
  USE Ogden family

Octets
  [M800-886]
  Here are entered collections of compositions for
eight instruments belonging to various families and in
various combinations; and compositions for eight
specific instruments belonging to various families,
followed by specification of instruments (including
the specification Unspecified instrument(s))
  Compositions for eight bowed stringed instruments are entered under String octets; for eight wind
instruments under Wind octets; for eight brass instruments under Brass octets; and for eight woodwind
instruments under Woodwind octets, with or without
specification of instruments in each case.
  Compositions for eight plectral instruments are
entered under Plectral ensembles, except those for
guitars and/or harps, which are entered under Octets
followed by specification of instruments.
  Compositions for eight percussionists are entered
under Percussion ensembles.
  Compositions for eight solo voices are entered
under Sacred octets or Vocal octets.
  Headings with specification of instruments are
printed below only if specific cross references are
needed.
  SA Suites, Variations, Waltzes, *and similar*
    headings with specification of
    instruments
Octets, Brass
  USE Brass octets
Octets, Sacred
  USE Sacred octets
Octets, Secular
  USE Vocal octets
Octets, String
  USE String octets
Octets, Vocal
  USE Vocal octets
Octets, Wind
  USE Wind octets
Octets, Woodwind
  USE Woodwind octets
Octets (Bassoon, clarinet, flute, horn, harp,
  violin, viola, double bass)
  [M880-882]
Octets (Bassoon, clarinet, flute, horn, oboe,
  trombone, trumpet, double bass)
  [M860-862]
Octets (Bassoon, clarinet, flute, horn, trumpet,
  violin, violoncello, double bass)
  [M860-862]
Octets (Bassoon, clarinet, flute, horn, trumpet,
  violin, violoncello, double bass), Arranged
  [M863-4]
Octets (Bassoon, clarinet, flute, horn, violin,
  viola, violoncello, double bass)
  [M860-862]
  NT Suites (Bassoon, clarinet, flute, horn,
    violin, viola, violoncello, double
    bass)
Octets (Bassoon, clarinet, flute, horn, violins
  (2), viola, violoncello)
  [M860-862]
  NT Variations (Bassoon, clarinet, flute,
    horn, violins (2), viola, violoncello)
Octets (Bassoon, clarinet, flute, horns (2),
  oboe, percussion)
  [M885]
Octets (Bassoon, clarinet, flute, horns (2),
  violin, viola, violoncello)
  [M860-862]
Octets (Bassoon, clarinet, flute, oboe, violin,
  viola, violoncello, double bass)
  [M860-862]
Octets (Bassoon, clarinet, flute, oboe, violins
  (2), viola, violoncello)
  [M860-862]
  NT Bassoon, clarinet, flute, oboe, violins
    (2), viola, violoncello with string
    orchestra
    Concertos (Bassoon, clarinet, flute,
    oboe, violins (2), viola, violoncello
    with string orchestra)

Suites (Bassoon, clarinet, flute, oboe, violins (2), viola, violoncello)

Octets (Bassoon, clarinet, horn, oboe, violin, viola, violoncello, double bass)
⌈M860-862⌉

Octets (Bassoon, clarinet, horn, oboe, violins (2), viola, violoncello)
⌈M860-862⌉

Octets (Bassoon, clarinet, horn, violin, violas (2), violoncello, double bass)
⌈M860-862⌉

Octets (Bassoon, clarinet, horn, violins (2), viola, violoncello, double bass)
⌈M860-862⌉

Octets (Bassoon, clarinets (2), flute, horn, oboe, violin, double bass)
⌈M860-862⌉

Octets (Clarinet, flute, horn, trumpet, percussion, vibraphone, violin, violoncello)
⌈M885⌉
NT Suites (Clarinet, flute, horn, trumpet, percussion, vibraphone, violin, violoncello)

Octets (Clarinet, flute, oboe, percussion, violin, viola, violoncello)
⌈M885⌉

Octets (Clarinet, flute, saxophone, percussion, vibraphone, violin, voice)
⌈M885⌉

Octets (Clarinet, horns (2), violin, violas (2), violoncello, double bass)
⌈M860-862⌉

Octets (Clarinets (2), flute, drums, percussion, viola, violoncello, double bass)
⌈M885⌉
NT Suites (Clarinets (2), flute, drums, percussion, viola, violoncello, double bass)

Octets (Clarinets (2), harp, violins (2), viola, violoncello, double bass)
⌈M880-882⌉

Octets (Clarinets (2), horns (2), violins (2), viola, double bass)
⌈M860-862⌉
NT Suites (Clarinets (2), horns (2), violins (2), viola, double bass)

Octets (Clarinets (2), horns (4), harp, double bass)
⌈M880-882⌉

Octets (Clarinets (2), horns (4), harp, double bass), Arranged
⌈M883-4⌉

Octets (Flute, horns (2), oboes (2), violins (2), violoncello)
⌈M860-862⌉

Octets (Flute, horns (2), violins (2), viola, violoncello, double bass)
⌈M860-862⌉
NT Suites (Flute, horns (2), violins (2), viola, violoncello, double bass)

Octets (Flutes (2), trumpets (5), percussion)
⌈M885⌉
NT Suites (Flutes (2), trumpets (5), percussion)

Octets (Harpsichord, bassoon, clarinet, flute, horn, oboe, viola, violoncello)
⌈M820-822⌉

Octets (Harpsichord, guitar, violins (6))
⌈M830-832⌉

Octets (Harpsichord, recorders (7))
⌈M815-817⌉
BT Octets (Piano, flutes (7))

Octets (Horns (2), oboes (2), violins (2), viola, violoncello)
⌈M860-862⌉
NT Suites (Horns (2), oboes (2), violins (2), viola, violoncello)

Octets (Horns (2), trombones (2), trumpets (2), tuba, percussion)
⌈M885⌉

Octets (Horns (2), trombones (2), trumpets (2), tuba, percussion), Arranged
⌈M885⌉

Octets (Organ, trombones (3), trumpets (3), percussion)
⌈M885⌉

Octets (Percussion, violins (2), viola, violoncello)
⌈M885⌉

Octets (Piano, bassoon, clarinet, flute, trumpet, percussion, violin, violoncello)
⌈M845-7⌉

Octets (Piano, clarinet, cymbals (2), violins (2), viola, violoncello)
⌈M845-849⌉
BT Cymbal music

Octets (Piano, clarinet, flute, guitar, mandolin, accordion, percussion, double bass)
⌈M832⌉

Octets (Piano, clarinet, flute, violins (2), viola, violoncello, double bass)
⌈M820-822⌉

Octets (Piano, clarinets (2), flute, trombone, trumpets (2), percussion)
⌈M845-7⌉

Octets (Piano, flute, horn, oboe, violin, viola, violoncello, double bass)
⌈M820-822⌉

Octets (Piano, flute, violins (2), violas (2), violoncellos (2))
⌈M820-822⌉

Octets (Piano, flutes (7))
⌈M815-817⌉
NT Octets (Harpsichord, recorders (7))

Octets (Piano, horn, violins (2), violas (2), violoncello, double bass)
⌈M820-822⌉

Octets (Piano, horns (2), trombone, trumpets (2), percussion)
⌈M845-7⌉

Octets (Piano, percussion, vibraphone, violins (2), viola, violoncello, double bass)
⌈M845-7⌉

Octets (Piano, recorders (3), violins (2), viola, violoncello)
⌈M820-822⌉
NT Variations (Piano, recorders (3), violins (2), viola, violoncello)

Octets (Piano, recorders (6), guitar)
⌈M835⌉

Octets (Piano, trombones (2), trumpets (3), percussion, double bass)
⌈M845-7⌉

Octets (Piano, trombones (3), trumpets (4))
⌈M815-817⌉

Octets (Piano, trombones (3), trumpets (4)), Arranged
⌈M818-819⌉

Octets (Pianos (2), bassoon, clarinets (2), English horn, horn, trombone)
⌈M815-817⌉

Octets (Pianos (2), chimes (2), violins (2), violoncellos (2))
⌈M845-7⌉

Octets (Pianos (2), percussion, violoncellos (4))
⌈M835⌉

Octets (Recorder, percussion, double bass)
NT Variations (Recorder, percussion, double bass)

Octets (Trombones (3), trumpets (3), percussion)
⌈M885⌉

Octets (Trumpets (4), percussion)
⌈M885⌉
NT Suites (Trumpets (4), percussion)

Octets (Trumpets (5), percussion)
⌈M885⌉
NT Concertos (Trumpets (5), percussion with string orchestra)

Trumpets (5), percussion with string orchestra

Octimal system
USE Octal system

October Incident, 1931 (Japan)
USE Japan—History—March and October Incidents, 1931

October Middle East War, 1973
USE Israel-Arab War, 1973

October Mountain Lake (Mass.)
BT Lakes—Massachusetts
Reservoirs—Massachusetts
Washington Mountain Brook (Mass.)

October Revolt, Thailand, 1973
USE Thailand—History—Student Uprising, 1973

October Revolution, Guatemala, 1944
USE Guatemala—History—October Revolution, 1944

October Revolution Monument (Kiev, Ukraine)
USE Pamiātnik Velikomu Oktiābriū (Kiev, Ukraine)

October twenty-eighth (Greek holiday)
USE Hēmera tou Ochi (Greek holiday)

Octoberfest
USE Oktoberfest

Octocorallia
USE Alcyonaria

Octopoda (May Subd Geog)
⌈QL430.2⌉
BT Cephalopoda
NT Octopodidae
Octopus

Octopodidae (May Subd Geog)
⌈QL430.3.O2⌉
UF Octopuses
BT Octopoda

Octopus
⌈QL430.3.O2⌉
UF Devilfish
BT Octopoda
NT Octopus vulgaris

Octopus, Common
USE Octopus vulgaris

Octopus dofleini
⌈QL430.3.02⌉

Octopus fisheries (May Subd Geog)
UF Cephalopod fisheries
BT Fisheries

Octopus vulgaris (May Subd Geog)
⌈QL430.3.O2⌉
UF Octopus, Common
BT Octopus

Octopuses
USE Octopodidae

Octoroons
USE Mulattoes

Octosyllable

Octroi (May Subd Geog)
⌈HJ9120⌉
UF Customs duties, Internal
Duties
Tariff, Internal
BT Internal revenue
Local taxation
Municipal finance
Tariff
Taxation
RT Taxation of articles of consumption
Tolls

Ocuiltec language
UF Atzinca language
Maclatzinca language
Ocuilteca language
Ocuilteco language
Tlahuica language
BT Indians of Mexico—Languages
Mexico—Languages
Otomian languages

Ocuilteca language
USE Ocuiltec language

2653

Ocuilteco language
USE Ocuiltec language
Ocular accommodation
USE Eye—Accommodation and refraction
Ocular adaptation
USE Eye—Adaptation
Ocular adnexa
USE Adnexa oculi
Ocular biomicroscopy
UF Biomicroscopy, Ocular
Ocular slit-lamp microscopy
Slit-lamp microscopy, Ocular
BT Eye—Examination
Microscopy, Medical
Ocular emergencies
USE Ophthalmologic emergencies
Ocular exercises
USE Orthoptics
Ocular fundus
USE Fundus oculi
Ocular histoplasmosis
USE Histoplasmosis, Ocular
Ocular hypotony
UF Hypotonia oculi
Hypotony, Ocular
Intraocular pressure, Low
Low intraocular pressure
BT Eye—Diseases and defects
Ocular manifestations of general diseases
[RE65]
UF Ocular symptoms of general diseases
Ophthalmological manifestations of
general diseases
Ophthalmological symptoms of general
diseases
BT Eye—Diseases and defects
Symptomatology
Ocular motility
USE Eye—Movements
Ocular motility disorders
USE Eye—Movement disorders
Ocular pharmacology (May Subd Geog)
[RE994]
UF Eye—Drug effects
Eye, Effect of drugs on
Ophthalmopharmacology
BT Eye—Diseases and defects
Pharmacology
NT Materia medica, Ophthalmological
Ocular refraction
USE Eye—Accommodation and refraction
Ocular slit-lamp microscopy
USE Ocular biomicroscopy
Ocular symptoms of general diseases
USE Ocular manifestations of general
diseases
Ocular tension
USE Intraocular pressure
Ocular therapeutics
USE Therapeutics, Ophthalmological
Ocular toxoplasmosis
USE Toxoplasmosis, Ocular
Oculinidae
[QL377.C5]
BT Scleractinia
Oculists
USE Ophthalmologists
Optometrists
Oculo-cerebro-renal syndrome
USE Lowe's syndrome
Oculocerebrorenal syndrome
USE Lowe's syndrome
Oculomotor disorders
USE Eye—Movement disorders
Oculomotor paralysis
UF Paralysis, Oculomotor
BT Eye—Paralysis
Neuro-ophthalmology
Oculomotor system
USE Eye—Movements

Ocumé
USE Aucoumea klaineana
Ocypoda gigantea
USE Cardisoma guanhumi
Ocypode
USE Ghost crabs
Od
USE Bhovis
Od (Punjab tribe)
BT Ethnology—India
Oda family (Not Subd Geog)
Odacanthidae
USE Carabidae
Odae Mountain (Korea) (Not Subd Geog)
UF Godaizan (Korea)
Gotaizan (Korea)
Mount Odae (Korea)
Odae-san (Korea)
Odaesan (Korea)
BT Mountains—Korea (South)
Odae-san (Korea)
USE Odae Mountain (Korea)
Odaesan (Korea)
USE Odae Mountain (Korea)
Odaesan Kungnip Kongwŏn (Korea)
BT National parks and reserves—Korea
(South)
Odakyū Dentetsu
BT Railroads—Japan
Street-railroads—Japan
Odam family
USE Odom family
O'dam language
USE Tepehuan language
Ōdate Cave (Takahata-machi, Japan)
(Not Subd Geog)
UF Ōdate Dōgetsu (Takahata-machi,
Japan)
BT Caves—Japan
Japan—Antiquities
Ōdate Dōgetsu (Takahata-machi, Japan)
USE Ōdate Cave (Takahata-machi, Japan)
Odawara, Japan, Battle of, 1590
[DS869.5]
UF Odawara gassen, 1590
Odawara seibatsu, 1590
BT Japan—History—Azuchi-Momoyama
period, 1568-1603
Odawara gassen, 1590
USE Odawara, Japan, Battle of, 1590
Odawara seibatsu, 1590
USE Odawara, Japan, Battle of, 1590
Odd-Fellows, Independent Order of
USE Independent Order of Odd Fellows
Odd-toed ungulates
USE Perissodactyla
Oddars
USE Bhovis
Oddē
USE Bhovis
Oddershede family (Not Subd Geog)
Oddfellows Home Cemetery (Mason City,
Iowa)
USE Mason City Oddfellows Home
Cemetery (Mason City, Iowa)
Oddi's muscle
USE Sphincter of Oddi
Oddi's sphincter
USE Sphincter of Oddi
Oddities
USE Curiosities and wonders
Oddle family
USE O'Dell family
Odekirk family
USE Ouderkerk family
Odel family
USE O'Dell family

O'Dell family (Not Subd Geog)
UF Oadell family
Oddle family
Odel family
Odelle family
Odil family
Odle family
Odelle family
USE O'Dell family
Odem family
USE Odom family
Oden family (Not Subd Geog)
Odense (Denmark). Albanikvarteret
USE Albanikvarteret (Odense, Denmark)
Odense (Denmark). Vesterbrokvarteret
USE Vesterbrokvarteret (Odense, Denmark)
Odense-Svendborg banen
BT Railroads—Denmark
Odenwald (Germany)
BT Mountains—Germany (West)
RT Naturpark Bergstrasse-Odenwald
(Germany)
Odenwald, Naturpark Bergstrasse (Germany)
USE Naturpark Bergstrasse-Odenwald
(Germany)
Oder-Neisse Line (Germany and Poland)
BT Germany (East)—Boundaries—Poland
Neisse River
Oder River
Poland—Boundaries—Germany (East)
World War, 1939-1945—Territorial
questions—Germany
World War, 1939-1945—Territorial
questions—Poland
NT Western and Northern Territories
(Poland)
Oder River
UF Odra River
BT Rivers—Czechoslovakia
Rivers—Germany (East)
Rivers—Poland
NT Oder-Neisse Line (Germany and
Poland)
Oderhaff (Poland and Germany)
USE Szczeciński Lagoon (Poland and
Germany)
Oderkirk family
USE Ouderkerk family
Odes
[PN1371 (History: general)]
[PN6110.O4 (Collections: general)]
[PR509.O3 (English)]
[PR1195.O3 (English)]
BT Lyric poetry
Poetry
Odescalchi family (Not Subd Geog)
Odessa, Battle of, 1941
[D764]
BT World War, 1939-1945—Campaigns—
Ukraine
Odessa, Battle of, 1944
BT World War, 1939-1945—Campaigns—
Ukraine
Odesskaiā oblast' (Ukraine)
— History
— — Revolution, 1917-1921
Odh
USE Bhovis
Odia
USE Bhovis
Odian family
USE Oldham family
Odil family
USE O'Dell family
Odina
USE Lannea
Odinia
[QL537.O3]
BT Odiniidae
Odinidae
USE Odiniidae

Odiniidae
　[QL537.O3]
　UF　Odinidae
　BT　Diptera
　NT　Odinia
Odissi dance
　[GV1796.O34]
　UF　Orissi dance
　BT　Dancing—India
Odle family
　USE　O'Dell family
Odo pottery　(May Subd Geog)
　[NK4168.K]
　UF　Pottery, Odo
　BT　Pottery, Japanese
　RT　Nōsayama pottery
Odoard family　(Not Subd Geog)
Odobenidae
　[QL737.P62]
　BT　Pinnipedia
　NT　Odobenus
Odobenus
　[QL737.P62]
　BT　Odobenidae
Odobenus rosmarus
　USE　Walruses
Odocoileus columbianus
　USE　Mule deer
Odocoileus hemionus
　USE　Mule deer
Odocoileus hemionus sitkensis
　USE　Mule deer
Odocoileus virginianus
　USE　White-tailed deer
Odom family　(Not Subd Geog)
　UF　Odam family
　　　Odem family
　　　Odum family
　RT　Oldham family
Odomari Harbor (R.S.F.S.R.)
　USE　Korsakov Harbor (R.S.F.S.R.)
Odometers for automobiles
　USE　Automobiles—Odometers
Odonata　(May Subd Geog)
　[QL520-520.42]
　UF　Libelluloidea
　　　Paraneuroptera
　BT　Insects
　NT　Aeshnidae
　　　Agrionidae
　　　Calopterygidae
　　　Chlorocyphidae
　　　Coenagrionidae
　　　Corduliidae
　　　Damselflies
　　　Dragonflies
　　　Epiophlebiidae
　　　Gomphidae
　　　Libellulidae
　　　Platycnemididae
　　　Synlestidae
O'Donill family
　USE　O'Donnell family
O'Donnell, Peter　(Not Subd Geog)
　— Characters
　— — Modesty Blaise
　　　RT　Blaise, Modesty (Fictitious
　　　　　character)
O'Donnell Camp (Luzon, Philippines :
　Concentration camp)
　[D805.P5]
　UF　Camp O'Donnell (Luzon, Philippines :
　　　　Concentration camp)
　BT　World War, 1939-1945—
　　　　Concentration camps—Philippines

O'Donnell family　(Not Subd Geog)
　UF　Donals family
　　　Donell family
　　　Donnal family
　　　Donnel family
　　　Donnell family
　　　Donnels family
　　　O'Donill family
O'Donnoghue family
　USE　Donahue family
O'Donoghue family
　USE　Donahue family
O'Donohue family
　USE　Donahue family
Odontaspidae
　USE　Odontaspididae
Odontaspididae
　[QL638.95.O3]
　UF　Carchariidae
　　　Odontaspidae
　BT　Lamniformes
　NT　Odontaspis
Odontaspis
　[QL638.95.O3]
　UF　Carcharias
　BT　Odontaspididae
Odontaspis Kamoharai
　[QL638.95.O3]
Odontaspis taurus
　USE　Sand tiger shark
Odontesthes
　[QL638.A8]
　UF　Odonthestes
　BT　Silversides
　RT　Pejerrey fishing
Odontesthes bonariensis
　[QL638.A8]
　UF　Basilichthys bonariensis
Odontesthes regia
　[QL638.A8]
　UF　Austromenidia regia
Odonthestes
　USE　Odontesthes
Odontites
　[QK495.S43]
　BT　Scrophulariaceae
Odontogenesis imperfecta
　USE　Dentinogenesis imperfecta
Odontogenic cysts
　BT　Cysts
　　　Jaws—Tumors
　　　Mouth—Tumors
　NT　Dentigerous cyst
　　　Radicular cyst
Odontogenic tumors
　BT　Jaws—Tumors
　　　Mouth—Tumors
　　　Tumors
Odontoglossae
　USE　Flamingos
Odontoglossum
　[QK495.O64]
　BT　Orchids
Odontoglossum subcruciforme
　[QK495.O64]
Odontograph
　[TJ186]
　BT　Gearing
Odontography
　USE　Teeth
Odontology
　USE　Dentistry
　　　Teeth
Odontophorus
　[QL696.G27]
　UF　Wood quails
　BT　Phasianidae
　　　Quails
　NT　Odontophorus gujanensis
Odontophorus gujanensis
　[QL696.G27]

　UF　Marbled wood quail
　BT　Odontophorus
Odontotermes
　[QL529.3.T4]
　BT　Termitidae
　NT　Odontotermes magdalenae
Odontotermes magdalenae
　[QL529.3.T4]
　BT　Odontotermes
Odor control
　[TD886]
　UF　Odors—Control
　BT　Air—Pollution
　　　Odors
　NT　Animal housing—Odor control
　　　Cat litter boxes—Odor control
　　　Cattle—Housing—Odor control
　　　Chemical plants—Odor control
　　　Deodorization
　　　Farm manure, Liquid—Odor control
　　　Fish handling—Odor control
　　　Fishery processing industries—Odor
　　　　control
　　　Paper mills—Odor control
　　　Pulp mills—Odor control
Odor of fishes
　USE　Fishes—Odor
Ōdōri (Sapporo-shi, Japan)
　BT　Streets—Japan
Odorizing of gas
　USE　Gas—Odorizing
Odors
　[BF271 (Psychology)]
　[QP458 (Physiology)]
　UF　Aromas
　　　Fragrances
　　　Scents
　　　Smells
　BT　Air—Pollution
　　　Nuisances
　　　Smell
　NT　Alcoholic beverages—Flavor and odor
　　　Beer—Flavor and odor
　　　Butter—Flavor and odor
　　　Dairy products—Flavor and odor
　　　Deodorization
　　　Feeds—Flavor and odor
　　　Fishes—Odor
　　　Flowers—Odor
　　　Food—Odor
　　　Fruit—Flavor and odor
　　　Fruit juices—Flavor and odor
　　　Gas—Odorizing
　　　Glands, Odoriferous
　　　Incense
　　　Liquors—Flavor and odor
　　　Meat, Precooked—Flavor and odor
　　　Milk—Flavor and odor
　　　Milk, Remade—Flavor and odor
　　　Odor control
　　　Oils and fats—Flavor and odor
　　　Orange juice—Flavor and odor
　　　Perfumes
　　　Stench fire-warning system in mines
　— Control
　　　USE　Odor control
Odors in literature
Odors in the Bible
　[BS680.O34]
　UF　Bible—Fragrances
　　　Bible—Odors
　　　Fragrances in the Bible
Odostemon
　USE　Mahonia
ODRA computer
　[QA76.8]
　BT　Electronic digital computers
　— Programming
Odra River
　USE　Oder River

2655

Odschi language
 USE Twi language
Odual language
  [PL8598.O29]
 UF Saka language (Nigeria)
 BT Abua-Ogbia languages
Odum family
 USE Odom family
Odumbaras
 USE Audumbaras
Odysseus (Greek mythology)
 BT Mythology, Greek
ODYSSEY (Computer programs)
 BT Cartography—Computer programs
   Computer programs
Odyssey (Dune buggy)
 BT Dune buggies
   Honda automobile
Ōe family *(Not Subd Geog)*
Oecanthinae
 USE Tree crickets
Oecanthus
 USE Tree crickets
OECD Compatible Trade and Production Data
  Base
 USE COMTAP (Information retrieval
    system)
Oecioa, Fossil
 USE Anthozoa, Fossil
Oecobiidae
  [QL458.42.O4]
 BT Spiders
Oecology
 USE Ecology
Oecophoridae
  [QL561.O43]
 UF Aecophoridae
   Ashinagidae
   Asphinagidae
   Depessariidae
   Depressariidae
   Metachandidae
   Oeocophoridae
   Thalamarchidae
 BT Lepidoptera
   Moths
 NT Agonopteryx
   Depressaria
   Peleopoda
Oecumenical councils and synods
 USE Councils and synods, Ecumenical
Oedaleus
  [QL508.A2]
 BT Acrididae
Oedaleus senegalensis
  [QL508.A2]
 UF Senegalese grasshopper
Oedanes River
 USE Brahmaputra River
Oedema
 USE Edema
Oedemeridae
  [QL596.O4]
 BT Beetles
 NT Vasaces
Oedionychis
  [QL596.C5]
 BT Chrysomelidae
Oedipoda
  [QL508.A2]
 BT Acrididae
Oedipomidas
 USE Saguinus
Oedipus (Greek mythology)
 UF Oidipos (Greek mythology)
 BT Mythology, Greek
Oedipus (Salamander)
 USE Bolitoglossa
Oedipus (Tale) *(May Subd Geog)*
  [GR75.O3]
 BT Tales

Oedipus complex
 UF Edipus complex
 BT Complexes (Psychology)
   Mothers and sons
   Parent and child
   Psychoanalysis
   Psychology, Pathological
   Sex (Psychology)
 RT Electra complex
Oedipus complex in art
Oedipus complex in literature
Oedogoniaceae
  [QK569.O4]
 BT Oedogoniales
 NT Oedogonium
Oedogoniales *(May Subd Geog)*
  [QK569.O4]
 BT Green algae
 NT Oedogoniaceae
Oedogonium
  [QK569.O4]
 BT Oedogoniaceae
Oehlke family
 USE Oelke family
Oehoendoeni (Indonesian people)
 USE Uhunduni (Indonesian people)
Oehserchestes
  [QL458.2.O]
 BT Oehserchestidae
Oehserchestidae
  [QL458.2.L]
 UF Hybalicidae
 NT Oehserchestes
Oelgart family
 USE Øllgaard family
Oelke family *(Not Subd Geog)*
 UF Oehlke family
Oelknitz Site (Germany)
 BT Germany (East)—Antiquities
Oelwes family
 USE Alves family
Oenanthe oenanthe
 USE Northern wheatear
Œnectria pilleriana
 USE Sparganothis pilleriana
Oenocarpus
  [QK495.P17]
 BT Palms
Oenocarpus bataua
  [QK495.P17]
 UF Jessenia bataua
Oenochoes *(May Subd Geog)*
 UF Oinochoai
 BT Pottery, Greek
Oenochromidae
 USE Geometridae
Oenochromiidae
 USE Geometridae
Oenophilidae
 USE Tineidae
Œnophthira pilleriana
 USE Sparganothis pilleriana
Oenothera
  [QK495.O46]
 UF Anogra
   Onagra
 BT Onagraceae
Oenothera biennis
 USE Evening primrose
Oenothera lamarkiana
  [QK495.O46 (Botany)]
Oenothera muricata
 USE Evening primrose
Oenothera whitneyi
 USE Clarkia amoenia
Oenotheraceae
 USE Onagraceae
Oenotherapy
 USE Wine—Therapeutic use
Oeocophoridae
 USE Oecophoridae

Oerter family
 USE Arthur family
Oerther family
 USE Arthur family
Oertley family
 USE Oertli family
Oertli family *(Not Subd Geog)*
 UF Oertley family
   Oertly family
Oertly family
 USE Oertli family
Oescus River (Bulgaria)
 USE Iskŭr River (Bulgaria)
Oesophagus
 USE Esophagus
Oestradiol
 USE Estradiol
Oestradiol monobenzoate
 USE Estradiol benzoate
Oestridae *(May Subd Geog)*
  [QL537.O4]
 UF Hypodermatidae
 BT Botflies
   Diptera
 NT Oestrus (Insect)
Oestrone
 USE Estrone
Oestrum
 USE Estrus
Oestrus
 USE Estrus
Oestrus (Insect) *(May Subd Geog)*
  [QL537.O4]
 BT Oestridae
Oestrus ovis
 USE Sheep botfly
Oetzel family *(Not Subd Geog)*
 UF Oezel family
Oever family
 USE Vanover family
Oezel family
 USE Oetzel family
Off-Broadway theater
  Here are entered works on regular productions at
 New York City theaters usually having fewer than
 300 seats and located outside the main Broadway
 theater district. Works on experimental or showcase
 performances at small theaters, lofts, churches and
 changeable locations in the New York City area gen-
 erally produced at wage scales below those normally
 prescribed by theatrical unions are entered under Off
 Off-Broadway theater.
 BT Theater—New York (N.Y.)
Off-budget government entities
  (May Subd Geog)
  Here are entered works on government-chartered
 entities whose financial transactions do not appear in
 official budgets and are not subject to debt or spend-
 ing limitations.
 BT Administrative agencies
   Budget
   Government business enterprises
Off-design performance of pumps
 USE Pumping machinery—Performance
Off family
 USE Eoff family
Off-limits areas
 USE Travel restrictions
Off Off-Broadway theater
  Here are entered works on experimental or show-
 case performances at small theaters, lofts, churches
 and changeable locations in the New York City area
 generally produced at wage scales below those nor-
 mally prescribed by theatrical unions. Works on regu-
 lar productions at New York City theaters usually
 having fewer than 300 seats and located outside the
 main Broadway theater district are entered under
 Off-Broadway theater.
 BT Experimental theater—New York
    (N.Y.)
   Theater—New York (N.Y.)
Off road operation of automobiles
 USE Automobiles—Off road operation

Off-road vehicles
  USE All terrain vehicles
Off-track betting
  USE Horse race betting
Offa's Dyke (Wales and England)
  BT Dikes (Engineering)—England
    Dikes (Engineering)—Wales
    Fortification—England
    Fortification—Wales
Offender-Based State Corrections Information
  System
  USE OBSCIS (Information retrieval system)
Offenders, Aged
  USE Aged offenders
Offenders, Female
  USE Female offenders
Offenders, Repeat
  USE Recidivists
Offenders, Sex
  USE Sex offenders
Offenses, Classification of
  USE Classification of crimes
Offenses, Compound
  USE Compound offenses
Offenses, Military
  USE Military offenses
Offenses, Naval
  USE Naval offenses
Offenses, Religious
  USE Offenses against religion
Offenses, Repeat
  USE Recidivism
Offenses affecting the public trade
  USE Commercial crimes
Offenses against foreign heads of state
  (May Subd Geog)
  UF Crimes against foreign heads of state
    Foreign heads of state, Crimes against
    Foreign heads of state, Offenses
      against
  BT Criminal law
    Heads of state
Offenses against heads of state
  (May Subd Geog)
  BT Heads of state
    Offenses against the person
    Personality (Law)
    Political crimes and offenses
  RT Assassination
  NT Regicides
Offenses against property *(May Subd Geog)*
  UF Crimes against property
    Property, Crimes against
    Property, Offenses against
  BT Criminal law
  NT Arson
    Burglary
    Embezzlement
    Extortion
    Forcible entry and detainer
    Forgery
    Fraud
    Larceny
    Malicious mischief
    Offenses against socialist property
    Poaching
    Receiving stolen goods
    Robbery
    White collar crimes
Offenses against property (Islamic law)
Offenses against public morality
  USE Crimes without victims
Offenses against public safety
  (May Subd Geog)
  UF Crimes against public safety
    Public safety, Crimes against
    Public safety, Offenses against
  BT Criminal law
  NT Bombings
    Crimes aboard aircraft
    Crimes aboard buses

    Local transit crime
    Riots
    Sabotage
Offenses against religion *(May Subd Geog)*
  UF Crimes, Religious
    Crimes against religion
    Offenses, Religious
    Religion, Crimes against
    Religion, Offenses against
  BT Criminal law
  NT Apostasy
    Blasphemy
    Heresy
    Offenses in the Bible
    Sacrilege
    Simony
Offenses against religion (Canon law)
Offenses against socialist property
  (May Subd Geog)
  UF Crimes against socialist property
    Socialist property, Crimes against
    Socialist property, Offenses against
  BT Criminal law
    Offenses against property
Offenses against the person
  (May Subd Geog)
  UF Abuse of persons
    Crimes against the person
    Person, Crimes against the
    Person, Offenses against the
    Persons, Abuse of
  BT Criminal law
  SA *subdivisions* Abuse of *and* Crimes
    against *under classes of persons and
    ethnic groups*
  NT Abduction
    Abortion—Law and legislation
    Assassination
    Assault and battery
    Conjugal violence
    Exposure (Criminal law)
    False imprisonment
    Homicide
    Infanticide
    Kidnapping
    Mugging
    Murder
    Offenses against heads of state
    Rape
    Sex crimes
    Suicide
    Trials (Offenses against the person)
    Violent deaths
Offenses against the person (Islamic law)
Offenses in the Bible
  UF Bible—Offenses
  BT Offenses against religion
Offensive (Military strategy)
  ₍U162₎
  UF Military offensive (Military strategy)
  BT Military policy
    Strategy
  RT Attack and defense (Military science)
Offensive backs (Football)
  USE Running backs (Football)
Offensive basketball
  USE Basketball—Offense
Offensive football
  USE Football—Offense
Offensive hockey
  USE Hockey—Offense
Offensive soccer
  USE Soccer—Offense
Offer and acceptance *(May Subd Geog)*
  UF Acceptance (Contracts)
  BT Contracts
  NT Option (Contract)
Offer and acceptance (Jewish law)
Offer to purchase (Securities)
  USE Tender offers (Securities)

Offering to Love (Painting)
  USE Vanloo, Carle, 1705-1765. Offering
    to Love
Offerings, Votive
  USE Votive offerings
Offers, Job
  USE Job offers
Offertories
  Here, without subdivision, are entered works on
  the place of the offertory in the Mass of the Catholic
  Church; also general works of an inclusive nature.
  UF Offertory
  **— Anglican Communion, ₍Lutheran Church,
    etc.₎**
Offertories (Music)
  BT Propers (Music)
    Sacred vocal music
Offertory
  USE Offertories
Office, Applications for
  USE Applications for office
Office, Appointment to
  USE *subdivision* Officials and employees—
    Selection and appointment *under
    names of countries, cities, etc. and
    names of individual government
    agencies; and subdivision* Selection
    and appointment *under types of
    officials*
Office, Divine
  USE Divine office
Office, Ecclesiastical
  USE Clergy—Office
Office, Nominations for
  USE Nominations for office
Office, Qualifications for
  USE *subdivision* Officials and employees—
    Selection and appointment *under
    names of countries, cities, etc. and
    names of individual government
    agencies; and subdivision* Selection
    and appointment *under types of
    officials*
    Nominations for office
Office, Rabbinical
  USE Rabbis—Office
Office, Resignation from
  USE *subdivision* Resignation from office
    under names of individual persons
Office accidents
  BT Accidents
Office administration
  USE Office management
Office buildings *(May Subd Geog)*
  ₍NA6230-NA6233₎
  UF Buildings, Office
  BT Commercial buildings
    Industrial buildings
  NT Condominium office buildings
    Employees' buildings and facilities
    Offices
    Real estate management
    Real estate office buildings
    Skyscrapers
  — Conservation and restoration
    NT Office buildings—Remodeling for
      other use
  — Law and legislation *(May Subd Geog)*
  — Lighting
    ₍TK4399.O35₎
  — Live loads
    UF Live loads in office buildings
    BT Structural dynamics
  — Remodeling for other use
    UF Office buildings—Renovation
    BT Buildings—Remodeling for other
      use
      Office buildings—Conservation and
        restoration
  — Renovation

Office buildings
— Renovation *(Continued)*
  USE Office buildings—Remodeling for
    other use
— **Illinois**
  NT Frank Lloyd Wright Studio (Oak
    Park, Ill.)
— **India**
— **Kentucky**
  NT Humana, Inc. Headquarters
    (Louisville, Ky.)
— **New York (State)**
  NT Empire State Building (New York,
    N.Y.)
    Granite Building (Rochester, N.Y.)
    Larkin Building (Buffalo, N.Y.)
    Six hundred Lexington Avenue
      (New York, N.Y.)
— **Texas**
  NT Southwest Center (Houston, Tex.)
    Transco Tower (Houston, Tex.)
— **Wisconsin**
  NT Germania Building (Milwaukee,
    Wis.)
Office decoration *(May Subd Geog)*
  UF Offices—Decoration
  BT Interior decoration
  NT House plants in office decoration
Office employees
  USE Clerks
Office equipment and supplies
  [HF5548]
  UF Business machines
    Office machines
    Office supplies
  BT Bookkeeping
    Industrial equipment
    Office management
    Office practice
  NT Accounting machines
    Blank-books
    Calculators
    Card system in business
    Cash registers
    Copying machines
    Dictating machines
    Dictograph
    Electronic office machines
    Magnetic recorders and recording—
      Business applications
    Marking devices
    Office furniture
    Plastics in business machines
    Point-of-sale systems industry
    Rubber stamps
    Selling—Office equipment and supplies
    Stationery
    Ticket selling registers
    Time clocks
    Typewriters
    Writing—Materials and instruments
— **Parts**
Office equipment and supplies industry
  (May Subd Geog)
  [HD9999.O4]
Office equipment leases *(May Subd Geog)*
  [HD9800.4]
  UF Equipment leasing
    Leases, Office equipment
  BT Industrial equipment leases
    Lease and rental services
Office etiquette
  USE Business etiquette
Office furniture
  [HF5521-5541]
  BT Furniture
    Office equipment and supplies
Office furniture industry *(May Subd Geog)*
  [HD9803]
Office house plants
  USE House plants in office decoration

Office landscaping
  USE Office layout
Office layout
  UF Layout, Office
    Office landscaping
    Office planning
  BT Interior architecture
  NT Medical offices—Planning
Office leases *(May Subd Geog)*
  BT Building leases
    Leases
    Offices
Office machines
  USE Electronic office machines
    Office equipment and supplies
Office mail procedures *(May Subd Geog)*
  UF Mail procedures, Office
  BT Office procedures
Office management
  [HF5546-HF5547]
  UF Office administration
  BT Management
  NT Business records
    Letter services
    Office equipment and supplies
    Office practice
    Office practice in government
    Office procedures
    Organization charts
    Public records
    Receptionists
— **Research** *(May Subd Geog)*
  UF Office management research
Office management research
  USE Office management—Research
Office nursing, Medical
  USE Medical office nursing
Office planning
  USE Office layout
Office politics *(May Subd Geog)*
  UF Corporate politics
    Politics, Office
  BT Industrial sociology
    Organizational behavior
Office practice
  UF Secretarial practice
  BT Office management
  RT Clerks
  NT Filing systems
    Office equipment and supplies
    Paperwork (Office practice)
    Shorthand
    Typewriting
— **Automation**
  RT Electronic data processing
    Electronic filing systems
    Electronic office machines
  NT Word processing
Office practice in churches
  [BV4379]
  BT Church work
Office practice in government
  (May Subd Geog)
  UF Government office practice
  BT Office management
    Public administration
  NT Congressional secretaries
    Government paperwork
Office procedures
  BT Office management
  NT Office mail procedures
Office records
  USE Business records
Office signs *(May Subd Geog)*
  UF Signs, Office
  BT Signs and signboards
Office sounds
  BT Sounds
Office supplies
  USE Office equipment and supplies

Officer, Resistance to
  USE Resisting an officer
Officer efficiency reports (United States Army)
  USE United States. Army—Officer
    efficiency reports
Officer personnel
  USE *subdivision* Officers *under armies,*
    navies, etc., e.g. United States.
    Army—Officers
Officers, Church
  USE Church officers
Officers, Congressional
  USE United States. Congress—Officials
    and employees
Officers' clubs
  USE *subdivision* Officers' clubs *under*
    armed forces, armies, navies, etc.,
    e.g. United States—Armed Forces—
    Officers' clubs
Officers' wives *(May Subd Geog)*
  BT Military dependents
    Wives
  NT Generals' wives
Offices
  BT Office buildings
  NT Dental offices
    Law offices
    Medical offices
    Office leases
— Decoration
  USE Office decoration
— **Location** *(May Subd Geog)*
  UF Location of offices
Offices, Sale of
  USE Sale of public office
Official gazettes
  USE Gazettes
Official jargon
  USE *subdivision* Government jargon *under*
    names of languages, e.g. English
    language—Government jargon
Official libraries
  USE Libraries, Governmental,
    administrative, etc.
Official misconduct
  USE Misconduct in office
Official Production System Version 5
  (Computer system)
  USE OPS5 (Computer system)
Official publications
  USE *subdivision* Government publications
    under names of countries, cities,
    etc., e.g. United States—
    Government publications
    Government publications
Official secrets *(May Subd Geog)*
  UF Disclosing official secrets
    Government secrecy
    Secrecy in government
    Secrets, Official
    Secrets of state
  BT Confidential communications
    Criminal law
    Government and the press
    Government information
    Ministerial responsibility
    Secrecy
  NT Defense information, Classified
    Executive privilege (Government
      information)
    Security classification (Government
      documents)
Officialese
  USE English language—Government jargon
Officials
  USE Public officers

Officials and employees
USE *subdivision* Officials and employees
under names of countries, cities,
etc., also under types of government
agencies and names of individual
international and governmental
agencies; and phrase headings for
particular types of officials and
employees
Officials and employees, Honorary
USE *subdivision* Officials and employees,
Honorary *under names of countries*
Officials and employees, International
USE International officials and employees
Officiating, Sports
USE Sports officiating
Officiating of soccer
USE Soccer—Officiating
Offill family *(Not Subd Geog)*
Offizierslager VI C (Osnabrück, Germany :
Concentration camp)
USE Oflag VI C (Osnabrück, Germany :
Concentration camp)
Offizierslager XIII B (Hammelburg, Germany :
Concentration camp)
USE Oflag XIII B (Hammelburg, Germany :
Concentration camp)
Offset (Accounting)
UF Offset accounts
BT Accounting
Offset accounts
USE Offset (Accounting)
Offset lithography *(May Subd Geog)*
UF Lithography, Offset
Offset prints
Prints, Offset
BT Lithography—20th century
Lithography—Metal plate processes
Offset printing
NT Camera-ready copy
Offset lithography, American
(May Subd Geog)
UF American offset lithography
Offset printing
UF Lithoprinting
Printing, Offset
BT Lithography
Lithography—Metal plate processes
Printing
RT Lithography, Direct
NT Offset lithography
— **Industrial capacity**
Offset printing of newspapers
UF Newspaper printing, Offset
BT Newspapers
Offset prints
USE Offset lithography
Offshore assembly industry
(May Subd Geog)
[HD9720-HD9739]
Here are entered works on the industry in which
unfinished goods are delivered to foreign factories
where they are assembled and exported.
UF Assembly industry, Offshore
Export assembly industry
In-bond industry
Maquiladora industry
Maquiladoras
RT Export processing zones
— Strikes and lockouts
USE Strikes and lockouts—Offshore
assembly industry
Offshore atomic power plants
USE Offshore nuclear power plants
Offshore banking (Finance)
USE Banks and banking, Foreign
Banks and banking, International
Offshore bar
USE Barrier islands
Offshore commercial radio
USE Pirate radio broadcasting

Offshore drilling (Petroleum)
USE Oil well drilling, Submarine
Offshore electric power plants
USE Electric power-plants, Offshore
Offshore gas fields
USE Gas, Natural, in submerged lands
Offshore gas industry *(May Subd Geog)*
BT Gas industry
RT Gas, Natural, in submerged lands
Offshore oil industry
Offshore installations
USE Offshore structures
Offshore nuclear power plants
(May Subd Geog)
UF Atomic power plants, Offshore
Offshore atomic power plants
BT Electric power-plants, Offshore
Nuclear power plants
NT Submerged nuclear power plants
Offshore oil field equipment industry
(May Subd Geog)
[HD9560-9579]
BT Offshore oil industry—Equipment and
supplies
Offshore oil fields
USE Petroleum in submerged lands
Offshore oil industry *(May Subd Geog)*
UF Oil industry, Offshore
Petroleum in submerged lands industry
Tidelands oil industry
BT Petroleum industry and trade
RT Offshore gas industry
Petroleum in submerged lands
NT Oil well drilling, Submarine
— **Equipment and supplies**
NT Offshore oil field equipment
industry
Offshore oil operations
USE Oil well drilling, Submarine
Offshore oil storage
USE Petroleum—Offshore storage
Offshore petroleum shipping terminals
USE Petroleum shipping terminals
Offshore pipe lines
USE Underwater pipe lines
Offshore procurement program, 1951-
BT Economic assistance, American
Military assistance, American
Munitions
Mutual security program, 1951-
United States—Armed Forces—
Procurement
Offshore radio broadcasting
USE Pirate radio broadcasting
Offshore structures *(May Subd Geog)*
UF Artificial islands
Marine structures
Offshore installations
Structures, Offshore
BT Hydraulic engineering
Ocean engineering
NT Drilling platforms
Electric power-plants, Offshore
Satellite launching ships
— **Aerodynamics**
[TC1665]
BT Aerodynamics
— **Anchorage**
BT Anchorage
Deep-sea moorings
— **Dynamics**
— **Hydrodynamics**
BT Hydrodynamics
— **Joints**
BT Joints (Engineering)
— **Law and legislation** *(May Subd Geog)*
BT Maritime law
— **Welding**
Offshore structures (International law)
[JX4427]

BT Islands—Law and legislation
Jurisdiction, Territorial
Maritime law
NT Oil well drilling, Submarine—Law and
legislation
Offshore support vessels *(May Subd Geog)*
[VM466.O35]
UF Ships, Offshore support
Supply vessels, Offshore
Support vessels, Offshore
BT Oil well drilling, Submarine
Work boats
— **Law and legislation** *(May Subd Geog)*
BT Maritime law
Offshore water pollution
USE Marine pollution
Oflag II C (Dobiegniew, Poland :
Concentration camp)
UF Oflag II C Woldenberg (Dobiegniew,
Poland : Concentration camp)
BT World War, 1939-1945—
Concentration camps—Poland
Oflag II C Woldenberg (Dobiegniew, Poland :
Concentration camp)
USE Oflag II C (Dobiegniew, Poland :
Concentration camp)
Oflag VI C (Osnabrück, Germany :
Concentration camp) *(Not Subd Geog)*
UF Offizierslager VI C (Osnabrück,
Germany : Concentration camp)
BT Concentration camps—Germany
(West)
World War, 1939-1945—
Concentration camps—Germany
(West)
World War, 1939-1945—Prisoners and
prisons, German
Oflag XIII B (Hammelburg, Germany :
Concentration camp) *(Not Subd Geog)*
[D805.G3]
UF Offizierslager XIII B (Hammelburg,
Germany : Concentration camp)
BT Concentration camps—Germany
(West)
World War, 1939-1945—
Concentration camps—Germany
(West)
Ofo language
USE Ofogoula language
Ofogoula language
[PM2049.O3]
UF Ofo language
BT Siouan languages
O'Friel family
USE Friel family
OFT (Flight simulator)
USE Flight simulators
Ōga family *(Not Subd Geog)*
Oga-hantō (Japan)
USE Oga Peninsula (Japan)
Oga Peninsula (Japan)
UF Oga-hantō (Japan)
BT Peninsulas—Japan
O'Gallagher family
USE Gallagher family
Ogallala Aquifer
UF Ogallala Formation
BT Aquifers—Great Plains
Ogallala Formation
USE Ogallala Aquifer
Ogallalla Indians
USE Oglala Indians
Ogam alphabet
USE Ogham alphabet
Ogan dialect
BT Malay language
Ogan folk literature
USE Folk literature, Ogan
Ogan literature *(May Subd Geog)*
BT Indonesia—Literatures
NT Folk literature, Ogan

Ogasawara family
Ogasawara-guntō (Japan)
  USE Bonin Islands (Japan)
Ogawa Castle (Shigaraki-chō, Japan)
  USE Ogawajō (Shigaraki-chō, Japan)
Ogawa Castle (Tsukiyono-machi, Japan)
  USE Ogawajō (Tsukiyono-machi, Japan)
Ogawa family (Not Subd Geog)
Ogawajō (Shigaraki-chō, Japan)
  UF Ogawa Castle (Shigaraki-chō, Japan)
  BT Castles—Japan
Ogawajō (Tsukiyono-machi, Japan)
  UF Ogawa Castle (Tsukiyono-machi,
        Japan)
  BT Castles—Japan
Ogbia dialect
  USE Abua-Ogbia languages
Ogboni (Cult)
    ⌜BL2480.Y6⌝
  BT Cults—Nigeria
        Yorubas—Religion
Ogborn family
  USE Ogburn family
Ogborne family
  USE Ogburn family
Ogbourn family
  USE Ogburn family
Ogbourne family
  USE Ogburn family
Ogburn family (Not Subd Geog)
  UF Ogborn family
        Ogborne family
        Ogbourn family
        Ogbourne family
        Ogburne family
Ogburne family
  USE Ogburn family
Ogcocephalidae
    ⌜QL638.O3⌝
  UF Batfishes
        Maltheidae
        Malthidae
        Onchocephalidae
        Oncocephalidae
  BT Anglerfishes
  NT Dibranchus
Ogcodes
    ⌜QL537.A3⌝
  UF Oncodes
        Onkodes
  BT Acroceridae
Ogden family (Not Subd Geog)
  UF Octdon family
        Ogdon family
Ogdon family
  USE Ogden family
Ogee wings (Airplanes)
  USE Airplanes—Wings, Ogee
Ogeechee River (Ga.)
  UF Big Ogeechee River (Ga.)
        Great Hogoheeche River (Ga.)
        Great Ogeechee River (Ga.)
  BT Rivers—Georgia
Ogelsby family
  USE Ogilvie family
Ogg family (Not Subd Geog)
Ogham alphabet (May Subd Geog)
    ⌜PB1217⌝
  UF Ogam alphabet
        Ogum alphabet
  BT Inscriptions, Irish
        Irish language—Alphabet
Oghuz
  UF Ghuzz
        Guzy
        Oguz
        Toquz Oghuz
        Uzy
  BT Ethnology—Asia, Central
        Turks
  NT Gagauzi

Kashkai tribe
  Seljuks
  Turkmen
Oghuz epic literature
  USE Epic literature, Oghuz
Oghuz language
  BT Turkic languages
        Turkic languages, Southwest
Oghuz literature
  NT Epic literature, Oghuz
Oghuz Turkic languages
  USE Turkic languages, Southwest
Ogiek
  USE Dorobo (African people)
Ōgijō (Hōrai-chō, Japan)
  USE Nagashinojō (Hōrai-chō, Japan)
Ogilby family
  USE Ogilvie family
Ogilvie family (Not Subd Geog)
  UF Ogelsby family
        Ogilby family
        Ogilvy family
        Oglebay family
        Oglesbee family
        Oglesby family
Ogilvy family
  USE Ogilvie family
Ogino family (Not Subd Geog)
Ōgiyama Iseki (Tokyo, Japan)
  USE Ōgiyama Site (Tokyo, Japan)
Ōgiyama Site (Tokyo, Japan)
    (Not Subd Geog)
  UF Ōgiyama Iseki (Tokyo, Japan)
  BT Japan—Antiquities
Oglala Indians
    ⌜E99.O3⌝
  UF Ogallalla Indians
  BT Dakota Indians
        Indians of North America
        Siouan Indians
  — Government relations
      NT Wounded Knee (S.D.)—History—
            Indian occupation, 1973
Ogle family (Not Subd Geog)
  UF Ogles family
Oglebay family
  USE Ogilvie family
Ogles family
  USE Ogle family
Oglesbee family
  USE Ogilvie family
Oglesby family
  USE Ogilvie family
Ogletree family (Not Subd Geog)
Ogmore River (Wales)
  USE Ogwr River (Wales)
OGO
  USE Orbiting geophysical observatories
Ōgo Castle (Kōbe-shi, Japan)
  USE Ōgojō (Kōbe-shi, Japan)
Ōgojō (Kōbe-shi, Japan)
  UF Kamiyamajō (Kōbe-shi, Japan)
        Ōgo Castle (Kōbe-shi, Japan)
  BT Castles—Japan
Ogoni language
  USE Kana language
Ogontz plan
  BT Students, Interchange of
Ogopogo
    ⌜QL89.2.O34⌝
  BT Sea monsters
O'Gorman family
  USE Gorman family
Ogōshibaru Iseki (Nishigōshi-machi, Japan)
  USE Ogōshibaru Site (Nishigōshi-machi,
        Japan)
Ogōshibaru Site (Nishigōshi-machi, Japan)
    (Not Subd Geog)
  UF Ogōshibaru Iseki (Nishigōshi-machi,
        Japan)
  BT Japan—Antiquities

O'Grady family
  USE Grady family
Ogram family (Not Subd Geog)
Ogre-faced spiders
  USE Dinopidae
Ogres
  USE Ghouls and ogres
Ogrizović family
  USE Ogrizovich family
Ogrizovich family (Not Subd Geog)
  UF Ogrizović family
Ogum alphabet
  USE Ogham alphabet
Ogura family (Not Subd Geog)
Ogura hyakunin isshu karuta (Game)
  USE Utagaruta (Game)
Oguz
  USE Oghuz
Ogwr River (Wales)
  UF Ogmore River (Wales)
  BT Rivers—Wales
Ohai Railway
  BT Railroads—New Zealand
Ohanian family (Not Subd Geog)
O'Hanrahan family
  USE Hanrahan family
O'Hara family (Not Subd Geog)
  UF Harrah family
        O'Harra family
Ohara ikebana
  USE Flower arrangement, Japanese—Ohara
        school
O'Harra family
  USE O'Hara family
Ohel Moshe (Jerusalem) (Not Subd Geog)
    ⌜DS109.8.O33⌝
  UF Jerusalem. Ohel Moshe
        Jerusalem. Ohel Mosheh
        Jerusalem. Shekhunat Ohel Mosheh
        Ohel Mosheh (Jerusalem)
        Shekhunat Ohel Mosheh (Jerusalem)
Ohel Mosheh (Jerusalem)
  USE Ohel Moshe (Jerusalem)
Ohia dieback (May Subd Geog)
  BT Dieback
        Ohia-lehua—Diseases and pests
        Ohia-lehua—Ecology
Ohia-lehua (May Subd Geog)
    ⌜QK495.M9⌝
  UF Lehua tree
        Metrosideros collina
        Metrosideros polymorpha
        Ohia tree
  — Diseases and pests
      NT Ohia dieback
  — Ecology
      NT Ohia dieback
Ohia tree
  USE Ohia-lehua
Ohio
  — Antiquities
      NT Edwin Harness Mound (Ohio)
            Kramer Village Site (Ohio)
            Locust Site (Ohio)
            Tower Site (Ohio)
            White Rocks Rockshelter (Ohio)
            Wise Rockshelter (Ohio)
  — Description and travel
  — — 1951-1980
  — — 1981-
  — History
      ⌜F486-500⌝
  — — To 1787
  — — Revolution, 1775-1783
        ⌜E263.O⌝
      NT Crawford's Indian Campaign,
            1782
  — — 1787-1865
  — — War of 1812
        ⌜E359.5.O2⌝
  — — War with Mexico, 1845-1848

2660

[E409.5.O]
— — Civil War, 1861-1865
[E525]
— — 1865-
[F496]
— — War of 1898
[E726.O3]
— Politics and government
— — 1787-1865
— — Civil War, 1861-1865
— — 1865-1950
— — 1951-
Ohio and Erie Canal (Ohio)
BT Canals—Ohio
Ohio River
— Navigation
Ohio River Valley
UF Ohio Valley
— **Antiquities** *(Not Subd Geog)*
NT Fort Ancient culture
— **Description and travel**
— — 1951-1980
— — 1981-
— **History**
— — To 1795
[F517]
— — Revolution, 1775-1783
[E230.5]
— — Civil War, 1861-1865
[E470.4]
Ohio Tests of Articulation and Perception of Sounds
UF OTAPS
BT Children—Language—Testing
Educational tests and measurements
Ohio Valley
USE Ohio River Valley
Ohlhausen family *(Not Subd Geog)*
UF Von Ohlhausen family
Ohlone Indians
USE Costanoan Indians
Ohmic contacts
[TK7872.C67]
BT Electric contactors
Semiconductor-metal boundaries
Semiconductors
Ohmmeter
BT Electric meters
RT Voltohmmeter
Ohm's law
[QC607]
NT Electric measurements
Ohod, Battle of, 625
USE Uḥud, Battle of, 625
Ohōtsuku culture
USE Okhotsk culture
Ohotsuku-kai
USE Okhotsk, Sea of
Ohrid trout
[QL638.S2]
UF Salmo letnica
Trutta balcanica
BT Salmo
Trout
Ohrig family
USE Orwig family
O'Hurley family
USE Hurley family
Oiampi language
USE Oyampi language
Oidiomycosis
USE Candidiasis
Oidipos (Greek mythology)
USE Oedipus (Greek mythology)
Oikos (The Greek word)
BT Greek language, Biblical—Etymology
Oikos tou Dionysou (New Paphos)
USE House of Dionysus (New Paphos)
Oil
USE Mineral oils
Oils and fats

Petroleum
Oil, Holy
USE Holy oils
Oil adjuvant vaccines, Inactivated
USE Inactivated oil adjuvant vaccines
Oil analysis
[TP671]
UF Analysis of oil
BT Oils and fats
Oil and gas law
USE Gas, Natural—Law and legislation
Petroleum law and legislation
Oil and gas leases *(May Subd Geog)*
UF Gas and oil leases
Gas leases
Oil leases
Oil royalties
BT Gas, Natural—Law and legislation
Mining leases
Petroleum law and legislation
Oil as pesticide
[SB952.O4]
UF Oil pesticides
Oil spray pesticides
Petroleum pesticides
Spray oil as pesticide
BT Pesticides
Petroleum
Oil-bearing sands
USE Oil sands
Oil burner industry
[HD9999.O5]
BT Oil burners
Oil burners
[TH7466.O6 (Heating of buildings)]
UF Fuel oil burners
BT Heating
Petroleum as fuel
NT Argand burner
Oil burner industry
Oil cake
UF Oilcake
BT Oils and fats
Oilseed plants
Organic fertilizers
NT Cottonseed cake
Neem cake
Oil cake as feed
Oil cans, Tariff on
USE Tariff on oil cans
Oil-cloth
[TS1779.O5]
Oil conservation
USE Petroleum conservation
Oil-cups
USE Oil-feeders
Oil drilling platforms
USE Drilling platforms
Oil drums
USE Drums (Containers)
Oil emulsion vaccines, Inactivated
USE Inactivated oil adjuvant vaccines
Oil engines
USE Diesel motor
Oil-feeders
[TJ1079]
UF Oil-cups
BT Lubrication and lubricants
Lubrication systems
Oil field brines
UF Formation waters (Oil fields)
Oil field waters
BT Petroleum—Geology
Petroleum engineering
Saline waters
Water, Underground
Oil field chemicals
UF Chemicals, Oil field
BT Chemicals
NT Drilling muds

Oil field chemicals industry
(May Subd Geog)
Oil field equipment
USE Oil fields—Equipment and supplies
Oil field equipment and supplies industry
(May Subd Geog)
[HD9560-9579]
BT Oil fields—Equipment and supplies
Oil field flooding *(May Subd Geog)*
UF Oil wells—Flooding
Water flooding of oil wells
Water injection in oil fields
BT Oil fields—Production methods
Oil wells
Secondary recovery of oil
NT Miscible displacement (Petroleum engineering)
Oil field waters
USE Oil field brines
Oil field workers
USE Petroleum workers
Oil fields *(May Subd Geog)*
[TN860-879]
UF Oil lands
Oil pools
Petroleum fields
RT Petroleum
SA *headings beginning with the phrase* Oil field
NT Gas condensate reservoirs
Oil seepage
Oil wells
Petroleum—Reserves
Petroleum in submerged lands
Secondary recovery of oil
— **Equipment and supplies**
[TN871.5]
UF Oil field equipment
Petroleum—Equipment and supplies
BT Petroleum industry and trade—Equipment and supplies
NT Oil field equipment and supplies industry
Oil well pumps
Oil wells—Equipment and supplies
Paraffin deposition
Petroleum—Pipe lines
— — Appraisal
USE Oil fields—Equipment and supplies—Valuation
— — Valuation
[TN871.5]
UF Oil fields—Equipment and supplies—Appraisal
— **Hydraulic equipment**
— **Production methods**
[TN870]
BT Oil reservoir engineering
NT Oil field flooding
Oil well completion
Oil well drilling
Oil well pumps
Oil well shooting
Oil wells—Acidization
Oil wells—Artificial lift
Oil wells—Gas lift
Oil wells—Hydraulic fracturing
Petroleum mining
Secondary recovery of oil
— Repressuring
USE Secondary recovery of oil
— **Safety measures**
UF Oil wells—Safety measures
BT Petroleum industry and trade—Safety measures
— Secondary recovery operations
USE Secondary recovery of oil
— Unit operation
USE Unit operation of oil fields
— **Valuation** *(May Subd Geog)*

Oil fields
— Valuation *(Continued)*
    UF Oil land valuation
        Oil properties valuation
        Petroleum—Valuation
    BT Petroleum—Reserves
        Petroleum engineering
— Great Plains
    NT Williston Basin
— Peru
    NT Brea y Pariñas (Peru)
Oil fields, Offshore
  USE Petroleum in submerged lands
Oil fields, Unit operation of
  USE Unit operation of oil fields
Oil filters
    [TJ1081]
  BT Filters and filtration
      Lubricating oils
  NT Airplanes—Motors—Oil filters
      Automobiles—Motors—Oil filters
      Diesel locomotives—Oil filters
      Diesel motor—Oil filters
      Tractors—Motors—Oil filters
Oil flower plants *(May Subd Geog)*
  BT Flowers
      Oils and fats
      Plants
Oil-fuel
  USE Petroleum as fuel
Oil gas
  BT Cracking process
      Gas as fuel
  NT Oil gasification
Oil gasification
    [TP759]
  UF Gasification of oil
      Petroleum—Gasification
      Petroleum gasification
  BT Gas manufacture and works
      Oil gas
Oil gushers
  USE Gushers
Oil hydraulic machinery
    [TJ843]
  UF Hydraulic transmission
  BT Hydraulic machinery
      Hydraulic motors
      Power transmission
      Pumping machinery
  NT Diesel locomotives—Hydraulic drive
      Hydraulic couplings
      Hydraulic cylinders
      Hydraulic servomechanisms
      Hydraulic torque converters
      Machine-tools—Hydraulic drive
— Dynamics
— Fluid dynamics
— Vibration
    [TJ843]
Oil hydraulic machinery industry
(May Subd Geog)
Oil industries *(May Subd Geog)*
    [HD9490 (Economics)]
    [TP670-TP692]
    Here are entered works on the economic aspects
of oils and fats. Works on fat in its relation to the
animal organism are entered under Fat. Works on the
technological aspects of oils and fats are entered
under Oils and fats.
  UF Oilseed industry
      Vegetable oils
  RT Petroleum industry and trade
  SA *names of individual oils and oil*
      industries, e.g. Cottonseed oil;
      Linseed oil; Soybean oil industry
  NT Castor oil industry
      Mineral oils
      Oil industry workers
      Wages—Oil industries
— Collective labor agreements

  USE Collective labor agreements—Oil
       industries
— Taxation *(May Subd Geog)*
    RT Oils and fats—Taxation
Oil industry, Offshore
  USE Offshore oil industry
Oil industry workers *(May Subd Geog)*
  UF Oil workers
  BT Oil industries
  NT Petroleum workers
      Women oil industry workers
Oil inspection *(May Subd Geog)*
    [HD9560.9 (State reports)]
    [TP691 (Technology)]
  UF Gasoline inspection
      Inspection of oil
      Petroleum inspection
  RT Inflammable liquids
  NT Oil tagging
— Law and legislation *(May Subd Geog)*
    BT Petroleum law and legislation
Oil land valuation
  USE Oil fields—Valuation
Oil lands
  USE Oil fields
Oil leases
  USE Oil and gas leases
Oil migration
  USE Petroleum—Migration
Oil mills *(May Subd Geog)*
  BT Milling machinery
  NT Cottonseed oil mills
      Olive oil mills
      Soybean oil mills
Oil of guaiac wood
  USE Guaiac wood oil
Oil of henbane
  USE Hyoscyamus (Drug)
Oil of katchung
  USE Peanut oil
Oil of lavender
  USE Lavender oil
Oil of peppermint
  USE Peppermint-oil
Oil of petitgrain
  USE Petitgrain oil
Oil of rose
  USE Attar of roses
Oil-painting
  USE Painting
Oil-palm *(May Subd Geog)*
    [SB299.P3]
  UF African oil-palm
  BT Oilseed plants
      Palms
  NT Palm-oil
— Diseases and pests *(May Subd Geog)*
    NT Oil palm wilt
Oil palm wilt *(May Subd Geog)*
    [SB608.O27]
  UF Fusarium wilt of oil palm
      Wilt, Oil palm
  BT Oil-palm—Diseases and pests
      Wilt diseases
  RT Fusarium oxysporum
Oil pesticides
  USE Oil as pesticide
Oil platforms
  USE Drilling platforms
Oil pollution damages, Liability for
  USE Liability for oil pollution damages
Oil pollution of rivers, harbors, etc.
(May Subd Geog)
  BT Oil pollution of water
  RT Oil spills
  NT Oil spill booms
      Oil spills and wildlife
      Oil tagging
— Law and legislation *(May Subd Geog)*
    NT Liability for oil pollution damages

Oil pollution of soils
    [TD879.P4]
  UF Petroleum pollution of soils
      Soils—Oil pollution
  BT Soil pollution
Oil pollution of the sea *(May Subd Geog)*
  UF Marine oil pollution
  BT Marine pollution
      Oil pollution of water
  RT Oil spills
— Law and legislation *(May Subd Geog)*
    BT Maritime law
    NT Liability for oil pollution damages
Oil pollution of water *(May Subd Geog)*
    [TD427.P4]
  UF Petroleum pollution of water
      Water—Oil pollution
  BT Oil spills
      Petroleum waste
      Water—Pollution
  NT Oil pollution of rivers, harbors, etc.
      Oil pollution of the sea
      Oil separators
Oil pools
  USE Oil fields
Oil poppy
  USE Opium poppy
Oil properties valuation
  USE Oil fields—Valuation
Oil reclamation
  USE Petroleum waste—Recycling
Oil recovery, Thermal
  USE Thermal oil recovery
Oil refineries
  USE Petroleum refineries
Oil removal (Sewage purification)
  USE Sewage—Purification—Oil removal
Oil reserves
  USE Petroleum—Reserves
Oil reservoir engineering
    [TN871]
  BT Petroleum engineering
  NT Oil fields—Production methods
      Oil saturation in reservoirs
      Reservoir oil pressure
Oil royalties
  USE Oil and gas leases
Oil sands *(May Subd Geog)*
  UF Bituminous sand
      Oil-bearing sands
      Tar sand
  BT Oil-shales
      Petroleum—Geology
— Law and legislation *(May Subd Geog)*
    BT Petroleum law and legislation
— Permeability
    NT Formation damage (Petroleum
       engineering)
Oil sands extraction plants
(May Subd Geog)
  BT Oil sands industry
      Petroleum refineries
Oil sands industry *(May Subd Geog)*
  BT Petroleum industry and trade
  NT Oil sands extraction plants
Oil sardine, Indian
  USE Sardinella longiceps
Oil saturation in reservoirs
  UF Reservoir oil saturation
      Residual oil saturation in reservoirs
      Saturation of oil in reservoirs
  BT Oil reservoir engineering
      Secondary recovery of oil
Oil seed plants
  USE Oilseed plants
Oil seeds
  USE Oilseeds
Oil seep
  USE Oil seepage
Oil seepage *(May Subd Geog)*
  UF Oil seep

BT Oil fields
  Petroleum
  Seepage
Oil separators
  UF Oil skimmers
    Oil-water separators
    Separators, Oil
  BT Oil pollution of water
    Separators (Machines)
    Water—Purification
  NT Oil spill booms
Oil-shale industry *(May Subd Geog)*
  BT Oil-shales
    Petroleum industry and trade
  NT Shale oils—Refining
  — Equipment and supplies
    [TP699]
Oil shale reserves
  USE Oil-shales—Reserves
Oil-shales *(May Subd Geog)*
  [TN858-859]
  BT Caustobioliths
    Energy minerals
    Fossil fuels
  NT Kerogen
    Oil sands
    Oil-shale industry
    Petroleum
    Sapropelites
    Shale oils
  — Reserves
    UF Oil shale reserves
      Reserves of oil-shale
Oil silk
  [TS1669]
  UF Oilsilk
    Silk, Oiled
  BT Silk
    Waterproofing of fabrics
Oil skimmers
  USE Oil separators
Oil slick containment booms
  USE Oil spill booms
Oil spill booms *(May Subd Geog)*
  UF Booms, Oil spill
    Oil slick containment booms
  BT Oil pollution of rivers, harbors, etc.
    Oil separators
    Oil spills
Oil spill damages, Liability for
  USE Liability for oil pollution damages
Oil spills *(May Subd Geog)*
  BT Waste spills
  RT Oil pollution of rivers, harbors, etc.
    Oil pollution of the sea
  NT Oil pollution of water
    Oil spill booms
    Oil spills and wildlife
  — Claims
    UF Claims against oil spill damage
    RT Liability for oil pollution damages
  — Environmental aspects
    (May Subd Geog)
    NT Oil spills and wildlife
  — Law and legislation *(May Subd Geog)*
    BT Environmental law
      Petroleum law and legislation
    NT Liability for oil pollution damages
Oil spills and wildlife *(May Subd Geog)*
  BT Oil pollution of rivers, harbors, etc.
    Oil spills
    Oil spills—Environmental aspects
    Wildlife conservation
Oil spray pesticides
  USE Oil as pesticide
Oil storage tanks
  [TP692.5]
  BT Petroleum—Storage
    Storage tanks
  RT Petroleum—Offshore storage
  — Evaporation control

[TP692.5]
  BT Evaporation control
— Insulation
  BT Insulation (Heat)
Oil stoves
  USE Stoves, Oil
Oil tagging
  [TD427.P4]
  BT Oil inspection
    Oil pollution of rivers, harbors, etc.
    Petroleum products—Analysis
Oil tankers
  USE Tankers
Oil-water separators
  USE Oil separators
Oil well blowouts
  USE Oil wells—Blowouts
Oil well boring
  USE Oil well drilling
Oil well casing
  UF Casing, Oil well
  BT Oil well drilling
    Oil wells—Equipment and supplies
  NT Casinghead gas
  — Cathodic protection
  — Welding
Oil well cementing
  UF Oil well plugging
  BT Oil well drilling
    Oil wells—Maintenance and repair
Oil well completion
  UF Oil wells—Completion
  BT Oil fields—Production methods
    Oil well drilling
Oil well drilling *(May Subd Geog)*
  [TN871.2]
  UF Drilling, Oil well
    Oil well boring
    Petroleum—Well-boring
    Well drilling, Oil
  BT Boring
    Oil fields—Production methods
    Petroleum engineering
  NT Air drilling (Petroleum engineering)
    Drilling muds
    Formation damage (Petroleum
      engineering)
    Gas drilling (Petroleum engineering)
    Oil well casing
    Oil well cementing
    Oil well completion
    Oil wells—Blowouts
  — Automation
    UF Oil well drilling rigs—Automatic
      control
  — Finance
  — — Law and legislation
    (May Subd Geog)
  — Law and legislation *(May Subd Geog)*
    BT Petroleum law and legislation
  — Lost circulation
    UF Lost circulation in oil well drilling
    BT Drilling muds
Oil well drilling, Electric
  [TN871.2]
Oil well drilling, Submarine
  (May Subd Geog)
  [TN871.3]
  UF Deep-water drilling (Petroleum)
    Marine oil operations
    Offshore drilling (Petroleum)
    Offshore oil operations
    Subaqueous well-boring (Petroleum)
    Submarine oil well drilling
    Underwater drilling (Petroleum)
  BT Ocean bottom (Maritime law)
    Ocean mining
    Offshore oil industry
    Petroleum engineering
    Petroleum in submerged lands
  NT Drilling platforms

Offshore support vessels
    Riser pipe
  — Law and legislation *(May Subd Geog)*
    BT Offshore structures (International
      law)
      Petroleum law and legislation
Oil well drilling fluids
  USE Drilling muds
Oil well drilling muds
  USE Drilling muds
Oil well drilling rigs
  [TN871.5]
  UF Drilling rigs, Oil well
    Rigs, Oil well drilling
  BT Cranes, derricks, etc.
    Oil wells—Equipment and supplies
  NT Bits (Drilling and boring)
    Drill pipe
    Drill stem
    Drilling platforms
    Ocean Ranger (Drilling rig)
  — Automatic control
    USE Oil well drilling—Automation
  — Electric driving
  — Vibration
Oil well equipment
  USE Oil wells—Equipment and supplies
Oil well logging *(May Subd Geog)*
  [TN871.35]
  UF Logging, Oil well
    Well logging, Oil
  BT Borings
    Geology, Stratigraphic
    Petroleum—Geology
    Petroleum engineering
  NT Mud logging
Oil well logging, Acoustic
  UF Acoustic logging (Oil wells)
    Acoustic well logging
    Sonic well logging
  BT Acoustical engineering
    Petroleum—Geology
    Petroleum engineering
Oil well logging, Electric
  [TN871.35]
  UF Electric logging (Oil wells)
    Electric well logging
  BT Electric measurements
    Petroleum—Geology
    Petroleum engineering
Oil well logging, Radiation
  [TN871.35]
  UF Radiation logging (Oil wells)
    Radioactivity logs
  BT Petroleum—Geology
    Petroleum engineering
    Radiation well logging
    Radioactive prospecting
Oil well maintenance
  USE Oil wells—Maintenance and repair
Oil well plugging
  USE Oil well cementing
Oil well pumps
  UF Petroleum—Pumping
  BT Oil fields—Equipment and supplies
    Oil fields—Production methods
    Oil wells—Artificial lift
    Oil wells—Equipment and supplies
    Pumping machinery
  NT Sucker rods
  — Electric driving
  — Transmission devices
    [TN871.5]
    BT Gearing
      Power transmission
Oil well servicing
  USE Oil wells—Maintenance and repair
Oil well shooting
  UF Oil well torpedoing
  BT Oil fields—Production methods

Oil well torpedoing
USE Oil well shooting
Oil well workover
USE Oil wells—Maintenance and repair
Oil wells *(May Subd Geog)*
  UF Wells, Oil
  BT Oil fields
     Petroleum engineering
  RT Gas wells
  SA *headings beginning with the phrase* Oil
     well
  NT Condensate oil wells
     Gushers
     Oil field flooding
  — Acidization
    UF Acidization of oil wells
    BT Oil fields—Production methods
  — Artificial lift
    UF Artificial lift (Oil wells)
    BT Oil fields—Production methods
    NT Oil well pumps
      Oil wells—Gas lift
  — Blowouts
    UF Blow outs, Oil well
      Blowouts, Oil well
      Oil well blowouts
    BT Oil well drilling
  — Completion
    USE Oil well completion
  — Equipment and supplies
    UF Oil well equipment
    BT Oil fields—Equipment and supplies
    NT Boring machinery
      Inclinometer
      Mud pumps
      Oil well casing
      Oil well drilling rigs
      Oil well pumps
      Turbodrills
      Well packers
  — — Repairing
      USE Oil wells—Maintenance and
        repair
  — Flooding
    USE Oil field flooding
  — Gas lift
    UF Gas-lift (Petroleum)
      Petroleum—Pumping
    BT Air lift pumps
      Oil fields—Production methods
      Oil wells—Artificial lift
      Secondary recovery of oil
    RT Gas lift pumps
  — Hydraulic fracturing
    BT Hydraulic fracturing
      Oil fields—Production methods
  — Maintenance and repair
    UF Oil well maintenance
      Oil well servicing
      Oil well workover
      Oil wells—Equipment and supplies
        —Repairing
      Oil wells—Repairing
      Oil wells—Servicing
      Oil wells—Workover
    NT Oil well cementing
  — Repairing
    USE Oil wells—Maintenance and
      repair
  — Safety measures
    USE Oil fields—Safety measures
  — Sand control
    UF Sand control in oil wells
      Sand exclusion in oil wells
      Silt control in oil wells
    BT Soil stabilization
  — Servicing
    USE Oil wells—Maintenance and
      repair
  — Testing
    NT Drill stem testing

— Workover
    USE Oil wells—Maintenance and
      repair
Oil workers
  USE Oil industry workers
     Petroleum workers
Oilcake
  USE Oil cake
Oilcloth flowers
  USE Anthuriums
Oilfishes, Baikal
  USE Comephoridae
Oils, Essential
  USE Essences and essential oils
Oils, Insulating
  USE Electric insulators and insulation—Oils
Oils, Lubricating
  USE Lubricating oils
Oils, Synthetic
  USE Synthetic lubricants
Oils and fats
  [TP670-TP695]
  Here are entered works on the technological aspects of oils and fats. Works on the economic aspects of oils and fats are entered under Oil industries. Works on fat in its relation to the animal organism are entered under Fat.
  UF Animal oils
     Fats
     Grease
     Oil
     Vegetable oils
  RT Lubrication and lubricants
     Rendering industry
     Seed products
  SA *particular oils, e.g.* Cottonseed oil,
     Linseed-oil, Rosin-oil
  NT Butterfat
     Cashew oil
     Castor oil
     Corn oil
     Drying oils
     Electric insulators and insulation—Oils
     Essences and essential oils
     Evening primrose oil
     Marine animal oils
     Mineral oils
     Oil analysis
     Oil cake
     Oil flower plants
     Oilseed plants
     Oilseeds
     Ointments
     Oleoresins
     Petroleum
     Rancidity
     Rape oil
     Rice oil
     Sal seed oil
     Silkworm oil
     Stearin
     Sulphonated oils
     Tallow
     Vegetable oils as fuel
     Wheat germ oil
     Wool-fat
  — Analysis
    [TP671]
    NT Oilseeds—Analysis
  — Bacteriology
    USE Oils and fats—Microbiology
  — Flavor and odor
    BT Flavor
      Odors
  — Law and legislation *(May Subd Geog)*
  — Microbiology
    UF Oils and fats—Bacteriology
  — Permeability
  — Spectra
  — Taxation
    RT Oil industries—Taxation

Oils and fats, Edible
  UF Edible oils and fats
     Shortenings
  SA *particular fats and oils, e.g.* Butter;
     Olive-oil
  NT Cocoa butter
     Essences and essential oils
     Food—Fat content
     Margarine
     Suet
  — Deterioration
    [TX560.O3]
    UF Deterioration of edible oils and fats
  — Tariff
    USE Tariff on edible oils and fats
Oils and fats in animal nutrition
  (May Subd Geog)
  [SF98.O34]
  BT Animal nutrition
Oilseed industry
  USE Oil industries
Oilseed plants *(May Subd Geog)*
  [SB298-SB299]
  UF Oil seed plants
  BT Botany, Economic
     Field crops
     Food crops
     Hydrocarbon-producing plants
     Oils and fats
     Plants, Cultivated
     Seed crops
  NT Camellia oleifera
     Candlenut tree
     Castor oil plant
     Cnidoscolus marcgravii
     Coconut palm
     Cotton
     Flax
     Jojoba
     Margosa
     Oil cake
     Oil-palm
     Oiticica tree
     Olive
     Opium poppy
     Peanuts
     Rape (Plant)
     Safflower
     Sal
     Sesame
     Soybean
     Sunflowers
     Tung tree
  — Diseases and pests *(May Subd Geog)*
  — Research *(May Subd Geog)*
  — Seed
    USE Oilseeds
Oilseeds *(May Subd Geog)*
  UF Oil seeds
     Oilseed plants—Seed
  BT Oils and fats
     Seeds
  NT Castor beans
     Flaxseed
  — Analysis
    BT Oils and fats—Analysis
Oilsilk
  USE Oil silk
Oinochoai
  USE Oenochoes
Oinophilia
  [QL561.T55]
  BT Tineidae
Oinophilidae
  USE Tineidae
Ointments
  [RS201.O3]
  UF Salves

BT Cosmetics
    Drugs—Dosage forms
    Oils and fats
    Solid dosage forms
NT Barrier creams
    Mollin

Oirat language
    [PL431.O]
UF Oyrat language
BT China—Languages
    Mongolia—Languages
    Mongolian languages
RT Kalmyk language
Oirat language (Turkic)
   USE Altai language

Oirats *(May Subd Geog)*
    [DS798.42]
UF Mongols, Western
    Oyrats
BT Ethnology—China
    Ethnology—Mongolia
    Mongols
NT Kalmyks
Oirot language
   USE Altai language
Oirots
   USE Altais
Oisans (France) *(Not Subd Geog)*
Oiseau River (Ont. and Man.)
BT Rivers—Manitoba
    Rivers—Ontario
Ōishi family *(Not Subd Geog)*
Ōishidaira Iseki (Rokkasho-mura, Japan)
   USE Ōishidaira Site (Rokkasho-mura,
     Japan)
Ōishidaira Site (Rokkasho-mura, Japan)
   (Not Subd Geog)
UF Ōishidaira Iseki (Rokkasho-mura,
    Japan)
BT Japan—Antiquities
Oithona
    [QL444.C73]
BT Oithonidae
Oithonidae
    [QL444.C73]
BT Cyclopoida
NT Oithona
    Paroithona
Oiticica oil
BT Drying oils
    Oiticica tree
Oiticica tree
BT Oilseed plants
NT Oiticica oil
Oittisen family *(Not Subd Geog)*
Ojai Valley (Calif.)
BT Valleys—California
Ojarikoelle Indians
   USE Oyaricoulet Indians
Ojców National Park (Poland)
   USE Ojcowski Park Narodowy (Poland)
Ojcowski Park Narodowy (Poland)
UF Ojców National Park (Poland)
BT National parks and reserves—Poland
Oji language
   USE Twi language
Oji Seishi Strike, 1958
Ojibwa Indians
   USE Chippewa Indians
Ojibwa language
   USE Chippewa language
Ojime *(May Subd Geog)*
    [NK3650 (Art industries)]
    [TS2301.B4 (Technology)]
BT Art objects, Japanese
    Beads
    Inro
    Netsukes
Ojito Wilderness (N.M.) *(Not Subd Geog)*
UF Ojito Wilderness Study Area (N.M.)

BT National parks and reserves—New
    Mexico
    Wilderness areas—New Mexico
Ojito Wilderness Study Area (N.M.)
   USE Ojito Wilderness (N.M.)
Ojo de Dios (Talisman)
UF Crosses, String (Talisman)
    Eye of God (Talisman)
    God's eye (Talisman)
    String crosses (Talisman)
BT Eye—Religious aspects
    Indian craft
    Indians of Mexico—Textile industry
     and fabrics
    Indians of North America—Southwest,
     New—Textile industry and fabrics
    Talismans
Ojo language
   USE Ijo language
Ojocaliente Hacienda (Mexico)
   (Not Subd Geog)
UF Hacienda de Ojocaliente (Mexico)
BT Haciendas—Mexico
Ok (Papua New Guinea people)
    [DU740.42]
BT Ethnology—Papua New Guinea
Oka family *(Not Subd Geog)*
Oka Indians
    [E99.O]
BT Algonquian Indians
    Indians of North America
    Iroquoian Indians
    Iroquois Indians
    Nipissing Indians
Oka River (R.S.F.S.R.)
BT Rivers—Russian S.F.S.R.
Okaina language
   USE Ocaina language
Okamura Iseki (Japan)
   USE Okamura Site (Japan)
Okamura Site (Japan) *(Not Subd Geog)*
UF Okamura Iseki (Japan)
BT Japan—Antiquities
Okanagan River (B.C. and Wash.)
UF Okanogan River (B.C. and Wash.)
    Okinakane River (B.C. and Wash.)
BT Rivers—British Columbia
    Rivers—Washington (State)
Okanogan Indians
   USE Okinagan Indians
Okanogan River (B.C. and Wash.)
   USE Okanagan River (B.C. and Wash.)
Okapi
    [QL737.U5]
BT Giraffes
Okara-Dipalpur Road (Pakistan)
   USE Dipalpur-Okara Road (Pakistan)
Okatibbee Lake (Miss.) *(Not Subd Geog)*
UF Okatibbee Reservoir (Miss.)
BT Lakes—Mississippi
    Reservoirs—Mississippi
Okatibbee Reservoir (Miss.)
   USE Okatibbee Lake (Miss.)
Okavango River
UF Cubango River
    Kubango River
    Okovanggo River
    Rio Cubango
BT Rivers—Angola
    Rivers—Botswana
    Rivers—Namibia
Ōkawa family *(Not Subd Geog)*
Ōkawachi family
   USE Ōkōchi family
Okayama Castle (Minakuchi-chō, Japan)
   USE Okayamajō (Minakuchi-chō, Japan)
Okayamajō (Japan)
   USE Mizukuki Okayamajō (Japan)

Okayamajō (Minakuchi-chō, Japan)
UF Minakuchijō (Minakuchi-chō, Japan)
    Okayama Castle (Minakuchi-chō,
     Japan)
BT Castles—Japan
Okayamajō (Okayama-shi, Japan)
UF Ishiyamajō (Okayama-shi, Japan)
    Karasujō (Okayama-shi, Japan)
BT Castles—Japan
Okazaki family *(Not Subd Geog)*
Okechobee, Battle of, 1837
    [E83.835]
BT Seminole War, 2d, 1835-1842
Okeechobee, Lake (Fla.)
UF Lake Okeechobee (Fla.)
BT Lakes—Florida
O'Keefe family *(Not Subd Geog)*
UF O'Keeffe family
O'Keeffe family
   USE O'Keefe family
Okefenoke Swamp (Ga. and Fla.)
   USE Okefenokee Swamp (Ga. and Fla.)
Okefenokee Swamp (Ga. and Fla.)
UF Okefenoke Swamp (Ga. and Fla.)
    Okefinokee Swamp (Ga. and Fla.)
BT Swamps—Florida
    Swamps—Georgia
Okefinokee Swamp (Ga. and Fla.)
   USE Okefenokee Swamp (Ga. and Fla.)
Okehazama (Japan), Battle of, 1560
UF Okehazama no kassen, Japan, 1560
    Okehazama no tatakai, Japan, 1560
BT Japan—History—Period of civil wars,
    1480-1603
Okehazama no kassen, Japan, 1560
   USE Okehazama (Japan), Battle of, 1560
Okehazama no tatakai, Japan, 1560
   USE Okehazama (Japan), Battle of, 1560
Okeina language
   USE Korape language
Okela language
   USE Kela language
Okeley family
   USE Oakley family
O'Kelia family
   USE Kelley family
O'Kelley family
   USE Kelley family
O'Kelly (Name)
O'Kelly family
   USE Kelley family
Okely family
   USE Oakley family
Okes family
   USE Oakes family
Okhotsk, Sea of
UF Lamutski
    Ohotsuku-kai
    Okhotskoe More
    Okhotskoye More
    Sea of Okhotsk
    Tungunski
BT Pacific Ocean
Okhotsk culture *(May Subd Geog)*
    [GN776.3.O35]
UF Ohōtsuku culture
BT Neolithic period
— **Japan**
Okhotskoe More
   USE Okhotsk, Sea of
Okhotskoye More
   USE Okhotsk, Sea of
Oki Archipelago (Japan)
   USE Oki Islands (Japan)
Ōki family *(Not Subd Geog)*
Oki Guntō (Japan)
   USE Oki Islands (Japan)

Oki Islands (Japan)
UF Oki Archipelago (Japan)
   Oki Guntō (Japan)
   Oki no Shima (Japan)
   Oki Rettō (Japan)
   Oki-shotō (Japan)
BT Archipelagoes—Japan
   Islands—Japan
Oki-kaikyō (Japan)
USE Oki Strait (Japan)
Oki no Shima (Japan)
USE Oki Islands (Japan)
Oki Rettō (Japan)
USE Oki Islands (Japan)
Oki-shotō (Japan)
USE Oki Islands (Japan)
Oki Strait (Japan) *(Not Subd Geog)*
UF Oki-kaikyō (Japan)
BT Straits—Japan
Oki Unomarujō (Yunotsu-machi, Japan)
USE Unomarujō (Yunotsu-machi, Japan)
Okidata printers
BT Printers (Data processing systems)
Okierabu Island (Japan)
USE Okinoerabu Island (Japan)
O'Killey family
USE Kelley family
O'Killia family
USE Kelley family
Okimijo (Shingū-shi, Japan)
USE Shingūjō (Shingū-shi, Japan)
Okinaga family *(Not Subd Geog)*
Okinagan Indians
   [E99.O]
UF Okanogan Indians
BT Indians of North America
   Salishan Indians
Okinagan language
   [PM2066]
RT Salishan languages
Okinakane River (B.C. and Wash.)
USE Okanagan River (B.C. and Wash.)
Okinawa, Battle of, 1945
USE World War, 1939-1945—Campaigns—
   Japan—Okinawa Island
Okinawa Island (Japan)
BT Islands—Japan
Okinawa woodpecker
USE Sapheopipo noguchii
Okinawan art
USE Art, Ryukyu
Okinawan fiction
USE Ryukyu fiction
Okinawan language
USE Ryukyu language
Okinawan poetry
USE Ryukyu poetry
Okinawans
USE Ryukyuans
Okininoerabu Island (Japan)
USE Okinoerabu Island (Japan)
Okinnarabe Island (Japan)
USE Okinoerabu Island (Japan)
Okino-daitō Island, Battle of, 1945
BT World War, 1939-1945—Campaigns—
   Japan
Okinoerabu Island (Japan)
UF Okierabu Island (Japan)
   Okininoerabu Island (Japan)
   Okinnarabe Island (Japan)
   Okinoerabu-jima (Japan)
   Okinoerabu-shima (Japan)
BT Amami Islands (Japan)
   Islands—Japan
Okinoerabu-jima (Japan)
USE Okinoerabu Island (Japan)
Okinoerabu-shima (Japan)
USE Okinoerabu Island (Japan)
Okishio Castle (Yumesaki-chō, Japan)
USE Okishiojō (Yumesaki-chō, Japan)

Okishiojō (Yumesaki-chō, Japan)
UF Fujimarujō (Yumesaki-chō, Japan)
   Okishio Castle (Yumesaki-chō, Japan)
BT Castles—Japan
Okisuga Iseki (Tamano-shi, Japan)
USE Okisuga Site (Tamano-shi, Japan)
Okisuga Site (Tamano-shi, Japan)
UF Okisuga Iseki (Tamano-shi, Japan)
BT Japan—Antiquities
Okitama Region (Japan)
Okitsuke Iseki (Rokkasho-mura, Japan)
USE Okitsuke Site (Rokkasho-mura, Japan)
Okitsuke Site (Rokkasho-mura, Japan)
(Not Subd Geog)
UF Okitsuke Iseki (Rokkasho-mura,
   Japan)
BT Japan—Antiquities
Okkaligas
   [DS432.O4]
BT Caste—India
   Ethnology—India
Oklahoma
— Antiquities
   NT Bug Hill Site (Okla.)
      Edwards I Site (Okla.)
      Ferdinandina Site (Okla.)
      Grobin Davis Site (Okla.)
      Mahaffey Site (Okla.)
      Panhandle culture
      Roden Site (Okla.)
      Sallee G. Site (Okla.)
      Spiro Site (Okla.)
      Uncas Site (Okla.)
— Description and travel
— — 1951-1980
— — 1981-
— History
— — Land Rush, 1889
      [F699]
      UF Land Rush, Oklahoma, 1889
         Oklahoma Land Rush of 1889
— Languages
   NT Mikasuki language
— Politics and government
— — To 1907
— — 1907-
Oklahoma (Game)
   [GV1295.O4]
BT Rummy (Game)
Oklahoma Land Rush of 1889
USE Oklahoma—History—Land Rush, 1889
Oklawaha River (Fla.)
UF Ocklawaha River (Fla.)
   Oclawaha River (Fla.)
BT Rivers—Florida
Ōkōchi family *(Not Subd Geog)*
UF Ōkawachi family
Okochi Memorial Prize
Okototen
USE Kunten
Okouahou (African people)
USE Kwahu (African people)
Okoume
USE Aucoumea klaineana
Okovanggo River
USE Okavango River
Okpe language
   [PL8598.O357]
BT Kwa languages
   Nigeria—Languages
— Vowel harmony
   BT Grammar, Comparative and
      general—Vowel harmony
Okra
   [SB351.O]
UF Gumbo
RT Cookery (Okra)
Okrika dialect
   [PL8276.95.O]
BT Ijo language

Okrouhlé Hradiště Site (Czechoslovakia)
BT Czechoslovakia—Antiquities
Oksapmin (Papua New Guinea people)
   [DU740.42]
BT Ethnology—Papua New Guinea
— Children
   BT Children
Oksapmin language *(May Subd Geog)*
BT Papua New Guinea—Languages
   Papuan languages
Oksywie Hill (Poland)
UF Kępa Oksywska (Poland)
BT Moraines—Poland
Oksywie Hill (Poland), Battle of, 1939
BT World War, 1939-1945—Campaigns—
   Poland
Oktoberfest *(May Subd Geog)*
   [GT4380]
UF Octoberfest
BT Harvest festivals
Oktogon (Kassel, Germany)
USE Herkules-Bauwerk (Kassel, Germany)
Oku Tama Lake (Japan)
USE Okutama Lake (Japan)
Okuda family *(Not Subd Geog)*
Okujiri-jima (Japan)
USE Okushiri Island (Japan)
Ōkuma family *(Not Subd Geog)*
Okume
USE Aucoumea klaineana
Ōkuninushi no kami
   [BL2226.2.O48]
UF Ōnamuchi no kami
BT Gods, Shinto
   Mythology, Japanese
Ōkura Zaibatsu
   [HD2907]
BT Trusts, Industrial—Japan
Okusaka Iseki (Okayama-shi, Japan)
USE Okusaka Site (Okayama-shi, Japan)
Okusaka Site (Okayama-shi, Japan)
(Not Subd Geog)
UF Okusaka Iseki (Okayama-shi, Japan)
BT Japan—Antiquities
Okushibetsu-gawa (Japan)
USE Okushibetsu River (Japan)
Okushibetsu River (Japan)
UF Okushibetsu-gawa (Japan)
   Okushibetsugawa (Japan)
BT Rivers—Japan
Okushibetsugawa (Japan)
USE Okushibetsu River (Japan)
Okushiri Island (Japan)
UF Okujiri-jima (Japan)
   Okushiri-shima (Japan)
BT Islands—Japan
Okushiri-shima (Japan)
USE Okushiri Island (Japan)
Okushōgonji Iseki (Hōfu-shi, Japan)
USE Okushōgonji Site (Hōfu-shi, Japan)
Okushōgonji Site (Hōfu-shi, Japan)
(Not Subd Geog)
UF Okushōgonji Iseki (Hōfu-shi, Japan)
BT Japan—Antiquities
Okutadami-ko (Japan)
USE Okutadami Lake (Japan)
Okutadami Lake (Japan)
UF Ginzan-ko (Japan)
   Ginzan Lake (Japan)
   Okutadami-ko (Japan)
BT Lakes—Japan
Okutama-ko (Japan)
USE Okutama Lake (Japan)
Okutama Lake (Japan) *(Not Subd Geog)*
UF Oku Tama Lake (Japan)
   Okutama-ko (Japan)
   Okutamako (Japan)
BT Lakes—Japan
Okutamako (Japan)
USE Okutama Lake (Japan)

Okwasar language
USE Saberi language

Okwe
USE Ayo (Game)

Okwoga (African people)
USE Idoma (African people)

OL/2 (Computer program language)
[QA76.73.O]
UF Operator language/2

Ol alphabet
[PL4563.1]
BT Alphabet
Santali language—Alphabet

Olacaceae
[QK495.O35 (Botany)]
UF Aptandraceae
Cathedraceae
Chaunochitonaceae
Coulaceae
Heisteriaceae
Schoepfiaceae
Tetrastylidiaceae
Ximeniaceae
BT Santalales
NT Liriosma

Olacales
USE Santalales

Olallie Scenic Area (Or.)
BT Recreation areas—Oregon

Öland (Sweden)
BT Islands—Sweden

Olbers' comet *(Not Subd Geog)*
[QB723.O4]
BT Comets

Olbers' paradox
UF Paradox, Olbers'
BT Astronomy

Olbia (Ancient city) *(Not Subd Geog)*
UF Borysthenes (Ancient city)
Ol'biia (Ancient city)
Olbiopolis (Ancient city)
Ol'viia (Ancient city)
BT Cities and towns, Ruined, extinct, etc.
—Ukraine
Ukraine—Antiquities

Ol'biia (Ancient city)
USE Olbia (Ancient city)

Olbiopolis (Ancient city)
USE Olbia (Ancient city)

Olča language
USE Olcha language

Olcha
[DK759.O4]
UF Mangoon
Mangun
Ulcha
Ulchi
BT Ethnology—Russian S.F.S.R.
Tunguses

Olcha language *(May Subd Geog)*
[PL481.043]
UF Olča language
Ulcha language
BT Soviet Union—Languages
Tungus-Manchu languages

Old age *(May Subd Geog)*
[BJ1691 (Ethics)]
[HV1451-HV1493 (Charities)]
[QP86 (Physiology)]
UF Senescence
BT Adulthood
Age
Death—Causes
Gerontology
Life cycle, Human
Physiology
RT Longevity
Middle age

SA *subdivision* Biography—Last years and
death *under names of individual
literary authors; and subdivision*
Last years *under names of other
individual persons*
NT Aged
Aged, Killing of the
Aging
Retirement
— Diseases
USE Aged—Diseases
— Periodicals
USE Aged—Periodicals
— Psychological aspects
USE Aged—Psychology
— **Research**
UF Aged—Research
— **Simulation games**
BT Simulation methods

Old age and employment
USE Aged—Employment

Old age assistance *(May Subd Geog)*
BT Public welfare
Supplemental security income program
NT Aged—Energy assistance
Aged—Medical care
Aged—Pharmaceutical assistance
Old age homes
Old age pensions
— **Law and legislation** *(May Subd Geog)*

Old age depression
USE Depression in the aged

Old age homes *(May Subd Geog)*
[HV1454-HV1454.2]
Here are entered works on old age homes in gen-
eral, and when divided by place, old age homes locat-
ed in a particular place. The heading may be qualified
by ethnic group to indicate old age homes for a par-
ticular group of people located outside their place of
origin.
UF Homes (Institutions)
Homes for the aged
BT Aged—Dwellings
Aged—Institutional care
Asylums
Charities
Old age assistance
Public institutions
RT Almshouses
— **Law and legislation** *(May Subd Geog)*
BT Building laws
Charity laws and legislation

Old age homes, Jewish *(May Subd Geog)*
UF Jewish old age homes
BT Jews—Charities

Old age homes, Ukrainian *(May Subd Geog)*
UF Ukrainian old age homes

Old age in art
[N8234.O4]

Old age in literature
UF Aged in literature
BT Characters and characteristics in
literature
NT Shakespeare, William, 1564-1616—
Characters—Aged

Old age pensions *(May Subd Geog)*
[HD7105.3-HD7105.35]
Here are entered works on regular payments of
money to individuals who have retired from employ-
ment because of age, including payments to survivors
upon the death of the retiree. Works on benefits from
any source, public or private, made to survivors, are
entered under Survivors' benefits.
UF Labor and laboring classes—Insurance
Retirement pensions
Survivors' benefits (Old age pensions)
BT Employee fringe benefits
Old age assistance
Pensions
Retirement income
Social security
RT Welfare funds (Trade-union)

SA *subdivision* Pensions *under classes of
persons and ethnic groups*
NT Disability evaluation
Survivors' benefits
— **Cost-of-living adjustments**
(May Subd Geog)
— **Effect of inflation on**
BT Inflation (Finance)
— **Law and legislation** *(May Subd Geog)*
— **Retirement test**
Here are entered works on the provision in
pension plans by which one's pension benefits
are reduced in proportion as one's earned income
increases.
UF Earnings test (Old age pensions)
Retirement test (Old age pensions)
Social security—Earnings test
Social security—Retirement test
Social security—Work clause
— **Taxation** *(May Subd Geog)*
UF Taxation of pensions
BT Income tax
— — **Law and legislation**
(May Subd Geog)

Old age, survivors and disability insurance
USE Insurance, Disability
Social security

Old Anatolian Turkish language
USE Turkish language—To 1500

Old Appomattox Court House, Va.

Old Armenian language
USE Armenian language, Classical

Old Bactrian language
USE Avesta language

Old Believers
USE Raskolniks

Old Bond Street (London, England)
USE Bond Street (London, England)

Old Boston Post Road
USE Boston Post Roads

Old Boston Post Roads
USE Boston Post Roads

Old Bulgarian language
USE Church Slavic language

Old Burmese language
USE Burmese language—To 1500

Old Burying Ground (Athens, Pa.)
BT Cemeteries—Pennsylvania

Old Burying Ground (Beaufort, N.C.)
BT Cemeteries—North Carolina

Old Burying Ground (Fredericton, N.B.)
BT Cemeteries—New Brunswick

Old Burying Ground (South Windsor, Conn.)
BT Cemeteries—Connecticut

Old Byelorussian language
USE Byelorussian language—To 1700

Old Calendarists *(May Subd Geog)*
[BX620]
UF Calendarists, Old
Palaioimerologites
BT Christian sects

Old Castle (Erlangen, Germany)
USE Alte Schloss (Erlangen, Germany)

Old Catholic Church *(May Subd Geog)*
[BX4751-4793]
BT Jansenists
Old Catholicism
— **United States**

Old Catholicism
[BX4751-4793]
UF Catholicism, Old
Christian Catholicism
NT Old Catholic Church

Old Cemetery (Carmi, Ill.)
BT Cemeteries—Illinois

Old Cemetery (Pa.)
USE Stone Church Cemetery (Pa.)

Old Church Slavic language
USE Church Slavic language

Old City Cemetery (Nephi, Utah)
USE Nephi City Cemetery (Nephi, Utah)

Old City Cemetery (Vancouver, Wash.)
    BT Cemeteries—Washington (State)
Old City Hall (Lowell, Mass.)
    UF City Hall, Old (Lowell, Mass.)
        Lowell Town House (Lowell, Mass.)
        Town House (Lowell, Mass.)
    BT City halls—Massachusetts
        Lowell National Historical Park
        (Mass.)
Old City Hall (Munich, Germany)
    USE Altes Rathaus (Munich, Germany)
Old City Palace (Rio de Janeiro, Brazil)
    USE Paço da Cidade (Rio de Janeiro,
        Brazil)
Old Colony Mennonites
    [BX8129.04]
    BT Mennonites
Old Crossing treaty, 1863
    BT Chippewa Indians—Treaties
Old Danish proverbs
    USE Proverbs, Danish—To 1500
Old East Slavic language
    USE Russian language—To 1300
Old Ebenezer Cemetery (Washington, D.C.)
    USE Eastern Methodist Cemetery
        (Washington, D.C.)
Old English authors
    USE Authors, English—Old English, ca.
        450-1100
Old English Christian literature
    USE Christian literature, English (Old)
Old English Christian poetry
    USE Christian poetry, English (Old)
Old English dialogues
    USE Dialogues, English (Old)
Old English didactic poetry
    USE Didactic poetry, English (Old)
Old English elegiac poetry
    USE Elegiac poetry, English (Old)
Old English epic poetry
    USE Epic poetry, English (Old)
Old English folk poetry
    USE Folk poetry, English (Old)
Old English Game (Chickens)
    [SF502.8-503.52]
    UF Game cocks
    BT Chicken breeds
        Game fowl
    NT Old English Game bantams
Old English Game bantams
    [SF489.O]
    BT Bantams
        Chicken breeds
        Game fowl
        Old English Game (Chickens)
Old English gnomic poetry
    USE Gnomic poetry, English (Old)
Old English inscriptions
    USE Inscriptions, English (Old)
Old English language
    USE English language—Old English, ca.
        450-1100
Old English literature
    USE English literature—Old English, ca.
        450-1100
Old English manuscripts
    USE Manuscripts, English (Old)
Old English mastiff
    USE Mastiff
Old English names
    USE Names, English (Old)
Old English philology
    USE English philology—Old English, ca.
        450-1100
Old English poetry
    USE English poetry—Old English, ca. 450-
        1100
Old English poets
    USE Poets, English—Old English, ca. 450-
        1100

Old English prose literature
    USE English prose literature—Old English,
        ca. 450-1100
Old English riddles
    USE Riddles, English (Old)
Old English sermons
    USE Sermons, English (Old)
Old English sheepdog
    [SF429.04]
    UF Bobtail dog
        English sheepdog, Old
        Sheepdog, Old English
    BT Sheep dogs
Old English type
    USE Type and type-founding—Old English
        type
Old Erie Canal State Park (N.Y.)
    BT Erie Canal (N.Y.)
        Parks—New York (State)
**Old Exchange Building and Provost Dungeon
(Charleston, S.C.)**
    UF Exchange and Provost (Charleston,
        S.C.)
        Exchange Building and Provost
        Dungeon (Charleston, S.C.)
        Provost and Exchange (Charleston,
        S.C.)
    BT Commercial buildings—South Carolina
Old family
    USE Olds family
Old fashioned roses
    USE Old roses
Old Fort Mifflin (Philadelphia, Pa.)
    USE Fort Mifflin (Philadelphia, Pa.)
Old Fort Niagara (N.Y.)   *(Not Subd Geog)*
    UF Fort Niagara (N.Y.)
        Niagara, Fort (N.Y.)
    BT Fortification—New York (State)
Old French folk-songs
    USE Folk-songs, Old French
Old French language
    USE French language—To 1500
Old French literature
    USE French literature—To 1500
Old French part-songs
    USE Part-songs, Old French
Old French poetry
    USE French poetry—To 1500
Old French songs
    USE Songs, Old French
Old garden roses
    USE Old roses
Old Government Road (Calif. and Nev.)
    USE Mojave Road (Calif. and Nev.)
Old Greenville Cemetery (Greenville, Miss.)
    BT Cemeteries—Mississippi
Old growth forests   *(May Subd Geog)*
    [QK938.F6 (Botany, QK108-474.5)]
    [SD387.O43 (Forestry)]
    UF Forests, Old growth
        Forests, Virgin
        Virgin forests
    BT Forest ecology
        Forests and forestry
Old High German language
    USE German language—Old High German,
        750-1050
Old High German literature
    USE German literature—Old High German,
        750-1050
Old Hundredth (Tune)
    [ML3186]
    BT Doxology
        Hymn tunes
Old Icelandic language
    USE Old Norse language
Old Indic language
    USE Vedic language
Old Khotanese language
    USE Khotanese language

Old Kirghiz language
    USE Old Turkic language
Old Korean
    USE Korean language—To 935
Old Kukis
    USE Hmar (Hill tribe)
Old lesbians
    USE Aged lesbians
Old Lillie's Cemetery (Bastard, Ont.)
    USE Lillie's Cemetery (Bastard, Ont.)
Old Low Franconian language
    USE Dutch language—To 1500
Old Lutheran Cemetery (Salisbury, N.C.)
    UF Lutheran Cemetery (Salisbury, N.C.)
    BT Cemeteries—North Carolina
Old Man Mountain (Colo.)
    BT Mountains—Colorado
Old Man of the Mountain (N.H.)
    UF Great Stone Face (N.H.)
        Profile (N.H.)
    BT Cannon Mountain (N.H.)
        Natural monuments—New Hampshire
Old man's beard (Plant)
    USE Spanish moss
Old Manse (Concord, Mass.)
    BT Dwellings—Massachusetts
        Emerson, Ralph Waldo, 1803-1882—
        Homes and haunts—Massachusetts
        Hawthorne, Nathaniel, 1804-1864—
        Homes and haunts—Massachusetts
Old Melbourne Cemetery (Melbourne, Vic.)
    UF Melbourne Cemetery, Old (Melbourne,
        Vic.)
    BT Cemeteries—Australia
Old men
    USE Aged men
Old Methodist Burial Ground (Washington,
D.C.)
    USE Mount Zion Cemetery (Washington,
        D.C.)
Old Methodist Cemetery (Greenwood, S.C.)
    USE Greenwood Cemetery (Greenwood,
        S.C.)
Old National Pike
    USE Cumberland Road
Old Norse authors
    USE Authors, Old Norse
Old Norse ballads
    USE Ballads, Old Norse
Old Norse language
    [PD2201-PD2392]
    Here are entered works about the Old Norse
   (Western Norse) language in general, as well as the
   Icelandic language to 1550 and the Norwegian lan-
   guage to 1350. Works about the East Norse lan-
   guages, i.e. Old Danish and Old Swedish, are entered
   under Danish language and Swedish language with
   the appropriate period subdivision.
    UF Icelandic language—To 1550
        Norse languages
        Norwegian language—To 1350
        Old Icelandic language
        Old Norwegian language
    BT Scandinavian languages
    NT Faroese dialect
        Norn dialect
   — Etymology
      NT Níd (The Old Norse word)
Old Norse letters   *(May Subd Geog)*
Old Norse literature   *(May Subd Geog)*
    [PT7101-PT7211 (History)]
    [PT7220-PT7262 (Collections)]
    BT Icelandic literature
        Norwegian literature
        Scandinavian literature
    NT Manuscripts, Old Norse
        Old Norse prose literature
        Sagas
Old Norse manuscripts
    USE Manuscripts, Old Norse
Old Norse paleography
    USE Paleography, Old Norse

Old Norse philology
Old Norse poetry (May Subd Geog)
  ₁PT7170-PT7174 (History)₁
  ₁PT7230-PT7252 (Collections)₁
  BT Scandinavian poetry
  NT Eddas
      Lausavísur
      Religious poetry, Old Norse
      Rímur
      Scalds and scaldic poetry
Old Norse prose literature
    (May Subd Geog)
  BT Old Norse literature
Old Norse religious poetry
  USE Religious poetry, Old Norse
Old Norse romances
  USE Romances, Old Norse
Old North Road (W.A.) (Not Subd Geog)
  BT Roads—Australia
Old Norwegian language
  USE Old Norse language
Old Oghuz language
  USE Old Turkic language
Old Order Amish
  USE Amish
      Mennonites
Old Order Mennonites (May Subd Geog)
  ₁BX8129.O43₁
      Here are entered works on those Mennonites who
  especially emphasize a strict adherence to the Ana-
  baptist inheritance in doctrine and worship, and who
  strongly resist assimilation and acculturation, espe-
  cially in the areas of traditional dress, modes of trans-
  portation, and language.
  BT Christian sects
      Mennonites
Old Osmanic language
  USE Turkish language—To 1500
Old Ottoman Turkish language
  USE Turkish language—To 1500
Old Persian inscriptions
  ₁PK6128₁
  UF Behistun inscriptions
      Cuneiform inscriptions, Persian
      Inscriptions, Behistun
      Inscriptions, Persian (Old)
      Persian cuneiform inscriptions
      Persian literature—Old Persian
  RT Cuneiform inscriptions
      Old Persian language
  NT Achaemenian inscriptions
Old Persian language
  ₁PK6121-9₁
  UF Persian language—Old Persian
  BT Iranian languages
  RT Avesta language
      Old Persian inscriptions
  — Writing
      ₁PK6122₁
      BT Cuneiform writing
Old Pike
  USE Cumberland Road
Old Polish language
  USE Polish language—To 1500
Old Polish literature
  USE Polish literature—To 1500
Old Post Office and Clock Tower
    (Washington, D.C.)
  BT Buildings—Washington (D.C.)
Old Prussian language
  USE Prussian language
Old Rajasthani language
  USE Rajasthani language—To 1500
Old red sandstone (Geology)
  USE Geology, Stratigraphic—Devonian
Old Rhine River (Netherlands)
  UF Oude Rijn River (Netherlands)
      Oude Ryn River (Netherlands)
  BT Rivers—Netherlands
Old roses (May Subd Geog)
  ₁SB411.65.O55₁

  UF Old fashioned roses
      Old garden roses
      Old shrub roses
  BT Roses
  NT Damask roses
Old Russian inscriptions
  USE Inscriptions, Russian (Old)
Old Russian language
  USE Russian language—To 1300
Old Russian letters
  USE Russian letters—To 1700
Old Russian literature
  USE Russian literature—To 1700
Old Russian manuscripts
  USE Manuscripts, Russian (Old)
Old Russian poetry
  USE Russian poetry—To 1700
Old Saxon language
  ₁PF3992-4000₁
  UF Low German language—Old Low
      German, 750-1050
  RT Low German language—To 1500
  NT English language—Old English, ca.
      450-1100
Old Serbo-Croatian language
  USE Serbo-Croatian language—To 1500
Old Settler's Cemetery (Pearland, Tex.)
    (Not Subd Geog)
  BT Cemeteries—Texas
Old shrub roses
  USE Old roses
Old Slavic language
  USE Church Slavic language
      Proto-Slavic language
Old Slovenian language
  USE Church Slavic language
Old-squaw
  UF Clangula hyemalis
      Long-tailed duck
      Oldsquaw
  BT Ducks
Old Standard Theatre (Shoreditch, London,
    England)
  USE Standard Theatre (Shoreditch, London,
      England)
Old Stone age
  USE Paleolithic period
Old Stone Church Cemetery (Clemson, S.C.)
  BT Cemeteries—South Carolina
Old Stone Church Cemetery (Pa.)
  USE Stone Church Cemetery (Pa.)
Old Stone Fort (Nacogdoches, Tex.)
  UF Stone Fort (Nacogdoches, Tex.)
      Stone House (Nacogdoches, Tex.)
      YBarbo's Stone House (Nacogdoches,
      Tex.)
  BT Buildings—Texas
Old Tatar language
  USE Tatar language—To 1500
Old Testament apocryphal books
  USE Apocryphal books (Old Testament)
Old Testament scholars (May Subd Geog)
  ₁BS1161₁
  UF Bible scholars (Old Testament)
      Scholars, Old Testament
  BT Biblical scholars
Old Testament Trinity (Icon)
  USE Rublev, Andrei, d. ca. 1430.   Trinity
Old Town (Alexandria, Va.)
    (Not Subd Geog)
  UF Alexandria (Va.).   Old Town
Old Town (Mombasa, Kenya)
    (Not Subd Geog)
  UF Mombasa (Kenya).   Old Town
Old Town (Portland, Or.) (Not Subd Geog)
  UF Oldtown (Portland, Or.)
      Portland (Or.).   Old Town
Old Town (Prague, Czechoslovakia)
  USE Staré Město (Prague, Czechoslovakia)
Old Town (Riga, Latvia)
  USE Vecrīga (Riga, Latvia)

Old Town (Stockholm, Sweden)
  USE Gamla Stan (Stockholm, Sweden)
Old Town (Warsaw, Poland)
  USE Stare Miasto (Warsaw, Poland)
Old Town Hall (Amsterdam, Netherlands)
  USE Koninklijk Paleis (Amsterdam,
      Netherlands)
Old Turkic inscriptions
  USE Inscriptions, Old Turkic
Old Turkic language (May Subd Geog)
  UF Kök-Türk language
      Old Kirghiz language
      Old Oghuz language
      Old Uighur language
      Uighur language—To 900
  BT Inscriptions, Old Turkic
      Turkic languages, Northeast
Old Turkic paleography
  USE Paleography, Old Turkic
Old Uighur language
  USE Old Turkic language
Old Ukrainian language
  USE Ukrainian language—1300-1700
Old Uzbek language
  USE Chagatai language
Old Vic Theatre (London, England)
  UF Coburg Theatre (London, England)
      Royal Victoria Hall (London, England)
  BT Theaters—England
Old Vriesland Cemetery (Zeeland, Mich.)
  BT Cemeteries—Michigan
Old Wolfville Cemetery (Wolfville, N.S.)
  BT Cemeteries—Nova Scotia
Old women
  USE Aged women
Old World badger (May Subd Geog)
  ₁QL737.C25₁
  UF Badger, Old World
      Eurasian badger
      European badger
      Meles meles
  BT Meles
Old World badger as carriers of disease
    (May Subd Geog)
  BT Animals as carriers of disease
Old World fruit bats
  USE Pteropodidae
Old-World monkeys
  USE Cercopithecidae
Old World orioles
  USE Oriolus
Old World rabbit
  USE Oryctolagus cuniculus
Old World warblers
  USE Sylviidae
Old World woodcock
  USE Woodcock, Eurasian
Oldacre family
  USE Oldaker family
Oldaker family (Not Subd Geog)
  UF Oldacre family
Oldam family
  USE Oldham family
Oldenburg, House of (Not Subd Geog)
  BT Denmark—Kings and rulers
Oldenburg (Germany : Landkreis)
  — History
  — — Revolution, 1848-1849
      ₁DD209.O₁
      BT Germany—History—Revolution,
          1848-1849
Oldenburger horse
  ₁SF293.O4₁
Oldendorf, Battle of, 1633
  ₁D267.O6₁
  BT Thirty Years' War, 1618-1648
Older lesbians
  USE Aged lesbians
Older men
  USE Aged men
      Middle aged men

Older persons
  USE Aged
Older women
  USE Aged women
      Middle aged women
Older workers
  USE Aged—Employment
Oldfield mouse
  UF Beach mouse
      Peromyscus polionotus
  BT Mice
Oldham family *(Not Subd Geog)*
  UF Oaldham family
      Oaldhum family
      Odian family
      Oldam family
  RT Odom family
Oldis family
  USE Olds family
Oldman River (Alta.) *(Not Subd Geog)*
  BT Rivers—Alberta
Olds family *(Not Subd Geog)*
  UF Oalds family
      Old family
      Oldis family
      Ould family
Oldsmobile automobile
  BT General Motors automobiles
  NT Calais automobile
      Cutlass automobile
      Omega automobile
Oldsquaw
  USE Old-squaw
Oldtown (Portland, Or.)
  USE Old Town (Portland, Or.)
Olea
  USE Olive
Oleaceae
    ⌜QK495.O44⌝
  NT Forsythia
      Jasmine
      Lilacs
      Olive
Oleander, Yellow
  USE Thevetia peruviana
Olearius family *(Not Subd Geog)*
  UF Ulearius family
      Von Olearius family
O'Leary family *(Not Subd Geog)*
  RT Leary family
Oleaster
  NT Russian olive
Oleates
    ⌜RS201.O5⌝
Olefer family
  USE Oliver family
Olefines
  USE Olefins
Olefins
  UF Alkenes
      Ethene series
      Ethylene series
      Olefines
  BT Hydrocarbons
  NT Cumulenes
      Diolefins
      Ethylene
      Isopentenoids
      Oxo process
      Polyolefins
      Propene
      Unsaturated fatty acids
Oleic acid
    ⌜QD305.A2 (Organic chemistry)⌝
  UF Octadecanoic acid
      Octadecenoic acid
      Oleinic acid
      Red oil
  BT Acids, Fatty
Oleinic acid
  USE Oleic acid

Olenek River (R.S.F.S.R.)
  UF Reka Olenek (R.S.F.S.R)
  BT Rivers—Russian S.F.S.R.
Oleneothyris
    ⌜QE797.T3⌝
  BT Terebratulidae, Fossil
Oleneothyris fragilis
    ⌜QE797.T3⌝
Oleomargarine
  USE Margarine
Oleoresins
    ⌜RS201.O6 (Pharmacy)⌝
  BT Gums and resins
      Oils and fats
Oléron, Ile d' (France)
  UF Ile d'Oléron (France)
      Uliarus Island (France)
  BT Islands—France
Olerud family *(Not Subd Geog)*
Olesen family
  USE Olson family
Oleson family
  USE Olson family
Olethreutidae
  USE Tortricidae
Oleum
  USE Sulphuric acid
Oleum hyoscyami
  USE Hyoscyamus (Drug)
Oleum ligni guaiaci
  USE Guaiac wood oil
Oleum rosae
  USE Attar of roses
Oleum sinapis volatile
  USE Mustard oils
OLF (Computer program)
  UF On-line filing (Computer program)
Olfaction
  USE Smell
Olfactometry
    ⌜QP458⌝
  UF Smell—Measurement
      Smell—Testing
  BT Smell
Olfactory brain
  USE Rhinencephalon
Olfactory disorders
  USE Smell disorders
Olfactory mucosa
    ⌜QL947 (Comparative anatomy)⌝
    ⌜QM561 (Histology)⌝
    ⌜QP458 (Physiology)⌝
  BT Nasal mucosa
Olfactory nerve
    ⌜QL947 (Comparative anatomy,
      QL939)⌝
    ⌜QM505 (Human anatomy, QM471)⌝
  BT Nerves, Cranial
      Nose
      Smell
  NT Septum (Brain)
Olfactory threshold
  USE Smell—Threshold
Ølgaard family
  USE Øllgaard family
Olifer family
  USE Oliver family
Oligacanthorhynchida *(May Subd Geog)*
    ⌜QL391.A2⌝
  BT Archiacanthocephala
  NT Oligacanthorhynchidae
Oligacanthorhynchidae *(May Subd Geog)*
    ⌜QL391.A2⌝
  BT Oligacanthorhynchida
  NT Macracanthorhynchus
Oligarchy *(May Subd Geog)*
    ⌜JC419⌝
  BT Political science
Oligoadenylates
    ⌜QP625.O45⌝
  UF Adenyladenosine oligonucleotides

  BT Adenylic acid
Oligocardia
  USE Bradycardia
Oligocene period
  USE Geology, Stratigraphic—Oligocene
      Paleobotany—Oligocene
      Paleontology—Oligocene
Oligochaeta *(May Subd Geog)*
    ⌜QL391.O4⌝
  UF Chaetopoda
      Clitellata
  BT Annelida
  NT Komarekionidae
      Opisthopora
      Plesiopora
      Prosopora
Oligodendroglia
  UF Mesoglia
  BT Nervous system
Oligolophinae
  USE Phalangiidae
Oligolychus
  USE Nothosaurus
Oligopeptides
    ⌜QP552.O⌝
  BT Peptides
  NT Amanitins
      Angiotensin
      Anserine
      Carnosine
      Glutathione
      Kallidin
      Oxytocin
      Phalloidine
      Tuftsin
Oligophrenia, Phenylpyruvic
  USE Phenylketonuria
Oligopolies *(May Subd Geog)*
    ⌜HD2757.3⌝
  UF Economic concentration
      Monopolies, Partial
      Partial monopolies
  BT Competition
      Competition, Imperfect
      Interorganizational relations
      Monopolies
      Prices
  RT Duopolies
  NT Industrial concentration
Oligosaccharides
  BT Glucosides
      Monosaccharides
  NT Sucrose
Oligospermia *(May Subd Geog)*
    ⌜RC889.5⌝
  UF Oligozoospermatism
      Oligozoospermia
  BT Infertility, Male
      Semen
      Spermatozoa
Oligozoospermatism
  USE Oligospermia
Oligozoospermia
  USE Oligospermia
Oliguresia
  USE Oliguria
Oliguria
  UF Oliguresia
Olimbos, Mount (Greece)
  USE Olympus, Mount (Greece)
Olindiidae *(May Subd Geog)*
    ⌜QL377.H9⌝
  BT Hydroida
  NT Craspedacusta
Olingo (Artificial language)
  BT Languages, Artificial
Oliphant family *(Not Subd Geog)*
  UF Olivant family
Olipher family
  USE Oliver family

Oliva (Mollusks) *(May Subd Geog)*
  ₍QL430.5.O5₎
  BT Olividae
Oliva (Neurology)
  USE Olivary nucleus
Olivant family
  USE Oliphant family
Olivar family
  USE Oliver family
Olivary body
  USE Olivary nucleus
Olivary nucleus
  UF Inferior olivary body
    Inferior olivary nucleus
    Nucleus, Olivary
    Oliva (Neurology)
    Olivary body
    Olive (Neurology)
  BT Medulla oblongata
    Neurons
Olivas family *(Not Subd Geog)*
Olive *(May Subd Geog)*
  ₍SB367₎
  UF Olea
  BT Oilseed plants
    Oleaceae
  NT Cookery (Olives)
  — **Diseases and pests** *(May Subd Geog)*
    ₍SB608.O4₎
    SA *names of specific diseases and*
        pests, e.g. Olive fly
    NT Prays oleae
  — Tariff
    USE Tariff on olives
  — **Varieties**
Olive (Neurology)
  USE Olivary nucleus
Olive baboon
  ₍QL737.P93₎
  UF Papio anubis
  BT Papio
Olive-backed pocket mouse
  USE Perognathus fasciatus
Olive fly
  UF Dacus oleae
Olive in literature
  BT Trees in literature
Olive industry and trade *(May Subd Geog)*
  ₍HD9019.O4 (Economics)₎
  ₍SB367 (Agriculture)₎
  BT Fruit-culture
    Fruit trade
Olive kernel borer
  USE Prays oleae
Olive loggerhead turtle
  USE Lepidochelys olivacea
Olive moth
  USE Prays oleae
Olive-oil *(May Subd Geog)*
  ₍TP683₎
  NT Cookery (Olive oil)
  — **Law and legislation** *(May Subd Geog)*
Olive-oil industry *(May Subd Geog)*
  ₍HD9490.5.O46₎
Olive oil mills *(May Subd Geog)*
  BT Oil mills
Olive oil presses *(May Subd Geog)*
  UF Presses, Olive oil
Olive tinea
  USE Prays oleae
Olive Township Cemetery (Olive, Ottawa
  County, Mich.)
  BT Cemeteries—Michigan
Oliveira family *(Not Subd Geog)*
  RT Oliver family
Oliver (Name)
  BT Names, Personal
Oliver Dam (Ala.)
  UF William Bacon Oliver Dam (Ala.)
  BT Dams—Alabama

Oliver family *(Not Subd Geog)*
  UF Olefer family
    Olifer family
    Olipher family
    Olivar family
    Olivier family
    Ollavor family
    Ollefer family
    Olliver family
    Ollivier family
    Ollivor family
    Olover family
    Olver family
  RT Oliveira family
Olives, Mount of (Jerusalem)
  USE Mount of Olives (Jerusalem)
Olivet, Mount of (Jerusalem)
  USE Mount of Olives (Jerusalem)
Olivetti M-10 (Computer)
  ₍QA76.8.O₎
  BT Microcomputers
Olivetti M-24 (Computer)
  BT Microcomputers
Olividae *(May Subd Geog)*
  ₍QL430.5.O5₎
  BT Gasteropoda
  NT Oliva (Mollusks)
Olivier family
  USE Oliver family
Olivin-diabase
  ₍QE461₎
  BT Rocks, Igneous
Olivine *(May Subd Geog)*
  ₍QE391.O45₎
  UF Chrysolite
    Chrysolith
  BT Silicate minerals
  NT Forsterite
Olivopontocerebellar atrophies
  (May Subd Geog)
  ₍RC394.O45₎
  UF Atrophies, Olivopontocerebellar
    Olivopontocerebellar degenerations
  BT Ataxia
    Brain stem—Diseases
    Cerebellum—Diseases
    Degeneration (Pathology)
Olivopontocerebellar degenerations
  USE Olivopontocerebellar atrophies
Oliwa, Battle of, 1627
  BT Swedish-Polish War, 1617-1629—
    Campaigns—Poland
Oliwa, Peace of, 1660
  ₍DL725₎
  BT Swedish-Polish War, 1655-1660
Ollar (Indic people)
  USE Gadaba (Indic people)
Ollari language
  USE Gadaba language (Dravidian)
Ollavor family
  USE Oliver family
Ollefer family
  USE Oliver family
Øllgaard family *(Not Subd Geog)*
  UF Oelgart family
    Ølgaard family
Olliver family
  USE Oliver family
Ollivier family
  USE Oliver family
Ollivor family
  USE Oliver family
Olm
  ₍QL668.C277₎
  UF Proteus (Amphibian)
    Proteus anguinus
  BT Cave fauna
    Proteidae
Olmec Indians
  USE Olmecs

Olmecas
  USE Olmecs
Olmecs
  ₍F219₎
  UF Hulmecas
    Olmec Indians
    Olmecas
    Ulmecas
  BT Indians of Mexico
Olmested family
  USE Olmstead family
Olmscheid family *(Not Subd Geog)*
Olmstead family *(Not Subd Geog)*
  UF Olmested family
    Olmsted family
    Olmstord family
    Omstead family
    Omsted family
    Onstead family
    Ormstead family
    Ormstid family
    Ulmsted family
    Umpstead family
    Umstad family
    Umstead family
    Umsted family
Olmsted family
  USE Olmstead family
Olmsted National Historic Site (Brookline,
  Mass.)
  USE Frederick Law Olmsted National
      Historic Site (Brookline, Mass.)
Olmstord family
  USE Olmstead family
Olo language
  ₍PL6621.O44₎
  UF Orlei language
    Wape language (West Sepik Province,
      Papua New Guinea)
    Wapi language (West Sepik Province,
      Papua New Guinea)
  BT Papua New Guinea—Languages
    Papuan languages
Olo Ngadjoe (Indonesian people)
  USE Ngaju (Indonesian people)
Olofson family
  USE Olson family
Olofsson family
  USE Olson family
Olon-ko Indians
  USE Moquelumnan Indians
Olonets dialect
  ₍PH521-529₎
  UF Olonetsian language
  BT Karelian language
    Russian S.F.S.R.—Languages
Olonetsian language
  USE Olonets dialect
Olover family
  USE Oliver family
Olpes
Olschwanger family *(Not Subd Geog)*
  UF Olshwanger family
    Olswanger family
Olsen family
  USE Olson family
Olshwanger family
  USE Olschwanger family
Olson, Christina
  — Portraits
    UF Olson, Christina—Portraits,
        caricatures, etc.
  — Portraits, caricatures, etc.
    USE Olson, Christina—Portraits
Olson family *(Not Subd Geog)*
  UF Olesen family
    Oleson family
    Olofson family
    Olofsson family
    Olsen family
    Olsson family

Olsson family
  USE Olson family
Olswanger family
  USE Olschwanger family
Olszanica Site (Poland) *(Not Subd Geog)*
  UF Cracow-Olszanica Site (Poland)
     Kraków-Olszanica Site (Poland)
  BT Poland—Antiquities
Olt River (Romania)
  UF Alt River (Romania)
     Aluta River (Romania)
     Oltul (Romania)
  BT Rivers—Romania
Olten Stadthaus (Olten, Switzerland)
  USE Stadthaus Olten (Olten, Switzerland)
Oltenitza, Battle of, 1853
  ₍DK215.8.O6₎
  BT Crimean War, 1853-1856
Oltis River (France)
  USE Lot River (France)
Oltman family
  USE Oltmanns family
Oltmann family
  USE Oltmanns family
Oltmanns family *(Not Subd Geog)*
  UF Oltman family
     Oltmann family
Oltul (Romania)
  USE Olt River (Romania)
Oluhanga dialect
  USE Hanga dialect (Kenya)
Oluluyia language
  USE Luyia language
Olunyaneka language
  USE Nyaneka language
Olunyore language
  USE Nyore language
Olushisa dialect
  USE Kisa dialect
Oluwanga dialect
  USE Hanga dialect (Kenya)
Olver family
  USE Oliver family
Olvey family
  USE Alvey family
Ol'viia (Ancient city)
  USE Olbia (Ancient city)
Olymbos, Mount (Greece)
  USE Olympus, Mount (Greece)
Olympia (Wash.). Washington State Capitol
  Historic District
  USE Washington State Capitol Historic
     District (Olympia, Wash.)
Olympia (Greece : Ancient sanctuary)
  (Not Subd Geog)
  ₍DF261.O5₎
  BT Greece—Antiquities
     Temples—Greece
Olympia automobile
  USE Opel automobile
Olympia HHC (Computer)
  USE HHC (Computer)
Olympic elk
  USE Roosevelt elk
**Olympic Games (21st : 1976 : Montréal,
  Québec)**
Olympic games
  USE Olympics
Olympic games (Ancient)
  BT Olympics
Olympic games (in numismatics)
  USE Olympics (in numismatics)
Olympic games in art
  USE Olympics in art
Olympic ideal
  USE Olympics—Philosophy
Olympic Mountains (Wash.)
  BT Coast Ranges
     Mountains—Washington (State)

Olympic National Park (Wash.)
  UF Mount Olympus National Monument
     (Wash.)
     Mount Olympus National Park
     (Wash.)
  BT National parks and reserves—United
     States
     Parks—Washington (State)
Olympic Park (N.J.)
  BT Amusement parks—New Jersey
Olympic Peninsula (Wash.)
  BT Peninsulas—Washington (State)
Olympic Theater (New York, N.Y.)
  BT Theaters—New York (State)
Olympic torch relay *(May Subd Geog)*
  ₍GV721.92₎
  UF Torch run, Olympic
  BT Relay racing
Olympics
  Here are entered comprehensive works on the
  Olympics. Works on the Olympic events of a particu-
  lar year are entered under the appropriate name
  heading, e.g. Olympic Games (21st : 1976 : Montréal,
  Québec).
  UF Games, Olympic
     Olympic games
  BT Sports
  NT Grand Prix de Dressage
     Olympic games (Ancient)
     Prix des Nations
     Winter Olympics
  — **Law and legislation** *(May Subd Geog)*
  — **Philosophy**
     UF Olympic ideal
  — **Programs**
     UF Programs, Olympics
  — **Records**
     ₍GV721.8₎
  — **Revival, 1896-**
Olympics, Senior
  USE Senior Olympics
Olympics (in numismatics)
  UF Olympic games (in numismatics)
  BT Numismatics
Olympics in art
  UF Olympic games in art
Olympus, Mount (Greece) *(Not Subd Geog)*
  UF Mount Olympus (Greece)
     Olimbos, Mount (Greece)
     Olymbos, Mount (Greece)
     Óros Ólimbos (Greece)
  BT Mountains—Greece
Olympus camera
Olympus Cumulus Project
  BT Cloud physics
Olympus Mountains (Cyprus)
  USE Troodos Mountains (Cyprus)
Om (Hinduism)
  UF Oṅkāra
  BT Bijas
     Mantras
     Meditation (Hinduism)
     Mysticism—Hinduism
     Prayer (Hinduism)
Om (Sikhism)
  UF Oṅkāra
  BT Mantras
     Mysticism—Sikhism
     Prayer (Sikhism)
Om soils
  USE Fluvisols
Omagua Indians
  USE Carijona Indians
Omaha Beach (France)
  USE Operation Neptune
Omaha Indians
  ₍E99.O4₎
  BT Dhegiha Indians
     Indians of North America
     Siouan Indians
  — **Land transfers**

  ₍HD234.O5₎
  — **Social life and customs**
  — **Tribal citizenship**
Omaha language
  ₍PM2071₎
Omalidae
  USE Staphylinidae
Oman
  — **History**
  — — **Dhofar War, 1964-1976**
     (May Subd Geog)
     ₍DS247.O68₎
     UF Dhofar (Oman) Rebellion, 1964-
        1976
        Zufar (Oman) Rebellion, 1964-
        1976
     BT Dhofar (Oman)—History
Oman, Gulf of
  UF Baḥr-i Makran
     Baḥr 'Umān
     Daryā-yi 'Umān
     Gulf of Oman
     Khalīj 'Umān
  BT Arabian Sea
Omaña (Spain)
  UF La Omaña (Spain)
Omas River (Peru)
  UF Río de Omas (Peru)
     Río Omas (Peru)
  BT Rivers—Peru
Omayyad coins
  USE Coins, Omayyad
Omayyads
  ₍DS97.2₎
  UF Banū 'Umajja
     Omeyyades
     Ommiads
     Umayyads
  BT Caliphs
     Islamic Empire
     Syria—History—634-750
Omayyads in Spain
  ₍DP105-113₎
  BT Spain—History—711-1516
Ombeke (African people)
  USE Orungu (African people)
Omber (Game)
  USE Ombre (Game)
Ombo language
  UF Hombo language
     Loombo language
     Songola language
  BT Bantu languages
Ombosi (Bantu people)
  USE Mbosi (Bantu people)
Ombre (Game)
  ₍GV1295.O5₎
  UF Omber (Game)
     Tresillo (Game)
Ombrone River (Italy)
  UF Umbro River (Italy)
  BT Rivers—Italy
Ombu
  ₍QK495.P₎
  UF Ombutree pokeberry
Ombudsman *(May Subd Geog)*
  UF Citizen's defender
  BT Abuse of administrative power
     Administrative remedies
  NT Patient representatives
Ombutree pokeberry
  USE Ombu
Omdurman, Battle of, 1898
  ₍DT108.5₎
  BT Sudan—History—1862-1899
Ōme Kaidō (Japan) *(Not Subd Geog)*
  BT Roads—Japan
Omega-3 EFA
  USE Omega-3 fatty acids
Omega-3 essential fatty acids
  USE Omega-3 fatty acids

Omega-3 fatty acids
UF Fatty acids, Omega-3
    N-3 fatty acids
    Omega-3 EFA
    Omega-3 essential fatty acids
BT Unsaturated fatty acids
Omega automobile
    [TL215.O]
BT General Motors X-cars
    Oldsmobile automobile
Omega Navigation System
    [VR560]
BT Electronics in navigation
Omega Point
UF Point Omega
BT Evolution
Omei Shan (China)
USE O-mei Mountain (China)
Omelets
UF Omelettes
BT Cookery (Eggs)
Omelettes
USE Omelets
Omens
    [BF1777]
UF Portents
    Prodigies (Omens)
    Signs (Omens)
BT Superstition
RT Signs and symbols
Omentum
    [QL864 (Comparative anatomy)]
    [QM367 (Human anatomy)]
BT Intestines
    Peritoneum
NT Bursa omentalis
— **Tumors**
Omer days
USE Sefirah period
Ometepe Island (Nicaragua)
BT Islands—Nicaragua
Omeya, Palacio ('Ammān, Jordan)
USE Qaṣr al-Umawī ('Ammān, Jordan)
Omeyyades
USE Omayyads
Ōmi-Fuji (Shiga-ken, Japan)
USE Mikami Mountain (Shiga-ken, Japan)
Ōmi Hinojō (Hino-chō, Shiga-ken, Japan)
USE Hinojō (Hino-chō, Shiga-ken, Japan)
Ōmi Mizukukijō (Japan)
USE Mizukuki Okayamajō (Japan)
Ōmi Okayamajō (Japan)
USE Mizukuki Okayamajō (Japan)
Ōmi Onoejō (Kohoku-chō, Japan)
USE Onoejō (Kohoku-chō, Japan)
Omi Shan (China)
USE O-mei Mountain (China)
Omie language
USE Aomie language
Ōmine Mountains (Japan)
UF Ōmine Sammyaku (Japan)
    Ōmine-san (Japan)
    Ōmine Sanmyaku (Japan)
    Ōminesan (Japan)
    Yamato Alps (Japan)
    Yamato Arupusu (Japan)
BT Mountains—Japan
Ōmine Sammyaku (Japan)
USE Ōmine Mountains (Japan)
Ōmine-san (Japan)
USE Ōmine Mountains (Japan)
Ōmine Sanmyaku (Japan)
USE Ōmine Mountains (Japan)
Ōminesan (Japan)
USE Ōmine Mountains (Japan)
Omission, Criminal *(May Subd Geog)*
UF Criminal omission
    Nonfeasance
BT Criminal act
    Criminal law
    Negligence

NT Misprision
Omizutori
UF Mizutori
    Nigatsudō shunie
    Shu-ni-e
    Shunie
BT Buddhism—Rituals
Ommastrephes *(May Subd Geog)*
    [QL430.3.O5 (Zoology)]
    [SH374.5 (Fisheries)]
BT Ommastrephidae
NT Ommastrephes bartrami
Ommastrephes argentinus
USE Illex illecebrosus
Ommastrephes bartrami *(May Subd Geog)*
    [QL430.3.O5 (Zoology)]
    [SH374.5 (Fisheries)]
BT Ommastrephes
Ommastrephidae
    [QL430.3.O5]
BT Cephalopoda
    Squids
NT Illex
    Ommastrephes
    Todarodes
Ommatophoca
    [QL737.P64]
BT Seals (Animals)
Ommatophoca rossi
USE Ross seal
Ommiads
USE Omayyads
Ommyōdō
USE Yin-yang cults
Omnes gentes, plaudite (Music)
USE Psalms (Music)—47th Psalm
Omni automobile
USE Dodge Omni automobile
Omnibus bill, 1850
USE Compromise of 1850
Omnibus service
USE Bus lines
    Cab and omnibus service
Omnibuses
    [HE5601-HE5720]
    Here are entered works on horse-drawn carriers
    used in local passenger transportation.
BT Cab and omnibus service
    Carriages and carts
    Vehicles
NT Buses
Omnidata (Computer system)
BT Data base management
    Information storage and retrieval
    systems
    Interactive computer systems
Omnidirectional range system
USE Omnirange system
Omnirange system
    [TL969.O]
UF Omnidirectional range system
    VAR
    Visual-aural range
    VOR
BT Aeronautical instruments
    Air traffic control
    Electronics in aeronautics
    Instrument flying
    Navigation (Aeronautics)
NT Distance measuring equipment
    (Aircraft to ground station)
Omnis 3 (Computer program)
BT Data base management—Computer
    programs
Omniscience (Theory of knowledge)
BT Knowledge, Theory of
Omniscience of God
USE God—Omniscience
OMNITAB (Computer program)
Omo language
USE Tigak language

Omobranchus
    [QL638.B6]
BT Blenniidae
Omolon River (R.S.F.S.R.)
UF Reka Omolon (R.S.F.S.R.)
BT Rivers—Russian S.F.S.R.
Omomyidae
    [QE882.P7]
BT Primates, Fossil
Omophronidae
USE Carabidae
Ōmori Iseki (Tokyo, Japan)
USE Ōmori Shell Mounds (Tokyo, Japan)
Ōmori Kaizuka (Tokyo, Japan)
USE Ōmori Shell Mounds (Tokyo, Japan)
Ōmori Shell Mounds (Tokyo, Japan)
    (Not Subd Geog)
UF Ōmori Iseki (Tokyo, Japan)
    Ōmori Kaizuka (Tokyo, Japan)
BT Japan—Antiquities
    Kitchen-middens—Japan
Omoshiroshi (The Japanese word)
    [PL669.O]
BT Japanese language—Etymology
Omote Nihon (Japan)
USE Pacific Coast (Japan)
Omote Nippon (Japan)
USE Pacific Coast (Japan)
Omotedate Iseki (Rokkasho-mura, Japan)
USE Omotedate Site (Rokkasho-mura,
    Japan)
Omotedate Site (Rokkasho-mura, Japan)
    (Not Subd Geog)
UF Omotedate Iseki (Rokkasho-mura,
    Japan)
BT Japan—Antiquities
Omotic languages
    [PJ2561-2594]
UF West Cushitic languages
BT Afroasiatic languages
    Cushitic languages
NT Kaffa language
    Mocha language
    Walamo language
Omoto
USE Rohdea japonica
Ōmoto (Religious organization) members
    (May Subd Geog)
Omphalocele
USE Navel—Hernia
Omphalometridae
    [QL391.P7]
BT Digenea
Omphalorrhagia
USE Navel—Hemorrhage
Omphalos
USE Navel
Omphralidae
USE Scenopinidae
OMR
USE Organic moderated reactors
Omri dynasty, 9th century B.C.
    (Not Subd Geog)
    [DS121.6]
UF Omride dynasty
BT Jews—History—953-586 B.C.
    Jews—Kings and rulers
Omride dynasty
USE Omri dynasty, 9th century B.C.
Omsk hemorrhagic fever
USE Hemorrhagic fever, Omsk
Omstead family
USE Olmstead family
Omsted family
USE Olmstead family
Omt'ae-do Island (Korea)
USE Amt'ae Island (Korea)
Omulu (Cultus)
USE Umbanda (Cultus)

Omuro ikebana
USE Flower arrangement, Japanese—
Omuro school
Omuroryū ikebana
USE Flower arrangement, Japanese—
Omuro school
Omweso (Game)
_[GV1469.O4]_
Omyene (African people)
USE Myene (African people)
On (Ancient city)
USE Heliopolis (Ancient city)
On-farm research, Agricultural
USE Agriculture—Research—On-farm
On-farm trials, Agricultural
USE Agriculture—Research—On-farm
ON GUARD, INC. (Computer program)
_[HF5630]_
BT Accounting—Computer-assisted
instruction—Computer programs
On-line bibliographic searching
(May Subd Geog)
_[Z699.3]_
UF Bibliographic searching, On-line
Online bibliographic searching
BT Data base searching
Machine-readable bibliographic data
On-line data processing
Searching, Bibliographical
NT Catalogs, On-line
Catalogs, On-line—User education
On-line catalogs
USE Catalogs, On-line
On-line data processing
UF In-line data processing
Online data processing
BT Electronic data processing
RT Real-time data processing
Teleprocessing monitors (Computer
programs)
Time-sharing computer systems
NT ADSO (Computer system)
Computer bulletin boards
CRTMAINT (Computer program)
GAMMA (Electronic computer
system)
GRAIL (Electronic computer system)
GRASS (Electronic computer system)
ICES (Electronic computer system)
Interactive computer systems
JOSS (Electronic computer system)
Network Access Machine (Computer)
OCLC Cataloging Subsystem
On-line bibliographic searching
PEG (Electronic computer system)
PROCSY (Computer system)
SOURCE (Information retrieval
system)
VIMCOS (Electronic computer
system)
— Downloading
_[QA76.55]_
UF Down loading in on-line data
processing
Downloading in on-line data
processing
BT Data transmission systems
— Uploading
_[QA76.55]_
UF Up loading in on-line data
processing
Uploading in on-line data
processing
BT Data transmission systems
On-line filing (Computer program)
USE OLF (Computer program)
On-line publishing
USE Electronic publishing

On-site electric power production (Total
energy systems)
USE Total energy systems (On-site electric
power production)
On-the-job stress
USE Job stress
On the river during the Spring Festival (Scroll)
USE Chang, Tse-tuan, fl. 1111-1120.
Going up the river at Ch'ing-ming
Festival time
On the wallaby track (Painting)
USE McCubbin, Frederick, 1855-1917. On
the wallaby track
Ona Indians
_[F2823.O5]_
UF Aonas
Selknam Indians
BT Fuegians
Indians of South America
Ona language
_[PM6691]_
UF Aonik language
Selknam language
BT Indians of South America—Languages
Onagra
USE Oenothera
Onagraceae
_[QK495.O46]_
UF Epilobiaceae
Oenotheraceae
BT Myrtales
NT Camissonia
Clarkia
Epilobium
Fuchsia
Gaura
Oenothera
Onagraceae, Fossil
_[QE983]_
BT Myrtales, Fossil
NT Hartziella
Ōnamuchi no kami
USE Ōkuninushi no kami
Onanism
USE Coitus interruptus
Masturbation
Onc genes
USE Oncogenes
Oncaeidae
_[QL444.C73]_
BT Cyclopoida
NT Lubbockia
Onchocephalidae
USE Ogcocephalidae
Onchocerciasis _(May Subd Geog)_
[RA644.O53 (Public health)]
[RC142.5 (Internal medicine)]
UF Onchocercosis
River blindness
Robles' disease
BT Filariasis
Onchocercosis
USE Onchocerciasis
Oncidium
[QK495.O64 (Botany)]
[SB409 (Culture)]
UF Butterfly orchids
Butterfly plants
BT Orchids
Oncocephalidae
USE Ogcocephalidae
Oncodes
USE Ogcodes
Oncodevelopmental antigens
USE Carcinoembryonic antigens
Oncodevelopmental markers
USE Carcinoembryonic antigens
Oncodidae
USE Acroceridae
Oncogenes
_[RC268.42]_

UF Cancer genes
Genes, Cancer
Onc genes
BT Cancer—Genetic aspects
Viral genetics
RT Oncogenic viruses
Oncogenic viruses
UF Tumor viruses
Viral oncology
BT Oncology
Viruses
RT Oncogenes
NT Epstein-Barr virus
Papovaviruses
Retroviruses
Viral carcinogenesis
— **Reproduction**
BT Reproduction
Oncogens
USE Carcinogens
Oncologists _(May Subd Geog)_
UF Cancer specialists
Cancerologists
BT Medical scientists
Physicians
Oncology _(May Subd Geog)_
_[RC254-282]_
RT Tumors
NT Anesthesia in oncology
Cancer
Forensic oncology
Geriatric oncology
Oncogenic viruses
Oncology, Experimental
Veterinary oncology
— Classification
USE Tumors—Classification
— Information storage and retrieval systems
USE Information storage and retrieval
systems—Oncology
— **Nomenclature**
UF Cancer—Nomenclature
Tumors—Nomenclature
— Staging
USE Tumors—Classification
Oncology, Experimental
UF Experimental oncology
BT Oncology
NT Carcinogenicity testing
Leukemia, Experimental
Tumors—Transplantation
Oncology, Forensic
USE Forensic oncology
Oncopeltus
_[QL523.L9]_
BT Lygaeidae
NT Oncopeltus fasciatus
Oncopeltus fasciatus _(May Subd Geog)_
_[QL523.L9]_
UF Milkweed bug
BT Oncopeltus
Oncorhynchus
USE Pacific salmon
Oncorhynchus gorbuscha
USE Pink salmon
Oncorhynchus keta
USE Chum salmon
Oncorhynchus kisutch
USE Coho salmon
Oncorhynchus nerka
USE Sockeye salmon
Oncorhynchus tshawytscha
USE Chinook salmon
Oncornaviruses
USE Retroviruses
Oncoviruses
USE Retroviruses
Onda pottery _(May Subd Geog)_
_[NK4168.H]_
UF Onta pottery
Pottery, Onda

BT Pottery, Japanese
Ondaine River (France)
  BT Rivers—France
Ondatra
  [QL737.R638]
  BT Cricetidae
Ondatra zibethica
  USE Muskrats
Ondes Martenot
  [ML1092]
  UF Martenot (Musical instrument)
    Martenot's ondes musicales
    Ondes musicales
    Ondium Martenot
  BT Musical instruments, Electronic
Ondes Martenot and percussion music
  [M298]
  UF Percussion and ondes Martenot music
Ondes Martenot and piano music
  [M284.O5]
  [M285.O5]
  UF Piano and ondes Martenot music
  NT Sonatas (Ondes Martenot and piano)
    Suites (Ondes Martenot and piano)
Ondes Martenot and piano music, Arranged
  [M284.O5]
  [M285.O5]
  NT Concertos (Ondes Martenot with
    string orchestra)—Solo with piano
Ondes Martenot music
  [M175.O5]
  NT Concertos (Ondes Martenot)
    Concertos (Ondes Martenot with
    string orchestra)
    Ondes Martenot with orchestra
    Ondes Martenot with string orchestra
    Quartets (Ondes Martenot (2), guitar,
    percussion)
    Quartets (Ondes Martenot (4))
    Sextets (Ondes Martenot (6))
    Trios (Ondes Martenot (2), percussion)
    Trios (Piano, ondes Martenot,
    percussion)
Ondes Martenot music (Ondes martenot (2))
  [M298]
Ondes Martenot music (Ondes Martenot (3))
  USE Trios (Ondes Martenot (3))
Ondes Martenot music (Ondes Martenot (6))
  USE Sextets (Ondes Martenot (6))
Ondes Martenot with orchestra
  [M1039.4.O5]
  BT Ondes Martenot music
  RT Concertos (Ondes Martenot)
Ondes Martenot with string orchestra
  [M1105-6]
  BT Ondes Martenot music
  RT Concertos (Ondes Martenot with
    string orchestra)
Ondes musicales
  USE Ondes Martenot
Ondine's curse
  USE Sleep apnea syndromes
Ondium Martenot
  USE Ondes Martenot
Ondonga (African people)
  USE Ndonga (African people)
Ondoumbo language
  USE Ndumu language
One, Cookery for
  USE Cookery for one
One (The number)
  BT Symbolism of numbers
One (The One in philosophy)
  [BD395]
  BT Idea (Philosophy)
    Ontology
    Philosophy
  RT Absolute, The
One-act plays
  UF Short plays
  BT Drama

— Technique
  BT Authorship
One-act plays, American (May Subd Geog)
  UF American one-act plays
  BT American drama
One-act plays, American, [English, etc.]
  (May Subd Geog)
One-act plays, Arabic (May Subd Geog)
  UF Arabic one-act plays
  BT Arabic drama
One-act plays, Assamese (May Subd Geog)
  UF Assamese one-act plays
  BT Assamese drama
One-act plays, Australian (May Subd Geog)
  UF Australian one-act plays
  BT Australian drama
One-act plays, Bengali (May Subd Geog)
  UF Bengali one-act plays
  BT Bengali drama
One-act plays, Chinese (May Subd Geog)
  [PL2368.O53 (History)]
  [PL2579.O53 (Collections)]
  UF Chinese one-act plays
  BT Chinese drama
One-act plays, Dogri (May Subd Geog)
  UF Dogri one-act plays
  BT Dogri drama
One-act plays, English (May Subd Geog)
  UF English one-act plays
  BT English drama
  — Indic authors
    USE One-act plays, Indic (English)
  — Philippine authors
    USE One-act plays, Philippine
      (English)
  — West Indian authors
    USE One-act plays, West Indian
      (English)
One-act plays, French-Canadian
  (May Subd Geog)
  [PQ3911 (History)]
  [PQ3915 (Collections)]
  UF French-Canadian one-act plays
  BT French-Canadian drama
One-act plays, Greek (Modern)
  (May Subd Geog)
  UF Greek one-act plays, Modern
    Modern Greek one-act plays
  BT Greek drama, Modern
One-act plays, Guatemalan
  (May Subd Geog)
  [PQ7493 (History)]
  [PQ7497 (Collections)]
  UF Guatemalan one-act plays
  BT Guatemalan drama
One-act plays, Gujarati (May Subd Geog)
  UF Gujarati one-act plays
  BT Gujarati drama
One-act plays, Hindi (May Subd Geog)
  UF Hindi one-act plays
  BT Hindi drama
One-act plays, Indic (English)
  (May Subd Geog)
  UF Indic one-act plays (English)
    One-act plays, English—Indic authors
  BT Indic drama (English)
One-act plays, Kashmiri (May Subd Geog)
  UF Kashmiri one-act plays
  BT Kashmiri drama
One-act plays, Marathi (May Subd Geog)
  UF Marathi one-act plays
  BT Marathi drama
One-act plays, Nepali (May Subd Geog)
  UF Nepali one-act plays
  BT Nepali drama
One-act plays, Oriya (May Subd Geog)
  UF Oriya one-act plays
  BT Oriya drama
One-act plays, Panjabi (May Subd Geog)
  UF Panjabi one-act plays
  BT Panjabi drama

One-act plays, Philippine (English)
  (May Subd Geog)
  UF One-act plays, English—Philippine
    authors
    Philippine one-act plays (English)
  BT Philippine drama (English)
One-act plays, Romanian (May Subd Geog)
  UF Romanian one-act plays
  BT Romanian drama
One-act plays, Russian (May Subd Geog)
  UF Russian one-act plays
  BT Russian drama
One-act plays, Sanskrit (May Subd Geog)
  UF Sanskrit one-act plays
  BT Sanskrit drama
One-act plays, Scandinavian
  (May Subd Geog)
  UF Scandinavian one-act plays
  BT Scandinavian drama
One-act plays, Shona (May Subd Geog)
  UF Shona one-act plays
  BT Shona drama
One-act plays, Sindhi (May Subd Geog)
  UF Sindhi one-act plays
  BT Sindhi drama
One-act plays, Spanish (May Subd Geog)
  UF Spanish one-act plays
  BT Spanish drama
  NT Sainetes
One-act plays, Tamil (May Subd Geog)
  UF Tamil one-act plays
  BT Tamil drama
One-act plays, Ukrainian (May Subd Geog)
  UF Ukrainian one-act plays
  BT Ukrainian drama
One-act plays, Urdu (May Subd Geog)
  UF Urdu one-act plays
  BT Urdu drama
One-act plays, West Indian (English)
  (May Subd Geog)
  UF One-act plays, English—West Indian
    authors
    West Indian one-act plays (English)
  BT West Indian drama (English)
One-act plays, Yiddish (May Subd Geog)
  UF Yiddish one-act plays
  BT Yiddish drama
One-armed bandits
  USE Slot machines
One-basket basketball
  USE Halfcourt basketball
One-dimensional conductors
  [QC176.8.E4]
  UF Conductors, One-dimensional
  BT Electric conductors
    Energy-band theory of solids
    Free electron theory of metals
    Salts
  NT Organic conductors
One-dimensional flow
  UF Flow, One-dimensional
  BT Fluid dynamics
One-eyed vision
  USE Vision, Monocular
One-family houses
  USE Architecture, Domestic
    Dwellings
One-hand typewriting
  USE Typewriting, One-hand
One-humped camel
  USE Dromedary
One hundred cranes (Painting)
  USE Pai ho t'u (Painting)
One-leg resting position
  [GN231]
  UF Nilotic position
    Standing on one foot
  BT Posture
    Rest
One-man companies (May Subd Geog)
  UF Companies, One-man

One-man companies *(Continued)*
  BT Corporation law
      Corporations
      Private companies
  NT Sole proprietorship
One-parent family
  USE Single-parent family
One party systems *(May Subd Geog)*
  UF Single party systems
  BT Political parties
One-person households
  USE Living alone
One-room schools
  USE Rural schools
One-teacher schools
  USE Rural schools
One thousand, A.D.
  UF Year one thousand
  BT End of the world
      Millennium
  RT Tenth century
One thousand automobile
  USE Pontiac 1000 automobile
One Tree Island (Qld.)
  BT Coral reefs and islands—Australia
      Great Barrier Reef (Qld.)
      Islands—Australia
One-way streets *(May Subd Geog)*
  BT Streets
      Traffic engineering
O'Neail family
  USE O'Neill family
O'Neal family
  USE O'Neill family
O'Neale family
  USE O'Neill family
O'Neall family
  USE O'Neill family
O'Neals family
  USE O'Neill family
Onega Lake (R.S.F.S.R.)
  UF Lake Onega (R.S.F.S.R.)
      Onezhskoe ozero (R.S.F.S.R.)
      Onezhskoye ozero (R.S.F.S.R.)
  BT Lakes—Russian S.F.S.R.
  NT Bol'shoe Onego (R.S.F.S.R.)
Onega River (R.S.F.S.R.)
  UF Reka Onega (R.S.F.S.R.)
  BT Rivers—Russian S.F.S.R.
Oneida Community
  [HX656.O5]
  UF Perfectionists
Oneida Indians
  [E99.O45]
  UF Oneota Indians (New York)
      Onneiout Indians
  BT Indians of North America
      Iroquoian Indians
      Iroquois Indians
  NT Caughnawaga Indians
Oneida language
  [PM2073]
  RT Iroquoian languages
O'Neil family
  USE O'Neill family
O'Neill, Eugene, 1888-1953
  — **Homes and haunts**
  — — **California**
      NT Tao House (Calif.)
O'Neill family *(Not Subd Geog)*
  UF O'Neail family
      O'Neal family
      O'Neale family
      O'Neall family
      O'Neals family
      O'Neil family
  RT Neal family
O'Neill Ranch (Calif.)
  USE Rancho Santa Margarita (Calif.)
Oneirodes
  [QL638.O5]

BT Oneirodidae
Oneirodidae
  [QL638.O5]
  UF Deepsea anglerfishes
  BT Anglerfishes
  NT Chaenophryne
      Oneirodes
Oneiromancy
  USE Dreams
Oneness doctrine (Pentecostalism)
  UF Doctrine of Oneness (Pentecostalism)
      Jesus only doctrine (Pentecostalism)
      Oneness movement (Pentecostalism)
      Oneness Pentecostalism
      Oneness theology (Pentecostalism)
  BT Jesus Christ—Person and offices
      Pentecostalism
Oneness movement (Pentecostalism)
  USE Oneness doctrine (Pentecostalism)
Oneness of God
  USE God—Simplicity
Oneness Pentecostalism
  USE Oneness doctrine (Pentecostalism)
Oneness theology (Pentecostalism)
  USE Oneness doctrine (Pentecostalism)
Oneota Indians (Great Plains)
  [E99.O5]
  BT Dakota Indians
      Indians of North America
      Mississippian culture
  — **Antiquities**
Oneota Indians (New York)
  USE Oneida Indians
Onespa
  [QL561.H5]
  BT Hesperiidae
Oness family *(Not Subd Geog)*
Onezhskoe ozero (R.S.F.S.R.)
  USE Onega Lake (R.S.F.S.R.)
Onezhskoye ozero (R.S.F.S.R.)
  USE Onega Lake (R.S.F.S.R.)
Onffroy family *(Not Subd Geog)*
  UF Onfroy family
Onfroy family
  USE Onffroy family
Onian (Senegal-Guinea people)
  USE Bassari (Senegal-Guinea people)
Ōnie no Matsuri
  [BL2224.25.O5]
  UF Daijō-sai
      Feast of kingship (Shinto rite)
  BT Shinto—Rituals
Ōnin Bummei no ran, 1467-1477
  USE Ōnin War, 1467-1477
Ōnin no ran, 1467-1477
  USE Ōnin War, 1467-1477
Ōnin War, 1467-1477
  UF Ōnin Bummei no ran, 1467-1477
      Ōnin no ran, 1467-1477
  BT Japan—History—1333-1600
Onion industry *(May Subd Geog)*
  [HD9235.O6-62]
  BT Onions
Onion pink-root disease
  USE Pink-root disease
Onion sets
  [SB341]
  RT Onions
Onion smudge
  [SB608.O5]
Onion thrips
  UF Thrips tabaci
  BT Thrips
Onions *(May Subd Geog)*
  [QK495.L72 (Botany)]
  [SB341 (Vegetables)]
  UF Allium cepa
  RT Onion sets
  NT Cookery (Onions)
      Leeks
      Onion industry

      Shallot
  — **Diseases and pests** *(May Subd Geog)*
    [SB608.O5]
    SA *names of specific diseases and*
       pests, e.g. Pink-root disease;
       Onion thrips
Oniscidae
  [QL444.M34]
  BT Isopoda
  NT Acanthoniscus
      Armadilloniscus
      Oniscus
      Trichorhina
Oniscigastridae
  USE Siphlonuridae
Oniscoidea
  USE Isopoda
Oniscus
  [QL444.M34]
  BT Oniscidae
Oniscus asellus
  [QL444.M34]
Onitis
  [QL596.S3]
  BT Scarabaeidae
Onji Site (Japan) *(Not Subd Geog)*
  BT Japan—Antiquities
Oṅkāra
  USE Om (Hinduism)
      Om (Sikhism)
Onkodes
  USE Ogcodes
Online Application System Interactive
    Software (Computer operating system)
  USE THEOS (Computer operating system)
Online bibliographic searching
  USE On-line bibliographic searching
Online catalogs
  USE Catalogs, On-line
Online data processing
  USE On-line data processing
Only child
  BT Family
Onna no Hi (Kyoto, Japan)
  BT Monuments—Japan
      Single women—Japan—Monuments
Onneiout Indians
  USE Oneida Indians
Ono family *(Not Subd Geog)*
Ono Kofun (Isahaya-shi, Japan)
  USE Ono Site (Isahaya-shi, Japan)
Ono Site (Isahaya-shi, Japan)
  (Not Subd Geog)
  UF Ono Kofun (Isahaya-shi, Japan)
  BT Japan—Antiquities
Onoe Castle (Kohoku-chō, Japan)
  USE Onoejō (Kohoku-chō, Japan)
Onoejō (Kohoku-chō, Japan)
  UF Ōmi Onoejō (Kohoku-chō, Japan)
      Onoe Castle (Kohoku-chō, Japan)
  BT Castles—Japan
Ōnogō Iseki (Mitsukaidō-shi, Japan)
  USE Ōnogō Site (Mitsukaidō-shi, Japan)
Ōnogō Site (Mitsukaidō-shi, Japan)
  (Not Subd Geog)
  UF Ōnogō Iseki (Mitsukaidō-shi, Japan)
  BT Japan—Antiquities
Ōnojō (Ōnojō-shi, Japan)
  UF Ōnojō Castle (Ōnojō-shi, Japan)
  BT Castles—Japan
Ōnojō Castle (Ōnojō-shi, Japan)
  USE Ōnojō (Ōnojō-shi, Japan)
Onomasiology
  [P325.5.O55]
  UF Naming (Semantics)
      Nomination (Semantics)
  BT Semantics
      Semiotics
  NT Onomastics
      Reference (Linguistics)

Onomastics *(May Subd Geog)*
⌐P321.8-323.5⌐
　UF　Onomatology
　BT　Language and languages—Etymology
　　　Names
　　　Onomasiology
　SA　*subdivision* Etymology—Names *under*
　　　names of languages and groups of
　　　languages, e.g. English language—
　　　Etymology—Names
　NT　Names, Ethnological
　　　Names, Geographical
　　　Names, Personal
　　　Names derived from animals
Onomatology
　USE　Onomastics
Onomatopoeia
⌐P119⌐
　BT　Language and languages
　　　Sound symbolism
　　　Sounds, Words for
　SA　*subdivision* Onomatopoeic words
　　　under names of languages and
　　　groups of languages, e.g., English
　　　language—Onomatopoeic words
Onondaga Indians
⌐E99.O58⌐
　BT　Indians of North America
　　　Iroquoian Indians
　　　Iroquois Indians
　— Missions
Onondaga language
⌐PM2076⌐
　RT　Iroquoian languages
Ons Island (Spain)
　UF　Isla Ons (Spain)
　BT　Islands—Spain
Onstead family
　USE　Olmstead family
Onta pottery
　USE　Onda pottery
Ontake Mountain (Japan)
　UF　Ontake-san (Japan)
　BT　Japanese Alps (Japan)
　　　Mountains—Japan
　　　Volcanoes—Japan
　— Eruption, 1979
　　　⌐QE523.O⌐
Ontake-san (Japan)
　USE　Ontake Mountain (Japan)
Ontario
　— Antiquities
　　　NT　Beckstead Site (Ont.)
　　　　　Bruner-Colasanti Site (Ont.)
　　　　　Christianson Site (Ont.)
　　　　　Draper Site (Ont.)
　　　　　Fisk Site (Ont.)
　　　　　Glenbrook Site (Ont.)
　　　　　Hamilton Site (Ont.)
　　　　　Lady Rapids Site (Ont.)
　　　　　McIntyre Site (Ont.)
　　　　　Robin Hood Site (Ont.)
　　　　　Walker Site (Ont.)
　　　　　Wenasaga Rapids Site (Ont.)
　— History
　— — War of 1812
Ontario, Lake (N.Y. and Ont.)
　UF　Lake Ontario (N.Y. and Ont.)
　BT　Great Lakes
　　　Lakes—New York (State)
　　　Lakes—Ontario
Ontario, Lake, Region (N.Y. and Ont.)
　NT　Golden Horseshoe (Ont.)
Ontario, Southern
　UF　Southern Ontario
Ontiveros Adobe Site (Santa Fe Springs,
Calif.) *(Not Subd Geog)*
　BT　Adobe houses—California
　　　California—Antiquities

Ontiveros family *(Not Subd Geog)*
Ontogenesis
　USE　Ontogeny
Ontogeny
⌐QH491⌐
　UF　Ontogenesis
　BT　Biology
　　　Embryology
　RT　Developmental biology
　　　Evolution
　NT　Plants—Ontogeny
Ontological argument
　USE　God—Proof, Ontological
Ontologism
　BT　Philosophy
Ontology
⌐BD300-BD444⌐
　UF　Being
　BT　Philosophy
　RT　Metaphysics
　　　Necessity (Philosophy)
　　　Substance (Philosophy)
　NT　Absolute, The
　　　All (Philosophy)
　　　Catastrophical, The
　　　Categories (Philosophy)
　　　Chain of being (Philosophy)
　　　Change
　　　Concrete (Philosophy)
　　　Ding an sich
　　　Existentialism
　　　Finite, The
　　　Four elements (Philosophy)
　　　God—Proof, Ontological
　　　Identity
　　　Intersubjectivity
　　　Nothing (Philosophy)
　　　One (The One in philosophy)
　　　Perspective (Philosophy)
　　　Philosophical anthropology
　　　Relation (Philosophy)
　　　Situation (Philosophy)
　　　Spiritualism (Philosophy)
Onu (Ancient city)
　USE　Heliopolis (Ancient city)
Onuphidae
⌐QL391.A6⌐
　BT　Eunicida
Onus probandi
　USE　Burden of proof
Onychiuridae
⌐QL503.O⌐
　UF　Aphoruridae
　　　Lipuridae
　　　Onychiurinae
　BT　Collembola
　NT　Onychiurus
Onychiurinae
　USE　Onychiuridae
Onychiurus
⌐QL503.O⌐
　BT　Onychiuridae
Onychocellidae
⌐QL398.C5⌐
　BT　Cheilostomata
　NT　Inversaria
　　　Solenonychocella
Onychodactylus
⌐QL668.C25⌐
　BT　Hynobiidae
　NT　Onychodactylus japonicus
Onychodactylus japonicus
⌐QL668.C25⌐
　BT　Onychodactylus
Onychomys
⌐QL737.R638⌐
　UF　Grasshopper mice
　BT　Cricetidae
Onychomys leucogaster
　USE　Grasshopper mouse

Onychophora
⌐QL448⌐
On'yōdō
　USE　Yin-yang cults
Onyx marble *(May Subd Geog)*
⌐TN967⌐
　BT　Marble
Onza de oro
　USE　Doubloons
Onze de setembre (Catalan holiday)
　UF　Eleventh of September (Catalan
　　　holiday)
　BT　Holidays—Spain
Onze-Lieve-Vrouw Virga Jesse (Sculpture)
　USE　Virga Jesse (Sculpture)
Oochoristica
⌐QL391.P7⌐
　BT　Anoplocephalidae
Oochoristica deserti
⌐QL391.P7⌐
Oocytin
⌐QP91⌐
　BT　Blood
　　　Serum
Oogenesis
⌐QL965⌐
　BT　Gametogenesis
　RT　Germ cells
　　　Ovum
Oohenonpa Indians
⌐E99.O63⌐
　UF　Two Kettle Indians
　BT　Dakota Indians
　　　Indians of North America
　　　Teton Indians
Ōoka family *(Not Subd Geog)*
Oolite *(May Subd Geog)*
⌐QE471 (Petrology)⌐
　BT　Sedimentary structures
　NT　Geology, Stratigraphic—Jurassic
Oologah Lake (Okla.)
　UF　Oologah Reservoir (Okla.)
　BT　Lakes—Oklahoma
　　　Reservoirs—Oklahoma
　　　Verdigris River (Kan. and Okla.)
Oologah Reservoir (Okla.)
　USE　Oologah Lake (Okla.)
Oomiaks
　USE　Umiaks
Oomycetes
⌐QK621.A1 (Botany)⌐
　BT　Phycomycetes
　NT　Lagenidiales
　　　Leptomitales
　　　Peronosporales
　　　Saprolegniales
Oonopidae
⌐QL458.42.O6⌐
　BT　Spiders
Oort cloud
　UF　Cloud, Oort
　BT　Comets
　　　Interstellar matter
Oost-Friesland (Germany)
　USE　East Friesland (Germany)
Ooster Schelde (Netherlands)
　USE　Oosterschelde (Netherlands)
Oosterhout family
　USE　Osterhout family
Oosterschelde (Netherlands)
　UF　East Schelde (Netherlands)
　　　Eastern Scheldt (Netherlands)
　　　Ooster Schelde (Netherlands)
　BT　Estuaries—Netherlands
　　　Inlets—Netherlands
Ootheca (Zoology)
　USE　Egg cases (Zoology)
Oothoudt family *(Not Subd Geog)*
Ŏou language
　USE　Tsou language

OP3VAR (Computer program)
Op art
   USE Optical art
Op-ed pages of newspapers
   USE Newspapers—Sections, columns, etc.—
      Op-ed pages
Op 't Eijnde family   *(Not Subd Geog)*
   UF Obdeijn family
      Opdien family
Opah
   [QL638.L24]
   UF Lampris guttatus
      Lampris luna
      Lampris regius
   BT Lampris
Opaina language
   USE Yahuna language
Opal glass   *(May Subd Geog)*
   UF Glass, Opal
      Opalescent glass
      Opaline glass
   BT Glassware
Opal mines and mining   *(May Subd Geog)*
   [TN997.O7]
Opalescence, Critical
   USE Critical opalescence
Opalescent dentin, Hereditary
   USE Dentinogenesis imperfecta
Opalescent glass
   USE Opal glass
Opaline glass
   USE Opal glass
Opals   *(May Subd Geog)*
   [QE391.O6 (Mineralogy)]
   [TN997.O7 (Mineral resources)]
   [TS755.O (Jewelry)]
Opaque glass
   USE Milk glass
Opaque porcelain
   USE Ironstone china
Oparanthus
   [QK495.C74]
   BT Compositae
Opat family   *(Not Subd Geog)*
Opata Indians
   [F1221.O6]
   UF Teguima Indians
   BT Indians of Mexico
      Piman Indians
Opata language
   BT Eudeve language
Opdien family
   USE Op 't Eijnde family
OPDOS4 (Computer program)
Opdyke family   *(Not Subd Geog)*
Opel (Adam) A.G., Strike, 1973
   [HD5379.A82. 1973B]
   BT Strikes and lockouts—Automobile
      industry—Germany (West)
Opel automobile
   UF Olympia automobile
      Opel-Olympia automobile
Opel-Olympia automobile
   USE Opel automobile
Opelousas Bay (La.)   *(Not Subd Geog)*
   BT Bays—Louisiana
Open admission to universities and colleges
   USE Universities and colleges—Open
      admission
Open-air institutions
   [RA793 (Hygiene)]
   UF Institutions, Open-air
   RT Open-air treatment
   NT Open-air museums
      Open-air schools
Open-air museums   *(May Subd Geog)*
   [AM111]
   UF Outdoor museums
   BT Museums
      Open-air institutions

Open-air schools   *(May Subd Geog)*
   [LB3481-3495]
   UF Outdoor schools
   BT Open-air institutions
      Public schools
      School hygiene
      Schools
Open-air theater
   USE Theater, Open-air
Open-air treatment
   [RA793]
   BT Climatotherapy
      Outdoor life
      Tuberculosis
   RT Open-air institutions
Open-air zoos   *(May Subd Geog)*
   UF Jungle zoos
      Outdoor zoos
      Zoos, Open-air
   BT Wildlife refuges
      Zoos
   — New Jersey
      NT Six Flags Great Adventure Safari
         Park (N.J.)
Open and closed collections in archives
   USE Restricted collections in archives
Open and closed shelves   *(May Subd Geog)*
   [Z711]
   UF Access to books in libraries
      Closed shelves in libraries
      Closed stacks in libraries
      Open shelves in libraries
      Open stacks in libraries
      Stack access in libraries
   BT Library science
Open and closed shop   *(May Subd Geog)*
   [HD6488-HD6488.2]
   UF Agency shop
      Closed shop
      Open shop
      Right to labor (Union membership)
      Right to work and trade-unions
      Shop, Open and closed
      Trade-unions and right to work
      Union shop
   BT Collective labor agreements
      Trade-unions
      Union security
   NT Yellow dog contract
   — **Law and legislation**   *(May Subd Geog)*
      BT Labor laws and legislation
   — — **United States**
         UF Right-to-work laws
   — **Religious aspects**
   — — **Baptists, [Catholic Church, etc.]**
Open angle glaucoma
   USE Glaucoma, Open angle
Open Arms Program
   USE Chieu Hoi Program
Open caissons
   [TC199]
   UF Sunk wells
   BT Caissons
      Foundations
Open-cast mining
   USE Strip mining
Open city (International law)
   UF City, Open (International law)
   BT War—Protection of civilians
      War (International law)
Open classroom approach to teaching
   USE Classroom learning centers
      Open plan schools
Open clusters
   USE Stars—Open clusters
Open code dating of food
   USE Food—Shelf-life dating
Open college admission
   USE Universities and colleges—Open
      admission

Open communion
   USE Close and open communion
Open-cut mining
   USE Strip mining
Open dating of food
   USE Food—Shelf-life dating
Open-door college admission
   USE Universities and colleges—Open
      admission
Open door policy (Far East)
   USE Eastern question (Far East)
Open education
   USE Open plan schools
Open-end mutual funds
   USE Mutual funds
Open forum
   USE Forums (Discussion and debate)
Open fractures
   USE Fractures, Open
Open-heart surgery
   USE Heart—Surgery
Open-hearth furnaces
   [TN740]
   UF Siemens-Martin furnace
   BT Metallurgical furnaces
   — Drawing
      USE Open-hearth furnaces—Drawings
   — **Drawings**
      UF Open-hearth furnaces—Drawing
      BT Mechanical drawing
Open-hearth process
   [TN740-742]
   BT Steel
      Steel—Metallurgy
Open housing
   USE Discrimination in housing
Open market operations   *(May Subd Geog)*
   BT Banks and banking, Central
      Credit
      Currency question
      Finance
   — **Law and legislation**   *(May Subd Geog)*
Open meetings
   USE Public meetings
Open meetings of administrative agencies
   USE Administrative agencies—Public
      meetings
Open meetings of legislative bodies
   USE Legislative bodies—Public meetings
Open-pit mining
   USE Strip mining
Open plan schools   *(May Subd Geog)*
   [LB1029.O6]
   UF Interest centers approach to teaching
      Learning center approach to teaching
      Open classroom approach to teaching
      Open education
      Open-space plan schools
   BT Education—Experimental methods
   RT Classroom learning centers
      Free schools
      Individualized instruction
Open price system   *(May Subd Geog)*
   BT Pricing
   RT Competition
Open prisons   *(May Subd Geog)*
   BT Prisons
Open pulpit
   UF Pulpit, Open
   BT Christian union
      Preaching
Open rain screens
   UF Rain barriers
      Rain screens, Open
      Two-stage weathertightening
   BT Waterproofing
Open sea (Mare liberum)
   USE Freedom of the seas
Open shelf-life dating of food
   USE Food—Shelf-life dating

Open shelves in libraries
  USE Open and closed shelves
Open shop
  USE Open and closed shop
Open space, Fear of
  USE Agoraphobia
Open-space plan schools
  USE Open plan schools
Open spaces *(May Subd Geog)*
  BT City planning
     Land use
     Metropolitan areas
     Regional planning
  RT Development rights transfer
  NT Greenbelts
     Planned unit developments
     Recreation areas
  — **Law and legislation** *(May Subd Geog)*
  — **Great Britain**
  — — **Competitions**
  — — **Exhibitions**
Open spaces, Fear of
  USE Agoraphobia
Open stacks in libraries
  USE Open and closed shelves
Open systems (Physics)
  [QC174.85.O6]
  UF Systems, Open (Physics)
  BT Irreversible processes
     Physics
     Statistical mechanics
     Statistical physics
Open-timbered roofs
  USE Roofs, Open-timbered
Open-web beams
  USE Castellated beams
Open-web expanded beams
  USE Castellated beams
Openers (Implements) *(May Subd Geog)*
  [NK8459.O64 (Applied arts)]
  BT Implements, utensils, etc.
**Opening of the eyes of one blind at Bethsaida
  (Miracle)**
  UF Bethsaida, Blind man at (Miracle)
  BT Jesus Christ—Miracles
Opening sentences
  USE Openings (Rhetoric)
Openings (Games)
  USE Checkers—Openings
     Chess—Openings
     Chinese chess—Openings
     Go (Game)—Openings
     Shogi—Openings
Openings (Holes)
  USE Holes
Openings (Rhetoric)
  UF Beginnings (Rhetoric)
     First lines (Rhetoric)
     Opening sentences
  BT Rhetoric
Opera *(May Subd Geog)*
  [ML1700-ML2110 (History and
     criticism)]
  [ML3858 (Aesthetics)]
  Here are entered works about opera. Musical
  works composed in this form are entered under the
  heading Operas.
  UF Comic opera
     Lyric drama
     Opera—History and criticism
     Opera, Comic
     Operas—History and criticism
  BT Drama
     Dramatic music
  NT Acting in opera
     Ballad opera
     Ballet
     Curses in opera
     Gluck-Piccinni controversy
     Greek drama—Incidental music
     Guerre des Bouffons

     Impresarios
     Leitmotiv
     Liturgical drama
     Melodrama
     Operetta
     Overture
     Turks in opera
     Women in opera
  — **Biography**
     NT Opera producers and directors
  — **Costume**
     USE Costume
  — **Dictionaries**
     [ML102]
     NT Operas—Stories, plots, etc.
  — Direction
     USE Opera—Production and direction
  — **Dramaturgy**
     [ML3858]
     Here are entered discussions of the technique
     of writing operas.
     UF Dramaturgy
     RT Operas—Stage guides
     SA subdivision Dramaturgy under
        names of composers, e.g.
        Wagner, Richard, 1813-1883—
        Dramaturgy
  — History and criticism
     USE Opera
  — **Juvenile**
     UF Children's opera
        Juvenile opera
        Opera, Children's
        Opera, Juvenile
        School opera
  — Librettists
     USE Librettists
  — Librettos
     USE Operas—Librettos
  — **Production and direction**
     [MT955]
     UF Opera—Direction
        Opera direction
        Opera production
     NT Opera producers and directors
  — Stories, plots, etc.
     USE Operas—Stories, plots, etc.
  — **China**
     NT Operas, Chinese—History and
        criticism
  — **Korea**
     NT Ch'anggŭk
        P'ansori
Opera, Children's
  USE Opera—Juvenile
Opera, Comic
  USE Opera
     Operetta
     Zarzuela
Opera, Juvenile
  USE Opera—Juvenile
Opera companies *(May Subd Geog)*
  UF Companies, Opera
Opera direction
  USE Opera—Production and direction
Opera directors and producers
  USE Opera producers and directors
Opera-glasses
  [GT2370 (Manners and customs)]
Opera-houses
  USE Theaters
Opera producers and directors
  (May Subd Geog)
  UF Directors, Opera
     Opera directors and producers
     Producers, Opera
  BT Opera—Biography
     Opera—Production and direction
Opera production
  USE Opera—Production and direction

Operant behavior
  [BF319.5.O6]
  UF Behavior, Instrumental
     Behavior, Operant
     Instrumental behavior
     Intervention (Psychology)
  BT Conditioned response
     Psychology
Operant conditioning
  [BF319.5.O6]
  UF Conditioned operant response
     Conditioning, Instrumental
     Conditioning, Operant
     Instrumental conditioning
  BT Conditioned response
  NT Biofeedback training
Operas
  [M1500-M1508]
  Here are entered musical works composed in this
  form. Works about opera are entered under the head-
  ing Opera.
  UF Operettas
     Puppet operas
     Singspiels
  BT Dramatic music
  NT Ballad operas
     College operas, revues, etc.
     Operatic scenes
     Radio operas
     Revolutionary operas
     Television operas
     Tonadillas
     Zarzuelas
  — **To 500**
  — **500-1400**
  — **15th century**
  — **16th century**
  — **17th century**
  — **18th century**
  — **19th century**
  — **20th century**
  — **Analysis, appreciation**
     [MT95]
     [MT100]
  — **Bibliography**
  — — **Graded lists**
  — **Cadenzas**
  — **Chorus scores with piano**
  — **Chorus scores without accompaniment**
     [M1502]
  — Copyright
     USE Copyright—Operas
  — **Discography**
     [ML156.4.O46]
  — — **Methodology**
     [ML110-112]
  — **Excerpts**
     [M1505-8]
     NT Overtures
        Suites (Orchestra)
  — — **Parts**
     [M1505-6]
     UF Operas—Parts—Excerpts
  — — **Scores**
     [M1505-6]
     UF Operas—Scores—Excerpts
  — — **Vocal scores with guitar**
     [M1508]
     UF Operas—Vocal scores with
        guitar—Excerpts
  — — **Vocal scores with piano**
     [M1507-8]
     UF Operas—Vocal scores with
        piano—Excerpts
  — **Excerpts, Arranged**
  — **Film and video adaptations**
     BT Film adaptations
        Moving-pictures, Musical
  — **First performances** *(May Subd Geog)*
  — History and criticism
     USE Opera

Operas (continued)
 — Instructive editions
 — Instrumental settings
 — Interpretation (Phrasing, dynamics, etc.)
 — Juvenile
  [M1995]
 — Librettos
  [ML48]
  UF Opera—Librettos
  NT Operas—Scenarios
    Operas—Stories, plots, etc.
 — Parts
  [M1500]
 — — Excerpts
   USE Operas—Excerpts—Parts
 — Parts (solo)
 — Piano scores
  [M33]
  BT Piano music, Arranged
 — Piano scores (4 hands)
  [M208]
 — Programs
  [ML40]
  BT Concerts—Programs
 — Scenarios
  [ML48-50.2]
  BT Operas—Librettos
 — Scores
  [M1500]
 — — Excerpts
   USE Operas—Excerpts—Scores
 — Scores and parts
  [M1500]
 — Scores and parts (solo)
 — Simplified editions
 — Stage guides
  [MT955]
  BT Theaters—Stage-setting and
    scenery
  RT Opera—Dramaturgy
 — Stories, plots, etc.
  [MT95]
  [MT100]
  UF Opera—Stories, plots, etc.
    Operetta—Stories, plots, etc.
    Stories of operas
  BT Opera—Dictionaries
    Operas—Librettos
    Plots (Drama, novel, etc.)
  SA subdivision Stories of operas under
    names of individual composers,
    e.g. Wagner, Richard, 1813-
    1883—Stories of operas
 — Teaching pieces
 — Themes, motives, Literary
 — Vocal scores with accordion
 — Vocal scores with continuo
 — Vocal scores with guitar
  [M1503]
 — — Excerpts
   USE Operas—Excerpts—Vocal
    scores with guitar
 — Vocal scores with harpsichord
  [M1503]
 — Vocal scores with keyboard instrument
  [M1503]
 — Vocal scores with organ
 — Vocal scores with piano
  [M1503]
 — — Excerpts
   USE Operas—Excerpts—Vocal
    scores with piano
 — Vocal scores with piano (4 hands)
  [M1503]
 — Vocal scores with piano and organ
 — Vocal scores with pianos (2)
  [M1503]
 — Vocal scores without accompaniment
  [M1502]
Operas, Chinese (May Subd Geog)
  [M1805.3-M1805.4]

Here are entered Chinese musical dramas, includ-
ing Peking operas, and, with local subdivision, re-
gional operas written and performed in the style of a
particular locality.
  UF Chinese operas
    Ching chü
    Jingju
    Operas, Peking
    Peking operas
    P'ing chü (Chinese operas)
  BT Chinese drama
 — History and criticism
  BT Opera—China
 — Production and direction
  [MT955]
Operas, Peking
  USE Operas, Chinese
Operas arranged for flute
  [M64]
  BT Flute music, Arranged
Operas arranged for flute, violin, viola, and
  violoncello
  [M463-4]
  BT Quartets (Flute, violin, viola,
    violoncello), Arranged
Operas arranged for string quartets
  [M453-4]
  BT String quartets, Arranged
Operas arranged for violin and piano
  [M222-3]
  BT Violin and piano music, Arranged
Operatic moving-pictures
  USE Moving-pictures, Musical
Operatic scenes
  [M1509]
  BT Operas
  RT College operas, revues, etc.
Operating life (Engineering)
  USE Service life (Engineering)
Operating room nursing (May Subd Geog)
  [RD32.3]
  RT Surgical nursing
  NT Nurse anesthetists
 — Law and legislation (May Subd Geog)
Operating room personnel (May Subd Geog)
  BT Medical personnel
  NT Anesthesiologists
    Nurse anesthetists
    Operating room technicians
    Surgeons
Operating room technicians
  (May Subd Geog)
  UF Surgical technologists
  BT Biomedical technicians
    Operating room personnel
    Surgery, Operative
    Surgical technology
Operating room technology
  USE Surgical technology
Operating rooms
  [RD63]
  UF Rooms, Operating
  BT Hospitals
    Surgery
 — Environmental engineering
  BT Environmental engineering
 — Exhaust systems
  BT Exhaust systems
Operating statements
  USE Financial statements
Operating System/8 (Computer system)
  USE OS/8 (Computer system)
Operating System Pub (Electronic computer
  system)
  USE OSPub (Electronic computer system)
Operating systems (Computers)
  [QA76.76.O63]
  UF Computer operating systems
    Computers—Operating systems

  BT Computer software
    Electronic digital computers—
    Programming
  NT AmigaDOS (Computer operating
    system)
    Concurrent PC DOS (Computer
    operating system)
    Coroutines (Computer programs)
    CP/68 (Computer operating system)
    CP/M (Computer operating system)
    CP/M-80 (Computer operating
    system)
    CP/M-86 (Computer operating
    system)
    CP/M Plus (Computer operating
    system)
    DISP (Computer operating system)
    GEM (Computer operating system)
    GEOS (Computer operating system)
    IBM VSE (Computer operating
    system)
    Kernal (Computer operating system)
    LDOS (Computer operating system)
    LOCUS (Computer operating system)
    Medusa (Computer system)
    MP/M (Computer operating system)
    MS-DOS (Computer operating system)
    MVS (Computer system)
    NetWare (Computer operating system)
    OS-9 (Computer operating system)
    OS-1100 (Computer operating system)
    OS BAMOS (Computer operating
    system)
    OS DISPAK (Computer operating
    system)
    OS ES (Computer operating system)
    PATHOS (Computer operating
    system)
    PC DOS (Computer operating system)
    PICK (Computer operating system)
    Polylith (Computer operating system)
    ProDOS (Computer operating system)
    PULSE (Computer operating system)
    RSTS (Computer operating system)
    RSX (Computer operating system)
    RT-11 (Computer operating system)
    SIRIS (Computer system)
    THEOS (Computer operating system)
    TopView (Computer operating system)
    UCSD p-System (Computer operating
    system)
    UNIX (Computer operating system)
    UNIX System V (Computer operating
    system)
    VAX/VMS (Computer operating
    system)
    Vil'nīūs (Computer operating system)
    XENIX (Computer operating system)
    Xinu (Computer operating system)
Operation Blue Star, Amritsar, India, 1984
  USE India—History—Golden Temple
    (Amritsar) Assault, 1984
Operation Cerberus, 1942
  UF Cerberus, Operation, 1942
  BT World War, 1939-1945—Campaigns—
    English Channel
    World War, 1939-1945—Naval
    operations, German
Operation Citadel
  [D764.3.K]
  UF Citadel Operation
  BT Kursk, Battle of, 1943
    World War, 1939-1945—Campaigns—
    Russian S.F.S.R.
    World War, 1939-1945—Tank warfare
Operation Coronet
  UF Coronet, Operation
  BT World War, 1939-1945—Campaigns—
    Japan
Operation Corporate, 1982
  USE Falkland Islands War, 1982

Operation Crossroads, 1946
  UF Bikini Nuclear Tests, 1946
       Crossroads, Operation, 1946
  BT Nuclear weapons—Testing
Operation Crossroads Africa
  USE Crossroads Africa
Operation Edelweiss
  UF Edelweiss, Operation
  BT Nuremberg Trial of Major German
       War Criminals, 1945-1946
Operation Goodwood
  [D756.5.B]
  UF Goodwood Operation
  BT World War, 1939-1945—Campaigns—
       France—Normandy
Operation Hardtack, 1958
  UF Hardtack, Operation, 1958
  BT Nuclear weapons—Testing
Operation Husky, 1943
  Here are entered works on the military planning
and strategy for the Sicily invasion. Works on the
Sicily invasion and campaign of 1943 are entered
under World War, 1939-1945—Campaigns—Italy—
Sicily.
  UF Husky, Operation, 1943
       Sicily Invasion, 1943 (Planning)
  BT World War, 1939-1945—Campaigns—
       Italy—Sicily
Operation Identification (Burglary protection)
  (May Subd Geog)
  [HV8061]
  BT Burglary protection
       Personal property—Marking
Operation Independence (Project)
  UF Independence Operation (Project)
  BT Aged—United States
       Social work with the aged—United
        States
       Voluntary health agencies—United
        States
       Volunteer workers in social service—
        United States
Operation Jaywick
  UF Jaywick, Operation
  BT World War, 1939-1945—Naval
       operations
Operation Jericho
  UF Jericho Operation
  BT World War, 1939-1945—Aerial
       operations, British
       World War, 1939-1945—Campaigns—
       France
Operation Jonathan, 1976
  USE Entebbe Airport Raid, 1976
Operation Lazarus, 1982
  BT Prisoners of war—United States
       Vietnamese Conflict, 1961-1975—
        Prisoners and prisons, Laotian
       Vietnamese Conflict, 1961-1975—
        Search and rescue operations—Laos
Operation Lila, 1942
  UF Lila, Operation, 1942
  BT World War, 1939-1945—Naval
       operations, German
       World War, 1939-1945—France
Operation Long Jump
  UF Long Jump, Operation
  BT World War, 1939-1945—Diplomatic
       history
Operation Match
Operation Menace
  [D766.99]
  UF Menace, Operation
  BT World War, 1939-1945—Campaigns—
       Africa, French-speaking West
       World War, 1939-1945—Naval
       operations
  NT Dakar, Battle of, 1940
Operation MENDEX
  UF MENDEX Operation

  BT Disaster medicine—Study and teaching
      —Texas
       Emergency medical services—Study
       and teaching—Texas
       Medicine, Military—Study and
       teaching—Texas
       United States. Army—Civic action
Operation Mercury, 1941
  [D764.3.O]
  UF Mercury, Operation, 1941
  BT World War, 1939-1945—Campaigns—
       Greece
Operation Mincemeat
  UF Mincemeat, Operation
  BT World War, 1939-1945—Secret service
      —Great Britain
Operation Moses, 1984-1985
  USE Falasha Rescue, 1984-1985
Operation Neptune
  UF Omaha Beach (France)
  BT World War, 1939-1945—Amphibious
       operations
       World War, 1939-1945—Campaigns—
       France—Normandy
Operation Overlord
  Here are entered works on the military planning
and diplomatic negotiations for the Normandy inva-
sion. Works on the Normandy invasion and cam-
paign of 1944 are entered under World War, 1939-
1945—Campaigns—France—Normandy.
  UF Normandy Invasion, 1944 (Planning)
       Overlord, Operation
  BT World War, 1939-1945—Campaigns—
       France—Normandy
Operation Plowshare
  USE Project Plowshare
Operation Pluto
  USE Cuba—History—Invasion, 1961
Operation Ranch Hand
  [DS559.8.C5]
  UF Ranch Hand, Operation
       Ranch Hand Project
  BT Herbicides—War use
       Vietnamese Conflict, 1961-1975—
       Chemical warfare
Operation Rimau
  UF Rimau, Operation
  BT World War, 1939-1945—Naval
       operations
Operation Rosario, 1982
  USE Falkland Islands War, 1982
Operation Sail
  USE Operation Sail, 1976
Operation Sail, 1976 *(May Subd Geog)*
  UF Operation Sail
       OpSail, 1976
  BT American Revolution Bicentennial,
       1776-1976
Operation Sail, 1986 *(May Subd Geog)*
  UF OpSail, 1986
  BT Statue of Liberty (New York, N.Y.)—
       Centennial celebrations, etc.
Operation Sandstone, 1948
  UF Sandstone, Operation, 1948
  BT Enewetak Atoll (Marshall Islands)
       Nuclear weapons—Testing
Operation Sea Lion
  UF Operation Sealion
       Sea Lion Operation
       Sealion Operation
  BT World War, 1939-1945—Campaigns—
       England
Operation Sealion
  USE Operation Sea Lion
Operation Stella Polaris, 1944
  UF Stella Polaris, Operation, 1944
  BT World War, 1939-1945—Campaigns—
       Sweden
       World War, 1939-1945—Naval
       operations, Finnish

Operation Sunrise
  [D748]
  UF Sunrise, Operation
  BT World War, 1939-1945—Campaigns—
       Italy
       World War, 1939-1945—Diplomatic
       history
Operation Susannah
  UF Susannah Operation
  BT Espionage, Israeli—Egypt
Operation Torch
  UF Torch, Operation
  RT World War, 1939-1945—Campaigns—
       Africa, North
Operation Urgent Fury, 1983
  USE Grenada—History—American
       invasion, 1983
Operation Victor Search
  UF Victor Search Operation
  BT Airplanes—Salvaging
       Victor (Jet planes)
Operational amplifiers
Operational analysis
  USE Operations research
Operational auditing
  USE Management audit
Operational calculus
  USE Calculus, Operational
Operational rations (Military supplies)
  (May Subd Geog)
  UF Combat rations
       Field rations
       Rations
       Soldiers—Food
       Soldiers—Rations
  BT Armies—Commissariat
       Food
  NT Survival and emergency rations
Operational readiness (Military science)
  Here are entered works on the capability and
readiness of military equipment and personnel to per-
form the mission or functions for which they were
organized or designed. Works on the capability of
military equipment and personnel to maintain the
necessary level and duration of combat activity are
entered under Combat sustainability (Military
science).
  UF Combat readiness (Military science)
       Preparedness (Military science)
       Readiness (Military science)
  BT Military art and science
  SA *subdivision* Operational readiness
       under names of individual military
       services, e.g. United States—Armed
       Forces—Operational readiness
Operational research
  USE Operations research
Operationalism
  [B828.35]
  BT Philosophy
Operations, Calculus of
  USE Calculus of operations
Operations, Elective (Surgery)
  USE Surgery, Elective
Operations, Low-intensity (Military science)
  USE Low-intensity conflicts (Military
       science)
Operations, Naval
  USE Sea control
Operations, Surgical *(May Subd Geog)*
  [RD]
  Here is entered literature relating to the risks and
accidents of surgical operations, treatment of patients
after operations, mortality, and other generalities.
Works on the details of the operations themselves are
entered under Surgery, Operative. Works relating
especially to methods of securing asepsis are entered
under Surgery, Aseptic and antiseptic.
  UF Surgical operations
  BT Surgery
       Surgery, Operative
  RT Surgery—Complications and sequelae

Operations, Surgical *(Continued)*
  NT Postoperative care
    Preoperative care
    Shock
    Surgery, Elective
    Surgical nursing
  — Anecdotes, facetiae, satire, etc.
    USE Medicine—Anecdotes, facetiae,
      satire, etc.
  — **Classification**
    ₍RD16₎
    BT Nosology
  — Psychological aspects
    USE Surgery—Psychological aspects
Operations, Undercover
  USE Undercover operations
Operations, Word processing
  USE Word processing operations
Operations auditing
  USE Management audit
Operations officers (United States Navy)
  USE United States. Navy—Operations
    officers
Operations research
  UF Operational analysis
    Operational research
  BT Industrial engineering
    Research
    System theory
  RT Management science
    Systems engineering
  NT Decomposition method
    Maintainability (Engineering)
    Management—Simulation methods
    Mathematical optimization
    Network analysis (Planning)
    Programming (Mathematics)
    Queuing theory
    Research, Industrial
    Resource allocation
    Scheduling (Management)
    Search theory
    Simulation methods
    Statistical decision
    Technological forecasting
Operations specialists (United States Navy)
  USE United States. Navy—Operations
    specialists
Operative ankylosis
  USE Arthrodesis
Operative dentistry
  USE Dentistry, Operative
Operative endoscopy
  USE Endoscopic surgery
Operative gynecology
  USE Gynecology, Operative
Operative obstetrics
  USE Obstetrics—Surgery
Operative orthopedics
  USE Orthopedic surgery
Operative otolaryngology
  USE Otolaryngology, Operative
Operative surgery
  USE Surgery, Operative
Operative urology
  USE Genitourinary organs—Surgery
Operative wound infections
  USE Surgical wound infections
Operator, D'Alembertian
  USE D'Alembertian operator
Operator, Hamiltonian
  USE Hamiltonian operator
Operator, Laplacian
  USE Laplacian operator
Operator, Schrödinger
  USE Schrödinger operator
Operator 5 (Fictitious character)
  UF Christopher, Jimmy (Fictitious
    character)
    Jimmy Christopher (Fictitious
    character)

  BT Characters and characteristics in
    literature
  RT Steele, Curtis—Characters—Operator 5
Operator algebras
  ₍QA326₎
  UF Algebras, Operator
  BT Operator theory
    Topological algebras
  NT Triangular operator algebras
Operator equations
  UF Equations, Operator
  BT Differential equations, Partial
  — Numerical solutions
    BT Numerical analysis
Operator equations, Nonlinear
  UF Nonlinear operator equations
  — Numerical solutions
    BT Numerical analysis
Operator ideals
  BT Ideals (Algebra)
Operator language/2
  USE OL/2 (Computer program language)
Operator product expansions
  UF Expansions, Operator product
    Product expansions, Operator
  BT Operator theory
Operator theory
  BT Functional analysis
  NT Differential operators
    Dilation theory (Operator theory)
    Eigenfunction expansions
    Factorization of operators
    Hecke operators
    Integral operators
    Linear operators
    Mellin operators
    Monotone operators
    Nonlinear operators
    Operator algebras
    Operator product expansions
    Operator-valued measures
    Polynomial operators
    Product formulas (Operator theory)
    Pseudodifferential operators
    Random operators
    Resolvents (Mathematics)
    Scattering operator
    Semigroups of operators
    Transmutation operators
    Unitary operators
Operator-valued measures
  UF Measures, Operator-valued
  BT Measure theory
    Operator theory
Operatories, Dental
  USE Dental offices
Operators, Closed
  USE Closed operators
Operators, Closure
  USE Closure operators
Operators, Contracting
  USE Contraction operators
Operators, Contraction
  USE Contraction operators
Operators, Differential
  USE Differential operators
Operators, Elliptic
  USE Elliptic operators
Operators, Factorization of
  USE Factorization of operators
Operators, Fredholm
  USE Fredholm operators
Operators, Hankel
  USE Hankel operators
Operators, Hecke
  USE Hecke operators
Operators, Hypoelliptic
  USE Hypoelliptic operators
Operators, Hyponormal
  USE Hyponormal operators

Operators, Integral
  USE Integral operators
Operators, Linear
  USE Linear operators
Operators, Markov
  USE Markov operators
Operators, Mellin
  USE Mellin operators
Operators, Motor vehicle
  USE Motor vehicle drivers
Operators, Nonlinear
  USE Nonlinear operators
Operators, Nonselfadjoint
  USE Nonselfadjoint operators
Operators, Normal
  USE Normal operators
Operators, Nuclear power plant
  USE Nuclear power plant operators
Operators, Parabolic
  USE Parabolic operators
Operators, Polynomial
  USE Polynomial operators
Operators, Positive
  USE Positive operators
Operators, Pseudodifferential
  USE Pseudodifferential operators
Operators, Random
  USE Random operators
Operators, Selfadjoint
  USE Selfadjoint operators
Operators, Semigroups of
  USE Semigroups of operators
Operators, Shift (Operator theory)
  USE Shift operators (Operator theory)
Operators, Subnormal
  USE Subnormal operators
Operators, Symmetric
  USE Symmetric operators
Operators, Toeplitz
  USE Toeplitz operators
Operators, Transmutation
  USE Transmutation operators
Operators, Unitary
  USE Unitary operators
Operators, Wiener-Hopf
  USE Wiener-Hopf operators
Operators' permits, Automobile
  USE Automobile drivers' licenses
Operculates
  USE Discomycetes
Operetta *(May Subd Geog)*
  ₍ML1900₎
  UF Comic opera
    Musical farce
    Opera, Comic
  BT Opera
  NT Melodrama
    Singspiel
    Zarzuela
  — Stories, plots, etc.
    USE Operas—Stories, plots, etc.
Operettas
  USE Musical revues, comedies, etc.
    Operas
    Tonadillas
    Zarzuelas
Operons
  ₍QH450.2₎
  BT Genetic regulation
    Genetic transcription
  NT Promoters (Genetics)
    Repressors, Genetic
Operophtera
  USE Operophthera
Operophtera brumata
  USE Winter moth
Operophthera
  ₍QL561.G6 (Zoology)₎
  UF Cheimatobia
    Operophtera
    Opheroptera

BT Geometridae
Operophthera boreata
USE Operophthera fagata
Operophthera fagata
    ₁QL561.G6 (Zoology)₁
    UF Geometra boreata
        Northern winter moth
        Operophthera boreata
        Winter moth, Northern
Ophelia (Annelida)
    ₁QL391.A6₁
    BT Opheliidae
Ophelia (Fictitious character)
    BT Characters and characteristics in
        literature
    RT Shakespeare, William, 1564-1616—
        Characters—Ophelia
Opheliida
    ₁QL391.A6₁
    BT Polychaeta
    NT Opheliidae
Opheliidae
    ₁QL391.A6₁
    BT Opheliida
    NT Ophelia (Annelida)
Opheodrys
    ₁QL666.O636₁
    BT Colubridae
    NT Opheodrys vernalis
Opheodrys vernalis
    ₁QL666.O636₁
    UF Smooth green snake
    BT Opheodrys
Opheroptera
    USE Operophthera
Ophibolus
    USE Lampropeltis
Ophichthidae
    USE Snake eels
Ophichthyidae
    USE Snake eels
Ophicleide
    ₁ML990.O₁
    BT Brass instruments
        Serpent (Musical instrument)
        Tuba
Ophidia
    USE Snakes
Ophidiidae
    ₁QL638.O637₁
    UF Aphyonidae
        Brotulidae
        Brotulophidae
        Cusk eels
        Cuskeels
    BT Gadiformes
    NT Parabassogigas
Ophiobolus graminis
    USE Gaeumannomyces graminis
Ophiochaeta graminis
    USE Gaeumannomyces graminis
Ophiodon
    USE Lingcod
Ophiodon elongatus
    USE Lingcod
Ophiodontidae
    USE Hexagrammidae
        Lingcod
Ophiolites *(May Subd Geog)*
    BT Rocks, Igneous
Ophiology
    USE Snakes
Ophiomorus
    ₁QL666.L28₁
    BT Skinks
Ophionyssus
    ₁QL458.2.M3₁
    BT Macronyssidae
    NT Ophionyssus natricis
Ophionyssus natricis
    ₁QL458.2.M3₁

BT Ophionyssus
Ophiophagus hannah
    USE King cobra
Ophiorhiza
    USE Ophiorrhiza
Ophiorrhiza
    ₁QK495.R85 (Botany)₁
    UF Ophiorhiza
Ophioscion
    ₁QL638.S34₁
    BT Sciaenidae
Ophiostoma
    ₁QK623.O6₁
    BT Ophiostomataceae
Ophiostoma multiannulatum
    ₁QK623.O6₁
Ophiostomataceae
    ₁QK623.O6₁
    BT Ascomycetes
        Sphaeriales
    NT Ceratocystiopsis
        Ceratocystis
        Ophiostoma
Ophioxylon serpentinum
    USE Rauvolfia serpentina
Ophisaurus
    ₁QL666.L2254₁
    UF Glass lizards
    BT Anguidae
    NT Ophisaurus apodus
Ophisaurus apodus
    ₁QL666.L2254₁
    BT Ophisaurus
Ophisternon
    ₁QL638.S893₁
    BT Synbranchidae
Ophisternon aenigmaticum
    ₁QL638.S893₁
Ophistonema
    USE Opisthonema
Ophites
    ₁BT1390₁
    BT Gnosticism
Ophiuroidea *(May Subd Geog)*
    ₁QL384.O6₁
    UF Brittle-stars
        Serpent stars
    BT Echinodermata
Ophiuroidea, Fossil
    NT Stenurida
Ophiusa (Spain)
    USE Formentera (Spain)
Ophphikia
    BT Church officers
        Orthodox Eastern Church—
        Government
Ophryoglena
    ₁QL368.H87₁
    BT Ophryoglenidae
Ophryoglenidae
    NT Ophryoglena
Ophryotrocha
    ₁QL391.A6₁
    BT Dorvilleidae
Ophrys
    ₁QK495.O64₁
    UF Listera
    BT Orchids
Ophrys cernua
    USE Spiranthes cernua
Ophthalmia
    USE Conjunctiva—Diseases
        Eye—Inflammation
Ophthalmia neonatorum
    USE Conjunctivitis, Infantile
Ophthalmic and aural dispensaries
    USE Dispensaries, Ophthalmic and aural
Ophthalmic and aural hospitals
    USE Hospitals, Ophthalmic and aural

Ophthalmic assistants
    BT Allied health personnel
        Ophthalmologists
        Ophthalmology—Practice
Ophthalmic dispensing
    USE Opticianry
Ophthalmic echography
    USE Ultrasonics in ophthalmology
Ophthalmic emergencies
    USE Ophthalmologic emergencies
Ophthalmic lasers
    USE Lasers in ophthalmology
Ophthalmic lenses *(May Subd Geog)*
    ₁RE961-2₁
    UF Corrective lenses
        Prosthetic lenses
    BT Lenses
        Opticianry
        Optometry
    NT Contact lenses
        Eyeglasses
        Intraocular lenses
Ophthalmic mallein
Ophthalmic nursing
    ₁RE88₁
    UF Eye—Diseases and defects—Nursing
    BT Eye—Diseases and defects
        Nursing
Ophthalmic opticians
    USE Optometrists
Ophthalmic photography
    USE Photography, Ophthalmic
Ophthalmodynamometry
    BT Blood pressure—Measurement
        Ophthalmoscope and ophthalmoscopy
        Retina—Blood-vessels
Ophthalmologic emergencies
    (May Subd Geog)
    ₁RE48₁
    UF Emergency ophthalmology
        Ocular emergencies
        Ophthalmic emergencies
    BT Medical emergencies
    NT Eye—Wounds and injuries
Ophthalmological instruments and apparatus
    USE Eye, Instruments and apparatus for
Ophthalmological manifestations of general
    diseases
    USE Ocular manifestations of general
        diseases
Ophthalmological materia medica
    USE Materia medica, Ophthalmological
Ophthalmological symptoms of general diseases
    USE Ocular manifestations of general
        diseases
Ophthalmological therapeutics
    USE Therapeutics, Ophthalmological
Ophthalmologists *(May Subd Geog)*
    UF Oculists
    BT Ophthalmology
        Physicians
    NT Ophthalmic assistants
        Ophthalmology—Vocational guidance
    — **Malpractice** *(May Subd Geog)*
        UF Tort liability of ophthalmologists
        BT Malpractice
            Medical laws and legislation
Ophthalmology *(May Subd Geog)*
    ₁RE₁
    BT Eye—Diseases and defects
    NT Eye
        Geriatric ophthalmology
        Hypnotism in ophthalmology
        Lasers in ophthalmology
        Neuro-ophthalmology
        Ophthalmologists
        Pediatric ophthalmology
        Radioisotopes in ophthalmology
        Sports ophthalmology
        Ultrasonics in ophthalmology
    — **Atlases**

Ophthalmology
— **Atlases** *(Continued)*
  BT Ophthalmoscope and
      ophthalmoscopy
— **Early works to 1800**
  [RE41]
  UF Eye—Diseases and defects—Early
      works to 1800
— **Formulae, receipts, prescriptions**
  BT Therapeutics, Ophthalmological
— Jurisprudence
  USE Forensic ophthalmology
— **Law and legislation** *(May Subd Geog)*
  BT Medical laws and legislation
— **Periodicals**
  UF Eye—Periodicals
— **Popular works**
  [RE51]
— **Practice**
  NT Ophthalmic assistants
— **Vocational guidance**
  [RE56]
  BT Ophthalmologists
Ophthalmology, Anesthetics in
  USE Anesthesia in ophthalmology
Ophthalmology, Forensic
  USE Forensic ophthalmology
Ophthalmology, Industrial
  USE Industrial ophthalmology
Ophthalmology, Veterinary
  USE Veterinary ophthalmology
Ophthalmology in sports
  USE Sports ophthalmology
Ophthalmometry
  USE Eye—Examination
Ophthalmopharmacology
  USE Ocular pharmacology
Ophthalmoplegia
  USE Eye—Paralysis
Ophthalmoscope and ophthalmoscopy
  [RE78]
  BT Eye—Examination
  NT Fundus oculi
      Ophthalmodynamometry
      Ophthalmology—Atlases
Ophthalmothripidae
  USE Phlaeothripidae
Ophthalmoxerosis
  USE Xerophthalmia
Opiate receptors
  USE Endorphins—Receptors
Opiates
  USE Narcotics
Opiates, Endogenous
  USE Endorphins
Opici
  USE Oscans
Opiliaceae
  [QK495.O62 (Botany)]
  BT Santalales
  NT Cansjera
Opilioacariformes
  USE Mites
Opiliones
  [QL458.5]
  UF Daddy longlegs
      Granddaddy longlegs
      Harvest spiders
      Harvestmen (Animals)
      Phalangida
      Phalangidea
      Phalangides
      Phalangiida
  BT Arachnida
  NT Nemastomatidae
      Phalangiidae
      Phalangodidae
      Triaenonychidae
Opinion, Public
  USE Public opinion

Opinion (Philosophy)
  BT Philosophy
Opinion evidence
  USE Evidence, Expert
Opinion polls
  USE Public opinion polls
Opinions, Auditors'
  USE Auditors' reports
Opinions, Judicial
  USE Judicial opinions
Opioid habit
  [RC568.O58]
  BT Opioids
      Opium habit
Opioid peptides
  USE Endorphins
Opioid receptors
  USE Opioids—Receptors
Opioids
  [RC483.5.O64 (Psychotherapy)]
  [RD86.O64 (Anesthesiology)]
  UF Opium-like agents
  BT Psychotropic drugs
  RT Opium
  NT Endorphins
      Opioid habit
— **Receptors**
  UF Opioid receptors
      Receptors, Opioid
  BT Cell receptors
      Drug receptors
Opisthobranchia
  [QL430.4]
  UF Opisthobranchiata
  BT Gasteropoda
Opisthobranchia, Fossil
  [QE809.O6]
  BT Gasteropoda, Fossil
  NT Actaeonellidae
Opisthobranchiata
  USE Opisthobranchia
Opisthocentridae
  USE Gunnels
Opisthocomi
  USE Hoactzin
Opisthocomidae
  USE Hoactzin
Opisthoglyphia
  [QL666.O636]
  BT Colubridae
Opisthognathidae
  [QL638.O65]
  UF Jawfishes
  BT Perciformes
  NT Gnathypops
      Lonchistium
Opisthonema
  [QL638.C64]
  UF Ophistonema
  BT Clupeidae
Opisthopora *(May Subd Geog)*
  [QL391.A6]
  Here are entered works on earthworms as a group.
  Works on the common earthworm (Lumbricus terrestris) are entered under Earthworms.
  BT Oligochaeta
  NT Megascolecidae
Opisthorchiasis
  BT Helminthiasis
Opisthotropis
  [QL666.O636]
  BT Colubridae
Opium
  [SB295.O6]
  BT Narcotics
  RT Morphine
      Opioids
Opium habit *(May Subd Geog)*
  [HV5816 (Social aspects)]
  [RC568.O6 (Psychiatry)]
  BT Narcotic habit

  NT Opioid habit
Opium-like agents
  USE Opioids
Opium poppy *(May Subd Geog)*
  [QK495.P22 (Botany)]
  [SB295.O65 (Medicinal plant)]
  [SB299.O65 (Oilseed plant)]
  UF Oil poppy
      Papaver setigerum
      Papaver somniferum
      Poppy, Oil
      Poppy, Opium
      Poppy, Seed
      Seed poppy
  BT Medicinal plants
      Oilseed plants
      Poppies
      Psychotropic plants
  NT Opium trade
Opium trade *(May Subd Geog)*
  [HV5816]
  BT Opium poppy
— **Law and legislation** *(May Subd Geog)*
  BT Narcotic laws
Opium War, China, 1840-1842
  USE China—History—Opium War, 1840-
      1842
Opius
  [QL568.B8]
  BT Braconidae
Oplandsplads family *(Not Subd Geog)*
Opogona
  [QL561.T55]
  BT Tineidae
Opomyza
  [QL537.O7]
  BT Opomyzidae
Opomyzidae
  [QL537.O7]
  UF Geomyzidae
  BT Diptera
  NT Opomyza
Oporabia
  USE Oporinia
Oporinia
  [QL561.G6 (Zoology)]
  UF Cidaria
      Epirrita
      Larentia
      Oporabia
  BT Geometridae
Oporinia autumnata
  [QL561.G6 (Zoology)]
  [SB945.O57 (Pest)]
  UF Autumnal moth
Opossum Creek (Hanover County, Va.)
  USE Totopotomoy Creek (Va.)
Opossum-shrew
  [QL737.I5]
Opossum shrimps
  USE Mysidacea
Opossums *(May Subd Geog)*
  [QL737.M34]
  UF Didelphidae
  BT Marsupialia
  NT Didelphis
      Metachirus
— **Anatomy**
Opossums, Australasian
  USE Phalangeridae
Opossums, Fossil
  [QE882.M3]
Opotherapy
  USE Animal extracts
      Organotherapy
Oppanol
  USE Rubber, Artificial
Oppatajō (Japan)
  BT Castles—Japan

Oppenheim, Dennis, 1938- **Power passage**
  (for Indianapolis)
  UF Power passage (for Indianapolis)
       (Conceptual art)
Oppenheim-Ziehen disease
  USE Dystonia musculorum deformans
Opple family
  USE Appel family
Opponents
  USE *subdivision* Adversaries *under names*
      of individual persons
Opportunistic infections (May Subd Geog)
  BT Infection
Opposites
  USE Polarity
Opposition, Theory of
  [BC199.O6 (Logic)]
  [BF455 (Psychology)]
  UF Contrariety
  BT Philosophy
      Psychology
  RT Polarity
Opposition (Political science)
  (May Subd Geog)
  [JF518 (Legislative bodies)]
  UF Political opposition
  BT Political science
Opposition (Political science) in the Bible
  UF Bible—Opposition (Political science)
  BT Politics in the Bible
Opposition in literature
  USE Polarity in literature
Oppression (Psychology)
  BT Criminal psychology
      Personality
      Psychology
      Social psychology
Oppression (Psychology) in mass media
  (May Subd Geog)
  BT Mass media
Ops (Roman deity)
  [BL820.O6]
  BT Gods, Roman
      Mythology, Roman
OPS5 (Computer system)
  UF Official Production System Version 5
      (Computer system)
  BT Electronic digital computers—
      Programming
      Expert systems (Computer science)
      Problem solving—Data processing
OpSail, 1976
  USE Operation Sail, 1976
OpSail, 1986
  USE Operation Sail, 1986
Opsanus (May Subd Geog)
  [QL638.B3]
  BT Toadfishes
Opsanus tau
  USE Oyster toadfish
Opsiphanes
  [QL561.S3]
  BT Satyridae
Opsiphanes tamarindi
  [QL561.S3]
Opsodexia
  [QL537.M8]
  BT Muscidae
Opsonins and opsonic index
  [RM751]
  RT Serumtherapy
Opsopoeodus emiliae
  USE Pugnose minnow
Optic chiasm
  [QL937]
  [QM455]
  [QP381]
  BT Brain
      Optic nerve
      Visual pathways
  — Wounds and injuries

Optic disc
  UF Blind spot
      Blindspot
      Disc, Optic
      Optic papills
      Papills, Optic
  BT Optic nerve
      Retina
Optic ganglion
  USE Optic lobes
Optic lobes
  [QL937]
  [QM455]
  [QP381]
  UF Optic ganglion
  BT Brain
Optic nerve
  [QL949]
  [QM511]
  [QP475]
  BT Eye
      Nerves, Cranial
      Visual pathways
  NT Optic chiasm
      Optic disc
  — Cytology
    RT Retinal ganglion cells
  — Diseases (May Subd Geog)
    [RE701]
    BT Neuro-ophthalmology
    NT Optic neuritis
  — Inflammation
    USE Optic neuritis
  — Tumors
    [RC280.E9]
  — Wounds and injuries
Optic neuritis
  [RE702.O]
  UF Optic nerve—Inflammation
  BT Optic nerve—Diseases
  NT Subacute myelooptic neuropathy
Optic papills
  USE Optic disc
Optic thalamus
  USE Thalamus
Optical alignment
  USE Optical tooling
Optical antipodes
  USE Enantiomers
Optical art (May Subd Geog)
  UF Art, Optical
      Op art
  BT Art, Modern—20th century
      Concrete art
      Kinetic art
      Visual perception
Optical bistability
  UF Bistability, Optical
  BT Quantum optics
      Statistical physics
Optical bleaches
  USE Optical brighteners
Optical brighteners
  UF Brighteners, Optical
      Fluorescent bleaches
      Fluorescent brighteners
      Fluorescent whitening agents
      Optical bleaches
      Optical whiteners
  BT Bleaching materials
      Dyes and dyeing
      Fluorescence
Optical character recognition device industry
  (May Subd Geog)
  BT Optical character recognition devices
Optical character recognition devices
  UF Character recognition devices, Optical
      OCR devices

  BT Computers—Optical equipment
      Optical pattern recognition
      Optical scanners
      Optoelectronic devices
      Pattern recognition systems
      Reading machines (Data processing
       equipment)
  NT Optical character recognition device
      industry
  — Library applications
    [Z678.93.O68]
    UF Libraries and optical character
       recognition devices
      Library applications of optical
       character recognition devices
Optical coatings
  Here are entered works on coatings applied to
  optical surfaces.
  BT Coatings
      Optical materials
Optical coherence
  USE Coherence (Optics)
Optical communication systems, Laser-based
  USE Laser communication systems
Optical communications
  [TK5103.59]
  UF Communications, Optical
      Light communications
  BT Photonics
      Telecommunication
  NT Astronautics—Optical communication
      systems
      Fiber optics
      Laser communication systems
      Light emitting diodes
      Optical radar
      Optical wave guides
      Retrometer
Optical computers
  USE Computers, Optical
Optical computing
  USE Optical data processing
Optical crystallography
  USE Crystal optics
Optical data processing
  UF Optical computing
      Visual data processing
  BT Bionics
      Electronic data processing
      Integrated optics
      Photonics
  RT Computers—Optical equipment
  NT Acoustooptical devices
      Astronautics—Optical communication
      systems
      Computers, Optical
      Flying spot scanners
      Image processing
      Image transmission
      Information display systems
      Laser recording
      Optical pattern recognition
      Radar—Optical equipment
      Show-and-Tell (Electronic computer
      system)
      Stellar inertial navigation systems
      Television bandwidth compression
      United States. Air Force translator
Optical detectors
  UF Detectors, Optical
  BT Light
  NT Bolometer
      Photoelectronic devices
      Photography—Films
      Thermocouples
Optical discs
  USE Optical disks
Optical disks (May Subd Geog)
  UF Discs, Optical
      Disks, Optical
      Optical discs

Optical disks (Continued)
  BT Optical storage devices
  — **Library applications**
      [Z681.3.O67]
      UF Libraries and optical disks
          Library applications of optical disks
Optical fibers
  UF Light guides (Optical fibers)
  BT Fiber optics
      Fibers
      Optical materials
      Optical wave guides
  — Connectors
      USE Optical fibers—Joints
  — Contacts
      USE Optical fibers—Joints
  — Joints
      UF Connectors, Optical fiber
          Contacts, Optical fiber
          Optical fibers—Connectors
          Optical fibers—Contacts
          Optical fibers—Splices
          Splices, Optical fiber
      BT Joints (Engineering)
  — Splices
      USE Optical fibers—Joints
Optical fibers in biochemistry
  (May Subd Geog)
  BT Biological chemistry
Optical fibers in medicine (May Subd Geog)
      [R857.O6]
  BT Medicine
Optical films
  UF Films, Optical
  BT Optical materials
      Thin films
Optical furnaces
  USE Image furnaces
Optical glass
  USE Glass, Optical
Optical gyroscopes
      [TL589.2.O6]
  UF Laser gyroscopes
  BT Gyroscopes
Optical illusions
      [QP495]
  UF Illusions, Optical
  BT Hallucinations and illusions
      Optics, Physiological
      Psychology, Physiological
      Vision
      Visual perception
  NT Anamorphosis (Visual perception)
      Autokinesis
      Black box theaters
Optical images
  USE Images, Optical
Optical industry (May Subd Geog)
      [TS510-TS518]
      Here are entered works on the manufacture of
      optical instruments and systems for scientific and en-
      gineering applications. Works on the optometrist's
      and optician's trade are entered under Optical trade.
  BT Instrument industry
  RT Optical instruments
  NT Laser industry
Optical inertial navigation systems
  USE Stellar inertial navigation systems
Optical inspection
  USE Quality control—Optical methods
Optical instruments (May Subd Geog)
      [QC371-QC376 (Optics)]
      [RE73 (Examination of eye)]
  UF Aberration, Chromatic and spherical
      Instruments, Optical
  BT Glass manufacture
      Physical instruments
      Scientific apparatus and instruments
      Space optics
  RT Optical industry
      Optical trade

  SA individual optical instruments, e.g.
      Eriometer, Spectroscope
  NT Achromatism
      Airplanes—Optical equipment
      Astronomical instruments
      Beam splitters
      Binoculars
      Computers—Optical equipment
      Crime prevention—Optical equipment
      Diffraction gratings
      Eriometer
      Fire control (Gunnery)—Optical
        equipment
      Glass
      Glass, Optical
      Law enforcement—Optical equipment
      Lenses
      Light deflectors
      Manipulators (Mechanism)—Optical
        equipment
      Microscope and microscopy
      Mining machinery—Blind-area viewers
      Mirrors
      Night vision devices
      Optical spectrometers
      Petrographic microscope
      Polariscope
      Polarizers (Light)
      Radar—Optical equipment
      Resolution (Optics)
      Reticles
      Rockets (Aeronautics)—Optical
        equipment
      Telescope
  — **Design and construction**
  — — **Computer programs**
  — Drawing
      USE Optical instruments—Drawings
  — **Drawings**
      UF Optical instruments—Drawing
      BT Mechanical drawing
Optical isomers
  UF Isomers, Optical
      Isomers, Optically active
      Optically active isomers
  BT Stereoisomers
  NT Enantiomers
Optical laboratories (May Subd Geog)
  UF Laboratories, Optical
      Optics laboratories
  BT Optics
      Physical laboratories
Optical masers
  USE Lasers
Optical materials
      [QC374]
  BT Materials
  RT Laser materials
  NT Optical coatings
      Optical fibers
      Optical films
Optical measurements
      [QC367]
  UF Measurements, Optical
  BT Optics—Laboratory manuals
  NT Air—Pollution—Measurement—
        Optical methods
      Densitometry
      Interferometry
      Optical tooling
      Optical transfer function
      Photometry, Ultraviolet
      Polarimetry
      Pollution—Measurement—Optical
        methods
      Quality control—Optical methods
      Speckle metrology
Optical mineralogy
      [QE369.O6]
  UF Mineralogy, Optical
  BT Mineralogy, Determinative

  NT Refractive index of minerals
Optical models, Nuclear
  USE Nuclear optical models
Optical oceanography (May Subd Geog)
      [GC178]
  UF Optics of the sea
  BT Oceanography
  NT Photography, Submarine
      Sea-water—Optical properties
      Underwater television
Optical pattern recognition
  BT Optical data processing
      Pattern perception
      Perceptrons
      Visual discrimination
  NT LINDA (Computer system)
      Optical character recognition devices
Optical phase conjugation
      [QC446.3.O67]
  UF Phase conjugation, Optical
  BT Beam optics
      Nonlinear optics
Optical phenomena, Influence of magnetism on
  USE Magneto-optics
Optical potentials, Nuclear
  USE Nuclear optical potentials
Optical properties of materials
  USE subdivision Optical properties under
      names of particular materials or
      substances, e.g. Metallic films—
      Optical properties; Metals—Optical
      properties
Optical pumping
  UF Pumping, Optical
  BT Atoms
      Light
  NT Lasers
      Masers
Optical pyrometers
      [QC277]
  BT Pyrometers and pyrometry
  RT Radiation pyrometers
Optical quality control
  USE Quality control—Optical methods
Optical radar
  UF Laser radar
      Lidar
  BT Laser communication systems
      Optical communications
      Optoelectronic devices
      Radar
  NT Radar—Optical equipment
      Shuttle Atmosphere Lidar Research
        Program
Optical range finders
  UF Range finders, Optical
  BT Range-finding
Optical resolution
  USE Resolution (Chemistry)
Optical resolving power
  USE Resolution (Optics)
Optical resonance
      [QC476.5]
  BT Luminescence
      Quantum optics
      Resonance
Optical rotation
      [QD651]
  BT Molecular rotation
      Polariscope
  RT Polarization (Light)
  NT Optical rotatory dispersion
      Walden inversion
Optical rotatory dispersion
      [QD473]
  BT Dispersion
      Optical rotation
Optical scanners
  BT Laser recording
      Scanning systems
  NT CHLOE scanner

Optical character recognition devices
Optical space communication systems
  USE Astronautics—Optical communication
       systems
Optical spectrometers
  BT Optical instruments
     Spectrometer
Optical storage device industry
  (May Subd Geog)
  BT Optical storage devices
Optical storage devices
  [TK7895.M4]
  BT Computer storage devices
     Computers—Optical equipment
  RT Laser recording
  NT CD-I technology
     CD-ROM
     Compact discs
     Documents in optical storage
     Optical disks
     Optical storage device industry
     Photoferroelectric effect
  — **Library applications**
     UF Libraries and optical storage
        devices
        Library applications of optical
          storage devices
Optical storage of documents
  USE Documents in optical storage
Optical synthetic apertures
  USE Synthetic apertures
Optical tooling
  UF Alignment, Optical
     Optical alignment
     Tooling, Optical
  BT Engineering inspection
     Machinery—Alignment
     Optical measurements
Optical trade *(May Subd Geog)*
  [HD9707-HD9707.5]
  Here are entered works on the optometrist's and
  optician's trade. Works on the manufacture of optical
  instruments and systems for scientific and engineer-
  ing applications are entered under Optical industry.
  RT Optical instruments
  NT Opticianry
  — Advertising
     USE Advertising—Optical trade
  — Collective labor agreements
     USE Collective labor agreements—
        Optical trade
Optical transducers
  UF Transducers, Optical
  BT Transducers
Optical transfer function
  UF Function, Optical transfer
  BT Fourier transformations
     Optical measurements
     Optics
     Transfer functions
Optical transforms
  USE Diffraction patterns
Optical wave guides
  BT Integrated optics
     Optical communications
     Optoelectronic devices
     Wave guides
  NT Optical fibers
Optical whiteners
  USE Optical brighteners
Optically active isomers
  USE Optical isomers
Optically stored documents
  USE Documents in optical storage
Opticianry *(May Subd Geog)*
  [RE940-981]
  UF Dispensing, Ophthalmic
     Ophthalmic dispensing
  BT Optical trade
     Optometry
  NT Eyeglasses

Ophthalmic lenses
  Opticians
— **Vocational guidance**
  BT Opticians
Opticians *(May Subd Geog)*
  [RE940]
  UF Dispensing opticians
  BT Opticianry
  RT Optometrists
  NT Collective labor agreements—Optical
     trade
     Opticianry—Vocational guidance
Optics *(May Subd Geog)*
  [QC350-467]
  Here are entered general works dealing with geo-
  metrical, physical, and physiological optics. Works
  dealing with special branches are entered under spe-
  cific headings, e.g. Optics, Geometrical; Optics,
  Physical; Optics, Physiological.
  BT Physics
  RT Light
     Photometry
  SA *headings beginning with the word*
     Optical
  NT Aberration
     Absorption of light
     Achromatism
     Acoustooptics
     Beam optics
     Blackbody radiation
     Cherenkov radiation
     Coherence (Optics)
     Color
     Diffraction
     Dispersion
     Electron optics
     Focal planes
     Fourier transform optics
     Grazing incidence
     Imaging systems
     Information theory in optics
     Interference (Light)
     Kerr effect
     Light, Corpuscular theory of
     Light, Wave theory of
     Light deflectors
     Light filters
     Magneto-optics
     Optical laboratories
     Optical transfer function
     Perspective
     Photochemistry
     Photonics
     Photoplasticity
     Polarization (Light)
     Quantum optics
     Radiation
     Reflection (Optics)
     Refraction
     Scanning systems
     Schlieren photography
     Space optics
     Speckle
     Spectrum analysis
  — **Atlases**
     [QC366]
     UF Atlases, Optical
     BT Photography—Scientific
        applications
        Photomicrography
  — **Laboratory manuals**
     [QC365-7]
     NT Optical measurements
  — **Tables**
     [QC369]
     UF Optics—Tables, etc.
  — Tables, etc.
     USE Optics—Tables
Optics, Adaptive
  UF Adaptive optics
  BT Aberration

Optics, Electronic
  USE Electron optics
Optics, Fiber
  USE Fiber optics
Optics, Geometrical
  [QC381-9]
  UF Geometrical optics
  NT Diffraction, Geometrical
     Eikonal equation
     Images, Optical
     Mangin mirror
     Resolution (Optics)
Optics, Hadamard transform
  USE Hadamard transform spectroscopy
Optics, Meteorological
  USE Meteorological optics
Optics, Microwave
  USE Microwave optics
Optics, Nonlinear
  USE Nonlinear optics
Optics, Photographic
  USE Photographic optics
Optics, Physical
  [QC401-495]
  UF Physical optics
  BT Light, Wave theory of
     Mathematical physics
  RT Electromagnetic theory
  NT Crystal optics
     Microwave optics
     Photoelasticity
     Visibility
     X-ray optics
Optics, Physiological
  [QP474-495]
  UF Physiological optics
  RT Vision
  NT Color vision
     Eye
     Eye—Accommodation and refraction
     Images, Optical
     Mach bands
     Optical illusions
     Phosphenes
     Talbot's law (Optics)
  — **Experiments**
Optics, Psychological
  USE Visual perception
Optics, Quantum
  USE Quantum optics
Optics laboratories
  USE Optical laboratories
Optics of the sea
  USE Optical oceanography
OPTIMA (Computer program)
Optima camera
Optimal regulator algorithms for the control of
  linear systems (Computer program)
  USE ORACLS (Computer program)
Optimal stopping (Mathematical statistics)
  [QA279.7]
  UF Stopping, Optimal (Mathematical
     statistics)
  BT Sequential analysis
Optimisation of Crystal Positions (Computer
  program)
  USE OCRYSP (Computer program)
Optimism
  [B829 (Philosophy)]
  [BJ1477 (Ethics)]
  BT Philosophy
  RT Cheerfulness
Optimism in literature
Optimization, Combinatorial
  USE Combinatorial optimization
Optimization, Trajectory
  USE Trajectory optimization
Optimization (Mathematics)
  USE Mathematical optimization
Optimization techniques
  USE Mathematical optimization

Optimization theory
USE Mathematical optimization
Optimum currency areas
USE Monetary unions
Optimum ship routing
[VK570]
UF Least-time ship routing
Ship routing
BT Meteorology, Maritime
Navigation
Shipping
Trade routes
Option, Fundamental (Ethics)
USE Fundamental option (Ethics)
Option (Contract) (May Subd Geog)
BT Contracts
Offer and acceptance
NT Put and call transactions—Law and
legislation
Restricted stock options
Option (Contract law, Islamic)
(May Subd Geog)
BT Contracts (Islamic law)
Option of nationality (May Subd Geog)
[JX4231.O7]
UF Nationality, Option of
BT Citizenship (International law)
Option value
BT Value
Options, Stock
USE Employee stock options
Put and call transactions
Restricted stock options
Opto-acoustic devices
USE Acoustooptical devices
Optoacoustic devices
USE Acoustooptical devices
Optoacoustic spectroscopy
[QD96.O6]
UF Photoacoustic spectroscopy
Spectroscopy, Optoacoustic
BT Atomic absorption spectroscopy
Laser spectroscopy
Optoelectronic devices
BT Electronic apparatus and appliances
Solid state electronics
NT Acoustooptical devices
Electroluminescent display systems
Electrooptical devices
Fiber optics
Imaging systems
Information display systems
Infrared equipment
Lasers
Light emitting diodes
Optical character recognition devices
Optical radar
Optical wave guides
Photoelectronic devices
Television
Optoelectronics
BT Electronics
Electrooptics
Photonics
Optoelectronics industry (May Subd Geog)
[HD9696.O67-674]
Optometric assistants (May Subd Geog)
[RE959.5]
BT Allied health personnel
Optometrists
Optometry
— **Supply and demand**
Optometric services insurance
USE Insurance, Optometric services
Optometrists (May Subd Geog)
UF Oculists
Ophthalmic opticians
Refractionists
RT Opticians
NT Optometric assistants
Optometry—Vocational guidance

— **Fees**
[RE959.3]
BT Medical fees
— **Malpractice** (May Subd Geog)
BT Optometry—Practice
— **Supply and demand**
Optometry (May Subd Geog)
[RE940-981]
RT Eye—Accommodation and refraction
NT Ophthalmic lenses
Opticianry
Optometric assistants
Vision—Testing
— **Economic aspects**
NT Insurance, Optometric services
— **Practice**
[RE959.3]
NT Optometrists—Malpractice
— **Vocational guidance**
[RE956]
BT Optometrists
Opulus (The Latin word)
BT Latin language—Etymology
Opuntiales
USE Cactus
O'Quin family
USE Quin family
OR GHX (Computer program)
Or Islands (France)
USE Hyères Islands (France)
Orach
[QK495.C46 (Botany)]
[SB351.O7 (Crop)]
UF French spinach
Garden orach
Mountain spinach
ORACLE (Computer system)
[QA76.9.D3]
UF ORACLE RDBMS (Computer system)
ORACLE Relational Database
Management System (Computer
system)
BT Data base management
Oracle bone style writing of Chinese
USE Chinese language—Writing, Chia-ku
style
Oracle bones (May Subd Geog)
BT Bone carving
Divination
Inscriptions, Chinese
ORACLE RDBMS (Computer system)
USE ORACLE (Computer system)
ORACLE Relational Database Management
System (Computer system)
USE ORACLE (Computer system)
Oracles
[BF1745-BF1779 (Occult sciences)]
[BL613 (Comparative religion)]
BT Mysteries, Religious
Occultism
Oracles, Egyptian, [Tibetan, etc.]
(May Subd Geog)
Oracles, Greek (May Subd Geog)
[DF125]
UF Greek oracles
BT Cults—Greece
NT Delphian oracle
Oracles, Hittite
UF Hittite oracles
ORACLS (Computer program)
UF Optimal regulator algorithms for the
control of linear systems (Computer
program)
BT Automatic control—Computer
programs
Computer programs
Oradour-sur-Glane Massacre, 1944
BT World War, 1939-1945—Atrocities
Öraefi (Iceland)
BT Plateaus—Iceland

Orak Lawoi' language
USE Urak Lawoi' language
Orakaiva language
USE Orokaiva language
Orakzais
Oral anovulants
USE Oral contraceptives
Oral antiseptics
USE Mouthwashes
Oral biography
[CT22]
Here are entered works on the technique of re-
cording the oral recollections of persons concerning
their lives and the lives of their families, as well as
collections of such recollections. Individual oral bio-
graphies are entered under the name of the individual
interviewed.
BT Biography
NT Oral history
Oral communication (May Subd Geog)
Here are entered works on speaking as a means of
communication. Works on the oral production of
meaningful sounds in language are entered under
Speech.
UF Oral transmission
Speech communication
BT Communication
RT Speech
NT Communication in small groups
Conversation
Folklore—Performance
Oral interpretation
Oral tradition
Paralinguistics
Public speaking
Speech processing systems
Verbal ability
Whistle speech
Oral contraceptives (May Subd Geog)
[RG137.5]
UF Anovulants, Oral
Birth control pills
Contraceptives, Oral
Oral anovulants
Oral contraceptives, Female
Pill, Birth control
Pill, The
BT Contraceptive drugs
Gynecologic drugs
Progestational hormones
NT Ethinyl estradiol
Mestranol
Norethindrone
— **Religious aspects**
— — **Baptists, [Catholic Church, etc.]**
— — **Buddhism, [Christianity, etc.]**
— **Side effects** (May Subd Geog)
— **Social aspects** (May Subd Geog)
UF Society and oral contraceptives
Oral contraceptives, Female
USE Oral contraceptives
Oral contraceptives, Male (May Subd Geog)
UF Birth control pills, Male
Male birth control pills
Male oral contraceptives
BT Contraceptive drugs
Male contraceptives
Oral diagnosis
USE Mouth—Diseases—Diagnosis
Teeth—Diseases—Diagnosis
Oral examination (Medicine)
USE Mouth—Examination
Oral examinations (May Subd Geog)
Here are entered works on tests of acquired
knowledge given orally. Works on oral examinations
on specific subjects are entered under two headings:
1. [subject]—Examinations, or [subject]—Ex-
aminations, questions, etc. 2. Oral examinations.
BT Examinations
Oral-formulaic analysis
[GR44.O72]
UF Formulaic analysis, Oral

BT Folk literature—History and criticism
    Folklore—Methodology
    Oral tradition

Oral habits *(May Subd Geog)*
    [BF637.O72]
  UF Mouth habits
      Oral motor behavior
  BT Habit
      Mouth
  RT Drinking behavior
      Food habits
  NT Bruxism
      Chewing gum
      Finger-sucking
      Mastication
      Mouth breathing
      Nail-biting
      Smoking
      Tongue thrust

Oral hemorrhage
  UF Mouth—Hemorrhage
  BT Hemorrhage

Oral history
    Here are entered works on the technique of recording the oral recollections of persons concerning their knowledge of historical events, as well as collections of such recollections. Individual oral histories are entered under the appropriate subject, e.g. United States—Civilization—1918-1945.
  BT History—Methodology
      Oral biography
  RT Oral tradition
  NT Appalachian Oral History Project

Oral hygiene
  USE Mouth—Care and hygiene

Oral hygiene products *(May Subd Geog)*
  UF Dental hygiene products
      Products, Oral hygiene
  BT Health products
  RT Mouth—Care and hygiene
  NT Dentifrices
      Mouthwashes
      Toothbrushes
      Toothpicks

Oral implantology
  USE Implant dentures

Oral intercourse
  UF Cunnilingus
      Fellatio
      Intercourse, Oral
      Sex, Oral
  BT Sexual intercourse

Oral interpretation
    [PN4145]
    Here are entered works on understanding and appreciation of various forms of literature through oral presentation. Works on the art and technical skill of reading aloud are entered under Oral reading.
  UF Interpretative reading
      Interpretative speech
      Reading, Interpretative
      Speech, Interpretative
  BT Oral communication
      Oral reading
      Reading
  RT Intonation (Phonetics)
      Recitations
  SA Chants (Anglican); Chants (Byzantine); Chants (Hindu); Chants (Jewish); Chants (Plain, Gregorian, etc.); *and similar headings*
  NT Cantillation
      Chamber theater
      Chants (Anglican)
      Chants (Byzantine)
      Chants (Hindu)
      Chants (Jewish)
      Chants (Plain, Gregorian, etc.)
      Choral speaking
      Koran—Recitation
      Readers' theater
      Storytelling

    Vedas—Recitation

Oral interpretation of fiction
  UF Fiction—Oral interpretation
      Fiction reading
      Reading fiction aloud
  BT Fiction
  RT Storytelling

Oral interpretation of poetry
    [PN4151]
  UF Poetry—Oral interpretation
      Poetry reading
      Reading poetry aloud

Oral irrigators *(May Subd Geog)*
  UF Irrigators, Oral
      Water irrigators (Dentistry)
  BT Dental instruments and apparatus

Oral law (Judaism)
  USE Tradition (Judaism)

Oral leukoplakia
  USE Leukoplakia, Oral

Oral literature
  USE Folk literature

Oral manifestations of general diseases
  UF Oral symptoms of general diseases
  BT Gums—Diseases
      Mouth—Diseases
      Symptomatology

Oral medication *(May Subd Geog)*
    [RM162]
  UF Drugs by mouth
      Medication, Oral
      Mouth, Medication by
      Peroral medication
  BT Drugs—Administration
      Therapeutics
  NT Diabetes—Oral therapy

Oral microbiology
  USE Mouth—Microbiology

Oral moniliasis
  USE Thrush (Mouth disease)

Oral motor behavior
  USE Oral habits

Oral mucosa
  UF Mucosa, Oral
  BT Mouth
      Mucous membrane
  — **Diseases** *(May Subd Geog)*
      NT Leukoplakia, Oral

Oral pleading *(May Subd Geog)*
  UF Pleading, Oral
  BT Pleading
      Trial practice
  NT Forensic orations
      Forensic oratory

Oral pleading (Canon law)
Oral poetry
  USE Folk poetry

Oral poliomyelitis vaccine
  USE Poliomyelitis vaccine, Oral

Oral prophylaxis
  USE Dental prophylaxis

Oral radiology
  USE Teeth—Radiography

Oral reading
    [LB1573.5]
    Here are entered works on the art and technical skill of reading aloud. Works on understanding and appreciation of various literary forms through oral presentation are entered under Oral interpretation.
  UF Reading, Oral
      Reading aloud
      Reading out loud
  BT Elocution
      Reading
  NT Oral interpretation

Oral reading in public worship
  USE Reading in public worship

Oral self-defense
  USE Verbal self-defense

Oral sepsis
  USE Mouth—Sepsis

Oral surgeons *(May Subd Geog)*
  BT Dentists
      Mouth—Surgery
      Surgeons

Oral surgery
  USE Mouth—Surgery

Oral symptoms of general diseases
  USE Oral manifestations of general diseases

Oral tobacco
  USE Smokeless tobacco

Oral tradition *(May Subd Geog)*
  UF Tradition, Oral
  BT Oral communication
  RT Folklore
      Oral history
  NT Communication in folklore
      Oral-formulaic analysis
  — **Japan**
      NT Kataribe

Oral tradition (Judaism)
  USE Tradition (Judaism)

Oral transmission
  USE Oral communication

Oral ulcerations
  USE Mouth—Ulcers

Oral vaccines *(May Subd Geog)*
  BT Vaccines

Oram family *(Not Subd Geog)*
  UF Orem family
      Orum family

Orana Region (N.S.W.)
Orang Abong
  USE Orang Abung

Orang Abung
  UF Orang Abong
  BT Ethnology—Indonesia

Orang Gunung (Indonesian people)
  USE Atoni (Indonesian people)

Orang Hulu (Malayan people)
  BT Ethnology—Malaysia
      Jakun (Malayan people)

Orang Laut (Southeast Asian people)
  USE Bajau (Southeast Asian people)
      Selung (Southeast Asian people)

Orang Laut language (Indonesia)
  USE Bajau language

Orang Laut language (Thailand and Malaysia)
  USE Urak Lawoi' language

Orang Melayu (Asian people)
  USE Malays (Asian people)

Orang-outang
  USE Orangutan

Orang-utan
  USE Orangutan

Orange *(May Subd Geog)*
    [SB370.O7]
  UF Orange tree
      Oranges
  BT Citrus fruits
  NT Citrus aurantium
      Cookery (Oranges)
      Orange juice
      Tangerine
  — **Diseases and pests** *(May Subd Geog)*
      [SB608.O6]
      NT Orange thrips
  — **Irrigation**
  — **Packaging**
      NT Orange wrappers
  — Tariff
      USE Tariff on oranges
  — **Varieties**

Orange, Agent
  USE Agent Orange

Orange, Herbicide
  USE Agent Orange

Orange (Color)
Orange Bowl Game, Miami, Fla.
    [GV957.O72]
  BT Football—Florida

Orange box labels *(May Subd Geog)*
  ₍NC1002.L3₎
  BT Labels
Orange Coast National Urban Park (Calif.)
  BT National parks and reserves—United
      States
      Recreation areas—California
Orange-flanked parakeet
  USE Gray-cheeked parakeet
Orange Free State (South Africa)
  — **Description and travel**
  — — **To 1854**
  — **History**
  — — **To 1854**
  — — **1854-1900**
          NT Sotho-Free State War, 1865-
              1866
Orange industry *(May Subd Geog)*
  ₍HD9259.O7-8₎
Orange juice
  ₍TX558.O7₎
  BT Citrus juices
      Fruit juices
      Orange
  — **Flavor and odor**
      UF Orange juice—Odor
      BT Flavor
          Odors
  — **Odor**
      USE Orange juice—Flavor and odor
Orange juice, Canned
  BT Fruit, Canned
      Fruit juices
Orange juice, Frozen concentrated
  (May Subd Geog)
  UF Frozen concentrated orange juice
  BT Fruit juices, Concentrated
      Fruit juices, Frozen
Orange juice industry *(May Subd Geog)*
  ₍HD9348.5.O72-724₎
Orange-leaf scab
  USE Sour orange scab
Orange-Nassau, House of *(Not Subd Geog)*
  BT Netherlands—Kings and rulers
Orange oil *(May Subd Geog)*
  ₍TP959.O7₎
  UF Orange peel oil
  BT Citrus oils
  NT Bitter orange oil
Orange peel
Orange peel oil
  USE Orange oil
Orange River
  UF Oranjerivier
  BT Rivers—Lesotho
      Rivers—Namibia
      Rivers—South Africa
Orange River Project
  BT Water resources development—South
      Africa
Orange sneezeweed
  USE Helenium hoopesii
Orange thrips
  ₍SB608.O6₎
  BT Orange—Diseases and pests
Orange tree
  USE Orange
Orange-winged parakeet
  USE Gray-cheeked parakeet
Orange worm, Navel
  USE Navel orangeworm
Orange wrappers *(May Subd Geog)*
  ₍NC1002.W72 (Commercial art)₎
  BT Orange—Packaging
      Wrappers
Orangemen *(May Subd Geog)*
  BT Irish
      Protestants—Northern Ireland
Orangeries *(May Subd Geog)*
  ₍NA8360₎
  BT Conservatories

Oranges
  USE Orange
Orangespotted sunfish
  ₍QL638.C3₎
  UF Lepomis humilis
Orangestriped oakworm
  USE Anisota senatoria
Orangeworm, Navel
  USE Navel orangeworm
Orangutan *(May Subd Geog)*
  ₍QL737.P96₎
  UF Orang-outang
      Orang-utan
      Pongo pygmaeus
      Simia satyrus
  BT Apes
Oranjerivier
  USE Orange River
Oraon language
  USE Kurukh language
Oraon poetry
  USE Kurukh poetry
Oraon songs
  USE Songs, Oraon
Oraons
  ₍DS432.O₎
  UF Uraons
  NT Missions to Oraons
Orations
  USE Speeches, addresses, etc.
Oratories *(May Subd Geog)*
  ₍NA4910₎
  BT Chapels
      Churches
Oratories (Canon law)
  ₍BX1939.O75₎
  BT Churches (Canon law)
      Sacred places (Canon law)
Oratorio *(May Subd Geog)*
  ₍ML3201-ML3251 (History and
      criticism)₎
  ₍ML3867 (Aesthetics)₎
  BT Church music
  NT Cantata
      Passion-music—History and criticism
Oratorio della Santissima Trinità frescoes
  (Painting)
  USE Salimbeni, Ventura, 1568-1613.
        Apocalypse frescoes
Oratorios
  ₍M2000-M2007₎
  BT Sacred vocal music
  NT Pantomimes with music, Sacred
  — **Analytical guides**
      ₍MT110-115₎
  — **Excerpts, Arranged**
  — **Juvenile**
      ₍M2190₎
      UF Children's oratorios
  — **Librettos**
Oratorios arranged for string quartets
  ₍M453-4₎
  BT String quartets, Arranged
Oratorios arranged for string quintets
  ₍M553-4₎
  BT String quintets, Arranged
Orators *(May Subd Geog)*
  ₍PN4057 (Collective biography)₎
  UF Speakers
  BT Elocutionists
  NT Women orators
Orators, Afro-American
  USE Afro-American orators
Oratory *(May Subd Geog)*
  ₍PN4001-4355₎
    Here are entered works dealing with the rhetorical
  aspects of speeches. Works dealing with the problems
  of speaking effectively in public are entered under
  Public speaking.
  UF Argumentation
      Speaking

  BT Language and languages
      Rhetoric
      Speeches, addresses, etc.
      Voice
  RT Debates and debating
      Elocution
      Eloquence
      Lectures and lecturing
      Persuasion (Rhetoric)
      Public speaking
  SA *subdivision* Oratory *under names of*
      persons
  NT Expression
      Forensic oratory
      Forensics (Public speaking)
      Gesture
      Indians of North America—Oratory
      Introduction of speakers
      Political oratory
      Rhetorical criticism
      Speechwriting
      Voice culture
  — **1500-1800**
Oratory, Ancient
  ₍PA6083 (History, PA3038, PA3263-
      4)₎
  ₍PA6138 (Collections, PA3479-3842)₎
  ₍PA6144 (Criticism, PA3561)₎
Oratory, Extemporaneous
  USE Extemporaneous speaking
Oratory, Primitive
  BT Communication, Primitive
  NT Indians of North America—Oratory
Oratosquilla
  ₍QL444.M375₎
  BT Squillidae
Oratosquilla ornata
  ₍QL444.M375₎
Oratosquilla tweediei
  ₍QL444.M375₎
Orava River (Czechoslovakia)
  BT Rivers—Czechoslovakia
Orb weavers
  USE Araneidae
Orb-web spiders
  USE Araneidae
Ørbaek family *(Not Subd Geog)*
Orbiculus ciliaris
  USE Pars plana
Orbig family
  USE Orwig family
Orbignya
  ₍QK495.P17 (Botany)₎
  BT Palms
  NT Babassu
Orbignya barbosiana
  USE Babassu
Orbignya martiana
  USE Babassu
Orbignya speciosa
  USE Babassu
Orbiniida
  ₍QL391.A6₎
  BT Polychaeta
  NT Orbiniidae
Orbiniidae
  ₍QL391.A6₎
  UF Ariciidae
  BT Orbiniida
Orbiston Community
  ₍HX698.O₎
Orbit (Eye)
  USE Eye-sockets
ORBIT (Information retrieval system)
  BT Information storage and retrieval
      systems
Orbit transfer (Space flight)
  USE Orbital transfer (Space flight)
Orbital cavity (Eye)
  USE Eye-sockets

Orbital debris
USE Space debris
Orbital Motorway, London (England)
USE London Orbital Motorway (England)
Orbital rendezvous (Space flight)
UF Rendezvous, Orbital
Rendezvous (Space)
Rendezvous in space
Space orbital rendezvous
BT Space flight
Space ships
Space stations
NT Apollo Soyuz Test Project
Project Apollo
Project Gemini
Orbital space suits
USE Extravehicular space suits
Orbital spacing of geostationary satellites
USE Geostationary satellites—Spacing
Orbital symmetry, Conservation of
USE Conservation of orbital symmetry
Orbital transfer (Space flight)
UF Orbit transfer (Space flight)
Transfer orbits (Space flight)
Transfer trajectories
BT Space flight
Space trajectories
Orbitals, Atomic
USE Atomic orbitals
Orbitals, Molecular
USE Molecular orbitals
Orbiting astronomical observatories
UF OAO
BT Astronautics in astronomy
Astronomical observatories
NT EXOSAT (Artificial satellite)
HEAO (Artificial satellite)
Hubble Space Telescope
Orbiting solar observatories
Orbiting geophysical observatories
UF OGO
BT Geophysical observatories
Orbiting Satellite Carrying Amateur Radio
USE OSCAR (Artificial satellite)
Orbiting solar observatories
UF OSO
Solar observatories, Orbiting
BT Orbiting astronomical observatories
Sun—Observations
Orbiting vehicles
USE Artificial satellites
Space stations
Orbitoides, Fossil
BT Orbitoididae, Fossil
Orbitoididae, Fossil
BT Foraminifera, Fossil
NT Orbitoides, Fossil
Orbits
[QB355-QB357 (Theoretical astronomy)]
UF Kepler's equation
Kepler's laws
BT Astronomy
Rotational motion
Solar system
RT Mechanics, Celestial
NT Artificial satellites—Orbits
Artificial satellites—Moon—Orbits
Comets—Orbits
K stars—Orbits
Lagrangian points
Meteors—Orbits
Moon—Orbit
Planets—Orbits
Planets, Minor—Orbits
Stars—Orbits
Stars, Double—Orbits
Orbits of stars
USE Stars—Orbits
Orbituliporidae
[QL398.C5]

BT Cheilostomata
Orbituliporidae, Fossil
[QE799.C5]
BT Cheilostomata, Fossil
Orbivirus
USE Orbiviruses
Orbiviruses (May Subd Geog)
UF Orbivirus
BT Reoviruses
NT Bluetongue virus
Orbs
[CR4485.O7]
BT Regalia (Insignia)
RT Globes
Sphere
Orca Group (Alaska) (Not Subd Geog)
BT Geology—Alaska
Geology, Stratigraphic—Eocene
Geology, Stratigraphic—Paleocene
Orca orca
USE Killer whale
Orchard grass (May Subd Geog)
[QK495.G74 (Botany)]
[SB201.O6 (Culture)]
UF Cocksfoot grass
Orchards (May Subd Geog)
BT Farms
Orchards, Seed
USE Seed orchards
Orcheitis
USE Orchitis
Orchesella
[QL503.E5]
BT Entomobryidae
Orchestra
[ML1200-1251]
BT Chamber music—History and criticism
Instrumental music—History and criticism
Musical instruments
RT Bands (Music)
Conducting
SA subdivision Orchestras and bands under names of individual universities and colleges, e.g. Harvard University—Orchestras and bands
NT Chamber orchestra
Chapels (Music)
Conductors (Music)
Dance orchestras
Gamelan
Instrumentation and orchestration
Mandolin orchestras
Orchestral music
Pīphāt
Rhythm bands and orchestras
Symphony orchestras
Orchestra music
USE Orchestral music
Orchestral bells
USE Glockenspiel
Orchestral music
[M1000-1049]
UF Orchestra music
BT Instrumental music
Orchestra
SA [Solo instrument(s)] with orchestra
NT Accordion with orchestra
Band music
Bassoon, clarinet, flute, horn, oboe with orchestra
Bassoon, clarinet, flute, oboe, harp with orchestra
Canons, fugues, etc. (Orchestra)
Chamber-orchestra music
Chorale preludes (Orchestra)
Concertos
Concertos (Bassoon, clarinet, English horn, flute)
Concertos (Clarinets (2))

Concertos (Jazz octet)
Concertos (Jazz quartet)
Concertos (Piano, trumpet, vibraphone, double bass)
Cornet with orchestra
Dance-orchestra music
Flute with orchestra
Guitar with orchestra
Guitars (4) with orchestra
Harpsichord with orchestra
Horn with orchestra
Marches (Orchestra)
Marimba with orchestra
Minuets (Orchestra)
Monologues with music (Orchestra)
Oboe and violin with orchestra
Overtures
Passacaglias (Orchestra)
Piano (4 hands) with orchestra
Pianos (3) with orchestra
Polkas (Orchestra)
Polonaises (Orchestra)
Potpourris (Orchestra)
Recorder with orchestra
Rondos (Orchestra)
Sacred monologues with music (Orchestra)
Salon-orchestra music
String-orchestra music
String quartet with orchestra
Suites (Orchestra)
Symphonic poems
Symphonies
Trautonium with orchestra
Trombone with orchestra
Trumpet and piano with orchestra
Variations (Orchestra)
Viola da gamba with orchestra
Viola d'amore with orchestra
Violin and harpsichord with orchestra
Violin and piano with orchestra
Violin and viola with orchestra
Violins (2) with orchestra
Vocal ensembles with orchestra
Waltzes (Orchestra)
— **Analysis, appreciation**
[MT125]
[MT130]
— **Parts**
[M1045]
— **Scores**
[M1045]
— **Scores and parts**
[M1045]
Orchestral music, Arranged
[M1060-1075]
Subdivided in the same manner as the heading Orchestral music.
Orchestration
USE Instrumentation and orchestration
Orchid culture (May Subd Geog)
[SB409]
BT Floriculture
Orchids
Orchid industry (May Subd Geog)
[SB409.5-409.55]
BT Orchids
Orchid Island (Taiwan)
USE Lan Island (Taiwan)
Orchidaceae
USE Orchids
Orchidopexy
USE Orchiopexy
Orchids (May Subd Geog)
[QK495.O64 (Botany)]
UF Orchidaceae
NT Aceras
Anacamptis
Brassavola
Bulbophyllum
Calanthe

Orchids *(Continued)*
    Cattleyas
    Cleisostoma
    Coelogyne
    Cymbidium
    Cypripedium
    Dactylorhiza
    Dendrobium
    Epipactis
    Eulophia
    Eurystyles
    Gastrodia
    Goodyera
    Habenaria
    Himantoglossum
    Leochilus
    Luisia
    Miniature orchids
    Oberonia
    Odontoglossum
    Oncidium
    Ophrys
    Orchid culture
    Orchid industry
    Orchis
    Paphiopedilum
    Phalaenopsis
    Phragmipedium
    Pleurothallis
    Polystachya
    Rhizanthella
    Schomburgkia
    Selenipedium
    Spiranthes
    Vanda
    Vanilla
    Yoania
  — **Diseases and pests** *(May Subd Geog)*
    NT Cymbidium mosaic diseases
       Cymbidium mosaic virus
  — **Flowering time**
  — **Varieties**
Orchids in art
Orchil
    [TP925.L7]
  UF Archil
Orchiopexy *(May Subd Geog)*
    [RD592]
  UF Orchidopexy
      Orchiorrhaphy
  BT Cryptorchism—Surgery
Orchiorrhaphy
  USE Orchiopexy
Orchis
    [QK495.O64]
  BT Orchids
Orchitis *(May Subd Geog)*
    [RC898.3]
  UF Orcheitis
      Testis—Inflammation
  BT Inflammation
      Testis—Diseases
Orcia River (Italy)
  UF Fiume Orcia (Italy)
  BT Rivers—Italy
Orcin
    [TP925.L7]
Orcinus orca
  USE Killer whale
Orcutt family *(Not Subd Geog)*
  RT Urquhart family
Ord River (W.A. : River)
  BT Rivers—Australia
Ord River Dam (W.A.) *(Not Subd Geog)*
  BT Dams—Australia
Orday family
  USE Ordway family
Ordeal *(May Subd Geog)*
    [GN493 (Primitive)]
  UF Trial by ordeal

  BT Civilization, Medieval
      Criminal procedure
      Evidence (Law)
      Manners and customs
      Superstition
      Witchcraft
Ordeal bean
  USE Calabar bean
Orden al Mérito en el Trabajo
  BT Decorations of honor—Venezuela
Orden de la Santa Faz *(May Subd Geog)*
    [BX4795.O73]
  BT Catholic Church—Spain
Orden Otechestvennoĭ voĭny
Orden Pour le Mérite
    [CR5327]
  UF Blue Max
      Order Pour le Mérite
      Pour le Mérite
  BT Decorations of honor—Germany
      Decorations of honor—Prussia
        (Germany)
      Germany—Armed Forces—Medals,
        badges, decorations, etc.
      Prussia (Germany)—Armed Forces—
        Medals, badges, decorations, etc.
Orden Slavy
  UF Order of Glory
      Slavy, Orden
  BT Soviet Union—Armed Forces—
        Medals, badges, decorations, etc.
Order
  NT Hierarchies
      Orderliness
  — **Religious aspects**
  — — **Baptists,** [**Catholic Church, etc.**]
  — — **Buddhism,** [**Christianity, etc.**]
Order (Grammar)
    [P299.O73]
  UF Linear ordering (Grammar)
      Ordering constraints (Grammar)
  BT Grammar, Comparative and general
  NT Grammar, Comparative and general—
        Word order
Order (Philosophy)
    [B105.O7]
  BT Philosophy
Order-books
  USE *subdivision* Order-books *under names*
        of armies or armed forces, e.g.
        United States—Armed Forces—
        Order-books
Order Budowniczych Polski Ludowej
Order-disorder in alloys
    [TN690]
  UF Ordering in alloys
  BT Alloys
      Domain structure
      Order-disorder models
      Phase rule and equilibrium
      Physical metallurgy
Order-disorder models
  UF Disorder models
      Models, Order-disorder
  BT Matter
  NT Anderson model
      Long range order (Solid state physics)
      Order-disorder in alloys
Order Entry and Invoicing (Computer
program)
  BT Accounting—Computer programs
Order filling systems
  USE Order picking systems
Order of Glory
  USE Orden Slavy
Order of Merit of the Prussian Crown
  UF Preussischer Verdienstorden
      Verdienstorden der Preussischen
        Krone
  BT Decorations of honor—Prussia
        (Germany)

Order of the Crown of Italy
    [CR5511]
  UF Crown of Italy, Order of the
      Iron Crown of Italy
Order Orła Białego
  BT Decorations of honor—Poland
Order picking systems
  UF Order filling systems
  BT Physical distribution of goods
      Warehouses
Order Pour le Mérite
  USE Orden Pour le Mérite
Order statistics
    [QA278.7]
  UF Statistics, Order
  BT Nonparametric statistics
  RT Ranking and selection (Statistics)
Orderable groups
  UF Groups, Orderable
  BT Infinite groups
      Ordered groups
Ordered algebraic structures
    [QA172-172.4]
  UF Algebraic structures, Ordered
      Structures, Ordered algebraic
  BT Algebra
Ordered Computer Collation of Unprepared
  Literary Text
  USE OCCULT (Computer program)
Ordered fields
  BT Topological fields
Ordered groups
  BT Groups, Theory of
  RT Solvable groups
  NT Groups of divisibility
      Orderable groups
Ordered groups, Lattice
  USE Lattice ordered groups
Ordered linear topological spaces
  USE Linear topological spaces, Ordered
Ordered rings, Lattice
  USE Lattice ordered rings
Ordered sets
    [QA171.48]
  UF Sets, Ordered
  BT Set theory
  NT Partially ordered sets
      Semilattices
Ordered topological spaces
    [QA611.23]
  UF Spaces, Ordered topological
  BT Topological spaces
  NT Linear topological spaces, Ordered
      Partially ordered spaces
Ordered topological vector spaces
  USE Linear topological spaces, Ordered
Ordering constraints (Grammar)
  USE Order (Grammar)
Ordering in alloys
  USE Order-disorder in alloys
Orderings, Linear
  USE Linear orderings
Orderliness
  UF Neatness
      Tidiness
  BT Order
Orderly books
  USE *subdivision* Order-books *under names*
        of armies or armed forces, e.g.
        United States—Armed Forces—
        Order-books
Orders, Anglican
  USE Anglican orders
Orders, Architectural
  USE Architecture—Orders
Orders, Major
  USE Bishops
      Clergy
Orders, Monastic
  USE Monasticism and religious orders

Orders, Preparation of (Military science)
　　[UB280-UB285 (Military)]
　　[VB255 (Naval)]
　　UF　Field orders
　　BT　Armies—Staffs
　　　　　Military art and science
Orders, Small
　　USE　Small orders
Orders, Speaking
　　USE　Speaking orders (Law)
Orders in council
　　[HF3505.9]
　　BT　International relations
　　RT　Continental system of Napoleon
Orders of knighthood and chivalry
　　(May Subd Geog)
　　[CR4501-6305]
　　UF　Knighthood, Orders of
　　BT　Decorations of honor
　　　　　Heraldry
　　RT　Knights and knighthood
　　SA　*subdivision* Nobility *under names of*
　　　　　countries, e.g. France—Nobility
　　NT　Chivalry
　　　　　Knights of Malta
　　　　　Military religious orders
　— **Insignia**
　　　　[CR4501-6305]
　　　BT　Insignia
　　　NT　Decorations of honor
Orders of knighthood and chivalry, Islamic
　　(May Subd Geog)
　　UF　Islamic orders of knighthood and
　　　　　chivalry
　　　　　Muslim orders of knighthood and
　　　　　chivalry
　　　　　Orders of knighthood and chivalry,
　　　　　Muslim
　　NT　Futuwwa (Islamic order)
Orders of knighthood and chivalry, Muslim
　　USE　Orders of knighthood and chivalry,
　　　　　Islamic
Orders of knighthood and chivalry, Papal
　　[CR4701-CR4731 (Military religious
　　　orders)]
　　[CR5547-CR5575 (Papal States)]
　　UF　Papal orders of knighthood and
　　　　　chivalry
Ordeway family
　　USE　Ordway family
Ordinal numbers
　　USE　Numbers, Ordinal
Ordinal position of children
　　USE　Birth order
Ordinals (Liturgical books)
　　BT　Liturgies
　　　　　Ordination (Liturgy)
Ordinance of Alsnö, 1280
　　USE　Alsnö, Ordinance of, 1280
Ordinances, Model
　　USE　Model ordinances
Ordinances, Municipal　*(May Subd Geog)*
　　　Here are entered nontopical collections of texts of
　　ordinances passed by municipal corporations and
　　works about these ordinances.
　　UF　By-laws, Municipal
　　　　　City ordinances
　　　　　Municipal ordinances
　　BT　Statutes
　　NT　Model ordinances
Ordinances for the dead (Mormon Church)
　　[BX8655.25]
　　BT　Dead—Religious aspects—Mormon
　　　　　Church
　　　　　Sacraments—Mormon Church
　　NT　Baptism for the dead

Ordinaries　*(May Subd Geog)*
　　BT　County officials and employees
　　　　　Courts—Officials and employees
　　　　　Guardian and ward
　　　　　Non-contentious jurisdiction
　　　　　Probate courts
Ordinary-language analysis
　　USE　Ordinary-language philosophy
Ordinary-language method
　　USE　Ordinary-language philosophy
Ordinary-language philosophy
　　[B828.36]
　　UF　Ordinary-language analysis
　　　　　Ordinary-language method
　　　　　Philosophy, Ordinary-language
　　BT　Analysis (Philosophy)
　　　　　Languages—Philosophy
Ordinary ray
　　USE　Refraction, Double
Ordinary's courts
　　USE　Probate courts
Ordination
　　[BV685]
　　[BV830 (Sacrament)]
　　BT　Bishops
　　　　　Clergy
　　　　　Rites and ceremonies
　　　　　Sacraments
　　NT　Chrism
　　　　　Consecration of bishops
　　　　　Imposition of hands
　　　　　Ordination of women
　　　　　Ordination sermons
　　　　　Priesthood
　　　　　Tonsure
　— **Anglican Communion, [Methodist**
　　　Church, etc.]
　— **Anniversary sermons**
　— **Judaism**
　　　USE　Rabbis—Ordination
Ordination (Buddhism)　*(May Subd Geog)*
　　UF　Buddhist ordination
　　　　　Monasticism and religious orders,
　　　　　　Buddhist—Ordination
　　BT　Buddhism
　　　　　Priests, Buddhist
Ordination (Canon law)
　　[BX1939.O82]
　　BT　Sacraments (Canon law)
　　NT　Incardination (Canon law)
　　　　　Irregularities (Canon law)
Ordination (Liturgy)
　　BT　Liturgics
　　　　　Sacraments (Liturgy)
　　NT　Ordinals (Liturgical books)
Ordination of plant communities
　　USE　Plant communities—Ordination
Ordination of women
　　[BV676]
　　UF　Women, Ordination of
　　BT　Ordination
　　　　　Women clergy
　— **Buddhism, [Christianity, etc.]**
　— **Catholic Church, [Church of England,**
　　　etc.]
Ordination sermons
　　[BV4285]
　　UF　Sermons, Ordination
　　BT　Occasional sermons
　　　　　Ordination
Ording family　*(Not Subd Geog)*
Ordnance
　　[UF520-630]
　　UF　Cannon
　　　　　Gun
　　　　　Guns
　　BT　Armaments
　　　　　Arms and armor
　　　　　Firearms
　　　　　Military art and science
　　　　　Shooting, Military

　　RT　Artillery
　　　　　Ballistics
　　　　　Gunnery
　　　　　Projectiles
　　SA　*subdivision* Ordnance and ordnance
　　　　　stores *under armies and navies, e.g.*
　　　　　United States.　Army—Ordnance
　　　　　and ordnance stores
　　NT　Antitank guns
　　　　　Antitank missiles
　　　　　Antitank weapons
　　　　　Armstrong gun
　　　　　Come and Take It Cannon
　　　　　Directed-energy weapons
　　　　　Fire control (Gunnery)—Optical
　　　　　　equipment
　　　　　Firearms—Sights
　　　　　Gun-carriages
　　　　　Howitzers
　　　　　Machine-guns
　　　　　Mortars (Ordnance)
　　　　　Nuclear weapons
　　　　　Ordnance disposal units
　　　　　Railway artillery
　　　　　Rocket launchers (Ordnance)
　　　　　Tear gas munitions
　　　　　Telescopic sights
　　　　　Trench mortars
　　　　　Weapons systems
　— **Decoration**
　　　[UF520-525]
　　　BT　Decoration and ornament
　— **Manufacture**
　　　[UF530-537]
　— **Research**　*(May Subd Geog)*
　　　[UF526-UF526.5]
　　　UF　Ordnance research
Ordnance, Coast　*(May Subd Geog)*
　　UF　Coast guns
　　　　　Coast ordnance
　　　　　Seacoast ordnance
　　BT　Artillery, Coast
　　　　　Coast defenses
Ordnance, Naval
　　[VF]
　　UF　Naval ordnance
　　BT　Naval art and science
　　NT　Depth charges
　　　　　Fire control (Naval gunnery)
　　　　　Naval gunnery
　　　　　Polaris (Missile)
　　　　　Ridgway's revolving battery
　　　　　Warships—Turrets
　— Drawing
　　　USE　Ordnance, Naval—Drawings
　— **Drawings**
　　　[VF580]
　　　UF　Ordnance, Naval—Drawing
　　　BT　Mechanical drawing
　— **Manufacture**
　　　[VF370-375]
Ordnance, Rapid-fire
　　[UF560-565]
　　UF　Rapid-fire guns
Ordnance disposal units　*(May Subd Geog)*
　　UF　Bomb disposal units
　　　　　Explosive ordnance disposal units
　　　　　Unexploded bomb disposal units
　　　　　UXB disposal units
　　BT　Ordnance
Ordnance research
　　USE　Ordnance—Research
Ordnance testing
　　[UF890 (Military)]
　　[VF540 (Naval)]
　　UF　Testing of ordnance
　　RT　Proving grounds
Ordo decurionum
　　USE　Decurions (Roman municipal
　　　　　government)

2693

Ordos (Mongolian tribe)
  BT Mongols
Ordos Desert (China)
  UF O-er-do-su Basin (China)
     O-er-do-su Desert (China)
     O-erh-to-ssu Basin (China)
     O-erh-to-ssu Desert (China)
  BT Deserts—China
Ordos dialect
  [PL431.O8]
  UF Ordos language
  BT Mongolian language
Ordos language
  USE Ordos dialect
Ordovician formation
  USE Geology, Stratigraphic—Ordovician
     Paleobotany—Ordovician
     Paleontology—Ordovician
Ordre national du Québec
  BT Decorations of honor—Québec
     (Province)
Ord's kangaroo rat
  USE Dipodomys ordii
Ordway family (Not Subd Geog)
  UF Orday family
     Ordeway family
Ore-bulk-oil ships (May Subd Geog)
  UF OBO ships
  BT Cargo ships
     Merchant ships
Ore carriers
  [VM457]
  UF Ore ships
  BT Bulk carrier cargo ships
     Cargo ships
Ore cars
  USE Mine railroads—Cars
Ore Data File Project for Northern Finland
  USE Pohjois-Suomen malmitiedostoprojekti
Ore-deposits (May Subd Geog)
  [TN263]
  UF Deposits, Ore
  BT Geology
     Mines and mineral resources
  RT Ores
  SA particular ores, e.g. Copper ores, Lead
     ores
  NT Disseminated deposits
     Hydrothermal deposits
     Placer deposits
     Tactite
  — Finland
     NT Pohjois-Suomen
        malmitiedostoprojekti
Ore-dressing
  [TN500-535]
  UF Beneficiation of ores
     Dressing of ores
     Jigging
     Milling (Metallurgy)
     Mineral dressing
     Ore treatment
  BT Smelting
  NT Dielectric separation
     Electrostatic separators
     Flotation
     Gravity concentrators
     Leaching
     Magnetic separation of ores
     Pelletizing (Ore-dressing)
     Screens (Mining)
     Spiral concentrators
     Tailings (Metallurgy)
     Tailings embankments
Ore-dressing plants (May Subd Geog)
  UF Ore-treatment plants
  — Electric equipment
  — Equipment and supplies
     NT Ball mills—Grinding media
        Electronic ore sorters

Ore-dressing plants equipment
     industry
     Radiometric ore sorters
  — — Appraisal
     USE Ore-dressing plants—
        Equipment and supplies—
        Valuation
  — — Valuation
     [TN504]
     UF Ore-dressing plants—Equipment
        and supplies—Appraisal
Ore-dressing plants equipment industry
  (May Subd Geog)
  [HD9506]
  BT Ore-dressing plants—Equipment and
     supplies
Ore family
  USE Orr family
Ore handling
  BT Bulk solids handling
     Loading and unloading
     Materials handling
     Ores—Transportation
Ore Mountains (Czechoslovakia and Germany)
  USE Erzgebirge (Czechoslovakia and
     Germany)
Ore ships
  USE Ore carriers
Ore sorters, Electronic
  USE Electronic ore sorters
Ore sorters, Radiometric
  USE Radiometric ore sorters
Ore transportation
  USE Ores—Transportation
Ore treatment
  USE Ore-dressing
Ore-treatment plants
  USE Ore-dressing plants
Oreamnos
  [QL737.U53]
  BT Bovidae
  NT Rocky Mountain goat
Oreamnos americanus
  USE Rocky Mountain goat
Oreamnos montanus
  USE Rocky Mountain goat
O'Rear family (Not Subd Geog)
Örebro, Treaty of, 1812
  [DA520.A25 1812]
Orectolobidae
  [QL638.95.O7]
  UF Wobbegong sharks
  BT Orectolobiformes
Orectolobiformes
  [QL638.9]
  UF Carpet sharks
  BT Chondrichthyes
     Sharks
  NT Orectolobidae
     Whale shark
O'Regan family
  USE Regan family
Oregon
  — Antiquities
     NT Hager's Grove Sites (Salem, Or.)
        Looney Site (Or.)
        Medicine Creek Site (Or.)
        Rigdon's Horse Pasture Cave Site
        (Or.)
        Wildcat Canyon Site (Or.)
  — Description and travel
  — — 1951-1980
  — — 1981-
  — History
     [F871-885]
  — — To 1859
  — — 1859-
  — — Civil War, 1861-1865
     [E526]
  — Politics and government
  — — To 1859

  — — 1859-1950
  — — 1951-
Oregon Caves National Monument (Or.)
  BT National monuments—Oregon
Oregon Coast Trail
  BT Trails—Oregon
Oregon Country
  USE Northwest, Pacific
Oregon garter snake
  USE Thamnophis couchii
Oregon Inlet (N.C.)
  BT Inlets—North Carolina
Oregon pine
  USE Douglas fir
Oregon question
  [F880]
  RT Northwest boundary of the United
     States
Oregon Trail
  [F592 (The West)]
  [F597 (Northwest)]
  [F880 (Oregon)]
  BT Trails—United States
Orejón language (Tucanoan)
  USE Coto language (Tucanoan)
Orel, Battle of, 1943
  BT World War, 1939-1945—Campaigns—
     Russian S.F.S.R.
Orelli family (Not Subd Geog)
Orem family
  USE Oram family
Oreocnemus
  [QL520.3.P53]
  BT Platycnemididae
Oreomyrrhis
  [QK495.U48]
  BT Umbelliferae
Oreophrynella
  [QL668.E227]
  BT Bufonidae
Oreotrochilus estella
  USE Andean hillstar
Ores (May Subd Geog)
  [TN265]
  BT Geology, Economic
  RT Ore-deposits
  SA particular ores, e.g. Copper ores, Lead
     ores
  NT Metallurgy
     Metals
     Mines and mineral resources
     Troilite ores
  — Analysis
     USE Ores—Sampling and estimation
  — Optical properties
  — Sampling and estimation
     [TN560]
     UF Ores—Analysis
        Sampling of ores
     BT Mineralogy, Determinative
        Mines and mineral resources
        Prospecting
     RT Assaying
  — Transportation
     UF Ore transportation
     NT Ore handling
Ores, Magnetic separation of
  USE Magnetic separation of ores
Ores family
  USE Orr family
Orestes (Greek mythology)
  BT Mythology, Greek
Orestias
  [QL638.P73]
  BT Poeciliidae
Oresund (Denmark and Sweden)
  USE Sound, The (Denmark and Sweden)
Orexigenic drugs
  USE Appetite stimulants
Orexigenics
  USE Appetite stimulants

Org Bê language
  USE Li language
Orga-sonic organ
  USE Baldwin organ
Organ
  [ML550-ML649 (History and
    criticism)]
  UF Enharmonic organ
    Pipe-organ
  BT Keyboard instruments
  RT Organs
  NT Archiphone
    Claviorganum
    Electronic organ
    Hammond organ
    Hydraulic organ
    Keyboards
    Kimball organ
    Mechanical organs
    Player-organ
    Reed-organ
    Welte-Lichtton-Orgel
    Wurlitzer organ
  — **Construction**
    [ML550-597]
    NT Organ-pipes
      Organ stops
  — **History**
    BT Church music
  — **Instruction and study**
    [MT180]
    NT Chants (Plain, Gregorian, etc.)—
      Accompaniment
      Organ music—Teaching pieces
  — **Methods**
    [MT182]
  — **Methods (Jazz)**
    [MT182]
  — **Registration**
    [MT189]
    UF Registration (Organ)
    BT Organ—Studies and exercises
    SA *subdivision* Registration *under
      individual types of organ, e.g.*
      Electronic organ—Registration;
      Hammond organ—Registration
    NT Organ stops
  — **Studies and exercises**
    [MT185-191]
    BT Organ music
    NT Organ—Registration
Organ, Electronic
  USE Electronic organ
Organ and alpenhorn music
  USE Alpenhorn and organ music
Organ and bass trombone music
  USE Bass trombone and organ music
Organ and bassoon music
  USE Bassoon and organ music
Organ and bugle music
  USE Bugle and organ music
Organ and clarinet music
  USE Clarinet and organ music
Organ and cornet music
  USE Cornet and organ music
Organ and double-bass music
  USE Double-bass and organ music
Organ and English-horn music
  USE English horn and organ music
Organ and fluegelhorn music
  USE Fluegelhorn and organ music
Organ and flute music
  USE Flute and organ music
Organ and guitar music
  USE Guitar and organ music
Organ and handbell music
  USE Handbell and organ music
Organ and harp music
  USE Harp and organ music
Organ and harpsichord music
  USE Harpsichord and organ music

Organ and horn music
  USE Horn and organ music
Organ and lute music
  USE Lute and organ music
Organ and marimba music
  USE Marimba and organ music
Organ and oboe music
  USE Oboe and organ music
Organ and percussion music
  USE Percussion and organ music
Organ and piano music
  USE Piano and organ music
Organ and recorder music
  USE Recorder and organ music
Organ and saxophone music
  USE Saxophone and organ music
Organ and timpani music
  USE Timpani and organ music
Organ and trombone music
  USE Trombone and organ music
Organ and trumpet music
  USE Trumpet and organ music
Organ and unspecified instrument music
  USE Duets (Unspecified instrument and
    organ)
Organ and viola da gamba music
  USE Viola da gamba and organ music
Organ and viola d'amore music
  USE Viola d'amore and organ music
Organ and viola music
  USE Viola and organ music
Organ and violin music
  USE Violin and organ music
Organ and violoncello music
  USE Violoncello and organ music
Organ banks
  USE Tissue banks
Organ-builders (May Subd Geog)
  BT Musical instrument makers
Organ culture
  USE Organs, Culture of
Organ donation
  USE Donation of organs, tissues, etc.
Organ donors (May Subd Geog)
  [RD129.5]
  UF Donors, Organ
  RT Donation of organs, tissues, etc.
Organ grinders (May Subd Geog)
  UF Barrel organ players
    Barrel organists
  BT Street music and musicians
Organ, harp, timpani with string orchestra
  [M1140-1141]
  BT Trios (Organ, harp, timpani)
  RT Concertos (Organ, harp, timpani with
    string orchestra)
Organ mass
  [ML647]
  BT Mass (Music)
Organ masses
  [M14.3]
  UF Instrumental masses
    Masses, Instrumental
    Masses, Organ
Organ Mountains (N.M.)
  BT Mountains—New Mexico
Organ music
  [M6-14]
  BT Church music
    Keyboard instrument music
  SA Concertos, Minuets, Sonatas, Suites,
    *and similar headings with
    specification of instruments;* Trios
    [Quartets, etc.] *followed by
    specifications which include the
    organ; also headings that begin with
    the words organ or organs*
  NT Calliope music
    Canons, fugues, etc. (Organ)
    Chaconnes (Organ)
    Chorale preludes

    Claviorganum music
    Marches (Organ)
    Minuets (Organ)
    Organ—Studies and exercises
    Overtures (Organ)
    Passacaglias (Organ)
    Player-organ music
    Reed-organ music
    Rondos (Organ)
    Sonatas (Organ)
    Suites (Organ)
    Symphonic poems (Organ)
    Symphonies (Organ)
    Tablature (Musical notation)
    Thorough bass—Realizations
    Variations (Organ)
  — **Bibliography**
  — — **Graded lists**
      [ML132.O]
      UF Organ music—Graded lists
  — Graded lists
      USE Organ music—Bibliography—
        Graded lists
  — **History and criticism**
  — **Instructive editions**
      [MT195-7]
  — **Teaching pieces**
      [MT193]
      BT Organ—Instruction and study
Organ music, Arranged
  [M12-13]
  NT Concerti grossi arranged for organ
    Overtures arranged for organ
    Symphonies arranged for organ
Organ music (4 hands)
  [M180-181]
  NT Canons, fugues, etc. (Organ, 4 hands)
    Sonatas (Organ, 4 hands)
    Suites (Organ, 4 hands)
    Variations (Organ, 4 hands)
Organ music (Jazz)
  NT Organ music (Ragtime)
Organ music (Organs (2))
  [M180-181]
  NT Canons, fugues, etc. (Organs (2))
    Sonatas (Organs (2))
Organ music (Organs (3))
  [M180-181]
  NT Concertos (Organs (3))
Organ music (Ragtime)
  [M6-13.5]
  BT Organ music (Jazz)
    Ragtime music
Organ of Corti
  USE Corti's organ
**Organ, piano, guitars (3), percussion with
  orchestra**
  [M1040-1041]
  BT Sextets (Organ, piano, guitars (3),
    percussion)
  RT Concertos (Organ, piano, guitars (3),
    percussion)
**Organ Pipe Cactus National Monument
  (Ariz.)**
  BT National monuments—Arizona
Organ-pipes
  [ML595]
  BT Musical pitch
    Organ—Construction
  RT Organ stops
  NT Flue pipes (Organ pipes)
    Reed pipes (Organ pipes)
Organ-player
  USE Player-organ
Organ-point
  [MT59]
  UF Pedal point
  BT Harmony
  RT Bourdon
Organ preservation (Anatomy)
  USE Preservation of organs, tissues, etc.

Organ realizations of thorough bass
USE Thorough bass—Realizations
Organ specificity (Immunology)
USE Tissue specific antigens
Organ stops
UF Stops, Organ
BT Organ—Construction
Organ—Registration
RT Organ-pipes
NT Mixture stops
Rohrflöte
Organ transplantation
USE Transplantation of organs, tissues, etc.
Organ with band
[M1205]
RT Concertos (Organ with band)
— **Solo with piano**
[M1206]
BT Piano and organ music, Arranged
Organ with brass ensemble
RT Concertos (Organ with brass ensemble)
Organ with chamber orchestra
[M1105-6]
RT Concertos (Organ with chamber
orchestra)
Organ with instrumental ensemble
RT Concertos (Organ with instrumental
ensemble)
Instrumental ensembles
NT Instrumental ensembles
Suites (Organ with instrumental
ensemble)
Organ with orchestra
[M1005-6]
RT Concertos (Organ)
NT Symphonies (Organ with orchestra)
— **Solo with piano**
[M1006]
BT Piano and organ music, Arranged
Organ with percussion ensemble
RT Concertos (Organ with percussion
ensemble)
Organ with string orchestra
[M1105-6]
RT Concertos (Organ with string
orchestra)
NT Passacaglias (Organ with string
orchestra)
Suites (Organ with string orchestra)
Symphonies (Organ with string
orchestra)
Variations (Organ with string
orchestra)
Organ with string orchestra, Arranged
[M1105-6]
— **Scores and parts**
[M1105]
Organ with wind ensemble
RT Concertos (Organ with wind ensemble)
Organa
Here are entered musical works composed in the
form of organum. Works on organum as a musical
form are entered under the heading Organum.
BT Part-songs, Sacred
Organa oculi accessoria
USE Adnexa oculi
Organelles, Cell
USE Cell organelles
Organelles, Plant
USE Plant organelles
Organic acids
USE Acids, Organic
Organic architecture (May Subd Geog)
UF Architecture, Organic
BT Architecture—Environmental aspects
Architecture, Modern—20th century
NT Usonian houses
Organic bases
BT Bases (Chemistry)
Chemistry, Organic

Organic chemicals
USE Organic compounds
Organic chemistry
USE Chemistry, Organic
Organic compounds
UF Compounds, Organic
Organic chemicals
BT Carbon compounds
Chemistry, Organic
SA *groups of organic compounds, e.g.*
Aldehydes, Esters; Phenols; *and*
individual organic compounds, e.g.
Carbolic acid, Toluene, Xylene
NT Allelopathic agents
Cyclic compounds
Disulfiram
Ionophores
Organic solvents
Polyenes
Soils—Organic compound content
— **Biodegradation**
BT Biodegradation
Organic compounds removal (Sewage
purification)
USE Sewage—Purification—Organic
compounds removal
Organic compounds removal (Water
purification)
USE Water—Purification—Organic
compounds removal
Organic conductor industry
(May Subd Geog)
[HD9662.O74-743]
RT Organic conductors
Organic conductors
UF Conductors, Organic
Molecular metals
Organic metals
Polymer metals
BT One-dimensional conductors
Organometallic compounds
RT Organic conductor industry
Organic cooled reactors
UF Reactors, Organic cooled
BT Nuclear reactors
Organic design (May Subd Geog)
UF Design, Organic
BT Design
Organic farming (May Subd Geog)
[S605.5]
UF Biodynamic farming
Organiculture
BT Agriculture
Horticulture
RT Organic gardening
— **Law and legislation** (May Subd Geog)
BT Agricultural laws and legislation
Organic fertilizers (May Subd Geog)
[S654]
BT Fertilizers
NT Bone-meal
Compost
Farm manure
Green manuring
Guano
Humus
Manures
Night soil
Oil cake
Organic wastes as fertilizer
Peat
Straw as fertilizer
Organic gardening (May Subd Geog)
[SB453.5]
UF Biodynamic gardening
Natural gardening
Organiculture
BT Gardening
RT Companion planting
Organic farming

Organic geochemistry (May Subd Geog)
[QE516.5]
BT Chemistry, Organic
Geochemistry
Organic matter in soil
USE Humus
Organic metals
USE Organic conductors
Organic moderated reactors
UF Moderated reactors, Organic
OMR
BT Nuclear reactors
Organic semiconductors
[QC611.8.O7]
BT Semiconductors
Organic soils
USE Histosols
Organic solvents
[QC463.S72 (Spectroscopy)]
[QD544.5 (Physical chemistry)]
[RA1270.S6 (Toxicology)]
[TP247.5 (Chemical technology)]
UF Solvents, Organic
BT Nonaqueous solvents
Organic compounds
Organic synthesis (Chemistry)
USE Chemistry, Organic—Synthesis
Organic waste as fuel
USE Waste products as fuel
Organic wastes (May Subd Geog)
UF Garbage
Wastes, Organic
BT Factory and trade waste
Refuse and refuse disposal
Sewage
Waste products
NT Agricultural wastes
Organic water pollutants
— **Burning**
UF Burning of organic wastes
BT Incineration
— **Recycling**
BT Recycling (Waste, etc.)
NT Organic wastes as feed
Organic wastes as fertilizer
Organic wastes as feed (May Subd Geog)
[SF99.W34 (Use)]
BT Feeds
Organic wastes—Recycling
Waste products as feed
NT Agricultural wastes as feed
Animal waste as feed
Garbage as feed
Sewage sludge as feed
Organic wastes as fertilizer
(May Subd Geog)
[S654 (Use)]
BT Fertilizers
Organic fertilizers
Organic wastes—Recycling
NT Farm manure
Fish-scrap fertilizer
Guano
Night soil
Sewage as fertilizer
Sewage irrigation
Wood waste as mulch, soil conditioner,
etc.
Organic wastes as soil amendments
(May Subd Geog)
[S654]
BT Soil amendments
NT Sewage as fertilizer
Wood waste as mulch, soil conditioner,
etc.
Organic water pollutants (May Subd Geog)
UF Contaminants, Organic water
Pollutants, Organic water
Water pollutants, Organic

BT Chemistry, Organic
      Organic wastes
      Pollutants
      Water—Pollution
RT Water—Purification—Organic
      compounds removal
   — Biodegradation
Organically grown food
  USE Food, Natural
Organiculture
  USE Organic farming
      Organic gardening
Organina
  [MT35]
  BT Musical instruments (Mechanical)
Organism (Philosophy)
  [B105.O74]
  BT Philosophy
Organists *(May Subd Geog)*
  [ML396 (Biography: collective)]
  [ML416 (individual)]
  UF Music—Biography
  BT Church musicians
Organization
  RT Management
  NT Communication in organizations
      Comparative organization
      Industrial organization
      Interorganizational relations
      Line and staff organization
      Matrix organization
      Organizational behavior
      Organizational change
      Organizational effectiveness
      Planning
      Resource allocation
      Secretariats
      Symbolism in organizations
   — Research *(May Subd Geog)*
      UF Organizational research
Organization, File (Computer science)
  USE File organization (Computer science)
Organization, Industrial
  USE Industrial organization
Organization, International
  USE International organization
Organization, Social
  USE Social structure
Organization center (Embryology)
  USE Organizer (Embryology)
Organization charts
  BT Business
      Graphic methods
      Office management
Organization development
  USE Organizational change
Organizational behavior
  [HD58.7]
  UF Behavior in organizations
  BT Management
      Organization
      Psychology, Industrial
      Social psychology
  NT Corporate culture
      Office politics
Organizational career development
  USE Career development
Organizational change *(May Subd Geog)*
  UF Organization development
      Organizational innovation
  BT Management
      Organization
  RT Manpower planning
  NT Job enrichment
Organizational communication
  USE Communication in organizations
Organizational culture
  USE Corporate culture
Organizational effectiveness
  [HD58.9]

BT Management
      Organization
Organizational innovation
  USE Organizational change
Organizational research
  USE Organization—Research
Organizational stress
  USE Job stress
Organizational symbolism
  USE Symbolism in organizations
Organizations
  USE Associations, institutions, etc.
Organizations, Business
  USE Business enterprises
Organizations, International
  USE *individual international congresses,*
        societies, etc.
      International agencies
Organizations, Non-governmental
  (International agencies)
  USE Non-governmental organizations
Organized camps
  USE Camps
Organized crime *(May Subd Geog)*
  UF Crime syndicates
  BT Crime and criminals
  NT Gambling
      Mafia
      Racketeering
      Vice
      Yakuza
   — Prevention
      UF Organized crime prevention
          Prevention of organized crime
      BT Crime prevention
   — United States
      NT Italian American criminals
Organized crime investigation
  (May Subd Geog)
  [HV8079.O73]
  BT Criminal investigation
Organized crime prevention
  USE Organized crime—Prevention
Organizer (Embryology)
  [QL971.2]
  UF Organization center (Embryology)
  BT Developmental biology
      Embryology
Organizing, Labor
  USE Trade-unions—Organizing
Organoaluminum compounds
  UF Aluminum organic compounds
Organoantimony compounds
  UF Antimony organic compounds
  BT Antimony compounds
Organoarsenic compounds
  UF Arsenic organic compounds
  BT Arsenic compounds
  NT Cacodylic acid
Organoberyllium compounds
  UF Beryllium organic compounds
Organobismuth compounds
  UF Bismuth organic compounds
Organoboron compounds
  UF Boron organic compounds
  NT Organoboron polymers
      Tetraphenylborates
Organoboron polymers
  UF Boron organic polymers
  BT Organoboron compounds
      Polymers and polymerization
Organobromine compounds
  NT Polybrominated biphenyls
Organocadmium compounds
  UF Cadmium organic compounds
  BT Cadmium compounds
Organochlorine compounds
  UF Chlorine organic compounds
  BT Chlorine compounds
  NT Chlordecone
      Chlorobenzene

      Chlorofluorocarbons
      Chlorophenols
      Dichloromethyl ether
      Dichloropropane
      Endosulfan
      Heptachlor
      Hexachlorocyclopentadiene
      Kelevan
      Mirex
      Polychlorinated biphenyls
      Polychlorinated dibenzofurans
      Polychlorinated terphenyls
      Tetrachlorodibenzodioxin
      Tetradifon
      Tioconazole
      Toxaphene
      Trichloroethane
      Trichloroethylene
Organochromium compounds
  UF Chromium organic compounds
Organocobalt compounds
  UF Cobalt organic compounds
Organocopper compounds
  UF Copper organic compounds
  NT Copper naphthenate
      Copper proteins
Organofluorine compounds
  UF Fluorine organic compounds
  BT Fluorine compounds
  NT Chlorofluorocarbons
      Electric insulators and insulation—
         Organofluorine compounds
      Fluorocarbons
      Fluoropyrimidines
      Sulindac
Organogallium compounds
  UF Gallium organic compounds
Organogenesis
  USE Morphogenesis
Organogermanium compounds
  UF Germanium organic compounds
Organogold compounds
  UF Gold organic compounds
  NT Auranofin
Organography
  USE Botany—Organography
      Natural history—Organography
Organohafnium compounds
  [QD412.H5]
  UF Hafnium organic compounds
Organohalogen compounds
  UF Halogen organic compounds
  BT Halogens
  NT Halocarbons
      Progabide
      Trihalomethanes
Organoids, Cell
  USE Cell organelles
Organoindium compounds
  [QD412.I5]
  UF Indium organic compounds
  BT Indium compounds
      Organometallic compounds
Organoiodine compounds
  UF Iodine organic compounds
  BT Iodine compounds
  NT Thyroglobulin
Organoiridium compounds
  [QD412.I7]
  UF Iridium organic compounds
  BT Iridium
Organoiron compounds
  UF Iron organic compounds
  NT Ferrocene
      Iron proteins
Organolead compounds
  UF Lead organic compounds
Organoleptic analysis of food
  USE Food—Sensory evaluation
Organolithium compounds
  UF Lithium organic compounds

Organology (Music)
USE Musical instruments
Organomagnesium compounds
UF Magnesium organic compounds
RT Grignard reagents
NT Protochlorophyllide
Organomanganese compounds
UF Manganese organic compounds
Organomercury compounds
UF Mercury organic compounds
NT Diuretics, Mercurial
Methylmercury
Organometallic chemistry *(May Subd Geog)*
[QD410-QD412.5]
UF Chemistry, Organometallic
Metallo-organic chemistry
BT Chemistry, Organic
Organometallic compounds
[QD411-412]
UF Metallo-organic compounds
Metalloids, Organic
Metalorganic compounds
Organometalloids
BT Sequestration (Chemistry)
SA *particular organometallic compounds,*
e.g. Organoantimony compounds;
Organomagnesium compounds
NT Metallocenes
Metalloproteins
Metallothionein
Organic conductors
Organoindium compounds
Organoosmium compounds
Organoruthenium compounds
Organothallium compounds
Sodium dihydrobismethoxyeth
anolatoaluminate
— Spectra
Organometalloids
USE Organometallic compounds
Organomolybdenum compounds
UF Molybdenum organic compounds
Organon vasculosum laminae terminalis
UF Lamina terminalis, Vascular organ of
Organum vasculosum laminae
terminalis
BT Brain
Organonickel compounds
UF Nickel organic compounds
Organonitrogen compounds
UF Nitrogen organic compounds
BT Nitrogen compounds
NT Azepines
Imines
Imino compounds
Nitroquinoline oxide
Pteridines
Pyrrole
Tetrazine
Organoosmium compounds
[QD412.O7]
UF Osmium organic compounds
BT Organometallic compounds
Osmium compounds
Organophosphorus compounds
UF Phosphorus organic compounds
BT Phosphorus compounds
NT Dibromopropanol phosphate
Fenitrothion
Glyphosate
Naled (Insecticide)
Phosphazo compounds
Phosphonic acids
Temephos
— Spectra
Organoplatinum compounds
UF Platinum organic compounds
Organorhodium compounds
[QD412.R5]
UF Rhodium organic compounds
BT Rhodium

Organoruthenium compounds
[QD412.R9]
UF Ruthenium organic compounds
BT Organometallic compounds
Ruthenium compounds
Organoselenium compounds
UF Selenium organic compounds
BT Selenium compounds
NT Benzoselenadiazole
Organosilicon compounds
UF Silicon organic compounds
BT Silicon compounds
NT Electric insulators and insulation—
Organosilicon compounds
Hydrosilyation
Silicones
Organosilver compounds
UF Silver organic compounds
Organosodium compounds
UF Sodium organic compounds
Organosulphur compounds
UF Sulphur organic compounds
BT Sulphur compounds
NT Auranofin
Dithiolylium
Iron sulphur proteins
Metallothionein
Penicillamine
Sulphilimines
Sulphones
Sulphoximines
Sulphur amino acids
Organotellurium compounds
UF Tellurium organic compounds
BT Tellurium compounds
Organothallium compounds
[QD412.T7]
UF Thallium organic compounds
BT Organometallic compounds
Thallium compounds
Organotherapy
[RM283-RM298]
UF Opotherapy
BT Therapeutics
RT Animal extracts
Serumtherapy
NT Cellular therapy
Rejuvenation
Thymus extract
Tissue extracts
Organotin compounds
UF Tin organic compounds
NT Tributyltin
Organotitanium compounds
UF Titanium organic compounds
Organotungsten compounds
UF Tungsten organic compounds
Organozinc compounds
UF Zinc organic compounds
Organozirconium compounds
[QD412.Z7]
UF Zirconium organic compounds
Organs *(May Subd Geog)*
RT Organ
SA *subdivisions* Organ *or* Organs *under*
names of churches, cathedrals, etc.
— France
NT Saint-Sernin de Toulouse (Church)
—Organ
Organs, Artificial
USE Artificial organs
Organs, Culture of
[QP88]
UF Organ culture
BT Cultures (Biology)
Organs (Anatomy)
RT Tissue culture
Organs (3) with orchestra
[M1005-6]
RT Concertos (Organs (3))

Organs (Anatomy)
UF Body organs
BT Anatomy
RT Tissues
NT Organs, Culture of
Viscera
— **Innervation**
— Perfusion
USE Isolation perfusion (Physiology)
— Preservation
USE Preservation of organs, tissues,
etc.
— Transplantation
USE Transplantation of organs, tissues,
etc.
Organs of Zuckerkandl
USE Aortic paraganglia
Organum
[ML174 (Musical history)]
Here are entered works on organum as a musical
form. Musical works composed in the form are en-
tered under the heading Organa.
BT Counterpoint
Music—500-1400
Organum vasculosum laminae terminalis
USE Organon vasculosum laminae
terminalis
Orgasm
BT Generative organs
Sexual excitement
Sexual intercourse
NT Anorgasmy
Orgasm, Female
UF Female orgasm
RT Frigidity (Psychology)
Orgasmic dysfunction
USE Anorgasmy
Orgies
USE Group sex
Orgilus
[QL568.B8]
BT Braconidae
Orgone energy
USE Orgonomy
Orgonomy
[RZ460]
UF Orgone energy
BT Radiation
Therapeutics
Orgueil meteorite
[QB756.O74]
UF Meteorite Orgueil
BT Chondrites (Meteorites)
Orgyia
[QL561.L9]
UF Notolophus
BT Lymantriidae
NT Orgyia antiqua
Orgyia antiqua *(May Subd Geog)*
[QL561.L9]
UF Notolophus antiqua
Phalaena antiqua
Rusty tussock moth
Tussock moth, Rusty
Vapourer moth
BT Orgyia
Orgyidae
USE Lymantriidae
Orgyiidae
USE Lymantriidae
Orh
USE Bhovis
Oriamendi, Battle of, 1837
BT Spain—History—Carlist War, 1833-
1840—Campaigns
Oribatei
USE Mites
Oribatidae
[QL458.2.O74]
BT Mites
NT Mucronothrus

Oribe pottery *(May Subd Geog)*
  [*NK4340.O*]
  UF Pottery, Oribe
  BT Pottery, Japanese
    Seto pottery
  RT Shino pottery
Oribe school of Japanese tea ceremony
  USE Japanese tea ceremony—Oribe school
Oric 1 (Computer)
  BT Microcomputers
  — **Programming**
Oric Atmos (Computer)
  [*QA76.8.O*]
  UF Atmos (Computer)
  BT Microcomputers
Oricellari, Orti, Conspiracy, 1522
  USE Orti Oricellari Conspiracy, 1522
Oricellari Gardens Group
  USE Orti Oricellari Group
Orichalc
  [*TN616 (Ancient metals)*]
  [*TS650 (Alloys)*]
  BT Brass
Oriels *(May Subd Geog)*
  BT Windows
Orient *(Not Subd Geog)*
    Here are entered works on the region that extends
  from the Mediterranean and Red Seas to the Pacific
  Ocean, encompassing the Middle East, South Asia,
  East Asia, Southeast Asia, etc., but excluding Siberia.
  Works that focus on a narrower region within the
  Orient are entered under the name of the more spe-
  cific region, e.g. East Asia.
  UF East
  BT Asia
  SA *subject headings beginning with the*
      word Oriental, *or headings qualified*
      by the term Oriental, *e.g.* Oriental
      antiquities; Art, Oriental
  NT Asia, Southeastern
    East Asia
    Latin Orient
    Middle East
    South Asia
Orient, Latin
  USE Latin Orient
Orient and Occident
  USE East and West
Orient Express (Express train)
  BT Railroads—Europe—Express-trains
Oriental aesthetics
  USE Aesthetics, Oriental
Oriental antiques
  USE Antiques, Oriental
Oriental antiquities
  [*DS11 (Asia)*]
  [*DS56 (Ancient Orient)*]
  [*N5343-N5345 (Art)*]
  UF Antiquities, Oriental
  BT Antiquities
  SA *subdivision* Antiquities *under names of*
      countries, cities, etc.
Oriental architecture
  USE Architecture, Oriental
Oriental art
  USE Art, Oriental
Oriental art metal-work
  USE Art metal-work, Oriental
Oriental art objects
  USE Art objects, Oriental
Oriental astrology
  USE Astrology, Oriental
Oriental bazaars
  USE Bazaars, Oriental
Oriental brush painting
  USE Ink painting
Oriental children *(May Subd Geog)*
  UF Children, Oriental
  BT Children
Oriental children's stories
  USE Children's stories, Oriental

Oriental chronology
  USE Chronology, Oriental
Oriental civilization
  USE Civilization, Oriental
Oriental coins
  USE Coins, Oriental
Oriental Cordillera (Peru)
  USE Cordillera Oriental (Peru)
Oriental drama
  [*PJ334 (History)*]
  [*PJ371 (Collections)*]
  [*PJ464 (Translations, PJ431-3)*]
  UF Drama, Oriental
Oriental ethics
  USE Ethics, Oriental
Oriental fables
  USE Fables, Oriental
Oriental fencing
  USE Fencing, Oriental
Oriental fiction
  NT Children's stories, Oriental
Oriental fruit fly
  [*SB945.O63*]
  UF Dacus dorsalis
  — **Biological control** *(May Subd Geog)*
    BT Oriental fruit fly—Control
  — **Control** *(May Subd Geog)*
    NT Oriental fruit fly—Biological
      control
  — **Host plants**
Oriental fruit moth
  [*SB945.O65*]
  UF Grapholitha molesta
    Oriental peach moth
  BT Grapholitha
Oriental gardens
  USE Gardens, Oriental
Oriental hand-to-hand fighting
  USE Hand-to-hand fighting, Oriental
Oriental hygiene
  USE Hygiene, Oriental
Oriental illumination of books and manuscripts
  USE Illumination of books and manuscripts,
    Oriental
Oriental inscriptions
  USE Inscriptions, Oriental
Oriental Jewish authors
  USE Jewish authors, Oriental
Oriental Jews
  USE Jews, Oriental
Oriental languages
  [*PJ*]
  UF Languages, Oriental
  BT Asia—Languages
  SA *names of languages and groups of*
      languages
Oriental law
  USE Law, Oriental
Oriental literature
  [*PJ301-PJ345 (History)*]
  [*PJ347-PJ598 (Collections)*]
  UF Asia—Literatures
    Asian literature
  BT Semitic literature
  SA *particular literatures, e.g.* Iranian
      literature
  NT Classification—Books—Oriental
      literature
    East Asian literature
    Literature, Comparative—Occidental
      and Oriental
    Literature, Comparative—Oriental and
      Occidental
  — Cataloging
      USE Cataloging of Oriental literature
Oriental literature (English)
  UF English literature—Asian authors
Oriental Lowestoft
  USE China trade porcelain
Oriental manuscripts
  USE Manuscripts, Oriental

Oriental maxims
  USE Maxims, Oriental
Oriental medicine
  USE Medicine, Oriental
Oriental mythology
  USE Mythology, Oriental
Oriental Orthodox churches
  (May Subd Geog)
    Here are entered works on the Syrian Jacobite,
  Armenian, Coptic, Ethiopian and Indian Orthodox
  churches treated collectively. Works on the followers
  of Eutyches are entered under Monophysites.
  UF Ancient Oriental churches
    Ante-Chalcedonian Orthodox churches
    Lesser Eastern Orthodox churches
    Orthodox Oriental churches
    Pre-Chalcedonian Orthodox churches
  BT Eastern churches
  RT Monophysites
Oriental Paraguay
  USE Paraguay, Eastern
Oriental peach moth
  USE Oriental fruit moth
Oriental persimmon
  USE Kaki persimmon
Oriental philology
  [*PJ*]
    Here are entered works on the ancient and/or
  modern Oriental languages and literatures of Asia as
  a whole, or of the Far East only. Works on the ancient
  and/or modern languages and literatures of the Mid-
  dle East are entered under Middle Eastern philology.
  UF Philology, Oriental
  NT Middle Eastern philology
Oriental philosophy
  USE Philosophy, Oriental
Oriental poetry
  [*PJ327 (History)*]
  [*PJ356 (Collections)*]
  [*PJ462-3 (Translations, PJ416-418)*]
  UF Poetry, Oriental
  NT Qasidas
    War poetry, Oriental
Oriental poetry (American)
  USE American poetry—Asian-American
    authors
Oriental poetry (English)
  UF English poetry—Oriental authors
Oriental poppy *(May Subd Geog)*
  [*QK495.P22 (Botany)*]
  UF Papaver bracteatum
    Papaver orientale
    Poppy, Oriental
  BT Poppies
Oriental porcelain
  USE Porcelain, Oriental
Oriental pottery
  USE Pottery, Oriental
Oriental proverbs
  USE Proverbs, Oriental
Oriental rat flea
  [*QL599.7.P8*]
  UF Rat flea, Oriental
    Xenopsylla cheopis
  BT Xenopsylla
Oriental rugs
  USE Rugs, Oriental
Oriental scrolls
  USE Scrolls, Oriental
Oriental silverwork
  USE Silverwork, Oriental
Oriental small-clawed otter
  [*QL737.C25*]
  UF Amblonyx cinerea
    Aonyx cinerea
    Asian short-clawed otter
    Small-clawed otter, Oriental
  BT Otters
Oriental sore
  USE Leishmaniasis, Cutaneous
Oriental spruce
  [*QK494.5.P66 (Botany)*]

Oriental spruce (Continued)
  ⌐SD397.O74 (Forestry)⌐
    UF Caucasian spruce
        Picea orientalis
    BT Spruce
Oriental studies
    USE Asia—Study and teaching
         Middle East—Study and teaching
Oriental swan goose
    USE Swan goose
Oriental temples
    USE Temples, Oriental
Oriental textile fabrics
    USE Textile fabrics, Oriental
Oriental war poetry
    USE War poetry, Oriental
Oriental wit and humor
  ⌐PN6222.O7⌐
Orientale sesame
    USE Sesame
Orientalism in art
    USE Exoticism in art
Orientalists (May Subd Geog)
    BT Asia—Study and teaching
        Scholars
    RT Middle East—Study and teaching
    NT Assyriologists
        Egyptologists
Orientals
    USE Asians
Orientanoplius
    USE Anoplius
Orientation (May Subd Geog)
  ⌐GV200.4 (Recreation)⌐
  ⌐QP443 (Physiology)⌐
    UF Direction, Sense of
        Orienteering
    BT Hiking
    NT Animal orientation
        Blind—Orientation and mobility
        Blind-deaf—Orientation and mobility
        Navigation
        Orientation (Physiology)
        Orientation (Psychology)
        Orienting reflex
  — **Judging**
    BT Sports officiating
  — **Testing**
    BT Perception—Testing
        Psychological tests
Orientation, Cross-cultural
    USE Cross-cultural orientation
Orientation (Architecture)
  ⌐NA2540⌐
  ⌐NA4800 (Churches)⌐
    BT Architecture
        Architecture and religion
        Church architecture
Orientation (College students)
    USE College student orientation
Orientation (Information services)
    USE Information services—User education
Orientation (Library use)
    USE Library orientation
Orientation (Military science)
    USE Range-finding
Orientation (Physiology)
  ⌐QP443⌐
    BT Instinct
        Orientation
        Physiology
        Proprioception
        Senses and sensation
    NT Phototropism
Orientation (Psychology)
  ⌐BF299.O7⌐
    BT Instinct
        Orientation
        Psychology
        Senses and sensation
        Spatial behavior

    RT Geographical perception
    NT Time perception
Orientation (Religion)
  ⌐BL619.O7⌐
    BT Cardinal points
        Christian art and symbolism
        Church architecture
        Cults
        Funeral rites and ceremonies
        Religion, Primitive
        Religion and geography
        Rites and ceremonies
        Sun worship
        Symbolism
        Worship
Orientation centers for visitors
    USE Visitors' centers
Orientation of teachers
    USE Teacher orientation
Orientation reaction
    USE Orienting reflex
Oriente (Bolivia)
    Here are entered works that deal collectively with
    the departments of Santa Cruz, Beni, and Pando in
    Bolivia.
    UF Bolivia, Eastern
        Eastern Bolivia
        Oriente Boliviano (Bolivia)
Oriente (Colombia)
    Here are entered works that deal collectively with
    the departments of Boyacá, Meta, Norte de Santand-
    er, and Santander in Colombia.
    UF Oriente Colombiano (Colombia)
Oriente (Ecuador)
    Here are entered works that deal collectively with
    the provinces of Napo, Pastaza, Morona-Santiago
    and Zamora-Chinchipe.
    UF Amazónica (Ecuador)
        Eastern Lowlands (Ecuador)
        Eastern Region (Ecuador)
        Ecuador Amazónico (Ecuador)
        Ecuadorian Oriente (Ecuador)
        La Región Oriental (Ecuador)
        Región Oriental (Ecuador)
        Transandina (Ecuador)
Oriente (Peru)
Oriente Boliviano (Bolivia)
    USE Oriente (Bolivia)
Oriente Colombiano (Colombia)
    USE Oriente (Colombia)
Orienteering
    USE Orientation
Orienting devices
    USE Orienting mechanisms
Orienting mechanisms
  ⌐TJ1317.5⌐
    UF Mechanisms, Orienting
        Orienting devices
    BT Assembling machines
        Mechanical movements
    RT Feed mechanisms
Orienting reaction
    USE Orienting reflex
Orienting reflex
  ⌐QP372⌐
    UF Orientation reaction
        Orienting reaction
        Orienting response
    BT Conditioned response
        Orientation
        Reflexes
Orienting response
    USE Orienting reflex
Orifices
    USE Holes
Orificial surgery
    USE Surgery, Orificial
Orig dialect (Sudan)
    BT Sudan—Languages
        Tagoi language
Origami
  ⌐TT870⌐

    UF Japanese paper folding
        Paper folding, Japanese
    BT Paper work
Origanum
  ⌐QK495.L25⌐
    UF Majorana
    BT Lamiaceae
Origin
    USE subdivision Origin under names of
         ethnic groups, races, religions, or
         certain topics, e.g. Buddhism—
         Origin; Life—Origin
Origin, Marks of
    USE Marks of origin
Origin and destination traffic statistics
    USE Origin and destination traffic surveys
Origin and destination traffic surveys
    (May Subd Geog)
    Here are entered works on the methods and tech-
    niques employed in conducting origin and destina-
    tion traffic surveys, and reports of individual surveys.
    For the latter, the heading may be subdivided by
    place.
    UF Origin and destination traffic statistics
        Origin-destination traffic surveys
    BT Traffic surveys
    NT Traffic assignment
        Trip generation
Origin-destination traffic surveys
    USE Origin and destination traffic surveys
Origin of agriculture
    USE Agriculture—Origin
Origin of languages
    USE Language and languages—Origin
Origin of life
    USE Life—Origin
Origin of man
    USE Man—Origin
Origin of species
    USE Evolution
Origin of the State
    USE State, The—Origin
Original Buddhism
    USE Buddhism—Doctrines—History—Early
         period, to ca. 250 B.C.
Original sin
    USE Sin, Original
Originality
  ⌐BF433.O7⌐
    BT Creative ability
        Genius
        Imagination
        Planning—Ability testing
    RT Creation (Literary, artistic, etc.)
Originality (Aesthetics)
  ⌐BH301.O75⌐
    BT Aesthetics
Originality (in literature)
    BT Authorship
        Imagination
        Literature
        Rhetoric
    RT Imitation (in literature)
    NT Influence (Literary, artistic, etc.)
        Plagiarism
Origins of country music (Painting)
    USE Benton, Thomas Hart, 1889-1975.
         Sources of country music
Orihashi family (Not Subd Geog)
Orikaka River (N.Z.)
    UF Mackley River (N.Z.)
    BT Rivers—New Zealand
Orimoto Nishihara Iseki (Yokohama-shi,
Japan)
    USE Orimoto Nishihara Site (Yokohama-
         shi, Japan)

Orimoto Nishihara Site (Yokohama-shi, Japan) *(Not Subd Geog)*
  UF Orimoto Nishihara Iseki (Yokohama-shi, Japan)
        Orimotonishihara Site (Yokohama-shi, Japan)
  BT Japan—Antiquities
Orimotonishihara Site (Yokohama-shi, Japan)
  USE Orimoto Nishihara Site (Yokohama-shi, Japan)
Orinoco River (Venezuela)
  UF Río Orinoco (Venezuela)
  BT Rivers—Venezuela
Oriole, Baltimore (Bird)
  USE Northern oriole
Oriole, Northern
  USE Northern oriole
Orioles
  [QL696.P2]
  BT Passeriformes
  NT Icterus (Birds)
        Oriolus
Orioles, New World
  USE Icterus (Birds)
Orioles, Old World
  USE Oriolus
Oriolidae
  [QL696.P2585]
  BT Passeriformes
  NT Oriolus
Oriolus
  [QL696.P2585]
  UF Old World orioles
        Orioles, Old World
  BT Orioles
        Oriolidae
  NT Golden oriole
Oriolus oriolus
  USE Golden oriole
Oriomo (Papua New Guinea people)
  USE Gidra (Papua New Guinea people)
Orion (Constellation)
  UF Hunter (Constellation)
        Warrior (Constellation)
  BT Constellations
Orion, Great nebula of
  USE Orion Nebula
Orion (Greek mythology)
  BT Mythology, Greek
Orion Nebula
  UF Great nebula of Orion
        M42 (Nebula)
        NGC 1976 (Nebula)
        Orion, Great nebula of
  BT Nebulae
Orion Project
  USE Project Orion
Orione (Fighter plane)
  UF C.205N (Fighter plane)
        Macchi C.205N (Fighter plane)
  BT Fighter planes
Oriskany, Battle of, 1777
  [E241.O6]
  BT New York (State)—History—Revolution, 1775-1783
        St. Leger's Expedition, 1777
        United States—History—Revolution, 1775-1783—Campaigns
Oriskany Campaign
  USE St. Leger's Expedition, 1777
Oriskany formation
  USE Geology, Stratigraphic—Devonian
        Paleobotany—Devonian
        Paleontology—Devonian
Orissa (India)
  — Civilization
  — — Islamic influences
        BT Civilization, Islamic
Orissi dance
  USE Odissi dance

Oriya art
  USE Art, Oriya
Oriya arts
  USE Arts, Oriya
Oriya authors
  USE Authors, Oriya
Oriya ballads
  USE Ballads, Oriya
Oriya bhajans
  USE Bhajans, Oriya
Oriya children's plays
  USE Children's plays, Oriya
Oriya didactic poetry
  USE Didactic poetry, Oriya
Oriya drama *(May Subd Geog)*
  NT Children's plays, Oriya
        Folk-drama, Oriya
        Historical drama, Oriya
        One-act plays, Oriya
Oriya dramatists
  USE Dramatists, Oriya
Oriya encyclopedias and dictionaries
  USE Encyclopedias and dictionaries, Oriya
Oriya essays *(May Subd Geog)*
Oriya fiction *(May Subd Geog)*
  NT Historical fiction, Oriya
        Short stories, Oriya
Oriya folk-drama
  USE Folk-drama, Oriya
Oriya folk literature
  USE Folk literature, Oriya
Oriya folk-songs
  USE Folk-songs, Oriya
Oriya historical drama
  USE Historical drama, Oriya
Oriya historical fiction
  USE Historical fiction, Oriya
Oriya imprints *(May Subd Geog)*
Oriya language
  [PK2561-9]
  UF Uriya language
  BT Indo-Aryan languages, Modern
  RT Halbi language
  NT Kotia dialect
        Sambalpuri dialect
  — Etymology
      NT Words, New—Oriya
  — Neologisms
      USE Words, New—Oriya
  — New words
      USE Words, New—Oriya
Oriya literature
  NT Folk literature, Oriya
        Religious literature, Oriya
  — To 1500
  — 20th century
  — Women authors
Oriya manuscripts
  USE Manuscripts, Oriya
Oriya mythology
  USE Mythology, Oriya
Oriya one-act plays
  USE One-act plays, Oriya
Oriya patriotic poetry
  USE Patriotic poetry, Oriya
Oriya periodicals *(May Subd Geog)*
Oriya philology
Oriya poetry
  NT Bhajans, Oriya
        Didactic poetry, Oriya
        Patriotic poetry, Oriya
        Quatrains, Oriya
        Religious poetry, Oriya
        Vaishnava poetry, Oriya
  — To 1500
  — 1500-1800
  — 20th century
  — Occidental influences
      BT Civilization, Occidental
Oriya poets
  USE Poets, Oriya

Oriya prose literature *(May Subd Geog)*
  — To 1500
Oriya quatrains
  USE Quatrains, Oriya
Oriya religious literature
  USE Religious literature, Oriya
Oriya religious poetry
  USE Religious poetry, Oriya
Oriya riddles
  USE Riddles, Oriya
Oriya short stories
  USE Short stories, Oriya
Oriya songs
  USE Songs, Oriya
Oriya Vaishnava poetry
  USE Vaishnava poetry, Oriya
Oriya wit and humor *(May Subd Geog)*
Oriyas
  [DS432.O8]
  UF Uriyas
Orkhon inscriptions (Turkic)
  USE Inscriptions, Old Turkic
Orkney
  NT Brough of Birsay (Scotland)
        North Ronaldsay (Scotland)
        Papa Westray (Scotland)
        Sanday (Scotland)
        Westray (Scotland)
Orlandini family *(Not Subd Geog)*
Orlando (Legendary character)
  USE Roland (Legendary character)
Orlean
  USE Annatto
Orlean tree
  USE Annatto tree
Orléans, House of *(Not Subd Geog)*
  [DC36.8.O7]
  BT France—Kings and rulers
Orléans, Forest of (France)
  UF Forest of Orléans (France)
        Forêt d'Orléans (France)
  BT Forests and forestry—France
Orléans, Isle of (Québec)
  UF Ile d'Orléans (Québec)
  BT Islands—Québec (Province)
Orléans, Battle of, 1870
  [DC305.6]
  BT Franco-German War, 1870-1871
  NT Loigny-Poupry, Battle of, 1870
Orlei language
  USE Olo language
Orleyl Site (Spain) *(Not Subd Geog)*
  UF Punta de Orleyl Site (Spain)
  BT Spain—Antiquities
Orlické Hory (Czechoslovakia)
  USE Orlické Mountains (Czechoslovakia)
Orlické Mountains (Czechoslovakia)
  UF Adler Gebirge (Czechoslovakia)
        Adlergebirge (Czechoslovakia)
        Gory Orlické (Czechoslovakia)
        Orlické Hory (Czechoslovakia)
  BT Mountains—Czechoslovakia
Orlicz lattice representations
  USE Representations of Orlicz lattices
Orlicz lattices
  UF Lattices, Orlicz
  BT Lattice theory
  NT Representations of Orlicz lattices
Orlicz spaces
  UF Spaces, Orlicz
  BT Function spaces
  NT Fenchel-Orlicz spaces
Orlon
  UF Acrylic fibers, Orlon
        Orlon acrylic fibers
  BT Textile fibers, Synthetic
Orlon acrylic fibers
  USE Orlon
Orlov trotter horse
  [SF293.O7]

Orma (African people)
  USE Oromo (African people)
Orman family
  USE Ormond family
Ormand family
  USE Ormond family
Ormaye, Bordeaux (France), 1652-1653
  USE Bordeaux (France)—History—
       Uprising, 1652-1653
Ormby family
  USE Ormsby family
Ormée, Bordeaux (France), 1652-1653
  USE Bordeaux (France)—History—
       Uprising, 1652-1653
Ormers
  USE Abalones
Ormond family *(Not Subd Geog)*
  UF Orman family
     Ormand family
Ormond's disease
  USE Retroperitoneal fibrosis
Ormsbe family
  USE Ormsby family
Ormsbee family
  USE Ormsby family
Ormsbey family
  USE Ormsby family
Ormsbry family
  USE Ormsby family
Ormsburg family
  USE Ormsby family
Ormsbury family
  USE Ormsby family
Ormsby family *(Not Subd Geog)*
  UF Ormby family
     Ormsbe family
     Ormsbee family
     Ormsbey family
     Ormsbry family
     Ormsburg family
     Ormsbury family
     Ornsbey family
     Ornsbough family
     Ornsby family
Ormsted family
  USE Olmstead family
Ormstid family
  USE Olmstead family
Ormuri language *(May Subd Geog)*
  UF Baraks language
     Bargista language
  BT Afghanistan—Languages
     Iranian languages
     Pakistan—Languages
Ormuz, Strait of
  USE Hormuz, Strait of
Ornament
  USE Decoration and ornament
Ornamental alphabets
  USE Alphabets
     Illumination of books and manuscripts
     Lettering
Ornamental birds
  USE Birds, Ornamental
Ornamental borders (Decorative arts)
  USE Borders, Ornamental (Decorative arts)
Ornamental borders (Gardening)
  USE Garden borders
Ornamental boxes
  USE Boxes, Ornamental
Ornamental carp *(May Subd Geog)*
  ⌈QL638.C94 (Zoology)⌉
  ⌈SF458.C37 (Culture)⌉
  UF Colored carp, Japanese
     Japanese colored carp
  BT Carp
     Ornamental fishes
  NT Goldfish
Ornamental climbing plants
  (May Subd Geog)
    ⌈SB427⌉

UF Garden vines
    Ornamental vines
  BT Climbing plants
    Ornamental woody plants
  RT Hanging plants
  NT Bougainvillea
    Wisteria
Ornamental combs
  USE Combs, Ornamental
Ornamental conifers *(May Subd Geog)*
  ⌈SB437.5.C6⌉
  BT Conifers
    Ornamental evergreens
    Ornamental trees
    Plants, Ornamental
  RT Ornamental shrubs
  NT Dwarf conifers
Ornamental evergreens *(May Subd Geog)*
  ⌈SB435⌉
  BT Evergreens
    Plants, Ornamental
  NT Ornamental conifers
Ornamental ferns
  USE Ferns, Ornamental
Ornamental fish trade *(May Subd Geog)*
  ⌈SF458.8-458.83⌉
  UF Aquarium fish trade
    Pet fish trade
    Tropical fish trade
  BT Fish trade
    Ornamental fishes
    Pet industry
    Wild animal trade
  NT Aquarium fish collecting
Ornamental fishes *(May Subd Geog)*
  ⌈SF456-458.83⌉
  UF Fishes as pets
    Pet fishes
  BT Fishes
  NT Aquarium fishes
    Goldfish
    Ornamental carp
    Ornamental fish trade
    Tropical fish
Ornamental grasses *(May Subd Geog)*
  ⌈SB431.7⌉
  BT Grasses
    Plants, Ornamental
Ornamental hair-work
  USE Hair-work, Ornamental
Ornamental heraldry
  USE Heraldry, Ornamental
Ornamental horticulture *(May Subd Geog)*
  BT Horticulture
  RT Landscape gardening
    Landscaping industry
    Plants, Ornamental
  NT Arboriculture
    Floriculture
    Florists
    Garden centers (Retail trade)
    Greenhouse management
    Grounds maintenance
    Horticultural service industry
    Landscape nurseries
    Nurseries (Horticulture)
Ornamental plant industry
  (May Subd Geog)
  BT Plants, Ornamental
  RT Bulb industry
    Floriculture
    Nurseries (Horticulture)
    Nursery stock
  NT Bedding plant industry
    Cut flower industry
    Florists
    Garden centers (Retail trade)
Ornamental plants
  USE Plants, Ornamental
Ornamental rocks *(May Subd Geog)*
  UF Rocks, Ornamental

BT Decoration and ornament
  NT Suiseki
Ornamental shrubs *(May Subd Geog)*
  ⌈SB435⌉
  UF Garden shrubs
  BT Ornamental woody plants
    Shrubs
  RT Ornamental conifers
  NT Dwarf shrubs
    Flowering shrubs
    Fullmoon maple
    Japanese maple
    Topiary work
Ornamental trees *(May Subd Geog)*
  ⌈SB435⌉
  UF Garden trees
  BT Ornamental woody plants
    Trees
  NT Flowering trees
    Fullmoon maple
    Japanese maple
    Ornamental conifers
    Shade trees
    Topiary work
Ornamental vines
  USE Ornamental climbing plants
Ornamental woody plants *(May Subd Geog)*
  ⌈SB435⌉
  BT Plants, Ornamental
    Woody plants
  RT Screens (Plants)
  NT Flowering woody plants
    Ornamental climbing plants
    Ornamental shrubs
    Ornamental trees
Ornaments (Music)
  USE Embellishment (Music)
Ornate box turtle
  UF Terrapene ornata
Orneodidae
  USE Alucitidae
Ornithischia
  BT Dinosaurs
  NT Ankylosauridae
    Ceratopsidae
    Hypsilophodontidae
    Iguanodontidae
    Protoceratopsidae
    Scutellosaurus lawleri
Ornithobilharzia
  ⌈QL391.P7⌉
  BT Schistosomatidae
Ornithobilharzia pricei
  ⌈QL391.P7⌉
Ornithodoros
  ⌈QL458.2.A74⌉
  BT Argasidae
    Relapsing fever
  NT Ornithodoros concanensis
    Ornithodoros coprophilus
    Ornithodoros coriaceus
    Ornithodoros hermsi
    Ornithodoros kelleyi
    Ornithodoros moubata
    Ornithodoros parkeri
    Ornithodoros turicata
    Ornithodoros viguerasi
Ornithodoros concanensis
  ⌈QL458.2.A74⌉
  BT Ornithodoros
Ornithodoros coprophilus
  ⌈QL458.2.A74⌉
  BT Ornithodoros
Ornithodoros coriaceus
  ⌈QL458.2.A74⌉
  UF Pajaroello tick
  BT Ornithodoros
Ornithodoros hermsi
  ⌈QL458.2.A74⌉
  BT Ornithodoros

Ornithodoros kelleyi
 ⌐QL458.2.A74¬
 BT Ornithodoros
Ornithodoros moubata
 ⌐QL458.2.A74¬
 BT Ornithodoros
Ornithodoros parkeri
 ⌐QL458.2.A74¬
 BT Ornithodoros
Ornithodoros turicata
 ⌐QL458.2.A74¬
 BT Ornithodoros
Ornithodoros viguerasi
 ⌐QL458.2.A74¬
 BT Ornithodoros
Ornithological literature
Ornithological research
 USE Birds—Research
Ornithological societies
 USE Birds—Societies, etc.
  Ornithology—Societies, etc.
Ornithologists *(May Subd Geog)*
 ⌐QL26¬
 BT Naturalists
  Scientists
  Zoologists
Ornithology *(May Subd Geog)*
 ⌐QL671-3¬
 BT Zoology
 RT Birds
 NT Bird-banding
  Radar in ornithology
 — Research
  USE Birds—Research
 — **Societies, etc.** *(May Subd Geog)*
  ⌐QL671¬
  UF Ornithological societies
 — **Study and teaching** *(May Subd Geog)*
  UF Birds—Study and teaching
Ornithology, Economic
 USE Beneficial birds
  Bird pests
Ornithoptera
 ⌐QL561.P2¬
 UF Birdwing butterflies
 BT Papilionidae
Ornithopters
 ⌐TL717¬
 UF Orthopters
 BT Flying-machines
Ornithorhynchidae
 USE Platypus
Ornithorhynchus
 USE Platypus
Ornithorhynchus anatinus
 USE Platypus
Ornithosis
Ornsbey family
 USE Ormsby family
Ornsbough family
 USE Ormsby family
Ornsby family
 USE Ormsby family
Ornstein-Uhlenbeck process
 BT Brownian motion processes
  Gaussian processes
  Stationary processes
Oro-facial pain
 USE Orofacial pain
Oroantral fistula
 USE Fistula, Oroantral
Orobanchaceae
 ⌐QK495.O74¬
 BT Tubiflorae
Oroch
 USE Oroches
Oroch language
 UF Orochee language
 BT Tungus-Manchu languages
Orochee language
 USE Oroch language

Oroches
 ⌐DK759.O7¬
 UF Oroch
  Orochi
 BT Ethnology—Russian S.F.S.R.
  Tunguses
 — Implements
Orochi
 USE Oroches
Orochon dialect
 ⌐PL461.O8¬
 BT Tungus-Manchu languages
Orodrassus
 ⌐QL458.42.G5¬
 BT Gnaphosidae
Orofacial pain *(May Subd Geog)*
 ⌐RK322¬
 UF Oro-facial pain
  Pain, Orofacial
 BT Face—Diseases
  Mouth—Diseases
  Pain
Orogenesis
 USE Orogeny
Orogeny *(May Subd Geog)*
 ⌐QE621¬
 UF Orogenesis
 BT Geology, Structural
  Mountains
Orographic clouds *(May Subd Geog)*
 BT Clouds
  Mountain climate
Orography
 USE Mountains
Orok language
 ⌐PL461.O85¬
 UF Ul'ta language
 BT Tungus-Manchu languages
Orokaiva
 USE Binandeli (Papuan people)
Orokaiva language *(May Subd Geog)*
 UF Orakaiva language
 BT Papua New Guinea—Languages
  Papuan languages
Orokolo dialect
 BT Papuan languages
 RT Toaripi dialect
Orology
 USE Mountains
Oromo (African people)
 ⌐DT390.G2¬
 UF Gala (African people)
  Galla (African people)
  Gallas
  Orma (African people)
 BT Ethnology—Ethiopia
  Ethnology—Kenya
 NT Boran (African people)
  Gabbra (African people)
  Missions to Oromo (African people)
Oromo language
 ⌐PJ2471-PJ2479¬
 UF Afan language
  Galla language
  Gallinya language
 BT Cushitic languages
  Ethiopia—Languages
  Kenya—Languages
 NT Boran dialect
  Qottu dialect
Orophaca
 USE Astragalus (Plants)
Óros Ólimbos (Greece)
 USE Olympus, Mount (Greece)
Oros Parnassos (Greece)
 USE Parnassus, Mount (Greece)
Óros Pílion (Greece)
 USE Pelion Mountains (Greece)
Orosháza (Bratislava, Czechoslovakia)
 USE Rusovce (Bratislava, Czechoslovakia)

Orosirá Rodhópis
 USE Rhodope Mountains
Orosius
 ⌐QL527.C49 (Zoology)¬
Orosius cellulosus
 ⌐QL527.C49 (Zoology)¬
 BT Cotton—Diseases and pests
 RT Cotton phyllody
Oroszvár (Bratislava, Czechoslovakia)
 USE Rusovce (Bratislava, Czechoslovakia)
Oroville, Lake (Calif.) *(Not Subd Geog)*
 UF Lake Oroville (Calif.)
 BT Lakes—California
  Reservoirs—California
Orovnik, Macedonia, Battle of, 1448
 ⌐DR960.5¬
 BT Albania—History—Turkish Wars, 15th
  century
  Albanian-Venetian War, 1447-1448—
  Campaigns
Oroya fever
 USE Verruga peruana
Orphan Annie (Fictitious character)
 USE Little Orphan Annie (Fictitious
  character)
Orphan asylums
 USE Orphanages
Orphan drugs *(May Subd Geog)*
  Here are entered works on drugs which appear to
 be useful for the treatment of rare disorders, but have
 difficulty in finding a sponsor for development and
 marketing because of insufficient anticipated finan-
 cial return.
 UF Drugs, Nonprofitable
  Drugs, Orphan
  Drugs of limited commercial value
  Nonprofitable drugs
 BT Drugs
Orphanages *(May Subd Geog)*
 ⌐HV959-1420.5¬
 UF Orphan asylums
 BT Charities
  Charity-schools
  Children—Institutional care
  Group homes for children
  Public welfare
  Youth—Dwellings
 NT Orphans
 — **Law and legislation** *(May Subd Geog)*
Orphanages, Jewish
 USE Jewish orphanages
Orphans *(May Subd Geog)*
 ⌐HV873-1420.5¬
 BT Child welfare
  Orphanages
 RT Abandoned children
  Children, Adopted
  Foundlings
Orphans, Jewish
 USE Jewish orphans
Orphans' courts
 USE Probate courts
Orpheus (Greek mythology)
 ⌐BL820.O7¬
 BT Mythology, Greek
Orphic mysteries
 USE Dionysia
Orphinidae
 USE Scarabaeidae
Orphism
 USE Dionysia
Orphism (Art) *(May Subd Geog)*
 BT Art, Modern—20th century
  Painting, Modern—20th century
Orpingtons
 ⌐SF489.O8¬
Orr family *(Not Subd Geog)*
 UF Oar family
  Ore family
  Ores family

2703

Orreries
USE Planetaria
Orsborn family
USE Osborne family
Orsborne family
USE Osborne family
Orsbourn family
USE Osborne family
Orsburn family
USE Osborne family
Őrség (Hungary)
Orser family *(Not Subd Geog)*
UF Aertszen family
Auser family
Orsera Valley (Switzerland)
USE Urseren Valley (Switzerland)
Orsi family
USE Orsini family
Orsini family *(Not Subd Geog)*
UF Orsi family
Orsino family
Orsino family
USE Orsini family
Orsodacnidae
USE Chrysomelidae
Országház (Budapest, Hungary)
UF Hungarian Parliament Building
(Budapest, Hungary)
Parliament Building (Budapest,
Hungary)
BT Hungary—Capital and capitol
Orta, Lake (Italy)
UF Lago d'Orta (Italy)
BT Lakes—Italy
Ortalidae
USE Otitidae
Ortalis
[QL696.G23]
BT Cracidae
NT Chachalaca
Ortalis vetula
USE Chachalaca
Ortega Adobe (Ventura, Calif.)
BT Dwellings—California
Ortega family *(Not Subd Geog)*
UF Ortego family
Ortego family
USE Ortega family
Orten family
USE Orton family
Orter family
USE Arthur family
Orthacanthacris aegyptia
USE Anacridium aegyptium
Orthagoriscus
BT Molidae
Orthez, Battle of, 1814
[DC233.O7]
BT Peninsular War, 1807-1814—
Campaigns—France
Orthida
[QE797.O7]
BT Brachiopoda, Fossil
NT Dalmanellidae
Plectorthidae
Orthidae, Fossil
NT Enteletacea
Orthite
USE Allanite
Orthocerida
[QE807.O]
BT Cephalopoda, Fossil
NT Lamellorthoceratidae
Orthochromatic photography
USE Photography, Orthochromatic
Orthocladius
[QL537.C56]
BT Chironomidae
Orthodiagraphy
UF Orthodiascopy

BT Heart—Dilatation
Heart—Hypertrophy
Heart—Measurement
Heart—Radiography
Orthodiascopy
USE Orthodiagraphy
Orthodontia
USE Orthodontics
Orthodontic appliances *(May Subd Geog)*
[RK527]
UF Braces, Orthodontic
BT Dental instruments and apparatus
Orthodontics
NT Begg appliance
Universal appliance (Dentistry)
Orthodontic appliances, Extraoral traction
[RK528.E98]
UF Extraoral orthodontic appliances
Extraoral traction appliances
BT Orthodontic appliances, Removable
Orthopedic traction
Orthodontic appliances, Removable
[RK528.R45]
UF Removable orthodontic appliances
NT Orthodontic appliances, Extraoral
traction
Splints, Bite plane
Orthodontics *(May Subd Geog)*
[RK521-528]
UF Dental orthopedics
Orthodontia
BT Dentistry
Orthopedia
NT Jaws—Abnormalities
Malocclusion
Orthodontic appliances
Orthodontists
Teeth—Abnormalities
— **Diagnosis**
[RK522]
Orthodontics, Corrective *(May Subd Geog)*
[RK527-528]
UF Corrective orthodontics
Tooth movement, Orthodontic
BT Therapeutics, Dental
NT Maxillary expansion
— **Complications and sequelae**
[RK527.4]
Orthodontics, Interceptive
(May Subd Geog)
[RK527.5]
UF Interceptive orthodontics
BT Pedodontics
Orthodontics, Preventive *(May Subd Geog)*
UF Malocclusion—Prevention
Preventive orthodontics
BT Preventive dentistry
Orthodontists *(May Subd Geog)*
BT Dentists
Orthodontics
Orthodox (Orthodox Eastern Church)
(May Subd Geog)
UF Eastern Orthodox
BT Orthodox Eastern Church
Orthodox Eastern Church *(May Subd Geog)*
[BX200-BX750]
Here are entered works on Orthodox Eastern
denominations treated collectively and works for
which the individual Orthodox denomination cannot
be identified.
UF Eastern Orthodox Church
Greek Church
Holy Orthodox Eastern Catholic and
Apostolic Church
BT Eastern churches
NT Monasteries, Orthodox Eastern
Orthodox (Orthodox Eastern Church)
Sakkos
— **Asceticism**
USE Asceticism—Orthodox Eastern
Church

— Confession
USE Confession—Orthodox Eastern
Church
— Converts
USE Converts, Orthodox Eastern
— **Finance**
— **Government**
NT Ophphikia
— **History**
NT Schism—Eastern and Western
Church
— **Hymns**
— Law
USE Canon law, Orthodox Eastern
— **Liturgical objects**
[BX341]
— **Liturgy**
NT Akathists
— **Relations**
[BX324]
— — **Catholic Church**
[BX324.3]
NT Schism—Eastern and Western
Church
Schism, Acacian, 484-519
— **Western rites** *(May Subd Geog)*
[BX756]
UF Western rites (Orthodox Eastern
Church)
— **Greece**
NT Zoe Movement (Christianity)
Orthodox Eastern Church and art
[N72.R4]
UF Art and the Orthodox Eastern Church
BT Art and religion
Christian art and symbolism
Orthodox Eastern church buildings
USE Churches, Orthodox Eastern
Orthodox Eastern churches
USE Churches, Orthodox Eastern
Orthodox Eastern converts
USE Converts, Orthodox Eastern
Orthodox Eastern monasteries
USE Monasteries, Orthodox Eastern
Orthodox Eastern monasticism and religious
orders
USE Monasticism and religious orders,
Orthodox Eastern
Orthodox Eastern monasticism and religious
orders for women
USE Monasticism and religious orders for
women, Orthodox Eastern
Orthodox Judaism *(May Subd Geog)*
UF Judaism, Orthodox
BT Jewish sects
Judaism
NT Jews—Return to Orthodox Judaism
Orthodox Oriental churches
USE Oriental Orthodox churches
Orthodox school of economics
USE Classical school of economics
Orthodox school of painting
[ND1043.53.O78]
UF Cheng t'ung hua p'ai
Standard school of painting
BT Painting, Chinese
Orthoepy
USE *subdivision* Pronunciation *under names
of languages, e.g.* English language
—Pronunciation
Phonetics
Orthoferrites
BT Ferrites (Magnetic materials)
Metallic oxides
Orthogeomys
[QL737.R654]
UF Heterogeomys
Macrogeomys
BT Pocket gophers
NT Orthogeomys cherriei

Orthogeomys cherriei
  [QL737.R654]
    UF Cherrie pocket gopher
    BT Orthogeomys
Orthogonal curves
  USE Curves, Orthogonal
Orthogonal functions
  USE Functions, Orthogonal
Orthogonal polynomials
  [QA404.5]
    BT Fourier analysis
       Functions, Orthogonal
       Polynomials
    NT Chebyshev polynomials
       Hermite polynomials
       Jacobi polynomials
       Laguerre polynomials
       Legendre's polynomials
  — Asymptotic theory
    [QA404.5]
      UF Asymptotic theory of orthogonal
         polynomials
Orthogonal projection
  USE Orthographic projection
Orthogonal series
  USE Series, Orthogonal
Orthogonal surfaces
  USE Surfaces, Orthogonal
Orthogonidae
  USE Carabidae
Orthogonoceros
  USE Megaloceros
Orthographic projection
  [GA115 (Cartography)]
  [QA503 (Mathematics)]
  [T363 (Mechanical drawing)]
    UF Orthogonal projection
       Projection, Orthographic
    BT Map-projection
       Projection
Orthographic shorthand
  USE Stenotypy
Orthography
  USE subdivision Orthography and spelling
      under names of languages, e.g.
      English language—Orthography and
         spelling
      Language and languages—Orthography
         and spelling
      Spelling reform
Orthomodular lattices
    UF Lattices, Orthomodular
    BT Modular lattices
Orthomolecular medicine
  USE Orthomolecular therapy
Orthomolecular therapy
    UF Meganutrition
       Megavitamin therapy
       Orthomolecular medicine
       Supernutrition therapy
    BT Psychotherapy
       Therapeutics
    NT Vitamin therapy
Orthomyxoviruses
  USE Myxoviruses
Orthopantomography
  USE Radiography, Panoramic
Orthopedia *(May Subd Geog)*
  [RD701-795]
    UF Orthopedics
    BT Surgery
    SA *special conditions to which orthopedic
       methods are applicable, e.g.* Hip
       joint—Diseases; Spine—
       Abnormalities
    NT Geriatric orthopedics
       Locomotion, Disordered
       Manipulation (Therapeutics)
       Orthodontics
       Orthopedic hospitals
       Orthopedic nursing

       Orthopedic surgery
       Orthopedic traction
       Orthopedists
       Osteoclasis
       Osteopathic orthopedics
       Osteotomy
       Pediatric orthopedia
       Veterinary orthopedics
  — Diagnosis
      BT Diagnosis
      NT Radiography in orthopedia
  — Hospitals and institutions
        USE Orthopedic hospitals
Orthopedia, Veterinary
  USE Veterinary orthopedics
Orthopedic apparatus *(May Subd Geog)*
  [RD755-757]
    UF Apparatus, Orthopedic
       Orthotics
    BT Crippled children
       Surgical instruments and apparatus
    NT Artificial limbs
       Crutches
       Orthopedic braces
       Orthopedic implants
       Orthopedic shoes
       Orthopedic slings
       Self-help devices for the disabled
       Splints (Surgery)
       Walkers (Orthopedic apparatus)
       Wheelchairs
Orthopedic apparatus industry
  (May Subd Geog)
    BT Medical instruments and apparatus
       industry
Orthopedic bone screws
  USE Bone screws (Orthopedics)
Orthopedic braces
    UF Braces, Orthopedic
    BT Orthopedic apparatus
  — Complications and sequelae
Orthopedic emergencies *(May Subd Geog)*
  [RD750]
    UF Emergency orthopedia
    BT Medical emergencies
Orthopedic hospitals *(May Subd Geog)*
  [RD705-706]
    UF Hospitals, Orthopedic
       Orthopedia—Hospitals and institutions
    BT Hospitals
       Orthopedia
Orthopedic implants *(May Subd Geog)*
  [RD755.5]
    UF Implants, Orthopedic
    BT Implants, Artificial
       Orthopedic apparatus
       Orthopedic surgery
       Prosthesis
    NT Artificial joints
       Bone nails (Orthopedics)
       Bone plates (Orthopedics)
       Bone screws (Orthopedics)
       Internal fixation in fractures
  — Complications and sequelae
Orthopedic manipulation
  USE Manipulation (Therapeutics)
Orthopedic nursing
  [RD737]
    BT Nursing
       Orthopedia
       Rehabilitation nursing
       Surgical nursing
Orthopedic plaster casts
  USE Plaster casts, Surgical
Orthopedic shoes *(May Subd Geog)*
  [RD757.S45]
    BT Orthopedic apparatus
       Shoes
    RT Foot—Abnormalities
Orthopedic slings
  [RD757.S5]

    UF Slings, Orthopedic
    BT Bandages and bandaging
       Orthopedic apparatus
Orthopedic surgeons
  USE Orthopedists
Orthopedic surgery *(May Subd Geog)*
  [RD701-733]
    UF Operative orthopedics
       Orthopedics, Operative
    BT Orthopedia
       Surgery
    NT Cerebral palsy—Surgery
       Orthopedic implants
       Synovectomy
       Tenotomy
  — Complications and sequelae
Orthopedic traction
    UF Traction (Orthopedia)
    BT Orthopedia
    NT Orthodontic appliances, Extraoral
       traction
Orthopedics
  USE Orthopedia
Orthopedics, Operative
  USE Orthopedic surgery
Orthopedics, Veterinary
  USE Veterinary orthopedics
Orthopedists *(May Subd Geog)*
    UF Orthopedic surgeons
       Orthopods
    BT Orthopedia
       Surgeons
  — Legal status, laws, etc.
    (May Subd Geog)
      BT Medical laws and legislation
      NT Orthopedists—Malpractice
  — Malpractice *(May Subd Geog)*
      UF Orthopedists—Tort liability
         Tort liability of orthopedists
      BT Malpractice
         Medical ethics
         Orthopedists—Legal status, laws,
            etc.
  — Tort liability
      USE Orthopedists—Malpractice
Orthoperidae
  USE Corylophidae
Orthoperus
  [QL596.C67]
    BT Corylophidae
Orthophotography
    BT Aerial photogrammetry
       Photography
    NT Orthophotomaps
Orthophotomaps
    BT Cartography
       Orthophotography
Orthopods
  USE Orthopedists
Orthopsychiatry *(May Subd Geog)*
    BT Mental health
       Psychiatry
Orthoptera *(May Subd Geog)*
  [QL506-9]
    UF Ensifera
       Saltatoria
    BT Insects
    NT Acrididae
       Crickets
       Eumastacidae
       Gryllacrididae
       Katydids
       Locusts
       Mantidae
       Mole-crickets
       Pyrgomorphidae
       Tetrigidae
       Tettigoniidae
       Thericleidae
       Tridactylidae

Orthoptera, Fossil
  UF Ensifera, Fossil
  BT Insects, Fossil
  NT Cockroaches, Fossil
Orthopters
  USE Ornithopters
Orthoptics
  ⌐RF992.O7⌐
  UF Exercises, Eye
    Exercises, Ocular
    Eye exercises
    Ocular exercises
    Visual training
  BT Exercise therapy
    Eye—Accommodation and refraction
    Eye—Movements
    Strabismus
    Therapeutics, Ophthalmological
  RT Binocular vision
Orthosphinctes
  ⌐QE807.A5⌐
  BT Perisphinctidae
Orthostatic hypotension
  USE Hypotension, Orthostatic
Orthostixidae
  USE Geometridae
Orthotaelidae
  USE Yponomeutidae
Orthotaeliidae
  USE Yponomeutidae
Orthotics
  USE Orthopedic apparatus
Orthotrichaceae
  ⌐QK539.O7⌐
  BT Isobryales
  NT Orthotrichum
Orthotrichum
  ⌐QK539.O7⌐
  BT Orthotrichaceae
Orti Oricellari Conspiracy, 1522
  ⌐DG738.13⌐
  UF Congiura degli Orti Oricellari, 1522
    Oricellari, Orti, Conspiracy, 1522
  BT Florence (Italy)—History—1421-1737
    Orti Oricellari Group
Orti Oricellari Group
  UF Oricellari Gardens Group
  BT Florence (Italy)—History—1421-1737
    Florence (Italy)—Intellectual life
  NT Orti Oricellari Conspiracy, 1522
Ortigara, Battle of, 1917
  ⌐D569.O⌐
  BT World War, 1914-1918—Campaigns—
    Italy
Ortiz family *(Not Subd Geog)*
Ortler (Italy) *(Not Subd Geog)*
  UF Ortles (Italy)
  BT Alps, Eastern
    Mountains—Italy
Ortles (Italy)
  USE Ortler (Italy)
Ortlibenses
  USE Brethren of the Free Spirit
Ortman family *(Not Subd Geog)*
  UF Ortmann family
Ortmann family
  USE Ortman family
Orto Botanico di Padova (Padua, Italy)
  UF Botanic Garden at Padua (Padua,
    Italy)
  BT Botanical gardens—Italy
Orto Botanico di Parma (Parma, Italy)
  BT Botanical gardens—Italy
Ortokids
  UF Ortugids
    Urtukis
  BT Syria—History—750-1260
Ortolan bunting
  ⌐QL696.P2438⌐
  UF Emberiza hortulana
  BT Emberiza

Orton family *(Not Subd Geog)*
  UF Orten family
Ortonal
  USE Methaqualone
Ortugids
  USE Ortokids
Oru language
  USE Ijo language
Orum family
  USE Oram family
Orungu (African people)
  ⌐DT546.142⌐
  UF Ombeke (African people)
  BT Ethnology—Gabon
    Myene (African people)
Orungu language
  ⌐PL8598.O8⌐
  UF Sekiani language
    Shekiani language
  BT Bantu languages
Orussidae
  ⌐QL568.O78⌐
  UF Oryssidae
    Parasitic wood wasps
  BT Hymenoptera
Orwick family
  USE Orwig family
Orwig family
  UF Ohrig family
    Orbig family
    Orwick family
    Urbig family
Oryctes
  ⌐QL596.S3⌐
  BT Scarabaeidae
  NT Oryctes rhinoceros
Oryctes rhinoceros
  ⌐QL596.S3⌐
  UF Indian rhinoceros beetle
    Rhinoceros beetle, Asiatic
    Rhinoceros beetle, Coconut
    Rhinoceros beetle, Indian
  BT Coconut palm—Diseases and pests
    Oryctes
Oryctolagus
  ⌐QL737.L32⌐
  BT Leporidae
  NT Oryctolagus cuniculus
Oryctolagus cuniculus
  ⌐QL737.L32⌐
  UF European rabbit
    Old World rabbit
  BT Oryctolagus
  RT Rabbits
Oryssidae
  USE Orussidae
Oryx
  ⌐QL737.U53⌐
  BT Antelopes
    Bovidae
  NT Arabian oryx
    Gemsbok
  — Religious aspects
Oryx gazella
  USE Gemsbok
Oryx leucoryx
  USE Arabian oryx
Oryza
  ⌐QK495.G74⌐
  BT Grasses
Oryza rufipogon
  USE Red rice
Oryza sativa
  USE Red rice
    Rice
Oryzaephilus
  ⌐QL596.C8⌐
  BT Cucujidae
  NT Oryzaephilus mercator
Oryzaephilus mercator
  ⌐QL596.C8⌐

  UF Merchant beetle
    Merchant grain beetle
  BT Grain—Storage—Diseases and injuries
    Oryzaephilus
Oryzaephilus surinamensis
  USE Sawtoothed grain beetle
Oryzias
  ⌐QL638.O78⌐
  BT Oryziatidae
Oryzias latipes
  ⌐QL638.O78⌐
  UF Aplocheilus latipes
    Haplochilus latipes
    Medaka
    Poecilia latipes
Oryziatidae
  ⌐QL638.O78⌐
  BT Atheriniformes
  NT Oryzias
Oryzomys
  ⌐QL737.R638⌐
  UF Rice rats
  BT Cricetidae
OS/8 (Computer system)
  UF Operating System/8 (Computer
    system)
  BT PDP-8 (Computer)—Programming
OS-9 (Computer operating system)
  BT Operating systems (Computers)
OS-1100 (Computer operating system)
  UF Sperry Series 1100 Operating System
  BT Operating systems (Computers)
OS BAMOS (Computer operating system)
  UF Batch Processing Multilanguage
    Operating System (Computer
    operating system)
  BT Operating systems (Computers)
Os calcis
  USE Heel bone
Os coccygis
  USE Coccyx
OS DISPAK (Computer operating system)
  BT Operating systems (Computers)
OS ES (Computer operating system)
  BT Operating systems (Computers)
Os sacrum
  USE Sacrum
Os sphenoidale
  USE Sphenoid bone
Os tarsi fibulare
  USE Heel bone
Os tarsi tibialis
  USE Anklebone
Os trigonum
  USE Anklebone
Osage, Fort (Mo.)
  USE Fort Osage (Mo.)
Osage Fork (Mo.)
  BT Rivers—Missouri
Osage Indians
  ⌐E99.O8⌐
  BT Dhegiha Indians
    Indians of North America
    Siouan Indians
  — Land transfers
    ⌐E99.O8⌐
    ⌐HD234.O⌐
  — Missions
Osage language
  ⌐PM2081⌐
  BT Siouan languages
Osage orange
  ⌐SD397.O8⌐
Osage River (Mo.)
  BT Rivers—Missouri
Osaka (Japan)
  — Civilization
  — — 1600-1868
  — History
  — — Meiji period, 1868-1912
  — — Taishō period, 1912-1926

— Siege, 1614
—— **Pictorial works**
    NT Ōsaka fuyu no jin zu (Screen
        painting)
— **Siege, 1615**
—— **Pictorial works**
    NT Ōsaka natsu no jin zu (Screen
        painting)
— **Social conditions**
—— **1600-1868**
Osaka (Japan). Kitahama
  USE Kitahama (Osaka, Japan)
Osaka Bay (Japan)
  UF Izumi Nada (Japan)
      Ōsaka-wan (Japan)
  BT Bays—Japan
Osaka Bay Route (Japan)
  USE Ōsaka fudō kōsoku wangansen (Japan)
Osaka Castle (Osaka, Japan)
  USE Ōsakajō (Osaka, Japan)
Ōsaka fudō kōsoku wangansen (Japan)
  UF Hyōgo kendō kōsoku wangansen
      (Japan)
      Kōsoku wangansen (Japan)
      Osaka Bay Route (Japan)
  BT Express highways—Japan
Ōsaka fuyu no jin zu (Screen painting)
    [ND1059.6]
  BT Osaka (Japan)—Siege, 1614—Pictorial
      works
      Painting, Japanese—Edo period, 1600-
      1868
      Screen painting, Japanese
Osaka Incident, Japan, 1885
  USE Japan—History—Osaka Incident, 1885
Ōsaka natsu no jin zu (Screen painting)
    [ND1059.6]
  BT Osaka (Japan)—Siege, 1615—Pictorial
      works
      Painting, Japanese—Edo period, 1600-
      1868
      Screen painting, Japanese
Ōsaka-wan (Japan)
  USE Osaka Bay (Japan)
Ōsakajō (Osaka, Japan)
  UF Osaka Castle (Osaka, Japan)
  BT Castles—Japan
Osaki Iseki (Tokyo, Japan)
  USE Osaki Site (Tokyo, Japan)
Ōsaki Maeyama Iseki (Yachiyo-machi, Ibaraki-
ken, Japan)
  USE Ōsaki Maeyama Site (Yachiyo-machi,
      Ibaraki-ken, Japan)
**Ōsaki Maeyama Site (Yachiyo-machi, Ibaraki-
ken, Japan)** *(Not Subd Geog)*
  UF Ōsaki Maeyama Iseki (Yachiyo-machi,
      Ibaraki-ken, Japan)
  BT Japan—Antiquities
Osaki Site (Tokyo, Japan) *(Not Subd Geog)*
  UF Osaki Iseki (Tokyo, Japan)
  BT Japan—Antiquities
Ōsato Iseki (Nose-chō, Japan)
  USE Ōsato Site (Nose-chō, Japan)
Ōsato Site (Nose-chō, Japan)
  (Not Subd Geog)
  UF Ōsato Iseki (Nose-chō, Japan)
  BT Japan—Antiquities
Osawatomie, Battle of, 1856
    [F685]
  BT Kansas—History—1854-1861
Osbäck family
  USE Osbeck family
Osband family
  USE Osman family
Osbeck family *(Not Subd Geog)*
  UF Osbäck family
      Ousbäck family
Osbeckia *(May Subd Geog)*
    [QK495.M514 (Botany)]
  BT Melastomataceae

Osborn family
  USE Osborne family
Osborne 1 (Computer)
  BT Microcomputers
      Portable computers
— **Programming**
Osborne computer
  BT Electronic digital computers
— **Programming**
    NT OSGLAS (Computer system)
Osborne family *(Not Subd Geog)*
  UF Orsborn family
      Orsborne family
      Orsbourn family
      Orsburn family
      Osborn family
      Osbourn family
      Osbourne family
      Osburn family
      Osburne family
  RT Osman family
Osborne House (Victor, N.Y.)
  UF D. H. Osborne House (Victor, N.Y.)
  BT Dwellings—New York (State)
Osbourn family
  USE Osborne family
Osbourne family
  USE Osborne family
Osburn family
  USE Osborne family
Osburne family
  USE Osborne family
Oscan coins
  USE Coins, Oscan
Oscan-Umbrian inscriptions
  USE Inscriptions, Oscan-Umbrian
Oscans
    [DG225.O8]
  UF Civilization, Oscan
      Obsci
      Opici
      Oschi
      Osci
  BT Ethnology—Italy
      Italic peoples
  RT Frentani (Italic people)
OSCAR (Artificial satellite)
  UF Orbiting Satellite Carrying Amateur
      Radio
  BT Amateur radio stations
      Artificial satellites in
        telecommunication
      Radio relay systems
Oscars (Moving-pictures)
  USE Academy awards (Moving-pictures)
Oscella (Medal)
  USE Osella (Medal)
Osceola doliata
  USE Lampropeltis triangulum
Osceola National Forest (Fla.)
  BT Forest reserves—Florida
      National parks and reserves—United
        States
Oschi
  USE Oscans
Oschrin family
  USE Oshrin family
Osci
  USE Oscans
Oscillating wings (Aerodynamics)
  UF Wings, Oscillating (Aerodynamics)
  BT Aerofoils
      Flutter (Aerodynamics)
      Oscillations
  RT Airplanes—Wings
Oscillations
    [QA871 (Dynamics)]
    [QA927 (Hydrodynamics)]
    [QA930 (Aerodynamics)]
    [QA935]
    [QC661 (Electric waves)]

  BT Cycles
      Fluctuations (Physics)
      Vibration
  NT Coupled mode theory
      Damping (Mechanics)
      Electric noise
      Flutter (Aerodynamics)
      Free earth oscillations
      Frequencies of oscillating systems
      Frequency response (Dynamics)
      Geomagnetic micropulsations
      Mechanical impedance
      Nonlinear oscillations
      Oscillating wings (Aerodynamics)
      Oscillometer
      Plasma oscillations
      Stellar oscillations
      Transients (Dynamics)
Oscillations, Betatron
  USE Betatron oscillations
Oscillations of stars
  USE Stellar oscillations
Oscillations of the sun
  USE Solar oscillations
Oscillatoriaceae
    [QK569.O8]
  BT Oscillatoriales
  NT Porphyrosiphon
      Spirulina
Oscillatoriales *(May Subd Geog)*
    [QR99.7.O82]
  UF Hormogonales
      Nostocales
  BT Cyanobacteria
  NT Nostocaceae
      Oscillatoriaceae
      Stigonemataceae
Oscillators, Audio-frequency
    [TK7872.O7]
  UF Audio-frequency oscillators
      Audio oscillators
  BT Audio frequency
      Oscillators, Electric
Oscillators, Blocking
  USE Blocking oscillators
Oscillators, Crystal
  UF Piezo-electric oscillators
      Quartz oscillators
      Quartz plate oscillators
      Quartz resonators
  BT Crystallography
      Crystals
      Electron tubes
      Electronics
      Frequency standards
      Oscillators, Electric
      Piezoelectric devices
      Quartz
  NT Frequency synthesizers
Oscillators, Electric
    [TK6565.O7 (Radio)]
  UF Electric oscillators
  BT Electric apparatus and appliances
      Electric machinery
      Radio
  NT Avalanche diode oscillators
      Blocking oscillators
      Feedback oscillators
      Magnetrons
      Noise generators (Electronics)
      Nonlinear oscillators
      Oscillators, Audio-frequency
      Oscillators, Crystal
      Oscillators, Microwave
      Oscillators, Resistance-capacitance
      Oscillators, Transistor
      Oscillators, Vacuum-tube
      Parametrons
      Phase-locked loops
      Pulse generators
      Relaxation oscillators

Oscillators, Electric *(Continued)*
 Signal generators
 Transients (Electricity)
 Tunnel diode oscillators
Oscillators, Feedback
 USE Feedback oscillators
Oscillators, Harmonic
 USE Harmonic oscillators
Oscillators, Linear
 USE Harmonic oscillators
Oscillators, Microwave
 UF Gunn oscillators
 Microwave oscillators
 BT Microwave devices
 Oscillators, Electric
 NT Gunn effect
Oscillators, Nonlinear
 USE Nonlinear oscillators
Oscillators, Relaxation
 USE Relaxation oscillators
Oscillators, Resistance-capacitance
 [TK7872.O7]
 UF Resistance-capacitance oscillators
 BT Electric capacity
 Electric resistance
 Oscillators, Electric
Oscillators, Simple
 USE Harmonic oscillators
Oscillators, Sweep
 [TK7872.O7]
 UF Sweep oscillators
 Time-base generators
 BT Cathode ray tubes
 Television scanning
Oscillators, Transistor
 UF Transistor oscillators
 BT Oscillators, Electric
Oscillators, Tunnel diode
 USE Tunnel diode oscillators
Oscillators, Vacuum-tube
 [TK6565.O7 (Radio)]
 [TK7872.O (Electronics)]
 UF Vacuum-tube oscillators
 BT Oscillators, Electric
 Vacuum-tubes
Oscillograph
 [TK381]
 NT Cathode ray oscillograph
 Light-beam oscillograph
Oscillograph, Cathode ray
 USE Cathode ray oscillograph
Oscillometer
 BT Oscillations
Oscilloscope
 USE Cathode ray oscilloscope
Oscinella *(May Subd Geog)*
 [QL537.C46]
 BT Chloropidae
Oscinella frit
 USE Frit-flies
Osculum, Battle of
 USE Ausculum, Battle of, 279 B.C.
Ose Marsh (Japan)
 USE Oze Marsh (Japan)
Ose-numa (Japan)
 USE Oze Lake (Japan)
Osehara (Japan)
 USE Oze Marsh (Japan)
Oseley family
 USE Ousley family
Osella (Medal)
 UF Oscella (Medal)
Oserhout family
 USE Osterhout family
Oseti language
 USE Ossetic language
OSGLAS (Computer system)
 UF General Ledger Accounting System for
 Osborne Computers (Computer
 system)

 BT Accounting—Data processing
 Osborne computer—Programming
 SuperCalc (Computer program)
Osgood family
 UF Ossgood family
O'Shay family
 USE Shea family
O'Shea family
 USE Shea family
O'Shee family
 USE Shea family
O'Shevelan family
 USE Shovlin family
O'Shiel family
 USE Shields family
Oshikuanjame (African people)
 USE Kuanyama (African people)
Ōshima (Yamaguchi-ken, Japan)
 USE Yashiro Island (Japan)
Ōshima Islands (Japan)
 USE Amami Islands (Japan)
Oshindonga language
 USE Ndonga language
Ōshio Heihachirō no Ran, Japan, 1837
 USE Japan—History—Ōshio Heihachirō
 Rebellion, 1837
Oshira-sama
 BT Folklore—Japan
Oshiwambo language
 USE Ndonga language
Oshrin family
 UF Oschrin family
 Oshrine family
Oshrine family
 USE Oshrin family
Osi language
 USE Ossetic language
Osiers *(May Subd Geog)*
 [SD397.O82]
 UF Basket willows
 BT Willows
 NT Basket making
Osikuanyame (African people)
 USE Kuanyama (African people)
Osing dialect *(May Subd Geog)*
 UF Banjuwangi dialect
 Banyuwangi dialect
 Using dialect
 BT Indonesia—Languages
 Javanese language
Osiris
 USE Osiris (Egyptian deity)
Osiris (Egyptian deity) *(May Subd Geog)*
 [BL2450.O7]
 UF Osiris
 BT Gods, Egyptian
 Mythology, Egyptian
OSIRIS (Electronic computer system)
Osismi (Celtic people)
 USE Osismii (Celtic people)
Osismii (Celtic people) *(May Subd Geog)*
 [DC62.2.O85]
 UF Osismi (Celtic people)
 BT Celts—France
 Ethnology—France
Osler-Vaquez disease
 USE Polycythemia vera
Oslerhout family
 USE Osterhout family
Oslo (Norway). Grefsenmarka
 USE Lillomarka (Oslo, Norway)
Oslo (Norway). Kampen
 USE Kampen (Oslo, Norway)
Oslo (Norway). Lillomarka
 USE Lillomarka (Oslo, Norway)
Oslo (Norway). Ulleväl Hageby
 USE Ulleväl Haveby (Oslo, Norway)
Oslo (Norway). Ulleväl Haveby
 USE Ulleväl Haveby (Oslo, Norway)
Oslo Fjord (Norway)
 USE Oslofjorden (Norway)

Oslofjorden (Norway)
 UF Oslo Fjord (Norway)
 BT Fjords—Norway
Oslofjorden, Battle of, 1940
 BT World War, 1939-1945—Campaigns—
 Norway
Osman family *(Not Subd Geog)*
 UF Osband family
 Osmon family
 RT Osbourne family
Osmanic language
 USE Turkish language
Osmanli language
 USE Turkish language
Osmeridae
 USE Smelts
Osmerus
 [QL638.O84]
 BT Smelts
 NT Osmerus eperlanus
Osmerus eperlanus
 [QL638.O84]
 BT Osmerus
Osmerus mordax
 USE American smelt
Osmia
 [QL568.M4]
 BT Megachilidae
Osminia
 [QL561.S47]
 BT Clearwing moths
Osmium
 [QD181.O7]
 BT Platinum group
 — Isotopes
 — — Decay
 — — Spectra
 — Spectra
Osmium compounds
 NT Organoosmium compounds
Osmium organic compounds
 USE Organoosmium compounds
Osmon family
 USE Osman family
Osmond-Hoffer diagnostic test
 USE Hoffer-Osmond diagnostic test
Osmoregulation
 UF Osmotic regulation
 Water balance (Physiology)
 BT Osmosis
 Salt in the body
 Water in the body
 RT Water-electrolyte balance (Physiology)
 NT Chloride cells
 Diuresis
 Physiologic salines
 Salt gland
Osmorhiza
 [QK495.U48]
 UF Washingtonia (Umbelliferae)
 BT Umbelliferae
Osmosis
 [QD543 (Chemistry)]
 [QH615 (Cytology)]
 BT Biological chemistry
 Body fluids
 Cells
 Fluids
 Gases
 Separation (Technology)
 RT Absorption (Physiology)
 Permeability
 Solution (Chemistry)
 NT Biological transport
 Chemiosmosis
 Dialysis
 Diosmosis
 Electro-osmosis
 Osmoregulation
 Porosity
 Reverse osmosis

Root pressure
Osmotic regulation
  USE Osmoregulation
Osmylidae
  [QL513.O8]
  BT Neuroptera
Osnaburg
  USE Mururoa Atoll
Osning (Germany)
  USE Teutoburg Forest (Germany)
OSO
  USE Orbiting solar observatories
Oso Bay (Tex.) *(Not Subd Geog)*
  BT Bays—Texas
Osona Region (Spain)
  UF Comarca de Osona (Spain)
Osore Mountains (Japan)
  UF Osore-yama (Japan)
    Osore-zan (Japan)
    Usori Mountains (Japan)
    Usori-yama (Japan)
  BT Mountains—Japan
    Volcanoes—Japan
Osore-yama (Japan)
  USE Osore Mountains (Japan)
Osore-zan (Japan)
  USE Osore Mountains (Japan)
Osphronemus goramy
  USE Gourami
Ospreys
  [QL696.A2]
  UF Fish-hawks
  BT Falconiformes
Ospriocerus
  [QL537.A85]
  BT Robber flies
OSPub (Electronic computer system)
  UF Operating System Pub (Electronic
    computer system)
Ossa motorcycle
  [TL448.O]
Ossa sesamoidea
  USE Sesamoid bones
Osseous manifestations of general diseases
  USE Osteal manifestations of general
    diseases
Ossetes
  BT Iranians
  NT Alani
Ossetian Military Road (Georgian S.S.R. and
  R.S.F.S.R.)
  USE Voenno-Osetinskaia doroga (Georgian
    S.S.R. and R.S.F.S.R.)
Ossetic epic literature
  USE Epic literature, Ossetic
Ossetic fiction
  [PK6958]
Ossetic folk literature
  USE Folk literature, Ossetic
Ossetic imprints *(May Subd Geog)*
Ossetic language
  [PK6951-9]
  UF Āsī language
    Oseti language
    Osi language
    Ūsatī language
  BT Iranian languages
Ossetic literature *(May Subd Geog)*
  [PK6958.5 (Collections and history)]
  NT Epic literature, Ossetic
    Folk literature, Ossetic
Ossetic philology
Ossetic poetry
Ossetic prose literature *(May Subd Geog)*
Ossetic proverbs
  USE Proverbs, Ossetic
Ossetic riddles
  USE Riddles, Ossetic
Ossetic songs
  USE Songs, Ossetic

Ossgood family
  USE Osgood family
Ossicles (Ear)
  USE Ear ossicles
Ossicula mentalia
Ossification
  [QP88.2]
  BT Bones
    Growth
  NT Endochondral ossification
    Metaplastic ossification
Ossipee Lake (N.H.)
  BT Lakes—New Hampshire
Ostariophyseae
  USE Cypriniformes
Ostariophysi
  USE Catfishes
    Cypriniformes
Ostdeutsche Musiktage
  [ML37.G3S36]
  BT Music festivals—Germany (West)
Ostdeutscher Literaturpreis
  USE Andreas-Gryphius-Preis
Osteal manifestations of general diseases
  UF Bone manifestations of general diseases
    Osseous manifestations of general
      diseases
    Osteological manifestations of general
      diseases
  BT Bones—Diseases
    Symptomatology
Osteichthyes
  [QL614-637.5]
  UF Bony fishes
    Malacopterygii
    Teleostomi
  BT Fishes
  NT Acipenseriformes
    Albuliformes
    Amiiformes
    Anglerfishes
    Atheriniformes
    Beryciformes
    Catfishes
    Characiformes
    Clupeiformes
    Cypriniformes
    Eels
    Elopiformes
    Flatfishes
    Gadiformes
    Gasterosteiformes
    Gobiesociformes
    Gonorynchiformes
    Lampriformes
    Mormyriformes
    Myctophiformes
    Notacanthiformes
    Osteoglossiformes
    Perciformes
    Percopsiformes
    Polypteriformes
    Salmoniformes
    Scorpaeniformes
    Semionotiformes
    Synbranchiformes
    Tetraodontiformes
    Toadfishes
    Zeiformes
Osteichthyes, Fossil
  NT Beryciformes, Fossil
    Clupeiformes, Fossil
    Coelacanthiformes, Fossil
    Crossopterygii, Fossil
    Cypriniformes, Fossil
    Eels, Fossil
    Gadiformes, Fossil
    Pholidophoriformes
Osteitis
  [RC931.O64]

  UF Bones—Inflammation
    Ostitis
  BT Bones—Diseases
  NT Osteitis deformans
    Osteitis fibrosa
    Osteomyelitis
Osteitis deformans *(May Subd Geog)*
  [RC931.O65]
  UF Paget's disease of bone
  BT Bones—Diseases
    Osteitis
Osteitis fibrosa
  BT Bones—Diseases
    Hyperparathyroidism
    Osteitis
    Parathyroid glands
Osten family
  UF Von der Osten family
Osteoarthritis *(May Subd Geog)*
  [RC931.O67]
  UF Degenerative arthritis
    Degenerative joint disease
    Joint disease, Degenerative
    Osteoarthrosis
  BT Arthritis
  NT Spinal osteophytosis
Osteoarthrosis
  USE Osteoarthritis
Osteocephalus
  [QL668.E24]
  BT Hylidae
Osteochondritis
  USE Osteochondrosis
Osteochondritis deformans juvenilis
  USE Legg-Calvé-Perthes disease
Osteochondroma
  BT Bones—Tumors
    Cartilage—Tumors
Osteochondrosis
  [RJ482.O]
  UF Epiphyseal ischemic necrosis
    Osteochondritis
  BT Bones—Necrosis
  NT Blount's disease
    Legg-Calvé-Perthes disease
    Scheuermann's disease
Osteochondrosis deformans tibiae
  USE Blount's disease
Osteoclasis
  BT Bones—Surgery
    Fractures
    Orthopedia
    Surgery, Operative
Osteodystrophy, Albright's hereditary
  USE Pseudo-pseudohypoparathyroidism
Osteogenesis
  USE Bone—Growth
Osteogenesis imperfecta
  USE Osteopsathyrosis
Osteogenic sarcoma
  USE Osteosarcoma
Osteoglossidae
  [QL638.O88]
  BT Osteoglossiformes
  NT Arapaima
    Osteoglossum
Osteoglossiformes
  [QL637.9.O8]
  BT Osteichthyes
  NT Osteoglossidae
Osteoglossiformes, Fossil
  [QE852.T2]
  BT Teleostei, Fossil
Osteoglossum
  [QL638.O88]
  BT Osteoglossidae
Osteoglossum ferreirai
  [QL638.O88]

Osteoglossum ferreirai *(Continued)*
  UF Arawana, Black
      Arowana, Black
      Aruana, Black (Fish)
      Black arawana
      Black arowana
      Black aruana (Fish)
Osteoid sarcoma
  USE Osteosarcoma
Osteological manifestations of general diseases
  USE Osteal manifestations of general
        diseases
Osteology
  USE Bones
      Skeleton
Osteology, Forensic
  USE Forensic osteology
Osteolysis
  USE Bone resorption
Osteolytic sarcoma
  USE Osteosarcoma
Osteomalacia *(May Subd Geog)*
  [*RC627.O7*]
  BT Bones—Diseases
      Vitamin D deficiency
Osteomyelitis
  BT Bones—Diseases
      Osteitis
Osteonecrosis
  USE Bones—Necrosis
Osteopathic hospitals *(May Subd Geog)*
  [*RZ302-304*]
  BT Hospitals
      Osteopathy
Osteopathic medicine
  USE Osteopathy
Osteopathic orthopedics *(May Subd Geog)*
  [*RZ397*]
  BT Orthopedia
      Osteopathy
Osteopathic physicians
  USE Osteopaths
Osteopathic schools *(May Subd Geog)*
  [*RZ337-338*]
  UF Schools, Osteopathic
  BT Health occupations schools
      Medical colleges
      Osteopathy—Study and teaching
      Universities and colleges
Osteopathic students *(May Subd Geog)*
  [*RZ337*]
  BT Health occupations students
      Students
Osteopaths *(May Subd Geog)*
  UF Osteopathic physicians
  BT Physicians
  NT Osteopathy—Vocational guidance
  — Legal status, laws, etc.
      USE Osteopathy—Law and legislation
  — Supply and demand
Osteopathy *(May Subd Geog)*
  [*RZ301-RZ397.5*]
  UF Medicine, Osteopathic
      Osteopathic medicine
  BT Therapeutic systems
  RT Massage
      Spondylotherapy
  NT Craniosacral therapy
      Gynecology, Osteopathic
      Mechanotherapy
      Neuropathy
      Osteopathic hospitals
      Osteopathic orthopedics
      Spinal adjustment
  — Fellowships
      USE Osteopathy—Scholarships,
          fellowships, etc.
  — Law and legislation *(May Subd Geog)*
      UF Osteopaths—Legal status, laws, etc.
      BT Medical laws and legislation

  — Scholarships, fellowships, etc.
      (May Subd Geog)
      [*RZ337*]
      UF Osteopathy—Fellowships
  — Study and teaching *(May Subd Geog)*
      NT Osteopathic schools
  — Vocational guidance
      [*RZ336*]
      BT Osteopaths
Osteopathy, Cranial
  USE Craniosacral therapy
Osteopenia *(May Subd Geog)*
  BT Bones—Diseases
Osteopetrosis
  [*RC931.O72*]
  UF Albers-Schoenberg disease
      Osteosclerosis fragilis
  BT Bones—Diseases
Osteoplasty
  USE Bone-grafting
      Bones—Surgery
Osteoporosis
  [*RC931.O73*]
  BT Bones—Diseases
      Vitamin D deficiency
  NT Sudeck's atrophy
Osteopsathyrosis
  [*RD684*]
  UF Osteogenesis imperfecta
  BT Bones—Diseases
  NT Dentinogenesis imperfecta
      Fractures, Spontaneous
Osteopygis
  [*QE862.C5*]
  BT Toxochelyidae
Osteosarcoma *(May Subd Geog)*
  [*RC280.B6*]
  UF Bone sarcoma
      Osteogenic sarcoma
      Osteoid sarcoma
      Osteolytic sarcoma
      Sarcoma, Osteogenic
      Sarcoma of bone
  BT Bones—Cancer
      Sarcoma
  NT Ewing's sarcoma
Osteosclerosis
  [*RC931.O8*]
  BT Bones—Diseases
  NT Hyperostosis corticalis generalisata
Osteosclerosis fragilis
  USE Osteopetrosis
Osteostraci
  [*QE852.O5*]
  UF Cephalaspida
  BT Agnatha, Fossil
Osteosynthesis
  USE Internal fixation in fractures
Osteosynthesis, Intramedullary
  USE Intramedullary fracture fixation
Osteotomy
  [*RD684*]
  BT Bones—Surgery
      Orthopedia
      Surgery, Operative
Oster family
Österbotten (Finland)
  USE Pohjanmaa (Finland)
Østerbro (Copenhagen, Denmark)
  (Not Subd Geog)
  UF Copenhagen (Denmark). Østerbro
Osterhant family
  USE Osterhout family
Osterhaus family
Osterhont family
  USE Osterhout family
Osterhoudt family
  USE Osterhout family

Osterhout family
  UF Oosterhout family
      Oserhout family
      Oslerhout family
      Osterhant family
      Osterhont family
      Osterhoudt family
Österlen (Sweden) *(Not Subd Geog)*
Östermalm (Stockholm, Sweden)
  (Not Subd Geog)
  UF Stockholm (Sweden). Östermalm
Ostfriesische Inseln (Germany)
  USE East Frisian Islands (Germany)
Ostfriesland (Germany)
  USE East Friesland (Germany)
Østgårdstrøen family
Ostgoths
  USE Goths
Osthannoversche Eisenbahn
  BT Railroads—Germany (West)
Ostia (Ancient city) *(Not Subd Geog)*
  [*DG70.O8*]
  BT Cities and towns, Ruined, extinct, etc.
          —Italy
      Italy—Antiquities
Ostiak language
  USE Khanty language
Ostiak poetry *(May Subd Geog)*
Ostiak Samoyeds
  USE Selkups
Ostiaks
  USE Khanty
Ostiaks of the Yenisei
  USE Kets
Ostinato
  USE Ground bass
Ostindiska huset (Göteborg, Sweden)
  BT Buildings—Sweden
Ostitis
  USE Osteitis
Ostium cardiacum
  USE Cardia
Ostler family
Ostomates *(May Subd Geog)*
  [*RD540*]
  UF Ostomy patients
  BT Enterostomy
      Physically handicapped
  — Sex counseling
      BT Sex counseling
Ostomatidae
  USE Trogositidae
Ostomidae
  USE Trogositidae
Ostomy, Intestinal
  USE Enterostomy
Ostomy, Renal
  USE Nephrostomy
Ostomy patients
  USE Ostomates
Ostpreussen (Poland and R.S.F.S.R.)
  USE Prussia, East (Poland and R.S.F.S.R.)
Ostpreussen cattle
  USE East Prussian cattle
Ostpreussisch Holländer cattle
  USE East Prussian cattle
Östra Södermanlands Järnväg
  BT Railroad museums—Sweden
      Railroads—Sweden
      Railroads, Narrow-gage—Sweden
Ostracoda *(May Subd Geog)*
  [*QL444.O8-86*]
  UF Ostracopoda
  BT Crustacea
      Entomostraca
  NT Myodocopida
      Podocopida
Ostracoda, Fossil
  [*QE817.O8*]
  NT Leperditicopida
      Myodocopida, Fossil

Palaeocopida
Podocopida, Fossil
Ostracopoda
USE Ostracoda
Ostraka
⌐PA3371 (Greek)¬
⌐PJ1675 (Egyptian)¬
UF Potsherds (Ostraka)
BT Paleography
Pottery
Writing—Materials and instruments
Ostrea
⌐QL430.7.O9¬
BT Ostreidae
Oysters
Ostrea chilensis
⌐QL430.7.O9¬
Ostrea edulis
USE European oyster
Ostrea gigantea
USE Crassostrea gigas
Ostrea rivularis
⌐QL430.7.O9¬
Ostrea virginica
USE American oyster
Ostreidae
⌐QL430.7.O9¬
BT Pterioida
NT Crassostrea
Ostrea
Ostreidae, Fossil
USE Oysters, Fossil
Ostrevant (France)
BT Plains—France
Ostrich farms and farming
⌐SF511¬
Ostrich fern
USE Fiddleheads
Ostriches
⌐QL696.S9¬
BT Ratitae
Ostriches, Fossil
UF Struthio
Struthionidae, Fossil
Ostrinia
⌐QL561.P9¬
BT Pyralidae
Ostrobothnia (Finland)
USE Pohjanmaa (Finland)
Ostrogoths
USE Goths
Ostrołęka (Ostrołęka, Poland), Battle of, 1831
BT Poland—History—Revolution, 1830-
1832—Campaigns
Ostrov Aėgna (Estonia)
USE Aegna Island (Estonia)
Ostrov Dolgiĭ (R.S.F.S.R.)
USE Dolgiĭ Island (R.S.F.S.R.)
Ostrov Dolgiy (R.S.F.S.R.)
USE Dolgiĭ Island (R.S.F.S.R.)
Ostrov Dolgoy (R.S.F.S.R.)
USE Dolgiĭ Island (R.S.F.S.R.)
Ostrov Moneron (R.S.F.S.R.)
USE Moneron Island (R.S.F.S.R.)
Ostrov Sakhalin (R.S.F.S.R.)
USE Sakhalin (R.S.F.S.R.)
Ostrov Vaĭgach (R.S.F.S.R.)
USE Vaigach Island (R.S.F.S.R.)
Ostrov Valaam (R.S.F.S.R.)
USE Valaam Island (R.S.F.S.R.)
Ostrov Valamo (R.S.F.S.R.)
USE Valaam Island (R.S.F.S.R.)
Ostrov Vaygach (R.S.F.S.R.)
USE Vaigach Island (R.S.F.S.R.)
Ostrov Vrangeli͡a (R.S.F.S.R.)
USE Wrangel Island (R.S.F.S.R.)
Ostrov Vrangelya (R.S.F.S.R.)
USE Wrangel Island (R.S.F.S.R.)
Østrupgård (Denmark)
BT Manors—Denmark

Ostrvo Korčula (Croatia)
USE Korčula Island (Croatia)
Østsjaellandske Jernbane
BT Railroads—Denmark
Ostyak language
USE Khanty language
Ostyaks
USE Khanty
O'Sullivan family
RT Sullivan family
Ōsumi-hantō (Japan)
USE Ōsumi Peninsula (Japan)
Ōsumi Islands (Japan)
UF Ōsumi-shoto (Japan)
BT Islands—Japan
NT Tanegashima (Japan)
Osumi Islands (Japan)
NT Yaku Island (Japan)
Ōsumi Peninsula (Japan)
UF Ōsumi-hantō (Japan)
BT Peninsulas—Japan
Ōsumi-shoto (Japan)
USE Ōsumi Islands (Japan)
Osvold family
USE Oswald family
Oswald family
UF Osvold family
Oswaldt family
Oswalt family
Oswold family
Oswaldt family
USE Oswald family
Oswalt family
USE Oswald family
Oswego, Fort (Oswego, N.Y.)
USE Fort Oswego (Oswego, N.Y.)
Oswego, Lake (Or.)
UF Lake Oswego (Or. : Lake)
BT Lakes—Oregon
NT Lake Oswego Dam (Or.)
Oswego, Fort, Capture of, 1756
USE Fort Oswego (Oswego, N.Y.)—
Capture, 1756
Oswidonga (African people)
USE Kuanyama (African people)
Oświęcim (Poland : Concentration camp)
USE Auschwitz (Poland : Concentration
camp)
Oswold family
USE Oswald family
Ōta family (Not Subd Geog)
Ōta Iseki (Maebaru-machi, Japan)
USE Ōta Site (Maebaru-machi, Japan)
Ōta Site (Maebaru-machi, Japan)
(Not Subd Geog)
UF Higashi Ōta Iseki (Maebaru-shi, Japan)
Ōta Iseki (Maebaru-machi, Japan)
BT Japan—Antiquities
Otachyrium
⌐QK495.G74 (Botany)¬
BT Grasses
Otago Harbor (N.Z.) (Not Subd Geog)
UF Harbour of Otago (N.Z.)
Otago Harbour (N.Z.)
BT Harbors—New Zealand
Otago Harbour (N.Z.)
USE Otago Harbor (N.Z.)
Ōtani Iseki (Kasuga-shi, Japan)
USE Ōtani Site (Kasuga-shi, Japan)
Ōtani pottery
UF Pottery, Ōtani
BT Pottery, Japanese
Ōtani Site (Kasuga-shi, Japan)
(Not Subd Geog)
UF Ōtani Iseki (Kasuga-shi, Japan)
BT Japan—Antiquities
OTAPS
USE Ohio Tests of Articulation and
Perception of Sounds
Otariidae
USE Eared seals

Otariinae
USE Sea lions
Otavalá Indians
USE Otavalo Indians
Otavalo Indians
⌐F3722.1.O¬
UF Otavalá Indians
BT Cara Indians
Indians of South America
OTC drugs
USE Drugs, Nonprescription
OTC markets
USE Over-the-counter markets
Otchipwe Indians
USE Chippewa Indians
Otchipwe language
USE Chippewa language
Otero Rodríguez, Alejandro.   Delta solar
UF Delta solar (Sculpture)
BT Art, Abstract—Venezuela
Steel sculpture, Venezuelan
Otetela language
USE Tetela language
OTH radar
USE Over-the-horizon radar
Othan (African people)
USE Uduk (African people)
Othello (Game)
⌐GV1469.O75¬
BT Board games
Other minds (Theory of knowledge)
⌐BD213¬
UF Minds of others (Theory of
knowledge)
BT Knowledge, Theory of
Mind and body
Othman family
USE Oatman family
Othoes
⌐QL458.82.G3¬
BT Galeodidae
NT Othoes saharae
Othoes saharae
⌐QL458.82.G3¬
BT Othoes
Othreis
⌐QL561.N7¬
UF Othryis
BT Noctuidae
Othryis
USE Othreis
Otic barotrauma
USE Barotrauma, Aural
Oties family
USE Otis family
Otiorhynchidae
USE Curculionidae
Otis family
UF Oties family
Ottis family
Otis quick-scoring mental ability tests
BT Intelligence tests
Otitic barotrauma
USE Barotrauma, Aural
Otitic hydrocephalus
USE Intracranial hypertension
Otitidae
⌐QL537.O8¬
UF Ortalidae
Picture-winged flies
Pterocallidae
Ulidiidae
BT Diptera
NT Pseudotephritis
Otitis externa (May Subd Geog)
⌐RF180¬
UF Ear, External—Inflammation
BT Ear, External—Diseases
Inflammation
Otitis media
BT Middle ear—Diseases

Otitis media *(Continued)*
  NT Acute otitis media
       Otitis media with effusion
— **Diagnosis**
Otitis media in children *(May Subd Geog)*
  [RF225]
  BT Pediatric otolaryngology
Otitis media with effusion *(May Subd Geog)*
  [RF225.7]
  UF Exudate otitis media
       Glue ear
       MEE (Otolaryngology)
       Middle ear effusion
       MOM (Otolaryngology)
       Mucous otitis media
       Secretory otitis media
       Serous otitis media
       SOM (Otolaryngology)
  BT Otitis media
Otji language
  USE Twi language
Otjiherero language
  USE Herero language
Otjisewa man
  USE Boskop man
Otkazniki
  USE Refuseniks
Otlukbeli, Battle of, 1473
  [DR502.5]
  BT Turkey—History—1453-1683
Otman family
  USE Oatman family
Oto Indians
  [E99.O87]
  UF Otoe Indians
       Ottoe Indians
  BT Dakota Indians
       Indians of North America
Oto language
  [PM2082.O8]
  UF Otoe language
       Watoto language
  RT Siouan languages
Oto-oculorenal syndrome
  USE Alport's syndrome
Otoconia
  USE Otoliths
Otoconites
  USE Otoliths
Otocorys
  USE Larks
Otocyon
  [QL737.C22]
  BT Canidae
Otocysts
  [QL948]
  BT Ear
Otoe Indians
  USE Oto Indians
Otoe language
  USE Oto language
Ōtohara Site (Japan) *(Not Subd Geog)*
  UF Hanamure Ōtohara Iseki (Japan)
  BT Japan—Antiquities
Otok Korčula (Croatia)
  USE Korčula Island (Croatia)
Otoko Mountain (Japan)
  UF Mount Otoko (Japan)
       Mt. Otoko (Japan)
       Otoko-yama (Japan)
       Otokoyama (Japan)
  BT Mountains—Japan
Otoko-yama (Japan)
  USE Otoko Mountain (Japan)
Otokoyama (Japan)
  USE Otoko Mountain (Japan)
Otolaryngologic emergencies
  (May Subd Geog)
  [RF90]
  UF Emergencies, Otolaryngologic

BT Medical emergencies
     Otolaryngology
Otolaryngologic examination
  [RF48]
  BT Otolaryngology—Diagnosis
       Physical diagnosis
  NT Ear—Examination
       Nose—Examination
       Rhinolaryngoscopy
       Throat—Examination
Otolaryngological nursing
  UF Ear, nose, and throat nursing
  BT Nursing
       Otolaryngology
Otolaryngological practice
  USE Otolaryngology—Practice
Otolaryngologists *(May Subd Geog)*
  BT Otolaryngology
— **Supply and demand**
  [RF85-85.7]
Otolaryngology *(May Subd Geog)*
  UF Ear, nose, and throat diseases
       ENT diseases
       Otorhinolaryngology
  NT Ear—Diseases
       Geriatric otolaryngology
       Leishmaniasis, Mucocutaneous
       Nose—Diseases
       Otolaryngologic emergencies
       Otolaryngological nursing
       Otolaryngologists
       Pediatric otolaryngology
       Radiography in otolaryngology
       Throat—Diseases
       Ultrasonics in otolaryngology
— **Chemotherapy**
  [RF55]
  BT Chemotherapy
— **Diagnosis**
  UF Diagnosis, Otolaryngological
  NT Otolaryngologic examination
— **Formulae, receipts, prescriptions**
— **Genetic aspects**
  BT Medical genetics
— **Immunological aspects**
— **Practice**
  UF Otolaryngological practice
— **Radiotherapy**
  [RF54.R]
Otolaryngology, Anesthetics in
  USE Anesthesia in otolaryngology
Otolaryngology, Operative
  UF Operative otolaryngology
  BT Surgery, Operative
       Surgery, Orificial
  NT Ear—Surgery
       Larynx—Surgery
       Nose—Surgery
       Throat—Surgery
— **Complications and sequelae**
Otoliths
  [QL948 (Zoology)]
  [QP471 (Physiology)]
  UF Ear-stones
       Otoconia
       Otoconites
       Otostea
  BT Ear
Otologic manifestations of general diseases
  BT Ear—Diseases
       Symptomatology
Otology
  USE Ear
Otomaco language
  [PM6703]
  UF Otomaque language
       Ottomacque language
       Ottomaku language
  BT Indians of South America—Languages
  NT Taparita language

Otomanguean languages
  [PM4145]
  BT Indians of Central America—
       Languages
       Indians of Mexico—Languages
  NT Chinantecan languages
       Mangue language
       Mixtec language
       Otomian languages
       Popolocan languages
       Proto-Popotecan language
       Zapotec language
Otomaque language
  USE Otomaco language
Otomari Harbor (R.S.F.S.R.)
  USE Korsakov Harbor (R.S.F.S.R.)
Ōtombe family
Otome Fudōhara Kitaura Iseki (Oyama-shi,
       Japan)
  USE Otome Fudōhara Kitaura Site (Oyama-
       shi, Japan)
**Otome Fudōhara Kitaura Site (Oyama-shi,
       Japan)** *(Not Subd Geog)*
  UF Otome Fudōhara Kitaura Iseki
       (Oyama-shi, Japan)
  BT Japan—Antiquities
Otomi Indians
  [F1221.O86]
  BT Indians of Central America
       Indians of Mexico
  NT Matlatzinca Indians
Otomi language
  [PM4146-9]
  BT Indians of Central America—
       Languages
       Otomian languages
Otomian languages
  [PM4146-9]
  BT Indians of Mexico—Languages
       Otomanguean languages
  NT Ocuiltec language
       Otomi language
Ōtomo family
Ōtomo Iseki (Ōtsu-shi, Japan)
  USE Ōtomo Site (Ōtsu-shi, Japan)
Ōtomo Site (Ōtsu-shi, Japan)
  (Not Subd Geog)
  UF Ōtomo Iseki (Ōtsu-shi, Japan)
  BT Japan—Antiquities
Otomops
  [QL737.C54]
  BT Molossidae
  NT Otomops martiensseni
Otomops martiensseni
  [QL737.C54]
  UF Martienssen's free-tailed bat
  BT Otomops
Otomycosis
  USE Ear—Fungi
O'Toole family
Otoplasty *(May Subd Geog)*
  [RF127]
  BT Ear—Surgery
       Surgery, Plastic
Otorhinolaryngology
  USE Otolaryngology
Otosazuka Kofun (Ushimado-chō, Japan)
  USE Otosazuka Site (Ushimado-chō, Japan)
Otosazuka Site (Ushimado-chō, Japan)
  (Not Subd Geog)
  UF Otosazuka Kofun (Ushimado-chō,
       Japan)
  BT Japan—Antiquities
Otosclerosis
  [RF270]
  UF Otospongiosis
  BT Deafness
       Labyrinth (Ear)—Diseases
Otoscope
  USE Otoscopes

Otoscopes (May Subd Geog)
  UF Otoscope
  BT Endoscopes
Otoscopy (May Subd Geog)
  [RF123]
  BT Ear—Examination
      Endoscopy
Otoshibanashi
  USE Rakugo
Otospongiosis
  USE Otosclerosis
Otostea
  USE Otoliths
Otostegia
  [QK495.L25]
  BT Lamiaceae
Ototoxic agents
  [RF285.O83]
  BT Ear—Diseases
      Hearing disorders
      Neurotoxic agents
      Poisons
Ototyphlonemertes
  [QL391.N6]
  BT Ototyphlonemertidae
Ototyphlonemertidae
  [QL391.N6]
  BT Hoplonemertea
  NT Ototyphlonemertes
Otranto mosaic
  [NA3790]
  UF Mosaik von Otranto
  BT Mosaics—Italy
Ots family
  USE Ott family
Ōtsubo Iseki (Okgaki-machi, Japan)
  USE Ōtsubo Site (Okagaki-machi, Japan)
Ōtsubo Site (Okagaki-machi, Japan)
  (Not Subd Geog)
  UF Ōtsubo Iseki (Okgaki-machi, Japan)
  BT Japan—Antiquities
Ōtsuka Iseki (Matsubara-shi, Japan)
  USE Ōtsuka Site (Matsubara-shi, Japan)
Ōtsuka Kofun (Tachibana-machi, Japan)
  USE Ōtsuka Site (Tachibana-machi, Japan)
Ōtsuka Kofun (Yamaguchi-shi, Japan)
  USE Ōtsuka Site (Yamaguchi-shi, Japan)
Ōtsuka Site (Matsubara-shi, Japan)
  (Not Subd Geog)
  UF Ōtsuka Iseki (Matsubara-shi, Japan)
  BT Japan—Antiquities
Ōtsuka Site (Tachibana-machi, Japan)
  UF Ōtsuka Kofun (Tachibana-machi,
      Japan)
  BT Japan—Antiquities
Ōtsuka Site (Yamaguchi-shi, Japan)
  UF Ōtsuka Kofun (Yamaguchi-shi, Japan)
  BT Japan—Antiquities
Ott family
  UF Ots family
      Otta family
      Otte family
      Utt family
      Utte family
      Utts family
      Utz family
Otta family
  USE Ott family
Ottar Nayakan
  USE Bhovis
Ottawa (Ont.). Britannia
  USE Britannia (Ottawa, Ont.)
Ottawa (Ont.). Lower Town
  USE Lower Town (Ottawa, Ont.)
Ottawa Indians
  [E99.O9]
  UF Outaouaks
  BT Algonquian Indians
      Indians of North America
  NT Pontiac's Conspiracy, 1763-1765
  — Missions

Ottawa language
  [PM2083]
  BT Algonquian languages
Ottawa National Forest (Mich.)
  BT Forest reserves—Michigan
      National parks and reserves—
        Michigan
Ottawa River (Québec and Ont.)
  UF Outaouais, Rivière des (Québec and
        Ont.)
      Rivière des Outaouais (Québec and
        Ont.)
  BT Rivers—Ontario
      Rivers—Québec (Province)
Otte family
  USE Ott family
Otter, Sea
  USE Sea otter
Otter Creek (Vt.)
  BT Rivers—Vermont
Otter hunting
  [SH364]
Otter-shrew
  [QL737.I5]
Otterbein family
Otterburn, Battle of, 1388
  [DA783.53]
  UF Chevy Chase, Battle of, 1388
  BT Scotland—History—Robert II, 1371-
        1390
Otterburn, Battle of, 1388, in literature
Otters
  [QL737.C2]
  UF Lutrinae
  BT Mustelidae
  NT Lutra
      Lutra canadensis
      Oriental small-clawed otter
      Sea otter
  — Food
Otters as pets (May Subd Geog)
  [SF459.O87]
Otting family
Ottis family
  USE Otis family
Otto-cycle engines
  USE Internal combustion engines, Spark
        ignition
Otto of roses
  USE Attar of roses
Ottoceros
  [QE882.U3]
  BT Antilocapridae, Fossil
Ottoceros peacevalleyensis
  [QE882.U3]
Ottoe Indians
  USE Oto Indians
Ottomacque language
  USE Otomaco language
Ottomaku language
  USE Otomaco language
Ottoman architecture
  USE Architecture, Ottoman
Ottoman art
  USE Art, Ottoman
Ottoman Empire
  USE Turkey—History—Ottoman Empire,
        1288-1918
Ottoman Turkish language (Arabic script)
  USE Turkish language
Ottonian art
  USE Art, Ottonian
Ottonian emperors
  USE Holy Roman Empire—History—Saxon
        House, 919-1024
Ottonian goldwork
  USE Goldwork, Ottonian
Ottonian House
  USE Germany—History—Saxon House,
        919-1024

Holy Roman Empire—History—Saxon
  House, 919-1024
Ottonian illumination of books and manuscripts
  USE Illumination of books and manuscripts,
        Ottonian
Ottonian ivories
  USE Ivories, Ottonian
Ottonian painting
  USE Painting, Ottonian
Ottonian sculpture
  USE Sculpture, Ottonian
Otuquis Indians
  [F3341.S2 (Santa Cruz, Bolivia)]
  BT Indians of South America
Oturkpo (African people)
  USE Idoma (African people)
Oturkpo dialect
  USE Idoma language
Otus
  [QL696.S83]
  BT Screech owls
      Strigidae
Otway Ranges (Vic.)
  UF Otways (Vic.)
  BT Mountains—Australia
Otways (Vic.)
  USE Otway Ranges (Vic.)
Ou family
Ōu Region (Japan)
  USE Tōhoku Region (Japan)
Ou-yang family
Ouabache State Park (Ind.)
  UF Ouabache State Recreation Area (Ind.)
  BT Parks—Indiana
      Recreation areas—Indiana
Ouabache State Recreation Area (Ind.)
  USE Ouabache State Park (Ind.)
Ouachita, Lake (Ark.)
  UF Lake Ouachita (Ark.)
  BT Lakes—Arkansas
Ouachita Mountains (Ark. and Okla.)
  (Not Subd Geog)
  BT Mountains—Arkansas
      Mountains—Oklahoma
Ouachita National Forest (Ark. and Okla.)
  (Not Subd Geog)
  BT Forest reserves—Arkansas
      Forest reserves—Oklahoma
      National parks and reserves—Arkansas
      National parks and reserves—
        Oklahoma
Ouachita National Recreation Trail (Ark. and
  Okla.) (Not Subd Geog)
  BT Trails—Arkansas
      Trails—Oklahoma
Ouachita River (Ark. and La.)
  UF Washita River (Ark. and La.)
  BT Rivers—Arkansas
      Rivers—Louisiana
Ouachita River (Tex. and Okla.)
  USE Washita River (Tex. and Okla.)
Oualan (Micronesia)
  USE Kosrae (Micronesia)
Ouananiche
  [SH685]
  UF Atlantic salmon, Landlocked
      Landlocked Atlantic salmon
      Sebago salmon
      Winninish
  BT Atlantic salmon
Ouapisiana Indians
  USE Wapisiana Indians
Ouașul (Romania)
  USE Oaș Mountains (Romania)
Ouayana Indians
  USE Oyana Indians
Ouayana language
  USE Oyana language
Ouayeoue Indians
  USE Waiwai Indians

Oubykh language
USE Ubykh language
Ouche River (France)
BT Rivers—France
Ōuchi family
Ōuchihikama Kofun (Yamaguchi-shi, Japan)
USE Ōuchihikami Site (Yamaguchi-shi, Japan)
Ōuchihikami Site (Yamaguchi-shi, Japan)
(Not Subd Geog)
UF Ōuchihikama Kofun (Yamaguchi-shi, Japan)
BT Japan—Antiquities
Tombs—Japan
Oud
[ML1015.O9]
UF 'Ud
BT Lute
Oud music
[M142.O9]
BT Lute music
NT Suites (Oud, violins (2), viola, violoncello)
Oud with string orchestra
[M1137.4.O9]
RT Concertos (Oud with string orchestra)
NT Suites (Oud with string orchestra)
Oudal family
UF Oudalstøl family
Oudalstøl family
USE Oudal family
Oude Rijn River (Netherlands)
USE Old Rhine River (Netherlands)
Oude Ryn River (Netherlands)
USE Old Rhine River (Netherlands)
Oude Stadthuis (Amsterdam, Netherlands)
USE Koninklijk Paleis (Amsterdam, Netherlands)
Oudenaarde (Belgium), Battle of, 1708
BT Spanish Succession, War of, 1701-1714
—Campaigns—Belgium
Ouderkerk family
UF Odekirk family
Oderkirk family
Ouderkirk family
Ouderkirk family
USE Ouderkerk family
Oued Drâa (Morocco)
USE Dra Wadi (Morocco)
Oued Massa (Morocco)
USE Massa River (Morocco)
Oued Noun (Morocco)
USE Nūn, Wādī (Morocco)
Ouedaou (Papua New Guinea people)
USE Wedau (Papua New Guinea people)
Ouedaou language
USE Wedau language
Oueds
USE Wadis
Oueili, Tall al- (Iraq)
UF Tall al-Oueili (Iraq)
Tall al-Uwayli (Iraq)
Tell el-Oueili (Iraq)
Tell el-Uwayli (Iraq)
Uwayli, Tall al- (Iraq)
BT Iraq—Antiquities
Ouellet family
USE Ouellette family
Ouellette family
UF Ouellet family
Ouénya (African people)
USE Genya (African people)
Ouessant, Battle of, 1778
[DA87.5 1778]
BT Anglo-French War, 1778-1783
Ouessant Island (France)
UF Eusa Island (France)
Ile d'Ouessant (France)
Ushant Island (France)
Uxisama Island (France)
BT Islands—France

Ouija board
[BF1343]
BT Automatism
Games
Spiritualism
NT Planchette
Ouitoto Indians
USE Witoto Indians
Ould family
USE Olds family
Oulé (African people)
USE LoWiili (African people)
Ouled Naïl
BT Arabs
Ethnology—Sahara
Oulema
[QL596.C5]
BT Chrysomelidae
NT Oulema melanopa
Oulema melanopa
[QL596.C5]
UF Cereal leaf beetle
BT Grain—Diseases and pests
Oulema
Oulu Lake (Finland)
USE Oulujärvi (Finland)
Ouluīarvi (Finland)
USE Oulujärvi (Finland)
Oulujarin (Finland)
USE Oulujärvi (Finland)
Oulujärvi (Finland)
UF Oulu Lake (Finland)
Ouluīarvi (Finland)
Oulujarin (Finland)
Oulunjärvi (Finland)
Oviujarvi (Finland)
Ozero Ouluīarvi (Finland)
Uleträsk (Finland)
BT Lakes—Finland
Oulunjärvi (Finland)
USE Oulujärvi (Finland)
Ouma Indians
USE Houma Indians
Ounce (Mammals)
USE Snow leopard
Ounû (Ancient city)
USE Heliopolis (Ancient city)
Ouobé (African people)
USE Wobe (African people)
Ouobé (African tribe)
USE Wobe (African people)
Ouobe language
USE Wobe language
Ouolof language
USE Wolof language
Our Gang films
[PN1995.9.O8]
BT Characters and characteristics in moving-pictures
Moving-pictures
Our Lady
USE Mary, Blessed Virgin, Saint
Our Lady of Beauraing
USE Beauraing, Notre-Dame de
Our Lady of Częstochowa (Icon)
USE Częstochowa, Our Lady of (Icon)
Our Lady of expectation (Mural painting)
USE Francesca, Piero della, 1416?-1492.
Madonna del parto
Our Lady of Fatima
USE Fatima, Our Lady of
Our Lady of Guadalupe
USE Guadalupe, Our Lady of
Our Lady of Luján
USE Luján, Our Lady of
Our Lady of the Conquest (Statue)
USE Conquistadora (Statue)
Our Lady of the Rosary
USE Rosary, Our Lady of the
Our Lady of Tongeren retable (Sculpture)
USE Mariaretabel van Tongeren (Sculpture)

Ouray, Mount (Colo.)
UF Mount Ouray (Colo.)
BT Mountains—Colorado
— Passes
NT Marshall Pass (Colo.)
Ouray National Wildlife Refuge (Utah)
(Not Subd Geog)
BT National parks and reserves—Utah
Wildlife refuges—Utah
Ouriaghel (Berber people)
USE Waryaghar (Berber people)
Ouricury palm
USE Syagrus coronata
Ourique, Battle of, 1139
[DP570]
UF Ourique, Battle of, July 25, 1139
BT Portugal—History—To 1385
Ourique, Battle of, July 25, 1139
USE Ourique, Battle of, 1139
Ourous
USE Puquina Indians
Ourry Island (Solomon Islands)
USE Vanikolo (Solomon Islands)
Ousbäck family
USE Osbeck family
Ouse, Great, River (England)
USE Great Ouse River (England)
Ouse, River (Northamptonshire-Norfolk, England)
USE Great Ouse River (England)
Ouselea family
USE Ousley family
Ouseley family
USE Ousley family
Ousiakē gē (The Greek phrase)
BT Land tenure—Law and legislation
Ousley family
UF Housley family
Oseley family
Ouselea family
Ouseley family
Owesley family
Owsley family
Out-of-date books, periodicals, etc.
USE Obsolescence of books, periodicals, etc.
Out-of-doors Christian education
USE Christian education, Outdoor
Out-of-doors education
USE Outdoor education
Out-of-print books
UF Bibliography—Out-of-print books
Books, Out-of-print
RT Antiquarian booksellers
Books—Want lists
Reprints (Publications)
Out-of-print books on microfilm
BT Microfilms
Out-of-state students *(May Subd Geog)*
BT State universities and colleges
Students
Out-of-the-body experiences
USE Astral projection
Out-of-work people
USE Unemployed
Outagami Indians
USE Fox Indians
Outakaihajime
USE Utakaihajime
Outaouais, Rivière des (Québec and Ont.)
USE Ottawa River (Québec and Ont.)
Outaouaks
USE Ottawa Indians
Outboard drives
USE Inboard-outboard engines
Outboard motor-boats
USE Outboard motorboats
Outboard motorboats *(May Subd Geog)*
[GV835.8 (Sports)]
[VM348 (Naval architecture)]
UF Outboard motor-boats

BT Motorboats
Outboard motors
  BT Motorboats—Gasoline engines
    Motorboats—Motors
    Motors
Outbuildings *(May Subd Geog)*
  UF Dependencies (Buildings)
  BT Buildings
  NT Privies
Outbursts, Gas
  USE Gas bursts
Outbursts, Rock
  USE Rock bursts
Outcasts
  ₁GT6550-GT6699 *(Manners and customs)*₁
  BT Brigands and robbers
    Ethnology
  RT Outlaws
  NT Pariahs
    Proscription
    Sanka (Social class)
Outcropping (Geology)
  USE Outcrops (Geology)
Outcrops (Geology) *(May Subd Geog)*
  UF Outcropping (Geology)
  BT Geology
  NT Granite outcrops
Outdoor advertising
  USE Advertising, Outdoor
Outdoor Christian education
  USE Christian education, Outdoor
Outdoor cookery
  ₁TX823₁
  UF Camp cookery
    Cookery, Camp
    Cookery, Outdoor
  BT Camping
    Cookery
    Picnicking
  RT Campfires
  NT Barbecue cookery
    Barbecues (Fireplaces)
    Camp stoves
    Cookery (Wild foods)
    Dutch oven cookery
Outdoor education *(May Subd Geog)*
  ₁LB1047₁
  UF Education, Outdoor
    Out-of-doors education
  NT Camping
    Christian education, Outdoor
    Natural history—Outdoor books
    Outward bound schools
    School camps
    School excursions
Outdoor electric wiring
  USE Electric wiring, Outdoor
Outdoor fireplaces
  USE Barbecues (Fireplaces)
Outdoor furniture *(May Subd Geog)*
  ₁TT197.5.O9₁
  BT Furniture
  NT Garden ornaments and furniture
Outdoor furniture industry
  (May Subd Geog)
Outdoor journalism
  USE Journalism, Outdoor
Outdoor life *(May Subd Geog)*
  ₁GV191.2-GV200.56₁
  UF Rural life
  BT Manners and customs
  RT Camping
    Sports
  NT Food, Wild
    Hiking
    Mountaineering
    Natural history—Outdoor books
    Open-air treatment
    Picnicking
    River life

Wayfaring life
    Wilderness survival
— **Accidents and injuries**
    ₁RC88.9.0₁
    UF Outdoor life—Injuries
    BT Sports—Accidents and injuries
      Wilderness survival
— Injuries
    USE Outdoor life—Accidents and injuries
— **Safety measures**
    BT Outdoor recreation—Safety measures
      Wilderness survival
Outdoor lighting
  USE Exterior lighting
Outdoor museums
  USE Open-air museums
Outdoor photography
  ₁TR659.5₁
  UF Field photography
    Photography, Outdoor
  RT Nature photography
    Travel photography
Outdoor pulpits *(May Subd Geog)*
  UF External pulpits
  BT Pulpits
Outdoor recreation *(May Subd Geog)*
  BT Recreation
  RT Recreation areas
  NT Camping
    Canals—Recreational use
    Coasts—Recreational use
    Dude ranches
    Farms—Recreational use
    Forest reserves—Recreational use
    Lakes—Recreational use
    Mountains—Recreational use
    Parks
    Picnicking
    Public lands—Recreational use
    Recreational vehicles
    Reservoirs—Recreational use
    Rivers—Recreational use
    Safaris
    Watersheds—Recreational use
    Wilderness areas—Recreational use
    Wildlife conservation
— Federal aid
    USE Federal aid to outdoor recreation
— **Finance**
    NT Federal aid to outdoor recreation
— **Law and legislation** *(May Subd Geog)*
    NT Federal aid to outdoor recreation
— **Safety measures**
    NT Outdoor life—Safety measures
Outdoor recreation areas
  USE Recreation areas
Outdoor recreation for children
  (May Subd Geog)
  ₁GV191.63₁
  UF Children—Recreation
  BT Children
Outdoor recreation for women
  (May Subd Geog)
  BT Women—Health and hygiene
    Women—Recreation
  RT Sports for women
Outdoor residential electric wiring
  USE Electric wiring, Outdoor
Outdoor schools
  USE Open-air schools
Outdoor sculpture *(May Subd Geog)*
  UF Sculpture, Outdoor
  BT Sculpture
Outdoor survival
  USE Wilderness survival
Outdoor theater
  USE Theater, Open-air
Outdoor zoos
  USE Open-air zoos

Outer Banks (N.C.)
  UF Banks, Outer (N.C.)
  BT Islands—North Carolina
  NT Bogue Banks (N.C.)
Outer Hebrides (Scotland)
  USE Western Isles (Scotland)
Outer planetary atmospheres
  USE Outer planets—Atmospheres
Outer planetary ionospheres
  USE Outer planets—Ionospheres
Outer planets
  ₁QB377-QB389 *(Theoretical astronomy)*₁
  ₁QB651-QB701 *(Descriptive astronomy)*₁
  BT Planets
  NT Jupiter (Planet)
    Neptune (Planet)
    Planets, Ultra-Neptunian
    Saturn (Planet)
    Uranus (Planet)
— **Atmospheres**
    UF Atmospheres, Outer planetary
      Outer planetary atmospheres
    BT Planetary meteorology
— **Ionospheres**
    UF Ionospheres, Outer planetary
      Outer planetary ionospheres
    BT Ionosphere
Outer self
  USE Self-presentation
Outer Shrine Shinto
  USE Ise Shintō
Outer space
  UF Space, Outer
  BT Astronautics
    Astronomy
    Space sciences
  NT Project Argus
    Space environment
    Space warfare
— **Anecdotes, facetiae, satire, etc.**
— **Caricatures and cartoons**
— Colonies
    USE Space colonies
— **Exploration** *(May Subd Geog)*
    UF Exploration of space
      Solar system—Exploration
      Space exploration (Astronautics)
      Space research
    BT Astronautics
      Interplanetary voyages
      Manned space flight
    NT Astronautics—International cooperation
      Extraterrestrial bases
      Jupiter probes
      Lunar probes
      Mars probes
      Mercury probes
      Planets—Exploration
      Project Orion
      Religion and astronautics
      Saturn probes
      Venus probes
— — **Juvenile literature**
— — **Public opinion**
— — **Supplies**
— — — **Mathematical models**
Outer space and civilization
  USE Astronautics and civilization
Outer space communication
  USE Interstellar communication
Outer space in art
Outfalls, Ocean
  USE Ocean outfalls
Outfield (Baseball)
  USE Fielding (Baseball)
Outlaw strikes
  USE Wildcat strikes

Outlawry
  BT Civil death
      Contempt of court
      Criminal procedure
  NT Proscription
Outlaws *(May Subd Geog)*
   [HV6441-6453]
  UF Bandits
  BT Crime and criminals
  RT Brigands and robbers
      Outcasts
  NT Women outlaws
Outlaws, Women
  USE Women outlaws
Outlaws in literature
Outlaws in motion pictures
   [PN1995.9.O84]
  BT Moving-pictures
Outlet boxes (Electric engineering)
  BT Electric apparatus and appliances
      Electric wiring
Outlet stores *(May Subd Geog)*
  UF Factory outlets
  BT Commerce
      Discount houses (Retail trade)
      Wholesale trade
Outlets, Manufacturers' retail
  USE Manufacturers' retail outlets
Outliers (Statistics)
   [HA31.2]
  BT Data editing
      Sampling (Statistics)
      Statistics
Outline maps
   [GA101-130]
  BT Maps
  SA *subdivision* Maps, Outline and base
      under names of countries, regions,
      etc., e.g. United States—Maps,
      Outline and base
  NT Plotting charts
      World maps, Outline and base
  — **Keys**
     [G129]
Outlines
  UF Syllabi
  SA *subdivision* Outlines, syllabi, etc. *under*
      topical headings for brief statements
      of the principal elements of a
      subject to be studied, usually
      arranged by headings and
      subheadings, e.g. History—Outlines,
      syllabi, etc.
  — **Computer programs**
     NT ThinkTank (Computer program)
Outman family
  USE Oatman family
Outpatient medical care
  USE Ambulatory medical care
Outpatient services in hospitals
  USE Hospitals—Outpatient services
Outpatient services in public hospitals
  USE Hospitals, Public—Outpatient services
Outpatient services in state hospitals
  USE Hospitals, State—Outpatient services
Outpatient services in veterans hospitals
  USE Hospitals, Veterans'—Outpatient
      services
Outpatient surgery
  USE Surgery, Outpatient
Outposts
  USE Guard duty
Output equipment (Computers)
  USE Computer input-output equipment
Output standards
  USE Production standards
Outrigger canoes *(May Subd Geog)*
   [GN440.2]
  BT Canoes and canoeing
Outside brokers
  USE Brokers

Outside employment
  USE Supplementary employment
Outside reading
  USE Supplementary reading
Outsiders in literature
Outsiders in the Bible
  USE Strangers in the Bible
Outward bound schools *(May Subd Geog)*
   [GV200.52-200.56]
  BT Outdoor education
      Wilderness survival—Study and
      teaching
Outzen family
  UF Autzen family
Ouvidor Street (Rio de Janeiro, Brazil)
  USE Rua do Ouvidor (Rio de Janeiro,
      Brazil)
Ouvirandra
  USE Aponogeton
Ovaguanyama (African people)
  USE Kuanyama (African people)
Ovaherero
  USE Hereros
Ovakuanyama (African people)
  USE Kuanyama (African people)
Oval pictures *(May Subd Geog)*
  UF Pictures, Oval
  BT Pictures
Ovalle family
  UF Ovalles family
Ovalles family
  USE Ovalle family
Ovals
  BT Curves
      Geometry, Differential
Ovambo (African people)
   [DT611.42 (Angola)]
   [DT709 (Namibia)]
  UF Ambo (Angolan and Namibian people)
      Ovampo (African people)
  BT Ethnology—Angola
      Ethnology—Namibia
  NT Kuanyama (African people)
      Ndonga (African people)
Ovambo language
  USE Kuanyama language
      Ndonga language
Ovambo proverbs
  USE Proverbs, Kuanyama
Ovampo (African people)
  USE Ovambo (African people)
Ovaries
   [QL881 (Comparative anatomy)]
   [QM421 (Human anatomy)]
   [QP261 (Physiology)]
  BT Adnexa uteri
      Gonads
      Ovum
  NT Corpus luteum
      Graafian follicle
      Inhibin
      Menstruation
      Ovulation
      Parovarium
      Progesterone
  — **Diseases** *(May Subd Geog)*
     [RG441-481]
    NT Anovulation
  — **Transplantation**
     [QP261]
  — **Tumors**
     [RC280.O8]
    NT Stein-Leventhal syndrome
Ovariotomy
   [RG481]
Ovenbirds, Neotropical
  USE Furnariidae
Ovens
  USE Stoves
Ovens, Gas
  USE Gas ovens

Ovens, Microwave
  USE Microwave ovens
Ovens, Solar
  USE Solar ovens
Ovens River (Vic.)
  BT Rivers—Australia
Over dosage of drugs
  USE Drugs—Overdosage
Over head projection
  USE Overhead projection
Over-the-counter drugs
  USE Drugs, Nonprescription
Over-the-counter markets *(May Subd Geog)*
  UF OTC markets
  BT Brokers
      Investment banking
      Securities
      Stock-exchange
Over-the-horizon radar
   [TK6592.O94]
  UF OTH radar
  BT Radar
Overactive children
  USE Hyperactive children
Overactivity
  USE Hyperkinesia
Overalls
  BT Clothing and dress
      Work clothes
Overberg (South Africa) *(Not Subd Geog)*
Overcoats
  USE Coats
Overcrowding of prisons
  USE Prisons—Overcrowding
Overdentures
  USE Overlay dentures
Overdosage of drugs
  USE Drugs—Overdosage
Overdosage of hypnotics
  USE Hypnotics—Overdosage
Overdosage of narcotics
  USE Narcotics—Overdosage
Overdosage of sedatives
  USE Sedatives—Overdosage
Overdose of drugs
  USE Drugs—Overdosage
Overeating disease of sheep
  USE Enterotoxemia
Overflows, Combined sewer
  USE Combined sewers—Overflows
Overgaard family
Overhauser effect (Nuclear physics)
  BT Nuclear magnetic resonance
      Spin-lattice relaxation
Overhead costs
  UF Fixed costs
      Indirect costs
  BT Costs, Industrial
Overhead electric lines
  USE Electric lines—Overhead
Overhead power lines
  USE Electric lines—Overhead
Overhead projection
   [LB1043.5 (Audio-visual education)]
   [TR738 (Projectors)]
  UF Over head projection
      Projection, Overhead
  BT Lantern projection
      Projectors
Overholser family
  USE Oberholtzer family
Overholt family
  USE Oberholtzer family
Overholts family
  USE Oberholtzer family
Overholtz family
  USE Oberholtzer family
Overholtzer family
  USE Oberholtzer family
Overholzer family
  USE Oberholtzer family

Overhults family
  USE Oberholtzer family
Overhydration
  USE Water intoxication
Overland family (Not Subd Geog)
Overland journeys to the Pacific
  ⌐F593⌐
    Here are entered accounts of the crossing of the continent under pioneer conditions, on foot, on horseback, by wagon, etc.
  UF Transcontinental journeys (United States)
     Travels
  BT Frontier and pioneer life
     Voyages and travels
     West (U.S.)—History—1848-1950
  NT Donner Party
Overland Telegraph Line (N.T. and S. Aust.)
  BT Telegraph lines—Australia
Overlap integral
  BT Integrals
     Quantum chemistry
     Wave function
  RT Chemical bonds
     Molecular orbitals
Overlay dentures
  ⌐RK656⌐
  UF Dental prosthesis, Telescopic
     Dentures, Overlay
     Overdentures
     Telescopic dental prosthesis
  BT Dentures
Overlay drafting systems
  BT Copying processes
     Mechanical drawing
Overlays on pavements
  USE Pavements—Overlays
Overlord, Operation
  USE Operation Overlord
Overlord embroidery (Tapestry)
  USE Lawrence, Sandra. Overlord embroidery
Overman
  USE Superman
Overmayer family
  USE Obermayer family
Overmeyer family
  USE Obermayer family
Overmiller family
Overmire family
  USE Obermayer family
Overmyer family
  USE Obermayer family
Overnight delivery service
  USE Express service
Overpasses
  USE Elevated highways
Overpotential
  USE Overvoltage
Overpressure (Education)
  ⌐LB3431⌐
  BT Education
     Fatigue, Mental
Overprints and surcharges (Philately)
  (May Subd Geog)
  ⌐HE6184.O93⌐
  UF Inscriptions (Philately)
     Surcharges and overprints (Philately)
  BT Postage-stamps
Overproduction
  ⌐HD61⌐
  UF Industrial production
  BT Business cycles
     Economics
     Prices
     Production (Economic theory)
  RT Supply and demand
  NT Depressions
     Technocracy
Overprotection, Parental
  USE Parental overprotection

Overruling, Prospective
  USE Prospective overruling
Overseas dependents schools
  USE Military post schools
Overseas employees
  USE subdivision Employment—Foreign countries under individual classes of persons; and subdivision Officials and employees—Foreign countries under countries, etc.
Overseas information libraries
  (May Subd Geog)
  UF Information libraries
     Libraries, Overseas information
     Overseas libraries
  BT Libraries, Governmental, administrative, etc.
Overseas information libraries, American
  (May Subd Geog)
  UF American overseas information libraries
     Libraries, American overseas information
Overseas information libraries, British
  (May Subd Geog)
  UF British overseas information libraries
     Libraries, British overseas information
Overseas libraries
  USE Overseas information libraries
Overseas students
  USE Returned students
Overseas teaching positions
  USE Teachers, Foreign—Employment
Oversight, Congressional
  USE Legislative oversight—United States
Oversight, Legislative
  USE Legislative oversight
Oversize books (May Subd Geog)
    Here are entered works on books too large to be shelved in normal shelf sequence.
  UF Bibliography—Oversize editions
     Books—Oversize editions
     Books, Oversize
     Oversized books
  BT Books—Sizes
Oversized books
  USE Oversize books
Overskei family (Not Subd Geog)
  UF Overskeid family
Overskeid family
  USE Overskei family
Overstolz family
Overstreet family
Overthrusts (Geology)
  USE Thrust faults (Geology)
Overtime (May Subd Geog)
  ⌐HD5111⌐
  BT Hours of labor
     Wages
— **Law and legislation** (May Subd Geog)
Overtone (Linguistics)
  USE Connotation (Linguistics)
Overtones (Music)
  USE Harmonics (Music)
Overture
  ⌐ML1261 (History and criticism)⌐
  BT Music, Incidental
     Opera
  NT Entr'acte music
Overtures
  ⌐M1004⌐
    Here are entered overtures for orchestra. Overtures for other media are entered under this heading followed by specification of medium, e.g. Overtures (Chamber orchestra)
  BT Ballets—Excerpts
     Operas—Excerpts
     Orchestral music
  RT Symphonic poems
Overtures, Arranged
  ⌐M1060⌐

Overtures (Band)
  ⌐M1204⌐
  BT Band music
Overtures (Band), Arranged
  ⌐M1255⌐
Overtures (Chamber orchestra)
  ⌐M1004⌐
  BT Chamber-orchestra music
Overtures (Clarinet and piano)
  ⌐M248-252⌐
  BT Clarinet and piano music
Overtures (Dance orchestra)
  ⌐M1356⌐
  BT Dance-orchestra music
— **Scores**
  ⌐M1356⌐
Overtures (Electronic music)
  ⌐M1473⌐
  BT Electronic music
Overtures (Guitar)
  ⌐M125-7⌐
  BT Guitar music
Overtures (Instrumental ensemble)
  ⌐M985⌐
  BT Instrumental ensembles
Overtures (Organ)
  ⌐M6-M7⌐
  ⌐M11⌐
  BT Organ music
Overtures (Organ), Arranged
  USE Overtures arranged for organ
Overtures (Piano)
  ⌐M25⌐
  BT Piano music
Overtures (Piano, 4 hands)
  ⌐M200-M201⌐
  ⌐M204⌐
  BT Piano music (4 hands)
Overtures (Piano, 4 hands), Arranged
  USE Overtures arranged for piano (4 hands)
Overtures (Piano), Arranged
  USE Overtures arranged for piano
Overtures (Pianos (2))
  ⌐M214-215⌐
  BT Piano music (Pianos (2))
Overtures (Recorders (5))
  ⌐M555-M556⌐
  ⌐M557.2⌐
  BT Woodwind quintets (Recorders (5))
Overtures (Salon orchestra)
  ⌐M1350⌐
  BT Salon-orchestra music
Overtures (String orchestra)
  ⌐M1104⌐
  BT String-orchestra music
Overtures (String orchestra), Arranged
  ⌐M1160⌐
— **Scores and parts**
Overtures (Trumpet with string orchestra)
  ⌐M1130-M1131⌐
  BT Trumpet with string orchestra
Overtures (Violin with orchestra)
  ⌐M1012-1013⌐
  BT Violin with orchestra
Overtures (Violin with string orchestra)
  ⌐M1112-M1113⌐
  BT Violin with string orchestra
Overtures (Wind ensemble)
  ⌐M955-7⌐
  BT Wind ensembles
Overtures arranged for accordion
  ⌐M175.A4⌐
  BT Accordion music
Overtures arranged for bassoons (3), clarinets (2), horns (2), oboes (2)
  ⌐M958-M959⌐
  BT Wind nonets (Bassoons (3), clarinets (2), horns (2), oboes (2)), Arranged
Overtures arranged for flute, guitar, viola
  ⌐M383-4⌐
  BT Trios (Flute, guitar, viola), Arranged

Overtures arranged for flute, guitar, violin
 [M383-4]
  BT Trios (Flute, guitar, violin), Arranged
Overtures arranged for flute, violin, viola, violoncello
 [M463-4]
  BT Quartets (Flute, violin, viola, violoncello), Arranged
Overtures arranged for flutes (2)
 [M288-9]
  BT Flute music (Flutes (2)), Arranged
Overtures arranged for flutes (4)
 [M458-459]
  BT Woodwind quartets (Flutes (4)), Arranged
Overtures arranged for guitar and piano
 [M276-7]
  BT Guitar and piano music, Arranged
Overtures arranged for guitar, violin, viola
 [M373-4]
  BT Trios (Guitar, violin, viola), Arranged
Overtures arranged for guitars (2)
 [M292-3]
  BT Guitar music (Guitars (2)), Arranged
Overtures arranged for harpsichord
 [M35]
  BT Harpsichord music, Arranged
     Overtures arranged for piano
Overtures arranged for organ
 [M12-13]
  UF Overtures (Organ), Arranged
  BT Organ music, Arranged
Overtures arranged for piano
 [M35]
  UF Overtures (Piano), Arranged
  BT Piano music, Arranged
  NT Overtures arranged for harpsichord
  — Excerpts
     [M35]
Overtures arranged for piano (4 hands)
 [M209]
  UF Overtures (Piano, 4 hands), Arranged
  BT Piano music (4 hands), Arranged
Overtures arranged for piano (6 hands)
 [M213]
  BT Piano music (6 hands), Arranged
Overtures arranged for piano (Pianos (2), 8 hands)
 [M216]
  BT Piano music (Pianos (2), 8 hands), Arranged
Overtures arranged for piano, flute, guitar
 [M338-9]
  BT Trios (Piano, flute, guitar), Arranged
Overtures arranged for piano trios
 [M313-314]
  BT Piano trios, Arranged
Overtures arranged for string quartets
 [M453-4]
  BT String quartets, Arranged
Overtures arranged for violin and piano
 [M222-3]
  BT Violin and piano music, Arranged
Overtures arranged for violins (2), violoncello
 [M352-3]
  BT String trios (Violins (2), violoncello), Arranged
Overuse injuries *(May Subd Geog)*
   Here are entered works on chronic inflammatory conditions caused by repeated microtraumas due to repetitious activities.
  UF Injuries, Overuse
     Overuse syndromes
     Repetition injuries
     Repetition strain injuries
     Repetition strain injury
     Repetitive microtrauma
     Repetitive strain injuries
     RSI (Injuries)
     Wear-and-tear injuries
  BT Wounds and injuries

Overuse syndromes
  USE Overuse injuries
Overvoltage
  UF Overpotential
  BT Electric apparatus and appliances— Protection
     Electrolysis
     Polarization (Electricity)
OverVUE (Computer program)
  BT Data base management—Computer programs
Overwater flying
  UF Flying, Overwater
     Flying over water
  BT Airplanes—Piloting
  NT Airplanes—Ditching
Overweight
  USE Obesity
Overwien family
  UF Overwijn family
Overwijn family
  USE Overwien family
Overwork, Mental
  USE Fatigue, Mental
Ovibos
  USE Musk ox
Oviduct
   [QL881 (Comparative anatomy)]
   [QP265 (Physiology)]
  BT Generative organs, Female
  NT Fallopian tubes
  — Diseases *(May Subd Geog)*
     NT Oviduct—Radiography
  — Radiography
     UF Salpingography
     BT Oviduct—Diseases
Oviedo (Spain : Province)
  USE Asturias (Spain)
Ovimbali (African people)
  USE Mbundu (African people)
Ovimbundu (African people)
  USE Mbundu (African people)
Ovine babesiosis
  USE Babesiosis in sheep
Ovine brucellosis
  USE Brucellosis in sheep
Ovine enterotoxemia
  USE Enterotoxemia
Ovis *(May Subd Geog)*
   [QL737.U53]
  BT Bovidae
Ovis ammon
  USE Argali
Ovis canadensis
  USE Bighorn sheep
Ovis dalli
  USE Dall sheep
Ovis jubata
  USE Argali
Ovis musimon
  USE Mouflon
Oviujarvi (Finland)
  USE Oulujärvi (Finland)
Ovoididae
  USE Tetraodontidae
Ovoviviparism
  USE Ovoviviparity
Ovoviviparity
  UF Ovoviviparism
  BT Embryology
Övre Fryken Lake (Sweden)
  USE Frykensjöarna (Sweden)
Ovulation
   [QP261]
  BT Embryology
     Menstrual cycle
     Ovaries
     Physiology
     Reproduction
  RT Corpus luteum
  NT Anovulation

     Estrus
  — Detection
     UF Detection of ovulation
        Ovulation—Time determination
        Time determination of ovulation
     NT Natural family planning— Ovulation method
  — Induction
     UF Induced ovulation
        Induction of ovulation
  — Regulation
     UF Regulation of ovulation
     BT Biological control systems
  — Time determination
     USE Ovulation—Detection
Ovulation method of birth control
  USE Natural family planning—Ovulation method
Ovules *(May Subd Geog)*
   [QK659]
  BT Plants—Reproduction
  RT Seeds
Ovum
   [QL965 (Zoology)]
   [QM611 (Human embryology)]
   [RG591 (Diseases)]
  BT Embryology
     Gametes
     Germ cells
  RT Oogenesis
  NT Cells
     Ovaries
Ovum implantation
  UF Implantation of ovum
     Nidation
  BT Biology, Experimental
     Pregnancy
     Pregnancy—Trimester, First
Owain Glyndŵr's Way (Wales)
   (Not Subd Geog)
  UF Glendower's Way (Wales)
     Glyndŵr's Way (Wales)
     Owen Glendower's Way (Wales)
  BT Trails—Wales
Owari Bay (Japan)
  USE Ise Bay (Japan)
Owari manzai
  USE Manzai (Dance)
Owen family
  UF Owens family
     Owin family
     Owing family
     Owings family
Owen Glendower's Way (Wales)
  USE Owain Glyndŵr's Way (Wales)
Owen Smith (Horse)
  BT Horses
Owenby family
  USE Ownby family
Owenke (Tribe)
  USE O-wen-k'o (Tribe)
Owenk'o (Tribe)
  USE O-wen-k'o (Tribe)
Owens family
  USE Owen family
Owen's Grove Cemetery (Owen, Iowa)
   (Not Subd Geog)
  BT Cemeteries—Iowa
Owens Peak Wilderness (Calif.)
  BT National parks and reserves— California
     Wilderness areas—California
Owens River (Calif.)
  BT Rivers—California
Owens sucker
   [QL638.C27]
  UF Catostomus fumeiventris
Owens Valley Formation (Calif.)
  USE Owens Valley Group (Calif.)
Owens Valley Group (Calif.)
  UF Owens Valley Formation (Calif.)

BT Geology—California
    Geology, Stratigraphic—Permian
Owesley family
  USE Ousley family
Owin family
  USE Owen family
Owing family
  USE Owen family
Owings family
  USE Owen family
Owl Creek (Wyo.)
  BT Rivers—Wyoming
Owl Creek Mountains (Wyo.)
  BT Mountains—Wyoming
    Rocky Mountains
Owl monkey
  USE Aotes trivirgatus
Owl parrot
  USE Kakapo
Owls
  [QL696.S8]
  UF Striges
    Strigiformes
  BT Birds
    Birds of prey
  NT Screech owls
    Strigidae
    Tytonidae
Owls, Barn
  USE Tytonidae
Owls, Fossil
  [QE872.S8]
Owls, Typical
  USE Strigidae
Owls as pets *(May Subd Geog)*
  [SF473.O85]
  BT Pets
Owls in art
  [N7666.O94]
Owls in literature
Owmby family
  USE Ownby family
Ownbey family
  USE Ownby family
Ownby family
  UF Owenby family
    Owmby family
    Ownbey family
Owners, Cat
  USE Cat owners
Owners, Dog
  USE Dog owners
Owners, Firearms
  USE Firearms owners
Owners, Forest
  USE Forest landowners
Owners, Home
  USE Homeowners
Owners, Horse
  USE Horse owners
Owners, Kennel
  USE Kennel owners
Owners, Pet
  USE Pet owners
Owners, Plantation
  USE Plantation owners
Owners of land
  USE Landowners
Ownership
  USE Property
Ownership, Employee
  USE Employee ownership
Ownership of firearms
  USE Firearms ownership
Ownership of homes
  USE Home ownership
Ownership of newspapers
  USE Newspapers—Ownership
Ownership of slaves
  USE Indians of North America—Slaves,
    Ownership of

    Slavery
Ownership of stock
  USE Stock ownership
Owsley family
  USE Ousley family
Owyhee Canyon Wilderness (Nev.)
  (Not Subd Geog)
  UF Owyhee Canyon Wilderness Study
    Area (Nev.)
  BT National parks and reserves—Nevada
    Wilderness areas—Nevada
Owyhee Canyon Wilderness (Or.)
  (Not Subd Geog)
  UF Owyhee Canyon Wilderness Study
    Area (Or.)
  BT National parks and reserves—Oregon
    Wilderness areas—Oregon
Owyhee Canyon Wilderness Study Area (Nev.)
  USE Owyhee Canyon Wilderness (Nev.)
Owyhee Canyon Wilderness Study Area (Or.)
  USE Owyhee Canyon Wilderness (Or.)
Owyhee River
  BT Rivers—Idaho
    Rivers—Nevada
    Rivers—Oregon
Owyhee River Canyon Wilderness (Idaho)
  UF Owyhee River Canyon Wilderness
    Study Area (Idaho)
  BT National parks and reserves—Idaho
    Wilderness areas—Idaho
Owyhee River Canyon Wilderness Study Area
  (Idaho)
  USE Owyhee River Canyon Wilderness
    (Idaho)
Owyhee River-Deep Creek Wilderness (Idaho)
  USE Deep Creek-Owyhee River Wilderness
    (Idaho)
Owyhee River-Deep Creek Wilderness Study
  Area (Idaho)
  USE Deep Creek-Owyhee River Wilderness
    (Idaho)
Owyhee River Wilderness, North Fork (Idaho)
  USE North Fork Owyhee River Wilderness
    (Idaho)
Owyhees
  USE Hawaiians
Ox
  USE Oxen
Ox driving *(May Subd Geog)*
  [HE153 (Transportation)]
  [SF209.5 (Animal culture)]
  UF Bullock driving
    Driving, Bullock
    Driving, Ox
  RT Bullockies
Ox-eye tarpon
  USE Oxeye tarpon
Ox-gall
  [QP197]
  BT Bile
Ox Hill, Battle of, 1862
  USE Chantilly (Va.), Battle of, 1862
Ox industry *(May Subd Geog)*
  UF Ox trade
  BT Animal industry
    Draft animals
    Oxen
Ox trade
  USE Ox industry
Oxaeidae *(May Subd Geog)*
  [QL568.O8]
  BT Hymenoptera
Oxalates
  BT Oxalic acid
Oxalic acid
  [QD305.A2]
  NT Oxalates
  — Excretion
    [QP211]
    BT Excretion

Oxalic acid in the body
  [QP801.O8]
  BT Biological chemistry
Oxalis
  [QK495.O98]
Oxaluria *(May Subd Geog)*
  [RC918.O9]
  BT Carbohydrates—Metabolism—
    Disorders
Oxazoles
  UF Furomonazoles
  BT Heterocyclic compounds
Oxen *(May Subd Geog)*
  [QL737.U5]
  UF Bullocks
    Ox
  BT Cattle
  NT Ox industry
  — Anatomy
Oxen, Fossil
  [QE882.U3]
Oxender family
  USE Oxenreider family
Oxenfrider family
  USE Oxenreider family
Oxenger family
  USE Oxenreider family
Oxenreider family
  UF Ochenrider family
    Ochsenreider family
    Ochsenreiter family
    Ochsenreither family
    Ochsenreuter family
    Ocksrider family
    Oxender family
    Oxenfrider family
    Oxenger family
    Oxenreiter family
    Oxrider family
Oxenreiter family
  USE Oxenreider family
Oxeye tarpon
  [QL638.M33]
  UF Megalops cyprinoides
    Ox-eye tarpon
Oxford and Cambridge Boat Race
  [GV799]
Oxford Canal (England)
  BT Canals—England
Oxford Group *(May Subd Geog)*
  [BV4915]
  UF Buchmanism
    First Century Christian Fellowship
  NT Moral rearmament
Oxford Hills (Me.)
  BT Mountains—Maine
Oxford movement *(May Subd Geog)*
  [BX5094-5100]
  UF Tractarianism
  BT Church of England—History—19th
    century
  RT Anglo-Catholicism
**Oxford, Worcester and Wolverhampton
Railway**
  BT Railroads—Great Britain
Oxholm family
Oxidants
  USE Oxidizing agents
Oxidants, Photochemical
  USE Photochemical oxidants
Oxidase test (Microbiology)
  UF Cytochrome oxidase test
  BT Bacteria—Identification
  RT Cytochrome oxidase—Analysis
Oxidases
  [QP601]
  NT Amine oxidase
    Cytochrome P-450
    Xanthine oxidase
Oxidation
  [QD63.O9 (Chemical operations)]

Oxidation (Continued)
⌐QD281.O9 (Organic chemistry)⌐
⌐QD501 (Physical chemistry)⌐
UF Autoxidation
NT Fretting corrosion
Krebs cycle
Nitrification
Oxidation-reduction reaction
Oxidizing agents
Peroxides
Soil oxidation
Oxidation, Biological
USE Oxidation, Physiological
Oxidation, Electrolytic
UF Electrolytic oxidation
BT Electrolysis
Reduction, Electrolytic
NT Metals—Anodic oxidation
Oxidation, Physiological
⌐QP177⌐
UF Biological oxidation
Oxidation, Biological
Physiological oxidation
BT Biological chemistry
NT Pentose phosphate pathway
Tissue respiration
Oxidation ditches
UF Continuous loop reactors (Sewage
treatment)
Ditches, Oxidation
Pasveer ditch process
Reactors, Continuous loop (Sewage
treatment)
BT Sewage—Purification—Activated
sludge process
Sewage lagoons
Oxidation lagoons
USE Sewage lagoons
Oxidation ponds
USE Sewage lagoons
Oxidation-reduction reaction
UF Oxido-reduction
Redox reaction
BT Chemical reactions
Oxidation
RT Reduction, Chemical
NT Reduction, Electrolytic
Oxide ceramics
BT Ceramics
Oxides
Oxide coating
Here are entered works on the coating produced
by oxidizing the surface of a metal.
BT Protective coatings
Thin films
NT Metals—Anodic oxidation
Oxide electrodes
USE Electrodes, Oxide
Oxides
⌐QD181.O1⌐
NT Alkaline earth oxides
Aluminum oxide
Bismuth trioxide
Cadmium oxysulphate
Cerium oxides
Chlorine oxides
Chrysoberyl
Dioxane
Hafnium oxide
Holmium oxide
Hydroxides
Manganese oxides
Metallic oxides
Nitrogen dioxide
Nitrogen oxides
Nitroquinoline oxide
Oxide ceramics
Polyethylene oxide
Rhenium trioxide
Silicon oxide
Stannic oxide

Sulphoxides
Sulphur oxides
Titanium dioxide
Vanadium oxide
Zirconium oxide
— Thermal properties
Oxidizers
USE Oxidizing agents
Oxidizing agents
UF Oxidants
Oxidizers
BT Oxidation
NT Photochemical oxidants
Oxido-reduction
USE Oxidation-reduction reaction
Oxidoreductase, Cholesterol
USE Cholesterol hydroxylase
Oxidoreductases
⌐QP602⌐
BT Enzymes
NT Aldose reductase
Cholesterol hydroxylase
Cytochrome oxidase
Laccase
Lactate dehydrogenase
Peroxidase
Superoxide dismutase
Oximetry
BT Blood gases—Analysis
Oxygen in the body
Oxirane
USE Ethylene oxide
Oxisols
USE Ferralsols
Oxo compounds
BT Oxygen
NT Aldehydes
Carbenicillin
Carbonyl compounds
Ketones
Oxo process
BT Alcohol
Aldehydes
Distillation, Destructive
Olefins
Oxoacid carboxylase
USE Pyruvate carboxylase
Oxon Hill Manor (Md.)
BT Maryland—Antiquities
Plantations—Maryland
Oxonium ions
UF Hydronium ions
BT Ions
Oxopropanoic acid
USE Pyruvic acid
Oxosulfamylchlorophenylhydroxyisoindoline
USE Chlorthalidone
Oxrider family
USE Oxenreider family
Oxuderces
USE Boleophthalmus
Oxuderces dentatus
USE Boleophthalmus cantoris
Oxudercidae
USE Gobiidae
Oxus River
USE Amu Darya
Oxya
⌐QL508.A2⌐
BT Acrididae
Oxyacetylene welding and cutting
⌐TS227⌐
UF Autogenous welding
Gas welding
BT Metal-cutting
Oxygen—Industrial applications
Welding
— Equipment and supplies
— Health aspects
USE Welding—Health aspects
— Safety measures

USE Welding—Safety measures
Oxyaldehydes
⌐QD305.A6⌐
⌐QD341.A6⌐
Oxybelidae
USE Sphecidae
Oxybelus
⌐QL568.S7⌐
BT Sphecidae
Oxybisethene
USE Vinyl ethers
Oxybismethane
USE Methyl ether
Oxycephaly
USE Craniosynostoses
Oxychlorides
NT Nitrogen oxychlorides
Oxycoccus
USE Vaccinium
Oxycoccus palustris
USE European cranberry
Oxycorynidae
USE Curculionidae
Oxydimorphine
⌐QP921 (Physiological effects)⌐
Oxygen
⌐QD181.O1⌐
⌐TP245.O9 (Chemical technology)⌐
BT Nonmetals
NT Active oxygen
Metals—Oxygen content
Oxo compounds
Ozone
Steel—Oxygen content
Superoxide
Water—Dissolved oxygen
Water—Electrolysis
— Industrial applications
BT Chemistry, Technical
NT Metallurgy
Nonferrous metals—Metallurgy—
Oxygen processes
Oxyacetylene welding and cutting
Steel—Metallurgy—Oxygen
processes
— Isotopes
— — Molecular rotation
— — Spectra
— Physiological effect
⌐QP913.O1⌐
NT Anaerobiosis
Anoxemia
— Therapeutic use
USE Oxygen therapy
Oxygen, Active
USE Active oxygen
Oxygen, Liquid
USE Liquid oxygen
Oxygen at low temperatures
BT Low temperatures
RT Liquid oxygen
Oxygen deficiency in the blood
USE Anoxemia
Oxygen electrodes
USE Electrodes, Oxygen
Oxygen equipment in airplanes
USE Airplanes—Oxygen equipment
Oxygen equipment in space vehicles
USE Space vehicles—Oxygen equipment
Oxygen in the body
RT Anoxemia
NT Active oxygen in the body
Oximetry
Oxygen transport (Physiology)
Oxygen index of materials
⌐TP265⌐
UF Flammability testing
Limiting oxygen index of materials
Materials—Oxygen index
BT Fire-testing
Materials—Testing

2720

Oxygen steelmaking
  USE Steel—Metallurgy—Oxygen processes
Oxygen therapy
  [RM666.O8]
  UF Oxygen—Therapeutic use
  BT Respiratory therapy
  NT Hyperbaric oxygenation
     Retrolental fibroplasia
     Spiroscope and spiroscopy
Oxygen therapy for children
  (May Subd Geog)
  BT Respiratory therapy for children
Oxygen transport (Physiology)
  UF Transport, Oxygen (Physiology)
  BT Biological transport
     Oxygen in the body
Oxygenases
  BT Hemoproteins
     Metalloenzymes
  NT Lipoxygenases
Oxygenation, Hyperbaric
  USE Hyperbaric oxygenation
Oxygenators
  UF Artificial lungs
     Blood oxygenation, Extracorporeal
     Lungs, Artificial
  BT Artificial organs
     Heart, Mechanical
  NT Oxygenators, Membrane
Oxygenators, Membrane
  UF Lungs, Membrane
     Membrane lungs
     Membrane oxygenators
  BT Oxygenators
Oxygyrus
  [QL430.5.A8]
  BT Atlantidae
Oxygyrus keraudreni
  [QL430.5.A8]
Oxyhemoglobin
  BT Hemoglobin
Oxylabracidae
  USE Centropomidae
Oxylebiidae
  USE Hexagrammidae
Oxymoron
  BT Figures of speech
Oxymuriatic acid
  USE Chlorine
Oxymyxteros breviceps
  USE Blarinomys breviceps
Oxynaphthoic acid
  [QD341.A2]
Oxyopidae
  [QL458.42.O9]
  UF Lynx spiders
  BT Spiders
  NT Hamataliva
Oxyrhyncha
  NT Majidae
Oxyrhynchites (Egypt)
  USE Oxyrhynchus (Egypt)
Oxyrhynchus (Egypt) *(Not Subd Geog)*
  [DT73.O8]
  UF Bahnasā (Egypt)
     Behenesa (Egypt)
     Behnesa (Egypt)
     Behnescha (Egypt)
     Oxyrhynchites (Egypt)
     Oxyrynkhos (Egypt)
     Pemdje (Egypt)
     Per-medjed (Egypt)
  BT Cities and towns, Ruined, extinct, etc.
     —Egypt
     Egypt—Antiquities
Oxyrynkhos (Egypt)
  USE Oxyrhynchus (Egypt)
Oxytelidae
  USE Staphylinidae
Oxytenia
  [QK495.C74]

  BT Compositae
Oxytenia acerosa
  [QK495.C74]
  BT Livestock poisoning plants
Oxytocin
  BT Oligopeptides
     Pituitary hormones
  — **Research** *(May Subd Geog)*
     UF Oxytocin research
Oxytocin research
  USE Oxytocin—Research
Oxytocinase
Oxyura jamaicensis
  USE Ruddy duck
Oxyuriasis
  UF Enterobiasis
     Pinworm infections
  BT Helminthiasis
Oxyuriasis in children *(May Subd Geog)*
  [RJ406.O]
  BT Infection in children
Oxyurida
  [QL391.N4]
  UF Oxyuroidea
  BT Nematoda
Oxyuroidea
  USE Oxyurida
Oya (Yoruba deity) *(May Subd Geog)*
  BT Goddesses, Yoruba
Oyacoulet Indians
  USE Oyaricoulet Indians
Oyama, Eruption of, 1962
  USE Miyake Island Earthquake, 1962
Ōyama Kaidō (Japan)
  UF Aoyama Kaidō (Japan)
     Atsugi Kaidō (Japan)
     Futako Kaidō (Japan)
     Ōyamadō (Japan)
     Sōshū Kaidō (Japan)
     Yagurasawa Kaidō (Japan)
     Yagurasawa Ōkan (Japan)
     Yagurazawa Kaidō (Japan)
     Yagurazawa Ōkan (Japan)
  BT Roads—Japan
Ōyamadō (Japan)
  USE Ōyama Kaidō (Japan)
Ōyamajō (Yamagata-shi, Japan)
  USE Yamagatajō (Yamagata-shi, Japan)
Oyambi Indians
  USE Oyampi Indians
Oyampi Indians
  [F2460.1.O9]
  UF Oyambi Indians
     Wayapi Indians
  BT Indians of South America
Oyampi language
  [PM6713]
  UF Oiampi language
     Oyapi language
     Wajapī language
     Wayapi language
  BT Brazil—Languages
     French Guiana—Languages
     Indians of South America—Languages
Oyana Indians
  [F2230.2.O8]
  UF Oajana Indians
     Ouayana Indians
     Rocouyenne Indians
     Roucouyenne Indians
     Waiana Indians
     Wayana Indians
  BT Carib Indians
     Indians of South America
Oyana language
  [PM6714]

  UF Ayana language
     Ouayana language
     Roucouyenne language
     Rucouyenne language
     Rukuyenne language
     Uayana language
     Upurui language
     Urucuiana language
  BT Indians of South America—Languages
Oyanagawa Iseki (Shichigashuku-machi, Japan)
  USE Oyanagawa Site (Shichigashuku-machi,
     Japan)
Oyanagawa Site (Shichigashuku-machi, Japan)
  (Not Subd Geog)
  UF Oyanagawa Iseki (Shichigashuku-
     machi, Japan)
  BT Japan—Antiquities
Oyapi language
  USE Oyampi language
Oyaricoulet Indians
  UF Ojarikoelle Indians
     Oyacoulet Indians
  BT Indians of South America
Oyasu Kaidō (Japan) *(Not Subd Geog)*
  UF Inaniwa Kaidō (Japan)
     Masuda Kaidō (Japan)
     Senboku Kaidō (Japan)
     Senbokudōri (Japan)
  BT Roads—Japan
Oyer family
Oyler family
Oyo Empire *(Not Subd Geog)*
  [DT515.45.Y67]
  BT Yorubas
Oyomei philosophy
  USE Yōmeigaku
Oyrat language
  USE Oirat language
Oyrats
  USE Oirats
Oyster cap (Fungus)
  USE Pleurotus ostreatus
Oyster catcher
  USE Oystercatcher
Oyster-culture *(May Subd Geog)*
  [SH365-SH371]
  Here are entered works on the techniques used in
culturing oysters. Works on the harvesting of oysters
are entered under Oyster fisheries.
  UF Oysters, Pearl
  BT Oyster fisheries
     Shellfish culture
  NT Oyster shell
  — **Law and legislation** *(May Subd Geog)*
     BT Fishery law and legislation
Oyster dredgers
  USE Bugeyes (Boats)
Oyster drill
  [QL430.5.M9]
  UF Urosalpinx cinerea
  BT Oysters—Diseases
Oyster drill, Southern
  USE Southern oyster drill
Oyster family
  UF Aister family
     Eyster family
Oyster fisheries *(May Subd Geog)*
  [SH371]
  Here are entered works on the harvesting of oys-
ters. Works on the techniques used in culturing oys-
ters are entered under Oyster-culture.
  BT Shellfish fisheries
  NT Oyster-culture
Oyster fishing boats
  USE Bugeyes (Boats)
Oyster mushroom
  USE Pleurotus ostreatus
Oyster plant
  USE Salsify
Oyster River (N.H.)
  BT Rivers—New Hampshire

Oyster shell *(May Subd Geog)*
 [SH379.5]
   BT Oyster-culture
       Shells
Oyster-shell scale
 [SB945.O9]
   UF Mussel scale
Oyster shucking
   USE Oysters—Shucking
Oyster toadfish
   UF Opsanus tau
   BT Toadfishes
Oystercatcher
   UF Common oystercatcher
       Haematopus ostralegus
       Oyster catcher
   BT Charadriiformes
Oystercatcher, Chatham Islands
   USE Chatham Islands oystercatcher
Oystercatcher, variable
   USE Variable oystercatcher
Oysters
 [QL430.7.O9 (Zoology)]
   NT American oyster
       Cookery (Oysters)
       Crassostrea
       European oyster
       Ostrea
   — Contamination
       UF Contamination of oysters
   — Diseases *(May Subd Geog)*
       NT Oyster drill
           Southern oyster drill
   — Shucking
       UF Oyster shucking
           Shucking of oysters
Oysters, Canned
   UF Canned oysters
   BT Fishery products, Canned
Oysters, Fossil
   UF Ostreidae, Fossil
Oysters, Pearl
   USE Oyster-culture
       Pearl-fisheries
Oz (Artificial language)
 [PM8707]
   BT Languages, Artificial
Ozaena
 [RF431.O9]
   UF Atrophic rhinitis
       Rhinitis, Atrophic
   BT Rhinitis
Ozaenidae
   USE Carabidae
Ozark Mountains
   UF Ozarks
   BT Mountains—Arkansas
       Mountains—Missouri
       Mountains—Oklahoma
Ozark National Forest (Ark.)
   BT Forest reserves—Arkansas
       National parks and reserves—United
       States
Ozark National Scenic Riverways (Mo.)
   BT Current River (Mo. and Ark.)
       Jacks Fork (Mo.)
       National parks and reserves—Missouri
       Wild and scenic rivers—Missouri
Ozarks
   USE Ozark Mountains
Ozarks, Lake of the (Mo.)
   UF Lake of the Ozarks (Mo.)
   BT Lakes—Missouri
       Reservoirs—Missouri
Oze-hara (Japan)
   USE Oze Marsh (Japan)
Oze Lake (Japan) *(Not Subd Geog)*
   UF Ose-numa (Japan)
       Oze-numa (Japan)
       Ozenuma (Japan)
   BT Lakes—Japan

Oze Marsh (Japan) *(Not Subd Geog)*
   UF Ose Marsh (Japan)
       Osehara (Japan)
       Oze-hara (Japan)
       Ozega-hara (Japan)
       Ozehara (Japan)
   BT Marshes—Japan
Oze-numa (Japan)
   USE Oze Lake (Japan)
Oze Region (Japan)
Ozega-hara (Japan)
   USE Oze Marsh (Japan)
Ozehara (Japan)
   USE Oze Marsh (Japan)
Ozenuma (Japan)
   USE Oze Lake (Japan)
Ozero Baykal (R.S.F.S.R.)
   USE Baikal Lake (R.S.F.S.R.)
Ozero Borovoe (Kazakh S.S.R.)
   USE Borovoe Lake (Kazakh S.S.R.)
Ozero Borovoye (Kazakh S.S.R.)
   USE Borovoe Lake (Kazakh S.S.R.)
Ozero Chany (R.S.F.S.R.)
   USE Chany Lake (R.S.F.S.R.)
Ozero Glubokoe (R.S.F.S.R.)
   USE Glubokoe Lake (R.S.F.S.R.)
Ozero Imandra (R.S.F.S.R.)
   USE Imandra, Lake (R.S.F.S.R.)
Ozero Inari (Finland)
   USE Inari Lake (Finland)
Ozero Issyk-Kul' (Kirghiz S.S.R.)
   USE Issyk-Kul' (Kirghiz S.S.R.)
Ozero Keĭtele (Finland)
   USE Keitele Lake (Finland)
Ozero Keytele (Finland)
   USE Keitele Lake (Finland)
Ozero Kubenskoe (R.S.F.S.R.)
   USE Kubenskoe Lake (R.S.F.S.R.)
Ozero Kubenskoye (R.S.F.S.R.)
   USE Kubenskoe Lake (R.S.F.S.R.)
Ozero Ouluĭärvi (Finland)
   USE Oulujärvi (Finland)
Ozero Saĭma (Finland)
   USE Saimaa Lake (Finland)
Ozero Sayma (Finland)
   USE Saimaa Lake (Finland)
Ozero Seliger (R.S.F.S.R.)
   USE Seliger, Lake (R.S.F.S.R.)
Ozero Siverskoe (R.S.F.S.R.)
   USE Siverskoe Lake (R.S.F.S.R.)
Ozero Siverskoye (R.S.F.S.R.)
   USE Siverskoe Lake (R.S.F.S.R.)
Ozero Zaĭsan (Kazakh S.S.R.)
   USE Zaisan Lake (Kazakh S.S.R.)
Ozero Zaysan (Kazakh S.S.R.)
   USE Zaisan Lake (Kazakh S.S.R.)
Ozokerite
 [TN857 (Mineral industries)]
 [TP695 (Chemical technology)]
   UF Mineral wax
       Wax, Mineral
   BT Ceresin
Ozonation
   USE Ozonization
Ozone
 [QD181.O1]
   BT Chemical tests and reagents
       Oxygen
   NT Atmospheric ozone
       Ozonization
       Ozonolysis
       Umkehr effect
   — Physiological effect
     [QP913.O1]
       NT Plants, Effect of ozone on
   — Spectra
Ozone sondes
   USE Ozonesondes
Ozonesondes
   UF Ozone sondes
       Sondes, Ozone

   BT Atmospheric ozone
       Meteorological instruments
   RT Radiosondes
Ozonization
 [QD281.O95]
   UF Ozonation
   BT Chemical reactions
       Ozone
   NT Sewage—Purification—Ozonization
       Water—Purification—Ozonization
Ozonolysis
   BT Ozone
Ozotype
   USE Photography—Printing processes—
       Ozotype
Ōzura Site (Japan) *(Not Subd Geog)*
   UF Ikarigaseki Ōzura Site (Japan)
   BT Japan—Antiquities